The College Blue Book®

38th Edition

Tabular Data

The College Blue Book®

38th Edition

Tabular Data

MACMILLAN REFERENCE USA
A part of Gale, Cengage Learning

GALE
CENGAGE Learning™

Detroit • New York • San Francisco • New Haven, Conn • Waterville, Maine • London

GALE
CENGAGE Learning

The College Blue Book, 38th Edition
Volume 2

Project Editor: Bohdan Romaniuk

Editorial Support Services: Wayne Fong

Composition and Electronic Prepress: Gary Leach

Manufacturing: Rita Wimberley

Product Management: Jerry Moore

A portion of the data was supplied by Peterson's Publishing, a Nelnet company.

For product information and technology assistance, contact us at
Gale Customer Support, 1-800-877-4253.
For permission to use material from this text or product,
submit all requests online at **www.cengage.com/permissions.**
Further permissions questions can be emailed to
permissionrequest@cengage.com

Gale
27500 Drake Rd.
Farmington Hills, MI, 48331-3535

ISBN-13: 978-0-02-866143-8 (6 vol. set)
ISBN-10: 0-02-866143-5 (6 vol. set)
ISBN-13: 978-0-02-866145-2 (vol. 2)
ISBN-10: 0-02-866145-1 (vol. 2)

ISSN 1082-7056

This title is also available as an e-book.
ISBN-13: 978-0-02-866172-8 (set)
ISBN-10: 0-02-866172-9 (set)
Contact your Gale sales representative for ordering information.

Printed in the United States of America
1 2 3 4 5 6 7 14 13 12 11 10

Contents

The College Blue Book® has been a standard, professional reference on higher education since it was first published in 1923. New features have been added during the intervening years to keep pace with the changing needs for information about our educational facilities. The information, especially in the areas of tuition, room and board, enrollment figures, library holdings, is constantly changing. It is difficult to maintain up-to-date figures in these areas, as many schools change tuition and related costs on an ongoing basis. We therefore urge our readers to check directly with the schools for the most current cost information.

CONTENTS OF EACH VOLUME

Volume 1: Narrative Descriptions

More than 4,300 colleges in the United States and Canada are fully described. Entrance requirements are detailed and campus facilities and costs are described. A map of each U.S. state and Canadian province is included and each college has a grid index for easy location. Web sites are also listed.

Volume 2: Tabular Data

Colleges are listed alphabetically by state or province. Information about costs, accreditation, enrollment figures, faculty, and names of the chief administrative officers are given for each school.

Volume 3: Degrees Offered by College and Subject

In Part I, the name of each college is listed alphabetically by state or province, with a list of the subject areas for which degrees are offered. Part II includes an alphabetical listing of subject areas for which degrees are granted by one or more institutions of higher education.

Volume 4: Occupational Education

More than 6,000 schools in the United States that provide occupational or technical training are fully described, offering such information as tuition costs, enrollment figures, and entrance requirements. Two indexes are provided: an alphabetical listing of schools in the "Index of Occupational Education Schools," in addition to the "Curricula and Areas of Instruction" index.

Volume 5: Scholarships, Fellowships, Grants, and Loans

This volume provides a listing of more than 5,000 different sources of financial aid for students wishing to further their education. Split alphabetically into eight broad subject areas (each containing several more specialized concentrations of study), as well as a general section, each listing provides basic information about a specific award, including eligibility requirements, amount of award, and application deadlines.

Volume 6: Distance Learning Programs

Responding to this rapidly growing trend in post-secondary education, this volume features comprehensive profiles of more than 900 institutions offering distance learning programs within the United States and Canada.

FOR MORE INFORMATION

We are always open to suggestions and recommendations for improvement of *The College Blue Book®* from our readers and from the educational professions. Please write or call: Editor,

The College Blue Book
Macmillan Reference USA
27500 Drake Rd.
Farmington Hills, MI 48331-3535 Phone: (248)699-4253
Toll-free: 800-347-GALE
Fax: (248)699-8075
Email: blue.book@gale.com
Web site: www.gale.cengage.com

Introduction

The decision to continue education beyond high school years, the selection of a collegiate institution, and the area of study to be pursued are some of the essential experiences necessary for students to determine their futures. Alternatives of choice institutions, work selection, job opportunities, professional training, or even discontinuing any further education are all selective decisions open to the students.

Nearly all students today have opportunities to continue education beyond high school. There are more schools accepting wider ranges of student ability and interest than ever before. This means more effort, more planning, and more personal study in making the college choice.

Self Appraisal

The best place to begin is with oneself. An appraisal with objective, honest answers is necessary. What are the personal potentials as a student? Where has the best performance been? What are the probabilities for improvement? What are the reasons for really wanting to go to college; is it for intellectual development, vocational preparation, or simply to satisfy a desire for status? What are the personal ideas of college? What is expected from the college experience? Have career plans been made? Where are the academic abilities? What subjects are preferred? What is the quality of performance in the preferred areas of study? What is the overall grade average? What is the class rank in high school? In what subject areas is there the greatest interest? What is the quality of work in these areas? Are interests and performance generally consistent? Are the expressed and recorded interests truly and accurately reflecting the inward wishes? What was liked best about the high school experience? Has the college preparatory program been followed in high school? What were the social and cultural experiences during high school years that were most meaningful? What was considered, if anything, to be lacking?

Well-thought-out answers to these and similar questions are helpful. Discussions of such topics with counselors, parents, and teachers increases the probability of success in college selection, attendance, and completion.

The counselor today is an extremely valued resource person available to assist the student. When an effective working team of counselor-student-parent actually exists, the probabilities for the student making selective choices that prove to be the "right" ones are unquestionably the greatest. The better the student and the counselor know one another, the more effective the guidance and counseling program will be. For this to occur, the opportunity for face-to- face student-counselor discussion needs to start in the latter elementary school years and continue through high school and college.

College Appraisals A

Research is continuing in the areas of college admissions and student success. The identification and understanding of causes of success and failure need professional study. However, one thing is apparent: the more careful the preparations and planning by the student, the better the chances of college admission and success.

Systemized planning should begin early. The more self-understanding and knowledge about available colleges one has, the better one can plan with corresponding success. Certainly, early in the high school career, students should be reviewing detailed information on colleges and universities with the counselor, noting academic requirements such as scholastic performance, course requirements, costs and other particular qualities of individual collegiate institutions. There is no single one-and-only college for the student. Colleges have personalities just as the students do. There are always several colleges with academic and social climates compatible and acceptable to each student.

Entrance requirements, courses available, costs, size of student body, academic pressure, special programs, geographical location, and specialty schools are some of the considerations of every student in appraising available colleges.

The College Blue Book® is dedicated to providing detailed information regarding collegiate institutions throughout the United States and Canada. Students and counselors should browse through *The College Blue Book®* and become familiar with the colleges of our country and neighboring Canada. As interest sharpens and narrows, a more selective and in-depth study of institutions should be made.

Where feasible, students should plan visits to college campuses. Campus visiting may begin during the summer between the sophomore and junior years of high school. The best time to be on a college campus, however, is during the regular term with a carefully planned visit in the spring semester of the junior year. Preparatory plans should be made with the high school counselor, reviewing discussions of earlier personal conferences. Advance arrangements should be made with admission officers of the colleges the student expects to visit. The admission officer's name and telephone number will be found in most instances in *The College Blue Book®* volume entitled *Tabular Data*. The admissions officer in many cases will want to know whether the student has actually applied for admission and probably the areas the student may plan to major in or other special interests the student has in the particular institution. The student should have prepared a summary of personal data. If possible, high school students should also talk to students of the colleges they wish to attend.

The growth of community colleges has opened up another avenue for students, especially those of limited finances or those who have not decided on their ultimate educational goals. Students will find many of these community colleges offer an excellent opportunity to gain a solid college background. Then one can choose a four-year institution to complete an undergraduate degree.

Any regular high school graduate can find a school that will accept him. Many students need to be encouraged to consider the smaller, private and public colleges of good standing.

Students entering professional training such as engineering or law might consider small schools that have cooperative programs with major universities. A knowledgeable student, through planning and guidance, can avoid unnecessary disappointment. A college career can be quite beneficial to the student who spends three to four years on a small campus and one, two, or three additional years of graduate work on another, larger campus.

Costs

Costs are continuing to rise. Tuition charges as listed herein should only be used as a guide. It would be wise to check with the institution of interest to be sure of having the most up-to-date information available.

Should the need for financial aid be a factor in selecting a college, a college-bound student should be aware that the best single source of financial assistance and information is the financial aid officer or admission director at the college. It is most important for the student to contact the finance office as early as possible during the student's senior year in high school. A principal source of financial assistance is the major federal undergraduate aid programs. Applications can be obtained from the college. Most colleges and universities also offer financial assistance in several forms including academic and general scholarships, grants-in-aid, student loans, and part-time work. For more information, see volume 5 of *The College Blue Book®*: *Scholarships, Fellowships, Grants, and Loans.*

Two-Year Colleges

Two-year colleges, referred to as junior colleges or community colleges, both public and private, offer programs that prepare students for technical and semiprofessional careers in business and technology fields, and for transfer to senior colleges. There are hundreds of two-year colleges providing comprehensive programs meeting the lower division requirements of virtually all four-year colleges and universities.

There are decided advantages for some students to enroll in a two-year college. Some of these are: less cost, home residence, availability of highly specialized programs, opportunity for the student to mature, a smaller student body, and generally a closer relationship to the faculty. The development of two-year colleges across the nation is one of the most vital forces in education today. The two-year college is neither an extension of high school, nor a little senior college. It has its own identity, sphere of service, and contribution to make to American education. The comprehensive community college is considered one of the best means of accommodating the demands of higher education, embracing the increasing variety of abilities of students graduating from high schools, preparing students in the technological and semiprofessional occupations, and all in an economical manner.

One very important caution needs to be heeded by students enrolling in two-year colleges who are planning to continue their work through a bachelor's program. Students expecting to transfer should very carefully study the requirements of the institution they ultimately plan to attend. In conference with the junior college counselor, a careful review of the planned program should be made to be sure the contemplated courses at the junior college will satisfy the requirements of the senior institution. Students who depart from prescribed courses stated by the senior institution or fail in any of these courses may experience difficulty with admission or normal progress toward the bachelor degree.

Liberal Arts Colleges

The liberal arts colleges offer four years of college and award the Bachelor of Arts and the Bachelor of Science degrees. The curriculum for the first two years is usually broad with an emphasis in the humanities, natural sciences, and cultural history of our society. The last two years may provide a concentration of specific programs such as premedicine or pre-law leading to graduate professional training.

Students considering professional training at the graduate level should keep this in mind as they plan their work at the liberal arts college. Graduate schools in some cases have strict preparatory requirements. Familiarity with these requirements can greatly assist in making the transfer to graduate level without loss of credit or time.

Specialized Institutions

Four-year institutions of technology are examples of the more specialized schools where concentration in a specialty is intensively pursued throughout the college career. Most of these institutions are quite selective in admission practice and may require more high school mathematics and science than most other schools for entrance. These programs lead to engineering degrees in many fields emphasizing technology and science. Recently there has been a broadening of the program of the first two years, but, in general, such a program is not nearly as comprehensive and varied as the liberal arts college. The demand for engineers and scientists with specially developed skills creates great competition for entrance into schools of technology.

There are other specialized institutions such as conservatories of music, seminaries, medical and law schools, institutions specializing in teacher training, or schools of the fine arts, most of which require specialized preparation for entrance.

Universities

The university is generally composed of a number of degree-granting colleges and schools where both bachelor and graduate degrees are grouped under one administrative head. Bachelor degrees at the university may be earned in liberal arts or one of the professions such as engineering or the physical sciences. The university, to some extent, combines what is available at the liberal arts college with the specialized institution. Complete professional training in such areas as law, medicine, and science is available on the university campus.

As a rule, universities have much larger student bodies than colleges. In order to meet the demand, most state universities have established several campuses. Many state universities are very selective in admitting students. This is particularly true for a student who is applying for admission from out- of-state.

Entrance Examinations

There are more applicants than there is room for students on many campuses. As this demand increases, colleges and universities attempt to identify those applicants who are most likely to succeed on their campuses. A quality scholastic record has more influence on acceptance and admission than any other single factor. High school grades predict with better accuracy than any other single measurement what college grades and success will be. The more selective colleges and universities may choose students who come out highest on quantitative criteria, that is, high school scholastic averages combined with test scores. Some institutions have far more applicants (whose scholastic records and test scores are of a maximum quality) than they can accept. In such cases, applicants are sometimes screened and accepted on the basis of categories according to residence in the state or region, special talents, minority groups, or relationship to alumni. Such procedures are used in an attempt to influence the makeup of the enrollment.

When investigating several schools, one of the most accurate ways for evaluation of an institution is to consider test scores and the high school rank order of the students actually on campus. In many instances this is more informative than the announced admission policies.

College testing is required by many colleges and universities for entering students; some have developed their own tests and over the years have established norms for such tests. Most institutions requiring tests for entrance, however, now use either the test of the American College Testing Program (ACT) or the examinations of the College Entrance Examination Board. The College Entrance Examination Board offers the Preliminary Scholastic Assessment Test/National Merit Scholarship Qualifying Test (PSAT/ NMSQT), the Scholastic Assessment Test I: Reasoning Test (Verbal and Math), and the SAT II: Subject Tests.

Coaching, tutoring, drill, and memorization of facts can do little to improve the scores of the standardized examinations. It is recommended that students not invest time and money in cramming in hopes of improving test scores. Students can do their best preparation in general reading, completing their school assignments, and arriving on the proper day of the test rested and refreshed.

American College Testing Assessment (ACT)

The ACT Assessment provided by the American College Testing Program covers four subject areas: English, mathematics, reading, and science reasoning. The ACT test is scored on a range of 1 to 36. The ACT is administered at various test sites in the United States and other countries on specified dates throughout the year. Many colleges and universities recommend that prospective students take the examination early in the senior year.

The tests provide estimates of the students' current level of educational development in knowledge skill areas often required in college work. The ACT college testing program was founded in 1959. It is a nonprofit educational service offering programs in testing and financial need analysis.

Scholastic Assessment Tests (SAT)

The SAT I: Reasoning Test is an examination to measure the verbal and mathematics abilities students have developed both in and out of school. The SAT II: Subject Tests, which some colleges require for admission or placement purposes, consist of 22 separate tests that cover subjects such as literature, history, math, languages, chemistry, biology, and physics. Unlike the SAT I, which measures more general abilities, the SAT II tests measure the students' knowledge of a particular subject and their ability to apply that knowledge. Because of this, students should try to take a SAT II Test as soon as possible after completion of their last course in that subject.

The SAT I and II tests are given on certain dates throughout the year at various test centers in the United States and foreign countries. The combination of the student's academic record and the SAT scores, along with other pertinent secondary information enables admissions officers to estimate how well the student will perform on a particular college campus. The SAT is scored on a scale of 200 minimum to 800 maximum.

Admission Policies

One of the most important considerations in planning is to note when colleges and universities request applications, and to be sure that the applications are complete and forwarded during the appropriate periods. Failure in any way in this procedure will usually automatically disqualify a student from acceptance.

Counselors can provide students with freshman profiles on many of the institutions. Studying *The College Blue Book®*, particularly the volume *Tabular Data,* provides a great amount of information on the kind of student bodies found on the campuses of American institutions. There are four general classifications of admission policies. An understanding of these provides valuable guidelines in identifying colleges for consideration.

Most Selective: Many more students apply who meet the announced admission requirements than the college could possibly accept. In addition to requiring outstanding academic records, personal recommendations are required from the high school, and identification of any special qualities of the student should be made known. In this regard, the high school recommendation made to the collegiate institution requires special attention.

Many times, particularly at selective institutions, the high school recommendation actually provides the necessary edge for admission. The recommendation should be on time, carefully providing all information called for, and finally, be precise and detailed in citing personal qualities of the applicant.

All these qualities, however, do not guarantee acceptance. It is strongly recommended that qualified students apply to more than one institution of this type, and that not all applicants should be made to the same type of institution.

Very Selective: Colleges having a very selective procedure in accepting students require ACT scores of 23 or over, or an SAT I score of 600 or more. Students should rank in the top 10 to 12 percent of their high school graduating classes. In addition, strong recommendations stressing particular talents and achievements are necessary. Applications should be made to several institutions of this type.

Selective: An ACT of 20 or over, or an SAT I score of 550 or more is generally necessary. Applications for admission to selective colleges and universities are usually called for in the spring prior to fall entry. In many situations, applications may be submitted in the fall of the senior year with final confirmation to be made after all grades are recorded and confirmed upon graduation from high school.

Least Selective: The fourth classification represents those institutions that will accept students with a C average on their high school work. In certain unusual instances, and under special situations, even the selective institutions may accept students who are in this category, particularly if the scores on the ACT are in the mid-20's or are in excess of 500 on the SAT I. Generally, for acceptance in the less selective schools, students should have an ACT composite score of 17 or a SAT I score of 450.

Entrance examinations may or may not be required. Occasionally, if examinations are required, the results are used for student placement rather than admission. Most high school graduates can meet the requirements for entry and will be accepted. It should be pointed out, however, that in some cases an institution may be liberal in acceptance but carefully screens candidates for graduation. In such an institution, a high attrition rate may occur.

Open Enrollment Policy: This is becoming more common, particularly with the public community colleges. Many students will find this privilege most helpful in continuing their formal education beyond high school. Such a policy enables those students to have a second chance who have failed to perform up to their ability during their high school years. Enrollment and attendance may enable the student to complete a most rewarding vocational program or to later transfer and complete the Bachelor degree, which otherwise might not have been possible because of the deficiency in the high school scholastic record.

A number of colleges and universities, particularly the publicly supported ones, have adopted the open enrollment policy. In response to a feeling of community responsibility, they accept any student who has a diploma (or G.E.D. equivalency certificate) from an accredited high school. This procedure allows students from disadvantaged and minority backgrounds, who might otherwise be denied such an opportunity, to acquire a college education and prepare for a meaningful occupation. These institutions have not lowered their graduation requirements; they have, instead, created opportunities for more students to satisfy these requirements.

Do not assume the erroneous generality that the tougher it is to get into an institution, the better the quality; or the easier to enter, the poorer the school. In fact, there is research evidence available indicating that it may be wise to re-examine some of our traditional notions and attitudes regarding admissions. Not all degree programs on any particular campus are equally outstanding. Every institution has its particular strengths in programs available. Certain institutions are excellent places for some kinds of students in some kinds of programs, but no institution is the one most suited for everyone.

More than 4,300 educational institutions of the United States and Canada are presented in this volume. The information presented has been collected by questionnaires submitted to these institutions. In addition the most recent college catalogs were often consulted.

ORGANIZATION

All institutions are arranged in alpha-geographic order. Beginning with the state of Alabama, each institution is listed in alphabetical order within each state. The states are followed by schools in Canada listed by province.

For easier, more comprehensive use this volume is in a ready-reference format that gives statistical data available on each institution. Another use for this volume is to provide easy comparisons of schools as to enrollment, tuition, and other data. Additional information may be obtained from consulting the individual school listing in the *Narrative Descriptions* volume.

USE

Most of the data in this volume are self-explanatory. A few elements, however, need some clarification:

Costs Per Year

Tuition charges are constantly changing and information reported here is as correct as possible. However, it is recommended that the institutions be contacted for the most current information on charges for tuition, room and board, and miscellaneous fees. Many schools will have several tuitions: in-district, instate, nonresident. See *Narrative Descriptions* volume for a more complete breakdown.

Athletics

An Index on Intercollegiate Athletics listed alphabetically by sport and then by school follows the main section of this volume.

Professional Accreditations

Due to space constraints, acronyms have been used. A list of these acronyms follows this section. An Index of Professional Accreditations follows the athletics index in this volume.

Admission Plans

Early admission: Exceptionally able students are admitted before high school graduation. *Early action plan:* Students apply and are notified of admission early; if accepted, the candidate is not committed to enroll. *Early decision:* The school accepts well-qualified students who are notified earlier than usual, generally by mid-December. *Rolling admission:* An admission decision will be given as soon as possible after all application materials are received. *Deferred admission:* A student who wants to work, travel, study abroad, etc., for one year, will be accepted for the following year. *Open admission:* Students are admitted without the usual record for standard qualifications. Almost all students with a high school diploma or equivalent are admitted.

Acronyms for Professional Accreditations

AABB American Association of Blood Banks
AACN American Association of Colleges of Nursing
AACSB AACSB International-The Association to Advance Collegiate Schools of Business
AAFCS American Association of Family and Consumer Sciences
AALE American Academy for Liberal Education
AALS Association of American Law Schools
AAMAE American Association of Medical Assistants Endowment
AAMFT American Association for Marriage and Family Therapy
AANA American Association of Nurse Anesthetists
AARTS Association of Advanced Rabbinical and Talmudic Schools
ABA American Bar Association
ABET Accreditation Board for Engineering and Technology, Inc.
ABFSE American Board of Funeral Service Education
ABHE Association for Biblical Higher Education
ABHES Accrediting Bureau of Health Education Schools
ACA American Counseling Association
ACAOM Accredition Commission for Acupuncture and Oriental Medicine
ACBSP Association of Collegiate Business Schools and Programs
ACCE American Council for Construction Education
ACCSCT Accrediting Commission of Career Schools and Colleges of Technology
ACEHSA Accrediting Commission on Education for Health Services Administration
ACEJMC Accrediting Council on Education in Journalism and Mass Communications
ACF American Culinary Federation, Inc.
ACICS Accrediting Council for Independent Colleges and Schools
ACIPE Association for Clinical Pastoral Education, Inc.
ACNM American College of Nurse-Midwives
ACPE Accreditation Committee for Perfusion Education
ACPhE American Council on Pharmaceutical Education
ACSP American Institute of Certified Planners/Association of Collegiate Schools of Planning
ADA American Dental Association
ADtA American Dietetic Association
AHIMA American Health Information Management Association
ALA American Library Association
AOA American Optometric Association
AOsA American Osteopathic Association
AOTA American Occupational Therapy Association
APA American Psychological Association
APMA American Podiatric Medical Association
APTA American Physical Therapy Association
ARCAA Accreditation Review Commission on Education for the Anesthesiologist Assistant
ARCEST Accreditation Review Committee on Education in Surgical Technology
ARCMI Accreditation Review Committee for the Medical Illustrator
ASC American Society of Cytopathology
ASLA American Society of Landscape Architects
ASLHA American Speech-Language-Hearing Association
ATS Association of Theological Schools in the United States and Canada
AVMA American Veterinary Medical Association
CAA Council on Aviation Accreditation
CAEPK Committee on Accreditation of Education Programs in Kinesiotherapy
CARC Committee on Accreditation for Respiratory Care
CCE Council on Chiropractic Education
CEPH Council on Education for Public Health
COE Council on Occupational Education
COpTA Commission on Opticianry Accreditation
CORE Council on Rehabilitation Education
CSWE Council on Social Work Education
DETC Distance Education and Training Council
FIDER Foundation for Interior Design Education Research
JCAHPO Joint Commission on Allied Health Personnel in Ophthalmology
JRCECT Joint Review Committee on Education in Cardiovascular Technology
JRCEDMS Joint Review Committee on Education in Diagnostic Medical Sonography
JRCEET Joint Review Committee on Education in Electroneurodiagnostic Technology
JRCEMT Joint Review Committee on Educational Programs for the EMT-Paramedic
JRCEPAT Joint Review Committee on Educational Programs in Athletic Training
JRCERT Joint Review Committee on Education in Radiological Technology
JRCNMT Joint Review Committee on Educational Programs in Nuclear Medicine Technology
LCMEAMA Liaison Committee on Medical Education/American Medical Association
MACTE Montessori Accreditation Council for Teacher Education
MEAC Midwifery Education Accreditation Council
NAACLS National Accrediting Agency for Clinical Laboratory Sciences

NAIT	National Association of Industrial Technology
NANPWH	National Association of Nurse Practitioners in Women's Health
NASAD	National Association of Schools of Art and Design
NASD	National Association of Schools of Dance
NASM	National Association of Schools of Music
NASPAA	National Association of Schools of Public Affairs and Administration
NAST	National Association of Schools of Theatre
NCATE	National Council for Accreditation of Teacher Education
NCCU	Northwest Commission on Colleges and Universities
NCOPE	National Commission on Orthotic and Prosthetic Education
NLN	National League for Nursing
NRPA	National Recreation and Park Association
NYSBR	New York State Board of Regents
SAF	Society of American Foresters
TACCS	Transnational Association of Christian Colleges and Schools
TEAC	Teacher Education Accreditation Council

ACT	American College Testing Program
FT	Full-time
GED	General Education Development
Grad	Graduate level
M	Math (SAT); Men
PT	Part-time
SAT I	Scholastic Assessment Test: Reasoning Test
SAT II	Scholastic Assessment Test: Subject Tests
V	Verbal
W	Women

ALABAMA AGRICULTURAL AND MECHANICAL UNIVERSITY
4900 Meridian St.
Huntsville, AL 35811
Tel: (256)372-5000; Free: 800-553-0816
Admissions: (256)372-5245
Fax: (256)372-5881
Web Site: http://www.aamu.edu/
President/CEO: Dr. Andrew Hugine, Jr.
Admissions: Dr. Evelyn Ellis
Financial Aid: Kai CampBell
Type: University **Sex:** Coed **Scores:** 43.16% ACT 18-23; 3.63% ACT 24-29 **% Accepted:** 47 **Admission Plans:** Deferred Admission **Application Deadline:** June 15 **Application Fee:** $10.00 **H.S. Requirements:** High school diploma required; GED accepted **Scholarships:** Available **Calendar System:** Semester, Summer Session Available **Enrollment:** FT 4,153, PT 343, Grad FT 320, Grad PT 511 **Faculty:** FT 314, PT 71 **Student-Faculty Ratio:** 14:1 **Exams:** ACT. **% Receiving Financial Aid:** 78 **Library Holdings:** 507,500 **Regional Accreditation:** Southern Association of Colleges and Schools **Credit Hours For Degree:** 128 semester hours, Bachelors **ROTC:** Army **Professional Accreditation:** ABET, AAFCS, ACSP, ASLHA, CORE, CSWE, NCATE, SAF **Intercollegiate Athletics:** Baseball M; Basketball M & W; Cross-Country Running M & W; Football M; Golf M; Soccer M; Tennis M & W; Track and Field M & W; Volleyball W

ALABAMA SOUTHERN COMMUNITY COLLEGE
PO Box 2000
Monroeville, AL 36461
Tel: (251)575-3156
E-mail: jhorton@ascc.edu
Web Site: http://www.ascc.edu/
President/CEO: William Blow
Admissions: Jana S. Horton
Type: Two-Year College **Sex:** Coed **Affiliation:** Alabama College System **Admission Plans:** Open Admission; Preferred Admission; Early Admission **Application Deadline:** September 10 **Application Fee:** $0.00 **H.S. Requirements:** High school diploma required; GED accepted **Scholarships:** Available **Calendar System:** Semester, Summer Session Available **Library Holdings:** 43,000 **Regional Accreditation:** Southern Association of Colleges and Schools **Credit Hours For Degree:** 64 semester hours, Associates **Intercollegiate Athletics:** Baseball M; Basketball M & W; Softball W

ALABAMA STATE UNIVERSITY
915 South Jackson St.
Montgomery, AL 36101-0271
Tel: (334)229-4100; Free: 800-253-5037
Admissions: (334)229-4291
Fax: (334)229-4984
E-mail: dtruss@alasu.edu
Web Site: http://www.alasu.edu/
President/CEO: Dr. William H. Harris
Admissions: Dr. Donta Truss
Financial Aid: Dorenda A. Adams
Type: Comprehensive **Sex:** Coed **Affiliation:** Alabama Commission on Higher Education **Scores:** 58.5% SAT V 400+; 43.1% SAT M 400+; 31.4% ACT 18-23; 2% ACT 24-29 **% Accepted:** 53 **Admission Plans:** Early Admission; Deferred Admission **Application Deadline:** July 31 **Application Fee:** $25.00 **H.S. Requirements:** High school diploma required; GED accepted **Costs Per Year:** Application fee: $25. One-time mandatory fee: $150. State resident tuition: $5616 full-time, $234 per credit hour part-time. Nonresident tuition: $11,232 full-time, $468 per credit hour part-time. Mandatory fees: $852 full-time, $213 per term part-time. College room and board: $4600. College room only: $2630. Room and board charges vary according to board plan and housing facility. **Scholarships:** Available **Calendar System:** Semester, Summer Session Available **Enrollment:** FT 4,216, PT 422, Grad FT 345, Grad PT 581 **Faculty:** FT 241, PT 167 **Student-Faculty Ratio:** 16:1 **Exams:** SAT I or ACT. ACT essay not being used. SAT essay not being used. **% Receiving Financial Aid:** 86 **% Residing in College-Owned, -Operated, or -Affiliated Housing:** 43 **Library Holdings:** 603,380 **Regional Accreditation:** Southern Association of Colleges and Schools **Credit Hours For Degree:** 129 credit hours, Bachelors **ROTC:** Army, Air Force **Professional Accreditation:** AOTA, APTA, ACBSP, CSWE, NASM, NCATE **Intercollegiate Athletics:** Baseball M; Basketball M & W; Bowling W; Cheerleading M & W; Cross-Country Running M & W; Football M; Golf M & W; Soccer W; Softball W; Tennis M & W; Track and Field M & W; Volleyball W

AMRIDGE UNIVERSITY
1200 Taylor Rd.
Montgomery, AL 36117
Tel: (334)387-3877; Free: 800-351-4040
Fax: (334)387-3878
E-mail: oradavis@amridgeuniversity.edu
Web Site: http://www.amridgeuniversity.edu/
President/CEO: Dr. Michael C. Turner
Admissions: Ora Davis
Financial Aid: Louise Hicks
Type: University **Sex:** Coed **Affiliation:** Church of Christ **Admission Plans:** Open Admission **Application Deadline:** Rolling **Application Fee:** $75.00 **H.S. Requirements:** High school diploma required; GED accepted **Costs Per Year:** Application fee: $75. Tuition: $6900 full-time, $300 per semester hour part-time. Mandatory fees: $800 full-time, $400 per term part-time. Full-time tuition and fees vary according to course load. Part-time tuition and fees vary according to course load. **Scholarships:** Available **Calendar System:** Semester, Summer Session Available **Enrollment:** FT 247, PT 143, Grad FT 141, Grad PT 235 **Faculty:** FT 63, PT 15 **Student-Faculty Ratio:** 11:1 **% Receiving Financial Aid:** 81 **Final Year or Final Semester Residency Requirement:** No **Library Holdings:** 80,000 **Regional Accreditation:** Southern Association of Colleges and Schools **Credit Hours For Degree:** 64 semester hours, Associates; 128 semester hours, Bachelors **Professional Accreditation:** ATS

ANDREW JACKSON UNIVERSITY
2919 John Hawkins Parkway
Birmingham, AL 35244
Tel: (205)871-9288
Fax: (205)871-9294
E-mail: admissions@aju.edu
Web Site: http://www.aju.edu/
President/CEO: E. Donald Kassner

Admissions: Tammy J. Kassner
Type: Comprehensive **Sex:** Coed **% Accepted:** 87 **Admission Plans:** Open Admission **Application Fee:** $75.00 **H.S. Requirements:** High school diploma required; GED accepted **Costs Per Year:** Application fee: $75. Tuition guaranteed not to increase for student's term of enrollment. **Enrollment:** , PT 230, Grad PT 242 **Faculty:** FT 0, PT 50 **Student-Faculty Ratio:** 11:1 **Final Year or Final Semester Residency Requirement:** No **Credit Hours For Degree:** 60 semester hours, Associates; 120 semester hours, Bachelors **Professional Accreditation:** DETC

ATHENS STATE UNIVERSITY
300 North Beaty St.
Athens, AL 35611
Tel: (256)233-8100; Free: 800-522-0272
Fax: (256)233-8164
E-mail: necedah.henderson@athens.edu
Web Site: http://www.athens.edu/
President/CEO: Robert Glenn
Admissions: Necedah Henderson
Financial Aid: Renee Stanford
Type: Two-Year Upper Division **Sex:** Coed **Affiliation:** Alabama College System **Admission Plans:** Open Admission; Deferred Admission **Application Deadline:** Rolling **Application Fee:** $30.00 **H.S. Requirements:** High school diploma required; GED accepted **Costs Per Year:** Application fee: $30. Area resident tuition: $120 per credit hour part-time. State resident tuition: $3600 full-time, $240 per credit hour part-time. Nonresident tuition: $7200 full-time. Mandatory fees: $750 full-time, $25 per credit hour part-time. **Scholarships:** Available **Calendar System:** Semester, Summer Session Available **Faculty:** FT 75, PT 102 **Student-Faculty Ratio:** 23:1 **Library Holdings:** 137,233 **Regional Accreditation:** Southern Association of Colleges and Schools **Credit Hours For Degree:** 124 credit hours, Bachelors **Professional Accreditation:** ACBSP, NCATE

AUBURN UNIVERSITY
Auburn University, AL 36849
Tel: (334)844-4000
Admissions: (334)844-4080
E-mail: admissions@auburn.edu
Web Site: http://www.auburn.edu/
President/CEO: Dr. Jay Gogue, PhD
Admissions: Cindy Singley
Financial Aid: Mike Reynolds
Type: University **Sex:** Coed **Scores:** 99.2% SAT V 400+; 99.5% SAT M 400+; 25.6% ACT 18-23; 51.2% ACT 24-29 **% Accepted:** 80 **Admission Plans:** Early Admission; Early Action; Deferred Admission **Application Deadline:** Rolling **Application Fee:** $40.00 **H.S. Requirements:** High school diploma required; GED accepted **Costs Per Year:** Application fee: $40. State resident tuition: $6240 full-time, $258 per credit hour part-time. Nonresident tuition: $18,720 full-time, $774 per credit hour part-time. Mandatory fees: $732 full-time. Full-time tuition and fees vary according to course load, program, and reciprocity agreements. Part-time tuition varies according to course load, program, and reciprocity agreements. College room and board: $8972. College room only: $4038. Room and board charges vary according to board plan and housing facility. **Scholarships:** Available **Calendar System:** Semester, Summer Session Available **Enrollment:** FT 18,387, PT 1,539, Grad FT 2,609, Grad PT 2,067 **Faculty:** FT 1,184, PT 159 **Student-Faculty Ratio:** 18:1 **Exams:** SAT I or ACT. **% Receiving Financial Aid:** 30 **% Residing in College-Owned, -Operated, or -Affiliated Housing:** 19 **Library Holdings:** 3,053,468 **Regional Accreditation:** Southern Association of Colleges and Schools **Credit Hours For Degree:** 120 semester hours, Bachelors **ROTC:** Army, Navy, Air Force **Professional Accreditation:** AACSB, ABET, ACPhE, ACEJMC, AAMFT, AAFCS, ACCE, ACA, ACSP, APA, ASLA, ASLHA, AVMA, CAA, FIDER, CORE, CSWE, NAAB, NASAD, NASM NASPAA, NAST, NCATE, NLN, SAF **Intercollegiate Athletics:** Baseball M; Basketball M & W; Cross-Country Running M & W; Equestrian Sports W; Football M; Golf M & W; Gymnastics W; Soccer W; Softball W; Swimming and Diving M & W; Tennis M & W; Track and Field M & W; Volleyball W

AUBURN UNIVERSITY MONTGOMERY
PO Box 244023
Montgomery, AL 36124-4023
Tel: (334)244-3000
Admissions: (334)244-3615
Fax: (334)244-3795
E-mail: rmckinne@aum.edu
Web Site: http://www.aum.edu/
President/CEO: Dr. John G. Veres, III
Admissions: Ronnie McKinney
Financial Aid: Anthony Richey
Type: Comprehensive **Sex:** Coed **Affiliation:** Auburn University **Scores:** 62% ACT 18-23; 20% ACT 24-29 **% Accepted:** 95 **Admission Plans:** Deferred Admission **Application Deadline:** Rolling **Application Fee:** $25.00 **H.S. Requirements:** High school diploma required; GED accepted **Costs Per Year:** Application fee: $25. State resident tuition: $5970 full-time, $188 per credit hour part-time. Nonresident tuition: $17,250 full-time, $564 per credit hour part-time. Mandatory fees: $330 full-time, $8 per semester hour part-time, $45 per term part-time. Full-time tuition and fees vary according to course load. Part-time tuition and fees vary according to course load. College room only: $3720. Room charges vary according to housing facility. **Scholarships:** Available **Calendar System:** Semester, Summer Session Available **Enrollment:** FT 3,140, PT 1,538, Grad FT 286, Grad PT 583 **Faculty:** FT 187, PT 121 **Student-Faculty Ratio:** 18:1 **Exams:** SAT I or ACT, SAT I. ACT essay not being used. SAT essay not being used. **% Receiving Financial Aid:** 35 **% Residing in College-Owned, -Operated, or -Affiliated Housing:** 12 **Library Holdings:** 367,620 **Regional Accreditation:** Southern Association of Colleges and Schools **Credit Hours For Degree:** 120 semester hours, Bachelors **ROTC:** Army, Air Force **Professional Accreditation:** AACSB, AACN, NAACLS, NASPAA, NCATE **Intercollegiate Athletics:** Baseball M; Basketball M & W; Cheerleading M & W; Soccer M & W; Softball W; Tennis M & W

BEVILL STATE COMMUNITY COLLEGE
PO Box 800
Sumiton, AL 35148
Tel: (205)648-3271
Admissions: (205)932-3221
Web Site: http://www.bscc.edu/
President/CEO: Dr. Anne McNutt
Admissions: Melissa Stowe
Type: Two-Year College **Sex:** Coed **Affiliation:** Alabama College System **Admission Plans:** Open Admission; Early Admission; Deferred Admission **Application Deadline:** Rolling **H.S. Requirements:** High school diploma required; GED accepted **Costs Per Year:** One-time mandatory fee: $40. State resident tuition: $2720 full-time, $85 per credit hour part-time. Nonresident tuition: $5440 full-time, $170 per credit hour part-time. Mandatory fees: $638 full-time, $11 per credit hour part-time, $15. Full-time tuition and fees vary according to course load. Part-time tuition and fees vary according to course load. College room and board: $1850. College room only: $1185. Room and board charges vary according to housing facility and location. **Scholarships:** Available **Calendar System:** Semester, Summer Session Available **Enrollment:** FT 2,544, PT 2,012 **Faculty:** FT 114, PT 215 **Library Holdings:** 31,690 **Regional Accreditation:** Southern Association of Colleges and Schools **Professional Accreditation:** NAACLS, NLN **Intercollegiate Athletics:** Baseball M; Basketball M; Cross-Country Running W; Softball W; Track and Field W

BIRMINGHAM-SOUTHERN COLLEGE
900 Arkadelphia Rd.
Birmingham, AL 35254
Tel: (205)226-4600; Free: 800-523-5793
Admissions: (205)226-4696
Fax: (205)226-3074
E-mail: admitme@bsc.edu
Web Site: http://www.bsc.edu/
President/CEO: Dr. G. David Pollick
Admissions: Sheri E. Salmon
Type: Comprehensive **Sex:** Coed **Affiliation:** Methodist **Scores:** 97.95% SAT V 400+; 98.41% SAT M 400+; 28.53% ACT 18-23; 51.94% ACT 24-29 **% Accepted:** 59 **Admission Plans:** Deferred Admission **Application Deadline:** Rolling **Application Fee:** $40.00 **H.S. Requirements:** High school diploma required; GED accepted **Scholarships:** Available **Calendar System:** 4-1-4, Summer Session Available **Enrollment:** FT 1,472, PT 36, Grad FT 20, Grad PT 21 **Faculty:** FT 111, PT 32 **Student-Faculty Ratio:** 12:1 **Exams:** SAT I or ACT. **% Receiving Financial Aid:** 53 **% Residing in College-Owned, -Operated, or -Affiliated Housing:** 84 **Regional Accreditation:** Southern Association of Colleges and Schools **Credit Hours For Degree:** 36 courses, Bachelors **ROTC:** Army, Air Force **Professional**

Accreditation: AACSB, NASM, NCATE **Intercollegiate Athletics:** Baseball M; Basketball M & W; Cheerleading M & W; Cross-Country Running M & W; Football M; Golf M & W; Lacrosse M & W; Riflery W; Soccer M & W; Softball W; Table Tennis M & W; Tennis M & W; Track and Field M & W; Volleyball W

BISHOP STATE COMMUNITY COLLEGE
351 North Broad St.
Mobile, AL 36603-5898
Tel: (251)690-6801
Admissions: (251)405-7000
Fax: (251)438-5403
E-mail: info@bishop.edu
Web Site: http://www.bscc.cc.al.us/
President/CEO: James Lowe
Admissions: Dr. Terry Hazzard
Type: Two-Year College **Sex:** Coed **Affiliation:** Alabama College System **Admission Plans:** Open Admission; Early Admission; Deferred Admission **Application Deadline:** Rolling **Application Fee:** $0.00 **H.S. Requirements:** High school diploma required; GED accepted **Costs Per Year:** Application fee: $0. State resident tuition: $1704 full-time, $71 per credit part-time. Nonresident tuition: $3408 full-time, $142 per credit part-time. Mandatory fees: $456 full-time, $19 per credit part-time. **Scholarships:** Available **Calendar System:** Semester, Summer Session Available **Enrollment:** FT 2,035, PT 2,035 **Faculty:** FT 121, PT 88 **Student-Faculty Ratio:** 17:1 **Library Holdings:** 53,883 **Regional Accreditation:** Southern Association of Colleges and Schools **Credit Hours For Degree:** 96 credit hours, Associates **Professional Accreditation:** ABFSE, ACF, AHIMA, APTA, ACBSP, NLN **Intercollegiate Athletics:** Baseball M; Basketball M & W; Softball W

CALHOUN COMMUNITY COLLEGE
PO Box 2216
Decatur, AL 35609-2216
Tel: (256)306-2500
Fax: (256)306-2877
E-mail: pml@calhoun.edu
Web Site: http://www.calhoun.edu/
President/CEO: Dr. Marilyn C. Beck
Admissions: Patricia Landers
Type: Two-Year College **Sex:** Coed **Affiliation:** Alabama College System **% Accepted:** 100 **Admission Plans:** Open Admission **Application Deadline:** Rolling **Application Fee:** $0.00 **H.S. Requirements:** High school diploma required; GED accepted **Costs Per Year:** Application fee: $0. State resident tuition: $1704 full-time, $71 per credit hour part-time. Nonresident tuition: $3408 full-time, $142 per credit hour part-time. Mandatory fees: $576 full-time, $24 per credit hour part-time. **Scholarships:** Available **Calendar System:** Semester, Summer Session Available **Enrollment:** FT 3,063, PT 5,486 **Faculty:** FT 117, PT 307 **Student-Faculty Ratio:** 21:1 **Exams:** SAT I or ACT. **Library Holdings:** 36,699 **Regional Accreditation:** Southern Association of Colleges and Schools **Credit Hours For Degree:** 64 semester hours, Associates **Professional Accreditation:** ADA, NLN

CENTRAL ALABAMA COMMUNITY COLLEGE
1675 Cherokee Rd.
Alexander City, AL 35011-0699
Tel: (256)234-6346
Fax: (256)234-0384
Web Site: http://www.cacc.edu/
President/CEO: Dr. Stephen Franks
Admissions: Donna Whaley
Financial Aid: Cindy Entrekin
Type: Two-Year College **Sex:** Coed **Affiliation:** Alabama College System **Admission Plans:** Open Admission; Early Admission **Application Deadline:** September 9 **Application Fee:** $0.00 **H.S. Requirements:** High school diploma required; GED accepted **Scholarships:** Available **Calendar System:** Semester, Summer Session Available **Enrollment:** FT 1,304, PT 873 **Faculty:** FT 52, PT 141 **Student-Faculty Ratio:** 15:1 **Exams:** SAT I or ACT. **Library Holdings:** 35,000 **Regional Accreditation:** Southern Association of Colleges and Schools **Professional Accreditation:** NLN **Intercollegiate Athletics:** Baseball M; Golf M; Softball W; Tennis M & W; Volleyball W

CHATTAHOOCHEE VALLEY COMMUNITY COLLEGE
2602 College Dr.
Phenix City, AL 36869-7928
Tel: (334)291-4900
Fax: (334)291-4994
E-mail: information@cv.edu
Web Site: http://www.cv.edu/
President/CEO: Dr. Laurel Blackwell
Admissions: Rita Cherry
Financial Aid: Joan B. Waters
Type: Two-Year College **Sex:** Coed **Admission Plans:** Open Admission; Preferred Admission; Early Admission **Application Deadline:** Rolling **Application Fee:** $0.00 **H.S. Requirements:** High school diploma required; GED accepted **Scholarships:** Available **Calendar System:** Semester, Summer Session Available **Enrollment:** FT 972, PT 1,062 **Faculty:** FT 28, PT 60 **Library Holdings:** 54,129 **Regional Accreditation:** Southern Association of Colleges and Schools **Professional Accreditation:** NLN **Intercollegiate Athletics:** Baseball M; Softball W

COLUMBIA SOUTHERN UNIVERSITY
21982 University Ln.
PO Box 3110
Orange Beach, AL 36561
Tel: (251)981-3771; Free: 800-977-8449
Fax: (251)981-3815
E-mail: admissions@columbiasouthern.edu
Web Site: http://www.columbiasouthern.edu/
President/CEO: Robert G. Mayes
Type: Comprehensive **Sex:** Coed **% Accepted:** 100 **Admission Plans:** Open Admission **Application Deadline:** Rolling **Application Fee:** $25.00 **H.S. Requirements:** High school diploma required; GED accepted **Calendar System:** Miscellaneous, Summer Session Not available **Enrollment:** FT 17,728, Grad FT 4,829 **Faculty:** FT 41, PT 205 **Final Year or Final Semester Residency Requirement:** No **Credit Hours For Degree:** 60 credit hours, Associates; 120 credit hours, Bachelors **Professional Accreditation:** DETC

COMMUNITY COLLEGE OF THE AIR FORCE
130 West Maxwell Blvd.
Maxwell Air Force Base, AL 36112-6613
Tel: (334)953-2223
Admissions: (334)649-5000
Fax: (334)953-8211
E-mail: ronald.hall@maxwell.af.mil
Web Site: http://www.au.af.mil/au/ccaf/
President/CEO: Timothy W. Albrecht
Admissions: C.M. Sgt. Robert McAlexander
Type: Two-Year College **Sex:** Coed **% Accepted:** 100 **Admission Plans:** Open Admission **Application Deadline:** Rolling **Application Fee:** $0.00 **H.S. Requirements:** High school diploma or equivalent not required **Calendar System:** Continuous, Summer Session Not available **Enrollment:** FT 351,715 **Faculty:** FT 6,720, PT 0 **Exams:** Other. **Library Holdings:** 5,000,000 **Regional Accreditation:** Southern Association of Colleges and Schools **Credit Hours For Degree:** 64 semester hours, Associates **Professional Accreditation:** APTA

CONCORDIA COLLEGE
1804 Green St.
Selma, AL 36703
Tel: (334)874-5700
Fax: (334)874-3728
E-mail: prichrdson@concordiaselma.edu
Web Site: http://www.concordiaselma.edu/
President/CEO: Dr. Portia Shields
Admissions: Phyllis Richardson
Financial Aid: T. H. Bridges
Type: Four-Year College **Sex:** Coed **Affiliation:** Lutheran; Concordia University System **Admission Plans:** Open Admission; Deferred Admission **Application Deadline:** August 15 **Application Fee:** $10.00 **H.S. Requirements:** High school diploma required; GED accepted **Scholarships:** Available **Calendar System:** Semester, Summer Session Not available **Exams:** ACT. **% Receiving Financial Aid:** 79 **Library Holdings:** 60,000 **Regional Accreditation:** Southern Association of Colleges and Schools **Credit Hours For Degree:** 64 credits, Associates; 130 credits, Bachelors

ENTERPRISE STATE COMMUNITY COLLEGE
PO Box 1300
Enterprise, AL 36331-1300
Tel: (334)347-2623
E-mail: gdeas@eocc.edu
Web Site: http://www.escc.edu/
President/CEO: Nancy Chandler, EdD
Admissions: Gary Deas
Type: Two-Year College **Sex:** Coed **Affiliation:** Alabama College System **Admission Plans:** Open Admission; Early Admission; Deferred Admission **Application Deadline:** Rolling **Application Fee:** $0.00 **H.S. Requirements:** High school diploma required; GED accepted **Scholarships:** Available **Calendar System:** Semester, Summer Session Available **Library Holdings:** 45,076 **Regional Accreditation:** Southern Association of Colleges and Schools **Intercollegiate Athletics:** Baseball M; Basketball M & W; Cheerleading M & W; Softball W

FAULKNER UNIVERSITY
5345 Atlanta Hwy.
Montgomery, AL 36109-3398
Tel: (334)386-7324; Free: 800-879-9816
Admissions: (334)386-7200
Fax: (334)386-7268
E-mail: admissions@faulkner.edu
Web Site: http://www.faulkner.edu/
President/CEO: Dr. Billy D. Hilyer
Admissions: Keith Mock
Financial Aid: William G. Jackson, II
Type: Comprehensive **Sex:** Coed **Affiliation:** Church of Christ **Scores:** 84.5% SAT V 400+; 86% SAT M 400+; 65.75% ACT 18-23; 15.5% ACT 24-29 **% Accepted:** 58 **Admission Plans:** Early Admission; Deferred Admission **Application Deadline:** Rolling **Application Fee:** $25.00 **H.S. Requirements:** High school diploma required; GED accepted **Costs Per Year:** Application fee: $25. Comprehensive fee: $21,380 includes full-time tuition ($13,740), mandatory fees ($1070), and college room and board ($6570). Full-time tuition and fees vary according to program. Room and board charges vary according to board plan and housing facility. Part-time tuition: $480 per semester hour. Part-time mandatory fees: $270 per semester hour, $60 per term. **Scholarships:** Available **Calendar System:** Semester, Summer Session Available **Enrollment:** FT 2,071, PT 768, Grad FT 450, Grad PT 60 **Faculty:** FT 125, PT 206 **Student-Faculty Ratio:** 12:1 **Exams:** SAT I or ACT. **Library Holdings:** 230,000 **Regional Accreditation:** Southern Association of Colleges and Schools **Credit Hours For Degree:** 64 semester hours, Associates; 126 semester hours, Bachelors **ROTC:** Army, Air Force **Professional Accreditation:** ABA **Intercollegiate Athletics:** Baseball M; Basketball M & W; Cheerleading M & W; Football M; Golf M & W; Soccer M & W; Softball W; Volleyball W

GADSDEN STATE COMMUNITY COLLEGE
PO Box 227
Gadsden, AL 35902-0227
Tel: (256)549-8200; Free: 800-226-5563
Admissions: (256)549-8210
Fax: (256)549-8444
E-mail: info@gadsdenstate.edu
Web Site: http://www.gadsdenstate.edu/
President/CEO: Dr. Darryl Harrison
Admissions: Dr. Teresa Rhea
Financial Aid: Kelly D'Eath
Type: Two-Year College **Sex:** Coed **Affiliation:** Alabama Community College System **Admission Plans:** Open Admission; Early Admission; Deferred Admission **Application Deadline:** Rolling **Application Fee:** $0.00 **H.S. Requirements:** High school diploma required; GED accepted. For autobody repair, auto service technology, carpentry, construction management, diesel mechanics, welding, cosmetology: High school diploma required; GED not accepted **Costs Per Year:** Application fee: $0. State resident tuition: $3240 full-time, $90 per credit hour part-time. Nonresident tuition: $6300 full-time, $175 per credit hour part-time. Mandatory fees: $684 full-time, $19 per credit hour part-time. Full-time tuition and fees vary according to reciprocity agreements. Part-time tuition and fees vary according to reciprocity agreements. College room and board: $3200. **Scholarships:** Available **Calendar System:** Semester, Summer Session Available **Enrollment:** FT 3,354, PT 2,449 **Faculty:** FT 150, PT 196 **Student-Faculty Ratio:** 17:1 **% Residing in College-Owned, -Operated, or -Affiliated Housing:** 2 **Final Year or Final Semester Residency Requirement:** No **Library Holdings:** 109,568 **Regional Accreditation:** Southern Association of Colleges and Schools **Credit Hours For Degree:** 60 credit hours, Associates **ROTC:** Army **Professional Accreditation:** ACBSP, JRCERT, JRCEMT, NAACLS, NLN **Intercollegiate Athletics:** Baseball M; Basketball M & W; Cross-Country Running W; Softball W; Tennis M; Volleyball W

GEORGE C. WALLACE COMMUNITY COLLEGE
1141 Wallace Dr.
Dothan, AL 36303-9234
Tel: (334)983-3521; Free: 800-543-2426
Fax: (334)983-3600
E-mail: ksaulsberry@wallace.edu
Web Site: http://www.wallace.edu/
President/CEO: Dr. Linda C. Young
Admissions: Keith Saulsberry
Type: Two-Year College **Sex:** Coed **Affiliation:** The Alabama Community College System **Admission Plans:** Open Admission; Early Admission **Application Deadline:** Rolling **Application Fee:** $0.00 **H.S. Requirements:** High school diploma required; GED accepted. For various technical programs: High school diploma required; GED not accepted **Costs Per Year:** Application fee: $0. State resident tuition: $4680 full-time, $90 per credit hour part-time. Nonresident tuition: $9630 full-time, $180 per credit hour part-time. Mandatory fees: $19 per credit hour part-time. **Scholarships:** Available **Calendar System:** Semester, Summer Session Not available **Enrollment:** FT 2,633, PT 2,022 **Faculty:** FT 126, PT 115 **Exams:** SAT I or ACT. **Library Holdings:** 45,000 **Regional Accreditation:** Southern Association of Colleges and Schools **Professional Accreditation:** AAMAE, APTA, CARC, JRCERT, JRCEMT, NLN **Intercollegiate Athletics:** Baseball M; Softball W

GEORGE CORLEY WALLACE STATE COMMUNITY COLLEGE
PO Box 2530
Selma, AL 36702
Tel: (334)876-9227
Fax: (334)876-9250
Web Site: http://www.wccs.edu/
President/CEO: Dr. James M. Mitchell
Admissions: Sunette Newman
Type: Two-Year College **Sex:** Coed **Affiliation:** Alabama College System **Admission Plans:** Open Admission; Early Admission; Deferred Admission **Application Deadline:** Rolling **Application Fee:** $0.00 **H.S. Requirements:** High school diploma required; GED accepted **Costs Per Year:** Application fee: $0. State resident tuition: $1704 full-time, $71 per credit hour part-time. Nonresident tuition: $3408 full-time, $142 per credit hour part-time. Mandatory fees: $456 full-time, $19 per credit hour part-time. Part-time tuition and fees vary according to course load. **Scholarships:** Available **Calendar System:** Semester, Summer Session Available **Library Holdings:** 16,598 **Regional Accreditation:** Southern Association of Colleges and Schools **Credit Hours For Degree:** 64 semester hours, Associates **Professional Accreditation:** NLN **Intercollegiate Athletics:** Baseball M; Basketball M

H. COUNCILL TRENHOLM STATE TECHNICAL COLLEGE
1225 Air Base Blvd.
Montgomery, AL 36108-2699
Tel: (334)420-4200
Admissions: (334)420-4306
Fax: (334)420-4201
E-mail: tmcbryde@trenholmstate.edu
Web Site: http://www.trenholmstate.edu/
President/CEO: Samuel Munnerlyn
Admissions: Tennie McBryde
Type: Two-Year College **Sex:** Coed **Affiliation:** Alabama Department of Postsecondary Education **% Accepted:** 55 **Admission Plans:** Open Admission; Early Admission **Application Deadline:** Rolling **Application Fee:** $0.00 **H.S. Requirements:** High school diploma required; GED accepted. For apparel and design, autobody repair, cosmetology, diesel mechanic, nursing assistant, truck driving, welding: High school diploma required; GED not accepted **Costs Per Year:** Application fee: $0. State resident tuition: $2550 full-time, $85 per credit hour part-time. Nonresident tuition: $5100 full-time, $170 per credit hour part-time. Mandatory fees: $570 full-time, $19 per credit hour part-time. **Scholarships:** Available **Calendar System:** Semester, Summer Session Available **Faculty:** FT 74, PT 73 **Student-Faculty Ratio:**

10:1 **Exams:** ACT. **Library Holdings:** 40,004 **Credit Hours For Degree:** 64 credit hours, Associates **Professional Accreditation:** COE

HERITAGE CHRISTIAN UNIVERSITY
PO Box HCU
Florence, AL 35630
Tel: (256)766-6610; Free: 800-367-3565
Fax: (256)760-0981
E-mail: ccollins@hcu.edu
Web Site: http://www.hcu.edu/
President/CEO: Dennis Jones
Admissions: Cory Collins
Financial Aid: Mechelle Thompson
Type: Comprehensive **Sex:** Coed **Affiliation:** Church of Christ **Admission Plans:** Open Admission; Preferred Admission; Early Admission; Deferred Admission **Application Deadline:** Rolling **Application Fee:** $25.00 **H.S. Requirements:** High school diploma required; GED accepted **Costs Per Year:** Application fee: $25. One-time mandatory fee: $300. Comprehensive fee: $17,265 includes full-time tuition ($11,360), mandatory fees ($480), and college room and board ($5425). College room only: $3000. Room and board charges vary according to housing facility. Part-time tuition: $355 per credit hour. Part-time mandatory fees: $20 per credit hour. **Scholarships:** Available **Calendar System:** Semester, Summer Session Available **Enrollment:** FT 45, PT 36, Grad FT 5, Grad PT 33 **Faculty:** FT 5, PT 15 **Exams:** Other. **% Residing in College-Owned, -Operated, or -Affiliated Housing:** 60 **Final Year or Final Semester Residency Requirement:** Yes **Library Holdings:** 70,501 **Credit Hours For Degree:** 65 semester hours, Associates; 128 semester hours, Bachelors **Professional Accreditation:** ABHE

HERZING COLLEGE
280 West Valley Ave.
Birmingham, AL 35209
Tel: (205)916-2800
Fax: (205)916-2807
E-mail: admiss@bhm.herzing.edu
Web Site: http://www.herzing.edu/birmingham/
President/CEO: Donald E. Lewis
Admissions: Tess Anderson
Type: Two-Year College **Sex:** Coed **Affiliation:** Herzing Institutes, Inc. **Admission Plans:** Early Admission; Deferred Admission **Application Deadline:** Rolling **Application Fee:** $0.00 **H.S. Requirements:** High school diploma required; GED accepted **Scholarships:** Available **Calendar System:** Semester, Summer Session Available **Professional Accreditation:** ACCSCT

HUNTINGDON COLLEGE
1500 East Fairview Ave.
Montgomery, AL 36106-2148
Tel: (334)833-4222; Free: 800-763-0313
Admissions: (334)833-4497
Fax: (334)833-4347
E-mail: admiss@huntingdon.edu
Web Site: http://www.huntingdon.edu/
President/CEO: Rev. J. Cameron West
Financial Aid: Belinda Goris Duett
Type: Four-Year College **Sex:** Coed **Affiliation:** United Methodist **Scores:** 100% SAT V 400+; 88% SAT M 400+; 72% ACT 18-23; 25% ACT 24-29 **% Accepted:** 67 **Admission Plans:** Deferred Admission **Application Deadline:** August 15 **Application Fee:** $0.00 **H.S. Requirements:** High school diploma required; GED accepted **Costs Per Year:** Application fee: $0. Comprehensive fee: $28,990 includes full-time tuition ($19,990), mandatory fees ($1000), and college room and board ($8000). Full-time tuition and fees vary according to course load, program, and student level. Room and board charges vary according to housing facility. Part-time tuition: $830 per credit hour. Part-time tuition varies according to course load and program. Tuition guaranteed not to increase for student's term of enrollment. **Scholarships:** Available **Calendar System:** Semester, Summer Session Available **Enrollment:** FT 857, PT 218 **Faculty:** FT 45, PT 75 **Student-Faculty Ratio:** 13:1 **Exams:** SAT I or ACT. **% Receiving Financial Aid:** 70 **% Residing in College-Owned, -Operated, or -Affiliated Housing:** 41 **Final Year or Final Semester Residency Requirement:** Yes **Library Holdings:** 170,439 **Regional Accreditation:** Southern Association of Colleges and Schools **Credit Hours For Degree:** 120 semester hours, Bachelors **ROTC:** Army, Air Force **Professional Accreditation:** NASM **Intercollegiate Athletics:** Baseball M; Basketball M & W; Cross-Country Running M & W; Football M; Golf M & W; Soccer M & W; Softball W; Tennis M & W; Volleyball W

ITT TECHNICAL INSTITUTE (BESSEMER)
6270 Park South Dr.
Bessemer, AL 35022
Tel: (205)497-5700
Fax: (205)991-5025
Web Site: http://www.itt-tech.edu/
President/CEO: Allen Rice
Type: Two-Year College **Sex:** Coed **Affiliation:** ITT Educational Services, Inc. **H.S. Requirements:** High school diploma required; GED accepted **Scholarships:** Available **Calendar System:** Quarter, Summer Session Not available **Professional Accreditation:** ACICS

ITT TECHNICAL INSTITUTE (MADISON)
9238 Madison Blvd., Ste. 500
Madison, AL 35758
Tel: (256)542-2900; Free: 877-210-4900
Admissions: (256)542-2900
Web Site: http://www.itt-tech.edu/
President/CEO: Kenya Cook
Type: Two-Year College **Sex:** Coed **Affiliation:** ITT Educational Services, Inc.

ITT TECHNICAL INSTITUTE (MOBILE)
Office Mall South
3100 Cottage Hill Rd., Bldg. 3
Mobile, AL 36606
Tel: (251)472-4760; Free: 877-327-1013
Admissions: (251)472-4760
Web Site: http://www.itt-tech.edu/
President/CEO: Marianne Rittner-Holmes
Type: Two-Year College **Sex:** Coed **Affiliation:** ITT Educational Services, Inc.

J. F. DRAKE STATE TECHNICAL COLLEGE
3421 Meridian St. North
Huntsville, AL 35811-1584
Tel: (256)539-8161; Free: 888-413-7253
E-mail: sudeall@drakestate.edu
Web Site: http://www.drakestate.edu/
President/CEO: Helen McAlpine, EdD
Admissions: Monica Sudeall
Type: Two-Year College **Sex:** Coed **Affiliation:** Alabama Department of Postsecondary Education **% Accepted:** 69 **Admission Plans:** Open Admission; Deferred Admission **Application Deadline:** Rolling **Application Fee:** $0.00 **H.S. Requirements:** High school diploma required; GED accepted **Costs Per Year:** Application fee: $0. State resident tuition: $2160 full-time, $72 per credit hour part-time. Nonresident tuition: $4320 full-time, $144 per credit hour part-time. Mandatory fees: $135 full-time, $18 per credit hour part-time. **Calendar System:** Semester, Summer Session Not available **Enrollment:** FT 754, PT 504 **Faculty:** FT 25, PT 47 **Student-Faculty Ratio:** 17:1 **Credit Hours For Degree:** 72 semester hours, Associates **Professional Accreditation:** COE

JACKSONVILLE STATE UNIVERSITY
700 Pelham Rd. North
Jacksonville, AL 36265-1602
Tel: (256)782-5781; Free: 800-231-5291
Admissions: (256)782-5363
Fax: (256)782-5291
E-mail: info@jsu.edu
Web Site: http://www.jsu.edu/
President/CEO: Dr. William Meehan
Admissions: Martha Mitchell
Financial Aid: Vickie Adams
Type: Comprehensive **Sex:** Coed **Scores:** 76.76% SAT V 400+; 78.84% SAT M 400+; 51.62% ACT 18-23; 15.85% ACT 24-29 **% Accepted:** 88 **Admission Plans:** Early Admission; Deferred Admission **Application Deadline:** Rolling **Application Fee:** $30.00 **H.S. Requirements:** High school diploma required; GED accepted **Costs Per Year:** Application fee: $30. State resident tuition: $6240 full-time, $208 per credit hour part-time. Nonresident tuition: $12,480 full-time, $416 per credit hour part-time. College

room and board: $5254. Room and board charges vary according to board plan and housing facility. **Scholarships:** Available **Calendar System:** Semester, Summer Session Available **Enrollment:** FT 5,957, PT 1,927, Grad FT 294, Grad PT 1,173 **Student-Faculty Ratio:** 20:1 **Exams:** SAT I or ACT. **% Receiving Financial Aid:** 78 **% Residing in College-Owned, -Operated, or -Affiliated Housing:** 22 **Library Holdings:** 685,991 **Regional Accreditation:** Southern Association of Colleges and Schools **Credit Hours For Degree:** 128 semester hours, Bachelors **ROTC:** Army **Professional Accreditation:** AACSB, AACN, AAFCS, CSWE, NASAD, NASM, NAST, NCATE, NAIT **Intercollegiate Athletics:** Baseball M; Basketball M & W; Cross-Country Running M & W; Football M; Golf M & W; Riflery M & W; Soccer W; Softball W; Tennis M & W; Volleyball W

JAMES H. FAULKNER STATE COMMUNITY COLLEGE
1900 Hwy. 31 South
Bay Minette, AL 36507
Tel: (251)580-2100; Free: 800-231-3752
Fax: (251)580-2285
E-mail: cmikkelsen@faulknerstate.edu
Web Site: http://www.faulknerstate.edu/
President/CEO: Gary Branch
Admissions: Carmelita Mikkelsen
Type: Two-Year College **Sex:** Coed **Affiliation:** Alabama College System **Admission Plans:** Open Admission; Early Admission; Deferred Admission **Application Deadline:** Rolling **Application Fee:** $0.00 **H.S. Requirements:** High school diploma required; GED accepted **Scholarships:** Available **Calendar System:** Semester, Summer Session Not available **Enrollment:** FT 2,139, PT 1,184 **Faculty:** FT 63, PT 130 **Student-Faculty Ratio:** 15:1 **% Residing in College-Owned, -Operated, or -Affiliated Housing:** 9 **Library Holdings:** 53,100 **Regional Accreditation:** Southern Association of Colleges and Schools **Credit Hours For Degree:** 60 semester hours, Associates **Professional Accreditation:** ARCEST, ACF, ADA **Intercollegiate Athletics:** Baseball M; Basketball M & W; Golf M; Softball W; Tennis M & W; Volleyball W

JEFFERSON DAVIS COMMUNITY COLLEGE
PO Box 958
Brewton, AL 36427-0958
Tel: (251)867-4832
Fax: (251)809-0178
Web Site: http://www.jdcc.edu/
President/CEO: Dr. Susan McBride
Admissions: Robin Sessions
Type: Two-Year College **Sex:** Coed **Admission Plans:** Open Admission; Early Admission **Application Deadline:** Rolling **Application Fee:** $0.00 **H.S. Requirements:** High school diploma required; GED accepted **Scholarships:** Available **Calendar System:** Semester, Summer Session Available **Library Holdings:** 926 **Regional Accreditation:** Southern Association of Colleges and Schools **Credit Hours For Degree:** 60 credit hours, Associates **Professional Accreditation:** NLN **Intercollegiate Athletics:** Baseball M; Basketball M; Softball W; Volleyball W

JEFFERSON STATE COMMUNITY COLLEGE
2601 Carson Rd.
Birmingham, AL 35215-3098
Tel: (205)853-1200
Fax: (205)856-8547
E-mail: lowens@jeffstateonline.com
Web Site: http://www.jeffstateonline.com/
President/CEO: Dr. Judy M. Merritt
Admissions: Lillian Owens
Type: Two-Year College **Sex:** Coed **Affiliation:** Alabama Community College System **Admission Plans:** Open Admission; Early Admission; Deferred Admission **Application Deadline:** Rolling **Application Fee:** $0.00 **H.S. Requirements:** High school diploma required; GED accepted **Costs Per Year:** Application fee: $0. State resident tuition: $3480 full-time, $116 per semester hour part-time. Nonresident tuition: $6030 full-time, $201 per semester hour part-time. Full-time tuition varies according to course load. Part-time tuition varies according to course load. **Scholarships:** Available **Calendar System:** Semester, Summer Session Available **Enrollment:** FT 3,270, PT 5,278 **Faculty:** FT 146, PT 295 **Student-Faculty Ratio:** 20:1 **Library Holdings:** 150,000 **Regional Accreditation:** Southern Association of Colleges and Schools **Credit Hours For Degree:** 60 semester hours, Associates **ROTC:** Army, Air Force **Professional Accreditation:** ABFSE, ACCE, ACF, APTA, ACBSP, JRCERT, NAACLS, NLN **Intercollegiate Athletics:** Baseball M; Softball W

JUDSON COLLEGE
302 Bibb St.
PO Box 120
Marion, AL 36756
Tel: (334)683-5100; Free: 800-447-9472
Admissions: (334)683-5110
Fax: (334)683-5158
E-mail: admissions@judson.edu
Web Site: http://www.judson.edu/
President/CEO: Dr. David E. Potts
Admissions: Charlotte S. Clements
Financial Aid: Doris A. Wilson
Type: Four-Year College **Sex:** Women **Affiliation:** Baptist **Scores:** 100% SAT V 400+; 80% SAT M 400+; 49% ACT 18-23; 45% ACT 24-29 **% Accepted:** 82 **Admission Plans:** Early Admission; Deferred Admission **Application Deadline:** Rolling **Application Fee:** $35.00 **H.S. Requirements:** High school diploma required; GED accepted **Costs Per Year:** Application fee: $35. One-time mandatory fee: $110. Comprehensive fee: $21,835 includes full-time tuition ($12,960), mandatory fees ($575), and college room and board ($8300). Full-time tuition and fees vary according to course load. Part-time tuition: $432 per semester hour. Part-time tuition varies according to course load. **Scholarships:** Available **Calendar System:** Semester, Summer Session Available **Enrollment:** FT 248, PT 65 **Faculty:** FT 19, PT 33 **Student-Faculty Ratio:** 9:1 **Exams:** SAT I or ACT. ACT essay not being used. SAT essay not being used. **% Receiving Financial Aid:** 85 **% Residing in College-Owned, -Operated, or -Affiliated Housing:** 62 **Final Year or Final Semester Residency Requirement:** No **Library Holdings:** 71,155 **Regional Accreditation:** Southern Association of Colleges and Schools **Credit Hours For Degree:** 128 semester hours, Bachelors **ROTC:** Army **Professional Accreditation:** NASM **Intercollegiate Athletics:** Basketball W; Equestrian Sports W; Soccer W; Softball W; Tennis W; Volleyball W

LAWSON STATE COMMUNITY COLLEGE
3060 Wilson Rd., SW
Birmingham, AL 35221-1798
Tel: (205)925-2515
Admissions: (205)929-6361
Fax: (205)929-6316
E-mail: jshelley@lawsonstate.edu
Web Site: http://www.lawsonstate.edu/
President/CEO: Perry W. Ward
Admissions: Jeff Shelley
Type: Two-Year College **Sex:** Coed **Affiliation:** Alabama Community College System **% Accepted:** 83 **Admission Plans:** Open Admission; Early Admission; Deferred Admission **Application Deadline:** Rolling **Application Fee:** $0.00 **H.S. Requirements:** High school diploma required; GED accepted **Costs Per Year:** Application fee: $0. State resident tuition: $2160 full-time. Nonresident tuition: $4320 full-time. Mandatory fees: $850 full-time. College room and board: $2000. Room and board charges vary according to board plan. **Scholarships:** Available **Calendar System:** Semester, Summer Session Available **Enrollment:** FT 2,542, PT 1,811 **Faculty:** FT 94, PT 124 **Student-Faculty Ratio:** 17:1 **% Residing in College-Owned, -Operated, or -Affiliated Housing:** 1 **Library Holdings:** 69,249 **Regional Accreditation:** Southern Association of Colleges and Schools **Credit Hours For Degree:** 60 credit hours, Associates **Professional Accreditation:** ACBSP, NLN **Intercollegiate Athletics:** Basketball M & W; Cross-Country Running M; Equestrian Sports M; Volleyball W

LURLEEN B. WALLACE COMMUNITY COLLEGE
PO Box 1418
Andalusia, AL 36420-1418
Tel: (334)222-6591
Admissions: (334)881-2273
E-mail: mstephens@lbwcc.edu
Web Site: http://www.lbwcc.edu/
President/CEO: Dr. Herbert H. J. Riedel
Admissions: Mackie Stephens
Type: Two-Year College **Sex:** Coed **Affiliation:** Alabama College System **Admission Plans:** Open Admission **Application Deadline:** Rolling **Application Fee:** $0.00 **H.S. Requirements:** High school diploma required;

GED accepted. For some technical programs: High school diploma required; GED not accepted **Costs Per Year:** Application fee: $0. State resident tuition: $3270 full-time, $109 per credit hour part-time. Nonresident tuition: $5820 full-time, $194 per credit hour part-time. Full-time tuition varies according to course load. Part-time tuition varies according to course load. **Scholarships:** Available **Calendar System:** Semester, Summer Session Available **Enrollment:** FT 1,088, PT 703 **Faculty:** FT 51, PT 59 **Student-Faculty Ratio:** 16:1 **Library Holdings:** 40,004 **Regional Accreditation:** Southern Association of Colleges and Schools **Credit Hours For Degree:** 60 credits, Associates **Professional Accreditation:** JRCEMT **Intercollegiate Athletics:** Baseball M; Basketball M & W; Softball W

MARION MILITARY INSTITUTE
1101 Washington St.
Marion, AL 36756
Tel: (334)683-2306
Admissions: 800-664-1842
Fax: (334)683-2380
Web Site: http://www.marionmilitary.org/
President/CEO: Col. David J. Mollahan
Type: Two-Year College **Sex:** Coed **% Accepted:** 84 **Admission Plans:** Deferred Admission **Application Deadline:** August 30 **Application Fee:** $35.00 **H.S. Requirements:** High school diploma required; GED accepted **Scholarships:** Available **Calendar System:** Semester, Summer Session Not available **Faculty:** FT 40, PT 4 **Student-Faculty Ratio:** 6:1 **% Residing in College-Owned, -Operated, or -Affiliated Housing:** 97 **Library Holdings:** 36,000 **Regional Accreditation:** Southern Association of Colleges and Schools **Credit Hours For Degree:** 64 credit hours, Associates **ROTC:** Army, Air Force **Intercollegiate Athletics:** Golf M & W; Soccer M & W; Tennis M & W

MILES COLLEGE
5500 Myron Massey Blvd.
Fairfield, AL 35064
Tel: (205)929-1000; Free: 800-445-0708
Admissions: (205)929-1657
E-mail: admissions@miles.edu
Web Site: http://www.miles.edu/
President/CEO: Dr. George T. French
Admissions: Christopher Robertson
Financial Aid: P. N. Lanier
Type: Four-Year College **Sex:** Coed **Affiliation:** Christian Methodist Episcopal **Scores:** 10% ACT 18-23; 1% ACT 24-29 **% Accepted:** 26 **Admission Plans:** Open Admission **Application Deadline:** August 23 **Application Fee:** $0.00 **H.S. Requirements:** High school diploma required; GED accepted **Scholarships:** Available **Calendar System:** Semester, Summer Session Available **Enrollment:** FT 1,589, PT 149 **Faculty:** FT 105, PT 42 **Student-Faculty Ratio:** 14:1 **Exams:** ACT, Other. **% Receiving Financial Aid:** 99 **% Residing in College-Owned, -Operated, or -Affiliated Housing:** 40 **Library Holdings:** 180,000 **Regional Accreditation:** Southern Association of Colleges and Schools **Credit Hours For Degree:** 124 semester hours, Bachelors **ROTC:** Army, Air Force **Professional Accreditation:** CSWE **Intercollegiate Athletics:** Baseball M; Basketball M & W; Cheerleading W; Cross-Country Running M; Football M; Softball W; Track and Field M

NORTHEAST ALABAMA COMMUNITY COLLEGE
PO Box 159
Rainsville, AL 35986-0159
Tel: (256)228-6001
E-mail: niblett@nacc.edu
Web Site: http://www.nacc.edu/
President/CEO: Dr. David Campbell
Admissions: Tonie Niblett
Type: Two-Year College **Sex:** Coed **Affiliation:** Alabama College System **Admission Plans:** Open Admission **Application Deadline:** Rolling **Application Fee:** $0.00 **H.S. Requirements:** High school diploma required; GED accepted **Costs Per Year:** Application fee: $0. State resident tuition: $2850 full-time, $95 per semester hour part-time. Nonresident tuition: $4980 full-time, $166 per semester hour part-time. **Calendar System:** Quarter, Summer Session Available **Enrollment:** FT 1,235, PT 1,278 **Faculty:** FT 43, PT 160 **Student-Faculty Ratio:** 30:1 **Library Holdings:** 45,000 **Regional Accreditation:** Southern Association of Colleges and Schools **Credit Hours For Degree:** 96 quarter hours, Associates **Professional Accreditation:** JRCEMT, NLN

NORTHWEST-SHOALS COMMUNITY COLLEGE
PO Box 2545
Muscle Shoals, AL 35662
Tel: (256)331-5200
Admissions: (256)331-5261
Fax: (256)331-5366
E-mail: berryk@nwscc.edu
Web Site: http://www.nwscc.edu/
President/CEO: Dr. Humphrey Lee
Admissions: Dr. Karen Berryhill
Financial Aid: Joel Parris
Type: Two-Year College **Sex:** Coed **Affiliation:** Alabama Department of Postsecondary Education **% Accepted:** 100 **Admission Plans:** Open Admission **Application Deadline:** Rolling **Application Fee:** $0.00 **H.S. Requirements:** High school diploma required; GED accepted **Costs Per Year:** Application fee: $0. State resident tuition: $2550 full-time, $85 per credit hour part-time. Nonresident tuition: $5100 full-time, $170 per credit hour part-time. Mandatory fees: $765 full-time, $25 per credit hour part-time. Full-time tuition and fees vary according to program. Part-time tuition and fees vary according to program. College room only: $1800. **Scholarships:** Available **Calendar System:** Semester, Summer Session Available **Enrollment:** FT 2,414, PT 2,123 **Faculty:** FT 91, PT 148 **Student-Faculty Ratio:** 22:1 **Exams:** Other. **% Residing in College-Owned, -Operated, or -Affiliated Housing:** 2 **Library Holdings:** 69,048 **Regional Accreditation:** Southern Association of Colleges and Schools **Credit Hours For Degree:** 64 credit hours, Associates **Professional Accreditation:** NLN **Intercollegiate Athletics:** Baseball M; Basketball M & W; Cheerleading M & W; Softball W; Volleyball W

OAKWOOD UNIVERSITY
7000 Adventist Blvd.
Huntsville, AL 35896
Tel: (256)726-7000
Admissions: (256)726-7354
Fax: (256)726-7404
E-mail: admission@oakwood.edu
Web Site: http://www.oakwood.edu/
President/CEO: Dr. Delbert W. Baker
Admissions: Jason McCracken
Type: Comprehensive **Sex:** Coed **Affiliation:** Seventh-day Adventist **Scores:** 82% SAT V 400+; 70% SAT M 400+; 41% ACT 18-23; 11% ACT 24-29 **% Accepted:** 57 **Admission Plans:** Early Action; Deferred Admission **Application Deadline:** Rolling **Application Fee:** $25.00 **H.S. Requirements:** High school diploma required; GED accepted **Scholarships:** Available **Calendar System:** Semester, Summer Session Not available **Enrollment:** FT 1,712, PT 112 **Faculty:** FT 103, PT 68 **Student-Faculty Ratio:** 14:1 **Exams:** SAT I or ACT. **% Receiving Financial Aid:** 90 **% Residing in College-Owned, -Operated, or -Affiliated Housing:** 64 **Library Holdings:** 133,106 **Regional Accreditation:** Southern Association of Colleges and Schools **Credit Hours For Degree:** 64 semester hours, Associates; 128 semester hours, Bachelors **Professional Accreditation:** ADtA, ACBSP, CSWE, NCATE **Intercollegiate Athletics:** Basketball M & W

PRINCE INSTITUTE OF PROFESSIONAL STUDIES
7735 Atlanta Hwy.
Montgomery, AL 36117-4231
Tel: (334)271-1670
Fax: (334)271-1671
E-mail: admissions@princeinstitute.edu
Web Site: http://www.princeinstitute.edu/
President/CEO: Patricia L. Hill
Admissions: Sherry Hill
Financial Aid: Reginald James
Type: Two-Year College **Sex:** Women **% Accepted:** 100 **Application Deadline:** October 1 **Application Fee:** $90.00 **H.S. Requirements:** High school diploma required; GED accepted **Scholarships:** Available **Calendar System:** Quarter **Enrollment:** FT 56, PT 38 **Faculty:** FT 5, PT 2 **Student-Faculty Ratio:** 15:1 **Professional Accreditation:** ACICS

REID STATE TECHNICAL COLLEGE
PO Box 588
Evergreen, AL 36401-0588
Tel: (251)578-1313
Fax: (251)578-5355

Web Site: http://www.rstc.edu/
President/CEO: Dr. Douglas M. Littles
Admissions: Dr. Alesia Stuart
Type: Two-Year College **Sex:** Coed **Affiliation:** Alabama College System **% Accepted:** 100 **Admission Plans:** Open Admission; Early Admission **Application Deadline:** Rolling **Application Fee:** $0.00 **H.S. Requirements:** High school diploma or equivalent not required. For industrial electricity/electronics, administration programs: High school diploma required; GED accepted **Costs Per Year:** Application fee: $0. State resident tuition: $2592 full-time. Nonresident tuition: $5184 full-time. Mandatory fees: $648 full-time. **Scholarships:** Available **Calendar System:** Semester, Summer Session Available **Enrollment:** FT 365, PT 245 **Faculty:** FT 25, PT 11 **Student-Faculty Ratio:** 12:1 **Library Holdings:** 3,800 **Credit Hours For Degree:** 114 credit hours, Associates **Professional Accreditation:** ACBSP, COE

REMINGTON COLLEGE—MOBILE CAMPUS
828 Downtowner Loop West
Mobile, AL 36609-5404
Tel: (251)343-8200; Free: 800-866-0850
Fax: (251)343-0577
E-mail: david.helveston@remingtoncollege.edu
Web Site: http://www.remingtoncollege.edu/
President/CEO: Steve Backman
Admissions: David Helveston
Financial Aid: Linda Calvanese
Type: Two-Year College **Sex:** Coed **H.S. Requirements:** High school diploma required; GED accepted **Scholarships:** Available **Calendar System:** Quarter, Summer Session Not available **Professional Accreditation:** ACCSCT

SAMFORD UNIVERSITY
800 Lakeshore Dr.
Birmingham, AL 35229
Tel: (205)726-2011; Free: 800-888-7218
Admissions: (205)726-3673
Fax: (205)726-2171
E-mail: jjblack@samford.edu
Web Site: http://www.samford.edu/
President/CEO: Dr. Andrew Westmoreland
Admissions: Jason J. Black
Financial Aid: Lane Smith
Type: University **Sex:** Coed **Affiliation:** Baptist **Scores:** 99% SAT V 400+; 99% SAT M 400+; 30% ACT 18-23; 48% ACT 24-29 **% Accepted:** 84 **Admission Plans:** Early Admission; Deferred Admission **Application Deadline:** Rolling **Application Fee:** $35.00 **H.S. Requirements:** High school diploma required; GED accepted **Costs Per Year:** Application fee: $35. Comprehensive fee: $27,044 includes full-time tuition ($20,200), mandatory fees ($220), and college room and board ($6624). College room only: $3240. Full-time tuition and fees vary according to course load, degree level, and program. Room and board charges vary according to board plan and housing facility. Part-time tuition: $675 per credit. Part-time mandatory fees: $220 per year. Part-time tuition and fees vary according to course load, degree level, and program. **Scholarships:** Available **Calendar System:** 4-1-4, Summer Session Available **Enrollment:** FT 2,702, PT 206, Grad FT 1,452, Grad PT 298 **Faculty:** FT 282, PT 137 **Student-Faculty Ratio:** 12:1 **Exams:** SAT I or ACT. ACT essay not being used. SAT essay not being used. **% Receiving Financial Aid:** 42 **% Residing in College-Owned, -Operated, or -Affiliated Housing:** 67 **Library Holdings:** 439,760 **Regional Accreditation:** Southern Association of Colleges and Schools **Credit Hours For Degree:** 64 semester hours, Associates; 128 semester hours, Bachelors **ROTC:** Army, Air Force **Professional Accreditation:** AACSB, ACPhE, AACN, AAFCS, AANA, ABA, AALS, ATS, FIDER, JRCEPAT, NASM, NCATE **Intercollegiate Athletics:** Baseball M; Basketball M & W; Cross-Country Running M & W; Football M; Golf M & W; Soccer M & W; Softball W; Tennis M & W; Track and Field M & W; Volleyball W

SHELTON STATE COMMUNITY COLLEGE
9500 Old Greensboro Rd.
Tuscaloosa, AL 35405
Tel: (205)391-2211
Admissions: (205)391-2347
Fax: (205)391-2426
Web Site: http://www.sheltonstate.edu/
President/CEO: Dr. Mark A. Heinrich
Admissions: Loretta Jones
Financial Aid: Cindy Green
Type: Two-Year College **Sex:** Coed **Affiliation:** Alabama College System **% Accepted:** 100 **Admission Plans:** Open Admission **Application Deadline:** Rolling **Application Fee:** $0.00 **H.S. Requirements:** High school diploma required; GED accepted **Costs Per Year:** Application fee: $0. State resident tuition: $2130 full-time, $71 per credit hour part-time. Nonresident tuition: $4260 full-time, $142 per credit hour part-time. Mandatory fees: $570 full-time, $18 per credit hour part-time. Full-time tuition and fees vary according to course load and reciprocity agreements. Part-time tuition and fees vary according to course load and reciprocity agreements. **Scholarships:** Available **Calendar System:** Semester, Summer Session Available **Enrollment:** FT 3,363, PT 2,391 **Faculty:** FT 82, PT 117 **Student-Faculty Ratio:** 30:1 **Library Holdings:** 50,123 **Regional Accreditation:** Southern Association of Colleges and Schools **Credit Hours For Degree:** 64 semester hours, Associates **ROTC:** Army, Air Force **Professional Accreditation:** CARC, NLN **Intercollegiate Athletics:** Baseball M; Basketball M & W; Cheerleading M & W; Soccer W; Softball W

SNEAD STATE COMMUNITY COLLEGE
220 N Walnut St., PO Box 734
Boaz, AL 35957-0734
Tel: (256)593-5120
Fax: (256)593-7180
E-mail: gchapman@snead.edu
Web Site: http://www.snead.edu/
President/CEO: Dr. Robert J. Exley
Admissions: Dr. Greg Chapman
Type: Two-Year College **Sex:** Coed **Affiliation:** Alabama College System **Admission Plans:** Open Admission; Early Admission; Deferred Admission **Application Deadline:** August 24 **Application Fee:** $0.00 **H.S. Requirements:** High school diploma required; GED accepted **Scholarships:** Available **Calendar System:** Semester, Summer Session Available **% Residing in College-Owned, -Operated, or -Affiliated Housing:** 2 **Library Holdings:** 40,690 **Regional Accreditation:** Southern Association of Colleges and Schools **Credit Hours For Degree:** 64 semester hours, Associates **Intercollegiate Athletics:** Baseball M; Basketball M & W; Softball W; Tennis W

SOUTH UNIVERSITY
5355 Vaughn Rd.
Montgomery, AL 36116-1120
Tel: (334)395-8800; Free: (866)629-2962
Fax: (334)395-8859
Web Site: http://www.southuniversity.edu/montgomery/
President/CEO: Victor K. Biebighauser
Type: Comprehensive **Sex:** Coed **Affiliation:** Education Management Corporation **Calendar System:** Quarter **Professional Accreditation:** AAMAE, APTA, ACBSP

SOUTHEASTERN BIBLE COLLEGE
2545 Valleydale Rd.
Birmingham, AL 35244-2083
Tel: (205)970-9200
Admissions: (205)970-9211
Fax: (205)970-9207
E-mail: wharrison@sebc.edu
Web Site: http://www.sebc.edu/
President/CEO: Dr. Don Hawkins
Admissions: Walker Harrison
Financial Aid: Jay Powell
Type: Four-Year College **Sex:** Coed **Affiliation:** nondenominational **Scores:** 55% ACT 18-23; 4% ACT 24-29 **% Accepted:** 100 **Admission Plans:** Deferred Admission **Application Deadline:** August 15 **Application Fee:** $30.00 **H.S. Requirements:** High school diploma required; GED accepted **Costs Per Year:** Application fee: $30. Tuition: $10,800 full-time, $360 per semester hour part-time. Mandatory fees: $350 full-time, $175 per term part-time. Full-time tuition and fees vary according to course load and program. Part-time tuition and fees vary according to course load and program. College room only: $2450. **Scholarships:** Available **Calendar System:** Semester, Summer Session Available **Enrollment:** FT 182, PT 21 **Faculty:** FT 8, PT 19 **Student-Faculty Ratio:** 14:1 **Exams:** SAT I or ACT. **% Residing in College-Owned, -Operated, or -Affiliated Housing:** 29 **Final Year or Final Semester Residency Requirement:** Yes **Library Holdings:**

50,000 **Credit Hours For Degree:** 65 semester hours, Associates; 128 semester hours, Bachelors **Professional Accreditation:** ABHE **Intercollegiate Athletics:** Basketball M

SOUTHERN UNION STATE COMMUNITY COLLEGE
PO Box 1000, Roberts St.
Wadley, AL 36276
Tel: (256)395-2211
Fax: (256)395-2215
E-mail: info@suscc.edu
Web Site: http://www.suscc.edu/
President/CEO: Amelia Pearson
Type: Two-Year College **Sex:** Coed **Affiliation:** Alabama College System **Admission Plans:** Open Admission; Early Admission; Deferred Admission **Application Deadline:** Rolling **H.S. Requirements:** High school diploma required; GED accepted **Costs Per Year:** State resident tuition: $3120 full-time, $104 per credit hour part-time. Nonresident tuition: $5670 full-time, $189 per credit hour part-time. **Scholarships:** Available **Calendar System:** Semester, Summer Session Available **Student-Faculty Ratio:** 25:1 **Regional Accreditation:** Southern Association of Colleges and Schools **Credit Hours For Degree:** 96 quarter hours, Associates **ROTC:** Air Force **Professional Accreditation:** JRCERT, JRCEMT, NLN

SPRING HILL COLLEGE
4000 Dauphin St.
Mobile, AL 36608-1791
Tel: (251)380-4000; Free: 800-SHC-6704
Admissions: (251)380-3030
Fax: (251)460-2186
E-mail: admit@shc.edu
Web Site: http://www.shc.edu/
President/CEO: Rev. Richard P. Salmi, SJ
Admissions: Ellen Richardson
Financial Aid: Ellen Foster
Type: Comprehensive **Sex:** Coed **Affiliation:** Roman Catholic (Jesuit) **Scores:** 96% SAT V 400+; 94% SAT M 400+; 46% ACT 18-23; 46% ACT 24-29 **% Accepted:** 55 **Admission Plans:** Early Admission; Deferred Admission **Application Deadline:** July 15 **Application Fee:** $25.00 **H.S. Requirements:** High school diploma required; GED accepted **Costs Per Year:** Application fee: $25. Comprehensive fee: $35,180 includes full-time tuition ($23,910), mandatory fees ($1540), and college room and board ($9730). College room only: $5100. Room and board charges vary according to board plan and housing facility. Part-time tuition: $890 per semester hour. Part-time mandatory fees: $50 per semester hour. **Scholarships:** Available **Calendar System:** Semester, Summer Session Available **Enrollment:** FT 1,184, PT 126, Grad FT 26, Grad PT 185 **Faculty:** FT 82, PT 51 **Student-Faculty Ratio:** 13:1 **Exams:** SAT I or ACT. ACT essay used for advising. SAT essay used for advising. **% Receiving Financial Aid:** 70 **% Residing in College-Owned, -Operated, or -Affiliated Housing:** 73 **Final Year or Final Semester Residency Requirement:** Yes **Library Holdings:** 193,638 **Regional Accreditation:** Southern Association of Colleges and Schools **Credit Hours For Degree:** 128 semester hours, Bachelors **ROTC:** Army, Air Force **Professional Accreditation:** AACN, ACBSP **Intercollegiate Athletics:** Baseball M; Basketball M & W; Cross-Country Running M & W; Golf M & W; Soccer M & W; Softball W; Tennis M & W; Volleyball W

STILLMAN COLLEGE
PO Drawer 1430, 3600 Stillman Blvd.
Tuscaloosa, AL 35403-9990
Tel: (205)349-4240; Free: 800-841-5722
Admissions: (205)366-8837
Fax: (205)366-8996
E-mail: mfinch@stillman.edu
Web Site: http://www.stillman.edu/
President/CEO: Dr. Ernest McNealey
Admissions: Monica Finch
Financial Aid: Jacqueline S. Morris
Type: Four-Year College **Sex:** Coed **Affiliation:** Presbyterian Church (U.S.A.) **Scores:** 67% SAT V 400+; 58% SAT M 400+; 33% ACT 18-23; 8% ACT 24-29 **% Accepted:** 45 **Admission Plans:** Early Admission; Early Decision Plan; Deferred Admission **Application Deadline:** Rolling **Application Fee:** $50.00 **H.S. Requirements:** High school diploma required; GED accepted **Costs Per Year:** Application fee: $50. Comprehensive fee: $19,798 includes full-time tuition ($12,160), mandatory fees ($1302), and college room and board ($6336). Room and board charges vary according to housing facility. Part-time tuition: $503 per credit hour. Part-time mandatory fees: $91 per term. **Scholarships:** Available **Calendar System:** Semester, Summer Session Available **Enrollment:** FT 1,028, PT 20 **Faculty:** FT 54, PT 9 **Student-Faculty Ratio:** 18:1 **Exams:** ACT, SAT I or ACT, SAT I and SAT II or ACT, SAT I, SAT II. **% Receiving Financial Aid:** 94 **% Residing in College-Owned, -Operated, or -Affiliated Housing:** 68 **Library Holdings:** 117,500 **Regional Accreditation:** Southern Association of Colleges and Schools **Credit Hours For Degree:** 124 semester hours, Bachelors **ROTC:** Army **Professional Accreditation:** NCATE **Intercollegiate Athletics:** Baseball M; Basketball M & W; Cross-Country Running M & W; Football M; Softball W; Tennis M & W; Track and Field M & W; Volleyball W

STRAYER UNIVERSITY - BIRMINGHAM CAMPUS
3570 Grandview Parkway
Ste. 200
Birmingham, AL 35243
Tel: (205)453-6300
Fax: (205)453-6330
Web Site: http://www.strayer.edu/birmingham/
Type: Comprehensive **Sex:** Coed **Application Fee:** $50.00 **Costs Per Year:** Application fee: $50. **Regional Accreditation:** Middle State Association of Colleges and Schools

STRAYER UNIVERSITY - HUNTSVILLE CAMPUS
4955 Corporate Dr., NW
Ste. 200
Huntsville, AL 35805
Tel: (256)665-9800
Fax: (256)665-9730
Web Site: http://www.strayer.edu/huntsville/
Type: Comprehensive **Sex:** Coed **Application Fee:** $50.00 **Costs Per Year:** Application fee: $50. **Regional Accreditation:** Middle State Association of Colleges and Schools

TALLADEGA COLLEGE
627 West Battle St.
Talladega, AL 35160-2354
Tel: (256)362-0206; Free: 800-633-2440
Admissions: (256)761-6415
Fax: (256)362-2268
E-mail: fdortch@talladega.edu
Web Site: http://www.talladega.edu/
President/CEO: Dr. Billy C. Hawkins
Admissions: Floretta Dortch
Financial Aid: K. Michael Francois
Type: Four-Year College **Sex:** Coed **% Accepted:** 52 **Admission Plans:** Early Admission **Application Deadline:** Rolling **Application Fee:** $25.00 **H.S. Requirements:** High school diploma required; GED accepted **Scholarships:** Available **Calendar System:** Semester, Summer Session Not available **Enrollment:** FT 673, PT 27 **Faculty:** FT 33, PT 11 **Student-Faculty Ratio:** 18:1 **Exams:** SAT I or ACT. **% Receiving Financial Aid:** 92 **% Residing in College-Owned, -Operated, or -Affiliated Housing:** 80 **Final Year or Final Semester Residency Requirement:** No **Regional Accreditation:** Southern Association of Colleges and Schools **Credit Hours For Degree:** 124 credit hours, Bachelors **ROTC:** Army **Professional Accreditation:** CSWE **Intercollegiate Athletics:** Golf M; Softball W; Tennis W

TROY UNIVERSITY
University Ave.
Troy, AL 36082
Tel: (334)670-3000; Free: 800-551-9716
Admissions: (334)670-3243
Fax: (334)670-3815
E-mail: bstar@troy.edu
Web Site: http://www.troy.edu/
President/CEO: Dr. Jack Hawkins, Jr.
Admissions: Buddy Starling
Financial Aid: Carol Ballard
Type: Comprehensive **Sex:** Coed **Affiliation:** Troy University System **Scores:** 55% ACT 18-23; 21% ACT 24-29 **% Accepted:** 66 **Admission Plans:** Deferred Admission **Application Deadline:** Rolling **Application Fee:** $30.00 **H.S. Requirements:** High school diploma required; GED accepted **Costs Per Year:** Application fee: $30. State resident tuition: $6176 full-time,

$193 per credit hour part-time. Nonresident tuition: $12,342 full-time, $386 per credit hour part-time. Mandatory fees: $840 full-time, $8 per credit hour part-time, $50 per term part-time. Full-time tuition and fees vary according to program. College room and board: $6042. Room and board charges vary according to board plan and housing facility. **Scholarships:** Available **Calendar System:** Semester, Summer Session Available **Enrollment:** FT 11,070, PT 11,141, Grad FT 2,151, Grad PT 4,965 **Faculty:** FT 518, PT 995 **Student-Faculty Ratio:** 21:1 **Exams:** SAT I or ACT. **% Receiving Financial Aid:** 71 **% Residing in College-Owned, -Operated, or -Affiliated Housing:** 30 **Library Holdings:** 571,172 **Regional Accreditation:** Southern Association of Colleges and Schools **Credit Hours For Degree:** 62 credit hours, Associates; 120 credit hours, Bachelors **ROTC:** Army, Air Force **Professional Accreditation:** ACA, ACBSP, CORE, CSWE, JRCEPAT, NASM, NASPAA, NCATE, NLN **Intercollegiate Athletics:** Baseball M; Basketball M & W; Cross-Country Running M & W; Football M; Golf M & W; Soccer W; Softball W; Tennis M & W; Track and Field M & W; Volleyball W

TUSKEGEE UNIVERSITY
Tuskegee, AL 36088
Tel: (334)727-8011; Free: 800-622-6531
Admissions: (334)727-8500
Web Site: http://www.tuskegee.edu/
President/CEO: Dr. Benjamin F. Payton
Admissions: Robert Laney, Jr.
Financial Aid: A. D. James, Jr.
Type: Comprehensive **Sex:** Coed **Scores:** 74% SAT V 400+; 73.6% SAT M 400+; 55.8% ACT 18-23; 8.6% ACT 24-29 **% Accepted:** 58 **Admission Plans:** Early Admission **Application Deadline:** April 15 **Application Fee:** $25.00 **H.S. Requirements:** High school diploma required; GED accepted **Costs Per Year:** Application fee: $25. Comprehensive fee: $24,320 includes full-time tuition ($16,100), mandatory fees ($650), and college room and board ($7570). Full-time tuition and fees vary according to course load and program. Room and board charges vary according to housing facility. Part-time tuition: $665 per credit hour. Part-time tuition varies according to course load and program. **Scholarships:** Available **Calendar System:** Semester, Summer Session Available **Enrollment:** FT 2,419, PT 56, Grad FT 435, Grad PT 21 **Faculty:** FT 267, PT 11 **Student-Faculty Ratio:** 11:1 **Exams:** SAT I or ACT. **% Receiving Financial Aid:** 72 **% Residing in College-Owned, -Operated, or -Affiliated Housing:** 63 **Library Holdings:** 623,824 **Regional Accreditation:** Southern Association of Colleges and Schools **Credit Hours For Degree:** 124 credit hours, Bachelors **ROTC:** Army, Air Force **Professional Accreditation:** AACSB, ABET, AAFCS, AOTA, AVMA, CSWE, NAACLS, NAAB, NCATE, NLN **Intercollegiate Athletics:** Baseball M; Basketball M & W; Cross-Country Running M & W; Football M; Golf M; Riflery M & W; Soccer M; Tennis M & W; Track and Field M & W; Volleyball W

UNITED STATES SPORTS ACADEMY
One Academy Dr.
Daphne, AL 36526-7055
Tel: (251)626-3303; Free: 800-223-2668
Fax: (251)621-2527
Web Site: http://www.ussa.edu/
President/CEO: Dr. Thomas Rosandich
Type: Two-Year Upper Division **Sex:** Coed **Application Fee:** $50.00 **Costs Per Year:** Application fee: $50. Tuition: $280 per semester hour part-time. **Calendar System:** Continuous **Student-Faculty Ratio:** 18:1 **Regional Accreditation:** Southern Association of Colleges and Schools

THE UNIVERSITY OF ALABAMA
Tuscaloosa, AL 35487
Tel: (205)348-6010; Free: 800-933-BAMA
Admissions: (205)348-5666
Fax: (205)348-9046
E-mail: admissions@ua.edu
Web Site: http://www.ua.edu/
President/CEO: Dr. Robert E. Witt
Admissions: Mary K. Spiegel
Financial Aid: Helen Leathers
Type: University **Sex:** Coed **Affiliation:** University of Alabama System **Scores:** 100% SAT V 400+; 99% SAT M 400+; 45% ACT 18-23; 36% ACT 24-29 **% Accepted:** 57 **Admission Plans:** Early Admission **Application Deadline:** February 1 **Application Fee:** $40.00 **H.S. Requirements:** High school diploma required; GED accepted **Costs Per Year:** Application fee: $40. State resident tuition: $7000 full-time. Nonresident tuition: $19,200 full-time. Full-time tuition varies according to course load. College room and board: $7796. College room only: $4400. Room and board charges vary according to board plan and housing facility. **Scholarships:** Available **Calendar System:** Semester, Summer Session Available **Enrollment:** FT 21,738, PT 1,962, Grad FT 3,197, Grad PT 1,802 **Faculty:** FT 1,068, PT 369 **Student-Faculty Ratio:** 20:1 **Exams:** SAT I or ACT. ACT essay used for admission. SAT essay used for admission. **% Receiving Financial Aid:** 38 **% Residing in College-Owned, -Operated, or -Affiliated Housing:** 29 **Final Year or Final Semester Residency Requirement:** No **Library Holdings:** 3,313,998 **Regional Accreditation:** Southern Association of Colleges and Schools **Credit Hours For Degree:** 120 semester hours, Bachelors **ROTC:** Army, Air Force **Professional Accreditation:** AACSB, ABET, ACEJMC, AACN, AAFCS, ABA, ACA, ADtA, ALA, APA, ASLHA, AALS, FIDER, CORE, CSWE, JRCEPAT, NASAD, NASD, NASM, NAST NCATE **Intercollegiate Athletics:** Baseball M; Basketball M & W; Cheerleading M & W; Crew W; Cross-Country Running M & W; Football M; Golf M & W; Gymnastics W; Soccer W; Softball W; Swimming and Diving M & W; Tennis M & W; Track and Field M & W; Volleyball W

THE UNIVERSITY OF ALABAMA AT BIRMINGHAM
1530 3rd Ave. South
Birmingham, AL 35294
Tel: (205)934-4011; Free: 800-421-8743
Admissions: (205)934-8221
Fax: (205)975-7114
E-mail: undergradadmit@uab.edu
Web Site: http://www.uab.edu/
President/CEO: Dr. Carol Z. Garrison
Admissions: Chenise Ryan
Financial Aid: Janet B. May
Type: University **Sex:** Coed **Affiliation:** University of Alabama System **Scores:** 46% ACT 18-23; 45% ACT 24-29 **% Accepted:** 84 **Admission Plans:** Early Admission; Deferred Admission **Application Deadline:** Rolling **Application Fee:** $35.00 **H.S. Requirements:** High school diploma required; GED accepted **Costs Per Year:** Application fee: $35. State resident tuition: $4224 full-time, $176 per credit hour part-time. Nonresident tuition: $10,560 full-time, $440 per credit hour part-time. Mandatory fees: $872 full-time. College room and board: $8142. College room only: $4492. **Scholarships:** Available **Calendar System:** Semester, Summer Session Available **Enrollment:** FT 7,938, PT 2,708, Grad FT 3,710, Grad PT 2,518 **Faculty:** FT 845, PT 71 **Student-Faculty Ratio:** 16:1 **Exams:** SAT I or ACT. ACT essay not being used. SAT essay not being used. **% Receiving Financial Aid:** 51 **% Residing in College-Owned, -Operated, or -Affiliated Housing:** 20 **Final Year or Final Semester Residency Requirement:** Yes **Library Holdings:** 1,365,041 **Regional Accreditation:** Southern Association of Colleges and Schools **Credit Hours For Degree:** 120 hours, Bachelors **ROTC:** Army, Air Force **Professional Accreditation:** AACSB, ABET, AACN, AANA, ADA, ADtA, AHIMA, AOTA, AOA, APTA, APA, ASC, ACIPE, ACEHSA, CARC, CEPH, CORE, CSWE, JRCERT, JRCEMT JRCNMT, LCMEAMA, NAACLS, NASAD, NASM, NASPAA, NCATE **Intercollegiate Athletics:** Baseball M; Basketball M & W; Cross-Country Running W; Football M; Golf M & W; Riflery M & W; Soccer M & W; Softball W; Tennis M & W; Track and Field W; Volleyball W

THE UNIVERSITY OF ALABAMA IN HUNTSVILLE
301 Sparkman Dr.
Huntsville, AL 35899
Tel: (256)824-1000; Free: 800-UAH-CALL
Admissions: (256)824-6070
Fax: (256)824-6073
E-mail: admitme@email.uah.edu
Web Site: http://www.uah.edu/
President/CEO: Dr. David B. Williams
Admissions: Sandra Patterson
Financial Aid: Andrew Weaver
Type: University **Sex:** Coed **Affiliation:** University of Alabama System **Scores:** 97.08% SAT V 400+; 98.24% SAT M 400+; 34.59% ACT 18-23; 48.51% ACT 24-29 **% Accepted:** 72 **Application Deadline:** August 19 **Application Fee:** $30.00 **H.S. Requirements:** High school diploma required; GED accepted **Costs Per Year:** Application fee: $30. State resident tuition: $6510 full-time, $227.95 per credit hour part-time. Nonresident tuition: $15,628 full-time, $551.47 per credit hour part-time. Mandatory fees: $31 per credit hour part-time. Full-time tuition varies according to course load. Part-

time tuition and fees vary according to course load. College room and board: $7208. College room only: $5084. Room and board charges vary according to board plan and housing facility. **Scholarships:** Available **Calendar System:** Semester, Summer Session Available **Enrollment:** FT 4,640, PT 1,479, Grad FT 444, Grad PT 1,118 **Faculty:** FT 303, PT 154 **Student-Faculty Ratio:** 17:1 **Exams:** SAT I or ACT. ACT essay not being used. SAT essay not being used. **% Receiving Financial Aid:** 49 **% Residing in College-Owned, -Operated, or -Affiliated Housing:** 20 **Final Year or Final Semester Residency Requirement:** No **Library Holdings:** 323,637 **Regional Accreditation:** Southern Association of Colleges and Schools **Credit Hours For Degree:** 128 semester hours, Bachelors **ROTC:** Army **Professional Accreditation:** AACSB, ABET, AACN, NASM, NLN **Intercollegiate Athletics:** Archery M & W; Badminton M & W; Baseball M; Basketball M & W; Bowling M & W; Cheerleading M & W; Crew M & W; Cross-Country Running M & W; Ice Hockey M; Soccer M & W; Softball W; Table Tennis M & W; Tennis M & W; Track and Field M & W; Volleyball W

UNIVERSITY OF MOBILE
5735 College Parkway
Mobile, AL 36613
Tel: (251)442-2773; Free: 800-946-7267
Admissions: (251)442-2221
Fax: (251)442-2498
E-mail: halig@umobile.edu
Web Site: http://www.umobile.edu/
President/CEO: Dr. Mark R. Foley
Admissions: Hali Givens
Financial Aid: Marie Thomas Baston
Type: Comprehensive **Sex:** Coed **Affiliation:** Southern Baptist **Scores:** 93. 33% SAT V 400+; 92.11% SAT M 400+; 57.73% ACT 18-23; 29.38% ACT 24-29 **% Accepted:** 78 **Admission Plans:** Deferred Admission **Application Deadline:** Rolling **Application Fee:** $50.00 **H.S. Requirements:** High school diploma required; GED accepted **Costs Per Year:** Application fee: $50. Comprehensive fee: $22,420 includes full-time tuition ($14,500), mandatory fees ($350), and college room and board ($7570). College room only: $4470. Full-time tuition and fees vary according to course load and program. Room and board charges vary according to housing facility. Part-time tuition: $515 per credit hour. Part-time mandatory fees: $98. Part-time tuition and fees vary according to course load. **Scholarships:** Available **Calendar System:** Semester, Summer Session Available **Enrollment:** FT 1,257, PT 160, Grad FT 44, Grad PT 111 **Faculty:** FT 84, PT 78 **Student-Faculty Ratio:** 12:1 **Exams:** SAT I or ACT, SAT I and SAT II or ACT, SAT II. ACT essay not being used. SAT essay not being used. **% Receiving Financial Aid:** 72 **% Residing in College-Owned, -Operated, or -Affiliated Housing:** 39 **Final Year or Final Semester Residency Requirement:** Yes **Library Holdings:** 111,285 **Regional Accreditation:** Southern Association of Colleges and Schools **Credit Hours For Degree:** 64 semester hours, Associates; 128 semester hours, Bachelors **ROTC:** Army, Air Force **Professional Accreditation:** AACN, APTA, ACBSP, NASM, NLN **Intercollegiate Athletics:** Baseball M; Basketball M & W; Cheerleading W; Cross-Country Running M & W; Golf M & W; Soccer M & W; Softball W; Tennis M & W; Track and Field M & W; Volleyball W

UNIVERSITY OF MONTEVALLO
Station 6001
Montevallo, AL 35115
Tel: (205)665-6000; Free: 800-292-4349
Admissions: (205)665-6030
E-mail: admissions@montevallo.edu
Web Site: http://www.montevallo.edu/
President/CEO: Dr. Philip C. Williams, PhD
Admissions: Ira Lynn Gurganus
Financial Aid: Maria Parker
Type: Comprehensive **Sex:** Coed **Scores:** 57% ACT 18-23; 36% ACT 24-29 **% Accepted:** 72 **Admission Plans:** Early Admission; Deferred Admission **Application Deadline:** August 1 **Application Fee:** $25.00 **H.S. Requirements:** High school diploma required; GED accepted **Costs Per Year:** Application fee: $25. State resident tuition: $7230 full-time, $241 per credit hour part-time. Nonresident tuition: $14,460 full-time, $482 per credit hour part-time. Mandatory fees: $520 full-time. Full-time tuition and fees vary according to course load. Part-time tuition varies according to course load. College room and board: $4924. Room and board charges vary according to housing facility. **Scholarships:** Available **Calendar System:** Semester, Summer Session Available **Enrollment:** FT 2,275, PT 296, Grad FT 219, Grad PT 258 **Faculty:** FT 137, PT 68 **Student-Faculty Ratio:** 16:1 **Exams:** ACT, SAT I or ACT. **% Receiving Financial Aid:** 52 **% Residing in College-Owned, -Operated, or -Affiliated Housing:** 43 **Library Holdings:** 265,877 **Regional Accreditation:** Southern Association of Colleges and Schools **Credit Hours For Degree:** 130 semester hours, Bachelors **ROTC:** Army, Air Force **Professional Accreditation:** AACSB, AAFCS, ACA, ASLHA, CSWE, NASAD, NASM, NCATE **Intercollegiate Athletics:** Baseball M; Basketball M & W; Golf M & W; Soccer M & W; Tennis W; Volleyball W

UNIVERSITY OF NORTH ALABAMA
One Harrison Plaza
Florence, AL 35632-0001
Tel: (256)765-4100; Free: 800-TAL-KUNA
Admissions: (256)765-4680
Fax: (256)765-4329
E-mail: admissions@una.edu
Web Site: http://www.una.edu/
President/CEO: Dr. William G. Cale, Jr.
Admissions: Kim O. Mauldin
Financial Aid: Ben Baker
Type: Comprehensive **Sex:** Coed **Scores:** 55% ACT 18-23; 25% ACT 24-29 **% Accepted:** 82 **Admission Plans:** Early Admission; Deferred Admission **Application Deadline:** Rolling **Application Fee:** $25.00 **H.S. Requirements:** High school diploma required; GED accepted **Costs Per Year:** Application fee: $25. State resident tuition: $5010 full-time, $167 per credit hour part-time. Nonresident tuition: $10,020 full-time, $334 per credit hour part-time. Mandatory fees: $1032 full-time. Full-time tuition and fees vary according to course load and program. Part-time tuition varies according to course load and program. College room and board: $4784. Room and board charges vary according to board plan and housing facility. **Scholarships:** Available **Calendar System:** Semester, Summer Session Available **Enrollment:** FT 5,023, PT 1,172, Grad FT 315, Grad PT 750 **Faculty:** FT 235, PT 121 **Student-Faculty Ratio:** 22:1 **Exams:** SAT I or ACT. **% Receiving Financial Aid:** 43 **% Residing in College-Owned, -Operated, or -Affiliated Housing:** 19 **Final Year or Final Semester Residency Requirement:** No **Library Holdings:** 393,457 **Regional Accreditation:** Southern Association of Colleges and Schools **Credit Hours For Degree:** 128 semester hours, Bachelors **ROTC:** Army **Professional Accreditation:** ABET, AACN, AAFCS, ACA, ACBSP, CSWE, NASAD, NASM, NCATE, NLN **Intercollegiate Athletics:** Baseball M; Basketball M & W; Cross-Country Running M & W; Football M; Golf M; Soccer W; Softball W; Tennis M & W; Volleyball W

UNIVERSITY OF PHOENIX—BIRMINGHAM CAMPUS
One Corporate Center, Ste. 400
Birmingham, AL 35244
Web Site: http://www.phoenix.edu/
Type: Comprehensive **Sex:** Coed **Regional Accreditation:** North Central Association of Colleges and Schools

UNIVERSITY OF SOUTH ALABAMA
307 University Blvd.
Mobile, AL 36688-0002
Tel: (251)460-6101; Free: 800-872-5247
Admissions: (251)460-6141
Fax: (251)460-7025
E-mail: admiss@usouthal.edu
Web Site: http://www.southalabama.edu/
President/CEO: V. Gordon Moulton
Admissions: Christopher A. Lynch
Type: University **Sex:** Coed **% Accepted:** 90 **Admission Plans:** Preferred Admission; Early Admission **Application Deadline:** July 15 **Application Fee:** $35.00 **H.S. Requirements:** High school diploma required; GED accepted **Costs Per Year:** Application fee: $35. State resident tuition: $4860 full-time, $162 per credit hour part-time. Nonresident tuition: $10,200 full-time, $340 per credit hour part-time. Mandatory fees: $1102 full-time, $363 per term part-time. Full-time tuition and fees vary according to class time, course level, course load, degree level, and program. Part-time tuition and fees vary according to class time, course level, course load, degree level, and program. College room and board: $5344. College room only: $2744. Room and board charges vary according to board plan, housing facility, and location. **Scholarships:** Available **Calendar System:** Semester, Summer Session Available **Enrollment:** FT 8,527, PT 2,881, Grad FT 2,407, Grad PT 707 **Faculty:** FT 743, PT 341 **Student-Faculty Ratio:** 14:1 **Exams:** SAT I or

ACT. **% Receiving Financial Aid:** 41 **% Residing in College-Owned, -Operated, or -Affiliated Housing:** 19 **Library Holdings:** 1,056,796 **Regional Accreditation:** Southern Association of Colleges and Schools **Credit Hours For Degree:** 128 semester hours, Bachelors **ROTC:** Army, Air Force **Professional Accreditation:** AACSB, ABET, AACN, AOTA, APTA, ASLHA, CARC, JRCEMT, LCMEAMA, NAACLS, NASAD, NASM, NCATE **Intercollegiate Athletics:** Baseball M; Basketball M & W; Cross-Country Running M & W; Fencing M & W; Football M; Golf M & W; Soccer W; Tennis M & W; Track and Field M & W; Volleyball W

THE UNIVERSITY OF WEST ALABAMA
Livingston, AL 35470
Tel: (205)652-3400; Free: 800-621-8044
Admissions: (205)652-3581
E-mail: db@uwa.edu
Web Site: http://www.uwa.edu/
President/CEO: Dr. Richard D. Holland
Admissions: Danny Buckalew
Financial Aid: Don Rainer
Type: Comprehensive **Sex:** Coed **Scores:** 62% ACT 18-23; 14% ACT 24-29 **% Accepted:** 61 **Admission Plans:** Early Admission; Deferred Admission **Application Deadline:** Rolling **Application Fee:** $50.00 **H.S. Requirements:** High school diploma required; GED accepted **Costs Per Year:** Application fee: $50. State resident tuition: $5060 full-time, $215 per semester hour part-time. Nonresident tuition: $10,120 full-time, $430 per semester hour part-time. Mandatory fees: $360 full-time. Full-time tuition and fees vary according to course load, degree level, and program. Part-time tuition varies according to course load, degree level, and program. College room and board: $3748. College room only: $2200. Room and board charges vary according to board plan and housing facility. **Scholarships:** Available **Calendar System:** Semester, Summer Session Available **Enrollment:** FT 1,541, PT 404, Grad FT 738, Grad PT 2,474 **Faculty:** FT 116, PT 131 **Student-Faculty Ratio:** 19:1 **Exams:** SAT I or ACT. **% Receiving Financial Aid:** 49 **% Residing in College-Owned, -Operated, or -Affiliated Housing:** 31 **Final Year or Final Semester Residency Requirement:** No **Library Holdings:** 161,991 **Regional Accreditation:** Southern Association of Colleges and Schools **Credit Hours For Degree:** 60 quarter hours, Associates; 120 quarter hours, Bachelors **ROTC:** Army, Air Force **Professional Accreditation:** ACBSP, JRCEPAT, NCATE, NLN **Intercollegiate Athletics:** Baseball M; Basketball M & W; Cross-Country Running M & W; Football M; Softball W; Volleyball W

VIRGINIA COLLEGE AT BIRMINGHAM
488 Palisades Blvd.
Birmingham, AL 35209
Tel: (205)802-1200
Fax: (205)802-1597
Web Site: http://www.vc.edu/
President/CEO: JoAnn Wilson
Type: Comprehensive **Sex:** Coed **Application Deadline:** Rolling **Application Fee:** $100.00 **H.S. Requirements:** High school diploma required; GED accepted **Scholarships:** Available **Calendar System:** Quarter **Library Holdings:** 3,900 **Credit Hours For Degree:** 96 quarter hours, Associates **Professional Accreditation:** ACICS, ACF

VIRGINIA COLLEGE AT HUNTSVILLE
2800-A Bob Wallace Ave.
Huntsville, AL 35805
Tel: (256)533-7387
Fax: (256)533-7785
Web Site: http://www.vc.edu/
President/CEO: James D. Foster
Type: Four-Year College **Sex:** Coed **Application Deadline:** Rolling **Application Fee:** $100.00 **H.S. Requirements:** High school diploma required; GED accepted **Scholarships:** Available **Calendar System:** Quarter **Credit Hours For Degree:** 90 quarter hours, Associates **Professional Accreditation:** ACICS

WALLACE STATE COMMUNITY COLLEGE
PO Box 2000
801 Main St.
Hanceville, AL 35077-2000
Tel: (256)352-8000; Free: (866)350-9722
Fax: (256)352-8228
Web Site: http://www.wallacestate.edu/
President/CEO: Vicki Hawsey
Admissions: Linda Sperling
Type: Two-Year College **Sex:** Coed **Scores:** 58% ACT 18-23; 13% ACT 24-29 **% Accepted:** 100 **Admission Plans:** Open Admission; Early Admission; Deferred Admission **Application Deadline:** Rolling **Application Fee:** $0.00 **H.S. Requirements:** High school diploma required; GED accepted **Scholarships:** Available **Calendar System:** Semester, Summer Session Available **Faculty:** FT 225, PT 387 **Student-Faculty Ratio:** 30:1 **% Residing in College-Owned, -Operated, or -Affiliated Housing:** 3 **Library Holdings:** 41,500 **Regional Accreditation:** Southern Association of Colleges and Schools **Credit Hours For Degree:** 60 semester hours, Associates **Professional Accreditation:** AAMAE, ADA, AHIMA, AOTA, APTA, CARC, JRCEDMS, JRCERT, JRCEMT, NAACLS, NLN **Intercollegiate Athletics:** Baseball M; Basketball M & W; Cross-Country Running M & W; Golf M; Soccer M & W; Softball W; Tennis M & W; Track and Field M & W; Volleyball W

ALASKA BIBLE COLLEGE
Box 289
Glennallen, AK 99588-0289
Tel: (907)822-3201; Free: 800-478-7884
Fax: (907)822-5027
E-mail: info@akbible.edu
Web Site: http://www.akbible.edu/
Admissions: Carol C. Ridley
Financial Aid: Jared Palmer
Type: Four-Year College **Sex:** Coed **Affiliation:** nondenominational **% Accepted:** 86 **Admission Plans:** Deferred Admission **Application Deadline:** July 1 **Application Fee:** $35.00 **H.S. Requirements:** High school diploma required; GED accepted **Scholarships:** Available **Calendar System:** Semester, Summer Session Not available **Enrollment:** FT 25, PT 13 **Faculty:** FT 3, PT 4 **Student-Faculty Ratio:** 7:1 **Exams:** SAT I or ACT. **% Receiving Financial Aid:** 27 **% Residing in College-Owned, -Operated, or -Affiliated Housing:** 87 **Library Holdings:** 30,764 **Credit Hours For Degree:** 61 credits, Associates; 120 credits, Bachelors **Professional Accreditation:** ABHE

ALASKA PACIFIC UNIVERSITY
4101 University Dr.
Anchorage, AK 99508-4672
Tel: (907)561-1266; Free: 800-252-7528
Admissions: (907)564-8248
Fax: (907)564-8317
E-mail: admissions@alaskapacific.edu
Web Site: http://www.alaskapacific.edu/
President/CEO: Dr. Don Bantz
Admissions: Jennifer Jensen
Financial Aid: Jo Holland
Type: Comprehensive **Sex:** Coed **Scores:** 101% SAT V 400+; 99% SAT M 400+; 44% ACT 18-23; 56% ACT 24-29 **% Accepted:** 10 **Admission Plans:** Deferred Admission **Application Deadline:** August 15 **Application Fee:** $25.00 **H.S. Requirements:** High school diploma required; GED accepted **Costs Per Year:** Application fee: $25. Comprehensive fee: $35,660 includes full-time tuition ($26,250), mandatory fees ($110), and college room and board ($9300). College room only: $4400. Full-time tuition and fees vary according to class time, degree level, location, and program. Room and board charges vary according to board plan and housing facility. Part-time tuition: $1100 per semester hour. Part-time mandatory fees: $55 per term. Part-time tuition and fees vary according to class time, course load, degree level, location, and program. Tuition guaranteed not to increase for student's term of enrollment. **Scholarships:** Available **Calendar System:** Semester, Summer Session Available **Enrollment:** FT 301, PT 233, Grad FT 107, Grad PT 140 **Faculty:** FT 50, PT 46 **Student-Faculty Ratio:** 10:1 **Exams:** SAT I or ACT. **% Receiving Financial Aid:** 77 **% Residing in College-Owned, -Operated, or -Affiliated Housing:** 26 **Final Year or Final Semester Residency Requirement:** Yes **Library Holdings:** 945,948 **Credit Hours For Degree:** 64 semester hours, Associates; 128 semester hours, Bachelors **ROTC:** Air Force **Professional Accreditation:** NCATE, NCCU

CHARTER COLLEGE
2221 East Northern Lights Blvd.
Ste. 120
Anchorage, AK 99508
Tel: (907)277-1000
Fax: (907)274-3342
Web Site: http://www.chartercollege.edu/
President/CEO: Terrance Harris
Admissions: Lily Sirianni
Type: Two-Year College **Sex:** Coed **Admission Plans:** Open Admission **Application Deadline:** Rolling **Application Fee:** $20.00 **H.S. Requirements:** High school diploma required; GED accepted **Scholarships:** Available **Calendar System:** Quarter, Summer Session Available **Faculty:** FT 10, PT 33 **Student-Faculty Ratio:** 15:1 **Library Holdings:** 1,000 **Credit Hours For Degree:** 90 credit hours, Associates **Professional Accreditation:** ACICS

ILISAGVIK COLLEGE
UIC/Narl
Barrow, AK 99723
Tel: (907)852-3333
Fax: (907)852-2729
E-mail: beverly.grinage@ilisagvik.cc
Web Site: http://www.ilisagvik.cc/
President/CEO: Beverly Patkotak Grinage
Admissions: Beverly Patkotak Grinage
Type: Two-Year College **Sex:** Coed **% Accepted:** 100 **Application Deadline:** August 1 **Application Fee:** $0.00 **Calendar System:** Semester **Enrollment:** FT 49, PT 214 **Faculty:** FT 12, PT 0 **Student-Faculty Ratio:** 10:1 **Exams:** Other. **Professional Accreditation:** NCCU

UNIVERSITY OF ALASKA ANCHORAGE
3211 Providence Dr.
Anchorage, AK 99508
Tel: (907)786-1800
Fax: (907)786-4888
E-mail: enroll@uaa.alaska.edu
Web Site: http://www.uaa.alaska.edu/
President/CEO: Fran Ulmer
Financial Aid: Theodore E. Malone
Type: Comprehensive **Sex:** Coed **Affiliation:** University of Alaska System **% Accepted:** 77 **Admission Plans:** Open Admission; Deferred Admission **Application Deadline:** July 1 **Application Fee:** $50.00 **H.S. Requirements:** High school diploma required; GED accepted. For applicants to associate degree programs, 18 or over, provided they complete Advisement and Assessment Program: High school diploma or equivalent not required. **Costs Per Year:** Application fee: $50. State resident tuition: $4020 full-time, $134 per term part-time. Nonresident tuition: $13,440 full-time, $448 per term part-time. Mandatory fees: $560 full-time. College room and board: $7962. **Scholarships:** Available **Calendar System:** Semester, Summer Session Available **Enrollment:** FT 7,641, PT 9,214, Grad FT 239, Grad PT 731 **Faculty:** FT 617, PT 661 **Exams:** SAT I or ACT. **% Receiving Financial Aid:** 44 **Credit Hours For Degree:** 60 semester credits, Associates; 120 semester credits, Bachelors **ROTC:** Army, Air Force **Professional Accreditation:** AACSB, ABET, ACEJMC, AAMAE, ADA, ADtA, CSWE, NAACLS, NASAD, NASM, NCATE, NLN, NCCU **Intercollegiate Athletics:** Basketball M & W; Cross-Country Running M & W; Gymnastics W; Ice Hockey M; Skiing (Cross-Country) M & W; Skiing (Downhill) M & W; Track and Field M & W; Volleyball W

UNIVERSITY OF ALASKA ANCHORAGE, KENAI PENINSULA COLLEGE
156 College Rd.
Soldotna, AK 99669-9798
Tel: (907)262-0300; Free: 877-262-0330
Admissions: (907)262-0311
Fax: (907)262-0322
Web Site: http://www.kpc.alaska.edu/
President/CEO: Gary J. Turner
Admissions: Shelly Love Blatchford
Type: Two-Year College **Sex:** Coed **Affiliation:** University of Alaska System **Admission Plans:** Open Admission **Application Deadline:** Rolling **Application Fee:** $40.00 **H.S. Requirements:** High school diploma required; GED accepted **Costs Per Year:** Application fee: $40. State resident tuition: $141 per credit hour part-time. Nonresident tuition: $141 per credit hour part-time. **Scholarships:** Available **Calendar System:** Semester, Summer Session Not available **Exams:** Other. SAT essay used for admission. **Final Year or Final Semester Residency Requirement:** Yes **Credit Hours For Degree:** 60 credits, Associates **Professional Accreditation:** NCCU

UNIVERSITY OF ALASKA ANCHORAGE, KODIAK COLLEGE
117 Benny Benson Dr.
Kodiak, AK 99615-6643
Tel: (907)486-4161
Admissions: (907)486-1235
Fax: (907)486-1257
E-mail: jmyrick@kodiak.alaska.edu
Web Site: http://www.koc.alaska.edu/
President/CEO: Barbara Bolson
Admissions: Jennifer Myrick
Type: Two-Year College **Sex:** Coed **Affiliation:** University of Alaska System **Admission Plans:** Open Admission **Application Deadline:** Rolling **Application Fee:** $40.00 **H.S. Requirements:** High school diploma required; GED accepted **Calendar System:** Semester, Summer Session Not available **Faculty:** FT 10, PT 30 **Student-Faculty Ratio:** 19:1 **Library Holdings:** 21,000 **Credit Hours For Degree:** 60 credits, Associates **Professional Accreditation:** NCCU

UNIVERSITY OF ALASKA ANCHORAGE, MATANUSKA-SUSITNA COLLEGE
PO Box 2889
Palmer, AK 99645-2889
Tel: (907)745-9774
Admissions: (907)745-9712
Fax: (907)745-9747
E-mail: info@matsu.alaska.edu
Web Site: http://www.matsu.alaska.edu/
President/CEO: Dennis Clark
Admissions: Sandra Gravley
Type: Two-Year College **Sex:** Coed **Affiliation:** University of Alaska System **Admission Plans:** Open Admission **Application Deadline:** September 15 **Application Fee:** $40.00 **H.S. Requirements:** High school diploma required; GED accepted **Costs Per Year:** Application fee: $40. State resident tuition: $147 per semester hour part-time. Nonresident tuition: $500 per semester hour part-time. Mandatory fees: $8 per semester hour part-time, $10 per term part-time. Part-time tuition and fees vary according to course level and course load. **Scholarships:** Available **Calendar System:** Semester, Summer Session Available **Enrollment:** FT 452, PT 1,330 **Faculty:** FT 26, PT 90 **Student-Faculty Ratio:** 16:1 **Library Holdings:** 50,000 **Credit Hours For Degree:** 60 credits, Associates **Professional Accreditation:** NCCU

UNIVERSITY OF ALASKA FAIRBANKS
PO Box 757500
Fairbanks, AK 99775-7520
Tel: (907)474-7211; Free: 800-478-1823
Admissions: (907)474-7500
Fax: (907)474-5379
E-mail: admissions@uaf.edu
Web Site: http://www.uaf.edu/
President/CEO: Brian Rogers
Admissions: Mike Earnest
Financial Aid: Deanna Dierenger
Type: University **Sex:** Coed **Affiliation:** University of Alaska System **Scores:** 86.8% SAT V 400+; 84.2% SAT M 400+; 45.65% ACT 18-23; 23.76% ACT 24-29 **% Accepted:** 74 **Admission Plans:** Open Admission; Deferred Admission **Application Deadline:** July 1 **Application Fee:** $50.00 **H.S. Requirements:** High school diploma required; GED not accepted. No HS diploma or equivalent is required for admission to an Associate degree program if the student is 18. **Costs Per Year:** Application fee: $50. State resident tuition: $4755 full-time, $147 per credit hour part-time. Nonresident tuition: $15,345 full-time, $500 per credit hour part-time. Mandatory fees: $913 full-time, $16 per credit hour part-time, $203 per term part-time. Full-time tuition and fees vary according to course level, course load, location, and reciprocity agreements. Part-time tuition and fees vary according to course level, course load, location, and reciprocity agreements. College room and board: $6800. College room only: $3610. Room and board charges vary according to board plan and housing facility. **Scholarships:** Available **Calendar System:** Semester, Summer Session Available **Enrollment:** FT 3,639, PT 4,338, Grad FT 648, Grad PT 512 **Faculty:** FT 341, PT 708 **Student-Faculty Ratio:** 12:1 **Exams:** SAT I or ACT. ACT essay used for advising. SAT essay used for advising. ACT essay used for placement. SAT essay used for placement. **% Receiving Financial Aid:** 43 **% Residing in College-Owned, -Operated, or -Affiliated Housing:** 25 **Final Year or Final Semester Residency Requirement:** No **Library Holdings:** 859,637 **Credit Hours For Degree:** 60 credits, Associates; 120 credits, Bachelors **ROTC:** Army **Professional Accreditation:** AACSB, ABET, ACEJMC, AAMAE, CSWE, NASM, NCATE, NCCU, SAF **Intercollegiate Athletics:** Basketball M & W; Cross-Country Running M & W; Ice Hockey M; Riflery M & W; Skiing (Cross-Country) M & W; Volleyball W

UNIVERSITY OF ALASKA, PRINCE WILLIAM SOUND COMMUNITY COLLEGE
PO Box 97
Valdez, AK 99686-0097
Tel: (907)834-1600
Admissions: (907)834-1631
Fax: (907)834-1627
E-mail: studentservices@pwscc.edu
Web Site: http://www.pwscc.edu/
President/CEO: Douglas A. Desorcie
Admissions: Nathan J. Platt
Financial Aid: Gianna Thornton
Type: Two-Year College **Sex:** Coed **Affiliation:** University of Alaska System **% Accepted:** 89 **Admission Plans:** Open Admission; Early Admission **Application Deadline:** Rolling **Application Fee:** $10.00 **Scholarships:** Available **Calendar System:** Semester, Summer Session Available **Faculty:** FT 6, PT 46 **Exams:** SAT I or ACT. **% Residing in College-Owned, -Operated, or -Affiliated Housing:** 2 **Library Holdings:** 40,870 **Credit Hours For Degree:** 60 credits, Associates **Professional Accreditation:** NCCU

UNIVERSITY OF ALASKA SOUTHEAST
11120 Glacier Hwy.
Juneau, AK 99801
Tel: (907)796-6457; Free: 877-796-4827
Admissions: (907)796-6294
Fax: (907)796-6365
E-mail: admissions@uas.alaska.edu
Web Site: http://www.uas.alaska.edu/
President/CEO: John Pugh
Admissions: Deema Ferguson
Financial Aid: Barbara Carlson Burnett
Type: Comprehensive **Sex:** Coed **Affiliation:** University of Alaska System **Scores:** 97.62% SAT V 400+; 90.48% SAT M 400+ **% Accepted:** 92 **Admission Plans:** Deferred Admission **H.S. Requirements:** High school diploma required; GED accepted **Scholarships:** Available **Calendar System:** Semester, Summer Session Available **Enrollment:** FT 775, PT 2,125, Grad FT 72, Grad PT 288 **Exams:** SAT I or ACT. ACT essay used for placement. SAT essay used for placement. **% Receiving Financial Aid:** 48 **Credit Hours For Degree:** 60 credits, Associates; 120 credits, Bachelors **Professional Accreditation:** NCATE, NCCU **Intercollegiate Athletics:** Riflery M & W

UNIVERSITY OF ALASKA SOUTHEAST, KETCHIKAN CAMPUS
2600 7th Ave.
Ketchikan, AK 99901-5798
Tel: (907)225-6177; Free: 888-550-6177
Fax: (907)225-3624

E-mail: ketch.info@uas.alaska.edu
Web Site: http://www.ketch.alaska.edu/
Type: Two-Year College **Sex:** Coed **Affiliation:** University of Alaska System **Application Deadline:** Rolling **Application Fee:** $50.00 **H.S. Requirements:** High school diploma required; GED accepted **Costs Per Year:** Application fee: $50. State resident tuition: $4230 full-time, $141 per credit part-time. Nonresident tuition: $14,130 full-time, $471 per credit part-time. Mandatory fees: $150 full-time, $6 per credit part-time. **Scholarships:** Available **Calendar System:** Semester, Summer Session Not available **Credit Hours For Degree:** 60 credits, Associates **Professional Accreditation:** NCCU

UNIVERSITY OF ALASKA SOUTHEAST, SITKA CAMPUS
1332 Seward Ave.
Sitka, AK 99835-9418
Tel: (907)747-6653
Admissions: (907)747-7705
Fax: (907)747-7747
E-mail: cynthia.rogers@uas.alaska.edu
Web Site: http://www.uas.alaska.edu/
Admissions: Cynthia Rogers
Type: Two-Year College **Sex:** Coed **Affiliation:** University of Alaska System **Admission Plans:** Open Admission; Early Admission **Application Deadline:** Rolling **Application Fee:** $35.00 **H.S. Requirements:** High school diploma required; GED accepted **Calendar System:** Semester, Summer Session Available **Student-Faculty Ratio:** 13:1 **Library Holdings:** 80,050 **Credit Hours For Degree:** 60 credits, Associates **Professional Accreditation:** AHIMA, NCCU

AMERICAN INDIAN COLLEGE OF THE ASSEMBLIES OF GOD, INC.
10020 North Fifteenth Ave.
Phoenix, AZ 85021-2199
Tel: (602)944-3335; Free: 800-933-3828
E-mail: sgonzales@aicag.edu
Web Site: http://www.aicag.edu/
President/CEO: Dr. David DeGarmo
Admissions: Sandra Gonzales
Financial Aid: Nadine Waldrop
Type: Four-Year College **Sex:** Coed **Affiliation:** Assemblies of God **Admission Plans:** Preferred Admission **Application Deadline:** August 15 **Application Fee:** $0.00 **H.S. Requirements:** High school diploma required; GED accepted **Scholarships:** Available **Calendar System:** Semester, Summer Session Not available **Exams:** SAT I or ACT. **Library Holdings:** 19,899 **Regional Accreditation:** North Central Association of Colleges and Schools **Credit Hours For Degree:** 73 semester hours, Associates; 128 semester hours, Bachelors

APOLLO COLLEGE—PHOENIX
8503 North 27th Ave.
Phoenix, AZ 85051
Tel: (602)864-1571
Admissions: (602)324-5505
Fax: (602)864-8207
Web Site: http://www.apollocollege.edu/
President/CEO: Jeffrey Gearhart
Type: Two-Year College **Sex:** Coed **Affiliation:** Apollo Colleges, Inc. **Application Fee:** $75.00 **H.S. Requirements:** High school diploma required; GED accepted **Scholarships:** Available **Calendar System:** Continuous, Summer Session Not available **Credit Hours For Degree:** 66 credit hours, Associates **Professional Accreditation:** ABHES, CARC

APOLLO COLLEGE—TRI-CITY, INC.
630 West Southern Ave.
Mesa, AZ 85210-5004
Tel: (480)831-6585; Free: 800-36-TRAIN
Admissions: (480)212-1600
Fax: (480)827-0022
E-mail: vcolmone@apollocollege.edu
Web Site: http://www.apollocollege.com/
Admissions: Valentina Colmone
Type: Two-Year College **Sex:** Coed **Affiliation:** Apollo Colleges, Inc. **Admission Plans:** Open Admission **Application Deadline:** Rolling **Scholarships:** Available **Calendar System:** Semester **Exams:** Other. **Credit Hours For Degree:** 66 credit hours, Associates **Professional Accreditation:** ABHES, CARC

APOLLO COLLEGE—TUCSON, INC.
3550 North Oracle Rd.
Tucson, AZ 85705-3227
Tel: (520)888-5885; Free: 800-36-TRAIN
E-mail: dwilson@apollo.edu
Web Site: http://www.apollocollege.com/
Admissions: Dennis C. Wilson
Type: Two-Year College **Sex:** Coed **Affiliation:** Apollo Colleges, Inc. **Application Fee:** $75.00 **H.S. Requirements:** High school diploma or equivalent not required. For Medical Office Management; Medical Laboratory Technician; Pharmacy Technician: High school diploma required; GED accepted **Calendar System:** Semester **Exams:** Other. **Credit Hours For Degree:** 67 credits, Associates **Professional Accreditation:** ABHES

APOLLO COLLEGE—WESTSIDE, INC.
2701 West Bethany Home Rd.
Phoenix, AZ 85017
Tel: (602)433-1333; Free: 800-36-TRAIN
Admissions: (602)433-1222
E-mail: cnestor@apollocollege.com
Web Site: http://www.apollocollege.com/
Type: Two-Year College **Sex:** Coed **Affiliation:** Apollo Colleges, Inc. **Admission Plans:** Open Admission **Application Deadline:** Rolling **Scholarships:** Available **Calendar System:** Semester **Exams:** Other. **Credit Hours For Degree:** 66 credit hours, Associates **Professional Accreditation:** ABHES

ARGOSY UNIVERSITY, PHOENIX
2233 West Dunlap Ave.
Phoenix, AZ 85021
Tel: (602)216-2600; Free: (866)216-2777
Fax: (602)216-2601
Web Site: http://www.argosy.edu/phoenix/
President/CEO: Bart Lerner, EdD
Type: University **Sex:** Coed **Calendar System:** Semester **Regional Accreditation:** North Central Association of Colleges and Schools **Professional Accreditation:** APA

ARIZONA AUTOMOTIVE INSTITUTE
6829 North 46th Ave.
Glendale, AZ 85301-3597
Tel: (602)934-7273
Admissions: 800-528-0717
Fax: (602)937-5000
E-mail: info@azautoinst.com
Web Site: http://www.aai.edu/
President/CEO: Dennis Del Valle
Type: Two-Year College **Sex:** Coed **Admission Plans:** Open Admission **Application Deadline:** Rolling **Application Fee:** $100.00 **Professional Accreditation:** ACCSCT

ARIZONA COLLEGE OF ALLIED HEALTH
4425 West Olive Ave.
Ste. 300
Glendale, AZ 85302-3843
Tel: (602)222-9300
Fax: (602)200-8726
E-mail: lhicks@arizonacollege.edu
Web Site: http://www.arizonacollege.edu/
President/CEO: C. Larkin Hicks
Type: Two-Year College **Sex:** Coed **Application Fee:** $25.00 **Calendar System:** Quarter **Professional Accreditation:** ABHES

ARIZONA STATE UNIVERSITY
Tempe, AZ 85287
Tel: (480)965-9011
Admissions: (480)965-7788
Fax: (482)965-1608
E-mail: ugradinq@asu.edu
Web Site: http://www.asu.edu/
President/CEO: Dr. Michael M. Crow
Admissions: Kent Hopkins
Financial Aid: Craig Fennell
Type: University **Sex:** Coed **Affiliation:** Arizona State University System **Scores:** 94.1% SAT V 400+; 94.7% SAT M 400+; 42.6% ACT 18-23; 39.5% ACT 24-29 **% Accepted:** 91 **Application Fee:** $55.00 **H.S. Requirements:** High school diploma required; GED accepted **Costs Per Year:** Application fee: $55. State resident tuition: $7793 full-time, $557 per credit hour part-time. Nonresident tuition: $20,257 full-time, $844 per credit hour part-time. Mandatory fees: $339 full-time. College room and board: $9706. College room only: $5640. **Scholarships:** Available **Calendar System:** Semester, Summer Session Available **Enrollment:** FT 45,597, PT 8,680, Grad FT 9,036, Grad PT 4,751 **Faculty:** FT 2,492, PT 237 **Student-Faculty Ratio:** 23:1 **Exams:** SAT I or ACT. **% Receiving Financial Aid:** 47 **% Residing in College-Owned, -Operated, or -Affiliated Housing:** 20 **Final Year or Final Semester Residency Requirement:** No **Library Holdings:** 4,393,156 **Regional Accreditation:** North Central Association of Colleges and Schools **Credit Hours For Degree:** 120 credits, Bachelors **ROTC:** Army, Air Force **Professional Accreditation:** AACSB, ABET, ACEJMC, AACN, ABA, ACCE, ACA, ACSP, APA, ASLA, ASLHA, AALS, ACEHSA, FIDER, CEPH, CSWE, NAACLS, NAAB, NASAD, NASM NASPAA, NLN, NRPA **Intercollegiate Athletics:** Baseball M; Basketball M & W; Cross-Country Running M & W; Football M; Golf M & W; Gymnastics W; Soccer W; Softball W; Swimming and Diving M & W; Tennis W; Track and Field M & W; Volleyball W; Water Polo W; Wrestling M

ARIZONA WESTERN COLLEGE
PO Box 929
Yuma, AZ 85366-0929
Tel: (928)317-6000; Free: 888-293-0392
Admissions: (928)317-7600
Fax: (928)344-7730
E-mail: amy.pignatore@azwestern.edu
Web Site: http://www.azwestern.edu/
President/CEO: Dr. Glen Mayle
Admissions: Amy Pignatore
Type: Two-Year College **Sex:** Coed **Affiliation:** Arizona State Community College System **Admission Plans:** Open Admission; Early Admission; Deferred Admission **Application Deadline:** Rolling **Application Fee:** $0.00 **H.S. Requirements:** High school diploma or equivalent not required. For applicants 18 or over: High school diploma required; GED accepted **Costs Per Year:** Application fee: $0. State resident tuition: $1440 full-time, $60 per credit hour part-time. Nonresident tuition: $6000 full-time, $66 per credit hour part-time. Full-time tuition varies according to course load and program. Part-time tuition varies according to course load and program. College room and board: $5140. College room only: $1990. Room and board charges vary according to board plan and housing facility. **Scholarships:** Available **Calendar System:** Semester, Summer Session Available **Enrollment:** FT 2,672, PT 5,312 **Student-Faculty Ratio:** 20:1 **Exams:** SAT I or ACT. **% Residing in College-Owned, -Operated, or -Affiliated Housing:** 3 **Final Year or Final Semester Residency Requirement:** No **Library Holdings:** 94,116 **Regional Accreditation:** North Central Association of Colleges and Schools **Credit Hours For Degree:** 64 credit hours, Associates **Professional Accreditation:** NLN **Intercollegiate Athletics:** Baseball M; Basketball M & W; Football M; Soccer M; Softball W; Volleyball W

THE ART CENTER DESIGN COLLEGE
2525 North Country Club Rd.
Tucson, AZ 85716-2505
Tel: (520)325-0123; Free: 800-825-8753
Fax: (520)325-5535
Web Site: http://www.theartcenter.edu/
President/CEO: Sharmon R. Woods
Admissions: Sarah LaVetter
Type: Four-Year College **Sex:** Coed **Application Deadline:** Rolling **Application Fee:** $25.00 **H.S. Requirements:** High school diploma required; GED accepted. For non-degree programs: High school diploma or equivalent not required **Costs Per Year:** Application fee: $25. One-time mandatory fee: $125. Tuition: $25,560 full-time, $710 per credit hour part-time. Full-time tuition varies according to course load, location, and program. Part-time tuition varies according to location and program. Tuition guaranteed not to increase for student's term of enrollment. **Scholarships:** Available **Calendar System:** Miscellaneous, Summer Session Available **Enrollment:** FT 164, PT 62 **Exams:** Other. **Regional Accreditation:** North Central Association of Colleges and Schools **ROTC:** Army **Professional Accreditation:** ACCSCT, FIDER

THE ART INSTITUTE OF PHOENIX
2233 West Dunlap Ave.
Phoenix, AZ 85021-2859
Tel: (602)331-7500; Free: 800-474-2479
Fax: (602)331-5301
Web Site: http://www.artinstitutes.edu/phoenix/
President/CEO: Kevin LaMountain
Type: Four-Year College **Sex:** Coed **Affiliation:** Education Management Corporation **Calendar System:** Quarter **Professional Accreditation:** ACICS

THE ART INSTITUTE OF TUCSON
5099 East Grant Rd.
Ste. 100
Tucson, AZ 85712
Tel: (520)881-2900; Free: (866)690-8850
Admissions: (520)318-2719
Fax: (520)881-4234
Web Site: http://www.artinstitutes.edu/tucson/
President/CEO: Karen Habblitz
Type: Four-Year College **Sex:** Coed

BROOKLINE COLLEGE (PHOENIX)
2445 West Dunlap Ave., Ste. 100
Phoenix, AZ 85021
Tel: (602)242-6265; Free: 800-793-2428
Fax: (602)973-2572
E-mail: obortman@brooklinecollege.edu
Web Site: http://brooklinecollege.edu/
President/CEO: Oleg Bortman
Admissions: Oleg Bortman
Type: Four-Year College **Sex:** Coed **Admission Plans:** Open Admission **Application Deadline:** Rolling **H.S. Requirements:** High school diploma required; GED accepted **Costs Per Year:** Tuition: $14,000 full-time. Full-time tuition varies according to degree level and program. Tuition guaranteed not to increase for student's term of enrollment. **Calendar System:** Continuous **Enrollment:** FT 1,186 **Faculty:** FT 46, PT 23 **Professional Accreditation:** ACICS

BROOKLINE COLLEGE (TEMPE)
1140-1150 South Priest Dr.
Tempe, AZ 85281
Tel: (480)545-8755; Free: 888-886-2428
Fax: (480)926-1371
E-mail: ckindred@brooklinecollege.edu
Web Site: http://brooklinecollege.edu/
President/CEO: Cheryl Kindred
Admissions: Cheryl Kindred
Type: Four-Year College **Sex:** Coed **Admission Plans:** Open Admission **Application Deadline:** Rolling **Application Fee:** $0.00 **H.S. Requirements:** High school diploma required; GED accepted **Costs Per Year:** Application fee: $0. Tuition: $14,000 full-time. Full-time tuition varies according to degree level and program. Tuition guaranteed not to increase for student's term of enrollment. **Calendar System:** Continuous **Enrollment:** FT 301 **Faculty:** FT 9, PT 12 **Student-Faculty Ratio:** 14:1 **Professional Accreditation:** ACICS

BROOKLINE COLLEGE (TUCSON)
5441 East 22nd St.
Ste. 125
Tucson, AZ 85711
Tel: (520)748-9799; Free: 888-292-2428
Fax: (520)748-9355
E-mail: lpechota@brooklinecollege.edu
Web Site: http://brooklinecollege.edu/

President/CEO: Leigh Anne Pechota
Admissions: Leigh Anne Pechota
Type: Four-Year College **Sex:** Coed **Admission Plans:** Open Admission **Application Deadline:** Rolling **H.S. Requirements:** High school diploma required; GED accepted **Costs Per Year:** Tuition: $14,000 full-time. Full-time tuition varies according to degree level and program. Tuition guaranteed not to increase for student's term of enrollment. **Calendar System:** Continuous **Enrollment:** FT 598 **Faculty:** FT 18, PT 8 **Student-Faculty Ratio:** 23:1 **Professional Accreditation:** ACICS

BROWN MACKIE COLLEGE—PHOENIX
13430 North Black Canyon Hwy.
Ste. 190
Phoenix, AZ 85029
Tel: (602)337-3044; Free: (866)824-4793
Web Site: http://www.brownmackie.edu/phoenix/
President/CEO: Deborah Thibodeaux
Type: Two-Year College **Sex:** Coed **Affiliation:** Education Management Corporation

BROWN MACKIE COLLEGE—TUCSON
4585 East Speedway, Ste. 204
Tucson, AZ 85712
Tel: (520)319-3300
Fax: (520)325-0108
Web Site: http://www.brownmackie.edu/tucson/
President/CEO: Holly Helscher, PhD
Type: Two-Year College **Sex:** Coed **Affiliation:** Education Management Corporation **Credit Hours For Degree:** 90 credit hours, Associates; 183 credit hours, Bachelors **Professional Accreditation:** ACICS

THE BRYMAN SCHOOL OF ARIZONA
2250 West Peoria Ave.
Phoenix, AZ 85029
Tel: (602)274-4300; Free: 800-729-4819
Fax: (602)248-9087
Web Site: http://www.brymanschool.edu/
President/CEO: Shawn Alexander
Type: Two-Year College **Sex:** Coed **Admission Plans:** Open Admission **Application Deadline:** Rolling **Application Fee:** $50.00 **H.S. Requirements:** High school diploma required; GED accepted **Scholarships:** Available **Calendar System:** Continuous, Summer Session Not available **Faculty:** FT 59, PT 0 **Student-Faculty Ratio:** 18:1 **Professional Accreditation:** ABHES, ACCSCT, AAMAE

CENTRAL ARIZONA COLLEGE
8470 North Overfield Rd.
Coolidge, AZ 85128
Tel: (520)494-5444
Admissions: (520)494-5261
Fax: (520)426-4234
E-mail: james.moore@centralaz.edu
Web Site: http://www.centralaz.edu/
President/CEO: Dennis Jenkins
Admissions: Dr. James Moore
Type: Two-Year College **Sex:** Coed **Admission Plans:** Open Admission; Early Admission; Deferred Admission **Application Deadline:** Rolling **Application Fee:** $0.00 **H.S. Requirements:** High school diploma or equivalent not required **Costs Per Year:** Application fee: $0. State resident tuition: $1560 full-time, $65 per credit hour part-time. Nonresident tuition: $6936 full-time, $130 per credit hour part-time. Full-time tuition varies according to course level, course load, program, reciprocity agreements, and student level. Part-time tuition varies according to course level, course load, program, and student level. College room and board: $4612. Room and board charges vary according to housing facility and location. **Scholarships:** Available **Calendar System:** Semester, Summer Session Available **Enrollment:** FT 2,976, PT 4,937 **Faculty:** FT 94, PT 116 **Student-Faculty Ratio:** 14:1 **% Residing in College-Owned, -Operated, or -Affiliated Housing:** 17 **Final Year or Final Semester Residency Requirement:** No **Library Holdings:** 77,709 **Regional Accreditation:** North Central Association of Colleges and Schools **Credit Hours For Degree:** 64 credits, Associates **Professional Accreditation:** NLN **Intercollegiate Athletics:** Baseball M; Basketball M & W; Cross-Country Running M & W; Equestrian Sports M & W; Softball W; Track and Field M & W

CHANDLER-GILBERT COMMUNITY COLLEGE
2626 East Pecos Rd.
Chandler, AZ 85225-2479
Tel: (480)732-7000
Web Site: http://www.cgc.maricopa.edu/
President/CEO: Dr. Linda Lujan
Admissions: Irene Pearl
Type: Two-Year College **Sex:** Coed **Affiliation:** Maricopa County Community College District System **Admission Plans:** Open Admission **Application Fee:** $0.00 **H.S. Requirements:** High school diploma or equivalent not required **Calendar System:** Semester, Summer Session Available **Enrollment:** FT 2,589, PT 6,831 **Faculty:** FT 92, PT 320 **Student-Faculty Ratio:** 19:1 **Library Holdings:** 26,060 **Regional Accreditation:** North Central Association of Colleges and Schools **Credit Hours For Degree:** 64 credits, Associates

COCHISE COLLEGE
901 North Colombo Ave.
Sierra Vista, AZ 85635-2317
Tel: (520)515-0500; Free: 800-593-9567
Admissions: (520)515-5412
Fax: (520)364-0206
E-mail: quickd@cochise.edu
Web Site: http://www.cochise.edu/
President/CEO: Dr. James Dale Rottweiler
Admissions: Debbie Quick
Type: Two-Year College **Sex:** Coed **% Accepted:** 100 **Admission Plans:** Open Admission; Deferred Admission **Application Deadline:** Rolling **H.S. Requirements:** High school diploma or equivalent not required. For applicants under 18, nursing program: High school diploma required; GED not accepted **Costs Per Year:** State resident tuition: $1560 full-time, $52 per credit hour part-time. Nonresident tuition: $8700 full-time, $290 per credit hour part-time. Mandatory fees: $70 full-time, $35 per term part-time. College room and board: $5300. Part-time tuition for nonresidents is $78 per credit for 1 to 6 credits, $290 per credit for students taking over 6 credits. **Scholarships:** Available **Calendar System:** Semester, Summer Session Available **Enrollment:** FT 1,109, PT 3,026 **Faculty:** FT 93, PT 227 **Student-Faculty Ratio:** 13:1 **Exams:** SAT I and SAT II or ACT. **% Residing in College-Owned, -Operated, or -Affiliated Housing:** 10 **Library Holdings:** 90,481 **Regional Accreditation:** North Central Association of Colleges and Schools **Credit Hours For Degree:** 64 credit hours, Associates **Intercollegiate Athletics:** Baseball M; Basketball M & W; Equestrian Sports M & W; Soccer W

COCONINO COMMUNITY COLLEGE
2800 South Lonetree Rd.
Flagstaff, AZ 86001
Tel: (928)527-1222; Free: 800-350-7122
Admissions: (928)226-4334
Fax: (928)526-1821
E-mail: veronica.hipolito@coconino.edu
Web Site: http://www.coconino.edu/
President/CEO: Dr. Leah Bornstein
Admissions: Veronica Hipolito
Type: Two-Year College **Sex:** Coed **Admission Plans:** Open Admission **Application Deadline:** Rolling **Application Fee:** $0.00 **H.S. Requirements:** High school diploma or equivalent not required **Costs Per Year:** Application fee: $0. State resident tuition: $1800 full-time, $75 per credit hour part-time. Nonresident tuition: $6000 full-time, $250 per credit hour part-time. **Scholarships:** Available **Calendar System:** Semester, Summer Session Available **Enrollment:** FT 840, PT 2,911 **Faculty:** FT 41, PT 230 **Student-Faculty Ratio:** 14:1 **Library Holdings:** 5,905 **Regional Accreditation:** North Central Association of Colleges and Schools **Credit Hours For Degree:** 60 credit hours, Associates **ROTC:** Army, Air Force

COLLEGE OF THE HUMANITIES AND SCIENCES, HARRISON MIDDLETON UNIVERSITY
1105 East Broadway
Tempe, AZ 85282
Tel: (480)317-5955; Free: 877-248-6724
Fax: (480)829-4999
Web Site: http://www.chumsci.edu/
President/CEO: Dr. David W. Curd
Financial Aid: Susan Chiaramonte

Type: Comprehensive **Sex:** Coed **Admission Plans:** Open Admission **Application Deadline:** Rolling **Application Fee:** $50.00 **H.S. Requirements:** High school diploma required; GED accepted **Costs Per Year:** Application fee: $50. Tuition: $27,200 full-time. **Calendar System:** Continuous, Summer Session Available **Faculty:** FT 17, PT 6 **Final Year or Final Semester Residency Requirement:** No **Credit Hours For Degree:** 60 credit hours, Associates; 120 credit hours, Bachelors **Professional Accreditation:** DETC

COLLEGEAMERICA—FLAGSTAFF
5200 East Cortland Blvd., Ste. A-19
Flagstaff, AZ 86004
Tel: (928)526-0763
Admissions: (928)213-6060
Fax: (928)526-3468
Web Site: http://www.collegeamerica.com/
President/CEO: Suzanne Scales
Type: Two-Year College **Sex:** Coed **Admission Plans:** Open Admission **Student-Faculty Ratio:** 24:1 **Professional Accreditation:** ABHES, ACCSCT

COLLINS COLLEGE: A SCHOOL OF DESIGN AND TECHNOLOGY
1140 South Priest Dr.
Tempe, AZ 85281-5206
Tel: (480)966-3000; Free: 800-876-7070
Fax: (480)966-2599
E-mail: contact@collinscollege.edu
Web Site: http://www.collinscollege.edu/
President/CEO: Joshua Padron
Financial Aid: Kari Yearwood
Type: Four-Year College **Sex:** Coed **Affiliation:** Career Education Corporation **Admission Plans:** Open Admission; Early Admission; Deferred Admission **Application Deadline:** Rolling **Application Fee:** $50.00 **H.S. Requirements:** High school diploma required; GED accepted **Scholarships:** Available **Calendar System:** Trimester **Enrollment:** FT 1,287 **Faculty:** FT 55, PT 47 **Student-Faculty Ratio:** 30:1 **Exams:** SAT I and SAT II or ACT. **% Receiving Financial Aid:** 90 **Library Holdings:** 1,000 **Professional Accreditation:** ACCSCT

DEVRY UNIVERSITY (MESA)
1201 South Alma School Rd.
Mesa, AZ 85210-2011
Tel: (480)827-1511
Fax: (480)827-2552
Web Site: http://www.devry.edu/
Type: Comprehensive **Sex:** Coed **Calendar System:** Semester **Regional Accreditation:** North Central Association of Colleges and Schools

DEVRY UNIVERSITY (PHOENIX)
2149 West Dunlap Ave.
Phoenix, AZ 85021-2995
Tel: (602)870-9222
Web Site: http://www.devry.edu/
President/CEO: Craig Jacob
Financial Aid: Kathy Wyse
Type: Comprehensive **Sex:** Coed **Affiliation:** DeVry University **Admission Plans:** Early Admission; Deferred Admission **Application Deadline:** Rolling **Application Fee:** $50.00 **H.S. Requirements:** High school diploma required; GED accepted **Costs Per Year:** Application fee: $50. Tuition: $14,080 full-time, $550 per credit hour part-time. **Scholarships:** Available **Calendar System:** Semester, Summer Session Available **Enrollment:** FT 819, PT 522, Grad FT 19, Grad PT 195 **Faculty:** FT 32, PT 87 **Student-Faculty Ratio:** 18:1 **Exams:** ACT essay used for admission. SAT essay used for admission. ACT essay used for placement. SAT essay used for placement. **% Receiving Financial Aid:** 82 **Regional Accreditation:** North Central Association of Colleges and Schools **ROTC:** Air Force **Professional Accreditation:** ABET

DINE COLLEGE
PO Box 98
Tsaile, AZ 86556
Tel: (520)724-6600
Admissions: (928)724-6633
Fax: (520)724-3349
E-mail: louise@dinecollege.edu
Web Site: http://www.dinecollege.edu/
President/CEO: Ferlin Clark
Admissions: Louise Litzin
Type: Two-Year College **Sex:** Coed **Admission Plans:** Open Admission; Preferred Admission; Early Admission **Application Deadline:** Rolling **Application Fee:** $20.00 **H.S. Requirements:** High school diploma required; GED accepted **Scholarships:** Available **Calendar System:** Semester, Summer Session Available **Enrollment:** FT 815, PT 842 **Library Holdings:** 50,000 **Regional Accreditation:** North Central Association of Colleges and Schools **Credit Hours For Degree:** 64 credit hours, Associates **Intercollegiate Athletics:** Archery M & W; Cross-Country Running M & W

DUNLAP-STONE UNIVERSITY
11225 North 28th Dr.
Ste. B-201
Phoenix, AZ 85029
Tel: (602)648-5750; Free: 800-474-8013
Fax: (602)648-5755
E-mail: director@expandglobal.com
Web Site: http://www.dunlap-stone.edu/
Admissions: Dr. Donald N. Burton
Type: Four-Year College **Sex:** Coed **Admission Plans:** Open Admission; Deferred Admission **Application Deadline:** Rolling **Application Fee:** $0.00 **H.S. Requirements:** High school diploma required; GED accepted **Costs Per Year:** Application fee: $0. Tuition: $7800 full-time, $310 per credit hour part-time. Mandatory fees: $50 full-time. Full-time tuition and fees vary according to course level, course load, degree level, and program. Part-time tuition varies according to course level, course load, degree level, and program. Tuition guaranteed not to increase for student's term of enrollment. **Calendar System:** Semester, Summer Session Not available **Faculty:** FT 0, PT 100 **Student-Faculty Ratio:** 15:1 **Final Year or Final Semester Residency Requirement:** No **Professional Accreditation:** DETC

EASTERN ARIZONA COLLEGE
PO Box 769
Thatcher, AZ 85552-0769
Tel: (928)428-8322
Admissions: (928)426-8354
Fax: (928)428-8462
E-mail: admissions@eac.edu
Web Site: http://www.eac.edu/
President/CEO: Mark Bryce, JD
Admissions: Dr. Gary Sorenson
Type: Two-Year College **Sex:** Coed **Affiliation:** Arizona State Community College System **% Accepted:** 100 **Admission Plans:** Open Admission; Early Admission; Deferred Admission **Application Deadline:** Rolling **Application Fee:** $0.00 **H.S. Requirements:** High school diploma or equivalent not required **Costs Per Year:** Application fee: $0. State resident tuition: $1520 full-time, $85 per credit hour part-time. Nonresident tuition: $8120 full-time, $140 per credit hour part-time. College room and board: $5075. College room only: $2690. Room and board charges vary according to board plan and housing facility. **Scholarships:** Available **Calendar System:** Semester, Summer Session Available **Enrollment:** FT 2,285, PT 4,956 **Faculty:** FT 94, PT 265 **Student-Faculty Ratio:** 22:1 **% Residing in College-Owned, -Operated, or -Affiliated Housing:** 5 **Regional Accreditation:** North Central Association of Colleges and Schools **Credit Hours For Degree:** 64 semester hours, Associates **Intercollegiate Athletics:** Baseball M; Basketball M & W; Football M; Golf M & W; Softball W; Volleyball W

EMBRY-RIDDLE AERONAUTICAL UNIVERSITY
3700 Willow Creek Rd.
Prescott, AZ 86301-3720
Tel: (928)777-3728; Free: 800-888-3728
Admissions: (928)777-6600
Fax: (928)777-3740
E-mail: pradmit@erau.edu
Web Site: http://www.embryriddle.edu/
President/CEO: Dr. John P. Johnson
Admissions: Debra Cates-Foster
Financial Aid: Dan Lupin
Type: Comprehensive **Sex:** Coed **Scores:** 97% SAT V 400+; 97% SAT M 400+; 35% ACT 18-23; 44% ACT 24-29 **% Accepted:** 85 **Admission Plans:** Deferred Admission **Application Deadline:** Rolling **Application Fee:** $50.00

H.S. Requirements: High school diploma required; GED accepted **Costs Per Year:** Application fee: $50. Comprehensive fee: $37,910 includes full-time tuition ($28,560), mandatory fees ($820), and college room and board ($8530). College room only: $4780. Room and board charges vary according to board plan and housing facility. Part-time tuition: $1190 per credit hour. **Scholarships:** Available **Calendar System:** Semester, Summer Session Available **Enrollment:** FT 1,498, PT 129, Grad FT 41, Grad PT 4 **Faculty:** FT 89, PT 29 **Student-Faculty Ratio:** 16:1 **Exams:** SAT I and SAT II or ACT. ACT essay not being used. SAT essay not being used. **% Receiving Financial Aid:** 67 **% Residing in College-Owned, -Operated, or -Affiliated Housing:** 45 **Final Year or Final Semester Residency Requirement:** No **Library Holdings:** 44,034 **Regional Accreditation:** Southern Association of Colleges and Schools **Credit Hours For Degree:** 120 credit hours, Bachelors **ROTC:** Army, Air Force **Professional Accreditation:** ABET, CAA **Intercollegiate Athletics:** Volleyball W; Wrestling M

ESTRELLA MOUNTAIN COMMUNITY COLLEGE
3000 North Dysart Rd.
Avondale, AZ 85392
Tel: (623)935-8000
Admissions: (623)935-8812
E-mail: debbie.kushibab@emcmail.maricopa.edu
Web Site: http://www.emc.maricopa.edu/
President/CEO: Dr. Ernesto Lara
Admissions: Dr. Debbie Kushibab
Type: Two-Year College **Sex:** Coed **Affiliation:** Maricopa County Community College District System **% Accepted:** 100 **Admission Plans:** Open Admission **Costs Per Year:** Area resident tuition: $1704 full-time, $71 per credit hour part-time. State resident tuition: $7488 full-time, $312 per credit hour part-time. Nonresident tuition: $7488 full-time, $312 per credit hour part-time. Mandatory fees: $30 full-time, $15 per term part-time. **Scholarships:** Available **Calendar System:** Semester, Summer Session Available **Enrollment:** FT 1,631, PT 4,727 **Faculty:** FT 70, PT 286 **Student-Faculty Ratio:** 22:1 **Library Holdings:** 57,000 **Regional Accreditation:** North Central Association of Colleges and Schools **Credit Hours For Degree:** 60 credits, Associates **ROTC:** Air Force

EVEREST COLLEGE
10400 North 25th Ave.
Ste. 190
Phoenix, AZ 85021
Tel: (602)942-4141
Fax: (602)943-0960
E-mail: jaskins@cci.edu
Web Site: http://www.everest.edu/
President/CEO: Todd McDonald
Admissions: Jim Askins
Type: Two-Year College **Sex:** Coed **Affiliation:** Corinthian Colleges, Inc. **% Accepted:** 78 **Admission Plans:** Deferred Admission **Application Deadline:** Rolling **Application Fee:** $0.00 **H.S. Requirements:** High school diploma required; GED accepted **Scholarships:** Available **Calendar System:** Miscellaneous **Enrollment:** FT 347, PT 205 **Faculty:** FT 15, PT 35 **Student-Faculty Ratio:** 16:1 **Library Holdings:** 17,515 **Regional Accreditation:** North Central Association of Colleges and Schools **Credit Hours For Degree:** 60 credits, Associates **Professional Accreditation:** ACICS

EVEREST ONLINE
8150 South Hardy Dr. No. 102
Tempe, AZ 85284-1117
Tel: 888-391-8881
Web Site: http://www.everestonline.edu/
Type: Comprehensive **Sex:** Coed

GATEWAY COMMUNITY COLLEGE
108 North 40th St.
Phoenix, AZ 85034-1795
Tel: (602)286-8000
Admissions: (602)392-5000
Fax: (602)286-8003
E-mail: cathy.gibson@gwmail.maricopa.edu
Web Site: http://www.gwc.maricopa.edu/
President/CEO: Eugene Giovannini, EdD
Admissions: Cathy Gibson
Type: Two-Year College **Sex:** Coed **Affiliation:** Maricopa County Community College District System **Admission Plans:** Open Admission; Early Admission; Deferred Admission **Application Deadline:** Rolling **Application Fee:** $0.00 **H.S. Requirements:** High school diploma or equivalent not required. For health science, nursing programs: High school diploma required; GED accepted **Scholarships:** Available **Calendar System:** Semester, Summer Session Available **Enrollment:** FT 976, PT 8,401 **Faculty:** FT 70, PT 189 **Student-Faculty Ratio:** 25:1 **Library Holdings:** 50,000 **Regional Accreditation:** North Central Association of Colleges and Schools **Credit Hours For Degree:** 60 credit hours, Associates **ROTC:** Army, Air Force **Professional Accreditation:** APTA, CARC, JRCERT, NLN **Intercollegiate Athletics:** Cross-Country Running M & W; Golf M & W; Tennis M & W

GLENDALE COMMUNITY COLLEGE
6000 West Olive Ave.
Glendale, AZ 85302-3090
Tel: (623)845-3000
Admissions: (623)435-3305
Fax: (623)845-3329
E-mail: info@gc.maricopa.edu
Web Site: http://www.gc.maricopa.edu/
President/CEO: Dr. Velvie Green
Admissions: Mary Blackwell
Type: Two-Year College **Sex:** Coed **Affiliation:** Maricopa County Community College District System **Admission Plans:** Open Admission **Application Deadline:** August 21 **Application Fee:** $0.00 **H.S. Requirements:** High school diploma or equivalent not required **Costs Per Year:** Application fee: $0. State resident tuition: $1704 full-time, $71 per semester hour part-time. Nonresident tuition: $7488 full-time, $312 per semester hour part-time. Mandatory fees: $30 full-time, $15 per term part-time. Full-time tuition and fees vary according to program and reciprocity agreements. Part-time tuition and fees vary according to course load, program, and reciprocity agreements. College room and board: $8352. **Scholarships:** Available **Calendar System:** Semester, Summer Session Available **Enrollment:** FT 7,131, PT 13,023 **Faculty:** FT 229, PT 813 **Student-Faculty Ratio:** 22:1 **Library Holdings:** 97,768 **Regional Accreditation:** North Central Association of Colleges and Schools **Credit Hours For Degree:** 60 credit hours, Associates **ROTC:** Army, Air Force **Professional Accreditation:** NLN **Intercollegiate Athletics:** Baseball M; Basketball M & W; Cross-Country Running M & W; Football M; Golf M; Soccer M & W; Softball W; Tennis M & W; Track and Field M & W; Volleyball W

GRAND CANYON UNIVERSITY
3300 West Camelback Rd., PO Box 11097
Phoenix, AZ 85017-1097
Tel: (602)249-3300
Admissions: 800-486-7085
Fax: (602)589-2580
E-mail: admissionsonline@gcu.edu
Web Site: http://www.gcu.edu/
President/CEO: Brent Richardson
Type: Comprehensive **Sex:** Coed **Affiliation:** Southern Baptist **% Accepted:** 73 **Admission Plans:** Early Admission; Deferred Admission **Application Deadline:** Rolling **Application Fee:** $100.00 **H.S. Requirements:** High school diploma required; GED accepted **Scholarships:** Available **Calendar System:** Semester, Summer Session Available **Enrollment:** FT 1,714, PT 3,108 **Faculty:** FT 46, PT 468 **Student-Faculty Ratio:** 13:1 **% Residing in College-Owned, -Operated, or -Affiliated Housing:** 40 **Regional Accreditation:** North Central Association of Colleges and Schools **Credit Hours For Degree:** 128 semester hours, Bachelors **ROTC:** Army, Air Force **Professional Accreditation:** AACN, ACBSP, NLN **Intercollegiate Athletics:** Baseball M; Basketball M & W; Cross-Country Running M; Golf M & W; Lacrosse M; Soccer M & W; Softball W; Swimming and Diving M & W; Tennis W; Volleyball W; Wrestling M

HIGH-TECH INSTITUTE
1515 East Indian School Rd.
Phoenix, AZ 85014-4901
Tel: (602)279-9700
Fax: (602)279-2999
Web Site: http://www.high-techinstitute.com/
President/CEO: Fred Pressel
Admissions: Glen Husband

Type: Two-Year College **Sex:** Coed **Admission Plans:** Open Admission **Application Deadline:** Rolling **Application Fee:** $50.00 **H.S. Requirements:** High school diploma required; GED accepted **Scholarships:** Available **Calendar System:** Semester **Credit Hours For Degree:** 75 credit hours, Associates **Professional Accreditation:** ACCSCT

INTERNATIONAL BAPTIST COLLEGE
2211 West Germann Rd.
Chandler, AZ 85286
Tel: (480)245-7903; Free: 800-422-4858
Web Site: http://www.ibconline.edu/ibc/
President/CEO: David W. Brock
Admissions: Rebecca M. Stertzbach
Type: Comprehensive **Sex:** Coed **Affiliation:** Baptist **Admission Plans:** Open Admission; Early Admission **Application Deadline:** August 20 **Application Fee:** $35.00 **H.S. Requirements:** High school diploma or equivalent not required **Scholarships:** Available **Calendar System:** 4-1-4 **Enrollment:** FT 47, PT 28 **Faculty:** FT 3, PT 10 **Student-Faculty Ratio:** 12:1 **Credit Hours For Degree:** 67 semester hours, Associates; 133 semester hours, Bachelors **Professional Accreditation:** TACCS

ITT TECHNICAL INSTITUTE (PHOENIX)
10220 North 25th Ave., Ste. 100
Phoenix, AZ 85021
Tel: (602)749-7900; Free: 877-221-1132
Admissions: (602)749-7900
Web Site: http://www.itt-tech.edu/
President/CEO: Gene McWhorter
Type: Two-Year College **Sex:** Coed **Affiliation:** ITT Educational Services, Inc. **H.S. Requirements:** High school diploma required; GED accepted **Scholarships:** Available **Calendar System:** Quarter, Summer Session Not available **Credit Hours For Degree:** 90 credit hours, Associates; 180 credit hours, Bachelors **Professional Accreditation:** ACICS

ITT TECHNICAL INSTITUTE (TEMPE)
5005 S. Wendler Dr.
Tempe, AZ 85282
Tel: (602)437-7500; Free: 800-879-4881
Web Site: http://www.itt-tech.edu/
President/CEO: Charles Wilson
Type: Four-Year College **Sex:** Coed **Affiliation:** ITT Educational Services, Inc.

ITT TECHNICAL INSTITUTE (TUCSON)
1455 West River Rd.
Tucson, AZ 85704
Tel: (520)408-7488; Free: 800-870-9730
Fax: (520)292-9899
Web Site: http://www.itt-tech.edu/
President/CEO: Annette Swanson
Type: Two-Year College **Sex:** Coed **Affiliation:** ITT Educational Services, Inc. **H.S. Requirements:** High school diploma required; GED accepted **Scholarships:** Available **Calendar System:** Quarter, Summer Session Not available **Credit Hours For Degree:** 96 credit hours, Associates; 180 credit hours, Bachelors **Professional Accreditation:** ACICS

KAPLAN COLLEGE, PHOENIX CAMPUS
13610 North Black Canyon Hwy.
Ste. 104
Phoenix, AZ 85029
Tel: (602)548-1955; Free: 877-548-1955
Fax: (602)548-1956
Web Site: http://www.kc-phoenix.com/
President/CEO: Shelley Donati
Type: Two-Year College **Sex:** Coed **H.S. Requirements:** High school diploma required; GED accepted **Calendar System:** Continuous **Professional Accreditation:** ACCSCT, ACICS, CARC

LAMSON COLLEGE
875 West Elliot Rd., Ste. 206
Tempe, AZ 85284
Tel: (480)898-7000; Free: 800-898-7017
Fax: (480)967-6645
Web Site: http://www.lamsoncollege.com/
President/CEO: Shannon Warren
Admissions: Brittany Staudt
Type: Two-Year College **Sex:** Coed **Affiliation:** National Career Education, Inc. **Application Deadline:** Rolling **Application Fee:** $25.00 **H.S. Requirements:** High school diploma required; GED accepted **Scholarships:** Available **Calendar System:** Quarter, Summer Session Available **Exams:** Other. **Library Holdings:** 4,400 **Credit Hours For Degree:** 92 quarter hours, Associates **Professional Accreditation:** ACICS

MESA COMMUNITY COLLEGE
1833 West Southern Ave.
Mesa, AZ 85202-4866
Tel: (480)461-7000
Admissions: (602)461-7000
Fax: (480)461-7805
E-mail: admissions@mc.maricopa.edu
Web Site: http://www.mc.maricopa.edu/
President/CEO: Dr. Shouan Pan
Admissions: Kathleen Perales
Type: Two-Year College **Sex:** Coed **Affiliation:** Maricopa County Community College District System **Admission Plans:** Open Admission; Early Admission; Deferred Admission **Application Deadline:** August 22 **Application Fee:** $0.00 **H.S. Requirements:** High school diploma or equivalent not required **Scholarships:** Available **Calendar System:** Semester, Summer Session Available **Faculty:** FT 265, PT 800 **Library Holdings:** 56,224 **Regional Accreditation:** North Central Association of Colleges and Schools **Credit Hours For Degree:** 60 credit hours, Associates **ROTC:** Army, Air Force **Professional Accreditation:** ABFSE, NLN **Intercollegiate Athletics:** Baseball M; Basketball M & W; Cross-Country Running M; Football M; Golf M & W; Soccer M & W; Softball W; Tennis M & W; Track and Field M & W; Volleyball W; Wrestling M

MOHAVE COMMUNITY COLLEGE
1971 Jagerson Ave.
Kingman, AZ 86409
Tel: (928)757-4331; Free: 888-664-2832
Admissions: (928)757-0803
Fax: (928)757-0808
E-mail: jwoods@mohave.edu
Web Site: http://www.mohave.edu/
President/CEO: Dr. Michael J. Kearns
Admissions: Jann Woods
Type: Two-Year College **Sex:** Coed **Admission Plans:** Open Admission; Early Admission; Deferred Admission **Application Deadline:** Rolling **H.S. Requirements:** High school diploma or equivalent not required **Costs Per Year:** State resident tuition: $2070 full-time, $69 per credit hour part-time. Nonresident tuition: $5910 full-time, $197 per credit hour part-time. Mandatory fees: $180 full-time, $6 per credit part-time. Full-time tuition and fees vary according to program. Part-time tuition and fees vary according to program. **Scholarships:** Available **Calendar System:** Semester, Summer Session Available **Enrollment:** FT 1,922, PT 4,780 **Faculty:** FT 64, PT 346 **Student-Faculty Ratio:** 19:1 **Library Holdings:** 45,849 **Regional Accreditation:** North Central Association of Colleges and Schools **Credit Hours For Degree:** 60 semester hours, Associates

NATIONAL PARALEGAL COLLEGE
6516 N 7th St.
Ste. 103
Phoenix, AZ 85014
Tel: (845)371-9101; Free: 800-371-6105
Web Site: http://nationalparalegal.edu/
Type: Four-Year College **Sex:** Coed **Professional Accreditation:** DETC

NORTHCENTRAL UNIVERSITY
10000 East University Dr.
Prescott Valley, AZ 86314
Tel: (928)541-7777; Free: 888-327-2877
Fax: (928)541-7817
E-mail: info@ncu.edu
Web Site: http://www.ncu.edu/
President/CEO: Dr. Clinton Gardner
Admissions: Eric Stoddard
Type: Comprehensive **Sex:** Coed **Application Deadline:** Rolling **Application Fee:** $75.00 **H.S. Requirements:** High school diploma required; GED

accepted **Calendar System:** Continuous, Summer Session Available **Enrollment:** FT 399, Grad FT 7,985 **Faculty:** FT 23, PT 447 **Student-Faculty Ratio:** 18:1 **Regional Accreditation:** North Central Association of Colleges and Schools **Credit Hours For Degree:** 120 semester hours, Bachelors

NORTHERN ARIZONA UNIVERSITY
South San Francisco St.
Flagstaff, AZ 86011
Tel: (928)523-9011; Free: 888-MORE-NAU
Admissions: (928)523-6080
Fax: (928)523-0226
E-mail: undergraduate.admissions@nau.edu
Web Site: http://www.nau.edu/
President/CEO: John Haeger
Admissions: James E. Casebeer
Financial Aid: Michelle Castillo
Type: University **Sex:** Coed **Affiliation:** Arizona State University System, under the Arizona Board of Regents **Scores:** 94% SAT V 400+; 93% SAT M 400+; 48% ACT 18-23; 36% ACT 24-29 **% Accepted:** 73 **Admission Plans:** Deferred Admission **Application Deadline:** Rolling **Application Fee:** $25.00 **H.S. Requirements:** High school diploma required; GED accepted **Costs Per Year:** Application fee: $25. State resident tuition: $6092 full-time. Nonresident tuition: $17,318 full-time. Mandatory fees: $540 full-time. Full-time tuition and fees vary according to location and program. College room and board: $7872. Room and board charges vary according to board plan, housing facility, and location. Tuition guaranteed not to increase for student's term of enrollment. **Scholarships:** Available **Calendar System:** Semester, Summer Session Available **Enrollment:** FT 15,391, PT 2,910, Grad FT 2,086, Grad PT 3,213 **Faculty:** FT 813, PT 601 **Student-Faculty Ratio:** 19:1 **Exams:** ACT, Other, SAT I or ACT, SAT I and SAT II or ACT, SAT I, SAT II. **% Receiving Financial Aid:** 49 **% Residing in College-Owned, -Operated, or -Affiliated Housing:** 37 **Final Year or Final Semester Residency Requirement:** No **Library Holdings:** 1,118,663 **Regional Accreditation:** North Central Association of Colleges and Schools **Credit Hours For Degree:** 120 semester hours, Bachelors **ROTC:** Army, Air Force **Professional Accreditation:** AACSB, ABET, AACN, ACCE, ACA, ADA, APTA, ASLHA, ACBSP, CEPH, CSWE, NASM, NRPA, SAF **Intercollegiate Athletics:** Basketball M & W; Cheerleading M & W; Cross-Country Running M & W; Football M; Golf W; Soccer W; Swimming and Diving W; Tennis M & W; Track and Field M & W; Volleyball W

NORTHERN ARIZONA UNIVERSITY—YUMA
2020 South Ave. 8E
PO Box 6236
Yuma, AZ 85365
Tel: (928)317-6400; Free: 888-NAU-Yuma
Admissions: (928)317-6431
E-mail: eileen.knight@nau.edu
Web Site: http://www.yuma.nau.edu/
President/CEO: Larry Gould
Admissions: Eileen Knight
Type: Two-Year Upper Division **Sex:** Coed **Affiliation:** Northern Arizona University **Application Fee:** $25.00 **H.S. Requirements:** High school diploma required; GED accepted **Costs Per Year:** Application fee: $25. State resident tuition: $5040 full-time, $263 per credit part-time. Nonresident tuition: $15,644 full-time, $652 per credit part-time. Mandatory fees: $199 full-time. **Regional Accreditation:** North Central Association of Colleges and Schools

NORTHLAND PIONEER COLLEGE
PO Box 610
Holbrook, AZ 86025
Tel: (928)524-7311; Free: 800-266-7845
Admissions: (928)536-6271
Fax: (928)524-7612
Web Site: http://www.npc.edu/
President/CEO: Dr. Jeanne Swarthout
Admissions: Suzette Willis
Type: Two-Year College **Sex:** Coed **Affiliation:** Arizona State Community College System **Admission Plans:** Open Admission; Early Admission **Application Deadline:** Rolling **Application Fee:** $0.00 **H.S. Requirements:** High school diploma or equivalent not required **Costs Per Year:** Application fee: $0. State resident tuition: $1248 full-time, $52 per credit hour part-time. Nonresident tuition: $6000 full-time, $85 per credit hour part-time. Mandatory fees: $35 full-time, $35 per term part-time. **Scholarships:** Available **Calendar System:** Semester, Summer Session Available **Enrollment:** FT 946, PT 3,690 **Faculty:** FT 73, PT 153 **Student-Faculty Ratio:** 17:1 **Final Year or Final Semester Residency Requirement:** No **Library Holdings:** 60,000 **Regional Accreditation:** North Central Association of Colleges and Schools **Credit Hours For Degree:** 64 semester hours, Associates

PARADISE VALLEY COMMUNITY COLLEGE
18401 North 32nd St.
Phoenix, AZ 85032-1200
Tel: (602)787-6500
Fax: (602)787-6625
E-mail: donna.simon@pvmail.maricopa.edu
Web Site: http://www.pvc.maricopa.edu/
President/CEO: Dr. Paul Dale
Type: Two-Year College **Sex:** Coed **Affiliation:** Maricopa County Community College District System **Admission Plans:** Open Admission; Early Admission **Application Deadline:** Rolling **Application Fee:** $0.00 **H.S. Requirements:** High school diploma or equivalent not required **Costs Per Year:** Application fee: $0. Area resident tuition: $2130 full-time, $71 per credit hour part-time. State resident tuition: $9360 full-time, $312 per credit hour part-time. Nonresident tuition: $9360 full-time, $312 per credit hour part-time. **Scholarships:** Available **Calendar System:** Semester, Summer Session Available **Enrollment:** FT 3,043, PT 6,908 **Faculty:** FT 98, PT 444 **Regional Accreditation:** North Central Association of Colleges and Schools **Credit Hours For Degree:** 60 credit hours, Associates **ROTC:** Army **Intercollegiate Athletics:** Baseball M; Cross-Country Running M & W; Golf M & W; Soccer M & W; Softball W; Tennis M & W; Track and Field M & W

THE PARALEGAL INSTITUTE, INC.
2933 West Indian School Rd.
Phoenix, AZ 85017
Tel: (602)212-0501; Free: 800-354-1254
E-mail: paralegalinst@mindspring.com
Web Site: http://www.theparalegalinstitute.edu/
Admissions: Patricia Yancy
Type: Two-Year College **Sex:** Coed **% Accepted:** 25 **Faculty:** FT 1, PT 3 **Credit Hours For Degree:** 60 credits, Associates **Professional Accreditation:** DETC

PENN FOSTER COLLEGE
14300 North Northsight Blvd., Ste. 111
Scottsdale, AZ 85260
Tel: (480)947-6644
Web Site: http://www.pennfostercollege.edu/
Type: Four-Year College **Sex:** Coed **Professional Accreditation:** DETC

PHOENIX COLLEGE
1202 West Thomas Rd.
Phoenix, AZ 85013-4234
Tel: (602)285-7800
Admissions: (602)285-7503
Fax: (602)285-7700
E-mail: kathy.french@pcmail.maricopa.edu
Web Site: http://www.pc.maricopa.edu/
President/CEO: Dr. Anna Solley
Admissions: Kathleen French
Type: Two-Year College **Sex:** Coed **Affiliation:** Maricopa County Community College District System **Admission Plans:** Open Admission; Early Admission; Deferred Admission **Application Deadline:** Rolling **Application Fee:** $0.00 **H.S. Requirements:** High school diploma or equivalent not required **Costs Per Year:** Application fee: $0. Area resident tuition: $1704 full-time, $71 per credit hour part-time. State resident tuition: $6432 full-time, $268 per credit hour part-time. Nonresident tuition: $6864 full-time, $286 per credit hour part-time. Mandatory fees: $30 full-time, $15 per term part-time. Full-time tuition and fees vary according to location, program, and reciprocity agreements. Part-time tuition and fees vary according to course load, location, program, and reciprocity agreements. **Scholarships:** Available **Calendar System:** Semester, Summer Session Available **Enrollment:** FT 3,054, PT 9,110 **Faculty:** FT 147, PT 567 **Student-Faculty Ratio:** 17:1 **Library Holdings:** 83,000 **Regional Accreditation:** North Central Association of Colleges and Schools **Credit Hours For Degree:** 64 credit hours, Associates **ROTC:** Army, Navy, Air Force **Professional Accreditation:**

ADA, AHIMA, NLN **Intercollegiate Athletics:** Baseball M; Basketball M & W; Cross-Country Running M & W; Football M; Golf M & W; Soccer M & W; Softball W; Tennis M & W; Track and Field M & W; Volleyball W

PIMA COMMUNITY COLLEGE
4905 East Broadway
Tucson, AZ 85709-1010
Tel: (520)206-4666
Admissions: (520)206-4640
Fax: (520)884-6728
E-mail: mtulino@pima.edu
Web Site: http://www.pima.edu/
President/CEO: Dr. Roy Flores
Admissions: Michael Tulino
Type: Two-Year College **Sex:** Coed **Admission Plans:** Open Admission **Application Deadline:** Rolling **Application Fee:** $0.00 **H.S. Requirements:** High school diploma or equivalent not required **Costs Per Year:** Application fee: $0. State resident tuition: $1284 full-time, $53.50 per credit hour part-time. Nonresident tuition: $6456 full-time, $90 per credit hour part-time. Mandatory fees: $128 full-time, $4.50 per credit hour part-time, $10 per term part-time. **Scholarships:** Available **Calendar System:** Semester, Summer Session Available **Enrollment:** FT 11,708, PT 24,172 **Faculty:** FT 330, PT 1,223 **Student-Faculty Ratio:** 21:1 **Final Year or Final Semester Residency Requirement:** No **Library Holdings:** 333,719 **Regional Accreditation:** North Central Association of Colleges and Schools **Credit Hours For Degree:** 60 credit hours, Associates **ROTC:** Army, Navy, Air Force **Professional Accreditation:** ADA, CARC, JRCERT, NLN **Intercollegiate Athletics:** Baseball M; Basketball M & W; Cheerleading W; Cross-Country Running M & W; Football M; Golf M & W; Soccer M & W; Softball W; Tennis M & W; Track and Field M & W; Volleyball W

PIMA MEDICAL INSTITUTE (MESA)
957 South Dobson Rd.
Mesa, AZ 85202
Tel: (480)644-0267; Free: 888-898-9048
Fax: (480)649-5249
Web Site: http://www.pmi.edu/
President/CEO: Kristen Torres
Type: Two-Year College **Sex:** Coed **Affiliation:** Vocational Training Institutes, Inc. **Calendar System:** Miscellaneous **Exams:** Other. **Professional Accreditation:** ABHES, ACCSCT, CARC, JRCERT

PIMA MEDICAL INSTITUTE (TUCSON)
3350 East Grant Rd.
Tucson, AZ 85716
Tel: (520)326-1600; Free: 888-898-9048
Fax: (520)326-4125
Web Site: http://www.pmi.edu/
President/CEO: Dale Berg
Type: Two-Year College **Sex:** Coed **Affiliation:** Vocational Training Institutes, Inc. **Admission Plans:** Early Admission **H.S. Requirements:** High school diploma required; GED accepted **Calendar System:** Miscellaneous, Summer Session Not available **Exams:** Other. **Credit Hours For Degree:** 66 credits, Associates **Professional Accreditation:** ABHES, CARC, JRCERT

PRESCOTT COLLEGE
220 Grove Ave.
Prescott, AZ 86301
Tel: (928)778-2090; Free: 800-628-6364
Admissions: (928)350-2100
Fax: (928)776-5157
E-mail: admissions@prescott.edu
Web Site: http://www.prescott.edu/
President/CEO: Dr. Daniel Garvey
Admissions: Nancy Simmons
Type: Comprehensive **Sex:** Coed **Scores:** 96% SAT V 400+; 100% SAT M 400+; 33% ACT 18-23; 53% ACT 24-29 **% Accepted:** 81 **Admission Plans:** Early Decision Plan; Deferred Admission **Application Deadline:** August 15 **Application Fee:** $25.00 **H.S. Requirements:** High school diploma required; GED accepted **Costs Per Year:** Application fee: $25. Tuition: $23,232 full-time, $968 per term part-time. Mandatory fees: $411 full-time, $205.50 per term part-time. Full-time tuition and fees vary according to course load and degree level. Part-time tuition and fees vary according to course load and degree level. College room only: $3630. Room charges vary according to housing facility. **Scholarships:** Available **Calendar System:** Quarter, Summer Session Available **Enrollment:** FT 636, PT 127, Grad FT 190, Grad PT 168 **Faculty:** FT 69, PT 52 **Student-Faculty Ratio:** 8:1 **Exams:** SAT I or ACT. **% Receiving Financial Aid:** 63 **% Residing in College-Owned, -Operated, or -Affiliated Housing:** 4 **Final Year or Final Semester Residency Requirement:** No **Library Holdings:** 35,293 **Regional Accreditation:** North Central Association of Colleges and Schools **Credit Hours For Degree:** 120 semester credits, Bachelors

THE REFRIGERATION SCHOOL
4210 East Washington St.
Phoenix, AZ 85034-1816
Tel: (602)275-7133
E-mail: heather@rsiaz.edu
Web Site: http://www.refrigerationschool.com/
President/CEO: Sherry Jones
Admissions: Heather Haskell
Type: Two-Year College **Sex:** Coed **Scholarships:** Available **Calendar System:** Continuous **Faculty:** FT 12, PT 10 **Student-Faculty Ratio:** 38:1 **Professional Accreditation:** ACCSCT

RIO SALADO COLLEGE
2323 West 14th St.
Tempe, AZ 85281-6950
Tel: (480)517-8000; Free: 800-729-1197
Admissions: (480)517-8563
Fax: (480)517-8199
E-mail: admission@riomail.maricopa.edu
Web Site: http://www.rio.maricopa.edu/
President/CEO: Dr. Chris Bustamante
Admissions: Laurel Redman
Type: Two-Year College **Sex:** Coed **Affiliation:** Maricopa County Community College District System **Admission Plans:** Open Admission; Early Admission; Deferred Admission **Application Deadline:** Rolling **Application Fee:** $0.00 **H.S. Requirements:** High school diploma or equivalent not required **Costs Per Year:** Application fee: $0. Area resident tuition: $1704 full-time, $71 per credit hour part-time. State resident tuition: $7488 full-time, $312 per credit hour part-time. Nonresident tuition: $7488 full-time, $312 per credit hour part-time. Mandatory fees: $30 full-time, $15 per term part-time. Full-time tuition and fees vary according to course load, program, and reciprocity agreements. Part-time tuition and fees vary according to course load and reciprocity agreements. **Scholarships:** Available **Calendar System:** Semester, Summer Session Available **Student-Faculty Ratio:** 25:1 **Library Holdings:** 16,000 **Regional Accreditation:** North Central Association of Colleges and Schools **Credit Hours For Degree:** 64 credit hours, Associates **Professional Accreditation:** ADA

SCOTTSDALE COMMUNITY COLLEGE
9000 East Chaparral Rd.
Scottsdale, AZ 85256-2626
Tel: (480)423-6000
Admissions: (480)423-6133
Fax: (480)423-6200
E-mail: fran.watkins@sccmail.maricopa.edu
Web Site: http://www.scottsdalecc.edu/
President/CEO: Dr. Jan L. Gehler
Admissions: Fran Watkins
Type: Two-Year College **Sex:** Coed **Affiliation:** Maricopa County Community College District System **% Accepted:** 100 **Admission Plans:** Open Admission; Early Admission **Application Deadline:** Rolling **Application Fee:** $0.00 **H.S. Requirements:** High school diploma or equivalent not required **Costs Per Year:** Application fee: $0. Area resident tuition: $2130 full-time, $71 per credit hour part-time. State resident tuition: $9360 full-time, $96 per credit hour part-time. Nonresident tuition: $9360 full-time, $96 per credit hour part-time. Mandatory fees: $30 full-time, $15 per term part-time. **Scholarships:** Available **Calendar System:** Semester, Summer Session Available **Enrollment:** FT 3,698, PT 7,225 **Faculty:** FT 165, PT 471 **Student-Faculty Ratio:** 19:1 **Final Year or Final Semester Residency Requirement:** No **Regional Accreditation:** North Central Association of Colleges and Schools **Credit Hours For Degree:** 64 credit hours, Associates **Professional Accreditation:** NLN **Intercollegiate Athletics:** Baseball

M; Basketball M & W; Cross-Country Running M & W; Football M; Golf M & W; Soccer M & W; Softball W; Tennis M & W; Track and Field M & W; Volleyball W

SCOTTSDALE CULINARY INSTITUTE
8100 East Camelback Rd.
Ste. 1001
Scottsdale, AZ 85251-3940
Tel: (480)990-3773; Free: 800-848-2433
Fax: (480)990-0351
Web Site: http://www.scichefs.com/
President/CEO: Jake Elsen
Type: Two-Year College **Sex:** Coed **Application Fee:** $50.00 **Scholarships:** Available **Calendar System:** Semester **Professional Accreditation:** ACCSCT, ACF

SESSIONS COLLEGE FOR PROFESSIONAL DESIGN
398 South MIll Ave., Ste. 300
Tempe, AZ 85281
Tel: (480)212-1704
Fax: (480)212-1705
Web Site: http://www.sessions.edu/
Type: Two-Year College **Sex:** Coed **Professional Accreditation:** DETC

SOUTH MOUNTAIN COMMUNITY COLLEGE
7050 South Twenty-fourth St.
Phoenix, AZ 85040
Tel: (602)243-8000
Admissions: (602)243-8120
Fax: (602)243-8329
Web Site: http://www.southmountaincc.edu/
President/CEO: Dr. Kenneth Atwater
Type: Two-Year College **Sex:** Coed **Affiliation:** Maricopa County Community College District System **Admission Plans:** Open Admission **Application Deadline:** August 22 **Costs Per Year:** Area resident tuition: $1704 full-time, $71 per credit hour part-time. State resident tuition: $7488 full-time, $312 per credit hour part-time. Nonresident tuition: $7488 full-time, $312 per credit hour part-time. Mandatory fees: $30 full-time, $15 per term part-time. **Scholarships:** Available **Calendar System:** Semester, Summer Session Available **Student-Faculty Ratio:** 20:1 **Regional Accreditation:** North Central Association of Colleges and Schools **Credit Hours For Degree:** 62 credit hours, Associates **ROTC:** Air Force **Intercollegiate Athletics:** Baseball M; Basketball M & W; Golf M & W; Soccer M; Softball W; Volleyball W

SOUTHWEST INSTITUTE OF HEALING ARTS
1100 East Apache Blvd.
Tempe, AZ 85281
Tel: (480)994-9244; Free: 888-504-9106
Fax: (480)994-3228
E-mail: joannl@swiha.net
Web Site: http://www.swiha.org/
President/CEO: K C. Miller
Admissions: Katie Yearous
Type: Two-Year College **Sex:** Coed **Application Fee:** $75.00 **Calendar System:** Quarter **Professional Accreditation:** ACCSCT

SOUTHWESTERN COLLEGE
2625 East Cactus Rd.
Phoenix, AZ 85032-7042
Tel: (602)992-6101; Free: 800-247-2697
Admissions: (602)386-4106
E-mail: rebekah@swcaz.edu
Web Site: http://www.swcaz.edu/
President/CEO: Dr. Brent D. Garrison
Admissions: Rebekah Dubina
Financial Aid: Pete Leonard
Type: Four-Year College **Sex:** Coed **Affiliation:** Conservative Baptist **% Accepted:** 48 **Admission Plans:** Deferred Admission **Application Deadline:** August 1 **Application Fee:** $30.00 **H.S. Requirements:** High school diploma required; GED accepted **Scholarships:** Available **Calendar System:** Miscellaneous, Summer Session Available **Faculty:** FT 9, PT 24 **Student-Faculty Ratio:** 17:1 **Exams:** SAT I and SAT II or ACT. **% Receiving Financial Aid:** 75 **% Residing in College-Owned, -Operated, or -Affiliated Housing:** 40 **Library Holdings:** 29,948 **Regional Accreditation:** North Central Association of Colleges and Schools **Credit Hours For Degree:** 62 semester hours, Associates; 128 semester hours, Bachelors **ROTC:** Air Force **Intercollegiate Athletics:** Basketball M & W; Soccer M; Volleyball W

TOHONO O'ODHAM COMMUNITY COLLEGE
PO Box 3129
Sells, AZ 85634
Tel: (520)383-8401
Fax: (520)383-8403
E-mail: info@tocc.cc.az.us
Web Site: http://www.tocc.cc.az.us/
President/CEO: Olivia Vanegas-Furcheon
Type: Two-Year College **Sex:** Coed **Admission Plans:** Open Admission **Application Deadline:** Rolling **Application Fee:** $25.00 **H.S. Requirements:** High school diploma required; GED accepted **Costs Per Year:** Application fee: $25. State resident tuition: $1008 full-time, $42 per credit hour part-time. Nonresident tuition: $5064 full-time, $72 per credit hour part-time. **Calendar System:** Semester, Summer Session Available **Enrollment:** FT 25, PT 229 **Faculty:** FT 17, PT 11 **Student-Faculty Ratio:** 4:1 **Library Holdings:** 7,886 **Regional Accreditation:** North Central Association of Colleges and Schools **Credit Hours For Degree:** 60 credits, Associates

UNIVERSAL TECHNICAL INSTITUTE
10695 West Pierce St.
Avondale, AZ 85323
Tel: (602)264-4164; Free: 800-859-1202
Admissions: (623)245-4600
Fax: (602)264-6412
Web Site: http://www.uti.edu/
President/CEO: Adrian Cordova
Type: Two-Year College **Sex:** Coed **Admission Plans:** Open Admission **H.S. Requirements:** High school diploma required; GED accepted **Scholarships:** Available **Student-Faculty Ratio:** 23:1 **Professional Accreditation:** ACCSCT

UNIVERSITY OF ADVANCING TECHNOLOGY
2625 West Baseline Rd.
Tempe, AZ 85283-1042
Tel: (602)383-8228; Free: 800-658-5744
Fax: (602)383-8222
E-mail: admissions@uat.edu
Web Site: http://www.uat.edu/
President/CEO: Dominic P. Pistillo
Type: Comprehensive **Sex:** Coed **Application Deadline:** Rolling **Application Fee:** $0.00 **H.S. Requirements:** High school diploma required; GED accepted **Costs Per Year:** Application fee: $0. Comprehensive fee: $29,934 includes full-time tuition ($18,800), mandatory fees ($100), and college room and board ($11,034). College room only: $7224. Room and board charges vary according to board plan. **Scholarships:** Available **Calendar System:** Semester, Summer Session Available **Enrollment:** FT 1,090, Grad FT 52, Grad PT 5 **Faculty:** FT 35, PT 68 **Student-Faculty Ratio:** 19:1 **Exams:** SAT I or ACT. **% Residing in College-Owned, -Operated, or -Affiliated Housing:** 22 **Library Holdings:** 27,500 **Regional Accreditation:** North Central Association of Colleges and Schools **Credit Hours For Degree:** 60 credits, Associates; 120 credits, Bachelors **Professional Accreditation:** ACICS

THE UNIVERSITY OF ARIZONA
Tucson, AZ 85721
Tel: (520)621-2211
Admissions: (520)621-3705
Fax: (520)621-9799
E-mail: admissions@arizona.edu
Web Site: http://www.arizona.edu/
President/CEO: Robert N. Shelton
Admissions: Paul Kohn
Financial Aid: John Nametz
Type: University **Sex:** Coed **Affiliation:** Arizona Board of Regents **Scores:** 96% SAT V 400+; 96% SAT M 400+; 41% ACT 18-23; 41% ACT 24-29 **% Accepted:** 78 **Admission Plans:** Preferred Admission; Early Admission **Application Deadline:** May 1 **Application Fee:** $50.00 **H.S. Requirements:** High school diploma required; GED accepted **Scholarships:** Available **Calendar System:** Semester, Summer Session Available **Enrollment:** FT

27,103, PT 3,243, Grad FT 6,003, Grad PT 2,418 **Faculty:** FT 1,546, PT 407 **Student-Faculty Ratio:** 20:1 **Exams:** SAT I or ACT. **% Receiving Financial Aid:** 40 **% Residing in College-Owned, -Operated, or -Affiliated Housing:** 20 **Regional Accreditation:** North Central Association of Colleges and Schools **Credit Hours For Degree:** 125 semester hours, Bachelors **ROTC:** Army, Navy, Air Force **Professional Accreditation:** AACSB, ABET, ACPhE, ACEJMC, AACN, AAFCS, ABA, ADtA, ACSP, ALA, APA, ASLA, ASLHA, AALS, CEPH, CORE, LCMEAMA, NAACLS, NAAB, NASAD NASD, NASM, NASPAA, NAST, NLN **Intercollegiate Athletics:** Baseball M; Basketball M & W; Cross-Country Running M & W; Football M; Golf M & W; Gymnastics W; Ice Hockey M; Lacrosse M & W; Rock Climbing M & W; Soccer M & W; Softball W; Swimming and Diving M & W; Tennis M & W; Track and Field M & W; Volleyball M & W; Wrestling M

UNIVERSITY OF PHOENIX
3157 East Elwood St.
Phoenix, AZ 85034-7209
Tel: (602)387-7000; Free: 800-228-7240
Admissions: (480)557-6151
E-mail: audra.mcquarie@phoenix.edu
Web Site: http://www.uopxonline.com/
President/CEO: William Pepicello
Admissions: Audra McQuarie
Type: Comprehensive **Sex:** Coed **Admission Plans:** Open Admission; Deferred Admission **Application Deadline:** Rolling **Application Fee:** $0.00 **H.S. Requirements:** High school diploma required; GED accepted **Costs Per Year:** Application fee: $0. Tuition: $12,550 full-time. Full-time tuition varies according to course level and course load. **Scholarships:** Available **Calendar System:** Continuous, Summer Session Not available **Enrollment:** FT 236,109 **Faculty:** FT 158, PT 11,319 **Regional Accreditation:** North Central Association of Colleges and Schools **Credit Hours For Degree:** 60 credits, Associates; 120 credits, Bachelors **Professional Accreditation:** AACN, ACBSP, NLN, TEAC

UNIVERSITY OF PHOENIX—PHOENIX CAMPUS
4635 East Elwood St.
Phoenix, AZ 85040-1958
Tel: (480)804-7600; Free: 800-228-7240
Admissions: (480)557-6151
E-mail: audra.mcquarie@phoenix.edu
Web Site: http://www.phoenix.edu/
President/CEO: William Pepicello
Admissions: Audra McQuarie
Type: Comprehensive **Sex:** Coed **Admission Plans:** Open Admission; Deferred Admission **Application Deadline:** Rolling **Application Fee:** $0.00 **H.S. Requirements:** High school diploma required; GED accepted **Costs Per Year:** Application fee: $0. Tuition: $11,450 full-time. Full-time tuition varies according to course level and course load. **Scholarships:** Available **Calendar System:** Continuous, Summer Session Not available **Enrollment:** FT 3,718 **Faculty:** FT 76, PT 909 **Regional Accreditation:** North Central Association of Colleges and Schools **Credit Hours For Degree:** 60 credits, Associates; 120 credits, Bachelors **Professional Accreditation:** ACA, NLN

UNIVERSITY OF PHOENIX—SOUTHERN ARIZONA CAMPUS
300 South Craycroft Rd.
Tucson, AZ 85711
Tel: (520)881-6512; Free: 800-228-7240
Admissions: (480)557-6151
Fax: (520)795-6177
E-mail: audra.mcquarie@phoenix.edu
Web Site: http://www.phoenix.edu/
President/CEO: William Pepicello
Admissions: Audra McQuarie
Type: Comprehensive **Sex:** Coed **Admission Plans:** Open Admission; Deferred Admission **Application Deadline:** Rolling **Application Fee:** $0.00 **H.S. Requirements:** High school diploma required; GED accepted **Costs Per Year:** Application fee: $0. Tuition: $11,425 full-time. Full-time tuition varies according to course level and course load. **Scholarships:** Available **Calendar System:** Continuous, Summer Session Not available **Enrollment:** FT 1,631 **Faculty:** FT 14, PT 270 **Regional Accreditation:** North Central Association of Colleges and Schools **Credit Hours For Degree:** 60 credits, Associates; 120 credits, Bachelors **Professional Accreditation:** ACA, NLN

WESTERN INTERNATIONAL UNIVERSITY
9215 North Black Canyon Hwy.
Phoenix, AZ 85021-2718
Tel: (602)943-2311
Admissions: (602)429-1063
E-mail: karen.janitell@west.edu
Web Site: http://www.wintu.edu/
President/CEO: Alan Drimmer, PhD
Admissions: Karen Janitell
Financial Aid: Ella Owen
Type: Comprehensive **Sex:** Coed **Affiliation:** Apollo Group, Inc. **% Accepted:** 78 **Admission Plans:** Deferred Admission **Application Deadline:** Rolling **Application Fee:** $25.00 **H.S. Requirements:** High school diploma required; GED accepted **Costs Per Year:** Application fee: $25. Tuition: $11,250 full-time, $375 per credit hour part-time. Full-time tuition varies according to course level, degree level, and student level. Part-time tuition varies according to course level, degree level, and student level. **Calendar System:** Continuous, Summer Session Available **Enrollment:** FT 2,258, Grad FT 763 **Faculty:** FT 0, PT 275 **Student-Faculty Ratio:** 10:1 **% Receiving Financial Aid:** 80 **Library Holdings:** 7,500 **Regional Accreditation:** North Central Association of Colleges and Schools **Credit Hours For Degree:** 60 credit hours, Associates; 126 credit hours, Bachelors

YAVAPAI COLLEGE
1100 East Sheldon St.
Prescott, AZ 86301-3297
Tel: (928)445-7300; Free: 800-922-6787
Fax: (928)776-2151
E-mail: registration@yc.edu
Web Site: http://www.yc.edu/
President/CEO: Dr. James Horton
Admissions: Sheila Jarrell
Type: Two-Year College **Sex:** Coed **Affiliation:** Arizona State Community College System **Admission Plans:** Open Admission; Early Admission; Deferred Admission **Application Deadline:** Rolling **H.S. Requirements:** High school diploma required; GED accepted **Costs Per Year:** State resident tuition: $1488 full-time. Nonresident tuition: $8158 full-time. College room and board: $5020. **Scholarships:** Available **Calendar System:** Semester, Summer Session Available **Enrollment:** FT 1,917, PT 6,359 **Faculty:** FT 112, PT 292 **Student-Faculty Ratio:** 15:1 **% Residing in College-Owned, -Operated, or -Affiliated Housing:** 5 **Library Holdings:** 81,144 **Regional Accreditation:** North Central Association of Colleges and Schools **Credit Hours For Degree:** 64 credits, Associates **ROTC:** Army, Air Force **Professional Accreditation:** NLN **Intercollegiate Athletics:** Baseball M; Basketball M & W; Soccer M; Softball W; Volleyball W

ARKANSAS BAPTIST COLLEGE
1621 Dr. Martin Luther King, Jr. Dr.
Little Rock, AR 72202-6067
Tel: (501)374-7856
Admissions: (501)244-5104
Web Site: http://www.arkansasbaptist.edu/
President/CEO: Fitzgerald Hill
Type: Four-Year College **Sex:** Coed **Affiliation:** Baptist **Admission Plans:** Open Admission; Deferred Admission **Application Deadline:** Rolling **Application Fee:** $25.00 **H.S. Requirements:** High school diploma required; GED accepted **Costs Per Year:** Application fee: $25. One-time mandatory fee: $100. Comprehensive fee: $14,624 includes full-time tuition ($6400), mandatory fees ($618), and college room and board ($7606). College room only: $3866. Room and board charges vary according to board plan and gender. Part-time tuition: $317 per credit hour. Part-time mandatory fees: $7 per credit hour. Part-time tuition and fees vary according to program. **Scholarships:** Available **Calendar System:** Semester, Summer Session Available **Enrollment:** FT 495, PT 131 **Faculty:** FT 18, PT 20 **Student-Faculty Ratio:** 22:1 **Exams:** ACT, Other. **% Residing in College-Owned, -Operated, or -Affiliated Housing:** 13 **Regional Accreditation:** North Central Association of Colleges and Schools **Credit Hours For Degree:** 124 semester hours, Bachelors **Intercollegiate Athletics:** Baseball M; Basketball M & W; Cheerleading W; Football M

ARKANSAS NORTHEASTERN COLLEGE
PO Box 1109
Blytheville, AR 72316-1109
Tel: (870)762-1020
Fax: (870)763-3704
E-mail: lwells@anc.edu
Web Site: http://www.anc.edu/
President/CEO: Dr. Robert Myers
Admissions: Leslie Wells
Type: Two-Year College **Sex:** Coed **% Accepted:** 100 **Admission Plans:** Open Admission; Deferred Admission **Application Deadline:** Rolling **Application Fee:** $0.00 **H.S. Requirements:** High school diploma required; GED accepted **Costs Per Year:** Application fee: $0. Area resident tuition: $1560 full-time, $52 per credit hour part-time. State resident tuition: $1860 full-time, $62 per credit hour part-time. Nonresident tuition: $3360 full-time, $112 per credit hour part-time. Mandatory fees: $220 full-time, $6 per credit hour part-time, $20 per term part-time. **Scholarships:** Available **Calendar System:** Semester, Summer Session Available **Enrollment:** FT 726, PT 1,074 **Faculty:** FT 76, PT 65 **Student-Faculty Ratio:** 18:1 **Library Holdings:** 15,493 **Regional Accreditation:** North Central Association of Colleges and Schools **Credit Hours For Degree:** 62 semester hours, Associates **Professional Accreditation:** ACBSP, NLN

ARKANSAS STATE UNIVERSITY - JONESBORO
PO Box 600
State University, AR 72467
Tel: (870)972-2100
Admissions: (870)972-3024
Fax: (870)972-2090
E-mail: admissions@astate.edu
Web Site: http://www.astate.edu/
President/CEO: Dr. Robert Potts
Admissions: Tammy Fowler
Financial Aid: Terry Finney
Type: University **Sex:** Coed **Affiliation:** Arkansas State University System **Scores:** 82.6% SAT V 400+; 89.3% SAT M 400+; 48.3% ACT 18-23; 28.1% ACT 24-29 **% Accepted:** 77 **Admission Plans:** Early Admission; Deferred Admission **Application Deadline:** Rolling **Application Fee:** $15.00 **H.S. Requirements:** High school diploma required; GED accepted **Costs Per Year:** Application fee: $15. State resident tuition: $4890 full-time, $163 per credit hour part-time. Nonresident tuition: $12,810 full-time, $427 per credit hour part-time. Mandatory fees: $1480 full-time, $47 per credit hour part-time, $25 per term part-time. Full-time tuition and fees vary according to course load, location, and program. Part-time tuition and fees vary according to course load, location, and program. College room and board: $5856. Room and board charges vary according to board plan, housing facility, and student level. **Scholarships:** Available **Calendar System:** Semester, Summer Session Available **Enrollment:** FT 7,732, PT 2,292, Grad FT 569, Grad PT 1,563 **Faculty:** FT 482, PT 172 **Student-Faculty Ratio:** 17:1 **Exams:** ACT, Other, SAT I or ACT. ACT essay not being used. SAT essay not being used. **% Receiving Financial Aid:** 73 **% Residing in College-Owned, -Operated, or -Affiliated Housing:** 24 **Final Year or Final Semester Residency Requirement:** Yes **Library Holdings:** 631,161 **Regional Accreditation:** North Central Association of Colleges and Schools **Credit Hours For Degree:** 62 credit hours, Associates; 124 credit hours, Bachelors **ROTC:** Army **Professional Accreditation:** AACSB, ABET, ACEJMC, AANA, ACA, APTA, ASLHA, CORE, CSWE, JRCERT, JRCEPAT, NAACLS, NASAD, NASM, NASPAA, NCATE, NLN **Intercollegiate Athletics:** Baseball M; Basketball M & W; Bowling W; Cross-Country Running M & W; Football M; Golf M & W; Soccer W; Tennis W; Track and Field M & W; Volleyball W

ARKANSAS STATE UNIVERSITY—BEEBE
PO Box 1000
Beebe, AR 72012-1000
Tel: (501)882-3600
Admissions: (501)882-8860
Fax: (501)882-8370
E-mail: rdhudson@asub.edu
Web Site: http://www.asub.edu/
President/CEO: Dr. Eugene McKay
Admissions: Ronald Hudson
Financial Aid: Linda Yelder
Type: Two-Year College **Sex:** Coed **Affiliation:** Arkansas State University System **% Accepted:** 54 **Admission Plans:** Open Admission; Deferred Admission **Application Deadline:** Rolling **Application Fee:** $0.00 **H.S. Requirements:** High school diploma required; GED accepted **Scholarships:** Available **Calendar System:** Semester, Summer Session Available **Enrollment:** FT 2,601, PT 1,890 **Faculty:** FT 63, PT 34 **Student-Faculty Ratio:** 30:1 **% Residing in College-Owned, -Operated, or -Affiliated Housing:** 12 **Library Holdings:** 90,000 **Regional Accreditation:** North Central Association of Colleges and Schools **Credit Hours For Degree:** 62 credit hours, Associates **ROTC:** Army **Professional Accreditation:** ABET, NAACLS

ARKANSAS STATE UNIVERSITY—MOUNTAIN HOME
1600 South College St.
Mountain Home, AR 72653

Tel: (870)508-6100
Admissions: (870)508-6168
E-mail: araney@asumh.edu
Web Site: http://www.asumh.edu/
President/CEO: Dr. William Edward Coulter
Admissions: Scott Raney
Financial Aid: Joyce Rone
Type: Two-Year College **Sex:** Coed **Affiliation:** Arkansas State University System **% Accepted:** 82 **Admission Plans:** Open Admission **Application Fee:** $0.00 **H.S. Requirements:** High school diploma required; GED accepted **Costs Per Year:** Application fee: $0. State resident tuition: $2310 full-time, $77 per credit hour part-time. Nonresident tuition: $3960 full-time, $132 per credit hour part-time. Mandatory fees: $450 full-time, $77 per credit hour part-time, $450. Full-time tuition and fees vary according to course load. Part-time tuition and fees vary according to course load. **Scholarships:** Available **Calendar System:** Semester, Summer Session Available **Enrollment:** FT 765, PT 467 **Faculty:** FT 43, PT 29 **Student-Faculty Ratio:** 22:1 **Exams:** Other, SAT I or ACT. ACT essay not being used. **Library Holdings:** 33,573 **Regional Accreditation:** North Central Association of Colleges and Schools **Credit Hours For Degree:** 60 credits, Associates **ROTC:** Army **Professional Accreditation:** ABFSE

ARKANSAS STATE UNIVERSITY—NEWPORT
7648 Victory Blvd.
Newport, AR 72112
Tel: (870)512-7800; Free: 800-976-1676
Web Site: http://www.asun.edu/
President/CEO: Larry Williams
Admissions: Tara Byrd
Financial Aid: Deana Tims
Type: Two-Year College **Sex:** Coed **Affiliation:** Arkansas State University System **Admission Plans:** Open Admission **H.S. Requirements:** High school diploma required; GED accepted **Scholarships:** Available **Calendar System:** Semester **Faculty:** FT 23, PT 27 **Student-Faculty Ratio:** 12:1 **Exams:** ACT, Other. **Regional Accreditation:** North Central Association of Colleges and Schools **Credit Hours For Degree:** 62 credits, Associates

ARKANSAS TECH UNIVERSITY
Russellville, AR 72801
Tel: (479)968-0389; Free: 800-582-6953
Admissions: (479)968-0343
Fax: (479)964-0522
E-mail: tech.enroll@atu.edu
Web Site: http://www.atu.edu/
President/CEO: Dr. Robert C. Brown
Admissions: Shauna Donnell
Type: Comprehensive **Sex:** Coed **Scores:** 72.72% SAT V 400+; 90.9% SAT M 400+; 40.9% ACT 18-23; 43.65% ACT 24-29 **% Accepted:** 94 **Admission Plans:** Deferred Admission **Application Fee:** $0.00 **H.S. Requirements:** High school diploma required; GED accepted **Costs Per Year:** Application fee: $0. State resident tuition: $5010 full-time, $167 per credit hour part-time. Nonresident tuition: $10,020 full-time, $334 per credit hour part-time. Mandatory fees: $600 full-time, $9 per credit hour part-time, $140 per term part-time. Full-time tuition and fees vary according to course load and location. Part-time tuition and fees vary according to course load and location. College room and board: $5156. College room only: $3076. Room and board charges vary according to board plan, housing facility, and location. **Scholarships:** Available **Calendar System:** Semester, Summer Session Available **Enrollment:** FT 6,377, PT 1,876, Grad FT 157, Grad PT 404 **Faculty:** FT 293, PT 163 **Student-Faculty Ratio:** 18:1 **Exams:** SAT I or ACT. ACT essay not being used. SAT essay not being used. **% Receiving Financial Aid:** 59 **% Residing in College-Owned, -Operated, or -Affiliated Housing:** 33 **Final Year or Final Semester Residency Requirement:** Yes **Library Holdings:** 289,158 **Regional Accreditation:** North Central Association of Colleges and Schools **Credit Hours For Degree:** 62 semester hours, Associates; 124 semester hours, Bachelors **ROTC:** Army **Professional Accreditation:** AACSB, ABET, AAMAE, AHIMA, NASM, NCATE, NLN, NRPA **Intercollegiate Athletics:** Baseball M; Basketball M & W; Cheerleading M & W; Cross-Country Running W; Football M; Golf M; Softball W; Tennis W; Volleyball W

BLACK RIVER TECHNICAL COLLEGE
1410 Hwy. 304 East
Pocahontas, AR 72455
Tel: (870)248-4000; Free: 800-919-3086
Fax: (870)248-4100
Web Site: http://www.blackrivertech.edu/
President/CEO: Richard Gaines
Type: Two-Year College **Sex:** Coed **Admission Plans:** Open Admission **Application Deadline:** Rolling **H.S. Requirements:** High school diploma required; GED accepted **Costs Per Year:** State resident tuition: $1680 full-time, $70 per credit hour part-time. Nonresident tuition: $4368 full-time, $182 per credit hour part-time. Mandatory fees: $72 full-time, $3 per credit hour part-time. Full-time tuition and fees vary according to course load. Part-time tuition and fees vary according to course load. **Scholarships:** Available **Calendar System:** Semester, Summer Session Available **Exams:** Other. **Library Holdings:** 10,000 **Regional Accreditation:** North Central Association of Colleges and Schools **Credit Hours For Degree:** 62 credit hours, Associates **Professional Accreditation:** CARC

CENTRAL BAPTIST COLLEGE
1501 College Ave.
Conway, AR 72032
Tel: (501)329-6872; Free: 800-205-6872
E-mail: rwaymire@cbc.edu
Web Site: http://www.cbc.edu/
President/CEO: Terry Kimbrow
Admissions: Rachel Waymire
Financial Aid: Christi Bell
Type: Four-Year College **Sex:** Coed **Affiliation:** Baptist **% Accepted:** 75 **Admission Plans:** Early Admission **Application Deadline:** August 15 **Application Fee:** $25.00 **H.S. Requirements:** High school diploma required; GED accepted **Costs Per Year:** Application fee: $25. Comprehensive fee: $16,480 includes full-time tuition ($9750), mandatory fees ($930), and college room and board ($5800). **Scholarships:** Available **Calendar System:** Semester, Summer Session Available **Enrollment:** FT 522, PT 103 **Faculty:** FT 19, PT 35 **Student-Faculty Ratio:** 21:1 **Exams:** ACT. **Library Holdings:** 50,448 **Regional Accreditation:** North Central Association of Colleges and Schools **Credit Hours For Degree:** 64 credit hours, Associates; 127 credit hours, Bachelors **ROTC:** Army **Intercollegiate Athletics:** Baseball M & W; Basketball M & W; Cross-Country Running M & W; Golf M & W; Softball W; Volleyball W

COSSATOT COMMUNITY COLLEGE OF THE UNIVERSITY OF ARKANSAS
PO Box 960
De Queen, AR 71832
Tel: (870)584-4471; Free: 800-844-4471
E-mail: ncowling@cccua.edu
Web Site: http://www.cccua.edu/
President/CEO: Frank G. Adams
Admissions: Nancy Cowling
Financial Aid: Denise Hammond
Type: Two-Year College **Sex:** Coed **Affiliation:** University of Arkansas System **Admission Plans:** Open Admission **Application Fee:** $0.00 **H.S. Requirements:** High school diploma required; GED accepted **Costs Per Year:** Application fee: $0. Area resident tuition: $1440 full-time, $48 per credit hour part-time. State resident tuition: $1740 full-time, $58 per credit hour part-time. Nonresident tuition: $4500 full-time, $150 per credit hour part-time. Mandatory fees: $280 full-time, $5 per credit hour part-time, $65. Full-time tuition and fees vary according to course load and program. Part-time tuition and fees vary according to course load and program. **Scholarships:** Available **Calendar System:** Semester, Summer Session Available **Faculty:** FT 34, PT 40 **Student-Faculty Ratio:** 12:1 **Regional Accreditation:** North Central Association of Colleges and Schools **Credit Hours For Degree:** 60 credit hours, Associates **Professional Accreditation:** ACBSP

CROWLEY'S RIDGE COLLEGE
100 College Dr.
Paragould, AR 72450-9731
Tel: (870)236-6901; Free: 800-264-1096
Fax: (870)236-7748
E-mail: njoneshi@crc.pioneer.paragould.ar.us
Web Site: http://www.crc.edu/
President/CEO: Ken Hoppe
Admissions: Amanda Drake
Type: Two-Year College **Sex:** Coed **Affiliation:** Church of Christ **Admission Plans:** Open Admission **Application Deadline:** Rolling **Application Fee:**

$0.00 **H.S. Requirements:** High school diploma required; GED accepted **Scholarships:** Available **Calendar System:** Semester, Summer Session Available **Regional Accreditation:** North Central Association of Colleges and Schools **Credit Hours For Degree:** 64 credit hours, Associates

EAST ARKANSAS COMMUNITY COLLEGE
1700 Newcastle Rd.
Forrest City, AR 72335-2204
Tel: (870)633-4480; Free: 877-797-3222
Fax: (870)633-7222
E-mail: dadams@eacc.edu
Web Site: http://www.eacc.edu/
President/CEO: Dr. Coy Grace
Admissions: DeAnna Adams
Type: Two-Year College **Sex:** Coed **Admission Plans:** Open Admission; Early Admission; Deferred Admission **Application Deadline:** Rolling **Application Fee:** $0.00 **H.S. Requirements:** High school diploma required; GED accepted. For applicants 18 or over who demonstrate ability to benefit from college: High school diploma or equivalent not required **Costs Per Year:** Application fee: $0. Area resident tuition: $1800 full-time, $60 per credit hour part-time. State resident tuition: $2040 full-time, $68 per credit hour part-time. Nonresident tuition: $2460 full-time, $82 per credit hour part-time. Mandatory fees: $240 full-time, $8 per credit hour part-time. **Scholarships:** Available **Calendar System:** Semester, Summer Session Available **Enrollment:** FT 779, PT 768 **Faculty:** FT 39, PT 56 **Student-Faculty Ratio:** 18:1 **Library Holdings:** 21,908 **Regional Accreditation:** North Central Association of Colleges and Schools **Credit Hours For Degree:** 64 credits, Associates **Professional Accreditation:** ACBSP, NLN

ECCLESIA COLLEGE
9653 Nations Dr.
Springdale, AR 72762
Tel: (479)248-7236; Free: 800-735-9926
E-mail: myfuture@ecollege.edu
Web Site: http://www.ecollege.edu/
President/CEO: Oren N. Paris, III
Admissions: Titus Hofer
Type: Four-Year College **Sex:** Coed **Application Fee:** $35.00 **H.S. Requirements:** High school diploma required; GED accepted **Costs Per Year:** Application fee: $35. Tuition: $14,250 full-time, $475 per credit hour part-time. **Calendar System:** Semester, Summer Session Not available **Student-Faculty Ratio:** 10:1 **Exams:** Other, SAT I or ACT. **Final Year or Final Semester Residency Requirement:** No **Credit Hours For Degree:** 64 credits, Associates; 128 credits, Bachelors **Professional Accreditation:** ABHE **Intercollegiate Athletics:** Baseball M; Basketball M & W

HARDING UNIVERSITY
915 East Market Ave.
Searcy, AR 72149-0001
Tel: (501)279-4000; Free: 800-477-4407
Admissions: (501)279-4407
Fax: (501)279-4865
E-mail: admissions@harding.edu
Web Site: http://www.harding.edu/
President/CEO: Dr. David B. Burks
Admissions: Glenn Dillard
Financial Aid: Dr. Jonathan C. Roberts
Type: University **Sex:** Coed **Affiliation:** Church of Christ **Scores:** 95% SAT V 400+; 94% SAT M 400+; 37% ACT 18-23; 43% ACT 24-29 **% Accepted:** 73 **Admission Plans:** Early Admission; Early Action; Deferred Admission **Application Deadline:** Rolling **Application Fee:** $40.00 **H.S. Requirements:** High school diploma required; GED accepted **Costs Per Year:** Application fee: $40. Comprehensive fee: $19,394 includes full-time tuition ($13,140), mandatory fees ($440), and college room and board ($5814). College room only: $2880. Full-time tuition and fees vary according to course load. Room and board charges vary according to board plan and housing facility. Part-time tuition: $438 per credit hour. Part-time mandatory fees: $22 per credit hour. Part-time tuition and fees vary according to course load. **Scholarships:** Available **Calendar System:** Semester, Summer Session Available **Enrollment:** FT 3,828, PT 258, Grad FT 484, Grad PT 1,914 **Faculty:** FT 248, PT 199 **Student-Faculty Ratio:** 17:1 **Exams:** SAT I or ACT. ACT essay not being used. SAT essay not being used. **% Receiving Financial Aid:** 57 **% Residing in College-Owned, -Operated, or -Affiliated Housing:** 77 **Final Year or Final Semester Residency Requirement:** No **Library Holdings:** 253,771 **Regional Accreditation:** North Central Association of Colleges and Schools **Credit Hours For Degree:** 128 semester hours, Bachelors **Professional Accreditation:** ACPhE, AAMFT, AAFCS, ACBSP, CSWE, NASM, NCATE, NLN **Intercollegiate Athletics:** Baseball M; Basketball M & W; Cheerleading W; Cross-Country Running M & W; Football M; Golf M & W; Lacrosse M; Rugby M; Soccer M & W; Tennis M & W; Track and Field M & W; Ultimate Frisbee M & W; Volleyball W

HENDERSON STATE UNIVERSITY
1100 Henderson St.
Arkadelphia, AR 71999-0001
Tel: (870)230-5000; Free: 800-228-7333
Admissions: (870)230-5028
Fax: (870)230-5144
E-mail: hardwrv@hsu.edu
Web Site: http://www.hsu.edu/
President/CEO: Dr. Charles Welch
Admissions: Vikita Hardwrick
Financial Aid: Vicki Taylor
Type: Comprehensive **Sex:** Coed **Scores:** 94% SAT M 400+; 45% ACT 18-23; 38% ACT 24-29 **% Accepted:** 65 **Admission Plans:** Deferred Admission **Application Deadline:** July 15 **Application Fee:** $0.00 **H.S. Requirements:** High school diploma required; GED accepted **Costs Per Year:** Application fee: $0. State resident tuition: $5100 full-time, $170 per credit hour part-time. Nonresident tuition: $10,200 full-time, $340 per credit hour part-time. Mandatory fees: $1104 full-time. Full-time tuition and fees vary according to course load. Part-time tuition varies according to course load. College room and board: $5034. Room and board charges vary according to board plan and housing facility. **Scholarships:** Available **Calendar System:** Semester, Summer Session Available **Enrollment:** FT 2,767, PT 340, Grad FT 99, Grad PT 372 **Faculty:** FT 170, PT 64 **Student-Faculty Ratio:** 18:1 **Exams:** ACT, SAT I or ACT. ACT essay not being used. SAT essay not being used. **% Receiving Financial Aid:** 74 **% Residing in College-Owned, -Operated, or -Affiliated Housing:** 45 **Library Holdings:** 264,367 **Regional Accreditation:** North Central Association of Colleges and Schools **Credit Hours For Degree:** 60 semester hours, Associates; 124 semester hours, Bachelors **ROTC:** Army **Professional Accreditation:** AACSB, AAFCS, ACA, NASM, NCATE, NLN **Intercollegiate Athletics:** Baseball M; Basketball M & W; Cross-Country Running M & W; Football M; Golf M & W; Softball W; Swimming and Diving M & W; Tennis M & W; Volleyball W

HENDRIX COLLEGE
1600 Washington Ave.
Conway, AR 72032-3080
Tel: (501)329-6811; Free: 800-277-9017
Admissions: (501)450-1362
Fax: (501)450-3843
E-mail: martinl@hendrix.edu
Web Site: http://www.hendrix.edu/
President/CEO: Dr. J. Timothy Cloyd
Admissions: Laura E. Martin
Financial Aid: Mark Bandre
Type: Comprehensive **Sex:** Coed **Affiliation:** United Methodist **Scores:** 100% SAT V 400+; 99% SAT M 400+; 8% ACT 18-23; 43% ACT 24-29 **% Accepted:** 80 **Admission Plans:** Deferred Admission **Application Deadline:** August 1 **Application Fee:** $40.00 **H.S. Requirements:** High school diploma required; GED accepted **Costs Per Year:** Application fee: $40. Comprehensive fee: $38,934 includes full-time tuition ($29,970), mandatory fees ($300), and college room and board ($8664). College room only: $4400. Full-time tuition and fees vary according to course load. Room and board charges vary according to board plan and housing facility. Part-time tuition: $3470 per course. Part-time tuition varies according to course load. **Scholarships:** Available **Calendar System:** Semester, Summer Session Not available **Enrollment:** FT 1,442, PT 14, Grad FT 7 **Faculty:** FT 102, PT 33 **Student-Faculty Ratio:** 13:1 **Exams:** SAT I or ACT. **% Receiving Financial Aid:** 61 **% Residing in College-Owned, -Operated, or -Affiliated Housing:** 86 **Library Holdings:** 218,390 **Regional Accreditation:** North Central Association of Colleges and Schools **Credit Hours For Degree:** 32 courses, Bachelors **ROTC:** Army **Professional Accreditation:** NASM, NCATE **Intercollegiate Athletics:** Baseball M; Basketball M & W; Cross-Country Running M & W; Field Hockey W; Golf M & W; Lacrosse M; Soccer M & W; Softball W; Swimming and Diving M & W; Tennis M & W; Track and Field M & W; Volleyball W

ITT TECHNICAL INSTITUTE
4520 South University Ave.
Little Rock, AR 72204
Tel: (501)565-5550
Web Site: http://www.itt-tech.edu/
President/CEO: Tom Olson
Type: Two-Year College **Sex:** Coed **Affiliation:** ITT Educational Services, Inc. **H.S. Requirements:** High school diploma required; GED accepted **Scholarships:** Available **Calendar System:** Quarter, Summer Session Not available **Professional Accreditation:** ACICS

JOHN BROWN UNIVERSITY
2000 West University St.
Siloam Springs, AR 72761-2121
Tel: (479)524-9500; Free: 877-JBU-INFO
Admissions: (479)524-7150
Fax: (479)524-9548
E-mail: dcrandal@jbu.edu
Web Site: http://www.jbu.edu/
President/CEO: Dr. Charles W. Pollard
Admissions: Don Crandall
Financial Aid: Kim Eldridge
Type: Comprehensive **Sex:** Coed **Affiliation:** interdenominational **Scores:** 97% SAT V 400+; 97% SAT M 400+; 35% ACT 18-23; 46% ACT 24-29 **% Accepted:** 73 **Admission Plans:** Deferred Admission **Application Deadline:** Rolling **Application Fee:** $25.00 **H.S. Requirements:** High school diploma required; GED accepted **Costs Per Year:** Application fee: $25. Comprehensive fee: $25,756 includes full-time tuition ($18,032), mandatory fees ($848), and college room and board ($6876). Full-time tuition and fees vary according to course load. Room and board charges vary according to board plan and housing facility. Part-time tuition: $720 per credit hour. Part-time tuition varies according to course load. **Scholarships:** Available **Calendar System:** Semester, Summer Session Not available **Enrollment:** FT 1,365, PT 348, Grad FT 84, Grad PT 276 **Faculty:** FT 75, PT 55 **Student-Faculty Ratio:** 13:1 **Exams:** SAT I or ACT. **% Receiving Financial Aid:** 65 **% Residing in College-Owned, -Operated, or -Affiliated Housing:** 71 **Library Holdings:** 106,283 **Regional Accreditation:** North Central Association of Colleges and Schools **Credit Hours For Degree:** 62 semester hours, Associates; 124 semester hours, Bachelors **ROTC:** Army, Air Force **Professional Accreditation:** ABET, ACCE, NCATE **Intercollegiate Athletics:** Basketball M & W; Golf M; Soccer M & W; Tennis M & W; Volleyball W

LYON COLLEGE
PO Box 2317
Batesville, AR 72503-2317
Tel: (870)793-9813; Free: 800-423-2542
Admissions: (870)307-7250
Fax: (870)698-4622
E-mail: admissions@lyon.edu
Web Site: http://www.lyon.edu/
President/CEO: Dr. Donald V. Weatherman
Financial Aid: Tommy Tucker
Type: Four-Year College **Sex:** Coed **Affiliation:** Presbyterian **Scores:** 95% SAT V 400+; 94% SAT M 400+; 41% ACT 18-23; 47% ACT 24-29 **% Accepted:** 67 **Admission Plans:** Early Admission; Early Action; Deferred Admission **Application Deadline:** Rolling **Application Fee:** $25.00 **H.S. Requirements:** High school diploma required; GED accepted **Costs Per Year:** Application fee: $25. Comprehensive fee: $27,308 includes full-time tuition ($19,424), mandatory fees ($544), and college room and board ($7340). Room and board charges vary according to board plan. Part-time tuition: $730 per credit hour. **Scholarships:** Available **Calendar System:** Semester, Summer Session Available **Enrollment:** FT 580, PT 34 **Faculty:** FT 41, PT 22 **Student-Faculty Ratio:** 12:1 **Exams:** SAT I or ACT. **% Receiving Financial Aid:** 75 **% Residing in College-Owned, -Operated, or -Affiliated Housing:** 94 **Final Year or Final Semester Residency Requirement:** No **Library Holdings:** 203,257 **Regional Accreditation:** North Central Association of Colleges and Schools **Credit Hours For Degree:** 120 credits, Bachelors **Professional Accreditation:** NCATE **Intercollegiate Athletics:** Baseball M; Basketball M & W; Cross-Country Running M & W; Golf M & W; Soccer M & W; Softball W; Volleyball W

MID-SOUTH COMMUNITY COLLEGE
2000 West Broadway
West Memphis, AR 72301
Tel: (870)733-6722
Admissions: (870)733-6786
Fax: (870)733-6719
E-mail: jreece@midsouthcc.edu
Web Site: http://www.midsouthcc.edu/
President/CEO: Dr. Glen F. Fenter
Admissions: Jeremy Reece
Type: Two-Year College **Sex:** Coed **% Accepted:** 100 **Admission Plans:** Open Admission; Early Admission **Application Deadline:** Rolling **Application Fee:** $0.00 **H.S. Requirements:** High school diploma required; GED accepted. For adults who demonstrate ability to benefit from college: High school diploma or equivalent not required **Scholarships:** Available **Calendar System:** Semester, Summer Session Available **Enrollment:** FT 408, PT 1,246 **Faculty:** FT 35, PT 69 **Student-Faculty Ratio:** 16:1 **Library Holdings:** 14,672 **Regional Accreditation:** North Central Association of Colleges and Schools **Credit Hours For Degree:** 64 credit hours, Associates

NATIONAL PARK COMMUNITY COLLEGE
101 College Dr.
Hot Springs, AR 71913
Tel: (501)760-4222; Free: 800-760-1825
Fax: (501)760-4100
E-mail: bmoody@npcc.edu
Web Site: http://www.npcc.edu/
President/CEO: Sally Carder
Admissions: Dr. Allen B. Moody
Type: Two-Year College **Sex:** Coed **Affiliation:** Arkansas Department of Higher Education **% Accepted:** 100 **Admission Plans:** Open Admission; Early Admission; Deferred Admission **Application Deadline:** Rolling **Application Fee:** $0.00 **H.S. Requirements:** High school diploma required; GED accepted **Costs Per Year:** Application fee: $0. Area resident tuition: $2340 full-time, $65 per credit hour part-time. State resident tuition: $2700 full-time, $75 per credit hour part-time. Nonresident tuition: $4824 full-time, $134 per credit hour part-time. Mandatory fees: $160 full-time, $3 per credit hour part-time, $80 per term part-time. Full-time tuition and fees vary according to course load. Part-time tuition and fees vary according to course load. **Scholarships:** Available **Calendar System:** Semester, Summer Session Available **Enrollment:** FT 1,237, PT 1,759 **Faculty:** FT 64, PT 83 **Student-Faculty Ratio:** 21:1 **Exams:** Other, SAT I and SAT II or ACT. **Library Holdings:** 17,800 **Regional Accreditation:** North Central Association of Colleges and Schools **Credit Hours For Degree:** 60 semester hours, Associates **Professional Accreditation:** AHIMA, ACBSP, JRCERT, NAACLS, NLN

NORTH ARKANSAS COLLEGE
1515 Pioneer Dr.
Harrison, AR 72601
Tel: (870)743-3000; Free: 800-679-6622
Admissions: (870)391-3221
Fax: (870)391-3339
E-mail: charlam@northark.edu
Web Site: http://www.northark.edu/
President/CEO: Dr. Jeff Olson
Admissions: Charla Jennings
Financial Aid: Jennifer Haddock
Type: Two-Year College **Sex:** Coed **Scores:** 60% ACT 18-23; 19.3% ACT 24-29 **% Accepted:** 100 **Admission Plans:** Open Admission; Deferred Admission **Application Deadline:** Rolling **Application Fee:** $0.00 **H.S. Requirements:** High school diploma required; GED accepted **Costs Per Year:** Application fee: $0. Area resident tuition: $1770 full-time, $59 per credit hour part-time. State resident tuition: $2430 full-time, $82 per credit hour part-time. Nonresident tuition: $4560 full-time, $152 per credit hour part-time. Mandatory fees: $150 full-time, $5 per credit hour part-time. Full-time tuition and fees vary according to course load. Part-time tuition and fees vary according to course load. **Scholarships:** Available **Calendar System:** Semester, Summer Session Available **Enrollment:** FT 1,491, PT 938 **Student-Faculty Ratio:** 19:1 **Final Year or Final Semester Residency Requirement:** No **Library Holdings:** 28,751 **Regional Accreditation:** North Central Association of Colleges and Schools **Credit Hours For Degree:** 62 credit hours, Associates **Professional Accreditation:** ARCEST, JRCERT, NAACLS, NLN **Intercollegiate Athletics:** Baseball M; Basketball M & W; Softball W

NORTHWEST ARKANSAS COMMUNITY COLLEGE
One College Dr.
Bentonville, AR 72712
Tel: (479)636-9222; Free: 800-995-6922
Fax: (479)619-4116
E-mail: admissions@nwacc.edu
Web Site: http://www.nwacc.edu/
President/CEO: Dr. Becky Paneitz
Type: Two-Year College **Sex:** Coed **Scores:** 57.4% ACT 18-23; 16.1% ACT 24-29 **% Accepted:** 100 **Admission Plans:** Open Admission **Application Deadline:** Rolling **Application Fee:** $10.00 **H.S. Requirements:** High school diploma required; GED accepted **Costs Per Year:** Application fee: $10. Area resident tuition: $1980 full-time, $66 per credit hour part-time. State resident tuition: $3090 full-time, $103 per credit hour part-time. Nonresident tuition: $4350 full-time, $145 per credit hour part-time. Mandatory fees: $512 full-time, $13.75 per credit hour part-time, $50 per term part-time. **Scholarships:** Available **Calendar System:** Semester, Summer Session Available **Enrollment:** FT 3,034, PT 4,972 **Faculty:** FT 121, PT 328 **Student-Faculty Ratio:** 20:1 **Final Year or Final Semester Residency Requirement:** No **Library Holdings:** 15,500 **Regional Accreditation:** North Central Association of Colleges and Schools **Credit Hours For Degree:** 62 credits, Associates **ROTC:** Army, Air Force **Professional Accreditation:** CARC, JRCEMT

OUACHITA BAPTIST UNIVERSITY
410 Ouachita St.
Arkadelphia, AR 71998-0001
Tel: (870)245-5000
Admissions: (870)245-5110
Fax: (870)245-5500
E-mail: motll@obu.edu
Web Site: http://www.obu.edu/
President/CEO: Dr. Rex M. Horne, Jr.
Admissions: Lori Motl
Financial Aid: Susan Hurst
Type: Four-Year College **Sex:** Coed **Affiliation:** Baptist **Scores:** 93% SAT V 400+; 97% SAT M 400+; 42% ACT 18-23; 42% ACT 24-29 **% Accepted:** 67 **Admission Plans:** Deferred Admission **Application Deadline:** August 15 **Application Fee:** $0.00 **H.S. Requirements:** High school diploma required; GED accepted **Costs Per Year:** Application fee: $0. Comprehensive fee: $25,660 includes full-time tuition ($19,360), mandatory fees ($460), and college room and board ($5840). Room and board charges vary according to housing facility. Part-time tuition: $560 per semester hour. **Scholarships:** Available **Calendar System:** Semester, Summer Session Available **Enrollment:** FT 1,416, PT 31 **Faculty:** FT 114, PT 35 **Student-Faculty Ratio:** 11:1 **Exams:** SAT I or ACT. ACT essay not being used. SAT essay not being used. **% Receiving Financial Aid:** 57 **% Residing in College-Owned, -Operated, or -Affiliated Housing:** 90 **Library Holdings:** 789,788 **Regional Accreditation:** North Central Association of Colleges and Schools **Credit Hours For Degree:** 64 semester hours, Associates; 128 semester hours, Bachelors **ROTC:** Army **Professional Accreditation:** AACSB, AAFCS, NASM, NCATE **Intercollegiate Athletics:** Baseball M; Basketball M & W; Cheerleading M & W; Cross-Country Running W; Football M; Golf M & W; Soccer M & W; Softball W; Swimming and Diving M & W; Tennis M & W; Volleyball W; Wrestling M

OUACHITA TECHNICAL COLLEGE
One College Circle
Malvern, AR 72104
Tel: (501)337-5000
Fax: (501)337-9382
E-mail: vkesterson@otcweb.edu
Web Site: http://www.otcweb.edu/
President/CEO: Barry Ballard
Admissions: Kathy Lazenby
Type: Two-Year College **Sex:** Coed **Scores:** 53% ACT 18-23; 9% ACT 24-29 **Admission Plans:** Open Admission; Early Admission; Deferred Admission **Application Deadline:** Rolling **H.S. Requirements:** High school diploma required; GED accepted **Scholarships:** Available **Calendar System:** Semester, Summer Session Available **Enrollment:** FT 605, PT 1,005 **Faculty:** FT 33, PT 66 **Student-Faculty Ratio:** 16:1 **Exams:** Other, SAT I or ACT. **Library Holdings:** 8,000 **Regional Accreditation:** North Central Association of Colleges and Schools **Credit Hours For Degree:** 60 credit hours, Associates

OZARKA COLLEGE
PO Box 10
Melbourne, AR 72556
Tel: (870)368-7371; Free: 800-821-4335
Fax: (870)368-4733
E-mail: zwilkerson@ozarka.edu
Web Site: http://www.ozarka.edu/
President/CEO: Dr. Dusty Johnston
Admissions: Zeda Wilkerson
Type: Two-Year College **Sex:** Coed **Admission Plans:** Open Admission; Deferred Admission **Application Deadline:** August 19 **Application Fee:** $0.00 **H.S. Requirements:** High school diploma required; GED accepted **Scholarships:** Available **Calendar System:** Semester, Summer Session Available **Faculty:** FT 31, PT 40 **Student-Faculty Ratio:** 20:1 **Library Holdings:** 10,500 **Regional Accreditation:** North Central Association of Colleges and Schools **Credit Hours For Degree:** 62 credit hours, Associates

PHILANDER SMITH COLLEGE
812 West 13th St.
Little Rock, AR 72202-3799
Tel: (501)375-9845; Free: 800-446-6772
Fax: (501)370-5225
E-mail: ggray@philander.edu
Web Site: http://www.philander.edu/
President/CEO: Dr. Walter Kimbrough
Admissions: George Gray
Financial Aid: David D. Page
Type: Four-Year College **Sex:** Coed **Affiliation:** United Methodist **Scores:** 20% SAT V 400+; 60% SAT M 400+; 33% ACT 18-23; 1% ACT 24-29 **% Accepted:** 30 **Admission Plans:** Open Admission; Deferred Admission **Application Deadline:** Rolling **Application Fee:** $25.00 **H.S. Requirements:** High school diploma required; GED accepted **Scholarships:** Available **Calendar System:** Semester, Summer Session Available **Enrollment:** FT 483, PT 97 **Faculty:** FT 37, PT 30 **Student-Faculty Ratio:** 11:1 **% Receiving Financial Aid:** 93 **% Residing in College-Owned, -Operated, or -Affiliated Housing:** 30 **Library Holdings:** 84,813 **Regional Accreditation:** North Central Association of Colleges and Schools **Credit Hours For Degree:** 124 semester hours, Bachelors **ROTC:** Army **Professional Accreditation:** ACBSP, CSWE, NCATE **Intercollegiate Athletics:** Basketball M & W; Volleyball W

PHILLIPS COMMUNITY COLLEGE OF THE UNIVERSITY OF ARKANSAS
PO Box 785
Helena, AR 72342-0785
Tel: (870)338-6474
Fax: (870)338-7542
Web Site: http://www.pccua.edu/
President/CEO: Dr. Steven Murray
Admissions: Lynn Boone
Type: Two-Year College **Sex:** Coed **Affiliation:** University of Arkansas System **Admission Plans:** Open Admission; Early Admission **Application Deadline:** August 25 **H.S. Requirements:** High school diploma required; GED accepted **Costs Per Year:** Area resident tuition: $1650 full-time, $55 per semester hour part-time. State resident tuition: $2300 full-time, $64 per semester hour part-time. Nonresident tuition: $3060 full-time, $102 per semester hour part-time. Mandatory fees: $400 full-time, $12 per semester hour part-time, $10 per term part-time. Full-time tuition and fees vary according to course load. Part-time tuition and fees vary according to course load. **Scholarships:** Available **Calendar System:** Semester, Summer Session Available **Library Holdings:** 39,000 **Regional Accreditation:** North Central Association of Colleges and Schools **Credit Hours For Degree:** 64 semester hours, Associates **Professional Accreditation:** ACBSP, NAACLS, NLN

PULASKI TECHNICAL COLLEGE
3000 West Scenic Dr.
North Little Rock, AR 72118
Tel: (501)812-2200
Admissions: (501)812-2734
Fax: (501)812-2316
E-mail: catkins@pulaskitech.edu
Web Site: http://www.pulaskitech.edu/
President/CEO: Dr. Dan Bakke

Admissions: Clark Atkins
Type: Two-Year College **Sex:** Coed **% Accepted:** 100 **Admission Plans:** Open Admission **Application Deadline:** Rolling **Application Fee:** $0.00 **H.S. Requirements:** High school diploma required; GED accepted **Costs Per Year:** Application fee: $0. State resident tuition: $1968 full-time, $82 per credit hour part-time. Nonresident tuition: $3240 full-time, $135 per credit hour part-time. Mandatory fees: $290 full-time, $10 per credit hour part-time, $25 per term part-time. Full-time tuition and fees vary according to course load. **Scholarships:** Available **Calendar System:** Semester, Summer Session Available **Enrollment:** FT 4,856, PT 5,399 **Faculty:** FT 153, PT 320 **Student-Faculty Ratio:** 25:1 **Final Year or Final Semester Residency Requirement:** Yes **Library Holdings:** 35,406 **Regional Accreditation:** North Central Association of Colleges and Schools **Credit Hours For Degree:** 62 semester hours, Associates **Professional Accreditation:** ADA, CARC

REMINGTON COLLEGE—LITTLE ROCK CAMPUS
19 Remington Dr.
Little Rock, AR 72204
Tel: (501)312-0007
Fax: (501)225-3819
E-mail: brian.maggio@remingtoncollege.edu
Web Site: http://www.remingtoncollege.edu/
President/CEO: Edna Higgins
Admissions: Brian Maggio
Type: Two-Year College **Sex:** Coed **Professional Accreditation:** ACCSCT

RICH MOUNTAIN COMMUNITY COLLEGE
1100 College Dr.
Mena, AR 71953
Tel: (479)394-7622
Fax: (479)394-2628
Web Site: http://www.rmcc.edu/
President/CEO: Dr. Wayne Hatcher
Admissions: Dr. Steve Rook
Type: Two-Year College **Sex:** Coed **Admission Plans:** Open Admission; Early Admission **Application Deadline:** August 25 **Application Fee:** $0.00 **H.S. Requirements:** High school diploma required; GED accepted **Scholarships:** Available **Calendar System:** Semester, Summer Session Available **Library Holdings:** 13,299 **Regional Accreditation:** North Central Association of Colleges and Schools **Credit Hours For Degree:** 60 credits, Associates

SOUTH ARKANSAS COMMUNITY COLLEGE
PO Box 7010
El Dorado, AR 71731-7010
Tel: (870)862-8131; Free: 800-955-2289
Admissions: (870)864-7142
Fax: (870)864-7122
E-mail: dinman@southark.edu
Web Site: http://www.southark.edu/
President/CEO: Dr. Alan Rasro
Admissions: Dean Inman
Financial Aid: Veronda C. Tatum
Type: Two-Year College **Sex:** Coed **Affiliation:** Arkansas Department of Higher Education **Admission Plans:** Open Admission; Early Admission; Deferred Admission **Application Deadline:** August 25 **H.S. Requirements:** High school diploma or equivalent not required **Scholarships:** Available **Calendar System:** Semester, Summer Session Available **Enrollment:** FT 612, PT 756 **Exams:** Other, SAT I or ACT. **Library Holdings:** 22,652 **Regional Accreditation:** North Central Association of Colleges and Schools **Credit Hours For Degree:** 60 semester hours, Associates **Professional Accreditation:** AOTA, APTA, JRCERT, NAACLS

SOUTHEAST ARKANSAS COLLEGE
1900 Hazel St.
Pine Bluff, AR 71603
Tel: (870)543-5900
Admissions: (870)543-5957
E-mail: bdunn@seark.edu
Web Site: http://www.seark.edu/
President/CEO: Phil E. Shirley
Admissions: Barbara Dunn
Financial Aid: Donna Cox
Type: Two-Year College **Sex:** Coed **Admission Plans:** Open Admission; Early Admission **H.S. Requirements:** High school diploma required; GED accepted **Scholarships:** Available **Calendar System:** Semester, Summer Session Available **Enrollment:** FT 1,017, PT 1,180 **Faculty:** FT 49, PT 80 **Student-Faculty Ratio:** 18:1 **Library Holdings:** 5,000 **Regional Accreditation:** North Central Association of Colleges and Schools **Credit Hours For Degree:** 62 credits, Associates **Professional Accreditation:** ARCEST, JRCERT, NLN

SOUTHERN ARKANSAS UNIVERSITY TECH
100 Carr Rd.
PO Box 3499
Camden, AR 71701
Tel: (870)574-4500
Admissions: (870)574-4558
E-mail: bellis@sautech.edu
Web Site: http://www.sautech.edu/
President/CEO: Dr. Corbet Lamkin
Admissions: Beverly Ellis
Financial Aid: John Jefferson
Type: Two-Year College **Sex:** Coed **Affiliation:** Southern Arkansas University System **Scores:** 100% SAT V 400+; 67% SAT M 400+; 57% ACT 18-23; 1% ACT 24-29 **% Accepted:** 100 **Admission Plans:** Open Admission; Deferred Admission **Application Deadline:** August 15 **Application Fee:** $0.00 **H.S. Requirements:** High school diploma required; GED accepted **Costs Per Year:** Application fee: $0. State resident tuition: $2550 full-time, $85 per credit hour part-time. Nonresident tuition: $3870 full-time, $129 per credit hour part-time. Mandatory fees: $1000 full-time, $21 per credit hour part-time. Full-time tuition and fees vary according to course load and program. Part-time tuition and fees vary according to course load and program. College room and board: $4875. College room only: $3000. Room and board charges vary according to housing facility. **Scholarships:** Available **Calendar System:** Semester, Summer Session Available **Enrollment:** FT 589, PT 1,228 **Faculty:** FT 29, PT 76 **Student-Faculty Ratio:** 19:1 **% Residing in College-Owned, -Operated, or -Affiliated Housing:** 2 **Library Holdings:** 17,389 **Regional Accreditation:** North Central Association of Colleges and Schools **Credit Hours For Degree:** 62 semester hours, Associates

SOUTHERN ARKANSAS UNIVERSITY—MAGNOLIA
100 East University
Magnolia, AR 71753
Tel: (870)235-4000
Admissions: (870)235-4040
Fax: (870)235-5005
E-mail: addanna@saumag.edu
Web Site: http://www.saumag.edu/
President/CEO: Dr. David Rankin, CFA
Admissions: Sarah Jennings
Financial Aid: Bronwyn C. Sneed
Type: Comprehensive **Sex:** Coed **Affiliation:** Southern Arkansas University System **Scores:** 86% SAT V 400+; 94% SAT M 400+; 49% ACT 18-23; 23% ACT 24-29 **% Accepted:** 73 **Admission Plans:** Early Admission; Deferred Admission **Application Deadline:** August 27 **Application Fee:** $0.00 **H.S. Requirements:** High school diploma required; GED accepted **Costs Per Year:** Application fee: $0. State resident tuition: $5100 full-time, $170 per hour part-time. Nonresident tuition: $7740 full-time, $258 per hour part-time. Mandatory fees: $966 full-time, $31 per hour part-time, $18 per term part-time. Full-time tuition and fees vary according to course load. Part-time tuition and fees vary according to course load. College room and board: $4400. College room only: $2236. Room and board charges vary according to board plan and housing facility. **Scholarships:** Available **Calendar System:** Semester, Summer Session Available **Enrollment:** FT 2,385, PT 392, Grad FT 116, Grad PT 333 **Faculty:** FT 162, PT 52 **Student-Faculty Ratio:** 15:1 **Exams:** ACT, SAT I or ACT. **% Receiving Financial Aid:** 64 **% Residing in College-Owned, -Operated, or -Affiliated Housing:** 44 **Library Holdings:** 151,166 **Regional Accreditation:** North Central Association of Colleges and Schools **Credit Hours For Degree:** 65 semester hours, Associates; 124 semester hours, Bachelors **Professional Accreditation:** CSWE, NASM, NCATE, NLN **Intercollegiate Athletics:** Baseball M; Basketball M & W; Cross-Country Running M & W; Football M; Golf M; Softball W; Tennis W; Track and Field M & W; Volleyball W

STRAYER UNIVERSITY - LITTLE ROCK CAMPUS
10825 Financial Centre Parkway
Ste. 131

Little Rock, AR 72211
Web Site: http://www.strayer.edu/little_rock
Type: Comprehensive **Sex:** Coed **Application Fee:** $50.00 **Costs Per Year:** Application fee: $50. **Regional Accreditation:** Middle State Association of Colleges and Schools

UNIVERSITY OF ARKANSAS
800 Hotz Hall
Fayetteville, AR 72701-1201
Tel: (479)575-2000; Free: 800-377-8632
Admissions: (479)575-5346
Fax: (479)575-7515
E-mail: uofa@uark.edu
Web Site: http://www.uark.edu/
President/CEO: G. David Gearhart
Financial Aid: Kattie Wing
Type: University **Sex:** Coed **Affiliation:** University of Arkansas System **Scores:** 98.3% SAT V 400+; 98.9% SAT M 400+; 31.8% ACT 18-23; 48.3% ACT 24-29 **% Accepted:** 56 **Admission Plans:** Early Admission; Early Action **Application Deadline:** August 1 **Application Fee:** $40.00 **H.S. Requirements:** High school diploma required; GED accepted **Costs Per Year:** Application fee: $40. State resident tuition: $5010 full-time, $167 per credit hour part-time. Nonresident tuition: $13,888 full-time, $463 per credit hour part-time. Mandatory fees: $1390 full-time. Full-time tuition and fees vary according to course load and program. Part-time tuition varies according to course load and program. College room and board: $7422. College room only: $4692. Room and board charges vary according to board plan and housing facility. **Scholarships:** Available **Calendar System:** Semester, Summer Session Available **Enrollment:** FT 13,783, PT 2,052, Grad FT 1,653, Grad PT 2,361 **Faculty:** FT 897, PT 86 **Student-Faculty Ratio:** 17:1 **Exams:** SAT I or ACT. **% Receiving Financial Aid:** 39 **% Residing in College-Owned, -Operated, or -Affiliated Housing:** 29 **Library Holdings:** 1,776,460 **Regional Accreditation:** North Central Association of Colleges and Schools **Credit Hours For Degree:** 124 credit hours, Bachelors **ROTC:** Army, Air Force **Professional Accreditation:** AACSB, ABET, ACEJMC, AACN, AAFCS, ABA, ACA, APA, ASLA, ASLHA, AALS, FIDER, CORE, CSWE, NAAB, NASM, NCATE, NLN, NRPA **Intercollegiate Athletics:** Baseball M; Basketball M & W; Cross-Country Running M & W; Football M; Golf M & W; Gymnastics W; Soccer W; Softball W; Swimming and Diving W; Tennis M & W; Track and Field M & W; Volleyball W

UNIVERSITY OF ARKANSAS COMMUNITY COLLEGE AT BATESVILLE
PO Box 3350
Batesville, AR 72503
Tel: (870)793-7581
Admissions: (870)612-2000
Fax: (870)793-4988
E-mail: sgage@uaccb.edu
Web Site: http://www.uaccb.edu/
President/CEO: Deborah Frazier
Admissions: Sharon Gage
Type: Two-Year College **Sex:** Coed **Affiliation:** University of Arkansas System **% Accepted:** 100 **Admission Plans:** Open Admission **Application Deadline:** Rolling **Application Fee:** $0.00 **H.S. Requirements:** High school diploma required; GED accepted **Costs Per Year:** Application fee: $0. Area resident tuition: $1296 full-time, $54 per credit hour part-time. State resident tuition: $1584 full-time, $66 per credit hour part-time. Nonresident tuition: $2880 full-time, $120 per credit hour part-time. Mandatory fees: $466 full-time, $19 per credit hour part-time, $10 per term part-time. Full-time tuition and fees vary according to course load and program. Part-time tuition and fees vary according to course load and program. **Scholarships:** Available **Calendar System:** Semester, Summer Session Available **Enrollment:** FT 757, PT 531 **Faculty:** FT 44, PT 73 **Student-Faculty Ratio:** 15:1 **Library Holdings:** 8,000 **Regional Accreditation:** North Central Association of Colleges and Schools **Credit Hours For Degree:** 60 credits, Associates **Professional Accreditation:** NLN

UNIVERSITY OF ARKANSAS COMMUNITY COLLEGE AT HOPE
PO Box 140
Hope, AR 71802
Tel: (870)777-5722
Admissions: (870)772-8174
Fax: (870)722-5957
E-mail: janderson@uacch.edu
Web Site: http://www.uacch.edu/
President/CEO: Chris Thomason
Admissions: Judy Anderson
Financial Aid: Becky Wilson
Type: Two-Year College **Sex:** Coed **Affiliation:** University of Arkansas System **Admission Plans:** Open Admission; Early Admission **Application Deadline:** Rolling **Application Fee:** $0.00 **H.S. Requirements:** High school diploma or equivalent not required **Costs Per Year:** Application fee: $0. Area resident tuition: $1296 full-time, $54 per credit hour part-time. State resident tuition: $1416 full-time, $59 per credit hour part-time. Nonresident tuition: $2760 full-time, $115 per credit hour part-time. Mandatory fees: $198 full-time, $8 per credit hour part-time, $3 per term part-time. **Scholarships:** Available **Calendar System:** Semester, Summer Session Available **Student-Faculty Ratio:** 17:1 **Regional Accreditation:** North Central Association of Colleges and Schools **Credit Hours For Degree:** 60 credits, Associates **Professional Accreditation:** ABFSE, CARC

UNIVERSITY OF ARKANSAS COMMUNITY COLLEGE AT MORRILTON
1537 University Blvd.
Morrilton, AR 72110
Tel: (501)977-2000
Admissions: (501)977-2174
Fax: (501)354-9948
E-mail: mullins@uaccm.edu
Web Site: http://www.uaccm.edu/
President/CEO: Nathan Crook
Admissions: Rachel Mullins
Type: Two-Year College **Sex:** Coed **Affiliation:** University of Arkansas System **Scores:** 56% ACT 18-23; 19% ACT 24-29 **% Accepted:** 74 **Admission Plans:** Open Admission; Early Admission; Deferred Admission **Application Deadline:** Rolling **Application Fee:** $0.00 **H.S. Requirements:** High school diploma required; GED accepted **Costs Per Year:** Application fee: $0. Area resident tuition: $2100 full-time, $70 per credit hour part-time. State resident tuition: $2310 full-time, $77 per credit hour part-time. Nonresident tuition: $3360 full-time, $112 per credit hour part-time. Mandatory fees: $540 full-time, $17 per credit hour part-time, $15 per term part-time. Full-time tuition and fees vary according to course load. Part-time tuition and fees vary according to course load. **Scholarships:** Available **Calendar System:** Semester, Summer Session Available **Enrollment:** FT 1,625, PT 796 **Faculty:** FT 59, PT 41 **Student-Faculty Ratio:** 19:1 **Final Year or Final Semester Residency Requirement:** No **Library Holdings:** 24,981 **Regional Accreditation:** North Central Association of Colleges and Schools **Credit Hours For Degree:** 60 credit hours, Associates

UNIVERSITY OF ARKANSAS AT FORT SMITH
PO Box 3649
Fort Smith, AR 72913-3649
Tel: (479)788-7000; Free: 888-512-5466
Admissions: (479)788-7120
Fax: (479)788-7003
E-mail: information@uafortsmith.edu
Web Site: http://www.uafortsmith.edu/
President/CEO: Paul B. Beran
Financial Aid: Tammy Malone
Type: Four-Year College **Sex:** Coed **Affiliation:** University of Arkansas System **Scores:** 53.6% ACT 18-23; 26.1% ACT 24-29 **% Accepted:** 61 **Admission Plans:** Open Admission; Early Admission; Deferred Admission **Application Deadline:** Rolling **Application Fee:** $0.00 **H.S. Requirements:** High school diploma required; GED accepted **Costs Per Year:** Application fee: $0. State resident tuition: $3420 full-time, $114 per credit hour part-time. Nonresident tuition: $8820 full-time, $294 per credit hour part-time. Mandatory fees: $1180 full-time, $35 per term part-time, $65 per term part-time. Full-time tuition and fees vary according to course load and program. Part-time tuition and fees vary according to course load and program. College room only: $4789. Room charges vary according to housing facility. **Scholarships:** Available **Calendar System:** Semester, Summer Session Available **Enrollment:** FT 4,962, PT 2,373 **Faculty:** FT 223, PT 176 **Student-Faculty Ratio:** 20:1 **Exams:** Other, SAT I or ACT. **% Receiving Financial Aid:** 57 **% Residing in College-Owned, -Operated, or -Affiliated Housing:** 6 **Final Year or Final Semester Residency Requirement:** No **Library Holdings:** 85,898 **Regional Accreditation:** North Central Association of Colleges and Schools **Credit Hours For Degree:** 60 credit

hours, Associates; 124 credit hours, Bachelors **ROTC:** Army, Air Force **Professional Accreditation:** ARCEST, ADA, JRCERT, NLN **Intercollegiate Athletics:** Baseball M; Basketball M & W; Cross-Country Running M & W; Golf M & W; Tennis M & W; Volleyball W

UNIVERSITY OF ARKANSAS AT LITTLE ROCK
2801 South University Ave.
Little Rock, AR 72204-1099
Tel: (501)569-3000
Fax: (501)569-8915
E-mail: twharrison@ualn.edu
Web Site: http://www.ualr.edu/
President/CEO: Joel E. Anderson
Admissions: Tammy Harrison
Type: University **Sex:** Coed **Affiliation:** University of Arkansas System **Scores:** 43.9% ACT 18-23; 16.9% ACT 24-29 **% Accepted:** 99 **Admission Plans:** Early Admission; Deferred Admission **Application Deadline:** Rolling **Application Fee:** $0.00 **H.S. Requirements:** High school diploma required; GED accepted **Scholarships:** Available **Calendar System:** Semester, Summer Session Available **Enrollment:** FT 5,669, PT 4,531, Grad FT 1,147, Grad PT 1,785 **Faculty:** FT 429, PT 320 **Student-Faculty Ratio:** 16:1 **Exams:** ACT. **% Residing in College-Owned, -Operated, or -Affiliated Housing:** 3 **Final Year or Final Semester Residency Requirement:** Yes **Regional Accreditation:** North Central Association of Colleges and Schools **Credit Hours For Degree:** 65 credit hours, Associates; 124 credit hours, Bachelors **ROTC:** Army **Professional Accreditation:** AACSB, ABET, ABA, ACCE, ASLHA, AALS, ACEHSA, CORE, CSWE, NASAD, NASM, NASPAA, NAST, NCATE, NLN **Intercollegiate Athletics:** Baseball M; Basketball M; Cross-Country Running M & W; Golf M & W; Soccer W; Swimming and Diving W; Tennis M & W; Track and Field M & W; Volleyball W

UNIVERSITY OF ARKANSAS FOR MEDICAL SCIENCES
4301 West Markham
Little Rock, AR 72205-7199
Tel: (501)686-5000
Admissions: (501)686-5730
Web Site: http://www.uams.edu/
President/CEO: I. Dodd Wilson
Admissions: Mona Stiles
Financial Aid: Paul Carter
Type: University **Sex:** Coed **Affiliation:** University of Arkansas System **H.S. Requirements:** High school diploma required; GED accepted **Scholarships:** Available **Calendar System:** Semester, Summer Session Not available **Enrollment:** FT 611, PT 223 **% Receiving Financial Aid:** 71 **Library Holdings:** 183,975 **Regional Accreditation:** North Central Association of Colleges and Schools **ROTC:** Army **Professional Accreditation:** ACPhE, ARCEST, AACN, ADA, ADtA, APA, ASC, ACIPE, CARC, CEPH, JRCERT, JRCEMT, JRCNMT, LCMEAMA, NAACLS, NLN **Intercollegiate Athletics:** Ultimate Frisbee M & W; Volleyball M & W

UNIVERSITY OF ARKANSAS AT MONTICELLO
Monticello, AR 71656
Tel: (870)367-6811
Admissions: (870)460-1026
Fax: (870)460-1321
E-mail: admissions@uamont.edu
Web Site: http://www.uamont.edu/
President/CEO: Dr. Jack Lassiter
Admissions: Mary Whiting
Financial Aid: Susan Brewer
Type: Comprehensive **Sex:** Coed **Affiliation:** University of Arkansas System **Scores:** 43% ACT 18-23; 16% ACT 24-29 **% Accepted:** 50 **Admission Plans:** Open Admission; Early Admission; Deferred Admission **Application Deadline:** August 1 **Application Fee:** $0.00 **H.S. Requirements:** High school diploma required; GED accepted **Costs Per Year:** Application fee: $0. State resident tuition: $3510 full-time, $117 per semester hour part-time. Nonresident tuition: $7770 full-time, $259 per semester hour part-time. Mandatory fees: $1230 full-time, $41 per semester hour part-time. Full-time tuition and fees vary according to location and program. Part-time tuition and fees vary according to location and program. College room and board: $3900. College room only: $1500. Room and board charges vary according to board plan and housing facility. **Scholarships:** Available **Calendar System:** Semester, Summer Session Available **Enrollment:** FT 2,481, PT 882, Grad FT 73, Grad PT 43 **Faculty:** FT 187, PT 87 **Student-Faculty Ratio:** 15:1 **Exams:** Other. **% Residing in College-Owned, -Operated, or -Affiliated Housing:** 25 **Final Year or Final Semester Residency Requirement:** Yes **Library Holdings:** 241,822 **Regional Accreditation:** North Central Association of Colleges and Schools **Credit Hours For Degree:** 62 hours, Associates; 124 hours, Bachelors **ROTC:** Army **Professional Accreditation:** CSWE, NASM, NCATE, NLN, SAF **Intercollegiate Athletics:** Baseball M; Basketball M & W; Cross-Country Running W; Football M; Golf M; Softball W; Tennis W

UNIVERSITY OF ARKANSAS AT PINE BLUFF
1200 North University Dr.
Pine Bluff, AR 71601-2799
Tel: (870)575-8000; Free: 800-264-6585
Fax: (870)543-2021
E-mail: jonesm@uapb.edu
Web Site: http://www.uapb.edu/
President/CEO: Lawrence A. Davis, Jr.
Admissions: Mary Jones
Financial Aid: Carolyn Iverson
Type: Comprehensive **Sex:** Coed **Affiliation:** University of Arkansas System **Scores:** 57% SAT V 400+; 64% SAT M 400+; 27% ACT 18-23; 2% ACT 24-29 **% Accepted:** 33 **Admission Plans:** Open Admission; Early Admission; Deferred Admission **Application Deadline:** Rolling **Application Fee:** $0.00 **H.S. Requirements:** High school diploma required; GED accepted **Costs Per Year:** Application fee: $0. State resident tuition: $3540 full-time, $118 per credit hour part-time. Nonresident tuition: $8220 full-time, $274 per credit hour part-time. Mandatory fees: $1256 full-time, $7.50 per credit hour part-time, $22.50. Full-time tuition and fees vary according to course level, degree level, and location. Part-time tuition and fees vary according to course level, degree level, and location. College room and board: $6168. College room only: $3510. Room and board charges vary according to board plan and housing facility. **Scholarships:** Available **Calendar System:** Semester, Summer Session Available **Enrollment:** FT 3,313, PT 338, Grad FT 55, Grad PT 86 **Faculty:** FT 173, PT 85 **Student-Faculty Ratio:** 17:1 **Exams:** SAT I or ACT. **% Receiving Financial Aid:** 96 **% Residing in College-Owned, -Operated, or -Affiliated Housing:** 46 **Final Year or Final Semester Residency Requirement:** No **Library Holdings:** 287,857 **Regional Accreditation:** North Central Association of Colleges and Schools **Credit Hours For Degree:** 62 semester hours, Associates; 124 semester hours, Bachelors **ROTC:** Army **Professional Accreditation:** AAFCS, CSWE, NASAD, NASM, NCATE, NLN, NAIT **Intercollegiate Athletics:** Baseball M; Basketball M & W; Cross-Country Running M & W; Football M; Golf M; Track and Field M & W; Volleyball W

UNIVERSITY OF CENTRAL ARKANSAS
201 Donaghey Ave.
Conway, AR 72035-0001
Tel: (501)450-5000
Admissions: (501)450-3170
Fax: (501)450-5228
E-mail: phatfield@uca.edu
Web Site: http://www.uca.edu/
President/CEO: Tom Courtway
Admissions: Penny Hatfield
Financial Aid: Cheryl Lyons
Type: University **Sex:** Coed **Scores:** 43.2% ACT 18-23; 35.1% ACT 24-29 **% Accepted:** 58 **Admission Plans:** Early Admission; Deferred Admission **Application Deadline:** Rolling **Application Fee:** $0.00 **H.S. Requirements:** High school diploma required; GED accepted **Costs Per Year:** Application fee: $0. State resident tuition: $5206 full-time. Nonresident tuition: $10,412 full-time. Mandatory fees: $1493 full-time. College room and board: $4880. College room only: $2780. Room and board charges vary according to board plan and housing facility. **Scholarships:** Available **Calendar System:** Semester, Summer Session Available **Enrollment:** FT 9,098, PT 1,950 **Faculty:** FT 510, PT 199 **Student-Faculty Ratio:** 19:1 **Exams:** SAT I or ACT. **% Residing in College-Owned, -Operated, or -Affiliated Housing:** 37 **Library Holdings:** 600,084 **Regional Accreditation:** North Central Association of Colleges and Schools **Credit Hours For Degree:** 60 credit hours, Associates; 124 credit hours, Bachelors **ROTC:** Army **Professional Accreditation:** AACSB, AACN, AAFCS, ADtA, AOTA, APTA, ASLHA, NASAD, NASM, NAST, NCATE, NLN **Intercollegiate Athletics:** Baseball M; Basketball M & W; Cheerleading M & W; Cross-Country Running M & W; Football M; Golf M & W; Soccer M & W; Softball W; Tennis W; Track and Field M & W; Volleyball W

UNIVERSITY OF THE OZARKS
415 North College Ave.
Clarksville, AR 72830-2880
Tel: (479)979-1000; Free: 800-264-8636
Admissions: (479)979-1227
Fax: (479)979-1355
E-mail: admiss@ozarks.edu
Web Site: http://www.ozarks.edu/
President/CEO: Dr. Rick Niece
Admissions: Kim Myrick
Financial Aid: Jana D. Hart
Type: Four-Year College **Sex:** Coed **Affiliation:** Presbyterian **Scores:** 82.93% SAT V 400+; 90.25% SAT M 400+; 52.03% ACT 18-23; 26.83% ACT 24-29 **% Accepted:** 89 **Admission Plans:** Deferred Admission **Application Deadline:** Rolling **Application Fee:** $30.00 **H.S. Requirements:** High school diploma required; GED accepted **Costs Per Year:** Application fee: $30. Comprehensive fee: $26,830 includes full-time tuition ($19,930), mandatory fees ($600), and college room and board ($6300). College room only: $2900. Room and board charges vary according to board plan and housing facility. **Scholarships:** Available **Calendar System:** Semester, Summer Session Available **Enrollment:** FT 590, PT 35 **Faculty:** FT 47, PT 34 **Student-Faculty Ratio:** 10:1 **Exams:** SAT I or ACT. **% Receiving Financial Aid:** 60 **% Residing in College-Owned, -Operated, or -Affiliated Housing:** 65 **Final Year or Final Semester Residency Requirement:** Yes **Library Holdings:** 132,500 **Regional Accreditation:** North Central Association of Colleges and Schools **Credit Hours For Degree:** 124 semester hours, Bachelors **Professional Accreditation:** NCATE **Intercollegiate Athletics:** Baseball M; Basketball M & W; Cheerleading M & W; Cross-Country Running M & W; Soccer M & W; Softball W; Tennis M & W

UNIVERSITY OF PHOENIX—LITTLE ROCK CAMPUS
10800 Financial Center Parkway
Little Rock, AR 72211-3500
Tel: (501)225-9337; Free: 800-228-7240
Admissions: (480)557-6151
E-mail: audra.mcquarie@phoenix.edu
Web Site: http://www.phoenix.edu/
President/CEO: William Pepicello
Admissions: Audra McQuarie
Type: Comprehensive **Sex:** Coed **Admission Plans:** Open Admission; Deferred Admission **Application Deadline:** Rolling **Application Fee:** $45.00 **H.S. Requirements:** High school diploma required; GED accepted **Costs Per Year:** Application fee: $45. Tuition: $10,800 full-time. Full-time tuition varies according to course level and course load. **Scholarships:** Available **Calendar System:** Continuous, Summer Session Not available **Enrollment:** FT 622 **Faculty:** FT 13, PT 109 **Regional Accreditation:** North Central Association of Colleges and Schools **Credit Hours For Degree:** 60 credits, Associates; 120 credits, Bachelors

UNIVERSITY OF PHOENIX—NORTHWEST ARKANSAS CAMPUS
903 North 47th St. - Barrington Centre 2
Rogers, AR 72756-9615
Tel: (479)986-0385
Web Site: http://www.phoenix.edu/
President/CEO: William Pepicello, PhD
Type: Comprehensive **Sex:** Coed **Regional Accreditation:** North Central Association of Colleges and Schools

WILLIAMS BAPTIST COLLEGE
60 West Fulbright Ave.
Walnut Ridge, AR 72476
Tel: (870)886-6741; Free: 800-722-4434
E-mail: admissions@wbcoll.edu
Web Site: http://www.wbcoll.edu/
President/CEO: Dr. Jerol Swaim
Admissions: Angela Flippo
Financial Aid: Barbara Turner
Type: Four-Year College **Sex:** Coed **Affiliation:** Southern Baptist **% Accepted:** 68 **Application Deadline:** Rolling **Application Fee:** $20.00 **H.S. Requirements:** High school diploma required; GED accepted **Costs Per Year:** Application fee: $20. Comprehensive fee: $16,600 includes full-time tuition ($10,600), mandatory fees ($800), and college room and board ($5200). **Scholarships:** Available **Calendar System:** Semester, Summer Session Available **Enrollment:** FT 517, PT 112 **Faculty:** FT 29, PT 16 **Student-Faculty Ratio:** 13:1 **Exams:** SAT I or ACT. **% Receiving Financial Aid:** 52 **% Residing in College-Owned, -Operated, or -Affiliated Housing:** 65 **Library Holdings:** 57,321 **Regional Accreditation:** North Central Association of Colleges and Schools **Credit Hours For Degree:** 60 hours, Associates; 128 hours, Bachelors **ROTC:** Army **Professional Accreditation:** NCATE **Intercollegiate Athletics:** Baseball M; Basketball M & W; Golf M; Soccer M & W; Softball W; Volleyball W

ACADEMY OF ART UNIVERSITY
79 New Montgomery St.
San Francisco, CA 94105-3410
Tel: (415)274-2200; Free: 800-544-ARTS
Admissions: 800-544-2787
Fax: (415)263-4130
E-mail: info@academyart.edu
Web Site: http://www.academyart.edu/
President/CEO: Dr. Elisa Stephens
Financial Aid: Joe Vollaro
Type: Comprehensive **Sex:** Coed **% Accepted:** 100 **Admission Plans:** Open Admission; Early Admission; Deferred Admission **Application Deadline:** Rolling **Application Fee:** $100.00 **H.S. Requirements:** High school diploma required; GED accepted **Costs Per Year:** Application fee: $100. Comprehensive fee: $35,890 includes full-time tuition ($22,200), mandatory fees ($290), and college room and board ($13,400). Full-time tuition and fees vary according to course load. Room and board charges vary according to housing facility. Part-time tuition: $740 per credit. Part-time tuition varies according to course load. **Scholarships:** Available **Calendar System:** Semester, Summer Session Available **Enrollment:** FT 6,557, PT 4,648, Grad FT 2,768, Grad PT 1,818 **Faculty:** FT 196, PT 1,105 **Student-Faculty Ratio:** 20:1 **% Receiving Financial Aid:** 52 **% Residing in College-Owned, -Operated, or -Affiliated Housing:** 13 **Library Holdings:** 36,000 **Regional Accreditation:** Western Association of Schools and Colleges **Credit Hours For Degree:** 132 units, Bachelors **Professional Accreditation:** ACICS, FIDER, NASAD **Intercollegiate Athletics:** Baseball M; Basketball M & W; Cross-Country Running M & W; Golf M & W; Soccer M & W; Softball W; Tennis W; Track and Field M & W; Volleyball W

ALLAN HANCOCK COLLEGE
800 South College Dr.
Santa Maria, CA 93454-6399
Tel: (805)922-6966; Free: (866)342-5242
Fax: (805)922-3477
Web Site: http://www.hancockcollege.edu/
President/CEO: Dr. Jose Ortiz
Admissions: Adela Esquivel Swinson
Type: Two-Year College **Sex:** Coed **Admission Plans:** Open Admission **Application Deadline:** Rolling **Application Fee:** $0.00 **H.S. Requirements:** High school diploma or equivalent not required **Costs Per Year:** Application fee: $0. State resident tuition: $0 full-time. Nonresident tuition: $4560 full-time, $190 per unit part-time. Mandatory fees: $673 full-time, $26 per unit part-time. Full-time tuition and fees vary according to course load. Part-time tuition and fees vary according to course load. **Scholarships:** Available **Calendar System:** Semester, Summer Session Available **Enrollment:** FT 2,996, PT 7,391 **Faculty:** FT 152, PT 442 **Student-Faculty Ratio:** 17:1 **Final Year or Final Semester Residency Requirement:** No **Library Holdings:** 47,370 **Regional Accreditation:** Western Association of Schools and Colleges **Credit Hours For Degree:** 60 units, Associates **Intercollegiate Athletics:** Baseball M; Basketball M & W; Cross-Country Running M & W; Football M; Golf M; Soccer M & W; Softball W; Tennis M & W; Track and Field M & W; Volleyball W

ALLIANT INTERNATIONAL UNIVERSITY
10455 Pomerado Rd.
San Diego, CA 92131-1799
Tel: (858)271-4300; Free: (866)825-5426
Admissions: (858)635-4772
Fax: (858)635-4739
E-mail: admissions@alliant.edu
Web Site: http://www.alliant.edu/
President/CEO: Geoffrey Cox, PhD
Financial Aid: Deborah Spindler
Type: University **Sex:** Coed **Affiliation:** Alliant International University **Admission Plans:** Deferred Admission **Application Fee:** $45.00 **H.S. Requirements:** High school diploma required; GED accepted **Costs Per Year:** Application fee: $45. Tuition: $15,000 full-time, $550 per unit part-time. Mandatory fees: $220 full-time. **Scholarships:** Available **Calendar System:** Semester, Summer Session Available **Enrollment:** FT 105, PT 51, Grad FT 2,643, Grad PT 1,544 **Faculty:** FT 236, PT 434 **Student-Faculty Ratio:** 13:1 **% Receiving Financial Aid:** 58 **% Residing in College-Owned, -Operated, or -Affiliated Housing:** 40 **Library Holdings:** 156,245 **Regional Accreditation:** Western Association of Schools and Colleges **Credit Hours For Degree:** 120 semester units, Bachelors **Professional Accreditation:** AAMFT

ALLIED AMERICAN UNIVERSITY
22952 Alcade Dr.
Laguna Hills, CA 92653
Tel: 888-384-0849
Fax: (949)707-2978
Web Site: http://allied.edu/
Type: Four-Year College **Sex:** Coed **Professional Accreditation:** DETC

AMERICAN ACADEMY OF DRAMATIC ARTS
1336 North La Brea Ave.
Hollywood, CA 90028
Tel: (323)464-2777; Free: 800-222-2867
Fax: (323)464-1250
E-mail: khigginbotham@ca.aada.org
Web Site: http://www.aada.org/
President/CEO: Roger Croucher
Admissions: Karen Higginbotham
Type: Two-Year College **Sex:** Coed **% Accepted:** 19 **Admission Plans:** Deferred Admission **Application Deadline:** Rolling **Application Fee:** $50.00 **H.S. Requirements:** High school diploma required; GED accepted **Costs Per Year:** Application fee: $50. Tuition: $28,620 full-time. Mandatory fees: $600 full-time. **Scholarships:** Available **Calendar System:** Continuous, Summer Session Not available **Enrollment:** FT 180 **Faculty:** FT 8, PT 22 **Student-Faculty Ratio:** 12:1 **Library Holdings:** 7,700 **Credit Hours For Degree:** 70 units, Associates **Professional Accreditation:** NAST

AMERICAN CAREER COLLEGE (ANAHEIM)
1200 North Magnolia Ave.
Anaheim, CA 92801
Tel: (714)763-9066; Free: 888-844-6522
Admissions: (714)952-9066
Web Site: http://www.americancareer.com/
President/CEO: David A. Pyle
Type: Two-Year College **Sex:** Coed

AMERICAN CAREER COLLEGE (LOS ANGELES)
4021 Rosewood Ave.
Los Angeles, CA 90004-2932
Tel: (323)668-7555; Free: 888-844-6522
Web Site: http://www.americancareer.com/
President/CEO: David Pyle
Type: Two-Year College **Sex:** Coed

AMERICAN CAREER COLLEGE (ONTARIO)
3130 East Sedona Ct.
Ontario, CA 91764
Tel: (909)218-3253; Free: 888-844-6522
Admissions: (951)739-0788
Web Site: http://www.americancareer.com/
President/CEO: David A. Pyle
Type: Two-Year College **Sex:** Coed

AMERICAN JEWISH UNIVERSITY
15600 Mulholland Dr.
Bel Air, CA 90077-1599
Tel: (310)476-9777; Free: 888-853-6763
Admissions: (310)440-1250
Fax: (310)471-3657
E-mail: admissions@ajula.edu
Web Site: http://www.ajula.edu/
President/CEO: Dr. Robert Wexler
Admissions: Matt Spooner
Financial Aid: Larisa Zadoyen
Type: Comprehensive **Sex:** Coed **Affiliation:** Jewish **Scores:** 84% SAT V 400+; 83% SAT M 400+; 67% ACT 18-23; 17% ACT 24-29 **% Accepted:** 96 **Admission Plans:** Deferred Admission **Application Deadline:** May 31 **Application Fee:** $35.00 **H.S. Requirements:** High school diploma required; GED accepted **Costs Per Year:** Application fee: $35. One-time mandatory fee: $200. Comprehensive fee: $33,568 includes full-time tuition ($21,408), mandatory fees ($944), and college room and board ($11,216). College room only: $5982. Full-time tuition and fees vary according to course load and degree level. Room and board charges vary according to board plan and housing facility. Part-time tuition: $892 per unit. Part-time tuition varies according to course load and degree level. **Scholarships:** Available **Calendar System:** Semester, Summer Session Available **Enrollment:** FT 106, PT 4, Grad FT 30 **Faculty:** FT 13, PT 67 **Student-Faculty Ratio:** 4:1 **Exams:** SAT I or ACT. ACT essay not being used. SAT essay not being used. **% Receiving Financial Aid:** 95 **% Residing in College-Owned, -Operated, or -Affiliated Housing:** 60 **Library Holdings:** 165,000 **Regional Accreditation:** Western Association of Schools and Colleges **Credit Hours For Degree:** 120 units, Bachelors

AMERICAN MUSICAL AND DRAMATIC ACADEMY, LOS ANGELES
6305 Yucca St.
Los Angeles, CA 90028
Tel: (323)469-3300; Free: (866)374-5300
Fax: (323)469-3350
E-mail: info@amda.edu
Web Site: http://www.amda.edu/
President/CEO: David Martin
Type: Four-Year College **Sex:** Coed **Application Fee:** $50.00 **Costs Per Year:** Application fee: $50. Comprehensive fee: $33,850 includes full-time tuition ($27,150) and college room and board ($6700).

AMERICAN RIVER COLLEGE
4700 College Oak Dr.
Sacramento, CA 95841-4286
Tel: (916)484-8011
E-mail: nealr@arc.losrios.edu
Web Site: http://www.arc.losrios.edu/
President/CEO: David Viar
Admissions: Robin Neal
Type: Two-Year College **Sex:** Coed **Affiliation:** Los Rios Community College District System **Admission Plans:** Open Admission; Early Admission; Deferred Admission **Application Deadline:** Rolling **H.S. Requirements:** High school diploma or equivalent not required. For nursing, respiratory therapy programs, applicants under 18: High school diploma required; GED accepted **Scholarships:** Available **Calendar System:** Semester, Summer Session Available **Library Holdings:** 78,400 **Regional Accreditation:** Western Association of Schools and Colleges **Credit Hours For Degree:** 60 units, Associates **Professional Accreditation:** ABFSE, CARC **Intercollegiate Athletics:** Baseball M; Basketball M & W; Cross-Country Running M & W; Football M & W; Golf M & W; Soccer M & W; Softball W; Swimming and Diving M & W; Tennis M & W; Track and Field M & W; Volleyball W; Water Polo M & W

ANTELOPE VALLEY COLLEGE
3041 West Ave. K
Lancaster, CA 93536-5426
Tel: (661)722-6300
Admissions: (661)722-6331
Fax: (661)943-5573
Web Site: http://www.avc.edu/
President/CEO: Dr. Jackie L. Fisher, Sr.
Type: Two-Year College **Sex:** Coed **Affiliation:** California Community College System **% Accepted:** 100 **Admission Plans:** Open Admission; Early Admission **Application Deadline:** Rolling **Application Fee:** $0.00 **H.S. Requirements:** High school diploma or equivalent not required **Costs Per Year:** Application fee: $0. State resident tuition: $0 full-time. Nonresident tuition: $4710 full-time, $157 per unit part-time. Mandatory fees: $780 full-time, $26 per unit part-time. Full-time tuition and fees vary according to course load. Part-time tuition and fees vary according to course load. **Scholarships:** Available **Calendar System:** Semester, Summer Session Available **Enrollment:** FT 4,802, PT 10,306 **Faculty:** FT 195, PT 423 **Student-Faculty Ratio:** 45:1 **Library Holdings:** 43,000 **Regional Accreditation:** Western Association of Schools and Colleges **Credit Hours For Degree:** 60 units, Associates **ROTC:** Air Force **Intercollegiate Athletics:** Baseball M; Basketball M & W; Cross-Country Running M & W; Football M; Soccer W; Softball W; Tennis W; Track and Field M & W; Volleyball W

ANTIOCH UNIVERSITY LOS ANGELES
400 Corporate Pointe
Culver City, CA 90230
Tel: (310)578-1080; Free: 800-7ANTIOCH
Fax: (310)827-4742
E-mail: admissions@antiochla.edu
Web Site: http://www.antiochla.edu/
President/CEO: Neal King
Type: Two-Year Upper Division **Sex:** Coed **Affiliation:** Antioch University **% Accepted:** 90 **Admission Plans:** Deferred Admission **Application Fee:** $60.00 **H.S. Requirements:** High school diploma required; GED accepted **Calendar System:** Quarter, Summer Session Available **Enrollment:** , PT 139 **Faculty:** FT 21, PT 151 **Student-Faculty Ratio:** 14:1 **Regional Accreditation:** North Central Association of Colleges and Schools **Credit Hours For Degree:** 180 units, Bachelors

ANTIOCH UNIVERSITY SANTA BARBARA
801 Garden St.
Santa Barbara, CA 93101-1581
Tel: (805)962-8179
Fax: (805)962-4786
E-mail: sweir@antiochsb.edu
Web Site: http://www.antiochsb.edu/
President/CEO: Michael Mulnix
Admissions: Steven Weir
Financial Aid: Cecilia Schneider
Type: Two-Year Upper Division **Sex:** Coed **Affiliation:** Antioch University **Admission Plans:** Deferred Admission **Application Fee:** $60.00 **H.S. Requirements:** High school diploma required; GED accepted **Costs Per Year:** Application fee: $60. Tuition: $15,840 full-time, $530 per unit part-time. Mandatory fees: $108 full-time. **Scholarships:** Available **Calendar System:** Quarter, Summer Session Available **Enrollment:** FT 37, PT 68 **Faculty:** FT 7, PT 51 **Student-Faculty Ratio:** 12:1 **Regional Accreditation:** North Central Association of Colleges and Schools **Credit Hours For Degree:** 180 quarter hours, Bachelors

APPLIED PROFESSIONAL TRAINING, INC.
5751 Palmer Way, Ste. D
PO Box 131717
Carlsbad, CA 92013
Tel: 800-431-8488
Fax: 888-431-8588
Web Site: http://www.aptc.edu/

Type: Two-Year College **Sex:** Coed **Professional Accreditation:** DETC

ARGOSY UNIVERSITY, INLAND EMPIRE
636 East Brier Dr., Ste. 120
San Bernardino, CA 92408
Tel: (909)915-3800; Free: (866)217-9075
Fax: (909)915-3810
Web Site: http://www.argosy.edu/inlandempire/
President/CEO: Darren Adamson
Type: University **Sex:** Coed **Regional Accreditation:** North Central Association of Colleges and Schools

ARGOSY UNIVERSITY, LOS ANGELES
5230 Pacific Concourse, Ste. 200
Santa Monica, CA 90045
Tel: (310)866-4000; Free: (866)505-0332
Web Site: http://www.argosy.edu/santamonica/
President/CEO: Darren Adamson
Type: University **Sex:** Coed **Regional Accreditation:** North Central Association of Colleges and Schools

ARGOSY UNIVERSITY, ORANGE COUNTY
601 South Lewis St.
Orange, CA 92868
Tel: (714)338-6200; Free: 800-716-9598
Admissions: (714)620-3700
Web Site: http://www.argosy.edu/orangecounty/
President/CEO: Dan Peterson
Type: University **Sex:** Coed **H.S. Requirements:** High school diploma required; GED accepted **Calendar System:** Semester **Regional Accreditation:** North Central Association of Colleges and Schools

ARGOSY UNIVERSITY, SAN DIEGO
1615 Murray Canyon Rd., Ste. 100
San Diego, CA 92108
Tel: (619)321-3000; Free: (866)505-0333
Web Site: http://www.argosy.edu/sandiego/
President/CEO: Darren Adamson
Type: University **Sex:** Coed **Regional Accreditation:** North Central Association of Colleges and Schools

ARGOSY UNIVERSITY, SAN FRANCISCO BAY AREA
1005 Atlantic Ave.
Alameda, CA 94501
Tel: (510)217-4700; Free: (866)215-2777
Fax: (510)217-4806
Web Site: http://www.argosy.edu/sanfrancisco/
President/CEO: Lucille H. Sansing, PhD
Type: University **Sex:** Coed **Affiliation:** Education Management Corporation **Calendar System:** Semester **Regional Accreditation:** North Central Association of Colleges and Schools **Professional Accreditation:** APA

ART CENTER COLLEGE OF DESIGN
1700 Lida St.
Pasadena, CA 91103
Tel: (626)396-2200
Admissions: (626)396-2322
Fax: (626)795-0578
E-mail: kit.baron@artcenter.edu
Web Site: http://www.artcenter.edu/
President/CEO: Lorne Buchman, PhD
Admissions: Kit Baron
Financial Aid: Clema McKenzie
Type: Comprehensive **Sex:** Coed **% Accepted:** 66 **Admission Plans:** Deferred Admission **Application Deadline:** Rolling **Application Fee:** $50.00 **H.S. Requirements:** High school diploma required; GED accepted **Costs Per Year:** Application fee: $50. Tuition: $31,076 full-time, $1173 per unit part-time. Mandatory fees: $250 full-time, $250. **Scholarships:** Available **Calendar System:** Trimester, Summer Session Available **Enrollment:** FT 1,321, Grad FT 134 **Faculty:** FT 85, PT 369 **Student-Faculty Ratio:** 8:1 **Exams:** SAT I or ACT. **% Receiving Financial Aid:** 82 **Library Holdings:** 90,038 **Regional Accreditation:** Western Association of Schools and Colleges **Credit Hours For Degree:** 135 credits, Bachelors **Professional Accreditation:** NASAD

THE ART INSTITUTE OF CALIFORNIA—HOLLYWOOD
5250 Lankershim Blvd.
North Hollywood, CA 91601
Tel: (818)299-5100; Free: 877-468-6232
Web Site: http://www.artinstitutes.edu/hollywood/
President/CEO: Sarah Peck
Type: Four-Year College **Sex:** Coed **Affiliation:** Education Management Corporation **Calendar System:** Quarter **Professional Accreditation:** ACICS

THE ART INSTITUTE OF CALIFORNIA—INLAND EMPIRE
674 East Brier Dr.
San Bernardino, CA 92408
Tel: (909)915-2100; Free: 800-353-0812
Web Site: http://www.artinstitutes.edu/inlandempire/
President/CEO: Emam Elhout
Type: Four-Year College **Sex:** Coed **Affiliation:** Education Management Corporation **Professional Accreditation:** ACCSCT

THE ART INSTITUTE OF CALIFORNIA—LOS ANGELES
2900 31st St.
Santa Monica, CA 90405-3035
Tel: (310)752-4700; Free: 888-646-4610
Fax: (310)752-4708
Web Site: http://www.artinstitutes.edu/losangeles/
President/CEO: Laura Soloff
Type: Four-Year College **Sex:** Coed **Affiliation:** Education Management Corporation **Calendar System:** Quarter **Professional Accreditation:** ACICS

THE ART INSTITUTE OF CALIFORNIA—ORANGE COUNTY
3601 West Sunflower Ave.
Santa Ana, CA 92704
Tel: (714)830-0200; Free: 888-549-3055
Web Site: http://www.artinstitutes.edu/orangecounty/
President/CEO: Daniel A. Levinson
Type: Four-Year College **Sex:** Coed **Affiliation:** Education Management Corporation **Calendar System:** Quarter **Professional Accreditation:** ACICS

THE ART INSTITUTE OF CALIFORNIA—SACRAMENTO
2850 Gateway Oaks Dr., Ste. 100
Sacramento, CA 95833
Free: 800-477-1957
Web Site: http://www.artinstitutes.edu/sacramento/
President/CEO: Roger Gomez
Type: Four-Year College **Sex:** Coed **Professional Accreditation:** ACICS

THE ART INSTITUTE OF CALIFORNIA—SAN DIEGO
7650 Mission Valley Rd.
San Diego, CA 92108
Tel: (858)598-1399; Free: (866)275-2422
Web Site: http://www.artinstitutes.edu/sandiego/
President/CEO: Elizabeth A. Erickson
Financial Aid: Monica McCormick
Type: Four-Year College **Sex:** Coed **Affiliation:** Education Management Corporation **Calendar System:** Quarter **Professional Accreditation:** ACCSCT

THE ART INSTITUTE OF CALIFORNIA—SAN FRANCISCO
1170 Market St.
San Francisco, CA 94102
Tel: (415)865-0198; Free: 888-493-3261
Fax: (415)863-6344
Web Site: http://www.artinstitutes.edu/sanfrancisco/
President/CEO: Byron Chung
Type: Comprehensive **Sex:** Coed **Affiliation:** Education Management Corporation **Calendar System:** Quarter **Professional Accreditation:** ACICS

THE ART INSTITUTE OF CALIFORNIA—SUNNYVALE
1120 Kifer Rd.
Sunnyvale, CA 94086
Tel: (408)962-6400; Free: (866)583-7961

Web Site: http://www.artinstitutes.edu/sunnyvale/
President/CEO: Jennifer Fuller
Type: Four-Year College **Sex:** Coed **Professional Accreditation:** ACICS

AVIATION & ELECTRONIC SCHOOLS OF AMERICA
111 South Railroad St.
PO Box 1810
Colfax, CA 95713-1810
Tel: (530)346-6792; Free: 800-345-2742
Fax: (530)346-8466
Web Site: http://www.aesa.com/
Type: Two-Year College **Sex:** Coed **Calendar System:** Continuous **Professional Accreditation:** COE

AZUSA PACIFIC UNIVERSITY
901 East Alosta Ave.
Azusa, CA 91702-7000
Tel: (626)969-3434; Free: 800-TALK-APU
Admissions: (626)815-6000
E-mail: admissions@apu.edu
Web Site: http://www.apu.edu/
President/CEO: Dr. Jon R. Wallace
Admissions: Lynnette Barnes
Financial Aid: Todd Ross
Type: University **Sex:** Coed **Affiliation:** nondenominational **Scores:** 98% SAT V 400+; 97% SAT M 400+ **% Accepted:** 59 **Admission Plans:** Early Admission; Early Action; Deferred Admission **Application Deadline:** June 1 **Application Fee:** $45.00 **H.S. Requirements:** High school diploma required; GED accepted **Costs Per Year:** Application fee: $45. Comprehensive fee: $36,064 includes full-time tuition ($26,950), mandatory fees ($800), and college room and board ($8314). College room only: $4840. **Scholarships:** Available **Calendar System:** Semester, Summer Session Available **Faculty:** FT 339, PT 651 **Student-Faculty Ratio:** 12:1 **Exams:** SAT I or ACT. ACT essay used for advising. SAT essay used for advising. ACT essay used for placement. SAT essay used for placement. **% Receiving Financial Aid:** 63 **% Residing in College-Owned, -Operated, or -Affiliated Housing:** 61 **Regional Accreditation:** Western Association of Schools and Colleges **Credit Hours For Degree:** 126 units, Bachelors **ROTC:** Army **Professional Accreditation:** AACN, APTA, APA, ATS, CSWE, JRCEPAT, NASAD, NASM, NCATE, NLN **Intercollegiate Athletics:** Baseball M; Basketball M & W; Cross-Country Running M & W; Football M; Golf M; Soccer M & W; Softball W; Tennis M; Track and Field M & W; Volleyball M & W

BAKERSFIELD COLLEGE
1801 Panorama Dr.
Bakersfield, CA 93305-1299
Tel: (661)395-4011
Fax: (661)395-4230
E-mail: svaughn@bakersfieldcollege.edu
Web Site: http://www.bakersfieldcollege.edu/
President/CEO: Dr. Greg A. Chamberlain
Admissions: Sue Vaughn
Type: Two-Year College **Sex:** Coed **Affiliation:** California Community College System **Admission Plans:** Open Admission; Preferred Admission **Application Deadline:** Rolling **Application Fee:** $0.00 **H.S. Requirements:** High school diploma or equivalent not required. For applicants under 18: High school diploma required; GED accepted **Scholarships:** Available **Calendar System:** Semester, Summer Session Available **Library Holdings:** 93,500 **Regional Accreditation:** Western Association of Schools and Colleges **Credit Hours For Degree:** 60 units, Associates **Professional Accreditation:** JRCERT **Intercollegiate Athletics:** Baseball M; Basketball M & W; Cross-Country Running M & W; Football M; Golf M; Soccer W; Softball W; Tennis M & W; Track and Field M & W; Volleyball W; Wrestling M

BARSTOW COLLEGE
2700 Barstow Rd.
Barstow, CA 92311-6699
Tel: (760)252-2411
Fax: (760)252-1875
Web Site: http://www.barstow.edu/
President/CEO: Thom Armstrong, PhD
Admissions: Don Low
Type: Two-Year College **Sex:** Coed **Affiliation:** California Community College System **Admission Plans:** Open Admission; Early Admission; Deferred Admission **Application Deadline:** Rolling **H.S. Requirements:** High school diploma or equivalent not required. For applicants under 18: High school diploma required; GED accepted **Scholarships:** Available **Calendar System:** Semester, Summer Session Available **Faculty:** FT 36, PT 91 **Student-Faculty Ratio:** 20:1 **Library Holdings:** 38,000 **Regional Accreditation:** Western Association of Schools and Colleges **Credit Hours For Degree:** 60 units, Associates **Intercollegiate Athletics:** Baseball M; Basketball M; Volleyball W

BERKELEY CITY COLLEGE
2050 Center St.
Berkeley, CA 94704-5102
Tel: (510)981-2800
Admissions: (510)981-2820
Fax: (510)841-7333
E-mail: mrivas@peralta.edu
Web Site: http://www.berkeleycitycollege.edu/
President/CEO: Dr. Betty Inclan
Admissions: Dr. May Kuang-chi Chen
Financial Aid: Loan Nguyen
Type: Two-Year College **Sex:** Coed **Affiliation:** Peralta Community College District; California Community College System **% Accepted:** 100 **Admission Plans:** Open Admission; Preferred Admission; Early Admission; Deferred Admission **Application Deadline:** Rolling **Application Fee:** $0.00 **H.S. Requirements:** High school diploma or equivalent not required. For applicants under 18: High school diploma required; GED accepted **Costs Per Year:** Application fee: $0. State resident tuition: $0 full-time. Nonresident tuition: $5880 full-time, $196 per unit part-time. Mandatory fees: $780 full-time, $26 per unit part-time. Full-time tuition and fees vary according to course load. Part-time tuition and fees vary according to course load. **Scholarships:** Available **Calendar System:** Semester, Summer Session Available **Faculty:** FT 49, PT 131 **Student-Faculty Ratio:** 35:1 **Regional Accreditation:** Western Association of Schools and Colleges **Credit Hours For Degree:** 60 semester hours, Associates

BETHANY UNIVERSITY
800 Bethany Dr.
Scotts Valley, CA 95066-2820
Tel: (831)438-3800; Free: 800-843-9410
Fax: (831)438-4517
E-mail: info@bethany.edu
Web Site: http://www.bethany.edu/
President/CEO: Lewis Shelton
Financial Aid: Deborah Snow
Type: Comprehensive **Sex:** Coed **Affiliation:** Assemblies of God **% Accepted:** 45 **Admission Plans:** Early Admission; Deferred Admission **Application Deadline:** July 31 **Application Fee:** $35.00 **H.S. Requirements:** High school diploma required; GED accepted **Costs Per Year:** Application fee: $35. One-time mandatory fee: $100. Comprehensive fee: $26,300 includes full-time tuition ($18,300), mandatory fees ($550), and college room and board ($7450). Full-time tuition and fees vary according to degree level and program. Room and board charges vary according to housing facility. Part-time tuition: $735 per unit. Part-time mandatory fees: $275 per term. Part-time tuition and fees vary according to course load, degree level, and program. **Scholarships:** Available **Calendar System:** Semester, Summer Session Available **Enrollment:** FT 344, PT 75, Grad FT 47, Grad PT 36 **Faculty:** FT 21, PT 13 **Student-Faculty Ratio:** 12:1 **Exams:** SAT I or ACT. ACT essay not being used. SAT essay not being used. **% Receiving Financial Aid:** 85 **% Residing in College-Owned, -Operated, or -Affiliated Housing:** 83 **Final Year or Final Semester Residency Requirement:** Yes **Library Holdings:** 59,453 **Regional Accreditation:** Western Association of Schools and Colleges **Credit Hours For Degree:** 66 credit hours, Associates; 124 credit hours, Bachelors **ROTC:** Army **Intercollegiate Athletics:** Baseball M; Basketball M & W; Cross-Country Running M & W; Soccer M & W; Softball W; Volleyball W

BETHESDA CHRISTIAN UNIVERSITY
730 North Euclid St.
Anaheim, CA 92801
Tel: (714)517-1945
Fax: (714)517-1948
E-mail: admission@bcu.edu
Web Site: http://www.bcu.edu/
President/CEO: Dr. John Stetz

Admissions: Jacquie Ha
Financial Aid: Grace Choi
Type: Comprehensive **Sex:** Coed **Affiliation:** Full Gospel World Mission **% Accepted:** 95 **Admission Plans:** Open Admission; Early Admission **Application Deadline:** August 11 **Application Fee:** $35.00 **H.S. Requirements:** High school diploma required; GED accepted **Scholarships:** Available **Calendar System:** Semester, Summer Session Available **% Receiving Financial Aid:** 24 **% Residing in College-Owned, -Operated, or -Affiliated Housing:** 0 **Library Holdings:** 27,763 **Credit Hours For Degree:** 125 units, Bachelors **Professional Accreditation:** ABHE, TACCS

BIOLA UNIVERSITY
13800 Biola Ave.
La Mirada, CA 90639-0001
Tel: (562)903-6000; Free: 800-652-4652
Admissions: (562)903-4752
Fax: (562)903-4709
E-mail: admissions@biola.edu
Web Site: http://www.biola.edu/
President/CEO: Dr. Barry H. Corey
Admissions: Andre Stephens
Financial Aid: Jonathan Choy
Type: University **Sex:** Coed **Affiliation:** interdenominational **Scores:** 98% SAT V 400+; 95% SAT M 400+; 41% ACT 18-23; 43% ACT 24-29 **% Accepted:** 82 **Admission Plans:** Early Action; Deferred Admission **Application Fee:** $45.00 **H.S. Requirements:** High school diploma required; GED accepted **Costs Per Year:** Application fee: $45. Comprehensive fee: $36,411 includes full-time tuition ($27,744), mandatory fees ($300), and college room and board ($8367). College room only: $4487. Room and board charges vary according to board plan and housing facility. Part-time tuition: $1156 per unit. Part-time tuition varies according to course load. **Scholarships:** Available **Calendar System:** 4-1-4, Summer Session Available **Enrollment:** FT 3,591, PT 345, Grad FT 777, Grad PT 1,235 **Faculty:** FT 220, PT 225 **Student-Faculty Ratio:** 17:1 **Exams:** SAT I or ACT. ACT essay not being used. SAT essay not being used. **% Receiving Financial Aid:** 64 **% Residing in College-Owned, -Operated, or -Affiliated Housing:** 69 **Regional Accreditation:** Western Association of Schools and Colleges **Credit Hours For Degree:** 130 units, Bachelors **ROTC:** Army, Air Force **Professional Accreditation:** APA, ACBSP, ATS, NASAD, NASM, NLN **Intercollegiate Athletics:** Baseball M; Basketball M & W; Cheerleading W; Cross-Country Running M & W; Golf M & W; Soccer M & W; Softball W; Swimming and Diving M & W; Tennis M & W; Track and Field M & W; Volleyball W

BROOKS INSTITUTE
27 East Cota St.
Santa Barbara, CA 93101
Tel: (805)966-3888; Free: 888-276-4999
Fax: (805)564-1475
E-mail: admissions@brooks.edu
Web Site: http://www.brooks.edu/
President/CEO: Roger Andersen
Financial Aid: Stacey Eymann
Type: Comprehensive **Sex:** Coed **Affiliation:** Career Education Corporation **Application Fee:** $100.00 **H.S. Requirements:** High school diploma required; GED accepted **Scholarships:** Available **Calendar System:** Trimester, Summer Session Not available **Student-Faculty Ratio:** 22:1 **Library Holdings:** 6,500 **Credit Hours For Degree:** 153 credits, Bachelors **Professional Accreditation:** ACICS

BRYAN COLLEGE
2317 Gold Meadow Way
Gold River, CA 95670
Tel: (916)649-2400; Free: (866)649-2400
Web Site: http://www.bryancollege.edu/
President/CEO: John Ledesma
Type: Two-Year College **Sex:** Coed **% Accepted:** 51 **Application Fee:** $35.00 **Scholarships:** Available **Professional Accreditation:** ACCSCT

BUTTE COLLEGE
3536 Butte Campus Dr.
Oroville, CA 95965-8399
Tel: (530)895-2511
Fax: (530)895-2345
Web Site: http://www.butte.edu/
President/CEO: Dr. Diana J. Van Der Ploeg
Admissions: Nancy Jenson
Type: Two-Year College **Sex:** Coed **Affiliation:** California Community College System **Admission Plans:** Open Admission; Early Admission; Deferred Admission **Application Deadline:** Rolling **Application Fee:** $0.00 **H.S. Requirements:** High school diploma or equivalent not required. For applicants under 18: High school diploma required; GED accepted **Costs Per Year:** Application fee: $0. State resident tuition: $0 full-time. Nonresident tuition: $4560 full-time, $190 per unit part-time. Mandatory fees: $804 full-time, $26 per unit part-time, $90 per term part-time. Full-time tuition and fees vary according to course level, course load, and program. Part-time tuition and fees vary according to course level, course load, and program. **Scholarships:** Available **Calendar System:** Semester, Summer Session Available **Library Holdings:** 50,000 **Regional Accreditation:** Western Association of Schools and Colleges **Credit Hours For Degree:** 60 semester hours, Associates **Professional Accreditation:** CARC **Intercollegiate Athletics:** Baseball M; Basketball M & W; Cross-Country Running M & W; Football M; Golf M & W; Soccer W; Softball W; Track and Field M & W; Volleyball W

CABRILLO COLLEGE
6500 Soquel Dr.
Aptos, CA 95003-3194
Tel: (831)479-6100
Fax: (831)479-6425
E-mail: esnee@cabrillo.edu
Web Site: http://www.cabrillo.edu/
President/CEO: Brian King
Admissions: Esperanza Nee
Type: Two-Year College **Sex:** Coed **Affiliation:** California Community College System **Admission Plans:** Open Admission; Early Admission **Application Deadline:** Rolling **Application Fee:** $0.00 **H.S. Requirements:** High school diploma or equivalent not required. For applicants under 18: High school diploma required; GED accepted **Scholarships:** Available **Calendar System:** Semester, Summer Session Available **Enrollment:** FT 3,993, PT 10,101 **Faculty:** FT 116, PT 535 **Library Holdings:** 60,000 **Regional Accreditation:** Western Association of Schools and Colleges **Credit Hours For Degree:** 60 semester hours, Associates **Professional Accreditation:** AAMAE, ADA, JRCERT **Intercollegiate Athletics:** Baseball M; Basketball M & W; Cross-Country Running M & W; Football M; Golf M & W; Soccer M & W; Softball W; Swimming and Diving M & W; Tennis M & W; Track and Field M & W; Volleyball M & W; Water Polo M & W; Wrestling M

CALIFORNIA BAPTIST UNIVERSITY
8432 Magnolia Ave.
Riverside, CA 92504-3206
Tel: (951)689-5771; Free: 877-228-8866
Admissions: (951)343-4212
E-mail: admissions@calbaptist.edu
Web Site: http://www.calbaptist.edu/
President/CEO: Dr. Ronald L. Ellis
Admissions: Allen Johnson
Financial Aid: Rebecca Sanchez
Type: Comprehensive **Sex:** Coed **Affiliation:** Southern Baptist **Scores:** 91.5% SAT V 400+; 89.1% SAT M 400+; 59% ACT 18-23; 24.9% ACT 24-29 **% Accepted:** 75 **Admission Plans:** Early Admission; Early Action; Deferred Admission **Application Deadline:** Rolling **Application Fee:** $45.00 **H.S. Requirements:** High school diploma required; GED accepted **Costs Per Year:** Application fee: $45. Comprehensive fee: $31,436 includes full-time tuition ($21,866), mandatory fees ($1400), and college room and board ($8170). College room only: $3960. Full-time tuition and fees vary according to class time and program. Room and board charges vary according to board plan and housing facility. Part-time tuition: $841 per semester hour. Part-time mandatory fees: $235 per term. Part-time tuition and fees vary according to class time and program. **Scholarships:** Available **Calendar System:** Miscellaneous, Summer Session Available **Enrollment:** FT 2,773, PT 449, Grad FT 361, Grad PT 520 **Faculty:** FT 164, PT 175 **Student-Faculty Ratio:** 18:1 **Exams:** SAT I or ACT. **% Receiving Financial Aid:** 69 **% Residing in College-Owned, -Operated, or -Affiliated Housing:** 52 **Final Year or Final Semester Residency Requirement:** No **Library Holdings:** 203,175 **Regional Accreditation:** Western Association of Schools and Colleges **Credit Hours For Degree:** 124 units, Bachelors **ROTC:** Army, Air Force **Professional Accreditation:** AACN, ACBSP, NASM **Intercollegiate Athletics:** Baseball M; Basketball M & W; Cheerleading M & W; Cross-

Country Running M & W; Golf M & W; Soccer M & W; Softball W; Swimming and Diving M & W; Volleyball M & W; Water Polo M & W; Wrestling M

CALIFORNIA CHRISTIAN COLLEGE
4881 East University Ave.
Fresno, CA 93703-3533
Tel: (559)251-4215
E-mail: cccadmissions@calchristiancollege.org
Web Site: http://www.calchristiancollege.org/
President/CEO: Wendell Walley
Admissions: Mallory Breshears
Financial Aid: Mindy Scroggins
Type: Four-Year College **Sex:** Coed **Admission Plans:** Open Admission **Application Deadline:** Rolling **Application Fee:** $40.00 **H.S. Requirements:** High school diploma required; GED accepted **Costs Per Year:** Application fee: $40. Comprehensive fee: $10,690 includes full-time tuition ($6840) and college room and board ($3850). Part-time tuition: $285 per unit. **Scholarships:** Available **Calendar System:** Semester, Summer Session Available **Enrollment:** FT 25, PT 3 **Faculty:** FT 2, PT 6 **Student-Faculty Ratio:** 6:1 **Exams:** Other, SAT I or ACT. **% Receiving Financial Aid:** 80 **% Residing in College-Owned, -Operated, or -Affiliated Housing:** 25 **Credit Hours For Degree:** 64 units, Associates; 128 units, Bachelors **Professional Accreditation:** TACCS

CALIFORNIA COAST UNIVERSITY
700 North Main St.
Santa Ana, CA 92701
Tel: (714)547-9625; Free: 888-CCU-UNIV
E-mail: admissions@calcoast.edu
Web Site: http://www.calcoast.edu/
Type: Comprehensive **Sex:** Coed **Application Fee:** $75.00 **Costs Per Year:** Application fee: $75. Tuition: $125 per unit part-time.

CALIFORNIA COLLEGE
2820 Camino del Rio South
Ste. 300
San Diego, CA 92108
Tel: (619)295-5785; Free: 800-622-3188
Admissions: (619)680-4430
Fax: (619)295-5985
Web Site: http://www.cc-sd.edu/
President/CEO: David Parker
Type: Four-Year College **Sex:** Coed **Admission Plans:** Open Admission **Student-Faculty Ratio:** 50:1 **Professional Accreditation:** ACCSCT

CALIFORNIA COLLEGE OF THE ARTS
1111 Eighth St.
San Francisco, CA 94107
Tel: (415)703-9500; Free: 800-447-1ART
Admissions: (415)703-9523
Fax: (415)703-9539
E-mail: enroll@cca.edu
Web Site: http://www.cca.edu/
President/CEO: Stephen Beal
Admissions: Robynne Royster
Type: Comprehensive **Sex:** Coed **Scores:** 91% SAT V 400+; 92% SAT M 400+; 60% ACT 18-23; 40% ACT 24-29 **% Accepted:** 75 **Admission Plans:** Deferred Admission **Application Deadline:** February 1 **Application Fee:** $60.00 **H.S. Requirements:** High school diploma required; GED accepted **Costs Per Year:** Application fee: $60. Tuition: $32,904 full-time, $1371 per unit part-time. Mandatory fees: $360 full-time. Full-time tuition and fees vary according to course load and degree level. Part-time tuition varies according to course load and degree level. College room only: $6600. Room charges vary according to housing facility. **Scholarships:** Available **Calendar System:** Semester, Summer Session Available **Enrollment:** FT 1,289, PT 115, Grad FT 409, Grad PT 18 **Faculty:** FT 81, PT 422 **Student-Faculty Ratio:** 8:1 **Exams:** SAT I or ACT. **% Receiving Financial Aid:** 68 **% Residing in College-Owned, -Operated, or -Affiliated Housing:** 19 **Final Year or Final Semester Residency Requirement:** Yes **Library Holdings:** 75,085 **Regional Accreditation:** Western Association of Schools and Colleges **Credit Hours For Degree:** 126 units, Bachelors **Professional Accreditation:** FIDER, NAAB, NASAD

CALIFORNIA CULINARY ACADEMY
625 Polk St.
San Francisco, CA 94102-3368
Tel: (415)771-3500; Free: 800-BAY-CHEF
Fax: (415)771-2194
Web Site: http://www.baychef.com/
President/CEO: Peter Lee
Admissions: Nancy Seyfert
Type: Two-Year College **Sex:** Coed **Admission Plans:** Open Admission **Application Deadline:** Rolling **Application Fee:** $65.00 **H.S. Requirements:** High school diploma required; GED accepted **Scholarships:** Available **Calendar System:** Continuous, Summer Session Not available **Library Holdings:** 3,000 **Credit Hours For Degree:** 78 credit hours, Associates **Professional Accreditation:** ACCSCT, ACF

CALIFORNIA INSTITUTE OF THE ARTS
24700 McBean Parkway
Valencia, CA 91355-2340
Tel: (661)255-1050; Free: 800-545-2787
E-mail: admiss@calarts.edu
Web Site: http://www.calarts.edu/
President/CEO: Steven D. Lavine
Admissions: Molly Ryan
Financial Aid: Bobbi Heuer
Type: Comprehensive **Sex:** Coed **% Accepted:** 33 **Application Deadline:** January 5 **Application Fee:** $70.00 **H.S. Requirements:** High school diploma required; GED accepted **Costs Per Year:** Application fee: $70. Comprehensive fee: $46,035 includes full-time tuition ($36,166), mandatory fees ($576), and college room and board ($9293). College room only: $5236. Room and board charges vary according to board plan, housing facility, and location. **Scholarships:** Available **Calendar System:** Semester, Summer Session Not available **Enrollment:** FT 882, PT 6, Grad FT 500, Grad PT 4 **Faculty:** FT 160, PT 143 **Student-Faculty Ratio:** 7:1 **% Receiving Financial Aid:** 67 **% Residing in College-Owned, -Operated, or -Affiliated Housing:** 43 **Final Year or Final Semester Residency Requirement:** Yes **Library Holdings:** 199,935 **Regional Accreditation:** Western Association of Schools and Colleges **Credit Hours For Degree:** 120 units, Bachelors **Professional Accreditation:** NASAD, NASD, NASM, NAST

CALIFORNIA INSTITUTE OF INTEGRAL STUDIES
1453 Mission St.
San Francisco, CA 94103
Tel: (415)575-6100
Fax: (415)575-1264
E-mail: info@ciis.edu
Web Site: http://www.ciis.edu/
President/CEO: Joseph Subbiondo
Type: Two-Year Upper Division **Sex:** Coed **Admission Plans:** Deferred Admission **Application Fee:** $65.00 **Scholarships:** Available **Calendar System:** Semester, Summer Session Not available **Student-Faculty Ratio:** 19:1 **Library Holdings:** 4,000 **Regional Accreditation:** Western Association of Schools and Colleges **Credit Hours For Degree:** 120 credits, Bachelors **Professional Accreditation:** APA

CALIFORNIA INSTITUTE OF TECHNOLOGY
1200 East California Blvd.
Pasadena, CA 91125-0001
Tel: (626)395-6811
Admissions: (626)395-6341
Fax: (626)683-3026
Web Site: http://www.caltech.edu/
President/CEO: Dr. Jean-Lou Chameau
Admissions: Ray Prado
Financial Aid: Don Crewell
Type: University **Sex:** Coed **Scores:** 100% SAT V 400+; 100% SAT M 400+ **% Accepted:** 15 **Admission Plans:** Early Admission; Early Action; Deferred Admission **Application Deadline:** January 1 **Application Fee:** $65.00 **H.S. Requirements:** High school diploma or equivalent not required **Scholarships:** Available **Calendar System:** Miscellaneous, Summer Session Not available **Enrollment:** FT 951, Grad FT 1,179 **Faculty:** FT 318, PT 28 **Student-Faculty Ratio:** 3:1 **Exams:** SAT I or ACT, SAT II. **% Receiving Financial Aid:** 55 **% Residing in College-Owned, -Operated, or -Affiliated Housing:** 95 **Library Holdings:** 346,648 **Regional Accreditation:** Western Association of Schools and Colleges **ROTC:** Army, Air Force

Professional Accreditation: ABET **Intercollegiate Athletics:** Baseball M; Basketball M & W; Cross-Country Running M & W; Fencing M & W; Ice Hockey M; Rugby M; Soccer M & W; Swimming and Diving M & W; Tennis M & W; Track and Field M & W; Volleyball M & W; Water Polo M & W

CALIFORNIA INTERCONTINENTAL UNIVERSITY
1470 Valley Vista Dr., Ste. 150
Diamond Bar, CA 91765
Tel: (909)396-6090; Free: (866)687-2258
Fax: (909)804-5151
E-mail: info@caluniversity.com
Web Site: http://caluniversity.edu/
Type: Comprehensive **Sex:** Coed **Application Fee:** $75.00 **Costs Per Year:** Application fee: $75. Tuition: $140 per credit part-time.

CALIFORNIA LUTHERAN UNIVERSITY
60 West Olsen Rd.
Thousand Oaks, CA 91360-2787
Tel: (805)492-2411; Free: 877-258-3678
Admissions: (805)493-3135
Fax: (805)493-3114
E-mail: cluadm@clunet.edu
Web Site: http://www.callutheran.edu/
President/CEO: Dr. Christopher Kimball
Admissions: Matthew Ward
Financial Aid: Rebecca Kennan
Type: Comprehensive **Sex:** Coed **Affiliation:** Lutheran **Scores:** 99% SAT V 400+; 99% SAT M 400+ **% Accepted:** 62 **Admission Plans:** Early Action; Deferred Admission **Application Deadline:** March 15 **Application Fee:** $45.00 **H.S. Requirements:** High school diploma required; GED accepted **Costs Per Year:** Application fee: $45. Comprehensive fee: $41,580 includes full-time tuition ($30,750), mandatory fees ($250), and college room and board ($10,580). College room only: $5690. Room and board charges vary according to board plan. Part-time tuition: $990 per unit. Part-time mandatory fees: $250 per year. **Scholarships:** Available **Calendar System:** Semester, Summer Session Available **Enrollment:** FT 2,276, PT 76, Grad FT 884, Grad PT 478 **Faculty:** FT 144, PT 180 **Student-Faculty Ratio:** 15:1 **Exams:** SAT I or ACT. **% Receiving Financial Aid:** 64 **% Residing in College-Owned, -Operated, or -Affiliated Housing:** 63 **Library Holdings:** 132,744 **Regional Accreditation:** Western Association of Schools and Colleges **Credit Hours For Degree:** 124 units, Bachelors **ROTC:** Army, Air Force **Professional Accreditation:** NCATE **Intercollegiate Athletics:** Baseball M; Basketball M & W; Cheerleading M & W; Cross-Country Running M & W; Football M; Golf M; Soccer M & W; Softball W; Swimming and Diving M & W; Tennis M & W; Track and Field M & W; Volleyball W; Water Polo M & W

CALIFORNIA MARITIME ACADEMY
200 Maritime Academy Dr.
Vallejo, CA 94590
Tel: (707)654-1000; Free: 800-561-1945
Admissions: (707)654-1330
Fax: (707)648-4204
E-mail: admission@csum.edu
Web Site: http://www.csum.edu/
President/CEO: Dr. William B. Eisenhardt
Admissions: Marc McGee
Financial Aid: Ken Walsh
Type: Four-Year College **Sex:** Coed **Affiliation:** California State University System **% Accepted:** 73 **Admission Plans:** Preferred Admission **Application Fee:** $55.00 **H.S. Requirements:** High school diploma required; GED accepted **Costs Per Year:** Application fee: $55. State resident tuition: $0 full-time. Nonresident tuition: $10,170 full-time. Mandatory fees: $4400 full-time. College room and board: $9750. **Scholarships:** Available **Calendar System:** Semester, Summer Session Available **Enrollment:** FT 823 **Student-Faculty Ratio:** 22:1 **Exams:** SAT I or ACT. **% Residing in College-Owned, -Operated, or -Affiliated Housing:** 85 **Final Year or Final Semester Residency Requirement:** Yes **Library Holdings:** 28,377 **Regional Accreditation:** Western Association of Schools and Colleges **Credit Hours For Degree:** 126 units, Bachelors **ROTC:** Navy **Professional Accreditation:** ABET **Intercollegiate Athletics:** Basketball M & W; Crew M & W; Golf M & W; Rugby M; Sailing M & W; Soccer M; Volleyball W; Water Polo M & W

CALIFORNIA MIRAMAR UNIVERSITY
9750 Miramar Rd.
Ste. 180
San Diego, CA 92126
Tel: (858)653-3000; Free: 877-570-5678
Fax: (858)653-6786
Web Site: http://www.calmu.edu/
Type: Comprehensive **Sex:** Coed **Professional Accreditation:** ACICS

CALIFORNIA NATIONAL UNIVERSITY FOR ADVANCED STUDIES
8550 Balboa Blvd., Ste. 210
Northridge, CA 91325
Tel: (818)830-2411; Free: 800-782-2422
Fax: (818)830-2418
E-mail: cnuadms@mail.cnuas.edu
Web Site: http://www.cnuas.edu/
Admissions: Stephanie Smith
Type: Comprehensive **Sex:** Coed **Admission Plans:** Open Admission; Deferred Admission **Application Deadline:** Rolling **Application Fee:** $75.00 **H.S. Requirements:** High school diploma required; GED accepted **Calendar System:** Trimester **Faculty:** FT 0, PT 98 **Student-Faculty Ratio:** 10:1 **Credit Hours For Degree:** 120 per semester hour, Bachelors **Professional Accreditation:** DETC

CALIFORNIA POLYTECHNIC STATE UNIVERSITY, SAN LUIS OBISPO
1 Grand Ave.
San Luis Obispo, CA 93407
Tel: (805)756-1111
Admissions: (805)756-2311
E-mail: admissions@calpoly.edu
Web Site: http://www.calpoly.edu/
President/CEO: Dr. Warren J. Baker
Admissions: James Maraviglia
Financial Aid: Lois Kelly
Type: Comprehensive **Sex:** Coed **Affiliation:** California State University System **Scores:** 99% SAT V 400+; 100% SAT M 400+; 20.5% ACT 18-23; 58.5% ACT 24-29 **% Accepted:** 37 **Admission Plans:** Early Admission; Early Decision Plan **Application Deadline:** November 30 **Application Fee:** $55.00 **H.S. Requirements:** High school diploma required; GED accepted **Costs Per Year:** Application fee: $55. State resident tuition: $0 full-time. Nonresident tuition: $11,160 full-time, $248 per unit part-time. Mandatory fees: $6198 full-time, $1371 per term part-time. Full-time tuition and fees vary according to course load, degree level, and program. Part-time tuition and fees vary according to course load, degree level, and program. College room and board: $9623. College room only: $5383. Room and board charges vary according to board plan and housing facility. **Scholarships:** Available **Calendar System:** Quarter, Summer Session Available **Enrollment:** FT 17,623, PT 679, Grad FT 713, Grad PT 310 **Faculty:** FT 824, PT 411 **Student-Faculty Ratio:** 19:1 **Exams:** SAT I or ACT. ACT essay not being used. SAT essay not being used. **% Receiving Financial Aid:** 31 **% Residing in College-Owned, -Operated, or -Affiliated Housing:** 35 **Library Holdings:** 763,651 **Regional Accreditation:** Western Association of Schools and Colleges **Credit Hours For Degree:** 186 units, Bachelors **ROTC:** Army **Professional Accreditation:** AACSB, ABET, ACCE, ACA, ACSP, ASLA, NAAB, NASAD, NASM, NRPA, SAF, NAIT **Intercollegiate Athletics:** Baseball M; Basketball M & W; Cross-Country Running M & W; Football M; Golf M & W; Soccer M & W; Softball W; Swimming and Diving M & W; Tennis M & W; Track and Field M & W; Volleyball W; Wrestling M

CALIFORNIA SCHOOL OF CULINARY ARTS
521 East Green St.
Pasadena, CA 91101
Tel: (626)229-1300
Web Site: http://www.csca.edu/
President/CEO: Anthony Bondi
Type: Two-Year College **Sex:** Coed **Application Fee:** $75.00

CALIFORNIA STATE POLYTECHNIC UNIVERSITY, POMONA
3801 West Temple Ave.
Pomona, CA 91768-2557
Tel: (909)869-7659
Admissions: (909)869-3258
Fax: (909)869-4529

E-mail: admissions@csupomona.edu
Web Site: http://www.csupomona.edu/
President/CEO: Dr. J. Michael Ortiz
Admissions: Scott J. Duncan
Financial Aid: Diana Minor
Type: Comprehensive **Sex:** Coed **Affiliation:** California State University System **Scores:** 92.93% SAT V 400+; 95.18% SAT M 400+; 45.09% ACT 18-23; 40.17% ACT 24-29 **% Accepted:** 61 **Application Deadline:** November 30 **Application Fee:** $55.00 **H.S. Requirements:** High school diploma required; GED accepted. For applicants out of high school 5 years or more: High school diploma or equivalent not required **Costs Per Year:** Application fee: $55. State resident tuition: $0 full-time. Nonresident tuition: $11,160 full-time, $248 per unit part-time. Mandatory fees: $4551 full-time, $2859 per year part-time. Full-time tuition and fees vary according to degree level and program. Part-time tuition and fees vary according to course load, degree level, and program. College room and board: $9570. College room only: $6027. Room and board charges vary according to board plan and housing facility. **Scholarships:** Available **Calendar System:** Quarter, Summer Session Available **Enrollment:** FT 16,641, PT 3,495, Grad FT 835, Grad PT 1,302 **Faculty:** FT 565, PT 455 **Student-Faculty Ratio:** 25:1 **Exams:** SAT I or ACT. ACT essay used for admission. SAT essay used for admission. ACT essay used for placement. SAT essay used for placement. **% Receiving Financial Aid:** 54 **% Residing in College-Owned, -Operated, or -Affiliated Housing:** 9 **Final Year or Final Semester Residency Requirement:** Yes **Library Holdings:** 670,580 **Regional Accreditation:** Western Association of Schools and Colleges **Credit Hours For Degree:** 180 units, Bachelors **ROTC:** Army **Professional Accreditation:** AACSB, ABET, ADtA, ACSP, ASLA, NAAB, NASAD, NASPAA **Intercollegiate Athletics:** Baseball M; Basketball M & W; Cross-Country Running M & W; Soccer M & W; Tennis M & W; Track and Field M & W; Volleyball W

CALIFORNIA STATE UNIVERSITY, BAKERSFIELD

9001 Stockdale Hwy.
Bakersfield, CA 93311
Tel: (661)664-2011
Admissions: (661)654-2782
Fax: (661)664-3188
E-mail: admissions@csub.edu
Web Site: http://www.csub.edu/
President/CEO: Horace Mitchell
Admissions: Debra Blowers
Financial Aid: Ron Radney
Type: Comprehensive **Sex:** Coed **Affiliation:** California State University System **Scores:** 71.4% SAT V 400+; 74.1% SAT M 400+; 48.7% ACT 18-23; 10% ACT 24-29 **% Accepted:** 70 **Admission Plans:** Preferred Admission; Deferred Admission **Application Deadline:** March 1 **Application Fee:** $55.00 **H.S. Requirements:** High school diploma required; GED not accepted **Scholarships:** Available **Calendar System:** Quarter, Summer Session Available **Enrollment:** FT 5,540, PT 954, Grad FT 1,000, Grad PT 509 **Faculty:** FT 284, PT 157 **Exams:** SAT I or ACT. **% Receiving Financial Aid:** 63 **% Residing in College-Owned, -Operated, or -Affiliated Housing:** 3 **Regional Accreditation:** Western Association of Schools and Colleges **Credit Hours For Degree:** 186 quarter units, Bachelors **Professional Accreditation:** AACSB, AACN, CSWE, NASPAA, NCATE, NLN **Intercollegiate Athletics:** Basketball M; Golf M; Soccer M; Softball W; Swimming and Diving M & W; Tennis W; Track and Field M & W; Volleyball W; Water Polo W; Wrestling M

CALIFORNIA STATE UNIVERSITY CHANNEL ISLANDS

One University Dr.
Camarillo, CA 93012
Tel: (805)437-8400
Fax: (805)437-8951
E-mail: prospective.student@csuci.edu
Web Site: http://www.csuci.edu/
President/CEO: Richard R. Rush
Admissions: Ginger Reyes
Type: Comprehensive **Sex:** Coed **Affiliation:** California State University System **% Accepted:** 53 **Application Fee:** $50.00 **Faculty:** FT 89, PT 205 **Student-Faculty Ratio:** 15:1 **Exams:** SAT I or ACT. **% Residing in College-Owned, -Operated, or -Affiliated Housing:** 23 **Regional Accreditation:** Western Association of Schools and Colleges

CALIFORNIA STATE UNIVERSITY, CHICO

400 West First St.
Chico, CA 95929-0722
Tel: (530)898-6116; Free: 800-542-4426
Admissions: (530)898-4428
Fax: (530)898-6456
E-mail: info@csuchico.edu
Web Site: http://www.csuchico.edu/
President/CEO: Paul J. Zingg
Admissions: Allan Bee
Financial Aid: Dan Reed
Type: Comprehensive **Sex:** Coed **Affiliation:** California State University System **Scores:** 93% SAT V 400+; 94% SAT M 400+; 57% ACT 18-23; 26% ACT 24-29 **% Accepted:** 88 **Admission Plans:** Deferred Admission **Application Deadline:** November 30 **Application Fee:** $55.00 **H.S. Requirements:** High school diploma required; GED accepted **Costs Per Year:** Application fee: $55. State resident tuition: $0 full-time. Nonresident tuition: $11,160 full-time, $372 per unit part-time. Mandatory fees: $5336 full-time. Full-time tuition and fees vary according to degree level. Part-time tuition varies according to course load and degree level. College room and board: $9404. College room only: $6692. Room and board charges vary according to board plan and housing facility. **Scholarships:** Available **Calendar System:** Semester, Summer Session Available **Enrollment:** FT 14,407, PT 1,371, Grad FT 826, Grad PT 491 **Faculty:** FT 501, PT 387 **Student-Faculty Ratio:** 23:1 **Exams:** SAT I or ACT. **% Receiving Financial Aid:** 46 **% Residing in College-Owned, -Operated, or -Affiliated Housing:** 1 **Library Holdings:** 951,276 **Regional Accreditation:** Western Association of Schools and Colleges **Credit Hours For Degree:** 120 units, Bachelors **Professional Accreditation:** AACSB, ABET, ACEJMC, AACN, ACCE, ADtA, ASLHA, CSWE, NASAD, NASM, NASPAA, NCATE, NLN, NRPA, NAIT **Intercollegiate Athletics:** Baseball M; Basketball M & W; Cross-Country Running M & W; Field Hockey W; Golf M & W; Racquetball M & W; Rugby M; Soccer M & W; Softball W; Tennis M & W; Track and Field M & W; Ultimate Frisbee M; Volleyball W; Water Polo M & W

CALIFORNIA STATE UNIVERSITY, DOMINGUEZ HILLS

1000 East Victoria St.
Carson, CA 90747-0001
Tel: (310)243-3300
Admissions: (310)243-3696
Web Site: http://www.csudh.edu/
President/CEO: Dr. Mildred Garcia
Financial Aid: Delores S. Lee
Type: Comprehensive **Sex:** Coed **Affiliation:** California State University System **Scores:** 61.3% SAT V 400+; 55.4% SAT M 400+; 35.9% ACT 18-23; 2.93% ACT 24-29 **% Accepted:** 84 **Admission Plans:** Preferred Admission **Application Deadline:** Rolling **Application Fee:** $55.00 **H.S. Requirements:** High school diploma required; GED accepted **Costs Per Year:** Application fee: $55. State resident tuition: $0 full-time. Nonresident tuition: $11,160 full-time, $372 per unit part-time. Mandatory fees: $4645 full-time, $1479 per term part-time. College room and board: $10,085. College room only: $5693. Room and board charges vary according to housing facility. **Scholarships:** Available **Calendar System:** Semester, Summer Session Available **Enrollment:** FT 6,746, PT 4,134, Grad FT 1,653, Grad PT 1,944 **Faculty:** FT 318, PT 392 **Student-Faculty Ratio:** 23:1 **Exams:** SAT I or ACT. **% Receiving Financial Aid:** 63 **% Residing in College-Owned, -Operated, or -Affiliated Housing:** 5 **Final Year or Final Semester Residency Requirement:** No **Library Holdings:** 442,893 **Regional Accreditation:** Western Association of Schools and Colleges **Credit Hours For Degree:** 124 semester units, Bachelors **ROTC:** Army, Air Force **Professional Accreditation:** ABET, AACN, AOTA, ACBSP, CSWE, NAACLS, NASM, NASPAA, NAST, NCOPE, NCATE, NLN **Intercollegiate Athletics:** Baseball M; Basketball M & W; Cross-Country Running W; Golf M; Soccer M & W; Softball W; Track and Field W; Volleyball W

CALIFORNIA STATE UNIVERSITY, EAST BAY

25800 Carlos Bee Blvd.
Hayward, CA 94542-3000
Tel: (510)885-3000
Admissions: (510)885-2784
Fax: (510)885-3816
E-mail: admissions@csueastbay.edu
Web Site: http://www.csueastbay.edu/
President/CEO: Dr. Mohammad H. Qayoumi, PhD

Admissions: Dr. Colin Ormsby
Type: Comprehensive **Sex:** Coed **Affiliation:** California State University System **Scores:** 77.4% SAT V 400+; 78.6% SAT M 400+; 43.7% ACT 18-23; 12.7% ACT 24-29 **% Accepted:** 73 **Application Deadline:** November 30 **Application Fee:** $55.00 **H.S. Requirements:** High school diploma required; GED accepted **Costs Per Year:** Application fee: $55. State resident tuition: $0 full-time. Nonresident tuition: $13,800 full-time. Mandatory fees: $4872 full-time. College room and board: $10,029. **Scholarships:** Available **Calendar System:** Quarter, Summer Session Available **Enrollment:** FT 9,713, PT 1,969, Grad FT 1,585, Grad PT 1,482 **Faculty:** FT 366, PT 454 **Student-Faculty Ratio:** 24:1 **Exams:** SAT I or ACT. **% Receiving Financial Aid:** 49 **Regional Accreditation:** Western Association of Schools and Colleges **Credit Hours For Degree:** 186 units, Bachelors **Professional Accreditation:** AACSB, ASLHA, CSWE, NASAD, NASM, NASPAA, NCATE, NLN **Intercollegiate Athletics:** Baseball M; Basketball M & W; Cross-Country Running M & W; Soccer M & W; Softball W; Swimming and Diving W; Volleyball W; Water Polo W

CALIFORNIA STATE UNIVERSITY, FRESNO
5241 North Maple Ave.
Fresno, CA 93740-8027
Tel: (559)278-4240
Admissions: (559)278-6115
Fax: (559)278-4715
E-mail: andyhe@csufresno.edu
Web Site: http://www.csufresno.edu/
President/CEO: Dr. John Welty
Admissions: Andy Hernandez
Financial Aid: Maria Hernandez
Type: Comprehensive **Sex:** Coed **Affiliation:** California State University System **Scores:** 78.7% SAT V 400+; 82.7% SAT M 400+; 48.6% ACT 18-23; 15.7% ACT 24-29 **% Accepted:** 72 **Admission Plans:** Preferred Admission **Application Deadline:** November 30 **Application Fee:** $55.00 **H.S. Requirements:** High school diploma required; GED accepted **Costs Per Year:** Application fee: $55. State resident tuition: $0 full-time. Nonresident tuition: $10,170 full-time. Mandatory fees: $3687 full-time. College room and board: $8590. College room only: $4100. Room and board charges vary according to board plan. **Scholarships:** Available **Calendar System:** Semester, Summer Session Available **Enrollment:** FT 15,420, PT 2,796, Grad FT 2,048, Grad PT 1,236 **Faculty:** FT 645, PT 493 **Student-Faculty Ratio:** 20:1 **Exams:** SAT I or ACT. ACT essay not being used. SAT essay not being used. **% Receiving Financial Aid:** 62 **% Residing in College-Owned, -Operated, or -Affiliated Housing:** 6 **Final Year or Final Semester Residency Requirement:** Yes **Library Holdings:** 1,870,645 **Regional Accreditation:** Western Association of Schools and Colleges **Credit Hours For Degree:** 124 units, Bachelors **ROTC:** Army, Air Force **Professional Accreditation:** AACSB, ABET, AACN, AAFCS, ACCE, ACA, ADtA, APTA, ASLHA, FIDER, CEPH, CORE, CSWE, JRCEPAT, NASM, NASPAA, NAST, NCATE, NLN, NRPA **Intercollegiate Athletics:** Baseball M; Basketball M & W; Cross-Country Running M & W; Equestrian Sports W; Football M; Golf M & W; Lacrosse W; Soccer W; Softball W; Swimming and Diving W; Tennis M & W; Track and Field M & W; Volleyball W

CALIFORNIA STATE UNIVERSITY, FULLERTON
PO Box 34080
Fullerton, CA 92834-9480
Tel: (657)278-2011
Admissions: (657)278-2370
E-mail: admissions@fullerton.edu
Web Site: http://www.fullerton.edu/
President/CEO: Dr. Milton A. Gordon
Admissions: Nancy J. Dority
Financial Aid: Jessica Schutte
Type: Comprehensive **Sex:** Coed **Affiliation:** California State University System **Scores:** 91% SAT V 400+; 90% SAT M 400+; 59% ACT 18-23; 22% ACT 24-29 **% Accepted:** 55 **Admission Plans:** Preferred Admission **Application Deadline:** November 30 **Application Fee:** $55.00 **H.S. Requirements:** High school diploma required; GED accepted **Costs Per Year:** Application fee: $55. State resident tuition: $0 full-time. Nonresident tuition: $15,822 full-time, $3717 per term part-time. Mandatory fees: $4662 full-time, $1485 per term part-time. Full-time tuition and fees vary according to course load. Part-time tuition and fees vary according to course load. College room and board: $9242. College room only: $5775. **Scholarships:** Available **Calendar System:** Semester, Summer Session Available **Enrollment:** FT 22,962, PT 7,775, Grad FT 2,474, Grad PT 3,051 **Faculty:** FT 867, PT 748 **Student-Faculty Ratio:** 26:1 **Exams:** SAT I or ACT, SAT I. **% Receiving Financial Aid:** 51 **% Residing in College-Owned, -Operated, or -Affiliated Housing:** 3 **Library Holdings:** 1,258,571 **Regional Accreditation:** Western Association of Schools and Colleges **Credit Hours For Degree:** 120 semester units, Bachelors **ROTC:** Army **Professional Accreditation:** AACSB, ABET, ACEJMC, AACN, AANA, ACNM, ACA, ASLHA, CSWE, JRCEPAT, NASAD, NASD, NASM, NASPAA, NAST, NCATE, NLN **Intercollegiate Athletics:** Baseball M; Basketball M & W; Cross-Country Running M & W; Golf M & W; Gymnastics W; Soccer M & W; Softball W; Tennis W; Track and Field M & W; Volleyball W; Wrestling M

CALIFORNIA STATE UNIVERSITY, LONG BEACH
1250 Bellflower Blvd.
Long Beach, CA 90840
Tel: (562)985-4111
Admissions: (562)985-4641
Web Site: http://www.csulb.edu/
President/CEO: Dr. F. King Alexander
Admissions: Thomas Enders
Financial Aid: Nicolas Valdivia
Type: Comprehensive **Sex:** Coed **Affiliation:** California State University System **Scores:** 90.32% SAT V 400+; 91.06% SAT M 400+; 48.86% ACT 18-23; 27.52% ACT 24-29 **% Accepted:** 32 **Admission Plans:** Preferred Admission **Application Deadline:** November 30 **Application Fee:** $55.00 **H.S. Requirements:** High school diploma required; GED accepted **Costs Per Year:** Application fee: $55. State resident tuition: $0 full-time. Nonresident tuition: $11,160 full-time. Mandatory fees: $4606 full-time. Full-time tuition and fees vary according to program. College room and board: $11,038. Room and board charges vary according to board plan. **Scholarships:** Available **Calendar System:** Semester, Summer Session Available **Enrollment:** FT 23,695, PT 5,531, Grad FT 3,078, Grad PT 3,253 **Faculty:** FT 1,021, PT 963 **Student-Faculty Ratio:** 21:1 **Exams:** SAT I or ACT. **% Receiving Financial Aid:** 61 **% Residing in College-Owned, -Operated, or -Affiliated Housing:** 7 **Regional Accreditation:** Western Association of Schools and Colleges **Credit Hours For Degree:** 124 units, Bachelors **ROTC:** Army **Professional Accreditation:** AACSB, ABET, AACN, AAFCS, ADtA, APTA, APA, ASLHA, ACEHSA, CAEPK, CEPH, CSWE, JRCERT, NASAD, NASD, NASM, NASPAA, NAST, NCATE, NRPA **Intercollegiate Athletics:** Archery M & W; Badminton M & W; Basketball M & W; Bowling M & W; Crew M & W; Cross-Country Running M & W; Fencing M & W; Golf M & W; Rugby M; Sailing M & W; Skiing (Downhill) M & W; Soccer M & W; Softball W; Table Tennis M; Tennis W; Track and Field M & W; Volleyball M & W; Water Polo M & W

CALIFORNIA STATE UNIVERSITY, LOS ANGELES
5151 State University Dr.
Los Angeles, CA 90032-8530
Tel: (323)343-3000
Admissions: (323)343-3839
Fax: (323)343-2670
E-mail: admission@calstatela.edu
Web Site: http://www.calstatela.edu/
President/CEO: Dr. James M. Rosser
Admissions: Vince Lopez
Financial Aid: Tamie L. Nguyen
Type: Comprehensive **Sex:** Coed **Affiliation:** California State University System **Scores:** 67.6% SAT V 400+; 68% SAT M 400+; 37.4% ACT 18-23; 8.5% ACT 24-29 **% Accepted:** 68 **Admission Plans:** Early Admission **Application Deadline:** June 15 **Application Fee:** $55.00 **H.S. Requirements:** High school diploma required; GED accepted **Costs Per Year:** Application fee: $55. State resident tuition: $0 full-time. Nonresident tuition: $8928 full-time, $248 per unit part-time. Mandatory fees: $4640 full-time, $983.90 per term part-time. Full-time tuition and fees vary according to course level and course load. Part-time tuition and fees vary according to course level and course load. College room and board: $9105. Room and board charges vary according to housing facility. **Scholarships:** Available **Calendar System:** Quarter, Summer Session Available **Enrollment:** FT 11,751, PT 3,983, Grad FT 2,018, Grad PT 2,867 **Faculty:** FT 580, PT 458 **Student-Faculty Ratio:** 21:1 **Exams:** SAT I or ACT. **% Receiving Financial Aid:** 73 **% Residing in College-Owned, -Operated, or -Affiliated Housing:** 6 **Library Holdings:** 1,250,042 **Regional Accreditation:** Western Association of Schools and Colleges **Credit Hours For Degree:** 186 quarter units, Bachelors **ROTC:** Army, Air Force **Professional Accreditation:** AACSB, ABET, AACN, ACA,

ADtA, ASLHA, CORE, CSWE, NASAD, NASM, NASPAA, NCATE, NLN **Intercollegiate Athletics:** Baseball M; Basketball M & W; Cross-Country Running W; Soccer M & W; Tennis W; Track and Field M & W; Volleyball W

CALIFORNIA STATE UNIVERSITY, MONTEREY BAY

100 Campus Center
Seaside, CA 93955-8001
Tel: (831)582-3000
Admissions: (831)582-3738
Fax: (831)582-3540
E-mail: admissions@csumb.edu
Web Site: http://www.csumb.edu/
President/CEO: Dr. Dianne F. Harrison, PhD
Admissions: John Larsen

Type: Comprehensive **Sex:** Coed **Affiliation:** California State University System **Scores:** 88% SAT V 400+; 86% SAT M 400+; 53% ACT 18-23; 23% ACT 24-29 **% Accepted:** 81 **Admission Plans:** Deferred Admission **Application Deadline:** November 30 **Application Fee:** $55.00 **H.S. Requirements:** High school diploma required; GED accepted **Costs Per Year:** Application fee: $55. State resident tuition: $0 full-time. Nonresident tuition: $11,160 full-time, $372 per unit part-time. Mandatory fees: $4517 full-time, $1167 per term part-time. Full-time tuition and fees vary according to degree level. Part-time tuition and fees vary according to degree level. College room and board: $8290. College room only: $5340. Room and board charges vary according to board plan and housing facility. **Scholarships:** Available **Calendar System:** Semester, Summer Session Available **Enrollment:** FT 3,933, PT 345, Grad FT 183, Grad PT 227 **Faculty:** FT 114, PT 163 **Student-Faculty Ratio:** 27:1 **Exams:** Other, SAT I or ACT. SAT essay used for placement. ACT essay not being used. **% Receiving Financial Aid:** 51 **% Residing in College-Owned, -Operated, or -Affiliated Housing:** 54 **Final Year or Final Semester Residency Requirement:** No **Library Holdings:** 106,510 **Regional Accreditation:** Western Association of Schools and Colleges **Credit Hours For Degree:** 120 units, Bachelors **Professional Accreditation:** NCATE **Intercollegiate Athletics:** Baseball M; Basketball M & W; Cross-Country Running M & W; Golf M & W; Sailing M & W; Soccer M & W; Softball W; Volleyball W; Water Polo W

CALIFORNIA STATE UNIVERSITY, NORTHRIDGE

18111 Nordhoff St.
Northridge, CA 91330
Tel: (818)677-1200
Admissions: (818)677-3777
Fax: (818)677-3766
E-mail: admissions.records@csun.edu
Web Site: http://www.csun.edu/
President/CEO: Dr. Jolene Koester
Admissions: Mary Baxton
Financial Aid: Lili Vidal

Type: Comprehensive **Sex:** Coed **Affiliation:** California State University System **Scores:** 79.9% SAT V 400+; 77.7% SAT M 400+ **% Accepted:** 73 **Admission Plans:** Preferred Admission **Application Deadline:** November 30 **Application Fee:** $55.00 **H.S. Requirements:** High school diploma required; GED accepted **Scholarships:** Available **Calendar System:** Semester, Summer Session Available **Enrollment:** FT 21,738, PT 7,537, Grad FT 2,784, Grad PT 3,139 **Faculty:** FT 814, PT 993 **Student-Faculty Ratio:** 24:1 **Exams:** SAT I or ACT. **% Receiving Financial Aid:** 62 **Regional Accreditation:** Western Association of Schools and Colleges **Credit Hours For Degree:** 124 units, Bachelors **ROTC:** Army, Air Force **Professional Accreditation:** AACSB, ABET, ACEJMC, AACN, AAFCS, ACA, ADtA, APTA, ASLHA, FIDER, CEPH, CSWE, JRCERT, JRCEPAT, NASAD, NASM, NAST, NCATE, NRPA **Intercollegiate Athletics:** Baseball M; Basketball M & W; Cross-Country Running M & W; Football M; Golf M; Soccer M; Softball W; Swimming and Diving M & W; Tennis W; Track and Field M & W; Volleyball M & W

CALIFORNIA STATE UNIVERSITY, SACRAMENTO

6000 J St.
Sacramento, CA 95819
Tel: (916)278-6011
Admissions: (916)278-3901
E-mail: admissions@csus.edu
Web Site: http://www.csus.edu/
President/CEO: Alexander Gonzalez
Admissions: Emiliano Diaz

Type: Comprehensive **Sex:** Coed **Affiliation:** California State University System **Scores:** 80.6% SAT V 400+; 85.57% SAT M 400+; 52.01% ACT 18-23; 18.82% ACT 24-29 **% Accepted:** 80 **Admission Plans:** Early Action; Deferred Admission **Application Fee:** $55.00 **H.S. Requirements:** High school diploma required; GED accepted **Scholarships:** Available **Calendar System:** Semester, Summer Session Available **Enrollment:** FT 19,824, PT 4,564, Grad FT 2,728, Grad PT 2,125 **Faculty:** FT 688, PT 818 **Student-Faculty Ratio:** 26:1 **Exams:** SAT I or ACT. ACT essay not being used. SAT essay not being used. **% Receiving Financial Aid:** 77 **% Residing in College-Owned, -Operated, or -Affiliated Housing:** 5 **Regional Accreditation:** Western Association of Schools and Colleges **Credit Hours For Degree:** 124 units, Bachelors **ROTC:** Army, Air Force **Professional Accreditation:** AACSB, ABET, AACN, ACCE, ACA, ADtA, APTA, ASLHA, FIDER, CORE, CSWE, JRCEPAT, NASAD, NASM, NAST, NRPA **Intercollegiate Athletics:** Baseball M; Basketball M & W; Bowling M & W; Cheerleading M & W; Crew M & W; Cross-Country Running M & W; Football M; Golf M & W; Gymnastics W; Ice Hockey M; Lacrosse M & W; Racquetball M & W; Rugby M; Skiing (Downhill) M & W; Soccer M & W; Softball W; Tennis M & W; Track and Field M & W; Volleyball M & W

CALIFORNIA STATE UNIVERSITY, SAN BERNARDINO

5500 University Parkway
San Bernardino, CA 92407-2397
Tel: (909)537-5000
Admissions: (909)537-5211
E-mail: moreinfo@mail.csusb.edu
Web Site: http://www.csusb.edu/
President/CEO: Dr. Albert Karnig
Admissions: Julie Mellen
Financial Aid: Roseanna Ruiz

Type: Comprehensive **Sex:** Coed **Affiliation:** California State University System **Scores:** 77% SAT V 400+; 75.6% SAT M 400+; 47.1% ACT 18-23; 8.9% ACT 24-29 **% Accepted:** 70 **Admission Plans:** Early Admission **Application Deadline:** Rolling **Application Fee:** $55.00 **H.S. Requirements:** High school diploma required; GED accepted **Costs Per Year:** Application fee: $55. State resident tuition: $0 full-time. Nonresident tuition: $11,445 full-time, $226 per unit part-time. Mandatory fees: $5373 full-time. Part-time tuition varies according to course load. **Scholarships:** Available **Calendar System:** Quarter, Summer Session Available **Enrollment:** FT 12,298, PT 2,118, Grad FT 2,106, Grad PT 1,320 **Faculty:** FT 471, PT 424 **Student-Faculty Ratio:** 21:1 **Exams:** SAT I or ACT. **% Receiving Financial Aid:** 71 **% Residing in College-Owned, -Operated, or -Affiliated Housing:** 10 **Library Holdings:** 731,259 **Regional Accreditation:** Western Association of Schools and Colleges **Credit Hours For Degree:** 186 units, Bachelors **ROTC:** Army, Air Force **Professional Accreditation:** AACSB, ABET, AACN, CORE, CSWE, NASAD, NASM, NASPAA, NAST, NCATE, NLN **Intercollegiate Athletics:** Baseball M; Basketball M & W; Cross-Country Running W; Golf M; Soccer M & W; Softball W; Swimming and Diving M & W; Tennis W; Volleyball W; Water Polo M & W

CALIFORNIA STATE UNIVERSITY, SAN MARCOS

333 South Twin Oaks Valley Rd.
San Marcos, CA 92096-0001
Tel: (760)750-4000
Admissions: (760)750-4848
Fax: (760)750-4030
E-mail: apply@csusm.edu
Web Site: http://www.csusm.edu/
President/CEO: Dr. Karen S. Haynes
Admissions: Darren Bush
Financial Aid: Addalou Davis

Type: Comprehensive **Sex:** Coed **Affiliation:** California State University System **Scores:** 87.8% SAT V 400+; 88% SAT M 400+ **% Accepted:** 71 **Application Deadline:** November 30 **Application Fee:** $55.00 **H.S. Requirements:** High school diploma required; GED accepted **Costs Per Year:** Application fee: $55. State resident tuition: $0 full-time. Nonresident tuition: $9136 full-time, $339 per credit hour part-time. Mandatory fees: $4650 full-time. Part-time tuition varies according to course load. College room only: $6250. Room charges vary according to housing facility. **Scholarships:** Available **Calendar System:** Semester, Summer Session Available **Enrollment:** FT 6,125, PT 2,602, Grad FT 490, Grad PT 528 **Faculty:** FT 202, PT 311 **Student-Faculty Ratio:** 25:1 **Exams:** SAT I or ACT. **% Receiving Financial Aid:** 39 **% Residing in College-Owned, -Operated, or -Affiliated Housing:** 6 **Library Holdings:** 326,393 **Regional**

Accreditation: Western Association of Schools and Colleges **Credit Hours For Degree:** 124 units, Bachelors **ROTC:** Army, Navy, Air Force **Professional Accreditation:** NCATE **Intercollegiate Athletics:** Baseball M; Cross-Country Running M & W; Golf M & W; Soccer M & W; Track and Field M & W

CALIFORNIA STATE UNIVERSITY, STANISLAUS

One University Circle
Turlock, CA 95382
Tel: (209)667-3122
Fax: (209)667-3333
E-mail: outreach_help_desk@csustan.edu
Web Site: http://www.csustan.edu/
President/CEO: Dr. Ham Shirvani
Financial Aid: Noelia Gonzalez

Type: Comprehensive **Sex:** Coed **Affiliation:** California State University System **Scores:** 82.7% SAT V 400+; 80.5% SAT M 400+; 54.1% ACT 18-23; 14.8% ACT 24-29 **% Accepted:** 37 **Application Deadline:** March 1 **Application Fee:** $55.00 **H.S. Requirements:** High school diploma required; GED accepted **Costs Per Year:** Application fee: $55. State resident tuition: $0 full-time. Nonresident tuition: $11,160 full-time, $372 per unit part-time. Mandatory fees: $4840 full-time. Full-time tuition and fees vary according to course load, degree level, reciprocity agreements, and student level. Part-time tuition varies according to course load, degree level, reciprocity agreements, and student level. College room and board: $8880. College room only: $6038. Room and board charges vary according to board plan and housing facility. **Scholarships:** Available **Calendar System:** 4-1-4, Summer Session Available **Enrollment:** FT 4,889, PT 2,198, Grad FT 686, Grad PT 813 **Faculty:** FT 279, PT 111 **Student-Faculty Ratio:** 21:1 **Exams:** SAT I or ACT. **% Receiving Financial Aid:** 81 **% Residing in College-Owned, -Operated, or -Affiliated Housing:** 7 **Library Holdings:** 375,662 **Regional Accreditation:** Western Association of Schools and Colleges **Credit Hours For Degree:** 120 units, Bachelors **Professional Accreditation:** AACSB, AACN, CSWE, NASAD, NASM, NASPAA, NAST, NCATE, NLN **Intercollegiate Athletics:** Baseball M; Basketball M & W; Cheerleading M & W; Cross-Country Running M & W; Golf M; Soccer M & W; Softball W; Tennis W; Track and Field M & W; Volleyball W

CAMBRIDGE CAREER COLLEGE

990-A Klamath Ln.
Yuba City, CA 95993
Tel: (530)674-9199
Web Site: http://cambridge.edu/
President/CEO: Daniel Flores

Type: Two-Year College **Sex:** Coed **Application Fee:** $100.00 **H.S. Requirements:** High school diploma required; GED accepted **Enrollment:** FT 162

CAÑADA COLLEGE

4200 Farm Hill Blvd.
Redwood City, CA 94061-1099
Tel: (650)306-3100
Fax: (650)306-3457
Web Site: http://www.canadacollege.net/
President/CEO: Tom Mohr
Admissions: Phyllis Lucas Woods

Type: Two-Year College **Sex:** Coed **Affiliation:** San Mateo County Community College District System **% Accepted:** 100 **Admission Plans:** Open Admission; Early Admission **Application Deadline:** Rolling **Application Fee:** $0.00 **H.S. Requirements:** High school diploma required; GED accepted **Costs Per Year:** Application fee: $0. State resident tuition: $0 full-time. Nonresident tuition: $5730 full-time, $191 per unit part-time. Mandatory fees: $600 full-time, $20 per unit part-time. **Scholarships:** Available **Calendar System:** Semester, Summer Session Available **Library Holdings:** 53,417 **Regional Accreditation:** Western Association of Schools and Colleges **Credit Hours For Degree:** 60 credits, Associates **Professional Accreditation:** JRCERT **Intercollegiate Athletics:** Baseball M

CERRITOS COLLEGE

11110 Alondra Blvd.
Norwalk, CA 90650-6298
Tel: (562)860-2451
E-mail: smurguia@cerritos.edu
Web Site: http://www.cerritos.edu/
President/CEO: Dr. Noelia Vela
Admissions: Stephanie Murguia

Type: Two-Year College **Sex:** Coed **Affiliation:** California Community College System **Admission Plans:** Open Admission; Early Admission; Deferred Admission **Application Deadline:** Rolling **Application Fee:** $0.00 **H.S. Requirements:** High school diploma or equivalent not required. For applicants under 18: High school diploma required; GED accepted **Costs Per Year:** Application fee: $0. State resident tuition: $0 full-time. Nonresident tuition: $5730 full-time, $191 per unit part-time. Mandatory fees: $847 full-time, $26 per unit part-time. **Scholarships:** Available **Calendar System:** Semester, Summer Session Available **Enrollment:** FT 5,107, PT 14,673 **Faculty:** FT 250, PT 440 **Library Holdings:** 74,502 **Regional Accreditation:** Western Association of Schools and Colleges **Credit Hours For Degree:** 64 units, Associates **Professional Accreditation:** ADA, APTA, NLN **Intercollegiate Athletics:** Baseball M; Basketball M & W; Cross-Country Running M & W; Football M; Golf M; Soccer M; Softball W; Swimming and Diving M & W; Tennis M & W; Track and Field M & W; Volleyball W; Water Polo M; Wrestling M

CERRO COSO COMMUNITY COLLEGE

3000 College Heights Blvd.
Ridgecrest, CA 93555-9571
Tel: (760)384-6100
Fax: (760)375-4776
E-mail: hostash@cerrocoso.edu
Web Site: http://www.cerrocoso.edu/
President/CEO: Dr. Mary Retterer
Admissions: Heather Ootash

Type: Two-Year College **Sex:** Coed **Affiliation:** Kern Community College District System **Admission Plans:** Open Admission; Early Admission **Application Deadline:** Rolling **Application Fee:** $0.00 **H.S. Requirements:** High school diploma or equivalent not required. For nursing program: High school diploma required; GED accepted **Scholarships:** Available **Calendar System:** Semester, Summer Session Available **Library Holdings:** 25,000 **Regional Accreditation:** Western Association of Schools and Colleges **Credit Hours For Degree:** 60 semester hours, Associates **Intercollegiate Athletics:** Baseball M; Basketball W

CHABOT COLLEGE

25555 Hesperian Blvd.
Hayward, CA 94545-5001
Tel: (510)723-6600
Web Site: http://www.chabotcollege.edu/
President/CEO: Dr. Celia Barberena
Admissions: Judy Young

Type: Two-Year College **Sex:** Coed **Affiliation:** California Community College System **Admission Plans:** Open Admission; Preferred Admission **Application Fee:** $0.00 **H.S. Requirements:** High school diploma required; GED accepted **Scholarships:** Available **Calendar System:** Semester, Summer Session Available **Library Holdings:** 100,000 **Regional Accreditation:** Western Association of Schools and Colleges **Credit Hours For Degree:** 60 semester hours, Associates **ROTC:** Army, Air Force **Professional Accreditation:** AAMAE, ADA, AHIMA **Intercollegiate Athletics:** Baseball M; Basketball M & W; Cross-Country Running M & W; Football M; Golf M; Soccer M & W; Softball W; Swimming and Diving M & W; Tennis M & W; Track and Field M & W; Volleyball W; Water Polo W; Wrestling M

CHAFFEY COLLEGE

5885 Haven Ave.
Rancho Cucamonga, CA 91737-3002
Tel: (909)987-1737
Fax: (909)941-2783
Web Site: http://www.chaffey.edu/
President/CEO: Henry D. Shannon, PhD
Admissions: Cecilia Carerra
Financial Aid: Karen Sanders

Type: Two-Year College **Sex:** Coed **Affiliation:** California Community College System **Admission Plans:** Open Admission; Early Admission **Application Deadline:** Rolling **Application Fee:** $0.00 **H.S. Requirements:** High school diploma or equivalent not required. For applicants under 18: High school diploma required; GED accepted **Costs Per Year:** Application fee: $0. Nonresident tuition: $190 per unit part-time. Mandatory fees: $20 per unit part-time, $3. Part-time tuition and fees vary according to course load. **Scholarships:** Available **Calendar System:** Semester, Summer Session

Available **Faculty:** FT 182, PT 501 **Library Holdings:** 72,000 **Regional Accreditation:** Western Association of Schools and Colleges **Credit Hours For Degree:** 60 units, Associates **ROTC:** Army **Professional Accreditation:** ADA, JRCERT, NLN **Intercollegiate Athletics:** Baseball M; Basketball M & W; Football M; Soccer M & W; Softball W; Swimming and Diving M & W; Tennis M & W; Track and Field M & W; Volleyball W; Water Polo M & W

CHAPMAN UNIVERSITY
One University Dr.
Orange, CA 92866
Tel: (714)997-6815; Free: 888-CUAPPLY
Admissions: (714)997-6711
Fax: (714)997-6713
E-mail: admit@chapman.edu
Web Site: http://www.chapman.edu/
President/CEO: Dr. James L. Doti
Admissions: Marcela Mejia-Martinez
Financial Aid: Gregory L. Ball
Type: Comprehensive **Sex:** Coed **Affiliation:** Christian Church (Disciples of Christ); Brandman University **Scores:** 100% SAT V 400+; 100% SAT M 400+; 17% ACT 18-23; 67% ACT 24-29 **% Accepted:** 56 **Admission Plans:** Early Action **Application Deadline:** January 15 **Application Fee:** $55.00 **H.S. Requirements:** High school diploma required; GED accepted **Costs Per Year:** Application fee: $55. Comprehensive fee: $51,481 includes full-time tuition ($37,500), mandatory fees ($1024), and college room and board ($12,957). College room only: $9255. Room and board charges vary according to board plan and housing facility. Part-time tuition: $1170 per credit. Part-time tuition varies according to course load. **Scholarships:** Available **Calendar System:** 4-1-4, Summer Session Available **Enrollment:** FT 4,264, PT 212, Grad FT 1,357, Grad PT 565 **Faculty:** FT 356, PT 297 **Student-Faculty Ratio:** 14:1 **Exams:** SAT I or ACT, SAT II. **% Receiving Financial Aid:** 62 **% Residing in College-Owned, -Operated, or -Affiliated Housing:** 41 **Final Year or Final Semester Residency Requirement:** No **Library Holdings:** 249,503 **Regional Accreditation:** Western Association of Schools and Colleges **Credit Hours For Degree:** 124 semester credits, Bachelors **ROTC:** Army, Air Force **Professional Accreditation:** AACSB, AAMFT, ABA, APTA, NASM, TEAC **Intercollegiate Athletics:** Baseball M; Basketball M & W; Cheerleading M & W; Crew M & W; Cross-Country Running M & W; Football M; Golf M; Lacrosse M & W; Sailing M & W; Soccer M & W; Softball W; Swimming and Diving M & W; Tennis M & W; Track and Field W; Volleyball W; Water Polo M & W

CHARLES DREW UNIVERSITY OF MEDICINE AND SCIENCE
1731 East 120th St.
Los Angeles, CA 90059
Tel: (323)563-4800
E-mail: yvettelane@cdrewu.edu
Web Site: http://www.cdrewu.edu/
President/CEO: Keith Norris, MD
Admissions: Yvette Lane
Type: Comprehensive **Sex:** Coed **% Accepted:** 21 **Application Deadline:** April 30 **Application Fee:** $35.00 **H.S. Requirements:** High school diploma required; GED accepted **Costs Per Year:** Application fee: $35. Comprehensive fee: $22,104 includes full-time tuition ($11,232) and college room and board ($10,872). College room only: $7398. Full-time tuition varies according to course level, course load, degree level, program, and student level. Part-time tuition: $5616 per term. Part-time tuition varies according to course level, course load, degree level, program, and student level. **Scholarships:** Available **Calendar System:** Semester **Enrollment:** FT 126, PT 104, Grad FT 20, Grad PT 11 **Faculty:** FT 22, PT 3 **Student-Faculty Ratio:** 9:1 **Exams:** SAT I or ACT. **Library Holdings:** 84,336 **Regional Accreditation:** Western Association of Schools and Colleges **Professional Accreditation:** AAMAE, ACNM, AHIMA, JRCERT

CITRUS COLLEGE
1000 West Foothill Blvd.
Glendora, CA 91741-1899
Tel: (626)963-0323
Admissions: (626)914-8511
E-mail: admissions@citruscollege.edu
Web Site: http://www.citruscollege.edu/
President/CEO: Michael J. Viera, PhD
Type: Two-Year College **Sex:** Coed **Affiliation:** California Community College System **Admission Plans:** Open Admission **Application Fee:** $0.00 **H.S. Requirements:** High school diploma required; GED accepted **Scholarships:** Available **Calendar System:** Semester, Summer Session Available **Enrollment:** FT 4,957, PT 6,619 **Faculty:** FT 171, PT 276 **Student-Faculty Ratio:** 26:1 **Library Holdings:** 45,091 **Regional Accreditation:** Western Association of Schools and Colleges **Credit Hours For Degree:** 60 units, Associates **Professional Accreditation:** ADA **Intercollegiate Athletics:** Baseball M; Basketball M & W; Cross-Country Running M & W; Football M; Golf M & W; Soccer M & W; Softball W; Swimming and Diving M & W; Tennis M & W; Track and Field M & W; Volleyball W; Water Polo M & W

CITY COLLEGE OF SAN FRANCISCO
50 Phelan Ave.
San Francisco, CA 94112-1821
Tel: (415)239-3000
Fax: (415)239-3936
E-mail: mleyba@ccsf.edu
Web Site: http://www.ccsf.edu/
President/CEO: Don Q. Griffin
Admissions: Mary Lou Leyba-Frank
Type: Two-Year College **Sex:** Coed **Affiliation:** California Community College System **Admission Plans:** Open Admission; Early Admission **Application Deadline:** August 9 **H.S. Requirements:** High school diploma or equivalent not required. For applicants under 18: High school diploma required; GED accepted **Costs Per Year:** State resident tuition: $0 full-time. Nonresident tuition: $4847 full-time, $179 per unit part-time. Mandatory fees: $738 full-time, $26 per unit part-time. Full-time tuition and fees vary according to course load. Part-time tuition and fees vary according to course load. **Scholarships:** Available **Calendar System:** Semester, Summer Session Available **Faculty:** FT 770, PT 1,547 **Library Holdings:** 93,518 **Regional Accreditation:** Western Association of Schools and Colleges **Credit Hours For Degree:** 60 units, Associates **Professional Accreditation:** AAMAE, ACF, ADA, AHIMA, JRCERT **Intercollegiate Athletics:** Archery W; Basketball M; Cross-Country Running M & W; Fencing W; Football M; Golf M; Gymnastics W; Soccer M; Swimming and Diving M; Tennis M & W; Track and Field M & W; Volleyball M & W; Water Polo M

CLAREMONT MCKENNA COLLEGE
500 East 9th St.
Claremont, CA 91711
Tel: (909)621-8000
Admissions: (909)621-8088
E-mail: admission@claremontmckenna.edu
Web Site: http://www.claremontmckenna.edu/
President/CEO: Pamela Brooks Gann
Admissions: Richard C. Vos
Financial Aid: Georgette R. DeVeres
Type: Comprehensive **Sex:** Coed **Affiliation:** The Claremont Colleges Consortium **Scores:** 100% SAT V 400+; 100% SAT M 400+ **% Accepted:** 18 **Admission Plans:** Early Decision Plan; Deferred Admission **Application Deadline:** January 2 **Application Fee:** $60.00 **H.S. Requirements:** High school diploma required; GED accepted **Costs Per Year:** Application fee: $60. One-time mandatory fee: $235. Comprehensive fee: $51,270 includes full-time tuition ($38,510), mandatory fees ($235), and college room and board ($12,525). College room only: $6470. Full-time tuition and fees vary according to reciprocity agreements. Room and board charges vary according to board plan and housing facility. Part-time tuition: $6,379.17 per course. Part-time tuition varies according to reciprocity agreements. **Scholarships:** Available **Calendar System:** Semester, Summer Session Not available **Enrollment:** FT 1,216, PT 1, Grad FT 20 **Faculty:** FT 128, PT 21 **Student-Faculty Ratio:** 9:1 **Exams:** SAT I or ACT. ACT essay not being used. SAT essay not being used. **% Receiving Financial Aid:** 44 **% Residing in College-Owned, -Operated, or -Affiliated Housing:** 98 **Regional Accreditation:** Western Association of Schools and Colleges **Credit Hours For Degree:** 32 courses, Bachelors **ROTC:** Army, Air Force **Intercollegiate Athletics:** Badminton M & W; Baseball M; Basketball M & W; Cheerleading M & W; Cross-Country Running M & W; Football M; Golf M; Lacrosse M & W; Rugby M & W; Skiing (Downhill) M & W; Soccer M & W; Softball W; Swimming and Diving M & W; Tennis M & W; Track and Field M & W; Volleyball M & W; Water Polo M & W

CLEVELAND CHIROPRACTIC COLLEGE—LOS ANGELES CAMPUS
590 North Vermont Ave.
Los Angeles, CA 90004-2196
Tel: (323)660-6166; Free: 800-446-CCLA

Admissions: (323)906-2162
Fax: (323)660-5387
E-mail: la.admissions@cleveland.edu
Web Site: http://www.clevelandchiropractic.edu/
President/CEO: Dr. Carl S. Cleveland, III
Admissions: Brian Kane
Type: Comprehensive **Sex:** Coed **Affiliation:** Cleveland Chiropractic College-Kansas City **Scores:** 100% SAT M 400+; 100% ACT 18-23 **% Accepted:** 67 **Application Deadline:** August 29 **Application Fee:** $50.00 **H.S. Requirements:** High school diploma required; GED accepted **Costs Per Year:** Application fee: $50. Tuition: $6465 full-time, $268 per credit part-time. Mandatory fees: $270 full-time, $90 per year part-time. **Calendar System:** Trimester, Summer Session Available **Enrollment:** FT 52, PT 21, Grad FT 240, Grad PT 33 **Faculty:** FT 22, PT 11 **Student-Faculty Ratio:** 7:1 **Exams:** SAT I or ACT. ACT essay used for admission. SAT essay used for admission. **Final Year or Final Semester Residency Requirement:** Yes **Library Holdings:** 24,576 **Credit Hours For Degree:** 60 credits, Associates; 123 credits, Bachelors **Professional Accreditation:** CCE

COASTLINE COMMUNITY COLLEGE
11460 Warner Ave.
Fountain Valley, CA 92708-2597
Tel: (714)546-7600
Fax: (714)241-6288
Web Site: http://coastline.cccd.edu/
President/CEO: Vangie Meneses
Admissions: Jennifer McDonald
Type: Two-Year College **Sex:** Coed **Affiliation:** Coast Community College District System **Admission Plans:** Open Admission; Early Admission **Application Deadline:** Rolling **Application Fee:** $0.00 **H.S. Requirements:** High school diploma or equivalent not required. For applicants under 18: High school diploma required; GED accepted **Scholarships:** Available **Calendar System:** Semester, Summer Session Available **Regional Accreditation:** Western Association of Schools and Colleges **Credit Hours For Degree:** 60 units, Associates

COGSWELL POLYTECHNICAL COLLEGE
1175 Bordeaux Dr.
Sunnyvale, CA 94089-1299
Tel: (408)541-0100; Free: 800-264-7955
Fax: (408)747-0764
E-mail: bking@cogswell.edu
Web Site: http://www.cogswell.edu/
President/CEO: Dr. Chester D. Haskell
Admissions: Brandace King
Financial Aid: Andrew Hagedorn
Type: Four-Year College **Sex:** Coed **Scores:** 88% SAT V 400+; 100% SAT M 400+ **% Accepted:** 94 **Admission Plans:** Deferred Admission **Application Deadline:** March 1 **Application Fee:** $55.00 **H.S. Requirements:** High school diploma required; GED accepted **Costs Per Year:** Application fee: $55. Comprehensive fee: $28,908 includes full-time tuition ($17,856), mandatory fees ($180), and college room and board ($10,872). Full-time tuition and fees vary according to course load. Room and board charges vary according to housing facility. Part-time tuition: $744 per credit. Part-time mandatory fees: $90 per term. Part-time tuition and fees vary according to course load. **Scholarships:** Available **Calendar System:** Semester, Summer Session Available **Enrollment:** FT 113, PT 86 **Faculty:** FT 10, PT 31 **Student-Faculty Ratio:** 6:1 **Exams:** SAT I or ACT. **% Receiving Financial Aid:** 74 **% Residing in College-Owned, -Operated, or -Affiliated Housing:** 14 **Final Year or Final Semester Residency Requirement:** No **Regional Accreditation:** Western Association of Schools and Colleges **Credit Hours For Degree:** 120 semester hours, Bachelors

THE COLBURN SCHOOL CONSERVATORY OF MUSIC
200 South Grand Ave.
Los Angeles, CA 90012
Tel: (213)621-2200
Admissions: (213)621-4534
Fax: (213)621-2110
E-mail: admissions@colburnschool.edu
Web Site: http://www.colburnschool.edu/
President/CEO: Sel Kardan
Admissions: Kathleen Tesar
Financial Aid: Kathleen Tesar
Type: Four-Year College **Sex:** Coed **% Accepted:** 17 **Admission Plans:** Deferred Admission **Application Deadline:** January 15 **Application Fee:** $110.00 **H.S. Requirements:** High school diploma required; GED accepted **Costs Per Year:** Application fee: $110. One-time mandatory fee: $500. Comprehensive fee: $0 includes full-time tuition ($0) and college room and board ($0). The Colburn School does not charge its Conservatory students for tuition, room or board.. **Calendar System:** Semester **Enrollment:** FT 67 **Faculty:** FT 8, PT 21 **Student-Faculty Ratio:** 4:1 **Exams:** SAT I or ACT. **% Residing in College-Owned, -Operated, or -Affiliated Housing:** 100 **Final Year or Final Semester Residency Requirement:** No **Library Holdings:** 20,171 **Credit Hours For Degree:** 120 credits, Bachelors **Professional Accreditation:** NASM

COLEMAN UNIVERSITY (SAN DIEGO)
8888 Balboa Ave.
San Diego, CA 92123
Tel: (858)499-0202
Fax: (858)499-0233
E-mail: jschafer@cts.com
Web Site: http://www.coleman.edu/
President/CEO: Pritpal Panesar
Type: Comprehensive **Sex:** Coed **% Accepted:** 100 **Admission Plans:** Deferred Admission **Application Deadline:** August 1 **Application Fee:** $100.00 **H.S. Requirements:** High school diploma required; GED accepted **Scholarships:** Available **Calendar System:** Quarter, Summer Session Available **Library Holdings:** 66,800 **Credit Hours For Degree:** 108 quarter hours, Associates; 180 quarter hours, Bachelors **Professional Accreditation:** ACICS

COLEMAN UNIVERSITY (SAN MARCOS)
1284 West San Marcos Blvd.
San Marcos, CA 92078
Tel: (760)747-3990
Fax: (760)752-9808
Web Site: http://www.coleman.edu/
Type: Two-Year College **Sex:** Coed **Calendar System:** Quarter **Professional Accreditation:** ACICS

COLLEGE OF ALAMEDA
555 Ralph Appezzato Memorial Parkway
Alameda, CA 94501-2109
Tel: (510)522-7221
Admissions: (510)748-2334
E-mail: hperdue@peralta.cc.ca.us
Web Site: http://www.peralta.cc.ca.us/
President/CEO: Dr. George Herring
Admissions: Barbara Simmons
Type: Two-Year College **Sex:** Coed **Affiliation:** Peralta Community College District System **Admission Plans:** Open Admission **Application Deadline:** Rolling **Application Fee:** $0.00 **H.S. Requirements:** High school diploma required; GED accepted. For applicants 18 or over: High school diploma or equivalent not required **Scholarships:** Available **Calendar System:** Semester, Summer Session Available **Faculty:** FT 80, PT 86 **Library Holdings:** 40,000 **Regional Accreditation:** Western Association of Schools and Colleges **Credit Hours For Degree:** 60 semester hours, Associates **Professional Accreditation:** ADA **Intercollegiate Athletics:** Basketball M & W; Bowling M & W

COLLEGE OF THE CANYONS
26455 Rockwell Canyon Rd.
Santa Clarita, CA 91355
Tel: (661)259-7800; Free: 888-206-7827
Admissions: (661)362-3280
Fax: (661)362-5300
E-mail: jasmine.ruys@canyons.edu
Web Site: http://www.canyons.edu/
President/CEO: Dr. Dianne G. Van Hook
Admissions: Jasmine Ruys
Type: Two-Year College **Sex:** Coed **Affiliation:** California Community College System **Admission Plans:** Open Admission; Early Admission **Application Deadline:** Rolling **Application Fee:** $0.00 **H.S. Requirements:** High school diploma or equivalent not required **Costs Per Year:** Application fee: $0. State resident tuition: $0 full-time. Nonresident tuition: $5142 full-time, $180 per unit part-time. Mandatory fees: $774 full-time, $26 per unit part-

time. **Scholarships:** Available **Calendar System:** Semester, Summer Session Available **Faculty:** FT 169, PT 448 **Student-Faculty Ratio:** 36:1 **Library Holdings:** 57,433 **Regional Accreditation:** Western Association of Schools and Colleges **Credit Hours For Degree:** 60 units, Associates **Professional Accreditation:** NLN **Intercollegiate Athletics:** Baseball M; Basketball M & W; Cross-Country Running M & W; Football M; Golf M & W; Ice Hockey M; Soccer M & W; Softball W; Swimming and Diving M & W; Track and Field M & W; Volleyball W

COLLEGE OF THE DESERT
43-500 Monterey Ave.
Palm Desert, CA 92260-9305
Tel: (760)346-8041
Web Site: http://www.collegeofthedesert.edu/
President/CEO: Jerry R. Patton
Admissions: Kathi Westerfield
Type: Two-Year College **Sex:** Coed **Affiliation:** California Community College System **Admission Plans:** Open Admission; Preferred Admission; Early Admission **Application Deadline:** Rolling **Application Fee:** $0.00 **H.S. Requirements:** High school diploma required; GED accepted. For applicants 18 or over: High school diploma or equivalent not required **Costs Per Year:** Application fee: $0. State resident tuition: $0 full-time. Nonresident tuition: $5190 full-time, $173 per unit part-time. Mandatory fees: $780 full-time, $26 per unit part-time. Full-time tuition and fees vary according to course load. **Scholarships:** Available **Calendar System:** Semester, Summer Session Available **Faculty:** FT 103, PT 235 **Library Holdings:** 58,000 **Regional Accreditation:** Western Association of Schools and Colleges **Credit Hours For Degree:** 60 units, Associates **Professional Accreditation:** NLN **Intercollegiate Athletics:** Baseball M; Basketball M & W; Cross-Country Running M & W; Football M; Golf M & W; Soccer M; Softball W; Tennis M & W; Track and Field M & W; Volleyball W

COLLEGE OF MARIN
835 College Ave.
Kentfield, CA 94904
Tel: (415)457-8811
Fax: (415)883-2632
E-mail: gina.longo@marin.edu
Web Site: http://www.marin.edu/
President/CEO: Frances L. White
Admissions: Gina Longo
Financial Aid: Adm. David Cook
Type: Two-Year College **Sex:** Coed **Affiliation:** California Community College System **Admission Plans:** Open Admission; Early Admission **Application Deadline:** Rolling **H.S. Requirements:** High school diploma or equivalent not required **Costs Per Year:** State resident tuition: $0 full-time. Nonresident tuition: $4560 full-time, $190 per unit part-time. Mandatory fees: $660 full-time, $26 per unit part-time. **Scholarships:** Available **Calendar System:** Semester, Summer Session Available **Enrollment:** FT 1,419, PT 5,188 **Faculty:** FT 145, PT 344 **Library Holdings:** 85,000 **Regional Accreditation:** Western Association of Schools and Colleges **Credit Hours For Degree:** 60 units, Associates **Professional Accreditation:** ADA, NLN **Intercollegiate Athletics:** Basketball M & W; Cross-Country Running M & W; Football M; Golf M & W; Soccer M & W; Swimming and Diving M & W; Tennis M & W; Track and Field M & W; Volleyball M & W; Water Polo M & W

COLLEGE OF THE REDWOODS
7351 Tompkins Hill Rd.
Eureka, CA 95501-9300
Tel: (707)476-4100
Web Site: http://www.redwoods.edu/
President/CEO: Dr. Jeff Marsee
Admissions: Kathy Goodlive
Type: Two-Year College **Sex:** Coed **Affiliation:** California Community College System **% Accepted:** 100 **Admission Plans:** Open Admission; Early Admission **Application Deadline:** Rolling **Application Fee:** $0.00 **H.S. Requirements:** High school diploma required; GED accepted. For applicants 18 or over: High school diploma or equivalent not required **Costs Per Year:** Application fee: $0. State resident tuition: $0 full-time. Nonresident tuition: $5424 full-time. Mandatory fees: $648 full-time. Full-time tuition and fees vary according to reciprocity agreements. College room and board: $6558. Room and board charges vary according to board plan. **Scholarships:** Available **Calendar System:** Semester, Summer Session Available **Faculty:** FT 104, PT 310 **Student-Faculty Ratio:** 21:1 **Library Holdings:** 50,266 **Regional Accreditation:** Western Association of Schools and Colleges **Credit Hours For Degree:** 60 units, Associates **Professional Accreditation:** ADA, NAIT **Intercollegiate Athletics:** Baseball M; Basketball M & W; Cross-Country Running M & W; Football M; Golf M; Soccer W; Softball W; Track and Field M & W; Volleyball W

COLLEGE OF SAN MATEO
1700 West Hillsdale Blvd.
San Mateo, CA 94402-3784
Tel: (650)574-6161
E-mail: csmadmission@smcccd.cc.ca.us
Web Site: http://www.collegeofsanmateo.edu/
President/CEO: Michael Claire
Admissions: Henry Villareal
Type: Two-Year College **Sex:** Coed **Affiliation:** California Community College System **Admission Plans:** Open Admission; Early Admission **Application Deadline:** Rolling **Application Fee:** $0.00 **H.S. Requirements:** High school diploma or equivalent not required. For applicants under 18: High school diploma required; GED accepted **Calendar System:** Semester, Summer Session Available **Faculty:** FT 184, PT 292 **Student-Faculty Ratio:** 15:1 **Library Holdings:** 85,085 **Regional Accreditation:** Western Association of Schools and Colleges **Credit Hours For Degree:** 60 semester hours, Associates **ROTC:** Army, Navy, Air Force **Professional Accreditation:** ADA **Intercollegiate Athletics:** Basketball M & W; Cross-Country Running M & W; Football M; Golf M; Soccer W; Tennis W; Track and Field M & W

COLLEGE OF THE SEQUOIAS
915 South Mooney Blvd.
Visalia, CA 93277-2234
Tel: (559)730-3700
Admissions: (559)737-4844
Web Site: http://www.cos.edu/
President/CEO: Dr. William Scroggins
Admissions: Lisa Hott
Type: Two-Year College **Sex:** Coed **Affiliation:** California Community College System **Admission Plans:** Open Admission **Application Deadline:** August 15 **Application Fee:** $0.00 **H.S. Requirements:** High school diploma or equivalent not required. For applicants under 18: High school diploma required; GED accepted **Costs Per Year:** Application fee: $0. State resident tuition: $0 full-time. Nonresident tuition: $5352 full-time, $223 per unit part-time. Mandatory fees: $658 full-time, $26 per unit part-time, $34 per term part-time. Full-time tuition and fees vary according to course load. Part-time tuition and fees vary according to course load. **Scholarships:** Available **Calendar System:** Semester, Summer Session Available **Enrollment:** FT 5,147, PT 8,302 **Faculty:** FT 185, PT 325 **Student-Faculty Ratio:** 27:1 **Library Holdings:** 73,557 **Regional Accreditation:** Western Association of Schools and Colleges **Credit Hours For Degree:** 60 units, Associates **ROTC:** Air Force **Intercollegiate Athletics:** Baseball M; Basketball M & W; Cross-Country Running M & W; Football M; Golf M; Soccer W; Softball W; Swimming and Diving M & W; Tennis M & W; Track and Field M & W; Volleyball W; Water Polo M

COLLEGE OF THE SISKIYOUS
800 College Ave.
Weed, CA 96094-2899
Tel: (530)938-5555
Fax: (530)938-5227
Web Site: http://www.siskiyous.edu/
President/CEO: Randall Lawrence, EdD
Admissions: Christina Bruck
Financial Aid: Vicki R. Wrobel
Type: Two-Year College **Sex:** Coed **Affiliation:** California Community College System **% Accepted:** 100 **Admission Plans:** Open Admission; Early Admission; Deferred Admission **Application Deadline:** Rolling **H.S. Requirements:** High school diploma or equivalent not required. For applicants under 18: High school diploma required; GED accepted **Costs Per Year:** State resident tuition: $0 full-time. Nonresident tuition: $4776 full-time, $199 per unit part-time. Mandatory fees: $624 full-time, $26 per unit part-time. Full-time tuition and fees vary according to course load and reciprocity agreements. Part-time tuition and fees vary according to reciprocity agreements. **Scholarships:** Available **Calendar System:** Semester, Summer Session Available **Faculty:** FT 50, PT 102 **Student-Faculty Ratio:** 21:1 **% Residing in College-Owned, -Operated, or -Affiliated Housing:** 10 **Library Holdings:** 34,708 **Regional Accreditation:** Western Association of

Schools and Colleges **Credit Hours For Degree:** 60 units, Associates **Intercollegiate Athletics:** Baseball M; Basketball M & W; Cross-Country Running M & W; Football M; Softball W; Track and Field M & W; Volleyball W

COLUMBIA COLLEGE
11600 Columbia College Dr.
Sonora, CA 95370
Tel: (209)588-5100
E-mail: smithk@yosemite.edu
Web Site: http://www.gocolumbia.org/
President/CEO: Joan Smith
Admissions: Dr. Kathleen Smith
Type: Two-Year College **Sex:** Coed **Affiliation:** Yosemite Community College District System **% Accepted:** 100 **Admission Plans:** Open Admission; Preferred Admission; Early Admission **Application Deadline:** Rolling **Application Fee:** $0.00 **H.S. Requirements:** High school diploma required; GED accepted. For applicants 18 or over: High school diploma or equivalent not required **Costs Per Year:** Application fee: $0. State resident tuition: $0 full-time. Nonresident tuition: $4560 full-time, $190 per unit part-time. Mandatory fees: $652 full-time, $26 per unit part-time, $28 per term part-time. **Scholarships:** Available **Calendar System:** Semester, Summer Session Available **Enrollment:** FT 903, PT 1,767 **Faculty:** FT 54, PT 109 **% Residing in College-Owned, -Operated, or -Affiliated Housing:** 7 **Library Holdings:** 34,892 **Regional Accreditation:** Western Association of Schools and Colleges **Credit Hours For Degree:** 60 units, Associates **Professional Accreditation:** ACF, JRCEMT **Intercollegiate Athletics:** Basketball M; Cross-Country Running M & W; Tennis M & W; Volleyball W

COLUMBIA COLLEGE HOLLYWOOD
18618 Oxnard St.
Tarzana, CA 91356
Tel: (818)345-8414
Fax: (818)345-9053
E-mail: admissions@columbiacollege.edu
Web Site: http://www.columbiacollege.edu/
President/CEO: Dr. Steve Martinez
Admissions: Carmen Munoz
Financial Aid: Jan Hastings
Type: Four-Year College **Sex:** Coed **% Accepted:** 60 **Admission Plans:** Deferred Admission **Application Deadline:** Rolling **Application Fee:** $50.00 **H.S. Requirements:** High school diploma required; GED accepted **Scholarships:** Available **Calendar System:** Quarter, Summer Session Available **Enrollment:** FT 301 **Faculty:** FT 52 **% Receiving Financial Aid:** 68 **Library Holdings:** 9,000 **Credit Hours For Degree:** 96 units, Associates; 192 units, Bachelors **Professional Accreditation:** ACCSCT

COMMUNITY CHRISTIAN COLLEGE
251 Tennessee St.
Redlands, CA 92373
Tel: (909)335-8863
Fax: (909)335-9101
Web Site: http://www.cccollege.edu/
President/CEO: Friedhelm K. Randant
Admissions: Ruth Pena
Type: Two-Year College **Sex:** Coed **Admission Plans:** Open Admission **Application Fee:** $25.00 **Costs Per Year:** Application fee: $25. Tuition: $9675 full-time, $215 per unit part-time. Mandatory fees: $300 full-time. **Professional Accreditation:** TACCS

CONCORDE CAREER COLLEGE
12951 Euclid St.
Ste. 101
Garden Grove, CA 92840
Tel: (714)703-1900
Fax: (714)530-4737
Web Site: http://www.concorde.edu/
President/CEO: Cindy Gordon
Type: Two-Year College **Sex:** Coed **% Accepted:** 100

CONCORDE CAREER INSTITUTE
12412 Victory Blvd.
North Hollywood, CA 91606
Tel: (818)766-8151
Fax: (818)766-1587
Web Site: http://www.concordecareercolleges.com/
President/CEO: Madeline Volker
Type: Two-Year College **Sex:** Coed **% Accepted:** 100 **Professional Accreditation:** ACCSCT, CARC

CONCORDIA UNIVERSITY
1530 Concordia West
Irvine, CA 92612-3299
Tel: (949)854-8002; Free: 800-229-1200
Fax: (949)854-6894
E-mail: admission@cui.edu
Web Site: http://www.cui.edu/
President/CEO: Rev. Loren T. Kramer
Admissions: Scott Rhodes
Financial Aid: Lori McDonald
Type: Comprehensive **Sex:** Coed **Affiliation:** Lutheran Church–Missouri Synod; The Concordia University System **Scores:** 95.1% SAT V 400+; 90.3% SAT M 400+; 57.5% ACT 18-23; 31.9% ACT 24-29 **% Accepted:** 62 **Admission Plans:** Early Action; Deferred Admission **Application Deadline:** Rolling **Application Fee:** $50.00 **H.S. Requirements:** High school diploma required; GED accepted. For home-schooled applicant: We review each file on an individual basis. Some documentation may be required. **Costs Per Year:** Application fee: $50. Comprehensive fee: $34,380 includes full-time tuition ($25,400), mandatory fees ($600), and college room and board ($8380). College room only: $4800. Full-time tuition and fees vary according to course load. Room and board charges vary according to board plan and housing facility. Part-time tuition: $775 per semester hour. Part-time tuition varies according to course load. **Scholarships:** Available **Calendar System:** Semester, Summer Session Available **Enrollment:** FT 1,365, PT 66, Grad FT 908, Grad PT 225 **Faculty:** FT 65, PT 173 **Student-Faculty Ratio:** 19:1 **Exams:** SAT I or ACT. ACT essay not being used. SAT essay not being used. **% Receiving Financial Aid:** 67 **% Residing in College-Owned, -Operated, or -Affiliated Housing:** 64 **Final Year or Final Semester Residency Requirement:** Yes **Library Holdings:** 77,783 **Regional Accreditation:** Western Association of Schools and Colleges **Credit Hours For Degree:** 64 semester hours, Associates; 128 semester hours, Bachelors **ROTC:** Army **Intercollegiate Athletics:** Baseball M; Basketball M & W; Cross-Country Running M & W; Lacrosse M; Soccer M & W; Softball W; Swimming and Diving M & W; Tennis M & W; Track and Field M & W; Volleyball W; Water Polo M & W

CONTRA COSTA COLLEGE
2600 Mission Bell Dr.
San Pablo, CA 94806-3195
Tel: (510)235-7800
Web Site: http://www.contracosta.edu/
President/CEO: McKinley Williams
Admissions: Ken Blustajn
Type: Two-Year College **Sex:** Coed **Affiliation:** Contra Costa Community College District and California Community College System **Admission Plans:** Open Admission; Early Admission **Application Deadline:** Rolling **Application Fee:** $0.00 **H.S. Requirements:** High school diploma or equivalent not required. For dental assisting, nursing programs: High school diploma required; GED accepted **Costs Per Year:** Application fee: $0. State resident tuition: $0 full-time. Nonresident tuition: $4368 full-time, $182 per unit part-time. Mandatory fees: $624 full-time, $26 per unit part-time. **Scholarships:** Available **Calendar System:** Semester, Summer Session Available **Enrollment:** FT 3,973, PT 4,861 **Faculty:** FT 115, PT 300 **Library Holdings:** 57,017 **Regional Accreditation:** Western Association of Schools and Colleges **Credit Hours For Degree:** 60 units, Associates **Professional Accreditation:** ADA, MACTE **Intercollegiate Athletics:** Baseball M; Basketball M & W; Cross-Country Running M & W; Football M; Softball W; Track and Field M & W; Volleyball W

COPPER MOUNTAIN COLLEGE
6162 Rotary Way
Joshua Tree, CA 92252
Tel: (760)366-3791
Web Site: http://www.cmccd.edu/
President/CEO: Dr. Roger Wagner
Admissions: Dr. Laraine Turk
Type: Two-Year College **Sex:** Coed **Admission Plans:** Open Admission **Calendar System:** Semester

COSUMNES RIVER COLLEGE
8401 Center Parkway
Sacramento, CA 95823-5799
Tel: (916)691-7344
Admissions: (916)688-7344
Fax: (916)691-7375
Web Site: http://www.crc.losrios.edu/
President/CEO: Dr. Deborah Travis
Admissions: Dianna L. Moore
Type: Two-Year College **Sex:** Coed **Affiliation:** Los Rios Community College District System **Admission Plans:** Open Admission; Early Admission **Application Deadline:** August 1 **Application Fee:** $0.00 **H.S. Requirements:** High school diploma required; GED accepted. For applicants 18 or over: High school diploma or equivalent not required **Scholarships:** Available **Calendar System:** Semester, Summer Session Available **Faculty:** FT 150, PT 400 **Library Holdings:** 55,447 **Regional Accreditation:** Western Association of Schools and Colleges **Credit Hours For Degree:** 60 units, Associates **Professional Accreditation:** AAMAE, AHIMA **Intercollegiate Athletics:** Baseball M; Basketball M & W; Soccer M & W; Softball W; Swimming and Diving M & W; Tennis M & W; Track and Field M & W; Volleyball W; Water Polo M & W

CRAFTON HILLS COLLEGE
11711 Sand Canyon Rd.
Yucaipa, CA 92399-1799
Tel: (909)794-2161
Fax: (909)389-9141
Web Site: http://www.craftonhills.edu/
President/CEO: Gloria Macías Harrison
Admissions: Joe Caabrales
Type: Two-Year College **Sex:** Coed **Affiliation:** California Community College System **Admission Plans:** Open Admission; Preferred Admission; Early Admission; Deferred Admission **Application Deadline:** Rolling **Application Fee:** $0.00 **H.S. Requirements:** High school diploma required; GED accepted **Scholarships:** Available **Calendar System:** Semester, Summer Session Available **Faculty:** FT 77, PT 131 **Library Holdings:** 65,731 **Regional Accreditation:** Western Association of Schools and Colleges **Credit Hours For Degree:** 60 credits, Associates **Professional Accreditation:** CARC, JRCEMT

CRIMSON TECHNICAL COLLEGE
8911 Aviation Blvd.
Inglewood, CA 90301
Free: (866)451-0818
Fax: (866)451-0818
Web Site: http://www.crimsontechnicalcollege.com/
Type: Two-Year College **Sex:** Coed **Admission Plans:** Open Admission **Application Fee:** $100.00 **Calendar System:** Quarter **Student-Faculty Ratio:** 19:1 **Professional Accreditation:** ACCSCT

CUESTA COLLEGE
PO Box 8106
San Luis Obispo, CA 93403-8106
Tel: (805)546-3100
Admissions: (805)546-3140
E-mail: jsiu@cuesta.edu
Web Site: http://www.cuesta.edu/
Admissions: Julieta Siu
Type: Two-Year College **Sex:** Coed **Affiliation:** San Luis Obispo County Community College District **Admission Plans:** Open Admission; Preferred Admission; Early Admission; Deferred Admission **Application Deadline:** Rolling **Application Fee:** $0.00 **H.S. Requirements:** High school diploma or equivalent not required **Scholarships:** Available **Calendar System:** Semester, Summer Session Available **Faculty:** FT 140, PT 415 **Student-Faculty Ratio:** 24:1 **Library Holdings:** 67,018 **Regional Accreditation:** Western Association of Schools and Colleges **Credit Hours For Degree:** 60 units, Associates **ROTC:** Army **Intercollegiate Athletics:** Baseball M; Basketball M & W; Cross-Country Running M & W; Soccer W; Softball W; Swimming and Diving M & W; Tennis W; Track and Field M & W; Volleyball W; Water Polo M & W; Wrestling M

CUYAMACA COLLEGE
900 Rancho San Diego Parkway
El Cajon, CA 92019-4304
Tel: (619)660-4000
Admissions: (619)660-4302
E-mail: susan.topham@gcccd.edu
Web Site: http://www.cuyamaca.net/
President/CEO: Tim O'Hare
Admissions: Susan Topham
Type: Two-Year College **Sex:** Coed **Affiliation:** Grossmont-Cuyamaca Community College District **Admission Plans:** Open Admission; Early Admission **Application Deadline:** Rolling **Application Fee:** $0.00 **H.S. Requirements:** High school diploma required; GED accepted. For applicants 18 or over: High school diploma or equivalent not required **Costs Per Year:** Application fee: $0. State resident tuition: $0 full-time. Nonresident tuition: $5700 full-time, $190 per unit part-time. Mandatory fees: $820 full-time, $26 per unit part-time, $20 per term part-time. Full-time tuition and fees vary according to course load. Part-time tuition and fees vary according to course load. **Scholarships:** Available **Calendar System:** Semester, Summer Session Available **Enrollment:** FT 1,636, PT 6,070 **Faculty:** FT 84, PT 561 **Library Holdings:** 81,304 **Regional Accreditation:** Western Association of Schools and Colleges **Credit Hours For Degree:** 60 units, Associates **ROTC:** Army, Air Force **Intercollegiate Athletics:** Basketball M & W; Cross-Country Running M & W; Golf M; Soccer M & W; Tennis W; Track and Field M & W; Volleyball W

CYPRESS COLLEGE
9200 Valley View
Cypress, CA 90630-5897
Tel: (714)484-7000
Fax: (714)761-3934
E-mail: dwassenaar@cypresscollege.edu
Web Site: http://www.cypresscollege.edu/
President/CEO: Michael Kasler
Admissions: David Wassenaar
Type: Two-Year College **Sex:** Coed **Affiliation:** California Community College System **Admission Plans:** Open Admission **Application Deadline:** August 25 **Application Fee:** $0.00 **H.S. Requirements:** High school diploma or equivalent not required **Scholarships:** Available **Calendar System:** Semester, Summer Session Available **Faculty:** FT 230, PT 360 **Library Holdings:** 76,696 **Regional Accreditation:** Western Association of Schools and Colleges **Credit Hours For Degree:** 60 units, Associates **Professional Accreditation:** ABFSE, ADA, AHIMA, JRCERT, NLN **Intercollegiate Athletics:** Baseball M; Basketball M & W; Golf M & W; Soccer M & W; Softball W; Swimming and Diving M & W; Tennis M & W; Volleyball W; Water Polo M & W; Wrestling M

DE ANZA COLLEGE
21250 Stevens Creek Blvd.
Cupertino, CA 95014-5793
Tel: (408)864-5678
Fax: (408)864-8329
E-mail: webregda@mercury.fhda.edu
Web Site: http://www.deanza.fhda.edu/
President/CEO: Brian Murphy
Admissions: Kathleen Moberg
Type: Two-Year College **Sex:** Coed **Affiliation:** California Community College System **Admission Plans:** Open Admission; Early Admission **Application Deadline:** Rolling **Application Fee:** $22.00 **H.S. Requirements:** High school diploma required; GED accepted **Scholarships:** Available **Calendar System:** Quarter, Summer Session Available **Enrollment:** FT 8,860, PT 14,484 **Faculty:** FT 512, PT 300 **Library Holdings:** 80,000 **Regional Accreditation:** Western Association of Schools and Colleges **Credit Hours For Degree:** 90 units, Associates **ROTC:** Army, Air Force **Professional Accreditation:** AAMAE, APTA **Intercollegiate Athletics:** Baseball M; Basketball M & W; Cross-Country Running M & W; Football M; Golf M & W; Soccer M & W; Softball W; Swimming and Diving M & W; Tennis M & W; Track and Field M & W; Volleyball M & W; Water Polo M

DEEP SPRINGS COLLEGE
HC 72, Box 45001
Deep Springs, CA 89010-9803
Tel: (760)872-2000
E-mail: apcom@deepsprings.edu
Web Site: http://www.deepsprings.edu/
President/CEO: David Neidorf
Admissions: David Neidorf

Type: Two-Year College **Sex:** Men **Scores:** 100% SAT V 400+; 100% SAT M 400+ **% Accepted:** 8 **Application Deadline:** November 15 **Application Fee:** $0.00 **H.S. Requirements:** High school diploma required; GED accepted **Costs Per Year:** Application fee: $0. **Calendar System:** Miscellaneous, Summer Session Available **Enrollment:** FT 24 **Faculty:** FT 4, PT 3 **Student-Faculty Ratio:** 4:1 **Exams:** SAT I and SAT II or ACT. **% Residing in College-Owned, -Operated, or -Affiliated Housing:** 100 **Library Holdings:** 20,000 **Regional Accreditation:** Western Association of Schools and Colleges **Credit Hours For Degree:** 60 hours, Associates

DESIGN INSTITUTE OF SAN DIEGO
8555 Commerce Ave.
San Diego, CA 92121-2685
Tel: (858)566-1200; Free: 800-619-4337
Fax: (858)566-2711
E-mail: admissions@disd.edu
Web Site: http://www.disd.edu/
President/CEO: Margot Blank Doucette
Admissions: Paula Parrish
Type: Four-Year College **Sex:** Coed **% Accepted:** 54 **Application Deadline:** Rolling **Application Fee:** $25.00 **H.S. Requirements:** High school diploma required; GED accepted **Scholarships:** Available **Calendar System:** Semester, Summer Session Not available **Library Holdings:** 5,000 **Professional Accreditation:** ACICS, FIDER

DEVRY UNIVERSITY (ALHAMBRA)
Unit 100, Bldg. A-11, First Floor
1000 South Fremont Ave.
Alhambra, CA 91803
Tel: (626)293-4300
Web Site: http://www.devry.edu/
Type: Comprehensive **Sex:** Coed **Regional Accreditation:** North Central Association of Colleges and Schools

DEVRY UNIVERSITY (ANAHEIM)
1900 South State College Blvd., Ste. 150
Anaheim, CA 92806-6136
Tel: (714)935-3200
Web Site: http://www.devry.edu/
Type: Comprehensive **Sex:** Coed

DEVRY UNIVERSITY (BAKERSFIELD)
3000 Ming Ave.
Bakersfield, CA 93304-4136
Tel: (661)833-7120
Web Site: http://www.devry.edu/
Type: Four-Year College **Sex:** Coed **Regional Accreditation:** North Central Association of Colleges and Schools

DEVRY UNIVERSITY (DALY CITY)
2001 Junipero Serra Blvd.
Ste. 161
Daly City, CA 94014-3899
Tel: (650)991-3520
Web Site: http://www.devry.edu/
Type: Comprehensive **Sex:** Coed **Regional Accreditation:** North Central Association of Colleges and Schools

DEVRY UNIVERSITY (ELK GROVE)
Sacramento Center
2216 Kausen Dr.
Elk Grove, CA 95758
Tel: (916)478-2847; Free: (866)573-3879
Fax: (916)478-2849
Web Site: http://www.devry.edu/
Type: Comprehensive **Sex:** Coed **Calendar System:** Semester **Regional Accreditation:** North Central Association of Colleges and Schools

DEVRY UNIVERSITY (FREMONT)
6600 Dumbarton Circle
Fremont, CA 94555
Tel: (510)574-1100
Fax: (510)742-0868
Web Site: http://www.devry.edu/
Financial Aid: Kim Kane
Type: Comprehensive **Sex:** Coed **Affiliation:** DeVry University **Admission Plans:** Early Admission; Deferred Admission **Application Deadline:** Rolling **Application Fee:** $50.00 **H.S. Requirements:** High school diploma required; GED accepted **Costs Per Year:** Application fee: $50. Tuition: $14,720 full-time, $575 per credit hour part-time. **Scholarships:** Available **Calendar System:** Semester, Summer Session Available **Enrollment:** FT 754, PT 587, Grad FT 14, Grad PT 198 **Faculty:** FT 35, PT 196 **Student-Faculty Ratio:** 10:1 **Exams:** ACT essay used for admission. SAT essay used for admission. ACT essay used for placement. SAT essay used for placement. **% Receiving Financial Aid:** 80 **Regional Accreditation:** North Central Association of Colleges and Schools **Credit Hours For Degree:** 67 credit hours, Associates; 122 credit hours, Bachelors **Professional Accreditation:** ABET

DEVRY UNIVERSITY (IRVINE)
430 Exchange, Ste. 250
Irvine, CA 92602-1303
Tel: (949)752-5631
Fax: (949)752-5637
Web Site: http://www.devry.edu/
Type: Comprehensive **Sex:** Coed **Calendar System:** Semester **Regional Accreditation:** North Central Association of Colleges and Schools

DEVRY UNIVERSITY (LONG BEACH)
3880 Kilroy Airport Way
Long Beach, CA 90806
Tel: (562)427-0861
Web Site: http://www.devry.edu/
Financial Aid: Kathy Odom
Type: Comprehensive **Sex:** Coed **Affiliation:** DeVry University **Admission Plans:** Early Admission; Deferred Admission **Application Deadline:** Rolling **Application Fee:** $50.00 **H.S. Requirements:** High school diploma required; GED accepted **Costs Per Year:** Application fee: $50. Tuition: $14,080 full-time, $550 per credit hour part-time. **Scholarships:** Available **Calendar System:** Semester, Summer Session Available **Enrollment:** FT 405, PT 512, Grad FT 5, Grad PT 250 **Faculty:** FT 20, PT 81 **Student-Faculty Ratio:** 14:1 **Exams:** ACT essay used for admission. SAT essay used for admission. ACT essay used for placement. SAT essay used for placement. **% Receiving Financial Aid:** 75 **Regional Accreditation:** North Central Association of Colleges and Schools **Credit Hours For Degree:** 66 credit hours, Associates; 122 credit hours, Bachelors **Professional Accreditation:** ABET

DEVRY UNIVERSITY (OAKLAND)
505 14th St.
Oakland, CA 94612
Tel: (866)473-3879
Web Site: http://www.devry.edu/
Type: Comprehensive **Sex:** Coed

DEVRY UNIVERSITY (PALMDALE)
One 39115 Trade Center Dr.
Ste. 100
Palmdale, CA 93551
Free: (866)986-9388
Web Site: http://www.devry.edu/
Financial Aid: Ann Logan
Type: Comprehensive **Sex:** Coed **Affiliation:** DeVry University **Admission Plans:** Deferred Admission **Application Deadline:** Rolling **Application Fee:** $50.00 **H.S. Requirements:** High school diploma required; GED accepted **Scholarships:** Available **Calendar System:** Semester, Summer Session Available **Enrollment:** FT 329, PT 342 **Faculty:** FT 17, PT 44 **Student-Faculty Ratio:** 16:1 **% Receiving Financial Aid:** 74 **Library Holdings:** 16,177 **Regional Accreditation:** North Central Association of Colleges and Schools **Credit Hours For Degree:** 66 credit hours, Associates; 122 credit hours, Bachelors **Professional Accreditation:** ABET

DEVRY UNIVERSITY (POMONA)
901 Corporate Center Dr.
Pomona, CA 91768-2642
Tel: (909)622-8866
Fax: (909)623-5666
Web Site: http://www.devry.edu/

President/CEO: Bill Van Zwol
Financial Aid: Kathy Odom
Type: Comprehensive **Sex:** Coed **Affiliation:** DeVry University **Admission Plans:** Early Admission; Deferred Admission **Application Deadline:** Rolling **Application Fee:** $50.00 **H.S. Requirements:** High school diploma required; GED accepted **Costs Per Year:** Application fee: $50. Tuition: $14,080 full-time, $550 per credit hour part-time. **Scholarships:** Available **Calendar System:** Semester, Summer Session Available **Enrollment:** FT 885, PT 1,135, Grad FT 41, Grad PT 262 **Faculty:** FT 25, PT 138 **Student-Faculty Ratio:** 20:1 **Exams:** ACT essay used for admission. SAT essay used for admission. ACT essay used for placement. SAT essay used for placement. **% Receiving Financial Aid:** 72 **Regional Accreditation:** North Central Association of Colleges and Schools **Credit Hours For Degree:** 66 credit hours, Associates; 122 credit hours, Bachelors **Professional Accreditation:** ABET

DEVRY UNIVERSITY (SAN DIEGO)
2655 Camino Del Rio North, Ste. 201
San Diego, CA 92108-1633
Tel: (619)683-2446
Fax: (619)683-2448
Web Site: http://www.devry.edu/
Type: Comprehensive **Sex:** Coed **Calendar System:** Semester **Regional Accreditation:** North Central Association of Colleges and Schools

DEVRY UNIVERSITY (SHERMAN OAKS)
15301 Ventura Blvd., D-100
Sherman Oaks, CA 91403
Tel: 888-610-0800; Free: 888-610-0800
Web Site: http://www.devry.edu/
Type: Comprehensive **Sex:** Coed **Admission Plans:** Early Admission; Deferred Admission **Application Deadline:** Rolling **Application Fee:** $50.00 **H.S. Requirements:** High school diploma required; GED accepted **Costs Per Year:** Application fee: $50. Tuition: $14,080 full-time, $550 per credit hour part-time. **Scholarships:** Available **Enrollment:** FT 456, PT 272, Grad FT 36, Grad PT 167 **Faculty:** FT 8, PT 61 **Student-Faculty Ratio:** 23:1 **Exams:** ACT essay used for admission. SAT essay used for admission. ACT essay used for placement. SAT essay used for placement. **% Receiving Financial Aid:** 65 **Regional Accreditation:** North Central Association of Colleges and Schools

DIABLO VALLEY COLLEGE
321 Golf Club Rd.
Pleasant Hill, CA 94523
Tel: (925)685-1230
Fax: (925)685-1551
E-mail: idorn@dvc.edu
Web Site: http://www.dvc.edu/
President/CEO: Judy Walters
Admissions: Ileana Dorn
Type: Two-Year College **Sex:** Coed **Affiliation:** Contra Costa Community College District **Admission Plans:** Open Admission; Early Admission **Application Deadline:** August 15 **Application Fee:** $0.00 **H.S. Requirements:** High school diploma or equivalent not required. For applicants under 18: High school diploma required; GED accepted **Costs Per Year:** Application fee: $0. State resident tuition: $0 full-time. Nonresident tuition: $4440 full-time, $185 per unit part-time. Mandatory fees: $634 full-time, $26 per unit part-time. **Scholarships:** Available **Calendar System:** Semester, Summer Session Available **Enrollment:** FT 7,340, PT 15,227 **Faculty:** FT 255, PT 550 **Student-Faculty Ratio:** 17:1 **Library Holdings:** 88,286 **Regional Accreditation:** Western Association of Schools and Colleges **Credit Hours For Degree:** 60 units, Associates **ROTC:** Air Force **Professional Accreditation:** ACF, ADA **Intercollegiate Athletics:** Basketball M & W; Cross-Country Running M & W; Football M; Soccer W; Softball W; Swimming and Diving M & W; Tennis M & W; Track and Field M & W; Volleyball W; Water Polo M & W

DOMINICAN UNIVERSITY OF CALIFORNIA
50 Acacia Ave.
San Rafael, CA 94901-2298
Tel: (415)457-4440; Free: 888-323-6763
Admissions: (415)485-3204
Fax: (415)485-3214
E-mail: enroll@dominican.edu
Web Site: http://www.dominican.edu/
President/CEO: Joseph R. Fink
Admissions: Rebecca Finn Kenney
Financial Aid: Shanon Little
Type: Comprehensive **Sex:** Coed **Affiliation:** Roman Catholic Church **Scores:** 93.9% SAT V 400+; 58.1% ACT 18-23; 25.8% ACT 24-29 **% Accepted:** 12 **Admission Plans:** Deferred Admission **Application Deadline:** February 1 **Application Fee:** $40.00 **H.S. Requirements:** High school diploma required; GED accepted **Costs Per Year:** Application fee: $40. Comprehensive fee: $49,147 includes full-time tuition ($35,220), mandatory fees ($367), and college room and board ($13,560). College room only: $7720. Full-time tuition and fees vary according to course load, degree level, and program. Room and board charges vary according to board plan. Part-time tuition: $1470 per unit. Part-time mandatory fees: $300 per term. Part-time tuition and fees vary according to degree level and program. **Scholarships:** Available **Calendar System:** Semester, Summer Session Available **Enrollment:** FT 1,171, PT 278, Grad FT 382, Grad PT 265 **Faculty:** FT 83, PT 272 **Student-Faculty Ratio:** 11:1 **Exams:** SAT I or ACT. ACT essay used for placement. SAT essay used for placement. **% Receiving Financial Aid:** 73 **% Residing in College-Owned, -Operated, or -Affiliated Housing:** 46 **Library Holdings:** 120,646 **Regional Accreditation:** Western Association of Schools and Colleges **Credit Hours For Degree:** 124 units, Bachelors **Professional Accreditation:** AACN, AOTA, NLN **Intercollegiate Athletics:** Basketball M & W; Golf M & W; Lacrosse M; Soccer M & W; Softball W; Tennis W; Volleyball W

EAST LOS ANGELES COLLEGE
1301 Avenida Cesar Chavez
Monterey Park, CA 91754
Tel: (323)265-8650
Admissions: (323)265-8801
Fax: (323)265-8763
E-mail: allredjp@elac.edu
Web Site: http://www.elac.edu/
President/CEO: Ernest H. Moreno
Admissions: Jeremy Allred
Type: Two-Year College **Sex:** Coed **Affiliation:** Los Angeles Community College District System **Admission Plans:** Early Admission **Application Deadline:** Rolling **Application Fee:** $0.00 **H.S. Requirements:** High school diploma or equivalent not required **Costs Per Year:** Application fee: $0. State resident tuition: $0 full-time. Nonresident tuition: $5790 full-time, $193 per unit part-time. Mandatory fees: $780 full-time, $26 per unit part-time. Tuition guaranteed not to increase for student's term of enrollment. **Scholarships:** Available **Calendar System:** Semester, Summer Session Available **Enrollment:** FT 8,640, PT 21,509 **Faculty:** FT 212, PT 816 **Student-Faculty Ratio:** 44:1 **Exams:** Other. **Library Holdings:** 102,000 **Regional Accreditation:** Western Association of Schools and Colleges **Credit Hours For Degree:** 60 units, Associates **Professional Accreditation:** AHIMA, CARC **Intercollegiate Athletics:** Baseball M; Basketball M & W; Cheerleading W; Cross-Country Running M & W; Football M; Soccer M & W; Softball W; Track and Field M & W; Volleyball W; Wrestling M

EL CAMINO COLLEGE
16007 Crenshaw Blvd.
Torrance, CA 90506-0001
Tel: (310)532-3670; Free: (866)ELCAMINO
Admissions: (310)660-3418
Fax: (310)660-3818
E-mail: wmulrooney@elcamino.edu
Web Site: http://www.elcamino.edu/
President/CEO: Dr. Thomas Fallo
Admissions: William Mulrooney
Type: Two-Year College **Sex:** Coed **Affiliation:** California Community College System **Admission Plans:** Open Admission; Early Admission **Application Deadline:** Rolling **Application Fee:** $0.00 **H.S. Requirements:** High school diploma or equivalent not required. For applicants under 18: High school diploma required; GED accepted **Calendar System:** Semester, Summer Session Available **Enrollment:** FT 7,729, PT 17,166 **Faculty:** FT 333, PT 650 **Student-Faculty Ratio:** 15:1 **Library Holdings:** 116,051 **Regional Accreditation:** Western Association of Schools and Colleges **Credit Hours For Degree:** 60 units, Associates **Professional Accreditation:** CARC, JRCERT, NLN **Intercollegiate Athletics:** Baseball M; Basketball M & W; Cross-Country Running M & W; Football M; Golf M; Gymnastics W; Soccer M; Swimming and Diving M & W; Tennis M & W; Track and Field M & W; Volleyball M & W; Water Polo M; Wrestling M

EMMANUEL BIBLE COLLEGE
1605 East Elizabeth St.
Pasadena, CA 91104
Tel: (626)791-2575
Admissions: (626)446-0300
Fax: (626)398-2424
E-mail: info@ebcministry.edu
Web Site: http://www.ebcministry.edu/
Type: Four-Year College **Sex:** Coed **Affiliation:** Church of the Nazarene **% Accepted:** 100 **Admission Plans:** Open Admission; Early Admission **Application Deadline:** September 15 **Application Fee:** $25.00 **Calendar System:** Quarter, Summer Session Not available **Enrollment:** FT 6, PT 14 **Faculty:** FT 1, PT 5 **Student-Faculty Ratio:** 10:1 **Library Holdings:** 15,000 **Credit Hours For Degree:** 96 credits, Associates; 192 credits, Bachelors **Professional Accreditation:** ABHE

EMPIRE COLLEGE
3035 Cleveland Ave.
Santa Rosa, CA 95403
Tel: (707)546-4000
Fax: (707)546-4058
Web Site: http://www.empcol.com/
President/CEO: Roy O. Hurd
Admissions: Dahnja Barker
Type: Two-Year College **Sex:** Coed **Application Deadline:** Rolling **Application Fee:** $75.00 **H.S. Requirements:** High school diploma required; GED accepted **Scholarships:** Available **Calendar System:** Continuous, Summer Session Not available **Exams:** Other. **Credit Hours For Degree:** 105 units, Associates **Professional Accreditation:** ACICS

EPIC BIBLE COLLEGE
5225 Hillsdale Blvd.
Sacramento, CA 95842
Tel: (916)348-4689
Fax: (916)334-2315
E-mail: kclarke@tlbc.edu
Web Site: http://epic.edu/
President/CEO: Ronald W. Harden
Admissions: Sheila Knoll
Type: Four-Year College **Sex:** Coed **Affiliation:** nondenominational **Application Fee:** $50.00 **Calendar System:** Quarter **Professional Accreditation:** TACCS

EVEREST COLLEGE (CITY OF INDUSTRY)
12801 Crossroads Parkway South
City of Industry, CA 91746
Tel: (562)908-2500; Free: 888-741-4270
Fax: (562)908-7656
Web Site: http://www.everest.edu/
President/CEO: Michelle Lisoskie
Type: Two-Year College **Sex:** Coed **Calendar System:** Quarter **Student-Faculty Ratio:** 20:1

EVEREST COLLEGE (ONTARIO)
1819 South Excise Ave.
Ontario, CA 91761
Tel: (909)484-4311
Fax: (909)484-1162
Web Site: http://www.everest.edu/campus/ontario/
President/CEO: Richard P. Mallow
Type: Two-Year College **Sex:** Coed **% Accepted:** 87 **Application Fee:** $25.00

EVEREST INSTITUTE
2161 Technology Place
Long Beach, CA 90810
Tel: (562)437-0501
Admissions: (562)624-9530
Fax: (562)432-3721
Web Site: http://www.everest.edu/
President/CEO: John Andrews
Type: Two-Year College **Sex:** Coed **% Accepted:** 63 **Calendar System:** Quarter **Professional Accreditation:** ACCSCT

EVERGREEN VALLEY COLLEGE
3095 Yerba Buena Rd.
San Jose, CA 95135-1598
Tel: (408)274-7900
Fax: (408)223-9351
Web Site: http://www.evc.edu/
President/CEO: David Wain Coon, EdD
Admissions: Cindy Tayag
Type: Two-Year College **Sex:** Coed **Affiliation:** California Community College System **% Accepted:** 100 **Admission Plans:** Open Admission; Early Admission **Application Deadline:** Rolling **H.S. Requirements:** High school diploma or equivalent not required. For applicants under 18: High school diploma required; GED accepted **Scholarships:** Available **Calendar System:** Semester, Summer Session Available **Enrollment:** FT 11,751 **Faculty:** FT 125, PT 176 **Library Holdings:** 42,782 **Regional Accreditation:** Western Association of Schools and Colleges **Credit Hours For Degree:** 60 units, Associates **ROTC:** Army **Professional Accreditation:** NLN **Intercollegiate Athletics:** Soccer M

FASHION CAREERS COLLEGE
1923 Morena Blvd.
San Diego, CA 92110
Tel: (619)275-4700; Free: 888-FCCC999
Fax: (619)275-0635
E-mail: ronny@fashioncareerscollege.com
Web Site: http://www.fashioncareerscollege.com/
President/CEO: Judith Thacker
Admissions: Ronny Catarcio
Type: Two-Year College **Sex:** Coed **Application Deadline:** Rolling **Application Fee:** $25.00 **H.S. Requirements:** High school diploma required; GED accepted **Costs Per Year:** Application fee: $25. Tuition: $19,900 full-time. Mandatory fees: $525 full-time. Full-time tuition and fees vary according to class time, course load, degree level, and program. **Scholarships:** Available **Calendar System:** Quarter, Summer Session Not available **Enrollment:** FT 91 **Faculty:** FT 1, PT 8 **Exams:** Other. **Library Holdings:** 800 **Credit Hours For Degree:** 91 credits, Associates **Professional Accreditation:** ACICS

FEATHER RIVER COLLEGE
570 Golden Eagle Ave.
Quincy, CA 95971-9124
Tel: (530)283-0202; Free: 800-442-9799
Fax: (530)283-3757
E-mail: info@frc.edu
Web Site: http://www.frc.edu/
President/CEO: Ron Taylor
Admissions: Karen Sue Hayden
Type: Two-Year College **Sex:** Coed **Affiliation:** California Community College System **Admission Plans:** Open Admission **Application Fee:** $0.00 **H.S. Requirements:** High school diploma or equivalent not required **Costs Per Year:** Application fee: $0. State resident tuition: $0 full-time. Nonresident tuition: $5700 full-time, $190 per unit part-time. Mandatory fees: $859 full-time, $27.50 per unit part-time, $17 per term part-time. **Scholarships:** Available **Calendar System:** Semester, Summer Session Available **Enrollment:** FT 732, PT 982 **Faculty:** FT 27, PT 66 **Student-Faculty Ratio:** 18:1 **% Residing in College-Owned, -Operated, or -Affiliated Housing:** 24 **Library Holdings:** 20,782 **Regional Accreditation:** Western Association of Schools and Colleges **Credit Hours For Degree:** 60 units, Associates **Intercollegiate Athletics:** Baseball M; Basketball M & W; Equestrian Sports M & W; Football M; Soccer M & W; Softball W

FIDM/THE FASHION INSTITUTE OF DESIGN & MERCHANDISING, LOS ANGELES CAMPUS
919 South Grand Ave.
Los Angeles, CA 90015-1421
Tel: (213)624-1200; Free: 800-624-1200
Admissions: (213)624-1201
Fax: (213)624-4799
E-mail: saronson@fidm.com
Web Site: http://www.fidm.edu/
President/CEO: Tonian Hohberg
Admissions: Susan Aronson
Type: Two-Year College **Sex:** Coed **Affiliation:** The Fashion Institute of Design and Merchandising/FIDM **% Accepted:** 71 **Admission Plans:** Deferred Admission **Application Deadline:** Rolling **Application Fee:**

$225.00 **H.S. Requirements:** High school diploma required; GED accepted **Costs Per Year:** Application fee: $225. Tuition guaranteed not to increase for student's term of enrollment. **Scholarships:** Available **Calendar System:** Quarter, Summer Session Available **Enrollment:** FT 4,013, PT 549 **Faculty:** FT 67, PT 250 **Student-Faculty Ratio:** 17:1 **Exams:** SAT I or ACT. **Library Holdings:** 24,564 **Regional Accreditation:** Western Association of Schools and Colleges **Credit Hours For Degree:** 90 quarter hours, Associates; 181 units, Bachelors **Professional Accreditation:** NASAD

FIDM/THE FASHION INSTITUTE OF DESIGN & MERCHANDISING, ORANGE COUNTY CAMPUS
17590 Gillette Ave.
Irvine, CA 92614
Tel: (949)851-6200
Fax: (949)851-6808
Web Site: http://www.fidm.com/
President/CEO: Tonian Hohberg
Type: Two-Year College **Sex:** Coed **Affiliation:** The Fashion Institute of Design and Merchandising/FIDM Orange County **% Accepted:** 75 **Admission Plans:** Deferred Admission **Application Deadline:** Rolling **Application Fee:** $225.00 **H.S. Requirements:** High school diploma required; GED accepted **Costs Per Year:** Application fee: $225. **Calendar System:** Quarter, Summer Session Available **Enrollment:** FT 469, PT 36 **Faculty:** FT 7, PT 31 **Student-Faculty Ratio:** 18:1 **Library Holdings:** 24,755 **Regional Accreditation:** Western Association of Schools and Colleges **Professional Accreditation:** NASAD

FIDM/THE FASHION INSTITUTE OF DESIGN & MERCHANDISING, SAN DIEGO CAMPUS
1010 Second Ave., Ste. 200
San Diego, CA 92101
Tel: (619)235-2049; Free: 800-243-3436
Admissions: (213)624-1200
Fax: (619)232-4322
E-mail: info@fidm.com
Web Site: http://www.fidm.com/
President/CEO: Tonian Hohberg
Admissions: Susan Aronson
Type: Two-Year College **Sex:** Coed **Affiliation:** The Fashion Institute of Design and Merchandising/FIDM San Diego **% Accepted:** 59 **Admission Plans:** Deferred Admission **Application Deadline:** Rolling **Application Fee:** $225.00 **H.S. Requirements:** High school diploma required; GED accepted **Costs Per Year:** Application fee: $225. Tuition guaranteed not to increase for student's term of enrollment. **Calendar System:** Quarter, Summer Session Available **Enrollment:** FT 262, PT 25 **Faculty:** FT 3, PT 16 **Student-Faculty Ratio:** 18:1 **Exams:** SAT I or ACT. **Library Holdings:** 4,777 **Regional Accreditation:** Western Association of Schools and Colleges **Credit Hours For Degree:** 90 units, Associates **Professional Accreditation:** NASAD

FIDM/THE FASHION INSTITUTE OF DESIGN & MERCHANDISING, SAN FRANCISCO CAMPUS
55 Stockton St.
San Francisco, CA 94108-5829
Tel: (415)675-5200; Free: 800-711-7175
Admissions: (213)624-1201
Fax: (415)296-7299
E-mail: info@fidm.com
Web Site: http://www.fidm.edu/
President/CEO: Tonian Hohberg
Admissions: Susan Aronson
Type: Two-Year College **Sex:** Coed **Affiliation:** The Fashion Institute of Design and Merchandising/FIDM **% Accepted:** 61 **Admission Plans:** Deferred Admission **Application Deadline:** Rolling **Application Fee:** $225.00 **H.S. Requirements:** High school diploma required; GED accepted **Calendar System:** Quarter, Summer Session Available **Faculty:** FT 9, PT 64 **Student-Faculty Ratio:** 16:1 **Exams:** SAT I or ACT. **Library Holdings:** 6,928 **Regional Accreditation:** Western Association of Schools and Colleges **Credit Hours For Degree:** 90 quarter hours, Associates **Professional Accreditation:** NASAD

FOLSOM LAKE COLLEGE
10 College Parkway
Folsom, CA 95630
Tel: (916)608-6500
Web Site: http://www.flc.losrios.edu/
President/CEO: Dr. Thelma Scott-Skilman
Type: Two-Year College **Sex:** Coed **Affiliation:** Los Rios Community College District System **Application Deadline:** Rolling **Application Fee:** $0.00 **H.S. Requirements:** High school diploma or equivalent not required. For for students under 18: High school diploma required; GED accepted **Costs Per Year:** Application fee: $0. State resident tuition: $0 full-time. Nonresident tuition: $4560 full-time, $190 per unit part-time. Mandatory fees: $624 full-time, $26 per unit part-time. **Faculty:** FT 109, PT 186 **Student-Faculty Ratio:** 32:1 **Library Holdings:** 26,100 **Regional Accreditation:** Western Association of Schools and Colleges **Credit Hours For Degree:** 60 semester units, Associates

FOOTHILL COLLEGE
12345 El Monte Rd.
Los Altos Hills, CA 94022-4599
Tel: (650)949-7777
Web Site: http://www.foothill.edu/
President/CEO: Judy C. Miner
Admissions: Penny Johnson
Type: Two-Year College **Sex:** Coed **Affiliation:** Foothill-DeAnza Community College District **% Accepted:** 100 **Admission Plans:** Open Admission **Application Deadline:** September 15 **H.S. Requirements:** High school diploma or equivalent not required **Scholarships:** Available **Calendar System:** Quarter, Summer Session Available **Enrollment:** FT 3,728, PT 14,614 **Faculty:** FT 201, PT 432 **Student-Faculty Ratio:** 34:1 **Library Holdings:** 70,000 **Regional Accreditation:** Western Association of Schools and Colleges **Credit Hours For Degree:** 90 quarter hours, Associates **ROTC:** Army, Air Force **Professional Accreditation:** ADA, CARC, JRCERT **Intercollegiate Athletics:** Basketball M & W; Football M; Golf M & W; Soccer M & W; Softball W; Swimming and Diving M & W; Tennis M; Volleyball W; Water Polo M & W

FRESNO CITY COLLEGE
1101 East University Ave.
Fresno, CA 93741-0002
Tel: (559)442-4600
Web Site: http://www.fresnocitycollege.edu/
President/CEO: Dr. Cynthia Azari
Admissions: Stephanie Pauhi
Financial Aid: Frank Ramon
Type: Two-Year College **Sex:** Coed **Affiliation:** California Community College System **% Accepted:** 100 **Admission Plans:** Open Admission; Early Admission; Deferred Admission **Application Deadline:** Rolling **Application Fee:** $0.00 **H.S. Requirements:** High school diploma or equivalent not required. For applicants under 18: High school diploma required; GED accepted **Costs Per Year:** Application fee: $0. State resident tuition: $0 full-time. Nonresident tuition: $4560 full-time, $190 per unit part-time. Mandatory fees: $658 full-time, $26 per unit part-time. Full-time tuition and fees vary according to course load. Part-time tuition and fees vary according to course load. **Scholarships:** Available **Calendar System:** Semester, Summer Session Available **Faculty:** FT 276, PT 1,200 **Student-Faculty Ratio:** 16:1 **Library Holdings:** 67,500 **Regional Accreditation:** Western Association of Schools and Colleges **Credit Hours For Degree:** 60 units, Associates **ROTC:** Army, Air Force **Professional Accreditation:** ADA, AHIMA, CARC, JRCERT **Intercollegiate Athletics:** Baseball M; Basketball M & W; Cross-Country Running M & W; Football M; Golf M & W; Soccer M & W; Softball W; Tennis M & W; Track and Field M & W; Volleyball W; Wrestling M

FRESNO PACIFIC UNIVERSITY
1717 South Chestnut Ave.
Fresno, CA 93702-4709
Tel: (559)453-2000
Admissions: 800-660-6089
Fax: (559)453-2007
E-mail: ugadmis@fresno.edu
Web Site: http://www.fresno.edu/
President/CEO: Dr. D. Merrill Ewert
Financial Aid: April Powell
Type: Comprehensive **Sex:** Coed **Affiliation:** Mennonite Brethren Church **Scores:** 81% SAT V 400+; 90% SAT M 400+; 46% ACT 18-23; 22% ACT 24-29 **% Accepted:** 68 **Admission Plans:** Early Admission; Deferred Admission **Application Deadline:** Rolling **Application Fee:** $40.00 **H.S.**

Requirements: High school diploma required; GED accepted **Scholarships:** Available **Calendar System:** Semester, Summer Session Available **Enrollment:** FT 1,311, PT 228 **Faculty:** FT 93, PT 262 **Student-Faculty Ratio:** 11:1 **Exams:** SAT I and SAT II or ACT. **% Receiving Financial Aid:** 82 **% Residing in College-Owned, -Operated, or -Affiliated Housing:** 49 **Library Holdings:** 196,000 **Regional Accreditation:** Western Association of Schools and Colleges **Credit Hours For Degree:** 60 units, Associates; 124 units, Bachelors **Intercollegiate Athletics:** Baseball M; Basketball M & W; Cheerleading W; Cross-Country Running M & W; Soccer M & W; Swimming and Diving M & W; Tennis M & W; Track and Field M & W; Volleyball M & W; Water Polo M & W

FULLERTON COLLEGE
321 East Chapman Ave.
Fullerton, CA 92832-2095
Tel: (714)992-7000
Web Site: http://www.fullcoll.edu/
President/CEO: Kathleen O'Connell Hodge, EdD
Admissions: Peter Fong
Type: Two-Year College **Sex:** Coed **Affiliation:** California Community College System **Admission Plans:** Open Admission; Early Admission **Application Deadline:** Rolling **H.S. Requirements:** High school diploma or equivalent not required **Scholarships:** Available **Calendar System:** Semester, Summer Session Available **Faculty:** FT 324, PT 511 **Library Holdings:** 113,236 **Regional Accreditation:** Western Association of Schools and Colleges **Credit Hours For Degree:** 60 semester hours, Associates **ROTC:** Army, Navy, Air Force **Intercollegiate Athletics:** Basketball M & W; Cross-Country Running M & W; Football M; Golf M & W; Soccer M; Swimming and Diving M & W; Tennis M & W; Track and Field M & W; Volleyball W; Water Polo M

GAVILAN COLLEGE
5055 Santa Teresa Blvd.
Gilroy, CA 95020-9599
Tel: (408)847-1400
Admissions: (408)848-4800
Fax: (408)848-4801
Web Site: http://www.gavilan.edu/
President/CEO: Steve Kinsella
Admissions: Joy Parker
Type: Two-Year College **Sex:** Coed **Affiliation:** California Community College System **Admission Plans:** Open Admission **Application Deadline:** Rolling **Application Fee:** $0.00 **H.S. Requirements:** High school diploma required; GED accepted. For applicants 18 or over: High school diploma or equivalent not required **Costs Per Year:** Application fee: $0. State resident tuition: $0 full-time. Nonresident tuition: $5280 full-time, $220 per unit part-time. Mandatory fees: $708 full-time, $26 per unit part-time, $42 per term part-time. Full-time tuition and fees vary according to course load and program. Part-time tuition and fees vary according to course load and program. **Scholarships:** Available **Calendar System:** Semester, Summer Session Available **Enrollment:** FT 1,212, PT 4,852 **Faculty:** FT 74, PT 90 **Library Holdings:** 55,440 **Regional Accreditation:** Western Association of Schools and Colleges **Credit Hours For Degree:** 60 units, Associates **Intercollegiate Athletics:** Basketball M & W; Football M; Golf M; Soccer M & W; Softball W; Tennis M; Volleyball W

GLENDALE COMMUNITY COLLEGE
1500 North Verdugo Rd.
Glendale, CA 91208-2894
Tel: (818)240-1000
Fax: (818)549-9436
E-mail: scombs@glendale.edu
Web Site: http://www.glendale.edu/
President/CEO: Dawn Lindsay
Admissions: Sharon Combs
Type: Two-Year College **Sex:** Coed **Affiliation:** California Community College System **% Accepted:** 52 **Admission Plans:** Open Admission; Early Admission; Deferred Admission **Application Deadline:** Rolling **Application Fee:** $0.00 **H.S. Requirements:** High school diploma required; GED accepted. For applicants 18 or over: High school diploma or equivalent not required **Scholarships:** Available **Calendar System:** Semester, Summer Session Available **Enrollment:** FT 4,730, PT 9,535 **Faculty:** FT 249, PT 605 **Library Holdings:** 91,371 **Regional Accreditation:** Western Association of Schools and Colleges **Credit Hours For Degree:** 60 units, Associates **Intercollegiate Athletics:** Baseball M; Basketball M & W; Cross-Country Running M & W; Football M; Soccer M & W; Softball W; Tennis M & W; Track and Field M & W; Volleyball W

GOLDEN GATE UNIVERSITY
536 Mission St.
San Francisco, CA 94105-2968
Tel: (415)442-7000; Free: 800-448-3381
Admissions: (415)442-7800
Fax: (415)442-7807
E-mail: info@ggu.edu
Web Site: http://www.ggu.edu/
President/CEO: Dan Angel
Admissions: Louis D. Riccardi, Jr.
Financial Aid: Ken Walsh
Type: University **Sex:** Coed **Admission Plans:** Deferred Admission **Application Deadline:** Rolling **Application Fee:** $55.00 **H.S. Requirements:** High school diploma required; GED accepted **Costs Per Year:** Application fee: $55. Tuition: $15,120 full-time, $1680 per course part-time. Full-time tuition varies according to course load, degree level, and program. Part-time tuition varies according to course load and program. **Scholarships:** Available **Calendar System:** Trimester, Summer Session Available **Enrollment:** FT 67, PT 347 **Faculty:** FT 30, PT 459 **Student-Faculty Ratio:** 16:1 **% Receiving Financial Aid:** 66 **Library Holdings:** 79,204 **Regional Accreditation:** Western Association of Schools and Colleges **Credit Hours For Degree:** 123 units, Bachelors **Professional Accreditation:** ABA, AALS

GOLDEN WEST COLLEGE
PO Box 2748, 15744 Golden West St.
Huntington Beach, CA 92647-2748
Tel: (714)892-7711
Web Site: http://www.goldenwestcollege.edu/
President/CEO: Wes Bryan
Admissions: Shirley Donnelly
Type: Two-Year College **Sex:** Coed **Affiliation:** Coast Community College District System **Admission Plans:** Open Admission; Early Admission **Application Deadline:** Rolling **Application Fee:** $0.00 **H.S. Requirements:** High school diploma required; GED accepted. For applicants 18 or over: High school diploma required; GED not accepted **Costs Per Year:** Application fee: $0. State resident tuition: $0 full-time. Nonresident tuition: $4940 full-time, $190 per unit part-time. Mandatory fees: $800 full-time, $26 per unit part-time, $30 per term part-time. **Scholarships:** Available **Calendar System:** Semester, Summer Session Available **Enrollment:** FT 4,291, PT 8,935 **Faculty:** FT 164, PT 246 **Student-Faculty Ratio:** 34:1 **Final Year or Final Semester Residency Requirement:** No **Library Holdings:** 95,000 **Regional Accreditation:** Western Association of Schools and Colleges **Credit Hours For Degree:** 60 units, Associates **ROTC:** Air Force **Professional Accreditation:** NLN **Intercollegiate Athletics:** Baseball M; Cross-Country Running M & W; Football M; Soccer M & W; Softball W; Swimming and Diving M & W; Track and Field M & W; Volleyball M & W; Water Polo M & W

GROSSMONT COLLEGE
8800 Grossmont College Dr.
El Cajon, CA 92020-1799
Tel: (619)644-7000
Fax: (619)644-7922
Web Site: http://www.grossmont.edu/
President/CEO: Sunita V. Cooke
Admissions: Sharon Clark
Type: Two-Year College **Sex:** Coed **Affiliation:** California Community College System **Admission Plans:** Open Admission; Early Admission **Application Deadline:** August 12 **Application Fee:** $0.00 **H.S. Requirements:** High school diploma or equivalent not required. For applicants under 18: High school diploma required; GED accepted **Scholarships:** Available **Calendar System:** Semester, Summer Session Available **Faculty:** FT 220, PT 574 **Student-Faculty Ratio:** 17:1 **Library Holdings:** 105,000 **Regional Accreditation:** Western Association of Schools and Colleges **Credit Hours For Degree:** 60 units, Associates **ROTC:** Army, Air Force **Professional Accreditation:** AOTA, CARC, JRCECT, NLN **Intercollegiate Athletics:** Baseball M; Basketball M & W; Cross-Country Running M; Football M; Golf M; Soccer W; Softball W; Swimming and Diving M & W; Tennis M & W; Track and Field M; Volleyball M & W; Water Polo M & W

HARTNELL COLLEGE
156 Homestead Ave.
Salinas, CA 93901-1697
Tel: (831)755-6700
Web Site: http://www.hartnell.edu/
President/CEO: Phoebe K. Helm
Admissions: Mary Dominguez
Type: Two-Year College **Sex:** Coed **Affiliation:** California Community College System **Admission Plans:** Open Admission; Early Admission; Deferred Admission **Application Deadline:** Rolling **Application Fee:** $0.00 **H.S. Requirements:** High school diploma required; GED accepted **Costs Per Year:** Application fee: $0. State resident tuition: $0 full-time. Nonresident tuition: $4632 full-time, $193 per unit part-time. Mandatory fees: $632 full-time, $26 per unit part-time, $4 per term part-time. **Scholarships:** Available **Calendar System:** Semester, Summer Session Available **Faculty:** FT 105, PT 273 **Library Holdings:** 70,000 **Regional Accreditation:** Western Association of Schools and Colleges **Credit Hours For Degree:** 60 semester hours, Associates **Professional Accreditation:** NAACLS **Intercollegiate Athletics:** Baseball M; Basketball M & W; Cross-Country Running M & W; Football M; Golf M; Soccer M & W; Softball W; Swimming and Diving M & W; Tennis M & W; Track and Field M & W; Volleyball W; Water Polo M

HARVEY MUDD COLLEGE
301 Platt Blvd.
Claremont, CA 91711-5994
Tel: (909)621-8000
Admissions: (909)621-8011
Fax: (909)621-8360
E-mail: admission@hmc.edu
Web Site: http://www.hmc.edu/
President/CEO: Maria Klawe
Admissions: Peter Osgood
Financial Aid: Gilma Lopez
Type: Four-Year College **Sex:** Coed **Affiliation:** The Claremont Colleges Consortium **Scores:** 100% SAT V 400+; 100% SAT M 400+; 1% ACT 24-29 **% Accepted:** 34 **Admission Plans:** Early Admission; Early Decision Plan; Deferred Admission **Application Deadline:** January 2 **Application Fee:** $60.00 **H.S. Requirements:** High school diploma or equivalent not required **Costs Per Year:** Application fee: $60. Comprehensive fee: $53,588 includes full-time tuition ($40,133), mandatory fees ($257), and college room and board ($13,198). College room only: $6935. Room and board charges vary according to board plan. Part-time tuition: $1194 per credit hour. **Scholarships:** Available **Calendar System:** Semester, Summer Session Not available **Enrollment:** FT 756, PT 1 **Student-Faculty Ratio:** 8:1 **Exams:** Other, SAT I or ACT, SAT II. ACT essay used for admission. SAT essay used for admission. **% Receiving Financial Aid:** 54 **% Residing in College-Owned, -Operated, or -Affiliated Housing:** 99 **Library Holdings:** 3,203,500 **Regional Accreditation:** Western Association of Schools and Colleges **Credit Hours For Degree:** 128 credit hours, Bachelors **ROTC:** Army, Air Force **Professional Accreditation:** ABET **Intercollegiate Athletics:** Baseball M; Basketball M & W; Cross-Country Running M & W; Football M; Golf M; Lacrosse W; Soccer M & W; Softball W; Swimming and Diving M & W; Tennis M & W; Track and Field M & W; Volleyball W; Water Polo M & W

HEALD COLLEGE—CONCORD
5130 Commercial Circle
Concord, CA 94520
Tel: (925)288-5800
Fax: (925)288-5896
E-mail: kwoodman@heald.edu
Web Site: http://www.heald.edu/
Admissions: Keith Woodman
Type: Two-Year College **Sex:** Coed **Admission Plans:** Open Admission; Early Admission; Deferred Admission **Application Deadline:** Rolling **Application Fee:** $40.00 **H.S. Requirements:** High school diploma required; GED accepted **Calendar System:** Quarter, Summer Session Available **Enrollment:** FT 524, PT 115 **Faculty:** FT 25, PT 19 **Student-Faculty Ratio:** 18:1 **Exams:** Other. **Regional Accreditation:** Western Association of Schools and Colleges

HEALD COLLEGE—FRESNO
255 West Bullard Ave.
Fresno, CA 93704-1706
Tel: (559)438-4222
Admissions: (209)438-4222
E-mail: tmathis@heald.edu
Web Site: http://www.heald.edu/
President/CEO: Carolyn Kovalski
Admissions: Tina Mathis
Type: Two-Year College **Sex:** Coed **Admission Plans:** Open Admission; Early Admission; Deferred Admission **Application Deadline:** Rolling **Application Fee:** $40.00 **H.S. Requirements:** High school diploma required; GED accepted **Scholarships:** Available **Calendar System:** Quarter, Summer Session Available **Enrollment:** FT 547, PT 182 **Faculty:** FT 26, PT 12 **Student-Faculty Ratio:** 20:1 **Exams:** Other. **Regional Accreditation:** Western Association of Schools and Colleges

HEALD COLLEGE—HAYWARD
25500 Industrial Blvd.
Hayward, CA 94545
Tel: (510)783-2100
Fax: (510)783-3287
E-mail: bgordon@heald.edu
Web Site: http://www.heald.edu/
President/CEO: Nick Davis
Admissions: Barbara Gordon
Type: Two-Year College **Sex:** Coed **Admission Plans:** Open Admission; Early Admission; Deferred Admission **Application Deadline:** Rolling **Application Fee:** $40.00 **H.S. Requirements:** High school diploma required; GED accepted **Scholarships:** Available **Calendar System:** Quarter, Summer Session Available **Enrollment:** FT 637, PT 227 **Faculty:** FT 23, PT 13 **Student-Faculty Ratio:** 26:1 **Exams:** Other. **Regional Accreditation:** Western Association of Schools and Colleges

HEALD COLLEGE—RANCHO CORDOVA
2910 Prospect Park Dr.
Rancho Cordova, CA 95670-6005
Tel: (916)638-1616
Admissions: (916)414-2700
Fax: (916)853-8282
E-mail: info@heald.edu
Web Site: http://www.heald.edu/
President/CEO: Ada Gerard
Type: Two-Year College **Sex:** Coed **Admission Plans:** Open Admission; Early Admission; Deferred Admission **Application Deadline:** Rolling **Application Fee:** $40.00 **H.S. Requirements:** High school diploma required; GED accepted **Scholarships:** Available **Calendar System:** Quarter, Summer Session Available **Enrollment:** FT 349, PT 122 **Faculty:** FT 19, PT 3 **Student-Faculty Ratio:** 20:1 **Exams:** Other. **Regional Accreditation:** Western Association of Schools and Colleges

HEALD COLLEGE—ROSEVILLE
Seven Sierra Gate Plaza
Roseville, CA 95678
Tel: (916)789-8600
E-mail: kculpepp@heald.edu
Web Site: http://www.heald.edu/
President/CEO: Guy R. Adams
Admissions: Kristi Culpepper
Type: Two-Year College **Sex:** Coed **Admission Plans:** Early Admission; Deferred Admission **Application Fee:** $40.00 **H.S. Requirements:** High school diploma required; GED accepted **Scholarships:** Available **Calendar System:** Quarter, Summer Session Available **Enrollment:** FT 376, PT 152 **Faculty:** FT 21, PT 2 **Student-Faculty Ratio:** 19:1 **Exams:** Other. **Regional Accreditation:** Western Association of Schools and Colleges

HEALD COLLEGE—SALINAS
1450 North Main St.
Salinas, CA 93906
Tel: (831)443-1700
Fax: (831)443-1050
E-mail: jferguso@heald.edu
Web Site: http://www.heald.edu/
President/CEO: Maria Embry
Admissions: Jason Ferguson
Type: Two-Year College **Sex:** Coed **Admission Plans:** Open Admission; Early Admission; Deferred Admission **Application Deadline:** Rolling **Application Fee:** $40.00 **H.S. Requirements:** High school diploma required;

GED accepted **Calendar System:** Quarter, Summer Session Available **Enrollment:** FT 329, PT 85 **Faculty:** FT 14, PT 4 **Student-Faculty Ratio:** 24:1 **Exams:** Other. **Regional Accreditation:** Western Association of Schools and Colleges

HEALD COLLEGE—SAN FRANCISCO
350 Mission St.
San Francisco, CA 94105-2206
Tel: (415)808-3000
Fax: (415)808-3003
E-mail: jennifer_dunckel@heald.edu
Web Site: http://www.heald.edu/
President/CEO: Daniel Waterman
Admissions: Jennifer Dunckel
Type: Two-Year College **Sex:** Coed **Admission Plans:** Open Admission; Early Admission; Deferred Admission **Application Deadline:** Rolling **Application Fee:** $40.00 **H.S. Requirements:** High school diploma required; GED accepted **Calendar System:** Quarter, Summer Session Available **Enrollment:** FT 273, PT 116 **Faculty:** FT 18, PT 6 **Student-Faculty Ratio:** 16:1 **Exams:** Other. **Regional Accreditation:** Western Association of Schools and Colleges

HEALD COLLEGE—SAN JOSE
341 Great Mall Parkway
Milpitas, CA 95035
Tel: (408)934-4900
Fax: (408)934-7777
E-mail: chardima@heald.edu
Web Site: http://www.heald.edu/
President/CEO: John Luotto
Admissions: Clarence Hardiman
Type: Two-Year College **Sex:** Coed **Admission Plans:** Open Admission; Early Admission; Deferred Admission **Application Deadline:** Rolling **Application Fee:** $40.00 **H.S. Requirements:** High school diploma required; GED accepted **Scholarships:** Available **Calendar System:** Quarter, Summer Session Available **Enrollment:** FT 502, PT 137 **Faculty:** FT 25, PT 7 **Student-Faculty Ratio:** 20:1 **Exams:** Other. **Regional Accreditation:** Western Association of Schools and Colleges

HEALD COLLEGE—STOCKTON
1605 East March Ln.
Stockton, CA 95210
Tel: (209)473-5200
Fax: (209)477-2739
E-mail: info@heald.edu
Web Site: http://www.heald.edu/
President/CEO: Bob Nodolf
Type: Two-Year College **Sex:** Coed **Admission Plans:** Open Admission; Early Admission; Deferred Admission **Application Deadline:** Rolling **Application Fee:** $40.00 **H.S. Requirements:** High school diploma required; GED accepted **Calendar System:** Quarter, Summer Session Available **Enrollment:** FT 398, PT 132 **Faculty:** FT 20, PT 17 **Student-Faculty Ratio:** 17:1 **Exams:** Other. **Regional Accreditation:** Western Association of Schools and Colleges

HENLEY-PUTNAM UNIVERSITY
25 Metro Dr.
Ste. 500
San Jose, CA 95110
Tel: (408)453-9900
Fax: (408)453-9700
Web Site: http://www.henley-putnam.edu/
Type: Comprehensive **Sex:** Coed **Professional Accreditation:** DETC

HIGH-TECH INSTITUTE
9738 Lincoln Village Dr.
Ste. 100
Sacramento, CA 95827
Tel: (916)929-9700; Free: 800-322-4128
Fax: (916)929-9703
Web Site: http://www.high-techinstitute.com/
President/CEO: Gordon Kent
Type: Two-Year College **Sex:** Coed **Application Fee:** $50.00 **Professional Accreditation:** ACCSCT

HOLY NAMES UNIVERSITY
3500 Mountain Blvd.
Oakland, CA 94619-1699
Tel: (510)436-1000; Free: 800-430-1321
Admissions: (510)436-1430
Fax: (510)436-1325
E-mail: admissions@hnu.edu
Web Site: http://www.hnu.edu/
President/CEO: Dr. Rosemarie T. Nassif, SSND
Admissions: Murad Dibbini
Financial Aid: Christina Miller
Type: Comprehensive **Sex:** Coed **Affiliation:** Roman Catholic **% Accepted:** 68 **Admission Plans:** Deferred Admission **Application Deadline:** August 15 **Application Fee:** $20.00 **H.S. Requirements:** High school diploma required; GED accepted **Costs Per Year:** Application fee: $20. One-time mandatory fee: $340. Comprehensive fee: $36,660 includes full-time tuition ($27,000), mandatory fees ($340), and college room and board ($9320). College room only: $4880. Full-time tuition and fees vary according to course load. Room and board charges vary according to board plan and housing facility. Part-time tuition: $905 per term. Part-time mandatory fees: $170 per term. Part-time tuition and fees vary according to course load. **Scholarships:** Available **Calendar System:** Semester, Summer Session Available **Enrollment:** FT 536, PT 157, Grad FT 99, Grad PT 343 **Faculty:** FT 37, PT 126 **Student-Faculty Ratio:** 16:1 **Exams:** SAT I or ACT. **% Receiving Financial Aid:** 41 **% Residing in College-Owned, -Operated, or -Affiliated Housing:** 47 **Library Holdings:** 117,760 **Regional Accreditation:** Western Association of Schools and Colleges **Credit Hours For Degree:** 120 units, Bachelors **ROTC:** Army, Air Force **Professional Accreditation:** AACN, NLN **Intercollegiate Athletics:** Basketball M & W; Cross-Country Running M & W; Golf M; Soccer M & W; Softball W; Volleyball M & W

HOPE INTERNATIONAL UNIVERSITY
2500 East Nutwood Ave.
Fullerton, CA 92831-3138
Tel: (714)879-3901; Free: 800-762-1294
Fax: (714)526-0231
E-mail: mfmadden@hiu.edu
Web Site: http://www.hiu.edu/
President/CEO: Dr. John Derry
Admissions: Midge Madden
Financial Aid: Shannon O'Shields
Type: Comprehensive **Sex:** Coed **Affiliation:** Christian Churches and Churches of Christ **Scores:** 86.7% SAT V 400+; 90.7% SAT M 400+; 50% ACT 18-23; 27.3% ACT 24-29 **% Accepted:** 80 **Admission Plans:** Early Admission; Early Action; Early Decision Plan; Deferred Admission **Application Deadline:** May 1 **Application Fee:** $40.00 **H.S. Requirements:** High school diploma required; GED accepted **Costs Per Year:** Application fee: $40. One-time mandatory fee: $300. Comprehensive fee: $30,965 includes full-time tuition ($22,220), mandatory fees ($1345), and college room and board ($7400). College room only: $4300. Full-time tuition and fees vary according to course load, location, and program. Room and board charges vary according to board plan and student level. Part-time tuition: $825 per unit. Part-time mandatory fees: $825 per unit. Part-time tuition and fees vary according to course load, location, and program. **Scholarships:** Available **Calendar System:** 4-1-4, Summer Session Available **Enrollment:** FT 592, PT 202 **Faculty:** FT 39, PT 81 **Student-Faculty Ratio:** 10:1 **Exams:** SAT I or ACT, SAT I. **% Receiving Financial Aid:** 37 **Library Holdings:** 94,646 **Regional Accreditation:** Western Association of Schools and Colleges **Credit Hours For Degree:** 62 units, Associates; 124 units, Bachelors **Intercollegiate Athletics:** Basketball M & W; Cheerleading M & W; Soccer M & W; Softball W; Tennis M & W; Ultimate Frisbee M & W; Volleyball M & W

HUMBOLDT STATE UNIVERSITY
1 Harpst St.
Arcata, CA 95521-8299
Tel: (707)826-3011
Admissions: (707)826-4402
Fax: (707)826-6194
E-mail: hsuinfo@humboldt.edu
Web Site: http://www.humboldt.edu/
President/CEO: Dr. Rollin C. Richmond
Admissions: Rebecca Kalal
Financial Aid: Kim Coughlin-Lamphear

Type: Comprehensive **Sex:** Coed **Affiliation:** California State University System **Scores:** 94% SAT V 400+; 91% SAT M 400+; 41% ACT 18-23; 30% ACT 24-29 **% Accepted:** 84 **Admission Plans:** Preferred Admission **Application Deadline:** November 30 **Application Fee:** $55.00 **H.S. Requirements:** High school diploma required; GED accepted **Costs Per Year:** Application fee: $55. State resident tuition: $0 full-time. Nonresident tuition: $14,094 full-time, $372 per unit part-time. Mandatory fees: $5166 full-time, $247 per unit part-time. Full-time tuition and fees vary according to degree level. Part-time tuition and fees vary according to course load and degree level. College room and board: $9510. Room and board charges vary according to board plan and housing facility. **Scholarships:** Available **Calendar System:** Semester, Summer Session Available **Enrollment:** FT 6,536, PT 633, Grad FT 562, Grad PT 223 **Faculty:** FT 254, PT 254 **Student-Faculty Ratio:** 22:1 **Exams:** SAT I or ACT. ACT essay not being used. SAT essay not being used. **% Receiving Financial Aid:** 59 **% Residing in College-Owned, -Operated, or -Affiliated Housing:** 23 **Final Year or Final Semester Residency Requirement:** No **Library Holdings:** 2,024,665 **Regional Accreditation:** Western Association of Schools and Colleges **Credit Hours For Degree:** 124 semester units, Bachelors **Professional Accreditation:** ABET, AACN, CSWE, NASAD, NASM, NAST, SAF **Intercollegiate Athletics:** Basketball M & W; Cheerleading W; Crew M & W; Cross-Country Running M & W; Football M; Lacrosse M; Soccer M & W; Softball W; Track and Field M & W; Volleyball W

HUMPHREYS COLLEGE
6650 Inglewood Ave.
Stockton, CA 95207-3896
Tel: (209)478-0800
Fax: (209)478-8721
E-mail: ugadmission@humphreys.edu
Web Site: http://www.humphreys.edu/
President/CEO: Robert Humphreys
Financial Aid: Rita Franco
Type: Comprehensive **Sex:** Coed **Admission Plans:** Open Admission; Early Admission; Deferred Admission **Application Deadline:** Rolling **Application Fee:** $35.00 **H.S. Requirements:** High school diploma required; GED accepted **Scholarships:** Available **Calendar System:** Quarter, Summer Session Available **Library Holdings:** 20,500 **Regional Accreditation:** Western Association of Schools and Colleges **Credit Hours For Degree:** 90 units, Associates; 180 units, Bachelors

IMPERIAL VALLEY COLLEGE
380 East Aten Rd.
PO Box 158
Imperial, CA 92251-0158
Tel: (760)352-8320
Web Site: http://www.imperial.edu/
President/CEO: Ed Gould
Admissions: Dawn Chun
Financial Aid: Janis L. Magno
Type: Two-Year College **Sex:** Coed **Affiliation:** California Community College System **Admission Plans:** Open Admission **Application Deadline:** Rolling **Application Fee:** $23.00 **H.S. Requirements:** High school diploma or equivalent not required **Scholarships:** Available **Calendar System:** Semester, Summer Session Available **Library Holdings:** 55,875 **Regional Accreditation:** Western Association of Schools and Colleges **Credit Hours For Degree:** 60 units, Associates **Intercollegiate Athletics:** Baseball M; Basketball M & W; Soccer M & W; Softball W; Tennis M & W

INTERIOR DESIGNERS INSTITUTE
1061 Camelback Rd.
Newport Beach, CA 92660
Tel: (949)675-4451
Fax: (949)759-0667
E-mail: contact@idi.edu
Web Site: http://www.idi.edu/
President/CEO: Judy Deaton
Type: Comprehensive **Sex:** Coed **Application Fee:** $95.00 **H.S. Requirements:** High school diploma required; GED accepted **Professional Accreditation:** ACCSCT, FIDER

INTERNATIONAL TECHNOLOGICAL UNIVERSITY
1650 Warburton Ave.
Santa Clara, CA 95050
Tel: (408)556-9010
Admissions: (408)331-1014
Fax: (408)556-9016
E-mail: mpai@itu.edu
Web Site: http://www.itu.edu/
President/CEO: Dr. Shu-Park Chan
Admissions: Manisha Pai
Type: Comprehensive **Sex:** Coed **Admission Plans:** Open Admission **Application Fee:** $80.00 **H.S. Requirements:** High school diploma required; GED accepted **Costs Per Year:** Application fee: $80. Tuition: $275 per unit part-time. **Calendar System:** Trimester **Credit Hours For Degree:** 60 per semester, Bachelors **Professional Accreditation:** ACICS

IRVINE VALLEY COLLEGE
5500 Irvine Center Dr.
Irvine, CA 92618
Tel: (949)451-5100
Fax: (949)559-3443
Web Site: http://www.ivc.edu/
President/CEO: Glenn R. Roquemore, PhD
Admissions: John Edwards
Type: Two-Year College **Sex:** Coed **Affiliation:** Saddleback Community College District **Admission Plans:** Open Admission; Early Admission **Application Deadline:** Rolling **Application Fee:** $0.00 **H.S. Requirements:** High school diploma or equivalent not required **Costs Per Year:** Application fee: $0. State resident tuition: $0 full-time. Nonresident tuition: $4560 full-time, $190 per unit part-time. Mandatory fees: $658 full-time, $26 per unit part-time, $17 per term part-time. Full-time tuition and fees vary according to course load. Part-time tuition and fees vary according to course load. **Scholarships:** Available **Calendar System:** Semester, Summer Session Available **Faculty:** FT 94, PT 250 **Library Holdings:** 24,000 **Regional Accreditation:** Western Association of Schools and Colleges **Credit Hours For Degree:** 60 units, Associates **Intercollegiate Athletics:** Basketball M & W; Cross-Country Running M & W; Soccer M & W; Tennis M & W; Volleyball M

ITT TECHNICAL INSTITUTE (ANAHEIM)
525 North Muller St.
Anaheim, CA 92801-9938
Tel: (714)535-3700
Web Site: http://www.itt-tech.edu/
President/CEO: Sam Russell
Type: Two-Year College **Sex:** Coed **Affiliation:** ITT Educational Services, Inc. **H.S. Requirements:** High school diploma required; GED accepted **Scholarships:** Available **Calendar System:** Quarter, Summer Session Not available **Credit Hours For Degree:** 96 credit hours, Associates; 180 credit hours, Bachelors **Professional Accreditation:** ACICS

ITT TECHNICAL INSTITUTE (CLOVIS)
362 N. Clovis Ave.
Clovis, CA 93612
Tel: (559)325-5400
Web Site: http://www.itt-tech.edu/
President/CEO: Michael McClenic
Type: Four-Year College **Sex:** Coed **Affiliation:** ITT Educational Services, Inc. **Calendar System:** Quarter

ITT TECHNICAL INSTITUTE (CONCORD)
1140 Galaxy Way
Ste. 400
Concord, CA 94520
Tel: (925)674-8200; Free: 800-211-7062
Web Site: http://www.itt-tech.edu/
President/CEO: Kristina Lopez
Type: Four-Year College **Sex:** Coed **Affiliation:** ITT Educational Services, Inc. **Calendar System:** Quarter **Professional Accreditation:** ACICS

ITT TECHNICAL INSTITUTE (CORONA)
4160 Temescal Canyon Rd.
Ste. 100
Corona, CA 92883
Tel: (951)277-5400; Free: 877-764-9661
Web Site: http://www.itt-tech.edu/
Type: Four-Year College **Sex:** Coed **Professional Accreditation:** ACICS

ITT TECHNICAL INSTITUTE (LATHROP)
16916 South Harlan Rd.
Lathrop, CA 95330
Tel: (209)858-0077
Web Site: http://www.itt-tech.edu/
President/CEO: Jason Halasa
Type: Two-Year College **Sex:** Coed **Affiliation:** ITT Educational Services, Inc. **H.S. Requirements:** High school diploma required; GED accepted **Scholarships:** Available **Calendar System:** Quarter, Summer Session Not available **Credit Hours For Degree:** 96 credit hours, Associates; 180 credit hours, Bachelors **Professional Accreditation:** ACICS

ITT TECHNICAL INSTITUTE (OXNARD)
2051 Solar Dr., Ste. 150
Oxnard, CA 93036
Tel: (805)988-0143
Fax: (805)988-1813
Web Site: http://www.itt-tech.edu/
President/CEO: Lorraine Bunt
Type: Two-Year College **Sex:** Coed **Affiliation:** ITT Educational Services, Inc. **H.S. Requirements:** High school diploma required; GED accepted **Scholarships:** Available **Calendar System:** Quarter, Summer Session Not available **Professional Accreditation:** ACICS

ITT TECHNICAL INSTITUTE (RANCHO CORDOVA)
10863 Gold Center Dr.
Rancho Cordova, CA 95670-6034
Tel: (916)851-3900; Free: 800-488-8466
Fax: (916)366-9225
Web Site: http://www.itt-tech.edu/
President/CEO: Jeff Wilkinson
Type: Two-Year College **Sex:** Coed **Affiliation:** ITT Educational Services, Inc. **H.S. Requirements:** High school diploma required; GED accepted **Scholarships:** Available **Calendar System:** Quarter, Summer Session Not available **Professional Accreditation:** ACICS

ITT TECHNICAL INSTITUTE (SAN BERNARDINO)
670 East Carnegie Dr.
San Bernardino, CA 92408
Tel: (909)806-4600
Fax: (909)888-6970
Web Site: http://www.itt-tech.edu/
President/CEO: Terrell W. Lorenz
Type: Two-Year College **Sex:** Coed **Affiliation:** ITT Educational Services, Inc. **H.S. Requirements:** High school diploma required; GED accepted **Scholarships:** Available **Calendar System:** Quarter, Summer Session Not available **Professional Accreditation:** ACICS

ITT TECHNICAL INSTITUTE (SAN DIEGO)
9680 Granite Ridge Dr.
San Diego, CA 92123
Tel: (858)571-8500
Fax: (858)571-1277
Web Site: http://www.itt-tech.edu/
President/CEO: Jackie Parma
Type: Two-Year College **Sex:** Coed **Affiliation:** ITT Educational Services, Inc. **H.S. Requirements:** High school diploma required; GED accepted **Scholarships:** Available **Calendar System:** Quarter, Summer Session Not available **Credit Hours For Degree:** 96 credit hours, Associates; 180 credit hours, Bachelors **Professional Accreditation:** ACICS

ITT TECHNICAL INSTITUTE (SAN DIMAS)
650 West Cienega Ave.
San Dimas, CA 91773
Tel: (909)971-2300
Web Site: http://www.itt-tech.edu/
President/CEO: Maria Alamat
Type: Two-Year College **Sex:** Coed **Affiliation:** ITT Educational Services, Inc. **H.S. Requirements:** High school diploma required; GED accepted **Scholarships:** Available **Calendar System:** Quarter, Summer Session Not available **Credit Hours For Degree:** 96 credit hours, Associates; 180 credit hours, Bachelors **Professional Accreditation:** ACICS

ITT TECHNICAL INSTITUTE (SYLMAR)
12669 Encinitas Ave.
Sylmar, CA 91342-3664
Tel: (818)364-5151
Web Site: http://www.itt-tech.edu/
President/CEO: Dana Martin
Type: Two-Year College **Sex:** Coed **Affiliation:** ITT Educational Services, Inc. **H.S. Requirements:** High school diploma required; GED accepted **Scholarships:** Available **Calendar System:** Quarter, Summer Session Not available **Professional Accreditation:** ACICS

ITT TECHNICAL INSTITUTE (TORRANCE)
20050 South Vermont Ave.
Torrance, CA 90502
Tel: (310)380-1555
Fax: (310)380-1557
Web Site: http://www.itt-tech.edu/
President/CEO: Arnulfo Runas
Type: Two-Year College **Sex:** Coed **Affiliation:** ITT Educational Services, Inc. **H.S. Requirements:** High school diploma required; GED accepted **Scholarships:** Available **Calendar System:** Quarter, Summer Session Not available **Professional Accreditation:** ACICS

JOHN F. KENNEDY UNIVERSITY
100 Ellinwood Way
Pleasant Hill, CA 94523-4817
Tel: (925)969-3300; Free: 800-696-JFKU
Admissions: (925)969-3584
Fax: (925)254-6964
E-mail: jmhogg@jfku.edu
Web Site: http://www.jfku.edu/
President/CEO: Dr. Steven Stargardter
Admissions: Jen Miller-Hogg
Financial Aid: Mindy Bergeron
Type: Two-Year Upper Division **Sex:** Coed **Affiliation:** National University System **Admission Plans:** Open Admission; Deferred Admission **Application Fee:** $60.00 **H.S. Requirements:** High school diploma required; GED accepted **Scholarships:** Available **Calendar System:** Quarter, Summer Session Available **Enrollment:** FT 54, PT 233 **Student-Faculty Ratio:** 8:1 **% Receiving Financial Aid:** 22 **Library Holdings:** 104,360 **Regional Accreditation:** Western Association of Schools and Colleges **Credit Hours For Degree:** 180 quarter hours, Bachelors **Professional Accreditation:** APA

KAPLAN COLLEGE, BAKERSFIELD CAMPUS
1914 Wible Rd.
Bakersfield, CA 93304
Tel: (661)836-6300
Web Site: http://www.kc-bakersfield.com/
President/CEO: Becky Anderson
Type: Two-Year College **Sex:** Coed **H.S. Requirements:** High school diploma required; GED accepted **Professional Accreditation:** ACICS

KAPLAN COLLEGE, CHULA VISTA CAMPUS
555 Broadway
Chula Vista, CA 91910
Tel: 877-473-3052; Free: (887)473-3052
Admissions: 877-473-3052
Web Site: http://www.kc-chulavista.com/
Type: Two-Year College **Sex:** Coed **H.S. Requirements:** High school diploma required; GED accepted **Professional Accreditation:** ACCSCT

KAPLAN COLLEGE, FRESNO CAMPUS
44 Shaw Ave.
Rodeo Plaza Shopping Center
Clovis, CA 93612
Tel: (559)325-5100; Free: 800-526-0256
Web Site: http://www.kc-fresno.com/
President/CEO: Chris VanEs
Type: Two-Year College **Sex:** Coed **H.S. Requirements:** High school diploma required; GED accepted **Professional Accreditation:** ACCSCT

KAPLAN COLLEGE, MODESTO CAMPUS
5172 Kiernan Ct.
Salida, CA 95368
Tel: (209)543-7000; Free: 800-526-0256
Fax: (209)571-9836
Web Site: http://www.kc-modesto.com/
President/CEO: Kevin Puls
Type: Two-Year College **Sex:** Coed **H.S. Requirements:** High school diploma required; GED accepted **Calendar System:** Semester

KAPLAN COLLEGE, PALM SPRINGS CAMPUS
2475 East Tahquitz Canyon Way
Palm Springs, CA 92262
Tel: (760)778-3540
Web Site: http://www.kc-palmsprings.com/
President/CEO: Kevin Quirk
Type: Two-Year College **Sex:** Coed **H.S. Requirements:** High school diploma required; GED accepted **Professional Accreditation:** ACCSCT

KAPLAN COLLEGE, PANORAMA CITY CAMPUS
14355 Roscoe Blvd.
Panorama City, CA 91402
Tel: (818)672-3000; Free: 800-526-0256
Web Site: http://www.kc-panoramacity.com/
President/CEO: Alojz A. Koscak
Type: Two-Year College **Sex:** Coed **H.S. Requirements:** High school diploma required; GED accepted **Professional Accreditation:** ACICS

KAPLAN COLLEGE, RIVERSIDE CAMPUS
4040 Vine St.
Riverside, CA 92507
Tel: (951)276-1704
Web Site: http://www.kc-riverside.com/
President/CEO: Carl Christopher
Type: Two-Year College **Sex:** Coed **H.S. Requirements:** High school diploma required; GED accepted **Professional Accreditation:** ACCSCT

KAPLAN COLLEGE, SACRAMENTO CAMPUS
4330 Watt Ave.
Ste. 400
Sacramento, CA 95821
Tel: (916)649-8168; Free: 800-526-0256
Fax: (916)649-8344
Web Site: http://www.kc-sacramento.com/
President/CEO: Joseph File
Type: Two-Year College **Sex:** Coed **H.S. Requirements:** High school diploma required; GED accepted **Calendar System:** Semester **Professional Accreditation:** ACICS

KAPLAN COLLEGE, SAN DIEGO CAMPUS
9055 Balboa Ave.
San Diego, CA 92123
Tel: (858)279-4500; Free: 800-526-0256
Fax: (858)279-4885
Web Site: http://www.kc-sandiego.com/
President/CEO: Mike Seifert
Type: Two-Year College **Sex:** Coed **H.S. Requirements:** High school diploma required; GED accepted **Calendar System:** Semester **Professional Accreditation:** ACCSCT

KAPLAN COLLEGE, STOCKTON CAMPUS
722 West March Ln.
Stockton, CA 95207
Tel: (209)462-8777
Fax: (209)462-3219
Web Site: http://www.kc-stockton.com/
President/CEO: Bill Jones
Type: Two-Year College **Sex:** Coed **H.S. Requirements:** High school diploma required; GED accepted

KAPLAN COLLEGE, VISTA CAMPUS
2022 University Dr.
Vista, CA 92083
Tel: (760)630-1555
Fax: (760)630-1656
Web Site: http://www.kc-vista.com/
President/CEO: Jann Underwood-Mitchell
Type: Two-Year College **Sex:** Coed **H.S. Requirements:** High school diploma required; GED accepted

THE KING'S COLLEGE AND SEMINARY
14800 Sherman Way
Van Nuys, CA 91405-8040
Tel: (818)779-8040
Fax: (818)779-8241
E-mail: mchappell@kingscollege.edu
Web Site: http://www.kingscollege.edu/
President/CEO: Paul Chappell, PhD
Admissions: Marilyn J. Chappell
Type: Comprehensive **Sex:** Coed **Affiliation:** International Church of the Foursquare Gospel **Application Fee:** $45.00 **Costs Per Year:** Application fee: $45. Tuition: $7020 full-time, $195 per credit hour part-time. Mandatory fees: $375 full-time, $45 per course part-time. Full-time tuition and fees vary according to course load. Part-time tuition and fees vary according to course load. **Calendar System:** Quarter **Professional Accreditation:** ABHE, TACCS

LA COLLEGE INTERNATIONAL
3200 Wilshire Blvd., No. 400
Los Angeles, CA 90010-1308
Tel: (213)381-3333
Fax: (213)383-9369
Web Site: http://www.lac.edu/
President/CEO: Dean Dunbar
Type: Four-Year College **Sex:** Coed **Admission Plans:** Open Admission **Application Fee:** $75.00 **H.S. Requirements:** High school diploma required; GED accepted **Scholarships:** Available **Calendar System:** Quarter, Summer Session Not available **Enrollment:** FT 85 **Faculty:** PT 25 **Student-Faculty Ratio:** 5:1 **Exams:** Other. **Library Holdings:** 2,000 **Professional Accreditation:** ACICS

LA SIERRA UNIVERSITY
4500 Riverwalk Parkway
Riverside, CA 92515
Tel: (951)785-2000; Free: 800-874-5587
Admissions: (951)785-2176
Fax: (951)785-2901
E-mail: admissions@lasierra.edu
Web Site: http://www.lasierra.edu/
President/CEO: Randal Wisbey
Admissions: Faye Swayze
Type: Comprehensive **Sex:** Coed **Affiliation:** Seventh-day Adventist; WASC (Western Association of Schools and Colleges) **Scores:** 86% SAT V 400+; 85% SAT M 400+; 58% ACT 18-23; 17% ACT 24-29 **% Accepted:** 55 **Admission Plans:** Preferred Admission; Deferred Admission **Application Deadline:** Rolling **Application Fee:** $30.00 **H.S. Requirements:** High school diploma required; GED accepted **Costs Per Year:** Application fee: $30. Comprehensive fee: $31,563 includes full-time tuition ($23,637), mandatory fees ($936), and college room and board ($6990). Full-time tuition and fees vary according to course load. Room and board charges vary according to board plan and housing facility. Part-time tuition: $657 per quarter hour. Part-time tuition varies according to course load. **Scholarships:** Available **Calendar System:** Quarter, Summer Session Available **Enrollment:** FT 1,309, PT 186 **Faculty:** FT 96, PT 91 **Student-Faculty Ratio:** 13:1 **Exams:** SAT I or ACT. **% Receiving Financial Aid:** 70 **% Residing in College-Owned, -Operated, or -Affiliated Housing:** 40 **Library Holdings:** 255,050 **Regional Accreditation:** Western Association of Schools and Colleges **Credit Hours For Degree:** 190 units, Bachelors **Professional Accreditation:** ATS, CSWE, NASM **Intercollegiate Athletics:** Baseball M; Basketball M & W; Golf M; Soccer M & W; Softball W; Tennis M & W; Volleyball W

LAGUNA COLLEGE OF ART & DESIGN
2222 Laguna Canyon Rd.
Laguna Beach, CA 92651-1136
Tel: (949)376-6000; Free: 800-255-0762
Fax: (949)376-6009
Web Site: http://www.lagunacollege.edu/

President/CEO: Dr. Dennis Power
Admissions: Mike Rivas
Financial Aid: Christopher Brown
Type: Comprehensive **Sex:** Coed **Scores:** 98% SAT V 400+; 100% SAT M 400+; 20% ACT 18-23; 70% ACT 24-29 **% Accepted:** 88 **Admission Plans:** Deferred Admission **Application Fee:** $45.00 **H.S. Requirements:** High school diploma required; GED accepted **Scholarships:** Available **Calendar System:** Semester, Summer Session Available **Enrollment:** FT 310 **Faculty:** FT 10, PT 62 **Student-Faculty Ratio:** 10:1 **Exams:** SAT I or ACT. **% Receiving Financial Aid:** 88 **Library Holdings:** 16,000 **Regional Accreditation:** Western Association of Schools and Colleges **Credit Hours For Degree:** 122 units, Bachelors **Professional Accreditation:** NASAD **Intercollegiate Athletics:** Ultimate Frisbee M & W; Volleyball M & W

LAKE TAHOE COMMUNITY COLLEGE
One College Dr.
South Lake Tahoe, CA 96150-4524
Tel: (530)541-4660
Fax: (530)541-7852
E-mail: admissions@ltcc.edu
Web Site: http://www.ltcc.edu/
President/CEO: Paul Killpatrick
Type: Two-Year College **Sex:** Coed **Affiliation:** California Community College System **% Accepted:** 100 **Admission Plans:** Open Admission; Early Admission **Application Deadline:** Rolling **Application Fee:** $0.00 **H.S. Requirements:** High school diploma or equivalent not required. For applicants under 18: High school diploma required; GED accepted **Costs Per Year:** Application fee: $0. State resident tuition: $0 full-time. Nonresident tuition: $6075 full-time, $135 per unit part-time. Mandatory fees: $765 full-time, $17 per unit part-time, $4 per term part-time. Full-time tuition and fees vary according to course load and reciprocity agreements. Part-time tuition and fees vary according to course load and reciprocity agreements. **Scholarships:** Available **Calendar System:** Quarter, Summer Session Available **Faculty:** FT 41, PT 159 **Library Holdings:** 20,000 **Regional Accreditation:** Western Association of Schools and Colleges **Credit Hours For Degree:** 90 units, Associates **Intercollegiate Athletics:** Skiing (Cross-Country) M & W; Volleyball W

LANEY COLLEGE
900 Fallon St.
Oakland, CA 94607-4893
Tel: (510)834-5740
Web Site: http://www.peralta.cc.ca.us/
President/CEO: Dr. Frank Chong
Admissions: Barbara Simmons
Type: Two-Year College **Sex:** Coed **Affiliation:** Peralta Community College District System **Admission Plans:** Open Admission; Early Admission **Application Deadline:** Rolling **Application Fee:** $0.00 **H.S. Requirements:** High school diploma required; GED accepted. For applicants 18 or over: High school diploma or equivalent not required **Scholarships:** Available **Calendar System:** Semester, Summer Session Available **Enrollment:** FT 2,424, PT 11,039 **Faculty:** FT 118, PT 333 **Library Holdings:** 78,054 **Regional Accreditation:** Western Association of Schools and Colleges **Credit Hours For Degree:** 60 semester hours, Associates **Intercollegiate Athletics:** Baseball M; Football M; Golf M; Softball W; Volleyball W

LAS POSITAS COLLEGE
3000 Campus Hill Dr.
Livermore, CA 94551
Tel: (925)424-1000
Fax: (925)443-0742
Web Site: http://www.laspositascollege.edu/
President/CEO: Dr. DeRionne Pollard
Admissions: Sylvia R. Rodriguez
Type: Two-Year College **Sex:** Coed **Affiliation:** California Community College System **Admission Plans:** Open Admission **Application Fee:** $0.00 **H.S. Requirements:** High school diploma required; GED accepted **Scholarships:** Available **Calendar System:** Semester, Summer Session Available **Regional Accreditation:** Western Association of Schools and Colleges **Credit Hours For Degree:** 60 units, Associates **Intercollegiate Athletics:** Cross-Country Running M & W; Soccer M & W

LASSEN COMMUNITY COLLEGE DISTRICT
Hwy. 139
PO Box 3000
Susanville, CA 96130
Tel: (530)257-6181
Fax: (530)257-8964
Web Site: http://www.lassencollege.edu/
President/CEO: Douglas Houston
Admissions: Chris J. Alberico
Type: Two-Year College **Sex:** Coed **Affiliation:** California Community College System **Admission Plans:** Open Admission; Early Admission **Application Deadline:** Rolling **H.S. Requirements:** High school diploma or equivalent not required. For applicants under 18: High school diploma required; GED accepted **Scholarships:** Available **Calendar System:** Semester, Summer Session Available **Faculty:** FT 44, PT 160 **Library Holdings:** 15,000 **Regional Accreditation:** Western Association of Schools and Colleges **Credit Hours For Degree:** 60 units, Associates **Intercollegiate Athletics:** Basketball M & W; Cross-Country Running M & W; Golf M & W; Riflery M & W; Softball W; Track and Field M & W; Volleyball W; Wrestling M

LIFE PACIFIC COLLEGE
1100 Covina Blvd.
San Dimas, CA 91773-3298
Tel: (909)599-5433; Free: 877-886-5433
Fax: (909)599-6690
E-mail: adm@lifepacific.edu
Web Site: http://www.lifepacific.edu/
President/CEO: Dr. Robert Flores
Admissions: Dorienne Elston
Financial Aid: Becky Huyck
Type: Four-Year College **Sex:** Coed **Affiliation:** International Church of the Foursquare Gospel **Scores:** 88% SAT V 400+; 76% SAT M 400+; 42% ACT 18-23; 25% ACT 24-29 **% Accepted:** 100 **Admission Plans:** Deferred Admission **Application Deadline:** May 1 **Application Fee:** $35.00 **H.S. Requirements:** High school diploma required; GED accepted **Costs Per Year:** Application fee: $35. Comprehensive fee: $18,500 includes full-time tuition ($12,000), mandatory fees ($500), and college room and board ($6000). Part-time tuition: $400 per unit. Part-time mandatory fees: $400 per semester hour, $250 per term. **Scholarships:** Available **Calendar System:** Semester, Summer Session Available **Enrollment:** FT 323, PT 191 **Faculty:** FT 16, PT 22 **Student-Faculty Ratio:** 16:1 **Exams:** SAT I or ACT. **% Receiving Financial Aid:** 74 **% Residing in College-Owned, -Operated, or -Affiliated Housing:** 50 **Regional Accreditation:** Western Association of Schools and Colleges **Credit Hours For Degree:** 64 semester hours, Associates; 128 semester hours, Bachelors **Professional Accreditation:** ABHE

LINCOLN UNIVERSITY
401 15th St.
Oakland, CA 94612
Tel: (510)628-8010
Fax: (510)628-8026
E-mail: admissions@lincolnuca.edu
Web Site: http://www.lincolnuca.edu/
President/CEO: Dr. Mikhail Brodsky
Admissions: Reenu Shrestha
Type: Comprehensive **Sex:** Coed **% Accepted:** 91 **Admission Plans:** Deferred Admission **Application Deadline:** August 22 **Application Fee:** $75.00 **H.S. Requirements:** High school diploma required; GED accepted **Costs Per Year:** Application fee: $75. Tuition: $8630 full-time, $345 per unit part-time. **Calendar System:** Semester, Summer Session Available **Enrollment:** FT 144, PT 51, Grad FT 421, Grad PT 8 **Faculty:** FT 10, PT 15 **Student-Faculty Ratio:** 14:1 **Final Year or Final Semester Residency Requirement:** No **Library Holdings:** 17,752 **Credit Hours For Degree:** 71 units, Associates; 124 units, Bachelors **Professional Accreditation:** ACICS

LOMA LINDA UNIVERSITY
Loma Linda, CA 92350
Tel: (909)558-1000
Fax: (909)558-4577
Web Site: http://www.llu.edu/
President/CEO: Richard Hart
Financial Aid: Verdell Schaefer
Type: University **Sex:** Coed **Affiliation:** Seventh-day Adventist **Admission Plans:** Deferred Admission **Application Fee:** $60.00 **H.S. Requirements:** High school diploma required; GED accepted **Scholarships:** Available **Calendar System:** Quarter, Summer Session Not available **Enrollment:** FT

885, PT 347 **Faculty:** FT 557, PT 283 **Student-Faculty Ratio:** 8:1 **% Receiving Financial Aid:** 77 **% Residing in College-Owned, -Operated, or -Affiliated Housing:** 27 **Library Holdings:** 338,418 **Regional Accreditation:** Western Association of Schools and Colleges **Professional Accreditation:** ACPhE, ARCEST, AAMFT, AACN, ADA, ADtA, AHIMA, AOTA, APTA, APA, ASC, ASLHA, ACIPE, CARC, CEPH, CSWE, JRCERT, LCMEAMA, NAACLS

LONG BEACH CITY COLLEGE
4901 East Carson St.
Long Beach, CA 90808-1780
Tel: (562)938-4353
Admissions: (562)938-4111
Web Site: http://www.lbcc.edu/
President/CEO: Eloy Oakley
Admissions: Ross Miyashiro
Type: Two-Year College **Sex:** Coed **Affiliation:** California Community College System **Admission Plans:** Open Admission; Early Admission **Application Deadline:** Rolling **Application Fee:** $0.00 **H.S. Requirements:** High school diploma or equivalent not required. For applicants under 18, international students: High school diploma required; GED accepted **Costs Per Year:** Application fee: $0. State resident tuition: $0 full-time. Nonresident tuition: $4560 full-time, $190 per unit part-time. Mandatory fees: $654 full-time, $26 per unit part-time, $156 per term part-time. Full-time tuition and fees vary according to course load. Part-time tuition and fees vary according to course load. **Scholarships:** Available **Calendar System:** Semester, Summer Session Available **Enrollment:** FT 9,580, PT 16,716 **Faculty:** FT 356, PT 777 **Student-Faculty Ratio:** 24:1 **Library Holdings:** 151,367 **Regional Accreditation:** Western Association of Schools and Colleges **Credit Hours For Degree:** 60 units, Associates **Professional Accreditation:** JRCERT, NLN **Intercollegiate Athletics:** Badminton M & W; Baseball M; Basketball M & W; Cross-Country Running M & W; Football M; Golf M & W; Soccer M & W; Softball W; Swimming and Diving M & W; Tennis M & W; Track and Field M & W; Volleyball M & W; Water Polo M & W

LOS ANGELES CITY COLLEGE
855 North Vermont Ave.
Los Angeles, CA 90029-3590
Tel: (323)953-4000
Fax: (323)953-4536
Web Site: http://www.lacitycollege.edu/
President/CEO: Jamillah Moore
Admissions: Elaine Geismar
Type: Two-Year College **Sex:** Coed **Affiliation:** Los Angeles Community College District System **Admission Plans:** Open Admission **Application Deadline:** September 5 **Application Fee:** $0.00 **H.S. Requirements:** High school diploma or equivalent not required **Calendar System:** Semester, Summer Session Available **Faculty:** FT 249, PT 323 **Library Holdings:** 150,000 **Regional Accreditation:** Western Association of Schools and Colleges **Credit Hours For Degree:** 60 units, Associates **ROTC:** Army, Air Force **Professional Accreditation:** ADA, JRCERT **Intercollegiate Athletics:** Basketball M; Cross-Country Running M; Football M; Gymnastics M; Track and Field M & W; Volleyball M & W

LOS ANGELES COUNTY COLLEGE OF NURSING AND ALLIED HEALTH
1237 North Mission Rd.
Los Angeles, CA 90033
Tel: (323)226-4911
Fax: (323)226-6427
Web Site: http://www.dhs.co.la.ca.us/wps/portal/collegeofnursing/
President/CEO: Nancy Miller
Type: Two-Year College **Sex:** Coed **Application Fee:** $5.00 **Scholarships:** Available **Calendar System:** Semester **Student-Faculty Ratio:** 2:1 **Regional Accreditation:** Western Association of Schools and Colleges

LOS ANGELES HARBOR COLLEGE
1111 Figueroa Place
Wilmington, CA 90744-2397
Tel: (310)233-4000
Admissions: (310)233-4091
Fax: (310)233-4223
E-mail: chingdm@lahc.edu
Web Site: http://www.lahc.edu/
President/CEO: Dr. Linda M. Spink
Admissions: David Ching
Type: Two-Year College **Sex:** Coed **Affiliation:** Los Angeles Community College District System **Admission Plans:** Open Admission; Early Admission; Deferred Admission **Application Deadline:** September 3 **Application Fee:** $0.00 **H.S. Requirements:** High school diploma or equivalent not required. For applicants under 18: High school diploma required; GED accepted **Costs Per Year:** Application fee: $0. State resident tuition: $0 full-time. Nonresident tuition: $4512 full-time, $188 per unit part-time. Mandatory fees: $646 full-time, $26 per unit part-time, $11 per term part-time. **Scholarships:** Available **Calendar System:** Semester, Summer Session Available **Enrollment:** FT 2,872, PT 7,211 **Faculty:** FT 110, PT 160 **Student-Faculty Ratio:** 40:1 **Library Holdings:** 110,433 **Regional Accreditation:** Western Association of Schools and Colleges **Credit Hours For Degree:** 60 units, Associates **Professional Accreditation:** NLN **Intercollegiate Athletics:** Baseball M; Basketball M; Football M; Soccer M & W; Softball W; Volleyball W

LOS ANGELES MISSION COLLEGE
13356 Eldridge Ave.
Sylmar, CA 91342-3245
Tel: (818)364-7600
Web Site: http://www.lamission.edu/
President/CEO: Judith Valles
Admissions: Angela Merrill
Type: Two-Year College **Sex:** Coed **Affiliation:** Los Angeles Community College District System **Admission Plans:** Open Admission; Early Admission **H.S. Requirements:** High school diploma or equivalent not required. For applicants under 18: High school diploma required; GED accepted **Scholarships:** Available **Calendar System:** Semester, Summer Session Available **Faculty:** FT 85, PT 185 **Student-Faculty Ratio:** 33:1 **Library Holdings:** 40,000 **Regional Accreditation:** Western Association of Schools and Colleges **Credit Hours For Degree:** 60 credits, Associates

LOS ANGELES PIERCE COLLEGE
6201 Winnetka Ave.
Woodland Hills, CA 91371-0001
Tel: (818)710-4123
Admissions: (818)347-6401
Fax: (818)710-9844
Web Site: http://www.piercecollege.edu/
President/CEO: Dr. Joy McCaslin
Admissions: Shelley L. Gerstl
Type: Two-Year College **Sex:** Coed **Affiliation:** Los Angeles Community College District System **% Accepted:** 100 **Admission Plans:** Open Admission; Early Admission **Application Deadline:** August 20 **Application Fee:** $0.00 **H.S. Requirements:** High school diploma or equivalent not required. For applicants under 18, nursing program: High school diploma required; GED accepted **Scholarships:** Available **Calendar System:** Semester, Summer Session Available **Library Holdings:** 106,122 **Regional Accreditation:** Western Association of Schools and Colleges **Credit Hours For Degree:** 60 credits, Associates **Professional Accreditation:** NLN **Intercollegiate Athletics:** Baseball M; Basketball W; Football M; Softball W; Swimming and Diving M & W; Tennis M & W; Volleyball M & W; Water Polo M

LOS ANGELES SOUTHWEST COLLEGE
1600 West Imperial Hwy.
Los Angeles, CA 90047-4810
Tel: (323)241-5225
Web Site: http://www.lasc.edu/
President/CEO: Dr. Jack E. Daniels, III
Admissions: Dan W. Walden
Type: Two-Year College **Sex:** Coed **Affiliation:** Los Angeles Community College District System **Admission Plans:** Open Admission; Early Admission **Application Deadline:** September 9 **H.S. Requirements:** High school diploma or equivalent not required. For applicants under 18: High school diploma required; GED accepted **Costs Per Year:** Nonresident tuition: $214 per unit part-time. Mandatory fees: $26 per unit part-time. **Scholarships:** Available **Calendar System:** Semester, Summer Session Available **Faculty:** FT 75, PT 148 **Library Holdings:** 60,000 **Regional Accreditation:** Western Association of Schools and Colleges **Credit Hours For Degree:** 60 units, Associates **Intercollegiate Athletics:** Basketball M & W; Cross-Country Running M & W; Football M; Track and Field M & W

LOS ANGELES TRADE-TECHNICAL COLLEGE
400 West Washington Blvd.
Los Angeles, CA 90015-4108
Tel: (213)744-9500
Admissions: (213)763-5301
Fax: (213)748-7334
E-mail: CardozaRJ@lattc.edu
Web Site: http://www.lattc.edu/
President/CEO: Dr. Roland Chapdelaine
Admissions: Dr. Raul Cardoza
Type: Two-Year College **Sex:** Coed **Affiliation:** Los Angeles Community College District System **Application Deadline:** September 7 **Application Fee:** $0.00 **H.S. Requirements:** High school diploma or equivalent not required. For nursing program: High school diploma required; GED accepted **Scholarships:** Available **Calendar System:** Semester, Summer Session Available **Enrollment:** FT 4,160, PT 9,034 **Faculty:** FT 200, PT 243 **Library Holdings:** 98,000 **Regional Accreditation:** Western Association of Schools and Colleges **Credit Hours For Degree:** 60 units, Associates **Professional Accreditation:** ACF, NLN **Intercollegiate Athletics:** Basketball M & W; Cross-Country Running M & W; Tennis M; Track and Field M & W

LOS ANGELES VALLEY COLLEGE
5800 Fulton Ave.
Van Nuys, CA 91401-4096
Tel: (818)947-2600
Fax: (818)947-2610
E-mail: manzanf@lavc.edu
Web Site: http://www.lavc.cc.ca.us/
President/CEO: Dr. A. Sue Carleo
Admissions: Florentino Manzano
Type: Two-Year College **Sex:** Coed **Affiliation:** Los Angeles Community College District System **Admission Plans:** Open Admission; Early Admission **Application Deadline:** Rolling **Application Fee:** $0.00 **H.S. Requirements:** High school diploma or equivalent not required **Scholarships:** Available **Calendar System:** Semester, Summer Session Available **Library Holdings:** 124,000 **Regional Accreditation:** Western Association of Schools and Colleges **Credit Hours For Degree:** 60 units, Associates **Professional Accreditation:** CARC, NLN **Intercollegiate Athletics:** Baseball M; Basketball M & W; Cross-Country Running M & W; Football M; Soccer W; Softball W; Swimming and Diving M & W; Track and Field M & W; Volleyball M & W; Water Polo M & W

LOS MEDANOS COLLEGE
2700 East Leland Rd.
Pittsburg, CA 94565-5197
Tel: (925)439-2181
Fax: (925)439-8797
Web Site: http://www.losmedanos.net/
President/CEO: Peter Garcia
Admissions: Gail Newman
Type: Two-Year College **Sex:** Coed **Affiliation:** California Community College System **Admission Plans:** Open Admission **Application Deadline:** August 29 **Application Fee:** $0.00 **H.S. Requirements:** High school diploma required; GED accepted. For applicants 18 or over: High school diploma or equivalent not required **Scholarships:** Available **Calendar System:** Semester, Summer Session Available **Faculty:** FT 104, PT 140 **Library Holdings:** 15,439 **Regional Accreditation:** Western Association of Schools and Colleges **Credit Hours For Degree:** 60 units, Associates **Intercollegiate Athletics:** Baseball M; Basketball M & W; Football M; Soccer M; Softball W; Volleyball W

LOYOLA MARYMOUNT UNIVERSITY
One LMU Dr.
Los Angeles, CA 90045-2659
Tel: (310)338-2700; Free: 800-LMU-INFO
Admissions: (310)338-2750
Fax: (310)338-2797
E-mail: admissions@lmu.edu
Web Site: http://www.lmu.edu/
President/CEO: Dr. Robert B. Lawton, SJ
Admissions: Matthew Fissinger
Type: Comprehensive **Sex:** Coed **Affiliation:** Roman Catholic **Scores:** 99.9% SAT V 400+; 99.4% SAT M 400+; 23.6% ACT 18-23; 60.8% ACT 24-29 **% Accepted:** 59 **Admission Plans:** Early Admission; Early Action; Deferred Admission **Application Deadline:** January 15 **Application Fee:** $60.00 **H.S. Requirements:** High school diploma required; GED accepted **Costs Per Year:** Application fee: $60. One-time mandatory fee: $214. Comprehensive fee: $47,444 includes full-time tuition ($34,730), mandatory fees ($689), and college room and board ($12,025). College room only: $9260. Room and board charges vary according to board plan and housing facility. Part-time tuition: $1447 per credit hour. Part-time mandatory fees: $5 per credit hour, $55 per term. Part-time tuition and fees vary according to course load. **Scholarships:** Available **Calendar System:** Semester, Summer Session Available **Enrollment:** FT 5,522, PT 311, Grad FT 2,427, Grad PT 750 **Faculty:** FT 507, PT 502 **Student-Faculty Ratio:** 11:1 **Exams:** SAT I or ACT. **% Receiving Financial Aid:** 49 **% Residing in College-Owned, -Operated, or -Affiliated Housing:** 57 **Final Year or Final Semester Residency Requirement:** No **Library Holdings:** 541,112 **Regional Accreditation:** Western Association of Schools and Colleges **Credit Hours For Degree:** 120 units, Bachelors **ROTC:** Army, Navy, Air Force **Professional Accreditation:** AACSB, ABET, ABA, AALS, ATS, NASAD, NASD, NASM, NAST, NCATE **Intercollegiate Athletics:** Baseball M; Basketball M & W; Cheerleading M & W; Crew M & W; Cross-Country Running M & W; Golf M; Soccer M & W; Softball W; Swimming and Diving W; Tennis M & W; Track and Field M & W; Volleyball W; Water Polo M & W

MARYMOUNT COLLEGE, PALOS VERDES, CALIFORNIA
30800 Palos Verdes Dr. East
Rancho Palos Verdes, CA 90275-6299
Tel: (310)377-5501
Fax: (310)377-6223
E-mail: admissions@marymountpv.edu
Web Site: http://www.marymountpv.edu/
President/CEO: Dr. Michael S. Brophy
Admissions: Paula Avery
Type: Four-Year College **Sex:** Coed **Affiliation:** Roman Catholic **Scores:** 85.61% SAT V 400+; 76.3% SAT M 400+ **% Accepted:** 61 **Admission Plans:** Early Admission **Application Deadline:** July 1 **Application Fee:** $40.00 **H.S. Requirements:** High school diploma required; GED accepted **Costs Per Year:** Application fee: $40. Comprehensive fee: $35,142 includes full-time tuition ($24,052), mandatory fees ($490), and college room and board ($10,600). Part-time tuition: $825 per credit hour. Part-time mandatory fees: $825 per credit hour. **Scholarships:** Available **Calendar System:** Semester, Summer Session Available **Enrollment:** FT 555, PT 6 **Faculty:** FT 26, PT 36 **Student-Faculty Ratio:** 15:1 **Exams:** SAT I or ACT. ACT essay used for admission. SAT essay used for admission. **% Residing in College-Owned, -Operated, or -Affiliated Housing:** 60 **Final Year or Final Semester Residency Requirement:** Yes **Library Holdings:** 42,104 **Regional Accreditation:** Western Association of Schools and Colleges **Credit Hours For Degree:** 60 units, Associates; 120 units, Bachelors **Intercollegiate Athletics:** Golf M & W; Soccer M; Tennis M & W

THE MASTER'S COLLEGE AND SEMINARY
21726 Placerita Canyon Rd.
Santa Clarita, CA 91321-1200
Tel: (661)259-3540; Free: 800-568-6248
E-mail: admissions@masters.edu
Web Site: http://www.masters.edu/
President/CEO: Dr. John MacArthur
Admissions: Hollie Gorsh
Financial Aid: Gary Edwards
Type: Comprehensive **Sex:** Coed **Affiliation:** nondenominational **% Accepted:** 83 **Admission Plans:** Early Admission; Early Action; Deferred Admission **Application Deadline:** September 1 **Application Fee:** $40.00 **H.S. Requirements:** High school diploma required; GED accepted **Costs Per Year:** Application fee: $40. Comprehensive fee: $32,650 includes full-time tuition ($24,280), mandatory fees ($370), and college room and board ($8000). College room only: $4480. Full-time tuition and fees vary according to course load, degree level, and program. Room and board charges vary according to board plan. Part-time tuition: $1015 per credit hour. Part-time mandatory fees: $1015 per credit hour. Part-time tuition and fees vary according to course load, degree level, and program. **Scholarships:** Available **Calendar System:** Semester, Summer Session Available **Enrollment:** FT 876, PT 110, Grad FT 165, Grad PT 197 **Faculty:** FT 64, PT 133 **Student-Faculty Ratio:** 9:1 **Exams:** SAT I or ACT. **% Receiving Financial Aid:** 88 **% Residing in College-Owned, -Operated, or -Affiliated Housing:** 82 **Library Holdings:** 170,136 **Regional Accreditation:** Western Association of Schools and Colleges **Credit Hours For Degree:** 122 units, Bachelors

Professional Accreditation: AAFCS **Intercollegiate Athletics:** Baseball M; Basketball M & W; Cross-Country Running M & W; Golf M; Soccer M & W; Tennis W; Track and Field M & W; Volleyball W

MENDOCINO COLLEGE
1000 Hensley Creek Rd.
Ukiah, CA 95482-0300
Tel: (707)468-3000
Admissions: (707)468-3103
Fax: (707)468-3430
E-mail: kanderson@mendocino.edu
Web Site: http://www.mendocino.edu/
President/CEO: Kathryn Lehner
Admissions: Kristie Anderson
Type: Two-Year College **Sex:** Coed **Affiliation:** California Community College System **% Accepted:** 100 **Admission Plans:** Open Admission; Preferred Admission; Early Admission; Deferred Admission **Application Deadline:** Rolling **Application Fee:** $0.00 **H.S. Requirements:** High school diploma or equivalent not required **Costs Per Year:** Application fee: $0. State resident tuition: $0 full-time. Nonresident tuition: $5700 full-time, $190 per unit part-time. Mandatory fees: $780 full-time, $26 per unit part-time. Full-time tuition and fees vary according to course load. Part-time tuition and fees vary according to course load. **Scholarships:** Available **Calendar System:** Semester, Summer Session Available **Enrollment:** FT 1,247, PT 3,520 **Faculty:** FT 50, PT 255 **Student-Faculty Ratio:** 12:1 **Final Year or Final Semester Residency Requirement:** No **Library Holdings:** 27,441 **Regional Accreditation:** Western Association of Schools and Colleges **Credit Hours For Degree:** 60 units, Associates **Intercollegiate Athletics:** Baseball M; Basketball M & W; Football M; Soccer W; Volleyball W

MENLO COLLEGE
1000 El Camino Real
Atherton, CA 94027-4301
Tel: (650)688-3753; Free: 800-556-3656
Admissions: (650)543-3940
Fax: (650)617-2395
E-mail: admissions@menlo.edu
Web Site: http://www.menlo.edu/
President/CEO: Timothy G. Haight
Admissions: Cindy McGrew
Financial Aid: Anne Heaton-Dunlap
Type: Four-Year College **Sex:** Coed **Scores:** 86.5% SAT V 400+; 92.8% SAT M 400+; 49.1% ACT 18-23; 24.5% ACT 24-29 **% Accepted:** 52 **Admission Plans:** Early Admission; Early Action; Deferred Admission **Application Deadline:** Rolling **Application Fee:** $40.00 **H.S. Requirements:** High school diploma required; GED accepted **Costs Per Year:** Application fee: $40. Comprehensive fee: $44,880 includes full-time tuition ($33,150), mandatory fees ($400), and college room and board ($11,330). Full-time tuition and fees vary according to program. Room and board charges vary according to housing facility. Part-time tuition: $1381 per credit hour. Part-time tuition varies according to program. **Scholarships:** Available **Calendar System:** Semester, Summer Session Available **Enrollment:** FT 569, PT 25 **Faculty:** FT 25, PT 47 **Student-Faculty Ratio:** 14:1 **Exams:** SAT I or ACT, SAT I and SAT II or ACT. SAT essay used for admission. **% Receiving Financial Aid:** 59 **% Residing in College-Owned, -Operated, or -Affiliated Housing:** 61 **Final Year or Final Semester Residency Requirement:** Yes **Library Holdings:** 81,600 **Regional Accreditation:** Western Association of Schools and Colleges **Credit Hours For Degree:** 124 units, Bachelors **ROTC:** Army **Intercollegiate Athletics:** Baseball M; Basketball M & W; Cross-Country Running M & W; Football M; Golf M; Soccer M & W; Softball W; Volleyball W; Wrestling M & W

MERCED COLLEGE
3600 M St.
Merced, CA 95348-2898
Tel: (209)384-6000
Fax: (209)384-6339
Web Site: http://www.mccd.edu/
President/CEO: Benjamin T. Duran
Admissions: Cherie Davis
Financial Aid: Judy Leufgen
Type: Two-Year College **Sex:** Coed **Affiliation:** California Community College System **% Accepted:** 100 **Admission Plans:** Open Admission; Early Admission **Application Deadline:** Rolling **H.S. Requirements:** High school diploma or equivalent not required. For applicants under 18: High school diploma required; GED accepted **Scholarships:** Available **Calendar System:** Semester, Summer Session Available **Enrollment:** FT 4,598, PT 7,927 **Faculty:** FT 145, PT 276 **Library Holdings:** 45,000 **Regional Accreditation:** Western Association of Schools and Colleges **Credit Hours For Degree:** 60 units, Associates **ROTC:** Army **Professional Accreditation:** JRCERT **Intercollegiate Athletics:** Baseball M; Basketball M & W; Bowling M & W; Cross-Country Running M; Equestrian Sports M & W; Football M; Golf M & W; Soccer M; Softball W; Swimming and Diving M & W; Tennis M & W; Track and Field M & W; Volleyball W; Water Polo M

MERRITT COLLEGE
12500 Campus Dr.
Oakland, CA 94619-3196
Tel: (510)531-4911
E-mail: hperdue@peralta.cc.ca.us
Web Site: http://www.merritt.edu/
President/CEO: Dr. Robert Adams
Admissions: Barbara Simmons
Type: Two-Year College **Sex:** Coed **Affiliation:** Peralta Community College District System **Admission Plans:** Open Admission; Early Admission; Deferred Admission **Application Deadline:** August 28 **H.S. Requirements:** High school diploma required; GED accepted. For applicants 18 or over: High school diploma or equivalent not required **Calendar System:** Semester, Summer Session Available **Library Holdings:** 80,000 **Regional Accreditation:** Western Association of Schools and Colleges **Credit Hours For Degree:** 60 semester hours, Associates **Professional Accreditation:** JRCERT **Intercollegiate Athletics:** Basketball M & W; Cross-Country Running M & W; Track and Field M & W

MILLS COLLEGE
5000 MacArthur Blvd.
Oakland, CA 94613-1000
Tel: (510)430-2255; Free: 800-87-MILLS
Admissions: (510)430-2135
Fax: (510)430-3314
E-mail: admission@mills.edu
Web Site: http://www.mills.edu/
President/CEO: Janet L. Holmgren
Admissions: Giulietta Aquino
Financial Aid: David Gin
Type: Comprehensive **Scores:** 100% SAT V 400+; 100% SAT M 400+; 37.7% ACT 18-23; 49.2% ACT 24-29 **% Accepted:** 57 **Admission Plans:** Early Action; Deferred Admission **Application Deadline:** February 1 **Application Fee:** $50.00 **H.S. Requirements:** High school diploma required; GED accepted **Costs Per Year:** Application fee: $50. Comprehensive fee: $49,249 includes full-time tuition ($36,428), mandatory fees ($1177), and college room and board ($11,644). Full-time tuition and fees vary according to course load. Room and board charges vary according to board plan and housing facility. Part-time tuition: $6072 per course. Part-time mandatory fees: $1177 per year. Part-time tuition and fees vary according to course load. **Scholarships:** Available **Calendar System:** Semester, Summer Session Not available **Enrollment:** FT 870, PT 51, Grad FT 505, Grad PT 75 **Faculty:** FT 93, PT 88 **Student-Faculty Ratio:** 12:1 **Exams:** SAT I or ACT, SAT II. ACT essay used for admission. SAT essay used for admission. ACT essay used as a validity check on application essay. SAT essay used as a validity check on application essay. **% Receiving Financial Aid:** 84 **% Residing in College-Owned, -Operated, or -Affiliated Housing:** 56 **Final Year or Final Semester Residency Requirement:** Yes **Library Holdings:** 331,940 **Regional Accreditation:** Western Association of Schools and Colleges **Credit Hours For Degree:** 34 semester course credits, Bachelors **ROTC:** Army **Intercollegiate Athletics:** Crew W; Cross-Country Running W; Soccer W; Swimming and Diving W; Tennis W; Volleyball W

MIRACOSTA COLLEGE
One Barnard Dr.
Oceanside, CA 92056-3899
Tel: (760)757-2121; Free: 888-201-8480
Fax: (760)795-6609
Web Site: http://www.miracosta.edu/
President/CEO: Dr. Francisco Rodriguez
Financial Aid: Priscilla Tarver
Type: Two-Year College **Sex:** Coed **Affiliation:** California Community College System **Admission Plans:** Open Admission; Early Admission; Deferred

Admission **Application Deadline:** Rolling **Application Fee:** $0.00 **H.S. Requirements:** High school diploma or equivalent not required **Scholarships:** Available **Calendar System:** Semester, Summer Session Available **Faculty:** FT 135, PT 394 **Student-Faculty Ratio:** 23:1 **Library Holdings:** 113,810 **Regional Accreditation:** Western Association of Schools and Colleges **Credit Hours For Degree:** 60 units, Associates **Intercollegiate Athletics:** Basketball M; Cross-Country Running M & W; Soccer W; Track and Field W

MISSION COLLEGE
3000 Mission College Blvd.
Santa Clara, CA 95054-1897
Tel: (408)988-2200
Web Site: http://www.missioncollege.org/
President/CEO: Harriett Robles
Admissions: Daniel Sanidad
Financial Aid: Rita Grogan
Type: Two-Year College **Sex:** Coed **Affiliation:** California Community College System **Admission Plans:** Open Admission; Preferred Admission; Early Admission **Application Deadline:** Rolling **H.S. Requirements:** High school diploma or equivalent not required. For applicants under 18, nursing program: High school diploma required; GED accepted **Costs Per Year:** State resident tuition: $0 full-time. Nonresident tuition: $5572 full-time, $199 per unit part-time. Mandatory fees: $786 full-time, $26 per unit part-time, $29 per term part-time. Full-time tuition and fees vary according to course load. Part-time tuition and fees vary according to course load. **Scholarships:** Available **Calendar System:** Semester, Summer Session Available **Enrollment:** FT 4,000, PT 6,500 **Faculty:** FT 180, PT 210 **Student-Faculty Ratio:** 26:1 **Library Holdings:** 43,456 **Regional Accreditation:** Western Association of Schools and Colleges **Credit Hours For Degree:** 60 semester hours, Associates **ROTC:** Army, Air Force **Intercollegiate Athletics:** Badminton M & W; Baseball M; Basketball W; Soccer M & W; Softball W; Tennis M & W

MODESTO JUNIOR COLLEGE
435 College Ave.
Modesto, CA 95350-5800
Tel: (209)575-6498
Admissions: (209)575-6470
E-mail: mjcadmissions@mail.yosemite.cc.ca.us
Web Site: http://www.mjc.edu/
President/CEO: Dr. Richard Rose
Admissions: Susie Agostini
Type: Two-Year College **Sex:** Coed **Affiliation:** Yosemite Community College District System **Admission Plans:** Open Admission **Application Deadline:** Rolling **Application Fee:** $0.00 **H.S. Requirements:** High school diploma or equivalent not required. For applicants under 18: High school diploma required; GED accepted **Costs Per Year:** Application fee: $0. State resident tuition: $0 full-time. Nonresident tuition: $4868 full-time, $190 per unit part-time. Mandatory fees: $722 full-time, $26 per unit part-time, $74 per year part-time. **Scholarships:** Available **Calendar System:** Semester, Summer Session Available **Enrollment:** FT 6,874, PT 12,433 **Faculty:** FT 267, PT 345 **Student-Faculty Ratio:** 29:1 **Library Holdings:** 69,865 **Regional Accreditation:** Western Association of Schools and Colleges **Credit Hours For Degree:** 62 units, Associates **Professional Accreditation:** AAMAE, ADA, CARC **Intercollegiate Athletics:** Baseball M; Basketball M & W; Cross-Country Running M & W; Football M; Golf M; Gymnastics W; Soccer M & W; Softball W; Swimming and Diving M & W; Tennis M & W; Track and Field M & W; Volleyball W; Water Polo M & W; Wrestling M

MONTEREY PENINSULA COLLEGE
980 Fremont St.
Monterey, CA 93940-4799
Tel: (831)646-4000
Fax: (831)655-2627
E-mail: vcoleman@mpc.edu
Web Site: http://www.mpc.edu/
President/CEO: Douglas Garrison
Admissions: Vera Coleman
Type: Two-Year College **Sex:** Coed **Affiliation:** California Community College System **Admission Plans:** Open Admission; Early Admission **Application Deadline:** Rolling **Application Fee:** $0.00 **H.S. Requirements:** High school diploma or equivalent not required. For international students: High school diploma required; GED accepted **Scholarships:** Available **Calendar System:** Semester, Summer Session Available **Faculty:** FT 136, PT 181 **Library Holdings:** 52,000 **Regional Accreditation:** Western Association of Schools and Colleges **Credit Hours For Degree:** 60 credits, Associates **Professional Accreditation:** ADA, NLN **Intercollegiate Athletics:** Baseball M; Basketball M; Cross-Country Running M & W; Football M; Golf M & W; Softball W; Swimming and Diving M & W; Tennis M & W; Track and Field M & W; Volleyball W

MOORPARK COLLEGE
7075 Campus Rd.
Moorpark, CA 93021-1695
Tel: (805)378-1400
Admissions: (805)378-1415
Web Site: http://www.moorparkcollege.edu/
President/CEO: Dr. Pam Eddinger
Admissions: Katherine Colborn
Type: Two-Year College **Sex:** Coed **Affiliation:** Ventura County Community College District System **Admission Plans:** Open Admission; Early Admission; Deferred Admission **Application Deadline:** Rolling **Application Fee:** $0.00 **H.S. Requirements:** High school diploma required; GED accepted. For nursing program: High school diploma required; GED not accepted **Scholarships:** Available **Calendar System:** Semester, Summer Session Available **Enrollment:** FT 6,021, PT 7,729 **Faculty:** FT 176, PT 401 **Student-Faculty Ratio:** 30:1 **Library Holdings:** 50,000 **Regional Accreditation:** Western Association of Schools and Colleges **Credit Hours For Degree:** 60 units, Associates **Professional Accreditation:** JRCERT, NLN **Intercollegiate Athletics:** Baseball M; Basketball M & W; Cross-Country Running M & W; Football M; Golf M & W; Soccer M & W; Softball W; Track and Field M & W; Volleyball M & W; Wrestling M

MOUNT ST. MARY'S COLLEGE
12001 Chalon Rd.
Los Angeles, CA 90049-1599
Tel: (310)954-4000; Free: 800-999-9893
Admissions: (310)954-4250
E-mail: admissions@msmc.la.edu
Web Site: http://www.msmc.la.edu/
President/CEO: Dr. Jacqueline Powers Doud
Admissions: Yvonne Berumen
Financial Aid: La Royce Dodd
Type: Comprehensive **Sex:** Coed **Affiliation:** Roman Catholic; Sister of St. Joseph Carondelet **Scores:** 81% SAT V 400+; 67% SAT M 400+; 49% ACT 18-23; 13% ACT 24-29 **% Accepted:** 79 **Admission Plans:** Early Action; Deferred Admission **Application Deadline:** February 15 **Application Fee:** $40.00 **H.S. Requirements:** High school diploma required; GED accepted **Costs Per Year:** Application fee: $40. Comprehensive fee: $39,962 includes full-time tuition ($29,232), mandatory fees ($900), and college room and board ($9830). Full-time tuition and fees vary according to degree level and program. Room and board charges vary according to board plan and housing facility. Part-time tuition: $1218 per unit. Part-time tuition varies according to degree level and program. **Scholarships:** Available **Calendar System:** Semester, Summer Session Available **Enrollment:** FT 1,489, PT 491, Grad FT 355, Grad PT 147 **Faculty:** FT 89, PT 263 **Student-Faculty Ratio:** 11:1 **Exams:** SAT I or ACT. **% Receiving Financial Aid:** 63 **% Residing in College-Owned, -Operated, or -Affiliated Housing:** 69 **Final Year or Final Semester Residency Requirement:** No **Library Holdings:** 140,000 **Regional Accreditation:** Western Association of Schools and Colleges **Credit Hours For Degree:** 60 units, Associates; 129 units, Bachelors **Professional Accreditation:** AACN, APTA, NASM

MT. SAN ANTONIO COLLEGE
1100 North Grand Ave.
Walnut, CA 91789-1399
Tel: (909)594-5611; Free: 800-672-2463
Web Site: http://www.mtsac.edu/
President/CEO: Dean John S. Nixon
Admissions: Dr. George Bradshaw
Financial Aid: Christian Alvarado
Type: Two-Year College **Sex:** Coed **Affiliation:** California Community College System **Admission Plans:** Open Admission; Early Admission; Deferred Admission **H.S. Requirements:** High school diploma or equivalent not required **Costs Per Year:** State resident tuition: $0 full-time. Nonresident tuition: $4560 full-time. Mandatory fees: $658 full-time. Full-time tuition and fees vary according to course load and program. **Scholarships:** Available **Calendar System:** Semester, Summer Session Available **Enrollment:** FT

9,827, PT 20,199 **Faculty:** FT 432, PT 893 **Student-Faculty Ratio:** 23:1 **Library Holdings:** 64,291 **Regional Accreditation:** Western Association of Schools and Colleges **Credit Hours For Degree:** 60 units, Associates **ROTC:** Army, Air Force **Professional Accreditation:** CARC, JRCERT, NAACLS **Intercollegiate Athletics:** Badminton W; Baseball M; Basketball M & W; Cheerleading M & W; Cross-Country Running M & W; Football M; Golf M & W; Soccer M & W; Softball W; Swimming and Diving M & W; Tennis M & W; Track and Field M & W; Volleyball M & W; Water Polo M & W; Wrestling M

MT. SAN JACINTO COLLEGE
1499 North State St.
San Jacinto, CA 92583-2399
Tel: (909)487-6752
Admissions: (951)639-5212
Fax: (909)654-6738
E-mail: SLoomis@msjc.edu
Web Site: http://www.msjc.edu/
President/CEO: Roger Schultz
Admissions: Susan Loomis
Type: Two-Year College **Sex:** Coed **Affiliation:** California Community College System **Admission Plans:** Open Admission; Early Admission **Application Deadline:** Rolling **Application Fee:** $0.00 **H.S. Requirements:** High school diploma or equivalent not required **Scholarships:** Available **Calendar System:** Semester, Summer Session Available **Enrollment:** FT 6,356, PT 11,227 **Library Holdings:** 28,000 **Regional Accreditation:** Western Association of Schools and Colleges **Credit Hours For Degree:** 60 units, Associates **Intercollegiate Athletics:** Baseball M; Basketball M & W; Football M; Golf M; Soccer W; Softball W; Tennis M & W; Volleyball W

MT. SIERRA COLLEGE
101 East Huntington Dr.
Monrovia, CA 91016
Tel: (626)873-2144; Free: 888-828-8800.
Fax: (626)359-5528
E-mail: enroll@mtsierra.edu
Web Site: http://www.mtsierra.edu/
President/CEO: Vaughn Hartunian
Type: Four-Year College **Sex:** Coed **Application Fee:** $50.00 **H.S. Requirements:** High school diploma required; GED accepted **Calendar System:** Quarter, Summer Session Available **Library Holdings:** 6,000 **Credit Hours For Degree:** 199 credits, Bachelors **Professional Accreditation:** ACCSCT

MTI COLLEGE OF BUSINESS & TECHNOLOGY
5221 Madison Ave.
Sacramento, CA 95841
Tel: (916)339-1500
Fax: (916)339-0305
E-mail: mmiller@mticollege.edu
Web Site: http://www.mticollege.com/
President/CEO: John Zimmerman
Admissions: Marije Miller
Type: Two-Year College **Sex:** Coed **Application Fee:** $75.00 **Scholarships:** Available **Calendar System:** Continuous **Exams:** Other. **Regional Accreditation:** Western Association of Schools and Colleges

MUSICIANS INSTITUTE
1655 North McCadden Place
Hollywood, CA 90028
Tel: (323)462-1384; Free: 800-255-PLAY
Fax: (323)462-6978
E-mail: admissions@mi.edu
Web Site: http://www.mi.edu/
President/CEO: Hisatake Shibuya
Admissions: Steve Lunn
Type: Four-Year College **Sex:** Coed **% Accepted:** 100 **Application Deadline:** Rolling **Application Fee:** $100.00 **H.S. Requirements:** High school diploma required; GED accepted **Scholarships:** Available **Calendar System:** Quarter **% Receiving Financial Aid:** 61 **Professional Accreditation:** NASM

NAPA VALLEY COLLEGE
2277 Napa-Vallejo Hwy.
Napa, CA 94558-6236
Tel: (707)253-3000
Fax: (707)253-3064
E-mail: odeharo@napavalley.edu
Web Site: http://www.napavalley.edu/
President/CEO: Dr. Christopher McCarthy
Admissions: Oscar De Haro
Type: Two-Year College **Sex:** Coed **Affiliation:** California Community College System **% Accepted:** 100 **Admission Plans:** Open Admission **Application Deadline:** Rolling **Application Fee:** $0.00 **H.S. Requirements:** High school diploma or equivalent not required. For allied health programs: High school diploma required; GED accepted **Scholarships:** Available **Calendar System:** Semester, Summer Session Available **Enrollment:** FT 1,909, PT 4,999 **Faculty:** FT 99, PT 212 **Student-Faculty Ratio:** 22:1 **Library Holdings:** 42,000 **Regional Accreditation:** Western Association of Schools and Colleges **Credit Hours For Degree:** 60 units, Associates **Professional Accreditation:** CARC **Intercollegiate Athletics:** Baseball M; Basketball M & W; Cross-Country Running M & W; Soccer M; Softball W; Swimming and Diving M & W; Tennis M & W; Volleyball W; Wrestling M

THE NATIONAL HISPANIC UNIVERSITY
14271 Story Rd.
San Jose, CA 95127-3823
Tel: (408)254-6900
E-mail: chernandez@nhu.edu
Web Site: http://www.nhu.edu/
President/CEO: Dr. David P. Lopez
Admissions: Pamela Bustillo
Financial Aid: Takeo Kubo
Type: Four-Year College **Sex:** Coed **Application Deadline:** August 15 **Application Fee:** $50.00 **H.S. Requirements:** High school diploma required; GED accepted **Scholarships:** Available **Calendar System:** Semester, Summer Session Available **Exams:** SAT I and SAT II or ACT. **% Receiving Financial Aid:** 79 **Library Holdings:** 10,000 **Regional Accreditation:** Western Association of Schools and Colleges **Credit Hours For Degree:** 64 units, Associates; 124 units, Bachelors **Professional Accreditation:** ACICS

NATIONAL POLYTECHNIC COLLEGE OF SCIENCE
272 South Fries Ave.
Wilmington, CA 90744-6399
Tel: (310)834-2501; Free: 800-432-DIVE
Admissions: (310)816-5700
Fax: (310)834-7132
Web Site: http://www.natpoly.edu/
President/CEO: Troy Roland
Admissions: Tony Rodriquez
Type: Two-Year College **Sex:** Coed **Admission Plans:** Deferred Admission **Application Deadline:** Rolling **Application Fee:** $60.00 **H.S. Requirements:** High school diploma required; GED accepted. For applicants sponsored by foreign governments: High school diploma or equivalent not required **Scholarships:** Available **Calendar System:** Continuous, Summer Session Not available **Regional Accreditation:** Western Association of Schools and Colleges **Credit Hours For Degree:** 90 quarter hours, Associates

NATIONAL UNIVERSITY
11255 North Torrey Pines Rd.
La Jolla, CA 92037-1011
Tel: (619)563-7100; Free: 800-NAT-UNIV
Admissions: (858)628-8648
Fax: (619)563-7299
E-mail: dgiovann@nu.edu
Web Site: http://www.nu.edu/
President/CEO: Dr. Dana Gibson
Admissions: Dominick Giovanniello
Financial Aid: Valerie Ryan
Type: Comprehensive **Sex:** Coed **Affiliation:** National University System **% Accepted:** 100 **Admission Plans:** Open Admission; Deferred Admission **Application Deadline:** Rolling **Application Fee:** $60.00 **H.S. Requirements:** High school diploma required; GED accepted **Costs Per Year:** Application fee: $60. Tuition: $10,728 full-time, $298 per unit part-time. Mandatory fees: $60 full-time. Full-time tuition and fees vary according to course load and location. Part-time tuition varies according to course load and location. **Scholarships:** Available **Calendar System:** Continuous, Summer Session Available **Enrollment:** FT 2,378, PT 3,861, Grad FT 5,532, Grad PT

5,270 **Faculty:** FT 271, PT 2,678 **Student-Faculty Ratio:** 19:1 **% Receiving Financial Aid:** 35 **Library Holdings:** 303,000 **Regional Accreditation:** Western Association of Schools and Colleges **Credit Hours For Degree:** 90 quarter hours, Associates; 180 quarter hours, Bachelors **ROTC:** Army, Air Force **Professional Accreditation:** AACN

NEW YORK FILM ACADEMY
3801 Barham Blvd.
Los Angeles, CA 90068
Tel: (818)733-2600
Fax: (818)733-4074
E-mail: studios@nyfa.edu
Web Site: http://www.nyfa.com/
Type: Two-Year College **Sex:** Coed **Application Fee:** $50.00

NEWSCHOOL OF ARCHITECTURE & DESIGN
1249 F St.
San Diego, CA 92101-6634
Tel: (619)235-4100
Admissions: (619)684-8800
Web Site: http://www.newschoolarch.edu/
President/CEO: Steven Altman
Admissions: Lexi Rogers
Financial Aid: Matt Wakeman
Type: Comprehensive **Sex:** Coed **% Accepted:** 100 **Admission Plans:** Early Decision Plan **Application Deadline:** Rolling **Application Fee:** $75.00 **H.S. Requirements:** High school diploma required; GED accepted **Scholarships:** Available **Calendar System:** Quarter, Summer Session Available **Library Holdings:** 7,500 **Credit Hours For Degree:** 100 quarter hours, Associates; 235 quarter hours, Bachelors **Professional Accreditation:** ACICS, NAAB

NORTHWESTERN POLYTECHNIC UNIVERSITY
47671 Westinghouse Dr.
Fremont, CA 94539-7482
Tel: (510)657-5913
Fax: (510)657-8975
E-mail: admission@npu.edu
Web Site: http://www.npu.edu/
President/CEO: George T.C. Hsieh
Admissions: Michael Tang
Type: Comprehensive **Sex:** Coed **% Accepted:** 100 **Admission Plans:** Deferred Admission **Application Deadline:** August 2 **Application Fee:** $60.00 **H.S. Requirements:** High school diploma required; GED accepted **Costs Per Year:** Application fee: $60. Tuition: $7200 full-time, $300 per unit part-time. Mandatory fees: $140 full-time. College room only: $4800. **Calendar System:** Trimester, Summer Session Available **Enrollment:** FT 142, PT 22, Grad FT 652, Grad PT 109 **Faculty:** FT 31, PT 56 **Student-Faculty Ratio:** 16:1 **Exams:** SAT I. **% Residing in College-Owned, -Operated, or -Affiliated Housing:** 12 **Library Holdings:** 12,000 **Professional Accreditation:** ACICS **Intercollegiate Athletics:** Table Tennis M

NOTRE DAME DE NAMUR UNIVERSITY
1500 Ralston Ave.
Belmont, CA 94002-1908
Tel: (650)508-3500; Free: 800-263-0545
Admissions: (650)508-3600
Fax: (650)508-3660
E-mail: rgort@ndnu.edu
Web Site: http://www.ndnu.edu/
President/CEO: Judith Maxwell Greig, PhD
Admissions: Rejeetha Gort
Financial Aid: Susan Pace
Type: Comprehensive **Sex:** Coed **Affiliation:** Roman Catholic **Scores:** 81% SAT V 400+; 82% SAT M 400+; 68% ACT 18-23; 6% ACT 24-29 **% Accepted:** 79 **Admission Plans:** Early Action; Deferred Admission **Application Deadline:** Rolling **Application Fee:** $50.00 **H.S. Requirements:** High school diploma required; GED accepted **Costs Per Year:** Application fee: $50. Comprehensive fee: $40,100 includes full-time tuition ($28,200), mandatory fees ($300), and college room and board ($11,600). College room only: $7610. Full-time tuition and fees vary according to degree level. Room and board charges vary according to board plan and housing facility. Part-time tuition: $700 per unit. Part-time mandatory fees: $3 per unit, $35 per term. Part-time tuition and fees vary according to degree level and program. **Scholarships:** Available **Calendar System:** Semester, Summer Session Available **Enrollment:** FT 522, PT 353, Grad FT 198, Grad PT 540 **Student-Faculty Ratio:** 11:1 **Exams:** SAT I or ACT. ACT essay used for admission. SAT essay used for admission. ACT essay used for advising. SAT essay used for advising. ACT essay used for placement. SAT essay used for placement. **% Receiving Financial Aid:** 75 **% Residing in College-Owned, -Operated, or -Affiliated Housing:** 40 **Final Year or Final Semester Residency Requirement:** Yes **Library Holdings:** 91,389 **Regional Accreditation:** Western Association of Schools and Colleges **Credit Hours For Degree:** 124 credit hours, Bachelors **Professional Accreditation:** ACBSP, NASM **Intercollegiate Athletics:** Basketball M & W; Cross-Country Running M & W; Golf M; Lacrosse M; Soccer M & W; Softball W; Tennis W; Volleyball W

OCCIDENTAL COLLEGE
1600 Campus Rd.
Los Angeles, CA 90041-3314
Tel: (323)259-2500; Free: 800-825-5262
Admissions: (323)259-2700
Fax: (323)341-4875
E-mail: admission@oxy.edu
Web Site: http://www.oxy.edu/
President/CEO: Dr. Jonathan Veitch
Admissions: Vince Cuseo
Financial Aid: Maureen McRae
Type: Comprehensive **Sex:** Coed **Scores:** 100% SAT V 400+; 100% SAT M 400+; 3% ACT 18-23; 46% ACT 24-29 **% Accepted:** 44 **Admission Plans:** Early Admission; Early Decision Plan; Deferred Admission **Application Deadline:** January 10 **Application Fee:** $50.00 **H.S. Requirements:** High school diploma required; GED accepted **Costs Per Year:** Application fee: $50. Comprehensive fee: $52,263 includes full-time tuition ($39,870), mandatory fees ($1033), and college room and board ($11,360). College room only: $6460. Room and board charges vary according to board plan. Part-time tuition: $1585 per credit. **Scholarships:** Available **Calendar System:** Semester, Summer Session Available **Enrollment:** FT 1,957, PT 15 **Faculty:** FT 163, PT 90 **Student-Faculty Ratio:** 10:1 **Exams:** SAT I or ACT, SAT II. **% Receiving Financial Aid:** 55 **% Residing in College-Owned, -Operated, or -Affiliated Housing:** 79 **Final Year or Final Semester Residency Requirement:** No **Library Holdings:** 497,161 **Regional Accreditation:** Western Association of Schools and Colleges **Credit Hours For Degree:** 128 units, Bachelors **ROTC:** Army, Air Force **Intercollegiate Athletics:** Baseball M; Basketball M & W; Cheerleading W; Cross-Country Running M & W; Football M; Golf M & W; Lacrosse M & W; Rugby M & W; Soccer M & W; Softball W; Swimming and Diving M & W; Tennis M & W; Track and Field M & W; Ultimate Frisbee M & W; Volleyball W; Water Polo M & W

OHLONE COLLEGE
43600 Mission Blvd.
Fremont, CA 94539-5884
Tel: (510)659-6000
Admissions: (510)659-6518
E-mail: cwilliamson@ohlone.edu
Web Site: http://www.ohlone.edu/
President/CEO: Dr. Gari Browing
Admissions: Christopher Williamson
Type: Two-Year College **Sex:** Coed **Affiliation:** California Community College System **Admission Plans:** Open Admission; Early Admission **Application Deadline:** Rolling **Application Fee:** $0.00 **H.S. Requirements:** High school diploma required; GED accepted. For part-time programs: High school diploma or equivalent not required **Scholarships:** Available **Calendar System:** Semester, Summer Session Available **Enrollment:** FT 3,473, PT 7,394 **Faculty:** FT 144, PT 286 **Student-Faculty Ratio:** 24:1 **Library Holdings:** 65,000 **Regional Accreditation:** Western Association of Schools and Colleges **Credit Hours For Degree:** 60 units, Associates **ROTC:** Army, Air Force **Professional Accreditation:** APTA, CARC, NLN **Intercollegiate Athletics:** Baseball M; Basketball M & W; Soccer M & W; Softball W; Swimming and Diving M & W; Tennis M & W; Volleyball M & W; Water Polo M

ORANGE COAST COLLEGE
2701 Fairview Rd., PO Box 5005
Costa Mesa, CA 92628-5005
Tel: (714)432-0202

Admissions: (714)432-5788
Fax: (714)432-5072
E-mail: kclark@occ.cccd.edu
Web Site: http://www.orangecoastcollege.com/
President/CEO: Dr. Dennis Harkins
Admissions: Kristin Clark
Type: Two-Year College **Sex:** Coed **Affiliation:** Coast Community College District System **Admission Plans:** Open Admission **Application Deadline:** Rolling **Application Fee:** $0.00 **H.S. Requirements:** High school diploma or equivalent not required **Costs Per Year:** Application fee: $0. State resident tuition: $0 full-time. Nonresident tuition: $5700 full-time, $190 per unit part-time. Mandatory fees: $902 full-time, $26 per unit part-time. **Scholarships:** Available **Calendar System:** Semester, Summer Session Available **Enrollment:** FT 9,776, PT 14,966 **Faculty:** FT 286, PT 495 **Student-Faculty Ratio:** 33:1 **Final Year or Final Semester Residency Requirement:** No **Library Holdings:** 112,018 **Regional Accreditation:** Western Association of Schools and Colleges **Credit Hours For Degree:** 60 units, Associates **ROTC:** Army, Air Force **Professional Accreditation:** ACF, ADA, CARC, JRCECT, JRCEDMS, JRCEET, JRCERT **Intercollegiate Athletics:** Baseball M; Basketball M & W; Bowling M & W; Crew M & W; Cross-Country Running M & W; Football M; Golf M & W; Soccer M & W; Softball W; Swimming and Diving M & W; Tennis M & W; Track and Field M & W; Volleyball W; Water Polo M & W

OTIS COLLEGE OF ART AND DESIGN

9045 Lincoln Blvd.
Los Angeles, CA 90045-9785
Tel: (310)665-6800; Free: 800-527-OTIS
Admissions: (310)665-6820
Fax: (310)665-6805
E-mail: admissions@otis.edu
Web Site: http://www.otis.edu/
President/CEO: Samuel Hoi
Admissions: Marc D. Meredith
Financial Aid: Jessika Huerta
Type: Comprehensive **Sex:** Coed **Scores:** 45% ACT 18-23; 40% ACT 24-29 **% Accepted:** 44 **Admission Plans:** Early Admission **Application Deadline:** Rolling **Application Fee:** $50.00 **H.S. Requirements:** High school diploma required; GED accepted **Costs Per Year:** Application fee: $50. Tuition: $30,660 full-time, $1022 per unit part-time. Mandatory fees: $700 full-time. **Scholarships:** Available **Calendar System:** Semester, Summer Session Available **Enrollment:** FT 1,141, PT 12, Grad FT 53, Grad PT 15 **Faculty:** FT 56, PT 222 **Student-Faculty Ratio:** 9:1 **Exams:** SAT I or ACT. ACT essay not being used. SAT essay not being used. **% Receiving Financial Aid:** 67 **% Residing in College-Owned, -Operated, or -Affiliated Housing:** 9 **Library Holdings:** 42,000 **Regional Accreditation:** Western Association of Schools and Colleges **Credit Hours For Degree:** 134 credits, Bachelors **Professional Accreditation:** NASAD

OXNARD COLLEGE

4000 South Rose Ave.
Oxnard, CA 93033-6699
Tel: (805)986-5800
Admissions: (805)986-5843
Fax: (805)986-5806
E-mail: scabral@vcccd.edu
Web Site: http://www.oxnardcollege.edu/
President/CEO: Dr. Richard Duran
Admissions: Susan Cabral
Type: Two-Year College **Sex:** Coed **Affiliation:** Ventura County Community College District System **Admission Plans:** Open Admission; Early Admission **Application Deadline:** Rolling **Application Fee:** $0.00 **H.S. Requirements:** High school diploma required; GED accepted. For applicants 18 or over: High school diploma or equivalent not required **Costs Per Year:** Application fee: $0. State resident tuition: $0 full-time. Nonresident tuition: $4536 full-time, $189 per unit part-time. Mandatory fees: $680 full-time, $26 per unit part-time. Full-time tuition and fees vary according to course load. Part-time tuition and fees vary according to course load. **Scholarships:** Available **Calendar System:** Semester, Summer Session Available **Enrollment:** FT 2,078, PT 4,725 **Faculty:** FT 99, PT 170 **Student-Faculty Ratio:** 24:1 **Library Holdings:** 31,500 **Regional Accreditation:** Western Association of Schools and Colleges **Credit Hours For Degree:** 60 units, Associates **Professional Accreditation:** ADA **Intercollegiate Athletics:** Baseball M; Basketball M & W; Cross-Country Running M & W; Soccer M & W; Softball W; Track and Field M & W; Volleyball W

PACIFIC OAKS COLLEGE

5 Westmoreland Place
Pasadena, CA 91103
Tel: (626)397-1300; Free: 800-684-0900
Fax: (626)397-1317
E-mail: admissions@pacificoaks.edu
Web Site: http://www.pacificoaks.edu/
President/CEO: Cynthia Carter, PhD
Admissions: Augusta Pickens
Financial Aid: Rosie Tristan
Type: Two-Year Upper Division **Sex:** Coed **% Accepted:** 77 **Admission Plans:** Deferred Admission **Application Fee:** $55.00 **H.S. Requirements:** High school diploma required; GED accepted **Scholarships:** Available **Calendar System:** Semester, Summer Session Available **Enrollment:** FT 17, PT 240 **Faculty:** FT 27, PT 98 **Student-Faculty Ratio:** 22:1 **Library Holdings:** 36,000 **Regional Accreditation:** Western Association of Schools and Colleges **Credit Hours For Degree:** 124 units, Bachelors

PACIFIC STATES UNIVERSITY

1516 South Western Ave.
Los Angeles, CA 90006
Tel: (323)731-2383; Free: 888-200-0383
Fax: (323)731-7276
E-mail: ryanray@psuca.edu
Web Site: http://www.psuca.edu/
President/CEO: Dr. Mark L. Hopkins
Admissions: Ryan Ray
Type: Comprehensive **Sex:** Coed **% Accepted:** 80 **Admission Plans:** Open Admission; Deferred Admission **Application Deadline:** Rolling **Application Fee:** $100.00 **H.S. Requirements:** High school diploma required; GED accepted **Costs Per Year:** Application fee: $100. Tuition: $14,080 full-time. Mandatory fees: $600 full-time. Full-time tuition and fees vary according to course load. College room only: $9000. **Calendar System:** Quarter, Summer Session Available **Enrollment:** FT 46, Grad FT 151 **Faculty:** FT 8, PT 23 **Student-Faculty Ratio:** 12:1 **Credit Hours For Degree:** 180 units, Bachelors **Professional Accreditation:** ACICS

PACIFIC UNION COLLEGE

One Angwin Ave.
Angwin, CA 94508-9707
Tel: (707)965-6311; Free: 800-862-7080
Admissions: (707)965-6425
Fax: (707)965-6390
E-mail: enroll@puc.edu
Web Site: http://www.puc.edu/
President/CEO: Dr. Heather Knight
Admissions: Darren Hagen
Financial Aid: Laurie Wheeler
Type: Comprehensive **Sex:** Coed **Affiliation:** Seventh-day Adventist **Scores:** 90% SAT V 400+; 90% SAT M 400+; 36% ACT 18-23; 32% ACT 24-29 **% Accepted:** 71 **Admission Plans:** Deferred Admission **Application Deadline:** Rolling **Application Fee:** $30.00 **H.S. Requirements:** High school diploma required; GED accepted **Costs Per Year:** Application fee: $30. Comprehensive fee: $30,729 includes full-time tuition ($23,844), mandatory fees ($135), and college room and board ($6750). College room only: $3975. Full-time tuition and fees vary according to course load. Part-time tuition: $695 per quarter hour. Part-time tuition varies according to course load. Tuition guaranteed not to increase for student's term of enrollment. **Scholarships:** Available **Calendar System:** Quarter, Summer Session Available **Enrollment:** FT 1,270, PT 257, Grad PT 1 **Faculty:** FT 84, PT 11 **Student-Faculty Ratio:** 15:1 **Exams:** SAT I or ACT. **% Receiving Financial Aid:** 97 **% Residing in College-Owned, -Operated, or -Affiliated Housing:** 70 **Final Year or Final Semester Residency Requirement:** Yes **Regional Accreditation:** Western Association of Schools and Colleges **Credit Hours For Degree:** 90 quarter hours, Associates; 192 quarter hours, Bachelors **Professional Accreditation:** CSWE, NASM, NLN **Intercollegiate Athletics:** Basketball M & W; Cross-Country Running M & W; Volleyball M & W

PALO VERDE COLLEGE

One College Dr.
Blythe, CA 92225

Tel: (760)921-5500
Fax: (760)921-5590
Web Site: http://www.paloverde.edu/
President/CEO: James Hottois
Admissions: Pat Koester
Type: Two-Year College **Sex:** Coed **Affiliation:** California Community College System **% Accepted:** 100 **Admission Plans:** Open Admission; Early Admission **Application Deadline:** Rolling **Application Fee:** $0.00 **H.S. Requirements:** High school diploma or equivalent not required **Scholarships:** Available **Calendar System:** Semester, Summer Session Available **Enrollment:** FT 3,648 **Faculty:** FT 33, PT 128 **Library Holdings:** 21,457 **Regional Accreditation:** Western Association of Schools and Colleges **Credit Hours For Degree:** 60 units, Associates

PALOMAR COLLEGE
1140 West Mission Rd.
San Marcos, CA 92069-1487
Tel: (760)744-1150
Fax: (760)744-2932
E-mail: admissions@palomar.edu
Web Site: http://www.palomar.edu/
President/CEO: Robert Deegan
Admissions: Herman Lee
Type: Two-Year College **Sex:** Coed **Affiliation:** California Community College System **Admission Plans:** Open Admission **Application Deadline:** Rolling **Application Fee:** $0.00 **H.S. Requirements:** High school diploma or equivalent not required **Scholarships:** Available **Calendar System:** Semester, Summer Session Available **Library Holdings:** 108,000 **Regional Accreditation:** Western Association of Schools and Colleges **Credit Hours For Degree:** 60 units, Associates **Professional Accreditation:** ADA, NLN **Intercollegiate Athletics:** Baseball M; Basketball M & W; Football M; Golf M; Soccer M & W; Softball W; Swimming and Diving M & W; Tennis M & W; Track and Field M & W; Volleyball M & W; Water Polo M & W; Wrestling M

PASADENA CITY COLLEGE
1570 East Colorado Blvd.
Pasadena, CA 91106-2041
Tel: (626)585-7123
Admissions: (626)585-7805
Fax: (626)585-7915
E-mail: mbramey@pasadena.edu
Web Site: http://www.pasadena.edu/
President/CEO: Dr. Paulette J. Perfumo
Admissions: Dr. Margaret Ramey
Type: Two-Year College **Sex:** Coed **Affiliation:** California Community College System **Admission Plans:** Open Admission **Application Deadline:** Rolling **H.S. Requirements:** High school diploma or equivalent not required. For applicants under 18: High school diploma required; GED accepted **Costs Per Year:** Nonresident tuition: $190 per unit part-time. Mandatory fees: $26 per unit part-time, $14 per term part-time. Part-time tuition and fees vary according to course load. **Calendar System:** Semester, Summer Session Available **Enrollment:** FT 27,000 **Faculty:** FT 425, PT 900 **Student-Faculty Ratio:** 20:1 **Library Holdings:** 120,000 **Regional Accreditation:** Western Association of Schools and Colleges **Credit Hours For Degree:** 60 units, Associates **Professional Accreditation:** ADA, JRCERT, NLN **Intercollegiate Athletics:** Baseball M; Basketball M & W; Cross-Country Running M & W; Football M; Soccer M & W; Softball W; Swimming and Diving M & W; Tennis M & W; Track and Field M & W; Volleyball W; Water Polo M

PATTEN UNIVERSITY
2433 Coolidge Ave.
Oakland, CA 94601-2699
Tel: (510)261-8500
Fax: (510)534-8564
Web Site: http://www.patten.edu/
President/CEO: Dr. Gary Moncher
Admissions: Kim Guerra
Financial Aid: Robert A. Olivera
Type: Comprehensive **Sex:** Coed **Affiliation:** interdenominational **Scores:** 100% ACT 18-23 **Admission Plans:** Open Admission; Early Admission; Deferred Admission **Application Deadline:** Rolling **Application Fee:** $30.00 **H.S. Requirements:** High school diploma required; GED accepted **Costs Per Year:** Application fee: $30. Comprehensive fee: $20,530 includes full-time tuition ($13,440) and college room and board ($7090). Full-time tuition varies according to course load. Part-time tuition: $560 per unit. **Scholarships:** Available **Calendar System:** Semester, Summer Session Available **Enrollment:** FT 487, PT 507, Grad FT 14, Grad PT 42 **Faculty:** FT 26, PT 99 **Student-Faculty Ratio:** 17:1 **Exams:** SAT I or ACT. **% Residing in College-Owned, -Operated, or -Affiliated Housing:** 34 **Library Holdings:** 36,160 **Regional Accreditation:** Western Association of Schools and Colleges **Credit Hours For Degree:** 63 units, Associates; 125 units, Bachelors **Intercollegiate Athletics:** Baseball M; Softball W

PEPPERDINE UNIVERSITY
24255 Pacific Coast Hwy.
Malibu, CA 90263
Tel: (310)506-4000
Admissions: (310)506-4392
Fax: (310)506-4861
E-mail: kristin.paredes@pepperdine.edu
Web Site: http://www.pepperdine.edu/
President/CEO: Dr. Andrew K. Benton
Admissions: Kristin Paredes-Collins
Financial Aid: Janet Lockhart
Type: University **Sex:** Coed **Affiliation:** Church of Christ **Scores:** 99.9% SAT V 400+; 99.8% SAT M 400+; 14.5% ACT 18-23; 52.2% ACT 24-29 **% Accepted:** 41 **Application Deadline:** January 15 **Application Fee:** $65.00 **H.S. Requirements:** High school diploma required; GED accepted **Costs Per Year:** Application fee: $65. Comprehensive fee: $48,750 includes full-time tuition ($37,730), mandatory fees ($120), and college room and board ($10,900). College room only: $8380. Room and board charges vary according to board plan and housing facility. Part-time tuition: $1170 per credit hour. **Scholarships:** Available **Calendar System:** Semester, Summer Session Available **Enrollment:** FT 3,052, PT 387, Grad FT 2,384, Grad PT 1,910 **Faculty:** FT 367, PT 312 **Student-Faculty Ratio:** 14:1 **Exams:** SAT I or ACT. **% Receiving Financial Aid:** 53 **% Residing in College-Owned, -Operated, or -Affiliated Housing:** 58 **Regional Accreditation:** Western Association of Schools and Colleges **Credit Hours For Degree:** 128 units, Bachelors **ROTC:** Army, Air Force **Professional Accreditation:** AACSB, ABA, AALS, NASM **Intercollegiate Athletics:** Baseball M; Basketball M & W; Cheerleading M & W; Crew M & W; Cross-Country Running M & W; Field Hockey W; Golf M & W; Lacrosse M; Rugby M; Sailing M & W; Soccer M & W; Swimming and Diving W; Tennis M & W; Volleyball M & W; Water Polo M & W

PERELANDRA COLLEGE
8697-C La Mesa Blvd.
PMB 21
La Mesa, CA 91941
Tel: (619)677-3308
Fax: (619)677-3304
Web Site: http://www.perelandra.edu/
Type: Comprehensive **Sex:** Coed

PIMA MEDICAL INSTITUTE
780 Bay Blvd.
Ste. 101
Chula Vista, CA 91910
Tel: (619)425-3200; Free: 888-898-9048
Fax: (619)425-3450
Web Site: http://www.pmi.edu/
President/CEO: Jim Volpe
Type: Two-Year College **Sex:** Coed **Affiliation:** Vocational Training Institutes, Inc. **H.S. Requirements:** High school diploma required; GED accepted **Exams:** Other. **Credit Hours For Degree:** 88 credits, Associates **Professional Accreditation:** ABHES

PITZER COLLEGE
1050 North Mills Ave.
Claremont, CA 91711-6101
Tel: (909)621-8000; Free: 800-748-9371
Admissions: (909)621-8129
Fax: (909)621-8770
E-mail: admission@pitzer.edu
Web Site: http://www.pitzer.edu/
President/CEO: Dr. Laura Skandera Trombley
Admissions: Angel Perez

Financial Aid: Margaret Carothers
Type: Four-Year College **Sex:** Coed **Affiliation:** The Claremont Colleges Consortium **Scores:** 99% SAT V 400+; 100% SAT M 400+; 6% ACT 18-23; 59% ACT 24-29 **% Accepted:** 20 **Admission Plans:** Early Decision Plan; Deferred Admission **Application Deadline:** January 1 **Application Fee:** $60.00 **H.S. Requirements:** High school diploma required; GED accepted **Costs Per Year:** Application fee: $60. Comprehensive fee: $50,770 includes full-time tuition ($35,840), mandatory fees ($3490), and college room and board ($11,440). College room only: $7240. Full-time tuition and fees vary according to course load. Room and board charges vary according to board plan. Part-time tuition: $4480 per course. Part-time tuition varies according to course load. **Scholarships:** Available **Calendar System:** Semester, Summer Session Available **Enrollment:** FT 986, PT 57 **Faculty:** FT 73, PT 24 **Student-Faculty Ratio:** 11:1 **Exams:** SAT I or ACT. **% Receiving Financial Aid:** 40 **% Residing in College-Owned, -Operated, or -Affiliated Housing:** 74 **Final Year or Final Semester Residency Requirement:** No **Library Holdings:** 2,500,000 **Regional Accreditation:** Western Association of Schools and Colleges **Credit Hours For Degree:** 32 courses, Bachelors **ROTC:** Army, Air Force **Intercollegiate Athletics:** Baseball M; Basketball M & W; Cross-Country Running M & W; Football M; Golf M; Lacrosse W; Soccer M & W; Softball W; Swimming and Diving M & W; Tennis M & W; Track and Field M & W; Volleyball W; Water Polo M & W

PLATT COLLEGE (CERRITOS)
10900 East 183rd St., Ste. 290
Cerritos, CA 90703-5342
Tel: (562)809-5100; Free: 800-807-5288
Fax: (562)809-7100
Web Site: http://www.platt.edu/
President/CEO: Sabrina Kay
Admissions: Ilene Holt
Type: Two-Year College **Sex:** Coed **H.S. Requirements:** High school diploma required; GED accepted **Scholarships:** Available **Calendar System:** Continuous **Faculty:** PT 30 **Student-Faculty Ratio:** 12:1 **Exams:** Other. **Professional Accreditation:** ACCSCT

PLATT COLLEGE (HUNTINGTON BEACH)
7755 Center Ave., Ste. 600
Huntington Beach, CA 92647
Tel: (714)373-3240; Free: 888-866-6697
Admissions: (949)833-2300
Web Site: http://www.plattcollege.edu/
Admissions: Lisa Rhodes
Type: Two-Year College **Sex:** Coed **Application Deadline:** Rolling **Application Fee:** $75.00 **H.S. Requirements:** High school diploma required; GED accepted **Calendar System:** Continuous, Summer Session Available **Exams:** Other. **Library Holdings:** 1,100 **Credit Hours For Degree:** 96 credits, Associates **Professional Accreditation:** ACCSCT

PLATT COLLEGE (ONTARIO)
3700 Inland Empire Blvd.
Ste. 400
Ontario, CA 91764
Tel: (909)941-9410; Free: 888-866-6697
Fax: (909)989-8974
Web Site: http://www.plattcollege.edu/
President/CEO: Daryl Goldberg
Admissions: Jennifer Abandonato
Type: Two-Year College **Sex:** Coed **Application Deadline:** Rolling **Application Fee:** $75.00 **H.S. Requirements:** High school diploma required; GED accepted **Calendar System:** Continuous, Summer Session Available **Exams:** Other. **Library Holdings:** 2,800 **Credit Hours For Degree:** 96 credit hours, Associates **Professional Accreditation:** ACCSCT

PLATT COLLEGE SAN DIEGO
6250 El Cajon Blvd.
San Diego, CA 92115-3919
Tel: (619)265-0107; Free: (866)752-8826
Fax: (619)265-8655
E-mail: sgallup@platt.edu
Web Site: http://www.platt.edu/
President/CEO: Robert D. Leiker
Admissions: Steve Gallup
Type: Four-Year College **Sex:** Coed **Admission Plans:** Open Admission; Early Admission; Deferred Admission **Application Deadline:** Rolling **Application Fee:** $110.00 **H.S. Requirements:** High school diploma required; GED accepted **Costs Per Year:** Application fee: $110. One-time mandatory fee: $110. Tuition: $25,040 full-time. **Calendar System:** Continuous, Summer Session Not available **Enrollment:** FT 292 **Faculty:** FT 6, PT 23 **Student-Faculty Ratio:** 21:1 **Exams:** Other, SAT I or ACT, SAT I and SAT II or ACT, SAT II. **Final Year or Final Semester Residency Requirement:** No **Library Holdings:** 775 **Credit Hours For Degree:** 65 semester credit hours, Associates; 128 semester credit hours, Bachelors **Professional Accreditation:** ACCSCT

PLATT COLLEGE—LOS ANGELES
1000 South Fremont A9W
Alhambra, CA 91803
Tel: (323)258-8050
Admissions: (626)300-5444
Fax: (323)258-8532
Web Site: http://www.plattcollege.edu/
President/CEO: Sam Alahmad
Admissions: Detroit Whiteside
Type: Two-Year College **Sex:** Coed **Application Deadline:** Rolling **Application Fee:** $75.00 **H.S. Requirements:** High school diploma required; GED accepted **Calendar System:** Continuous, Summer Session Available **Exams:** Other. **Library Holdings:** 808 **Credit Hours For Degree:** 96 credits, Associates **Professional Accreditation:** ACCSCT

POINT LOMA NAZARENE UNIVERSITY
3900 Lomaland Dr.
San Diego, CA 92106-2899
Tel: (619)849-2200; Free: 800-733-7770
Admissions: (619)849-2273
Fax: (619)849-2579
E-mail: admissions@pointloma.edu
Web Site: http://www.pointloma.edu/
President/CEO: Dr. Bob Brower
Admissions: Eric Groves
Type: Comprehensive **Sex:** Coed **Affiliation:** Nazarene **Scores:** 99.5% SAT V 400+; 98.1% SAT M 400+; 44.8% ACT 18-23; 41.9% ACT 24-29 **% Accepted:** 74 **Admission Plans:** Early Action **Application Fee:** $50.00 **H.S. Requirements:** High school diploma required; GED accepted **Costs Per Year:** Application fee: $50. Comprehensive fee: $36,100 includes full-time tuition ($26,500), mandatory fees ($600), and college room and board ($9000). College room only: $5000. Full-time tuition and fees vary according to course load. Room and board charges vary according to board plan. Part-time tuition: $1105 per credit hour. Part-time tuition varies according to course load. **Scholarships:** Available **Calendar System:** Semester, Summer Session Available **Enrollment:** FT 2,306, PT 81, Grad FT 458, Grad PT 532 **Exams:** SAT I or ACT, SAT I. ACT essay used as a validity check on application essay. SAT essay used as a validity check on application essay. **% Receiving Financial Aid:** 64 **% Residing in College-Owned, -Operated, or -Affiliated Housing:** 68 **Final Year or Final Semester Residency Requirement:** Yes **Regional Accreditation:** Western Association of Schools and Colleges **Credit Hours For Degree:** 128 semester units, Bachelors **ROTC:** Army, Navy, Air Force **Professional Accreditation:** AACN, AAFCS, ACBSP, NASM, NLN **Intercollegiate Athletics:** Baseball M; Basketball M & W; Cross-Country Running M & W; Golf M; Soccer M & W; Softball W; Tennis M & W; Track and Field M & W; Volleyball W

POMONA COLLEGE
333 North College Way
Claremont, CA 91711
Tel: (909)621-8000
Admissions: (909)621-8134
Fax: (909)621-8403
E-mail: admissions@pomona.edu
Web Site: http://www.pomona.edu/
President/CEO: Dr. David W. Oxtoby
Admissions: Bruce Poch
Financial Aid: Mary Booker
Type: Four-Year College **Sex:** Coed **Scores:** 100% SAT V 400+; 100% SAT M 400+; 1% ACT 18-23; 16% ACT 24-29 **% Accepted:** 16 **Admission Plans:** Early Admission; Early Decision Plan; Deferred Admission **Application Deadline:** January 2 **Application Fee:** $65.00 **H.S. Requirements:** High school diploma or equivalent not required **Costs Per Year:** Application

fee: $65. Comprehensive fee: $51,330 includes full-time tuition ($38,087), mandatory fees ($307), and college room and board ($12,936). Room and board charges vary according to board plan. **Scholarships:** Available **Calendar System:** Semester, Summer Session Not available **Enrollment:** FT 1,535, PT 15 **Faculty:** FT 188, PT 37 **Student-Faculty Ratio:** 7:1 **Exams:** SAT I and SAT II or ACT. ACT essay used for admission. SAT essay used for admission. ACT essay used for advising. SAT essay used for advising. ACT essay used as a validity check on application essay. SAT essay used as a validity check on application essay. **% Receiving Financial Aid:** 54 **% Residing in College-Owned, -Operated, or -Affiliated Housing:** 98 **Library Holdings:** 2,500,000 **Regional Accreditation:** Western Association of Schools and Colleges **Credit Hours For Degree:** 32 courses, Bachelors **ROTC:** Army, Air Force **Intercollegiate Athletics:** Baseball M; Basketball M & W; Cross-Country Running M & W; Football M; Golf M & W; Lacrosse W; Soccer M & W; Softball W; Swimming and Diving M & W; Tennis M & W; Track and Field M & W; Ultimate Frisbee M & W; Volleyball M & W; Water Polo M & W

PORTERVILLE COLLEGE
100 East College Ave.
Porterville, CA 93257-6058
Tel: (559)791-2200
Fax: (559)791-2349
Web Site: http://www.pc.cc.ca.us/
President/CEO: Dr. Rosa Carlson
Admissions: Judy Pope
Type: Two-Year College **Sex:** Coed **Affiliation:** Kern Community College District System **% Accepted:** 100 **Admission Plans:** Open Admission; Early Admission **Application Deadline:** Rolling **Application Fee:** $0.00 **H.S. Requirements:** High school diploma or equivalent not required. For licensed vocational nursing program: High school diploma required; GED accepted **Calendar System:** Semester, Summer Session Available **Faculty:** FT 60, PT 80 **Library Holdings:** 31,557 **Regional Accreditation:** Western Association of Schools and Colleges **Credit Hours For Degree:** 60 units, Associates **Intercollegiate Athletics:** Baseball M; Basketball M & W; Soccer M & W; Softball W; Tennis M & W; Volleyball W

PROFESSIONAL GOLFERS CAREER COLLEGE
PO Box 892319
Temecula, CA 92589
Tel: (909)693-2963; Free: 800-877-4380
Admissions: (951)719-2994
Fax: (909)693-2863
E-mail: Mark@golfcollege.edu
Web Site: http://www.golfcollege.edu/
President/CEO: Dr. Tim Somerville
Admissions: Mark Bland
Type: Two-Year College **Sex:** Coed **% Accepted:** 100 **Admission Plans:** Open Admission; Early Admission; Deferred Admission **Application Deadline:** Rolling **Application Fee:** $75.00 **H.S. Requirements:** High school diploma required; GED accepted **Calendar System:** Semester **Enrollment:** FT 318 **Faculty:** FT 5, PT 18 **Student-Faculty Ratio:** 15:1 **% Residing in College-Owned, -Operated, or -Affiliated Housing:** 26 **Library Holdings:** 2,291 **Credit Hours For Degree:** 66 credits, Associates **Professional Accreditation:** ACICS

REEDLEY COLLEGE
995 North Reed Ave.
Reedley, CA 93654-2099
Tel: (559)638-3641
Web Site: http://www.reedleycollege.edu/
President/CEO: Dr. Barbara Hioco
Type: Two-Year College **Sex:** Coed **Affiliation:** State Center Community College District System **% Accepted:** 100 **Admission Plans:** Open Admission **Application Deadline:** Rolling **Application Fee:** $0.00 **H.S. Requirements:** High school diploma required; GED accepted **Costs Per Year:** Application fee: $0. State resident tuition: $0 full-time. Nonresident tuition: $5700 full-time. Mandatory fees: $1496 full-time. College room and board: $2502. College room only: $1402. **Scholarships:** Available **Calendar System:** Semester, Summer Session Available **Enrollment:** FT 4,423, PT 7,359 **Faculty:** FT 180, PT 354 **Student-Faculty Ratio:** 14:1 **Library Holdings:** 36,000 **Regional Accreditation:** Western Association of Schools and Colleges **Credit Hours For Degree:** 60 units, Associates **ROTC:** Air Force **Intercollegiate Athletics:** Baseball M; Basketball M & W; Football M; Golf M; Softball W; Tennis M & W; Track and Field M & W; Volleyball W

RIO HONDO COLLEGE
3600 Workman Mill Rd.
Whittier, CA 90601-1699
Tel: (562)692-0921
Fax: (562)692-9318
Web Site: http://www.riohondo.edu/
President/CEO: Dr. Ted Martinez, Jr.
Admissions: Judy G. Pearson
Type: Two-Year College **Sex:** Coed **Affiliation:** California Community College System **Admission Plans:** Open Admission; Early Admission **Application Deadline:** July 10 **Application Fee:** $0.00 **H.S. Requirements:** High school diploma or equivalent not required **Scholarships:** Available **Calendar System:** Semester, Summer Session Available **Faculty:** FT 210, PT 500 **Library Holdings:** 94,143 **Regional Accreditation:** Western Association of Schools and Colleges **Credit Hours For Degree:** 62 units, Associates **ROTC:** Army, Navy, Air Force **Intercollegiate Athletics:** Baseball M; Basketball M & W; Cross-Country Running M & W; Softball W; Swimming and Diving M & W; Tennis M & W; Volleyball W; Water Polo M & W; Wrestling M

RIVERSIDE COMMUNITY COLLEGE DISTRICT
4800 Magnolia Ave.
Riverside, CA 92506-1299
Tel: (909)222-8000
Admissions: (951)222-8600
Fax: (909)222-8037
E-mail: admissions@rcc.edu
Web Site: http://www.rcc.edu/
President/CEO: Dr. Irving Hendrick
Admissions: Lorraine Anderson
Type: Two-Year College **Sex:** Coed **Affiliation:** California Community College System **% Accepted:** 100 **Admission Plans:** Open Admission **Application Deadline:** Rolling **Application Fee:** $0.00 **H.S. Requirements:** High school diploma or equivalent not required. For registered nursing program: High school diploma required; GED accepted **Scholarships:** Available **Calendar System:** Semester, Summer Session Available **Enrollment:** FT 10,771, PT 27,734 **Faculty:** FT 250, PT 1,335 **Library Holdings:** 101,243 **Regional Accreditation:** Western Association of Schools and Colleges **Credit Hours For Degree:** 60 units, Associates **ROTC:** Army, Air Force **Professional Accreditation:** ADA, NLN **Intercollegiate Athletics:** Baseball M; Basketball M & W; Cross-Country Running M & W; Football M; Golf M; Soccer M & W; Softball W; Swimming and Diving M & W; Tennis M & W; Track and Field M & W; Volleyball W; Water Polo M & W

SACRAMENTO CITY COLLEGE
3835 Freeport Blvd.
Sacramento, CA 95822-1386
Tel: (916)558-2111
Fax: (916)558-2190
Web Site: http://www.scc.losrios.edu/
President/CEO: Kathryn E. Jeffrey
Admissions: Sam T. Sandusky
Type: Two-Year College **Sex:** Coed **Affiliation:** California Community College System **Admission Plans:** Open Admission **Application Deadline:** Rolling **Application Fee:** $0.00 **H.S. Requirements:** High school diploma or equivalent not required **Scholarships:** Available **Calendar System:** Semester, Summer Session Available **Student-Faculty Ratio:** 30:1 **Library Holdings:** 68,462 **Regional Accreditation:** Western Association of Schools and Colleges **Credit Hours For Degree:** 60 units, Associates **Professional Accreditation:** ADA, AOTA, APTA **Intercollegiate Athletics:** Baseball M; Basketball M & W; Cross-Country Running M & W; Football M; Golf M & W; Soccer W; Softball W; Swimming and Diving M & W; Tennis M & W; Track and Field M & W; Volleyball W; Water Polo W; Wrestling M

SADDLEBACK COLLEGE
28000 Marguerite Parkway
Mission Viejo, CA 92692
Tel: (949)582-4500
Admissions: (949)582-4555
Fax: (949)347-8315
E-mail: earaiza@saddleback.edu

Web Site: http://www.saddleback.edu/
President/CEO: Dr. Richard D. McCullough
Type: Two-Year College **Sex:** Coed **Admission Plans:** Open Admission; Early Admission **Application Deadline:** Rolling **Application Fee:** $0.00 **H.S. Requirements:** High school diploma or equivalent not required **Costs Per Year:** Application fee: $0. State resident tuition: $0 full-time. Nonresident tuition: $4560 full-time, $190 per unit part-time. Mandatory fees: $762 full-time, $26 per unit part-time. **Scholarships:** Available **Calendar System:** Semester, Summer Session Available **Enrollment:** FT 6,621, PT 11,750 **Faculty:** FT 215, PT 539 **Library Holdings:** 109,000 **Regional Accreditation:** Western Association of Schools and Colleges **Credit Hours For Degree:** 64 units, Associates **Professional Accreditation:** NLN **Intercollegiate Athletics:** Baseball M; Basketball M & W; Cross-Country Running M & W; Football M; Golf M & W; Softball W; Swimming and Diving M & W; Tennis M & W; Track and Field M & W; Volleyball W; Water Polo M & W

SAGE COLLEGE

12125 Day St., Bldg. L
Moreno Valley, CA 92557-6720
Tel: (951)781-2727; Free: 888-781-2727
Fax: (951)781-0570
Web Site: http://www.sagecollege.edu/
President/CEO: Lauren Somma
Type: Two-Year College **Sex:** Coed **% Accepted:** 100 **Application Fee:** $100.00 **Calendar System:** Quarter **Professional Accreditation:** ACICS

SAINT MARY'S COLLEGE OF CALIFORNIA

1928 Saint Mary's Rd.
Moraga, CA 94556
Tel: (925)631-4000; Free: 800-800-4SMC
Admissions: (925)631-4224
Fax: (925)376-7193
E-mail: smcadmit@stmarys-ca.edu
Web Site: http://www.stmarys-ca.edu/
President/CEO: Br. Ronald Gallagher, PhD
Admissions: Michael McKeon
Financial Aid: Priscilla Muha
Type: Comprehensive **Sex:** Coed **Affiliation:** Roman Catholic **Scores:** 99.8% SAT V 400+; 99.8% SAT M 400+ **% Accepted:** 79 **Admission Plans:** Early Action; Deferred Admission **Application Deadline:** February 1 **Application Fee:** $55.00 **H.S. Requirements:** High school diploma required; GED accepted **Costs Per Year:** Application fee: $55. Comprehensive fee: $45,850 includes full-time tuition ($33,760), mandatory fees ($150), and college room and board ($11,940). College room only: $6570. Room and board charges vary according to board plan and housing facility. Part-time tuition: $4220 per course. **Scholarships:** Available **Calendar System:** 4-1-4, Summer Session Available **Enrollment:** FT 2,294, PT 245, Grad FT 322, Grad PT 775 **Faculty:** FT 202, PT 201 **Student-Faculty Ratio:** 12:1 **Exams:** SAT I or ACT. **% Receiving Financial Aid:** 76 **% Residing in College-Owned, -Operated, or -Affiliated Housing:** 67 **Final Year or Final Semester Residency Requirement:** No **Library Holdings:** 230,133 **Regional Accreditation:** Western Association of Schools and Colleges **Credit Hours For Degree:** 18 courses, Associates; 36 courses, Bachelors **ROTC:** Army, Air Force **Professional Accreditation:** AACN, MACTE **Intercollegiate Athletics:** Baseball M; Basketball M & W; Crew M & W; Cross-Country Running M & W; Golf M; Lacrosse M & W; Rugby M & W; Soccer M & W; Softball W; Tennis M & W; Volleyball M & W; Water Polo M & W

THE SALVATION ARMY COLLEGE FOR OFFICER TRAINING AT CRESTMONT

30840 Hawthorne Blvd.
Rancho Palos Verdes, CA 90275
Tel: (310)377-0481
Admissions: (310)544-6442
Fax: (310)265-6565
Web Site: http://www.crestmont.edu/
Admissions: Capt. Kevin Jackson
Type: Two-Year College **Sex:** Coed **Affiliation:** The Salvation Army **% Accepted:** 67 **Admission Plans:** Preferred Admission **Application Deadline:** June 1 **Application Fee:** $15.00 **H.S. Requirements:** High school diploma required; GED accepted **Calendar System:** Quarter, Summer Session Not available **Enrollment:** FT 27 **Faculty:** FT 13, PT 22 **Student-Faculty Ratio:** 1:1 **% Residing in College-Owned, -Operated, or -Affiliated Housing:** 100 **Library Holdings:** 35,700 **Regional Accreditation:** Western Association of Schools and Colleges **Credit Hours For Degree:** 90 quarter units, Associates

SAMUEL MERRITT UNIVERSITY

370 Hawthorne Ave.
Oakland, CA 94609-3108
Tel: (510)869-6511; Free: 800-607-MERRITT
Admissions: (510)869-6610
Fax: (510)869-6525
E-mail: admission@samuelmerritt.edu
Web Site: http://www.samuelmerritt.edu/
President/CEO: Dr. Sharon Diaz
Admissions: Anne Seed
Financial Aid: Adel Mareghni
Type: Two-Year Upper Division **Sex:** Coed **% Accepted:** 32 **Admission Plans:** Deferred Admission **Application Fee:** $50.00 **H.S. Requirements:** High school diploma required; GED accepted **Costs Per Year:** Application fee: $50. One-time mandatory fee: $1323. Tuition: $34,148 full-time, $1439 per unit part-time. Full-time tuition varies according to degree level and program. Part-time tuition varies according to degree level and program. **Scholarships:** Available **Calendar System:** Trimester, Summer Session Available **Enrollment:** FT 512, PT 67, Grad FT 616, Grad PT 205 **Faculty:** FT 119, PT 121 **Student-Faculty Ratio:** 10:1 **% Receiving Financial Aid:** 85 **Final Year or Final Semester Residency Requirement:** No **Library Holdings:** 45,040 **Regional Accreditation:** Western Association of Schools and Colleges **Credit Hours For Degree:** 128 units, Bachelors **ROTC:** Army, Air Force **Professional Accreditation:** AACN, AANA, AOTA, APTA

SAN BERNARDINO VALLEY COLLEGE

701 South Mount Vernon Ave.
San Bernardino, CA 92410-2748
Tel: (909)384-4400
Web Site: http://www.valleycollege.edu/
President/CEO: Debra Daniels
Admissions: Helena Johnson
Financial Aid: Nancy Davis
Type: Two-Year College **Sex:** Coed **Affiliation:** San Bernardino Community College District System **Admission Plans:** Open Admission **Application Deadline:** August 29 **H.S. Requirements:** High school diploma required; GED accepted **Scholarships:** Available **Calendar System:** Semester, Summer Session Available **Faculty:** FT 175, PT 200 **Library Holdings:** 122,802 **Regional Accreditation:** Western Association of Schools and Colleges **Credit Hours For Degree:** 60 semester hours, Associates **Professional Accreditation:** NLN **Intercollegiate Athletics:** Basketball M & W; Cross-Country Running M & W; Football M; Golf M; Soccer M & W; Tennis M & W; Track and Field M & W; Volleyball W; Wrestling M

SAN DIEGO CHRISTIAN COLLEGE

2100 Greenfield Dr.
El Cajon, CA 92019-1157
Tel: (619)441-2200; Free: 800-676-2242
Admissions: (619)588-7747
Fax: (619)440-0209
E-mail: cdelgiudice@sdcc.edu
Web Site: http://www.sdcc.edu/
President/CEO: Dr. Paul Ague
Admissions: Candice Del Giudice
Financial Aid: Susie Parks
Type: Four-Year College **Sex:** Coed **Affiliation:** nondenominational **Scores:** 85% SAT V 400+; 75% SAT M 400+; 59% ACT 18-23; 7% ACT 24-29 **% Accepted:** 60 **Admission Plans:** Deferred Admission **Application Deadline:** July 1 **Application Fee:** $25.00 **H.S. Requirements:** High school diploma required; GED accepted **Costs Per Year:** Application fee: $25. One-time mandatory fee: $100. Comprehensive fee: $30,952 includes full-time tuition ($21,610), mandatory fees ($1082), and college room and board ($8260). Full-time tuition and fees vary according to class time, course load, and program. Part-time tuition: $874 per unit. Part-time mandatory fees: $204 per term. Part-time tuition and fees vary according to class time, course load, and program. **Scholarships:** Available **Calendar System:** Semester, Summer Session Available **Enrollment:** FT 387, PT 34, Grad FT 12, Grad PT 6 **Faculty:** FT 13, PT 42 **Student-Faculty Ratio:** 15:1 **Exams:** SAT I or ACT. ACT essay not being used. SAT essay not being used. **% Receiving Financial Aid:** 78 **% Residing in College-Owned, -Operated,**

or -Affiliated Housing: 39 **Library Holdings:** 121,605 **Regional Accreditation:** Western Association of Schools and Colleges **Credit Hours For Degree:** 124 semester credits, Bachelors **ROTC:** Army, Air Force **Professional Accreditation:** TACCS **Intercollegiate Athletics:** Baseball M; Basketball M & W; Cross-Country Running M & W; Soccer M & W; Volleyball W

SAN DIEGO CITY COLLEGE
1313 Park Blvd.
San Diego, CA 92101-4787
Tel: (619)388-3400
Admissions: (619)388-3474
Fax: (619)388-3063
E-mail: lhumphri@sdccd.edu
Web Site: http://www.sdcity.edu/
President/CEO: Dr. Terrence J. Burgess
Admissions: Lou Humphries
Financial Aid: Gregory Sanchez
Type: Two-Year College **Sex:** Coed **Affiliation:** San Diego Community College District System **Admission Plans:** Open Admission **Application Deadline:** Rolling **Application Fee:** $0.00 **H.S. Requirements:** High school diploma or equivalent not required. For applicants under 18: High school diploma required; GED accepted **Costs Per Year:** Application fee: $0. State resident tuition: $0 full-time. Nonresident tuition: $5700 full-time, $190 per unit part-time. Mandatory fees: $780 full-time. **Scholarships:** Available **Calendar System:** Semester, Summer Session Available **Faculty:** FT 160, PT 325 **Student-Faculty Ratio:** 35:1 **Library Holdings:** 73,000 **Regional Accreditation:** Western Association of Schools and Colleges **Credit Hours For Degree:** 60 semester hours, Associates **ROTC:** Air Force **Professional Accreditation:** NLN **Intercollegiate Athletics:** Baseball M; Basketball M & W; Cross-Country Running M & W; Football M; Golf M & W; Soccer M & W; Softball W; Tennis M & W; Track and Field M & W; Volleyball M & W

SAN DIEGO GOLF ACADEMY
1910 Shadowridge Dr., Ste. 111
Vista, CA 92083
Tel: (760)734-1208; Free: 800-342-7342
Fax: (760)734-1642
E-mail: sdga@sdgagolf.com
Web Site: http://www.sdgagolf.com/
President/CEO: Chris Hunkler
Admissions: Deborah Wells
Type: Two-Year College **Sex:** Coed **Application Deadline:** Rolling **Application Fee:** $50.00 **H.S. Requirements:** High school diploma required; GED accepted **Scholarships:** Available **Calendar System:** Semester **Credit Hours For Degree:** 66 credits, Associates **Professional Accreditation:** ACICS

SAN DIEGO MESA COLLEGE
7250 Mesa College Dr.
San Diego, CA 92111-4998
Tel: (619)388-2600
Admissions: (619)388-2604
Fax: (619)388-2968
E-mail: csawyer@sdccd.edu
Web Site: http://www.sdmesa.edu/
President/CEO: Rita Cepeda
Admissions: Cheri Sawyer
Type: Two-Year College **Sex:** Coed **Affiliation:** San Diego Community College District System **% Accepted:** 100 **Admission Plans:** Open Admission; Early Admission **Application Deadline:** Rolling **Application Fee:** $0.00 **H.S. Requirements:** High school diploma or equivalent not required **Scholarships:** Available **Calendar System:** Semester, Summer Session Available **Enrollment:** FT 24,250 **Faculty:** FT 287, PT 553 **Library Holdings:** 84,353 **Regional Accreditation:** Western Association of Schools and Colleges **Credit Hours For Degree:** 60 semester hours, Associates **Professional Accreditation:** AAMAE, ADA, AHIMA, APTA **Intercollegiate Athletics:** Baseball M; Basketball M & W; Cross-Country Running M & W; Football M; Soccer M & W; Softball W; Swimming and Diving M & W; Tennis M & W; Track and Field M & W; Volleyball M & W; Water Polo M & W

SAN DIEGO MIRAMAR COLLEGE
10440 Black Mountain Rd.
San Diego, CA 92126-2999
Tel: (619)388-7800
Fax: (619)388-7801
E-mail: dmaxwell@sdccd.cc.ca.us
Web Site: http://www.sdmiramar.edu/
President/CEO: Patricia Hsieh
Admissions: Dana Andras
Type: Two-Year College **Sex:** Coed **Affiliation:** San Diego Community College District System **Admission Plans:** Open Admission **Application Fee:** $0.00 **H.S. Requirements:** High school diploma or equivalent not required **Scholarships:** Available **Calendar System:** Semester, Summer Session Available **Library Holdings:** 19,301 **Regional Accreditation:** Western Association of Schools and Colleges **Credit Hours For Degree:** 60 credits, Associates **Intercollegiate Athletics:** Basketball M; Water Polo M & W

SAN DIEGO STATE UNIVERSITY
5500 Campanile Dr.
San Diego, CA 92182
Tel: (619)594-5200
E-mail: admissions@sdsu.edu
Web Site: http://www.sdsu.edu/
President/CEO: Stephen L. Weber
Admissions: Beverly Arata
Financial Aid: Chrys Dutton
Type: University **Sex:** Coed **Affiliation:** California State University System **Scores:** 91.5% SAT V 400+; 91.8% SAT M 400+; 46.6% ACT 18-23; 36.9% ACT 24-29 **% Accepted:** 36 **Application Deadline:** November 30 **Application Fee:** $55.00 **H.S. Requirements:** High school diploma required; GED accepted **Costs Per Year:** Application fee: $55. State resident tuition: $0 full-time. Nonresident tuition: $11,160 full-time, $372 per unit part-time. Mandatory fees: $4902 full-time, $1605 per term part-time. Full-time tuition and fees vary according to degree level. Part-time tuition and fees vary according to course load and degree level. College room and board: $11,485. Room and board charges vary according to board plan and housing facility. **Scholarships:** Available **Calendar System:** Semester, Summer Session Available **Enrollment:** FT 23,264, PT 4,273, Grad FT 3,303, Grad PT 2,950 **Faculty:** FT 841, PT 689 **Student-Faculty Ratio:** 22:1 **Exams:** SAT I or ACT. ACT essay used for placement. SAT essay used for placement. **% Receiving Financial Aid:** 52 **% Residing in College-Owned, -Operated, or -Affiliated Housing:** 12 **Final Year or Final Semester Residency Requirement:** No **Library Holdings:** 1,342,735 **Regional Accreditation:** Western Association of Schools and Colleges **Credit Hours For Degree:** 120 units, Bachelors **ROTC:** Army, Navy, Air Force **Professional Accreditation:** AACSB, ABET, AACN, ACNM, ADtA, APA, ASLHA, ACEHSA, CAEPK, CEPH, CORE, CSWE, JRCEPAT, NASAD, NASPAA, NAST, NCATE, NRPA **Intercollegiate Athletics:** Baseball M; Basketball M & W; Crew W; Cross-Country Running W; Football M; Golf M & W; Soccer M & W; Softball W; Swimming and Diving W; Tennis M & W; Track and Field W; Volleyball W; Water Polo W

SAN DIEGO STATE UNIVERSITY—IMPERIAL VALLEY CAMPUS
720 Heber Ave.
Calexico, CA 92231
Tel: (760)768-5500
Web Site: http://www.ivcampus.sdsu.edu/
President/CEO: Stephen Roeder
Type: Comprehensive **Sex:** Coed **Application Fee:** $55.00 **Costs Per Year:** Application fee: $55. Nonresident tuition: $372 per unit part-time. Mandatory fees: $1284 per term part-time. **Regional Accreditation:** Western Association of Schools and Colleges

SAN FRANCISCO ART INSTITUTE
800 Chestnut St.
San Francisco, CA 94133
Tel: (415)771-7020; Free: 800-345-SFAI
Admissions: (415)749-4500
E-mail: admissions@sfai.edu
Web Site: http://www.sfai.edu/
President/CEO: Chris Bratton
Financial Aid: Erin Zagaski
Type: Comprehensive **Sex:** Coed **Scores:** 97% SAT V 400+; 85% SAT M 400+; 37% ACT 18-23; 63% ACT 24-29 **% Accepted:** 74 **Admission Plans:** Early Admission; Early Action; Deferred Admission **Application Deadline:** Rolling **Application Fee:** $65.00 **H.S. Requirements:** High school diploma required; GED accepted **Costs Per Year:** Application fee: $65. Comprehen-

sive fee: $41,400 includes full-time tuition ($30,880), mandatory fees ($470), and college room and board ($10,050). College room only: $9050. Room and board charges vary according to housing facility. Part-time tuition: $1378 per unit. Part-time mandatory fees: $470 per year. **Scholarships:** Available **Calendar System:** Semester, Summer Session Available **Enrollment:** FT 318, PT 35 **Faculty:** FT 48, PT 99 **Student-Faculty Ratio:** 11:1 **Exams:** SAT I or ACT. **% Receiving Financial Aid:** 63 **% Residing in College-Owned, -Operated, or -Affiliated Housing:** 24 **Library Holdings:** 35,500 **Regional Accreditation:** Western Association of Schools and Colleges **Credit Hours For Degree:** 120 units, Bachelors **Professional Accreditation:** NASAD

SAN FRANCISCO CONSERVATORY OF MUSIC
50 Oak St.
San Francisco, CA 94102
Tel: (415)864-7326
Admissions: 800-899-7326
Fax: (415)503-6299
E-mail: admit@sfcm.edu
Web Site: http://www.sfcm.edu/
President/CEO: Colin Murdoch
Admissions: Alexander Brose
Financial Aid: Doris Howard
Type: Comprehensive **Sex:** Coed **% Accepted:** 44 **Application Deadline:** December 1 **Application Fee:** $100.00 **H.S. Requirements:** High school diploma required; GED accepted **Costs Per Year:** Application fee: $100. Tuition: $34,900 full-time, $1540 per credit hour part-time. Mandatory fees: $280 full-time, $280 per year part-time. Part-time tuition and fees vary according to course load. **Scholarships:** Available **Calendar System:** Semester, Summer Session Not available **Enrollment:** FT 201, PT 6, Grad FT 203, Grad PT 5 **Faculty:** FT 32, PT 78 **Student-Faculty Ratio:** 7:1 **Exams:** SAT I or ACT. ACT essay not being used. SAT essay not being used. **% Receiving Financial Aid:** 60 **% Residing in College-Owned, -Operated, or -Affiliated Housing:** 33 **Final Year or Final Semester Residency Requirement:** No **Library Holdings:** 60,000 **Regional Accreditation:** Western Association of Schools and Colleges **Credit Hours For Degree:** 127 semester hours, Bachelors **Professional Accreditation:** AOTA, NASM

SAN FRANCISCO STATE UNIVERSITY
1600 Holloway Ave.
San Francisco, CA 94132-1722
Tel: (415)338-1100
Admissions: (415)338-1113
E-mail: ugadmit@sfsu.edu
Web Site: http://www.sfsu.edu/
President/CEO: Dr. Robert A. Corrigan
Financial Aid: Barbara Hubler
Type: University **Sex:** Coed **Affiliation:** California State University System **Scores:** 89.6% SAT V 400+; 89.8% SAT M 400+; 54.2% ACT 18-23; 28.5% ACT 24-29 **% Accepted:** 73 **Application Deadline:** November 30 **Application Fee:** $55.00 **H.S. Requirements:** High school diploma required; GED accepted **Costs Per Year:** Application fee: $55. State resident tuition: $0 full-time. Nonresident tuition: $11,160 full-time, $372 per unit part-time. Mandatory fees: $4740 full-time, $1524 per term part-time. College room and board: $10,904. College room only: $7116. Room and board charges vary according to board plan and housing facility. **Scholarships:** Available **Calendar System:** Semester, Summer Session Available **Enrollment:** FT 19,877, PT 5,124, Grad FT 3,190, Grad PT 2,278 **Faculty:** FT 818, PT 748 **Student-Faculty Ratio:** 26:1 **Exams:** SAT I or ACT. ACT essay not being used. SAT essay not being used. **% Receiving Financial Aid:** 55 **% Residing in College-Owned, -Operated, or -Affiliated Housing:** 11 **Library Holdings:** 1,143,765 **Regional Accreditation:** Western Association of Schools and Colleges **Credit Hours For Degree:** 124 units, Bachelors **ROTC:** Army, Navy, Air Force **Professional Accreditation:** AACSB, ABET, ACEJMC, AACN, AAFCS, ACA, ADtA, APTA, ASLHA, CEPH, CORE, CSWE, NAACLS, NASAD, NASM, NASPAA, NAST, NCATE, NLN, NRPA **Intercollegiate Athletics:** Baseball M; Basketball M & W; Cross-Country Running M & W; Soccer M & W; Softball W; Track and Field W; Volleyball W; Wrestling M

SAN JOAQUIN DELTA COLLEGE
5151 Pacific Ave.
Stockton, CA 95207-6370
Tel: (209)954-5151
Admissions: (209)954-5635
Fax: (209)954-5600
E-mail: admissions@deltacollege.edu
Web Site: http://www.deltacollege.edu/
President/CEO: Dr. Raul Rodriguez
Admissions: Catherine Mooney
Type: Two-Year College **Sex:** Coed **Affiliation:** California Community College System **% Accepted:** 100 **Admission Plans:** Open Admission; Early Admission **Application Deadline:** Rolling **Application Fee:** $0.00 **H.S. Requirements:** High school diploma or equivalent not required. For applicants under 18: High school diploma required; GED accepted **Costs Per Year:** Application fee: $0. Nonresident tuition: $190 per unit part-time. Mandatory fees: $26 per unit part-time, $1 per term part-time. Part-time tuition and fees vary according to course load. **Scholarships:** Available **Calendar System:** Semester, Summer Session Available **Faculty:** FT 235, PT 408 **Student-Faculty Ratio:** 31:1 **Library Holdings:** 124,755 **Regional Accreditation:** Western Association of Schools and Colleges **Credit Hours For Degree:** 60 units, Associates **Professional Accreditation:** ACF, NLN **Intercollegiate Athletics:** Baseball M; Basketball M & W; Cross-Country Running M & W; Fencing M & W; Football M; Golf M & W; Soccer M & W; Softball W; Swimming and Diving M & W; Tennis M & W; Track and Field M & W; Volleyball W; Water Polo M & W; Wrestling M

SAN JOAQUIN VALLEY COLLEGE (BAKERSFIELD)
201 New Stine Rd.
Bakersfield, CA 93309
Tel: (661)834-0126; Free: (866)544-7898
E-mail: admissions@sjvc.edu
Web Site: http://www.sjvc.edu/
President/CEO: Mark Perry
Type: Two-Year College **Sex:** Coed **Affiliation:** San Joaquin Valley College **Application Deadline:** Rolling **H.S. Requirements:** High school diploma required; GED accepted **Enrollment:** FT 541 **Faculty:** FT 36, PT 31 **Student-Faculty Ratio:** 12:1

SAN JOAQUIN VALLEY COLLEGE (VISALIA)
8400 West Mineral King Ave.
Visalia, CA 93291
Tel: (559)651-2500
E-mail: admissions@sjvc.edu
Web Site: http://www.sjvc.edu/
President/CEO: Mark Perry
Type: Two-Year College **Sex:** Coed **Affiliation:** San Joaquin Valley College **Application Deadline:** Rolling **H.S. Requirements:** High school diploma required; GED accepted **Scholarships:** Available **Calendar System:** Semester, Summer Session Not available **Enrollment:** FT 895 **Faculty:** FT 68, PT 61 **Student-Faculty Ratio:** 9:1 **Library Holdings:** 4,720 **Regional Accreditation:** Western Association of Schools and Colleges **Credit Hours For Degree:** 60 credits, Associates **Professional Accreditation:** ARCEST, ADA, CARC

SAN JOAQUIN VALLEY COLLEGE—FRESNO AVIATION CAMPUS
4985 East Anderson Ave.
Fresno, CA 93727
Tel: (559)453-0123
Admissions: (559)453-0123
E-mail: admissions@sjvc.edu
Web Site: http://www.sjvc.edu/
President/CEO: Mark A. Perry
Type: Two-Year College **Sex:** Coed **Affiliation:** San Joaquin Valley College **Application Deadline:** Rolling **H.S. Requirements:** High school diploma required; GED accepted **Enrollment:** FT 59 **Faculty:** FT 5, PT 0 **Student-Faculty Ratio:** 12:1

SAN JOAQUIN VALLEY COLLEGE—ONLINE
3808 West Caldwell Ave.
Ste. A
Visalia, CA 93277
Tel: (559)734-7582
E-mail: admissions@sjvc.edu
Web Site: http://www.sjvconline.edu/
President/CEO: Mark Perry
Type: Two-Year College **Sex:** Coed **Affiliation:** San Joaquin Valley College

Application Deadline: Rolling **H.S. Requirements:** High school diploma required; GED accepted **Enrollment:** FT 887 **Faculty:** FT 1, PT 40 **Student-Faculty Ratio:** 21:1 **Regional Accreditation:** Western Association of Schools and Colleges

SAN JOSE CITY COLLEGE
2100 Moorpark Ave.
San Jose, CA 95128-2799
Tel: (408)298-2181
Web Site: http://www.sjcc.edu/
President/CEO: Dr. Michael Burke
Admissions: Carlo Santos
Type: Two-Year College **Sex:** Coed **Affiliation:** San Jose/Evergreen Community College District System **Admission Plans:** Open Admission; Preferred Admission; Early Admission; Deferred Admission **Application Deadline:** Rolling **Application Fee:** $0.00 **H.S. Requirements:** High school diploma or equivalent not required. For applicants under 18: High school diploma required; GED accepted **Scholarships:** Available **Calendar System:** Semester, Summer Session Available **Library Holdings:** 54,075 **Regional Accreditation:** Western Association of Schools and Colleges **Credit Hours For Degree:** 60 units, Associates **ROTC:** Army, Air Force **Professional Accreditation:** ADA **Intercollegiate Athletics:** Baseball M; Basketball M & W; Cross-Country Running M & W; Football M; Golf M; Softball W; Track and Field M & W; Volleyball W

SAN JOSE STATE UNIVERSITY
One Washington Square
San Jose, CA 95192-0001
Tel: (408)924-1000
Admissions: (408)283-7500
Fax: (408)924-2050
E-mail: contact@sjsu.edu
Web Site: http://www.sjsu.edu/
President/CEO: Jon Whitmore
Financial Aid: Coleetta McElroy
Type: Comprehensive **Sex:** Coed **Affiliation:** California State University System **Scores:** 88.8% SAT V 400+; 92% SAT M 400+; 55.2% ACT 18-23; 22.7% ACT 24-29 **% Accepted:** 74 **Admission Plans:** Preferred Admission **Application Deadline:** November 30 **Application Fee:** $55.00 **H.S. Requirements:** High school diploma required; GED accepted **Costs Per Year:** Application fee: $55. State resident tuition: $0 full-time. Nonresident tuition: $10,170 full-time, $339 per unit part-time. Mandatory fees: $3992 full-time, $1399 per term part-time. College room and board: $8663. College room only: $4968. **Scholarships:** Available **Calendar System:** Semester, Summer Session Available **Enrollment:** FT 18,304, PT 5,969, Grad FT 3,589, Grad PT 3,418 **Faculty:** FT 683, PT 1,002 **Student-Faculty Ratio:** 25:1 **Exams:** SAT I or ACT. ACT essay used for placement. SAT essay used for placement. **% Receiving Financial Aid:** 53 **% Residing in College-Owned, -Operated, or -Affiliated Housing:** 12 **Regional Accreditation:** Western Association of Schools and Colleges **Credit Hours For Degree:** 120 units, Bachelors **ROTC:** Army, Air Force **Professional Accreditation:** AACSB, ABET, ACEJMC, AACN, ADtA, ACSP, ALA, AOTA, ASLHA, CEPH, CSWE, JRCEPAT, NASAD, NASD, NASM, NASPAA, NAST, NCATE, NRPA, NAIT **Intercollegiate Athletics:** Badminton M & W; Baseball M; Basketball M & W; Bowling M & W; Cheerleading M & W; Cross-Country Running M & W; Football M; Golf M & W; Gymnastics W; Ice Hockey M & W; Rugby M; Sailing M & W; Soccer M & W; Softball W; Swimming and Diving W; Tennis W; Volleyball M & W; Water Polo W; Wrestling M & W

SANTA ANA COLLEGE
1530 West 17th St.
Santa Ana, CA 92706-3398
Tel: (714)564-6000
Web Site: http://www.sac.edu/
President/CEO: Erlinda Martinez
Admissions: Christie Steward
Type: Two-Year College **Sex:** Coed **Affiliation:** California Community College System **Admission Plans:** Open Admission; Early Admission **Application Deadline:** August 21 **H.S. Requirements:** High school diploma required; GED accepted **Scholarships:** Available **Calendar System:** Semester, Summer Session Available **Faculty:** FT 249, PT 1,047 **Student-Faculty Ratio:** 20:1 **Library Holdings:** 99,473 **Regional Accreditation:** Western Association of Schools and Colleges **Credit Hours For Degree:** 60 credits, Associates **ROTC:** Air Force **Professional Accreditation:** AOTA, NLN **Intercollegiate Athletics:** Baseball M; Basketball M & W; Cross-Country Running M & W; Football M; Golf M; Soccer M; Softball W; Swimming and Diving M; Tennis M & W; Track and Field M & W; Volleyball W; Water Polo M; Wrestling M

SANTA BARBARA CITY COLLEGE
721 Cliff Dr.
Santa Barbara, CA 93109-2394
Tel: (805)965-0581
Fax: (805)963-SBCC
E-mail: admissions@sbcc.edu
Web Site: http://www.sbcc.edu/
President/CEO: Dr. Andreea Serban
Admissions: Allison Curtis
Type: Two-Year College **Sex:** Coed **Affiliation:** California Community College System **Admission Plans:** Open Admission; Early Admission **Application Deadline:** August 22 **Application Fee:** $0.00 **H.S. Requirements:** High school diploma required; GED accepted. For applicants 18 or over: High school diploma or equivalent not required **Costs Per Year:** Application fee: $0. State resident tuition: $0 full-time. Nonresident tuition: $5700 full-time, $190 per unit part-time. Mandatory fees: $866 full-time, $26 per unit part-time, $86 per year part-time. Full-time tuition and fees vary according to course load. Part-time tuition and fees vary according to course load. **Scholarships:** Available **Calendar System:** Semester, Summer Session Available **Enrollment:** FT 6,823, PT 9,594 **Faculty:** FT 259, PT 598 **Student-Faculty Ratio:** 28:1 **Library Holdings:** 131,918 **Regional Accreditation:** Western Association of Schools and Colleges **Credit Hours For Degree:** 60 units, Associates **ROTC:** Army **Professional Accreditation:** ACF, AHIMA, JRCERT, NLN **Intercollegiate Athletics:** Baseball M; Basketball M & W; Cross-Country Running M & W; Football M; Golf M & W; Soccer M & W; Softball W; Tennis M & W; Track and Field M & W; Volleyball M & W

SANTA CLARA UNIVERSITY
500 El Camino Real
Santa Clara, CA 95053
Tel: (408)554-4000
Admissions: (408)554-4700
Fax: (408)554-5255
E-mail: ugadmissions@scu.edu
Web Site: http://www.scu.edu/
President/CEO: Rev. Michael E. Engh, SJ
Admissions: Sandra Hayes
Financial Aid: Marta I. Murchison
Type: University **Sex:** Coed **Affiliation:** Roman Catholic (Jesuit) **Scores:** 100% SAT V 400+; 100% SAT M 400+; 14% ACT 18-23; 56% ACT 24-29 **% Accepted:** 59 **Admission Plans:** Early Action; Deferred Admission **Application Deadline:** January 7 **Application Fee:** $55.00 **H.S. Requirements:** High school diploma required; GED not accepted **Costs Per Year:** Application fee: $55. Comprehensive fee: $47,400 includes full-time tuition ($36,000) and college room and board ($11,400). Room and board charges vary according to housing facility and student level. Part-time tuition: $1200 per unit. Part-time tuition varies according to course load. **Scholarships:** Available **Calendar System:** Quarter, Summer Session Available **Enrollment:** FT 5,087, PT 113, Grad FT 1,682, Grad PT 1,964 **Faculty:** FT 436, PT 362 **Student-Faculty Ratio:** 13:1 **Exams:** SAT I or ACT. ACT essay not being used. SAT essay not being used. **% Receiving Financial Aid:** 38 **% Residing in College-Owned, -Operated, or -Affiliated Housing:** 48 **Library Holdings:** 803,280 **Regional Accreditation:** Western Association of Schools and Colleges **Credit Hours For Degree:** 175 units, Bachelors **ROTC:** Army, Air Force **Professional Accreditation:** AACSB, ABET, ABA, AALS **Intercollegiate Athletics:** Baseball M; Basketball M & W; Crew M & W; Cross-Country Running M & W; Golf M & W; Soccer M & W; Tennis M & W; Track and Field M & W; Volleyball W; Water Polo M & W

SANTA MONICA COLLEGE
1900 Pico Blvd.
Santa Monica, CA 90405-1628
Tel: (310)434-4000
Web Site: http://www.smc.edu/
President/CEO: Chui L. Tsang
Admissions: Teresita Rodriguez
Type: Two-Year College **Sex:** Coed **Affiliation:** California Community College System **Admission Plans:** Open Admission; Early Admission **Applica-**

tion Deadline: August 30 **Application Fee:** $0.00 **H.S. Requirements:** High school diploma required; GED accepted. For international students: High school diploma required; GED not accepted **Scholarships:** Available **Calendar System:** Miscellaneous, Summer Session Available **Library Holdings:** 101,317 **Regional Accreditation:** Western Association of Schools and Colleges **Credit Hours For Degree:** 60 units, Associates **ROTC:** Army **Professional Accreditation:** CARC, NLN **Intercollegiate Athletics:** Basketball M & W; Cross-Country Running M & W; Football M; Soccer W; Softball W; Swimming and Diving M & W; Tennis W; Track and Field M & W; Volleyball M & W; Water Polo M & W

SANTA ROSA JUNIOR COLLEGE
1501 Mendocino Ave.
Santa Rosa, CA 95401-4395
Tel: (707)527-4011
Admissions: (707)527-4510
E-mail: admininfo@santarosa.edu
Web Site: http://www.santarosa.edu/
President/CEO: Dr. Robert F. Agrella
Admissions: Diane Traversi
Financial Aid: Lynn McMullin
Type: Two-Year College **Sex:** Coed **Affiliation:** California Community College System **% Accepted:** 100 **Admission Plans:** Open Admission; Early Admission **Application Deadline:** Rolling **Application Fee:** $0.00 **H.S. Requirements:** High school diploma or equivalent not required. For applicants under 18, allied health programs: High school diploma required; GED accepted **Costs Per Year:** Application fee: $0. One-time mandatory fee: $34. State resident tuition: $0 full-time. Nonresident tuition: $4392 full-time, $183 per unit part-time. Mandatory fees: $624 full-time, $26 per unit part-time. **Scholarships:** Available **Calendar System:** Semester, Summer Session Available **Enrollment:** FT 8,801, PT 16,518 **Faculty:** FT 305, PT 1,116 **Student-Faculty Ratio:** 22:1 **Library Holdings:** 127,394 **Regional Accreditation:** Western Association of Schools and Colleges **Credit Hours For Degree:** 60 units, Associates **Professional Accreditation:** ADA, JRCERT **Intercollegiate Athletics:** Baseball M; Basketball M & W; Cross-Country Running M & W; Football M; Golf M; Ice Hockey M; Rugby M; Soccer M & W; Softball W; Swimming and Diving M & W; Tennis M & W; Track and Field M & W; Volleyball W; Water Polo M & W; Wrestling M

SANTIAGO CANYON COLLEGE
8045 East Chapman Ave.
Orange, CA 92869
Tel: (714)628-4900
Fax: (714)564-4379
Web Site: http://www.sccollege.edu/
President/CEO: Juan Vazquez
Admissions: Denise Pennock
Type: Two-Year College **Sex:** Coed **Affiliation:** California Community College System **Admission Plans:** Open Admission; Early Admission **Application Deadline:** August 21 **H.S. Requirements:** High school diploma required; GED accepted **Calendar System:** Semester, Summer Session Available **Faculty:** FT 92, PT 325 **Student-Faculty Ratio:** 23:1 **Library Holdings:** 31,000 **Regional Accreditation:** Western Association of Schools and Colleges **Credit Hours For Degree:** 60 credits, Associates

SCHOOL OF URBAN MISSIONS
735 105th Ave.
Oakland, CA 94603
Tel: (510)567-6174; Free: 800-385-6364
Web Site: http://www.sum.edu/
President/CEO: Rev. George Neau
Type: Two-Year College **Sex:** Coed **Affiliation:** interdenominational **% Accepted:** 59 **Admission Plans:** Deferred Admission **Application Deadline:** Rolling **Application Fee:** $25.00 **H.S. Requirements:** High school diploma required; GED accepted **Calendar System:** Trimester **Enrollment:** FT 133, PT 6 **Faculty:** FT 4, PT 18 **Student-Faculty Ratio:** 11:1 **Professional Accreditation:** ABHE

SCRIPPS COLLEGE
1030 Columbia Ave.
Claremont, CA 91711-3948
Tel: (909)621-8000; Free: 800-770-1333
Admissions: (909)621-8149
Fax: (909)621-8323
E-mail: admission@scrippscollege.edu
Web Site: http://www.scrippscollege.edu/
President/CEO: Lori Bettison-Varga
Admissions: Patricia F. Goldsmith
Financial Aid: David Levy
Type: Four-Year College **Sex:** Women **Affiliation:** The Claremont Colleges Consortium **Scores:** 100% SAT V 400+; 100% SAT M 400+; 4% ACT 18-23; 43% ACT 24-29 **% Accepted:** 33 **Admission Plans:** Early Admission; Early Decision Plan; Deferred Admission **Application Deadline:** January 1 **Application Fee:** $60.00 **H.S. Requirements:** High school diploma required; GED accepted **Costs Per Year:** Application fee: $60. Comprehensive fee: $50,910 includes full-time tuition ($38,846), mandatory fees ($214), and college room and board ($11,850). Full-time tuition and fees vary according to program. Room and board charges vary according to board plan. Part-time tuition: $4811 per course. Part-time tuition varies according to program. **Scholarships:** Available **Calendar System:** Semester, Summer Session Not available **Enrollment:** FT 902, PT 5, Grad FT 13, Grad PT 2 **Faculty:** FT 81, PT 23 **Student-Faculty Ratio:** 10:1 **Exams:** SAT I or ACT. **% Receiving Financial Aid:** 41 **% Residing in College-Owned, -Operated, or -Affiliated Housing:** 96 **Library Holdings:** 2,604,795 **Regional Accreditation:** Western Association of Schools and Colleges **Credit Hours For Degree:** 32 courses, Bachelors **ROTC:** Army, Air Force **Intercollegiate Athletics:** Basketball W; Cross-Country Running W; Fencing W; Golf W; Lacrosse W; Rock Climbing W; Rugby W; Skiing (Downhill) W; Soccer W; Softball W; Swimming and Diving W; Tennis W; Track and Field W; Ultimate Frisbee W; Volleyball W; Water Polo W

SHASTA BIBLE COLLEGE
2951 Goodwater Ave.
Redding, CA 96002
Tel: (530)221-4275; Free: 800-800-6929
E-mail: registrar@shasta.edu
Web Site: http://www.shasta.edu/
President/CEO: David R. Nicholas
Admissions: Connie Barton
Financial Aid: Connie Barton
Type: Comprehensive **Sex:** Coed **Affiliation:** nondenominational **% Accepted:** 83 **Admission Plans:** Open Admission; Early Admission **Application Deadline:** Rolling **Application Fee:** $50.00 **H.S. Requirements:** High school diploma required; GED accepted **Costs Per Year:** Application fee: $50. Tuition: $8800 full-time, $275 per unit part-time. Mandatory fees: $620 full-time, $480 per year part-time. College room only: $2400. **Scholarships:** Available **Calendar System:** Semester, Summer Session Available **Enrollment:** FT 36, PT 13, Grad FT 3, Grad PT 7 **Faculty:** FT 9, PT 28 **Student-Faculty Ratio:** 3:1 **% Receiving Financial Aid:** 44 **% Residing in College-Owned, -Operated, or -Affiliated Housing:** 77 **Final Year or Final Semester Residency Requirement:** No **Library Holdings:** 30,983 **Credit Hours For Degree:** 64 credit hours, Associates; 128 credit hours, Bachelors **Professional Accreditation:** TACCS

SHASTA COLLEGE
PO Box 496006
11555 Old Oregon Trail
Redding, CA 96049-6006
Tel: (530)242-7500
Web Site: http://www.shastacollege.edu/
President/CEO: Gary Lewis
Admissions: Dr. Kevin O'Rorke
Type: Two-Year College **Sex:** Coed **Affiliation:** California Community College System **% Accepted:** 100 **Admission Plans:** Open Admission; Early Admission **Application Deadline:** Rolling **Application Fee:** $0.00 **H.S. Requirements:** High school diploma or equivalent not required **Costs Per Year:** Application fee: $0. State resident tuition: $0 full-time. Nonresident tuition: $4632 full-time, $193 per unit part-time. Mandatory fees: $699 full-time, $26 per unit part-time, $37.50 per term part-time. College room and board: $4659. College room only: $3229. Room and board charges vary according to board plan. **Scholarships:** Available **Calendar System:** Semester, Summer Session Available **Enrollment:** FT 4,336, PT 5,904 **Faculty:** FT 146, PT 345 **Library Holdings:** 67,500 **Regional Accreditation:** Western Association of Schools and Colleges **Credit Hours For Degree:** 60 semester hours, Associates **Professional Accreditation:** ADA **Intercollegiate Athletics:** Baseball M; Basketball M & W; Cross-Country Running M & W; Football M; Golf M & W; Soccer M & W; Softball W; Swimming and Diving M & W; Tennis M & W; Track and Field M & W; Volleyball W

SIERRA COLLEGE
5000 Rocklin Rd.
Rocklin, CA 95677-3397
Tel: (916)624-3333
Admissions: (916)660-7341
E-mail: gmodder@sierracollege.edu
Web Site: http://www.sierracollege.edu/
President/CEO: Dr. Leo Chavez
Admissions: Gail Modder
Financial Aid: Linda S. Williams
Type: Two-Year College **Sex:** Coed **Affiliation:** California Community College System **% Accepted:** 100 **Admission Plans:** Open Admission; Early Admission **Application Deadline:** Rolling **Application Fee:** $0.00 **H.S. Requirements:** High school diploma or equivalent not required. For applicants 18 or over: High school diploma required; GED accepted **Costs Per Year:** Application fee: $0. State resident tuition: $0 full-time. Nonresident tuition: $5320 full-time, $190 per unit part-time. Mandatory fees: $772 full-time, $26 per unit part-time, $22 per term part-time. Full-time tuition and fees vary according to course load. Part-time tuition and fees vary according to course load. College room and board: $6700. **Scholarships:** Available **Calendar System:** Semester, Summer Session Available **Enrollment:** FT 5,355, PT 14,061 **Faculty:** FT 158, PT 712 **Student-Faculty Ratio:** 25:1 **% Residing in College-Owned, -Operated, or -Affiliated Housing:** 1 **Library Holdings:** 69,879 **Regional Accreditation:** Western Association of Schools and Colleges **Credit Hours For Degree:** 60 units, Associates **Intercollegiate Athletics:** Baseball M; Basketball M & W; Football M; Golf M & W; Soccer W; Softball W; Swimming and Diving M & W; Tennis M & W; Volleyball W; Water Polo M & W; Wrestling M

SILICON VALLEY UNIVERSITY
2160 Lundy Ave.
Ste. 110
San Jose, CA 95131
Tel: (408)435-8989
Fax: (408)435-8989
E-mail: admission-office@svuca.edu
Web Site: http://www.svuca.edu/
President/CEO: Dr. Jerry Shiao
Type: Comprehensive **Sex:** Coed **Admission Plans:** Deferred Admission **Application Fee:** $50.00 **H.S. Requirements:** High school diploma required; GED accepted **Costs Per Year:** Application fee: $50. Tuition: $250 per unit part-time. Part-time tuition varies according to course level, course load, degree level, program, and student level. **Calendar System:** Trimester, Summer Session Available **Faculty:** FT 1, PT 30 **Student-Faculty Ratio:** 24:1 **Exams:** ACT, Other, SAT I or ACT, SAT I. **Library Holdings:** 1,683 **Credit Hours For Degree:** 120 credit hours, Bachelors **Professional Accreditation:** ACICS

SIMPSON UNIVERSITY
2211 College View Dr.
Redding, CA 96003-8606
Tel: (530)226-4606; Free: 800-598-2493
Admissions: (530)226-5600
Fax: (530)226-4861
E-mail: admissions@simpsonu.edu
Web Site: http://www.simpsonu.edu/
President/CEO: Dr. Larry J. McKinney
Admissions: Kendell Kluttz
Financial Aid: Melissa Hudson
Type: Comprehensive **Sex:** Coed **Affiliation:** The Christian and Missionary Alliance **Scores:** 89% SAT V 400+; 88% SAT M 400+; 48% ACT 18-23; 29% ACT 24-29 **% Accepted:** 59 **Admission Plans:** Deferred Admission **Application Deadline:** Rolling **Application Fee:** $50.00 **H.S. Requirements:** High school diploma required; GED accepted **Costs Per Year:** Application fee: $50. Comprehensive fee: $28,000 includes full-time tuition ($21,000) and college room and board ($7000). College room only: $6000. Full-time tuition varies according to course load and program. Room and board charges vary according to board plan. Part-time tuition: $875 per unit. Part-time tuition varies according to course load and program. **Scholarships:** Available **Calendar System:** Semester, Summer Session Available **Enrollment:** FT 926, PT 30, Grad FT 40, Grad PT 147 **Faculty:** FT 39, PT 82 **Student-Faculty Ratio:** 16:1 **Exams:** SAT I or ACT, SAT II. **% Receiving Financial Aid:** 96 **% Residing in College-Owned, -Operated, or -Affiliated Housing:** 70 **Library Holdings:** 136,202 **Regional Accreditation:** Western Association of Schools and Colleges **Credit Hours For Degree:** 62 credits, Associates; 124 credits, Bachelors **ROTC:** Army **Intercollegiate Athletics:** Baseball M; Basketball M & W; Cross-Country Running M & W; Golf M & W; Soccer M & W; Softball W; Volleyball W

SKYLINE COLLEGE
3300 College Dr.
San Bruno, CA 94066-1698
Tel: (650)738-4100
Admissions: (650)738-4251
E-mail: stats@smccd.net
Web Site: http://skylinecollege.net/
President/CEO: Dr. Victoria P. Morrow
Admissions: Terry Stats
Financial Aid: Regina Morrison
Type: Two-Year College **Sex:** Coed **Affiliation:** San Mateo County Community College District System **Admission Plans:** Open Admission **Application Deadline:** Rolling **Application Fee:** $0.00 **H.S. Requirements:** High school diploma or equivalent not required. For applicants under 18, international students: High school diploma required; GED accepted **Costs Per Year:** Application fee: $0. State resident tuition: $0 full-time. Nonresident tuition: $5348 full-time, $191 per unit part-time. Mandatory fees: $790 full-time, $26 per unit part-time, $31 per term part-time. Full-time tuition and fees vary according to course load. Part-time tuition and fees vary according to course load. **Scholarships:** Available **Calendar System:** Semester, Summer Session Available **Enrollment:** FT 2,486, PT 5,873 **Faculty:** FT 119, PT 214 **Student-Faculty Ratio:** 25:1 **Library Holdings:** 50,000 **Regional Accreditation:** Western Association of Schools and Colleges **Credit Hours For Degree:** 60 credits, Associates **Professional Accreditation:** ARCEST, CARC **Intercollegiate Athletics:** Baseball M; Basketball M; Cross-Country Running M & W; Soccer M; Softball W; Track and Field M & W; Volleyball W; Wrestling M

SOKA UNIVERSITY OF AMERICA
1 University Dr.
Aliso Viejo, CA 92656
Tel: (949)480-4000; Free: 888-600-SOKA
Admissions: (949)480-4131
Fax: (949)480-4001
E-mail: admission@soka.edu
Web Site: http://www.soka.edu/
President/CEO: Danny Habuki
Admissions: Marilyn Grove
Type: Comprehensive **Sex:** Coed **Scores:** 93% SAT V 400+; 100% SAT M 400+; 44% ACT 18-23; 56% ACT 24-29 **% Accepted:** 26 **Admission Plans:** Early Admission; Early Action; Deferred Admission **Application Deadline:** January 15 **Application Fee:** $45.00 **H.S. Requirements:** High school diploma required; GED accepted **Costs Per Year:** Application fee: $45. Comprehensive fee: $35,750 includes full-time tuition ($25,344), mandatory fees ($766), and college room and board ($9640). Full-time tuition and fees vary according to course load. **Calendar System:** Semester **Enrollment:** FT 361 **Faculty:** FT 38, PT 17 **Student-Faculty Ratio:** 9:1 **Exams:** SAT I or ACT. ACT essay used for admission. SAT essay used for admission. **% Residing in College-Owned, -Operated, or -Affiliated Housing:** 99 **Library Holdings:** 63,806 **Regional Accreditation:** Western Association of Schools and Colleges **Credit Hours For Degree:** 120 units, Bachelors **Professional Accreditation:** AALE **Intercollegiate Athletics:** Cross-Country Running M & W; Soccer M & W; Swimming and Diving M & W; Track and Field M & W; Water Polo M & W

SOLANO COMMUNITY COLLEGE
4000 Suisun Valley Rd.
Fairfield, CA 94534
Tel: (707)864-7000
Fax: (707)864-7175
E-mail: barbara.fountain@solano.edu
Web Site: http://www.solano.edu/
President/CEO: Jowel C. Laguerre, PhD
Admissions: Barbara Fountain
Type: Two-Year College **Sex:** Coed **Affiliation:** California Community College System **Admission Plans:** Open Admission; Early Admission; Deferred Admission **Application Deadline:** Rolling **Application Fee:** $0.00 **H.S. Requirements:** High school diploma required; GED accepted **Costs Per Year:** Application fee: $0. State resident tuition: $0 full-time. Nonresident

tuition: $4584 full-time, $191 per unit part-time. Mandatory fees: $660 full-time, $26 per unit part-time, $13 per term part-time. Full-time tuition and fees vary according to course load. Part-time tuition and fees vary according to course load. **Scholarships:** Available **Calendar System:** Semester, Summer Session Available **Faculty:** FT 147, PT 227 **Student-Faculty Ratio:** 27:1 **Library Holdings:** 32,000 **Regional Accreditation:** Western Association of Schools and Colleges **Credit Hours For Degree:** 60 credits, Associates **Intercollegiate Athletics:** Baseball M; Basketball M & W; Football M; Softball W; Swimming and Diving M & W; Volleyball W; Water Polo M & W

SONOMA STATE UNIVERSITY
1801 East Cotati Ave.
Rohnert Park, CA 94928-3609
Tel: (707)664-2880
Admissions: (707)664-2778
E-mail: gustavo.flores@sonoma.edu
Web Site: http://www.sonoma.edu/
President/CEO: Dr. Ruben Armiñana
Admissions: Gustavo Flores
Financial Aid: Susan Gutierrez
Type: Comprehensive **Sex:** Coed **Affiliation:** California State University System **Scores:** 94.5% SAT V 400+; 54% ACT 18-23; 34% ACT 24-29 **% Accepted:** 77 **Admission Plans:** Early Admission **Application Deadline:** Rolling **Application Fee:** $55.00 **H.S. Requirements:** High school diploma required; GED accepted **Costs Per Year:** Application fee: $55. State resident tuition: $0 full-time. Nonresident tuition: $10,347 full-time, $372 per unit part-time. Mandatory fees: $5290 full-time, $1799 per term part-time. Full-time tuition and fees vary according to course load and degree level. Part-time tuition and fees vary according to course load and degree level. College room and board: $10,086. Room and board charges vary according to housing facility. **Scholarships:** Available **Calendar System:** Semester, Summer Session Available **Enrollment:** FT 6,866, PT 843 **Faculty:** FT 278, PT 263 **Student-Faculty Ratio:** 23:1 **Exams:** SAT I or ACT. **% Receiving Financial Aid:** 41 **% Residing in College-Owned, -Operated, or -Affiliated Housing:** 40 **Library Holdings:** 678,474 **Regional Accreditation:** Western Association of Schools and Colleges **Credit Hours For Degree:** 124 units, Bachelors **ROTC:** Army, Air Force **Professional Accreditation:** AACSB, ACA, NASAD, NASM, NCATE, NLN **Intercollegiate Athletics:** Baseball M; Basketball M & W; Cross-Country Running M; Golf M & W; Soccer M & W; Softball W; Tennis M & W; Volleyball W; Water Polo W

SOUTH COAST COLLEGE
2011 West Chapman Ave.
Orange, CA 92868
Tel: (714)867-5009; Free: 800-337-8366
Fax: (714)867-5026
Web Site: http://www.southcoastcollege.com/
Type: Two-Year College **Sex:** Coed **Application Fee:** $99.00 **Professional Accreditation:** ACICS

SOUTHERN CALIFORNIA INSTITUTE OF ARCHITECTURE
960 East Third St.
Los Angeles, CA 90013
Tel: (213)613-2200; Free: 800-774-7242
Fax: (213)613-0524
E-mail: jj@sciarc.edu
Web Site: http://www.sciarc.edu/
President/CEO: Eric Owen Moss
Admissions: J.J. Jackman
Financial Aid: Lina Johnson
Type: Comprehensive **Sex:** Coed **Scores:** 100% SAT V 400+; 100% SAT M 400+; 100% ACT 18-23 **% Accepted:** 82 **Admission Plans:** Deferred Admission **Application Deadline:** February 1 **Application Fee:** $75.00 **H.S. Requirements:** High school diploma required; GED accepted. If applying with more than 24 completed undergraduate credits, High School Transcript and ACT/SAT not required. **Costs Per Year:** Application fee: $75. Tuition: $27,500 full-time. Mandatory fees: $250 full-time. **Scholarships:** Available **Calendar System:** Semester, Summer Session Available **Enrollment:** FT 238, Grad FT 228 **Student-Faculty Ratio:** 15:1 **Exams:** SAT I or ACT. ACT essay not being used. SAT essay not being used. **% Receiving Financial Aid:** 72 **Library Holdings:** 30,000 **Regional Accreditation:** Western Association of Schools and Colleges **Credit Hours For Degree:** 150 units, Bachelors **Professional Accreditation:** NAAB

SOUTHERN CALIFORNIA INSTITUTE OF TECHNOLOGY
222 Soouth Harbor Blvd.
Ste. 200
Anaheim, CA 92805
Tel: (714)520-5552
Admissions: (714)300-0300
E-mail: admissions@scitech.edu
Web Site: http://www.scitcollege.com/
President/CEO: Parviz Shams
Type: Four-Year College **Sex:** Coed **Admission Plans:** Open Admission **Application Fee:** $100.00 **H.S. Requirements:** High school diploma required; GED accepted **Scholarships:** Available **Enrollment:** FT 600 **Exams:** Other. **Professional Accreditation:** ACCSCT

SOUTHERN CALIFORNIA SEMINARY
2075 East Madison Ave.
El Cajon, CA 92019
Tel: (619)442-9841
Admissions: 888-389-7244
Fax: (619)442-4510
E-mail: thpittman@socalsem.edu
Web Site: http://www.socalsem.edu/
President/CEO: Dr. Gary F. Coombs
Admissions: Thomas Pittman
Type: Comprehensive **Sex:** Coed **Affiliation:** interdenominational **% Accepted:** 88 **Admission Plans:** Early Admission; Deferred Admission **Application Deadline:** August 13 **H.S. Requirements:** High school diploma required; GED accepted **Costs Per Year:** Tuition: $12,204 full-time, $339 per credit hour part-time. Mandatory fees: $372 full-time, $31 per course part-time. College room only: $5110. **Faculty:** FT 11, PT 44 **Student-Faculty Ratio:** 10:1 **% Residing in College-Owned, -Operated, or -Affiliated Housing:** 9 **Professional Accreditation:** TACCS

SOUTHWESTERN COLLEGE
900 Otay Lakes Rd.
Chula Vista, CA 91910-7299
Tel: (619)421-6700
Web Site: http://www.swc.edu/
President/CEO: Dr. Raj Chopra
Type: Two-Year College **Sex:** Coed **Affiliation:** California Community College System **Admission Plans:** Open Admission; Early Admission **Application Deadline:** Rolling **H.S. Requirements:** High school diploma or equivalent not required. For applicants under 18: High school diploma required; GED accepted **Costs Per Year:** State resident tuition: $0 full-time. Nonresident tuition: $4560 full-time, $190 per unit part-time. Mandatory fees: $642 full-time, $1 per unit part-time, $8 per year part-time. **Scholarships:** Available **Calendar System:** Semester, Summer Session Available **Student-Faculty Ratio:** 22:1 **Regional Accreditation:** Western Association of Schools and Colleges **Credit Hours For Degree:** 60 units, Associates **Professional Accreditation:** ARCEST, ADA, NLN **Intercollegiate Athletics:** Baseball M; Basketball M & W; Cross-Country Running M & W; Football M; Soccer M & W; Softball W; Swimming and Diving M & W; Tennis M & W; Track and Field M & W; Volleyball W; Water Polo M & W

STANBRIDGE COLLEGE
2041 Business Center Dr.
Irvine, CA 92612
Tel: (949)794-9090
Fax: (949)794-9094
Web Site: http://www.stanbridge.edu/
President/CEO: Yasith Weerasuriya
Type: Two-Year College **Sex:** Coed **% Accepted:** 95 **Professional Accreditation:** ACCSCT

STANFORD UNIVERSITY
Stanford, CA 94305-9991
Tel: (650)723-2300
Admissions: (650)723-2091
Fax: (650)725-2846
E-mail: admission@stanford.edu
Web Site: http://www.stanford.edu/
President/CEO: John Hennessy
Admissions: Rick Shaw
Type: University **Sex:** Coed **Scores:** 100% SAT V 400+; 100% SAT M

400+ **% Accepted:** 8 **Admission Plans:** Early Action; Deferred Admission **Application Deadline:** January 1 **Application Fee:** $90.00 **H.S. Requirements:** High school diploma required; GED accepted **Costs Per Year:** Application fee: $90. Comprehensive fee: $49,344 includes full-time tuition ($37,380), mandatory fees ($501), and college room and board ($11,463). College room only: $6411. Room and board charges vary according to housing facility. **Scholarships:** Available **Calendar System:** Quarter, Summer Session Available **Enrollment:** FT 6,565, PT 37, Grad FT 7,997, Grad PT 3,899 **Faculty:** FT 1,008, PT 15 **Student-Faculty Ratio:** 6:1 **Exams:** SAT I or ACT, SAT II. ACT essay not being used. SAT essay not being used. **% Receiving Financial Aid:** 48 **% Residing in College-Owned, -Operated, or -Affiliated Housing:** 95 **Final Year or Final Semester Residency Requirement:** No **Library Holdings:** 8,500,000 **Regional Accreditation:** Western Association of Schools and Colleges **Credit Hours For Degree:** 180 quarter hours, Bachelors **ROTC:** Army, Navy, Air Force **Professional Accreditation:** AACSB, ABET, ABA, APA, ACIPE, AALS, LCMEAMA, NCATE **Intercollegiate Athletics:** Archery M & W; Baseball M; Basketball M & W; Cheerleading M & W; Crew M & W; Cross-Country Running M & W; Equestrian Sports M & W; Fencing M & W; Field Hockey W; Football M; Golf M & W; Gymnastics M & W; Ice Hockey M; Lacrosse M & W; Racquetball M & W; Rugby M & W; Sailing M & W; Skiing (Downhill) M & W; Soccer M & W; Softball W; Squash M & W; Swimming and Diving M & W; Tennis M & W; Track and Field M & W; Ultimate Frisbee M & W; Volleyball M & W; Water Polo M & W; Wrestling M

TAFT COLLEGE
29 Emmons Park Dr.
Taft, CA 93268-2317
Tel: (661)763-7700
Fax: (661)763-7705
E-mail: hrussell@taft.org
Web Site: http://www.taftcollege.edu/
President/CEO: William Duncan
Admissions: Harold Russell, III
Financial Aid: Ruthie Welborn
Type: Two-Year College **Sex:** Coed **Affiliation:** California Community College System **% Accepted:** 100 **Admission Plans:** Open Admission **Application Deadline:** Rolling **Application Fee:** $0.00 **H.S. Requirements:** High school diploma required; GED accepted. For applicants under 18: High school diploma or equivalent not required **Scholarships:** Available **Calendar System:** Semester, Summer Session Available **Enrollment:** FT 505, PT 8,995 **Faculty:** FT 37, PT 54 **% Residing in College-Owned, -Operated, or -Affiliated Housing:** 6 **Library Holdings:** 28,500 **Regional Accreditation:** Western Association of Schools and Colleges **Credit Hours For Degree:** 60 units, Associates **Professional Accreditation:** ADA **Intercollegiate Athletics:** Baseball M; Basketball W; Soccer M; Softball W; Volleyball W

THOMAS AQUINAS COLLEGE
10000 North Ojai Rd.
Santa Paula, CA 93060
Tel: (805)525-4417; Free: 800-634-9797
Fax: (805)525-9342
E-mail: admissions@thomasaqinas.edu
Web Site: http://www.thomasaquinas.edu/
President/CEO: Dr. Michael F. McLean
Admissions: Jonathan P. Daly
Financial Aid: Gregory Becher
Type: Four-Year College **Sex:** Coed **Affiliation:** Roman Catholic **Scores:** 100% SAT V 400+; 100% SAT M 400+; 12% ACT 18-23; 50% ACT 24-29 **% Accepted:** 78 **Admission Plans:** Early Admission; Deferred Admission **Application Deadline:** Rolling **Application Fee:** $0.00 **H.S. Requirements:** High school diploma required; GED accepted **Costs Per Year:** Application fee: $0. Comprehensive fee: $29,800 includes full-time tuition ($22,400) and college room and board ($7400). Part-time tuition: $622 per credit hour. **Scholarships:** Available **Calendar System:** Semester, Summer Session Not available **Enrollment:** FT 345 **Faculty:** FT 28, PT 7 **Student-Faculty Ratio:** 11:1 **Exams:** SAT I or ACT. **% Receiving Financial Aid:** 76 **% Residing in College-Owned, -Operated, or -Affiliated Housing:** 99 **Library Holdings:** 63,000 **Regional Accreditation:** Western Association of Schools and Colleges **Credit Hours For Degree:** 146 hours, Bachelors **Professional Accreditation:** AALE

TUI UNIVERSITY
5665 Plaza Dr., 3rd Floor
Cypress, CA 90630
Tel: (714)816-0366
Fax: (714)816-0367
E-mail: registration@tuiu.edu
Web Site: http://www.tuiu.edu/
President/CEO: Ken Sobaski
Admissions: Wei Ren
Type: University **Sex:** Coed **% Accepted:** 72 **Admission Plans:** Open Admission **Application Deadline:** Rolling **Application Fee:** $0.00 **H.S. Requirements:** High school diploma required; GED accepted **Costs Per Year:** Application fee: $0. Tuition: $9440 full-time, $295 per semester hour part-time. Part-time tuition varies according to degree level. **Calendar System:** Miscellaneous, Summer Session Available **Enrollment:** FT 1,958, PT 2,043, Grad FT 1,359, Grad PT 2,686 **Faculty:** FT 73, PT 196 **Student-Faculty Ratio:** 18:1 **Final Year or Final Semester Residency Requirement:** No **Library Holdings:** 30,692 **Regional Accreditation:** Western Association of Schools and Colleges **Credit Hours For Degree:** 120 credits, Bachelors

UNITED STATES UNIVERSITY
140 West 16th St.
National City, CA 91950
Tel: (619)477-6310; Free: 888-422-3381
Fax: (619)477-7340
Web Site: http://www.usuniversity.edu/
Type: Comprehensive **Sex:** Coed **Regional Accreditation:** Western Association of Schools and Colleges

UNIVERSITY OF CALIFORNIA, BERKELEY
Berkeley, CA 94720-1500
Tel: (510)642-6000
Admissions: (510)642-2316
Fax: (510)642-7333
Web Site: http://www.berkeley.edu/
President/CEO: Dr. Robert J. Birgeneau
Admissions: Walter Robinson
Financial Aid: Kathy Bradley
Type: University **Sex:** Coed **Affiliation:** University of California System **Scores:** 100% SAT V 400+; 99% SAT M 400+ **% Accepted:** 22 **Admission Plans:** Preferred Admission **Application Deadline:** November 30 **Application Fee:** $60.00 **H.S. Requirements:** High school diploma required; GED accepted **Costs Per Year:** Application fee: $60. State resident tuition: $6888 full-time. Nonresident tuition: $29,557 full-time. Mandatory fees: $2929 full-time. Full-time tuition and fees vary according to course load and program. College room and board: $15,308. Room and board charges vary according to board plan and housing facility. **Scholarships:** Available **Calendar System:** Semester, Summer Session Available **Student-Faculty Ratio:** 15:1 **Exams:** SAT I and SAT II or ACT. ACT essay used for admission. SAT essay used for admission. ACT essay used for advising. SAT essay used for advising. **% Receiving Financial Aid:** 51 **% Residing in College-Owned, -Operated, or -Affiliated Housing:** 35 **Regional Accreditation:** Western Association of Schools and Colleges **Credit Hours For Degree:** 120 credits, Bachelors **ROTC:** Army, Navy, Air Force **Professional Accreditation:** AACSB, ABET, ACEJMC, ABA, ADtA, ACSP, AOA, APA, ASLA, AALS, ACEHSA, FIDER, CEPH, CSWE, NAAB, SAF **Intercollegiate Athletics:** Baseball M; Basketball M & W; Crew M & W; Cross-Country Running M & W; Field Hockey W; Football M; Golf M & W; Gymnastics M & W; Lacrosse W; Rugby M; Soccer M & W; Softball W; Swimming and Diving M & W; Tennis M & W; Track and Field M & W; Volleyball W; Water Polo M & W

UNIVERSITY OF CALIFORNIA, DAVIS
One Shields Ave.
Davis, CA 95616
Tel: (530)752-1011
Fax: (530)752-6363
E-mail: undergraduateadmissions@ucdavis.edu
Web Site: http://www.ucdavis.edu/
President/CEO: Linda P.B. Katehi
Admissions: Frank Wada
Financial Aid: Katy Maloney
Type: University **Sex:** Coed **Affiliation:** University of California System **Scores:** 97.07% SAT V 400+; 98.87% SAT M 400+; 18.64% ACT 18-23; 49.05% ACT 24-29 **% Accepted:** 47 **Admission Plans:** Preferred Admission **Application Deadline:** November 30 **Application Fee:** $60.00 **H.S. Requirements:** High school diploma required; GED accepted **Costs Per**

Year: Application fee: $60. State resident tuition: $0 full-time. Nonresident tuition: $22,021 full-time. Mandatory fees: $9364 full-time. College room and board: $12,361. Room and board charges vary according to board plan. **Scholarships:** Available **Calendar System:** Quarter, Summer Session Available **Enrollment:** FT 24,351, PT 304, Grad FT 6,416, Grad PT 176 **Faculty:** FT 1,568, PT 311 **Student-Faculty Ratio:** 19:1 **Exams:** SAT I or ACT, SAT II. **% Receiving Financial Aid:** 57 **% Residing in College-Owned, -Operated, or -Affiliated Housing:** 19 **Library Holdings:** 3,650,774 **Regional Accreditation:** Western Association of Schools and Colleges **Credit Hours For Degree:** 180 units, Bachelors **ROTC:** Army, Navy, Air Force **Professional Accreditation:** AACSB, ABET, ABA, ADtA, APA, ASLA, AVMA, ACIPE, AALS, LCMEAMA, NAACLS **Intercollegiate Athletics:** Baseball M; Basketball M & W; Crew W; Cross-Country Running M & W; Field Hockey W; Football M; Golf M & W; Gymnastics W; Lacrosse W; Soccer M & W; Softball W; Swimming and Diving M & W; Tennis M & W; Track and Field M & W; Volleyball W; Water Polo M & W; Wrestling M

UNIVERSITY OF CALIFORNIA, IRVINE

Irvine, CA 92697
Tel: (949)824-5011
Admissions: (949)824-6703
Web Site: http://www.uci.edu/
President/CEO: Michael Drake
Financial Aid: Penny Harrell
Type: University **Sex:** Coed **Affiliation:** University of California System **Scores:** 99% SAT V 400+; 100% SAT M 400+ **% Accepted:** 44 **Application Deadline:** November 30 **Application Fee:** $60.00 **H.S. Requirements:** High school diploma required; GED accepted **Costs Per Year:** Application fee: $60. State resident tuition: $0 full-time. Nonresident tuition: $22,879 full-time. Mandatory fees: $11,913 full-time. College room and board: $10,655. Room and board charges vary according to board plan and housing facility. **Scholarships:** Available **Calendar System:** Quarter, Summer Session Available **Enrollment:** FT 21,705, PT 521, Grad FT 4,331, Grad PT 585 **Faculty:** FT 1,464, PT 428 **Student-Faculty Ratio:** 19:1 **Exams:** SAT I and SAT II or ACT. ACT essay used for admission. SAT essay used for admission. **% Receiving Financial Aid:** 53 **% Residing in College-Owned, -Operated, or -Affiliated Housing:** 35 **Final Year or Final Semester Residency Requirement:** Yes **Library Holdings:** 3,049,706 **Regional Accreditation:** Western Association of Schools and Colleges **Credit Hours For Degree:** 180 units, Bachelors **ROTC:** Army, Air Force **Professional Accreditation:** AACSB, ABET, ACSP, APA, LCMEAMA, NAACLS **Intercollegiate Athletics:** Baseball M; Basketball M & W; Cross-Country Running M & W; Golf M & W; Sailing M & W; Soccer M & W; Tennis M & W; Track and Field M & W; Volleyball M & W; Water Polo M & W

UNIVERSITY OF CALIFORNIA, LOS ANGELES

405 Hilgard Ave.
Los Angeles, CA 90095
Tel: (310)825-4321
Admissions: (310)825-3101
E-mail: ugadm@saonet.ucla.edu
Web Site: http://www.ucla.edu/
President/CEO: Dr. Gene D. Block
Admissions: Dr. Vu T. Tran
Financial Aid: Yolanda Tan
Type: University **Sex:** Coed **Affiliation:** University of California System **Scores:** 99.59% SAT V 400+; 99.38% SAT M 400+; 18.53% ACT 18-23; 39.83% ACT 24-29 **% Accepted:** 22 **Application Deadline:** November 30 **Application Fee:** $60.00 **H.S. Requirements:** High school diploma required; GED accepted **Costs Per Year:** Application fee: $60. State resident tuition: $0 full-time. Nonresident tuition: $22,021 full-time. Mandatory fees: $9151 full-time. College room and board: $13,314. Room and board charges vary according to board plan and housing facility. **Scholarships:** Available **Calendar System:** Quarter, Summer Session Available **Enrollment:** FT 25,756, PT 931, Grad FT 12,829, Grad PT 468 **Faculty:** FT 2,035, PT 676 **Student-Faculty Ratio:** 16:1 **Exams:** SAT I or ACT, SAT II. ACT essay used for advising. SAT essay used for advising. ACT essay used for placement. SAT essay used for placement. **% Receiving Financial Aid:** 53 **% Residing in College-Owned, -Operated, or -Affiliated Housing:** 40 **Final Year or Final Semester Residency Requirement:** No **Library Holdings:** 9,045,818 **Regional Accreditation:** Western Association of Schools and Colleges **Credit Hours For Degree:** 180 quarter units, Bachelors **ROTC:** Army, Navy, Air Force **Professional Accreditation:** AACSB, ABET, AACN, ABA, ADA, ADtA, ACSP, ALA, APA, ASC, ACIPE, AALS, ACEHSA, FIDER, CEPH, CSWE, LCMEAMA, NAAB, NAST, NLN **Intercollegiate Athletics:** Baseball M; Basketball M & W; Crew W; Cross-Country Running M & W; Football M; Golf M & W; Gymnastics W; Soccer M & W; Softball W; Swimming and Diving W; Tennis M & W; Track and Field M & W; Volleyball M & W; Water Polo M & W

UNIVERSITY OF CALIFORNIA, MERCED

5200 North Lake Rd.
Merced, CA 95343
Tel: (209)228-4400
Admissions: (209)228-4241
Web Site: http://www.ucmerced.edu/
President/CEO: Dr. Sung-Mo Kang
Admissions: Susan Fauroat
Type: University **Sex:** Coed **Affiliation:** University of California System **Scores:** 90% SAT V 400+; 92% SAT M 400+ **% Accepted:** 91 **Application Deadline:** January 1 **Application Fee:** $60.00 **H.S. Requirements:** High school diploma required; GED accepted **Enrollment:** FT 3,161, PT 29, Grad FT 219, Grad PT 5 **Faculty:** FT 184, PT 33 **Student-Faculty Ratio:** 16:1 **Exams:** SAT I or ACT, SAT II. ACT essay used for admission. SAT essay used for admission. **% Residing in College-Owned, -Operated, or -Affiliated Housing:** 37 **Final Year or Final Semester Residency Requirement:** Yes **Regional Accreditation:** Western Association of Schools and Colleges **Credit Hours For Degree:** 120 units, Bachelors

UNIVERSITY OF CALIFORNIA, RIVERSIDE

900 University Ave.
Riverside, CA 92521-0102
Tel: (951)827-1012
Admissions: (951)827-3986
Fax: (951)827-6344
E-mail: discover@ucr.edu
Web Site: http://www.ucr.edu/
President/CEO: Dr. Timothy White
Admissions: Emily Engelschall
Financial Aid: Sheryl Hayes
Type: University **Sex:** Coed **Affiliation:** University of California System **Scores:** 93% SAT V 400+; 93% SAT M 400+; 52% ACT 18-23; 30% ACT 24-29 **% Accepted:** 80 **Application Deadline:** November 30 **Application Fee:** $60.00 **H.S. Requirements:** High school diploma required; GED accepted **Costs Per Year:** Application fee: $60. State resident tuition: $0 full-time. Nonresident tuition: $22,671 full-time. Mandatory fees: $8507 full-time. College room and board: $10,900. Room and board charges vary according to board plan and housing facility. **Scholarships:** Available **Calendar System:** Quarter, Summer Session Available **Enrollment:** FT 16,515, PT 481, Grad FT 2,401, Grad PT 42 **Faculty:** FT 765, PT 154 **Student-Faculty Ratio:** 19:1 **Exams:** SAT I or ACT, SAT II. ACT essay not being used. SAT essay not being used. **% Receiving Financial Aid:** 69 **% Residing in College-Owned, -Operated, or -Affiliated Housing:** 33 **Library Holdings:** 2,955,171 **Regional Accreditation:** Western Association of Schools and Colleges **Credit Hours For Degree:** 180 quarter hours, Bachelors **ROTC:** Army, Air Force **Professional Accreditation:** AACSB, ABET **Intercollegiate Athletics:** Baseball M; Basketball M & W; Cross-Country Running M & W; Golf M & W; Soccer M & W; Softball W; Tennis M & W; Track and Field M & W; Volleyball W

UNIVERSITY OF CALIFORNIA, SAN DIEGO

9500 Gilman Dr.
La Jolla, CA 92093
Tel: (858)534-2230
Admissions: (858)534-4831
E-mail: admissionsreply@ucsd.edu
Web Site: http://www.ucsd.edu/
President/CEO: Dr. Marye Anne Fox
Admissions: Mae Brown
Financial Aid: Ann Klein
Type: University **Sex:** Coed **Affiliation:** University of California System **Scores:** 100% SAT V 400+; 100% SAT M 400+; 18% ACT 18-23; 50% ACT 24-29 **% Accepted:** 42 **Admission Plans:** Preferred Admission **Application Deadline:** November 30 **Application Fee:** $60.00 **H.S. Requirements:** High school diploma required; GED accepted **Costs Per Year:** Application fee: $60. State resident tuition: $0 full-time. Nonresident tuition: $22,669 full-time. Mandatory fees: $9698 full-time. College room and board: $11,057. **Scholarships:** Available **Calendar System:** Quarter, Summer Session

Available **Enrollment:** FT 22,205, PT 313, Grad FT 4,112, Grad PT 93 **Faculty:** FT 943, PT 201 **Student-Faculty Ratio:** 19:1 **Exams:** Other, SAT I or ACT. ACT essay used for admission. SAT essay used for admission. **% Receiving Financial Aid:** 60 **Regional Accreditation:** Western Association of Schools and Colleges **Credit Hours For Degree:** 180 credit hours, Bachelors **ROTC:** Army **Professional Accreditation:** ABET, ACPhE, APA, ASLHA, LCMEAMA **Intercollegiate Athletics:** Baseball M; Basketball M & W; Crew M & W; Cross-Country Running M & W; Fencing M & W; Golf M; Soccer M & W; Softball W; Swimming and Diving M & W; Tennis M & W; Track and Field M & W; Volleyball M & W; Water Polo M & W

UNIVERSITY OF CALIFORNIA, SANTA BARBARA
1210 Cheadle Hall
Santa Barbara, CA 93106-2014
Tel: (805)893-8000
Admissions: (805)893-2881
E-mail: admissions@sa.ucsb.edu
Web Site: http://www.ucsb.edu/
President/CEO: Dr. Henry T. Yang
Type: University **Sex:** Coed **Affiliation:** University of California System **Scores:** 100% SAT V 400+; 99% SAT M 400+; 21% ACT 18-23; 49% ACT 24-29 **% Accepted:** 48 **Application Deadline:** November 30 **Application Fee:** $60.00 **H.S. Requirements:** High school diploma required; GED accepted **Costs Per Year:** Application fee: $60. State resident tuition: $0 full-time. Nonresident tuition: $21,669 full-time. Mandatory fees: $9055 full-time. College room and board: $12,765. Room and board charges vary according to board plan and housing facility. **Scholarships:** Available **Calendar System:** Quarter, Summer Session Available **Enrollment:** FT 19,307, PT 489, Grad FT 3,040, Grad PT 14 **Faculty:** FT 919, PT 167 **Student-Faculty Ratio:** 17:1 **Exams:** SAT I or ACT, SAT II. ACT essay used for admission. SAT essay used for admission. **% Receiving Financial Aid:** 50 **% Residing in College-Owned, -Operated, or -Affiliated Housing:** 31 **Final Year or Final Semester Residency Requirement:** No **Library Holdings:** 3,423,732 **Regional Accreditation:** Western Association of Schools and Colleges **Credit Hours For Degree:** 180 quarter units, Bachelors **ROTC:** Army **Professional Accreditation:** ABET, APA, NASD **Intercollegiate Athletics:** Baseball M; Basketball M & W; Bowling M & W; Crew M & W; Cross-Country Running M & W; Equestrian Sports M & W; Fencing M & W; Field Hockey W; Golf M; Gymnastics M & W; Lacrosse M & W; Rugby M; Sailing M & W; Skiing (Downhill) M & W; Soccer M & W; Softball W; Swimming and Diving M & W; Tennis M & W; Track and Field M & W; Ultimate Frisbee M & W; Volleyball M & W; Water Polo M & W

UNIVERSITY OF CALIFORNIA, SANTA CRUZ
1156 High St.
Santa Cruz, CA 95064
Tel: (831)459-0111
Admissions: (831)459-1372
Fax: (831)459-4452
E-mail: admissions@ucsc.edu
Web Site: http://www.ucsc.edu/
President/CEO: George Blumenthal
Admissions: Michelle Whittingham
Financial Aid: Ann Draper
Type: University **Sex:** Coed **Affiliation:** University of California System **Scores:** 98% SAT V 400+; 97% SAT M 400+; 28% ACT 18-23; 56% ACT 24-29 **% Accepted:** 64 **Admission Plans:** Preferred Admission **Application Deadline:** November 30 **Application Fee:** $60.00 **H.S. Requirements:** High school diploma required; GED accepted **Costs Per Year:** Application fee: $60. State resident tuition: $0 full-time. Nonresident tuition: $22,020 full-time. Mandatory fees: $10,095 full-time. Full-time tuition and fees vary according to course load. College room and board: $13,641. Room and board charges vary according to board plan and housing facility. **Scholarships:** Available **Calendar System:** Quarter, Summer Session Available **Faculty:** FT 566, PT 237 **Student-Faculty Ratio:** 19:1 **Exams:** Other, SAT I or ACT, SAT I and SAT II or ACT. **% Receiving Financial Aid:** 53 **% Residing in College-Owned, -Operated, or -Affiliated Housing:** 48 **Final Year or Final Semester Residency Requirement:** No **Library Holdings:** 2,080,000 **Regional Accreditation:** Western Association of Schools and Colleges **Credit Hours For Degree:** 180 credits, Bachelors **ROTC:** Army, Navy, Air Force **Professional Accreditation:** ABET, APA **Intercollegiate Athletics:** Badminton M & W; Baseball M & W; Basketball M & W; Cross-Country Running M & W; Equestrian Sports M & W; Fencing M & W; Golf W; Lacrosse M & W; Rugby M & W; Soccer M & W; Swimming and Diving M & W; Table Tennis M & W; Tennis M & W; Track and Field M & W; Ultimate Frisbee M & W; Volleyball M & W; Water Polo M & W

UNIVERSITY OF LA VERNE
1950 Third St.
La Verne, CA 91750-4443
Tel: (909)593-3511; Free: 800-876-4858
Fax: (909)593-0965
E-mail: admissions@ulv.edu
Web Site: http://www.laverne.edu/
President/CEO: Dr. Stephen C. Morgan
Admissions: Ana Liza V. Zell
Financial Aid: Leatha Webster
Type: University **Sex:** Coed **Scores:** 93% SAT V 400+; 88% SAT M 400+; 52% ACT 18-23; 18% ACT 24-29 **% Accepted:** 68 **Admission Plans:** Deferred Admission **Application Deadline:** February 1 **Application Fee:** $50.00 **H.S. Requirements:** High school diploma required; GED accepted **Costs Per Year:** Application fee: $50. Comprehensive fee: $40,240 includes full-time tuition ($29,800) and college room and board ($10,440). College room only: $5620. Full-time tuition varies according to course load, degree level, location, program, and student level. Room and board charges vary according to board plan and housing facility. Part-time tuition: $845 per unit. Part-time tuition varies according to course load, degree level, location, program, and student level. **Scholarships:** Available **Calendar System:** 4-1-4, Summer Session Available **Enrollment:** FT 1,435, PT 105, Grad FT 1,395, Grad PT 1,125 **Faculty:** FT 190, PT 204 **Student-Faculty Ratio:** 12:1 **Exams:** SAT I or ACT. **% Receiving Financial Aid:** 83 **% Residing in College-Owned, -Operated, or -Affiliated Housing:** 29 **Library Holdings:** 196,842 **Regional Accreditation:** Western Association of Schools and Colleges **Credit Hours For Degree:** 128 semester hours, Bachelors **ROTC:** Army **Professional Accreditation:** ABA, APA, NASPAA **Intercollegiate Athletics:** Baseball M; Basketball M & W; Cross-Country Running M & W; Football M; Golf M; Soccer M & W; Softball W; Swimming and Diving M & W; Tennis M & W; Track and Field M & W; Volleyball W; Water Polo M & W

UNIVERSITY OF THE PACIFIC
3601 Pacific Ave.
Stockton, CA 95211-0197
Tel: (209)946-2344; Free: 800-959-2867
Admissions: (209)946-2211
Fax: (209)946-2413
E-mail: admissions@pacific.edu
Web Site: http://www.pacific.edu/
President/CEO: Dr. Pamela A. Eibeck
Admissions: Rich Toledo
Financial Aid: Lynn Fox
Type: University **Sex:** Coed **Scores:** 98.1% SAT V 400+; 99% SAT M 400+; 29.4% ACT 18-23; 42% ACT 24-29 **% Accepted:** 42 **Admission Plans:** Early Action **Application Deadline:** January 15 **Application Fee:** $60.00 **H.S. Requirements:** High school diploma required; GED accepted **Costs Per Year:** Application fee: $60. Comprehensive fee: $42,846 includes full-time tuition ($31,730), mandatory fees ($500), and college room and board ($10,616). Room and board charges vary according to board plan and housing facility. **Scholarships:** Available **Calendar System:** Semester, Summer Session Available **Enrollment:** FT 3,384, PT 117, Grad FT 2,144, Grad PT 756 **Faculty:** FT 434, PT 341 **Student-Faculty Ratio:** 13:1 **Exams:** SAT I or ACT. **% Receiving Financial Aid:** 69 **% Residing in College-Owned, -Operated, or -Affiliated Housing:** 56 **Library Holdings:** 376,012 **Regional Accreditation:** Western Association of Schools and Colleges **Credit Hours For Degree:** 124 units, Bachelors **ROTC:** Air Force **Professional Accreditation:** AACSB, ABET, ACPhE, ABA, ADA, APTA, ASLHA, AALS, NASAD, NASM, NCATE **Intercollegiate Athletics:** Baseball M; Basketball M & W; Cross-Country Running W; Field Hockey W; Golf M; Soccer W; Softball W; Swimming and Diving M & W; Tennis M & W; Volleyball M & W; Water Polo M & W

UNIVERSITY OF PHOENIX—BAY AREA CAMPUS
Stoneridge Business Center
Pleasanton, CA 94588-3677
Tel: (925)416-4100; Free: 877-4-STUDENT
Admissions: (480)557-6151
E-mail: audra.mcquarie@phoenix.edu
Web Site: http://www.phoenix.edu/
President/CEO: William Pepicello

Admissions: Audra McQuarie
Type: Comprehensive **Sex:** Coed **Admission Plans:** Open Admission; Deferred Admission **Application Deadline:** Rolling **Application Fee:** $0.00 **H.S. Requirements:** High school diploma required; GED accepted **Costs Per Year:** Application fee: $0. Tuition: $13,380 full-time. Full-time tuition varies according to course level and course load. **Scholarships:** Available **Calendar System:** Continuous, Summer Session Not available **Enrollment:** FT 1,676 **Faculty:** FT 29, PT 289 **Regional Accreditation:** North Central Association of Colleges and Schools **Credit Hours For Degree:** 60 credits, Associates; 120 credits, Bachelors **Professional Accreditation:** NLN

UNIVERSITY OF PHOENIX—CENTRAL VALLEY CAMPUS
45 River Park Place West
Ste. 101
Fresno, CA 93720-1562
Tel: (480)557-6151; Free: 888-228-7240
Admissions: (480)557-6151
E-mail: audra.mcquarie@phoenix.edu
Web Site: http://phoenix.edu/
President/CEO: William Pepicello
Admissions: Audra McQuarie
Type: Comprehensive **Sex:** Coed **Admission Plans:** Open Admission; Deferred Admission **Application Deadline:** Rolling **Application Fee:** $0.00 **H.S. Requirements:** High school diploma required; GED accepted **Costs Per Year:** Application fee: $0. Tuition: $13,380 full-time. Full-time tuition varies according to course level and course load. **Scholarships:** Available **Enrollment:** FT 1,928 **Faculty:** FT 31, PT 241 **Regional Accreditation:** North Central Association of Colleges and Schools **Credit Hours For Degree:** 60 credits, Associates; 120 credits, Bachelors

UNIVERSITY OF PHOENIX—SACRAMENTO VALLEY CAMPUS
2890 Gateway Oaks Dr.
Ste. 200
Sacramento, CA 95833-3632
Tel: (916)923-2107; Free: 800-228-7240
Admissions: (480)557-6151
Fax: (916)923-3914
E-mail: audra.mcquarie@phoenix.edu
Web Site: http://www.phoenix.edu/
President/CEO: William Pepicello
Admissions: Audra McQuarie
Type: Comprehensive **Sex:** Coed **Admission Plans:** Open Admission; Deferred Admission **Application Deadline:** Rolling **Application Fee:** $0.00 **H.S. Requirements:** High school diploma required; GED accepted **Costs Per Year:** Application fee: $0. Tuition: $13,380 full-time. Full-time tuition varies according to course level and course load. **Scholarships:** Available **Calendar System:** Continuous, Summer Session Not available **Enrollment:** FT 3,162 **Faculty:** FT 49, PT 469 **Regional Accreditation:** North Central Association of Colleges and Schools **Credit Hours For Degree:** 60 credits, Associates; 120 credits, Bachelors **Professional Accreditation:** NLN

UNIVERSITY OF PHOENIX—SAN DIEGO CAMPUS
3870 Murphy Canyon Rd.
Ste. 100
San Diego, CA 92123
Tel: 800-473-4346; Free: 888-228-7240
Admissions: (480)557-6151
Fax: (858)576-0032
E-mail: audra.mcquarie@phoenix.edu
Web Site: http://www.phoenix.edu/
President/CEO: William Pepicello
Admissions: Audra McQuarie
Type: Comprehensive **Sex:** Coed **Admission Plans:** Open Admission; Deferred Admission **Application Deadline:** Rolling **Application Fee:** $0.00 **H.S. Requirements:** High school diploma required; GED accepted **Costs Per Year:** Application fee: $0. Tuition: $13,200 full-time. Full-time tuition varies according to course level and course load. **Scholarships:** Available **Calendar System:** Continuous, Summer Session Not available **Enrollment:** FT 2,500 **Faculty:** FT 30, PT 369 **Regional Accreditation:** North Central Association of Colleges and Schools **Credit Hours For Degree:** 60 credits, Associates; 120 credits, Bachelors **Professional Accreditation:** NLN

UNIVERSITY OF PHOENIX—SOUTHERN CALIFORNIA CAMPUS
3150 Bristol St.
Ste. 340
Costa Mesa, CA 92626
Tel: 800-GO-TO-UOP; Free: 800-228-7240
Admissions: (480)557-6151
E-mail: audra.mcquarie@phoenix.edu
Web Site: http://www.phoenix.edu/
President/CEO: William Pepicello
Admissions: Audra McQuarie
Type: Comprehensive **Sex:** Coed **Admission Plans:** Open Admission; Deferred Admission **Application Deadline:** Rolling **Application Fee:** $0.00 **H.S. Requirements:** High school diploma required; GED accepted **Costs Per Year:** Application fee: $0. Tuition: $14,100 full-time. Full-time tuition varies according to course level and course load. **Scholarships:** Available **Calendar System:** Continuous, Summer Session Not available **Enrollment:** FT 9,196 **Faculty:** FT 64, PT 1,276 **Regional Accreditation:** North Central Association of Colleges and Schools **Credit Hours For Degree:** 60 credits, Associates; 120 credits, Bachelors **Professional Accreditation:** NLN

UNIVERSITY OF REDLANDS
1200 East Colton Ave.
PO Box 3080
Redlands, CA 92373-0999
Tel: (909)793-2121; Free: 800-455-5064
Admissions: (909)748-8159
Fax: (909)335-4089
E-mail: admissions@redlands.edu
Web Site: http://www.redlands.edu/
President/CEO: Dr. Stuart Dorsey
Admissions: Paul Driscoll
Financial Aid: Bethann Corey
Type: Comprehensive **Sex:** Coed **Scores:** 99% SAT V 400+; 99% SAT M 400+; 45% ACT 18-23; 48% ACT 24-29 **% Accepted:** 70 **Admission Plans:** Deferred Admission **Application Deadline:** March 1 **Application Fee:** $30.00 **H.S. Requirements:** High school diploma required; GED accepted **Costs Per Year:** Application fee: $30. Comprehensive fee: $44,366 includes full-time tuition ($33,594), mandatory fees ($300), and college room and board ($10,472). College room only: $5814. Full-time tuition and fees vary according to program. Room and board charges vary according to board plan and housing facility. Part-time tuition: $1050 per credit. Part-time mandatory fees: $150 per term. Part-time tuition and fees vary according to course load and program. **Scholarships:** Available **Calendar System:** Miscellaneous, Summer Session Not available **Enrollment:** FT 2,269, PT 681, Grad FT 101, Grad PT 1,406 **Faculty:** FT 221, PT 286 **Student-Faculty Ratio:** 14:1 **Exams:** SAT I or ACT. ACT essay used for placement. SAT essay used for placement. **% Receiving Financial Aid:** 76 **% Residing in College-Owned, -Operated, or -Affiliated Housing:** 53 **Final Year or Final Semester Residency Requirement:** Yes **Library Holdings:** 280,503 **Regional Accreditation:** Western Association of Schools and Colleges **Credit Hours For Degree:** 132 units, Bachelors **ROTC:** Army, Air Force **Professional Accreditation:** ASLHA, NASM **Intercollegiate Athletics:** Baseball M; Basketball M & W; Cross-Country Running M & W; Football M; Golf M & W; Lacrosse W; Soccer M & W; Softball W; Swimming and Diving M & W; Tennis M & W; Track and Field M & W; Volleyball W; Water Polo M & W

UNIVERSITY OF SAN DIEGO
5998 Alcala Park
San Diego, CA 92110-2492
Tel: (619)260-4600; Free: 800-248-4873
Admissions: (619)260-4506
E-mail: admissions@sandiego.edu
Web Site: http://www.sandiego.edu/
President/CEO: Dr. Mary E. Lyons
Admissions: Stephen Pultz
Financial Aid: Judith Lewis Logue
Type: University **Sex:** Coed **Affiliation:** Roman Catholic **Scores:** 99% SAT V 400+; 99% SAT M 400+; 12% ACT 18-23; 66% ACT 24-29 **% Accepted:** 49 **Admission Plans:** Early Action; Deferred Admission **Application Deadline:** January 15 **Application Fee:** $55.00 **H.S. Requirements:** High school diploma required; GED accepted **Costs Per Year:** Application fee: $55. Comprehensive fee: $48,894 includes full-time tuition ($35,870), mandatory fees ($422), and college room and board ($12,602). Room and

board charges vary according to board plan and housing facility. Part-time tuition: $1240 per unit. Part-time mandatory fees: $151 per term. Part-time tuition and fees vary according to course load. **Scholarships:** Available **Calendar System:** 4-1-4, Summer Session Available **Enrollment:** FT 4,896, PT 215, Grad FT 1,575, Grad PT 1,182 **Faculty:** FT 381, PT 427 **Student-Faculty Ratio:** 15:1 **Exams:** SAT I or ACT. ACT essay used for advising. SAT essay used for advising. ACT essay used for placement. SAT essay used for placement. **% Receiving Financial Aid:** 48 **% Residing in College-Owned, -Operated, or -Affiliated Housing:** 48 **Final Year or Final Semester Residency Requirement:** Yes **Library Holdings:** 704,887 **Regional Accreditation:** Western Association of Schools and Colleges **Credit Hours For Degree:** 124 units, Bachelors **ROTC:** Army, Navy, Air Force **Professional Accreditation:** AACSB, ABET, AAMFT, AACN, ABA, APA, AALS, NCATE **Intercollegiate Athletics:** Baseball M; Basketball M & W; Crew M & W; Cross-Country Running M & W; Equestrian Sports W; Football M; Golf M; Lacrosse M & W; Rock Climbing M; Rugby M & W; Soccer M & W; Softball W; Swimming and Diving W; Tennis M & W; Track and Field W; Ultimate Frisbee M & W; Volleyball M & W

UNIVERSITY OF SAN FRANCISCO
2130 Fulton St.
San Francisco, CA 94117-1080
Tel: (415)422-5555; Free: 800-CAL-LUSF
Admissions: (415)422-6563
Fax: (415)422-2217
E-mail: admissions@usfca.edu
Web Site: http://www.usfca.edu/
President/CEO: Rev. Stephen A. Privett, SJ
Admissions: Michael Hughes
Financial Aid: Susan Murphy
Type: University **Sex:** Coed **Affiliation:** Roman Catholic (Jesuit) **Scores:** 99% SAT V 400+; 99% SAT M 400+; 43% ACT 18-23; 46% ACT 24-29 **% Accepted:** 71 **Admission Plans:** Early Action; Deferred Admission **Application Deadline:** January 15 **Application Fee:** $55.00 **H.S. Requirements:** High school diploma required; GED accepted **Costs Per Year:** Application fee: $55. Comprehensive fee: $48,370 includes full-time tuition ($36,000), mandatory fees ($380), and college room and board ($11,990). College room only: $8080. Full-time tuition and fees vary according to course load, degree level, program, and reciprocity agreements. Room and board charges vary according to board plan and housing facility. Part-time tuition: $1280 per credit hour. Part-time mandatory fees: $380 per year. Part-time tuition and fees vary according to course load, degree level, program, and reciprocity agreements. **Scholarships:** Available **Calendar System:** 4-1-4, Summer Session Available **Enrollment:** FT 5,314, PT 211, Grad FT 2,916, Grad PT 571 **Faculty:** FT 386, PT 553 **Student-Faculty Ratio:** 15:1 **Exams:** SAT I or ACT. ACT essay used for placement. SAT essay used for placement. **% Receiving Financial Aid:** 56 **% Residing in College-Owned, -Operated, or -Affiliated Housing:** 73 **Library Holdings:** 1,148,737 **Regional Accreditation:** Western Association of Schools and Colleges **Credit Hours For Degree:** 128 units, Bachelors **ROTC:** Army, Air Force **Professional Accreditation:** AACSB, AACN, ABA, AALS, NLN **Intercollegiate Athletics:** Baseball M; Basketball M & W; Cross-Country Running M & W; Golf M & W; Soccer M & W; Softball M & W; Tennis M & W; Track and Field M & W; Volleyball M & W

UNIVERSITY OF SOUTHERN CALIFORNIA
University Park Campus
Los Angeles, CA 90089
Tel: (213)740-2311
Admissions: (213)740-1111
Fax: (213)740-6364
E-mail: admitusc@usc.edu
Web Site: http://www.usc.edu/
President/CEO: Steven B. Sample
Admissions: Timothy Brunold
Financial Aid: Katharine Harrington
Type: University **Sex:** Coed **Scores:** 100% SAT V 400+; 100% SAT M 400+; 2% ACT 18-23; 33% ACT 24-29 **% Accepted:** 24 **Application Deadline:** January 10 **Application Fee:** $65.00 **H.S. Requirements:** High school diploma required; GED not accepted. **Costs Per Year:** Application fee: $65. One-time mandatory fee: $150. Comprehensive fee: $50,642 includes full-time tuition ($38,570), mandatory fees ($614), and college room and board ($11,458). College room only: $6416. Full-time tuition and fees vary according to program. Room and board charges vary according to board plan and housing facility. Part-time tuition: $1299 per unit. Part-time tuition varies according to course load and program. **Scholarships:** Available **Calendar System:** Semester, Summer Session Available **Enrollment:** FT 16,096, PT 655, Grad FT 14,481, Grad PT 3,592 **Faculty:** FT 1,638, PT 1,133 **Student-Faculty Ratio:** 9:1 **Exams:** SAT I or ACT. ACT essay used for admission. SAT essay used for admission. ACT essay used for advising. SAT essay used for advising. ACT essay used as a validity check on application essay. SAT essay used as a validity check on application essay. **% Receiving Financial Aid:** 42 **% Residing in College-Owned, -Operated, or -Affiliated Housing:** 42 **Final Year or Final Semester Residency Requirement:** No **Library Holdings:** 4,397,851 **Regional Accreditation:** Western Association of Schools and Colleges **Credit Hours For Degree:** 128 units, Bachelors **ROTC:** Army, Navy, Air Force **Professional Accreditation:** AACSB, ABET, ACPhE, ACEJMC, AACN, AANA, ABA, ADA, ADtA, ACSP, AOTA, APTA, APA, AALS, ACEHSA, CEPH, CSWE, LCMEAMA, NAAB, NASM NASPAA **Intercollegiate Athletics:** Archery M & W; Badminton M & W; Baseball M; Basketball M & W; Cheerleading W; Crew M & W; Cross-Country Running M & W; Equestrian Sports M & W; Fencing M & W; Football M; Golf M & W; Ice Hockey M & W; Lacrosse M & W; Racquetball M & W; Rock Climbing M & W; Rugby M & W; Skiing (Downhill) M & W; Soccer M & W; Softball W; Squash M & W; Swimming and Diving M & W; Table Tennis M & W; Tennis M & W; Track and Field M & W; Ultimate Frisbee M & W; Volleyball M & W; Water Polo M & W; Wrestling M

UNIVERSITY OF THE WEST
1409 North Walnut Grove Ave.
Rosemead, CA 91770
Tel: (626)571-8811
Fax: (626)571-1413
E-mail: graceh@uwest.edu
Web Site: http://www.uwest.edu/
President/CEO: Dr. Allen Huang
Admissions: Grace Hsiao
Financial Aid: Dr. Teresa Ku
Type: Comprehensive **Sex:** Coed **% Accepted:** 85 **Admission Plans:** Deferred Admission **Application Deadline:** June 1 **Application Fee:** $50.00 **H.S. Requirements:** High school diploma required; GED accepted **Costs Per Year:** Application fee: $50. One-time mandatory fee: $75. Comprehensive fee: $14,322 includes full-time tuition ($7680), mandatory fees ($460), and college room and board ($6182). Full-time tuition and fees vary according to course load and program. Room and board charges vary according to board plan and housing facility. Part-time tuition: $320 per unit. Part-time mandatory fees: $230 per term. Part-time tuition and fees vary according to course load and program. **Scholarships:** Available **Calendar System:** Semester, Summer Session Available **Faculty:** FT 10, PT 52 **Student-Faculty Ratio:** 8:1 **% Receiving Financial Aid:** 25 **% Residing in College-Owned, -Operated, or -Affiliated Housing:** 35 **Regional Accreditation:** Western Association of Schools and Colleges

VANGUARD UNIVERSITY OF SOUTHERN CALIFORNIA
55 Fair Dr.
Costa Mesa, CA 92626-9601
Tel: (714)556-3610; Free: 800-722-6279
Fax: (714)966-5460
E-mail: admissions@vanguard.edu
Web Site: http://www.vanguard.edu/
President/CEO: Carol Taylor
Admissions: Kristi Pruett
Type: Comprehensive **Sex:** Coed **Affiliation:** Assemblies of God **% Accepted:** 79 **Admission Plans:** Preferred Admission; Early Admission; Early Action; Deferred Admission **Application Deadline:** January 15 **Application Fee:** $45.00 **H.S. Requirements:** High school diploma required; GED accepted **Costs Per Year:** Application fee: $45. Comprehensive fee: $34,616 includes full-time tuition ($26,342) and college room and board ($8274). College room only: $4074. Full-time tuition varies according to course load. Room and board charges vary according to board plan and housing facility. Part-time tuition: $1098 per unit. Part-time tuition varies according to course load. **Scholarships:** Available **Calendar System:** Semester, Summer Session Available **Enrollment:** FT 1,293, PT 359, Grad FT 114, Grad PT 157 **Faculty:** FT 65, PT 85 **Student-Faculty Ratio:** 17:1 **Exams:** SAT I or ACT. **% Receiving Financial Aid:** 79 **% Residing in College-Owned, -Operated, or -Affiliated Housing:** 68 **Library Holdings:** 164,333 **Regional Accreditation:** Western Association of Schools and Colleges **Credit Hours For Degree:** 124 credits, Bachelors **ROTC:** Air Force **Professional Accredita-**

tion: JRCEPAT **Intercollegiate Athletics:** Baseball M; Basketball M & W; Cross-Country Running M & W; Soccer M & W; Softball W; Swimming and Diving M & W; Tennis M & W; Track and Field M & W; Volleyball W

VENTURA COLLEGE
4667 Telegraph Rd.
Ventura, CA 93003-3899
Tel: (805)654-6400
Admissions: (805)654-6456
Fax: (805)654-6466
E-mail: sbricker@vcccd.net
Web Site: http://www.venturacollege.edu/
President/CEO: Dr. Robin Calote
Admissions: Susan Bricker
Type: Two-Year College **Sex:** Coed **Affiliation:** California Community College System **Admission Plans:** Open Admission **Application Deadline:** Rolling **Application Fee:** $0.00 **H.S. Requirements:** High school diploma required; GED accepted **Costs Per Year:** Application fee: $0. State resident tuition: $0 full-time. Nonresident tuition: $5670 full-time, $189 per unit part-time. Mandatory fees: $780 full-time, $26 per unit part-time. **Scholarships:** Available **Calendar System:** Semester, Summer Session Available **Faculty:** FT 136, PT 386 **Student-Faculty Ratio:** 26:1 **Library Holdings:** 63,529 **Regional Accreditation:** Western Association of Schools and Colleges **Credit Hours For Degree:** 60 semester hours, Associates **Intercollegiate Athletics:** Baseball M; Basketball M & W; Cheerleading M & W; Football M; Golf M; Soccer W; Softball W; Swimming and Diving M & W; Tennis M & W; Track and Field M & W; Volleyball W; Water Polo M & W

VICTOR VALLEY COLLEGE
18422 Bear Valley Rd.
Victorville, CA 92395
Tel: (760)245-4271
Fax: (760)245-9745
E-mail: moong@vvc.edu
Web Site: http://www.vvc.edu/
President/CEO: Dr. Robert M. Silverman
Admissions: Greta Moon
Financial Aid: Maria Gonzalez
Type: Two-Year College **Sex:** Coed **Affiliation:** California Community College System **Admission Plans:** Open Admission **Application Deadline:** Rolling **H.S. Requirements:** High school diploma or equivalent not required. For applicants under 18: High school diploma required; GED accepted **Costs Per Year:** State resident tuition: $0 full-time. Nonresident tuition: $4560 full-time, $190 per unit part-time. Mandatory fees: $624 full-time, $26 per unit part-time. **Scholarships:** Available **Calendar System:** Semester, Summer Session Available **Faculty:** FT 133, PT 441 **Student-Faculty Ratio:** 28:1 **Regional Accreditation:** Western Association of Schools and Colleges **Credit Hours For Degree:** 60 units, Associates **Professional Accreditation:** CARC **Intercollegiate Athletics:** Baseball M; Basketball M & W; Cross-Country Running M & W; Football M; Golf M; Soccer M & W; Softball W; Tennis M & W; Track and Field M & W; Volleyball W; Wrestling M

WEST COAST UNIVERSITY
12215 Victory Blvd.
North Hollywood, CA 91606
Tel: (323)315-5207
E-mail: info@katz.wcula.edu
Web Site: http://www.westcoastuniversity.edu/
President/CEO: David A. Pyle
Admissions: Roger A. Miller
Type: Four-Year College **Sex:** Coed **Calendar System:** Miscellaneous **Professional Accreditation:** ACICS

WEST HILLS COMMUNITY COLLEGE
300 Cherry Ln.
Coalinga, CA 93210-1399
Tel: (559)934-2000; Free: 800-266-1114
Fax: (559)934-1511
E-mail: sandradagnino@westhillscollege.com
Web Site: http://www.westhillscollege.com/
President/CEO: Willard Lewallen
Admissions: Sandra Dagnino
Type: Two-Year College **Sex:** Coed **Affiliation:** California Community College System **Admission Plans:** Open Admission; Preferred Admission; Early Admission **Application Deadline:** Rolling **Application Fee:** $0.00 **H.S. Requirements:** High school diploma or equivalent not required **Scholarships:** Available **Calendar System:** Semester, Summer Session Available **Enrollment:** FT 1,956, PT 4,132 **Faculty:** FT 87, PT 176 **Student-Faculty Ratio:** 20:1 **% Residing in College-Owned, -Operated, or -Affiliated Housing:** 20 **Library Holdings:** 32,000 **Regional Accreditation:** Western Association of Schools and Colleges **Credit Hours For Degree:** 60 units, Associates **Intercollegiate Athletics:** Baseball M; Basketball M; Equestrian Sports M & W; Football M; Softball W; Tennis W; Volleyball W

WEST LOS ANGELES COLLEGE
9000 Overland Ave.
Culver City, CA 90230-3519
Tel: (310)287-4200
Fax: (310)841-0396
Web Site: http://www.lacolleges.net/
President/CEO: Mark W. Rocha
Admissions: Len Isaksen
Financial Aid: Ludwig Perez
Type: Two-Year College **Sex:** Coed **Affiliation:** Los Angeles Community College District System **Admission Plans:** Open Admission; Early Admission **Application Deadline:** August 16 **H.S. Requirements:** High school diploma or equivalent not required **Scholarships:** Available **Calendar System:** Semester, Summer Session Available **Faculty:** FT 120, PT 200 **Library Holdings:** 51,000 **Regional Accreditation:** Western Association of Schools and Colleges **Credit Hours For Degree:** 60 units, Associates **ROTC:** Army, Air Force **Professional Accreditation:** ADA **Intercollegiate Athletics:** Basketball M; Football M; Golf M; Track and Field M & W; Volleyball W

WEST VALLEY COLLEGE
14000 Fruitvale Ave.
Saratoga, CA 95070-5698
Tel: (408)867-2200
Fax: (408)867-5033
E-mail: barbara_ogilvie@westvalley.edu
Web Site: http://www.westvalley.edu/
President/CEO: Lori Gaskin
Admissions: Barbara Ogilive
Type: Two-Year College **Sex:** Coed **Affiliation:** California Community College System **Admission Plans:** Open Admission; Preferred Admission; Early Admission **Application Deadline:** Rolling **Application Fee:** $0.00 **H.S. Requirements:** High school diploma or equivalent not required **Scholarships:** Available **Calendar System:** Semester, Summer Session Available **Faculty:** FT 210, PT 350 **Library Holdings:** 82,959 **Regional Accreditation:** Western Association of Schools and Colleges **Credit Hours For Degree:** 60 units, Associates **ROTC:** Army, Air Force **Professional Accreditation:** AAMAE, FIDER **Intercollegiate Athletics:** Basketball M & W; Cross-Country Running M & W; Football M; Golf M; Soccer M; Swimming and Diving M & W; Tennis M & W; Track and Field M; Volleyball M & W; Water Polo M; Wrestling M

WESTERN CAREER COLLEGE (EMERYVILLE)
1400 65th St.
Ste. 200
Emeryville, CA 94608
Tel: (510)601-0133
Fax: (510)601-0793
Web Site: http://www.westerncollege.edu/
President/CEO: Jeff Akens
Type: Two-Year College **Sex:** Coed **% Accepted:** 100 **Application Fee:** $100.00 **H.S. Requirements:** High school diploma required; GED accepted **Calendar System:** Semester, Summer Session Not available **Exams:** ACT. **Regional Accreditation:** Western Association of Schools and Colleges **Professional Accreditation:** ACCSCT

WESTERN CAREER COLLEGE (FREMONT)
41350 Christy St.
Fremont, CA 94538
Tel: (510)623-9966
Fax: (510)623-9822
Web Site: http://www.westerncollege.edu/
Admissions: Anton Croos
Type: Two-Year College **Sex:** Coed **Admission Plans:** Open Admission **Ap-**

plication Fee: $125.00 **H.S. Requirements:** High school diploma required; GED accepted **Calendar System:** Semester, Summer Session Not available **Enrollment:** FT 460 **Faculty:** FT 22, PT 4 **Student-Faculty Ratio:** 18:1 **Exams:** ACT. **Library Holdings:** 1,000 **Professional Accreditation:** ACCSCT

WESTERN CAREER COLLEGE (PLEASANT HILL)
380 Civic Dr.
Ste. 300
Pleasant Hill, CA 94523
Tel: (925)609-6650; Free: 888-203-9947
Fax: (925)609-6666
Web Site: http://www.westerncollege.edu/
President/CEO: Jeff Akens
Type: Two-Year College **Sex:** Coed **% Accepted:** 90 **Application Fee:** $100.00 **Calendar System:** Semester **Regional Accreditation:** Western Association of Schools and Colleges **Professional Accreditation:** AAMAE

WESTERN CAREER COLLEGE (SACRAMENTO)
8909 Folsom Blvd.
Sacramento, CA 95826
Tel: (916)361-1660; Free: 888-203-9947
Fax: (916)361-6666
Web Site: http://www.westerncollege.edu/
President/CEO: Jeff Akens
Type: Two-Year College **Sex:** Coed **% Accepted:** 79 **Application Fee:** $100.00 **Calendar System:** Semester **Regional Accreditation:** Western Association of Schools and Colleges **Professional Accreditation:** AAMAE

WESTERN CAREER COLLEGE (SAN JOSE)
6201 San Ignacio Blvd.
San Jose, CA 95119
Tel: (408)360-0840
Fax: (408)360-0840
Web Site: http://www.westerncollege.edu/
President/CEO: Jeff Akens
Type: Two-Year College **Sex:** Coed **% Accepted:** 100 **Application Fee:** $100.00 **H.S. Requirements:** High school diploma required; GED accepted **Calendar System:** Semester, Summer Session Not available **Student-Faculty Ratio:** 22:1 **Regional Accreditation:** Western Association of Schools and Colleges **Professional Accreditation:** ACCSCT

WESTERN CAREER COLLEGE (SAN LEANDRO)
15555 East 14th St.
Ste. 500
San Leandro, CA 94578
Tel: (510)276-3888; Free: 888-203-9947
Fax: (510)276-3854
Web Site: http://www.westerncollege.edu/
President/CEO: Jeff Akens
Type: Two-Year College **Sex:** Coed **% Accepted:** 75 **Application Fee:** $100.00 **Calendar System:** Semester **Regional Accreditation:** Western Association of Schools and Colleges **Professional Accreditation:** AAMAE, AOTA

WESTERN CAREER COLLEGE (WALNUT CREEK)
2800 Mitchell Dr.
Walnut Creek, CA 94598
Tel: (925)280-0235
Admissions: (925)522-7777
Web Site: http://www.westerncollege.edu/
President/CEO: Jeff Akens
Type: Two-Year College **Sex:** Coed **% Accepted:** 100 **Application Fee:** $100.00 **Calendar System:** Continuous, Summer Session Not available **Exams:** Other. **Professional Accreditation:** ACCSCT

WESTMONT COLLEGE
955 La Paz Rd.
Santa Barbara, CA 93108-1099
Tel: (805)565-6000; Free: 800-777-9011
Admissions: (805)565-6200
Fax: (805)565-6234
E-mail: admissions@westmont.edu
Web Site: http://www.westmont.edu/
President/CEO: Dr. Gayle Beebe
Admissions: Joyce Luy
Financial Aid: Diane L. Horvath
Type: Four-Year College **Sex:** Coed **Affiliation:** nondenominational **Scores:** 99% SAT V 400+; 99% SAT M 400+; 33% ACT 18-23; 46% ACT 24-29 **% Accepted:** 80 **Admission Plans:** Early Action **Application Deadline:** February 20 **Application Fee:** $35.00 **H.S. Requirements:** High school diploma required; GED accepted **Costs Per Year:** Application fee: $35. Comprehensive fee: $45,420 includes full-time tuition ($33,400), mandatory fees ($1060), and college room and board ($10,960). College room only: $6810. **Scholarships:** Available **Calendar System:** Semester, Summer Session Available **Enrollment:** FT 1,293, PT 11, Grad FT 4 **Faculty:** FT 93, PT 40 **Student-Faculty Ratio:** 12:1 **Exams:** SAT I or ACT. ACT essay used for admission. SAT essay used for admission. ACT essay used for advising. SAT essay used for advising. ACT essay used for placement. SAT essay used for placement. **% Receiving Financial Aid:** 62 **% Residing in College-Owned, -Operated, or -Affiliated Housing:** 80 **Library Holdings:** 174,246 **Regional Accreditation:** Western Association of Schools and Colleges **Credit Hours For Degree:** 124 units, Bachelors **ROTC:** Army, Air Force **Intercollegiate Athletics:** Baseball M; Basketball M & W; Cross-Country Running M & W; Equestrian Sports M; Lacrosse W; Rugby M; Soccer M & W; Tennis M & W; Track and Field M & W; Volleyball M & W

WESTWOOD COLLEGE—ANAHEIM
1551 South Douglass Rd.
Anaheim, CA 92806
Tel: (714)226-9990
Admissions: (714)704-2720
Fax: (714)826-7398
Web Site: http://www.westwood.edu/
President/CEO: Lou Osborn
Type: Four-Year College **Sex:** Coed **Scholarships:** Available **Calendar System:** Continuous **Professional Accreditation:** ACCSCT

WESTWOOD COLLEGE—INLAND EMPIRE
20 West 7th St.
Upland, CA 91786
Tel: (909)931-7550
Fax: (909)931-9195
Web Site: http://www.westwood.edu/
President/CEO: Tina Miller
Type: Four-Year College **Sex:** Coed **Scholarships:** Available **Calendar System:** Continuous **Professional Accreditation:** ACCSCT

WESTWOOD COLLEGE—LOS ANGELES
3250 Wilshire Blvd., 4th Floor
Los Angeles, CA 90010
Tel: (213)739-9999
Fax: (213)382-2468
Web Site: http://www.westwood.edu/
President/CEO: DeWayne Johnson
Type: Four-Year College **Sex:** Coed **Scholarships:** Available **Calendar System:** Continuous **Professional Accreditation:** ACICS

WESTWOOD COLLEGE—SOUTH BAY CAMPUS
19700 South Vermont Ave.
Ste. 100
Torrance, CA 90502
Tel: (310)522-2088; Free: 800-281-2978
Admissions: (310)525-1263
Fax: (310)522-4318
Web Site: http://www.westwood.edu/
President/CEO: Chris Turen
Type: Four-Year College **Sex:** Coed **Affiliation:** Association of Independent Technological Universities (AITU) **H.S. Requirements:** High school diploma required; GED accepted **Scholarships:** Available **Calendar System:** Continuous **Professional Accreditation:** ACCSCT

WHITTIER COLLEGE
13406 East Philadelphia St.
Whittier, CA 90608-0634
Tel: (562)907-4200
Admissions: (562)907-4238
Fax: (562)907-4870

E-mail: admission@whittier.edu
Web Site: http://www.whittier.edu/
President/CEO: Sharon D. Herzberger, PhD
Admissions: Kieron Miller
Financial Aid: David Carnevale
Type: Comprehensive **Sex:** Coed **Scores:** 97% SAT V 400+; 96% SAT M 400+; 52% ACT 18-23; 32% ACT 24-29 **% Accepted:** 72 **Admission Plans:** Early Action; Deferred Admission **Application Deadline:** Rolling **Application Fee:** $50.00 **H.S. Requirements:** High school diploma required; GED accepted. For transfer students with at least 30 units: High school diploma or equivalent not required **Costs Per Year:** Application fee: $50. Comprehensive fee: $44,146 includes full-time tuition ($33,868), mandatory fees ($520), and college room and board ($9758). Room and board charges vary according to board plan. Part-time tuition: $1430 per unit. **Scholarships:** Available **Calendar System:** 4-1-4, Summer Session Available **Enrollment:** FT 1,354, PT 17, Grad FT 362, Grad PT 276 **Faculty:** FT 96, PT 34 **Student-Faculty Ratio:** 13:1 **Exams:** SAT I or ACT, SAT II. ACT essay used for admission. SAT essay used for admission. ACT essay used as a validity check on application essay. SAT essay used as a validity check on application essay. ACT essay used for placement. SAT essay used for placement. **% Receiving Financial Aid:** 67 **% Residing in College-Owned, -Operated, or -Affiliated Housing:** 63 **Library Holdings:** 225,337 **Regional Accreditation:** Western Association of Schools and Colleges **Credit Hours For Degree:** 120 credits, Bachelors **ROTC:** Army, Air Force **Professional Accreditation:** ABA, AALS, CSWE **Intercollegiate Athletics:** Baseball M; Basketball M & W; Cross-Country Running M & W; Football M; Golf M; Lacrosse M & W; Soccer M & W; Softball W; Swimming and Diving M & W; Tennis M & W; Track and Field M & W; Volleyball W; Water Polo M & W

WILLIAM JESSUP UNIVERSITY
333 Sunset Blvd.
Rocklin, CA 95765
Tel: (916)577-1800; Free: 800-355-7522
Admissions: (916)577-2222
Fax: (916)577-1813
E-mail: admissions@jessup.edu
Web Site: http://www.jessup.edu/
President/CEO: Dr. Bryce Jessup
Admissions: Vance Pascua
Financial Aid: Kristi Kindberg
Type: Four-Year College **Sex:** Coed **Affiliation:** nondenominational **Scores:** 95% SAT V 400+; 90% SAT M 400+; 55% ACT 18-23; 28% ACT 24-29 **% Accepted:** 76 **Application Deadline:** April 1 **Application Fee:** $45.00 **H.S. Requirements:** High school diploma required; GED accepted **Costs Per Year:** Application fee: $45. Comprehensive fee: $27,820 includes full-time tuition ($19,980) and college room and board ($7840). Full-time tuition varies according to course load. Room and board charges vary according to housing facility. Part-time tuition: $850 per semester hour. Part-time tuition varies according to course load. **Scholarships:** Available **Calendar System:** Semester, Summer Session Available **Enrollment:** FT 412, PT 142, Grad PT 24 **Faculty:** FT 18, PT 50 **Student-Faculty Ratio:** 14:1 **Exams:** SAT I or ACT. **% Receiving Financial Aid:** 70 **% Residing in College-Owned, -Operated, or -Affiliated Housing:** 38 **Final Year or Final Semester Residency Requirement:** Yes **Library Holdings:** 52,294 **Regional Accreditation:** Western Association of Schools and Colleges **Credit Hours For Degree:** 64 semester hours, Associates; 128 semester hours, Bachelors **Professional Accreditation:** ABHE **Intercollegiate Athletics:** Basketball M & W; Cross-Country Running M & W; Soccer M & W; Softball W; Volleyball W

WOODBURY UNIVERSITY
7500 Glenoaks Blvd.
Burbank, CA 91504-1099
Tel: (818)767-0888; Free: 800-784-WOOD
Admissions: 800-784-9663
Fax: (818)504-9320
E-mail: admissions@woodbury.edu
Web Site: http://www.woodbury.edu/
President/CEO: Dr. Kenneth Nielsen
Admissions: Sabrina Taylor
Financial Aid: Celeastia Williams
Type: Comprehensive **Sex:** Coed **Scores:** 73.4% SAT V 400+; 78.5% SAT M 400+; 46% ACT 18-23; 23% ACT 24-29 **% Accepted:** 41 **Admission Plans:** Deferred Admission **Application Deadline:** Rolling **Application Fee:** $50.00 **H.S. Requirements:** High school diploma required; GED accepted **Costs Per Year:** Application fee: $50. Comprehensive fee: $38,148 includes full-time tuition ($28,465), mandatory fees ($390), and college room and board ($9293). College room only: $5788. Full-time tuition and fees vary according to course load and degree level. Part-time tuition: $965 per credit hour. Part-time tuition varies according to course load and degree level. **Scholarships:** Available **Calendar System:** Semester, Summer Session Available **Enrollment:** FT 1,079, PT 222, Grad FT 289, Grad PT 24 **Faculty:** FT 59, PT 221 **Student-Faculty Ratio:** 11:1 **Exams:** SAT I or ACT. **% Receiving Financial Aid:** 86 **% Residing in College-Owned, -Operated, or -Affiliated Housing:** 16 **Library Holdings:** 66,648 **Regional Accreditation:** Western Association of Schools and Colleges **Credit Hours For Degree:** 120 units, Bachelors **Professional Accreditation:** ACBSP, FIDER, NAAB

WOODLAND COMMUNITY COLLEGE
2300 East Gibson Rd.
Woodland, CA 95776
Tel: (530)661-5700
Web Site: http://www.yccd.edu/woodland/
President/CEO: Angela Fairchilds
Type: Two-Year College **Sex:** Coed **Regional Accreditation:** Western Association of Schools and Colleges

WYOTECH (FREMONT)
200 Whitney Place
Fremont, CA 94539-7663
Tel: (510)490-6900; Free: 800-248-8585
Fax: (510)490-8599
Web Site: http://www.wyotech.edu/
President/CEO: Joe Pappaly
Type: Two-Year College **Sex:** Coed **Affiliation:** Corinthian Colleges, Inc. **% Accepted:** 84 **Calendar System:** Continuous **Enrollment:** FT 1,926 **Faculty:** FT 96, PT 12 **Student-Faculty Ratio:** 25:1 **Exams:** Other. **Professional Accreditation:** ACCSCT

WYOTECH (WEST SACRAMENTO)
980 Riverside Parkway
West Sacramento, CA 95605-1507
Tel: (916)376-8888; Free: 888-577-7559
Web Site: http://www.wyotech.com/
President/CEO: John Hurd
Type: Two-Year College **Sex:** Coed **Admission Plans:** Open Admission **Calendar System:** Miscellaneous **Student-Faculty Ratio:** 16:1 **Professional Accreditation:** ACCSCT

YESHIVA OHR ELCHONON CHABAD/WEST COAST TALMUDICAL SEMINARY
7215 Waring Ave.
Los Angeles, CA 90046-7660
Tel: (213)937-3763
Admissions: (323)937-3763
E-mail: roshyeshiva@yoec.edu
President/CEO: Rabbi Ezra Schochet
Admissions: Rabbi Ezra Binyomin Schochet
Financial Aid: Hendy Tauber
Type: Four-Year College **Sex:** Men **Affiliation:** Jewish **% Accepted:** 100 **Admission Plans:** Preferred Admission; Early Admission; Deferred Admission **Application Deadline:** Rolling **Application Fee:** $0.00 **H.S. Requirements:** High school diploma required; GED accepted **Calendar System:** Semester, Summer Session Available **Library Holdings:** 12,000 **Credit Hours For Degree:** 120 credits, Bachelors **Professional Accreditation:** AARTS

YUBA COLLEGE
2088 North Beale Rd.
Marysville, CA 95901-7699
Tel: (530)741-6700
Fax: (530)741-3541
Web Site: http://www.yccd.edu/
President/CEO: Virginia Harrington
Admissions: Dr. David Farrell
Type: Two-Year College **Sex:** Coed **Affiliation:** California Community Col-

lege System **Admission Plans:** Open Admission **Application Deadline:** Rolling **Application Fee:** $0.00 **H.S. Requirements:** High school diploma required; GED accepted. For applicants 18 or over: High school diploma required; GED accepted **Scholarships:** Available **Calendar System:** Semester, Summer Session Available **Faculty:** FT 135, PT 375 **Library Holdings:** 65,000 **Regional Accreditation:** Western Association of Schools and Colleges **Credit Hours For Degree:** 60 units, Associates **Professional Accreditation:** JRCERT **Intercollegiate Athletics:** Baseball M; Basketball M & W; Cross-Country Running M & W; Football M; Soccer M & W; Softball W; Tennis M & W; Track and Field M & W; Volleyball W

ADAMS STATE COLLEGE
208 Edgemont Blvd.
Alamosa, CO 81102
Tel: (719)587-7011; Free: 800-824-6494
Admissions: (719)587-7712
Fax: (719)587-7522
E-mail: ascadmit@adams.edu
Web Site: http://www.adams.edu/
President/CEO: Dr. David Svaldi
Admissions: Eric Carpio
Financial Aid: Phil Schroeder
Type: Comprehensive **Sex:** Coed **Scores:** 79.51% SAT V 400+; 84.33% SAT M 400+; 52.7% ACT 18-23; 15.12% ACT 24-29 **% Accepted:** 57 **Admission Plans:** Early Admission; Deferred Admission **Application Deadline:** August 1 **Application Fee:** $30.00 **H.S. Requirements:** High school diploma required; GED accepted **Costs Per Year:** Application fee: $30. State resident tuition: $2712 full-time, $113 per credit hour part-time. Nonresident tuition: $11,856 full-time, $494 per credit hour part-time. Mandatory fees: $1742 full-time, $73 per credit hour part-time. Full-time tuition and fees vary according to course load. Part-time tuition and fees vary according to course load. College room and board: $7020. College room only: $3560. Room and board charges vary according to board plan and housing facility. **Scholarships:** Available **Calendar System:** Semester, Summer Session Available **Enrollment:** FT 1,914, PT 455, Grad FT 160, Grad PT 595 **Faculty:** FT 111, PT 55 **Student-Faculty Ratio:** 20:1 **Exams:** SAT I or ACT. **% Receiving Financial Aid:** 78 **% Residing in College-Owned, -Operated, or -Affiliated Housing:** 40 **Final Year or Final Semester Residency Requirement:** No **Library Holdings:** 125,288 **Regional Accreditation:** North Central Association of Colleges and Schools **Credit Hours For Degree:** 60 semester hours, Associates; 120 semester hours, Bachelors **Professional Accreditation:** ACA, NASM, TEAC **Intercollegiate Athletics:** Basketball M & W; Cross-Country Running M & W; Football M; Golf M & W; Soccer M & W; Softball W; Swimming and Diving W; Track and Field M & W; Volleyball W; Wrestling M

AIMS COMMUNITY COLLEGE
Box 69
5401 West 20th St.
Greeley, CO 80632-0069
Tel: (970)330-8008
E-mail: wgreen@chiron.aims.edu
Web Site: http://www.aims.edu/
President/CEO: Dr. Marilynn Liddell
Admissions: Susie Gallardo
Type: Two-Year College **Sex:** Coed **Admission Plans:** Open Admission; Early Admission; Deferred Admission **Application Deadline:** Rolling **H.S. Requirements:** High school diploma or equivalent not required **Scholarships:** Available **Calendar System:** Semester, Summer Session Available **Enrollment:** FT 1,701, PT 2,887 **Faculty:** FT 91, PT 182 **Student-Faculty Ratio:** 18:1 **Library Holdings:** 39,129 **Regional Accreditation:** North Central Association of Colleges and Schools **Credit Hours For Degree:** 96 quarter hours, Associates **ROTC:** Air Force **Professional Accreditation:** JRCERT

AMERICAN SENTINEL UNIVERSITY
385 Inverness Parkway
Englewood, CO 80112
Free: 800-729-2427
E-mail: info@AmericanSentinel.edu
Web Site: http://www.americansentinel.edu/
President/CEO: Mary Adams
Type: Comprehensive **Sex:** Coed **Costs Per Year:** Tuition: $8850 full-time, $295 per credit hour part-time.

ANTHEM COLLEGE AURORA
350 Blackhawk St.
Aurora, CO 80011
Tel: (720)859-7900
Web Site: http://www.anthem.edu/locations/anthem-college-aurora/
President/CEO: Erin Henry
Type: Two-Year College **Sex:** Coed **Application Fee:** $50.00 **Professional Accreditation:** ABHES, ACCSCT

ARAPAHOE COMMUNITY COLLEGE
5900 South Santa Fe Dr., PO Box 9002
Littleton, CO 80160-9002
Tel: (303)797-4222
Fax: (303)797-5970
E-mail: hfukaye@arapahoe.edu
Web Site: http://www.arapahoe.edu/
President/CEO: Bert Glandon
Admissions: Emily Dovi
Type: Two-Year College **Sex:** Coed **Affiliation:** Colorado Community College and Occupational Education System **% Accepted:** 100 **Admission Plans:** Open Admission; Early Admission; Deferred Admission **Application Deadline:** Rolling **Application Fee:** $0.00 **H.S. Requirements:** High school diploma or equivalent not required. For medical laboratory technology, medical assistant technology, nursing, medical records technology, police & fire science academy, mortuary science: High school diploma required; GED accepted **Scholarships:** Available **Calendar System:** Semester, Summer Session Available **Enrollment:** FT 2,312, PT 5,248 **Faculty:** FT 114, PT 300 **Student-Faculty Ratio:** 19:1 **Library Holdings:** 45,000 **Regional Accreditation:** North Central Association of Colleges and Schools **Credit Hours For Degree:** 61 credit hours, Associates **ROTC:** Army, Air Force **Professional Accreditation:** ABFSE, AHIMA, APTA, NAACLS

ARGOSY UNIVERSITY, DENVER
7600 East Eastman Ave.
Denver, CO 80231
Tel: (303)923-4110; Free: (866)431-5981
Admissions: (303)248-2700
Fax: (303)923-4111
Web Site: http://www.argosy.edu/denver/
President/CEO: Marcia Bankirer, PhD
Type: University **Sex:** Coed **Regional Accreditation:** North Central Association of Colleges and Schools

THE ART INSTITUTE OF COLORADO
1200 Lincoln St.
Denver, CO 80203
Tel: (303)837-0825; Free: 800-275-2420
Fax: (303)860-8520

Web Site: http://www.artinstitutes.edu/denver/
President/CEO: David C. Zorn
Type: Four-Year College **Sex:** Coed **Affiliation:** Education Management Corporation **Calendar System:** Quarter **Regional Accreditation:** North Central Association of Colleges and Schools **Professional Accreditation:** ACICS, ACF

ASPEN UNIVERSITY
501 South Cherry St., Ste. 350
Denver, CO 80246
Tel: (303)333-4224
Fax: (303)336-1144
E-mail: admissions@aspen.edu
Web Site: http://www.aspen.edu/
President/CEO: David Lady
Financial Aid: Jennifer Quinn
Type: Comprehensive **Sex:** Coed **Application Fee:** $50.00 **Costs Per Year:** Application fee: $50. Tuition: $750 per course part-time. **Scholarships:** Available **Calendar System:** Miscellaneous **Professional Accreditation:** DETC

BEL—REA INSTITUTE OF ANIMAL TECHNOLOGY
1681 South Dayton St.
Denver, CO 80247
Tel: (303)751-8700; Free: 800-950-8001
Fax: (303)751-9969
E-mail: admissions@bel-rea.com
Web Site: http://www.bel-rea.com/
President/CEO: Marc Schapiro
Admissions: Paulette Kaufman
Type: Two-Year College **Sex:** Coed **Application Deadline:** Rolling **H.S. Requirements:** High school diploma required; GED accepted **Scholarships:** Available **Calendar System:** Quarter, Summer Session Not available **Library Holdings:** 1,800 **Credit Hours For Degree:** 125 credits, Associates **Professional Accreditation:** ACCSCT

BOULDER COLLEGE OF MASSAGE THERAPY
6255 Longbow Dr.
Boulder, CO 80301
Tel: (303)530-2100; Free: 800-442-5131
Fax: (303)530-2204
Web Site: http://www.bcmt.org/
President/CEO: Jan Combs
Type: Two-Year College **Sex:** Coed **Application Fee:** $75.00 **Calendar System:** Quarter **Professional Accreditation:** ACCSCT

COLLEGEAMERICA—COLORADO SPRINGS
3645 Citadel Dr. South
Colorado Springs, CO 80909
Tel: (719)637-0600
Admissions: (719)622-3600
Fax: (719)637-0806
Web Site: http://www.collegeamerica.edu/
President/CEO: Rozann Kunstle
Type: Two-Year College **Sex:** Coed **Professional Accreditation:** ACCSCT

COLLEGEAMERICA—DENVER
1385 South Colorado Blvd.
Denver, CO 80222
Tel: (303)691-9756
Admissions: (303)300-8740
Fax: (303)692-9156
Web Site: http://www.collegeamerica.com/
President/CEO: Nathan Larson
Type: Two-Year College **Sex:** Coed **Scholarships:** Available **Professional Accreditation:** ACCSCT

COLLEGEAMERICA—FORT COLLINS
4601 South Mason St.
Fort Collins, CO 80525-3740
Tel: (970)223-6060
Admissions: (970)225-4860
Fax: (970)223-6060
Web Site: http://www.collegeamerica.edu/
President/CEO: Joel V. Scimeca
Admissions: Anna DiTorrice-Mull
Type: Two-Year College **Sex:** Coed **Admission Plans:** Open Admission **Application Fee:** $0.00 **H.S. Requirements:** High school diploma required; GED accepted **Calendar System:** Continuous, Summer Session Not available **Professional Accreditation:** ACCSCT

COLORADO CHRISTIAN UNIVERSITY
8787 West Alameda
Lakewood, CO 80226
Tel: (303)202-0100; Free: 800-44-FAITH
Admissions: (303)963-3200
Fax: (303)238-2191
E-mail: admission@ccu.edu
Web Site: http://www.ccu.edu/
President/CEO: Bill Armstrong
Admissions: Jeff Cazer
Financial Aid: Steve Woodburn
Type: Comprehensive **Sex:** Coed **Affiliation:** interdenominational **Scores:** 100% SAT V 400+; 92% SAT M 400+; 46% ACT 18-23; 37% ACT 24-29 **% Accepted:** 65 **Admission Plans:** Deferred Admission **Application Deadline:** August 21 **Application Fee:** $50.00 **H.S. Requirements:** High school diploma required; GED accepted **Scholarships:** Available **Calendar System:** Semester, Summer Session Available **Enrollment:** FT 1,169, PT 728 **Faculty:** FT 43, PT 3 **Student-Faculty Ratio:** 21:1 **Exams:** SAT I or ACT. **% Receiving Financial Aid:** 67 **% Residing in College-Owned, -Operated, or -Affiliated Housing:** 65 **Library Holdings:** 71,565 **Regional Accreditation:** North Central Association of Colleges and Schools **Credit Hours For Degree:** 64 semester hours, Associates; 128 semester hours, Bachelors **ROTC:** Army **Intercollegiate Athletics:** Basketball M & W; Cross-Country Running M & W; Golf M; Soccer M & W; Tennis M & W; Volleyball W

THE COLORADO COLLEGE
14 East Cache La Poudre
Colorado Springs, CO 80903-3294
Tel: (719)389-6000; Free: 800-542-7214
Admissions: (719)389-6344
Fax: (719)389-6282
E-mail: admission@coloradocollege.edu
Web Site: http://www.coloradocollege.edu/
President/CEO: Richard Celeste
Admissions: Matt Bonser
Financial Aid: James M. Swanson
Type: Comprehensive **Sex:** Coed **Scores:** 100.01% SAT V 400+; 100.01% SAT M 400+; 6.06% ACT 18-23; 45.02% ACT 24-29 **% Accepted:** 32 **Admission Plans:** Early Action; Early Decision Plan; Deferred Admission **Application Deadline:** January 15 **Application Fee:** $50.00 **H.S. Requirements:** High school diploma or equivalent not required **Costs Per Year:** Application fee: $50. One-time mandatory fee: $150. Comprehensive fee: $47,102 includes full-time tuition ($37,278), mandatory fees ($200), and college room and board ($9624). College room only: $5184. Full-time tuition and fees vary according to degree level. Room and board charges vary according to board plan and housing facility. Part-time tuition: $6213 per course. Part-time tuition varies according to course load and degree level. **Scholarships:** Available **Calendar System:** Miscellaneous, Summer Session Available **Enrollment:** FT 1,966, PT 34, Grad FT 29, Grad PT 3 **Faculty:** FT 164, PT 33 **Student-Faculty Ratio:** 10:1 **Exams:** SAT I or ACT. ACT essay not being used. SAT essay not being used. **% Receiving Financial Aid:** 37 **% Residing in College-Owned, -Operated, or -Affiliated Housing:** 76 **Final Year or Final Semester Residency Requirement:** No **Library Holdings:** 550,622 **Regional Accreditation:** North Central Association of Colleges and Schools **Credit Hours For Degree:** 128 semester hours, Bachelors **ROTC:** Army **Intercollegiate Athletics:** Baseball M; Basketball M & W; Cross-Country Running M & W; Equestrian Sports M & W; Field Hockey M & W; Ice Hockey M & W; Lacrosse M & W; Rugby M & W; Skiing (Downhill) M & W; Soccer M & W; Swimming and Diving M & W; Tennis M & W; Track and Field M & W; Ultimate Frisbee M & W; Volleyball M & W

COLORADO HEIGHTS UNIVERSITY
3001 South Federal Blvd.
Denver, CO 80236-2711
Tel: (303)937-4200

E-mail: admissions@tlhu.edu
Web Site: http://www.chu.edu/
President/CEO: Tony Sanichara
Admissions: Ashley Henderson
Type: Four-Year College **Sex:** Coed **Affiliation:** Teikyo University Group **% Accepted:** 100 **Application Fee:** $50.00 **Scholarships:** Available **Professional Accreditation:** ACICS

COLORADO MOUNTAIN COLLEGE
831 Grand Ave.
Glenwood Springs, CO 81601
Tel: (970)945-7481; Free: 800-621-8559
Admissions: (970)947-8276
E-mail: joinus@coloradomtn.edu
Web Site: http://www.coloradomtn.edu/
President/CEO: Carla Malmquist
Admissions: Vicky Butler
Type: Two-Year College **Sex:** Coed **Affiliation:** Colorado Mountain College District System **Admission Plans:** Open Admission; Early Admission; Deferred Admission **Application Deadline:** Rolling **Application Fee:** $0.00 **H.S. Requirements:** High school diploma required; GED accepted. For some adult applicants: High school diploma or equivalent not required **Costs Per Year:** Application fee: $0. Area resident tuition: $1350 full-time, $45 per credit part-time. State resident tuition: $2250 full-time, $75 per credit part-time. Nonresident tuition: $7050 full-time, $235 per credit part-time. Mandatory fees: $180 full-time. Full-time tuition and fees vary according to course load, location, and program. Part-time tuition varies according to course load, location, and program. College room and board: $7400. College room only: $3660. Room and board charges vary according to board plan and location. **Scholarships:** Available **Calendar System:** Semester, Summer Session Available **Faculty:** FT 28 **Student-Faculty Ratio:** 12:1 **Exams:** SAT I or ACT. **% Residing in College-Owned, -Operated, or -Affiliated Housing:** 44 **Library Holdings:** 36,000 **Regional Accreditation:** North Central Association of Colleges and Schools **Credit Hours For Degree:** 62 credits, Associates **Intercollegiate Athletics:** Soccer M & W

COLORADO MOUNTAIN COLLEGE, ALPINE CAMPUS
1330 Bob Adams Dr.
Steamboat Springs, CO 80487
Tel: (970)870-4444; Free: 800-621-8559
Admissions: (970)870-4417
E-mail: joinus@coloradomtn.edu
Web Site: http://www.coloradomtn.edu/
President/CEO: Dr. Kerry Hart
Admissions: Janice Bell
Type: Two-Year College **Sex:** Coed **Affiliation:** Colorado Mountain College District System **Admission Plans:** Open Admission; Early Admission; Deferred Admission **Application Deadline:** Rolling **Application Fee:** $0.00 **H.S. Requirements:** High school diploma required; GED accepted **Costs Per Year:** Application fee: $0. Area resident tuition: $1350 full-time, $45 per credit part-time. State resident tuition: $2250 full-time, $75 per credit part-time. Nonresident tuition: $7050 full-time, $235 per credit part-time. Mandatory fees: $180 full-time. Full-time tuition and fees vary according to course load. Part-time tuition varies according to course load. College room and board: $7040. College room only: $3660. Room and board charges vary according to board plan and location. **Scholarships:** Available **Calendar System:** Semester, Summer Session Available **Faculty:** FT 25 **Student-Faculty Ratio:** 12:1 **Exams:** SAT I or ACT. **% Residing in College-Owned, -Operated, or -Affiliated Housing:** 44 **Library Holdings:** 17,000 **Regional Accreditation:** North Central Association of Colleges and Schools **Credit Hours For Degree:** 62 credits, Associates **Intercollegiate Athletics:** Skiing (Downhill) M & W

COLORADO MOUNTAIN COLLEGE, TIMBERLINE CAMPUS
901 South Hwy. 24
Leadville, CO 80461
Tel: (719)486-2015; Free: 800-621-8559
Admissions: (719)486-4292
E-mail: joinus@coloradomtn.edu
Web Site: http://www.coloradomtn.edu/
President/CEO: John Marrin
Admissions: Mary Laing
Type: Two-Year College **Sex:** Coed **Affiliation:** Colorado Mountain College District System **Admission Plans:** Open Admission; Early Admission; Deferred Admission **Application Deadline:** Rolling **Application Fee:** $0.00 **H.S. Requirements:** High school diploma required; GED accepted **Costs Per Year:** Application fee: $0. Area resident tuition: $1350 full-time, $45 per credit part-time. State resident tuition: $2250 full-time, $75 per credit part-time. Nonresident tuition: $7050 full-time, $235 per credit part-time. Mandatory fees: $180 full-time. Full-time tuition and fees vary according to course load, location, and program. Part-time tuition varies according to course load, location, and program. College room and board: $7400. College room only: $3660. Room and board charges vary according to board plan and housing facility. **Scholarships:** Available **Calendar System:** Semester, Summer Session Available **Faculty:** FT 16 **Student-Faculty Ratio:** 12:1 **Exams:** SAT I or ACT. **% Residing in College-Owned, -Operated, or -Affiliated Housing:** 30 **Library Holdings:** 25,000 **Regional Accreditation:** North Central Association of Colleges and Schools **Credit Hours For Degree:** 62 credits, Associates

COLORADO NORTHWESTERN COMMUNITY COLLEGE
500 Kennedy Dr.
Rangely, CO 81648-3598
Tel: (970)675-2261; Free: 800-562-1105
Fax: (970)675-3343
E-mail: gene.bilodeau@cncc.edu
Web Site: http://www.cncc.edu/
President/CEO: John Boyd
Admissions: Gene Bilodeau
Financial Aid: Merrie Byers
Type: Two-Year College **Sex:** Coed **Affiliation:** Colorado Community College and Occupational Education System **Admission Plans:** Open Admission; Early Admission; Deferred Admission **Application Deadline:** Rolling **Application Fee:** $0.00 **H.S. Requirements:** High school diploma required; GED accepted **Costs Per Year:** Application fee: $0. State resident tuition: $2649 full-time, $88.29 per credit hour part-time. Nonresident tuition: $5450 full-time, $181.65 per credit hour part-time. Mandatory fees: $249 full-time, $7.53 per credit hour part-time, $11.48 per term part-time. Full-time tuition and fees vary according to program. Part-time tuition and fees vary according to course load, program, and reciprocity agreements. College room and board: $5868. College room only: $2306. Room and board charges vary according to board plan and housing facility. **Scholarships:** Available **Calendar System:** Semester, Summer Session Available **Library Holdings:** 20,063 **Regional Accreditation:** North Central Association of Colleges and Schools **Credit Hours For Degree:** 60 semester hours, Associates **Professional Accreditation:** ADA **Intercollegiate Athletics:** Baseball M; Basketball M & W; Cross-Country Running W; Softball W

COLORADO SCHOOL OF HEALING ARTS
7655 West Mississippi Ave.
Ste. 100
Lakewood, CO 80226
Tel: (303)986-2320; Free: 800-233-7114
Fax: (303)980-6594
Web Site: http://www.csha.net/
President/CEO: Victoria Steere
Admissions: Victoria Steere
Type: Two-Year College **Sex:** Coed **% Accepted:** 100 **Application Deadline:** October 1 **Application Fee:** $50.00 **Calendar System:** Quarter **Enrollment:** FT 149, PT 91 **Faculty:** FT 4, PT 31 **Student-Faculty Ratio:** 13:1 **Professional Accreditation:** ACCSCT

COLORADO SCHOOL OF MINES
1500 Illinois St.
Golden, CO 80401-1887
Tel: (303)273-3000; Free: 800-446-9488
Admissions: (303)273-3220
Fax: (303)273-3509
E-mail: admit@mines.edu
Web Site: http://www.mines.edu/
President/CEO: Dr. Myles W. Scoggins
Admissions: Joanne Lambert
Financial Aid: Jill Robertson
Type: University **Sex:** Coed **Scores:** 100% SAT V 400+; 101% SAT M 400+; 8% ACT 18-23; 62% ACT 24-29 **% Accepted:** 63 **Admission Plans:** Deferred Admission **Application Deadline:** May 1 **Application Fee:** $45.00 **H.S. Requirements:** High school diploma required; GED accepted **Costs Per Year:** Application fee: $45. State resident tuition: $10,590 full-time, $353

per credit hour part-time. Nonresident tuition: $24,750 full-time, $825 per credit hour part-time. Mandatory fees: $1654 full-time. Part-time tuition varies according to course load. College room and board: $8120. Room and board charges vary according to board plan and housing facility. **Scholarships:** Available **Calendar System:** Semester, Summer Session Available **Enrollment:** FT 3,488, PT 187, Grad FT 886, Grad PT 288 **Faculty:** FT 235, PT 96 **Student-Faculty Ratio:** 15:1 **Exams:** SAT I or ACT. **% Receiving Financial Aid:** 43 **% Residing in College-Owned, -Operated, or -Affiliated Housing:** 43 **Final Year or Final Semester Residency Requirement:** Yes **Library Holdings:** 412,560 **Regional Accreditation:** North Central Association of Colleges and Schools **Credit Hours For Degree:** 130.5 semester hours, Bachelors **ROTC:** Army, Air Force **Professional Accreditation:** ABET **Intercollegiate Athletics:** Baseball M; Basketball M & W; Bowling M & W; Cross-Country Running M & W; Football M; Golf M; Ice Hockey M & W; Lacrosse M; Rugby M & W; Skiing (Downhill) M & W; Soccer M & W; Softball W; Swimming and Diving M & W; Track and Field M & W; Ultimate Frisbee M & W; Volleyball M & W; Wrestling M

COLORADO SCHOOL OF TRADES
1575 Hoyt St.
Lakewood, CO 80215-2996
Tel: (303)233-4697; Free: 800-234-4594
Fax: (303)233-4723
Web Site: http://www.schooloftrades.com/
President/CEO: Robert E. Martin
Admissions: Robert Martin
Financial Aid: Robert E. Martin
Type: Two-Year College **Sex:** Coed **% Accepted:** 87 **Application Fee:** $25.00 **H.S. Requirements:** High school diploma required; GED accepted **Scholarships:** Available **Enrollment:** FT 125 **Faculty:** FT 10 **Student-Faculty Ratio:** 12:1 **Professional Accreditation:** ACCSCT

COLORADO STATE UNIVERSITY
Fort Collins, CO 80523-0015
Tel: (970)491-1101
Admissions: (970)491-6909
Fax: (970)491-7799
E-mail: admissions@colostate.edu
Web Site: http://www.colostate.edu/
President/CEO: Dr. Anthony A. Frank
Admissions: Jim Rawlins
Type: University **Sex:** Coed **Affiliation:** Colorado State University System **Scores:** 97.9% SAT V 400+; 98.6% SAT M 400+; 38.4% ACT 18-23; 51.6% ACT 24-29 **% Accepted:** 72 **Admission Plans:** Deferred Admission **Application Deadline:** February 1 **Application Fee:** $50.00 **H.S. Requirements:** High school diploma required; GED accepted **Costs Per Year:** Application fee: $50. State resident tuition: $4822 full-time, $241.10 per credit hour part-time. Nonresident tuition: $20,744 full-time, $1,037 per credit hour part-time. Mandatory fees: $1496 full-time, $24.60 per credit hour part-time, $123 per term part-time. Full-time tuition and fees vary according to course load. Part-time tuition and fees vary according to course load. College room and board: $8378. College room only: $4238. Room and board charges vary according to board plan and housing facility. **Scholarships:** Available **Calendar System:** Semester, Summer Session Available **Enrollment:** FT 19,936, PT 2,222, Grad FT 2,971, Grad PT 3,418 **Faculty:** FT 944, PT 45 **Student-Faculty Ratio:** 17:1 **Exams:** SAT I or ACT. **% Receiving Financial Aid:** 42 **% Residing in College-Owned, -Operated, or -Affiliated Housing:** 26 **Library Holdings:** 2,366,608 **Regional Accreditation:** North Central Association of Colleges and Schools **Credit Hours For Degree:** 120 credits, Bachelors **ROTC:** Army, Air Force **Professional Accreditation:** AACSB, ABET, ACEJMC, AAMFT, AAFCS, ACCE, ACA, ADtA, AOTA, APA, ASLA, AVMA, FIDER, CSWE, NASM, NCATE, NRPA, SAF, TEAC **Intercollegiate Athletics:** Baseball M; Basketball M & W; Crew M & W; Cross-Country Running M & W; Field Hockey M & W; Football M; Golf M & W; Ice Hockey M & W; Lacrosse M & W; Rugby M & W; Skiing (Downhill) M & W; Soccer M & W; Softball W; Swimming and Diving W; Tennis M & W; Track and Field M & W; Ultimate Frisbee M & W; Volleyball W; Water Polo M & W; Wrestling M & W

COLORADO STATE UNIVERSITY—PUEBLO
2200 Bonforte Blvd.
Pueblo, CO 81001-4901
Tel: (719)549-2100
Admissions: (719)549-2391
Fax: (719)549-2419
E-mail: dana.trujillo@colostate-pueblo.edu
Web Site: http://www.colostate-pueblo.edu/
President/CEO: Joseph Garcia
Admissions: Dana Trujillo
Financial Aid: Sean McGivney
Type: Comprehensive **Sex:** Coed **Affiliation:** Colorado State University System **Scores:** 78% SAT V 400+; 85% SAT M 400+; 59% ACT 18-23; 19% ACT 24-29 **% Accepted:** 95 **Admission Plans:** Deferred Admission **Application Deadline:** August 1 **Application Fee:** $25.00 **H.S. Requirements:** High school diploma required; GED accepted **Costs Per Year:** Application fee: $25. State resident tuition: $3732 full-time, $148.30 per credit hour part-time. Nonresident tuition: $14,124 full-time, $564.30 per credit hour part-time. Mandatory fees: $1478 full-time, $49.25 per credit hour part-time. Full-time tuition and fees vary according to course load. Part-time tuition and fees vary according to course load. College room and board: $6750. College room only: $3520. Room and board charges vary according to board plan. **Scholarships:** Available **Calendar System:** Semester, Summer Session Available **Enrollment:** FT 3,894, PT 1,685, Grad FT 203, Grad PT 1,428 **Faculty:** FT 192, PT 226 **Student-Faculty Ratio:** 16:1 **Exams:** SAT I or ACT. ACT essay not being used. SAT essay not being used. **% Receiving Financial Aid:** 68 **% Residing in College-Owned, -Operated, or -Affiliated Housing:** 19 **Library Holdings:** 274,890 **Regional Accreditation:** North Central Association of Colleges and Schools **Credit Hours For Degree:** 120 semester hours, Bachelors **ROTC:** Army **Professional Accreditation:** AACSB, ABET, CSWE, NASM, NLN, TEAC **Intercollegiate Athletics:** Baseball M; Basketball M & W; Bowling M & W; Cheerleading M & W; Cross-Country Running W; Football M; Golf M & W; Ice Hockey M; Soccer M & W; Softball W; Tennis M & W; Track and Field W; Volleyball W; Wrestling M

COLORADO TECHNICAL UNIVERSITY COLORADO SPRINGS
4435 North Chestnut St.
Colorado Springs, CO 80907-3896
Tel: (719)598-0200
Admissions: 888-404-7555
E-mail: bbraaten@coloradotech.edu
Web Site: http://www.coloradotech.edu/
President/CEO: Dr. Wallace K. Pond
Admissions: Beth Braaten
Financial Aid: Jacqueline Harris
Type: University **Sex:** Coed **Affiliation:** Colorado Technical University **Admission Plans:** Deferred Admission **Application Deadline:** Rolling **Application Fee:** $50.00 **H.S. Requirements:** High school diploma required; GED accepted **Costs Per Year:** Application fee: $50. **Scholarships:** Available **Calendar System:** Quarter, Summer Session Available **Enrollment:** FT 679, PT 1,217 **% Receiving Financial Aid:** 69 **Regional Accreditation:** North Central Association of Colleges and Schools **Credit Hours For Degree:** 90 quarter hours, Associates; 178 quarter hours, Bachelors **ROTC:** Army **Professional Accreditation:** ABET, ACBSP

COLORADO TECHNICAL UNIVERSITY DENVER
5775 Denver Tech Center Blvd.
Greenwood Village, CO 80111
Tel: (303)694-6600
Admissions: 888-404-7555
Fax: (303)694-6673
E-mail: rgiboney@coloradotech.edu
Web Site: http://www.coloradotech.edu/
President/CEO: Dr. Wallace Pond
Admissions: Rosaland Giboney
Financial Aid: Natalie Dietsch
Type: Comprehensive **Sex:** Coed **Affiliation:** Colorado Technical University **Admission Plans:** Deferred Admission **Application Deadline:** Rolling **Application Fee:** $50.00 **H.S. Requirements:** High school diploma required; GED accepted **Costs Per Year:** Application fee: $50. **Scholarships:** Available **Calendar System:** Quarter, Summer Session Available **Enrollment:** FT 229, PT 344 **Regional Accreditation:** North Central Association of Colleges and Schools **Credit Hours For Degree:** 90 credit hours, Associates; 178 credit hours, Bachelors

COLORADO TECHNICAL UNIVERSITY ONLINE
4435 North Chestnut St.
Ste. E

Colorado Springs, CO 80907
Tel: (303)362-2900
Admissions: 888-404-7555
Fax: (303)362-2945
Web Site: http://www.coloradotech.edu/
President/CEO: Dr. Wallace Pond
Admissions: William Beckley
Type: Comprehensive **Sex:** Coed **Affiliation:** Colorado Technical University **Admission Plans:** Deferred Admission **Application Deadline:** Rolling **Application Fee:** $50.00 **H.S. Requirements:** High school diploma required; GED accepted **Calendar System:** Quarter **Enrollment:** FT 23,094 **Regional Accreditation:** North Central Association of Colleges and Schools

COMMUNITY COLLEGE OF AURORA
16000 East Centre Tech Parkway
Aurora, CO 80011-9036
Tel: (303)360-4700
Web Site: http://www.ccaurora.edu/
President/CEO: Linda S. Bowman
Admissions: Connie Simpson
Type: Two-Year College **Sex:** Coed **% Accepted:** 100 **Admission Plans:** Open Admission; Early Admission **Application Deadline:** Rolling **Application Fee:** $0.00 **H.S. Requirements:** High school diploma or equivalent not required **Scholarships:** Available **Calendar System:** Semester, Summer Session Available **Enrollment:** FT 1,412, PT 4,065 **Faculty:** FT 27, PT 320 **Student-Faculty Ratio:** 21:1 **Library Holdings:** 7,440 **Regional Accreditation:** North Central Association of Colleges and Schools **Credit Hours For Degree:** 60 semester hours, Associates **Professional Accreditation:** CARC

COMMUNITY COLLEGE OF DENVER
PO Box 173363
Denver, CO 80217-3363
Tel: (303)556-2600
Admissions: (303)556-6325
E-mail: enrollment_services@ccd.edu
Web Site: http://www.ccd.edu/
President/CEO: Karen Clos Bleeker
Admissions: Michael Rusk
Financial Aid: Karla Nash
Type: Two-Year College **Sex:** Coed **Affiliation:** Colorado Community College System **Admission Plans:** Open Admission; Early Admission; Deferred Admission **Application Deadline:** Rolling **Application Fee:** $0.00 **H.S. Requirements:** High school diploma or equivalent not required **Costs Per Year:** Application fee: $0. State resident tuition: $2119 full-time, $88 per credit part-time. Nonresident tuition: $9453 full-time, $394 per credit part-time. Mandatory fees: $664 full-time. Full-time tuition and fees vary according to location, program, and reciprocity agreements. Part-time tuition varies according to location, program, and reciprocity agreements. **Scholarships:** Available **Calendar System:** Semester, Summer Session Available **Enrollment:** FT 2,740, PT 8,178 **Faculty:** FT 90, PT 346 **Student-Faculty Ratio:** 27:1 **Regional Accreditation:** North Central Association of Colleges and Schools **Credit Hours For Degree:** 60 credit hours, Associates **ROTC:** Army, Air Force **Professional Accreditation:** ARCEST, ADA, JRCERT

DENVER ACADEMY OF COURT REPORTING
9051 Harlan St., Unit 20
Westminster, CO 80031
Tel: (303)427-5292; Free: 800-574-2087
Fax: (303)427-5383
Web Site: http://www.denveracademy.edu/
President/CEO: Susan Kuhl
Admissions: Howard Brookner
Type: Two-Year College **Sex:** Coed **Admission Plans:** Open Admission **Application Deadline:** Rolling **Application Fee:** $150.00 **H.S. Requirements:** High school diploma required; GED accepted **Scholarships:** Available **Calendar System:** Quarter **Credit Hours For Degree:** 99 credits, Associates **Professional Accreditation:** ACICS

DEVRY UNIVERSITY (COLORADO SPRINGS)
1175 Kelly Johnson Blvd.
Colorado Springs, CO 80920
Tel: (719)632-3000; Free: (866)338-7934
Web Site: http://www.devry.edu/
Financial Aid: Carol Oppman
Type: Comprehensive **Sex:** Coed **Affiliation:** DeVry University **Admission Plans:** Deferred Admission **Application Deadline:** Rolling **Application Fee:** $50.00 **H.S. Requirements:** High school diploma required; GED accepted **Scholarships:** Available **Calendar System:** Semester, Summer Session Available **Enrollment:** FT 89, PT 127 **Faculty:** FT 1, PT 41 **Student-Faculty Ratio:** 9:1 **% Receiving Financial Aid:** 73 **Regional Accreditation:** North Central Association of Colleges and Schools **Credit Hours For Degree:** 67 credit hours, Associates; 122 credit hours, Bachelors

DEVRY UNIVERSITY (WESTMINSTER)
1870 West 122nd Ave.
Westminster, CO 80234-2010
Tel: (303)280-7400
Web Site: http://www.devry.edu/
President/CEO: James Caldwell
Type: Comprehensive **Sex:** Coed **Affiliation:** DeVry, Inc. **Admission Plans:** Deferred Admission **Application Deadline:** Rolling **Application Fee:** $50.00 **H.S. Requirements:** High school diploma required; GED accepted **Costs Per Year:** Application fee: $50. Tuition: $14,080 full-time, $550 per credit hour part-time. **Scholarships:** Available **Calendar System:** Semester, Summer Session Available **Enrollment:** FT 320, PT 539, Grad FT 8, Grad PT 74 **Faculty:** FT 13, PT 87 **Student-Faculty Ratio:** 13:1 **Exams:** ACT essay used for admission. SAT essay used for admission. ACT essay used for placement. SAT essay used for placement. **% Receiving Financial Aid:** 72 **Regional Accreditation:** North Central Association of Colleges and Schools

EVEREST COLLEGE (AURORA)
14280 East Jewell Ave.
Ste. 100
Aurora, CO 80014
Tel: (303)745-6244
Fax: (303)745-6245
Web Site: http://www.everest.edu/
President/CEO: Patricia Schlotter
Type: Two-Year College **Sex:** Coed **Calendar System:** Quarter **Professional Accreditation:** ACICS

EVEREST COLLEGE (COLORADO SPRINGS)
1815 Jet Wing Dr.
Colorado Springs, CO 80916
Tel: (719)638-6580; Free: 888-741-4271
Fax: (719)638-6818
Web Site: http://www.everest.edu/
President/CEO: James Hadley, PhD
Type: Two-Year College **Sex:** Coed **Affiliation:** Corinthian Colleges, Inc. **Application Deadline:** Rolling **H.S. Requirements:** High school diploma required; GED accepted **Scholarships:** Available **Calendar System:** Quarter, Summer Session Not available **Exams:** Other. **Credit Hours For Degree:** 96 credit hours, Associates **Professional Accreditation:** ACICS, AAMAE

EVEREST COLLEGE (DENVER)
9065 Grant St.
Denver, CO 80229-4339
Tel: (303)457-2757
Web Site: http://www.everest.edu/
President/CEO: Bruce Pileggi
Type: Two-Year College **Sex:** Coed **Application Deadline:** Rolling **H.S. Requirements:** High school diploma required; GED accepted **Scholarships:** Available **Calendar System:** Quarter, Summer Session Available **Exams:** Other. **Credit Hours For Degree:** 96 credits, Associates **Professional Accreditation:** ACICS, AAMAE

FORT LEWIS COLLEGE
1000 Rim Dr.
Durango, CO 81301-3999
Tel: (970)247-7010
Admissions: (970)247-7184
Fax: (970)247-7179
E-mail: burns_a@fortlewis.edu
Web Site: http://www.fortlewis.edu/
President/CEO: Dr. Brad Bartel
Admissions: Andrew Burns

Financial Aid: Elaine Redwine
Type: Four-Year College **Sex:** Coed **Scores:** 95% SAT V 400+; 96% SAT M 400+; 59% ACT 18-23; 32% ACT 24-29 **% Accepted:** 68 **Admission Plans:** Deferred Admission **Application Deadline:** August 1 **Application Fee:** $40.00 **H.S. Requirements:** High school diploma required; GED accepted **Costs Per Year:** Application fee: $40. One-time mandatory fee: $135. State resident tuition: $6204 full-time, $155 per credit hour part-time. Nonresident tuition: $16,072 full-time, $803 per credit hour part-time. Mandatory fees: $1428 full-time, $51.45 per credit hour part-time. Full-time tuition and fees vary according to reciprocity agreements. Part-time tuition and fees vary according to course load and reciprocity agreements. College room and board: $8304. College room only: $4800. Room and board charges vary according to board plan and housing facility. **Scholarships:** Available **Calendar System:** Miscellaneous, Summer Session Available **Enrollment:** FT 3,380, PT 305 **Faculty:** FT 171, PT 89 **Student-Faculty Ratio:** 17:1 **Exams:** SAT I or ACT. **% Receiving Financial Aid:** 51 **% Residing in College-Owned, -Operated, or -Affiliated Housing:** 37 **Library Holdings:** 213,506 **Regional Accreditation:** North Central Association of Colleges and Schools **Credit Hours For Degree:** 120 credit hours, Bachelors **Professional Accreditation:** AACSB, JRCEPAT, NASM **Intercollegiate Athletics:** Baseball M; Basketball M & W; Cheerleading M & W; Cross-Country Running M & W; Fencing M & W; Football M; Golf M; Ice Hockey M & W; Lacrosse M & W; Rock Climbing M & W; Rugby M & W; Skiing (Cross-Country) M & W; Skiing (Downhill) M & W; Soccer M & W; Softball W; Ultimate Frisbee M & W; Volleyball W; Wrestling M & W

FRONT RANGE COMMUNITY COLLEGE
3645 West 112th Ave.
Westminster, CO 80030
Tel: (303)466-8811
Admissions: (303)404-5000
E-mail: yolanda.espinoza@frontrange.edu
Web Site: http://frcc.cc.co.us/
President/CEO: Andrew R. Dorsey
Admissions: Yolanda Espinoza
Type: Two-Year College **Sex:** Coed **Affiliation:** Community Colleges of Colorado System **Admission Plans:** Open Admission; Early Admission; Deferred Admission **Application Deadline:** Rolling **Application Fee:** $0.00 **H.S. Requirements:** High school diploma or equivalent not required **Costs Per Year:** Application fee: $0. State resident tuition: $2649 full-time. Nonresident tuition: $11,817 full-time. Mandatory fees: $244 full-time. Full-time tuition and fees vary according to location. **Scholarships:** Available **Calendar System:** Semester, Summer Session Available **Enrollment:** FT 6,905, PT 11,808 **Faculty:** FT 204, PT 863 **Student-Faculty Ratio:** 22:1 **Final Year or Final Semester Residency Requirement:** No **Regional Accreditation:** North Central Association of Colleges and Schools **Credit Hours For Degree:** 60 credit hours, Associates **ROTC:** Army, Air Force **Professional Accreditation:** ADA, CARC

HERITAGE COLLEGE
12 Lakeside Ln.
Denver, CO 80212-7413
Tel: (303)477-7240
Fax: (303)477-7276
Web Site: http://www.heritage-education.com/
President/CEO: Jennifer Sprague
Type: Two-Year College **Sex:** Coed **% Accepted:** 53 **Professional Accreditation:** ACCSCT

INSTITUTE OF BUSINESS & MEDICAL CAREERS
3842 South Mason St.
Fort Collins, CO 80525
Tel: (970)223-2669
E-mail: kmcneil@ibmc.edu
Web Site: http://www.ibmc.edu/
President/CEO: Steve Steele
Admissions: Kevin McNeil
Financial Aid: Jackie Gresham
Type: Two-Year College **Sex:** Coed **Affiliation:** Institute of Business & Medical Careers- Greeley, Colorado and Cheyenne, Wyoming **% Accepted:** 100 **Admission Plans:** Open Admission **Application Deadline:** Rolling **Application Fee:** $75.00 **H.S. Requirements:** High school diploma required; GED accepted **Costs Per Year:** Application fee: $75. Tuition: $10,800 full-time, $300 per credit hour part-time. Full-time tuition varies according to course load and program. Part-time tuition varies according to course load and program. Tuition guaranteed not to increase for student's term of enrollment. **Scholarships:** Available **Calendar System:** Continuous, Summer Session Not available **Enrollment:** FT 302 **Faculty:** FT 11, PT 23 **Student-Faculty Ratio:** 14:1 **Final Year or Final Semester Residency Requirement:** No **Credit Hours For Degree:** 96 credits, Associates **Professional Accreditation:** ACICS

INTELLITEC COLLEGE (COLORADO SPRINGS)
2315 East Pikes Peak Ave.
Colorado Springs, CO 80909-6030
Tel: (719)632-7626; Free: 800-748-2282
Fax: (719)632-7451
Web Site: http://www.intelliteccollege.edu/
President/CEO: Edwin Kraus
Type: Two-Year College **Sex:** Coed **Affiliation:** Technical Trades Institute, Inc. **Admission Plans:** Open Admission **Application Deadline:** Rolling **Application Fee:** $30.00 **H.S. Requirements:** High school diploma required; GED accepted **Scholarships:** Available **Calendar System:** Miscellaneous **Library Holdings:** 274 **Credit Hours For Degree:** 90 credit hours, Associates **Professional Accreditation:** ACCSCT

INTELLITEC COLLEGE (GRAND JUNCTION)
772 Horizon Dr.
Grand Junction, CO 81506
Tel: (970)245-8101
Fax: (970)243-8074
Web Site: http://www.intelliteccollege.edu/
President/CEO: Ed Kraus
Type: Two-Year College **Sex:** Coed **% Accepted:** 100 **Application Fee:** $0.00 **Scholarships:** Available **Calendar System:** Continuous **Enrollment:** FT 486 **Faculty:** FT 26, PT 20 **Professional Accreditation:** ACCSCT

INTELLITEC MEDICAL INSTITUTE
2345 North Academy Blvd.
Colorado Springs, CO 80909
Tel: (719)596-7400
Fax: (719)596-2464
Web Site: http://www.intelliteccollege.edu/
President/CEO: Todd Matthews
Admissions: Michelle Squibb
Type: Two-Year College **Sex:** Coed **Admission Plans:** Open Admission **Application Deadline:** Rolling **Application Fee:** $0.00 **H.S. Requirements:** High school diploma required; GED accepted **Scholarships:** Available **Calendar System:** Miscellaneous, Summer Session Not available **Credit Hours For Degree:** 99 credit hours, Associates **Professional Accreditation:** ABHES

ITT TECHNICAL INSTITUTE (AURORA)
12500 East Iliff Ave.
Ste. 100
Aurora, CO 80014
Tel: (303)695-6317
Web Site: http://www.itt-tech.edu/
Type: Two-Year College **Sex:** Coed **Professional Accreditation:** ACICS

ITT TECHNICAL INSTITUTE (THORNTON)
500 East 84th Ave., Ste. B12
Thornton, CO 80229
Tel: (303)288-4488; Free: 800-395-4488
Fax: (303)288-8166
Web Site: http://www.itt-tech.edu/
President/CEO: Fred Hansen
Financial Aid: Brad J. Hettich
Type: Two-Year College **Sex:** Coed **Affiliation:** ITT Educational Services, Inc. **H.S. Requirements:** High school diploma required; GED accepted **Scholarships:** Available **Calendar System:** Quarter, Summer Session Not available **Professional Accreditation:** ACICS

JOHNSON & WALES UNIVERSITY
7150 Montview Blvd.
Denver, CO 80220
Tel: (303)256-9300; Free: 877-598-3368
Fax: (303)256-9333

E-mail: den.admissions@jwu.edu
Web Site: http://www.jwu.edu/
President/CEO: Bette Matkowski
Admissions: Kim Ostrowski
Financial Aid: Lynn Robinson
Type: Four-Year College **Sex:** Coed **Affiliation:** Johnson & Wales University (RI) **Scores:** 85.8% SAT V 400+; 92.5% SAT M 400+ **% Accepted:** 72 **Admission Plans:** Early Admission; Deferred Admission **Application Deadline:** Rolling **Application Fee:** $0.00 **H.S. Requirements:** High school diploma required; GED accepted **Costs Per Year:** Application fee: $0. One-time mandatory fee: $288. Comprehensive fee: $33,045 includes full-time tuition ($23,034), mandatory fees ($1107), and college room and board ($8904). Room and board charges vary according to board plan, housing facility, and location. **Scholarships:** Available **Calendar System:** Quarter, Summer Session Available **Enrollment:** FT 1,430, PT 31 **Faculty:** FT 46, PT 35 **Student-Faculty Ratio:** 25:1 **Exams:** SAT I or ACT. **% Receiving Financial Aid:** 74 **% Residing in College-Owned, -Operated, or -Affiliated Housing:** 41 **Regional Accreditation:** New England Association of Schools and Colleges **Credit Hours For Degree:** 90 credits, Associates; 180 credits, Bachelors **Intercollegiate Athletics:** Baseball M; Basketball M & W; Cheerleading M & W; Golf M; Soccer M; Tennis M & W

JONES INTERNATIONAL UNIVERSITY
9697 East Mineral Ave.
Centennial, CO 80112
Tel: (303)784-8904; Free: 800-811-5663
Fax: (303)784-8547
E-mail: admissions@international.edu
Web Site: http://www.jiu.edu/
President/CEO: Dr. D Terry Rawls
Financial Aid: Stacy Broadus
Type: University **Sex:** Coed **Admission Plans:** Open Admission; Deferred Admission **Application Deadline:** Rolling **Application Fee:** $60.00 **H.S. Requirements:** High school diploma required; GED accepted **Costs Per Year:** Application fee: $60. Tuition: $11,400 full-time, $475 per credit hour part-time. Full-time tuition varies according to course level, course load, degree level, and program. Part-time tuition varies according to course level, course load, degree level, and program. **Scholarships:** Available **Calendar System:** Continuous, Summer Session Available **Enrollment:** FT 147, PT 880, Grad FT 1,040, Grad PT 1,794 **Faculty:** FT 0, PT 137 **Student-Faculty Ratio:** 8:1 **% Receiving Financial Aid:** 74 **% Residing in College-Owned, -Operated, or -Affiliated Housing:** 0 **Final Year or Final Semester Residency Requirement:** No **Library Holdings:** 215,000 **Regional Accreditation:** North Central Association of Colleges and Schools **Credit Hours For Degree:** 60 semester hours, Associates; 120 semester hours, Bachelors **Professional Accreditation:** NCATE

KAPLAN COLLEGE, DENVER CAMPUS
500 East 84th Ave.
Ste. W-200
Thornton, CO 80229
Tel: (303)295-0550
Web Site: http://www.kc-denver.com/
President/CEO: Todd Smith
Type: Two-Year College **Sex:** Coed **H.S. Requirements:** High school diploma required; GED accepted **Calendar System:** Continuous **Professional Accreditation:** ACCSCT

LAMAR COMMUNITY COLLEGE
2401 South Main St.
Lamar, CO 81052-3999
Tel: (719)336-2248; Free: 800-968-6920
Fax: (719)336-2448
E-mail: admissions@lamarcc.edu
Web Site: http://www.lamarcc.edu/
President/CEO: John Marrin
Type: Two-Year College **Sex:** Coed **Affiliation:** Colorado Community College and Occupational Education System **% Accepted:** 100 **Admission Plans:** Open Admission; Preferred Admission; Early Admission **Application Deadline:** September 16 **Application Fee:** $0.00 **H.S. Requirements:** High school diploma required; GED accepted **Scholarships:** Available **Calendar System:** Semester, Summer Session Available **Faculty:** FT 24, PT 24 **Library Holdings:** 27,729 **Regional Accreditation:** North Central Association of Colleges and Schools **Credit Hours For Degree:** 64 semester hours, Associates **Intercollegiate Athletics:** Baseball M; Basketball M; Cross-Country Running W; Equestrian Sports M & W; Golf M; Softball W; Volleyball W

LINCOLN TECHNICAL INSTITUTE
460 South Lipan St.
Denver, CO 80223-2025
Tel: (303)722-5724; Free: 800-347-3232
Fax: (303)778-8264
Web Site: http://www.lincolnedu.com/campus/denver-co/
President/CEO: Robert Lantzy
Admissions: Jennifer Hash
Type: Two-Year College **Sex:** Coed **% Accepted:** 100 **Application Deadline:** Rolling **Application Fee:** $150.00 **H.S. Requirements:** High school diploma required; GED accepted **Scholarships:** Available **Calendar System:** Miscellaneous, Summer Session Available **Library Holdings:** 1,050 **Credit Hours For Degree:** 108 credit hours, Associates **Professional Accreditation:** ACCSCT

MESA STATE COLLEGE
1100 North Ave.
Grand Junction, CO 81501-3122
Tel: (970)248-1020; Free: 800-982-MESA
Admissions: (970)248-1802
Fax: (970)248-1973
E-mail: rlarsen@mesastate.edu
Web Site: http://www.mesastate.edu/
President/CEO: Timothy Foster
Admissions: Rance Larsen
Financial Aid: Curt Martin
Type: Comprehensive **Sex:** Coed **Scores:** 90.6% SAT V 400+; 87.1% SAT M 400+; 55.7% ACT 18-23; 16.5% ACT 24-29 **% Accepted:** 81 **Admission Plans:** Open Admission; Deferred Admission **Application Deadline:** Rolling **Application Fee:** $30.00 **H.S. Requirements:** High school diploma required; GED accepted **Scholarships:** Available **Calendar System:** Semester, Summer Session Available **Enrollment:** FT 4,383, PT 1,782 **Faculty:** FT 225, PT 177 **Student-Faculty Ratio:** 18:1 **Exams:** SAT I or ACT. **% Receiving Financial Aid:** 56 **% Residing in College-Owned, -Operated, or -Affiliated Housing:** 22 **Library Holdings:** 260,784 **Regional Accreditation:** North Central Association of Colleges and Schools **Credit Hours For Degree:** 60 credit hours, Associates; 123 credit hours, Bachelors **Professional Accreditation:** AACN, JRCERT, NCATE **Intercollegiate Athletics:** Baseball M; Basketball M & W; Cross-Country Running W; Football M; Golf W; Ice Hockey M; Soccer M & W; Softball W; Tennis M & W; Track and Field W; Volleyball W; Wrestling M

METROPOLITAN STATE COLLEGE OF DENVER
PO Box 173362
Denver, CO 80217-3362
Tel: (303)556-2400
Admissions: (303)556-2615
Fax: (303)556-6345
Web Site: http://www.mscd.edu/
President/CEO: Stephen Jordan
Admissions: Michelle Brown
Type: Four-Year College **Sex:** Coed **Scores:** 96% SAT V 400+; 90% SAT M 400+; 62% ACT 18-23; 21% ACT 24-29 **% Accepted:** 72 **Admission Plans:** Open Admission; Deferred Admission **Application Fee:** $25.00 **H.S. Requirements:** High school diploma required; GED accepted **Costs Per Year:** Application fee: $25. State resident tuition: $2850 full-time, $118.75 per credit hour part-time. Nonresident tuition: $12,343 full-time, $514.30 per credit hour part-time. Mandatory fees: $789 full-time, $320.10 per term part-time. Full-time tuition and fees vary according to course load and location. Part-time tuition and fees vary according to course load and location. **Scholarships:** Available **Calendar System:** Semester, Summer Session Available **Enrollment:** FT 14,321, PT 8,516 **Faculty:** FT 509, PT 808 **Student-Faculty Ratio:** 22:1 **Exams:** ACT, SAT I or ACT, SAT I. ACT essay not being used. SAT essay not being used. **% Receiving Financial Aid:** 48 **Final Year or Final Semester Residency Requirement:** No **Library Holdings:** 607,971 **Regional Accreditation:** North Central Association of Colleges and Schools **Credit Hours For Degree:** 120 semester hours, Bachelors **ROTC:** Army, Air Force **Professional Accreditation:** ABET, APA, CSWE, NASAD, NASM, NCATE, NLN, NRPA **Intercollegiate Athletics:** Baseball M; Basketball M & W; Cheerleading M & W; Golf M & W; Ice

Hockey M; Soccer M & W; Softball W; Squash M & W; Swimming and Diving M & W; Tennis M & W; Track and Field M & W; Volleyball W

MORGAN COMMUNITY COLLEGE
920 Barlow Rd.
Fort Morgan, CO 80701-4399
Tel: (970)542-3100; Free: 800-622-0216
Admissions: (970)542-3111
E-mail: kim.maxwell@morgancc.edu
Web Site: http://www.morgancc.edu/
President/CEO: Dr. Kerry Hart
Admissions: Kim Maxwell
Type: Two-Year College **Sex:** Coed **Affiliation:** Colorado Community College and Occupational Education System **% Accepted:** 100 **Admission Plans:** Open Admission; Early Admission; Deferred Admission **Application Deadline:** Rolling **H.S. Requirements:** High school diploma or equivalent not required **Scholarships:** Available **Calendar System:** Semester, Summer Session Available **Enrollment:** FT 501, PT 1,142 **Faculty:** FT 36, PT 114 **Student-Faculty Ratio:** 11:1 **Library Holdings:** 13,800 **Regional Accreditation:** North Central Association of Colleges and Schools **Credit Hours For Degree:** 60 credit hours, Associates **Professional Accreditation:** APTA

NAROPA UNIVERSITY
2130 Arapahoe Ave.
Boulder, CO 80302-6697
Tel: (303)444-0202; Free: 800-772-0410
Admissions: (303)546-5285
Fax: (303)444-0410
E-mail: admissions@naropa.edu
Web Site: http://www.naropa.edu/
President/CEO: Dr. Stuart Lord
Admissions: Amy Atkins
Financial Aid: Nancy Morrell
Type: Comprehensive **Sex:** Coed **% Accepted:** 75 **Admission Plans:** Deferred Admission **Application Deadline:** July 15 **Application Fee:** $50.00 **H.S. Requirements:** High school diploma required; GED accepted **Costs Per Year:** Application fee: $50. Comprehensive fee: $31,998 includes full-time tuition ($23,420), mandatory fees ($100), and college room and board ($8478). College room only: $6174. Full-time tuition and fees vary according to course load. Room and board charges vary according to board plan. Part-time tuition: $760 per credit hour. Part-time mandatory fees: $300 per term. Part-time tuition and fees vary according to course load. **Scholarships:** Available **Calendar System:** Semester, Summer Session Available **Enrollment:** FT 432, PT 48, Grad FT 400, Grad PT 201 **Faculty:** FT 51, PT 148 **Student-Faculty Ratio:** 9:1 **% Receiving Financial Aid:** 66 **% Residing in College-Owned, -Operated, or -Affiliated Housing:** 15 **Library Holdings:** 30,000 **Regional Accreditation:** North Central Association of Colleges and Schools **Credit Hours For Degree:** 120 semester hours, Bachelors

NATIONAL AMERICAN UNIVERSITY (COLORADO SPRINGS)
5125 North Academy Blvd.
Colorado Springs, CO 80918
Tel: (719)277-0588
Admissions: (719)590-8300
Fax: (719)277-0589
E-mail: csadmissions@national.edu
Web Site: http://www.national.edu/
President/CEO: Dr. Jerry Gallentine
Type: Four-Year College **Sex:** Coed **Admission Plans:** Open Admission; Deferred Admission **Application Deadline:** Rolling **Application Fee:** $25.00 **H.S. Requirements:** High school diploma required; GED accepted **Scholarships:** Available **Calendar System:** Quarter, Summer Session Available **Library Holdings:** 15,000 **Regional Accreditation:** North Central Association of Colleges and Schools **Credit Hours For Degree:** 96 quarter hours, Associates; 193 quarter hours, Bachelors

NATIONAL AMERICAN UNIVERSITY (DENVER)
1325 South Colorado Blvd, Ste. 100
Denver, CO 80222
Tel: (303)758-6700
Admissions: (303)876-7100
Fax: (303)758-6810
E-mail: jhaack@national.edu
Web Site: http://www.national.edu/
President/CEO: Dr. Jerry Gallentine
Admissions: Jacklyn Haack
Financial Aid: Cheryl Schunneman
Type: Comprehensive **Sex:** Coed **Admission Plans:** Open Admission; Early Admission; Deferred Admission **Application Deadline:** Rolling **Application Fee:** $25.00 **H.S. Requirements:** High school diploma required; GED accepted **Scholarships:** Available **Calendar System:** Quarter, Summer Session Available **Enrollment:** FT 54, PT 146 **Faculty:** FT 0, PT 35 **Student-Faculty Ratio:** 10:1 **Library Holdings:** 400 **Regional Accreditation:** North Central Association of Colleges and Schools **Credit Hours For Degree:** 97 quarter credits, Associates; 193 quarter credits, Bachelors

NAZARENE BIBLE COLLEGE
1111 Academy Park Loop
Colorado Springs, CO 80910-3704
Tel: (719)884-5000; Free: 800-873-3873
Fax: (719)884-5199
Web Site: http://www.nbc.edu/
President/CEO: Harold B. Graves
Admissions: Dr. Laurel Matson
Financial Aid: Malcolm Britton
Type: Four-Year College **Sex:** Coed **Affiliation:** Church of the Nazarene **% Accepted:** 20 **Admission Plans:** Open Admission; Deferred Admission **Application Deadline:** July 31 **Application Fee:** $0.00 **H.S. Requirements:** High school diploma required; GED accepted **Costs Per Year:** Application fee: $0. Tuition: $8100 full-time, $300 per credit hour part-time. Mandatory fees: $540 full-time, $20 per credit hour part-time. **Scholarships:** Available **Calendar System:** Quarter, Summer Session Available **Enrollment:** FT 212, PT 783 **Faculty:** FT 14, PT 65 **Student-Faculty Ratio:** 10:1 **% Receiving Financial Aid:** 81 **Library Holdings:** 64,651 **Regional Accreditation:** North Central Association of Colleges and Schools **Credit Hours For Degree:** 64 semester hours, Associates; 128 semester hours, Bachelors **Professional Accreditation:** ABHE

NORTHEASTERN JUNIOR COLLEGE
100 College Ave.
Sterling, CO 80751-2399
Tel: (970)521-6600
Admissions: (970)521-7000
Fax: (970)522-4945
E-mail: andy.long@njc.edu
Web Site: http://www.njc.edu/
President/CEO: Dr. Lance Bolton
Admissions: Andy Long
Type: Two-Year College **Sex:** Coed **Affiliation:** Colorado Community College and Occupational Education System **% Accepted:** 100 **Admission Plans:** Open Admission; Preferred Admission; Early Admission; Deferred Admission **Application Deadline:** August 1 **Application Fee:** $0.00 **H.S. Requirements:** High school diploma or equivalent not required **Costs Per Year:** Application fee: $0. State resident tuition: $2310 full-time, $96.25 per credit hour part-time. Nonresident tuition: $8242 full-time, $343.41 per credit hour part-time. Mandatory fees: $574 full-time, $10 per semester hour part-time, $11.45. Full-time tuition and fees vary according to course load. Part-time tuition and fees vary according to course load. College room and board: $5654. College room only: $2580. Room and board charges vary according to board plan and housing facility. **Scholarships:** Available **Calendar System:** Semester, Summer Session Available **Enrollment:** FT 910, PT 1,788 **Faculty:** FT 53, PT 62 **Student-Faculty Ratio:** 36:1 **% Residing in College-Owned, -Operated, or -Affiliated Housing:** 44 **Final Year or Final Semester Residency Requirement:** No **Library Holdings:** 29,549 **Regional Accreditation:** North Central Association of Colleges and Schools **Credit Hours For Degree:** 60 credit hours, Associates **Intercollegiate Athletics:** Baseball M; Basketball M & W; Equestrian Sports M & W; Volleyball W

OTERO JUNIOR COLLEGE
1802 Colorado Ave.
La Junta, CO 81050-3415
Tel: (719)384-6831
Admissions: (719)384-6833
Fax: (719)384-6880
E-mail: jan.schiro@ojc.edu

Web Site: http://www.ojc.edu/
President/CEO: James T. Rizzuto
Admissions: Jeff Paolucci
Type: Two-Year College **Sex:** Coed **Affiliation:** Colorado Community College and Occupational Education System **Admission Plans:** Open Admission; Early Admission **Application Deadline:** August 30 **Application Fee:** $0.00 **H.S. Requirements:** High school diploma required; GED accepted **Costs Per Year:** Application fee: $0. State resident tuition: $2310 full-time. Nonresident tuition: $4578 full-time. Mandatory fees: $206 full-time. College room and board: $5354. **Scholarships:** Available **Calendar System:** Semester, Summer Session Available **Enrollment:** FT 870, PT 790 **Faculty:** FT 33, PT 42 **% Residing in College-Owned, -Operated, or -Affiliated Housing:** 17 **Library Holdings:** 36,701 **Regional Accreditation:** North Central Association of Colleges and Schools **Credit Hours For Degree:** 60 semester hours, Associates **Professional Accreditation:** NLN **Intercollegiate Athletics:** Baseball M; Basketball M & W; Golf M & W; Soccer M; Softball W; Volleyball W

PIKES PEAK COMMUNITY COLLEGE
5675 South Academy Blvd.
Colorado Springs, CO 80906-5498
Tel: (719)576-7711; Free: (866)411-7722
Admissions: (719)502-2000
Fax: (719)540-7614
Web Site: http://www.ppcc.edu/
President/CEO: Dr. Tony Kinkel
Type: Two-Year College **Sex:** Coed **Affiliation:** Colorado Community College and Occupational Education System **Admission Plans:** Open Admission **Application Deadline:** Rolling **H.S. Requirements:** High school diploma or equivalent not required **Scholarships:** Available **Calendar System:** Semester, Summer Session Available **Library Holdings:** 34,332 **Regional Accreditation:** North Central Association of Colleges and Schools **Credit Hours For Degree:** 60 credit hours, Associates **ROTC:** Army **Professional Accreditation:** ADA

PIMA MEDICAL INSTITUTE
1701 West 72nd Ave.
Ste. 130
Denver, CO 80221
Tel: (303)426-1800; Free: 888-898-9048
Fax: (303)412-8752
Web Site: http://www.pmi.edu/
President/CEO: Susan Anderson
Type: Two-Year College **Sex:** Coed **Affiliation:** Vocational Training Institutes, Inc. **Scholarships:** Available **Calendar System:** Miscellaneous, Summer Session Not available **Exams:** Other. **Credit Hours For Degree:** 76 credits, Associates **Professional Accreditation:** ABHES, CARC, JRCERT

PLATT COLLEGE
3100 South Parker Rd., Ste. 200
Aurora, CO 80014-3141
Tel: (303)369-5151
Web Site: http://www.plattcolorado.edu/
President/CEO: Jerald B. Sirbu
Type: Two-Year College **Sex:** Coed **Application Deadline:** Rolling **Application Fee:** $75.00 **H.S. Requirements:** High school diploma required; GED accepted **Scholarships:** Available **Calendar System:** Continuous **Credit Hours For Degree:** 96 quarter hours, Associates; 200 quarter hours, Bachelors **Professional Accreditation:** ACCSCT

PUEBLO COMMUNITY COLLEGE
900 West Orman Ave.
Pueblo, CO 81004-1499
Tel: (719)549-3200
Admissions: (719)549-3039
Fax: (719)549-3012
Web Site: http://www.pueblocc.edu/
President/CEO: Dr. John Garvin
Admissions: Barbara Benedict
Type: Two-Year College **Sex:** Coed **Affiliation:** Colorado Community College System **Scores:** 100% SAT V 400+; 100% SAT M 400+; 34% ACT 18-23; 11% ACT 24-29 **% Accepted:** 100 **Admission Plans:** Open Admission; Early Admission; Deferred Admission **Application Deadline:** Rolling **Application Fee:** $0.00 **H.S. Requirements:** High school diploma required; GED accepted **Costs Per Year:** Application fee: $0. One-time mandatory fee: $10. State resident tuition: $2700 full-time, $173 per credit part-time. Nonresident tuition: $11,525 full-time, $375.15 per credit part-time. Mandatory fees: $271 full-time, $8.64 per course part-time, $62.89 per term part-time. Full-time tuition and fees vary according to location and program. Part-time tuition and fees vary according to location and program. **Scholarships:** Available **Calendar System:** Semester, Summer Session Available **Enrollment:** FT 2,772, PT 3,756 **Faculty:** FT 99, PT 340 **Student-Faculty Ratio:** 19:1 **Library Holdings:** 38,956 **Regional Accreditation:** North Central Association of Colleges and Schools **Credit Hours For Degree:** 60 credits, Associates **Professional Accreditation:** ACF, ADA, AOTA, APTA, CARC, JCAHPO, JRCEMT, NLN

RED ROCKS COMMUNITY COLLEGE
13300 West 6th Ave.
Lakewood, CO 80228-1255
Tel: (303)914-6600
Admissions: (303)914-6360
Fax: (303)914-6666
E-mail: admissions@rrcc.edu
Web Site: http://www.rrcc.edu/
President/CEO: Dr. Michele Haney
Type: Two-Year College **Sex:** Coed **Affiliation:** Colorado Community College and Occupational Education System **% Accepted:** 100 **Admission Plans:** Open Admission; Early Admission **Application Deadline:** Rolling **Application Fee:** $0.00 **H.S. Requirements:** High school diploma or equivalent not required **Costs Per Year:** Application fee: $0. State resident tuition: $2649 full-time, $88.30 per credit hour part-time. Nonresident tuition: $11,817 full-time, $393.90 per credit hour part-time. Mandatory fees: $298 full-time, $9.15 per credit hour part-time, $11.45 per term part-time. Full-time tuition and fees vary according to program and reciprocity agreements. Part-time tuition and fees vary according to program and reciprocity agreements. **Scholarships:** Available **Calendar System:** Semester, Summer Session Available **Enrollment:** FT 3,058, PT 6,047 **Faculty:** FT 79, PT 429 **Student-Faculty Ratio:** 23:1 **Library Holdings:** 40,909 **Regional Accreditation:** North Central Association of Colleges and Schools **Credit Hours For Degree:** 60 credit hours, Associates **Professional Accreditation:** AAMAE

REDSTONE COLLEGE—DENVER
10851 West 120th Ave.
Broomfield, CO 80021
Tel: (303)466-1714; Free: 877-801-1025
Admissions: 800-888-3995
Fax: (303)469-3797
Web Site: http://www.redstone.edu/
President/CEO: Mike Couling
Type: Two-Year College **Sex:** Coed **H.S. Requirements:** High school diploma required; GED accepted **Scholarships:** Available **Calendar System:** Continuous **Professional Accreditation:** ACCSCT

REGIS UNIVERSITY
3333 Regis Blvd.
Denver, CO 80221-1099
Tel: (303)458-4100; Free: 800-388-2366
Admissions: (303)458-4905
Fax: (303)964-5534
E-mail: regisadm@regis.edu
Web Site: http://www.regis.edu/
President/CEO: Rev. Michael J. Sheeran, SJ
Admissions: Vic Davolt
Financial Aid: Ellie Miller
Type: Comprehensive **Sex:** Coed **Affiliation:** Roman Catholic (Jesuit) **Scores:** 97% SAT V 400+; 95.3% SAT M 400+; 44.7% ACT 18-23; 43.7% ACT 24-29 **% Accepted:** 74 **Application Deadline:** Rolling **Application Fee:** $40.00 **H.S. Requirements:** High school diploma required; GED accepted **Scholarships:** Available **Calendar System:** Semester, Summer Session Available **Enrollment:** FT 2,288, PT 3,417 **Faculty:** FT 206, PT 761 **Student-Faculty Ratio:** 14:1 **Exams:** SAT I or ACT, SAT II. **% Receiving Financial Aid:** 60 **% Residing in College-Owned, -Operated, or -Affiliated Housing:** 45 **Library Holdings:** 350,000 **Regional Accreditation:** North Central Association of Colleges and Schools **Credit Hours For Degree:** 128 semester hours, Bachelors **ROTC:** Army, Air Force **Professional Accreditation:** AACN, ACA, AHIMA, APTA, NLN, TEAC **Intercol-**

legiate Athletics: Baseball M; Basketball M & W; Golf M & W; Lacrosse W; Soccer M & W; Softball W; Volleyball W

REMINGTON COLLEGE—COLORADO SPRINGS CAMPUS
6050 Erin Park Dr., No. 250
Colorado Springs, CO 80918
Tel: (719)532-1234
Fax: (719)264-1234
E-mail: larry.schafer@remingtoncollege.edu
Web Site: http://www.remingtoncollege.edu/
Admissions: Larry Schafer
Type: Two-Year College **Sex:** Coed **Calendar System:** Quarter **Professional Accreditation:** ACICS

ROCKY MOUNTAIN COLLEGE OF ART DESIGN
1600 Pierce St.
Lakewood, CO 80214
Tel: (303)753-6046; Free: 800-888-ARTS
Admissions: (303)225-8567
Fax: (303)759-4970
E-mail: admit@rmcad.edu
Web Site: http://www.rmcad.edu/
President/CEO: Dr. James Schoemer
Admissions: John Meurer
Financial Aid: Tammy Dybdahl
Type: Four-Year College **Sex:** Coed **Scores:** 86% SAT V 400+; 82% SAT M 400+; 61% ACT 18-23; 20% ACT 24-29 **% Accepted:** 99 **Application Deadline:** Rolling **Application Fee:** $50.00 **H.S. Requirements:** High school diploma required; GED accepted **Costs Per Year:** Application fee: $50. Tuition: $26,832 full-time, $1118 per credit hour part-time. **Scholarships:** Available **Calendar System:** Trimester, Summer Session Available **Enrollment:** FT 523, PT 63 **Faculty:** FT 28, PT 61 **Student-Faculty Ratio:** 12:1 **Exams:** SAT I or ACT. ACT essay used for admission. SAT essay used for admission. ACT essay used for advising. SAT essay used for advising. ACT essay used for placement. SAT essay used for placement. **% Receiving Financial Aid:** 66 **Library Holdings:** 12,800 **Regional Accreditation:** North Central Association of Colleges and Schools **Credit Hours For Degree:** 120 credits, Bachelors **Professional Accreditation:** FIDER, NASAD

TRINIDAD STATE JUNIOR COLLEGE
600 Prospect
Trinidad, CO 81082-2396
Tel: (719)846-5011; Free: 800-621-8752
Admissions: (719)846-5559
Fax: (719)846-5667
E-mail: sandy.veltri@trinidadstate.edu
Web Site: http://www.trinidadstate.edu/
President/CEO: Ruth Ann Woods
Admissions: Dr. Sandra Veltri
Type: Two-Year College **Sex:** Coed **Affiliation:** Colorado Community College and Occupational Education System **Admission Plans:** Open Admission; Deferred Admission **Application Deadline:** Rolling **Application Fee:** $0.00 **H.S. Requirements:** High school diploma required; GED accepted **Costs Per Year:** Application fee: $0. State resident tuition: $2119 full-time, $88.30 per credit hour part-time. Nonresident tuition: $4359 full-time, $181.65 per credit hour part-time. Mandatory fees: $491 full-time, $8.90 per credit hour part-time, $11.05 per term part-time. Part-time tuition and fees vary according to course load. College room and board: $4874. College room only: $1344. Room and board charges vary according to board plan. **Scholarships:** Available **Calendar System:** Semester, Summer Session Available **Enrollment:** FT 794, PT 966 **Faculty:** FT 37, PT 85 **Student-Faculty Ratio:** 17:1 **Library Holdings:** 54,255 **Regional Accreditation:** North Central Association of Colleges and Schools **Credit Hours For Degree:** 60 semester hours, Associates **Professional Accreditation:** ABET **Intercollegiate Athletics:** Baseball M; Basketball M; Golf M & W; Softball W; Volleyball W

UNITED STATES AIR FORCE ACADEMY
HQ USAFA/XPA
2304 Cadet Dr., Ste. 3800
USAF Academy, CO 80840-5025
Tel: (719)333-1818; Free: 800-443-9266
Fax: (719)333-3012
Web Site: http://www.usafa.edu/
President/CEO: Lt. Gen. Michael C. Gould
Type: Four-Year College **Sex:** Coed **Scores:** 100% SAT V 400+; 100% SAT M 400+ **% Accepted:** 14 **Application Deadline:** January 31 **Application Fee:** $0.00 **H.S. Requirements:** High school diploma required; GED accepted **Costs Per Year:** Application fee: $0. Comprehensive fee: $0. Tuition, room and board, and medical and dental care are provided by the U.S. government. Each cadet receives a salary from which to pay for uniforms, supplies, and personal expenses.. **Calendar System:** Semester, Summer Session Available **Enrollment:** FT 4,620 **Faculty:** FT 506, PT 21 **Student-Faculty Ratio:** 9:1 **Exams:** SAT I or ACT. **% Residing in College-Owned, -Operated, or -Affiliated Housing:** 100 **Final Year or Final Semester Residency Requirement:** Yes **Library Holdings:** 575,741 **Regional Accreditation:** North Central Association of Colleges and Schools **Credit Hours For Degree:** 132 semester hours, Bachelors **Professional Accreditation:** AACSB, ABET **Intercollegiate Athletics:** Archery M & W; Baseball M; Basketball M & W; Cheerleading M & W; Cross-Country Running M & W; Equestrian Sports M & W; Fencing M & W; Football M; Golf M; Gymnastics M & W; Ice Hockey M; Lacrosse M & W; Racquetball M & W; Riflery M & W; Rock Climbing M & W; Rugby M & W; Skiing (Cross-Country) M & W; Skiing (Downhill) M & W; Soccer M & W; Softball W; Squash M & W; Swimming and Diving M & W; Track and Field M & W; Ultimate Frisbee M & W; Volleyball M & W; Water Polo M & W; Weight Lifting M & W; Wrestling M

UNIVERSITY OF COLORADO AT BOULDER
Boulder, CO 80309
Tel: (303)492-1411
Admissions: (303)492-6301
Fax: (303)492-7115
E-mail: apply@colorado.edu
Web Site: http://www.colorado.edu/
President/CEO: Philip P. DiStefano
Financial Aid: Gwen E. Pomper
Type: University **Sex:** Coed **Affiliation:** University of Colorado System **Scores:** 98% SAT V 400+; 100% SAT M 400+; 21% ACT 18-23; 60% ACT 24-29 **% Accepted:** 84 **Admission Plans:** Early Action; Deferred Admission **Application Deadline:** January 15 **Application Fee:** $50.00 **H.S. Requirements:** High school diploma required; GED accepted **Costs Per Year:** Application fee: $50. One-time mandatory fee: $182. State resident tuition: $6446 full-time. Nonresident tuition: $26,700 full-time. Mandatory fees: $1486 full-time. Full-time tuition and fees vary according to program. College room and board: $10,378. Room and board charges vary according to board plan, housing facility, and location. **Scholarships:** Available **Calendar System:** Semester, Summer Session Available **Enrollment:** FT 24,847, PT 2,222, Grad FT 2,478, Grad PT 3,204 **Faculty:** FT 1,392, PT 699 **Student-Faculty Ratio:** 18:1 **Exams:** SAT I or ACT. ACT essay not being used. SAT essay not being used. **% Receiving Financial Aid:** 34 **% Residing in College-Owned, -Operated, or -Affiliated Housing:** 24 **Final Year or Final Semester Residency Requirement:** Yes **Library Holdings:** 4,348,639 **Regional Accreditation:** North Central Association of Colleges and Schools **Credit Hours For Degree:** 120 semester hours, Bachelors **ROTC:** Army, Navy, Air Force **Professional Accreditation:** AACSB, ABET, ACEJMC, ABA, APA, ASLHA, AALS, NASM, NCATE **Intercollegiate Athletics:** Baseball M; Basketball M & W; Crew M & W; Cross-Country Running M & W; Equestrian Sports M & W; Fencing M & W; Field Hockey M & W; Football M; Golf M & W; Ice Hockey M & W; Lacrosse M & W; Racquetball M & W; Rugby M & W; Skiing (Cross-Country) M & W; Skiing (Downhill) M & W; Soccer M & W; Softball W; Swimming and Diving M & W; Tennis M & W; Track and Field M & W; Ultimate Frisbee M & W; Volleyball M & W; Water Polo M & W; Wrestling M

UNIVERSITY OF COLORADO AT COLORADO SPRINGS
1420 Austin Bluffs Parkway
PO Box 7150
Colorado Springs, CO 80933-7150
Tel: (719)255-3000; Free: 800-990-8227
Admissions: (719)255-3795
E-mail: john.salnaitis@uccs.edu
Web Site: http://www.uccs.edu/
President/CEO: Dr. Pamela Shockley-Zalabak
Admissions: John Salnaitis
Financial Aid: Robert Bode
Type: University **Sex:** Coed **Affiliation:** University of Colorado System **Scores:** 98% SAT V 400+; 98% SAT M 400+; 49% ACT 18-23; 43% ACT

24-29 **% Accepted:** 62 **Admission Plans:** Deferred Admission **Application Deadline:** July 1 **Application Fee:** $50.00 **H.S. Requirements:** High school diploma required; GED accepted **Costs Per Year:** Application fee: $50. State resident tuition: $4680 full-time. Nonresident tuition: $15,600 full-time. Mandatory fees: $1013 full-time. Full-time tuition and fees vary according to course load, degree level, program, reciprocity agreements, and student level. College room and board: $7490. Room and board charges vary according to board plan and housing facility. **Scholarships:** Available **Calendar System:** Semester, Summer Session Available **Enrollment:** FT 5,459, PT 1,461, Grad FT 1,107, Grad PT 2,061 **Faculty:** FT 367, PT 54 **Student-Faculty Ratio:** 16:1 **Exams:** SAT I or ACT. **% Receiving Financial Aid:** 55 **% Residing in College-Owned, -Operated, or -Affiliated Housing:** 13 **Library Holdings:** 391,638 **Regional Accreditation:** North Central Association of Colleges and Schools **Credit Hours For Degree:** 120 credit hours, Bachelors **ROTC:** Army **Professional Accreditation:** AACSB, ABET, AACN, ACA, NASPAA, NCATE, NLN **Intercollegiate Athletics:** Baseball M; Basketball M & W; Cross-Country Running M & W; Golf M; Soccer M & W; Softball W; Track and Field M & W; Volleyball M & W

UNIVERSITY OF COLORADO DENVER
PO Box 173364
Denver, CO 80217-3364
Tel: (303)556-2400
Admissions: (303)556-3287
Fax: (303)556-2398
E-mail: admissions@castle.cudenver.edu
Web Site: http://www.ucdenver.edu/
Admissions: Barbara Edwards
Financial Aid: Patrick McTee
Type: University **Sex:** Coed **Affiliation:** University of Colorado System **Scores:** 97.58% SAT V 400+; 95.16% SAT M 400+; 51.72% ACT 18-23; 38.55% ACT 24-29 **% Accepted:** 61 **Admission Plans:** Deferred Admission **Application Deadline:** July 22 **Application Fee:** $50.00 **H.S. Requirements:** High school diploma required; GED accepted **Costs Per Year:** Application fee: $50. State resident tuition: $5712 full-time, $238 per credit hour part-time. Nonresident tuition: $18,744 full-time, $781 per credit hour part-time. Mandatory fees: $945 full-time. Full-time tuition and fees vary according to program and student level. Part-time tuition varies according to program and student level. College room and board: $11,374. College room only: $6739. **Scholarships:** Available **Calendar System:** Semester, Summer Session Available **Enrollment:** FT 7,247, PT 5,999, Grad FT 3,620, Grad PT 7,253 **Faculty:** FT 2,420, PT 516 **Student-Faculty Ratio:** 15:1 **Exams:** SAT I or ACT. ACT essay not being used. SAT essay not being used. **% Receiving Financial Aid:** 79 **Regional Accreditation:** North Central Association of Colleges and Schools **Credit Hours For Degree:** 120 semester hours, Bachelors **ROTC:** Army, Air Force **Professional Accreditation:** AACSB, ABET, ACPhE, AACN, ACNM, ACA, ADA, ACSP, APTA, ASLA, ACEHSA, LCMEAMA, NAAB, NASM, NASPAA, NCATE, NLN

UNIVERSITY OF DENVER
2199 South University Blvd.
Denver, CO 80208
Tel: (303)871-2000; Free: 800-525-9495
Admissions: (303)871-3125
Fax: (303)871-3301
E-mail: admission@du.edu
Web Site: http://www.du.edu/
President/CEO: Dr. Robert D. Coombe
Admissions: Todd R. Rinehart
Financial Aid: Julia Benz
Type: University **Sex:** Coed **Scores:** 99.14% SAT V 400+; 99.43% SAT M 400+; 19.55% ACT 18-23; 58.33% ACT 24-29 **% Accepted:** 70 **Admission Plans:** Early Admission; Early Action; Deferred Admission **Application Deadline:** January 15 **Application Fee:** $50.00 **H.S. Requirements:** High school diploma required; GED accepted **Costs Per Year:** Application fee: $50. Comprehensive fee: $46,725 includes full-time tuition ($35,604), mandatory fees ($897), and college room and board ($10,224). College room only: $6240. Part-time tuition: $989 per quarter hour. **Scholarships:** Available **Calendar System:** Quarter, Summer Session Available **Enrollment:** FT 4,825, PT 518, Grad FT 3,394, Grad PT 2,907 **Faculty:** FT 615, PT 644 **Student-Faculty Ratio:** 9:1 **Exams:** SAT I or ACT. ACT essay not being used. SAT essay not being used. **% Receiving Financial Aid:** 43 **% Residing in College-Owned, -Operated, or -Affiliated Housing:** 43 **Library Holdings:** 1,499,212 **Regional Accreditation:** North Central Association of Colleges and Schools **Credit Hours For Degree:** 183 quarter hours, Bachelors **ROTC:** Army, Air Force **Professional Accreditation:** AACSB, ABET, ABA, ALA, APA, AALS, CSWE, NASAD, NASM **Intercollegiate Athletics:** Baseball M; Basketball M & W; Cross-Country Running M & W; Equestrian Sports M & W; Golf M & W; Gymnastics W; Ice Hockey M & W; Lacrosse M & W; Racquetball M & W; Skiing (Cross-Country) M & W; Skiing (Downhill) M & W; Soccer M & W; Softball W; Swimming and Diving M & W; Tennis M & W; Volleyball W; Water Polo M & W

UNIVERSITY OF NORTHERN COLORADO
Greeley, CO 80639
Tel: (970)351-1890
Admissions: (970)351-2881
E-mail: admissions.help@unco.edu
Web Site: http://www.unco.edu/
President/CEO: Kay Norton
Admissions: Randall Langston
Financial Aid: Marty Somero
Type: University **Sex:** Coed **Scores:** 96% SAT V 400+; 96% SAT M 400+; 57% ACT 18-23; 33% ACT 24-29 **% Accepted:** 92 **Admission Plans:** Deferred Admission **Application Deadline:** August 1 **Application Fee:** $45.00 **H.S. Requirements:** High school diploma required; GED accepted **Costs Per Year:** Application fee: $45. State resident tuition: $4296 full-time, $179 per credit hour part-time. Nonresident tuition: $14,544 full-time, $606 per credit hour part-time. Mandatory fees: $820 full-time, $41 per credit hour part-time. Full-time tuition and fees vary according to program. Part-time tuition and fees vary according to program. College room and board: $8370. College room only: $3950. Room and board charges vary according to board plan, housing facility, and student level. **Scholarships:** Available **Calendar System:** Semester, Summer Session Available **Enrollment:** FT 8,996, PT 977, Grad FT 976, Grad PT 1,199 **Faculty:** FT 491, PT 214 **Student-Faculty Ratio:** 19:1 **Exams:** SAT I or ACT. **% Receiving Financial Aid:** 44 **% Residing in College-Owned, -Operated, or -Affiliated Housing:** 32 **Library Holdings:** 1,046,197 **Regional Accreditation:** North Central Association of Colleges and Schools **Credit Hours For Degree:** 120 semester hours, Bachelors **ROTC:** Army, Air Force **Professional Accreditation:** AACSB, AACN, ACA, ADtA, APA, ASLHA, CEPH, CORE, JRCEPAT, NASM, NCATE, NLN **Intercollegiate Athletics:** Baseball M; Basketball M & W; Cross-Country Running W; Football M; Golf M & W; Ice Hockey M; Lacrosse M; Rugby M & W; Soccer M & W; Softball W; Swimming and Diving W; Tennis M & W; Track and Field M & W; Volleyball W; Wrestling M

UNIVERSITY OF PHOENIX—DENVER CAMPUS
10004 Park Meadows Dr.
Lone Tree, CO 80124-5453
Tel: (303)694-9093; Free: 800-228-7240
Admissions: (480)557-6151
E-mail: audra.mcquarie@phoenix.edu
Web Site: http://www.phoenix.edu/
President/CEO: William Pepicello
Admissions: Audra McQuarie
Type: Comprehensive **Sex:** Coed **Admission Plans:** Open Admission; Deferred Admission **Application Deadline:** Rolling **Application Fee:** $0.00 **H.S. Requirements:** High school diploma required; GED accepted **Costs Per Year:** Application fee: $0. Tuition: $11,000 full-time. Full-time tuition varies according to course level and course load. **Scholarships:** Available **Calendar System:** Continuous, Summer Session Not available **Enrollment:** FT 1,289 **Faculty:** FT 27, PT 275 **Regional Accreditation:** North Central Association of Colleges and Schools **Credit Hours For Degree:** 60 credits, Associates; 120 credits, Bachelors **Professional Accreditation:** NLN

UNIVERSITY OF PHOENIX—SOUTHERN COLORADO CAMPUS
5725 Mark Dabling Blvd.
Ste. 150
Colorado Springs, CO 80919-2335
Tel: (719)599-5282; Free: 800-228-7240
Admissions: (480)557-6151
E-mail: audra.mcquarie@phoenix.edu
Web Site: http://www.phoenix.edu/
President/CEO: William Pepicello
Admissions: Audra McQuarie
Type: Comprehensive **Sex:** Coed **Admission Plans:** Open Admission; Deferred Admission **Application Deadline:** Rolling **Application Fee:** $0.00 **H.S. Requirements:** High school diploma required; GED accepted **Costs**

Per Year: Application fee: $0. Tuition: $11,000 full-time. Full-time tuition varies according to course level and course load. **Scholarships:** Available **Calendar System:** Continuous, Summer Session Not available **Faculty:** FT 9, PT 117 **Regional Accreditation:** North Central Association of Colleges and Schools **Credit Hours For Degree:** 60 credits, Associates; 120 credits, Bachelors **Professional Accreditation:** NLN

WESTERN STATE COLLEGE OF COLORADO
600 North Adams St.
Gunnison, CO 81231
Tel: (970)943-0120; Free: 800-876-5309
Admissions: (970)943-2119
Fax: (970)943-7069
E-mail: admissions@western.edu
Web Site: http://www.western.edu/
President/CEO: Dr. Jay W. Helman
Admissions: Timothy Albers
Financial Aid: Eric Cronkright
Type: Comprehensive **Sex:** Coed **Scores:** 93% SAT V 400+; 95% SAT M 400+; 58% ACT 18-23; 18% ACT 24-29 **% Accepted:** 72 **Admission Plans:** Deferred Admission **Application Deadline:** July 1 **Application Fee:** $40.00 **H.S. Requirements:** High school diploma required; GED accepted **Costs Per Year:** Application fee: $40. State resident tuition: $3140 full-time, $130.84 per credit hour part-time. Nonresident tuition: $12,336 full-time, $514 per credit hour part-time. Mandatory fees: $924 full-time, $289 per term part-time. Full-time tuition and fees vary according to course load. Part-time tuition and fees vary according to course load. College room and board: $8324. College room only: $4292. Room and board charges vary according to board plan and housing facility. **Scholarships:** Available **Calendar System:** Semester, Summer Session Available **Enrollment:** FT 1,873, PT 320 **Faculty:** FT 107, PT 43 **Student-Faculty Ratio:** 17:1 **Exams:** SAT I or ACT. ACT essay not being used. SAT essay not being used. **% Receiving Financial Aid:** 38 **Library Holdings:** 162,127 **Regional Accreditation:** North Central Association of Colleges and Schools **Credit Hours For Degree:** 120 credits, Bachelors **Professional Accreditation:** NASM **Intercollegiate Athletics:** Baseball M; Basketball M & W; Cheerleading M & W; Cross-Country Running M & W; Football M; Ice Hockey M; Lacrosse M & W; Rock Climbing M & W; Rugby M & W; Skiing (Cross-Country) M & W; Skiing (Downhill) M & W; Soccer M & W; Track and Field M & W; Volleyball M & W; Wrestling M & W

WESTWOOD COLLEGE—DENVER NORTH
7350 North Broadway
Denver, CO 80221-3653
Tel: (303)650-5050; Free: 800-992-5050
Admissions: (303)426-7000
Fax: (303)426-0702
Web Site: http://www.westwood.edu/
President/CEO: Natalie Williams
Type: Four-Year College **Sex:** Coed **H.S. Requirements:** High school diploma required; GED accepted **Scholarships:** Available **Calendar System:** Miscellaneous **Professional Accreditation:** ACCSCT, AAMAE

WESTWOOD COLLEGE—DENVER SOUTH
3150 South Sheridan Blvd.
Denver, CO 80227
Tel: (303)934-2790; Free: 800-281-2978
Admissions: (303)934-1122
Fax: (303)934-2583
Web Site: http://www.westwood.edu/
President/CEO: Daniel Snyder
Type: Four-Year College **Sex:** Coed **Scholarships:** Available **Calendar System:** Continuous **Professional Accreditation:** ACCSCT

WESTWOOD COLLEGE—ONLINE CAMPUS
10249 Church Ranch Way
Broomfield, CO 80021
Tel: (303)650-5050; Free: 800-875-6050
Admissions: (720)887-8888
Fax: (303)426-0702
Web Site: http://www.westwood.edu/
Type: Comprehensive **Sex:** Coed **Professional Accreditation:** ACCSCT

YESHIVA TORAS CHAIM TALMUDICAL SEMINARY
1555 Stuart St.
Denver, CO 80204-1415
Tel: (303)629-8200
Fax: (303)623-5949
President/CEO: Rabbi Isaac Wasserman
Admissions: Rabbi Israel Kagan
Type: Comprehensive **Sex:** Men **Affiliation:** Jewish **% Accepted:** 100 **Admission Plans:** Early Admission **H.S. Requirements:** High school diploma required; GED accepted **Calendar System:** Trimester **Credit Hours For Degree:** 168 credits, Bachelors **Professional Accreditation:** AARTS

YORKTOWN UNIVERSITY
4340 East Kentucky Ave.
Ste. 457
Denver, CO 80246
Tel: 877-757-0059
Fax: (720)528-7761
Web Site: http://yorktownuniversity.edu/
Type: Comprehensive **Sex:** Coed

ALBERTUS MAGNUS COLLEGE
700 Prospect St.
New Haven, CT 06511-1189
Tel: (203)773-8550; Free: 800-578-9160
Admissions: (203)773-8501
Fax: (203)785-8652
E-mail: admissions@albertus.edu
Web Site: http://www.albertus.edu/
President/CEO: Dr. Julia M. McNamara
Admissions: Jessica Van Deren
Financial Aid: Andrew Foster
Type: Comprehensive **Sex:** Coed **Affiliation:** Roman Catholic **Scores:** 85% SAT V 400+; 80% SAT M 400+ **% Accepted:** 83 **Admission Plans:** Deferred Admission **Application Deadline:** August 20 **Application Fee:** $35.00 **H.S. Requirements:** High school diploma required; GED accepted **Costs Per Year:** Application fee: $35. Comprehensive fee: $33,040 includes full-time tuition ($22,656), mandatory fees ($470), and college room and board ($9914). Full-time tuition and fees vary according to program. Part-time tuition: $944 per credit. Part-time mandatory fees: $75 per term. Part-time tuition and fees vary according to program. **Scholarships:** Available **Calendar System:** Semester, Summer Session Available **Enrollment:** FT 1,505, PT 108, Grad FT 273, Grad PT 137 **Faculty:** FT 43, PT 26 **Student-Faculty Ratio:** 15:1 **Exams:** SAT I or ACT, SAT II. **% Receiving Financial Aid:** 76 **% Residing in College-Owned, -Operated, or -Affiliated Housing:** 55 **Library Holdings:** 10,600 **Regional Accreditation:** New England Association of Schools and Colleges **Intercollegiate Athletics:** Baseball M; Basketball M & W; Cross-Country Running M & W; Soccer M & W; Softball W; Tennis M & W; Volleyball M & W

ASNUNTUCK COMMUNITY COLLEGE
170 Elm St.
Enfield, CT 06082-3800
Tel: (860)253-3000; Free: 800-501-3967
Fax: (860)253-9310
E-mail: dshaw@acc.commnet.edu
Web Site: http://www.acc.commnet.edu/
President/CEO: Martha McLeod
Admissions: Donna Shaw
Financial Aid: Donna Jones-Searle
Type: Two-Year College **Sex:** Coed **Affiliation:** Connecticut Community–Technical College System **% Accepted:** 100 **Admission Plans:** Open Admission; Deferred Admission **Application Deadline:** Rolling **Application Fee:** $20.00 **H.S. Requirements:** High school diploma required; GED accepted **Costs Per Year:** Application fee: $20. State resident tuition: $2832 full-time, $118 per credit hour part-time. Nonresident tuition: $8496 full-time, $354 per credit hour part-time. Mandatory fees: $368 full-time, $64 per credit hour part-time. Full-time tuition and fees vary according to course load. Part-time tuition and fees vary according to course load. **Scholarships:** Available **Calendar System:** Semester, Summer Session Available **Enrollment:** FT 568, PT 1,070 **Faculty:** FT 26, PT 94 **Student-Faculty Ratio:** 15:1 **Library Holdings:** 31,700 **Regional Accreditation:** New England Association of Schools and Colleges **Credit Hours For Degree:** 60 credits, Associates

BAIS BINYOMIN ACADEMY
132 Prospect St.
Stamford, CT 06901-1202
Tel: (203)325-4351
President/CEO: Michoel Bender
Type: Four-Year College **Sex:** Men **Affiliation:** Jewish **% Accepted:** 100 **H.S. Requirements:** High school diploma required; GED accepted **Calendar System:** Trimester **Student-Faculty Ratio:** 9:1 **Professional Accreditation:** AARTS

CAPITAL COMMUNITY COLLEGE
950 Main St.
Hartford, CT 06103
Tel: (860)906-5000
E-mail: mballj-davis@ccc.commnet.edu
Web Site: http://www.ccc.commnet.edu/
President/CEO: Calvin E. Woodland
Admissions: Jackie Phillips
Type: Two-Year College **Sex:** Coed **Affiliation:** Connecticut Community–Technical College System **Admission Plans:** Open Admission **Application Deadline:** Rolling **Application Fee:** $20.00 **H.S. Requirements:** High school diploma required; GED accepted. For students with baccalaureate degrees: High school diploma or equivalent not required **Costs Per Year:** Application fee: $20. State resident tuition: $2832 full-time, $118 per credit hour part-time. Nonresident tuition: $8496 full-time, $354 per credit hour part-time. Mandatory fees: $368 full-time, $64 per term part-time. Full-time tuition and fees vary according to program. Part-time tuition and fees vary according to program. **Scholarships:** Available **Calendar System:** Semester, Summer Session Available **Enrollment:** FT 896, PT 2,654 **Library Holdings:** 46,760 **Regional Accreditation:** New England Association of Schools and Colleges **Credit Hours For Degree:** 60 credit hours, Associates **Professional Accreditation:** AAMAE, APTA, JRCERT, JRCEMT, NLN

CENTRAL CONNECTICUT STATE UNIVERSITY
1615 Stanley St.
New Britain, CT 06050-4010
Tel: (860)832-2278
Admissions: (860)832-2285
Fax: (860)832-2522
E-mail: admissions@ccsu.edu
Web Site: http://www.ccsu.edu/
President/CEO: John W. Miller
Financial Aid: Dennis Williams
Type: Comprehensive **Sex:** Coed **Affiliation:** Connecticut State University System **Scores:** 96% SAT V 400+; 96% SAT M 400+ **% Accepted:** 54 **Application Deadline:** June 1 **Application Fee:** $50.00 **H.S. Requirements:** High school diploma required; GED accepted **Costs Per Year:** Application fee: $50. State resident tuition: $3742 full-time, $350 per credit part-time. Nonresident tuition: $12,112 full-time, $350 per credit part-time. Mandatory fees: $3672 full-time, $55 per term part-time. Full-time tuition and fees vary according to course level, course load, program, and reciprocity agreements. Part-time tuition and fees vary according to course level, course load, and program. College room and board: $9122. College room only: $5308. Room and board charges vary according to board plan. **Scholarships:** Available **Calendar System:** Semester, Summer Session Available **Enrollment:** FT 7,859, PT 2,130, Grad FT 564, Grad PT 1,908 **Faculty:** FT 433, PT 491 **Student-Faculty Ratio:** 16:1 **Exams:** SAT I. %

Receiving Financial Aid: 57 **% Residing in College-Owned, -Operated, or -Affiliated Housing:** 22 **Library Holdings:** 725,978 **Regional Accreditation:** New England Association of Schools and Colleges **Credit Hours For Degree:** 122 credit hours, Bachelors **ROTC:** Army, Air Force **Professional Accreditation:** ABET, AAMFT, AACN, AANA, ACCE, CSWE, JRCEPAT, NASM, NCATE, NAIT **Intercollegiate Athletics:** Baseball M; Basketball M & W; Cross-Country Running M & W; Fencing M & W; Football M; Golf M & W; Lacrosse M & W; Soccer M & W; Softball W; Swimming and Diving W; Track and Field M & W; Volleyball W

CHARTER OAK STATE COLLEGE
55 Paul Manafort Dr.
New Britain, CT 06053-2142
Tel: (860)832-3800
Admissions: (860)832-3858
Fax: (860)832-3999
E-mail: info@charteroak.edu
Web Site: http://www.charteroak.edu/
President/CEO: Ed Klonoski
Admissions: Lori Pendleton
Financial Aid: Velma Walters
Type: Four-Year College **Sex:** Coed **Admission Plans:** Open Admission; Deferred Admission **Application Fee:** $75.00 **H.S. Requirements:** High school diploma or equivalent not required **Costs Per Year:** Application fee: $75. State resident tuition: $195 per credit hour part-time. Nonresident tuition: $265 per credit hour part-time. Mandatory fees: $45 per term part-time. **Scholarships:** Available **Calendar System:** Continuous, Summer Session Available **Enrollment:** FT 168, PT 1,911 **Faculty:** FT 0, PT 107 **Student-Faculty Ratio:** 11:1 **% Receiving Financial Aid:** 14 **Regional Accreditation:** New England Association of Schools and Colleges **Credit Hours For Degree:** 60 credits, Associates; 120 credits, Bachelors

CONNECTICUT COLLEGE
270 Mohegan Ave.
New London, CT 06320-4196
Tel: (860)447-1911
Admissions: (860)439-2200
Fax: (860)439-4301
E-mail: admission@conncoll.edu
Web Site: http://www.conncoll.edu/
President/CEO: Leo I. Higdon, Jr.
Admissions: Martha C. Merrill
Financial Aid: Elaine Solinga
Type: Comprehensive **Sex:** Coed **Scores:** 100% SAT V 400+; 100% SAT M 400+; 15% ACT 18-23; 58% ACT 24-29 **% Accepted:** 37 **Admission Plans:** Early Decision Plan; Deferred Admission **Application Deadline:** January 1 **Application Fee:** $60.00 **H.S. Requirements:** High school diploma required; GED accepted **Costs Per Year:** Application fee: $60. Comprehensive fee: $51,115. Part-time tuition: $1186 per credit hour. Tuition: $1186 per credit hour part-time. **Scholarships:** Available **Calendar System:** Semester, Summer Session Available **Enrollment:** FT 1,839, PT 67, Grad FT 4, Grad PT 1 **Faculty:** FT 177, PT 65 **Student-Faculty Ratio:** 9:1 **% Receiving Financial Aid:** 45 **% Residing in College-Owned, -Operated, or -Affiliated Housing:** 99 **Library Holdings:** 496,817 **Regional Accreditation:** New England Association of Schools and Colleges **Credit Hours For Degree:** 128 semester hours, Bachelors **Intercollegiate Athletics:** Baseball M; Basketball M & W; Crew M & W; Cross-Country Running M & W; Equestrian Sports M & W; Field Hockey W; Ice Hockey M & W; Lacrosse M & W; Rugby W; Sailing M & W; Skiing (Cross-Country) M & W; Skiing (Downhill) M & W; Soccer M & W; Squash M & W; Swimming and Diving M & W; Tennis M & W; Track and Field M & W; Ultimate Frisbee M & W; Volleyball M & W; Water Polo M & W

EASTERN CONNECTICUT STATE UNIVERSITY
83 Windham St.
Willimantic, CT 06226-2295
Tel: (860)465-5000; Free: 877-353-3278
Admissions: (860)465-5286
E-mail: admissions@easternct.edu
Web Site: http://www.easternct.edu/
President/CEO: Dr. Elsa M. Nunez
Admissions: Kimberly M. Crone
Type: Comprehensive **Sex:** Coed **Affiliation:** Connecticut State University System **Scores:** 94% SAT V 400+; 93% SAT M 400+ **% Accepted:** 62 **Admission Plans:** Early Admission; Deferred Admission **Application Deadline:** Rolling **Application Fee:** $50.00 **H.S. Requirements:** High school diploma required; GED accepted **Costs Per Year:** Application fee: $50. State resident tuition: $3742 full-time, $400 per credit hour part-time. Nonresident tuition: $12,112 full-time, $400 per credit hour part-time. Mandatory fees: $3901 full-time. Full-time tuition and fees vary according to reciprocity agreements. College room and board: $10,048. College room only: $5674. Room and board charges vary according to board plan. **Scholarships:** Available **Calendar System:** Semester, Summer Session Available **Enrollment:** FT 4,326, PT 916, Grad FT 100, Grad PT 232 **Faculty:** FT 202, PT 244 **Student-Faculty Ratio:** 16:1 **Exams:** SAT I or ACT. **% Receiving Financial Aid:** 48 **% Residing in College-Owned, -Operated, or -Affiliated Housing:** 53 **Final Year or Final Semester Residency Requirement:** No **Library Holdings:** 239,218 **Regional Accreditation:** New England Association of Schools and Colleges **Credit Hours For Degree:** 60 credit hours, Associates; 120 credit hours, Bachelors **ROTC:** Army, Air Force **Professional Accreditation:** CSWE, NCATE **Intercollegiate Athletics:** Baseball M; Basketball M & W; Cheerleading W; Cross-Country Running M & W; Field Hockey W; Lacrosse M & W; Soccer M & W; Softball W; Swimming and Diving W; Track and Field M & W; Volleyball W

FAIRFIELD UNIVERSITY
1073 North Benson Rd.
Fairfield, CT 06824-5195
Tel: (203)254-4000
Admissions: (203)254-4100
Fax: (203)254-4199
E-mail: admis@fairfield.edu
Web Site: http://www.fairfield.edu/
President/CEO: Rev. Jeffrey P. von Arx, SJ
Admissions: Karen Pellegrino
Financial Aid: Erin Chiaro
Type: Comprehensive **Sex:** Coed **Affiliation:** Roman Catholic (Jesuit) **Scores:** 94% SAT V 400+; 93% SAT M 400+ **% Accepted:** 65 **Admission Plans:** Early Admission; Early Action; Deferred Admission **Application Deadline:** January 15 **Application Fee:** $60.00 **H.S. Requirements:** High school diploma required; GED not accepted **Costs Per Year:** Application fee: $60. One-time mandatory fee: $60. Comprehensive fee: $48,760 includes full-time tuition ($36,900), mandatory fees ($590), and college room and board ($11,270). College room only: $6730. Room and board charges vary according to board plan and housing facility. Part-time tuition: $495 per credit hour. Part-time mandatory fees: $25 per term. Part-time tuition and fees vary according to course load. **Scholarships:** Available **Calendar System:** Semester, Summer Session Available **Enrollment:** FT 3,320, PT 566, Grad FT 351, Grad PT 837 **Faculty:** FT 253, PT 221 **Student-Faculty Ratio:** 13:1 **Exams:** ACT essay used for admission. SAT essay used for admission. **% Receiving Financial Aid:** 55 **% Residing in College-Owned, -Operated, or -Affiliated Housing:** 80 **Final Year or Final Semester Residency Requirement:** Yes **Library Holdings:** 394,600 **Regional Accreditation:** New England Association of Schools and Colleges **Credit Hours For Degree:** 120 credits, Bachelors **ROTC:** Army, Air Force **Professional Accreditation:** AACSB, ABET, AAMFT, AACN, AANA, ACA, NCATE, NLN **Intercollegiate Athletics:** Baseball M; Basketball M & W; Cheerleading M & W; Crew M & W; Cross-Country Running M & W; Equestrian Sports M & W; Field Hockey W; Golf M & W; Ice Hockey M & W; Lacrosse M & W; Rugby M & W; Sailing M & W; Skiing (Downhill) M & W; Soccer M & W; Softball W; Swimming and Diving M & W; Tennis M & W; Track and Field M & W; Volleyball M & W

GATEWAY COMMUNITY COLLEGE
60 Sargent Dr.
New Haven, CT 06511
Tel: (203)285-2000; Free: 800-390-7723
Admissions: (203)789-7043
Fax: (203)285-2018
E-mail: gateway_ctc@commnet.edu
Web Site: http://www.gwcc.commnet.edu/
President/CEO: Dr. Dorsey L. Kendrick
Admissions: Kim Shea
Financial Aid: Raymond R. Zeek
Type: Two-Year College **Sex:** Coed **Affiliation:** Connecticut Community–Technical College System **% Accepted:** 100 **Admission Plans:** Open Admission; Early Admission; Deferred Admission **Application**

Deadline: September 1 **Application Fee:** $20.00 **H.S. Requirements:** High school diploma required; GED accepted **Costs Per Year:** Application fee: $20. State resident tuition: $3024 full-time, $126 per credit part-time. Nonresident tuition: $9072 full-time, $378 per credit part-time. Mandatory fees: $382 full-time. **Scholarships:** Available **Calendar System:** Semester, Summer Session Available **Enrollment:** FT 2,474, PT 4,373 **Faculty:** FT 86, PT 321 **Student-Faculty Ratio:** 9:1 **Library Holdings:** 45,409 **Regional Accreditation:** New England Association of Schools and Colleges **Credit Hours For Degree:** 60 credit hours, Associates **Professional Accreditation:** ABET, JRCERT, JRCNMT **Intercollegiate Athletics:** Baseball M; Basketball M & W; Soccer M; Softball W

GOODWIN COLLEGE
One Riverside Dr.
East Hartford, CT 06118
Tel: (860)528-4111
Fax: (860)291-9550
E-mail: nlantino@goodwin.edu
Web Site: http://www.goodwin.edu/
President/CEO: Mark Scheinberg
Admissions: Nicholas Lantino
Financial Aid: Pat Hickey
Type: Two-Year College **Sex:** Coed **% Accepted:** 100 **Admission Plans:** Open Admission; Early Action; Early Decision Plan; Deferred Admission **Application Deadline:** Rolling **Application Fee:** $50.00 **H.S. Requirements:** High school diploma required; GED accepted **Costs Per Year:** Application fee: $50. Tuition: $15,920 full-time, $530 per credit hour part-time. Mandatory fees: $500 full-time. Full-time tuition and fees vary according to course load and program. Part-time tuition varies according to course load and program. **Scholarships:** Available **Calendar System:** Semester, Summer Session Available **Enrollment:** FT 523, PT 1,560 **Faculty:** FT 44, PT 135 **Student-Faculty Ratio:** 12:1 **Exams:** ACT essay not being used. SAT essay not being used. **Regional Accreditation:** New England Association of Schools and Colleges **Credit Hours For Degree:** 62 semester hours, Associates **Professional Accreditation:** ACICS, AAMAE

HOLY APOSTLES COLLEGE AND SEMINARY
33 Prospect Hill Rd.
Cromwell, CT 06416-2005
Tel: (860)632-3010; Free: 800-330-7272
Fax: (860)632-3030
E-mail: admissions@holyapostles.edu
Web Site: http://www.holyapostles.edu/
President/CEO: Very Rev. Douglas L. Mosey, CSB
Admissions: Very Rev. Douglas Mosey, CSB
Type: Comprehensive **Sex:** Coed **Affiliation:** Roman Catholic **% Accepted:** 100 **Admission Plans:** Open Admission; Deferred Admission **Application Deadline:** Rolling **Application Fee:** $50.00 **H.S. Requirements:** High school diploma required; GED accepted **Costs Per Year:** Application fee: $50. Tuition: $9360 full-time, $390 per credit part-time. Part-time tuition varies according to course load. **Calendar System:** Semester, Summer Session Available **Enrollment:** FT 32, PT 24, Grad FT 82, Grad PT 179 **Faculty:** FT 17, PT 12 **Student-Faculty Ratio:** 2:1 **Exams:** SAT I. **Library Holdings:** 85,000 **Regional Accreditation:** New England Association of Schools and Colleges **Credit Hours For Degree:** 60 credit hours, Associates; 120 credit hours, Bachelors

HOUSATONIC COMMUNITY COLLEGE
900 Lafayette Blvd.
Bridgeport, CT 06604-4704
Tel: (203)332-5000
Admissions: (203)332-5102
Web Site: http://www.hctc.commnet.edu/
President/CEO: Anita T. Gliniecki
Admissions: Delores Y. Curtis
Type: Two-Year College **Sex:** Coed **Affiliation:** Connecticut Community–Technical College System **Admission Plans:** Open Admission; Deferred Admission **Application Deadline:** Rolling **Application Fee:** $20.00 **H.S. Requirements:** High school diploma required; GED accepted **Scholarships:** Available **Calendar System:** Semester, Summer Session Available **Faculty:** FT 71, PT 320 **Student-Faculty Ratio:** 14:1 **Library Holdings:** 30,000 **Regional Accreditation:** New England Association of Schools and Colleges **Credit Hours For Degree:** 60 credits, Associates **ROTC:** Army **Professional Accreditation:** AOTA, APTA, NAACLS

LINCOLN COLLEGE OF NEW ENGLAND (SOUTHINGTON)
2279 Mount Vernon Rd.
Southington, CT 06489-1057
Tel: (860)628-4751
Fax: (860)628-6444
E-mail: areich@lincolncollegene.edu
Web Site: http://www.lincolncollegene.edu/
President/CEO: Lynn Alan Brooks
Admissions: Anthony Reich
Type: Four-Year College **Sex:** Coed **Scores:** 58% SAT V 400+; 32% SAT M 400+ **% Accepted:** 73 **Application Deadline:** Rolling **Application Fee:** $30.00 **H.S. Requirements:** High school diploma required; GED accepted **Costs Per Year:** Application fee: $30. Tuition: $18,400 full-time, $615 per credit hour part-time. Mandatory fees: $600 full-time, $150 per term part-time. Part-time tuition and fees vary according to course load. College room only: $4400. **Scholarships:** Available **Calendar System:** Semester, Summer Session Available **Enrollment:** FT 378, PT 394 **Faculty:** FT 29, PT 66 **Student-Faculty Ratio:** 8:1 **% Residing in College-Owned, -Operated, or -Affiliated Housing:** 21 **Library Holdings:** 11,500 **Regional Accreditation:** New England Association of Schools and Colleges **Credit Hours For Degree:** 60 credit hours, Associates; 120 credit hours, Bachelors **Professional Accreditation:** AAMAE, ABFSE, ADA, AHIMA, AOTA

LINCOLN COLLEGE OF NEW ENGLAND (SUFFIELD)
1760 Mapleton Ave.
Suffield, CT 06078
Tel: (860)668-3515; Free: 800-955-0809
Fax: (860)668-7369
E-mail: admissions@ichm.edu
Web Site: http://www.clemenscollege.edu/
President/CEO: Tad Graham Handley
Admissions: Jolie Swanson
Type: Two-Year College **Sex:** Coed **% Accepted:** 77 **Admission Plans:** Deferred Admission **Application Deadline:** Rolling **Application Fee:** $100.00 **H.S. Requirements:** High school diploma required; GED accepted **Scholarships:** Available **Calendar System:** Continuous, Summer Session Not available **Enrollment:** FT 116 **Faculty:** FT 7, PT 6 **Exams:** SAT I. **% Residing in College-Owned, -Operated, or -Affiliated Housing:** 90 **Library Holdings:** 10,000 **Regional Accreditation:** New England Association of Schools and Colleges **Credit Hours For Degree:** 66 credits, Associates

LYME ACADEMY COLLEGE OF FINE ARTS
84 Lyme St.
Old Lyme, CT 06371
Tel: (860)434-5232
Admissions: (860)434-3571
Fax: (860)434-8725
E-mail: kshaffer@lymeacademy.edu
Web Site: http://www.lymeacademy.edu/
President/CEO: Debra Petke
Admissions: Krissy Shaffer
Financial Aid: James Falconer
Type: Four-Year College **Sex:** Coed **Scores:** 100% SAT V 400+; 81% SAT M 400+ **% Accepted:** 93 **Admission Plans:** Deferred Admission **Application Deadline:** Rolling **Application Fee:** $55.00 **H.S. Requirements:** High school diploma required; GED accepted **Costs Per Year:** Application fee: $55. Tuition: $23,384 full-time, $974.33 per credit part-time. Mandatory fees: $1476 full-time, $50 per term part-time. Full-time tuition and fees vary according to course load. Part-time tuition and fees vary according to course load. **Scholarships:** Available **Calendar System:** Semester, Summer Session Not available **Enrollment:** FT 68, PT 28, Grad FT 1 **Faculty:** FT 8, PT 16 **Student-Faculty Ratio:** 3:1 **Exams:** SAT I or ACT. **% Receiving Financial Aid:** 59 **Final Year or Final Semester Residency Requirement:** Yes **Regional Accreditation:** New England Association of Schools and Colleges **Credit Hours For Degree:** 120 credits, Bachelors **Professional Accreditation:** NASAD

MANCHESTER COMMUNITY COLLEGE
PO Box 1046
Manchester, CT 06045-1046
Tel: (860)512-3000
Fax: (860)647-6238
Web Site: http://www.mcc.commnet.edu/

President/CEO: Gena Glickman
Admissions: Peter Harris
Type: Two-Year College **Sex:** Coed **Affiliation:** Connecticut Community–Technical College System **% Accepted:** 99 **Admission Plans:** Open Admission **Application Deadline:** Rolling **Application Fee:** $20.00 **H.S. Requirements:** High school diploma required; GED accepted **Costs Per Year:** Application fee: $20. State resident tuition: $3200 full-time, $118 per credit hour part-time. Nonresident tuition: $9560 full-time, $354 per credit hour part-time. **Scholarships:** Available **Calendar System:** Semester, Summer Session Available **Enrollment:** FT 3,430, PT 3,936 **Regional Accreditation:** New England Association of Schools and Colleges **Credit Hours For Degree:** 60 credit hours, Associates **Professional Accreditation:** ARCEST, ACF, AOTA, APTA, CARC, NAACLS **Intercollegiate Athletics:** Baseball M; Basketball M & W; Soccer M & W; Softball W

MIDDLESEX COMMUNITY COLLEGE
100 Training Hill Rd.
Middletown, CT 06457-4889
Tel: (860)343-5800
Admissions: (860)343-5742
Fax: (860)344-7488
E-mail: mshabazz@mxcc.commnet.edu
Web Site: http://www.mxcc.commnet.edu/
President/CEO: Dr. Wilfredo Nieves
Admissions: Mensimah Shabazz
Type: Two-Year College **Sex:** Coed **Affiliation:** Connecticut Community–Technical College System **% Accepted:** 97 **Admission Plans:** Open Admission; Early Admission; Deferred Admission **Application Deadline:** Rolling **Application Fee:** $20.00 **H.S. Requirements:** High school diploma required; GED accepted **Costs Per Year:** Application fee: $20. State resident tuition: $3024 full-time, $126 per credit hour part-time. Nonresident tuition: $9796 full-time, $378 per credit hour part-time. Mandatory fees: $382 full-time. Full-time tuition and fees vary according to course load, degree level, program, and reciprocity agreements. Part-time tuition varies according to course load, degree level, program, and reciprocity agreements. **Scholarships:** Available **Calendar System:** Semester, Summer Session Available **Enrollment:** FT 1,222, PT 1,692 **Faculty:** FT 41, PT 138 **Student-Faculty Ratio:** 20:1 **Exams:** Other. **Final Year or Final Semester Residency Requirement:** No **Library Holdings:** 70,265 **Regional Accreditation:** New England Association of Schools and Colleges **Credit Hours For Degree:** 60 credits, Associates **Professional Accreditation:** COptA, JRCERT

MITCHELL COLLEGE
437 Pequot Ave.
New London, CT 06320-4498
Tel: (860)701-5000; Free: 800-443-2811
Admissions: (860)701-5038
Fax: (860)444-1209
E-mail: admissions@mitchell.edu
Web Site: http://www.mitchell.edu/
President/CEO: Dr. Mary Ellen Jukoski
Admissions: Kimberly Hodges
Financial Aid: Jacklyn Stoltz
Type: Four-Year College **Sex:** Coed **% Accepted:** 83 **Admission Plans:** Early Admission; Early Decision Plan; Deferred Admission **Application Deadline:** Rolling **Application Fee:** $35.00 **H.S. Requirements:** High school diploma required; GED accepted **Costs Per Year:** Application fee: $35. Comprehensive fee: $37,175 includes full-time tuition ($24,035), mandatory fees ($1592), and college room and board ($11,548). College room only: $6005. Full-time tuition and fees vary according to course load. Room and board charges vary according to housing facility. Part-time tuition: $275 per credit hour. Part-time mandatory fees: $35 per term. **Scholarships:** Available **Calendar System:** Semester, Summer Session Available **Enrollment:** FT 818, PT 143 **Faculty:** FT 35, PT 72 **Student-Faculty Ratio:** 15:1 **% Residing in College-Owned, -Operated, or -Affiliated Housing:** 59 **Final Year or Final Semester Residency Requirement:** No **Library Holdings:** 89,363 **Regional Accreditation:** New England Association of Schools and Colleges **Credit Hours For Degree:** 60 credit hours, Associates; 120 credit hours, Bachelors **Intercollegiate Athletics:** Baseball M; Basketball M & W; Cross-Country Running M & W; Golf M & W; Lacrosse M; Sailing M & W; Soccer M & W; Softball W; Volleyball W

NAUGATUCK VALLEY COMMUNITY COLLEGE
750 Chase Parkway
Waterbury, CT 06708-3000
Tel: (203)575-8040
Fax: (203)596-8766
E-mail: lsveda@nvcc.commnet.edu
Web Site: http://www.nvcc.commnet.edu/
President/CEO: Daisy Cocco de Filippis
Admissions: Lucretia Sveda
Type: Two-Year College **Sex:** Coed **Affiliation:** Connecticut Community–Technical College System **% Accepted:** 39 **Admission Plans:** Open Admission; Deferred Admission **Application Deadline:** Rolling **Application Fee:** $20.00 **H.S. Requirements:** High school diploma required; GED accepted **Costs Per Year:** Application fee: $20. One-time mandatory fee: $20. State resident tuition: $3200 full-time, $118 per semester hour part-time. Nonresident tuition: $9560 full-time, $354 per semester hour part-time. Mandatory fees: $368 full-time. Full-time tuition and fees vary according to course load and reciprocity agreements. Part-time tuition varies according to course load and reciprocity agreements. **Scholarships:** Available **Calendar System:** Semester, Summer Session Available **Enrollment:** FT 2,266, PT 3,393 **Student-Faculty Ratio:** 5:1 **Exams:** Other. **Library Holdings:** 35,000 **Regional Accreditation:** New England Association of Schools and Colleges **Credit Hours For Degree:** 60 credits, Associates **Professional Accreditation:** ABET, APTA, CARC, JRCERT, NLN

NORTHWESTERN CONNECTICUT COMMUNITY COLLEGE
Park Place East
Winsted, CT 06098-1798
Tel: (860)738-6300
Admissions: (860)738-6330
Fax: (860)379-4465
E-mail: admissions@nwcc.commnet.edu
Web Site: http://www.nwcc.commnet.edu/
President/CEO: Dr. Barbara Douglass
Type: Two-Year College **Sex:** Coed **Affiliation:** Connecticut Community–Technical College System **Admission Plans:** Open Admission; Deferred Admission **Application Deadline:** Rolling **Application Fee:** $20.00 **H.S. Requirements:** High school diploma required; GED accepted **Costs Per Year:** Application fee: $20. State resident tuition: $2832 full-time, $118 per credit hour part-time. Nonresident tuition: $8496 full-time, $354 per credit hour part-time. Mandatory fees: $368 full-time, $64 per credit hour part-time. Full-time tuition and fees vary according to reciprocity agreements. Part-time tuition and fees vary according to course load and reciprocity agreements. **Scholarships:** Available **Calendar System:** Semester, Summer Session Available **Enrollment:** FT 591, PT 1,120 **Library Holdings:** 37,666 **Regional Accreditation:** New England Association of Schools and Colleges **Credit Hours For Degree:** 62 credits, Associates **Professional Accreditation:** AAMAE, APTA

NORWALK COMMUNITY COLLEGE
188 Richards Ave.
Norwalk, CT 06854-1655
Tel: (203)857-7000
Admissions: (203)857-7060
Fax: (203)857-3335
E-mail: admissions@commnet.edu
Web Site: http://www.ncc.commnet.edu/
President/CEO: David Levinson
Admissions: Curtis Antrum
Type: Two-Year College **Sex:** Coed **Affiliation:** Connecticut Community–Technical College System **Admission Plans:** Open Admission; Deferred Admission **Application Deadline:** Rolling **Application Fee:** $20.00 **H.S. Requirements:** High school diploma required; GED accepted **Scholarships:** Available **Calendar System:** Semester, Summer Session Available **Enrollment:** FT 2,197, PT 4,034 **Faculty:** FT 100, PT 312 **Student-Faculty Ratio:** 17:1 **Library Holdings:** 66,080 **Regional Accreditation:** New England Association of Schools and Colleges **Credit Hours For Degree:** 60 credits, Associates **Professional Accreditation:** CARC, NLN

PAIER COLLEGE OF ART, INC.
20 Gorham Ave.
Hamden, CT 06514-3902
Tel: (203)287-3030
Admissions: (203)287-3031
E-mail: paier.admission@snet.net
Web Site: http://www.paiercollegeofart.edu/
President/CEO: Jonathan E. Paier

Admissions: Lynn Pascale
Financial Aid: John DeRose
Type: Four-Year College **Sex:** Coed **Scores:** 64% SAT V 400+; 57% SAT M 400+ **% Accepted:** 78 **Admission Plans:** Deferred Admission **Application Deadline:** Rolling **Application Fee:** $25.00 **H.S. Requirements:** High school diploma required; GED accepted **Scholarships:** Available **Calendar System:** Semester, Summer Session Available **Enrollment:** FT 168, PT 81 **Faculty:** FT 9, PT 37 **Student-Faculty Ratio:** 7:1 **Exams:** SAT I or ACT. **% Receiving Financial Aid:** 88 **Library Holdings:** 12,000 **Credit Hours For Degree:** 64 semester hours, Associates; 130 semester hours, Bachelors **Professional Accreditation:** ACCSCT

POST UNIVERSITY
800 Country Club Rd.
Waterbury, CT 06723-2540
Tel: (203)596-4500; Free: 800-345-2562
Fax: (203)756-5810
E-mail: admiss@post.edu
Web Site: http://www.post.edu/
President/CEO: Kenneth Zirkle
Admissions: Jay Murray
Financial Aid: Regina Faulds
Type: Comprehensive **Sex:** Coed **Scores:** 76% SAT V 400+; 74% SAT M 400+; 33% ACT 18-23; 17% ACT 24-29 **% Accepted:** 59 **Admission Plans:** Deferred Admission **Application Deadline:** Rolling **Application Fee:** $40.00 **H.S. Requirements:** High school diploma required; GED accepted **Costs Per Year:** Application fee: $40. Comprehensive fee: $34,750 includes full-time tuition ($24,000), mandatory fees ($1050), and college room and board ($9700). College room only: $5335. Full-time tuition and fees vary according to degree level and program. Room and board charges vary according to housing facility. Part-time tuition: $800 per credit hour. Part-time tuition varies according to class time, course load, degree level, and program. **Scholarships:** Available **Calendar System:** Semester, Summer Session Available **Enrollment:** FT 1,228, PT 969, Grad FT 120, Grad PT 273 **Faculty:** FT 30, PT 188 **Student-Faculty Ratio:** 19:1 **Exams:** SAT I or ACT. **% Receiving Financial Aid:** 99 **% Residing in College-Owned, -Operated, or -Affiliated Housing:** 54 **Library Holdings:** 64,889 **Regional Accreditation:** New England Association of Schools and Colleges **Credit Hours For Degree:** 60 credits, Associates; 120 credits, Bachelors **Intercollegiate Athletics:** Baseball M; Basketball M & W; Cross-Country Running M & W; Equestrian Sports M & W; Golf M; Soccer M & W; Softball W; Volleyball W

QUINEBAUG VALLEY COMMUNITY COLLEGE
742 Upper Maple St.
Danielson, CT 06239-1440
Tel: (860)774-1130
Fax: (860)774-7768
E-mail: qu_isd@commnet.edu
Web Site: http://www.qvcc.commnet.edu/
President/CEO: Dianne Williams
Admissions: Dr. Toni Moumouris
Type: Two-Year College **Sex:** Coed **Affiliation:** Connecticut Community–Technical College System **% Accepted:** 98 **Admission Plans:** Open Admission; Early Admission; Deferred Admission **Application Deadline:** September 1 **Application Fee:** $20.00 **H.S. Requirements:** High school diploma required; GED accepted **Scholarships:** Available **Calendar System:** Semester, Summer Session Available **Enrollment:** FT 669, PT 1,110 **Faculty:** FT 29, PT 97 **Student-Faculty Ratio:** 18:1 **Library Holdings:** 31,000 **Regional Accreditation:** New England Association of Schools and Colleges **Credit Hours For Degree:** 60 credit hours, Associates **Professional Accreditation:** AAMAE

QUINNIPIAC UNIVERSITY
275 Mount Carmel Ave.
Hamden, CT 06518-1940
Tel: (203)582-8200; Free: 800-462-1944
Admissions: (203)582-8600
Fax: (203)582-6347
E-mail: admissions@quinnipiac.edu
Web Site: http://www.quinnipiac.edu/
President/CEO: Dr. John L. Lahey
Admissions: Joan Isaac Mohr
Financial Aid: Dominic Yoia
Type: Comprehensive **Sex:** Coed **Scores:** 100% SAT V 400+; 100% SAT M 400+; 20% ACT 18-23; 61% ACT 24-29 **% Accepted:** 69 **Admission Plans:** Early Action; Deferred Admission **Application Deadline:** February 1 **Application Fee:** $45.00 **H.S. Requirements:** High school diploma required; GED accepted **Costs Per Year:** Application fee: $45. Comprehensive fee: $46,980 includes full-time tuition ($32,850), mandatory fees ($1400), and college room and board ($12,730). Room and board charges vary according to housing facility. Part-time tuition: $790 per credit hour. Part-time mandatory fees: $35 per credit hour. Part-time tuition and fees vary according to class time and course load. **Scholarships:** Available **Calendar System:** Semester, Summer Session Available **Enrollment:** FT 5,686, PT 285, Grad FT 1,101, Grad PT 686 **Faculty:** FT 304, PT 541 **Student-Faculty Ratio:** 12:1 **Exams:** SAT I or ACT. **% Receiving Financial Aid:** 59 **% Residing in College-Owned, -Operated, or -Affiliated Housing:** 78 **Final Year or Final Semester Residency Requirement:** Yes **Library Holdings:** 285,000 **Regional Accreditation:** New England Association of Schools and Colleges **Credit Hours For Degree:** 120 semester hours, Bachelors **ROTC:** Army, Air Force **Professional Accreditation:** AACSB, ABA, AOTA, APTA, AALS, CARC, JRCERT, NAACLS, NCATE, NLN **Intercollegiate Athletics:** Baseball M; Basketball M & W; Cross-Country Running M & W; Field Hockey W; Golf M; Ice Hockey M & W; Lacrosse M & W; Soccer M & W; Softball W; Tennis M & W; Track and Field W; Volleyball W

SACRED HEART UNIVERSITY
5151 Park Ave.
Fairfield, CT 06825-1000
Tel: (203)371-7999
Admissions: (203)371-7880
Fax: (203)371-7889
E-mail: enroll@sacredheart.edu
Web Site: http://www.sacredheart.edu/
President/CEO: Dr. Anthony Cernera, PhD
Admissions: Karen N. Guastelle
Financial Aid: Julie B. Savino
Type: Comprehensive **Sex:** Coed **Affiliation:** Roman Catholic **Scores:** 99% SAT V 400+; 99% SAT M 400+ **% Accepted:** 66 **Admission Plans:** Early Admission; Early Decision Plan; Deferred Admission **Application Fee:** $50.00 **H.S. Requirements:** High school diploma required; GED accepted **Costs Per Year:** Application fee: $50. Comprehensive fee: $41,982 includes full-time tuition ($30,090), mandatory fees ($208), and college room and board ($11,684). College room only: $8840. Full-time tuition and fees vary according to program and student level. Room and board charges vary according to board plan and housing facility. Part-time tuition: $460 per credit hour. Part-time mandatory fees: $80 per term. Part-time tuition and fees vary according to program. **Scholarships:** Available **Calendar System:** Semester, Summer Session Available **Enrollment:** FT 3,534, PT 658, Grad FT 680, Grad PT 1,151 **Faculty:** FT 204, PT 363 **Student-Faculty Ratio:** 13:1 **Exams:** ACT essay used for advising. SAT essay used for advising. ACT essay used for placement. SAT essay used for placement. **% Receiving Financial Aid:** 69 **% Residing in College-Owned, -Operated, or -Affiliated Housing:** 60 **Library Holdings:** 148,803 **Regional Accreditation:** New England Association of Schools and Colleges **Credit Hours For Degree:** 60 credits, Associates; 120 credits, Bachelors **ROTC:** Army **Professional Accreditation:** AACSB, AACN, AOTA, APTA, CSWE, JRCEPAT, NCATE, NLN **Intercollegiate Athletics:** Baseball M; Basketball M & W; Bowling W; Cheerleading W; Crew W; Cross-Country Running M & W; Equestrian Sports W; Fencing M & W; Field Hockey W; Football M; Golf M & W; Ice Hockey M & W; Lacrosse M & W; Soccer M & W; Softball W; Swimming and Diving W; Tennis M & W; Track and Field M & W; Volleyball M & W; Wrestling M

SAINT JOSEPH COLLEGE
1678 Asylum Ave.
West Hartford, CT 06117-2700
Tel: (860)232-4571; Free: (866)442-8752
Fax: (860)233-5695
E-mail: admissions@sjc.edu
Web Site: http://www.sjc.edu/
President/CEO: Dr. Pamela Trotman Reid
Financial Aid: Beth Baker
Type: Comprehensive **Affiliation:** Roman Catholic **Scores:** 95% SAT V 400+; 91% SAT M 400+ **% Accepted:** 84 **Admission Plans:** Deferred Admission **Application Deadline:** Rolling **Application Fee:** $50.00 **H.S. Requirements:** High school diploma required; GED accepted **Costs Per Year:** Application fee: $50. Comprehensive fee: $39,639 includes full-time

tuition ($26,502), mandatory fees ($700), and college room and board ($12,437). College room only: $5671. Full-time tuition and fees vary according to course load, degree level, program, and student level. Room and board charges vary according to board plan and housing facility. Part-time tuition: $595 per credit. Part-time mandatory fees: $30 per credit. Part-time tuition and fees vary according to course load, degree level, program, and student level. **Scholarships:** Available **Calendar System:** Semester, Summer Session Available **Enrollment:** FT 768, PT 195, Grad FT 167, Grad PT 805 **Faculty:** FT 78, PT 140 **Student-Faculty Ratio:** 10:1 **Exams:** SAT I or ACT, SAT I. **% Receiving Financial Aid:** 85 **% Residing in College-Owned, -Operated, or -Affiliated Housing:** 40 **Regional Accreditation:** New England Association of Schools and Colleges **Credit Hours For Degree:** 120 credits, Bachelors **Professional Accreditation:** AAMFT, AACN, AAFCS, ADtA, CSWE, NLN **Intercollegiate Athletics:** Basketball W; Cross-Country Running W; Lacrosse W; Soccer W; Softball W; Swimming and Diving W; Tennis W; Volleyball W

ST. VINCENT'S COLLEGE
2800 Main St.
Bridgeport, CT 06606-4292
Tel: (203)576-5235; Free: 800-873-1013
Admissions: (203)576-5515
E-mail: jmarrone@stvincentscollege.edu
Web Site: http://www.stvincentscollege.edu/
President/CEO: Martha K. Shouldis
Admissions: Joseph Marrone
Type: Two-Year College **Sex:** Coed **Affiliation:** Roman Catholic Church **Admission Plans:** Deferred Admission **Application Deadline:** Rolling **Application Fee:** $50.00 **H.S. Requirements:** High school diploma required; GED accepted **Costs Per Year:** Application fee: $50. Tuition: $11,088 full-time, $396 per credit hour part-time. Mandatory fees: $850 full-time, $850 per year part-time. Full-time tuition and fees vary according to class time, course level, course load, program, and student level. Part-time tuition and fees vary according to class time, course level, course load, program, and student level. **Scholarships:** Available **Calendar System:** Semester, Summer Session Available **Student-Faculty Ratio:** 7:1 **Regional Accreditation:** New England Association of Schools and Colleges **Credit Hours For Degree:** 72 credits, Associates **Professional Accreditation:** AAMAE, NLN

SOUTHERN CONNECTICUT STATE UNIVERSITY
501 Crescent St.
New Haven, CT 06515-1355
Tel: (203)392-5200
Admissions: (203)392-5651
Fax: (203)392-5727
Web Site: http://www.southernct.edu/
President/CEO: Dr. Cheryl J. Norton
Admissions: Paula Kennedy
Financial Aid: Avon Dennis
Type: Comprehensive **Sex:** Coed **Affiliation:** Connecticut State University System **Scores:** 90.7% SAT V 400+; 89.1% SAT M 400+ **% Accepted:** 71 **Admission Plans:** Deferred Admission **Application Deadline:** April 1 **Application Fee:** $50.00 **H.S. Requirements:** High school diploma required; GED accepted **Costs Per Year:** Application fee: $50. State resident tuition: $4023 full-time, $403 per credit part-time. Nonresident tuition: $13,020 full-time, $416 per credit part-time. Mandatory fees: $4027 full-time, $55 per term part-time. Full-time tuition and fees vary according to course load. Part-time tuition and fees vary according to course load. College room and board: $9983. College room only: $5541. Room and board charges vary according to board plan and housing facility. **Scholarships:** Available **Calendar System:** Semester, Summer Session Available **Enrollment:** FT 7,366, PT 1,228, Grad FT 980, Grad PT 2,241 **Faculty:** FT 403, PT 678 **Student-Faculty Ratio:** 16:1 **Exams:** SAT I or ACT. SAT essay not being used. **% Receiving Financial Aid:** 55 **% Residing in College-Owned, -Operated, or -Affiliated Housing:** 32 **Final Year or Final Semester Residency Requirement:** No **Library Holdings:** 495,660 **Regional Accreditation:** New England Association of Schools and Colleges **Credit Hours For Degree:** 122 semester hours, Bachelors **ROTC:** Army, Air Force **Professional Accreditation:** ABET, AAMFT, AACN, AANA, ACA, ALA, ASLHA, CEPH, CSWE, JRCEPAT, NCATE, NLN **Intercollegiate Athletics:** Baseball M; Basketball M & W; Cheerleading M & W; Cross-Country Running M & W; Field Hockey W; Football M; Gymnastics W; Lacrosse W; Rugby M & W; Soccer M & W; Softball W; Swimming and Diving M & W; Track and Field M & W; Ultimate Frisbee M & W; Volleyball W

THREE RIVERS COMMUNITY COLLEGE
574 New London Turnpike
Norwich, CT 06360
Tel: (860)886-0177
Admissions: (860)383-5260
Fax: (860)886-0691
E-mail: admissions@trcc.commnet.edu
Web Site: http://www.trcc.commnet.edu/
President/CEO: Dr. Grace S. Jones
Admissions: Aida Garcia
Type: Two-Year College **Sex:** Coed **Affiliation:** Connecticut Community-Technical College System **% Accepted:** 98 **Admission Plans:** Open Admission; Early Admission; Deferred Admission **Application Deadline:** Rolling **Application Fee:** $20.00 **H.S. Requirements:** High school diploma required; GED accepted **Costs Per Year:** Application fee: $20. State resident tuition: $3200 full-time, $118 per credit hour part-time. Nonresident tuition: $9560 full-time, $354 per credit hour part-time. Mandatory fees: $368 full-time, $64 per credit hour part-time, $182. **Scholarships:** Available **Calendar System:** Semester, Summer Session Available **Student-Faculty Ratio:** 20:1 **Exams:** SAT I. **Final Year or Final Semester Residency Requirement:** No **Library Holdings:** 48,000 **Regional Accreditation:** New England Association of Schools and Colleges **Credit Hours For Degree:** 60 credits, Associates **Professional Accreditation:** ABET, ACBSP, MACTE, NLN

TRINITY COLLEGE
300 Summit St.
Hartford, CT 06106-3100
Tel: (860)297-2000
Admissions: (860)297-2180
Fax: (860)297-2287
E-mail: admissions.office@trincoll.edu
Web Site: http://www.trincoll.edu/
President/CEO: James F. Jones, Jr.
Admissions: Larry Dow
Financial Aid: Kelly O'Brien
Type: Comprehensive **Sex:** Coed **Scores:** 100% SAT V 400+; 100% SAT M 400+; 8.1% ACT 18-23; 65.1% ACT 24-29 **% Accepted:** 41 **Admission Plans:** Early Admission; Early Decision Plan; Deferred Admission **Application Deadline:** January 1 **Application Fee:** $60.00 **H.S. Requirements:** High school diploma required; GED accepted **Costs Per Year:** Application fee: $60. One-time mandatory fee: $25. Comprehensive fee: $53,330 includes full-time tuition ($40,360), mandatory fees ($2010), and college room and board ($10,960). College room only: $7120. Full-time tuition and fees vary according to course load and program. Room and board charges vary according to board plan. Part-time tuition: $4484 per course. Part-time tuition varies according to course load and program. **Scholarships:** Available **Calendar System:** Semester, Summer Session Available **Enrollment:** FT 2,207, PT 134, Grad FT 7, Grad PT 166 **Faculty:** FT 195, PT 72 **Student-Faculty Ratio:** 9:1 **Exams:** SAT I or ACT, SAT II. **% Receiving Financial Aid:** 42 **% Residing in College-Owned, -Operated, or -Affiliated Housing:** 95 **Library Holdings:** 904,988 **Regional Accreditation:** New England Association of Schools and Colleges **Credit Hours For Degree:** 36 courses, Bachelors **ROTC:** Army **Professional Accreditation:** ABET **Intercollegiate Athletics:** Baseball M; Basketball M & W; Crew M & W; Cross-Country Running M & W; Equestrian Sports M & W; Fencing M & W; Football M; Golf M; Ice Hockey M & W; Lacrosse M & W; Rugby M & W; Sailing M & W; Skiing (Downhill) M & W; Soccer M & W; Softball W; Squash M & W; Swimming and Diving M & W; Tennis M & W; Track and Field M & W; Ultimate Frisbee M & W; Volleyball W; Water Polo M & W; Wrestling M

TUNXIS COMMUNITY COLLEGE
271 Scott Swamp Rd.
Farmington, CT 06032-3026
Tel: (860)255-3500
Admissions: (860)255-3550
E-mail: pmccluskey@txcc.commnet.edu
Web Site: http://www.tunxis.commnet.edu/
President/CEO: Dr. Cathryn Addy
Admissions: Peter McCluskey
Type: Two-Year College **Sex:** Coed **Affiliation:** Connecticut Community-Technical College System **Admission Plans:** Open Admission; Preferred Admission; Deferred Admission **Application Deadline:** Rolling **Application Fee:** $20.00 **H.S. Requirements:** High school diploma

required; GED accepted **Costs Per Year:** Application fee: $20. State resident tuition: $3024 full-time, $126 per credit hour part-time. Nonresident tuition: $9072 full-time, $189 per credit hour part-time. Mandatory fees: $382 full-time. **Calendar System:** Semester, Summer Session Available **Enrollment:** FT 1,874, PT 2,622 **Faculty:** FT 67, PT 172 **Student-Faculty Ratio:** 19:1 **Library Holdings:** 33,866 **Regional Accreditation:** New England Association of Schools and Colleges **Credit Hours For Degree:** 60 credits, Associates **Professional Accreditation:** ADA, APTA

UNITED STATES COAST GUARD ACADEMY
15 Mohegan Ave.
New London, CT 06320-8100
Tel: (860)444-8444; Free: 800-883-8724
Admissions: (860)444-8500
Fax: (860)444-8289
E-mail: admissions@uscga.edu
Web Site: http://www.uscga.edu/
President/CEO: Adm. J. S. Burboe
Admissions: Capt. Susan Bibeau
Type: Four-Year College **Sex:** Coed **Scores:** 100% SAT V 400+; 100% SAT M 400+; 18% ACT 18-23; 56% ACT 24-29 **% Accepted:** 25 **Admission Plans:** Early Action **Application Deadline:** February 1 **Application Fee:** $0.00 **H.S. Requirements:** High school diploma required; GED accepted. For home schooled applicants: High school diploma or equivalent not required **Costs Per Year:** Application fee: $0. **Calendar System:** Semester, Summer Session Available **Enrollment:** FT 973 **Faculty:** FT 116, PT 14 **Student-Faculty Ratio:** 8:1 **Exams:** SAT I or ACT. ACT essay not being used. SAT essay not being used. **% Residing in College-Owned, -Operated, or -Affiliated Housing:** 100 **Final Year or Final Semester Residency Requirement:** Yes **Library Holdings:** 155,000 **Regional Accreditation:** New England Association of Schools and Colleges **Credit Hours For Degree:** 126 credit hours, Bachelors **Professional Accreditation:** ABET **Intercollegiate Athletics:** Baseball M; Basketball M & W; Bowling M & W; Crew M & W; Cross-Country Running M & W; Football M; Golf M & W; Ice Hockey M; Lacrosse M & W; Riflery M & W; Rugby M & W; Sailing M & W; Soccer M & W; Softball W; Swimming and Diving M & W; Tennis M & W; Track and Field M & W; Volleyball W; Water Polo M; Wrestling M

UNIVERSITY OF BRIDGEPORT
126 Park Ave.
Bridgeport, CT 06604
Tel: (203)576-4000; Free: 800-243-9496
Admissions: (203)576-4552
Fax: (203)576-4941
E-mail: admit@bridgeport.edu
Web Site: http://www.bridgeport.edu/
President/CEO: Neil Albert Salonen
Financial Aid: Kathleen E. Gailor
Type: Comprehensive **Sex:** Coed **Scores:** 81% SAT V 400+; 80% SAT M 400+; 41% ACT 18-23; 7% ACT 24-29 **% Accepted:** 55 **Admission Plans:** Early Admission; Deferred Admission **Application Deadline:** Rolling **Application Fee:** $25.00 **H.S. Requirements:** High school diploma required; GED accepted **Costs Per Year:** Application fee: $25. Comprehensive fee: $36,545 includes full-time tuition ($23,400), mandatory fees ($2065), and college room and board ($11,080). Full-time tuition and fees vary according to course load and program. Room and board charges vary according to board plan and student level. Part-time tuition: $780 per credit hour. Part-time mandatory fees: $80 per term. Part-time tuition and fees vary according to course load and program. **Scholarships:** Available **Calendar System:** Semester, Summer Session Available **Enrollment:** FT 1,504, PT 744, Grad FT 1,531, Grad PT 1,324 **Faculty:** FT 125, PT 368 **Student-Faculty Ratio:** 12:1 **Exams:** SAT I or ACT. ACT essay used for admission. SAT essay used for admission. ACT essay used for advising. SAT essay used for advising. ACT essay used for placement. SAT essay used for placement. **% Receiving Financial Aid:** 79 **% Residing in College-Owned, -Operated, or -Affiliated Housing:** 47 **Final Year or Final Semester Residency Requirement:** Yes **Library Holdings:** 293,440 **Regional Accreditation:** New England Association of Schools and Colleges **Credit Hours For Degree:** 60 credits, Associates; 120 credits, Bachelors **ROTC:** Army **Professional Accreditation:** ABET, NACSCAO, ADA, ACBSP, CCE, NASAD **Intercollegiate Athletics:** Baseball M; Basketball M & W; Cross-Country Running M & W; Gymnastics W; Lacrosse W; Soccer M & W; Softball W; Swimming and Diving M & W; Volleyball W

UNIVERSITY OF CONNECTICUT
Storrs, CT 06269
Tel: (860)486-2000
Admissions: (860)486-3137
Fax: (860)486-1476
E-mail: beahusky@uconnvm.uconn.edu
Web Site: http://www.uconn.edu/
President/CEO: Dr. Michael J. Hogan
Admissions: Brian Usher
Financial Aid: Jean D. Main
Type: University **Sex:** Coed **Scores:** 99% SAT V 400+; 100% SAT M 400+; 13% ACT 18-23; 66% ACT 24-29 **% Accepted:** 50 **Admission Plans:** Early Action; Deferred Admission **Application Deadline:** February 1 **Application Fee:** $70.00 **H.S. Requirements:** High school diploma required; GED accepted **Costs Per Year:** Application fee: $70. State resident tuition: $8064 full-time, $336 per credit part-time. Nonresident tuition: $24,528 full-time, $1022 per credit part-time. Mandatory fees: $2352 full-time. Part-time tuition varies according to course load. College room and board: $10,782. College room only: $5774. Room and board charges vary according to board plan and housing facility. **Scholarships:** Available **Calendar System:** Semester, Summer Session Available **Enrollment:** FT 16,336, PT 672, Grad FT 4,855, Grad PT 3,166 **Faculty:** FT 1,003, PT 330 **Student-Faculty Ratio:** 18:1 **Exams:** SAT I or ACT. **% Receiving Financial Aid:** 52 **% Residing in College-Owned, -Operated, or -Affiliated Housing:** 73 **Library Holdings:** 2,987,772 **Regional Accreditation:** New England Association of Schools and Colleges **Credit Hours For Degree:** 120 credits, Bachelors **ROTC:** Army, Air Force **Professional Accreditation:** AACSB, ABET, ACPhE, ACEJMC, AAMFT, AACN, ABA, ACA, ADtA, APTA, APA, ASLA, ASLHA, AALS, CSWE, NAACLS, NASAD, NASM, NASPAA, NAST NCATE, NLN **Intercollegiate Athletics:** Baseball M; Basketball M & W; Crew W; Cross-Country Running M & W; Field Hockey W; Football M; Golf M; Ice Hockey M & W; Lacrosse W; Soccer M & W; Softball W; Swimming and Diving M & W; Tennis M & W; Track and Field M & W; Volleyball W

UNIVERSITY OF HARTFORD
200 Bloomfield Ave.
West Hartford, CT 06117-1599
Tel: (860)768-4100; Free: 800-947-4303
Admissions: (860)768-4296
Fax: (860)768-4961
E-mail: admissions@hartford.edu
Web Site: http://www.hartford.edu/
President/CEO: Dr. Walter Harrison
Admissions: Richard Zeiser
Type: Comprehensive **Sex:** Coed **Scores:** 98% SAT V 400+; 98% SAT M 400+; 68% ACT 18-23; 22% ACT 24-29 **% Accepted:** 69 **Admission Plans:** Early Admission; Deferred Admission **Application Deadline:** Rolling **Application Fee:** $35.00 **H.S. Requirements:** High school diploma required; GED accepted **Costs Per Year:** Application fee: $35. Comprehensive fee: $41,424 includes full-time tuition ($28,582), mandatory fees ($1270), and college room and board ($11,572). College room only: $7114. Full-time tuition and fees vary according to program. Room and board charges vary according to board plan and housing facility. Part-time tuition: $420 per credit hour. Part-time mandatory fees: $420 per credit hour. Part-time tuition and fees vary according to course load and program. **Scholarships:** Available **Calendar System:** Semester, Summer Session Available **Enrollment:** FT 4,697, PT 819, Grad FT 677, Grad PT 1,019 **Faculty:** FT 345, PT 576 **Student-Faculty Ratio:** 12:1 **Exams:** SAT I or ACT. ACT essay not being used. SAT essay not being used. **% Receiving Financial Aid:** 78 **% Residing in College-Owned, -Operated, or -Affiliated Housing:** 64 **Library Holdings:** 481,685 **Regional Accreditation:** New England Association of Schools and Colleges **Credit Hours For Degree:** 60 credits, Associates; 120 credits, Bachelors **ROTC:** Army, Air Force **Professional Accreditation:** AACSB, ABET, AACN, AOTA, APTA, APA, CARC, JRCERT, NAACLS, NASAD, NASD, NASM, NCATE, NLN **Intercollegiate Athletics:** Badminton M & W; Baseball M; Basketball M & W; Cross-Country Running M & W; Golf M & W; Lacrosse M; Racquetball M & W; Rugby M & W; Soccer M & W; Softball W; Squash M & W; Tennis M & W; Track and Field M & W; Volleyball M & W

UNIVERSITY OF NEW HAVEN
300 Boston Post Rd.
West Haven, CT 06516-1916
Tel: (203)932-7000; Free: 800-DIAL-UNH

Admissions: (203)932-7318
Fax: (203)937-0756
E-mail: adminfo@newhaven.edu
Web Site: http://www.newhaven.edu/
President/CEO: Dr. Steven Kaplan, PhD
Admissions: Kevin Phillips
Financial Aid: Karen Flynn
Type: Comprehensive **Sex:** Coed **Scores:** 93% SAT V 400+; 94% SAT M 400+; 51% ACT 18-23; 33% ACT 24-29 **% Accepted:** 61 **Admission Plans:** Early Action **Application Deadline:** Rolling **Application Fee:** $75.00 **H.S. Requirements:** High school diploma required; GED accepted **Costs Per Year:** Application fee: $75. One-time mandatory fee: $350. Comprehensive fee: $41,674 includes full-time tuition ($28,250), mandatory fees ($1220), and college room and board ($12,204). College room only: $7600. Full-time tuition and fees vary according to course load. Room and board charges vary according to board plan and housing facility. Part-time tuition: $470 per credit hour. Part-time mandatory fees: $70 per term. Part-time tuition and fees vary according to course load. **Scholarships:** Available **Calendar System:** 4-1-4, Summer Session Available **Enrollment:** FT 3,540, PT 473, Grad FT 1,000, Grad PT 757 **Faculty:** FT 200, PT 362 **Student-Faculty Ratio:** 15:1 **Exams:** SAT I or ACT. SAT essay used for placement. **% Receiving Financial Aid:** 79 **% Residing in College-Owned, -Operated, or -Affiliated Housing:** 69 **Library Holdings:** 408,619 **Regional Accreditation:** New England Association of Schools and Colleges **Credit Hours For Degree:** 60 credit hours, Associates; 120 credit hours, Bachelors **ROTC:** Army, Air Force **Professional Accreditation:** ABET, ADA **Intercollegiate Athletics:** Baseball M; Basketball M & W; Cheerleading M & W; Cross-Country Running M & W; Football M; Golf M; Lacrosse W; Soccer M & W; Softball W; Tennis W; Track and Field M & W; Volleyball M & W

UNIVERSITY OF PHOENIX—FAIRFIELD COUNTY CAMPUS
535 Connecticut Ave. Ste. 400
Norwalk, CT 06854-1799
Tel: (203)523-4700
Web Site: http://www.phoenix.edu/
President/CEO: William Pepicello, PhD
Type: Comprehensive **Sex:** Coed **Regional Accreditation:** North Central Association of Colleges and Schools

WESLEYAN UNIVERSITY
Middletown, CT 06459
Tel: (860)685-2000
Admissions: (860)685-3000
Fax: (860)685-3001
E-mail: admissions@wesleyan.edu
Web Site: http://www.wesleyan.edu/
President/CEO: Dr. Michael Roth
Admissions: Nancy Meislahn
Financial Aid: Jennifer Garratt Lawton
Type: University **Sex:** Coed **Scores:** 100% SAT V 400+; 100% SAT M 400+; 1.56% ACT 18-23; 26.04% ACT 24-29 **% Accepted:** 22 **Admission Plans:** Early Admission; Early Decision Plan; Deferred Admission **Application Deadline:** January 1 **Application Fee:** $55.00 **H.S. Requirements:** High school diploma required; GED accepted **Costs Per Year:** Application fee: $55. One-time mandatory fee: $300. Comprehensive fee: $51,132 includes full-time tuition ($39,822), mandatory fees ($270), and college room and board ($11,040). Room and board charges vary according to board plan and housing facility. **Scholarships:** Available **Calendar System:** Semester, Summer Session Available **Enrollment:** FT 2,774, PT 13, Grad FT 194, Grad PT 167 **Faculty:** FT 330, PT 31 **Student-Faculty Ratio:** 9:1 **Exams:** SAT I and SAT II or ACT. ACT essay not being used. SAT essay not being used. **% Receiving Financial Aid:** 47 **% Residing in College-Owned, -Operated, or -Affiliated Housing:** 98 **Library Holdings:** 1,661,056 **Regional Accreditation:** New England Association of Schools and Colleges **Credit Hours For Degree:** 32 courses, Bachelors **ROTC:** Air Force **Intercollegiate Athletics:** Baseball M; Basketball M & W; Crew M & W; Cross-Country Running M & W; Equestrian Sports M & W; Field Hockey W; Football M; Golf M; Ice Hockey M & W; Lacrosse M & W; Rugby M & W; Sailing M & W; Skiing (Cross-Country) M & W; Skiing (Downhill) M & W; Soccer M & W; Softball W; Squash M & W; Swimming and Diving M & W; Tennis M & W; Track and Field M & W; Volleyball M & W; Water Polo M; Wrestling M

WESTERN CONNECTICUT STATE UNIVERSITY
181 White St.
Danbury, CT 06810-6885
Tel: (203)837-8200; Free: 877-837-WCSU
Admissions: (203)837-9000
Fax: (203)837-8320
E-mail: admissions@wcsu.edu
Web Site: http://www.wcsu.edu/
President/CEO: Dr. James W. Schmotter
Financial Aid: Nancy Barton
Type: Comprehensive **Sex:** Coed **Affiliation:** Connecticut State University System **Scores:** 95% SAT V 400+; 93% SAT M 400+ **% Accepted:** 62 **Admission Plans:** Preferred Admission; Early Admission; Deferred Admission **Application Fee:** $50.00 **H.S. Requirements:** High school diploma required; GED accepted **Costs Per Year:** Application fee: $50. State resident tuition: $4023 full-time, $364 per credit hour part-time. Nonresident tuition: $13,020 full-time, $367 per credit hour part-time. Mandatory fees: $3886 full-time. Full-time tuition and fees vary according to reciprocity agreements. College room only: $5858. Room charges vary according to housing facility. **Scholarships:** Available **Calendar System:** Semester, Summer Session Available **Enrollment:** FT 4,756, PT 1,113, Grad FT 126, Grad PT 622 **Faculty:** FT 218, PT 364 **Student-Faculty Ratio:** 15:1 **Exams:** SAT I or ACT. SAT essay used for placement. **% Receiving Financial Aid:** 55 **% Residing in College-Owned, -Operated, or -Affiliated Housing:** 29 **Regional Accreditation:** New England Association of Schools and Colleges **Credit Hours For Degree:** 62 semester hours, Associates; 122 semester hours, Bachelors **ROTC:** Army, Air Force **Professional Accreditation:** AACN, ACA, CSWE, NASM, NCATE, NLN **Intercollegiate Athletics:** Baseball M; Basketball M & W; Cheerleading W; Field Hockey W; Football M; Lacrosse M & W; Soccer M & W; Softball W; Swimming and Diving W; Tennis M & W; Volleyball W

YALE UNIVERSITY
New Haven, CT 06520
Tel: (203)432-4771
Admissions: (203)432-9300
Fax: (203)432-9392
E-mail: student.questions@yale.edu
Web Site: http://www.yale.edu/
President/CEO: Richard C. Levin
Financial Aid: Caesar T. Storlazzi
Type: University **Sex:** Coed **Scores:** 100% SAT V 400+; 100% SAT M 400+ **% Accepted:** 8 **Admission Plans:** Early Admission; Early Action; Deferred Admission **Application Deadline:** December 31 **Application Fee:** $75.00 **H.S. Requirements:** High school diploma or equivalent not required **Costs Per Year:** Application fee: $75. Comprehensive fee: $47,500 includes full-time tuition ($36,500) and college room and board ($11,000). College room only: $6000. Room and board charges vary according to board plan. **Scholarships:** Available **Calendar System:** Semester, Summer Session Available **Enrollment:** FT 5,260, PT 15, Grad FT 6,194, Grad PT 124 **Faculty:** FT 1,158, PT 495 **Student-Faculty Ratio:** 6:1 **Exams:** SAT I and SAT II or ACT. ACT essay used for admission. SAT essay used for admission. **% Receiving Financial Aid:** 54 **% Residing in College-Owned, -Operated, or -Affiliated Housing:** 88 **Final Year or Final Semester Residency Requirement:** No **Library Holdings:** 12,500,000 **Regional Accreditation:** New England Association of Schools and Colleges **Credit Hours For Degree:** 36 courses, Bachelors **ROTC:** Army, Air Force **Professional Accreditation:** AACSB, ABET, AACN, ABA, ACNM, ADtA, APA, ACIPE, AALS, ATS, ACEHSA, CEPH, LCMEAMA, NAAB, NASM, NLN, SAF **Intercollegiate Athletics:** Archery M & W; Baseball M; Basketball M & W; Crew M & W; Cross-Country Running M & W; Equestrian Sports M & W; Fencing M & W; Field Hockey W; Football M; Golf M & W; Gymnastics W; Ice Hockey M & W; Lacrosse M & W; Riflery M & W; Rock Climbing M & W; Rugby M & W; Sailing M & W; Skiing (Cross-Country) M & W; Skiing (Downhill) M & W; Soccer M & W; Softball W; Squash M & W; Swimming and Diving M & W; Table Tennis M & W; Tennis M & W; Track and Field M & W; Ultimate Frisbee M & W; Volleyball M & W; Water Polo M & W; Wrestling M

DELAWARE COLLEGE OF ART AND DESIGN
600 North Market St.
Wilmington, DE 19801
Tel: (302)622-8000
Admissions: (302)622-8867
Fax: (302)622-8870
E-mail: agullo@dcad.edu
Web Site: http://www.dcad.edu/
President/CEO: James P. Lecky
Admissions: Allison Gullo
Type: Two-Year College **Sex:** Coed **Affiliation:** Corcoran College of Art and Design **% Accepted:** 58 **Admission Plans:** Deferred Admission **Application Deadline:** Rolling **Application Fee:** $25.00 **H.S. Requirements:** High school diploma required; GED accepted **Costs Per Year:** Application fee: $25. Tuition: $17,100 full-time, $750 per credit hour part-time. Mandatory fees: $1110 full-time, $715 per year part-time. Full-time tuition and fees vary according to program. Part-time tuition and fees vary according to course load and program. College room only: $6700. Room charges vary according to housing facility. **Calendar System:** Semester, Summer Session Available **Enrollment:** FT 192, PT 18 **Faculty:** FT 7, PT 20 **Student-Faculty Ratio:** 8:1 **% Residing in College-Owned, -Operated, or -Affiliated Housing:** 50 **Library Holdings:** 8,000 **Regional Accreditation:** Middle State Association of Colleges and Schools **Credit Hours For Degree:** 68 semester hours, Associates

DELAWARE STATE UNIVERSITY
1200 North DuPont Hwy.
Dover, DE 19901-2277
Tel: (302)857-6290; Free: 800-845-2544
Admissions: (302)857-6351
Fax: (302)857-6352
E-mail: gcheatha@desu.edu
Web Site: http://www.desu.edu/
President/CEO: Dr. Harry L. Williams
Admissions: Lawita G. Scott-Cheatham
Type: University **Sex:** Coed **Affiliation:** Delaware Higher Education Commission **Scores:** 77% SAT V 400+; 74% SAT M 400+; 42% ACT 18-23; 7% ACT 24-29 **% Accepted:** 39 **Admission Plans:** Preferred Admission; Early Admission **Application Fee:** $25.00 **H.S. Requirements:** High school diploma required; GED accepted **Costs Per Year:** Application fee: $25. State resident tuition: $6481 full-time, $238 per credit hour part-time. Nonresident tuition: $13,742 full-time, $540 per credit hour part-time. Mandatory fees: $780 full-time, $50 per term part-time. Full-time tuition and fees vary according to reciprocity agreements. Part-time tuition and fees vary according to reciprocity agreements. College room and board: $8752. College room only: $5935. Room and board charges vary according to board plan and housing facility. **Scholarships:** Available **Calendar System:** Semester, Summer Session Available **Enrollment:** FT 2,818, PT 404, Grad FT 295, Grad PT 92 **Faculty:** FT 190, PT 66 **Student-Faculty Ratio:** 16:1 **Exams:** SAT I or ACT. **% Receiving Financial Aid:** 79 **% Residing in College-Owned, -Operated, or -Affiliated Housing:** 64 **Library Holdings:** 187,045 **Regional Accreditation:** Middle State Association of Colleges and Schools **Credit Hours For Degree:** 121 credit hours, Bachelors **ROTC:** Army, Air Force **Professional Accreditation:** AACSB, AACN, CSWE, NCATE, NLN **Intercollegiate Athletics:** Baseball M; Basketball M & W; Bowling W; Cheerleading W; Cross-Country Running M & W; Equestrian Sports W; Football M; Soccer W; Softball W; Tennis M & W; Track and Field M & W; Volleyball W; Wrestling M

DELAWARE TECHNICAL & COMMUNITY COLLEGE, JACK F. OWENS CAMPUS
PO Box 610
Georgetown, DE 19947
Tel: (302)856-5400
Fax: (302)856-9461
Web Site: http://www.dtcc.edu/
President/CEO: Dr. Orlando George
Admissions: Claire McDonald
Type: Two-Year College **Sex:** Coed **Affiliation:** Delaware Technical and Community College System **Admission Plans:** Open Admission; Preferred Admission; Early Admission; Deferred Admission **Application Deadline:** Rolling **Application Fee:** $10.00 **H.S. Requirements:** High school diploma or equivalent not required. For nursing program: High school diploma required; GED accepted **Costs Per Year:** Application fee: $10. State resident tuition: $2472 full-time, $103 per credit hour part-time. Nonresident tuition: $6180 full-time, $257.50 per credit hour part-time. Mandatory fees: $516 full-time, $7 per credit hour part-time, $25 per term part-time. **Scholarships:** Available **Calendar System:** Semester, Summer Session Available **Enrollment:** FT 2,382, PT 2,405 **Faculty:** FT 117, PT 237 **Student-Faculty Ratio:** 16:1 **Library Holdings:** 62,663 **Regional Accreditation:** Middle State Association of Colleges and Schools **Professional Accreditation:** AOTA, APTA, ACBSP, CARC, JRCERT, NAACLS, NLN **Intercollegiate Athletics:** Baseball M; Golf M; Softball W

DELAWARE TECHNICAL & COMMUNITY COLLEGE, STANTON/ WILMINGTON CAMPUS
400 Stanton-Christiana Rd.
Newark, DE 19713
Tel: (302)454-3900
Admissions: (302)571-5343
Fax: (302)577-2548
Web Site: http://www.dtcc.edu/
President/CEO: Dr. Orlando George
Admissions: Rebecca Bailey
Type: Two-Year College **Sex:** Coed **Affiliation:** Delaware Technical and Community College System **Admission Plans:** Open Admission; Preferred Admission; Early Admission; Deferred Admission **Application Deadline:** Rolling **Application Fee:** $10.00 **H.S. Requirements:** High school diploma or equivalent not required. For nursing and particular allied health programs: High school diploma required; GED accepted **Costs Per Year:** Application fee: $10. State resident tuition: $2472 full-time, $103 per credit hour part-time. Nonresident tuition: $6180 full-time, $257.50 per credit hour part-time. Mandatory fees: $516 full-time, $7 per credit hour part-time, $25 per term part-time. **Scholarships:** Available **Calendar System:** Semester, Summer Session Available **Enrollment:** FT 3,290, PT 4,198 **Faculty:** FT 178, PT 346 **Student-Faculty Ratio:** 16:1 **Library Holdings:** 74,259 **Regional Accreditation:** Middle State Association of Colleges and Schools **ROTC:** Air Force **Professional Accreditation:** ABET, AAMAE, ADA, AOTA, APTA, ACBSP, CARC, JRCEDMS, JRCERT, JRCNMT, NAACLS, NLN **Intercollegiate Athletics:** Basketball M & W; Soccer M; Softball W

DELAWARE TECHNICAL & COMMUNITY COLLEGE, TERRY CAMPUS
100 Campus Dr.
Dover, DE 19901
Tel: (302)857-1000
Admissions: (302)857-1020
Fax: (302)857-1296
E-mail: mharris@outland.dtcc.edu
Web Site: http://www.dtcc.edu/terry/
President/CEO: Dr. Orlando George
Admissions: Maria Harris
Type: Two-Year College **Sex:** Coed **Affiliation:** Delaware Technical and Community College System **Admission Plans:** Open Admission; Preferred Admission; Early Admission; Deferred Admission **Application Deadline:** Rolling **Application Fee:** $10.00 **H.S. Requirements:** High school diploma or equivalent not required. For nursing program: High school diploma required; GED accepted **Costs Per Year:** Application fee: $10. State resident tuition: $2472 full-time, $103 per credit hour part-time. Nonresident tuition: $6180 full-time, $257.50 per credit hour part-time. Mandatory fees: $516 full-time, $7 per credit hour part-time, $25 per term part-time. **Scholarships:** Available **Calendar System:** Semester, Summer Session Available **Enrollment:** FT 1,607, PT 1,799 **Faculty:** FT 81, PT 163 **Student-Faculty Ratio:** 16:1 **Library Holdings:** 15,327 **Regional Accreditation:** Middle State Association of Colleges and Schools **Professional Accreditation:** ACBSP, JRCEMT, NLN **Intercollegiate Athletics:** Lacrosse M; Soccer M & W; Softball W

GOLDEY-BEACOM COLLEGE
4701 Limestone Rd.
Wilmington, DE 19808-1999
Tel: (302)998-8814; Free: 800-833-4877
Admissions: (302)225-6289
Fax: (302)996-5408
E-mail: admissions@gbc.edu
Web Site: http://www.gbc.edu/
President/CEO: Dr. Mohammad Ilyas
Admissions: Larry Eby
Financial Aid: Jane H. Lysle
Type: Comprehensive **Sex:** Coed **Scores:** 77% SAT V 400+; 83% SAT M 400+; 50% ACT 18-23 **% Accepted:** 76 **Admission Plans:** Early Admission; Deferred Admission **Application Deadline:** Rolling **Application Fee:** $0.00 **H.S. Requirements:** High school diploma required; GED accepted **Costs Per Year:** Application fee: $0. Tuition: $18,360 full-time, $612 per credit hour part-time. Mandatory fees: $300 full-time, $10 per credit hour part-time. Full-time tuition and fees vary according to course load. Part-time tuition and fees vary according to course load. College room only: $5021. Room charges vary according to housing facility. **Scholarships:** Available **Calendar System:** Semester, Summer Session Available **Enrollment:** FT 487, PT 236, Grad FT 70, Grad PT 473 **Faculty:** FT 20, PT 28 **Student-Faculty Ratio:** 26:1 **Exams:** SAT I or ACT. ACT essay used for admission. SAT essay used for admission. **% Residing in College-Owned, -Operated, or -Affiliated Housing:** 21 **Final Year or Final Semester Residency Requirement:** No **Library Holdings:** 54,744 **Regional Accreditation:** Middle State Association of Colleges and Schools **Credit Hours For Degree:** 66 credits, Associates; 131 credits, Bachelors **ROTC:** Air Force **Professional Accreditation:** ACBSP **Intercollegiate Athletics:** Basketball M & W; Cross-Country Running M & W; Golf M & W; Soccer M & W; Softball W; Tennis W; Volleyball W

STRAYER UNIVERSITY - CHRISTIANA CAMPUS
240 Continental Dr.
Ste. 108
Newark, DE 19713
Tel: (302)292-6100
Fax: (302)292-6130
Web Site: http://www.strayer.edu/christiana
Type: Comprehensive **Sex:** Coed **Application Fee:** $50.00 **Costs Per Year:** Application fee: $50. **Regional Accreditation:** Middle State Association of Colleges and Schools

UNIVERSITY OF DELAWARE
Newark, DE 19716
Tel: (302)831-2000
Fax: (302)831-6905
E-mail: admissions@udel.edu
Web Site: http://www.udel.edu/
President/CEO: Patrick T. Harker
Admissions: Lou Hirsh
Financial Aid: James Holloway
Type: University **Sex:** Coed **Scores:** 99% SAT V 400+; 100% SAT M 400+; 21% ACT 18-23; 62% ACT 24-29 **% Accepted:** 57 **Admission Plans:** Preferred Admission; Early Admission; Deferred Admission **Application Deadline:** January 15 **Application Fee:** $75.00 **H.S. Requirements:** High school diploma required; GED accepted **Costs Per Year:** Application fee: $75. State resident tuition: $8540 full-time, $356 per credit part-time. Nonresident tuition: $22,240 full-time, $927 per credit part-time. Mandatory fees: $946 full-time. College room and board: $9066. College room only: $5466. Room and board charges vary according to board plan, housing facility, and student level. **Scholarships:** Available **Calendar System:** 4-1-4, Summer Session Available **Faculty:** FT 1,159, PT 281 **Student-Faculty Ratio:** 12:1 **Exams:** SAT I or ACT, SAT II. ACT essay used for admission. SAT essay used for admission. ACT essay used as a validity check on application essay. SAT essay used as a validity check on application essay. ACT essay used for placement. SAT essay used for placement. **% Receiving Financial Aid:** 57 **% Residing in College-Owned, -Operated, or -Affiliated Housing:** 46 **Regional Accreditation:** Middle State Association of Colleges and Schools **Credit Hours For Degree:** 60 credit hours, Associates; 120 credit hours, Bachelors **ROTC:** Army, Air Force **Professional Accreditation:** AACSB, ABET, AACN, ADtA, APTA, APA, JRCEPAT, NAACLS, NASM, NASPAA, NCATE, NLN **Intercollegiate Athletics:** Baseball M; Basketball M & W; Bowling M & W; Cheerleading M & W; Crew M & W; Cross-Country Running M & W; Equestrian Sports M & W; Field Hockey W; Football M; Golf M; Ice Hockey M; Lacrosse M & W; Rugby W; Sailing M & W; Soccer M & W; Softball W; Swimming and Diving M & W; Tennis M & W; Track and Field M & W; Volleyball W; Wrestling M

WESLEY COLLEGE
120 North State St.
Dover, DE 19901-3875
Tel: (302)736-2300; Free: 800-937-5398
Admissions: (302)736-2400
Fax: (302)736-2301
E-mail: admissions@wesley.edu
Web Site: http://www.wesley.edu/
President/CEO: Dr. J. Thomas Sturgis
Admissions: Arthur Jacobs
Financial Aid: James Marks
Type: Comprehensive **Sex:** Coed **Affiliation:** United Methodist **Scores:** 88% SAT V 400+; 90% SAT M 400+ **% Accepted:** 67 **Application Deadline:** Rolling **Application Fee:** $25.00 **H.S. Requirements:** High school diploma required; GED accepted **Scholarships:** Available **Calendar System:** Semester, Summer Session Available **Enrollment:** FT 1,459, PT 308 **Faculty:** FT 69, PT 88 **Student-Faculty Ratio:** 17:1 **Exams:** Other, SAT I. **% Receiving Financial Aid:** 86 **% Residing in College-Owned, -Operated, or -Affiliated Housing:** 66 **Library Holdings:** 104,636 **Regional Accreditation:** Middle State Association of Colleges and Schools **Credit Hours For Degree:** 64 credit hours, Associates; 124 credit hours, Bachelors **ROTC:** Army **Professional Accreditation:** NCATE, NLN **Intercollegiate Athletics:** Baseball M; Basketball M & W; Field Hockey W; Football M; Golf M & W; Lacrosse M & W; Soccer M & W; Softball W; Tennis M & W

WILMINGTON UNIVERSITY
320 North DuPont Hwy.
New Castle, DE 19720-6491
Tel: (302)328-9401; Free: 877-967-5464
Admissions: (302)356-6745
Fax: (302)328-5902
E-mail: inquire@wilmcoll.edu
Web Site: http://www.wilmu.edu/
President/CEO: Dr. Jack P. Varsalona
Admissions: Christopher Ferguson
Financial Aid: J. Lynn Iocono
Type: Comprehensive **Sex:** Coed **% Accepted:** 97 **Admission Plans:** Open Admission; Early Admission; Deferred Admission **Application Deadline:** Rolling **Application Fee:** $25.00 **H.S. Requirements:** High school diploma required; GED accepted **Costs Per Year:** Application fee: $25. Tuition: $7224 full-time. Mandatory fees: $50 full-time. **Scholarships:** Available

Calendar System: Semester, Summer Session Available **Enrollment:** FT 3,217, PT 2,701, Grad FT 1,069, Grad PT 2,671 **Faculty:** FT 92, PT 994 **Student-Faculty Ratio:** 17:1 **% Receiving Financial Aid:** 40 **Library Holdings:** 98,713 **Regional Accreditation:** Middle State Association of Colleges and Schools **Credit Hours For Degree:** 60 credit hours, Associates; 120 credit hours, Bachelors **ROTC:** Army, Air Force **Professional Accreditation:** AACN, ACA, NCATE, NLN **Intercollegiate Athletics:** Baseball M; Basketball M & W; Cross-Country Running M & W; Softball W; Volleyball W

AMERICAN UNIVERSITY
4400 Massachusetts Ave., NW
Washington, DC 20016-8001
Tel: (202)885-1000
Fax: (202)885-6014
E-mail: admissions@american.edu
Web Site: http://www.american.edu/
President/CEO: Dr. Cornelius M. Kerwin
Admissions: Greg Grauman
Financial Aid: Brian Lee Sang
Type: University **Sex:** Coed **Affiliation:** Methodist **Scores:** 100% SAT V 400+; 99% SAT M 400+; 10% ACT 18-23; 55% ACT 24-29 **% Accepted:** 53 **Admission Plans:** Early Decision Plan; Deferred Admission **Application Deadline:** January 15 **Application Fee:** $60.00 **H.S. Requirements:** High school diploma required; GED accepted **Costs Per Year:** Application fee: $60. Comprehensive fee: $50,165 includes full-time tuition ($36,180), mandatory fees ($517), and college room and board ($13,468). Full-time tuition and fees vary according to degree level. Room and board charges vary according to board plan, housing facility, and location. Part-time tuition: $1205 per credit hour. Part-time tuition varies according to course load. **Scholarships:** Available **Calendar System:** Semester, Summer Session Available **Enrollment:** FT 6,404, PT 244, Grad FT 3,043, Grad PT 2,550 **Faculty:** FT 626, PT 549 **Student-Faculty Ratio:** 13:1 **Exams:** SAT I or ACT, SAT II. ACT essay not being used. SAT essay not being used. **% Receiving Financial Aid:** 50 **% Residing in College-Owned, -Operated, or -Affiliated Housing:** 64 **Final Year or Final Semester Residency Requirement:** No **Library Holdings:** 1,000,000 **Regional Accreditation:** Middle State Association of Colleges and Schools **ROTC:** Army, Air Force **Professional Accreditation:** AACSB, ACEJMC, ABA, APA, AALS, NASM, NASPAA, NCATE **Intercollegiate Athletics:** Basketball M & W; Cross-Country Running M & W; Field Hockey W; Lacrosse W; Soccer M & W; Swimming and Diving M & W; Track and Field M & W; Volleyball W; Wrestling M

THE CATHOLIC UNIVERSITY OF AMERICA
Cardinal Station
Washington, DC 20064
Tel: (202)319-5000; Free: 800-673-2772
Admissions: (202)319-5305
Fax: (202)319-6533
E-mail: cua-admissions@cua.edu
Web Site: http://www.cua.edu/
President/CEO: Very Rev. David M. O'Connell, CM
Admissions: Christine Mica
Financial Aid: Donald Bosse
Type: University **Sex:** Coed **Affiliation:** Roman Catholic Church **Scores:** 99% SAT V 400+; 100% SAT M 400+; 50% ACT 18-23; 40% ACT 24-29 **% Accepted:** 86 **Admission Plans:** Early Action; Deferred Admission **Application Deadline:** February 15 **Application Fee:** $55.00 **H.S. Requirements:** High school diploma required; GED accepted **Costs Per Year:** Application fee: $55. One-time mandatory fee: $425. Comprehensive fee: $44,024 includes full-time tuition ($31,740), mandatory fees ($150), and college room and board ($12,134). College room only: $7340. Full-time tuition and fees vary according to program. Room and board charges vary according to board plan and housing facility. Part-time tuition: $1170 per credit hour. Part-time mandatory fees: $75 per year. Part-time tuition and fees vary according to course load. **Scholarships:** Available **Calendar System:** Semester, Summer Session Available **Enrollment:** FT 3,234, PT 232, Grad FT 1,423, Grad PT 1,879 **Faculty:** FT 354, PT 349 **Student-Faculty Ratio:** 10:1 **Exams:** SAT I or ACT, SAT II. ACT essay used for advising. SAT essay used for advising. ACT essay used as a validity check on application essay. SAT essay used as a validity check on application essay. **% Receiving Financial Aid:** 58 **% Residing in College-Owned, -Operated, or -Affiliated Housing:** 70 **Library Holdings:** 1,642,234 **Regional Accreditation:** Middle State Association of Colleges and Schools **Credit Hours For Degree:** 120 credits, Bachelors **ROTC:** Army, Navy, Air Force **Professional Accreditation:** ABET, AACN, ABA, ALA, APA, AALS, ATS, CSWE, NAAB, NASM, NCATE, NLN **Intercollegiate Athletics:** Baseball M; Basketball M & W; Cross-Country Running M & W; Field Hockey W; Football M; Lacrosse M & W; Soccer M & W; Softball W; Swimming and Diving M & W; Tennis M & W; Track and Field M & W; Volleyball W

CORCORAN COLLEGE OF ART AND DESIGN
500 17th St. NW
Washington, DC 20006-4804
Tel: (202)639-1800; Free: 888-CORCORAN
Admissions: (202)639-1814
E-mail: admissions@corcoran.org
Web Site: http://www.corcoran.edu/
President/CEO: Paul Greenhalgh
Admissions: Elizabeth Smith Paladino
Financial Aid: Diane Morris
Type: Comprehensive **Sex:** Coed **Scores:** 90% SAT V 400+; 86% SAT M 400+; 54% ACT 18-23; 38% ACT 24-29 **% Accepted:** 53 **Admission Plans:** Early Admission; Deferred Admission **Application Deadline:** Rolling **Application Fee:** $45.00 **H.S. Requirements:** High school diploma required; GED accepted **Scholarships:** Available **Calendar System:** Semester, Summer Session Available **Enrollment:** FT 309, PT 86, Grad FT 133, Grad PT 97 **Faculty:** FT 22, PT 147 **Student-Faculty Ratio:** 4:1 **Exams:** SAT I or ACT. **% Receiving Financial Aid:** 71 **% Residing in College-Owned, -Operated, or -Affiliated Housing:** 21 **Library Holdings:** 29,413 **Regional Accreditation:** Middle State Association of Colleges and Schools **Credit Hours For Degree:** 66 credits, Associates; 126 credits, Bachelors **Professional Accreditation:** NASAD **Intercollegiate Athletics:** Ultimate Frisbee M & W; Volleyball M & W

GALLAUDET UNIVERSITY
800 Florida Ave., NE
Washington, DC 20002-3625
Tel: (202)651-5000; Free: 800-995-0550
Admissions: (202)651-5750
Fax: (202)651-5774
E-mail: charity.reedy-hines@gallaudet.edu
Web Site: http://www.gallaudet.edu/
President/CEO: Dr. Alan Hurwitz
Admissions: Charity Reedy-Hines
Financial Aid: Nancy C. Goodman
Type: University **Sex:** Coed **Scores:** 32.5% ACT 18-23; 9.5% ACT 24-29 **% Accepted:** 68 **Admission Plans:** Deferred Admission **Application Deadline:** Rolling **Application Fee:** $50.00 **H.S. Requirements:** High school diploma required; GED accepted **Costs Per Year:** Application fee:

$50. Comprehensive fee: $20,886 includes full-time tuition ($10,850), mandatory fees ($376), and college room and board ($9660). College room only: $5460. Full-time tuition and fees vary according to degree level. Room and board charges vary according to board plan. Part-time tuition: $542.50 per credit hour. Part-time tuition varies according to degree level. **Scholarships:** Available **Calendar System:** Semester, Summer Session Available **Enrollment:** FT 1,000, PT 81, Grad FT 267, Grad PT 140 **Student-Faculty Ratio:** 5:1 **Exams:** SAT I or ACT. ACT essay used for placement. **% Receiving Financial Aid:** 72 **Library Holdings:** 260,000 **Regional Accreditation:** Middle State Association of Colleges and Schools **Credit Hours For Degree:** 120 credit hours, Bachelors **Professional Accreditation:** ACA, APA, ASLHA, ACBSP, CSWE, NCATE, NRPA **Intercollegiate Athletics:** Baseball M; Basketball M & W; Cross-Country Running M & W; Football M; Soccer M & W; Softball W; Swimming and Diving M & W; Tennis M; Track and Field M & W; Volleyball W; Wrestling M

THE GEORGE WASHINGTON UNIVERSITY
2121 Eye St., NW
Washington, DC 20052
Tel: (202)994-1000
E-mail: gwadm@gwis2.circ.gwu.edu
Web Site: http://www.gwu.edu/
President/CEO: Steven Knapp
Admissions: Dr. Kathryn M. Napper
Financial Aid: Dan Small
Type: University **Sex:** Coed **Scores:** 100% SAT V 400+; 100% SAT M 400+; 5.61% ACT 18-23; 62.88% ACT 24-29 **% Accepted:** 37 **Admission Plans:** Early Admission; Early Decision Plan; Deferred Admission **Application Deadline:** January 10 **Application Fee:** $65.00 **H.S. Requirements:** High school diploma required; GED not accepted **Costs Per Year:** Application fee: $65. Comprehensive fee: $51,775 includes full-time tuition ($41,610), mandatory fees ($45), and college room and board ($10,120). College room only: $6720. Full-time tuition and fees vary according to student level. Room and board charges vary according to housing facility. Part-time tuition: $1157 per credit hour. Part-time mandatory fees: $1.50 per credit hour, $22.50 per term. Part-time tuition and fees vary according to course load. Tuition guaranteed not to increase for student's term of enrollment. **Scholarships:** Available **Calendar System:** Semester, Summer Session Available **Enrollment:** FT 9,640, PT 918, Grad FT 6,621, Grad PT 7,882 **Faculty:** FT 903, PT 1,416 **Student-Faculty Ratio:** 13:1 **Exams:** SAT I or ACT. **% Receiving Financial Aid:** 39 **% Residing in College-Owned, -Operated, or -Affiliated Housing:** 67 **Regional Accreditation:** Middle State Association of Colleges and Schools **Credit Hours For Degree:** 60 semester hours, Associates; 120 semester hours, Bachelors **ROTC:** Army, Navy, Air Force **Professional Accreditation:** AACSB, ABET, AABB, ABA, ACA, APTA, APA, ASLHA, AALS, ACEHSA, FIDER, CEPH, CORE, JRCEDMS, JRCEPAT, LCMEAMA, NAACLS, NASM, NASPAA, NCATE **Intercollegiate Athletics:** Baseball M; Basketball M & W; Crew M & W; Cross-Country Running M & W; Golf M; Gymnastics W; Soccer M & W; Swimming and Diving M & W; Tennis M & W; Volleyball W; Water Polo M

GEORGETOWN UNIVERSITY
37th and O Sts., NW
Washington, DC 20057
Tel: (202)687-5055
Admissions: (202)687-3600
Fax: (202)687-6660
Web Site: http://www.georgetown.edu/
President/CEO: John J. Degioia
Admissions: Charles A. Deacon
Financial Aid: Patricia A. McWade
Type: University **Sex:** Coed **Affiliation:** Roman Catholic (Jesuit) **Scores:** 99.86% SAT V 400+; 99.86% SAT M 400+ **% Accepted:** 20 **Admission Plans:** Early Action; Deferred Admission **Application Deadline:** January 10 **Application Fee:** $65.00 **H.S. Requirements:** High school diploma required; GED accepted **Scholarships:** Available **Calendar System:** Semester, Summer Session Available **Enrollment:** FT 7,115, PT 318, Grad FT 6,572, Grad PT 2,432 **Faculty:** FT 873, PT 904 **Student-Faculty Ratio:** 10:1 **Exams:** SAT I or ACT, SAT II. **% Receiving Financial Aid:** 43 **% Residing in College-Owned, -Operated, or -Affiliated Housing:** 70 **Regional Accreditation:** Middle State Association of Colleges and Schools **Credit Hours For Degree:** 120 credit hours, Bachelors **ROTC:** Army, Navy, Air Force **Professional Accreditation:** AACSB, AACN, AANA, ABA, ACNM, ACIPE, AALS, LCMEAMA, NLN **Intercollegiate Athletics:** Baseball M; Basketball M & W; Crew M & W; Cross-Country Running M & W; Field Hockey W; Football M; Golf M; Ice Hockey M; Lacrosse M & W; Rugby M & W; Sailing M & W; Soccer M & W; Softball W; Swimming and Diving M & W; Tennis M & W; Track and Field M & W; Ultimate Frisbee M & W; Volleyball M & W; Water Polo M

HOWARD UNIVERSITY
2400 Sixth St., NW
Washington, DC 20059-0002
Tel: (202)806-6100; Free: 800-HOWARD-U
Admissions: (202)806-2700
E-mail: lsanders-hawkins@howard.edu
Web Site: http://www.howard.edu/
President/CEO: Dr. Sidney A. Ribeau
Admissions: Linda Sanders-Hawkins
Financial Aid: Derek Kindle
Type: University **Sex:** Coed **Scores:** 99% SAT M 400+ **% Accepted:** 49 **Admission Plans:** Early Admission; Early Action; Deferred Admission **Application Deadline:** February 15 **Application Fee:** $45.00 **H.S. Requirements:** High school diploma required; GED accepted **Costs Per Year:** Application fee: $45. Comprehensive fee: $24,041 includes full-time tuition ($15,270), mandatory fees ($805), and college room and board ($7966). College room only: $4898. Full-time tuition and fees vary according to course load. Room and board charges vary according to board plan and housing facility. Part-time tuition: $637 per credit hour. Part-time mandatory fees: $805 per year. Part-time tuition and fees vary according to course load. **Scholarships:** Available **Calendar System:** Semester, Summer Session Available **Enrollment:** FT 6,653, PT 316 **Faculty:** FT 1,064, PT 456 **Student-Faculty Ratio:** 8:1 **Exams:** SAT I or ACT. **% Receiving Financial Aid:** 38 **% Residing in College-Owned, -Operated, or -Affiliated Housing:** 56 **Library Holdings:** 2,455,985 **Regional Accreditation:** Middle State Association of Colleges and Schools **Credit Hours For Degree:** 127 credit hours, Bachelors **ROTC:** Army, Air Force **Professional Accreditation:** AACSB, ABET, ACPhE, ACEJMC, AACN, ABA, ADA, ADtA, AOTA, APTA, APA, ASLHA, ACIPE, AALS, ATS, CSWE, JRCERT, LCMEAMA, NAAB, NASAD NASM, NASPAA, NAST, NCATE, NLN **Intercollegiate Athletics:** Baseball M & W; Basketball M & W; Bowling W; Cross-Country Running M & W; Football M; Lacrosse W; Soccer M; Swimming and Diving M & W; Tennis M & W; Track and Field M & W; Volleyball W

POTOMAC COLLEGE
4000 Chesapeake St., NW
Washington, DC 20016
Tel: (202)686-0876; Free: 888-686-0876
Fax: (202)686-0818
E-mail: info@potomac.edu
Web Site: http://www.potomac.edu/
President/CEO: Glenn Johanessen
Admissions: Asha Ellison
Financial Aid: Phyllis Crews
Type: Four-Year College **Sex:** Coed **% Accepted:** 76 **Admission Plans:** Open Admission **Application Deadline:** Rolling **Application Fee:** $15.00 **H.S. Requirements:** High school diploma required; GED accepted **Scholarships:** Available **Calendar System:** Miscellaneous, Summer Session Available **Enrollment:** FT 87, PT 311 **Faculty:** FT 14, PT 33 **Student-Faculty Ratio:** 15:1 **Library Holdings:** 5,565 **Regional Accreditation:** Middle State Association of Colleges and Schools **Credit Hours For Degree:** 123 semester credits, Bachelors

STRAYER UNIVERSITY - TAKOMA PARK CAMPUS
6830 Laurel St., NW
Washington, DC 20012
Tel: (202)722-8100
Web Site: http://www.strayer.edu/takoma_park
Type: Comprehensive **Sex:** Coed **Application Fee:** $50.00 **Costs Per Year:** Application fee: $50. **Regional Accreditation:** Middle State Association of Colleges and Schools

STRAYER UNIVERSITY - WASHINGTON CAMPUS
1133 15th St., NW
Washington, DC 20005
Tel: (202)408-2400
Fax: (202)419-1425
Web Site: http://www.strayer.edu/washington_dc

Type: Comprehensive **Sex:** Coed **Application Fee:** $50.00 **Costs Per Year:** Application fee: $50. **Regional Accreditation:** Middle State Association of Colleges and Schools

TRINITY (WASHINGTON) UNIVERSITY
125 Michigan Ave., NE
Washington, DC 20017-1094
Tel: (202)884-9000; Free: 800-IWA-NTTC
Admissions: (202)884-9050
Fax: (202)884-9229
E-mail: admissions@trinitydc.edu
Web Site: http://www.trinitydc.edu/
President/CEO: Patricia A. McGuire
Financial Aid: Catherine H. Geier
Type: Comprehensive **Affiliation:** Roman Catholic **Admission Plans:** Early Action; Deferred Admission **Application Deadline:** March 1 **Application Fee:** $40.00 **H.S. Requirements:** High school diploma required; GED accepted **Scholarships:** Available **Calendar System:** Semester, Summer Session Available **Exams:** SAT I or ACT. **% Receiving Financial Aid:** 87 **Library Holdings:** 207,000 **Regional Accreditation:** Middle State Association of Colleges and Schools **Credit Hours For Degree:** 128 credit hours, Bachelors **ROTC:** Army **Professional Accreditation:** NCATE **Intercollegiate Athletics:** Basketball W; Field Hockey W; Lacrosse W; Soccer W; Softball W; Swimming and Diving W; Tennis W; Volleyball W

UNIVERSITY OF THE DISTRICT OF COLUMBIA
4200 Connecticut Ave., NW
Washington, DC 20008-1175
Tel: (202)274-5000
Admissions: (202)274-6110
Web Site: http://www.udc.edu/
President/CEO: Dr. Allen L. Sessoms
Admissions: Ann Marie Waterman
Financial Aid: Willis Parker
Type: Comprehensive **Sex:** Coed **% Accepted:** 67 **Admission Plans:** Open Admission; Preferred Admission; Deferred Admission **Application Deadline:** August 1 **Application Fee:** $35.00 **H.S. Requirements:** High school diploma required; GED accepted **Costs Per Year:** Application fee: $35. District resident tuition: $4750 full-time, $198 per credit hour part-time. Nonresident tuition: $11,680 full-time, $487 per credit hour part-time. Mandatory fees: $620 full-time, $30 per credit hour part-time, $30. Part-time tuition and fees vary according to course load. **Scholarships:** Available **Calendar System:** Semester, Summer Session Available **Enrollment:** FT 2,181, PT 2,589, Grad FT 97, Grad PT 93 **Faculty:** FT 241, PT 199 **Student-Faculty Ratio:** 13:1 **Exams:** SAT I. **% Receiving Financial Aid:** 67 **Library Holdings:** 544,412 **Regional Accreditation:** Middle State Association of Colleges and Schools **Credit Hours For Degree:** 60 semester hours, Associates; 120 semester hours, Bachelors **ROTC:** Army, Air Force **Professional Accreditation:** ABET, ABA, ABFSE, ASLHA, ACBSP, CARC, CSWE, JRCERT, NAAB, NCATE, NLN **Intercollegiate Athletics:** Golf M; Soccer M; Tennis M & W; Track and Field M & W; Volleyball W

UNIVERSITY OF PHOENIX—WASHINGTON D.C. CAMPUS
25 Massachusetts Ave. NW, Ste. 150
Washington, DC 20001
Tel: (480)557-6151
Admissions: (480)557-6151
E-mail: audra.mcquarie@phoenix.edu
Web Site: http://www.phoenix.edu/
President/CEO: William Pepicello
Admissions: Audra McQuarie
Type: Comprehensive **Sex:** Coed **Admission Plans:** Open Admission; Deferred Admission **Application Fee:** $0.00 **H.S. Requirements:** High school diploma required; GED accepted **Costs Per Year:** Application fee: $0. Tuition: $13,200 full-time. Full-time tuition varies according to course level and course load. **Enrollment:** FT 14 **Faculty:** FT 3, PT 22 **Regional Accreditation:** North Central Association of Colleges and Schools

AMERICAN INTERCONTINENTAL UNIVERSITY SOUTH FLORIDA
2250 North Commerce Parkway, Ste. 100
Weston, FL 33326
Tel: (954)446-6100; Free: 888-603-4888
Admissions: 877-564-6248
Fax: (954)835-1020
Web Site: http://www.aiuniv.edu/
President/CEO: Stephen J. Tober
Admissions: Piera Brum
Type: Comprehensive **Sex:** Coed **Affiliation:** American InterContinental University **Admission Plans:** Deferred Admission **Application Deadline:** Rolling **Application Fee:** $50.00 **H.S. Requirements:** High school diploma required; GED accepted **Costs Per Year:** Application fee: $50. **Calendar System:** Miscellaneous, Summer Session Available **Enrollment:** FT 671, PT 127 **Regional Accreditation:** North Central Association of Colleges and Schools **Credit Hours For Degree:** 100 quarter hours, Associates; 200 quarter hours, Bachelors

ANGLEY COLLEGE
230 North Woodland Blvd.
Ste. 310
Deland, FL 32720
Tel: (386)740-1215
E-mail: admissions@angley.edu
Web Site: http://www.angley.edu/
President/CEO: Joseph T. Angley
Type: Two-Year College **Sex:** Coed **% Accepted:** 97 **Application Fee:** $25.00 **Calendar System:** Continuous

ARGOSY UNIVERSITY, SARASOTA
5250 17th St.
Sarasota, FL 34235
Tel: (941)379-0404; Free: 800-331-5995
Fax: (941)379-9464
Web Site: http://www.argosy.edu/sarasota/
Type: University **Sex:** Coed **Affiliation:** Education Management Corporation **Calendar System:** Semester **Regional Accreditation:** North Central Association of Colleges and Schools

ARGOSY UNIVERSITY, TAMPA
1403 North Howard Ave.
Tampa, FL 33607
Tel: (813)393-5290; Free: 800-850-6488
Fax: (813)246-4045
Web Site: http://www.argosy.edu/tampa/
President/CEO: Melanie Storms, PsyD
Type: University **Sex:** Coed **Affiliation:** Education Management Corporation **Calendar System:** Semester **Regional Accreditation:** North Central Association of Colleges and Schools **Professional Accreditation:** APA

THE ART INSTITUTE OF FORT LAUDERDALE
1799 Southeast 17th St.
Fort Lauderdale, FL 33316
Tel: (954)527-1799; Free: 800-275-7603
Admissions: (954)463-3000
Fax: (954)728-8637
Web Site: http://www.artinstitutes.edu/fortlauderdale/
President/CEO: Charles J. Nagele
Type: Four-Year College **Sex:** Coed **Affiliation:** Education Management Corporation **Calendar System:** Quarter **Professional Accreditation:** ACICS, ACF

THE ART INSTITUTE OF JACKSONVILLE
8775 Baypine Rd.
Jacksonville, FL 32256
Tel: (904)732-9393; Free: 800-924-1589
Admissions: (904)486-3000
Fax: (904)732-9423
Web Site: http://www.artinstitutes.edu/jacksonville/
Type: Four-Year College **Sex:** Coed **Affiliation:** Education Management Corporation **Regional Accreditation:** Southern Association of Colleges and Schools

THE ART INSTITUTE OF TAMPA
Parkside at Tampa Bay Park
4401 North Himes Ave., Ste. 150
Tampa, FL 33614
Tel: (813)873-2112; Free: (866)703-3277
Fax: (813)873-2171
Web Site: http://www.artinstitutes.edu/tampa/
Type: Four-Year College **Sex:** Coed **Affiliation:** Education Management Corporation **Calendar System:** Quarter **Regional Accreditation:** Southern Association of Colleges and Schools

ATI CAREER TRAINING CENTER (FORT LAUDERDALE)
2880 NW 62nd St.
Fort Lauderdale, FL 33309-9731
Tel: (954)973-4760
Fax: (954)973-6422
Web Site: http://www.aticareertraining.com/
President/CEO: Kimberly Stone
Type: Two-Year College **Sex:** Coed **% Accepted:** 100 **Application Fee:** $100.00 **H.S. Requirements:** High school diploma required; GED accepted **Scholarships:** Available **Calendar System:** Quarter **Professional Accreditation:** ACCSCT

ATI CAREER TRAINING CENTER (OAKLAND PARK)
3501 NW 9th Ave.
Oakland Park, FL 33309-9612
Tel: (954)563-5899
Web Site: http://www.aticareertraining.edu/
President/CEO: John F. Walsch
Type: Two-Year College **Sex:** Coed **Application Fee:** $100.00 **Professional Accreditation:** ACCSCT

ATI COLLEGE OF HEALTH
1395 NW 167th St., Ste. 200
Miami, FL 33169-5742
Tel: (305)628-1000
E-mail: admissions@atienterprises.edu

Web Site: http://www.aticareertraining.edu/
President/CEO: David Wagner
Type: Two-Year College **Sex:** Coed **Affiliation:** ATI Enterprises, Inc. of Florida **Admission Plans:** Open Admission **Application Deadline:** Rolling **Application Fee:** $100.00 **H.S. Requirements:** High school diploma required; GED accepted **Scholarships:** Available **Calendar System:** Semester, Summer Session Not available **Credit Hours For Degree:** 86 semester hours, Associates **Professional Accreditation:** ACCSCT, CARC

AVE MARIA UNIVERSITY
5050 Ave Maria Blvd.
Ave Maria, FL 34142
Tel: (239)280-2556; Free: 877-283-8648
Admissions: (239)280-2487
Fax: (239)352-2392
E-mail: brett.ormandy@avemaria.edu
Web Site: http://www.avemaria.edu/
President/CEO: Nicholas Healy, Jr.
Admissions: Brett Ormandy
Financial Aid: Anne Hart
Type: Comprehensive **Sex:** Coed **Affiliation:** Roman Catholic **Scores:** 100% SAT V 400+; 96% SAT M 400+; 44% ACT 18-23; 27% ACT 24-29 **% Accepted:** 56 **Admission Plans:** Early Admission; Early Decision Plan; Deferred Admission **Application Deadline:** Rolling **Application Fee:** $0.00 **H.S. Requirements:** High school diploma required; GED accepted **Costs Per Year:** Application fee: $0. Comprehensive fee: $25,725 includes full-time tuition ($17,165), mandatory fees ($580), and college room and board ($7980). College room only: $4355. Part-time tuition: $536.40 per credit hour. **Scholarships:** Available **Calendar System:** Semester, Summer Session Available **Enrollment:** FT 525, PT 7 **Faculty:** FT 56, PT 17 **Student-Faculty Ratio:** 10:1 **Exams:** SAT I or ACT. **% Receiving Financial Aid:** 63 **% Residing in College-Owned, -Operated, or -Affiliated Housing:** 90 **Library Holdings:** 200,000 **Credit Hours For Degree:** 128 credit hours, Bachelors **Professional Accreditation:** AALE **Intercollegiate Athletics:** Basketball M & W; Golf M; Soccer M & W; Volleyball W

THE BAPTIST COLLEGE OF FLORIDA
5400 College Dr.
Graceville, FL 32440-1898
Tel: (850)263-3261; Free: 800-328-2660
Fax: (850)263-7506
E-mail: skrichards@baptistcollege.edu
Web Site: http://www.baptistcollege.edu/
President/CEO: Dr. Thomas A. Kinchen
Admissions: Sandra Richards
Financial Aid: Angela Rathel
Type: Four-Year College **Sex:** Coed **Affiliation:** Southern Baptist **% Accepted:** 52 **Admission Plans:** Open Admission; Preferred Admission; Deferred Admission **Application Deadline:** August 11 **Application Fee:** $25.00 **H.S. Requirements:** High school diploma required; GED accepted **Costs Per Year:** Application fee: $25. Comprehensive fee: $12,566 includes full-time tuition ($8100), mandatory fees ($400), and college room and board ($4066). Full-time tuition and fees vary according to course load and location. Room and board charges vary according to board plan and housing facility. Part-time tuition: $270 per semester hour. Part-time tuition varies according to course load and location. **Scholarships:** Available **Calendar System:** Semester, Summer Session Available **Enrollment:** FT 414, PT 174 **Faculty:** FT 23, PT 41 **Student-Faculty Ratio:** 13:1 **Exams:** SAT I or ACT. **% Receiving Financial Aid:** 56 **% Residing in College-Owned, -Operated, or -Affiliated Housing:** 37 **Final Year or Final Semester Residency Requirement:** No **Library Holdings:** 117,277 **Regional Accreditation:** Southern Association of Colleges and Schools **Credit Hours For Degree:** 66 semester hours, Associates; 120 semester hours, Bachelors **Professional Accreditation:** NASM **Intercollegiate Athletics:** Golf M; Volleyball W

BARRY UNIVERSITY
11300 Northeast Second Ave.
Miami Shores, FL 33161-6695
Tel: (305)899-3000; Free: 800-695-2279
Admissions: (305)899-3100
Fax: (305)899-2971
E-mail: admissions@mail.barry.edu
Web Site: http://www.barry.edu/
President/CEO: Sr. Linda M. Bevilacqua, OP,PhD
Admissions: Magda Castineyra
Financial Aid: Dart Humeston
Type: University **Sex:** Coed **Affiliation:** Roman Catholic **Scores:** 92% SAT V 400+; 90% SAT M 400+; 69% ACT 18-23; 7% ACT 24-29 **% Accepted:** 62 **Admission Plans:** Early Admission; Deferred Admission **Application Deadline:** Rolling **Application Fee:** $30.00 **H.S. Requirements:** High school diploma required; GED accepted **Costs Per Year:** Application fee: $30. Comprehensive fee: $33,986 includes full-time tuition ($25,500) and college room and board ($8486). **Scholarships:** Available **Calendar System:** Semester, Summer Session Available **Enrollment:** FT 4,156, PT 942, Grad FT 2,033, Grad PT 1,715 **Faculty:** FT 341, PT 539 **Student-Faculty Ratio:** 18:1 **Exams:** SAT I or ACT. **% Receiving Financial Aid:** 76 **% Residing in College-Owned, -Operated, or -Affiliated Housing:** 37 **Library Holdings:** 316,517 **Regional Accreditation:** Southern Association of Colleges and Schools **Credit Hours For Degree:** 120 credits, Bachelors **ROTC:** Army, Air Force **Professional Accreditation:** AACSB, ACPE, AACN, AANA, ABA, ACA, AOTA, APMA, ATS, CSWE, JRCEPAT, MACTE **Intercollegiate Athletics:** Baseball M; Basketball M & W; Crew W; Golf M & W; Soccer M & W; Softball W; Tennis M & W; Volleyball W

BEACON COLLEGE
105 East Main St.
Leesburg, FL 34748
Tel: (352)787-7660
Fax: (352)787-0721
E-mail: ccorrad@beaconcollege.edu
Web Site: http://www.beaconcollege.edu/
President/CEO: Deborah Brodbeck
Admissions: Celia Corrad
Type: Four-Year College **Sex:** Coed **% Accepted:** 85 **Admission Plans:** Early Admission; Early Decision Plan; Deferred Admission **Application Deadline:** Rolling **Application Fee:** $50.00 **H.S. Requirements:** High school diploma required; GED accepted **Costs Per Year:** Application fee: $50. One-time mandatory fee: $400. Comprehensive fee: $36,860 includes full-time tuition ($27,810), mandatory fees ($900), and college room and board ($8150). College room only: $5150. Room and board charges vary according to board plan and housing facility. Part-time tuition: $610 per credit hour. **Calendar System:** Semester, Summer Session Available **Enrollment:** FT 128 **Faculty:** FT 20, PT 1 **Student-Faculty Ratio:** 6:1 **Exams:** SAT I or ACT. **% Residing in College-Owned, -Operated, or -Affiliated Housing:** 95 **Final Year or Final Semester Residency Requirement:** Yes **Library Holdings:** 59,879 **Regional Accreditation:** Southern Association of Colleges and Schools **Credit Hours For Degree:** 60 credits, Associates; 120 credits, Bachelors

BELHAVEN UNIVERSITY
Maitland 200 Ste. 165
2301 Maitland Center Parkway
Maitland, FL 32751
Tel: (407)804-1424; Free: 877-804-1424
Fax: (407)661-1732
Web Site: http://www.belhaven.edu/
Type: Comprehensive **Sex:** Coed **Affiliation:** Presbyterian **Costs Per Year:** Comprehensive fee: $22,900 includes full-time tuition ($16,780) and college room and board ($6120). Part-time tuition: $350 per hour. **Calendar System:** Semester **Regional Accreditation:** Southern Association of Colleges and Schools

BETHUNE-COOKMAN UNIVERSITY
640 Dr Mary McLeod Bethune Blvd
Daytona Beach, FL 32114-3099
Tel: (386)481-2000; Free: 800-448-0228
Admissions: (386)481-2600
Fax: (386)481-2010
E-mail: admissions@cookman.edu
Web Site: http://www.bethune.cookman.edu/
President/CEO: Dr. Trudie Kibbe Reed
Admissions: Aixa Melendez
Financial Aid: Joseph Coleman
Type: Comprehensive **Sex:** Coed **Affiliation:** Methodist **Scores:** 86% SAT V 400+; 69% SAT M 400+; 24% ACT 18-23; 1% ACT 24-29 **% Accepted:** 69 **Admission Plans:** Early Admission; Deferred Admission **Application Deadline:** June 30 **Application Fee:** $25.00 **H.S. Requirements:** High

school diploma required; GED accepted **Costs Per Year:** Application fee: $25. Comprehensive fee: $20,608 includes full-time tuition ($12,936) and college room and board ($7672). Full-time tuition varies according to course load. **Scholarships:** Available **Calendar System:** Semester, Summer Session Available **Enrollment:** FT 3,450, PT 144, Grad FT 11, Grad PT 9 **Faculty:** FT 202, PT 28 **Student-Faculty Ratio:** 16:1 **Exams:** SAT I or ACT. **% Receiving Financial Aid:** 94 **% Residing in College-Owned, -Operated, or -Affiliated Housing:** 54 **Library Holdings:** 164,874 **Regional Accreditation:** Southern Association of Colleges and Schools **Credit Hours For Degree:** 124 credit hours, Bachelors **ROTC:** Army, Air Force **Professional Accreditation:** NCATE, NLN **Intercollegiate Athletics:** Baseball M; Basketball M & W; Bowling W; Cheerleading W; Cross-Country Running M & W; Football M; Golf M & W; Softball W; Tennis M & W; Track and Field M & W; Volleyball W

BREVARD COMMUNITY COLLEGE
1519 Clearlake Rd.
Cocoa, FL 32922-6597
Tel: (321)632-1111
Admissions: (321)433-7271
Fax: (321)633-4565
E-mail: cocoaadmissions@brevardcc.edu
Web Site: http://www.brevardcc.edu/
President/CEO: Dr. James A. Drake
Admissions: Stephanie Burnette
Type: Two-Year College **Sex:** Coed **Affiliation:** Florida Community College System **% Accepted:** 100 **Admission Plans:** Open Admission; Early Admission **Application Deadline:** Rolling **Application Fee:** $30.00 **H.S. Requirements:** High school diploma required; GED accepted **Costs Per Year:** Application fee: $30. State resident tuition: $1622 full-time. Nonresident tuition: $6484 full-time. Mandatory fees: $526 full-time. **Scholarships:** Available **Calendar System:** Semester, Summer Session Available **Enrollment:** FT 6,125, PT 9,482 **Faculty:** FT 215, PT 822 **Student-Faculty Ratio:** 19:1 **Library Holdings:** 213,873 **Regional Accreditation:** Southern Association of Colleges and Schools **Credit Hours For Degree:** 60 credit hours, Associates **ROTC:** Army, Air Force **Professional Accreditation:** ADA, CARC, JRCERT, JRCEMT, MACTE, NAACLS **Intercollegiate Athletics:** Baseball M; Basketball M & W; Golf M; Softball W; Volleyball W

BROWARD COLLEGE
225 East Las Olas Blvd.
Fort Lauderdale, FL 33301-2298
Tel: (954)761-7450
Admissions: (954)201-7400
Fax: (954)761-7484
Web Site: http://www.broward.edu/
President/CEO: J. David Armstrong, Jr.
Admissions: Willie J. Alexander
Type: Two-Year College **Sex:** Coed **Affiliation:** Florida Community College System **Scores:** 73% SAT V 400+; 74% SAT M 400+ **% Accepted:** 100 **Admission Plans:** Open Admission; Preferred Admission; Early Admission; Deferred Admission **Application Fee:** $35.00 **H.S. Requirements:** High school diploma required; GED accepted **Costs Per Year:** Application fee: $35. State resident tuition: $1552 full-time, $64.65 per credit hour part-time. Nonresident tuition: $6210 full-time, $258.75 per credit hour part-time. Mandatory fees: $559 full-time, $23.30 per credit hour part-time. Full-time tuition and fees vary according to course level, course load, and degree level. Part-time tuition and fees vary according to course level, course load, and degree level. **Scholarships:** Available **Calendar System:** Trimester, Summer Session Available **Enrollment:** FT 10,006, PT 21,024 **Faculty:** FT 441, PT 1,120 **Library Holdings:** 200,000 **Regional Accreditation:** Southern Association of Colleges and Schools **Credit Hours For Degree:** 60 semester hours, Associates **ROTC:** Army **Professional Accreditation:** ADA, AHIMA, APTA, CARC, JRCEDMS, JRCEMT, JRCNMT, NASM, NLN **Intercollegiate Athletics:** Baseball M; Basketball M & W; Soccer W; Softball W; Swimming and Diving M & W; Tennis W; Volleyball W; Wrestling M

BROWN MACKIE COLLEGE—MIAMI
One Herald Plaza
Miami, FL 33132
Tel: (305)341-6600; Free: (866)505-0335
Web Site: http://www.brownmackie.edu/miami/
President/CEO: Julia Denniston
Type: Two-Year College **Sex:** Coed **Affiliation:** Education Management Corporation

CARLOS ALBIZU UNIVERSITY, MIAMI CAMPUS
2173 NW 99th Ave.
Miami, FL 33172-2209
Tel: (305)593-1223; Free: 888-672-3246
Fax: (305)592-7930
E-mail: mtriana@albizu.edu
Web Site: http://www.mia.albizu.edu/
President/CEO: Dr. Ileana Rodriguez-Garcia, EdD
Admissions: Mildred Triana
Financial Aid: Maria V. Chavez
Type: Comprehensive **Sex:** Coed **Affiliation:** Carlos Albizu University **% Accepted:** 88 **Admission Plans:** Open Admission **Application Deadline:** Rolling **Application Fee:** $25.00 **H.S. Requirements:** High school diploma required; GED accepted **Costs Per Year:** Application fee: $25. Tuition: $10,980 full-time, $305 per credit part-time. Mandatory fees: $744 full-time, $248 per term part-time. Full-time tuition and fees vary according to course load, degree level, and program. Part-time tuition and fees vary according to course load, degree level, and program. **Scholarships:** Available **Calendar System:** Trimester, Summer Session Available **Enrollment:** FT 176, PT 205, Grad FT 529, Grad PT 171 **Faculty:** FT 8, PT 55 **Student-Faculty Ratio:** 9:1 **% Receiving Financial Aid:** 94 **Library Holdings:** 32,724 **Regional Accreditation:** Middle State Association of Colleges and Schools **Credit Hours For Degree:** 120 credits, Bachelors **Professional Accreditation:** APA, ACBSP

CENTRAL FLORIDA COMMUNITY COLLEGE
PO Box 1388
Ocala, FL 34478-1388
Tel: (352)854-2322
Admissions: (352)237-2111
Fax: (352)237-3747
E-mail: jonesch@cf.edu
Web Site: http://www.cf.edu/
President/CEO: Dr. Charles Dassance
Admissions: Christy Jones
Type: Two-Year College **Sex:** Coed **Affiliation:** Florida Community College System **Admission Plans:** Open Admission; Early Admission **Application Deadline:** Rolling **Application Fee:** $20.00 **H.S. Requirements:** High school diploma required; GED accepted **Scholarships:** Available **Calendar System:** Semester, Summer Session Available **Enrollment:** FT 2,667, PT 3,543 **Faculty:** FT 114, PT 488 **Student-Faculty Ratio:** 15:1 **Library Holdings:** 82,112 **Regional Accreditation:** Southern Association of Colleges and Schools **Credit Hours For Degree:** 60 credit hours, Associates **Professional Accreditation:** APTA, JRCEMT, NLN **Intercollegiate Athletics:** Baseball M; Basketball M & W; Softball W; Tennis W

CENTRAL FLORIDA INSTITUTE
60522 US Hwy. 19 North
Ste. 200
Palm Harbor, FL 34684
Tel: (727)786-4707
Fax: (727)781-9421
Web Site: http://www.cfinstitute.com/
President/CEO: Olivia T. Fields
Admissions: Carol Bruno
Type: Two-Year College **Sex:** Coed **Admission Plans:** Open Admission **Application Fee:** $50.00 **Calendar System:** Continuous **Professional Accreditation:** ARCEST, ABHES

CENTURA INSTITUTE
6359 Edgewater Dr.
Orlando, FL 32810
Tel: (407)275-9696
Fax: (407)275-4499
Web Site: http://www.centurainstitute.edu/
President/CEO: Deborah Harrison
Type: Two-Year College **Sex:** Coed **Professional Accreditation:** ACCSCT

CHIPOLA COLLEGE
3094 Indian Circle
Marianna, FL 32446-3065

Tel: (850)526-2761
Admissions: (850)718-2233
Fax: (850)718-2388
E-mail: rehbergk@chipola.edu
Web Site: http://www.chipola.edu/
President/CEO: Dr. Gene Prough
Admissions: Kathy L. Rehberg
Type: Two-Year College **Sex:** Coed **Scores:** 76% SAT V 400+; 72% SAT M 400+; 56% ACT 18-23; 22% ACT 24-29 **% Accepted:** 78 **Admission Plans:** Open Admission; Early Admission **Application Deadline:** Rolling **Application Fee:** $0.00 **H.S. Requirements:** High school diploma required; GED accepted **Costs Per Year:** Application fee: $0. State resident tuition: $2550 full-time, $85 per semester hour part-time. Nonresident tuition: $7314 full-time, $244 per credit hour part-time. Full-time tuition varies according to degree level. Part-time tuition varies according to degree level. **Scholarships:** Available **Calendar System:** Semester, Summer Session Available **Enrollment:** FT 1,112, PT 1,229 **Faculty:** FT 54, PT 15 **Student-Faculty Ratio:** 24:1 **Final Year or Final Semester Residency Requirement:** No **Library Holdings:** 37,740 **Regional Accreditation:** Southern Association of Colleges and Schools **Credit Hours For Degree:** 60 semester hours, Associates; 120 semester hours, Bachelors **Intercollegiate Athletics:** Baseball M; Basketball M & W; Softball W

CITY COLLEGE (CASSELBERRY)
853 Semoran Blvd., Ste. 200
Casselberry, FL 32707-5342
Tel: (407)831-8466
Admissions: (352)335-4000
Fax: (407)831-1147
E-mail: kbowden@citycollege.edu
Web Site: http://www.citycollegeorlando.edu/
President/CEO: Steve Schwab
Admissions: Kimberly Bowden
Type: Two-Year College **Sex:** Coed **Application Fee:** $25.00 **H.S. Requirements:** High school diploma required; GED accepted **Calendar System:** Semester **Enrollment:** FT 217 **Faculty:** FT 2, PT 35 **Student-Faculty Ratio:** 17:1 **Exams:** Other. **Professional Accreditation:** ACICS

CITY COLLEGE (FORT LAUDERDALE)
2000 West Commercial Blvd.
Ste. 200
Fort Lauderdale, FL 33309
Tel: (954)492-5353
Fax: (954)491-1965
Web Site: http://www.citycollege.edu/
President/CEO: R. Esther Fike
Financial Aid: Ginger Ruback
Type: Two-Year College **Sex:** Coed **% Accepted:** 77 **Application Fee:** $25.00 **Scholarships:** Available **Calendar System:** Semester **Faculty:** FT 14, PT 47 **Professional Accreditation:** ACICS

CITY COLLEGE (GAINESVILLE)
2400 Southwest 13th St.
Gainesville, FL 32608
Tel: (352)335-4000
Fax: (352)335-4303
Web Site: http://www.citycollege.edu/
President/CEO: Steve Schwab
Type: Two-Year College **Sex:** Coed **% Accepted:** 100 **Application Fee:** $25.00 **Calendar System:** Semester **Professional Accreditation:** ACICS

CITY COLLEGE (MIAMI)
9300 South Dadeland Blvd.
Ste. PH
Miami, FL 33156
Tel: (305)666-9242
Fax: (305)666-9243
Web Site: http://www.citycollege.edu/
President/CEO: Maricela Howard
Type: Two-Year College **Sex:** Coed **% Accepted:** 79 **Application Fee:** $25.00 **Calendar System:** Semester **Professional Accreditation:** ACICS

CLEARWATER CHRISTIAN COLLEGE
3400 Gulf-to-Bay Blvd.
Clearwater, FL 33759-4595
Tel: (727)726-1153; Free: 800-348-4463
Fax: (727)726-8597
E-mail: admissions@clearwater.edu
Web Site: http://www.clearwater.edu/
President/CEO: Dr. Richard A. Stratton
Admissions: Dr. Keith Hutchison
Financial Aid: Ruth Strum
Type: Comprehensive **Sex:** Coed **Affiliation:** nondenominational **Scores:** 100% SAT V 400+; 100% SAT M 400+; 25% ACT 18-23; 75% ACT 24-29 **% Accepted:** 89 **Admission Plans:** Early Admission; Deferred Admission **Application Deadline:** Rolling **Application Fee:** $35.00 **H.S. Requirements:** High school diploma required; GED accepted **Costs Per Year:** Application fee: $35. Comprehensive fee: $21,450 includes full-time tuition ($14,710) and college room and board ($6740). College room only: $4140. Room and board charges vary according to board plan. Part-time tuition: $580 per credit hour. Tuition guaranteed not to increase for student's term of enrollment. **Scholarships:** Available **Calendar System:** Semester, Summer Session Available **Enrollment:** FT 555, PT 15, Grad PT 1 **Faculty:** FT 32, PT 17 **Student-Faculty Ratio:** 15:1 **Exams:** SAT I or ACT. **% Receiving Financial Aid:** 73 **% Residing in College-Owned, -Operated, or -Affiliated Housing:** 80 **Library Holdings:** 112,000 **Regional Accreditation:** Southern Association of Colleges and Schools **Credit Hours For Degree:** 64 credit hours, Associates; 128 credit hours, Bachelors **ROTC:** Army, Navy, Air Force **Intercollegiate Athletics:** Baseball M; Basketball M & W; Golf M & W; Soccer M & W; Softball W; Volleyball W

COLLEGE OF BUSINESS AND TECHNOLOGY
8991 Southwest 107th Ave.
Ste. 200
Miami, FL 33176
Tel: (305)273-4499
Fax: (305)273-5216
E-mail: admissions@cbt.edu
Web Site: http://www.cbt.edu/
President/CEO: Luis Llerena
Admissions: Ivis Delgado
Type: Two-Year College **Sex:** Coed **% Accepted:** 98 **Admission Plans:** Open Admission **Application Fee:** $25.00 **H.S. Requirements:** High school diploma required; GED accepted **Calendar System:** Semester, Summer Session Available **Enrollment:** FT 382 **Faculty:** FT 12, PT 16 **Student-Faculty Ratio:** 15:1 **Library Holdings:** 700,000 **Credit Hours For Degree:** 68 credits, Associates **Professional Accreditation:** COE

DAYTONA STATE COLLEGE
1200 West International Speedway Blvd.
Daytona Beach, FL 32120-2811
Tel: (386)506-3000
Admissions: (386)506-3050
E-mail: sanderk@daytonastate.edu
Web Site: http://www.daytonastate.edu/
President/CEO: Dr. D. Kent Sharples
Admissions: Karen Sanders
Type: Two-Year College **Sex:** Coed **Affiliation:** Florida Community College System **% Accepted:** 100 **Admission Plans:** Open Admission; Early Admission; Deferred Admission **Application Deadline:** Rolling **H.S. Requirements:** High school diploma required; GED accepted. For a small number of vocational programs: High school diploma required; GED not accepted **Costs Per Year:** One-time mandatory fee: $20. State resident tuition: $2253 full-time, $93.88 per credit hour part-time. Nonresident tuition: $8098 full-time, $337.40 per credit hour part-time. Mandatory fees: $60 full-time, $30 per term part-time. Full-time tuition and fees vary according to course load, degree level, and program. Part-time tuition and fees vary according to course load, degree level, and program. **Scholarships:** Available **Calendar System:** Semester, Summer Session Available **Enrollment:** FT 8,083, PT 9,696 **Faculty:** FT 316, PT 663 **Student-Faculty Ratio:** 19:1 **Library Holdings:** 91,000 **Regional Accreditation:** Southern Association of Colleges and Schools **Credit Hours For Degree:** 60 semester hours, Associates **ROTC:** Army, Air Force **Professional Accreditation:** ADA, AHIMA, AOTA, APTA, CARC, JRCEMT, NLN **Intercollegiate Athletics:** Baseball M; Basketball M & W; Golf W; Softball W; Swimming and Diving M & W

DEVRY UNIVERSITY (JACKSONVILLE)
5200 Belfort Rd.
Jacksonville, FL 32256-6040
Web Site: http://www.devry.edu/locations/campuses/loc_jacksonville.jsp
Type: Comprehensive **Sex:** Coed

DEVRY UNIVERSITY (MIAMI)
8700 West Flagler St., Ste. 100
Miami, FL 33174-2535
Tel: (305)229-4833
Web Site: http://www.devry.edu/
Type: Comprehensive **Sex:** Coed **Calendar System:** Semester **Regional Accreditation:** North Central Association of Colleges and Schools

DEVRY UNIVERSITY (MIRAMAR)
2300 Southwest 145th Ave.
Miramar, FL 33027-4150
Tel: (954)499-9700
Web Site: http://www.devry.edu/
President/CEO: Julio Torres
Type: Comprehensive **Sex:** Coed **Affiliation:** DeVry University **Admission Plans:** Deferred Admission **Application Deadline:** Rolling **Application Fee:** $50.00 **H.S. Requirements:** High school diploma required; GED accepted **Costs Per Year:** Application fee: $50. Tuition: $14,080 full-time, $550 per credit hour part-time. **Scholarships:** Available **Calendar System:** Semester **Enrollment:** FT 515, PT 586, Grad FT 18, Grad PT 142 **Faculty:** FT 21, PT 70 **Student-Faculty Ratio:** 17:1 **Exams:** ACT essay used for admission. SAT essay used for admission. ACT essay used for placement. SAT essay used for placement. **% Receiving Financial Aid:** 68 **Regional Accreditation:** North Central Association of Colleges and Schools **Credit Hours For Degree:** 66 credit hours, Associates; 122 credit hours, Bachelors

DEVRY UNIVERSITY (ORLANDO)
4000 Millenia Blvd.
Orlando, FL 32839
Tel: (407)370-3131
Web Site: http://www.devry.edu/
Financial Aid: Estrella Velazquez-Domenech
Type: Comprehensive **Sex:** Coed **Affiliation:** DeVry University **Admission Plans:** Early Admission; Deferred Admission **Application Deadline:** Rolling **Application Fee:** $50.00 **H.S. Requirements:** High school diploma required; GED accepted **Costs Per Year:** Application fee: $50. Tuition: $14,080 full-time, $550 per credit part-time. **Scholarships:** Available **Calendar System:** Semester, Summer Session Available **Enrollment:** FT 898, PT 831, Grad FT 30, Grad PT 170 **Faculty:** FT 27, PT 181 **Student-Faculty Ratio:** 14:1 **Exams:** ACT essay used for admission. SAT essay used for admission. ACT essay used for placement. SAT essay used for placement. **% Receiving Financial Aid:** 73 **Regional Accreditation:** North Central Association of Colleges and Schools **Credit Hours For Degree:** 67 credit hours, Associates; 122 credit hours, Bachelors

DEVRY UNIVERSITY (TAMPA)
3030 North Rocky Point Dr. West, Ste. 100
Tampa, FL 33607-5901
Tel: (813)288-8994
Fax: (813)288-8980
Web Site: http://www.devry.edu/
Type: Comprehensive **Sex:** Coed **Calendar System:** Semester **Regional Accreditation:** North Central Association of Colleges and Schools

ECKERD COLLEGE
4200 54th Ave. South
St. Petersburg, FL 33711
Tel: (727)867-1166; Free: 800-456-9009
Admissions: (727)864-8331
Fax: (727)866-2304
E-mail: admissions@eckerd.edu
Web Site: http://www.eckerd.edu/
President/CEO: Donald R. Eastman, III
Admissions: Donna Grosso
Financial Aid: Dr. Pat Garrett Watkins
Type: Four-Year College **Sex:** Coed **Affiliation:** Presbyterian **Scores:** 99% SAT V 400+; 100% SAT M 400+; 33% ACT 18-23; 50% ACT 24-29 **% Accepted:** 72 **Admission Plans:** Deferred Admission **Application Deadline:** Rolling **Application Fee:** $35.00 **H.S. Requirements:** High school diploma required; GED accepted **Costs Per Year:** Application fee: $35. Comprehensive fee: $42,554 includes full-time tuition ($32,932), mandatory fees ($296), and college room and board ($9326). College room only: $4716. Room and board charges vary according to board plan and housing facility. **Scholarships:** Available **Calendar System:** 4-1-4, Summer Session Available **Enrollment:** FT 1,845, PT 18 **Faculty:** FT 110, PT 52 **Student-Faculty Ratio:** 14:1 **Exams:** SAT I or ACT, SAT II. ACT essay not being used. SAT essay not being used. **% Residing in College-Owned, -Operated, or -Affiliated Housing:** 78 **Final Year or Final Semester Residency Requirement:** Yes **Library Holdings:** 169,029 **Regional Accreditation:** Southern Association of Colleges and Schools **Credit Hours For Degree:** 36 courses, Bachelors **ROTC:** Army, Air Force **Intercollegiate Athletics:** Baseball M; Basketball M & W; Golf M & W; Sailing M & W; Soccer M & W; Softball W; Tennis M & W; Volleyball M & W

EDISON STATE COLLEGE
8099 College Parkway
Fort Myers, FL 33919
Tel: (239)489-9300; Free: 800-749-2ECC
Fax: (239)489-9399
E-mail: registrar@edison.edu
Web Site: http://www.edison.edu/
President/CEO: Kenneth Walker
Admissions: Pat Armstrong
Type: Two-Year College **Sex:** Coed **Affiliation:** Florida Community College System **Admission Plans:** Open Admission; Early Admission; Deferred Admission **Application Deadline:** August 18 **Application Fee:** $30.00 **H.S. Requirements:** High school diploma required; GED accepted **Scholarships:** Available **Calendar System:** Semester, Summer Session Available **Enrollment:** FT 4,570, PT 8,437 **Exams:** SAT I or ACT. **Library Holdings:** 181,085 **Regional Accreditation:** Southern Association of Colleges and Schools **Credit Hours For Degree:** 60 credits, Associates; 120 credits, Bachelors **Professional Accreditation:** ADA, CARC, JRCECT, JRCERT, JRCEMT, NLN

EDWARD WATERS COLLEGE
1658 Kings Rd.
Jacksonville, FL 32209-6199
Tel: (904)470-8000; Free: 888-898-3191
Fax: (904)470-8039
E-mail: Lmorris@ewc.edu
Web Site: http://www.ewc.edu/
President/CEO: Dr. Claudette H. Williams
Admissions: Lonnie Morris
Financial Aid: Gabriel Mbomeh
Type: Four-Year College **Sex:** Coed **Affiliation:** African Methodist Episcopal **% Accepted:** 31 **Admission Plans:** Open Admission **Application Deadline:** Rolling **Application Fee:** $25.00 **H.S. Requirements:** High school diploma required; GED accepted **Costs Per Year:** Application fee: $25. Tuition: $9990 full-time. **Scholarships:** Available **Calendar System:** Semester, Summer Session Available **Enrollment:** FT 812, PT 19 **Faculty:** FT 29, PT 33 **Student-Faculty Ratio:** 13:1 **% Receiving Financial Aid:** 91 **Library Holdings:** 65,798 **Regional Accreditation:** Southern Association of Colleges and Schools **Credit Hours For Degree:** 120 semester hours, Bachelors **ROTC:** Army **Intercollegiate Athletics:** Basketball M & W; Tennis M & W; Track and Field M & W

EMBRY-RIDDLE AERONAUTICAL UNIVERSITY
600 South Clyde Morris Blvd.
Daytona Beach, FL 32114-3900
Tel: (386)226-6000; Free: 800-862-2416
Admissions: (386)226-6100
Fax: (386)226-7070
E-mail: dbadmit@erau.edu
Web Site: http://www.embryriddle.edu/
President/CEO: Dr. John P. Johnson
Financial Aid: Barbara Dryden
Type: Comprehensive **Sex:** Coed **Scores:** 92% SAT V 400+; 96% SAT M 400+; 42% ACT 18-23; 39% ACT 24-29 **% Accepted:** 81 **Admission Plans:** Deferred Admission **Application Deadline:** Rolling **Application Fee:** $50.00 **H.S. Requirements:** High school diploma required; GED accepted **Costs Per Year:** Application fee: $50. Comprehensive fee: $38,564 includes full-time tuition ($28,560), mandatory fees ($1164), and college room and board

($8840). College room only: $5300. Room and board charges vary according to board plan and housing facility. Part-time tuition: $1190 per credit hour. **Scholarships:** Available **Calendar System:** Semester, Summer Session Available **Enrollment:** FT 4,158, PT 272, Grad FT 373, Grad PT 132 **Faculty:** FT 242, PT 82 **Student-Faculty Ratio:** 16:1 **Exams:** SAT I or ACT. **% Receiving Financial Aid:** 61 **% Residing in College-Owned, -Operated, or -Affiliated Housing:** 37 **Final Year or Final Semester Residency Requirement:** No **Library Holdings:** 137,472 **Regional Accreditation:** Southern Association of Colleges and Schools **Credit Hours For Degree:** 63 credit hours, Associates; 120 credit hours, Bachelors **ROTC:** Army, Navy, Air Force **Professional Accreditation:** ABET, ACBSP, CAA **Intercollegiate Athletics:** Baseball M; Basketball M; Cheerleading M & W; Cross-Country Running M & W; Golf M & W; Soccer M & W; Tennis M & W; Track and Field M & W; Volleyball W

EMBRY-RIDDLE AERONAUTICAL UNIVERSITY WORLDWIDE
600 South Clyde Morris Blvd.
Daytona Beach, FL 32114-3900
Tel: (386)226-6910; Free: 800-522-6787
Admissions: (866)509-0743
Fax: (386)226-6984
E-mail: ecinfo@erau.edu
Web Site: http://www.embryriddle.edu/
President/CEO: Dr. John P. Johnson
Financial Aid: Frederic Ndiaye
Type: Comprehensive **Sex:** Coed **Admission Plans:** Deferred Admission **Application Deadline:** Rolling **Application Fee:** $50.00 **H.S. Requirements:** High school diploma required; GED accepted **Costs Per Year:** Application fee: $50. Tuition: $5520 full-time. **Scholarships:** Available **Calendar System:** Miscellaneous, Summer Session Not available **Enrollment:** FT 2,092, PT 9,809, Grad FT 1,695, Grad PT 2,579 **Faculty:** FT 122, PT 2,762 **% Receiving Financial Aid:** 25 **Library Holdings:** 137,472 **Regional Accreditation:** Southern Association of Colleges and Schools **Credit Hours For Degree:** 60 credit hours, Associates; 120 credit hours, Bachelors **Professional Accreditation:** ACBSP

EVEREST INSTITUTE (FORT LAUDERDALE)
1040 Bayview Dr.
Fort Lauderdale, FL 33304
Tel: (954)630-0066; Free: 888-741-4270
Fax: (954)630-0076
Web Site: http://www.everest.edu/
President/CEO: Edward Galizia
Type: Two-Year College **Sex:** Coed **Calendar System:** Continuous **Student-Faculty Ratio:** 7:1 **Professional Accreditation:** ABHES

EVEREST INSTITUTE (HIALEAH)
530 West 49th St.
Hialeah, FL 33012
Tel: (305)558-9500; Free: 888-741-4270
Fax: (305)558-4419
E-mail: dalonso@cci.edu
Web Site: http://www.everest.edu/
President/CEO: Michael Escalante
Admissions: Daniel Alonso
Type: Two-Year College **Sex:** Coed **% Accepted:** 67 **Calendar System:** Continuous **Professional Accreditation:** ARCEST, ABHES

EVEREST INSTITUTE (MIAMI)
111 Northwest 183rd St., Second Floor
Miami, FL 33169
Tel: (305)949-9500
Fax: (305)956-5758
Web Site: http://www.everest.edu/
President/CEO: Mario Miro
Type: Two-Year College **Sex:** Coed **Calendar System:** Continuous **Professional Accreditation:** ABHES

EVEREST INSTITUTE (MIAMI)
9020 Southwest 137th Ave.
Miami, FL 33186
Tel: (305)386-9900
Fax: (305)388-1740
Web Site: http://www.everest.edu/
President/CEO: Darrell Rhoten
Type: Two-Year College **Sex:** Coed **Calendar System:** Continuous **Student-Faculty Ratio:** 8:1 **Professional Accreditation:** ARCEST, ABHES

EVEREST UNIVERSITY (CLEARWATER)
2471 McMullen Booth Rd.
Clearwater, FL 33759
Tel: (727)725-2688; Free: 800-353-FMUS
Fax: (727)796-3722
E-mail: kbuskirk@cci.edu
Web Site: http://www.everest.edu/
President/CEO: John Buck
Admissions: Kevin Buskirk
Financial Aid: Will Scott
Type: Comprehensive **Sex:** Coed **Affiliation:** Corinthian Colleges, Inc. **Admission Plans:** Early Admission; Deferred Admission **Application Deadline:** Rolling **Application Fee:** $25.00 **H.S. Requirements:** High school diploma required; GED accepted **Scholarships:** Available **Calendar System:** Quarter, Summer Session Available **Exams:** Other, SAT I or ACT. **% Receiving Financial Aid:** 98 **Library Holdings:** 6,721 **Credit Hours For Degree:** 96 quarter hours, Associates; 192 quarter hours, Bachelors **Professional Accreditation:** ACICS, AAMAE

EVEREST UNIVERSITY (JACKSONVILLE)
8226 Phillips Hwy.
Jacksonville, FL 32256
Tel: (904)731-4949; Free: 888-741-4270
Fax: (904)731-0599
E-mail: rmanning@cci.edu
Web Site: http://www.everest.edu/
President/CEO: Peter Neigler
Admissions: Robin Manning
Type: Comprehensive **Sex:** Coed **Calendar System:** Quarter **Professional Accreditation:** ACICS

EVEREST UNIVERSITY (LAKELAND)
995 East Memorial Blvd.
Ste. 110
Lakeland, FL 33801
Tel: (863)686-1444
Fax: (863)688-9881
E-mail: psabol@cci.edu
Web Site: http://www.everest.edu/
President/CEO: Silvina Lamoureux
Admissions: Patricia Sabol
Financial Aid: Brian Jones
Type: Comprehensive **Sex:** Coed **Affiliation:** Corinthian Colleges, Inc. **Admission Plans:** Early Admission **Application Fee:** $25.00 **H.S. Requirements:** High school diploma required; GED accepted **Scholarships:** Available **Calendar System:** Quarter, Summer Session Available **Enrollment:** FT 343, PT 340 **Faculty:** FT 10, PT 26 **Student-Faculty Ratio:** 18:1 **Exams:** Other, SAT I or ACT. **% Receiving Financial Aid:** 86 **Library Holdings:** 5,000 **Credit Hours For Degree:** 96 quarter hours, Associates; 192 quarter hours, Bachelors **Professional Accreditation:** ACICS, AAMAE

EVEREST UNIVERSITY (MELBOURNE)
2401 North Harbor City Blvd.
Melbourne, FL 32935-6657
Tel: (321)253-2929
Fax: (321)255-2017
Web Site: http://www.everest.edu/
President/CEO: Mark W. Judge
Admissions: Timothy Alexander
Financial Aid: Ida C. Liska
Type: Comprehensive **Sex:** Coed **Affiliation:** Corinthian Colleges, Inc. **Admission Plans:** Deferred Admission **Application Deadline:** Rolling **H.S. Requirements:** High school diploma required; GED accepted **Scholarships:** Available **Calendar System:** Quarter, Summer Session Available **Exams:** Other. **Library Holdings:** 5,000 **Credit Hours For Degree:** 96 quarter hours, Associates; 192 quarter hours, Bachelors **Professional Accreditation:** ACICS, AAMAE

EVEREST UNIVERSITY (ORANGE PARK)
805 Wells Rd.
Orange Park, FL 32073
Tel: (904)264-9122
Fax: (904)264-9952
Web Site: http://www.everest.edu/
President/CEO: Bruce Jones
Type: Two-Year College **Sex:** Coed **% Accepted:** 69 **Calendar System:** Quarter **Professional Accreditation:** ACICS

EVEREST UNIVERSITY (ORLANDO)
9200 South Park Center Loop
Orlando, FL 32819
Tel: (407)851-2525; Free: 888-471-4270
Fax: (407)851-1477
Web Site: http://www.everest.edu/
President/CEO: John Buck
Admissions: Annette Cloin
Financial Aid: Sherri Williams
Type: Comprehensive **Sex:** Coed **Application Deadline:** Rolling **H.S. Requirements:** High school diploma required; GED accepted **Scholarships:** Available **Calendar System:** Quarter, Summer Session Not available **Library Holdings:** 5,113 **Credit Hours For Degree:** 96 quarter hours, Associates; 192 quarter hours, Bachelors **Professional Accreditation:** ACICS, AAMAE

EVEREST UNIVERSITY (ORLANDO)
5421 Diplomat Circle
Orlando, FL 32810-5674
Tel: (407)628-5870; Free: 800-628-5870
Fax: (407)628-2616
Web Site: http://www.everest.edu/
President/CEO: Michael Beaty
Admissions: Joann Derosa-Weber
Financial Aid: Linda Kaisrlik
Type: Comprehensive **Sex:** Coed **Affiliation:** Corinthian Colleges, Inc. **Admission Plans:** Deferred Admission **Application Deadline:** Rolling **Application Fee:** $0.00 **H.S. Requirements:** High school diploma required; GED accepted **Scholarships:** Available **Calendar System:** Quarter, Summer Session Available **Faculty:** FT 10, PT 86 **Student-Faculty Ratio:** 15:1 **Library Holdings:** 18,000 **Credit Hours For Degree:** 96 credit hours, Associates; 192 credit hours, Bachelors **Professional Accreditation:** ACICS

EVEREST UNIVERSITY (POMPANO BEACH)
225 North Federal Hwy.
Pompano Beach, FL 33062
Tel: (954)783-7339; Free: 800-468-0168
Fax: (954)568-2008
Web Site: http://www.everest.edu/
President/CEO: Dr. Ilia Martin
Admissions: Fran Heaston
Financial Aid: Sharon Scheible
Type: Comprehensive **Sex:** Coed **Affiliation:** Corinthian Colleges, Inc. **% Accepted:** 70 **Admission Plans:** Deferred Admission **Application Deadline:** Rolling **Application Fee:** $25.00 **H.S. Requirements:** High school diploma required; GED accepted **Scholarships:** Available **Calendar System:** Quarter, Summer Session Available **Enrollment:** FT 573, PT 709 **Faculty:** FT 15, PT 46 **Student-Faculty Ratio:** 19:1 **Exams:** Other, SAT I or ACT. **Library Holdings:** 14,500 **Credit Hours For Degree:** 96 quarter hours, Associates; 192 quarter hours, Bachelors **Professional Accreditation:** ACICS

EVEREST UNIVERSITY (TAMPA)
3924 Coconut Palm Dr.
Tampa, FL 33619
Tel: (813)621-0041; Free: 877-338-0068
E-mail: spointer@cci.edu
Web Site: http://www.everest.edu/
President/CEO: David Splitstone
Admissions: Shandretta Pointer
Financial Aid: Ginger Waymire
Type: Comprehensive **Sex:** Coed **Affiliation:** Corinthian Colleges, Inc. **Admission Plans:** Early Admission; Deferred Admission **Application Deadline:** Rolling **Application Fee:** $25.00 **H.S. Requirements:** High school diploma required; GED accepted. For ATB (Ability to Benefit) students who pass the entrance evaluation: High school diploma or equivalent not required **Scholarships:** Available **Calendar System:** Quarter, Summer Session Available **Enrollment:** FT 1,199, PT 4,457 **Faculty:** FT 26, PT 40 **Student-Faculty Ratio:** 17:1 **Exams:** Other, SAT I or ACT. **% Receiving Financial Aid:** 75 **Library Holdings:** 5,076 **Credit Hours For Degree:** 96 quarter hours, Associates; 192 quarter hours, Bachelors **Professional Accreditation:** ACICS, AAMAE

EVEREST UNIVERSITY (TAMPA)
3319 West Hillsborough Ave.
Tampa, FL 33614-5899
Tel: (813)879-6000
Fax: (813)871-2483
Web Site: http://www.everest.edu/
President/CEO: Mike Barlow
Admissions: Donnie Broughton
Financial Aid: Rod Kirkwood
Type: Comprehensive **Sex:** Coed **Affiliation:** Corinthian Colleges, Inc. **Admission Plans:** Deferred Admission **Application Deadline:** Rolling **Application Fee:** $25.00 **H.S. Requirements:** High school diploma required; GED accepted **Scholarships:** Available **Calendar System:** Quarter, Summer Session Available **Faculty:** FT 13, PT 48 **Student-Faculty Ratio:** 20:1 **Exams:** ACT, Other, SAT I. **% Receiving Financial Aid:** 85 **Library Holdings:** 4,000 **Credit Hours For Degree:** 96 quarter hours, Associates; 192 quarter hours, Bachelors **Professional Accreditation:** ACICS, AAMAE

EVERGLADES UNIVERSITY (ALTAMONTE SPRINGS)
887 East Altamonte Dr.
Altamonte Springs, FL 32701
Tel: (407)277-0311; Free: (866)289-1078
Fax: (407)482-9801
Web Site: http://www.evergladesuniversity.edu/
Type: Comprehensive **Sex:** Coed **Application Fee:** $50.00 **Professional Accreditation:** ACCSCT

EVERGLADES UNIVERSITY (BOCA RATON)
5002 T-Rex Ave., Ste. 100
Boca Raton, FL 33431
Tel: (561)912-1211; Free: 888-772-6077
Fax: (561)912-1191
E-mail: admissions-boca@evergladesuniversity.edu
Web Site: http://www.evergladesuniversity.edu/
President/CEO: Kristi Mollis
Admissions: Jean Graham
Financial Aid: Seeta Singh Moonilal
Type: Comprehensive **Sex:** Coed **Admission Plans:** Open Admission **Application Deadline:** Rolling **Application Fee:** $50.00 **H.S. Requirements:** High school diploma required; GED accepted **Scholarships:** Available **Calendar System:** Continuous, Summer Session Available **Enrollment:** FT 519, PT 125 **Faculty:** FT 64, PT 54 **Exams:** Other, SAT I or ACT. **Regional Accreditation:** Southern Association of Colleges and Schools **Professional Accreditation:** ACCSCT

EVERGLADES UNIVERSITY (SARASOTA)
6151 Lake Osprey Dr.
Sarasota, FL 34240
Tel: (941)907-2262; Free: (866)907-2262
Fax: (941)907-6634
E-mail: bbrewer@evergladesuniversity.edu
Web Site: http://www.evergladesuniversity.edu/
Admissions: Kathleen Cornett
Type: Comprehensive **Sex:** Coed **Calendar System:** Continuous **Professional Accreditation:** ACCSCT

FLAGLER COLLEGE
74 King St.
PO Box 1027
St. Augustine, FL 32085-1027
Tel: (904)829-6481; Free: 800-304-4208
Admissions: (904)819-6220
Fax: (904)826-0094
E-mail: admiss@flagler.edu
Web Site: http://www.flagler.edu/

President/CEO: Dr. William T. Abare, Jr.
Admissions: Marc Williar
Financial Aid: Sheia Pleasant
Type: Four-Year College **Sex:** Coed **Scores:** 100% SAT V 400+; 99% SAT M 400+; 59% ACT 18-23; 38% ACT 24-29 **% Accepted:** 44 **Admission Plans:** Early Admission; Early Decision Plan; Deferred Admission **Application Deadline:** March 1 **Application Fee:** $40.00 **H.S. Requirements:** High school diploma required; GED accepted **Costs Per Year:** Application fee: $40. Comprehensive fee: $20,520 includes full-time tuition ($13,330) and college room and board ($7190). Room and board charges vary according to board plan. Part-time tuition: $445 per credit hour. **Scholarships:** Available **Calendar System:** Semester, Summer Session Available **Enrollment:** FT 2,640, PT 76 **Faculty:** FT 95, PT 102 **Student-Faculty Ratio:** 20:1 **Exams:** SAT I or ACT. **% Receiving Financial Aid:** 52 **% Residing in College-Owned, -Operated, or -Affiliated Housing:** 40 **Library Holdings:** 187,945 **Regional Accreditation:** Southern Association of Colleges and Schools **Credit Hours For Degree:** 120 credit hours, Bachelors **Intercollegiate Athletics:** Baseball M; Basketball M & W; Cross-Country Running M & W; Golf M & W; Lacrosse M; Soccer M & W; Softball W; Tennis M & W; Volleyball M & W

FLORIDA AGRICULTURAL AND MECHANICAL UNIVERSITY

Tallahassee, FL 32307-3200
Tel: (850)599-3000
Admissions: (850)599-3796
Fax: (850)561-2428
E-mail: admission@famu.edu
Web Site: http://www.famu.edu/
President/CEO: James H. Ammons
Admissions: Barbara Cox
Financial Aid: Dr. Marcia D. Boyd
Type: University **Sex:** Coed **Affiliation:** State University System of Florida **Scores:** 82.9% SAT V 400+; 79.3% SAT M 400+; 55.7% ACT 18-23; 7.3% ACT 24-29 **% Accepted:** 61 **Admission Plans:** Preferred Admission; Early Admission; Deferred Admission **Application Deadline:** May 15 **Application Fee:** $30.00 **H.S. Requirements:** High school diploma required; GED accepted **Scholarships:** Available **Calendar System:** Semester, Summer Session Available **Enrollment:** FT 9,268, PT 976, Grad FT 1,710, Grad PT 320 **Faculty:** FT 590, PT 140 **Student-Faculty Ratio:** 18:1 **Exams:** SAT I or ACT. **% Receiving Financial Aid:** 75 **% Residing in College-Owned, -Operated, or -Affiliated Housing:** 70 **Final Year or Final Semester Residency Requirement:** No **Library Holdings:** 889,272 **Regional Accreditation:** Southern Association of Colleges and Schools **Credit Hours For Degree:** 60 semester hours, Associates; 120 semester hours, Bachelors **ROTC:** Army, Navy, Air Force **Professional Accreditation:** ABET, ACPhE, ACEJMC, ABA, AHIMA, AOTA, APTA, CARC, CEPH, CSWE, NAAB, NCATE, NLN **Intercollegiate Athletics:** Baseball M; Basketball M & W; Bowling W; Cheerleading M & W; Cross-Country Running M & W; Football M; Golf M & W; Softball W; Swimming and Diving M & W; Tennis M & W; Track and Field M & W; Volleyball W

FLORIDA ATLANTIC UNIVERSITY

777 Glades Rd., PO Box 3091
Boca Raton, FL 33431-0991
Tel: (561)297-3000; Free: 800-299-4FAU
Admissions: (561)297-3040
Web Site: http://www.fau.edu/
President/CEO: Dr. John Pritchett
Financial Aid: Carole Pfeilsticker
Type: University **Sex:** Coed **Affiliation:** State University System of Florida **Scores:** 99.8% SAT V 400+; 99.9% SAT M 400+; 60.1% ACT 18-23; 34.3% ACT 24-29 **% Accepted:** 46 **Admission Plans:** Early Admission; Deferred Admission **Application Deadline:** June 1 **Application Fee:** $30.00 **H.S. Requirements:** High school diploma required; GED accepted **Costs Per Year:** Application fee: $30. State resident tuition: $4187 full-time, $139.55 per credit hour part-time. Nonresident tuition: $17,532 full-time, $584.41 per credit hour part-time. Full-time tuition varies according to course load. Part-time tuition varies according to course load. College room and board: $9582. Room and board charges vary according to board plan and housing facility. **Scholarships:** Available **Calendar System:** Semester, Summer Session Available **Enrollment:** FT 13,096, PT 9,212, Grad FT 1,671, Grad PT 3,721 **Faculty:** FT 785, PT 498 **Student-Faculty Ratio:** 20:1 **Exams:** SAT I or ACT. **% Receiving Financial Aid:** 51 **% Residing in College-Owned, -Operated, or -Affiliated Housing:** 4 **Final Year or Final Semester Residency Requirement:** No **Library Holdings:** 1,330,817 **Regional Accreditation:** Southern Association of Colleges and Schools **Credit Hours For Degree:** 60 semester hours, Associates; 120 semester hours, Bachelors **ROTC:** Army, Air Force **Professional Accreditation:** AACSB, ABET, AACN, ACA, ACSP, ASLHA, CSWE, NASM, NASPAA, NCATE, NLN, TEAC **Intercollegiate Athletics:** Baseball M; Basketball M & W; Cheerleading M & W; Cross-Country Running M & W; Football M; Golf M & W; Soccer M & W; Softball W; Swimming and Diving M & W; Tennis M & W; Track and Field W; Volleyball W

FLORIDA CAREER COLLEGE

1321 Southwest 107 Ave.
Ste. 201B
Miami, FL 33174
Tel: (305)553-6065
Admissions: (954)535-8678
Fax: (305)225-0128
Web Site: http://www.careercollege.edu/
President/CEO: Pedro DeGuzman
Admissions: David Knobel
Type: Two-Year College **Sex:** Coed **Admission Plans:** Open Admission; Deferred Admission **Application Deadline:** Rolling **Application Fee:** $100.00 **H.S. Requirements:** High school diploma required; GED accepted **Scholarships:** Available **Calendar System:** Quarter, Summer Session Available **Library Holdings:** 1,200 **Credit Hours For Degree:** 90 credits, Associates **Professional Accreditation:** ACICS

FLORIDA CHRISTIAN COLLEGE

1011 Bill Beck Blvd.
Kissimmee, FL 34744-5301
Tel: (407)847-8966
Fax: (407)847-3925
E-mail: admissionsforms@fcc.edu
Web Site: http://www.fcc.edu/
President/CEO: William Behrman
Financial Aid: Sandra Peppard
Type: Four-Year College **Sex:** Coed **Affiliation:** Christian Churches and Churches of Christ **Admission Plans:** Early Admission; Deferred Admission **Application Deadline:** July 15 **Application Fee:** $35.00 **H.S. Requirements:** High school diploma required; GED accepted **Scholarships:** Available **Calendar System:** Semester, Summer Session Available **% Receiving Financial Aid:** 100 **Library Holdings:** 31,000 **Regional Accreditation:** Southern Association of Colleges and Schools **Credit Hours For Degree:** 65 credits, Associates; 135 credits, Bachelors **Professional Accreditation:** ABHE

FLORIDA COLLEGE

119 North Glen Arven Ave.
Temple Terrace, FL 33617
Tel: (813)988-5131; Free: 800-326-7655
Fax: (813)899-6772
E-mail: admissions@floridacollege.edu
Web Site: http://www.floridacollege.edu/
President/CEO: Dr. Harry E. Payne, IHM
Admissions: Shay Angelo
Financial Aid: Lisa McClister
Type: Four-Year College **Sex:** Coed **Scores:** 43% ACT 18-23; 33% ACT 24-29 **% Accepted:** 61 **Application Deadline:** August 1 **Application Fee:** $30.00 **H.S. Requirements:** High school diploma required; GED accepted **Costs Per Year:** Application fee: $30. One-time mandatory fee: $150. Comprehensive fee: $18,590 includes full-time tuition ($11,400), mandatory fees ($750), and college room and board ($6440). Room and board charges vary according to board plan and housing facility. Part-time tuition: $450 per credit hour. Part-time tuition varies according to course load. **Scholarships:** Available **Calendar System:** Semester, Summer Session Available **Enrollment:** FT 452, PT 15 **Faculty:** FT 37, PT 17 **Student-Faculty Ratio:** 15:1 **Exams:** SAT I or ACT. ACT essay not being used. SAT essay not being used. **% Receiving Financial Aid:** 54 **% Residing in College-Owned, -Operated, or -Affiliated Housing:** 75 **Library Holdings:** 114,938 **Regional Accreditation:** Southern Association of Colleges and Schools **Credit Hours For Degree:** 64 semester hours, Associates; 124 semester hours, Bachelors **ROTC:** Army, Air Force **Intercollegiate Athletics:** Basketball M; Cheerleading W; Cross-Country Running M & W; Volleyball W

FLORIDA COLLEGE OF NATURAL HEALTH (BRADENTON)
616 67th St. Circle East
Bradenton, FL 34208
Tel: (941)744-1244; Free: 800-966-7117
Fax: (941)744-1242
Web Site: http://www.fcnh.com/
President/CEO: Stephen Lazarus
Type: Two-Year College **Sex:** Coed **Professional Accreditation:** ACCSCT

FLORIDA COLLEGE OF NATURAL HEALTH (MAITLAND)
2600 Lake Lucien Dr.
Ste. 140
Maitland, FL 32751
Tel: (407)261-0319; Free: 800-393-7337
Fax: (407)261-0342
Web Site: http://www.fcnh.com/
President/CEO: Stephen Lazarus
Type: Two-Year College **Sex:** Coed **Professional Accreditation:** ACCSCT

FLORIDA COLLEGE OF NATURAL HEALTH (MIAMI)
7925 Northwest 12th St.
Ste. 201
Miami, FL 33126
Tel: (305)597-9599; Free: 800-599-9599
Fax: (305)597-9110
E-mail: miami@fcnh.com
Web Site: http://www.fcnh.com/
President/CEO: Stephen Lazarus
Admissions: Lissette Vidal
Type: Two-Year College **Sex:** Coed **Professional Accreditation:** ACCSCT

FLORIDA COLLEGE OF NATURAL HEALTH (POMPANO BEACH)
2001 West Sample Rd.
Ste. 100
Pompano Beach, FL 33064
Tel: (954)975-6400; Free: 800-541-9299
Fax: (954)975-9633
Web Site: http://www.fcnh.com/
President/CEO: Stephen Lazarus
Type: Two-Year College **Sex:** Coed **Professional Accreditation:** ACCSCT

FLORIDA CULINARY INSTITUTE
2400 Metrocenter Blvd.
West Palm Beach, FL 33407
Tel: (561)688-2001
Admissions: (561)842-8324
E-mail: info@floridaculinary.com
Web Site: http://www.floridaculinary.com/
Admissions: David Conway
Type: Four-Year College **Sex:** Coed **Affiliation:** Lincoln Educational Services **Scholarships:** Available **Enrollment:** FT 600 **Professional Accreditation:** ACF, COE

FLORIDA GULF COAST UNIVERSITY
10501 FGCU Blvd. South
Fort Myers, FL 33965-6565
Tel: (239)590-1000; Free: 888-889-1095
Admissions: (239)590-7878
Fax: (239)590-7894
Web Site: http://www.fgcu.edu/
President/CEO: Wilson Bradshaw
Admissions: Marc Laviolette
Financial Aid: Jorge Lopez-Rosado
Type: Comprehensive **Sex:** Coed **Affiliation:** State University System of Florida **Scores:** 97% SAT V 400+; 98% SAT M 400+; 70% ACT 18-23; 23% ACT 24-29 **% Accepted:** 66 **Admission Plans:** Deferred Admission **Application Deadline:** June 1 **Application Fee:** $30.00 **H.S. Requirements:** High school diploma required; GED accepted **Costs Per Year:** Application fee: $30. State resident tuition: $4191 full-time. Nonresident tuition: $19,450 full-time. Mandatory fees: $1533 full-time. Full-time tuition and fees vary according to course load. College room and board: $7642. Room and board charges vary according to board plan. **Scholarships:** Available **Calendar System:** Semester, Summer Session Available **Enrollment:** FT 7,854, PT 1,859, Grad FT 456, Grad PT 935 **Faculty:** FT 348, PT 208 **Student-Faculty Ratio:** 22:1 **Exams:** SAT I and SAT II or ACT. **% Receiving Financial Aid:** 33 **% Residing in College-Owned, -Operated, or -Affiliated Housing:** 29 **Library Holdings:** 387,860 **Regional Accreditation:** Southern Association of Colleges and Schools **Credit Hours For Degree:** 60 credits, Associates; 120 credits, Bachelors **Professional Accreditation:** AACSB, AACN, AANA, ACA, AOTA, APTA, CSWE, NAACLS, NASPAA, NLN **Intercollegiate Athletics:** Baseball M; Basketball M & W; Cheerleading W; Cross-Country Running M & W; Golf M & W; Soccer M & W; Softball W; Swimming and Diving W; Tennis M & W; Volleyball W

FLORIDA HOSPITAL COLLEGE OF HEALTH SCIENCES
671 Winyah Dr.
Orlando, FL 32803
Tel: (407)303-7747; Free: 800-500-7747
Admissions: (407)303-7742
E-mail: katie.shaw@fhchs.edu
Web Site: http://www.fhchs.edu/
President/CEO: David E. Greenlaw
Admissions: Katie Shaw
Financial Aid: Starr Bender
Type: Comprehensive **Sex:** Coed **Scores:** 56% ACT 18-23; 12% ACT 24-29 **Admission Plans:** Open Admission **Application Deadline:** July 18 **Application Fee:** $20.00 **H.S. Requirements:** High school diploma required; GED accepted **Scholarships:** Available **Calendar System:** Semester, Summer Session Not available **Faculty:** FT 44, PT 40 **Exams:** SAT I or ACT. **Library Holdings:** 74,581 **Regional Accreditation:** Southern Association of Colleges and Schools **Credit Hours For Degree:** 60 credits, Associates; 120 credits, Bachelors **ROTC:** Air Force **Professional Accreditation:** AOTA, JRCEDMS, JRCERT, JRCNMT, NLN

FLORIDA INSTITUTE OF TECHNOLOGY
150 West University Blvd.
Melbourne, FL 32901-6975
Tel: (321)674-8000; Free: 800-888-4348
Admissions: (321)674-8030
Fax: (321)723-9468
E-mail: admission@fit.edu
Web Site: http://www.fit.edu/
President/CEO: Anthony J. Catanese
Admissions: Michael J. Perry
Financial Aid: Melissa Todd
Type: University **Sex:** Coed **Scores:** 99% SAT V 400+; 98% SAT M 400+; 31% ACT 18-23; 52% ACT 24-29 **% Accepted:** 74 **Admission Plans:** Early Admission; Deferred Admission **Application Deadline:** Rolling **Application Fee:** $50.00 **H.S. Requirements:** High school diploma required; GED accepted **Costs Per Year:** Application fee: $50. Comprehensive fee: $42,150 includes full-time tuition ($31,020), mandatory fees ($500), and college room and board ($10,630). College room only: $6220. Full-time tuition and fees vary according to course load, location, and program. Room and board charges vary according to board plan and housing facility. Part-time tuition: $930 per credit hour. Part-time tuition varies according to course load, location, and program. **Scholarships:** Available **Calendar System:** Semester, Summer Session Available **Enrollment:** FT 3,929, PT 1,093, Grad FT 794, Grad PT 2,411 **Faculty:** FT 240, PT 338 **Exams:** SAT I or ACT. ACT essay not being used. SAT essay not being used. **% Receiving Financial Aid:** 61 **% Residing in College-Owned, -Operated, or -Affiliated Housing:** 54 **Library Holdings:** 342,791 **Regional Accreditation:** Southern Association of Colleges and Schools **Credit Hours For Degree:** 120 credits, Bachelors **ROTC:** Army **Professional Accreditation:** ABET, APA, CAA **Intercollegiate Athletics:** Baseball M; Basketball M & W; Crew W; Cross-Country Running M & W; Golf M & W; Soccer M & W; Softball W; Tennis M & W; Volleyball W

FLORIDA INTERNATIONAL UNIVERSITY
11200 Southwest 8th St.
Miami, FL 33199
Tel: (305)348-2000
Admissions: (305)348-3675
Fax: (305)348-3648
E-mail: admiss@fiu.edu
Web Site: http://www.fiu.edu/
President/CEO: Dr. Mark Rosenberg
Admissions: Valerire Peterson
Financial Aid: Francisco Valines
Type: University **Sex:** Coed **Affiliation:** State University System of Florida

Scores: 99.87% SAT V 400+; 99.93% SAT M 400+; 22.47% ACT 18-23; 70.78% ACT 24-29 **% Accepted:** 35 **Application Deadline:** Rolling **Application Fee:** $30.00 **H.S. Requirements:** High school diploma required; GED accepted **Costs Per Year:** Application fee: $30. State resident tuition: $4261 full-time, $142.04 per credit hour part-time. Nonresident tuition: $16,660 full-time, $555.34 per credit hour part-time. Mandatory fees: $319 full-time, $319. Full-time tuition and fees vary according to course load. Part-time tuition and fees vary according to course load. College room and board: $11,946. College room only: $7536. Room and board charges vary according to housing facility. **Scholarships:** Available **Calendar System:** Semester, Summer Session Available **Enrollment:** FT 19,513, PT 12,277, Grad FT 4,483, Grad PT 3,445 **Faculty:** FT 871, PT 683 **Student-Faculty Ratio:** 27:1 **Exams:** Other, SAT I or ACT, SAT I and SAT II or ACT, SAT II. SAT essay used for admission. **% Receiving Financial Aid:** 54 **% Residing in College-Owned, -Operated, or -Affiliated Housing:** 8 **Final Year or Final Semester Residency Requirement:** Yes **Library Holdings:** 2,095,131 **Regional Accreditation:** Southern Association of Colleges and Schools **Credit Hours For Degree:** 120 credit hours, Bachelors **ROTC:** Army, Air Force **Professional Accreditation:** AACSB, ABET, ACEJMC, AACN, AANA, ABA, ACCE, ACA, ADtA, AHIMA, AOTA, APTA, ASLA, ASLHA, ACEHSA, CEPH, CSWE, NASAD, NASM, NASPAA NAST, NCATE, NLN, NRPA **Intercollegiate Athletics:** Baseball M; Basketball M & W; Cross-Country Running M & W; Football M; Golf W; Soccer M & W; Softball W; Swimming and Diving W; Tennis W; Track and Field M & W; Volleyball W

FLORIDA KEYS COMMUNITY COLLEGE
5901 College Rd.
Key West, FL 33040-4397
Tel: (305)296-9081
Web Site: http://www.fkcc.edu/
President/CEO: Jill Landesberg-Boyle
Admissions: Cheryl A. Malsheimer
Type: Two-Year College **Sex:** Coed **Affiliation:** Florida Community College System **Admission Plans:** Open Admission; Early Admission; Deferred Admission **Application Deadline:** Rolling **Application Fee:** $20.00 **H.S. Requirements:** High school diploma required; GED accepted **Scholarships:** Available **Calendar System:** Trimester, Summer Session Available **Library Holdings:** 29,402 **Regional Accreditation:** Southern Association of Colleges and Schools **Credit Hours For Degree:** 60 credits, Associates

FLORIDA MEMORIAL UNIVERSITY
15800 NW 42nd Ave.
Miami-Dade, FL 33054
Tel: (305)626-3600; Free: 800-822-1362
Admissions: (305)626-3147
Web Site: http://www.fmuniv.edu/
President/CEO: Dr. Karl S. Wright
Admissions: Peggy Murray Martin
Financial Aid: Brian Phillip
Type: Comprehensive **Sex:** Coed **Affiliation:** Baptist Church **% Accepted:** 39 **Admission Plans:** Open Admission **Application Deadline:** July 1 **Application Fee:** $15.00 **H.S. Requirements:** High school diploma required; GED accepted **Scholarships:** Available **Calendar System:** Semester, Summer Session Available **Enrollment:** FT 1,516, PT 153 **Faculty:** FT 105, PT 68 **Student-Faculty Ratio:** 12:1 **Exams:** SAT I or ACT. **% Receiving Financial Aid:** 82 **Library Holdings:** 122,919 **Regional Accreditation:** Southern Association of Colleges and Schools **Credit Hours For Degree:** 124 credit hours, Bachelors **ROTC:** Army, Air Force **Professional Accreditation:** ACBSP, NCATE **Intercollegiate Athletics:** Baseball M; Basketball M & W; Cross-Country Running M & W; Track and Field M & W; Volleyball M & W

FLORIDA NATIONAL COLLEGE
4425 West 20th Ave.
Hialeah, FL 33012
Tel: (305)821-3333
Fax: (305)362-0595
E-mail: admissions@fnc.edu
Web Site: http://www.fnc.edu/
President/CEO: Maria Cristina Regueiro
Admissions: Guillermo Araya
Type: Four-Year College **Sex:** Coed **% Accepted:** 81 **Admission Plans:** Open Admission; Deferred Admission **Application Deadline:** Rolling **H.S. Requirements:** High school diploma required; GED accepted **Costs Per Year:** Tuition: $12,600 full-time, $525 per credit part-time. Mandatory fees: $570 full-time. Tuition guaranteed not to increase for student's term of enrollment. **Scholarships:** Available **Calendar System:** Semester, Summer Session Available **Enrollment:** FT 2,061, PT 750 **Faculty:** FT 45, PT 51 **Student-Faculty Ratio:** 26:1 **Library Holdings:** 33,857 **Regional Accreditation:** Southern Association of Colleges and Schools **Credit Hours For Degree:** 60 credits, Associates; 120 credits, Bachelors

THE FLORIDA SCHOOL OF MIDWIFERY
PO Box 5505
Gainesville, FL 32627-5505
Tel: (352)338-0766
Fax: (352)338-2013
E-mail: info@midwiferyschool.org
Web Site: http://www.midwiferyschool.org/
Type: Two-Year College **Sex:** Women **Calendar System:** Quarter **Professional Accreditation:** MEAC

FLORIDA SOUTHERN COLLEGE
111 Lake Hollingsworth Dr.
Lakeland, FL 33801-5698
Tel: (863)680-4111; Free: 800-274-4131
Admissions: (863)680-4131
Fax: (863)680-4120
E-mail: fscadm@flsouthern.edu
Web Site: http://www.flsouthern.edu/
President/CEO: Dr. Anne B. Kerr
Admissions: Bill C. Langston
Financial Aid: William L. Healy
Type: Comprehensive **Sex:** Coed **Affiliation:** United Methodist Church **Scores:** 100% SAT V 400+; 99% SAT M 400+; 61% ACT 18-23; 35% ACT 24-29 **% Accepted:** 69 **Admission Plans:** Early Admission; Early Decision Plan; Deferred Admission **Application Deadline:** March 1 **Application Fee:** $30.00 **H.S. Requirements:** High school diploma required; GED accepted **Costs Per Year:** Application fee: $30. Comprehensive fee: $32,972 includes full-time tuition ($24,112), mandatory fees ($550), and college room and board ($8310). College room only: $4700. Room and board charges vary according to board plan and housing facility. Part-time tuition: $700 per credit hour. Part-time mandatory fees: $50 per term. Part-time tuition and fees vary according to class time. **Scholarships:** Available **Calendar System:** Semester, Summer Session Available **Enrollment:** FT 1,832, PT 79, Grad FT 24, Grad PT 124 **Faculty:** FT 109, PT 107 **Student-Faculty Ratio:** 13:1 **Exams:** SAT I or ACT. ACT essay not being used. SAT essay not being used. **% Receiving Financial Aid:** 67 **% Residing in College-Owned, -Operated, or -Affiliated Housing:** 70 **Final Year or Final Semester Residency Requirement:** No **Library Holdings:** 175,213 **Regional Accreditation:** Southern Association of Colleges and Schools **Credit Hours For Degree:** 124 semester hours, Bachelors **ROTC:** Army, Air Force **Professional Accreditation:** AACN, JRCEPAT **Intercollegiate Athletics:** Baseball M; Basketball M & W; Cheerleading W; Cross-Country Running M & W; Golf M & W; Lacrosse M; Soccer M & W; Softball W; Swimming and Diving M & W; Tennis M & W; Track and Field M & W; Volleyball M & W

FLORIDA STATE COLLEGE AT JACKSONVILLE
501 West State St.
Jacksonville, FL 32202-4030
Tel: (904)632-3000
Admissions: (904)632-3131
Fax: (904)632-3393
E-mail: admissions@fccj.edu
Web Site: http://www.fscj.edu/
President/CEO: Dr. Steven R. Wallace
Admissions: Peter Biegel
Type: Two-Year College **Sex:** Coed **Affiliation:** Florida Community College System **Scores:** 94.94% SAT V 400+; 78.15% SAT M 400+; 33.95% ACT 18-23; 5.86% ACT 24-29 **% Accepted:** 48 **Admission Plans:** Open Admission; Early Admission; Deferred Admission **Application Deadline:** Rolling **Application Fee:** $15.00 **H.S. Requirements:** High school diploma required; GED accepted **Costs Per Year:** Application fee: $15. State resident tuition: $2044 full-time, $85.16 per credit hour part-time. Nonresident tuition: $7797 full-time, $324.89 per credit hour part-time. Mandatory fees: $525 full-time. Full-time tuition and fees vary according to degree level and program. Part-time tuition varies according to degree level and program. **Calendar System:** Semester, Summer Session Available

Enrollment: FT 8,080, PT 17,823 **Faculty:** FT 378, PT 780 **Student-Faculty Ratio:** 22:1 **Library Holdings:** 302,146 **Regional Accreditation:** Southern Association of Colleges and Schools **Credit Hours For Degree:** 60 semester hours, Associates; 120 semester hours, Bachelors **ROTC:** Navy **Professional Accreditation:** ABFSE, ACF, ADA, AHIMA, APTA, ACBSP, CARC, JRCEMT, NAACLS, NLN **Intercollegiate Athletics:** Baseball M; Basketball M & W; Softball W; Tennis W; Volleyball W

FLORIDA STATE UNIVERSITY
Tallahassee, FL 32306
Tel: (850)644-2525
Admissions: (850)644-6200
Fax: (850)644-0197
E-mail: admissions@admin.fsu.edu
Web Site: http://www.fsu.edu/
President/CEO: Dr. Eric J. Barron
Admissions: Janice V. Finney
Financial Aid: Darryl Marshall
Type: University **Sex:** Coed **Affiliation:** State University System of Florida **Scores:** 99.9% SAT V 400+; 99.9% SAT M 400+; 15.5% ACT 18-23; 71.4% ACT 24-29 **% Accepted:** 61 **Admission Plans:** Early Admission **Application Deadline:** January 19 **Application Fee:** $30.00 **H.S. Requirements:** High school diploma required; GED accepted **Costs Per Year:** Application fee: $30. State resident tuition: $2933 full-time, $97.77 per credit hour part-time. Nonresident tuition: $17,171 full-time, $579.25 per credit hour part-time. Mandatory fees: $1633 full-time, $53.10 per credit hour part-time, $20 per term part-time. College room and board: $8000. College room only: $4800. Room and board charges vary according to board plan and housing facility. **Scholarships:** Available **Calendar System:** Semester, Summer Session Available **Enrollment:** FT 27,705, PT 3,098, Grad FT 5,982, Grad PT 3,000 **Faculty:** FT 1,293, PT 329 **Student-Faculty Ratio:** 22:1 **Exams:** SAT I or ACT. ACT essay used for admission. SAT essay used for admission. **% Receiving Financial Aid:** 34 **% Residing in College-Owned, -Operated, or -Affiliated Housing:** 20 **Library Holdings:** 3,034,491 **Regional Accreditation:** Southern Association of Colleges and Schools **Credit Hours For Degree:** 60 semester hours, Associates; 120 semester hours, Bachelors **ROTC:** Army, Navy, Air Force **Professional Accreditation:** AACSB, ABET, AAMFT, AACN, AAFCS, ABA, ACA, ADtA, ACSP, ALA, APA, ASLHA, AALS, FIDER, CORE, CSWE, LCMEAMA, NASAD, NASD, NASM NASPAA, NAST, NCATE, NLN, NRPA **Intercollegiate Athletics:** Baseball M; Basketball M & W; Bowling M & W; Cheerleading M & W; Cross-Country Running M & W; Football M; Golf M & W; Rugby M & W; Soccer M & W; Softball W; Swimming and Diving M & W; Table Tennis M & W; Tennis M & W; Track and Field M & W; Volleyball M & W; Wrestling M & W

FLORIDA TECHNICAL COLLEGE (AUBURNDALE)
298 Havendale Blvd.
Auburndale, FL 33823
Tel: (863)967-8822
Fax: (863)967-4972
Web Site: http://www.flatech.edu/
Admissions: Charles Owens
Type: Two-Year College **Sex:** Coed **% Accepted:** 100 **Scholarships:** Available **Calendar System:** Quarter **Faculty:** FT 5, PT 3 **Professional Accreditation:** ACICS

FLORIDA TECHNICAL COLLEGE (DELAND)
1450 South Woodland Blvd., 3rd Floor
DeLand, FL 32720
Tel: (904)734-3303
Admissions: (386)734-3303
Fax: (904)734-5150
Web Site: http://www.flatech.edu/
Admissions: Bill Atkinson
Type: Two-Year College **Sex:** Coed **Application Fee:** $25.00 **Calendar System:** Quarter **Enrollment:** FT 260 **Faculty:** FT 11, PT 2 **Student-Faculty Ratio:** 22:1 **Professional Accreditation:** ACICS

FLORIDA TECHNICAL COLLEGE (JACKSONVILLE)
8711 Lone Star Rd.
Jacksonville, FL 32211
Tel: (904)724-2229
Fax: (904)720-0920
Web Site: http://www.flatech.edu/
President/CEO: Don Slayter
Admissions: Bryan Gulebiam
Type: Two-Year College **Sex:** Coed **Application Deadline:** Rolling **Application Fee:** $25.00 **Scholarships:** Available **Calendar System:** Quarter **Professional Accreditation:** ACICS

FLORIDA TECHNICAL COLLEGE (ORLANDO)
12689 Challenger Parkway
Orlando, FL 32826
Tel: (407)678-5600
Admissions: (407)447-7300
Fax: (407)678-1149
Web Site: http://www.flatech.edu/
President/CEO: Gabe Garces
Admissions: Jeanette E. Muschlitz
Type: Two-Year College **Sex:** Coed **Affiliation:** Fore Front Education, Inc. **Application Fee:** $25.00 **H.S. Requirements:** High school diploma required; GED accepted **Scholarships:** Available **Calendar System:** Quarter, Summer Session Not available **Credit Hours For Degree:** 90 quarter hours, Associates **Professional Accreditation:** ACICS

FORTIS COLLEGE
1573 West Fairbanks Ave.
Ste. 100
Winter Park, FL 32789
Tel: (407)843-3984
Fax: (407)843-9828
Web Site: http://www.fortis.edu/
President/CEO: Mark Gutmann
Type: Two-Year College **Sex:** Coed **Application Fee:** $50.00 **Professional Accreditation:** ACCSCT

FULL SAIL UNIVERSITY
3300 University Blvd.
Winter Park, FL 32792-7437
Tel: (407)679-6333; Free: 800-226-7625
Fax: (407)678-0070
E-mail: admissions@fullsail.com
Web Site: http://www.fullsail.edu/
President/CEO: Garry Jones
Admissions: Mary Beth Plank
Type: Comprehensive **Sex:** Coed **Admission Plans:** Open Admission **Application Deadline:** Rolling **Application Fee:** $150.00 **H.S. Requirements:** High school diploma required; GED accepted **Costs Per Year:** Application fee: $150. **Scholarships:** Available **Calendar System:** Miscellaneous, Summer Session Available **Student-Faculty Ratio:** 8:1 **% Receiving Financial Aid:** 56 **Library Holdings:** 2,531 **Professional Accreditation:** ACCSCT

GULF COAST COLLEGE
3910 US Hwy. 301 North
Ste. 200
Tampa, FL 33619-1259
Tel: (813)620-1446; Free: 888-729-7247
Web Site: http://gulfcoastcollege.edu/
President/CEO: Tracey Schoonmaker
Type: Two-Year College **Sex:** Coed **Admission Plans:** Open Admission **Application Fee:** $75.00 **H.S. Requirements:** High school diploma required; GED accepted **Scholarships:** Available **Calendar System:** Quarter **Student-Faculty Ratio:** 12:1 **Library Holdings:** 2,063 **Credit Hours For Degree:** 90 quarter hours, Associates **Professional Accreditation:** ACICS

GULF COAST COMMUNITY COLLEGE
5230 West Hwy. 98
Panama City, FL 32401-1058
Tel: (850)769-1551; Free: 800-311-3628
Fax: (850)913-3308
Web Site: http://www.gulfcoast.edu/
President/CEO: A. James Kerley
Admissions: Jackie Kuczenski
Type: Two-Year College **Sex:** Coed **Admission Plans:** Open Admission; Early Admission; Deferred Admission **Application Deadline:** Rolling **Application Fee:** $0.00 **H.S. Requirements:** High school diploma required; GED accepted **Scholarships:** Available **Calendar System:** Semester, Summer Session Available **Library Holdings:** 80,000 **Regional Accreditation:**

Southern Association of Colleges and Schools **Credit Hours For Degree:** 60 credit hours, Associates **Professional Accreditation:** ACF, ADA, APTA, CARC, JRCERT, JRCEMT, NLN **Intercollegiate Athletics:** Baseball M; Basketball M & W; Cheerleading M & W; Softball W; Volleyball W

HERZING COLLEGE
1595 South Semoran Blvd.
Ste. 1501
Winter Park, FL 32792
Tel: (407)380-6315
Admissions: (407)478-0500
Fax: (407)380-0269
Web Site: http://www.herzing.edu/
President/CEO: Heather Antonacci
Admissions: Tessie Uranga
Type: Two-Year College **Sex:** Coed **Scholarships:** Available **Calendar System:** Semester **Professional Accreditation:** ACICS

HIGH-TECH INSTITUTE
3710 Maguire Blvd.
Orlando, FL 32803
Tel: (407)893-7400; Free: (866)326-1985
Fax: (407)895-1804
Web Site: http://www.high-techinstitute.com/
President/CEO: David Champlain
Type: Two-Year College **Sex:** Coed **Application Fee:** $50.00 **Professional Accreditation:** ACCSCT

HILLSBOROUGH COMMUNITY COLLEGE
PO Box 31127
Tampa, FL 33631-3127
Tel: (813)253-7000
Admissions: (813)253-7032
Fax: (813)253-7196
E-mail: eolmo2@hccfl.edu
Web Site: http://www.hccfl.edu/
President/CEO: Gwendolyn W. Stephenson, PhD
Admissions: Edwin Olmo
Type: Two-Year College **Sex:** Coed **Affiliation:** Florida Community College System **% Accepted:** 100 **Admission Plans:** Open Admission; Early Admission **Application Deadline:** August 10 **Application Fee:** $20.00 **H.S. Requirements:** High school diploma required; GED accepted **Costs Per Year:** Application fee: $20. State resident tuition: $2097 full-time, $87.68 per credit hour part-time. Nonresident tuition: $7640 full-time, $318.35 per credit hour part-time. **Scholarships:** Available **Calendar System:** Semester, Summer Session Available **Enrollment:** FT 11,277, PT 15,687 **Faculty:** FT 283, PT 1,002 **Exams:** Other. **Final Year or Final Semester Residency Requirement:** No **Library Holdings:** 170,615 **Regional Accreditation:** Southern Association of Colleges and Schools **Credit Hours For Degree:** 60 credit hours, Associates **ROTC:** Army, Air Force **Professional Accreditation:** ACF, ADA, COptA, CARC, JRCEDMS, JRCERT, JRCEMT, JRCNMT, NLN **Intercollegiate Athletics:** Baseball M; Basketball M & W; Softball W; Tennis W; Volleyball W

HOBE SOUND BIBLE COLLEGE
PO Box 1065
Hobe Sound, FL 33475-1065
Tel: (561)546-5534; Free: 800-881-5534
Admissions: (772)546-5534
Fax: (561)545-1422
E-mail: hsbcuwin@aol.com
Web Site: http://www.hsbc.edu/
President/CEO: P. Daniel Stetler
Admissions: Ann French
Type: Four-Year College **Sex:** Coed **Affiliation:** nondenominational **Scores:** 75% SAT V 400+; 100% SAT M 400+; 70% ACT 18-23; 20% ACT 24-29 **% Accepted:** 92 **Admission Plans:** Open Admission; Preferred Admission; Early Admission **Application Deadline:** Rolling **Application Fee:** $25.00 **H.S. Requirements:** High school diploma required; GED accepted **Scholarships:** Available **Calendar System:** Semester, Summer Session Available **Faculty:** FT 10, PT 11 **Student-Faculty Ratio:** 7:1 **Exams:** SAT I or ACT. **% Residing in College-Owned, -Operated, or -Affiliated Housing:** 75 **Library Holdings:** 35,468 **Credit Hours For Degree:** 70 semester hours, Associates; 128 semester hours, Bachelors **Professional Accreditation:** ABHE

HODGES UNIVERSITY
2655 Northbrooke Dr.
Naples, FL 34119
Tel: (239)513-1122; Free: 800-466-8017
Fax: (239)513-9071
E-mail: rlampus@hodges.edu
Web Site: http://www.hodges.edu/
President/CEO: Dr. Terry McMahan
Admissions: Rita Lampus
Financial Aid: Joe Gilchrist
Type: Comprehensive **Sex:** Coed **% Accepted:** 94 **Admission Plans:** Deferred Admission **Application Deadline:** Rolling **Application Fee:** $20.00 **H.S. Requirements:** High school diploma required; GED accepted **Costs Per Year:** Application fee: $20. Tuition: $16,560 full-time, $460 per semester hour part-time. Mandatory fees: $380 full-time. **Scholarships:** Available **Calendar System:** Trimester, Summer Session Available **Enrollment:** FT 1,587, PT 451, Grad FT 37, Grad PT 217 **Faculty:** FT 58, PT 57 **Student-Faculty Ratio:** 23:1 **Exams:** ACT, Other, SAT I. **% Receiving Financial Aid:** 74 **Final Year or Final Semester Residency Requirement:** Yes **Library Holdings:** 38,008 **Regional Accreditation:** Southern Association of Colleges and Schools **Credit Hours For Degree:** 60 semester hour credits, Associates; 120 semester hour credits, Bachelors **Professional Accreditation:** AAMAE, AHIMA

INDIAN RIVER STATE COLLEGE
3209 Virginia Ave.
Fort Pierce, FL 34981-5596
Tel: (772)462-4700
Admissions: (772)462-7805
Fax: (772)462-4796
E-mail: spayne@ircc.edu
Web Site: http://www.irsc.edu/
President/CEO: Dr. Edwin R. Massey
Admissions: Steven Payne
Type: Two-Year College **Sex:** Coed **Affiliation:** Florida Community College System **Admission Plans:** Open Admission; Early Admission; Deferred Admission **Application Deadline:** Rolling **Application Fee:** $0.00 **H.S. Requirements:** High school diploma required; GED accepted **Scholarships:** Available **Calendar System:** Semester, Summer Session Available **Enrollment:** FT 5,966, PT 11,144 **Faculty:** FT 200, PT 643 **Student-Faculty Ratio:** 24:1 **Final Year or Final Semester Residency Requirement:** No **Library Holdings:** 88,397 **Regional Accreditation:** Southern Association of Colleges and Schools **Credit Hours For Degree:** 60 semester hours, Associates; 120 semester hours, Bachelors **Professional Accreditation:** AAMAE, ADA, AHIMA, APTA, CARC, JRCERT, JRCEMT, NAACLS, NLN **Intercollegiate Athletics:** Baseball M; Basketball M & W; Softball W; Swimming and Diving M & W; Volleyball W

INTERNATIONAL ACADEMY OF DESIGN & TECHNOLOGY
5104 Eisenhower Blvd.
Tampa, FL 33634-7350
Tel: (813)881-0007; Free: 800-ACA-DEMY
Fax: (813)881-0008
E-mail: admissions@academy.edu
Web Site: http://www.academy.edu/
President/CEO: Mark A. Page
Admissions: Debbie Love
Type: Four-Year College **Sex:** Coed **Affiliation:** Career Education Corporation **Admission Plans:** Open Admission; Early Admission; Deferred Admission **Application Deadline:** Rolling **Application Fee:** $50.00 **H.S. Requirements:** High school diploma required; GED accepted **Costs Per Year:** Application fee: $50. Comprehensive fee: $23,007 includes full-time tuition ($13,860), mandatory fees ($600), and college room and board ($8547). College room only: $4186. Part-time tuition: $385 per credit hour. Part-time mandatory fees: $200 per term. **Scholarships:** Available **Calendar System:** Quarter, Summer Session Available **Faculty:** FT 18, PT 180 **Student-Faculty Ratio:** 16:1 **Library Holdings:** 6,000 **Credit Hours For Degree:** 90 quarter hours, Associates; 180 quarter hours, Bachelors **Professional Accreditation:** ACICS, FIDER

ITT TECHNICAL INSTITUTE (FORT LAUDERDALE)
3401 South University Dr.
Fort Lauderdale, FL 33328-2021
Tel: (954)476-9300
Fax: (954)476-6889
Web Site: http://www.itt-tech.edu/
President/CEO: Nanell Lough
Type: Two-Year College **Sex:** Coed **Affiliation:** ITT Educational Services, Inc. **H.S. Requirements:** High school diploma required; GED accepted **Scholarships:** Available **Calendar System:** Quarter, Summer Session Not available **Professional Accreditation:** ACICS

ITT TECHNICAL INSTITUTE (FORT MYERS)
13500 Powers Ct.
Ste. 100
Fort Myers, FL 33912
Tel: (239)603-8700; Free: 877-485-5313
Web Site: http://www.itt-tech.edu/
President/CEO: Micehlle Lawrence
Type: Two-Year College **Sex:** Coed **Professional Accreditation:** ACICS

ITT TECHNICAL INSTITUTE (JACKSONVILLE)
7011 A.C. Skinner Parkway
Ste. 140
Jacksonville, FL 32256
Tel: (904)573-9100
Web Site: http://www.itt-tech.edu/
President/CEO: Scot Haynes
Type: Two-Year College **Sex:** Coed **Affiliation:** ITT Educational Services, Inc. **H.S. Requirements:** High school diploma required; GED accepted **Scholarships:** Available **Calendar System:** Quarter, Summer Session Not available **Professional Accreditation:** ACICS

ITT TECHNICAL INSTITUTE (LAKE MARY)
1400 South International Parkway
Lake Mary, FL 32746
Tel: (407)660-2900
Web Site: http://www.itt-tech.edu/
President/CEO: Melinda Matheus
Type: Two-Year College **Sex:** Coed **Affiliation:** ITT Educational Services, Inc. **H.S. Requirements:** High school diploma required; GED accepted **Scholarships:** Available **Calendar System:** Quarter, Summer Session Not available **Professional Accreditation:** ACICS

ITT TECHNICAL INSTITUTE (MIAMI)
7955 NW 12th St.
Miami, FL 33126
Tel: (305)477-3080
Web Site: http://www.itt-tech.edu/
President/CEO: Robert T. Hayward
Type: Two-Year College **Sex:** Coed **Affiliation:** ITT Educational Services, Inc. **H.S. Requirements:** High school diploma required; GED accepted **Scholarships:** Available **Calendar System:** Quarter, Summer Session Not available **Professional Accreditation:** ACICS

ITT TECHNICAL INSTITUTE (PINELLAS PARK)
3491 Gandy Blvd.
Ste. 101
Pinellas Park, FL 33781-2658
Tel: (727)209-4700; Free: (866)488-5084
Web Site: http://www.itt-tech.edu/
President/CEO: Sheryl Gunning
Type: Two-Year College **Sex:** Coed **Affiliation:** ITT Educational Services, Inc.

ITT TECHNICAL INSTITUTE (TALLAHASSEE)
2639 North Monroe St.
Tallahassee, FL 32303
Tel: (850)422-6300; Free: 877-230-3559
Web Site: http://www.itt-tech.edu/
Type: Two-Year College **Sex:** Coed **Professional Accreditation:** ACICS

ITT TECHNICAL INSTITUTE (TAMPA)
4809 Memorial Hwy.
Tampa, FL 33634-7151
Tel: (813)885-2244
Fax: (813)888-6078
Web Site: http://www.itt-tech.edu/
President/CEO: Dennis W. Alspaugh
Type: Two-Year College **Sex:** Coed **Affiliation:** ITT Educational Services, Inc. **H.S. Requirements:** High school diploma required; GED accepted **Scholarships:** Available **Calendar System:** Quarter, Summer Session Not available **Professional Accreditation:** ACICS

JACKSONVILLE UNIVERSITY
2800 University Blvd. North
Jacksonville, FL 32211
Tel: (904)256-8000; Free: 800-225-2027
Admissions: (904)256-7000
Fax: (904)256-7086
E-mail: admissions@ju.edu
Web Site: http://www.ju.edu/
President/CEO: Dr. Kerry D. Romesburg
Admissions: Lisa Hannasch
Financial Aid: Catherine Huntress
Type: Comprehensive **Sex:** Coed **Scores:** 97.3% SAT V 400+; 98% SAT M 400+; 61.6% ACT 18-23; 31% ACT 24-29 **% Accepted:** 54 **Admission Plans:** Early Admission; Deferred Admission **Application Deadline:** Rolling **H.S. Requirements:** High school diploma required; GED accepted **Costs Per Year:** Comprehensive fee: $34,360 includes full-time tuition ($25,300) and college room and board ($9060). College room only: $5300. Room and board charges vary according to board plan and housing facility. Part-time tuition: $840 per credit hour. **Scholarships:** Available **Calendar System:** Semester, Summer Session Available **Enrollment:** FT 2,316, PT 857, Grad FT 125, Grad PT 256 **Faculty:** FT 166, PT 105 **Student-Faculty Ratio:** 14:1 **Exams:** SAT I or ACT. SAT essay used for admission. SAT essay used for advising. SAT essay used for placement. **% Receiving Financial Aid:** 71 **% Residing in College-Owned, -Operated, or -Affiliated Housing:** 43 **Regional Accreditation:** Southern Association of Colleges and Schools **Credit Hours For Degree:** 128 credit hours, Bachelors **ROTC:** Navy **Professional Accreditation:** AACN, ADA, NASD, NASM, NLN **Intercollegiate Athletics:** Baseball M; Basketball M & W; Crew M & W; Cross-Country Running M & W; Football M; Golf M & W; Soccer M & W; Softball W; Tennis M & W; Track and Field W; Volleyball W

JOHNSON & WALES UNIVERSITY
1701 Northeast 127th St.
North Miami, FL 33181
Tel: (305)892-7000; Free: 800-232-2433
Admissions: (305)892-7002
Fax: (305)892-7030
E-mail: admissions.mia@jwu.edu
Web Site: http://www.jwu.edu/northmiami/
President/CEO: Donald G. McGregor, JD
Admissions: Jeff Greenip
Financial Aid: Lynn Robinson
Type: Four-Year College **Sex:** Coed **Affiliation:** Johnson & Wales University (RI) **Scores:** 74.4% SAT V 400+; 78.9% SAT M 400+ **% Accepted:** 60 **Admission Plans:** Early Admission; Deferred Admission **Application Deadline:** Rolling **Application Fee:** $0.00 **H.S. Requirements:** High school diploma required; GED accepted **Costs Per Year:** Application fee: $0. Comprehensive fee: $33,333 includes full-time tuition ($23,034), mandatory fees ($1395), and college room and board ($8904). Room and board charges vary according to board plan and housing facility. **Scholarships:** Available **Calendar System:** Quarter, Summer Session Available **Enrollment:** FT 1,977, PT 56 **Faculty:** FT 60, PT 32 **Student-Faculty Ratio:** 28:1 **Exams:** SAT I or ACT. **% Receiving Financial Aid:** 78 **% Residing in College-Owned, -Operated, or -Affiliated Housing:** 45 **Regional Accreditation:** New England Association of Schools and Colleges **Credit Hours For Degree:** 90 quarter credit hours, Associates; 180 quarter credit hours, Bachelors

JONES COLLEGE
5353 Arlington Expressway
Jacksonville, FL 32211
Tel: (904)743-1122

E-mail: lvaughn@jones.edu
Web Site: http://www.jones.edu/
President/CEO: Frank McCafferty
Admissions: Linda Vaughn
Financial Aid: Becky Davis
Type: Four-Year College **Sex:** Coed **% Accepted:** 69 **Admission Plans:** Open Admission **Application Deadline:** Rolling **Application Fee:** $0.00 **H.S. Requirements:** High school diploma required; GED accepted **Costs Per Year:** Application fee: $0. Tuition: $6600 full-time. Mandatory fees: $90 full-time. **Scholarships:** Available **Calendar System:** Trimester, Summer Session Available **Enrollment:** FT 263, PT 485 **Faculty:** FT 5, PT 109 **Student-Faculty Ratio:** 12:1 **Exams:** Other. **Library Holdings:** 34,000 **Credit Hours For Degree:** 60 credit hours, Associates; 120 credit hours, Bachelors **Professional Accreditation:** ACICS

KAPLAN COLLEGE, PEMBROKE PINES
10131 Pines Blvd.
Pembroke Pines, FL 33026
Tel: (954)885-3500
Web Site: http://www.kc-pembrokepines.com/
Type: Two-Year College **Sex:** Coed **H.S. Requirements:** High school diploma required; GED accepted **Professional Accreditation:** ACICS

KEISER CAREER COLLEGE—GREENACRES
6812 Forest Hill Blvd.
Ste. D-1
Greenacres, FL 33413
Tel: (561)433-2330
Web Site: http://www.keisercareer.edu/kcc2009/ga_campus.htm
President/CEO: Carole Fuller
Type: Two-Year College **Sex:** Coed **% Accepted:** 98 **Application Fee:** $55.00

KEISER UNIVERSITY
1500 NW 49th St.
Fort Lauderdale, FL 33309
Tel: (954)776-4456; Free: 888-KEISER-9
E-mail: admissions@keisercollege.edu
Web Site: http://www.keiseruniversity.edu/
President/CEO: Dr. Arthur Keiser
Admissions: LaFrawn Mays
Financial Aid: Judy Martin
Type: Comprehensive **Sex:** Coed **Admission Plans:** Open Admission **Application Deadline:** Rolling **Application Fee:** $50.00 **H.S. Requirements:** High school diploma required; GED accepted **Scholarships:** Available **Calendar System:** Miscellaneous, Summer Session Not available **Faculty:** FT 352, PT 485 **Student-Faculty Ratio:** 11:1 **Exams:** Other. **Regional Accreditation:** Southern Association of Colleges and Schools **Credit Hours For Degree:** 60 semester hours, Associates; 120 semester hours, Bachelors **Professional Accreditation:** ABHES, AOTA, APTA, JRCEDMS, JRCERT, NAACLS

KEY COLLEGE
225 East Dania Beach Blvd.
Dania, FL 33004
Tel: (954)581-2223; Free: 800-581-8292
Admissions: (954)923-4440
Fax: (954)583-9458
Web Site: http://www.keycollege.edu/
President/CEO: Ronald Dooley
Admissions: Ronald H. Dooley
Type: Two-Year College **Sex:** Coed **% Accepted:** 100 **Admission Plans:** Deferred Admission **Application Deadline:** Rolling **Application Fee:** $35.00 **H.S. Requirements:** High school diploma required; GED accepted **Scholarships:** Available **Calendar System:** Quarter, Summer Session Not available **Exams:** Other. **Credit Hours For Degree:** 90 credits, Associates **Professional Accreditation:** ACICS

LAKE CITY COMMUNITY COLLEGE
149 SE College Place
Lake City, FL 32025
Tel: (386)752-1822
Fax: (386)755-1521
E-mail: admissions@mail.lakecity.cc.fl.us
Web Site: http://www.lakecitycc.edu/
President/CEO: Dr. Charles Hall
Financial Aid: Bobbie Starling
Type: Two-Year College **Sex:** Coed **Affiliation:** Florida Community College System **Admission Plans:** Open Admission **Application Deadline:** Rolling **Application Fee:** $15.00 **H.S. Requirements:** High school diploma required; GED accepted. For cosmetology, heating and air conditioning, patient care assistant, phlebotomy, welding: NRH **Costs Per Year:** Application fee: $15. State resident tuition: $2447 full-time, $81.58 per credit hour part-time. Nonresident tuition: $9571 full-time, $319.03 per credit hour part-time. Full-time tuition varies according to course load and program. Part-time tuition varies according to course load and program. **Scholarships:** Available **Calendar System:** Semester, Summer Session Available **Enrollment:** FT 1,175, PT 1,674 **Faculty:** FT 62, PT 150 **Student-Faculty Ratio:** 16:1 **Library Holdings:** 42,000 **Regional Accreditation:** Southern Association of Colleges and Schools **Credit Hours For Degree:** 60 semester hours, Associates **Professional Accreditation:** APTA, JRCEMT, NAACLS, NLN

LAKE-SUMTER COMMUNITY COLLEGE
9501 US Hwy. 441
Leesburg, FL 34788-8751
Tel: (352)787-3747
Admissions: (352)365-3561
E-mail: admissinquiry@lscc.edu
Web Site: http://www.lscc.edu/
President/CEO: Dr. Charles R. Mojock
Admissions: Bonnie Yanick
Type: Two-Year College **Sex:** Coed **Affiliation:** Florida Community College System **% Accepted:** 100 **Admission Plans:** Open Admission **Application Deadline:** Rolling **Application Fee:** $25.00 **H.S. Requirements:** High school diploma required; GED accepted **Costs Per Year:** Application fee: $25. State resident tuition: $2556 full-time, $85.20 per credit hour part-time. Nonresident tuition: $9627 full-time, $320.90 per credit hour part-time. Full-time tuition varies according to course load. Part-time tuition varies according to course load. **Scholarships:** Available **Calendar System:** Semester, Summer Session Available **Enrollment:** FT 1,513, PT 2,987 **Faculty:** FT 74, PT 263 **Student-Faculty Ratio:** 15:1 **Library Holdings:** 82,908 **Regional Accreditation:** Southern Association of Colleges and Schools **Credit Hours For Degree:** 60 semester hours, Associates **Professional Accreditation:** AHIMA **Intercollegiate Athletics:** Baseball M; Softball W; Volleyball W

LE CORDON BLEU COLLEGE OF CULINARY ARTS, MIAMI
3221 Enterprise Way
Miramar, FL 33025
Tel: (954)628-4000; Free: 888-569-3222
Admissions: (954)628-4000
Web Site: http://www.miamiculinary.com/
President/CEO: Robert Kane
Type: Two-Year College **Sex:** Coed **Admission Plans:** Open Admission **Application Fee:** $50.00 **Student-Faculty Ratio:** 26:1 **Professional Accreditation:** ACCSCT

LINCOLN COLLEGE OF TECHNOLOGY
2410 Metro Centre Blvd.
West Palm Beach, FL 33407
Tel: (561)842-8324; Free: 800-826-9986
Fax: (561)842-9503
Web Site: http://www.lincolnedu.com/
President/CEO: Charles Halliday
Admissions: Kevin Cassidy
Type: Two-Year College **Sex:** Coed **Admission Plans:** Open Admission; Early Admission **Application Deadline:** Rolling **Application Fee:** $25.00 **H.S. Requirements:** High school diploma required; GED accepted **Scholarships:** Available **Calendar System:** Quarter, Summer Session Not available **Credit Hours For Degree:** 90 quarter hours, Associates **Professional Accreditation:** AAMAE, COE

LYNN UNIVERSITY
3601 North Military Trail
Boca Raton, FL 33431-5598
Tel: (561)237-7000; Free: 800-888-5966
Admissions: (561)237-7304
Fax: (561)241-3552
E-mail: jtamayo@lynn.edu

Web Site: http://www.lynn.edu/
President/CEO: Dr. Kevin M. Ross
Admissions: Juan Camilo Tamayo
Financial Aid: Chan Park
Type: Comprehensive **Sex:** Coed **Affiliation:** American College Dublin **Scores:** 85.46% SAT V 400+; 84.37% SAT M 400+; 52.25% ACT 18-23; 14.66% ACT 24-29 **% Accepted:** 72 **Admission Plans:** Early Admission; Deferred Admission **Application Deadline:** Rolling **Application Fee:** $35.00 **H.S. Requirements:** High school diploma required; GED accepted **Costs Per Year:** Application fee: $35. Comprehensive fee: $41,000 includes full-time tuition ($28,600), mandatory fees ($1500), and college room and board ($10,900). Room and board charges vary according to housing facility. Part-time tuition: $825 per credit hour. Part-time mandatory fees: $30 per term. Part-time tuition and fees vary according to class time and course load. **Scholarships:** Available **Calendar System:** Semester, Summer Session Available **Enrollment:** FT 1,576, PT 210, Grad FT 236, Grad PT 202 **Faculty:** FT 103, PT 57 **Student-Faculty Ratio:** 16:1 **Exams:** SAT I or ACT. ACT essay used for admission. SAT essay used for admission. ACT essay used for advising. SAT essay used for advising. ACT essay used for placement. SAT essay used for placement. **% Receiving Financial Aid:** 42 **% Residing in College-Owned, -Operated, or -Affiliated Housing:** 42 **Regional Accreditation:** Southern Association of Colleges and Schools **Credit Hours For Degree:** 120 credit hours, Bachelors **ROTC:** Air Force **Professional Accreditation:** NASM

MEDVANCE INSTITUTE
170 JFK Dr.
Atlantis, FL 33462
Tel: (561)304-3466; Free: 877-606-3382
Fax: (561)304-3471
Web Site: http://www.medvance.edu/
President/CEO: John Hopkins
Type: Two-Year College **Sex:** Coed **Application Fee:** $25.00 **Calendar System:** Quarter **Professional Accreditation:** ABHES, COE

MIAMI DADE COLLEGE
300 Northeast Second Ave.
Miami, FL 33132-2296
Tel: (305)237-3000
Admissions: (305)237-2103
Fax: (305)237-3761
E-mail: dbeltran@mdc.edu
Web Site: http://www.mdc.edu/
President/CEO: Dr. Eduardo J. Padron
Admissions: Dulce Beltran
Type: Two-Year College **Sex:** Coed **Affiliation:** Florida Community College System **Admission Plans:** Open Admission; Early Admission **Application Deadline:** Rolling **Application Fee:** $20.00 **H.S. Requirements:** High school diploma required; GED accepted **Costs Per Year:** Application fee: $20. One-time mandatory fee: $20. State resident tuition: $2028 full-time, $67.60 per credit hour part-time. Nonresident tuition: $8116 full-time, $270.53 per credit hour part-time. Mandatory fees: $558 full-time, $18.59 per credit hour part-time. Full-time tuition and fees vary according to course load. Part-time tuition and fees vary according to course load. **Scholarships:** Available **Calendar System:** Miscellaneous, Summer Session Available **Enrollment:** FT 21,768, PT 35,454 **Faculty:** FT 662, PT 1,548 **Student-Faculty Ratio:** 30:1 **Final Year or Final Semester Residency Requirement:** Yes **Library Holdings:** 363,432 **Regional Accreditation:** Southern Association of Colleges and Schools **Credit Hours For Degree:** 60 credit hours, Associates; 120 credit hours, Bachelors **ROTC:** Army, Air Force **Professional Accreditation:** ABFSE, ADA, AHIMA, APTA, COptA, CARC, JRCEDMS, JRCERT, JRCEMT, MEAC, NAACLS, NLN **Intercollegiate Athletics:** Baseball M; Basketball M & W; Softball W; Volleyball W

MIAMI INTERNATIONAL UNIVERSITY OF ART & DESIGN
1501 Biscayne Blvd., Ste. 100
Miami, FL 33132-1418
Tel: (305)428-5700; Free: 800-225-9023
Fax: (305)374-7946
Web Site: http://www.artinstitutes.edu/miami
President/CEO: Erika Fleming
Financial Aid: Mitzie Forrest
Type: Comprehensive **Sex:** Coed **Affiliation:** Education Management Corporation **Calendar System:** Quarter **Regional Accreditation:** Southern Association of Colleges and Schools

NEW COLLEGE OF FLORIDA
5800 Bay Shore Rd.
Sarasota, FL 34243
Tel: (941)359-4269
Admissions: (941)487-5000
Fax: (941)359-4435
E-mail: admissions@ncf.edu
Web Site: http://www.ncf.edu/
President/CEO: Dr. Gordon E. Michalson, Jr.
Financial Aid: Monica Baldwin
Type: Four-Year College **Sex:** Coed **Affiliation:** State University System of Florida **Scores:** 100% SAT V 400+; 100% SAT M 400+; 8% ACT 18-23; 48% ACT 24-29 **% Accepted:** 53 **Admission Plans:** Early Admission; Deferred Admission **Application Deadline:** April 15 **Application Fee:** $30.00 **H.S. Requirements:** High school diploma required; GED accepted **Costs Per Year:** Application fee: $30. State resident tuition: $4784 full-time. Nonresident tuition: $26,386 full-time. College room and board: $7783. College room only: $5252. Room and board charges vary according to board plan and housing facility. **Scholarships:** Available **Calendar System:** 4-1-4, Summer Session Not available **Enrollment:** FT 825 **Faculty:** FT 71, PT 23 **Student-Faculty Ratio:** 10:1 **Exams:** SAT I or ACT. ACT essay used for admission. SAT essay used for admission. **% Receiving Financial Aid:** 45 **% Residing in College-Owned, -Operated, or -Affiliated Housing:** 79 **Final Year or Final Semester Residency Requirement:** Yes **Library Holdings:** 285,897 **Regional Accreditation:** Southern Association of Colleges and Schools **Intercollegiate Athletics:** Sailing M & W

NEW WORLD SCHOOL OF THE ARTS
300 NE 2nd Ave.
Miami, FL 33132
Tel: (305)237-3135
Admissions: (305)237-7007
Fax: (305)237-3794
E-mail: nwsaadm@mdc.edu
Web Site: http://www.mdc.edu/nwsa/
President/CEO: Mercedes Quiroga
Admissions: Pamela Neumann
Type: Four-Year College **Sex:** Coed **Affiliation:** Miami Dade College and University of Florida **% Accepted:** 52 **Application Deadline:** Rolling **Application Fee:** $0.00 **H.S. Requirements:** High school diploma required; GED accepted **Calendar System:** Semester, Summer Session Available **Enrollment:** FT 416 **Faculty:** FT 22, PT 55 **Student-Faculty Ratio:** 5:1 **Credit Hours For Degree:** 72 credit hours, Associates; 136 credit hours, Bachelors **Professional Accreditation:** NASAD, NASD, NASM, NAST

NORTH FLORIDA COMMUNITY COLLEGE
325 Northwest Turner Davis Dr.
Madison, FL 32340
Tel: (850)973-2288
Admissions: (850)973-9450
Fax: (850)973-1696
Web Site: http://www.nfcc.edu/
President/CEO: John Grosskopf
Admissions: Bobby Scott
Type: Two-Year College **Sex:** Coed **Admission Plans:** Open Admission; Early Admission **Application Deadline:** Rolling **Application Fee:** $20.00 **H.S. Requirements:** High school diploma required; GED accepted **Costs Per Year:** Application fee: $20. State resident tuition: $2466 full-time, $82.20 per credit hour part-time. Nonresident tuition: $9240 full-time, $308 per credit hour part-time. Full-time tuition varies according to course load. Part-time tuition varies according to course load. **Scholarships:** Available **Calendar System:** Semester, Summer Session Available **Enrollment:** FT 593, PT 704 **Faculty:** FT 25, PT 19 **Student-Faculty Ratio:** 18:1 **Library Holdings:** 30,137 **Regional Accreditation:** Southern Association of Colleges and Schools **Credit Hours For Degree:** 60 semester hours, Associates

NORTHWEST FLORIDA STATE COLLEGE
100 College Blvd.
Niceville, FL 32578-1295
Tel: (850)678-5111

E-mail: registrar@nwfsc.edu
Web Site: http://www.nwfsc.edu/
President/CEO: Dr. Jill J. White
Admissions: Christine Bishop
Type: Two-Year College **Sex:** Coed **Affiliation:** Florida Community College System **Admission Plans:** Open Admission; Preferred Admission **Application Deadline:** Rolling **Application Fee:** $0.00 **H.S. Requirements:** High school diploma required; GED accepted. For for limited certificate programs: High school diploma or equivalent not required **Costs Per Year:** Application fee: $0. State resident tuition: $2272 full-time, $75.73 per credit hour part-time. Nonresident tuition: $9198 full-time, $306.59 per credit hour part-time. Full-time tuition varies according to course load, degree level, and reciprocity agreements. Part-time tuition varies according to course load, degree level, and reciprocity agreements. **Scholarships:** Available **Calendar System:** Semester, Summer Session Available **Faculty:** FT 92, PT 191 **Student-Faculty Ratio:** 15:1 **Exams:** Other. **Final Year or Final Semester Residency Requirement:** No **Library Holdings:** 106,383 **Regional Accreditation:** Southern Association of Colleges and Schools **Credit Hours For Degree:** 60 semester hours, Associates; 120 semester hours, Bachelors **ROTC:** Army **Professional Accreditation:** ADA **Intercollegiate Athletics:** Baseball M; Basketball M & W; Softball W

NORTHWOOD UNIVERSITY, FLORIDA CAMPUS

2600 North Military Trail
West Palm Beach, FL 33409-2911
Tel: (561)478-5500; Free: 800-458-8325
Fax: (561)640-3328
E-mail: fladmit@northwood.edu
Web Site: http://www.northwood.edu/
President/CEO: Keith A. Pretty, JD
Admissions: John (Jack) M. Letvinchuck
Financial Aid: Teresa A. Palmer
Type: Four-Year College **Sex:** Coed **Affiliation:** Northwood University (MI) **Scores:** 74% SAT V 400+; 79% SAT M 400+; 68% ACT 18-23 **% Accepted:** 61 **Admission Plans:** Early Admission; Deferred Admission **Application Deadline:** Rolling **Application Fee:** $25.00 **H.S. Requirements:** High school diploma required; GED accepted **Costs Per Year:** Application fee: $25. Comprehensive fee: $26,970 includes full-time tuition ($17,430), mandatory fees ($978), and college room and board ($8562). Full-time tuition and fees vary according to class time. Room and board charges vary according to board plan. Part-time tuition: $363 per credit hour. Part-time tuition varies according to class time. **Scholarships:** Available **Calendar System:** Quarter, Summer Session Available **Enrollment:** FT 604, PT 16 **Faculty:** FT 18, PT 45 **Student-Faculty Ratio:** 18:1 **Exams:** SAT I or ACT. **% Receiving Financial Aid:** 45 **% Residing in College-Owned, -Operated, or -Affiliated Housing:** 40 **Library Holdings:** 793 **Regional Accreditation:** North Central Association of Colleges and Schools **Credit Hours For Degree:** 90 credit hours, Associates; 180 credit hours, Bachelors **Intercollegiate Athletics:** Baseball M; Basketball M & W; Golf M & W; Soccer M & W; Softball W; Tennis M & W; Volleyball W

NOVA SOUTHEASTERN UNIVERSITY

3301 College Ave.
Fort Lauderdale, FL 33314-7796
Tel: (954)262-7300; Free: 800-541-NOVA
Admissions: (954)262-8000
Fax: (954)262-3967
E-mail: nsuinfo@nova.edu
Web Site: http://www.nova.edu/
President/CEO: Ray Ferrero, Jr.
Admissions: Maria Dillard
Financial Aid: Stephanie G. Brown, EdD
Type: University **Sex:** Coed **Scores:** 97% SAT V 400+; 96% SAT M 400+; 67% ACT 18-23; 20% ACT 24-29 **% Accepted:** 48 **Admission Plans:** Deferred Admission **Application Deadline:** Rolling **Application Fee:** $50.00 **H.S. Requirements:** High school diploma required; GED accepted **Costs Per Year:** Application fee: $50. Comprehensive fee: $29,460 includes full-time tuition ($20,550), mandatory fees ($550), and college room and board ($8360). Full-time tuition and fees vary according to class time and program. Room and board charges vary according to board plan and housing facility. Part-time tuition: $680 per credit hour. Part-time tuition varies according to class time, course load, and program. **Scholarships:** Available **Calendar System:** Trimester, Summer Session Available **Enrollment:** FT 3,879, PT 1,989, Grad FT 10,969, Grad PT 12,317 **Faculty:** FT 712, PT 1,001 **Exams:** SAT I or ACT. **% Receiving Financial Aid:** 75 **% Residing in College-Owned, -Operated, or -Affiliated Housing:** 9 **Library Holdings:** 850,095 **Regional Accreditation:** Southern Association of Colleges and Schools **Credit Hours For Degree:** 60 credits, Associates; 120 credits, Bachelors **Professional Accreditation:** ACPhE, AAMFT, AACN, ABA, ADA, AOTA, AOA, AOsA, APTA, APA, ASLHA, AALS, CEPH **Intercollegiate Athletics:** Baseball M; Basketball M & W; Cheerleading W; Crew W; Cross-Country Running M & W; Golf M & W; Soccer M & W; Softball W; Swimming and Diving M & W; Tennis W; Track and Field M; Volleyball W

ORLANDO CULINARY ACADEMY

8511 Commodity Circle
Ste. 100
Orlando, FL 32819
Tel: (407)888-4000; Free: 888-793-3222
Fax: (407)888-4019
Web Site: http://www.orlandoculinary.com/
President/CEO: Joe Hardiman
Type: Two-Year College **Sex:** Coed **Application Fee:** $50.00 **Professional Accreditation:** ACICS

PALM BEACH ATLANTIC UNIVERSITY

901 South Flagler Dr., PO Box 24708
West Palm Beach, FL 33416-4708
Tel: (561)803-2000; Free: 800-238-3998
Admissions: (561)803-2102
E-mail: admit@pba.edu
Web Site: http://www.pba.edu/
President/CEO: Lu Hardin
Admissions: Joe Sharp
Type: Comprehensive **Sex:** Coed **Affiliation:** nondenominational **Scores:** 97.28% SAT V 400+; 93.66% SAT M 400+; 54.72% ACT 18-23; 30.85% ACT 24-29 **% Accepted:** 69 **Admission Plans:** Early Admission; Early Action; Deferred Admission **Application Deadline:** Rolling **Application Fee:** $35.00 **H.S. Requirements:** High school diploma required; GED accepted **Costs Per Year:** Application fee: $35. Comprehensive fee: $30,920 includes full-time tuition ($22,400), mandatory fees ($300), and college room and board ($8220). College room only: $4570. Full-time tuition and fees vary according to course load, degree level, location, program, and reciprocity agreements. Room and board charges vary according to board plan and housing facility. Part-time tuition: $540 per credit hour. Part-time mandatory fees: $99 per term. Part-time tuition and fees vary according to course load, degree level, location, program, and reciprocity agreements. **Scholarships:** Available **Calendar System:** Semester, Summer Session Available **Enrollment:** FT 2,244, PT 190, Grad FT 566, Grad PT 260 **Faculty:** FT 157, PT 173 **Student-Faculty Ratio:** 14:1 **Exams:** SAT I or ACT. ACT essay used for placement. SAT essay used for placement. **% Receiving Financial Aid:** 75 **% Residing in College-Owned, -Operated, or -Affiliated Housing:** 55 **Library Holdings:** 160,714 **Regional Accreditation:** Southern Association of Colleges and Schools **Credit Hours For Degree:** 60 credit hours, Associates; 120 credit hours, Bachelors **ROTC:** Army **Professional Accreditation:** ACPhE, NASM **Intercollegiate Athletics:** Baseball M; Basketball M & W; Cheerleading M & W; Cross-Country Running M & W; Fencing M & W; Lacrosse M & W; Soccer M & W; Softball W; Tennis M & W; Volleyball W

PALM BEACH STATE COLLEGE

4200 Congress Ave.
Lake Worth, FL 33461-4796
Tel: (561)967-7222
Admissions: (561)868-3032
E-mail: enrollmt@palmbeachstate.edu
Web Site: http://www.palmbeachstate.edu/
President/CEO: Dr. Dennis P. Gallon
Admissions: Anne Guiler
Type: Two-Year College **Sex:** Coed **Affiliation:** Florida State College System **% Accepted:** 100 **Admission Plans:** Open Admission; Preferred Admission; Early Admission; Deferred Admission **Application Deadline:** August 20 **Application Fee:** $20.00 **H.S. Requirements:** High school diploma required; GED accepted **Costs Per Year:** Application fee: $20. One-time mandatory fee: $20. State resident tuition: $1980 full-time, $82.50 per credit hour part-time. Nonresident tuition: $7185 full-time, $299.36 per credit hour part-time. Mandatory fees: $10 full-time, $10 per term part-time. Full-time tuition and fees vary according to course level, course load, and student level. Part-time tuition and fees vary according to course level,

course load, and student level. **Scholarships:** Available **Calendar System:** Semester, Summer Session Available **Enrollment:** FT 10,725, PT 17,862 **Faculty:** FT 273, PT 1,083 **Student-Faculty Ratio:** 21:1 **Library Holdings:** 151,000 **Regional Accreditation:** Southern Association of Colleges and Schools **Credit Hours For Degree:** 60 semester hours, Associates **Professional Accreditation:** ADA, CARC, JRCERT, JRCEMT, MACTE, NLN **Intercollegiate Athletics:** Baseball M; Basketball M & W; Softball W; Volleyball M & W

PASCO-HERNANDO COMMUNITY COLLEGE
10230 Ridge Rd.
New Port Richey, FL 34654-5199
Tel: (727)847-2727
Fax: (727)816-3450
E-mail: bullard@phcc.edu
Web Site: http://www.phcc.edu/
President/CEO: Katherine M. Johnson, EdD
Admissions: Debra Bullard
Type: Two-Year College **Sex:** Coed **Affiliation:** Florida Community College System **Admission Plans:** Open Admission **Application Deadline:** Rolling **Application Fee:** $25.00 **H.S. Requirements:** High school diploma required; GED accepted **Costs Per Year:** Application fee: $25. State resident tuition: $2438 full-time, $81.28 per credit part-time. Nonresident tuition: $9272 full-time, $309.08 per credit part-time. **Scholarships:** Available **Calendar System:** Semester, Summer Session Available **Faculty:** FT 109, PT 287 **Student-Faculty Ratio:** 26:1 **Exams:** Other, SAT I and SAT II or ACT. **Regional Accreditation:** Southern Association of Colleges and Schools **Credit Hours For Degree:** 60 semester hours, Associates **ROTC:** Army **Professional Accreditation:** ADA, JRCEMT, NLN **Intercollegiate Athletics:** Baseball M; Basketball M; Cross-Country Running W; Softball W; Volleyball W

PENSACOLA JUNIOR COLLEGE
1000 College Blvd.
Pensacola, FL 32504-8998
Tel: (850)484-1000
Fax: (850)484-1826
Web Site: http://www.pjc.edu/
President/CEO: Dr. Ed Meadows
Admissions: Martha Caughey
Type: Two-Year College **Sex:** Coed **Affiliation:** Florida Community College System **Admission Plans:** Open Admission; Early Admission **Application Deadline:** August 30 **Application Fee:** $30.00 **H.S. Requirements:** High school diploma required; GED accepted **Costs Per Year:** Application fee: $30. State resident tuition: $3026 full-time, $84.06 per semester hour part-time. Nonresident tuition: $11,412 full-time, $317 per semester hour part-time. **Scholarships:** Available **Calendar System:** Semester, Summer Session Available **Enrollment:** FT 4,901, PT 6,697 **Regional Accreditation:** Southern Association of Colleges and Schools **Credit Hours For Degree:** 60 semester hours, Associates **ROTC:** Army **Professional Accreditation:** ACF, ADA, AHIMA, APTA, CARC, JRCERT, JRCEMT **Intercollegiate Athletics:** Baseball M; Basketball M & W; Softball W; Volleyball W

POLK STATE COLLEGE
999 Ave. H, NE
Winter Haven, FL 33881-4299
Tel: (863)297-1000
Admissions: (863)297-1010
Fax: (863)297-1060
E-mail: kbucklew@polk.edu
Web Site: http://www.polk.edu/
President/CEO: Eileen Holden, EdD
Admissions: Kathy Bucklew
Type: Two-Year College **Sex:** Coed **Affiliation:** Florida Community College System **Admission Plans:** Open Admission; Early Admission; Deferred Admission **Application Deadline:** Rolling **Application Fee:** $20.00 **H.S. Requirements:** High school diploma required; GED accepted **Costs Per Year:** Application fee: $20. State resident tuition: $2585 full-time, $86.10 per credit hour part-time. Nonresident tuition: $9596 full-time, $319.88 per credit hour part-time. Full-time tuition varies according to course load and degree level. Part-time tuition varies according to course load and degree level. **Scholarships:** Available **Calendar System:** Semester, Summer Session Available **Enrollment:** FT 3,262, PT 6,175 **Faculty:** FT 154, PT 356 **Student-Faculty Ratio:** 19:1 **Library Holdings:** 151,274 **Regional Accreditation:** Southern Association of Colleges and Schools **Credit Hours For Degree:** 60 credit hours, Associates **ROTC:** Army **Professional Accreditation:** AHIMA, AOTA, APTA, JRCERT, JRCEMT, NLN **Intercollegiate Athletics:** Baseball M; Basketball M; Soccer W; Softball W; Volleyball W

POLYTECHNIC UNIVERSITY OF THE AMERICAS—MIAMI CAMPUS
8180 Northwest 36th St.
Ste. 401
Miami, FL 33166
Tel: (305)592-7659; Free: 888-729-7659
Admissions: (305)418-4220
Web Site: http://www.pupr.edu/miami/
President/CEO: Ernesto Vazquez-Barquet
Financial Aid: Maria Victoria Shehadeh
Type: Comprehensive **Sex:** Coed **Application Fee:** $30.00 **Costs Per Year:** Application fee: $30. Tuition: $315 per credit hour part-time. Mandatory fees: $150 per term part-time. **Scholarships:** Available **Regional Accreditation:** Middle State Association of Colleges and Schools

POLYTECHNIC UNIVERSITY OF THE AMERICAS—ORLANDO CAMPUS
4800 Howell Branch Rd.
Winter Park, FL 32792
Tel: (407)677-5661; Free: 888-729-7659
Fax: (407)677-5082
Web Site: http://www.pupr.edu/orlando/
President/CEO: Ernest Vazquez-Barquet
Financial Aid: Maria Victoria Shehadeh
Type: Comprehensive **Sex:** Coed **Application Fee:** $30.00 **Costs Per Year:** Application fee: $30. Tuition: $315 per credit hour part-time. Mandatory fees: $50 per term part-time. tuition is $315 per credit hour for business and general courses, $345 per credit hour for engineering courses. **Scholarships:** Available **Regional Accreditation:** Middle State Association of Colleges and Schools

RASMUSSEN COLLEGE FORT MYERS
9160 Forum Corporate Parkway
Ste. 100
Fort Myers, FL 33905
Tel: (239)477-2100; Free: (866)344-0229
Fax: (239)477-2101
Web Site: http://www.rasmussen.edu/
President/CEO: Eric Whitehouse
Type: Two-Year College **Sex:** Coed **Costs Per Year:** Tuition: $365 per course part-time. **Regional Accreditation:** North Central Association of Colleges and Schools

RASMUSSEN COLLEGE OCALA
2221 Southwest 19th Ave. Rd.
Ocala, FL 34471
Tel: (352)629-1941; Free: 877-593-2783
Fax: (352)629-0926
Web Site: http://www.rasmussen.edu/
President/CEO: Pete Beasley
Type: Two-Year College **Sex:** Coed **Admission Plans:** Open Admission; Deferred Admission **Application Deadline:** Rolling **Application Fee:** $60.00 **H.S. Requirements:** High school diploma required; GED accepted **Costs Per Year:** Application fee: $60. Tuition: $365 per credit part-time. Part-time tuition varies according to program. **Scholarships:** Available **Calendar System:** Quarter, Summer Session Available **Library Holdings:** 2,400 **Credit Hours For Degree:** 90 credits, Associates **Professional Accreditation:** ACICS

RASMUSSEN COLLEGE PASCO COUNTY
2127 Grand Blvd.
Holiday, FL 34690
Tel: (727)942-0069; Free: 888-729-7247
Fax: (727)938-5709
Web Site: http://www.rasmussen.edu/
President/CEO: Claire Walker
Admissions: Claire L. Walker
Type: Two-Year College **Sex:** Coed **Application Deadline:** Rolling **Application Fee:** $60.00 **Costs Per Year:** Application fee: $60. Tuition: $365 per

credit part-time. Part-time tuition varies according to course level and program. **Scholarships:** Available **Exams:** Other. **Professional Accreditation:** ACICS

REMINGTON COLLEGE—LARGO CAMPUS
8550 Ulmerton Rd.
Largo, FL 33771
Tel: (727)532-1999; Free: 888-900-2343
Fax: (727)530-7710
E-mail: kathy.mccabe@remingtoncollege.edu
Web Site: http://www.remingtoncollege.edu/
President/CEO: Michael Seltzer
Admissions: Kathy McCabe
Type: Two-Year College **Sex:** Coed **Calendar System:** Continuous **Professional Accreditation:** ACCSCT

REMINGTON COLLEGE—TAMPA CAMPUS
2410 East Busch Blvd.
Tampa, FL 33612-8410
Tel: (813)932-0701
Fax: (813)935-7415
E-mail: raymond.johnson@remingtoncollege.edu
Web Site: http://www.remingtoncollege.edu/
President/CEO: Rosalie Lampone
Admissions: Raymond Johnson
Type: Two-Year College **Sex:** Coed **H.S. Requirements:** High school diploma required; GED accepted **Scholarships:** Available **Calendar System:** Quarter, Summer Session Not available **Library Holdings:** 4,100 **Credit Hours For Degree:** 99 quarter hours, Associates; 90 quarter hours, Bachelors **Professional Accreditation:** ACCSCT

RINGLING COLLEGE OF ART AND DESIGN
2700 North Tamiami Trail
Sarasota, FL 34234-5895
Tel: (941)351-5100; Free: 800-255-7695
Admissions: (941)359-7526
Fax: (941)359-7517
E-mail: admissions@ringling.edu
Web Site: http://www.ringling.edu/
President/CEO: Dr. Larry R. Thompson
Admissions: Tracy Stephanski
Financial Aid: Micah Jordan
Type: Four-Year College **Sex:** Coed **% Accepted:** 73 **Admission Plans:** Deferred Admission **Application Deadline:** Rolling **Application Fee:** $70.00 **H.S. Requirements:** High school diploma required; GED accepted **Costs Per Year:** Application fee: $70. Comprehensive fee: $38,940 includes full-time tuition ($27,620), mandatory fees ($850), and college room and board ($10,470). College room only: $5520. Full-time tuition and fees vary according to course load, program, and student level. Room and board charges vary according to board plan and housing facility. Part-time tuition: $1304 per semester hour. Part-time tuition varies according to course load, program, and student level. **Scholarships:** Available **Calendar System:** Semester, Summer Session Not available **Enrollment:** FT 1,268, PT 50 **Faculty:** FT 83, PT 65 **Student-Faculty Ratio:** 12:1 **% Receiving Financial Aid:** 88 **% Residing in College-Owned, -Operated, or -Affiliated Housing:** 53 **Final Year or Final Semester Residency Requirement:** Yes **Library Holdings:** 96,041 **Regional Accreditation:** Southern Association of Colleges and Schools **Credit Hours For Degree:** 123 semester hours, Bachelors **Professional Accreditation:** FIDER, NASAD

ROLLINS COLLEGE
1000 Holt Ave.
Winter Park, FL 32789-4499
Tel: (407)646-2000
Admissions: (407)646-2161
Fax: (407)646-2600
E-mail: admission@rollins.edu
Web Site: http://www.rollins.edu/
President/CEO: Dr. Lewis Duncan
Admissions: David Erdmann
Financial Aid: Steve Booker
Type: Comprehensive **Sex:** Coed **Scores:** 100.01% SAT V 400+; 99.72% SAT M 400+; 18.58% ACT 18-23; 61.06% ACT 24-29 **% Accepted:** 62 **Admission Plans:** Early Admission; Early Decision Plan; Deferred Admission **Application Deadline:** February 15 **Application Fee:** $40.00 **H.S. Requirements:** High school diploma required; GED accepted **Costs Per Year:** Application fee: $40. Comprehensive fee: $47,540 includes full-time tuition ($36,220) and college room and board ($11,320). College room only: $6660. **Scholarships:** Available **Calendar System:** Semester, Summer Session Not available **Enrollment:** FT 1,773, Grad FT 384, Grad PT 329 **Faculty:** FT 196, PT 40 **Student-Faculty Ratio:** 10:1 **Exams:** SAT I or ACT. **% Receiving Financial Aid:** 47 **% Residing in College-Owned, -Operated, or -Affiliated Housing:** 67 **Library Holdings:** 311,366 **Regional Accreditation:** Southern Association of Colleges and Schools **Credit Hours For Degree:** 35 courses, Bachelors **Professional Accreditation:** AACSB, ACA, NASM **Intercollegiate Athletics:** Baseball M; Basketball M & W; Crew M & W; Cross-Country Running M & W; Golf M & W; Lacrosse M & W; Sailing M & W; Soccer M & W; Softball W; Swimming and Diving M & W; Tennis M & W; Volleyball W

ST. JOHN VIANNEY COLLEGE SEMINARY
2900 Southwest 87th Ave.
Miami, FL 33165-3244
Tel: (305)223-4561
Web Site: http://www.sjvcs.edu/
President/CEO: Michael Carruthers
Admissions: Br. Edward Van Merrienboer
Financial Aid: Bonnie DeAngulo
Type: Four-Year College **Sex:** Coed **Affiliation:** Roman Catholic **% Accepted:** 100 **Admission Plans:** Preferred Admission **Application Deadline:** Rolling **Application Fee:** $0.00 **H.S. Requirements:** High school diploma required; GED accepted **Scholarships:** Available **Calendar System:** Semester, Summer Session Not available **Exams:** SAT I or ACT. **Library Holdings:** 54,000 **Regional Accreditation:** Southern Association of Colleges and Schools **Credit Hours For Degree:** 128 semester hours, Bachelors

ST. JOHNS RIVER COMMUNITY COLLEGE
5001 Saint Johns Ave.
Palatka, FL 32177-3897
Tel: (386)312-4200
Admissions: (386)312-4032
Fax: (386)312-4292
Web Site: http://www.sjrcc.edu/
President/CEO: Dr. R. L. McLendon, Jr.
Admissions: O'Neal Williams
Type: Two-Year College **Sex:** Coed **Admission Plans:** Open Admission; Early Admission **Application Deadline:** Rolling **Application Fee:** $30.00 **H.S. Requirements:** High school diploma required; GED accepted **Costs Per Year:** Application fee: $30. State resident tuition: $85 per semester hour part-time. Nonresident tuition: $319.50 per semester hour part-time. **Scholarships:** Available **Calendar System:** Semester, Summer Session Available **Faculty:** FT 111, PT 154 **Student-Faculty Ratio:** 24:1 **Library Holdings:** 56,925 **Regional Accreditation:** Southern Association of Colleges and Schools **Credit Hours For Degree:** 60 credit hours, Associates **Intercollegiate Athletics:** Baseball M; Basketball M; Softball W; Volleyball W

SAINT LEO UNIVERSITY
PO Box 6665
St. Leo, FL 33574-6665
Tel: (352)588-8200; Free: 800-334-5532
Admissions: (352)588-8283
Fax: (352)588-8257
E-mail: admissions@saintleo.edu
Web Site: http://www.saintleo.edu/
President/CEO: Dr. Arthur F. Kirk, Jr.
Admissions: Christine O'Donnell
Type: Comprehensive **Sex:** Coed **Affiliation:** Roman Catholic **Scores:** 95% SAT V 400+; 97% SAT M 400+; 71% ACT 18-23; 26% ACT 24-29 **% Accepted:** 76 **Admission Plans:** Early Admission; Deferred Admission **Application Deadline:** August 15 **Application Fee:** $35.00 **H.S. Requirements:** High school diploma required; GED accepted **Costs Per Year:** Application fee: $35. Comprehensive fee: $26,370 includes full-time tuition ($16,996), mandatory fees ($650), and college room and board ($8724). College room only: $4584. Room and board charges vary according to board plan and housing facility. **Scholarships:** Available **Calendar System:** Semester, Summer Session Available **Enrollment:** FT 1,640, PT 104, Grad

FT 2,343, Grad PT 40 **Faculty:** FT 106, PT 51 **Student-Faculty Ratio:** 15:1 **Exams:** SAT I or ACT. ACT essay used for admission. SAT essay used for admission. ACT essay used for advising. SAT essay used for advising. ACT essay used in place of application essay. SAT essay used in place of application essay. ACT essay used as a validity check on application essay. SAT essay used as a validity check on application essay. ACT essay used for placement. SAT essay used for placement. **% Receiving Financial Aid:** 72 **% Residing in College-Owned, -Operated, or -Affiliated Housing:** 72 **Final Year or Final Semester Residency Requirement:** No **Library Holdings:** 176,684 **Regional Accreditation:** Southern Association of Colleges and Schools **Credit Hours For Degree:** 62 semester hours, Associates; 122 semester hours, Bachelors **ROTC:** Army, Air Force **Professional Accreditation:** CSWE **Intercollegiate Athletics:** Baseball M; Basketball M & W; Cross-Country Running M & W; Golf M & W; Lacrosse M; Soccer M & W; Softball W; Swimming and Diving M & W; Tennis M & W; Volleyball W

ST. PETERSBURG COLLEGE
PO Box 13489
St. Petersburg, FL 33733-3489
Tel: (727)341-3600
Admissions: (727)341-3166
Fax: (727)341-3150
E-mail: information@spcollege.edu
Web Site: http://www.spjc.edu/
President/CEO: Dr. Thomas E. Furlong
Admissions: Susan Fell
Type: Four-Year College **Sex:** Coed **Admission Plans:** Open Admission; Early Admission **Application Deadline:** Rolling **Application Fee:** $40.00 **H.S. Requirements:** High school diploma required; GED accepted **Scholarships:** Available **Calendar System:** Semester, Summer Session Available **Enrollment:** FT 9,555, PT 19,727 **Faculty:** FT 309, PT 1,425 **Library Holdings:** 334,769 **Regional Accreditation:** Southern Association of Colleges and Schools **Credit Hours For Degree:** 60 credit hours, Associates; 120 credit hours, Bachelors **Professional Accreditation:** ABFSE, ADA, AHIMA, APTA, CARC, JRCEMT, NAACLS, NLN **Intercollegiate Athletics:** Baseball M; Basketball M & W; Softball W; Volleyball W

ST. THOMAS UNIVERSITY
16401 Northwest 37th Ave.
Miami Gardens, FL 33054-6459
Tel: (305)625-6000; Free: 800-367-9010
Fax: (305)628-6591
E-mail: signup@stu.edu
Web Site: http://www.stu.edu/
President/CEO: Msgr. Franklyn M. Casale
Admissions: Andre Lightbourne
Financial Aid: Anh Do
Type: Comprehensive **Sex:** Coed **Affiliation:** Roman Catholic **Scores:** 74.3% SAT V 400+; 71.3% SAT M 400+; 42.2% ACT 18-23; 1.1% ACT 24-29 **% Accepted:** 59 **Admission Plans:** Deferred Admission **Application Deadline:** Rolling **Application Fee:** $40.00 **H.S. Requirements:** High school diploma required; GED accepted **Costs Per Year:** Application fee: $40. Comprehensive fee: $28,206 includes full-time tuition ($21,690) and college room and board ($6516). Full-time tuition varies according to program. Room and board charges vary according to board plan and housing facility. Part-time tuition: $434 per credit hour. **Scholarships:** Available **Calendar System:** Semester, Summer Session Available **Enrollment:** FT 1,109, PT 67, Grad FT 921, Grad PT 379 **Faculty:** FT 100, PT 131 **Student-Faculty Ratio:** 13:1 **Exams:** SAT I or ACT. ACT essay not being used. SAT essay not being used. **% Receiving Financial Aid:** 72 **% Residing in College-Owned, -Operated, or -Affiliated Housing:** 19 **Regional Accreditation:** Southern Association of Colleges and Schools **Credit Hours For Degree:** 120 credits, Bachelors **Professional Accreditation:** ABA, AALS **Intercollegiate Athletics:** Baseball M; Cross-Country Running M & W; Golf M & W; Soccer M & W; Softball W; Tennis M & W; Volleyball W

SANFORD-BROWN INSTITUTE (FORT LAUDERDALE)
1201 West Cypress Creek Rd.
Fort Lauderdale, FL 33309
Tel: (954)733-8900
Admissions: (954)308-7400
Fax: (954)733-8994
E-mail: snelowet@sbjacksonville.com
Web Site: http://www.sbftlauderdale.com/
President/CEO: Michael Labelle
Admissions: Scott Nelowet
Type: Two-Year College **Sex:** Coed **Affiliation:** Career Education Corporation **% Accepted:** 29 **Application Deadline:** Rolling **Application Fee:** $0.00 **Faculty:** FT 25, PT 5 **Student-Faculty Ratio:** 10:1 **Library Holdings:** 4,000

SANFORD-BROWN INSTITUTE (JACKSONVILLE)
10255 Fortune Parkway
Ste. 501
Jacksonville, FL 32256
Tel: (904)363-6221
Admissions: (904)380-2912
Fax: (904)363-6824
E-mail: dneal@sbjacksonville.com
Web Site: http://www.sbjacksonville.com/
President/CEO: Scott Nelowet
Admissions: Denise Neal
Type: Two-Year College **Sex:** Coed **% Accepted:** 52 **Admission Plans:** Open Admission; Early Admission **Application Fee:** $25.00 **H.S. Requirements:** High school diploma required; GED accepted **Enrollment:** FT 358, PT 60 **Professional Accreditation:** ABHES, ACICS

SANFORD-BROWN INSTITUTE (TAMPA)
5701 East Hillsborough Ave.
Tampa, FL 33610
Tel: (813)393-4250; Free: 888-450-0333
Admissions: (813)621-0072
Fax: (813)626-0392
Web Site: http://www.sbtampa.com/
President/CEO: Steeve Dumerve
Type: Two-Year College **Sex:** Coed **Application Fee:** $25.00 **Professional Accreditation:** ACICS

SANTA FE COLLEGE
3000 Northwest 83rd St.
Gainesville, FL 32606
Tel: (352)395-5000
Admissions: (352)395-4177
Fax: (352)395-5581
E-mail: michael.hutley@sfcollege.edu
Web Site: http://www.sfcollege.edu/
President/CEO: Dr. Jackson N. Sasser, PhD
Admissions: Mike Hutley
Type: Four-Year College **Sex:** Coed **Affiliation:** Florida Community College System **Admission Plans:** Open Admission; Early Admission **Application Deadline:** Rolling **Application Fee:** $0.00 **H.S. Requirements:** High school diploma required; GED accepted **Costs Per Year:** Application fee: $0. State resident tuition: $2031 full-time. Nonresident tuition: $7620 full-time. Full-time tuition varies according to degree level. **Scholarships:** Available **Calendar System:** Semester, Summer Session Available **Enrollment:** FT 6,743, PT 8,053 **Faculty:** FT 254, PT 567 **Final Year or Final Semester Residency Requirement:** No **Library Holdings:** 81,832 **Regional Accreditation:** Southern Association of Colleges and Schools **Credit Hours For Degree:** 60 semester hours, Associates **ROTC:** Army, Air Force **Professional Accreditation:** ACCE, ADA, AHIMA, CARC, JRCERT, JRCEMT, JRCNMT, NLN **Intercollegiate Athletics:** Baseball M; Basketball M & W; Softball W

SCHILLER INTERNATIONAL UNIVERSITY
300 East Bay Dr.
Largo, FL 33770
Tel: (727)736-5082; Free: 800-336-4133
Admissions: (727)738-6365
Fax: (727)734-0359
E-mail: admissions@schiller.edu
Web Site: http://www.schiller.edu/
President/CEO: Dr. Geoffery Bannister
Admissions: Donald Trippe
Type: Comprehensive **Sex:** Coed **Affiliation:** Schiller International University **Admission Plans:** Deferred Admission **Application Deadline:** Rolling **Application Fee:** $65.00 **H.S. Requirements:** High school diploma required; GED accepted **Costs Per Year:** Application fee: $65. Tuition: $18,320 full-time, $535 per credit hour part-time. Mandatory fees: $535 per credit hour part-time. **Calendar System:** Semester, Summer Session Avail-

able **Enrollment:** FT 153, PT 38 **Faculty:** FT 2, PT 64 **Student-Faculty Ratio:** 16:1 **% Residing in College-Owned, -Operated, or -Affiliated Housing:** 85 **Library Holdings:** 1,918 **Credit Hours For Degree:** 62 credits, Associates; 124 credits, Bachelors **Professional Accreditation:** ACICS

SEMINOLE STATE COLLEGE OF FLORIDA
100 Weldon Blvd.
Sanford, FL 32773-6199
Tel: (407)708-4722
Admissions: (407)708-2050
Fax: (407)328-2395
E-mail: admissions@scc-fl.edu
Web Site: http://www.seminolestate.edu/
President/CEO: Dr. E. Ann McGee
Admissions: Pamela Mennechey
Type: Two-Year College **Sex:** Coed **% Accepted:** 100 **Admission Plans:** Open Admission; Early Admission; Deferred Admission **Application Deadline:** Rolling **Application Fee:** $0.00 **H.S. Requirements:** High school diploma required; GED accepted **Costs Per Year:** Application fee: $0. State resident tuition: $2028 full-time, $91.43 per credit hour part-time. Nonresident tuition: $8116 full-time, $326.90 per credit hour part-time. Mandatory fees: $23.83 per credit hour part-time. **Scholarships:** Available **Calendar System:** Semester, Summer Session Available **Enrollment:** FT 7,019, PT 9,430 **Faculty:** FT 208, PT 515 **Student-Faculty Ratio:** 27:1 **Exams:** ACT, Other. **Library Holdings:** 93,296 **Regional Accreditation:** Southern Association of Colleges and Schools **Credit Hours For Degree:** 60 credit hours, Associates **ROTC:** Army **Professional Accreditation:** APTA, CARC, JRCEMT, NLN **Intercollegiate Athletics:** Baseball M; Golf W; Softball W

SOUTH FLORIDA COMMUNITY COLLEGE
600 West College Dr.
Avon Park, FL 33825-9356
Tel: (863)453-6661
Fax: (863)453-0165
Web Site: http://www.sfcc.cc.fl.us/
President/CEO: Dr. Norman L. Stephens, Jr.
Admissions: Annie Alexander-Harvey
Type: Two-Year College **Sex:** Coed **Affiliation:** Florida Community College System **Admission Plans:** Open Admission; Early Admission; Deferred Admission **Application Deadline:** Rolling **Application Fee:** $0.00 **H.S. Requirements:** High school diploma required; GED accepted **Scholarships:** Available **Calendar System:** Semester, Summer Session Available **Enrollment:** FT 813, PT 1,263 **Faculty:** FT 46, PT 157 **Student-Faculty Ratio:** 15:1 **Library Holdings:** 42,000 **Regional Accreditation:** Southern Association of Colleges and Schools **Credit Hours For Degree:** 60 semester hours, Associates **Professional Accreditation:** ADA **Intercollegiate Athletics:** Baseball M; Tennis W; Volleyball W

SOUTH UNIVERSITY (ROYAL PALM BEACH)
University Centre
9801 Belvedere Rd.
Royal Palm Beach, FL 33411
Tel: (561)697-9200; Free: (866)629-2902
Fax: (561)697-9944
Web Site: http://www.southuniversity.edu/west-palm-beach/
President/CEO: David McGuire
Type: Comprehensive **Sex:** Coed **Affiliation:** Education Management Corporation **Calendar System:** Quarter **Professional Accreditation:** AAMAE, APTA, ACBSP

SOUTH UNIVERSITY (TAMPA)
4401 North Himes Ave.
Ste. 175
Tampa, FL 33614
Tel: (813)393-3800; Free: 800-846-1472
Web Site: http://www.southuniversity.edu/tampa/
President/CEO: Dan Coble, RN,PhD
Type: Comprehensive **Sex:** Coed **Affiliation:** Education Management Corporation **Regional Accreditation:** Southern Association of Colleges and Schools

SOUTHEASTERN UNIVERSITY
1000 Longfellow Blvd.
Lakeland, FL 33801-6099
Tel: (863)667-5000; Free: 800-500-8760
Fax: (863)667-5200
E-mail: admission@seuniversity.edu
Web Site: http://www.seuniversity.edu/
President/CEO: Dr. Charles Kelly
Admissions: Chris Diaz
Financial Aid: Carol B. Bradley
Type: Comprehensive **Sex:** Coed **Affiliation:** Assemblies of God **Scores:** 90.08% SAT V 400+; 81.39% SAT M 400+; 51.53% ACT 18-23; 22.09% ACT 24-29 **% Accepted:** 76 **Admission Plans:** Open Admission; Early Admission; Deferred Admission **Application Deadline:** July 1 **Application Fee:** $40.00 **H.S. Requirements:** High school diploma required; GED accepted **Costs Per Year:** Application fee: $40. Comprehensive fee: $22,566 includes full-time tuition ($14,450), mandatory fees ($550), and college room and board ($7566). Full-time tuition and fees vary according to class time, degree level, program, and reciprocity agreements. Room and board charges vary according to board plan and housing facility. Part-time tuition: $605 per credit. Part-time mandatory fees: $140 per term. Part-time tuition and fees vary according to class time, course load, degree level, program, and reciprocity agreements. **Scholarships:** Available **Calendar System:** Semester, Summer Session Available **Enrollment:** FT 2,348, PT 317, Grad FT 168, Grad PT 117 **Faculty:** FT 83, PT 71 **Student-Faculty Ratio:** 25:1 **Exams:** SAT I or ACT. ACT essay used for placement. SAT essay used for placement. **% Receiving Financial Aid:** 73 **% Residing in College-Owned, -Operated, or -Affiliated Housing:** 80 **Final Year or Final Semester Residency Requirement:** No **Library Holdings:** 110,675 **Regional Accreditation:** Southern Association of Colleges and Schools **Credit Hours For Degree:** 125 credits, Bachelors **ROTC:** Army, Air Force **Intercollegiate Athletics:** Baseball M; Basketball M & W; Cheerleading M & W; Golf M; Soccer M & W; Tennis W; Volleyball W

SOUTHWEST FLORIDA COLLEGE (FORT MYERS)
1685 Medical Ln.
Fort Myers, FL 33907
Tel: (239)939-4766; Free: (866)SWFC-NOW
Fax: (239)936-4040
E-mail: kreynolds@swfc.edu
Web Site: http://www.swfc.edu/
President/CEO: Raul Valdes Pages
Admissions: Ken Reynolds
Type: Four-Year College **Sex:** Coed **Admission Plans:** Open Admission **Application Deadline:** Rolling **H.S. Requirements:** High school diploma required; GED accepted **Scholarships:** Available **Calendar System:** Quarter **Library Holdings:** 1,000 **Credit Hours For Degree:** 96 quarter hours, Associates **Professional Accreditation:** ACICS

SOUTHWEST FLORIDA COLLEGE (TAMPA)
3910 Riga Blvd.
Tampa, FL 33619
Tel: (813)630-4401; Free: 877-907-2456
Web Site: http://www.swfc.edu/
Type: Two-Year College **Sex:** Coed **Calendar System:** Quarter

STATE COLLEGE OF FLORIDA MANATEE-SARASOTA
5840 26th St. West, PO Box 1849
Bradenton, FL 34206-7046
Tel: (941)752-5000
Admissions: (941)752-5384
Fax: (941)727-6177
E-mail: lewym@scf.edu
Web Site: http://www.scf.edu/
President/CEO: Dr. Lars Hafner
Admissions: MariLynn Lewy
Type: Two-Year College **Sex:** Coed **Affiliation:** Florida Community College System **Scores:** 85.61% SAT V 400+; 84.3% SAT M 400+; 37.52% ACT 18-23; 14.9% ACT 24-29 **% Accepted:** 100 **Admission Plans:** Open Admission; Early Admission **Application Deadline:** August 20 **Application Fee:** $0.00 **H.S. Requirements:** High school diploma required; GED accepted **Costs Per Year:** Application fee: $0. State resident tuition: $2636 full-time, $87.88 per credit hour part-time. Nonresident tuition: $9942 full-time, $331.40 per credit hour part-time. Mandatory fees: $40 full-time. **Scholar-**

ships: Available **Calendar System:** Semester, Summer Session Available **Enrollment:** FT 5,419, PT 5,813 **Faculty:** FT 169, PT 355 **Library Holdings:** 65,386 **Regional Accreditation:** Southern Association of Colleges and Schools **Credit Hours For Degree:** 60 credit hours, Associates **Professional Accreditation:** ADA, AOTA, APTA, CARC, JRCERT, NLN **Intercollegiate Athletics:** Baseball M; Basketball M; Softball W; Volleyball W

STETSON UNIVERSITY
421 North Woodland Blvd.
DeLand, FL 32723
Tel: (386)822-7000; Free: 800-688-0101
Admissions: (386)822-7100
Fax: (386)822-8832
E-mail: admissions@stetson.edu
Web Site: http://www.stetson.edu/
President/CEO: Dr. Wendy B. Libby
Admissions: Deborah Thompson
Financial Aid: Robert D. Stewart
Type: Comprehensive **Sex:** Coed **Scores:** 99% SAT V 400+; 98% SAT M 400+; 51% ACT 18-23; 37% ACT 24-29 **% Accepted:** 53 **Admission Plans:** Early Admission; Early Decision Plan; Deferred Admission **Application Deadline:** March 15 **Application Fee:** $40.00 **H.S. Requirements:** High school diploma required; GED accepted **Costs Per Year:** Application fee: $40. Comprehensive fee: $43,229 includes full-time tuition ($31,374), mandatory fees ($2050), and college room and board ($9805). College room only: $5620. Room and board charges vary according to board plan and housing facility. Part-time tuition: $960 per credit hour. **Scholarships:** Available **Calendar System:** Semester, Summer Session Available **Enrollment:** FT 2,079, PT 83, Grad FT 229, Grad PT 251 **Faculty:** FT 229, PT 124 **Student-Faculty Ratio:** 11:1 **Exams:** SAT I or ACT. **% Receiving Financial Aid:** 64 **% Residing in College-Owned, -Operated, or -Affiliated Housing:** 69 **Library Holdings:** 404,061 **Regional Accreditation:** Southern Association of Colleges and Schools **Credit Hours For Degree:** 128 hours, Bachelors **ROTC:** Army **Professional Accreditation:** AACSB, ABA, ACA, AALS, JRCEPAT, NASM, NCATE **Intercollegiate Athletics:** Baseball M; Basketball M & W; Crew M & W; Cross-Country Running M & W; Golf M & W; Soccer M & W; Softball W; Tennis M & W; Volleyball W

STRAYER UNIVERSITY - BAYMEADOWS CAMPUS
8375 Dix Ellis Trail
Ste. 200
Jacksonville, FL 32256
Tel: (904)538-1000
Fax: (904)538-1030
Web Site: http://www.strayer.edu/baymeadows/
Type: Comprehensive **Sex:** Coed **Application Fee:** $50.00 **Costs Per Year:** Application fee: $50. **Regional Accreditation:** Middle State Association of Colleges and Schools

STRAYER UNIVERSITY - BRICKELL CAMPUS
1201 Brickell Ave.
Ste. 700
Miami, FL 33131
Tel: (305)507-5800
Fax: (305)416-2970
E-mail: brickell@strayer.edu
Web Site: http://www.strayer.edu/brickell
Type: Comprehensive **Sex:** Coed **Application Fee:** $50.00 **Costs Per Year:** Application fee: $50. **Regional Accreditation:** Middle State Association of Colleges and Schools

STRAYER UNIVERSITY - CORAL SPRINGS CAMPUS
5830 Coral Ridge Dr.
Ste. 300
Coral Springs, FL 33076
Tel: (954)369-0700
Fax: (954)369-0730
Web Site: http://www.strayer.edu/coral_springs/
Type: Comprehensive **Sex:** Coed **Application Fee:** $50.00 **Costs Per Year:** Application fee: $50. **Regional Accreditation:** Middle State Association of Colleges and Schools

STRAYER UNIVERSITY - DORAL CAMPUS
11430 Northwest 20th St.
Ste. 150
Miami, FL 33172
Tel: (305)507-5700
Fax: (305)470-3988
E-mail: doral@strayer.edu
Web Site: http://www.strayer.edu/doral
Type: Comprehensive **Sex:** Coed **Application Fee:** $50.00 **Costs Per Year:** Application fee: $50. **Regional Accreditation:** Middle State Association of Colleges and Schools

STRAYER UNIVERSITY - FORT LAUDERDALE CAMPUS
2307 West Broward Blvd.
Ste. 100
Fort Lauderdale, FL 33312
Tel: (954)745-6960
Fax: (954)745-6930
Web Site: http://www.strayer.edu/fort_lauderdale/
Type: Comprehensive **Sex:** Coed **Application Fee:** $50.00 **Costs Per Year:** Application fee: $50. **Regional Accreditation:** Middle State Association of Colleges and Schools

STRAYER UNIVERSITY - MAITLAND CAMPUS
850 Trafalgar Ct.
Ste. 360
Maitland, FL 32751
Tel: (407)618-5900
Fax: (407)618-5930
Web Site: http://www.strayer.edu/maitland/
Type: Comprehensive **Sex:** Coed **Application Fee:** $50.00 **Costs Per Year:** Application fee: $50. **Regional Accreditation:** Middle State Association of Colleges and Schools

STRAYER UNIVERSITY - MIRAMAR CAMPUS
15620 Southwest 29th St.
Miramar, FL 33027
Tel: (954)378-2400
Fax: (305)207-3042
Web Site: http://www.strayer.edu/miramar
Type: Comprehensive **Sex:** Coed **Application Fee:** $50.00 **Costs Per Year:** Application fee: $50. **Regional Accreditation:** Middle State Association of Colleges and Schools

STRAYER UNIVERSITY - ORLANDO EAST CAMPUS
2200 North Alafaya Trail
Ste. 500
Orlando, FL 32826
Tel: (407)926-2000
Fax: (407)926-2030
Web Site: http://www.strayer.edu/orlando_east/
Type: Comprehensive **Sex:** Coed **Application Fee:** $50.00 **Costs Per Year:** Application fee: $50. **Regional Accreditation:** Middle State Association of Colleges and Schools

STRAYER UNIVERSITY - PALM BEACH GARDENS CAMPUS
11025 RCA Center Dr.
Ste. 200
Palm Beach Gardens, FL 33410
Tel: (561)904-3000
Fax: (561)904-3030
Web Site: http://www.strayer.edu/palm_beach_gardens
Type: Comprehensive **Sex:** Coed **Application Fee:** $50.00 **Costs Per Year:** Application fee: $50. **Regional Accreditation:** Middle State Association of Colleges and Schools

STRAYER UNIVERSITY - SAND LAKE CAMPUS
8541 South Park Circle
Bldg. 900
Orlando, FL 32819
Tel: (407)264-9400
Fax: (407)264-9430
Web Site: http://www.strayer.edu/sand_lake/

Type: Comprehensive **Sex:** Coed **Application Fee:** $50.00 **Costs Per Year:** Application fee: $50. **Regional Accreditation:** Middle State Association of Colleges and Schools

STRAYER UNIVERSITY - TAMPA EAST CAMPUS
6302 East Martin Luther King Blvd., Ste. 450
Tampa, FL 33619
Tel: (813)663-0100
Fax: (813)626-2245
Web Site: http://www.strayer.edu/tampa_east
Type: Comprehensive **Sex:** Coed **Application Fee:** $50.00 **Costs Per Year:** Application fee: $50. **Regional Accreditation:** Middle State Association of Colleges and Schools

STRAYER UNIVERSITY - TAMPA WESTSHORE CAMPUS
4902 Eisenhower Blvd., Ste. 100
Tampa, FL 33634
Tel: (813)882-0100
Fax: (813)249-2483
Web Site: http://www.strayer.edu/tampa_westshore
Type: Comprehensive **Sex:** Coed **Application Fee:** $50.00 **Costs Per Year:** Application fee: $50. **Regional Accreditation:** Middle State Association of Colleges and Schools

TALLAHASSEE COMMUNITY COLLEGE
444 Appleyard Dr.
Tallahassee, FL 32304-2895
Tel: (850)201-6200
Admissions: (850)201-8555
E-mail: admissions@tcc.fl.edu
Web Site: http://www.tcc.fl.edu/
President/CEO: Dr. William D. Law, Jr.
Type: Two-Year College **Sex:** Coed **Affiliation:** Florida Community College System **% Accepted:** 100 **Admission Plans:** Open Admission; Early Admission; Deferred Admission **Application Deadline:** August 1 **Application Fee:** $0.00 **H.S. Requirements:** High school diploma required; GED accepted **Costs Per Year:** Application fee: $0. State resident tuition: $2232 full-time, $85.85 per credit hour part-time. Nonresident tuition: $7887 full-time, $303.35 per credit hour part-time. Full-time tuition varies according to course load. Part-time tuition varies according to course load. **Scholarships:** Available **Calendar System:** Semester, Summer Session Available **Enrollment:** FT 7,553, PT 6,973 **Faculty:** FT 184, PT 658 **Student-Faculty Ratio:** 25:1 **Library Holdings:** 120,152 **Regional Accreditation:** Southern Association of Colleges and Schools **Credit Hours For Degree:** 60 semester hours, Associates **ROTC:** Army, Navy, Air Force **Professional Accreditation:** ADA, CARC, JRCEMT **Intercollegiate Athletics:** Baseball M; Basketball M & W; Softball W

TALMUDIC COLLEGE OF FLORIDA
1910 Alton Rd.
Miami Beach, FL 33139
Tel: (305)534-7050; Free: 888-825-6834
Fax: (305)534-8444
E-mail: yandtg@gmail,com
Web Site: http://www.talmudicu.edu/
President/CEO: Rabbi Yitzchak Zweig
Admissions: Rabbi Yeshaya Greenberg
Financial Aid: Rabbi Ira Hill
Type: Comprehensive **Sex:** Men **Affiliation:** Jewish **% Accepted:** 80 **Admission Plans:** Early Admission; Deferred Admission **Application Deadline:** Rolling **Application Fee:** $250.00 **H.S. Requirements:** High school diploma required; GED accepted **Scholarships:** Available **Calendar System:** Semester, Summer Session Available **Enrollment:** FT 30 **Faculty:** FT 6, PT 0 **Student-Faculty Ratio:** 5:1 **% Receiving Financial Aid:** 70 **% Residing in College-Owned, -Operated, or -Affiliated Housing:** 99 **Library Holdings:** 25,000 **Credit Hours For Degree:** 120 credits, Bachelors **Professional Accreditation:** AARTS

TRINITY BAPTIST COLLEGE
800 Hammond Blvd.
Jacksonville, FL 32221
Tel: (904)596-2400; Free: 800-786-2206
Fax: (904)596-2531
E-mail: trinity@tbc.edu
Web Site: http://www.tbc.edu/
President/CEO: Charles Shoemaker
Admissions: Larry Appleby
Financial Aid: Donald Schaffer
Type: Comprehensive **Sex:** Coed **Affiliation:** Baptist **Scores:** 88% SAT V 400+; 87% SAT M 400+ **% Accepted:** 100 **Application Deadline:** Rolling **Application Fee:** $30.00 **H.S. Requirements:** High school diploma required; GED accepted **Scholarships:** Available **Calendar System:** Semester, Summer Session Available **Enrollment:** FT 282, PT 37 **Faculty:** FT 13, PT 40 **Student-Faculty Ratio:** 6:1 **Exams:** SAT I or ACT. **% Receiving Financial Aid:** 48 **% Residing in College-Owned, -Operated, or -Affiliated Housing:** 57 **Library Holdings:** 35,070 **Credit Hours For Degree:** 64 semester hours, Associates; 130 semester hours, Bachelors **Professional Accreditation:** TACCS **Intercollegiate Athletics:** Basketball M & W; Track and Field M

TRINITY COLLEGE OF FLORIDA
2430 Welbilt Blvd.
New Port Richey, FL 34655
Tel: (727)376-6911; Free: 800-388-0869
Fax: (727)376-0781
E-mail: msawyer@trinitycollege.edu
Web Site: http://www.trinitycollege.edu/
President/CEO: Mark T. O'Farrell
Admissions: Mark A. Sawyer
Financial Aid: Sue Wayne
Type: Four-Year College **Sex:** Coed **Affiliation:** nondenominational **Scores:** 88% SAT V 400+; 64% SAT M 400+; 63% ACT 18-23; 25% ACT 24-29 **% Accepted:** 85 **Admission Plans:** Early Admission; Deferred Admission **Application Deadline:** August 8 **Application Fee:** $25.00 **H.S. Requirements:** High school diploma required; GED accepted **Costs Per Year:** Application fee: $25. Comprehensive fee: $18,480 includes full-time tuition ($11,024), mandatory fees ($800), and college room and board ($6656). Part-time tuition: $430 per credit hour. Part-time mandatory fees: $400 per term. Part-time tuition and fees vary according to course load. **Scholarships:** Available **Calendar System:** Semester, Summer Session Available **Enrollment:** FT 185, PT 26 **Faculty:** FT 6, PT 18 **Student-Faculty Ratio:** 14:1 **Exams:** SAT I or ACT. **% Receiving Financial Aid:** 86 **% Residing in College-Owned, -Operated, or -Affiliated Housing:** 41 **Library Holdings:** 37,457 **Credit Hours For Degree:** 60 credit hours, Associates; 123 credit hours, Bachelors **Professional Accreditation:** ABHE **Intercollegiate Athletics:** Basketball M; Volleyball W

UNIVERSIDAD FLET
14540 Southwest 136th St.
Ste. 108
Miami, FL 33186
Tel: (305)232-5880; Free: 888-376-3538
Admissions: (305)378-8700
Fax: (305)232-3592
E-mail: admissiones@flet.edu
Web Site: http://www.flet.edu/
President/CEO: Jeffrey De Leon
Admissions: Dalia Sosa
Type: Comprehensive **Sex:** Coed **Admission Plans:** Open Admission **Application Fee:** $20.00 **H.S. Requirements:** High school diploma required; GED accepted **Costs Per Year:** Application fee: $20. Tuition: $1800 full-time, $100 per credit hour part-time. Mandatory fees: $20 full-time, $20 per year part-time. **Enrollment:** , PT 696 **Faculty:** FT 4, PT 16 **Student-Faculty Ratio:** 33:1 **Professional Accreditation:** DETC

UNIVERSITY OF CENTRAL FLORIDA
4000 Central Florida Blvd.
Orlando, FL 32816
Tel: (407)823-2000
Admissions: (407)823-3000
Fax: (407)823-3419
E-mail: admission@mail.ucf.edu
Web Site: http://www.ucf.edu/
President/CEO: Dr. John Hitt
Admissions: Dr. Gordon Chavis, Jr.
Financial Aid: Inez Ford
Type: University **Sex:** Coed **Affiliation:** State University System of Florida **Scores:** 99.8% SAT V 400+; 100% SAT M 400+; 24.9% ACT 18-23; 65.5%

ACT 24-29 **% Accepted:** 47 **Admission Plans:** Preferred Admission; Early Admission **Application Deadline:** March 1 **Application Fee:** $30.00 **H.S. Requirements:** High school diploma required; GED accepted **Costs Per Year:** Application fee: $30. State resident tuition: $4526 full-time, $150.85 per credit part-time. Nonresident tuition: $20,005 full-time, $666.83 per credit part-time. Full-time tuition varies according to course load. Part-time tuition varies according to course load. College room and board: $8540. College room only: $4940. Room and board charges vary according to board plan and housing facility. **Scholarships:** Available **Calendar System:** Semester, Summer Session Available **Enrollment:** FT 34,095, PT 11,206, Grad FT 3,824, Grad PT 4,412 **Faculty:** FT 1,240, PT 467 **Student-Faculty Ratio:** 31:1 **Exams:** SAT I or ACT. ACT essay used for admission. SAT essay used for admission. **% Receiving Financial Aid:** 42 **% Residing in College-Owned, -Operated, or -Affiliated Housing:** 21 **Library Holdings:** 1,936,014 **Regional Accreditation:** Southern Association of Colleges and Schools **Credit Hours For Degree:** 60 semester hours, Associates; 120 semester hours, Bachelors **ROTC:** Army, Air Force **Professional Accreditation:** AACSB, ABET, AACN, ACA, AHIMA, APTA, APA, ASLHA, ACEHSA, CARC, CSWE, JRCERT, JRCEPAT, NAACLS, NASM, NASPAA, NCATE, NLN **Intercollegiate Athletics:** Baseball M; Basketball M & W; Cheerleading M & W; Crew W; Cross-Country Running M & W; Football M; Golf M & W; Soccer M & W; Tennis M & W; Track and Field W; Volleyball W

UNIVERSITY OF FLORIDA
Gainesville, FL 32611
Tel: (352)392-3261
Admissions: (352)392-1365
Web Site: http://www.ufl.edu/
President/CEO: Dr. Bernard James Machen
Financial Aid: Karen L. Fooks
Type: University **Sex:** Coed **Scores:** 100% SAT V 400+; 99% SAT M 400+; 11% ACT 18-23; 51% ACT 24-29 **% Accepted:** 42 **Admission Plans:** Preferred Admission; Early Admission **Application Deadline:** November 1 **Application Fee:** $30.00 **H.S. Requirements:** High school diploma required; GED accepted **Costs Per Year:** Application fee: $30. State resident tuition: $4373 full-time, $145.76 per credit hour part-time. Nonresident tuition: $23,744 full-time, $791.47 per credit hour part-time. College room and board: $7500. College room only: $4860. **Scholarships:** Available **Calendar System:** Semester, Summer Session Available **Enrollment:** FT 31,304, PT 2,324, Grad FT 12,644, Grad PT 4,419 **Faculty:** FT 3,372, PT 224 **Student-Faculty Ratio:** 20:1 **Exams:** SAT I or ACT. ACT essay used for admission. SAT essay used for admission. **% Receiving Financial Aid:** 41 **Final Year or Final Semester Residency Requirement:** Yes **Library Holdings:** 5,554,505 **Regional Accreditation:** Southern Association of Colleges and Schools **Credit Hours For Degree:** 120 semester hours, Bachelors **ROTC:** Army, Navy, Air Force **Professional Accreditation:** AACSB, ABET, ACPhE, ACEJMC, AACN, AAFCS, ABA, ACNM, ACCE, ACA, ADA, ADtA, ACSP, AOTA, APTA, APA, ASLA, ASLHA, AVMA, AALS ACEHSA, FIDER, CORE, JRCEPAT, LCMEAMA, NAAB, NASAD, NASM, NAST, NCATE, NRPA, SAF **Intercollegiate Athletics:** Baseball M; Basketball M & W; Cross-Country Running M & W; Football M; Golf M & W; Gymnastics W; Lacrosse W; Racquetball M & W; Soccer M & W; Softball W; Swimming and Diving M & W; Tennis M & W; Track and Field M & W; Ultimate Frisbee M & W; Volleyball M & W

UNIVERSITY OF MIAMI
University of Miami Branch
Coral Gables, FL 33124
Tel: (305)284-2211
Admissions: (305)284-4323
Fax: (305)284-2507
E-mail: admission@miami.edu
Web Site: http://www.miami.edu/
President/CEO: Donna E. Shalala
Financial Aid: James M. Bauer
Type: University **Sex:** Coed **Scores:** 99% SAT V 400+; 101% SAT M 400+; 7% ACT 18-23; 46% ACT 24-29 **% Accepted:** 44 **Admission Plans:** Early Admission; Early Action; Early Decision Plan; Deferred Admission **Application Deadline:** January 15 **Application Fee:** $65.00 **H.S. Requirements:** High school diploma required; GED accepted **Costs Per Year:** Application fee: $65. Comprehensive fee: $48,898 includes full-time tuition ($36,962), mandatory fees ($874), and college room and board ($11,062). College room only: $6448. Full-time tuition and fees vary according to course load, degree level, and program. Room and board charges vary according to board plan and housing facility. Part-time tuition: $1538 per credit hour. Part-time tuition varies according to course load, degree level, and program. **Scholarships:** Available **Calendar System:** Semester, Summer Session Available **Enrollment:** FT 9,451, PT 919, Grad FT 4,761, Grad PT 498 **Faculty:** FT 961, PT 335 **Student-Faculty Ratio:** 11:1 **Exams:** SAT I or ACT, SAT I and SAT II or ACT, SAT II. ACT essay not being used. SAT essay not being used. **% Receiving Financial Aid:** 48 **% Residing in College-Owned, -Operated, or -Affiliated Housing:** 43 **Final Year or Final Semester Residency Requirement:** No **Library Holdings:** 3,300,000 **Regional Accreditation:** Southern Association of Colleges and Schools **Credit Hours For Degree:** 120 credits, Bachelors **ROTC:** Army, Air Force **Professional Accreditation:** AACSB, ABET, ACEJMC, AACN, AANA, ABA, ACNM, APTA, APA, AALS, ACEHSA, CEPH, LCMEAMA, NAAB, NASM, NCATE, NLN **Intercollegiate Athletics:** Baseball M; Basketball M & W; Cheerleading M & W; Crew M; Cross-Country Running M & W; Football M; Golf W; Soccer W; Swimming and Diving W; Tennis M & W; Track and Field M & W; Volleyball W

UNIVERSITY OF NORTH FLORIDA
1 UNF Dr.
Jacksonville, FL 32224
Tel: (904)620-1000
Admissions: (904)620-2624
Fax: (904)620-1040
E-mail: admissions@unf.edu
Web Site: http://www.unf.edu/
President/CEO: John A. Delaney
Admissions: John Yancey
Financial Aid: Anissa Agne
Type: Comprehensive **Sex:** Coed **Affiliation:** State University System of Florida **Scores:** 100% SAT V 400+; 100% SAT M 400+; 71% ACT 18-23; 26% ACT 24-29 **% Accepted:** 64 **Admission Plans:** Deferred Admission **Application Deadline:** June 11 **Application Fee:** $30.00 **H.S. Requirements:** High school diploma required; GED accepted **Costs Per Year:** Application fee: $30. State resident tuition: $4193 full-time, $139.78 per credit hour part-time. Nonresident tuition: $17,582 full-time, $586.06 per credit hour part-time. College room and board: $9982. Room and board charges vary according to board plan and housing facility. **Scholarships:** Available **Calendar System:** Semester, Summer Session Available **Enrollment:** FT 10,453, PT 4,042, Grad FT 801, Grad PT 1,181 **Faculty:** FT 495, PT 246 **Student-Faculty Ratio:** 23:1 **Exams:** SAT I or ACT. ACT essay used for placement. SAT essay used for placement. ACT essay not being used. SAT essay not being used. **% Receiving Financial Aid:** 45 **% Residing in College-Owned, -Operated, or -Affiliated Housing:** 17 **Library Holdings:** 957,625 **Regional Accreditation:** Southern Association of Colleges and Schools **Credit Hours For Degree:** 60 semester hours, Associates; 120 semester hours, Bachelors **ROTC:** Army, Navy **Professional Accreditation:** AACSB, ABET, AACN, AANA, ACCE, ACA, ADtA, APTA, CORE, JRCEPAT, NASM, NASPAA, NCATE, NLN **Intercollegiate Athletics:** Baseball M; Basketball M & W; Cross-Country Running M & W; Golf M; Soccer M & W; Softball W; Swimming and Diving W; Tennis M & W; Track and Field M & W; Volleyball W

UNIVERSITY OF PHOENIX—CENTRAL FLORIDA CAMPUS
2290 Lucien Way
Ste. 400
Maitland, FL 32751-7057
Tel: (407)667-0555; Free: 800-228-7240
Admissions: (480)557-6151
E-mail: audra.mcquarie@phoenix.edu
Web Site: http://www.phoenix.edu/
President/CEO: William Pepicello
Admissions: Audra McQuarie
Type: Comprehensive **Sex:** Coed **Admission Plans:** Open Admission; Deferred Admission **Application Deadline:** Rolling **Application Fee:** $0.00 **H.S. Requirements:** High school diploma required; GED accepted **Costs Per Year:** Application fee: $0. Tuition: $11,500 full-time. Full-time tuition varies according to course level and course load. **Scholarships:** Available **Calendar System:** Continuous, Summer Session Not available **Enrollment:** FT 1,174 **Faculty:** FT 33, PT 182 **Regional Accreditation:** North Central Association of Colleges and Schools **Credit Hours For Degree:** 60 credits, Associates; 120 credits, Bachelors **Professional Accreditation:** NLN

UNIVERSITY OF PHOENIX—NORTH FLORIDA CAMPUS
4500 Salisbury Rd.
Jacksonville, FL 32216-0959

Tel: (904)636-6645; Free: 800-894-1758
Admissions: (480)557-6151
E-mail: audra.mcquarie@phoenix.edu
Web Site: http://www.phoenix.edu/
President/CEO: William Pepicello
Admissions: Audra McQuarie
Type: Comprehensive **Sex:** Coed **Admission Plans:** Open Admission; Deferred Admission **Application Deadline:** Rolling **Application Fee:** $0.00 **H.S. Requirements:** High school diploma required; GED accepted **Costs Per Year:** Application fee: $0. Tuition: $11,500 full-time. Full-time tuition varies according to course level and course load. **Scholarships:** Available **Calendar System:** Continuous, Summer Session Not available **Enrollment:** FT 1,019 **Faculty:** FT 24, PT 186 **Regional Accreditation:** North Central Association of Colleges and Schools **Credit Hours For Degree:** 60 credits, Associates; 120 credits, Bachelors **Professional Accreditation:** NLN

UNIVERSITY OF PHOENIX—SOUTH FLORIDA CAMPUS
600 North Pine Island Rd.
Fort Lauderdale, FL 33309
Tel: (954)382-5303; Free: 800-228-7240
Admissions: (480)557-6151
E-mail: audra.mcquarie@phoenix.edu
Web Site: http://www.phoenix.edu/
President/CEO: William Pepicello
Admissions: Audra McQuarie
Type: Comprehensive **Sex:** Coed **Admission Plans:** Open Admission; Deferred Admission **Application Deadline:** Rolling **Application Fee:** $0.00 **H.S. Requirements:** High school diploma required; GED accepted **Costs Per Year:** Application fee: $0. Tuition: $11,600 full-time. Full-time tuition varies according to course level and course load. **Scholarships:** Available **Calendar System:** Continuous, Summer Session Not available **Enrollment:** FT 1,961 **Faculty:** FT 22, PT 211 **Regional Accreditation:** North Central Association of Colleges and Schools **Credit Hours For Degree:** 60 credits, Associates; 120 credits, Bachelors **Professional Accreditation:** NLN

UNIVERSITY OF PHOENIX—WEST FLORIDA CAMPUS
12802 Tampa Oaks Blvd.
Ste. 200
Temple Terrace, FL 33637
Tel: (813)626-7911; Free: 800-228-7240
Admissions: (480)557-3303
Fax: (813)977-1449
E-mail: evelyn.gaskin@phoenix.edu
Web Site: http://www.phoenix.edu/
President/CEO: William Pepicello
Admissions: Evelyn Gaskin
Type: Comprehensive **Sex:** Coed **% Accepted:** 100 **Admission Plans:** Open Admission; Deferred Admission **Application Deadline:** Rolling **Application Fee:** $0.00 **H.S. Requirements:** High school diploma required; GED accepted **Costs Per Year:** Application fee: $0. Tuition: $11,500 full-time. Full-time tuition varies according to course level and course load. **Scholarships:** Available **Calendar System:** Continuous, Summer Session Not available **Enrollment:** FT 740 **Faculty:** FT 25, PT 176 **Regional Accreditation:** North Central Association of Colleges and Schools **Credit Hours For Degree:** 60 credits, Associates; 120 credits, Bachelors **Professional Accreditation:** NLN

UNIVERSITY OF SOUTH FLORIDA
4202 East Fowler Ave.
Tampa, FL 33620-9951
Tel: (813)974-2011
Admissions: (813)974-3350
Fax: (813)974-9689
E-mail: bullseye@admin.usf.edu
Web Site: http://www.usf.edu/
President/CEO: Dr. Judy Genshaft, PhD
Admissions: Alicia Kornowa
Financial Aid: Billie Jo Hamilton
Type: University **Sex:** Coed **Affiliation:** State University System of Florida **Scores:** 99.84% SAT V 400+; 99.88% SAT M 400+; 38.14% ACT 18-23; 53.13% ACT 24-29 **% Accepted:** 43 **Admission Plans:** Early Admission **Application Deadline:** April 15 **Application Fee:** $30.00 **H.S. Requirements:** High school diploma required; GED accepted **Costs Per Year:** Application fee: $30. One-time mandatory fee: $74. State resident tuition: $4503 full-time, $150.10 per credit hour part-time. Nonresident tuition: $15,312 full-time, $510.41 per credit hour part-time. Mandatory fees: $74 full-time, $37 per term part-time. Full-time tuition and fees vary according to course level, course load, and location. Part-time tuition and fees vary according to course level, course load, and location. College room and board: $8080. College room only: $4552. Room and board charges vary according to board plan, housing facility, and location. **Scholarships:** Available **Calendar System:** Semester, Summer Session Available **Enrollment:** FT 25,978, PT 10,617, Grad FT 4,825, Grad PT 5,604 **Student-Faculty Ratio:** 27:1 **Exams:** SAT I or ACT. ACT essay used for admission. SAT essay used for admission. ACT essay used for placement. SAT essay used for placement. **% Receiving Financial Aid:** 48 **% Residing in College-Owned, -Operated, or -Affiliated Housing:** 12 **Final Year or Final Semester Residency Requirement:** Yes **Library Holdings:** 2,257,058 **Regional Accreditation:** Southern Association of Colleges and Schools **Credit Hours For Degree:** 60 semester hours, Associates; 120 semester hours, Bachelors **ROTC:** Army, Navy, Air Force **Professional Accreditation:** AACSB, ABET, ACEJMC, AACN, AANA, ACA, ALA, APTA, APA, ASLHA, CEPH, CORE, CSWE, LCMEAMA, NAAB, NASAD, NASM, NASPAA, NAST, NCATE NLN **Intercollegiate Athletics:** Baseball M; Basketball M & W; Cross-Country Running M & W; Football M; Golf M & W; Soccer M & W; Softball W; Tennis M & W; Track and Field M & W; Volleyball W

THE UNIVERSITY OF TAMPA
401 West Kennedy Blvd.
Tampa, FL 33606-1490
Tel: (813)253-3333; Free: 888-MINARET
Admissions: (813)257-1808
Fax: (813)254-4955
E-mail: admissions@ut.edu
Web Site: http://www.ut.edu/
President/CEO: Dr. Ronald L. Vaughn
Admissions: Dennis Nostrand
Type: Comprehensive **Sex:** Coed **Scores:** 99% SAT V 400+; 99% SAT M 400+; 58% ACT 18-23; 35% ACT 24-29 **% Accepted:** 62 **Admission Plans:** Early Admission; Early Action; Deferred Admission **Application Deadline:** May 1 **Application Fee:** $40.00 **H.S. Requirements:** High school diploma required; GED accepted **Costs Per Year:** Application fee: $40. Comprehensive fee: $30,778 includes full-time tuition ($21,420), mandatory fees ($1062), and college room and board ($8296). College room only: $4430. Full-time tuition and fees vary according to class time. Room and board charges vary according to board plan and housing facility. Part-time tuition: $455 per credit hour. Part-time mandatory fees: $35 per term. Part-time tuition and fees vary according to class time. **Scholarships:** Available **Calendar System:** Semester, Summer Session Available **Enrollment:** FT 5,196, PT 363, Grad FT 246, Grad PT 501 **Faculty:** FT 238, PT 293 **Student-Faculty Ratio:** 17:1 **Exams:** SAT I or ACT. ACT essay used for advising. SAT essay used for advising. ACT essay used for placement. SAT essay used for placement. **% Receiving Financial Aid:** 55 **% Residing in College-Owned, -Operated, or -Affiliated Housing:** 59 **Final Year or Final Semester Residency Requirement:** Yes **Library Holdings:** 292,202 **Regional Accreditation:** Southern Association of Colleges and Schools **Credit Hours For Degree:** 62 semester hours, Associates; 124 semester hours, Bachelors **ROTC:** Army, Navy, Air Force **Professional Accreditation:** AACSB, NASM, NLN **Intercollegiate Athletics:** Baseball M; Basketball M & W; Crew W; Cross-Country Running M & W; Golf M; Soccer M & W; Softball W; Swimming and Diving M & W; Tennis W; Volleyball W

UNIVERSITY OF WEST FLORIDA
11000 University Parkway
Pensacola, FL 32514-5750
Tel: (850)474-2000; Free: 800-263-1074
Admissions: (850)474-2230
Fax: (850)474-2096
E-mail: admissions@uwf.edu
Web Site: http://www.uwf.edu/
President/CEO: Dr. Judy A. Bense
Financial Aid: Georganne E. Major
Type: Comprehensive **Sex:** Coed **Affiliation:** State University System of Florida **Scores:** 99% SAT V 400+; 98% SAT M 400+; 58% ACT 18-23; 37% ACT 24-29 **% Accepted:** 70 **Admission Plans:** Preferred Admission; Early Admission; Deferred Admission **Application Deadline:** June 30 **Application Fee:** $30.00 **H.S. Requirements:** High school diploma required; GED accepted **Costs Per Year:** Application fee: $30. State resident tuition: $2658

full-time, $140.34 per semester hour part-time. Nonresident tuition: $14,926 full-time, $569.73 per semester hour part-time. Mandatory fees: $1552 full-time. Full-time tuition and fees vary according to location and reciprocity agreements. Part-time tuition varies according to location and reciprocity agreements. College room and board: $6900. Room and board charges vary according to housing facility. **Scholarships:** Available **Calendar System:** Semester, Summer Session Available **Enrollment:** FT 6,533, PT 2,592, Grad FT 472, Grad PT 1,546 **Faculty:** FT 312, PT 197 **Student-Faculty Ratio:** 22:1 **Exams:** SAT I or ACT. ACT essay used for admission. SAT essay used for admission. ACT essay used for advising. SAT essay used for advising. ACT essay used for placement. SAT essay used for placement. **% Residing in College-Owned, -Operated, or -Affiliated Housing:** 15 **Library Holdings:** 1,000,558 **Regional Accreditation:** Southern Association of Colleges and Schools **Credit Hours For Degree:** 60 semester hours, Associates; 120 semester hours, Bachelors **ROTC:** Army, Air Force **Professional Accreditation:** AACSB, AACN, CSWE, NAACLS, NASM, NASPAA, NCATE, NLN **Intercollegiate Athletics:** Baseball M; Basketball M & W; Cross-Country Running M & W; Golf M; Soccer M & W; Softball W; Tennis M & W; Track and Field W; Volleyball W

VALENCIA COMMUNITY COLLEGE
PO Box 3028
Orlando, FL 32802-3028
Tel: (407)299-5000
Admissions: (407)299-2187
E-mail: rsimpson@valenciacc.edu
Web Site: http://www.valencia.cc.fl.us/
President/CEO: Sanford C. Shugart, PhD
Admissions: Dr. Renee Simpson
Type: Two-Year College **Sex:** Coed **Affiliation:** Florida Community College System **Scores:** 80.1% SAT V 400+; 79.8% SAT M 400+ **% Accepted:** 100 **Admission Plans:** Open Admission; Preferred Admission; Early Admission **Application Deadline:** August 10 **Application Fee:** $25.00 **H.S. Requirements:** High school diploma required; GED accepted **Costs Per Year:** Application fee: $25. State resident tuition: $2097 full-time, $87.36 per credit hour part-time. Nonresident tuition: $7941 full-time, $330.88 per credit hour part-time. **Scholarships:** Available **Calendar System:** Semester, Summer Session Available **Enrollment:** FT 12,522, PT 17,723 **Faculty:** FT 383, PT 832 **Student-Faculty Ratio:** 24:1 **Library Holdings:** 183,264 **Regional Accreditation:** Southern Association of Colleges and Schools **Credit Hours For Degree:** 60 semester hours, Associates **ROTC:** Army **Professional Accreditation:** ADA, CARC, JRCEDMS, JRCERT, JRCEMT, NLN

WARNER UNIVERSITY
13895 US Hwy. 27
Lake Wales, FL 33859
Tel: (863)638-1426
E-mail: admissions@warner.edu
Web Site: http://www.warner.edu/
President/CEO: Gregory V. Hall
Admissions: Jason Roe
Type: Comprehensive **Sex:** Coed **Affiliation:** Church of God **Scores:** 76% SAT V 400+; 75% SAT M 400+; 48% ACT 18-23; 6% ACT 24-29 **% Accepted:** 58 **Admission Plans:** Deferred Admission **Application Deadline:** Rolling **Application Fee:** $20.00 **H.S. Requirements:** High school diploma required; GED accepted. For a portfolio of standardized tests for home schooled students: High school diploma required; GED accepted **Costs Per Year:** Application fee: $20. One-time mandatory fee: $50. Comprehensive fee: $21,580 includes full-time tuition ($15,120), mandatory fees ($200), and college room and board ($6260). College room only: $3320. Full-time tuition and fees vary according to course load, degree level, and program. Room and board charges vary according to board plan and housing facility. Part-time tuition: $290 per credit hour. Part-time mandatory fees: $25 per term. Part-time tuition and fees vary according to course load, degree level, and program. **Scholarships:** Available **Calendar System:** Semester, Summer Session Available **Enrollment:** FT 778, PT 143 **Faculty:** FT 35, PT 64 **Student-Faculty Ratio:** 16:1 **Exams:** SAT I or ACT. **% Receiving Financial Aid:** 66 **% Residing in College-Owned, -Operated, or -Affiliated Housing:** 41 **Library Holdings:** 56,419 **Regional Accreditation:** Southern Association of Colleges and Schools **Credit Hours For Degree:** 64 credit hours, Associates; 128 credit hours, Bachelors **Intercollegiate Athletics:** Baseball M; Basketball M & W; Cheerleading M & W; Cross-Country Running M & W; Golf M & W; Soccer M & W; Softball W; Tennis M & W; Track and Field M & W; Volleyball W

WEBBER INTERNATIONAL UNIVERSITY
PO Box 96, 1200 North Scenic Hwy.
Babson Park, FL 33827-0096
Tel: (863)638-1431; Free: 800-741-1844
Admissions: (863)638-2910
Fax: (863)638-2823
E-mail: admissions@webber.edu
Web Site: http://www.webber.edu/
President/CEO: Dr. Keith Wade
Admissions: Mike Mattison
Financial Aid: Kathleen Wilson
Type: Comprehensive **Sex:** Coed **Scores:** 85% SAT V 400+; 90% SAT M 400+; 72% ACT 18-23; 11% ACT 24-29 **% Accepted:** 53 **Admission Plans:** Early Action **Application Deadline:** August 1 **Application Fee:** $35.00 **H.S. Requirements:** High school diploma required; GED accepted **Costs Per Year:** Application fee: $35. Comprehensive fee: $24,822 includes full-time tuition ($17,850) and college room and board ($6972). College room only: $4500. Full-time tuition varies according to class time and course load. Room and board charges vary according to board plan and gender. Part-time tuition: $247 per credit hour. Part-time tuition varies according to course load. **Scholarships:** Available **Calendar System:** Semester, Summer Session Available **Enrollment:** FT 553, PT 52, Grad FT 52, Grad PT 12 **Faculty:** FT 19, PT 22 **Student-Faculty Ratio:** 22:1 **Exams:** SAT I or ACT. **% Receiving Financial Aid:** 63 **% Residing in College-Owned, -Operated, or -Affiliated Housing:** 58 **Final Year or Final Semester Residency Requirement:** No **Library Holdings:** 15,000 **Regional Accreditation:** Southern Association of Colleges and Schools **Credit Hours For Degree:** 60 credit hours, Associates; 120 credit hours, Bachelors **Intercollegiate Athletics:** Baseball M; Basketball M & W; Bowling M & W; Cross-Country Running M & W; Football M; Golf M & W; Soccer M & W; Softball W; Tennis M & W; Track and Field M & W; Volleyball M & W

YESHIVA GEDOLAH RABBINICAL COLLEGE
1140 Alton Rd.
Miami Beach, FL 33139
Tel: (305)673-5664
Admissions: (305)653-8770
Fax: (305)532-9820
President/CEO: Rabbi Abraham Korf
Type: Comprehensive **Sex:** Men **Affiliation:** Jewish **Admission Plans:** Open Admission **Professional Accreditation:** AARTS

ABRAHAM BALDWIN AGRICULTURAL COLLEGE
2802 Moore Hwy.
Tifton, GA 31793
Tel: (229)391-5001; Free: 800-733-3653
Admissions: (229)391-5004
Fax: (229)386-7006
E-mail: dwebb@abac.edu
Web Site: http://www.abac.edu/
President/CEO: Dr. David C. Bridges
Admissions: Donna Webb
Financial Aid: Jenelle L. Handcox
Type: Four-Year College **Sex:** Coed **Affiliation:** University System of Georgia **% Accepted:** 79 **Admission Plans:** Open Admission; Early Admission; Deferred Admission **Application Fee:** $20.00 **H.S. Requirements:** High school diploma required; GED accepted **Scholarships:** Available **Calendar System:** Semester, Summer Session Available **Enrollment:** FT 2,475, PT 852 **Faculty:** FT 94, PT 68 **Student-Faculty Ratio:** 24:1 **% Residing in College-Owned, -Operated, or -Affiliated Housing:** 32 **Library Holdings:** 72,149 **Regional Accreditation:** Southern Association of Colleges and Schools **Professional Accreditation:** NLN **Intercollegiate Athletics:** Baseball M; Golf M; Soccer W; Softball W; Tennis M & W

AGNES SCOTT COLLEGE
141 East College Ave.
Decatur, GA 30030-3797
Tel: (404)471-6000; Free: 800-868-8602
Admissions: (404)471-6285
Fax: (404)471-6414
E-mail: admission@agnesscott.edu
Web Site: http://www.agnesscott.edu/
President/CEO: Dr. Elizabeth Kiss
Admissions: Alexa Gaeta
Financial Aid: Patrick Bonones
Type: Comprehensive **Affiliation:** Presbyterian Church (U.S.A.) **Scores:** 99.5% SAT V 400+; 98.98% SAT M 400+; 35.85% ACT 18-23; 46.23% ACT 24-29 **% Accepted:** 46 **Admission Plans:** Early Admission; Early Action; Deferred Admission **Application Deadline:** March 1 **Application Fee:** $35.00 **H.S. Requirements:** High school diploma required; GED accepted **Costs Per Year:** Application fee: $35. Comprehensive fee: $41,133 includes full-time tuition ($31,068), mandatory fees ($215), and college room and board ($9850). College room only: $4925. Full-time tuition and fees vary according to course load. Room and board charges vary according to board plan and housing facility. Part-time tuition: $1,295 per hour. Part-time tuition varies according to course load. **Scholarships:** Available **Calendar System:** Semester, Summer Session Available **Enrollment:** FT 810, PT 32, Grad FT 18, Grad PT 8 **Faculty:** FT 82, PT 26 **Student-Faculty Ratio:** 9:1 **Exams:** Other, SAT I and SAT II or ACT. ACT essay used for admission. SAT essay used for admission. **% Receiving Financial Aid:** 74 **% Residing in College-Owned, -Operated, or -Affiliated Housing:** 86 **Final Year or Final Semester Residency Requirement:** Yes **Library Holdings:** 231,399 **Regional Accreditation:** Southern Association of Colleges and Schools **Credit Hours For Degree:** 128 semester hours, Bachelors **ROTC:** Army, Air Force **Intercollegiate Athletics:** Basketball W; Lacrosse W; Soccer W; Softball W; Tennis W; Volleyball W

ALBANY STATE UNIVERSITY
504 College Dr.
Albany, GA 31705-2717
Tel: (229)430-4600
Admissions: (229)430-4646
Fax: (229)430-3936
E-mail: admissions@asurams.edu
Web Site: http://www.asurams.edu/
President/CEO: Dr. Everette Freeman
Financial Aid: Kathleen J. Caldwell
Type: Comprehensive **Sex:** Coed **Affiliation:** University System of Georgia **Scores:** 82.7% SAT V 400+; 82.2% SAT M 400+; 55.2% ACT 18-23; 2% ACT 24-29 **% Accepted:** 42 **Admission Plans:** Early Admission; Early Action; Deferred Admission **Application Deadline:** July 1 **Application Fee:** $20.00 **H.S. Requirements:** High school diploma required; GED accepted **Costs Per Year:** Application fee: $20. State resident tuition: $3874 full-time, $130 per semester hour part-time. Nonresident tuition: $15,488 full-time, $517 per semester hour part-time. Mandatory fees: $962 full-time, $130 per semester hour part-time. Full-time tuition and fees vary according to location. Part-time tuition and fees vary according to location. College room and board: $5240. College room only: $2890. Room and board charges vary according to board plan and housing facility. **Scholarships:** Available **Calendar System:** Semester, Summer Session Available **Enrollment:** FT 3,366, PT 651, Grad FT 140, Grad PT 316 **Faculty:** FT 152, PT 132 **Student-Faculty Ratio:** 21:1 **Exams:** SAT I or ACT. ACT essay used for placement. SAT essay used for placement. **% Receiving Financial Aid:** 82 **% Residing in College-Owned, -Operated, or -Affiliated Housing:** 35 **Library Holdings:** 196,411 **Regional Accreditation:** Southern Association of Colleges and Schools **Credit Hours For Degree:** 120 credits, Bachelors **ROTC:** Army **Professional Accreditation:** ACBSP, CSWE, NASPAA, NCATE, NLN **Intercollegiate Athletics:** Baseball M; Basketball M & W; Cheerleading W; Cross-Country Running M & W; Football M; Softball W; Tennis W; Track and Field M & W; Volleyball W

ALBANY TECHNICAL COLLEGE
1704 South Slappey Blvd.
Albany, GA 31701
Tel: (229)430-3500
Fax: (229)430-5155
E-mail: ldejesus@albanytech.edu
Web Site: http://www.albanytech.edu/
President/CEO: Anthony O. Parker
Type: Two-Year College **Sex:** Coed **Affiliation:** Technical College System of Georgia **Admission Plans:** Open Admission; Early Admission **Application Fee:** $15.00 **H.S. Requirements:** High school diploma required; GED accepted **Calendar System:** Quarter **Enrollment:** FT 2,526, PT 1,436 **Regional Accreditation:** Southern Association of Colleges and Schools **Professional Accreditation:** ADA, COE, JRCERT

ALTAMAHA TECHNICAL COLLEGE
1777 West Cherry St.
Jesup, GA 31545
Tel: (912)427-5800
Fax: (912)427-5823
E-mail: cjeancake@altamahatech.edu

Web Site: http://www.altamahatech.edu/
President/CEO: Lorette M. Hoover
Type: Two-Year College **Sex:** Coed **Affiliation:** Technical College System of Georgia **Admission Plans:** Open Admission; Early Admission **Application Fee:** $15.00 **H.S. Requirements:** High school diploma required; GED accepted **Calendar System:** Quarter **Enrollment:** FT 641, PT 910 **Professional Accreditation:** COE

AMERICAN INTERCONTINENTAL UNIVERSITY BUCKHEAD CAMPUS
3330 Peachtree Rd., NE
Atlanta, GA 30326-1016
Tel: (404)965-5700; Free: 888-591-7888
Admissions: 877-564-6248
Fax: (404)231-1062
Web Site: http://www.aiuniv.edu/
President/CEO: Stephen Tober
Admissions: Harold Saulsby
Financial Aid: Sherry Rizzi
Type: Comprehensive **Sex:** Coed **Affiliation:** American InterContinental University **Admission Plans:** Deferred Admission **Application Deadline:** Rolling **H.S. Requirements:** High school diploma required; GED accepted **Scholarships:** Available **Calendar System:** Miscellaneous, Summer Session Available **Enrollment:** FT 321, PT 593 **Credit Hours For Degree:** 90 credit hours, Associates; 180 credit hours, Bachelors **Professional Accreditation:** FIDER

AMERICAN INTERCONTINENTAL UNIVERSITY DUNWOODY CAMPUS
6600 Peachtree-Dunwoody Rd.
500 Embassy Row
Atlanta, GA 30328
Tel: (404)965-6500; Free: 800-353-1744
Admissions: 877-564-6248
Fax: (404)965-6501
Web Site: http://www.aiuniv.edu/
President/CEO: Stephen J. Tober
Admissions: Harold Saulsby
Type: Comprehensive **Sex:** Coed **Affiliation:** American InterContinental University **Admission Plans:** Deferred Admission **Application Deadline:** Rolling **Application Fee:** $50.00 **H.S. Requirements:** High school diploma required; GED accepted **Costs Per Year:** Application fee: $50. **Calendar System:** Miscellaneous **Enrollment:** FT 315, PT 119 **Regional Accreditation:** North Central Association of Colleges and Schools

ANDREW COLLEGE
501 College St.
Cuthbert, GA 39840
Tel: (229)732-2171; Free: 800-664-9250
Admissions: (229)732-5986
Fax: (229)732-2176
E-mail: admissions@andrewcollege.edu
Web Site: http://www.andrewcollege.edu/
President/CEO: Dr. David Seyle
Admissions: Bridget Kurkowski
Type: Two-Year College **Sex:** Coed **Affiliation:** United Methodist **Admission Plans:** Early Admission; Deferred Admission **Application Deadline:** August 15 **Application Fee:** $20.00 **H.S. Requirements:** High school diploma required; GED accepted **Costs Per Year:** Application fee: $20. Comprehensive fee: $18,584 includes full-time tuition ($11,415) and college room and board ($7169). **Scholarships:** Available **Calendar System:** Semester, Summer Session Available **Faculty:** FT 17, PT 5 **Student-Faculty Ratio:** 12:1 **Exams:** SAT I or ACT. **Library Holdings:** 40,000 **Regional Accreditation:** Southern Association of Colleges and Schools **Credit Hours For Degree:** 64 credit hours, Associates **Intercollegiate Athletics:** Baseball M; Basketball W; Cross-Country Running M & W; Golf M & W; Soccer M & W; Softball W

ARGOSY UNIVERSITY, ATLANTA
980 Hammond Dr.
Ste. 100
Atlanta, GA 30328
Tel: (770)671-1200; Free: 888-671-4777
Fax: (770)671-0476
Web Site: http://www.argosy.edu/atlanta/
President/CEO: Michael Falotico
Type: University **Sex:** Coed **Affiliation:** Education Management Corporation **Calendar System:** Semester **Regional Accreditation:** North Central Association of Colleges and Schools **Professional Accreditation:** APA

ARMSTRONG ATLANTIC STATE UNIVERSITY
11935 Abercorn St.
Savannah, GA 31419-1997
Tel: (912)927-5211; Free: 800-633-2349
Admissions: (912)344-2503
Fax: (912)921-5462
E-mail: adm-info@mail.armstrong.edu
Web Site: http://www.armstrong.edu/
President/CEO: Dr. Linda M. Bleicken
Admissions: Stephanie Whaley
Financial Aid: Lee Ann Kirkland
Type: Comprehensive **Sex:** Coed **Affiliation:** University System of Georgia **Scores:** 97% SAT V 400+; 95.8% SAT M 400+; 64.2% ACT 18-23; 22.6% ACT 24-29 **% Accepted:** 60 **Admission Plans:** Early Admission; Deferred Admission **Application Deadline:** August 1 **Application Fee:** $25.00 **H.S. Requirements:** High school diploma required; GED accepted **Costs Per Year:** Application fee: $25. State resident tuition: $3120 full-time, $130 per credit hour part-time. Nonresident tuition: $12,408 full-time, $517 per credit hour part-time. Mandatory fees: $928 full-time, $464 per term part-time. Full-time tuition and fees vary according to program and student level. Part-time tuition and fees vary according to course load and program. College room and board: $5398. College room only: $4998. Room and board charges vary according to board plan and housing facility. **Scholarships:** Available **Calendar System:** Semester, Summer Session Available **Enrollment:** FT 4,623, PT 1,964, Grad FT 305, Grad PT 615 **Faculty:** FT 289, PT 145 **Student-Faculty Ratio:** 17:1 **Exams:** SAT I or ACT, SAT II. ACT essay used for advising. SAT essay used for advising. **% Receiving Financial Aid:** 3 **% Residing in College-Owned, -Operated, or -Affiliated Housing:** 13 **Library Holdings:** 231,500 **Regional Accreditation:** Southern Association of Colleges and Schools **Credit Hours For Degree:** 60 semester hours, Associates; 123 semester hours, Bachelors **ROTC:** Army, Navy **Professional Accreditation:** ABET, AACN, ADA, APTA, ACEHSA, CARC, CEPH, JRCERT, NAACLS, NASM, NCATE, NLN **Intercollegiate Athletics:** Baseball M; Basketball M & W; Cheerleading M & W; Golf M & W; Softball W; Tennis M & W; Volleyball W

THE ART INSTITUTE OF ATLANTA
6600 Peachtree Dunwoody Rd., NE
100 Embassy Row
Atlanta, GA 30328
Tel: (770)394-8300; Free: 800-275-4242
Fax: (770)394-0008
Web Site: http://www.artinstitutes.edu/atlanta/
President/CEO: Janet S. Day
Type: Four-Year College **Sex:** Coed **Affiliation:** Education Management Corporation **Calendar System:** Quarter **Regional Accreditation:** Southern Association of Colleges and Schools **Professional Accreditation:** ACF, FIDER

THE ART INSTITUTE OF ATLANTA—DECATUR
One West Ct. Square, Ste. 110
Decatur, GA 30030
Tel: (404)942-1800; Free: (866)856-6203
Admissions: (404)942-1800
Web Site: http://www.artinstitutes.edu/decatur/
Type: Four-Year College **Sex:** Coed **Affiliation:** Education Management Corporation **Calendar System:** Quarter **Regional Accreditation:** Southern Association of Colleges and Schools

ASHWORTH COLLEGE
430 Technology Parkway
Norcross, GA 30092
Tel: (770)729-8400; Free: 800-957-5412
Fax: (770)729-9296
E-mail: registrar@ashworthcollege.edu
Web Site: http://www.ashworthcollege.edu/
Type: Comprehensive **Sex:** Coed **Affiliation:** Professional Career Development, LLC **H.S. Requirements:** High school diploma required; GED ac-

cepted **Calendar System:** Semester, Summer Session Available **Credit Hours For Degree:** 20 courses, Associates **Professional Accreditation:** DETC

ATHENS TECHNICAL COLLEGE
800 US Hwy. 29 North
Athens, GA 30601-1500
Tel: (706)355-5000
Fax: (706)369-5753
E-mail: lreid@athenstech.edu
Web Site: http://www.athenstech.edu/
President/CEO: Flora W. Tydings
Admissions: Lenzy Reid
Type: Two-Year College **Sex:** Coed **Affiliation:** Technical College System of Georgia **Admission Plans:** Open Admission; Early Admission **Application Fee:** $20.00 **H.S. Requirements:** High school diploma required; GED accepted **Scholarships:** Available **Calendar System:** Quarter, Summer Session Available **Enrollment:** FT 2,099, PT 3,068 **Regional Accreditation:** Southern Association of Colleges and Schools **Professional Accreditation:** ADA, APTA, ACBSP, CARC, JRCERT, NLN

ATLANTA CHRISTIAN COLLEGE
2605 Ben Hill Rd.
East Point, GA 30344-1999
Tel: (404)761-8861; Free: 800-776-1ACC
Admissions: (404)669-4000
E-mail: admissions@acc.edu
Web Site: http://www.acc.edu/
President/CEO: Dean Collins
Admissions: Stacy Bartlett
Financial Aid: Blair Walker
Type: Four-Year College **Sex:** Coed **Affiliation:** Christian **Admission Plans:** Early Admission; Early Decision Plan; Deferred Admission **Application Deadline:** August 1 **Application Fee:** $25.00 **H.S. Requirements:** High school diploma required; GED accepted **Costs Per Year:** Application fee: $25. Comprehensive fee: $20,650 includes full-time tuition ($14,450), mandatory fees ($700), and college room and board ($5500). **Scholarships:** Available **Calendar System:** Semester, Summer Session Available **Enrollment:** FT 664, PT 26 **Exams:** SAT I or ACT. ACT essay not being used. SAT essay not being used. **Library Holdings:** 50,000 **Regional Accreditation:** Southern Association of Colleges and Schools **Credit Hours For Degree:** 64 semester hours, Associates; 128 semester hours, Bachelors **Professional Accreditation:** NCATE **Intercollegiate Athletics:** Baseball M; Basketball M & W; Soccer M & W; Volleyball W

ATLANTA METROPOLITAN COLLEGE
1630 Metropolitan Parkway, SW
Atlanta, GA 30310-4498
Tel: (404)756-4000
E-mail: admissions@atlm.edu
Web Site: http://www.atlm.edu/
President/CEO: Dr. Gary McGaha
Admissions: Audrey Reid
Type: Two-Year College **Sex:** Coed **Affiliation:** University System of Georgia **% Accepted:** 27 **Application Deadline:** July 15 **Application Fee:** $20.00 **H.S. Requirements:** High school diploma required; GED accepted **Scholarships:** Available **Calendar System:** Semester, Summer Session Available **Enrollment:** FT 826, PT 840 **Faculty:** FT 43, PT 42 **Student-Faculty Ratio:** 20:1 **Library Holdings:** 49,585 **Regional Accreditation:** Southern Association of Colleges and Schools **Credit Hours For Degree:** 60 credit hours, Associates **Professional Accreditation:** ACBSP **Intercollegiate Athletics:** Basketball M & W; Cheerleading M & W

ATLANTA TECHNICAL COLLEGE
1560 Metropolitan Parkway, SW
Atlanta, GA 30310
Tel: (404)225-4601
Fax: (404)752-0809
E-mail: vbillups@atlantatech.edu
Web Site: http://www.atlantatech.org/
President/CEO: Alvetta Thomas, EdD
Type: Two-Year College **Sex:** Coed **Affiliation:** Technical College System of Georgia **Admission Plans:** Open Admission; Early Admission **Application Fee:** $20.00 **H.S. Requirements:** High school diploma required; GED accepted **Calendar System:** Quarter **Enrollment:** FT 2,395, PT 2,345 **Regional Accreditation:** Southern Association of Colleges and Schools **Professional Accreditation:** ADA, COE

AUGUSTA STATE UNIVERSITY
2500 Walton Way
Augusta, GA 30904-2200
Tel: (706)737-1400; Free: 800-341-4373
Admissions: (706)737-1632
Fax: (706)737-1774
E-mail: admissions@aug.edu
Web Site: http://www.aug.edu/
President/CEO: Dr. William A. Bloodworth, Jr.
Admissions: Jody Wilson
Financial Aid: Roxanne Padgett
Type: Comprehensive **Sex:** Coed **Affiliation:** University System of Georgia **Scores:** 90.4% SAT V 400+; 92.4% SAT M 400+; 58.8% ACT 18-23; 10.2% ACT 24-29 **% Accepted:** 61 **Admission Plans:** Deferred Admission **Application Fee:** $30.00 **H.S. Requirements:** High school diploma required; GED accepted **Costs Per Year:** Application fee: $30. One-time mandatory fee: $75. State resident tuition: $3120 full-time, $130 per credit hour part-time. Nonresident tuition: $12,408 full-time, $517 per credit hour part-time. Mandatory fees: $610 full-time, $610. College room only: $5250. **Scholarships:** Available **Calendar System:** Semester, Summer Session Available **Enrollment:** FT 4,181, PT 1,654, Grad FT 585, Grad PT 641 **Faculty:** FT 243, PT 192 **Student-Faculty Ratio:** 18:1 **Exams:** SAT I or ACT. **% Receiving Financial Aid:** 51 **% Residing in College-Owned, -Operated, or -Affiliated Housing:** 7 **Regional Accreditation:** Southern Association of Colleges and Schools **Credit Hours For Degree:** 60 credits, Associates; 120 credits, Bachelors **ROTC:** Army **Professional Accreditation:** AACSB, ACA, NASAD, NASM, NCATE, NLN **Intercollegiate Athletics:** Baseball M; Basketball M & W; Cross-Country Running M & W; Softball W; Tennis M & W; Volleyball W

AUGUSTA TECHNICAL COLLEGE
3200 Augusta Tech Dr.
Augusta, GA 30906
Tel: (706)771-4000
Fax: (706)771-4016
E-mail: bcrobert@augustatech.edu
Web Site: http://www.augustatech.edu/
President/CEO: Terry Elam
Admissions: Brian Roberts
Type: Two-Year College **Sex:** Coed **Affiliation:** Technical College System of Georgia **Admission Plans:** Open Admission; Early Admission **Application Fee:** $20.00 **H.S. Requirements:** High school diploma required; GED accepted **Scholarships:** Available **Calendar System:** Quarter **Enrollment:** FT 2,398, PT 2,630 **Regional Accreditation:** Southern Association of Colleges and Schools **Professional Accreditation:** ABET, ARCEST, ADA, AOTA, CARC, JRCECT

BAINBRIDGE COLLEGE
2500 East Shotwell St.
Bainbridge, GA 39819
Tel: (229)248-2500
Admissions: (229)248-2504
Fax: (229)248-2525
E-mail: csnyder@bainbridge.edu
Web Site: http://www.bainbridge.edu/
President/CEO: Dr. Tom Wilkerson
Admissions: Connie Snyder
Type: Two-Year College **Sex:** Coed **Affiliation:** University System of Georgia **% Accepted:** 80 **Admission Plans:** Early Admission **Application Deadline:** August 1 **Application Fee:** $0.00 **H.S. Requirements:** High school diploma required; GED accepted **Costs Per Year:** Application fee: $0. State resident tuition: $1838 full-time, $77 per credit hour part-time. Nonresident tuition: $7340 full-time, $306 per credit hour part-time. Mandatory fees: $488 full-time. Full-time tuition and fees vary according to course load. Part-time tuition varies according to course load. Tuition guaranteed not to increase for student's term of enrollment. **Scholarships:** Available **Calendar System:** Semester, Summer Session Available **Enrollment:** FT 1,745, PT 1,800 **Faculty:** FT 71, PT 98 **Exams:** Other, SAT I or ACT.

Library Holdings: 40,950 **Regional Accreditation:** Southern Association of Colleges and Schools **Credit Hours For Degree:** 60 semester hours, Associates

BAUDER COLLEGE
384 Northyards Blvd. NW
Suites 190 and 400
Atlanta, GA 30313
Tel: (404)237-7573; Free: 800-241-3797
Fax: (404)237-1642
Web Site: http://www.bauder.edu/
President/CEO: Reginald Morton
Type: Four-Year College **Sex:** Coed **Affiliation:** Kaplan Higher Education **H.S. Requirements:** High school diploma required; GED accepted **Scholarships:** Available **Calendar System:** Quarter **Regional Accreditation:** Southern Association of Colleges and Schools

BERRY COLLEGE
PO Box 490159
Mount Berry, GA 30149-0159
Tel: (706)232-5374; Free: 800-237-7942
Admissions: (706)236-2215
Fax: (706)236-2248
E-mail: admissions@berry.edu
Web Site: http://www.berry.edu/
President/CEO: Dr. Stephen R. Briggs
Admissions: Timothy Tarpley
Financial Aid: Marcia McConnell
Type: Comprehensive **Sex:** Coed **Affiliation:** interdenominational **Scores:** 99% SAT V 400+; 100% SAT M 400+; 35% ACT 18-23; 50% ACT 24-29 **% Accepted:** 67 **Admission Plans:** Early Admission; Deferred Admission **Application Deadline:** July 23 **Application Fee:** $50.00 **H.S. Requirements:** High school diploma required; GED accepted **Costs Per Year:** Application fee: $50. Comprehensive fee: $31,700 includes full-time tuition ($23,160), mandatory fees ($200), and college room and board ($8340). College room only: $4660. Room and board charges vary according to board plan and housing facility. Part-time tuition: $772 per credit hour. **Scholarships:** Available **Calendar System:** Semester, Summer Session Available **Enrollment:** FT 1,737, PT 40, Grad FT 8, Grad PT 137 **Faculty:** FT 145, PT 59 **Student-Faculty Ratio:** 12:1 **Exams:** SAT I or ACT. **% Receiving Financial Aid:** 68 **% Residing in College-Owned, -Operated, or -Affiliated Housing:** 84 **Final Year or Final Semester Residency Requirement:** Yes **Library Holdings:** 347,056 **Regional Accreditation:** Southern Association of Colleges and Schools **Credit Hours For Degree:** 124 semester hours, Bachelors **Professional Accreditation:** AACSB, AAFCS, NASM, NCATE **Intercollegiate Athletics:** Baseball M; Basketball M & W; Cross-Country Running M & W; Equestrian Sports W; Golf M & W; Lacrosse M & W; Soccer M & W; Softball W; Swimming and Diving M & W; Tennis M & W; Volleyball W

BEULAH HEIGHTS UNIVERSITY
892 Berne St., SE, PO Box 18145
Atlanta, GA 30316
Tel: (404)627-2681; Free: 888-777-BHBC
Fax: (404)627-0702
E-mail: john.dreher@beulah.org
Web Site: http://www.beulah.org/
President/CEO: Dr. Benson Karanja
Admissions: John Dreher
Financial Aid: Patricia Banks
Type: Comprehensive **Sex:** Coed **Affiliation:** Pentecostal **Admission Plans:** Open Admission; Early Admission **Application Deadline:** Rolling **Application Fee:** $20.00 **H.S. Requirements:** High school diploma required; GED accepted **Costs Per Year:** Application fee: $20. Tuition: $6900 full-time, $230 per credit hour part-time. Mandatory fees: $200 full-time. College room only: $3200. **Scholarships:** Available **Calendar System:** Semester, Summer Session Available **Enrollment:** FT 291, PT 480, Grad FT 54, Grad PT 76 **Faculty:** FT 8, PT 46 **Student-Faculty Ratio:** 12:1 **Exams:** SAT I or ACT. **% Receiving Financial Aid:** 58 **% Residing in College-Owned, -Operated, or -Affiliated Housing:** 10 **Final Year or Final Semester Residency Requirement:** No **Library Holdings:** 48,000 **Credit Hours For Degree:** 66 semester hours, Associates; 129 semester hours, Bachelors **Professional Accreditation:** ABHE, TACCS **Intercollegiate Athletics:** Ultimate Frisbee M & W; Volleyball M & W

BRENAU UNIVERSITY
500 Washington St. SE
Gainesville, GA 30501
Tel: (770)534-6299; Free: 800-252-5119
Admissions: (770)538-4704
Fax: (770)534-6114
E-mail: admissions@brenau.edu
Web Site: http://www.brenau.edu/
President/CEO: Dr. Ed Schrader
Admissions: Scott Briell
Financial Aid: Pam Barrett
Type: Comprehensive **Sex:** Women **Scores:** 98% SAT V 400+; 90% SAT M 400+ **% Accepted:** 38 **Admission Plans:** Deferred Admission **Application Deadline:** Rolling **Application Fee:** $35.00 **H.S. Requirements:** High school diploma required; GED accepted **Costs Per Year:** Application fee: $35. Comprehensive fee: $30,195 includes full-time tuition ($19,870), mandatory fees ($260), and college room and board ($10,065). Full-time tuition and fees vary according to location and program. Part-time tuition: $662 per credit hour. Part-time mandatory fees: $130 per term. Part-time tuition and fees vary according to course load, location, and program. **Scholarships:** Available **Calendar System:** Semester, Summer Session Available **Enrollment:** FT 766, PT 67, Grad FT 54 **Faculty:** FT 73, PT 89 **Student-Faculty Ratio:** 8:1 **Exams:** SAT I or ACT. SAT essay used for advising. SAT essay used for placement. **% Receiving Financial Aid:** 73 **% Residing in College-Owned, -Operated, or -Affiliated Housing:** 55 **Library Holdings:** 89,016 **Regional Accreditation:** Southern Association of Colleges and Schools **Credit Hours For Degree:** 120 semester hours, Bachelors **Professional Accreditation:** AOTA, FIDER, NCATE, NLN **Intercollegiate Athletics:** Basketball W; Crew W; Cross-Country Running W; Soccer W; Softball W; Swimming and Diving W; Tennis W; Volleyball W

BREWTON-PARKER COLLEGE
201 David-Eliza Fountain Circle
PO Box 197
Mt. Vernon, GA 30445
Tel: (912)583-2241; Free: 800-342-1087
Admissions: (912)583-3245
Fax: (912)583-4498
E-mail: kwuerzberger@bpc.edu
Web Site: http://www.bpc.edu/
President/CEO: Dr. David R. Smith
Admissions: Ken Wuerzberger
Financial Aid: Shannon Mullins
Type: Four-Year College **Sex:** Coed **Affiliation:** Southern Baptist **Scores:** 84% SAT V 400+; 86% SAT M 400+; 36% ACT 18-23; 11% ACT 24-29 **% Accepted:** 96 **Admission Plans:** Early Admission **Application Deadline:** Rolling **Application Fee:** $25.00 **H.S. Requirements:** High school diploma required; GED accepted **Costs Per Year:** Application fee: $25. Comprehensive fee: $21,543 includes full-time tuition ($13,920), mandatory fees ($1370), and college room and board ($6253). College room only: $2620. Room and board charges vary according to board plan and housing facility. Part-time tuition: $435 per credit hour. **Scholarships:** Available **Calendar System:** Semester, Summer Session Available **Enrollment:** FT 736, PT 281 **Faculty:** FT 57, PT 142 **Student-Faculty Ratio:** 9:1 **Exams:** SAT I or ACT. **% Receiving Financial Aid:** 80 **% Residing in College-Owned, -Operated, or -Affiliated Housing:** 34 **Library Holdings:** 89,833 **Regional Accreditation:** Southern Association of Colleges and Schools **Credit Hours For Degree:** 61 semesters, Associates; 121 semesters, Bachelors **Professional Accreditation:** NASM **Intercollegiate Athletics:** Baseball M; Basketball M & W; Cheerleading M & W; Soccer M & W; Softball W; Volleyball W

BROWN MACKIE COLLEGE—ATLANTA
4370 Peachtree Rd., NE
Atlanta, GA 30319
Tel: (404)799-4500
Admissions: (404)799-4504
Web Site: http://www.brownmackie.edu/atlanta/
President/CEO: Sidney Sattler
Type: Two-Year College **Sex:** Coed **Affiliation:** Education Management Corporation **Professional Accreditation:** COE

CARVER BIBLE COLLEGE
437 Nelson St.
Atlanta, GA 30313

Tel: (404)527-4520
Fax: (404)527-4526
E-mail: info@carver.edu
Web Site: http://www.carver.edu/
Admissions: Bertha Mack
Type: Four-Year College **Sex:** Coed **Affiliation:** nondenominational **Admission Plans:** Open Admission **Application Fee:** $35.00 **H.S. Requirements:** High school diploma required; GED accepted **Calendar System:** Semester, Summer Session Available **Credit Hours For Degree:** 65 hours, Associates; 130 hours, Bachelors **Professional Accreditation:** ABHE **Intercollegiate Athletics:** Basketball M

CENTRAL GEORGIA TECHNICAL COLLEGE
3300 Macon Tech Dr.
Macon, GA 31206
Tel: (478)757-3400
Fax: (478)757-3454
E-mail: tcarter@centralgatech.edu
Web Site: http://www.centralgatech.edu/
President/CEO: Dr. Flora Tydings
Type: Two-Year College **Sex:** Coed **Affiliation:** Technical College System of Georgia **Admission Plans:** Open Admission; Early Admission **Application Fee:** $15.00 **H.S. Requirements:** High school diploma required; GED accepted **Scholarships:** Available **Calendar System:** Quarter, Summer Session Not available **Enrollment:** FT 3,913, PT 3,037 **Regional Accreditation:** Southern Association of Colleges and Schools **Professional Accreditation:** ADA, COE, NAACLS

CHATTAHOOCHEE TECHNICAL COLLEGE
980 South Cobb Dr., SE
Marietta, GA 30060
Tel: (770)528-4525
Fax: (770)528-4578
E-mail: mcusack@chattahoocheetech.edu
Web Site: http://www.chattahoocheetech.edu/
President/CEO: Sanford Chandler
Type: Two-Year College **Sex:** Coed **Affiliation:** Technical College System of Georgia **Admission Plans:** Open Admission; Early Admission **Application Fee:** $15.00 **H.S. Requirements:** High school diploma required; GED accepted **Scholarships:** Available **Calendar System:** Quarter, Summer Session Not available **Enrollment:** FT 5,335, PT 6,056 **Regional Accreditation:** Southern Association of Colleges and Schools **Professional Accreditation:** ABET, ACF, ACBSP

CLARK ATLANTA UNIVERSITY
223 James P. Brawley Dr., SW
Atlanta, GA 30314
Tel: (404)880-8000; Free: 800-688-3228
Admissions: (404)880-8918
Fax: (404)880-6174
E-mail: cauadmissions@cau.edu
Web Site: http://www.cau.edu/
President/CEO: Dr. Carlton E. Brown
Admissions: Michelle Davis
Type: University **Sex:** Coed **Affiliation:** United Methodist **Scores:** 85% SAT V 400+; 79% SAT M 400+; 81% ACT 18-23; 4% ACT 24-29 **% Accepted:** 59 **Admission Plans:** Early Admission; Deferred Admission **Application Deadline:** June 1 **Application Fee:** $35.00 **H.S. Requirements:** High school diploma required; GED accepted **Costs Per Year:** Application fee: $35. Comprehensive fee: $24,658 includes full-time tuition ($16,328), mandatory fees ($710), and college room and board ($7620). Room and board charges vary according to board plan and housing facility. Part-time tuition: $680 per credit hour. Part-time mandatory fees: $355 per term. **Scholarships:** Available **Calendar System:** Semester, Summer Session Available **Enrollment:** FT 3,067, PT 135, Grad FT 323, Grad PT 348 **Faculty:** FT 178, PT 98 **Student-Faculty Ratio:** 17:1 **Exams:** SAT I or ACT. **% Receiving Financial Aid:** 90 **% Residing in College-Owned, -Operated, or -Affiliated Housing:** 34 **Final Year or Final Semester Residency Requirement:** Yes **Library Holdings:** 375,956 **Regional Accreditation:** Southern Association of Colleges and Schools **Credit Hours For Degree:** 122 credits, Bachelors **ROTC:** Army, Navy **Professional Accreditation:** AACSB, AHIMA, ALA, CSWE, NASPAA, NCATE **Intercollegiate Athletics:** Baseball M; Basketball M & W; Cross-Country Running M & W; Football M; Softball W; Tennis W; Track and Field M & W; Volleyball W

CLAYTON STATE UNIVERSITY
2000 Clayton State Blvd.
Morrow, GA 30260-0285
Tel: (678)466-4000
Admissions: (678)466-4115
E-mail: csc-info@clayton.edu
Web Site: http://www.clayton.edu/
President/CEO: Dr. Thomas J. Hynes, Jr.
Admissions: Carol S. Montgomery
Financial Aid: Pat Barton
Type: Comprehensive **Sex:** Coed **Affiliation:** University System of Georgia **Scores:** 95.8% SAT V 400+; 95.8% SAT M 400+; 42.9% ACT 18-23; 9.8% ACT 24-29 **% Accepted:** 62 **Admission Plans:** Early Admission; Deferred Admission **Application Deadline:** July 17 **Application Fee:** $40.00 **H.S. Requirements:** High school diploma or equivalent not required **Scholarships:** Available **Calendar System:** Semester, Summer Session Available **Enrollment:** FT 3,674, PT 2,738, Grad FT 83, Grad PT 91 **Faculty:** FT 196, PT 172 **Student-Faculty Ratio:** 19:1 **Exams:** SAT I or ACT, SAT II. **% Receiving Financial Aid:** 71 **% Residing in College-Owned, -Operated, or -Affiliated Housing:** 7 **Library Holdings:** 77,043 **Regional Accreditation:** Southern Association of Colleges and Schools **Credit Hours For Degree:** 60 credit hours, Associates; 120 credit hours, Bachelors **ROTC:** Army, Navy, Air Force **Professional Accreditation:** AACSB, AACN, ADA, NCATE, NLN **Intercollegiate Athletics:** Basketball M & W; Cheerleading W; Cross-Country Running M & W; Golf M; Soccer M & W; Tennis W; Track and Field M & W

COLLEGE OF COASTAL GEORGIA
3700 Altama Ave.
Brunswick, GA 31520
Tel: (912)264-7235; Free: 800-675-7235
Admissions: (912)264-7253
Fax: (912)262-3072
E-mail: admiss@ccga.edu
Web Site: http://www.ccga.edu/
President/CEO: Dr. Dorothy L. Lord
Admissions: Lisa Lessig
Type: Four-Year College **Sex:** Coed **Affiliation:** University System of Georgia **% Accepted:** 66 **Admission Plans:** Deferred Admission **Application Deadline:** August 15 **Application Fee:** $20.00 **H.S. Requirements:** High school diploma required; GED accepted **Costs Per Year:** Application fee: $20. State resident tuition: $1838 full-time, $77 per credit hour part-time. Nonresident tuition: $7340 full-time, $306 per credit hour part-time. Mandatory fees: $316 full-time, $91.50 per credit hour part-time. Full-time tuition and fees vary according to student level. Part-time tuition and fees vary according to course load and student level. Tuition guaranteed not to increase for student's term of enrollment. **Scholarships:** Available **Calendar System:** Semester, Summer Session Available **Enrollment:** FT 1,082, PT 1,860 **Faculty:** FT 80, PT 64 **Student-Faculty Ratio:** 18:1 **Regional Accreditation:** Southern Association of Colleges and Schools **Credit Hours For Degree:** 60 semester hours, Associates **Professional Accreditation:** JRCERT, NAACLS, NLN **Intercollegiate Athletics:** Basketball M; Softball W

COLUMBUS STATE UNIVERSITY
4225 University Ave.
Columbus, GA 31907-5645
Tel: (706)568-2001; Free: (866)264-2035
Admissions: (706)507-8806
Fax: (706)568-2123
E-mail: lovell_susan@colstate.edu
Web Site: http://www.colstate.edu/
President/CEO: Dr. Timothy Mescon
Admissions: Susan Lovell
Financial Aid: Janis Bowles
Type: Comprehensive **Sex:** Coed **Affiliation:** University System of Georgia **Scores:** 85.2% SAT V 400+; 86.1% SAT M 400+; 58.1% ACT 18-23; 11.8% ACT 24-29 **% Accepted:** 64 **Admission Plans:** Early Admission; Deferred Admission **Application Deadline:** July 1 **Application Fee:** $30.00 **H.S. Requirements:** High school diploma required; GED not accepted **Costs Per Year:** Application fee: $30. State resident tuition: $3874 full-time, $130 per semester hour part-time. Nonresident tuition: $15,488 full-time, $517 per semester hour part-time. Mandatory fees: $1150 full-time. Full-time tuition and fees vary according to course level and student level. Part-time tuition varies according to course level and student level. College room and board:

$7090. Room and board charges vary according to board plan and location. **Scholarships:** Available **Calendar System:** Semester, Summer Session Available **Enrollment:** FT 4,908, PT 2,061, Grad FT 427, Grad PT 783 **Faculty:** FT 276, PT 192 **Student-Faculty Ratio:** 18:1 **Exams:** SAT I or ACT. **% Receiving Financial Aid:** 60 **% Residing in College-Owned, -Operated, or -Affiliated Housing:** 18 **Final Year or Final Semester Residency Requirement:** No **Library Holdings:** 368,486 **Regional Accreditation:** Southern Association of Colleges and Schools **Credit Hours For Degree:** 63 credits, Associates; 123 credits, Bachelors **ROTC:** Army **Professional Accreditation:** AACSB, ACA, NASAD, NASM, NAST, NCATE, NLN **Intercollegiate Athletics:** Baseball M; Basketball M & W; Cross-Country Running M & W; Golf M & W; Riflery M & W; Soccer W; Softball W; Tennis M & W

COLUMBUS TECHNICAL COLLEGE
928 Manchester Expressway
Columbus, GA 31904-6572
Tel: (706)649-1800
Fax: (706)649-1937
E-mail: taskew@columbustech.edu
Web Site: http://www.columbustech.edu/
President/CEO: J. Robert Jones
Type: Two-Year College **Sex:** Coed **Affiliation:** Technical College System of Georgia **Admission Plans:** Open Admission; Early Admission **Application Fee:** $25.00 **H.S. Requirements:** High school diploma required; GED accepted **Scholarships:** Available **Calendar System:** Quarter **Enrollment:** FT 1,791, PT 2,381 **Regional Accreditation:** Southern Association of Colleges and Schools **Professional Accreditation:** ARCEST, ADA

COVENANT COLLEGE
14049 Scenic Hwy.
Lookout Mountain, GA 30750
Tel: (706)820-1560; Free: 888-451-2683
Admissions: (706)419-1158
E-mail: admissions@covenant.edu
Web Site: http://www.covenant.edu/
President/CEO: Dr. Neil B. Nielson
Admissions: David Gambrell
Financial Aid: Margaret Stewart
Type: Comprehensive **Sex:** Coed **Affiliation:** Presbyterian Church in America **Scores:** 99.5% SAT V 400+; 98% SAT M 400+; 32% ACT 18-23; 51% ACT 24-29 **% Accepted:** 60 **Admission Plans:** Early Admission; Deferred Admission **Application Deadline:** Rolling **Application Fee:** $35.00 **H.S. Requirements:** High school diploma required; GED accepted **Costs Per Year:** Application fee: $35. Comprehensive fee: $32,440 includes full-time tuition ($24,520), mandatory fees ($750), and college room and board ($7170). Full-time tuition and fees vary according to course load. Part-time tuition: $1025 per credit hour. Part-time tuition varies according to course load. **Scholarships:** Available **Calendar System:** Semester, Summer Session Available **Enrollment:** FT 965, PT 33, Grad FT 41, Grad PT 22 **Faculty:** FT 58, PT 29 **Student-Faculty Ratio:** 14:1 **Exams:** SAT I or ACT. **% Receiving Financial Aid:** 61 **% Residing in College-Owned, -Operated, or -Affiliated Housing:** 86 **Library Holdings:** 90,000 **Regional Accreditation:** Southern Association of Colleges and Schools **Credit Hours For Degree:** 62 units, Associates; 126 units, Bachelors **ROTC:** Army **Intercollegiate Athletics:** Baseball M; Basketball M & W; Cross-Country Running M & W; Golf M & W; Soccer M & W; Softball W; Tennis M & W; Volleyball W

DALTON STATE COLLEGE
650 College Dr.
Dalton, GA 30720
Tel: (706)272-4436; Free: 800-829-4436
Admissions: (706)272-4476
Fax: (706)272-2530
E-mail: aharris@daltonstate.edu
Web Site: http://www.daltonstate.edu/
President/CEO: Dr. John O. Schwenn
Admissions: Dr. Angela Harris
Financial Aid: Holly Woods
Type: Four-Year College **Sex:** Coed **Affiliation:** University System of Georgia **Scores:** 53% ACT 18-23; 20% ACT 24-29 **% Accepted:** 60 **Admission Plans:** Open Admission; Deferred Admission **Application Deadline:** July 15 **Application Fee:** $30.00 **H.S. Requirements:** High school diploma required; GED accepted **Costs Per Year:** Application fee: $30. State resident tuition: $2016 full-time, $84 per credit hour part-time. Nonresident tuition: $7992 full-time, $333 per credit hour part-time. Mandatory fees: $276 full-time, $7.33 per credit hour part-time, $50 per term part-time. **Scholarships:** Available **Calendar System:** Semester, Summer Session Available **Enrollment:** FT 3,414, PT 2,308 **Faculty:** FT 137, PT 97 **Student-Faculty Ratio:** 25:1 **% Receiving Financial Aid:** 57 **% Residing in College-Owned, -Operated, or -Affiliated Housing:** 1 **Regional Accreditation:** Southern Association of Colleges and Schools **Credit Hours For Degree:** 60 semester hours, Associates; 120 semester hours, Bachelors **Professional Accreditation:** AAMAE, NAACLS, NLN **Intercollegiate Athletics:** Basketball M & W; Golf W; Softball M & W; Table Tennis M & W; Tennis M & W; Volleyball M & W

DARTON COLLEGE
2400 Gillionville Rd.
Albany, GA 31707-3098
Tel: (229)317-6000
Admissions: (229)430-6740
Fax: (229)430-2926
E-mail: info@darton.edu
Web Site: http://www.darton.edu/
President/CEO: Dr. Peter Sireno
Admissions: Susan Bowen
Type: Two-Year College **Sex:** Coed **Affiliation:** University System of Georgia **Scores:** 75.1% SAT M 400+; 40% ACT 18-23; 6.2% ACT 24-29 **Admission Plans:** Open Admission **Application Deadline:** July 20 **Application Fee:** $20.00 **H.S. Requirements:** High school diploma required; GED accepted **Costs Per Year:** Application fee: $20. State resident tuition: $1848 full-time, $77 per credit hour part-time. Nonresident tuition: $7344 full-time, $306 per credit hour part-time. Mandatory fees: $694 full-time, $252.50 per term part-time. College room only: $5040. $2,298 if 15 credits/semester in-state; $7,340 if 15 credits/semester out-of-state. **Scholarships:** Available **Calendar System:** Semester, Summer Session Available **Enrollment:** FT 2,874, PT 2,980 **Faculty:** FT 118, PT 153 **Student-Faculty Ratio:** 21:1 **Exams:** SAT I or ACT, SAT II. **Final Year or Final Semester Residency Requirement:** No **Library Holdings:** 67,507 **Regional Accreditation:** Southern Association of Colleges and Schools **Credit Hours For Degree:** 60 semester hours, Associates **ROTC:** Army **Professional Accreditation:** ADA, AHIMA, AOTA, APTA, CARC, NAACLS, NLN **Intercollegiate Athletics:** Baseball M; Basketball W; Cross-Country Running M & W; Golf M; Soccer M & W; Softball W; Swimming and Diving M & W; Wrestling M

DEKALB TECHNICAL COLLEGE
495 North Indian Creek Dr.
Clarkston, GA 30021-2397
Tel: (404)297-9522
Fax: (404)294-4234
E-mail: richardt@dekalbtech.org
Web Site: http://www.dekalbtech.edu/
President/CEO: Robin Hoffman
Admissions: Terry Richardson
Type: Two-Year College **Sex:** Coed **Affiliation:** Technical College System of Georgia **Admission Plans:** Open Admission; Early Admission **Application Fee:** $25.00 **H.S. Requirements:** High school diploma required; GED accepted **Scholarships:** Available **Calendar System:** Quarter **Enrollment:** FT 1,971, PT 2,771 **Regional Accreditation:** Southern Association of Colleges and Schools **Professional Accreditation:** ABET, COptA, NAACLS

DEVRY UNIVERSITY (ALPHARETTA)
2555 Northwinds Parkway
Alpharetta, GA 30009
Tel: (770)521-4900; Free: 800-346-5420
Web Site: http://www.devry.edu/
Financial Aid: David Pickett
Type: Comprehensive **Sex:** Coed **Affiliation:** DeVry University **Admission Plans:** Early Admission; Deferred Admission **Application Deadline:** Rolling **Application Fee:** $50.00 **H.S. Requirements:** High school diploma required; GED accepted **Costs Per Year:** Application fee: $50. Tuition: $14,080 full-time, $550 per credit part-time. **Scholarships:** Available **Calendar System:** Semester, Summer Session Available **Enrollment:** FT 343, PT 369, Grad FT 14, Grad PT 166 **Faculty:** FT 27, PT 31 **Student-Faculty Ratio:** 14:1 **Exams:** ACT essay used for admission. SAT essay used for admission. ACT essay used for placement. SAT essay used for placement. **% Receiving Financial Aid:** 74 **Regional Accreditation:** North

Central Association of Colleges and Schools **Credit Hours For Degree:** 66 credit hours, Associates; 122 credit hours, Bachelors **Professional Accreditation:** ABET

DEVRY UNIVERSITY (DECATUR)
1 West Ct. Square
Decatur, GA 30030-2556
Tel: (404)292-7900
Admissions: (404)270-2700
Fax: (404)292-2321
Web Site: http://www.devry.edu/
President/CEO: Chris Chavez
Financial Aid: Robin Winston
Type: Comprehensive **Sex:** Coed **Affiliation:** DeVry University **Admission Plans:** Early Admission; Deferred Admission **Application Deadline:** Rolling **Application Fee:** $50.00 **H.S. Requirements:** High school diploma required; GED accepted **Costs Per Year:** Application fee: $50. Tuition: $14,080 full-time, $550 per credit hour part-time. **Scholarships:** Available **Calendar System:** Semester, Summer Session Available **Enrollment:** FT 1,300, PT 1,461, Grad FT 53, Grad PT 343 **Faculty:** FT 35, PT 162 **Student-Faculty Ratio:** 22:1 **Exams:** ACT essay used for admission. SAT essay used for admission. ACT essay used for placement. SAT essay used for placement. **% Receiving Financial Aid:** 88 **Regional Accreditation:** North Central Association of Colleges and Schools **Credit Hours For Degree:** 66 credit hours, Associates; 122 credit hours, Bachelors **Professional Accreditation:** ABET

DEVRY UNIVERSITY (DULUTH)
3505 Koger Blvd., Ste. 170
Duluth, GA 30096-7671
Tel: (678)380-9780
Fax: (678)924-0958
Web Site: http://www.devry.edu/
Type: Comprehensive **Sex:** Coed **Calendar System:** Semester **Regional Accreditation:** North Central Association of Colleges and Schools

EAST CENTRAL TECHNICAL COLLEGE
667 Perry House Rd.
Fitzgerald, GA 31750
Tel: (229)468-2000
Fax: (229)468-2110
E-mail: tspires@eastcentraltech.edu
Web Site: http://www.eastcentraltech.edu/
President/CEO: Lisa Tomberlin
Type: Two-Year College **Sex:** Coed **Affiliation:** Technical College System of Georgia **Admission Plans:** Open Admission; Early Admission **Application Fee:** $15.00 **H.S. Requirements:** High school diploma required; GED accepted **Calendar System:** Quarter **Enrollment:** FT 952, PT 809 **Professional Accreditation:** COE

EAST GEORGIA COLLEGE
131 College Circle
Swainsboro, GA 30401-2699
Tel: (478)289-2000
Fax: (478)289-2038
Web Site: http://www.ega.edu/
President/CEO: Dr. John B. Black
Admissions: Linda Connelly
Type: Two-Year College **Sex:** Coed **Affiliation:** University System of Georgia **Scores:** 70% SAT V 400+; 61% SAT M 400+ **% Accepted:** 65 **Admission Plans:** Early Admission; Deferred Admission **Application Deadline:** Rolling **Application Fee:** $20.00 **H.S. Requirements:** High school diploma required; GED accepted **Scholarships:** Available **Calendar System:** Semester, Summer Session Available **Enrollment:** FT 887, PT 431 **Faculty:** FT 33, PT 28 **Student-Faculty Ratio:** 23:1 **Library Holdings:** 43,780 **Regional Accreditation:** Southern Association of Colleges and Schools **Credit Hours For Degree:** 64 semester hours, Associates

EMMANUEL COLLEGE
PO Box 129
181 Springs St.
Franklin Springs, GA 30639-0129
Tel: (706)245-7226
E-mail: admissions@ec.edu
Web Site: http://www.ec.edu/
President/CEO: Michael S. Stewart
Admissions: Mariella Lora
Financial Aid: Gloria Hambrick
Type: Four-Year College **Sex:** Coed **Affiliation:** Pentecostal Holiness Church **% Accepted:** 32 **Admission Plans:** Early Admission; Deferred Admission **Application Deadline:** August 1 **Application Fee:** $25.00 **H.S. Requirements:** High school diploma required; GED accepted **Costs Per Year:** Application fee: $25. Comprehensive fee: $18,400 includes full-time tuition ($12,880) and college room and board ($5520). Part-time tuition: $530 per hour. **Scholarships:** Available **Calendar System:** Semester, Summer Session Available **Enrollment:** FT 660, PT 72 **Faculty:** FT 36, PT 33 **Student-Faculty Ratio:** 15:1 **Exams:** SAT I or ACT. **% Receiving Financial Aid:** 79 **% Residing in College-Owned, -Operated, or -Affiliated Housing:** 46 **Final Year or Final Semester Residency Requirement:** No **Library Holdings:** 84,328 **Regional Accreditation:** Southern Association of Colleges and Schools **Credit Hours For Degree:** 64 semester hours, Associates; 124 semester hours, Bachelors **Intercollegiate Athletics:** Baseball M; Basketball M & W; Soccer M & W; Softball W; Tennis M & W

EMORY UNIVERSITY
201 Dowman Dr.
Atlanta, GA 30322-1100
Tel: (404)727-6123; Free: 800-727-6036
Admissions: (404)727-6036
E-mail: admiss@emory.edu
Web Site: http://www.emory.edu/
President/CEO: Dr. James W. Wagner
Admissions: Jean Jordan
Financial Aid: Dean Bentley
Type: University **Sex:** Coed **Affiliation:** Methodist **Scores:** 100% SAT V 400+; 100% SAT M 400+; 1% ACT 18-23; 24% ACT 24-29 **% Accepted:** 30 **Admission Plans:** Early Admission; Early Decision Plan; Deferred Admission **Application Deadline:** January 15 **Application Fee:** $50.00 **H.S. Requirements:** High school diploma required; GED not accepted. For transfer students with a full year of college credit: High school diploma or equivalent not required **Costs Per Year:** Application fee: $50. Comprehensive fee: $50,900 includes full-time tuition ($38,064), mandatory fees ($536), and college room and board ($12,300). College room only: $7503. Full-time tuition and fees vary according to location. Room and board charges vary according to board plan, housing facility, location, and student level. **Scholarships:** Available **Calendar System:** Semester, Summer Session Available **Enrollment:** FT 6,884, PT 96, Grad FT 5,175, Grad PT 775 **Faculty:** FT 1,229, PT 332 **Student-Faculty Ratio:** 7:1 **Exams:** SAT I or ACT, SAT II. ACT essay used for admission. SAT essay used for admission. ACT essay used as a validity check on application essay. SAT essay used as a validity check on application essay. **% Receiving Financial Aid:** 45 **% Residing in College-Owned, -Operated, or -Affiliated Housing:** 67 **Final Year or Final Semester Residency Requirement:** No **Library Holdings:** 3,479,536 **Regional Accreditation:** Southern Association of Colleges and Schools **Credit Hours For Degree:** 132 semester hours, Bachelors **ROTC:** Army, Air Force **Professional Accreditation:** AACSB, ARCAA, AACN, ABA, ACNM, ADtA, APTA, APA, ACIPE, AALS, ATS, CEPH, JCAHPO, JRCERT, LCMEAMA, NANPWH, NASM, NCATE **Intercollegiate Athletics:** Badminton M & W; Baseball M; Basketball M & W; Cheerleading M & W; Crew M & W; Cross-Country Running M & W; Equestrian Sports W; Fencing M & W; Field Hockey W; Golf M; Gymnastics M & W; Ice Hockey M; Lacrosse M & W; Rock Climbing M & W; Rugby M & W; Sailing M & W; Soccer M & W; Softball W; Swimming and Diving M & W; Tennis M & W; Track and Field M & W; Ultimate Frisbee M & W; Volleyball M & W; Water Polo M & W; Weight Lifting M & W; Wrestling M & W

EMORY UNIVERSITY, OXFORD COLLEGE
100 Hamill St., PO Box 1328
Oxford, GA 30054
Tel: (770)784-8888; Free: 800-723-8328
Admissions: (770)784-8328
Fax: (770)784-8359
E-mail: oxadmission@emory.edu
Web Site: http://oxford.emory.edu/
President/CEO: Dr. Stephen Bowen
Admissions: Jennifer B. Taylor
Type: Two-Year College **Sex:** Coed **Affiliation:** Methodist; Emory University **Scores:** 100% SAT V 400+; 27% ACT 18-23; 59% ACT 24-29 **Admission**

Plans: Early Admission; Early Action; Deferred Admission **Application Deadline:** January 15 **Application Fee:** $50.00 **H.S. Requirements:** High school diploma required; GED not accepted **Costs Per Year:** Application fee: $50. Comprehensive fee: $42,734 includes full-time tuition ($32,800), mandatory fees ($462), and college room and board ($9472). Full-time tuition and fees vary according to course load. Room and board charges vary according to board plan. Part-time tuition: $1000 per credit hour. Part-time tuition varies according to course load. **Scholarships:** Available **Calendar System:** Semester, Summer Session Available **Enrollment:** FT 755, PT 1 **Faculty:** FT 57, PT 14 **Student-Faculty Ratio:** 10:1 **Exams:** SAT I or ACT, SAT II. ACT essay used for advising. SAT essay used for advising. ACT essay used for placement. SAT essay used for placement. ACT essay not being used. SAT essay not being used. **% Residing in College-Owned, -Operated, or -Affiliated Housing:** 95 **Final Year or Final Semester Residency Requirement:** Yes **Library Holdings:** 92,681 **Regional Accreditation:** Southern Association of Colleges and Schools **Credit Hours For Degree:** 67 semester hours, Associates **Intercollegiate Athletics:** Basketball M; Soccer W; Tennis M & W

EVEREST INSTITUTE
1706 Northeast Expressway
Atlanta, GA 30329
Tel: (404)327-8787; Free: 888-741-4270
Fax: (404)327-8980
Web Site: http://www.everest.edu/
President/CEO: Tira Harney Clay
Type: Two-Year College **Sex:** Coed **Calendar System:** Continuous **Professional Accreditation:** ACCSCT

FLINT RIVER TECHNICAL COLLEGE
1533 US Hwy. 19 South
Thomaston, GA 30286
Tel: (706)646-6148; Free: 800-752-9681
Fax: (706)646-6163
Web Site: http://www.flintrivertech.edu/
President/CEO: Jim Wheeless
Type: Two-Year College **Sex:** Coed **Affiliation:** Technical College System of Georgia **Admission Plans:** Open Admission; Early Admission **Application Fee:** $15.00 **H.S. Requirements:** High school diploma required; GED accepted **Calendar System:** Quarter **Enrollment:** FT 554, PT 405 **Professional Accreditation:** COE

FORT VALLEY STATE UNIVERSITY
1005 State University Dr.
Fort Valley, GA 31030
Tel: (478)825-6211; Free: 877-462-3878
Fax: (478)825-6394
E-mail: admissap@fvsu.edu
Web Site: http://www.fvsu.edu/
President/CEO: Larry E. Rivers
Admissions: Donald Moore
Type: Comprehensive **Sex:** Coed **Affiliation:** University System of Georgia **Scores:** 79% SAT V 400+; 81% SAT M 400+; 51% ACT 18-23; 2% ACT 24-29 **% Accepted:** 40 **Admission Plans:** Early Admission; Deferred Admission **Application Deadline:** July 19 **Application Fee:** $30.00 **H.S. Requirements:** High school diploma required; GED accepted **Scholarships:** Available **Calendar System:** Semester, Summer Session Available **Enrollment:** FT 3,001, PT 420, Grad FT 67, Grad PT 83 **Faculty:** FT 153, PT 49 **Student-Faculty Ratio:** 19:1 **Exams:** SAT I or ACT. ACT essay not being used. SAT essay not being used. **% Receiving Financial Aid:** 84 **% Residing in College-Owned, -Operated, or -Affiliated Housing:** 62 **Regional Accreditation:** Southern Association of Colleges and Schools **Credit Hours For Degree:** 60 hours, Associates; 120 hours, Bachelors **ROTC:** Army **Professional Accreditation:** ABET, AAFCS, CORE, MACTE, NCATE **Intercollegiate Athletics:** Basketball M & W; Football M; Golf M; Tennis M & W; Track and Field M & W; Volleyball W

GAINESVILLE STATE COLLEGE
PO Box 1358
Gainesville, GA 30503-1358
Tel: (770)718-3639
Admissions: (678)717-3641
Fax: (770)718-3859
E-mail: admissions@gsc.edu
Web Site: http://www.gsc.edu/
President/CEO: Dr. Martha T. Nesbitt
Admissions: Mack Palmour
Type: Two-Year College **Sex:** Coed **Affiliation:** University System of Georgia **% Accepted:** 83 **Admission Plans:** Early Admission **Application Deadline:** July 1 **Application Fee:** $35.00 **H.S. Requirements:** High school diploma required; GED accepted **Costs Per Year:** Application fee: $35. State resident tuition: $2016 full-time, $84 per credit hour part-time. Nonresident tuition: $7992 full-time, $333 per credit hour part-time. Mandatory fees: $554 full-time, $484 per year part-time. **Scholarships:** Available **Calendar System:** Semester, Summer Session Available **Enrollment:** FT 6,068, PT 2,733 **Faculty:** FT 196, PT 205 **Student-Faculty Ratio:** 26:1 **Exams:** SAT I or ACT. **Final Year or Final Semester Residency Requirement:** No **Library Holdings:** 70,000 **Regional Accreditation:** Southern Association of Colleges and Schools **Credit Hours For Degree:** 60 semester hours, Associates **ROTC:** Army, Air Force **Professional Accreditation:** ADA, ACBSP

GEORGIA COLLEGE & STATE UNIVERSITY
Hancock St.
Milledgeville, GA 31061
Tel: (478)445-5004
Admissions: (478)445-1283
Fax: (478)445-6795
E-mail: info@gcsu.edu
Web Site: http://www.gcsu.edu/
President/CEO: Dr. Dorothy Leland
Admissions: Mike Augustine
Financial Aid: Cathy Crawley
Type: Comprehensive **Sex:** Coed **Affiliation:** University System of Georgia **Scores:** 100% SAT V 400+; 100% SAT M 400+; 50% ACT 18-23; 47% ACT 24-29 **% Accepted:** 59 **Admission Plans:** Early Admission; Early Action; Deferred Admission **Application Deadline:** April 1 **Application Fee:** $40.00 **H.S. Requirements:** High school diploma required; GED accepted **Costs Per Year:** Application fee: $40. State resident tuition: $5684 full-time, $190 per credit hour part-time. Nonresident tuition: $22,722 full-time, $758 per credit hour part-time. Mandatory fees: $1218 full-time, $609 per term part-time. Full-time tuition and fees vary according to location and student level. Part-time tuition and fees vary according to course load and location. College room and board: $8228. College room only: $4568. Room and board charges vary according to board plan and housing facility. **Scholarships:** Available **Calendar System:** Semester, Summer Session Available **Enrollment:** FT 4,954, PT 536 **Faculty:** FT 297, PT 115 **Student-Faculty Ratio:** 17:1 **Exams:** SAT I or ACT, SAT II. **% Receiving Financial Aid:** 43 **% Residing in College-Owned, -Operated, or -Affiliated Housing:** 39 **Library Holdings:** 199,506 **Regional Accreditation:** Southern Association of Colleges and Schools **Credit Hours For Degree:** 120 semester hours, Bachelors **ROTC:** Army **Professional Accreditation:** AACSB, NASM, NASPAA, NCATE, NLN **Intercollegiate Athletics:** Baseball M; Basketball M & W; Cheerleading M & W; Cross-Country Running M & W; Golf M; Soccer W; Softball W; Tennis M & W

GEORGIA GWINNETT COLLEGE
1000 University Center Ln.
Lawrenceville, GA 30043
Tel: (678)407-5000
Web Site: http://www.ggc.usg.edu/
President/CEO: Dr. Daniel J. Kaufman
Type: Four-Year College **Sex:** Coed **Regional Accreditation:** Southern Association of Colleges and Schools

GEORGIA HIGHLANDS COLLEGE
3175 Cedartown Hwy.
Rome, GA 30161
Tel: (706)802-5000; Free: 800-332-2406
Admissions: (706)295-6339
Fax: (706)295-6610
E-mail: tjones@highlands.edu
Web Site: http://www.highlands.edu/
President/CEO: Dr. J. Randy Pierce
Admissions: Todd Jones
Type: Two-Year College **Sex:** Coed **Affiliation:** University System of Georgia **% Accepted:** 78 **Admission Plans:** Deferred Admission **Application Deadline:** Rolling **Application Fee:** $20.00 **H.S. Requirements:** High

school diploma required; GED accepted **Costs Per Year:** Application fee: $20. State resident tuition: $1848 full-time, $77 per credit hour part-time. Nonresident tuition: $7344 full-time, $306 per credit hour part-time. Mandatory fees: $434 full-time, $217 per term part-time, $217 per term part-time. Part-time tuition and fees vary according to course load. **Scholarships:** Available **Calendar System:** Semester, Summer Session Available **Enrollment:** FT 3,184, PT 2,062 **Faculty:** FT 115, PT 99 **Student-Faculty Ratio:** 25:1 **Exams:** ACT essay not being used. SAT essay not being used. **Final Year or Final Semester Residency Requirement:** No **Library Holdings:** 68,346 **Regional Accreditation:** Southern Association of Colleges and Schools **Credit Hours For Degree:** 60 semester hours, Associates **Professional Accreditation:** ADA, NLN

GEORGIA INSTITUTE OF TECHNOLOGY
225 North Ave., NW
Atlanta, GA 30332-0001
Tel: (404)894-2000
Admissions: (404)894-4154
Fax: (404)853-9163
E-mail: admission@gatech.edu
Web Site: http://www.gatech.edu/
President/CEO: Dr. G.P. (Bud) Peterson
Admissions: Rick A. Clark, Jr.
Financial Aid: Marie Mons
Type: University **Sex:** Coed **Affiliation:** University System of Georgia **Scores:** 99.84% SAT V 400+; 99.8% SAT M 400+; 3.56% ACT 18-23; 52.09% ACT 24-29 **% Accepted:** 59 **Admission Plans:** Preferred Admission; Early Admission; Early Action **Application Deadline:** January 15 **Application Fee:** $65.00 **H.S. Requirements:** High school diploma required; GED accepted **Costs Per Year:** Application fee: $65. State resident tuition: $6070 full-time, $300 per credit hour part-time. Nonresident tuition: $24,480 full-time, $1200 per credit hour part-time. Mandatory fees: $1436 full-time, $275 per course part-time, $718 per term part-time. Full-time tuition and fees vary according to course load and reciprocity agreements. Part-time tuition and fees vary according to course load and reciprocity agreements. College room and board: $8384. College room only: $5054. Room and board charges vary according to board plan and housing facility. **Scholarships:** Available **Calendar System:** Semester, Summer Session Available **Enrollment:** FT 12,422, PT 1,093, Grad FT 5,506, Grad PT 1,270 **Faculty:** FT 939, PT 125 **Exams:** SAT I or ACT. ACT essay used for admission. SAT essay used for admission. ACT essay used for advising. SAT essay used for advising. **% Receiving Financial Aid:** 34 **% Residing in College-Owned, -Operated, or -Affiliated Housing:** 60 **Final Year or Final Semester Residency Requirement:** No **Library Holdings:** 2,541,880 **Regional Accreditation:** Southern Association of Colleges and Schools **Credit Hours For Degree:** 120 semester hours, Bachelors **ROTC:** Army, Navy, Air Force **Professional Accreditation:** AACSB, ABET, ACCE, ACSP, NAAB **Intercollegiate Athletics:** Baseball M; Basketball M & W; Cheerleading M & W; Cross-Country Running M & W; Football M; Golf M; Ice Hockey M; Lacrosse M & W; Rugby M; Soccer M & W; Softball W; Swimming and Diving M & W; Tennis M & W; Track and Field M & W; Volleyball W; Wrestling M

GEORGIA MILITARY COLLEGE
201 East Greene St.
Milledgeville, GA 31061-3398
Tel: (478)387-4900; Free: 800-342-0413
Admissions: (478)387-4948
Fax: (478)445-2688
E-mail: dfindley@gmc.cc.ga.us
Web Site: http://www.gmc.cc.ga.us/
President/CEO: Gen. Peter Boylan
Admissions: Donna W. Findley
Type: Two-Year College **Sex:** Coed **% Accepted:** 100 **Admission Plans:** Early Admission; Deferred Admission **Application Deadline:** Rolling **Application Fee:** $35.00 **H.S. Requirements:** High school diploma required; GED accepted **Costs Per Year:** Application fee: $35. One-time mandatory fee: $900. State resident tuition: $12,510 full-time, $105 per quarter hour part-time. Mandatory fees: $652 full-time. Part-time tuition varies according to course load. College room and board: $5835. **Scholarships:** Available **Calendar System:** Quarter, Summer Session Available **Enrollment:** FT 4,035, PT 1,689 **Faculty:** FT 82, PT 149 **Student-Faculty Ratio:** 20:1 **Exams:** SAT I or ACT. **Library Holdings:** 57,000 **Regional Accreditation:** Southern Association of Colleges and Schools **Credit Hours For Degree:** 90 quarter hours, Associates **ROTC:** Army **Intercollegiate Athletics:** Football M; Riflery M & W

GEORGIA NORTHWESTERN TECHNICAL COLLEGE
One Maurice Culberson Dr.
Rome, GA 30161
Tel: (706)295-6963
Fax: (706)295-6944
E-mail: dmcburnett@gntc.edu
Web Site: http://www.gntc.edu/
President/CEO: F. Craig McDaniel, EdD
Type: Two-Year College **Sex:** Coed **Affiliation:** Technical College System of Georgia **Admission Plans:** Open Admission; Early Admission **Application Fee:** $15.00 **H.S. Requirements:** High school diploma required; GED accepted **Calendar System:** Quarter **Enrollment:** FT 3,053, PT 2,941 **Regional Accreditation:** Southern Association of Colleges and Schools **Professional Accreditation:** COE

GEORGIA PERIMETER COLLEGE
3251 Panthersville Rd.
Decatur, GA 30034-3897
Tel: (404)244-5090; Free: 888-696-2780
Admissions: (678)891-2300
Fax: (404)244-2996
Web Site: http://www.gpc.edu/
President/CEO: Anthony S. Tricoli
Admissions: Doug Ruch
Type: Two-Year College **Sex:** Coed **Affiliation:** University System of Georgia **% Accepted:** 59 **Admission Plans:** Early Admission **Application Deadline:** July 1 **Application Fee:** $20.00 **H.S. Requirements:** High school diploma required; GED accepted **Costs Per Year:** Application fee: $20. State resident tuition: $2298 full-time, $77 per credit hour part-time. Nonresident tuition: $9176 full-time, $306 per credit hour part-time. Mandatory fees: $544 full-time, $272 per term part-time. Full-time tuition and fees vary according to course load. Part-time tuition and fees vary according to course load. **Scholarships:** Available **Calendar System:** Semester, Summer Session Available **Enrollment:** FT 11,522, PT 13,027 **Faculty:** FT 351, PT 563 **Student-Faculty Ratio:** 24:1 **Exams:** SAT I or ACT. ACT essay not being used. SAT essay not being used. **Library Holdings:** 369,969 **Regional Accreditation:** Southern Association of Colleges and Schools **Credit Hours For Degree:** 62 semester hours, Associates **ROTC:** Army **Professional Accreditation:** ADA, NLN **Intercollegiate Athletics:** Baseball M; Basketball M & W; Soccer M & W; Softball W; Tennis W

GEORGIA SOUTHERN UNIVERSITY
PO Box 8126
Statesboro, GA 30460
Tel: (912)681-5611
Admissions: (912)478-5391
Fax: (912)681-5635
E-mail: admissions@georgiasouthern.edu
Web Site: http://www.georgiasouthern.edu/
President/CEO: Dr. Brooks A. Keel
Admissions: Sarah Smith
Financial Aid: Elise Boyett
Type: University **Sex:** Coed **Affiliation:** University System of Georgia **Scores:** 100% SAT V 400+; 100% SAT M 400+; 63% ACT 18-23; 34% ACT 24-29 **% Accepted:** 56 **Admission Plans:** Early Admission; Deferred Admission **Application Deadline:** May 1 **Application Fee:** $30.00 **H.S. Requirements:** High school diploma required; GED not accepted. For applicants out of high school at least 5 years: High school diploma or equivalent not required **Costs Per Year:** Application fee: $30. State resident tuition: $3996 full-time, $134 per semester hour part-time. Nonresident tuition: $15,972 full-time, $533 per semester hour part-time. Mandatory fees: $1444 full-time, $722 per term part-time. Full-time tuition and fees vary according to degree level, location, and program. Part-time tuition and fees vary according to course load, degree level, location, and program. College room and board: $7900. College room only: $5070. Room and board charges vary according to board plan and housing facility. **Scholarships:** Available **Calendar System:** Semester, Summer Session Available **Enrollment:** FT 14,799, PT 1,687, Grad FT 972, Grad PT 1,628 **Faculty:** FT 728, PT 109 **Student-Faculty Ratio:** 22:1 **Exams:** SAT I or ACT. ACT essay used as a validity check on application essay. SAT essay used as a validity check on application essay. **% Receiving Financial Aid:** 54 **% Residing in College-Owned, -Operated, or -Affiliated Housing:** 27 **Final Year or Final Semester Residency Requirement:** Yes **Library Holdings:** 607,542 **Regional Accreditation:** Southern Association of Colleges and Schools

Credit Hours For Degree: 126 semester hours, Bachelors **ROTC:** Army **Professional Accreditation:** AACSB, ABET, AACN, AAFCS, ACCE, ACA, FIDER, JRCEPAT, NASAD, NASM, NASPAA, NCATE, NLN, NRPA, NAIT **Intercollegiate Athletics:** Baseball M; Basketball M & W; Bowling M & W; Cheerleading M & W; Cross-Country Running W; Equestrian Sports M & W; Fencing M & W; Football M; Golf M; Lacrosse M; Rugby M & W; Soccer M & W; Softball W; Swimming and Diving W; Tennis M & W; Track and Field W; Ultimate Frisbee M & W; Volleyball W; Wrestling M & W

GEORGIA SOUTHWESTERN STATE UNIVERSITY
800 Georgia Southwestern State University Dr.
Americus, GA 31709-4693
Tel: (229)928-1273; Free: 800-338-0082
Fax: (229)931-2983
E-mail: gswapps@canes.gsw.edu
Web Site: http://www.gsw.edu/
President/CEO: Dr. Kendall A. Blanchard
Admissions: David Jenkins
Financial Aid: Angela Bryant
Type: Comprehensive **Sex:** Coed **Affiliation:** University System of Georgia **Scores:** 99% SAT V 400+; 96% SAT M 400+; 62% ACT 18-23; 9% ACT 24-29 **% Accepted:** 79 **Admission Plans:** Early Admission; Early Decision Plan **Application Deadline:** July 21 **Application Fee:** $25.00 **H.S. Requirements:** High school diploma required; GED accepted **Scholarships:** Available **Calendar System:** Semester, Summer Session Available **Enrollment:** FT 1,680, PT 541 **Faculty:** FT 99, PT 56 **Student-Faculty Ratio:** 20:1 **Exams:** SAT I or ACT. **% Receiving Financial Aid:** 68 **% Residing in College-Owned, -Operated, or -Affiliated Housing:** 31 **Regional Accreditation:** Southern Association of Colleges and Schools **Credit Hours For Degree:** 60 semester hours, Associates; 120 semester hours, Bachelors **Professional Accreditation:** AACSB, ACBSP, NCATE, NLN **Intercollegiate Athletics:** Baseball M; Basketball M & W; Golf M; Soccer M & W; Softball W; Tennis M & W

GEORGIA STATE UNIVERSITY
33 Gilmer St.
Atlanta, GA 30302-3083
Tel: (404)651-2000
Admissions: (404)413-2500
E-mail: dniccum@gsu.edu
Web Site: http://www.gsu.edu/
President/CEO: Dr. Mark P. Becker
Admissions: Daniel Niccum
Financial Aid: Louis Scott
Type: University **Sex:** Coed **Affiliation:** University System of Georgia **Scores:** 99.49% SAT V 400+; 99.79% SAT M 400+; 54.04% ACT 18-23; 36.45% ACT 24-29 **% Accepted:** 41 **Admission Plans:** Early Admission; Early Action; Deferred Admission **Application Deadline:** March 1 **Application Fee:** $60.00 **H.S. Requirements:** High school diploma required; GED accepted **Costs Per Year:** Application fee: $60. State resident tuition: $6070 full-time, $203 per credit hour part-time. Nonresident tuition: $24,280 full-time, $810 per credit hour part-time. Mandatory fees: $1428 full-time, $714 per term part-time. Part-time tuition and fees vary according to course load. College room and board: $10,140. College room only: $6950. Room and board charges vary according to housing facility. **Scholarships:** Available **Calendar System:** Semester, Summer Session Available **Enrollment:** FT 16,973, PT 5,411, Grad FT 5,038, Grad PT 3,009 **Faculty:** FT 1,096, PT 407 **Student-Faculty Ratio:** 19:1 **Exams:** SAT I or ACT, SAT II. **% Receiving Financial Aid:** 63 **% Residing in College-Owned, -Operated, or -Affiliated Housing:** 13 **Library Holdings:** 1,758,343 **Regional Accreditation:** Southern Association of Colleges and Schools **Credit Hours For Degree:** 120 semester hours, Bachelors **ROTC:** Army, Navy, Air Force **Professional Accreditation:** AACSB, AACN, ABA, ACA, ADtA, APTA, APA, ASLHA, AALS, ACEHSA, CARC, CORE, CSWE, NASAD, NASM, NASPAA, NCATE, NLN **Intercollegiate Athletics:** Baseball M; Basketball M & W; Cross-Country Running M & W; Football M; Golf M & W; Soccer M & W; Softball W; Tennis M & W; Track and Field M & W; Volleyball W

GORDON COLLEGE
419 College Dr.
Barnesville, GA 30204-1762
Tel: (770)358-5000
Fax: (770)358-3031
E-mail: gordon@gdn.edu
Web Site: http://www.gdn.edu/
President/CEO: Lawrence V. Weill
Type: Two-Year College **Sex:** Coed **Affiliation:** University System of Georgia **Scores:** 64% SAT V 400+; 55% SAT M 400+; 33% ACT 18-23; 33% ACT 24-29 **% Accepted:** 91 **Admission Plans:** Open Admission; Early Admission; Deferred Admission **Application Deadline:** Rolling **Application Fee:** $20.00 **H.S. Requirements:** High school diploma required; GED accepted **Scholarships:** Available **Calendar System:** Semester, Summer Session Available **Enrollment:** FT 2,365, PT 1,230 **Faculty:** FT 97, PT 64 **Student-Faculty Ratio:** 24:1 **% Residing in College-Owned, -Operated, or -Affiliated Housing:** 20 **Library Holdings:** 122,918 **Regional Accreditation:** Southern Association of Colleges and Schools **Credit Hours For Degree:** 64 semester hours, Associates **Professional Accreditation:** NLN **Intercollegiate Athletics:** Baseball M; Soccer M & W; Softball W; Tennis W

GRIFFIN TECHNICAL COLLEGE
501 Varsity Rd.
Griffin, GA 30223
Tel: (770)228-7348
Fax: (770)229-3227
E-mail: tkinard@griffintech.edu
Web Site: http://www.griffintech.edu/
President/CEO: Dr. Robert H. Arnold
Type: Two-Year College **Sex:** Coed **Affiliation:** Technical College System of Georgia **Admission Plans:** Open Admission; Early Admission **Application Fee:** $26.00 **H.S. Requirements:** High school diploma required; GED accepted **Scholarships:** Available **Calendar System:** Quarter, Summer Session Not available **Enrollment:** FT 2,546, PT 2,639 **% Residing in College-Owned, -Operated, or -Affiliated Housing:** 0 **Regional Accreditation:** Southern Association of Colleges and Schools **Professional Accreditation:** ARCEST, COE

GUPTON-JONES COLLEGE OF FUNERAL SERVICE
5141 Snapfinger Woods Dr.
Decatur, GA 30035-4022
Tel: (770)593-2257; Free: 800-848-5352
Fax: (770)593-1891
Web Site: http://www.gupton-jones.edu/
President/CEO: Patty Hutcheson
Admissions: Beverly Wheaton
Type: Two-Year College **Sex:** Coed **Affiliation:** Pierce Mortuary Colleges, Inc. **Admission Plans:** Open Admission **Application Deadline:** Rolling **Application Fee:** $50.00 **H.S. Requirements:** High school diploma required; GED accepted **Scholarships:** Available **Calendar System:** Quarter, Summer Session Available **Library Holdings:** 3,500 **Credit Hours For Degree:** 107 quarter hours, Associates **Professional Accreditation:** ABFSE

GWINNETT TECHNICAL COLLEGE
5150 Sugarloaf Parkway
PO Box 1505
Lawrenceville, GA 30043-5702
Tel: (770)962-7580
E-mail: fhalloran@gwinnetttech.edu
Web Site: http://www.gwinnetttech.edu/
President/CEO: Sharon Bartels
Type: Two-Year College **Sex:** Coed **Affiliation:** Technical College System of Georgia **Admission Plans:** Open Admission; Early Admission **Application Fee:** $20.00 **H.S. Requirements:** High school diploma required; GED accepted **Scholarships:** Available **Calendar System:** Quarter **Enrollment:** FT 3,066, PT 3,583 **Regional Accreditation:** Southern Association of Colleges and Schools **Professional Accreditation:** ADA, APTA, CARC, JRCERT

HEART OF GEORGIA TECHNICAL COLLEGE
560 Pinehill Rd.
Dublin, GA 31021
Tel: (478)275-6589
Fax: (478)275-6642
E-mail: bhutcheson@heartofgatech.edu
Web Site: http://www.heartofgatech.edu/
President/CEO: Randall Peters
Type: Two-Year College **Sex:** Coed **Affiliation:** Technical College System of Georgia **Admission Plans:** Open Admission; Early Admission **Application**

Fee: $15.00 **H.S. Requirements:** High school diploma required; GED accepted **Calendar System:** Quarter **Enrollment:** FT 811, PT 1,004 **Professional Accreditation:** COE

HERZING UNIVERSITY
3393 Peachtree Rd.
Ste. 1003
Atlanta, GA 30326
Tel: (404)816-4533; Free: 800-573-4533
Fax: (404)816-5576
E-mail: info@ath.herzing.edu
Web Site: http://www.herzing.edu/atlanta/
President/CEO: Frank Webster
Admissions: Rose White
Type: Four-Year College **Sex:** Coed **Affiliation:** Herzing, Inc. **% Accepted:** 75 **Application Deadline:** Rolling **Application Fee:** $25.00 **H.S. Requirements:** High school diploma required; GED accepted **Costs Per Year:** Application fee: $25. One-time mandatory fee: $100. Tuition: $9840 full-time, $410 per credit hour part-time. Full-time tuition varies according to course load. **Scholarships:** Available **Calendar System:** Semester **Enrollment:** FT 426, PT 183 **Faculty:** FT 10, PT 15 **Student-Faculty Ratio:** 8:1 **Exams:** Other. **Final Year or Final Semester Residency Requirement:** No **Library Holdings:** 6,000 **Credit Hours For Degree:** 63 credit hours, Associates; 124 credit hours, Bachelors **Professional Accreditation:** ACICS

HIGH-TECH INSTITUTE
1090 Northchase Parkway, Ste. 150
Marietta, GA 30067
Tel: (770)988-9877; Free: 800-987-0110
Admissions: (678)279-7000
Fax: (770)988-8824
E-mail: ckusema@hightechschools.com
Web Site: http://www.high-techinstitute.com/
President/CEO: Melissa Gray
Admissions: Frank Webster
Type: Two-Year College **Sex:** Coed **Calendar System:** Semester **Professional Accreditation:** ACCSCT

INTERACTIVE COLLEGE OF TECHNOLOGY
5303 New Peachtree Rd.
Chamblee, GA 30341
Tel: (770)216-2960; Free: 800-550-3475
Fax: (770)216-2989
Web Site: http://www.ict-ils.edu/
President/CEO: Elmer R. Smith
Admissions: Nicole Caruso
Type: Two-Year College **Sex:** Coed **Affiliation:** Interactive Learning Systems **Admission Plans:** Open Admission **Application Deadline:** Rolling **Application Fee:** $50.00 **H.S. Requirements:** High school diploma required; GED accepted **Enrollment:** FT 1,063, PT 6 **Faculty:** FT 18, PT 44 **Student-Faculty Ratio:** 18:1 **Library Holdings:** 1,600 **Professional Accreditation:** COE

ITT TECHNICAL INSTITUTE (ATLANTA)
485 Oak Place
Ste. 800
Atlanta, GA 30349
Tel: (770)909-4606
Admissions: (770)909-4606
Web Site: http://www.itt-tech.edu/
President/CEO: Kim Ingram
Type: Two-Year College **Sex:** Coed **Affiliation:** ITT Educational Services, Inc. **Professional Accreditation:** ACICS

ITT TECHNICAL INSTITUTE (DULUTH)
10700 Abbotts Bridge Rd.
Duluth, GA 30097
Tel: (678)957-8510; Free: (866)489-8818
Web Site: http://www.itt-tech.edu/
President/CEO: Nicholas Karimi
Type: Two-Year College **Sex:** Coed **Affiliation:** ITT Educational Services, Inc. **H.S. Requirements:** High school diploma required; GED accepted **Scholarships:** Available **Calendar System:** Quarter, Summer Session Not available **Professional Accreditation:** ACICS

ITT TECHNICAL INSTITUTE (KENNESAW)
2065 ITT Tech Way
Kennesaw, GA 30144
Tel: (770)426-2300
Web Site: http://www.itt-tech.edu/
President/CEO: Nasser Salmanzadeh
Type: Two-Year College **Sex:** Coed **Affiliation:** ITT Educational Services, Inc. **Calendar System:** Quarter

KENNESAW STATE UNIVERSITY
1000 Chastain Rd.
Kennesaw, GA 30144-5591
Tel: (770)423-6000
Admissions: (770)423-6300
Fax: (770)423-6541
E-mail: ksuadmit@kennesaw.edu
Web Site: http://www.kennesaw.edu/
President/CEO: Dr. Daniel Papp
Financial Aid: Ron H. Day
Type: Comprehensive **Sex:** Coed **Affiliation:** University System of Georgia **Scores:** 100% SAT V 400+; 100% SAT M 400+; 69% ACT 18-23; 28% ACT 24-29 **% Accepted:** 64 **Admission Plans:** Early Admission; Deferred Admission **Application Deadline:** May 14 **Application Fee:** $40.00 **H.S. Requirements:** High school diploma required; GED not accepted **Costs Per Year:** Application fee: $40. State resident tuition: $4196 full-time, $134 per credit hour part-time. Nonresident tuition: $16,172 full-time, $533 per credit hour part-time. Mandatory fees: $948 full-time. Part-time tuition varies according to course load. College room and board: $6593. Room and board charges vary according to board plan and housing facility. **Scholarships:** Available **Calendar System:** Semester, Summer Session Available **Enrollment:** FT 15,508, PT 4,796, Grad FT 1,027, Grad PT 1,058 **Faculty:** FT 701, PT 533 **Student-Faculty Ratio:** 21:1 **Exams:** SAT I or ACT. **% Receiving Financial Aid:** 54 **% Residing in College-Owned, -Operated, or -Affiliated Housing:** 15 **Library Holdings:** 556,325 **Regional Accreditation:** Southern Association of Colleges and Schools **Credit Hours For Degree:** 123 semester hours, Bachelors **ROTC:** Army, Air Force **Professional Accreditation:** AACSB, AACN, CSWE, NASAD, NASM, NASPAA, NAST, NCATE, NLN **Intercollegiate Athletics:** Baseball M; Basketball M & W; Cheerleading W; Cross-Country Running M & W; Golf M & W; Soccer M & W; Softball W; Tennis M & W; Track and Field M & W; Ultimate Frisbee M; Volleyball M & W

LAGRANGE COLLEGE
601 Broad St.
LaGrange, GA 30240-2999
Tel: (706)880-8000; Free: 800-593-2885
Admissions: (706)880-8253
Fax: (706)880-8040
E-mail: lgcadmis@lagrange.edu
Web Site: http://www.lagrange.edu/
President/CEO: Dr. Dan McAlexander
Admissions: Dana Paul
Financial Aid: Michelle Reeves
Type: Comprehensive **Sex:** Coed **Affiliation:** United Methodist **Scores:** 96.2% SAT V 400+; 96.8% SAT M 400+; 63.2% ACT 18-23; 36.8% ACT 24-29 **% Accepted:** 65 **Admission Plans:** Early Admission; Early Action; Deferred Admission **Application Deadline:** Rolling **Application Fee:** $30.00 **H.S. Requirements:** High school diploma required; GED accepted **Costs Per Year:** Application fee: $30. Comprehensive fee: $29,745 includes full-time tuition ($21,094), mandatory fees ($75), and college room and board ($8576). College room only: $5022. Full-time tuition and fees vary according to class time, course load, degree level, and program. Room and board charges vary according to board plan and housing facility. Part-time tuition: $869 per hour. Part-time tuition varies according to class time, course load, degree level, and program. **Scholarships:** Available **Calendar System:** 4-1-4, Summer Session Available **Enrollment:** FT 776, PT 89, Grad FT 145, Grad PT 17 **Faculty:** FT 65, PT 82 **Student-Faculty Ratio:** 10:1 **Exams:** SAT I or ACT. **% Residing in College-Owned, -Operated, or -Affiliated Housing:** 62 **Library Holdings:** 116,300 **Regional Accreditation:** Southern Association of Colleges and Schools **Credit Hours For Degree:** 108 semester hours, Bachelors **Professional Accreditation:** ACBSP, NCATE, NLN **Intercollegiate Athletics:** Baseball M; Basketball M & W; Cheerleading

M & W; Cross-Country Running M & W; Football M; Golf M; Lacrosse W; Soccer M & W; Softball W; Swimming and Diving M & W; Tennis M & W; Volleyball W

LANIER TECHNICAL COLLEGE
2990 Landrum Education Dr.
PO Box 58
Oakwood, GA 30566
Tel: (770)531-6300
Fax: (770)531-6328
E-mail: mike@laniertech.edu
Web Site: http://www.laniertech.edu/
President/CEO: Dr. Michael D. Moye
Admissions: Mike Marlowe
Type: Two-Year College **Sex:** Coed **Affiliation:** Technical College System of Georgia **Admission Plans:** Open Admission; Early Admission **Application Fee:** $15.00 **H.S. Requirements:** High school diploma required; GED accepted **Calendar System:** Quarter **Enrollment:** FT 1,646, PT 2,469 **Professional Accreditation:** ADA, COE, NAACLS

LE CORDON BLEU COLLEGE OF CULINARY ARTS, ATLANTA
1957 Lakeside Parkway
Tucker, GA 30084
Tel: (770)938-4711; Free: 888-549-8222
Web Site: http://www.atlantaculinary.com/
President/CEO: Glenn Mack
Type: Two-Year College **Sex:** Coed **Application Fee:** $50.00

LIFE UNIVERSITY
1269 Barclay Circle
Marietta, GA 30060-2903
Tel: (770)426-2600
Admissions: 800-543-3202
E-mail: admissions@life.edu
Web Site: http://www.life.edu/
Admissions: Brian Gipson
Financial Aid: Melissa Waters
Type: Comprehensive **Sex:** Coed **Scores:** 78% SAT V 400+; 83% SAT M 400+; 55% ACT 18-23; 18% ACT 24-29 **% Accepted:** 82 **Application Deadline:** September 1 **Application Fee:** $50.00 **H.S. Requirements:** High school diploma required; GED accepted **Costs Per Year:** Application fee: $50. Comprehensive fee: $20,832 includes full-time tuition ($7605), mandatory fees ($747), and college room and board ($12,480). College room only: $6300. Full-time tuition and fees vary according to course load. Part-time tuition: $169 per credit hour. Part-time mandatory fees: $249 per term. Part-time tuition and fees vary according to course load. **Scholarships:** Available **Calendar System:** Quarter, Summer Session Available **Enrollment:** FT 528, PT 199, Grad FT 1,473, Grad PT 101 **Faculty:** FT 119, PT 47 **Student-Faculty Ratio:** 14:1 **Exams:** SAT I or ACT. ACT essay used for placement. SAT essay used for placement. **% Receiving Financial Aid:** 75 **Library Holdings:** 72,480 **Regional Accreditation:** Southern Association of Colleges and Schools **Professional Accreditation:** ADtA, CCE

LUTHER RICE UNIVERSITY
3038 Evans Mill Rd.
Lithonia, GA 30038-2454
Tel: (770)484-1204; Free: 800-442-1577
E-mail: admissions@lru.edu
Web Site: http://www.lru.edu/
President/CEO: James Flanagan
Admissions: Steve Pray
Financial Aid: Gary W. Cook
Type: Comprehensive **Sex:** Coed **Affiliation:** Baptist **Admission Plans:** Open Admission; Early Admission **Application Deadline:** Rolling **Application Fee:** $50.00 **H.S. Requirements:** High school diploma required; GED accepted **Scholarships:** Available **Calendar System:** Semester **Exams:** Other. **% Receiving Financial Aid:** 72 **Library Holdings:** 45,200 **Credit Hours For Degree:** 126 semester hours, Bachelors **Professional Accreditation:** TACCS

MACON STATE COLLEGE
100 College Station Dr.
Macon, GA 31206
Tel: (478)471-2800; Free: 800-272-7619
Admissions: (478)471-2700
Fax: (478)471-2846
E-mail: mscinfo@mail.maconstate.edu
Web Site: http://www.maconstate.edu/
President/CEO: David A. Bell
Admissions: Ryan Tucker
Type: Four-Year College **Sex:** Coed **Affiliation:** University System of Georgia **Admission Plans:** Early Admission **Application Deadline:** Rolling **Application Fee:** $20.00 **H.S. Requirements:** High school diploma required; GED accepted **Costs Per Year:** Application fee: $20. State resident tuition: $2016 full-time, $84 per semester hour part-time. Nonresident tuition: $7992 full-time, $333 per semester hour part-time. Mandatory fees: $376 full-time, $94 per term part-time. **Scholarships:** Available **Calendar System:** Semester, Summer Session Available **Enrollment:** FT 2,876, PT 3,368 **Faculty:** FT 193, PT 100 **Student-Faculty Ratio:** 21:1 **Exams:** SAT I or ACT, SAT II. **% Receiving Financial Aid:** 55 **Library Holdings:** 80,000 **Regional Accreditation:** Southern Association of Colleges and Schools **Credit Hours For Degree:** 64 semester hours, Associates; 124 semester hours, Bachelors **Professional Accreditation:** AHIMA, CARC, NLN

MEDICAL COLLEGE OF GEORGIA
1120 15th St.
Augusta, GA 30912
Tel: (706)721-0211
Admissions: (706)721-2725
Fax: (706)721-3461
E-mail: underadm@mail.mcg.edu
Web Site: http://www.mcg.edu/
President/CEO: Dr. James N. Thompson
Admissions: Dr. Beverly Boggs
Financial Aid: Dr. Beverly Boggs
Type: Two-Year Upper Division **Sex:** Coed **Affiliation:** University System of Georgia **% Accepted:** 41 **Admission Plans:** Preferred Admission **Application Fee:** $30.00 **H.S. Requirements:** High school diploma required; GED accepted **Costs Per Year:** Application fee: $30. State resident tuition: $6070 full-time, $203 per credit hour part-time. Nonresident tuition: $24,280 full-time, $810 per credit hour part-time. Mandatory fees: $712 full-time. Full-time tuition and fees vary according to location. Part-time tuition varies according to course load and location. **Scholarships:** Available **Calendar System:** Semester, Summer Session Available **Enrollment:** FT 506, PT 32, Grad FT 1,851, Grad PT 126 **Faculty:** FT 688, PT 143 **% Receiving Financial Aid:** 84 **% Residing in College-Owned, -Operated, or -Affiliated Housing:** 10 **Library Holdings:** 165,901 **Regional Accreditation:** Southern Association of Colleges and Schools **Professional Accreditation:** ARCMI, AACN, AANA, ADA, AHIMA, AOTA, APTA, APA, CARC, JRCEDMS, JRCERT, JRCNMT, LCMEAMA, NAACLS, NLN

MERCER UNIVERSITY
1400 Coleman Ave.
Macon, GA 31207-0003
Tel: (478)301-2700; Free: 800-840-8577
Admissions: (478)301-2312
Fax: (478)301-2828
E-mail: dunn_e@mercer.edu
Web Site: http://www.mercer.edu/
President/CEO: William D. Underwood
Admissions: Emory Dunn
Financial Aid: Carol Williams
Type: University **Sex:** Coed **Affiliation:** Baptist **Scores:** 100% SAT V 400+; 100% SAT M 400+; 17% ACT 18-23; 60% ACT 24-29 **% Accepted:** 62 **Admission Plans:** Early Admission; Early Action; Deferred Admission **Application Deadline:** July 1 **Application Fee:** $50.00 **H.S. Requirements:** High school diploma required; GED accepted **Costs Per Year:** Application fee: $50. Comprehensive fee: $38,328 includes full-time tuition ($29,340), mandatory fees ($200), and college room and board ($8788). Full-time tuition and fees vary according to class time and location. Room and board charges vary according to board plan, housing facility, and location. Part-time tuition: $978 per credit hour. Part-time mandatory fees: $8.50 per credit hour. Part-time tuition and fees vary according to class time, course load, and location. **Scholarships:** Available **Calendar System:** Semester, Summer Session Available **Enrollment:** FT 2,267, PT 41, Grad FT 2,347, Grad PT 1,194 **Faculty:** FT 370, PT 264 **Student-Faculty Ratio:** 14:1 **Exams:** SAT I or ACT. **% Receiving Financial Aid:** 71 **% Residing in College-**

Owned, -Operated, or -Affiliated Housing: 70 **Library Holdings:** 796,693 **Regional Accreditation:** Southern Association of Colleges and Schools **Credit Hours For Degree:** 120 semester hours, Bachelors **ROTC:** Army **Professional Accreditation:** AACSB, ABET, ACPhE, AAMFT, AACN, AANA, ABA, AALS, ATS, LCMEAMA, NASM, NCATE **Intercollegiate Athletics:** Baseball M; Basketball M & W; Cross-Country Running M & W; Golf M & W; Lacrosse M & W; Riflery M; Soccer M & W; Softball W; Tennis M & W; Volleyball W

MIDDLE GEORGIA COLLEGE
1100 Second St., SE
Cochran, GA 31014-1599
Tel: (478)934-6221
Admissions: (478)934-3103
Fax: (478)934-3199
E-mail: admissions@mgc.edu
Web Site: http://www.mgc.edu/
President/CEO: Dr. Michael Stoy
Admissions: Jennifer Brannon
Type: Two-Year College **Sex:** Coed **Affiliation:** University System of Georgia **Scores:** 77% SAT V 400+; 73% SAT M 400+; 33% ACT 18-23; 7% ACT 24-29 **% Accepted:** 89 **Admission Plans:** Early Admission; Deferred Admission **Application Deadline:** Rolling **Application Fee:** $20.00 **H.S. Requirements:** High school diploma required; GED accepted **Costs Per Year:** Application fee: $20. State resident tuition: $2494 full-time, $84 per credit hour part-time. Nonresident tuition: $9976 full-time, $333 per credit hour part-time. Mandatory fees: $474 full-time. Full-time tuition and fees vary according to course load and program. Part-time tuition varies according to course load and program. College room and board: $6800. Room and board charges vary according to board plan and housing facility. Tuition guaranteed not to increase for student's term of enrollment. **Scholarships:** Available **Calendar System:** Semester, Summer Session Available **Enrollment:** FT 2,586, PT 1,028 **Faculty:** FT 115, PT 55 **Student-Faculty Ratio:** 22:1 **Exams:** SAT I or ACT. **% Residing in College-Owned, -Operated, or -Affiliated Housing:** 35 **Library Holdings:** 105,568 **Regional Accreditation:** Southern Association of Colleges and Schools **Credit Hours For Degree:** 60 semester hours, Associates; 125 semester hours, Bachelors **Professional Accreditation:** AOTA, NLN **Intercollegiate Athletics:** Baseball M; Basketball M & W; Soccer M & W; Softball W

MIDDLE GEORGIA TECHNICAL COLLEGE
80 Cohen Walker Dr.
Warner Robins, GA 31088
Tel: (478)988-6800; Free: 800-474-1031
E-mail: cjackson@middlegatech.edu
Web Site: http://www.middlegatech.edu/
President/CEO: Ivan H. Allen
Admissions: Craig B. Jackson
Type: Two-Year College **Sex:** Coed **Affiliation:** Technical College System of Georgia **Admission Plans:** Open Admission; Early Admission **Application Fee:** $15.00 **H.S. Requirements:** High school diploma required; GED accepted **Scholarships:** Available **Calendar System:** Quarter **Enrollment:** FT 2,199, PT 1,344 **Regional Accreditation:** Southern Association of Colleges and Schools **Professional Accreditation:** ADA, COE

MOREHOUSE COLLEGE
830 Westview Dr., SW
Atlanta, GA 30314
Tel: (404)681-2800; Free: 800-851-1254
Admissions: (404)215-2632
Fax: (404)659-6536
Web Site: http://www.morehouse.edu/
President/CEO: Dr. Robert Franklin
Admissions: Terrance Dixon
Financial Aid: James A. Stotts
Type: Four-Year College **Sex:** Men **Scores:** 95% SAT V 400+; 93% SAT M 400+; 60% ACT 18-23; 26% ACT 24-29 **% Accepted:** 67 **Admission Plans:** Early Admission; Early Action; Early Decision Plan; Deferred Admission **Application Deadline:** February 15 **Application Fee:** $45.00 **H.S. Requirements:** High school diploma required; GED accepted **Costs Per Year:** Application fee: $45. Comprehensive fee: $32,322 includes full-time tuition ($19,424), mandatory fees ($1952), and college room and board ($10,946). College room only: $6238. Full-time tuition and fees vary according to course load and student level. Room and board charges vary according to board plan. Part-time tuition: $809 per credit hour. Part-time mandatory fees: $976 per term. Part-time tuition and fees vary according to course load. **Scholarships:** Available **Calendar System:** Semester, Summer Session Available **Enrollment:** FT 2,512, PT 177 **Faculty:** FT 158, PT 55 **Student-Faculty Ratio:** 15:1 **Exams:** SAT I or ACT. ACT essay used for admission. **% Receiving Financial Aid:** 97 **% Residing in College-Owned, -Operated, or -Affiliated Housing:** 96 **Regional Accreditation:** Southern Association of Colleges and Schools **Credit Hours For Degree:** 120 semester hours, Bachelors **ROTC:** Army, Navy, Air Force **Professional Accreditation:** AACSB **Intercollegiate Athletics:** Basketball M; Cross-Country Running M; Football M; Tennis M; Track and Field M

MOULTRIE TECHNICAL COLLEGE
800 Veterans Parkway North
Moultrie, GA 31788
Tel: (229)891-7000
Fax: (229)891-7010
E-mail: lgriffin@moultrietech.edu
Web Site: http://www.moultrietech.edu/
President/CEO: Dr. Tina Anderson
Type: Two-Year College **Sex:** Coed **Affiliation:** Technical College System of Georgia **Admission Plans:** Open Admission; Early Admission **Application Fee:** $15.00 **H.S. Requirements:** High school diploma required; GED accepted **Calendar System:** Quarter **Enrollment:** FT 1,286, PT 1,121 **Professional Accreditation:** COE

NORTH GEORGIA COLLEGE & STATE UNIVERSITY
82 College Circle
Dahlonega, GA 30597
Tel: (706)864-1400; Free: 800-498-9581
Admissions: (706)864-1800
Fax: (706)864-1478
E-mail: admissions@northgeorgia.edu
Web Site: http://www.northgeorgia.edu/
President/CEO: Dr. David Potter
Admissions: Jennifer Chadwick
Financial Aid: Jill Rayner
Type: Comprehensive **Sex:** Coed **Affiliation:** University System of Georgia **Scores:** 100% SAT V 400+; 99% SAT M 400+; 58% ACT 18-23; 36% ACT 24-29 **% Accepted:** 54 **Admission Plans:** Early Admission **Application Deadline:** July 1 **Application Fee:** $30.00 **H.S. Requirements:** High school diploma required; GED accepted **Costs Per Year:** Application fee: $30. State resident tuition: $3874 full-time, $130 per credit hour part-time. Nonresident tuition: $15,488 full-time, $517 per credit hour part-time. Mandatory fees: $1162 full-time. Part-time tuition varies according to course load. College room and board: $5248. College room only: $2758. Room and board charges vary according to board plan and housing facility. **Scholarships:** Available **Calendar System:** Semester, Summer Session Available **Enrollment:** FT 4,111, PT 903, Grad FT 90, Grad PT 548 **Faculty:** FT 218, PT 121 **Student-Faculty Ratio:** 20:1 **Exams:** SAT I or ACT, SAT I and SAT II or ACT. **% Receiving Financial Aid:** 38 **% Residing in College-Owned, -Operated, or -Affiliated Housing:** 31 **Library Holdings:** 173,074 **Regional Accreditation:** Southern Association of Colleges and Schools **Credit Hours For Degree:** 60 semester hours, Associates; 120 semester hours, Bachelors **ROTC:** Army **Professional Accreditation:** APTA, ACBSP, NCATE, NLN **Intercollegiate Athletics:** Baseball M; Basketball M & W; Cheerleading W; Cross-Country Running M & W; Equestrian Sports M & W; Riflery M & W; Soccer M & W; Softball W; Tennis M & W; Track and Field M & W

NORTH GEORGIA TECHNICAL COLLEGE
1500 Georgia Hwy. 197, North
PO Box 65
Clarkesville, GA 30523
Tel: (706)754-7700
Fax: (706)754-7777
E-mail: amitchell@northgatech.edu
Web Site: http://www.northgatech.edu/
President/CEO: Steve Dougherty
Type: Two-Year College **Sex:** Coed **Affiliation:** Technical College System of Georgia **Admission Plans:** Open Admission; Early Admission **Application Fee:** $15.00 **H.S. Requirements:** High school diploma required; GED accepted **Calendar System:** Quarter **Enrollment:** FT 1,814, PT 1,051

Regional Accreditation: Southern Association of Colleges and Schools **Professional Accreditation:** COE, NAACLS

OGEECHEE TECHNICAL COLLEGE
One Joe Kennedy Blvd.
Statesboro, GA 30458
Tel: (912)681-5500; Free: 800-646-1316
E-mail: rfoley@ogeecheetech.edu
Web Site: http://www.ogeecheetech.edu/
President/CEO: Dr. Dawn Cartee
Admissions: Ryan Foley
Type: Two-Year College **Sex:** Coed **Affiliation:** Technical College System of Georgia **Admission Plans:** Open Admission; Early Admission **Application Fee:** $20.00 **H.S. Requirements:** High school diploma required; GED accepted **Calendar System:** Quarter **Enrollment:** FT 1,242, PT 1,177 **Professional Accreditation:** ABFSE, ADA, COptA, COE

OGLETHORPE UNIVERSITY
4484 Peachtree Rd., NE
Atlanta, GA 30319-2797
Tel: (404)261-1441; Free: 800-428-4484
Admissions: (404)364-8307
Fax: (404)364-8500
E-mail: admission@oglethorpe.edu
Web Site: http://www.oglethorpe.edu/
President/CEO: Dr. Lawrence Miller Schall
Admissions: Lucy Leusch
Financial Aid: Meg McGinnis
Type: Comprehensive **Sex:** Coed **Scores:** 100% SAT V 400+; 100% SAT M 400+; 34% ACT 18-23; 58% ACT 24-29 **% Accepted:** 42 **Admission Plans:** Early Admission; Early Action; Deferred Admission **Application Deadline:** Rolling **Application Fee:** $35.00 **H.S. Requirements:** High school diploma required; GED accepted **Costs Per Year:** Application fee: $35. Comprehensive fee: $36,690 includes full-time tuition ($26,450), mandatory fees ($250), and college room and board ($9990). Full-time tuition and fees vary according to degree level and program. Room and board charges vary according to housing facility and location. Part-time tuition: $1217 per credit hour. Part-time tuition varies according to course load, degree level, and program. **Scholarships:** Available **Calendar System:** Semester, Summer Session Available **Enrollment:** FT 923, PT 107, Grad FT 27, Grad PT 42 **Faculty:** FT 46, PT 53 **Student-Faculty Ratio:** 16:1 **Exams:** SAT I or ACT. ACT essay used for admission. SAT essay used for admission. **% Receiving Financial Aid:** 58 **% Residing in College-Owned, -Operated, or -Affiliated Housing:** 61 **Final Year or Final Semester Residency Requirement:** Yes **Library Holdings:** 150,000 **Regional Accreditation:** Southern Association of Colleges and Schools **Credit Hours For Degree:** 120 semester hours, Bachelors **ROTC:** Air Force **Intercollegiate Athletics:** Baseball M; Basketball M & W; Cross-Country Running M & W; Golf M & W; Lacrosse M; Soccer M & W; Tennis M & W; Track and Field M & W; Volleyball W

OKEFENOKEE TECHNICAL COLLEGE
1701 Carswell Ave.
Waycross, GA 31503
Tel: (912)287-6584
Fax: (912)287-4865
E-mail: nmurphy@okefenokeetech.edu
Web Site: http://www.okefenokeetech.edu/
President/CEO: Gail Thaxton
Type: Two-Year College **Sex:** Coed **Affiliation:** Technical College System of Georgia **Admission Plans:** Open Admission; Early Admission **Application Fee:** $20.00 **H.S. Requirements:** High school diploma required; GED accepted **Calendar System:** Quarter **Enrollment:** FT 684, PT 1,050 **Regional Accreditation:** Southern Association of Colleges and Schools **Professional Accreditation:** COE, NAACLS

PAINE COLLEGE
1235 15th St.
Augusta, GA 30901-3182
Tel: (706)821-8200; Free: 800-476-7703
Admissions: (706)821-8320
Fax: (706)821-8293
E-mail: jtinsley@paine.edu
Web Site: http://www.paine.edu/
President/CEO: Dr. George C. Bradley
Admissions: Joseph D. Tinsley
Financial Aid: Gerri Bogan
Type: Four-Year College **Sex:** Coed **Affiliation:** Methodist **Scores:** 43% SAT V 400+; 37% SAT M 400+; 21% ACT 18-23; 1% ACT 24-29 **% Accepted:** 39 **Admission Plans:** Early Admission; Deferred Admission **Application Deadline:** August 1 **Application Fee:** $25.00 **H.S. Requirements:** High school diploma required; GED accepted **Costs Per Year:** Application fee: $25. Comprehensive fee: $17,542 includes full-time tuition ($10,896), mandatory fees ($898), and college room and board ($5748). Full-time tuition and fees vary according to course load, location, and reciprocity agreements. Room and board charges vary according to housing facility. Part-time tuition: $454 per credit hour. Part-time tuition varies according to course load, location, and reciprocity agreements. **Scholarships:** Available **Calendar System:** Semester, Summer Session Available **Enrollment:** FT 855, PT 53 **Faculty:** FT 58, PT 20 **Student-Faculty Ratio:** 13:1 **Exams:** SAT I or ACT. ACT essay used for placement. SAT essay used for placement. **% Residing in College-Owned, -Operated, or -Affiliated Housing:** 60 **Final Year or Final Semester Residency Requirement:** Yes **Library Holdings:** 76,157 **Regional Accreditation:** Southern Association of Colleges and Schools **Credit Hours For Degree:** 124 semester hours, Bachelors **ROTC:** Army **Professional Accreditation:** ACBSP **Intercollegiate Athletics:** Baseball M; Basketball M & W; Cross-Country Running M & W; Golf M; Softball W; Track and Field M & W; Volleyball W

PIEDMONT COLLEGE
PO Box 10
165 Central Ave.
Demorest, GA 30535-0010
Tel: (706)778-3000; Free: 800-277-7020
Admissions: (706)776-0103
Fax: (706)776-6635
E-mail: cpeterson@piedmont.edu
Web Site: http://www.piedmont.edu/
President/CEO: W. Ray Cleere
Admissions: Cynthia L. Peterson
Financial Aid: Kim Lovell
Type: Comprehensive **Sex:** Coed **Affiliation:** United Church of Christ **Scores:** 91% SAT V 400+; 86.5% SAT M 400+; 61.8% ACT 18-23; 19.1% ACT 24-29 **% Accepted:** 60 **Admission Plans:** Early Admission; Deferred Admission **Application Deadline:** July 1 **Application Fee:** $0.00 **H.S. Requirements:** High school diploma required; GED accepted. For home schooled students can submit a portfolio in lieu of transcripts: High school diploma or equivalent not required **Costs Per Year:** Application fee: $0. Tuition: $18,000 full-time, $750 per semester hour part-time. Full-time tuition varies according to course load, degree level, location, and program. Part-time tuition varies according to course load, degree level, location, and program. **Scholarships:** Available **Calendar System:** Semester, Summer Session Available **Enrollment:** FT 1,116, PT 152, Grad FT 458, Grad PT 1,085 **Faculty:** FT 113, PT 134 **Exams:** SAT I or ACT. **% Receiving Financial Aid:** 59 **% Residing in College-Owned, -Operated, or -Affiliated Housing:** 42 **Library Holdings:** 115,400 **Regional Accreditation:** Southern Association of Colleges and Schools **Credit Hours For Degree:** 120 semester hours, Bachelors **Professional Accreditation:** ACBSP **Intercollegiate Athletics:** Baseball M; Basketball M & W; Cross-Country Running M & W; Golf M & W; Soccer M & W; Softball W; Tennis M & W; Volleyball W

REINHARDT UNIVERSITY
7300 Reinhardt College Circle
Waleska, GA 30183-2981
Tel: (770)720-5600
Admissions: (770)720-5526
Fax: (770)720-5602
E-mail: admissions@mail.reinhardt.edu
Web Site: http://www.reinhardt.edu/
President/CEO: J. Thomas Isherwood
Admissions: Julie Fleming
Financial Aid: Angela D. Harlow
Type: Comprehensive **Sex:** Coed **Affiliation:** United Methodist Church **Scores:** 87% SAT V 400+; 81.3% SAT M 400+; 50% ACT 18-23; 27.3% ACT 24-29 **% Accepted:** 68 **Admission Plans:** Early Admission; Deferred Admission **Application Deadline:** Rolling **Application Fee:** $25.00 **H.S. Requirements:** High school diploma required; GED accepted **Costs Per**

Year: Application fee: $25. Comprehensive fee: $22,942 includes full-time tuition ($16,500), mandatory fees ($170), and college room and board ($6272). Full-time tuition and fees vary according to degree level, location, and program. Room and board charges vary according to board plan and housing facility. Part-time tuition: $550 per credit hour. Part-time mandatory fees: $85 per term. Part-time tuition and fees vary according to degree level, location, and program. **Scholarships:** Available **Calendar System:** Semester, Summer Session Available **Enrollment:** FT 978, PT 78, Grad FT 64, Grad PT 3 **Faculty:** FT 60, PT 100 **Student-Faculty Ratio:** 12:1 **Exams:** SAT I or ACT. **% Receiving Financial Aid:** 69 **% Residing in College-Owned, -Operated, or -Affiliated Housing:** 44 **Final Year or Final Semester Residency Requirement:** No **Library Holdings:** 60,278 **Regional Accreditation:** Southern Association of Colleges and Schools **Credit Hours For Degree:** 60 credit hours, Associates; 120 credit hours, Bachelors **Professional Accreditation:** NASM **Intercollegiate Athletics:** Baseball M; Basketball M & W; Cross-Country Running M & W; Golf M; Lacrosse M & W; Soccer M & W; Softball W; Tennis M & W; Volleyball W

SANDERSVILLE TECHNICAL COLLEGE
1189 Deepstep Rd.
Sandersville, GA 31082
Tel: (478)553-2050
Fax: (478)553-2118
E-mail: tchapman@sandervilletech.edu
Web Site: http://www.sandersvilletech.edu/
President/CEO: Lloyd Horadan
Type: Two-Year College **Sex:** Coed **Affiliation:** Technical College System of Georgia **Admission Plans:** Open Admission; Early Admission **Application Fee:** $15.00 **H.S. Requirements:** High school diploma required; GED accepted **Calendar System:** Quarter **Enrollment:** FT 389, PT 727 **Professional Accreditation:** COE

SAVANNAH COLLEGE OF ART AND DESIGN
342 Bull St., PO Box 3146
Savannah, GA 31402-3146
Tel: (912)525-5000; Free: 800-869-7223
Admissions: (912)525-5100
Fax: (912)238-2436
E-mail: admission@scad.edu
Web Site: http://www.scad.edu/
President/CEO: Paula S. Wallace
Admissions: Ginger Hansen
Financial Aid: Brenda Clark
Type: Comprehensive **Sex:** Coed **Scores:** 97% SAT V 400+; 95% SAT M 400+; 47% ACT 18-23; 40% ACT 24-29 **% Accepted:** 68 **Admission Plans:** Early Admission; Deferred Admission **Application Deadline:** Rolling **Application Fee:** $50.00 **H.S. Requirements:** High school diploma required; GED accepted **Costs Per Year:** Application fee: $50. Comprehensive fee: $41,320 includes full-time tuition ($29,070), mandatory fees ($500), and college room and board ($11,750). Full-time tuition and fees vary according to course load and degree level. Room and board charges vary according to board plan, housing facility, and location. Part-time tuition: $646 per quarter hour. Part-time tuition varies according to course load and degree level. **Scholarships:** Available **Calendar System:** Quarter, Summer Session Available **Enrollment:** FT 7,194, PT 994, Grad FT 1,451, Grad PT 267 **Faculty:** FT 491, PT 167 **Student-Faculty Ratio:** 17:1 **Exams:** SAT I or ACT. ACT essay used for admission. SAT essay used for admission. **% Receiving Financial Aid:** 56 **% Residing in College-Owned, -Operated, or -Affiliated Housing:** 35 **Final Year or Final Semester Residency Requirement:** No **Library Holdings:** 203,002 **Regional Accreditation:** Southern Association of Colleges and Schools **Credit Hours For Degree:** 180 quarter credit hours, Bachelors **ROTC:** Army **Professional Accreditation:** NAAB **Intercollegiate Athletics:** Baseball M; Cheerleading M & W; Cross-Country Running M & W; Equestrian Sports M & W; Fencing M & W; Golf M & W; Lacrosse W; Soccer M & W; Softball W; Swimming and Diving M & W; Tennis M & W; Volleyball W

SAVANNAH RIVER COLLEGE
2528 Center West Parkway
Augusta, GA 30909
Tel: (706)738-5046
Fax: (706)736-3599
Web Site: http://www.savannahrivercollege.edu/
President/CEO: Darryl Kerr
Type: Two-Year College **Sex:** Coed **% Accepted:** 86 **Application Fee:** $50.00

SAVANNAH STATE UNIVERSITY
3219 College Ave.
Savannah, GA 31404
Tel: (912)356-2186; Free: 800-788-0478
Admissions: (912)356-2345
Fax: (912)356-2529
E-mail: dolanc@savannahstate.edu
Web Site: http://www.savannahstate.edu/
President/CEO: Dr. Earl G. Yarbrough, PhD
Admissions: Carol Dolan
Financial Aid: Adrienne Brown
Type: Comprehensive **Sex:** Coed **Affiliation:** University System of Georgia **Scores:** 83% SAT V 400+; 80% SAT M 400+; 55.74% ACT 18-23; 1.91% ACT 24-29 **% Accepted:** 40 **Admission Plans:** Early Admission; Deferred Admission **Application Deadline:** July 15 **Application Fee:** $20.00 **H.S. Requirements:** High school diploma required; GED accepted **Scholarships:** Available **Calendar System:** Semester, Summer Session Available **Enrollment:** FT 3,171, PT 515, Grad FT 84, Grad PT 50 **Faculty:** FT 151, PT 29 **Student-Faculty Ratio:** 21:1 **Exams:** SAT I or ACT, SAT I, SAT II. ACT essay not being used. SAT essay not being used. **% Residing in College-Owned, -Operated, or -Affiliated Housing:** 73 **Library Holdings:** 187,916 **Regional Accreditation:** Southern Association of Colleges and Schools **Credit Hours For Degree:** 125 semester hours, Bachelors **ROTC:** Army, Navy **Professional Accreditation:** AACSB, ABET, CSWE, NASPAA **Intercollegiate Athletics:** Baseball M; Basketball M & W; Cheerleading M & W; Cross-Country Running M & W; Football M; Golf M & W; Softball W; Tennis W; Track and Field M & W; Volleyball W

SAVANNAH TECHNICAL COLLEGE
5717 White Bluff Rd.
Savannah, GA 31405
Tel: (912)443-5700
Fax: (912)352-4362
E-mail: jhoze@savannahtech.edu
Web Site: http://www.savannahtech.edu/
President/CEO: Dr. Kathy Love
Type: Two-Year College **Sex:** Coed **Affiliation:** Technical College System of Georgia **Admission Plans:** Open Admission; Early Admission **Application Fee:** $20.00 **H.S. Requirements:** High school diploma required; GED accepted **Scholarships:** Available **Calendar System:** Quarter **Enrollment:** FT 2,430, PT 3,053 **Regional Accreditation:** Southern Association of Colleges and Schools **Professional Accreditation:** ABET, ACF, ADA

SHORTER UNIVERSITY
315 Shorter Ave.
Rome, GA 30165
Tel: (706)291-2121; Free: 800-868-6980
Admissions: (706)233-7342
Fax: (706)236-1515
E-mail: admissions@shorter.edu
Web Site: http://www.shorter.edu/
President/CEO: Dr. Harold E. Newman
Admissions: John Head
Financial Aid: Tara Jones
Type: Comprehensive **Sex:** Coed **Affiliation:** Baptist **Scores:** 91.4% SAT V 400+; 87.8% SAT M 400+; 55.7% ACT 18-23; 22.7% ACT 24-29 **% Accepted:** 65 **Admission Plans:** Early Admission; Deferred Admission **Application Deadline:** August 25 **Application Fee:** $25.00 **H.S. Requirements:** High school diploma required; GED accepted **Costs Per Year:** Application fee: $25. Tuition: $440 per credit hour part-time. **Scholarships:** Available **Calendar System:** Semester, Summer Session Available **Enrollment:** FT 1,167, PT 38 **Faculty:** FT 83, PT 66 **Student-Faculty Ratio:** 11:1 **Exams:** SAT I or ACT. ACT essay used for admission. SAT essay used for admission. ACT essay used for advising. SAT essay used for advising. ACT essay used for placement. SAT essay used for placement. **% Receiving Financial Aid:** 73 **% Residing in College-Owned, -Operated, or -Affiliated Housing:** 54 **Library Holdings:** 144,475 **Regional Accreditation:** Southern Association of Colleges and Schools **Credit Hours For Degree:** 126 semester hours, Bachelors **Professional Accreditation:** NASM **Intercollegiate Athletics:** Baseball M; Basketball M & W; Cheerlead-

ing M & W; Cross-Country Running M & W; Football M; Golf M & W; Soccer M & W; Softball W; Tennis M & W; Track and Field M & W; Volleyball W

SOUTH GEORGIA COLLEGE
100 West College Park Dr.
Douglas, GA 31533-5098
Tel: (912)260-4200
Fax: (912)389-4392
E-mail: danielle.buehrer@sgc.edu
Web Site: http://www.sgc.edu/
President/CEO: Dr. Virginia Carson
Admissions: Danielle S. Buehrer
Type: Two-Year College **Sex:** Coed **Affiliation:** University System of Georgia **Scores:** 72.7% SAT M 400+; 34.3% ACT 18-23; 6.3% ACT 24-29 **Admission Plans:** Early Admission; Deferred Admission **Application Deadline:** Rolling **Application Fee:** $20.00 **H.S. Requirements:** High school diploma required; GED accepted **Costs Per Year:** Application fee: $20. State resident tuition: $2298 full-time, $77 per credit hour part-time. Nonresident tuition: $9176 full-time, $306 per credit hour part-time. Mandatory fees: $540 full-time, $540 per term part-time. College room and board: $7600. College room only: $4250. Room and board charges vary according to board plan and housing facility. **Scholarships:** Available **Calendar System:** Semester, Summer Session Available **Enrollment:** FT 1,487, PT 513 **Faculty:** FT 42, PT 58 **Student-Faculty Ratio:** 27:1 **Regional Accreditation:** Southern Association of Colleges and Schools **Credit Hours For Degree:** 64 semester hours, Associates **Professional Accreditation:** NLN **Intercollegiate Athletics:** Baseball M; Soccer M; Softball W

SOUTH GEORGIA TECHNICAL COLLEGE
900 South Georgia Tech Parkway
Americus, GA 31709
Tel: (229)931-2394
Fax: (229)931-2459
E-mail: wcrisp@southgatech.edu
Web Site: http://www.southgatech.edu/
President/CEO: Sparky Reeves
Type: Two-Year College **Sex:** Coed **Affiliation:** Technical College System of Georgia **Admission Plans:** Open Admission; Early Admission **Application Fee:** $20.00 **H.S. Requirements:** High school diploma required; GED accepted **Calendar System:** Quarter **Enrollment:** FT 1,597, PT 965 **Professional Accreditation:** COE

SOUTH UNIVERSITY
709 Mall Blvd.
Savannah, GA 31406
Tel: (912)201-8000; Free: (866)629-2901
Fax: (912)201-8070
Web Site: http://www.southuniversity.edu/savannah/
President/CEO: Todd Cellini
Type: Comprehensive **Sex:** Coed **Affiliation:** Education Management Corporation **Calendar System:** Quarter **Regional Accreditation:** Southern Association of Colleges and Schools **Professional Accreditation:** ACPhE, AAMAE, APTA, ACBSP

SOUTHEASTERN TECHNICAL COLLEGE
3001 East First St.
Vidalia, GA 30474
Tel: (912)538-3100
Fax: (912)538-3156
E-mail: brhart @southeasterntech.edu
Web Site: http://www.southeasterntech.edu/
President/CEO: Cathryn T. Mitchell
Type: Two-Year College **Sex:** Coed **Affiliation:** Technical College System of Georgia **Admission Plans:** Open Admission; Early Admission **Application Fee:** $15.00 **H.S. Requirements:** High school diploma required; GED accepted **Calendar System:** Quarter **Enrollment:** FT 899, PT 1,073 **Regional Accreditation:** Southern Association of Colleges and Schools **Professional Accreditation:** COE

SOUTHERN POLYTECHNIC STATE UNIVERSITY
1100 South Marietta Parkway
Marietta, GA 30060-2896
Tel: (678)915-7778; Free: 800-635-3204
Admissions: (678)915-7468
E-mail: gbush@spsu.edu
Web Site: http://www.spsu.edu/
President/CEO: Dr. Lisa A. Rossbacher
Admissions: Gary Bush
Financial Aid: Gary Mann
Type: Comprehensive **Sex:** Coed **Affiliation:** University System of Georgia **Scores:** 100% SAT V 400+; 100% SAT M 400+; 60% ACT 18-23; 36% ACT 24-29 **% Accepted:** 61 **Admission Plans:** Deferred Admission **Application Deadline:** July 1 **Application Fee:** $20.00 **H.S. Requirements:** High school diploma required; GED not accepted **Costs Per Year:** Application fee: $20. State resident tuition: $3502 full-time, $146 per credit hour part-time. Nonresident tuition: $13,998 full-time, $584 per credit hour part-time. Mandatory fees: $996 full-time, $498 per term part-time. Full-time tuition and fees vary according to course load and degree level. Part-time tuition and fees vary according to course load and degree level. College room and board: $6350. College room only: $3550. Room and board charges vary according to board plan. **Scholarships:** Available **Calendar System:** Semester, Summer Session Available **Enrollment:** FT 3,317, PT 1,247, Grad FT 195, Grad PT 427 **Faculty:** FT 177, PT 101 **Student-Faculty Ratio:** 18:1 **Exams:** SAT I or ACT. **% Receiving Financial Aid:** 50 **% Residing in College-Owned, -Operated, or -Affiliated Housing:** 25 **Final Year or Final Semester Residency Requirement:** Yes **Library Holdings:** 128,560 **Regional Accreditation:** Southern Association of Colleges and Schools **Credit Hours For Degree:** 60 semester hours, Associates; 120 semester hours, Bachelors **ROTC:** Army, Navy, Air Force **Professional Accreditation:** ABET, ACCE, ACBSP, NAAB **Intercollegiate Athletics:** Baseball M; Basketball M & W; Cheerleading M & W; Soccer M

SOUTHWEST GEORGIA TECHNICAL COLLEGE
15689 US 19 North
Thomasville, GA 31792
Tel: (229)225-4096
Fax: (229)225-4330
E-mail: whancock@southwestgatech.edu
Web Site: http://www.southwestgatech.edu/
President/CEO: Dr. Glenn Deibert
Type: Two-Year College **Sex:** Coed **Affiliation:** Technical College System of Georgia **Admission Plans:** Open Admission; Early Admission **Application Fee:** $20.00 **H.S. Requirements:** High school diploma required; GED accepted **Scholarships:** Available **Calendar System:** Quarter **Enrollment:** FT 689, PT 1,032 **Regional Accreditation:** Southern Association of Colleges and Schools **Professional Accreditation:** APTA, CARC, COE, NAACLS

SPELMAN COLLEGE
350 Spelman Ln., SW
Atlanta, GA 30314-4399
Tel: (404)681-3643; Free: 800-982-2411
Fax: (404)215-7788
E-mail: admiss@spelman.edu
Web Site: http://www.spelman.edu/
President/CEO: Dr. Beverly Daniel Tatum, PhD
Admissions: Arlene Cash
Financial Aid: Lenora J. Jackson
Type: Four-Year College **Sex:** Women **Scores:** 96.75% SAT M 400+; 64.89% ACT 18-23; 28.21% ACT 24-29 **% Accepted:** 40 **Admission Plans:** Early Action; Early Decision Plan **Application Deadline:** February 1 **Application Fee:** $35.00 **H.S. Requirements:** High school diploma required; GED accepted **Costs Per Year:** Application fee: $35. One-time mandatory fee: $250. Comprehensive fee: $32,072 includes full-time tuition ($18,709), mandatory fees ($3301), and college room and board ($10,062). College room only: $6706. **Scholarships:** Available **Calendar System:** Semester, Summer Session Not available **Enrollment:** FT 2,121, PT 108 **Faculty:** FT 172, PT 76 **Student-Faculty Ratio:** 11:1 **Exams:** SAT I or ACT. **% Receiving Financial Aid:** 72 **% Residing in College-Owned, -Operated, or -Affiliated Housing:** 43 **Library Holdings:** 727,767 **Regional Accreditation:** Southern Association of Colleges and Schools **Credit Hours For Degree:** 124 hours, Bachelors **ROTC:** Army, Navy, Air Force **Professional Accreditation:** NASM, NCATE **Intercollegiate Athletics:** Basketball W; Cross-Country Running W; Golf W; Soccer W; Tennis W; Track and Field W; Volleyball W

STRAYER UNIVERSITY - AUGUSTA CAMPUS
1330 Augusta West Parkway
Augusta, GA 30909

Tel: (706)855-8233
Fax: (706)855-8234
Web Site: http://www.strayer.edu/augusta/
Type: Comprehensive **Sex:** Coed **Application Fee:** $50.00 **Costs Per Year:** Application fee: $50. **Regional Accreditation:** Middle State Association of Colleges and Schools

STRAYER UNIVERSITY - CHAMBLEE CAMPUS
3355 Northeast Expressway
Ste. 100
Atlanta, GA 30341
Tel: (770)454-9270
Fax: (770)457-6958
Web Site: http://www.strayer.edu/chamblee/
Type: Comprehensive **Sex:** Coed **Application Fee:** $50.00 **Costs Per Year:** Application fee: $50. **Regional Accreditation:** Middle State Association of Colleges and Schools

STRAYER UNIVERSITY - COBB COUNTY CAMPUS
3101 Towercreek Parkway, SE
Ste. 700
Atlanta, GA 30339-3256
Tel: (770)612-2170
Fax: (770)956-7241
Web Site: http://www.strayer.edu/cobb_county/
Type: Comprehensive **Sex:** Coed **Application Fee:** $50.00 **Costs Per Year:** Application fee: $50. **Regional Accreditation:** Middle State Association of Colleges and Schools

STRAYER UNIVERSITY - DOUGLASVILLE CAMPUS
4655 Timber Ridge Dr.
Douglasville, GA 30135
Tel: (678)715-2200
Fax: (678)715-2230
Web Site: http://www.strayer.edu/douglasville/
Type: Comprehensive **Sex:** Coed **Application Fee:** $50.00 **Costs Per Year:** Application fee: $50. **Regional Accreditation:** Middle State Association of Colleges and Schools

STRAYER UNIVERSITY - LITHONIA CAMPUS
3120 Stonecrest Blvd.
Ste. 200
Lithonia, GA 30038
Tel: (678)323-7700
Fax: (678)323-7730
Web Site: http://www.strayer.edu/lithonia/
Type: Comprehensive **Sex:** Coed **Application Fee:** $50.00 **Costs Per Year:** Application fee: $50. **Regional Accreditation:** Middle State Association of Colleges and Schools

STRAYER UNIVERSITY - MORROW CAMPUS
3000 Corporate Center Dr., Ste. 100
Morrow, GA 30260
Tel: (678)422-4100
Fax: (678)422-4130
Web Site: http://www.strayer.edu/morrow
Type: Comprehensive **Sex:** Coed **Application Fee:** $50.00 **Costs Per Year:** Application fee: $50. **Regional Accreditation:** Middle State Association of Colleges and Schools

STRAYER UNIVERSITY - ROSWELL CAMPUS
100 Mansell Ct. East, Ste. 100
Roswell, GA 30076
Tel: (770)650-3000
Fax: (770)650-3030
Web Site: http://www.strayer.edu/roswell
Type: Comprehensive **Sex:** Coed **Application Fee:** $50.00 **Costs Per Year:** Application fee: $50. **Regional Accreditation:** Middle State Association of Colleges and Schools

STRAYER UNIVERSITY - SAVANNAH CAMPUS
20 Martin Ct.
Savannah, GA 31419
Tel: (912)921-2900
Fax: (912)291-2930
Web Site: http://www.strayer.edu/savannah/
Type: Comprehensive **Sex:** Coed **Application Fee:** $50.00 **Costs Per Year:** Application fee: $50. **Regional Accreditation:** Middle State Association of Colleges and Schools

THOMAS UNIVERSITY
1501 Millpond Rd.
Thomasville, GA 31792-7499
Tel: (229)226-1621; Free: 800-538-9784
E-mail: hmueller@thomasu.edu
Web Site: http://www.thomasu.edu/
President/CEO: Gary Bonvillian
Financial Aid: Angela Keys
Type: Comprehensive **Sex:** Coed **% Accepted:** 63 **Admission Plans:** Open Admission; Early Admission; Deferred Admission **Application Deadline:** Rolling **Application Fee:** $25.00 **H.S. Requirements:** High school diploma required; GED accepted **Scholarships:** Available **Calendar System:** Semester, Summer Session Available **Enrollment:** FT 390, PT 204 **Faculty:** FT 41, PT 41 **Student-Faculty Ratio:** 12:1 **Exams:** SAT I and SAT II or ACT, SAT I. **% Receiving Financial Aid:** 86 **% Residing in College-Owned, -Operated, or -Affiliated Housing:** 9 **Library Holdings:** 41,467 **Regional Accreditation:** Southern Association of Colleges and Schools **Credit Hours For Degree:** 60 semester hours, Associates; 120 semester hours, Bachelors **Professional Accreditation:** CORE, NLN **Intercollegiate Athletics:** Baseball M; Golf M & W; Soccer M & W; Softball W

TOCCOA FALLS COLLEGE
107 North Chapel Dr.
Toccoa Falls, GA 30598
Tel: (706)886-6831
Admissions: 888-785-5624
Fax: (706)282-6012
E-mail: admissions@tfc.edu
Web Site: http://www.tfc.edu/
President/CEO: Dr. Wayne Gardner
Admissions: Mike Davis
Financial Aid: Vince Welch
Type: Four-Year College **Sex:** Coed **Affiliation:** interdenominational **Scores:** 93% SAT V 400+; 85% SAT M 400+; 54% ACT 18-23; 22% ACT 24-29 **Admission Plans:** Early Admission; Deferred Admission **Application Deadline:** Rolling **Application Fee:** $25.00 **H.S. Requirements:** High school diploma required; GED accepted **Costs Per Year:** Application fee: $25. One-time mandatory fee: $25. Comprehensive fee: $21,225 includes full-time tuition ($15,450), mandatory fees ($125), and college room and board ($5650). Room and board charges vary according to board plan. Part-time tuition: $644 per credit hour. Part-time mandatory fees: $62.50 per term. **Scholarships:** Available **Calendar System:** 4-1-4, Summer Session Available **Enrollment:** FT 788, PT 71 **Faculty:** FT 46, PT 30 **Student-Faculty Ratio:** 14:1 **Exams:** SAT I or ACT. **% Receiving Financial Aid:** 78 **% Residing in College-Owned, -Operated, or -Affiliated Housing:** 63 **Library Holdings:** 142,674 **Regional Accreditation:** Southern Association of Colleges and Schools **Credit Hours For Degree:** 54 credit hours, Associates; 126 credit hours, Bachelors **Professional Accreditation:** ABHE, NASM **Intercollegiate Athletics:** Baseball M; Basketball M & W; Golf M & W; Soccer M & W; Volleyball W

TRUETT-MCCONNELL COLLEGE
100 Alumni Dr.
Cleveland, GA 30528
Tel: (706)865-2134
Fax: (706)219-3339
E-mail: agailey@truett.edu
Web Site: http://www.truett.edu/
President/CEO: Dr. Emir Caner
Admissions: Andrew Gailey
Financial Aid: Becky Moore
Type: Four-Year College **Sex:** Coed **Affiliation:** Baptist **Scores:** 63.1% SAT V 400+; 70.8% SAT M 400+; 35.3% ACT 18-23; 3.5% ACT 24-29 **% Accepted:** 62 **Admission Plans:** Early Admission; Deferred Admission **Application Deadline:** August 1 **Application Fee:** $25.00 **H.S. Requirements:** High school diploma required; GED accepted **Costs Per Year:** Application fee: $25. Comprehensive fee: $19,700 includes full-time tuition ($13,500), mandatory fees ($500), and college room and board ($5700).

Full-time tuition and fees vary according to course load. Room and board charges vary according to housing facility. Part-time tuition: $450 per semester hour. Part-time mandatory fees: $250 per term. Part-time tuition and fees vary according to course load. **Scholarships:** Available **Calendar System:** Semester, Summer Session Available **Enrollment:** FT 357, PT 162 **Faculty:** FT 23, PT 41 **Student-Faculty Ratio:** 11:1 **Exams:** SAT I or ACT. **% Receiving Financial Aid:** 79 **% Residing in College-Owned, -Operated, or -Affiliated Housing:** 72 **Regional Accreditation:** Southern Association of Colleges and Schools **Credit Hours For Degree:** 61 semester hours, Associates; 120 semester hours, Bachelors **Professional Accreditation:** NASM **Intercollegiate Athletics:** Baseball M; Basketball M & W; Cross-Country Running M & W; Golf M & W; Soccer M & W; Softball W

UNIVERSITY OF ATLANTA
6685 Peachtree Industrial Blvd.
Atlanta, GA 30360
Tel: (770)368-8877; Free: 800-533-3378
Admissions: (404)424-8410
Fax: 888-368-8667
E-mail: bkay@uofa.edu
Web Site: http://www.uofa.edu/
President/CEO: Nick Mithani
Admissions: Bill Kay
Type: Comprehensive **Sex:** Coed **% Accepted:** 48 **Admission Plans:** Early Admission; Deferred Admission **Application Deadline:** Rolling **Application Fee:** $100.00 **H.S. Requirements:** High school diploma required; GED accepted **Costs Per Year:** Application fee: $100. Tuition: $3150 full-time. Mandatory fees: $150 full-time. Tuition guaranteed not to increase for student's term of enrollment. **Enrollment:** FT 701, Grad FT 709 **Faculty:** FT 73, PT 226 **Student-Faculty Ratio:** 6:1 **Exams:** SAT I or ACT. **Credit Hours For Degree:** 120 semester credit hours, Bachelors

UNIVERSITY OF GEORGIA
Athens, GA 30602
Tel: (706)542-3000
Admissions: (706)542-8776
E-mail: undergrad@admissions.uga.edu
Web Site: http://www.uga.edu/
President/CEO: Michael F. Adams
Admissions: Charles Carabello
Financial Aid: Bonnie C. Joerschke
Type: Comprehensive **Sex:** Coed **Affiliation:** University System of Georgia **Scores:** 99.89% SAT M 400+; 12.81% ACT 18-23; 62.59% ACT 24-29 **% Accepted:** 54 **Admission Plans:** Early Admission; Early Action; Deferred Admission **Application Deadline:** January 15 **Application Fee:** $60.00 **H.S. Requirements:** High school diploma required; GED accepted **Costs Per Year:** Application fee: $60. State resident tuition: $6070 full-time, $203 per credit part-time. Nonresident tuition: $24,280 full-time, $882 per credit part-time. Mandatory fees: $1460 full-time, $730 per term part-time. Full-time tuition and fees vary according to course load, location, and program. Part-time tuition and fees vary according to course load, location, and program. College room and board: $8046. College room only: $4524. Room and board charges vary according to board plan and housing facility. Tuition guaranteed not to increase for student's term of enrollment. **Scholarships:** Available **Calendar System:** Semester, Summer Session Available **Enrollment:** FT 24,670, PT 1,472, Grad FT 6,340, Grad PT 2,403 **Faculty:** FT 1,775, PT 438 **Student-Faculty Ratio:** 18:1 **Exams:** SAT I or ACT, SAT II. ACT essay used for admission. SAT essay used for admission. ACT essay used as a validity check on application essay. SAT essay used as a validity check on application essay. **% Receiving Financial Aid:** 32 **% Residing in College-Owned, -Operated, or -Affiliated Housing:** 27 **Final Year or Final Semester Residency Requirement:** No **Library Holdings:** 4,559,220 **Regional Accreditation:** Southern Association of Colleges and Schools **Credit Hours For Degree:** 65 semester hours, Associates; 120 semester hours, Bachelors **ROTC:** Army, Air Force **Professional Accreditation:** AACSB, ABET, ACPhE, ACEJMC, AAMFT, AAFCS, ABA, ACA, ADtA, APA, ASLA, ASLHA, AVMA, AALS, FIDER, CSWE, JRCEPAT, NASAD, NASM, NASPAA NAST, NCATE, NRPA, SAF **Intercollegiate Athletics:** Baseball M; Basketball M & W; Cross-Country Running M & W; Equestrian Sports W; Football M; Golf M & W; Gymnastics W; Soccer W; Softball W; Swimming and Diving M & W; Tennis M & W; Track and Field M & W; Volleyball W

UNIVERSITY OF PHOENIX—ATLANTA CAMPUS
8200 Roberts Dr., Ste. 300
Sandy Springs, GA 30350-4153
Tel: (678)731-0555; Free: 800-228-7240
Admissions: (480)557-6151
Fax: (770)821-5399
E-mail: audra.mcquarie@phoenix.edu
Web Site: http://www.phoenix.edu/
President/CEO: William Pepicello
Admissions: Audra McQuarie
Type: Comprehensive **Sex:** Coed **Admission Plans:** Open Admission; Deferred Admission **Application Deadline:** Rolling **Application Fee:** $0.00 **H.S. Requirements:** High school diploma required; GED accepted **Costs Per Year:** Application fee: $0. Tuition: $12,090 full-time. Full-time tuition varies according to course level and course load. **Scholarships:** Available **Calendar System:** Continuous, Summer Session Not available **Enrollment:** FT 1,196 **Faculty:** FT 17, PT 203 **Regional Accreditation:** North Central Association of Colleges and Schools **Credit Hours For Degree:** 60 credits, Associates; 120 credits, Bachelors **Professional Accreditation:** NLN

UNIVERSITY OF PHOENIX—AUGUSTA CAMPUS
3150 Perimeter Parkway
Augusta, GA 30909-4583
Tel: (706)868-2000
Web Site: http://www.phoenix.edu/
Type: Comprehensive **Sex:** Coed **Regional Accreditation:** North Central Association of Colleges and Schools

UNIVERSITY OF PHOENIX—COLUMBUS GEORGIA CAMPUS
4747 Hamilton Rd., Ste. E
Columbus, GA 31904-6321
Tel: (706)320-1266; Free: 800-228-7240
Admissions: (480)557-6151
E-mail: audra.mcquarie@phoenix.edu
Web Site: http://www.phoenix.edu/
President/CEO: William Pepicello
Admissions: Audra McQuarie
Type: Comprehensive **Sex:** Coed **Admission Plans:** Open Admission; Deferred Admission **Application Deadline:** Rolling **Application Fee:** $0.00 **H.S. Requirements:** High school diploma required; GED accepted **Costs Per Year:** Application fee: $0. Tuition: $11,775 full-time. Full-time tuition varies according to course level and course load. **Scholarships:** Available **Calendar System:** Continuous, Summer Session Not available **Enrollment:** FT 704 **Faculty:** FT 12, PT 95 **Regional Accreditation:** North Central Association of Colleges and Schools **Credit Hours For Degree:** 60 credits, Associates; 120 credits, Bachelors

UNIVERSITY OF PHOENIX—SAVANNAH CAMPUS
8001 Chatham Center Dr., Ste. 200
Savannah, GA 31405-7400
Tel: (912)232-0531
Web Site: http://www.phoenix.edu/
President/CEO: William Pepicello, PhD
Type: Comprehensive **Sex:** Coed **Regional Accreditation:** North Central Association of Colleges and Schools

UNIVERSITY OF WEST GEORGIA
1601 Maple St.
Carrollton, GA 30118
Tel: (678)839-5000
Admissions: (678)839-4000
E-mail: admiss@westga.edu
Web Site: http://www.westga.edu/
President/CEO: Dr. Beheruz N. Sethna
Admissions: Justin Barlow
Financial Aid: Kimberly Jordan
Type: Comprehensive **Sex:** Coed **Affiliation:** University System of Georgia **Scores:** 99.7% SAT V 400+; 99.5% SAT M 400+; 72.8% ACT 18-23; 10.9% ACT 24-29 **% Accepted:** 58 **Admission Plans:** Early Admission; Deferred Admission **Application Deadline:** June 1 **Application Fee:** $30.00 **H.S. Requirements:** High school diploma required; GED not accepted. For nontraditional students: High school diploma or equivalent not required **Costs Per Year:** Application fee: $30. State resident tuition: $3196 full-time, $134 per semester hour part-time. Nonresident tuition: $12,778 full-time, $533 per semester hour part-time. Mandatory fees: $1386 full-time, $42.90 per semester hour part-time, $307 per term part-time. Full-time tuition and fees vary according to course load. Part-time tuition and fees vary according

to course load. College room and board: $6254. College room only: $3300. Room and board charges vary according to board plan and housing facility. **Scholarships:** Available **Calendar System:** Semester, Summer Session Available **Enrollment:** FT 8,126, PT 1,496, Grad FT 549, Grad PT 1,329 **Faculty:** FT 431, PT 134 **Student-Faculty Ratio:** 20:1 **Exams:** SAT I or ACT. ACT essay not being used. SAT essay not being used. **% Receiving Financial Aid:** 60 **% Residing in College-Owned, -Operated, or -Affiliated Housing:** 28 **Library Holdings:** 541,488 **Regional Accreditation:** Southern Association of Colleges and Schools **Credit Hours For Degree:** 120 semester hours, Bachelors **ROTC:** Army **Professional Accreditation:** AACSB, ABET, AACN, ACA, NASAD, NASM, NASPAA, NAST, NCATE, NLN **Intercollegiate Athletics:** Baseball M; Basketball M & W; Cheerleading M & W; Cross-Country Running M & W; Football M; Golf M & W; Soccer W; Softball W; Volleyball W

VALDOSTA STATE UNIVERSITY
1500 North Patterson St.
Valdosta, GA 31698
Tel: (229)333-5800; Free: 800-618-1878
Admissions: (229)333-5791
Fax: (229)333-5482
E-mail: wpeacock@valdosta.edu
Web Site: http://www.valdosta.edu/
President/CEO: Dr. Patrick J. Schloss
Admissions: Walter Peacock
Financial Aid: Douglas R. Tanner
Type: University **Sex:** Coed **Affiliation:** University System of Georgia **Scores:** 99% SAT V 400+; 80% ACT 18-23; 12% ACT 24-29 **% Accepted:** 71 **Admission Plans:** Deferred Admission **Application Deadline:** June 15 **Application Fee:** $40.00 **H.S. Requirements:** High school diploma required; GED not accepted **Costs Per Year:** Application fee: $40. State resident tuition: $2978 full-time, $125 per credit hour part-time. Nonresident tuition: $11,907 full-time, $497 per credit hour part-time. Mandatory fees: $1510 full-time. Part-time tuition varies according to course load. College room and board: $6480. College room only: $3250. Room and board charges vary according to board plan and housing facility. **Scholarships:** Available **Calendar System:** Semester, Summer Session Available **Enrollment:** FT 9,019, PT 1,309, Grad FT 823, Grad PT 1,240 **Faculty:** FT 456, PT 120 **Student-Faculty Ratio:** 23:1 **Exams:** SAT I or ACT. ACT essay not being used. SAT essay not being used. **% Receiving Financial Aid:** 64 **% Residing in College-Owned, -Operated, or -Affiliated Housing:** 28 **Final Year or Final Semester Residency Requirement:** No **Library Holdings:** 636,608 **Regional Accreditation:** Southern Association of Colleges and Schools **Credit Hours For Degree:** 60 semester hours, Associates; 120 semester hours, Bachelors **ROTC:** Air Force **Professional Accreditation:** AACSB, AAMFT, AACN, ADA, ALA, ASLHA, CSWE, JRCEPAT, NASAD, NASM, NASPAA, NAST, NCATE, NLN **Intercollegiate Athletics:** Baseball M; Basketball M & W; Cross-Country Running M & W; Football M; Golf M; Softball W; Tennis M & W; Volleyball W

VALDOSTA TECHNICAL COLLEGE
4089 Val Tech Rd.
Valdosta, GA 31602
Tel: (229)333-2100
Fax: (229)333-2129
E-mail: chesters@valdostatech.edu
Web Site: http://www.valdostatech.edu/
President/CEO: Ray Perren
Type: Two-Year College **Sex:** Coed **Affiliation:** Technical College System of Georgia **Admission Plans:** Open Admission; Early Admission **Application Fee:** $15.00 **H.S. Requirements:** High school diploma required; GED accepted **Calendar System:** Quarter **Enrollment:** FT 1,875, PT 1,710 **Regional Accreditation:** Southern Association of Colleges and Schools **Professional Accreditation:** ADA, COE, JRCERT, NAACLS

WAYCROSS COLLEGE
2001 South Georgia Parkway
Waycross, GA 31503-9248
Tel: (912)285-6133
Admissions: (912)449-7600
Fax: (912)287-4909
E-mail: rwing@waycross.edu
Web Site: http://www.waycross.edu/
President/CEO: David A. Palmer
Admissions: Robert Wingfield
Type: Two-Year College **Sex:** Coed **Affiliation:** University System of Georgia **% Accepted:** 100 **Admission Plans:** Early Admission; Deferred Admission **Application Deadline:** Rolling **Application Fee:** $20.00 **H.S. Requirements:** High school diploma required; GED accepted **Costs Per Year:** Application fee: $20. State resident tuition: $2298 full-time, $77 per hour part-time. Nonresident tuition: $9176 full-time, $306 per hour part-time. Mandatory fees: $140 full-time, $6 per hour part-time, $77 per term part-time. Full-time tuition and fees vary according to course load. Part-time tuition and fees vary according to course load. **Scholarships:** Available **Calendar System:** Semester, Summer Session Available **Student-Faculty Ratio:** 19:1 **Exams:** SAT I or ACT. **Regional Accreditation:** Southern Association of Colleges and Schools **Credit Hours For Degree:** 60 semester hours, Associates **Intercollegiate Athletics:** Basketball M; Softball W

WESLEYAN COLLEGE
4760 Forsyth Rd.
Macon, GA 31210-4462
Tel: (478)477-1110; Free: 800-447-6610
Admissions: (478)757-3700
Fax: (478)757-4030
E-mail: admissions@wesleyancollege.edu
Web Site: http://www.wesleyancollege.edu/
President/CEO: Ruth A. Knox
Financial Aid: Kizzy K. Holmes
Type: Comprehensive **Affiliation:** United Methodist **Scores:** 99% SAT V 400+; 92% SAT M 400+; 30% ACT 18-23; 61% ACT 24-29 **% Accepted:** 51 **Admission Plans:** Early Admission; Early Action; Early Decision Plan; Deferred Admission **Application Deadline:** Rolling **Application Fee:** $30.00 **H.S. Requirements:** High school diploma required; GED accepted **Costs Per Year:** Application fee: $30. Comprehensive fee: $25,500 includes full-time tuition ($17,500) and college room and board ($8000). Full-time tuition varies according to class time, course load, and program. Room and board charges vary according to board plan and housing facility. Part-time tuition: $415 per credit hour. Part-time tuition varies according to class time, course load, and program. **Scholarships:** Available **Calendar System:** Semester, Summer Session Available **Enrollment:** FT 385, PT 222, Grad FT 33, Grad PT 31 **Faculty:** FT 46, PT 31 **Student-Faculty Ratio:** 10:1 **Exams:** SAT I or ACT. **% Receiving Financial Aid:** 60 **% Residing in College-Owned, -Operated, or -Affiliated Housing:** 82 **Library Holdings:** 145,571 **Regional Accreditation:** Southern Association of Colleges and Schools **Credit Hours For Degree:** 120 semester hours, Bachelors **Professional Accreditation:** NASM **Intercollegiate Athletics:** Basketball W; Cross-Country Running W; Equestrian Sports W; Soccer W; Softball W; Tennis W; Volleyball W

WEST GEORGIA TECHNICAL COLLEGE
176 Murphy Campus Blvd.
Waco, GA 30182
Tel: (706)845-4323
Fax: (706)845-4339
E-mail: mary.aderhold@westgatech.edu
Web Site: http://www.westgatech.edu/
President/CEO: Perrin Alford
Type: Two-Year College **Sex:** Coed **Affiliation:** Technical College System of Georgia **Admission Plans:** Open Admission; Early Admission **Application Fee:** $25.00 **H.S. Requirements:** High school diploma required; GED accepted **Scholarships:** Available **Calendar System:** Quarter **Enrollment:** FT 2,833, PT 4,480 **Regional Accreditation:** Southern Association of Colleges and Schools **Professional Accreditation:** COE

WESTWOOD COLLEGE—ATLANTA MIDTOWN
1100 Spring St.
Atlanta, GA 30309
Tel: (404)745-9096
Admissions: (404)745-9862
Fax: (404)892-7253
Web Site: http://www.westwood.edu/
President/CEO: Gary Sullenger
Type: Four-Year College **Sex:** Coed **Calendar System:** Continuous **Professional Accreditation:** ACCSCT

WESTWOOD COLLEGE—ATLANTA NORTHLAKE
2309 Parklake Dr., NE
Bldg. 10

Atlanta, GA 30345
Tel: (404)962-2999
Web Site: http://www.westwood.edu/
President/CEO: Tira Harney Clay
Type: Four-Year College **Sex:** Coed **Affiliation:** Alta College, Inc. **Intercollegiate Athletics:** Ultimate Frisbee M & W; Volleyball M & W

YOUNG HARRIS COLLEGE
PO Box 98
Young Harris, GA 30582-0098
Tel: (706)379-3111
Fax: (706)379-4306
E-mail: admissions@yhc.edu
Web Site: http://www.yhc.edu/
President/CEO: Cathy Cox
Admissions: Clinton G. Hobbs
Type: Four-Year College **Sex:** Coed **Affiliation:** United Methodist **Scores:** 93% SAT V 400+; 90% SAT M 400+; 65% ACT 18-23; 19% ACT 24-29 % **Accepted:** 58 **Application Deadline:** Rolling **Application Fee:** $0.00 **H.S. Requirements:** High school diploma required; GED accepted **Costs Per Year:** Application fee: $0. Comprehensive fee: $27,609 includes full-time tuition ($20,280), mandatory fees ($245), and college room and board ($7084). College room only: $3200. Full-time tuition and fees vary according to student level. Room and board charges vary according to housing facility. Part-time tuition: $650 per credit hour. Part-time tuition varies according to course load. **Scholarships:** Available **Calendar System:** Semester, Summer Session Available **Enrollment:** FT 622, PT 27 **Faculty:** FT 54, PT 16 **Student-Faculty Ratio:** 10:1 **Exams:** SAT I or ACT. ACT essay not being used. SAT essay not being used. **% Residing in College-Owned, -Operated, or -Affiliated Housing:** 83 **Library Holdings:** 92,454 **Regional Accreditation:** Southern Association of Colleges and Schools **Credit Hours For Degree:** 62 semester hours, Associates; 120 semester hours, Bachelors **Professional Accreditation:** NASM **Intercollegiate Athletics:** Baseball M; Cross-Country Running M & W; Golf M & W; Soccer M & W; Softball W; Tennis M & W

GUAM COMMUNITY COLLEGE
PO Box 23069 Guam Main Facility
Barrigada, GU 96921-3069
Tel: (671)735-4422
Admissions: (671)735-5500
Fax: (671)734-5238
E-mail: pclymer@guamcc.edu
Web Site: http://www.guamcc.net/
President/CEO: Mary A.Y. Okada
Admissions: Patrick L. Clymer
Type: Two-Year College **Sex:** Coed **Admission Plans:** Open Admission; Early Admission **Application Deadline:** Rolling **Application Fee:** $0.00 **H.S. Requirements:** High school diploma required; GED accepted. For some adult applicants: High school diploma or equivalent not required **Scholarships:** Available **Calendar System:** Semester, Summer Session Available **Enrollment:** FT 504, PT 2,337 **Faculty:** FT 74, PT 46 **Library Holdings:** 15,806 **Regional Accreditation:** Western Association of Schools and Colleges **Credit Hours For Degree:** 60 semester hours, Associates **ROTC:** Army **Professional Accreditation:** AAMAE

PACIFIC ISLANDS UNIVERSITY
172 Kinney's Rd.
Mangilao, GU 96913
Tel: (671)734-1812
Fax: (671)734-1813
E-mail: guamcampus@pibc.edu
Web Site: http://www.piu.edu/
Admissions: Ethel Laco
Type: Four-Year College **Sex:** Coed **Affiliation:** interdenominational **Application Deadline:** August 25 **Application Fee:** $25.00 **Calendar System:** Semester **Enrollment:** FT 132, PT 56 **Faculty:** FT 12, PT 10 **Student-Faculty Ratio:** 7:1 **Exams:** Other. **Professional Accreditation:** TACCS

UNIVERSITY OF GUAM
UOG Station
Mangilao, GU 96923
Tel: (671)735-2350
Admissions: (671)735-2201
Fax: (671)734-6005
E-mail: admitme@uguam.uog.edu
Web Site: http://www.uog.edu/
President/CEO: Dr. Robert A. Underwood
Admissions: Angelica Anthonio
Type: Comprehensive **Sex:** Coed **% Accepted:** 86 **Admission Plans:** Open Admission; Early Admission; Deferred Admission **Application Deadline:** June 1 **Application Fee:** $49.00 **H.S. Requirements:** High school diploma required; GED accepted. For applicants 18 or over admitted as special students: High school diploma or equivalent not required **Costs Per Year:** Application fee: $49. Territory resident tuition: $5320 full-time, $190 per credit part-time. Nonresident tuition: $15,820 full-time, $565 per credit part-time. Mandatory fees: $450 full-time, $225 per term part-time. Part-time tuition and fees vary according to course load and degree level. College room and board: $9102. College room only: $1620. Room and board charges vary according to housing facility. **Scholarships:** Available **Calendar System:** Semester, Summer Session Available **Enrollment:** FT 2,511, PT 768, Grad FT 107, Grad PT 164 **Faculty:** FT 182, PT 76 **Student-Faculty Ratio:** 14:1 **% Residing in College-Owned, -Operated, or -Affiliated Housing:** 5 **Final Year or Final Semester Residency Requirement:** Yes **Library Holdings:** 309,528 **Regional Accreditation:** Western Association of Schools and Colleges **Credit Hours For Degree:** 92 credits, Associates; 124 credits, Bachelors **ROTC:** Army **Professional Accreditation:** CSWE, NCATE, NLN

ARGOSY UNIVERSITY, HAWAI'I
400 ASBTower, 1001 Bishop St.
Honolulu, HI 96813
Tel: (808)536-5555; Free: 888-323-2777
Fax: (808)536-5505
Web Site: http://www.argosy.edu/hawaii/
President/CEO: Warren Evans
Type: University **Sex:** Coed **Affiliation:** Education Management Corporation **Calendar System:** Semester **Regional Accreditation:** North Central Association of Colleges and Schools **Professional Accreditation:** APA

BRIGHAM YOUNG UNIVERSITY—HAWAII
55-220 Kulanui St.
Laie, HI 96762-1294
Tel: (808)293-3211
Admissions: (808)675-3731
E-mail: admissions@byuh.edu
Web Site: http://www.byuh.edu/
President/CEO: Dr. Steven C. Wheelwright
Admissions: Arapata P. Meha
Financial Aid: Wes Duke
Type: Four-Year College **Sex:** Coed **Affiliation:** Latter-day Saints; Brigham Young University **Scores:** 89% SAT V 400+; 98% SAT M 400+; 43% ACT 18-23; 48% ACT 24-29 **% Accepted:** 58 **Admission Plans:** Preferred Admission; Early Admission; Deferred Admission **Application Deadline:** February 15 **Application Fee:** $30.00 **H.S. Requirements:** High school diploma required; GED not accepted **Costs Per Year:** Application fee: $30. Comprehensive fee: $9086 includes full-time tuition ($4330) and college room and board ($4756). Room and board charges vary according to board plan and housing facility. **Scholarships:** Available **Calendar System:** Semester, Summer Session Available **Enrollment:** FT 2,380, PT 175 **Faculty:** FT 121, PT 107 **Student-Faculty Ratio:** 15:1 **Exams:** ACT, SAT I or ACT. **% Receiving Financial Aid:** 89 **% Residing in College-Owned, -Operated, or -Affiliated Housing:** 57 **Library Holdings:** 358,513 **Regional Accreditation:** Western Association of Schools and Colleges **Credit Hours For Degree:** 60 credits, Associates; 120 credits, Bachelors **ROTC:** Army, Navy, Air Force **Professional Accreditation:** CSWE **Intercollegiate Athletics:** Basketball M & W; Cross-Country Running M & W; Golf M; Soccer M & W; Softball W; Tennis M & W; Volleyball W

CHAMINADE UNIVERSITY OF HONOLULU
3140 Waialae Ave.
Honolulu, HI 96816-1578
Tel: (808)735-4711; Free: 800-735-3733
Admissions: (808)735-4735
Fax: (808)739-4647
E-mail: admissions@chaminade.edu
Web Site: http://www.chaminade.edu/
President/CEO: Dr. Bernard Ploeger
Admissions: Martin Motooka
Financial Aid: Eric Nemoto
Type: Comprehensive **Sex:** Coed **Affiliation:** Roman Catholic **Scores:** 87% SAT V 400+; 86% SAT M 400+; 67% ACT 18-23; 8% ACT 24-29 **% Accepted:** 95 **Admission Plans:** Deferred Admission **Application Deadline:** Rolling **Application Fee:** $50.00 **H.S. Requirements:** High school diploma required; GED accepted **Costs Per Year:** Application fee: $50. Comprehensive fee: $28,160 includes full-time tuition ($17,600), mandatory fees ($140), and college room and board ($10,420). College room only: $5170. Full-time tuition and fees vary according to course load. Room and board charges vary according to board plan and housing facility. Part-time tuition: $587 per credit hour. Part-time tuition varies according to course load. **Scholarships:** Available **Calendar System:** Semester, Summer Session Available **Enrollment:** FT 989, PT 39, Grad FT 459, Grad PT 268 **Faculty:** FT 70, PT 50 **Student-Faculty Ratio:** 12:1 **Exams:** Other, SAT I or ACT. ACT essay used for advising. SAT essay used for advising. ACT essay used for placement. SAT essay used for placement. **% Residing in College-Owned, -Operated, or -Affiliated Housing:** 32 **Final Year or Final Semester Residency Requirement:** Yes **Library Holdings:** 78,000 **Regional Accreditation:** Western Association of Schools and Colleges **Credit Hours For Degree:** 60 credit hours, Associates; 124 credit hours, Bachelors **ROTC:** Army, Air Force **Professional Accreditation:** MACTE **Intercollegiate Athletics:** Basketball M; Cross-Country Running M & W; Golf M & W; Softball W; Tennis M & W; Volleyball W; Water Polo M

HAWAII COMMUNITY COLLEGE
200 West Kawili St.
Hilo, HI 96720-4091
Tel: (808)974-7611
Fax: (808)974-7692
Web Site: http://www.hawcc.hawaii.edu/
President/CEO: Rockne Freitas
Admissions: Tammy M. Tanaka
Type: Two-Year College **Sex:** Coed **Affiliation:** University of Hawaii System **Admission Plans:** Open Admission; Early Admission **Application Deadline:** August 1 **Application Fee:** $25.00 **H.S. Requirements:** High school diploma or equivalent not required. For nursing program: High school diploma required; GED accepted **Calendar System:** Semester, Summer Session Available **Regional Accreditation:** Western Association of Schools and Colleges **Credit Hours For Degree:** 60 credit hours, Associates **Professional Accreditation:** NLN

HAWAI'I PACIFIC UNIVERSITY
1164 Bishop St.
Honolulu, HI 96813
Tel: (808)544-0200; Free: (866)225-5478
Admissions: (808)544-0238
Fax: (808)544-1136
E-mail: admissions@hpu.edu
Web Site: http://www.hpu.edu/
President/CEO: Dr. Chatt G. Wright
Admissions: Scott Stensrud
Financial Aid: Adam Hatch
Type: Comprehensive **Sex:** Coed **Scores:** 87.8% SAT V 400+; 88.7% SAT M 400+; 54.1% ACT 18-23; 23% ACT 24-29 **% Accepted:** 73 **Admission Plans:** Early Admission; Deferred Admission **Application Deadline:** Rolling **Application Fee:** $50.00 **H.S. Requirements:** High school diploma required; GED accepted **Costs Per Year:** Application fee: $50. Comprehensive fee: $26,054 includes full-time tuition ($14,860), mandatory fees ($100), and college room and board ($11,094). Full-time tuition and fees vary according to course load, program, and student level. Room and board

charges vary according to housing facility. Part-time tuition: $300 per credit. Part-time tuition varies according to course load. **Scholarships:** Available **Calendar System:** Semester, Summer Session Available **Enrollment:** FT 3,849, PT 3,057, Grad FT 622, Grad PT 585 **Faculty:** FT 253, PT 346 **Student-Faculty Ratio:** 15:1 **Exams:** SAT I or ACT. **% Receiving Financial Aid:** 46 **% Residing in College-Owned, -Operated, or -Affiliated Housing:** 10 **Library Holdings:** 160,800 **Regional Accreditation:** Western Association of Schools and Colleges **Credit Hours For Degree:** 60 credits, Associates; 124 credits, Bachelors **ROTC:** Army, Air Force **Professional Accreditation:** CSWE, NLN **Intercollegiate Athletics:** Baseball M; Basketball M & W; Cheerleading M & W; Cross-Country Running M & W; Golf M; Soccer M & W; Softball W; Tennis M & W; Volleyball W

HAWAII TOKAI INTERNATIONAL COLLEGE
2241 Kapiolani Blvd.
Honolulu, HI 96826-4310
Tel: (808)983-4100
Admissions: (808)983-4187
Fax: (808)983-4107
E-mail: studentservices@tokai.edu
Web Site: http://www.hawaiitokai.edu/
President/CEO: Dr. Naoto Yoshikawa, PhD
Admissions: Morna Dexter
Type: Two-Year College **Sex:** Coed **Affiliation:** Tokai University Educational System (Japan) **% Accepted:** 100 **Admission Plans:** Deferred Admission **Application Deadline:** Rolling **Application Fee:** $50.00 **H.S. Requirements:** High school diploma required; GED accepted **Costs Per Year:** Application fee: $50. Comprehensive fee: $22,840 includes full-time tuition ($13,400), mandatory fees ($560), and college room and board ($8880). College room only: $6000. Full-time tuition and fees vary according to course load and program. Room and board charges vary according to board plan. Part-time tuition: $400 per credit hour. Part-time mandatory fees: $140 per term. Part-time tuition and fees vary according to course load and program. **Scholarships:** Available **Calendar System:** Quarter, Summer Session Available **Enrollment:** FT 59, PT 1 **Faculty:** FT 6, PT 11 **Student-Faculty Ratio:** 4:1 **Exams:** Other. **% Residing in College-Owned, -Operated, or -Affiliated Housing:** 60 **Final Year or Final Semester Residency Requirement:** Yes **Library Holdings:** 7,000 **Regional Accreditation:** Western Association of Schools and Colleges **Credit Hours For Degree:** 60 credits, Associates

HEALD COLLEGE—HONOLULU
1500 Kapiolani Blvd.
Honolulu, HI 96814-3797
Tel: (808)955-1500
Fax: (808)955-6964
E-mail: wnishimu@heald.edu
Web Site: http://www.heald.edu/
President/CEO: Evelyn A. Schemmel
Admissions: Wendy Nishimura
Type: Two-Year College **Sex:** Coed **Admission Plans:** Open Admission; Early Admission; Deferred Admission **Application Deadline:** Rolling **Application Fee:** $40.00 **H.S. Requirements:** High school diploma required; GED accepted **Scholarships:** Available **Calendar System:** Quarter, Summer Session Available **Enrollment:** FT 591, PT 216 **Faculty:** FT 30, PT 31 **Student-Faculty Ratio:** 17:1 **Exams:** Other. **Regional Accreditation:** Western Association of Schools and Colleges **Professional Accreditation:** AAMAE

HONOLULU COMMUNITY COLLEGE
874 Dillingham Blvd.
Honolulu, HI 96817-4598
Tel: (808)845-9211
Admissions: (808)845-9129
E-mail: admission@hccadb.hcc.hawaii.edu
Web Site: http://www.honolulu.hawaii.edu/
President/CEO: Michael Rota
Financial Aid: Jannine Oyama
Type: Two-Year College **Sex:** Coed **Affiliation:** University of Hawaii System **Admission Plans:** Open Admission; Early Admission **Application Deadline:** August 15 **Application Fee:** $0.00 **H.S. Requirements:** High school diploma or equivalent not required. For cosmetology program: High school diploma required; GED accepted **Costs Per Year:** Application fee: $0. State resident tuition: $2142 full-time, $88 per credit hour part-time. Nonresident tuition: $6774 full-time, $281 per credit hour part-time. Mandatory fees: $.50 per credit hour part-time, $10. Full-time tuition varies according to course load. Part-time tuition and fees vary according to course load. **Scholarships:** Available **Calendar System:** Semester, Summer Session Available **Enrollment:** FT 1,481, PT 2,737 **Faculty:** FT 125, PT 73 **Student-Faculty Ratio:** 16:1 **Exams:** Other. **Final Year or Final Semester Residency Requirement:** No **Library Holdings:** 54,902 **Regional Accreditation:** Western Association of Schools and Colleges **Credit Hours For Degree:** 60 semester hours, Associates **ROTC:** Army, Air Force

KAPIOLANI COMMUNITY COLLEGE
4303 Diamond Head Rd.
Honolulu, HI 96816-4421
Tel: (808)734-9111
Admissions: (808)734-9000
E-mail: kapinfo@hawaii.edu
Web Site: http://www.kcc.hawaii.edu/
President/CEO: Leon Richards
Admissions: Jerilynn Lorenzo
Type: Two-Year College **Sex:** Coed **Affiliation:** University of Hawaii System **% Accepted:** 92 **Admission Plans:** Open Admission; Preferred Admission; Early Admission **Application Deadline:** July 1 **H.S. Requirements:** High school diploma or equivalent not required. For nursing, health sciences, paralegal programs: High school diploma required; GED accepted **Scholarships:** Available **Calendar System:** Semester, Summer Session Available **Enrollment:** FT 2,833, PT 4,341 **Faculty:** FT 200, PT 144 **Library Holdings:** 50,000 **Regional Accreditation:** Western Association of Schools and Colleges **Credit Hours For Degree:** 60 credits, Associates **ROTC:** Army, Air Force **Professional Accreditation:** AAMAE, ACF, AOTA, APTA, CARC, JRCERT, NAACLS, NLN

KAUAI COMMUNITY COLLEGE
3-1901 Kaumualii Hwy.
Lihue, HI 96766
Tel: (808)245-8311
Fax: (808)245-8297
E-mail: arkauai@hawaii.edu
Web Site: http://kauai.hawaii.edu/
President/CEO: Helen Cox
Admissions: Leighton Oride
Type: Two-Year College **Sex:** Coed **Affiliation:** University of Hawaii System **Admission Plans:** Open Admission; Preferred Admission; Early Admission **Application Deadline:** August 1 **Application Fee:** $0.00 **H.S. Requirements:** High school diploma or equivalent not required. For nursing program: High school diploma required; GED accepted **Scholarships:** Available **Calendar System:** Semester, Summer Session Available **Library Holdings:** 51,875 **Regional Accreditation:** Western Association of Schools and Colleges **Credit Hours For Degree:** 60 credits, Associates **Professional Accreditation:** NLN

LEEWARD COMMUNITY COLLEGE
96-045 Ala Ike
Pearl City, HI 96782-3393
Tel: (808)455-0011
Fax: (808)455-0471
Web Site: http://www.lcc.hawaii.edu/
President/CEO: Manuel Cabral
Admissions: Anna Donald
Type: Two-Year College **Sex:** Coed **Affiliation:** University of Hawaii System **Admission Plans:** Open Admission; Preferred Admission; Early Admission **Application Deadline:** August 1 **Application Fee:** $25.00 **H.S. Requirements:** High school diploma required; GED accepted. For applicants 18 or over: High school diploma required; GED not accepted **Scholarships:** Available **Calendar System:** Semester, Summer Session Available **Faculty:** FT 179, PT 57 **Library Holdings:** 62,000 **Regional Accreditation:** Western Association of Schools and Colleges **Credit Hours For Degree:** 60 credits, Associates **ROTC:** Army, Air Force **Professional Accreditation:** ACF

MAUI COMMUNITY COLLEGE
310 Kaahumanu Ave.
Kahului, HI 96732
Tel: (808)984-3500; Free: 800-479-6692
Admissions: (808)984-3267
Fax: (808)242-9618

E-mail: kameda@hawaii.edu
Web Site: http://maui.hawaii.edu/
President/CEO: Clyde Sakamoto
Admissions: Stephen Kameda
Type: Two-Year College **Sex:** Coed **Affiliation:** University of Hawaii System **Admission Plans:** Open Admission; Early Admission **Application Deadline:** Rolling **Application Fee:** $25.00 **H.S. Requirements:** High school diploma or equivalent not required **Costs Per Year:** Application fee: $25. State resident tuition: $1896 full-time, $79 per credit part-time. Nonresident tuition: $9600 full-time, $400 per credit part-time. Mandatory fees: $126 full-time, $5 per credit part-time, $12 per term part-time. College room and board: $10,043. College room only: $6111. **Scholarships:** Available **Calendar System:** Semester, Summer Session Available **Enrollment:** FT 1,258, PT 1,996 **Faculty:** FT 116, PT 1 **% Residing in College-Owned, -Operated, or -Affiliated Housing:** 1 **Library Holdings:** 49,812 **Regional Accreditation:** Western Association of Schools and Colleges **Credit Hours For Degree:** 60 credits, Associates **Professional Accreditation:** ACF, ADA, NLN

REMINGTON COLLEGE—HONOLULU CAMPUS
1111 Bishop St.
Ste. 400
Honolulu, HI 96813
Tel: (808)942-1000
Fax: (808)533-3064
E-mail: louis.lamair@remingtoncollege.edu
Web Site: http://www.remingtoncollege.edu/
President/CEO: Kenneth Heinemann
Admissions: Louis LaMair
Type: Two-Year College **Sex:** Coed **Professional Accreditation:** ACICS

UNIVERSITY OF HAWAII AT HILO
200 West Kawili St.
Hilo, HI 96720-4091
Tel: (808)974-7311; Free: 800-897-4456
Admissions: (808)974-7414
Fax: (808)933-0861
E-mail: uhhao@hawaii.edu
Web Site: http://www.uhh.hawaii.edu/
President/CEO: Dr. Rose Y. Tseng
Admissions: James Cromwell
Type: Comprehensive **Sex:** Coed **Affiliation:** University of Hawaii System **Scores:** 81% SAT V 400+; 86% SAT M 400+; 54% ACT 18-23; 26% ACT 24-29 **% Accepted:** 50 **Admission Plans:** Deferred Admission **Application Deadline:** July 1 **Application Fee:** $50.00 **H.S. Requirements:** High school diploma required; GED accepted **Scholarships:** Available **Calendar System:** Semester, Summer Session Available **Enrollment:** FT 2,821, PT 623, Grad FT 353, Grad PT 177 **Faculty:** FT 271, PT 76 **Student-Faculty Ratio:** 14:1 **Exams:** SAT I or ACT. **% Receiving Financial Aid:** 69 **% Residing in College-Owned, -Operated, or -Affiliated Housing:** 22 **Library Holdings:** 250,000 **Regional Accreditation:** Western Association of Schools and Colleges **Credit Hours For Degree:** 120 semester hours, Bachelors **Professional Accreditation:** NLN **Intercollegiate Athletics:** Baseball M; Basketball M; Cross-Country Running M & W; Golf M; Softball W; Tennis M & W; Volleyball W

UNIVERSITY OF HAWAII AT MANOA
2500 Campus Rd.
Honolulu, HI 96822
Tel: (808)956-8111; Free: 800-823-9771
Admissions: (808)956-8975
E-mail: ar-info@hawaii.edu
Web Site: http://manoa.hawaii.edu/
President/CEO: Dr. Virginia Hinshaw
Admissions: Lisa Buto
Financial Aid: Linda Clemons
Type: University **Sex:** Coed **Affiliation:** University of Hawaii System **Scores:** 98.4% SAT V 400+; 99.7% SAT M 400+; 52.9% ACT 18-23; 38.7% ACT 24-29 **% Accepted:** 67 **Admission Plans:** Preferred Admission **Application Deadline:** May 1 **Application Fee:** $50.00 **H.S. Requirements:** High school diploma required; GED accepted **Costs Per Year:** Application fee: $50. State resident tuition: $7584 full-time, $316 per credit hour part-time. Nonresident tuition: $21,024 full-time, $876 per credit hour part-time. Mandatory fees: $399 full-time, $199.70 per term part-time. Full-time tuition and fees vary according to class time, course level, course load, degree level, program, reciprocity agreements, and student level. Part-time tuition and fees vary according to class time, course level, course load, degree level, program, reciprocity agreements, and student level. College room and board: $8493. College room only: $5775. Room and board charges vary according to board plan and housing facility. **Scholarships:** Available **Calendar System:** Semester, Summer Session Available **Enrollment:** FT 11,361, PT 2,591, Grad FT 3,365, Grad PT 3,118 **Faculty:** FT 1,200, PT 70 **Student-Faculty Ratio:** 14:1 **Exams:** SAT I or ACT. ACT essay used for admission. SAT essay used for admission. ACT essay used for placement. SAT essay used for placement. **% Receiving Financial Aid:** 32 **% Residing in College-Owned, -Operated, or -Affiliated Housing:** 13 **Library Holdings:** 3,366,361 **Regional Accreditation:** Western Association of Schools and Colleges **Credit Hours For Degree:** 124 semester hours, Bachelors **ROTC:** Army, Air Force **Professional Accreditation:** AACSB, ABET, ACEJMC, AACN, ABA, ACA, ADA, ACSP, ALA, APA, ASLHA, AALS, CEPH, CORE, CSWE, LCMEAMA, NAACLS, NAAB, NASM, NCATE NLN **Intercollegiate Athletics:** Archery M; Baseball M; Basketball M & W; Cheerleading M & W; Cross-Country Running W; Football M; Golf M & W; Sailing M & W; Soccer W; Softball W; Swimming and Diving M & W; Tennis M & W; Track and Field W; Volleyball M & W; Water Polo W

UNIVERSITY OF HAWAII—WEST OAHU
96-129 Ala Ike
Pearl City, HI 96782-3366
Tel: (808)454-4700
E-mail: robyno@hawaii.edu
Web Site: http://www.uhwo.hawaii.edu/
President/CEO: Dr. Gene I. Awakuni
Admissions: Robyn Oshiro
Type: Four-Year College **Sex:** Coed **Affiliation:** University of Hawaii System **% Accepted:** 81 **Admission Plans:** Preferred Admission; Deferred Admission **Application Deadline:** April 1 **Application Fee:** $50.00 **H.S. Requirements:** High school diploma required; GED accepted **Costs Per Year:** Application fee: $50. State resident tuition: $4656 full-time, $194 per credit part-time. Nonresident tuition: $14,352 full-time, $598 per credit part-time. Mandatory fees: $10 full-time. **Scholarships:** Available **Calendar System:** Semester, Summer Session Available **Enrollment:** FT 408, PT 885 **Faculty:** FT 46, PT 28 **Student-Faculty Ratio:** 13:1 **Exams:** SAT I or ACT. **% Receiving Financial Aid:** 51 **Regional Accreditation:** Western Association of Schools and Colleges **Credit Hours For Degree:** 120 credits, Bachelors **ROTC:** Army, Air Force

UNIVERSITY OF PHOENIX—HAWAII CAMPUS
827 Fort St.
Honolulu, HI 96813-4317
Tel: (808)536-2686; Free: 800-228-7240
Admissions: (480)557-6151
E-mail: audra.mcquarie@phoenix.edu
Web Site: http://www.phoenix.edu/
President/CEO: William Pepicello
Admissions: Audra McQuarie
Type: Comprehensive **Sex:** Coed **Admission Plans:** Open Admission; Deferred Admission **Application Deadline:** Rolling **Application Fee:** $0.00 **H.S. Requirements:** High school diploma required; GED accepted **Costs Per Year:** Application fee: $0. Tuition: $13,200 full-time. Full-time tuition varies according to course level and course load. **Scholarships:** Available **Calendar System:** Continuous, Summer Session Not available **Enrollment:** FT 743 **Faculty:** FT 20, PT 158 **Regional Accreditation:** North Central Association of Colleges and Schools **Credit Hours For Degree:** 60 credits, Associates; 120 credits, Bachelors **Professional Accreditation:** NLN

WINDWARD COMMUNITY COLLEGE
45-720 Keaahala Rd.
Kaneohe, HI 96744-3528
Tel: (808)235-7400
E-mail: gerii@hawaii.edu
Web Site: http://www.wcc.hawaii.edu/
President/CEO: Douglas Dykstra
Admissions: Geri Imai
Type: Two-Year College **Sex:** Coed **Affiliation:** University of Hawaii System **Admission Plans:** Open Admission; Preferred Admission; Early Admission **Application Deadline:** Rolling **Application Fee:** $25.00 **H.S. Require-**

ments: High school diploma or equivalent not required **Costs Per Year:** Application fee: $25. Area resident tuition: $1896 full-time. State resident tuition: $6528 full-time, $79 per credit part-time. Nonresident tuition: $272 per credit part-time. Mandatory fees: $20 full-time, $2 per credit part-time. **Scholarships:** Available **Calendar System:** Semester, Summer Session Available **Student-Faculty Ratio:** 15:1 **Regional Accreditation:** Western Association of Schools and Colleges **Credit Hours For Degree:** 60 credits, Associates **ROTC:** Army, Air Force

APOLLO COLLEGE—BOISE
1200 North Liberty Rd.
Boise, ID 83704
Tel: (208)377-8080; Free: 800-473-4365
Fax: (208)322-7658
Web Site: http://www.apollocollege.edu/
President/CEO: Robert Robichaud
Type: Two-Year College **Sex:** Coed **Affiliation:** U.S. Education Corporation **Admission Plans:** Open Admission **Application Deadline:** March 1 **Application Fee:** $100.00 **H.S. Requirements:** High school diploma required; GED accepted **Scholarships:** Available **Calendar System:** Semester, Summer Session Not available **Exams:** Other. **Library Holdings:** 20,000 **Professional Accreditation:** ABHES, ADA

BOISE BIBLE COLLEGE
8695 West Marigold St.
Boise, ID 83714-1220
Tel: (208)376-7731; Free: 800-893-7755
Fax: (208)376-7743
E-mail: martinf@boisebible.edu
Web Site: http://www.boisebible.edu/
President/CEO: Terry Stine
Admissions: Martin Flaherty
Financial Aid: Beth Turner
Type: Four-Year College **Sex:** Coed **Affiliation:** nondenominational **Scores:** 86% SAT V 400+; 82% SAT M 400+; 48% ACT 18-23; 10% ACT 24-29 **% Accepted:** 99 **Admission Plans:** Deferred Admission **Application Deadline:** August 1 **Application Fee:** $25.00 **H.S. Requirements:** High school diploma required; GED accepted **Scholarships:** Available **Calendar System:** Semester, Summer Session Not available **Enrollment:** FT 168, PT 16 **Faculty:** FT 8, PT 8 **Student-Faculty Ratio:** 16:1 **Exams:** SAT I or ACT. **% Receiving Financial Aid:** 81 **% Residing in College-Owned, -Operated, or -Affiliated Housing:** 55 **Library Holdings:** 29,431 **Credit Hours For Degree:** 64 semester hours, Associates; 128 semester hours, Bachelors **Professional Accreditation:** ABHE

BOISE STATE UNIVERSITY
1910 University Dr.
Boise, ID 83725-0399
Tel: (208)426-1011; Free: 800-824-7017
Admissions: (208)426-1177
E-mail: bsuinfo@boisestate.edu
Web Site: http://www.boisestate.edu/
President/CEO: Dr. Robert Kustra
Admissions: Jenny Cerda
Type: University **Sex:** Coed **Affiliation:** Idaho System of Higher Education **Scores:** 94% SAT V 400+; 94% SAT M 400+; 55% ACT 18-23; 30% ACT 24-29 **% Accepted:** 87 **Application Deadline:** June 30 **Application Fee:** $40.00 **H.S. Requirements:** High school diploma required; GED accepted **Costs Per Year:** Application fee: $40. One-time mandatory fee: $75. State resident tuition: $3106 full-time, $168.52 per credit hour part-time. Nonresident tuition: $12,110 full-time, $248.52 per credit hour part-time. Mandatory fees: $1758 full-time, $83.48 per credit hour part-time. Full-time tuition and fees vary according to reciprocity agreements. Part-time tuition and fees vary according to course load. College room and board: $5602. College room only: $2650. Room and board charges vary according to board plan and housing facility. **Scholarships:** Available **Calendar System:** Semester, Summer Session Available **Enrollment:** FT 12,142, PT 4,551, Grad FT 732, Grad PT 1,508 **Faculty:** FT 542, PT 461 **Student-Faculty Ratio:** 21:1 **Exams:** SAT I or ACT. ACT essay not being used. SAT essay not being used. **% Receiving Financial Aid:** 67 **% Residing in College-Owned, -Operated, or -Affiliated Housing:** 12 **Library Holdings:** 838,932 **Credit Hours For Degree:** 64 semester hours, Associates; 128 semester hours, Bachelors **ROTC:** Army **Professional Accreditation:** AACSB, ABET, ACCE, ACA, ACF, ADA, AHIMA, CARC, CSWE, JRCEDMS, JRCERT, JRCEPAT, NASAD, NASM, NASPAA, NAST, NCATE, NLN, NCCU **Intercollegiate Athletics:** Basketball M & W; Cross-Country Running M & W; Football M; Golf M & W; Gymnastics W; Soccer W; Softball W; Tennis M & W; Track and Field M & W; Volleyball W; Wrestling M

BRIGHAM YOUNG UNIVERSITY—IDAHO
Rexburg, ID 83460
Tel: (208)496-2011
Admissions: (208)496-2411
Fax: (208)496-1220
E-mail: daviss@byui.edu
Web Site: http://www.byui.edu/
President/CEO: Kim Bryce Clark
Admissions: Steven Davis
Type: Two-Year College **Sex:** Coed **Affiliation:** The Church of Jesus Christ of Latter-day Saints **Scores:** 49.4% ACT 18-23; 41.4% ACT 24-29 **% Accepted:** 95 **Admission Plans:** Preferred Admission **Application Deadline:** February 15 **Application Fee:** $30.00 **H.S. Requirements:** High school diploma required; GED accepted **Scholarships:** Available **Calendar System:** Semester, Summer Session Available **Student-Faculty Ratio:** 25:1 **Exams:** SAT I or ACT. **% Residing in College-Owned, -Operated, or -Affiliated Housing:** 20 **Library Holdings:** 134,423 **Credit Hours For Degree:** 64 semester hours, Associates **ROTC:** Army **Professional Accreditation:** ABET, FIDER, NASM, NLN, NCCU

BROWN MACKIE COLLEGE—BOISE
9050 West Overland Rd., Ste. 100
Boise, ID 83709
Tel: (208)321-8800
Admissions: (208)321-8800
Web Site: http://www.brownmackie.edu/boise/
President/CEO: Richard Murphree
Type: Two-Year College **Sex:** Coed

THE COLLEGE OF IDAHO
2112 Cleveland Blvd.
Caldwell, ID 83605
Tel: (208)459-5011; Free: 800-244-3246
Admissions: (208)459-5319
Fax: (208)454-2077
E-mail: admission@collegeofidaho.edu
Web Site: http://www.collegeofidaho.edu/
President/CEO: Dr. Marvin Henberg
Admissions: Brian Bava
Financial Aid: Juanitta M. Pearson

Type: Comprehensive **Sex:** Coed **Scores:** 86.9% SAT V 400+; 94.6% SAT M 400+; 41.8% ACT 18-23; 42.3% ACT 24-29 **% Accepted:** 62 **Admission Plans:** Early Admission; Early Action; Deferred Admission **Application Deadline:** August 1 **Application Fee:** $0.00 **H.S. Requirements:** High school diploma required; GED accepted **Costs Per Year:** Application fee: $0. One-time mandatory fee: $330. Comprehensive fee: $28,750 includes full-time tuition ($20,600), mandatory fees ($450), and college room and board ($7700). College room only: $3513. Room and board charges vary according to board plan and housing facility. Part-time tuition: $850 per credit hour. Part-time tuition varies according to course load. **Scholarships:** Available **Calendar System:** Miscellaneous, Summer Session Not available **Enrollment:** FT 945, PT 57, Grad FT 11 **Faculty:** FT 74, PT 26 **Student-Faculty Ratio:** 12:1 **Exams:** SAT I or ACT. ACT essay used for admission. SAT essay used for admission. ACT essay used for advising. SAT essay used for advising. ACT essay used for placement. SAT essay used for placement. **% Receiving Financial Aid:** 64 **% Residing in College-Owned, -Operated, or -Affiliated Housing:** 58 **Final Year or Final Semester Residency Requirement:** Yes **Library Holdings:** 155,000 **Credit Hours For Degree:** 124 credits, Bachelors **ROTC:** Army **Professional Accreditation:** NCCU **Intercollegiate Athletics:** Baseball M; Basketball M & W; Cross-Country Running M & W; Golf M & W; Skiing (Downhill) M & W; Soccer M & W; Softball W; Swimming and Diving M & W; Tennis M & W; Track and Field M & W; Volleyball W

COLLEGE OF SOUTHERN IDAHO
PO Box 1238
Twin Falls, ID 83303-1238
Tel: (208)733-9554
Admissions: (208)732-6232
Fax: (208)736-3014
Web Site: http://www.csi.edu/
President/CEO: Dr. Gerald Beck
Type: Two-Year College **Sex:** Coed **Admission Plans:** Open Admission **Application Deadline:** Rolling **H.S. Requirements:** High school diploma required; GED accepted **Costs Per Year:** State resident tuition: $2400 full-time, $100 per credit hour part-time. Nonresident tuition: $6720 full-time, $280 per credit hour part-time. College room and board: $3980. Room and board charges vary according to board plan. **Scholarships:** Available **Calendar System:** Semester, Summer Session Available **Enrollment:** FT 2,812, PT 4,306 **Faculty:** FT 160, PT 201 **Student-Faculty Ratio:** 19:1 **Exams:** ACT, Other. **% Residing in College-Owned, -Operated, or -Affiliated Housing:** 10 **Library Holdings:** 62,556 **Credit Hours For Degree:** 64 credits, Associates **Professional Accreditation:** AAMAE, NLN, NCCU **Intercollegiate Athletics:** Baseball M; Basketball M & W; Cheerleading M & W; Equestrian Sports M & W; Softball W; Volleyball M & W

EASTERN IDAHO TECHNICAL COLLEGE
1600 South 25th East
Idaho Falls, ID 83404-5788
Tel: (208)524-3000; Free: 800-662-0261
Fax: (208)524-3007
E-mail: steven.albiston@my.eitc.edu
Web Site: http://www.eitc.edu/
President/CEO: Burton Waite
Admissions: Dr. Steve Albiston
Type: Two-Year College **Sex:** Coed **% Accepted:** 59 **Admission Plans:** Open Admission; Deferred Admission **Application Deadline:** Rolling **Application Fee:** $10.00 **H.S. Requirements:** High school diploma required; GED accepted **Costs Per Year:** Application fee: $10. State resident tuition: $1750 full-time, $84 per credit part-time. Nonresident tuition: $6414 full-time, $168 per credit part-time. Mandatory fees: $130 full-time, $15 per term part-time. **Scholarships:** Available **Calendar System:** Semester, Summer Session Available **Enrollment:** FT 296, PT 470 **Faculty:** FT 41, PT 46 **Student-Faculty Ratio:** 11:1 **Exams:** Other. **Library Holdings:** 18,000 **Credit Hours For Degree:** 60 credits, Associates **Professional Accreditation:** ARCEST, AAMAE, NCCU

IDAHO STATE UNIVERSITY
921 South 8th Ave.
Pocatello, ID 83209
Tel: (208)282-0211
Admissions: (208)282-2475
E-mail: info@isu.edu
Web Site: http://www.isu.edu/
President/CEO: Dr. Arthur C. Vailas
Financial Aid: Kent Larson
Type: University **Sex:** Coed **Scores:** 92% SAT M 400+; 52% ACT 18-23; 27% ACT 24-29 **% Accepted:** 73 **Admission Plans:** Open Admission; Early Admission; Deferred Admission **Application Deadline:** August 1 **Application Fee:** $40.00 **H.S. Requirements:** High school diploma required; GED accepted **Costs Per Year:** Application fee: $40. One-time mandatory fee: $40. State resident tuition: $3318 full-time, $253 per credit hour part-time. Nonresident tuition: $13,120 full-time, $393 per credit hour part-time. Mandatory fees: $1650 full-time. Full-time tuition and fees vary according to course load, program, and reciprocity agreements. Part-time tuition varies according to course load and reciprocity agreements. College room and board: $5050. College room only: $2350. Room and board charges vary according to board plan and housing facility. **Scholarships:** Available **Calendar System:** Semester, Summer Session Available **Enrollment:** FT 7,638, PT 3,620, Grad FT 1,229, Grad PT 1,006 **Faculty:** FT 602, PT 236 **Student-Faculty Ratio:** 15:1 **Exams:** ACT, SAT I or ACT. ACT essay not being used. SAT essay not being used. **% Residing in College-Owned, -Operated, or -Affiliated Housing:** 7 **Final Year or Final Semester Residency Requirement:** No **Library Holdings:** 2,164,443 **Credit Hours For Degree:** 64 credits, Associates; 128 credits, Bachelors **ROTC:** Army **Professional Accreditation:** AACSB, ABET, ACPhE, AACN, AAMAE, ACA, ACF, ADA, ADtA, AHIMA, AOTA, APTA, APA, ASLHA, CEPH, CSWE, NAACLS, NASM, NCATE, NCCU **Intercollegiate Athletics:** Basketball M & W; Cross-Country Running M & W; Football M; Golf W; Soccer W; Softball W; Tennis M & W; Track and Field M & W; Volleyball W

ITT TECHNICAL INSTITUTE
12302 West Explorer Dr.
Boise, ID 83713
Tel: (208)322-8844
Fax: (208)322-0173
Web Site: http://www.itt-tech.edu/
President/CEO: Erica Bisch
Type: Two-Year College **Sex:** Coed **Affiliation:** ITT Educational Services, Inc. **H.S. Requirements:** High school diploma required; GED accepted **Scholarships:** Available **Calendar System:** Quarter, Summer Session Not available **Credit Hours For Degree:** 96 credit hours, Associates; 180 credit hours, Bachelors **Professional Accreditation:** ACICS

LEWIS-CLARK STATE COLLEGE
500 Eighth Ave.
Lewiston, ID 83501-2698
Tel: (208)792-5272; Free: 800-933-5272
Fax: (208)799-2063
E-mail: admissions@lcsc.edu
Web Site: http://www.lcsc.edu/
President/CEO: Dene Kay Thomas
Admissions: Soo Lee Bruce-Smith
Financial Aid: Laura Hughes
Type: Four-Year College **Sex:** Coed **Scores:** 88.68% SAT V 400+; 84.91% SAT M 400+; 43.14% ACT 18-23; 17.71% ACT 24-29 **% Accepted:** 98 **Admission Plans:** Deferred Admission **Application Deadline:** Rolling **Application Fee:** $35.00 **H.S. Requirements:** High school diploma required; GED accepted **Scholarships:** Available **Calendar System:** Semester, Summer Session Available **Enrollment:** FT 2,534, PT 1,666 **Student-Faculty Ratio:** 15:1 **Exams:** Other, SAT I or ACT. ACT essay not being used. SAT essay not being used. **% Receiving Financial Aid:** 65 **Credit Hours For Degree:** 64 credit hours, Associates; 128 credit hours, Bachelors **ROTC:** Army, Navy, Air Force **Professional Accreditation:** AACN, CSWE, NCCU **Intercollegiate Athletics:** Baseball M; Basketball M & W; Cross-Country Running M & W; Golf M & W; Tennis M & W; Volleyball W

NEW SAINT ANDREWS COLLEGE
PO Box 9025
Moscow, ID 83843
Tel: (208)882-1566
Fax: (208)882-4293
E-mail: info@nsa.edu
Web Site: http://www.nsa.edu/
President/CEO: Dr. Roy Atwood
Admissions: Lindsey Tollefson
Type: Comprehensive **Sex:** Coed **Scores:** 100% SAT V 400+; 97% SAT M 400+; 31% ACT 18-23; 46% ACT 24-29 **% Accepted:** 69 **Admission Plans:**

Early Action; Deferred Admission **Application Deadline:** February 15 **Application Fee:** $40.00 **H.S. Requirements:** High school diploma required; GED accepted **Costs Per Year:** Application fee: $40. Tuition: $9890 full-time, $800 per course part-time. Tuition guaranteed not to increase for student's term of enrollment. **Calendar System:** Miscellaneous, Summer Session Available **Enrollment:** FT 146, PT 17, Grad FT 17, Grad PT 1 **Faculty:** FT 10, PT 4 **Student-Faculty Ratio:** 14:1 **Exams:** SAT I or ACT. ACT essay not being used. SAT essay not being used. **Final Year or Final Semester Residency Requirement:** Yes **Library Holdings:** 58,720 **Professional Accreditation:** TACCS

NORTH IDAHO COLLEGE
1000 West Garden Ave.
Coeur d'Alene, ID 83814-2199
Tel: (208)769-3300; Free: 877-404-4536
Fax: (208)769-3273
E-mail: admit@nic.edu
Web Site: http://www.nic.edu/
President/CEO: Dr. Priscilla Bell
Type: Two-Year College **Sex:** Coed **Admission Plans:** Early Admission; Deferred Admission **Application Deadline:** August 20 **Application Fee:** $25.00 **H.S. Requirements:** High school diploma or equivalent not required **Costs Per Year:** Application fee: $25. Area resident tuition: $1464 full-time, $83 per credit part-time. State resident tuition: $2464 full-time, $124 per credit part-time. Nonresident tuition: $6016 full-time, $273 per credit part-time. Mandatory fees: $1050 full-time, $1050 per term part-time. College room and board: $5750. **Scholarships:** Available **Calendar System:** Semester, Summer Session Available **Enrollment:** FT 2,575, PT 1,748 **Faculty:** FT 153, PT 154 **Student-Faculty Ratio:** 17:1 **Library Holdings:** 60,893 **Credit Hours For Degree:** 64 credit hours, Associates **ROTC:** Army **Professional Accreditation:** NLN, NCCU **Intercollegiate Athletics:** Basketball M & W; Cheerleading M & W; Soccer M & W; Softball W; Volleyball W; Wrestling M

NORTHWEST NAZARENE UNIVERSITY
623 Holly St.
Nampa, ID 83686-5897
Tel: (208)467-8011; Free: 877-668-4968
Admissions: (208)467-8648
Fax: (208)467-8645
E-mail: slberggren@nnu.edu
Web Site: http://www.nnu.edu/
President/CEO: Dr. David Alexander
Admissions: Stacey Berggren
Financial Aid: Wes Maggard
Type: Comprehensive **Sex:** Coed **Affiliation:** Church of the Nazarene **Scores:** 95% SAT V 400+; 93% SAT M 400+; 48% ACT 18-23; 34% ACT 24-29 **% Accepted:** 58 **Admission Plans:** Early Action; Deferred Admission **Application Deadline:** August 15 **Application Fee:** $25.00 **H.S. Requirements:** High school diploma required; GED accepted **Costs Per Year:** Application fee: $25. Comprehensive fee: $29,110 includes full-time tuition ($22,810), mandatory fees ($280), and college room and board ($6020). Full-time tuition and fees vary according to course load, degree level, program, and reciprocity agreements. Room and board charges vary according to board plan. **Scholarships:** Available **Calendar System:** Semester, Summer Session Available **Enrollment:** FT 1,181, PT 131, Grad FT 487, Grad PT 135 **Faculty:** FT 98, PT 6 **Student-Faculty Ratio:** 14:1 **Exams:** SAT I or ACT. **% Receiving Financial Aid:** 72 **% Residing in College-Owned, -Operated, or -Affiliated Housing:** 84 **Library Holdings:** 127,036 **Credit Hours For Degree:** 124 semester credits, Bachelors **ROTC:** Army **Professional Accreditation:** AACN, ACA, ACBSP, CSWE, NASM, NCATE, NCCU **Intercollegiate Athletics:** Baseball M; Basketball M & W; Cheerleading W; Cross-Country Running M & W; Golf M; Soccer M & W; Softball W; Track and Field M & W; Volleyball W

STEVENS-HENAGER COLLEGE
730 Americana Blvd.
Boise, ID 83702
Tel: (801)345-0700
Fax: (801)621-0866
Web Site: http://www.stevenshenager.edu/
Financial Aid: Jaime L. Davis
Type: Four-Year College **Sex:** Coed **Scholarships:** Available **% Receiving Financial Aid:** 75

UNIVERSITY OF IDAHO
875 Perimeter Dr., PO Box 442282
Moscow, ID 83844-2282
Tel: (208)885-6111; Free: 888-884-3246
Admissions: (208)885-6326
Fax: (208)885-6911
E-mail: admissions@uidaho.edu
Web Site: http://www.uidaho.edu/
President/CEO: Dr. M. Duane Nellis
Admissions: Dan Davenport
Financial Aid: Dan Davenport
Type: University **Sex:** Coed **Scores:** 95.58% SAT V 400+; 97.03% SAT M 400+; 48.07% ACT 18-23; 35.68% ACT 24-29 **% Accepted:** 80 **Admission Plans:** Deferred Admission **Application Deadline:** August 1 **Application Fee:** $40.00 **H.S. Requirements:** High school diploma required; GED accepted **Costs Per Year:** Application fee: $40. State resident tuition: $0 full-time. Nonresident tuition: $10,080 full-time, $504 per credit part-time. Mandatory fees: $4932 full-time, $251 per credit part-time. Full-time tuition and fees vary according to course load, degree level, and program. Part-time tuition and fees vary according to course load, degree level, and program. College room and board: $7242. Room and board charges vary according to board plan and housing facility. **Scholarships:** Available **Calendar System:** Semester, Summer Session Available **Enrollment:** FT 8,288, PT 1,055, Grad FT 1,337, Grad PT 1,277 **Faculty:** FT 545, PT 122 **Student-Faculty Ratio:** 17:1 **Exams:** SAT I or ACT. ACT essay not being used. SAT essay not being used. **% Receiving Financial Aid:** 58 **% Residing in College-Owned, -Operated, or -Affiliated Housing:** 21 **Library Holdings:** 1,299,257 **Credit Hours For Degree:** 128 credits, Bachelors **ROTC:** Army, Navy, Air Force **Professional Accreditation:** AACSB, ABET, AAFCS, ABA, ACA, ADtA, ASLA, AALS, CORE, NAAB, NASAD, NASM, NCATE, NRPA, NCCU, SAF **Intercollegiate Athletics:** Badminton M & W; Baseball M; Basketball M & W; Cross-Country Running M & W; Football M; Golf M & W; Gymnastics M & W; Ice Hockey M; Riflery M & W; Rugby M & W; Skiing (Cross-Country) M & W; Skiing (Downhill) M & W; Soccer M & W; Table Tennis M & W; Tennis M & W; Track and Field M & W; Ultimate Frisbee M & W; Volleyball W

UNIVERSITY OF PHOENIX—IDAHO CAMPUS
3080 Gentry Way, Ste. 150
Meridian, ID 83642-3014
Tel: (208)888-1505; Free: 800-228-7240
Admissions: (480)557-6151
Fax: (208)888-4775
E-mail: audra.mcquarie@phoenix.edu
Web Site: http://www.phoenix.edu/
President/CEO: William Pepicello
Admissions: Audra McQuarie
Type: Comprehensive **Sex:** Coed **Admission Plans:** Open Admission; Deferred Admission **Application Deadline:** Rolling **Application Fee:** $0.00 **H.S. Requirements:** High school diploma required; GED accepted **Costs Per Year:** Application fee: $0. Tuition: $11,625 full-time. Full-time tuition varies according to course level and course load. **Scholarships:** Available **Calendar System:** Continuous, Summer Session Not available **Enrollment:** FT 456 **Faculty:** FT 22, PT 98 **Regional Accreditation:** North Central Association of Colleges and Schools **Credit Hours For Degree:** 60 credits, Associates; 120 credits, Bachelors

AMERICAN ACADEMY OF ART
332 South Michigan Ave, Ste. 300
Chicago, IL 60604-4302
Tel: (312)461-0600
E-mail: srosenbloom@aaart.edu
Web Site: http://www.aaart.edu/
President/CEO: Richard H. Otto
Admissions: Stuart Rosenbloom
Financial Aid: Ione Fitzgerald
Type: Four-Year College **Sex:** Coed **Application Deadline:** Rolling **Application Fee:** $25.00 **H.S. Requirements:** High school diploma required; GED accepted **Costs Per Year:** Application fee: $25. Tuition: $11,940 full-time, $746 per credit hour part-time. Full-time tuition varies according to course load. Part-time tuition varies according to course load. **Scholarships:** Available **Calendar System:** Trimester, Summer Session Available **Enrollment:** FT 338, PT 58 **Faculty:** FT 25, PT 10 **Student-Faculty Ratio:** 10:1 **Library Holdings:** 1,730 **Regional Accreditation:** North Central Association of Colleges and Schools **Credit Hours For Degree:** 133 semester hours, Bachelors **Professional Accreditation:** ACCSCT

AMERICAN INTERCONTINENTAL UNIVERSITY ONLINE
5550 Prairie Stone Parkway, Ste. 400
Hoffman Estates, IL 60192
Tel: (847)851-5000; Free: 877-701-3800
Admissions: 877-564-6248
Fax: (847)851-6002
E-mail: jziegenmier@aiuonline.edu
Web Site: http://www.aiuniv.edu/
President/CEO: Steve Tober
Admissions: Jennifer Ziegenmier
Type: Comprehensive **Sex:** Coed **Affiliation:** American InterContinental University **Admission Plans:** Deferred Admission **Application Deadline:** Rolling **Application Fee:** $50.00 **H.S. Requirements:** High school diploma required; GED accepted **Costs Per Year:** Application fee: $50. **Calendar System:** Miscellaneous **Enrollment:** FT 20,341 **Regional Accreditation:** North Central Association of Colleges and Schools

ARGOSY UNIVERSITY, CHICAGO
225 North Michigan Ave., Ste. 1300
Chicago, IL 60601
Tel: (312)777-7600; Free: 800-626-4123
Fax: (312)201-1907
Web Site: http://www.argosy.edu/chicago/
President/CEO: C. Ronald Kimberling, PhD
Type: University **Sex:** Coed **H.S. Requirements:** High school diploma required; GED accepted **Calendar System:** Semester **Regional Accreditation:** North Central Association of Colleges and Schools **Professional Accreditation:** APA, ACBSP

ARGOSY UNIVERSITY, SCHAUMBURG
999 North Plaza Dr., Ste. 111
Schaumburg, IL 60173-5403
Tel: (847)969-4900; Free: (866)290-2777
Fax: (847)598-6191
Web Site: http://www.argosy.edu/schaumburg/
President/CEO: James Chitwood, MBA
Type: University **Sex:** Coed **Calendar System:** Semester **Regional Accreditation:** North Central Association of Colleges and Schools **Professional Accreditation:** ACA, APA

AUGUSTANA COLLEGE
639 38th St.
Rock Island, IL 61201-2296
Tel: (309)794-7000; Free: 800-798-8100
Admissions: (309)794-7341
Fax: (309)794-7431
E-mail: admissions@augustana.edu
Web Site: http://www.augustana.edu/
President/CEO: Steven C. Bahls
Admissions: Megan Cooley
Financial Aid: Sue Standley
Type: Four-Year College **Sex:** Coed **Affiliation:** Evangelical Lutheran Church in America **Scores:** 31% ACT 18-23; 52% ACT 24-29 **% Accepted:** 73 **Admission Plans:** Deferred Admission **Application Deadline:** Rolling **Application Fee:** $35.00 **H.S. Requirements:** High school diploma required; GED accepted **Costs Per Year:** Application fee: $35. Comprehensive fee: $39,276 includes full-time tuition ($31,326) and college room and board ($7950). Full-time tuition varies according to student level. Room and board charges vary according to board plan and housing facility. Part-time tuition: $1350 per credit hour. Part-time tuition varies according to course load. **Scholarships:** Available **Calendar System:** Quarter, Summer Session Available **Enrollment:** FT 2,446, PT 26 **Student-Faculty Ratio:** 11:1 **Exams:** SAT I or ACT. **% Receiving Financial Aid:** 69 **% Residing in College-Owned, -Operated, or -Affiliated Housing:** 70 **Library Holdings:** 209,688 **Regional Accreditation:** North Central Association of Colleges and Schools **Credit Hours For Degree:** 123 credits, Bachelors **Professional Accreditation:** NASM, NCATE **Intercollegiate Athletics:** Baseball M; Basketball M & W; Cheerleading M & W; Cross-Country Running M & W; Football M; Golf M & W; Lacrosse M & W; Soccer M & W; Softball W; Swimming and Diving M & W; Tennis M & W; Track and Field M & W; Ultimate Frisbee M & W; Volleyball M & W; Wrestling M

AURORA UNIVERSITY
347 South Gladstone Ave.
Aurora, IL 60506-4892
Tel: (630)892-6431; Free: 800-742-5281
Admissions: (630)844-5533
Fax: (630)844-5535
E-mail: admission@aurora.edu
Web Site: http://www.aurora.edu/
President/CEO: Dr. Rebecca L. Sherrick
Admissions: James Lancaster
Financial Aid: Heather McKane
Type: Comprehensive **Sex:** Coed **Scores:** 100% SAT V 400+; 100% SAT M 400+; 66% ACT 18-23; 30% ACT 24-29 **% Accepted:** 71 **Admission Plans:** Deferred Admission **Application Deadline:** May 1 **Application Fee:** $25.00 **H.S. Requirements:** High school diploma required; GED accepted **Costs Per Year:** Application fee: $25. Comprehensive fee: $27,500 includes full-time tuition ($18,600), mandatory fees ($100), and college room and board ($8800). Full-time tuition and fees vary according to location. Room and

board charges vary according to board plan, housing facility, and location. Part-time tuition: $550 per semester hour. Part-time tuition varies according to course load, location, and program. **Scholarships:** Available **Calendar System:** Semester, Summer Session Available **Enrollment:** FT 2,066, PT 325, Grad FT 436, Grad PT 1,528 **Faculty:** FT 120, PT 298 **Student-Faculty Ratio:** 14:1 **Exams:** SAT I or ACT. ACT essay not being used. SAT essay not being used. **% Receiving Financial Aid:** 78 **% Residing in College-Owned, -Operated, or -Affiliated Housing:** 25 **Final Year or Final Semester Residency Requirement:** Yes **Library Holdings:** 95,869 **Regional Accreditation:** North Central Association of Colleges and Schools **ROTC:** Army **Professional Accreditation:** AACN, ACBSP, CSWE, NCATE, NRPA **Intercollegiate Athletics:** Baseball M; Basketball M & W; Cross-Country Running M & W; Football M; Golf M & W; Lacrosse M; Soccer M & W; Softball W; Tennis M & W; Track and Field M & W; Volleyball W

BENEDICTINE UNIVERSITY
5700 College Rd.
Lisle, IL 60532-0900
Tel: (630)829-6000; Free: 888-829-6363
Admissions: (630)829-6300
Fax: (630)960-1126
E-mail: admissions@ben.edu
Web Site: http://www.ben.edu/
President/CEO: Dr. William J. Carroll
Admissions: Kari Gibbons
Financial Aid: Diane Battistella
Type: Comprehensive **Sex:** Coed **Affiliation:** Roman Catholic **Scores:** 53% ACT 18-23; 33% ACT 24-29 **% Accepted:** 79 **Admission Plans:** Deferred Admission **Application Deadline:** Rolling **Application Fee:** $40.00 **H.S. Requirements:** High school diploma required; GED accepted **Costs Per Year:** Application fee: $40. Comprehensive fee: $29,670 includes full-time tuition ($21,600), mandatory fees ($710), and college room and board ($7360). Full-time tuition and fees vary according to class time, degree level, and location. Room and board charges vary according to board plan and housing facility. Part-time tuition: $720 per credit hour. Part-time mandatory fees: $15 per credit hour. Part-time tuition and fees vary according to class time and degree level. **Scholarships:** Available **Calendar System:** Semester, Summer Session Available **Enrollment:** FT 2,262, PT 1,093, Grad FT 716, Grad PT 1,765 **Faculty:** FT 103, PT 459 **Student-Faculty Ratio:** 13:1 **Exams:** SAT I or ACT. **% Receiving Financial Aid:** 68 **% Residing in College-Owned, -Operated, or -Affiliated Housing:** 31 **Library Holdings:** 126,358 **Regional Accreditation:** North Central Association of Colleges and Schools **Credit Hours For Degree:** 60 semester hours, Associates; 120 semester hours, Bachelors **ROTC:** Army **Professional Accreditation:** ADtA, NLN **Intercollegiate Athletics:** Baseball M; Basketball M & W; Cross-Country Running M & W; Football M; Golf M & W; Soccer M & W; Softball W; Tennis W; Track and Field M & W; Volleyball W

BLACK HAWK COLLEGE
6600 34th Ave.
Moline, IL 61265-5899
Tel: (309)796-5000
Admissions: (309)796-5341
E-mail: berryv@bhc.edu
Web Site: http://www.bhc.edu/
President/CEO: Dr. Richard Underbakke
Admissions: Vashti Berry
Financial Aid: Joanna Dye
Type: Two-Year College **Sex:** Coed **Affiliation:** Black Hawk College District System **Scores:** 42% ACT 18-23; 10% ACT 24-29 **% Accepted:** 100 **Admission Plans:** Open Admission; Early Admission; Deferred Admission **Application Deadline:** Rolling **Application Fee:** $0.00 **H.S. Requirements:** High school diploma or equivalent not required **Scholarships:** Available **Calendar System:** Semester, Summer Session Available **Enrollment:** FT 2,715, PT 3,552 **Faculty:** FT 134, PT 195 **Student-Faculty Ratio:** 19:1 **Exams:** ACT essay not being used. SAT essay not being used. **Final Year or Final Semester Residency Requirement:** No **Library Holdings:** 59,840 **Regional Accreditation:** North Central Association of Colleges and Schools **Credit Hours For Degree:** 60 semester hours, Associates **Professional Accreditation:** APTA, NLN **Intercollegiate Athletics:** Baseball M; Basketball M & W; Golf M; Softball W; Volleyball W

BLACKBURN COLLEGE
700 College Ave.
Carlinville, IL 62626-1498
Tel: (217)854-3231; Free: 800-233-3550
Fax: (217)854-3713
E-mail: admit@mail.blackburn.edu
Web Site: http://www.blackburn.edu/
President/CEO: Dr. Miriam R. Pride
Admissions: John Malin
Financial Aid: Jane Kelsey
Type: Four-Year College **Sex:** Coed **Affiliation:** Presbyterian **Scores:** 53% ACT 18-23; 28% ACT 24-29 **% Accepted:** 64 **Admission Plans:** Deferred Admission **Application Deadline:** Rolling **Application Fee:** $0.00 **H.S. Requirements:** High school diploma required; GED accepted **Scholarships:** Available **Calendar System:** Semester, Summer Session Available **Enrollment:** FT 585, PT 22 **Faculty:** FT 36, PT 34 **Student-Faculty Ratio:** 13:1 **Exams:** SAT I or ACT. **% Receiving Financial Aid:** 83 **% Residing in College-Owned, -Operated, or -Affiliated Housing:** 66 **Library Holdings:** 61,586 **Regional Accreditation:** North Central Association of Colleges and Schools **Credit Hours For Degree:** 122 semester hours, Bachelors **Intercollegiate Athletics:** Baseball M; Basketball M & W; Cheerleading M & W; Cross-Country Running M & W; Golf M; Soccer M & W; Softball W; Tennis W; Volleyball W

BLESSING-RIEMAN COLLEGE OF NURSING
Broadway at 11th St., POB 7005
Quincy, IL 62305-7005
Tel: (217)228-5520; Free: 800-877-9140
Fax: (217)223-6400
E-mail: admissions@brcn.edu
Web Site: http://www.brcn.edu/
President/CEO: Dr. Pamela S. Brown
Admissions: Heather Mutter
Financial Aid: Misty McBee
Type: Comprehensive **Sex:** Coed **Scores:** 33% ACT 18-23; 67% ACT 24-29 **% Accepted:** 77 **Admission Plans:** Deferred Admission **Application Deadline:** Rolling **Application Fee:** $0.00 **H.S. Requirements:** High school diploma required; GED accepted **Costs Per Year:** Application fee: $0. Comprehensive fee: $30,180 includes full-time tuition ($21,775), mandatory fees ($515), and college room and board ($7890). College room only: $3910. Full-time tuition and fees vary according to course load, location, and student level. Room and board charges vary according to board plan, location, and student level. Part-time tuition: $498 per credit hour. Part-time tuition varies according to course load, location, and student level. **Scholarships:** Available **Calendar System:** Semester, Summer Session Available **Enrollment:** FT 198, PT 13 **Faculty:** FT 18, PT 0 **Student-Faculty Ratio:** 12:1 **Exams:** SAT I or ACT. **% Receiving Financial Aid:** 100 **% Residing in College-Owned, -Operated, or -Affiliated Housing:** 82 **Library Holdings:** 3,767 **Regional Accreditation:** North Central Association of Colleges and Schools **Credit Hours For Degree:** 124 semester hours, Bachelors **Professional Accreditation:** AACN, NLN **Intercollegiate Athletics:** Baseball M & W; Basketball M & W; Football M; Soccer M & W; Volleyball M & W

BRADLEY UNIVERSITY
1501 West Bradley Ave.
Peoria, IL 61625-0002
Tel: (309)676-7611; Free: 800-447-6460
Admissions: (309)677-1000
E-mail: admissions@bradley.edu
Web Site: http://www.bradley.edu/
President/CEO: Joanne K. Glasser, Esq.
Admissions: Rodney San Jose
Financial Aid: David L. Pardieck
Type: Comprehensive **Sex:** Coed **Scores:** 96% SAT V 400+; 96% SAT M 400+; 35% ACT 18-23; 52% ACT 24-29 **% Accepted:** 73 **Admission Plans:** Early Admission; Deferred Admission **Application Deadline:** Rolling **Application Fee:** $35.00 **H.S. Requirements:** High school diploma required; GED accepted **Costs Per Year:** Application fee: $35. Comprehensive fee: $31,874 includes full-time tuition ($23,950), mandatory fees ($274), and college room and board ($7650). Part-time tuition: $650 per credit hour. Part-time tuition varies according to course load. **Scholarships:** Available **Calendar System:** Semester, Summer Session Available **Enrollment:** FT 4,801, PT 260, Grad FT 304, Grad PT 435 **Faculty:** FT 345, PT 204 **Student-Faculty Ratio:** 13:1 **Exams:** SAT I or ACT. ACT essay not being used. SAT essay not being used. **% Receiving Financial Aid:** 71 **% Residing in College-Owned, -Operated, or -Affiliated Housing:** 70 **Library Holdings:** 511,000 **Regional Accreditation:** North Central Association of

Colleges and Schools **Credit Hours For Degree:** 124 credits, Bachelors **Professional Accreditation:** AACSB, ABET, AAFCS, AANA, ACCE, ACA, APTA, CSWE, NASAD, NASM, NAST, NCATE, NLN **Intercollegiate Athletics:** Baseball M; Basketball M & W; Cheerleading M & W; Cross-Country Running M & W; Golf M & W; Soccer M; Softball M & W; Tennis M & W; Track and Field W; Volleyball W

BROWN MACKIE COLLEGE—QUAD CITIES
1527 47th Ave.
Moline, IL 61265-7062
Tel: (309)762-2100
Web Site: http://www.brownmackie.edu/quad-cities/
President/CEO: Kareem Odukale
Type: Two-Year College **Sex:** Coed **Affiliation:** Education Management Corporation

CARL SANDBURG COLLEGE
2400 Tom L. Wilson Blvd.
Galesburg, IL 61401-9576
Tel: (309)344-2518
Fax: (309)344-1395
Web Site: http://www.sandburg.edu/
President/CEO: Thomas A. Schmidt
Admissions: Carol Kreider
Financial Aid: Lisa Hanson
Type: Two-Year College **Sex:** Coed **Affiliation:** Illinois Community College Board **Admission Plans:** Open Admission; Early Admission; Deferred Admission **Application Deadline:** Rolling **Application Fee:** $0.00 **H.S. Requirements:** High school diploma or equivalent not required. For allied health programs: High school diploma required; GED accepted **Scholarships:** Available **Calendar System:** Semester, Summer Session Available **Library Holdings:** 39,900 **Regional Accreditation:** North Central Association of Colleges and Schools **Credit Hours For Degree:** 64 semester hours, Associates **ROTC:** Army **Professional Accreditation:** ABFSE, ADA, JRCERT, NLN **Intercollegiate Athletics:** Baseball M; Basketball M & W; Volleyball W

CHICAGO STATE UNIVERSITY
9501 South King Dr.
Chicago, IL 60628
Tel: (773)995-2000
Admissions: (773)995-2513
E-mail: ug-admissions@csu.edu
Web Site: http://www.csu.edu/
President/CEO: Dr. Elnora D. Daniel
Admissions: Addie Epps
Type: Comprehensive **Sex:** Coed **Scores:** 77.2% ACT 18-23; 4.1% ACT 24-29 **% Accepted:** 57 **Application Fee:** $25.00 **H.S. Requirements:** High school diploma required; GED accepted **Scholarships:** Available **Calendar System:** Semester, Summer Session Available **Enrollment:** FT 3,308, PT 1,909 **Faculty:** FT 313, PT 120 **Student-Faculty Ratio:** 13:1 **Exams:** SAT I or ACT. **Library Holdings:** 426,691 **Regional Accreditation:** North Central Association of Colleges and Schools **Credit Hours For Degree:** 120 credit hours, Bachelors **ROTC:** Army, Navy, Air Force **Professional Accreditation:** ACA, AHIMA, AOTA, CSWE, NASM, NCATE, NLN **Intercollegiate Athletics:** Baseball M; Basketball M & W; Cross-Country Running M & W; Golf M & W; Tennis M & W; Track and Field M & W; Volleyball W

CHRISTIAN LIFE COLLEGE
400 East Gregory St.
Mount Prospect, IL 60056
Tel: (847)259-1840
E-mail: mail@christianlifecollege.edu
Web Site: http://www.christianlifecollege.edu/
President/CEO: Harry Schmidt
Financial Aid: Jeanna Wilson
Type: Four-Year College **Sex:** Coed **Admission Plans:** Early Admission; Deferred Admission **Application Deadline:** Rolling **Application Fee:** $40.00 **H.S. Requirements:** High school diploma required; GED accepted **Costs Per Year:** Application fee: $40. Tuition: $9120 full-time, $365 per credit hour part-time. Mandatory fees: $950 full-time, $365 per term part-time. Full-time tuition and fees vary according to class time, course load, and program. Part-time tuition and fees vary according to class time, course load, and program. College room only: $3700. **Scholarships:** Available **Enrollment:** FT 36, PT 8 **Faculty:** FT 6, PT 9 **Student-Faculty Ratio:** 10:1 **Exams:** SAT I or ACT. **% Receiving Financial Aid:** 60 **Final Year or Final Semester Residency Requirement:** No **Credit Hours For Degree:** 64 units, Associates; 128 units, Bachelors **Professional Accreditation:** TACCS

CITY COLLEGES OF CHICAGO, HAROLD WASHINGTON COLLEGE
30 East Lake St.
Chicago, IL 60601-2449
Tel: (312)553-5600
Fax: (312)553-6077
Web Site: http://hwashington.ccc.edu/
President/CEO: John R. Wozniak
Admissions: Terry Pendleton
Type: Two-Year College **Sex:** Coed **Affiliation:** City Colleges of Chicago **Admission Plans:** Open Admission; Early Admission; Deferred Admission **Application Deadline:** Rolling **Application Fee:** $0.00 **H.S. Requirements:** High school diploma required; GED accepted **Scholarships:** Available **Calendar System:** Semester, Summer Session Available **Enrollment:** FT 2,608, PT 5,826 **Faculty:** FT 117, PT 114 **Student-Faculty Ratio:** 23:1 **Library Holdings:** 65,926 **Regional Accreditation:** North Central Association of Colleges and Schools **Credit Hours For Degree:** 60 credit hours, Associates **Professional Accreditation:** ACBSP

CITY COLLEGES OF CHICAGO, HARRY S. TRUMAN COLLEGE
1145 West Wilson Ave.
Chicago, IL 60640-5616
Tel: (773)907-4000
Admissions: (773)907-4700
Fax: (773)907-4464
Web Site: http://www.trumancollege.cc/
President/CEO: Lynn Walker
Admissions: Kelly O'Malley
Type: Two-Year College **Sex:** Coed **Affiliation:** City Colleges of Chicago **Admission Plans:** Open Admission; Early Admission; Deferred Admission **Application Deadline:** Rolling **Application Fee:** $0.00 **H.S. Requirements:** High school diploma required; GED accepted **Scholarships:** Available **Calendar System:** Semester, Summer Session Available **Faculty:** FT 116, PT 387 **Student-Faculty Ratio:** 61:1 **Library Holdings:** 59,750 **Regional Accreditation:** North Central Association of Colleges and Schools **Credit Hours For Degree:** 60 semester hours, Associates **Professional Accreditation:** NLN **Intercollegiate Athletics:** Baseball M; Basketball M & W; Tennis M & W; Wrestling M

CITY COLLEGES OF CHICAGO, KENNEDY-KING COLLEGE
6800 South Wentworth Ave.
Chicago, IL 60621-3733
Tel: (773)602-5000
Web Site: http://kennedyking.ccc.edu/
President/CEO: John Dozier
Admissions: Joyce Collins
Type: Two-Year College **Sex:** Coed **Affiliation:** City Colleges of Chicago **Admission Plans:** Open Admission; Preferred Admission **Application Deadline:** Rolling **Application Fee:** $0.00 **H.S. Requirements:** High school diploma or equivalent not required **Scholarships:** Available **Calendar System:** Semester, Summer Session Available **Faculty:** FT 61, PT 86 **Library Holdings:** 45,000 **Regional Accreditation:** North Central Association of Colleges and Schools **Credit Hours For Degree:** 90 quarter credits, Associates **Professional Accreditation:** ADA, NLN **Intercollegiate Athletics:** Basketball M & W; Soccer M; Track and Field M & W; Wrestling M

CITY COLLEGES OF CHICAGO, MALCOLM X COLLEGE
1900 West Van Buren St.
Chicago, IL 60612-3145
Tel: (312)850-7000
Admissions: (312)850-7120
Fax: (312)850-7092
E-mail: khollingsworth@ccc.edu
Web Site: http://malcolmx.ccc.edu/
President/CEO: Ghingo Brooks
Admissions: Kimberly Hollingsworth
Type: Two-Year College **Sex:** Coed **Affiliation:** City Colleges of Chicago **Admission Plans:** Open Admission; Preferred Admission **Application Deadline:** Rolling **Application Fee:** $0.00 **H.S. Requirements:** High school diploma required; GED accepted **Costs Per Year:** Application fee: $0. Area

resident tuition: $2370 full-time, $79 per credit hour part-time. State resident tuition: $7775 full-time, $259 per credit hour part-time. Nonresident tuition: $9257 full-time, $309 per credit hour part-time. Mandatory fees: $350 full-time. Full-time tuition and fees vary according to program. Part-time tuition varies according to program. **Scholarships:** Available **Calendar System:** Semester, Summer Session Available **Enrollment:** FT 2,522, PT 3,509 **Faculty:** FT 75, PT 165 **Student-Faculty Ratio:** 25:1 **Final Year or Final Semester Residency Requirement:** Yes **Library Holdings:** 50,000 **Regional Accreditation:** North Central Association of Colleges and Schools **Credit Hours For Degree:** 60 credit hours, Associates **Professional Accreditation:** ARCEST, ABFSE, JRCERT, NLN **Intercollegiate Athletics:** Basketball M & W; Cross-Country Running M

CITY COLLEGES OF CHICAGO, OLIVE-HARVEY COLLEGE
10001 South Woodlawn Ave.
Chicago, IL 60628-1645
Tel: (773)291-6100
Fax: (773)291-6304
E-mail: OH_admissions@ccc.edu
Web Site: http://oliveharvey.ccc.edu/
President/CEO: Clyde El-Amin
Admissions: Michelle Adams
Type: Two-Year College **Sex:** Coed **Affiliation:** City Colleges of Chicago **% Accepted:** 100 **Admission Plans:** Open Admission; Preferred Admission; Early Admission; Deferred Admission **Application Deadline:** Rolling **Application Fee:** $0.00 **H.S. Requirements:** High school diploma required; GED accepted **Scholarships:** Available **Calendar System:** Semester, Summer Session Available **Enrollment:** FT 795, PT 1,393 **Faculty:** FT 80, PT 50 **Student-Faculty Ratio:** 19:1 **Library Holdings:** 56,318 **Regional Accreditation:** North Central Association of Colleges and Schools **Credit Hours For Degree:** 60 credit hours, Associates **Intercollegiate Athletics:** Baseball M; Basketball M; Volleyball W

CITY COLLEGES OF CHICAGO, RICHARD J. DALEY COLLEGE
7500 South Pulaski Rd.
Chicago, IL 60652-1242
Tel: (773)838-7500
Admissions: (773)838-7606
Fax: (773)838-7524
E-mail: mwright@ccc.edu
Web Site: http://daley.ccc.edu/
President/CEO: Dr. Jose Aybar
Admissions: Milton Wright
Type: Two-Year College **Sex:** Coed **Affiliation:** City Colleges of Chicago **% Accepted:** 100 **Admission Plans:** Open Admission; Preferred Admission; Early Admission; Deferred Admission **Application Deadline:** Rolling **Application Fee:** $0.00 **H.S. Requirements:** High school diploma required; GED accepted **Costs Per Year:** Application fee: $0. Area resident tuition: $2370 full-time. State resident tuition: $7775 full-time. Nonresident tuition: $9257 full-time. Mandatory fees: $350 full-time. Full-time tuition and fees vary according to course load. **Scholarships:** Available **Calendar System:** Semester, Summer Session Available **Enrollment:** FT 3,507, PT 6,204 **Faculty:** FT 56, PT 106 **Student-Faculty Ratio:** 44:1 **Exams:** ACT essay used for placement. **Library Holdings:** 53,201 **Regional Accreditation:** North Central Association of Colleges and Schools **Credit Hours For Degree:** 60 credit hours, Associates **ROTC:** Air Force **Professional Accreditation:** NLN **Intercollegiate Athletics:** Basketball M & W; Soccer M & W

CITY COLLEGES OF CHICAGO, WILBUR WRIGHT COLLEGE
4300 North Narragansett Ave.
Chicago, IL 60634-1591
Tel: (773)777-7900
Admissions: (773)481-8207
E-mail: aaiello@ccc.edu
Web Site: http://wright.ccc.edu/
President/CEO: Dr. Charles Guengerich
Admissions: Amy Aiello
Type: Two-Year College **Sex:** Coed **Affiliation:** City Colleges of Chicago **% Accepted:** 100 **Admission Plans:** Open Admission; Preferred Admission; Early Admission; Deferred Admission **Application Deadline:** Rolling **Application Fee:** $0.00 **H.S. Requirements:** High school diploma required; GED accepted. For applicants 18 or over: High school diploma or equivalent not required **Scholarships:** Available **Calendar System:** Semester, Summer Session Available **Enrollment:** FT 2,214, PT 4,612 **Faculty:** FT 112, PT 150 **Student-Faculty Ratio:** 23:1 **Library Holdings:** 60,000 **Regional Accreditation:** North Central Association of Colleges and Schools **Credit Hours For Degree:** 64 credit hours, Associates **Professional Accreditation:** AOTA, ACBSP, JRCERT **Intercollegiate Athletics:** Basketball M & W; Wrestling M

COLLEGE OF DUPAGE
425 Fawell Blvd.
Glen Ellyn, IL 60137-6599
Tel: (630)942-2800
Fax: (630)790-2686
E-mail: hauenstein@cod.edu
Web Site: http://www.cod.edu/
President/CEO: Dr. Robert Breuder
Admissions: Amy Hauenstein
Type: Two-Year College **Sex:** Coed **Admission Plans:** Open Admission; Early Admission; Deferred Admission **Application Deadline:** Rolling **Application Fee:** $20.00 **H.S. Requirements:** High school diploma or equivalent not required **Costs Per Year:** Application fee: $20. Area resident tuition: $3870 full-time, $129 per credit hour part-time. State resident tuition: $9480 full-time, $316 per credit hour part-time. Nonresident tuition: $11,580 full-time, $386 per credit hour part-time. **Scholarships:** Available **Calendar System:** Semester, Summer Session Available **Enrollment:** FT 10,591, PT 16,492 **Faculty:** FT 273, PT 861 **Student-Faculty Ratio:** 24:1 **Library Holdings:** 203,300 **Regional Accreditation:** North Central Association of Colleges and Schools **Credit Hours For Degree:** 60 semester hours, Associates **Professional Accreditation:** ACF, ADA, AHIMA, APTA, CARC, JRCERT, NLN **Intercollegiate Athletics:** Baseball M; Basketball M & W; Cheerleading M & W; Cross-Country Running M & W; Football M; Golf M; Soccer M & W; Softball W; Swimming and Diving M & W; Tennis M & W; Track and Field M & W; Volleyball W

COLLEGE OF LAKE COUNTY
19351 West Washington St.
Grayslake, IL 60030-1198
Tel: (847)543-2000
Admissions: (847)543-2383
Fax: (847)223-1017
Web Site: http://www.clcillinois.edu/
President/CEO: Dr. Girard Weber
Type: Two-Year College **Sex:** Coed **Affiliation:** Illinois Community College Board **% Accepted:** 100 **Admission Plans:** Open Admission; Preferred Admission; Early Admission; Deferred Admission **Application Deadline:** Rolling **Application Fee:** $0.00 **H.S. Requirements:** High school diploma or equivalent not required. For health programs: High school diploma required; GED accepted **Costs Per Year:** Application fee: $0. Area resident tuition: $1944 full-time, $81 per credit hour part-time. State resident tuition: $4944 full-time, $206 per credit hour part-time. Nonresident tuition: $6648 full-time, $277 per credit hour part-time. Mandatory fees: $336 full-time, $14 per credit hour part-time. **Scholarships:** Available **Calendar System:** Semester, Summer Session Available **Faculty:** FT 201, PT 762 **Student-Faculty Ratio:** 19:1 **Library Holdings:** 106,842 **Regional Accreditation:** North Central Association of Colleges and Schools **Credit Hours For Degree:** 60 credits, Associates **Professional Accreditation:** ADA, AHIMA, JRCERT, NLN **Intercollegiate Athletics:** Baseball M; Basketball M & W; Cross-Country Running M & W; Golf M; Soccer M & W; Softball W; Tennis M & W; Volleyball W

THE COLLEGE OF OFFICE TECHNOLOGY
1520 West Division St.
Chicago, IL 60622
Tel: (773)278-0042; Free: 800-953-6161
Fax: (773)278-0143
E-mail: bbolton@cotedu.com
Web Site: http://www.cotedu.com/
President/CEO: Pedro Galva
Admissions: William Bolton
Type: Two-Year College **Sex:** Coed **Application Fee:** $50.00 **Scholarships:** Available **Professional Accreditation:** ACICS

COLUMBIA COLLEGE CHICAGO
600 South Michigan Ave.
Chicago, IL 60605-1996

Tel: (312)663-1600
Admissions: (312)369-7133
E-mail: admissions@colum.edu
Web Site: http://www.colum.edu/
President/CEO: Dr. Warrick L. Carter
Admissions: Murphy Monroe
Financial Aid: Jennifer Waters
Type: Comprehensive **Sex:** Coed **Scores:** 90% SAT V 400+; 83% SAT M 400+; 50% ACT 18-23; 28% ACT 24-29 **% Accepted:** 84 **Admission Plans:** Deferred Admission **Application Deadline:** Rolling **Application Fee:** $35.00 **H.S. Requirements:** High school diploma required; GED accepted **Costs Per Year:** Application fee: $35. Tuition: $19,140 full-time, $661 per credit hour part-time. Mandatory fees: $710 full-time, $300 per semester hour part-time. Full-time tuition and fees vary according to course load. Part-time tuition and fees vary according to course load. College room only: $10,780. Room charges vary according to housing facility. **Scholarships:** Available **Calendar System:** Semester, Summer Session Available **Enrollment:** FT 10,410, PT 1,182, Grad FT 338, Grad PT 197 **Faculty:** FT 354, PT 1,381 **Student-Faculty Ratio:** 15:1 **Exams:** SAT I or ACT. ACT essay not being used. SAT essay not being used. **% Receiving Financial Aid:** 59 **% Residing in College-Owned, -Operated, or -Affiliated Housing:** 26 **Final Year or Final Semester Residency Requirement:** Yes **Library Holdings:** 290,556 **Regional Accreditation:** North Central Association of Colleges and Schools **Credit Hours For Degree:** 120 credits, Bachelors **Intercollegiate Athletics:** Baseball M; Basketball M; Lacrosse M

CONCORDIA UNIVERSITY CHICAGO
7400 Augusta St.
River Forest, IL 60305-1499
Tel: (708)771-8300; Free: 800-285-2668
Admissions: (708)209-3101
Fax: (708)209-3176
E-mail: gwen.kanelos@cuchicago.edu
Web Site: http://www.cuchicago.edu/
President/CEO: Dr. John F. Johnson
Admissions: Gwen Kanelos
Financial Aid: Aida Asencio-Pinto
Type: Comprehensive **Sex:** Coed **Affiliation:** Lutheran Church–Missouri Synod; Concordia University System **Scores:** 60% ACT 18-23; 28% ACT 24-29 **% Accepted:** 83 **Admission Plans:** Deferred Admission **Application Deadline:** Rolling **Application Fee:** $0.00 **H.S. Requirements:** High school diploma required; GED accepted **Costs Per Year:** Application fee: $0. Comprehensive fee: $32,581 includes full-time tuition ($23,918), mandatory fees ($663), and college room and board ($8000). Full-time tuition and fees vary according to program. Part-time tuition: $747 per semester hour. Part-time tuition varies according to program. **Scholarships:** Available **Calendar System:** Semester, Summer Session Available **Enrollment:** FT 1,180, PT 90, Grad FT 501, Grad PT 3,278 **Faculty:** FT 122, PT 200 **Student-Faculty Ratio:** 17:1 **Exams:** SAT I or ACT. **% Receiving Financial Aid:** 79 **% Residing in College-Owned, -Operated, or -Affiliated Housing:** 60 **Library Holdings:** 159,716 **Regional Accreditation:** North Central Association of Colleges and Schools **Credit Hours For Degree:** 128 semester hours, Bachelors **Professional Accreditation:** ACA, NASM, NCATE, NLN **Intercollegiate Athletics:** Baseball M; Basketball M & W; Cheerleading M & W; Cross-Country Running M & W; Football M; Golf M; Soccer M & W; Softball W; Tennis M & W; Track and Field M & W; Volleyball W

DANVILLE AREA COMMUNITY COLLEGE
2000 East Main St.
Danville, IL 61832-5199
Tel: (217)443-3222
Admissions: (217)443-8800
Fax: (217)443-8560
E-mail: stacy@dacc.edu
Web Site: http://www.dacc.cc.il.us/
President/CEO: Dr. Alice Marie Jacobs
Admissions: Stacy L. Ehmen
Financial Aid: Janet Ingargiola
Type: Two-Year College **Sex:** Coed **Affiliation:** Illinois Community College Board **Admission Plans:** Open Admission; Early Admission; Deferred Admission **Application Deadline:** Rolling **Application Fee:** $0.00 **H.S. Requirements:** High school diploma required; GED accepted **Costs Per Year:** Application fee: $0. Area resident tuition: $2670 full-time, $89 per credit hour part-time. State resident tuition: $5250 full-time, $175 per credit hour part-time. Nonresident tuition: $5250 full-time, $175 per credit hour part-time. Mandatory fees: $360 full-time, $12 per credit hour part-time. Full-time tuition and fees vary according to program. Part-time tuition and fees vary according to program. **Scholarships:** Available **Calendar System:** Semester, Summer Session Available **Enrollment:** FT 1,486, PT 2,098 **Faculty:** FT 51, PT 100 **Student-Faculty Ratio:** 26:1 **Library Holdings:** 50,000 **Regional Accreditation:** North Central Association of Colleges and Schools **Credit Hours For Degree:** 61 semester hours, Associates **Intercollegiate Athletics:** Baseball M; Basketball M & W; Cross-Country Running M & W; Golf M; Soccer M; Softball W; Volleyball W

DEPAUL UNIVERSITY
1 East Jackson Blvd.
Chicago, IL 60604-2287
Tel: (312)362-8000
Admissions: (312)362-8300
Fax: (312)362-3322
E-mail: admission@depaul.edu
Web Site: http://www.depaul.edu/
President/CEO: Rev. Dennis H. Holtschneider, CM
Admissions: Carlene Klaas-Kennelly
Financial Aid: Christopher Rone
Type: University **Sex:** Coed **Affiliation:** Roman Catholic **Scores:** 98.9% SAT V 400+; 99.6% SAT M 400+; 39.4% ACT 18-23; 49.2% ACT 24-29 **% Accepted:** 74 **Admission Plans:** Early Action; Deferred Admission **Application Deadline:** February 1 **Application Fee:** $40.00 **H.S. Requirements:** High school diploma required; GED accepted **Costs Per Year:** Application fee: $40. Comprehensive fee: $37,959 includes full-time tuition ($26,765), mandatory fees ($577), and college room and board ($10,617). College room only: $7827. Full-time tuition and fees vary according to program. Room and board charges vary according to board plan, housing facility, and location. Part-time tuition: $475 per quarter hour. Part-time tuition varies according to program. **Scholarships:** Available **Calendar System:** Quarter, Summer Session Available **Enrollment:** FT 13,213, PT 2,986, Grad FT 5,576, Grad PT 3,297 **Faculty:** FT 919, PT 906 **Student-Faculty Ratio:** 16:1 **Exams:** SAT I or ACT. ACT essay not being used. SAT essay not being used. **% Receiving Financial Aid:** 64 **% Residing in College-Owned, -Operated, or -Affiliated Housing:** 17 **Library Holdings:** 927,400 **Regional Accreditation:** North Central Association of Colleges and Schools **Credit Hours For Degree:** 192 quarter hours, Bachelors **ROTC:** Army **Professional Accreditation:** AACSB, AACN, AANA, ABA, APA, AALS, NASM, NASPAA, NCATE **Intercollegiate Athletics:** Basketball M & W; Cross-Country Running M & W; Golf M; Soccer M & W; Softball W; Tennis M & W; Track and Field M & W; Volleyball W

DEVRY UNIVERSITY (ADDISON)
1221 North Swift Rd.
Addison, IL 60101-6106
Tel: (630)953-1300; Free: 800-346-5420
Fax: (630)953-1236
Web Site: http://www.devry.edu/
Financial Aid: Sejal Amin
Type: Four-Year College **Sex:** Coed **Affiliation:** DeVry University **Admission Plans:** Early Admission; Deferred Admission **Application Deadline:** Rolling **Application Fee:** $50.00 **H.S. Requirements:** High school diploma required; GED accepted **Costs Per Year:** Application fee: $50. Tuition: $14,080 full-time, $550 per credit hour part-time. **Scholarships:** Available **Calendar System:** Semester, Summer Session Available **Enrollment:** FT 919, PT 589 **Faculty:** FT 45, PT 109 **Student-Faculty Ratio:** 14:1 **Exams:** ACT essay used for admission. SAT essay used for admission. ACT essay used for placement. SAT essay used for placement. **% Receiving Financial Aid:** 70 **Regional Accreditation:** North Central Association of Colleges and Schools **Credit Hours For Degree:** 67 credit hours, Associates; 122 credit hours, Bachelors **Professional Accreditation:** ABET

DEVRY UNIVERSITY (CHICAGO)
3300 North Campbell Ave.
Chicago, IL 60618-5994
Tel: (773)929-8500
Web Site: http://www.devry.edu/
President/CEO: Candace Goodwin
Financial Aid: Milena Dobrina
Type: Four-Year College **Sex:** Coed **Affiliation:** DeVry University **Admission Plans:** Deferred Admission **Application Deadline:** Rolling **Application**

Fee: $50.00 **H.S. Requirements:** High school diploma required; GED accepted **Costs Per Year:** Application fee: $50. Tuition: $14,080 full-time, $550 per credit hour part-time. **Scholarships:** Available **Calendar System:** Semester, Summer Session Available **Enrollment:** FT 1,170, PT 905 **Faculty:** FT 40, PT 163 **Student-Faculty Ratio:** 16:1 **Exams:** ACT essay used for admission. SAT essay used for admission. ACT essay used for placement. SAT essay used for placement. **% Receiving Financial Aid:** 72 **Regional Accreditation:** North Central Association of Colleges and Schools **Credit Hours For Degree:** 67 credit hours, Associates; 122 credit hours, Bachelors **Professional Accreditation:** ABET

DEVRY UNIVERSITY (DOWNERS GROVE)
3005 Highland Parkway
Downers Grove, IL 60515
Tel: (630)515-3000
Admissions: (630)515-7700
Web Site: http://www.devry.edu/
President/CEO: David Pauldine
Type: Comprehensive **Sex:** Coed **Calendar System:** Semester **Regional Accreditation:** North Central Association of Colleges and Schools

DEVRY UNIVERSITY (ELGIN)
Randall Point
2250 Point Blvd., Ste. 250
Elgin, IL 60123
Tel: (847)649-3980
Web Site: http://www.devry.edu/
Type: Comprehensive **Sex:** Coed **Calendar System:** Semester **Regional Accreditation:** North Central Association of Colleges and Schools

DEVRY UNIVERSITY (GURNEE)
1075 Tri-State Parkway, Ste. 800
Gurnee, IL 60031-9126
Tel: (847)855-2649; Free: (866)563-3879
Fax: (847)855-5932
Web Site: http://www.devry.edu/
Type: Comprehensive **Sex:** Coed **Calendar System:** Semester **Regional Accreditation:** North Central Association of Colleges and Schools

DEVRY UNIVERSITY (NAPERVILLE)
2056 Westings Ave., Ste. 40
Naperville, IL 60563-2361
Tel: (630)428-9086; Free: 877-496-9050
Fax: (630)428-4721
Web Site: http://www.devry.edu/
Type: Comprehensive **Sex:** Coed **Application Deadline:** Rolling **Application Fee:** $50.00 **Calendar System:** Semester **Enrollment:** FT 2,196, PT 3,887 **Faculty:** FT 0, PT 2,248 **Student-Faculty Ratio:** 6:1 **Regional Accreditation:** North Central Association of Colleges and Schools

DEVRY UNIVERSITY ONLINE
1221 North Swift Rd.
Addison, IL 60101-6106
Tel: 877-496-9050
Web Site: http://www.devry.edu/
Type: Comprehensive **Sex:** Coed **Admission Plans:** Deferred Admission **Application Deadline:** Rolling **Application Fee:** $50.00 **H.S. Requirements:** High school diploma required; GED accepted **Scholarships:** Available **Calendar System:** Semester **Enrollment:** FT 5,217, PT 11,831, Grad FT 659, Grad PT 4,123 **Faculty:** FT 4, PT 3,062 **Student-Faculty Ratio:** 11:1 **Exams:** ACT essay used for admission. SAT essay used for admission. ACT essay used for placement. SAT essay used for placement. **% Receiving Financial Aid:** 52 **Regional Accreditation:** North Central Association of Colleges and Schools

DEVRY UNIVERSITY (TINLEY PARK)
18624 West Creek Dr.
Tinley Park, IL 60477
Tel: (708)342-3300
Web Site: http://www.devry.edu/
Type: Comprehensive **Sex:** Coed **Affiliation:** DeVry University **Admission Plans:** Deferred Admission **Application Deadline:** Rolling **Application Fee:** $50.00 **H.S. Requirements:** High school diploma required; GED accepted **Costs Per Year:** Application fee: $50. Tuition: $14,080 full-time, $550 per credit hour part-time. **Scholarships:** Available **Calendar System:** Semester, Summer Session Available **Enrollment:** FT 589, PT 552, Grad FT 42, Grad PT 288 **Faculty:** FT 32, PT 47 **Student-Faculty Ratio:** 19:1 **Exams:** ACT essay used for admission. SAT essay used for admission. ACT essay used for placement. SAT essay used for placement. **% Receiving Financial Aid:** 83 **Regional Accreditation:** North Central Association of Colleges and Schools **Credit Hours For Degree:** 67 credit hours, Associates; 122 credit hours, Bachelors

DOMINICAN UNIVERSITY
7900 West Division St.
River Forest, IL 60305-1099
Tel: (708)366-2490; Free: 800-828-8475
Admissions: (708)524-6800
Fax: (708)366-5360
E-mail: domadmis@dom.edu
Web Site: http://www.dom.edu/
President/CEO: Dr. Donna M. Carroll
Admissions: Glenn Hamilton
Financial Aid: Michael Shields
Type: Comprehensive **Sex:** Coed **Affiliation:** Roman Catholic **Scores:** 88% SAT V 400+; 80% SAT M 400+; 63% ACT 18-23; 29% ACT 24-29 **% Accepted:** 72 **Admission Plans:** Deferred Admission **Application Deadline:** Rolling **Application Fee:** $25.00 **H.S. Requirements:** High school diploma required; GED accepted **Costs Per Year:** Application fee: $25. One-time mandatory fee: $150. Comprehensive fee: $32,320 includes full-time tuition ($24,600), mandatory fees ($100), and college room and board ($7620). Full-time tuition and fees vary according to program. Room and board charges vary according to board plan and housing facility. Part-time tuition: $820 per semester hour. Part-time mandatory fees: $10 per course. Part-time tuition and fees vary according to location and program. **Scholarships:** Available **Calendar System:** Semester, Summer Session Available **Enrollment:** FT 1,707, PT 197, Grad FT 679, Grad PT 1,326 **Faculty:** FT 142, PT 298 **Student-Faculty Ratio:** 12:1 **Exams:** SAT I or ACT. ACT essay not being used. SAT essay not being used. **% Receiving Financial Aid:** 83 **% Residing in College-Owned, -Operated, or -Affiliated Housing:** 40 **Library Holdings:** 348,474 **Regional Accreditation:** North Central Association of Colleges and Schools **Credit Hours For Degree:** 124 credit hours, Bachelors **Professional Accreditation:** ALA, ACBSP, CSWE, NCATE **Intercollegiate Athletics:** Baseball M; Basketball M & W; Cross-Country Running M & W; Golf M; Soccer M & W; Softball W; Tennis M & W; Volleyball M & W

EAST-WEST UNIVERSITY
816 South Michigan Ave.
Chicago, IL 60605-2103
Tel: (312)939-0111
Fax: (312)939-0083
E-mail: ho@eastwest.edu
Web Site: http://www.eastwest.edu/
President/CEO: Dr. M. Wasiullah Khan
Admissions: Ho Chung
Financial Aid: Elizabeth Guzman
Type: Four-Year College **Sex:** Coed **Scores:** 35% ACT 18-23; 4% ACT 24-29 **% Accepted:** 89 **Admission Plans:** Early Decision Plan **Application Deadline:** Rolling **Application Fee:** $40.00 **H.S. Requirements:** High school diploma required; GED accepted **Costs Per Year:** Application fee: $40. One-time mandatory fee: $45. Tuition: $15,000 full-time, $500 per credit hour part-time. Mandatory fees: $750 full-time. Full-time tuition and fees vary according to degree level and program. **Scholarships:** Available **Calendar System:** Quarter, Summer Session Available **Enrollment:** FT 1,143, PT 27 **Faculty:** FT 18, PT 49 **Student-Faculty Ratio:** 15:1 **Exams:** ACT. **% Receiving Financial Aid:** 100 **Final Year or Final Semester Residency Requirement:** No **Library Holdings:** 32,820 **Regional Accreditation:** North Central Association of Colleges and Schools **Credit Hours For Degree:** 92 quarter hours, Associates; 180 quarter hours, Bachelors **Intercollegiate Athletics:** Basketball M

EASTERN ILLINOIS UNIVERSITY
600 Lincoln Ave.
Charleston, IL 61920-3099
Tel: (217)581-5000; Free: 800-252-5711
Admissions: (217)581-2223
Fax: (217)581-7060

E-mail: admissions@eiu.edu
Web Site: http://www.eiu.edu/
President/CEO: Dr. William Perry
Admissions: Brenda Major
Financial Aid: Tracy L. Hall
Type: Comprehensive **Sex:** Coed **Scores:** 64% ACT 18-23; 24% ACT 24-29 **% Accepted:** 68 **Admission Plans:** Deferred Admission **Application Deadline:** Rolling **Application Fee:** $30.00 **H.S. Requirements:** High school diploma required; GED accepted **Costs Per Year:** Application fee: $30. State resident tuition: $7170 full-time, $239 per credit hour part-time. Nonresident tuition: $21,510 full-time, $717 per credit hour part-time. Mandatory fees: $2370 full-time, $82 per credit hour part-time. Full-time tuition and fees vary according to course load and student level. Part-time tuition and fees vary according to course load and student level. College room and board: $8078. Room and board charges vary according to board plan and housing facility. **Scholarships:** Available **Calendar System:** Semester, Summer Session Available **Enrollment:** FT 9,205, PT 1,020, Grad FT 735, Grad PT 1,006 **Faculty:** FT 629, PT 163 **Student-Faculty Ratio:** 16:1 **Exams:** SAT I or ACT. ACT essay not being used. **% Receiving Financial Aid:** 52 **% Residing in College-Owned, -Operated, or -Affiliated Housing:** 41 **Final Year or Final Semester Residency Requirement:** Yes **Library Holdings:** 992,487 **Regional Accreditation:** North Central Association of Colleges and Schools **Credit Hours For Degree:** 120 semester hours, Bachelors **ROTC:** Army **Professional Accreditation:** AACSB, ACEJMC, AAFCS, ACA, ADtA, ASLHA, JRCEPAT, NASAD, NASM, NCATE, NRPA, NAIT **Intercollegiate Athletics:** Badminton M & W; Baseball M; Basketball M & W; Cross-Country Running M & W; Football M; Golf M & W; Racquetball M & W; Rugby M & W; Soccer M & W; Softball W; Swimming and Diving M & W; Tennis M & W; Track and Field M & W; Ultimate Frisbee M & W; Volleyball M & W; Wrestling M & W

ELGIN COMMUNITY COLLEGE

1700 Spartan Dr.
Elgin, IL 60123-7193
Tel: (847)697-1000
Admissions: (847)214-7414
E-mail: admissions@elgin.edu
Web Site: http://www.elgin.edu/
President/CEO: Dr. David Sam
Type: Two-Year College **Sex:** Coed **Affiliation:** Illinois Community College Board **Admission Plans:** Open Admission; Early Admission **Application Deadline:** Rolling **Application Fee:** $0.00 **H.S. Requirements:** High school diploma or equivalent not required. For nursing, selected health programs: High school diploma required; GED accepted **Costs Per Year:** Application fee: $0. Area resident tuition: $2730 full-time, $91 per credit hour part-time. State resident tuition: $10,742 full-time, $358.08 per credit hour part-time. Nonresident tuition: $13,280 full-time, $442.65 per credit hour part-time. Mandatory fees: $10 full-time. Full-time tuition and fees vary according to program. Part-time tuition varies according to program. **Calendar System:** Semester, Summer Session Available **Enrollment:** FT 3,624, PT 6,197 **Faculty:** FT 127 **Student-Faculty Ratio:** 23:1 **Library Holdings:** 71,561 **Regional Accreditation:** North Central Association of Colleges and Schools **Credit Hours For Degree:** 60 credit hours, Associates **Professional Accreditation:** ACF, ADA, NAACLS, NLN **Intercollegiate Athletics:** Baseball M; Basketball M & W; Cross-Country Running M & W; Golf M; Soccer M & W; Softball W; Tennis M & W; Volleyball W

ELLIS UNIVERSITY

111 North Canal St.
Ste. 380
Chicago, IL 60606-7204
Free: 877-355-4762
Web Site: http://www.ellis.edu/
President/CEO: Dr. Roger Widmer
Type: Comprehensive **Sex:** Coed

ELMHURST COLLEGE

190 Prospect Ave.
Elmhurst, IL 60126-3296
Tel: (630)617-3500; Free: 800-697-1871
Admissions: (630)617-3400
Fax: (630)617-5501
E-mail: admit@elmhurst.edu
Web Site: http://www.elmhurst.edu/
President/CEO: Dr. S. Alan Ray
Admissions: Stephanie Levenson
Financial Aid: Ruth A. Pusich
Type: Comprehensive **Sex:** Coed **Affiliation:** United Church of Christ **Scores:** 98% SAT V 400+; 98% SAT M 400+; 46% ACT 18-23; 42% ACT 24-29 **% Accepted:** 70 **Admission Plans:** Deferred Admission **Application Deadline:** Rolling **Application Fee:** $0.00 **H.S. Requirements:** High school diploma required; GED accepted **Costs Per Year:** Application fee: $0. Comprehensive fee: $36,876 includes full-time tuition ($28,600), mandatory fees ($60), and college room and board ($8216). College room only: $4956. Room and board charges vary according to board plan and housing facility. **Scholarships:** Available **Calendar System:** 4-1-4, Summer Session Available **Enrollment:** FT 2,851, PT 242, Grad FT 24, Grad PT 246 **Faculty:** FT 125, PT 215 **Student-Faculty Ratio:** 14:1 **Exams:** SAT I or ACT. **% Receiving Financial Aid:** 69 **% Residing in College-Owned, -Operated, or -Affiliated Housing:** 38 **Library Holdings:** 228,015 **Regional Accreditation:** North Central Association of Colleges and Schools **Credit Hours For Degree:** 32 courses, Bachelors **ROTC:** Army, Air Force **Professional Accreditation:** AACN, NCATE **Intercollegiate Athletics:** Baseball M; Basketball M & W; Bowling W; Cross-Country Running M & W; Football M; Golf M & W; Soccer M & W; Softball W; Tennis M & W; Track and Field M & W; Volleyball W; Wrestling M

EUREKA COLLEGE

300 East College Ave.
Eureka, IL 61530
Tel: (309)467-3721; Free: 888-4-EUREKA
Fax: (309)467-6576
E-mail: admissions@eureka.edu
Web Site: http://www.eureka.edu/
President/CEO: Dr. J. David Arnold
Admissions: Dr. Brian Sajko
Financial Aid: Ellen Rigsby
Type: Four-Year College **Sex:** Coed **Affiliation:** Christian Church (Disciples of Christ) **Admission Plans:** Deferred Admission **Application Deadline:** August 1 **Application Fee:** $0.00 **H.S. Requirements:** High school diploma required; GED accepted **Scholarships:** Available **Calendar System:** Miscellaneous, Summer Session Available **Exams:** SAT I or ACT. **% Receiving Financial Aid:** 72 **Library Holdings:** 75,000 **Regional Accreditation:** North Central Association of Colleges and Schools **Credit Hours For Degree:** 124 semester hours, Bachelors **Intercollegiate Athletics:** Baseball M; Basketball M & W; Football M; Golf M; Softball W; Swimming and Diving M & W; Tennis M & W; Volleyball W

FOX COLLEGE

6640 South Cicero
Bedford Park, IL 60638
Tel: (708)636-7700
Admissions: (708)444-4500
Fax: (708)636-8078
Web Site: http://www.foxcollege.edu/
President/CEO: Carey Cranston
Type: Two-Year College **Sex:** Coed **% Accepted:** 62 **Regional Accreditation:** North Central Association of Colleges and Schools **Professional Accreditation:** ACICS

GEM CITY COLLEGE

PO Box 179
Quincy, IL 62301
Tel: (217)222-0391
Fax: (217)222-1557
Web Site: http://www.gemcitycollege.com/
President/CEO: Russell H. Hagenah
Type: Two-Year College **Sex:** Coed **Admission Plans:** Open Admission; Early Admission; Deferred Admission **Application Deadline:** Rolling **Application Fee:** $50.00 **H.S. Requirements:** High school diploma required; GED accepted **Scholarships:** Available **Calendar System:** Quarter, Summer Session Available **Library Holdings:** 2,700 **Professional Accreditation:** ACICS

GOVERNORS STATE UNIVERSITY

One University Parkway
University Park, IL 60466-0975
Tel: (708)534-5000

Fax: (708)534-1640
E-mail: gsunow@govst.edu
Web Site: http://www.govst.edu/
President/CEO: Elaine P. Maimon
Admissions: Sharon Evans
Type: Two-Year Upper Division **Sex:** Coed **Admission Plans:** Deferred Admission **Application Fee:** $25.00 **Scholarships:** Available **Calendar System:** Trimester, Summer Session Available **Enrollment:** FT 1,022, PT 1,769, Grad FT 642, Grad PT 2,241 **Faculty:** FT 212, PT 186 **Student-Faculty Ratio:** 12:1 **Final Year or Final Semester Residency Requirement:** No **Library Holdings:** 462,924 **Regional Accreditation:** North Central Association of Colleges and Schools **Credit Hours For Degree:** 120 credit hours, Bachelors **ROTC:** Army, Air Force **Professional Accreditation:** ACA, AOTA, APTA, ASLHA, ACBSP, ACEHSA, CSWE, NASPAA, NCATE, NLN

GREENVILLE COLLEGE
315 East College Ave., PO Box 159
Greenville, IL 62246-0159
Tel: (618)664-2800; Free: 800-345-4440
Admissions: (618)664-7100
Fax: (618)664-9841
E-mail: admissions@greenville.edu
Web Site: http://www.greenville.edu/
President/CEO: Dr. Larry H. Linamen
Admissions: Jen McMahon
Financial Aid: Marilae Latham
Type: Comprehensive **Sex:** Coed **Affiliation:** Free Methodist **Scores:** 85% SAT V 400+; 79% SAT M 400+; 41% ACT 18-23; 40% ACT 24-29 **% Accepted:** 78 **Admission Plans:** Early Admission; Deferred Admission **Application Deadline:** August 1 **Application Fee:** $25.00 **H.S. Requirements:** High school diploma required; GED accepted **Costs Per Year:** Application fee: $25. Comprehensive fee: $27,958 includes full-time tuition ($20,766), mandatory fees ($158), and college room and board ($7034). College room only: $3374. Room and board charges vary according to housing facility. Part-time tuition: $437 per credit hour. Part-time tuition varies according to course load. **Scholarships:** Available **Calendar System:** 4-1-4, Summer Session Available **Enrollment:** FT 1,330, PT 52, Grad FT 121, Grad PT 73 **Faculty:** FT 67, PT 111 **Student-Faculty Ratio:** 16:1 **Exams:** SAT I or ACT. **% Receiving Financial Aid:** 87 **% Residing in College-Owned, -Operated, or -Affiliated Housing:** 68 **Library Holdings:** 135,210 **Regional Accreditation:** North Central Association of Colleges and Schools **Credit Hours For Degree:** 126 credits, Bachelors **Intercollegiate Athletics:** Baseball M; Basketball M & W; Cross-Country Running M & W; Football M; Soccer M & W; Softball W; Tennis M & W; Track and Field M & W; Volleyball W

HARPER COLLEGE
1200 West Algonquin Rd.
Palatine, IL 60067-7398
Tel: (847)925-6000
Admissions: (847)925-6700
Fax: (847)925-6044
E-mail: admissions@harpercollege.edu
Web Site: http://www.harpercollege.edu/
President/CEO: Dr. Robert L. Breuder
Type: Two-Year College **Sex:** Coed **Affiliation:** Illinois Community College Board **% Accepted:** 100 **Admission Plans:** Open Admission; Preferred Admission; Early Admission; Deferred Admission **Application Deadline:** Rolling **Application Fee:** $25.00 **H.S. Requirements:** High school diploma required; GED accepted **Costs Per Year:** Application fee: $25. Area resident tuition: $2160 full-time, $90 per credit hour part-time. State resident tuition: $7776 full-time, $324 per credit hour part-time. Nonresident tuition: $9768 full-time, $407 per credit hour part-time. Mandatory fees: $450 full-time, $120 per term part-time. Full-time tuition and fees vary according to course load. Part-time tuition and fees vary according to course load. **Scholarships:** Available **Calendar System:** Semester, Summer Session Available **Enrollment:** FT 6,538, PT 8,618 **Faculty:** FT 191, PT 643 **Student-Faculty Ratio:** 23:1 **Library Holdings:** 141,124 **Regional Accreditation:** North Central Association of Colleges and Schools **Credit Hours For Degree:** 60 semester hours, Associates **Professional Accreditation:** AAMAE, ADA, ACBSP, NASM, NLN **Intercollegiate Athletics:** Baseball M; Basketball M & W; Cross-Country Running M & W; Football M; Soccer M & W; Softball W; Track and Field M & W; Volleyball W; Wrestling M

HARRINGTON COLLEGE OF DESIGN
200 West Madison St.
Chicago, IL 60605-1496
Tel: (312)939-4975; Free: 877-939-4975
Admissions: (312)697-8022
Fax: (312)939-8005
E-mail: rhacker@harringtoncollege.com
Web Site: http://www.interiordesign.edu/
President/CEO: Erik Parks
Admissions: Rian Hacker
Financial Aid: Renee Darosky
Type: Comprehensive **Sex:** Coed **Affiliation:** Career Education Corporation **Admission Plans:** Open Admission **Application Deadline:** Rolling **Application Fee:** $60.00 **H.S. Requirements:** High school diploma required; GED accepted **Costs Per Year:** Application fee: $60. Tuition: $17,550 full-time, $4550 per term part-time. Mandatory fees: $1050 full-time, $410 per term part-time. Full-time tuition and fees vary according to course load, degree level, and program. Part-time tuition and fees vary according to course load, degree level, and program. **Scholarships:** Available **Calendar System:** Semester, Summer Session Not available **Enrollment:** FT 449, PT 615, Grad FT 37, Grad PT 15 **Faculty:** FT 20, PT 89 **Student-Faculty Ratio:** 10:1 **Final Year or Final Semester Residency Requirement:** Yes **Library Holdings:** 25,000 **Regional Accreditation:** North Central Association of Colleges and Schools **Credit Hours For Degree:** 65 credit hours, Associates; 130 credit hours, Bachelors **Professional Accreditation:** FIDER, NASAD

HEARTLAND COMMUNITY COLLEGE
1500 West Raab Rd.
Normal, IL 61761
Tel: (309)268-8000
Admissions: (309)268-8041
Fax: (309)268-7999
E-mail: candace.brownlee@heartland.edu
Web Site: http://www.heartland.edu/
President/CEO: Dr. Jonathan M. Astroth
Admissions: Candace Brownlee
Type: Two-Year College **Sex:** Coed **Affiliation:** Illinois Community College Board **Admission Plans:** Open Admission **Application Deadline:** Rolling **Application Fee:** $0.00 **H.S. Requirements:** High school diploma required; GED accepted **Costs Per Year:** Application fee: $0. Area resident tuition: $2640 full-time, $88 per semester hour part-time. State resident tuition: $5280 full-time, $176 per semester hour part-time. Nonresident tuition: $7920 full-time, $264 per semester hour part-time. Mandatory fees: $210 full-time, $7 per semester hour part-time. Full-time tuition and fees vary according to reciprocity agreements. Part-time tuition and fees vary according to reciprocity agreements. **Scholarships:** Available **Calendar System:** Semester, Summer Session Available **Faculty:** FT 70, PT 183 **Student-Faculty Ratio:** 19:1 **Library Holdings:** 5,000 **Regional Accreditation:** North Central Association of Colleges and Schools **Credit Hours For Degree:** 60 semester hours, Associates **ROTC:** Army **Professional Accreditation:** NLN **Intercollegiate Athletics:** Baseball M; Soccer M & W; Softball W

HEBREW THEOLOGICAL COLLEGE
7135 North Carpenter Rd.
Skokie, IL 60077-3263
Tel: (847)982-2500
Web Site: http://www.htc.edu/
President/CEO: Rabbi Jerold Isenberg, PhD
Admissions: Rabbi Berish Cardash
Financial Aid: Rhoda Morris
Type: Four-Year College **Affiliation:** Jewish **Application Deadline:** August 15 **Application Fee:** $75.00 **H.S. Requirements:** High school diploma required; GED accepted **Calendar System:** Semester, Summer Session Available **Exams:** SAT I or ACT. **Library Holdings:** 63,000 **Regional Accreditation:** North Central Association of Colleges and Schools **Credit Hours For Degree:** 120 credit hours, Bachelors

HIGHLAND COMMUNITY COLLEGE
2998 West Pearl City Rd.
Freeport, IL 61032-9341
Tel: (815)235-6121
Fax: (815)235-6130

E-mail: jeremy.bradt@highland.edu
Web Site: http://www.highland.edu/
President/CEO: Dr. Joe Kanosky
Admissions: Jeremy Bradt
Financial Aid: Kathy Bangasser
Type: Two-Year College **Sex:** Coed **Affiliation:** Illinois Community College Board **Scores:** 50% ACT 18-23; 21% ACT 24-29 **% Accepted:** 100 **Admission Plans:** Open Admission; Preferred Admission; Early Admission; Deferred Admission **Application Deadline:** Rolling **Application Fee:** $0.00 **H.S. Requirements:** High school diploma required; GED accepted **Scholarships:** Available **Calendar System:** Semester, Summer Session Available **Enrollment:** FT 1,269, PT 1,186 **Faculty:** FT 46, PT 115 **Student-Faculty Ratio:** 20:1 **Regional Accreditation:** North Central Association of Colleges and Schools **Credit Hours For Degree:** 62 credit hours, Associates **Intercollegiate Athletics:** Baseball M; Basketball M & W; Golf M & W; Softball W; Volleyball W

ILLINOIS CENTRAL COLLEGE
One College Dr.
East Peoria, IL 61635-0001
Tel: (309)694-5011
Admissions: (309)694-5422
Fax: (309)694-5450
E-mail: info@icc.edu
Web Site: http://www.icc.edu/
President/CEO: Dr. John S. Erwin
Admissions: John Avendano
Type: Two-Year College **Sex:** Coed **Affiliation:** Illinois Community College Board **Admission Plans:** Open Admission; Early Admission **Application Deadline:** Rolling **Application Fee:** $0.00 **H.S. Requirements:** High school diploma or equivalent not required **Costs Per Year:** Application fee: $0. Area resident tuition: $2088 full-time, $87 per credit hour part-time. State resident tuition: $4584 full-time, $191 per credit hour part-time. Nonresident tuition: $4584 full-time, $191 per credit hour part-time. **Scholarships:** Available **Calendar System:** Semester, Summer Session Available **Enrollment:** FT 4,907, PT 7,436 **Faculty:** FT 172, PT 486 **Library Holdings:** 82,492 **Regional Accreditation:** North Central Association of Colleges and Schools **Credit Hours For Degree:** 64 semester hours, Associates **Professional Accreditation:** ADA, AOTA, APTA, CARC, JRCERT, NAACLS, NASM, NLN **Intercollegiate Athletics:** Baseball M; Basketball M & W; Golf M & W; Soccer M & W; Softball W; Volleyball W

ILLINOIS COLLEGE
1101 West College Ave.
Jacksonville, IL 62650-2299
Tel: (217)245-3000; Free: (866)464-5265
Admissions: (217)245-3030
Fax: (217)245-3034
E-mail: admissions@ic.edu
Web Site: http://www.ic.edu/
President/CEO: Dr. Axel D. Steuer
Admissions: Rick Bystry
Financial Aid: Kate Taylor
Type: Four-Year College **Sex:** Coed **Affiliation:** interdenominational **Scores:** 44% ACT 18-23; 45% ACT 24-29 **% Accepted:** 55 **Admission Plans:** Early Admission; Deferred Admission **Application Deadline:** Rolling **Application Fee:** $0.00 **H.S. Requirements:** High school diploma required; GED accepted **Costs Per Year:** Application fee: $0. Comprehensive fee: $28,900 includes full-time tuition ($20,900), mandatory fees ($400), and college room and board ($7600). College room only: $3800. Full-time tuition and fees vary according to student level. Room and board charges vary according to board plan and housing facility. Part-time tuition: $700 per semester hour. Part-time mandatory fees: $200 per year. **Scholarships:** Available **Calendar System:** Semester, Summer Session Available **Faculty:** FT 74, PT 17 **Student-Faculty Ratio:** 11:1 **Exams:** SAT I or ACT. ACT essay not being used. SAT essay not being used. **% Receiving Financial Aid:** 82 **% Residing in College-Owned, -Operated, or -Affiliated Housing:** 78 **Regional Accreditation:** North Central Association of Colleges and Schools **Credit Hours For Degree:** 120 credits, Bachelors **Intercollegiate Athletics:** Baseball M; Cheerleading W; Cross-Country Running M & W; Football M; Golf M & W; Soccer M & W; Softball W; Swimming and Diving M & W; Tennis M & W; Track and Field M & W; Volleyball W

ILLINOIS EASTERN COMMUNITY COLLEGES, FRONTIER COMMUNITY COLLEGE
Frontier Dr.
Fairfield, IL 62837-2601
Tel: (618)842-3711
Fax: (618)842-6340
E-mail: atkinsm@iecc.edu
Web Site: http://www.iecc.edu/fcc/
President/CEO: Dr. Chuck Novak
Admissions: Mary Atkins
Financial Aid: Adam Bowles
Type: Two-Year College **Sex:** Coed **Affiliation:** Illinois Eastern Community College System **Admission Plans:** Open Admission; Preferred Admission; Early Admission; Deferred Admission **Application Deadline:** Rolling **Application Fee:** $10.00 **H.S. Requirements:** High school diploma required; GED accepted **Costs Per Year:** Application fee: $10. One-time mandatory fee: $10. Area resident tuition: $2272 full-time, $71 per semester hour part-time. State resident tuition: $6341 full-time, $198.15 per semester hour part-time. Nonresident tuition: $7969 full-time, $249.04 per semester hour part-time. Mandatory fees: $170 full-time, $5 per semester hour part-time, $5 per term part-time. **Scholarships:** Available **Calendar System:** Semester, Summer Session Available **Enrollment:** FT 330, PT 1,679 **Faculty:** FT 6, PT 199 **Library Holdings:** 19,875 **Regional Accreditation:** North Central Association of Colleges and Schools **Credit Hours For Degree:** 64 credit hours, Associates **Professional Accreditation:** NLN

ILLINOIS EASTERN COMMUNITY COLLEGES, LINCOLN TRAIL COLLEGE
11220 State Hwy. 1
Robinson, IL 62454
Tel: (618)544-8657
Fax: (618)544-7423
E-mail: mikeworthb@iecc.edu
Web Site: http://www.iecc.edu/ltc/
President/CEO: Dr. Bev Turkal
Admissions: Becky Mikeworth
Financial Aid: Jennifer Barthelemy
Type: Two-Year College **Sex:** Coed **Affiliation:** Illinois Eastern Community College System **Admission Plans:** Open Admission; Preferred Admission; Early Admission; Deferred Admission **Application Deadline:** Rolling **Application Fee:** $10.00 **H.S. Requirements:** High school diploma required; GED accepted **Costs Per Year:** Application fee: $10. One-time mandatory fee: $10. Area resident tuition: $2272 full-time, $71 per semester hour part-time. State resident tuition: $6341 full-time, $198.15 per semester hour part-time. Nonresident tuition: $7969 full-time, $249.04 per semester hour part-time. Mandatory fees: $170 full-time, $5 per semester hour part-time, $5 per term part-time. **Scholarships:** Available **Calendar System:** Semester, Summer Session Available **Enrollment:** FT 564, PT 667 **Faculty:** FT 21, PT 71 **Library Holdings:** 16,240 **Regional Accreditation:** North Central Association of Colleges and Schools **Credit Hours For Degree:** 64 credit hours, Associates **Professional Accreditation:** NLN **Intercollegiate Athletics:** Baseball M; Basketball M & W; Softball W; Volleyball W

ILLINOIS EASTERN COMMUNITY COLLEGES, OLNEY CENTRAL COLLEGE
305 North West St.
Olney, IL 62450
Tel: (618)395-7777
Fax: (618)392-5212
E-mail: webberc@iecc.edu
Web Site: http://www.iecc.edu/occ/
President/CEO: Dr. Jack Davis
Admissions: Chris Webber
Financial Aid: Vicki Stuckey
Type: Two-Year College **Sex:** Coed **Affiliation:** Illinois Eastern Community College System **Admission Plans:** Open Admission; Preferred Admission; Early Admission; Deferred Admission **Application Deadline:** Rolling **Application Fee:** $10.00 **H.S. Requirements:** High school diploma required; GED accepted **Costs Per Year:** Application fee: $10. One-time mandatory fee: $10. Area resident tuition: $2272 full-time, $71 per semester hour part-time. State resident tuition: $6341 full-time, $198.15 per semester hour part-time. Nonresident tuition: $7969 full-time, $249.04 per semester hour part-time. Mandatory fees: $170 full-time, $5 per semester hour part-time, $5 per term part-time. **Scholarships:** Available **Calendar System:** Semester, Sum-

mer Session Available **Enrollment:** FT 924, PT 703 **Faculty:** FT 49, PT 76 **Library Holdings:** 22,652 **Regional Accreditation:** North Central Association of Colleges and Schools **Credit Hours For Degree:** 64 credit hours, Associates **Professional Accreditation:** JRCERT, NLN **Intercollegiate Athletics:** Baseball M; Basketball M & W; Softball W; Volleyball W

ILLINOIS EASTERN COMMUNITY COLLEGES, WABASH VALLEY COLLEGE

2200 College Dr.
Mount Carmel, IL 62863-2657
Tel: (618)262-8641
Fax: (618)262-8641
E-mail: speard@iecc.edu
Web Site: http://www.iecc.edu/wvc/
President/CEO: Matt Fowler
Admissions: Diana Spear
Financial Aid: Melinda Silvernale

Type: Two-Year College **Sex:** Coed **Affiliation:** Illinois Eastern Community College System **Admission Plans:** Open Admission; Preferred Admission; Early Admission; Deferred Admission **Application Deadline:** Rolling **Application Fee:** $10.00 **H.S. Requirements:** High school diploma required; GED accepted **Costs Per Year:** Application fee: $10. One-time mandatory fee: $10. Area resident tuition: $2272 full-time, $71 per semester hour part-time. State resident tuition: $6341 full-time, $198.15 per semester hour part-time. Nonresident tuition: $7969 full-time, $249.04 per semester hour part-time. Mandatory fees: $170 full-time, $5 per semester hour part-time, $5 per term part-time. **Scholarships:** Available **Calendar System:** Semester, Summer Session Available **Enrollment:** FT 868, PT 3,942 **Faculty:** FT 39, PT 111 **Library Holdings:** 32,237 **Regional Accreditation:** North Central Association of Colleges and Schools **Credit Hours For Degree:** 64 credit hours, Associates **Professional Accreditation:** NLN **Intercollegiate Athletics:** Baseball M; Basketball M & W; Softball W; Tennis M; Volleyball W

THE ILLINOIS INSTITUTE OF ART—CHICAGO

350 North Orleans St.
Chicago, IL 60654
Tel: (312)280-3500; Free: 800-351-3450
Fax: (312)280-3528
Web Site: http://www.artinstitutes.edu/chicago/
President/CEO: John Jenkins

Type: Four-Year College **Sex:** Coed **Affiliation:** Education Management Corporation **Calendar System:** Quarter **Regional Accreditation:** North Central Association of Colleges and Schools **Professional Accreditation:** ACCSCT, ACF, FIDER

THE ILLINOIS INSTITUTE OF ART—SCHAUMBURG

1000 North Plaza Dr., Ste. 100
Schaumburg, IL 60173
Tel: (847)619-3450; Free: 800-314-3450
Fax: (847)619-3064
Web Site: http://www.artinstitutes.edu/schaumburg/
President/CEO: David Ray

Type: Four-Year College **Sex:** Coed **Affiliation:** Education Management Corporation **Calendar System:** Quarter **Professional Accreditation:** ACCSCT, FIDER

ILLINOIS INSTITUTE OF TECHNOLOGY

3300 South Federal St.
Chicago, IL 60616-3793
Tel: (312)567-3000; Free: 800-448-2329
Admissions: (312)567-3025
Fax: (312)567-6939
E-mail: admission@iit.edu
Web Site: http://www.iit.edu/
President/CEO: John L. Anderson
Admissions: Gerald Doyle
Financial Aid: Nareth Phin

Type: University **Sex:** Coed **Scores:** 98.38% SAT V 400+; 13.86% ACT 18-23; 47.79% ACT 24-29 **% Accepted:** 60 **Admission Plans:** Early Admission; Early Action; Early Decision Plan; Deferred Admission **Application Deadline:** Rolling **Application Fee:** $0.00 **H.S. Requirements:** High school diploma required; GED accepted **Costs Per Year:** Application fee: $0. Comprehensive fee: $42,537 includes full-time tuition ($31,363), mandatory fees ($1080), and college room and board ($10,094). College room only: $5384. Full-time tuition and fees vary according to student level. Room and board charges vary according to board plan and housing facility. Part-time tuition: $975 per credit hour. Part-time mandatory fees: $8.50 per credit hour, $100 per term. Part-time tuition and fees vary according to student level. **Scholarships:** Available **Calendar System:** Semester, Summer Session Available **Enrollment:** FT 2,480, PT 185, Grad FT 3,160, Grad PT 1,882 **Faculty:** FT 385, PT 270 **Student-Faculty Ratio:** 10:1 **Exams:** SAT I or ACT. ACT essay used for advising. SAT essay used for advising. ACT essay used as a validity check on application essay. SAT essay used as a validity check on application essay. ACT essay used for placement. SAT essay used for placement. **% Receiving Financial Aid:** 63 **% Residing in College-Owned, -Operated, or -Affiliated Housing:** 46 **Final Year or Final Semester Residency Requirement:** Yes **Library Holdings:** 1,765,169 **Regional Accreditation:** North Central Association of Colleges and Schools **Credit Hours For Degree:** 126 semester hours, Bachelors **ROTC:** Army, Navy, Air Force **Professional Accreditation:** AACSB, ABET, ABA, APA, AALS, CORE, NAAB **Intercollegiate Athletics:** Baseball M; Cross-Country Running M & W; Soccer M & W; Swimming and Diving M & W; Volleyball W

ILLINOIS STATE UNIVERSITY

Normal, IL 61790-2200
Tel: (309)438-2111
Admissions: (309)438-2478
Fax: (309)438-3932
E-mail: admissions@ilstu.edu
Web Site: http://www.illinoisstate.edu/
President/CEO: Dr. C. Alvin Bowman
Admissions: Molly Arnold
Financial Aid: David Krueger

Type: University **Sex:** Coed **Scores:** 39.7% ACT 18-23; 53.4% ACT 24-29 **% Accepted:** 62 **Application Deadline:** March 1 **Application Fee:** $40.00 **H.S. Requirements:** High school diploma required; GED accepted **Costs Per Year:** Application fee: $40. State resident tuition: $8220 full-time, $276 per credit hour part-time. Nonresident tuition: $14,310 full-time, $477 per credit hour part-time. Mandatory fees: $2251 full-time, $64.30 per credit hour part-time, $964.50 per term part-time. Full-time tuition and fees vary according to course load and degree level. Part-time tuition and fees vary according to course load and degree level. College room and board: $8093. College room only: $4190. Room and board charges vary according to board plan, housing facility, and location. Tuition guaranteed not to increase for student's term of enrollment. **Scholarships:** Available **Calendar System:** Semester, Summer Session Available **Enrollment:** FT 17,290, PT 1,099, Grad FT 1,204, Grad PT 1,591 **Faculty:** FT 876, PT 304 **Student-Faculty Ratio:** 19:1 **Exams:** SAT I or ACT. ACT essay not being used. SAT essay not being used. **% Receiving Financial Aid:** 52 **% Residing in College-Owned, -Operated, or -Affiliated Housing:** 33 **Library Holdings:** 1,604,061 **Regional Accreditation:** North Central Association of Colleges and Schools **Credit Hours For Degree:** 120 credits, Bachelors **ROTC:** Army **Professional Accreditation:** AACSB, ABET, AACN, AAFCS, ACA, ADtA, AHIMA, APA, ASLHA, FIDER, CSWE, JRCEPAT, NAACLS, NASAD, NASM, NAST, NCATE, NLN, NRPA, NAIT **Intercollegiate Athletics:** Baseball M; Basketball M & W; Cross-Country Running M & W; Football M; Golf M & W; Gymnastics W; Soccer W; Softball W; Swimming and Diving W; Tennis M & W; Track and Field M & W; Volleyball W

ILLINOIS VALLEY COMMUNITY COLLEGE

815 North Orlando Smith Ave.
Oglesby, IL 61348-9692
Tel: (815)224-2720
Admissions: (815)224-0437
Fax: (815)224-3033
E-mail: tracy_morris@ivcc.edu
Web Site: http://www.ivcc.edu/
President/CEO: Dr. Jerome Corcoran
Admissions: Tracy Morris

Type: Two-Year College **Sex:** Coed **Affiliation:** Illinois Community College Board **Admission Plans:** Open Admission; Early Admission; Deferred Admission **Application Deadline:** Rolling **H.S. Requirements:** High school diploma or equivalent not required **Costs Per Year:** Area resident tuition: $2188 full-time, $68.36 per credit hour part-time. State resident tuition: $7879 full-time, $246.21 per credit hour part-time. Nonresident tuition: $8943 full-time, $279.47 per credit hour part-time. Mandatory fees: $2434 full-time, $7.39 per credit hour part-time. **Scholarships:** Available **Calendar System:** Semester, Summer Session Available **Enrollment:** FT 2,082, PT 2,447

Faculty: FT 90, PT 152 **Exams:** ACT. **Final Year or Final Semester Residency Requirement:** No **Library Holdings:** 58,248 **Regional Accreditation:** North Central Association of Colleges and Schools **Credit Hours For Degree:** 64 semester hours, Associates **Professional Accreditation:** ADA, NLN **Intercollegiate Athletics:** Baseball M; Basketball M & W; Golf M; Softball W; Tennis M & W

ILLINOIS WESLEYAN UNIVERSITY
PO Box 2900
Bloomington, IL 61702-2900
Tel: (309)556-1000; Free: 800-332-2498
Admissions: (309)556-3031
Fax: (309)556-3411
E-mail: iwuadmit@iwu.edu
Web Site: http://www.iwu.edu/
President/CEO: Dr. Richard F. Wilson
Admissions: Tony Bankston
Financial Aid: Scott Seibring
Type: Four-Year College **Sex:** Coed **Scores:** 100% SAT V 400+; 100% SAT M 400+; 8% ACT 18-23; 58% ACT 24-29 **% Accepted:** 54 **Admission Plans:** Early Admission; Early Action; Deferred Admission **Application Deadline:** Rolling **Application Fee:** $0.00 **H.S. Requirements:** High school diploma required; GED accepted **Costs Per Year:** Application fee: $0. Comprehensive fee: $41,758 includes full-time tuition ($33,808), mandatory fees ($174), and college room and board ($7776). College room only: $4800. Room and board charges vary according to board plan and housing facility. Part-time tuition: $1057 per credit hour. **Scholarships:** Available **Calendar System:** Miscellaneous, Summer Session Not available **Enrollment:** FT 2,057, PT 9 **Faculty:** FT 162, PT 67 **Student-Faculty Ratio:** 11:1 **Exams:** SAT I or ACT. ACT essay not being used. SAT essay not being used. **% Receiving Financial Aid:** 59 **% Residing in College-Owned, -Operated, or -Affiliated Housing:** 75 **Regional Accreditation:** North Central Association of Colleges and Schools **Credit Hours For Degree:** 32 courses, Bachelors **ROTC:** Army **Professional Accreditation:** AACN, NASM **Intercollegiate Athletics:** Baseball M; Basketball M & W; Cheerleading M & W; Cross-Country Running M & W; Football M; Golf M & W; Lacrosse M; Soccer M & W; Softball W; Swimming and Diving M & W; Tennis M & W; Track and Field M & W; Ultimate Frisbee M & W; Volleyball M & W; Water Polo M

INTERNATIONAL ACADEMY OF DESIGN & TECHNOLOGY
One North State St., Ste. 500
Chicago, IL 60602-9736
Tel: (312)980-9200; Free: 877-ACADEMY
Fax: (312)828-9405
E-mail: sreichart@iadtchicago.edu
Web Site: http://www.iadtchicago.edu/
President/CEO: Bob Nachtsheim
Admissions: Suzanne Reichart
Financial Aid: Barbara Williams
Type: Four-Year College **Sex:** Coed **Affiliation:** Career Education Corporation **% Accepted:** 52 **Admission Plans:** Early Admission **Application Deadline:** Rolling **Application Fee:** $20.00 **H.S. Requirements:** High school diploma required; GED accepted **Costs Per Year:** Application fee: $20. One-time mandatory fee: $150. Tuition: $14,580 full-time, $405 per credit hour part-time. Mandatory fees: $450 full-time, $150 per term part-time. Full-time tuition and fees vary according to course load and program. Part-time tuition and fees vary according to course load and program. **Scholarships:** Available **Calendar System:** Quarter, Summer Session Available **Enrollment:** FT 1,482, PT 350 **Faculty:** FT 14, PT 99 **Student-Faculty Ratio:** 27:1 **Library Holdings:** 10,000 **Credit Hours For Degree:** 90 quarter hours, Associates; 180 quarter hours, Bachelors **Professional Accreditation:** ACICS, FIDER

ITT TECHNICAL INSTITUTE (BURR RIDGE)
7040 High Grove Blvd.
Burr Ridge, IL 60527
Tel: (630)455-6470
Web Site: http://www.itt-tech.edu/
President/CEO: Larry Brueck
Type: Two-Year College **Sex:** Coed **Affiliation:** ITT Educational Services, Inc. **H.S. Requirements:** High school diploma required; GED accepted **Scholarships:** Available **Calendar System:** Quarter, Summer Session Not available **Professional Accreditation:** ACICS

ITT TECHNICAL INSTITUTE (MOUNT PROSPECT)
1401 Feehanville Dr.
Mount Prospect, IL 60056
Tel: (847)375-8800
Web Site: http://www.itt-tech.edu/
President/CEO: Kristine Ginley
Type: Two-Year College **Sex:** Coed **Affiliation:** ITT Educational Services, Inc. **H.S. Requirements:** High school diploma required; GED accepted **Scholarships:** Available **Calendar System:** Quarter, Summer Session Not available **Credit Hours For Degree:** 96 credit hours, Associates; 180 credit hours, Bachelors **Professional Accreditation:** ACICS

ITT TECHNICAL INSTITUTE (ORLAND PARK)
11551 184th Place
Orland Park, IL 60467
Tel: (708)326-3200
Web Site: http://www.itt-tech.edu/
President/CEO: Elvis Parker
Type: Two-Year College **Sex:** Coed **Affiliation:** ITT Educational Services, Inc. **H.S. Requirements:** High school diploma required; GED accepted **Scholarships:** Available **Calendar System:** Quarter, Summer Session Not available **Professional Accreditation:** ACICS

JOHN A. LOGAN COLLEGE
700 Logan College Rd.
Carterville, IL 62918-9900
Tel: (618)985-3741
Fax: (618)985-2248
E-mail: terrycrain@jalc.edu
Web Site: http://www.jalc.edu/
President/CEO: Dr. Robert Mees
Admissions: Terry Crain
Type: Two-Year College **Sex:** Coed **Affiliation:** Illinois Community College Board **Admission Plans:** Open Admission; Early Admission **Application Deadline:** August 25 **Application Fee:** $0.00 **H.S. Requirements:** High school diploma required; GED accepted **Costs Per Year:** Application fee: $0. Area resident tuition: $2280 full-time, $76 per credit hour part-time. State resident tuition: $5880 full-time, $196 per credit hour part-time. Nonresident tuition: $7890 full-time, $263 per credit hour part-time. **Scholarships:** Available **Calendar System:** Semester, Summer Session Available **Enrollment:** FT 2,368, PT 5,191 **Faculty:** FT 103, PT 210 **Student-Faculty Ratio:** 24:1 **Library Holdings:** 33,306 **Regional Accreditation:** North Central Association of Colleges and Schools **Credit Hours For Degree:** 62 semester hours, Associates **ROTC:** Army, Air Force **Professional Accreditation:** ACCE, ADA, AHIMA, AOTA, NAACLS **Intercollegiate Athletics:** Baseball M; Basketball M & W; Golf M & W; Softball W; Volleyball W

JOHN WOOD COMMUNITY COLLEGE
1301 South 48th St.
Quincy, IL 62301-9147
Tel: (217)224-6500
Admissions: (217)641-4339
Fax: (217)224-4208
E-mail: admissions@jwcc.edu
Web Site: http://www.jwcc.edu/
President/CEO: Dr. Thomas Klincar
Admissions: Lee Wibbell
Type: Two-Year College **Sex:** Coed **Affiliation:** Illinois Community College Board **Scores:** 54% ACT 18-23; 8% ACT 24-29 **Admission Plans:** Open Admission; Preferred Admission; Early Admission **Application Deadline:** Rolling **Application Fee:** $0.00 **H.S. Requirements:** High school diploma required; GED accepted **Costs Per Year:** Application fee: $0. Area resident tuition: $2910 full-time, $97 per credit hour part-time. State resident tuition: $5910 full-time, $197 per credit hour part-time. Nonresident tuition: $5910 full-time, $197 per credit hour part-time. Mandatory fees: $300 full-time, $10 per credit hour part-time. Full-time tuition and fees vary according to reciprocity agreements. Part-time tuition and fees vary according to reciprocity agreements. **Scholarships:** Available **Calendar System:** Semester, Summer Session Available **Enrollment:** FT 1,216, PT 1,187 **Faculty:** FT 53, PT 177 **Student-Faculty Ratio:** 14:1 **Exams:** ACT. **Library Holdings:** 18,000 **Regional Accreditation:** North Central Association of Colleges and Schools **Credit Hours For Degree:** 64 credit hours, Associates **Intercollegiate Athletics:** Baseball M; Basketball M & W; Golf M; Softball W; Volleyball W

JOLIET JUNIOR COLLEGE
1215 Houbolt Rd.
Joliet, IL 60431-8938
Tel: (815)729-9020
E-mail: admission@jjc.edu
Web Site: http://www.jjc.edu/
President/CEO: Dr. Eugenia Proulx
Admissions: Jennifer Kloberdanz
Type: Two-Year College **Sex:** Coed **Affiliation:** Illinois Community College Board **% Accepted:** 100 **Admission Plans:** Open Admission; Preferred Admission; Early Admission; Deferred Admission **Application Deadline:** Rolling **Application Fee:** $0.00 **H.S. Requirements:** High school diploma or equivalent not required. For nursing and veterinary technician programs: High school diploma required; GED accepted **Costs Per Year:** Application fee: $0. Area resident tuition: $2010 full-time, $67 per credit hour part-time. State resident tuition: $6767 full-time, $225.58 per credit hour part-time. Nonresident tuition: $7626 full-time, $254.19 per credit hour part-time. Mandatory fees: $780 full-time, $26 per credit hour part-time. Full-time tuition and fees vary according to course load and program. Part-time tuition and fees vary according to course load and program. **Scholarships:** Available **Calendar System:** Semester, Summer Session Available **Enrollment:** FT 5,103, PT 7,821 **Faculty:** FT 190, PT 364 **Student-Faculty Ratio:** 25:1 **Library Holdings:** 60,364 **Regional Accreditation:** North Central Association of Colleges and Schools **Credit Hours For Degree:** 64 credits, Associates **Professional Accreditation:** ACF, ACBSP, NASM, NLN **Intercollegiate Athletics:** Basketball M & W; Football M; Golf M; Softball W; Tennis M & W; Volleyball W

JUDSON UNIVERSITY
1151 North State St.
Elgin, IL 60123-1498
Tel: (847)628-2500; Free: 800-879-5376
Admissions: (847)695-2522
Fax: (847)695-0712
E-mail: bdean@judsonu.edu
Web Site: http://www.judsonu.edu/
President/CEO: Jerry B. Cain
Admissions: William W. Dean
Financial Aid: Michael Davis
Type: Comprehensive **Sex:** Coed **Affiliation:** Baptist **Scores:** 100% SAT V 400+; 100% SAT M 400+; 60% ACT 18-23; 28% ACT 24-29 **% Accepted:** 71 **Admission Plans:** Early Admission; Deferred Admission **Application Deadline:** Rolling **Application Fee:** $50.00 **H.S. Requirements:** High school diploma required; GED accepted **Costs Per Year:** Application fee: $50. Comprehensive fee: $31,700 includes full-time tuition ($22,950), mandatory fees ($550), and college room and board ($8200). Room and board charges vary according to board plan. Part-time tuition: $850 per credit hour. Part-time mandatory fees: $275 per term. Part-time tuition and fees vary according to course load. **Scholarships:** Available **Calendar System:** Semester, Summer Session Not available **Enrollment:** FT 860, PT 253, Grad FT 75, Grad PT 43 **Student-Faculty Ratio:** 14:1 **Exams:** SAT I or ACT. **% Receiving Financial Aid:** 78 **Regional Accreditation:** North Central Association of Colleges and Schools **Credit Hours For Degree:** 126 semester hours, Bachelors **ROTC:** Army **Intercollegiate Athletics:** Baseball M; Basketball M & W; Cheerleading W; Cross-Country Running M & W; Golf M & W; Soccer M & W; Softball W; Tennis M & W; Track and Field M & W; Volleyball W

KANKAKEE COMMUNITY COLLEGE
100 College Dr.
Kankakee, IL 60901
Tel: (815)802-8100
Admissions: (815)802-8520
Fax: (815)933-0217
E-mail: mdriscoll@kcc.edu
Web Site: http://www.kcc.edu/
President/CEO: Dr. John Avendano
Admissions: Michelle Driscoll
Type: Two-Year College **Sex:** Coed **Affiliation:** Illinois Community College Board **Admission Plans:** Open Admission; Preferred Admission; Early Admission **Application Deadline:** Rolling **Application Fee:** $0.00 **H.S. Requirements:** High school diploma required; GED accepted **Costs Per Year:** Application fee: $0. Area resident tuition: $2970 full-time. State resident tuition: $5125 full-time. Nonresident tuition: $12,355 full-time. Mandatory fees: $300 full-time. **Scholarships:** Available **Calendar System:** Semester, Summer Session Available **Enrollment:** FT 1,835, PT 2,192 **Faculty:** FT 65, PT 109 **Student-Faculty Ratio:** 20:1 **Final Year or Final Semester Residency Requirement:** Yes **Library Holdings:** 42,861 **Regional Accreditation:** North Central Association of Colleges and Schools **Credit Hours For Degree:** 64 semester hours, Associates **ROTC:** Army **Professional Accreditation:** CARC, NAACLS **Intercollegiate Athletics:** Baseball M; Basketball M & W; Soccer M; Softball W; Volleyball W

KASKASKIA COLLEGE
27210 College Rd.
Centralia, IL 62801-7878
Tel: (618)545-3000
Admissions: (618)545-3041
Fax: (618)532-1135
E-mail: jripperda@kaskaskia.edu
Web Site: http://www.kaskaskia.edu/
President/CEO: Dr. James Underwood
Admissions: Jan Ripperda
Type: Two-Year College **Sex:** Coed **Affiliation:** Illinois Community College Board **% Accepted:** 100 **Admission Plans:** Open Admission; Preferred Admission; Early Admission; Deferred Admission **Application Deadline:** Rolling **Application Fee:** $0.00 **H.S. Requirements:** High school diploma required; GED accepted **Costs Per Year:** Application fee: $0. Area resident tuition: $2240 full-time, $70 per credit hour part-time. State resident tuition: $4320 full-time, $135 per credit hour part-time. Nonresident tuition: $9920 full-time, $310 per credit hour part-time. Mandatory fees: $352 full-time, $11 per credit hour part-time. Full-time tuition and fees vary according to location and program. Part-time tuition and fees vary according to location and program. **Scholarships:** Available **Calendar System:** Semester, Summer Session Available **Enrollment:** FT 2,425, PT 2,912 **Faculty:** FT 75, PT 162 **Student-Faculty Ratio:** 23:1 **Exams:** ACT. **Library Holdings:** 21,096 **Regional Accreditation:** North Central Association of Colleges and Schools **Credit Hours For Degree:** 64 semester hours, Associates **Professional Accreditation:** ADA, APTA, CARC, JRCERT, NLN **Intercollegiate Athletics:** Baseball M; Basketball M & W; Cheerleading M & W; Golf M & W; Soccer M & W; Softball W; Tennis M; Volleyball W

KENDALL COLLEGE
900 North Branch St.
Chicago, IL 60201-2899
Tel: (312)752-2000; Free: 877-588-8860
Admissions: (312)752-2020
E-mail: admissions@kendall.edu
Web Site: http://www.kendall.edu/
President/CEO: Dr. Karen Gersten
Admissions: Lisa Marrello
Financial Aid: Chris Miller
Type: Four-Year College **Sex:** Coed **Affiliation:** United Methodist; Laureate International Universities **% Accepted:** 99 **Application Deadline:** Rolling **Application Fee:** $50.00 **H.S. Requirements:** High school diploma required; GED accepted **Costs Per Year:** Application fee: $50. **Scholarships:** Available **Calendar System:** Quarter, Summer Session Available **Enrollment:** FT 1,421, PT 968 **Faculty:** FT 43, PT 154 **Student-Faculty Ratio:** 19:1 **Exams:** SAT I or ACT. ACT essay used for admission. SAT essay used for admission. ACT essay used for advising. SAT essay used for advising. ACT essay used for placement. SAT essay used for placement. **% Residing in College-Owned, -Operated, or -Affiliated Housing:** 14 **Library Holdings:** 33,000 **Regional Accreditation:** North Central Association of Colleges and Schools **Credit Hours For Degree:** 96 quarter hours, Associates; 180 hours, Bachelors **Professional Accreditation:** ACF

KISHWAUKEE COLLEGE
21193 Malta Rd.
Malta, IL 60150
Tel: (815)825-2086
Fax: (815)825-2306
Web Site: http://www.kishwaukeecollege.edu/
President/CEO: Tom Choice
Admissions: Sally Misciasci
Type: Two-Year College **Sex:** Coed **Affiliation:** Illinois Community College Board **Admission Plans:** Open Admission; Early Admission; Deferred Admission **Application Deadline:** Rolling **Application Fee:** $0.00 **H.S. Requirements:** High school diploma required; GED accepted **Costs Per**

Year: Application fee: $0. Area resident tuition: $2250 full-time, $75 per credit hour part-time. State resident tuition: $8070 full-time, $269 per credit hour part-time. Nonresident tuition: $9330 full-time, $311 per credit hour part-time. Mandatory fees: $300 full-time, $8 per credit hour part-time, $6. Full-time tuition and fees vary according to program and reciprocity agreements. Part-time tuition and fees vary according to program and reciprocity agreements. **Scholarships:** Available **Calendar System:** Semester, Summer Session Available **Library Holdings:** 52,075 **Regional Accreditation:** North Central Association of Colleges and Schools **Credit Hours For Degree:** 64 semester hours, Associates **Professional Accreditation:** JRCERT **Intercollegiate Athletics:** Baseball M; Basketball M & W; Soccer M; Softball W; Volleyball W

KNOX COLLEGE
2 East South St.
Galesburg, IL 61401
Tel: (309)341-7000; Free: 800-678-KNOX
Admissions: (309)341-7100
Fax: (309)341-7070
E-mail: admission@knox.edu
Web Site: http://www.knox.edu/
President/CEO: Roger Taylor
Admissions: Paul Steenis
Financial Aid: Ann M. Brill
Type: Four-Year College **Sex:** Coed **Scores:** 100% SAT V 400+; 100% SAT M 400+; 7% ACT 18-23; 52% ACT 24-29 **% Accepted:** 74 **Admission Plans:** Early Admission; Early Action; Deferred Admission **Application Deadline:** February 1 **Application Fee:** $40.00 **H.S. Requirements:** High school diploma required; GED accepted **Costs Per Year:** Application fee: $40. Comprehensive fee: $39,075 includes full-time tuition ($31,575), mandatory fees ($336), and college room and board ($7164). College room only: $3603. Room and board charges vary according to board plan. Part-time tuition: $3508 per credit. Part-time tuition varies according to course load. **Scholarships:** Available **Calendar System:** Trimester, Summer Session Not available **Enrollment:** FT 1,384, PT 23 **Faculty:** FT 108, PT 29 **Student-Faculty Ratio:** 12:1 **Exams:** ACT essay used for admission. SAT essay used for admission. ACT essay used for advising. SAT essay used for advising. ACT essay used as a validity check on application essay. SAT essay used as a validity check on application essay. **% Receiving Financial Aid:** 70 **% Residing in College-Owned, -Operated, or -Affiliated Housing:** 87 **Final Year or Final Semester Residency Requirement:** Yes **Library Holdings:** 329,977 **Regional Accreditation:** North Central Association of Colleges and Schools **Credit Hours For Degree:** 36 credits, Bachelors **Intercollegiate Athletics:** Baseball M; Basketball M & W; Cross-Country Running M & W; Football M; Golf M & W; Soccer M & W; Softball W; Swimming and Diving M & W; Tennis M & W; Track and Field M & W; Volleyball W; Wrestling M

LAKE FOREST COLLEGE
555 North Sheridan Rd.
Lake Forest, IL 60045
Tel: (847)234-3100; Free: 800-828-4751
Admissions: (847)735-5000
Fax: (847)735-6271
E-mail: admissions@lakeforest.edu
Web Site: http://www.lakeforest.edu/
President/CEO: Stephen D. Schutt
Admissions: William Motzer
Financial Aid: Jerry Cebrzynski
Type: Comprehensive **Sex:** Coed **% Accepted:** 69 **Admission Plans:** Early Admission; Early Action; Early Decision Plan; Deferred Admission **Application Deadline:** Rolling **Application Fee:** $40.00 **H.S. Requirements:** High school diploma required; GED accepted **Costs Per Year:** Application fee: $40. Comprehensive fee: $42,212 includes full-time tuition ($33,576), mandatory fees ($630), and college room and board ($8006). College room only: $3966. Full-time tuition and fees vary according to course load. Room and board charges vary according to board plan and housing facility. Part-time tuition: $4200 per course. Part-time tuition varies according to course load. **Scholarships:** Available **Calendar System:** Semester, Summer Session Available **Enrollment:** FT 1,384, PT 14, Grad FT 3, Grad PT 14 **Faculty:** FT 95, PT 76 **Student-Faculty Ratio:** 12:1 **Exams:** SAT I or ACT. **% Receiving Financial Aid:** 76 **% Residing in College-Owned, -Operated, or -Affiliated Housing:** 77 **Final Year or Final Semester Residency Requirement:** No **Library Holdings:** 281,079 **Regional Accreditation:** North Central Association of Colleges and Schools **Credit Hours For Degree:** 32 courses, Bachelors **Intercollegiate Athletics:** Baseball M; Basketball M & W; Cheerleading M & W; Cross-Country Running M & W; Fencing M & W; Football M; Golf M & W; Ice Hockey M & W; Lacrosse M; Rock Climbing M & W; Rugby M & W; Sailing M & W; Soccer M & W; Softball W; Swimming and Diving M & W; Table Tennis M & W; Tennis M & W; Track and Field M & W; Ultimate Frisbee M & W; Volleyball W; Water Polo M & W

LAKE LAND COLLEGE
5001 Lake Land Blvd.
Mattoon, IL 61938-9366
Tel: (217)234-5253
Admissions: (217)234-5378
E-mail: admissions@lakeland.cc.il.us
Web Site: http://www.lakelandcollege.edu/
President/CEO: Scott Lensink
Admissions: Jon VanDyke
Type: Two-Year College **Sex:** Coed **Affiliation:** Illinois Community College Board **% Accepted:** 100 **Admission Plans:** Open Admission; Early Admission **Application Deadline:** Rolling **Application Fee:** $0.00 **H.S. Requirements:** High school diploma or equivalent not required **Costs Per Year:** Application fee: $0. Area resident tuition: $2025 full-time, $67.50 per credit hour part-time. State resident tuition: $4890 full-time, $163 per credit hour part-time. Nonresident tuition: $9300 full-time, $310 per credit hour part-time. Mandatory fees: $519 full-time, $17.30 per credit hour part-time. **Scholarships:** Available **Calendar System:** Semester, Summer Session Available **Enrollment:** FT 3,160, PT 4,271 **Faculty:** FT 116, PT 75 **Student-Faculty Ratio:** 21:1 **Exams:** ACT. **Library Holdings:** 28,000 **Regional Accreditation:** North Central Association of Colleges and Schools **Credit Hours For Degree:** 64 semester hours, Associates **Professional Accreditation:** ADA, APTA, NLN **Intercollegiate Athletics:** Baseball M; Basketball M & W; Cheerleading W; Softball W; Tennis M & W; Volleyball W

LAKEVIEW COLLEGE OF NURSING
903 North Logan Ave.
Danville, IL 61832
Tel: (217)443-5238
Fax: (217)431-4015
E-mail: admission@lakeviewcol.edu
Web Site: http://www.lakeviewcol.edu/
President/CEO: Dick Shockey
Financial Aid: Janet Ingargiola
Type: Two-Year Upper Division **Sex:** Coed **Admission Plans:** Early Admission; Early Decision Plan; Deferred Admission **Application Fee:** $100.00 **H.S. Requirements:** High school diploma required; GED accepted **Costs Per Year:** Application fee: $100. Tuition: $10,880 full-time, $340 per credit hour part-time. Mandatory fees: $1920 full-time, $60 per credit hour part-time. **Scholarships:** Available **Calendar System:** Semester, Summer Session Available **Enrollment:** FT 239 **Faculty:** FT 25, PT 26 **Student-Faculty Ratio:** 7:1 **Regional Accreditation:** North Central Association of Colleges and Schools **Credit Hours For Degree:** 124 credit hours, Bachelors **ROTC:** Army **Professional Accreditation:** AACN, NLN

LE CORDON BLEU COLLEGE OF CULINARY ARTS IN CHICAGO
361 West Chestnut
Chicago, IL 60610-3050
Tel: (312)944-0882
Fax: (312)944-8557
E-mail: mverratti@chicnet.org
Web Site: http://www.chefs.edu/chicago/
President/CEO: Lloyd Kirsch
Admissions: Matthew Verratti
Type: Two-Year College **Sex:** Coed **Affiliation:** Career Education Corporation **Admission Plans:** Open Admission; Deferred Admission **Application Fee:** $100.00 **H.S. Requirements:** High school diploma required; GED accepted **Scholarships:** Available **Calendar System:** Continuous, Summer Session Not available **Enrollment:** FT 721, PT 177 **Faculty:** FT 28, PT 40 **Student-Faculty Ratio:** 19:1 **Library Holdings:** 11,000 **Regional Accreditation:** North Central Association of Colleges and Schools **Credit Hours For Degree:** 69 credits, Associates **Professional Accreditation:** ACCSCT, ACF

LEWIS AND CLARK COMMUNITY COLLEGE
5800 Godfrey Rd.
Godfrey, IL 62035-2466

Tel: (618)466-7000
Admissions: (618)468-7000
Fax: (618)466-2798
Web Site: http://www.lc.edu/
President/CEO: Dale T. Chapman
Admissions: Peggy Hudson
Type: Two-Year College **Sex:** Coed **Affiliation:** Illinois Community College Board **Admission Plans:** Open Admission; Early Admission; Deferred Admission **Application Deadline:** Rolling **Application Fee:** $0.00 **H.S. Requirements:** High school diploma or equivalent not required. For nursing, dental assisting, dental hygiene, occupational therapy programs: High school diploma required; GED accepted **Scholarships:** Available **Calendar System:** Semester, Summer Session Available **Library Holdings:** 47,000 **Regional Accreditation:** North Central Association of Colleges and Schools **Credit Hours For Degree:** 60 credit hours, Associates **ROTC:** Army **Professional Accreditation:** ADA, AOTA, NLN **Intercollegiate Athletics:** Baseball M; Basketball M & W; Golf M; Soccer M & W; Softball W; Tennis M & W; Volleyball W

LEWIS UNIVERSITY
One University Parkway
Romeoville, IL 60446
Tel: (815)838-0500; Free: 800-897-9000
Fax: (815)838-9456
E-mail: admissions@lewisu.edu
Web Site: http://www.lewisu.edu/
President/CEO: Br. James Gaffney, FSC
Admissions: Ryan Cockerill
Financial Aid: Janeen Decharinte
Type: Comprehensive **Sex:** Coed **Affiliation:** Roman Catholic Church **Scores:** 94.74% SAT V 400+; 100% SAT M 400+; 61.46% ACT 18-23; 29. 94% ACT 24-29 **% Accepted:** 74 **Admission Plans:** Deferred Admission **Application Deadline:** August 1 **Application Fee:** $40.00 **H.S. Requirements:** High school diploma required; GED accepted **Costs Per Year:** Application fee: $40. Comprehensive fee: $31,340 includes full-time tuition ($22,990) and college room and board ($8350). College room only: $5450. Full-time tuition varies according to course level, course load, and program. Room and board charges vary according to board plan and housing facility. Part-time tuition: $720 per credit hour. Part-time tuition varies according to course level, course load, and program. **Scholarships:** Available **Calendar System:** Semester, Summer Session Available **Enrollment:** FT 3,252, PT 827, Grad FT 436, Grad PT 1,332 **Faculty:** FT 187, PT 384 **Student-Faculty Ratio:** 14:1 **Exams:** SAT I or ACT. ACT essay not being used. SAT essay not being used. **% Receiving Financial Aid:** 72 **% Residing in College-Owned, -Operated, or -Affiliated Housing:** 31 **Library Holdings:** 149,870 **Regional Accreditation:** North Central Association of Colleges and Schools **Credit Hours For Degree:** 77 credit hours, Associates; 128 credit hours, Bachelors **ROTC:** Army, Air Force **Professional Accreditation:** AACN, ACBSP, NCATE, NLN **Intercollegiate Athletics:** Baseball M; Basketball M & W; Cheerleading M & W; Cross-Country Running M & W; Golf M & W; Soccer M & W; Softball W; Swimming and Diving M & W; Tennis M & W; Track and Field M & W; Volleyball M & W

LEXINGTON COLLEGE
310 South Peoria St., Ste. 512
Chicago, IL 60607-3534
Tel: (312)226-6294
Fax: (312)226-6405
E-mail: admissions@lexingtoncollege.edu
Web Site: http://www.lexingtoncollege.edu/
President/CEO: Dr. Susan E. Mangels
Admissions: Carmen Larios
Financial Aid: Maria Lebron
Type: Four-Year College **Sex:** Women **% Accepted:** 47 **Admission Plans:** Open Admission **Application Deadline:** Rolling **Application Fee:** $30.00 **H.S. Requirements:** High school diploma required; GED accepted **Costs Per Year:** Application fee: $30. One-time mandatory fee: $50. Tuition: $22,800 full-time, $760 per credit hour part-time. Mandatory fees: $1000 full-time. Full-time tuition and fees vary according to course load. Part-time tuition varies according to course load. **Scholarships:** Available **Calendar System:** Semester, Summer Session Not available **Enrollment:** FT 52, PT 2 **Faculty:** FT 4, PT 15 **Student-Faculty Ratio:** 6:1 **Exams:** SAT I or ACT. **Library Holdings:** 3,500 **Regional Accreditation:** North Central Association of Colleges and Schools **Credit Hours For Degree:** 66 credits, Associates; 129 credits, Bachelors

LINCOLN CHRISTIAN UNIVERSITY
100 Campus View Dr.
Lincoln, IL 62656-2167
Tel: (217)732-3168; Free: 888-522-5228
Fax: (217)732-5914
E-mail: coladmis@lincolnchristian.edu
Web Site: http://www.lincolnchristian.edu/
President/CEO: Keith Ray
Admissions: Mary K. Davis
Financial Aid: Nancy Siddens
Type: Four-Year College **Sex:** Coed **Affiliation:** Christian Churches and Churches of Christ **Scores:** 59% ACT 18-23; 22% ACT 24-29 **% Accepted:** 78 **Admission Plans:** Preferred Admission; Deferred Admission **Application Deadline:** Rolling **Application Fee:** $20.00 **H.S. Requirements:** High school diploma required; GED accepted **Costs Per Year:** Application fee: $20. Comprehensive fee: $18,803 includes full-time tuition ($13,020) and college room and board ($5783). Part-time tuition: $434 per semester hour. **Scholarships:** Available **Calendar System:** Semester, Summer Session Available **Enrollment:** FT 538, PT 105 **Faculty:** FT 29, PT 30 **Student-Faculty Ratio:** 13:1 **Exams:** SAT I or ACT. ACT essay not being used. SAT essay not being used. **% Receiving Financial Aid:** 70 **% Residing in College-Owned, -Operated, or -Affiliated Housing:** 50 **Final Year or Final Semester Residency Requirement:** No **Library Holdings:** 127,000 **Regional Accreditation:** North Central Association of Colleges and Schools **Credit Hours For Degree:** 65 semester hours, Associates; 130 semester hours, Bachelors **Professional Accreditation:** ABHE **Intercollegiate Athletics:** Baseball M; Basketball M & W; Cheerleading M & W; Cross-Country Running M & W; Soccer M & W; Volleyball W

LINCOLN COLLEGE
300 Keokuk St.
Lincoln, IL 62656-1699
Tel: (217)732-3155; Free: 800-569-0556
Fax: (217)732-8859
Web Site: http://www.lincolncollege.edu/
President/CEO: John Hutchinson
Admissions: Tony Schilling
Type: Two-Year College **Sex:** Coed **Scores:** 40% ACT 18-23; 8% ACT 24-29 **% Accepted:** 65 **Admission Plans:** Early Admission; Deferred Admission **Application Deadline:** Rolling **Application Fee:** $25.00 **H.S. Requirements:** High school diploma required; GED accepted **Costs Per Year:** Application fee: $25. Comprehensive fee: $27,750 includes full-time tuition ($21,000), mandatory fees ($250), and college room and board ($6500). College room only: $2500. Room and board charges vary according to housing facility and student level. Part-time tuition: $250 per credit hour. Tuition guaranteed not to increase for student's term of enrollment. **Scholarships:** Available **Calendar System:** Semester, Summer Session Available **Enrollment:** FT 700, PT 58 **Faculty:** FT 34, PT 19 **Student-Faculty Ratio:** 16:1 **Exams:** SAT I or ACT. **% Residing in College-Owned, -Operated, or -Affiliated Housing:** 90 **Library Holdings:** 42,500 **Regional Accreditation:** North Central Association of Colleges and Schools **Credit Hours For Degree:** 64 semester hours, Associates **Intercollegiate Athletics:** Baseball M; Basketball M & W; Golf M & W; Soccer M & W; Softball W; Swimming and Diving M & W; Tennis M & W; Volleyball W; Wrestling M

LINCOLN COLLEGE—NORMAL
715 West Raab Rd.
Normal, IL 61761
Tel: (309)452-0500; Free: 800-569-0558
Admissions: (309)268-4314
Fax: (309)454-5652
E-mail: spuck@lincolncollege.edu
Web Site: http://www.lincolncollege.edu/normal/
President/CEO: John Hutchinson
Admissions: Steve Puck
Type: Four-Year College **Sex:** Coed **Scores:** 28% ACT 18-23; 3% ACT 24-29 **% Accepted:** 72 **Admission Plans:** Deferred Admission **Application Deadline:** September 1 **Application Fee:** $25.00 **H.S. Requirements:** High school diploma required; GED accepted **Costs Per Year:** Application fee: $25. Tuition: $21,000 full-time. Full-time tuition varies according to location

and program. College room only: $3500. **Scholarships:** Available **Calendar System:** Miscellaneous, Summer Session Available **Enrollment:** FT 290, PT 237 **Faculty:** FT 9, PT 49 **Student-Faculty Ratio:** 14:1 **Exams:** Other, SAT I or ACT. ACT essay not being used. SAT essay not being used. **% Residing in College-Owned, -Operated, or -Affiliated Housing:** 35 **Library Holdings:** 1,800,000 **Regional Accreditation:** North Central Association of Colleges and Schools **Credit Hours For Degree:** 63 credit hours, Associates; 123 credit hours, Bachelors

LINCOLN LAND COMMUNITY COLLEGE
5250 Shepherd Rd.
PO Box 19256
Springfield, IL 62794-9256
Tel: (217)786-2200
Admissions: (217)786-2243
Fax: (217)786-2492
E-mail: ron.gregoire@llcc.edu
Web Site: http://www.llcc.edu/
President/CEO: Dr. Charlotte Warren
Admissions: Ron Gregoire
Type: Two-Year College **Sex:** Coed **Affiliation:** Illinois Community College Board **Scores:** 50% ACT 18-23; 14% ACT 24-29 **Admission Plans:** Open Admission; Early Admission; Deferred Admission **Application Deadline:** Rolling **Application Fee:** $0.00 **H.S. Requirements:** High school diploma or equivalent not required. For allied health programs: High school diploma required; GED accepted **Costs Per Year:** Application fee: $0. Area resident tuition: $2370 full-time, $79 per credit hour part-time. State resident tuition: $4740 full-time, $158 per credit hour part-time. Nonresident tuition: $7110 full-time, $237 per credit hour part-time. Mandatory fees: $330 full-time, $11 per credit hour part-time. **Scholarships:** Available **Calendar System:** Semester, Summer Session Available **Enrollment:** FT 3,264, PT 4,413 **Faculty:** FT 125, PT 220 **Student-Faculty Ratio:** 17:1 **Library Holdings:** 65,000 **Regional Accreditation:** North Central Association of Colleges and Schools **Credit Hours For Degree:** 60 credit hours, Associates **Professional Accreditation:** AOTA, CARC, JRCERT, NLN **Intercollegiate Athletics:** Baseball M; Basketball M & W; Soccer M; Softball W; Volleyball W

LOYOLA UNIVERSITY CHICAGO
1032 West Sheridan Rd.
Chicago, IL 60660
Tel: (773)274-3000; Free: 800-262-2373
Admissions: (773)508-3079
Fax: (773)915-6414
E-mail: admission@luc.edu
Web Site: http://www.luc.edu/
President/CEO: Rev. Michael Garanzini, SJ
Admissions: Lori Greene
Financial Aid: Eric Weems
Type: University **Sex:** Coed **Affiliation:** Roman Catholic (Jesuit) **Scores:** 99.3% SAT V 400+; 99.4% SAT M 400+; 19.4% ACT 18-23; 60.8% ACT 24-29 **% Accepted:** 78 **Application Deadline:** April 1 **Application Fee:** $0.00 **H.S. Requirements:** High school diploma required; GED accepted **Costs Per Year:** Application fee: $0. Comprehensive fee: $43,334 includes full-time tuition ($31,040), mandatory fees ($1074), and college room and board ($11,220). College room only: $7370. Full-time tuition and fees vary according to course load, location, program, and student level. Room and board charges vary according to board plan and housing facility. Part-time tuition: $630 per credit hour. Part-time tuition varies according to course load. **Scholarships:** Available **Calendar System:** Semester, Summer Session Available **Enrollment:** FT 9,348, PT 729, Grad FT 4,278, Grad PT 1,524 **Faculty:** FT 629, PT 723 **Student-Faculty Ratio:** 15:1 **Exams:** SAT I or ACT. ACT essay not being used. SAT essay not being used. **% Receiving Financial Aid:** 73 **% Residing in College-Owned, -Operated, or -Affiliated Housing:** 40 **Final Year or Final Semester Residency Requirement:** No **Library Holdings:** 1,731,343 **Regional Accreditation:** North Central Association of Colleges and Schools **Credit Hours For Degree:** 128 semester hours, Bachelors **ROTC:** Army, Navy, Air Force **Professional Accreditation:** AACSB, AACN, ABA, ADtA, APA, ACIPE, AALS, ATS, CSWE, LCMEAMA, NAST, NCATE, NLN **Intercollegiate Athletics:** Basketball M & W; Cheerleading M & W; Cross-Country Running M & W; Golf M & W; Soccer M & W; Softball W; Track and Field M & W; Volleyball M & W

MACCORMAC COLLEGE
506 South Wabash Ave.
Chicago, IL 60605-1667
Tel: (312)922-1884
Fax: (312)922-3196
Web Site: http://www.maccormac.edu/
President/CEO: Leo Loughead
Admissions: David Grassi
Type: Two-Year College **Sex:** Coed **Admission Plans:** Deferred Admission **Application Deadline:** Rolling **Application Fee:** $20.00 **H.S. Requirements:** High school diploma required; GED accepted **Scholarships:** Available **Calendar System:** Semester, Summer Session Available **Enrollment:** FT 159, PT 218 **Faculty:** FT 4, PT 30 **Student-Faculty Ratio:** 9:1 **Exams:** ACT, SAT I. **Library Holdings:** 11,000 **Regional Accreditation:** North Central Association of Colleges and Schools **Credit Hours For Degree:** 96 quarter hours, Associates

MACMURRAY COLLEGE
447 East College Ave.
Jacksonville, IL 62650
Tel: (217)479-7000
Admissions: (217)479-7059
Fax: (217)245-0405
E-mail: alicia.zeone@mac.edu
Web Site: http://www.mac.edu/
President/CEO: Dr. Colleen Hester
Admissions: Alicia Zeone
Financial Aid: Charles R. Carothers
Type: Four-Year College **Sex:** Coed **Affiliation:** United Methodist **Scores:** 57% SAT V 400+; 71% SAT M 400+; 33% ACT 18-23; 12% ACT 24-29 **% Accepted:** 60 **Admission Plans:** Early Admission **Application Deadline:** Rolling **Application Fee:** $0.00 **H.S. Requirements:** High school diploma required; GED accepted **Costs Per Year:** Application fee: $0. Comprehensive fee: $25,703 includes full-time tuition ($17,940), mandatory fees ($225), and college room and board ($7538). College room only: $3430. Room and board charges vary according to board plan. Part-time tuition: $600 per credit hour. Part-time mandatory fees: $25 per credit hour. Part-time tuition and fees vary according to course load. **Scholarships:** Available **Calendar System:** 4-1-4, Summer Session Available **Enrollment:** FT 540, PT 62 **Faculty:** FT 35, PT 31 **Student-Faculty Ratio:** 14:1 **Exams:** SAT I or ACT. **% Receiving Financial Aid:** 95 **% Residing in College-Owned, -Operated, or -Affiliated Housing:** 50 **Library Holdings:** 1,813,620 **Regional Accreditation:** North Central Association of Colleges and Schools **Credit Hours For Degree:** 60 semester hours, Associates; 120 semester hours, Bachelors **Professional Accreditation:** AACN, CSWE **Intercollegiate Athletics:** Baseball M; Basketball M & W; Cheerleading M & W; Football M; Golf M & W; Soccer M & W; Softball W; Swimming and Diving M & W; Volleyball W

MCHENRY COUNTY COLLEGE
8900 US Hwy. 14
Crystal Lake, IL 60012-2761
Tel: (815)455-3700
E-mail: admissions@mchenry.edu
Web Site: http://www.mchenry.edu/
President/CEO: Larry Tyree
Admissions: Fran Duwaldt
Type: Two-Year College **Sex:** Coed **Affiliation:** Illinois Community College Board **Admission Plans:** Open Admission; Early Admission; Deferred Admission **Application Deadline:** Rolling **Application Fee:** $15.00 **H.S. Requirements:** High school diploma or equivalent not required **Scholarships:** Available **Calendar System:** Semester, Summer Session Available **Library Holdings:** 40,000 **Regional Accreditation:** North Central Association of Colleges and Schools **Credit Hours For Degree:** 60 semester hours, Associates **Professional Accreditation:** ACBSP **Intercollegiate Athletics:** Baseball M; Basketball M & W; Soccer M; Softball W; Tennis M & W; Volleyball W

MCKENDREE UNIVERSITY
701 College Rd.
Lebanon, IL 62254-1299
Tel: (618)537-4481; Free: 800-232-7228
Fax: (618)537-6259
E-mail: inquiry@mckendree.edu
Web Site: http://www.mckendree.edu/
President/CEO: James M. Dennis
Admissions: Chris Hall

Financial Aid: James A. Myers
Type: Comprehensive **Sex:** Coed **Affiliation:** United Methodist Church **Scores:** 76.3% SAT V 400+; 82.2% SAT M 400+ **% Accepted:** 71 **Admission Plans:** Deferred Admission **Application Deadline:** Rolling **Application Fee:** $40.00 **H.S. Requirements:** High school diploma required; GED accepted **Costs Per Year:** Application fee: $40. Comprehensive fee: $29,920 includes full-time tuition ($21,370), mandatory fees ($700), and college room and board ($7850). College room only: $4180. Full-time tuition and fees vary according to course load, degree level, and location. Room and board charges vary according to board plan and housing facility. Part-time tuition: $690 per hour. Part-time tuition varies according to course load, degree level, and location. **Scholarships:** Available **Calendar System:** Semester, Summer Session Available **Enrollment:** FT 1,529, PT 665, Grad FT 193, Grad PT 820 **Faculty:** FT 94, PT 300 **Student-Faculty Ratio:** 13:1 **Exams:** SAT I or ACT. ACT essay used for admission. SAT essay used for admission. **% Receiving Financial Aid:** 77 **% Residing in College-Owned, -Operated, or -Affiliated Housing:** 50 **Final Year or Final Semester Residency Requirement:** No **Library Holdings:** 109,000 **Regional Accreditation:** North Central Association of Colleges and Schools **Credit Hours For Degree:** 128 credit hours, Bachelors **ROTC:** Army, Air Force **Professional Accreditation:** AACN, NCATE, NLN **Intercollegiate Athletics:** Baseball M; Basketball M & W; Bowling M & W; Cheerleading M & W; Cross-Country Running M & W; Football M; Golf M & W; Ice Hockey M; Soccer M & W; Softball W; Tennis M & W; Track and Field M & W; Volleyball W; Wrestling M

MIDSTATE COLLEGE
411 West Northmoor Rd.
Peoria, IL 61614
Tel: (309)692-4092
Fax: (309)692-3893
E-mail: jhancock2@midstate.edu
Web Site: http://www.midstate.edu/
President/CEO: R. Dale Bunch
Admissions: Jessica Hancock
Type: Four-Year College **Sex:** Coed **Admission Plans:** Early Admission; Deferred Admission **Application Deadline:** Rolling **Application Fee:** $25.00 **H.S. Requirements:** High school diploma required; GED accepted **Scholarships:** Available **Calendar System:** Quarter, Summer Session Available **Exams:** Other. **Library Holdings:** 8,724 **Regional Accreditation:** North Central Association of Colleges and Schools **Credit Hours For Degree:** 92 quarter hours, Associates **Professional Accreditation:** AAMAE

MILLIKIN UNIVERSITY
1184 West Main St.
Decatur, IL 62522-2084
Tel: (217)424-6211; Free: 800-373-7733
Admissions: (217)424-6210
Fax: (217)425-4669
E-mail: admis@millikin.edu
Web Site: http://www.millikin.edu/
President/CEO: Douglas E. Zemke
Admissions: Joe Havis
Financial Aid: Cheryl Howerton
Type: Comprehensive **Sex:** Coed **Affiliation:** Presbyterian Church (U.S.A.) **Scores:** 98% SAT V 400+; 91% SAT M 400+; 50% ACT 18-23; 39% ACT 24-29 **% Accepted:** 60 **Admission Plans:** Deferred Admission **Application Deadline:** Rolling **Application Fee:** $0.00 **H.S. Requirements:** High school diploma required; GED accepted **Costs Per Year:** Application fee: $0. Comprehensive fee: $34,211 includes full-time tuition ($25,750), mandatory fees ($595), and college room and board ($7866). College room only: $4306. Room and board charges vary according to board plan and housing facility. Part-time tuition: $860 per credit hour. Part-time mandatory fees: $75 per term. **Scholarships:** Available **Calendar System:** Semester, Summer Session Available **Enrollment:** FT 2,157, PT 119, Grad FT 26, Grad PT 12 **Faculty:** FT 154, PT 123 **Student-Faculty Ratio:** 11:1 **Exams:** SAT I or ACT. **% Receiving Financial Aid:** 79 **% Residing in College-Owned, -Operated, or -Affiliated Housing:** 69 **Final Year or Final Semester Residency Requirement:** No **Library Holdings:** 218,618 **Regional Accreditation:** North Central Association of Colleges and Schools **Credit Hours For Degree:** 124 credits, Bachelors **Professional Accreditation:** AACN, ACBSP, NASM, NLN **Intercollegiate Athletics:** Baseball M; Basketball M & W; Cheerleading M & W; Cross-Country Running M & W; Football M; Golf M & W; Soccer M & W; Softball W; Swimming and Diving M & W; Tennis W; Track and Field M & W; Volleyball W

MONMOUTH COLLEGE
700 East Broadway
Monmouth, IL 61462-1998
Tel: (309)457-2311; Free: 800-747-2687
Admissions: (309)457-2210
Fax: (309)457-2141
E-mail: admit@monm.edu
Web Site: http://www.monm.edu/
President/CEO: Dr. Mauri Ditzler
Admissions: Christine Johnston
Financial Aid: Jayne Schreck
Type: Four-Year College **Sex:** Coed **Affiliation:** Presbyterian Church **Scores:** 59% ACT 18-23; 31% ACT 24-29 **% Accepted:** 70 **Admission Plans:** Deferred Admission **Application Deadline:** Rolling **Application Fee:** $0.00 **H.S. Requirements:** High school diploma required; GED accepted **Costs Per Year:** Application fee: $0. Comprehensive fee: $32,250 includes full-time tuition ($24,950) and college room and board ($7300). College room only: $4250. Full-time tuition varies according to course load. Room and board charges vary according to board plan and housing facility. Part-time tuition: $830 per credit hour. **Scholarships:** Available **Calendar System:** Semester, Summer Session Not available **Enrollment:** FT 1,366, PT 13 **Faculty:** FT 83, PT 43 **Student-Faculty Ratio:** 14:1 **Exams:** SAT I or ACT. **% Receiving Financial Aid:** 84 **% Residing in College-Owned, -Operated, or -Affiliated Housing:** 95 **Final Year or Final Semester Residency Requirement:** Yes **Library Holdings:** 191,866 **Regional Accreditation:** North Central Association of Colleges and Schools **Credit Hours For Degree:** 124 semester hours, Bachelors **ROTC:** Army **Intercollegiate Athletics:** Baseball M; Basketball M & W; Cross-Country Running M & W; Football M; Golf M & W; Soccer M & W; Softball W; Swimming and Diving M & W; Tennis M & W; Track and Field M & W; Volleyball W

MOODY BIBLE INSTITUTE
820 North LaSalle Blvd.
Chicago, IL 60610-3284
Tel: (312)329-4000; Free: 800-967-4MBI
Admissions: (312)329-4307
Fax: (312)329-8987
E-mail: admissions@moody.edu
Web Site: http://www.moody.edu/
President/CEO: Dr. J. Paul Nyquist
Admissions: Jacqueline Holman
Financial Aid: Esther Kim
Type: Comprehensive **Sex:** Coed **Affiliation:** nondenominational **% Accepted:** 75 **Admission Plans:** Early Admission; Early Decision Plan **Application Deadline:** March 1 **H.S. Requirements:** High school diploma required; GED accepted **Costs Per Year:** Comprehensive fee: $9515 includes full-time tuition ($0), mandatory fees ($1275), and college room and board ($8240). College room only: $4810. Full-time fees vary according to course load and degree level. Room and board charges vary according to board plan, housing facility, and location. the college meets all of the tuition cost for each student. **Scholarships:** Available **Calendar System:** Semester, Summer Session Available **Enrollment:** FT 1,897, PT 649, Grad FT 150, Grad PT 295 **Faculty:** FT 85, PT 98 **Student-Faculty Ratio:** 15:1 **Exams:** SAT I and SAT II or ACT. ACT essay not being used. SAT essay not being used. **Final Year or Final Semester Residency Requirement:** No **Library Holdings:** 135,000 **Regional Accreditation:** North Central Association of Colleges and Schools **Credit Hours For Degree:** 60 semester hours, Associates; 130 semester hours, Bachelors **Professional Accreditation:** ABHE, NASM **Intercollegiate Athletics:** Basketball M & W; Soccer M; Volleyball M & W

MORAINE VALLEY COMMUNITY COLLEGE
9000 West College Parkway
Palos Hills, IL 60465
Tel: (708)974-4300
Admissions: (708)974-5357
Fax: (708)974-0681
E-mail: roselli@morainevalley.edu
Web Site: http://www.morainevalley.edu/
President/CEO: Dr. Vernon O. Crawley, EdD
Admissions: Claudia Roselli
Financial Aid: Laurie Anema
Type: Two-Year College **Sex:** Coed **Affiliation:** Illinois Community College Board **Scores:** 58.3% ACT 18-23; 14.6% ACT 24-29 **% Accepted:** 100

Admission Plans: Open Admission; Preferred Admission; Early Admission; Deferred Admission **Application Deadline:** Rolling **Application Fee:** $0.00 **H.S. Requirements:** High school diploma required; GED accepted **Costs Per Year:** Application fee: $0. Area resident tuition: $2610 full-time, $87 per credit hour part-time. State resident tuition: $6960 full-time, $232 per credit hour part-time. Nonresident tuition: $8160 full-time, $272 per credit hour part-time. Mandatory fees: $156 full-time, $5 per credit hour part-time, $3. **Scholarships:** Available **Calendar System:** Semester, Summer Session Available **Enrollment:** FT 7,761, PT 10,013 **Faculty:** FT 183, PT 580 **Student-Faculty Ratio:** 30:1 **Exams:** ACT essay not being used. SAT essay not being used. **Library Holdings:** 71,069 **Regional Accreditation:** North Central Association of Colleges and Schools **Credit Hours For Degree:** 62 semester hours, Associates **Professional Accreditation:** AHIMA, CARC, JRCERT, NLN **Intercollegiate Athletics:** Baseball M; Basketball M & W; Cross-Country Running M & W; Golf M; Soccer M & W; Softball W; Tennis M & W; Volleyball W

MORRISON INSTITUTE OF TECHNOLOGY
701 Portland Ave.
Morrison, IL 61270-0410
Tel: (815)772-7218
Fax: (815)772-7584
E-mail: admissions@morrison.tec.il.us
Web Site: http://www.morrison.tec.il.us/
President/CEO: Richard C. Parkinson
Admissions: Tammy Pruis
Financial Aid: Julie Damhoff
Type: Two-Year College **Sex:** Coed **% Accepted:** 100 **Admission Plans:** Open Admission; Deferred Admission **Application Deadline:** Rolling **Application Fee:** $100.00 **H.S. Requirements:** High school diploma required; GED accepted **Scholarships:** Available **Calendar System:** Semester, Summer Session Not available **Enrollment:** FT 142, PT 2 **Faculty:** FT 10, PT 1 **Student-Faculty Ratio:** 13:1 **Exams:** SAT I or ACT. **% Residing in College-Owned, -Operated, or -Affiliated Housing:** 55 **Library Holdings:** 7,946 **Credit Hours For Degree:** 67 semester hours, Associates **Professional Accreditation:** ABET, COE

MORTON COLLEGE
3801 South Central Ave.
Cicero, IL 60804-4398
Tel: (708)656-8000
Fax: (708)656-9592
Web Site: http://www.morton.edu/
President/CEO: Leslie Navarro
Admissions: Roslyn Castro
Type: Two-Year College **Sex:** Coed **Affiliation:** Illinois Community College Board **Admission Plans:** Open Admission; Preferred Admission **Application Deadline:** Rolling **Application Fee:** $10.00 **H.S. Requirements:** High school diploma required; GED accepted **Scholarships:** Available **Calendar System:** Semester, Summer Session Available **Enrollment:** FT 1,278, PT 3,771 **Faculty:** FT 52, PT 176 **Student-Faculty Ratio:** 21:1 **Library Holdings:** 40,972 **Regional Accreditation:** North Central Association of Colleges and Schools **Credit Hours For Degree:** 62 semester hours, Associates **Professional Accreditation:** APTA **Intercollegiate Athletics:** Baseball M; Basketball M & W; Cross-Country Running M & W; Soccer M; Softball W; Volleyball W

NATIONAL-LOUIS UNIVERSITY
122 South Michigan Ave.
Chicago, IL 60603
Tel: (312)621-9650; Free: 800-443-5522
Admissions: 888-NLU-TODA
Fax: (312)261-3057
Web Site: http://www.nl.edu/
President/CEO: Dr. Richard Pappas
Financial Aid: Janet Jazwiec
Type: University **Sex:** Coed **Admission Plans:** Deferred Admission **Application Deadline:** Rolling **Application Fee:** $25.00 **H.S. Requirements:** High school diploma required; GED accepted **Costs Per Year:** Application fee: $25. Tuition: $19,035 full-time, $423 per credit hour part-time. Mandatory fees: $120 full-time. Full-time tuition and fees vary according to course level, course load, degree level, location, and program. Part-time tuition varies according to course level, course load, degree level, location, and program. **Scholarships:** Available **Calendar System:** Quarter, Summer Session Available **Enrollment:** FT 1,233, PT 516 **Faculty:** FT 254, PT 472 **Student-Faculty Ratio:** 9:1 **Exams:** SAT I or ACT. **% Receiving Financial Aid:** 69 **Regional Accreditation:** North Central Association of Colleges and Schools **Credit Hours For Degree:** 180 quarter hours, Bachelors **Professional Accreditation:** CARC, JRCERT, NCATE

NORTH CENTRAL COLLEGE
30 North Brainard St., PO Box 3063
Naperville, IL 60566-7063
Tel: (630)637-5100; Free: 800-411-1861
Admissions: (630)637-5800
E-mail: admissions@noctrl.edu
Web Site: http://www.noctrl.edu/
President/CEO: Dr. Harold R. Wilde
Admissions: Martha Stolze
Financial Aid: Marty Rossman
Type: Comprehensive **Sex:** Coed **Affiliation:** United Methodist **Scores:** 40.7% ACT 18-23; 45.6% ACT 24-29 **% Accepted:** 67 **Admission Plans:** Deferred Admission **Application Deadline:** Rolling **Application Fee:** $25.00 **H.S. Requirements:** High school diploma required; GED accepted **Costs Per Year:** Application fee: $25. Comprehensive fee: $35,481 includes full-time tuition ($26,676), mandatory fees ($240), and college room and board ($8565). Room and board charges vary according to housing facility. Part-time tuition: $645 per credit hour. Part-time mandatory fees: $20 per term. Part-time tuition and fees vary according to course load. **Scholarships:** Available **Calendar System:** Quarter, Summer Session Available **Enrollment:** FT 2,333, PT 189, Grad FT 83, Grad PT 193 **Faculty:** FT 118, PT 134 **Student-Faculty Ratio:** 16:1 **Exams:** ACT, SAT I or ACT. **% Receiving Financial Aid:** 76 **% Residing in College-Owned, -Operated, or -Affiliated Housing:** 53 **Final Year or Final Semester Residency Requirement:** Yes **Library Holdings:** 151,296 **Regional Accreditation:** North Central Association of Colleges and Schools **Credit Hours For Degree:** 120 semester hours, Bachelors **ROTC:** Army, Air Force **Intercollegiate Athletics:** Baseball M; Basketball M & W; Cheerleading W; Cross-Country Running M & W; Football M; Golf M & W; Lacrosse W; Soccer M & W; Softball W; Swimming and Diving M & W; Tennis M & W; Track and Field M & W; Volleyball W; Wrestling M

NORTH PARK UNIVERSITY
3225 West Foster Ave.
Chicago, IL 60625-4895
Tel: (773)244-6200; Free: 800-888-NPC8
Admissions: (773)244-5500
Fax: (773)583-0858
E-mail: afao@northpark.edu
Web Site: http://www.northpark.edu/
President/CEO: Daivd L. Parkyn
Financial Aid: Dr. Lucy Shaker
Type: Comprehensive **Sex:** Coed **Affiliation:** Evangelical Covenant Church **Admission Plans:** Early Admission **Application Deadline:** Rolling **Application Fee:** $40.00 **H.S. Requirements:** High school diploma required; GED accepted **Costs Per Year:** Application fee: $40. Comprehensive fee: $26,380 includes full-time tuition ($18,800) and college room and board ($7580). College room only: $4180. Full-time tuition varies according to program. Room and board charges vary according to board plan and housing facility. Part-time tuition: $730 per credit hour. Part-time tuition varies according to program. **Scholarships:** Available **Calendar System:** Semester, Summer Session Available **Enrollment:** FT 1,252, PT 321 **Exams:** SAT I or ACT. **Library Holdings:** 260,685 **Regional Accreditation:** North Central Association of Colleges and Schools **Credit Hours For Degree:** 120 semester hours, Bachelors **Professional Accreditation:** AACN, NASM **Intercollegiate Athletics:** Baseball M; Basketball M & W; Cross-Country Running M & W; Football M; Golf M & W; Soccer M & W; Softball W; Track and Field M & W; Volleyball W

NORTHEASTERN ILLINOIS UNIVERSITY
5500 North St Louis Ave.
Chicago, IL 60625-4699
Tel: (773)583-4050
Admissions: (773)442-4026
Fax: (773)794-6243
E-mail: admrec@neiu.edu
Web Site: http://www.neiu.edu/
President/CEO: Dr. Sharon K. Hahs

Admissions: Zarrin Kerwell
Type: Comprehensive **Sex:** Coed **Scores:** 51.8% ACT 18-23; 11.2% ACT 24-29 **% Accepted:** 74 **Admission Plans:** Deferred Admission **Application Deadline:** July 1 **Application Fee:** $25.00 **H.S. Requirements:** High school diploma required; GED accepted **Costs Per Year:** Application fee: $25. State resident tuition: $7350 full-time, $245 per credit hour part-time. Nonresident tuition: $14,700 full-time, $490 per credit hour part-time. Mandatory fees: $1158 full-time, $49.85 per credit hour part-time, $3 per term part-time. Full-time tuition and fees vary according to location and student level. Part-time tuition and fees vary according to course load and location. Tuition guaranteed not to increase for student's term of enrollment. **Scholarships:** Available **Calendar System:** Semester, Summer Session Available **Enrollment:** FT 5,350, PT 3,841, Grad FT 427, Grad PT 2,013 **Faculty:** FT 404, PT 295 **Student-Faculty Ratio:** 15:1 **Exams:** ACT. **% Receiving Financial Aid:** 58 **Library Holdings:** 705,949 **Regional Accreditation:** North Central Association of Colleges and Schools **Credit Hours For Degree:** 120 credit hours, Bachelors **ROTC:** Army, Air Force **Professional Accreditation:** ACA, CSWE, NCATE

NORTHERN ILLINOIS UNIVERSITY
De Kalb, IL 60115-2854
Tel: (815)753-1000
Admissions: (815)753-0446
E-mail: admission-info@niu.edu
Web Site: http://www.niu.edu/
President/CEO: Dr. John G. Peters
Admissions: Dr. Robert Burk
Financial Aid: Kathleen D. Brunson
Type: University **Sex:** Coed **Scores:** 57% ACT 18-23; 29% ACT 24-29 **% Accepted:** 61 **Application Deadline:** August 1 **H.S. Requirements:** High school diploma required; GED accepted **Costs Per Year:** State resident tuition: $7260 full-time, $269 per credit hour part-time. Nonresident tuition: $14,520 full-time, $538 per credit hour part-time. Mandatory fees: $1819 full-time, $75.77 per credit hour part-time. Full-time tuition and fees vary according to course load, location, and student level. Part-time tuition and fees vary according to course load, location, and student level. College room and board: $9588. Room and board charges vary according to board plan and housing facility. Tuition guaranteed not to increase for student's term of enrollment. **Scholarships:** Available **Calendar System:** Semester, Summer Session Available **Enrollment:** FT 16,940, PT 1,977 **Faculty:** FT 908, PT 272 **Student-Faculty Ratio:** 17:1 **Exams:** SAT I or ACT. **% Receiving Financial Aid:** 64 **% Residing in College-Owned, -Operated, or -Affiliated Housing:** 33 **Library Holdings:** 3,119,829 **Regional Accreditation:** North Central Association of Colleges and Schools **Credit Hours For Degree:** 124 credit hours, Bachelors **ROTC:** Army, Air Force **Professional Accreditation:** AACSB, ABET, AAMFT, AACN, AAFCS, ABA, ACA, ADtA, APTA, APA, ASLHA, AALS, CEPH, CORE, JRCEPAT, NAACLS, NASAD, NASM, NASPAA, NAST NCATE, NLN, NAIT **Intercollegiate Athletics:** Baseball M; Basketball M & W; Cross-Country Running W; Football M; Golf M & W; Gymnastics W; Soccer M & W; Softball W; Swimming and Diving M & W; Tennis M & W; Volleyball W; Wrestling M

NORTHWESTERN COLLEGE
9700 West Higgins Rd.
Ste. 750
Rosemont, IL 60018
Tel: (847)318-8550; Free: 800-396-5613
Admissions: (773)777-4220
Web Site: http://www.northwesterncollege.edu/
President/CEO: Lawrence Schumacher
Admissions: Mark Sliz
Type: Two-Year College **Sex:** Coed **Application Deadline:** Rolling **Application Fee:** $25.00 **H.S. Requirements:** High school diploma required; GED accepted **Costs Per Year:** Application fee: $25. Tuition: $410 per credit hour part-time. **Scholarships:** Available **Calendar System:** Quarter, Summer Session Available **Enrollment:** FT 706, PT 1,056 **Exams:** SAT I or ACT. **Library Holdings:** 2,000 **Regional Accreditation:** North Central Association of Colleges and Schools **Credit Hours For Degree:** 100 quarter hours, Associates **Professional Accreditation:** AAMAE, AHIMA, ACBSP

NORTHWESTERN UNIVERSITY
Evanston, IL 60208
Tel: (847)491-3741
Admissions: (847)491-7271
E-mail: ug-admission@northwestern.edu
Web Site: http://www.northwestern.edu/
President/CEO: Henry Bienen
Admissions: Christopher Watson
Type: University **Sex:** Coed **Scores:** 100% SAT V 400+; 100% SAT M 400+; 3% ACT 18-23; 24% ACT 24-29 **% Accepted:** 26 **Admission Plans:** Early Admission; Early Decision Plan; Deferred Admission **Application Deadline:** January 1 **Application Fee:** $65.00 **H.S. Requirements:** High school diploma required; GED not accepted **Costs Per Year:** Application fee: $65. Comprehensive fee: $50,164 includes full-time tuition ($38,088), mandatory fees ($373), and college room and board ($11,703). College room only: $6657. **Scholarships:** Available **Calendar System:** Semester, Summer Session Available **Enrollment:** FT 8,273, PT 203 **Faculty:** FT 1,027, PT 126 **Student-Faculty Ratio:** 7:1 **Exams:** SAT I or ACT, SAT II. **% Receiving Financial Aid:** 43 **% Residing in College-Owned, -Operated, or -Affiliated Housing:** 65 **Library Holdings:** 4,842,949 **Regional Accreditation:** North Central Association of Colleges and Schools **Credit Hours For Degree:** 45 courses, Bachelors **ROTC:** Army, Navy, Air Force **Professional Accreditation:** AACSB, ABET, ACEJMC, AAMFT, ABA, APTA, APA, ASLHA, AALS, ACEHSA, CEPH, LCMEAMA, NASM, NAST **Intercollegiate Athletics:** Baseball M; Basketball M & W; Cheerleading M & W; Cross-Country Running W; Fencing W; Field Hockey W; Football M; Golf M & W; Lacrosse W; Soccer M & W; Softball W; Swimming and Diving M & W; Tennis M & W; Volleyball W; Wrestling M

OAKTON COMMUNITY COLLEGE
1600 East Golf Rd.
Des Plaines, IL 60016-1268
Tel: (847)635-1600
Fax: (847)635-1706
E-mail: dcohen@oakton.edu
Web Site: http://www.oakton.edu/
President/CEO: Margaret B. Lee
Admissions: Dale Cohen
Financial Aid: Christina Coines
Type: Two-Year College **Sex:** Coed **Affiliation:** Illinois Community College Board **Admission Plans:** Open Admission **Application Deadline:** Rolling **Application Fee:** $25.00 **H.S. Requirements:** High school diploma required; GED accepted **Scholarships:** Available **Calendar System:** Semester, Summer Session Available **Library Holdings:** 92,000 **Regional Accreditation:** North Central Association of Colleges and Schools **Credit Hours For Degree:** 60 semester hours, Associates **Professional Accreditation:** AHIMA, APTA, NAACLS, NLN **Intercollegiate Athletics:** Baseball M; Basketball M & W; Cross-Country Running M & W; Soccer M & W; Softball W; Tennis M & W; Track and Field M & W; Volleyball W

OLIVET NAZARENE UNIVERSITY
One University Ave.
Bourbonnais, IL 60914
Tel: (815)939-5011; Free: 800-648-1463
E-mail: swolfe@olivet.edu
Web Site: http://www.olivet.edu/
President/CEO: John C. Bowling
Admissions: Susan Wolfe
Financial Aid: Greg Bruner
Type: Comprehensive **Sex:** Coed **Affiliation:** Church of the Nazarene **Admission Plans:** Deferred Admission **Application Deadline:** Rolling **Application Fee:** $25.00 **H.S. Requirements:** High school diploma required; GED accepted **Scholarships:** Available **Calendar System:** Semester, Summer Session Available **Exams:** ACT. **% Receiving Financial Aid:** 76 **Library Holdings:** 160,039 **Regional Accreditation:** North Central Association of Colleges and Schools **Credit Hours For Degree:** 64 semester hours, Associates; 128 semester hours, Bachelors **ROTC:** Army **Professional Accreditation:** ABET, AACN, AAFCS, CSWE, NASM, NCATE **Intercollegiate Athletics:** Baseball M; Basketball M & W; Cheerleading M & W; Cross-Country Running M & W; Football M; Golf M; Soccer M & W; Softball W; Tennis M & W; Track and Field M & W; Volleyball W

PARKLAND COLLEGE
2400 West Bradley Ave.
Champaign, IL 61821-1899
Tel: (217)351-2200
Admissions: (217)351-2482
Fax: (217)351-7640

E-mail: mhenry@parkland.edu
Web Site: http://www.parkland.edu/
President/CEO: Thomas Ramage
Financial Aid: Tim Wendt
Type: Two-Year College **Sex:** Coed **Affiliation:** Illinois Community College Board **Scores:** 45% ACT 18-23; 15% ACT 24-29 **% Accepted:** 92 **Admission Plans:** Open Admission; Deferred Admission **Application Deadline:** Rolling **Application Fee:** $0.00 **H.S. Requirements:** High school diploma required; GED accepted **Costs Per Year:** Application fee: $0. Area resident tuition: $2670 full-time, $89 per credit hour part-time. State resident tuition: $7200 full-time, $240 per credit hour part-time. Nonresident tuition: $11,250 full-time, $375 per credit hour part-time. Mandatory fees: $90 full-time. **Scholarships:** Available **Calendar System:** Semester, Summer Session Available **Enrollment:** FT 4,345, PT 5,062 **Faculty:** FT 169, PT 350 **Student-Faculty Ratio:** 22:1 **Exams:** ACT. **Regional Accreditation:** North Central Association of Colleges and Schools **Credit Hours For Degree:** 60 semester hours, Associates **ROTC:** Army, Navy, Air Force **Professional Accreditation:** ARCEST, ADA, AOTA, CARC, JRCERT, NLN **Intercollegiate Athletics:** Baseball M; Basketball M & W; Golf M; Soccer M & W; Softball W; Volleyball W

PRAIRIE STATE COLLEGE
202 South Halsted St.
Chicago Heights, IL 60411-8226
Tel: (708)709-3500
E-mail: webmaster@prairiestate.edu
Web Site: http://www.prairiestate.edu/
President/CEO: Eric Radtke
Admissions: Marietta Turner
Type: Two-Year College **Sex:** Coed **Affiliation:** Illinois Community College Board **% Accepted:** 100 **Admission Plans:** Open Admission; Deferred Admission **Application Deadline:** Rolling **Application Fee:** $10.00 **H.S. Requirements:** High school diploma or equivalent not required. For transfer associate programs: High school diploma or equivalent not required **Costs Per Year:** Application fee: $10. Area resident tuition: $2760 full-time, $83 per credit hour part-time. State resident tuition: $7470 full-time, $240 per credit hour part-time. Nonresident tuition: $9840 full-time, $328 per credit hour part-time. Mandatory fees: $20 full-time, $9 per credit hour part-time, $10 per term part-time. Full-time tuition and fees vary according to course load, program, and reciprocity agreements. Part-time tuition and fees vary according to course load, program, and reciprocity agreements. **Scholarships:** Available **Calendar System:** Semester, Summer Session Available **Enrollment:** FT 1,714, PT 3,369 **Faculty:** FT 80, PT 283 **Student-Faculty Ratio:** 16:1 **Library Holdings:** 45,000 **Regional Accreditation:** North Central Association of Colleges and Schools **Credit Hours For Degree:** 62 credit hours, Associates **Professional Accreditation:** ADA, NLN **Intercollegiate Athletics:** Baseball M; Basketball M & W; Football M; Golf M & W; Soccer M & W; Softball M & W; Tennis W

PRINCIPIA COLLEGE
One Maybeck Place
Elsah, IL 62028-9799
Tel: (618)374-2131; Free: 800-277-4648 Ext. 2802
Fax: (618)374-4000
Web Site: http://www.prin.edu/college/
President/CEO: Jonathan W. Palmer
Admissions: Brian McCauley
Financial Aid: Tami Gavaletz
Type: Four-Year College **Sex:** Coed **Affiliation:** Christian Science **Scores:** 98.8% SAT V 400+; 94.12% SAT M 400+; 30% ACT 18-23; 42% ACT 24-29 **% Accepted:** 61 **Admission Plans:** Deferred Admission **Application Deadline:** Rolling **Application Fee:** $0.00 **H.S. Requirements:** High school diploma required; GED accepted **Costs Per Year:** Application fee: $0. One-time mandatory fee: $300. Comprehensive fee: $32,625 includes full-time tuition ($23,625) and college room and board ($9000). College room only: $4380. Full-time tuition varies according to course load. **Scholarships:** Available **Calendar System:** Quarter, Summer Session Not available **Enrollment:** FT 536, PT 6 **Faculty:** FT 55, PT 11 **Student-Faculty Ratio:** 8:1 **Exams:** SAT I or ACT, SAT II. **% Receiving Financial Aid:** 70 **% Residing in College-Owned, -Operated, or -Affiliated Housing:** 100 **Library Holdings:** 211,460 **Regional Accreditation:** North Central Association of Colleges and Schools **Credit Hours For Degree:** 180 quarter hours, Bachelors **Intercollegiate Athletics:** Baseball M; Basketball M & W; Cross-Country Running M & W; Soccer M & W; Softball W; Swimming and Diving M & W; Tennis M & W; Track and Field M & W; Volleyball W

QUINCY UNIVERSITY
1800 College Ave.
Quincy, IL 62301-2699
Tel: (217)222-8020; Free: 800-688-4295
Admissions: (217)228-5210
Fax: (217)228-5479
E-mail: admissions@quincy.edu
Web Site: http://www.quincy.edu/
President/CEO: Dr. Robert A. Gervasi
Admissions: Syndi Peck
Financial Aid: Lisa Flack
Type: Comprehensive **Sex:** Coed **Affiliation:** Roman Catholic **Scores:** 95% SAT V 400+; 95% SAT M 400+; 63% ACT 18-23; 23% ACT 24-29 **% Accepted:** 90 **Admission Plans:** Early Admission; Deferred Admission **Application Deadline:** Rolling **Application Fee:** $25.00 **H.S. Requirements:** High school diploma required; GED accepted **Costs Per Year:** Application fee: $25. Comprehensive fee: $30,410 includes full-time tuition ($21,300), mandatory fees ($730), and college room and board ($8380). College room only: $4520. Room and board charges vary according to board plan and housing facility. Part-time tuition: $480 per credit hour. Part-time mandatory fees: $15 per credit hour. **Scholarships:** Available **Calendar System:** Semester, Summer Session Available **Enrollment:** FT 1,094, PT 147, Grad FT 342, Grad PT 262 **Faculty:** FT 53, PT 116 **Student-Faculty Ratio:** 14:1 **Exams:** SAT I or ACT. ACT essay not being used. SAT essay not being used. **% Receiving Financial Aid:** 80 **% Residing in College-Owned, -Operated, or -Affiliated Housing:** 54 **Library Holdings:** 212,930 **Regional Accreditation:** North Central Association of Colleges and Schools **Credit Hours For Degree:** 64 credit hours, Associates; 124 credit hours, Bachelors **Professional Accreditation:** NASM **Intercollegiate Athletics:** Baseball M; Basketball M & W; Cheerleading M & W; Football M; Golf M & W; Soccer M & W; Softball W; Tennis M & W; Volleyball M & W

RASMUSSEN COLLEGE AURORA
2363 Sequoia Dr.
Aurora, IL 60506
Tel: (630)888-3500; Free: 877-888-4110
Fax: (630)888-3501
Web Site: http://www.rasmussen.edu/
President/CEO: Susan Cheney
Type: Two-Year College **Sex:** Coed **Costs Per Year:** Tuition: $365 per credit part-time. Part-time tuition varies according to course load and program. **Regional Accreditation:** North Central Association of Colleges and Schools

RASMUSSEN COLLEGE ROCKFORD, ILLINOIS
6000 East State St., Fourth Floor
Rockford, IL 61108-2513
Tel: (815)316-4800; Free: 877-533-5825
Fax: (815)316-4801
Web Site: http://www.rasmussen.edu/
President/CEO: Scott Vukoder
Type: Two-Year College **Sex:** Coed **Costs Per Year:** Tuition: $365 per credit part-time. Part-time tuition varies according to course load and program. **Regional Accreditation:** North Central Association of Colleges and Schools

REND LAKE COLLEGE
468 North Ken Gray Parkway
Ina, IL 62846-9801
Tel: (618)437-5321
Fax: (618)437-5677
E-mail: swannj@rlc.edu
Web Site: http://www.rlc.edu/
President/CEO: Charley Holstein
Admissions: Jason Swann
Type: Two-Year College **Sex:** Coed **Affiliation:** Illinois Community College Board **Admission Plans:** Open Admission; Deferred Admission **Application Deadline:** August 18 **Application Fee:** $0.00 **H.S. Requirements:** High school diploma required; GED accepted **Scholarships:** Available **Calendar System:** Semester, Summer Session Available **Library Holdings:** 35,426 **Regional Accreditation:** North Central Association of Colleges and Schools **Credit Hours For Degree:** 64 semester hours, Associates **Professional Accreditation:** AHIMA, AOTA, NAACLS **Intercollegiate Athletics:** Baseball

M; Basketball M & W; Cross-Country Running M; Golf M & W; Softball W; Tennis W; Track and Field M & W; Volleyball W

RICHLAND COMMUNITY COLLEGE
One College Park
Decatur, IL 62521-8513
Tel: (217)875-7200
Fax: (217)875-6991
E-mail: jwirey@richland.edu
Web Site: http://www.richland.edu/
President/CEO: Dr. Gayle Saunders
Admissions: JoAnn Wirey
Type: Two-Year College **Sex:** Coed **Affiliation:** Illinois Community College Board **Admission Plans:** Open Admission; Early Admission **Application Deadline:** Rolling **Application Fee:** $0.00 **H.S. Requirements:** High school diploma required; GED accepted **Costs Per Year:** Application fee: $0. Area resident tuition: $2355 full-time, $78.50 per credit hour part-time. State resident tuition: $11,596 full-time, $386.53 per credit hour part-time. Nonresident tuition: $17,411 full-time, $580.36 per credit hour part-time. Mandatory fees: $155 full-time, $4.50 per credit hour part-time. Full-time tuition and fees vary according to program and reciprocity agreements. Part-time tuition and fees vary according to program and reciprocity agreements. **Scholarships:** Available **Calendar System:** Semester, Summer Session Available **Enrollment:** FT 1,003, PT 2,149 **Faculty:** FT 96, PT 146 **Student-Faculty Ratio:** 14:1 **Exams:** ACT. **Library Holdings:** 39,452 **Regional Accreditation:** North Central Association of Colleges and Schools **Credit Hours For Degree:** 60 semester hours, Associates **Professional Accreditation:** ARCEST, NLN

ROBERT MORRIS UNIVERSITY ILLINOIS
401 South State St.
Chicago, IL 60605
Tel: (312)935-6800; Free: 800-RMC-5960
Admissions: (312)935-4141
Fax: (312)836-4599
E-mail: enroll@robertmorris.edu
Web Site: http://www.robertmorris.edu/
President/CEO: Michael P. Viollt
Admissions: Connie Esparza
Financial Aid: Leigh Taylor
Type: Comprehensive **Sex:** Coed **Scores:** 40.17% ACT 18-23; 10.84% ACT 24-29 **% Accepted:** 81 **Admission Plans:** Deferred Admission **Application Deadline:** Rolling **Application Fee:** $30.00 **H.S. Requirements:** High school diploma required; GED accepted **Costs Per Year:** Application fee: $30. Comprehensive fee: $30,045 includes full-time tuition ($20,100) and college room and board ($9945). College room only: $7800. Full-time tuition varies according to location. Room and board charges vary according to housing facility and location. Part-time tuition: $558 per credit hour. Part-time tuition varies according to course load and location. **Scholarships:** Available **Calendar System:** Miscellaneous, Summer Session Available **Enrollment:** FT 3,949, PT 201, Grad FT 51, Grad PT 418 **Faculty:** FT 113, PT 179 **Student-Faculty Ratio:** 23:1 **Exams:** SAT I or ACT. **% Receiving Financial Aid:** 91 **% Residing in College-Owned, -Operated, or -Affiliated Housing:** 5 **Final Year or Final Semester Residency Requirement:** Yes **Library Holdings:** 149,673 **Regional Accreditation:** North Central Association of Colleges and Schools **Credit Hours For Degree:** 92 quarter hours, Associates; 188 quarter hours, Bachelors **ROTC:** Army **Professional Accreditation:** AAMAE **Intercollegiate Athletics:** Baseball M; Basketball M & W; Bowling M & W; Cheerleading M & W; Crew W; Cross-Country Running M & W; Golf M & W; Ice Hockey M & W; Lacrosse W; Sailing M & W; Soccer M & W; Softball W; Swimming and Diving W; Tennis W; Track and Field W; Volleyball M & W

ROCK VALLEY COLLEGE
3301 North Mulford Rd.
Rockford, IL 61114-5699
Tel: (815)921-7821; Free: 800-973-7821
Fax: (815)654-5568
E-mail: a.diaz@rockvalleycollege.edu
Web Site: http://www.rockvalleycollege.edu/
President/CEO: Jack Becherer
Admissions: Amy Diaz
Type: Two-Year College **Sex:** Coed **Affiliation:** Illinois Community College Board **Admission Plans:** Open Admission **Application Deadline:** August 29 **Application Fee:** $0.00 **H.S. Requirements:** High school diploma or equivalent not required. For nursing, respiratory therapy programs: High school diploma required; GED accepted **Costs Per Year:** Application fee: $0. Area resident tuition: $1980 full-time, $66 per credit hour part-time. State resident tuition: $8430 full-time, $281 per credit hour part-time. Nonresident tuition: $13,320 full-time, $444 per credit hour part-time. Mandatory fees: $302 full-time, $8 per credit hour part-time, $55 per term part-time. Full-time tuition and fees vary according to course load. Part-time tuition and fees vary according to course load. **Scholarships:** Available **Calendar System:** Semester, Summer Session Available **Enrollment:** FT 3,508, PT 4,637 **Faculty:** FT 139, PT 152 **Student-Faculty Ratio:** 25:1 **Library Holdings:** 67,168 **Regional Accreditation:** North Central Association of Colleges and Schools **Credit Hours For Degree:** 64 semester hours, Associates **Professional Accreditation:** ADA, CARC **Intercollegiate Athletics:** Baseball M; Basketball M & W; Football M; Golf M; Softball W; Tennis M & W; Volleyball W

ROCKFORD BUSINESS COLLEGE
730 North Church St.
Rockford, IL 61103
Tel: (815)965-8616
Fax: (815)965-0360
Web Site: http://www.rbcsuccess.com/
President/CEO: Steve W. Gibson
Admissions: Barbara Holliman
Type: Two-Year College **Sex:** Coed **Admission Plans:** Open Admission; Early Admission **Application Deadline:** September 4 **Application Fee:** $50.00 **H.S. Requirements:** High school diploma required; GED accepted **Scholarships:** Available **Calendar System:** Quarter, Summer Session Available **Enrollment:** FT 243, PT 185 **Faculty:** FT 8, PT 18 **Student-Faculty Ratio:** 15:1 **Library Holdings:** 1,823 **Credit Hours For Degree:** 100 credits, Associates **Professional Accreditation:** ACICS, AAMAE

ROCKFORD COLLEGE
5050 East State St.
Rockford, IL 61108-2393
Tel: (815)226-4000; Free: 800-892-2984
Admissions: (815)226-4050
Fax: (815)226-4119
E-mail: rcadmissions@rockford.edu
Web Site: http://www.rockford.edu/
President/CEO: Dr. Robert Head
Admissions: Rebecca Miziniak
Financial Aid: Todd M. Free
Type: Comprehensive **Sex:** Coed **Scores:** 87.5% SAT V 400+; 75% SAT M 400+; 60.67% ACT 18-23; 29.21% ACT 24-29 **Admission Plans:** Early Admission; Deferred Admission **Application Deadline:** August 15 **Application Fee:** $35.00 **H.S. Requirements:** High school diploma required; GED accepted **Costs Per Year:** Application fee: $35. Comprehensive fee: $31,700 includes full-time tuition ($24,750) and college room and board ($6950). College room only: $3950. Room and board charges vary according to board plan and housing facility. Part-time tuition: $650 per credit hour. Part-time mandatory fees: $40 per term. **Scholarships:** Available **Calendar System:** Semester, Summer Session Available **Enrollment:** FT 753, PT 116, Grad FT 73, Grad PT 398 **Faculty:** FT 69, PT 87 **Student-Faculty Ratio:** 9:1 **Exams:** SAT I or ACT. ACT essay not being used. SAT essay not being used. **% Receiving Financial Aid:** 90 **% Residing in College-Owned, -Operated, or -Affiliated Housing:** 30 **Final Year or Final Semester Residency Requirement:** No **Library Holdings:** 140,000 **Regional Accreditation:** North Central Association of Colleges and Schools **Credit Hours For Degree:** 124 credits, Bachelors **ROTC:** Army **Professional Accreditation:** NLN **Intercollegiate Athletics:** Baseball M; Basketball M & W; Football M; Golf M & W; Soccer M & W; Softball W; Tennis M & W; Volleyball M & W

ROOSEVELT UNIVERSITY
430 South Michigan Ave.
Chicago, IL 60605
Tel: (312)341-3500; Free: 877-APPLYRU
Admissions: (312)341-6733
E-mail: bgierach@roosevelt.edu
Web Site: http://www.roosevelt.edu/
President/CEO: Dr. Charles R. Middleton
Admissions: Beth Gierach

Financial Aid: Walter J. H. O'Neill
Type: Comprehensive **Sex:** Coed **Scores:** 100% SAT V 400+; 93.7% SAT M 400+; 66% ACT 18-23; 29.9% ACT 24-29 **% Accepted:** 50 **Admission Plans:** Deferred Admission **Application Deadline:** August 1 **Application Fee:** $25.00 **H.S. Requirements:** High school diploma required; GED accepted **Costs Per Year:** Application fee: $25. Comprehensive fee: $34,200 includes full-time tuition ($23,000) and college room and board ($11,200). Full-time tuition varies according to course load and program. Room and board charges vary according to board plan and housing facility. Part-time tuition: $689 per credit hour. Part-time mandatory fees: $125 per term. Part-time tuition and fees vary according to course load and program. **Scholarships:** Available **Calendar System:** Semester, Summer Session Available **Enrollment:** FT 2,834, PT 1,348, Grad FT 1,220, Grad PT 1,904 **Student-Faculty Ratio:** 13:1 **Exams:** SAT I or ACT. ACT essay used for advising. SAT essay used for advising. **% Receiving Financial Aid:** 66 **% Residing in College-Owned, -Operated, or -Affiliated Housing:** 18 **Final Year or Final Semester Residency Requirement:** Yes **Library Holdings:** 211,000 **Regional Accreditation:** North Central Association of Colleges and Schools **Credit Hours For Degree:** 120 semester hours, Bachelors **Professional Accreditation:** ACA, APA, ACBSP, NASM, NCATE **Intercollegiate Athletics:** Baseball M; Basketball M & W; Cross-Country Running M & W; Tennis M & W

RUSH UNIVERSITY
600 South Paulina
Chicago, IL 60612-3832
Tel: (312)942-5000
Admissions: (312)942-7100
Fax: (312)942-2100
E-mail: hicela_castruita@rush.edu
Web Site: http://www.rushu.rush.edu/
President/CEO: Dr. Larry J. Goodman
Admissions: Hicela Castruita Woods
Financial Aid: David Nelson
Type: Two-Year Upper Division **Sex:** Coed **% Accepted:** 37 **Admission Plans:** Preferred Admission **Application Fee:** $40.00 **Scholarships:** Available **Calendar System:** Quarter, Summer Session Not available **Enrollment:** FT 159, PT 7 **Faculty:** FT 796, PT 0 **Student-Faculty Ratio:** 8:1 **% Receiving Financial Aid:** 70 **% Residing in College-Owned, -Operated, or -Affiliated Housing:** 10 **Library Holdings:** 120,042 **Regional Accreditation:** North Central Association of Colleges and Schools **Credit Hours For Degree:** 180 quarter hours, Bachelors **Professional Accreditation:** ACPE, AACN, AANA, ADtA, AOTA, ASLHA, ACIPE, ACEHSA, LCMEAMA, NAACLS, NLN

SAINT ANTHONY COLLEGE OF NURSING
5658 East State St.
Rockford, IL 61108-2468
Tel: (815)395-5091
E-mail: info@sacn.edu
Web Site: http://www.sacn.edu/
President/CEO: Terese Ann Burch
Admissions: Nancy Sanders
Financial Aid: Serrita Woods
Type: Two-Year Upper Division **Sex:** Coed **Affiliation:** Roman Catholic **Admission Plans:** Deferred Admission **Application Fee:** $50.00 **H.S. Requirements:** High school diploma or equivalent not required **Costs Per Year:** Application fee: $50. Tuition: $18,846 full-time, $590 per semester hour part-time. Mandatory fees: $404 full-time, $30 per term part-time. Full-time tuition and fees vary according to course load and degree level. Part-time tuition and fees vary according to course load and degree level. **Scholarships:** Available **Calendar System:** Semester, Summer Session Available **Enrollment:** FT 129, PT 17 **Faculty:** FT 12, PT 3 **Student-Faculty Ratio:** 9:1 **% Receiving Financial Aid:** 94 **Library Holdings:** 1,258 **Regional Accreditation:** North Central Association of Colleges and Schools **Credit Hours For Degree:** 128 credits, Bachelors **Professional Accreditation:** AACN, NLN

ST. AUGUSTINE COLLEGE
1333-1345 West Argyle
Chicago, IL 60640-3501
Tel: (773)878-8756
Admissions: (773)878-3256
E-mail: info@staugustine.edu
Web Site: http://www.staugustine.edu/
President/CEO: Andrew C. Sund
Admissions: Gloria Quiroz
Financial Aid: Maria Zambonino
Type: Four-Year College **Sex:** Coed **Admission Plans:** Open Admission **Application Deadline:** Rolling **Application Fee:** $0.00 **H.S. Requirements:** High school diploma required; GED accepted. For international students: High school diploma or equivalent not required **Costs Per Year:** Application fee: $0. Tuition: $8400 full-time, $350 per credit hour part-time. **Scholarships:** Available **Calendar System:** Semester, Summer Session Available **Enrollment:** FT 1,218, PT 212 **Faculty:** FT 20, PT 134 **Student-Faculty Ratio:** 20:1 **% Receiving Financial Aid:** 83 **Library Holdings:** 24,007 **Regional Accreditation:** North Central Association of Colleges and Schools **Credit Hours For Degree:** 60 semester hours, Associates; 128 semester hours, Bachelors **Professional Accreditation:** CARC

SAINT FRANCIS MEDICAL CENTER COLLEGE OF NURSING
511 Northeast Greenleaf St.
Peoria, IL 61603-3783
Tel: (309)655-2201
Admissions: (309)624-8980
E-mail: janice.farquharson@osfhealthcare.org
Web Site: http://www.sfmccon.edu/
President/CEO: Lois J. Hamilton
Admissions: Janice Farquharson
Financial Aid: Nancy Perryman
Type: Two-Year Upper Division **Sex:** Coed **Affiliation:** Roman Catholic **% Accepted:** 67 **Admission Plans:** Deferred Admission **Application Fee:** $50.00 **H.S. Requirements:** High school diploma required; GED accepted **Costs Per Year:** Application fee: $50. Tuition: $14,880 full-time, $480 per semester hour part-time. Mandatory fees: $556 full-time, $130 per term part-time. Full-time tuition and fees vary according to course load. Part-time tuition and fees vary according to course load. College room only: $2400. **Scholarships:** Available **Calendar System:** Semester, Summer Session Available **Enrollment:** FT 282, PT 81, Grad FT 8, Grad PT 128 **Faculty:** FT 31, PT 20 **% Receiving Financial Aid:** 76 **% Residing in College-Owned, -Operated, or -Affiliated Housing:** 3 **Final Year or Final Semester Residency Requirement:** No **Library Holdings:** 6,790 **Regional Accreditation:** North Central Association of Colleges and Schools **Credit Hours For Degree:** 124 semester hours, Bachelors **Professional Accreditation:** NLN

ST. JOHN'S COLLEGE
729 East Carpenter St.
Springfield, IL 62702
Tel: (217)525-5628
E-mail: college@st-johns.org
Web Site: http://www.stjohnscollegespringfield.edu/
President/CEO: Marjorie Beyers
Financial Aid: Mary M. Deatherage
Type: Two-Year Upper Division **Sex:** Coed **Affiliation:** Roman Catholic **Admission Plans:** Early Action **Application Fee:** $50.00 **H.S. Requirements:** High school diploma required; GED accepted **Scholarships:** Available **Calendar System:** Semester, Summer Session Not available **Student-Faculty Ratio:** 6:1 **% Receiving Financial Aid:** 72 **Regional Accreditation:** North Central Association of Colleges and Schools **Credit Hours For Degree:** 125 semester hours, Bachelors **Professional Accreditation:** NLN

SAINT XAVIER UNIVERSITY
3700 West 103rd St.
Chicago, IL 60655-3105
Tel: (773)298-3000; Free: 800-462-9288
Admissions: (773)298-3305
Fax: (773)298-3076
E-mail: carlson@sxu.edu
Web Site: http://www.sxu.edu/
President/CEO: Dr. Judith A. Dwyer
Admissions: Dr. Kathleen Carlson
Financial Aid: Susan Swisher
Type: Comprehensive **Sex:** Coed **Affiliation:** Roman Catholic **Scores:** 95.5% SAT V 400+; 95.4% SAT M 400+; 59.6% ACT 18-23; 30.8% ACT 24-29 **% Accepted:** 87 **Admission Plans:** Deferred Admission **Application Deadline:** Rolling **Application Fee:** $25.00 **H.S. Requirements:** High school diploma required; GED accepted **Costs Per Year:** Application fee:

$25. Comprehensive fee: $32,748 includes full-time tuition ($23,610), mandatory fees ($730), and college room and board ($8408). College room only: $4897. Room and board charges vary according to board plan and housing facility. Part-time tuition: $790 per credit hour. Part-time mandatory fees: $490 per year. **Scholarships:** Available **Calendar System:** Semester, Summer Session Available **Enrollment:** FT 2,495, PT 589, Grad FT 310, Grad PT 1,660 **Faculty:** FT 280, PT 226 **Student-Faculty Ratio:** 15:1 **Exams:** SAT I or ACT. ACT essay used for placement. **% Receiving Financial Aid:** 84 **% Residing in College-Owned, -Operated, or -Affiliated Housing:** 21 **Library Holdings:** 170,753 **Regional Accreditation:** North Central Association of Colleges and Schools **Credit Hours For Degree:** 120 semester hours, Bachelors **ROTC:** Air Force **Professional Accreditation:** AACN, ASLHA, ACBSP, NASM, NCATE, NLN **Intercollegiate Athletics:** Baseball M; Basketball M; Cross-Country Running W; Football M; Golf M; Soccer M & W; Softball W; Volleyball W

SAUK VALLEY COMMUNITY COLLEGE

173 Illinois Route 2
Dixon, IL 61021
Tel: (815)288-5511
E-mail: medemap@svcc.edu
Web Site: http://www.svcc.edu/
President/CEO: Dr. George J. Mihel
Admissions: Pamela Medema
Financial Aid: Debra Stiefel

Type: Two-Year College **Sex:** Coed **Affiliation:** Illinois Community College Board **% Accepted:** 100 **Admission Plans:** Open Admission; Early Admission; Deferred Admission **Application Deadline:** Rolling **Application Fee:** $0.00 **H.S. Requirements:** High school diploma or equivalent not required **Costs Per Year:** Application fee: $0. Area resident tuition: $2848 full-time, $89 per credit hour part-time. State resident tuition: $8000 full-time, $250 per credit hour part-time. Nonresident tuition: $9152 full-time, $286 per credit hour part-time. College room only: $4131. Room charges vary according to housing facility. **Scholarships:** Available **Calendar System:** Semester, Summer Session Available **Enrollment:** FT 1,092, PT 1,301 **Faculty:** FT 43 **Student-Faculty Ratio:** 11:1 **Exams:** ACT. **Library Holdings:** 55,000 **Regional Accreditation:** North Central Association of Colleges and Schools **Credit Hours For Degree:** 64 semester hours, Associates **Professional Accreditation:** JRCERT **Intercollegiate Athletics:** Baseball M; Basketball M & W; Cross-Country Running M & W; Softball W; Tennis M & W

SCHOOL OF THE ART INSTITUTE OF CHICAGO

37 South Wabash
Chicago, IL 60603-3103
Tel: (312)899-5100; Free: 800-232-SAIC
Admissions: (312)629-6100
Fax: (312)263-0141
E-mail: ugadmiss@saic.edu
Web Site: http://www.saic.edu/
President/CEO: Tony Jones
Admissions: Scott Ramon

Type: Comprehensive **Sex:** Coed **% Accepted:** 81 **Admission Plans:** Early Action; Deferred Admission **Application Deadline:** June 1 **Application Fee:** $65.00 **H.S. Requirements:** High school diploma required; GED accepted **Costs Per Year:** Application fee: $65. Tuition: $35,550 full-time, $1185 per semester hour part-time. Mandatory fees: $400 full-time. College room only: $9800. **Scholarships:** Available **Calendar System:** Semester, Summer Session Available **Enrollment:** FT 2,219, PT 226, Grad FT 677, Grad PT 48 **Faculty:** FT 135, PT 462 **Student-Faculty Ratio:** 8:1 **Exams:** SAT I or ACT. **% Receiving Financial Aid:** 55 **% Residing in College-Owned, -Operated, or -Affiliated Housing:** 31 **Library Holdings:** 10,000 **Regional Accreditation:** North Central Association of Colleges and Schools **Credit Hours For Degree:** 132 semester hours, Bachelors **Professional Accreditation:** NASAD

SHAWNEE COMMUNITY COLLEGE

8364 Shawnee College Rd.
Ullin, IL 62992
Tel: (618)634-3200
Fax: (618)634-3300
E-mail: erink@shawneecc.edu
Web Site: http://www.shawneecc.edu/
President/CEO: Dr. Larry Peterson
Admissions: Erin King

Type: Two-Year College **Sex:** Coed **Affiliation:** Illinois Community College Board **Admission Plans:** Open Admission; Preferred Admission; Early Admission; Deferred Admission **Application Deadline:** Rolling **Application Fee:** $0.00 **H.S. Requirements:** High school diploma required; GED accepted **Costs Per Year:** Application fee: $0. Area resident tuition: $2610 full-time, $87 per credit hour part-time. State resident tuition: $3930 full-time, $131 per credit hour part-time. Nonresident tuition: $4350 full-time, $145 per credit hour part-time. Full-time tuition varies according to program and reciprocity agreements. Part-time tuition varies according to program and reciprocity agreements. **Scholarships:** Available **Calendar System:** Semester, Summer Session Available **Enrollment:** FT 942, PT 2,248 **Faculty:** FT 42, PT 170 **Student-Faculty Ratio:** 20:1 **Exams:** ACT. ACT essay not being used. **Final Year or Final Semester Residency Requirement:** No **Library Holdings:** 46,313 **Regional Accreditation:** North Central Association of Colleges and Schools **Credit Hours For Degree:** 64 semester hours, Associates **Professional Accreditation:** AHIMA, AOTA, NAACLS **Intercollegiate Athletics:** Baseball M; Basketball M & W; Cheerleading M & W; Golf M & W; Softball W; Volleyball W

SHIMER COLLEGE

3424 South State St.
Chicago, IL 60616
Tel: (312)235-3500; Free: 800-215-7173
Admissions: (312)235-3504
Fax: (312)235-3501
E-mail: a.pritts@shimer.edu
Web Site: http://www.shimer.edu/
President/CEO: Ed Noonan
Admissions: Amy Pritts
Financial Aid: Janet Henthorn

Type: Four-Year College **Sex:** Coed **Scores:** 100% SAT V 400+; 100% SAT M 400+; 8% ACT 18-23; 66% ACT 24-29 **% Accepted:** 29 **Application Deadline:** July 31 **Application Fee:** $25.00 **H.S. Requirements:** High school diploma or equivalent not required **Costs Per Year:** Application fee: $25. Comprehensive fee: $40,660 includes full-time tuition ($26,510), mandatory fees ($1300), and college room and board ($12,850). College room only: $7526. Full-time tuition and fees vary according to class time, course load, and program. Room and board charges vary according to housing facility. Part-time tuition: $970 per credit hour. Part-time mandatory fees: $400 per term. Part-time tuition and fees vary according to class time, course load, and program. **Scholarships:** Available **Calendar System:** Semester, Summer Session Available **Enrollment:** FT 91, PT 13 **Faculty:** FT 9, PT 4 **Student-Faculty Ratio:** 10:1 **Exams:** SAT I or ACT. **% Receiving Financial Aid:** 83 **% Residing in College-Owned, -Operated, or -Affiliated Housing:** 42 **Library Holdings:** 200,000 **Regional Accreditation:** North Central Association of Colleges and Schools **Credit Hours For Degree:** 125 credit hours, Bachelors

SOLEX COLLEGE

350 East Dundee Rd.
Wheeling, IL 60090
Tel: (847)229-9595
Web Site: http://www.solex.edu/

Type: Two-Year College **Sex:** Coed **Affiliation:** The School of Massage Therapy at SOLEX **Application Fee:** $150.00 **H.S. Requirements:** High school diploma required; GED accepted **Exams:** SAT I or ACT. ACT essay used for admission. SAT essay used for admission. ACT essay used for placement. SAT essay used for placement. **Final Year or Final Semester Residency Requirement:** No **Credit Hours For Degree:** 60 credit hours, Associates **Professional Accreditation:** ACICS

SOUTH SUBURBAN COLLEGE

15800 South State St.
South Holland, IL 60473-1270
Tel: (708)596-2000
E-mail: admissionsquestions@southsuburbancollege.edu
Web Site: http://www.ssc.edu/
President/CEO: George Dammer

Type: Two-Year College **Sex:** Coed **Affiliation:** Illinois Community College Board **Admission Plans:** Open Admission; Preferred Admission; Early Admission; Deferred Admission **Application Deadline:** Rolling **H.S. Requirements:** High school diploma required; GED accepted **Costs Per Year:** Area resident tuition: $2700 full-time, $90 per credit hour part-time. State resident tuition: $8040 full-time, $268 per credit hour part-time.

Nonresident tuition: $9690 full-time, $325 per credit hour part-time. Mandatory fees: $413 full-time, $13.75 per credit hour part-time. **Scholarships:** Available **Calendar System:** Semester, Summer Session Available **Enrollment:** FT 2,428, PT 4,851 **Faculty:** FT 120, PT 217 **Student-Faculty Ratio:** 22:1 **Regional Accreditation:** North Central Association of Colleges and Schools **Credit Hours For Degree:** 60 semester hours, Associates **Professional Accreditation:** AOTA, ACBSP, JRCERT, NASM, NLN **Intercollegiate Athletics:** Baseball M; Basketball M & W; Soccer M & W; Softball W; Volleyball W

SOUTHEASTERN ILLINOIS COLLEGE
3575 College Rd.
Harrisburg, IL 62946-4925
Tel: (618)252-5400; Free: (866)338-2742
Web Site: http://www.sic.edu/
President/CEO: Jonah Rice
Admissions: Dr. David Nudo
Type: Two-Year College **Sex:** Coed **Affiliation:** Illinois Community College Board **Scores:** 39% ACT 18-23; 22% ACT 24-29 **% Accepted:** 100 **Admission Plans:** Open Admission; Preferred Admission; Early Admission; Deferred Admission **Application Deadline:** September 1 **Application Fee:** $0.00 **H.S. Requirements:** High school diploma required; GED accepted **Scholarships:** Available **Calendar System:** Semester, Summer Session Available **Enrollment:** FT 795, PT 1,764 **Faculty:** FT 53, PT 200 **Student-Faculty Ratio:** 12:1 **Library Holdings:** 58,030 **Regional Accreditation:** North Central Association of Colleges and Schools **Credit Hours For Degree:** 62 semester hours, Associates **Professional Accreditation:** AHIMA, AOTA, NAACLS **Intercollegiate Athletics:** Baseball M; Basketball M & W; Softball W

SOUTHERN ILLINOIS UNIVERSITY CARBONDALE
Carbondale, IL 62901-4701
Tel: (618)453-2121
Admissions: (618)536-4405
Fax: (618)453-3250
E-mail: pradmit@siu.edu
Web Site: http://www.siuc.edu/
President/CEO: Dr. Samuel Goldman
Admissions: Patsy Reynolds
Financial Aid: Linda Joy Clemons
Type: University **Sex:** Coed **Affiliation:** Southern Illinois University **Scores:** 86% SAT M 400+; 55% ACT 18-23; 26% ACT 24-29 **% Accepted:** 69 **Admission Plans:** Deferred Admission **Application Deadline:** Rolling **Application Fee:** $30.00 **H.S. Requirements:** High school diploma required; GED accepted **Costs Per Year:** Application fee: $30. State resident tuition: $7290 full-time, $243 per credit hour part-time. Nonresident tuition: $18,225 full-time, $607.50 per credit hour part-time. Mandatory fees: $3121 full-time, $288 per credit hour part-time. Full-time tuition and fees vary according to course load. Part-time tuition and fees vary according to course load. College room and board: $7673. College room only: $4405. Room and board charges vary according to board plan and housing facility. Tuition guaranteed not to increase for student's term of enrollment. **Scholarships:** Available **Calendar System:** Semester, Summer Session Available **Enrollment:** FT 13,619, PT 1,932, Grad FT 2,642, Grad PT 2,157 **Faculty:** FT 958, PT 136 **Student-Faculty Ratio:** 16:1 **Exams:** SAT I or ACT. **% Receiving Financial Aid:** 60 **% Residing in College-Owned, -Operated, or -Affiliated Housing:** 25 **Final Year or Final Semester Residency Requirement:** No **Library Holdings:** 3,513,542 **Regional Accreditation:** North Central Association of Colleges and Schools **Credit Hours For Degree:** 60 semester hours, Associates; 120 semester hours, Bachelors **ROTC:** Army, Air Force **Professional Accreditation:** AACSB, ABET, ACEJMC, ABA, ABFSE, ACA, ADA, ADtA, APTA, APA, ASLHA, AALS, CARC, FIDER, CORE, CSWE, JRCEPAT, LCMEAMA, NAACLS, NASAD NASM, NASPAA, NAST, NCATE, NRPA, SAF, NAIT **Intercollegiate Athletics:** Baseball M; Basketball M & W; Cheerleading M & W; Cross-Country Running M & W; Football M; Golf M & W; Softball W; Swimming and Diving M & W; Tennis M & W; Track and Field M & W; Volleyball W

SOUTHERN ILLINOIS UNIVERSITY EDWARDSVILLE
Edwardsville, IL 62026-0001
Tel: (618)650-2000; Free: 800-447-SIUE
Admissions: (618)650-3705
Fax: (618)692-2081
E-mail: admissions@siue.edu
Web Site: http://www.siue.edu/
President/CEO: Dr. Vaughn Vandegrift
Admissions: Todd Burrell
Financial Aid: Sharon Berry
Type: Comprehensive **Sex:** Coed **Affiliation:** Southern Illinois University **Scores:** 54.9% ACT 18-23; 34.8% ACT 24-29 **% Accepted:** 84 **Admission Plans:** Early Admission; Deferred Admission **Application Deadline:** May 1 **Application Fee:** $30.00 **H.S. Requirements:** High school diploma required; GED accepted **Costs Per Year:** Application fee: $30. State resident tuition: $6201 full-time, $206.70 per semester hour part-time. Nonresident tuition: $15,503 full-time. Mandatory fees: $2135 full-time, $250.60 per semester hour part-time. Full-time tuition and fees vary according to course load. Part-time tuition and fees vary according to course load. College room and board: $7461. Room and board charges vary according to board plan and housing facility. Tuition guaranteed not to increase for student's term of enrollment. **Scholarships:** Available **Calendar System:** Semester, Summer Session Available **Enrollment:** FT 9,491, PT 1,653, Grad FT 1,232, Grad PT 1,564 **Faculty:** FT 622, PT 248 **Student-Faculty Ratio:** 17:1 **Exams:** SAT I or ACT. **% Receiving Financial Aid:** 63 **% Residing in College-Owned, -Operated, or -Affiliated Housing:** 30 **Library Holdings:** 1,413,823 **Regional Accreditation:** North Central Association of Colleges and Schools **Credit Hours For Degree:** 124 semester hours, Bachelors **ROTC:** Army, Air Force **Professional Accreditation:** AACSB, ABET, ACPhE, ACEJMC, AACN, AANA, ACCE, ADA, ASLHA, CSWE, NAACLS, NASM, NASPAA, NCATE, NLN **Intercollegiate Athletics:** Baseball M; Basketball M & W; Cross-Country Running M & W; Golf M & W; Soccer M & W; Softball W; Tennis M & W; Track and Field M & W; Volleyball W; Wrestling M

SOUTHWESTERN ILLINOIS COLLEGE
2500 Carlyle Rd.
Belleville, IL 62221-5899
Tel: (618)235-2700
Fax: (618)235-1578
Web Site: http://www.southwestern.cc.il.us/
President/CEO: Georgia Costello
Admissions: Mike Leiker
Type: Two-Year College **Sex:** Coed **Affiliation:** Illinois Community College Board **Admission Plans:** Open Admission; Early Admission; Deferred Admission **Application Deadline:** Rolling **Application Fee:** $10.00 **H.S. Requirements:** High school diploma required; GED accepted **Scholarships:** Available **Calendar System:** Semester, Summer Session Available **Enrollment:** FT 5,296, PT 9,183 **Faculty:** FT 125, PT 704 **Student-Faculty Ratio:** 17:1 **Exams:** Other. **Library Holdings:** 82,537 **Regional Accreditation:** North Central Association of Colleges and Schools **Credit Hours For Degree:** 64 credit hours, Associates **ROTC:** Army, Air Force **Professional Accreditation:** AAMAE, ACF, AHIMA, APTA, ACBSP, CARC, JRCERT, NAACLS, NLN **Intercollegiate Athletics:** Baseball M; Basketball M & W; Soccer M; Softball W; Tennis M & W; Volleyball W

SPOON RIVER COLLEGE
23235 North County 22
Canton, IL 61520-9801
Tel: (309)647-4645
Fax: (309)649-6235
E-mail: info@spoonrivercollege.edu
Web Site: http://www.spoonrivercollege.net/
President/CEO: Dr. Robert Ritschel
Admissions: Missy Wilkinson
Type: Two-Year College **Sex:** Coed **Affiliation:** Illinois Community College Board **Scores:** 52% ACT 18-23; 12% ACT 24-29 **Admission Plans:** Open Admission; Early Admission **Application Deadline:** Rolling **Application Fee:** $0.00 **H.S. Requirements:** High school diploma required; GED accepted **Costs Per Year:** Application fee: $0. Area resident tuition: $2670 full-time, $89 per credit hour part-time. State resident tuition: $6300 full-time, $210 per credit hour part-time. Nonresident tuition: $7380 full-time, $246 per credit hour part-time. Full-time tuition varies according to course load. Part-time tuition varies according to course load. **Scholarships:** Available **Calendar System:** Semester, Summer Session Available **Enrollment:** FT 1,053, PT 1,280 **Faculty:** FT 41, PT 101 **Student-Faculty Ratio:** 20:1 **Library Holdings:** 34,799 **Regional Accreditation:** North Central Association of Colleges and Schools **Credit Hours For Degree:** 64 semester hours, Associates **ROTC:** Army **Intercollegiate Athletics:** Baseball M; Basketball M & W; Softball W; Track and Field M & W; Volleyball W

SPRINGFIELD COLLEGE IN ILLINOIS
1500 North Fifth St.
Springfield, IL 62702
Tel: (217)525-1420; Free: 800-635-7289
Fax: (217)789-1698
E-mail: khinkle@sci.edu
Web Site: http://www.sci.edu/
President/CEO: Michael D. Bromberg
Admissions: Kevin Hinkle
Type: Two-Year College **Sex:** Coed **Affiliation:** Roman Catholic Church **Application Deadline:** Rolling **Application Fee:** $20.00 **H.S. Requirements:** High school diploma required; GED accepted **Scholarships:** Available **Calendar System:** Semester, Summer Session Available **Enrollment:** FT 286, PT 322 **Faculty:** FT 25, PT 44 **Student-Faculty Ratio:** 10:1 **Exams:** SAT I and SAT II or ACT. **Library Holdings:** 19,951 **Regional Accreditation:** North Central Association of Colleges and Schools **Credit Hours For Degree:** 60 semester hours, Associates **Intercollegiate Athletics:** Baseball M; Golf M; Soccer M & W; Softball W; Volleyball W

TAYLOR BUSINESS INSTITUTE
318 West Adams
Chicago, IL 60606
Tel: (312)658-5100
Fax: (312)658-0867
Web Site: http://www.tbiil.edu/
President/CEO: Janice C. Parker
Type: Two-Year College **Sex:** Coed **% Accepted:** 78 **Application Fee:** $25.00 **Professional Accreditation:** ACICS

TELSHE YESHIVA—CHICAGO
3535 West Foster Ave.
Chicago, IL 60625-5598
Tel: (773)463-7738
President/CEO: Rabbi Avrohom C. Levin
Type: Comprehensive **Sex:** Men **Affiliation:** Jewish **% Accepted:** 100 **Application Fee:** $100.00 **H.S. Requirements:** High school diploma required; GED not accepted **Calendar System:** Semester, Summer Session Available **Credit Hours For Degree:** 150 credits, Bachelors **Professional Accreditation:** AARTS

TRINITY CHRISTIAN COLLEGE
6601 West College Dr.
Palos Heights, IL 60463-0929
Tel: (708)597-3000; Free: 800-748-0085
Admissions: (708)239-4708
Fax: (708)239-3995
E-mail: admissions@trnty.edu
Web Site: http://www.trnty.edu/
President/CEO: Dr. Steven Timmermans
Admissions: Jeremy Klyn
Financial Aid: L. Denise Coleman
Type: Four-Year College **Sex:** Coed **Affiliation:** Christian Reformed **Scores:** 100% SAT V 400+; 94% SAT M 400+; 36% ACT 18-23; 32% ACT 24-29 **% Accepted:** 86 **Admission Plans:** Deferred Admission **Application Deadline:** Rolling **Application Fee:** $20.00 **H.S. Requirements:** High school diploma required; GED accepted **Costs Per Year:** Application fee: $20. Comprehensive fee: $29,460 includes full-time tuition ($21,225), mandatory fees ($110), and college room and board ($8125). College room only: $4225. Room and board charges vary according to board plan. Part-time tuition: $710 per semester hour. Part-time tuition varies according to course load. **Scholarships:** Available **Calendar System:** Semester, Summer Session Not available **Enrollment:** FT 1,081, PT 369 **Faculty:** FT 79, PT 72 **Student-Faculty Ratio:** 12:1 **Exams:** ACT, SAT I or ACT. **% Receiving Financial Aid:** 86 **% Residing in College-Owned, -Operated, or -Affiliated Housing:** 61 **Library Holdings:** 66,232 **Regional Accreditation:** North Central Association of Colleges and Schools **Credit Hours For Degree:** 125 credit hours, Bachelors **Professional Accreditation:** AACN, ACBSP, NLN **Intercollegiate Athletics:** Baseball M; Basketball M & W; Cross-Country Running M & W; Soccer M & W; Softball W; Track and Field M & W; Volleyball W

TRINITY COLLEGE OF NURSING AND HEALTH SCIENCES
2122 25th Ave.
Rock Island, IL 61201
Tel: (309)779-7700
Fax: (309)779-7796
E-mail: kimpeb@trintyqc.com
Web Site: http://www.trinitycollegeqc.edu/
President/CEO: Lori Rodrigues-Fisher, EdD
Admissions: Barbara Kimpe
Financial Aid: Kris Hodgerson
Type: Four-Year College **Sex:** Coed **Affiliation:** Trinity Medical Center **Scores:** 90% ACT 18-23; 5% ACT 24-29 **% Accepted:** 33 **Admission Plans:** Preferred Admission **Application Deadline:** Rolling **Application Fee:** $50.00 **H.S. Requirements:** High school diploma required; GED accepted **Costs Per Year:** Application fee: $50. Tuition: $4836 full-time, $403 per credit hour part-time. Mandatory fees: $350 full-time. Full-time tuition and fees vary according to degree level. Part-time tuition varies according to degree level. **Scholarships:** Available **Calendar System:** Semester, Summer Session Available **Enrollment:** FT 108, PT 103 **Faculty:** FT 13, PT 5 **Student-Faculty Ratio:** 10:1 **Exams:** SAT I or ACT. **% Receiving Financial Aid:** 85 **Library Holdings:** 8,500 **Regional Accreditation:** North Central Association of Colleges and Schools **Credit Hours For Degree:** 70 credits, Associates; 122 credits, Bachelors

TRINITY INTERNATIONAL UNIVERSITY
2065 Half Day Rd.
Deerfield, IL 60015-1284
Tel: (847)945-8800; Free: 800-822-3225
Admissions: (847)317-7000
Fax: (847)317-7081
E-mail: tcadmissions@tiu.edu
Web Site: http://www.tiu.edu/
President/CEO: Dr. Jeanette Hsieh
Admissions: Aaron Mahl
Financial Aid: Pat Coles
Type: University **Sex:** Coed **Affiliation:** Evangelical Free Church of America; Evangelical Free Church of America **Scores:** 89% SAT V 400+; 93% SAT M 400+; 50% ACT 18-23; 29% ACT 24-29 **% Accepted:** 63 **Admission Plans:** Deferred Admission **Application Deadline:** Rolling **Application Fee:** $25.00 **H.S. Requirements:** High school diploma required; GED accepted **Costs Per Year:** Application fee: $25. Comprehensive fee: $29,410 includes full-time tuition ($21,980) and college room and board ($7430). College room only: $4050. **Scholarships:** Available **Calendar System:** Semester, Summer Session Not available **Enrollment:** FT 841, PT 127 **Faculty:** FT 43, PT 39 **Student-Faculty Ratio:** 12:1 **Exams:** SAT I or ACT. **% Receiving Financial Aid:** 77 **% Residing in College-Owned, -Operated, or -Affiliated Housing:** 70 **Library Holdings:** 266,586 **Regional Accreditation:** North Central Association of Colleges and Schools **Credit Hours For Degree:** 126 hours, Bachelors **Professional Accreditation:** ATS **Intercollegiate Athletics:** Baseball M; Basketball M & W; Football M; Soccer M & W; Softball W; Track and Field M & W; Volleyball W

TRITON COLLEGE
2000 5th Ave.
River Grove, IL 60171
Tel: (708)456-0300; Free: 800-942-7404
Fax: (708)583-3121
E-mail: mpatrice@triton.edu
Web Site: http://www.triton.edu/
President/CEO: Dr. Patricia Granados
Admissions: Mary-Rita Moore
Type: Two-Year College **Sex:** Coed **Affiliation:** Illinois Community College Board **Admission Plans:** Open Admission; Preferred Admission; Deferred Admission **Application Deadline:** Rolling **Application Fee:** $10.00 **H.S. Requirements:** High school diploma required; GED accepted **Scholarships:** Available **Calendar System:** Semester, Summer Session Available **Enrollment:** FT 3,893, PT 11,765 **Faculty:** FT 123, PT 521 **Student-Faculty Ratio:** 24:1 **Library Holdings:** 70,859 **Regional Accreditation:** North Central Association of Colleges and Schools **Credit Hours For Degree:** 64 credit hours, Associates **Professional Accreditation:** CARC, JCAHPO, JRCEDMS, JRCERT, JRCNMT, NLN **Intercollegiate Athletics:** Baseball M; Basketball M & W; Soccer M; Softball W; Volleyball W; Wrestling M

UNIVERSITY OF CHICAGO
5801 South Ellis Ave.
Chicago, IL 60637-1513

Tel: (773)702-1234
Admissions: (773)702-8650
Fax: (773)702-4199
E-mail: collegeadmissions@uchicago.edu
Web Site: http://www.uchicago.edu/
President/CEO: Robert Zimmer
Admissions: James G. Nondorf
Type: University **Sex:** Coed **Scores:** 100% SAT V 400+; 100% SAT M 400+; 5% ACT 18-23; 28% ACT 24-29 **% Accepted:** 27 **Admission Plans:** Early Admission; Early Action; Deferred Admission **Application Deadline:** January 2 **Application Fee:** $65.00 **H.S. Requirements:** High school diploma or equivalent not required **Costs Per Year:** Application fee: $65. Comprehensive fee: $51,129 includes full-time tuition ($38,550), mandatory fees ($882), and college room and board ($11,697). Room and board charges vary according to board plan and housing facility. **Scholarships:** Available **Calendar System:** Quarter, Summer Session Available **Enrollment:** FT 5,017, PT 49, Grad FT 4,387, Grad PT 2,879 **Faculty:** FT 1,082, PT 580 **Student-Faculty Ratio:** 6:1 **Exams:** SAT I or ACT. ACT essay not being used. SAT essay not being used. **% Receiving Financial Aid:** 49 **Library Holdings:** 7,000,000 **Regional Accreditation:** North Central Association of Colleges and Schools **Credit Hours For Degree:** 42 courses, Bachelors **ROTC:** Army, Air Force **Professional Accreditation:** AACSB, ABA, APA, ACIPE, AALS, ATS, CSWE, LCMEAMA **Intercollegiate Athletics:** Baseball M; Basketball M & W; Cross-Country Running M & W; Football M; Soccer M & W; Softball W; Swimming and Diving M & W; Tennis M & W; Track and Field M & W; Volleyball W; Wrestling M

UNIVERSITY OF ILLINOIS AT CHICAGO
601 South Morgan St.
Chicago, IL 60607-7128
Tel: (312)996-7000
Admissions: (312)996-5133
E-mail: uic.admit@uic.edu
Web Site: http://www.uic.edu/
President/CEO: Dr. Paula Allen-Meares
Admissions: Thomas Glenn
Financial Aid: Deidre Rush
Type: University **Sex:** Coed **Affiliation:** University of Illinois System **Scores:** 46.9% ACT 18-23; 44.1% ACT 24-29 **% Accepted:** 63 **Application Deadline:** January 15 **Application Fee:** $40.00 **H.S. Requirements:** High school diploma required; GED accepted **Costs Per Year:** Application fee: $40. State resident tuition: $8342 full-time, $1390 per term part-time. Nonresident tuition: $20,732 full-time, $3455 per term part-time. Mandatory fees: $3692 full-time, $1147 per term part-time. Full-time tuition and fees vary according to program. Part-time tuition and fees vary according to course load and program. College room and board: $9435. College room only: $6650. Room and board charges vary according to board plan and housing facility. Tuition guaranteed not to increase for student's term of enrollment. **Scholarships:** Available **Calendar System:** Semester, Summer Session Available **Enrollment:** FT 14,898, PT 1,146, Grad FT 6,072, Grad PT 4,724 **Faculty:** FT 1,160, PT 380 **Student-Faculty Ratio:** 18:1 **Exams:** SAT I or ACT, SAT I and SAT II or ACT, SAT II. **% Receiving Financial Aid:** 62 **% Residing in College-Owned, -Operated, or -Affiliated Housing:** 21 **Final Year or Final Semester Residency Requirement:** No **Library Holdings:** 3,324,390 **Regional Accreditation:** North Central Association of Colleges and Schools **Credit Hours For Degree:** 120 semester hours, Bachelors **ROTC:** Army, Navy, Air Force **Professional Accreditation:** AACSB, ABET, ACPhE, ARCMI, AABB, AACN, ACNM, ADA, ADtA, AHIMA, ACSP, AOTA, APTA, APA, CEPH, CSWE, LCMEAMA, NAAB, NASAD, NASPAA **Intercollegiate Athletics:** Baseball M; Basketball M & W; Cross-Country Running M & W; Gymnastics M & W; Soccer M; Softball W; Swimming and Diving M & W; Tennis M & W; Track and Field M & W; Volleyball W

UNIVERSITY OF ILLINOIS AT SPRINGFIELD
One University Plaza
Springfield, IL 62703-5407
Tel: (217)206-6600; Free: 888-977-4847
Admissions: (217)206-4847
Fax: (217)206-7279
E-mail: admissions@uis.edu
Web Site: http://www.uis.edu/
President/CEO: Dr. Richard D. Ringeisen
Admissions: Dr. Lori Giordano
Financial Aid: Gerard Joseph
Type: Comprehensive **Sex:** Coed **Affiliation:** University of Illinois System **Scores:** 47.2% ACT 18-23; 37% ACT 24-29 **% Accepted:** 58 **Admission Plans:** Deferred Admission **Application Deadline:** Rolling **Application Fee:** $40.00 **H.S. Requirements:** High school diploma required; GED accepted **Costs Per Year:** Application fee: $40. State resident tuition: $7402 full-time, $246.75 per credit hour part-time. Nonresident tuition: $16,552 full-time, $551.75 per credit hour part-time. Mandatory fees: $2130 full-time, $5 per credit hour part-time, $726.50 per term part-time. Full-time tuition and fees vary according to course load. Part-time tuition and fees vary according to course load. College room and board: $9200. College room only: $6250. Room and board charges vary according to board plan and housing facility. Tuition guaranteed not to increase for student's term of enrollment. **Scholarships:** Available **Calendar System:** Semester, Summer Session Available **Enrollment:** FT 1,954, PT 1,073, Grad FT 504, Grad PT 1,430 **Faculty:** FT 211, PT 147 **Student-Faculty Ratio:** 13:1 **Exams:** SAT I or ACT. ACT essay not being used. SAT essay not being used. **% Receiving Financial Aid:** 61 **% Residing in College-Owned, -Operated, or -Affiliated Housing:** 27 **Library Holdings:** 612,417 **Regional Accreditation:** North Central Association of Colleges and Schools **Credit Hours For Degree:** 120 semester hours, Bachelors **Professional Accreditation:** AACSB, ACA, CSWE, NAACLS, NASPAA **Intercollegiate Athletics:** Baseball M; Basketball M & W; Cheerleading W; Golf M & W; Soccer M & W; Softball W; Tennis M & W; Volleyball W

UNIVERSITY OF ILLINOIS AT URBANA—CHAMPAIGN
601 East John St.
Champaign, IL 61820
Tel: (217)333-1000
Admissions: (217)333-0302
Fax: (217)244-7278
E-mail: ugradadmissions@uiuc.edu
Web Site: http://www.illinois.edu/
President/CEO: Dr. Richard Herman
Admissions: Stacey Kostell
Financial Aid: Daniel Mann
Type: University **Sex:** Coed **Affiliation:** University of Illinois System **Scores:** 98.68% SAT V 400+; 99.68% SAT M 400+; 9.86% ACT 18-23; 50.03% ACT 24-29 **% Accepted:** 65 **Admission Plans:** Early Admission; Deferred Admission **Application Deadline:** January 2 **Application Fee:** $40.00 **H.S. Requirements:** High school diploma required; GED accepted **Costs Per Year:** Application fee: $40. State resident tuition: $9484 full-time. Nonresident tuition: $23,626 full-time. Mandatory fees: $3176 full-time. Full-time tuition and fees vary according to course load, program, and student level. College room and board: $9284. Room and board charges vary according to board plan, housing facility, and location. Tuition guaranteed not to increase for student's term of enrollment. **Scholarships:** Available **Calendar System:** Semester, Summer Session Available **Enrollment:** FT 30,639, PT 838, Grad FT 9,238, Grad PT 3,166 **Faculty:** FT 1,880, PT 57 **Student-Faculty Ratio:** 16:1 **Exams:** SAT I or ACT. ACT essay used for admission. SAT essay used for admission. **% Receiving Financial Aid:** 42 **% Residing in College-Owned, -Operated, or -Affiliated Housing:** 50 **Regional Accreditation:** North Central Association of Colleges and Schools **Credit Hours For Degree:** 120 semester hours, Bachelors **ROTC:** Army, Navy, Air Force **Professional Accreditation:** AACSB, ABET, ACEJMC, ABA, ADtA, ACSP, ALA, APA, ASLA, ASLHA, AVMA, AALS, CORE, CSWE, JRCEPAT, NAAB, NASAD, NASD, NASM, NAST NRPA, SAF **Intercollegiate Athletics:** Baseball M; Basketball M & W; Cheerleading M & W; Cross-Country Running M & W; Football M; Golf M & W; Gymnastics M & W; Soccer W; Softball W; Swimming and Diving W; Tennis M & W; Track and Field M & W; Volleyball W; Wrestling M

UNIVERSITY OF PHOENIX—CHICAGO CAMPUS
1500 McConner Parkway
Ste. 700
Schaumburg, IL 60173-4399
Tel: (847)413-1922; Free: 800-228-7240
Admissions: (480)557-6151
Fax: (847)413-8706
E-mail: audra.mcquarie@phoenix.edu
Web Site: http://www.phoenix.edu/
President/CEO: William Pepicello
Admissions: Audra McQuarie
Type: Comprehensive **Sex:** Coed **Admission Plans:** Open Admission; Deferred Admission **Application Deadline:** Rolling **Application Fee:** $0.00

H.S. Requirements: High school diploma required; GED accepted **Costs Per Year:** Application fee: $0. Tuition: $12,225 full-time. Full-time tuition varies according to course level and course load. **Scholarships:** Available **Calendar System:** Continuous, Summer Session Not available **Enrollment:** FT 1,025 **Faculty:** FT 16, PT 175 **Regional Accreditation:** North Central Association of Colleges and Schools **Credit Hours For Degree:** 60 credits, Associates; 120 credits, Bachelors

UNIVERSITY OF ST. FRANCIS
500 Wilcox St.
Joliet, IL 60435-6169
Tel: (815)740-3400; Free: 800-735-7500
Fax: (815)740-4285
E-mail: jmarlatt@stfrancis.edu
Web Site: http://www.stfrancis.edu/
President/CEO: Dr. Michael J. Vinciguerra
Admissions: Julie Marlatt
Financial Aid: Mary V. Shaw
Type: Comprehensive **Sex:** Coed **Affiliation:** Roman Catholic **Scores:** 53% ACT 18-23; 40% ACT 24-29 **% Accepted:** 50 **Admission Plans:** Deferred Admission **Application Deadline:** August 1 **Application Fee:** $30.00 **H.S. Requirements:** High school diploma required; GED accepted **Costs Per Year:** Application fee: $30. Comprehensive fee: $30,636 includes full-time tuition ($22,288), mandatory fees ($410), and college room and board ($7938). Room and board charges vary according to board plan and housing facility. Part-time tuition: $743 per credit hour. **Scholarships:** Available **Calendar System:** Semester, Summer Session Available **Enrollment:** FT 1,210, PT 66, Grad FT 145, Grad PT 736 **Faculty:** FT 88, PT 147 **Student-Faculty Ratio:** 12:1 **Exams:** SAT I or ACT. **% Receiving Financial Aid:** 81 **% Residing in College-Owned, -Operated, or -Affiliated Housing:** 30 **Final Year or Final Semester Residency Requirement:** No **Library Holdings:** 134,400 **Regional Accreditation:** North Central Association of Colleges and Schools **Credit Hours For Degree:** 128 credits, Bachelors **Professional Accreditation:** AACN, ACBSP, CSWE, NCATE, NLN, NRPA **Intercollegiate Athletics:** Baseball M; Basketball M & W; Cheerleading W; Cross-Country Running M & W; Football M; Golf M & W; Soccer M & W; Softball W; Tennis M & W; Track and Field M & W; Volleyball W

VANDERCOOK COLLEGE OF MUSIC
3140 South Federal St.
Chicago, IL 60616-3731
Tel: (312)225-6288; Free: 800-448-2655
Fax: (312)225-5211
E-mail: admissions@vandercook.edu
Web Site: http://www.vandercook.edu/
President/CEO: Dr. Charles Menghini
Admissions: Amy Lenting
Financial Aid: D. Denny
Type: Comprehensive **Sex:** Coed **Scores:** 100% SAT M 400+; 56% ACT 18-23; 24% ACT 24-29 **% Accepted:** 98 **Admission Plans:** Deferred Admission **Application Deadline:** Rolling **Application Fee:** $35.00 **H.S. Requirements:** High school diploma required; GED accepted **Costs Per Year:** Application fee: $35. Comprehensive fee: $32,114 includes full-time tuition ($21,060), mandatory fees ($960), and college room and board ($10,094). College room only: $5384. Part-time tuition: $855 per semester hour. **Scholarships:** Available **Calendar System:** Semester, Summer Session Not available **Enrollment:** FT 135, PT 40, Grad FT 20, Grad PT 208 **Faculty:** FT 13, PT 17 **Student-Faculty Ratio:** 8:1 **Exams:** SAT I or ACT. SAT essay used for admission. SAT essay used for advising. SAT essay used for placement. **Library Holdings:** 13,000 **Regional Accreditation:** North Central Association of Colleges and Schools **Credit Hours For Degree:** 140.5 semester hours, Bachelors **Professional Accreditation:** NASM

VET TECH INSTITUTE AT FOX COLLEGE
18020 South Oak Park Ave.
Tinley Park, IL 60477
Tel: (708)444-4500
Admissions: 888-884-3694
Web Site: http://www.vettechinstitute.edu/camp_fox.php
Type: Two-Year College **Sex:** Coed **% Accepted:** 61 **Professional Accreditation:** AVMA

WAUBONSEE COMMUNITY COLLEGE
Route 47 at Waubonsee Dr.
Sugar Grove, IL 60554-9799
Tel: (630)466-7900
Fax: (630)466-4964
E-mail: recruitment@waubonsee.edu
Web Site: http://www.waubonsee.edu/
President/CEO: Christine J. Sobek
Type: Two-Year College **Sex:** Coed **Affiliation:** Illinois Community College Board **% Accepted:** 100 **Admission Plans:** Open Admission; Preferred Admission **Application Deadline:** Rolling **Application Fee:** $0.00 **H.S. Requirements:** High school diploma or equivalent not required. For financial aid recipients: High school diploma required; GED accepted **Costs Per Year:** Application fee: $0. Area resident tuition: $2550 full-time, $85 per semester hour part-time. State resident tuition: $7877 full-time, $263 per semester hour part-time. Nonresident tuition: $8688 full-time, $290 per semester hour part-time. Mandatory fees: $150 full-time, $5 per semester hour part-time. Full-time tuition and fees vary according to course load. Part-time tuition and fees vary according to course load. **Scholarships:** Available **Calendar System:** Semester, Summer Session Available **Enrollment:** FT 2,624, PT 6,210 **Faculty:** FT 92, PT 785 **Student-Faculty Ratio:** 17:1 **Library Holdings:** 53,679 **Regional Accreditation:** North Central Association of Colleges and Schools **Credit Hours For Degree:** 64 semester hours, Associates **ROTC:** Army **Intercollegiate Athletics:** Baseball M; Basketball M & W; Cross-Country Running M & W; Golf M; Soccer M; Softball W; Tennis M & W; Volleyball W; Wrestling M

WEST SUBURBAN COLLEGE OF NURSING
3 Erie Ct.
Oak Park, IL 60302
Tel: (708)763-6530
Fax: (708)763-1531
Web Site: http://www.wscn.edu/
President/CEO: Dr. Steven Langdon
Admissions: Cynthia Valdez
Financial Aid: Shirley Howell
Type: Two-Year Upper Division **Sex:** Coed **Admission Plans:** Deferred Admission **Application Fee:** $30.00 **H.S. Requirements:** High school diploma required; GED accepted **Costs Per Year:** Application fee: $30. Tuition: $20,986 full-time, $711 per credit hour part-time. Mandatory fees: $550 full-time, $135 per term part-time. Full-time tuition and fees vary according to program. Part-time tuition and fees vary according to course load and program. **Scholarships:** Available **Calendar System:** Semester, Summer Session Available **Enrollment:** FT 189, PT 47, Grad PT 16 **Faculty:** FT 23, PT 2 **Student-Faculty Ratio:** 10:1 **% Receiving Financial Aid:** 80 **Regional Accreditation:** North Central Association of Colleges and Schools **Credit Hours For Degree:** 120 semester hours, Bachelors **Professional Accreditation:** AACN, NLN

WESTERN ILLINOIS UNIVERSITY
1 University Circle
Macomb, IL 61455-1390
Tel: (309)298-1414; Free: 877-742-5948
Admissions: (309)298-3157
Fax: (309)298-3111
E-mail: e-campbell@wiu.edu
Web Site: http://www.wiu.edu/
President/CEO: Dr. Al Goldfarb
Admissions: Eric Campbell
Type: Comprehensive **Sex:** Coed **Scores:** 66% ACT 18-23; 21% ACT 24-29 **% Accepted:** 64 **Admission Plans:** Deferred Admission **Application Deadline:** May 15 **Application Fee:** $30.00 **H.S. Requirements:** High school diploma required; GED accepted **Costs Per Year:** Application fee: $30. State resident tuition: $6779 full-time, $226 per credit hour part-time. Nonresident tuition: $10,168 full-time, $339 per credit hour part-time. Mandatory fees: $2179 full-time, $72.62 per credit hour part-time. Full-time tuition and fees vary according to course load, location, and student level. Part-time tuition and fees vary according to course load, location, and student level. College room and board: $7642. College room only: $4612. Room and board charges vary according to board plan, housing facility, and student level. Tuition guaranteed not to increase for student's term of enrollment. **Scholarships:** Available **Calendar System:** Semester, Summer Session Available **Enrollment:** FT 9,556, PT 997, Grad FT 890, Grad PT 1,236 **Faculty:** FT 672, PT 82 **Student-Faculty Ratio:** 16:1 **Exams:** SAT I or ACT.

% Receiving Financial Aid: 65 **% Residing in College-Owned, -Operated, or -Affiliated Housing:** 44 **Final Year or Final Semester Residency Requirement:** Yes **Library Holdings:** 998,041 **Regional Accreditation:** North Central Association of Colleges and Schools **Credit Hours For Degree:** 120 credit hours, Bachelors **ROTC:** Army **Professional Accreditation:** AACSB, AAFCS, ACA, ASLHA, CSWE, JRCEPAT, NASM, NAST, NCATE, NRPA **Intercollegiate Athletics:** Baseball M; Basketball M & W; Cross-Country Running M & W; Football M; Golf M & W; Soccer M & W; Softball W; Swimming and Diving M & W; Tennis M & W; Track and Field M & W; Volleyball W

WESTWOOD COLLEGE—CHICAGO DU PAGE
7155 Janes Ave.
Woodridge, IL 60517
Tel: (630)434-8244
Admissions: (630)434-8250
Fax: (630)434-8255
Web Site: http://www.westwood.edu/
President/CEO: Kelly Thumm Moore
Financial Aid: Patty Zavala
Type: Four-Year College **Sex:** Coed **Scholarships:** Available **Calendar System:** Continuous **Professional Accreditation:** ACICS

WESTWOOD COLLEGE—CHICAGO LOOP CAMPUS
17 North State St., Ste. 300
Chicago, IL 60602
Tel: (312)739-0850
Fax: (312)739-1004
Web Site: http://www.westwood.edu/
President/CEO: Brian Olson
Type: Four-Year College **Sex:** Coed **Professional Accreditation:** ACICS

WESTWOOD COLLEGE—CHICAGO O'HARE AIRPORT
8501 West Higgins Rd.
Ste. 100
Chicago, IL 60631
Tel: (773)380-6801
Web Site: http://www.westwood.edu/
Type: Four-Year College **Sex:** Coed **Scholarships:** Available **Calendar System:** Continuous **Professional Accreditation:** ACCSCT, ACICS

WESTWOOD COLLEGE—CHICAGO RIVER OAKS
80 River Oaks Dr.
Ste. D-49
Calumet City, IL 60409
Tel: (708)832-1988
Fax: (708)832-9617
Web Site: http://www.westwood.edu/
President/CEO: Bruce McKenzie
Type: Four-Year College **Sex:** Coed **Scholarships:** Available **Calendar System:** Continuous **Professional Accreditation:** ACICS

WHEATON COLLEGE
501 College Ave.
Wheaton, IL 60187-5593
Tel: (630)752-5000; Free: 800-222-2419
Admissions: (630)752-5011
Fax: (630)752-5285
E-mail: admissions@wheaton.edu
Web Site: http://www.wheaton.edu/
President/CEO: Dr. Duane Litfin
Admissions: Shawn Leftwich
Financial Aid: Karen Belling
Type: Comprehensive **Sex:** Coed **Affiliation:** nondenominational **Scores:** 100% SAT V 400+; 100% SAT M 400+; 7.8% ACT 18-23; 48.7% ACT 24-29 **% Accepted:** 71 **Admission Plans:** Preferred Admission; Early Action **Application Deadline:** January 10 **Application Fee:** $50.00 **H.S. Requirements:** High school diploma required; GED accepted **Costs Per Year:** Application fee: $50. Comprehensive fee: $35,630 includes full-time tuition ($27,580) and college room and board ($8050). College room only: $4750. Part-time tuition: $1149 per credit hour. Part-time tuition varies according to course load. **Scholarships:** Available **Calendar System:** Semester, Summer Session Available **Enrollment:** FT 2,332, PT 67, Grad FT 251, Grad PT 270 **Faculty:** FT 202, PT 104 **Student-Faculty Ratio:** 11:1 **Exams:** SAT I or ACT. ACT essay used for admission. SAT essay used for admission. ACT essay used as a validity check on application essay. SAT essay used as a validity check on application essay. **% Receiving Financial Aid:** 54 **% Residing in College-Owned, -Operated, or -Affiliated Housing:** 90 **Final Year or Final Semester Residency Requirement:** Yes **Library Holdings:** 473,968 **Regional Accreditation:** North Central Association of Colleges and Schools **Credit Hours For Degree:** 124 hours, Bachelors **ROTC:** Army, Air Force **Professional Accreditation:** APA, NASM, NCATE **Intercollegiate Athletics:** Baseball M; Basketball M & W; Cheerleading W; Crew M & W; Cross-Country Running M & W; Football M; Golf M & W; Ice Hockey M; Lacrosse M & W; Soccer M & W; Softball W; Swimming and Diving M & W; Tennis M & W; Track and Field M & W; Volleyball M & W; Water Polo M & W; Wrestling M

WORSHAM COLLEGE OF MORTUARY SCIENCE
495 Northgate Parkway
Wheeling, IL 60090-2646
Tel: (847)808-8444
Fax: (847)808-8493
Web Site: http://www.worshamcollege.com/
President/CEO: Karl Kann
Type: Two-Year College **Sex:** Coed **Application Fee:** $30.00 **Costs Per Year:** Application fee: $30. Tuition: $16,606 full-time. Mandatory fees: $900 full-time. **Scholarships:** Available **Calendar System:** Quarter **Student-Faculty Ratio:** 21:1 **Professional Accreditation:** ABFSE

ANCILLA COLLEGE
Union Rd., PO Box 1
Donaldson, IN 46513
Tel: (574)936-8898
Fax: (574)935-1773
E-mail: admissions@ancilla.edu
Web Site: http://www.ancilla.edu/
President/CEO: Dr. Ronald L. May
Admissions: Erin Alonzo
Type: Two-Year College **Sex:** Coed **Affiliation:** Roman Catholic **Scores:** 60% SAT V 400+; 66% SAT M 400+; 40% ACT 18-23; 1% ACT 24-29 **% Accepted:** 80 **Admission Plans:** Open Admission **Application Deadline:** Rolling **Application Fee:** $0.00 **H.S. Requirements:** High school diploma required; GED accepted **Costs Per Year:** Application fee: $0. Tuition: $12,450 full-time, $415 per credit hour part-time. Mandatory fees: $230 full-time, $55 per term part-time. Full-time tuition and fees vary according to course load and program. Part-time tuition and fees vary according to course load and program. **Scholarships:** Available **Calendar System:** Semester, Summer Session Available **Enrollment:** FT 352, PT 159 **Faculty:** FT 22, PT 26 **Student-Faculty Ratio:** 13:1 **Exams:** SAT I or ACT. **Library Holdings:** 27,859 **Regional Accreditation:** North Central Association of Colleges and Schools **Credit Hours For Degree:** 64 semester hours, Associates **Intercollegiate Athletics:** Baseball M; Basketball M & W; Cheerleading M & W; Golf M & W; Soccer M; Softball W; Volleyball W

ANDERSON UNIVERSITY
1100 East Fifth St.
Anderson, IN 46012-3495
Tel: (765)649-9071; Free: 800-428-6414
Admissions: (765)641-4080
Fax: (765)641-3851
E-mail: info@anderson.edu
Web Site: http://www.anderson.edu/
President/CEO: Dr. James L. Edwards
Admissions: Jim King
Financial Aid: Kenneth Nieman
Type: Comprehensive **Sex:** Coed **Affiliation:** Church of God **Scores:** 91% SAT V 400+; 92% SAT M 400+; 44% ACT 18-23; 41% ACT 24-29 **% Accepted:** 60 **Admission Plans:** Deferred Admission **Application Deadline:** July 1 **Application Fee:** $25.00 **H.S. Requirements:** High school diploma required; GED accepted **Costs Per Year:** Application fee: $25. Comprehensive fee: $32,320 includes full-time tuition ($23,940), mandatory fees ($30), and college room and board ($8350). College room only: $5350. Room and board charges vary according to board plan and housing facility. Part-time tuition: $998 per semester hour. Part-time tuition varies according to course load. **Scholarships:** Available **Calendar System:** Semester, Summer Session Available **Enrollment:** FT 1,927, PT 207, Grad FT 99, Grad PT 458 **Faculty:** FT 138, PT 166 **Student-Faculty Ratio:** 12:1 **Exams:** SAT I or ACT. ACT essay used for advising. SAT essay used for advising. ACT essay used for placement. SAT essay used for placement. **% Receiving Financial Aid:** 81 **% Residing in College-Owned, -Operated, or -Affiliated Housing:** 76 **Library Holdings:** 307,239 **Regional Accreditation:** North Central Association of Colleges and Schools **Credit Hours For Degree:** 62 semester hours, Associates; 124 semester hours, Bachelors **Professional Accreditation:** ACIPE, ACBSP, ATS, CSWE, JRCEPAT, NASM, NCATE, NLN **Intercollegiate Athletics:** Baseball M; Basketball M & W; Cross-Country Running M & W; Football M; Golf M & W; Soccer M & W; Softball W; Tennis M & W; Track and Field M & W; Volleyball W

THE ART INSTITUTE OF INDIANAPOLIS
3500 Depauw Blvd.
Ste. 1010
Indianapolis, IN 46268
Tel: (317)613-4800
Web Site: http://www.artinstitutes.edu/indianapolis/
President/CEO: Madeleine Slutsky
Type: Four-Year College **Sex:** Coed **Affiliation:** Education Management Corporation **Professional Accreditation:** ACICS

AVIATION INSTITUTE OF MAINTENANCE—INDIANAPOLIS
7251 West McCarty St.
Indianapolis, IN 46241
Tel: (317)243-4519; Free: 888-349-5387
Fax: (317)243-4569
Web Site: http://www.aviationmaintenance.edu/
President/CEO: Mark Holloway
Type: Two-Year College **Sex:** Coed **Admission Plans:** Open Admission **Application Fee:** $25.00 **Calendar System:** Semester **Professional Accreditation:** ACCSCT

BALL STATE UNIVERSITY
2000 West University Ave.
Muncie, IN 47306-1099
Tel: (765)289-1241; Free: 800-482-4BSU
Admissions: (765)285-8300
Fax: (765)285-1632
E-mail: askus@bsu.edu
Web Site: http://www.bsu.edu/
President/CEO: Dr. Jo Ann M. Gora
Admissions: Christopher T. Munchel
Financial Aid: John McPherson
Type: University **Sex:** Coed **Scores:** 98% SAT V 400+; 98% SAT M 400+; 65% ACT 18-23; 26% ACT 24-29 **% Accepted:** 74 **Admission Plans:** Deferred Admission **Application Deadline:** August 15 **Application Fee:** $25.00 **H.S. Requirements:** High school diploma required; GED accepted **Costs Per Year:** Application fee: $25. State resident tuition: $7228 full-time, $278 per credit hour part-time. Nonresident tuition: $19,796 full-time, $728 per credit hour part-time. Mandatory fees: $602 full-time. Full-time tuition and fees vary according to course level and reciprocity agreements. Part-time tuition varies according to course level and course load. College room and board: $7932. Room and board charges vary according to board plan and housing facility. **Scholarships:** Available **Calendar System:** Semester, Summer Session Available **Enrollment:** FT 16,412, PT 1,325, Grad FT 1,281, Grad PT 2,383 **Faculty:** FT 940, PT 240 **Student-Faculty Ratio:** 18:1 **Exams:** SAT I or ACT. ACT essay used for admission. SAT essay used for admission. ACT essay used for advising. SAT essay used for advising. ACT essay used for placement. SAT essay used for placement. **% Receiving Financial Aid:** 63 **% Residing in College-Owned, -Operated, or -Affiliated Housing:** 44 **Library Holdings:** 1,071,492 **Regional Accreditation:** North Central Association of Colleges and Schools **Credit Hours For Degree:** 63 credit hours, Associates; 126 credit hours, Bachelors **ROTC:**

Army **Professional Accreditation:** AACSB, ABET, ACEJMC, AACN, AAFCS, ACA, ADtA, ACSP, APA, ASLA, ASLHA, CORE, CSWE, JRCERT, JRCEPAT, NAAB, NASAD, NASM, NAST, NCATE NLN **Intercollegiate Athletics:** Baseball M & W; Basketball M & W; Bowling M & W; Cheerleading M & W; Cross-Country Running M & W; Equestrian Sports M & W; Fencing M & W; Field Hockey W; Football M; Golf M & W; Gymnastics W; Lacrosse M & W; Racquetball M & W; Rock Climbing M & W; Rugby M & W; Soccer M & W; Softball W; Swimming and Diving M & W; Tennis M & W; Track and Field W; Ultimate Frisbee M & W; Volleyball M & W; Water Polo M & W; Wrestling M

BETHEL COLLEGE
1001 Bethel Circle
Mishawaka, IN 46545-5591
Tel: (574)259-8511; Free: 800-422-4101
Admissions: (574)807-7600
Fax: (574)257-3326
E-mail: admissions@bethelcollege.edu
Web Site: http://www.bethelcollege.edu/
President/CEO: Dr. Steven R. Cramer
Admissions: Krista Wong
Financial Aid: Guy A. Fisher
Type: Comprehensive **Sex:** Coed **Affiliation:** Missionary Church **Scores:** 93% SAT V 400+; 92% SAT M 400+; 48% ACT 18-23; 33% ACT 24-29 **% Accepted:** 78 **Admission Plans:** Early Admission; Deferred Admission **Application Deadline:** August 15 **Application Fee:** $25.00 **H.S. Requirements:** High school diploma required; GED accepted **Costs Per Year:** Application fee: $25. One-time mandatory fee: $600. Comprehensive fee: $27,228 includes full-time tuition ($20,978) and college room and board ($6250). College room only: $3150. Full-time tuition varies according to program. Room and board charges vary according to board plan and housing facility. Part-time tuition: $450 per credit hour. Part-time tuition varies according to course load and program. **Scholarships:** Available **Calendar System:** Semester, Summer Session Available **Enrollment:** FT 1,482, PT 446, Grad FT 52, Grad PT 183 **Faculty:** FT 91, PT 114 **Student-Faculty Ratio:** 13:1 **Exams:** SAT I or ACT. ACT essay not being used. SAT essay not being used. **% Receiving Financial Aid:** 80 **% Residing in College-Owned, -Operated, or -Affiliated Housing:** 46 **Final Year or Final Semester Residency Requirement:** Yes **Library Holdings:** 136,958 **Regional Accreditation:** North Central Association of Colleges and Schools **Credit Hours For Degree:** 62 semester hours, Associates; 124 semester hours, Bachelors **ROTC:** Army, Air Force **Professional Accreditation:** NCATE, NLN **Intercollegiate Athletics:** Baseball M; Basketball M & W; Cheerleading M & W; Cross-Country Running M & W; Golf M & W; Soccer M & W; Softball W; Tennis M & W; Track and Field M & W; Volleyball W

BROWN MACKIE COLLEGE—FORT WAYNE
3000 East Coliseum Blvd.
Fort Wayne, IN 46805
Tel: (219)484-4400; Free: (866)433-2289
Admissions: (260)484-4400
Fax: (219)484-2678
Web Site: http://www.brownmackie.edu/fortwayne/
President/CEO: Jim Bishop
Type: Two-Year College **Sex:** Coed **Affiliation:** Education Management Corporation **Calendar System:** Quarter **Professional Accreditation:** ACICS, AOTA

BROWN MACKIE COLLEGE—INDIANAPOLIS
1200 North Meridian St.
Ste. 100
Indianapolis, IN 46204
Tel: (317)554-8301; Free: (866)255-0279
Admissions: (317)554-8301
Web Site: http://www.brownmackie.edu/indianapolis/
President/CEO: William Rooney
Type: Two-Year College **Sex:** Coed **Affiliation:** Education Management Corporation

BROWN MACKIE COLLEGE—MERRILLVILLE
1000 East 80th Place
Ste. 205S
Merrillville, IN 46410
Tel: (219)769-3321; Free: 800-258-3321
Fax: (219)258-3321
Web Site: http://www.brownmackie.edu/merrillville/
President/CEO: Sheryl Elston
Type: Two-Year College **Sex:** Coed **Affiliation:** Education Management Corporation **Calendar System:** Quarter **Professional Accreditation:** ABHES, ACICS

BROWN MACKIE COLLEGE—MICHIGAN CITY
325 East US Hwy. 20
Michigan City, IN 46360
Tel: (219)877-3100; Free: 800-519-2416
Fax: (219)877-3110
Web Site: http://www.brownmackie.edu/michigancity/
President/CEO: Eric Rudie
Type: Two-Year College **Sex:** Coed **Affiliation:** Education Management Corporation **Calendar System:** Quarter **Professional Accreditation:** ABHES, ACICS

BROWN MACKIE COLLEGE—SOUTH BEND
3454 Douglas Rd.
South Bend, IN 46635
Tel: (574)237-0774; Free: 800-743-2447
Fax: (219)237-3585
Web Site: http://www.brownmackie.edu/southbend/
President/CEO: Louise Stienkeoway
Type: Two-Year College **Sex:** Coed **Affiliation:** Education Management Corporation **Calendar System:** Quarter **Professional Accreditation:** ACICS, AAMAE, AOTA, APTA

BUTLER UNIVERSITY
4600 Sunset Ave.
Indianapolis, IN 46208-3485
Tel: (317)940-8000; Free: 888-940-8100
Admissions: (317)940-8100
Fax: (317)940-8150
E-mail: admission@butler.edu
Web Site: http://www.butler.edu/
President/CEO: Dr. Bobby Fong
Admissions: Scott Ham
Financial Aid: Kristine Butz
Type: Comprehensive **Sex:** Coed **Scores:** 100% SAT V 400+; 99.7% SAT M 400+; 14.6% ACT 18-23; 56.9% ACT 24-29 **% Accepted:** 79 **Admission Plans:** Early Action; Deferred Admission **Application Deadline:** Rolling **Application Fee:** $35.00 **H.S. Requirements:** High school diploma required; GED accepted **Costs Per Year:** Application fee: $35. Comprehensive fee: $38,986 includes full-time tuition ($28,460), mandatory fees ($786), and college room and board ($9740). College room only: $4770. Full-time tuition and fees vary according to course load, degree level, and program. Room and board charges vary according to housing facility. Part-time tuition: $1200 per credit hour. Part-time tuition varies according to course load, degree level, and program. **Scholarships:** Available **Calendar System:** Semester, Summer Session Available **Enrollment:** FT 3,670, PT 56, Grad FT 346, Grad PT 433 **Faculty:** FT 327, PT 139 **Student-Faculty Ratio:** 11:1 **Exams:** SAT I or ACT. ACT essay used for admission. SAT essay used for admission. ACT essay used for advising. SAT essay used for advising. SAT essay used for placement. **% Receiving Financial Aid:** 66 **% Residing in College-Owned, -Operated, or -Affiliated Housing:** 66 **Library Holdings:** 339,944 **Regional Accreditation:** North Central Association of Colleges and Schools **Credit Hours For Degree:** 63 semester hours, Associates; 126 semester hours, Bachelors **ROTC:** Army, Air Force **Professional Accreditation:** AACSB, ACPhE, ACA, APA, NASD, NASM, NAST, NCATE **Intercollegiate Athletics:** Baseball M; Basketball M & W; Crew M & W; Cross-Country Running M & W; Football M; Golf M & W; Ice Hockey M; Rugby M; Soccer M & W; Softball W; Swimming and Diving W; Tennis M & W; Track and Field M & W; Volleyball W

CALUMET COLLEGE OF SAINT JOSEPH
2400 New York Ave.
Whiting, IN 46394-2195
Tel: (219)473-7770; Free: 877-700-9100
Admissions: (219)473-4215
Fax: (219)473-4259
E-mail: admissions@ccsj.edu
Web Site: http://www.ccsj.edu/

President/CEO: Dr. Dennis C. Rittenmeyer
Admissions: Rebecca Leevey
Financial Aid: Gina Pirtle
Type: Comprehensive **Sex:** Coed **Affiliation:** Roman Catholic **Scores:** 64% SAT V 400+; 63% SAT M 400+; 47% ACT 18-23; 3% ACT 24-29 **% Accepted:** 51 **Admission Plans:** Deferred Admission **Application Deadline:** Rolling **Application Fee:** $0.00 **H.S. Requirements:** High school diploma required; GED accepted **Costs Per Year:** Application fee: $0. Tuition: $13,050 full-time, $410 per credit hour part-time. Mandatory fees: $170 full-time, $80 per term part-time. **Scholarships:** Available **Calendar System:** Semester, Summer Session Available **Enrollment:** FT 561, PT 554, Grad FT 36, Grad PT 141 **Faculty:** FT 33, PT 93 **Student-Faculty Ratio:** 12:1 **Exams:** Other, SAT I or ACT. ACT essay not being used. SAT essay not being used. **% Receiving Financial Aid:** 78 **Library Holdings:** 110,000 **Regional Accreditation:** North Central Association of Colleges and Schools **Credit Hours For Degree:** 60 credit hours, Associates; 124 credit hours, Bachelors **Intercollegiate Athletics:** Baseball M; Basketball M & W; Bowling M & W; Cross-Country Running M & W; Golf M & W; Soccer M & W; Softball W; Tennis M & W; Track and Field M & W; Volleyball W

COLLEGE OF COURT REPORTING
111 West Tenth St.
Ste. 111
Hobart, IN 46342
Tel: (219)942-1459; Free: (866)294-3974
Fax: (219)942-1631
E-mail: nrodriquez@ccredu.com
Web Site: http://www.ccredu.com/
President/CEO: Jeff Moody
Admissions: Nicky Rodriquez
Type: Two-Year College **Sex:** Coed **% Accepted:** 88 **Enrollment:** FT 89, PT 67 **Faculty:** FT 8, PT 8 **Student-Faculty Ratio:** 8:1 **Professional Accreditation:** ACICS

CROSSROADS BIBLE COLLEGE
601 North Shortridge Rd.
Indianapolis, IN 46219
Tel: (317)352-8736; Free: 800-273-2224
Fax: (317)352-9145
Web Site: http://www.crossroads.edu/
President/CEO: Dr. A. Charles Ware
Admissions: Michael Garrison
Financial Aid: Phyllis Dodson
Type: Four-Year College **Sex:** Coed **Affiliation:** Baptist **Admission Plans:** Open Admission; Deferred Admission **Application Deadline:** August 8 **Application Fee:** $10.00 **H.S. Requirements:** High school diploma required; GED accepted **Costs Per Year:** Application fee: $10. Tuition: $9480 full-time. Mandatory fees: $370 full-time. College room only: $3000. **Scholarships:** Available **Calendar System:** Semester, Summer Session Available **Faculty:** FT 3, PT 24 **Exams:** SAT I and SAT II or ACT. **Final Year or Final Semester Residency Requirement:** No **Credit Hours For Degree:** 69 credit hours, Associates; 129 credit hours, Bachelors **Professional Accreditation:** ABHE

DEPAUW UNIVERSITY
313 South Locust St.
Greencastle, IN 46135
Tel: (765)658-4800; Free: 800-447-2495
Fax: (765)658-4007
E-mail: admission@depauw.edu
Web Site: http://www.depauw.edu/
President/CEO: Brian W. Casey
Admissions: Brett Kennedy
Financial Aid: Craig Slaughter
Type: Four-Year College **Sex:** Coed **Affiliation:** United Methodist Church **Scores:** 99.6% SAT V 400+; 99.8% SAT M 400+; 19.3% ACT 18-23; 56.8% ACT 24-29 **% Accepted:** 66 **Admission Plans:** Early Admission; Early Action; Early Decision Plan; Deferred Admission **Application Deadline:** February 1 **Application Fee:** $40.00 **H.S. Requirements:** High school diploma required; GED accepted **Costs Per Year:** Application fee: $40. Comprehensive fee: $41,990 includes full-time tuition ($32,800), mandatory fees ($450), and college room and board ($8740). **Scholarships:** Available **Calendar System:** 4-1-4, Summer Session Not available **Enrollment:** FT 2,368, PT 28 **Faculty:** FT 224, PT 55 **Student-Faculty Ratio:** 10:1 **Exams:** SAT I or ACT. ACT essay used as a validity check on application essay. SAT essay used as a validity check on application essay. **% Receiving Financial Aid:** 53 **% Residing in College-Owned, -Operated, or -Affiliated Housing:** 95 **Regional Accreditation:** North Central Association of Colleges and Schools **Credit Hours For Degree:** 31 courses, Bachelors **ROTC:** Army, Air Force **Professional Accreditation:** JRCEPAT, NASM, NCATE **Intercollegiate Athletics:** Baseball M; Basketball M & W; Cheerleading M & W; Crew M & W; Cross-Country Running M & W; Field Hockey W; Football M; Golf M & W; Rugby M; Soccer M & W; Softball W; Swimming and Diving M & W; Tennis M & W; Track and Field M & W; Volleyball W

DEVRY UNIVERSITY (INDIANAPOLIS)
9100 Keystone Crossing, Ste. 350
Indianapolis, IN 46240-2158
Tel: (317)581-8854
Web Site: http://www.devry.edu/
President/CEO: Bill Coit
Type: Comprehensive **Sex:** Coed **Affiliation:** DeVry University **Admission Plans:** Deferred Admission **Application Deadline:** Rolling **Application Fee:** $50.00 **H.S. Requirements:** High school diploma required; GED accepted **Costs Per Year:** Application fee: $50. Tuition: $14,080 full-time, $550 per credit hour part-time. **Scholarships:** Available **Calendar System:** Semester, Summer Session Available **Enrollment:** FT 99, PT 132, Grad FT 15, Grad PT 119 **Faculty:** FT 0, PT 33 **Student-Faculty Ratio:** 18:1 **Exams:** ACT essay used for admission. SAT essay used for admission. ACT essay used for placement. SAT essay used for placement. **% Receiving Financial Aid:** 82 **Regional Accreditation:** North Central Association of Colleges and Schools **Credit Hours For Degree:** 122 credit hours, Bachelors

DEVRY UNIVERSITY (MERRILLVILLE)
Twin Towers
1000 East 80th Place, Ste. 222 Mall
Merrillville, IN 46410-5673
Tel: (219)736-7440
Fax: (219)736-7874
Web Site: http://www.devry.edu/
Type: Comprehensive **Sex:** Coed **Calendar System:** Semester **Regional Accreditation:** North Central Association of Colleges and Schools

EARLHAM COLLEGE
801 National Rd. West
Richmond, IN 47374-4095
Tel: (765)983-1200; Free: 800-327-5426
Admissions: (765)983-1600
Fax: (765)983-1560
E-mail: admission@earlham.edu
Web Site: http://www.earlham.edu/
President/CEO: Douglas Bennett
Admissions: Jeff Rickey
Financial Aid: Robert W. Arnold
Type: Comprehensive **Sex:** Coed **Affiliation:** Society of Friends **Scores:** 96% SAT V 400+; 96% SAT M 400+; 21% ACT 18-23; 50% ACT 24-29 **% Accepted:** 75 **Admission Plans:** Preferred Admission; Early Admission; Early Action; Early Decision Plan; Deferred Admission **Application Deadline:** February 15 **Application Fee:** $0.00 **H.S. Requirements:** High school diploma required; GED accepted. For home schooled students: High school diploma or equivalent not required **Costs Per Year:** Application fee: $0. Comprehensive fee: $43,894 includes full-time tuition ($35,720), mandatory fees ($774), and college room and board ($7400). College room only: $3750. Part-time tuition: $1194 per credit. **Scholarships:** Available **Calendar System:** Semester, Summer Session Not available **Enrollment:** FT 1,168, PT 16 **Faculty:** FT 94, PT 10 **Student-Faculty Ratio:** 12:1 **Exams:** SAT I or ACT. **% Receiving Financial Aid:** 58 **% Residing in College-Owned, -Operated, or -Affiliated Housing:** 81 **Library Holdings:** 406,316 **Regional Accreditation:** North Central Association of Colleges and Schools **Credit Hours For Degree:** 120 semester hours, Bachelors **Intercollegiate Athletics:** Baseball M; Basketball M & W; Cheerleading W; Cross-Country Running M & W; Equestrian Sports W; Field Hockey W; Football M; Lacrosse M & W; Rugby W; Soccer M & W; Tennis M & W; Track and Field M & W; Ultimate Frisbee M & W; Volleyball M & W

FRANKLIN COLLEGE
101 Branigin Blvd.
Franklin, IN 46131

Tel: (317)738-8000; Free: 800-852-0232
Admissions: (317)738-8062
Fax: (317)738-8274
E-mail: jacosta@franklincollege.edu
Web Site: http://www.franklincollege.edu/
President/CEO: James Moseley
Admissions: Jacqueline Acosta
Financial Aid: Elizabeth Sappenfield
Type: Four-Year College **Sex:** Coed **Affiliation:** American Baptist Churches in the U.S.A. **Scores:** 91% SAT V 400+; 94% SAT M 400+; 61% ACT 18-23; 27% ACT 24-29 **% Accepted:** 67 **Admission Plans:** Deferred Admission **Application Deadline:** Rolling **Application Fee:** $30.00 **H.S. Requirements:** High school diploma required; GED accepted **Costs Per Year:** Application fee: $30. Comprehensive fee: $30,160 includes full-time tuition ($23,100), mandatory fees ($175), and college room and board ($6885). College room only: $4085. Room and board charges vary according to board plan and housing facility. Part-time tuition: $325 per credit hour. Part-time tuition varies according to course load. **Scholarships:** Available **Calendar System:** 4-1-4, Summer Session Available **Enrollment:** FT 1,018, PT 135 **Faculty:** FT 69, PT 36 **Student-Faculty Ratio:** 12:1 **Exams:** SAT I or ACT. ACT essay used for admission. SAT essay used for admission. ACT essay used for advising. SAT essay used for advising. ACT essay used in place of application essay. SAT essay used in place of application essay. ACT essay used for placement. SAT essay used for placement. **% Receiving Financial Aid:** 80 **% Residing in College-Owned, -Operated, or -Affiliated Housing:** 69 **Library Holdings:** 25,434 **Regional Accreditation:** North Central Association of Colleges and Schools **Credit Hours For Degree:** 128 semester hours, Bachelors **ROTC:** Army **Professional Accreditation:** NCATE **Intercollegiate Athletics:** Baseball M; Basketball M & W; Cross-Country Running M & W; Football M; Golf M & W; Soccer M & W; Softball W; Tennis M & W; Track and Field M & W; Volleyball W

GOSHEN COLLEGE
1700 South Main St.
Goshen, IN 46526-4794
Tel: (574)535-7000; Free: 800-348-7422
Admissions: (574)535-7535
Fax: (574)535-7060
E-mail: lynnj@goshen.edu
Web Site: http://www.goshen.edu/
President/CEO: Dr. James E. Brenneman
Admissions: Lynn Jackson
Financial Aid: Galen Graber
Type: Comprehensive **Sex:** Coed **Affiliation:** Mennonite **Scores:** 96% SAT V 400+; 98% SAT M 400+; 33% ACT 18-23; 45% ACT 24-29 **% Accepted:** 68 **Admission Plans:** Deferred Admission **Application Deadline:** August 15 **Application Fee:** $25.00 **H.S. Requirements:** High school diploma required; GED accepted **Costs Per Year:** Application fee: $25. Comprehensive fee: $31,300 includes full-time tuition ($23,400) and college room and board ($7900). College room only: $4150. Room and board charges vary according to board plan and housing facility. Part-time tuition: $890 per credit hour. Part-time tuition varies according to course load. **Scholarships:** Available **Calendar System:** Semester, Summer Session Available **Enrollment:** FT 903, PT 71, Grad FT 8, Grad PT 35 **Faculty:** FT 68, PT 54 **Student-Faculty Ratio:** 11:1 **Exams:** SAT I or ACT. **% Receiving Financial Aid:** 78 **% Residing in College-Owned, -Operated, or -Affiliated Housing:** 70 **Final Year or Final Semester Residency Requirement:** Yes **Library Holdings:** 137,000 **Regional Accreditation:** North Central Association of Colleges and Schools **Credit Hours For Degree:** 120 credit hours, Bachelors **Professional Accreditation:** AACN, CSWE, NCATE, NLN **Intercollegiate Athletics:** Baseball M; Basketball M & W; Cross-Country Running M & W; Golf M; Soccer M & W; Softball W; Tennis M & W; Track and Field M & W; Volleyball W

GRACE COLLEGE
200 Seminary Dr.
Winona Lake, IN 46590-1294
Tel: (574)372-5100; Free: 800-54 GRACE
Fax: (574)372-5139
E-mail: enroll@grace.edu
Web Site: http://www.grace.edu/
President/CEO: Dr. Ronald E. Manahan
Admissions: Jessica Hauck
Financial Aid: Charlette Sauders
Type: Comprehensive **Sex:** Coed **Affiliation:** Fellowship of Grace Brethren Churches; Grace Theological Seminary **Scores:** 89.9% SAT V 400+; 91.8% SAT M 400+; 35.5% ACT 18-23; 45.5% ACT 24-29 **% Accepted:** 97 **Admission Plans:** Early Admission; Early Action; Deferred Admission **Application Deadline:** August 1 **Application Fee:** $30.00 **H.S. Requirements:** High school diploma required; GED accepted **Costs Per Year:** Application fee: $30. Comprehensive fee: $27,980 includes full-time tuition ($21,100) and college room and board ($6880). Full-time tuition varies according to program. Room and board charges vary according to board plan and housing facility. Part-time tuition: $466 per credit hour. Part-time tuition varies according to course load. **Scholarships:** Available **Calendar System:** Semester, Summer Session Available **Enrollment:** FT 1,296, PT 170, Grad FT 60, Grad PT 115 **Faculty:** FT 57, PT 71 **Student-Faculty Ratio:** 18:1 **Exams:** SAT I or ACT. ACT essay not being used. SAT essay not being used. **% Residing in College-Owned, -Operated, or -Affiliated Housing:** 69 **Final Year or Final Semester Residency Requirement:** No **Library Holdings:** 158,622 **Regional Accreditation:** North Central Association of Colleges and Schools **Credit Hours For Degree:** 73 semester hours, Associates; 124 semester hours, Bachelors **Professional Accreditation:** ACA, CSWE, NASM, NCATE **Intercollegiate Athletics:** Baseball M; Basketball M & W; Cheerleading M & W; Cross-Country Running M & W; Golf M; Soccer M & W; Softball W; Tennis M & W; Track and Field M & W; Volleyball W

HANOVER COLLEGE
PO Box 108
Hanover, IN 47243-0108
Tel: (812)866-7000; Free: 800-213-2178
Admissions: (812)866-7021
Fax: (812)866-7098
E-mail: admission@hanover.edu
Web Site: http://www.hanover.edu/
President/CEO: Dr. Sue Dewine
Admissions: Christopher Gage
Financial Aid: Richard A. Nash
Type: Four-Year College **Sex:** Coed **Affiliation:** Presbyterian **Scores:** 99% SAT V 400+; 99% SAT M 400+; 43% ACT 18-23; 42% ACT 24-29 **% Accepted:** 61 **Admission Plans:** Early Admission; Early Action; Deferred Admission **Application Deadline:** March 1 **Application Fee:** $40.00 **H.S. Requirements:** High school diploma required; GED not accepted **Costs Per Year:** Application fee: $40. One-time mandatory fee: $250. Comprehensive fee: $34,250 includes full-time tuition ($25,800), mandatory fees ($550), and college room and board ($7900). College room only: $3850. Full-time tuition and fees vary according to reciprocity agreements. Room and board charges vary according to housing facility and location. Part-time tuition: $2860 per unit. Part-time tuition varies according to course load and reciprocity agreements. **Scholarships:** Available **Calendar System:** Miscellaneous, Summer Session Not available **Enrollment:** FT 932, PT 6 **Faculty:** FT 91, PT 4 **Student-Faculty Ratio:** 10:1 **Exams:** SAT I or ACT. **% Receiving Financial Aid:** 76 **% Residing in College-Owned, -Operated, or -Affiliated Housing:** 95 **Final Year or Final Semester Residency Requirement:** Yes **Library Holdings:** 224,478 **Regional Accreditation:** North Central Association of Colleges and Schools **Credit Hours For Degree:** 37 units, Bachelors **Professional Accreditation:** NCATE **Intercollegiate Athletics:** Baseball M; Basketball M & W; Cross-Country Running M & W; Football M; Golf M & W; Lacrosse M; Soccer M & W; Softball W; Tennis M & W; Track and Field M & W; Volleyball W

HARRISON COLLEGE (ANDERSON)
140 East 53rd St.
Anderson, IN 46013
Tel: (765)644-7514
E-mail: kynan.simison@harrison.edu
Web Site: http://www.harrison.edu/
President/CEO: Charlene Stacy
Admissions: Kynan Simison
Type: Two-Year College **Sex:** Coed **Admission Plans:** Early Admission **Application Deadline:** Rolling **Application Fee:** $50.00 **H.S. Requirements:** High school diploma required; GED accepted **Costs Per Year:** Application fee: $50. **Calendar System:** Quarter **Student-Faculty Ratio:** 16:1 **Exams:** Other. **Professional Accreditation:** ACICS

HARRISON COLLEGE (COLUMBUS)
2222 Poshard Dr.
Columbus, IN 47203-1843

Tel: (812)379-9000
E-mail: gina.pate@harrison.edu
Web Site: http://www.harrison.edu/
President/CEO: Angela Rentmeesters
Admissions: Gina Pate
Type: Two-Year College **Sex:** Coed **Application Deadline:** Rolling **Application Fee:** $50.00 **H.S. Requirements:** High school diploma required; GED accepted **Costs Per Year:** Application fee: $50. **Scholarships:** Available **Calendar System:** Quarter **Student-Faculty Ratio:** 15:1 **Exams:** Other. **Professional Accreditation:** ACICS

HARRISON COLLEGE (ELKHART)
56075 Parkway Ave.
Elkhart, IN 46516
Tel: (574)522-0397; Free: 888-544-4422
E-mail: matt.brady@harrison.edu
Web Site: http://www.harrison.edu/
President/CEO: Justin Elliott
Admissions: Matt Brady
Type: Two-Year College **Sex:** Coed **Application Deadline:** Rolling **Application Fee:** $50.00 **H.S. Requirements:** High school diploma required; GED accepted **Costs Per Year:** Application fee: $50. **Calendar System:** Quarter **Student-Faculty Ratio:** 25:1 **Exams:** Other. **Professional Accreditation:** ACICS

HARRISON COLLEGE (EVANSVILLE)
4601 Theatre Dr.
Evansville, IN 47715-4601
Tel: (812)476-6000
E-mail: bryan.barber@harrison.edu
Web Site: http://www.harrison.edu/
President/CEO: Steve Hardin
Admissions: Bryan Barber
Type: Two-Year College **Sex:** Coed **Application Deadline:** Rolling **Application Fee:** $50.00 **H.S. Requirements:** High school diploma required; GED accepted **Costs Per Year:** Application fee: $50. **Scholarships:** Available **Calendar System:** Quarter **Student-Faculty Ratio:** 15:1 **Exams:** Other. **Professional Accreditation:** ACICS, AAMAE

HARRISON COLLEGE (FORT WAYNE)
6413 North Clinton St.
Fort Wayne, IN 46825
Tel: (260)471-7667
E-mail: matt.wallace@harrison.edu
Web Site: http://www.harrison.edu/
President/CEO: Janet Herman
Admissions: Matt Wallace
Type: Two-Year College **Sex:** Coed **Application Deadline:** Rolling **Application Fee:** $50.00 **H.S. Requirements:** High school diploma required; GED accepted **Costs Per Year:** Application fee: $50. **Scholarships:** Available **Calendar System:** Quarter **Student-Faculty Ratio:** 15:1 **Exams:** Other. **Professional Accreditation:** ACICS

HARRISON COLLEGE (INDIANAPOLIS)
6300 Technology Center Dr.
Indianapolis, IN 46278
Tel: (317)873-6500
E-mail: matthew.stein@harrison.edu
Web Site: http://www.harrison.edu/
President/CEO: Rod Allee
Admissions: Matt Stein
Type: Two-Year College **Sex:** Coed **Application Deadline:** Rolling **Application Fee:** $50.00 **Costs Per Year:** Application fee: $50. **Calendar System:** Quarter **Student-Faculty Ratio:** 15:1 **Exams:** Other. **Professional Accreditation:** ACICS

HARRISON COLLEGE (INDIANAPOLIS)
8150 Brookville Rd.
Indianapolis, IN 46239
Tel: (317)375-8000
Fax: (317)351-1871
E-mail: jan.carter@harrison.edu
Web Site: http://www.harrison.edu/
President/CEO: Gary McGee
Admissions: Jan Carter
Type: Two-Year College **Sex:** Coed **Application Deadline:** Rolling **Application Fee:** $50.00 **H.S. Requirements:** High school diploma required; GED accepted **Costs Per Year:** Application fee: $50. **Calendar System:** Quarter **Student-Faculty Ratio:** 15:1 **Exams:** Other. **Professional Accreditation:** ACICS

HARRISON COLLEGE (INDIANAPOLIS)
550 East Washington St.
Indianapolis, IN 46204
Tel: (317)264-5656
Fax: (317)264-5650
E-mail: ted.lukomski@ibcschools.edu
Web Site: http://www.harrison.edu/
President/CEO: Greg Reger
Admissions: Ted Lukomski
Type: Two-Year College **Sex:** Coed **Application Deadline:** Rolling **Application Fee:** $50.00 **H.S. Requirements:** High school diploma required; GED accepted **Costs Per Year:** Application fee: $50. **Scholarships:** Available **Calendar System:** Quarter, Summer Session Available **Student-Faculty Ratio:** 16:1 **Exams:** Other. **Professional Accreditation:** ACICS

HARRISON COLLEGE (LAFAYETTE)
4705 Meijer Ct.
Lafayette, IN 47905
Tel: (765)447-9550
E-mail: stacy.golleher@harrison.edu
Web Site: http://www.harrison.edu/
President/CEO: Timothy Parsons
Admissions: Stacy Golleher
Type: Two-Year College **Sex:** Coed **Application Deadline:** Rolling **Application Fee:** $50.00 **H.S. Requirements:** High school diploma required; GED accepted **Costs Per Year:** Application fee: $50. **Scholarships:** Available **Calendar System:** Quarter **Student-Faculty Ratio:** 15:1 **Exams:** Other. **Professional Accreditation:** ACICS

HARRISON COLLEGE (MUNCIE)
411 West Riggin Rd.
Muncie, IN 47303
Tel: (765)288-8681
Fax: (765)288-8797
E-mail: Jeremy.linder@harrison.edu
Web Site: http://www.harrison.edu/
President/CEO: Charlene Purtlebaugh
Admissions: Jeremy Linder
Type: Two-Year College **Sex:** Coed **Application Deadline:** Rolling **Application Fee:** $50.00 **H.S. Requirements:** High school diploma required; GED accepted **Costs Per Year:** Application fee: $50. **Scholarships:** Available **Calendar System:** Quarter **Student-Faculty Ratio:** 16:1 **Exams:** Other. **Professional Accreditation:** ACICS

HARRISON COLLEGE (TERRE HAUTE)
1378 South State Rd. 46
Terre Haute, IN 47803
Tel: (812)232-4458
Admissions: (812)877-2100
E-mail: sarah.stultz@harrison.edu
Web Site: http://www.harrison.edu/
President/CEO: Pat Mozley
Admissions: Sarah Stultz
Type: Two-Year College **Sex:** Coed **Application Deadline:** Rolling **Application Fee:** $50.00 **H.S. Requirements:** High school diploma required; GED accepted **Costs Per Year:** Application fee: $50. **Calendar System:** Quarter **Student-Faculty Ratio:** 15:1 **Exams:** Other. **Professional Accreditation:** ACICS

HOLY CROSS COLLEGE
PO Box 308, 54515 State Rd. 933 North
Notre Dame, IN 46556-0308
Tel: (574)239-8400
Fax: (574)239-8323
E-mail: vduke@hcc-nd.edu
Web Site: http://www.hcc-nd.edu/
President/CEO: Richard Gilman

Financial Aid: Robert Benjamin
Type: Four-Year College **Sex:** Coed **Affiliation:** Roman Catholic **% Accepted:** 97 **Admission Plans:** Deferred Admission **Application Deadline:** Rolling **Application Fee:** $50.00 **H.S. Requirements:** High school diploma required; GED accepted **Costs Per Year:** Application fee: $50. Comprehensive fee: $26,700 includes full-time tuition ($17,700), mandatory fees ($1000), and college room and board ($8000). Room and board charges vary according to housing facility. Part-time tuition: $590 per semester hour. **Scholarships:** Available **Calendar System:** Semester, Summer Session Available **Faculty:** FT 26, PT 12 **Student-Faculty Ratio:** 12:1 **Exams:** SAT I or ACT. **% Residing in College-Owned, -Operated, or -Affiliated Housing:** 54 **Library Holdings:** 15,000 **Regional Accreditation:** North Central Association of Colleges and Schools **Credit Hours For Degree:** 61 semester hours, Associates; 122 semester hours, Bachelors **ROTC:** Army, Air Force **Intercollegiate Athletics:** Basketball M; Crew M & W; Cross-Country Running M & W; Lacrosse M; Soccer M & W

HUNTINGTON UNIVERSITY

2303 College Ave.
Huntington, IN 46750-1299
Tel: (260)356-6000; Free: 800-642-6493
Fax: (260)356-9448
E-mail: jberggren@huntington.edu
Web Site: http://www.huntington.edu/
President/CEO: Dr. G. Blair Dowden
Admissions: Jeff Berggren
Financial Aid: Sharon Woods
Type: Comprehensive **Sex:** Coed **Affiliation:** Church of the United Brethren in Christ **Scores:** 90% SAT V 400+; 92% SAT M 400+; 49% ACT 18-23; 40% ACT 24-29 **% Accepted:** 89 **Admission Plans:** Deferred Admission **Application Deadline:** August 1 **Application Fee:** $20.00 **H.S. Requirements:** High school diploma required; GED accepted **Costs Per Year:** Application fee: $20. Comprehensive fee: $29,760 includes full-time tuition ($21,850), mandatory fees ($480), and college room and board ($7430). Full-time tuition and fees vary according to course load, degree level, and program. Room and board charges vary according to board plan. Part-time tuition: $650 per credit hour. Part-time mandatory fees: $240 per term. Part-time tuition and fees vary according to course load, degree level, and program. **Scholarships:** Available **Calendar System:** 4-1-4, Summer Session Available **Enrollment:** FT 1,050, PT 140, Grad FT 32, Grad PT 75 **Faculty:** FT 62, PT 41 **Student-Faculty Ratio:** 13:1 **Exams:** SAT I or ACT. ACT essay used for admission. SAT essay used for admission. ACT essay used for advising. SAT essay used for advising. ACT essay used as a validity check on application essay. SAT essay used as a validity check on application essay. ACT essay used for placement. SAT essay used for placement. **% Receiving Financial Aid:** 74 **% Residing in College-Owned, -Operated, or -Affiliated Housing:** 80 **Library Holdings:** 181,291 **Regional Accreditation:** North Central Association of Colleges and Schools **Credit Hours For Degree:** 64 semester hours, Associates; 128 semester hours, Bachelors **Professional Accreditation:** NASM, NCATE **Intercollegiate Athletics:** Baseball M; Basketball M & W; Cross-Country Running M & W; Golf M; Soccer M & W; Softball W; Tennis M & W; Track and Field M & W; Volleyball W

INDIANA STATE UNIVERSITY

210 North Seventh St.
Terre Haute, IN 47809
Tel: (812)237-6311; Free: 800-742-0891
Admissions: (812)237-2121
Fax: (812)237-8023
E-mail: admisu@isugw.indstate.edu
Web Site: http://www.indstate.edu/
President/CEO: Daniel J. Bradley
Admissions: Richard Toomey
Financial Aid: Kim Donat
Type: University **Sex:** Coed **Scores:** 80.7% SAT V 400+; 82.9% SAT M 400+; 47.7% ACT 18-23; 16.3% ACT 24-29 **% Accepted:** 68 **Admission Plans:** Deferred Admission **Application Deadline:** August 15 **Application Fee:** $25.00 **H.S. Requirements:** High school diploma required; GED accepted **Costs Per Year:** Application fee: $25. State resident tuition: $7226 full-time, $262 per credit hour part-time. Nonresident tuition: $15,802 full-time, $558 per credit hour part-time. Mandatory fees: $200 full-time, $100 per term part-time. Part-time tuition and fees vary according to course load. College room and board: $7463. College room only: $4254. Room and board charges vary according to board plan, housing facility, and student level. **Scholarships:** Available **Calendar System:** Semester, Summer Session Available **Enrollment:** FT 7,301, PT 1,159, Grad FT 824, Grad PT 1,250 **Faculty:** FT 430, PT 213 **Student-Faculty Ratio:** 18:1 **Exams:** SAT I or ACT. ACT essay not being used. SAT essay not being used. **% Receiving Financial Aid:** 67 **% Residing in College-Owned, -Operated, or -Affiliated Housing:** 37 **Library Holdings:** 1,246,771 **Regional Accreditation:** North Central Association of Colleges and Schools **Credit Hours For Degree:** 62 credit hours, Associates; 124 credit hours, Bachelors **ROTC:** Army, Air Force **Professional Accreditation:** AACSB, AAMFT, AAFCS, ACCE, ACA, ADtA, APA, ASLHA, CSWE, JRCEPAT, NASAD, NASM, NCATE, NLN, NRPA, NAIT **Intercollegiate Athletics:** Baseball M; Basketball M & W; Cross-Country Running M & W; Football M; Golf W; Soccer W; Softball W; Track and Field M & W; Volleyball W

INDIANA TECH

1600 East Washington Blvd.
Fort Wayne, IN 46803-1297
Tel: (260)422-5561; Free: 888-666-TECH
Fax: (260)422-7696
E-mail: admissions@indianatech.edu
Web Site: http://www.indianatech.edu/
President/CEO: Dr. Arthur E. Snyder
Admissions: Monica Chamberlain
Type: Comprehensive **Sex:** Coed **Scores:** 76% SAT V 400+; 85% SAT M 400+; 56% ACT 18-23; 13% ACT 24-29 **% Accepted:** 74 **Admission Plans:** Early Admission; Deferred Admission **Application Fee:** $50.00 **H.S. Requirements:** High school diploma required; GED accepted **Costs Per Year:** Application fee: $50. Comprehensive fee: $29,440 includes full-time tuition ($21,080), mandatory fees ($320), and college room and board ($8040). **Scholarships:** Available **Calendar System:** Semester, Summer Session Available **Enrollment:** FT 2,398, PT 1,252, Grad FT 317, Grad PT 55 **Faculty:** FT 38, PT 173 **Exams:** SAT I or ACT. ACT essay used for advising. SAT essay used for advising. ACT essay used for placement. SAT essay used for placement. **% Residing in College-Owned, -Operated, or -Affiliated Housing:** 45 **Final Year or Final Semester Residency Requirement:** Yes **Library Holdings:** 40,000 **Regional Accreditation:** North Central Association of Colleges and Schools **Credit Hours For Degree:** 60 credit hours, Associates; 123 credit hours, Bachelors **ROTC:** Army **Professional Accreditation:** ABET **Intercollegiate Athletics:** Baseball M; Basketball M & W; Cheerleading M & W; Cross-Country Running M & W; Golf M & W; Soccer M & W; Softball W; Track and Field M & W; Volleyball W

INDIANA UNIVERSITY BLOOMINGTON

107 South Indiana Ave.
Bloomington, IN 47405-7000
Tel: (812)855-4848
Admissions: (812)855-0661
Fax: (812)855-1871
E-mail: iuadmit@indiana.edu
Web Site: http://www.iub.edu/
President/CEO: Dr. Michael A. McRobbie
Admissions: Mary Ellen Anderson
Financial Aid: Susan Pugh
Type: University **Sex:** Coed **Affiliation:** Indiana University System **Scores:** 98.5% SAT V 400+; 99.1% SAT M 400+; 16.6% ACT 18-23; 58.4% ACT 24-29 **% Accepted:** 73 **Admission Plans:** Preferred Admission; Deferred Admission **Application Deadline:** Rolling **Application Fee:** $55.00 **H.S. Requirements:** High school diploma required; GED accepted **Costs Per Year:** Application fee: $55. State resident tuition: $7722 full-time, $241.10 per credit hour part-time. Nonresident tuition: $25,269 full-time, $789.80 per credit hour part-time. Mandatory fees: $891 full-time. Full-time tuition and fees vary according to location and program. Part-time tuition varies according to course load, location, and program. College room and board: $7546. College room only: $4646. Room and board charges vary according to board plan and housing facility. **Scholarships:** Available **Calendar System:** Semester, Summer Session Available **Enrollment:** FT 31,061, PT 1,429, Grad FT 6,411, Grad PT 3,446 **Faculty:** FT 1,917, PT 368 **Student-Faculty Ratio:** 19:1 **Exams:** SAT I or ACT, SAT II. SAT essay used for placement. **% Receiving Financial Aid:** 41 **% Residing in College-Owned, -Operated, or -Affiliated Housing:** 36 **Library Holdings:** 7,600,000 **Regional Accreditation:** North Central Association of Colleges and Schools **Credit Hours For Degree:** 60 credit hours, Associates; 122 credit hours, Bachelors **ROTC:** Army, Air Force **Professional Accreditation:** AACSB, ACEJMC, ABA, ACA, ALA, AOA, APA, ASLHA, COptA, FIDER, CEPH, CSWE,

JRCEPAT, NASAD, NASM, NASPAA, NAST, NCATE, NLN, NRPA **Intercollegiate Athletics:** Baseball M; Basketball M & W; Crew W; Cross-Country Running M & W; Field Hockey W; Football M; Golf M & W; Soccer M & W; Softball W; Swimming and Diving M & W; Tennis M & W; Track and Field M & W; Volleyball W; Water Polo W; Wrestling M

INDIANA UNIVERSITY EAST
2325 Chester Blvd.
Richmond, IN 47374-1289
Tel: (765)973-8200; Free: 800-959-EAST
Admissions: (765)973-8415
Fax: (765)973-8288
Web Site: http://www.iue.edu/
President/CEO: Nasser H. Paydar
Admissions: Molly Vanderpool
Financial Aid: William Gill
Type: Comprehensive **Sex:** Coed **Affiliation:** Indiana University System **Scores:** 80% SAT V 400+; 83.5% SAT M 400+; 54.8% ACT 18-23; 16.3% ACT 24-29 **% Accepted:** 74 **Admission Plans:** Early Admission; Deferred Admission **Application Deadline:** Rolling **Application Fee:** $35.00 **H.S. Requirements:** High school diploma required; GED accepted **Costs Per Year:** Application fee: $35. State resident tuition: $5416 full-time, $180.54 per credit hour part-time. Nonresident tuition: $14,572 full-time, $485.72 per credit hour part-time. Mandatory fees: $385 full-time. Full-time tuition and fees vary according to course load, location, program, and reciprocity agreements. Part-time tuition varies according to course load, location, program, and reciprocity agreements. **Scholarships:** Available **Calendar System:** Semester, Summer Session Available **Enrollment:** FT 1,514, PT 1,313, Grad FT 10, Grad PT 87 **Faculty:** FT 86, PT 119 **Student-Faculty Ratio:** 16:1 **Exams:** SAT I or ACT. **% Receiving Financial Aid:** 79 **Library Holdings:** 67,036 **Regional Accreditation:** North Central Association of Colleges and Schools **Credit Hours For Degree:** 60 credit hours, Associates; 120 credit hours, Bachelors **Professional Accreditation:** ACBSP, CSWE, NCATE, NLN **Intercollegiate Athletics:** Basketball M; Cheerleading W; Cross-Country Running M & W; Golf M & W; Tennis M & W; Track and Field M & W; Volleyball W

INDIANA UNIVERSITY KOKOMO
PO Box 9003
Kokomo, IN 46904-9003
Tel: (765)453-2000; Free: 888-875-4485
Admissions: (765)455-9217
Fax: (765)455-9537
E-mail: iuadmis@iuk.edu
Web Site: http://www.iuk.edu/
President/CEO: Stuart M. Green
Admissions: Reeta Piirala-Skoglund
Financial Aid: Jolane Rohr
Type: Comprehensive **Sex:** Coed **Affiliation:** Indiana University System **Scores:** 82.6% SAT V 400+; 87.9% SAT M 400+; 54.7% ACT 18-23; 11.6% ACT 24-29 **% Accepted:** 81 **Admission Plans:** Deferred Admission **Application Deadline:** Rolling **Application Fee:** $45.00 **H.S. Requirements:** High school diploma required; GED accepted **Costs Per Year:** Application fee: $45. State resident tuition: $5408 full-time, $180.25 per credit hour part-time. Nonresident tuition: $14,097 full-time, $469.89 per credit hour part-time. Mandatory fees: $430 full-time. Full-time tuition and fees vary according to course load, location, and program. Part-time tuition varies according to course load, location, and program. **Scholarships:** Available **Calendar System:** Semester, Summer Session Available **Enrollment:** FT 1,549, PT 1,299, Grad FT 52, Grad PT 92 **Faculty:** FT 89, PT 86 **Student-Faculty Ratio:** 17:1 **Exams:** SAT I or ACT. ACT essay used for placement. SAT essay used for placement. **% Receiving Financial Aid:** 67 **Library Holdings:** 132,424 **Regional Accreditation:** North Central Association of Colleges and Schools **Credit Hours For Degree:** 60 credit hours, Associates; 120 credit hours, Bachelors **ROTC:** Army **Professional Accreditation:** AACSB, AACN, NCATE, NLN

INDIANA UNIVERSITY NORTHWEST
3400 Broadway
Gary, IN 46408-1197
Tel: (219)980-6500; Free: 800-968-7486
Admissions: (219)980-6991
Fax: (219)981-4219
E-mail: admit@iun.edu
Web Site: http://www.iun.edu/
President/CEO: Dr. Bruce Bergland
Admissions: Dr. Linda B. Templeton
Financial Aid: Harold Burtley
Type: Comprehensive **Sex:** Coed **Affiliation:** Indiana University System **Scores:** 77.1% SAT V 400+; 70.2% SAT M 400+; 45.4% ACT 18-23; 14.2% ACT 24-29 **% Accepted:** 79 **Admission Plans:** Early Admission; Deferred Admission **Application Deadline:** Rolling **Application Fee:** $25.00 **H.S. Requirements:** High school diploma required; GED accepted **Costs Per Year:** Application fee: $25. State resident tuition: $5478 full-time, $182.61 per credit hour part-time. Nonresident tuition: $14,583 full-time, $486.11 per credit hour part-time. Mandatory fees: $441 full-time. Full-time tuition and fees vary according to course load, location, and program. Part-time tuition varies according to course load, location, and program. **Scholarships:** Available **Calendar System:** Semester, Summer Session Available **Enrollment:** FT 3,098, PT 1,781, Grad FT 153, Grad PT 528 **Faculty:** FT 177, PT 182 **Student-Faculty Ratio:** 16:1 **Exams:** SAT I or ACT. **% Receiving Financial Aid:** 67 **Library Holdings:** 251,508 **Regional Accreditation:** North Central Association of Colleges and Schools **Credit Hours For Degree:** 60 credits, Associates; 120 credits, Bachelors **ROTC:** Army **Professional Accreditation:** AACSB, AACN, ADA, AHIMA, CARC, CSWE, JRCERT, NAACLS, NASPAA, NCATE, NLN **Intercollegiate Athletics:** Baseball M; Basketball M & W; Volleyball W

INDIANA UNIVERSITY SOUTH BEND
1700 Mishawaka Ave., PO Box 7111
South Bend, IN 46634-7111
Tel: (574)520-4872; Free: 877-GO-2-IUSB
Admissions: (574)520-4839
Fax: (574)520-4834
E-mail: admissio@iusb.edu
Web Site: http://www.iusb.edu/
President/CEO: Dr. Una Mae Reck
Admissions: Michael Renfrow
Financial Aid: Bev Cooper
Type: Comprehensive **Sex:** Coed **Affiliation:** Indiana University System **Scores:** 82.4% SAT V 400+; 84.3% SAT M 400+; 50.3% ACT 18-23; 20.7% ACT 24-29 **% Accepted:** 80 **Admission Plans:** Deferred Admission **Application Deadline:** Rolling **Application Fee:** $45.00 **H.S. Requirements:** High school diploma required; GED accepted **Costs Per Year:** Application fee: $45. State resident tuition: $5573 full-time, $185.75 per credit hour part-time. Nonresident tuition: $15,270 full-time, $509 per credit hour part-time. Mandatory fees: $442 full-time. Full-time tuition and fees vary according to course load, location, and program. Part-time tuition varies according to course load, location, and program. **Scholarships:** Available **Calendar System:** Semester, Summer Session Available **Enrollment:** FT 4,328, PT 3,168, Grad FT 207, Grad PT 691 **Faculty:** FT 292, PT 254 **Student-Faculty Ratio:** 15:1 **Exams:** SAT I or ACT. **% Receiving Financial Aid:** 68 **Library Holdings:** 300,202 **Regional Accreditation:** North Central Association of Colleges and Schools **Credit Hours For Degree:** 60 credit hours, Associates; 120 credit hours, Bachelors **ROTC:** Army, Navy, Air Force **Professional Accreditation:** AACSB, AACN, ACA, ADA, CSWE, JRCERT, MACTE, NASPAA, NCATE, NLN **Intercollegiate Athletics:** Basketball M & W

INDIANA UNIVERSITY SOUTHEAST
4201 Grant Line Rd.
New Albany, IN 47150-6405
Tel: (812)941-2000
Admissions: (812)941-2212
E-mail: admissions@ius.edu
Web Site: http://www.ius.edu/
President/CEO: Dr. Sandra R. Patterson-Randles
Admissions: Anne Skuce
Financial Aid: Brittany Hubbard
Type: Comprehensive **Sex:** Coed **Affiliation:** Indiana University System **Scores:** 82.8% SAT V 400+; 82.8% SAT M 400+; 55.3% ACT 18-23; 15.1% ACT 24-29 **% Accepted:** 85 **Admission Plans:** Early Admission; Deferred Admission **Application Deadline:** Rolling **Application Fee:** $30.00 **H.S. Requirements:** High school diploma required; GED accepted **Costs Per Year:** Application fee: $30. State resident tuition: $5417 full-time, $180.58 per credit hour part-time. Nonresident tuition: $14,105 full-time, $470.15 per credit hour part-time. Mandatory fees: $473 full-time. Full-time tuition and fees vary according to course load, location, program, and reciprocity agree-

ments. Part-time tuition varies according to course load, location, program, and reciprocity agreements. College room only: $5630. Room charges vary according to housing facility. **Scholarships:** Available **Calendar System:** Semester, Summer Session Available **Enrollment:** FT 3,899, PT 2,044, Grad FT 39, Grad PT 858 **Faculty:** FT 200, PT 265 **Student-Faculty Ratio:** 17:1 **Exams:** SAT I or ACT. **% Receiving Financial Aid:** 62 **Library Holdings:** 215,429 **Regional Accreditation:** North Central Association of Colleges and Schools **Credit Hours For Degree:** 63 credit hours, Associates; 120 credit hours, Bachelors **ROTC:** Army **Professional Accreditation:** AACSB, AACN, NCATE **Intercollegiate Athletics:** Baseball M; Basketball M & W; Cheerleading W; Softball W; Tennis M & W; Volleyball W

INDIANA UNIVERSITY—PURDUE UNIVERSITY FORT WAYNE
2101 East Coliseum Blvd.
Fort Wayne, IN 46805-1499
Tel: (260)481-6100
Admissions: (260)481-6142
E-mail: morrena@ipfw.edu
Web Site: http://www.ipfw.edu/
President/CEO: Dr. Michael A. Wartell
Admissions: Angela Morren
Financial Aid: Judith Cramer
Type: Comprehensive **Sex:** Coed **Affiliation:** Indiana University System and Purdue University System **Scores:** 85.4% SAT V 400+; 88% SAT M 400+; 53.1% ACT 18-23; 24.7% ACT 24-29 **% Accepted:** 96 **Admission Plans:** Deferred Admission **Application Deadline:** August 1 **Application Fee:** $50.00 **H.S. Requirements:** High school diploma required; GED accepted **Costs Per Year:** Application fee: $50. State resident tuition: $5441 full-time, $202 per credit hour part-time. Nonresident tuition: $14,037 full-time, $520 per credit hour part-time. Mandatory fees: $792 full-time, $29.35 per credit hour part-time. Full-time tuition and fees vary according to course load. Part-time tuition and fees vary according to course load. College room only: $5620. Room charges vary according to housing facility. **Scholarships:** Available **Calendar System:** Semester, Summer Session Available **Enrollment:** FT 8,389, PT 4,487, Grad FT 151, Grad PT 648 **Faculty:** FT 407, PT 405 **Student-Faculty Ratio:** 18:1 **Exams:** SAT I or ACT. ACT essay used for placement. SAT essay used for placement. **% Receiving Financial Aid:** 64 **% Residing in College-Owned, -Operated, or -Affiliated Housing:** 5 **Final Year or Final Semester Residency Requirement:** No **Library Holdings:** 441,647 **Regional Accreditation:** North Central Association of Colleges and Schools **Credit Hours For Degree:** 60 semester hours, Associates; 120 semester hours, Bachelors **ROTC:** Army **Professional Accreditation:** AACSB, ABET, ADA, AHIMA, NASM, NASPAA, NCATE, NLN **Intercollegiate Athletics:** Baseball M; Basketball M & W; Cross-Country Running M & W; Golf M & W; Soccer M & W; Softball W; Tennis M & W; Track and Field W; Volleyball M & W

INDIANA UNIVERSITY—PURDUE UNIVERSITY INDIANAPOLIS
355 North Lansing
Indianapolis, IN 46202-2896
Tel: (317)274-5555
Admissions: (317)274-4591
Fax: (317)278-1862
E-mail: apply@iupui.edu
Web Site: http://www.iupui.edu/
President/CEO: Dr. Charles R. Bantz
Admissions: Chris J. Foley
Financial Aid: Kathy Purris
Type: University **Sex:** Coed **Affiliation:** Indiana University System **Scores:** 89.1% SAT V 400+; 91.8% SAT M 400+; 54.7% ACT 18-23; 27% ACT 24-29 **% Accepted:** 67 **Admission Plans:** Deferred Admission **Application Deadline:** June 1 **Application Fee:** $50.00 **H.S. Requirements:** High school diploma required; GED accepted **Costs Per Year:** Application fee: $50. State resident tuition: $6923 full-time, $230.76 per credit hour part-time. Nonresident tuition: $21,820 full-time, $727.33 per credit hour part-time. Mandatory fees: $600 full-time. Full-time tuition and fees vary according to course load, location, and program. Part-time tuition varies according to course load, location, and program. College room only: $3370. Room charges vary according to housing facility. **Scholarships:** Available **Calendar System:** Semester, Summer Session Available **Enrollment:** FT 15,696, PT 6,423, Grad FT 4,045, Grad PT 4,219 **Faculty:** FT 2,116, PT 980 **Student-Faculty Ratio:** 16:1 **Exams:** SAT I or ACT. SAT essay used for advising. SAT essay used for placement. **% Receiving Financial Aid:** 65 **% Residing in College-Owned, -Operated, or -Affiliated Housing:** 5 **Library Holdings:** 1,481,216 **Regional Accreditation:** North Central Association of Colleges and Schools **Credit Hours For Degree:** 60 credit hours, Associates; 120 credit hours, Bachelors **ROTC:** Army, Air Force **Professional Accreditation:** AACSB, ABET, AACN, ABA, ADA, ADtA, AHIMA, AOTA, APTA, APA, ASC, ACIPE, ACEHSA, CARC, CEPH, CSWE, JRCERT, JRCNMT, LCMEAMA, NAACLS NASAD, NASPAA, NLN **Intercollegiate Athletics:** Basketball M & W; Cross-Country Running M & W; Golf M & W; Soccer M & W; Softball W; Swimming and Diving M & W; Tennis M & W; Volleyball W

INDIANA WESLEYAN UNIVERSITY
4201 South Washington St.
Marion, IN 46953-4974
Tel: (765)674-6901; Free: 800-332-6901
Admissions: (866)468-6498
Fax: (765)677-2333
E-mail: admissions@indwes.edu
Web Site: http://www.indwes.edu/
President/CEO: Dr. Henry Smith
Admissions: Daniel Solms
Type: Comprehensive **Sex:** Coed **Affiliation:** Wesleyan **Scores:** 97% SAT V 400+; 95% SAT M 400+; 38% ACT 18-23; 47% ACT 24-29 **% Accepted:** 76 **Admission Plans:** Deferred Admission **Application Deadline:** Rolling **Application Fee:** $25.00 **H.S. Requirements:** High school diploma required; GED accepted **Costs Per Year:** Application fee: $25. Comprehensive fee: $28,221 includes full-time tuition ($21,213) and college room and board ($7008). College room only: $3390. Room and board charges vary according to board plan. **Scholarships:** Available **Calendar System:** Semester, Summer Session Available **Enrollment:** FT 2,980, PT 265 **Faculty:** FT 161, PT 153 **Student-Faculty Ratio:** 15:1 **Exams:** Other, SAT I or ACT. **% Receiving Financial Aid:** 69 **% Residing in College-Owned, -Operated, or -Affiliated Housing:** 82 **Final Year or Final Semester Residency Requirement:** No **Library Holdings:** 164,272 **Regional Accreditation:** North Central Association of Colleges and Schools **Credit Hours For Degree:** 62 semester hours, Associates; 124 semester hours, Bachelors **ROTC:** Army **Professional Accreditation:** AACN, ACA, CSWE, NASM, NCATE **Intercollegiate Athletics:** Baseball M; Basketball M & W; Cheerleading M & W; Cross-Country Running M & W; Golf M; Soccer M & W; Softball W; Tennis M & W; Track and Field M & W; Volleyball W

INTERNATIONAL BUSINESS COLLEGE (FORT WAYNE)
5699 Coventry Ln.
Fort Wayne, IN 46804
Tel: (219)459-4500; Free: 800-589-6363
Admissions: (260)459-4500
Fax: (219)436-1896
Web Site: http://www.ibcfortwayne.edu/
President/CEO: Jim Zillman
Type: Four-Year College **Sex:** Coed **% Accepted:** 78 **H.S. Requirements:** High school diploma required; GED accepted **Scholarships:** Available **Calendar System:** Semester, Summer Session Not available **Credit Hours For Degree:** 69 semester credits, Associates; 127 semester credits, Bachelors **Professional Accreditation:** ACICS, AAMAE

INTERNATIONAL BUSINESS COLLEGE (INDIANAPOLIS)
7205 Shadeland Station
Indianapolis, IN 46256
Tel: (317)841-6400; Free: 800-589-6500
Admissions: (317)813-2300
Fax: (317)841-6419
Web Site: http://www.ibcindianapolis.edu/
President/CEO: Kathy Chiudioni
Type: Two-Year College **Sex:** Coed **% Accepted:** 77 **H.S. Requirements:** High school diploma required; GED accepted **Scholarships:** Available **Calendar System:** Semester **Professional Accreditation:** ACICS

ITT TECHNICAL INSTITUTE (FORT WAYNE)
2810 Dupont Commerce Ct.
Fort Wayne, IN 46825
Tel: (260)497-6200; Free: 800-866-4488
Web Site: http://www.itt-tech.edu/
President/CEO: Alois Johnson
Type: Two-Year College **Sex:** Coed **Affiliation:** ITT Educational Services, Inc. **H.S. Requirements:** High school diploma required; GED accepted

Scholarships: Available **Calendar System:** Quarter, Summer Session Not available **Professional Accreditation:** ACICS

ITT TECHNICAL INSTITUTE (INDIANAPOLIS)
9511 Angola Ct.
Indianapolis, IN 46268-1119
Tel: (317)875-8640; Free: 800-937-4488
Fax: (317)875-8641
Web Site: http://www.itt-tech.edu/
President/CEO: Karen Larson-Reuter
Type: Two-Year College **Sex:** Coed **Affiliation:** ITT Educational Services, Inc. **H.S. Requirements:** High school diploma required; GED accepted **Scholarships:** Available **Calendar System:** Quarter, Summer Session Not available **Credit Hours For Degree:** 96 credit hours, Associates; 180 credit hours, Bachelors **Professional Accreditation:** ACICS

ITT TECHNICAL INSTITUTE (MERRILLVILLE)
8488 Georgia St.
Merrillville, IN 46410
Tel: (219)738-6100; Free: 877-418-8134
Web Site: http://www.itt-tech.edu/
Type: Two-Year College **Sex:** Coed **Professional Accreditation:** ACICS

ITT TECHNICAL INSTITUTE (NEWBURGH)
10999 Stahl Rd.
Newburgh, IN 47630-7430
Tel: (812)858-1600
Web Site: http://www.itt-tech.edu/
President/CEO: Roseanna Dodson
Type: Two-Year College **Sex:** Coed **Affiliation:** ITT Educational Services, Inc. **H.S. Requirements:** High school diploma required; GED accepted **Scholarships:** Available **Calendar System:** Quarter, Summer Session Not available **Credit Hours For Degree:** 96 credit hours, Associates; 180 credit hours, Bachelors **Professional Accreditation:** ACICS

ITT TECHNICAL INSTITUTE (SOUTH BEND)
17390 Dugdale Dr.
Ste. 100
South Bend, IN 46635
Tel: (574)247-8300; Free: 877-474-1926
Web Site: http://www.itt-tech.edu/
President/CEO: Leon Baker
Type: Four-Year College **Sex:** Coed **Affiliation:** ITT Educational Services, Inc. **Calendar System:** Quarter

IVY TECH COMMUNITY COLLEGE—BLOOMINGTON
200 Daniels Way
Bloomington, IN 47404
Tel: (812)332-1559
Fax: (812)332-8147
E-mail: nfrederi@ivytech.edu
Web Site: http://www.ivytech.edu/
President/CEO: John Whikehart
Admissions: Neil Frederick
Type: Two-Year College **Sex:** Coed **Affiliation:** Ivy Tech Community College System **% Accepted:** 100 **Admission Plans:** Open Admission; Preferred Admission; Deferred Admission **Application Deadline:** Rolling **Application Fee:** $0.00 **Costs Per Year:** Application fee: $0. State resident tuition: $104.55 per credit hour part-time. Nonresident tuition: $221.35 per credit hour part-time. Mandatory fees: $60 per term part-time. **Scholarships:** Available **Calendar System:** Semester, Summer Session Available **Enrollment:** FT 2,237, PT 2,483 **Faculty:** FT 57, PT 269 **Library Holdings:** 5,516 **Regional Accreditation:** North Central Association of Colleges and Schools **Credit Hours For Degree:** 60 credits, Associates **Professional Accreditation:** ACBSP, NLN

IVY TECH COMMUNITY COLLEGE—CENTRAL INDIANA
50 West Fall Creek Parkway North Dr.
Indianapolis, IN 46206-1763
Tel: (317)921-4800; Free: 888-IVYLINE
E-mail: tfunk@ivytech.edu
Web Site: http://www.ivytech.edu/
President/CEO: Hank Dunn
Admissions: Tracy Funk
Type: Two-Year College **Sex:** Coed **Affiliation:** Ivy Tech Community College System **Admission Plans:** Open Admission; Preferred Admission; Early Admission; Deferred Admission **Application Deadline:** Rolling **Application Fee:** $0.00 **H.S. Requirements:** High school diploma or equivalent not required. For allied health programs: High school diploma required; GED accepted **Costs Per Year:** Application fee: $0. State resident tuition: $104.55 per credit hour part-time. Nonresident tuition: $221.35 per credit hour part-time. Mandatory fees: $60 per term part-time. **Scholarships:** Available **Calendar System:** Semester, Summer Session Available **Enrollment:** FT 7,053, PT 14,448 **Faculty:** FT 153, PT 552 **Library Holdings:** 20,247 **Regional Accreditation:** North Central Association of Colleges and Schools **Credit Hours For Degree:** 60 credits, Associates **Professional Accreditation:** ARCEST, AAMAE, ACF, ACBSP, CARC, JRCERT, NLN, NAIT

IVY TECH COMMUNITY COLLEGE—COLUMBUS
4475 Central Ave.
Columbus, IN 47203-1868
Tel: (812)372-9925; Free: 800-922-4838
Fax: (812)372-0311
E-mail: nbagadio@ivytech.edu
Web Site: http://www.ivytech.edu/
President/CEO: John Hogan
Admissions: Neil Bagadiong
Type: Two-Year College **Sex:** Coed **Affiliation:** Ivy Tech Community College System **Admission Plans:** Open Admission; Preferred Admission; Early Admission; Deferred Admission **Application Deadline:** Rolling **Application Fee:** $0.00 **H.S. Requirements:** High school diploma or equivalent not required. For allied health programs: High school diploma required; GED accepted **Costs Per Year:** Application fee: $0. State resident tuition: $104.55 per credit hour part-time. Nonresident tuition: $221.35 per credit hour part-time. Mandatory fees: $60 per term part-time. **Scholarships:** Available **Calendar System:** Semester, Summer Session Available **Enrollment:** FT 1,940, PT 3,004 **Faculty:** FT 48, PT 211 **Library Holdings:** 7,855 **Regional Accreditation:** North Central Association of Colleges and Schools **Credit Hours For Degree:** 60 credits, Associates **Professional Accreditation:** ARCEST, AAMAE, ADA, ACBSP

IVY TECH COMMUNITY COLLEGE—EAST CENTRAL
4301 South Cowan Rd., PO Box 3100
Muncie, IN 47302-9448
Tel: (765)289-2291
E-mail: mlewelle@ivytech.edu
Web Site: http://www.ivytech.edu/
President/CEO: Gail Chesterfield
Admissions: Mary Lewellen
Type: Two-Year College **Sex:** Coed **Affiliation:** Ivy Tech Community College System **Admission Plans:** Open Admission; Preferred Admission; Early Admission; Deferred Admission **Application Deadline:** Rolling **Application Fee:** $0.00 **H.S. Requirements:** High school diploma or equivalent not required. For allied health programs: High school diploma required; GED accepted **Costs Per Year:** Application fee: $0. State resident tuition: $104.55 per credit hour part-time. Nonresident tuition: $231.35 per credit hour part-time. Mandatory fees: $60 per term part-time. **Scholarships:** Available **Calendar System:** Semester, Summer Session Not available **Enrollment:** FT 4,069, PT 4,510 **Faculty:** FT 93, PT 393 **Library Holdings:** 5,779 **Regional Accreditation:** North Central Association of Colleges and Schools **Credit Hours For Degree:** 60 credits, Associates **Professional Accreditation:** ARCEST, AAMAE, APTA, ACBSP

IVY TECH COMMUNITY COLLEGE—KOKOMO
1815 East Morgan St, PO Box 1373
Kokomo, IN 46903-1373
Tel: (765)459-0561
E-mail: sdillman@ivytech.edu
Web Site: http://www.ivytech.edu/
President/CEO: Steve Daily
Admissions: Suzanne Dillman
Type: Two-Year College **Sex:** Coed **Affiliation:** Ivy Tech Community College System **Admission Plans:** Open Admission; Preferred Admission; Early Admission **Application Deadline:** Rolling **Application Fee:** $0.00 **H.S. Requirements:** High school diploma or equivalent not required. For allied health programs: High school diploma required; GED accepted **Costs Per Year:** Application fee: $0. State resident tuition: $104.55 per credit hour part-time. Nonresident tuition: $221.35 per credit hour part-time. Mandatory fees:

$60 per term part-time. **Scholarships:** Available **Calendar System:** Semester, Summer Session Available **Enrollment:** FT 2,265, PT 3,169 **Faculty:** FT 67, PT 253 **Library Holdings:** 5,177 **Regional Accreditation:** North Central Association of Colleges and Schools **Credit Hours For Degree:** 60 credits, Associates **Professional Accreditation:** AAMAE, ACBSP

IVY TECH COMMUNITY COLLEGE—LAFAYETTE
3101 South Creasy Ln.
Lafayette, IN 47905-5266
Tel: (765)772-9100
Admissions: (765)269-5000
E-mail: jdopplef@ivytech.edu
Web Site: http://www.ivytech.edu/
President/CEO: Dr. David Bathe
Admissions: Judy Doppelfeld
Type: Two-Year College **Sex:** Coed **Affiliation:** Ivy Tech Community College System **Admission Plans:** Open Admission; Preferred Admission **Application Deadline:** Rolling **Application Fee:** $0.00 **H.S. Requirements:** High school diploma or equivalent not required. For allied health programs: High school diploma required; GED accepted **Costs Per Year:** Application fee: $0. State resident tuition: $104.55 per credit hour part-time. Nonresident tuition: $221.35 per credit hour part-time. Mandatory fees: $60 per term part-time. **Scholarships:** Available **Calendar System:** Semester, Summer Session Available **Enrollment:** FT 3,768, PT 4,537 **Faculty:** FT 87, PT 289 **Library Holdings:** 8,043 **Regional Accreditation:** North Central Association of Colleges and Schools **Credit Hours For Degree:** 60 credits, Associates **Professional Accreditation:** ARCEST, AAMAE, ADA, ACBSP, CARC, NLN, NAIT

IVY TECH COMMUNITY COLLEGE—NORTH CENTRAL
220 Dean Johnson Blvd.
South Bend, IN 46601
Tel: (574)289-7001
Fax: (574)236-7181
E-mail: pdecker@ivytech.edu
Web Site: http://www.ivytech.edu/
President/CEO: Virginia Calvin
Admissions: Pam Decker
Type: Two-Year College **Sex:** Coed **Affiliation:** Ivy Tech Community College System **Admission Plans:** Open Admission; Preferred Admission; Early Admission; Deferred Admission **Application Deadline:** Rolling **Application Fee:** $0.00 **H.S. Requirements:** High school diploma or equivalent not required. For allied health programs: High school diploma required; GED accepted **Costs Per Year:** Application fee: $0. State resident tuition: $104.55 per credit hour part-time. Nonresident tuition: $221.35 per credit hour part-time. Mandatory fees: $60 per term part-time. **Scholarships:** Available **Calendar System:** Semester, Summer Session Available **Enrollment:** FT 2,765, PT 5,900 **Faculty:** FT 82, PT 288 **Library Holdings:** 6,246 **Regional Accreditation:** North Central Association of Colleges and Schools **Credit Hours For Degree:** 60 credits, Associates **Professional Accreditation:** AAMAE, ACF, ACBSP, NAACLS, NLN

IVY TECH COMMUNITY COLLEGE—NORTHEAST
3800 North Anthony Blvd.
Fort Wayne, IN 46805-1430
Tel: (260)482-9171; Free: 800-859-4882
Fax: (260)480-4177
E-mail: sscheer@ivytech.edu
Web Site: http://www.ivytech.edu/
President/CEO: Mark Keen
Admissions: Steve Scheer
Type: Two-Year College **Sex:** Coed **Affiliation:** Ivy Tech Community College System **Admission Plans:** Open Admission; Preferred Admission; Early Admission **Application Deadline:** Rolling **Application Fee:** $0.00 **H.S. Requirements:** High school diploma or equivalent not required. For allied health programs: High school diploma required; GED accepted **Costs Per Year:** Application fee: $0. State resident tuition: $104.55 per credit hour part-time. Nonresident tuition: $221.35 per credit hour part-time. Mandatory fees: $60 per term part-time. **Scholarships:** Available **Calendar System:** Semester, Summer Session Available **Enrollment:** FT 4,771, PT 6,726 **Faculty:** FT 113, PT 383 **Library Holdings:** 18,389 **Regional Accreditation:** North Central Association of Colleges and Schools **Credit Hours For Degree:** 60 credits, Associates **Professional Accreditation:** AAMAE, ACF, ACBSP, CARC, NAIT

IVY TECH COMMUNITY COLLEGE—NORTHWEST
1440 East 35th Ave.
Gary, IN 46409-1499
Tel: (219)981-1111
E-mail: tlewis@ivytech.edu
Web Site: http://www.ivytech.edu/
President/CEO: J. Guadalupe Valtierra
Admissions: Twilla Lewis
Type: Two-Year College **Sex:** Coed **Affiliation:** Ivy Tech Community College System **Admission Plans:** Open Admission; Preferred Admission; Deferred Admission **Application Deadline:** Rolling **Application Fee:** $0.00 **H.S. Requirements:** High school diploma or equivalent not required. For allied health programs: High school diploma required; GED accepted **Costs Per Year:** Application fee: $0. State resident tuition: $104.55 per credit hour part-time. Nonresident tuition: $221.35 per credit hour part-time. Mandatory fees: $60 per term part-time. **Scholarships:** Available **Calendar System:** Semester, Summer Session Available **Enrollment:** FT 3,518, PT 5,783 **Faculty:** FT 106, PT 277 **Library Holdings:** 13,805 **Regional Accreditation:** North Central Association of Colleges and Schools **Credit Hours For Degree:** 60 credits, Associates **Professional Accreditation:** ARCEST, AAMAE, ACF, APTA, ACBSP, CARC

IVY TECH COMMUNITY COLLEGE—RICHMOND
2325 Chester Blvd.
Richmond, IN 47374-1220
Tel: (765)966-2656
E-mail: jplaster@ivytech.edu
Web Site: http://www.ivytech.edu/richmond/
President/CEO: James Steck
Admissions: Jeff Plasterer
Type: Two-Year College **Sex:** Coed **Affiliation:** Ivy Tech Community College System **Admission Plans:** Open Admission; Preferred Admission; Early Admission **Application Deadline:** Rolling **Application Fee:** $0.00 **H.S. Requirements:** High school diploma or equivalent not required. For allied health programs: High school diploma required; GED accepted **Costs Per Year:** Application fee: $0. State resident tuition: $104.55 per credit hour part-time. Nonresident tuition: $221.35 per credit hour part-time. Mandatory fees: $60 per term part-time. **Scholarships:** Available **Calendar System:** Semester, Summer Session Available **Enrollment:** FT 1,347, PT 2,438 **Faculty:** FT 35, PT 136 **Regional Accreditation:** North Central Association of Colleges and Schools **Credit Hours For Degree:** 60 credits, Associates **Professional Accreditation:** AAMAE, ACBSP, NLN, NAIT

IVY TECH COMMUNITY COLLEGE—SOUTHEAST
590 Ivy Tech Dr., PO Box 209
Madison, IN 47250-1883
Tel: (812)265-4028
Admissions: (812)265-2580
E-mail: chutcher@ivytech.edu
Web Site: http://www.ivytech.edu/
President/CEO: James Helms
Admissions: Cindy Hutcherson
Type: Two-Year College **Sex:** Coed **Affiliation:** Ivy Tech Community College System **Admission Plans:** Open Admission; Preferred Admission **Application Deadline:** Rolling **Application Fee:** $0.00 **H.S. Requirements:** High school diploma or equivalent not required. For allied health programs: High school diploma required; GED accepted **Costs Per Year:** Application fee: $0. State resident tuition: $104.55 per credit hour part-time. Nonresident tuition: $221.35 per credit hour part-time. Mandatory fees: $60 per term part-time. **Scholarships:** Available **Calendar System:** Semester, Summer Session Available **Enrollment:** FT 1,213, PT 1,867 **Faculty:** FT 41, PT 134 **Library Holdings:** 9,027 **Regional Accreditation:** North Central Association of Colleges and Schools **Credit Hours For Degree:** 60 credits, Associates **Professional Accreditation:** ACBSP

IVY TECH COMMUNITY COLLEGE—SOUTHERN INDIANA
8204 Hwy. 311
Sellersburg, IN 47172-1829
Tel: (812)246-3301
E-mail: msteinbe@ivytech.edu

Web Site: http://www.ivytech.edu/
President/CEO: Rita Shourds
Admissions: Mindy Steinberg
Type: Two-Year College **Sex:** Coed **Affiliation:** Ivy Tech Community College System **Admission Plans:** Open Admission; Preferred Admission; Early Admission; Deferred Admission **Application Deadline:** Rolling **Application Fee:** $0.00 **H.S. Requirements:** High school diploma or equivalent not required. For allied health programs: High school diploma required; GED accepted **Costs Per Year:** Application fee: $0. State resident tuition: $104.55 per credit hour part-time. Nonresident tuition: $221.35 per credit hour part-time. Mandatory fees: $60 per term part-time. **Scholarships:** Available **Calendar System:** Semester, Summer Session Available **Enrollment:** FT 1,861, PT 2,982 **Faculty:** FT 51, PT 145 **Library Holdings:** 7,634 **Regional Accreditation:** North Central Association of Colleges and Schools **Credit Hours For Degree:** 60 credits, Associates **Professional Accreditation:** AAMAE, ACBSP, NAIT

IVY TECH COMMUNITY COLLEGE—SOUTHWEST
3501 First Ave.
Evansville, IN 47710-3398
Tel: (812)426-2865
E-mail: ajohnson@ivytech.edu
Web Site: http://www.ivytech.edu/
President/CEO: Daniel L. Schenk
Admissions: Denise Johnson-Kincade
Type: Two-Year College **Sex:** Coed **Affiliation:** Ivy Tech Community College System **Admission Plans:** Open Admission; Preferred Admission; Early Admission; Deferred Admission **Application Deadline:** Rolling **Application Fee:** $0.00 **H.S. Requirements:** High school diploma or equivalent not required. For allied health programs: High school diploma required; GED accepted **Costs Per Year:** Application fee: $0. State resident tuition: $104.55 per credit hour part-time. Nonresident tuition: $221.35 per credit hour part-time. Mandatory fees: $60 per term part-time. **Scholarships:** Available **Calendar System:** Semester, Summer Session Available **Enrollment:** FT 2,402, PT 4,099 **Faculty:** FT 79, PT 249 **Library Holdings:** 7,082 **Regional Accreditation:** North Central Association of Colleges and Schools **Credit Hours For Degree:** 60 credits, Associates **Professional Accreditation:** ARCEST, AAMAE, ACBSP, JRCEMT, NLN, NAIT

IVY TECH COMMUNITY COLLEGE—WABASH VALLEY
7999 US Hwy. 41, South
Terre Haute, IN 47802
Tel: (812)299-1121
E-mail: mfisher@ivytech.edu
Web Site: http://www.ivytech.edu/
President/CEO: Jeff Pittman
Admissions: Michael Fisher
Type: Two-Year College **Sex:** Coed **Affiliation:** Ivy Tech Community College System **Admission Plans:** Open Admission; Preferred Admission; Early Admission; Deferred Admission **Application Deadline:** Rolling **Application Fee:** $0.00 **H.S. Requirements:** High school diploma or equivalent not required. For allied health programs: High school diploma required; GED accepted **Costs Per Year:** Application fee: $0. State resident tuition: $104.55 per credit hour part-time. Nonresident tuition: $221.35 per credit hour part-time. Mandatory fees: $60 per term part-time. **Scholarships:** Available **Calendar System:** Semester, Summer Session Available **Enrollment:** FT 2,784, PT 3,862 **Faculty:** FT 82, PT 203 **Library Holdings:** 4,403 **Regional Accreditation:** North Central Association of Colleges and Schools **Credit Hours For Degree:** 60 credits, Associates **Professional Accreditation:** ARCEST, AAMAE, ACBSP, JRCERT, NAACLS, NAIT

KAPLAN COLLEGE, HAMMOND CAMPUS
7833 Indianapolis Blvd.
Hammond, IN 46324
Tel: (219)844-0100
Web Site: http://www.kc-hammond.com/
President/CEO: Linda Yednak
Type: Two-Year College **Sex:** Coed **H.S. Requirements:** High school diploma required; GED accepted **Scholarships:** Available **Calendar System:** Quarter **Professional Accreditation:** ACICS

KAPLAN COLLEGE, MERRILLVILLE CAMPUS
3803 East Lincoln Hwy.
Merrillville, IN 46410
Tel: (219)947-8400
Web Site: http://www.kc-merrillville.com/
President/CEO: Chris Artim
Type: Two-Year College **Sex:** Coed **H.S. Requirements:** High school diploma required; GED accepted **Professional Accreditation:** ACICS

KAPLAN COLLEGE, NORTHWEST INDIANAPOLIS CAMPUS
7302 Woodland Dr.
Indianapolis, IN 46278
Tel: (317)299-6001; Free: 800-849-4995
Web Site: http://www.kc-indy.com/
President/CEO: Harry Strong
Type: Two-Year College **Sex:** Coed **H.S. Requirements:** High school diploma required; GED accepted **Scholarships:** Available **Professional Accreditation:** ACCSCT, ADA

LINCOLN TECHNICAL INSTITUTE
7225 Winton Dr.
Bldg. 128
Indianapolis, IN 46268
Tel: (317)632-5553; Free: 800-554-4465
Web Site: http://www.lincolnedu.com/
President/CEO: Mary Jo Greco
Admissions: Cindy Ryan
Type: Two-Year College **Sex:** Coed **Affiliation:** Lincoln Technical Institute, Inc **Application Deadline:** Rolling **H.S. Requirements:** High school diploma required; GED accepted **Scholarships:** Available **Calendar System:** Miscellaneous, Summer Session Available **Library Holdings:** 800 **Credit Hours For Degree:** 59 credits, Associates **Professional Accreditation:** ACCSCT

MANCHESTER COLLEGE
604 East College Ave.
North Manchester, IN 46962-1225
Tel: (260)982-5000; Free: 800-852-3648
Admissions: (260)982-5055
Fax: (260)982-5043
E-mail: admitinfo@manchester.edu
Web Site: http://www.manchester.edu/
President/CEO: Dr. Jo Young Switzer
Admissions: Adam Hohman
Financial Aid: Sherri Shockey
Type: Four-Year College **Sex:** Coed **Affiliation:** Church of the Brethren **Scores:** 90% SAT V 400+; 94% SAT M 400+; 49% ACT 18-23; 35% ACT 24-29 **% Accepted:** 77 **Admission Plans:** Deferred Admission **Application Deadline:** Rolling **Application Fee:** $25.00 **H.S. Requirements:** High school diploma required; GED accepted **Costs Per Year:** Application fee: $25. One-time mandatory fee: $250. Comprehensive fee: $32,340 includes full-time tuition ($23,000), mandatory fees ($790), and college room and board ($8550). College room only: $5250. Room and board charges vary according to board plan and housing facility. Part-time mandatory fees: $350 per year. Part-time fees vary according to course load. **Scholarships:** Available **Calendar System:** 4-1-4, Summer Session Available **Enrollment:** FT 1,182, PT 41 **Faculty:** FT 67, PT 26 **Student-Faculty Ratio:** 16:1 **Exams:** SAT I or ACT. ACT essay used in place of application essay. SAT essay used in place of application essay. ACT essay used for placement. SAT essay used for placement. **% Receiving Financial Aid:** 84 **% Residing in College-Owned, -Operated, or -Affiliated Housing:** 75 **Regional Accreditation:** North Central Association of Colleges and Schools **Credit Hours For Degree:** 64 semester hours, Associates; 128 semester hours, Bachelors **Professional Accreditation:** CSWE, JRCEPAT, NCATE **Intercollegiate Athletics:** Baseball M; Basketball M & W; Cheerleading M & W; Cross-Country Running M & W; Football M; Golf M & W; Soccer M & W; Softball W; Tennis M & W; Track and Field M & W; Volleyball W; Wrestling M

MARIAN UNIVERSITY
3200 Cold Spring Rd.
Indianapolis, IN 46222-1997
Tel: (317)955-6000
Admissions: (317)955-6300
E-mail: admissions@marian.edu
Web Site: http://www.marian.edu/
President/CEO: Daniel Elsener
Financial Aid: John E. Shelton

Type: Comprehensive **Sex:** Coed **Affiliation:** Roman Catholic **Scores:** 95% SAT V 400+; 98% SAT M 400+; 70% ACT 18-23; 11% ACT 24-29 **% Accepted:** 54 **Admission Plans:** Deferred Admission **Application Deadline:** August 1 **Application Fee:** $35.00 **H.S. Requirements:** High school diploma required; GED accepted **Costs Per Year:** Application fee: $35. Comprehensive fee: $32,770 includes full-time tuition ($24,960) and college room and board ($7810). Room and board charges vary according to board plan and housing facility. Part-time tuition: $1050 per credit hour. **Scholarships:** Available **Calendar System:** Semester, Summer Session Available **Enrollment:** FT 1,488, PT 550, Grad FT 26, Grad PT 223 **Faculty:** FT 86, PT 116 **Student-Faculty Ratio:** 14:1 **Exams:** SAT I or ACT. ACT essay used for admission. SAT essay used for admission. ACT essay used for advising. SAT essay used for advising. ACT essay used for placement. SAT essay used for placement. **% Receiving Financial Aid:** 81 **% Residing in College-Owned, -Operated, or -Affiliated Housing:** 36 **Final Year or Final Semester Residency Requirement:** Yes **Library Holdings:** 102,237 **Regional Accreditation:** North Central Association of Colleges and Schools **Credit Hours For Degree:** 64 credit hours, Associates; 128 credit hours, Bachelors **ROTC:** Army **Professional Accreditation:** NCATE, NLN **Intercollegiate Athletics:** Baseball M; Basketball M & W; Bowling M & W; Cheerleading M & W; Cross-Country Running M & W; Football M; Golf M & W; Soccer M & W; Softball W; Tennis M & W; Track and Field M & W; Volleyball W

MARTIN UNIVERSITY
2171 Avondale Place, PO Box 18567
Indianapolis, IN 46218-3867
Tel: (317)543-3235
Admissions: (317)543-3237
Fax: (317)543-3257
Web Site: http://www.martin.edu/
President/CEO: Dr. Algeania Freeman
Admissions: Brenda Shaheed
Financial Aid: Berdia Marshall
Type: Comprehensive **Sex:** Coed **% Accepted:** 96 **Admission Plans:** Open Admission; Early Admission; Deferred Admission **Application Deadline:** Rolling **Application Fee:** $25.00 **H.S. Requirements:** High school diploma required; GED accepted **Costs Per Year:** Application fee: $25. One-time mandatory fee: $25. Tuition: $13,200 full-time, $440 per credit part-time. Mandatory fees: $320 full-time, $160 per term part-time. **Scholarships:** Available **Calendar System:** Semester, Summer Session Available **Enrollment:** FT 336, PT 738 **Faculty:** FT 26, PT 17 **Student-Faculty Ratio:** 21:1 **% Receiving Financial Aid:** 89 **Regional Accreditation:** North Central Association of Colleges and Schools **Credit Hours For Degree:** 134 credits, Bachelors

MID-AMERICA COLLEGE OF FUNERAL SERVICE
3111 Hamburg Pike
Jeffersonville, IN 47130-9630
Tel: (812)288-8878; Free: 800-221-6158
Fax: (812)288-5942
E-mail: macfs@mindspring.com
Web Site: http://www.mid-america.edu/
President/CEO: John R. Braboy
Admissions: Richard Nelson
Type: Two-Year College **Sex:** Coed **Admission Plans:** Open Admission; Deferred Admission **Application Deadline:** Rolling **Application Fee:** $25.00 **H.S. Requirements:** High school diploma required; GED accepted **Costs Per Year:** Application fee: $25. Tuition: $9000 full-time, $3000 per term part-time. **Scholarships:** Available **Calendar System:** Quarter, Summer Session Not available **Enrollment:** FT 120 **Faculty:** FT 6, PT 1 **Student-Faculty Ratio:** 13:1 **Library Holdings:** 1,500 **Credit Hours For Degree:** 133 quarter hours, Associates **Professional Accreditation:** ABFSE **Intercollegiate Athletics:** Softball M & W

OAKLAND CITY UNIVERSITY
138 North Lucretia St.
Oakland City, IN 47660-1099
Tel: (812)749-4781; Free: 800-737-5125
Admissions: (812)749-1222
Fax: (812)749-1233
Web Site: http://www.oak.edu/
President/CEO: Dr. Ray Barber
Admissions: Kim Heldt
Financial Aid: Caren K. Richeson
Type: Comprehensive **Sex:** Coed **Affiliation:** General Baptist **Scores:** 80% SAT V 400+; 82% SAT M 400+; 53% ACT 18-23; 17% ACT 24-29 **% Accepted:** 44 **Admission Plans:** Early Admission; Deferred Admission **Application Deadline:** Rolling **Application Fee:** $35.00 **H.S. Requirements:** High school diploma required; GED accepted **Costs Per Year:** Application fee: $35. Comprehensive fee: $22,700 includes full-time tuition ($15,600), mandatory fees ($400), and college room and board ($6700). College room only: $2400. Full-time tuition and fees vary according to degree level. Room and board charges vary according to board plan and housing facility. Part-time tuition: $500 per credit hour. **Scholarships:** Available **Calendar System:** Semester, Summer Session Available **Enrollment:** FT 1,228, PT 1,154, Grad FT 33, Grad PT 135 **Faculty:** FT 55, PT 123 **Student-Faculty Ratio:** 14:1 **Exams:** SAT I or ACT. **% Residing in College-Owned, -Operated, or -Affiliated Housing:** 49 **Library Holdings:** 87,724 **Regional Accreditation:** North Central Association of Colleges and Schools **Credit Hours For Degree:** 64 semester hours, Associates; 128 semester hours, Bachelors **Professional Accreditation:** ATS, NCATE **Intercollegiate Athletics:** Baseball M; Basketball M & W; Cheerleading W; Cross-Country Running M & W; Golf M & W; Soccer M & W; Softball W; Tennis M & W; Volleyball W

PURDUE UNIVERSITY
West Lafayette, IN 47907
Tel: (765)494-4600
Admissions: (765)494-1776
Fax: (765)494-0544
E-mail: admissions@purdue.edu
Web Site: http://www.purdue.edu/
President/CEO: France A. Cordova
Admissions: Pamela T. Horne
Financial Aid: Joyce Hall
Type: University **Sex:** Coed **Affiliation:** Purdue University System **Scores:** 100% SAT V 400+; 100% SAT M 400+; 27% ACT 18-23; 50% ACT 24-29 **% Accepted:** 73 **Admission Plans:** Early Admission; Deferred Admission **Application Deadline:** March 1 **Application Fee:** $50.00 **H.S. Requirements:** High school diploma required; GED accepted **Costs Per Year:** Application fee: $50. State resident tuition: $8183 full-time, $309 per credit hour part-time. Nonresident tuition: $24,663 full-time, $835 per credit hour part-time. Mandatory fees: $455 full-time. Full-time tuition and fees vary according to course load and program. Part-time tuition varies according to course load. College room and board: $8710. College room only: $3994. Room and board charges vary according to board plan and housing facility. **Scholarships:** Available **Calendar System:** Semester, Summer Session Available **Enrollment:** FT 29,646, PT 1,499, Grad FT 6,088, Grad PT 2,464 **Faculty:** FT 2,367, PT 353 **Student-Faculty Ratio:** 14:1 **Exams:** SAT I or ACT. ACT essay used for admission. SAT essay used for admission. **% Receiving Financial Aid:** 46 **% Residing in College-Owned, -Operated, or -Affiliated Housing:** 38 **Library Holdings:** 2,506,158 **Regional Accreditation:** North Central Association of Colleges and Schools **Credit Hours For Degree:** 63 semester hours, Associates; 126 semester hours, Bachelors **ROTC:** Army, Navy, Air Force **Professional Accreditation:** AACSB, ABET, ACPhE, AAMFT, AACN, AAFCS, ACCE, ACA, ADtA, APA, ASLA, ASLHA, AVMA, CAA, FIDER, JRCEPAT, NASAD, NAST, NCATE, NLN SAF, NAIT **Intercollegiate Athletics:** Baseball M; Basketball M & W; Cross-Country Running M & W; Football M; Golf M & W; Soccer W; Softball W; Swimming and Diving M & W; Tennis M & W; Track and Field M & W; Volleyball W; Wrestling M

PURDUE UNIVERSITY CALUMET
2200 169th St.
Hammond, IN 46323-2094
Tel: (219)989-2400
Admissions: (219)989-2213
Fax: (219)989-2775
E-mail: mcguinn@calumet.purdue.edu
Web Site: http://www.calumet.purdue.edu/
President/CEO: Dr. Howard Cohen
Admissions: Paul McGuinness
Financial Aid: Tanika House
Type: Comprehensive **Sex:** Coed **Affiliation:** Purdue University System **Scores:** 89.5% SAT V 400+; 88.1% SAT M 400+; 56.98% ACT 18-23; 20.35% ACT 24-29 **% Accepted:** 69 **Admission Plans:** Deferred Admission **Application Deadline:** Rolling **Application Fee:** $0.00 **H.S. Requirements:**

High school diploma required; GED accepted **Costs Per Year:** Application fee: $0. State resident tuition: $6337 full-time, $210.25 per credit hour part-time. Nonresident tuition: $13,624 full-time, $470.50 per credit hour part-time. Mandatory fees: $20.65 per credit hour part-time. Full-time tuition varies according to course load and program. Part-time tuition and fees vary according to course load and program. College room and board: $6653. College room only: $4680. Room and board charges vary according to housing facility. **Scholarships:** Available **Calendar System:** Semester, Summer Session Available **Enrollment:** FT 5,858, PT 3,147, Grad FT 293, Grad PT 835 **Faculty:** FT 268, PT 250 **Student-Faculty Ratio:** 21:1 **Exams:** SAT I or ACT. **% Receiving Financial Aid:** 56 **% Residing in College-Owned, -Operated, or -Affiliated Housing:** 6 **Regional Accreditation:** North Central Association of Colleges and Schools **Credit Hours For Degree:** 61 credit hours, Associates; 120 credit hours, Bachelors **Professional Accreditation:** ABET, AAMFT, NCATE, NLN **Intercollegiate Athletics:** Basketball M & W

PURDUE UNIVERSITY NORTH CENTRAL
1401 South US Hwy. 421
Westville, IN 46391-9542
Tel: (219)785-5200
Admissions: (219)785-5283
Fax: (219)785-5538
E-mail: acardenas@pnc.edu
Web Site: http://www.pnc.edu/
President/CEO: Dr. James B. Dworkin
Admissions: Anthony Cardenas
Financial Aid: Anthony Cardenas
Type: Comprehensive **Sex:** Coed **Affiliation:** Purdue University System **Scores:** 81.8% SAT V 400+; 84.49% SAT M 400+; 56.39% ACT 18-23; 18.09% ACT 24-29 **% Accepted:** 86 **Admission Plans:** Deferred Admission **Application Deadline:** August 15 **Application Fee:** $0.00 **H.S. Requirements:** High school diploma required; GED accepted **Costs Per Year:** Application fee: $0. State resident tuition: $6128 full-time, $204.25 per credit hour part-time. Nonresident tuition: $15,384 full-time, $512.80 per credit hour part-time. Mandatory fees: $576 full-time, $19.20 per credit hour part-time. Full-time tuition and fees vary according to course load, location, program, and reciprocity agreements. Part-time tuition and fees vary according to course load, location, program, and reciprocity agreements. **Scholarships:** Available **Calendar System:** Semester, Summer Session Available **Enrollment:** FT 2,761, PT 1,618, Grad PT 84 **Faculty:** FT 121, PT 193 **Student-Faculty Ratio:** 18:1 **Exams:** SAT I or ACT. ACT essay not being used. SAT essay not being used. **% Receiving Financial Aid:** 58 **Library Holdings:** 88,379 **Regional Accreditation:** North Central Association of Colleges and Schools **Credit Hours For Degree:** 60 credit hours, Associates; 123 credit hours, Bachelors **Professional Accreditation:** ABET, ACBSP, NCATE, NLN **Intercollegiate Athletics:** Baseball M; Basketball M; Cheerleading M & W; Softball W; Volleyball W

ROSE-HULMAN INSTITUTE OF TECHNOLOGY
5500 Wabash Ave.
Terre Haute, IN 47803-3999
Tel: (812)877-1511; Free: 800-248-7448
Admissions: (812)877-8894
Fax: (812)877-8941
E-mail: admissions@rose-hulman.edu
Web Site: http://www.rose-hulman.edu/
President/CEO: Matthew Branam
Admissions: James Goecker
Financial Aid: Melinda L. Middleton
Type: Comprehensive **Sex:** Coed **Scores:** 99.7% SAT V 400+; 100% SAT M 400+; 8.4% ACT 18-23; 44.1% ACT 24-29 **% Accepted:** 70 **Admission Plans:** Deferred Admission **Application Deadline:** March 1 **Application Fee:** $40.00 **H.S. Requirements:** High school diploma required; GED not accepted **Costs Per Year:** Application fee: $40. One-time mandatory fee: $2800. Comprehensive fee: $44,001 includes full-time tuition ($33,900), mandatory fees ($660), and college room and board ($9441). College room only: $5529. Full-time tuition and fees vary according to course load. Room and board charges vary according to board plan. Part-time tuition: $987 per credit hour. Part-time tuition varies according to course load. **Scholarships:** Available **Calendar System:** Quarter, Summer Session Available **Enrollment:** FT 1,835, PT 9, Grad FT 61, Grad PT 59 **Faculty:** FT 160, PT 8 **Student-Faculty Ratio:** 12:1 **Exams:** SAT I or ACT. **% Receiving Financial Aid:** 70 **% Residing in College-Owned, -Operated, or -Affiliated Housing:** 60 **Final Year or Final Semester Residency Requirement:** Yes **Library Holdings:** 79,708 **Regional Accreditation:** North Central Association of Colleges and Schools **Credit Hours For Degree:** 188 quarter hours, Bachelors **ROTC:** Army, Air Force **Professional Accreditation:** ABET **Intercollegiate Athletics:** Baseball M; Basketball M & W; Cross-Country Running M & W; Football M; Golf M & W; Riflery M & W; Soccer M & W; Softball W; Swimming and Diving M & W; Tennis M & W; Track and Field M & W; Volleyball W

SAINT JOSEPH'S COLLEGE
U.S. Hwy. 231, PO Box 890
Rensselaer, IN 47978
Tel: (219)866-6000; Free: 800-447-8781
Admissions: (219)866-6170
Fax: (219)866-6122
E-mail: admissions@saintjoe.edu
Web Site: http://www.saintjoe.edu/
President/CEO: Ernest R. Mills, III,Jr
Admissions: Karen Raftus
Financial Aid: Debra Sizemore
Type: Comprehensive **Sex:** Coed **Affiliation:** Roman Catholic **Scores:** 86% SAT V 400+; 86% SAT M 400+; 59% ACT 18-23; 24% ACT 24-29 **% Accepted:** 74 **Admission Plans:** Deferred Admission **Application Deadline:** Rolling **Application Fee:** $25.00 **H.S. Requirements:** High school diploma required; GED accepted **Costs Per Year:** Application fee: $25. Comprehensive fee: $31,950 includes full-time tuition ($24,350), mandatory fees ($180), and college room and board ($7420). Full-time tuition and fees vary according to reciprocity agreements. Room and board charges vary according to housing facility. Part-time tuition: $810 per credit hour. Part-time tuition varies according to course load and reciprocity agreements. **Scholarships:** Available **Calendar System:** Semester, Summer Session Available **Enrollment:** FT 1,017, PT 59 **Faculty:** FT 59, PT 48 **Student-Faculty Ratio:** 15:1 **Exams:** SAT I or ACT. **% Receiving Financial Aid:** 87 **% Residing in College-Owned, -Operated, or -Affiliated Housing:** 67 **Library Holdings:** 228,858 **Regional Accreditation:** North Central Association of Colleges and Schools **Credit Hours For Degree:** 60 credits, Associates; 120 credits, Bachelors **Professional Accreditation:** NCATE **Intercollegiate Athletics:** Baseball M; Basketball M & W; Cheerleading M & W; Cross-Country Running M & W; Football M; Golf M & W; Soccer M & W; Softball W; Tennis M & W; Track and Field M & W; Volleyball W

SAINT MARY-OF-THE-WOODS COLLEGE
St. Mary-of-the-Woods, IN 47876
Tel: (812)535-5151; Free: 800-926-SMWC
Admissions: (812)535-5107
Fax: (812)535-5215
E-mail: smwcadms@smwc.edu
Web Site: http://www.smwc.edu/
President/CEO: Dr. David Behrs
Admissions: Aaron Kelley
Financial Aid: Jan Benton
Type: Comprehensive **Sex:** Coed **Affiliation:** Roman Catholic **Scores:** 90% SAT V 400+; 83% SAT M 400+; 35% ACT 18-23; 30% ACT 24-29 **% Accepted:** 67 **Admission Plans:** Early Admission; Deferred Admission **Application Deadline:** August 1 **Application Fee:** $30.00 **H.S. Requirements:** High school diploma required; GED accepted **Costs Per Year:** Application fee: $30. One-time mandatory fee: $70. Comprehensive fee: $31,510 includes full-time tuition ($22,360), mandatory fees ($700), and college room and board ($8450). College room only: $3300. Full-time tuition and fees vary according to program. Part-time tuition: $424 per hour. Part-time mandatory fees: $150 per year. Part-time tuition and fees vary according to program. **Scholarships:** Available **Calendar System:** Semester, Summer Session Available **Enrollment:** FT 592, PT 873, Grad FT 85, Grad PT 127 **Faculty:** FT 66, PT 108 **Student-Faculty Ratio:** 8:1 **Exams:** SAT I or ACT. ACT essay not being used. SAT essay not being used. **% Receiving Financial Aid:** 98 **% Residing in College-Owned, -Operated, or -Affiliated Housing:** 15 **Final Year or Final Semester Residency Requirement:** No **Library Holdings:** 92,429 **Regional Accreditation:** North Central Association of Colleges and Schools **Credit Hours For Degree:** 62 credit hours, Associates; 125 credit hours, Bachelors **ROTC:** Army, Air Force **Professional Accreditation:** NASM, NCATE **Intercollegiate Athletics:** Basketball W; Cross-Country Running W; Equestrian Sports W; Golf W; Soccer W; Softball W

SAINT MARY'S COLLEGE
Notre Dame, IN 46556
Tel: (574)284-4000; Free: 800-551-7621
Admissions: (574)284-4587
Fax: (574)284-4713
E-mail: admission@saintmarys.edu
Web Site: http://www.saintmarys.edu/
President/CEO: Carol Mooney
Admissions: Mona Bowe
Financial Aid: Kathleen M. Brown
Type: Four-Year College **Sex:** Women **Affiliation:** Roman Catholic **Scores:** 99.63% SAT V 400+; 98.89% SAT M 400+; 31.85% ACT 18-23; 55.1% ACT 24-29 **% Accepted:** 86 **Admission Plans:** Early Admission; Early Decision Plan; Deferred Admission **Application Deadline:** February 15 **Application Fee:** $30.00 **H.S. Requirements:** High school diploma required; GED accepted **Costs Per Year:** Application fee: $30. Comprehensive fee: $38,822 includes full-time tuition ($28,980), mandatory fees ($636), and college room and board ($9206). College room only: $5672. Room and board charges vary according to board plan and housing facility. Part-time tuition: $1146 per credit hour. Part-time mandatory fees: $318 per term. **Scholarships:** Available **Calendar System:** Semester, Summer Session Available **Enrollment:** FT 1,647, PT 17 **Faculty:** FT 129, PT 62 **Student-Faculty Ratio:** 11:1 **Exams:** SAT I or ACT. ACT essay used for admission. SAT essay used for admission. ACT essay used for advising. SAT essay used for advising. **% Receiving Financial Aid:** 69 **% Residing in College-Owned, -Operated, or -Affiliated Housing:** 85 **Final Year or Final Semester Residency Requirement:** No **Library Holdings:** 271,161 **Regional Accreditation:** North Central Association of Colleges and Schools **Credit Hours For Degree:** 128 semester hours, Bachelors **ROTC:** Army, Navy, Air Force **Professional Accreditation:** CSWE, NASAD, NASM, NCATE, NLN **Intercollegiate Athletics:** Basketball W; Cross-Country Running W; Equestrian Sports W; Field Hockey W; Golf W; Gymnastics W; Skiing (Downhill) W; Soccer W; Softball W; Swimming and Diving W; Tennis W; Ultimate Frisbee W; Volleyball W; Water Polo W

TAYLOR UNIVERSITY
236 West Reade Ave.
Upland, IN 46989-1001
Tel: (765)998-2751; Free: 800-882-3456
Admissions: (765)998-5565
Fax: (765)998-4925
E-mail: admissions@taylor.edu
Web Site: http://www.taylor.edu/
President/CEO: Dr. Eugene Habecker
Admissions: Amy Barnett
Financial Aid: Timothy A. Nace
Type: Comprehensive **Sex:** Coed **Affiliation:** interdenominational **Scores:** 99% SAT V 400+; 95% SAT M 400+; 21% ACT 18-23; 45% ACT 24-29 **% Accepted:** 83 **Admission Plans:** Preferred Admission; Early Action; Deferred Admission **Application Deadline:** Rolling **Application Fee:** $25.00 **H.S. Requirements:** High school diploma required; GED accepted **Costs Per Year:** Application fee: $25. Comprehensive fee: $32,104 includes full-time tuition ($25,164), mandatory fees ($232), and college room and board ($6708). College room only: $3320. Full-time tuition and fees vary according to course load. Room and board charges vary according to board plan and housing facility. Part-time tuition: $901 per credit hour. Part-time mandatory fees: $36 per term. Part-time tuition and fees vary according to course load. **Scholarships:** Available **Calendar System:** 4-1-4, Summer Session Available **Enrollment:** FT 1,900, PT 536, Grad FT 116, Grad PT 8 **Faculty:** FT 129, PT 117 **Student-Faculty Ratio:** 12:1 **Exams:** SAT I or ACT. **% Receiving Financial Aid:** 62 **% Residing in College-Owned, -Operated, or -Affiliated Housing:** 81 **Final Year or Final Semester Residency Requirement:** No **Library Holdings:** 185,623 **Regional Accreditation:** North Central Association of Colleges and Schools **Credit Hours For Degree:** 64 credit hours, Associates; 128 credit hours, Bachelors **Professional Accreditation:** ACBSP, CSWE, NASM, NCATE **Intercollegiate Athletics:** Baseball M; Basketball M & W; Cross-Country Running M & W; Football M; Golf M; Soccer M & W; Softball W; Tennis M & W; Track and Field M & W; Volleyball W

TRINE UNIVERSITY
1 University Ave.
Angola, IN 46703-1764
Tel: (260)665-4100; Free: 800-347-4TSU
Admissions: (260)665-4365
Fax: (260)665-4292
E-mail: admit@trine.edu
Web Site: http://www.trine.edu/
President/CEO: Dr. Earl D. Brooks, II
Admissions: Scott Goplin
Financial Aid: Kim Bennett
Type: Comprehensive **Sex:** Coed **Scores:** 92% SAT V 400+; 96% SAT M 400+; 53% ACT 18-23; 34% ACT 24-29 **% Accepted:** 75 **Admission Plans:** Deferred Admission **Application Deadline:** August 1 **Application Fee:** $0.00 **H.S. Requirements:** High school diploma required; GED accepted **Costs Per Year:** Application fee: $0. Comprehensive fee: $33,900 includes full-time tuition ($25,300), mandatory fees ($100), and college room and board ($8500). Full-time tuition and fees vary according to degree level and location. Room and board charges vary according to board plan and housing facility. Part-time tuition: $786 per credit hour. Part-time tuition varies according to degree level and location. **Scholarships:** Available **Calendar System:** Semester, Summer Session Available **Enrollment:** FT 1,479, PT 129, Grad FT 6, Grad PT 2 **Faculty:** FT 72, PT 30 **Student-Faculty Ratio:** 15:1 **Exams:** SAT I or ACT. **% Receiving Financial Aid:** 71 **% Residing in College-Owned, -Operated, or -Affiliated Housing:** 85 **Final Year or Final Semester Residency Requirement:** Yes **Library Holdings:** 48,845 **Regional Accreditation:** North Central Association of Colleges and Schools **Credit Hours For Degree:** 61 semester hours, Associates; 120 semester hours, Bachelors **ROTC:** Air Force **Professional Accreditation:** ABET **Intercollegiate Athletics:** Baseball M; Basketball M & W; Cross-Country Running M & W; Field Hockey W; Football M; Golf M & W; Lacrosse M & W; Soccer M & W; Softball W; Tennis M & W; Track and Field M & W; Volleyball W; Wrestling M

UNIVERSITY OF EVANSVILLE
1800 Lincoln Ave.
Evansville, IN 47722
Tel: (812)488-2000; Free: 800-423-8633
Admissions: (812)488-2468
Fax: (812)474-4076
E-mail: admission@evansville.edu
Web Site: http://www.evansville.edu/
President/CEO: Dr. Stephen G. Jennings
Admissions: Don Vos
Financial Aid: JoAnn E. Laugel
Type: Comprehensive **Sex:** Coed **Affiliation:** United Methodist Church **Scores:** 99% SAT V 400+; 99% SAT M 400+; 31% ACT 18-23; 49% ACT 24-29 **% Accepted:** 86 **Admission Plans:** Early Action; Deferred Admission **Application Deadline:** February 1 **Application Fee:** $35.00 **H.S. Requirements:** High school diploma required; GED accepted **Costs Per Year:** Application fee: $35. Comprehensive fee: $35,426 includes full-time tuition ($26,010), mandatory fees ($746), and college room and board ($8670). College room only: $4470. Room and board charges vary according to board plan and housing facility. Part-time tuition: $725 per hour. Part-time mandatory fees: $45 per term. Part-time tuition and fees vary according to course load. **Scholarships:** Available **Calendar System:** Semester, Summer Session Available **Enrollment:** FT 2,476, PT 240, Grad FT 159, Grad PT 9 **Faculty:** FT 172, PT 49 **Student-Faculty Ratio:** 14:1 **Exams:** SAT I or ACT. ACT essay used for advising. SAT essay used for advising. **% Receiving Financial Aid:** 72 **% Residing in College-Owned, -Operated, or -Affiliated Housing:** 69 **Final Year or Final Semester Residency Requirement:** Yes **Library Holdings:** 277,330 **Regional Accreditation:** North Central Association of Colleges and Schools **Credit Hours For Degree:** 69 semester hours, Associates; 120 semester hours, Bachelors **Professional Accreditation:** AACSB, ABET, APTA, NASM, NCATE, NLN **Intercollegiate Athletics:** Baseball M; Basketball M & W; Cross-Country Running M & W; Golf M & W; Soccer M & W; Softball W; Swimming and Diving M & W; Tennis W; Volleyball W

UNIVERSITY OF INDIANAPOLIS
1400 East Hanna Ave.
Indianapolis, IN 46227-3697
Tel: (317)788-3368; Free: 800-232-8634
Admissions: (317)788-3216
Fax: (317)788-3300
E-mail: admissions@uindy.edu
Web Site: http://www.uindy.edu/
President/CEO: Beverley Pitts

Admissions: Ronald Wilks
Financial Aid: Linda B. Handy
Type: Comprehensive **Sex:** Coed **Affiliation:** United Methodist Church **Scores:** 93% SAT V 400+; 94% SAT M 400+; 47% ACT 18-23; 31% ACT 24-29 **% Accepted:** 80 **Admission Plans:** Deferred Admission **Application Deadline:** Rolling **Application Fee:** $25.00 **H.S. Requirements:** High school diploma required; GED accepted **Costs Per Year:** Application fee: $25. Comprehensive fee: $29,210 includes full-time tuition ($20,970), mandatory fees ($200), and college room and board ($8040). College room only: $3820. Room and board charges vary according to board plan and housing facility. Part-time tuition: $874 per credit hour. Part-time tuition varies according to course load. **Scholarships:** Available **Calendar System:** Semester, Summer Session Available **Enrollment:** FT 2,880, PT 912, Grad FT 480, Grad PT 717 **Faculty:** FT 205, PT 232 **Student-Faculty Ratio:** 13:1 **Exams:** SAT I or ACT. ACT essay used for advising. SAT essay used for advising. ACT essay used for placement. SAT essay used for placement. **% Receiving Financial Aid:** 72 **% Residing in College-Owned, -Operated, or -Affiliated Housing:** 38 **Final Year or Final Semester Residency Requirement:** No **Library Holdings:** 173,363 **Regional Accreditation:** North Central Association of Colleges and Schools **Credit Hours For Degree:** 62 credit hours, Associates; 124 credit hours, Bachelors **ROTC:** Army **Professional Accreditation:** AACN, ACNM, AOTA, APTA, APA, ACBSP, CSWE, JRCEPAT, NASAD, NASM, NCATE, NLN **Intercollegiate Athletics:** Baseball M; Basketball M & W; Cross-Country Running M & W; Football M; Golf M & W; Soccer M & W; Softball W; Swimming and Diving M & W; Tennis M & W; Track and Field M & W; Volleyball W; Wrestling M

UNIVERSITY OF NOTRE DAME

Notre Dame, IN 46556
Tel: (574)631-5000
Admissions: (574)631-7505
Fax: (574)631-8865
E-mail: admissions@nd.edu
Web Site: http://www.nd.edu/
President/CEO: Rev. John I. Jenkins, CSC
Financial Aid: Joseph A. Russo
Type: University **Sex:** Coed **Affiliation:** Roman Catholic **% Accepted:** 29 **Admission Plans:** Early Action; Deferred Admission **Application Deadline:** December 31 **Application Fee:** $65.00 **H.S. Requirements:** High school diploma required; GED not accepted **Costs Per Year:** Application fee: $65. Comprehensive fee: $48,845 includes full-time tuition ($37,970), mandatory fees ($507), and college room and board ($10,368). Part-time tuition: $1582 per credit. **Scholarships:** Available **Calendar System:** Semester, Summer Session Available **Enrollment:** FT 8,356, PT 16, Grad FT 3,334, Grad PT 110 **Faculty:** FT 947, PT 108 **Student-Faculty Ratio:** 12:1 **Exams:** SAT I or ACT, SAT II. **% Receiving Financial Aid:** 49 **% Residing in College-Owned, -Operated, or -Affiliated Housing:** 77 **Library Holdings:** 3,469,001 **Regional Accreditation:** North Central Association of Colleges and Schools **Credit Hours For Degree:** 120 credit hours, Bachelors **ROTC:** Army, Navy, Air Force **Professional Accreditation:** AACSB, ABET, ABA, APA, ACIPE, AALS, ATS, NAAB, NASAD **Intercollegiate Athletics:** Baseball M; Basketball M & W; Crew W; Cross-Country Running M & W; Fencing M & W; Football M; Golf M & W; Ice Hockey M; Lacrosse M & W; Soccer M & W; Softball W; Swimming and Diving M & W; Tennis M & W; Track and Field M & W; Volleyball W

UNIVERSITY OF PHOENIX—INDIANAPOLIS CAMPUS

7999 Knue Rd. Dr.
Ste. 100 and 500
Indianapolis, IN 46250-1932
Tel: (317)585-8610; Free: 800-228-7240
Admissions: (480)557-6151
E-mail: audra.mcquarie@phoenix.edu
Web Site: http://www.phoenix.edu/
President/CEO: William Pepicello
Admissions: Audra McQuarie
Type: Comprehensive **Sex:** Coed **% Accepted:** 100 **Admission Plans:** Open Admission; Deferred Admission **Application Deadline:** Rolling **Application Fee:** $0.00 **H.S. Requirements:** High school diploma required; GED accepted **Costs Per Year:** Application fee: $0. Tuition: $11,438 full-time. Full-time tuition varies according to course level and course load. **Scholarships:** Available **Calendar System:** Continuous, Summer Session Not available **Enrollment:** FT 271 **Faculty:** FT 15, PT 65 **Regional Accreditation:** North Central Association of Colleges and Schools **Credit Hours For Degree:** 60 credits, Associates; 120 credits, Bachelors

UNIVERSITY OF PHOENIX—NORTHWEST INDIANA CAMPUS

359 East 81st Ave.
Merrillville, IN 46410
Tel: (219)769-6418
Admissions: (219)794-1500
Web Site: http://www.phoenix.edu/
President/CEO: William Pepicello, PhD
Type: Comprehensive **Sex:** Coed **Regional Accreditation:** North Central Association of Colleges and Schools

UNIVERSITY OF SAINT FRANCIS

2701 Spring St.
Fort Wayne, IN 46808-3994
Tel: (260)434-3100; Free: 800-729-4732
Admissions: (260)434-3279
E-mail: admis@sf.edu
Web Site: http://www.sf.edu/
President/CEO: Sr. M. Elise Kriss
Admissions: Ron Schumacher
Type: Comprehensive **Sex:** Coed **Affiliation:** Roman Catholic **Scores:** 89% SAT V 400+; 90% SAT M 400+; 61% ACT 18-23; 24% ACT 24-29 **% Accepted:** 47 **Admission Plans:** Deferred Admission **Application Deadline:** Rolling **Application Fee:** $20.00 **H.S. Requirements:** High school diploma required; GED accepted **Costs Per Year:** Application fee: $20. Comprehensive fee: $28,510 includes full-time tuition ($20,950), mandatory fees ($810), and college room and board ($6750). Full-time tuition and fees vary according to course load. Room and board charges vary according to board plan and housing facility. Part-time tuition: $660 per semester hour. Part-time mandatory fees: $20 per semester hour, $135 per term. Part-time tuition and fees vary according to course load. **Scholarships:** Available **Calendar System:** Semester, Summer Session Available **Enrollment:** FT 1,461, PT 339 **Faculty:** FT 106, PT 116 **Student-Faculty Ratio:** 12:1 **Exams:** SAT I or ACT. **% Receiving Financial Aid:** 87 **% Residing in College-Owned, -Operated, or -Affiliated Housing:** 23 **Library Holdings:** 95,991 **Regional Accreditation:** North Central Association of Colleges and Schools **Credit Hours For Degree:** 64 semester hours, Associates; 128 semester hours, Bachelors **Professional Accreditation:** ARCEST, AACN, AOTA, APTA, ACBSP, CSWE, JRCERT, NASAD, NCATE, NLN **Intercollegiate Athletics:** Baseball M; Basketball M & W; Cheerleading M & W; Cross-Country Running M & W; Football M; Golf M & W; Soccer M & W; Softball W; Tennis W; Track and Field M & W; Volleyball W

UNIVERSITY OF SOUTHERN INDIANA

8600 University Blvd.
Evansville, IN 47712-3590
Tel: (812)464-8600; Free: 800-467-1965
Admissions: (812)464-1765
Fax: (812)465-7154
E-mail: enroll@usi.edu
Web Site: http://www.usi.edu/
President/CEO: Dr. Linda L.M. Bennett
Admissions: Eric Otto
Type: Comprehensive **Sex:** Coed **Affiliation:** Indiana Commission for Higher Education **Scores:** 85.13% SAT V 400+; 87.3% SAT M 400+; 57.38% ACT 18-23; 18.37% ACT 24-29 **% Accepted:** 88 **Application Deadline:** August 15 **Application Fee:** $25.00 **H.S. Requirements:** High school diploma required; GED accepted **Costs Per Year:** Application fee: $25. State resident tuition: $5274 full-time, $175.80 per credit hour part-time. Nonresident tuition: $12,555 full-time, $418.50 per credit hour part-time. Mandatory fees: $200 full-time, $22.75 per term part-time. Full-time tuition and fees vary according to course load and reciprocity agreements. Part-time tuition and fees vary according to course load and reciprocity agreements. College room and board: $6700. College room only: $3450. Room and board charges vary according to board plan and housing facility. **Scholarships:** Available **Calendar System:** Semester, Summer Session Available **Enrollment:** FT 8,033, PT 1,615, Grad FT 116, Grad PT 752 **Faculty:** FT 338, PT 330 **Student-Faculty Ratio:** 18:1 **Exams:** SAT I or ACT. ACT essay used for advising. SAT essay used for advising. ACT essay used for placement. SAT essay used for placement. **% Receiving Financial Aid:** 60 **% Residing in College-Owned, -Operated, or -Affiliated Housing:** 28 **Final Year or Final Semester Residency Requirement:** No

Library Holdings: 328,129 **Regional Accreditation:** North Central Association of Colleges and Schools **Credit Hours For Degree:** 62 semester hours, Associates; 124 semester hours, Bachelors **ROTC:** Army **Professional Accreditation:** AACSB, ABET, AACN, ADA, AOTA, CARC, CSWE, JRCERT, NCATE **Intercollegiate Athletics:** Baseball M; Basketball M & W; Cheerleading M & W; Cross-Country Running M & W; Golf M & W; Ice Hockey M; Lacrosse M; Rugby M & W; Soccer M & W; Softball W; Tennis M & W; Volleyball W; Wrestling M

VALPARAISO UNIVERSITY
1700 Chapel Dr.
Valparaiso, IN 46383
Tel: (219)464-5000; Free: 888-GO-VALPO
Admissions: (219)464-5011
Fax: (219)464-6898
E-mail: Undergrad.Admissions@valpo.edu
Web Site: http://www.valpo.edu/
President/CEO: Mark Heckler
Financial Aid: Robert Helgeson
Type: University **Sex:** Coed **Affiliation:** Lutheran Church **Scores:** 99% SAT V 400+; 99% SAT M 400+; 33% ACT 18-23; 43% ACT 24-29 **% Accepted:** 91 **Admission Plans:** Early Action; Deferred Admission **Application Deadline:** August 15 **Application Fee:** $30.00 **H.S. Requirements:** High school diploma required; GED accepted **Costs Per Year:** Application fee: $30. Comprehensive fee: $36,280 includes full-time tuition ($27,360), mandatory fees ($960), and college room and board ($7960). College room only: $4910. Full-time tuition and fees vary according to course load. Room and board charges vary according to housing facility and student level. Part-time tuition: $1240 per credit hour. Part-time mandatory fees: $25 per credit hour. Part-time tuition and fees vary according to course load. **Scholarships:** Available **Calendar System:** Semester, Summer Session Available **Enrollment:** FT 2,733, PT 155, Grad FT 874, Grad PT 303 **Faculty:** FT 242, PT 114 **Student-Faculty Ratio:** 14:1 **Exams:** SAT I or ACT. **% Receiving Financial Aid:** 72 **% Residing in College-Owned, -Operated, or -Affiliated Housing:** 66 **Final Year or Final Semester Residency Requirement:** Yes **Library Holdings:** 537,234 **Regional Accreditation:** North Central Association of Colleges and Schools **Credit Hours For Degree:** 60 credits, Associates; 124 credits, Bachelors **ROTC:** Army, Air Force **Professional Accreditation:** AACSB, ABET, AACN, ABA, AALS, CSWE, NASM, NCATE **Intercollegiate Athletics:** Baseball M; Basketball M & W; Bowling W; Cross-Country Running M & W; Football M; Golf M & W; Soccer M & W; Softball W; Swimming and Diving M & W; Tennis M & W; Track and Field M & W; Volleyball W

VET TECH INSTITUTE AT INTERNATIONAL BUSINESS COLLEGE (FORT WAYNE)
5699 Coventry Ln.
Fort Wayne, IN 46804
Tel: (260)459-4500; Free: 800-589-6363
Web Site: http://www.vettechinstitute.edu/
Type: Two-Year College **Sex:** Coed **% Accepted:** 51 **Professional Accreditation:** AVMA

VET TECH INSTITUTE AT INTERNATIONAL BUSINESS COLLEGE (INDIANAPOLIS)
7205 Shadeland Station
Indianapolis, IN 46256
Tel: (317)813-2300; Free: 800-589-6500
Fax: (317)841-6419
Web Site: http://www.vettechinstitute.edu/
Type: Two-Year College **Sex:** Coed **% Accepted:** 55 **Professional Accreditation:** AVMA

VINCENNES UNIVERSITY
1002 North First St.
Vincennes, IN 47591-5202
Tel: (812)888-8888
Admissions: 800-742-9198
Fax: (812)888-5868
E-mail: cblome@vinu.edu
Web Site: http://www.vinu.edu/
President/CEO: Dr. Dick Helton
Admissions: Christian Blome
Type: Two-Year College **Sex:** Coed **Admission Plans:** Open Admission; Early Admission; Deferred Admission **Application Deadline:** Rolling **Application Fee:** $20.00 **H.S. Requirements:** High school diploma required; GED accepted **Costs Per Year:** Application fee: $20. State resident tuition: $4360 full-time, $138.66 per credit hour part-time. Nonresident tuition: $10,304 full-time, $336.78 per credit hour part-time. Mandatory fees: $200 full-time, $100 per term part-time. Full-time tuition and fees vary according to course level, degree level, program, reciprocity agreements, and student level. Part-time tuition and fees vary according to course level, degree level, program, reciprocity agreements, and student level. College room and board: $7316. Room and board charges vary according to board plan and housing facility. **Scholarships:** Available **Calendar System:** Semester, Summer Session Available **Student-Faculty Ratio:** 16:1 **Regional Accreditation:** North Central Association of Colleges and Schools **Credit Hours For Degree:** 64 credits, Associates **ROTC:** Army, Air Force **Professional Accreditation:** ARCEST, ABFSE, AHIMA, APTA, ACBSP, CARC, NASAD, NAST, NLN **Intercollegiate Athletics:** Baseball M; Basketball M & W; Bowling M; Cross-Country Running M & W; Golf M; Swimming and Diving M & W; Tennis M; Track and Field M & W; Volleyball W

VINCENNES UNIVERSITY JASPER CAMPUS
850 College Ave.
Jasper, IN 47546-9393
Tel: (812)482-3030; Free: 800-809-VUJC
Fax: (812)481-5960
E-mail: lagilbert@vinu.edu
Web Site: http://vujc.vinu.edu/
Admissions: Louann Gilbert
Type: Two-Year College **Sex:** Coed **Affiliation:** Vincennes University **Admission Plans:** Open Admission **Application Deadline:** Rolling **Application Fee:** $20.00 **H.S. Requirements:** High school diploma required; GED accepted **Scholarships:** Available **Calendar System:** Semester, Summer Session Available **Faculty:** FT 20, PT 31 **Student-Faculty Ratio:** 16:1 **Library Holdings:** 14,000 **Regional Accreditation:** North Central Association of Colleges and Schools **Credit Hours For Degree:** 62 credit hours, Associates

WABASH COLLEGE
PO Box 352
Crawfordsville, IN 47933-0352
Tel: (765)361-6100; Free: 800-345-5385
Admissions: (765)361-6225
Fax: (765)361-6437
E-mail: admissions@wabash.edu
Web Site: http://www.wabash.edu/
President/CEO: Dr. Patrick E. White
Admissions: Steven J. Klein
Financial Aid: Clint Gasaway
Type: Four-Year College **Sex:** Men **Scores:** 97% SAT V 400+; 99% SAT M 400+; 37% ACT 18-23; 48% ACT 24-29 **% Accepted:** 49 **Admission Plans:** Early Admission; Early Action; Early Decision Plan; Deferred Admission **Application Deadline:** Rolling **Application Fee:** $40.00 **H.S. Requirements:** High school diploma required; GED accepted **Costs Per Year:** Application fee: $40. Comprehensive fee: $37,350 includes full-time tuition ($29,100), mandatory fees ($650), and college room and board ($7600). College room only: $3500. Full-time tuition and fees vary according to reciprocity agreements. Room and board charges vary according to board plan and housing facility. Part-time tuition: $4850 per course. Part-time mandatory fees: $450 per year. Part-time tuition and fees vary according to course load and reciprocity agreements. **Scholarships:** Available **Calendar System:** Semester, Summer Session Not available **Enrollment:** FT 874, PT 9 **Faculty:** FT 90, PT 2 **Student-Faculty Ratio:** 10:1 **Exams:** SAT I or ACT. ACT essay used for admission. SAT essay used for admission. **% Receiving Financial Aid:** 80 **% Residing in College-Owned, -Operated, or -Affiliated Housing:** 91 **Final Year or Final Semester Residency Requirement:** No **Library Holdings:** 304,082 **Regional Accreditation:** North Central Association of Colleges and Schools **Credit Hours For Degree:** 34 courses, Bachelors **Professional Accreditation:** NCATE **Intercollegiate Athletics:** Baseball M; Basketball M; Crew M; Cross-Country Running M; Football M; Golf M; Lacrosse M; Rugby M; Sailing M; Soccer M; Swimming and Diving M; Tennis M; Track and Field M; Water Polo M; Wrestling M

AIB COLLEGE OF BUSINESS
2500 Fleur Dr.
Des Moines, IA 50321-1799
Tel: (515)244-4221; Free: 800-444-1921
Fax: (515)244-6773
E-mail: thompsonm@aib.edu
Web Site: http://www.aib.edu/
President/CEO: Nancy Williams
Admissions: Mark Thompson
Type: Four-Year College **Sex:** Coed **% Accepted:** 70 **Application Deadline:** Rolling **Application Fee:** $25.00 **H.S. Requirements:** High school diploma required; GED accepted **Costs Per Year:** Application fee: $25. Tuition: $12,900 full-time, $240 per quarter hour part-time. Mandatory fees: $240 full-time, $80 per term part-time. Full-time tuition and fees vary according to course load. Part-time tuition and fees vary according to course load. College room only: $4311. Room charges vary according to housing facility. Tuition guaranteed not to increase for student's term of enrollment. **Scholarships:** Available **Calendar System:** Quarter, Summer Session Available **Enrollment:** FT 595, PT 374 **Faculty:** FT 24, PT 50 **Student-Faculty Ratio:** 18:1 **Exams:** ACT. ACT essay not being used. **% Residing in College-Owned, -Operated, or -Affiliated Housing:** 43 **Final Year or Final Semester Residency Requirement:** No **Library Holdings:** 6,274 **Regional Accreditation:** North Central Association of Colleges and Schools **Credit Hours For Degree:** 126 quarter hours, Associates; 198 quarter hours, Bachelors **Intercollegiate Athletics:** Basketball W; Cheerleading M & W; Golf M & W

ALLEN COLLEGE
1825 Logan Ave.
Waterloo, IA 50703
Tel: (319)226-2000
Fax: (319)226-2020
E-mail: allencollegeadmissions@ihs.org
Web Site: http://www.allencollege.edu/
President/CEO: Dr. Jerry Durham
Admissions: Dina Dowden
Financial Aid: Kathie S. Walters
Type: Comprehensive **Sex:** Coed **Scores:** 33.33% ACT 18-23; 66.67% ACT 24-29 **% Accepted:** 40 **Application Deadline:** July 1 **Application Fee:** $50.00 **H.S. Requirements:** High school diploma required; GED accepted **Costs Per Year:** Application fee: $50. Tuition: $13,458 full-time, $500 per credit hour part-time. Mandatory fees: $1537 full-time, $68 per credit hour part-time. Full-time tuition and fees vary according to course load, degree level, program, and student level. Part-time tuition and fees vary according to course load, degree level, program, and student level. **Scholarships:** Available **Calendar System:** Semester, Summer Session Not available **Enrollment:** FT 249, PT 65, Grad FT 37, Grad PT 103 **Faculty:** FT 29, PT 9 **Student-Faculty Ratio:** 12:1 **Exams:** SAT I or ACT. ACT essay not being used. SAT essay not being used. **% Receiving Financial Aid:** 85 **% Residing in College-Owned, -Operated, or -Affiliated Housing:** 6 **Library Holdings:** 3,300 **Regional Accreditation:** North Central Association of Colleges and Schools **Credit Hours For Degree:** 73 credit hours, Associates; 124 credit hours, Bachelors **ROTC:** Army **Professional Accreditation:** AACN, JRCERT, NLN

ASHFORD UNIVERSITY
400 North Bluff Blvd., PO Box 2967
Clinton, IA 52733-2967
Tel: (563)242-4023; Free: 800-242-4153
Fax: (563)242-2003
E-mail: admissns@tfu.edu
Web Site: http://www.ashford.edu/
President/CEO: Dr. Jane McAuliffe
Admissions: Waunita M. Sullivan
Financial Aid: Lisa Kramer
Type: Comprehensive **Sex:** Coed **Scores:** 49% ACT 18-23; 9% ACT 24-29 **Admission Plans:** Early Admission; Deferred Admission **Application Deadline:** Rolling **Application Fee:** $20.00 **H.S. Requirements:** High school diploma required; GED accepted **Scholarships:** Available **Calendar System:** Semester, Summer Session Available **Enrollment:** FT 9,761, PT 105 **Faculty:** FT 45, PT 703 **Student-Faculty Ratio:** 37:1 **Exams:** SAT I or ACT. **Library Holdings:** 98,974 **Regional Accreditation:** North Central Association of Colleges and Schools **Credit Hours For Degree:** 62 credit hours, Associates; 122 credit hours, Bachelors **Intercollegiate Athletics:** Baseball M; Basketball M & W; Cross-Country Running M & W; Golf M & W; Soccer M & W; Softball W; Track and Field M & W; Volleyball W

BRIAR CLIFF UNIVERSITY
3303 Rebecca St.
Sioux City, IA 51104-0100
Tel: (712)279-5321; Free: 800-662-3303
Admissions: (712)279-5200
Fax: (712)279-5410
E-mail: admissions@briarcliff.edu
Web Site: http://www.briarcliff.edu/
President/CEO: Beverly A. Wharton
Type: Comprehensive **Sex:** Coed **Affiliation:** Roman Catholic **% Accepted:** 62 **Admission Plans:** Early Admission; Deferred Admission **Application Deadline:** Rolling **Application Fee:** $20.00 **H.S. Requirements:** High school diploma required; GED accepted **Costs Per Year:** Application fee: $20. Comprehensive fee: $29,514 includes full-time tuition ($21,867), mandatory fees ($669), and college room and board ($6978). College room only: $3357. Room and board charges vary according to board plan and housing facility. Part-time tuition: $729 per credit hour. Part-time mandatory fees: $22 per credit hour. Part-time tuition and fees vary according to class time and course load. **Scholarships:** Available **Calendar System:** Miscellaneous, Summer Session Available **Enrollment:** FT 893, PT 186, Grad FT 10, Grad PT 69 **Faculty:** FT 60, PT 48 **Student-Faculty Ratio:** 13:1 **Exams:** SAT I or ACT. **% Receiving Financial Aid:** 70 **% Residing in College-Owned, -Operated, or -Affiliated Housing:** 52 **Library Holdings:** 81,794 **Regional Accreditation:** North Central Association of Colleges and Schools **Credit Hours For Degree:** 60 credit hours, Associates; 120 credit hours, Bachelors **Professional Accreditation:** CSWE, NLN **Intercollegiate Athletics:** Baseball M; Basketball M & W; Cross-Country Running M & W; Football M; Golf M & W; Soccer M & W; Softball W; Tennis M & W; Track and Field M & W; Volleyball W; Wrestling M

BUENA VISTA UNIVERSITY
610 West Fourth St.
Storm Lake, IA 50588

Tel: (712)749-2351; Free: 800-383-9600
Admissions: (712)749-2235
Fax: (712)749-2037
E-mail: admissions@bvu.edu
Web Site: http://www.bvu.edu/
President/CEO: Dr. Frederick V. Moore
Admissions: Marcia Nance
Financial Aid: Leanne Valentine
Type: Comprehensive **Sex:** Coed **Affiliation:** Presbyterian Church (U.S.A.) **Scores:** 56% ACT 18-23; 25% ACT 24-29 **% Accepted:** 72 **Admission Plans:** Deferred Admission **Application Fee:** $0.00 **H.S. Requirements:** High school diploma required; GED accepted **Costs Per Year:** Application fee: $0. Comprehensive fee: $32,832 includes full-time tuition ($25,540) and college room and board ($7292). Full-time tuition varies according to location. Room and board charges vary according to board plan. Part-time tuition: $858 per credit hour. Part-time tuition varies according to location. Tuition guaranteed not to increase for student's term of enrollment. **Scholarships:** Available **Calendar System:** 4-1-4, Summer Session Available **Enrollment:** FT 943, PT 14, Grad PT 57 **Faculty:** FT 83, PT 23 **Student-Faculty Ratio:** 10:1 **Exams:** SAT I or ACT. **% Receiving Financial Aid:** 87 **% Residing in College-Owned, -Operated, or -Affiliated Housing:** 85 **Library Holdings:** 144,000 **Regional Accreditation:** North Central Association of Colleges and Schools **Credit Hours For Degree:** 128 semester hours, Bachelors **ROTC:** Army **Professional Accreditation:** CSWE, TEAC **Intercollegiate Athletics:** Baseball M; Basketball M & W; Cross-Country Running M & W; Football M; Golf M & W; Soccer M & W; Softball W; Tennis M & W; Track and Field M & W; Volleyball W; Wrestling M

CENTRAL COLLEGE
812 University St.
Pella, IA 50219
Tel: (641)628-9000; Free: 877-462-3689
Admissions: (641)628-7600
Fax: (641)628-5316
E-mail: admissions@central.edu
Web Site: http://www.central.edu/
President/CEO: Dr. David Roe
Admissions: Carol Williamson
Financial Aid: Jean L. Vander Wert
Type: Four-Year College **Sex:** Coed **Affiliation:** Reformed Church in America **Scores:** 100% SAT V 400+; 100% SAT M 400+; 43% ACT 18-23; 44% ACT 24-29 **% Accepted:** 74 **Admission Plans:** Deferred Admission **Application Deadline:** Rolling **Application Fee:** $25.00 **H.S. Requirements:** High school diploma required; GED accepted **Costs Per Year:** Application fee: $25. Comprehensive fee: $33,378 includes full-time tuition ($24,630), mandatory fees ($380), and college room and board ($8368). College room only: $4104. Room and board charges vary according to board plan. Part-time tuition: $855 per semester hour. Part-time tuition varies according to course load. **Scholarships:** Available **Calendar System:** Semester, Summer Session Available **Enrollment:** FT 1,597, PT 39 **Faculty:** FT 88, PT 76 **Student-Faculty Ratio:** 13:1 **Exams:** SAT I or ACT. **% Receiving Financial Aid:** 82 **% Residing in College-Owned, -Operated, or -Affiliated Housing:** 93 **Final Year or Final Semester Residency Requirement:** Yes **Library Holdings:** 249,709 **Regional Accreditation:** North Central Association of Colleges and Schools **Credit Hours For Degree:** 120 semester hours, Bachelors **Professional Accreditation:** NASM **Intercollegiate Athletics:** Baseball M; Basketball M & W; Cross-Country Running M & W; Football M; Golf M & W; Soccer M & W; Softball W; Tennis M & W; Track and Field M & W; Volleyball W; Wrestling M

CLARKE COLLEGE
1550 Clarke Dr.
Dubuque, IA 52001-3198
Tel: (563)588-6300; Free: 800-383-2345
Admissions: (563)588-6436
Fax: (563)588-6789
E-mail: admissions@clarke.edu
Web Site: http://www.clarke.edu/
President/CEO: Sr. Joanne Burrows, SC
Admissions: Emily Kruse
Financial Aid: Sharon Willenborg
Type: Comprehensive **Sex:** Coed **Affiliation:** Roman Catholic **Scores:** 47% ACT 18-23; 42% ACT 24-29 **% Accepted:** 77 **Admission Plans:** Deferred Admission **Application Deadline:** Rolling **Application Fee:** $25.00 **H.S. Requirements:** High school diploma required; GED accepted **Costs Per Year:** Application fee: $25. Comprehensive fee: $30,360 includes full-time tuition ($22,800), mandatory fees ($720), and college room and board ($6840). College room only: $3360. Room and board charges vary according to board plan and housing facility. Part-time tuition: $578 per credit hour. **Scholarships:** Available **Calendar System:** Semester, Summer Session Available **Enrollment:** FT 802, PT 180, Grad FT 126, Grad PT 94 **Faculty:** FT 75, PT 60 **Student-Faculty Ratio:** 11:1 **Exams:** SAT I or ACT. ACT essay not being used. SAT essay not being used. **% Receiving Financial Aid:** 87 **% Residing in College-Owned, -Operated, or -Affiliated Housing:** 60 **Library Holdings:** 110,000 **Regional Accreditation:** North Central Association of Colleges and Schools **Credit Hours For Degree:** 62 credits, Associates; 124 credits, Bachelors **ROTC:** Army **Professional Accreditation:** AACN, APTA, CSWE, NASM, NLN **Intercollegiate Athletics:** Baseball M; Basketball M & W; Bowling M & W; Cheerleading W; Cross-Country Running M & W; Golf M & W; Soccer M & W; Softball W; Tennis W; Track and Field M & W; Volleyball M & W

CLINTON COMMUNITY COLLEGE
1000 Lincoln Blvd.
Clinton, IA 52732-6299
Tel: (563)244-7001
Admissions: (563)336-3322
Fax: (563)244-7107
E-mail: gmohr@eicc.edu
Web Site: http://www.eicc.edu/ccc/
President/CEO: Dean Karen Vickers
Admissions: Gary Mohr
Financial Aid: Teresa Thiede
Type: Two-Year College **Sex:** Coed **Affiliation:** Eastern Iowa Community College District **% Accepted:** 100 **Admission Plans:** Open Admission; Early Admission; Deferred Admission **Application Deadline:** Rolling **Application Fee:** $0.00 **H.S. Requirements:** High school diploma or equivalent not required **Costs Per Year:** Application fee: $0. State resident tuition: $2688 full-time, $112 per credit hour part-time. Nonresident tuition: $4032 full-time, $168 per credit hour part-time. Full-time tuition varies according to class time, program, and reciprocity agreements. Part-time tuition varies according to class time, program, and reciprocity agreements. **Scholarships:** Available **Calendar System:** Semester, Summer Session Available **Enrollment:** FT 571, PT 669 **Faculty:** FT 30, PT 13 **Student-Faculty Ratio:** 23:1 **Library Holdings:** 18,701 **Regional Accreditation:** North Central Association of Colleges and Schools **Credit Hours For Degree:** 62 semester hours, Associates **Intercollegiate Athletics:** Basketball M; Cheerleading M & W; Soccer M & W; Softball W; Volleyball W

COE COLLEGE
1220 1st Ave., NE
Cedar Rapids, IA 52402-5092
Tel: (319)399-8000; Free: 877-225-5263
Admissions: (319)399-8500
Fax: (319)399-8816
E-mail: admission@coe.edu
Web Site: http://www.coe.edu/
President/CEO: James R. Phifer
Admissions: John Grundig
Financial Aid: Barbara Hoffman
Type: Comprehensive **Sex:** Coed **Affiliation:** Presbyterian Church **Scores:** 97% SAT V 400+; 100% SAT M 400+; 29% ACT 18-23; 56% ACT 24-29 **Admission Plans:** Early Admission; Early Action; Deferred Admission **Application Deadline:** March 1 **Application Fee:** $30.00 **H.S. Requirements:** High school diploma required; GED accepted **Costs Per Year:** Application fee: $30. Comprehensive fee: $36,420 includes full-time tuition ($28,950), mandatory fees ($320), and college room and board ($7150). College room only: $3210. Room and board charges vary according to board plan and housing facility. Part-time tuition: $3620 per course. **Scholarships:** Available **Calendar System:** Miscellaneous, Summer Session Available **Enrollment:** FT 1,249, PT 61 **Student-Faculty Ratio:** 11:1 **% Receiving Financial Aid:** 77 **Regional Accreditation:** North Central Association of Colleges and Schools **Credit Hours For Degree:** 32 courses, Bachelors **ROTC:** Army, Air Force **Professional Accreditation:** AACN, NASM **Intercollegiate Athletics:** Baseball M; Basketball M & W; Cheerleading W; Cross-Country Running M & W; Football M; Golf M & W; Soccer M & W; Softball W; Swimming and Diving M & W; Tennis M & W; Track and Field M & W; Volleyball W; Wrestling M

CORNELL COLLEGE

600 First St. West
Mount Vernon, IA 52314-1098
Tel: (319)895-4000; Free: 800-747-1112
Admissions: (319)895-4167
Fax: (319)895-4492
E-mail: twhite@cornellcollege.edu
Web Site: http://www.cornellcollege.edu/
President/CEO: Dr. Leslie H. Garner, Jr.
Admissions: Todd White
Financial Aid: Cindi P. Reints

Type: Four-Year College **Sex:** Coed **Affiliation:** Methodist **Scores:** 101% SAT V 400+; 100% SAT M 400+; 22% ACT 18-23; 54% ACT 24-29 **% Accepted:** 44 **Admission Plans:** Early Admission; Early Action; Deferred Admission **Application Deadline:** February 1 **Application Fee:** $30.00 **H.S. Requirements:** High school diploma required; GED accepted **Costs Per Year:** Application fee: $30. Comprehensive fee: $36,900 includes full-time tuition ($29,400) and college room and board ($7500). College room only: $3500. Room and board charges vary according to board plan and housing facility. **Scholarships:** Available **Calendar System:** Miscellaneous, Summer Session Not available **Enrollment:** FT 1,133, PT 8 **Faculty:** FT 87, PT 5 **Student-Faculty Ratio:** 12:1 **Exams:** SAT I or ACT, SAT II. ACT essay not being used. SAT essay not being used. **% Receiving Financial Aid:** 74 **% Residing in College-Owned, -Operated, or -Affiliated Housing:** 90 **Library Holdings:** 194,131 **Regional Accreditation:** North Central Association of Colleges and Schools **Credit Hours For Degree:** 128 semester hours, Bachelors **Intercollegiate Athletics:** Baseball M; Basketball M & W; Cross-Country Running M & W; Football M; Golf M & W; Lacrosse M & W; Soccer M & W; Softball W; Tennis M & W; Track and Field M & W; Volleyball M & W; Wrestling M

DES MOINES AREA COMMUNITY COLLEGE

2006 South Ankeny Blvd.
Ankeny, IA 50021-8995
Tel: (515)964-6200
Admissions: (515)964-6216
E-mail: mjleutsch@dmacc.edu
Web Site: http://www.dmacc.edu/
President/CEO: Dr. Robert J. Denson
Admissions: Michael Lentsch

Type: Two-Year College **Sex:** Coed **Affiliation:** Iowa Area Community Colleges System **Admission Plans:** Open Admission; Early Admission; Deferred Admission **Application Deadline:** Rolling **Application Fee:** $0.00 **H.S. Requirements:** High school diploma or equivalent not required. For health programs: High school diploma required; GED accepted **Costs Per Year:** Application fee: $0. State resident tuition: $3450 full-time, $115 per credit hour part-time. Nonresident tuition: $6900 full-time, $230 per credit hour part-time. Full-time tuition varies according to course load and reciprocity agreements. Part-time tuition varies according to course load and reciprocity agreements. **Scholarships:** Available **Calendar System:** Semester, Summer Session Available **Enrollment:** FT 8,947, PT 13,377 **Faculty:** FT 322, PT 4 **Student-Faculty Ratio:** 33:1 **Exams:** Other, SAT I or ACT. **Library Holdings:** 62,986 **Regional Accreditation:** North Central Association of Colleges and Schools **Credit Hours For Degree:** 64 semester hours, Associates **Professional Accreditation:** ACF, ADA, CARC, NAACLS, NLN **Intercollegiate Athletics:** Baseball M; Basketball M & W; Cross-Country Running W; Golf M & W; Volleyball W

DIVINE WORD COLLEGE

102 Jacoby Dr. SW
Epworth, IA 52045-0380
Tel: (563)876-3353; Free: 800-553-3321
Fax: (563)876-3407
E-mail: luhal@dwci.edu
Web Site: http://www.dwci.edu/
President/CEO: Rev. Michael Hutchins, SVD
Admissions: Len Uhal

Type: Four-Year College **Sex:** Coed **Affiliation:** Roman Catholic **Admission Plans:** Early Admission **Application Deadline:** July 15 **Application Fee:** $25.00 **H.S. Requirements:** High school diploma required; GED accepted **Costs Per Year:** Application fee: $25. One-time mandatory fee: $25. Comprehensive fee: $13,750 includes full-time tuition ($10,800), mandatory fees ($100), and college room and board ($2850). Part-time tuition: $360 per credit hour. **Calendar System:** Semester, Summer Session Not available **Exams:** SAT I or ACT. **Library Holdings:** 94,583 **Regional Accreditation:** North Central Association of Colleges and Schools **Credit Hours For Degree:** 60 semester hours, Associates; 128 semester hours, Bachelors

DORDT COLLEGE

498 4th Ave., NE
Sioux Center, IA 51250-1697
Tel: (712)722-6000; Free: 800-343-6738
Admissions: (712)722-6080
Fax: (712)722-1967
E-mail: admissions@dordt.edu
Web Site: http://www.dordt.edu/
President/CEO: Dr. Carl E. Zylstra
Admissions: Quentin Van Essen
Financial Aid: Michael Epema

Type: Comprehensive **Sex:** Coed **Affiliation:** Christian Reformed **Scores:** 93.2% SAT V 400+; 37.8% ACT 18-23; 43.5% ACT 24-29 **% Accepted:** 84 **Admission Plans:** Deferred Admission **Application Deadline:** August 1 **Application Fee:** $25.00 **H.S. Requirements:** High school diploma required; GED accepted **Costs Per Year:** Application fee: $25. Comprehensive fee: $28,090 includes full-time tuition ($21,720), mandatory fees ($360), and college room and board ($6010). College room only: $3170. Full-time tuition and fees vary according to course load. Room and board charges vary according to board plan and housing facility. Part-time tuition: $880 per semester hour. Part-time mandatory fees: $160 per term. **Scholarships:** Available **Calendar System:** Semester, Summer Session Not available **Enrollment:** FT 1,298, PT 33 **Faculty:** FT 79, PT 27 **Student-Faculty Ratio:** 15:1 **Exams:** SAT I or ACT. **% Receiving Financial Aid:** 74 **% Residing in College-Owned, -Operated, or -Affiliated Housing:** 90 **Library Holdings:** 170,000 **Regional Accreditation:** North Central Association of Colleges and Schools **Credit Hours For Degree:** 63 credits, Associates; 126 credits, Bachelors **Professional Accreditation:** ABET, CSWE, TEAC **Intercollegiate Athletics:** Baseball M; Basketball M & W; Cross-Country Running M & W; Football M; Golf M & W; Ice Hockey M; Lacrosse M; Soccer M & W; Softball W; Track and Field M & W; Volleyball W

DRAKE UNIVERSITY

2507 University Ave.
Des Moines, IA 50311-4516
Tel: (515)271-2011; Free: 800-44D-RAKE
Admissions: (515)271-3181
Fax: (515)271-2831
E-mail: admission@drake.edu
Web Site: http://www.drake.edu/
President/CEO: Dr. David Maxwell
Admissions: Laura Linn

Type: University **Sex:** Coed **Scores:** 97% SAT V 400+; 97% SAT M 400+; 20% ACT 18-23; 56% ACT 24-29 **% Accepted:** 74 **Admission Plans:** Early Admission; Deferred Admission **Application Deadline:** March 1 **Application Fee:** $25.00 **H.S. Requirements:** High school diploma required; GED accepted **Costs Per Year:** Application fee: $25. Comprehensive fee: $33,422 includes full-time tuition ($25,160), mandatory fees ($462), and college room and board ($7800). College room only: $4100. Full-time tuition and fees vary according to course load, program, and student level. Room and board charges vary according to board plan. Part-time tuition: $520 per hour. Part-time mandatory fees: $44 per term. Part-time tuition and fees vary according to class time and program. **Scholarships:** Available **Calendar System:** Semester, Summer Session Available **Enrollment:** FT 3,326, PT 222, Grad FT 1,056, Grad PT 1,049 **Faculty:** FT 275, PT 145 **Student-Faculty Ratio:** 13:1 **Exams:** SAT I or ACT. ACT essay not being used. SAT essay not being used. **% Receiving Financial Aid:** 57 **% Residing in College-Owned, -Operated, or -Affiliated Housing:** 76 **Library Holdings:** 534,531 **Regional Accreditation:** North Central Association of Colleges and Schools **Credit Hours For Degree:** 124 semester hours, Bachelors **ROTC:** Army, Air Force **Professional Accreditation:** AACSB, ACPhE, ACEJMC, ABA, AALS, CORE, NASAD, NASM, NLN **Intercollegiate Athletics:** Basketball M & W; Cheerleading M & W; Crew W; Cross-Country Running M & W; Football M; Golf M & W; Soccer M & W; Softball W; Tennis M & W; Track and Field M & W; Volleyball W

ELLSWORTH COMMUNITY COLLEGE

1100 College Ave.
Iowa Falls, IA 50126-1199
Tel: (641)648-4611; Free: 800-ECC-9235

Admissions: 800-322-9235
Fax: (641)648-3128
Web Site: http://www.iavalley.cc.ia.us/ecc/
President/CEO: Tim Wynes
Admissions: Nancy Walters
Type: Two-Year College **Sex:** Coed **Affiliation:** Iowa Valley Community College District System **Admission Plans:** Open Admission; Early Admission; Deferred Admission **Application Deadline:** Rolling **H.S. Requirements:** High school diploma required; GED accepted **Scholarships:** Available **Calendar System:** Semester, Summer Session Available **Library Holdings:** 25,500 **Regional Accreditation:** North Central Association of Colleges and Schools **Credit Hours For Degree:** 64 semester hours, Associates **Intercollegiate Athletics:** Baseball M; Basketball M & W; Football M; Golf M & W; Softball W; Track and Field M & W; Volleyball W; Wrestling M

EMMAUS BIBLE COLLEGE
2570 Asbury Rd.
Dubuque, IA 52001-3097
Tel: (319)588-8000; Free: 800-397-2425
Admissions: (563)588-8000
Fax: (319)588-1216
E-mail: ichavez@emmaus.edu
Web Site: http://www.emmaus.edu/
President/CEO: Kenneth A. Daughters
Admissions: Israel Chavez
Financial Aid: Steve Seeman
Type: Four-Year College **Sex:** Coed **Affiliation:** nondenominational **Admission Plans:** Open Admission; Deferred Admission **Application Deadline:** June 1 **Application Fee:** $25.00 **H.S. Requirements:** High school diploma required; GED accepted **Costs Per Year:** Application fee: $25. Comprehensive fee: $16,974 includes full-time tuition ($10,916), mandatory fees ($662), and college room and board ($5396). Full-time tuition and fees vary according to course load. Part-time mandatory fees: $490 per credit hour. Part-time fees vary according to course load. **Scholarships:** Available **Calendar System:** Semester, Summer Session Not available **% Receiving Financial Aid:** 47 **Library Holdings:** 86,000 **Regional Accreditation:** North Central Association of Colleges and Schools **Credit Hours For Degree:** 101 semester hours, Associates; 132 semester hours, Bachelors **Professional Accreditation:** ABHE **Intercollegiate Athletics:** Basketball M & W

FAITH BAPTIST BIBLE COLLEGE AND THEOLOGICAL SEMINARY
1900 Northwest 4th St.
Ankeny, IA 50023
Tel: (515)964-0601; Free: 888-FAITH 4U
Fax: (515)964-1638
E-mail: admissions@faith.edu
Web Site: http://www.faith.edu/
President/CEO: Dr. James Maxwell
Admissions: Carrie Johnson
Financial Aid: Breck Appell
Type: Comprehensive **Sex:** Coed **Affiliation:** General Association of Regular Baptist Churches **Scores:** 100% SAT V 400+; 100.01% SAT M 400+; 52% ACT 18-23; 33.33% ACT 24-29 **% Accepted:** 94 **Admission Plans:** Deferred Admission **Application Deadline:** August 1 **Application Fee:** $25.00 **H.S. Requirements:** High school diploma required; GED accepted **Costs Per Year:** Application fee: $25. One-time mandatory fee: $50. Comprehensive fee: $18,770 includes full-time tuition ($12,860), mandatory fees ($400), and college room and board ($5510). College room only: $2390. Full-time tuition and fees vary according to course load. Room and board charges vary according to board plan. Part-time tuition: $470 per credit hour. Part-time mandatory fees: $200 per term. Part-time tuition and fees vary according to course load. **Scholarships:** Available **Calendar System:** Semester, Summer Session Available **Enrollment:** FT 306, PT 45, Grad FT 31, Grad PT 35 **Faculty:** FT 21, PT 15 **Student-Faculty Ratio:** 12:1 **Exams:** SAT I or ACT. **% Receiving Financial Aid:** 91 **% Residing in College-Owned, -Operated, or -Affiliated Housing:** 90 **Library Holdings:** 63,840 **Regional Accreditation:** North Central Association of Colleges and Schools **Credit Hours For Degree:** 64 semester hours, Associates; 126 semester hours, Bachelors **Professional Accreditation:** ABHE **Intercollegiate Athletics:** Basketball M & W; Cross-Country Running M & W; Soccer M & W; Track and Field M; Volleyball W

GRACELAND UNIVERSITY
1 University Place
Lamoni, IA 50140
Tel: (641)784-5000; Free: (866)GRACELAND
Admissions: (641)784-5110
Fax: (641)784-5480
E-mail: sutherla@graceland.edu
Web Site: http://www.graceland.edu/
President/CEO: Dr. John Sellars
Admissions: Greg Sutherland
Type: Comprehensive **Sex:** Coed **Affiliation:** Community of Christ **Scores:** 93% SAT V 400+; 79% SAT M 400+; 54% ACT 18-23; 24% ACT 24-29 **% Accepted:** 88 **Admission Plans:** Deferred Admission **Application Deadline:** Rolling **Application Fee:** $50.00 **H.S. Requirements:** High school diploma required; GED accepted **Costs Per Year:** Application fee: $50. Comprehensive fee: $28,020 includes full-time tuition ($20,680), mandatory fees ($300), and college room and board ($7040). College room only: $2810. Room and board charges vary according to board plan, housing facility, and location. Part-time tuition: $650 per semester hour. **Scholarships:** Available **Calendar System:** 4-1-4, Summer Session Available **Enrollment:** FT 1,177, PT 345, Grad FT 650, Grad PT 183 **Faculty:** FT 85, PT 34 **Student-Faculty Ratio:** 16:1 **Exams:** SAT I or ACT. ACT essay not being used. SAT essay not being used. **% Receiving Financial Aid:** 72 **% Residing in College-Owned, -Operated, or -Affiliated Housing:** 69 **Final Year or Final Semester Residency Requirement:** No **Library Holdings:** 123,990 **Regional Accreditation:** North Central Association of Colleges and Schools **Credit Hours For Degree:** 124 credits, Bachelors **Professional Accreditation:** AACN, NCATE, NLN **Intercollegiate Athletics:** Baseball M; Basketball M & W; Cross-Country Running M & W; Football M; Golf M & W; Racquetball M & W; Soccer M & W; Softball W; Swimming and Diving M & W; Tennis M & W; Track and Field M & W; Ultimate Frisbee M & W; Volleyball M & W

GRAND VIEW UNIVERSITY
1200 Grandview Ave.
Des Moines, IA 50316-1599
Tel: (515)263-2800; Free: 800-444-6083
Admissions: (515)263-2810
Fax: (515)263-2974
E-mail: admissions@grandview.edu
Web Site: http://www.grandview.edu/
President/CEO: Kent Henning
Admissions: Diane Schaefer
Financial Aid: Michele Dunne
Type: Comprehensive **Sex:** Coed **Affiliation:** Evangelical Lutheran Church in America **Scores:** 92% SAT V 400+; 75% SAT M 400+; 69% ACT 18-23; 18% ACT 24-29 **% Accepted:** 95 **Application Deadline:** August 15 **Application Fee:** $35.00 **H.S. Requirements:** High school diploma required; GED accepted **Costs Per Year:** Application fee: $35. Comprehensive fee: $25,766 includes full-time tuition ($18,944), mandatory fees ($380), and college room and board ($6442). Full-time tuition and fees vary according to class time and course load. Room and board charges vary according to board plan and housing facility. Part-time tuition: $485 per hour. Part-time tuition varies according to class time and course load. **Scholarships:** Available **Calendar System:** Semester, Summer Session Available **Enrollment:** FT 1,601, PT 384, Grad PT 54 **Faculty:** FT 87, PT 116 **Student-Faculty Ratio:** 14:1 **Exams:** SAT I or ACT. ACT essay used for admission. SAT essay used for admission. ACT essay used for advising. SAT essay used for advising. ACT essay used for placement. SAT essay used for placement. **% Receiving Financial Aid:** 82 **% Residing in College-Owned, -Operated, or -Affiliated Housing:** 29 **Library Holdings:** 137,138 **Regional Accreditation:** North Central Association of Colleges and Schools **Credit Hours For Degree:** 62 semester hours, Associates; 124 semester hours, Bachelors **ROTC:** Army, Air Force **Professional Accreditation:** AACN **Intercollegiate Athletics:** Baseball M; Basketball M & W; Cross-Country Running M & W; Football M; Golf M & W; Soccer M & W; Softball W; Track and Field M & W; Volleyball W; Wrestling M

GRINNELL COLLEGE
1103 Park St.
Grinnell, IA 50112-1690
Tel: (641)269-4000; Free: 800-247-0113
Admissions: (641)269-3600
Fax: (641)269-3408
E-mail: askgrin@grinnell.edu
Web Site: http://www.grinnell.edu/
President/CEO: Russell K. Osgood

Admissions: Seth Allen
Financial Aid: Arnold Woods
Type: Four-Year College **Sex:** Coed **Scores:** 99.5% SAT V 400+; 99.5% SAT M 400+; 3.6% ACT 18-23; 36.2% ACT 24-29 **% Accepted:** 34 **Admission Plans:** Early Admission; Early Decision Plan; Deferred Admission **Application Deadline:** January 2 **Application Fee:** $30.00 **H.S. Requirements:** High school diploma required; GED accepted **Costs Per Year:** Application fee: $30. Comprehensive fee: $45,012 includes full-time tuition ($35,976), mandatory fees ($500), and college room and board ($8536). College room only: $3968. Full-time tuition and fees vary according to student level. Room and board charges vary according to board plan and housing facility. Part-time tuition: $1124 per credit. Part-time tuition varies according to student level. **Scholarships:** Available **Calendar System:** Semester, Summer Session Not available **Enrollment:** FT 1,633, PT 55 **Faculty:** FT 157, PT 46 **Student-Faculty Ratio:** 9:1 **Exams:** SAT I or ACT. ACT essay not being used. SAT essay not being used. **% Receiving Financial Aid:** 64 **% Residing in College-Owned, -Operated, or -Affiliated Housing:** 87 **Library Holdings:** 1,230,201 **Regional Accreditation:** North Central Association of Colleges and Schools **Credit Hours For Degree:** 124 credits, Bachelors **Intercollegiate Athletics:** Baseball M; Basketball M & W; Cross-Country Running M & W; Football M; Golf M & W; Soccer M & W; Softball W; Swimming and Diving M & W; Tennis M & W; Track and Field M & W; Volleyball W

HAMILTON TECHNICAL COLLEGE
1011 East 53rd St.
Davenport, IA 52807-2653
Tel: (563)386-3570
Fax: (563)386-6756
E-mail: servin@hamiltontechcollege.com
Web Site: http://www.hamiltontechcollege.com/
President/CEO: Maryanne Hamilton
Admissions: Scott Ervin
Financial Aid: Lisa Boyd
Type: Four-Year College **Sex:** Coed **Admission Plans:** Open Admission; Deferred Admission **Application Deadline:** Rolling **Application Fee:** $25.00 **H.S. Requirements:** High school diploma required; GED accepted **Scholarships:** Available **Calendar System:** Continuous, Summer Session Not available **Faculty:** FT 11, PT 1 **Student-Faculty Ratio:** 20:1 **Library Holdings:** 4,500 **Credit Hours For Degree:** 75 credit hours, Associates; 120 credit hours, Bachelors **Professional Accreditation:** ACCSCT

HAWKEYE COMMUNITY COLLEGE
PO Box 8015
Waterloo, IA 50704-8015
Tel: (319)296-2320; Free: 800-670-4769
Admissions: (319)296-4277
Fax: (319)296-2874
E-mail: hgrimm-see@hawkeyecollege.edu
Web Site: http://www.hawkeyecollege.edu/
President/CEO: Greg Schmitz
Admissions: Holly Grimm-See
Type: Two-Year College **Sex:** Coed **Scores:** 37.5% ACT 18-23; 10% ACT 24-29 **% Accepted:** 67 **Admission Plans:** Open Admission; Deferred Admission **Application Deadline:** Rolling **Application Fee:** $0.00 **H.S. Requirements:** High school diploma required; GED accepted **Costs Per Year:** Application fee: $0. State resident tuition: $3630 full-time, $121 per credit hour part-time. Nonresident tuition: $4380 full-time, $146 per credit hour part-time. Mandatory fees: $210 full-time, $7 per credit hour part-time. Full-time tuition and fees vary according to course load and program. Part-time tuition and fees vary according to course load and program. **Scholarships:** Available **Calendar System:** Semester, Summer Session Available **Enrollment:** FT 3,189, PT 3,132 **Faculty:** FT 116, PT 180 **Student-Faculty Ratio:** 24:1 **Exams:** ACT. ACT essay not being used. SAT essay not being used. **Final Year or Final Semester Residency Requirement:** Yes **Library Holdings:** 94,295 **Regional Accreditation:** North Central Association of Colleges and Schools **Credit Hours For Degree:** 62 credits, Associates **ROTC:** Army **Professional Accreditation:** ADA, CARC, NAACLS

INDIAN HILLS COMMUNITY COLLEGE
525 Grandview Ave., Bldg. No. 1
Ottumwa, IA 52501-1398
Tel: (641)683-5111; Free: 800-726-2585
Web Site: http://www.ihcc.cc.ia.us/
President/CEO: Jim Lindenmayer
Admissions: Jane Sapp
Type: Two-Year College **Sex:** Coed **Affiliation:** Iowa Area Community Colleges System **Admission Plans:** Open Admission; Early Admission **Application Deadline:** Rolling **Application Fee:** $0.00 **H.S. Requirements:** High school diploma required; GED accepted **Scholarships:** Available **Calendar System:** Quarter, Summer Session Available **Library Holdings:** 53,073 **Regional Accreditation:** North Central Association of Colleges and Schools **Credit Hours For Degree:** 61 credit hours, Associates **Professional Accreditation:** ACF, AHIMA, APTA, JRCERT **Intercollegiate Athletics:** Baseball M; Basketball M; Golf M; Softball W; Volleyball W

INSTE BIBLE COLLEGE
2302 SW 3rd St.
Ankeny, IA 50023
Tel: (515)289-9200
Fax: (515)289-9201
Web Site: http://www.inste.edu/
Type: Four-Year College **Sex:** Coed **Professional Accreditation:** DETC

IOWA CENTRAL COMMUNITY COLLEGE
330 Ave. M
Fort Dodge, IA 50501-5798
Tel: (515)576-7201
Admissions: (515)576-0099
Fax: (515)576-7724
E-mail: bahls@iowacentral.com
Web Site: http://www.iccc.cc.ia.us/
President/CEO: Dr. Robert A. Paxton
Admissions: Deb Bahis
Type: Two-Year College **Sex:** Coed **Affiliation:** Iowa Department of Education Division of Community Colleges **Admission Plans:** Open Admission; Early Admission; Deferred Admission **Application Deadline:** Rolling **Application Fee:** $0.00 **H.S. Requirements:** High school diploma required; GED accepted **Scholarships:** Available **Calendar System:** Semester, Summer Session Available **Enrollment:** FT 2,590, PT 3,141 **Faculty:** FT 73, PT 207 **Student-Faculty Ratio:** 18:1 **% Residing in College-Owned, -Operated, or -Affiliated Housing:** 22 **Library Holdings:** 55,000 **Regional Accreditation:** North Central Association of Colleges and Schools **Credit Hours For Degree:** 60 semester hours, Associates **Professional Accreditation:** JRCERT, NAACLS, NLN **Intercollegiate Athletics:** Baseball M; Basketball M & W; Cross-Country Running M & W; Football M; Golf M & W; Soccer M & W; Softball W; Volleyball W; Wrestling M

IOWA LAKES COMMUNITY COLLEGE
19 South 7th St.
Estherville, IA 51334-2295
Tel: (712)362-2604; Free: 800-521-5054
Admissions: (712)852-5254
E-mail: info@iowalakes.edu
Web Site: http://www.iowalakes.edu/
President/CEO: Valerie Newhouse
Admissions: Anne Stansbury Johnson
Type: Two-Year College **Sex:** Coed **Affiliation:** Iowa Community College System **% Accepted:** 96 **Admission Plans:** Open Admission **Application Deadline:** Rolling **Application Fee:** $0.00 **H.S. Requirements:** High school diploma required; GED accepted **Costs Per Year:** Application fee: $0. State resident tuition: $4363 full-time, $128 per credit hour part-time. Nonresident tuition: $4423 full-time, $130 per credit hour part-time. Mandatory fees: $556 full-time, $17 per credit hour part-time, $17. Full-time tuition and fees vary according to course load, program, and reciprocity agreements. Part-time tuition and fees vary according to course load, program, and reciprocity agreements. College room and board: $4800. Room and board charges vary according to housing facility and location. **Scholarships:** Available **Calendar System:** Semester, Summer Session Available **Enrollment:** FT 1,839, PT 1,330 **Faculty:** FT 88, PT 41 **Student-Faculty Ratio:** 24:1 **% Residing in College-Owned, -Operated, or -Affiliated Housing:** 35 **Library Holdings:** 42,867 **Regional Accreditation:** North Central Association of Colleges and Schools **Credit Hours For Degree:** 64 credit hours, Associates **Professional Accreditation:** AAMAE **Intercollegiate Athletics:** Baseball M; Basketball M & W; Cross-Country Running M & W; Golf M & W; Soccer M & W; Softball W; Volleyball W; Wrestling M

IOWA STATE UNIVERSITY OF SCIENCE AND TECHNOLOGY
Ames, IA 50011
Tel: (515)294-4111; Free: 800-262-3810
Admissions: (515)294-5836
Fax: (515)294-2592
E-mail: admissions@iastate.edu
Web Site: http://www.iastate.edu/
President/CEO: Dr. Gregory L. Geoffroy
Admissions: Phil Caffrey
Financial Aid: Roberta Johnson
Type: University **Sex:** Coed **Scores:** 93% SAT V 400+; 98% SAT M 400+; 37.5% ACT 18-23; 48.5% ACT 24-29 **% Accepted:** 85 **Admission Plans:** Early Admission; Deferred Admission **Application Deadline:** July 1 **Application Fee:** $40.00 **H.S. Requirements:** High school diploma required; GED accepted **Costs Per Year:** Application fee: $40. State resident tuition: $6102 full-time, $255 per semester hour part-time. Nonresident tuition: $17,668 full-time, $736 per semester hour part-time. Mandatory fees: $895 full-time. Full-time tuition and fees vary according to class time, degree level, and program. Part-time tuition varies according to class time, course load, degree level, and program. **Scholarships:** Available **Calendar System:** Semester, Summer Session Available **Enrollment:** FT 21,394, PT 1,127, Grad FT 3,344, Grad PT 2,080 **Faculty:** FT 1,435, PT 228 **Student-Faculty Ratio:** 16:1 **Exams:** SAT I or ACT. ACT essay not being used. SAT essay not being used. **% Receiving Financial Aid:** 52 **% Residing in College-Owned, -Operated, or -Affiliated Housing:** 38 **Library Holdings:** 2,578,144 **Regional Accreditation:** North Central Association of Colleges and Schools **Credit Hours For Degree:** 120.5 semester hours, Bachelors **ROTC:** Army, Navy, Air Force **Professional Accreditation:** AACSB, ABET, ACEJMC, AAMFT, AAFCS, ADtA, ACSP, APA, ASLA, AVMA, FIDER, JRCEPAT, NAAB, NASM, NASPAA, SAF, NAIT **Intercollegiate Athletics:** Basketball M & W; Cross-Country Running M & W; Football M; Golf M & W; Gymnastics W; Soccer W; Softball W; Swimming and Diving M & W; Tennis W; Track and Field M & W; Volleyball W; Wrestling M

IOWA WESLEYAN COLLEGE
601 North Main St.
Mount Pleasant, IA 52641-1398
Tel: (319)385-8021; Free: 800-582-2383
Admissions: (319)385-6231
Fax: (319)385-6296
E-mail: mpetty@iwc.edu
Web Site: http://www.iwc.edu/
President/CEO: Jay K. Simmons
Admissions: Mark T. Petty
Financial Aid: Debra Morrissey
Type: Four-Year College **Sex:** Coed **Affiliation:** United Methodist **Scores:** 73% SAT V 400+; 70% SAT M 400+; 53% ACT 18-23; 15% ACT 24-29 **% Accepted:** 68 **Admission Plans:** Early Admission; Deferred Admission **Application Deadline:** August 15 **Application Fee:** $20.00 **H.S. Requirements:** High school diploma required; GED accepted **Costs Per Year:** Application fee: $20. Comprehensive fee: $27,654 includes full-time tuition ($21,000) and college room and board ($6654). College room only: $2710. Room and board charges vary according to board plan and housing facility. Part-time tuition: $520 per credit hour. Part-time tuition varies according to class time and course load. **Scholarships:** Available **Calendar System:** Semester, Summer Session Available **Enrollment:** FT 662, PT 196 **Faculty:** FT 49, PT 38 **Student-Faculty Ratio:** 14:1 **Exams:** SAT I or ACT. ACT essay used for advising. SAT essay used for advising. **% Residing in College-Owned, -Operated, or -Affiliated Housing:** 68 **Library Holdings:** 102,869 **Regional Accreditation:** North Central Association of Colleges and Schools **Credit Hours For Degree:** 124 credit hours, Bachelors **Professional Accreditation:** NLN **Intercollegiate Athletics:** Baseball M; Basketball M & W; Cross-Country Running M & W; Football M; Golf M & W; Soccer M & W; Softball W; Track and Field M & W; Volleyball W

IOWA WESTERN COMMUNITY COLLEGE
2700 College Rd., Box 4-C
Council Bluffs, IA 51502
Tel: (712)325-3200; Free: 800-432-5852
Fax: (712)325-3720
E-mail: admissions@iwcc.edu
Web Site: http://www.iwcc.edu/
President/CEO: Dan Kinney
Admissions: Tori Christie
Type: Two-Year College **Sex:** Coed **Affiliation:** Iowa Department of Education Division of Community Colleges **Admission Plans:** Open Admission; Early Admission; Deferred Admission **Application Deadline:** Rolling **H.S. Requirements:** High school diploma required; GED accepted **Scholarships:** Available **Calendar System:** Semester, Summer Session Available **Library Holdings:** 59,200 **Regional Accreditation:** North Central Association of Colleges and Schools **Credit Hours For Degree:** 64 credit hours, Associates **ROTC:** Army, Air Force **Professional Accreditation:** ABET, ACF, ADA **Intercollegiate Athletics:** Baseball M; Basketball M & W; Golf M & W; Softball W; Track and Field M & W; Volleyball W

ITT TECHNICAL INSTITUTE (CEDAR RAPIDS)
3735 Queen Ct. SW
Cedar Rapids, IA 52404
Tel: (319)297-3400; Free: 877-320-4625
Web Site: http://www.itt-tech.edu/
Type: Two-Year College **Sex:** Coed **Professional Accreditation:** ACICS

ITT TECHNICAL INSTITUTE (CLIVE)
1860 Northwest 118th St., Ste. 110
Clive, IA 50325
Tel: (515)327-5500; Free: 877-526-7312
Admissions: (515)327-5500
Web Site: http://www.itt-tech.edu/
President/CEO: Jodi Clendenen
Type: Two-Year College **Sex:** Coed **Affiliation:** ITT Educational Services, Inc.

KAPLAN UNIVERSITY, CEDAR FALLS
7009 Nordic Dr.
Cedar Falls, IA 50613
Tel: (319)277-0220; Free: 800-728-1220
Web Site: http://www.cedarfalls.kaplanuniversity.edu/
President/CEO: Gwen Bramlet-Hecker
Type: Two-Year College **Sex:** Coed **Application Deadline:** Rolling **H.S. Requirements:** High school diploma required; GED accepted **Calendar System:** Quarter **Regional Accreditation:** North Central Association of Colleges and Schools

KAPLAN UNIVERSITY, CEDAR RAPIDS
3165 Edgewood Parkway, SW
Cedar Rapids, IA 52404
Tel: (319)363-0481; Free: 800-728-0481
Fax: (319)363-3812
Web Site: http://www.cedarrapids.kaplanuniversity.edu/
President/CEO: Susan Spivey
Type: Two-Year College **Sex:** Coed **Affiliation:** Kaplan University - Davenport Campus **H.S. Requirements:** High school diploma required; GED accepted **Scholarships:** Available **Calendar System:** Quarter **Regional Accreditation:** North Central Association of Colleges and Schools **Credit Hours For Degree:** 92 credit hours, Associates **Professional Accreditation:** AAMAE

KAPLAN UNIVERSITY, COUNCIL BLUFFS
1751 Madison Ave.
Council Bluffs, IA 51503
Tel: (712)328-4212; Free: 800-518-4212
Web Site: http://www.councilbluffs.kaplanuniversity.edu/
President/CEO: Michael Zawisky
Type: Two-Year College **Sex:** Coed **H.S. Requirements:** High school diploma required; GED accepted **Exams:** Other. **Regional Accreditation:** North Central Association of Colleges and Schools

KAPLAN UNIVERSITY, DAVENPORT CAMPUS
1801 East Kimberly Rd.
Ste. 1
Davenport, IA 52807-2095
Tel: (563)355-3500
Web Site: http://www.davenport.kaplanuniversity.edu/
President/CEO: Ron Blumenthal
Type: Comprehensive **Sex:** Coed **H.S. Requirements:** High school diploma required; GED accepted **Scholarships:** Available **Calendar System:** Quarter **Regional Accreditation:** North Central Association of Colleges and Schools **Professional Accreditation:** AAMAE

KAPLAN UNIVERSITY, DES MOINES
4655 121st St.
Urbandale, IA 50323
Tel: (515)727-2100
Web Site: http://www.desmoines.kaplanuniversity.edu/
President/CEO: Jeremy Wells
Type: Two-Year College **Sex:** Coed **H.S. Requirements:** High school diploma required; GED accepted

KAPLAN UNIVERSITY, MASON CITY CAMPUS
2570 4th St., SW
Mason City, IA 50401
Tel: (641)423-2530
Web Site: http://masoncity.kaplanuniversity.edu/Pages/Homepage.aspx
President/CEO: Joe Albers
Type: Four-Year College **Sex:** Coed **H.S. Requirements:** High school diploma required; GED accepted

KIRKWOOD COMMUNITY COLLEGE
PO Box 2068
Cedar Rapids, IA 52406-2068
Tel: (319)398-5411; Free: 800-332-2055
Admissions: (319)398-5517
Fax: (319)398-1244
E-mail: dbannon@kirkwood.cc.ia.us
Web Site: http://www.kirkwood.cc.ia.us/
President/CEO: Dr. Mick Starcevich
Admissions: Doug Bannon
Type: Two-Year College **Sex:** Coed **Affiliation:** Iowa Department of Education Division of Community Colleges **Admission Plans:** Open Admission; Early Admission **Application Deadline:** Rolling **Application Fee:** $0.00 **H.S. Requirements:** High school diploma or equivalent not required **Costs Per Year:** Application fee: $0. State resident tuition: $2664 full-time, $111 per credit hour part-time. Nonresident tuition: $3264 full-time, $136 per credit hour part-time. **Scholarships:** Available **Calendar System:** Semester, Summer Session Available **Enrollment:** FT 9,715, PT 8,126 **Faculty:** FT 288, PT 680 **Student-Faculty Ratio:** 24:1 **Library Holdings:** 60,622 **Regional Accreditation:** North Central Association of Colleges and Schools **Credit Hours For Degree:** 62 semester hours, Associates **Professional Accreditation:** ARCEST, AAMAE, ACF, ADA, AHIMA, AOTA, APTA, CARC, JRCEET **Intercollegiate Athletics:** Baseball M; Basketball M & W; Golf M; Soccer M & W; Softball W; Volleyball W

LORAS COLLEGE
1450 Alta Vista
Dubuque, IA 52004-0178
Tel: (563)588-7100; Free: 800-245-6727
Admissions: (563)588-7829
Fax: (563)588-7964
E-mail: adms@loras.edu
Web Site: http://www.loras.edu/
President/CEO: James E. Collins
Admissions: Sharon Lyons
Financial Aid: Julie A. Dunn
Type: Comprehensive **Sex:** Coed **Affiliation:** Roman Catholic **Scores:** 56% ACT 18-23; 36% ACT 24-29 **% Accepted:** 61 **Admission Plans:** Deferred Admission **Application Deadline:** Rolling **Application Fee:** $25.00 **H.S. Requirements:** High school diploma required; GED accepted **Costs Per Year:** Application fee: $25. Comprehensive fee: $33,505 includes full-time tuition ($24,912), mandatory fees ($1322), and college room and board ($7271). College room only: $3643. Full-time tuition and fees vary according to course load and degree level. Room and board charges vary according to board plan and housing facility. Part-time tuition: $470 per credit hour. Part-time mandatory fees: $25 per credit hour. **Scholarships:** Available **Calendar System:** Semester, Summer Session Available **Enrollment:** FT 1,458, PT 41, Grad FT 4, Grad PT 65 **Faculty:** FT 111, PT 48 **Student-Faculty Ratio:** 12:1 **Exams:** SAT I or ACT. **% Receiving Financial Aid:** 76 **% Residing in College-Owned, -Operated, or -Affiliated Housing:** 67 **Library Holdings:** 392,859 **Regional Accreditation:** North Central Association of Colleges and Schools **Credit Hours For Degree:** 60 credits, Associates; 120 credits, Bachelors **ROTC:** Army **Professional Accreditation:** CSWE **Intercollegiate Athletics:** Baseball M; Basketball M & W; Cross-Country Running M & W; Football M; Golf M & W; Ice Hockey M; Rugby M; Skiing (Downhill) M; Soccer M & W; Softball W; Swimming and Diving M & W; Tennis M & W; Track and Field M & W; Volleyball M & W; Water Polo M; Wrestling M

LUTHER COLLEGE
700 College Dr.
Decorah, IA 52101
Tel: (563)387-2000; Free: 800-458-8437
Admissions: (563)387-1287
Fax: (563)387-2159
E-mail: admissions@luther.edu
Web Site: http://www.luther.edu/
President/CEO: Dr. Richard L. Torgerson
Admissions: Kirk Neubauer
Financial Aid: Janice Cordell
Type: Four-Year College **Sex:** Coed **Affiliation:** Evangelical Lutheran Church in America **Scores:** 90.9% SAT V 400+; 95.5% SAT M 400+; 25.3% ACT 18-23; 50% ACT 24-29 **% Accepted:** 70 **Admission Plans:** Deferred Admission **Application Fee:** $25.00 **H.S. Requirements:** High school diploma required; GED accepted **Costs Per Year:** Application fee: $25. Comprehensive fee: $39,280 includes full-time tuition ($33,330), mandatory fees ($150), and college room and board ($5800). College room only: $2880. Full-time tuition and fees vary according to course load. Room and board charges vary according to board plan and housing facility. Part-time tuition: $1190 per credit hour. Part-time tuition varies according to course load. **Scholarships:** Available **Calendar System:** 4-1-4, Summer Session Available **Enrollment:** FT 2,470, PT 49 **Faculty:** FT 177, PT 74 **Student-Faculty Ratio:** 12:1 **Exams:** SAT I or ACT. **% Receiving Financial Aid:** 69 **% Residing in College-Owned, -Operated, or -Affiliated Housing:** 88 **Library Holdings:** 329,949 **Regional Accreditation:** North Central Association of Colleges and Schools **Credit Hours For Degree:** 128 semester hours, Bachelors **Professional Accreditation:** AACN, CSWE, NASM, NCATE **Intercollegiate Athletics:** Baseball M; Basketball M & W; Cross-Country Running M & W; Football M; Golf M & W; Soccer M & W; Softball W; Swimming and Diving M & W; Tennis M & W; Track and Field M & W; Volleyball W; Wrestling M

MAHARISHI UNIVERSITY OF MANAGEMENT
1000 North 4th St.
Fairfield, IA 52557
Tel: (641)472-7000; Free: 800-369-6480
Admissions: (641)472-1110
Fax: (641)472-1189
E-mail: admissions@mum.edu
Web Site: http://www.mum.edu/
President/CEO: Dr. Bevan Morris
Admissions: Michelle Paton
Financial Aid: Bill Christensen
Type: University **Sex:** Coed **Admission Plans:** Preferred Admission; Early Admission; Deferred Admission **Application Deadline:** August 1 **Application Fee:** $30.00 **H.S. Requirements:** High school diploma required; GED accepted **Costs Per Year:** Application fee: $30. Comprehensive fee: $30,000 includes full-time tuition ($24,000) and college room and board ($6000). College room only: $2800. Part-time tuition: $12,000 per year. Part-time tuition varies according to course load. **Scholarships:** Available **Calendar System:** Semester, Summer Session Not available **Enrollment:** FT 252, PT 21, Grad FT 438, Grad PT 496 **Student-Faculty Ratio:** 16:1 **Exams:** SAT I or ACT. **% Receiving Financial Aid:** 92 **% Residing in College-Owned, -Operated, or -Affiliated Housing:** 60 **Library Holdings:** 137,775 **Regional Accreditation:** North Central Association of Colleges and Schools **Credit Hours For Degree:** 166 units, Bachelors **Intercollegiate Athletics:** Soccer M & W; Ultimate Frisbee M & W; Volleyball M & W

MARSHALLTOWN COMMUNITY COLLEGE
3700 South Center St.
Marshalltown, IA 50158-4760
Tel: (641)752-7106; Free: (866)622-4748
Fax: (641)752-8149
Web Site: http://www.marshalltowncommunitycollege.com/
President/CEO: Tim Wynes
Admissions: Deana Inman
Type: Two-Year College **Sex:** Coed **Affiliation:** Iowa Valley Community College District System **Admission Plans:** Open Admission; Early Admission **Application Deadline:** Rolling **Application Fee:** $0.00 **H.S. Requirements:**

High school diploma required; GED accepted **Scholarships:** Available **Calendar System:** Semester, Summer Session Available **Exams:** ACT, Other. **Library Holdings:** 39,348 **Regional Accreditation:** North Central Association of Colleges and Schools **Credit Hours For Degree:** 64 credits, Associates **ROTC:** Air Force **Professional Accreditation:** ADA **Intercollegiate Athletics:** Baseball M; Basketball M & W; Cheerleading M & W; Golf M & W; Soccer M & W; Softball W; Volleyball W

MERCY COLLEGE OF HEALTH SCIENCES
928 Sixth Ave.
Des Moines, IA 50309-1239
Tel: (515)643-3180; Free: 800-637-2994
Fax: (515)643-6698
E-mail: kscholten@mercydesmoines.org
Web Site: http://www.mchs.edu/
President/CEO: Barbara Q. Decker, JD
Admissions: Kara Scholten
Financial Aid: Lisa Croat
Type: Four-Year College **Sex:** Coed **Affiliation:** Roman Catholic Church; Catholic Health Initiatives, Mercy Medial Center **Admission Plans:** Open Admission **Application Deadline:** Rolling **Application Fee:** $25.00 **H.S. Requirements:** High school diploma required; GED accepted **Costs Per Year:** Application fee: $25. Tuition: $13,000 full-time, $440 per credit hour part-time. Full-time tuition varies according to course load. Part-time tuition varies according to course load. **Scholarships:** Available **Calendar System:** Semester, Summer Session Available **Enrollment:** FT 458, PT 320 **Faculty:** FT 48 **Student-Faculty Ratio:** 12:1 **Exams:** ACT. **% Receiving Financial Aid:** 84 **Library Holdings:** 20,334 **Regional Accreditation:** North Central Association of Colleges and Schools **Professional Accreditation:** ARCEST, AACN, JRCEDMS, NLN

MORNINGSIDE COLLEGE
1501 Morningside Ave.
Sioux City, IA 51106
Tel: (712)274-5000; Free: 800-831-0806
Admissions: (712)274-5111
E-mail: mscadm@morningside.edu
Web Site: http://www.morningside.edu/
President/CEO: John Reynders
Admissions: Amy Williams
Financial Aid: Karen Gagnon
Type: Comprehensive **Sex:** Coed **Affiliation:** United Methodist Church **Scores:** 58% ACT 18-23; 35% ACT 24-29 **% Accepted:** 71 **Admission Plans:** Deferred Admission **Application Deadline:** Rolling **Application Fee:** $0.00 **H.S. Requirements:** High school diploma required; GED accepted. For home-schooled students must also provide transcript/record of courses and grades.: High school diploma required; GED accepted **Costs Per Year:** Application fee: $0. Comprehensive fee: $30,020 includes full-time tuition ($21,810), mandatory fees ($1170), and college room and board ($7040). College room only: $3610. Full-time tuition and fees vary according to degree level, program, and student level. Room and board charges vary according to housing facility. **Scholarships:** Available **Calendar System:** Semester, Summer Session Available **Enrollment:** FT 1,198, PT 41, Grad FT 2, Grad PT 795 **Faculty:** FT 70, PT 103 **Student-Faculty Ratio:** 14:1 **Exams:** SAT I or ACT. ACT essay not being used. SAT essay not being used. **% Receiving Financial Aid:** 86 **% Residing in College-Owned, -Operated, or -Affiliated Housing:** 64 **Final Year or Final Semester Residency Requirement:** Yes **Library Holdings:** 91,926 **Regional Accreditation:** North Central Association of Colleges and Schools **Credit Hours For Degree:** 124 semester hours, Bachelors **ROTC:** Army **Professional Accreditation:** NASM, NCATE, NLN **Intercollegiate Athletics:** Baseball M; Basketball M & W; Cross-Country Running M & W; Football M; Golf M & W; Soccer M & W; Softball W; Swimming and Diving M & W; Tennis M & W; Track and Field M & W; Volleyball W; Wrestling M

MOUNT MERCY COLLEGE
1330 Elmhurst Dr., NE
Cedar Rapids, IA 52402-4797
Tel: (319)363-8213; Free: 800-248-4504
Admissions: (319)368-6460
Fax: (319)368-6492
E-mail: emetz@mtmercy.edu
Web Site: http://www.mtmercy.edu/
President/CEO: Dr. Christopher R. Blake
Admissions: Liz Metz
Financial Aid: Bethany Rinderknecht
Type: Comprehensive **Sex:** Coed **Affiliation:** Roman Catholic **Scores:** 62.8% ACT 18-23; 33% ACT 24-29 **% Accepted:** 78 **Admission Plans:** Deferred Admission **Application Deadline:** August 15 **Application Fee:** $0.00 **H.S. Requirements:** High school diploma required; GED accepted **Costs Per Year:** Application fee: $0. Comprehensive fee: $29,084 includes full-time tuition ($22,100) and college room and board ($6984). Full-time tuition varies according to course load. Room and board charges vary according to board plan and housing facility. Part-time tuition: $610 per credit hour. Part-time tuition varies according to course load. **Scholarships:** Available **Calendar System:** 4-1-4, Summer Session Available **Enrollment:** FT 939, PT 559, Grad FT 33, Grad PT 135 **Faculty:** FT 81, PT 71 **Student-Faculty Ratio:** 13:1 **Exams:** SAT I or ACT. ACT essay not being used. SAT essay not being used. **% Receiving Financial Aid:** 84 **% Residing in College-Owned, -Operated, or -Affiliated Housing:** 29 **Final Year or Final Semester Residency Requirement:** Yes **Library Holdings:** 140,319 **Regional Accreditation:** North Central Association of Colleges and Schools **Credit Hours For Degree:** 123 credit hours, Bachelors **Professional Accreditation:** AACN, CSWE **Intercollegiate Athletics:** Baseball M; Basketball M & W; Cross-Country Running M & W; Golf M & W; Soccer M & W; Softball W; Track and Field M & W; Volleyball W

MUSCATINE COMMUNITY COLLEGE
152 Colorado St.
Muscatine, IA 52761-5396
Tel: (563)288-6001
Admissions: (563)336-3322
Fax: (563)288-6074
E-mail: gmohr@eicc.edu
Web Site: http://www.eicc.edu/
President/CEO: Dr. Jeffrey Armstrong, PhD
Admissions: Gary Mohr
Financial Aid: Robin Jennings
Type: Two-Year College **Sex:** Coed **Affiliation:** Eastern Iowa Community College District **Scores:** 56% ACT 18-23; 23% ACT 24-29 **% Accepted:** 100 **Admission Plans:** Open Admission **Application Deadline:** Rolling **H.S. Requirements:** High school diploma or equivalent not required **Costs Per Year:** State resident tuition: $2688 full-time, $112 per credit hour part-time. Nonresident tuition: $4032 full-time, $168 per credit hour part-time. Full-time tuition varies according to class time, program, and reciprocity agreements. Part-time tuition varies according to class time, program, and reciprocity agreements. College room only: $3780. **Scholarships:** Available **Calendar System:** Semester, Summer Session Available **Enrollment:** FT 608, PT 1,016 **Faculty:** FT 32, PT 59 **% Residing in College-Owned, -Operated, or -Affiliated Housing:** 4 **Library Holdings:** 19,588 **Regional Accreditation:** North Central Association of Colleges and Schools **Credit Hours For Degree:** 62 credits, Associates **Intercollegiate Athletics:** Baseball M; Softball W

NORTH IOWA AREA COMMUNITY COLLEGE
500 College Dr.
Mason City, IA 50401-7299
Tel: (641)423-1264; Free: 888-GO NIACC
Admissions: (641)422-4104
Fax: (641)423-1711
E-mail: request@niacc.edu
Web Site: http://www.niacc.edu/
President/CEO: Dr. Debra Derr
Admissions: Rachel McGuire
Type: Two-Year College **Sex:** Coed **Affiliation:** Iowa Community College System **Admission Plans:** Open Admission **Application Deadline:** Rolling **Application Fee:** $0.00 **H.S. Requirements:** High school diploma required; GED accepted **Costs Per Year:** Application fee: $0. State resident tuition: $3292 full-time, $109 per semester hour part-time. Nonresident tuition: $4939 full-time, $164 per semester hour part-time. Mandatory fees: $398 full-time, $13.28 per semester hour part-time. Full-time tuition and fees vary according to course load. Part-time tuition and fees vary according to course load. College room and board: $4806. Room and board charges vary according to housing facility. **Scholarships:** Available **Calendar System:** Semester, Summer Session Available **Enrollment:** FT 1,990, PT 1,739 **Faculty:** FT 84, PT 172 **Library Holdings:** 29,540 **Regional Accreditation:** North Central Association of Colleges and Schools **Credit Hours For Degree:** 60 semester hours, Associates **Professional Accreditation:**

APTA, NLN **Intercollegiate Athletics:** Baseball M; Basketball M & W; Cross-Country Running M & W; Golf M & W; Soccer M; Softball W; Track and Field M & W; Volleyball W; Wrestling M

NORTHEAST IOWA COMMUNITY COLLEGE
Box 400
Calmar, IA 52132-0480
Tel: (563)562-3263; Free: 800-728-CALMAR
Fax: (563)562-3719
E-mail: keunem@nicc.edu
Web Site: http://www.nicc.edu/
President/CEO: Dr. Penelope Wills
Admissions: Martha Keune
Type: Two-Year College **Sex:** Coed **Affiliation:** Iowa Area Community Colleges System **% Accepted:** 74 **Admission Plans:** Open Admission **Application Deadline:** Rolling **Application Fee:** $0.00 **H.S. Requirements:** High school diploma or equivalent not required **Costs Per Year:** Application fee: $0. State resident tuition: $4352 full-time, $136 per credit hour part-time. Nonresident tuition: $4352 full-time, $136 per credit hour part-time. Mandatory fees: $416 full-time, $13 per credit hour part-time. **Scholarships:** Available **Calendar System:** Semester, Summer Session Available **Enrollment:** FT 2,564, PT 2,825 **Faculty:** FT 115, PT 166 **Student-Faculty Ratio:** 18:1 **Final Year or Final Semester Residency Requirement:** No **Library Holdings:** 21,337 **Regional Accreditation:** North Central Association of Colleges and Schools **Credit Hours For Degree:** 64 credit hours, Associates **Professional Accreditation:** AHIMA, CARC

NORTHWEST IOWA COMMUNITY COLLEGE
603 West Park St.
Sheldon, IA 51201-1046
Tel: (712)324-5061; Free: 800-352-4907
Fax: (712)324-4136
E-mail: lstory@nwicc.edu
Web Site: http://www.nwicc.edu/
President/CEO: Dr. William G. Giddings
Admissions: Lisa Story
Type: Two-Year College **Sex:** Coed **Affiliation:** Iowa Department of Education Division of Community Colleges **Admission Plans:** Open Admission **Application Deadline:** Rolling **Application Fee:** $10.00 **H.S. Requirements:** High school diploma required; GED accepted **Costs Per Year:** Application fee: $10. State resident tuition: $3570 full-time, $119 per credit part-time. Nonresident tuition: $4620 full-time, $154 per credit part-time. Mandatory fees: $840 full-time, $28 per credit part-time. Full-time tuition and fees vary according to course load. Part-time tuition and fees vary according to course load. College room and board: $4400. College room only: $3200. Room and board charges vary according to housing facility. **Scholarships:** Available **Calendar System:** Semester **Faculty:** FT 40, PT 99 **Student-Faculty Ratio:** 11:1 **Exams:** Other. **Library Holdings:** 16,300 **Regional Accreditation:** North Central Association of Colleges and Schools **Credit Hours For Degree:** 60 credit hours, Associates **Professional Accreditation:** AHIMA

NORTHWESTERN COLLEGE
101 Seventh St., SW
Orange City, IA 51041-1996
Tel: (712)707-7000; Free: 800-747-4757
Admissions: (712)737-7130
Fax: (712)707-7247
E-mail: admissions@nwciowa.edu
Web Site: http://www.nwciowa.edu/
President/CEO: Greg Christy
Admissions: Mark Bloemendaal
Financial Aid: Gerry Korver
Type: Four-Year College **Sex:** Coed **Affiliation:** Reformed Church in America **Scores:** 37.5% ACT 18-23; 52% ACT 24-29 **% Accepted:** 75 **Admission Plans:** Early Admission; Deferred Admission **Application Deadline:** Rolling **Application Fee:** $25.00 **H.S. Requirements:** High school diploma required; GED accepted **Costs Per Year:** Application fee: $25. Comprehensive fee: $28,996 includes full-time tuition ($22,240) and college room and board ($6756). Full-time tuition varies according to program. Room and board charges vary according to board plan and housing facility. **Scholarships:** Available **Calendar System:** Semester, Summer Session Available **Enrollment:** FT 1,164, PT 42 **Faculty:** FT 82, PT 53 **Student-Faculty Ratio:** 14:1 **Exams:** SAT I or ACT. **% Receiving Financial Aid:** 79 **% Residing in College-Owned, -Operated, or -Affiliated Housing:** 89 **Final Year or Final Semester Residency Requirement:** No **Library Holdings:** 125,000 **Regional Accreditation:** North Central Association of Colleges and Schools **Credit Hours For Degree:** 124 credit hours, Bachelors **Professional Accreditation:** CSWE, NCATE **Intercollegiate Athletics:** Baseball M; Basketball M & W; Cross-Country Running M & W; Football M; Golf M & W; Soccer M & W; Softball W; Tennis M & W; Track and Field M & W; Volleyball W; Wrestling M

PALMER COLLEGE OF CHIROPRACTIC
1000 Brady St.
Davenport, IA 52803-5287
Tel: (563)884-5000; Free: 800-722-3648
Admissions: (563)884-5743
Fax: (563)884-5897
E-mail: lisa.gisel@palmer.edu
Web Site: http://www.palmer.edu/
President/CEO: Dr. Donald Kern, DC
Admissions: Lisa Gisel
Financial Aid: Sue McCabe
Type: Comprehensive **Sex:** Coed **% Accepted:** 67 **Admission Plans:** Open Admission; Deferred Admission **Application Deadline:** Rolling **Application Fee:** $50.00 **H.S. Requirements:** High school diploma required; GED accepted **Scholarships:** Available **Calendar System:** Trimester, Summer Session Available **Enrollment:** FT 65, PT 3 **Library Holdings:** 55,278 **Regional Accreditation:** North Central Association of Colleges and Schools **Credit Hours For Degree:** 60 credit hours, Associates; 120 credit hours, Bachelors **Professional Accreditation:** CCE **Intercollegiate Athletics:** Rugby M & W

ST. AMBROSE UNIVERSITY
518 West Locust St.
Davenport, IA 52803-2898
Tel: (563)333-6000; Free: 800-383-2627
Admissions: (563)333-6300
Fax: (563)383-8791
E-mail: higginsmegf@sau.edu
Web Site: http://www.sau.edu/
President/CEO: Sr. Joan Lescinski, CSJ
Admissions: Meg Halligan
Financial Aid: Julie Haack
Type: Comprehensive **Sex:** Coed **Affiliation:** Roman Catholic **Scores:** 61.18% ACT 18-23; 28.62% ACT 24-29 **% Accepted:** 82 **Admission Plans:** Deferred Admission **Application Deadline:** Rolling **Application Fee:** $25.00 **H.S. Requirements:** High school diploma required; GED accepted **Costs Per Year:** Application fee: $25. Comprehensive fee: $32,495 includes full-time tuition ($23,670), mandatory fees ($240), and college room and board ($8585). College room only: $4375. Full-time tuition and fees vary according to course load, location, program, and reciprocity agreements. Room and board charges vary according to board plan and housing facility. Part-time tuition: $735 per credit hour. Part-time mandatory fees: $60 per term. Part-time tuition and fees vary according to course load and location. **Scholarships:** Available **Calendar System:** 4-1-4, Summer Session Available **Enrollment:** FT 2,414, PT 473, Grad FT 285, Grad PT 557 **Faculty:** FT 186, PT 220 **Student-Faculty Ratio:** 11:1 **Exams:** ACT, SAT I or ACT. ACT essay not being used. SAT essay not being used. **% Receiving Financial Aid:** 74 **% Residing in College-Owned, -Operated, or -Affiliated Housing:** 52 **Library Holdings:** 156,303 **Regional Accreditation:** North Central Association of Colleges and Schools **Credit Hours For Degree:** 120 credit hours, Bachelors **Professional Accreditation:** ABET, AACN, AOTA, APTA, ACBSP, CSWE, TEAC **Intercollegiate Athletics:** Baseball M; Basketball M & W; Bowling M & W; Cheerleading M & W; Cross-Country Running M & W; Football M; Golf M & W; Soccer M & W; Softball W; Tennis M & W; Track and Field M & W; Volleyball M & W

ST. LUKE'S COLLEGE
2720 Stone Park Blvd.
Sioux City, IA 51104
Tel: (712)279-3149; Free: 800-352-4660
Fax: (712)233-8017
E-mail: mccartsj@stlukes.org
Web Site: http://stlukescollege.edu/
President/CEO: Michael D. Stiles
Admissions: Sherry McCarthy

Type: Two-Year College **Sex:** Coed **Affiliation:** St. Luke's Regional Medical Center **% Accepted:** 48 **Application Deadline:** August 1 **Application Fee:** $50.00 **H.S. Requirements:** High school diploma required; GED accepted **Costs Per Year:** Application fee: $50. Tuition: $14,580 full-time, $405 per credit hour part-time. Mandatory fees: $920 full-time. Full-time tuition and fees vary according to course load, degree level, and program. Part-time tuition varies according to course load and degree level. **Scholarships:** Available **Calendar System:** Semester, Summer Session Available **Enrollment:** FT 135, PT 44 **Faculty:** FT 19, PT 13 **Student-Faculty Ratio:** 8:1 **Exams:** SAT I or ACT. ACT essay not being used. SAT essay not being used. **Final Year or Final Semester Residency Requirement:** No **Library Holdings:** 2,724 **Regional Accreditation:** North Central Association of Colleges and Schools **Credit Hours For Degree:** 71 credit hours, Associates

SCOTT COMMUNITY COLLEGE
500 Belmont Rd.
Bettendorf, IA 52722-6804
Tel: (563)441-4001
Admissions: (563)336-3322
Fax: (563)441-4066
E-mail: gmohr@eicc.edu
Web Site: http://www.eicc.edu/scc/
President/CEO: Dr. Thomas Coley
Admissions: Gary Mohr
Financial Aid: Jeannine Ingelson
Type: Two-Year College **Sex:** Coed **Affiliation:** Eastern Iowa Community College District **% Accepted:** 100 **Admission Plans:** Open Admission **Application Deadline:** Rolling **H.S. Requirements:** High school diploma or equivalent not required **Costs Per Year:** State resident tuition: $2688 full-time, $112 per credit hour part-time. Nonresident tuition: $4032 full-time, $168 per credit hour part-time. **Scholarships:** Available **Calendar System:** Semester, Summer Session Available **Enrollment:** FT 2,059, PT 2,052 **Faculty:** FT 86, PT 164 **Student-Faculty Ratio:** 20:1 **Library Holdings:** 22,700 **Regional Accreditation:** North Central Association of Colleges and Schools **Credit Hours For Degree:** 62 credits, Associates **Professional Accreditation:** ADA, JRCEET, JRCERT **Intercollegiate Athletics:** Golf M & W; Soccer M & W

SIMPSON COLLEGE
701 North C St.
Indianola, IA 50125-1297
Tel: (515)961-6251; Free: 800-362-2454
Admissions: (515)961-1624
Fax: (515)961-1498
E-mail: admiss@simpson.edu
Web Site: http://www.simpson.edu/
President/CEO: John W. Byrd
Admissions: Deborah Tierney
Financial Aid: Tracie Lynn Pavon
Type: Comprehensive **Sex:** Coed **Affiliation:** United Methodist **Scores:** 45.3% ACT 18-23; 47.1% ACT 24-29 **% Accepted:** 89 **Admission Plans:** Deferred Admission **Application Deadline:** August 15 **Application Fee:** $0.00 **H.S. Requirements:** High school diploma required; GED accepted **Costs Per Year:** Application fee: $0. One-time mandatory fee: $200. Comprehensive fee: $32,994 includes full-time tuition ($25,366), mandatory fees ($367), and college room and board ($7261). College room only: $3485. Full-time tuition and fees vary according to course load, degree level, and program. Room and board charges vary according to board plan and housing facility. Part-time tuition: $290 per credit hour. Part-time tuition varies according to course load and degree level. **Scholarships:** Available **Calendar System:** Miscellaneous, Summer Session Available **Enrollment:** FT 1,481, PT 507, Grad FT 3, Grad PT 32 **Faculty:** FT 99, PT 96 **Student-Faculty Ratio:** 14:1 **Exams:** SAT I or ACT. ACT essay not being used. SAT essay not being used. **% Receiving Financial Aid:** 86 **% Residing in College-Owned, -Operated, or -Affiliated Housing:** 84 **Final Year or Final Semester Residency Requirement:** No **Library Holdings:** 162,197 **Regional Accreditation:** North Central Association of Colleges and Schools **Credit Hours For Degree:** 128 credit hours, Bachelors **Professional Accreditation:** NASM **Intercollegiate Athletics:** Baseball M; Basketball M & W; Cheerleading M & W; Cross-Country Running M & W; Football M; Golf M & W; Soccer M & W; Softball W; Swimming and Diving M & W; Tennis M & W; Track and Field M & W; Volleyball W; Wrestling M

SOUTHEASTERN COMMUNITY COLLEGE
1500 West Agency Rd.
PO Box 180
West Burlington, IA 52655-0180
Tel: (319)752-2731
Fax: (319)752-4957
E-mail: admoff@scciowa.edu
Web Site: http://www.secc.cc.ia.us/
President/CEO: Dr. Beverly Simone
Admissions: Stacy White
Financial Aid: Gwen Scholer
Type: Two-Year College **Sex:** Coed **Affiliation:** Iowa Department of Education Division of Community Colleges **Admission Plans:** Open Admission; Early Admission; Deferred Admission **Application Deadline:** Rolling **Application Fee:** $0.00 **H.S. Requirements:** High school diploma or equivalent not required **Costs Per Year:** Application fee: $0. State resident tuition: $3450 full-time, $115 per credit hour part-time. Nonresident tuition: $3600 full-time, $120 per credit hour part-time. College room and board: $3856. **Scholarships:** Available **Calendar System:** Semester, Summer Session Available **Enrollment:** FT 2,087, PT 1,667 **Exams:** ACT essay not being used. SAT essay not being used. **% Residing in College-Owned, -Operated, or -Affiliated Housing:** 2 **Regional Accreditation:** North Central Association of Colleges and Schools **Credit Hours For Degree:** 62 credit hours, Associates **Professional Accreditation:** AAMAE **Intercollegiate Athletics:** Baseball M; Basketball M; Softball W; Volleyball W

SOUTHWESTERN COMMUNITY COLLEGE
1501 West Townline St.
Creston, IA 50801
Tel: (641)782-7081; Free: 800-247-4023
Fax: (641)782-3312
E-mail: carstens@swcciowa.edu
Web Site: http://www.swcciowa.edu/
President/CEO: Dr. Barb Crittenden
Admissions: Lisa Carstens
Type: Two-Year College **Sex:** Coed **Affiliation:** Iowa Department of Education Division of Community Colleges **Admission Plans:** Open Admission; Early Admission **Application Deadline:** September 5 **H.S. Requirements:** High school diploma required; GED accepted **Costs Per Year:** State resident tuition: $4096 full-time. Nonresident tuition: $4635 full-time. College room and board: $4900. Room and board charges vary according to housing facility. **Scholarships:** Available **Calendar System:** Semester, Summer Session Available **Enrollment:** FT 839, PT 841 **Faculty:** FT 43, PT 80 **Student-Faculty Ratio:** 13:1 **Exams:** Other, SAT I or ACT. **% Residing in College-Owned, -Operated, or -Affiliated Housing:** 3 **Final Year or Final Semester Residency Requirement:** No **Library Holdings:** 20,500 **Regional Accreditation:** North Central Association of Colleges and Schools **Credit Hours For Degree:** 64 credit hours, Associates **Intercollegiate Athletics:** Baseball M; Basketball M & W

UNIVERSITY OF DUBUQUE
2000 University Ave.
Dubuque, IA 52001-5099
Tel: (563)589-3000
Admissions: (563)589-3214
Fax: (563)589-3690
E-mail: admissns@dbq.edu
Web Site: http://www.dbq.edu/
President/CEO: Rev. Jeffrey F. Bullock
Admissions: Jesse James
Financial Aid: Timothy Kremer
Type: Comprehensive **Sex:** Coed **Affiliation:** Presbyterian **Scores:** 90% SAT V 400+; 87% SAT M 400+; 56% ACT 18-23; 20% ACT 24-29 **% Accepted:** 75 **Application Deadline:** Rolling **Application Fee:** $25.00 **H.S. Requirements:** High school diploma required; GED accepted **Costs Per Year:** Application fee: $25. One-time mandatory fee: $100. Comprehensive fee: $28,960 includes full-time tuition ($21,000), mandatory fees ($590), and college room and board ($7370). College room only: $3640. Room and board charges vary according to board plan, housing facility, and location. Part-time tuition: $460 per credit hour. **Scholarships:** Available **Calendar System:** Semester, Summer Session Available **Enrollment:** FT 1,355, PT 85, Grad FT 149, Grad PT 129 **Faculty:** FT 83, PT 81 **Student-Faculty Ratio:** 14:1 **Exams:** SAT I or ACT. **% Receiving Financial Aid:** 89 **% Residing in College-Owned, -Operated, or -Affiliated Housing:** 70 **Library Holdings:** 184,728 **Regional Accreditation:** North Central Association of Colleges and Schools **Credit Hours For Degree:** 120 semester hours, Bachelors **ROTC:** Army **Professional Accreditation:** ACIPE, ATS **Intercol-**

legiate Athletics: Baseball M; Basketball M & W; Cross-Country Running M & W; Football M; Golf M & W; Soccer M & W; Softball W; Tennis M & W; Track and Field M & W; Volleyball W; Wrestling M

THE UNIVERSITY OF IOWA
Iowa City, IA 52242-1316
Tel: (319)335-3500; Free: 800-553-4692
Admissions: (319)335-3847
Fax: (319)335-1535
E-mail: admissions@uiowa.edu
Web Site: http://www.uiowa.edu/
President/CEO: Dr. Sally Mason
Admissions: Michael Barron
Financial Aid: Mark Warner
Type: University **Sex:** Coed **Scores:** 100% SAT M 400+; 29% ACT 18-23; 56% ACT 24-29 **% Accepted:** 83 **Admission Plans:** Early Admission; Deferred Admission **Application Deadline:** April 1 **Application Fee:** $40.00 **H.S. Requirements:** High school diploma required; GED accepted **Costs Per Year:** Application fee: $40. State resident tuition: $6128 full-time, $255 per semester hour part-time. Nonresident tuition: $22,424 full-time, $934 per semester hour part-time. Mandatory fees: $1289 full-time, $69 per semester hour part-time. Full-time tuition and fees vary according to course load and program. Part-time tuition and fees vary according to course load and program. College room and board: $8331. Room and board charges vary according to board plan and housing facility. **Scholarships:** Available **Calendar System:** Semester, Summer Session Available **Enrollment:** FT 18,476, PT 2,098, Grad FT 5,837, Grad PT 2,576 **Faculty:** FT 1,586, PT 93 **Student-Faculty Ratio:** 15:1 **Exams:** SAT I or ACT. **% Receiving Financial Aid:** 46 **% Residing in College-Owned, -Operated, or -Affiliated Housing:** 29 **Final Year or Final Semester Residency Requirement:** No **Library Holdings:** 4,134,268 **Regional Accreditation:** North Central Association of Colleges and Schools **Credit Hours For Degree:** 120 semester hours, Bachelors **ROTC:** Army, Air Force **Professional Accreditation:** AACSB, ABET, ACPhE, ACEJMC, AACN, AANA, ABA, ACA, ADA, ADtA, ACSP, ALA, APTA, APA, ASLHA, ACIPE, AALS, ACEHSA, CEPH, CORE CSWE, JRCEPAT, JRCNMT, LCMEAMA, NAACLS, NASM, NAST, NRPA **Intercollegiate Athletics:** Baseball M; Basketball M & W; Crew M & W; Cross-Country Running M & W; Field Hockey W; Football M; Golf M & W; Gymnastics M & W; Ice Hockey M; Lacrosse M & W; Rugby M & W; Sailing M & W; Soccer M & W; Softball W; Swimming and Diving M & W; Table Tennis M & W; Tennis M & W; Track and Field M & W; Ultimate Frisbee M & W; Volleyball M & W; Wrestling M

UNIVERSITY OF NORTHERN IOWA
1227 West 27th St.
Cedar Falls, IA 50614
Tel: (319)273-2311; Free: 800-772-2037
Admissions: (319)273-2281
Fax: (319)273-2885
E-mail: admissions@uni.edu
Web Site: http://www.uni.edu/
President/CEO: Benjamin J. Allen
Admissions: Christie Kangas
Financial Aid: Heather Soesbe
Type: Comprehensive **Sex:** Coed **Affiliation:** Board of Regents, State of Iowa **Scores:** 53.95% ACT 18-23; 36.63% ACT 24-29 **% Accepted:** 85 **Admission Plans:** Deferred Admission **Application Deadline:** August 15 **Application Fee:** $40.00 **H.S. Requirements:** High school diploma required; GED accepted **Costs Per Year:** Application fee: $40. State resident tuition: $6102 full-time, $254.25 per hour part-time. Nonresident tuition: $14,442 full-time, $395.55 per hour part-time. Mandatory fees: $906 full-time. Full-time tuition and fees vary according to course load and program. Part-time tuition varies according to course load and program. College room and board: $7189. College room only: $3435. Room and board charges vary according to board plan and housing facility. **Scholarships:** Available **Calendar System:** Semester, Summer Session Available **Enrollment:** FT 10,227, PT 1,154, Grad FT 696, Grad PT 1,226 **Faculty:** FT 632, PT 178 **Student-Faculty Ratio:** 17:1 **Exams:** ACT, SAT I or ACT, SAT I. ACT essay not being used. SAT essay not being used. **% Receiving Financial Aid:** 57 **% Residing in College-Owned, -Operated, or -Affiliated Housing:** 38 **Final Year or Final Semester Residency Requirement:** Yes **Library Holdings:** 1,251,947 **Regional Accreditation:** North Central Association of Colleges and Schools **Credit Hours For Degree:** 120 semester hours, Bachelors **ROTC:** Army **Professional Accreditation:** AACSB, AAFCS, ACA, ASLHA, CSWE, JRCEPAT, NASAD, NASM, NRPA, NAIT **Intercollegiate Athletics:** Basketball M & W; Cross-Country Running M & W; Football M; Golf M & W; Soccer W; Softball W; Swimming and Diving W; Tennis W; Track and Field M & W; Volleyball W; Wrestling M

UNIVERSITY OF PHOENIX—DES MOINES CAMPUS
6600 Westown Parkway
Des Moines, IA 50266
Tel: (515)267-8218; Free: (866)229-5743
Web Site: http://www.phoenix.edu/
President/CEO: William Pepicello, PhD
Type: Comprehensive **Sex:** Coed **Regional Accreditation:** North Central Association of Colleges and Schools

UPPER IOWA UNIVERSITY
605 Washington St., Box 1857
Fayette, IA 52142-1857
Tel: (563)425-5200; Free: 800-553-4150
Fax: (563)425-5277
E-mail: admission@uiu.edu
Web Site: http://www.uiu.edu/
President/CEO: Dr. Alan G. Walker, PhD
Admissions: Renee Lape
Financial Aid: Jobyna Johnston
Type: Comprehensive **Sex:** Coed **% Accepted:** 42 **Admission Plans:** Early Admission; Deferred Admission **Application Deadline:** Rolling **Application Fee:** $15.00 **H.S. Requirements:** High school diploma required; GED accepted **Costs Per Year:** Application fee: $15. Comprehensive fee: $29,220 includes full-time tuition ($22,350) and college room and board ($6870). College room only: $2850. Full-time tuition varies according to degree level, location, and program. Room and board charges vary according to board plan, housing facility, and location. Part-time tuition: $745 per credit hour. **Scholarships:** Available **Calendar System:** Miscellaneous, Summer Session Available **Enrollment:** FT 3,119, PT 3,039, Grad FT 438, Grad PT 9 **Faculty:** FT 60, PT 402 **Student-Faculty Ratio:** 24:1 **Exams:** SAT I or ACT. **% Residing in College-Owned, -Operated, or -Affiliated Housing:** 70 **Final Year or Final Semester Residency Requirement:** Yes **Library Holdings:** 73,237 **Regional Accreditation:** North Central Association of Colleges and Schools **Credit Hours For Degree:** 60 semester hours, Associates; 120 semester hours, Bachelors **Intercollegiate Athletics:** Baseball M; Basketball M & W; Football M; Golf M & W; Soccer M & W; Softball W; Tennis M & W; Volleyball W; Wrestling M

VATTEROTT COLLEGE
6100 Thornton Ave.
Ste. 290
Des Moines, IA 50321
Tel: (515)309-9000; Free: 800-353-7264
Fax: (515)309-0366
Web Site: http://www.vatterott-college.edu/
President/CEO: Daniel Nieland
Admissions: Henry Franken
Type: Two-Year College **Sex:** Coed **Calendar System:** Miscellaneous **Faculty:** FT 8, PT 6 **Student-Faculty Ratio:** 15:1 **Professional Accreditation:** ACCSCT

WALDORF COLLEGE
106 South 6th St.
Forest City, IA 50436-1713
Tel: (641)585-2450; Free: 800-292-1903
Fax: (641)585-8194
E-mail: admissions@waldorf.edu
Web Site: http://www.waldorf.edu/
President/CEO: Dr. Joseph Manjone
Financial Aid: Duane Polsdofer
Type: Four-Year College **Sex:** Coed **Affiliation:** Lutheran **Scores:** 64% ACT 18-23; 14% ACT 24-29 **% Accepted:** 59 **Admission Plans:** Early Admission **Application Deadline:** Rolling **Application Fee:** $0.00 **H.S. Requirements:** High school diploma required; GED accepted **Costs Per Year:** Application fee: $0. Comprehensive fee: $24,714 includes full-time tuition ($17,900), mandatory fees ($860), and college room and board ($5954). Full-time tuition and fees vary according to class time, course load, and program. Room and board charges vary according to board plan and housing facility. **Scholarships:** Available **Calendar System:** Semester, Summer Session

Available **Enrollment:** FT 493, PT 65 **Faculty:** FT 34, PT 6 **Student-Faculty Ratio:** 14:1 **Exams:** SAT I or ACT. ACT essay not being used. SAT essay not being used. **% Receiving Financial Aid:** 81 **% Residing in College-Owned, -Operated, or -Affiliated Housing:** 70 **Final Year or Final Semester Residency Requirement:** No **Library Holdings:** 55,325 **Regional Accreditation:** North Central Association of Colleges and Schools **Credit Hours For Degree:** 64 semester hours, Associates; 124 semester hours, Bachelors **Intercollegiate Athletics:** Baseball M; Basketball M & W; Cheerleading W; Football M; Golf M & W; Soccer M & W; Softball W; Volleyball W; Wrestling M

WARTBURG COLLEGE
100 Wartburg Blvd., PO Box 1003
Waverly, IA 50677-0903
Tel: (319)352-8200; Free: 800-772-2085
Admissions: (319)352-8264
Fax: (319)352-8279
E-mail: admissions@wartburg.edu
Web Site: http://www.wartburg.edu/
President/CEO: Dr. Darrel D. Colson
Admissions: Todd Coleman
Financial Aid: Jennifer Sassman
Type: Four-Year College **Sex:** Coed **Affiliation:** Lutheran **Scores:** 78% SAT V 400+; 89% SAT M 400+; 43% ACT 18-23; 41% ACT 24-29 **% Accepted:** 73 **Admission Plans:** Early Action; Deferred Admission **Application Deadline:** Rolling **Application Fee:** $0.00 **H.S. Requirements:** High school diploma required; GED accepted **Costs Per Year:** Application fee: $0. Comprehensive fee: $36,995 includes full-time tuition ($28,220), mandatory fees ($800), and college room and board ($7975). College room only: $3810. **Scholarships:** Available **Calendar System:** Miscellaneous, Summer Session Available **Enrollment:** FT 1,736, PT 64 **Faculty:** FT 109, PT 72 **Student-Faculty Ratio:** 12:1 **Exams:** SAT I or ACT. **% Receiving Financial Aid:** 77 **% Residing in College-Owned, -Operated, or -Affiliated Housing:** 81 **Library Holdings:** 194,178 **Regional Accreditation:** North Central Association of Colleges and Schools **Credit Hours For Degree:** 126 semester hours, Bachelors **Professional Accreditation:** CSWE, NASM, NCATE **Intercollegiate Athletics:** Baseball M; Basketball M & W; Cheerleading W; Cross-Country Running M & W; Football M; Golf M & W; Soccer M & W; Softball W; Tennis M & W; Track and Field M & W; Volleyball W; Wrestling M

WESTERN IOWA TECH COMMUNITY COLLEGE
4647 Stone Ave., PO Box 5199
Sioux City, IA 51102-5199
Tel: (712)274-6400
Fax: (712)274-6412
Web Site: http://www.witcc.edu/
President/CEO: Robert Dunker
Admissions: Lora Vanderzwaag
Type: Two-Year College **Sex:** Coed **Affiliation:** Iowa Department of Education Division of Community Colleges **Scores:** 46.4% ACT 18-23; 8.2% ACT 24-29 **% Accepted:** 100 **Admission Plans:** Open Admission; Early Admission; Deferred Admission **Application Deadline:** Rolling **Application Fee:** $20.00 **H.S. Requirements:** High school diploma required; GED accepted **Costs Per Year:** Application fee: $20. State resident tuition: $3168 full-time, $115 per credit hour part-time. Nonresident tuition: $3552 full-time, $133 per credit hour part-time. Mandatory fees: $372 full-time, $15.50 per credit hour part-time. College room and board: $4977. **Scholarships:** Available **Calendar System:** Semester, Summer Session Available **Enrollment:** FT 2,086, PT 3,248 **Faculty:** FT 88, PT 218 **Student-Faculty Ratio:** 20:1 **% Residing in College-Owned, -Operated, or -Affiliated Housing:** 2 **Library Holdings:** 25,696 **Regional Accreditation:** North Central Association of Colleges and Schools **Credit Hours For Degree:** 64 semester hours, Associates **Professional Accreditation:** ADA, APTA, NLN

WILLIAM PENN UNIVERSITY
201 Trueblood Ave.
Oskaloosa, IA 52577-1799
Tel: (641)673-1001; Free: 800-779-7366
Admissions: (641)673-1012
Fax: (641)673-1396
E-mail: admissions@wmpenn.edu
Web Site: http://www.wmpenn.edu/
President/CEO: Dr. Ann M. Fields
Admissions: John Ottosson
Financial Aid: Cyndi Peiffer
Type: Comprehensive **Sex:** Coed **Affiliation:** Society of Friends **Scores:** 58% ACT 18-23; 10% ACT 24-29 **Admission Plans:** Deferred Admission **Application Fee:** $20.00 **H.S. Requirements:** High school diploma required; GED accepted **Costs Per Year:** Application fee: $20. Comprehensive fee: $25,626 includes full-time tuition ($19,864), mandatory fees ($370), and college room and board ($5392). Full-time tuition and fees vary according to location. Part-time tuition: $450 per credit hour. Part-time tuition varies according to location. **Scholarships:** Available **Calendar System:** Semester, Summer Session Available **Enrollment:** FT 1,817, PT 44 **Faculty:** FT 35, PT 17 **Student-Faculty Ratio:** 15:1 **Exams:** SAT I or ACT. ACT essay not being used. SAT essay not being used. **% Receiving Financial Aid:** 94 **% Residing in College-Owned, -Operated, or -Affiliated Housing:** 40 **Library Holdings:** 72,907 **Regional Accreditation:** North Central Association of Colleges and Schools **Credit Hours For Degree:** 64 credit hours, Associates; 124 credit hours, Bachelors **Intercollegiate Athletics:** Baseball M; Basketball M & W; Bowling M & W; Cheerleading M & W; Cross-Country Running M & W; Football M; Golf M & W; Soccer M & W; Softball W; Track and Field M & W; Volleyball W; Wrestling M

ALLEN COMMUNITY COLLEGE
1801 North Cottonwood St.
Iola, KS 66749-1607
Tel: (620)365-5116
Fax: (620)365-7406
E-mail: weber@allencc.edu
Web Site: http://www.allencc.edu/
President/CEO: John Masterson
Admissions: Randall Weber
Financial Aid: Vicki Curry
Type: Two-Year College **Sex:** Coed **Affiliation:** Kansas State Board of Regents **Admission Plans:** Open Admission; Early Admission; Deferred Admission **Application Deadline:** August 24 **Application Fee:** $0.00 **H.S. Requirements:** High school diploma required; GED accepted **Costs Per Year:** Application fee: $0. State resident tuition: $1410 full-time, $47 per credit hour part-time. Nonresident tuition: $1410 full-time, $47 per credit hour part-time. Mandatory fees: $540 full-time, $18 per credit hour part-time. Full-time tuition and fees vary according to course load. Part-time tuition and fees vary according to course load. College room and board: $4300. College room only: $3600. Room and board charges vary according to housing facility. **Scholarships:** Available **Calendar System:** Semester, Summer Session Available **Enrollment:** FT 1,164, PT 1,612 **Faculty:** FT 35, PT 120 **Student-Faculty Ratio:** 17:1 **Library Holdings:** 49,416 **Regional Accreditation:** North Central Association of Colleges and Schools **Credit Hours For Degree:** 64 credit hours, Associates **Intercollegiate Athletics:** Baseball M; Basketball M & W; Cheerleading M & W; Cross-Country Running M & W; Golf M; Soccer M & W; Softball W; Track and Field M & W; Volleyball W

THE ART INSTITUTES INTERNATIONAL—KANSAS CITY
8208 Melrose Dr.
Lenexa, KS 66214
Free: (866)530-8508
Web Site: http://www.artinstitutes.edu/kansascity/
President/CEO: Susanne Behrens
Type: Four-Year College **Sex:** Coed **Affiliation:** Education Management Corporation

BAKER UNIVERSITY
PO Box 65
Baldwin City, KS 66006-0065
Tel: (785)594-6451; Free: 800-873-4282
Fax: (785)594-6721
E-mail: admissions@bakeru.edu
Web Site: http://www.bakeru.edu/
President/CEO: Dr. Patricia N. Long
Admissions: Daniel McKinney
Financial Aid: Jeanne Mott
Type: Comprehensive **Sex:** Coed **Affiliation:** United Methodist **Scores:** 51% ACT 18-23; 38% ACT 24-29 **% Accepted:** 56 **Admission Plans:** Deferred Admission **Application Deadline:** Rolling **Application Fee:** $0.00 **H.S. Requirements:** High school diploma required; GED accepted **Costs Per Year:** Application fee: $0. One-time mandatory fee: $80. Comprehensive fee: $27,850 includes full-time tuition ($21,050) and college room and board ($6800). College room only: $3100. Full-time tuition varies according to course load, degree level, location, and program. Room and board charges vary according to board plan and housing facility. Part-time tuition: $640 per credit hour. Part-time tuition varies according to course load, degree level, location, and program. **Scholarships:** Available **Calendar System:** Miscellaneous, Summer Session Available **Enrollment:** FT 899, PT 93 **Faculty:** FT 65, PT 36 **Student-Faculty Ratio:** 12:1 **Exams:** SAT I or ACT. ACT essay not being used. SAT essay not being used. **% Residing in College-Owned, -Operated, or -Affiliated Housing:** 84 **Library Holdings:** 103,243 **Regional Accreditation:** North Central Association of Colleges and Schools **Credit Hours For Degree:** 132 credit hours, Bachelors **ROTC:** Army, Air Force **Professional Accreditation:** AACN, ACBSP, NASM, NCATE, NLN **Intercollegiate Athletics:** Baseball M; Basketball M & W; Bowling W; Cheerleading M & W; Cross-Country Running M & W; Football M; Golf M & W; Soccer M & W; Softball W; Tennis M & W; Track and Field M & W; Volleyball W; Wrestling M

BARCLAY COLLEGE
607 North Kingman
Haviland, KS 67059-0288
Tel: (620)862-5252; Free: 800-862-0226
Fax: (620)862-5403
E-mail: jkendall@barclaycollege.edu
Web Site: http://www.barclaycollege.edu/
President/CEO: Dr. Herb Frazier
Admissions: Justin Kendall
Financial Aid: Christina Foster
Type: Four-Year College **Sex:** Coed **Affiliation:** Society of Friends **Scores:** 100% SAT V 400+; 68% ACT 18-23; 9% ACT 24-29 **% Accepted:** 73 **Admission Plans:** Early Admission; Deferred Admission **Application Deadline:** September 1 **Application Fee:** $15.00 **H.S. Requirements:** High school diploma required; GED accepted **Costs Per Year:** Application fee: $15. Comprehensive fee: $20,290 includes full-time tuition ($11,000), mandatory fees ($2690), and college room and board ($6600). Room and board charges vary according to board plan and housing facility. Part-time tuition: $250 per credit hour. Part-time tuition varies according to course load. **Scholarships:** Available **Calendar System:** Semester, Summer Session Not available **Enrollment:** FT 171, PT 23 **Faculty:** FT 7, PT 24 **Student-Faculty Ratio:** 12:1 **Exams:** SAT I or ACT. **% Receiving Financial Aid:** 97 **% Residing in College-Owned, -Operated, or -Affiliated Housing:** 38 **Library Holdings:** 63,759 **Credit Hours For Degree:** 65 credit hours, Associates; 128 credit hours, Bachelors **Professional Accreditation:** ABHE **Intercollegiate Athletics:** Basketball M & W; Cheerleading M & W; Soccer M; Tennis M & W; Volleyball W

BARTON COUNTY COMMUNITY COLLEGE
245 Northeast 30th Rd.
Great Bend, KS 67530-9283
Tel: (620)792-2701; Free: 800-722-6842
Admissions: (620)792-9241
Fax: (620)792-3238
E-mail: admissions@bartonccc.edu
Web Site: http://www.bartonccc.edu/
President/CEO: Dr. Carl R. Heilman
Admissions: Todd Moore
Type: Two-Year College **Sex:** Coed **Affiliation:** Kansas Board of Regents **Scores:** 55% ACT 18-23; 16% ACT 24-29 **Admission Plans:** Open Admis-

sion; Early Admission **Application Deadline:** Rolling **Application Fee:** $0.00 **H.S. Requirements:** High school diploma required; GED accepted **Costs Per Year:** Application fee: $0. State resident tuition: $1470 full-time, $49 per credit hour part-time. Nonresident tuition: $2100 full-time, $70 per credit hour part-time. Mandatory fees: $750 full-time, $25 per credit hour part-time. Full-time tuition and fees vary according to course load. Part-time tuition and fees vary according to course load. College room and board: $4342. Room and board charges vary according to board plan. **Scholarships:** Available **Calendar System:** Semester, Summer Session Available **Enrollment:** FT 1,028, PT 3,695 **Faculty:** FT 68, PT 128 **Student-Faculty Ratio:** 23:1 **% Residing in College-Owned, -Operated, or -Affiliated Housing:** 8 **Library Holdings:** 49,204 **Regional Accreditation:** North Central Association of Colleges and Schools **Credit Hours For Degree:** 64 credit hours, Associates **Professional Accreditation:** NAACLS, NLN **Intercollegiate Athletics:** Baseball M; Basketball M & W; Cheerleading M & W; Cross-Country Running M & W; Golf M & W; Soccer M & W; Softball W; Tennis M & W; Track and Field M & W; Volleyball W

BENEDICTINE COLLEGE
1020 North 2nd St.
Atchison, KS 66002-1499
Tel: (913)367-5340; Free: 800-467-5340
Fax: (913)367-3673
E-mail: phelgesen@benedictine.edu
Web Site: http://www.benedictine.edu/
President/CEO: Stephen Minnis, JD
Admissions: Pete Helgesen
Financial Aid: Tony Tanking
Type: Comprehensive **Sex:** Coed **Affiliation:** Roman Catholic **Scores:** 44% ACT 18-23; 31% ACT 24-29 **% Accepted:** 61 **Admission Plans:** Deferred Admission **Application Fee:** $25.00 **H.S. Requirements:** High school diploma required; GED accepted **Costs Per Year:** Application fee: $25. Comprehensive fee: $26,075 includes full-time tuition ($19,500) and college room and board ($6575). College room only: $3480. Full-time tuition varies according to course load and degree level. Room and board charges vary according to board plan and housing facility. Part-time tuition: $540 per credit hour. Part-time tuition varies according to course load and degree level. **Scholarships:** Available **Calendar System:** Semester, Summer Session Available **Enrollment:** FT 1,470, PT 344, Grad FT 32, Grad PT 28 **Faculty:** FT 74, PT 57 **Student-Faculty Ratio:** 15:1 **Exams:** SAT I or ACT. **% Receiving Financial Aid:** 73 **% Residing in College-Owned, -Operated, or -Affiliated Housing:** 77 **Library Holdings:** 207,316 **Regional Accreditation:** North Central Association of Colleges and Schools **Credit Hours For Degree:** 65 credit hours, Associates; 128 credit hours, Bachelors **ROTC:** Army **Professional Accreditation:** NASM, NCATE **Intercollegiate Athletics:** Baseball M; Basketball M & W; Cheerleading M & W; Cross-Country Running M & W; Football M; Golf M & W; Soccer M & W; Softball W; Track and Field M & W; Volleyball W

BETHANY COLLEGE
335 East Swensson St.
Lindsborg, KS 67456-1897
Tel: (785)227-3311; Free: 800-826-2281
Fax: (785)227-2860
E-mail: admissions@bethanylb.edu
Web Site: http://www.bethanylb.edu/
President/CEO: Edward F. Leonard, III
Admissions: Tricia Hawk
Financial Aid: Amber Maneth
Type: Four-Year College **Sex:** Coed **Affiliation:** Lutheran **Scores:** 67% SAT V 400+; 93% SAT M 400+; 52% ACT 18-23; 30% ACT 24-29 **% Accepted:** 65 **Admission Plans:** Deferred Admission **Application Deadline:** Rolling **Application Fee:** $20.00 **H.S. Requirements:** High school diploma required; GED accepted **Costs Per Year:** Application fee: $20. Comprehensive fee: $26,200 includes full-time tuition ($19,426), mandatory fees ($600), and college room and board ($6174). College room only: $3309. Room and board charges vary according to board plan and housing facility. Part-time tuition: $405 per credit hour. Part-time mandatory fees: $75 per term. Part-time tuition and fees vary according to course load. **Scholarships:** Available **Calendar System:** 4-1-4, Summer Session Available **Enrollment:** FT 555, PT 32 **Faculty:** FT 44, PT 43 **Student-Faculty Ratio:** 9:1 **Exams:** SAT I or ACT. **% Receiving Financial Aid:** 78 **% Residing in College-Owned, -Operated, or -Affiliated Housing:** 64 **Library Holdings:** 90,230 **Regional Accreditation:** North Central Association of Colleges and Schools **Credit Hours For Degree:** 128 semester hours, Bachelors **Professional Accreditation:** CSWE, NASM, NCATE **Intercollegiate Athletics:** Baseball M; Basketball M & W; Cross-Country Running M & W; Football M; Golf M; Soccer M & W; Softball W; Tennis M & W; Track and Field M & W; Volleyball W

BETHEL COLLEGE
300 East 27th St.
North Newton, KS 67117
Tel: (316)283-2500; Free: 800-522-1887
Admissions: (316)284-5230
Fax: (316)284-5286
E-mail: admissions@bethelks.edu
Web Site: http://www.bethelks.edu/
President/CEO: John K. Sheriff
Admissions: Todd H. Moore
Financial Aid: Tony Graber
Type: Four-Year College **Sex:** Coed **Affiliation:** Mennonite Church USA **Scores:** 100% SAT V 400+; 90% SAT M 400+; 30% ACT 18-23; 39% ACT 24-29 **% Accepted:** 75 **Admission Plans:** Deferred Admission **Application Deadline:** Rolling **Application Fee:** $20.00 **H.S. Requirements:** High school diploma required; GED accepted **Costs Per Year:** Application fee: $20. Comprehensive fee: $26,760 includes full-time tuition ($19,990) and college room and board ($6770). College room only: $3620. Full-time tuition varies according to course load. Room and board charges vary according to board plan and housing facility. Part-time tuition: $720 per credit hour. Part-time tuition varies according to course load. **Scholarships:** Available **Calendar System:** 4-1-4, Summer Session Not available **Enrollment:** FT 416, PT 21 **Faculty:** FT 40, PT 20 **Student-Faculty Ratio:** 9:1 **Exams:** SAT I or ACT. **% Receiving Financial Aid:** 76 **% Residing in College-Owned, -Operated, or -Affiliated Housing:** 72 **Library Holdings:** 1,147,965 **Regional Accreditation:** North Central Association of Colleges and Schools **Credit Hours For Degree:** 124 credit hours, Bachelors **Professional Accreditation:** AACN, CSWE **Intercollegiate Athletics:** Basketball M & W; Cross-Country Running M & W; Football M; Golf M & W; Soccer M & W; Tennis M & W; Track and Field M & W; Volleyball W

BROWN MACKIE COLLEGE—KANSAS CITY
9705 Lenexa Dr.
Lenexa, KS 66215
Tel: (913)768-1900; Free: 800-635-9101
Fax: (913)823-7448
Web Site: http://www.brownmackie.edu/kansascity/
President/CEO: Susan Naples
Type: Two-Year College **Sex:** Coed **Affiliation:** Education Management Corporation **Calendar System:** Quarter **Regional Accreditation:** North Central Association of Colleges and Schools

BROWN MACKIE COLLEGE—SALINA
2106 South 9th St.
Salina, KS 67401-2810
Tel: (785)825-5422; Free: 800-365-0433
Fax: (785)827-7623
Web Site: http://www.brownmackie.edu/salina/
President/CEO: Danny Finuf
Type: Two-Year College **Sex:** Coed **Affiliation:** Education Management Corporation **Calendar System:** Miscellaneous **Regional Accreditation:** North Central Association of Colleges and Schools

BUTLER COMMUNITY COLLEGE
901 South Haverhill Rd.
El Dorado, KS 67042-3280
Tel: (316)321-2222
Fax: (316)322-3109
E-mail: admissions@butlercc.edu
Web Site: http://www.butlercc.edu/
President/CEO: Dr. Jacqueline Vietti
Admissions: Glenn Lygrisse
Type: Two-Year College **Sex:** Coed **Affiliation:** Kansas State Board of Education **Scores:** 52% ACT 18-23; 22% ACT 24-29 **Admission Plans:** Open Admission; Early Admission; Deferred Admission **Application Deadline:** August 19 **Application Fee:** $0.00 **H.S. Requirements:** High school diploma required; GED accepted **Scholarships:** Available **Calendar System:** Semester, Summer Session Available **Enrollment:** FT 3,543, PT 4,553 **Faculty:** FT 151, PT 431 **Student-Faculty Ratio:** 17:1 **% Residing in**

College-Owned, -Operated, or -Affiliated Housing: 4 **Library Holdings:** 38,000 **Regional Accreditation:** North Central Association of Colleges and Schools **Credit Hours For Degree:** 62 credit hours, Associates **Professional Accreditation:** NLN **Intercollegiate Athletics:** Baseball M; Basketball M & W; Cross-Country Running M & W; Football M; Soccer W; Softball W; Tennis M & W; Track and Field M & W; Volleyball W

CENTRAL CHRISTIAN COLLEGE OF KANSAS
1200 South Main
PO Box 1403
McPherson, KS 67460-5799
Tel: (620)241-0723; Free: 800-835-0078
Fax: (620)241-6032
E-mail: rick.wyatt@centralchristian.edu
Web Site: http://www.centralchristian.edu/
President/CEO: Hal Hoxie
Admissions: Rick Wyatt
Financial Aid: Mike Reimer
Type: Four-Year College **Sex:** Coed **Affiliation:** Free Methodist **Scores:** 53% ACT 18-23; 24% ACT 24-29 **% Accepted:** 99 **Admission Plans:** Deferred Admission **Application Deadline:** Rolling **Application Fee:** $20.00 **H.S. Requirements:** High school diploma required; GED accepted **Costs Per Year:** Application fee: $20. Comprehensive fee: $23,900 includes full-time tuition ($17,800), mandatory fees ($200), and college room and board ($5900). College room only: $2700. Full-time tuition and fees vary according to course load and program. Room and board charges vary according to board plan and gender. Part-time tuition: $500 per credit hour. Part-time tuition varies according to course load and program. **Scholarships:** Available **Calendar System:** 4-1-4, Summer Session Not available **Enrollment:** FT 328, PT 138 **Faculty:** FT 19, PT 27 **Student-Faculty Ratio:** 14:1 **Exams:** SAT I or ACT. **% Receiving Financial Aid:** 80 **% Residing in College-Owned, -Operated, or -Affiliated Housing:** 85 **Library Holdings:** 35,027 **Regional Accreditation:** North Central Association of Colleges and Schools **Credit Hours For Degree:** 64 credit hours, Associates; 128 credit hours, Bachelors **Intercollegiate Athletics:** Baseball M; Basketball M & W; Cheerleading M & W; Golf M & W; Soccer M & W; Softball W; Tennis M & W; Volleyball W

CLEVELAND CHIROPRACTIC COLLEGE—KANSAS CITY CAMPUS
10850 Lowell Ave.
Overland Park, KS 66210
Tel: (913)234-0600; Free: 800-467-2252
Admissions: (913)234-0750
Fax: (913)234-0912
E-mail: kc.admissions@cleveland.edu
Web Site: http://www.cleveland.edu/
President/CEO: Dr. Carl S. Cleveland, III
Admissions: Melissa Denton
Type: Comprehensive **Sex:** Coed **Affiliation:** Cleveland Chiropractic College-Los Angeles Campus **Scores:** 50% ACT 18-23; 50% ACT 24-29 **Admission Plans:** Open Admission; Deferred Admission **Application Deadline:** August 28 **Application Fee:** $50.00 **H.S. Requirements:** High school diploma required; GED accepted **Calendar System:** Trimester, Summer Session Available **Enrollment:** FT 66, PT 21 **Faculty:** FT 43, PT 10 **Student-Faculty Ratio:** 11:1 **Exams:** SAT I or ACT. **Library Holdings:** 15,000 **Regional Accreditation:** North Central Association of Colleges and Schools **Credit Hours For Degree:** 123 credits, Bachelors **Professional Accreditation:** CCE

CLOUD COUNTY COMMUNITY COLLEGE
2221 Campus Dr., PO Box 1002
Concordia, KS 66901-1002
Tel: (785)243-1435; Free: 800-729-5101
Fax: (785)243-1043
Web Site: http://www.cloud.edu/
President/CEO: Dr. Richard Underbakke
Admissions: Kim Reynolds
Type: Two-Year College **Sex:** Coed **Affiliation:** Kansas Community College System **Admission Plans:** Open Admission; Early Admission; Deferred Admission **Application Deadline:** September 11 **Application Fee:** $0.00 **H.S. Requirements:** High school diploma required; GED accepted **Scholarships:** Available **Calendar System:** Semester, Summer Session Available **Library Holdings:** 18,010 **Regional Accreditation:** North Central Association of Colleges and Schools **Credit Hours For Degree:** 64 credit hours, Associates **Professional Accreditation:** NLN **Intercollegiate Athletics:** Baseball M; Basketball M & W; Cross-Country Running M & W; Soccer M & W; Softball W; Tennis M & W; Track and Field M & W; Volleyball W

COFFEYVILLE COMMUNITY COLLEGE
400 West 11th St.
Coffeyville, KS 67337-5063
Tel: (620)251-7700
Fax: (620)252-7098
E-mail: kellib@coffeyville.edu
Web Site: http://www.coffeyville.edu/
President/CEO: Don A. Woodburn
Admissions: Kelli Baur
Type: Two-Year College **Sex:** Coed **Affiliation:** Kansas State Board of Education **Scores:** 41% ACT 18-23; 12% ACT 24-29 **% Accepted:** 100 **Admission Plans:** Open Admission; Early Admission; Deferred Admission **Application Deadline:** Rolling **Application Fee:** $0.00 **H.S. Requirements:** High school diploma or equivalent not required **Scholarships:** Available **Calendar System:** Semester, Summer Session Available **Enrollment:** FT 1,095, PT 951 **Faculty:** FT 51, PT 34 **Student-Faculty Ratio:** 20:1 **% Residing in College-Owned, -Operated, or -Affiliated Housing:** 28 **Library Holdings:** 27,928 **Regional Accreditation:** North Central Association of Colleges and Schools **Credit Hours For Degree:** 64 credit hours, Associates **Intercollegiate Athletics:** Baseball M; Basketball M & W; Cross-Country Running M & W; Football M; Golf M; Softball W; Track and Field M & W; Volleyball W

COLBY COMMUNITY COLLEGE
1255 South Range
Colby, KS 67701-4099
Tel: (785)462-3984
Fax: (785)462-4600
E-mail: admissions@colbycc.edu
Web Site: http://www.colbycc.edu/
President/CEO: Dr. Lynn Kreider
Admissions: Nikol Nolan
Type: Two-Year College **Sex:** Coed **Affiliation:** Kansas State Board of Education **Scores:** 55% ACT 18-23; 10% ACT 24-29 **% Accepted:** 100 **Admission Plans:** Open Admission; Early Admission; Deferred Admission **Application Deadline:** Rolling **Application Fee:** $0.00 **H.S. Requirements:** High school diploma required; GED accepted **Costs Per Year:** Application fee: $0. State resident tuition: $1664 full-time, $52 per credit hour part-time. Nonresident tuition: $3104 full-time, $97 per credit hour part-time. Mandatory fees: $1152 full-time, $36 per credit hour part-time. Full-time tuition and fees vary according to course load and program. Part-time tuition and fees vary according to course load and program. College room and board: $4690. Room and board charges vary according to housing facility. **Scholarships:** Available **Calendar System:** Semester, Summer Session Available **Enrollment:** FT 759, PT 806 **Faculty:** FT 58, PT 95 **Student-Faculty Ratio:** 11:1 **Exams:** SAT I or ACT. ACT essay not being used. SAT essay not being used. **% Residing in College-Owned, -Operated, or -Affiliated Housing:** 30 **Library Holdings:** 34,000 **Regional Accreditation:** North Central Association of Colleges and Schools **Credit Hours For Degree:** 62 semester hours, Associates **Professional Accreditation:** APTA, NLN **Intercollegiate Athletics:** Baseball M; Basketball M & W; Cheerleading M & W; Cross-Country Running M & W; Equestrian Sports M & W; Golf M & W; Softball W; Track and Field M & W; Volleyball W; Wrestling M

COWLEY COUNTY COMMUNITY COLLEGE AND AREA VOCATIONAL—TECHNICAL SCHOOL
125 South Second, PO Box 1147
Arkansas City, KS 67005-1147
Tel: (620)442-0430; Free: 800-593-CCCC
Admissions: (620)441-5368
Fax: (620)441-5350
E-mail: admissions@cowley.edu
Web Site: http://www.cowley.edu/
President/CEO: Dr. Patrick J. McAtee
Admissions: Ben Schears
Type: Two-Year College **Sex:** Coed **Affiliation:** Kansas State Board of Education **Scores:** 54% ACT 18-23; 20% ACT 24-29 **% Accepted:** 100 **Admission Plans:** Open Admission; Early Admission **Application Deadline:** Rolling **Application Fee:** $0.00 **H.S. Requirements:** High school diploma required; GED accepted **Costs Per Year:** Application fee: $0. Area

resident tuition: $1440 full-time, $45 per credit hour part-time. State resident tuition: $1760 full-time, $55 per credit hour part-time. Nonresident tuition: $3328 full-time, $104 per credit hour part-time. Mandatory fees: $690 full-time, $23 per credit hour part-time. College room and board: $4375. Room and board charges vary according to board plan. **Scholarships:** Available **Calendar System:** Semester, Summer Session Available **Enrollment:** FT 2,019, PT 1,995 **Faculty:** FT 48, PT 151 **Student-Faculty Ratio:** 27:1 **Exams:** ACT. **% Residing in College-Owned, -Operated, or -Affiliated Housing:** 10 **Final Year or Final Semester Residency Requirement:** No **Library Holdings:** 30,000 **Regional Accreditation:** North Central Association of Colleges and Schools **Credit Hours For Degree:** 62 credit hours, Associates **Intercollegiate Athletics:** Baseball M; Basketball M & W; Cross-Country Running M & W; Soccer M & W; Softball W; Tennis M & W; Track and Field M & W; Volleyball W

DODGE CITY COMMUNITY COLLEGE
2501 North 14th Ave.
Dodge City, KS 67801-2399
Tel: (620)225-1321
Fax: (620)225-0918
E-mail: admin@dc3.edu
Web Site: http://www.dc3.edu/
President/CEO: Richard K. Burke, PhD
Admissions: Tammy Tabor
Type: Two-Year College **Sex:** Coed **Affiliation:** Kansas State Board of Education **Admission Plans:** Open Admission; Early Admission; Deferred Admission **Application Deadline:** Rolling **Application Fee:** $0.00 **H.S. Requirements:** High school diploma or equivalent not required **Costs Per Year:** Application fee: $0. State resident tuition: $35 per credit hour part-time. Nonresident tuition: $45 per credit hour part-time. Part-time tuition varies according to course load. College room and board: $4502. Room and board charges vary according to board plan. **Scholarships:** Available **Calendar System:** Semester, Summer Session Available **Enrollment:** FT 1,766 **Faculty:** FT 55, PT 108 **Student-Faculty Ratio:** 18:1 **% Residing in College-Owned, -Operated, or -Affiliated Housing:** 20 **Library Holdings:** 30,000 **Regional Accreditation:** North Central Association of Colleges and Schools **Credit Hours For Degree:** 62 credit hours, Associates **Professional Accreditation:** NLN **Intercollegiate Athletics:** Baseball M; Basketball M & W; Cross-Country Running M & W; Equestrian Sports M & W; Football M; Golf M; Softball W; Volleyball W

DONNELLY COLLEGE
608 North 18th St.
Kansas City, KS 66102-4298
Tel: (913)621-8700
Admissions: (913)621-8713
Fax: (913)621-0354
E-mail: admissions@donnelly.edu
Web Site: http://www.donnelly.edu/
President/CEO: Dr. Steven M. LaNasa
Admissions: Edward Marquez
Type: Two-Year College **Sex:** Coed **Affiliation:** Roman Catholic **Admission Plans:** Open Admission; Early Admission; Deferred Admission **Application Deadline:** Rolling **Application Fee:** $0.00 **H.S. Requirements:** High school diploma required; GED accepted **Scholarships:** Available **Calendar System:** Semester, Summer Session Available **Enrollment:** FT 291, PT 370 **Faculty:** FT 15, PT 33 **Student-Faculty Ratio:** 16:1 **% Residing in College-Owned, -Operated, or -Affiliated Housing:** 2 **Final Year or Final Semester Residency Requirement:** Yes **Library Holdings:** 33,752 **Regional Accreditation:** North Central Association of Colleges and Schools **Credit Hours For Degree:** 64 credits, Associates; 124 credits, Bachelors

EMPORIA STATE UNIVERSITY
1200 Commercial St.
Emporia, KS 66801-5087
Tel: (620)341-1200; Free: 877-468-6378
Admissions: (620)341-5465
E-mail: go2esu@emporia.edu
Web Site: http://www.emporia.edu/
President/CEO: Michael Lane
Admissions: Laura Eddy
Financial Aid: Elaine Henrie
Type: Comprehensive **Sex:** Coed **Affiliation:** Kansas State Board of Regents **Scores:** 49% ACT 18-23; 33% ACT 24-29 **% Accepted:** 88 **Admission Plans:** Early Admission; Deferred Admission **Application Deadline:** Rolling **Application Fee:** $30.00 **H.S. Requirements:** High school diploma required; GED accepted **Costs Per Year:** Application fee: $30. State resident tuition: $3426 full-time, $114 per credit hour part-time. Nonresident tuition: $12,630 full-time, $421 per credit hour part-time. Mandatory fees: $948 full-time, $58 per credit hour part-time. Full-time tuition and fees vary according to course load, degree level, and location. Part-time tuition and fees vary according to course load, degree level, and location. College room and board: $6146. College room only: $3146. Room and board charges vary according to board plan and housing facility. **Scholarships:** Available **Calendar System:** Semester, Summer Session Available **Enrollment:** FT 3,734, PT 474, Grad FT 334, Grad PT 1,772 **Faculty:** FT 253, PT 25 **Student-Faculty Ratio:** 18:1 **Exams:** SAT I or ACT. ACT essay not being used. SAT essay not being used. **% Receiving Financial Aid:** 60 **% Residing in College-Owned, -Operated, or -Affiliated Housing:** 23 **Final Year or Final Semester Residency Requirement:** No **Library Holdings:** 2,457,985 **Regional Accreditation:** North Central Association of Colleges and Schools **Credit Hours For Degree:** 124 credit hours, Bachelors **Professional Accreditation:** AACSB, ACA, ALA, CORE, JRCEPAT, NASAD, NASM, NCATE, NLN **Intercollegiate Athletics:** Baseball M; Basketball M & W; Cheerleading M & W; Cross-Country Running M & W; Football M; Soccer W; Softball W; Tennis M & W; Track and Field M & W; Volleyball W

FLINT HILLS TECHNICAL COLLEGE
3301 West 18th Ave.
Emporia, KS 66801
Tel: (620)343-4600; Free: 800-711-6947
Web Site: http://www.fhtc.net/
President/CEO: Dr. Dean Hollenbeck
Type: Two-Year College **Sex:** Coed **Application Fee:** $0.00 **H.S. Requirements:** High school diploma required; GED accepted **Calendar System:** Semester **Enrollment:** FT 259, PT 222 **Faculty:** FT 27, PT 45 **Student-Faculty Ratio:** 15:1 **Exams:** SAT I or ACT. **Regional Accreditation:** North Central Association of Colleges and Schools **Professional Accreditation:** ADA, COE

FORT HAYS STATE UNIVERSITY
600 Park St.
Hays, KS 67601-4099
Tel: (785)628-4000; Free: 800-628-FHSU
Admissions: (785)628-4091
Fax: (785)628-4014
E-mail: tcline@fhsu.edu
Web Site: http://www.fhsu.edu/
President/CEO: Dr. Edward Hammond
Admissions: Tricia Cline
Financial Aid: Craig Karlin
Type: Comprehensive **Sex:** Coed **Affiliation:** Kansas State Board of Education **Admission Plans:** Open Admission; Deferred Admission **Application Deadline:** Rolling **Application Fee:** $35.00 **H.S. Requirements:** High school diploma required; GED accepted **Costs Per Year:** Application fee: $35. State resident tuition: $3762 full-time, $125.40 per credit hour part-time. Nonresident tuition: $11,915 full-time, $397.15 per credit hour part-time. Full-time tuition varies according to course load. Part-time tuition varies according to course load. College room and board: $6370. College room only: $3335. Room and board charges vary according to board plan and housing facility. **Scholarships:** Available **Calendar System:** Semester, Summer Session Available **Student-Faculty Ratio:** 17:1 **Exams:** SAT I or ACT. **% Receiving Financial Aid:** 65 **Regional Accreditation:** North Central Association of Colleges and Schools **Credit Hours For Degree:** 60 credit hours, Associates **Professional Accreditation:** AACN, ASLHA, CSWE, JRCERT, NASM, NCATE **Intercollegiate Athletics:** Baseball M; Basketball M & W; Cross-Country Running M & W; Football M; Golf M; Softball W; Tennis W; Track and Field M & W; Volleyball W; Wrestling M

FORT SCOTT COMMUNITY COLLEGE
2108 South Horton
Fort Scott, KS 66701
Tel: (316)223-2700; Free: 800-874-3722
Admissions: (620)223-2700
Fax: (316)223-4927
Web Site: http://www.fortscott.edu/
President/CEO: Dr. Clayton Tatro
Admissions: Mert Barrows

Type: Two-Year College **Sex:** Coed **Admission Plans:** Open Admission; Early Admission; Deferred Admission **Application Deadline:** August 15 **Application Fee:** $0.00 **H.S. Requirements:** High school diploma required; GED accepted **Costs Per Year:** Application fee: $0. State resident tuition: $1776 full-time, $74 per credit hour part-time. Nonresident tuition: $3120 full-time, $130 per credit hour part-time. Full-time tuition varies according to course load. Part-time tuition varies according to course load. College room and board: $4600. Room and board charges vary according to housing facility. **Scholarships:** Available **Calendar System:** Semester, Summer Session Available **Library Holdings:** 25,308 **Regional Accreditation:** North Central Association of Colleges and Schools **Credit Hours For Degree:** 60 semester hours, Associates **ROTC:** Army **Professional Accreditation:** NLN **Intercollegiate Athletics:** Baseball M; Basketball M & W; Football M; Softball W; Track and Field M & W; Volleyball W

FRIENDS UNIVERSITY
2100 West University St.
Wichita, KS 67213
Tel: (316)295-5000; Free: 800-577-2233
Admissions: (316)794-6945
Fax: (316)262-5027
E-mail: haneberg@friends.edu
Web Site: http://www.friends.edu/
President/CEO: Dr. Biff Green
Admissions: Erin Haneberg
Financial Aid: Brandon Pierce
Type: Comprehensive **Sex:** Coed **Scores:** 41.2% ACT 18-23; 23.7% ACT 24-29 **% Accepted:** 66 **Admission Plans:** Early Admission **Application Deadline:** Rolling **Application Fee:** $35.00 **H.S. Requirements:** High school diploma required; GED accepted **Costs Per Year:** Application fee: $35. Comprehensive fee: $25,830 includes full-time tuition ($19,890), mandatory fees ($150), and college room and board ($5790). College room only: $2650. Full-time tuition and fees vary according to course load, location, and program. Room and board charges vary according to board plan and housing facility. Part-time tuition: $663 per credit hour. Part-time mandatory fees: $5 per credit hour, $75 per term. Part-time tuition and fees vary according to course load, location, and program. **Scholarships:** Available **Calendar System:** Semester, Summer Session Available **Enrollment:** FT 1,683, PT 405, Grad FT 139, Grad PT 626 **Faculty:** FT 74, PT 268 **Student-Faculty Ratio:** 13:1 **Exams:** SAT I or ACT. **% Receiving Financial Aid:** 82 **% Residing in College-Owned, -Operated, or -Affiliated Housing:** 33 **Final Year or Final Semester Residency Requirement:** No **Library Holdings:** 110,945 **Regional Accreditation:** North Central Association of Colleges and Schools **Credit Hours For Degree:** 62 semester hours, Associates; 124 semester hours, Bachelors **Professional Accreditation:** AAMFT, NASM, NCATE **Intercollegiate Athletics:** Baseball M; Basketball M & W; Cheerleading M & W; Cross-Country Running M & W; Football M; Golf M; Soccer M & W; Softball W; Tennis M & W; Track and Field M & W; Volleyball W

GARDEN CITY COMMUNITY COLLEGE
801 Campus Dr.
Garden City, KS 67846-6399
Tel: (316)276-7611
Admissions: (620)276-7611
E-mail: admissions@gcccks.edu
Web Site: http://www.gcccks.edu/
President/CEO: Carol Ballantyne
Type: Two-Year College **Sex:** Coed **Affiliation:** Kansas Board of Regents **Admission Plans:** Open Admission **Application Deadline:** Rolling **Application Fee:** $0.00 **H.S. Requirements:** High school diploma required; GED accepted **Scholarships:** Available **Calendar System:** Semester, Summer Session Available **Exams:** ACT, Other. **Library Holdings:** 44,985 **Regional Accreditation:** North Central Association of Colleges and Schools **Credit Hours For Degree:** 64 credit hours, Associates **Professional Accreditation:** NLN **Intercollegiate Athletics:** Baseball M; Basketball M & W; Cheerleading M & W; Cross-Country Running M & W; Football M; Soccer M & W; Softball W; Track and Field M & W; Volleyball W

HASKELL INDIAN NATIONS UNIVERSITY
155 Indian Ave., No. 5031
Lawrence, KS 66046-4800
Tel: (785)749-8404
Fax: (785)749-8429
Web Site: http://www.haskell.edu/
President/CEO: Linda Sue Warner
Admissions: Patty Grant
Financial Aid: Reta Beaver Brewer
Type: Four-Year College **Sex:** Coed **Admission Plans:** Preferred Admission **Application Deadline:** July 30 **Application Fee:** $10.00 **H.S. Requirements:** High school diploma required; GED accepted **Scholarships:** Available **Calendar System:** Semester, Summer Session Available **Exams:** ACT. **Library Holdings:** 50,000 **Regional Accreditation:** North Central Association of Colleges and Schools **Credit Hours For Degree:** 61 credit hours, Associates; 128 credit hours, Bachelors **ROTC:** Air Force **Intercollegiate Athletics:** Basketball M & W; Cheerleading M & W; Cross-Country Running M & W; Football M; Golf M; Softball W; Track and Field M & W; Volleyball W

HESSTON COLLEGE
Box 3000
Hesston, KS 67062-2093
Tel: (620)327-4221; Free: 800-995-2757
Admissions: (620)327-8222
Fax: (620)327-8300
E-mail: admissions@hesston.edu
Web Site: http://www.hesston.edu/
President/CEO: Howard Keim
Admissions: Joel Kauffman
Type: Two-Year College **Sex:** Coed **Affiliation:** Mennonite **Scores:** 88% SAT V 400+; 88% SAT M 400+; 50% ACT 18-23; 27% ACT 24-29 **% Accepted:** 100 **Admission Plans:** Open Admission; Early Admission; Deferred Admission **Application Deadline:** Rolling **Application Fee:** $15.00 **H.S. Requirements:** High school diploma required; GED accepted **Costs Per Year:** Application fee: $15. Comprehensive fee: $26,496 includes full-time tuition ($19,610), mandatory fees ($296), and college room and board ($6590). Full-time tuition and fees vary according to program. Part-time tuition: $817 per hour. Part-time mandatory fees: $74 per term. Part-time tuition and fees vary according to course load and program. **Scholarships:** Available **Calendar System:** Semester, Summer Session Available **Enrollment:** FT 383, PT 51 **Faculty:** FT 24, PT 19 **Student-Faculty Ratio:** 13:1 **Exams:** SAT I or ACT. **% Residing in College-Owned, -Operated, or -Affiliated Housing:** 71 **Library Holdings:** 35,000 **Regional Accreditation:** North Central Association of Colleges and Schools **Credit Hours For Degree:** 60 credit hours, Associates **Professional Accreditation:** NLN **Intercollegiate Athletics:** Baseball M; Basketball M & W; Soccer M & W; Softball W; Tennis M & W; Volleyball W

HIGHLAND COMMUNITY COLLEGE
606 West Main St.
Highland, KS 66035
Tel: (785)442-6000
Fax: (785)442-6100
Web Site: http://www.highlandcc.edu/
President/CEO: David E. Reist
Admissions: Cheryl Rasmussen
Type: Two-Year College **Sex:** Coed **Affiliation:** Kansas Community College System **Admission Plans:** Open Admission; Preferred Admission; Early Admission **Application Deadline:** August 20 **Application Fee:** $0.00 **H.S. Requirements:** High school diploma required; GED accepted **Scholarships:** Available **Calendar System:** Semester, Summer Session Available **Library Holdings:** 30,000 **Regional Accreditation:** North Central Association of Colleges and Schools **Credit Hours For Degree:** 62 credit hours, Associates **ROTC:** Army **Intercollegiate Athletics:** Baseball M; Basketball M & W; Cross-Country Running M & W; Football M; Softball W; Track and Field M & W; Volleyball W

HUTCHINSON COMMUNITY COLLEGE AND AREA VOCATIONAL SCHOOL
1300 North Plum St.
Hutchinson, KS 67501-5894
Tel: (620)665-3500; Free: 800-289-3501
Admissions: (620)665-3536
Fax: (620)665-3310
E-mail: strobelc@hutchcc.edu
Web Site: http://www.hutchcc.edu/
President/CEO: Dr. Edward E. Berger
Admissions: Corbin Strobel
Type: Two-Year College **Sex:** Coed **Affiliation:** Kansas Board of Regents

Admission Plans: Open Admission; Early Admission; Deferred Admission **Application Deadline:** Rolling **Application Fee:** $0.00 **H.S. Requirements:** High school diploma required; GED accepted. For continuing education program: High school diploma required; GED not accepted **Costs Per Year:** Application fee: $0. State resident tuition: $1920 full-time, $60 per credit hour part-time. Nonresident tuition: $3008 full-time, $94 per credit hour part-time. Mandatory fees: $512 full-time, $16 per credit hour part-time. College room and board: $4816. Room and board charges vary according to board plan. **Scholarships:** Available **Calendar System:** Semester, Summer Session Available **Enrollment:** FT 2,415, PT 3,038 **Faculty:** FT 116, PT 231 **Student-Faculty Ratio:** 18:1 **% Residing in College-Owned, -Operated, or -Affiliated Housing:** 7 **Final Year or Final Semester Residency Requirement:** No **Library Holdings:** 42,500 **Regional Accreditation:** North Central Association of Colleges and Schools **Credit Hours For Degree:** 64 credit hours, Associates **ROTC:** Army **Professional Accreditation:** AHIMA, JRCERT, NLN **Intercollegiate Athletics:** Baseball M; Basketball M & W; Cheerleading M & W; Cross-Country Running M & W; Football M; Golf M; Soccer W; Softball W; Track and Field M & W; Volleyball W

INDEPENDENCE COMMUNITY COLLEGE
Brookside Dr. and College Ave.
PO Box 708
Independence, KS 67301-0708
Tel: (620)331-4100; Free: 800-842-6063
Fax: (620)331-5344
E-mail: sciufulescu@indycc.edu
Web Site: http://www.indycc.edu/
President/CEO: Daniel Bain
Admissions: Sally A. Ciufulescu
Type: Two-Year College **Sex:** Coed **Affiliation:** Kansas State Board of Education **Admission Plans:** Open Admission; Early Admission **Application Deadline:** Rolling **Application Fee:** $0.00 **H.S. Requirements:** High school diploma required; GED accepted **Costs Per Year:** Application fee: $0. Area resident tuition: $720 full-time, $30 per credit hour part-time. State resident tuition: $780 full-time, $32.50 per credit hour part-time. Nonresident tuition: $1740 full-time, $72.50 per credit hour part-time. Mandatory fees: $780 full-time, $32.50 per credit hour part-time. College room and board: $4600. **Scholarships:** Available **Calendar System:** Semester, Summer Session Available **Enrollment:** FT 478, PT 428 **Faculty:** FT 29, PT 65 **Student-Faculty Ratio:** 17:1 **% Residing in College-Owned, -Operated, or -Affiliated Housing:** 10 **Library Holdings:** 32,408 **Regional Accreditation:** North Central Association of Colleges and Schools **Credit Hours For Degree:** 64 semester hours, Associates **Intercollegiate Athletics:** Baseball M; Basketball M & W; Cheerleading M & W; Football M; Softball W; Tennis M & W; Track and Field M & W; Volleyball W

ITT TECHNICAL INSTITUTE
One Brittany Place, Ste. 100
2024 North Woodlawn
Wichita, KS 67208
Tel: (316)681-8400; Free: 877-207-1047
Web Site: http://www.itt-tech.edu/
President/CEO: Michael Hauser
Type: Four-Year College **Sex:** Coed **Affiliation:** ITT Educational Services, Inc. **Calendar System:** Quarter **Professional Accreditation:** ACICS

JOHNSON COUNTY COMMUNITY COLLEGE
12345 College Blvd.
Overland Park, KS 66210-1299
Tel: (913)469-8500
Web Site: http://www.johnco.cc.ks.us/
President/CEO: Terry Calaway
Admissions: Dr. Charles J. Carlsen
Type: Two-Year College **Sex:** Coed **Affiliation:** Kansas State Board of Education **Admission Plans:** Open Admission; Early Admission **Application Deadline:** Rolling **H.S. Requirements:** High school diploma required; GED accepted **Scholarships:** Available **Calendar System:** Semester, Summer Session Available **Library Holdings:** 89,400 **Regional Accreditation:** North Central Association of Colleges and Schools **Credit Hours For Degree:** 64 credit hours, Associates **Professional Accreditation:** ACF, ADA, ACBSP, CARC, JRCEMT, NLN **Intercollegiate Athletics:** Baseball M; Basketball M & W; Cross-Country Running M & W; Golf M; Soccer M & W; Softball W; Tennis M & W; Track and Field M & W; Volleyball W

KANSAS CITY KANSAS COMMUNITY COLLEGE
7250 State Ave.
Kansas City, KS 66112-3003
Tel: (913)334-1100
Admissions: (913)288-7694
Fax: (913)696-9646
E-mail: dmcdowell@kckcc.edu
Web Site: http://www.kckcc.edu/
President/CEO: Dr. Thomas R. Burke
Admissions: Dr. Denise McDowell
Type: Two-Year College **Sex:** Coed **Admission Plans:** Open Admission **Application Deadline:** Rolling **Application Fee:** $0.00 **H.S. Requirements:** High school diploma required; GED accepted. For partnership and dual enrollment students still in high school: High school diploma required; GED accepted **Costs Per Year:** Application fee: $0. State resident tuition: $1470 full-time, $49 per credit hour part-time. Nonresident tuition: $4410 full-time, $147 per credit hour part-time. Mandatory fees: $300 full-time, $10 per credit hour part-time. Full-time tuition and fees vary according to course load. Part-time tuition and fees vary according to course load. **Scholarships:** Available **Calendar System:** Semester, Summer Session Available **Enrollment:** FT 2,053, PT 3,767 **Faculty:** FT 120, PT 240 **Student-Faculty Ratio:** 15:1 **Library Holdings:** 75,000 **Regional Accreditation:** North Central Association of Colleges and Schools **Credit Hours For Degree:** 60 credit hours, Associates **Professional Accreditation:** ABFSE, APTA, ACBSP, CARC, NLN **Intercollegiate Athletics:** Baseball M; Basketball M & W; Cross-Country Running M & W; Golf M; Soccer M; Softball W; Track and Field M & W; Volleyball W

KANSAS STATE UNIVERSITY
Manhattan, KS 66506
Tel: (785)532-6011
Admissions: (785)532-6250
Fax: (785)532-6393
E-mail: k-state@k-state.edu
Web Site: http://www.k-state.edu/
President/CEO: Dr. Kirk Schulz
Admissions: Molly McGaughey
Financial Aid: Larry Moeder
Type: University **Sex:** Coed **Affiliation:** Kansas Board of Regents **Scores:** 39.2% ACT 18-23; 42.8% ACT 24-29 **% Accepted:** 55 **Admission Plans:** Early Admission **Application Deadline:** Rolling **Application Fee:** $30.00 **H.S. Requirements:** High school diploma required; GED accepted **Costs Per Year:** Application fee: $30. State resident tuition: $6186 full-time. Nonresident tuition: $16,893 full-time. Mandatory fees: $684 full-time. Full-time tuition and fees vary according to course load, location, program, and reciprocity agreements. College room and board: $6752. Room and board charges vary according to board plan, housing facility, and location. **Scholarships:** Available **Calendar System:** Semester, Summer Session Available **Enrollment:** FT 16,510, PT 2,268, Grad FT 2,341, Grad PT 2,462 **Faculty:** FT 973, PT 138 **Student-Faculty Ratio:** 20:1 **Exams:** SAT I or ACT. **% Receiving Financial Aid:** 49 **% Residing in College-Owned, -Operated, or -Affiliated Housing:** 37 **Library Holdings:** 1,929,015 **Regional Accreditation:** North Central Association of Colleges and Schools **Credit Hours For Degree:** 60 semester hours, Associates; 120 semester hours, Bachelors **ROTC:** Army, Air Force **Professional Accreditation:** AACSB, ABET, ACEJMC, AAMFT, AAFCS, ACCE, ACA, ADtA, ACSP, APA, ASLA, ASLHA, AVMA, FIDER, CSWE, JRCEPAT, NAAB, NASAD, NASM, NASPAA NAST, NCATE, NRPA **Intercollegiate Athletics:** Baseball M; Basketball M & W; Crew W; Cross-Country Running M & W; Football M; Golf M & W; Tennis W; Track and Field M & W; Volleyball W

KANSAS WESLEYAN UNIVERSITY
100 East Claflin Ave.
Salina, KS 67401-6196
Tel: (785)827-5541; Free: 800-874-1154
Fax: (785)827-0927
E-mail: jallen@kwu.edu
Web Site: http://www.kwu.edu/
President/CEO: Dr. Philip P. Kerstetter
Admissions: Jim Allen
Financial Aid: Glenna Alexander
Type: Comprehensive **Sex:** Coed **Affiliation:** United Methodist **Scores:** 70% ACT 18-23; 28% ACT 24-29 **% Accepted:** 63 **Admission Plans:** Deferred Admission **Application Deadline:** Rolling **Application Fee:** $20.00

H.S. Requirements: High school diploma required; GED accepted **Costs Per Year:** Application fee: $20. Comprehensive fee: $25,800 includes full-time tuition ($19,200) and college room and board ($6600). College room only: $2400. Part-time tuition: $220 per credit hour. Part-time tuition varies according to course load. **Scholarships:** Available **Calendar System:** Miscellaneous, Summer Session Available **Faculty:** FT 43, PT 37 **Student-Faculty Ratio:** 14:1 **Exams:** SAT I or ACT. **% Receiving Financial Aid:** 90 **% Residing in College-Owned, -Operated, or -Affiliated Housing:** 92 **Library Holdings:** 97,060 **Regional Accreditation:** North Central Association of Colleges and Schools **Credit Hours For Degree:** 63 credit hours, Associates; 126 credit hours, Bachelors **Professional Accreditation:** NCATE, NLN **Intercollegiate Athletics:** Baseball M; Basketball M & W; Cheerleading M & W; Cross-Country Running M & W; Football M; Golf M & W; Soccer M & W; Softball W; Tennis M & W; Track and Field M & W; Volleyball W

LABETTE COMMUNITY COLLEGE
200 South 14th St.
Parsons, KS 67357-4299
Tel: (620)421-6700
Web Site: http://www.labette.edu/
President/CEO: Dr. George C. Knox
Admissions: Tammy Fuentez
Type: Two-Year College **Sex:** Coed **Affiliation:** Kansas State Board of Education **% Accepted:** 100 **Admission Plans:** Open Admission; Early Admission **Application Deadline:** Rolling **Application Fee:** $0.00 **H.S. Requirements:** High school diploma required; GED accepted **Scholarships:** Available **Calendar System:** Semester, Summer Session Available **Enrollment:** FT 466, PT 935 **Faculty:** FT 31, PT 177 **Library Holdings:** 26,000 **Regional Accreditation:** North Central Association of Colleges and Schools **Credit Hours For Degree:** 62 credit hours, Associates **ROTC:** Army **Professional Accreditation:** CARC, JRCERT, NLN **Intercollegiate Athletics:** Baseball M; Basketball M & W; Cheerleading W; Softball W; Tennis W; Volleyball W; Wrestling M

MANHATTAN AREA TECHNICAL COLLEGE
3136 Dickens Ave.
Manhattan, KS 66503
Tel: (785)587-2800; Free: 800-352-7575
Web Site: http://www.matc.net/
President/CEO: Dr. Robert J. Edleston
Admissions: Rick Smith
Type: Two-Year College **Sex:** Coed **Application Fee:** $40.00 **H.S. Requirements:** High school diploma required; GED accepted **Calendar System:** Semester **Enrollment:** FT 343, PT 130 **Faculty:** FT 27, PT 8 **Student-Faculty Ratio:** 11:1 **Regional Accreditation:** North Central Association of Colleges and Schools **Credit Hours For Degree:** 62 credit hours, Associates **Professional Accreditation:** NLN

MANHATTAN CHRISTIAN COLLEGE
1415 Anderson Ave.
Manhattan, KS 66502-4081
Tel: (785)539-3571; Free: 877-246-4622
Fax: (785)539-0832
E-mail: admit@mccks.edu
Web Site: http://www.mccks.edu/
President/CEO: Kevin Ingram
Admissions: Eric Ingmire
Financial Aid: Margaret Carlisle
Type: Four-Year College **Sex:** Coed **Affiliation:** Christian Churches and Churches of Christ **Application Deadline:** August 1 **Application Fee:** $25.00 **H.S. Requirements:** High school diploma required; GED accepted **Scholarships:** Available **Calendar System:** Semester, Summer Session Available **Exams:** SAT I or ACT. **% Receiving Financial Aid:** 73 **Library Holdings:** 3,300 **Regional Accreditation:** North Central Association of Colleges and Schools **Credit Hours For Degree:** 62 credit hours, Associates; 120 credit hours, Bachelors **ROTC:** Army, Air Force **Professional Accreditation:** ABHE **Intercollegiate Athletics:** Baseball M; Basketball M & W; Soccer M & W; Volleyball W

MCPHERSON COLLEGE
1600 East Euclid, PO Box 1402
McPherson, KS 67460-1402
Tel: (620)241-0731; Free: 800-365-7402
Fax: (620)241-8443
E-mail: admiss@mcpherson.edu
Web Site: http://www.mcpherson.edu/
President/CEO: Michael Schnieder
Admissions: Matt Pfannenstiel
Financial Aid: Steven Frick
Type: Four-Year College **Sex:** Coed **Affiliation:** Church of the Brethren **Scores:** 90% SAT V 400+; 95% SAT M 400+; 64.96% ACT 18-23; 29.91% ACT 24-29 **% Accepted:** 87 **Admission Plans:** Deferred Admission **Application Deadline:** Rolling **Application Fee:** $25.00 **H.S. Requirements:** High school diploma required; GED accepted **Costs Per Year:** Application fee: $25. Comprehensive fee: $25,310 includes full-time tuition ($17,900), mandatory fees ($500), and college room and board ($6910). College room only: $2735. Full-time tuition and fees vary according to course load and program. Part-time tuition: $250 per credit hour. Part-time mandatory fees: $30 per credit hour. **Scholarships:** Available **Calendar System:** 4-1-4, Summer Session Available **Enrollment:** FT 542, PT 87 **Faculty:** FT 34, PT 20 **Student-Faculty Ratio:** 15:1 **Exams:** ACT, SAT I or ACT. ACT essay not being used. SAT essay not being used. **% Receiving Financial Aid:** 85 **% Residing in College-Owned, -Operated, or -Affiliated Housing:** 74 **Final Year or Final Semester Residency Requirement:** No **Library Holdings:** 81,917 **Regional Accreditation:** North Central Association of Colleges and Schools **Credit Hours For Degree:** 65 credit hours, Associates; 124 credit hours, Bachelors **Professional Accreditation:** NCATE **Intercollegiate Athletics:** Basketball M & W; Cheerleading M & W; Cross-Country Running M & W; Football M; Soccer M & W; Softball W; Tennis M & W; Track and Field M & W; Volleyball W

MIDAMERICA NAZARENE UNIVERSITY
2030 East College Way
Olathe, KS 66062-1899
Tel: (913)782-3750; Free: 800-800-8887
Admissions: (913)971-3380
Fax: (913)791-3481
E-mail: admissions@mnu.edu
Web Site: http://www.mnu.edu/
President/CEO: Dr. Ed Robinson
Admissions: Dennis Miller
Financial Aid: Rhonda L. Cole
Type: Comprehensive **Sex:** Coed **Affiliation:** Church of the Nazarene **Scores:** 90% SAT V 400+; 86% SAT M 400+; 48% ACT 18-23; 33% ACT 24-29 **% Accepted:** 74 **Admission Plans:** Deferred Admission **Application Deadline:** August 1 **Application Fee:** $25.00 **H.S. Requirements:** High school diploma required; GED accepted **Costs Per Year:** Application fee: $25. Comprehensive fee: $27,000 includes full-time tuition ($19,250), mandatory fees ($1000), and college room and board ($6750). Full-time tuition and fees vary according to course load. Room and board charges vary according to board plan and housing facility. Part-time tuition: $645 per hour. Part-time mandatory fees: $365 per term. Part-time tuition and fees vary according to course load. **Scholarships:** Available **Calendar System:** Semester, Summer Session Available **Enrollment:** FT 1,045, PT 290, Grad FT 189, Grad PT 254 **Faculty:** FT 81, PT 194 **Student-Faculty Ratio:** 8:1 **Exams:** SAT I or ACT. ACT essay not being used. SAT essay not being used. **% Receiving Financial Aid:** 72 **% Residing in College-Owned, -Operated, or -Affiliated Housing:** 55 **Final Year or Final Semester Residency Requirement:** Yes **Library Holdings:** 133,140 **Regional Accreditation:** North Central Association of Colleges and Schools **Credit Hours For Degree:** 63 semester hours, Associates; 126 semester hours, Bachelors **ROTC:** Army, Air Force **Professional Accreditation:** AACN, NASM, NCATE, NLN **Intercollegiate Athletics:** Baseball M; Basketball M & W; Cheerleading M & W; Football M; Soccer M & W; Softball W; Volleyball W

NATIONAL AMERICAN UNIVERSITY
10310 Mastin
Overland Park, KS 66212
Tel: (913)981-8700
Web Site: http://www.national.edu/
President/CEO: Dr. Jerry Gallentine
Type: Two-Year College **Sex:** Coed **Application Fee:** $25.00 **Regional Accreditation:** North Central Association of Colleges and Schools

NEOSHO COUNTY COMMUNITY COLLEGE
800 West 14th St.
Chanute, KS 66720-2699

Tel: (620)431-6222
Admissions: (620)431-2820
Fax: (620)431-0082
E-mail: llast@neosho.edu
Web Site: http://www.neosho.edu/
President/CEO: Dr. Vicky Smith
Admissions: Lisa Last
Type: Two-Year College **Sex:** Coed **Affiliation:** Kansas State Board of Education **% Accepted:** 100 **Admission Plans:** Open Admission; Early Admission **Application Deadline:** September 15 **Application Fee:** $0.00 **H.S. Requirements:** High school diploma required; GED accepted **Scholarships:** Available **Calendar System:** Semester, Summer Session Available **Enrollment:** FT 615, PT 1,211 **Faculty:** FT 40, PT 86 **% Residing in College-Owned, -Operated, or -Affiliated Housing:** 5 **Library Holdings:** 33,000 **Regional Accreditation:** North Central Association of Colleges and Schools **Credit Hours For Degree:** 62 semester hours, Associates **Professional Accreditation:** NLN **Intercollegiate Athletics:** Baseball M; Basketball M & W; Cross-Country Running M & W; Softball W; Track and Field M; Volleyball W

NEWMAN UNIVERSITY
3100 McCormick Ave.
Wichita, KS 67213-2097
Tel: (316)942-4291; Free: 877-NEWMANU
Fax: (316)942-4483
E-mail: reusserj@newmanu.edu
Web Site: http://www.newmanu.edu/
President/CEO: Noreen Carrocci
Admissions: Jann Reusser
Financial Aid: Kara Schwinn
Type: Comprehensive **Sex:** Coed **Affiliation:** Roman Catholic **Scores:** 88% SAT V 400+; 91% SAT M 400+; 53% ACT 18-23; 27% ACT 24-29 **% Accepted:** 42 **Admission Plans:** Early Admission; Deferred Admission **Application Deadline:** Rolling **Application Fee:** $20.00 **H.S. Requirements:** High school diploma required; GED accepted. For international students: High school diploma or equivalent not required **Costs Per Year:** Application fee: $20. Comprehensive fee: $27,650 includes full-time tuition ($19,872), mandatory fees ($840), and college room and board ($6938). College room only: $3520. Full-time tuition and fees vary according to class time, course load, location, and program. Room and board charges vary according to board plan and housing facility. Part-time tuition: $662 per credit hour. Part-time mandatory fees: $15 per credit hour, $40 per year. Part-time tuition and fees vary according to class time, course load, location, and program. **Scholarships:** Available **Calendar System:** Semester, Summer Session Available **Enrollment:** FT 997, PT 871, Grad FT 125, Grad PT 564 **Faculty:** FT 77, PT 106 **Student-Faculty Ratio:** 14:1 **Exams:** SAT I or ACT. **% Receiving Financial Aid:** 85 **% Residing in College-Owned, -Operated, or -Affiliated Housing:** 26 **Library Holdings:** 110,167 **Regional Accreditation:** North Central Association of Colleges and Schools **Credit Hours For Degree:** 62 semester hours, Associates; 124 semester hours, Bachelors **Professional Accreditation:** AACN, AANA, CARC, CSWE, JRCERT, NCATE **Intercollegiate Athletics:** Baseball M; Basketball M & W; Bowling M & W; Cross-Country Running M & W; Golf M & W; Soccer M & W; Softball W; Tennis M & W; Volleyball W; Wrestling M

NORTH CENTRAL KANSAS TECHNICAL COLLEGE
PO Box 507, 3033 US Hwy. 24
Beloit, KS 67420
Tel: (913)738-2276; Free: 800-658-4655
Admissions: (785)738-2276
E-mail: jheidrick@ncktc.tec.ks.us
Web Site: http://www.ncktc.edu/
President/CEO: Clark Coco
Admissions: Judy Heidrick
Type: Two-Year College **Sex:** Coed **Application Fee:** $50.00 **Calendar System:** Semester **Regional Accreditation:** North Central Association of Colleges and Schools

NORTHEAST KANSAS TECHNICAL CENTER OF HIGHLAND COMMUNITY COLLEGE
1501 West Riley St.
Atchison, KS 66002
Tel: (913)367-6204; Free: 800-567-4890
Fax: (913)367-3107
Web Site: http://www.nektc.net/
President/CEO: Michael B. Rogg
Type: Two-Year College **Sex:** Coed **Admission Plans:** Open Admission **Application Fee:** $25.00 **Calendar System:** Semester **Professional Accreditation:** COE

NORTHWEST KANSAS TECHNICAL COLLEGE
PO Box 668, 1209 Harrison St.
Goodland, KS 67735
Tel: (785)899-3641; Free: 800-316-4127
Admissions: (785)890-3641
Fax: (785)899-5711
Web Site: http://www.nwktc.edu/
President/CEO: Guy E. Mills
Type: Two-Year College **Sex:** Coed **Application Fee:** $50.00 **Costs Per Year:** Application fee: $50. One-time mandatory fee: $25. State resident tuition: $3150 full-time, $75 per credit hour part-time. Nonresident tuition: $5880 full-time, $140 per credit hour part-time. Mandatory fees: $650 full-time, $325 per term part-time. Full-time tuition and fees vary according to course load and program. Part-time tuition and fees vary according to course load and program. **Calendar System:** Semester **Regional Accreditation:** North Central Association of Colleges and Schools **Professional Accreditation:** COE

OTTAWA UNIVERSITY
1001 South Cedar
Ottawa, KS 66067-3399
Tel: (785)242-5200; Free: 800-755-5200
Admissions: (785)229-1051
Fax: (785)242-7429
E-mail: june.unrein@ottawa.edu
Web Site: http://www.ottawa.edu/
President/CEO: Dr. Kevin C. Eichner
Admissions: June Unrein
Type: Four-Year College **Sex:** Coed **Affiliation:** American Baptist Churches in the USA **Scores:** 80% SAT V 400+; 86% SAT M 400+; 61% ACT 18-23; 23% ACT 24-29 **% Accepted:** 70 **Application Deadline:** Rolling **Application Fee:** $25.00 **H.S. Requirements:** High school diploma required; GED accepted **Costs Per Year:** Application fee: $25. Comprehensive fee: $27,414 includes full-time tuition ($20,000), mandatory fees ($400), and college room and board ($7014). Full-time tuition and fees vary according to course load. Room and board charges vary according to board plan and housing facility. Part-time tuition: $833 per credit hour. Part-time mandatory fees: $17 per credit hour. Part-time tuition and fees vary according to course load. **Scholarships:** Available **Calendar System:** Semester, Summer Session Available **Enrollment:** FT 511, PT 20 **Faculty:** FT 25, PT 11 **Student-Faculty Ratio:** 18:1 **Exams:** SAT I or ACT. **% Residing in College-Owned, -Operated, or -Affiliated Housing:** 63 **Final Year or Final Semester Residency Requirement:** No **Library Holdings:** 82,069 **Regional Accreditation:** North Central Association of Colleges and Schools **Credit Hours For Degree:** 124 credit hours, Bachelors **Professional Accreditation:** NCATE **Intercollegiate Athletics:** Baseball M; Basketball M & W; Cross-Country Running M & W; Football M; Golf M; Soccer M & W; Softball W; Track and Field M & W; Volleyball W

PITTSBURG STATE UNIVERSITY
1701 South Broadway
Pittsburg, KS 66762
Tel: (620)231-7000; Free: 800-854-7488
Admissions: (620)235-4251
Fax: (620)235-4080
E-mail: psuadmit@pittstate.edu
Web Site: http://www.pittstate.edu/
President/CEO: Dr. Steve Scott
Financial Aid: Tammy Higgins
Type: Comprehensive **Sex:** Coed **Affiliation:** Kansas State Board of Regents **Scores:** 57% ACT 18-23; 28% ACT 24-29 **% Accepted:** 80 **Application Deadline:** Rolling **Application Fee:** $30.00 **H.S. Requirements:** High school diploma required; GED accepted **Costs Per Year:** Application fee: $30. State resident tuition: $3652 full-time, $122 per credit hour part-time. Nonresident tuition: $12,176 full-time, $406 per credit hour part-time. Mandatory fees: $940 full-time, $43 per credit hour part-time. Part-time tuition and fees vary according to course load. College room and board: $5744. Room and board charges vary according to board plan and housing

facility. **Scholarships:** Available **Calendar System:** Semester, Summer Session Available **Enrollment:** FT 5,615, PT 319, Grad FT 528, Grad PT 815 **Faculty:** FT 308, PT 96 **Student-Faculty Ratio:** 19:1 **Exams:** ACT. ACT essay not being used. **% Receiving Financial Aid:** 58 **% Residing in College-Owned, -Operated, or -Affiliated Housing:** 15 **Final Year or Final Semester Residency Requirement:** Yes **Library Holdings:** 712,681 **Regional Accreditation:** North Central Association of Colleges and Schools **Credit Hours For Degree:** 60 semester hours, Associates; 124 semester hours, Bachelors **ROTC:** Army **Professional Accreditation:** AACSB, ABET, AACN, AAFCS, ACA, CSWE, NASM, NCATE, NLN **Intercollegiate Athletics:** Baseball M; Basketball M & W; Cheerleading M & W; Cross-Country Running M & W; Football M; Golf M; Softball W; Track and Field M & W; Volleyball W

PRATT COMMUNITY COLLEGE
348 NE State Rd. 61
Pratt, KS 67124-8317
Tel: (620)672-9800
Admissions: (620)450-2217
Fax: (620)672-5288
E-mail: theresaz@prattcc.edu
Web Site: http://www.prattcc.edu/
President/CEO: Dr. William Wojciechowski
Admissions: Theresa Ziehr
Type: Two-Year College **Sex:** Coed **Affiliation:** Kansas State Board of Education **% Accepted:** 100 **Admission Plans:** Open Admission; Early Admission **Application Deadline:** Rolling **Application Fee:** $0.00 **H.S. Requirements:** High school diploma required; GED accepted **Costs Per Year:** Application fee: $0. State resident tuition: $1536 full-time, $48 per credit hour part-time. Nonresident tuition: $1696 full-time, $53 per credit hour part-time. Mandatory fees: $992 full-time, $31 per credit hour part-time. Full-time tuition and fees vary according to program. Part-time tuition and fees vary according to program. College room and board: $4176. College room only: $1769. Room and board charges vary according to board plan and housing facility. **Scholarships:** Available **Calendar System:** Semester, Summer Session Available **Enrollment:** FT 743, PT 795 **Faculty:** FT 45, PT 84 **Student-Faculty Ratio:** 14:1 **Exams:** Other. **% Residing in College-Owned, -Operated, or -Affiliated Housing:** 35 **Library Holdings:** 33,000 **Regional Accreditation:** North Central Association of Colleges and Schools **Credit Hours For Degree:** 64 credit hours, Associates **Professional Accreditation:** ACBSP, NLN **Intercollegiate Athletics:** Baseball M; Basketball M & W; Cheerleading W; Cross-Country Running M & W; Golf M & W; Softball W; Track and Field M & W; Volleyball W; Wrestling M

SEWARD COUNTY COMMUNITY COLLEGE
PO Box 1137
Liberal, KS 67905-1137
Tel: (620)624-1951; Free: 800-373-9951
Fax: (620)629-2725
Web Site: http://www.sccc.edu/
President/CEO: Dr. Duane Dunn
Admissions: Dr. Gerald Harris
Type: Two-Year College **Sex:** Coed **Affiliation:** Kansas State Board of Regents **Admission Plans:** Open Admission; Early Admission; Deferred Admission **Application Deadline:** August 15 **Application Fee:** $0.00 **H.S. Requirements:** High school diploma required; GED accepted **Scholarships:** Available **Calendar System:** Semester, Summer Session Available **Library Holdings:** 32,926 **Regional Accreditation:** North Central Association of Colleges and Schools **Credit Hours For Degree:** 64 semester hours, Associates **Professional Accreditation:** ARCEST, CARC, NAACLS, NLN **Intercollegiate Athletics:** Baseball M; Basketball M & W; Softball W; Tennis M & W; Volleyball W

SOUTHWESTERN COLLEGE
100 College St.
Winfield, KS 67156-2499
Tel: (620)229-6000; Free: 800-846-1543
Admissions: (620)229-6364
Fax: (620)229-6224
E-mail: scadmit@sckans.edu
Web Site: http://www.sckans.edu/
President/CEO: Dr. W. Richard Merriman, Jr.
Admissions: Marla Sexson
Financial Aid: Brenda D. Hicks
Type: Comprehensive **Sex:** Coed **Affiliation:** United Methodist **Scores:** 76% SAT V 400+; 88% SAT M 400+; 48% ACT 18-23; 29% ACT 24-29 **% Accepted:** 90 **Admission Plans:** Deferred Admission **Application Deadline:** August 25 **Application Fee:** $25.00 **H.S. Requirements:** High school diploma required; GED accepted **Costs Per Year:** Application fee: $25. Comprehensive fee: $25,380 includes full-time tuition ($19,530), mandatory fees ($100), and college room and board ($5750). College room only: $2716. Full-time tuition and fees vary according to class time, course load, degree level, location, and program. Room and board charges vary according to board plan and housing facility. Part-time tuition: $814 per semester hour. Part-time tuition varies according to class time, course load, degree level, location, and program. **Scholarships:** Available **Calendar System:** Semester, Summer Session Available **Enrollment:** FT 575, PT 950, Grad FT 22, Grad PT 263 **Faculty:** FT 47, PT 55 **Student-Faculty Ratio:** 12:1 **Exams:** SAT I or ACT. ACT essay used for admission. SAT essay used for admission. ACT essay used in place of application essay. SAT essay used in place of application essay. **% Receiving Financial Aid:** 80 **% Residing in College-Owned, -Operated, or -Affiliated Housing:** 72 **Final Year or Final Semester Residency Requirement:** Yes **Library Holdings:** 56,237 **Regional Accreditation:** North Central Association of Colleges and Schools **Credit Hours For Degree:** 124 semester hours, Bachelors **Professional Accreditation:** AACN, NASM, NCATE, NLN **Intercollegiate Athletics:** Badminton M & W; Basketball M & W; Cheerleading M & W; Cross-Country Running M & W; Football M; Golf M & W; Soccer M & W; Softball W; Swimming and Diving M & W; Tennis M & W; Track and Field M & W; Volleyball W

STERLING COLLEGE
125 West Cooper
Sterling, KS 67579-0098
Tel: (620)278-2173; Free: 800-346-1017
Admissions: (620)278-4275
Fax: (620)278-3690
E-mail: admissions@sterling.edu
Web Site: http://www.sterling.edu/
President/CEO: Paul Maurer
Admissions: Marge Jones
Financial Aid: Jodi Lightner
Type: Four-Year College **Sex:** Coed **Affiliation:** Presbyterian **Scores:** 82% SAT V 400+; 93% SAT M 400+; 59% ACT 18-23; 25% ACT 24-29 **% Accepted:** 55 **Admission Plans:** Early Action; Deferred Admission **Application Deadline:** July 15 **Application Fee:** $25.00 **H.S. Requirements:** High school diploma required; GED accepted **Costs Per Year:** Application fee: $25. One-time mandatory fee: $100. Comprehensive fee: $25,830 includes full-time tuition ($19,000) and college room and board ($6830). Room and board charges vary according to board plan and housing facility. Part-time tuition: $365 per credit hour. **Scholarships:** Available **Calendar System:** 4-1-4, Summer Session Not available **Enrollment:** FT 602, PT 120 **Faculty:** FT 37, PT 20 **Student-Faculty Ratio:** 14:1 **Exams:** SAT I or ACT. **% Receiving Financial Aid:** 81 **% Residing in College-Owned, -Operated, or -Affiliated Housing:** 72 **Final Year or Final Semester Residency Requirement:** Yes **Library Holdings:** 76,637 **Regional Accreditation:** North Central Association of Colleges and Schools **Credit Hours For Degree:** 124 credit hours, Bachelors **Intercollegiate Athletics:** Baseball M; Basketball M & W; Cross-Country Running M & W; Football M; Golf M & W; Soccer M & W; Softball W; Tennis M & W; Track and Field M & W; Volleyball W

TABOR COLLEGE
400 South Jefferson
Hillsboro, KS 67063
Tel: (620)947-3121; Free: 800-822-6799
Fax: (620)947-2607
E-mail: lindac@tabor.edu
Web Site: http://www.tabor.edu/
President/CEO: Dr. Jules Glanzer
Admissions: Dr. Linda Cantwell
Financial Aid: Scott Franz
Type: Comprehensive **Sex:** Coed **Affiliation:** Mennonite Brethren **Scores:** 50% ACT 18-23; 28% ACT 24-29 **% Accepted:** 94 **Admission Plans:** Early Admission; Early Decision Plan; Deferred Admission **Application Deadline:** August 1 **Application Fee:** $30.00 **H.S. Requirements:** High school diploma required; GED accepted **Costs Per Year:** Application fee: $30. One-time mandatory fee: $100. Comprehensive fee: $26,530 includes full-

time tuition ($19,200), mandatory fees ($460), and college room and board ($6870). College room only: $2700. Full-time tuition and fees vary according to course load. Room and board charges vary according to board plan, housing facility, and location. Part-time tuition: $800 per credit hour. Part-time mandatory fees: $10 per credit hour. Part-time tuition and fees vary according to course load. **Scholarships:** Available **Calendar System:** 4-1-4, Summer Session Not available **Enrollment:** FT 515, PT 103, Grad FT 6, Grad PT 16 **Faculty:** FT 30, PT 51 **Student-Faculty Ratio:** 12:1 **Exams:** SAT I or ACT. ACT essay not being used. SAT essay not being used. **% Receiving Financial Aid:** 85 **% Residing in College-Owned, -Operated, or -Affiliated Housing:** 87 **Library Holdings:** 80,099 **Regional Accreditation:** North Central Association of Colleges and Schools **Credit Hours For Degree:** 64 credit hours, Associates; 124 credit hours, Bachelors **Professional Accreditation:** AACN, NASM **Intercollegiate Athletics:** Baseball M; Basketball M & W; Cheerleading M & W; Cross-Country Running M & W; Football M; Golf M & W; Soccer M & W; Softball W; Tennis M & W; Track and Field M & W; Volleyball W

THE UNIVERSITY OF KANSAS
Lawrence, KS 66045
Tel: (785)864-2700
Admissions: (785)864-3911
Fax: (785)864-5006
E-mail: adm@ku.edu
Web Site: http://www.ku.edu/
President/CEO: Dr. Bernadette Gray-Little
Admissions: Lisa Pinamonti Kress
Financial Aid: Brenda Maigaard
Type: University **Sex:** Coed **Affiliation:** Kansas Board of Regents System **Scores:** 38% ACT 18-23; 47% ACT 24-29 **% Accepted:** 91 **Application Deadline:** April 1 **Application Fee:** $30.00 **H.S. Requirements:** High school diploma required; GED accepted **Costs Per Year:** Application fee: $30. State resident tuition: $7359 full-time, $245.30 per credit hour part-time. Nonresident tuition: $19,327 full-time, $644.25 per credit hour part-time. Mandatory fees: $847 full-time, $70.56 per credit hour part-time. Full-time tuition and fees vary according to program, reciprocity agreements, and student level. Part-time tuition and fees vary according to program, reciprocity agreements, and student level. College room and board: $6802. College room only: $3554. Room and board charges vary according to board plan and housing facility. Tuition guaranteed not to increase for student's term of enrollment. **Scholarships:** Available **Calendar System:** Semester, Summer Session Available **Enrollment:** FT 18,930, PT 2,136, Grad FT 5,562, Grad PT 2,614 **Faculty:** FT 1,246, PT 69 **Student-Faculty Ratio:** 20:1 **Exams:** SAT I or ACT. **% Receiving Financial Aid:** 39 **% Residing in College-Owned, -Operated, or -Affiliated Housing:** 22 **Final Year or Final Semester Residency Requirement:** Yes **Library Holdings:** 5,012,773 **Regional Accreditation:** North Central Association of Colleges and Schools **Credit Hours For Degree:** 124 credit hours, Bachelors **ROTC:** Army, Navy, Air Force **Professional Accreditation:** AACSB, ABET, ACPhE, ACEJMC, AACN, AANA, ABA, ACNM, ADtA, AHIMA, ACSP, AOTA, APTA, APA, ASC, ASLHA, AALS, ACEHSA, CARC, CEPH CSWE, LCMEAMA, NAACLS, NAAB, NASAD, NASM, NASPAA, NCATE **Intercollegiate Athletics:** Baseball M; Basketball M & W; Crew W; Cross-Country Running M & W; Football M; Golf M & W; Ice Hockey M; Rugby M; Soccer W; Softball W; Swimming and Diving W; Tennis W; Track and Field M & W; Ultimate Frisbee M & W; Volleyball W

UNIVERSITY OF PHOENIX—WICHITA CAMPUS
3020 North Cypress Dr., Ste. 150
Wichita, KS 67226-4011
Tel: (316)630-8121; Free: 800-228-7240
Admissions: (480)557-6151
E-mail: audra.mcquarie@phoenix.edu
Web Site: http://www.phoenix.edu/
President/CEO: William Pepicello
Admissions: Audra McQuarie
Type: Comprehensive **Sex:** Coed **Admission Plans:** Open Admission; Deferred Admission **Application Deadline:** Rolling **Application Fee:** $0.00 **H.S. Requirements:** High school diploma required; GED accepted **Costs Per Year:** Application fee: $0. Tuition: $11,775 full-time. Full-time tuition varies according to course level and course load. **Scholarships:** Available **Calendar System:** Continuous, Summer Session Not available **Enrollment:** FT 125 **Faculty:** FT 4, PT 45 **Regional Accreditation:** North Central Association of Colleges and Schools **Credit Hours For Degree:** 60 credits, Associates; 120 credits, Bachelors

UNIVERSITY OF SAINT MARY
4100 South Fourth St. Trafficway
Leavenworth, KS 66048-5082
Tel: (913)682-5151; Free: 800-752-7043
Admissions: (913)758-6118
Fax: (913)758-6140
E-mail: admiss@stmary.edu
Web Site: http://www.stmary.edu/
President/CEO: Sr. Diane Steele
Admissions: Brandon Johnson
Financial Aid: Judy Wiedower
Type: Comprehensive **Sex:** Coed **Affiliation:** Roman Catholic **Scores:** 85% SAT V 400+; 91% SAT M 400+; 55% ACT 18-23; 24% ACT 24-29 **% Accepted:** 70 **Application Deadline:** Rolling **Application Fee:** $25.00 **H.S. Requirements:** High school diploma required; GED accepted **Costs Per Year:** Application fee: $25. Comprehensive fee: $26,310 includes full-time tuition ($19,500), mandatory fees ($460), and college room and board ($6350). Full-time tuition and fees vary according to class time, course load, location, and program. Room and board charges vary according to board plan and housing facility. Part-time tuition: $375 per credit hour. Part-time mandatory fees: $90 per term. Part-time tuition and fees vary according to class time, course load, location, and program. **Scholarships:** Available **Calendar System:** Semester, Summer Session Available **Enrollment:** FT 513, PT 266, Grad FT 30, Grad PT 263 **Faculty:** FT 43, PT 67 **Student-Faculty Ratio:** 11:1 **Exams:** SAT I or ACT. **% Residing in College-Owned, -Operated, or -Affiliated Housing:** 33 **Final Year or Final Semester Residency Requirement:** Yes **Library Holdings:** 120,753 **Regional Accreditation:** North Central Association of Colleges and Schools **Credit Hours For Degree:** 64 semester hours, Associates; 128 semester hours, Bachelors **ROTC:** Army, Air Force **Professional Accreditation:** NCATE **Intercollegiate Athletics:** Baseball M; Basketball M & W; Football M; Soccer M & W; Softball W; Volleyball W

WASHBURN UNIVERSITY
1700 Southwest College Ave.
Topeka, KS 66621
Tel: (785)670-1010
Admissions: (785)670-1030
Fax: (785)231-1089
E-mail: admissions@washburn.edu
Web Site: http://www.washburn.edu/
President/CEO: Dr. Jerry Farley
Financial Aid: Gail Palmer
Type: Comprehensive **Sex:** Coed **Scores:** 52% ACT 18-23; 29% ACT 24-29 **% Accepted:** 100 **Admission Plans:** Early Admission **Application Deadline:** July 31 **Application Fee:** $20.00 **H.S. Requirements:** High school diploma required; GED accepted **Costs Per Year:** Application fee: $20. State resident tuition: $6030 full-time, $201 per credit hour part-time. Nonresident tuition: $13,680 full-time, $456 per credit hour part-time. Mandatory fees: $86 full-time, $21 per term part-time. Full-time tuition and fees vary according to program. Part-time tuition and fees vary according to program. College room and board: $5792. College room only: $3242. Room and board charges vary according to board plan and housing facility. **Scholarships:** Available **Calendar System:** Semester, Summer Session Available **Enrollment:** FT 3,906, PT 1,860, Grad FT 578, Grad PT 308 **Faculty:** FT 256, PT 243 **Student-Faculty Ratio:** 16:1 **Exams:** ACT. ACT essay not being used. SAT essay not being used. **% Receiving Financial Aid:** 62 **% Residing in College-Owned, -Operated, or -Affiliated Housing:** 13 **Final Year or Final Semester Residency Requirement:** No **Library Holdings:** 356,990 **Regional Accreditation:** North Central Association of Colleges and Schools **Credit Hours For Degree:** 62 credit hours, Associates; 124 credit hours, Bachelors **ROTC:** Army, Navy, Air Force **Professional Accreditation:** AACSB, AACN, ABA, AHIMA, APTA, AALS, CARC, CSWE, JRCERT, NASAD, NASM, NCATE **Intercollegiate Athletics:** Baseball M; Basketball M & W; Cheerleading M & W; Football M; Golf M; Soccer W; Softball W; Tennis M & W; Volleyball W

WICHITA AREA TECHNICAL COLLEGE
301 South Grove St.
Wichita, KS 67211
Tel: (316)677-9282
Admissions: (316)677-9400
E-mail: info@watc.edu
Web Site: http://www.wichitatech.com/

President/CEO: Pete Gustaf
Admissions: Jessica Ross
Type: Two-Year College **Sex:** Coed **Application Deadline:** Rolling **Application Fee:** $16.00 **Costs Per Year:** Application fee: $16. State resident tuition: $1650 full-time, $55 per credit hour part-time. Nonresident tuition: $1650 full-time, $55 per credit hour part-time. Mandatory fees: $810 full-time, $27 per credit hour part-time. Full-time tuition and fees vary according to program. Part-time tuition and fees vary according to program. **Calendar System:** Semester **Enrollment:** FT 317, PT 376 **Faculty:** FT 44, PT 14 **Student-Faculty Ratio:** 12:1 **Exams:** Other. **Library Holdings:** 3,696 **Professional Accreditation:** ARCEST, ADA, COE, NAACLS

WICHITA STATE UNIVERSITY
1845 North Fairmount
Wichita, KS 67260
Tel: (316)978-3456; Free: 800-362-2594
Admissions: (316)978-3085
Fax: (316)978-3795
E-mail: bobby.gandu@wichita.edu
Web Site: http://www.wichita.edu/
President/CEO: Donald Beggs
Admissions: Bobby Gandu
Financial Aid: Deborah D. Byers
Type: University **Sex:** Coed **Affiliation:** Kansas State Board of Education **Scores:** 98% SAT V 400+; 99% SAT M 400+; 48% ACT 18-23; 37% ACT 24-29 **% Accepted:** 89 **Admission Plans:** Open Admission; Deferred Admission **Application Deadline:** Rolling **Application Fee:** $30.00 **H.S. Requirements:** High school diploma required; GED accepted **Costs Per Year:** Application fee: $30. State resident tuition: $4497 full-time, $149.90 per credit hour part-time. Nonresident tuition: $12,531 full-time, $417.70 per credit hour part-time. Mandatory fees: $953 full-time, $31.20 per credit hour part-time, $17 per term part-time. Full-time tuition and fees vary according to course load and degree level. Part-time tuition and fees vary according to course load and degree level. College room and board: $6700. Room and board charges vary according to board plan and housing facility. **Scholarships:** Available **Calendar System:** Semester, Summer Session Available **Enrollment:** FT 8,138, PT 3,566, Grad FT 1,290, Grad PT 1,829 **Faculty:** FT 448, PT 40 **Student-Faculty Ratio:** 20:1 **Exams:** Other, SAT I or ACT. **% Receiving Financial Aid:** 37 **% Residing in College-Owned, -Operated, or -Affiliated Housing:** 8 **Final Year or Final Semester Residency Requirement:** No **Library Holdings:** 1,772,590 **Regional Accreditation:** North Central Association of Colleges and Schools **Credit Hours For Degree:** 65 credit hours, Associates; 124 credit hours, Bachelors **Professional Accreditation:** AACSB, ABET, AACN, ADA, APTA, APA, ASLHA, CEPH, CSWE, NAACLS, NASD, NASM, NASPAA, NCATE **Intercollegiate Athletics:** Baseball M; Basketball M & W; Cheerleading M & W; Cross-Country Running M & W; Golf M & W; Softball W; Swimming and Diving M & W; Tennis M & W; Track and Field M & W; Volleyball M & W

ALICE LLOYD COLLEGE
100 Purpose Rd.
Pippa Passes, KY 41844
Tel: (606)368-2101
Admissions: (606)368-6036
Fax: (606)368-2125
E-mail: ronniecollins@alc.edu
Web Site: http://www.alc.edu/
President/CEO: Dr. Joe A. Stepp
Admissions: Ronnie Collins
Financial Aid: Jacqueline Stewart
Type: Four-Year College **Sex:** Coed **Scores:** 92% SAT V 400+; 92% SAT M 400+ **% Accepted:** 10 **Admission Plans:** Deferred Admission **Application Deadline:** Rolling **Application Fee:** $0.00 **H.S. Requirements:** High school diploma required; GED accepted **Costs Per Year:** Application fee: $0. One-time mandatory fee: $50. Comprehensive fee: $5850 includes full-time tuition ($0), mandatory fees ($1400), and college room and board ($4450). College room only: $2070. Full-time fees vary according to course load and location. Room and board charges vary according to location. Part-time tuition: $212 per credit hour. full-time students in the 108-county service area are granted guaranteed tuition. **Scholarships:** Available **Calendar System:** Semester, Summer Session Not available **Enrollment:** FT 584, PT 25 **Faculty:** FT 29, PT 9 **Student-Faculty Ratio:** 18:1 **Exams:** SAT I or ACT. **% Receiving Financial Aid:** 82 **% Residing in College-Owned, -Operated, or -Affiliated Housing:** 80 **Library Holdings:** 72,781 **Regional Accreditation:** Southern Association of Colleges and Schools **Credit Hours For Degree:** 128 credit hours, Bachelors **Intercollegiate Athletics:** Baseball M; Basketball M & W; Cheerleading W; Golf M & W; Softball W

ASBURY UNIVERSITY
1 Macklem Dr.
Wilmore, KY 40390-1198
Tel: (859)858-3511; Free: 800-888-1818
Fax: (859)858-3921
E-mail: admissions@asbury.edu
Web Site: http://www.asbury.edu/
President/CEO: Dr. Sandra C. Gray
Admissions: Lisa D. Harper
Financial Aid: Ronald Anderson
Type: Comprehensive **Sex:** Coed **Affiliation:** nondenominational **Scores:** 97.17% SAT V 400+; 94.34% SAT M 400+; 40.74% ACT 18-23; 43.06% ACT 24-29 **% Accepted:** 57 **Admission Plans:** Early Admission; Deferred Admission **Application Deadline:** Rolling **Application Fee:** $0.00 **H.S. Requirements:** High school diploma required; GED accepted **Costs Per Year:** Application fee: $0. Comprehensive fee: $28,869 includes full-time tuition ($23,132), mandatory fees ($171), and college room and board ($5566). College room only: $3270. Full-time tuition and fees vary according to course load and program. Room and board charges vary according to board plan, housing facility, and location. Part-time tuition: $889 per credit hour. Part-time tuition varies according to course load and program. **Scholarships:** Available **Calendar System:** Semester, Summer Session Available **Enrollment:** FT 1,377, PT 93, Grad FT 48, Grad PT 90 **Faculty:** FT 83, PT 84 **Student-Faculty Ratio:** 15:1 **Exams:** SAT I or ACT. **% Receiving Financial Aid:** 74 **% Residing in College-Owned, -Operated, or -Affiliated Housing:** 87 **Final Year or Final Semester Residency Requirement:** Yes **Library Holdings:** 162,467 **Regional Accreditation:** Southern Association of Colleges and Schools **Credit Hours For Degree:** 60 semester hours, Associates; 124 semester hours, Bachelors **ROTC:** Army, Air Force **Professional Accreditation:** NASM, NCATE **Intercollegiate Athletics:** Baseball M; Basketball M & W; Cross-Country Running M & W; Soccer M & W; Softball W; Swimming and Diving M & W; Tennis M & W; Volleyball W

ASHLAND COMMUNITY AND TECHNICAL COLLEGE
1400 College Dr.
Ashland, KY 41101-3683
Tel: (606)329-2999; Free: 800-370-7191
Admissions: (606)326-2000
Fax: (606)325-8124
E-mail: willie.mccullough@kctcs.net
Web Site: http://www.ashland.kctcs.edu/
President/CEO: Dr. Gregory D. Adkins
Admissions: Willie G. McCullough
Type: Two-Year College **Sex:** Coed **Affiliation:** Kentucky Community and Technical College System **Scores:** 46% ACT 18-23; 7% ACT 24-29 **% Accepted:** 100 **Admission Plans:** Open Admission; Early Admission; Deferred Admission **Application Deadline:** August 20 **Application Fee:** $0.00 **H.S. Requirements:** High school diploma required; GED accepted **Scholarships:** Available **Calendar System:** Semester, Summer Session Available **Student-Faculty Ratio:** 19:1 **Library Holdings:** 41,379 **Regional Accreditation:** Southern Association of Colleges and Schools **Credit Hours For Degree:** 60 credit hours, Associates **Professional Accreditation:** ARCEST, ACBSP, CARC, COE, NLN

ATA CAREER EDUCATION
10180 Linn Station Rd.
Ste. A200
Louisville, KY 40223
Tel: (502)371-8330
Web Site: http://www.atai.com/
President/CEO: Donald Jones
Type: Two-Year College **Sex:** Coed **Admission Plans:** Open Admission **Application Fee:** $25.00 **Student-Faculty Ratio:** 14:1

BECKFIELD COLLEGE
16 Spiral Dr.
Florence, KY 41042
Tel: (859)371-9393
Fax: (859)371-5096
E-mail: lboerger@beckfield.edu
Web Site: http://www.beckfield.edu/
President/CEO: Dr. Ronald A. Swanson
Admissions: Leah Boerger
Type: Two-Year College **Sex:** Coed **Admission Plans:** Open Admission **Application Fee:** $150.00 **H.S. Requirements:** High school diploma required; GED accepted **Scholarships:** Available **Calendar System:** Quarter **Professional Accreditation:** ACICS

BELLARMINE UNIVERSITY
2001 Newburg Rd.
Louisville, KY 40205-0671

Tel: (502)452-8000; Free: 800-274-4723
Admissions: (502)452-8131
Fax: (502)452-8002
E-mail: admissions@bellarmine.edu
Web Site: http://www.bellarmine.edu/
President/CEO: Dr. Joseph J. McGowan
Admissions: Timothy A. Sturgeon
Financial Aid: Heather Boutell
Type: Comprehensive **Sex:** Coed **Affiliation:** Roman Catholic **Scores:** 98% SAT V 400+; 99% SAT M 400+; 39% ACT 18-23; 51% ACT 24-29 **% Accepted:** 53 **Admission Plans:** Early Admission; Early Action; Deferred Admission **Application Deadline:** August 15 **Application Fee:** $25.00 **H.S. Requirements:** High school diploma required; GED accepted **Costs Per Year:** Application fee: $25. One-time mandatory fee: $300. Comprehensive fee: $38,860 includes full-time tuition ($29,160), mandatory fees ($1150), and college room and board ($8550). College room only: $4960. Room and board charges vary according to board plan and housing facility. Part-time tuition: $690 per credit hour. Part-time mandatory fees: $45 per course. **Scholarships:** Available **Calendar System:** Semester, Summer Session Available **Enrollment:** FT 2,047, PT 370, Grad FT 290, Grad PT 383 **Faculty:** FT 138, PT 162 **Student-Faculty Ratio:** 12:1 **Exams:** SAT I or ACT. **% Receiving Financial Aid:** 74 **% Residing in College-Owned, -Operated, or -Affiliated Housing:** 47 **Final Year or Final Semester Residency Requirement:** No **Library Holdings:** 132,323 **Regional Accreditation:** Southern Association of Colleges and Schools **Credit Hours For Degree:** 126 credits, Bachelors **ROTC:** Army, Air Force **Professional Accreditation:** AACSB, AACN, APTA, ASC, CARC, NAACLS, NCATE, NLN **Intercollegiate Athletics:** Baseball M; Basketball M & W; Bowling M & W; Cross-Country Running M & W; Field Hockey W; Golf M & W; Lacrosse M; Soccer M & W; Softball W; Swimming and Diving M & W; Tennis M & W; Track and Field M & W; Volleyball W

BEREA COLLEGE
Berea, KY 40404
Tel: (859)985-3000; Free: 800-326-5948
Admissions: (859)985-3500
E-mail: admissions@berea.edu
Web Site: http://www.berea.edu/
President/CEO: Dr. Larry D. Shinn
Admissions: Luke Hodson
Financial Aid: Nancy Melton
Type: Four-Year College **Sex:** Coed **Scores:** 98.4% SAT V 400+; 98.4% SAT M 400+; 45.5% ACT 18-23; 45.2% ACT 24-29 **% Accepted:** 14 **Admission Plans:** Preferred Admission **Application Deadline:** April 30 **Application Fee:** $0.00 **H.S. Requirements:** High school diploma required; GED accepted **Costs Per Year:** Application fee: $0. Comprehensive fee: $6644 includes full-time tuition ($0), mandatory fees ($876), and college room and board ($5768). financial aid is provided to all students for tuition costs. **Scholarships:** Available **Calendar System:** 4-1-4, Summer Session Available **Enrollment:** FT 1,501, PT 47 **Faculty:** FT 130, PT 46 **Student-Faculty Ratio:** 10:1 **Exams:** SAT I or ACT. **% Receiving Financial Aid:** 100 **% Residing in College-Owned, -Operated, or -Affiliated Housing:** 90 **Final Year or Final Semester Residency Requirement:** No **Library Holdings:** 381,418 **Regional Accreditation:** Southern Association of Colleges and Schools **Credit Hours For Degree:** 33 courses, Bachelors **Professional Accreditation:** AACN, AAFCS, NCATE, NLN **Intercollegiate Athletics:** Baseball M; Basketball M & W; Cross-Country Running M & W; Golf M; Soccer M & W; Softball W; Swimming and Diving M & W; Tennis M & W; Track and Field M & W; Volleyball W

BIG SANDY COMMUNITY AND TECHNICAL COLLEGE
One Bert T. Combs Dr.
Prestonsburg, KY 41653-1815
Tel: (606)886-3863; Free: 888-641-4132
Fax: (606)886-6943
E-mail: jimmy.wright@kctcs.edu
Web Site: http://www.bigsandy.kctcs.edu/
President/CEO: Dr. George D. Edwards
Admissions: Jimmy Wright
Type: Two-Year College **Sex:** Coed **Affiliation:** Kentucky Community and Technical College System **Admission Plans:** Open Admission; Early Admission; Deferred Admission **Application Deadline:** Rolling **H.S. Requirements:** High school diploma required; GED accepted **Costs Per Year:** State resident tuition: $3750 full-time, $125 per credit hour part-time. Nonresident tuition: $12,750 full-time, $425 per credit hour part-time. **Scholarships:** Available **Calendar System:** Semester, Summer Session Available **Library Holdings:** 34,668 **Regional Accreditation:** Southern Association of Colleges and Schools **Credit Hours For Degree:** 60 credit hours, Associates **Professional Accreditation:** ADA, COE

BLUEGRASS COMMUNITY AND TECHNICAL COLLEGE
470 Cooper Dr.
Lexington, KY 40506-0235
Tel: (859)246-0235
Admissions: (859)246-6216
E-mail: shelbie.hugle@kctcs.edu
Web Site: http://www.bluegrass.kctcs.edu/
President/CEO: Dr. Augusta Julian
Admissions: Shelbie Hugle
Type: Two-Year College **Sex:** Coed **Affiliation:** Kentucky Community and Technical College System **Admission Plans:** Open Admission; Preferred Admission; Early Admission **Application Deadline:** August 2 **Application Fee:** $20.00 **H.S. Requirements:** High school diploma required; GED accepted **Costs Per Year:** Application fee: $20. State resident tuition: $3000 full-time, $125 per credit hour part-time. Nonresident tuition: $10,200 full-time, $425 per credit hour part-time. Mandatory fees: $60 full-time, $30 per term part-time. Full-time tuition and fees vary according to location. Part-time tuition and fees vary according to location. College room and board: $8017. College room only: $5903. Room and board charges vary according to board plan and housing facility. **Scholarships:** Available **Calendar System:** Semester, Summer Session Available **Enrollment:** FT 5,539, PT 6,057 **Faculty:** FT 260, PT 586 **% Residing in College-Owned, -Operated, or -Affiliated Housing:** 3 **Library Holdings:** 27,000 **Regional Accreditation:** Southern Association of Colleges and Schools **Credit Hours For Degree:** 60 credit hours, Associates **ROTC:** Army, Air Force **Professional Accreditation:** ADA, CARC, NLN

BOWLING GREEN TECHNICAL COLLEGE
1845 Loop Dr.
Bowling Green, KY 42101
Tel: (270)901-1000; Free: 800-790.0990
Fax: (270)746-7466
Web Site: http://www.bowlinggreen.kctcs.edu/
President/CEO: Dr. Nathan L. Hodges
Admissions: Mark Garrett
Type: Two-Year College **Sex:** Coed **Admission Plans:** Open Admission **Calendar System:** Semester **Regional Accreditation:** Southern Association of Colleges and Schools **Professional Accreditation:** CARC, COE

BRESCIA UNIVERSITY
717 Frederica St.
Owensboro, KY 42301-3023
Tel: (270)685-3131; Free: 877-273-7242
Admissions: (270)686-4241
Fax: (270)686-6422
E-mail: admissions@brescia.edu
Web Site: http://www.brescia.edu/
President/CEO: Rev. Larry Hostetter
Admissions: Chris Houk
Financial Aid: Britton Hibbitt
Type: Comprehensive **Sex:** Coed **Affiliation:** Roman Catholic **Scores:** 83% SAT M 400+; 53% ACT 18-23; 27% ACT 24-29 **% Accepted:** 67 **Admission Plans:** Deferred Admission **Application Deadline:** Rolling **Application Fee:** $25.00 **H.S. Requirements:** High school diploma required; GED accepted **Costs Per Year:** Application fee: $25. One-time mandatory fee: $120. Comprehensive fee: $25,390 includes full-time tuition ($16,950), mandatory fees ($440), and college room and board ($8000). Full-time tuition and fees vary according to class time. Room and board charges vary according to board plan and housing facility. Part-time tuition: $495 per credit hour. Part-time tuition varies according to class time. **Scholarships:** Available **Calendar System:** Semester, Summer Session Available **Enrollment:** FT 489, PT 181, Grad FT 21, Grad PT 34 **Faculty:** FT 41, PT 38 **Student-Faculty Ratio:** 11:1 **Exams:** SAT I or ACT. ACT essay not being used. SAT essay not being used. **% Receiving Financial Aid:** 89 **% Residing in College-Owned, -Operated, or -Affiliated Housing:** 41 **Final Year or Final Semester Residency Requirement:** No **Library Holdings:** 161,814 **Regional Accreditation:** Southern Association of Colleges and Schools **Credit Hours For Degree:** 63 credit hours, Associates; 128 credit hours,

Bachelors **Professional Accreditation:** CSWE **Intercollegiate Athletics:** Baseball M; Basketball M & W; Cross-Country Running M & W; Golf M & W; Soccer M & W; Softball W; Track and Field M & W; Volleyball W

BROWN MACKIE COLLEGE—HOPKINSVILLE
4001 Fort Cambell Blvd.
Hopkinsville, KY 42240
Tel: (270)886-1302; Free: 800-359-4753
Fax: (270)886-3544
Web Site: http://www.brownmackie.edu/Hopkinsville/
President/CEO: Lesley Wilbert
Type: Two-Year College **Sex:** Coed **Affiliation:** Education Management Corporation **Calendar System:** Quarter **Professional Accreditation:** ACCSCT, ACICS

BROWN MACKIE COLLEGE—LOUISVILLE
3605 Fern Valley Rd.
Louisville, KY 40219
Tel: (502)968-7191; Free: 800-999-7387
Fax: (502)968-1727
Web Site: http://www.brownmackie.edu/louisville/
President/CEO: Elyane Harney
Type: Two-Year College **Sex:** Coed **Affiliation:** Education Management Corporation **Calendar System:** Quarter **Professional Accreditation:** ACCSCT, ACICS

BROWN MACKIE COLLEGE—NORTHERN KENTUCKY
309 Buttermilk Pike
Fort Mitchell, KY 41017-2191
Tel: (859)341-5627; Free: 800-888-1445
Fax: (859)341-6483
Web Site: http://www.brownmackie.edu/northernkentucky/
President/CEO: Christine Knouff
Type: Two-Year College **Sex:** Coed **Affiliation:** Education Management Corporation **Calendar System:** Quarter **Professional Accreditation:** ACICS

CAMPBELLSVILLE UNIVERSITY
1 University Dr.
Campbellsville, KY 42718-2799
Tel: (270)789-5000; Free: 800-264-6014
Admissions: (270)789-5220
Fax: (270)789-5071
E-mail: admissions@campbellsville.edu
Web Site: http://www.campbellsville.edu/
President/CEO: Dr. Michael V. Carter
Admissions: David Walters
Financial Aid: Aaron Gabehart
Type: Comprehensive **Sex:** Coed **Affiliation:** Kentucky Baptist Convention **Scores:** 89% SAT V 400+; 89% SAT M 400+; 55% ACT 18-23; 20% ACT 24-29 **% Accepted:** 67 **Admission Plans:** Deferred Admission **Application Deadline:** Rolling **Application Fee:** $20.00 **H.S. Requirements:** High school diploma required; GED accepted **Costs Per Year:** Application fee: $20. Comprehensive fee: $26,450 includes full-time tuition ($19,310), mandatory fees ($400), and college room and board ($6740). Room and board charges vary according to housing facility. Part-time tuition: $805 per credit hour. **Scholarships:** Available **Calendar System:** Semester, Summer Session Available **Enrollment:** FT 1,710, PT 1,023, Grad FT 39, Grad PT 406 **Faculty:** FT 115, PT 179 **Student-Faculty Ratio:** 13:1 **Exams:** SAT I or ACT. **% Receiving Financial Aid:** 84 **% Residing in College-Owned, -Operated, or -Affiliated Housing:** 56 **Library Holdings:** 172,000 **Regional Accreditation:** Southern Association of Colleges and Schools **Credit Hours For Degree:** 64 credits, Associates; 128 credits, Bachelors **ROTC:** Army **Professional Accreditation:** CSWE, NASM, NCATE **Intercollegiate Athletics:** Baseball M; Basketball M & W; Bowling M & W; Cheerleading M & W; Cross-Country Running M & W; Football M; Golf M & W; Soccer M & W; Softball W; Swimming and Diving W; Tennis M & W; Track and Field M & W; Volleyball W; Wrestling M

CENTRE COLLEGE
600 West Walnut St.
Danville, KY 40422-1394
Tel: (859)238-5200; Free: 800-423-6236
Admissions: (859)238-5350
Fax: (859)238-5456
E-mail: admission@centre.edu
Web Site: http://www.centre.edu/
President/CEO: Dr. John A. Roush
Admissions: Bob Nesmith
Financial Aid: Elaine Larson
Type: Four-Year College **Sex:** Coed **Affiliation:** Presbyterian Church (U.S.A.) **Scores:** 98.82% SAT V 400+; 100.01% SAT M 400+; 3.69% ACT 18-23; 60.66% ACT 24-29 **% Accepted:** 69 **Admission Plans:** Early Admission; Early Action; Deferred Admission **Application Deadline:** February 1 **Application Fee:** $40.00 **H.S. Requirements:** High school diploma or equivalent not required **Scholarships:** Available **Calendar System:** 4-1-4, Summer Session Not available **Enrollment:** FT 1,216 **Faculty:** FT 103, PT 17 **Student-Faculty Ratio:** 11:1 **Exams:** SAT I or ACT. ACT essay not being used. SAT essay not being used. **% Receiving Financial Aid:** 59 **% Residing in College-Owned, -Operated, or -Affiliated Housing:** 99 **Regional Accreditation:** Southern Association of Colleges and Schools **Credit Hours For Degree:** 111 semester hours, Bachelors **ROTC:** Army, Air Force **Intercollegiate Athletics:** Baseball M; Basketball M & W; Cheerleading W; Cross-Country Running M & W; Field Hockey W; Football M; Golf M & W; Soccer M & W; Softball W; Swimming and Diving M & W; Tennis M & W; Track and Field M & W; Volleyball W

CLEAR CREEK BAPTIST BIBLE COLLEGE
300 Clear Creek Rd.
Pineville, KY 40977-9754
Tel: (606)337-3196
E-mail: bhowell@ccbbc.edu
Web Site: http://www.ccbbc.edu/
President/CEO: Dr. Donnie Fox
Admissions: Billy Howell
Financial Aid: Sam Risner
Type: Four-Year College **Sex:** Coed **Affiliation:** Southern Baptist **Admission Plans:** Open Admission; Deferred Admission **Application Deadline:** July 15 **Application Fee:** $40.00 **H.S. Requirements:** High school diploma or equivalent not required. For bachelor's degree program: High school diploma required; GED accepted **Costs Per Year:** Application fee: $40. Tuition: $8700 full-time. **Scholarships:** Available **Calendar System:** Semester, Summer Session Available **Enrollment:** FT 117, PT 58 **Faculty:** FT 8, PT 8 **Student-Faculty Ratio:** 13:1 **% Receiving Financial Aid:** 78 **Library Holdings:** 38,000 **Regional Accreditation:** Southern Association of Colleges and Schools **Credit Hours For Degree:** 66 semester hours, Associates; 130 semester hours, Bachelors **Professional Accreditation:** ABHE

DAYMAR COLLEGE (BELLEVUE)
119 Fairfield Ave.
Bellevue, KY 41073
Tel: (859)291-0800; Free: 877-258-7796
Web Site: http://www.daymarcollege.edu/
President/CEO: Mark Gabis
Type: Two-Year College **Sex:** Coed **Admission Plans:** Open Admission

DAYMAR COLLEGE (BOWLING GREEN)
2421 Fitzgerald Industrial Dr.
Bowling Green, KY 42101
Tel: (270)843-6750
Fax: (270)843-6976
Web Site: http://www.draughons.edu/
President/CEO: Melva Hale
Admissions: Traci Henderson
Type: Two-Year College **Sex:** Coed **Affiliation:** Draughons Junior College, Inc. **% Accepted:** 100 **Admission Plans:** Open Admission **H.S. Requirements:** High school diploma required; GED accepted **Scholarships:** Available **Calendar System:** Semester **Enrollment:** FT 285, PT 225 **Faculty:** FT 10, PT 14 **Student-Faculty Ratio:** 13:1 **Library Holdings:** 5,000 **Credit Hours For Degree:** 63 credit hours, Associates **Professional Accreditation:** ACICS

DAYMAR COLLEGE (LOUISVILLE)
4400 Breckenridge Ln.
Ste. 415
Louisville, KY 40218
Tel: (502)495-1040

Web Site: http://www.daymarcollege.edu/
President/CEO: Mark A. Gabis
Admissions: Patrick Carney
Type: Two-Year College **Sex:** Coed **Admission Plans:** Open Admission **Calendar System:** Quarter **Professional Accreditation:** ACICS

DAYMAR COLLEGE (OWENSBORO)
3361 Buckland Square
Owensboro, KY 42301
Tel: (270)926-4040; Free: 800-960-4090
Fax: (270)685-4090
E-mail: info@daymarcollege.edu
Web Site: http://www.daymarcollege.edu/
President/CEO: Mark A. Gabis
Admissions: Vickie McDougal
Type: Two-Year College **Sex:** Coed **Admission Plans:** Open Admission; Deferred Admission **Application Deadline:** Rolling **Application Fee:** $150.00 **H.S. Requirements:** High school diploma required; GED accepted **Scholarships:** Available **Calendar System:** Quarter, Summer Session Available **Exams:** Other, SAT I or ACT. **Library Holdings:** 3,215 **Credit Hours For Degree:** 96 quarter hours, Associates **Professional Accreditation:** ACICS

DAYMAR COLLEGE (PADUCAH)
509 South 30th St.
Paducah, KY 42001
Tel: 877-258-7796; Free: 877-258-7796
Admissions: (270)444-9950
Web Site: http://www.daymarcollege.edu/
President/CEO: Mark A. Gabis
Type: Two-Year College **Sex:** Coed **Admission Plans:** Open Admission **Application Fee:** $75.00

DEVRY UNIVERSITY
10172 Linn Station Rd.
Ste. 300
Louisville, KY 40223
Free: (866)906-9388
Web Site: http://www.devry.edu/
President/CEO: Mary Hawkins
Type: Four-Year College **Sex:** Coed **Admission Plans:** Deferred Admission **Application Deadline:** Rolling **Application Fee:** $50.00 **H.S. Requirements:** High school diploma required; GED accepted **Costs Per Year:** Application fee: $50. Tuition: $14,080 full-time, $550 per credit hour part-time. **Scholarships:** Available **Enrollment:** FT 49, PT 40 **Faculty:** FT 0, PT 21 **Student-Faculty Ratio:** 9:1 **Exams:** ACT essay used for admission. SAT essay used for admission. ACT essay used for placement. SAT essay used for placement. **Regional Accreditation:** North Central Association of Colleges and Schools

EASTERN KENTUCKY UNIVERSITY
521 Lancaster Ave.
Richmond, KY 40475-3102
Tel: (859)622-1000
Admissions: (859)622-2106
Fax: (859)622-1020
E-mail: admissions@eku.edu
Web Site: http://www.eku.edu/
President/CEO: Dr. Doug Whitlock
Admissions: Stephen Byrn
Type: Comprehensive **Sex:** Coed **% Accepted:** 69 **Admission Plans:** Open Admission; Deferred Admission **Application Deadline:** August 1 **Application Fee:** $30.00 **H.S. Requirements:** High school diploma required; GED accepted **Costs Per Year:** Application fee: $30. State resident tuition: $6312 full-time, $263 per credit hour part-time. Nonresident tuition: $17,280 full-time, $720 per credit hour part-time. Part-time tuition varies according to course load. College room and board: $6020. College room only: $3074. Room and board charges vary according to board plan and housing facility. **Scholarships:** Available **Calendar System:** Semester, Summer Session Available **Enrollment:** FT 11,025, PT 2,634 **Faculty:** FT 584, PT 455 **Student-Faculty Ratio:** 17:1 **Exams:** SAT I or ACT. **% Receiving Financial Aid:** 63 **Library Holdings:** 799,496 **Regional Accreditation:** Southern Association of Colleges and Schools **Credit Hours For Degree:** 64 semester hours, Associates; 128 semester hours, Bachelors **ROTC:** Army, Air Force **Professional Accreditation:** AACSB, ABET, AACN, AAFCS, AAMAE, ACCE, ACA, ADtA, AHIMA, AOTA, ASC, ASLHA, CSWE, JRCEMT, JRCEPAT, NAACLS, NASM, NASPAA, NCATE, NLN NRPA, NAIT **Intercollegiate Athletics:** Baseball M; Basketball M & W; Cheerleading M & W; Cross-Country Running M & W; Football M; Golf M & W; Softball W; Tennis M & W; Track and Field M & W; Volleyball W

ELIZABETHTOWN COMMUNITY AND TECHNICAL COLLEGE
620 College St. Rd.
Elizabethtown, KY 42701
Tel: (270)769-2371; Free: 877-246-2322
Admissions: (270)706-8800
Fax: (270)769-0736
E-mail: bryan.smith@kctcs.edu
Web Site: http://www.elizabethtown.kctcs.edu/
President/CEO: Dr. Thelma White
Admissions: Bryan Smith
Type: Two-Year College **Sex:** Coed **Affiliation:** Kentucky Community and Technical College System **Application Deadline:** Rolling **H.S. Requirements:** High school diploma required; GED accepted **Calendar System:** Semester, Summer Session Available **Enrollment:** FT 2,441, PT 3,065 **Faculty:** FT 124, PT 163 **Student-Faculty Ratio:** 19:1 **Exams:** ACT. **Regional Accreditation:** Southern Association of Colleges and Schools **Professional Accreditation:** COE

GATEWAY COMMUNITY AND TECHNICAL COLLEGE
1025 Amsterdam Rd.
Covington, KY 41011
Tel: (859)441-4500
Fax: (859)292-6415
E-mail: andre.washington@kctcs.edu
Web Site: http://www.gateway.kctcs.edu/
President/CEO: Dr. G. Edward Hughes
Type: Two-Year College **Sex:** Coed **Affiliation:** Kentucky Community and Technical College System **Admission Plans:** Open Admission; Early Admission **Application Deadline:** Rolling **H.S. Requirements:** High school diploma required; GED accepted **Costs Per Year:** State resident tuition: $3750 full-time, $125 per credit hour part-time. Nonresident tuition: $12,750 full-time, $425 per credit hour part-time. Full-time tuition varies according to course load. Part-time tuition varies according to course load. **Calendar System:** Semester, Summer Session Available **Enrollment:** FT 1,477, PT 2,729 **Faculty:** FT 83, PT 159 **Student-Faculty Ratio:** 18:1 **Exams:** Other. **Regional Accreditation:** Southern Association of Colleges and Schools **Professional Accreditation:** COE

GEORGETOWN COLLEGE
400 East College St.
Georgetown, KY 40324-1696
Tel: (502)863-8000; Free: 800-788-9985
Admissions: (502)863-8015
Fax: (502)868-8891
E-mail: admissions@georgetowncollege.edu
Web Site: http://www.georgetowncollege.edu/
President/CEO: Dr. William H. Crouch, Jr.
Admissions: Garvel Kindrick
Financial Aid: Rhyan Conyers
Type: Comprehensive **Sex:** Coed **Affiliation:** Baptist Church **Scores:** 88% SAT V 400+; 100% SAT M 400+; 50% ACT 18-23; 39% ACT 24-29 **% Accepted:** 79 **Admission Plans:** Deferred Admission **Application Deadline:** August 1 **Application Fee:** $30.00 **H.S. Requirements:** High school diploma required; GED accepted **Costs Per Year:** Application fee: $30. Comprehensive fee: $33,110 includes full-time tuition ($26,080) and college room and board ($7030). College room only: $3390. Full-time tuition varies according to course load. Room and board charges vary according to board plan and housing facility. Part-time tuition: $1080 per credit hour. **Scholarships:** Available **Calendar System:** Semester, Summer Session Available **Enrollment:** FT 1,281, PT 54, Grad FT 27, Grad PT 520 **Faculty:** FT 110, PT 53 **Student-Faculty Ratio:** 11:1 **Exams:** ACT, SAT I or ACT. ACT essay not being used. SAT essay not being used. **% Receiving Financial Aid:** 77 **% Residing in College-Owned, -Operated, or -Affiliated Housing:** 87 **Final Year or Final Semester Residency Requirement:** Yes **Library Holdings:** 180,711 **Regional Accreditation:** Southern Association of Colleges and Schools **Credit Hours For Degree:** 120 semester hours, Bachelors **ROTC:** Army, Air Force **Professional Accreditation:** NCATE **Intercol-**

legiate Athletics: Baseball M; Basketball M & W; Cheerleading W; Cross-Country Running M & W; Football M; Golf M & W; Soccer M & W; Softball W; Tennis M & W; Track and Field M & W; Volleyball W

HAZARD COMMUNITY AND TECHNICAL COLLEGE
1 Community College Dr.
Hazard, KY 41701-2403
Tel: (606)436-5721; Free: 800-246-7521
Fax: (606)439-2988
Web Site: http://www.hazard.kctcs.edu/
President/CEO: Dr. Allen F. Goben
Type: Two-Year College **Sex:** Coed **Affiliation:** Kentucky Community and Technical College System **Scores:** 49% ACT 18-23; 6% ACT 24-29 **Admission Plans:** Open Admission; Early Admission **Application Deadline:** Rolling **Application Fee:** $0.00 **H.S. Requirements:** High school diploma required; GED accepted **Costs Per Year:** Application fee: $0. State resident tuition: $3000 full-time, $125 per credit hour part-time. Nonresident tuition: $10,200 full-time, $425 per credit hour part-time. **Scholarships:** Available **Calendar System:** Semester **Enrollment:** FT 1,806, PT 2,908 **Faculty:** FT 80, PT 90 **Student-Faculty Ratio:** 25:1 **Regional Accreditation:** Southern Association of Colleges and Schools **Credit Hours For Degree:** 60 credit hours, Associates **Professional Accreditation:** APTA, JRCERT, NAACLS

HENDERSON COMMUNITY COLLEGE
2660 South Green St.
Henderson, KY 42420-4623
Tel: (270)827-1867
Web Site: http://www.henderson.kctcs.edu/
President/CEO: Dr. Patrick Lake
Admissions: Teresa Hamiton
Type: Two-Year College **Sex:** Coed **Affiliation:** Kentucky Community and Technical College System **Admission Plans:** Open Admission **Application Deadline:** September 1 **H.S. Requirements:** High school diploma required; GED accepted **Scholarships:** Available **Calendar System:** Semester, Summer Session Available **Library Holdings:** 30,206 **Regional Accreditation:** Southern Association of Colleges and Schools **Credit Hours For Degree:** 60 credit hours, Associates **Professional Accreditation:** ADA, NAACLS, NLN

HOPKINSVILLE COMMUNITY COLLEGE
PO Box 2100
Hopkinsville, KY 42241-2100
Tel: (270)707-3700
Admissions: (270)707-3918
E-mail: janet.level@kctcs.edu
Web Site: http://hopkinsville.kctcs.edu/
President/CEO: Dr. James E. Selbe
Admissions: Janet Level
Type: Two-Year College **Sex:** Coed **Affiliation:** Kentucky Community and Technical College System **Scores:** 50% SAT V 400+; 86% SAT M 400+; 44% ACT 18-23; 11% ACT 24-29 **% Accepted:** 100 **Admission Plans:** Open Admission; Deferred Admission **Application Deadline:** Rolling **Application Fee:** $0.00 **H.S. Requirements:** High school diploma required; GED accepted **Costs Per Year:** Application fee: $0. State resident tuition: $3250 full-time, $125 per credit hour part-time. Nonresident tuition: $11,050 full-time, $425 per credit hour part-time. **Scholarships:** Available **Calendar System:** Semester, Summer Session Available **Enrollment:** FT 1,771, PT 1,982 **Faculty:** FT 65, PT 98 **Student-Faculty Ratio:** 25:1 **Regional Accreditation:** Southern Association of Colleges and Schools **Credit Hours For Degree:** 60 credit hours, Associates **Professional Accreditation:** NLN

ITT TECHNICAL INSTITUTE (LEXINGTON)
2473 Fortune Dr., Ste. 180
Lexington, KY 40509
Tel: (859)246-3300; Free: 800-519-8151
Web Site: http://www.itt-tech.edu/
President/CEO: Jennifer Gripshover
Type: Four-Year College **Sex:** Coed **Affiliation:** ITT Educational Services, Inc.

ITT TECHNICAL INSTITUTE (LOUISVILLE)
9500 Ormsby Station Rd.
Louisville, KY 40223
Tel: (502)327-7424
Web Site: http://www.itt-tech.edu/
President/CEO: David Ritz
Type: Two-Year College **Sex:** Coed **Affiliation:** ITT Educational Services, Inc. **H.S. Requirements:** High school diploma required; GED accepted **Scholarships:** Available **Calendar System:** Quarter, Summer Session Not available **Professional Accreditation:** ACICS

JEFFERSON COMMUNITY AND TECHNICAL COLLEGE
109 East Broadway
Louisville, KY 40202-2005
Tel: (502)213-5333
Admissions: (502)213-4000
Fax: (502)213-2115
Web Site: http://www.jefferson.kctcs.edu/
President/CEO: Dr. Anthony Newberry
Admissions: Melanie Vaughan-Cooke
Type: Two-Year College **Sex:** Coed **Affiliation:** Kentucky Community and Technical College System **Admission Plans:** Open Admission; Early Admission **Application Deadline:** Rolling **Application Fee:** $0.00 **H.S. Requirements:** High school diploma or equivalent not required. For allied health programs: High school diploma required; GED accepted **Scholarships:** Available **Calendar System:** Semester, Summer Session Available **Enrollment:** FT 4,879, PT 10,596 **Faculty:** FT 292, PT 360 **Student-Faculty Ratio:** 19:1 **Library Holdings:** 76,578 **Regional Accreditation:** Southern Association of Colleges and Schools **Credit Hours For Degree:** 60 credits, Associates **ROTC:** Army **Professional Accreditation:** ACF, AOTA, APTA, CARC, NLN

KENTUCKY CHRISTIAN UNIVERSITY
100 Academic Parkway
Grayson, KY 41143-2205
Tel: (606)474-3000; Free: 800-522-3181
Admissions: (606)474-3266
Fax: (606)474-3155
E-mail: kbomer@kcu.edu
Web Site: http://www.kcu.edu/
President/CEO: Dr. Keith P. Keeran
Admissions: Kara Bomer
Financial Aid: Jennie M. Bender
Type: Comprehensive **Sex:** Coed **Affiliation:** Christian Churches and Churches of Christ **Scores:** 65% SAT V 400+; 75% SAT M 400+; 55% ACT 18-23; 14% ACT 24-29 **% Accepted:** 71 **Admission Plans:** Deferred Admission **Application Deadline:** Rolling **Application Fee:** $30.00 **H.S. Requirements:** High school diploma required; GED accepted **Costs Per Year:** Application fee: $30. One-time mandatory fee: $165. Comprehensive fee: $19,888 includes full-time tuition ($13,888), mandatory fees ($200), and college room and board ($5800). Full-time tuition and fees vary according to course load. Room and board charges vary according to housing facility. Part-time tuition: $434 per credit hour. Part-time tuition varies according to course load. **Scholarships:** Available **Calendar System:** Semester, Summer Session Available **Enrollment:** FT 570, PT 60 **Faculty:** FT 34, PT 25 **Student-Faculty Ratio:** 14:1 **Exams:** SAT I or ACT. **% Receiving Financial Aid:** 77 **Library Holdings:** 103,323 **Regional Accreditation:** Southern Association of Colleges and Schools **Credit Hours For Degree:** 66 credit hours, Associates; 132 credit hours, Bachelors **Professional Accreditation:** CSWE **Intercollegiate Athletics:** Basketball M & W; Cheerleading W; Cross-Country Running M & W; Football M; Soccer M & W; Volleyball W

KENTUCKY MOUNTAIN BIBLE COLLEGE
PO Box 10
Vancleve, KY 41385
Tel: (606)693-5000; Free: 800-879-KMBC
Fax: (606)693-7744
E-mail: kmbc@kmbc.edu
Web Site: http://www.kmbc.edu/
President/CEO: Dr. Philip Speas
Admissions: David Lorimer
Financial Aid: Rosita Marshall
Type: Four-Year College **Sex:** Coed **Affiliation:** interdenominational **Application Deadline:** Rolling **Application Fee:** $25.00 **H.S. Requirements:** High school diploma required; GED accepted **Scholarships:** Available **Calendar System:** Semester, Summer Session Not available **Faculty:** FT 0, PT 15 **Student-Faculty Ratio:** 6:1 **Exams:** ACT. **Final Year or Final**

Semester Residency Requirement: No **Credit Hours For Degree:** 65 semester credit, Associates; 130 semester credits, Bachelors **Professional Accreditation:** ABHE

KENTUCKY STATE UNIVERSITY
400 East Main St.
Frankfort, KY 40601
Tel: (502)597-6000; Free: 800-325-1716
Admissions: (502)597-6813
Fax: (502)597-6239
E-mail: james.burrell@kysu.edu
Web Site: http://www.kysu.edu/
President/CEO: Dr. Mary Evans Sias
Admissions: James Burrell
Financial Aid: Myrna C. Bryant
Type: Comprehensive **Sex:** Coed **Scores:** 61% SAT V 400+; 53% SAT M 400+; 37% ACT 18-23; 6% ACT 24-29 **% Accepted:** 24 **Admission Plans:** Early Admission **Application Deadline:** Rolling **Application Fee:** $30.00 **H.S. Requirements:** High school diploma required; GED accepted **Costs Per Year:** Application fee: $30. State resident tuition: $5170 full-time, $172 per credit hour part-time. Nonresident tuition: $13,458 full-time, $449 per credit hour part-time. Mandatory fees: $750 full-time, $25 per credit hour part-time. Part-time tuition and fees vary according to course load. College room and board: $6480. College room only: $3240. Room and board charges vary according to board plan and housing facility. **Scholarships:** Available **Calendar System:** Semester, Summer Session Available **Enrollment:** FT 2,106, PT 532, Grad FT 98, Grad PT 98 **Faculty:** FT 128, PT 52 **Student-Faculty Ratio:** 15:1 **Exams:** SAT I or ACT. ACT essay not being used. SAT essay not being used. **% Receiving Financial Aid:** 76 **% Residing in College-Owned, -Operated, or -Affiliated Housing:** 39 **Library Holdings:** 333,642 **Regional Accreditation:** Southern Association of Colleges and Schools **Credit Hours For Degree:** 64 credit hours, Associates; 128 credit hours, Bachelors **ROTC:** Army, Air Force **Professional Accreditation:** ACBSP, CSWE, NASM, NASPAA, NCATE, NLN **Intercollegiate Athletics:** Baseball M; Basketball M & W; Cheerleading W; Cross-Country Running M & W; Football M; Golf M; Softball W; Track and Field M & W; Volleyball W

KENTUCKY WESLEYAN COLLEGE
3000 Frederica St.
Owensboro, KY 42301
Tel: (270)926-3111; Free: 800-990-0592
Admissions: (270)852-3120
Fax: (270)926-3196
E-mail: admitme@kwc.edu
Web Site: http://www.kwc.edu/
President/CEO: Dr. Cheryl King
Admissions: Scott Kramer
Financial Aid: Samantha Hays
Type: Four-Year College **Sex:** Coed **Affiliation:** Methodist **Scores:** 90% SAT V 400+; 95% SAT M 400+; 57% ACT 18-23; 24% ACT 24-29 **% Accepted:** 67 **Admission Plans:** Early Admission; Deferred Admission **Application Fee:** $0.00 **H.S. Requirements:** High school diploma required; GED accepted **Costs Per Year:** Application fee: $0. Comprehensive fee: $23,310 includes full-time tuition ($16,870) and college room and board ($6440). College room only: $2920. Full-time tuition varies according to course load. Room and board charges vary according to board plan and housing facility. **Scholarships:** Available **Calendar System:** Semester, Summer Session Available **Enrollment:** FT 834, PT 42 **Faculty:** FT 43, PT 44 **Student-Faculty Ratio:** 15:1 **Exams:** SAT I or ACT. **% Receiving Financial Aid:** 83 **% Residing in College-Owned, -Operated, or -Affiliated Housing:** 45 **Final Year or Final Semester Residency Requirement:** Yes **Library Holdings:** 106,000 **Regional Accreditation:** Southern Association of Colleges and Schools **Credit Hours For Degree:** 128 semester hours, Bachelors **ROTC:** Army **Intercollegiate Athletics:** Baseball M; Basketball M & W; Cheerleading M & W; Cross-Country Running M & W; Football M; Golf M & W; Soccer M & W; Softball W; Tennis W; Volleyball W

LINDSEY WILSON COLLEGE
210 Lindsey Wilson St.
Columbia, KY 42728
Tel: (270)384-2126; Free: 800-264-0138
Admissions: (270)384-8100
Fax: (270)384-8200
Web Site: http://www.lindsey.edu/
President/CEO: Dr. William T. Luckey, Jr.
Admissions: Charity Ferguson
Financial Aid: Marilyn D. Radford
Type: Comprehensive **Sex:** Coed **Affiliation:** United Methodist **Scores:** 48.3% ACT 18-23; 14.4% ACT 24-29 **% Accepted:** 78 **Admission Plans:** Open Admission **Application Deadline:** Rolling **Application Fee:** $0.00 **H.S. Requirements:** High school diploma required; GED accepted **Costs Per Year:** Application fee: $0. Comprehensive fee: $26,595 includes full-time tuition ($18,720), mandatory fees ($230), and college room and board ($7645). Part-time tuition: $780 per credit hour. **Scholarships:** Available **Calendar System:** Semester, Summer Session Available **Enrollment:** FT 1,900, PT 92, Grad FT 322, Grad PT 35 **Faculty:** FT 90, PT 88 **Student-Faculty Ratio:** 16:1 **Exams:** SAT I or ACT. **% Receiving Financial Aid:** 91 **% Residing in College-Owned, -Operated, or -Affiliated Housing:** 43 **Library Holdings:** 80,000 **Regional Accreditation:** Southern Association of Colleges and Schools **Credit Hours For Degree:** 64 semester hours, Associates; 128 semester hours, Bachelors **Professional Accreditation:** ACA **Intercollegiate Athletics:** Baseball M; Basketball M & W; Bowling M & W; Cheerleading M & W; Cross-Country Running M & W; Football M & W; Golf M & W; Soccer M & W; Softball W; Swimming and Diving M & W; Tennis M & W; Track and Field M & W; Volleyball W; Wrestling M

MADISONVILLE COMMUNITY COLLEGE
2000 College Dr.
Madisonville, KY 42431-9185
Tel: (270)821-2250
Fax: (270)824-1866
Web Site: http://www.madcc.kctcs.edu/
President/CEO: Dr. Judith Rhoads
Admissions: Jay Parent
Type: Two-Year College **Sex:** Coed **Affiliation:** Kentucky Community and Technical College System **Admission Plans:** Open Admission; Early Admission; Deferred Admission **Application Deadline:** Rolling **Application Fee:** $0.00 **H.S. Requirements:** High school diploma required; GED accepted **Scholarships:** Available **Calendar System:** Semester, Summer Session Available **Faculty:** FT 95, PT 89 **Library Holdings:** 26,793 **Regional Accreditation:** Southern Association of Colleges and Schools **Credit Hours For Degree:** 60 credit hours, Associates **Professional Accreditation:** AOTA, APTA, CARC, NLN

MAYSVILLE COMMUNITY AND TECHNICAL COLLEGE (MAYSVILLE)
1755 US 68
Maysville, KY 41056
Tel: (606)759-7141
E-mail: ccsmayrg@ukcc.uky.edu
Web Site: http://www.maysville.kctcs.edu/
President/CEO: Dr. Edward Story
Admissions: Patee Massie
Type: Two-Year College **Sex:** Coed **Affiliation:** Kentucky Community and Technical College System **Admission Plans:** Open Admission; Early Admission **Application Deadline:** Rolling **Application Fee:** $0.00 **H.S. Requirements:** High school diploma required; GED accepted **Scholarships:** Available **Calendar System:** Semester, Summer Session Available **Library Holdings:** 36,600 **Regional Accreditation:** Southern Association of Colleges and Schools **Credit Hours For Degree:** 60 credit hours, Associates **Professional Accreditation:** CARC

MAYSVILLE COMMUNITY AND TECHNICAL COLLEGE (MOREHEAD)
609 Viking Dr.
Morehead, KY 40351
Tel: (606)783-1538
Admissions: (606)759-7141
Fax: (606)784-9876
Web Site: http://www.maysville.kctcs.edu/
Admissions: Patee Massie
Type: Two-Year College **Sex:** Coed **Calendar System:** Semester **Professional Accreditation:** CARC, COE

MID-CONTINENT UNIVERSITY
99 Powell Rd. East
Mayfield, KY 42066-9007
Tel: (270)247-8521
Fax: (270)247-3115

E-mail: admissions@midcontinent.edu
Web Site: http://www.midcontinent.edu/
President/CEO: Dr. Robert Imhoff
Admissions: Debbie Smith
Financial Aid: Kent Youngblood
Type: Comprehensive **Sex:** Coed **Affiliation:** Southern Baptist **Scores:** 64% ACT 18-23; 13% ACT 24-29 **% Accepted:** 57 **Admission Plans:** Early Admission **Application Deadline:** Rolling **Application Fee:** $20.00 **H.S. Requirements:** High school diploma required; GED accepted **Costs Per Year:** Application fee: $20. Comprehensive fee: $20,200 includes full-time tuition ($12,450), mandatory fees ($1250), and college room and board ($6500). Full-time tuition and fees vary according to course load and program. Room and board charges vary according to board plan and housing facility. Part-time tuition: $415 per credit hour. Part-time tuition varies according to course load and program. **Scholarships:** Available **Calendar System:** Semester, Summer Session Available **Enrollment:** FT 1,576, PT 247 **Faculty:** FT 33, PT 113 **Student-Faculty Ratio:** 16:1 **Exams:** SAT I or ACT. **% Receiving Financial Aid:** 95 **% Residing in College-Owned, -Operated, or -Affiliated Housing:** 5 **Final Year or Final Semester Residency Requirement:** No **Library Holdings:** 35,893 **Regional Accreditation:** Southern Association of Colleges and Schools **Credit Hours For Degree:** 60 semester hours, Associates; 128 semester hours, Bachelors **Intercollegiate Athletics:** Baseball M; Basketball M & W; Soccer M; Softball W; Volleyball W

MIDWAY COLLEGE
512 East Stephens St.
Midway, KY 40347-1120
Tel: (859)846-4421; Free: 800-755-0031
Admissions: (859)846-5799
Fax: (859)846-5823
Web Site: http://www.midway.edu/
President/CEO: Dr. William B. Drake, Jr.
Admissions: Dr. Jim Wombles
Financial Aid: Katie Conrad
Type: Comprehensive **Sex:** Coed **Affiliation:** Christian Church (Disciples of Christ) **Scores:** 90% SAT V 400+; 83% SAT M 400+; 52% ACT 18-23; 18% ACT 24-29 **% Accepted:** 71 **Admission Plans:** Early Admission; Deferred Admission **Application Deadline:** Rolling **Application Fee:** $25.00 **H.S. Requirements:** High school diploma required; GED accepted **Costs Per Year:** Application fee: $25. Comprehensive fee: $24,940 includes full-time tuition ($18,000) and college room and board ($6940). Full-time tuition varies according to class time, location, and program. Room and board charges vary according to housing facility. Part-time tuition: $600 per semester hour. Part-time mandatory fees: $150 per year. Part-time tuition and fees vary according to class time, location, and program. **Scholarships:** Available **Calendar System:** Semester, Summer Session Available **Faculty:** FT 53, PT 61 **Student-Faculty Ratio:** 15:1 **Exams:** SAT I or ACT. **% Receiving Financial Aid:** 81 **% Residing in College-Owned, -Operated, or -Affiliated Housing:** 14 **Library Holdings:** 96,236 **Regional Accreditation:** Southern Association of Colleges and Schools **Credit Hours For Degree:** 65 semester hours, Associates; 130 semester hours, Bachelors **ROTC:** Army **Professional Accreditation:** NLN **Intercollegiate Athletics:** Basketball W; Equestrian Sports W; Soccer W; Softball W; Tennis W; Track and Field W; Volleyball W

MOREHEAD STATE UNIVERSITY
University Blvd.
Morehead, KY 40351
Tel: (606)783-2221; Free: 800-585-6781
Admissions: (606)783-2000
Fax: (606)783-5038
E-mail: admissions@moreheadstate.edu
Web Site: http://www.moreheadstate.edu/
President/CEO: Dr. Wayne Andrews
Admissions: Jeffrey Liles
Financial Aid: Donna King
Type: Comprehensive **Sex:** Coed **Scores:** 94% SAT V 400+; 98% SAT M 400+; 61% ACT 18-23; 25% ACT 24-29 **% Accepted:** 80 **Admission Plans:** Early Admission; Deferred Admission **Application Deadline:** Rolling **Application Fee:** $30.00 **H.S. Requirements:** High school diploma required; GED accepted **Costs Per Year:** Application fee: $30. State resident tuition: $6036 full-time, $234 per credit hour part-time. Nonresident tuition: $15,096 full-time, $585 per credit hour part-time. Full-time tuition varies according to course load and reciprocity agreements. College room and board: $6192. Room and board charges vary according to board plan and housing facility. **Scholarships:** Available **Calendar System:** Semester, Summer Session Available **Enrollment:** FT 5,586, PT 1,964, Grad FT 289, Grad PT 1,207 **Faculty:** FT 371, PT 96 **Student-Faculty Ratio:** 17:1 **Exams:** ACT, SAT I or ACT. ACT essay not being used. SAT essay not being used. **% Receiving Financial Aid:** 70 **% Residing in College-Owned, -Operated, or -Affiliated Housing:** 33 **Library Holdings:** 537,675 **Regional Accreditation:** Southern Association of Colleges and Schools **Credit Hours For Degree:** 64 credit hours, Associates; 128 credit hours, Bachelors **ROTC:** Army **Professional Accreditation:** AACSB, AAFCS, ADtA, ACBSP, CARC, CSWE, JRCERT, NASM, NCATE, NLN, NAIT **Intercollegiate Athletics:** Baseball M; Basketball M & W; Bowling M & W; Cross-Country Running M & W; Equestrian Sports M & W; Football M; Golf M; Riflery M & W; Soccer W; Softball W; Tennis M & W; Track and Field M & W; Volleyball W

MURRAY STATE UNIVERSITY
113 Sparks Hall
Murray, KY 42071
Tel: (270)762-3011; Free: 800-272-4678
Admissions: (270)809-3035
Fax: (270)762-3413
E-mail: admissions@murraystate.edu
Web Site: http://www.murraystate.edu/
President/CEO: Dr. Randy Dunn
Admissions: Stacy Bell
Financial Aid: Lori Mitchum
Type: Comprehensive **Sex:** Coed **Affiliation:** Kentucky Council on Post Secondary Education **Scores:** 55% ACT 18-23; 37% ACT 24-29 **% Accepted:** 73 **Application Fee:** $30.00 **H.S. Requirements:** High school diploma required; GED accepted **Costs Per Year:** Application fee: $30. State resident tuition: $5130 full-time, $214 per credit hour part-time. Nonresident tuition: $8006 full-time, $301 per credit hour part-time. Mandatory fees: $846 full-time, $35 per credit hour part-time. Full-time tuition and fees vary according to reciprocity agreements. Part-time tuition and fees vary according to reciprocity agreements. College room and board: $6562. College room only: $3590. Room and board charges vary according to board plan and housing facility. **Scholarships:** Available **Calendar System:** Semester, Summer Session Available **Enrollment:** FT 6,816, PT 1,426, Grad FT 656, Grad PT 1,173 **Faculty:** FT 406, PT 161 **Student-Faculty Ratio:** 16:1 **Exams:** ACT. **% Receiving Financial Aid:** 56 **% Residing in College-Owned, -Operated, or -Affiliated Housing:** 36 **Library Holdings:** 933,635 **Regional Accreditation:** Southern Association of Colleges and Schools **Credit Hours For Degree:** 64 credit hours, Associates; 120 credit hours, Bachelors **ROTC:** Army **Professional Accreditation:** AACSB, ABET, ACEJMC, AACN, AAFCS, AANA, ACA, ADtA, AOTA, ASLHA, CSWE, NASAD, NASM, NCATE, NLN **Intercollegiate Athletics:** Baseball M; Basketball M & W; Bowling M & W; Cheerleading M & W; Crew M & W; Cross-Country Running M & W; Equestrian Sports M & W; Football M; Golf M & W; Riflery M & W; Soccer W; Softball W; Tennis M & W; Track and Field M & W; Volleyball W

NATIONAL COLLEGE (DANVILLE)
115 East Lexington Ave.
Danville, KY 40422
Tel: (859)236-6991; Free: 800-664-1886
Web Site: http://www.national-college.edu/
Admissions: James McGuire
Type: Two-Year College **Sex:** Coed **Affiliation:** National College of Business and Technology **Admission Plans:** Open Admission **Application Deadline:** Rolling **H.S. Requirements:** High school diploma required; GED accepted **Scholarships:** Available **Calendar System:** Quarter, Summer Session Available **Credit Hours For Degree:** 96 credit hours, Associates **Professional Accreditation:** ACICS, AAMAE

NATIONAL COLLEGE (FLORENCE)
7627 Ewing Blvd.
Florence, KY 41042
Tel: (859)525-6510; Free: 800-664-1886
Fax: (859)525-8961
Web Site: http://www.national-college.edu/
Admissions: Terry Kovacs
Type: Two-Year College **Sex:** Coed **Affiliation:** National College of Business and Technology **Admission Plans:** Open Admission **Application**

Deadline: Rolling **H.S. Requirements:** High school diploma required; GED accepted **Scholarships:** Available **Calendar System:** Quarter, Summer Session Available **Credit Hours For Degree:** 96 credit hours, Associates **Professional Accreditation:** ACICS, AAMAE

NATIONAL COLLEGE (LEXINGTON)
2376 Sir Barton Way
Lexington, KY 40509
Tel: (859)253-0621; Free: 800-664-1886
Web Site: http://www.national-college.edu/
President/CEO: Frank Longaker
Admissions: Kim Thomasson
Type: Two-Year College **Sex:** Coed **Affiliation:** National College of Business and Technology **Admission Plans:** Open Admission **Application Deadline:** Rolling **H.S. Requirements:** High school diploma required; GED accepted **Scholarships:** Available **Calendar System:** Quarter, Summer Session Available **Credit Hours For Degree:** 96 credit hours, Associates **Professional Accreditation:** ACICS, AAMAE

NATIONAL COLLEGE (LOUISVILLE)
3950 Dixie Hwy.
Louisville, KY 40216
Tel: (502)447-7634; Free: 800-664-1886
Web Site: http://www.national-college.edu/
Admissions: Vincent C. Tinebra
Type: Two-Year College **Sex:** Coed **Affiliation:** National College of Business and Technology **Admission Plans:** Open Admission **Application Deadline:** Rolling **H.S. Requirements:** High school diploma required; GED accepted **Scholarships:** Available **Calendar System:** Quarter, Summer Session Available **Credit Hours For Degree:** 96 credit hours, Associates **Professional Accreditation:** ACICS, AAMAE, AHIMA

NATIONAL COLLEGE (PIKEVILLE)
288 South Mayo Trail, Ste. 2
Pikeville, KY 41501
Tel: (606)432-5477; Free: 800-664-1886
Admissions: (606)478-7200
Fax: (606)437-4952
Web Site: http://www.national-college.edu/
Admissions: Tammy Riley
Type: Two-Year College **Sex:** Coed **Affiliation:** National College of Business and Technology **Admission Plans:** Open Admission **Application Deadline:** Rolling **H.S. Requirements:** High school diploma required; GED accepted **Scholarships:** Available **Calendar System:** Quarter, Summer Session Available **Credit Hours For Degree:** 96 credit hours, Associates **Professional Accreditation:** ACICS, AAMAE

NATIONAL COLLEGE (RICHMOND)
139 South Killarney Ln.
Richmond, KY 40475
Tel: (859)623-8956; Free: 800-664-1886
Fax: (859)624-5544
Web Site: http://www.national-college.edu/
Admissions: Keeley Gadd
Type: Two-Year College **Sex:** Coed **Affiliation:** National College of Business and Technology **Admission Plans:** Open Admission **Application Deadline:** Rolling **H.S. Requirements:** High school diploma required; GED accepted **Scholarships:** Available **Calendar System:** Quarter, Summer Session Available **Credit Hours For Degree:** 96 credit hours, Associates **Professional Accreditation:** ACICS, AAMAE

NORTHERN KENTUCKY UNIVERSITY
Louie B Nunn Dr.
Highland Heights, KY 41099
Tel: (859)572-5100; Free: 800-637-9948
Admissions: (859)572-5220
E-mail: admitnku@nku.edu
Web Site: http://www.nku.edu/
President/CEO: Dr. James C. Votruba
Admissions: Melissa Gorbandt
Financial Aid: Leah Stewart
Type: Comprehensive **Sex:** Coed **Scores:** 87.73% SAT V 400+; 87.19% SAT M 400+; 61.63% ACT 18-23; 24.47% ACT 24-29 **% Accepted:** 69 **Admission Plans:** Early Admission; Early Action; Deferred Admission **Application Deadline:** August 1 **Application Fee:** $40.00 **H.S. Requirements:** High school diploma required; GED accepted **Costs Per Year:** Application fee: $40. State resident tuition: $6792 full-time, $283 per credit hour part-time. Nonresident tuition: $12,792 full-time, $533 per credit hour part-time. Full-time tuition varies according to course load and reciprocity agreements. Part-time tuition varies according to course load and reciprocity agreements. **Scholarships:** Available **Calendar System:** Semester, Summer Session Available **Enrollment:** FT 9,948, PT 3,225, Grad FT 571, Grad PT 1,628 **Faculty:** FT 536, PT 615 **Student-Faculty Ratio:** 17:1 **Exams:** SAT I or ACT. ACT essay used for admission. SAT essay used for admission. ACT essay used for advising. SAT essay used for advising. ACT essay used for placement. SAT essay used for placement. **% Receiving Financial Aid:** 53 **% Residing in College-Owned, -Operated, or -Affiliated Housing:** 14 **Final Year or Final Semester Residency Requirement:** No **Library Holdings:** 871,092 **Regional Accreditation:** Southern Association of Colleges and Schools **Credit Hours For Degree:** 60 semester hours, Associates; 120 semester hours, Bachelors **ROTC:** Army, Air Force **Professional Accreditation:** AACSB, ABET, ABA, ACCE, AALS, CARC, CSWE, JRCERT, NASM, NASPAA, NCATE, NLN **Intercollegiate Athletics:** Baseball M; Basketball M & W; Cheerleading M & W; Cross-Country Running M & W; Golf M & W; Soccer M & W; Softball W; Tennis M & W; Volleyball W

OWENSBORO COMMUNITY AND TECHNICAL COLLEGE
4800 New Hartford Rd.
Owensboro, KY 42303-1899
Tel: (270)686-4400; Free: (866)755-6282
Admissions: (270)686-4530
Fax: (270)686-4496
E-mail: barb.tipmore@kctcs.edu
Web Site: http://www.octc.kctcs.edu/
President/CEO: Dr. Larry Durrence
Admissions: Barbara Tipmore
Financial Aid: Bernice T. Ayer
Type: Two-Year College **Sex:** Coed **Affiliation:** Kentucky Community and Technical College System **Admission Plans:** Open Admission **Application Deadline:** Rolling **Application Fee:** $0.00 **H.S. Requirements:** High school diploma required; GED accepted **Costs Per Year:** Application fee: $0. State resident tuition: $3750 full-time, $125 per credit hour part-time. Nonresident tuition: $12,750 full-time, $425 per credit hour part-time. Full-time tuition varies according to location and reciprocity agreements. Part-time tuition varies according to location and reciprocity agreements. **Scholarships:** Available **Calendar System:** Semester **Enrollment:** FT 2,136, PT 4,192 **Faculty:** FT 104, PT 103 **Student-Faculty Ratio:** 26:1 **Exams:** SAT I or ACT. **Library Holdings:** 25,600 **Regional Accreditation:** Southern Association of Colleges and Schools **Credit Hours For Degree:** 60 semester hours, Associates **Professional Accreditation:** COE, JRCERT

PIKEVILLE COLLEGE
147 Sycamore St.
Pikeville, KY 41501
Tel: (606)218-5250; Free: (866)232-7700
Admissions: (606)218-5251
Fax: (606)218-5269
E-mail: wewantyou@pc.edu
Web Site: http://www.pc.edu/
President/CEO: Hon. Paul E. Patton
Admissions: Amanda Slone
Financial Aid: Judy Vance Bradley
Type: Comprehensive **Sex:** Coed **Affiliation:** Presbyterian Church (U.S.A.) **Scores:** 55% ACT 18-23; 16% ACT 24-29 **% Accepted:** 100 **Admission Plans:** Open Admission; Deferred Admission **Application Deadline:** August 15 **Application Fee:** $0.00 **H.S. Requirements:** High school diploma required; GED accepted. For some part-time and nontraditional students: High school diploma or equivalent not required **Costs Per Year:** Application fee: $0. Comprehensive fee: $20,535 includes full-time tuition ($14,535) and college room and board ($6000). Full-time tuition varies according to course load. Part-time tuition: $606 per credit hour. **Scholarships:** Available **Calendar System:** Semester, Summer Session Available **Enrollment:** FT 624, PT 81, Grad FT 300 **Faculty:** FT 53, PT 17 **Student-Faculty Ratio:** 11:1 **% Receiving Financial Aid:** 93 **% Residing in College-Owned, -Operated, or -Affiliated Housing:** 44 **Final Year or Final Semester Residency Requirement:** Yes **Library Holdings:** 72,673 **Regional Accreditation:** Southern Association of Colleges and Schools **Credit Hours For Degree:** 64 semester hours, Associates; 128 semester hours, Bachelors

ROTC: Army **Professional Accreditation:** AOsA, NAACLS **Intercollegiate Athletics:** Baseball M; Basketball M & W; Bowling M & W; Cheerleading M & W; Cross-Country Running M & W; Football M; Golf M & W; Soccer M & W; Softball W; Tennis M & W; Volleyball W

ST. CATHARINE COLLEGE
2735 Bardstown Rd.
St. Catharine, KY 40061-9499
Tel: (859)336-5082
Fax: (859)336-5031
Web Site: http://www.sccky.edu/
President/CEO: William D. Huston
Admissions: Amy C. Carrico
Type: Two-Year College **Sex:** Coed **Affiliation:** Roman Catholic **% Accepted:** 45 **Admission Plans:** Early Admission **Application Deadline:** Rolling **Application Fee:** $15.00 **H.S. Requirements:** High school diploma required; GED accepted **Scholarships:** Available **Calendar System:** Semester, Summer Session Available **Faculty:** FT 35, PT 14 **Student-Faculty Ratio:** 15:1 **% Residing in College-Owned, -Operated, or -Affiliated Housing:** 19 **Library Holdings:** 25,000 **Regional Accreditation:** Southern Association of Colleges and Schools **Credit Hours For Degree:** 66 semester hours, Associates **Intercollegiate Athletics:** Baseball M; Basketball M & W; Softball W

SOMERSET COMMUNITY COLLEGE
808 Monticello St.
Somerset, KY 42501-2973
Tel: (606)679-8501
Admissions: (606)451-6630
E-mail: somerset-admissions@kctcs.edu
Web Site: http://www.somerset.kctcs.edu/
President/CEO: Dr. Jo Marshall
Financial Aid: Shawn Renee Anderson
Type: Two-Year College **Sex:** Coed **Affiliation:** Kentucky Community and Technical College System **Admission Plans:** Open Admission; Early Admission **Application Deadline:** August 14 **Application Fee:** $0.00 **H.S. Requirements:** High school diploma required; GED accepted **Scholarships:** Available **Calendar System:** Semester, Summer Session Available **Student-Faculty Ratio:** 23:1 **Regional Accreditation:** Southern Association of Colleges and Schools **Credit Hours For Degree:** 60 credit hours, Associates **Professional Accreditation:** APTA, COE, NAACLS, NLN

SOUTHEAST KENTUCKY COMMUNITY AND TECHNICAL COLLEGE
700 College Rd.
Cumberland, KY 40823-1099
Tel: (606)589-2145; Free: 888-274-SECC
Fax: (606)589-5423
E-mail: cookie.baldwin@kctcs.edu
Web Site: http://www.soucc.kctcs.net/
President/CEO: Dr. W. Bruce Ayers
Admissions: Cookie Baldwin
Type: Two-Year College **Sex:** Coed **Affiliation:** Kentucky Community and Technical College System **Scores:** 45% ACT 18-23; 10% ACT 24-29 **% Accepted:** 98 **Admission Plans:** Open Admission **Application Deadline:** August 20 **Application Fee:** $0.00 **H.S. Requirements:** High school diploma required; GED accepted **Costs Per Year:** Application fee: $0. State resident tuition: $3900 full-time, $130 per credit hour part-time. Nonresident tuition: $13,000 full-time, $430 per credit hour part-time. Mandatory fees: $144 full-time. Full-time tuition and fees vary according to reciprocity agreements. Part-time tuition varies according to reciprocity agreements. **Scholarships:** Available **Calendar System:** Semester, Summer Session Available **Enrollment:** FT 1,943, PT 3,016 **Faculty:** FT 106, PT 108 **Student-Faculty Ratio:** 19:1 **Exams:** ACT. **Library Holdings:** 25,921 **Regional Accreditation:** Southern Association of Colleges and Schools **Credit Hours For Degree:** 60 credit hours, Associates **Professional Accreditation:** APTA, CARC, NAACLS, NLN

SOUTHERN BAPTIST THEOLOGICAL SEMINARY
2825 Lexington Rd.
Louisville, KY 40280-0004
Tel: (502)897-4011
Web Site: http://www.sbts.edu/
President/CEO: Dr. R. Albert Mohler, Jr.
Admissions: Dr. Scott Davis
Financial Aid: Erin Joiner
Type: Comprehensive **Sex:** Coed **Affiliation:** Southern Baptist **% Accepted:** 71 **Admission Plans:** Open Admission **Application Deadline:** July 15 **Application Fee:** $35.00 **H.S. Requirements:** High school diploma required; GED accepted **Scholarships:** Available **Enrollment:** FT 412, PT 256 **Exams:** SAT I or ACT. **% Receiving Financial Aid:** 18 **Regional Accreditation:** Southern Association of Colleges and Schools **Professional Accreditation:** ACIPE, ATS, NASM **Intercollegiate Athletics:** Basketball M

SOUTHWESTERN COLLEGE OF BUSINESS
8095 Connector Dr.
Florence, KY 41042
Tel: (859)282-9999
Web Site: http://www.swcollege.net/
President/CEO: Peter Martinello
Type: Two-Year College **Sex:** Coed **Application Fee:** $20.00 **Scholarships:** Available **Calendar System:** Quarter **Student-Faculty Ratio:** 19:1 **Professional Accreditation:** ACICS

SPALDING UNIVERSITY
845 South Third St.
Louisville, KY 40203-2188
Tel: (502)585-9911; Free: 800-896-8941
Fax: (502)585-7158
E-mail: admissions@spalding.edu
Web Site: http://www.spalding.edu/
President/CEO: Dr. Jo Ann Rooney
Admissions: Matt Elder
Type: Comprehensive **Sex:** Coed **Affiliation:** Roman Catholic Church **Scores:** 75% SAT V 400+; 75% SAT M 400+ **% Accepted:** 49 **Admission Plans:** Deferred Admission **Application Deadline:** Rolling **Application Fee:** $20.00 **H.S. Requirements:** High school diploma required; GED accepted **Scholarships:** Available **Calendar System:** Miscellaneous, Summer Session Available **Enrollment:** FT 841, PT 339, Grad FT 590, Grad PT 299 **Faculty:** FT 88, PT 222 **Student-Faculty Ratio:** 17:1 **Exams:** SAT I or ACT. ACT essay not being used. SAT essay not being used. **% Residing in College-Owned, -Operated, or -Affiliated Housing:** 11 **Final Year or Final Semester Residency Requirement:** Yes **Library Holdings:** 109,292 **Regional Accreditation:** Southern Association of Colleges and Schools **Credit Hours For Degree:** 64 semester hours, Associates; 125 semester hours, Bachelors **ROTC:** Army, Air Force **Professional Accreditation:** AACN, AOTA, APA, CSWE, NCATE, NLN **Intercollegiate Athletics:** Baseball M; Basketball M & W; Bowling W; Cross-Country Running M & W; Golf M & W; Soccer M & W; Softball W; Volleyball W

SPENCERIAN COLLEGE
4627 Dixie Hwy.
Louisville, KY 40216
Tel: (502)447-1000; Free: 800-264-1799
Fax: (502)447-4574
E-mail: kbelanger@spencerian.edu
Web Site: http://www.spencerian.edu/
President/CEO: Jan Gordon
Admissions: Kathleen Belanger
Type: Two-Year College **Sex:** Coed **Affiliation:** The Sullivan University System **Admission Plans:** Open Admission **Application Fee:** $100.00 **H.S. Requirements:** High school diploma required; GED accepted **Costs Per Year:** Application fee: $100. Tuition: $14,580 full-time, $245 per credit hour part-time. Mandatory fees: $2070 full-time, $50 per course part-time. Full-time tuition and fees vary according to program. Part-time tuition and fees vary according to program. College room only: $4950. Tuition guaranteed not to increase for student's term of enrollment. **Scholarships:** Available **Calendar System:** Quarter, Summer Session Available **Enrollment:** FT 939, PT 343 **Faculty:** FT 49, PT 81 **Student-Faculty Ratio:** 13:1 **Final Year or Final Semester Residency Requirement:** Yes **Library Holdings:** 1,650 **Credit Hours For Degree:** 90 credits, Associates **Professional Accreditation:** ACICS

SPENCERIAN COLLEGE—LEXINGTON
1575 Winchester Rd.
Lexington, KY 40505
Tel: (859)223-9608
Fax: (859)224-7744
E-mail: dprofita@spencerian.edu

Web Site: http://www.spencerian.edu/
President/CEO: Buddy Hoskinson
Admissions: David Profita
Financial Aid: Shauna West
Type: Two-Year College **Sex:** Coed **Affiliation:** Sullivan Colleges System **Application Deadline:** Rolling **Application Fee:** $90.00 **H.S. Requirements:** High school diploma required; GED accepted **Costs Per Year:** Application fee: $90. Tuition: $15,500 full-time, $287.50 per credit hour part-time. Mandatory fees: $1600 full-time. Full-time tuition and fees vary according to class time, course load, program, and student level. Part-time tuition varies according to class time, course load, program, and student level. College room only: $4950. **Scholarships:** Available **Calendar System:** Quarter, Summer Session Available **Enrollment:** FT 453, PT 203 **Faculty:** FT 24, PT 20 **Student-Faculty Ratio:** 11:1 **Exams:** Other. **Library Holdings:** 450 **Credit Hours For Degree:** 96 credit hours, Associates **Professional Accreditation:** ACICS

STRAYER UNIVERSITY - FLORENCE CAMPUS
7300 Turfway Rd.
Ste. 250
Florence, KY 41042
Tel: (859)692-2800
Fax: (859)282-8078
Web Site: http://strayer.edu/florence
Type: Comprehensive **Sex:** Coed **Application Fee:** $50.00 **Costs Per Year:** Application fee: $50. **Regional Accreditation:** Middle State Association of Colleges and Schools

STRAYER UNIVERSITY - LEXINGTON CAMPUS
220 Lexington Green Circle
Ste. 550
Lexington, KY 40503
Tel: (859)971-4400
Fax: (859)971-4430
Web Site: http://www.strayer.edu/lexington/
Type: Comprehensive **Sex:** Coed **Application Fee:** $50.00 **Costs Per Year:** Application fee: $50. **Regional Accreditation:** Middle State Association of Colleges and Schools

STRAYER UNIVERSITY - LOUISVILLE CAMPUS
2650 Eastpoint Parkway
Ste. 100
Louisville, KY 40223
Tel: (502)253-5000
Fax: (502)253-5030
Web Site: http://www.strayer.edu/louisville/
Type: Comprehensive **Sex:** Coed **Application Fee:** $50.00 **Costs Per Year:** Application fee: $50. **Regional Accreditation:** Middle State Association of Colleges and Schools

SULLIVAN COLLEGE OF TECHNOLOGY AND DESIGN
3901 Atkinson Square Dr.
Louisville, KY 40218-4528
Tel: (502)456-6509; Free: 800-884-6528
Fax: (502)456-2341
E-mail: achauhdri@sctd.edu
Web Site: http://www.louisvilletech.com/
President/CEO: David Winkler
Admissions: Aamer Z. Chauhdri
Type: Two-Year College **Sex:** Coed **Affiliation:** The Sullivan University System, Inc. **Admission Plans:** Deferred Admission **Application Deadline:** Rolling **Application Fee:** $100.00 **H.S. Requirements:** High school diploma required; GED accepted **Costs Per Year:** Application fee: $100. One-time mandatory fee: $100. Tuition: $15,570 full-time, $395 per credit hour part-time. Mandatory fees: $540 full-time, $50 per course part-time. Full-time tuition and fees vary according to course load and program. Part-time tuition and fees vary according to course load and program. College room only: $4950. Tuition guaranteed not to increase for student's term of enrollment. **Scholarships:** Available **Calendar System:** Quarter, Summer Session Available **Enrollment:** FT 413, PT 249 **Faculty:** FT 31, PT 41 **Student-Faculty Ratio:** 14:1 **Exams:** Other, SAT I or ACT. **Final Year or Final Semester Residency Requirement:** No **Library Holdings:** 2,332 **Credit Hours For Degree:** 103 quarter hours, Associates; 184 quarter hours, Bachelors **Professional Accreditation:** ACICS

SULLIVAN UNIVERSITY
3101 Bardstown Rd.
Louisville, KY 40205
Tel: (502)456-6504; Free: 800-844-1354
Admissions: (502)456-6505
Fax: (502)456-0040
E-mail: admissions@sullivan.edu
Web Site: http://www.sullivan.edu/
President/CEO: Glenn D. Sullivan
Admissions: Terri Thomas
Financial Aid: Charlene Geiser
Type: Comprehensive **Sex:** Coed **Affiliation:** Sullivan University System **Application Deadline:** Rolling **Application Fee:** $100.00 **H.S. Requirements:** High school diploma required; GED accepted **Scholarships:** Available **Calendar System:** Quarter, Summer Session Available **Enrollment:** FT 3,562, PT 639 **Faculty:** FT 116, PT 153 **Student-Faculty Ratio:** 20:1 **Exams:** Other. **% Receiving Financial Aid:** 71 **% Residing in College-Owned, -Operated, or -Affiliated Housing:** 9 **Library Holdings:** 22,500 **Regional Accreditation:** Southern Association of Colleges and Schools **Credit Hours For Degree:** 95 quarter hours, Associates; 180 quarter hours, Bachelors **Professional Accreditation:** AAMAE, ACF

THOMAS MORE COLLEGE
333 Thomas More Parkway
Crestview Hills, KY 41017-3495
Tel: (859)341-5800; Free: 800-825-4557
Admissions: (859)344-3332
Fax: (859)344-3638
E-mail: admissions@thomasmore.edu
Web Site: http://www.thomasmore.edu/
President/CEO: Sr. Margaret Stallmeyer, CDP
Admissions: Billy Sarge
Financial Aid: Mary Givhan
Type: Comprehensive **Sex:** Coed **Affiliation:** Roman Catholic **Scores:** 92% SAT V 400+; 91% SAT M 400+; 63% ACT 18-23; 31% ACT 24-29 **% Accepted:** 93 **Admission Plans:** Deferred Admission **Application Deadline:** August 1 **Application Fee:** $25.00 **H.S. Requirements:** High school diploma required; GED accepted **Costs Per Year:** Application fee: $25. Comprehensive fee: $31,250 includes full-time tuition ($24,000), mandatory fees ($720), and college room and board ($6530). College room only: $3200. Full-time tuition and fees vary according to program and student level. Room and board charges vary according to board plan and housing facility. Part-time tuition: $545 per credit hour. Part-time mandatory fees: $30 per credit hour, $15 per term. Part-time tuition and fees vary according to course load and program. **Scholarships:** Available **Calendar System:** Semester, Summer Session Available **Enrollment:** FT 1,327, PT 384, Grad FT 117, Grad PT 30 **Faculty:** FT 75, PT 58 **Student-Faculty Ratio:** 18:1 **Exams:** SAT I or ACT. **% Receiving Financial Aid:** 70 **% Residing in College-Owned, -Operated, or -Affiliated Housing:** 21 **Final Year or Final Semester Residency Requirement:** Yes **Library Holdings:** 110,565 **Regional Accreditation:** Southern Association of Colleges and Schools **Credit Hours For Degree:** 64 credit hours, Associates; 128 credit hours, Bachelors **ROTC:** Army, Air Force **Professional Accreditation:** NLN **Intercollegiate Athletics:** Baseball M; Basketball M & W; Cross-Country Running M & W; Football M; Golf M & W; Soccer M & W; Softball W; Tennis M & W; Volleyball W

TRANSYLVANIA UNIVERSITY
300 North Broadway
Lexington, KY 40508-1797
Tel: (859)233-8300; Free: 800-872-6798
Admissions: (859)233-4242
Fax: (859)233-8797
E-mail: admissions@transy.edu
Web Site: http://www.transy.edu/
President/CEO: Dr. Charles L. Shearer
Admissions: Bradley Goan
Financial Aid: Dave Cecil
Type: Four-Year College **Sex:** Coed **Affiliation:** Christian Church (Disciples of Christ) **Scores:** 99% SAT V 400+; 100% SAT M 400+; 24% ACT 18-23; 52% ACT 24-29 **% Accepted:** 80 **Admission Plans:** Early Admission; Early Action; Deferred Admission **Application Deadline:** February 1 **Application Fee:** $30.00 **H.S. Requirements:** High school diploma required; GED accepted **Costs Per Year:** Application fee: $30. Comprehensive fee: $33,050

includes full-time tuition ($24,250), mandatory fees ($1030), and college room and board ($7770). Room and board charges vary according to board plan and location. Part-time tuition: $2805 per course. Part-time tuition varies according to course load. **Scholarships:** Available **Calendar System:** Miscellaneous, Summer Session Available **Enrollment:** FT 1,086, PT 6 **Faculty:** FT 86, PT 10 **Student-Faculty Ratio:** 13:1 **Exams:** SAT I or ACT. **% Receiving Financial Aid:** 65 **% Residing in College-Owned, -Operated, or -Affiliated Housing:** 76 **Final Year or Final Semester Residency Requirement:** Yes **Library Holdings:** 137,000 **Regional Accreditation:** Southern Association of Colleges and Schools **Credit Hours For Degree:** 36 units, Bachelors **ROTC:** Army, Air Force **Professional Accreditation:** NCATE **Intercollegiate Athletics:** Baseball M; Basketball M & W; Cheerleading M & W; Cross-Country Running M & W; Field Hockey W; Golf M & W; Soccer M & W; Softball W; Swimming and Diving M & W; Tennis M & W; Track and Field M & W; Volleyball W

UNION COLLEGE
310 College St.
Barbourville, KY 40906-1499
Tel: (606)546-4151; Free: 800-489-8646
Admissions: (606)546-1222
Fax: (606)546-1667
E-mail: enroll@unionky.edu
Web Site: http://www.unionky.edu/
President/CEO: Edward deRosset
Admissions: Jerry Jackson
Financial Aid: Jessica Cook
Type: Comprehensive **Sex:** Coed **Affiliation:** United Methodist **Scores:** 83% SAT V 400+; 92% SAT M 400+; 52.24% ACT 18-23; 13% ACT 24-29 **% Accepted:** 28 **Admission Plans:** Early Admission; Deferred Admission **Application Fee:** $10.00 **H.S. Requirements:** High school diploma required; GED accepted **Costs Per Year:** Application fee: $10. Comprehensive fee: $24,810 includes full-time tuition ($18,260), mandatory fees ($600), and college room and board ($5950). College room only: $2550. Full-time tuition and fees vary according to course load. Room and board charges vary according to board plan and housing facility. Part-time tuition: $305 per credit hour. Part-time tuition varies according to course load. **Scholarships:** Available **Calendar System:** Semester, Summer Session Available **Enrollment:** FT 765, PT 60, Grad FT 176, Grad PT 420 **Faculty:** FT 61, PT 43 **Student-Faculty Ratio:** 12:1 **Exams:** SAT I or ACT. **% Receiving Financial Aid:** 86 **% Residing in College-Owned, -Operated, or -Affiliated Housing:** 50 **Final Year or Final Semester Residency Requirement:** No **Library Holdings:** 113,995 **Regional Accreditation:** Southern Association of Colleges and Schools **Credit Hours For Degree:** 128 credit hours, Bachelors **ROTC:** Army **Intercollegiate Athletics:** Baseball M; Basketball M & W; Bowling M & W; Cheerleading M & W; Cross-Country Running M & W; Football M; Golf M & W; Soccer M & W; Softball W; Swimming and Diving M & W; Tennis M & W; Track and Field M & W; Volleyball W

UNIVERSITY OF THE CUMBERLANDS
6178 College Station Dr.
Williamsburg, KY 40769-1372
Tel: (606)549-2200; Free: 800-343-1609
Admissions: (606)539-4241
Fax: (606)539-4303
E-mail: admiss@ucumberlands.edu
Web Site: http://www.ucumberlands.edu/
President/CEO: Dr. James Taylor
Admissions: Erica Harris
Financial Aid: Steve Allen
Type: Comprehensive **Sex:** Coed **Affiliation:** Kentucky Baptist **Scores:** 93% SAT V 400+; 97% SAT M 400+; 67% ACT 18-23; 28% ACT 24-29 **% Accepted:** 73 **Application Deadline:** Rolling **Application Fee:** $30.00 **H.S. Requirements:** High school diploma required; GED accepted **Costs Per Year:** Application fee: $30. Comprehensive fee: $23,826 includes full-time tuition ($16,640), mandatory fees ($360), and college room and board ($6826). Part-time tuition: $7829 per term. Part-time mandatory fees: $530 per credit hour. Part-time tuition and fees vary according to course load. **Scholarships:** Available **Calendar System:** Semester, Summer Session Available **Enrollment:** FT 1,432, PT 328, Grad FT 345, Grad PT 850 **Faculty:** FT 96, PT 58 **Student-Faculty Ratio:** 19:1 **Exams:** SAT I or ACT. ACT essay not being used. SAT essay not being used. **% Receiving Financial Aid:** 81 **% Residing in College-Owned, -Operated, or -Affiliated Housing:** 62 **Final Year or Final Semester Residency Requirement:** No **Library Holdings:** 205,631 **Regional Accreditation:** Southern Association of Colleges and Schools **Credit Hours For Degree:** 128 credit hours, Bachelors **ROTC:** Army **Intercollegiate Athletics:** Baseball M; Basketball M & W; Cheerleading M & W; Cross-Country Running M & W; Football M; Golf M & W; Soccer M & W; Softball M & W; Swimming and Diving M & W; Tennis M & W; Track and Field M & W; Volleyball W; Wrestling M & W

UNIVERSITY OF KENTUCKY
Lexington, KY 40506-0032
Tel: (859)257-9000
Admissions: (859)257-2000
Fax: (859)257-4000
E-mail: admissio@uky.edu
Web Site: http://www.uky.edu/
President/CEO: Dr. Lee T. Todd, Jr.
Admissions: Michelle Nordin
Financial Aid: Lynda S. George
Type: University **Sex:** Coed **Scores:** 96.68% SAT V 400+; 97.57% SAT M 400+; 40.63% ACT 18-23; 44.72% ACT 24-29 **% Accepted:** 74 **Admission Plans:** Preferred Admission; Deferred Admission **Application Deadline:** February 15 **Application Fee:** $50.00 **H.S. Requirements:** High school diploma required; GED accepted **Costs Per Year:** Application fee: $50. State resident tuition: $7214 full-time, $301 per credit hour part-time. Nonresident tuition: $15,769 full-time, $658 per credit hour part-time. Mandatory fees: $909 full-time, $21.50 per credit hour part-time. Full-time tuition and fees vary according to degree level, program, reciprocity agreements, and student level. Part-time tuition and fees vary according to degree level, program, reciprocity agreements, and student level. College room and board: $9125. College room only: $3975. Room and board charges vary according to board plan and housing facility. **Scholarships:** Available **Calendar System:** Semester, Summer Session Available **Enrollment:** FT 17,619, PT 1,564, Grad FT 5,654, Grad PT 1,458 **Faculty:** FT 1,301, PT 382 **Student-Faculty Ratio:** 18:1 **Exams:** SAT I or ACT. **% Receiving Financial Aid:** 39 **% Residing in College-Owned, -Operated, or -Affiliated Housing:** 28 **Regional Accreditation:** Southern Association of Colleges and Schools **Credit Hours For Degree:** 120 semester hours, Bachelors **ROTC:** Army, Air Force **Professional Accreditation:** AACSB, ABET, ACPhE, ACEJMC, AAMFT, AACN, AAFCS, ABA, ADA, ADtA, ALA, AOTA, APTA, APA, ASLA, ASLHA, ACIPE, AALS, ACEHSA, FIDER CORE, CSWE, LCMEAMA, NAACLS, NAAB, NASAD, NASM, NASPAA, NCATE, NLN, SAF **Intercollegiate Athletics:** Baseball M; Basketball M & W; Cross-Country Running M & W; Football M; Golf M & W; Gymnastics W; Riflery M & W; Soccer M & W; Softball W; Swimming and Diving M & W; Tennis M & W; Track and Field M & W; Volleyball W

UNIVERSITY OF LOUISVILLE
2301 South Third St.
Louisville, KY 40292-0001
Tel: (502)852-5555; Free: 800-334-8635
Admissions: (502)852-6531
Fax: (502)852-4776
E-mail: admitme@louisville.edu
Web Site: http://www.louisville.edu/
President/CEO: Dr. James R. Ramsey
Admissions: Jenny L. Sawyer
Financial Aid: Patricia O. Arauz
Type: University **Sex:** Coed **Scores:** 97.95% SAT V 400+; 97.26% SAT M 400+; 43.75% ACT 18-23; 40.76% ACT 24-29 **% Accepted:** 73 **Admission Plans:** Deferred Admission **Application Deadline:** February 15 **Application Fee:** $40.00 **H.S. Requirements:** High school diploma required; GED accepted **Costs Per Year:** Application fee: $40. Area resident tuition: $331 per credit hour part-time. State resident tuition: $7944 full-time. Nonresident tuition: $19,272 full-time, $803 per credit hour part-time. Full-time tuition varies according to reciprocity agreements. Part-time tuition varies according to course load and reciprocity agreements. College room and board: $5437. Room and board charges vary according to board plan and housing facility. **Scholarships:** Available **Calendar System:** Semester, Summer Session Available **Enrollment:** FT 11,981, PT 3,496, Grad FT 3,631, Grad PT 1,908 **Faculty:** FT 867, PT 489 **Student-Faculty Ratio:** 18:1 **Exams:** SAT I or ACT. **% Receiving Financial Aid:** 55 **% Residing in College-Owned, -Operated, or -Affiliated Housing:** 17 **Final Year or Final Semester Residency Requirement:** No **Library Holdings:** 2,244,103 **Regional Accreditation:** Southern Association of Colleges and Schools **Credit Hours**

For Degree: 63 credit hours, Associates; 121 credit hours, Bachelors **ROTC:** Army, Air Force **Professional Accreditation:** AACSB, ABET, AAMFT, AACN, ABA, ADA, ACSP, APTA, APA, ASLHA, ACIPE, AALS, FIDER, CSWE, JRCERT, LCMEAMA, NASM, NASPAA, NAST, NCATE **Intercollegiate Athletics:** Baseball M; Basketball M & W; Cheerleading M & W; Crew W; Cross-Country Running M & W; Field Hockey W; Football M; Golf M & W; Lacrosse W; Soccer M & W; Softball W; Swimming and Diving M & W; Tennis M & W; Track and Field M & W; Volleyball W

UNIVERSITY OF PHOENIX—LOUISVILLE CAMPUS
10400 Linn Station Rd.
Louisville, KY 40223-3839
Tel: (502)423-0149; Free: 800-697-8223
Web Site: http://www.phoenix.edu/
President/CEO: William Pepicello, PhD
Type: Comprehensive **Sex:** Coed **Regional Accreditation:** North Central Association of Colleges and Schools

WEST KENTUCKY COMMUNITY AND TECHNICAL COLLEGE
4810 Alben Barkley Dr.
PO Box 7380
Paducah, KY 42002-7380
Tel: (270)554-9200
Admissions: (270)554-3266
Fax: (270)554-6217
E-mail: jerry.anderson@kctcs.edu
Web Site: http://www.westkentucky.kctcs.edu/
President/CEO: Dr. Barbara Veazey
Admissions: Jerry Anderson
Type: Two-Year College **Sex:** Coed **Affiliation:** Kentucky Community and Technical College System **Scores:** 53.7% ACT 18-23; 30.2% ACT 24-29 **Admission Plans:** Open Admission; Early Admission **Application Deadline:** Rolling **H.S. Requirements:** High school diploma required; GED accepted **Costs Per Year:** State resident tuition: $3750 full-time, $125 per credit hour part-time. Nonresident tuition: $12,750 full-time, $425 per credit hour part-time. **Scholarships:** Available **Calendar System:** Semester, Summer Session Not available **Enrollment:** FT 2,072, PT 1,439 **Faculty:** FT 132, PT 237 **Student-Faculty Ratio:** 17:1 **Library Holdings:** 74,676 **Regional Accreditation:** Southern Association of Colleges and Schools **Credit Hours For Degree:** 60 credit hours, Associates **Professional Accreditation:** ADA, APTA, COE, NLN

WESTERN KENTUCKY UNIVERSITY
1906 College Heights Blvd.
Bowling Green, KY 42101
Tel: (270)745-0111
Admissions: (270)745-2551
Fax: (270)745-6133
E-mail: admission@wku.edu
Web Site: http://www.wku.edu/
President/CEO: Gary A. Ransdell
Admissions: Scott S. Gordon
Financial Aid: Cindy Burnette
Type: Comprehensive **Sex:** Coed **Scores:** 87% SAT V 400+; 85% SAT M 400+; 49% ACT 18-23; 26% ACT 24-29 **% Accepted:** 95 **Application Deadline:** August 1 **Application Fee:** $40.00 **H.S. Requirements:** High school diploma required; GED accepted **Costs Per Year:** Application fee: $40. State resident tuition: $7200 full-time, $300 per hour part-time. Nonresident tuition: $17,784 full-time, $741 per hour part-time. Full-time tuition varies according to course level, course load, location, program, and reciprocity agreements. Part-time tuition varies according to course level, course load, location, program, and reciprocity agreements. College room and board: $6351. College room only: $3645. Room and board charges vary according to board plan and housing facility. **Scholarships:** Available **Calendar System:** Semester, Summer Session Available **Enrollment:** FT 14,024, PT 3,621, Grad FT 912, Grad PT 2,155 **Faculty:** FT 735, PT 415 **Student-Faculty Ratio:** 19:1 **Exams:** SAT I or ACT. ACT essay not being used. SAT essay not being used. **% Receiving Financial Aid:** 58 **% Residing in College-Owned, -Operated, or -Affiliated Housing:** 28 **Library Holdings:** 1,779,657 **Regional Accreditation:** Southern Association of Colleges and Schools **Credit Hours For Degree:** 60 hours, Associates; 120 hours, Bachelors **ROTC:** Army, Air Force **Professional Accreditation:** AACSB, ABET, ACEJMC, AACN, AAFCS, ACA, ADA, AHIMA, AOTA, ASLHA, CEPH, CSWE, NASAD, NASM, NCATE, NLN, NRPA, NAIT **Intercollegiate Athletics:** Baseball M; Basketball M & W; Cheerleading M & W; Cross-Country Running M & W; Football M; Golf M & W; Riflery M & W; Softball W; Swimming and Diving M & W; Tennis M & W; Track and Field M & W; Volleyball W

BATON ROUGE COMMUNITY COLLEGE
5310 Florida Blvd.
Baton Rouge, LA 70806
Tel: (225)216-8000; Free: 800-601-4558
Fax: (225)216-8100
Web Site: http://www.mybrcc.edu/
President/CEO: Myrtle E.B. Dorsey
Admissions: Nancy Clay
Type: Two-Year College **Sex:** Coed **Admission Plans:** Open Admission **Application Fee:** $7.00 **Calendar System:** Semester **Regional Accreditation:** Southern Association of Colleges and Schools **Intercollegiate Athletics:** Baseball M

BATON ROUGE SCHOOL OF COMPUTERS
10425 Plaza Americana
Baton Rouge, LA 70816
Tel: (504)923-2525
Admissions: (225)923-2524
Fax: (504)923-2979
E-mail: admissions@brsc.net
Web Site: http://www.brsc.edu/
President/CEO: Betty D. Truxillo
Admissions: Brenda Boss
Type: Two-Year College **Sex:** Coed **Professional Accreditation:** ACCSCT

BLUE CLIFF COLLEGE—LAFAYETTE
100 Asma Blvd.
Ste. 350
Lafayette, LA 70508-3862
Tel: (337)269-0620
Web Site: http://www.bluecliffcollege.com/
President/CEO: Theresa Rice
Type: Two-Year College **Sex:** Coed **Admission Plans:** Open Admission **Application Fee:** $25.00

BLUE CLIFF COLLEGE—SHREVEPORT
8731 Park Plaza Dr.
Shreveport, LA 71105
Tel: (318)425-7941
Web Site: http://www.bluecliffcollege.com/
President/CEO: Michael Rowan
Type: Two-Year College **Sex:** Coed **Application Fee:** $0.00 **H.S. Requirements:** High school diploma required; GED accepted **Faculty:** FT 19, PT 2 **Student-Faculty Ratio:** 12:1 **Final Year or Final Semester Residency Requirement:** No

BOSSIER PARISH COMMUNITY COLLEGE
2719 Airline Dr. North
Bossier City, LA 71111-5801
Tel: (318)746-9851
Admissions: (318)678-6000
Fax: (318)742-8664
Web Site: http://www.bpcc.edu/
President/CEO: James B. Henderson
Admissions: Ann Jampole
Type: Two-Year College **Sex:** Coed **Affiliation:** Louisiana Community and Technical College System **Admission Plans:** Open Admission; Early Admission **Application Deadline:** August 10 **Application Fee:** $15.00 **H.S. Requirements:** High school diploma required; GED accepted **Scholarships:** Available **Calendar System:** Semester, Summer Session Available **Library Holdings:** 29,600 **Regional Accreditation:** Southern Association of Colleges and Schools **Credit Hours For Degree:** 66 semester hours, Associates **Professional Accreditation:** AAMAE, ACF, APTA, CARC **Intercollegiate Athletics:** Baseball M; Basketball M; Soccer W; Softball W

CAMELOT COLLEGE
2618 Wooddale Blvd.
Ste. A
Baton Rouge, LA 70805
Tel: (225)928-3005; Free: 800-470-3320
Fax: (225)927-3794
Web Site: http://www.camelotcollege.com/
President/CEO: Ronnie L. Williams
Type: Two-Year College **Sex:** Coed **Scholarships:** Available **Professional Accreditation:** ACICS

CAMERON COLLEGE
2740 Canal St.
New Orleans, LA 70119
Tel: (504)821-5881
Web Site: http://www.cameroncollege.com/
President/CEO: Eleanor Cameron
Type: Two-Year College **Sex:** Coed **Admission Plans:** Open Admission **Application Fee:** $100.00 **Professional Accreditation:** COE

CAREER TECHNICAL COLLEGE
2319 Louisville Ave.
Monroe, LA 71201
Tel: (318)323-2889; Free: 800-234-6766
Fax: (318)324-9883
Web Site: http://www.careertc.edu/
President/CEO: Cheryl Lokey
Type: Two-Year College **Sex:** Coed **% Accepted:** 84 **Application Fee:** $35.00 **Calendar System:** Quarter **Professional Accreditation:** ARCEST, COE

CENTENARY COLLEGE OF LOUISIANA
2911 Centenary Blvd., PO Box 41188
Shreveport, LA 71104
Tel: (318)869-5011; Free: 800-234-4448
Admissions: (318)869-5134
Fax: (318)869-5005
E-mail: dvoskuil@centenary.edu
Web Site: http://www.centenary.edu/
President/CEO: Dr. B. David Rowe
Admissions: David Voskuil
Financial Aid: Mary Sue Rix
Type: Comprehensive **Sex:** Coed **Affiliation:** United Methodist **Scores:** 98.2% SAT V 400+; 95.5% SAT M 400+; 38.5% ACT 18-23; 50.49% ACT 24-29 **% Accepted:** 54 **Admission Plans:** Early Admission; Early Action;

Deferred Admission **Application Deadline:** August 1 **Application Fee:** $30.00 **H.S. Requirements:** High school diploma required; GED accepted **Costs Per Year:** Application fee: $30. Comprehensive fee: $31,220 includes full-time tuition ($22,080), mandatory fees ($1200), and college room and board ($7940). College room only: $4020. Room and board charges vary according to board plan and housing facility. **Scholarships:** Available **Calendar System:** Miscellaneous, Summer Session Available **Enrollment:** FT 875, PT 12, Grad FT 4, Grad PT 83 **Faculty:** FT 71, PT 39 **Student-Faculty Ratio:** 12:1 **Exams:** SAT I or ACT. ACT essay not being used. SAT essay not being used. **% Receiving Financial Aid:** 63 **% Residing in College-Owned, -Operated, or -Affiliated Housing:** 68 **Final Year or Final Semester Residency Requirement:** Yes **Library Holdings:** 186,564 **Regional Accreditation:** Southern Association of Colleges and Schools **Credit Hours For Degree:** 124 semester credit hours, Bachelors **Professional Accreditation:** NASM, NCATE **Intercollegiate Athletics:** Baseball M; Basketball M & W; Cheerleading M & W; Cross-Country Running M & W; Golf M & W; Gymnastics W; Soccer M & W; Softball W; Swimming and Diving M & W; Tennis M & W; Volleyball W

DELGADO COMMUNITY COLLEGE
501 City Park Ave.
New Orleans, LA 70119-4399
Tel: (504)483-4400
Admissions: (504)671-5010
Fax: (504)483-1986
E-mail: enroll@dcc.edu
Web Site: http://www.dcc.edu/
President/CEO: Debbie Lea
Admissions: Gwen Boute
Type: Two-Year College **Sex:** Coed **Affiliation:** Louisiana Community and Technical College System **% Accepted:** 100 **Admission Plans:** Open Admission **Application Deadline:** Rolling **Application Fee:** $15.00 **H.S. Requirements:** High school diploma required; GED accepted **Scholarships:** Available **Calendar System:** Semester, Summer Session Available **Enrollment:** FT 6,068, PT 7,149 **Faculty:** FT 389, PT 239 **Student-Faculty Ratio:** 20:1 **Library Holdings:** 110,000 **Regional Accreditation:** Southern Association of Colleges and Schools **Credit Hours For Degree:** 66 semester hours, Associates **ROTC:** Army, Air Force **Professional Accreditation:** ABET, ABFSE, ACF, AHIMA, AOTA, APTA, ACBSP, CARC, JRCERT, JRCEMT, NAACLS, NLN, NAIT **Intercollegiate Athletics:** Baseball M; Basketball M & W; Track and Field W

DELTA COLLEGE OF ARTS AND TECHNOLOGY
7380 Exchange Place
Baton Rouge, LA 70806-3851
Tel: (504)928-7770
Admissions: (225)928-7770
Fax: (504)927-9096
E-mail: bbrown@deltacollege.com
Web Site: http://www.deltacollege.com/
President/CEO: Billy L. Clark
Admissions: Beulah Laverghe-Brown
Type: Two-Year College **Sex:** Coed **Admission Plans:** Open Admission **Application Fee:** $100.00 **Calendar System:** Continuous **Professional Accreditation:** ACCSCT

DELTA SCHOOL OF BUSINESS & TECHNOLOGY
517 Broad St.
Lake Charles, LA 70601
Tel: (337)439-5765; Free: 800-259-5627
Fax: (337)436-5151
E-mail: gholt@deltatech.edu
Web Site: http://www.deltatech.edu/
President/CEO: Gary Holt
Admissions: Gary J. Holt
Type: Two-Year College **Sex:** Coed **Scholarships:** Available **Calendar System:** Quarter **Professional Accreditation:** ACICS

DILLARD UNIVERSITY
2601 Gentilly Blvd.
New Orleans, LA 70122-3097
Tel: (504)283-8822; Free: 800-216-6637
Admissions: (504)816-4670
Fax: (504)286-4895
E-mail: mreed@dillard.edu
Web Site: http://www.dillard.edu/
President/CEO: Dr. Marvalene Hughes
Admissions: Meredith Reed
Financial Aid: Shannon Neal
Type: Four-Year College **Sex:** Coed **Affiliation:** interdenominational **Scores:** 64% SAT V 400+; 53% SAT M 400+; 46% ACT 18-23; 7% ACT 24-29 **% Accepted:** 48 **Admission Plans:** Early Admission; Early Decision Plan **Application Deadline:** Rolling **Application Fee:** $30.00 **H.S. Requirements:** High school diploma required; GED accepted **Costs Per Year:** Application fee: $30. Comprehensive fee: $22,266 includes full-time tuition ($13,000), mandatory fees ($880), and college room and board ($8386). College room only: $5360. Room and board charges vary according to housing facility. Part-time tuition: $542 per credit hour. Part-time tuition varies according to course load. **Scholarships:** Available **Calendar System:** Semester, Summer Session Available **Enrollment:** FT 949, PT 62 **Faculty:** FT 94, PT 23 **Student-Faculty Ratio:** 10:1 **Exams:** Other, SAT I or ACT. ACT essay not being used. SAT essay not being used. **% Receiving Financial Aid:** 94 **% Residing in College-Owned, -Operated, or -Affiliated Housing:** 41 **Final Year or Final Semester Residency Requirement:** Yes **Library Holdings:** 105,128 **Regional Accreditation:** Southern Association of Colleges and Schools **Credit Hours For Degree:** 124 credit hours, Bachelors **ROTC:** Army, Air Force **Professional Accreditation:** NCATE, NLN **Intercollegiate Athletics:** Basketball M & W; Cross-Country Running M & W; Softball W; Track and Field M & W; Volleyball W

ELAINE P. NUNEZ COMMUNITY COLLEGE
3710 Paris Rd.
Chalmette, LA 70043-1249
Tel: (504)278-6200
Admissions: (504)278-6477
Fax: (504)680-2243
E-mail: bmaillet@nunez.edu
Web Site: http://www.nunez.edu/
President/CEO: Dr. Thomas R. Warner
Admissions: Becky Maillet
Type: Two-Year College **Sex:** Coed **Affiliation:** Louisiana Community and Technical College System **Admission Plans:** Open Admission; Deferred Admission **Application Deadline:** Rolling **Application Fee:** $10.00 **H.S. Requirements:** High school diploma or equivalent not required. For practical nursing and EMT programs: High school diploma required; GED accepted **Costs Per Year:** Application fee: $10. State resident tuition: $1582 full-time. Nonresident tuition: $4102 full-time. Mandatory fees: $368 full-time. **Scholarships:** Available **Calendar System:** Semester, Summer Session Available **Enrollment:** FT 729, PT 1,105 **Faculty:** FT 40, PT 27 **Student-Faculty Ratio:** 22:1 **Library Holdings:** 68,000 **Regional Accreditation:** Southern Association of Colleges and Schools **Credit Hours For Degree:** 60 semester hours, Associates **Professional Accreditation:** NAIT

GRAMBLING STATE UNIVERSITY
403 Main St.
Grambling, LA 71245
Tel: (318)247-3811
Admissions: (318)274-6183
Fax: (318)274-6172
E-mail: mossa@gram.edu
Web Site: http://www.gram.edu/
President/CEO: Dr. Frank G. Pogue
Admissions: Annie L. Moss
Type: University **Sex:** Coed **Affiliation:** University of Louisiana System **Scores:** 62% SAT V 400+; 68% SAT M 400+; 43% ACT 18-23; 3% ACT 24-29 **% Accepted:** 33 **Admission Plans:** Early Admission **Application Deadline:** June 30 **Application Fee:** $20.00 **H.S. Requirements:** High school diploma required; GED not accepted **Costs Per Year:** Application fee: $20. State resident tuition: $2606 full-time, $109 per credit hour part-time. Nonresident tuition: $8492 full-time, $109 per credit hour part-time. Mandatory fees: $1410 full-time, $440 per term part-time. Part-time tuition and fees vary according to course load. College room and board: $7168. College room only: $4456. Room and board charges vary according to housing facility. **Scholarships:** Available **Calendar System:** Semester, Summer Session Available **Enrollment:** FT 4,228, PT 310, Grad FT 282, Grad PT 172 **Faculty:** FT 242, PT 17 **Student-Faculty Ratio:** 19:1 **Exams:** SAT I or ACT. ACT essay not being used. SAT essay not being used. **% Receiving Financial Aid:** 90 **% Residing in College-Owned, -Operated, or**

-Affiliated Housing: 50 **Final Year or Final Semester Residency Requirement:** No **Library Holdings:** 322,995 **Regional Accreditation:** Southern Association of Colleges and Schools **Credit Hours For Degree:** 60 credit hours, Associates; 128 credit hours, Bachelors **ROTC:** Army, Air Force **Professional Accreditation:** AACSB, ABET, ACEJMC, CSWE, NASM, NASPAA, NAST, NCATE, NLN, NRPA **Intercollegiate Athletics:** Baseball M; Basketball M & W; Bowling W; Cross-Country Running M & W; Football M; Golf M & W; Tennis M & W; Track and Field M & W; Volleyball W

GRETNA CAREER COLLEGE
1415 Whitney Ave.
Gretna, LA 70053-5835
Tel: (504)366-5409
Fax: (504)365-1004
Web Site: http://www.gretnacareercollege.com/
President/CEO: Nick Randazzo
Type: Two-Year College **Sex:** Coed **Professional Accreditation:** ACCSCT

HERZING COLLEGE
2500 Williams Blvd.
Kenner, LA 70062
Tel: (504)733-0074
Fax: (504)733-0020
Web Site: http://www.herzing.edu/
President/CEO: Mark Aspiazu
Admissions: Genny Bordelon
Type: Two-Year College **Sex:** Coed **% Accepted:** 100 **Calendar System:** Semester **Professional Accreditation:** ACICS

ITI TECHNICAL COLLEGE
13944 Airline Hwy.
Baton Rouge, LA 70817
Tel: (225)752-4233; Free: 800-467-4484
Admissions: (225)752-4230
Fax: (225)756-0903
E-mail: mstevens@iticollege.edu
Web Site: http://www.iticollege.edu/
President/CEO: Joe Martin
Admissions: Marcia Stevens
Type: Two-Year College **Sex:** Coed **% Accepted:** 85 **Admission Plans:** Open Admission **Application Fee:** $0.00 **H.S. Requirements:** High school diploma or equivalent not required **Costs Per Year:** Application fee: $0. **Calendar System:** Continuous **Enrollment:** FT 393 **Faculty:** FT 24, PT 27 **Student-Faculty Ratio:** 15:1 **Professional Accreditation:** ACCSCT

ITT TECHNICAL INSTITUTE (BATON ROUGE)
14111 Airline Hwy.
Ste. 101
Baton Rouge, LA 70817
Tel: (225)754-5800; Free: 800-295-8485
Web Site: http://www.itt-tech.edu/
President/CEO: Susie Schowen
Type: Two-Year College **Sex:** Coed

ITT TECHNICAL INSTITUTE (ST. ROSE)
140 James Dr. East
St. Rose, LA 70087
Tel: (504)463-0338
Web Site: http://www.itt-tech.edu/
President/CEO: Heather Alleman
Type: Two-Year College **Sex:** Coed **Affiliation:** ITT Educational Services, Inc. **H.S. Requirements:** High school diploma required; GED accepted **Scholarships:** Available **Calendar System:** Quarter **Professional Accreditation:** ACICS

LOUISIANA COLLEGE
1140 College Dr.
Pineville, LA 71359-0001
Tel: (318)487-7011; Free: 800-487-1906
Admissions: (318)487-7439
Fax: (318)487-7550
E-mail: admissions@lacollege.edu
Web Site: http://www.lacollege.edu/
President/CEO: Dr. Joe Aguillard
Admissions: Byron McGee
Financial Aid: Shelley Jinks
Type: Comprehensive **Sex:** Coed **Affiliation:** Southern Baptist **% Accepted:** 51 **Admission Plans:** Early Admission **Application Deadline:** August 15 **Application Fee:** $25.00 **H.S. Requirements:** High school diploma required; GED accepted **Costs Per Year:** Application fee: $25. Comprehensive fee: $16,796 includes full-time tuition ($11,100), mandatory fees ($1380), and college room and board ($4316). Full-time tuition and fees vary according to program. Room and board charges vary according to board plan and housing facility. Part-time tuition: $370 per hour. Part-time tuition varies according to program. **Scholarships:** Available **Calendar System:** Semester, Summer Session Available **Enrollment:** FT 960, PT 77, Grad FT 106, Grad PT 318 **Faculty:** FT 63 **Exams:** SAT I or ACT. **% Receiving Financial Aid:** 59 **% Residing in College-Owned, -Operated, or -Affiliated Housing:** 48 **Library Holdings:** 348,673 **Regional Accreditation:** Southern Association of Colleges and Schools **Credit Hours For Degree:** 127 credit hours, Bachelors **ROTC:** Army **Professional Accreditation:** AACN, ACBSP, CSWE, NLN **Intercollegiate Athletics:** Baseball M; Basketball M & W; Cheerleading M & W; Cross-Country Running W; Football M; Golf M; Soccer M & W; Softball W; Tennis W

LOUISIANA STATE UNIVERSITY AND AGRICULTURAL AND MECHANICAL COLLEGE
Baton Rouge, LA 70803
Tel: (225)578-3202
Admissions: (225)578-3113
Fax: (225)578-4433
E-mail: admissions@lsu.edu
Web Site: http://www.lsu.edu/
President/CEO: Dr. Michael Martin
Admissions: Mary G. Parker
Financial Aid: Mary G. Parker
Type: University **Sex:** Coed **Affiliation:** Louisiana State University System **Scores:** 98.45% SAT V 400+; 99.38% SAT M 400+; 31.06% ACT 18-23; 55.35% ACT 24-29 **% Accepted:** 69 **Admission Plans:** Early Admission; Deferred Admission **Application Deadline:** April 15 **Application Fee:** $40.00 **H.S. Requirements:** High school diploma required; GED accepted **Costs Per Year:** Application fee: $40. State resident tuition: $3469 full-time. Nonresident tuition: $12,619 full-time. Mandatory fees: $1764 full-time. College room and board: $7738. College room only: $4610. Room and board charges vary according to board plan and housing facility. **Scholarships:** Available **Calendar System:** Semester, Summer Session Available **Enrollment:** FT 21,539, PT 1,473, Grad FT 4,299, Grad PT 1,332 **Faculty:** FT 1,309, PT 146 **Student-Faculty Ratio:** 20:1 **Exams:** SAT I or ACT. ACT essay used in place of application essay. SAT essay used in place of application essay. **% Receiving Financial Aid:** 32 **% Residing in College-Owned, -Operated, or -Affiliated Housing:** 25 **Library Holdings:** 4,085,637 **Regional Accreditation:** Southern Association of Colleges and Schools **Credit Hours For Degree:** 119 semester hours, Bachelors **ROTC:** Army, Navy, Air Force **Professional Accreditation:** AACSB, ABET, ACEJMC, AAFCS, ABA, ACCE, ACA, ADtA, ALA, APA, ASLA, ASLHA, AVMA, AALS, FIDER, CSWE, NAAB, NASAD, NASM, NAST NCATE, SAF **Intercollegiate Athletics:** Baseball M; Basketball M & W; Cheerleading M & W; Cross-Country Running M & W; Football M; Golf M & W; Gymnastics W; Soccer W; Softball W; Swimming and Diving M & W; Tennis M & W; Track and Field M & W; Volleyball W

LOUISIANA STATE UNIVERSITY AT ALEXANDRIA
8100 Hwy. 71 South
Alexandria, LA 71302-9121
Tel: (318)445-3672; Free: 888-473-6417
Fax: (318)473-6418
E-mail: skieffer@isua.edu
Web Site: http://www.lsua.edu/
President/CEO: David P. Manuel
Admissions: Shelly Kieffer
Type: Two-Year College **Sex:** Coed **Affiliation:** Louisiana State University System **Scores:** 49.7% ACT 18-23; 11.3% ACT 24-29 **% Accepted:** 77 **Admission Plans:** Open Admission; Early Admission **Application Deadline:** Rolling **Application Fee:** $20.00 **H.S. Requirements:** High school diploma required; GED accepted **Scholarships:** Available **Calendar System:** Semester, Summer Session Available **Enrollment:** FT 1,572, PT 1,416 **Faculty:** FT 105, PT 75 **Student-Faculty Ratio:** 16:1 **Exams:** ACT.

Library Holdings: 154,935 **Regional Accreditation:** Southern Association of Colleges and Schools **ROTC:** Army **Professional Accreditation:** NAACLS, NLN

LOUISIANA STATE UNIVERSITY AT EUNICE
PO Box 1129
Eunice, LA 70535-1129
Tel: (337)457-7311
Fax: (337)457-7311
Web Site: http://www.lsue.edu/
President/CEO: William Nunez
Admissions: Gracie Guillory
Type: Two-Year College **Sex:** Coed **Affiliation:** Louisiana State University System **Scores:** 54% ACT 18-23; 20% ACT 24-29 **% Accepted:** 99 **Admission Plans:** Open Admission; Early Admission **Application Deadline:** August 7 **Application Fee:** $25.00 **H.S. Requirements:** High school diploma required; GED accepted **Scholarships:** Available **Calendar System:** Semester, Summer Session Available **Library Holdings:** 100,000 **Regional Accreditation:** Southern Association of Colleges and Schools **Credit Hours For Degree:** 66 credit hours, Associates **Professional Accreditation:** CARC, JRCERT, NLN **Intercollegiate Athletics:** Baseball M; Basketball W

LOUISIANA STATE UNIVERSITY HEALTH SCIENCES CENTER
433 Bolivar St.
New Orleans, LA 70112-2223
Tel: (504)568-4808
Admissions: (504)568-4829
Web Site: http://www.lsuhsc.edu/
President/CEO: Dr. Larry Hollier, MD
Admissions: William Bryant Faust, IV
Financial Aid: Patrick Gorman
Type: University **Sex:** Coed **Affiliation:** Louisiana State University System **Application Fee:** $50.00 **H.S. Requirements:** High school diploma required; GED accepted **Costs Per Year:** Application fee: $50. State resident tuition: $3303 full-time, $165 per hour part-time. Nonresident tuition: $5645 full-time, $282 per hour part-time. Mandatory fees: $893 full-time, $39 per credit hour part-time. Full-time tuition and fees vary according to course load, degree level, location, and program. Part-time tuition and fees vary according to course load, degree level, location, and program. College room only: $6396. Room charges vary according to housing facility. **Scholarships:** Available **Calendar System:** Miscellaneous, Summer Session Available **Enrollment:** FT 644, PT 186, Grad FT 1,207, Grad PT 607 **Faculty:** FT 726, PT 167 **% Residing in College-Owned, -Operated, or -Affiliated Housing:** 10 **Final Year or Final Semester Residency Requirement:** Yes **Regional Accreditation:** Southern Association of Colleges and Schools **Credit Hours For Degree:** 60 credits, Associates; 120 credits, Bachelors **ROTC:** Army, Navy, Air Force **Professional Accreditation:** AACN, AANA, ADA, AOTA, APTA, APA, ASLHA, CARC, CEPH, CORE, JCAHPO, LCMEAMA, NAACLS

LOUISIANA STATE UNIVERSITY IN SHREVEPORT
1 University Place
Shreveport, LA 71115-2399
Tel: (318)797-5000
Admissions: (318)797-5063
Fax: (318)797-5286
E-mail: admissions@pilot.lsus.edu
Web Site: http://www.lsus.edu/
President/CEO: Dr. Vincent J. Marsala
Admissions: Mickey Diez
Type: Comprehensive **Sex:** Coed **Affiliation:** Louisiana State University System **Scores:** 63.3% ACT 18-23; 27.9% ACT 24-29 **Admission Plans:** Early Admission **Application Deadline:** August 1 **Application Fee:** $10.00 **H.S. Requirements:** High school diploma required; GED accepted **Costs Per Year:** Application fee: $10. State resident tuition: $2978 full-time, $117.85 per credit hour part-time. Nonresident tuition: $7748 full-time, $316.58 per credit hour part-time. Mandatory fees: $947 full-time, $41.70 per credit hour part-time. **Scholarships:** Available **Calendar System:** Semester, Summer Session Available **Enrollment:** FT 2,511, PT 1,709, Grad FT 128, Grad PT 319 **Exams:** ACT, SAT I or ACT. **Regional Accreditation:** Southern Association of Colleges and Schools **Credit Hours For Degree:** 128 semester hours, Bachelors **ROTC:** Army **Professional Accreditation:** AACSB, ABET, APTA, LCMEAMA, NCATE **Intercollegiate Athletics:** Baseball M; Basketball M & W; Soccer W

LOUISIANA TECH UNIVERSITY
PO Box 3168
Ruston, LA 71272
Tel: (318)257-0211; Free: 800-528-3241
Admissions: (318)257-3036
E-mail: bulldog@latech.edu
Web Site: http://www.latech.edu/
President/CEO: Dr. Daniel D. Reneau
Admissions: Jan B. Albritton
Type: University **Sex:** Coed **Affiliation:** University of Louisiana System **Scores:** 51% ACT 18-23; 38% ACT 24-29 **% Accepted:** 63 **Admission Plans:** Early Admission **Application Deadline:** July 31 **Application Fee:** $20.00 **H.S. Requirements:** High school diploma required; GED accepted **Costs Per Year:** Application fee: $20. State resident tuition: $5220 full-time, $180.75 per semester hour part-time. Nonresident tuition: $10,617 full-time, $180.75 per semester hour part-time. Full-time tuition varies according to course load, location, and program. Part-time tuition varies according to course load, location, and program. College room and board: $5055. College room only: $2580. Room and board charges vary according to board plan and housing facility. **Scholarships:** Available **Calendar System:** Quarter, Summer Session Available **Enrollment:** FT 6,484, PT 2,264, Grad FT 996, Grad PT 1,520 **Faculty:** FT 378, PT 98 **Student-Faculty Ratio:** 21:1 **Exams:** ACT, SAT I or ACT. **% Receiving Financial Aid:** 46 **% Residing in College-Owned, -Operated, or -Affiliated Housing:** 15 **Regional Accreditation:** Southern Association of Colleges and Schools **Credit Hours For Degree:** 60 credit hours, Associates; 126 credit hours, Bachelors **ROTC:** Army, Air Force **Professional Accreditation:** AACSB, ABET, AAFCS, ADtA, AHIMA, APA, ASLHA, CAA, FIDER, NAAB, NASAD, NASM, NCATE, NLN, SAF **Intercollegiate Athletics:** Baseball M; Basketball M & W; Cross-Country Running M & W; Football M; Golf M; Softball W; Tennis W; Track and Field M & W; Volleyball W; Weight Lifting M & W

LOUISIANA TECHNICAL COLLEGE
3250 North Acadian Thruway, E
Baton Rouge, LA 70805
Tel: (225)359-9201; Free: 800-351-7611
Admissions: (225)359-9201
E-mail: aaguillard@ltc.edu
Web Site: http://region2.ltc.edu/
President/CEO: Dr. Kay McDaniel
Admissions: Amber Aguillard
Type: Two-Year College **Sex:** Coed **Affiliation:** Louisiana Community and Technical College System **% Accepted:** 100 **Application Fee:** $5.00 **Enrollment:** FT 7,264, PT 6,150 **Faculty:** FT 780, PT 573 **Student-Faculty Ratio:** 10:1 **Exams:** Other. **Professional Accreditation:** COE

LOUISIANA TECHNICAL COLLEGE—FLORIDA PARISHES CAMPUS
PO Box 1300
Greensburg, LA 70441
Tel: (225)222-4251
Web Site: http://www.ltc.edu/
President/CEO: Sharon Hornsby
Admissions: Sharon G. Hornsby
Type: Two-Year College **Sex:** Coed **Affiliation:** Louisiana Community and Technical College System **Admission Plans:** Open Admission; Early Action **Application Fee:** $5.00 **H.S. Requirements:** High school diploma or equivalent not required. For for practical nursing, EMT, and associates degree programs: High school diploma required; GED accepted **Costs Per Year:** Application fee: $5. State resident tuition: $630 full-time, $26.25 per credit hour part-time. Nonresident tuition: $1260 full-time, $52.50 per credit hour part-time. Mandatory fees: $374 full-time, $14 per credit hour part-time, $25 per term part-time. Full-time tuition and fees vary according to course load. Part-time tuition and fees vary according to course load. **Scholarships:** Available **Calendar System:** Semester **Professional Accreditation:** COE

LOUISIANA TECHNICAL COLLEGE—NORTHEAST LOUISIANA CAMPUS
1710 Warren St.
Winnsboro, LA 71295
Tel: (318)485-2163

Admissions: (318)435-2163
Web Site: http://www.ltc.edu/
President/CEO: Debbie M. Price
Type: Two-Year College **Sex:** Coed **Application Fee:** $5.00 **Scholarships:** Available **Calendar System:** Semester **Faculty:** FT 9, PT 9 **Professional Accreditation:** COE

LOUISIANA TECHNICAL COLLEGE—YOUNG MEMORIAL CAMPUS
900 Youngs Rd.
Morgan City, LA 70381
Tel: (504)380-2436
Admissions: (985)380-2436
Web Site: http://www.ltc.edu/
President/CEO: Karl Young
Admissions: Melanie Henry
Type: Two-Year College **Sex:** Coed **Application Fee:** $5.00 **Scholarships:** Available **Calendar System:** Semester **Faculty:** FT 39, PT 24 **Professional Accreditation:** COE

LOYOLA UNIVERSITY NEW ORLEANS
6363 Saint Charles Ave.
New Orleans, LA 70118-6195
Tel: (504)865-2011; Free: 800-4-LOYOLA
Admissions: (504)865-3240
Fax: (504)865-3383
E-mail: admit@loyno.edu
Web Site: http://www.loyno.edu/
President/CEO: Rev. Kevin W. Wildes, SJ
Admissions: Keith E. Gramling
Financial Aid: Catherine M. Simoneaux
Type: Comprehensive **Sex:** Coed **Affiliation:** Roman Catholic (Jesuit) **Scores:** 100% SAT V 400+; 100% SAT M 400+; 22.2% ACT 18-23; 59.8% ACT 24-29 **% Accepted:** 58 **Admission Plans:** Early Admission **Application Deadline:** Rolling **Application Fee:** $20.00 **H.S. Requirements:** High school diploma required; GED accepted **Costs Per Year:** Application fee: $20. Comprehensive fee: $41,892 includes full-time tuition ($30,468), mandatory fees ($1036), and college room and board ($10,388). College room only: $6160. Room and board charges vary according to board plan and housing facility. Part-time tuition: $869 per credit hour. **Scholarships:** Available **Calendar System:** Semester, Summer Session Available **Enrollment:** FT 2,463, PT 301, Grad FT 899, Grad PT 1,051 **Faculty:** FT 283, PT 158 **Student-Faculty Ratio:** 11:1 **Exams:** SAT I or ACT. ACT essay used for placement. SAT essay used for placement. **% Receiving Financial Aid:** 64 **% Residing in College-Owned, -Operated, or -Affiliated Housing:** 35 **Final Year or Final Semester Residency Requirement:** Yes **Library Holdings:** 623,596 **Regional Accreditation:** Southern Association of Colleges and Schools **Credit Hours For Degree:** 120 credit hours, Bachelors **ROTC:** Army, Navy, Air Force **Professional Accreditation:** AACSB, ABA, ACA, AALS, NASM, NLN **Intercollegiate Athletics:** Baseball M; Basketball M & W; Cheerleading M & W; Cross-Country Running M & W; Golf M & W; Ice Hockey M & W; Lacrosse M; Racquetball M & W; Rugby M; Sailing M & W; Soccer M & W; Swimming and Diving M & W; Tennis M & W; Track and Field M & W; Ultimate Frisbee M & W; Volleyball W; Wrestling M

MCNEESE STATE UNIVERSITY
4205 Ryan St.
Lake Charles, LA 70609
Tel: (337)475-5000; Free: 800-622-3352
Admissions: (337)475-5504
E-mail: ksmith2@mcneese.edu
Web Site: http://www.mcneese.edu/
President/CEO: Dr. Robert D. Hebert
Admissions: Kara Smith
Financial Aid: Taina J. Savoit
Type: Comprehensive **Sex:** Coed **Affiliation:** University of Louisiana System **Scores:** 65% ACT 18-23; 22% ACT 24-29 **% Accepted:** 67 **Admission Plans:** Early Admission **Application Deadline:** Rolling **Application Fee:** $20.00 **H.S. Requirements:** High school diploma required; GED accepted **Scholarships:** Available **Calendar System:** Semester, Summer Session Available **Enrollment:** FT 5,967, PT 1,568, Grad FT 439, Grad PT 671 **Faculty:** FT 307, PT 102 **Student-Faculty Ratio:** 21:1 **Exams:** SAT I or ACT. **% Receiving Financial Aid:** 57 **% Residing in College-Owned, -Operated, or -Affiliated Housing:** 10 **Regional Accreditation:** Southern Association of Colleges and Schools **Credit Hours For Degree:** 60 semester hours, Associates; 120 semester hours, Bachelors **ROTC:** Army **Professional Accreditation:** AACSB, ABET, AACN, AAFCS, ADtA, JRCERT, NAACLS, NASM, NCATE, NLN **Intercollegiate Athletics:** Baseball M; Basketball M & W; Cross-Country Running M & W; Football M; Golf M & W; Soccer W; Softball W; Tennis W; Track and Field M & W; Volleyball W

MEDVANCE INSTITUTE
9255 Interline Ave.
Baton Rouge, LA 70809
Tel: (225)248-1015
Fax: (225)248-9571
Web Site: http://www.medvance.org/
Admissions: Sheri Kirley
Type: Two-Year College **Sex:** Coed **Application Deadline:** Rolling **Application Fee:** $25.00 **H.S. Requirements:** High school diploma required; GED accepted **Scholarships:** Available **Calendar System:** Quarter, Summer Session Not available **Exams:** Other. **Credit Hours For Degree:** 96 quarter hours, Associates **Professional Accreditation:** COE, NAACLS

NEW ORLEANS BAPTIST THEOLOGICAL SEMINARY
3939 Gentilly Blvd.
New Orleans, LA 70126-4858
Tel: (504)282-4455; Free: 800-662-8701
Web Site: http://www.nobts.edu/
President/CEO: Charles S. Kelley, Jr.
Admissions: Dr. Paul E. Gregoire, Jr.
Financial Aid: Owen Nease
Type: Comprehensive **Sex:** Coed **Affiliation:** Southern Baptist **Admission Plans:** Open Admission; Deferred Admission **Application Deadline:** August 9 **Application Fee:** $25.00 **H.S. Requirements:** High school diploma required; GED accepted **Scholarships:** Available **Calendar System:** Semester, Summer Session Available **% Receiving Financial Aid:** 33 **Library Holdings:** 206,321 **Regional Accreditation:** Southern Association of Colleges and Schools **Credit Hours For Degree:** 69 hours, Associates; 126 hours, Bachelors **Professional Accreditation:** ACIPE, ATS, NASM

NICHOLLS STATE UNIVERSITY
906 East First St.
Thibodaux, LA 70310
Tel: (985)446-8111; Free: 877-NICHOLLS
Admissions: (985)448-4507
Fax: (985)448-4929
E-mail: nicholls@nicholls.edu
Web Site: http://www.nicholls.edu/
President/CEO: Dr. Stephen T. Hulbert
Admissions: Becky L. Durocher
Financial Aid: Casie Triche
Type: Comprehensive **Sex:** Coed **Affiliation:** University of Louisiana System **Scores:** 67% ACT 18-23; 23% ACT 24-29 **% Accepted:** 78 **Admission Plans:** Early Admission; Deferred Admission **Application Deadline:** Rolling **Application Fee:** $20.00 **H.S. Requirements:** High school diploma required; GED accepted **Costs Per Year:** Application fee: $20. State resident tuition: $3965 full-time. Nonresident tuition: $10,433 full-time. College room and board: $7310. College room only: $4850. Room and board charges vary according to board plan and housing facility. **Scholarships:** Available **Calendar System:** Semester, Summer Session Available **Enrollment:** FT 5,177, PT 1,347, Grad FT 131, Grad PT 526 **Faculty:** FT 265, PT 6 **Student-Faculty Ratio:** 22:1 **Exams:** SAT I or ACT. **% Receiving Financial Aid:** 46 **% Residing in College-Owned, -Operated, or -Affiliated Housing:** 19 **Library Holdings:** 254,683 **Regional Accreditation:** Southern Association of Colleges and Schools **Credit Hours For Degree:** 60 semester hours, Associates; 120 semester hours, Bachelors **Professional Accreditation:** AACSB, ABET, ACEJMC, AACN, AAFCS, ADtA, ASC, CARC, JRCEMT, NASAD, NASM, NCATE, NLN **Intercollegiate Athletics:** Baseball M; Basketball M & W; Cross-Country Running M & W; Football M; Golf M & W; Soccer W; Softball W; Tennis M & W; Track and Field M & W; Volleyball W

NORTHWESTERN STATE UNIVERSITY OF LOUISIANA
University Parkway
Natchitoches, LA 71497
Tel: (318)357-6361; Free: 800-327-1903
Admissions: (318)357-4503

E-mail: recruiting@nsula.edu
Web Site: http://www.nsula.edu/
President/CEO: Dr. Randall Webb
Admissions: Jana Lucky
Financial Aid: Misti Adams
Type: Comprehensive **Sex:** Coed **Affiliation:** University of Louisiana System **Scores:** 79.25% SAT V 400+; 86.8% SAT M 400+; 61.92% ACT 18-23; 18.83% ACT 24-29 **% Accepted:** 81 **Admission Plans:** Deferred Admission **Application Deadline:** July 6 **Application Fee:** $20.00 **H.S. Requirements:** High school diploma required; GED accepted **Costs Per Year:** Application fee: $20. State resident tuition: $2594 full-time, $399 per credit hour part-time. Nonresident tuition: $9280 full-time, $678 per credit hour part-time. Mandatory fees: $1192 full-time. Full-time tuition and fees vary according to course load and location. Part-time tuition varies according to course load and location. College room and board: $6682. College room only: $4288. Room and board charges vary according to board plan, housing facility, and location. **Scholarships:** Available **Calendar System:** Semester, Summer Session Available **Enrollment:** FT 5,411, PT 2,730, Grad FT 215, Grad PT 891 **Faculty:** FT 318, PT 213 **Student-Faculty Ratio:** 18:1 **Exams:** SAT I or ACT. ACT essay not being used. SAT essay not being used. **% Receiving Financial Aid:** 60 **% Residing in College-Owned, -Operated, or -Affiliated Housing:** 17 **Final Year or Final Semester Residency Requirement:** Yes **Library Holdings:** 777,027 **Regional Accreditation:** Southern Association of Colleges and Schools **Credit Hours For Degree:** 63 credit hours, Associates; 120 credit hours, Bachelors **ROTC:** Army, Air Force **Professional Accreditation:** AACSB, ABET, ACEJMC, AACN, AAFCS, ACA, CSWE, JRCERT, NASAD, NASM, NAST, NCATE, NLN **Intercollegiate Athletics:** Baseball M; Basketball M & W; Cross-Country Running M & W; Football M; Soccer W; Softball W; Tennis W; Track and Field M & W; Volleyball W

OUR LADY OF HOLY CROSS COLLEGE
4123 Woodland Dr.
New Orleans, LA 70131-7399
Tel: (504)394-7744; Free: 800-259-7744
Fax: (504)391-2421
E-mail: dkennedy@olhcc.edu
Web Site: http://www.olhcc.edu/
President/CEO: Rev. Anthony J. de Conciliis, PhD
Admissions: Donna Kennedy
Financial Aid: Kristine Hatfield
Type: Comprehensive **Sex:** Coed **Affiliation:** Roman Catholic **Admission Plans:** Open Admission; Deferred Admission **Application Deadline:** July 20 **Application Fee:** $15.00 **H.S. Requirements:** High school diploma required; GED accepted **Costs Per Year:** Application fee: $15. Tuition: $3720 full-time, $310 per semester hour part-time. Mandatory fees: $315 full-time. Full-time tuition and fees vary according to course load and degree level. Part-time tuition varies according to course load and degree level. **Scholarships:** Available **Calendar System:** Semester, Summer Session Available **% Receiving Financial Aid:** 82 **Library Holdings:** 83,631 **Regional Accreditation:** Southern Association of Colleges and Schools **Credit Hours For Degree:** 60 semester hours, Associates; 125 semester hours, Bachelors **ROTC:** Army, Air Force **Professional Accreditation:** ACA, CARC, NCATE, NLN

OUR LADY OF THE LAKE COLLEGE
7434 Perkins Rd.
Baton Rouge, LA 70808
Tel: (225)768-1700; Free: 877-242-3509
Admissions: (225)768-1718
Fax: (225)768-1726
E-mail: admissions@ololcollege.edu
Web Site: http://www.ololcollege.edu/
President/CEO: Dr. Sandra Harper
Financial Aid: Tiffany D. Magee
Type: Comprehensive **Sex:** Coed **Affiliation:** Roman Catholic **Scores:** 82.3% ACT 18-23; 10.1% ACT 24-29 **% Accepted:** 88 **Admission Plans:** Open Admission; Early Admission; Deferred Admission **Application Deadline:** August 15 **Application Fee:** $35.00 **H.S. Requirements:** High school diploma required; GED accepted **Scholarships:** Available **Calendar System:** Semester, Summer Session Available **Enrollment:** FT 1,136, PT 587, Grad FT 106, Grad PT 43 **Faculty:** FT 84, PT 61 **Exams:** Other, SAT I or ACT. **% Receiving Financial Aid:** 66 **Regional Accreditation:** Southern Association of Colleges and Schools **Credit Hours For Degree:** 63 credit hours, Associates; 129 credit hours, Bachelors **ROTC:** Army, Air Force **Professional Accreditation:** ARCEST, APTA, JRCERT, NAACLS, NLN

REMINGTON COLLEGE—BATON ROUGE CAMPUS
10551 Coursey Blvd.
Baton Rouge, LA 70816
Tel: (225)922-3990
Admissions: (225)236-3200
Fax: (225)922-6569
E-mail: monica.johnson@remingtoncollege.edu
Web Site: http://www.remingtoncollege.edu/
President/CEO: Mike Smith
Admissions: Monica Butler-Johnson
Type: Two-Year College **Sex:** Coed **Calendar System:** Continuous **Professional Accreditation:** ACICS

REMINGTON COLLEGE—LAFAYETTE CAMPUS
303 Rue Louis XIV
Lafayette, LA 70508
Tel: (337)981-4010
Fax: (337)983-7130
E-mail: shannon.williams@remingtoncollege.edu
Web Site: http://www.remingtoncollege.edu/
President/CEO: Jo Ann Boudreaux
Admissions: Shannon Lee Williams
Type: Two-Year College **Sex:** Coed **H.S. Requirements:** High school diploma required; GED accepted **Scholarships:** Available **Calendar System:** Continuous, Summer Session Not available **Library Holdings:** 15,435 **Professional Accreditation:** ACICS

REMINGTON COLLEGE—SHREVEPORT
2106 Bert Kouns Industrial Loop
Shreveport, LA 71118
Tel: (318)671-4000
Admissions: (318)671-4000
E-mail: marc.wright@remingtoncollege.edu
Web Site: http://www.remingtoncollege.edu/shreveport/
President/CEO: Jerry Driskill
Admissions: Marc Wright
Type: Two-Year College **Sex:** Coed **Professional Accreditation:** ACCSCT

RIVER PARISHES COMMUNITY COLLEGE
PO Box 310
Sorrento, LA 70778
Tel: (225)675-8270
Fax: (225)675-5478
E-mail: adauzat@rpcc.cc.la.us
Web Site: http://www.rpcc.edu/
President/CEO: Dr. Joe Ben Welch
Admissions: Allison Dauzat
Type: Two-Year College **Sex:** Coed **Application Fee:** $10.00 **Calendar System:** Semester **Regional Accreditation:** Southern Association of Colleges and Schools **Credit Hours For Degree:** 61 credits, Associates

SAINT JOSEPH SEMINARY COLLEGE
St. Benedict, LA 70457
Tel: (985)867-2299
E-mail: acdean@sjasc.edu
Web Site: http://www.sjasc.edu/
President/CEO: Rev. Gregory Boquet, OSB
Financial Aid: George J. Binder, Jr.
Type: Four-Year College **Sex:** Coed **Affiliation:** Roman Catholic **Scores:** 33% ACT 18-23; 22% ACT 24-29 **Admission Plans:** Preferred Admission; Early Admission; Deferred Admission **Application Deadline:** Rolling **Application Fee:** $0.00 **H.S. Requirements:** High school diploma required; GED accepted **Costs Per Year:** Application fee: $0. One-time mandatory fee: $150. Comprehensive fee: $24,050 includes full-time tuition ($11,582), mandatory fees ($1300), and college room and board ($11,168). College room only: $5896. Part-time tuition: $185 per credit hour. **Scholarships:** Available **Calendar System:** Semester, Summer Session Not available **Enrollment:** FT 83, PT 38 **Faculty:** FT 9, PT 15 **Student-Faculty Ratio:** 3:1 **Exams:** ACT. ACT essay not being used. **% Receiving Financial Aid:** 43 **% Residing in College-Owned, -Operated, or -Affiliated Housing:** 100 **Final Year or Final Semester Residency Requirement:** Yes **Library Holdings:**

70,000 **Regional Accreditation:** Southern Association of Colleges and Schools **Credit Hours For Degree:** 124 semester hours, Bachelors

SOUTHEASTERN LOUISIANA UNIVERSITY
548 Western Ave.
Hammond, LA 70402
Tel: (985)549-2000; Free: 800-222-7358
Admissions: (985)549-5067
Fax: (985)549-5095
E-mail: admissions@selu.edu
Web Site: http://www.selu.edu/
President/CEO: Dr. John Crain
Admissions: Dr. Jeff Rhodes
Financial Aid: Sarah Schillage
Type: Comprehensive **Sex:** Coed **Affiliation:** University of Louisiana System **Scores:** 65.9% ACT 18-23; 26% ACT 24-29 **% Accepted:** 93 **Admission Plans:** Early Admission; Deferred Admission **Application Deadline:** August 1 **Application Fee:** $20.00 **H.S. Requirements:** High school diploma required; GED accepted **Costs Per Year:** Application fee: $20. State resident tuition: $2546 full-time, $106 per credit hour part-time. Nonresident tuition: $9802 full-time, $106 per credit hour part-time. Mandatory fees: $1386 full-time, $105 per credit hour part-time. Full-time tuition and fees vary according to course load. Part-time tuition and fees vary according to course load. College room and board: $6450. College room only: $4020. Room and board charges vary according to board plan and housing facility. **Scholarships:** Available **Calendar System:** Semester, Summer Session Available **Enrollment:** FT 11,196, PT 2,588, Grad FT 456, Grad PT 920 **Faculty:** FT 526, PT 118 **Student-Faculty Ratio:** 25:1 **Exams:** SAT I or ACT. ACT essay not being used. SAT essay not being used. **% Receiving Financial Aid:** 50 **% Residing in College-Owned, -Operated, or -Affiliated Housing:** 16 **Library Holdings:** 714,423 **Regional Accreditation:** Southern Association of Colleges and Schools **Credit Hours For Degree:** 60 semester hours, Associates; 120 semester hours, Bachelors **ROTC:** Army **Professional Accreditation:** AACSB, ABET, AACN, ACA, ASLHA, CSWE, NASM, NCATE, NLN, NAIT **Intercollegiate Athletics:** Baseball M; Basketball M & W; Cross-Country Running M & W; Football M; Golf M; Soccer W; Softball W; Tennis W; Track and Field M & W; Volleyball W

SOUTHERN UNIVERSITY AND AGRICULTURAL AND MECHANICAL COLLEGE
Baton Rouge, LA 70813
Tel: (225)771-4500; Free: 800-256-1531
Admissions: (225)771-2430
E-mail: velva_thomas@subr.edu
Web Site: http://www.subr.edu/
President/CEO: Dr. Kofi Lomotey
Admissions: Velva Thomas
Financial Aid: Phillip Rodgers, Sr.
Type: University **Sex:** Coed **Affiliation:** Southern University System **Scores:** 71.6% SAT M 400+; 53.7% ACT 18-23; 10% ACT 24-29 **% Accepted:** 57 **Admission Plans:** Early Admission **Application Deadline:** July 1 **Application Fee:** $20.00 **H.S. Requirements:** High school diploma required; GED accepted **Costs Per Year:** Application fee: $20. State resident tuition: $4100 full-time. Nonresident tuition: $9892 full-time. Full-time tuition varies according to course load and location. College room and board: $5666. Room and board charges vary according to board plan, gender, and housing facility. **Scholarships:** Available **Calendar System:** Semester, Summer Session Available **Enrollment:** FT 5,763, PT 696 **Faculty:** FT 405, PT 141 **Student-Faculty Ratio:** 16:1 **Exams:** SAT I or ACT. **% Receiving Financial Aid:** 85 **% Residing in College-Owned, -Operated, or -Affiliated Housing:** 31 **Library Holdings:** 880,098 **Regional Accreditation:** Southern Association of Colleges and Schools **Credit Hours For Degree:** 65 credits, Associates; 124 credits, Bachelors **ROTC:** Army, Navy, Air Force **Professional Accreditation:** AACSB, ABET, ACEJMC, AACN, AAFCS, ABA, ACA, ADtA, ASLHA, CORE, CSWE, NASM, NASPAA, NCATE, NLN **Intercollegiate Athletics:** Baseball M; Basketball M & W; Bowling W; Cross-Country Running M; Football M; Golf M & W; Softball W; Tennis M & W; Track and Field M & W; Volleyball W

SOUTHERN UNIVERSITY AT NEW ORLEANS
6400 Press Dr.
New Orleans, LA 70126-1009
Tel: (504)286-5000
Admissions: (504)286-5033
E-mail: llatimor@suno.edu
Web Site: http://www.suno.edu/
President/CEO: Dr. Victor Ukpolo
Admissions: Leatrice D. Latimore
Type: Comprehensive **Sex:** Coed **Affiliation:** Southern University System **% Accepted:** 79 **Admission Plans:** Early Admission; Early Action; Early Decision Plan; Deferred Admission **Application Deadline:** July 1 **Application Fee:** $20.00 **H.S. Requirements:** High school diploma required; GED accepted **Costs Per Year:** Application fee: $20. State resident tuition: $2038 full-time. Nonresident tuition: $5776 full-time. Mandatory fees: $1034 full-time. **Scholarships:** Available **Calendar System:** Semester, Summer Session Available **Enrollment:** FT 2,048, PT 542, Grad FT 228, Grad PT 323 **Faculty:** FT 100, PT 2 **Exams:** ACT, SAT I or ACT. ACT essay used for admission. ACT essay used for advising. ACT essay used for placement. ACT essay not being used. **Regional Accreditation:** Southern Association of Colleges and Schools **Credit Hours For Degree:** 62 semester hours, Associates; 124 semester hours, Bachelors **ROTC:** Army, Air Force **Professional Accreditation:** CSWE, NCATE **Intercollegiate Athletics:** Basketball M & W; Cross-Country Running M & W; Track and Field M & W; Ultimate Frisbee M & W; Volleyball M & W

SOUTHERN UNIVERSITY AT SHREVEPORT
3050 Martin Luther King, Jr. Dr.
Shreveport, LA 71107
Tel: (318)674-3300
Admissions: (318)670-6000
Fax: (318)674-3489
Web Site: http://www.susla.edu/
President/CEO: Dr. Ray L. Belton
Admissions: Juanita Johnson
Type: Two-Year College **Sex:** Coed **Affiliation:** Southern University System **Scores:** 7.7% ACT 18-23 **Admission Plans:** Open Admission; Early Admission **Application Deadline:** Rolling **Application Fee:** $5.00 **H.S. Requirements:** High school diploma required; GED accepted **Scholarships:** Available **Calendar System:** Semester, Summer Session Available **Enrollment:** FT 921, PT 403 **Faculty:** FT 49, PT 49 **Student-Faculty Ratio:** 16:1 **Exams:** ACT. **Regional Accreditation:** Southern Association of Colleges and Schools **Credit Hours For Degree:** 68 credits, Associates **Professional Accreditation:** ARCEST, ADA, AHIMA, CARC, JRCERT, NAACLS, NAIT **Intercollegiate Athletics:** Basketball M & W

SOUTHWEST UNIVERSITY
2200 Veterans Memorial Blvd.
Kenner, LA 70062
Tel: (504)468-2900; Free: 800-433-5923
Web Site: http://www.southwest.edu/
Type: Comprehensive **Sex:** Coed **Professional Accreditation:** DETC

STRAYER UNIVERSITY - METAIRIE CAMPUS
111 Veterans Memorial Blvd.
Ste. 420
Metairie, LA 70005
Tel: (504)799-1700
Fax: (504)849-9980
E-mail: metairie@strayer.edu
Web Site: http://www.strayer.edu/metairie
Type: Comprehensive **Sex:** Coed **Application Fee:** $50.00 **Costs Per Year:** Application fee: $50. **Regional Accreditation:** Middle State Association of Colleges and Schools

TULANE UNIVERSITY
6823 St Charles Ave.
New Orleans, LA 70118-5669
Tel: (504)865-5000; Free: 800-873-9283
Admissions: (504)865-5731
Fax: (504)862-8715
E-mail: undergrad.admission@tulane.edu
Web Site: http://www.tulane.edu/
President/CEO: Scott S. Cowen
Admissions: Earl Retif
Financial Aid: Michael T. Goodman
Type: University **Sex:** Coed **Scores:** 99.73% SAT V 400+; 99.06% SAT M 400+; 4.57% ACT 18-23; 39.61% ACT 24-29 **% Accepted:** 26 **Admission**

Plans: Early Action; Deferred Admission **Application Deadline:** January 15 **Application Fee:** $0.00 **H.S. Requirements:** High school diploma required; GED accepted **Costs Per Year:** Application fee: $0. Comprehensive fee: $50,190 includes full-time tuition ($37,200), mandatory fees ($3384), and college room and board ($9606). College room only: $5506. Room and board charges vary according to board plan and housing facility. **Scholarships:** Available **Calendar System:** Semester, Summer Session Available **Enrollment:** FT 5,452, PT 1,758, Grad FT 4,026, Grad PT 675 **Faculty:** FT 572, PT 612 **Student-Faculty Ratio:** 8:1 **Exams:** SAT I or ACT. **% Receiving Financial Aid:** 40 **% Residing in College-Owned, -Operated, or -Affiliated Housing:** 46 **Library Holdings:** 3,207,609 **Regional Accreditation:** Southern Association of Colleges and Schools **Credit Hours For Degree:** 120 credit hours, Bachelors **ROTC:** Army, Navy, Air Force **Professional Accreditation:** AACSB, ABET, ABA, ADtA, APA, AALS, ACEHSA, CEPH, CSWE, LCMEAMA, NAAB, TEAC **Intercollegiate Athletics:** Baseball M; Basketball M & W; Crew M & W; Cross-Country Running M & W; Football M; Golf W; Gymnastics M & W; Ice Hockey M & W; Lacrosse M & W; Rugby M; Sailing M & W; Soccer M & W; Swimming and Diving M & W; Tennis M & W; Track and Field M & W; Volleyball M & W; Water Polo M & W

UNIVERSITY OF LOUISIANA AT LAFAYETTE
104 University Circle
PO Drawer 41008
Lafayette, LA 70504
Tel: (337)482-1000
Admissions: (337)482-6473
Fax: (337)482-6195
E-mail: admissions@louisiana.edu
Web Site: http://www.louisiana.edu/
President/CEO: Dr. Ray P. Authement
Admissions: Leroy Broussard, Jr.
Financial Aid: Cindy S. Perez
Type: University **Sex:** Coed **Affiliation:** University of Louisiana System **Scores:** 67% ACT 18-23; 25% ACT 24-29 **% Accepted:** 70 **Admission Plans:** Early Admission; Deferred Admission **Application Deadline:** Rolling **Application Fee:** $25.00 **H.S. Requirements:** High school diploma required; GED accepted. For applicants 21 or over: High school diploma or equivalent not required **Scholarships:** Available **Calendar System:** Semester, Summer Session Available **Enrollment:** FT 12,539, PT 2,392 **Faculty:** FT 577, PT 166 **Student-Faculty Ratio:** 23:1 **Exams:** SAT I or ACT. **% Receiving Financial Aid:** 48 **% Residing in College-Owned, -Operated, or -Affiliated Housing:** 12 **Library Holdings:** 999,913 **Regional Accreditation:** Southern Association of Colleges and Schools **Credit Hours For Degree:** 124 semester hours, Bachelors **ROTC:** Army **Professional Accreditation:** AACSB, ABET, ACEJMC, AACN, AAFCS, ADtA, AHIMA, ASLHA, FIDER, NAAB, NASAD, NASM, NCATE, NLN, NAIT **Intercollegiate Athletics:** Baseball M; Basketball M & W; Cross-Country Running M & W; Football M; Golf M; Soccer W; Softball W; Tennis M & W; Track and Field M & W; Volleyball W

UNIVERSITY OF LOUISIANA AT MONROE
700 University Ave.
Monroe, LA 71209-0001
Tel: (318)342-1000; Free: 800-372-5127
Admissions: (318)342-5430
Fax: (318)342-1049
E-mail: admissions@ulm.edu
Web Site: http://www.ulm.edu/
President/CEO: Dr. James E. Cofer, Sr.
Admissions: Frances Self
Financial Aid: Teresa Smith
Type: University **Sex:** Coed **Affiliation:** University of Louisiana System **Scores:** 80% SAT V 400+; 93% SAT M 400+; 68% ACT 18-23; 22% ACT 24-29 **% Accepted:** 74 **Admission Plans:** Early Admission; Deferred Admission **Application Deadline:** Rolling **Application Fee:** $20.00 **H.S. Requirements:** High school diploma required; GED accepted **Scholarships:** Available **Calendar System:** Semester, Summer Session Available **Enrollment:** FT 6,019, PT 1,800, Grad FT 693, Grad PT 492 **Faculty:** FT 345, PT 40 **Student-Faculty Ratio:** 18:1 **Exams:** SAT I or ACT. **% Residing in College-Owned, -Operated, or -Affiliated Housing:** 22 **Library Holdings:** 639,133 **Regional Accreditation:** Southern Association of Colleges and Schools **Credit Hours For Degree:** 60 credit hours, Associates; 128 credit hours, Bachelors **ROTC:** Army **Professional Accreditation:** AACSB, ABET, ACPhE, ACEJMC, AAMFT, AACN, AAFCS, ACCE, ACA, ADA, AOTA, ASLHA, CSWE, JRCERT, NASM, NCATE **Intercollegiate Athletics:** Baseball M; Basketball M & W; Cheerleading M & W; Cross-Country Running M & W; Football M; Golf M & W; Racquetball M & W; Soccer M & W; Softball W; Swimming and Diving M & W; Tennis M & W; Track and Field M & W; Volleyball M & W; Weight Lifting M & W

UNIVERSITY OF NEW ORLEANS
2000 Lakeshore Dr.
New Orleans, LA 70148
Tel: (504)280-6000; Free: 800-256-5866
Admissions: (504)280-7013
Fax: (504)280-5522
E-mail: admissions@uno.edu
Web Site: http://www.uno.edu/
President/CEO: Dr. Timothy P. Ryan
Admissions: Andy Benoit
Financial Aid: Emily London-Jones
Type: University **Sex:** Coed **Affiliation:** Louisiana State University System **Scores:** 95.75% SAT V 400+; 95.74% SAT M 400+; 62.74% ACT 18-23; 29.35% ACT 24-29 **% Accepted:** 57 **Admission Plans:** Early Admission; Deferred Admission **Application Deadline:** July 1 **Application Fee:** $40.00 **H.S. Requirements:** High school diploma required; GED accepted **Costs Per Year:** Application fee: $40. State resident tuition: $3704 full-time, $123.47 per credit hour part-time. Nonresident tuition: $11,860 full-time, $395.33 per credit hour part-time. Mandatory fees: $668 full-time. Full-time tuition and fees vary according to course load. Part-time tuition varies according to course load. College room and board: $6700. Room and board charges vary according to board plan and housing facility. **Scholarships:** Available **Calendar System:** Semester, Summer Session Available **Enrollment:** FT 6,724, PT 2,022, Grad FT 1,392, Grad PT 1,586 **Faculty:** FT 442, PT 188 **Student-Faculty Ratio:** 18:1 **Exams:** SAT I or ACT. ACT essay not being used. SAT essay not being used. **% Receiving Financial Aid:** 62 **% Residing in College-Owned, -Operated, or -Affiliated Housing:** 3 **Library Holdings:** 959,987 **Regional Accreditation:** Southern Association of Colleges and Schools **Credit Hours For Degree:** 128 semester hours, Bachelors **ROTC:** Army, Navy, Air Force **Professional Accreditation:** AACSB, ABET, ACA, ACSP, NASAD, NASM, NAST, NCATE **Intercollegiate Athletics:** Baseball M; Basketball M & W; Golf M; Swimming and Diving M & W; Tennis M & W; Volleyball W

UNIVERSITY OF PHOENIX—LOUISIANA CAMPUS
1 Galleria Blvd.
Ste. 725
Metairie, LA 70001-2082
Tel: (504)461-8852; Free: 800-228-7240
Admissions: (480)557-6151
E-mail: audra.mcquarie@phoenix.edu
Web Site: http://www.phoenix.edu/
President/CEO: William Pepicello
Admissions: Audra McQuarie
Type: Comprehensive **Sex:** Coed **Admission Plans:** Open Admission; Deferred Admission **Application Deadline:** Rolling **Application Fee:** $0.00 **H.S. Requirements:** High school diploma required; GED accepted **Costs Per Year:** Application fee: $0. Tuition: $11,025 full-time. Full-time tuition varies according to course level and course load. **Scholarships:** Available **Calendar System:** Continuous, Summer Session Not available **Enrollment:** FT 1,530 **Faculty:** FT 18, PT 228 **Regional Accreditation:** North Central Association of Colleges and Schools **Credit Hours For Degree:** 60 credits, Associates; 120 credits, Bachelors **Professional Accreditation:** NLN

XAVIER UNIVERSITY OF LOUISIANA
1 Drexel Dr.
New Orleans, LA 70125-1098
Tel: (504)486-7411; Free: 877-XAVIERU
E-mail: apply@xula.edu
Web Site: http://www.xula.edu/
President/CEO: Dr. Norman C. Francis
Admissions: Winston Brown
Financial Aid: Mildred Higgins
Type: Comprehensive **Sex:** Coed **Affiliation:** Roman Catholic **Scores:** 83% SAT V 400+; 79% SAT M 400+; 56% ACT 18-23; 24% ACT 24-29 **% Accepted:** 67 **Admission Plans:** Early Action **Application Deadline:** July 1 **Application Fee:** $25.00 **H.S. Requirements:** High school diploma required; GED accepted **Costs Per Year:** Application fee: $25. One-time

mandatory fee: $150. Comprehensive fee: $22,300 includes full-time tuition ($15,300) and college room and board ($7000). Room and board charges vary according to housing facility. Part-time tuition: $700 per semester hour. Part-time tuition varies according to course load. **Scholarships:** Available **Calendar System:** Semester, Summer Session Available **Enrollment:** FT 2,565, PT 101, Grad FT 615, Grad PT 57 **Faculty:** FT 227, PT 31 **Student-Faculty Ratio:** 13:1 **Exams:** SAT I or ACT. ACT essay used for advising. SAT essay used for advising. **% Receiving Financial Aid:** 81 **% Residing in College-Owned, -Operated, or -Affiliated Housing:** 43 **Library Holdings:** 251,757 **Regional Accreditation:** Southern Association of Colleges and Schools **Credit Hours For Degree:** 128 semester hours, Bachelors **ROTC:** Army, Navy, Air Force **Professional Accreditation:** ACPhE, AANA, ACBSP, NASM, NCATE **Intercollegiate Athletics:** Basketball M & W; Cross-Country Running M & W; Tennis M & W

BATES COLLEGE
2 Andrews Rd.
Lewiston, ME 04240-6028
Tel: (207)786-6255
Admissions: (207)786-6000
Fax: (207)786-6025
E-mail: admissions@bates.edu
Web Site: http://www.bates.edu/
President/CEO: Dr. Elaine T. Hansen
Admissions: Wylie Mitchell
Financial Aid: Wendy G. Glass
Type: Four-Year College **Sex:** Coed **Scores:** 100% SAT V 400+; 99.99% SAT M 400+; 40.74% ACT 24-29 **% Accepted:** 27 **Admission Plans:** Early Admission; Early Decision Plan; Deferred Admission **Application Deadline:** January 1 **Application Fee:** $60.00 **H.S. Requirements:** High school diploma required; GED not accepted **Costs Per Year:** Application fee: $60. Comprehensive fee: $51,300. **Scholarships:** Available **Calendar System:** Miscellaneous, Summer Session Not available **Enrollment:** FT 1,738 **Faculty:** FT 163, PT 31 **Student-Faculty Ratio:** 10:1 **Exams:** ACT essay used for admission. SAT essay used for admission. **% Receiving Financial Aid:** 43 **% Residing in College-Owned, -Operated, or -Affiliated Housing:** 93 **Library Holdings:** 803,500 **Regional Accreditation:** New England Association of Schools and Colleges **Credit Hours For Degree:** 32 courses and 2 short terms, Bachelors **Intercollegiate Athletics:** Baseball M; Basketball M & W; Crew M & W; Cross-Country Running M & W; Equestrian Sports M & W; Fencing M & W; Field Hockey W; Football M; Golf M & W; Ice Hockey M & W; Lacrosse M & W; Rugby M & W; Sailing M & W; Skiing (Cross-Country) M & W; Skiing (Downhill) M & W; Soccer M & W; Softball W; Squash M & W; Swimming and Diving M & W; Tennis M & W; Track and Field M & W; Ultimate Frisbee M & W; Volleyball M & W; Water Polo M & W

BEAL COLLEGE
99 Farm Rd.
Bangor, ME 04401
Tel: (207)947-4591
Web Site: http://www.bealcollege.edu/
President/CEO: Allen T. Stehle
Admissions: Susan Palmer
Type: Two-Year College **Sex:** Coed **Admission Plans:** Open Admission; Deferred Admission **Application Deadline:** Rolling **Application Fee:** $25.00 **H.S. Requirements:** High school diploma required; GED accepted **Scholarships:** Available **Calendar System:** Miscellaneous, Summer Session Available **Enrollment:** FT 239, PT 134 **Faculty:** FT 6, PT 10 **Student-Faculty Ratio:** 16:1 **Library Holdings:** 7,275 **Credit Hours For Degree:** 72 credit hours, Associates **Professional Accreditation:** ACICS, AAMAE

BOWDOIN COLLEGE
5000 College Station
Brunswick, ME 04011
Tel: (207)725-3000
Admissions: (207)725-3190
Fax: (207)725-3003
E-mail: admissions@bowdoin.edu
Web Site: http://www.bowdoin.edu/
President/CEO: Barry Mills
Admissions: Peter T. Wiley
Financial Aid: Stephen H. Joyce
Type: Four-Year College **Sex:** Coed **Scores:** 100% SAT V 400+; 100% SAT M 400+; 3% ACT 18-23; 21% ACT 24-29 **% Accepted:** 19 **Admission Plans:** Early Admission; Early Decision Plan; Deferred Admission **Application Deadline:** January 1 **Application Fee:** $60.00 **H.S. Requirements:** High school diploma required; GED not accepted **Costs Per Year:** Application fee: $60. One-time mandatory fee: $100. Comprehensive fee: $50,900 includes full-time tuition ($39,605), mandatory fees ($415), and college room and board ($10,880). College room only: $5085. Room and board charges vary according to board plan. **Scholarships:** Available **Calendar System:** Semester, Summer Session Not available **Enrollment:** FT 1,771, PT 6 **Faculty:** FT 177, PT 40 **Student-Faculty Ratio:** 9:1 **Exams:** ACT essay used for admission. SAT essay used for admission. ACT essay used for advising. SAT essay used for advising. ACT essay used for placement. SAT essay used for placement. **% Receiving Financial Aid:** 43 **% Residing in College-Owned, -Operated, or -Affiliated Housing:** 94 **Final Year or Final Semester Residency Requirement:** No **Library Holdings:** 1,034,567 **Regional Accreditation:** New England Association of Schools and Colleges **Credit Hours For Degree:** 32 courses, Bachelors **Intercollegiate Athletics:** Baseball M; Basketball M & W; Crew M & W; Cross-Country Running M & W; Equestrian Sports M & W; Fencing M & W; Field Hockey W; Football M; Golf M & W; Ice Hockey M & W; Lacrosse M & W; Riflery M & W; Rugby M & W; Sailing M & W; Skiing (Cross-Country) M & W; Skiing (Downhill) M & W; Soccer M & W; Softball W; Squash M & W; Swimming and Diving M & W; Tennis M & W; Track and Field M & W; Ultimate Frisbee M & W; Volleyball M & W; Water Polo M & W

CENTRAL MAINE COMMUNITY COLLEGE
1250 Turner St.
Auburn, ME 04210-6498
Tel: (207)755-5100; Free: 800-891-2002
Fax: (207)755-5491
E-mail: jnichols@cmcc.edu
Web Site: http://www.cmcc.edu/
President/CEO: Scott E. Knapp
Admissions: Joan Nichols
Type: Two-Year College **Sex:** Coed **Affiliation:** Maine Technical College System **Scores:** 69% SAT V 400+; 73% SAT M 400+ **% Accepted:** 54 **Admission Plans:** Deferred Admission **Application Deadline:** Rolling **Application Fee:** $20.00 **H.S. Requirements:** High school diploma required; GED accepted **Scholarships:** Available **Calendar System:** Semester, Summer Session Available **Faculty:** FT 53, PT 82 **Student-Faculty Ratio:** 18:1 **% Residing in College-Owned, -Operated, or -Affiliated Housing:** 11 **Library Holdings:** 15,000 **Regional Accreditation:** New England Association of Schools and Colleges **Credit Hours For Degree:** 66 credits, Associates **Professional Accreditation:** ABET, ACBSP, NAACLS, NLN **Intercollegiate Athletics:** Baseball M; Basketball M & W; Soccer M & W; Softball W

CENTRAL MAINE MEDICAL CENTER COLLEGE OF NURSING AND HEALTH PROFESSIONS
70 Middle St.
Lewiston, ME 04240-0305
Tel: (207)795-2840
Admissions: (207)795-2843

Fax: (207)795-2849
E-mail: jenisod@cmhc.org
Web Site: http://www.cmmcson.edu/
President/CEO: Susan C. Balturs
Admissions: Dagmar Jenison
Type: Two-Year College **Sex:** Coed **Application Deadline:** February 15 **Application Fee:** $40.00 **H.S. Requirements:** High school diploma required; GED accepted **Costs Per Year:** Application fee: $40. Tuition: $7140 full-time, $210 per credit hour part-time. Mandatory fees: $1430 full-time. College room only: $1900. Room charges vary according to housing facility. **Scholarships:** Available **Calendar System:** Semester, Summer Session Available **Enrollment:** FT 23, PT 134 **Faculty:** FT 15, PT 4 **Student-Faculty Ratio:** 12:1 **Exams:** SAT I or ACT. ACT essay not being used. SAT essay not being used. **% Residing in College-Owned, -Operated, or -Affiliated Housing:** 6 **Final Year or Final Semester Residency Requirement:** No **Library Holdings:** 1,975 **Regional Accreditation:** New England Association of Schools and Colleges **Credit Hours For Degree:** 69 credits, Associates **Professional Accreditation:** NLN

COLBY COLLEGE
Mayflower Hill
Waterville, ME 04901-8840
Tel: (207)872-3000; Free: 800-723-3032
Admissions: (207)859-4800
Fax: (207)872-3474
E-mail: admissions@colby.edu
Web Site: http://www.colby.edu/
President/CEO: William D. Adams
Admissions: Steve Thomas
Financial Aid: Lucia Whittelsey
Type: Four-Year College **Sex:** Coed **Scores:** 100% SAT V 400+; 100% SAT M 400+; 2% ACT 18-23; 45% ACT 24-29 **% Accepted:** 34 **Admission Plans:** Early Admission; Early Decision Plan; Deferred Admission **Application Deadline:** January 1 **Application Fee:** $65.00 **H.S. Requirements:** High school diploma or equivalent not required **Costs Per Year:** Application fee: $65. Comprehensive fee: $50,320. **Scholarships:** Available **Calendar System:** 4-1-4, Summer Session Not available **Enrollment:** FT 1,838 **Faculty:** FT 165, PT 37 **Student-Faculty Ratio:** 10:1 **Exams:** SAT I or ACT, SAT II. ACT essay used for admission. SAT essay used for admission. **% Receiving Financial Aid:** 38 **% Residing in College-Owned, -Operated, or -Affiliated Housing:** 93 **Final Year or Final Semester Residency Requirement:** Yes **Library Holdings:** 926,539 **Regional Accreditation:** New England Association of Schools and Colleges **Credit Hours For Degree:** 128 semester hours, Bachelors **ROTC:** Army **Intercollegiate Athletics:** Badminton M & W; Baseball M; Basketball M & W; Crew M & W; Cross-Country Running M & W; Equestrian Sports M & W; Fencing M & W; Field Hockey W; Football M; Golf M & W; Ice Hockey M & W; Lacrosse M & W; Rugby M & W; Sailing M & W; Skiing (Cross-Country) M & W; Skiing (Downhill) M & W; Soccer M & W; Softball W; Squash M & W; Swimming and Diving M & W; Tennis M & W; Track and Field M & W; Ultimate Frisbee M & W; Volleyball M & W; Water Polo M & W

COLLEGE OF THE ATLANTIC
105 Eden St.
Bar Harbor, ME 04609-1198
Tel: (207)288-5015; Free: 800-528-0025
Admissions: (207)801-5640
Fax: (207)288-4126
E-mail: inquiry@coa.edu
Web Site: http://www.coa.edu/
President/CEO: David F. Hales
Admissions: Sarah Baker
Financial Aid: Bruce Hazam
Type: Comprehensive **Sex:** Coed **Scores:** 100% SAT V 400+; 98% SAT M 400+; 30% ACT 18-23; 60% ACT 24-29 **% Accepted:** 75 **Admission Plans:** Early Admission; Early Decision Plan; Deferred Admission **Application Deadline:** February 15 **Application Fee:** $45.00 **H.S. Requirements:** High school diploma required; GED accepted **Costs Per Year:** Application fee: $45. Comprehensive fee: $42,630 includes full-time tuition ($33,885), mandatory fees ($495), and college room and board ($8250). College room only: $5400. Room and board charges vary according to board plan. Part-time tuition: $3765 per credit. **Scholarships:** Available **Calendar System:** Trimester, Summer Session Not available **Enrollment:** FT 312, PT 24, Grad FT 5 **Faculty:** FT 25, PT 14 **Student-Faculty Ratio:** 11:1 **Exams:** SAT I or ACT. **% Receiving Financial Aid:** 85 **% Residing in College-Owned, -Operated, or -Affiliated Housing:** 43 **Final Year or Final Semester Residency Requirement:** No **Library Holdings:** 50,000 **Regional Accreditation:** New England Association of Schools and Colleges **Credit Hours For Degree:** 36 credits, Bachelors

EASTERN MAINE COMMUNITY COLLEGE
354 Hogan Rd.
Bangor, ME 04401-4206
Tel: (207)974-4600
Fax: (207)974-4683
E-mail: admissions@emcc.edu
Web Site: http://www.emcc.edu/
President/CEO: Joyce B. Hedlund
Admissions: W. Gregory Swett
Type: Two-Year College **Sex:** Coed **Affiliation:** Maine Community College System **Admission Plans:** Preferred Admission; Deferred Admission **Application Deadline:** Rolling **Application Fee:** $20.00 **H.S. Requirements:** High school diploma required; GED accepted **Scholarships:** Available **Calendar System:** Semester, Summer Session Available **Exams:** Other, SAT I. **Library Holdings:** 17,554 **Regional Accreditation:** New England Association of Schools and Colleges **Credit Hours For Degree:** 62 credit hours, Associates **Professional Accreditation:** JRCERT, NLN **Intercollegiate Athletics:** Basketball M & W; Golf M

HUSSON UNIVERSITY
One College Circle
Bangor, ME 04401-2999
Tel: (207)941-7000; Free: 800-4-HUSSON
Admissions: (207)941-7067
Fax: (207)941-7935
E-mail: beanc@husson.edu
Web Site: http://www.husson.edu/
President/CEO: Dr. Robert Clark
Admissions: Carlena Bean
Financial Aid: Linda B. Conant
Type: Comprehensive **Sex:** Coed **Scores:** 84% SAT V 400+; 84% SAT M 400+; 52% ACT 18-23; 15% ACT 24-29 **% Accepted:** 87 **Admission Plans:** Early Admission; Deferred Admission **Application Deadline:** August 1 **Application Fee:** $25.00 **H.S. Requirements:** High school diploma required; GED accepted **Costs Per Year:** Application fee: $25. Comprehensive fee: $20,689 includes full-time tuition ($13,140), mandatory fees ($310), and college room and board ($7239). Full-time tuition and fees vary according to class time. Part-time tuition: $438 per credit hour. Part-time tuition varies according to class time and course load. **Scholarships:** Available **Calendar System:** Semester, Summer Session Available **Enrollment:** FT 1,903, PT 568, Grad FT 316, Grad PT 189 **Faculty:** FT 101, PT 8 **Student-Faculty Ratio:** 19:1 **Exams:** SAT I or ACT. ACT essay used as a validity check on application essay. SAT essay used as a validity check on application essay. **% Receiving Financial Aid:** 85 **% Residing in College-Owned, -Operated, or -Affiliated Housing:** 48 **Library Holdings:** 40,814 **Regional Accreditation:** New England Association of Schools and Colleges **Credit Hours For Degree:** 60 semester hours, Associates; 120 semester hours, Bachelors **ROTC:** Army, Navy **Professional Accreditation:** AACN, AOTA, APTA, NLN **Intercollegiate Athletics:** Baseball M; Basketball M & W; Field Hockey W; Football M; Golf M & W; Lacrosse M & W; Soccer M & W; Softball W; Swimming and Diving W; Volleyball W

KAPLAN UNIVERSITY (LEWISTON)
475 Lisbon St.
Lewiston, ME 04240
Tel: (207)333-3300
Web Site: http://www.kaplanuniversity.edu/
Type: Two-Year College **Sex:** Coed **H.S. Requirements:** High school diploma required; GED accepted **Regional Accreditation:** New England Association of Schools and Colleges

KAPLAN UNIVERSITY (SOUTH PORTLAND)
265 Western Ave.
South Portland, ME 04106
Tel: (207)774-6126; Free: 800-639-3110
Fax: (207)774-1715
Web Site: http://www.kaplanuniversity.edu/
President/CEO: Dr. Christopher Quinn

Type: Two-Year College **Sex:** Coed **H.S. Requirements:** High school diploma required; GED accepted **Scholarships:** Available **Calendar System:** Miscellaneous **Regional Accreditation:** New England Association of Schools and Colleges

KENNEBEC VALLEY COMMUNITY COLLEGE
92 Western Ave.
Fairfield, ME 04937-1367
Tel: (207)453-5000
Admissions: (207)453-5035
E-mail: admissions@kvcc.me.edu
Web Site: http://www.kvcc.me.edu/
President/CEO: Dr. Barbara Woodlee
Admissions: Jim Bourgoin
Type: Two-Year College **Sex:** Coed **Affiliation:** Maine Community College System **% Accepted:** 72 **Admission Plans:** Open Admission; Deferred Admission **Application Deadline:** Rolling **Application Fee:** $20.00 **H.S. Requirements:** High school diploma required; GED accepted **Costs Per Year:** Application fee: $20. State resident tuition: $2520 full-time, $84 per credit hour part-time. Nonresident tuition: $5040 full-time, $168 per credit hour part-time. Mandatory fees: $756 full-time. **Scholarships:** Available **Calendar System:** Semester, Summer Session Available **Enrollment:** FT 730, PT 1,568 **Faculty:** FT 42, PT 159 **Exams:** Other, SAT I or ACT. **Final Year or Final Semester Residency Requirement:** No **Library Holdings:** 17,454 **Regional Accreditation:** New England Association of Schools and Colleges **Credit Hours For Degree:** 61 credits, Associates **Professional Accreditation:** AHIMA, AOTA, APTA, ACBSP, CARC, NLN **Intercollegiate Athletics:** Ice Hockey M & W

MAINE COLLEGE OF ART
522 Congress St.
Portland, ME 04101
Tel: (207)775-3052; Free: 800-639-4808
Admissions: (207)699-5026
Fax: (207)772-5069
E-mail: admissions@meca.edu
Web Site: http://www.meca.edu/
President/CEO: Jim Baker
Admissions: Blaise Maccarrone
Financial Aid: Adrienne J. Amari
Type: Comprehensive **Sex:** Coed **Scores:** 90% SAT V 400+; 85% SAT M 400+; 58% ACT 18-23; 42% ACT 24-29 **% Accepted:** 77 **Admission Plans:** Early Admission; Early Action; Deferred Admission **Application Deadline:** Rolling **Application Fee:** $40.00 **H.S. Requirements:** High school diploma required; GED accepted **Costs Per Year:** Application fee: $40. One-time mandatory fee: $50. Comprehensive fee: $38,445 includes full-time tuition ($27,965), mandatory fees ($680), and college room and board ($9800). Room and board charges vary according to board plan and housing facility. Part-time tuition: $1165 per credit hour. **Scholarships:** Available **Calendar System:** Semester, Summer Session Not available **Enrollment:** FT 295, PT 9, Grad FT 21 **Faculty:** FT 5, PT 40 **Student-Faculty Ratio:** 10:1 **% Receiving Financial Aid:** 86 **% Residing in College-Owned, -Operated, or -Affiliated Housing:** 34 **Final Year or Final Semester Residency Requirement:** No **Library Holdings:** 33,000 **Regional Accreditation:** New England Association of Schools and Colleges **Credit Hours For Degree:** 120 credits, Bachelors **Professional Accreditation:** NASAD

MAINE MARITIME ACADEMY
Castine, ME 04420
Tel: (207)326-4311; Free: 800-227-8465
Admissions: (207)326-2215
Fax: (207)326-2515
E-mail: jeff.wright@mma.edu
Web Site: http://www.mainemaritime.edu/
President/CEO: Leonard H. Tyler, Jr.
Admissions: Jeffrey C. Wright
Financial Aid: Holly Bayle
Type: Comprehensive **Sex:** Coed **% Accepted:** 67 **Admission Plans:** Early Admission; Early Decision Plan; Deferred Admission **Application Deadline:** July 1 **Application Fee:** $15.00 **H.S. Requirements:** High school diploma required; GED accepted **Costs Per Year:** Application fee: $15. State resident tuition: $7900 full-time, $300 per credit hour part-time. Nonresident tuition: $15,600 full-time, $550 per credit hour part-time. Mandatory fees: $2205 full-time. Full-time tuition and fees vary according to course load and program. Part-time tuition varies according to course load and program. College room and board: $8450. College room only: $5250. Room and board charges vary according to board plan. **Scholarships:** Available **Calendar System:** Semester, Summer Session Not available **Enrollment:** FT 822, PT 20 **Faculty:** FT 69, PT 21 **Student-Faculty Ratio:** 12:1 **Exams:** SAT I or ACT. **% Receiving Financial Aid:** 67 **% Residing in College-Owned, -Operated, or -Affiliated Housing:** 80 **Library Holdings:** 427,532 **Regional Accreditation:** New England Association of Schools and Colleges **Credit Hours For Degree:** 78 credit hours, Associates; 140 credit hours, Bachelors **ROTC:** Army, Navy **Professional Accreditation:** ABET **Intercollegiate Athletics:** Basketball M & W; Cross-Country Running M & W; Football M; Lacrosse M; Sailing M & W; Soccer M & W; Softball W; Volleyball W

NEW ENGLAND SCHOOL OF COMMUNICATIONS
1 College Circle
Bangor, ME 04401-2999
Tel: (207)941-7176; Free: 888-877-1876
Fax: (207)947-3987
E-mail: info@nescom.edu
Web Site: http://www.nescom.edu/
President/CEO: Thomas Johnston
Admissions: Louise Grant
Financial Aid: Nicole Vachon
Type: Four-Year College **Sex:** Coed **Affiliation:** Husson University **% Accepted:** 64 **Admission Plans:** Deferred Admission **Application Deadline:** Rolling **Application Fee:** $25.00 **H.S. Requirements:** High school diploma required; GED accepted **Costs Per Year:** Application fee: $25. Comprehensive fee: $18,494 includes full-time tuition ($10,700), mandatory fees ($800), and college room and board ($6994). Part-time tuition: $360 per credit. Part-time tuition varies according to course load. **Scholarships:** Available **Calendar System:** Semester, Summer Session Available **Enrollment:** FT 471, PT 28 **Faculty:** FT 20, PT 49 **Student-Faculty Ratio:** 14:1 **Exams:** Other, SAT I or ACT. **% Receiving Financial Aid:** 87 **% Residing in College-Owned, -Operated, or -Affiliated Housing:** 50 **Final Year or Final Semester Residency Requirement:** No **Library Holdings:** 40,814 **Credit Hours For Degree:** 120 credits, Bachelors **ROTC:** Army **Professional Accreditation:** ACCSCT

NORTHERN MAINE COMMUNITY COLLEGE
33 Edgemont Dr.
Presque Isle, ME 04769-2016
Tel: (207)768-2700
Admissions: (207)768-2785
Fax: (207)768-2831
E-mail: ngagnon@nmcc.edu
Web Site: http://www.nmcc.edu/
President/CEO: Timothy Crowley
Admissions: Nancy Gagnon
Financial Aid: Norma Smith
Type: Two-Year College **Sex:** Coed **Affiliation:** Maine Community College System **% Accepted:** 53 **Admission Plans:** Open Admission; Early Admission; Deferred Admission **Application Deadline:** Rolling **Application Fee:** $20.00 **H.S. Requirements:** High school diploma required; GED accepted **Costs Per Year:** Application fee: $20. One-time mandatory fee: $100. State resident tuition: $2856 full-time, $84 per credit hour part-time. Nonresident tuition: $4250 full-time, $168 per credit hour part-time. Mandatory fees: $995 full-time, $33 per credit hour part-time, $71 per term part-time. Full-time tuition and fees vary according to course level, course load, degree level, program, reciprocity agreements, and student level. Part-time tuition and fees vary according to course level, course load, degree level, program, reciprocity agreements, and student level. College room and board: $5780. College room only: $2230. Room and board charges vary according to board plan and housing facility. **Scholarships:** Available **Calendar System:** Semester, Summer Session Available **Faculty:** FT 45, PT 32 **Student-Faculty Ratio:** 18:1 **Exams:** Other. **% Residing in College-Owned, -Operated, or -Affiliated Housing:** 63 **Library Holdings:** 14,600 **Regional Accreditation:** New England Association of Schools and Colleges **Credit Hours For Degree:** 64 credit hours, Associates **Professional Accreditation:** ACBSP, NLN **Intercollegiate Athletics:** Golf M & W; Soccer M & W

SAINT JOSEPH'S COLLEGE OF MAINE
278 Whites Bridge Rd.
Standish, ME 04084

Tel: (207)892-6766; Free: 800-338-7057
Fax: (207)893-7862
E-mail: admission@sjcme.edu
Web Site: http://www.sjcme.edu/
President/CEO: Joseph Lee
Admissions: Vincent J. Kloskowski
Type: Comprehensive **Sex:** Coed **Affiliation:** Roman Catholic Church **Scores:** 92% SAT V 400+; 91% SAT M 400+ **% Accepted:** 82 **Admission Plans:** Early Action; Deferred Admission **Application Deadline:** Rolling **Application Fee:** $50.00 **H.S. Requirements:** High school diploma required; GED accepted **Costs Per Year:** Application fee: $50. Comprehensive fee: $36,400 includes full-time tuition ($25,150), mandatory fees ($900), and college room and board ($10,350). Part-time tuition: $450 per credit hour. Part-time tuition varies according to course load. **Scholarships:** Available **Calendar System:** Semester, Summer Session Available **Enrollment:** FT 1,015, PT 35 **Faculty:** FT 68, PT 58 **Student-Faculty Ratio:** 15:1 **Exams:** SAT I or ACT. **% Receiving Financial Aid:** 83 **% Residing in College-Owned, -Operated, or -Affiliated Housing:** 82 **Library Holdings:** 113,453 **Regional Accreditation:** New England Association of Schools and Colleges **Credit Hours For Degree:** 128 credit hours, Bachelors **ROTC:** Army **Professional Accreditation:** AACN **Intercollegiate Athletics:** Baseball M; Basketball M & W; Cheerleading M & W; Cross-Country Running M & W; Field Hockey W; Golf M; Ice Hockey M & W; Soccer M & W; Softball W; Volleyball W

SOUTHERN MAINE COMMUNITY COLLEGE
2 Fort Rd.
South Portland, ME 04106
Tel: (207)741-5500
Admissions: (207)741-5515
Fax: (207)741-5751
E-mail: sgrasky@smccme.edu
Web Site: http://www.smccme.edu/
President/CEO: Dr. James O. Ortiz
Admissions: Staci Grasky
Type: Two-Year College **Sex:** Coed **Affiliation:** Maine Community College System **Admission Plans:** Preferred Admission **Application Deadline:** Rolling **Application Fee:** $20.00 **H.S. Requirements:** High school diploma required; GED accepted **Costs Per Year:** Application fee: $20. State resident tuition: $2520 full-time, $84 per credit hour part-time. Nonresident tuition: $5040 full-time, $168 per credit hour part-time. Mandatory fees: $845 full-time, $19.10 per credit hour part-time, $25 per term part-time. College room and board: $8212. College room only: $5212. **Scholarships:** Available **Calendar System:** Semester, Summer Session Available **Enrollment:** FT 2,993, PT 3,268 **Faculty:** FT 107, PT 308 **Student-Faculty Ratio:** 19:1 **Exams:** Other, SAT I or ACT. **% Residing in College-Owned, -Operated, or -Affiliated Housing:** 5 **Library Holdings:** 18,500 **Regional Accreditation:** New England Association of Schools and Colleges **Credit Hours For Degree:** 60 credit hours, Associates **Professional Accreditation:** CARC, JRCERT, NLN **Intercollegiate Athletics:** Baseball M; Basketball M; Golf M & W; Soccer M & W; Softball W; Volleyball M & W

THOMAS COLLEGE
180 West River Rd.
Waterville, ME 04901-5097
Tel: (207)859-1111; Free: 800-339-7001
Fax: (207)859-1114
E-mail: admiss@thomas.edu
Web Site: http://www.thomas.edu/
President/CEO: George R. Spann
Admissions: James Love
Financial Aid: Jeannine Bosse
Type: Comprehensive **Sex:** Coed **Scores:** 75% SAT V 400+; 70% SAT M 400+; 44% ACT 18-23; 12% ACT 24-29 **% Accepted:** 81 **Admission Plans:** Early Action; Deferred Admission **Application Deadline:** Rolling **Application Fee:** $50.00 **H.S. Requirements:** High school diploma required; GED accepted **Scholarships:** Available **Calendar System:** Semester, Summer Session Available **Enrollment:** FT 633, PT 132 **Faculty:** FT 21, PT 60 **Student-Faculty Ratio:** 18:1 **Exams:** SAT I. **% Receiving Financial Aid:** 90 **% Residing in College-Owned, -Operated, or -Affiliated Housing:** 64 **Library Holdings:** 20,000 **Regional Accreditation:** New England Association of Schools and Colleges **Credit Hours For Degree:** 60 credits, Associates; 120 credits, Bachelors **Intercollegiate Athletics:** Baseball M; Basketball M & W; Field Hockey W; Golf M; Lacrosse M & W; Soccer M & W; Softball W; Tennis M; Volleyball W

UNITY COLLEGE
90 Quaker Hill Rd.
Unity, ME 04988
Tel: (207)948-3131
Fax: (207)948-6277
E-mail: gzane@unity.edu
Web Site: http://www.unity.edu/
President/CEO: Dr. Mitchell Thomashow
Admissions: Gary Zane
Financial Aid: Rand E. Newell
Type: Four-Year College **Sex:** Coed **Scores:** 88% SAT V 400+; 85.95% SAT M 400+ **% Accepted:** 88 **Admission Plans:** Early Admission; Early Action; Deferred Admission **Application Deadline:** Rolling **Application Fee:** $25.00 **H.S. Requirements:** High school diploma required; GED accepted **Scholarships:** Available **Calendar System:** Semester, Summer Session Available **Enrollment:** FT 556, PT 6 **Faculty:** FT 34, PT 10 **Student-Faculty Ratio:** 14:1 **Exams:** SAT I or ACT. **% Receiving Financial Aid:** 82 **% Residing in College-Owned, -Operated, or -Affiliated Housing:** 62 **Library Holdings:** 46,000 **Regional Accreditation:** New England Association of Schools and Colleges **Credit Hours For Degree:** 120 semester hours, Bachelors **ROTC:** Army **Intercollegiate Athletics:** Basketball M; Cross-Country Running M & W; Soccer M; Volleyball W

UNIVERSITY OF MAINE
Orono, ME 04469
Tel: (207)581-1110; Free: 877-486-2364
Admissions: (207)581-1561
Fax: (207)581-1213
E-mail: um-admit@maine.edu
Web Site: http://www.umaine.edu/
President/CEO: Dr. Robert A. Kennedy
Admissions: Sharon Oliver
Financial Aid: Peggy L. Crawford
Type: University **Sex:** Coed **Affiliation:** University of Maine System **Scores:** 97% SAT V 400+; 97% SAT M 400+; 51% ACT 18-23; 33% ACT 24-29 **% Accepted:** 80 **Admission Plans:** Early Admission; Early Action; Deferred Admission **Application Deadline:** Rolling **Application Fee:** $40.00 **H.S. Requirements:** High school diploma required; GED accepted. For early admission program: High school diploma required; GED accepted **Costs Per Year:** Application fee: $40. State resident tuition: $7590 full-time, $253 per credit hour part-time. Nonresident tuition: $21,840 full-time, $728 per credit hour part-time. Mandatory fees: $2036 full-time. Full-time tuition and fees vary according to course load and program. Part-time tuition varies according to course load and program. College room and board: $8008. Room and board charges vary according to board plan and housing facility. **Scholarships:** Available **Calendar System:** Semester, Summer Session Available **Enrollment:** FT 8,004, PT 1,480, Grad FT 772, Grad PT 1,611 **Faculty:** FT 567, PT 231 **Student-Faculty Ratio:** 15:1 **Exams:** SAT I or ACT. ACT essay not being used. SAT essay not being used. **% Residing in College-Owned, -Operated, or -Affiliated Housing:** 40 **Final Year or Final Semester Residency Requirement:** Yes **Library Holdings:** 1,148,891 **Regional Accreditation:** New England Association of Schools and Colleges **Credit Hours For Degree:** 120 credit hours, Bachelors **ROTC:** Army, Navy **Professional Accreditation:** AACSB, ABET, AACN, ADtA, AHIMA, APA, ASLHA, AALS, CSWE, NASM, NASPAA, NCATE, SAF **Intercollegiate Athletics:** Baseball M; Basketball M & W; Cheerleading M & W; Crew W; Cross-Country Running M & W; Field Hockey W; Football M; Ice Hockey M & W; Soccer W; Softball W; Swimming and Diving M & W; Tennis M & W; Track and Field M & W

UNIVERSITY OF MAINE AT AUGUSTA
46 University Dr.
Augusta, ME 04330-9410
Tel: (207)621-3000
Admissions: (207)621-3465
Fax: (207)621-3116
E-mail: umaadm@maine.edu
Web Site: http://www.uma.maine.edu/
President/CEO: Allyson Handley
Admissions: Jonathan Henry

Financial Aid: Sherry McCollett
Type: Four-Year College **Sex:** Coed **Affiliation:** University of Maine System **% Accepted:** 93 **Admission Plans:** Early Admission; Deferred Admission **Application Deadline:** August 31 **Application Fee:** $40.00 **H.S. Requirements:** High school diploma required; GED accepted **Costs Per Year:** Application fee: $40. State resident tuition: $6000 full-time, $200 per credit hour part-time. Nonresident tuition: $14,520 full-time, $484 per credit hour part-time. Mandatory fees: $855 full-time, $28.50 per credit hour part-time. Full-time tuition and fees vary according to reciprocity agreements. Part-time tuition and fees vary according to reciprocity agreements. **Scholarships:** Available **Calendar System:** Semester, Summer Session Available **Enrollment:** FT 1,699, PT 3,355 **Faculty:** FT 104, PT 192 **Student-Faculty Ratio:** 18:1 **Exams:** SAT I or ACT. **% Receiving Financial Aid:** 85 **Final Year or Final Semester Residency Requirement:** No **Regional Accreditation:** New England Association of Schools and Colleges **Credit Hours For Degree:** 60 credits, Associates; 120 credits, Bachelors **ROTC:** Army, Navy, Air Force **Professional Accreditation:** ADA, NAACLS, NLN **Intercollegiate Athletics:** Basketball M & W; Golf M & W; Soccer W

UNIVERSITY OF MAINE AT FARMINGTON
224 Main St.
Farmington, ME 04938-1990
Tel: (207)778-7000
Admissions: (207)778-7050
Fax: (207)778-8182
E-mail: umfadmit@maine.edu
Web Site: http://www.umf.maine.edu/
President/CEO: Dr. Theodora J. Kalikow
Admissions: James G. Collins
Financial Aid: Ronald P. Milliken
Type: Comprehensive **Sex:** Coed **Affiliation:** University of Maine System **Scores:** 93.8% SAT V 400+; 91% SAT M 400+ **% Accepted:** 80 **Admission Plans:** Early Admission; Early Action; Deferred Admission **Application Deadline:** Rolling **Application Fee:** $40.00 **H.S. Requirements:** High school diploma required; GED accepted **Costs Per Year:** Application fee: $40. State resident tuition: $7744 full-time, $241 per credit hour part-time. Nonresident tuition: $16,128 full-time, $504 per credit hour part-time. Mandatory fees: $966 full-time. Full-time tuition and fees vary according to course load, reciprocity agreements, and student level. Part-time tuition varies according to course load, reciprocity agreements, and student level. College room and board: $7552. College room only: $4020. Room and board charges vary according to board plan and housing facility. **Scholarships:** Available **Calendar System:** Semester, Summer Session Available **Enrollment:** FT 1,971, PT 220, Grad PT 47 **Faculty:** FT 120, PT 49 **Student-Faculty Ratio:** 14:1 **Exams:** SAT I or ACT. **% Receiving Financial Aid:** 70 **% Residing in College-Owned, -Operated, or -Affiliated Housing:** 50 **Library Holdings:** 98,935 **Regional Accreditation:** New England Association of Schools and Colleges **Credit Hours For Degree:** 120 credit hours, Bachelors **Professional Accreditation:** NCATE **Intercollegiate Athletics:** Baseball M; Basketball M & W; Cross-Country Running M & W; Field Hockey W; Golf M; Ice Hockey M; Lacrosse M & W; Soccer M & W; Softball W; Tennis M & W; Ultimate Frisbee M & W; Volleyball W

UNIVERSITY OF MAINE AT FORT KENT
23 University Dr.
Fort Kent, ME 04743-1292
Tel: (207)834-7500; Free: 888-TRY-UMFK
Admissions: (207)834-7600
Fax: (207)834-7609
E-mail: jillb@maine.edu
Web Site: http://www.umfk.maine.edu/
President/CEO: Dr. Richard W. Cost
Admissions: Jill Cairns
Financial Aid: Ellen Cost
Type: Four-Year College **Sex:** Coed **Affiliation:** University of Maine System **Scores:** 74% SAT V 400+; 73% SAT M 400+ **% Accepted:** 78 **Admission Plans:** Early Admission; Early Decision Plan; Deferred Admission **Application Deadline:** Rolling **Application Fee:** $40.00 **H.S. Requirements:** High school diploma required; GED accepted **Costs Per Year:** Application fee: $40. State resident tuition: $6030 full-time. Nonresident tuition: $15,180 full-time. Mandatory fees: $773 full-time. College room and board: $7080. College room only: $4000. **Scholarships:** Available **Calendar System:** Semester, Summer Session Available **Enrollment:** FT 577, PT 549 **Faculty:** FT 41, PT 31 **Student-Faculty Ratio:** 15:1 **Exams:** SAT I and SAT II or ACT, SAT I. **% Receiving Financial Aid:** 57 **% Residing in College-Owned, -Operated, or -Affiliated Housing:** 20 **Library Holdings:** 58,298 **Regional Accreditation:** New England Association of Schools and Colleges **Credit Hours For Degree:** 60 credit hours, Associates; 120 credit hours, Bachelors **Professional Accreditation:** AACN, NLN **Intercollegiate Athletics:** Basketball M & W; Golf M & W; Skiing (Cross-Country) M & W; Skiing (Downhill) M & W; Soccer M & W; Volleyball W

UNIVERSITY OF MAINE AT MACHIAS
9 O'Brien Ave.
Machias, ME 04654
Tel: (207)255-1200; Free: 888-468-6866
Fax: (207)255-1363
E-mail: ummadmissions@maine.edu
Web Site: http://umm.maine.edu/
President/CEO: Cynthia E. Huggins
Admissions: David Dollins
Financial Aid: Stephanie Larrabee
Type: Four-Year College **Sex:** Coed **Affiliation:** University of Maine System **Scores:** 85.1% SAT V 400+; 71.3% SAT M 400+; 39.1% ACT 18-23; 17.4% ACT 24-29 **% Accepted:** 74 **Admission Plans:** Early Admission; Early Action; Deferred Admission **Application Deadline:** August 15 **Application Fee:** $40.00 **H.S. Requirements:** High school diploma required; GED accepted **Costs Per Year:** Application fee: $40. State resident tuition: $5700 full-time, $190 per semester hour part-time. Nonresident tuition: $15,840 full-time, $528 per semester hour part-time. Mandatory fees: $1171 full-time. College room and board: $6574. College room only: $3308. **Scholarships:** Available **Calendar System:** Semester, Summer Session Available **Enrollment:** FT 452, PT 512 **Faculty:** FT 30, PT 40 **Student-Faculty Ratio:** 14:1 **Exams:** SAT I or ACT. **% Receiving Financial Aid:** 77 **% Residing in College-Owned, -Operated, or -Affiliated Housing:** 44 **Regional Accreditation:** New England Association of Schools and Colleges **Credit Hours For Degree:** 60 credits, Associates; 120 credits, Bachelors **Professional Accreditation:** NRPA **Intercollegiate Athletics:** Basketball M & W; Cross-Country Running M & W; Lacrosse M & W; Soccer M & W; Volleyball W

UNIVERSITY OF MAINE AT PRESQUE ISLE
181 Main St.
Presque Isle, ME 04769-2888
Tel: (207)768-9400
Admissions: (207)768-9453
Fax: (207)768-9608
E-mail: erin.benson@umpi.edu
Web Site: http://www.umpi.edu/
President/CEO: Donald Zillman
Admissions: Erin V. Benson
Financial Aid: Christopher A. R. Bell
Type: Four-Year College **Sex:** Coed **Affiliation:** University of Maine System **Scores:** 73% SAT V 400+; 74% SAT M 400+ **% Accepted:** 87 **Admission Plans:** Early Admission; Early Action; Deferred Admission **Application Deadline:** Rolling **Application Fee:** $40.00 **H.S. Requirements:** High school diploma required; GED accepted **Costs Per Year:** Application fee: $40. State resident tuition: $6030 full-time. Nonresident tuition: $15,180 full-time. Mandatory fees: $845 full-time. Full-time tuition and fees vary according to course load and reciprocity agreements. College room and board: $7300. College room only: $3752. Room and board charges vary according to board plan and housing facility. **Scholarships:** Available **Calendar System:** Semester, Summer Session Available **Enrollment:** FT 919, PT 493 **Faculty:** FT 59, PT 60 **Student-Faculty Ratio:** 20:1 **% Receiving Financial Aid:** 66 **% Residing in College-Owned, -Operated, or -Affiliated Housing:** 92 **Regional Accreditation:** New England Association of Schools and Colleges **Credit Hours For Degree:** 61 credit hours, Associates; 120 credit hours, Bachelors **Professional Accreditation:** CSWE, NAACLS, NRPA **Intercollegiate Athletics:** Baseball M; Basketball M & W; Cross-Country Running M & W; Golf M; Soccer M & W; Softball W; Volleyball W

UNIVERSITY OF NEW ENGLAND
Hills Beach Rd.
Biddeford, ME 04005-9526
Tel: (207)283-0171; Free: 800-477-4UNE
Admissions: (207)283-0170
E-mail: admissions@une.edu
Web Site: http://www.une.edu/

President/CEO: Dr. Danielle H. Ripich
Admissions: Robert J. Pecchia
Financial Aid: John R. Bowie
Type: Comprehensive **Sex:** Coed **Scores:** 97.47% SAT V 400+; 97.29% SAT M 400+; 44.68% ACT 18-23; 51.06% ACT 24-29 **% Accepted:** 80 **Admission Plans:** Deferred Admission **Application Deadline:** February 15 **Application Fee:** $40.00 **H.S. Requirements:** High school diploma required; GED accepted **Costs Per Year:** Application fee: $40. Comprehensive fee: $38,790 includes full-time tuition ($26,940), mandatory fees ($980), and college room and board ($10,870). Room and board charges vary according to board plan, housing facility, and location. Part-time tuition: $970 per credit hour. **Scholarships:** Available **Calendar System:** Semester, Summer Session Available **Enrollment:** FT 2,059, PT 382, Grad FT 1,791, Grad PT 261 **Faculty:** FT 197, PT 173 **Student-Faculty Ratio:** 13:1 **Exams:** SAT I or ACT. **% Receiving Financial Aid:** 82 **% Residing in College-Owned, -Operated, or -Affiliated Housing:** 45 **Library Holdings:** 156,752 **Regional Accreditation:** New England Association of Schools and Colleges **Credit Hours For Degree:** 68 credits, Associates; 120 credits, Bachelors **ROTC:** Army **Professional Accreditation:** AANA, ADA, AOTA, AOsA, APTA, CSWE, NLN **Intercollegiate Athletics:** Basketball M & W; Cross-Country Running M & W; Field Hockey W; Golf M; Lacrosse M & W; Soccer M & W; Softball W; Swimming and Diving W; Volleyball W

UNIVERSITY OF SOUTHERN MAINE
96 Falmouth St., PO Box 9300
Portland, ME 04104-9300
Tel: (207)780-4141; Free: 800-800-4USM
Admissions: (207)780-5724
Fax: (207)780-5640
E-mail: usmadm@usm.maine.edu
Web Site: http://www.usm.maine.edu/
President/CEO: Dr. Selma Botman
Admissions: Jonathan Barker
Financial Aid: Keith P. Dubois
Type: Comprehensive **Sex:** Coed **Affiliation:** University of Maine System **Scores:** 94% SAT V 400+; 92% SAT M 400+; 57% ACT 18-23; 20% ACT 24-29 **% Accepted:** 84 **Admission Plans:** Early Admission; Deferred Admission **Application Deadline:** February 15 **Application Fee:** $40.00 **H.S. Requirements:** High school diploma required; GED accepted **Scholarships:** Available **Calendar System:** Semester, Summer Session Available **Enrollment:** FT 4,831, PT 2,787, Grad FT 798, Grad PT 1,239 **Faculty:** FT 335, PT 292 **Student-Faculty Ratio:** 13:1 **Exams:** SAT I or ACT. **% Receiving Financial Aid:** 82 **% Residing in College-Owned, -Operated, or -Affiliated Housing:** 15 **Library Holdings:** 455,129 **Regional Accreditation:** New England Association of Schools and Colleges **Credit Hours For Degree:** 60 credit hours, Associates; 120 credit hours, Bachelors **ROTC:** Army, Air Force **Professional Accreditation:** AACSB, ABET, AACN, ABA, ACA, AOTA, ACEHSA, CORE, CSWE, JRCEPAT, NASAD, NASM, NASPAA, NCATE, NLN, TEAC, NAIT **Intercollegiate Athletics:** Baseball M; Basketball M & W; Cheerleading M & W; Cross-Country Running M & W; Field Hockey W; Golf M & W; Ice Hockey M & W; Lacrosse M & W; Sailing M & W; Soccer M & W; Softball W; Tennis M & W; Track and Field M & W; Volleyball W; Wrestling M

WASHINGTON COUNTY COMMUNITY COLLEGE
One College Dr.
Calais, ME 04619
Tel: (207)454-1000
Fax: (207)454-1026
Web Site: http://www.wccc.me.edu/
President/CEO: William Cassidy
Admissions: Kent Lyons
Type: Two-Year College **Sex:** Coed **Affiliation:** Maine Technical College System **% Accepted:** 98 **Admission Plans:** Open Admission; Deferred Admission **Application Deadline:** Rolling **Application Fee:** $20.00 **H.S. Requirements:** High school diploma required; GED accepted **Scholarships:** Available **Calendar System:** Semester **Faculty:** FT 29, PT 10 **Student-Faculty Ratio:** 9:1 **% Residing in College-Owned, -Operated, or -Affiliated Housing:** 22 **Library Holdings:** 26,370 **Regional Accreditation:** New England Association of Schools and Colleges **Credit Hours For Degree:** 64 credits, Associates

YORK COUNTY COMMUNITY COLLEGE
112 College Dr.
Wells, ME 04090
Tel: (207)646-9282; Free: 800-580-3820
Fax: (207)641-0837
E-mail: fquistgard@yccc.edu
Web Site: http://www.yccc.edu/
President/CEO: Charles Lyons
Admissions: Fred Quistgard
Type: Two-Year College **Sex:** Coed **Affiliation:** Maine Community College System **% Accepted:** 74 **Admission Plans:** Open Admission **Application Deadline:** Rolling **Application Fee:** $20.00 **H.S. Requirements:** High school diploma required; GED accepted **Costs Per Year:** Application fee: $20. State resident tuition: $84 per credit hour part-time. Nonresident tuition: $168 per credit hour part-time. Part-time tuition varies according to course load and program. **Scholarships:** Available **Calendar System:** Semester, Summer Session Available **Faculty:** FT 17, PT 60 **Student-Faculty Ratio:** 15:1 **Library Holdings:** 4,000 **Regional Accreditation:** New England Association of Schools and Colleges **Credit Hours For Degree:** 63 credit hours, Associates **Intercollegiate Athletics:** Golf M

ALLEGANY COLLEGE OF MARYLAND
12401 Willowbrook Rd., SE
Cumberland, MD 21502-2596
Tel: (301)784-5000
Fax: (301)784-5024
E-mail: cnolan@allegany.edu
Web Site: http://www.allegany.edu/
President/CEO: Gary Durr
Admissions: Cathy Nolan
Financial Aid: Deborah D. Yonker
Type: Two-Year College **Sex:** Coed **Affiliation:** Maryland State Community Colleges System **Admission Plans:** Open Admission; Early Admission **Application Deadline:** Rolling **Application Fee:** $0.00 **H.S. Requirements:** High school diploma required; GED accepted. For Dislocated Workers Program: High school diploma required; GED not accepted **Costs Per Year:** Application fee: $0. Area resident tuition: $3234 full-time. State resident tuition: $5714 full-time. Nonresident tuition: $6824 full-time. Mandatory fees: $194 full-time. Full-time tuition and fees vary according to course load and location. College room and board: $8000. College room only: $6000. Room and board charges vary according to housing facility. **Scholarships:** Available **Calendar System:** Semester, Summer Session Available **Faculty:** FT 114, PT 118 **Student-Faculty Ratio:** 16:1 **Exams:** ACT. **% Residing in College-Owned, -Operated, or -Affiliated Housing:** 7 **Library Holdings:** 86,636 **Regional Accreditation:** Middle State Association of Colleges and Schools **Credit Hours For Degree:** 60 credits, Associates **ROTC:** Army **Professional Accreditation:** ADA, AOTA, APTA, CARC, JRCERT, NAACLS, NLN **Intercollegiate Athletics:** Baseball M; Basketball M & W; Soccer M & W; Softball W; Tennis M & W; Volleyball W

ANNE ARUNDEL COMMUNITY COLLEGE
101 College Parkway
Arnold, MD 21012-1895
Tel: (410)647-7100
Admissions: (410)777-2240
Fax: (410)541-2245
E-mail: 4info@aacc.edu
Web Site: http://www.aacc.edu/
President/CEO: Dr. Martha A. Smith
Admissions: Thomas McGinn
Financial Aid: Richard C. Heath
Type: Two-Year College **Sex:** Coed **Admission Plans:** Open Admission; Early Admission; Deferred Admission **Application Deadline:** Rolling **Application Fee:** $0.00 **H.S. Requirements:** High school diploma or equivalent not required. For certain allied health programs: High school diploma required; GED accepted **Costs Per Year:** Application fee: $0. Area resident tuition: $2640 full-time, $88 per credit hour part-time. State resident tuition: $5070 full-time, $169 per credit hour part-time. Nonresident tuition: $8970 full-time, $299 per credit hour part-time. Mandatory fees: $370 full-time, $11 per credit hour part-time, $20 per term part-time. Full-time tuition and fees vary according to course load. Part-time tuition and fees vary according to course load. **Scholarships:** Available **Calendar System:** Semester, Summer Session Available **Enrollment:** FT 5,957, PT 10,784 **Faculty:** FT 262, PT 754 **Student-Faculty Ratio:** 18:1 **Library Holdings:** 144,694 **Regional Accreditation:** Middle State Association of Colleges and Schools **Credit Hours For Degree:** 60 credit hours, Associates **ROTC:** Army, Air Force **Professional Accreditation:** ACF, APTA, JRCERT, NLN **Intercollegiate Athletics:** Baseball M; Basketball M & W; Cross-Country Running M & W; Golf M; Lacrosse M & W; Soccer M & W; Softball W; Volleyball W

BALTIMORE CITY COMMUNITY COLLEGE
2901 Liberty Heights Ave.
Baltimore, MD 21215-7893
Tel: (410)462-8300
Fax: (410)462-7677
E-mail: sforman@bccc.edu
Web Site: http://www.bccc.edu/
President/CEO: Dr. Carolane Williams
Admissions: Scheherazade Forman
Type: Two-Year College **Sex:** Coed **Admission Plans:** Open Admission; Early Admission; Deferred Admission **Application Deadline:** August 9 **Application Fee:** $10.00 **H.S. Requirements:** High school diploma required; GED accepted **Scholarships:** Available **Calendar System:** Semester, Summer Session Available **Faculty:** FT 121, PT 315 **Student-Faculty Ratio:** 17:1 **Library Holdings:** 72,413 **Regional Accreditation:** Middle State Association of Colleges and Schools **Credit Hours For Degree:** 62 credits, Associates **Professional Accreditation:** ARCEST, ADA, AHIMA, APTA, ACBSP, CARC, NLN **Intercollegiate Athletics:** Basketball M & W; Cross-Country Running M & W; Track and Field M & W

BALTIMORE INTERNATIONAL COLLEGE
Commerce Exchange
17 Commerce St.
Baltimore, MD 21202-3230
Tel: (410)752-4710; Free: 800-624-9926
Fax: (410)752-3730
E-mail: admissions@bic.edu
Web Site: http://www.bic.edu/
President/CEO: Roger Chylinski
Admissions: Kristin Ciarlo
Financial Aid: Kim Wittler
Type: Two-Year College **Sex:** Coed **Admission Plans:** Early Action; Deferred Admission **Application Deadline:** Rolling **Application Fee:** $35.00 **H.S. Requirements:** High school diploma required; GED accepted **Costs Per Year:** Application fee: $35. Comprehensive fee: $32,650 includes full-time tuition ($17,930), mandatory fees ($5458), and college room and board ($9262). Full-time tuition and fees vary according to course load, degree level, and program. Room and board charges vary according to board plan. **Scholarships:** Available **Calendar System:** Semester, Summer Session Not available **Enrollment:** FT 486, PT 30 **Faculty:** FT 14, PT 18 **Exams:** Other, SAT I or ACT. **% Residing in College-Owned, -Operated, or -Affiliated Housing:** 24 **Library Holdings:** 13,000 **Regional Accreditation:** Middle State Association of Colleges and Schools **Credit Hours For Degree:** 60 credits, Associates; 120 credits, Bachelors

BOWIE STATE UNIVERSITY
14000 Jericho Park Rd.
Bowie, MD 20715-9465
Tel: (301)860-4000; Free: 877-772-6943
Admissions: (301)860-3415
Fax: (301)860-3510

E-mail: sholt@bowiestate.edu
Web Site: http://www.bowiestate.edu/
President/CEO: Mickey L. Burnim
Admissions: Don Kiah
Financial Aid: Deborah Stanley
Type: Comprehensive **Sex:** Coed **Affiliation:** University System of Maryland **Scores:** 79% SAT V 400+; 75.2% SAT M 400+ **% Accepted:** 48 **Admission Plans:** Preferred Admission **Application Deadline:** April 1 **Application Fee:** $40.00 **H.S. Requirements:** High school diploma required; GED accepted **Costs Per Year:** Application fee: $40. State resident tuition: $4286 full-time, $189 per credit hour part-time. Nonresident tuition: $14,725 full-time, $620 per credit hour part-time. Mandatory fees: $1754 full-time, $88.30 per credit hour part-time. Part-time tuition and fees vary according to course load. College room and board: $7536. Room and board charges vary according to board plan and housing facility. **Scholarships:** Available **Calendar System:** Semester, Summer Session Available **Enrollment:** FT 3,710, PT 690, Grad FT 401, Grad PT 816 **Faculty:** FT 294, PT 223 **Student-Faculty Ratio:** 16:1 **Exams:** SAT I or ACT. **% Receiving Financial Aid:** 79 **% Residing in College-Owned, -Operated, or -Affiliated Housing:** 33 **Library Holdings:** 331,640 **Regional Accreditation:** Middle State Association of Colleges and Schools **Credit Hours For Degree:** 120 credits, Bachelors **Professional Accreditation:** ABET, ACBSP, CSWE, NCATE, NLN **Intercollegiate Athletics:** Basketball M & W; Bowling W; Cross-Country Running M & W; Football M; Softball W; Tennis W; Track and Field M & W; Volleyball W

CAPITOL COLLEGE
11301 Springfield Rd.
Laurel, MD 20708-9759
Tel: (301)369-2800; Free: 800-950-1992
Admissions: (301)953-3200
E-mail: ghwalls@capitol-college.edu
Web Site: http://www.capitol-college.edu/
President/CEO: Michael T. Wood, PhD
Admissions: George Walls
Financial Aid: Suzanne Thompson
Type: Comprehensive **Sex:** Coed **Admission Plans:** Deferred Admission **Application Deadline:** Rolling **Application Fee:** $25.00 **H.S. Requirements:** High school diploma required; GED accepted **Costs Per Year:** Application fee: $25. Tuition: $619 per credit part-time. Mandatory fees: $25 per credit part-time. **Scholarships:** Available **Calendar System:** Semester, Summer Session Available **Student-Faculty Ratio:** 12:1 **Exams:** SAT I or ACT. **Regional Accreditation:** Middle State Association of Colleges and Schools **Credit Hours For Degree:** 62 semester hours, Associates; 122 semester hours, Bachelors **ROTC:** Army **Professional Accreditation:** ABET

CARROLL COMMUNITY COLLEGE
1601 Washington Rd.
Westminster, MD 21157
Tel: (410)386-8000
Admissions: (410)386-8430
Fax: (410)876-8855
E-mail: cedwards@carrollcc.edu
Web Site: http://www.carrollcc.edu/
President/CEO: Dr. Faye Pappalardo
Admissions: Candace Edwards
Financial Aid: Lori Henry
Type: Two-Year College **Sex:** Coed **Affiliation:** Maryland Higher Education Commission **% Accepted:** 100 **Admission Plans:** Open Admission; Early Admission **Application Deadline:** Rolling **Application Fee:** $0.00 **H.S. Requirements:** High school diploma or equivalent not required **Costs Per Year:** Application fee: $0. Area resident tuition: $3565 full-time, $119 per credit hour part-time. State resident tuition: $5158 full-time, $172 per credit hour part-time. Nonresident tuition: $7246 full-time, $242 per credit hour part-time. **Scholarships:** Available **Calendar System:** Semester, Summer Session Available **Enrollment:** FT 1,730, PT 2,183 **Faculty:** FT 69, PT 219 **Student-Faculty Ratio:** 17:1 **Library Holdings:** 68,038 **Regional Accreditation:** Middle State Association of Colleges and Schools **Credit Hours For Degree:** 62 credits, Associates **Professional Accreditation:** APTA

CECIL COLLEGE
One Seahawk Dr.
North East, MD 21901-1999
Tel: (410)287-6060
Admissions: (410)287-1002
Fax: (410)287-1026
E-mail: dlane@cecil.edu
Web Site: http://www.cecil.edu/
President/CEO: Dr. Stephen Pannill
Admissions: Dr. Diane Lane
Financial Aid: Kate Lockhart
Type: Two-Year College **Sex:** Coed **% Accepted:** 100 **Admission Plans:** Open Admission; Early Admission; Deferred Admission **Application Deadline:** Rolling **H.S. Requirements:** High school diploma required; GED accepted **Costs Per Year:** Area resident tuition: $2550 full-time, $85 per credit hour part-time. State resident tuition: $5250 full-time, $175 per credit hour part-time. Nonresident tuition: $6600 full-time, $220 per credit hour part-time. Mandatory fees: $362 full-time. **Scholarships:** Available **Calendar System:** Semester, Summer Session Available **Enrollment:** FT 874, PT 1,514 **Faculty:** FT 47, PT 179 **Student-Faculty Ratio:** 13:1 **Library Holdings:** 38,105 **Regional Accreditation:** Middle State Association of Colleges and Schools **Credit Hours For Degree:** 60 credits, Associates **Professional Accreditation:** NLN **Intercollegiate Athletics:** Baseball M; Basketball M & W; Cheerleading W; Soccer W; Softball W; Tennis W; Volleyball W

CHESAPEAKE COLLEGE
PO Box 8
Wye Mills, MD 21679-0008
Tel: (410)822-5400
Fax: (410)827-9466
E-mail: kpetrichenko@chesapeake.edu
Web Site: http://www.chesapeake.edu/
President/CEO: Barbara Viniar
Admissions: Kathy Petrichenko
Type: Two-Year College **Sex:** Coed **Admission Plans:** Open Admission; Early Admission; Deferred Admission **Application Deadline:** Rolling **Application Fee:** $0.00 **H.S. Requirements:** High school diploma required; GED accepted **Scholarships:** Available **Calendar System:** Semester, Summer Session Available **Faculty:** FT 54, PT 76 **Student-Faculty Ratio:** 16:1 **Library Holdings:** 44,049 **Regional Accreditation:** Middle State Association of Colleges and Schools **Credit Hours For Degree:** 63 credit hours, Associates **Professional Accreditation:** APTA, JRCERT **Intercollegiate Athletics:** Baseball M; Basketball M & W; Soccer M & W; Softball W; Tennis M & W; Volleyball W

COLLEGE OF NOTRE DAME OF MARYLAND
4701 North Charles St.
Baltimore, MD 21210-2476
Tel: (410)435-0100; Free: 800-435-0300
Admissions: (410)532-5332
Fax: (410)532-6287
E-mail: sbogdon@ndm.edu
Web Site: http://www.ndm.edu/
President/CEO: Dr. Mary Pat Seurkamp
Admissions: Sharon Bogdan
Financial Aid: Zhanna Goltser
Type: Comprehensive **Sex:** Coed **Affiliation:** Roman Catholic **% Accepted:** 65 **Admission Plans:** Early Admission; Early Action; Deferred Admission **Application Deadline:** February 15 **Application Fee:** $45.00 **H.S. Requirements:** High school diploma required; GED accepted **Costs Per Year:** Application fee: $45. Comprehensive fee: $37,850 includes full-time tuition ($27,600), mandatory fees ($750), and college room and board ($9500). Room and board charges vary according to board plan. Part-time tuition: $425 per credit hour. **Scholarships:** Available **Calendar System:** 4-1-4, Summer Session Available **Enrollment:** FT 493, PT 761, Grad FT 180, Grad PT 1,537 **Faculty:** FT 102, PT 136 **Student-Faculty Ratio:** 12:1 **Exams:** SAT I or ACT. **% Receiving Financial Aid:** 84 **% Residing in College-Owned, -Operated, or -Affiliated Housing:** 55 **Final Year or Final Semester Residency Requirement:** Yes **Library Holdings:** 999,295 **Regional Accreditation:** Middle State Association of Colleges and Schools **Credit Hours For Degree:** 120 credits, Bachelors **ROTC:** Army **Professional Accreditation:** NCATE, NLN **Intercollegiate Athletics:** Basketball W; Field Hockey W; Lacrosse W; Soccer W; Softball W; Swimming and Diving W; Tennis W; Volleyball W

COLLEGE OF SOUTHERN MARYLAND
8730 Mitchell Rd., PO Box 910
La Plata, MD 20646-0910
Tel: (301)934-2251; Free: 800-933-9177
Admissions: (301)934-7520
Fax: (301)934-5255
E-mail: info@csmd.edu
Web Site: http://www.csmd.edu/
President/CEO: Dr. Bradley Gottfried
Type: Two-Year College **Sex:** Coed **% Accepted:** 100 **Admission Plans:** Open Admission; Early Admission; Deferred Admission **Application Deadline:** Rolling **Application Fee:** $0.00 **H.S. Requirements:** High school diploma or equivalent not required. For nursing program: High school diploma required; GED accepted **Costs Per Year:** Application fee: $0. Area resident tuition: $3690 full-time, $100 per credit hour part-time. State resident tuition: $6420 full-time, $174 per credit hour part-time. Nonresident tuition: $8303 full-time, $225 per credit hour part-time. **Scholarships:** Available **Calendar System:** Semester, Summer Session Available **Enrollment:** FT 3,595, PT 5,215 **Faculty:** FT 123, PT 448 **Final Year or Final Semester Residency Requirement:** No **Library Holdings:** 44,896 **Regional Accreditation:** Middle State Association of Colleges and Schools **Credit Hours For Degree:** 62 credits, Associates **Professional Accreditation:** APTA, ACBSP, NLN **Intercollegiate Athletics:** Baseball M; Basketball M & W; Golf M; Soccer M & W; Softball W; Tennis M; Volleyball W

THE COMMUNITY COLLEGE OF BALTIMORE COUNTY
7201 Rossville Blvd.
Baltimore, MD 21228
Tel: (443)840-2999
Admissions: (443)840-4392
E-mail: ddrake@ccbcmd.edu
Web Site: http://www.ccbcmd.edu/
President/CEO: Dr. Sandra Kurtinitis, PhD
Admissions: Diane Drake
Type: Two-Year College **Sex:** Coed **Application Deadline:** Rolling **H.S. Requirements:** High school diploma required; GED accepted **Costs Per Year:** Area resident tuition: $2700 full-time. State resident tuition: $5490 full-time. Nonresident tuition: $8220 full-time. Mandatory fees: $402 full-time. **Calendar System:** Semester, Summer Session Available **Enrollment:** FT 8,558, PT 15,026 **Faculty:** FT 403, PT 845 **Exams:** SAT I or ACT. **Regional Accreditation:** Middle State Association of Colleges and Schools **Professional Accreditation:** ABFSE, AOTA, CARC, JRCERT, NASM, NAST, NLN **Intercollegiate Athletics:** Baseball M; Basketball M & W; Lacrosse M & W; Soccer M & W; Softball W; Track and Field W; Volleyball W

COPPIN STATE UNIVERSITY
2500 West North Ave.
Baltimore, MD 21216-3698
Tel: (410)951-3000; Free: 800-635-3674
Admissions: (410)951-3600
Fax: (410)523-7238
E-mail: mgross@coppin.edu
Web Site: http://www.coppin.edu/
President/CEO: Dr. Reginald S. Avery
Admissions: Michelle Gross
Financial Aid: Fay Tayree
Type: Comprehensive **Sex:** Coed **Affiliation:** University System of Maryland **Scores:** 79% SAT V 400+; 73% SAT M 400+ **% Accepted:** 50 **Admission Plans:** Early Admission; Deferred Admission **Application Deadline:** July 15 **Application Fee:** $35.00 **H.S. Requirements:** High school diploma required; GED accepted **Costs Per Year:** Application fee: $35. State resident tuition: $3527 full-time, $151 per credit hour part-time. Nonresident tuition: $12,222 full-time, $420 per credit hour part-time. Mandatory fees: $1749 full-time, $27.18 per credit hour part-time. Full-time tuition and fees vary according to course load. Part-time tuition and fees vary according to course load. College room and board: $7496. College room only: $4686. Room and board charges vary according to board plan. **Scholarships:** Available **Calendar System:** Semester, Summer Session Available **Enrollment:** FT 2,575, PT 726, Grad FT 142, Grad PT 358 **Faculty:** FT 159, PT 173 **Student-Faculty Ratio:** 16:1 **Exams:** SAT I or ACT. **% Receiving Financial Aid:** 78 **Library Holdings:** 134,983 **Regional Accreditation:** Middle State Association of Colleges and Schools **Credit Hours For Degree:** 120 credit hours, Bachelors **ROTC:** Army **Professional Accreditation:** CORE, CSWE, NCATE, NLN **Intercollegiate Athletics:** Baseball M; Basketball M & W; Bowling W; Cross-Country Running M & W; Rugby M; Softball W; Tennis M & W; Track and Field M & W; Volleyball W

DEVRY UNIVERSITY
4550 Montgomery Ave.. Ste. 100 North
Bethesda, MD 20814-3304
Tel: (301)652-8477
Fax: (301)652-8577
Web Site: http://www.devry.edu/
President/CEO: Mary Kay Porter
Type: Comprehensive **Sex:** Coed **Affiliation:** DeVry University **Admission Plans:** Deferred Admission **Application Deadline:** Rolling **Application Fee:** $50.00 **H.S. Requirements:** High school diploma required; GED accepted **Costs Per Year:** Application fee: $50. Tuition: $14,080 full-time, $550 per credit part-time. **Scholarships:** Available **Calendar System:** Semester, Summer Session Available **Enrollment:** FT 29, PT 39, Grad FT 9, Grad PT 65 **Faculty:** FT 0, PT 21 **Student-Faculty Ratio:** 10:1 **Exams:** ACT essay used for admission. SAT essay used for admission. ACT essay used for placement. SAT essay used for placement. **% Receiving Financial Aid:** 33 **Regional Accreditation:** North Central Association of Colleges and Schools **Credit Hours For Degree:** 122 credits, Bachelors

FAITH THEOLOGICAL SEMINARY
529 Walker Ave.
Baltimore, MD 21212
Tel: (410)323-6211
Fax: (410)323-6331
Web Site: http://www.faiththeological.org/
Type: Comprehensive **Sex:** Coed

FREDERICK COMMUNITY COLLEGE
7932 Opossumtown Pike
Frederick, MD 21702-2097
Tel: (301)846-2400
Admissions: (301)846-2468
E-mail: admissions@frederick.edu
Web Site: http://www.frederick.edu/
President/CEO: Dr. Carol W. Eaton
Admissions: Lisa A. Freel
Type: Two-Year College **Sex:** Coed **Admission Plans:** Open Admission **Application Deadline:** September 1 **Application Fee:** $0.00 **H.S. Requirements:** High school diploma or equivalent not required **Costs Per Year:** Application fee: $0. Area resident tuition: $3000 full-time. State resident tuition: $6400 full-time. Nonresident tuition: $8600 full-time. Mandatory fees: $400 full-time. **Scholarships:** Available **Calendar System:** Semester, Summer Session Available **Enrollment:** FT 2,359, PT 3,874 **Faculty:** FT 97, PT 425 **Student-Faculty Ratio:** 12:1 **Final Year or Final Semester Residency Requirement:** No **Library Holdings:** 40,000 **Regional Accreditation:** Middle State Association of Colleges and Schools **Credit Hours For Degree:** 60 credit hours, Associates **ROTC:** Army **Professional Accreditation:** ARCEST, CARC **Intercollegiate Athletics:** Baseball M; Basketball M & W; Golf M & W; Soccer M & W; Softball W; Volleyball W

FROSTBURG STATE UNIVERSITY
101 Braddock Rd.
Frostburg, MD 21532-1099
Tel: (301)687-4000
Admissions: (301)687-4201
Fax: (301)687-7074
E-mail: fsuadmissions@frostburg.edu
Web Site: http://www.frostburg.edu/
President/CEO: Dr. Jonathan Gibralter
Admissions: Trish Gregory
Financial Aid: Angela Hovatter
Type: Comprehensive **Sex:** Coed **Affiliation:** University System of Maryland **Scores:** 92% SAT V 400+; 89% SAT M 400+; 53% ACT 18-23; 7% ACT 24-29 **% Accepted:** 59 **Admission Plans:** Early Admission **Application Deadline:** February 15 **Application Fee:** $30.00 **H.S. Requirements:** High school diploma required; GED accepted **Costs Per Year:** Application fee: $30. State resident tuition: $5000 full-time, $207 per credit hour part-time. Nonresident tuition: $15,196 full-time, $427 per credit hour part-time. Mandatory fees: $1684 full-time, $82 per credit hour part-time, $11 per term part-time. Full-time tuition and fees vary according to location. Part-time tuition and fees vary according to course load and location. College room and

board: $7304. College room only: $3474. Room and board charges vary according to board plan and housing facility. **Scholarships:** Available **Calendar System:** Semester, Summer Session Available **Enrollment:** FT 4,439, PT 316, Grad FT 243, Grad PT 387 **Faculty:** FT 242, PT 118 **Student-Faculty Ratio:** 17:1 **Exams:** SAT I or ACT. **% Receiving Financial Aid:** 56 **% Residing in College-Owned, -Operated, or -Affiliated Housing:** 35 **Library Holdings:** 261,712 **Regional Accreditation:** Middle State Association of Colleges and Schools **Credit Hours For Degree:** 120 credit hours, Bachelors **Professional Accreditation:** AACSB, CSWE, NCATE, NRPA **Intercollegiate Athletics:** Baseball M; Basketball M & W; Cross-Country Running M & W; Field Hockey W; Football M; Lacrosse M & W; Soccer M & W; Softball W; Swimming and Diving M & W; Tennis M & W; Track and Field M & W; Volleyball W

GARRETT COLLEGE
687 Mosser Rd.
McHenry, MD 21541
Tel: (301)387-3000
Fax: (301)387-3055
E-mail: admissions@garrettcollege.edu
Web Site: http://www.garrettcollege.edu/
President/CEO: Dr. Jeanne H. Neff
Admissions: Connie Meyers
Type: Two-Year College **Sex:** Coed **Admission Plans:** Open Admission; Early Admission; Deferred Admission **Application Deadline:** Rolling **Application Fee:** $0.00 **H.S. Requirements:** High school diploma or equivalent not required **Costs Per Year:** Application fee: $0. Area resident tuition: $2580 full-time, $86 per credit hour part-time. State resident tuition: $6480 full-time, $216 per credit hour part-time. Nonresident tuition: $7650 full-time, $255 per credit hour part-time. Mandatory fees: $630 full-time, $20 per credit hour part-time, $15 per term part-time. Full-time tuition and fees vary according to course load. Part-time tuition and fees vary according to course load. College room and board: $8345. College room only: $6365. Room and board charges vary according to board plan and housing facility. **Scholarships:** Available **Calendar System:** Semester, Summer Session Available **Enrollment:** FT 450, PT 284 **Faculty:** FT 17, PT 45 **Student-Faculty Ratio:** 10:1 **% Residing in College-Owned, -Operated, or -Affiliated Housing:** 12 **Library Holdings:** 24,105 **Regional Accreditation:** Middle State Association of Colleges and Schools **Credit Hours For Degree:** 64 credit hours, Associates **Intercollegiate Athletics:** Baseball M; Basketball M & W; Golf M; Skiing (Downhill) M & W; Volleyball W

GOUCHER COLLEGE
1021 Dulaney Valley Rd.
Baltimore, MD 21204-2794
Tel: (410)337-6000; Free: 800-468-2437
Admissions: (410)337-6100
Fax: (410)337-6236
E-mail: admissions@goucher.edu
Web Site: http://www.goucher.edu/
President/CEO: Sanford J. Ungar
Admissions: Carlton E. Surbeck, III
Financial Aid: Sharon Hassan
Type: Comprehensive **Sex:** Coed **Scores:** 99.35% SAT V 400+; 21.65% ACT 18-23; 53.61% ACT 24-29 **% Accepted:** 73 **Admission Plans:** Early Admission; Early Action; Early Decision Plan; Deferred Admission **Application Deadline:** February 1 **Application Fee:** $55.00 **H.S. Requirements:** High school diploma required; GED accepted **Costs Per Year:** Application fee: $55. Comprehensive fee: $45,898 includes full-time tuition ($34,626), mandatory fees ($516), and college room and board ($10,756). Room and board charges vary according to board plan and housing facility. Part-time tuition: $1154 per credit hour. **Scholarships:** Available **Calendar System:** Semester, Summer Session Not available **Enrollment:** FT 1,446, PT 35, Grad FT 132, Grad PT 666 **Faculty:** FT 130, PT 83 **Student-Faculty Ratio:** 9:1 **% Receiving Financial Aid:** 58 **% Residing in College-Owned, -Operated, or -Affiliated Housing:** 82 **Library Holdings:** 280,000 **Regional Accreditation:** Middle State Association of Colleges and Schools **Credit Hours For Degree:** 120 semester hours, Bachelors **ROTC:** Army **Intercollegiate Athletics:** Basketball M & W; Cross-Country Running M & W; Equestrian Sports M & W; Field Hockey W; Lacrosse M & W; Soccer M & W; Swimming and Diving M & W; Tennis M & W; Track and Field M & W; Volleyball W

GRIGGS UNIVERSITY
PO Box 4437, 12501 Old Columbia Pk
Silver Spring, MD 20914-4437
Tel: (301)680-6570
Admissions: (301)680-6590
Fax: (301)680-6577
E-mail: LLundberg@griggs.edu
Web Site: http://www.griggs.edu/
Admissions: Linda Lundberg
Type: Four-Year College **Sex:** Coed **Affiliation:** Seventh-day Adventist; Seventh-day Adventist Parochial School System **% Accepted:** 100 **Admission Plans:** Early Admission; Deferred Admission **Application Deadline:** Rolling **Application Fee:** $80.00 **H.S. Requirements:** High school diploma required; GED accepted **Costs Per Year:** Application fee: $80. Tuition: $7800 full-time. Mandatory fees: $160 full-time. Full-time tuition and fees vary according to course load. **Calendar System:** Continuous, Summer Session Available **Enrollment:** FT 167, PT 698 **Faculty:** PT 38 **Credit Hours For Degree:** 60 semester hours, Associates; 120 semester hours, Bachelors **Professional Accreditation:** DETC

HAGERSTOWN COMMUNITY COLLEGE
11400 Robinwood Dr.
Hagerstown, MD 21742-6590
Tel: (301)790-2800
Fax: (301)739-0737
E-mail: bockd@hagerstowncc.edu
Web Site: http://www.hagerstowncc.edu/
President/CEO: Dr. Guy Altieri
Admissions: Dr. Daniel Bock
Type: Two-Year College **Sex:** Coed **Admission Plans:** Open Admission; Early Admission; Deferred Admission **Application Deadline:** Rolling **Application Fee:** $0.00 **H.S. Requirements:** High school diploma or equivalent not required. **Costs Per Year:** Application fee: $0. Area resident tuition: $2940 full-time, $98 per credit hour part-time. State resident tuition: $4590 full-time, $153 per credit hour part-time. Nonresident tuition: $6060 full-time, $202 per credit hour part-time. Mandatory fees: $330 full-time, $8 per credit hour part-time, $20 per term part-time. **Scholarships:** Available **Calendar System:** Semester, Summer Session Available **Enrollment:** FT 1,342, PT 2,660 **Faculty:** FT 71, PT 168 **Student-Faculty Ratio:** 18:1 **Library Holdings:** 45,705 **Regional Accreditation:** Middle State Association of Colleges and Schools **Credit Hours For Degree:** 64 credit hours, Associates **Professional Accreditation:** JRCERT **Intercollegiate Athletics:** Baseball M; Basketball M & W; Cross-Country Running M & W; Golf M & W; Soccer M & W; Softball W; Track and Field M & W; Volleyball W

HARFORD COMMUNITY COLLEGE
401 Thomas Run Rd.
Bel Air, MD 21015-1698
Tel: (443)412-2000
Admissions: (443)412-2311
E-mail: sendinfo@harford.edu
Web Site: http://www.harford.edu/
President/CEO: Dr. James La Calle
Admissions: Donna Strasavich
Type: Two-Year College **Sex:** Coed **Admission Plans:** Open Admission **Application Deadline:** Rolling **Application Fee:** $0.00 **H.S. Requirements:** High school diploma or equivalent not required **Costs Per Year:** Application fee: $0. Area resident tuition: $2310 full-time, $77 per credit hour part-time. State resident tuition: $4620 full-time, $154 per credit hour part-time. Nonresident tuition: $6930 full-time, $231 per credit hour part-time. Mandatory fees: $300 full-time. **Scholarships:** Available **Calendar System:** Semester, Summer Session Available **Enrollment:** FT 2,973, PT 3,683 **Faculty:** FT 102, PT 277 **Student-Faculty Ratio:** 20:1 **Final Year or Final Semester Residency Requirement:** No **Library Holdings:** 80,777 **Regional Accreditation:** Middle State Association of Colleges and Schools **Credit Hours For Degree:** 62 credit hours, Associates **Professional Accreditation:** NAACLS, NLN **Intercollegiate Athletics:** Baseball M; Basketball M & W; Cheerleading M & W; Cross-Country Running M & W; Golf M; Lacrosse M & W; Soccer M & W; Softball W; Tennis M & W; Volleyball W

HOOD COLLEGE
401 Rosemont Ave.
Frederick, MD 21701-8575
Tel: (301)663-3131; Free: 800-922-1599
Admissions: (301)696-3400
E-mail: admissions@hood.edu

Web Site: http://www.hood.edu/
President/CEO: Dr. Ronald J. Volpe
Admissions: David Adams
Financial Aid: Carol Schroyer
Type: Comprehensive **Sex:** Coed **Scores:** 99% SAT V 400+; 98% SAT M 400+; 56% ACT 18-23; 25% ACT 24-29 **% Accepted:** 72 **Admission Plans:** Early Action; Deferred Admission **Application Deadline:** Rolling **Application Fee:** $35.00 **H.S. Requirements:** High school diploma required; GED accepted **Costs Per Year:** Application fee: $35. Comprehensive fee: $39,761 includes full-time tuition ($29,440), mandatory fees ($420), and college room and board ($9901). College room only: $5171. Room and board charges vary according to board plan. Part-time tuition: $850 per credit hour. Part-time mandatory fees: $140 per term. **Scholarships:** Available **Calendar System:** Semester, Summer Session Available **Enrollment:** FT 1,259, PT 173, Grad FT 73, Grad PT 988 **Faculty:** FT 80, PT 177 **Student-Faculty Ratio:** 12:1 **Exams:** SAT I or ACT. ACT essay used for placement. SAT essay used for placement. **% Receiving Financial Aid:** 82 **% Residing in College-Owned, -Operated, or -Affiliated Housing:** 54 **Final Year or Final Semester Residency Requirement:** Yes **Library Holdings:** 205,825 **Regional Accreditation:** Middle State Association of Colleges and Schools **Credit Hours For Degree:** 124 credits, Bachelors **ROTC:** Army **Professional Accreditation:** ACBSP, CSWE **Intercollegiate Athletics:** Basketball M & W; Cross-Country Running M & W; Equestrian Sports M & W; Field Hockey W; Golf M & W; Lacrosse M & W; Soccer M & W; Softball W; Swimming and Diving M & W; Tennis M & W; Track and Field M & W; Volleyball W

HOWARD COMMUNITY COLLEGE
10901 Little Patuxent Parkway
Columbia, MD 21044-3197
Tel: (410)772-4800
Admissions: (410)772-4856
Fax: (410)772-4589
E-mail: hsinfo@howardcc.edu
Web Site: http://www.howardcc.edu/
President/CEO: Dr. Kate Hetherington
Admissions: Christy Thomson
Type: Two-Year College **Sex:** Coed **Admission Plans:** Open Admission; Early Admission; Deferred Admission **Application Deadline:** Rolling **Application Fee:** $25.00 **H.S. Requirements:** High school diploma or equivalent not required **Costs Per Year:** Application fee: $25. Area resident tuition: $3420 full-time, $114 per credit hour part-time. State resident tuition: $5910 full-time, $197 per credit hour part-time. Nonresident tuition: $7260 full-time, $242 per credit hour part-time. Mandatory fees: $572 full-time, $19.10 per credit hour part-time. **Scholarships:** Available **Calendar System:** Semester, Summer Session Available **Enrollment:** FT 3,443, PT 5,334 **Faculty:** FT 150, PT 477 **Student-Faculty Ratio:** 19:1 **Exams:** SAT I or ACT. ACT essay not being used. SAT essay not being used. **Final Year or Final Semester Residency Requirement:** No **Library Holdings:** 45,707 **Regional Accreditation:** Middle State Association of Colleges and Schools **Credit Hours For Degree:** 60 credit hours, Associates **Professional Accreditation:** NLN **Intercollegiate Athletics:** Basketball M & W; Cross-Country Running M & W; Lacrosse M & W; Soccer M & W; Track and Field M & W; Volleyball W

ITT TECHNICAL INSTITUTE
11301 Red Run Blvd.
Owings Mills, MD 21117
Tel: (443)394-7115
Admissions: (443)394-7115
Web Site: http://www.itt-tech.edu/
President/CEO: Shaher Shanti
Type: Two-Year College **Sex:** Coed **Calendar System:** Quarter

THE JOHNS HOPKINS UNIVERSITY
3400 North Charles St.
Baltimore, MD 21218-2699
Tel: (410)516-8000
Admissions: (410)516-8341
Fax: (410)516-6025
E-mail: gotojhu@jhu.edu
Web Site: http://www.jhu.edu/
President/CEO: Ronald J. Daniels
Admissions: Dr. John Latting
Financial Aid: Vincent Amoroso
Type: University **Sex:** Coed **Scores:** 100% SAT V 400+; 100% SAT M 400+; 2.07% ACT 18-23; 27.03% ACT 24-29 **% Accepted:** 27 **Admission Plans:** Early Admission; Early Decision Plan; Deferred Admission **Application Deadline:** January 1 **Application Fee:** $70.00 **H.S. Requirements:** High school diploma or equivalent not required **Costs Per Year:** Application fee: $70. One-time mandatory fee: $500. Comprehensive fee: $51,190 includes full-time tuition ($39,150) and college room and board ($12,040). College room only: $6882. Room and board charges vary according to board plan and housing facility. Part-time tuition: $1305 per credit hour. **Scholarships:** Available **Calendar System:** 4-1-4, Summer Session Available **Enrollment:** FT 4,965, PT 33, Grad FT 1,726, Grad PT 58 **Faculty:** FT 519, PT 73 **Student-Faculty Ratio:** 12:1 **Exams:** SAT I or ACT, SAT II. **% Receiving Financial Aid:** 46 **% Residing in College-Owned, -Operated, or -Affiliated Housing:** 56 **Final Year or Final Semester Residency Requirement:** Yes **Library Holdings:** 3,700,000 **Regional Accreditation:** Middle State Association of Colleges and Schools **Credit Hours For Degree:** 120 credits, Bachelors **ROTC:** Army, Air Force **Professional Accreditation:** ABET, ARCMI, AACN, ADtA, APA, ACIPE, ACEHSA, CEPH, LCMEAMA, NASM, NCATE, NLN **Intercollegiate Athletics:** Baseball M; Basketball M & W; Cross-Country Running M & W; Fencing M & W; Field Hockey W; Football M; Lacrosse M & W; Soccer M & W; Swimming and Diving M & W; Tennis M & W; Track and Field M & W; Volleyball W; Water Polo M; Wrestling M

KAPLAN UNIVERSITY, HAGERSTOWN CAMPUS
18618 Crestwood Dr.
Hagerstown, MD 21742-2797
Tel: (301)739-2670; Free: 800-422-2670
Fax: (301)791-7661
Web Site: http://www.ku-hagerstown.com/
President/CEO: W. Christopher Motz
Type: Two-Year College **Sex:** Coed **Affiliation:** Kaplan Higher Education **H.S. Requirements:** High school diploma required; GED accepted **Scholarships:** Available **Calendar System:** Quarter **% Residing in College-Owned, -Operated, or -Affiliated Housing:** 3 **Professional Accreditation:** ACICS, AHIMA

LOYOLA UNIVERSITY MARYLAND
4501 North Charles St.
Baltimore, MD 21210-2699
Tel: (410)617-2000
Admissions: (410)617-2251
Fax: (410)323-2768
Web Site: http://www.loyola.edu/
President/CEO: Fr. Brian Linnane
Admissions: Elena Hicks
Financial Aid: Mark L. Lindenmeyer
Type: University **Sex:** Coed **Affiliation:** Roman Catholic (Jesuit) **Scores:** 100% SAT V 400+; 99% SAT M 400+; 23% ACT 18-23; 66% ACT 24-29 **% Accepted:** 66 **Admission Plans:** Early Admission; Early Action; Deferred Admission **Application Deadline:** January 15 **Application Fee:** $50.00 **H.S. Requirements:** High school diploma required; GED accepted **Costs Per Year:** Application fee: $50. One-time mandatory fee: $165. Comprehensive fee: $48,890 includes full-time tuition ($36,510), mandatory fees ($1100), and college room and board ($11,280). College room only: $9260. Full-time tuition and fees vary according to course load. Room and board charges vary according to board plan, housing facility, and location. Part-time tuition: $590 per credit. Part-time tuition varies according to course load. **Scholarships:** Available **Calendar System:** Semester, Summer Session Available **Enrollment:** FT 3,719, PT 38, Grad FT 694, Grad PT 1,616 **Faculty:** FT 331, PT 230 **Student-Faculty Ratio:** 12:1 **Exams:** ACT essay not being used. SAT essay not being used. **% Receiving Financial Aid:** 49 **% Residing in College-Owned, -Operated, or -Affiliated Housing:** 84 **Final Year or Final Semester Residency Requirement:** No **Library Holdings:** 999,295 **Regional Accreditation:** Middle State Association of Colleges and Schools **Credit Hours For Degree:** 120 credits, Bachelors **ROTC:** Army, Air Force **Professional Accreditation:** AACSB, ABET, ACA, APA, ASLHA, NCATE **Intercollegiate Athletics:** Basketball M & W; Crew M & W; Cross-Country Running M & W; Golf M; Lacrosse M & W; Soccer M & W; Swimming and Diving M & W; Tennis M & W; Track and Field M & W; Volleyball W

MAPLE SPRINGS BAPTIST BIBLE COLLEGE AND SEMINARY
4130 Belt Rd.
Capitol Heights, MD 20743

Tel: (301)736-3631
Fax: (301)735-6507
Web Site: http://www.msbbcs.edu/
President/CEO: Larry W. Jordan
Admissions: Jeannie Bowman
Financial Aid: Fannie G. Thompson
Type: Comprehensive **Sex:** Coed **Affiliation:** Baptist **Admission Plans:** Open Admission; Deferred Admission **Application Deadline:** Rolling **Application Fee:** $40.00 **H.S. Requirements:** High school diploma required; GED accepted **Scholarships:** Available **Calendar System:** Semester **Exams:** Other. **Library Holdings:** 1,781 **Credit Hours For Degree:** 66 credit hours, Associates; 132 credit hours, Bachelors **Professional Accreditation:** TACCS

MARYLAND INSTITUTE COLLEGE OF ART
1300 Mount Royal Ave.
Baltimore, MD 21217
Tel: (410)669-9200
Admissions: (410)225-2222
Fax: (410)225-2337
E-mail: cgyland@mica.edu
Web Site: http://www.mica.edu/
President/CEO: Fred Lazarus, IV
Admissions: Christine Seese
Financial Aid: Diane Prengaman
Type: Comprehensive **Sex:** Coed **Scores:** 99% SAT V 400+; 96% SAT M 400+ **% Accepted:** 47 **Admission Plans:** Early Admission; Early Decision Plan; Deferred Admission **Application Deadline:** February 13 **Application Fee:** $60.00 **H.S. Requirements:** High school diploma required; GED accepted **Costs Per Year:** Application fee: $60. One-time mandatory fee: $140. Comprehensive fee: $43,540 includes full-time tuition ($33,000), mandatory fees ($1090), and college room and board ($9450). College room only: $7100. Room and board charges vary according to board plan and housing facility. Part-time tuition: $1375 per credit hour. Part-time mandatory fees: $545 per term. **Scholarships:** Available **Calendar System:** Semester, Summer Session Available **Enrollment:** FT 1,678, PT 24, Grad FT 150, Grad PT 67 **Faculty:** FT 129, PT 168 **Student-Faculty Ratio:** 10:1 **Exams:** SAT I or ACT. SAT essay used for admission. **% Residing in College-Owned, -Operated, or -Affiliated Housing:** 88 **Final Year or Final Semester Residency Requirement:** Yes **Library Holdings:** 85,100 **Regional Accreditation:** Middle State Association of Colleges and Schools **Credit Hours For Degree:** 126 credits, Bachelors **ROTC:** Army **Professional Accreditation:** NASAD

MCDANIEL COLLEGE
2 College Hill
Westminster, MD 21157-4390
Tel: (410)848-7000; Free: 800-638-5005
Admissions: (410)857-2230
Fax: (410)857-2729
E-mail: admissions@mcdaniel.edu
Web Site: http://www.mcdaniel.edu/
President/CEO: Dr. Joan Develin Coley
Admissions: Florence Hines
Financial Aid: Patricia Williams
Type: Comprehensive **Sex:** Coed **Scores:** 100% SAT V 400+; 100% SAT M 400+ **% Accepted:** 79 **Admission Plans:** Early Admission; Early Action; Deferred Admission **Application Deadline:** February 15 **Application Fee:** $50.00 **H.S. Requirements:** High school diploma required; GED accepted **Costs Per Year:** Application fee: $50. Comprehensive fee: $38,820 includes full-time tuition ($32,000) and college room and board ($6820). College room only: $3500. Room and board charges vary according to board plan and housing facility. Part-time tuition: $1000 per credit. Part-time tuition varies according to reciprocity agreements. **Scholarships:** Available **Calendar System:** 4-1-4, Summer Session Available **Enrollment:** FT 1,660, PT 47, Grad FT 175, Grad PT 1,741 **Faculty:** FT 103, PT 266 **Student-Faculty Ratio:** 12:1 **Exams:** SAT I or ACT. ACT essay not being used. SAT essay not being used. **% Receiving Financial Aid:** 69 **% Residing in College-Owned, -Operated, or -Affiliated Housing:** 79 **Library Holdings:** 440,760 **Regional Accreditation:** Middle State Association of Colleges and Schools **Credit Hours For Degree:** 128 semester hours, Bachelors **ROTC:** Army **Professional Accreditation:** CSWE, NCATE **Intercollegiate Athletics:** Baseball M; Basketball M & W; Cross-Country Running M & W; Field Hockey W; Football M; Golf M & W; Lacrosse M & W; Soccer M & W; Softball W; Swimming and Diving M & W; Tennis M & W; Track and Field M & W; Volleyball W; Wrestling M

MONTGOMERY COLLEGE
51 Mannakee St.
Rockville, MD 20850
Tel: (240)567-5000
Admissions: (240)567-5034
E-mail: rochelle.hopkins@montgomerycollege.edu
Web Site: http://www.montgomerycollege.edu/
President/CEO: DeRionne P. Pollard, PhD
Admissions: Rochelle I. Hopkins
Type: Two-Year College **Sex:** Coed **Affiliation:** Maryland Higher Education Commission **% Accepted:** 100 **Admission Plans:** Open Admission; Early Admission; Deferred Admission **Application Deadline:** Rolling **Application Fee:** $25.00 **H.S. Requirements:** High school diploma or equivalent not required **Costs Per Year:** Application fee: $25. One-time mandatory fee: $25. Area resident tuition: $3210 full-time, $107 per credit hour part-time. State resident tuition: $6570 full-time, $219 per credit hour part-time. Nonresident tuition: $8970 full-time, $299 per credit hour part-time. Mandatory fees: $1062 full-time, $64 per credit hour part-time. **Scholarships:** Available **Calendar System:** Semester, Summer Session Available **Enrollment:** FT 10,379, PT 15,768 **Faculty:** FT 516, PT 764 **Student-Faculty Ratio:** 20:1 **Final Year or Final Semester Residency Requirement:** No **Library Holdings:** 286,116 **Regional Accreditation:** Middle State Association of Colleges and Schools **Credit Hours For Degree:** 60 credits, Associates **Professional Accreditation:** ARCEST, AHIMA, APTA, NASM **Intercollegiate Athletics:** Baseball M; Basketball M; Cross-Country Running M & W; Golf M; Lacrosse M; Soccer M & W; Softball W; Tennis M & W; Track and Field M & W; Volleyball M & W

MORGAN STATE UNIVERSITY
1700 East Cold Spring Ln.
Baltimore, MD 21251
Tel: (443)885-3333; Free: 800-332-6674
Admissions: (443)885-3000
E-mail: shantell.saunders@morgan.edu
Web Site: http://www.morgan.edu/
President/CEO: Dr. Earl Richardson
Admissions: Shonda Gray
Type: University **Sex:** Coed **% Accepted:** 43 **Admission Plans:** Preferred Admission; Early Admission; Deferred Admission **Application Deadline:** April 15 **Application Fee:** $35.00 **H.S. Requirements:** High school diploma required; GED accepted **Scholarships:** Available **Calendar System:** Semester, Summer Session Available **Enrollment:** FT 5,472, PT 642 **Faculty:** FT 436, PT 122 **Student-Faculty Ratio:** 13:1 **Exams:** SAT I or ACT, SAT II. **% Residing in College-Owned, -Operated, or -Affiliated Housing:** 46 **Regional Accreditation:** Middle State Association of Colleges and Schools **Credit Hours For Degree:** 120 semester hours, Bachelors **ROTC:** Army **Professional Accreditation:** AACSB, ABET, ACSP, ASLA, CEPH, CSWE, NAACLS, NAAB, NASM, NCATE **Intercollegiate Athletics:** Basketball M & W; Bowling W; Cheerleading W; Cross-Country Running M & W; Football M; Softball W; Tennis M & W; Track and Field M & W; Volleyball W

MOUNT ST. MARY'S UNIVERSITY
16300 Old Emmitsburg Rd.
Emmitsburg, MD 21727-7799
Tel: (301)447-6122; Free: 800-448-4347
Admissions: (301)447-5214
E-mail: admissions@msmary.edu
Web Site: http://www.msmary.edu/
President/CEO: Dr. Thomas Powell
Admissions: Michael Post
Financial Aid: David C. Reeder
Type: Comprehensive **Sex:** Coed **Affiliation:** Roman Catholic **Scores:** 97% SAT V 400+; 95% SAT M 400+; 50% ACT 18-23; 32% ACT 24-29 **% Accepted:** 84 **Admission Plans:** Early Action; Deferred Admission **Application Deadline:** Rolling **Application Fee:** $35.00 **H.S. Requirements:** High school diploma required; GED accepted **Costs Per Year:** Application fee: $35. Comprehensive fee: $40,658 includes full-time tuition ($29,650), mandatory fees ($700), and college room and board ($10,308). College room only: $5044. Part-time tuition: $990 per credit hour. **Scholarships:**

Available **Calendar System:** Semester, Summer Session Available **Enrollment:** FT 1,501, PT 119, Grad FT 212, Grad PT 248 **Faculty:** FT 112, PT 75 **Student-Faculty Ratio:** 13:1 **Exams:** SAT I or ACT. **% Receiving Financial Aid:** 66 **% Residing in College-Owned, -Operated, or -Affiliated Housing:** 84 **Final Year or Final Semester Residency Requirement:** Yes **Library Holdings:** 216,740 **Regional Accreditation:** Middle State Association of Colleges and Schools **Credit Hours For Degree:** 120 credits, Bachelors **ROTC:** Army **Professional Accreditation:** ATS, NCATE **Intercollegiate Athletics:** Baseball M; Basketball M & W; Cheerleading W; Cross-Country Running M & W; Equestrian Sports M & W; Golf M & W; Ice Hockey M; Lacrosse M & W; Rugby M & W; Soccer M & W; Softball W; Swimming and Diving W; Tennis M & W; Track and Field M & W

NATIONAL LABOR COLLEGE
10000 New Hampshire Ave.
Silver Spring, MD 20903
Tel: (301)431-6400; Free: 800-GMC-4CDP
Admissions: (301)431-5422
Fax: (301)431-5411
E-mail: kbanks@nlc.edu
Web Site: http://www.nlc.edu/
President/CEO: William Scheuerman
Admissions: Karen Banks
Type: Two-Year Upper Division **Sex:** Coed **Application Fee:** $60.00 **Calendar System:** Quarter **Student-Faculty Ratio:** 5:1 **Regional Accreditation:** Middle State Association of Colleges and Schools

NER ISRAEL RABBINICAL COLLEGE
400 Mount Wilson Ln.
Baltimore, MD 21208
Tel: (410)484-7200
Fax: (410)484-3060
President/CEO: Sheftel Neuberger
Financial Aid: Moshe Pelberg
Type: Comprehensive **Sex:** Men **Affiliation:** Jewish **Admission Plans:** Early Admission; Deferred Admission **Application Deadline:** Rolling **Application Fee:** $50.00 **H.S. Requirements:** High school diploma required; GED accepted **Calendar System:** Semester, Summer Session Available **Credit Hours For Degree:** 120 credits, Bachelors **Professional Accreditation:** AARTS

PEABODY CONSERVATORY OF THE JOHNS HOPKINS UNIVERSITY
1 East Mount Vernon Place
Baltimore, MD 21202-2397
Tel: (410)659-8150; Free: 800-368-2521
Admissions: (410)659-8110
Web Site: http://www.peabody.jhu.edu/
President/CEO: Jeffrey Sharkey
Admissions: David Lane
Financial Aid: Tom McDermott
Type: Comprehensive **Sex:** Coed **Affiliation:** Johns Hopkins University **% Accepted:** 53 **Application Deadline:** December 1 **Application Fee:** $100.00 **H.S. Requirements:** High school diploma required; GED accepted **Costs Per Year:** Application fee: $100. One-time mandatory fee: $700. Comprehensive fee: $45,775 includes full-time tuition ($34,250), mandatory fees ($425), and college room and board ($11,100). Full-time tuition and fees vary according to program. Room and board charges vary according to board plan. Part-time tuition: $975 per semester hour. Part-time tuition varies according to course load. **Scholarships:** Available **Calendar System:** Semester, Summer Session Not available **Enrollment:** FT 332, PT 10, Grad FT 307, Grad PT 33 **Student-Faculty Ratio:** 4:1 **Exams:** SAT I or ACT. **% Receiving Financial Aid:** 62 **% Residing in College-Owned, -Operated, or -Affiliated Housing:** 40 **Library Holdings:** 99,700 **Regional Accreditation:** Middle State Association of Colleges and Schools **Credit Hours For Degree:** 149 semester hours, Bachelors **Professional Accreditation:** NASM

PRINCE GEORGE'S COMMUNITY COLLEGE
301 Largo Rd.
Largo, MD 20774-2199
Tel: (301)336-6000
Admissions: (301)322-0801
E-mail: enrollmentservices@pgcc.edu
Web Site: http://www.pgcc.edu/
President/CEO: Dr. Charlene Dukes
Admissions: Vera Bagley
Type: Two-Year College **Sex:** Coed **% Accepted:** 100 **Admission Plans:** Open Admission; Early Admission **Application Deadline:** Rolling **Application Fee:** $25.00 **H.S. Requirements:** High school diploma or equivalent not required. For nursing, allied health programs: High school diploma required; GED accepted **Scholarships:** Available **Calendar System:** Semester, Summer Session Available **Enrollment:** FT 3,007, PT 8,854 **Faculty:** FT 244, PT 451 **Student-Faculty Ratio:** 15:1 **Library Holdings:** 242,519 **Regional Accreditation:** Middle State Association of Colleges and Schools **Credit Hours For Degree:** 62 credits, Associates **ROTC:** Army **Professional Accreditation:** ABET, AHIMA, CARC, JRCERT, JRCNMT, NLN **Intercollegiate Athletics:** Baseball M; Basketball M & W; Bowling M & W; Golf M; Soccer M & W; Softball W; Tennis M & W; Volleyball W

ST. JOHN'S COLLEGE
PO Box 2800
Annapolis, MD 21404
Tel: (410)263-2371; Free: 800-727-9238
Admissions: (410)626-2522
E-mail: admissions@sjca.edu
Web Site: http://www.stjohnscollege.edu/
President/CEO: Christopher B. Nelson
Admissions: John Christensen
Financial Aid: Dana Kennedy
Type: Comprehensive **Sex:** Coed **Scores:** 100% SAT V 400+; 99% SAT M 400+; 4% ACT 18-23; 70% ACT 24-29 **% Accepted:** 81 **Admission Plans:** Early Admission; Deferred Admission **Application Deadline:** Rolling **Application Fee:** $0.00 **H.S. Requirements:** High school diploma required; GED accepted **Costs Per Year:** Application fee: $0. Comprehensive fee: $52,176 includes full-time tuition ($41,792), mandatory fees ($400), and college room and board ($9984). Room and board charges vary according to board plan. **Scholarships:** Available **Calendar System:** Semester, Summer Session Not available **Enrollment:** FT 489 **Faculty:** FT 76, PT 9 **Student-Faculty Ratio:** 8:1 **Exams:** SAT I or ACT. ACT essay not being used. SAT essay not being used. **% Receiving Financial Aid:** 57 **% Residing in College-Owned, -Operated, or -Affiliated Housing:** 80 **Final Year or Final Semester Residency Requirement:** Yes **Library Holdings:** 113,343 **Regional Accreditation:** Middle State Association of Colleges and Schools **Credit Hours For Degree:** 132 credits, Bachelors **Intercollegiate Athletics:** Crew M & W; Fencing M & W

ST. MARY'S COLLEGE OF MARYLAND
18952 East Fisher Rd.
St. Mary's City, MD 20686-3001
Tel: (240)895-2000; Free: 800-492-7181
Admissions: (240)895-5000
Fax: (240)895-5001
E-mail: admissions@smcm.edu
Web Site: http://www.smcm.edu/
President/CEO: Dr. Larry E. Vote
Admissions: Richard J. Edgar
Financial Aid: Tim Wolfe
Type: Comprehensive **Sex:** Coed **Scores:** 99.13% SAT V 400+; 98.91% SAT M 400+; 22% ACT 18-23; 54% ACT 24-29 **% Accepted:** 57 **Admission Plans:** Early Admission; Early Decision Plan **Application Deadline:** January 1 **Application Fee:** $50.00 **H.S. Requirements:** High school diploma required; GED accepted **Costs Per Year:** Application fee: $50. State resident tuition: $11,325 full-time, $185 per credit hour part-time. Nonresident tuition: $22,718 full-time, $185 per credit hour part-time. Mandatory fees: $2305 full-time. Full-time tuition and fees vary according to course load. Part-time tuition varies according to course load. College room and board: $10,245. College room only: $5745. Room and board charges vary according to board plan and housing facility. **Scholarships:** Available **Calendar System:** Semester, Summer Session Available **Enrollment:** FT 1,952, PT 65, Grad FT 43 **Faculty:** FT 142, PT 83 **Student-Faculty Ratio:** 12:1 **Exams:** SAT I or ACT. ACT essay not being used. SAT essay not being used. **% Receiving Financial Aid:** 46 **% Residing in College-Owned, -Operated, or -Affiliated Housing:** 82 **Library Holdings:** 167,872 **Regional Accreditation:** Middle State Association of Colleges and Schools **Credit Hours For Degree:** 128 credits, Bachelors **Intercollegiate Athletics:** Baseball M; Basketball M & W; Crew M & W; Cross-Country Running M & W; Equestrian Sports M & W; Fencing M & W; Field Hockey W; Golf M &

W; Lacrosse M & W; Rock Climbing M & W; Rugby M & W; Sailing M & W; Soccer M & W; Swimming and Diving M & W; Tennis M & W; Ultimate Frisbee M & W; Volleyball W

SALISBURY UNIVERSITY
1101 Camden Ave.
Salisbury, MD 21801-6837
Tel: (410)543-6000; Free: 888-543-0148
Admissions: (410)543-6161
Fax: (410)548-2587
E-mail: admissions@salisbury.edu
Web Site: http://www.salisbury.edu/
President/CEO: Dr. Janet Dudley-Eshbach
Admissions: Aaron Basko
Financial Aid: Elizabeth B. Zimmerman
Type: Comprehensive **Sex:** Coed **Affiliation:** University System of Maryland **Scores:** 99.6% SAT V 400+; 99.6% SAT M 400+; 48.7% ACT 18-23; 46.2% ACT 24-29 **% Accepted:** 54 **Admission Plans:** Early Admission; Early Action **Application Deadline:** January 15 **Application Fee:** $45.00 **H.S. Requirements:** High school diploma required; GED accepted **Costs Per Year:** Application fee: $45. State resident tuition: $4814 full-time, $200 per credit hour part-time. Nonresident tuition: $13,310 full-time, $553 per credit hour part-time. Mandatory fees: $1804 full-time, $61 per credit hour part-time. College room and board: $8070. College room only: $4150. Room and board charges vary according to board plan and housing facility. **Scholarships:** Available **Calendar System:** 4-1-4, Summer Session Available **Enrollment:** FT 6,954, PT 603, Grad FT 257, Grad PT 390 **Faculty:** FT 380, PT 191 **Student-Faculty Ratio:** 17:1 **Exams:** SAT I or ACT. ACT essay used for admission. SAT essay used for admission. **% Receiving Financial Aid:** 40 **% Residing in College-Owned, -Operated, or -Affiliated Housing:** 36 **Library Holdings:** 442,682 **Regional Accreditation:** Middle State Association of Colleges and Schools **Credit Hours For Degree:** 120 semester hours, Bachelors **ROTC:** Army, Air Force **Professional Accreditation:** AACSB, AACN, CARC, CSWE, JRCEPAT, NAACLS, NCATE, NLN **Intercollegiate Athletics:** Baseball M; Basketball M & W; Cross-Country Running M & W; Field Hockey W; Football M; Lacrosse M & W; Soccer M & W; Softball W; Swimming and Diving M & W; Tennis M & W; Track and Field M & W; Volleyball W

SOJOURNER-DOUGLASS COLLEGE
500 North Caroline St.
Baltimore, MD 21205-1814
Tel: (410)276-0306
Fax: (410)675-1810
E-mail: dsamuels@host.sdc.edu
Web Site: http://sdc.edu/
President/CEO: Charles W. Simmons
Admissions: Diana Samuels
Financial Aid: Rebecca Chalk
Type: Comprehensive **Sex:** Coed **Admission Plans:** Open Admission; Deferred Admission **Application Deadline:** Rolling **Application Fee:** $25.00 **H.S. Requirements:** High school diploma required; GED accepted **Scholarships:** Available **Calendar System:** Trimester, Summer Session Available **% Receiving Financial Aid:** 100 **Library Holdings:** 10,000 **Regional Accreditation:** Middle State Association of Colleges and Schools **Credit Hours For Degree:** 132 credits, Bachelors

STEVENSON UNIVERSITY
1525 Greenspring Valley Rd.
Stevenson, MD 21153
Tel: (410)486-7000; Free: 877-468-3852
Admissions: (410)486-7001
E-mail: admissions@stevenson.edu
Web Site: http://www.stevenson.edu/
President/CEO: Dr. Kevin J. Manning, PhD
Admissions: Mark Hergan
Financial Aid: Barbara L. Miller
Type: Comprehensive **Sex:** Coed **Scores:** 96.7% SAT V 400+; 90.87% SAT M 400+; 60.81% ACT 18-23; 14.86% ACT 24-29 **% Accepted:** 57 **Admission Plans:** Early Admission; Deferred Admission **Application Deadline:** Rolling **Application Fee:** $40.00 **H.S. Requirements:** High school diploma required; GED accepted **Costs Per Year:** Application fee: $40. Comprehensive fee: $30,940 includes full-time tuition ($19,234), mandatory fees ($1410), and college room and board ($10,296). College room only: $6750. Full-time tuition and fees vary according to degree level. Room and board charges vary according to board plan and housing facility. Part-time tuition: $487 per credit hour. Part-time mandatory fees: $75 per term. Part-time tuition and fees vary according to course load and degree level. **Scholarships:** Available **Calendar System:** Semester, Summer Session Available **Enrollment:** FT 2,619, PT 557, Grad FT 60, Grad PT 196 **Faculty:** FT 110, PT 239 **Student-Faculty Ratio:** 15:1 **Exams:** SAT I or ACT. ACT essay not being used. SAT essay not being used. **% Receiving Financial Aid:** 68 **% Residing in College-Owned, -Operated, or -Affiliated Housing:** 41 **Library Holdings:** 81,802 **Regional Accreditation:** Middle State Association of Colleges and Schools **Credit Hours For Degree:** 60 credits, Associates; 120 credits, Bachelors **ROTC:** Army **Professional Accreditation:** NAACLS, NLN **Intercollegiate Athletics:** Baseball M; Basketball M & W; Cheerleading M & W; Cross-Country Running M & W; Field Hockey W; Golf M & W; Lacrosse M & W; Soccer M & W; Softball W; Tennis M & W; Track and Field M & W; Volleyball M & W

STRAYER UNIVERSITY - ANNE ARUNDEL CAMPUS
1520 Jabez Run
Millersville, MD 21108
Tel: (410)923-4500
Fax: (410)923-4570
Web Site: http://www.strayer.edu/anne_arundel
Type: Comprehensive **Sex:** Coed **Application Fee:** $50.00 **Costs Per Year:** Application fee: $50.

STRAYER UNIVERSITY - OWINGS MILLS CAMPUS
500 Redland Ct., Ste. 100
Owings Mills, MD 21117
Tel: (443)394-3339
Fax: (443)394-3394
Web Site: http://www.strayer.edu/owings_mills
Type: Comprehensive **Sex:** Coed **Application Fee:** $50.00 **Costs Per Year:** Application fee: $50. **Regional Accreditation:** Middle State Association of Colleges and Schools

STRAYER UNIVERSITY - PRINCE GEORGE'S CAMPUS
4710 Auth Place
First Floor
Suitland, MD 20746
Tel: (301)423-3600
Fax: (301)423-3999
Web Site: http://www.strayer.edu/prince_georges
Type: Comprehensive **Sex:** Coed **Application Fee:** $50.00 **Costs Per Year:** Application fee: $50. **Regional Accreditation:** Middle State Association of Colleges and Schools

STRAYER UNIVERSITY - ROCKVILLE CAMPUS
4 Research Place, Ste. 100
Rockville, MD 20850
Tel: (301)548-5500
Fax: (301)548-5530
Web Site: http://www.strayer.edu/rockville
Type: Comprehensive **Sex:** Coed **Application Fee:** $50.00 **Costs Per Year:** Application fee: $50. **Regional Accreditation:** Middle State Association of Colleges and Schools

STRAYER UNIVERSITY - WHITE MARSH CAMPUS
9920 Franklin Square Dr.
Ste. 200
Baltimore, MD 21236
Tel: (410)238-9000
Fax: (410)238-9099
Web Site: http://www.strayer.edu/white_marsh
Type: Comprehensive **Sex:** Coed **Application Fee:** $50.00 **Costs Per Year:** Application fee: $50.

TESST COLLEGE OF TECHNOLOGY (BALTIMORE)
1520 South Caton Ave.
Baltimore, MD 21227
Tel: (410)644-6400; Free: 800-833-0209
Fax: (410)644-6481
Web Site: http://www.tesst.com/
President/CEO: Sandra Ugol

Type: Two-Year College **Sex:** Coed **H.S. Requirements:** High school diploma required; GED accepted **Calendar System:** Quarter **Professional Accreditation:** ACCSCT

TESST COLLEGE OF TECHNOLOGY (BELTSVILLE)
4600 Powder Mill Rd.
Beltsville, MD 20705
Tel: (301)937-8448; Free: 800-833-0209
Fax: (301)937-5327
Web Site: http://www.tesst.com/
President/CEO: Amy Beauregard
Type: Two-Year College **Sex:** Coed **Application Fee:** $20.00 **H.S. Requirements:** High school diploma required; GED accepted **Calendar System:** Quarter **Professional Accreditation:** ACCSCT

TESST COLLEGE OF TECHNOLOGY (TOWSON)
803 Glen Eagles Ct.
Towson, MD 21286
Tel: (410)296-5350; Free: 800-48-TESST
Fax: (410)296-5356
Web Site: http://www.tesst.com/
President/CEO: William DeFusco
Type: Two-Year College **Sex:** Coed **H.S. Requirements:** High school diploma required; GED accepted **Calendar System:** Quarter **Professional Accreditation:** ACCSCT

TOWSON UNIVERSITY
8000 York Rd.
Towson, MD 21252-0001
Tel: (410)704-2000; Free: 888-4TOWSON
Admissions: (410)704-2113
Fax: (410)704-3030
E-mail: admissions@towson.edu
Web Site: http://www.towson.edu/
President/CEO: Dr. Robert Caret
Admissions: Louise Shulack
Financial Aid: Vince Pecora
Type: University **Sex:** Coed **Affiliation:** University System of Maryland **Scores:** 98.8% SAT V 400+; 98.5% SAT M 400+; 62% ACT 18-23; 32% ACT 24-29 **% Accepted:** 63 **Admission Plans:** Early Admission; Deferred Admission **Application Deadline:** February 15 **Application Fee:** $45.00 **H.S. Requirements:** High school diploma required; GED accepted **Costs Per Year:** Application fee: $45. State resident tuition: $5180 full-time, $225 per credit part-time. Nonresident tuition: $15,994 full-time, $611 per credit part-time. Mandatory fees: $2238 full-time, $93 per credit part-time. Full-time tuition and fees vary according to course load. College room and board: $8670. College room only: $5256. Room and board charges vary according to board plan and housing facility. Tuition guaranteed not to increase for student's term of enrollment. **Scholarships:** Available **Calendar System:** Semester, Summer Session Available **Enrollment:** FT 15,281, PT 1,867, Grad FT 1,261, Grad PT 2,768 **Faculty:** FT 822, PT 723 **Student-Faculty Ratio:** 17:1 **Exams:** SAT I or ACT. ACT essay used for admission. SAT essay used for admission. ACT essay used for placement. SAT essay used for placement. **% Receiving Financial Aid:** 45 **% Residing in College-Owned, -Operated, or -Affiliated Housing:** 25 **Library Holdings:** 578,057 **Regional Accreditation:** Middle State Association of Colleges and Schools **Credit Hours For Degree:** 120 credit hours, Bachelors **ROTC:** Army, Air Force **Professional Accreditation:** AACSB, ABET, AACN, AOTA, APA, ASLHA, JRCEPAT, NASD, NASM, NAST, NCATE **Intercollegiate Athletics:** Badminton M & W; Baseball M; Basketball M & W; Cheerleading M & W; Cross-Country Running M & W; Equestrian Sports M & W; Field Hockey W; Football M; Golf M & W; Gymnastics W; Lacrosse M & W; Rugby M & W; Soccer M & W; Softball W; Swimming and Diving M & W; Tennis M & W; Track and Field M & W; Ultimate Frisbee M & W; Volleyball M & W; Wrestling M

UNITED STATES NAVAL ACADEMY
121 Blake Rd.
Annapolis, MD 21402-5000
Tel: (410)293-1000
Admissions: (410)293-4361
Fax: (410)293-4348
E-mail: webmail@usna.edu
Web Site: http://www.usna.edu/
President/CEO: Vice Adm. Jeffrey L. Fowler
Admissions: Capt. Pat L. Williams
Type: Four-Year College **Sex:** Coed **Scores:** 100% SAT V 400+; 100% SAT M 400+ **% Accepted:** 8 **Admission Plans:** Early Action **Application Deadline:** January 31 **Application Fee:** $0.00 **H.S. Requirements:** High school diploma or equivalent not required **Costs Per Year:** Application fee: $0. **Calendar System:** Semester, Summer Session Available **Enrollment:** FT 4,552 **Faculty:** FT 522 **Student-Faculty Ratio:** 9:1 **Exams:** SAT I or ACT. **% Residing in College-Owned, -Operated, or -Affiliated Housing:** 100 **Final Year or Final Semester Residency Requirement:** Yes **Library Holdings:** 716,676 **Regional Accreditation:** Middle State Association of Colleges and Schools **Credit Hours For Degree:** 137 semester hours, Bachelors **Professional Accreditation:** ABET **Intercollegiate Athletics:** Baseball M; Basketball M & W; Cheerleading M & W; Crew M & W; Cross-Country Running M & W; Fencing M & W; Field Hockey W; Football M; Golf M; Gymnastics M & W; Ice Hockey M; Lacrosse M & W; Riflery M & W; Rugby M & W; Sailing M & W; Skiing (Downhill) M & W; Soccer M & W; Softball W; Squash M; Swimming and Diving M & W; Tennis M & W; Track and Field M & W; Volleyball M & W; Water Polo M; Weight Lifting M & W; Wrestling M

UNIVERSITY OF BALTIMORE
1420 North Charles St.
Baltimore, MD 21201-5779
Tel: (410)837-4200; Free: 877-APPLYUB
Admissions: (410)837-4777
Fax: (410)837-4793
E-mail: admissions@ubalt.edu
Web Site: http://www.ubalt.edu/
President/CEO: Robert Bologomny
Admissions: Dr. Valarie J. Trimarchi
Type: Comprehensive **Sex:** Coed **Affiliation:** University System of Maryland **Admission Plans:** Deferred Admission **Application Deadline:** Rolling **Application Fee:** $30.00 **H.S. Requirements:** High school diploma required; GED accepted **Costs Per Year:** Application fee: $30. State resident tuition: $5484 full-time, $250 per credit hour part-time. Nonresident tuition: $15,000 full-time, $784 per credit hour part-time. Mandatory fees: $1846 full-time, $923 per term part-time. **Scholarships:** Available **Calendar System:** Semester, Summer Session Available **Enrollment:** FT 1,768, PT 1,236, Grad FT 1,519, Grad PT 1,742 **Faculty:** FT 178, PT 195 **Student-Faculty Ratio:** 20:1 **Exams:** SAT I or ACT. **% Receiving Financial Aid:** 69 **Library Holdings:** 258,747 **Regional Accreditation:** Middle State Association of Colleges and Schools **Credit Hours For Degree:** 120 semester hours, Bachelors **ROTC:** Army, Air Force **Professional Accreditation:** AACSB, ABA, AALS, NASPAA

UNIVERSITY OF MARYLAND, BALTIMORE COUNTY
1000 Hilltop Circle
Baltimore, MD 21250
Tel: (410)455-1000; Free: 800-862-2402
Admissions: (410)455-2291
Fax: (410)455-1210
E-mail: admissions@umbc.edu
Web Site: http://www.umbc.edu/
President/CEO: Dr. Freeman Hrabowski
Admissions: Dale Bittinger
Financial Aid: Stephanie Johnson
Type: University **Sex:** Coed **Affiliation:** University System of Maryland **Scores:** 99.3% SAT V 400+; 99.8% SAT M 400+; 35.5% ACT 18-23; 43.5% ACT 24-29 **% Accepted:** 69 **Admission Plans:** Early Admission; Early Action; Deferred Admission **Application Deadline:** February 1 **Application Fee:** $50.00 **H.S. Requirements:** High school diploma required; GED accepted **Costs Per Year:** Application fee: $50. One-time mandatory fee: $125. State resident tuition: $6484 full-time, $270 per credit hour part-time. Nonresident tuition: $15,825 full-time, $658 per credit hour part-time. Mandatory fees: $2388 full-time, $106 per credit hour part-time. Full-time tuition and fees vary according to location and program. Part-time tuition and fees vary according to location and program. College room and board: $9303. College room only: $5670. Room and board charges vary according to board plan and housing facility. **Scholarships:** Available **Calendar System:** 4-1-4, Summer Session Available **Enrollment:** FT 8,614, PT 1,333, Grad FT 1,042, Grad PT 1,881 **Faculty:** FT 480, PT 250 **Student-Faculty Ratio:** 19:1 **Exams:** SAT I or ACT. **% Receiving Financial Aid:** 46 **% Residing in College-Owned, -Operated, or -Affiliated Housing:** 37 **Final Year or Final**

Semester Residency Requirement: Yes **Library Holdings:** 1,020,060 **Regional Accreditation:** Middle State Association of Colleges and Schools **Credit Hours For Degree:** 120 credit hours, Bachelors **ROTC:** Army **Professional Accreditation:** ABET, APA, CSWE, JRCEMT, NASPAA, NCATE **Intercollegiate Athletics:** Badminton M & W; Baseball M; Basketball M & W; Bowling M & W; Crew M & W; Cross-Country Running M & W; Fencing M & W; Field Hockey W; Ice Hockey M; Lacrosse M & W; Rugby M & W; Sailing M & W; Skiing (Downhill) M & W; Soccer M & W; Softball W; Swimming and Diving M & W; Tennis M & W; Track and Field M & W; Ultimate Frisbee M & W; Volleyball M & W; Wrestling M

UNIVERSITY OF MARYLAND, COLLEGE PARK
College Park, MD 20742
Tel: (301)405-1000; Free: 800-422-5867
Admissions: (301)314-8385
Fax: (301)314-9693
Web Site: http://www.maryland.edu/
President/CEO: Dr. C.D. Mote, Jr.
Admissions: Barbara Gill
Financial Aid: Sarah Bauder
Type: University **Sex:** Coed **Affiliation:** University System of Maryland **Scores:** 99.7% SAT V 400+; 99.9% SAT M 400+ **% Accepted:** 42 **Admission Plans:** Preferred Admission; Early Admission; Early Action; Deferred Admission **Application Deadline:** January 20 **Application Fee:** $55.00 **H.S. Requirements:** High school diploma required; GED accepted **Costs Per Year:** Application fee: $55. State resident tuition: $6566 full-time, $273 per credit hour part-time. Nonresident tuition: $22,502 full-time, $938 per credit hour part-time. Mandatory fees: $1487 full-time, $338.94 per term part-time. Part-time tuition and fees vary according to course load. College room and board: $9377. College room only: $5549. Room and board charges vary according to board plan. **Scholarships:** Available **Calendar System:** Semester, Summer Session Available **Enrollment:** FT 24,583, PT 1,910, Grad FT 7,062, Grad PT 3,591 **Faculty:** FT 1,644, PT 629 **Student-Faculty Ratio:** 18:1 **Exams:** SAT I or ACT. SAT essay not being used. **% Receiving Financial Aid:** 37 **% Residing in College-Owned, -Operated, or -Affiliated Housing:** 42 **Library Holdings:** 3,767,653 **Regional Accreditation:** Middle State Association of Colleges and Schools **Credit Hours For Degree:** 120 semester hours, Bachelors **ROTC:** Army, Navy, Air Force **Professional Accreditation:** AACSB, ABET, ACEJMC, AAMFT, ACA, ADtA, ACSP, ALA, APA, ASLA, ASLHA, AVMA, CEPH, CORE, NAAB, NASM, NASPAA, NAST, NCATE **Intercollegiate Athletics:** Baseball M; Basketball M & W; Cheerleading W; Cross-Country Running M & W; Field Hockey W; Football M; Golf M & W; Gymnastics W; Lacrosse M & W; Soccer M & W; Softball W; Swimming and Diving M & W; Tennis M & W; Track and Field M & W; Volleyball W; Water Polo W; Wrestling M

UNIVERSITY OF MARYLAND EASTERN SHORE
Princess Anne, MD 21853-1299
Tel: (410)651-2200
Admissions: (410)651-6410
Fax: (410)651-7922
Web Site: http://www.umes.edu/
President/CEO: Dr. Thelma Thompson
Admissions: Tyrone Young
Financial Aid: James W. Kellam
Type: University **Sex:** Coed **Affiliation:** University System of Maryland **Scores:** 66.2% SAT V 400+; 60.2% SAT M 400+ **% Accepted:** 58 **Admission Plans:** Preferred Admission; Early Admission; Early Action; Deferred Admission **Application Deadline:** July 15 **Application Fee:** $25.00 **H.S. Requirements:** High school diploma required; GED accepted **Costs Per Year:** Application fee: $25. State resident tuition: $4112 full-time, $171 per credit hour part-time. Nonresident tuition: $11,336 full-time, $417 per credit hour part-time. Mandatory fees: $1970 full-time, $43 per term part-time. Full-time tuition and fees vary according to course load. Part-time tuition and fees vary according to course load. College room and board: $7230. College room only: $3930. Room and board charges vary according to board plan and housing facility. **Scholarships:** Available **Calendar System:** Semester, Summer Session Available **Enrollment:** FT 2,902, PT 424 **Faculty:** FT 172, PT 111 **Student-Faculty Ratio:** 20:1 **Exams:** Other, SAT I or ACT. **% Receiving Financial Aid:** 81 **% Residing in College-Owned, -Operated, or -Affiliated Housing:** 60 **Library Holdings:** 150,000 **Regional Accreditation:** Middle State Association of Colleges and Schools **Credit Hours For Degree:** 122 credits, Bachelors **Professional Accreditation:** AAFCS, ACCE, ADtA, APTA, CORE, NCATE **Intercollegiate Athletics:** Baseball M; Basketball M & W; Cheerleading M & W; Cross-Country Running M & W; Softball W; Tennis M & W; Track and Field M & W; Volleyball W; Wrestling M

UNIVERSITY OF MARYLAND UNIVERSITY COLLEGE
3501 University Blvd. East
Adelphi, MD 20783
Tel: (301)985-7000
Admissions: 800-888-UMUC
Fax: (301)985-7678
E-mail: enroll@umuc.edu
Web Site: http://www.umuc.edu/
President/CEO: Dr. Susan C. Aldridge
Financial Aid: Cheryl Storie
Type: Comprehensive **Sex:** Coed **Affiliation:** University System of Maryland **% Accepted:** 100 **Admission Plans:** Open Admission; Deferred Admission **Application Deadline:** Rolling **Application Fee:** $50.00 **H.S. Requirements:** High school diploma required; GED accepted **Costs Per Year:** Application fee: $50. State resident tuition: $5520 full-time, $230 per credit hour part-time. Nonresident tuition: $11,976 full-time, $499 per credit hour part-time. Mandatory fees: $240 full-time, $10 per credit hour part-time. **Scholarships:** Available **Calendar System:** Semester, Summer Session Available **Enrollment:** FT 3,408, PT 20,876, Grad FT 270, Grad PT 12,793 **Faculty:** FT 228, PT 1,730 **Student-Faculty Ratio:** 19:1 **% Receiving Financial Aid:** 59 **Library Holdings:** 1,247 **Regional Accreditation:** Middle State Association of Colleges and Schools **Credit Hours For Degree:** 60 semester hours, Associates; 120 semester hours, Bachelors

UNIVERSITY OF PHOENIX—MARYLAND CAMPUS
8830 Stanford Blvd.
Ste. 100
Columbia, MD 21045-5424
Tel: (410)872-9001; Free: 800-228-7240
Admissions: (480)557-6151
E-mail: audra.mcquarie@phoenix.edu
Web Site: http://www.phoenix.edu/
President/CEO: William Pepicello
Admissions: Audra McQuarie
Type: Comprehensive **Sex:** Coed **Admission Plans:** Open Admission; Deferred Admission **Application Deadline:** Rolling **Application Fee:** $0.00 **H.S. Requirements:** High school diploma required; GED accepted **Costs Per Year:** Application fee: $0. Tuition: $12,250 full-time. Full-time tuition varies according to course level and course load. **Scholarships:** Available **Calendar System:** Continuous, Summer Session Not available **Enrollment:** FT 615 **Faculty:** FT 22, PT 137 **Regional Accreditation:** North Central Association of Colleges and Schools **Credit Hours For Degree:** 60 credits, Associates; 120 credits, Bachelors

WASHINGTON ADVENTIST UNIVERSITY
7600 Flower Ave.
Takoma Park, MD 20912
Tel: (301)891-4000; Free: 800-835-4212
Admissions: (301)891-4502
Fax: (301)891-4230
E-mail: enroll@cuc.edu
Web Site: http://www.wau.edu/
President/CEO: Dr. Weymouth Spence
Admissions: Elaine Oliver
Financial Aid: Elaine Oliver
Type: Comprehensive **Sex:** Coed **Affiliation:** Seventh-day Adventist **% Accepted:** 41 **Admission Plans:** Early Admission; Deferred Admission **Application Deadline:** August 1 **Application Fee:** $25.00 **H.S. Requirements:** High school diploma required; GED accepted **Costs Per Year:** Application fee: $25. Comprehensive fee: $26,680 includes full-time tuition ($18,200), mandatory fees ($1280), and college room and board ($7200). Part-time tuition: $760 per semester hour. Part-time mandatory fees: $432.50 per term. Part-time tuition and fees vary according to class time and course load. **Scholarships:** Available **Calendar System:** Semester, Summer Session Available **Enrollment:** FT 805, PT 270, Grad FT 7, Grad PT 101 **Faculty:** FT 41, PT 68 **Student-Faculty Ratio:** 14:1 **Exams:** SAT I or ACT. ACT essay used for admission. SAT essay used for admission. ACT essay used for placement. SAT essay used for placement. **Regional Accreditation:** Middle State Association of Colleges and Schools **Credit Hours For Degree:** 64 semester hours, Associates; 128 semester hours, Bachelors **Professional Accreditation:** CARC, NLN **Intercollegiate Athlet-**

ics: Baseball M; Basketball M & W; Cross-Country Running M & W; Soccer M & W; Softball W; Track and Field M & W

WASHINGTON BIBLE COLLEGE
6511 Princess Garden Parkway
Lanham, MD 20706-3599
Tel: (301)552-1400; Free: 877-793-7227
Fax: (301)552-2775
E-mail: admissions@bible.edu
Web Site: http://www.bible.edu/
President/CEO: Dr. Larry A. Mercer
Admissions: Mark D. Johnson
Financial Aid: Nichole Sefiane
Type: Comprehensive **Sex:** Coed **Affiliation:** nondenominational; Capital Bible Seminary **% Accepted:** 65 **Admission Plans:** Early Admission; Deferred Admission **Application Deadline:** January 9 **Application Fee:** $25.00 **H.S. Requirements:** High school diploma required; GED accepted **Scholarships:** Available **Calendar System:** Semester, Summer Session Available **Enrollment:** FT 126, PT 128 **Faculty:** FT 14, PT 0 **Student-Faculty Ratio:** 13:1 **Exams:** SAT I or ACT. **% Receiving Financial Aid:** 80 **Regional Accreditation:** Middle State Association of Colleges and Schools **Credit Hours For Degree:** 64 credit hours, Associates; 120 credit hours, Bachelors **Professional Accreditation:** ABHE **Intercollegiate Athletics:** Basketball M & W; Volleyball W

WASHINGTON COLLEGE
300 Washington Ave.
Chestertown, MD 21620-1197
Tel: (410)778-2800; Free: 800-422-1782
Admissions: (410)778-7700
Fax: (410)778-7287
E-mail: admissions_office@washcoll.edu
Web Site: http://www.washcoll.edu/
President/CEO: Dr. Baird Tipson
Admissions: Kevin Coveney
Financial Aid: Jean M. Narcum
Type: Comprehensive **Sex:** Coed **Scores:** 100% SAT V 400+; 100% SAT M 400+; 36% ACT 18-23; 57% ACT 24-29 **% Accepted:** 72 **Admission Plans:** Early Admission; Early Action; Early Decision Plan; Deferred Admission **Application Deadline:** March 1 **Application Fee:** $55.00 **H.S. Requirements:** High school diploma required; GED accepted **Costs Per Year:** Application fee: $55. Comprehensive fee: $42,810 includes full-time tuition ($34,690), mandatory fees ($660), and college room and board ($7460). College room only: $3790. Room and board charges vary according to board plan and housing facility. Part-time tuition: $5780 per course. **Scholarships:** Available **Calendar System:** Semester, Summer Session Not available **Enrollment:** FT 1,285, PT 29, Grad FT 2, Grad PT 56 **Faculty:** FT 87, PT 66 **Student-Faculty Ratio:** 12:1 **Exams:** SAT I or ACT. ACT essay not being used. SAT essay not being used. **% Receiving Financial Aid:** 52 **% Residing in College-Owned, -Operated, or -Affiliated Housing:** 86 **Library Holdings:** 218,350 **Regional Accreditation:** Middle State Association of Colleges and Schools **Credit Hours For Degree:** 128 credits, Bachelors **Intercollegiate Athletics:** Baseball M; Basketball M & W; Cheerleading W; Crew M & W; Equestrian Sports M & W; Field Hockey W; Ice Hockey M; Lacrosse M & W; Rugby M & W; Sailing M & W; Soccer M & W; Softball W; Swimming and Diving M & W; Tennis M & W; Volleyball W; Water Polo M & W

WOR-WIC COMMUNITY COLLEGE
32000 Campus Dr.
Salisbury, MD 21804
Tel: (410)334-2800
Admissions: (410)334-2895
E-mail: admissions@worwic.edu
Web Site: http://www.worwic.edu/
President/CEO: Dr. Ray Hoy
Admissions: Richard Webster
Type: Two-Year College **Sex:** Coed **% Accepted:** 100 **Admission Plans:** Open Admission; Early Admission **Application Deadline:** Rolling **Application Fee:** $0.00 **H.S. Requirements:** High school diploma or equivalent not required **Costs Per Year:** Application fee: $0. Area resident tuition: $2670 full-time, $89 per credit hour part-time. State resident tuition: $5910 full-time, $197 per credit hour part-time. Nonresident tuition: $7290 full-time, $243 per credit hour part-time. Mandatory fees: $228 full-time, $7 per credit hour part-time, $15 per term part-time. **Calendar System:** Semester, Summer Session Available **Enrollment:** FT 1,290, PT 2,755 **Faculty:** FT 68, PT 113 **Student-Faculty Ratio:** 21:1 **Exams:** ACT. **Regional Accreditation:** Middle State Association of Colleges and Schools **Credit Hours For Degree:** 60 credit hours, Associates **Professional Accreditation:** JRCERT

YESHIVA COLLEGE OF THE NATION'S CAPITAL
1216 Arcola Ave.
Silver Spring, MD 20902
Tel: (301)593-2534
Fax: (301)949-7040
Web Site: http://www.yeshiva.edu/
President/CEO: Rabbi Yitzchok Merkin
Type: Four-Year College **Sex:** Men **Affiliation:** Jewish **Admission Plans:** Open Admission **Application Fee:** $50.00 **Professional Accreditation:** AARTS

AMERICAN INTERNATIONAL COLLEGE
1000 State St.
Springfield, MA 01109-3189
Tel: (413)737-7000
Admissions: (413)205-3275
Fax: (413)737-2803
E-mail: kim.lablanc@aic.edu
Web Site: http://www.aic.edu/
President/CEO: Dr. Vincent Maniaci
Admissions: Kim LaBlanc
Financial Aid: Douglas E. Fish
Type: Comprehensive **Sex:** Coed **Scores:** 76% SAT V 400+; 79% SAT M 400+; 49% ACT 18-23; 10% ACT 24-29 **% Accepted:** 79 **Admission Plans:** Early Admission; Deferred Admission **Application Deadline:** Rolling **Application Fee:** $25.00 **H.S. Requirements:** High school diploma required; GED accepted **Scholarships:** Available **Calendar System:** Semester, Summer Session Available **Enrollment:** FT 1,581, PT 148, Grad FT 311, Grad PT 1,361 **Faculty:** FT 89, PT 234 **Student-Faculty Ratio:** 15:1 **Exams:** SAT I or ACT. ACT essay used for advising. SAT essay used for advising. ACT essay used for placement. SAT essay used for placement. **% Receiving Financial Aid:** 88 **% Residing in College-Owned, -Operated, or -Affiliated Housing:** 51 **Library Holdings:** 70,741 **Regional Accreditation:** New England Association of Schools and Colleges **Credit Hours For Degree:** 60 credits, Associates; 120 credits, Bachelors **ROTC:** Army, Air Force **Professional Accreditation:** AACN, AOTA, APTA, NLN **Intercollegiate Athletics:** Baseball M; Basketball M & W; Cross-Country Running M & W; Field Hockey W; Football M; Golf M; Ice Hockey M; Lacrosse M & W; Soccer M & W; Softball W; Tennis M & W; Volleyball W; Wrestling M

AMHERST COLLEGE
PO Box 5000
Amherst, MA 01002-5000
Tel: (413)542-2000
Fax: (413)542-2040
E-mail: admission@amherst.edu
Web Site: http://www.amherst.edu/
President/CEO: Anthony W. Marx
Admissions: Thomas H. Parker
Financial Aid: Joe Paul Case
Type: Four-Year College **Sex:** Coed **Scores:** 100% SAT V 400+; 100% SAT M 400+; 0.7% ACT 18-23; 22.7% ACT 24-29 **% Accepted:** 16 **Admission Plans:** Early Admission; Early Decision Plan; Deferred Admission **Application Deadline:** January 1 **Application Fee:** $60.00 **H.S. Requirements:** High school diploma or equivalent not required **Costs Per Year:** Application fee: $60. Comprehensive fee: $49,078 includes full-time tuition ($38,250), mandatory fees ($678), and college room and board ($10,150). College room only: $5500. **Scholarships:** Available **Calendar System:** Semester, Summer Session Not available **Enrollment:** FT 1,744 **Faculty:** FT 206, PT 27 **Student-Faculty Ratio:** 8:1 **Exams:** SAT I and SAT II or ACT. ACT essay used for admission. SAT essay used for admission. **% Receiving Financial Aid:** 58 **% Residing in College-Owned, -Operated, or -Affiliated Housing:** 98 **Library Holdings:** 1,023,085 **Regional Accreditation:** New England Association of Schools and Colleges **Credit Hours For Degree:** 32 courses, Bachelors **Intercollegiate Athletics:** Baseball M; Basketball M & W; Crew M & W; Cross-Country Running M & W; Equestrian Sports M & W; Fencing M & W; Field Hockey W; Football M; Golf M & W; Ice Hockey M & W; Lacrosse M & W; Rugby M & W; Sailing M & W; Skiing (Downhill) M & W; Soccer M & W; Softball W; Squash M & W; Swimming and Diving M & W; Tennis M & W; Track and Field M & W; Ultimate Frisbee M & W; Volleyball M & W; Water Polo M & W; Wrestling M & W

ANNA MARIA COLLEGE
50 Sunset Ln.
Paxton, MA 01612
Tel: (508)849-3300; Free: 800-344-4586
Admissions: (508)849-3360
E-mail: admissions@annamaria.edu
Web Site: http://www.annamaria.edu/
President/CEO: Dr. Jack P. Calareso
Admissions: Jenna Noel
Financial Aid: Colleen King
Type: Comprehensive **Sex:** Coed **Affiliation:** Roman Catholic **Scores:** 76.6% SAT V 400+; 73.8% SAT M 400+; 68.4% ACT 18-23; 5.3% ACT 24-29 **% Accepted:** 71 **Admission Plans:** Deferred Admission **Application Deadline:** Rolling **Application Fee:** $40.00 **H.S. Requirements:** High school diploma required; GED accepted **Costs Per Year:** Application fee: $40. Comprehensive fee: $35,834 includes full-time tuition ($25,632) and college room and board ($10,202). Full-time tuition varies according to program. Room and board charges vary according to board plan and housing facility. Part-time tuition: $1068 per credit hour. Part-time tuition varies according to class time, course load, degree level, and program. **Scholarships:** Available **Calendar System:** Semester, Summer Session Available **Enrollment:** FT 959, PT 224, Grad FT 73, Grad PT 334 **Faculty:** FT 52, PT 147 **Student-Faculty Ratio:** 12:1 **Exams:** SAT I or ACT. ACT essay not being used. SAT essay not being used. **% Receiving Financial Aid:** 79 **% Residing in College-Owned, -Operated, or -Affiliated Housing:** 49 **Regional Accreditation:** New England Association of Schools and Colleges **Credit Hours For Degree:** 60 credit hours, Associates; 120 credit hours, Bachelors **ROTC:** Air Force **Professional Accreditation:** CSWE, NASM, NLN **Intercollegiate Athletics:** Baseball M; Basketball M & W; Cross-Country Running M; Field Hockey W; Football M; Golf M; Lacrosse M & W; Soccer M & W; Softball W; Tennis M & W; Volleyball W

THE ART INSTITUTE OF BOSTON AT LESLEY UNIVERSITY
700 Beacon St.
Boston, MA 02215-2598
Tel: (617)585-6600
Admissions: (617)585-6710
Fax: (617)437-1226
E-mail: admissions@aiboston.edu
Web Site: http://www.aiboston.edu/
President/CEO: Joseph B. Moore
Admissions: Bob Gielow
Financial Aid: Scott Jewell
Type: Comprehensive **Sex:** Coed **Affiliation:** Lesley University **Scores:** 97% SAT V 400+; 95% SAT M 400+; 53% ACT 18-23; 32% ACT 24-29 **% Accepted:** 67 **Admission Plans:** Early Action; Deferred Admission **Application Deadline:** Rolling **Application Fee:** $40.00 **H.S. Requirements:** High school diploma required; GED accepted **Costs Per Year:** Application fee: $40. Comprehensive fee: $40,400 includes full-time tuition ($26,850), mandatory fees ($750), and college room and board ($12,800). College

room only: $7950. Room and board charges vary according to housing facility. **Scholarships:** Available **Calendar System:** Semester, Summer Session Available **Enrollment:** FT 1,327, PT 50, Grad FT 943, Grad PT 3,144 **Faculty:** FT 73, PT 185 **Student-Faculty Ratio:** 10:1 **Exams:** SAT I or ACT. ACT essay used for admission. SAT essay used for admission. ACT essay used as a validity check on application essay. SAT essay used as a validity check on application essay. ACT essay used for placement. SAT essay used for placement. **% Residing in College-Owned, -Operated, or -Affiliated Housing:** 54 **Regional Accreditation:** New England Association of Schools and Colleges **Credit Hours For Degree:** 128 credits, Bachelors **Professional Accreditation:** NASAD **Intercollegiate Athletics:** Baseball M; Basketball M & W; Cross-Country Running M & W; Soccer M & W; Softball W; Volleyball M & W

ASSUMPTION COLLEGE
500 Salisbury St.
Worcester, MA 01609-1296
Tel: (508)767-7000; Free: 888-882-7786
Admissions: (508)767-7110
Fax: (508)799-4412
E-mail: admiss@assumption.edu
Web Site: http://www.assumption.edu/
President/CEO: Dr. Francesco C. Cesareo
Admissions: Kathleen Murphy
Financial Aid: Linda Mularczyk
Type: Comprehensive **Sex:** Coed **Affiliation:** Roman Catholic **Scores:** 97.8% SAT V 400+; 97.4% SAT M 400+; 51.3% ACT 18-23; 36.1% ACT 24-29 **% Accepted:** 79 **Admission Plans:** Early Action; Deferred Admission **Application Deadline:** February 15 **Application Fee:** $50.00 **H.S. Requirements:** High school diploma required; GED accepted **Costs Per Year:** Application fee: $50. Comprehensive fee: $36,511 includes full-time tuition ($29,806), mandatory fees ($365), and college room and board ($6340). College room only: $3730. Full-time tuition and fees vary according to course load and reciprocity agreements. Room and board charges vary according to housing facility. Part-time tuition: $993.53 per credit hour. Part-time mandatory fees: $365 per year. Part-time tuition and fees vary according to course load. **Scholarships:** Available **Calendar System:** Semester, Summer Session Available **Enrollment:** FT 2,114, PT 3, Grad FT 158, Grad PT 326 **Faculty:** FT 154, PT 70 **Student-Faculty Ratio:** 12:1 **% Receiving Financial Aid:** 75 **% Residing in College-Owned, -Operated, or -Affiliated Housing:** 90 **Final Year or Final Semester Residency Requirement:** No **Library Holdings:** 230,180 **Regional Accreditation:** New England Association of Schools and Colleges **Credit Hours For Degree:** 40 courses, Bachelors **ROTC:** Army, Air Force **Professional Accreditation:** CORE **Intercollegiate Athletics:** Baseball M; Basketball M & W; Crew W; Cross-Country Running M & W; Field Hockey W; Football M; Golf M; Ice Hockey M; Lacrosse M & W; Soccer M & W; Softball W; Swimming and Diving W; Tennis M & W; Track and Field M & W; Volleyball W

ATLANTIC UNION COLLEGE
PO Box 1000
South Lancaster, MA 01561-1000
Tel: (978)368-2000; Free: 800-282-2030
Admissions: (978)368-2239
Fax: (978)368-2015
E-mail: bordes.henry-saturne@auc.edu
Web Site: http://www.auc.edu/
President/CEO: Norman Wendth
Admissions: Dr. Bordes Henry-Saturne
Financial Aid: Sandra Pereira
Type: Comprehensive **Sex:** Coed **Affiliation:** Seventh-day Adventist **% Accepted:** 59 **Application Deadline:** August 1 **Application Fee:** $25.00 **H.S. Requirements:** High school diploma required; GED accepted **Costs Per Year:** Application fee: $25. Comprehensive fee: $22,216 includes full-time tuition ($15,408), mandatory fees ($1658), and college room and board ($5150). Full-time tuition and fees vary according to course load and program. Room and board charges vary according to board plan and housing facility. Tuition guaranteed not to increase for student's term of enrollment. **Scholarships:** Available **Calendar System:** Semester, Summer Session Available **Enrollment:** FT 371, PT 90 **Faculty:** FT 26, PT 46 **Student-Faculty Ratio:** 10:1 **Exams:** SAT I and SAT II or ACT. **% Receiving Financial Aid:** 81 **Library Holdings:** 153,827 **Regional Accreditation:** New England Association of Schools and Colleges **Credit Hours For Degree:** 64 hours, Associates; 128 hours, Bachelors **Professional Accreditation:** CSWE, NASM, NLN

BABSON COLLEGE
Babson Park, MA 02457-0310
Tel: (781)235-1200; Free: 800-488-3696
Fax: (781)239-5614
E-mail: ugradadmission@babson.edu
Web Site: http://www.babson.edu/
President/CEO: Leonard Schlesinger
Admissions: Adrienne Ramsey
Financial Aid: Melissa Shaak
Type: Comprehensive **Sex:** Coed **Scores:** 100% SAT V 400+; 100% SAT M 400+; 9% ACT 18-23; 69% ACT 24-29 **% Accepted:** 40 **Admission Plans:** Early Action; Early Decision Plan; Deferred Admission **Application Deadline:** January 15 **Application Fee:** $65.00 **H.S. Requirements:** High school diploma required; GED accepted **Costs Per Year:** Application fee: $65. Comprehensive fee: $51,324 includes full-time tuition ($37,824) and college room and board ($13,500). College room only: $8066. Room and board charges vary according to board plan and housing facility. **Scholarships:** Available **Calendar System:** Semester, Summer Session Available **Enrollment:** FT 1,898, Grad FT 968, Grad PT 579 **Faculty:** FT 174, PT 94 **Student-Faculty Ratio:** 13:1 **Exams:** SAT I or ACT. **% Receiving Financial Aid:** 44 **% Residing in College-Owned, -Operated, or -Affiliated Housing:** 86 **Final Year or Final Semester Residency Requirement:** No **Library Holdings:** 131,436 **Regional Accreditation:** New England Association of Schools and Colleges **Credit Hours For Degree:** 128 credit hours, Bachelors **ROTC:** Army, Navy, Air Force **Professional Accreditation:** AACSB **Intercollegiate Athletics:** Baseball M; Basketball M & W; Cheerleading W; Cross-Country Running M & W; Field Hockey W; Golf M; Ice Hockey M & W; Lacrosse M & W; Rugby M & W; Skiing (Downhill) M & W; Soccer M & W; Softball W; Swimming and Diving M & W; Tennis M & W; Track and Field M & W; Volleyball W

BARD COLLEGE AT SIMON'S ROCK
84 Alford Rd.
Great Barrington, MA 01230-9702
Tel: (413)528-0771; Free: 800-235-7186
Admissions: (413)528-7312
Fax: (413)528-7334
E-mail: admit@simons-rock.edu
Web Site: http://www.simons-rock.edu/
President/CEO: Dr. Mary B. Marcy
Admissions: Steven Coleman
Financial Aid: Ann Murtagh Gitto
Type: Four-Year College **Sex:** Coed **Affiliation:** Bard College **% Accepted:** 84 **Application Deadline:** May 31 **Application Fee:** $50.00 **H.S. Requirements:** High school diploma or equivalent not required **Costs Per Year:** Application fee: $50. Comprehensive fee: $51,130 includes full-time tuition ($39,380), mandatory fees ($790), and college room and board ($10,960). Full-time tuition and fees vary according to course load. Part-time tuition: $1550 per credit hour. Part-time tuition varies according to course load. **Scholarships:** Available **Calendar System:** Semester, Summer Session Not available **Enrollment:** FT 421, PT 10 **Faculty:** FT 43, PT 42 **Student-Faculty Ratio:** 8:1 **Exams:** ACT essay not being used. SAT essay not being used. **% Receiving Financial Aid:** 62 **% Residing in College-Owned, -Operated, or -Affiliated Housing:** 95 **Final Year or Final Semester Residency Requirement:** Yes **Library Holdings:** 106,788 **Regional Accreditation:** New England Association of Schools and Colleges **Credit Hours For Degree:** 60 credit hours, Associates; 120 credit hours, Bachelors **Intercollegiate Athletics:** Basketball M & W; Cheerleading M & W; Cross-Country Running M & W; Fencing M & W; Racquetball M & W; Soccer M & W; Swimming and Diving M & W

BAY PATH COLLEGE
588 Longmeadow St.
Longmeadow, MA 01106-2292
Tel: (413)565-1000; Free: 800-782-7284
Fax: (413)567-0501
E-mail: admiss@baypath.edu
Web Site: http://www.baypath.edu/
President/CEO: Dr. Carol A. Leary
Admissions: Diane Ranaldi
Financial Aid: Phyllis Brand
Type: Comprehensive **Scores:** 88% SAT V 400+; 81% SAT M 400+; 63% ACT 18-23; 19% ACT 24-29 **% Accepted:** 83 **Admission Plans:** Early Admission; Early Action; Deferred Admission **Application Deadline:** Rolling

Application Fee: $25.00 **H.S. Requirements:** High school diploma required; GED accepted **Costs Per Year:** Application fee: $25. Comprehensive fee: $34,565 includes full-time tuition ($24,530) and college room and board ($10,035). Room and board charges vary according to board plan. Part-time tuition: $455 per credit. **Scholarships:** Available **Calendar System:** Semester, Summer Session Available **Enrollment:** FT 1,199, PT 282, Grad FT 194, Grad PT 359 **Faculty:** FT 43, PT 154 **Student-Faculty Ratio:** 15:1 **Exams:** SAT I or ACT. ACT essay used as a validity check on application essay. SAT essay used as a validity check on application essay. **% Receiving Financial Aid:** 87 **% Residing in College-Owned, -Operated, or -Affiliated Housing:** 64 **Final Year or Final Semester Residency Requirement:** No **Library Holdings:** 63,234 **Regional Accreditation:** New England Association of Schools and Colleges **Credit Hours For Degree:** 60 credits, Associates; 120 credits, Bachelors **ROTC:** Army, Air Force **Professional Accreditation:** AOTA **Intercollegiate Athletics:** Basketball W; Cross-Country Running W; Field Hockey W; Soccer W; Softball W; Tennis W; Volleyball W

BAY STATE COLLEGE
122 Commonwealth Ave.
Boston, MA 02116-2975
Tel: (617)236-8000; Free: 800-81-LEARN
Admissions: (617)217-9000
Fax: (617)536-1735
E-mail: admissions@baystate.edu
Web Site: http://www.baystate.edu/
President/CEO: Craig F. Pfannenstiehl
Admissions: Kim Olds
Type: Two-Year College **Sex:** Coed **% Accepted:** 80 **Admission Plans:** Early Admission **Application Deadline:** Rolling **Application Fee:** $40.00 **H.S. Requirements:** High school diploma required; GED accepted **Scholarships:** Available **Calendar System:** Semester, Summer Session Not available **Enrollment:** FT 522, PT 235 **Faculty:** FT 19, PT 47 **Student-Faculty Ratio:** 13:1 **% Residing in College-Owned, -Operated, or -Affiliated Housing:** 21 **Library Holdings:** 4,490 **Regional Accreditation:** New England Association of Schools and Colleges **Credit Hours For Degree:** 60 credits, Associates **Professional Accreditation:** ABHES, APTA

BECKER COLLEGE
61 Sever St.
Worcester, MA 01609
Tel: (508)791-9241; Free: 877-5BECKER
Admissions: (508)373-9400
Fax: (508)831-7505
E-mail: admissions@beckercollege.edu
Web Site: http://www.becker.edu/
President/CEO: Dr. Joseph Bascuas
Financial Aid: Russ Romandini
Type: Four-Year College **Sex:** Coed **Scores:** 73% SAT V 400+; 71% SAT M 400+; 41% ACT 18-23; 13% ACT 24-29 **% Accepted:** 72 **Admission Plans:** Deferred Admission **Application Deadline:** Rolling **Application Fee:** $30.00 **H.S. Requirements:** High school diploma required; GED accepted **Costs Per Year:** Application fee: $30. Comprehensive fee: $37,508 includes full-time tuition ($24,780), mandatory fees ($2968), and college room and board ($9760). Full-time tuition and fees vary according to course load. Room and board charges vary according to board plan and housing facility. Part-time tuition: $1025 per credit hour. Part-time tuition varies according to course load and program. **Scholarships:** Available **Calendar System:** Semester, Summer Session Available **Enrollment:** FT 1,354, PT 398 **Faculty:** FT 41, PT 143 **Student-Faculty Ratio:** 16:1 **Exams:** SAT I or ACT. **% Receiving Financial Aid:** 72 **% Residing in College-Owned, -Operated, or -Affiliated Housing:** 50 **Library Holdings:** 75,000 **Regional Accreditation:** New England Association of Schools and Colleges **Credit Hours For Degree:** 60 credits, Associates; 122 credits, Bachelors **ROTC:** Army, Navy, Air Force **Professional Accreditation:** APTA, NLN **Intercollegiate Athletics:** Baseball M; Basketball M & W; Cheerleading M & W; Equestrian Sports M & W; Field Hockey W; Football M; Golf M; Ice Hockey M; Lacrosse M & W; Soccer M & W; Softball W; Tennis M & W; Volleyball W

BENJAMIN FRANKLIN INSTITUTE OF TECHNOLOGY
41 Berkeley St.
Boston, MA 02116-6296
Tel: (617)423-4630
Fax: (617)482-3706
E-mail: bjohnson@bfit.edu
Web Site: http://www.bfit.edu/
President/CEO: Michael Taylor
Admissions: Brittainy Johnson
Type: Two-Year College **Sex:** Coed **% Accepted:** 66 **Admission Plans:** Open Admission; Deferred Admission **Application Deadline:** August 15 **Application Fee:** $25.00 **H.S. Requirements:** High school diploma required; GED accepted **Costs Per Year:** Application fee: $25. Comprehensive fee: $23,884 includes full-time tuition ($13,950), mandatory fees ($334), and college room and board ($9600). Full-time tuition and fees vary according to course load, degree level, and program. Room and board charges vary according to housing facility. Part-time tuition: $581 per credit. Part-time mandatory fees: $581 per credit hour. Part-time tuition and fees vary according to course load, degree level, and program. **Calendar System:** Semester, Summer Session Available **Enrollment:** FT 416, PT 120 **Faculty:** FT 30, PT 40 **Student-Faculty Ratio:** 12:1 **% Residing in College-Owned, -Operated, or -Affiliated Housing:** 11 **Library Holdings:** 10,000 **Regional Accreditation:** New England Association of Schools and Colleges **Credit Hours For Degree:** 70 credits, Associates; 134 credits, Bachelors **Professional Accreditation:** ABET **Intercollegiate Athletics:** Soccer M

BENTLEY UNIVERSITY
175 Forest St.
Waltham, MA 02452-4705
Tel: (781)891-2000; Free: 800-523-2354
Admissions: (781)891-2244
Fax: (781)891-3414
E-mail: ugadmission@bentley.edu
Web Site: http://www.bentley.edu/
President/CEO: Gloria Cordes Larson
Financial Aid: Donna Kendall
Type: Comprehensive **Sex:** Coed **Scores:** 99% SAT V 400+; 100% SAT M 400+; 14% ACT 18-23; 74% ACT 24-29 **% Accepted:** 43 **Admission Plans:** Early Admission; Early Action; Early Decision Plan; Deferred Admission **Application Deadline:** January 15 **Application Fee:** $50.00 **H.S. Requirements:** High school diploma required; GED accepted **Costs Per Year:** Application fee: $50. Comprehensive fee: $47,568 includes full-time tuition ($34,360), mandatory fees ($1468), and college room and board ($11,740). College room only: $7010. Room and board charges vary according to board plan and housing facility. Part-time tuition: $1642 per course. Part-time mandatory fees: $45 per term. **Scholarships:** Available **Calendar System:** Semester, Summer Session Available **Enrollment:** FT 4,030, PT 205, Grad FT 451, Grad PT 930 **Faculty:** FT 279, PT 178 **Student-Faculty Ratio:** 14:1 **Exams:** SAT I or ACT. SAT essay used for admission. **% Receiving Financial Aid:** 48 **% Residing in College-Owned, -Operated, or -Affiliated Housing:** 83 **Library Holdings:** 170,300 **Regional Accreditation:** New England Association of Schools and Colleges **Credit Hours For Degree:** 122 credits, Bachelors **ROTC:** Army, Air Force **Professional Accreditation:** AACSB **Intercollegiate Athletics:** Baseball M; Basketball M & W; Cross-Country Running M & W; Field Hockey W; Football M; Golf M; Ice Hockey M; Lacrosse M & W; Soccer M & W; Softball W; Swimming and Diving M & W; Tennis M & W; Track and Field M & W; Volleyball W

BERKLEE COLLEGE OF MUSIC
1140 Boylston St.
Boston, MA 02215-3693
Tel: (617)266-1400; Free: 800-BER-KLEE
Admissions: (617)747-2222
Fax: (617)747-2047
E-mail: admissions@berklee.edu
Web Site: http://www.berklee.edu/
President/CEO: Roger H. Brown
Admissions: Damien Bracken
Financial Aid: Frank Mullen
Type: Four-Year College **Sex:** Coed **% Accepted:** 42 **Admission Plans:** Early Action; Deferred Admission **Application Deadline:** January 15 **Application Fee:** $150.00 **H.S. Requirements:** High school diploma required; GED accepted **Costs Per Year:** Application fee: $150. Comprehensive fee: $45,730 includes full-time tuition ($29,700), mandatory fees ($950), and college room and board ($15,080). Part-time tuition: $1053 per credit hour. there is a one-time $2,950 charge for laptop purchase required of all entering students. **Scholarships:** Available **Calendar System:** Semester, Summer Session Available **Enrollment:** FT 3,800, PT 345 **Faculty:** FT 234, PT 296 **Student-Faculty Ratio:** 12:1 **% Receiving Financial Aid:** 46 **% Residing**

in College-Owned, -Operated, or -Affiliated Housing: 18 **Regional Accreditation:** New England Association of Schools and Colleges **Credit Hours For Degree:** 120 credit hours, Bachelors

BERKSHIRE COMMUNITY COLLEGE
1350 West St.
Pittsfield, MA 01201-5786
Tel: (413)499-4660
Admissions: (413)236-1635
Fax: (606)224-7744
E-mail: tschetti@berkshirecc.edu
Web Site: http://www.berkshirecc.edu/
President/CEO: Paul E. Raverta
Admissions: Tina Schettini
Financial Aid: Janet Cormier
Type: Two-Year College **Sex:** Coed **Affiliation:** Massachusetts Public Higher Education System **% Accepted:** 100 **Admission Plans:** Open Admission; Deferred Admission **Application Deadline:** Rolling **Application Fee:** $10.00 **H.S. Requirements:** High school diploma required; GED accepted **Costs Per Year:** Application fee: $10. One-time mandatory fee: $10. State resident tuition: $624 full-time, $26 per credit part-time. Nonresident tuition: $6720 full-time, $280 per credit part-time. Mandatory fees: $3120 full-time, $130 per credit part-time. Full-time tuition and fees vary according to reciprocity agreements. Part-time tuition and fees vary according to reciprocity agreements. **Scholarships:** Available **Calendar System:** Semester, Summer Session Available **Enrollment:** FT 996, PT 1,279 **Faculty:** FT 55, PT 120 **Student-Faculty Ratio:** 15:1 **Library Holdings:** 77,497 **Regional Accreditation:** New England Association of Schools and Colleges **Credit Hours For Degree:** 60 credits, Associates **Professional Accreditation:** APTA, CARC, NLN

BOSTON ARCHITECTURAL COLLEGE
320 Newbury St.
Boston, MA 02115-2795
Tel: (617)262-5000; Free: 877-585-0100
Admissions: (617)585-0256
Fax: (617)585-0111
E-mail: admissions@the-bac.edu
Web Site: http://www.the-bac.edu/
President/CEO: Dr. Theodore C. Landsmark
Admissions: Richard Moyer
Financial Aid: Anne Downey
Type: Comprehensive **Sex:** Coed **% Accepted:** 71 **Application Deadline:** Rolling **Application Fee:** $50.00 **H.S. Requirements:** High school diploma required; GED accepted **Costs Per Year:** Application fee: $50. Tuition: $11,448 full-time, $954 per credit hour part-time. Mandatory fees: $20 full-time, $10 per term part-time. Full-time tuition and fees vary according to course load, degree level, program, and reciprocity agreements. Part-time tuition and fees vary according to course load, degree level, program, and reciprocity agreements. **Scholarships:** Available **Calendar System:** Semester, Summer Session Available **Enrollment:** FT 620, PT 15, Grad FT 505, Grad PT 6 **Faculty:** FT 11, PT 218 **Student-Faculty Ratio:** 4:1 **% Receiving Financial Aid:** 82 **Library Holdings:** 27,000 **Regional Accreditation:** New England Association of Schools and Colleges **Credit Hours For Degree:** 178.50 credit hours, Bachelors **Professional Accreditation:** FIDER, NAAB

BOSTON BAPTIST COLLEGE
950 Metropolitan Ave.
Boston, MA 02136
Tel: (617)364-3510; Free: 888-235-2014
Fax: (617)364-0723
E-mail: kfox@boston.edu
Web Site: http://www.boston.edu/
President/CEO: Rev. David V. Melton
Admissions: Karen Fox
Type: Four-Year College **Sex:** Coed **Affiliation:** Baptist **% Accepted:** 47 **Admission Plans:** Deferred Admission **Application Deadline:** Rolling **Application Fee:** $40.00 **H.S. Requirements:** High school diploma required; GED accepted **Costs Per Year:** Application fee: $40. Comprehensive fee: $18,495 includes full-time tuition ($9376), mandatory fees ($1453), and college room and board ($7666). College room only: $4570. Room and board charges vary according to board plan. Part-time tuition: $391 per credit hour. **Scholarships:** Available **Calendar System:** Semester, Summer Session Available **Enrollment:** FT 108, PT 40 **Faculty:** FT 2, PT 17 **Student-Faculty Ratio:** 8:1 **Exams:** SAT I or ACT. ACT essay used for placement. SAT essay used for placement. **% Residing in College-Owned, -Operated, or -Affiliated Housing:** 65 **Final Year or Final Semester Residency Requirement:** Yes **Credit Hours For Degree:** 64 credit hours, Associates; 128 credit hours, Bachelors **Professional Accreditation:** TACCS

BOSTON COLLEGE
140 Commonwealth Ave.
Chestnut Hill, MA 02467-3800
Tel: (617)552-8000; Free: 800-360-2522
Admissions: (617)552-3100
Fax: (617)552-0798
Web Site: http://www.bc.edu/
President/CEO: Fr. William P. Leahy
Type: University **Sex:** Coed **Affiliation:** Roman Catholic (Jesuit) **Scores:** 99.7% SAT V 400+; 99.9% SAT M 400+; 3.5% ACT 18-23; 28.5% ACT 24-29 **% Accepted:** 30 **Admission Plans:** Early Admission; Early Action; Deferred Admission **Application Deadline:** January 1 **Application Fee:** $70.00 **H.S. Requirements:** High school diploma required; GED accepted **Costs Per Year:** Application fee: $70. One-time mandatory fee: $438. Comprehensive fee: $52,039 includes full-time tuition ($38,530), mandatory fees ($600), and college room and board ($12,909). College room only: $8369. Room and board charges vary according to housing facility. **Scholarships:** Available **Calendar System:** Semester, Summer Session Available **Enrollment:** FT 9,171, Grad FT 2,642, Grad PT 2,318 **Faculty:** FT 708, PT 615 **Student-Faculty Ratio:** 13:1 **Exams:** SAT I and SAT II or ACT. ACT essay used for admission. SAT essay used for admission. ACT essay used as a validity check on application essay. SAT essay used as a validity check on application essay. **% Receiving Financial Aid:** 42 **% Residing in College-Owned, -Operated, or -Affiliated Housing:** 80 **Final Year or Final Semester Residency Requirement:** No **Library Holdings:** 2,547,714 **Regional Accreditation:** New England Association of Schools and Colleges **Credit Hours For Degree:** 38 courses, Bachelors **ROTC:** Army, Navy, Air Force **Professional Accreditation:** AACSB, AACN, AANA, ABA, APA, AALS, ATS, CSWE, NCATE, TEAC **Intercollegiate Athletics:** Baseball M; Basketball M & W; Cheerleading M & W; Crew W; Cross-Country Running M & W; Fencing M & W; Field Hockey W; Football M; Golf M & W; Ice Hockey M & W; Lacrosse W; Sailing M & W; Skiing (Downhill) M & W; Soccer M & W; Softball W; Swimming and Diving M & W; Tennis M & W; Track and Field M & W; Volleyball W

THE BOSTON CONSERVATORY
8 The Fenway
Boston, MA 02215
Tel: (617)536-6340
Admissions: (617)912-9153
Fax: (617)536-3176
E-mail: hshefler@bostonconservatory.edu
Web Site: http://www.bostonconservatory.edu/
President/CEO: Richard Ortner
Admissions: Halley Shefler
Financial Aid: Jessica Raine
Type: Comprehensive **Sex:** Coed **% Accepted:** 34 **Admission Plans:** Deferred Admission **Application Deadline:** December 1 **Application Fee:** $110.00 **H.S. Requirements:** High school diploma required; GED accepted **Costs Per Year:** Application fee: $110. Comprehensive fee: $49,580 includes full-time tuition ($31,900), mandatory fees ($1800), and college room and board ($15,880). College room only: $10,500. Full-time tuition and fees vary according to course load, degree level, and program. Room and board charges vary according to board plan and housing facility. Part-time tuition: $1320 per credit. Part-time mandatory fees: $390 per term. Part-time tuition and fees vary according to course load, degree level, and program. **Scholarships:** Available **Calendar System:** Semester, Summer Session Available **Enrollment:** FT 487, PT 2, Grad FT 180, Grad PT 7 **Faculty:** FT 74, PT 115 **Student-Faculty Ratio:** 4:1 **Exams:** SAT I or ACT. ACT essay not being used. SAT essay not being used. **% Receiving Financial Aid:** 59 **% Residing in College-Owned, -Operated, or -Affiliated Housing:** 30 **Library Holdings:** 30,261 **Regional Accreditation:** New England Association of Schools and Colleges **Credit Hours For Degree:** 125 credits, Bachelors **Professional Accreditation:** NASM

BOSTON UNIVERSITY
Boston, MA 02215
Tel: (617)353-2000

Admissions: (617)353-2300
Fax: (617)353-9695
E-mail: admissions@bu.edu
Web Site: http://www.bu.edu/
President/CEO: Dr. Robert A. Brown
Admissions: Kelly Walter
Financial Aid: Christine McGuire
Type: University **Sex:** Coed **Scores:** 100% SAT V 400+; 100% SAT M 400+; 7% ACT 18-23; 66% ACT 24-29 **% Accepted:** 58 **Admission Plans:** Early Admission; Early Decision Plan; Deferred Admission **Application Deadline:** January 1 **Application Fee:** $75.00 **H.S. Requirements:** High school diploma required; GED accepted **Costs Per Year:** Application fee: $75. Comprehensive fee: $52,124 includes full-time tuition ($39,314), mandatory fees ($550), and college room and board ($12,260). College room only: $7980. Full-time tuition and fees vary according to class time and degree level. Room and board charges vary according to board plan and housing facility. Part-time tuition: $1228 per credit. Part-time mandatory fees: $40 per term. Part-time tuition and fees vary according to class time, course load, and degree level. **Scholarships:** Available **Calendar System:** Semester, Summer Session Available **Enrollment:** FT 16,810, PT 1,473, Grad FT 8,935, Grad PT 4,742 **Faculty:** FT 1,549, PT 1,079 **Student-Faculty Ratio:** 13:1 **Exams:** SAT I and SAT II or ACT. ACT essay used for admission. SAT essay used for admission. **% Receiving Financial Aid:** 44 **% Residing in College-Owned, -Operated, or -Affiliated Housing:** 67 **Library Holdings:** 2,427,253 **Regional Accreditation:** New England Association of Schools and Colleges **Credit Hours For Degree:** 128 credits, Bachelors **ROTC:** Army, Navy, Air Force **Professional Accreditation:** AACSB, ABET, ABA, ACNM, ADA, ADtA, AOTA, APTA, APA, ASLHA, ACIPE, AALS, ATS, ACEHSA, CEPH, CORE, CSWE, JRCEPAT, LCMEAMA, NASM **Intercollegiate Athletics:** Badminton M & W; Baseball M; Basketball M & W; Cheerleading M & W; Crew M & W; Cross-Country Running M & W; Equestrian Sports M & W; Fencing M & W; Field Hockey W; Golf M & W; Gymnastics M & W; Ice Hockey M & W; Lacrosse M & W; Rugby M & W; Sailing M & W; Skiing (Downhill) M & W; Soccer M & W; Softball W; Swimming and Diving M & W; Tennis M & W; Track and Field M & W; Ultimate Frisbee M & W; Volleyball M & W; Water Polo W; Wrestling M

BRANDEIS UNIVERSITY
415 South St.
Waltham, MA 02454-9110
Tel: (781)736-2000; Free: 800-622-0622
Admissions: (781)736-3500
Fax: (781)736-3536
E-mail: admissions@brandeis.edu
Web Site: http://www.brandeis.edu/
President/CEO: Jehuda Reinharz
Admissions: Jean C. Eddy
Financial Aid: Peter Giumette
Type: University **Sex:** Coed **Scores:** 100% SAT V 400+; 100% SAT M 400+; 2.6% ACT 18-23; 48.3% ACT 24-29 **% Accepted:** 40 **Admission Plans:** Early Decision Plan; Deferred Admission **Application Deadline:** January 15 **Application Fee:** $55.00 **H.S. Requirements:** High school diploma required; GED accepted **Costs Per Year:** Application fee: $55. Comprehensive fee: $49,554 includes full-time tuition ($37,530), mandatory fees ($1232), and college room and board ($10,792). Room and board charges vary according to board plan and housing facility. **Scholarships:** Available **Calendar System:** Semester, Summer Session Available **Enrollment:** FT 3,296, PT 21, Grad FT 1,705, Grad PT 576 **Faculty:** FT 358, PT 128 **Student-Faculty Ratio:** 9:1 **Exams:** SAT I or ACT. **% Receiving Financial Aid:** 51 **% Residing in College-Owned, -Operated, or -Affiliated Housing:** 83 **Library Holdings:** 1,208,777 **Regional Accreditation:** New England Association of Schools and Colleges **Credit Hours For Degree:** 32 courses, Bachelors **ROTC:** Army, Air Force **Professional Accreditation:** AACSB **Intercollegiate Athletics:** Baseball M; Basketball M & W; Crew M; Cross-Country Running M & W; Fencing M & W; Field Hockey W; Golf M; Lacrosse M & W; Rugby M & W; Sailing M & W; Skiing (Downhill) M & W; Soccer W; Softball W; Squash M; Swimming and Diving M & W; Tennis M & W; Track and Field M & W; Volleyball W

BRIDGEWATER STATE COLLEGE
Bridgewater, MA 02325-0001
Tel: (508)531-1000
Admissions: (508)531-1237
Fax: (508)531-1707
E-mail: admission@bridgew.edu
Web Site: http://www.bridgew.edu/
President/CEO: Dr. Dana Mohler-Faria
Admissions: Gregg Meyer
Type: Comprehensive **Sex:** Coed **Affiliation:** Massachusetts Public Higher Education System **Scores:** 95.1% SAT V 400+; 95.8% SAT M 400+; 73.6% ACT 18-23; 22.6% ACT 24-29 **% Accepted:** 61 **Admission Plans:** Early Admission; Early Action; Deferred Admission **Application Deadline:** February 15 **Application Fee:** $25.00 **H.S. Requirements:** High school diploma required; GED accepted **Costs Per Year:** Application fee: $25. State resident tuition: $910 full-time, $38 per credit hour part-time. Nonresident tuition: $7050 full-time, $294 per credit hour part-time. Mandatory fees: $5694 full-time, $231.80 per credit hour part-time. College room and board: $9670. College room only: $6420. Room and board charges vary according to board plan and housing facility. **Scholarships:** Available **Calendar System:** Semester, Summer Session Available **Enrollment:** FT 7,516, PT 1,387, Grad FT 427, Grad PT 1,444 **Faculty:** FT 304, PT 260 **Student-Faculty Ratio:** 23:1 **Exams:** SAT I or ACT. ACT essay not being used. SAT essay not being used. **% Receiving Financial Aid:** 52 **% Residing in College-Owned, -Operated, or -Affiliated Housing:** 31 **Final Year or Final Semester Residency Requirement:** No **Library Holdings:** 343,382 **Regional Accreditation:** New England Association of Schools and Colleges **Credit Hours For Degree:** 120 semester hours, Bachelors **ROTC:** Army, Air Force **Professional Accreditation:** ACA, CSWE, JRCEPAT, NASPAA, NCATE **Intercollegiate Athletics:** Baseball M; Basketball M & W; Cross-Country Running M & W; Field Hockey W; Football M; Lacrosse M & W; Soccer M & W; Softball W; Swimming and Diving M & W; Tennis M & W; Track and Field M & W; Volleyball W; Water Polo M & W; Wrestling M

BRISTOL COMMUNITY COLLEGE
777 Elsbree St.
Fall River, MA 02720-7395
Tel: (508)678-2811
Fax: (508)674-8838
E-mail: rodney.clark@bristolcc.edu
Web Site: http://www.bristolcc.edu/
President/CEO: John J. Sbrega, PhD
Admissions: Rodney Clark
Type: Two-Year College **Sex:** Coed **Affiliation:** Massachusetts Community College System **Admission Plans:** Open Admission **Application Fee:** $10.00 **H.S. Requirements:** High school diploma required; GED accepted **Scholarships:** Available **Calendar System:** Semester, Summer Session Available **Enrollment:** FT 3,365, PT 4,023 **Faculty:** FT 105, PT 310 **Student-Faculty Ratio:** 17:1 **Library Holdings:** 65,000 **Regional Accreditation:** New England Association of Schools and Colleges **Credit Hours For Degree:** 60 credits, Associates **Professional Accreditation:** ADA, AHIMA, AOTA, NAACLS, NLN

BUNKER HILL COMMUNITY COLLEGE
250 New Rutherford Ave.
Boston, MA 02129
Tel: (617)228-2000
Admissions: (617)228-2346
Fax: (617)228-2120
Web Site: http://www.bhcc.mass.edu/
President/CEO: Mary L. Fifield, PhD
Admissions: David Gomes
Financial Aid: Melissa Holster
Type: Two-Year College **Sex:** Coed **% Accepted:** 85 **Admission Plans:** Open Admission; Deferred Admission **Application Deadline:** Rolling **Application Fee:** $10.00 **H.S. Requirements:** High school diploma required; GED accepted. For non-degree seeking students do not need proof of high school or GED: High school diploma or equivalent not required **Costs Per Year:** Application fee: $10. State resident tuition: $576 full-time, $24 per credit part-time. Nonresident tuition: $5520 full-time, $230 per credit part-time. Mandatory fees: $2448 full-time, $97 per credit part-time. Full-time tuition and fees vary according to course load. Part-time tuition and fees vary according to course load. **Scholarships:** Available **Calendar System:** Semester, Summer Session Available **Enrollment:** FT 3,767, PT 7,242 **Faculty:** FT 131, PT 447 **Student-Faculty Ratio:** 19:1 **Library Holdings:** 66,777 **Regional Accreditation:** New England Association of Schools and Colleges **Credit Hours For Degree:** 60 credits, Associates **Professional Accreditation:** ARCEST, JRCEDMS, JRCERT, NLN **Intercollegiate Athletics:** Baseball M; Basketball M & W; Golf M & W; Soccer M & W; Softball W

CAMBRIDGE COLLEGE
1000 Massachusetts Ave.
Cambridge, MA 02138-5304
Tel: (617)868-1000; Free: 800-877-4723
Admissions: (617)873-0167
Fax: (617)349-3545
E-mail: stephen.lyons@cambridgecollege.edu
Web Site: http://www.cambridgecollege.edu/
President/CEO: Dr. Tito Guerrero, III
Admissions: Stephen Lyons
Financial Aid: Dr. Frank Lauder
Type: Comprehensive **Sex:** Coed **% Accepted:** 100 **Admission Plans:** Open Admission; Deferred Admission **Application Deadline:** Rolling **Application Fee:** $30.00 **H.S. Requirements:** High school diploma required; GED accepted **Costs Per Year:** Application fee: $30. Tuition: $10,950 full-time, $365 per credit part-time. **Scholarships:** Available **Calendar System:** Trimester, Summer Session Available **Faculty:** FT 26, PT 545 **Student-Faculty Ratio:** 16:1 **% Receiving Financial Aid:** 72 **Library Holdings:** 45,628 **Regional Accreditation:** New England Association of Schools and Colleges **Credit Hours For Degree:** 120 credit hours, Bachelors **Professional Accreditation:** TEAC

CAPE COD COMMUNITY COLLEGE
2240 Iyannough Rd.
West Barnstable, MA 02668-1599
Tel: (508)362-2131
E-mail: admiss@capecod.edu
Web Site: http://www.capecod.edu/
President/CEO: Kathleen Schatzberg
Admissions: Susan Kline-Symington
Type: Two-Year College **Sex:** Coed **Affiliation:** Massachusetts Public Higher Education System **Admission Plans:** Open Admission; Preferred Admission; Deferred Admission **Application Deadline:** August 10 **Application Fee:** $10.00 **H.S. Requirements:** High school diploma required; GED accepted **Costs Per Year:** Application fee: $10. State resident tuition: $3264 full-time, $136 per credit hour part-time. Nonresident tuition: $8208 full-time, $342 per credit hour part-time. **Scholarships:** Available **Calendar System:** Semester, Summer Session Available **Enrollment:** FT 1,465, PT 2,747 **Faculty:** FT 65, PT 249 **Student-Faculty Ratio:** 16:1 **Library Holdings:** 54,342 **Regional Accreditation:** New England Association of Schools and Colleges **Credit Hours For Degree:** 60 credit hours, Associates **Professional Accreditation:** ADA, NLN

CLARK UNIVERSITY
950 Main St.
Worcester, MA 01610-1477
Tel: (508)793-7711; Free: 800-GO-CLARK
Admissions: (508)793-7431
Fax: (508)793-8821
E-mail: admissions@clarku.edu
Web Site: http://www.clarku.edu/
President/CEO: John Bassett
Admissions: Donald Honeman
Financial Aid: Mary Ellen Severance
Type: University **Sex:** Coed **Scores:** 99% SAT V 400+; 99% SAT M 400+; 21% ACT 18-23; 58% ACT 24-29 **% Accepted:** 64 **Admission Plans:** Early Admission; Early Decision Plan; Deferred Admission **Application Deadline:** January 15 **Application Fee:** $55.00 **H.S. Requirements:** High school diploma required; GED accepted **Costs Per Year:** Application fee: $55. Comprehensive fee: $43,370 includes full-time tuition ($36,100), mandatory fees ($320), and college room and board ($6950). College room only: $4000. Room and board charges vary according to board plan and housing facility. Part-time tuition: $1128 per course. Part-time mandatory fees: $1128 per credit hour. **Scholarships:** Available **Calendar System:** Semester, Summer Session Available **Enrollment:** FT 2,206, PT 127, Grad FT 747, Grad PT 336 **Faculty:** FT 187, PT 105 **Student-Faculty Ratio:** 10:1 **Exams:** SAT I or ACT. ACT essay not being used. SAT essay not being used. **% Receiving Financial Aid:** 55 **% Residing in College-Owned, -Operated, or -Affiliated Housing:** 70 **Final Year or Final Semester Residency Requirement:** Yes **Library Holdings:** 289,658 **Regional Accreditation:** New England Association of Schools and Colleges **Credit Hours For Degree:** 32 courses, Bachelors **ROTC:** Army, Navy, Air Force **Professional Accreditation:** AACSB, APA **Intercollegiate Athletics:** Baseball M; Basketball M & W; Crew M & W; Cross-Country Running M & W; Field Hockey W; Lacrosse M; Soccer M & W; Softball W; Swimming and Diving M & W; Tennis M & W; Volleyball W

COLLEGE OF THE HOLY CROSS
1 College St.
Worcester, MA 01610-2395
Tel: (508)793-2011; Free: 800-442-2421
Admissions: (508)793-2443
Fax: (508)793-3888
E-mail: admissions@holycross.edu
Web Site: http://www.holycross.edu/
President/CEO: Rev. Michael C. McFarland, SJ
Admissions: Ann McDermott
Financial Aid: Lynne Myers
Type: Four-Year College **Sex:** Coed **Affiliation:** Roman Catholic (Jesuit) **Scores:** 100% SAT V 400+; 100% SAT M 400+; 12% ACT 18-23; 50% ACT 24-29 **% Accepted:** 36 **Admission Plans:** Early Admission; Early Decision Plan; Deferred Admission **Application Deadline:** January 15 **Application Fee:** $60.00 **H.S. Requirements:** High school diploma required; GED accepted **Costs Per Year:** Application fee: $60. Comprehensive fee: $50,832 includes full-time tuition ($39,330), mandatory fees ($562), and college room and board ($10,940). College room only: $5700. Room and board charges vary according to board plan and housing facility. **Scholarships:** Available **Calendar System:** Semester, Summer Session Not available **Enrollment:** FT 2,897, PT 36 **Faculty:** FT 244, PT 62 **Student-Faculty Ratio:** 11:1 **Exams:** ACT essay not being used. SAT essay not being used. **% Receiving Financial Aid:** 54 **% Residing in College-Owned, -Operated, or -Affiliated Housing:** 88 **Final Year or Final Semester Residency Requirement:** Yes **Library Holdings:** 636,014 **Regional Accreditation:** New England Association of Schools and Colleges **Credit Hours For Degree:** 32 courses, Bachelors **ROTC:** Army, Navy, Air Force **Professional Accreditation:** NAST **Intercollegiate Athletics:** Baseball M; Basketball M & W; Crew M & W; Cross-Country Running M & W; Field Hockey W; Football M; Golf M & W; Ice Hockey M & W; Lacrosse M & W; Soccer M & W; Softball W; Swimming and Diving M & W; Tennis M & W; Track and Field M & W; Volleyball W

CURRY COLLEGE
1071 Blue Hill Ave.
Milton, MA 02186-9984
Tel: (617)333-0500; Free: 800-669-0686
Admissions: (617)333-2210
Fax: (617)333-6860
E-mail: curryadm@curry.edu
Web Site: http://www.curry.edu/
President/CEO: Kenneth Quigley
Admissions: Jane P. Fidler
Financial Aid: Dyan Teehan
Type: Comprehensive **Sex:** Coed **Scores:** 81% SAT V 400+; 80% SAT M 400+; 66% ACT 18-23; 11% ACT 24-29 **% Accepted:** 75 **Admission Plans:** Early Admission; Early Decision Plan; Deferred Admission **Application Deadline:** April 1 **Application Fee:** $50.00 **H.S. Requirements:** High school diploma required; GED accepted **Costs Per Year:** Application fee: $50. Tuition: $933 per credit hour part-time. Part-time tuition varies according to course load. **Scholarships:** Available **Calendar System:** Semester, Summer Session Available **Enrollment:** FT 1,988, PT 817, Grad FT 18, Grad PT 302 **Faculty:** FT 119, PT 302 **Student-Faculty Ratio:** 10:1 **Exams:** Other, SAT I or ACT. **% Receiving Financial Aid:** 69 **% Residing in College-Owned, -Operated, or -Affiliated Housing:** 75 **Library Holdings:** 139,600 **Regional Accreditation:** New England Association of Schools and Colleges **Credit Hours For Degree:** 120 credit hours, Bachelors **ROTC:** Army **Professional Accreditation:** AACN **Intercollegiate Athletics:** Baseball M; Basketball M & W; Cross-Country Running W; Football M; Ice Hockey M; Lacrosse M & W; Soccer M & W; Softball W; Tennis M & W

DEAN COLLEGE
99 Main St.
Franklin, MA 02038-1994
Tel: (508)541-1900; Free: 877-TRY-DEAN
Fax: (508)541-8726
E-mail: jfowler@dean.edu
Web Site: http://www.dean.edu/
President/CEO: Dr. Paula M. Rooney
Admissions: James Fowler
Type: Two-Year College **Sex:** Coed **Scores:** 72% SAT V 400+; 65% SAT M

400+; 41% ACT 18-23; 7% ACT 24-29 **% Accepted:** 73 **Admission Plans:** Deferred Admission **Application Deadline:** Rolling **Application Fee:** $35.00 **H.S. Requirements:** High school diploma required; GED accepted **Costs Per Year:** Application fee: $35. Comprehensive fee: $41,582 includes full-time tuition ($29,140) and college room and board ($12,442). College room only: $7868. Part-time tuition: $780 per course. **Scholarships:** Available **Calendar System:** Semester, Summer Session Available **Enrollment:** FT 975, PT 131 **Faculty:** FT 33, PT 79 **Student-Faculty Ratio:** 19:1 **Exams:** SAT I or ACT. **% Residing in College-Owned, -Operated, or -Affiliated Housing:** 88 **Library Holdings:** 45,565 **Regional Accreditation:** New England Association of Schools and Colleges **Credit Hours For Degree:** 63 credits, Associates **Intercollegiate Athletics:** Baseball M; Basketball M & W; Football M; Golf M; Lacrosse M & W; Soccer M & W; Softball W; Volleyball W

EASTERN NAZARENE COLLEGE
23 East Elm Ave.
Quincy, MA 02170
Tel: (617)745-3000; Free: 800-88-ENC88
Admissions: (617)745-3864
Fax: (617)745-3907
E-mail: andrew.wright@enc.edu
Web Site: http://www.enc.edu/
President/CEO: Dr. Corlis A. McGee
Admissions: Andrew R. Wright
Financial Aid: Dana LeRoy Parker
Type: Comprehensive **Sex:** Coed **Affiliation:** Church of the Nazarene **Scores:** 88% SAT V 400+; 84% SAT M 400+; 40% ACT 18-23; 32% ACT 24-29 **% Accepted:** 61 **Admission Plans:** Deferred Admission **Application Deadline:** Rolling **Application Fee:** $25.00 **H.S. Requirements:** High school diploma required; GED accepted **Costs Per Year:** Application fee: $25. Comprehensive fee: $31,772 includes full-time tuition ($22,982), mandatory fees ($790), and college room and board ($8000). Full-time tuition and fees vary according to course load, degree level, program, reciprocity agreements, and student level. Room and board charges vary according to board plan and housing facility. Part-time tuition: $901 per credit hour. Part-time mandatory fees: $102 per term. Part-time tuition and fees vary according to degree level, program, reciprocity agreements, and student level. **Scholarships:** Available **Calendar System:** Semester, Summer Session Available **Enrollment:** FT 810, PT 25 **Faculty:** FT 43, PT 60 **Student-Faculty Ratio:** 13:1 **Exams:** SAT I or ACT, SAT I and SAT II or ACT, SAT II. ACT essay used for admission. SAT essay used for admission. ACT essay used for advising. SAT essay used for advising. ACT essay used in place of application essay. SAT essay used in place of application essay. ACT essay used as a validity check on application essay. SAT essay used as a validity check on application essay. ACT essay used for placement. SAT essay used for placement. **% Receiving Financial Aid:** 66 **% Residing in College-Owned, -Operated, or -Affiliated Housing:** 75 **Library Holdings:** 117,540 **Regional Accreditation:** New England Association of Schools and Colleges **Credit Hours For Degree:** 65 hours, Associates; 130 hours, Bachelors **ROTC:** Army, Air Force **Professional Accreditation:** CSWE **Intercollegiate Athletics:** Baseball M; Basketball M & W; Cross-Country Running M & W; Lacrosse M; Skiing (Downhill) M; Soccer M & W; Softball W; Tennis M & W; Volleyball M & W

ELMS COLLEGE
291 Springfield St.
Chicopee, MA 01013-2839
Tel: (413)594-2761; Free: 800-255-ELMS
Fax: (413)594-2781
E-mail: admissions@elms.edu
Web Site: http://www.elms.edu/
President/CEO: Mary Reap, PhD
Admissions: Joseph Wagner
Financial Aid: April Arcouette
Type: Comprehensive **Sex:** Coed **Affiliation:** Roman Catholic **Scores:** 97% SAT V 400+; 99% SAT M 400+ **% Accepted:** 89 **Admission Plans:** Early Admission; Deferred Admission **Application Deadline:** Rolling **Application Fee:** $30.00 **H.S. Requirements:** High school diploma required; GED accepted **Scholarships:** Available **Calendar System:** Semester, Summer Session Available **Enrollment:** FT 681, PT 385 **Faculty:** FT 59, PT 87 **Student-Faculty Ratio:** 12:1 **Exams:** SAT I or ACT. **% Receiving Financial Aid:** 79 **% Residing in College-Owned, -Operated, or -Affiliated Housing:** 39 **Library Holdings:** 111,379 **Regional Accreditation:** New England Association of Schools and Colleges **Credit Hours For Degree:** 120 credits, Bachelors **ROTC:** Army, Air Force **Professional Accreditation:** AACN, CSWE **Intercollegiate Athletics:** Baseball M; Basketball M & W; Cross-Country Running M & W; Field Hockey W; Golf M; Lacrosse W; Soccer M & W; Softball W; Swimming and Diving M & W; Volleyball M & W

EMERSON COLLEGE
120 Boylston St.
Boston, MA 02116-4624
Tel: (617)824-8500
Admissions: (617)824-8600
Fax: (617)824-8609
E-mail: admission@emerson.edu
Web Site: http://www.emerson.edu/
President/CEO: Jacqueline W. Liebergott
Admissions: Sara S. Ramirez
Financial Aid: Michelle Smith
Type: Comprehensive **Sex:** Coed **Scores:** 100% SAT V 400+; 100% SAT M 400+; 20% ACT 18-23; 64% ACT 24-29 **% Accepted:** 42 **Admission Plans:** Early Admission; Early Action; Deferred Admission **Application Deadline:** January 5 **Application Fee:** $65.00 **H.S. Requirements:** High school diploma required; GED accepted **Costs Per Year:** Application fee: $65. Comprehensive fee: $42,198 includes full-time tuition ($29,408), mandatory fees ($510), and college room and board ($12,280). Part-time tuition: $919 per credit hour. **Scholarships:** Available **Calendar System:** Semester, Summer Session Available **Enrollment:** FT 3,422, PT 274 **Faculty:** FT 177, PT 254 **Student-Faculty Ratio:** 13:1 **Exams:** SAT I or ACT. ACT essay not being used. SAT essay not being used. **% Receiving Financial Aid:** 56 **% Residing in College-Owned, -Operated, or -Affiliated Housing:** 55 **Library Holdings:** 179,380 **Regional Accreditation:** New England Association of Schools and Colleges **Credit Hours For Degree:** 128 credits, Bachelors **Professional Accreditation:** ASLHA **Intercollegiate Athletics:** Baseball M; Basketball M & W; Cross-Country Running M & W; Golf M & W; Ice Hockey M; Lacrosse M & W; Soccer M & W; Softball W; Tennis M & W; Track and Field W; Volleyball M & W

EMMANUEL COLLEGE
400 The Fenway
Boston, MA 02115
Tel: (617)277-9340
Admissions: (617)735-9715
Fax: (617)735-9801
E-mail: enroll@emmanuel.edu
Web Site: http://www.emmanuel.edu/
President/CEO: Sr. Janet Eisner, SND
Admissions: Sandra Robbins
Financial Aid: Jennifer Porter
Type: Comprehensive **Sex:** Coed **Affiliation:** Roman Catholic **Scores:** 100% SAT V 400+; 99% SAT M 400+; 64% ACT 18-23; 29% ACT 24-29 **% Accepted:** 56 **Admission Plans:** Early Admission; Early Decision Plan; Deferred Admission **Application Deadline:** March 1 **Application Fee:** $40.00 **H.S. Requirements:** High school diploma required; GED accepted **Costs Per Year:** Application fee: $40. Comprehensive fee: $41,315 includes full-time tuition ($29,200), mandatory fees ($165), and college room and board ($11,950). Full-time tuition and fees vary according to course load, degree level, and program. Room and board charges vary according to housing facility. Part-time tuition: $912.50 per credit. Part-time tuition varies according to program. **Scholarships:** Available **Calendar System:** Semester, Summer Session Available **Enrollment:** FT 1,648, PT 359, Grad FT 17, Grad PT 262 **Faculty:** FT 82, PT 109 **Student-Faculty Ratio:** 16:1 **Exams:** SAT I or ACT. **% Receiving Financial Aid:** 79 **% Residing in College-Owned, -Operated, or -Affiliated Housing:** 71 **Library Holdings:** 138,000 **Regional Accreditation:** New England Association of Schools and Colleges **Credit Hours For Degree:** 128 credits, Bachelors **ROTC:** Army **Professional Accreditation:** NLN **Intercollegiate Athletics:** Basketball M & W; Cross-Country Running M & W; Golf M; Lacrosse W; Soccer M & W; Softball W; Tennis W; Track and Field M & W; Volleyball M & W

ENDICOTT COLLEGE
376 Hale St.
Beverly, MA 01915-2096
Tel: (978)927-0585; Free: 800-325-1114
Admissions: (978)921-1000
Fax: (978)927-0084

E-mail: admissio@endicott.edu
Web Site: http://www.endicott.edu/
President/CEO: Richard E. Wylie
Admissions: Thomas J. Redman
Financial Aid: Marcia Toomey
Type: Comprehensive **Sex:** Coed **Scores:** 99% SAT V 400+; 99% SAT M 400+; 58% ACT 18-23; 36% ACT 24-29 **% Accepted:** 53 **Application Deadline:** February 15 **Application Fee:** $40.00 **H.S. Requirements:** High school diploma required; GED accepted **Costs Per Year:** Application fee: $40. Comprehensive fee: $37,212 includes full-time tuition ($24,976), mandatory fees ($400), and college room and board ($11,836). College room only: $8248. Room and board charges vary according to board plan and housing facility. Part-time tuition: $766 per credit hour. Part-time mandatory fees: $150 per term. **Scholarships:** Available **Calendar System:** Semester, Summer Session Available **Enrollment:** FT 2,115, PT 176, Grad FT 197, Grad PT 1,656 **Faculty:** FT 77 **Student-Faculty Ratio:** 16:1 **Exams:** SAT I or ACT. ACT essay used for admission. SAT essay used for admission. **% Receiving Financial Aid:** 60 **% Residing in College-Owned, -Operated, or -Affiliated Housing:** 84 **Library Holdings:** 121,485 **Regional Accreditation:** New England Association of Schools and Colleges **Credit Hours For Degree:** 67 credits, Associates; 124 credits, Bachelors **ROTC:** Army, Air Force **Professional Accreditation:** FIDER, JRCEPAT, NLN **Intercollegiate Athletics:** Baseball M; Basketball M & W; Cheerleading W; Crew M & W; Cross-Country Running M & W; Equestrian Sports M & W; Field Hockey W; Football M; Golf M & W; Ice Hockey M & W; Lacrosse M & W; Sailing M & W; Soccer M & W; Softball W; Tennis M & W; Volleyball M & W

FINE MORTUARY COLLEGE, LLC
150 Kerry Place
Norwood, MA 02062
Tel: (781)762-1211
Fax: (781)762-7177
E-mail: mwise@fine-ne.com
Web Site: http://www.fine-ne.com/
President/CEO: Dr. Louis Misantone, PhD
Admissions: Dean Marsha Wise
Type: Two-Year College **Sex:** Coed **Application Fee:** $55.00 **H.S. Requirements:** High school diploma required; GED accepted **Calendar System:** Continuous, Summer Session Available **Faculty:** FT 2, PT 15 **Student-Faculty Ratio:** 5:1 **Exams:** Other. **Credit Hours For Degree:** 64 credits, Associates

FISHER COLLEGE
118 Beacon St.
Boston, MA 02116-1500
Tel: (617)236-8800; Free: 800-446-1226
Admissions: (617)236-8818
Fax: (617)236-8858
E-mail: admissions@fisher.edu
Web Site: http://www.fisher.edu/
President/CEO: Dr. Thomas McGovern
Admissions: Robert Melaragni
Type: Four-Year College **Sex:** Coed **Scores:** 68% SAT V 400+; 66% SAT M 400+; 38% ACT 18-23; 4% ACT 24-29 **% Accepted:** 60 **Admission Plans:** Deferred Admission **Application Deadline:** Rolling **Application Fee:** $50.00 **H.S. Requirements:** High school diploma required; GED accepted **Costs Per Year:** Application fee: $50. Comprehensive fee: $37,175 includes full-time tuition ($23,625), mandatory fees ($950), and college room and board ($12,600). Full-time tuition and fees vary according to class time, course level, course load, degree level, location, program, reciprocity agreements, and student level. **Scholarships:** Available **Calendar System:** Semester, Summer Session Available **Enrollment:** FT 895, PT 415 **Faculty:** FT 26, PT 77 **Student-Faculty Ratio:** 23:1 **Exams:** SAT I or ACT. **% Residing in College-Owned, -Operated, or -Affiliated Housing:** 53 **Final Year or Final Semester Residency Requirement:** No **Library Holdings:** 30,529 **Regional Accreditation:** New England Association of Schools and Colleges **Credit Hours For Degree:** 60 credits, Associates; 120 credits, Bachelors **ROTC:** Army **Professional Accreditation:** AHIMA **Intercollegiate Athletics:** Baseball M; Basketball M & W; Soccer M & W; Softball W

FITCHBURG STATE COLLEGE
160 Pearl St.
Fitchburg, MA 01420-2697
Tel: (978)345-2151; Free: 800-705-9692
Admissions: (978)665-3140
Fax: (978)665-4540
E-mail: admissions@fsc.edu
Web Site: http://www.fsc.edu/
President/CEO: Robert V. Antonucci
Admissions: Pamela McCafferty
Financial Aid: Lynn Beauregard
Type: Comprehensive **Sex:** Coed **Affiliation:** Massachusetts Public Higher Education System **Scores:** 96% SAT V 400+; 97% SAT M 400+; 64% ACT 18-23; 18% ACT 24-29 **% Accepted:** 64 **Admission Plans:** Deferred Admission **Application Deadline:** Rolling **Application Fee:** $25.00 **H.S. Requirements:** High school diploma required; GED accepted **Costs Per Year:** Application fee: $25. State resident tuition: $970 full-time, $40.42 per credit part-time. Nonresident tuition: $7050 full-time, $293.75 per credit part-time. Mandatory fees: $5930 full-time, $247.08 per credit part-time. Full-time tuition and fees vary according to reciprocity agreements. Part-time tuition and fees vary according to class time and reciprocity agreements. College room and board: $7632. Room and board charges vary according to board plan and housing facility. **Scholarships:** Available **Calendar System:** Semester, Summer Session Available **Enrollment:** FT 3,512, PT 711, Grad FT 308, Grad PT 2,512 **Faculty:** FT 179, PT 86 **Student-Faculty Ratio:** 17:1 **Exams:** SAT I or ACT. **% Receiving Financial Aid:** 54 **% Residing in College-Owned, -Operated, or -Affiliated Housing:** 42 **Final Year or Final Semester Residency Requirement:** No **Library Holdings:** 248,644 **Regional Accreditation:** New England Association of Schools and Colleges **Credit Hours For Degree:** 120 semester hours, Bachelors **ROTC:** Army **Professional Accreditation:** AACN, NAACLS, NCATE **Intercollegiate Athletics:** Baseball M; Basketball M & W; Cross-Country Running M & W; Field Hockey W; Football M; Ice Hockey M; Lacrosse W; Soccer M & W; Softball W; Track and Field M & W

FRAMINGHAM STATE COLLEGE
100 State St., PO Box 9101
Framingham, MA 01701-9101
Tel: (508)620-1220
Admissions: (508)626-4500
Fax: (508)626-4017
E-mail: admiss@framingham.edu
Web Site: http://www.framingham.edu/
President/CEO: Dr. Timothy J. Flanagan, PhD
Admissions: Shayna Bailey
Type: Comprehensive **Sex:** Coed **Affiliation:** Massachusetts Public Higher Education System **Scores:** 98% SAT V 400+; 97% SAT M 400+; 78% ACT 18-23; 4% ACT 24-29 **% Accepted:** 63 **Admission Plans:** Preferred Admission; Early Admission; Early Action; Deferred Admission **Application Deadline:** May 15 **Application Fee:** $45.00 **H.S. Requirements:** High school diploma required; GED accepted **Costs Per Year:** Application fee: $45. State resident tuition: $970 full-time, $162 per course part-time. Nonresident tuition: $7050 full-time, $1175 per course part-time. Mandatory fees: $5570 full-time, $993.50 per course part-time. Full-time tuition and fees vary according to class time. Part-time tuition and fees vary according to class time and course load. College room and board: $8148. College room only: $5248. Room and board charges vary according to board plan and housing facility. **Scholarships:** Available **Calendar System:** Semester, Summer Session Available **Enrollment:** FT 3,121, PT 726, Grad FT 74, Grad PT 2,068 **Faculty:** FT 164, PT 86 **Student-Faculty Ratio:** 17:1 **Exams:** SAT I or ACT. **% Receiving Financial Aid:** 40 **% Residing in College-Owned, -Operated, or -Affiliated Housing:** 50 **Final Year or Final Semester Residency Requirement:** No **Library Holdings:** 216,518 **Regional Accreditation:** New England Association of Schools and Colleges **Credit Hours For Degree:** 128 semester hours, Bachelors **Professional Accreditation:** AAFCS, ADtA, NLN **Intercollegiate Athletics:** Baseball M; Basketball M & W; Cross-Country Running M & W; Field Hockey W; Football M; Ice Hockey M; Lacrosse W; Soccer M & W; Softball W; Volleyball W

FRANKLIN W. OLIN COLLEGE OF ENGINEERING
Olin Way
Needham, MA 02492-1200
Tel: (781)292-2300
Admissions: (781)292-2250
E-mail: info@olin.edu
Web Site: http://www.olin.edu/
President/CEO: Dr. Richard K. Miller, PhD

Financial Aid: Jean Ricker
Type: Four-Year College **Sex:** Coed **Scores:** 100% SAT V 400+; 100% SAT M 400+; 1% ACT 24-29 **% Accepted:** 17 **Admission Plans:** Deferred Admission **Application Deadline:** January 1 **Application Fee:** $80.00 **H.S. Requirements:** High school diploma required; GED accepted **Costs Per Year:** Application fee: $80. Comprehensive fee: $51,275 includes full-time tuition ($36,400), mandatory fees ($1645), and college room and board ($13,230). College room only: $8500. Room and board charges vary according to board plan. all students are awarded full-tuition scholarships. **Scholarships:** Available **Enrollment:** FT 337 **Faculty:** FT 33, PT 8 **Student-Faculty Ratio:** 9:1 **Exams:** SAT I or ACT, SAT II. ACT essay used for admission. SAT essay used for admission. **% Receiving Financial Aid:** 11 **% Residing in College-Owned, -Operated, or -Affiliated Housing:** 100 **Final Year or Final Semester Residency Requirement:** No **Library Holdings:** 199,173 **Regional Accreditation:** New England Association of Schools and Colleges **Credit Hours For Degree:** 120 credits, Bachelors **Intercollegiate Athletics:** Soccer M & W; Ultimate Frisbee M & W

GORDON COLLEGE

255 Grapevine Rd.
Wenham, MA 01984-1899
Tel: (978)927-2300; Free: (866)464-6736
Admissions: (978)867-4217
Fax: (978)524-3704
E-mail: admissions@gordon.edu
Web Site: http://www.gordon.edu/
President/CEO: Dr. R. Judson Carlberg
Admissions: Brook Berry
Financial Aid: Daniel O'Connell
Type: Comprehensive **Sex:** Coed **Affiliation:** nondenominational **Scores:** 100% SAT V 400+; 98% SAT M 400+ **% Accepted:** 66 **Admission Plans:** Early Admission; Early Action; Early Decision Plan; Deferred Admission **Application Deadline:** Rolling **Application Fee:** $50.00 **H.S. Requirements:** High school diploma required; GED accepted **Costs Per Year:** Application fee: $50. Comprehensive fee: $37,558 includes full-time tuition ($28,210), mandatory fees ($1248), and college room and board ($8100). College room only: $5400. Full-time tuition and fees vary according to course load. Room and board charges vary according to board plan and housing facility. **Scholarships:** Available **Calendar System:** Semester, Summer Session Not available **Enrollment:** FT 1,554, PT 32, Grad FT 2, Grad PT 93 **Faculty:** FT 97, PT 52 **Student-Faculty Ratio:** 14:1 **Exams:** SAT I or ACT, SAT II. ACT essay used for admission. SAT essay used for admission. **% Receiving Financial Aid:** 67 **% Residing in College-Owned, -Operated, or -Affiliated Housing:** 88 **Library Holdings:** 142,688 **Regional Accreditation:** New England Association of Schools and Colleges **Credit Hours For Degree:** 124 semester hours, Bachelors **ROTC:** Army, Air Force **Professional Accreditation:** CSWE, NASM **Intercollegiate Athletics:** Baseball M; Basketball M & W; Cross-Country Running M & W; Field Hockey W; Golf M & W; Lacrosse M & W; Soccer M & W; Softball W; Swimming and Diving M & W; Tennis M & W; Track and Field M & W; Volleyball W

GREENFIELD COMMUNITY COLLEGE

1 College Dr.
Greenfield, MA 01301-9739
Tel: (413)775-1000
Fax: (413)773-5129
E-mail: admission@gcc.mass.edu
Web Site: http://www.gcc.mass.edu/
President/CEO: Robert L. Pura
Admissions: Herbert Hentz
Type: Two-Year College **Sex:** Coed **Affiliation:** Commonwealth of Massachusetts Department of Higher Education **% Accepted:** 100 **Admission Plans:** Open Admission; Preferred Admission **Application Deadline:** Rolling **Application Fee:** $10.00 **H.S. Requirements:** High school diploma required; GED accepted **Scholarships:** Available **Calendar System:** Semester, Summer Session Available **Enrollment:** FT 1,045, PT 1,501 **Faculty:** FT 59, PT 132 **Exams:** Other. **Library Holdings:** 52,690 **Regional Accreditation:** New England Association of Schools and Colleges **Credit Hours For Degree:** 60 credits, Associates **Professional Accreditation:** NLN

HAMPSHIRE COLLEGE

893 West St.
Amherst, MA 01002
Tel: (413)549-4600; Free: 877-937-4267
Admissions: (413)559-5471
Fax: (413)582-5631
E-mail: admissions@hampshire.edu
Web Site: http://www.hampshire.edu/
President/CEO: Dr. Ralph Hexter
Admissions: Karen S. Parker
Financial Aid: Kathleen Methot
Type: Four-Year College **Sex:** Coed **Scores:** 99% SAT V 400+; 99% SAT M 400+; 16% ACT 18-23; 61% ACT 24-29 **% Accepted:** 63 **Admission Plans:** Early Admission; Early Action; Early Decision Plan; Deferred Admission **Application Deadline:** January 1 **Application Fee:** $60.00 **H.S. Requirements:** High school diploma required; GED accepted **Costs Per Year:** Application fee: $60. Comprehensive fee: $50,345 includes full-time tuition ($39,112), mandatory fees ($800), and college room and board ($10,433). College room only: $6653. Room and board charges vary according to board plan. **Scholarships:** Available **Calendar System:** 4-1-4, Summer Session Not available **Enrollment:** FT 1,463 **Faculty:** FT 99, PT 60 **Student-Faculty Ratio:** 12:1 **Exams:** ACT essay not being used. SAT essay not being used. **% Receiving Financial Aid:** 61 **% Residing in College-Owned, -Operated, or -Affiliated Housing:** 89 **Final Year or Final Semester Residency Requirement:** Yes **Library Holdings:** 177,506 **Regional Accreditation:** New England Association of Schools and Colleges **ROTC:** Army **Intercollegiate Athletics:** Basketball M & W; Fencing M & W; Soccer M & W; Ultimate Frisbee M & W

HARVARD UNIVERSITY

Cambridge, MA 02138
Tel: (617)495-1000
Admissions: (617)495-1551
E-mail: college@harvard.edu
Web Site: http://www.harvard.edu/
President/CEO: Drew Gilpin Faust
Admissions: Dr. William R. Fitzsimmons
Type: University **Sex:** Coed **% Accepted:** 7 **Admission Plans:** Deferred Admission **Application Deadline:** January 1 **Application Fee:** $75.00 **H.S. Requirements:** High school diploma or equivalent not required **Costs Per Year:** Application fee: $75. Comprehensive fee: $48,684 includes full-time tuition ($33,696), mandatory fees ($3132), and college room and board ($11,856). **Scholarships:** Available **Calendar System:** Semester, Summer Session Available **Enrollment:** FT 6,650, PT 5, Grad FT 3,730, Grad PT 8 **Faculty:** FT 1,712, PT 410 **Student-Faculty Ratio:** 7:1 **Exams:** SAT I or ACT, SAT II. ACT essay used for admission. SAT essay used for admission. ACT essay used for advising. SAT essay used for advising. ACT essay used for placement. SAT essay used for placement. **% Receiving Financial Aid:** 60 **% Residing in College-Owned, -Operated, or -Affiliated Housing:** 99 **Library Holdings:** 16,254,755 **Regional Accreditation:** New England Association of Schools and Colleges **Credit Hours For Degree:** 16 courses, Bachelors **ROTC:** Army, Navy, Air Force **Professional Accreditation:** AACSB, ABET, ABA, ADA, ADtA, ACSP, APA, ASLA, ACIPE, AALS, ATS, CEPH, LCMEAMA, NAAB, NASPAA **Intercollegiate Athletics:** Baseball M; Basketball M & W; Crew M & W; Cross-Country Running M & W; Fencing M & W; Field Hockey W; Football M; Golf M & W; Ice Hockey M & W; Lacrosse M & W; Sailing M & W; Skiing (Cross-Country) M & W; Skiing (Downhill) M & W; Soccer M & W; Softball W; Squash M & W; Swimming and Diving M & W; Tennis M & W; Track and Field M & W; Volleyball M & W; Water Polo M & W; Wrestling M

HEBREW COLLEGE

160 Herrick Rd.
Newton Centre, MA 02459
Tel: (617)559-8600; Free: 800-866-4814
Admissions: (617)559-8610
Fax: (617)559-8601
E-mail: admissions@lhebrewcollege.edu
Web Site: http://www.hebrewcollege.edu/
President/CEO: Rabbi Daniel Lehmann
Admissions: Kristin Card
Financial Aid: Marilyn Jaye
Type: Comprehensive **Sex:** Coed **Affiliation:** Jewish **Admission Plans:** Open Admission; Early Admission; Early Decision Plan; Deferred Admission **Application Deadline:** Rolling **Application Fee:** $50.00 **H.S. Requirements:** High school diploma or equivalent not required **Scholarships:** Available **Calendar System:** Semester, Summer Session Available **Enrollment:**

FT 4, PT 4 **Faculty:** FT 20, PT 21 **Exams:** Other. **% Receiving Financial Aid:** 60 **Regional Accreditation:** New England Association of Schools and Colleges **Credit Hours For Degree:** 120 credits, Bachelors

HELLENIC COLLEGE
50 Goddard Ave.
Brookline, MA 02445-7496
Tel: (617)731-3500; Free: (866)424-2338
Admissions: (617)850-1285
Fax: (617)232-7819
E-mail: admissions@hchc.edu
Web Site: http://www.hchc.edu/
President/CEO: Rev. Nicholas C. Triantafilou
Admissions: Gregory Floor
Financial Aid: Gregory Floor
Type: Comprehensive **Sex:** Coed **Affiliation:** Greek Orthodox **Scores:** 100% SAT V 400+; 100% SAT M 400+ **% Accepted:** 57 **Admission Plans:** Early Action; Deferred Admission **Application Deadline:** Rolling **Application Fee:** $50.00 **H.S. Requirements:** High school diploma required; GED accepted **Costs Per Year:** Application fee: $50. Comprehensive fee: $30,630 includes full-time tuition ($18,400), mandatory fees ($450), and college room and board ($11,780). Room and board charges vary according to housing facility. Part-time tuition: $766.50 per credit hour. **Scholarships:** Available **Calendar System:** Semester, Summer Session Available **Enrollment:** FT 85, Grad FT 116, Grad PT 11 **Faculty:** FT 13, PT 22 **Student-Faculty Ratio:** 9:1 **Exams:** SAT I or ACT, SAT II. **% Receiving Financial Aid:** 88 **% Residing in College-Owned, -Operated, or -Affiliated Housing:** 90 **Library Holdings:** 115,805 **Regional Accreditation:** New England Association of Schools and Colleges **Credit Hours For Degree:** 128 credits, Bachelors

HOLYOKE COMMUNITY COLLEGE
303 Homestead Ave.
Holyoke, MA 01040-1099
Tel: (413)538-7000
Admissions: (413)552-2000
E-mail: admissions@hcc.edu
Web Site: http://www.hcc.edu/
President/CEO: Dr. William F. Messner
Admissions: Marcia Rosbury-Henne
Type: Two-Year College **Sex:** Coed **Affiliation:** Massachusetts Public Higher Education System **Admission Plans:** Open Admission; Early Admission; Deferred Admission **Application Deadline:** Rolling **Application Fee:** $0.00 **H.S. Requirements:** High school diploma or equivalent not required **Costs Per Year:** Application fee: $0. State resident tuition: $576 full-time, $121 per credit part-time. Nonresident tuition: $5520 full-time, $327 per credit part-time. Mandatory fees: $2496 full-time, $84 per term part-time. Full-time tuition and fees vary according to course load. Part-time tuition and fees vary according to course load. **Scholarships:** Available **Calendar System:** Semester, Summer Session Available **Enrollment:** FT 3,969, PT 3,500 **Faculty:** FT 128, PT 353 **Student-Faculty Ratio:** 21:1 **Library Holdings:** 88,149 **Regional Accreditation:** New England Association of Schools and Colleges **Credit Hours For Degree:** 60 credits, Associates **ROTC:** Army, Air Force **Professional Accreditation:** ACBSP, COptA, JRCERT, NASM, NLN **Intercollegiate Athletics:** Baseball M; Basketball M & W; Golf M & W; Skiing (Downhill) M & W; Soccer M & W; Softball W; Volleyball W

ITT TECHNICAL INSTITUTE (NORWOOD)
333 Providence Hwy.
Route 1
Norwood, MA 02062
Tel: (781)278-7200; Free: 800-879-8324
Web Site: http://www.itt-tech.edu/
President/CEO: Dennis Saccoia
Type: Two-Year College **Sex:** Coed **Affiliation:** ITT Educational Services, Inc. **H.S. Requirements:** High school diploma required; GED accepted **Scholarships:** Available **Calendar System:** Quarter, Summer Session Not available **Credit Hours For Degree:** 96 credit hours, Associates **Professional Accreditation:** ACICS

ITT TECHNICAL INSTITUTE (WOBURN)
10 Forbes Rd.
Woburn, MA 01801
Tel: (781)937-8324
Web Site: http://www.itt-tech.edu/
President/CEO: Thomas Ryan
Type: Two-Year College **Sex:** Coed **Affiliation:** ITT Educational Services, Inc. **H.S. Requirements:** High school diploma required; GED accepted **Scholarships:** Available **Calendar System:** Quarter, Summer Session Not available **Credit Hours For Degree:** 96 credit hours, Associates **Professional Accreditation:** ACICS

LABOURE COLLEGE
2120 Dorchester Ave.
Boston, MA 02124-5698
Tel: (617)296-8300
Web Site: http://www.laboure.edu/
President/CEO: Joseph W. McNabb
Admissions: Gina M. Morrissette
Type: Two-Year College **Sex:** Coed **Affiliation:** Roman Catholic **Admission Plans:** Deferred Admission **Application Deadline:** Rolling **Application Fee:** $25.00 **H.S. Requirements:** High school diploma required; GED accepted **Scholarships:** Available **Calendar System:** Semester, Summer Session Available **Library Holdings:** 10,975 **Regional Accreditation:** New England Association of Schools and Colleges **Credit Hours For Degree:** 60 credits, Associates **Professional Accreditation:** AHIMA, JRCEET, JRCERT, NLN

LASELL COLLEGE
1844 Commonwealth Ave.
Newton, MA 02466-2709
Tel: (617)243-2000; Free: 888-LASELL-4
Admissions: (617)243-2225
Fax: (617)796-4343
E-mail: info@lasell.edu
Web Site: http://www.lasell.edu/
President/CEO: Michael Alexander
Admissions: James Tweed
Financial Aid: Michele R. Kosboth
Type: Comprehensive **Sex:** Coed **Scores:** 94.34% SAT V 400+; 96.3% SAT M 400+; 72.92% ACT 18-23; 16.67% ACT 24-29 **% Accepted:** 64 **Admission Plans:** Deferred Admission **Application Deadline:** Rolling **Application Fee:** $40.00 **H.S. Requirements:** High school diploma required; GED accepted **Costs Per Year:** Application fee: $40. Comprehensive fee: $35,800 includes full-time tuition ($24,300), mandatory fees ($1000), and college room and board ($10,500). Room and board charges vary according to housing facility. Part-time tuition: $775 per credit. Part-time mandatory fees: $280 per term. **Scholarships:** Available **Calendar System:** Semester, Summer Session Not available **Enrollment:** FT 1,504, PT 27, Grad FT 31, Grad PT 110 **Faculty:** FT 67, PT 112 **Student-Faculty Ratio:** 14:1 **Exams:** SAT I or ACT. SAT essay not being used. **% Receiving Financial Aid:** 78 **% Residing in College-Owned, -Operated, or -Affiliated Housing:** 81 **Final Year or Final Semester Residency Requirement:** Yes **Library Holdings:** 52,466 **Regional Accreditation:** New England Association of Schools and Colleges **Credit Hours For Degree:** 120 credits, Bachelors **Professional Accreditation:** JRCEPAT **Intercollegiate Athletics:** Baseball M; Basketball M & W; Cross-Country Running M & W; Field Hockey W; Lacrosse M & W; Soccer M & W; Softball W; Track and Field M & W; Volleyball M & W

LESLEY UNIVERSITY
29 Everett St.
Cambridge, MA 02138-2790
Tel: (617)868-9600; Free: 800-999-1959
Admissions: (617)349-8800
Fax: (617)349-8150
E-mail: lcadmissions@lesley.edu
Web Site: http://www.lesley.edu/
President/CEO: Joseph B. Moore
Admissions: Deborah Kocar
Financial Aid: Scott A. Jewell
Type: Comprehensive **Sex:** Coed **Scores:** 97% SAT V 400+; 95% SAT M 400+; 53% ACT 18-23; 32% ACT 24-29 **% Accepted:** 67 **Admission Plans:** Early Action; Deferred Admission **Application Deadline:** Rolling **Application Fee:** $50.00 **H.S. Requirements:** High school diploma required; GED accepted **Costs Per Year:** Application fee: $50. Comprehensive fee: $42,200 includes full-time tuition ($29,150), mandatory fees ($250), and college room and board ($12,800). College room only: $7950. Room and board charges vary according to housing facility. **Scholarships:** Available **Calendar System:** Semester, Summer Session Available **Enrollment:** FT

1,327, PT 50, Grad FT 943, Grad PT 3,144 **Faculty:** FT 73, PT 185 **Student-Faculty Ratio:** 10:1 **Exams:** SAT I or ACT. ACT essay used for admission. SAT essay used for admission. ACT essay used as a validity check on application essay. SAT essay used as a validity check on application essay. ACT essay used for placement. SAT essay used for placement. **% Receiving Financial Aid:** 71 **% Residing in College-Owned, -Operated, or -Affiliated Housing:** 54 **Regional Accreditation:** New England Association of Schools and Colleges **Professional Accreditation:** TEAC **Intercollegiate Athletics:** Baseball M; Basketball M & W; Cross-Country Running M & W; Soccer M & W; Softball W; Volleyball M & W

MARIAN COURT COLLEGE
35 Little's Point Rd.
Swampscott, MA 01907-2840
Tel: (781)595-6768
Admissions: (781)309-5200
Fax: (781)595-3560
Web Site: http://www.mariancourt.edu/
President/CEO: Dr. Ghazi Darkazalli
Admissions: Bryan Boppert
Type: Two-Year College **Sex:** Coed **Affiliation:** Roman Catholic **% Accepted:** 74 **Admission Plans:** Deferred Admission **Application Deadline:** Rolling **Application Fee:** $0.00 **H.S. Requirements:** High school diploma required; GED accepted **Scholarships:** Available **Calendar System:** Semester, Summer Session Available **Student-Faculty Ratio:** 14:1 **Library Holdings:** 5,006 **Regional Accreditation:** New England Association of Schools and Colleges **Credit Hours For Degree:** 60 credits, Associates

MASSACHUSETTS BAY COMMUNITY COLLEGE
50 Oakland St.
Wellesley Hills, MA 02481
Tel: (781)239-3000
Fax: (781)239-1047
E-mail: info@massbay.edu
Web Site: http://www.massbay.edu/
President/CEO: Carole M. Berotte Joseph, PhD
Admissions: Donna Raposa
Financial Aid: Paula Ogden
Type: Two-Year College **Sex:** Coed **% Accepted:** 99 **Admission Plans:** Open Admission; Deferred Admission **Application Deadline:** Rolling **Application Fee:** $20.00 **H.S. Requirements:** High school diploma required; GED accepted **Costs Per Year:** Application fee: $20. State resident tuition: $3704 full-time, $24 per credit hour part-time. Nonresident tuition: $8648 full-time, $230 per credit hour part-time. Mandatory fees: $127 per credit hour part-time, $40 per term part-time. Full-time tuition varies according to program and reciprocity agreements. Part-time tuition and fees vary according to program and reciprocity agreements. **Scholarships:** Available **Calendar System:** Semester, Summer Session Available **Enrollment:** FT 2,035, PT 3,005 **Faculty:** FT 79, PT 264 **Student-Faculty Ratio:** 19:1 **Library Holdings:** 51,429 **Regional Accreditation:** New England Association of Schools and Colleges **Credit Hours For Degree:** 62 credits, Associates **Professional Accreditation:** APTA, CARC, JRCERT, NLN **Intercollegiate Athletics:** Baseball M; Basketball M & W; Cross-Country Running M & W; Golf M & W; Soccer M & W; Softball W; Tennis M & W; Volleyball W

MASSACHUSETTS COLLEGE OF ART AND DESIGN
621 Huntington Ave.
Boston, MA 02115-5882
Tel: (617)879-7000
Admissions: (617)879-7230
Fax: (617)879-7250
E-mail: admissions@massart.edu
Web Site: http://www.massart.edu/
President/CEO: Dr. Katherine Sloan
Financial Aid: Auelio Ramirez
Type: Comprehensive **Sex:** Coed **Affiliation:** Massachusetts Public Higher Education System **Scores:** 99% SAT V 400+; 98% SAT M 400+ **% Accepted:** 51 **Admission Plans:** Preferred Admission; Early Admission; Early Action; Deferred Admission **Application Deadline:** February 1 **Application Fee:** $65.00 **H.S. Requirements:** High school diploma required; GED accepted **Costs Per Year:** Application fee: $65. State resident tuition: $8400 full-time. Nonresident tuition: $24,400 full-time. Full-time tuition varies according to course load and degree level. College room and board: $11,288. Room and board charges vary according to board plan and housing facility. **Scholarships:** Available **Calendar System:** Semester, Summer Session Available **Enrollment:** FT 1,593, PT 652, Grad FT 121, Grad PT 39 **Faculty:** FT 101, PT 143 **Student-Faculty Ratio:** 13:1 **Exams:** SAT I or ACT. **% Receiving Financial Aid:** 59 **% Residing in College-Owned, -Operated, or -Affiliated Housing:** 23 **Library Holdings:** 258,675 **Regional Accreditation:** New England Association of Schools and Colleges **Credit Hours For Degree:** 120 credits, Bachelors **Professional Accreditation:** NASAD

MASSACHUSETTS COLLEGE OF LIBERAL ARTS
375 Church St.
North Adams, MA 01247-4100
Tel: (413)662-5000
Fax: (413)662-5179
E-mail: j.mendel@mcla.edu
Web Site: http://www.mcla.edu/
President/CEO: Dr. Mary K. Grant
Admissions: Joshua Mendal
Financial Aid: Elizabeth M. Petri
Type: Comprehensive **Sex:** Coed **Affiliation:** Massachusetts Public Higher Education System **Scores:** 92% SAT V 400+; 92% SAT M 400+ **% Accepted:** 70 **Admission Plans:** Early Admission; Early Action; Deferred Admission **Application Deadline:** Rolling **Application Fee:** $35.00 **H.S. Requirements:** High school diploma required; GED accepted **Costs Per Year:** Application fee: $35. One-time mandatory fee: $140. State resident tuition: $1030 full-time, $42.92 per credit part-time. Nonresident tuition: $9975 full-time, $415.63 per credit part-time. Mandatory fees: $5845 full-time, $198.01 per credit part-time. Full-time tuition and fees vary according to program. Part-time tuition and fees vary according to course load and program. College room and board: $7868. College room only: $3418. Room and board charges vary according to board plan and housing facility. **Scholarships:** Available **Calendar System:** Semester, Summer Session Available **Enrollment:** FT 1,467, PT 208, Grad FT 57, Grad PT 230 **Faculty:** FT 84, PT 79 **Student-Faculty Ratio:** 14:1 **Exams:** SAT I or ACT. **% Receiving Financial Aid:** 67 **% Residing in College-Owned, -Operated, or -Affiliated Housing:** 68 **Final Year or Final Semester Residency Requirement:** No **Library Holdings:** 180,000 **Regional Accreditation:** New England Association of Schools and Colleges **Credit Hours For Degree:** 120 credits, Bachelors **Intercollegiate Athletics:** Baseball M; Basketball M & W; Cross-Country Running M & W; Golf M; Soccer M & W; Softball W; Tennis W

MASSACHUSETTS COLLEGE OF PHARMACY AND HEALTH SCIENCES
179 Longwood Ave.
Boston, MA 02115-5896
Tel: (617)732-2800; Free: 800-225-5506
Admissions: (617)732-2850
Fax: (617)732-2801
E-mail: admissions@mcphs.edu
Web Site: http://www.mcphs.edu/
President/CEO: Charles F. Monahan
Admissions: Sandra Hernandez
Financial Aid: Carrie Glass
Type: University **Sex:** Coed **Scores:** 98.6% SAT V 400+; 99.2% SAT M 400+; 45% ACT 18-23; 48.9% ACT 24-29 **% Accepted:** 55 **Admission Plans:** Open Admission; Early Action; Deferred Admission **Application Deadline:** Rolling **Application Fee:** $70.00 **H.S. Requirements:** High school diploma required; GED accepted **Costs Per Year:** Application fee: $70. Comprehensive fee: $36,450 includes full-time tuition ($23,800), mandatory fees ($750), and college room and board ($11,900). Full-time tuition and fees vary according to course load, degree level, location, program, and student level. Room and board charges vary according to board plan, housing facility, and location. Part-time tuition: $875 per credit. Part-time mandatory fees: $190 per term. **Scholarships:** Available **Calendar System:** Semester, Summer Session Available **Enrollment:** FT 2,770, PT 139, Grad FT 1,200, Grad PT 169 **Faculty:** FT 206, PT 4 **Student-Faculty Ratio:** 18:1 **Exams:** SAT I or ACT. ACT essay not being used. SAT essay not being used. **% Receiving Financial Aid:** 84 **% Residing in College-Owned, -Operated, or -Affiliated Housing:** 26 **Regional Accreditation:** New England Association of Schools and Colleges **Credit Hours For Degree:** 120 semester hours, Bachelors **Professional Accreditation:** ACPhE, ADA, JRCNMT, NLN

MASSACHUSETTS INSTITUTE OF TECHNOLOGY
77 Massachusetts Ave.
Cambridge, MA 02139-4307

Tel: (617)253-1000
Admissions: (617)253-3400
Fax: (617)258-8304
E-mail: admissions@mit.edu
Web Site: http://web.mit.edu/
President/CEO: Susan Hockfield
Financial Aid: Elizabeth Hicks
Type: University **Sex:** Coed **Scores:** 100% SAT V 400+; 100% SAT M 400+; 10% ACT 24-29 **% Accepted:** 11 **Admission Plans:** Early Action; Deferred Admission **Application Deadline:** January 1 **Application Fee:** $75.00 **H.S. Requirements:** High school diploma or equivalent not required **Costs Per Year:** Application fee: $75. Comprehensive fee: $49,142 includes full-time tuition ($37,510), mandatory fees ($272), and college room and board ($11,360). College room only: $6850. Room and board charges vary according to board plan and housing facility. Part-time tuition: $585 per unit. Part-time tuition varies according to course load. **Scholarships:** Available **Calendar System:** 4-1-4 **Enrollment:** FT 4,201, PT 31, Grad FT 6,022, Grad PT 130 **Faculty:** FT 1,326, PT 452 **Student-Faculty Ratio:** 7:1 **Exams:** Other, SAT I or ACT. **% Receiving Financial Aid:** 61 **% Residing in College-Owned, -Operated, or -Affiliated Housing:** 92 **Library Holdings:** 3,057,604 **Regional Accreditation:** New England Association of Schools and Colleges **ROTC:** Army, Navy, Air Force **Professional Accreditation:** AACSB, ABET, ACSP, NAAB **Intercollegiate Athletics:** Badminton M & W; Baseball M; Basketball M & W; Cheerleading M & W; Crew M & W; Cross-Country Running M & W; Fencing M & W; Field Hockey W; Football M; Golf M & W; Gymnastics M & W; Ice Hockey M & W; Lacrosse M & W; Riflery M & W; Rugby M & W; Sailing M & W; Soccer M & W; Softball W; Squash M; Swimming and Diving M & W; Table Tennis M & W; Tennis M & W; Track and Field M & W; Ultimate Frisbee M & W; Volleyball M & W; Water Polo M & W; Wrestling M

MASSACHUSETTS MARITIME ACADEMY
101 Academy Dr.
Buzzards Bay, MA 02532-1803
Tel: (508)830-5000; Free: 800-544-3411
Admissions: (508)830-5031
Fax: (508)830-5077
E-mail: fuji@maritime.edu
Web Site: http://www.maritime.edu/
President/CEO: Adm. Richard G. Gurnon
Admissions: Roy Fulgueras
Financial Aid: Catherine Kedski
Type: Comprehensive **Sex:** Coed **Affiliation:** Massachusetts Public Higher Education System **Scores:** 97% SAT V 400+; 99% SAT M 400+; 57% ACT 18-23; 34% ACT 24-29 **% Accepted:** 61 **Admission Plans:** Early Admission; Early Decision Plan; Deferred Admission **Application Deadline:** Rolling **Application Fee:** $100.00 **H.S. Requirements:** High school diploma required; GED accepted **Costs Per Year:** Application fee: $100. One-time mandatory fee: $2285. State resident tuition: $1242 full-time, $255 per credit hour part-time. Nonresident tuition: $13,881 full-time, $782 per credit hour part-time. Mandatory fees: $5267 full-time. Full-time tuition and fees vary according to course load, program, reciprocity agreements, and student level. Part-time tuition varies according to class time, course load, program, reciprocity agreements, and student level. College room and board: $8917. College room only: $4978. Room and board charges vary according to location. Tuition guaranteed not to increase for student's term of enrollment. **Scholarships:** Available **Calendar System:** Semester, Summer Session Available **Enrollment:** FT 1,126, PT 65, Grad FT 23, Grad PT 74 **Faculty:** FT 65, PT 29 **Student-Faculty Ratio:** 15:1 **Exams:** SAT I and SAT II or ACT. ACT essay used for advising. SAT essay used for advising. ACT essay used for placement. SAT essay used for placement. **% Residing in College-Owned, -Operated, or -Affiliated Housing:** 98 **Final Year or Final Semester Residency Requirement:** Yes **Library Holdings:** 93,499 **Regional Accreditation:** New England Association of Schools and Colleges **Credit Hours For Degree:** 164 semester hours, Bachelors **ROTC:** Army, Navy **Intercollegiate Athletics:** Baseball M; Crew M & W; Cross-Country Running M & W; Football M; Lacrosse M; Riflery M & W; Sailing M & W; Soccer M; Softball W; Track and Field M & W; Volleyball W

MASSASOIT COMMUNITY COLLEGE
1 Massasoit Blvd.
Brockton, MA 02302-3996
Tel: (508)588-9100
Fax: (508)427-1220
Web Site: http://www.massasoit.mass.edu/
President/CEO: Charles Wall, PhD
Admissions: Michelle Hughes
Type: Two-Year College **Sex:** Coed **Admission Plans:** Open Admission; Preferred Admission **Application Deadline:** Rolling **Application Fee:** $0.00 **H.S. Requirements:** High school diploma required; GED accepted **Costs Per Year:** Application fee: $0. State resident tuition: $576 full-time, $24 per credit hour part-time. Nonresident tuition: $5520 full-time, $230 per credit hour part-time. Mandatory fees: $2712 full-time, $113 per credit hour part-time. Full-time tuition and fees vary according to program. Part-time tuition and fees vary according to program. **Scholarships:** Available **Calendar System:** Semester, Summer Session Available **Enrollment:** FT 3,631, PT 4,310 **Faculty:** FT 119, PT 384 **Final Year or Final Semester Residency Requirement:** Yes **Library Holdings:** 75,000 **Regional Accreditation:** New England Association of Schools and Colleges **Credit Hours For Degree:** 60 credits, Associates **Professional Accreditation:** ADA, CARC, JRCERT, NLN **Intercollegiate Athletics:** Baseball M; Basketball M & W; Soccer M & W; Softball W

MERRIMACK COLLEGE
315 Turnpike St.
North Andover, MA 01845-5800
Tel: (978)837-5000
Admissions: (978)837-5100
Fax: (978)837-5222
E-mail: admission@merrimack.edu
Web Site: http://www.merrimack.edu/
President/CEO: Dr. Ronald O. Champagne
Financial Aid: Christine A. Mordach
Type: Comprehensive **Sex:** Coed **Affiliation:** Roman Catholic **% Accepted:** 79 **Admission Plans:** Early Admission; Early Action; Deferred Admission **Application Deadline:** February 1 **Application Fee:** $60.00 **H.S. Requirements:** High school diploma required; GED accepted **Costs Per Year:** Application fee: $60. Comprehensive fee: $40,000 includes full-time tuition ($29,310), mandatory fees ($500), and college room and board ($10,190). College room only: $6040. Full-time tuition and fees vary according to program and student level. Room and board charges vary according to board plan and housing facility. Part-time tuition: $1045 per credit. Part-time mandatory fees: $62.50 per term. Part-time tuition and fees vary according to class time, course level, course load, and degree level. Tuition guaranteed not to increase for student's term of enrollment. **Scholarships:** Available **Calendar System:** Semester, Summer Session Available **Enrollment:** FT 1,884, PT 147, Grad FT 2, Grad PT 57 **Faculty:** FT 132, PT 110 **Student-Faculty Ratio:** 13:1 **% Receiving Financial Aid:** 61 **% Residing in College-Owned, -Operated, or -Affiliated Housing:** 85 **Regional Accreditation:** New England Association of Schools and Colleges **Credit Hours For Degree:** 20 courses, Associates; 40 courses, Bachelors **ROTC:** Air Force **Professional Accreditation:** ABET, JRCEPAT **Intercollegiate Athletics:** Baseball M; Basketball M & W; Cheerleading W; Cross-Country Running M & W; Field Hockey W; Football M; Ice Hockey M; Lacrosse M & W; Soccer M & W; Softball W; Tennis M & W; Track and Field M & W; Volleyball M & W

MIDDLESEX COMMUNITY COLLEGE
Springs Rd.
Bedford, MA 01730-1655
Tel: (781)280-3200
Admissions: (978)656-3200
Fax: (978)656-3322
E-mail: orellanad@middlesex.cc.ma.us
Web Site: http://www.middlesex.mass.edu/
President/CEO: Carole A. Cowan
Admissions: Laurie Dimitrov
Financial Aid: Rob Baumel
Type: Two-Year College **Sex:** Coed **Affiliation:** Massachusetts Public Higher Education System **Admission Plans:** Open Admission; Preferred Admission; Early Admission **Application Deadline:** Rolling **Application Fee:** $0.00 **H.S. Requirements:** High school diploma required; GED accepted **Scholarships:** Available **Calendar System:** Semester, Summer Session Available **Exams:** Other. **Library Holdings:** 52,960 **Regional Accreditation:** New England Association of Schools and Colleges **Credit Hours For Degree:** 60 credits, Associates **ROTC:** Air Force **Professional Accreditation:** AAMAE, ADA, JRCEDMS, JRCERT, NLN

MONTSERRAT COLLEGE OF ART
23 Essex St.
Beverly, MA 01915
Tel: (978)922-8222; Free: 800-836-0487
Admissions: (978)921-4242
Fax: (978)922-4268
E-mail: bbicknell@montserrat.edu
Web Site: http://www.montserrat.edu/
President/CEO: Dr. Helena Sturnick
Admissions: Brian Bicknell
Financial Aid: Creda Carney
Type: Four-Year College **Sex:** Coed **Scores:** 83% SAT M 400+ **% Accepted:** 68 **Admission Plans:** Deferred Admission **Application Deadline:** August 15 **Application Fee:** $50.00 **H.S. Requirements:** High school diploma required; GED accepted **Costs Per Year:** Application fee: $50. Tuition: $23,140 full-time, $964 per credit part-time. Mandatory fees: $850 full-time, $25 per credit part-time. Full-time tuition and fees vary according to course load. Part-time tuition and fees vary according to course load. College room only: $6180. Room charges vary according to housing facility. **Scholarships:** Available **Calendar System:** Semester, Summer Session Not available **Enrollment:** FT 260, PT 25 **Faculty:** FT 20, PT 28 **Student-Faculty Ratio:** 12:1 **% Receiving Financial Aid:** 76 **% Residing in College-Owned, -Operated, or -Affiliated Housing:** 52 **Library Holdings:** 12,025 **Regional Accreditation:** New England Association of Schools and Colleges **Credit Hours For Degree:** 120 credits, Bachelors **ROTC:** Air Force **Professional Accreditation:** NASAD

MOUNT HOLYOKE COLLEGE
50 College St.
South Hadley, MA 01075
Tel: (413)538-2000
Admissions: (413)538-2023
Fax: (413)538-2409
E-mail: admission@mtholyoke.edu
Web Site: http://www.mtholyoke.edu/
President/CEO: Dr. Joanne V. Creighton
Admissions: Diane Anci
Financial Aid: Kathryn Blaisdell
Type: Comprehensive **Sex:** Women **Scores:** 99.99% SAT V 400+; 100% SAT M 400+; 3.54% ACT 18-23; 53.98% ACT 24-29 **% Accepted:** 58 **Admission Plans:** Early Admission; Early Decision Plan; Deferred Admission **Application Deadline:** January 15 **Application Fee:** $60.00 **H.S. Requirements:** High school diploma required; GED accepted **Costs Per Year:** Application fee: $60. Comprehensive fee: $50,576 includes full-time tuition ($38,940), mandatory fees ($186), and college room and board ($11,450). College room only: $5610. Full-time tuition and fees vary according to reciprocity agreements. Part-time tuition: $1220 per credit hour. Part-time tuition varies according to reciprocity agreements. **Scholarships:** Available **Calendar System:** Semester, Summer Session Not available **Enrollment:** FT 2,224, PT 64, Grad FT 7, Grad PT 9 **Faculty:** FT 224, PT 63 **Student-Faculty Ratio:** 9:1 **Exams:** SAT II. ACT essay used for admission. SAT essay used for admission. **% Receiving Financial Aid:** 68 **% Residing in College-Owned, -Operated, or -Affiliated Housing:** 93 **Final Year or Final Semester Residency Requirement:** No **Library Holdings:** 1,123,338 **Regional Accreditation:** New England Association of Schools and Colleges **Credit Hours For Degree:** 128 credit hours, Bachelors **ROTC:** Army, Air Force **Intercollegiate Athletics:** Basketball W; Crew W; Cross-Country Running W; Equestrian Sports W; Field Hockey W; Golf W; Lacrosse W; Soccer W; Squash W; Swimming and Diving W; Tennis W; Track and Field W; Volleyball W

MOUNT IDA COLLEGE
777 Dedham St.
Newton, MA 02459-3310
Tel: (617)928-4500
Admissions: (617)928-4553
Fax: (617)928-4507
E-mail: admissions@mountida.edu
Web Site: http://www.mountida.edu/
President/CEO: Dr. Carol J. Matteson
Admissions: Jay Titus
Financial Aid: David L. Goldman
Type: Comprehensive **Sex:** Coed **Scores:** 76% SAT V 400+; 72% SAT M 400+; 46% ACT 18-23; 10% ACT 24-29 **% Accepted:** 74 **Admission Plans:** Deferred Admission **Application Deadline:** Rolling **Application Fee:** $45.00 **H.S. Requirements:** High school diploma required; GED accepted **Costs Per Year:** Application fee: $45. Comprehensive fee: $36,500 includes full-time tuition ($24,250), mandatory fees ($250), and college room and board ($12,000). **Scholarships:** Available **Calendar System:** Semester, Summer Session Available **Enrollment:** FT 1,399, PT 92, Grad PT 10 **Faculty:** FT 65, PT 135 **Student-Faculty Ratio:** 13:1 **Exams:** SAT I or ACT. **% Receiving Financial Aid:** 80 **% Residing in College-Owned, -Operated, or -Affiliated Housing:** 64 **Final Year or Final Semester Residency Requirement:** No **Library Holdings:** 94,464 **Regional Accreditation:** New England Association of Schools and Colleges **Credit Hours For Degree:** 60 credit hours, Associates; 120 credit hours, Bachelors **Professional Accreditation:** ABFSE, ADA, FIDER, NASAD **Intercollegiate Athletics:** Baseball M; Basketball M & W; Cheerleading M & W; Cross-Country Running M & W; Equestrian Sports W; Football M; Lacrosse M & W; Soccer M & W; Softball W; Tennis W; Volleyball M & W

MOUNT WACHUSETT COMMUNITY COLLEGE
444 Green St.
Gardner, MA 01440-1000
Tel: (978)632-6600
Fax: (978)632-8925
E-mail: admissions@mwcc.mass.edu
Web Site: http://www.mwcc.mass.edu/
President/CEO: Dr. Daniel M. Asquino
Admissions: John D. Walsh
Type: Two-Year College **Sex:** Coed **Affiliation:** Massachusetts Public Higher Education System **% Accepted:** 100 **Admission Plans:** Open Admission; Preferred Admission; Early Admission **Application Deadline:** Rolling **Application Fee:** $10.00 **H.S. Requirements:** High school diploma required; GED accepted **Costs Per Year:** Application fee: $10. State resident tuition: $600 full-time, $25 per credit hour part-time. Nonresident tuition: $5520 full-time, $230 per credit hour part-time. Mandatory fees: $3510 full-time, $140 per credit hour part-time, $75 per term part-time. Full-time tuition and fees vary according to program and reciprocity agreements. Part-time tuition and fees vary according to program and reciprocity agreements. **Scholarships:** Available **Calendar System:** Semester, Summer Session Available **Enrollment:** FT 1,987, PT 2,774 **Faculty:** FT 73, PT 138 **Student-Faculty Ratio:** 24:1 **Exams:** ACT, SAT I or ACT, SAT I and SAT II or ACT, SAT I, SAT II. ACT essay used for admission. SAT essay used for admission. ACT essay used for advising. SAT essay used for advising. ACT essay used for placement. SAT essay used for placement. **Library Holdings:** 53,763 **Regional Accreditation:** New England Association of Schools and Colleges **Credit Hours For Degree:** 60 credits, Associates **Professional Accreditation:** AAMAE, APTA, NLN

NEW ENGLAND COLLEGE OF BUSINESS
10 High St.
Ste. 204
Boston, MA 02111-2645
Tel: (617)951-2350; Free: 888-696-NECF
Fax: (617)951-2533
E-mail: Mina.Goldman@necb.edu
Web Site: http://www.finance.edu/
President/CEO: Howard Horton
Admissions: Mina Goldman
Type: Comprehensive **Sex:** Coed **Affiliation:** Whitney International University **Admission Plans:** Open Admission **Application Fee:** $0.00 **H.S. Requirements:** High school diploma required; GED accepted **Calendar System:** Miscellaneous, Summer Session Available **Faculty:** FT 1, PT 28 **Student-Faculty Ratio:** 38:1 **Final Year or Final Semester Residency Requirement:** No **Regional Accreditation:** New England Association of Schools and Colleges **Credit Hours For Degree:** 63 credits, Associates; 121 credits, Bachelors

NEW ENGLAND CONSERVATORY OF MUSIC
290 Huntington Ave.
Boston, MA 02115-5000
Tel: (617)585-1100
Admissions: (617)585-1103
Fax: (617)585-1115
E-mail: christina.daly@necmusic.edu
Web Site: http://necmusic.edu/
President/CEO: Tony Woodcock

Admissions: Christina Daly
Financial Aid: Lauren G. Urbanek
Type: Comprehensive **Sex:** Coed **% Accepted:** 33 **Admission Plans:** Deferred Admission **Application Deadline:** December 1 **Application Fee:** $105.00 **H.S. Requirements:** High school diploma required; GED accepted **Costs Per Year:** Application fee: $105. Comprehensive fee: $47,050 includes full-time tuition ($34,500), mandatory fees ($450), and college room and board ($12,100). Room and board charges vary according to board plan. Part-time tuition: $1100 per credit. **Scholarships:** Available **Calendar System:** Semester, Summer Session Available **Enrollment:** FT 377, PT 31, Grad FT 354, Grad PT 23 **Faculty:** FT 90, PT 124 **Student-Faculty Ratio:** 6:1 **% Receiving Financial Aid:** 55 **% Residing in College-Owned, -Operated, or -Affiliated Housing:** 30 **Library Holdings:** 95,000 **Regional Accreditation:** New England Association of Schools and Colleges **Credit Hours For Degree:** 120 credit hours, Bachelors **Professional Accreditation:** NASM

THE NEW ENGLAND INSTITUTE OF ART
10 Brookline Place West
Brookline, MA 02445
Tel: (617)267-7910; Free: 800-903-4425
Admissions: (617)739-1700
Fax: (617)236-7883
Web Site: http://www.artinstitutes.edu/boston/
President/CEO: Susan Lane
Type: Four-Year College **Sex:** Coed **Affiliation:** Education Management Corporation **Calendar System:** Semester **Regional Accreditation:** New England Association of Schools and Colleges

NEWBURY COLLEGE
129 Fisher Ave.
Brookline, MA 02445
Tel: (617)730-7000; Free: 800-NEW-BURY
Admissions: (617)730-7007
Fax: (617)731-9618
E-mail: info@newbury.edu
Web Site: http://www.newbury.edu/
President/CEO: Hannah McCarthy
Type: Four-Year College **Sex:** Coed **% Accepted:** 66 **Application Deadline:** September 1 **Application Fee:** $25.00 **H.S. Requirements:** High school diploma required; GED accepted **Costs Per Year:** Application fee: $25. One-time mandatory fee: $150. Comprehensive fee: $34,730 includes full-time tuition ($22,400), mandatory fees ($1100), and college room and board ($11,230). Full-time tuition and fees vary according to class time, program, and reciprocity agreements. Room and board charges vary according to board plan, housing facility, and location. Part-time tuition: $280 per credit. Part-time tuition varies according to class time, course load, program, and reciprocity agreements. **Scholarships:** Available **Calendar System:** Semester, Summer Session Available **Enrollment:** FT 863, PT 131 **Faculty:** FT 28, PT 79 **Student-Faculty Ratio:** 16:1 **% Receiving Financial Aid:** 69 **% Residing in College-Owned, -Operated, or -Affiliated Housing:** 40 **Final Year or Final Semester Residency Requirement:** No **Library Holdings:** 32,500 **Regional Accreditation:** New England Association of Schools and Colleges **Credit Hours For Degree:** 60 credits, Associates; 121 credits, Bachelors **Professional Accreditation:** FIDER **Intercollegiate Athletics:** Baseball M; Basketball M & W; Cross-Country Running M & W; Golf M & W; Soccer M & W; Softball W; Tennis M & W; Volleyball M & W

NICHOLS COLLEGE
PO Box 5000
Dudley, MA 01571-5000
Tel: (508)213-1560; Free: 800-470-3379
Admissions: (508)213-2203
Fax: (508)213-9885
E-mail: admissions@nichols.edu
Web Site: http://www.nichols.edu/
President/CEO: Dr. Debra Townsley, PhD
Admissions: Marie Keegan
Financial Aid: Denise Brindle
Type: Comprehensive **Sex:** Coed **Scores:** 80% SAT V 400+; 84% SAT M 400+; 56% ACT 18-23; 16% ACT 24-29 **% Accepted:** 74 **Admission Plans:** Deferred Admission **Application Deadline:** Rolling **Application Fee:** $25.00 **H.S. Requirements:** High school diploma required; GED accepted **Costs Per Year:** Application fee: $25. Comprehensive fee: $38,200 includes full-time tuition ($28,570), mandatory fees ($300), and college room and board ($9330). College room only: $4900. Part-time tuition: $275 per credit hour. Part-time tuition varies according to class time and course load. **Scholarships:** Available **Calendar System:** Semester, Summer Session Available **Enrollment:** FT 1,159, PT 178, Grad FT 25, Grad PT 185 **Faculty:** FT 36, PT 44 **Student-Faculty Ratio:** 18:1 **Exams:** SAT I or ACT. ACT essay not being used. SAT essay not being used. **% Receiving Financial Aid:** 90 **% Residing in College-Owned, -Operated, or -Affiliated Housing:** 80 **Final Year or Final Semester Residency Requirement:** No **Library Holdings:** 80,000 **Regional Accreditation:** New England Association of Schools and Colleges **Credit Hours For Degree:** 122 credit hours, Bachelors **ROTC:** Army **Intercollegiate Athletics:** Baseball M; Basketball M & W; Field Hockey W; Football M; Golf M; Ice Hockey M & W; Lacrosse M & W; Racquetball M & W; Rugby M & W; Soccer M & W; Softball W; Tennis M & W; Track and Field M & W; Volleyball M & W

NORTH SHORE COMMUNITY COLLEGE
1 Ferncroft Rd.
Danvers, MA 01923-4093
Tel: (978)762-4000
Fax: (978)762-4021
E-mail: info@northshore.edu
Web Site: http://www.northshore.edu/
President/CEO: Dr. Wayne M. Burton
Admissions: Dr. Joanne Light
Financial Aid: Margaret Miles
Type: Two-Year College **Sex:** Coed **% Accepted:** 78 **Admission Plans:** Open Admission; Preferred Admission; Early Admission **Application Deadline:** Rolling **Application Fee:** $0.00 **H.S. Requirements:** High school diploma required; GED accepted **Costs Per Year:** Application fee: $0. State resident tuition: $600 full-time, $25 per credit part-time. Nonresident tuition: $6168 full-time, $257 per credit part-time. Mandatory fees: $2688 full-time, $112 per credit part-time. **Scholarships:** Available **Calendar System:** Semester, Summer Session Available **Enrollment:** FT 3,120, PT 4,104 **Faculty:** FT 135, PT 361 **Student-Faculty Ratio:** 17:1 **Library Holdings:** 71,704 **Regional Accreditation:** New England Association of Schools and Colleges **Credit Hours For Degree:** 60 credits, Associates **Professional Accreditation:** AOTA, APTA, CAA, CARC, JRCERT, NLN

NORTHEASTERN UNIVERSITY
360 Huntington Ave.
Boston, MA 02115-5096
Tel: (617)373-2000
Admissions: (617)373-2200
Fax: (617)373-8780
E-mail: admissions@neu.edu
Web Site: http://www.northeastern.edu/
President/CEO: Dr. Joseph E. Aoun
Admissions: Ronne Turner
Financial Aid: Anthony Erwin
Type: University **Sex:** Coed **Scores:** 100% SAT V 400+; 100% SAT M 400+; 6% ACT 18-23; 55% ACT 24-29 **% Accepted:** 41 **Admission Plans:** Early Admission; Early Action; Deferred Admission **Application Deadline:** January 15 **Application Fee:** $70.00 **H.S. Requirements:** High school diploma required; GED accepted **Costs Per Year:** Application fee: $70. Comprehensive fee: $47,712 includes full-time tuition ($34,950), mandatory fees ($412), and college room and board ($12,350). College room only: $6530. Room and board charges vary according to board plan and housing facility. **Scholarships:** Available **Calendar System:** Semester, Summer Session Available **Enrollment:** FT 15,699, Grad FT 4,157, Grad PT 2,235 **Faculty:** FT 984, PT 439 **Student-Faculty Ratio:** 15:1 **Exams:** SAT I or ACT, SAT I and SAT II or ACT. ACT essay used for admission. SAT essay used for admission. **% Receiving Financial Aid:** 54 **% Residing in College-Owned, -Operated, or -Affiliated Housing:** 50 **Final Year or Final Semester Residency Requirement:** Yes **Library Holdings:** 1,285,092 **Regional Accreditation:** New England Association of Schools and Colleges **Credit Hours For Degree:** 128 semester hours, Bachelors **ROTC:** Army, Navy, Air Force **Professional Accreditation:** AACSB, ABET, ACPE, ACPhE, AACN, AANA, ABA, AHIMA, APTA, APA, ASLHA, AALS, CARC, CORE, JRCEPAT, NAACLS, NASPAA, NLN **Intercollegiate Athletics:** Baseball M; Basketball M & W; Crew M & W; Cross-Country Running M & W; Field Hockey W; Ice Hockey M & W; Soccer M & W; Swimming and Diving W; Track and Field M & W; Volleyball W

NORTHERN ESSEX COMMUNITY COLLEGE

100 Elliott St.
Haverhill, MA 01830
Tel: (978)556-3000; Free: 800-NECC-123
Admissions: (978)556-3616
Web Site: http://www.necc.mass.edu/
President/CEO: David F. Hartleb
Admissions: Nora Sheridan

Type: Two-Year College **Sex:** Coed **% Accepted:** 95 **Admission Plans:** Open Admission; Preferred Admission; Early Admission **Application Deadline:** Rolling **Application Fee:** $0.00 **H.S. Requirements:** High school diploma required; GED accepted **Costs Per Year:** Application fee: $0. State resident tuition: $600 full-time, $25 per credit hour part-time. Nonresident tuition: $6384 full-time, $266 per credit hour part-time. Mandatory fees: $2496 full-time, $104 per credit hour part-time. **Scholarships:** Available **Calendar System:** Semester, Summer Session Available **Enrollment:** FT 2,386, PT 4,140 **Faculty:** FT 99, PT 398 **Student-Faculty Ratio:** 21:1 **Exams:** Other. **Library Holdings:** 61,120 **Regional Accreditation:** New England Association of Schools and Colleges **Credit Hours For Degree:** 60 credits, Associates **ROTC:** Air Force **Professional Accreditation:** ADA, AHIMA, CARC, JRCERT, NLN **Intercollegiate Athletics:** Baseball M; Basketball M & W; Cross-Country Running M & W; Volleyball M & W

PINE MANOR COLLEGE

400 Heath St.
Chestnut Hill, MA 02467
Tel: (617)731-7000; Free: 800-762-1357
Fax: (617)731-7199
E-mail: admisson@pmc.edu
Web Site: http://www.pmc.edu/
President/CEO: Gloria Nemerowicz
Admissions: Robin Engel
Financial Aid: Adrienne Hynek

Type: Four-Year College **Sex:** Women **% Accepted:** 71 **Admission Plans:** Preferred Admission; Deferred Admission **Application Deadline:** Rolling **Application Fee:** $25.00 **H.S. Requirements:** High school diploma required; GED accepted **Costs Per Year:** Application fee: $25. Comprehensive fee: $31,859 includes full-time tuition ($20,189) and college room and board ($11,670). Full-time tuition varies according to course load. Part-time tuition: $615 per credit. Part-time tuition varies according to course load. **Scholarships:** Available **Calendar System:** Semester, Summer Session Available **Enrollment:** FT 484, PT 7 **Faculty:** FT 32, PT 44 **Student-Faculty Ratio:** 10:1 **Exams:** SAT I or ACT. **% Receiving Financial Aid:** 91 **% Residing in College-Owned, -Operated, or -Affiliated Housing:** 77 **Library Holdings:** 65,632 **Regional Accreditation:** New England Association of Schools and Colleges **Credit Hours For Degree:** 16 courses, Associates; 32 courses, Bachelors **Intercollegiate Athletics:** Basketball W; Cross-Country Running W; Lacrosse W; Soccer W; Softball W; Tennis W; Volleyball W

QUINCY COLLEGE

34 Coddington St.
Quincy, MA 02169-4522
Tel: (617)984-1700
Admissions: 800-698-1700
Fax: (617)984-1669
E-mail: psmith@quincycollege.edu
Web Site: http://www.quincycollege.edu/
President/CEO: Sue Harris
Admissions: Paula Smith

Type: Two-Year College **Sex:** Coed **Admission Plans:** Open Admission; Early Admission; Deferred Admission **Application Deadline:** Rolling **Application Fee:** $20.00 **H.S. Requirements:** High school diploma required; GED accepted **Scholarships:** Available **Calendar System:** Semester, Summer Session Available **Faculty:** FT 20, PT 384 **Library Holdings:** 32,000 **Regional Accreditation:** New England Association of Schools and Colleges **Credit Hours For Degree:** 60 credits, Associates **Professional Accreditation:** NLN

QUINSIGAMOND COMMUNITY COLLEGE

670 West Boylston St.
Worcester, MA 01606-2092
Tel: (508)853-2300
Admissions: (508)854-4260
Fax: (508)852-6943
E-mail: qccadm@qcc.mass.edu
Web Site: http://www.qcc.edu/
President/CEO: Dr. Gail Carberry
Admissions: Iris Godes
Financial Aid: Paula Ogden

Type: Two-Year College **Sex:** Coed **Affiliation:** Massachusetts System of Higher Education **% Accepted:** 100 **Admission Plans:** Open Admission **Application Deadline:** Rolling **Application Fee:** $20.00 **H.S. Requirements:** High school diploma required; GED accepted **Costs Per Year:** Application fee: $20. State resident tuition: $24 per credit part-time. Nonresident tuition: $230 per credit part-time. Part-time tuition varies according to course load and program. **Scholarships:** Available **Calendar System:** Semester, Summer Session Available **Enrollment:** FT 4,089, PT 4,260 **Faculty:** FT 121, PT 393 **Student-Faculty Ratio:** 22:1 **Library Holdings:** 60,000 **Regional Accreditation:** New England Association of Schools and Colleges **Credit Hours For Degree:** 62 credits, Associates **ROTC:** Army **Professional Accreditation:** AAMAE, ADA, AOTA, CARC, JRCERT, NLN **Intercollegiate Athletics:** Basketball M & W; Softball W

REGIS COLLEGE

235 Wellesley St.
Weston, MA 02493
Tel: (781)768-7000; Free: (866)438-7344
Admissions: (781)768-7100
Fax: (781)768-8339
E-mail: admission@regiscollege.edu
Web Site: http://www.regiscollege.edu/
President/CEO: Dr. Mary Jane England
Admissions: Wanda Suriel
Financial Aid: Dee J. Ludwick

Type: Comprehensive **Sex:** Coed **Affiliation:** Roman Catholic **Scores:** 83.92% SAT V 400+; 82.61% SAT M 400+; 64.29% ACT 18-23; 7.14% ACT 24-29 **% Accepted:** 73 **Admission Plans:** Deferred Admission **Application Deadline:** Rolling **Application Fee:** $50.00 **H.S. Requirements:** High school diploma required; GED accepted **Costs Per Year:** Application fee: $50. One-time mandatory fee: $195. Comprehensive fee: $41,090 includes full-time tuition ($28,900) and college room and board ($12,190). College room only: $6220. Full-time tuition varies according to course load. **Scholarships:** Available **Calendar System:** Semester, Summer Session Available **Enrollment:** FT 749, PT 223, Grad FT 179, Grad PT 435 **Faculty:** FT 69, PT 69 **Student-Faculty Ratio:** 13:1 **Exams:** SAT I or ACT. **% Receiving Financial Aid:** 72 **Final Year or Final Semester Residency Requirement:** No **Library Holdings:** 135,458 **Regional Accreditation:** New England Association of Schools and Colleges **Credit Hours For Degree:** 72 credits, Associates; 36 courses, Bachelors **ROTC:** Army **Professional Accreditation:** CSWE, NLN **Intercollegiate Athletics:** Basketball M & W; Cheerleading M & W; Field Hockey W; Lacrosse M & W; Soccer M & W; Softball W; Swimming and Diving M & W; Tennis W; Track and Field M & W; Volleyball M & W

ROXBURY COMMUNITY COLLEGE

1234 Columbus Ave.
Roxbury Crossing, MA 02120-3400
Tel: (617)427-0060
Web Site: http://www.rcc.mass.edu/
President/CEO: Terrence Gomes
Admissions: Milton Samuels

Type: Two-Year College **Sex:** Coed **Affiliation:** Massachusetts Public Higher Education System **% Accepted:** 83 **Admission Plans:** Open Admission; Preferred Admission; Deferred Admission **Application Deadline:** Rolling **Application Fee:** $10.00 **H.S. Requirements:** High school diploma required; GED accepted **Scholarships:** Available **Calendar System:** Semester, Summer Session Available **Enrollment:** FT 1,124, PT 1,258 **Faculty:** FT 65, PT 55 **Student-Faculty Ratio:** 16:1 **Library Holdings:** 12,800 **Regional Accreditation:** New England Association of Schools and Colleges **Credit Hours For Degree:** 60 credits, Associates **Professional Accreditation:** NLN **Intercollegiate Athletics:** Baseball M; Basketball M & W; Soccer M & W; Tennis M & W

SALEM STATE COLLEGE

352 Lafayette St.
Salem, MA 01970-5353
Tel: (978)542-6000

Admissions: (978)542-6202
Fax: (978)542-6126
E-mail: admissions@salemstate.edu
Web Site: http://www.salemstate.edu/
President/CEO: Dr. Patricia Maguire Meservey
Admissions: Mary Dunn
Financial Aid: Mary Benda
Type: Comprehensive **Sex:** Coed **Affiliation:** Massachusetts Public Higher Education System **Scores:** 91% SAT V 400+; 90% SAT M 400+ **% Accepted:** 55 **Application Deadline:** Rolling **Application Fee:** $30.00 **H.S. Requirements:** High school diploma required; GED accepted **Costs Per Year:** Application fee: $30. State resident tuition: $910 full-time, $37.92 per credit part-time. Nonresident tuition: $7050 full-time, $293.75 per credit part-time. Mandatory fees: $5880 full-time, $245 per credit part-time. Full-time tuition and fees vary according to class time and course load. Part-time tuition and fees vary according to class time and course load. College room only: $6625. Room charges vary according to housing facility. **Scholarships:** Available **Calendar System:** Semester, Summer Session Available **Enrollment:** FT 5,894, PT 1,869, Grad FT 343, Grad PT 2,019 **Faculty:** FT 331, PT 428 **Student-Faculty Ratio:** 14:1 **Exams:** SAT I or ACT. **% Residing in College-Owned, -Operated, or -Affiliated Housing:** 21 **Library Holdings:** 273,225 **Regional Accreditation:** New England Association of Schools and Colleges **Credit Hours For Degree:** 120 credits, Bachelors **ROTC:** Army, Air Force **Professional Accreditation:** AACN, AOTA, CSWE, JRCEPAT, JRCNMT, NASAD, NAST, NCATE, NLN **Intercollegiate Athletics:** Baseball M; Basketball M & W; Cross-Country Running M & W; Field Hockey W; Golf M; Ice Hockey M; Lacrosse M; Soccer M & W; Softball W; Tennis M & W; Track and Field M & W; Volleyball W

SCHOOL OF THE MUSEUM OF FINE ARTS, BOSTON
230 The Fenway
Boston, MA 02115
Tel: (617)267-6100
Admissions: (617)369-3626
Fax: (617)369-3679
E-mail: admissions@smfa.edu
Web Site: http://www.smfa.edu/
President/CEO: Deborah H. Dluhy
Admissions: Jesse Tarantino
Financial Aid: Elizabeth Goreham
Type: Comprehensive **Sex:** Coed **Affiliation:** Tufts University; Museum of Fine Arts, Boston; Northeastern University **Scores:** 96.8% SAT V 400+; 88.3% SAT M 400+; 36% ACT 18-23; 36% ACT 24-29 **% Accepted:** 81 **Admission Plans:** Deferred Admission **Application Deadline:** February 1 **Application Fee:** $65.00 **H.S. Requirements:** High school diploma required; GED accepted **Costs Per Year:** Application fee: $65. One-time mandatory fee: $125. Tuition: $29,540 full-time, $1240 per credit hour part-time. Mandatory fees: $1120 full-time. Full-time tuition and fees vary according to course load, degree level, and program. Part-time tuition varies according to class time, course load, and program. College room only: $13,046. Room charges vary according to housing facility. **Scholarships:** Available **Calendar System:** Semester, Summer Session Available **Enrollment:** FT 565, PT 80, Grad FT 110 **Faculty:** FT 46, PT 50 **Student-Faculty Ratio:** 10:1 **Exams:** Other. **% Receiving Financial Aid:** 79 **% Residing in College-Owned, -Operated, or -Affiliated Housing:** 10 **Library Holdings:** 1,042,180 **Credit Hours For Degree:** 162 credits, Bachelors **Professional Accreditation:** NASAD

SIMMONS COLLEGE
300 The Fenway
Boston, MA 02115
Tel: (617)521-2000; Free: 800-345-8468
Admissions: (617)521-2057
Fax: (617)521-3199
E-mail: ugadm@simmons.edu
Web Site: http://www.simmons.edu/
President/CEO: Helen Drinan
Admissions: Catherine Capolupo
Financial Aid: Diane M. Hallisey
Type: University **Scores:** 98% SAT V 400+; 99% SAT M 400+; 49% ACT 18-23; 45% ACT 24-29 **% Accepted:** 57 **Admission Plans:** Early Admission; Early Action; Deferred Admission **Application Deadline:** February 1 **Application Fee:** $55.00 **H.S. Requirements:** High school diploma or equivalent not required **Costs Per Year:** Application fee: $55. Comprehensive fee: $43,500 includes full-time tuition ($30,520), mandatory fees ($930), and college room and board ($12,050). Full-time tuition and fees vary according to course load and program. Room and board charges vary according to board plan. Part-time tuition: $954 per credit. Part-time tuition varies according to course load and program. **Scholarships:** Available **Calendar System:** Semester, Summer Session Available **Enrollment:** FT 1,746, PT 223, Grad FT 782, Grad PT 2,252 **Faculty:** FT 231, PT 317 **Student-Faculty Ratio:** 13:1 **Exams:** SAT I or ACT. SAT essay used for admission. **% Receiving Financial Aid:** 71 **% Residing in College-Owned, -Operated, or -Affiliated Housing:** 48 **Final Year or Final Semester Residency Requirement:** No **Library Holdings:** 206,238 **Regional Accreditation:** New England Association of Schools and Colleges **Credit Hours For Degree:** 128 semester hours, Bachelors **ROTC:** Army **Professional Accreditation:** AACN, ADtA, ALA, APTA, ACEHSA, CSWE, NLN **Intercollegiate Athletics:** Basketball W; Crew W; Field Hockey W; Lacrosse W; Soccer W; Softball W; Swimming and Diving W; Tennis W; Volleyball W

SMITH COLLEGE
Northampton, MA 01063
Tel: (413)584-2700; Free: 800-383-3232
Admissions: (413)585-2500
Fax: (413)585-2123
E-mail: admission@smith.edu
Web Site: http://www.smith.edu/
President/CEO: Carol T. Christ
Admissions: Debra Shaver
Financial Aid: David Belanger
Type: Comprehensive **Sex:** Women **Scores:** 100% SAT V 400+; 100.01% SAT M 400+; 9.14% ACT 18-23; 60.57% ACT 24-29 **% Accepted:** 47 **Admission Plans:** Early Admission; Early Decision Plan; Deferred Admission **Application Deadline:** January 15 **Application Fee:** $60.00 **H.S. Requirements:** High school diploma or equivalent not required **Costs Per Year:** Application fee: $60. Comprehensive fee: $50,380 includes full-time tuition ($37,510), mandatory fees ($248), and college room and board ($12,622). College room only: $6230. Part-time tuition: $1170 per credit hour. **Scholarships:** Available **Calendar System:** Semester, Summer Session Not available **Enrollment:** FT 2,593, PT 21, Grad FT 428, Grad PT 79 **Faculty:** FT 281, PT 25 **Student-Faculty Ratio:** 9:1 **Exams:** SAT I or ACT. ACT essay used for admission. SAT essay used for admission. ACT essay not being used. SAT essay not being used. **% Receiving Financial Aid:** 63 **% Residing in College-Owned, -Operated, or -Affiliated Housing:** 94 **Library Holdings:** 1,430,466 **Regional Accreditation:** New England Association of Schools and Colleges **Credit Hours For Degree:** 128 credits, Bachelors **ROTC:** Army, Air Force **Professional Accreditation:** CSWE **Intercollegiate Athletics:** Basketball W; Crew W; Cross-Country Running W; Equestrian Sports W; Field Hockey W; Lacrosse W; Skiing (Downhill) W; Soccer W; Softball W; Squash W; Swimming and Diving W; Tennis W; Track and Field W; Volleyball W

SPRINGFIELD COLLEGE
263 Alden St.
Springfield, MA 01109-3797
Tel: (413)748-3000; Free: 800-343-1257
Admissions: (413)748-3116
Fax: (413)748-3764
E-mail: admissions@spfldcol.edu
Web Site: http://www.spfldcol.edu/
President/CEO: Richard B. Flynn
Admissions: Mary DeAngelo
Financial Aid: Edward J. Ciosek
Type: Comprehensive **Sex:** Coed **% Accepted:** 69 **Admission Plans:** Preferred Admission; Early Admission; Early Decision Plan; Deferred Admission **Application Deadline:** April 1 **Application Fee:** $50.00 **H.S. Requirements:** High school diploma required; GED accepted **Costs Per Year:** Application fee: $50. Comprehensive fee: $35,990 includes full-time tuition ($26,480) and college room and board ($9510). Room and board charges vary according to board plan and housing facility. Part-time tuition: $790 per credit hour. **Scholarships:** Available **Calendar System:** Semester, Summer Session Available **Enrollment:** FT 2,172, PT 45 **Faculty:** FT 174, PT 168 **Student-Faculty Ratio:** 12:1 **Exams:** SAT I or ACT. **% Receiving Financial Aid:** 77 **% Residing in College-Owned, -Operated, or -Affiliated Housing:** 85 **Library Holdings:** 125,000 **Regional Accreditation:** New England Association of Schools and Colleges **Credit Hours For Degree:** 130 credit hours, Bachelors **ROTC:** Army, Air Force **Professional Accreditation:**

AOTA, APTA, CORE, CSWE, JRCEPAT, NRPA **Intercollegiate Athletics:** Baseball M; Basketball M & W; Cross-Country Running M & W; Field Hockey W; Football M; Golf M; Gymnastics M & W; Lacrosse M & W; Soccer M & W; Softball W; Swimming and Diving M & W; Tennis M & W; Track and Field M & W; Volleyball M & W; Wrestling M

SPRINGFIELD TECHNICAL COMMUNITY COLLEGE
1 Armory Square, Ste. One
PO Box 9000
Springfield, MA 01105
Tel: (413)781-7822
Fax: (413)781-5805
E-mail: rblair@stcc.edu
Web Site: http://www.stcc.edu/
President/CEO: Dr. Ira Rubenzahl
Admissions: Ray Blair
Financial Aid: Mary Forni
Type: Two-Year College **Sex:** Coed **% Accepted:** 83 **Admission Plans:** Open Admission **Application Deadline:** Rolling **Application Fee:** $10.00 **H.S. Requirements:** High school diploma required; GED accepted **Costs Per Year:** Application fee: $10. State resident tuition: $750 full-time, $25 per credit part-time. Nonresident tuition: $7260 full-time, $242 per credit part-time. Mandatory fees: $3186 full-time, $99 per credit part-time, $108 per term part-time. Full-time tuition and fees vary according to reciprocity agreements. Part-time tuition and fees vary according to reciprocity agreements. Tuition guaranteed not to increase for student's term of enrollment. **Scholarships:** Available **Calendar System:** Semester, Summer Session Available **Enrollment:** FT 2,952, PT 3,830 **Faculty:** FT 152, PT 274 **Student-Faculty Ratio:** 17:1 **Exams:** SAT I. **Library Holdings:** 59,369 **Regional Accreditation:** New England Association of Schools and Colleges **Credit Hours For Degree:** 60 credits, Associates **Professional Accreditation:** ARCEST, AAMAE, ADA, AOTA, APTA, CARC, JRCEDMS, JRCERT, JRCNMT, NAACLS, NLN **Intercollegiate Athletics:** Basketball M & W; Golf M; Lacrosse W; Soccer M & W; Wrestling M

STONEHILL COLLEGE
320 Washington St.
Easton, MA 02357
Tel: (508)565-1000
Admissions: (508)565-1373
Fax: (508)565-1500
E-mail: admissions@stonehill.edu
Web Site: http://www.stonehill.edu/
President/CEO: Mark T. Cregan, CSC
Financial Aid: Rhonda Nickley
Type: Four-Year College **Sex:** Coed **Affiliation:** Roman Catholic **Scores:** 100% SAT V 400+; 100% SAT M 400+; 14% ACT 18-23; 71% ACT 24-29 **% Accepted:** 56 **Admission Plans:** Early Action; Early Decision Plan; Deferred Admission **Application Deadline:** January 15 **Application Fee:** $60.00 **H.S. Requirements:** High school diploma required; GED accepted **Costs Per Year:** Application fee: $60. Comprehensive fee: $43,450 includes full-time tuition ($31,210) and college room and board ($12,240). College room only: $7468. Room and board charges vary according to board plan. Part-time tuition: $1040 per course. Part-time mandatory fees: $25 per term. Part-time tuition and fees vary according to course load. **Scholarships:** Available **Calendar System:** Semester, Summer Session Available **Enrollment:** FT 2,420, PT 48 **Faculty:** FT 151, PT 103 **Student-Faculty Ratio:** 13:1 **Exams:** ACT essay used for advising. SAT essay used for advising. ACT essay used for placement. SAT essay used for placement. **% Receiving Financial Aid:** 69 **% Residing in College-Owned, -Operated, or -Affiliated Housing:** 88 **Final Year or Final Semester Residency Requirement:** No **Library Holdings:** 246,055 **Regional Accreditation:** New England Association of Schools and Colleges **Credit Hours For Degree:** 40 courses, Bachelors **ROTC:** Army **Intercollegiate Athletics:** Baseball M; Basketball M & W; Bowling M & W; Cheerleading M & W; Cross-Country Running M & W; Equestrian Sports W; Field Hockey W; Football M; Golf M & W; Ice Hockey M; Lacrosse M & W; Rugby M & W; Soccer M & W; Softball W; Tennis M & W; Track and Field M & W; Ultimate Frisbee M & W; Volleyball M & W

SUFFOLK UNIVERSITY
8 Ashburton Place
Boston, MA 02108-2770
Tel: (617)573-8000; Free: 800-6-SUFFOLK
Admissions: (617)573-8460
Fax: (617)742-4291
E-mail: admission@suffolk.edu
Web Site: http://www.suffolk.edu/
President/CEO: David J. Sargent
Admissions: John Hamel
Financial Aid: Christine A. Perry
Type: Comprehensive **Sex:** Coed **Scores:** 58.9% ACT 18-23; 26% ACT 24-29 **% Accepted:** 85 **Admission Plans:** Early Action; Deferred Admission **Application Deadline:** March 1 **Application Fee:** $50.00 **H.S. Requirements:** High school diploma required; GED accepted **Costs Per Year:** Application fee: $50. Comprehensive fee: $41,752 includes full-time tuition ($27,100), mandatory fees ($108), and college room and board ($14,544). College room only: $12,204. Room and board charges vary according to board plan and housing facility. Part-time tuition: $665 per credit. Part-time mandatory fees: $10 per term. **Scholarships:** Available **Calendar System:** Semester, Summer Session Available **Enrollment:** FT 5,291, PT 481, Grad FT 1,693, Grad PT 1,992 **Faculty:** FT 425, PT 564 **Student-Faculty Ratio:** 13:1 **Exams:** SAT I or ACT. ACT essay used for admission. SAT essay not being used. **% Receiving Financial Aid:** 61 **% Residing in College-Owned, -Operated, or -Affiliated Housing:** 23 **Final Year or Final Semester Residency Requirement:** No **Library Holdings:** 134,401 **Regional Accreditation:** New England Association of Schools and Colleges **Credit Hours For Degree:** 66 semester hours, Associates; 122 semester hours, Bachelors **ROTC:** Army **Professional Accreditation:** AACSB, ABA, APA, AALS, FIDER, NASAD, NASPAA **Intercollegiate Athletics:** Baseball M; Basketball M & W; Cross-Country Running M & W; Golf M; Ice Hockey M; Soccer M; Softball W; Tennis M & W; Volleyball W

TUFTS UNIVERSITY
Medford, MA 02155
Tel: (617)628-5000
Admissions: (617)627-3170
Fax: (617)627-3860
E-mail: admissions.inquiry@ase.tufts.edu
Web Site: http://www.tufts.edu/
President/CEO: Lawrence S. Bacow
Admissions: Lee Coffin
Financial Aid: Patricia C. Reilly
Type: University **Sex:** Coed **Scores:** 100.2% SAT V 400+; 99.2% SAT M 400+; 1% ACT 18-23; 19% ACT 24-29 **% Accepted:** 27 **Admission Plans:** Early Admission; Early Decision Plan; Deferred Admission **Application Deadline:** January 1 **Application Fee:** $70.00 **H.S. Requirements:** High school diploma required; GED accepted **Costs Per Year:** Application fee: $70. Comprehensive fee: $51,088 includes full-time tuition ($39,432), mandatory fees ($910), and college room and board ($10,746). College room only: $5564. Room and board charges vary according to board plan. **Scholarships:** Available **Calendar System:** Semester, Summer Session Available **Enrollment:** FT 5,111, PT 53, Grad FT 4,286, Grad PT 802 **Faculty:** FT 675, PT 422 **Student-Faculty Ratio:** 9:1 **Exams:** SAT I and SAT II or ACT. **% Receiving Financial Aid:** 41 **% Residing in College-Owned, -Operated, or -Affiliated Housing:** 75 **Library Holdings:** 1,455,977 **Regional Accreditation:** New England Association of Schools and Colleges **Credit Hours For Degree:** 34 courses, Bachelors **ROTC:** Army, Navy, Air Force **Professional Accreditation:** ABET, ADA, ADtA, ACSP, AOTA, APA, AVMA, CEPH, LCMEAMA **Intercollegiate Athletics:** Baseball M; Basketball M & W; Crew M & W; Cross-Country Running M & W; Fencing W; Field Hockey W; Football M; Golf M; Ice Hockey M; Lacrosse M & W; Sailing M & W; Soccer M & W; Softball W; Squash M & W; Swimming and Diving M & W; Tennis M & W; Track and Field M & W; Volleyball W

UNIVERSITY OF MASSACHUSETTS AMHERST
Amherst, MA 01003
Tel: (413)545-0111
Admissions: (413)545-0222
Fax: (413)545-4312
E-mail: mail@admissions.umass.edu
Web Site: http://www.umass.edu/
President/CEO: Dr. Robert C. Holub
Admissions: Kevin Kelly
Type: University **Sex:** Coed **Affiliation:** University of Massachusetts **Scores:** 99.2% SAT V 400+; 99.8% SAT M 400+; 28.7% ACT 18-23; 59% ACT 24-29 **% Accepted:** 67 **Admission Plans:** Early Action; Deferred Admission **Application Deadline:** January 15 **Application Fee:** $40.00 **H.S.**

Requirements: High school diploma required; GED accepted **Costs Per Year:** Application fee: $40. One-time mandatory fee: $185. State resident tuition: $1714 full-time, $71.50 per credit part-time. Nonresident tuition: $9937 full-time, $414 per credit part-time. Mandatory fees: $10,203 full-time. Full-time tuition and fees vary according to class time, course load, degree level, location, program, reciprocity agreements, and student level. Part-time tuition varies according to class time, course load, degree level, location, program, reciprocity agreements, and student level. College room and board: $8276. College room only: $4612. Room and board charges vary according to board plan and housing facility. **Scholarships:** Available **Calendar System:** Semester, Summer Session Available **Enrollment:** FT 19,315, PT 1,558, Grad FT 2,200, Grad PT 3,943 **Faculty:** FT 1,170, PT 145 **Student-Faculty Ratio:** 18:1 **Exams:** SAT I or ACT. **% Receiving Financial Aid:** 51 **% Residing in College-Owned, -Operated, or -Affiliated Housing:** 63 **Final Year or Final Semester Residency Requirement:** Yes **Library Holdings:** 3,654,181 **Regional Accreditation:** New England Association of Schools and Colleges **Credit Hours For Degree:** 60 credits, Associates; 120 credits, Bachelors **ROTC:** Army, Air Force **Professional Accreditation:** AACSB, ABET, AACN, AAFCS, ADtA, ACSP, APA, ASLA, ASLHA, CEPH, NASM, NCATE, SAF **Intercollegiate Athletics:** Baseball M; Basketball M & W; Crew W; Cross-Country Running M & W; Field Hockey W; Football M; Ice Hockey M; Lacrosse M & W; Soccer M & W; Softball W; Swimming and Diving M & W; Tennis W; Track and Field M & W

UNIVERSITY OF MASSACHUSETTS BOSTON
100 Morrissey Blvd.
Boston, MA 02125-3393
Tel: (617)287-5000
Admissions: (617)287-6000
E-mail: enrollment.info@umb.edu
Web Site: http://www.umb.edu/
President/CEO: Dr. J. Keith Motley
Admissions: Liliana Mickle
Financial Aid: Judy L. Keyes
Type: University **Sex:** Coed **Affiliation:** University of Massachusetts **Scores:** 97% SAT V 400+; 99% SAT M 400+ **% Accepted:** 61 **Admission Plans:** Deferred Admission **Application Deadline:** June 1 **Application Fee:** $40.00 **H.S. Requirements:** High school diploma required; GED accepted **Costs Per Year:** Application fee: $40. State resident tuition: $1714 full-time, $71.50 per credit hour part-time. Nonresident tuition: $9758 full-time, $406.50 per credit hour part-time. Mandatory fees: $8897 full-time, $370 per credit hour part-time. Full-time tuition and fees vary according to class time, course load, program, reciprocity agreements, and student level. Part-time tuition and fees vary according to class time, course load, program, reciprocity agreements, and student level. **Scholarships:** Available **Calendar System:** Semester, Summer Session Available **Enrollment:** FT 7,681, PT 3,360, Grad FT 1,225, Grad PT 2,646 **Faculty:** FT 499, PT 465 **Student-Faculty Ratio:** 16:1 **Exams:** SAT I or ACT. SAT essay not being used. **% Receiving Financial Aid:** 60 **Library Holdings:** 600,000 **Regional Accreditation:** New England Association of Schools and Colleges **Credit Hours For Degree:** 120 credits, Bachelors **ROTC:** Army, Navy, Air Force **Professional Accreditation:** AACSB, AAMFT, AACN, APA, CORE, NCATE, TEAC **Intercollegiate Athletics:** Baseball M; Basketball M & W; Cross-Country Running M & W; Ice Hockey M; Lacrosse M; Soccer M & W; Softball W; Tennis M & W; Track and Field M & W; Volleyball W

UNIVERSITY OF MASSACHUSETTS DARTMOUTH
285 Old Westport Rd.
North Dartmouth, MA 02747-2300
Tel: (508)999-8000
Admissions: (508)999-8605
Fax: (508)999-8755
E-mail: admissions@umassd.edu
Web Site: http://www.umassd.edu/
President/CEO: Dr. Jean F. MacCormack
Financial Aid: Bruce Palmer
Type: University **Sex:** Coed **Affiliation:** University of Massachusetts **Scores:** 95% SAT V 400+; 97% SAT M 400+; 58% ACT 18-23; 34% ACT 24-29 **% Accepted:** 68 **Admission Plans:** Early Admission; Early Action; Deferred Admission **Application Deadline:** Rolling **Application Fee:** $40.00 **H.S. Requirements:** High school diploma required; GED accepted **Costs Per Year:** Application fee: $40. State resident tuition: $1417 full-time, $59.04 per credit part-time. Nonresident tuition: $8099 full-time, $337.46 per credit part-time. Mandatory fees: $8941 full-time, $372.54 per credit part-time. Full-time tuition and fees vary according to program and reciprocity agreements. Part-time tuition and fees vary according to course load, program, and reciprocity agreements. College room and board: $8950. College room only: $6133. Room and board charges vary according to board plan and housing facility. **Scholarships:** Available **Calendar System:** Semester, Summer Session Available **Enrollment:** FT 7,068, PT 914, Grad FT 452, Grad PT 868 **Faculty:** FT 369, PT 219 **Student-Faculty Ratio:** 18:1 **Exams:** SAT I or ACT. **% Receiving Financial Aid:** 65 **% Residing in College-Owned, -Operated, or -Affiliated Housing:** 56 **Final Year or Final Semester Residency Requirement:** No **Library Holdings:** 461,338 **Regional Accreditation:** New England Association of Schools and Colleges **Credit Hours For Degree:** 120 credit hours, Bachelors **ROTC:** Army **Professional Accreditation:** AACSB, ABET, NAACLS, NASAD, NLN **Intercollegiate Athletics:** Baseball M; Basketball M & W; Cheerleading W; Cross-Country Running M & W; Equestrian Sports W; Field Hockey W; Football M; Golf M; Ice Hockey M; Lacrosse M & W; Rugby M & W; Soccer M & W; Softball W; Swimming and Diving M & W; Tennis M & W; Track and Field M & W; Volleyball W

UNIVERSITY OF MASSACHUSETTS LOWELL
1 University Ave.
Lowell, MA 01854-2881
Tel: (978)934-4000; Free: 800-410-4607
Admissions: (978)934-3944
Fax: (978)934-3000
E-mail: admissions@uml.edu
Web Site: http://www.uml.edu/
President/CEO: Martin Meehan
Financial Aid: Joyce McLaughlin
Type: University **Sex:** Coed **Affiliation:** University of Massachusetts **Scores:** 97.04% SAT V 400+; 98.25% SAT M 400+ **% Accepted:** 73 **Admission Plans:** Deferred Admission **Application Deadline:** Rolling **Application Fee:** $40.00 **H.S. Requirements:** High school diploma required; GED accepted **Costs Per Year:** Application fee: $40. State resident tuition: $1454 full-time, $60.58 per credit part-time. Nonresident tuition: $13,474 full-time, $357 per credit part-time. Mandatory fees: $9227 full-time, $390.67 per credit part-time. Part-time tuition and fees vary according to course load. College room and board: $8635. College room only: $5596. Room and board charges vary according to board plan and housing facility. **Scholarships:** Available **Calendar System:** Semester, Summer Session Available **Enrollment:** FT 7,559, PT 2,989, Grad FT 873, Grad PT 2,181 **Faculty:** FT 402, PT 312 **Student-Faculty Ratio:** 15:1 **Exams:** SAT I or ACT. ACT essay not being used. SAT essay not being used. **% Receiving Financial Aid:** 52 **% Residing in College-Owned, -Operated, or -Affiliated Housing:** 40 **Library Holdings:** 382,599 **Regional Accreditation:** New England Association of Schools and Colleges **Credit Hours For Degree:** 60 credits, Associates; 120 credits, Bachelors **ROTC:** Air Force **Professional Accreditation:** AACSB, ABET, AACN, APTA, NAACLS, NASAD, NASM, NCATE **Intercollegiate Athletics:** Baseball M; Basketball M & W; Crew M & W; Cross-Country Running M & W; Field Hockey W; Ice Hockey M; Soccer M; Swimming and Diving M; Tennis M & W; Track and Field M & W; Volleyball W

UNIVERSITY OF PHOENIX—BOSTON CAMPUS
100 Grossman Dr.
Braintree, MA 02184-4949
Tel: (781)843-0844; Free: 800-228-7240
Admissions: (480)557-6151
E-mail: audra.mcquarie@phoenix.edu
Web Site: http://www.phoenix.edu/
President/CEO: William Pepicello
Admissions: Audra McQuarie
Type: Comprehensive **Sex:** Coed **Admission Plans:** Open Admission; Deferred Admission **Application Deadline:** Rolling **Application Fee:** $0.00 **H.S. Requirements:** High school diploma required; GED accepted **Costs Per Year:** Application fee: $0. Tuition: $13,875 full-time. Full-time tuition varies according to course level and course load. **Scholarships:** Available **Calendar System:** Continuous, Summer Session Not available **Enrollment:** FT 265 **Faculty:** FT 9, PT 98 **Regional Accreditation:** North Central Association of Colleges and Schools **Credit Hours For Degree:** 60 credits, Associates; 120 credits, Bachelors

UNIVERSITY OF PHOENIX—CENTRAL MASSACHUSETTS CAMPUS
One Research Dr.
Westborough, MA 01581-3906

Tel: (508)614-4100; Free: 800-228-7240
Admissions: (480)557-6151
E-mail: audra.mcquarie@phoenix.edu
Web Site: http://www.phoenix.edu/
President/CEO: William Pepicello
Admissions: Audra McQuarie
Type: Comprehensive **Sex:** Coed **Admission Plans:** Open Admission; Deferred Admission **Application Deadline:** Rolling **Application Fee:** $0.00 **H.S. Requirements:** High school diploma required; GED accepted **Costs Per Year:** Application fee: $0. Tuition: $13,875 full-time. Full-time tuition varies according to course level and course load. **Scholarships:** Available **Calendar System:** Continuous, Summer Session Not available **Enrollment:** FT 117 **Faculty:** FT 5, PT 75 **Regional Accreditation:** North Central Association of Colleges and Schools **Credit Hours For Degree:** 60 credits, Associates; 120 credits, Bachelors

URBAN COLLEGE OF BOSTON
178 Tremont St.
Boston, MA 02111
Tel: (617)292-4723
Admissions: (617)348-6353
Fax: (617)423-4758
Web Site: http://www.urbancollegeofboston.org/
President/CEO: Dr. Linda Edmonds Turner
Admissions: Dr. Henry J. Johnson
Type: Two-Year College **Sex:** Coed **Admission Plans:** Open Admission **Application Fee:** $10.00 **H.S. Requirements:** High school diploma required; GED accepted **Costs Per Year:** Application fee: $10. Tuition: $3984 full-time, $166 per credit hour part-time. Mandatory fees: $20 full-time, $10 per term part-time. Full-time tuition and fees vary according to course load. Part-time tuition and fees vary according to course load. **Scholarships:** Available **Calendar System:** Semester **Student-Faculty Ratio:** 13:1 **Regional Accreditation:** New England Association of Schools and Colleges **Credit Hours For Degree:** 65 credits, Associates

WELLESLEY COLLEGE
106 Central St.
Wellesley, MA 02481
Tel: (781)283-1000
Admissions: (781)283-2270
Fax: (781)283-3678
E-mail: admission@wellesley.edu
Web Site: http://www.wellesley.edu/
President/CEO: Kim Bottomly
Financial Aid: Kathryn Osmond
Type: Four-Year College **Sex:** Women **Scores:** 100% SAT V 400+; 100% SAT M 400+; 1.4% ACT 18-23; 31.2% ACT 24-29 **% Accepted:** 35 **Admission Plans:** Early Admission; Early Decision Plan; Deferred Admission **Application Deadline:** January 15 **Application Fee:** $50.00 **H.S. Requirements:** High school diploma or equivalent not required **Costs Per Year:** Application fee: $50. Comprehensive fee: $49,794 includes full-time tuition ($37,826), mandatory fees ($236), and college room and board ($11,732). College room only: $5980. Part-time tuition: $1182 per credit hour. Part-time mandatory fees: $30 per credit. Part-time tuition and fees vary according to course load. **Scholarships:** Available **Calendar System:** Semester, Summer Session Available **Enrollment:** FT 2,186, PT 138 **Faculty:** FT 259, PT 55 **Student-Faculty Ratio:** 8:1 **Exams:** SAT I and SAT II or ACT. ACT essay used for admission. SAT essay used for admission. ACT essay not being used. SAT essay not being used. **% Receiving Financial Aid:** 62 **% Residing in College-Owned, -Operated, or -Affiliated Housing:** 92 **Library Holdings:** 1,094,346 **Regional Accreditation:** New England Association of Schools and Colleges **Credit Hours For Degree:** 32 courses, Bachelors **ROTC:** Army, Air Force **Intercollegiate Athletics:** Basketball W; Crew W; Cross-Country Running W; Fencing W; Field Hockey W; Golf W; Lacrosse W; Rugby W; Sailing W; Skiing (Downhill) W; Soccer W; Softball W; Squash W; Swimming and Diving W; Tennis W; Track and Field W; Ultimate Frisbee W; Volleyball W

WENTWORTH INSTITUTE OF TECHNOLOGY
550 Huntington Ave.
Boston, MA 02115-5998
Tel: (617)989-4590; Free: 800-556-0610
Admissions: (617)989-4116
Fax: (617)989-4010
E-mail: dufoura@wit.edu
Web Site: http://www.wit.edu/
President/CEO: Dr. Zorica Pantic
Admissions: Amy Dufour
Financial Aid: Anne-marie Caruso
Type: Comprehensive **Sex:** Coed **Scores:** 95% SAT V 400+; 98% SAT M 400+; 54% ACT 18-23; 38% ACT 24-29 **% Accepted:** 67 **Admission Plans:** Deferred Admission **Application Deadline:** Rolling **Application Fee:** $50.00 **H.S. Requirements:** High school diploma required; GED accepted **Costs Per Year:** Application fee: $50. Comprehensive fee: $32,300 includes full-time tuition ($21,800) and college room and board ($10,500). Full-time tuition varies according to student level. Room and board charges vary according to board plan. Part-time tuition: $680 per credit hour. Part-time tuition varies according to class time, course load, and degree level. **Scholarships:** Available **Calendar System:** Miscellaneous, Summer Session Available **Enrollment:** FT 3,384, PT 424, Grad FT 84 **Faculty:** FT 139, PT 168 **Student-Faculty Ratio:** 15:1 **Exams:** SAT I or ACT. ACT essay used for admission. SAT essay used for admission. **% Receiving Financial Aid:** 67 **% Residing in College-Owned, -Operated, or -Affiliated Housing:** 51 **Final Year or Final Semester Residency Requirement:** Yes **Library Holdings:** 118,329 **Regional Accreditation:** New England Association of Schools and Colleges **Credit Hours For Degree:** 72 credits, Associates; 128 credits, Bachelors **ROTC:** Army, Air Force **Professional Accreditation:** ABET, ACCE, FIDER, NAAB **Intercollegiate Athletics:** Baseball M; Basketball M & W; Crew M & W; Golf M; Ice Hockey M; Lacrosse M; Riflery M & W; Rugby M & W; Soccer M & W; Softball W; Tennis M & W; Volleyball M & W

WESTERN NEW ENGLAND COLLEGE
1215 Wilbraham Rd.
Springfield, MA 01119
Tel: (413)782-3111; Free: 800-325-1122
Admissions: (413)782-1321
Fax: (413)782-1777
E-mail: ugradmis@wnec.edu
Web Site: http://www.wnec.edu/
President/CEO: Dr. Anthony S. Caprio
Admissions: Dr. Charles R. Pollock
Financial Aid: Kathy M. Chambers
Type: Comprehensive **Sex:** Coed **Scores:** 97% SAT V 400+; 98% SAT M 400+; 56% ACT 18-23; 37% ACT 24-29 **% Accepted:** 81 **Application Deadline:** Rolling **Application Fee:** $50.00 **H.S. Requirements:** High school diploma required; GED accepted **Costs Per Year:** Application fee: $50. Comprehensive fee: $39,796 includes full-time tuition ($26,822), mandatory fees ($1994), and college room and board ($10,980). Full-time tuition and fees vary according to program. Room and board charges vary according to board plan and housing facility. Part-time tuition: $505 per credit hour. Part-time tuition varies according to location and program. **Scholarships:** Available **Calendar System:** Semester, Summer Session Available **Enrollment:** FT 2,463, PT 276, Grad FT 396, Grad PT 575 **Faculty:** FT 188, PT 113 **Student-Faculty Ratio:** 15:1 **Exams:** SAT I or ACT. **% Receiving Financial Aid:** 75 **% Residing in College-Owned, -Operated, or -Affiliated Housing:** 79 **Library Holdings:** 130,900 **Regional Accreditation:** New England Association of Schools and Colleges **Credit Hours For Degree:** 60 semester hours, Associates; 122 semester hours, Bachelors **ROTC:** Army, Air Force **Professional Accreditation:** AACSB, ABET, ABA, AALS, CSWE **Intercollegiate Athletics:** Baseball M; Basketball M & W; Bowling M & W; Cross-Country Running M & W; Field Hockey W; Football M; Golf M; Ice Hockey M; Lacrosse M & W; Soccer M & W; Softball W; Swimming and Diving W; Tennis M & W; Volleyball W; Wrestling M

WESTFIELD STATE COLLEGE
Western Ave.
Westfield, MA 01086
Tel: (413)572-5300
Admissions: (413)572-5218
E-mail: admission@wsc.ma.edu
Web Site: http://www.wsc.ma.edu/
President/CEO: Dr. Evan Dobelle
Admissions: Emily Gibbings
Financial Aid: Catherine Ryan
Type: Comprehensive **Sex:** Coed **Affiliation:** Massachusetts Public Higher Education System **Scores:** 94.4% SAT V 400+; 95.6% SAT M 400+; 63% ACT 18-23; 21% ACT 24-29 **% Accepted:** 58 **Admission Plans:** Deferred

Admission **Application Deadline:** March 1 **Application Fee:** $50.00 **H.S. Requirements:** High school diploma required; GED accepted **Costs Per Year:** Application fee: $50. State resident tuition: $970 full-time, $85 per credit hour part-time. Nonresident tuition: $7050 full-time, $95 per credit hour part-time. Mandatory fees: $6046 full-time, $110 per credit hour part-time, $150 per term part-time. Full-time tuition and fees vary according to reciprocity agreements. College room and board: $7728. Room and board charges vary according to board plan, housing facility, and location. **Scholarships:** Available **Calendar System:** Semester, Summer Session Available **Enrollment:** FT 4,543, PT 500, Grad FT 89, Grad PT 543 **Faculty:** FT 208, PT 240 **Student-Faculty Ratio:** 17:1 **Exams:** SAT I or ACT. ACT essay not being used. SAT essay not being used. **% Receiving Financial Aid:** 53 **% Residing in College-Owned, -Operated, or -Affiliated Housing:** 55 **Final Year or Final Semester Residency Requirement:** No **Library Holdings:** 149,818 **Regional Accreditation:** New England Association of Schools and Colleges **Credit Hours For Degree:** 120 credit hours, Bachelors **ROTC:** Army, Air Force **Professional Accreditation:** CSWE, JRCEPAT, NCATE **Intercollegiate Athletics:** Baseball M; Basketball M & W; Cheerleading M & W; Cross-Country Running M & W; Equestrian Sports M & W; Field Hockey W; Football M; Golf M & W; Ice Hockey M; Lacrosse M & W; Soccer M & W; Softball W; Swimming and Diving W; Track and Field M & W; Volleyball W

WHEATON COLLEGE
26 East Main St.
Norton, MA 02766
Tel: (508)285-7722; Free: 800-394-6003
Admissions: (508)286-8251
Fax: (508)285-8271
E-mail: admission@wheatoncollege.edu
Web Site: http://www.wheatoncollege.edu/
President/CEO: Ronald A. Crutcher
Admissions: Gail Berson
Financial Aid: Susan Beard
Type: Four-Year College **Sex:** Coed **% Accepted:** 59 **Admission Plans:** Early Admission; Early Decision Plan; Deferred Admission **Application Deadline:** January 15 **Application Fee:** $55.00 **H.S. Requirements:** High school diploma required; GED accepted **Costs Per Year:** Application fee: $55. One-time mandatory fee: $50. Comprehensive fee: $51,264 includes full-time tuition ($40,790), mandatory fees ($294), and college room and board ($10,180). College room only: $5350. **Scholarships:** Available **Calendar System:** Semester, Summer Session Not available **Enrollment:** FT 1,627, PT 5 **Faculty:** FT 139, PT 30 **Student-Faculty Ratio:** 11:1 **Exams:** ACT essay not being used. SAT essay not being used. **% Receiving Financial Aid:** 56 **% Residing in College-Owned, -Operated, or -Affiliated Housing:** 93 **Library Holdings:** 376,616 **Regional Accreditation:** New England Association of Schools and Colleges **Credit Hours For Degree:** 32 courses, Bachelors **ROTC:** Army **Intercollegiate Athletics:** Baseball M; Basketball M & W; Cross-Country Running M & W; Field Hockey W; Lacrosse M & W; Soccer M & W; Softball W; Swimming and Diving M & W; Tennis M & W; Track and Field M & W; Volleyball W

WHEELOCK COLLEGE
200 The Riverway
Boston, MA 02215-4176
Tel: (617)879-2000; Free: 800-734-5212
Admissions: (617)879-2206
Fax: (617)566-7531
E-mail: kharrington@wheelock.edu
Web Site: http://www.wheelock.edu/
President/CEO: Jackie Jenkins-Scott
Admissions: Kristen Harrington
Financial Aid: Roxanne Dumas
Type: Comprehensive **Sex:** Coed **Scores:** 86% SAT V 400+; 87% SAT M 400+; 55% ACT 18-23; 24% ACT 24-29 **% Accepted:** 75 **Admission Plans:** Early Admission; Early Action; Deferred Admission **Application Deadline:** March 1 **H.S. Requirements:** High school diploma required; GED accepted **Costs Per Year:** One-time mandatory fee: $225. Comprehensive fee: $39,360 includes full-time tuition ($27,150), mandatory fees ($1010), and college room and board ($11,200). Full-time tuition and fees vary according to program. Part-time tuition: $850 per credit. Part-time tuition varies according to program. **Scholarships:** Available **Calendar System:** Semester, Summer Session Available **Enrollment:** FT 724, PT 27, Grad FT 143, Grad PT 161 **Faculty:** FT 63, PT 80 **Student-Faculty Ratio:** 10:1 **Exams:** SAT I or ACT. **% Receiving Financial Aid:** 84 **Final Year or Final Semester Residency Requirement:** No **Library Holdings:** 80,763 **Regional Accreditation:** New England Association of Schools and Colleges **Credit Hours For Degree:** 134 credits, Bachelors **Professional Accreditation:** CSWE, NCATE **Intercollegiate Athletics:** Basketball M & W; Cross-Country Running M & W; Field Hockey W; Lacrosse M & W; Soccer M & W; Softball W; Tennis M

WILLIAMS COLLEGE
PO Box 687
Williamstown, MA 01267
Tel: (413)597-3131
Admissions: (413)597-2211
Fax: (413)597-4018
E-mail: admission@williams.edu
Web Site: http://www.williams.edu/
President/CEO: Dean Adam Falk
Admissions: Richard L. Nesbitt
Financial Aid: Paul J. Boyer
Type: Comprehensive **Sex:** Coed **Scores:** 100.2% SAT V 400+; 101% SAT M 400+; 1% ACT 18-23; 23% ACT 24-29 **% Accepted:** 20 **Admission Plans:** Early Admission; Early Decision Plan; Deferred Admission **Application Deadline:** January 1 **Application Fee:** $60.00 **H.S. Requirements:** High school diploma or equivalent not required **Costs Per Year:** Application fee: $60. Comprehensive fee: $49,880 includes full-time tuition ($39,250), mandatory fees ($240), and college room and board ($10,390). College room only: $5280. Room and board charges vary according to board plan. **Scholarships:** Available **Calendar System:** 4-1-4, Summer Session Not available **Enrollment:** FT 2,033, PT 34, Grad FT 56 **Faculty:** FT 271, PT 34 **Student-Faculty Ratio:** 7:1 **Exams:** SAT I and SAT II or ACT. ACT essay not being used. SAT essay not being used. **% Receiving Financial Aid:** 52 **% Residing in College-Owned, -Operated, or -Affiliated Housing:** 94 **Library Holdings:** 945,691 **Regional Accreditation:** New England Association of Schools and Colleges **Credit Hours For Degree:** 36 courses, Bachelors **ROTC:** Air Force **Intercollegiate Athletics:** Baseball M; Basketball M & W; Crew M & W; Cross-Country Running M & W; Equestrian Sports M & W; Field Hockey W; Football M; Golf M & W; Ice Hockey M & W; Lacrosse M & W; Rugby M & W; Sailing M & W; Skiing (Cross-Country) M & W; Skiing (Downhill) M & W; Soccer M & W; Softball W; Squash M & W; Swimming and Diving M & W; Tennis M & W; Track and Field M & W; Volleyball M & W; Water Polo M & W; Wrestling M

WORCESTER POLYTECHNIC INSTITUTE
100 Institute Rd.
Worcester, MA 01609-2280
Tel: (508)831-5000
Admissions: (508)831-5286
Fax: (508)831-5875
E-mail: admissions@wpi.edu
Web Site: http://www.wpi.edu/
President/CEO: Dr. Dennis D. Berkey
Admissions: Edward J. Connor
Type: University **Sex:** Coed **Scores:** 99% SAT V 400+; 100% SAT M 400+; 11% ACT 18-23; 54% ACT 24-29 **% Accepted:** 63 **Admission Plans:** Early Admission; Early Action; Deferred Admission **Application Deadline:** February 1 **Application Fee:** $60.00 **H.S. Requirements:** High school diploma required; GED accepted **Costs Per Year:** Application fee: $60. One-time mandatory fee: $200. Comprehensive fee: $50,530 includes full-time tuition ($38,360), mandatory fees ($560), and college room and board ($11,610). College room only: $6790. Room and board charges vary according to board plan and housing facility. Part-time tuition: $1025 per credit hour. Part-time tuition varies according to course load. **Scholarships:** Available **Calendar System:** Miscellaneous, Summer Session Available **Enrollment:** FT 3,318, PT 135, Grad FT 439, Grad PT 1,086 **Faculty:** FT 263, PT 102 **Student-Faculty Ratio:** 14:1 **Exams:** Other, SAT I or ACT. ACT essay not being used. SAT essay not being used. **% Receiving Financial Aid:** 70 **% Residing in College-Owned, -Operated, or -Affiliated Housing:** 50 **Library Holdings:** 272,022 **Regional Accreditation:** New England Association of Schools and Colleges **Credit Hours For Degree:** 45 courses, Bachelors **ROTC:** Army, Navy, Air Force **Professional Accreditation:** AACSB, ABET **Intercollegiate Athletics:** Baseball M; Basketball M & W; Crew M & W; Cross-Country Running M & W; Field Hockey W; Football M; Soccer M & W; Softball W; Swimming and Diving M & W; Track and Field M & W; Volleyball W; Water Polo M & W; Wrestling M

WORCESTER STATE COLLEGE
486 Chandler St.
Worcester, MA 01602-2597
Tel: (508)929-8000; Free: (866)WSC-CALL
Admissions: (508)929-8040
Fax: (508)929-8131
E-mail: admissions@worcester.edu
Web Site: http://www.worcester.edu/
President/CEO: Dr. Janelle C. Ashley
Admissions: Kim Albro
Financial Aid: Jayne McGinn
Type: Comprehensive **Sex:** Coed **Affiliation:** Massachusetts Public Higher Education System **Scores:** 96.02% SAT V 400+; 96.31% SAT M 400+; 68. 75% ACT 18-23; 22.92% ACT 24-29 **% Accepted:** 59 **Admission Plans:** Deferred Admission **Application Deadline:** February 1 **Application Fee:** $40.00 **H.S. Requirements:** High school diploma required; GED accepted **Costs Per Year:** Application fee: $40. State resident tuition: $970 full-time, $40.42 per credit part-time. Nonresident tuition: $7050 full-time, $293.75 per credit part-time. Mandatory fees: $5635 full-time, $224.37 per credit part-time. Full-time tuition and fees vary according to class time, course load, degree level, and reciprocity agreements. Part-time tuition and fees vary according to class time, course load, degree level, and reciprocity agreements. College room and board: $9067. College room only: $6267. Room and board charges vary according to board plan and housing facility. **Scholarships:** Available **Calendar System:** Semester, Summer Session Available **Enrollment:** FT 3,494, PT 1,209, Grad FT 149, Grad PT 621 **Faculty:** FT 179, PT 199 **Student-Faculty Ratio:** 17:1 **Exams:** SAT I or ACT. **% Receiving Financial Aid:** 49 **% Residing in College-Owned, -Operated, or -Affiliated Housing:** 24 **Final Year or Final Semester Residency Requirement:** No **Library Holdings:** 201,975 **Regional Accreditation:** New England Association of Schools and Colleges **Credit Hours For Degree:** 120 credits, Bachelors **ROTC:** Army, Navy, Air Force **Professional Accreditation:** AACN, AOTA, ASLHA, JRCNMT, NLN **Intercollegiate Athletics:** Baseball M; Basketball M & W; Crew W; Cross-Country Running M & W; Field Hockey W; Football M; Golf M; Ice Hockey M; Lacrosse W; Skiing (Downhill) M & W; Soccer M & W; Softball W; Tennis W; Track and Field M & W; Volleyball M & W

ZION BIBLE COLLEGE
320 South Main St.
Haverhill, MA 01835
Tel: (978)478-3400; Free: 800-356-4014
E-mail: admissions@zbc.edu
Web Site: http://www.zbc.edu/
President/CEO: Dr. Charles Crabtree
Admissions: Helen Brouillette
Type: Four-Year College **Sex:** Coed **Affiliation:** Assembly of God Church **Admission Plans:** Open Admission **Application Fee:** $35.00 **Calendar System:** Semester **Professional Accreditation:** ABHE

ADRIAN COLLEGE
110 South Madison St.
Adrian, MI 49221-2575
Tel: (517)265-5161; Free: 800-877-2246
Fax: (517)265-3331
E-mail: admissions@adrian.edu
Web Site: http://www.adrian.edu/
President/CEO: Dr. Jeffrey R. Docking
Admissions: Carolyn Quinlan
Financial Aid: Andrew Spohn
Type: Four-Year College **Sex:** Coed **Affiliation:** United Methodist Church **Scores:** 56% ACT 18-23; 37% ACT 24-29 **% Accepted:** 58 **Admission Plans:** Deferred Admission **Application Deadline:** March 15 **Application Fee:** $0.00 **H.S. Requirements:** High school diploma required; GED accepted **Costs Per Year:** Application fee: $0. Comprehensive fee: $31,900 includes full-time tuition ($24,140), mandatory fees ($300), and college room and board ($7460). College room only: $3610. Part-time tuition: $685 per credit hour. Part-time mandatory fees: $75 per term. **Scholarships:** Available **Calendar System:** Semester, Summer Session Available **Enrollment:** FT 1,420, PT 49 **Faculty:** FT 80, PT 97 **Student-Faculty Ratio:** 13:1 **Exams:** ACT, SAT I or ACT. **% Receiving Financial Aid:** 81 **% Residing in College-Owned, -Operated, or -Affiliated Housing:** 85 **Library Holdings:** 145,742 **Regional Accreditation:** North Central Association of Colleges and Schools **Credit Hours For Degree:** 62 credit hours, Associates; 124 credit hours, Bachelors **Intercollegiate Athletics:** Baseball M; Basketball M & W; Bowling W; Cross-Country Running M & W; Football M; Golf M & W; Ice Hockey M & W; Lacrosse M & W; Soccer M & W; Softball W; Tennis M & W; Track and Field M & W; Volleyball W

ALBION COLLEGE
611 East Porter St.
Albion, MI 49224-1831
Tel: (517)629-1000; Free: 800-858-6770
Admissions: (517)629-0600
Fax: (517)629-0569
E-mail: admissions@albion.edu
Web Site: http://www.albion.edu/
President/CEO: Dr. Donna Randall
Admissions: Doug Kellar
Financial Aid: Ann Whitmer
Type: Four-Year College **Sex:** Coed **Affiliation:** Methodist **Scores:** 98% SAT V 400+; 98% SAT M 400+; 28% ACT 18-23; 59% ACT 24-29 **% Accepted:** 83 **Admission Plans:** Early Action; Deferred Admission **Application Deadline:** May 1 **Application Fee:** $20.00 **H.S. Requirements:** High school diploma required; GED accepted **Costs Per Year:** Application fee: $20. Comprehensive fee: $38,512 includes full-time tuition ($29,488), mandatory fees ($514), and college room and board ($8510). College room only: $4162. Room and board charges vary according to housing facility. **Scholarships:** Available **Calendar System:** Semester, Summer Session Available **Enrollment:** FT 1,842, PT 18 **Faculty:** FT 138, PT 33 **Student-Faculty Ratio:** 12:1 **Exams:** SAT I or ACT. **% Receiving Financial Aid:** 65 **% Residing in College-Owned, -Operated, or -Affiliated Housing:** 90 **Library Holdings:** 363,870 **Regional Accreditation:** North Central Association of Colleges and Schools **Credit Hours For Degree:** 32 units, Bachelors **Professional Accreditation:** NASM **Intercollegiate Athletics:** Baseball M; Basketball M & W; Cheerleading M & W; Cross-Country Running M & W; Equestrian Sports M & W; Football M; Golf M & W; Soccer M & W; Softball W; Swimming and Diving M & W; Tennis M & W; Track and Field M & W; Volleyball M & W

ALMA COLLEGE
614 West Superior St.
Alma, MI 48801-1599
Tel: (989)463-7111; Free: 800-321-ALMA
Admissions: 800-321-2562
Fax: (989)463-7057
E-mail: admissions@alma.edu
Web Site: http://www.alma.edu/
President/CEO: Dr. Saundra J. Tracy
Admissions: Bob Garcia
Financial Aid: Christopher A. Brown
Type: Four-Year College **Sex:** Coed **Affiliation:** Presbyterian **Scores:** 95. 46% SAT V 400+; 100% SAT M 400+; 43.08% ACT 18-23; 45.9% ACT 24-29 **% Accepted:** 75 **Admission Plans:** Deferred Admission **Application Deadline:** Rolling **Application Fee:** $25.00 **H.S. Requirements:** High school diploma required; GED accepted **Costs Per Year:** Application fee: $25. Comprehensive fee: $34,586 includes full-time tuition ($25,838), mandatory fees ($230), and college room and board ($8518). College room only: $4196. Room and board charges vary according to board plan and housing facility. Part-time tuition: $1000 per credit hour. Part-time tuition varies according to course load. **Scholarships:** Available **Calendar System:** Miscellaneous, Summer Session Available **Enrollment:** FT 1,377, PT 67 **Faculty:** FT 85, PT 49 **Student-Faculty Ratio:** 14:1 **Exams:** SAT I or ACT. ACT essay not being used. SAT essay not being used. **% Receiving Financial Aid:** 81 **% Residing in College-Owned, -Operated, or -Affiliated Housing:** 87 **Library Holdings:** 279,901 **Regional Accreditation:** North Central Association of Colleges and Schools **Credit Hours For Degree:** 136 credits, Bachelors **ROTC:** Army **Professional Accreditation:** NASM **Intercollegiate Athletics:** Baseball M; Basketball M & W; Cross-Country Running M & W; Football M; Golf M & W; Soccer M & W; Softball W; Swimming and Diving M & W; Tennis M & W; Track and Field M & W; Volleyball W

ALPENA COMMUNITY COLLEGE
665 Johnson St.
Alpena, MI 49707-1495
Tel: (989)356-9021
Fax: (989)358-7553
E-mail: kollienm@alpenacc.edu
Web Site: http://www.alpenacc.edu/
President/CEO: Olin Joynton
Admissions: Mike Kollien
Type: Two-Year College **Sex:** Coed **% Accepted:** 100 **Admission Plans:** Open Admission; Early Admission; Deferred Admission **Application Deadline:** Rolling **Application Fee:** $0.00 **H.S. Requirements:** High school diploma or equivalent not required. For nursing, utility technician programs: High school diploma required; GED accepted **Costs Per Year:** Application fee: $0. Area resident tuition: $2760 full-time, $92 per contact hour part-time. State resident tuition: $4140 full-time, $138 per contact hour part-time. Nonresident tuition: $4740 full-time, $184 per contact hour part-time. Mandatory fees: $500 full-time, $16 per contact hour part-time. College room only:

$3000. **Scholarships:** Available **Calendar System:** Semester, Summer Session Available **Faculty:** FT 51, PT 74 **Student-Faculty Ratio:** 17:1 **% Residing in College-Owned, -Operated, or -Affiliated Housing:** 2 **Library Holdings:** 29,000 **Regional Accreditation:** North Central Association of Colleges and Schools **Credit Hours For Degree:** 60 semester hours, Associates **Professional Accreditation:** AAMAE, ACBSP **Intercollegiate Athletics:** Basketball M & W; Golf M; Softball W; Volleyball W

ANDREWS UNIVERSITY
Berrien Springs, MI 49104
Tel: (269)471-7771; Free: 800-253-2874
Fax: (269)471-3228
E-mail: enroll@andrews.edu
Web Site: http://www.andrews.edu/
President/CEO: Dr. Niels-Erik Andreasen
Admissions: Shanna Leak
Financial Aid: Cynthia Gammon
Type: University **Sex:** Coed **Affiliation:** Seventh-day Adventist **Scores:** 91% SAT V 400+; 90% SAT M 400+; 41% ACT 18-23; 20% ACT 24-29 **% Accepted:** 49 **Admission Plans:** Deferred Admission **Application Deadline:** Rolling **Application Fee:** $30.00 **H.S. Requirements:** High school diploma required; GED accepted **Costs Per Year:** Application fee: $30. Comprehensive fee: $28,030 includes full-time tuition ($20,520), mandatory fees ($650), and college room and board ($6860). College room only: $3510. Full-time tuition and fees vary according to course load. Room and board charges vary according to board plan. Part-time tuition: $855 per credit hour. Part-time tuition varies according to course load. **Scholarships:** Available **Calendar System:** Semester, Summer Session Available **Enrollment:** FT 1,714, PT 250, Grad FT 694, Grad PT 931 **Faculty:** FT 218, PT 59 **Student-Faculty Ratio:** 13:1 **Exams:** SAT I or ACT. **% Receiving Financial Aid:** 67 **% Residing in College-Owned, -Operated, or -Affiliated Housing:** 57 **Library Holdings:** 727,764 **Regional Accreditation:** North Central Association of Colleges and Schools **Credit Hours For Degree:** 62 semester hours, Associates; 124 semester hours, Bachelors **Professional Accreditation:** ACA, ADtA, APTA, ATS, CSWE, NAACLS, NASM, NCATE, NLN

AQUINAS COLLEGE
1607 Robinson Rd., SE
Grand Rapids, MI 49506-1799
Tel: (616)459-8281; Free: 800-678-9593
Admissions: (616)632-2851
Fax: (616)459-2563
E-mail: admissions@aquinas.edu
Web Site: http://www.aquinas.edu/
President/CEO: Dr. C. Edward Balog
Admissions: Vicki Bassett
Financial Aid: David J. Steffee
Type: Comprehensive **Sex:** Coed **Affiliation:** Roman Catholic **Scores:** 53% ACT 18-23; 37% ACT 24-29 **% Accepted:** 80 **Admission Plans:** Early Admission; Deferred Admission **Application Deadline:** Rolling **Application Fee:** $0.00 **H.S. Requirements:** High school diploma required; GED not accepted **Costs Per Year:** Application fee: $0. Comprehensive fee: $29,328 includes full-time tuition ($22,314) and college room and board ($7014). College room only: $3238. Full-time tuition varies according to course load. Room and board charges vary according to board plan and housing facility. Part-time tuition: $452 per credit hour. Part-time tuition varies according to course load. **Scholarships:** Available **Calendar System:** Semester, Summer Session Available **Enrollment:** FT 1,635, PT 273, Grad FT 36, Grad PT 201 **Faculty:** FT 94, PT 150 **Student-Faculty Ratio:** 13:1 **Exams:** SAT I or ACT. ACT essay not being used. SAT essay not being used. **% Receiving Financial Aid:** 72 **% Residing in College-Owned, -Operated, or -Affiliated Housing:** 47 **Final Year or Final Semester Residency Requirement:** No **Library Holdings:** 100,014 **Regional Accreditation:** North Central Association of Colleges and Schools **Credit Hours For Degree:** 64 credits, Associates; 124 credits, Bachelors **Professional Accreditation:** TEAC **Intercollegiate Athletics:** Baseball M; Basketball M & W; Cross-Country Running M & W; Golf M & W; Lacrosse M & W; Soccer M & W; Softball W; Tennis M & W; Track and Field M & W; Volleyball W

THE ART INSTITUTE OF MICHIGAN
28125 Cabot Dr.
Ste. 120
Novi, MI 48377
Tel: (248)675-3800; Free: 800-479-0087
Fax: (248)675-3830
Web Site: http://www.artinstitutes.edu/detroit/
President/CEO: Marc Sherrod
Type: Four-Year College **Sex:** Coed **Affiliation:** Education Management Corporation **Regional Accreditation:** North Central Association of Colleges and Schools

BAKER COLLEGE OF ALLEN PARK
4500 Enterprise Dr.
Allen Park, MI 48101
Tel: (313)425-3700
E-mail: steve.peterson@baker.edu
Web Site: http://www.baker.edu/
President/CEO: Aaron Maike
Admissions: Steve Peterson
Type: Four-Year College **Sex:** Coed **Affiliation:** Baker College System **% Accepted:** 100 **Admission Plans:** Deferred Admission **Application Deadline:** September 24 **Application Fee:** $0.00 **H.S. Requirements:** High school diploma required; GED accepted **Costs Per Year:** Application fee: $0. Tuition: $7380 full-time, $205 per quarter hour part-time. Full-time tuition varies according to program. Part-time tuition varies according to program. **Calendar System:** Quarter, Summer Session Available **Enrollment:** FT 2,030, PT 1,354 **Faculty:** FT 2, PT 86 **Student-Faculty Ratio:** 34:1 **Exams:** SAT I or ACT. **Regional Accreditation:** North Central Association of Colleges and Schools **Credit Hours For Degree:** 90 quarter hours, Associates; 180 quarter hours, Bachelors

BAKER COLLEGE OF AUBURN HILLS
1500 University Dr.
Auburn Hills, MI 48326-1586
Tel: (248)340-0600
E-mail: jan.bohlen@baker.edu
Web Site: http://www.baker.edu/
President/CEO: Jeff Love
Admissions: Jan Bohlen
Type: Four-Year College **Sex:** Coed **Affiliation:** Baker College System **% Accepted:** 100 **Admission Plans:** Open Admission; Early Admission; Deferred Admission **Application Deadline:** Rolling **Application Fee:** $20.00 **H.S. Requirements:** High school diploma required; GED accepted **Costs Per Year:** Application fee: $20. Tuition: $7380 full-time, $205 per quarter hour part-time. **Calendar System:** Quarter, Summer Session Available **Enrollment:** FT 2,271, PT 2,014 **Faculty:** FT 11, PT 144 **Student-Faculty Ratio:** 41:1 **Exams:** SAT I or ACT. **Library Holdings:** 5,400 **Regional Accreditation:** North Central Association of Colleges and Schools **Credit Hours For Degree:** 90 quarter hours, Associates; 180 quarter hours, Bachelors **Professional Accreditation:** AAMAE

BAKER COLLEGE OF CADILLAC
9600 East 13th St.
Cadillac, MI 49601
Tel: (231)876-3100
Fax: (231)775-8505
E-mail: mike.tisdale@baker.edu
Web Site: http://www.baker.edu/
President/CEO: Robert Van Dellen
Admissions: Mike Tisdale
Type: Four-Year College **Sex:** Coed **Affiliation:** Baker College System **% Accepted:** 100 **Admission Plans:** Open Admission; Early Admission; Deferred Admission **Application Deadline:** September 24 **Application Fee:** $20.00 **H.S. Requirements:** High school diploma required; GED accepted **Costs Per Year:** Application fee: $20. Tuition: $7380 full-time, $205 per quarter hour part-time. Full-time tuition varies according to program. Part-time tuition varies according to program. **Calendar System:** Quarter, Summer Session Available **Enrollment:** FT 1,242, PT 828 **Faculty:** FT 4, PT 101 **Student-Faculty Ratio:** 42:1 **Exams:** SAT I or ACT. **Library Holdings:** 4,000 **Regional Accreditation:** North Central Association of Colleges and Schools **Credit Hours For Degree:** 90 quarter hours, Associates; 180 quarter hours, Bachelors **Professional Accreditation:** ARCEST, AAMAE

BAKER COLLEGE OF CLINTON TOWNSHIP
34950 Little Mack Ave.
Clinton Township, MI 48035-4701
Tel: (586)791-6610; Free: 888-272-2842
Admissions: (586)790-3000

Fax: (586)791-6611
E-mail: annette.looser@baker.edu
Web Site: http://www.baker.edu/
President/CEO: Donald Torline
Admissions: Annette Looser
Type: Four-Year College **Sex:** Coed **Affiliation:** Baker College System **% Accepted:** 100 **Admission Plans:** Open Admission; Early Admission; Deferred Admission **Application Deadline:** Rolling **Application Fee:** $20.00 **H.S. Requirements:** High school diploma required; GED accepted **Costs Per Year:** Application fee: $20. Tuition: $7380 full-time, $205 per quarter hour part-time. Full-time tuition varies according to program. Part-time tuition varies according to program. **Calendar System:** Quarter, Summer Session Available **Enrollment:** FT 3,744, PT 2,711 **Faculty:** FT 17, PT 191 **Student-Faculty Ratio:** 45:1 **Exams:** SAT I or ACT. **Library Holdings:** 8,000 **Regional Accreditation:** North Central Association of Colleges and Schools **Credit Hours For Degree:** 90 quarter hours, Associates; 180 quarter hours, Bachelors **Professional Accreditation:** ARCEST, AAMAE, AHIMA

BAKER COLLEGE OF FLINT
1050 West Bristol Rd.
Flint, MI 48507-5508
Tel: (810)767-7600; Free: 800-964-4299
Admissions: (810)766-4008
Fax: (810)766-4049
Web Site: http://www.baker.edu/
President/CEO: Dr. Julianne T. Princinsky
Admissions: Jodi Cunez
Type: Four-Year College **Sex:** Coed **Affiliation:** Baker College System **% Accepted:** 100 **Admission Plans:** Open Admission; Early Admission; Deferred Admission **Application Deadline:** September 20 **Application Fee:** $20.00 **H.S. Requirements:** High school diploma required; GED accepted **Costs Per Year:** Application fee: $20. Tuition: $7380 full-time, $205 per quarter hour part-time. Full-time tuition varies according to program. Part-time tuition varies according to program. College room only: $3000. Room charges vary according to housing facility. **Calendar System:** Quarter, Summer Session Available **Enrollment:** FT 4,456, PT 2,849 **Faculty:** FT 40, PT 275 **Student-Faculty Ratio:** 31:1 **Exams:** SAT I or ACT. **% Residing in College-Owned, -Operated, or -Affiliated Housing:** 2 **Library Holdings:** 168,700 **Regional Accreditation:** North Central Association of Colleges and Schools **Credit Hours For Degree:** 90 quarter hours, Associates; 180 quarter hours, Bachelors **Professional Accreditation:** ARCEST, AAMAE, AHIMA, APTA

BAKER COLLEGE OF JACKSON
2800 Springport Rd.
Jackson, MI 49202
Tel: (517)789-6123; Free: 888-343-3683
Admissions: (517)788-7800
E-mail: kevin.pnacek@baker.edu
Web Site: http://www.baker.edu/
President/CEO: Patty Kaufman
Admissions: Kevin Pnacek
Type: Four-Year College **Sex:** Coed **Affiliation:** Baker College System **% Accepted:** 100 **Admission Plans:** Open Admission; Early Admission; Deferred Admission **Application Deadline:** September 19 **Application Fee:** $20.00 **H.S. Requirements:** High school diploma required; GED accepted **Costs Per Year:** Application fee: $20. Tuition: $7380 full-time, $205 per quarter hour part-time. Mandatory fees: $20 full-time. Full-time tuition and fees vary according to program. Part-time tuition varies according to program. **Calendar System:** Quarter, Summer Session Available **Enrollment:** FT 1,386, PT 1,046 **Faculty:** FT 5, PT 80 **Student-Faculty Ratio:** 36:1 **Exams:** SAT I or ACT. **Library Holdings:** 7,000 **Regional Accreditation:** North Central Association of Colleges and Schools **Credit Hours For Degree:** 90 quarter hours, Associates; 180 quarter hours, Bachelors **Professional Accreditation:** ARCEST, AAMAE, AHIMA, JRCERT

BAKER COLLEGE OF MUSKEGON
1903 Marquette Ave.
Muskegon, MI 49442-3497
Tel: (231)777-5200
Admissions: (231)777-5207
Fax: (231)777-5201
E-mail: kathy.jacobson@baker.edu
Web Site: http://www.baker.edu/
President/CEO: Dr. Mary Ann Herbst
Admissions: Kathy Jacobson
Type: Four-Year College **Sex:** Coed **Affiliation:** Baker College System **% Accepted:** 100 **Admission Plans:** Open Admission; Early Admission; Deferred Admission **Application Deadline:** September 24 **Application Fee:** $20.00 **H.S. Requirements:** High school diploma required; GED accepted **Costs Per Year:** Application fee: $20. Tuition: $7380 full-time, $205 per quarter hour part-time. Mandatory fees: $20 full-time. Full-time tuition and fees vary according to program. Part-time tuition varies according to program. College room only: $3000. **Calendar System:** Quarter, Summer Session Available **Enrollment:** FT 3,864, PT 2,269 **Faculty:** FT 17, PT 160 **Student-Faculty Ratio:** 55:1 **Exams:** SAT I or ACT. **% Residing in College-Owned, -Operated, or -Affiliated Housing:** 11 **Library Holdings:** 32,000 **Regional Accreditation:** North Central Association of Colleges and Schools **Credit Hours For Degree:** 90 quarter hours, Associates; 180 quarter hours, Bachelors **Professional Accreditation:** ARCEST, AAMAE, ACF, AHIMA, AOTA, APTA

BAKER COLLEGE OF OWOSSO
1020 South Washington St.
Owosso, MI 48867-4400
Tel: (989)729-3300; Free: 800-879-3797
Admissions: (989)729-3350
Fax: (989)729-3411
E-mail: mike.konopacke@baker.edu
Web Site: http://www.baker.edu/
President/CEO: Pete Karsten
Admissions: Michael Konopacke
Type: Four-Year College **Sex:** Coed **Affiliation:** Baker College System **% Accepted:** 100 **Admission Plans:** Open Admission; Early Admission; Deferred Admission **Application Deadline:** Rolling **Application Fee:** $20.00 **H.S. Requirements:** High school diploma required; GED accepted **Costs Per Year:** Application fee: $20. Tuition: $7380 full-time, $205 per quarter hour part-time. Mandatory fees: $20 full-time. Full-time tuition and fees vary according to program. Part-time tuition varies according to program. College room only: $2700. Room charges vary according to housing facility. **Calendar System:** Quarter, Summer Session Available **Enrollment:** FT 2,473, PT 1,164 **Faculty:** FT 8, PT 136 **Student-Faculty Ratio:** 40:1 **Exams:** SAT I or ACT. **% Residing in College-Owned, -Operated, or -Affiliated Housing:** 15 **Library Holdings:** 35,424 **Regional Accreditation:** North Central Association of Colleges and Schools **Credit Hours For Degree:** 90 quarter hours, Associates; 180 quarter hours, Bachelors **Professional Accreditation:** AAMAE, JRCERT, NAACLS

BAKER COLLEGE OF PORT HURON
3403 Lapeer Rd.
Port Huron, MI 48060-2597
Tel: (810)985-7000; Free: 888-262-2442
Fax: (810)985-7066
E-mail: kenny_d@porthuron.baker.edu
Web Site: http://www.baker.edu/
President/CEO: Connie Harrison
Admissions: Daniel Kenny
Type: Four-Year College **Sex:** Coed **Affiliation:** Baker College System **% Accepted:** 100 **Admission Plans:** Open Admission; Early Admission; Deferred Admission **Application Deadline:** September 24 **Application Fee:** $20.00 **H.S. Requirements:** High school diploma required; GED accepted **Costs Per Year:** Application fee: $20. Tuition: $7380 full-time, $205 per quarter hour part-time. Full-time tuition varies according to program. Part-time tuition varies according to program. **Calendar System:** Quarter, Summer Session Available **Enrollment:** FT 1,369, PT 615 **Faculty:** FT 12, PT 114 **Student-Faculty Ratio:** 28:1 **Exams:** SAT I or ACT. **Library Holdings:** 16,823 **Regional Accreditation:** North Central Association of Colleges and Schools **Credit Hours For Degree:** 90 quarter hours, Associates; 180 quarter hours, Bachelors **Professional Accreditation:** ARCEST, AAMAE, ADA

BAY MILLS COMMUNITY COLLEGE
12214 West Lakeshore Dr.
Brimley, MI 49715
Tel: (906)248-3354; Free: 800-844-BMCC
Fax: (906)248-3351
Web Site: http://www.bmcc.edu/
President/CEO: Michael C. Parish

Admissions: Elaine Lehre
Type: Two-Year College **Sex:** Coed **Admission Plans:** Open Admission; Early Admission **Application Deadline:** Rolling **H.S. Requirements:** High school diploma required; GED accepted **Scholarships:** Available **Calendar System:** Semester **Regional Accreditation:** North Central Association of Colleges and Schools **Credit Hours For Degree:** 63 credits, Associates

BAY DE NOC COMMUNITY COLLEGE
2001 North Lincoln Rd.
Escanaba, MI 49829-2511
Tel: (906)786-5802; Free: 800-221-2001
Fax: (906)786-6555
E-mail: carterc@baycollege.edu
Web Site: http://www.baydenoc.cc.mi.us/
President/CEO: Dr. Laura Coleman
Admissions: Cindy Carter
Financial Aid: Susan Hebert
Type: Two-Year College **Sex:** Coed **Affiliation:** Michigan Department of Education **Admission Plans:** Open Admission; Early Admission **Application Deadline:** August 15 **Application Fee:** $25.00 **H.S. Requirements:** High school diploma required; GED accepted **Costs Per Year:** Application fee: $25. One-time mandatory fee: $25. Area resident tuition: $2475 full-time, $82.50 per contact hour part-time. State resident tuition: $4125 full-time, $137.50 per contact hour part-time. Nonresident tuition: $5235 full-time, $174.50 per contact hour part-time. Mandatory fees: $330 full-time, $11.25 per contact hour part-time. Full-time tuition and fees vary according to course load, location, and reciprocity agreements. Part-time tuition and fees vary according to course load, location, and reciprocity agreements. College room only: $2800. Room charges vary according to housing facility. **Scholarships:** Available **Calendar System:** Semester, Summer Session Available **Enrollment:** FT 1,400, PT 1,014 **Faculty:** FT 46, PT 117 **Student-Faculty Ratio:** 20:1 **% Residing in College-Owned, -Operated, or -Affiliated Housing:** 4 **Library Holdings:** 63,643 **Regional Accreditation:** North Central Association of Colleges and Schools **Credit Hours For Degree:** 62 credit hours, Associates

CALVIN COLLEGE
3201 Burton St., SE
Grand Rapids, MI 49546-4388
Tel: (616)526-6000; Free: 800-688-0122
Admissions: (616)526-6106
Fax: (616)526-8551
E-mail: admissions@calvin.edu
Web Site: http://www.calvin.edu/
President/CEO: Gaylen Byker
Admissions: Dale Kuiper
Financial Aid: Craig Heerema
Type: Comprehensive **Sex:** Coed **Affiliation:** Christian Reformed **Scores:** 98% SAT V 400+; 98.4% SAT M 400+; 28.6% ACT 18-23; 49.2% ACT 24-29 **% Accepted:** 93 **Admission Plans:** Deferred Admission **Application Deadline:** August 15 **Application Fee:** $35.00 **H.S. Requirements:** High school diploma required; GED accepted **Costs Per Year:** Application fee: $35. Comprehensive fee: $32,310 includes full-time tuition ($23,810), mandatory fees ($225), and college room and board ($8275). Full-time tuition and fees vary according to degree level and program. Room and board charges vary according to board plan. Part-time tuition: $570 per credit hour. Part-time tuition varies according to course load and degree level. **Scholarships:** Available **Calendar System:** 4-1-4, Summer Session Available **Enrollment:** FT 3,883, PT 132, Grad FT 12, Grad PT 65 **Faculty:** FT 326, PT 69 **Student-Faculty Ratio:** 11:1 **Exams:** SAT I or ACT. ACT essay not being used. SAT essay not being used. **% Receiving Financial Aid:** 65 **% Residing in College-Owned, -Operated, or -Affiliated Housing:** 57 **Final Year or Final Semester Residency Requirement:** No **Library Holdings:** 493,213 **Regional Accreditation:** North Central Association of Colleges and Schools **Credit Hours For Degree:** 124 semester hours, Bachelors **ROTC:** Army **Professional Accreditation:** ABET, CSWE, NASM, NCATE, NLN, TEAC **Intercollegiate Athletics:** Baseball M; Basketball M & W; Crew M & W; Cross-Country Running M & W; Golf M & W; Ice Hockey M; Lacrosse M & W; Rock Climbing M & W; Rugby M; Soccer M & W; Softball W; Swimming and Diving M & W; Tennis M & W; Track and Field M & W; Ultimate Frisbee M & W; Volleyball M & W

CENTRAL MICHIGAN UNIVERSITY
Mount Pleasant, MI 48859
Tel: (989)774-4000; Free: 888-292-5366
Admissions: (989)774-3076
Fax: (989)774-3537
Web Site: http://www.cmich.edu/x22.xml
President/CEO: Dr. George Ross
Admissions: Betty J. Wagner
Financial Aid: Kirk Yats
Type: University **Sex:** Coed **Scores:** 89.2% SAT V 400+; 90.5% SAT M 400+; 61% ACT 18-23; 30.4% ACT 24-29 **% Accepted:** 73 **Admission Plans:** Early Admission; Early Action; Deferred Admission **Application Deadline:** Rolling **Application Fee:** $35.00 **H.S. Requirements:** High school diploma required; GED accepted **Costs Per Year:** Application fee: $35. State resident tuition: $10,170 full-time, $339 per credit hour part-time. Nonresident tuition: $23,670 full-time, $789 per credit hour part-time. Full-time tuition varies according to student level. Part-time tuition varies according to student level. College room and board: $7896. College room only: $3948. Room and board charges vary according to board plan, housing facility, location, and student level. **Scholarships:** Available **Calendar System:** Semester, Summer Session Available **Enrollment:** FT 18,253, PT 2,327, Grad FT 1,899, Grad PT 4,767 **Faculty:** FT 752, PT 438 **Student-Faculty Ratio:** 21:1 **Exams:** ACT. ACT essay used for advising. ACT essay used for placement. **% Receiving Financial Aid:** 54 **% Residing in College-Owned, -Operated, or -Affiliated Housing:** 33 **Library Holdings:** 1,221,815 **Regional Accreditation:** North Central Association of Colleges and Schools **Credit Hours For Degree:** 124 credits, Bachelors **ROTC:** Army **Professional Accreditation:** AACSB, ACEJMC, ADtA, APTA, APA, ASLHA, CSWE, JRCEPAT, NASAD, NASM, NCATE, NRPA, TEAC **Intercollegiate Athletics:** Baseball M; Basketball M & W; Cross-Country Running M & W; Field Hockey W; Football M; Gymnastics W; Soccer W; Softball W; Track and Field M & W; Volleyball W; Wrestling M

CLEARY UNIVERSITY
3601 Plymouth Rd.
Ann Arbor, MI 48105-2659
Tel: (517)548-3670; Free: 888-5-CLEARY
Admissions: (517)338-3330
E-mail: admissions@cleary.edu
Web Site: http://www.cleary.edu/
President/CEO: Thomas P. Sullivan
Admissions: Charlotte Paquette
Financial Aid: Vesta Smith-Campbell
Type: Comprehensive **Sex:** Coed **Scores:** 50% ACT 18-23; 27% ACT 24-29 **% Accepted:** 85 **Admission Plans:** Early Admission; Deferred Admission **Application Deadline:** August 15 **Application Fee:** $25.00 **H.S. Requirements:** High school diploma required; GED accepted **Costs Per Year:** Application fee: $25. Tuition: $15,600 full-time, $325 per quarter hour part-time. Full-time tuition varies according to degree level. Tuition guaranteed not to increase for student's term of enrollment. **Scholarships:** Available **Calendar System:** Quarter, Summer Session Available **Enrollment:** FT 413, PT 240, Grad FT 100, Grad PT 21 **Faculty:** FT 4, PT 146 **Student-Faculty Ratio:** 10:1 **Exams:** SAT I or ACT, SAT II. **% Receiving Financial Aid:** 64 **Regional Accreditation:** North Central Association of Colleges and Schools **Credit Hours For Degree:** 90 quarter hours, Associates; 180 quarter hours, Bachelors

COLLEGE FOR CREATIVE STUDIES
201 East Kirby
Detroit, MI 48202-4034
Tel: (313)664-7400; Free: 800-872-2739
Fax: (313)872-2739
E-mail: admissions@ccscad.edu
Web Site: http://www.collegeforcreativestudies.edu/
President/CEO: Richard L. Rogers
Type: Comprehensive **Sex:** Coed **Scores:** 53% ACT 18-23; 25% ACT 24-29 **% Accepted:** 39 **Admission Plans:** Deferred Admission **Application Deadline:** August 1 **Application Fee:** $35.00 **H.S. Requirements:** High school diploma required; GED accepted **Costs Per Year:** Application fee: $35. Comprehensive fee: $39,775 includes full-time tuition ($29,940), mandatory fees ($1335), and college room and board ($8500). College room only: $4900. Full-time tuition and fees vary according to course load. Room and board charges vary according to board plan and housing facility. Part-time tuition: $998 per credit hour. Part-time tuition varies according to course load. **Scholarships:** Available **Calendar System:** Semester, Summer Session Available **Faculty:** FT 58, PT 190 **Student-Faculty Ratio:** 11:1 **Exams:** SAT I or ACT. **% Residing in College-Owned, -Operated, or -Affiliated**

Housing: 29 **Regional Accreditation:** North Central Association of Colleges and Schools **Credit Hours For Degree:** 126 credit hours, Bachelors **Professional Accreditation:** NASAD

CONCORDIA UNIVERSITY
4090 Geddes Rd.
Ann Arbor, MI 48105-2797
Tel: (734)995-7300; Free: 800-253-0680
Admissions: (734)995-7450
Fax: (734)995-4610
E-mail: admissions@cuaa.edu
Web Site: http://www.cuaa.edu/
President/CEO: Rev. Thomas Ahlersmeyer
Admissions: Amy Becher
Financial Aid: Karen Neuendorf
Type: Comprehensive **Sex:** Coed **Affiliation:** Lutheran Church–Missouri Synod; Concordia University System **Scores:** 100% SAT V 400+; 93% SAT M 400+; 48% ACT 18-23; 39% ACT 24-29 **% Accepted:** 66 **Admission Plans:** Deferred Admission **Application Deadline:** Rolling **Application Fee:** $25.00 **H.S. Requirements:** High school diploma required; GED accepted **Costs Per Year:** Application fee: $25. One-time mandatory fee: $125. Comprehensive fee: $27,996 includes full-time tuition ($20,390) and college room and board ($7606). Full-time tuition varies according to location and program. Room and board charges vary according to housing facility. Part-time tuition: $673 per credit hour. Part-time tuition varies according to course load, location, and program. **Scholarships:** Available **Calendar System:** Semester, Summer Session Available **Enrollment:** FT 428, PT 93 **Faculty:** FT 39, PT 56 **Student-Faculty Ratio:** 17:1 **Exams:** ACT, SAT I or ACT. **% Receiving Financial Aid:** 78 **Regional Accreditation:** North Central Association of Colleges and Schools **Credit Hours For Degree:** 60 semester hours, Associates; 128 semester hours, Bachelors **ROTC:** Army, Air Force **Professional Accreditation:** NCATE **Intercollegiate Athletics:** Baseball M; Basketball M & W; Cross-Country Running M & W; Golf M & W; Soccer M & W; Softball W; Volleyball W

CORNERSTONE UNIVERSITY
1001 East Beltline Ave., NE
Grand Rapids, MI 49525-5897
Tel: (616)949-5300; Free: 800-787-9778
Admissions: (616)222-1426
Fax: (616)222-1540
E-mail: admissions@cornerstone.edu
Web Site: http://www.cornerstone.edu/
President/CEO: Dr. Joseph Stowell, III
Financial Aid: Scott W. Stewart
Type: Comprehensive **Sex:** Coed **Affiliation:** nondenominational **Scores:** 96% SAT V 400+; 95% SAT M 400+; 52% ACT 18-23; 39% ACT 24-29 **% Accepted:** 79 **Admission Plans:** Deferred Admission **Application Deadline:** Rolling **Application Fee:** $25.00 **H.S. Requirements:** High school diploma required; GED accepted **Costs Per Year:** Application fee: $25. Comprehensive fee: $27,030 includes full-time tuition ($19,960), mandatory fees ($560), and college room and board ($6510). Full-time tuition and fees vary according to course load and reciprocity agreements. Room and board charges vary according to board plan. Part-time tuition: $765 per credit hour. Part-time tuition varies according to course load. **Scholarships:** Available **Calendar System:** Semester, Summer Session Available **Enrollment:** FT 1,427, PT 465, Grad FT 406, Grad PT 308 **Faculty:** FT 58, PT 70 **Student-Faculty Ratio:** 20:1 **Exams:** SAT I or ACT. ACT essay used for advising. ACT essay used for placement. **% Receiving Financial Aid:** 84 **% Residing in College-Owned, -Operated, or -Affiliated Housing:** 49 **Final Year or Final Semester Residency Requirement:** No **Library Holdings:** 160,815 **Regional Accreditation:** North Central Association of Colleges and Schools **Credit Hours For Degree:** 64 credit hours, Associates; 120 credit hours, Bachelors **ROTC:** Army **Professional Accreditation:** CSWE, NASM **Intercollegiate Athletics:** Basketball M & W; Cross-Country Running M & W; Golf M & W; Soccer M & W; Softball W; Track and Field M & W; Volleyball W

DAVENPORT UNIVERSITY
415 East Fulton
Grand Rapids, MI 49503
Tel: (616)451-3511; Free: 800-632-9569
Fax: (616)732-1142
E-mail: heather.knechtel@davenport.edu
Web Site: http://www.davenport.edu/
President/CEO: Dr. Richard Pappas
Admissions: Heather Knechtel
Financial Aid: David DeBoer
Type: Comprehensive **Sex:** Coed **Admission Plans:** Deferred Admission **Application Deadline:** Rolling **Application Fee:** $25.00 **H.S. Requirements:** High school diploma required; GED accepted **Costs Per Year:** Application fee: $25. Comprehensive fee: $20,741 includes full-time tuition ($11,016), mandatory fees ($225), and college room and board ($9500). Full-time tuition and fees vary according to location. Room and board charges vary according to board plan and housing facility. Part-time tuition: $459 per credit hour. Part-time tuition varies according to location. **Scholarships:** Available **Calendar System:** Semester, Summer Session Available **Enrollment:** FT 3,358, PT 6,672, Grad FT 938, Grad PT 538 **Faculty:** FT 157, PT 797 **Student-Faculty Ratio:** 14:1 **Exams:** SAT I or ACT. **% Residing in College-Owned, -Operated, or -Affiliated Housing:** 4 **Library Holdings:** 82,078 **Regional Accreditation:** North Central Association of Colleges and Schools **Credit Hours For Degree:** 90 credit hours, Associates; 184.5 credit hours, Bachelors **Professional Accreditation:** AAMAE **Intercollegiate Athletics:** Basketball M & W; Bowling M & W; Cheerleading W; Cross-Country Running M & W; Golf M & W; Ice Hockey M; Lacrosse M & W; Rugby M; Soccer M & W; Track and Field M & W; Volleyball W

DELTA COLLEGE
1961 Delta Rd.
University Center, MI 48710
Tel: (989)686-9000; Free: 800-285-1705
Admissions: (989)686-9590
Fax: (989)686-8736
E-mail: admit@delta.edu
Web Site: http://www.delta.edu/
President/CEO: Dr. Jean Goodnow
Admissions: Gary Brasseur
Type: Two-Year College **Sex:** Coed **% Accepted:** 100 **Admission Plans:** Open Admission; Early Admission; Deferred Admission **Application Deadline:** Rolling **Application Fee:** $20.00 **H.S. Requirements:** High school diploma or equivalent not required. For international students: High school diploma required; GED accepted **Costs Per Year:** Application fee: $20. Area resident tuition: $1968 full-time, $82 per credit hour part-time. State resident tuition: $2976 full-time, $124 per credit hour part-time. Nonresident tuition: $4320 full-time, $180 per credit hour part-time. Mandatory fees: $360 full-time, $30 per term part-time. Full-time tuition and fees vary according to course load. Part-time tuition and fees vary according to course load. **Scholarships:** Available **Calendar System:** Semester, Summer Session Available **Enrollment:** FT 4,499, PT 6,400 **Faculty:** FT 219, PT 308 **Student-Faculty Ratio:** 20:1 **Library Holdings:** 110,985 **Regional Accreditation:** North Central Association of Colleges and Schools **Credit Hours For Degree:** 62 semester hours, Associates **Professional Accreditation:** ABET, ARCEST, ADA, APTA, CARC, JRCEDMS, JRCERT, NLN **Intercollegiate Athletics:** Basketball M & W; Soccer M; Softball W; Volleyball W

DEVRY UNIVERSITY
26999 Central Park Blvd., Ste. 125
Southfield, MI 48076
Tel: (248)213-1610
Fax: (248)353-1804
Web Site: http://www.devry.edu/
President/CEO: Georgianna Bailey
Financial Aid: Stephen Haworth
Type: Four-Year College **Sex:** Coed **Admission Plans:** Deferred Admission **Application Deadline:** Rolling **Application Fee:** $50.00 **H.S. Requirements:** High school diploma required; GED accepted **Costs Per Year:** Application fee: $50. Tuition: $14,080 full-time, $550 per credit hour part-time. **Scholarships:** Available **Calendar System:** Semester **Enrollment:** FT 28, PT 60 **Faculty:** FT 0, PT 14 **Student-Faculty Ratio:** 10:1 **Exams:** ACT essay used for admission. SAT essay used for admission. ACT essay used for placement. SAT essay used for placement. **% Receiving Financial Aid:** 100 **Regional Accreditation:** North Central Association of Colleges and Schools

EASTERN MICHIGAN UNIVERSITY
Ypsilanti, MI 48197
Tel: (734)487-1849; Free: 800-GO TO EMU
Admissions: (734)487-3060

Fax: (734)487-1484
Web Site: http://www.emich.edu/
President/CEO: Dr. Susan W. Martin
Admissions: Kathy Orscheln
Financial Aid: Cynthia Van Pelt
Type: Comprehensive **Sex:** Coed **Scores:** 90.41% SAT V 400+; 89.04% SAT M 400+; 54.24% ACT 18-23; 23.88% ACT 24-29 **% Accepted:** 71 **Admission Plans:** Deferred Admission **Application Deadline:** Rolling **Application Fee:** $30.00 **H.S. Requirements:** High school diploma required; GED accepted **Costs Per Year:** Application fee: $30. One-time mandatory fee: $300. State resident tuition: $7148 full-time, $238 per credit hour part-time. Nonresident tuition: $21,053 full-time, $701.75 per credit hour part-time. Mandatory fees: $1230 full-time, $38 per credit hour part-time, $44.75 per term part-time. Full-time tuition and fees vary according to course level and reciprocity agreements. Part-time tuition and fees vary according to course level and reciprocity agreements. College room and board: $7785. College room only: $3656. Room and board charges vary according to board plan, housing facility, and location. **Scholarships:** Available **Calendar System:** Semester, Summer Session Available **Enrollment:** FT 12,816, PT 4,947, Grad FT 1,083, Grad PT 4,013 **Faculty:** FT 780, PT 535 **Student-Faculty Ratio:** 18:1 **Exams:** SAT I or ACT. ACT essay not being used. SAT essay not being used. **% Receiving Financial Aid:** 47 **% Residing in College-Owned, -Operated, or -Affiliated Housing:** 16 **Library Holdings:** 995,386 **Regional Accreditation:** North Central Association of Colleges and Schools **Credit Hours For Degree:** 124 semester hours, Bachelors **ROTC:** Army, Navy, Air Force **Professional Accreditation:** AACSB, AACN, ACCE, ACA, ADtA, ACSP, AOTA, ASLHA, FIDER, CSWE, JRCEPAT, NAACLS, NASM, NASPAA, NCATE, NRPA, NAIT **Intercollegiate Athletics:** Baseball M; Basketball M & W; Crew W; Cross-Country Running M & W; Football M; Golf M & W; Gymnastics W; Soccer W; Softball W; Swimming and Diving M & W; Tennis W; Track and Field M & W; Volleyball W; Wrestling M

FERRIS STATE UNIVERSITY
1201 South State St.
Big Rapids, MI 49307
Tel: (231)591-2000; Free: 800-433-7747
Fax: (231)591-2978
E-mail: admissions@ferris.edu
Web Site: http://www.ferris.edu/
President/CEO: Dr. David Eisler
Admissions: Troy Tissue
Financial Aid: Nancy Wencl
Type: Comprehensive **Sex:** Coed **Scores:** 53.53% ACT 18-23; 24.42% ACT 24-29 **% Accepted:** 55 **Admission Plans:** Open Admission **Application Deadline:** August 1 **Application Fee:** $30.00 **H.S. Requirements:** High school diploma required; GED accepted **Scholarships:** Available **Calendar System:** Semester, Summer Session Available **Enrollment:** FT 9,203, PT 3,389, Grad FT 775, Grad PT 498 **Faculty:** FT 613, PT 290 **Student-Faculty Ratio:** 16:1 **Exams:** SAT I or ACT. **% Receiving Financial Aid:** 71 **% Residing in College-Owned, -Operated, or -Affiliated Housing:** 29 **Library Holdings:** 411,778 **Regional Accreditation:** North Central Association of Colleges and Schools **ROTC:** Army **Professional Accreditation:** ABET, ACPhE, ACCE, ADA, AHIMA, AOA, ACBSP, CARC, CSWE, JRCERT, JRCNMT, NAACLS, NASAD, NLN, NRPA, TEAC **Intercollegiate Athletics:** Basketball M & W; Cross-Country Running M & W; Football M; Golf M & W; Ice Hockey M; Soccer M & W; Softball W; Tennis M & W; Track and Field M & W; Volleyball W

FINLANDIA UNIVERSITY
601 Quincy St.
Hancock, MI 49930-1882
Tel: (906)482-5300; Free: 877-202-5491
Admissions: (906)487-7352
Fax: (906)487-7300
E-mail: admissions@finlandia.edu
Web Site: http://www.finlandia.edu/
President/CEO: Dr. Philip Johnson
Admissions: Martin Kinard
Financial Aid: Sandra Turnquist
Type: Four-Year College **Sex:** Coed **Affiliation:** Evangelical Lutheran Church in America **Scores:** 51% ACT 18-23; 21% ACT 24-29 **% Accepted:** 67 **Admission Plans:** Early Admission **Application Deadline:** August 25 **Application Fee:** $30.00 **H.S. Requirements:** High school diploma required; GED accepted **Costs Per Year:** Application fee: $30. One-time mandatory fee: $100. Comprehensive fee: $24,410 includes full-time tuition ($17,936), mandatory fees ($500), and college room and board ($5974). Full-time tuition and fees vary according to program. Room and board charges vary according to housing facility. Part-time tuition: $598 per credit hour. Part-time tuition varies according to course load and program. **Scholarships:** Available **Calendar System:** Semester, Summer Session Available **Enrollment:** FT 485, PT 60 **Faculty:** FT 42, PT 28 **Student-Faculty Ratio:** 10:1 **Exams:** SAT I or ACT. **% Receiving Financial Aid:** 83 **% Residing in College-Owned, -Operated, or -Affiliated Housing:** 24 **Library Holdings:** 68,803 **Regional Accreditation:** North Central Association of Colleges and Schools **Credit Hours For Degree:** 60 credits, Associates; 129 credits, Bachelors **ROTC:** Army, Air Force **Professional Accreditation:** APTA **Intercollegiate Athletics:** Baseball M; Basketball M & W; Cross-Country Running M & W; Ice Hockey M & W; Soccer M & W; Softball W; Volleyball W

GLEN OAKS COMMUNITY COLLEGE
62249 Shimmel Rd.
Centreville, MI 49032-9719
Tel: (616)467-9945; Free: 888-994-7818
Admissions: (269)467-9945
Fax: (616)467-9068
Web Site: http://www.glenoaks.edu/
President/CEO: Gary Wheeler
Admissions: Beverly M. Andrews
Type: Two-Year College **Sex:** Coed **Affiliation:** Michigan Department of Career Development **Admission Plans:** Open Admission **Application Deadline:** Rolling **Application Fee:** $0.00 **H.S. Requirements:** High school diploma or equivalent not required **Scholarships:** Available **Calendar System:** Semester, Summer Session Available **Library Holdings:** 37,087 **Regional Accreditation:** North Central Association of Colleges and Schools **Credit Hours For Degree:** 62 credit hours, Associates **Intercollegiate Athletics:** Baseball M; Basketball M & W; Golf M; Softball W; Track and Field M & W

GOGEBIC COMMUNITY COLLEGE
E-4946 Jackson Rd.
Ironwood, MI 49938
Tel: (906)932-4231
Fax: (906)932-5541
E-mail: jeanneg@gogebic.edu
Web Site: http://www.gogebic.edu/
President/CEO: James Lorenson
Admissions: Jeanne Graham
Type: Two-Year College **Sex:** Coed **Affiliation:** Michigan Department of Education **Admission Plans:** Open Admission; Early Admission; Deferred Admission **Application Deadline:** Rolling **Application Fee:** $10.00 **H.S. Requirements:** High school diploma required; GED accepted **Scholarships:** Available **Calendar System:** Semester, Summer Session Available **Library Holdings:** 22,000 **Regional Accreditation:** North Central Association of Colleges and Schools **Credit Hours For Degree:** 63 credit hours, Associates **Professional Accreditation:** AHIMA **Intercollegiate Athletics:** Basketball M & W; Cheerleading M & W

GRACE BIBLE COLLEGE
1011 Aldon St. SW
PO Box 910
Grand Rapids, MI 49509-0910
Tel: (616)538-2330; Free: 800-968-1887
Fax: (616)538-0599
E-mail: gbc@gbcol.edu
Web Site: http://www.gbcol.edu/
President/CEO: Kenneth B. Kemper
Admissions: Kevin Gilliam
Financial Aid: Kurt Postma
Type: Four-Year College **Sex:** Coed **Affiliation:** Grace Gospel Fellowship **Scores:** 100% SAT V 400+; 100% SAT M 400+; 58% ACT 18-23; 26% ACT 24-29 **% Accepted:** 61 **Admission Plans:** Early Admission; Deferred Admission **Application Deadline:** July 15 **Application Fee:** $0.00 **H.S. Requirements:** High school diploma required; GED accepted **Costs Per Year:** Application fee: $0. Comprehensive fee: $20,500 includes full-time tuition ($14,250) and college room and board ($6250). College room only: $3150. Room and board charges vary according to housing facility. **Scholarships:** Available **Calendar System:** Semester, Summer Session Not avail-

able **Enrollment:** FT 181, PT 13 **Faculty:** FT 7, PT 9 **Student-Faculty Ratio:** 19:1 **Exams:** SAT I and SAT II or ACT. **% Receiving Financial Aid:** 87 **% Residing in College-Owned, -Operated, or -Affiliated Housing:** 52 **Final Year or Final Semester Residency Requirement:** No **Library Holdings:** 42,143 **Regional Accreditation:** North Central Association of Colleges and Schools **Credit Hours For Degree:** 64 semester hours, Associates; 124 semester hours, Bachelors **ROTC:** Army **Professional Accreditation:** ABHE **Intercollegiate Athletics:** Basketball M & W; Soccer M; Volleyball W

GRAND RAPIDS COMMUNITY COLLEGE
143 Bostwick Ave., NE
Grand Rapids, MI 49503-3201
Tel: (616)234-4000
Admissions: (616)234-4100
Fax: (616)234-4005
E-mail: dpatrick@grcc.edu
Web Site: http://www.grcc.edu/
President/CEO: Dr. Steven Ender
Admissions: Diane Patrick
Type: Two-Year College **Sex:** Coed **Affiliation:** Michigan Department of Education **% Accepted:** 79 **Admission Plans:** Open Admission; Early Admission; Deferred Admission **Application Deadline:** August 30 **Application Fee:** $20.00 **H.S. Requirements:** High school diploma required; GED accepted **Costs Per Year:** Application fee: $20. Area resident tuition: $2535 full-time. State resident tuition: $5430 full-time. Nonresident tuition: $8040 full-time. Mandatory fees: $220 full-time. **Scholarships:** Available **Calendar System:** Semester, Summer Session Available **Enrollment:** FT 7,546, PT 9,396 **Faculty:** FT 268, PT 579 **Student-Faculty Ratio:** 23:1 **Exams:** Other, SAT I or ACT. **Library Holdings:** 170,884 **Regional Accreditation:** North Central Association of Colleges and Schools **Credit Hours For Degree:** 62 credits, Associates **Professional Accreditation:** ACF, ADA, AOTA, JRCERT, NASM, NLN **Intercollegiate Athletics:** Baseball M; Basketball M & W; Football M; Golf M; Softball W; Swimming and Diving M & W; Tennis M & W; Track and Field M; Volleyball W; Wrestling M

GRAND VALLEY STATE UNIVERSITY
1 Campus Dr.
Allendale, MI 49401-9403
Tel: (616)331-5000; Free: 800-748-0246
Admissions: (616)331-2025
Fax: (616)331-2000
E-mail: go2gvsu@gvsu.edu
Web Site: http://www.gvsu.edu/
President/CEO: Dr. Thomas J. Haas
Admissions: Jodi Chycinski
Type: Comprehensive **Sex:** Coed **Scores:** 96.87% SAT V 400+; 98.48% SAT M 400+; 45.23% ACT 18-23; 45.94% ACT 24-29 **% Accepted:** 81 **Application Deadline:** May 1 **Application Fee:** $30.00 **H.S. Requirements:** High school diploma required; GED accepted **Costs Per Year:** Application fee: $30. State resident tuition: $8630 full-time, $375 per credit hour part-time. Nonresident tuition: $12,944 full-time, $551 per credit hour part-time. Full-time tuition varies according to degree level, program, and student level. Part-time tuition varies according to course load, degree level, program, and student level. College room and board: $7478. College room only: $5406. Room and board charges vary according to board plan, housing facility, and location. **Scholarships:** Available **Calendar System:** Semester, Summer Session Available **Enrollment:** FT 18,448, PT 2,402, Grad FT 941, Grad PT 2,617 **Faculty:** FT 1,051, PT 536 **Student-Faculty Ratio:** 17:1 **Exams:** SAT I or ACT. **% Receiving Financial Aid:** 61 **% Residing in College-Owned, -Operated, or -Affiliated Housing:** 25 **Library Holdings:** 664,000 **Regional Accreditation:** North Central Association of Colleges and Schools **Credit Hours For Degree:** 120 semester hours, Bachelors **Professional Accreditation:** AACSB, ABET, AACN, AOTA, APTA, APA, CSWE, JRCEPAT, NAACLS, NASAD, NASM, NASPAA, NCATE **Intercollegiate Athletics:** Baseball M; Basketball M & W; Cheerleading M & W; Crew M & W; Cross-Country Running M & W; Football M; Golf M & W; Ice Hockey M; Rugby M & W; Sailing M & W; Skiing (Downhill) M & W; Soccer M & W; Softball W; Swimming and Diving M & W; Tennis M & W; Track and Field M & W; Volleyball M & W; Water Polo M & W; Wrestling M

GREAT LAKES CHRISTIAN COLLEGE
6211 West Willow Hwy.
Lansing, MI 48917-1299
Tel: (517)321-0242; Free: 800-YES-GLCC
Fax: (517)321-5902
E-mail: lscharer@glcc.edu
Web Site: http://www.glcc.edu/
President/CEO: Lawrence L. Carter
Admissions: Lloyd Scharer
Type: Four-Year College **Sex:** Coed **Affiliation:** Christian Churches and Churches of Christ **Scores:** 60% ACT 18-23; 17% ACT 24-29 **Application Deadline:** August 1 **Application Fee:** $30.00 **H.S. Requirements:** High school diploma required; GED accepted **Costs Per Year:** Application fee: $30. One-time mandatory fee: $200. Comprehensive fee: $19,600 includes full-time tuition ($11,520), mandatory fees ($1080), and college room and board ($7000). Part-time tuition: $360 per credit hour. Part-time mandatory fees: $360 per credit hour. **Calendar System:** Semester, Summer Session Not available **Enrollment:** FT 174, PT 67 **Faculty:** FT 10, PT 13 **Student-Faculty Ratio:** 13:1 **Exams:** SAT I or ACT. **Regional Accreditation:** North Central Association of Colleges and Schools **Credit Hours For Degree:** 64 semester hours, Associates; 128 semester hours, Bachelors **Professional Accreditation:** ABHE **Intercollegiate Athletics:** Basketball M & W; Soccer M; Volleyball W

HENRY FORD COMMUNITY COLLEGE
5101 Evergreen Rd.
Dearborn, MI 48128-1495
Tel: (313)845-9615
Admissions: (313)845-9600
Fax: (313)845-9658
E-mail: dfreed@hfcc.edu
Web Site: http://www.hfcc.edu/
President/CEO: Gail Mee
Admissions: Doug Freed
Type: Two-Year College **Sex:** Coed **% Accepted:** 100 **Admission Plans:** Open Admission; Early Admission; Deferred Admission **Application Deadline:** Rolling **Application Fee:** $30.00 **H.S. Requirements:** High school diploma required; GED accepted **Scholarships:** Available **Calendar System:** Semester, Summer Session Available **Enrollment:** FT 13,000 **Faculty:** FT 220, PT 550 **Library Holdings:** 80,000 **Regional Accreditation:** North Central Association of Colleges and Schools **Credit Hours For Degree:** 60 credit hours, Associates **Professional Accreditation:** ARCEST, ACF, AHIMA, APTA, ACBSP, CARC, NLN **Intercollegiate Athletics:** Baseball M; Basketball M & W; Golf M; Softball W; Tennis W; Track and Field M; Volleyball W

HILLSDALE COLLEGE
33 East College St.
Hillsdale, MI 49242-1298
Tel: (517)437-7341
Admissions: (517)607-2327
Fax: (517)437-0190
E-mail: admissions@hillsdale.edu
Web Site: http://www.hillsdale.edu/
President/CEO: Dr. Larry Arnn
Admissions: Jeffrey S. Lantis
Financial Aid: Rich Moeggengberg
Type: Four-Year College **Sex:** Coed **Scores:** 100% SAT V 400+; 100% SAT M 400+; 10% ACT 18-23; 52% ACT 24-29 **% Accepted:** 62 **Admission Plans:** Early Admission; Early Action; Early Decision Plan; Deferred Admission **Application Deadline:** February 15 **Application Fee:** $0.00 **H.S. Requirements:** High school diploma required; GED accepted **Costs Per Year:** Application fee: $0. Comprehensive fee: $28,490 includes full-time tuition ($19,960), mandatory fees ($540), and college room and board ($7990). Room and board charges vary according to board plan. Part-time tuition: $785 per credit hour. **Scholarships:** Available **Calendar System:** Semester, Summer Session Available **Enrollment:** FT 1,282, PT 34 **Faculty:** FT 117, PT 37 **Student-Faculty Ratio:** 10:1 **Exams:** SAT I or ACT, SAT II. ACT essay used for admission. SAT essay used for admission. ACT essay used as a validity check on application essay. SAT essay used as a validity check on application essay. **% Receiving Financial Aid:** 40 **% Residing in College-Owned, -Operated, or -Affiliated Housing:** 75 **Final Year or Final Semester Residency Requirement:** No **Library Holdings:** 240,000 **Regional Accreditation:** North Central Association of Colleges and Schools **Credit Hours For Degree:** 124 semester hours, Bachelors **Intercollegiate Athletics:** Baseball M; Basketball M & W; Equestrian Sports

W; Football M; Ice Hockey M; Lacrosse M; Riflery M & W; Soccer M & W; Softball W; Swimming and Diving W; Track and Field M & W; Volleyball W

HOPE COLLEGE
141 East 12th St., PO Box 9000
Holland, MI 49422-9000
Tel: (616)395-7000; Free: 800-968-7850
Admissions: (616)395-7850
Fax: (616)395-7130
E-mail: admissions@hope.edu
Web Site: http://www.hope.edu/
President/CEO: Dr. James E. Bultman
Financial Aid: Phyllis Hooyman
Type: Four-Year College **Sex:** Coed **Affiliation:** Reformed Church in America **Scores:** 97.2% SAT V 400+; 98.6% SAT M 400+; 29.9% ACT 18-23; 51.4% ACT 24-29 **% Accepted:** 84 **Admission Plans:** Early Admission; Deferred Admission **Application Deadline:** Rolling **Application Fee:** $35.00 **H.S. Requirements:** High school diploma required; GED accepted **Costs Per Year:** Application fee: $35. Comprehensive fee: $34,620 includes full-time tuition ($26,350), mandatory fees ($160), and college room and board ($8110). College room only: $3710. Room and board charges vary according to board plan. **Scholarships:** Available **Calendar System:** Semester, Summer Session Available **Enrollment:** FT 3,114, PT 116 **Faculty:** FT 230, PT 73 **Student-Faculty Ratio:** 12:1 **Exams:** SAT I or ACT. ACT essay not being used. SAT essay not being used. **% Receiving Financial Aid:** 62 **% Residing in College-Owned, -Operated, or -Affiliated Housing:** 81 **Final Year or Final Semester Residency Requirement:** Yes **Library Holdings:** 371,987 **Regional Accreditation:** North Central Association of Colleges and Schools **Credit Hours For Degree:** 126 credit hours, Bachelors **ROTC:** Army **Professional Accreditation:** ABET, CSWE, JRCEPAT, NASAD, NASD, NASM, NAST, NCATE, NLN **Intercollegiate Athletics:** Baseball M; Basketball M & W; Cheerleading M & W; Cross-Country Running M & W; Football M; Golf M & W; Ice Hockey M; Lacrosse M & W; Sailing M & W; Soccer M & W; Softball W; Swimming and Diving M & W; Tennis M & W; Track and Field M & W; Volleyball W

ITT TECHNICAL INSTITUTE (CANTON)
1905 South Haggerty Rd.
Canton, MI 48188-2025
Tel: (734)397-7800; Free: 800-247-4477
Fax: (734)397-1945
Web Site: http://www.itt-tech.edu/
President/CEO: Nadine Palazzolo
Type: Two-Year College **Sex:** Coed **Affiliation:** ITT Educational Services, Inc. **H.S. Requirements:** High school diploma required; GED accepted **Scholarships:** Available **Calendar System:** Quarter, Summer Session Not available **Professional Accreditation:** ACICS

ITT TECHNICAL INSTITUTE (SWARTZ CREEK)
6359 Miller Rd.
Swartz Creek, MI 48473
Tel: (810)628-2500; Free: 800-514-6564
Web Site: http://www.itt-tech.edu/
President/CEO: Tracey Schaffer
Type: Two-Year College **Sex:** Coed **Affiliation:** ITT Educational Services, Inc. **Calendar System:** Quarter

ITT TECHNICAL INSTITUTE (TROY)
1522 East Big Beaver Rd.
Troy, MI 48083-1905
Tel: (248)524-1800
Web Site: http://www.itt-tech.edu/
President/CEO: James Pfaff
Type: Two-Year College **Sex:** Coed **Affiliation:** ITT Educational Services, Inc. **H.S. Requirements:** High school diploma required; GED accepted **Scholarships:** Available **Calendar System:** Quarter, Summer Session Not available **Credit Hours For Degree:** 96 credit hours, Associates **Professional Accreditation:** ACICS

ITT TECHNICAL INSTITUTE (WYOMING)
1980 Metro Ct. SW
Wyoming, MI 49519
Tel: (616)406-1200
Web Site: http://www.itt-tech.edu/
President/CEO: Dennis Hormel
Type: Two-Year College **Sex:** Coed **Affiliation:** ITT Educational Services, Inc. **H.S. Requirements:** High school diploma required; GED accepted **Scholarships:** Available **Calendar System:** Quarter, Summer Session Not available **Credit Hours For Degree:** 96 credit hours, Associates **Professional Accreditation:** ACICS

JACKSON COMMUNITY COLLEGE
2111 Emmons Rd.
Jackson, MI 49201-8399
Tel: (517)787-0800; Free: 888-522-7344
Admissions: (517)796-8425
E-mail: admissions@jccmi.edu
Web Site: http://www.jccmi.edu/
President/CEO: Daniel J. Phelan, PhD
Admissions: Julie Hand
Type: Two-Year College **Sex:** Coed **Scores:** 57% ACT 18-23; 17% ACT 24-29 **Admission Plans:** Open Admission; Early Admission **Application Deadline:** Rolling **Application Fee:** $0.00 **H.S. Requirements:** High school diploma required; GED accepted **Costs Per Year:** Application fee: $0. Area resident tuition: $2172 full-time, $90.50 per contact hour part-time. State resident tuition: $3048 full-time, $127 per contact hour part-time. Nonresident tuition: $4368 full-time, $182 per contact hour part-time. Mandatory fees: $612 full-time, $25.50 per contact hour part-time. Full-time tuition and fees vary according to course load. Part-time tuition and fees vary according to course load. College room only: $5900. **Scholarships:** Available **Calendar System:** Semester, Summer Session Available **Enrollment:** FT 2,673, PT 3,500 **Faculty:** FT 90, PT 302 **Student-Faculty Ratio:** 20:1 **Exams:** SAT I and SAT II or ACT. ACT essay not being used. **Final Year or Final Semester Residency Requirement:** No **Library Holdings:** 67,000 **Regional Accreditation:** North Central Association of Colleges and Schools **Credit Hours For Degree:** 60 credit hours, Associates **ROTC:** Army **Professional Accreditation:** AAMAE, ACBSP, JRCEDMS **Intercollegiate Athletics:** Baseball M; Basketball M & W; Cross-Country Running M & W; Golf M & W; Ice Hockey M; Soccer M & W; Softball W; Volleyball W

KALAMAZOO COLLEGE
1200 Academy St.
Kalamazoo, MI 49006-3295
Tel: (269)337-7000; Free: 800-253-3602
Admissions: (269)337-7166
Fax: (269)337-7251
E-mail: admission@kzoo.edu
Web Site: http://www.kzoo.edu/
President/CEO: Eileen Wilson-Oyelaran
Admissions: Linda Wirgau
Financial Aid: Judy Clark
Type: Four-Year College **Sex:** Coed **Affiliation:** American Baptist Churches in the U.S.A. **Scores:** 100% SAT V 400+; 100% SAT M 400+; 11% ACT 18-23; 59% ACT 24-29 **% Accepted:** 73 **Admission Plans:** Early Action; Early Decision Plan; Deferred Admission **Application Deadline:** February 1 **Application Fee:** $40.00 **H.S. Requirements:** High school diploma required; GED accepted **Costs Per Year:** Application fee: $40. One-time mandatory fee: $100. Comprehensive fee: $40,419 includes full-time tuition ($32,643) and college room and board ($7776). College room only: $3792. Room and board charges vary according to board plan. **Scholarships:** Available **Calendar System:** Quarter, Summer Session Not available **Enrollment:** FT 1,384 **Faculty:** FT 93, PT 18 **Student-Faculty Ratio:** 14:1 **Exams:** SAT I or ACT. **% Residing in College-Owned, -Operated, or -Affiliated Housing:** 78 **Library Holdings:** 342,939 **Regional Accreditation:** North Central Association of Colleges and Schools **Credit Hours For Degree:** 35 courses, Bachelors **ROTC:** Army **Intercollegiate Athletics:** Baseball M; Basketball M & W; Cross-Country Running M & W; Football M; Golf M & W; Soccer M & W; Softball W; Swimming and Diving M & W; Tennis M & W; Volleyball W

KALAMAZOO VALLEY COMMUNITY COLLEGE
PO Box 4070
Kalamazoo, MI 49003-4070
Tel: (269)488-4400
Admissions: (269)488-4100
Fax: (269)448-4555
Web Site: http://www.kvcc.edu/
President/CEO: Dr. Marilyn Schlack

Admissions: Michael McCall
Financial Aid: Sue Newington
Type: Two-Year College **Sex:** Coed **Admission Plans:** Open Admission **Application Deadline:** Rolling **Application Fee:** $0.00 **H.S. Requirements:** High school diploma required; GED accepted **Scholarships:** Available **Calendar System:** Semester, Summer Session Available **Exams:** ACT. **Library Holdings:** 88,791 **Regional Accreditation:** North Central Association of Colleges and Schools **Credit Hours For Degree:** 62 credit hours, Associates **ROTC:** Army **Professional Accreditation:** AAMAE, ADA, CARC **Intercollegiate Athletics:** Baseball M; Basketball M & W; Golf M; Softball W; Tennis W; Volleyball W

KELLOGG COMMUNITY COLLEGE
450 North Ave.
Battle Creek, MI 49017-3397
Tel: (616)965-3931
Admissions: (269)965-3931
Fax: (616)965-4133
E-mail: harriss@kellogg.edu
Web Site: http://www.kellogg.edu/
President/CEO: G. Edward Haring, PhD
Admissions: Denise Newman
Type: Two-Year College **Sex:** Coed **Affiliation:** Michigan Department of Education **% Accepted:** 100 **Admission Plans:** Open Admission; Early Admission **Application Deadline:** Rolling **Application Fee:** $0.00 **H.S. Requirements:** High school diploma or equivalent not required. For allied health and nursing programs: High school diploma required; GED accepted **Costs Per Year:** Application fee: $0. Area resident tuition: $2295 full-time, $78.50 per credit hour part-time. State resident tuition: $3720 full-time, $124 per credit hour part-time. Nonresident tuition: $5325 full-time, $177.50 per credit hour part-time. Mandatory fees: $210 full-time, $7 per credit hour part-time. **Scholarships:** Available **Calendar System:** Semester, Summer Session Available **Enrollment:** FT 2,053, PT 3,923 **Faculty:** FT 92, PT 293 **Student-Faculty Ratio:** 23:1 **Exams:** ACT, SAT I or ACT. **Final Year or Final Semester Residency Requirement:** No **Library Holdings:** 42,131 **Regional Accreditation:** North Central Association of Colleges and Schools **Credit Hours For Degree:** 62 credit hours, Associates **Professional Accreditation:** ADA, APTA, JRCERT, NAACLS **Intercollegiate Athletics:** Baseball M; Basketball M & W; Soccer M; Softball W; Volleyball W

KETTERING UNIVERSITY
1700 University Ave.
Flint, MI 48504
Tel: (810)762-9500; Free: 800-955-4464
Admissions: (810)762-7865
Fax: (810)762-9837
E-mail: admissions@kettering.edu
Web Site: http://www.kettering.edu/
President/CEO: Stanley R. Liberty
Admissions: Shari Luck
Financial Aid: Diane Bice
Type: Comprehensive **Sex:** Coed **Scores:** 100% SAT V 400+; 100% SAT M 400+; 12.24% ACT 18-23; 65.31% ACT 24-29 **% Accepted:** 64 **Admission Plans:** Deferred Admission **Application Deadline:** Rolling **Application Fee:** $35.00 **H.S. Requirements:** High school diploma required; GED not accepted **Costs Per Year:** Application fee: $35. One-time mandatory fee: $310. Comprehensive fee: $35,510 includes full-time tuition ($28,672), mandatory fees ($448), and college room and board ($6390). College room only: $4000. Part-time tuition: $896 per credit hour. **Scholarships:** Available **Calendar System:** Semester, Summer Session Available **Enrollment:** FT 2,029, PT 51, Grad FT 18, Grad PT 312 **Faculty:** FT 116, PT 35 **Student-Faculty Ratio:** 16:1 **Exams:** SAT I or ACT. ACT essay not being used. SAT essay not being used. **% Receiving Financial Aid:** 66 **% Residing in College-Owned, -Operated, or -Affiliated Housing:** 28 **Final Year or Final Semester Residency Requirement:** No **Library Holdings:** 148,600 **Regional Accreditation:** North Central Association of Colleges and Schools **Credit Hours For Degree:** 161 credit hours, Bachelors **Professional Accreditation:** ABET, ACBSP **Intercollegiate Athletics:** Ice Hockey M

KEWEENAW BAY OJIBWA COMMUNITY COLLEGE
111 Beartown Rd.
Baraga, MI 49908
Tel: (906)353-4600
Web Site: http://www.kbocc.org/
Type: Two-Year College **Sex:** Coed **Regional Accreditation:** North Central Association of Colleges and Schools

KIRTLAND COMMUNITY COLLEGE
10775 North St. Helen Rd.
Roscommon, MI 48653-9699
Tel: (989)275-5000
Fax: (989)275-8210
E-mail: registrar@kirtland.edu
Web Site: http://www.kirtland.edu/
President/CEO: Dr. Tom Quinn
Admissions: Luann Mabarak
Financial Aid: Christin Horndt
Type: Two-Year College **Sex:** Coed **Affiliation:** Michigan Department of Energy, Labor and Economic Growth - Community Colleges Service Unit **Scores:** 38% ACT 18-23; 7% ACT 24-29 **Admission Plans:** Open Admission **Application Deadline:** Rolling **Application Fee:** $0.00 **H.S. Requirements:** High school diploma required; GED accepted **Costs Per Year:** Application fee: $0. Area resident tuition: $2402 full-time, $81 per contact hour part-time. State resident tuition: $4402 full-time, $149 per contact hour part-time. Nonresident tuition: $5440 full-time, $184 per contact hour part-time. Mandatory fees: $270 full-time, $8 per contact hour part-time. **Scholarships:** Available **Calendar System:** Semester, Summer Session Available **Enrollment:** FT 925, PT 1,047 **Faculty:** FT 38, PT 101 **Student-Faculty Ratio:** 19:1 **Exams:** ACT. **Library Holdings:** 35,000 **Regional Accreditation:** North Central Association of Colleges and Schools **Credit Hours For Degree:** 60 credit hours, Associates **Professional Accreditation:** AAMAE **Intercollegiate Athletics:** Basketball M & W; Cross-Country Running M & W; Golf M & W

KUYPER COLLEGE
3333 East Beltline, NE
Grand Rapids, MI 49525-9749
Tel: (616)222-3000; Free: 800-511-3749
Fax: (616)222-3045
E-mail: admissions@kuyper.edu
Web Site: http://www.kuyper.edu/
President/CEO: Nicholas V. Kroeze
Financial Aid: Agnes Russell
Type: Four-Year College **Sex:** Coed **Scores:** 100% SAT V 400+; 84% SAT M 400+ **% Accepted:** 88 **Admission Plans:** Deferred Admission **Application Deadline:** Rolling **Application Fee:** $25.00 **H.S. Requirements:** High school diploma required; GED accepted **Costs Per Year:** Application fee: $25. Comprehensive fee: $22,696 includes full-time tuition ($15,866), mandatory fees ($550), and college room and board ($6280). Full-time tuition and fees vary according to course load. Room and board charges vary according to board plan, housing facility, and student level. Part-time tuition: $760 per credit hour. Part-time tuition varies according to course load. **Scholarships:** Available **Calendar System:** Semester, Summer Session Available **Enrollment:** FT 302, PT 45, Grad PT 1 **Faculty:** FT 14, PT 23 **Student-Faculty Ratio:** 15:1 **Exams:** SAT I or ACT. ACT essay not being used. SAT essay not being used. **% Receiving Financial Aid:** 85 **% Residing in College-Owned, -Operated, or -Affiliated Housing:** 60 **Final Year or Final Semester Residency Requirement:** Yes **Library Holdings:** 56,590 **Regional Accreditation:** North Central Association of Colleges and Schools **Credit Hours For Degree:** 63 credits, Associates; 124 credits, Bachelors **ROTC:** Army **Professional Accreditation:** ABHE **Intercollegiate Athletics:** Basketball M & W; Soccer M; Volleyball W

LAKE MICHIGAN COLLEGE
2755 East Napier
Benton Harbor, MI 49022-1899
Tel: (269)927-8100
Admissions: (616)927-8100
E-mail: skinner@lakemichigancollege.edu
Web Site: http://www.lakemichigancollege.edu/
President/CEO: Dr. Robert P. Harrison
Admissions: Sara Skinner
Financial Aid: Anne Tews
Type: Two-Year College **Sex:** Coed **Affiliation:** Michigan Department of Education **Admission Plans:** Open Admission **Application Deadline:** Rolling **Application Fee:** $0.00 **H.S. Requirements:** High school diploma or equivalent not required. For health science students: High school diploma required; GED accepted **Costs Per Year:** Application fee: $0. Area resident

tuition: $3105 full-time, $72.50 per contact hour part-time. State resident tuition: $4170 full-time, $102 per credit part-time. Nonresident tuition: $5190 full-time, $142 per contact hour part-time. **Scholarships:** Available **Calendar System:** Semester, Summer Session Available **Enrollment:** FT 1,616, PT 3,081 **Faculty:** FT 53, PT 278 **Student-Faculty Ratio:** 18:1 **Final Year or Final Semester Residency Requirement:** No **Library Holdings:** 93,803 **Regional Accreditation:** North Central Association of Colleges and Schools **Credit Hours For Degree:** 61 credit hours, Associates **Professional Accreditation:** ADA, AOTA, JRCERT, NLN **Intercollegiate Athletics:** Baseball M; Basketball M & W; Softball W; Volleyball W

LAKE SUPERIOR STATE UNIVERSITY
650 West Easterday Ave.
Sault Sainte Marie, MI 49783
Tel: (906)632-6841; Free: 888-800-LSSU
Admissions: (906)635-2231
Fax: (906)635-6669
E-mail: admissions@lssu.edu
Web Site: http://www.lssu.edu/
President/CEO: Dr. Tony McLain
Admissions: Susan Camp
Financial Aid: Deborah Faust
Type: Comprehensive **Sex:** Coed **Scores:** 53% ACT 18-23; 27% ACT 24-29 **% Accepted:** 29 **Admission Plans:** Deferred Admission **Application Deadline:** Rolling **Application Fee:** $35.00 **H.S. Requirements:** High school diploma required; GED accepted **Costs Per Year:** Application fee: $35. One-time mandatory fee: $125. State resident tuition: $8284 full-time, $341 per credit hour part-time. Nonresident tuition: $16,468 full-time, $682 per credit hour part-time. Mandatory fees: $100 full-time. Full-time tuition and fees vary according to reciprocity agreements. Part-time tuition varies according to course load and reciprocity agreements. College room and board: $7994. Room and board charges vary according to board plan and housing facility. **Scholarships:** Available **Calendar System:** Semester, Summer Session Available **Enrollment:** FT 2,097, PT 471, Grad PT 20 **Faculty:** FT 115, PT 69 **Student-Faculty Ratio:** 16:1 **Exams:** SAT I or ACT. **% Receiving Financial Aid:** 91 **Library Holdings:** 200,449 **Regional Accreditation:** North Central Association of Colleges and Schools **Credit Hours For Degree:** 62 semester hours, Associates; 124 semester hours, Bachelors **Professional Accreditation:** ABET, NLN **Intercollegiate Athletics:** Basketball M & W; Cross-Country Running M & W; Golf M & W; Ice Hockey M; Softball W; Tennis M & W; Track and Field M & W; Volleyball W

LANSING COMMUNITY COLLEGE
PO Box 40010
Lansing, MI 48901-7210
Tel: (517)483-1957; Free: 800-644-4LCC
Admissions: (517)483-9886
Fax: (517)483-9668
E-mail: grossbt@lcc.edu
Web Site: http://www.lcc.edu/
President/CEO: Dr. Brent Knight
Admissions: Tammy Grossbauer
Type: Two-Year College **Sex:** Coed **Affiliation:** Michigan Department of Education **Admission Plans:** Open Admission; Preferred Admission; Early Admission; Deferred Admission **Application Deadline:** Rolling **Application Fee:** $0.00 **H.S. Requirements:** High school diploma or equivalent not required. For allied health programs, international students: High school diploma required; GED accepted **Costs Per Year:** Application fee: $0. One-time mandatory fee: $35. Area resident tuition: $2190 full-time, $73 per contact hour part-time. State resident tuition: $4020 full-time, $134 per contact hour part-time. Nonresident tuition: $6030 full-time, $201 per contact hour part-time. Mandatory fees: $50 full-time, $35 per term part-time. **Scholarships:** Available **Calendar System:** Semester, Summer Session Available **Enrollment:** FT 7,815, PT 13,308 **Faculty:** FT 250, PT 1,670 **Student-Faculty Ratio:** 14:1 **Library Holdings:** 98,125 **Regional Accreditation:** North Central Association of Colleges and Schools **Credit Hours For Degree:** 60 semester hours, Associates **ROTC:** Army, Air Force **Professional Accreditation:** ADA, JRCERT, JRCEMT, NAACLS, NLN **Intercollegiate Athletics:** Basketball M & W; Cross-Country Running M & W; Golf M; Track and Field M & W; Volleyball W

LAWRENCE TECHNOLOGICAL UNIVERSITY
21000 West Ten Mile Rd.
Southfield, MI 48075-1058
Tel: (248)204-4000; Free: 800-225-5588
Admissions: (248)204-3160
Fax: (248)204-3727
E-mail: admissions@ltu.edu
Web Site: http://www.ltu.edu/
President/CEO: Dr. Lewis N. Walker
Admissions: Jane Rohrback
Financial Aid: Mark Martin
Type: University **Sex:** Coed **Scores:** 38% ACT 18-23; 44% ACT 24-29 **% Accepted:** 50 **Admission Plans:** Early Admission; Deferred Admission **Application Deadline:** August 15 **Application Fee:** $30.00 **H.S. Requirements:** High school diploma required; GED accepted **Costs Per Year:** Application fee: $30. Comprehensive fee: $32,361 includes full-time tuition ($22,638), mandatory fees ($370), and college room and board ($9353). College room only: $5573. Full-time tuition and fees vary according to course level, degree level, location, program, and student level. Room and board charges vary according to board plan and housing facility. Part-time tuition: $755 per credit hour. Part-time mandatory fees: $185 per term. Part-time tuition and fees vary according to course level, degree level, location, program, and student level. **Scholarships:** Available **Calendar System:** Semester, Summer Session Available **Enrollment:** FT 1,631, PT 1,556, Grad FT 40, Grad PT 1,291 **Faculty:** FT 129, PT 301 **Student-Faculty Ratio:** 11:1 **Exams:** Other. **% Receiving Financial Aid:** 60 **% Residing in College-Owned, -Operated, or -Affiliated Housing:** 16 **Final Year or Final Semester Residency Requirement:** No **Library Holdings:** 150,770 **Regional Accreditation:** North Central Association of Colleges and Schools **Credit Hours For Degree:** 60 credit hours, Associates; 120 credit hours, Bachelors **ROTC:** Air Force **Professional Accreditation:** ABET, ACBSP, FIDER, NAAB, NASAD

MACOMB COMMUNITY COLLEGE
14500 East Twelve Mile Rd.
Warren, MI 48088-3896
Tel: (586)445-7999; Free: (866)622-6624
Admissions: (586)445-7246
Fax: (586)445-7140
E-mail: stevensr@macomb.edu
Web Site: http://www.macomb.edu/
President/CEO: Dr. James Jacobs
Admissions: Brian Bouwman
Financial Aid: Judy L. Florian
Type: Two-Year College **Sex:** Coed **Affiliation:** Michigan Public Community College System **Admission Plans:** Open Admission; Early Admission; Deferred Admission **Application Deadline:** Rolling **Application Fee:** $0.00 **H.S. Requirements:** High school diploma or equivalent not required **Costs Per Year:** Application fee: $0. Area resident tuition: $2232 full-time, $72 per credit hour part-time. State resident tuition: $3410 full-time, $110 per credit hour part-time. Nonresident tuition: $4433 full-time, $143 per credit hour part-time. Mandatory fees: $40 full-time, $20. Full-time tuition and fees vary according to course load. Part-time tuition and fees vary according to course load. **Scholarships:** Available **Calendar System:** Semester, Summer Session Available **Enrollment:** FT 9,599, PT 14,777 **Faculty:** FT 232, PT 883 **Student-Faculty Ratio:** 28:1 **Library Holdings:** 159,226 **Regional Accreditation:** North Central Association of Colleges and Schools **Credit Hours For Degree:** 62 semester hours, Associates **Professional Accreditation:** ARCEST, AAMAE, ACF, AOTA, APTA, CARC, NLN **Intercollegiate Athletics:** Baseball M; Basketball M; Cross-Country Running M & W; Soccer M; Softball W; Track and Field M & W; Volleyball W

MADONNA UNIVERSITY
36600 Schoolcraft Rd.
Livonia, MI 48150-1173
Tel: (734)432-5300; Free: 800-852-4951
Admissions: (734)432-5341
Fax: (734)432-5393
E-mail: muinfo@madonna.edu
Web Site: http://www.madonna.edu/
President/CEO: Sr. Rose Marie Kujawa, CSSF
Admissions: Mike Quattro
Financial Aid: Cathy Durham
Type: Comprehensive **Sex:** Coed **Affiliation:** Roman Catholic **Scores:** 100% SAT V 400+; 100% SAT M 400+; 54% ACT 18-23; 33% ACT 24-29 **% Accepted:** 74 **Admission Plans:** Early Admission; Deferred Admission **Application Deadline:** Rolling **Application Fee:** $25.00 **H.S. Requirements:**

High school diploma required; GED accepted **Costs Per Year:** Application fee: $25. Comprehensive fee: $19,958 includes full-time tuition ($13,050), mandatory fees ($100), and college room and board ($6808). College room only: $3040. Room and board charges vary according to board plan. Part-time tuition: $435 per credit hour. Part-time mandatory fees: $50 per term. **Scholarships:** Available **Calendar System:** Semester, Summer Session Available **Enrollment:** FT 1,667, PT 1,466, Grad FT 79, Grad PT 1,255 **Faculty:** FT 120, PT 210 **Student-Faculty Ratio:** 11:1 **Exams:** SAT I or ACT. ACT essay used in place of application essay. ACT essay used for placement. **% Receiving Financial Aid:** 45 **% Residing in College-Owned, -Operated, or -Affiliated Housing:** 5 **Final Year or Final Semester Residency Requirement:** No **Library Holdings:** 108,000 **Regional Accreditation:** North Central Association of Colleges and Schools **Credit Hours For Degree:** 60 semester hours, Associates; 120 semester hours, Bachelors **ROTC:** Army **Professional Accreditation:** AACN, CSWE, NCATE, NLN **Intercollegiate Athletics:** Baseball M; Basketball M & W; Cross-Country Running M & W; Golf M & W; Soccer M & W; Softball W; Volleyball W

MARYGROVE COLLEGE
8425 West McNichols Rd.
Detroit, MI 48221-2599
Tel: (313)927-1200; Free: (866)313-1297
Fax: (313)927-1345
E-mail: info@marygrove.edu
Web Site: http://www.marygrove.edu/
President/CEO: David Fike
Admissions: John Ambrose
Financial Aid: Donald Hurt
Type: Comprehensive **Sex:** Coed **Affiliation:** Roman Catholic **% Accepted:** 42 **Admission Plans:** Early Admission; Deferred Admission **Application Deadline:** August 15 **Application Fee:** $25.00 **H.S. Requirements:** High school diploma required; GED accepted **Calendar System:** Semester, Summer Session Available **Enrollment:** FT 455, PT 325 **Faculty:** FT 56, PT 8 **Student-Faculty Ratio:** 22:1 **Exams:** ACT. **% Residing in College-Owned, -Operated, or -Affiliated Housing:** 12 **Library Holdings:** 86,268 **Regional Accreditation:** North Central Association of Colleges and Schools **Credit Hours For Degree:** 64 credits, Associates; 128 credits, Bachelors **Professional Accreditation:** AAFCS, CARC, CSWE, JRCERT, NCATE, TEAC **Intercollegiate Athletics:** Basketball M & W

MICHIGAN JEWISH INSTITUTE
25401 Coolidge Hwy.
Oak Park, MI 48237
Tel: (248)414-6900
Fax: (248)414-6907
E-mail: dstein@mji.edu
Web Site: http://www.mji.edu/
President/CEO: Rabbi Kasriel Shemtov
Admissions: Dov Stein
Type: Four-Year College **Sex:** Coed **Admission Plans:** Open Admission; Early Admission; Deferred Admission **Application Deadline:** Rolling **Application Fee:** $50.00 **H.S. Requirements:** High school diploma required; GED accepted **Calendar System:** Semester, Summer Session Available **Faculty:** FT 6, PT 18 **Credit Hours For Degree:** 62 credits, Associates; 120 credits, Bachelors **Professional Accreditation:** ACICS

MICHIGAN STATE UNIVERSITY
East Lansing, MI 48824
Tel: (517)355-1855
Admissions: (517)355-8332
E-mail: admis@msu.edu
Web Site: http://www.msu.edu/
President/CEO: Dr. LouAnna K. Simon
Admissions: James Cotter
Financial Aid: Keith Williams
Type: University **Sex:** Coed **Scores:** 91.1% SAT V 400+; 98.5% SAT M 400+; 27.5% ACT 18-23; 56.5% ACT 24-29 **% Accepted:** 73 **Admission Plans:** Early Action; Deferred Admission **Application Deadline:** Rolling **Application Fee:** $35.00 **H.S. Requirements:** High school diploma required; GED accepted **Costs Per Year:** Application fee: $35. State resident tuition: $10,410 full-time, $347 per credit hour part-time. Nonresident tuition: $26,873 full-time, $895.75 per credit hour part-time. Mandatory fees: $470 full-time, $235 per term part-time. Full-time tuition and fees vary according to course load, degree level, program, and student level. Part-time tuition and fees vary according to course load, degree level, program, and student level. College room and board: $7394. College room only: $3052. Room and board charges vary according to board plan and housing facility. **Scholarships:** Available **Calendar System:** Semester, Summer Session Available **Enrollment:** FT 33,618, PT 2,871, Grad FT 7,985, Grad PT 2,804 **Faculty:** FT 2,620, PT 352 **Student-Faculty Ratio:** 17:1 **Exams:** SAT I or ACT. **% Receiving Financial Aid:** 48 **% Residing in College-Owned, -Operated, or -Affiliated Housing:** 40 **Library Holdings:** 4,994,033 **Regional Accreditation:** North Central Association of Colleges and Schools **Credit Hours For Degree:** 120 semester hours, Bachelors **ROTC:** Army, Air Force **Professional Accreditation:** AACSB, ABET, ACEJMC, AALE, AAMFT, AACN, AAFCS, AANA, ACCE, ADtA, ACSP, AOsA, APA, ASLA, ASLHA, AVMA, FIDER, CORE, CSWE, LCMEAMA NAACLS, NASM, NASPAA, NRPA, SAF, TEAC **Intercollegiate Athletics:** Baseball M; Basketball M & W; Cheerleading M & W; Crew W; Cross-Country Running M & W; Equestrian Sports M & W; Field Hockey W; Football M; Golf M & W; Gymnastics W; Ice Hockey M & W; Lacrosse M & W; Racquetball M & W; Rugby M & W; Sailing M & W; Skiing (Cross-Country) M & W; Skiing (Downhill) M & W; Soccer M & W; Softball W; Swimming and Diving M & W; Tennis M & W; Track and Field M & W; Volleyball M & W; Water Polo M & W; Wrestling M

MICHIGAN TECHNOLOGICAL UNIVERSITY
1400 Townsend Dr.
Houghton, MI 49931
Tel: (906)487-1885; Free: 888-MTU-1885
Fax: (906)487-3343
E-mail: mtu4u@mtu.edu
Web Site: http://www.mtu.edu/
President/CEO: Glenn Mroz
Admissions: Allison Carter
Financial Aid: Bill Roberts
Type: University **Sex:** Coed **Scores:** 95.6% SAT V 400+; 100% SAT M 400+; 26.7% ACT 18-23; 55.3% ACT 24-29 **% Accepted:** 73 **Admission Plans:** Deferred Admission **Application Deadline:** Rolling **Application Fee:** $0.00 **H.S. Requirements:** High school diploma required; GED accepted **Costs Per Year:** Application fee: $0. State resident tuition: $10,500 full-time, $350 per credit hour part-time. Nonresident tuition: $22,770 full-time, $759 per credit hour part-time. Mandatory fees: $848 full-time, $423.75 per term part-time. Full-time tuition and fees vary according to course load and program. Part-time tuition and fees vary according to course load and program. College room and board: $8121. College room only: $4401. Room and board charges vary according to board plan and housing facility. **Scholarships:** Available **Calendar System:** Semester, Summer Session Available **Enrollment:** FT 5,559, PT 383, Grad FT 829, Grad PT 377 **Faculty:** FT 379, PT 66 **Student-Faculty Ratio:** 15:1 **Exams:** SAT I or ACT. ACT essay not being used. SAT essay not being used. **% Receiving Financial Aid:** 63 **% Residing in College-Owned, -Operated, or -Affiliated Housing:** 44 **Regional Accreditation:** North Central Association of Colleges and Schools **Credit Hours For Degree:** 64 credit hours, Associates; 120 credit hours, Bachelors **ROTC:** Army, Air Force **Professional Accreditation:** AACSB, ABET, SAF, TEAC **Intercollegiate Athletics:** Basketball M & W; Cross-Country Running M & W; Fencing M & W; Football M; Ice Hockey M & W; Racquetball M & W; Riflery M & W; Skiing (Cross-Country) M & W; Skiing (Downhill) M & W; Soccer M & W; Squash M & W; Swimming and Diving M & W; Table Tennis M & W; Tennis M & W; Track and Field M & W; Volleyball W; Water Polo M & W

MID MICHIGAN COMMUNITY COLLEGE
1375 South Clare Ave.
Harrison, MI 48625-9447
Tel: (989)386-6622
Admissions: (989)386-6661
Fax: (989)386-9088
E-mail: apply@midmich.edu
Web Site: http://www.midmich.edu/
President/CEO: Carol Churchill
Admissions: Tena Diamond
Type: Two-Year College **Sex:** Coed **Affiliation:** Michigan Department of Education **% Accepted:** 100 **Admission Plans:** Open Admission; Early Admission **Application Deadline:** Rolling **Application Fee:** $0.00 **H.S. Requirements:** High school diploma required; GED accepted **Costs Per Year:** Application fee: $0. Area resident tuition: $1920 full-time, $80 per

contact hour part-time. State resident tuition: $3576 full-time, $140 per credit part-time. Nonresident tuition: $6528 full-time, $272 per contact hour part-time. Mandatory fees: $120 full-time, $60 per term part-time. **Scholarships:** Available **Calendar System:** Semester, Summer Session Available **Enrollment:** FT 1,941, PT 1,977 **Faculty:** FT 38, PT 146 **Student-Faculty Ratio:** 30:1 **Library Holdings:** 29,450 **Regional Accreditation:** North Central Association of Colleges and Schools **Credit Hours For Degree:** 62 credit hours, Associates **Professional Accreditation:** JRCERT

MONROE COUNTY COMMUNITY COLLEGE
1555 South Raisinville Rd.
Monroe, MI 48161-9047
Tel: (734)242-7300
Admissions: (734)384-4261
Fax: (734)242-9711
E-mail: mhall@monroeccc.edu
Web Site: http://www.monroeccc.edu/
President/CEO: Dr. David E. Nixon
Admissions: Mark V. Hall
Type: Two-Year College **Sex:** Coed **Affiliation:** Michigan Department of Education **% Accepted:** 100 **Admission Plans:** Open Admission; Early Admission; Deferred Admission **Application Fee:** $25.00 **H.S. Requirements:** High school diploma required; GED accepted **Costs Per Year:** Application fee: $25. Area resident tuition: $73 per contact hour part-time. State resident tuition: $121 per contact hour part-time. Nonresident tuition: $134 per contact hour part-time. **Calendar System:** Semester, Summer Session Available **Enrollment:** FT 1,712, PT 2,721 **Faculty:** FT 54, PT 147 **Exams:** ACT, Other. **Library Holdings:** 47,352 **Regional Accreditation:** North Central Association of Colleges and Schools **Credit Hours For Degree:** 60 credit hours, Associates **Professional Accreditation:** ACF, CARC, NLN

MONTCALM COMMUNITY COLLEGE
2800 College Dr.
Sidney, MI 48885
Tel: (989)328-2111
Admissions: (989)328-1276
Fax: (989)328-2950
E-mail: admissions@montcalm.edu
Web Site: http://www.montcalm.edu/
President/CEO: Robert Ferrentino, JD
Admissions: Debra Alexander
Type: Two-Year College **Sex:** Coed **Affiliation:** Michigan Department of Education **Scores:** 59% ACT 18-23; 15% ACT 24-29 **% Accepted:** 100 **Admission Plans:** Open Admission; Early Admission; Deferred Admission **Application Deadline:** Rolling **Application Fee:** $0.00 **H.S. Requirements:** High school diploma required; GED accepted **Costs Per Year:** Application fee: $0. Area resident tuition: $2310 full-time, $77 per credit hour part-time. State resident tuition: $3990 full-time, $133 per credit hour part-time. Nonresident tuition: $5850 full-time, $195 per credit hour part-time. Mandatory fees: $195 full-time, $6.50 per credit hour part-time. Full-time tuition and fees vary according to course load. Part-time tuition and fees vary according to course load. **Scholarships:** Available **Calendar System:** Semester, Summer Session Available **Enrollment:** FT 937, PT 1,391 **Faculty:** FT 34, PT 145 **Student-Faculty Ratio:** 21:1 **Library Holdings:** 29,848 **Regional Accreditation:** North Central Association of Colleges and Schools **Credit Hours For Degree:** 60 credit hours, Associates

MOTT COMMUNITY COLLEGE
1401 East Ct. St.
Flint, MI 48503-2089
Tel: (810)762-0200
Admissions: (810)762-0315
Fax: (810)762-0292
Web Site: http://www.mcc.edu/
President/CEO: Dr. M. Richard Shaink
Admissions: Delores Deen
Type: Two-Year College **Sex:** Coed **Affiliation:** Michigan Labor and Economic Growth Department **Admission Plans:** Open Admission; Early Admission; Deferred Admission **Application Deadline:** August 31 **Application Fee:** $0.00 **H.S. Requirements:** High school diploma or equivalent not required. For nursing, allied health programs, applicants under 19: High school diploma required; GED accepted **Scholarships:** Available **Calendar System:** Semester, Summer Session Available **Enrollment:** FT 3,743, PT 6,712 **Faculty:** FT 141, PT 326 **Student-Faculty Ratio:** 24:1 **Library Holdings:** 96,910 **Regional Accreditation:** North Central Association of Colleges and Schools **Credit Hours For Degree:** 62 credit hours, Associates **Professional Accreditation:** ADA, AOTA, APTA, CARC, NLN **Intercollegiate Athletics:** Baseball M; Basketball M & W; Cross-Country Running M & W; Golf M; Softball W; Volleyball W

MUSKEGON COMMUNITY COLLEGE
221 South Quarterline Rd.
Muskegon, MI 49442-1493
Tel: (231)773-9131
Fax: (231)777-0255
Web Site: http://www.muskegoncc.edu/
President/CEO: Dr. Dale K. Nesbary
Admissions: Darlene Peklar
Type: Two-Year College **Sex:** Coed **Affiliation:** Michigan Department of Education **Admission Plans:** Open Admission; Early Admission; Deferred Admission **Application Deadline:** Rolling **Application Fee:** $0.00 **H.S. Requirements:** High school diploma required; GED accepted **Costs Per Year:** Application fee: $0. Area resident tuition: $72.25 per credit hour part-time. State resident tuition: $119 per credit hour part-time. Nonresident tuition: $161.50 per credit hour part-time. **Scholarships:** Available **Calendar System:** Semester, Summer Session Available **Faculty:** FT 100, PT 50 **Student-Faculty Ratio:** 20:1 **Library Holdings:** 48,597 **Regional Accreditation:** North Central Association of Colleges and Schools **Credit Hours For Degree:** 62 credit hours, Associates **Professional Accreditation:** CARC **Intercollegiate Athletics:** Baseball M; Basketball M & W; Golf M & W; Softball W; Tennis M & W; Volleyball W; Wrestling M

NORTH CENTRAL MICHIGAN COLLEGE
1515 Howard St.
Petoskey, MI 49770-8717
Tel: (231)348-6600; Free: 888-298-6605
Admissions: (231)439-6511
E-mail: jtobin@ncmich.edu
Web Site: http://www.ncmich.edu/
President/CEO: Dr. Cameron Brunet-Koch
Admissions: Julieanne Tobin
Type: Two-Year College **Sex:** Coed **Admission Plans:** Open Admission **Application Deadline:** Rolling **Application Fee:** $0.00 **H.S. Requirements:** High school diploma or equivalent not required. For nursing program: High school diploma required; GED accepted **Scholarships:** Available **Calendar System:** Semester, Summer Session Available **Faculty:** FT 31, PT 102 **Student-Faculty Ratio:** 17:1 **Exams:** ACT. **Library Holdings:** 29,249 **Regional Accreditation:** North Central Association of Colleges and Schools **Credit Hours For Degree:** 60 credit hours, Associates

NORTHERN MICHIGAN UNIVERSITY
1401 Presque Isle Ave.
Marquette, MI 49855-5301
Tel: (906)227-1000; Free: 800-682-9797
Admissions: (906)227-2650
Fax: (906)227-1747
E-mail: admiss@nmu.edu
Web Site: http://www.nmu.edu/
President/CEO: Dr. Leslie E. Wong
Admissions: Gerri Daniels
Financial Aid: Michael Rotundo
Type: Comprehensive **Sex:** Coed **Scores:** 57% ACT 18-23; 33% ACT 24-29 **% Accepted:** 73 **Admission Plans:** Deferred Admission **Application Deadline:** Rolling **Application Fee:** $30.00 **H.S. Requirements:** High school diploma required; GED accepted **Costs Per Year:** Application fee: $30. One-time mandatory fee: $225. State resident tuition: $6840 full-time, $285 per credit hour part-time. Nonresident tuition: $11,214 full-time, $467.25 per credit hour part-time. Mandatory fees: $614 full-time, $31.13 per term part-time. College room and board: $7846. College room only: $3948. Room and board charges vary according to board plan and housing facility. **Scholarships:** Available **Calendar System:** Semester, Summer Session Available **Enrollment:** FT 7,794, PT 784, Grad FT 183, Grad PT 497 **Faculty:** FT 317, PT 145 **Student-Faculty Ratio:** 23:1 **Exams:** SAT I or ACT. ACT essay not being used. SAT essay not being used. **% Receiving Financial Aid:** 57 **% Residing in College-Owned, -Operated, or -Affiliated Housing:** 35 **Library Holdings:** 631,244 **Regional Accreditation:** North Central Association of Colleges and Schools **Credit Hours For Degree:** 62 credit hours, Associates; 124 credit hours, Bachelors **ROTC:**

Army **Professional Accreditation:** AACSB, AACN, ASLHA, CSWE, NAACLS, NASM, NCATE, NAIT **Intercollegiate Athletics:** Crew M & W; Cross-Country Running W; Football M; Golf M; Ice Hockey M & W; Lacrosse M; Rugby M & W; Skiing (Cross-Country) M & W; Skiing (Downhill) M & W; Soccer M & W; Track and Field M & W; Ultimate Frisbee M & W; Volleyball W

NORTHWESTERN MICHIGAN COLLEGE
1701 East Front St.
Traverse City, MI 49686-3061
Tel: (231)995-1000; Free: 800-748-0566
Admissions: (231)995-1034
Fax: (231)995-1680
E-mail: welcome@nmc.edu
Web Site: http://www.nmc.edu/
President/CEO: Timothy Nelson
Admissions: James Bensley
Financial Aid: Deb Faas
Type: Two-Year College **Sex:** Coed **% Accepted:** 89 **Admission Plans:** Open Admission; Early Admission; Deferred Admission **Application Deadline:** Rolling **Application Fee:** $15.00 **H.S. Requirements:** High school diploma required; GED accepted **Scholarships:** Available **Calendar System:** Semester, Summer Session Available **Enrollment:** FT 2,011, PT 2,598 **Faculty:** FT 91, PT 189 **Student-Faculty Ratio:** 18:1 **% Residing in College-Owned, -Operated, or -Affiliated Housing:** 5 **Library Holdings:** 97,458 **Regional Accreditation:** North Central Association of Colleges and Schools **Credit Hours For Degree:** 64 credits, Associates **Professional Accreditation:** ACF, ADA, ACBSP

NORTHWOOD UNIVERSITY
4000 Whiting Dr.
Midland, MI 48640-2398
Tel: (989)837-4200; Free: 800-457-7878
Admissions: (989)837-4273
Fax: (989)837-4490
E-mail: miadmit@northwood.edu
Web Site: http://www.northwood.edu/
President/CEO: Keith A. Pretty, JD
Admissions: Daniel F. Toland
Financial Aid: Terri Mieler
Type: Comprehensive **Sex:** Coed **Scores:** 89% SAT V 400+; 97% SAT M 400+; 65% ACT 18-23; 21% ACT 24-29 **% Accepted:** 75 **Admission Plans:** Early Admission; Deferred Admission **Application Deadline:** Rolling **Application Fee:** $25.00 **H.S. Requirements:** High school diploma required; GED accepted **Costs Per Year:** Application fee: $25. Tuition: $17,430 full-time, $363 per quarter hour part-time. Mandatory fees: $978 full-time. Full-time tuition and fees vary according to class time. Part-time tuition varies according to class time. **Scholarships:** Available **Calendar System:** Quarter, Summer Session Available **Enrollment:** FT 1,888, PT 62 **Faculty:** FT 53, PT 76 **Student-Faculty Ratio:** 26:1 **Exams:** SAT I or ACT. **% Receiving Financial Aid:** 71 **% Residing in College-Owned, -Operated, or -Affiliated Housing:** 37 **Library Holdings:** 40,063 **Regional Accreditation:** North Central Association of Colleges and Schools **Credit Hours For Degree:** 90 credit hours, Associates; 180 credit hours, Bachelors **Intercollegiate Athletics:** Baseball M; Basketball M & W; Cheerleading M & W; Cross-Country Running M & W; Football M; Golf M & W; Soccer M & W; Softball W; Tennis M & W; Track and Field M & W; Volleyball W

OAKLAND COMMUNITY COLLEGE
2480 Opdyke Rd.
Bloomfield Hills, MI 48304-2266
Tel: (248)341-2000
Admissions: (248)341-2186
Fax: (248)341-2099
E-mail: mhmccall@oaklandcc.edu
Web Site: http://www.oaklandcc.edu/
President/CEO: Dr. Timothy Meyer
Admissions: Dr. Maurice McCall
Type: Two-Year College **Sex:** Coed **% Accepted:** 100 **Admission Plans:** Open Admission; Deferred Admission **Application Deadline:** Rolling **Application Fee:** $0.00 **H.S. Requirements:** High school diploma or equivalent not required. For allied health programs: High school diploma required; GED accepted **Costs Per Year:** Application fee: $0. Area resident tuition: $1803 full-time, $60.10 per credit hour part-time. State resident tuition: $3051 full-time, $101.70 per credit hour part-time. Nonresident tuition: $4281 full-time, $142.70 per credit hour part-time. Mandatory fees: $70 full-time, $35 per term part-time. Full-time tuition and fees vary according to course load. Part-time tuition and fees vary according to course load. **Scholarships:** Available **Calendar System:** Semester, Summer Session Available **Enrollment:** FT 10,032, PT 18,010 **Faculty:** FT 247, PT 811 **Student-Faculty Ratio:** 27:1 **Library Holdings:** 276,969 **Regional Accreditation:** North Central Association of Colleges and Schools **Credit Hours For Degree:** 62 credit hours, Associates **Professional Accreditation:** AAMAE, ACF, ADA, CARC, JRCEDMS, JRCERT, NLN **Intercollegiate Athletics:** Basketball M & W; Cross-Country Running M & W; Golf M; Soccer M; Softball W; Tennis W; Track and Field M & W; Volleyball W

OAKLAND UNIVERSITY
Rochester, MI 48309-4401
Tel: (248)370-2100; Free: 800-OAK-UNIV
Admissions: (248)370-3364
Fax: (248)370-4462
E-mail: ouinfo@oakland.edu
Web Site: http://www.oakland.edu/
President/CEO: Dr. Gary Russi
Admissions: Eleanor Reynolds
Financial Aid: Cindy Hermsen
Type: University **Sex:** Coed **Scores:** 50.6% ACT 18-23; 31.7% ACT 24-29 **% Accepted:** 69 **Admission Plans:** Deferred Admission **Application Deadline:** Rolling **Application Fee:** $0.00 **H.S. Requirements:** High school diploma required; GED accepted **Costs Per Year:** Application fee: $0. State resident tuition: $8783 full-time, $292.75 per credit part-time. Nonresident tuition: $20,498 full-time, $683.25 per credit hour part-time. Full-time tuition varies according to program and student level. Part-time tuition varies according to program and student level. College room and board: $7350. Room and board charges vary according to housing facility. **Scholarships:** Available **Calendar System:** Semester, Summer Session Available **Enrollment:** FT 11,335, PT 3,940, Grad FT 1,346, Grad PT 2,299 **Student-Faculty Ratio:** 21:1 **Exams:** ACT, SAT I or ACT. ACT essay used for placement. **% Receiving Financial Aid:** 48 **% Residing in College-Owned, -Operated, or -Affiliated Housing:** 13 **Library Holdings:** 856,760 **Regional Accreditation:** North Central Association of Colleges and Schools **Credit Hours For Degree:** 124 credits, Bachelors **ROTC:** Air Force **Professional Accreditation:** AACSB, ABET, AACN, AANA, ACA, APTA, ASC, NASD, NASM, NASPAA, NAST, NCATE, TEAC **Intercollegiate Athletics:** Baseball M; Basketball M & W; Cross-Country Running M & W; Golf M & W; Ice Hockey M; Soccer M & W; Softball W; Swimming and Diving M & W; Tennis W; Track and Field M & W; Volleyball W

OLIVET COLLEGE
320 South Main St.
Olivet, MI 49076-9701
Tel: (269)749-7000; Free: 800-456-7189
Fax: (616)749-3821
E-mail: lvallar@olivetcollege.edu
Web Site: http://www.olivetcollege.edu/
President/CEO: Dr. Donald L. Tuski
Admissions: Larry Vallar
Financial Aid: Libby M. Jean
Type: Comprehensive **Sex:** Coed **Affiliation:** Congregational Christian Church **Admission Plans:** Deferred Admission **Application Deadline:** Rolling **Application Fee:** $25.00 **H.S. Requirements:** High school diploma required; GED accepted **Costs Per Year:** Application fee: $25. Comprehensive fee: $26,800 includes full-time tuition ($19,138), mandatory fees ($790), and college room and board ($6872). College room only: $3472. Full-time tuition and fees vary according to reciprocity agreements. Room and board charges vary according to board plan and housing facility. Part-time tuition: $637 per semester hour. Part-time mandatory fees: $395 per term. Part-time tuition and fees vary according to course load and reciprocity agreements. **Scholarships:** Available **Calendar System:** Miscellaneous, Summer Session Available **Exams:** SAT I or ACT. **% Receiving Financial Aid:** 82 **Library Holdings:** 90,000 **Regional Accreditation:** North Central Association of Colleges and Schools **Credit Hours For Degree:** 120 semester hours, Bachelors **Professional Accreditation:** TEAC **Intercollegiate Athletics:** Baseball M; Basketball M & W; Cross-Country Running M & W; Football M; Golf M & W; Soccer M & W; Softball W; Swimming and Diving M & W; Tennis W; Track and Field M & W; Volleyball W; Wrestling M

ROCHESTER COLLEGE
800 West Avon Rd.
Rochester Hills, MI 48307-2764
Tel: (248)218-2000; Free: 800-521-6010
Admissions: (248)218-2190
Fax: (248)218-2005
E-mail: admissions@rc.edu
Web Site: http://www.rc.edu/
President/CEO: Dr. Michael W. Westerfield
Admissions: Larry Norman
Financial Aid: Kara Miller
Type: Comprehensive **Sex:** Coed **Affiliation:** Church of Christ **Scores:** 100% SAT V 400+; 83% SAT M 400+; 50% ACT 18-23; 32% ACT 24-29 **% Accepted:** 80 **Admission Plans:** Early Admission; Deferred Admission **Application Deadline:** Rolling **Application Fee:** $25.00 **H.S. Requirements:** High school diploma required; GED accepted **Costs Per Year:** Application fee: $25. One-time mandatory fee: $175. Comprehensive fee: $22,858 includes full-time tuition ($15,792), mandatory fees ($1570), and college room and board ($5496). College room only: $2904. Full-time tuition and fees vary according to course load. Room and board charges vary according to housing facility. Part-time tuition: $512 per credit hour. Part-time tuition varies according to course load. **Scholarships:** Available **Calendar System:** Semester, Summer Session Available **Enrollment:** FT 636, PT 334 **Faculty:** FT 46, PT 113 **Student-Faculty Ratio:** 6:1 **Exams:** SAT I or ACT. **% Residing in College-Owned, -Operated, or -Affiliated Housing:** 25 **Library Holdings:** 55,000 **Regional Accreditation:** North Central Association of Colleges and Schools **Credit Hours For Degree:** 64 credit hours, Associates; 128 credit hours, Bachelors **Intercollegiate Athletics:** Baseball M; Basketball M & W; Golf M; Soccer M & W; Softball W; Volleyball W

SACRED HEART MAJOR SEMINARY
2701 Chicago Blvd.
Detroit, MI 48206-1799
Tel: (313)883-8500
Admissions: (313)883-8552
Web Site: http://www.shms.edu/
President/CEO: Msgr. Jeffrey Monforton
Admissions: Fr. Michael Byrnes
Type: Comprehensive **Sex:** Coed **Affiliation:** Roman Catholic **Scores:** 40% ACT 18-23; 60% ACT 24-29 **% Accepted:** 100 **Admission Plans:** Preferred Admission; Early Admission; Deferred Admission **Application Deadline:** August 15 **Application Fee:** $30.00 **H.S. Requirements:** High school diploma required; GED accepted **Costs Per Year:** Application fee: $30. Comprehensive fee: $22,190 includes full-time tuition ($14,310), mandatory fees ($80), and college room and board ($7800). Part-time tuition: $335 per credit hour. Part-time mandatory fees: $40 per term. **Scholarships:** Available **Calendar System:** Semester, Summer Session Not available **Enrollment:** FT 50, PT 185, Grad FT 65, Grad PT 110 **Faculty:** FT 30, PT 39 **Student-Faculty Ratio:** 5:1 **Exams:** SAT I or ACT. ACT essay used for admission. SAT essay used for admission. **% Receiving Financial Aid:** 63 **% Residing in College-Owned, -Operated, or -Affiliated Housing:** 18 **Regional Accreditation:** North Central Association of Colleges and Schools **Credit Hours For Degree:** 64 credits, Associates; 120 credits, Bachelors **Professional Accreditation:** ACIPE, ATS

SAGINAW CHIPPEWA TRIBAL COLLEGE
2274 Enterprise Dr.
Mount Pleasant, MI 48858
Tel: (989)775-4123
Fax: (989)775-4528
E-mail: treed@sagchip.org
Web Site: http://www.sagchip.org/tribalcollege/
President/CEO: Betty Redleaf-Collett
Admissions: Tracy Reed
Type: Two-Year College **Sex:** Coed **% Accepted:** 100 **Application Fee:** $0.00 **Calendar System:** Semester **Enrollment:** FT 43, PT 80 **Faculty:** FT 4, PT 13 **Student-Faculty Ratio:** 9:1 **Regional Accreditation:** North Central Association of Colleges and Schools

SAGINAW VALLEY STATE UNIVERSITY
7400 Bay Rd.
University Center, MI 48710
Tel: (989)964-4000; Free: 800-968-9500
Admissions: (989)964-4200
Fax: (989)964-0180
E-mail: admissions@svsu.edu
Web Site: http://www.svsu.edu/
President/CEO: Dr. Eric R. Gilbertson
Admissions: Jennifer Pahl
Financial Aid: Robert Lemuel
Type: Comprehensive **Sex:** Coed **Scores:** 48.4% ACT 18-23; 26.9% ACT 24-29 **% Accepted:** 86 **Admission Plans:** Deferred Admission **Application Deadline:** Rolling **Application Fee:** $25.00 **H.S. Requirements:** High school diploma required; GED accepted **Costs Per Year:** Application fee: $25. State resident tuition: $6452 full-time, $215.40 per credit hour part-time. Nonresident tuition: $15,762 full-time, $525.40 per credit hour part-time. Mandatory fees: $438 full-time, $14.60 per credit hour part-time. Full-time tuition and fees vary according to course level, course load, location, and program. Part-time tuition and fees vary according to course level, course load, location, and program. College room and board: $7270. College room only: $4110. Room and board charges vary according to board plan, housing facility, and student level. **Scholarships:** Available **Calendar System:** Semester, Summer Session Available **Enrollment:** FT 7,373, PT 1,427, Grad FT 288, Grad PT 1,410 **Faculty:** FT 297, PT 300 **Student-Faculty Ratio:** 22:1 **Exams:** ACT. **% Receiving Financial Aid:** 63 **% Residing in College-Owned, -Operated, or -Affiliated Housing:** 30 **Final Year or Final Semester Residency Requirement:** Yes **Library Holdings:** 241,661 **Regional Accreditation:** North Central Association of Colleges and Schools **Credit Hours For Degree:** 124 credit hours, Bachelors **Professional Accreditation:** AACSB, ABET, AACN, AOTA, CSWE, NCATE, NLN **Intercollegiate Athletics:** Baseball M; Basketball M & W; Bowling M; Cheerleading M & W; Cross-Country Running M & W; Equestrian Sports M & W; Football M; Golf M; Gymnastics M & W; Ice Hockey M; Lacrosse M & W; Rugby M & W; Soccer M & W; Softball W; Tennis M & W; Track and Field M & W; Ultimate Frisbee M & W; Volleyball W; Wrestling M

ST. CLAIR COUNTY COMMUNITY COLLEGE
323 Erie St., PO Box 5015
Port Huron, MI 48061-5015
Tel: (810)984-3881
Admissions: (810)989-5552
Fax: (810)984-4730
Web Site: http://www.sc4.edu/
President/CEO: Dr. Kevin Pollock
Admissions: Pete Lacey
Type: Two-Year College **Sex:** Coed **Affiliation:** Michigan Department of Education **Admission Plans:** Open Admission; Early Admission **Application Deadline:** Rolling **Application Fee:** $0.00 **H.S. Requirements:** High school diploma required; GED accepted. Certain applicants 18 or over can be admitted as special tudents without a high school diploma or GED. **Scholarships:** Available **Calendar System:** Semester, Summer Session Available **Student-Faculty Ratio:** 22:1 **Regional Accreditation:** North Central Association of Colleges and Schools **Credit Hours For Degree:** 62 credits, Associates **Intercollegiate Athletics:** Baseball M; Basketball M & W; Golf M; Softball W; Volleyball W

SCHOOLCRAFT COLLEGE
18600 Haggerty Rd.
Livonia, MI 48152-2696
Tel: (734)462-4400
Fax: (734)462-4553
E-mail: admissions@schoolcraft.edu
Web Site: http://www.schoolcraft.edu/
President/CEO: Dr. Conway A. Jeffress
Admissions: Cheryl Hagen
Type: Two-Year College **Sex:** Coed **Affiliation:** Michigan Department of Education **Admission Plans:** Open Admission; Early Admission; Deferred Admission **Application Deadline:** Rolling **Application Fee:** $0.00 **H.S. Requirements:** High school diploma required; GED accepted **Scholarships:** Available **Calendar System:** Semester, Summer Session Available **Enrollment:** FT 4,035, PT 7,070 **Faculty:** FT 94, PT 335 **Student-Faculty Ratio:** 30:1 **Regional Accreditation:** North Central Association of Colleges and Schools **Credit Hours For Degree:** 60 credit hours, Associates **Professional Accreditation:** AHIMA **Intercollegiate Athletics:** Basketball M & W; Cross-Country Running W; Golf M & W; Soccer M & W; Volleyball W

SIENA HEIGHTS UNIVERSITY
1247 East Siena Heights Dr.
Adrian, MI 49221-1796

Tel: (517)263-0731; Free: 800-521-0009
Admissions: (517)264-7185
Fax: (517)264-7745
E-mail: sjohnson@sienaheights.edu
Web Site: http://www.sienaheights.edu/
President/CEO: Sr. Peg Albert, OP,PhD
Admissions: Sara Johnson
Type: Comprehensive **Sex:** Coed **Affiliation:** Roman Catholic **Scores:** 56% ACT 18-23; 13% ACT 24-29 **% Accepted:** 69 **Admission Plans:** Deferred Admission **Application Deadline:** Rolling **Application Fee:** $25.00 **H.S. Requirements:** High school diploma required; GED accepted **Costs Per Year:** Application fee: $25. Comprehensive fee: $26,280 includes full-time tuition ($18,610), mandatory fees ($600), and college room and board ($7070). Full-time tuition and fees vary according to degree level and location. Room and board charges vary according to board plan and housing facility. Part-time tuition: $375 per semester hour. Part-time mandatory fees: $125 per term. Part-time tuition and fees vary according to course load, degree level, and location. **Scholarships:** Available **Calendar System:** Semester, Summer Session Available **Enrollment:** FT 997, PT 1,031, Grad FT 35, Grad PT 288 **Faculty:** FT 68, PT 148 **Student-Faculty Ratio:** 12:1 **Exams:** SAT I or ACT. ACT essay not being used. SAT essay not being used. **% Residing in College-Owned, -Operated, or -Affiliated Housing:** 54 **Library Holdings:** 142,000 **Regional Accreditation:** North Central Association of Colleges and Schools **Credit Hours For Degree:** 60 semester hours, Associates; 120 semester hours, Bachelors **Professional Accreditation:** NASAD, TEAC **Intercollegiate Athletics:** Baseball M; Basketball M & W; Bowling M & W; Cross-Country Running M & W; Golf M & W; Lacrosse M; Soccer M & W; Softball W; Track and Field M & W; Volleyball M & W

SOUTHWESTERN MICHIGAN COLLEGE

58900 Cherry Grove Rd.
Dowagiac, MI 49047-9793
Tel: (269)782-1000; Free: 800-456-8675
Fax: (269)782-8414
E-mail: mhay@swmich.edu
Web Site: http://www.swmich.edu/
President/CEO: Dr. David Mathews
Admissions: Dr. Margaret Hay
Type: Two-Year College **Sex:** Coed **% Accepted:** 100 **Admission Plans:** Open Admission; Deferred Admission **Application Deadline:** Rolling **Application Fee:** $0.00 **H.S. Requirements:** High school diploma required; GED accepted **Costs Per Year:** Application fee: $0. Area resident tuition: $2648 full-time, $88.25 per credit hour part-time. State resident tuition: $3383 full-time, $112.75 per credit hour part-time. Nonresident tuition: $3668 full-time, $122.25 per credit hour part-time. Mandatory fees: $810 full-time, $27 per credit hour part-time. College room and board: $7160. College room only: $5000. **Scholarships:** Available **Calendar System:** Semester, Summer Session Available **Enrollment:** FT 1,458, PT 1,512 **Faculty:** FT 53, PT 101 **Student-Faculty Ratio:** 23:1 **% Residing in College-Owned, -Operated, or -Affiliated Housing:** 5 **Library Holdings:** 36,149 **Regional Accreditation:** North Central Association of Colleges and Schools **Credit Hours For Degree:** 62 credit hours, Associates

SPRING ARBOR UNIVERSITY

106 East Main St.
Spring Arbor, MI 49283-9799
Tel: (517)750-1200; Free: 800-968-0011
Fax: (517)750-1604
E-mail: admissions@arbor.edu
Web Site: http://www.arbor.edu/
President/CEO: Charles H. Webb
Admissions: Randy Comfort
Financial Aid: Geoff Marsh
Type: Comprehensive **Sex:** Coed **Affiliation:** Free Methodist **Scores:** 98% SAT V 400+; 91% SAT M 400+; 52% ACT 18-23; 31% ACT 24-29 **% Accepted:** 78 **Admission Plans:** Early Admission; Deferred Admission **Application Deadline:** August 1 **Application Fee:** $30.00 **H.S. Requirements:** High school diploma required; GED accepted **Costs Per Year:** Application fee: $30. Comprehensive fee: $26,740 includes full-time tuition ($19,250), mandatory fees ($540), and college room and board ($6950). College room only: $3250. Full-time tuition and fees vary according to course load, degree level, and program. Room and board charges vary according to board plan and housing facility. Part-time tuition: $485 per credit hour. Part-time mandatory fees: $225 per term. Part-time tuition and fees vary according to course load, degree level, program, and reciprocity agreements. **Scholarships:** Available **Calendar System:** 4-1-4, Summer Session Available **Enrollment:** FT 1,978, PT 888, Grad FT 617, Grad PT 637 **Faculty:** FT 83, PT 57 **Student-Faculty Ratio:** 15:1 **Exams:** ACT, SAT I or ACT. ACT essay not being used. SAT essay not being used. **% Receiving Financial Aid:** 86 **% Residing in College-Owned, -Operated, or -Affiliated Housing:** 71 **Final Year or Final Semester Residency Requirement:** No **Library Holdings:** 115,987 **Regional Accreditation:** North Central Association of Colleges and Schools **Credit Hours For Degree:** 62 credits, Associates; 124 credits, Bachelors **ROTC:** Army, Air Force **Professional Accreditation:** AACN, CSWE, NCATE, TEAC **Intercollegiate Athletics:** Baseball M; Basketball M & W; Cross-Country Running M & W; Golf M; Soccer M & W; Softball W; Tennis M & W; Track and Field M & W; Volleyball W

UNIVERSITY OF DETROIT MERCY

4001 West McNichols Rd.
Detroit, MI 48221
Tel: (313)993-1000; Free: 800-635-5020
Fax: (313)993-3326
E-mail: admissions@udmercy.edu
Web Site: http://www.udmercy.edu/
President/CEO: Fr. Gerard Stockhausen, SJ,PhD
Financial Aid: Sandy Ross
Type: University **Sex:** Coed **Affiliation:** Roman Catholic (Jesuit) **Admission Plans:** Deferred Admission **Application Deadline:** Rolling **Application Fee:** $25.00 **H.S. Requirements:** High school diploma required; GED accepted **Costs Per Year:** Application fee: $25. Comprehensive fee: $37,510 includes full-time tuition ($28,920) and college room and board ($8590). College room only: $5030. Full-time tuition varies according to program. Room and board charges vary according to board plan and housing facility. Part-time tuition: $735 per credit hour. Part-time tuition varies according to location and program. **Scholarships:** Available **Calendar System:** Semester, Summer Session Available **Student-Faculty Ratio:** 7:1 **Exams:** SAT I or ACT. **% Receiving Financial Aid:** 80 **Regional Accreditation:** North Central Association of Colleges and Schools **Credit Hours For Degree:** 63 credit hours, Associates; 126 credit hours, Bachelors **Professional Accreditation:** AACSB, ABET, AACN, AANA, ABA, ACA, ADA, APA, AALS, CSWE, NAAB, NLN, TEAC **Intercollegiate Athletics:** Basketball M & W; Cross-Country Running M & W; Fencing M & W; Golf M & W; Soccer M & W; Softball W; Tennis W; Track and Field M & W

UNIVERSITY OF MICHIGAN

Ann Arbor, MI 48109
Tel: (734)764-1817
Admissions: (734)764-7433
Fax: (734)936-0740
Web Site: http://www.umich.edu/
President/CEO: Dr. Mary Sue Coleman
Admissions: Theodore Spencer
Type: University **Sex:** Coed **Scores:** 100% SAT V 400+; 99% SAT M 400+; 6% ACT 18-23; 48% ACT 24-29 **% Accepted:** 50 **Admission Plans:** Early Action; Deferred Admission **Application Deadline:** February 1 **Application Fee:** $40.00 **H.S. Requirements:** High school diploma required; GED accepted **Costs Per Year:** Application fee: $40. State resident tuition: $12,400 full-time, $449 per credit hour part-time. Nonresident tuition: $36,163 full-time, $1419 per credit hour part-time. Mandatory fees: $189 full-time, $95 per term part-time. Full-time tuition and fees vary according to course load, program, and student level. Part-time tuition and fees vary according to course load, program, and student level. College room and board: $8924. Room and board charges vary according to board plan and housing facility. **Scholarships:** Available **Calendar System:** Trimester, Summer Session Available **Enrollment:** FT 25,342, PT 866, Grad FT 13,531, Grad PT 1,935 **Faculty:** FT 2,479, PT 595 **Student-Faculty Ratio:** 15:1 **Exams:** SAT I or ACT, SAT II. **% Receiving Financial Aid:** 46 **% Residing in College-Owned, -Operated, or -Affiliated Housing:** 37 **Final Year or Final Semester Residency Requirement:** No **Library Holdings:** 9,559,140 **Regional Accreditation:** North Central Association of Colleges and Schools **Credit Hours For Degree:** 120 credits, Bachelors **ROTC:** Army, Navy, Air Force **Professional Accreditation:** AACSB, ABET, ACPhE, ARCMI, AACN, ABA, ACNM, ADA, ADtA, ACSP, ALA, APA, ASLA, AALS, ACEHSA, CEPH, CSWE, LCMEAMA, NAAB, NASAD NASD, NASM, SAF, TEAC **Intercollegiate Athletics:** Baseball M; Basketball M & W; Cheerleading M & W; Crew M; Cross-Country Running M & W; Field Hockey W; Football M; Golf M

& W; Gymnastics M & W; Ice Hockey M; Soccer M & W; Softball W; Swimming and Diving M & W; Tennis M & W; Track and Field M & W; Volleyball W; Water Polo W; Wrestling M

UNIVERSITY OF MICHIGAN—DEARBORN
4901 Evergreen Rd.
Dearborn, MI 48128-1491
Tel: (313)593-5000
Admissions: (313)593-5100
E-mail: admissions@umd.umich.edu
Web Site: http://www.umd.umich.edu/
President/CEO: Dr. Daniel Little
Admissions: Christopher Tremblay
Financial Aid: Christopher W. Tremblay
Type: Comprehensive **Sex:** Coed **Affiliation:** University of Michigan System **Scores:** 47.1% ACT 18-23; 43.8% ACT 24-29 **% Accepted:** 67 **Admission Plans:** Deferred Admission **Application Deadline:** Rolling **Application Fee:** $30.00 **H.S. Requirements:** High school diploma required; GED accepted **Costs Per Year:** Application fee: $30. State resident tuition: $8573 full-time, $339.25 per credit hour part-time. Nonresident tuition: $19,356 full-time, $770.35 per credit hour part-time. Mandatory fees: $527 full-time, $163.25 per term part-time. Full-time tuition and fees vary according to course level, course load, program, and student level. Part-time tuition and fees vary according to course level, course load, program, and student level. **Scholarships:** Available **Calendar System:** Semester, Summer Session Available **Enrollment:** FT 4,729, PT 2,049, Grad FT 242, Grad PT 1,323 **Faculty:** FT 306, PT 201 **Student-Faculty Ratio:** 17:1 **Exams:** SAT I or ACT. ACT essay not being used. SAT essay not being used. **% Receiving Financial Aid:** 56 **Library Holdings:** 366,577 **Regional Accreditation:** North Central Association of Colleges and Schools **Credit Hours For Degree:** 120 credit hours, Bachelors **ROTC:** Army, Navy, Air Force **Professional Accreditation:** AACSB, ABET, TEAC **Intercollegiate Athletics:** Basketball M & W; Bowling M & W; Cheerleading M & W; Cross-Country Running M & W; Ice Hockey M; Rugby M; Soccer M & W; Softball W; Ultimate Frisbee M; Volleyball W

UNIVERSITY OF MICHIGAN—FLINT
303 East Kearsley St.
Flint, MI 48502-1950
Tel: (810)762-3000
Admissions: (810)762-3300
E-mail: admissions@umflint.edu
Web Site: http://www.umflint.edu/
President/CEO: Dr. Ruth J. Person
Admissions: Kimberley Buster-Williams
Financial Aid: Lori Vedder
Type: Comprehensive **Sex:** Coed **Affiliation:** University of Michigan System **Scores:** 75% SAT M 400+; 49.03% ACT 18-23; 27.43% ACT 24-29 **% Accepted:** 82 **Admission Plans:** Deferred Admission **Application Fee:** $30.00 **H.S. Requirements:** High school diploma required; GED accepted **Costs Per Year:** Application fee: $30. One-time mandatory fee: $30. State resident tuition: $7899 full-time, $311.40 per credit hour part-time. Nonresident tuition: $15,413 full-time, $622.75 per credit hour part-time. Mandatory fees: $380 full-time, $144.50 per term part-time. Full-time tuition and fees vary according to course level, course load, degree level, program, and student level. Part-time tuition and fees vary according to course level, course load, degree level, program, and student level. College room and board: $6874. College room only: $4274. Room and board charges vary according to board plan. **Scholarships:** Available **Calendar System:** Semester, Summer Session Available **Enrollment:** FT 4,358, PT 2,223, Grad FT 279, Grad PT 913 **Faculty:** FT 257, PT 237 **Student-Faculty Ratio:** 15:1 **Exams:** SAT I or ACT. **% Residing in College-Owned, -Operated, or -Affiliated Housing:** 5 **Final Year or Final Semester Residency Requirement:** No **Library Holdings:** 273,881 **Regional Accreditation:** North Central Association of Colleges and Schools **Credit Hours For Degree:** 120 credit hours, Bachelors **ROTC:** Army, Navy, Air Force **Professional Accreditation:** AACSB, AACN, AANA, APTA, CSWE, JRCERT, NASM, NLN

UNIVERSITY OF PHOENIX—DETROIT CAMPUS
26999 Central Park Blvd., Ste. 100
Southfield, MI 48076
Tel: (248)262-3003
Web Site: http://www.phoenix.edu/
Type: Comprehensive **Sex:** Coed **Scholarships:** Available **Professional Accreditation:** NLN

UNIVERSITY OF PHOENIX—METRO DETROIT CAMPUS
5480 Corporate Dr.
Ste. 240
Troy, MI 48098-2623
Tel: (248)925-4100; Free: 800-228-7240
Admissions: (480)557-6151
Fax: (248)267-0147
E-mail: audra.mcquarie@phoenix.edu
Web Site: http://www.phoenix.edu/
President/CEO: William Pepicello
Admissions: Audra McQuarie
Type: Comprehensive **Sex:** Coed **Admission Plans:** Open Admission; Deferred Admission **Application Deadline:** Rolling **Application Fee:** $0.00 **H.S. Requirements:** High school diploma required; GED accepted **Costs Per Year:** Application fee: $0. Tuition: $13,200 full-time. Full-time tuition varies according to course level and course load. **Scholarships:** Available **Calendar System:** Continuous, Summer Session Not available **Enrollment:** FT 2,018 **Faculty:** FT 39, PT 290 **Library Holdings:** 1,759 **Regional Accreditation:** North Central Association of Colleges and Schools **Credit Hours For Degree:** 60 credits, Associates; 120 credits, Bachelors **Professional Accreditation:** NLN

UNIVERSITY OF PHOENIX—WEST MICHIGAN CAMPUS
318 River Ridge Dr. NW
Walker, MI 49544
Tel: (616)647-5100; Free: 800-228-7240
Admissions: (480)557-6151
E-mail: audra.mcquarie@phoenix.edu
Web Site: http://www.phoenix.edu/
President/CEO: William Pepicello
Admissions: Audra McQuarie
Type: Comprehensive **Sex:** Coed **Admission Plans:** Open Admission; Deferred Admission **Application Deadline:** Rolling **H.S. Requirements:** High school diploma required; GED accepted **Costs Per Year:** Tuition: $12,525 full-time. Full-time tuition varies according to course level and course load. **Scholarships:** Available **Calendar System:** Continuous, Summer Session Not available **Enrollment:** FT 456 **Faculty:** FT 13, PT 136 **Regional Accreditation:** North Central Association of Colleges and Schools **Credit Hours For Degree:** 60 credits, Associates; 120 credits, Bachelors **Professional Accreditation:** NLN

WALSH COLLEGE OF ACCOUNTANCY AND BUSINESS ADMINISTRATION
3838 Livernois Rd., PO Box 7006
Troy, MI 48007-7006
Tel: (248)689-8282
Admissions: (248)823-1344
Fax: (248)524-2520
E-mail: jguc@walshcollege.edu
Web Site: http://www.walshcollege.edu/
President/CEO: Stephanie W. Bergeron, MBA
Admissions: Jeremy Guc
Financial Aid: Howard Thomas
Type: Two-Year Upper Division **Sex:** Coed **Admission Plans:** Open Admission; Deferred Admission **Application Fee:** $25.00 **Scholarships:** Available **Calendar System:** Miscellaneous, Summer Session Available **Enrollment:** FT 149, PT 876 **Faculty:** FT 18, PT 160 **Student-Faculty Ratio:** 17:1 **% Receiving Financial Aid:** 40 **Library Holdings:** 26,300 **Regional Accreditation:** North Central Association of Colleges and Schools **Credit Hours For Degree:** 127 credit hours, Bachelors

WASHTENAW COMMUNITY COLLEGE
4800 East Huron River Dr., PO Box D-1
Ann Arbor, MI 48106
Tel: (734)973-3300
Admissions: (734)973-3315
Fax: (734)677-5408
Web Site: http://www.wccnet.edu/
President/CEO: Larry Whitworth
Admissions: Sukanya J. Jett
Type: Two-Year College **Sex:** Coed **Admission Plans:** Open Admission;

Preferred Admission; Early Admission; Deferred Admission **Application Deadline:** Rolling **H.S. Requirements:** High school diploma required; GED accepted. For health occupations programs only, otherwise open enrollment: High school diploma required; GED accepted **Costs Per Year:** Area resident tuition: $2400 full-time, $80 per credit hour part-time. State resident tuition: $3930 full-time, $131 per credit hour part-time. Nonresident tuition: $5220 full-time, $174 per credit hour part-time. **Scholarships:** Available **Calendar System:** Semester, Summer Session Available **Student-Faculty Ratio:** 16:1 **Exams:** SAT I or ACT. **Regional Accreditation:** North Central Association of Colleges and Schools **Credit Hours For Degree:** 60 credit hours, Associates **ROTC:** Army, Navy, Air Force **Professional Accreditation:** ACF, ADA, JRCERT, NLN

WAYNE COUNTY COMMUNITY COLLEGE DISTRICT

801 West Fort St.
Detroit, MI 48226-3010
Tel: (313)496-2600
Admissions: (313)496-2634
Fax: (313)961-2791
E-mail: caafjh@wccc.edu
Web Site: http://www.wcccd.edu/
President/CEO: Dr. Curtis L. Ivery
Type: Two-Year College **Sex:** Coed **Admission Plans:** Open Admission; Early Admission; Deferred Admission **Application Deadline:** Rolling **H.S. Requirements:** High school diploma or equivalent not required. For applicants under 18, allied health program: High school diploma required; GED accepted **Costs Per Year:** Area resident tuition: $2030 full-time, $67.65 per credit hour part-time. State resident tuition: $3000 full-time, $100 per credit hour part-time. Nonresident tuition: $3900 full-time, $130 per credit hour part-time. Mandatory fees: $300 full-time, $7 per credit hour part-time, $45 per term part-time. **Scholarships:** Available **Calendar System:** Semester, Summer Session Available **Student-Faculty Ratio:** 21:1 **Regional Accreditation:** North Central Association of Colleges and Schools **Credit Hours For Degree:** 60 credits, Associates **Professional Accreditation:** ARCEST, ADA, AOTA, CARC **Intercollegiate Athletics:** Basketball M & W; Golf M; Track and Field M; Volleyball W

WAYNE STATE UNIVERSITY

656 West Kirby St.
Detroit, MI 48202
Tel: (313)577-2424; Free: 877-WSU-INFO
Admissions: (313)577-3577
Fax: (313)577-7536
E-mail: admissions@wayne.edu
Web Site: http://www.wayne.edu/
President/CEO: Dr. Jay Noren
Admissions: Judy Benfield Tatam
Financial Aid: Albert Hermsen
Type: University **Sex:** Coed **Scores:** 45% ACT 18-23; 21% ACT 24-29 **% Accepted:** 75 **Admission Plans:** Deferred Admission **Application Deadline:** August 1 **Application Fee:** $30.00 **H.S. Requirements:** High school diploma required; GED accepted **Costs Per Year:** Application fee: $30. State resident tuition: $7571 full-time, $252.35 per credit hour part-time. Nonresident tuition: $17,340 full-time, $578 per credit hour part-time. Mandatory fees: $1072 full-time, $23.70 per credit hour part-time, $180.45 per term part-time. Full-time tuition and fees vary according to course load, program, and student level. Part-time tuition and fees vary according to course load, program, and student level. College room and board: $7210. Room and board charges vary according to board plan and housing facility. **Scholarships:** Available **Calendar System:** Semester, Summer Session Available **Enrollment:** FT 13,202, PT 7,563, Grad FT 5,868, Grad PT 5,153 **Faculty:** FT 1,055, PT 988 **Student-Faculty Ratio:** 16:1 **Exams:** SAT I or ACT. **% Receiving Financial Aid:** 61 **% Residing in College-Owned, -Operated, or -Affiliated Housing:** 13 **Library Holdings:** 3,665,628 **Regional Accreditation:** North Central Association of Colleges and Schools **Credit Hours For Degree:** 120 credit hours, Bachelors **ROTC:** Air Force **Professional Accreditation:** AACSB, ABET, ACPhE, AACN, AANA, ABA, ABFSE, ACNM, ACA, ADtA, ACSP, ALA, AOTA, APTA, APA, ASC, ASLHA, AALS, CORE, CSWE JRCERT, LCMEAMA, NAACLS, NASD, NASM, NASPAA, NAST, NLN, TEAC **Intercollegiate Athletics:** Baseball M; Basketball M & W; Cross-Country Running M & W; Fencing M & W; Football M; Golf M; Ice Hockey W; Softball W; Swimming and Diving M & W; Tennis M & W; Volleyball W

WEST SHORE COMMUNITY COLLEGE

PO Box 277, 3000 North Stiles Rd.
Scottville, MI 49454-0277
Tel: (231)845-6211
Fax: (231)845-0207
E-mail: admissions@westshore.edu
Web Site: http://www.westshore.edu/
President/CEO: Charles T. Dillon
Admissions: Wendy Fought
Financial Aid: Victoria Oddo
Type: Two-Year College **Sex:** Coed **Affiliation:** Michigan Department of Education **% Accepted:** 100 **Admission Plans:** Open Admission; Early Admission; Deferred Admission **Application Deadline:** Rolling **Application Fee:** $15.00 **H.S. Requirements:** High school diploma or equivalent not required. For nursing program: High school diploma required; GED accepted **Scholarships:** Available **Calendar System:** Semester, Summer Session Available **Faculty:** FT 28, PT 72 **Library Holdings:** 2,500 **Regional Accreditation:** North Central Association of Colleges and Schools **Credit Hours For Degree:** 60 credits, Associates

WESTERN MICHIGAN UNIVERSITY

1903 West Michigan Ave.
Kalamazoo, MI 49008
Tel: (269)387-1000
Admissions: (269)387-2000
Fax: (269)387-2096
E-mail: ask-wmu@wmich.edu
Web Site: http://www.wmich.edu/
President/CEO: Dr. John M. Dunn
Admissions: Penny Bundy
Financial Aid: David Ladd
Type: University **Sex:** Coed **Scores:** 57.97% ACT 18-23; 29.53% ACT 24-29 **% Accepted:** 83 **Admission Plans:** Deferred Admission **Application Deadline:** Rolling **Application Fee:** $35.00 **H.S. Requirements:** High school diploma required; GED accepted **Costs Per Year:** Application fee: $35. One-time mandatory fee: $300. State resident tuition: $7654 full-time, $264.66 per credit hour part-time. Nonresident tuition: $18,774 full-time, $649.24 per credit hour part-time. Mandatory fees: $728 full-time, $195.25 per term part-time. Full-time tuition and fees vary according to course load, location, and student level. Part-time tuition and fees vary according to course load, location, and student level. College room and board: $7784. College room only: $3796. Room and board charges vary according to board plan. **Scholarships:** Available **Calendar System:** Semester, Summer Session Available **Enrollment:** FT 17,043, PT 2,504, Grad FT 1,024, Grad PT 4,005 **Faculty:** FT 908, PT 527 **Student-Faculty Ratio:** 19:1 **Exams:** SAT I or ACT. **% Receiving Financial Aid:** 50 **% Residing in College-Owned, -Operated, or -Affiliated Housing:** 24 **Final Year or Final Semester Residency Requirement:** No **Library Holdings:** 2,816,673 **Regional Accreditation:** North Central Association of Colleges and Schools **Credit Hours For Degree:** 122 credit hours, Bachelors **ROTC:** Army **Professional Accreditation:** AACSB, ABET, AACN, AAFCS, ACA, ADtA, AOTA, APA, ASLHA, CAA, FIDER, CORE, CSWE, NASAD, NASD, NASM, NASPAA, NAST, NCATE, NLN **Intercollegiate Athletics:** Baseball M; Basketball M & W; Cross-Country Running W; Football M; Golf W; Gymnastics W; Ice Hockey M; Soccer M & W; Softball W; Tennis M & W; Track and Field W; Volleyball W

YESHIVA GEDOLAH OF GREATER DETROIT

24600 Greenfield
Oak Park, MI 48237-1544
Tel: (810)968-3360
Admissions: (248)968-3360
President/CEO: Rabbi P. Rushnawitz
Admissions: Rabbi P. Rushnawitz
Financial Aid: Rabbi P. Rushnawitz
Type: Comprehensive **Sex:** Men **Affiliation:** Jewish **% Accepted:** 100 **H.S. Requirements:** High school diploma required; GED not accepted **Professional Accreditation:** AARTS

ACADEMY COLLEGE

1101 East 78th St.
Ste. 100
Minneapolis, MN 55420
Tel: (952)851-0066; Free: 800-292-9149
Fax: (952)851-0094
E-mail: admissions@academycollege.edu
Web Site: http://www.academycollege.edu/
President/CEO: Nancy Grazzini-Olson
Admissions: Tracey Schantz
Type: Four-Year College **Sex:** Coed **Admission Plans:** Open Admission; Early Admission; Deferred Admission **Application Fee:** $30.00 **H.S. Requirements:** High school diploma required; GED accepted **Scholarships:** Available **Calendar System:** Quarter, Summer Session Available **Enrollment:** FT 141, PT 9 **Faculty:** FT 4, PT 50 **Student-Faculty Ratio:** 7:1 **Library Holdings:** 1,309 **Credit Hours For Degree:** 102 credit hours, Associates; 180 credit hours, Bachelors **Professional Accreditation:** ACICS

ALEXANDRIA TECHNICAL COLLEGE

1601 Jefferson St.
Alexandria, MN 56308-3707
Tel: (320)762-0221; Free: 888-234-1222
Admissions: (320)762-4520
Fax: (320)762-4430
E-mail: admissionsrep@alextech.edu
Web Site: http://www.alextech.edu/
President/CEO: Kevin Kopischke
Admissions: Janet Dropik
Type: Two-Year College **Sex:** Coed **Affiliation:** Minnesota State Colleges and Universities System **% Accepted:** 67 **Admission Plans:** Open Admission; Early Admission; Deferred Admission **Application Deadline:** Rolling **Application Fee:** $20.00 **H.S. Requirements:** High school diploma required; GED accepted **Costs Per Year:** Application fee: $20. State resident tuition: $5278 full-time, $138.68 per credit part-time. Nonresident tuition: $5278 full-time, $138.68 per credit part-time. Mandatory fees: $563 full-time, $16.56 per credit hour part-time. **Scholarships:** Available **Calendar System:** Semester, Summer Session Available **Enrollment:** FT 1,562, PT 643 **Faculty:** FT 72, PT 31 **Student-Faculty Ratio:** 20:1 **Library Holdings:** 13,378 **Regional Accreditation:** North Central Association of Colleges and Schools **Professional Accreditation:** NAACLS

ANOKA-RAMSEY COMMUNITY COLLEGE

11200 Mississippi Blvd., NW
Coon Rapids, MN 55433-3470
Tel: (763)433-1100
Admissions: (763)433-1300
Fax: (763)576-5944
E-mail: admissions@anokaramsey.edu
Web Site: http://www.anokaramsey.edu/
President/CEO: Dr. Patrick M. Johns
Type: Two-Year College **Sex:** Coed **Affiliation:** Minnesota State Colleges and Universities System **% Accepted:** 92 **Admission Plans:** Open Admission; Early Admission; Deferred Admission **Application Deadline:** Rolling **Application Fee:** $20.00 **H.S. Requirements:** High school diploma required; GED accepted **Costs Per Year:** Application fee: $20. State resident tuition: $3704 full-time, $123.47 per credit part-time. Nonresident tuition: $3704 full-time, $123.47 per credit part-time. Mandatory fees: $504 full-time, $16.81 per credit part-time. Full-time tuition and fees vary according to course load and program. Part-time tuition and fees vary according to course load and program. **Scholarships:** Available **Calendar System:** Semester, Summer Session Available **Faculty:** FT 89, PT 161 **Student-Faculty Ratio:** 30:1 **Library Holdings:** 41,522 **Regional Accreditation:** North Central Association of Colleges and Schools **Credit Hours For Degree:** 64 semester credits, Associates **ROTC:** Air Force **Professional Accreditation:** APTA, NLN **Intercollegiate Athletics:** Baseball M; Basketball M & W; Soccer M & W; Softball W; Volleyball W

ANOKA-RAMSEY COMMUNITY COLLEGE, CAMBRIDGE CAMPUS

300 Spirit River Dr. South
Cambridge, MN 55008-5706
Tel: (763)433-1110
Admissions: (763)433-1300
Fax: (763)689-7050
E-mail: admissions@anokaramsey.edu
Web Site: http://www.anokaramsey.edu/
President/CEO: Dr. Patrick M. Johns
Type: Two-Year College **Sex:** Coed **Affiliation:** Minnesota State Colleges and Universities System **% Accepted:** 92 **Admission Plans:** Open Admission; Early Admission; Deferred Admission **Application Deadline:** Rolling **Application Fee:** $20.00 **H.S. Requirements:** High school diploma required; GED accepted **Costs Per Year:** Application fee: $20. State resident tuition: $3704 full-time, $123.47 per credit part-time. Nonresident tuition: $3704 full-time, $123.47 per credit part-time. Mandatory fees: $504 full-time, $16.81 per credit part-time. Full-time tuition and fees vary according to course load and program. Part-time tuition and fees vary according to course load and program. **Scholarships:** Available **Calendar System:** Semester, Summer Session Available **Enrollment:** FT 1,150, PT 1,486 **Faculty:** FT 26, PT 33 **Student-Faculty Ratio:** 31:1 **Library Holdings:** 15,739 **Regional Accreditation:** North Central Association of Colleges and Schools **Credit Hours For Degree:** 64 semester credits, Associates **ROTC:** Air Force **Intercollegiate Athletics:** Baseball M; Basketball M & W; Soccer M & W; Softball W; Volleyball W

ANOKA TECHNICAL COLLEGE

1355 West Hwy. 10
Anoka, MN 55303
Tel: (763)576-4700
E-mail: info@anokatech.edu
Web Site: http://www.anokatech.edu/
President/CEO: Anne Weyandt
Admissions: Robert Hoenie
Type: Two-Year College **Sex:** Coed **Affiliation:** Minnesota State Colleges and Universities System **Admission Plans:** Open Admission; Deferred Admission **Application Deadline:** August 1 **Application Fee:** $20.00 **H.S. Requirements:** High school diploma required; GED accepted **Scholarships:** Available **Calendar System:** Semester, Summer Session Not available **Regional Accreditation:** North Central Association of Colleges and Schools **Credit Hours For Degree:** 64 credits, Associates **Professional Accreditation:** AOTA

ARGOSY UNIVERSITY, TWIN CITIES
1515 Central Parkway
Eagan, MN 55121
Tel: (651)846-2882; Free: 888-844-2004
Fax: (952)844-0472
Web Site: http://www.argosy.edu/twincities/
President/CEO: Scott Tjaden, PhD
Type: University **Sex:** Coed **Affiliation:** Education Management Corporation **H.S. Requirements:** High school diploma required; GED accepted **Calendar System:** Semester **Professional Accreditation:** AAMAE, ADA, JRCERT, NAACLS

THE ART INSTITUTES INTERNATIONAL MINNESOTA
15 South 9th St.
Minneapolis, MN 55402
Tel: (612)332-3361; Free: 800-777-3643
Fax: (612)332-3934
Web Site: http://www.artinstitutes.edu/minneapolis/
President/CEO: William Johnson
Type: Four-Year College **Sex:** Coed **Affiliation:** Education Management Corporation **Calendar System:** Quarter **Professional Accreditation:** ACICS, ACF

AUGSBURG COLLEGE
2211 Riverside Ave.
Minneapolis, MN 55454-1351
Tel: (612)330-1000; Free: 800-788-5678
Admissions: (612)330-1001
Fax: (612)330-1649
E-mail: admissions@augsburg.edu
Web Site: http://www.augsburg.edu/
President/CEO: Paul C. Pribbenow
Admissions: Carrie Carroll
Financial Aid: Paul L. Terrio
Type: Comprehensive **Sex:** Coed **Affiliation:** Lutheran **Scores:** 94.33% SAT V 400+; 94.28% SAT M 400+; 49.3% ACT 18-23; 36.7% ACT 24-29 **% Accepted:** 52 **Admission Plans:** Deferred Admission **Application Deadline:** August 15 **Application Fee:** $25.00 **H.S. Requirements:** High school diploma required; GED accepted **Costs Per Year:** Application fee: $25. Comprehensive fee: $36,624 includes full-time tuition ($28,240), mandatory fees ($624), and college room and board ($7760). College room only: $3920. Full-time tuition and fees vary according to location. Room and board charges vary according to board plan and housing facility. Part-time tuition: $3457 per course. Part-time tuition varies according to course load and location. **Scholarships:** Available **Calendar System:** Semester, Summer Session Available **Enrollment:** FT 2,557, PT 544, Grad FT 554, Grad PT 338 **Faculty:** FT 200, PT 209 **Student-Faculty Ratio:** 13:1 **Exams:** SAT I or ACT. **% Receiving Financial Aid:** 82 **% Residing in College-Owned, -Operated, or -Affiliated Housing:** 54 **Library Holdings:** 146,166 **Regional Accreditation:** North Central Association of Colleges and Schools **Credit Hours For Degree:** 32 courses, Bachelors **ROTC:** Army, Navy, Air Force **Professional Accreditation:** AACN, ACBSP, CSWE, NASM, NCATE, NLN **Intercollegiate Athletics:** Baseball M; Basketball M & W; Cross-Country Running M & W; Football M; Golf M & W; Ice Hockey M & W; Soccer M & W; Softball W; Swimming and Diving W; Track and Field M & W; Volleyball W; Wrestling M

BEMIDJI STATE UNIVERSITY
1500 Birchmont Dr., NE
Bemidji, MN 56601-2699
Tel: (218)755-2000; Free: 800-652-9747
Admissions: (218)755-2040
Fax: (218)755-2074
E-mail: admissions@bemidjistate.edu
Web Site: http://www.bemidjistate.edu/
President/CEO: Dr. Jon E. Quistgaard
Admissions: Russ Kreager
Type: Comprehensive **Sex:** Coed **Affiliation:** Minnesota State Colleges and Universities System **Scores:** 64% ACT 18-23; 24% ACT 24-29 **% Accepted:** 81 **Admission Plans:** Deferred Admission **Application Deadline:** Rolling **Application Fee:** $20.00 **H.S. Requirements:** High school diploma required; GED accepted **Costs Per Year:** Application fee: $20. State resident tuition: $6575 full-time, $229 per credit hour part-time. Nonresident tuition: $6575 full-time, $229 per credit hour part-time. Mandatory fees: $935 full-time, $22 per credit hour part-time. Full-time tuition and fees vary according to course load, location, program, and reciprocity agreements. Part-time tuition and fees vary according to course load, location, program, and reciprocity agreements. College room and board: $6425. Room and board charges vary according to board plan and housing facility. **Scholarships:** Available **Calendar System:** Semester, Summer Session Available **Enrollment:** FT 3,582, PT 1,148, Grad FT 76, Grad PT 369 **Faculty:** FT 159, PT 110 **Student-Faculty Ratio:** 21:1 **Exams:** ACT. **% Receiving Financial Aid:** 64 **% Residing in College-Owned, -Operated, or -Affiliated Housing:** 26 **Library Holdings:** 554,087 **Regional Accreditation:** North Central Association of Colleges and Schools **Credit Hours For Degree:** 64 semester credits, Associates; 128 semester credits, Bachelors **Professional Accreditation:** AACN, CSWE, NASM, NCATE, NLN **Intercollegiate Athletics:** Baseball M; Basketball M & W; Cross-Country Running W; Football M; Golf M & W; Ice Hockey M & W; Soccer W; Softball W; Tennis W; Track and Field M & W; Volleyball W

BETHANY LUTHERAN COLLEGE
700 Luther Dr.
Mankato, MN 56001-6163
Tel: (507)344-7000; Free: 800-944-3066
Admissions: (507)344-7320
Fax: (507)344-7376
E-mail: dwestpha@blc.edu
Web Site: http://www.blc.edu/
President/CEO: Dr. Dan Bruss
Admissions: Donald Westphal
Type: Four-Year College **Sex:** Coed **Affiliation:** Lutheran **Scores:** 53% ACT 18-23; 25% ACT 24-29 **% Accepted:** 83 **Application Deadline:** July 1 **Application Fee:** $0.00 **H.S. Requirements:** High school diploma required; GED accepted **Costs Per Year:** Application fee: $0. Comprehensive fee: $27,150 includes full-time tuition ($20,650) and college room and board ($6500). College room only: $2890. Room and board charges vary according to board plan and housing facility. **Scholarships:** Available **Calendar System:** Semester, Summer Session Not available **Faculty:** FT 39 **Student-Faculty Ratio:** 12:1 **Exams:** SAT I or ACT. **% Receiving Financial Aid:** 80 **% Residing in College-Owned, -Operated, or -Affiliated Housing:** 73 **Final Year or Final Semester Residency Requirement:** Yes **Library Holdings:** 72,704 **Regional Accreditation:** North Central Association of Colleges and Schools **Credit Hours For Degree:** 128 credits, Bachelors **ROTC:** Army **Intercollegiate Athletics:** Baseball M; Basketball M & W; Cross-Country Running M & W; Equestrian Sports M & W; Golf M & W; Soccer M & W; Softball W; Tennis M & W; Track and Field M & W; Volleyball W

BETHEL UNIVERSITY
3900 Bethel Dr.
St. Paul, MN 55112-6999
Tel: (651)638-6400; Free: 800-255-8706
Admissions: (651)638-6242
E-mail: buadmissions-cas@bethel.edu
Web Site: http://www.bethel.edu/
President/CEO: Dr. James (Jay) H. Barnes, III
Financial Aid: Jeffrey D. Olson
Type: Comprehensive **Sex:** Coed **Affiliation:** Baptist General Conference **Scores:** 95.95% SAT V 400+; 95.94% SAT M 400+; 36.56% ACT 18-23; 45.52% ACT 24-29 **% Accepted:** 80 **Admission Plans:** Early Admission; Deferred Admission **Application Deadline:** Rolling **Application Fee:** $0.00 **H.S. Requirements:** High school diploma required; GED accepted **Costs Per Year:** Application fee: $0. Comprehensive fee: $36,300 includes full-time tuition ($27,950), mandatory fees ($130), and college room and board ($8220). College room only: $4900. Room and board charges vary according to board plan. Part-time tuition: $1165 per credit. Part-time tuition varies according to course load. **Scholarships:** Available **Calendar System:** 4-1-4, Summer Session Available **Enrollment:** FT 2,773, PT 648, Grad FT 1,250, Grad PT 767 **Faculty:** FT 188, PT 105 **Student-Faculty Ratio:** 12:1 **Exams:** SAT I or ACT. ACT essay not being used. SAT essay not being used. **% Receiving Financial Aid:** 73 **% Residing in College-Owned, -Operated, or -Affiliated Housing:** 70 **Final Year or Final Semester Residency Requirement:** No **Library Holdings:** 194,000 **Regional Accreditation:** North Central Association of Colleges and Schools **Credit Hours For Degree:** 61 credit hours, Associates; 122 credit hours, Bachelors **ROTC:** Army, Air Force **Professional Accreditation:** AACN, CSWE, JRCEPAT, NLN, TEAC **Intercollegiate Athletics:** Baseball M; Basketball M

& W; Cross-Country Running M & W; Football M; Golf M & W; Ice Hockey M & W; Soccer M & W; Softball W; Tennis M & W; Track and Field M & W; Volleyball M & W

BROWN COLLEGE
1440 Northland Dr.
Mendota Heights, MN 55120
Tel: (651)905-3400; Free: 800-6BR-OWN6
Fax: (651)905-3550
Web Site: http://www.browncollege.edu/
President/CEO: William Cowan, DVM
Admissions: Mark Fredrichs
Type: Two-Year College **Sex:** Coed **Affiliation:** Career Education Corporation **% Accepted:** 100 **Admission Plans:** Open Admission; Early Action; Early Decision Plan; Deferred Admission **Application Deadline:** Rolling **Application Fee:** $50.00 **H.S. Requirements:** High school diploma required; GED accepted **Scholarships:** Available **Calendar System:** Quarter, Summer Session Available **Enrollment:** FT 1,106, PT 127 **Faculty:** FT 78, PT 44 **Student-Faculty Ratio:** 11:1 **Library Holdings:** 768 **Credit Hours For Degree:** 105 credits, Associates **Professional Accreditation:** ACCSCT

CAPELLA UNIVERSITY
225 South 6th St., 9th Floor
Minneapolis, MN 55402
Tel: (612)252-4200; Free: 888-CAPELLA
Admissions: 888-227-3552
Fax: (612)337-5396
E-mail: info@capella.edu
Web Site: http://www.capella.edu/
President/CEO: Christopher Cassirer
Type: Two-Year Upper Division **Sex:** Coed **Application Deadline:** Rolling **Application Fee:** $75.00 **H.S. Requirements:** High school diploma required; GED accepted **Costs Per Year:** Application fee: $75. Tuition: $10,620 full-time. **Scholarships:** Available **Calendar System:** Quarter, Summer Session Available **Enrollment:** FT 907, PT 4,712, Grad FT 1,455, Grad PT 24,924 **Regional Accreditation:** North Central Association of Colleges and Schools **Professional Accreditation:** ACA, NCATE

CARLETON COLLEGE
One North College St.
Northfield, MN 55057-4001
Tel: (507)646-4000; Free: 800-995-2275
Admissions: (507)222-4190
Fax: (507)646-4526
E-mail: admissions@carleton.edu
Web Site: http://www.carleton.edu/
President/CEO: Dr. Robert A. Oden, Jr.
Admissions: Paul Thiboutot
Financial Aid: Rodney M. Oto
Type: Four-Year College **Sex:** Coed **Scores:** 100% SAT V 400+; 100% SAT M 400+; 4.53% ACT 18-23; 28.16% ACT 24-29 **% Accepted:** 30 **Admission Plans:** Early Admission; Early Decision Plan; Deferred Admission **Application Deadline:** January 15 **Application Fee:** $30.00 **H.S. Requirements:** High school diploma required; GED accepted **Costs Per Year:** Application fee: $30. Comprehensive fee: $52,110 includes full-time tuition ($41,076), mandatory fees ($228), and college room and board ($10,806). College room only: $5676. Room and board charges vary according to board plan. **Scholarships:** Available **Calendar System:** Miscellaneous, Summer Session Not available **Enrollment:** FT 1,996, PT 13 **Faculty:** FT 217, PT 21 **Student-Faculty Ratio:** 9:1 **Exams:** SAT I or ACT, SAT II. **% Receiving Financial Aid:** 56 **% Residing in College-Owned, -Operated, or -Affiliated Housing:** 95 **Final Year or Final Semester Residency Requirement:** No **Library Holdings:** 1,055,151 **Regional Accreditation:** North Central Association of Colleges and Schools **Credit Hours For Degree:** 210 credits, Bachelors **Intercollegiate Athletics:** Badminton M & W; Baseball M; Basketball M & W; Crew M & W; Cross-Country Running M & W; Equestrian Sports M & W; Fencing M & W; Field Hockey W; Football M; Golf M & W; Gymnastics W; Ice Hockey M & W; Lacrosse M & W; Rugby M & W; Sailing M & W; Skiing (Cross-Country) M & W; Skiing (Downhill) M & W; Soccer M & W; Softball W; Swimming and Diving M & W; Tennis M & W; Track and Field M & W; Ultimate Frisbee M & W; Volleyball M & W; Water Polo M & W

CENTRAL LAKES COLLEGE
501 West College Dr.
Brainerd, MN 56401-3904
Tel: (218)855-8000
Admissions: (218)855-8036
Fax: (218)855-8220
E-mail: cdaniels@clcmn.edu
Web Site: http://www.clcmn.edu/
President/CEO: Dr. Larry Lundblad
Admissions: Rose Tretter
Financial Aid: Mike Barnaby
Type: Two-Year College **Sex:** Coed **Affiliation:** Minnesota State Colleges and Universities System **Admission Plans:** Open Admission; Deferred Admission **Application Deadline:** Rolling **Application Fee:** $20.00 **H.S. Requirements:** High school diploma required; GED accepted **Costs Per Year:** Application fee: $20. State resident tuition: $4382 full-time, $136.93 per credit part-time. Nonresident tuition: $4382 full-time, $136.93 per credit part-time. Mandatory fees: $637 full-time, $19.91 per credit part-time. Full-time tuition and fees vary according to course load and program. Part-time tuition and fees vary according to course load and program. **Scholarships:** Available **Calendar System:** Semester, Summer Session Available **Enrollment:** FT 2,313, PT 1,697 **Faculty:** FT 87, PT 62 **Student-Faculty Ratio:** 17:1 **Final Year or Final Semester Residency Requirement:** No **Library Holdings:** 16,052 **Regional Accreditation:** North Central Association of Colleges and Schools **Credit Hours For Degree:** 60 credits, Associates **Professional Accreditation:** ADA **Intercollegiate Athletics:** Baseball M; Basketball M & W; Football M; Golf M & W; Softball W; Volleyball W

CENTURY COLLEGE
3300 Century Ave. North
White Bear Lake, MN 55110
Tel: (651)779-3200; Free: 800-228-1978
Admissions: (651)779-2619
Fax: (651)779-5810
E-mail: admissions@century.edu
Web Site: http://www.century.edu/
President/CEO: Lawrence Litecky
Admissions: Christine Paulos
Type: Two-Year College **Sex:** Coed **Affiliation:** Minnesota State Colleges and Universities System **% Accepted:** 100 **Admission Plans:** Open Admission; Deferred Admission **Application Deadline:** Rolling **Application Fee:** $20.00 **H.S. Requirements:** High school diploma required; GED accepted **Costs Per Year:** Application fee: $20. State resident tuition: $4162 full-time, $138.75 per credit hour part-time. Nonresident tuition: $4162 full-time, $138.75 per credit hour part-time. Mandatory fees: $527 full-time, $17.56 per credit hour part-time. Full-time tuition and fees vary according to program. Part-time tuition and fees vary according to program. **Scholarships:** Available **Calendar System:** Semester, Summer Session Available **Enrollment:** FT 4,937, PT 5,532 **Faculty:** FT 182, PT 184 **Student-Faculty Ratio:** 28:1 **Final Year or Final Semester Residency Requirement:** No **Library Holdings:** 67,214 **Regional Accreditation:** North Central Association of Colleges and Schools **Credit Hours For Degree:** 64 semester credits, Associates **ROTC:** Air Force **Professional Accreditation:** ADA, JRCEMT, NLN **Intercollegiate Athletics:** Golf M & W; Soccer M & W

COLLEGE OF SAINT BENEDICT
37 South College Ave.
St. Joseph, MN 56374
Tel: (320)363-5011; Free: 800-544-1489
Admissions: (320)363-2196
Fax: (320)363-5010
E-mail: admissions@csbsju.edu
Web Site: http://www.csbsju.edu/
President/CEO: Dr. Mary Ann Baenninger
Admissions: Karen Backes
Financial Aid: Jane Haugen
Type: Four-Year College **Sex:** Coed **Affiliation:** Roman Catholic **Scores:** 95% SAT V 400+; 99% SAT M 400+; 26% ACT 18-23; 54% ACT 24-29 **% Accepted:** 85 **Admission Plans:** Early Action; Deferred Admission **Application Deadline:** Rolling **Application Fee:** $0.00 **H.S. Requirements:** High school diploma required; GED accepted. For home schooled students with appropriate documentation of college preparatory curriculum: High school diploma or equivalent not required **Costs Per Year:** Application fee: $0. Comprehensive fee: $38,544 includes full-time tuition ($29,388), mandatory fees ($798), and college room and board ($8358). College room only: $4025. Room and board charges vary according to board plan and housing facility. Part-time tuition: $1225 per credit hour. Part-time tuition varies ac-

cording to course load. **Scholarships:** Available **Calendar System:** Semester, Summer Session Not available **Enrollment:** FT 2,057, PT 49 **Faculty:** FT 159, PT 34 **Student-Faculty Ratio:** 12:1 **Exams:** SAT I or ACT. ACT essay not being used. SAT essay not being used. **% Receiving Financial Aid:** 66 **% Residing in College-Owned, -Operated, or -Affiliated Housing:** 80 **Library Holdings:** 658,438 **Regional Accreditation:** North Central Association of Colleges and Schools **Credit Hours For Degree:** 124 credits, Bachelors **ROTC:** Army **Professional Accreditation:** AACN, ADtA, CSWE, NASM, NCATE, NLN **Intercollegiate Athletics:** Basketball W; Crew W; Cross-Country Running W; Golf W; Ice Hockey W; Lacrosse W; Riflery W; Rugby W; Skiing (Cross-Country) W; Soccer W; Softball W; Swimming and Diving W; Tennis W; Track and Field W; Ultimate Frisbee W; Volleyball W

THE COLLEGE OF ST. SCHOLASTICA

1200 Kenwood Ave.
Duluth, MN 55811-4199
Tel: (218)723-6000; Free: 800-249-6412
Admissions: (218)723-6053
Fax: (218)723-6290
E-mail: admissions@css.edu
Web Site: http://www.css.edu/
President/CEO: Dr. Larry Goodwin
Admissions: Eric Berg
Financial Aid: Jon P. Erickson

Type: Comprehensive **Sex:** Coed **Affiliation:** Roman Catholic Church **Scores:** 89% SAT V 400+; 47% ACT 18-23; 44% ACT 24-29 **% Accepted:** 85 **Admission Plans:** Early Admission; Deferred Admission **Application Deadline:** Rolling **Application Fee:** $25.00 **H.S. Requirements:** High school diploma required; GED accepted **Costs Per Year:** Application fee: $25. Comprehensive fee: $35,868 includes full-time tuition ($28,200), mandatory fees ($170), and college room and board ($7498). College room only: $4248. Full-time tuition and fees vary according to class time. Room and board charges vary according to board plan and housing facility. Part-time tuition: $881 per credit hour. Part-time tuition varies according to class time and course load. **Scholarships:** Available **Calendar System:** Semester, Summer Session Available **Enrollment:** FT 2,566, PT 255, Grad FT 618, Grad PT 307 **Faculty:** FT 166, PT 167 **Student-Faculty Ratio:** 14:1 **Exams:** SAT I or ACT. **% Receiving Financial Aid:** 78 **% Residing in College-Owned, -Operated, or -Affiliated Housing:** 51 **Library Holdings:** 152,843 **Regional Accreditation:** North Central Association of Colleges and Schools **Credit Hours For Degree:** 128 credits, Bachelors **ROTC:** Air Force **Professional Accreditation:** AACN, AHIMA, AOTA, APTA, CSWE, TEAC **Intercollegiate Athletics:** Baseball M; Basketball M & W; Cross-Country Running M & W; Football M; Ice Hockey M & W; Skiing (Cross-Country) M & W; Soccer M & W; Softball W; Tennis M & W; Track and Field M & W; Volleyball W

COLLEGE OF VISUAL ARTS

344 Summit Ave.
St. Paul, MN 55102-2124
Tel: (651)224-3416; Free: 800-224-1536
Admissions: (651)757-4049
Fax: (651)224-8854
E-mail: awhite@cva.edu
Web Site: http://www.cva.edu/
President/CEO: Ann Ledy
Admissions: Anne White
Financial Aid: David Woodward

Type: Four-Year College **Sex:** Coed **Scores:** 78.1% ACT 18-23; 7.3% ACT 24-29 **% Accepted:** 72 **Admission Plans:** Deferred Admission **Application Deadline:** Rolling **Application Fee:** $40.00 **H.S. Requirements:** High school diploma required; GED accepted **Costs Per Year:** Application fee: $40. Tuition: $23,488 full-time, $1174 per credit part-time. Mandatory fees: $500 full-time, $50. Full-time tuition and fees vary according to course load. Part-time tuition and fees vary according to course load. **Scholarships:** Available **Calendar System:** Semester, Summer Session Available **Enrollment:** FT 180, PT 6 **Faculty:** FT 7, PT 39 **Student-Faculty Ratio:** 9:1 **Exams:** SAT I or ACT. **% Receiving Financial Aid:** 87 **Final Year or Final Semester Residency Requirement:** No **Library Holdings:** 9,518 **Regional Accreditation:** North Central Association of Colleges and Schools **Credit Hours For Degree:** 126 credits, Bachelors

CONCORDIA COLLEGE

901 South 8th St.
Moorhead, MN 56562
Tel: (218)299-4000; Free: 800-699-9897
Admissions: (218)299-3004
Fax: (218)299-3947
E-mail: admissions@cord.edu
Web Site: http://www.concordiacollege.edu/
President/CEO: Dr. Pamela M. Jolicoeur
Admissions: Scott D. Ellingson
Financial Aid: Jane Williams

Type: Comprehensive **Sex:** Coed **Affiliation:** Evangelical Lutheran Church in America **Scores:** 99% SAT V 400+; 100% SAT M 400+; 35% ACT 18-23; 51% ACT 24-29 **% Accepted:** 79 **Admission Plans:** Early Admission; Deferred Admission **Application Deadline:** Rolling **Application Fee:** $20.00 **H.S. Requirements:** High school diploma required; GED accepted **Costs Per Year:** Application fee: $20. Comprehensive fee: $33,670 includes full-time tuition ($26,950), mandatory fees ($210), and college room and board ($6510). College room only: $2890. Full-time tuition and fees vary according to course load and degree level. Room and board charges vary according to board plan and housing facility. Part-time tuition: $1060 per credit hour. Part-time mandatory fees: $105 per term. Part-time tuition and fees vary according to course load and degree level. **Scholarships:** Available **Calendar System:** Semester, Summer Session Available **Enrollment:** FT 2,740, PT 48, Grad PT 23 **Faculty:** FT 194, PT 54 **Student-Faculty Ratio:** 13:1 **Exams:** SAT I or ACT. ACT essay not being used. SAT essay not being used. **% Receiving Financial Aid:** 69 **% Residing in College-Owned, -Operated, or -Affiliated Housing:** 67 **Final Year or Final Semester Residency Requirement:** Yes **Library Holdings:** 346,108 **Regional Accreditation:** North Central Association of Colleges and Schools **Credit Hours For Degree:** 126 semester hours, Bachelors **ROTC:** Army, Air Force **Professional Accreditation:** AACN, AAFCS, ADtA, CSWE, NASM, NLN **Intercollegiate Athletics:** Baseball M; Basketball M & W; Cheerleading W; Cross-Country Running M & W; Football M; Golf M & W; Ice Hockey M & W; Rugby M & W; Soccer M & W; Softball W; Swimming and Diving W; Tennis M & W; Track and Field M & W; Volleyball M & W; Wrestling M

CONCORDIA UNIVERSITY, ST. PAUL

275 Syndicate St. North
St. Paul, MN 55104-5494
Tel: (651)641-8278; Free: 800-333-4705
Admissions: (651)641-8230
Fax: (651)659-0207
E-mail: admission@csp.edu
Web Site: http://www.csp.edu/
President/CEO: Dr. Robert Holst
Admissions: Kristin Schoon
Financial Aid: Carolyn Chesebrough

Type: Comprehensive **Sex:** Coed **Affiliation:** Lutheran Church–Missouri Synod **Scores:** 51% ACT 18-23; 21% ACT 24-29 **% Accepted:** 56 **Admission Plans:** Early Admission; Deferred Admission **Application Deadline:** August 1 **Application Fee:** $30.00 **H.S. Requirements:** High school diploma required; GED accepted **Costs Per Year:** Application fee: $30. Comprehensive fee: $34,900 includes full-time tuition ($27,400) and college room and board ($7500). Full-time tuition varies according to program. Room and board charges vary according to housing facility. Part-time tuition: $580 per credit. Part-time tuition varies according to course load and program. **Scholarships:** Available **Calendar System:** Semester, Summer Session Available **Enrollment:** FT 1,423, PT 367, Grad FT 1,006, Grad PT 20 **Faculty:** FT 70, PT 242 **Student-Faculty Ratio:** 17:1 **Exams:** ACT. **% Receiving Financial Aid:** 71 **% Residing in College-Owned, -Operated, or -Affiliated Housing:** 30 **Library Holdings:** 154,742 **Regional Accreditation:** North Central Association of Colleges and Schools **Credit Hours For Degree:** 64 semester hours, Associates; 128 semester hours, Bachelors **ROTC:** Army, Navy, Air Force **Professional Accreditation:** ACBSP, NCATE **Intercollegiate Athletics:** Baseball M; Basketball M & W; Cross-Country Running M & W; Football M; Golf M & W; Soccer W; Softball W; Track and Field M & W; Volleyball W

CROSSROADS COLLEGE

920 Mayowood Rd., SW
Rochester, MN 55902-2382
Tel: (507)288-4563; Free: 800-456-7651
Fax: (507)288-9046
E-mail: admissions@crossroadscollege.edu
Web Site: http://www.crossroadscollege.edu/
President/CEO: Michael Kilgallin

Admissions: Scott Klaehn
Financial Aid: Polly Kellogg-Bradley
Type: Four-Year College **Sex:** Coed **Affiliation:** Christian Churches and Churches of Christ **Scores:** 100% SAT V 400+; 100% SAT M 400+; 53% ACT 18-23; 21% ACT 24-29 **Admission Plans:** Deferred Admission **Application Deadline:** August 15 **Application Fee:** $30.00 **H.S. Requirements:** High school diploma required; GED accepted **Scholarships:** Available **Calendar System:** Semester, Summer Session Not available **Enrollment:** FT 134, PT 26 **Faculty:** FT 7, PT 24 **Student-Faculty Ratio:** 9:1 **Exams:** SAT I or ACT. **% Residing in College-Owned, -Operated, or -Affiliated Housing:** 74 **Library Holdings:** 33,697 **Credit Hours For Degree:** 64 semester hours, Associates; 130 semester hours, Bachelors **Professional Accreditation:** ABHE **Intercollegiate Athletics:** Baseball M; Basketball M & W; Golf M & W; Softball W; Tennis M & W; Volleyball M & W

CROWN COLLEGE
8700 College View Dr.
St. Bonifacius, MN 55375-9001
Tel: (952)446-4100; Free: 800-68-CROWN
Admissions: (952)446-4144
Fax: (952)446-4149
E-mail: info@crown.edu
Web Site: http://www.crown.edu/
President/CEO: Dr. Richard P. Mann
Admissions: Bret Hyder
Financial Aid: Marla Rupp
Type: Comprehensive **Sex:** Coed **Affiliation:** The Christian and Missionary Alliance **Scores:** 100% SAT V 400+; 95% SAT M 400+; 59% ACT 18-23; 33% ACT 24-29 **% Accepted:** 66 **Admission Plans:** Early Admission; Deferred Admission **Application Deadline:** Rolling **Application Fee:** $35.00 **H.S. Requirements:** High school diploma required; GED accepted **Costs Per Year:** Application fee: $35. Comprehensive fee: $28,450 includes full-time tuition ($20,870) and college room and board ($7580). Part-time tuition: $870 per credit. **Scholarships:** Available **Calendar System:** Semester, Summer Session Available **Enrollment:** FT 819, PT 242, Grad FT 130, Grad PT 30 **Faculty:** FT 35, PT 83 **Student-Faculty Ratio:** 14:1 **Exams:** SAT I or ACT. **% Receiving Financial Aid:** 48 **% Residing in College-Owned, -Operated, or -Affiliated Housing:** 74 **Final Year or Final Semester Residency Requirement:** Yes **Library Holdings:** 104,859 **Regional Accreditation:** North Central Association of Colleges and Schools **Credit Hours For Degree:** 66 credit hours, Associates; 125 credit hours, Bachelors **ROTC:** Army **Intercollegiate Athletics:** Baseball M; Basketball M & W; Cross-Country Running M & W; Football M; Golf M; Soccer M & W; Softball W; Volleyball W

DAKOTA COUNTY TECHNICAL COLLEGE
1300 East 145th St.
Rosemount, MN 55068
Tel: (651)423-8000; Free: 877-YES-DCTC
Admissions: (651)423-8301
E-mail: admissions@dctc.mnscu.edu
Web Site: http://www.dctc.edu/
President/CEO: Ronald E. Thomas
Admissions: Patrick Lair
Type: Two-Year College **Sex:** Coed **Affiliation:** Minnesota State Colleges and Universities System **Admission Plans:** Open Admission **Application Fee:** $20.00 **H.S. Requirements:** High school diploma required; GED accepted **Costs Per Year:** Application fee: $20. State resident tuition: $5084 full-time, $149 per credit part-time. Nonresident tuition: $8920 full-time, $297 per credit part-time. Mandatory fees: $624 full-time, $21 per credit part-time. Full-time tuition and fees vary according to program and reciprocity agreements. Part-time tuition and fees vary according to program and reciprocity agreements. **Scholarships:** Available **Calendar System:** Semester, Summer Session Available **Library Holdings:** 15,693 **Regional Accreditation:** North Central Association of Colleges and Schools **Credit Hours For Degree:** 72 credits, Associates **Professional Accreditation:** AAMAE, ADA, FIDER **Intercollegiate Athletics:** Baseball M; Soccer M & W; Softball W; Wrestling M

DEVRY UNIVERSITY
7700 France Ave. South
Ste. 575
Edina, MN 55435
Tel: (952)838-1860
Admissions: (952)738-3100
Fax: (952)838-3737
Web Site: http://www.devry.edu/
President/CEO: Gina Quinn
Type: Comprehensive **Sex:** Coed **Admission Plans:** Deferred Admission **Application Deadline:** Rolling **Application Fee:** $50.00 **H.S. Requirements:** High school diploma required; GED accepted **Costs Per Year:** Application fee: $50. Tuition: $14,080 full-time, $550 per credit hour part-time. **Scholarships:** Available **Enrollment:** FT 56, PT 72, Grad FT 11, Grad PT 68 **Exams:** ACT essay used for admission. SAT essay used for admission. ACT essay used for placement. SAT essay used for placement. **% Receiving Financial Aid:** 74 **Regional Accreditation:** North Central Association of Colleges and Schools

DULUTH BUSINESS UNIVERSITY
4724 Mike Colalillo Dr.
Duluth, MN 55807
Tel: (218)722-4000; Free: 800-777-8406
E-mail: markt@dbumn.edu
Web Site: http://www.dbumn.edu/
President/CEO: James Gessner
Admissions: Mark Traux
Type: Two-Year College **Sex:** Coed **Application Fee:** $35.00 **Calendar System:** Quarter **Professional Accreditation:** ACICS, AAMAE, ADA

DUNWOODY COLLEGE OF TECHNOLOGY
818 Dunwoody Blvd.
Minneapolis, MN 55403
Tel: (612)374-5800; Free: 800-292-4625
Fax: (612)374-4128
E-mail: smanning@dunwoody.edu
Web Site: http://www.dunwoody.edu/
President/CEO: Dr. C. Ben Wright
Admissions: Shaun Manning
Type: Two-Year College **Sex:** Coed **Admission Plans:** Early Admission; Deferred Admission **Application Deadline:** Rolling **Application Fee:** $50.00 **H.S. Requirements:** High school diploma required; GED accepted **Scholarships:** Available **Calendar System:** Quarter, Summer Session Available **Enrollment:** FT 1,322, PT 249 **Faculty:** FT 81, PT 24 **Student-Faculty Ratio:** 15:1 **Exams:** Other. **Library Holdings:** 8,000 **Regional Accreditation:** North Central Association of Colleges and Schools

FOND DU LAC TRIBAL AND COMMUNITY COLLEGE
2101 14th St.
Cloquet, MN 55720
Tel: (218)879-0800; Free: 800-657-3712
Fax: (218)879-0814
E-mail: darla@asab.fdl.cc.mn.us
Web Site: http://www.fdltcc.edu/
President/CEO: Larry Anderson
Admissions: Nancy Gordon
Type: Two-Year College **Sex:** Coed **Affiliation:** Minnesota State Colleges and Universities System **% Accepted:** 100 **Admission Plans:** Open Admission; Early Admission; Deferred Admission **Application Fee:** $20.00 **H.S. Requirements:** High school diploma required; GED accepted **Costs Per Year:** Application fee: $20. State resident tuition: $4108 full-time, $136.93 per credit part-time. Nonresident tuition: $8216 full-time, $273.86 per credit part-time. Mandatory fees: $452 full-time, $15.06 per credit part-time. College room only: $3000. **Scholarships:** Available **Calendar System:** Semester, Summer Session Available **Enrollment:** FT 719, PT 1,016 **Faculty:** FT 28, PT 52 **Student-Faculty Ratio:** 21:1 **% Residing in College-Owned, -Operated, or -Affiliated Housing:** 10 **Library Holdings:** 3,482 **Regional Accreditation:** North Central Association of Colleges and Schools **Credit Hours For Degree:** 60 credits, Associates

GLOBE UNIVERSITY
8089 Globe Dr.
Woodbury, MN 55125
Tel: (651)730-5100
Admissions: (651)332-8000
Fax: (651)730-5151
Web Site: http://www.globeuniversity.edu/
President/CEO: Terry Myhre
Admissions: Christina Hilipipre

Type: Comprehensive **Sex:** Coed **Admission Plans:** Open Admission **Application Deadline:** October 5 **Application Fee:** $50.00 **H.S. Requirements:** High school diploma required; GED accepted **Scholarships:** Available **Calendar System:** Quarter, Summer Session Available **Enrollment:** FT 533, PT 312 **Student-Faculty Ratio:** 15:1 **Exams:** Other. **Library Holdings:** 1,432 **Credit Hours For Degree:** 90 credits, Associates; 180 credits, Bachelors **Professional Accreditation:** ACICS, AAMAE

GUSTAVUS ADOLPHUS COLLEGE
800 West College Ave.
St. Peter, MN 56082-1498
Tel: (507)933-8000; Free: 800-GUSTAVU(S)
Admissions: (507)933-7676
E-mail: admission@gac.edu
Web Site: http://www.gustavus.edu/
President/CEO: Jack Ohle
Admissions: Mark Anderson
Financial Aid: Doug Minter
Type: Four-Year College **Sex:** Coed **Affiliation:** Evangelical Lutheran Church in America **Scores:** 19% ACT 18-23; 58% ACT 24-29 **% Accepted:** 74 **Admission Plans:** Early Admission; Early Action; Deferred Admission **Application Deadline:** April 1 **Application Fee:** $0.00 **H.S. Requirements:** High school diploma required; GED accepted **Costs Per Year:** Application fee: $0. One-time mandatory fee: $400. Comprehensive fee: $41,800 includes full-time tuition ($33,100), mandatory fees ($300), and college room and board ($8400). College room only: $5400. **Scholarships:** Available **Calendar System:** 4-1-4, Summer Session Available **Enrollment:** FT 2,442, PT 33 **Faculty:** FT 200, PT 43 **Student-Faculty Ratio:** 11:1 **Exams:** SAT I or ACT. **% Receiving Financial Aid:** 65 **% Residing in College-Owned, -Operated, or -Affiliated Housing:** 95 **Library Holdings:** 357,186 **Regional Accreditation:** North Central Association of Colleges and Schools **Credit Hours For Degree:** 35 courses, Bachelors **ROTC:** Army **Professional Accreditation:** AACN, JRCEPAT, NASM, NCATE, NLN **Intercollegiate Athletics:** Baseball M; Basketball M & W; Cross-Country Running M & W; Football M; Golf M & W; Gymnastics W; Ice Hockey M & W; Lacrosse M; Rugby M & W; Skiing (Cross-Country) M & W; Soccer M & W; Softball W; Swimming and Diving M & W; Tennis M & W; Track and Field M & W; Ultimate Frisbee M & W; Volleyball M & W

HAMLINE UNIVERSITY
1536 Hewitt Ave.
St. Paul, MN 55104-1284
Tel: (651)523-2800; Free: 800-753-9753
Admissions: (651)523-2207
Fax: (651)523-2458
E-mail: admission@hamline.edu
Web Site: http://www.hamline.edu/
President/CEO: Dr. Linda N. Hanson
Admissions: Milyon Trulove
Financial Aid: Lynette Wahl
Type: Comprehensive **Sex:** Coed **Affiliation:** United Methodist Church **Scores:** 91% SAT V 400+; 100% SAT M 400+; 37% ACT 18-23; 46% ACT 24-29 **% Accepted:** 75 **Admission Plans:** Early Admission; Early Action; Deferred Admission **Application Deadline:** Rolling **Application Fee:** $0.00 **H.S. Requirements:** High school diploma required; GED accepted **Costs Per Year:** Application fee: $0. One-time mandatory fee: $260. Comprehensive fee: $38,899 includes full-time tuition ($30,016), mandatory fees ($487), and college room and board ($8396). College room only: $4172. Room and board charges vary according to board plan and housing facility. Part-time tuition: $938 per credit hour. Part-time mandatory fees: $356 per term. Part-time tuition and fees vary according to course load. **Scholarships:** Available **Calendar System:** 4-1-4, Summer Session Available **Enrollment:** FT 1,808, PT 113, Grad FT 1,433, Grad PT 1,812 **Faculty:** FT 192, PT 339 **Student-Faculty Ratio:** 12:1 **Exams:** SAT I or ACT. ACT essay used for admission. SAT essay used for admission. **% Receiving Financial Aid:** 79 **% Residing in College-Owned, -Operated, or -Affiliated Housing:** 41 **Final Year or Final Semester Residency Requirement:** Yes **Library Holdings:** 199,160 **Regional Accreditation:** North Central Association of Colleges and Schools **Credit Hours For Degree:** 128 credits, Bachelors **ROTC:** Army, Air Force **Professional Accreditation:** ABA, AALS, NASM, NCATE **Intercollegiate Athletics:** Baseball M; Basketball M & W; Cheerleading W; Cross-Country Running M & W; Football M; Gymnastics W; Ice Hockey M & W; Lacrosse W; Soccer M & W; Softball W; Swimming and Diving M & W; Tennis M & W; Track and Field M & W; Volleyball W

HENNEPIN TECHNICAL COLLEGE
9000 Brooklyn Blvd.
Brooklyn Park, MN 55445
Tel: (952)995-1300
Fax: (763)488-2944
Web Site: http://www.hennepintech.edu/
President/CEO: Cecilia Cervantes
Admissions: Joy Bodin
Type: Two-Year College **Sex:** Coed **Affiliation:** Minnesota State Colleges and Universities System **% Accepted:** 100 **Admission Plans:** Open Admission **Application Deadline:** Rolling **Application Fee:** $20.00 **H.S. Requirements:** High school diploma required; GED accepted **Costs Per Year:** Application fee: $20. State resident tuition: $157 per credit part-time. Nonresident tuition: $157 per credit part-time. **Scholarships:** Available **Calendar System:** Semester, Summer Session Available **Student-Faculty Ratio:** 25:1 **Final Year or Final Semester Residency Requirement:** No **Regional Accreditation:** North Central Association of Colleges and Schools **Credit Hours For Degree:** 60 credits, Associates **Professional Accreditation:** ACF, ADA

HERZING COLLEGE
5700 West Broadway
Minneapolis, MN 55428
Tel: (763)535-3000; Free: 800-878-DRAW
E-mail: info@mpls.herzing.edu
Web Site: http://www.herzing.edu/
President/CEO: John Slama
Admissions: Shelly Larson
Type: Two-Year College **Sex:** Coed **Affiliation:** Herzing College **% Accepted:** 75 **Admission Plans:** Open Admission **Application Fee:** $0.00 **H.S. Requirements:** High school diploma required; GED accepted **Calendar System:** Semester **Enrollment:** FT 242, PT 28 **Faculty:** FT 21, PT 11 **Student-Faculty Ratio:** 14:1 **Exams:** Other. **Credit Hours For Degree:** 80 credits, Associates **Professional Accreditation:** ACCSCT

HIBBING COMMUNITY COLLEGE
1515 East 25th St.
Hibbing, MN 55746-3300
Tel: (218)262-7200; Free: 800-224-4HCC
E-mail: admissions@hibbing.edu
Web Site: http://www.hcc.mnscu.edu/
President/CEO: Kenneth Simberg
Admissions: Shelly Corradi
Type: Two-Year College **Sex:** Coed **Affiliation:** Minnesota State Colleges and Universities System **% Accepted:** 100 **Admission Plans:** Open Admission; Early Admission; Deferred Admission **Application Deadline:** Rolling **Application Fee:** $20.00 **H.S. Requirements:** High school diploma required; GED accepted **Scholarships:** Available **Calendar System:** Semester, Summer Session Available **Faculty:** FT 63, PT 23 **Student-Faculty Ratio:** 14:1 **% Residing in College-Owned, -Operated, or -Affiliated Housing:** 10 **Library Holdings:** 19,536 **Regional Accreditation:** North Central Association of Colleges and Schools **Credit Hours For Degree:** 64 credits, Associates **Professional Accreditation:** ADA, NAACLS **Intercollegiate Athletics:** Baseball M; Basketball M & W; Football M; Golf M & W; Softball W; Volleyball W

HIGH-TECH INSTITUTE
5100 Gamble Dr.
St. Louis Park, MN 55416
Tel: (952)417-2200; Free: 888-324-9700
Fax: (952)545-6149
Web Site: http://www.high-techinstitute.com/
President/CEO: Elizabeth Beseke
Type: Two-Year College **Sex:** Coed **Application Fee:** $50.00 **Calendar System:** Semester **Professional Accreditation:** ACCSCT

INVER HILLS COMMUNITY COLLEGE
2500 East 80th St.
Inver Grove Heights, MN 55076-3224
Tel: (651)450-8500
Admissions: (651)450-3589
Fax: (651)450-8677
E-mail: admissions@inverhills.edu
Web Site: http://www.inverhills.edu/

President/CEO: Dr. Cheryl Frank
Admissions: Casey Carmody
Financial Aid: Steve Yang
Type: Two-Year College **Sex:** Coed **Affiliation:** Minnesota State Colleges and Universities System **% Accepted:** 81 **Admission Plans:** Open Admission **Application Deadline:** August 15 **Application Fee:** $20.00 **H.S. Requirements:** High school diploma required; GED accepted **Costs Per Year:** Application fee: $20. State resident tuition: $3459 full-time, $144.12 per credit hour part-time. Nonresident tuition: $3459 full-time, $144.12 per credit hour part-time. Mandatory fees: $390 full-time, $16.23 per credit part-time. Full-time tuition and fees vary according to course load, location, program, and reciprocity agreements. Part-time tuition and fees vary according to course load, location, program, and reciprocity agreements. **Scholarships:** Available **Calendar System:** Semester, Summer Session Available **Enrollment:** FT 2,541, PT 3,674 **Faculty:** FT 100, PT 135 **Student-Faculty Ratio:** 24:1 **Library Holdings:** 42,073 **Regional Accreditation:** North Central Association of Colleges and Schools **Credit Hours For Degree:** 60 credits, Associates **Professional Accreditation:** NLN

ITASCA COMMUNITY COLLEGE
1851 Hwy. 169 East
Grand Rapids, MN 55744
Tel: (218)322-2300; Free: 800-996-6422
Admissions: (218)322-2340
Fax: (218)327-4350
E-mail: iccinfo@itascacc.edu
Web Site: http://www.itascacc.edu/
President/CEO: Dr. Susan Collins
Admissions: Candace Perry
Financial Aid: Nathan Wright
Type: Two-Year College **Sex:** Coed **Affiliation:** Minnesota State Colleges and Universities System **% Accepted:** 100 **Admission Plans:** Open Admission **Application Deadline:** August 29 **Application Fee:** $20.00 **H.S. Requirements:** High school diploma required; GED accepted **Costs Per Year:** Application fee: $20. State resident tuition: $4282 full-time, $142.73 per credit part-time. Nonresident tuition: $5459 full-time, $181.97 per credit part-time. Mandatory fees: $572 full-time, $19.06 per credit part-time. Full-time tuition and fees vary according to course load and program. Part-time tuition and fees vary according to program. **Scholarships:** Available **Calendar System:** Semester, Summer Session Available **Enrollment:** FT 879, PT 251 **Faculty:** FT 43, PT 34 **Student-Faculty Ratio:** 15:1 **% Residing in College-Owned, -Operated, or -Affiliated Housing:** 10 **Library Holdings:** 28,790 **Regional Accreditation:** North Central Association of Colleges and Schools **Credit Hours For Degree:** 60 credits, Associates **Intercollegiate Athletics:** Baseball M; Basketball M & W; Football M; Softball W; Volleyball W; Wrestling M

ITT TECHNICAL INSTITUTE
8911 Columbine Rd.
Eden Prairie, MN 55347
Tel: (952)914-5300
Web Site: http://www.itt-tech.edu/
President/CEO: Jeffrey Georgeson
Type: Two-Year College **Sex:** Coed **Affiliation:** ITT Educational Services, Inc. **Calendar System:** Quarter **Professional Accreditation:** ACICS

LAKE SUPERIOR COLLEGE
2101 Trinity Rd.
Duluth, MN 55811
Tel: (218)733-7600; Free: 800-432-2884
Admissions: (218)723-4895
E-mail: enroll@lsc.edu
Web Site: http://www.lsc.edu/
President/CEO: Dr. Kathleen Nelson
Admissions: Melissa Leno
Type: Two-Year College **Sex:** Coed **Affiliation:** Minnesota State Colleges and Universities System **Admission Plans:** Open Admission; Early Admission; Deferred Admission **Application Deadline:** Rolling **Application Fee:** $20.00 **H.S. Requirements:** High school diploma or equivalent not required **Costs Per Year:** Application fee: $20. State resident tuition: $3770 full-time, $125.66 per credit part-time. Nonresident tuition: $7740 full-time, $258 per credit part-time. Mandatory fees: $634 full-time, $20.31 per credit part-time. Full-time tuition and fees vary according to course load and reciprocity agreements. Part-time tuition and fees vary according to course load and reciprocity agreements. **Scholarships:** Available **Calendar System:** Semester, Summer Session Available **Enrollment:** FT 2,246, PT 2,744 **Faculty:** FT 87, PT 162 **Student-Faculty Ratio:** 18:1 **Library Holdings:** 2,869 **Regional Accreditation:** North Central Association of Colleges and Schools **Credit Hours For Degree:** 60 credits, Associates **Professional Accreditation:** ADA, APTA, CARC, NAACLS

LE CORDON BLEU COLLEGE OF CULINARY ARTS
1315 Mendota Heights Rd.
St. Paul, MN 55120
Tel: (651)675-4700; Free: 888-348-5222
Admissions: (651)675-4700
Web Site: http://www.twincitiesculinary.com/
President/CEO: Kevin Sanderson
Type: Two-Year College **Sex:** Coed **Admission Plans:** Open Admission **Application Fee:** $50.00 **Professional Accreditation:** ACCSCT

LEECH LAKE TRIBAL COLLEGE
6945 Littlewolf Rd. NW
Cass Lake, MN 56633
Tel: (218)335-4200
Fax: (218)335-4282
E-mail: shelly.braford@lltc.edu
Web Site: http://www.lltc.edu/
President/CEO: Dr. Ginny Carney
Admissions: Shelly Braford
Type: Two-Year College **Sex:** Coed **Admission Plans:** Open Admission **Application Fee:** $15.00 **H.S. Requirements:** High school diploma required; GED accepted **Costs Per Year:** Application fee: $15. State resident tuition: $4200 full-time. Mandatory fees: $230 full-time. **Calendar System:** Semester, Summer Session Available **Enrollment:** FT 190, PT 53 **Faculty:** FT 9, PT 19 **Student-Faculty Ratio:** 16:1 **Final Year or Final Semester Residency Requirement:** No **Regional Accreditation:** North Central Association of Colleges and Schools **Credit Hours For Degree:** 64 semester credits, Associates

MACALESTER COLLEGE
1600 Grand Ave.
St. Paul, MN 55105-1899
Tel: (651)696-6000; Free: 800-231-7974
Admissions: (651)696-6357
Fax: (651)696-6500
E-mail: admissions@macalester.edu
Web Site: http://www.macalester.edu/
President/CEO: Dr. Brian Rosenberg
Admissions: Lorne T. Robinson
Type: Four-Year College **Sex:** Coed **Affiliation:** Presbyterian **Scores:** 100% SAT V 400+; 99% SAT M 400+; 1.9% ACT 18-23; 33.9% ACT 24-29 **% Accepted:** 46 **Admission Plans:** Early Admission; Early Decision Plan; Deferred Admission **Application Deadline:** January 15 **Application Fee:** $40.00 **H.S. Requirements:** High school diploma or equivalent not required **Costs Per Year:** Application fee: $40. Comprehensive fee: $49,124 includes full-time tuition ($39,846), mandatory fees ($200), and college room and board ($9078). College room only: $4854. Full-time tuition and fees vary according to reciprocity agreements. Room and board charges vary according to board plan and housing facility. Part-time tuition: $18,987 per term. Part-time mandatory fees: $1187 per credit hour. **Scholarships:** Available **Calendar System:** Semester, Summer Session Not available **Enrollment:** FT 1,958, PT 38 **Faculty:** FT 163, PT 73 **Student-Faculty Ratio:** 11:1 **Exams:** SAT I or ACT. ACT essay used as a validity check on application essay. SAT essay used as a validity check on application essay. **% Receiving Financial Aid:** 67 **% Residing in College-Owned, -Operated, or -Affiliated Housing:** 65 **Library Holdings:** 434,215 **Regional Accreditation:** North Central Association of Colleges and Schools **Credit Hours For Degree:** 128 semester hours, Bachelors **ROTC:** Army, Navy, Air Force **Intercollegiate Athletics:** Baseball M; Basketball M & W; Crew M & W; Cross-Country Running M & W; Fencing M & W; Football M; Golf M & W; Ice Hockey M & W; Rock Climbing M & W; Rugby M & W; Skiing (Cross-Country) M & W; Soccer M & W; Softball W; Swimming and Diving M & W; Tennis M & W; Track and Field M & W; Ultimate Frisbee M & W; Volleyball M & W; Water Polo M & W

MARTIN LUTHER COLLEGE
1995 Luther Ct.
New Ulm, MN 56073

Tel: (507)354-8221
Fax: (507)354-8225
E-mail: brutlaro@mlc-wels.edu
Web Site: http://www.mlc-wels.edu/
President/CEO: Mark G. Zarling
Admissions: Prof. Ronald B. Brutlag
Financial Aid: Gene Slettedahl
Type: Comprehensive **Sex:** Coed **Affiliation:** Wisconsin Evangelical Lutheran Synod **Scores:** 38% ACT 18-23; 52% ACT 24-29 **% Accepted:** 98 **Admission Plans:** Deferred Admission **Application Deadline:** April 15 **Application Fee:** $25.00 **H.S. Requirements:** High school diploma required; GED accepted **Costs Per Year:** Application fee: $25. Comprehensive fee: $15,250 includes full-time tuition ($10,990) and college room and board ($4260). **Scholarships:** Available **Calendar System:** Semester, Summer Session Available **Enrollment:** FT 702, PT 54, Grad PT 70 **Faculty:** FT 49, PT 26 **Student-Faculty Ratio:** 12:1 **Exams:** ACT. ACT essay used for admission. ACT essay used for advising. ACT essay used for placement. ACT essay not being used. **% Receiving Financial Aid:** 74 **% Residing in College-Owned, -Operated, or -Affiliated Housing:** 95 **Regional Accreditation:** North Central Association of Colleges and Schools **Credit Hours For Degree:** 134 semester hours, Bachelors **Intercollegiate Athletics:** Baseball M; Basketball M & W; Cross-Country Running M & W; Football M; Golf M; Soccer M & W; Softball W; Tennis M & W; Track and Field M & W; Volleyball W

MCNALLY SMITH COLLEGE OF MUSIC
19 Exchange St. East
St. Paul, MN 55101
Tel: (651)291-0177; Free: 800-594-9500
Admissions: (651)361-3450
Fax: (651)291-0366
E-mail: kathy.hawks@mcnallysmith.edu
Web Site: http://www.mcnallysmith.edu/
President/CEO: Harry Chalmiers
Admissions: Kathy Hawks
Financial Aid: Paul Haugen
Type: Four-Year College **Sex:** Coed **Application Deadline:** August 1 **Application Fee:** $75.00 **H.S. Requirements:** High school diploma required; GED accepted **Costs Per Year:** Application fee: $75. Tuition: $21,970 full-time, $845 per credit part-time. Mandatory fees: $1800 full-time, $400 per term part-time. Full-time tuition and fees vary according to course load. Part-time tuition and fees vary according to course load. **Scholarships:** Available **Calendar System:** Semester, Summer Session Available **Enrollment:** FT 611, PT 69 **Faculty:** FT 50, PT 62 **Student-Faculty Ratio:** 9:1 **Exams:** ACT. **Final Year or Final Semester Residency Requirement:** Yes **Library Holdings:** 6,000 **Credit Hours For Degree:** 60 semester credits, Associates; 120 semester credits, Bachelors **Professional Accreditation:** NASM

MESABI RANGE COMMUNITY AND TECHNICAL COLLEGE
1001 West Chestnut St.
Virginia, MN 55792-3448
Tel: (218)741-3095
Admissions: (218)749-0314
E-mail: b.kochevar@mr.mnscu.edu
Web Site: http://www.mesabirange.edu/
President/CEO: Dr. Tina Royer
Admissions: Brenda Kochevar
Type: Two-Year College **Sex:** Coed **Affiliation:** Minnesota State Colleges and Universities System **Admission Plans:** Open Admission; Early Admission; Deferred Admission **Application Deadline:** Rolling **Application Fee:** $20.00 **H.S. Requirements:** High school diploma required; GED accepted. For Minnesota high school students: High school diploma or equivalent not required **Costs Per Year:** Application fee: $20. State resident tuition: $4630 full-time, $135.53 per credit hour part-time. Nonresident tuition: $5630 full-time, $173.23 per credit hour part-time. Mandatory fees: $18.81 per credit hour part-time. College room only: $3776. **Scholarships:** Available **Calendar System:** Semester, Summer Session Available **Student-Faculty Ratio:** 24:1 **% Residing in College-Owned, -Operated, or -Affiliated Housing:** 10 **Library Holdings:** 23,000 **Regional Accreditation:** North Central Association of Colleges and Schools **Credit Hours For Degree:** 64 credits, Associates **Intercollegiate Athletics:** Baseball M; Basketball M & W; Football M; Softball W; Volleyball W

METROPOLITAN STATE UNIVERSITY
700 East 7th St.
St. Paul, MN 55106-5000
Tel: (651)793-1212
Admissions: (651)793-1303
Fax: (651)772-7632
E-mail: monir.johnson@metrostate.edu
Web Site: http://www.metrostate.edu/
President/CEO: William Lowe
Admissions: Monir Johnson
Financial Aid: Dr. Lois Larson
Type: Comprehensive **Sex:** Coed **Affiliation:** Minnesota State Colleges and Universities System **Scores:** 49% ACT 18-23; 16% ACT 24-29 **% Accepted:** 53 **Admission Plans:** Deferred Admission **Application Deadline:** June 15 **Application Fee:** $20.00 **H.S. Requirements:** High school diploma or equivalent not required. For non-transfer students: High school diploma required; GED accepted **Costs Per Year:** Application fee: $20. State resident tuition: $5314 full-time, $177.15 per credit hour part-time. Nonresident tuition: $10,860 full-time, $362 per credit hour part-time. Mandatory fees: $313 full-time, $10.43 per credit hour part-time. Full-time tuition and fees vary according to program and reciprocity agreements. Part-time tuition and fees vary according to course load, program, and reciprocity agreements. **Scholarships:** Available **Calendar System:** Semester, Summer Session Available **Enrollment:** FT 2,884, PT 5,353 **Faculty:** FT 135, PT 576 **Student-Faculty Ratio:** 12:1 **Exams:** SAT I or ACT. **Library Holdings:** 39,128 **Regional Accreditation:** North Central Association of Colleges and Schools **Credit Hours For Degree:** 120 credits, Bachelors **Professional Accreditation:** AACN, CSWE, NLN

MINNEAPOLIS BUSINESS COLLEGE
1711 West County Rd. B
Roseville, MN 55113
Tel: (612)636-7406; Free: 800-279-5200
Admissions: (651)636-7406
Fax: (612)636-8185
Web Site: http://www.minneapolisbusinesscollege.edu/
President/CEO: David B. Whitman
Type: Two-Year College **Sex:** Coed **% Accepted:** 89 **Professional Accreditation:** ACICS

MINNEAPOLIS COLLEGE OF ART AND DESIGN
2501 Stevens Ave.
Minneapolis, MN 55404-4347
Tel: (612)874-3700; Free: 800-874-6223
Admissions: (612)874-3762
Fax: (612)874-3704
E-mail: admissions@mn.mcad.edu
Web Site: http://www.mcad.edu/
President/CEO: Jay Coogan
Admissions: William Mullen
Financial Aid: Laura Link
Type: Comprehensive **Sex:** Coed **Scores:** 95% SAT V 400+; 100% SAT M 400+; 53% ACT 18-23; 35% ACT 24-29 **% Accepted:** 66 **Admission Plans:** Deferred Admission **Application Deadline:** May 1 **Application Fee:** $50.00 **H.S. Requirements:** High school diploma required; GED accepted **Costs Per Year:** Application fee: $50. Tuition: $29,500 full-time, $985 per credit hour part-time. Mandatory fees: $200 full-time, $100 per term part-time. Part-time tuition and fees vary according to course load. **Scholarships:** Available **Calendar System:** Semester, Summer Session Available **Enrollment:** FT 638, PT 65, Grad FT 30 **Faculty:** FT 42, PT 69 **Student-Faculty Ratio:** 13:1 **Exams:** SAT I or ACT. ACT essay not being used. SAT essay not being used. **% Receiving Financial Aid:** 80 **% Residing in College-Owned, -Operated, or -Affiliated Housing:** 45 **Final Year or Final Semester Residency Requirement:** No **Library Holdings:** 47,166 **Regional Accreditation:** North Central Association of Colleges and Schools **Credit Hours For Degree:** 120 credits, Bachelors **Professional Accreditation:** NASAD

MINNEAPOLIS COMMUNITY AND TECHNICAL COLLEGE
1501 Hennepin Ave.
Minneapolis, MN 55403-1779
Tel: (612)659-6000
Admissions: (612)659-6200
Fax: (612)659-6210

E-mail: admissions.office@minneapolis.edu
Web Site: http://www.mctc.mnscu.edu/
President/CEO: Phillip Davis
Type: Two-Year College **Sex:** Coed **Affiliation:** Minnesota State Colleges and Universities System **Admission Plans:** Open Admission; Early Admission; Deferred Admission **Application Deadline:** Rolling **Application Fee:** $20.00 **H.S. Requirements:** High school diploma required; GED accepted **Costs Per Year:** Application fee: $20. State resident tuition: $4305 full-time. Nonresident tuition: $4305 full-time. Mandatory fees: $669 full-time. **Scholarships:** Available **Calendar System:** Semester, Summer Session Available **Enrollment:** FT 4,477, PT 6,141 **Library Holdings:** 65,865 **Regional Accreditation:** North Central Association of Colleges and Schools **Credit Hours For Degree:** 64 credits, Associates **Professional Accreditation:** ADA, NLN

MINNESOTA SCHOOL OF BUSINESS—BLAINE
3680 Pheasant Ridge Dr. NE
Blaine, MN 55449
Tel: (763)225-8000
Admissions: (763)225-8003
Fax: (763)225-8001
E-mail: kswanson@msbcollege.edu
Web Site: http://www.msbcollege.edu/oncampus/blaine/
President/CEO: Diana Igo
Admissions: Kristen Swanson
Type: Four-Year College **Sex:** Coed **Affiliation:** Globe University/Minnesota School of Business **% Accepted:** 100 **Admission Plans:** Early Admission **Application Deadline:** October 5 **Application Fee:** $50.00 **H.S. Requirements:** High school diploma required; GED accepted. For High School Advantage Program, students who are current year graduating seniors and have at least 2.0 GPA: High school diploma or equivalent not required. **Costs Per Year:** Application fee: $50. Tuition: $19,920 full-time, $415 per credit part-time. Mandatory fees: $1100 full-time. Full-time tuition and fees vary according to course load, program, and student level. Part-time tuition varies according to course load, program, and student level. **Enrollment:** FT 221, PT 530 **Faculty:** FT 8, PT 29 **Student-Faculty Ratio:** 22:1 **Exams:** Other.

MINNESOTA SCHOOL OF BUSINESS—BROOKLYN CENTER
5910 Shingle Creek Parkway
Brooklyn Center, MN 55430
Tel: (763)566-7777
Admissions: (763)585-7777
Fax: (763)566-7030
Web Site: http://www.msbcollege.edu/
President/CEO: Lorrie Laurin
Admissions: Bruce Christman
Type: Two-Year College **Sex:** Coed **% Accepted:** 68 **Admission Plans:** Open Admission **Application Deadline:** October 6 **Application Fee:** $50.00 **H.S. Requirements:** High school diploma required; GED accepted **Costs Per Year:** Application fee: $50. Tuition: $14,940 full-time, $415 per credit hour part-time. Full-time tuition varies according to course load. Part-time tuition varies according to course load. **Calendar System:** Quarter **Student-Faculty Ratio:** 13:1 **Exams:** Other. **Library Holdings:** 1,534 **Professional Accreditation:** ACICS

MINNESOTA SCHOOL OF BUSINESS—PLYMOUTH
1455 Country Rd. 101 North
Minneapolis, MN 55447
Tel: (763)476-2000
Web Site: http://www.msbcollege.edu/
President/CEO: Lorrie Laurin
Type: Two-Year College **Sex:** Coed **% Accepted:** 74 **Admission Plans:** Open Admission **Application Deadline:** October 6 **Application Fee:** $50.00 **H.S. Requirements:** High school diploma required; GED accepted **Calendar System:** Quarter, Summer Session Available **Student-Faculty Ratio:** 10:1 **Exams:** Other. **Library Holdings:** 1,189 **Credit Hours For Degree:** 90 credits, Associates; 180 credits, Bachelors **Professional Accreditation:** ACICS

MINNESOTA SCHOOL OF BUSINESS—RICHFIELD
1401 West 76th St.
Ste. 500
Richfield, MN 55423
Tel: (612)861-2000
Fax: (612)861-5548
E-mail: pmurray@msbcollege.com
Web Site: http://www.msbcollege.edu/
President/CEO: Lorrie Laurin
Admissions: Patricia Murray
Type: Two-Year College **Sex:** Coed **Affiliation:** Globe University **% Accepted:** 99 **Admission Plans:** Open Admission **Application Deadline:** October 6 **Application Fee:** $50.00 **H.S. Requirements:** High school diploma required; GED accepted **Scholarships:** Available **Calendar System:** Quarter, Summer Session Available **Student-Faculty Ratio:** 14:1 **Exams:** Other. **Library Holdings:** 2,420 **Credit Hours For Degree:** 90 credits, Associates; 180 credits, Bachelors **Professional Accreditation:** ACICS, AAMAE

MINNESOTA SCHOOL OF BUSINESS—ROCHESTER
2521 Pennington Dr., NW
Rochester, MN 55901
Tel: (507)536-9500; Free: 888-662-8772
Fax: (507)535-8011
Web Site: http://www.msbcollege.edu/
President/CEO: Dave Tracy
Admissions: Shan Pollitt
Type: Comprehensive **Sex:** Coed **Affiliation:** Minnesota School of Business **% Accepted:** 82 **Application Deadline:** October 6 **Application Fee:** $50.00 **Calendar System:** Quarter, Summer Session Available **Enrollment:** FT 355, PT 180 **Faculty:** FT 2, PT 39 **Student-Faculty Ratio:** 13:1 **Exams:** Other. **Library Holdings:** 6,369

MINNESOTA SCHOOL OF BUSINESS—ST. CLOUD
1201 2nd St. South
Waite Park, MN 56387
Tel: (320)257-2000; Free: (866)403-3333
E-mail: cjanssen@msbcollege.edu
Web Site: http://www.msbcollege.edu/
President/CEO: Lorrie Laurin
Admissions: Candi Janssen
Type: Two-Year College **Sex:** Coed **% Accepted:** 100 **Admission Plans:** Open Admission **Application Deadline:** October 6 **Application Fee:** $50.00 **H.S. Requirements:** High school diploma required; GED accepted **Costs Per Year:** Application fee: $50. Tuition: $18,675 full-time, $415 per credit hour part-time. Full-time tuition varies according to course load. Part-time tuition varies according to course load. **Calendar System:** Quarter, Summer Session Available **Student-Faculty Ratio:** 13:1 **Exams:** Other. **Library Holdings:** 724 **Credit Hours For Degree:** 90 credits, Associates; 180 credits, Bachelors **Professional Accreditation:** ACICS

MINNESOTA SCHOOL OF BUSINESS—SHAKOPEE
1200 Shakopee Town Square
Shakopee, MN 55379
Tel: (952)345-1200; Free: (866)766-1200
Admissions: (952)516-7015
Fax: (952)345-1201
Web Site: http://www.msbcollege.edu/
President/CEO: Lorrie Laurin
Admissions: Gretchen Seifert
Type: Two-Year College **Sex:** Coed **% Accepted:** 99 **Admission Plans:** Open Admission **Application Deadline:** October 6 **Application Fee:** $50.00 **H.S. Requirements:** High school diploma required; GED accepted **Calendar System:** Quarter, Summer Session Available **Student-Faculty Ratio:** 12:1 **Exams:** Other. **Library Holdings:** 919 **Credit Hours For Degree:** 90 credits, Associates; 180 credits, Bachelors

MINNESOTA STATE COLLEGE—SOUTHEAST TECHNICAL
1250 Homer Rd., PO Box 409
Winona, MN 55987
Tel: (507)453-2700; Free: 800-372-8164
Admissions: 877-853-8324
Fax: (507)453-2715
E-mail: enrollmentservices@southeastmn.edu
Web Site: http://www.southeastmn.edu/
President/CEO: James Johnson
Type: Two-Year College **Sex:** Coed **Affiliation:** Minnesota State Colleges and Universities System **Admission Plans:** Open Admission **Application**

Deadline: Rolling **Application Fee:** $20.00 **H.S. Requirements:** High school diploma required; GED accepted **Costs Per Year:** Application fee: $20. State resident tuition: $5076 full-time, $152 per credit hour part-time. Nonresident tuition: $5076 full-time, $152 per credit hour part-time. Mandatory fees: $417 full-time. College room and board: $6412. **Scholarships:** Available **Calendar System:** Semester, Summer Session Available **Enrollment:** FT 1,524, PT 1,005 **Faculty:** FT 57, PT 39 **Student-Faculty Ratio:** 19:1 **Final Year or Final Semester Residency Requirement:** No **Regional Accreditation:** North Central Association of Colleges and Schools **Credit Hours For Degree:** 60 credits, Associates

MINNESOTA STATE COMMUNITY AND TECHNICAL COLLEGE
1414 College Way
Fergus Falls, MN 56537-1009
Tel: (218)736-1500; Free: 888-MY-MSCTC
Admissions: (218)736-1528
Fax: (218)739-7475
E-mail: carrie.brimhall@minnesota.edu
Web Site: http://www.minnesota.edu/
President/CEO: Dr. Ann Valentine
Admissions: Carrie Brimhall
Financial Aid: Tom Whelihan
Type: Two-Year College **Sex:** Coed **Affiliation:** Minnesota State Colleges and Universities System **Admission Plans:** Open Admission; Early Admission; Deferred Admission **Application Deadline:** Rolling **Application Fee:** $20.00 **H.S. Requirements:** High school diploma required; GED accepted **Costs Per Year:** Application fee: $20. State resident tuition: $4310 full-time, $143.67 per credit part-time. Nonresident tuition: $4310 full-time, $143.67 per credit part-time. Mandatory fees: $651 full-time, $22 per credit part-time. Full-time tuition and fees vary according to location and program. Part-time tuition and fees vary according to location and program. College room only: $3100. Room charges vary according to housing facility. **Scholarships:** Available **Calendar System:** Semester, Summer Session Available **Enrollment:** FT 3,462, PT 3,270 **Faculty:** FT 176, PT 148 **Student-Faculty Ratio:** 18:1 **Exams:** ACT essay not being used. **% Residing in College-Owned, -Operated, or -Affiliated Housing:** 2 **Final Year or Final Semester Residency Requirement:** No **Library Holdings:** 63,721 **Regional Accreditation:** North Central Association of Colleges and Schools **Credit Hours For Degree:** 64 semester hours, Associates **Professional Accreditation:** NAACLS **Intercollegiate Athletics:** Baseball M; Basketball M & W; Football M; Golf M & W; Softball W; Volleyball W

MINNESOTA STATE UNIVERSITY MANKATO
228 Wiecking Center
Mankato, MN 56001
Tel: (507)389-2463; Free: 800-722-0544
Admissions: (507)389-1822
E-mail: admissions@mnsu.edu
Web Site: http://www.mnsu.edu/
President/CEO: Dr. Richard Davenport
Financial Aid: Sandra Loerts
Type: University **Sex:** Coed **Affiliation:** Minnesota State Colleges and Universities System **Scores:** 61% ACT 18-23; 28% ACT 24-29 **% Accepted:** 88 **Admission Plans:** Early Admission; Deferred Admission **Application Deadline:** Rolling **Application Fee:** $20.00 **H.S. Requirements:** High school diploma required; GED accepted **Costs Per Year:** Application fee: $20. State resident tuition: $5631 full-time, $225.15 per credit hour part-time. Nonresident tuition: $12,063 full-time, $481.05 per credit hour part-time. Mandatory fees: $798 full-time, $33.14 per credit hour part-time. Full-time tuition and fees vary according to course load, location, and reciprocity agreements. Part-time tuition and fees vary according to course load, location, and reciprocity agreements. College room and board: $6019. Room and board charges vary according to board plan and housing facility. **Scholarships:** Available **Calendar System:** Semester, Summer Session Available **Enrollment:** FT 11,488, PT 1,337, Grad FT 583, Grad PT 1,213 **Faculty:** FT 499, PT 262 **Student-Faculty Ratio:** 22:1 **Exams:** SAT I or ACT. ACT essay not being used. **% Receiving Financial Aid:** 52 **% Residing in College-Owned, -Operated, or -Affiliated Housing:** 25 **Library Holdings:** 1,200,000 **Regional Accreditation:** North Central Association of Colleges and Schools **Credit Hours For Degree:** 64 credits, Associates; 128 credits, Bachelors **ROTC:** Army **Professional Accreditation:** AACSB, ABET, AACN, ACA, ADA, ASLHA, CORE, CSWE, JRCEPAT, NASAD, NASM, NCATE, NLN, NRPA **Intercollegiate Athletics:** Baseball M; Basketball M & W; Bowling W; Cheerleading M & W; Cross-Country Running M & W; Football M; Golf M & W; Ice Hockey M & W; Soccer W; Softball W; Swimming and Diving M & W; Tennis M & W; Track and Field M & W; Volleyball W; Wrestling M

MINNESOTA STATE UNIVERSITY MOORHEAD
1104 7th Ave. South
Moorhead, MN 56563-0002
Tel: (218)236-2011; Free: 800-593-7246
Admissions: (218)477-2161
Fax: (218)236-2168
E-mail: dragon@mnstate.edu
Web Site: http://www.mnstate.edu/
President/CEO: Dr. Edna Mora Szymanski
Admissions: Jeremy Johnson
Financial Aid: Carolyn Zehren
Type: Comprehensive **Sex:** Coed **Affiliation:** Minnesota State Colleges and Universities System **Scores:** 58.4% ACT 18-23; 29.1% ACT 24-29 **% Accepted:** 77 **Admission Plans:** Early Admission; Deferred Admission **Application Deadline:** August 1 **Application Fee:** $20.00 **H.S. Requirements:** High school diploma required; GED accepted **Costs Per Year:** Application fee: $20. State resident tuition: $6140 full-time. Nonresident tuition: $6140 full-time. Mandatory fees: $778 full-time. Full-time tuition and fees vary according to program and reciprocity agreements. College room and board: $6468. Room and board charges vary according to board plan and housing facility. **Scholarships:** Available **Calendar System:** Semester, Summer Session Available **Enrollment:** FT 5,773, PT 1,177, Grad FT 145, Grad PT 415 **Faculty:** FT 304, PT 180 **Student-Faculty Ratio:** 19:1 **Exams:** SAT I or ACT. ACT essay not being used. SAT essay not being used. **% Receiving Financial Aid:** 55 **% Residing in College-Owned, -Operated, or -Affiliated Housing:** 20 **Final Year or Final Semester Residency Requirement:** Yes **Library Holdings:** 645,544 **Regional Accreditation:** North Central Association of Colleges and Schools **Credit Hours For Degree:** 64 credits, Associates; 128 credits, Bachelors **ROTC:** Army, Air Force **Professional Accreditation:** AACN, ACCE, ACA, ASLHA, CSWE, NASAD, NASM, NCATE, NLN, NAIT **Intercollegiate Athletics:** Basketball M & W; Cross-Country Running M & W; Football M; Golf M & W; Soccer W; Softball W; Swimming and Diving W; Tennis W; Track and Field M & W; Volleyball W; Wrestling M

MINNESOTA WEST COMMUNITY AND TECHNICAL COLLEGE
1314 North Hiawatha Ave.
Pipestone, MN 56164
Tel: (507)825-6800; Free: 800-658-2330
Admissions: (320)564-4511
Fax: (507)825-4656
E-mail: crystal.strouth@mnwest.edu
Web Site: http://www.mnwest.edu/
President/CEO: Dr. Richard Shrubb
Admissions: Crystal Strouth
Type: Two-Year College **Sex:** Coed **Affiliation:** Minnesota State Colleges and Universities System **% Accepted:** 68 **Admission Plans:** Open Admission **Application Deadline:** Rolling **Application Fee:** $20.00 **H.S. Requirements:** High school diploma required; GED accepted **Costs Per Year:** Application fee: $20. State resident tuition: $4761 full-time, $148.79 per credit hour part-time. Nonresident tuition: $4761 full-time, $148.79 per credit hour part-time. Mandatory fees: $507 full-time, $15.85 per credit hour part-time. Full-time tuition and fees vary according to reciprocity agreements. Part-time tuition and fees vary according to reciprocity agreements. **Scholarships:** Available **Calendar System:** Semester, Summer Session Available **Enrollment:** FT 1,600, PT 1,263 **Faculty:** FT 90, PT 118 **Student-Faculty Ratio:** 13:1 **Library Holdings:** 46,057 **Regional Accreditation:** North Central Association of Colleges and Schools **Credit Hours For Degree:** 64 credits, Associates **Professional Accreditation:** AAMAE, ADA, NAACLS, NLN **Intercollegiate Athletics:** Baseball M; Basketball M & W; Cheerleading M & W; Football M; Golf M & W; Softball W; Volleyball W; Wrestling M

NATIONAL AMERICAN UNIVERSITY (BLOOMINGTON)
112 West Market
Bloomington, MN 55425
Tel: (605)394-4800
Admissions: (952)356-3600
E-mail: jmichaelson@national.edu
Web Site: http://www.national.edu/
President/CEO: Dr. Jerry Gallentine

Admissions: Jennifer Michaelson
Type: Two-Year College **Sex:** Coed **% Accepted:** 100 **Application Fee:** $25.00 **Enrollment:** FT 311, PT 163 **Faculty:** FT 15, PT 31 **Student-Faculty Ratio:** 19:1 **% Residing in College-Owned, -Operated, or -Affiliated Housing:** 18 **Regional Accreditation:** North Central Association of Colleges and Schools **ROTC:** Air Force

NATIONAL AMERICAN UNIVERSITY (BROOKLYN CENTER)
6120 Earle Brown Dr.
Ste. 100
Brooklyn Center, MN 55430
Tel: (763)852-7500
Fax: (763)549-9955
Web Site: http://www.national.edu/
President/CEO: Dr. Jerry Gallentine
Type: Two-Year College **Sex:** Coed **Regional Accreditation:** North Central Association of Colleges and Schools

NATIONAL AMERICAN UNIVERSITY (ROSEVILLE)
1500 West Hwy. 36
Roseville, MN 55113
Tel: (651)644-1265
Admissions: (651)855-6300
Fax: (651)644-0690
Web Site: http://www.national.edu/
President/CEO: Dr. Jerry Gallentine
Admissions: Steve Grunlan
Type: Four-Year College **Sex:** Coed **Affiliation:** National American University **% Accepted:** 100 **Application Deadline:** Rolling **Application Fee:** $25.00 **Calendar System:** Quarter **Faculty:** FT 5, PT 27 **Student-Faculty Ratio:** 10:1 **Regional Accreditation:** North Central Association of Colleges and Schools

NORMANDALE COMMUNITY COLLEGE
9700 France Ave. South
Bloomington, MN 55431-4399
Tel: (952)487-8200; Free: (866)880-8740
Admissions: (952)487-8201
Fax: (612)487-8101
E-mail: information@normandale.edu
Web Site: http://www.normandale.edu/
President/CEO: Dr. Joe Opatz
Type: Two-Year College **Sex:** Coed **Affiliation:** Minnesota State Colleges and Universities System **% Accepted:** 71 **Admission Plans:** Open Admission; Early Admission; Deferred Admission **Application Deadline:** Rolling **Application Fee:** $20.00 **H.S. Requirements:** High school diploma required; GED accepted **Costs Per Year:** Application fee: $20. State resident tuition: $4226 full-time, $140.87 per credit part-time. Nonresident tuition: $4226 full-time, $140.87 per credit part-time. Mandatory fees: $662 full-time, $22.06 per credit part-time. **Scholarships:** Available **Calendar System:** Semester, Summer Session Available **Faculty:** FT 170, PT 60 **Student-Faculty Ratio:** 28:1 **Library Holdings:** 98,141 **Regional Accreditation:** North Central Association of Colleges and Schools **Credit Hours For Degree:** 64 semester hours, Associates **ROTC:** Army, Air Force **Professional Accreditation:** ADA, NASM, NLN

NORTH CENTRAL UNIVERSITY
910 Elliot Ave.
Minneapolis, MN 55404-1322
Tel: (612)332-3491; Free: 800-289-6222
Admissions: (612)343-4460
Fax: (612)343-4778
E-mail: admissions@northcentral.edu
Web Site: http://www.northcentral.edu/
President/CEO: Dr. Gordon L. Anderson
Admissions: Sigi Shawa
Financial Aid: Donna Jager
Type: Four-Year College **Sex:** Coed **Affiliation:** Assemblies of God **Admission Plans:** Open Admission; Deferred Admission **Application Deadline:** June 1 **Application Fee:** $25.00 **H.S. Requirements:** High school diploma required; GED accepted **Costs Per Year:** Application fee: $25. Comprehensive fee: $21,201 includes full-time tuition ($14,640), mandatory fees ($1061), and college room and board ($5500). College room only: $2450. Part-time tuition: $488 per credit hour. **Scholarships:** Available **Calendar System:** Semester, Summer Session Available **Enrollment:** FT 1,125 **Faculty:** FT 40, PT 62 **Student-Faculty Ratio:** 19:1 **Exams:** SAT I or ACT. **% Residing in College-Owned, -Operated, or -Affiliated Housing:** 80 **Library Holdings:** 80,000 **Regional Accreditation:** North Central Association of Colleges and Schools **Credit Hours For Degree:** 62 credits, Associates; 127 credits, Bachelors **ROTC:** Army, Air Force **Intercollegiate Athletics:** Baseball M; Basketball M & W; Cross-Country Running M & W; Golf M; Soccer M & W; Softball W; Tennis M & W; Track and Field M & W; Volleyball W

NORTH HENNEPIN COMMUNITY COLLEGE
7411 85th Ave. North
Brooklyn Park, MN 55445-2231
Tel: (763)488-0391; Free: 800-818-0395
Admissions: (763)424-0702
Fax: (763)424-0929
E-mail: jlsummer@nhcc.edu
Web Site: http://www.nhcc.edu/
President/CEO: Ann Wynia
Admissions: Jennifer Lambrecht
Type: Two-Year College **Sex:** Coed **Affiliation:** Minnesota State Colleges and Universities System **Admission Plans:** Open Admission; Early Admission; Deferred Admission **Application Deadline:** Rolling **Application Fee:** $20.00 **H.S. Requirements:** High school diploma required; GED accepted **Costs Per Year:** Application fee: $20. State resident tuition: $3451 full-time, $143.79 per credit hour part-time. Nonresident tuition: $3451 full-time, $143.79 per credit hour part-time. Mandatory fees: $348 full-time, $14.51 per credit hour part-time. Full-time tuition and fees vary according to course load, location, and program. Part-time tuition and fees vary according to course load, location, and program. **Scholarships:** Available **Calendar System:** Semester, Summer Session Available **Enrollment:** FT 2,984, PT 4,460 **Faculty:** FT 105, PT 143 **Student-Faculty Ratio:** 29:1 **Final Year or Final Semester Residency Requirement:** No **Library Holdings:** 46,636 **Regional Accreditation:** North Central Association of Colleges and Schools **Credit Hours For Degree:** 60 credits, Associates **ROTC:** Army, Navy, Air Force **Professional Accreditation:** ACBSP, NAACLS, NLN

NORTHLAND COMMUNITY AND TECHNICAL COLLEGE—THIEF RIVER FALLS
1101 Hwy. One East
Thief River Falls, MN 56701
Tel: (218)681-0701; Free: 800-959-6282
Admissions: (218)683-8554
Fax: (218)681-6405
E-mail: eugene.klinke@northlandcollege.edu
Web Site: http://www.northlandcollege.edu/
President/CEO: Dr. Anne K. Temte
Admissions: Eugene Klinke
Type: Two-Year College **Sex:** Coed **Affiliation:** Minnesota State Colleges and Universities System **% Accepted:** 100 **Admission Plans:** Open Admission; Early Admission; Deferred Admission **Application Deadline:** August 27 **Application Fee:** $20.00 **H.S. Requirements:** High school diploma required; GED accepted **Costs Per Year:** Application fee: $20. State resident tuition: $4422 full-time, $147.40 per credit hour part-time. Nonresident tuition: $4422 full-time, $147.40 per credit hour part-time. Mandatory fees: $522 full-time, $17.41 per credit hour part-time. Full-time tuition and fees vary according to course load, location, program, and reciprocity agreements. Part-time tuition and fees vary according to course load, location, program, and reciprocity agreements. **Scholarships:** Available **Calendar System:** Semester, Summer Session Available **Enrollment:** FT 2,038, PT 2,205 **Faculty:** FT 123, PT 123 **Student-Faculty Ratio:** 21:1 **Final Year or Final Semester Residency Requirement:** No **Regional Accreditation:** North Central Association of Colleges and Schools **Credit Hours For Degree:** 64 semester hours, Associates **Intercollegiate Athletics:** Baseball M; Basketball M & W; Football M; Softball W; Volleyball W

NORTHWEST TECHNICAL COLLEGE
905 Grant Ave., SE
Bemidji, MN 56601
Tel: (218)333-6600; Free: 800-942-8324
Admissions: (218)333-6645
E-mail: kari.kantack@ntcmn.edu
Web Site: http://www.ntcmn.edu/
President/CEO: Dr. Jon E. Quistgaard, PhD

Admissions: Kari Kantack
Type: Two-Year College **Sex:** Coed **Affiliation:** Bemidji State University; Minnesota State Colleges and Universities System **% Accepted:** 100 **Admission Plans:** Open Admission **Application Deadline:** Rolling **Application Fee:** $20.00 **H.S. Requirements:** High school diploma required; GED accepted **Costs Per Year:** Application fee: $20. State resident tuition: $4616 full-time, $153.85 per credit hour part-time. Nonresident tuition: $4616 full-time, $153.85 per credit hour part-time. Mandatory fees: $296 full-time, $9.88 per credit hour part-time. Full-time tuition and fees vary according to course load, program, and reciprocity agreements. Part-time tuition and fees vary according to course load, program, and reciprocity agreements. College room and board: $6240. College room only: $3940. Room and board charges vary according to board plan. **Scholarships:** Available **Calendar System:** Semester, Summer Session Available **Enrollment:** FT 590, PT 1,013 **Faculty:** FT 27, PT 36 **Student-Faculty Ratio:** 24:1 **Regional Accreditation:** North Central Association of Colleges and Schools **Credit Hours For Degree:** 60 credits, Associates **Professional Accreditation:** ARCEST, AAMAE, ADA, AHIMA, CARC, JRCERT, NAACLS

NORTHWEST TECHNICAL INSTITUTE
950 Blue Gentian Rd.
Ste. 500
Eagan, MN 55121
Tel: (952)944-0080; Free: 800-443-4223
Fax: (952)944-9274
Web Site: http://www.nti.edu/
President/CEO: Keith Fossen
Admissions: John Hartman
Type: Two-Year College **Sex:** Coed **Admission Plans:** Open Admission **Application Deadline:** Rolling **Application Fee:** $25.00 **H.S. Requirements:** High school diploma required; GED accepted **Costs Per Year:** Application fee: $25. Tuition: $15,850 full-time. Tuition guaranteed not to increase for student's term of enrollment. **Scholarships:** Available **Calendar System:** Semester, Summer Session Not available **Library Holdings:** 565 **Credit Hours For Degree:** 64 credits, Associates **Professional Accreditation:** ACCSCT

NORTHWESTERN COLLEGE
3003 Snelling Ave. North
St. Paul, MN 55113-1598
Tel: (651)631-5100; Free: 800-827-6827
Admissions: (651)631-5111
Fax: (651)631-5680
E-mail: admissions@nwc.edu
Web Site: http://www.nwc.edu/
President/CEO: Dr. Alan S. Cureton
Admissions: Kenneth K. Faffler
Financial Aid: Richard L. Blatchley
Type: Comprehensive **Sex:** Coed **Affiliation:** nondenominational **Scores:** 97% SAT V 400+; 95% SAT M 400+; 42% ACT 18-23; 46% ACT 24-29 **% Accepted:** 98 **Admission Plans:** Early Admission; Deferred Admission **Application Deadline:** August 1 **Application Fee:** $30.00 **H.S. Requirements:** High school diploma required; GED accepted **Costs Per Year:** Application fee: $30. Comprehensive fee: $32,290 includes full-time tuition ($24,370), mandatory fees ($200), and college room and board ($7720). College room only: $4480. Full-time tuition and fees vary according to course load. Room and board charges vary according to board plan. Part-time tuition: $1040 per semester hour. Part-time mandatory fees: $55 per term. Part-time tuition and fees vary according to course load. **Scholarships:** Available **Calendar System:** Semester, Summer Session Available **Enrollment:** FT 1,805, PT 53, Grad FT 2, Grad PT 87 **Faculty:** FT 101, PT 81 **Student-Faculty Ratio:** 14:1 **Exams:** SAT I or ACT. SAT essay not being used. **% Receiving Financial Aid:** 82 **% Residing in College-Owned, -Operated, or -Affiliated Housing:** 67 **Final Year or Final Semester Residency Requirement:** No **Library Holdings:** 124,574 **Regional Accreditation:** North Central Association of Colleges and Schools **Credit Hours For Degree:** 60 semester hours, Associates; 125 semester hours, Bachelors **ROTC:** Army, Air Force **Professional Accreditation:** ACBSP, NASM **Intercollegiate Athletics:** Baseball M; Basketball M & W; Cross-Country Running M & W; Football M; Golf M & W; Ice Hockey M; Soccer M & W; Softball W; Tennis M & W; Track and Field M & W; Volleyball M & W

OAK HILLS CHRISTIAN COLLEGE
1600 Oak Hills Rd., SW
Bemidji, MN 56601-8832
Tel: (218)751-8670; Free: 888-751-8670
Fax: (218)751-8825
E-mail: admissions@oakhills.edu
Web Site: http://www.oakhills.edu/
President/CEO: Dr. Steve Hostetter
Admissions: Shelly Fast
Financial Aid: Daniel Hovestol
Type: Four-Year College **Sex:** Coed **Affiliation:** interdenominational **Scores:** 53% ACT 18-23; 15% ACT 24-29 **% Accepted:** 67 **Admission Plans:** Deferred Admission **Application Deadline:** Rolling **Application Fee:** $25.00 **H.S. Requirements:** High school diploma required; GED accepted **Costs Per Year:** Application fee: $25. Comprehensive fee: $18,320 includes full-time tuition ($13,480) and college room and board ($4840). College room only: $1936. Room and board charges vary according to board plan and housing facility. Part-time tuition: $395 per credit. Part-time tuition varies according to course load. Tuition guaranteed not to increase for student's term of enrollment. **Scholarships:** Available **Calendar System:** Semester, Summer Session Not available **Enrollment:** FT 124, PT 25 **Faculty:** FT 6, PT 11 **Student-Faculty Ratio:** 14:1 **Exams:** SAT I or ACT. **% Receiving Financial Aid:** 90 **% Residing in College-Owned, -Operated, or -Affiliated Housing:** 80 **Library Holdings:** 28,523 **Credit Hours For Degree:** 64 semester hours, Associates; 126 semester hours, Bachelors **Professional Accreditation:** ABHE **Intercollegiate Athletics:** Basketball M; Volleyball W

PINE TECHNICAL COLLEGE
900 4th St. SE
Pine City, MN 55063
Tel: (320)629-5100; Free: 800-521-7463
Fax: (320)629-5101
Web Site: http://www.pinetech.edu/
President/CEO: Robert Musgrove
Admissions: Nancy Mach
Type: Two-Year College **Sex:** Coed **Affiliation:** Minnesota State Colleges and Universities System **Admission Plans:** Open Admission; Early Admission **Application Deadline:** Rolling **Application Fee:** $20.00 **H.S. Requirements:** High school diploma required; GED accepted **Costs Per Year:** Application fee: $20. One-time mandatory fee: $20. State resident tuition: $4005 full-time. Nonresident tuition: $8010 full-time. Mandatory fees: $486 full-time. **Scholarships:** Available **Calendar System:** Semester, Summer Session Available **Enrollment:** FT 296, PT 516 **Faculty:** FT 18, PT 21 **Student-Faculty Ratio:** 18:1 **Library Holdings:** 6,000 **Regional Accreditation:** North Central Association of Colleges and Schools **Credit Hours For Degree:** 65 credits, Associates

RAINY RIVER COMMUNITY COLLEGE
1501 Hwy. 71
International Falls, MN 56649
Tel: (218)285-7722; Free: 800-456-3996
Admissions: (218)285-2207
Fax: (218)285-2239
E-mail: hagen_b@rrcc.mnscu.edu
Web Site: http://www.rrcc.mnscu.edu/
President/CEO: Dr. Wayne Merrell
Admissions: Berta Hagen
Financial Aid: Scott Riley
Type: Two-Year College **Sex:** Coed **Affiliation:** Minnesota State Colleges and Universities System **Admission Plans:** Open Admission; Early Admission; Deferred Admission **Application Deadline:** Rolling **Application Fee:** $20.00 **H.S. Requirements:** High school diploma required; GED accepted. For applicants who demonstrate ability to benefit from college: High school diploma or equivalent not required **Costs Per Year:** Application fee: $20. State resident tuition: $4066 full-time, $135.53 per credit hour part-time. Nonresident tuition: $5197 full-time, $173.23 per credit hour part-time. Mandatory fees: $594 full-time, $19.81 per credit hour part-time, $19.81. Full-time tuition and fees vary according to course load, program, and reciprocity agreements. Part-time tuition and fees vary according to course load, program, and reciprocity agreements. College room only: $2680. **Scholarships:** Available **Calendar System:** Semester, Summer Session Available **Enrollment:** FT 283, PT 138 **Faculty:** FT 15, PT 18 **Student-Faculty Ratio:** 15:1 **Library Holdings:** 20,000 **Regional Accreditation:** North Central Association of Colleges and Schools **Credit Hours For Degree:** 96 credits, Associates **Intercollegiate Athletics:** Basketball M & W; Softball W; Volleyball W

RASMUSSEN COLLEGE BROOKLYN PARK
8301 93rd Ave. North
Brooklyn Park, MN 55445-1512
Tel: (763)493-4500; Free: 877-495-4500
Fax: (763)425-4344
Web Site: http://www.rasmussen.edu/
President/CEO: Dwayne Bertotto
Type: Two-Year College **Sex:** Coed **Application Fee:** $60.00 **Costs Per Year:** Application fee: $60. Tuition: $420 per credit part-time. Part-time tuition varies according to course level, course load, and program. **Regional Accreditation:** North Central Association of Colleges and Schools

RASMUSSEN COLLEGE EAGAN
3500 Federal Dr.
Eagan, MN 55122-1346
Tel: (651)687-9000; Free: 800-852-6367
Fax: (651)687-0507
Web Site: http://www.rasmussen.edu/
President/CEO: Tammy Jackson
Admissions: Jacinda Miller
Type: Two-Year College **Sex:** Coed **Affiliation:** Rasmussen College System **Application Deadline:** Rolling **Application Fee:** $60.00 **H.S. Requirements:** High school diploma required; GED accepted **Costs Per Year:** Application fee: $60. Tuition: $420 per credit part-time. Part-time tuition varies according to course level, course load, and program. **Scholarships:** Available **Calendar System:** Quarter, Summer Session Not available **Faculty:** FT 10, PT 30 **Student-Faculty Ratio:** 12:1 **Exams:** Other. **Credit Hours For Degree:** 113 credits, Associates **Professional Accreditation:** ACICS, AHIMA

RASMUSSEN COLLEGE EDEN PRAIRIE
7905 Golden Triangle Dr.
Ste. 100
Eden Prairie, MN 55344
Tel: (952)545-2000
Web Site: http://www.rasmussen.edu/
President/CEO: Patty Sagert
Admissions: Jeff Hagy
Type: Two-Year College **Sex:** Coed **Affiliation:** Rasmussen College System **Admission Plans:** Early Admission; Deferred Admission **Application Deadline:** Rolling **Application Fee:** $60.00 **H.S. Requirements:** High school diploma required; GED accepted **Costs Per Year:** Application fee: $60. Tuition: $420 per credit part-time. Part-time tuition varies according to course load and program. **Scholarships:** Available **Calendar System:** Quarter, Summer Session Available **Enrollment:** FT 209, PT 154 **Faculty:** FT 15, PT 17 **Student-Faculty Ratio:** 11:1 **Exams:** Other. **Library Holdings:** 3,400 **Regional Accreditation:** North Central Association of Colleges and Schools **Credit Hours For Degree:** 116 credits, Associates **Professional Accreditation:** ACICS, AHIMA

RASMUSSEN COLLEGE LAKE ELMO/WOODBURY
8565 Eagle Point Circle
Lake Elmo, MN 55042
Tel: (651)259-6600; Free: 888-813-2358
Fax: (651)259-6601
Web Site: http://www.rasmussen.edu/
President/CEO: Phillip Kagol
Type: Two-Year College **Sex:** Coed **Costs Per Year:** Tuition: $420 per credit part-time. Part-time tuition varies according to course load and program. **Regional Accreditation:** North Central Association of Colleges and Schools

RASMUSSEN COLLEGE MANKATO
130 Saint Andrews Dr.
Mankato, MN 56001
Tel: (507)625-6556
Fax: (507)625-6557
E-mail: rascoll@ic.mankato.mn.us
Web Site: http://www.rasmussen.edu/
President/CEO: Douglas Gardner
Admissions: Kathy Clifford
Type: Two-Year College **Sex:** Coed **Affiliation:** Rasmussen College System **Admission Plans:** Deferred Admission **Application Fee:** $60.00 **H.S. Requirements:** High school diploma required; GED accepted **Costs Per Year:** Application fee: $60. Tuition: $420 per credit part-time. Part-time tuition varies according to program. **Scholarships:** Available **Calendar System:** Quarter, Summer Session Available **Enrollment:** FT 600 **Faculty:** FT 19, PT 32 **Student-Faculty Ratio:** 18:1 **Exams:** Other. **Library Holdings:** 1,000 **Credit Hours For Degree:** 64 credits, Associates **Professional Accreditation:** ACICS, AHIMA

RASMUSSEN COLLEGE MOORHEAD
1250 29th Ave. South
Moorhead, MN 56560
Tel: (218)304-6200; Free: (866)562-2758
Fax: (218)304-2601
Web Site: http://www.rasmussen.edu/
Type: Two-Year College **Sex:** Coed **Costs Per Year:** Tuition: $365 per credit part-time. Part-time tuition varies according to course level, course load, and program. **Regional Accreditation:** North Central Association of Colleges and Schools

RASMUSSEN COLLEGE ST. CLOUD
226 Park Ave. South
St. Cloud, MN 56301-3713
Tel: (320)251-5600
Fax: (320)251-3702
E-mail: admstc@rasmussen.edu
Web Site: http://www.rasmussen.edu/
President/CEO: Liz Rian
Admissions: Andrea Peters
Type: Two-Year College **Sex:** Coed **Affiliation:** Rasmussen College System **Admission Plans:** Early Admission; Deferred Admission **Application Deadline:** Rolling **Application Fee:** $60.00 **H.S. Requirements:** High school diploma required; GED accepted **Costs Per Year:** Application fee: $60. Tuition: $420 per credit part-time. Part-time tuition varies according to course load and program. **Scholarships:** Available **Calendar System:** Quarter, Summer Session Available **Exams:** Other. **Library Holdings:** 689 **Regional Accreditation:** North Central Association of Colleges and Schools **Credit Hours For Degree:** 102 credits, Associates **Professional Accreditation:** ACICS, AHIMA

RIDGEWATER COLLEGE
PO Box 1097
Willmar, MN 56201-1097
Tel: (320)235-5114; Free: 800-722-1151
Admissions: (320)222-5976
Fax: (320)231-6602
E-mail: linda.barron@ridgewater.edu
Web Site: http://www.ridgewater.edu/
President/CEO: Dr. Douglas Allen
Admissions: Linda Barron
Type: Two-Year College **Sex:** Coed **Affiliation:** Minnesota State Colleges and Universities System **Admission Plans:** Open Admission **Application Fee:** $20.00 **H.S. Requirements:** High school diploma required; GED accepted **Scholarships:** Available **Calendar System:** Semester, Summer Session Available **Enrollment:** FT 2,576, PT 1,601 **Faculty:** FT 122, PT 117 **Library Holdings:** 30,000 **Regional Accreditation:** North Central Association of Colleges and Schools **Credit Hours For Degree:** 64 semester hours, Associates **Professional Accreditation:** AHIMA, NLN **Intercollegiate Athletics:** Baseball M; Basketball M & W; Football M; Soccer M; Softball W; Volleyball W; Wrestling M

RIVERLAND COMMUNITY COLLEGE
1900 8th Ave., NW
Austin, MN 55912
Tel: (507)433-0600; Free: 800-247-5039
Admissions: (507)433-0820
Fax: (507)433-0515
E-mail: admissions@riverland.edu
Web Site: http://www.riverland.edu/
President/CEO: Dr. Terrence Leas
Admissions: Renee Njos
Type: Two-Year College **Sex:** Coed **Affiliation:** Minnesota State Colleges and Universities System **% Accepted:** 62 **Admission Plans:** Open Admission; Early Admission **Application Deadline:** Rolling **Application Fee:** $20.00 **H.S. Requirements:** High school diploma required; GED accepted **Costs Per Year:** Application fee: $20. State resident tuition: $4277 full-time, $142.55 per credit part-time. Nonresident tuition: $4277 full-time, $142.55

per credit part-time. Mandatory fees: $564 full-time, $18.81 per credit part-time. Full-time tuition and fees vary according to program and reciprocity agreements. Part-time tuition and fees vary according to program and reciprocity agreements. College room only: $2640. **Scholarships:** Available **Calendar System:** Semester, Summer Session Available **Enrollment:** FT 1,489, PT 2,197 **Student-Faculty Ratio:** 18:1 **% Residing in College-Owned, -Operated, or -Affiliated Housing:** 2 **Library Holdings:** 33,500 **Regional Accreditation:** North Central Association of Colleges and Schools **Credit Hours For Degree:** 64 semester hours, Associates **Professional Accreditation:** JRCERT, NLN **Intercollegiate Athletics:** Baseball M; Basketball M & W; Golf M & W; Softball W; Volleyball W

ROCHESTER COMMUNITY AND TECHNICAL COLLEGE
851 30th Ave., SE
Rochester, MN 55904-4999
Tel: (507)285-7210
Fax: (507)285-7496
Web Site: http://www.rctc.edu/
President/CEO: Donald Supalla
Admissions: Troy Tynsky
Type: Two-Year College **Sex:** Coed **Affiliation:** Minnesota State Colleges and Universities System **Admission Plans:** Open Admission; Early Admission **Application Deadline:** August 24 **Application Fee:** $20.00 **H.S. Requirements:** High school diploma required; GED accepted **Scholarships:** Available **Calendar System:** Semester, Summer Session Available **Library Holdings:** 62,000 **Regional Accreditation:** North Central Association of Colleges and Schools **Professional Accreditation:** ARCEST, AAMAE, ADA, AHIMA, CARC, NLN **Intercollegiate Athletics:** Baseball M; Basketball M & W; Football M; Golf M & W; Soccer W; Softball W; Volleyball W; Wrestling M

ST. CATHERINE UNIVERSITY
2004 Randolph Ave.
St. Paul, MN 55105
Tel: (651)690-6000
Fax: (651)690-6042
E-mail: stkate@stkate.edu
Web Site: http://www.stkate.edu/
President/CEO: Andrea J. Lee, IHM
Admissions: Cory Piper-Hauswirth
Financial Aid: Beth Stevens
Type: Comprehensive **Affiliation:** Roman Catholic **Scores:** 50% ACT 18-23; 42% ACT 24-29 **% Accepted:** 67 **Admission Plans:** Deferred Admission **Application Deadline:** Rolling **Application Fee:** $0.00 **H.S. Requirements:** High school diploma required; GED accepted **Costs Per Year:** Application fee: $0. One-time mandatory fee: $100. Comprehensive fee: $36,088 includes full-time tuition ($28,480), mandatory fees ($278), and college room and board ($7330). College room only: $4110. Full-time tuition and fees vary according to class time and degree level. Room and board charges vary according to board plan and housing facility. Part-time tuition: $890 per credit hour. Part-time mandatory fees: $890 per credit hour, $139 per term. Part-time tuition and fees vary according to class time and degree level. **Scholarships:** Available **Calendar System:** 4-1-4, Summer Session Available **Enrollment:** FT 2,468, PT 1,329, Grad FT 776, Grad PT 704 **Faculty:** FT 286, PT 161 **Student-Faculty Ratio:** 12:1 **Exams:** SAT I or ACT. **% Receiving Financial Aid:** 85 **% Residing in College-Owned, -Operated, or -Affiliated Housing:** 40 **Regional Accreditation:** North Central Association of Colleges and Schools **Credit Hours For Degree:** 130 semester credits, Bachelors **ROTC:** Army, Air Force **Professional Accreditation:** AOTA, APTA, CSWE, JRCEDMS, NASM, NLN **Intercollegiate Athletics:** Basketball W; Cross-Country Running W; Ice Hockey W; Soccer W; Softball W; Swimming and Diving W; Tennis W; Track and Field W; Volleyball W

ST. CLOUD STATE UNIVERSITY
720 4th Ave. South
St. Cloud, MN 56301-4498
Tel: (320)308-0121; Free: 877-654-7278
Admissions: (320)308-2244
E-mail: scsu4u@stcloudstate.edu
Web Site: http://www.stcloudstate.edu/
President/CEO: Dr. Earl H. Potter, III
Admissions: Richard Shearer
Financial Aid: Frank P. Morrissey
Type: Comprehensive **Sex:** Coed **Affiliation:** Minnesota State Colleges and Universities System **Scores:** 61.75% ACT 18-23; 25.01% ACT 24-29 **% Accepted:** 87 **Admission Plans:** Deferred Admission **Application Deadline:** June 1 **Application Fee:** $20.00 **H.S. Requirements:** High school diploma required; GED accepted **Costs Per Year:** Application fee: $20. State resident tuition: $5567 full-time, $185.55 per credit part-time. Nonresident tuition: $13,081 full-time, $410.60 per credit part-time. Mandatory fees: $733 full-time. Full-time tuition and fees vary according to course load and reciprocity agreements. Part-time tuition varies according to course load and reciprocity agreements. College room and board: $5984. College room only: $3824. Room and board charges vary according to board plan and housing facility. **Scholarships:** Available **Calendar System:** Semester, Summer Session Available **Enrollment:** FT 12,233, PT 3,547, Grad FT 686, Grad PT 1,319 **Faculty:** FT 668, PT 271 **Student-Faculty Ratio:** 19:1 **Exams:** SAT I or ACT. **% Receiving Financial Aid:** 50 **% Residing in College-Owned, -Operated, or -Affiliated Housing:** 20 **Library Holdings:** 947,787 **Regional Accreditation:** North Central Association of Colleges and Schools **Credit Hours For Degree:** 60 credit hours, Associates; 120 credit hours, Bachelors **ROTC:** Army **Professional Accreditation:** AACSB, ABET, ACEJMC, AAMFT, ACA, ASLHA, CAA, CORE, CSWE, NASAD, NASM, NAST, NCATE **Intercollegiate Athletics:** Baseball M; Basketball M & W; Bowling M & W; Cheerleading M & W; Crew M & W; Cross-Country Running M & W; Equestrian Sports M & W; Football M; Golf M & W; Ice Hockey M & W; Rock Climbing M & W; Skiing (Cross-Country) M & W; Skiing (Downhill) M & W; Soccer M & W; Softball W; Swimming and Diving M & W; Tennis M & W; Track and Field M & W; Ultimate Frisbee M & W; Volleyball M & W; Wrestling M

ST. CLOUD TECHNICAL COLLEGE
1540 Northway Dr.
St. Cloud, MN 56303-1240
Tel: (320)654-5000
Admissions: (320)308-5089
Fax: (320)654-5981
E-mail: jelness@sctc.edu
Web Site: http://www.sctc.edu/
President/CEO: Joyce Helens
Admissions: Jodi Elness
Type: Two-Year College **Sex:** Coed **Affiliation:** Minnesota State Colleges and Universities System **% Accepted:** 91 **Admission Plans:** Open Admission; Early Admission; Deferred Admission **Application Deadline:** Rolling **Application Fee:** $20.00 **H.S. Requirements:** High school diploma required; GED accepted **Costs Per Year:** Application fee: $20. State resident tuition: $4219 full-time, $140.64 per credit part-time. Nonresident tuition: $4219 full-time, $140.64 per credit part-time. Mandatory fees: $518 full-time, $17.26 per credit part-time. Full-time tuition and fees vary according to course load and program. Part-time tuition and fees vary according to course load and program. **Scholarships:** Available **Calendar System:** Semester, Summer Session Available **Enrollment:** FT 2,484, PT 1,465 **Faculty:** FT 117, PT 67 **Library Holdings:** 10,000 **Regional Accreditation:** North Central Association of Colleges and Schools **Credit Hours For Degree:** 60 credits, Associates **Professional Accreditation:** ARCEST, ADA **Intercollegiate Athletics:** Baseball M; Basketball M & W; Softball W; Volleyball W

SAINT JOHN'S UNIVERSITY
PO Box 2000
Collegeville, MN 56321
Tel: (320)363-2011; Free: 800-544-1489
Admissions: (320)363-2196
Fax: (320)363-3206
E-mail: admissions@csbsju.edu
Web Site: http://www.csbsju.edu/
President/CEO: Fr. Robert Koopmann, OSB
Admissions: Matt Beirne
Financial Aid: Mary Dehler
Type: Comprehensive **Sex:** Coed **Affiliation:** Roman Catholic **Scores:** 93% SAT V 400+; 97% SAT M 400+; 27% ACT 18-23; 54% ACT 24-29 **% Accepted:** 84 **Admission Plans:** Early Action; Deferred Admission **Application Deadline:** Rolling **Application Fee:** $0.00 **H.S. Requirements:** High school diploma required; GED accepted. For home schooled students with appropriate documentation of college preparatory curriculum: High school diploma or equivalent not required **Costs Per Year:** Application fee: $0. Comprehensive fee: $37,650 includes full-time tuition ($29,388), mandatory

fees ($548), and college room and board ($7714). College room only: $3884. Room and board charges vary according to board plan and housing facility. Part-time tuition: $1225 per credit hour. Part-time tuition varies according to course load. **Scholarships:** Available **Calendar System:** Semester, Summer Session Not available **Enrollment:** FT 1,867, PT 48, Grad FT 52, Grad PT 53 **Faculty:** FT 147, PT 30 **Student-Faculty Ratio:** 12:1 **Exams:** SAT I or ACT. ACT essay not being used. SAT essay not being used. **% Receiving Financial Aid:** 59 **% Residing in College-Owned, -Operated, or -Affiliated Housing:** 78 **Library Holdings:** 658,438 **Regional Accreditation:** North Central Association of Colleges and Schools **Credit Hours For Degree:** 124 credits, Bachelors **ROTC:** Army **Professional Accreditation:** AACN, ATS, CSWE, NASM, NCATE, NLN **Intercollegiate Athletics:** Baseball M; Basketball M; Crew M; Cross-Country Running M; Football M; Golf M; Ice Hockey M; Lacrosse M; Riflery M; Rugby M; Skiing (Cross-Country) M; Soccer M; Swimming and Diving M; Tennis M; Track and Field M; Ultimate Frisbee M; Volleyball M; Water Polo M; Wrestling M

SAINT MARY'S UNIVERSITY OF MINNESOTA

700 Terrace Heights
Winona, MN 55987-1399
Tel: (507)452-4430; Free: 800-635-5987
Admissions: (507)457-1700
Fax: (507)457-1722
E-mail: admission@smumn.edu
Web Site: http://www.smumn.edu/
President/CEO: Br. William Mann
Admissions: Anthony M. Piscitiello
Financial Aid: Jayne P. Wobig
Type: Comprehensive **Sex:** Coed **Affiliation:** Roman Catholic **Scores:** 100% SAT V 400+; 92% SAT M 400+; 48% ACT 18-23; 38% ACT 24-29 **% Accepted:** 72 **Admission Plans:** Early Admission; Deferred Admission **Application Deadline:** May 1 **Application Fee:** $25.00 **H.S. Requirements:** High school diploma required; GED accepted **Costs Per Year:** Application fee: $25. Comprehensive fee: $33,030 includes full-time tuition ($25,600), mandatory fees ($490), and college room and board ($6940). College room only: $3880. Full-time tuition and fees vary according to course load, degree level, location, and program. Room and board charges vary according to housing facility. Part-time tuition: $850 per credit. Part-time mandatory fees: $490 per year. Part-time tuition and fees vary according to course load, degree level, location, and program. **Scholarships:** Available **Calendar System:** Semester, Summer Session Available **Enrollment:** FT 1,455, PT 658, Grad FT 601, Grad PT 2,851 **Faculty:** FT 103, PT 482 **Student-Faculty Ratio:** 12:1 **Exams:** SAT I or ACT. ACT essay used in place of application essay. SAT essay used in place of application essay. **% Receiving Financial Aid:** 73 **% Residing in College-Owned, -Operated, or -Affiliated Housing:** 83 **Final Year or Final Semester Residency Requirement:** No **Library Holdings:** 241,470 **Regional Accreditation:** North Central Association of Colleges and Schools **Credit Hours For Degree:** 122 credits, Bachelors **ROTC:** Army **Professional Accreditation:** AANA, JRCNMT **Intercollegiate Athletics:** Baseball M; Basketball M & W; Cross-Country Running M & W; Golf M & W; Ice Hockey M & W; Soccer M & W; Softball W; Swimming and Diving M & W; Tennis M & W; Track and Field M & W; Volleyball W

ST. OLAF COLLEGE

1520 St. Olaf Ave.
Northfield, MN 55057-1098
Tel: (507)646-2222; Free: 800-800-3025
Admissions: (507)786-3025
Fax: (507)646-3832
E-mail: admissions@stolaf.edu
Web Site: http://www.stolaf.edu/
President/CEO: David R. Anderson
Admissions: Derek Gueldenzoph
Financial Aid: Katharine Ruby
Type: Four-Year College **Sex:** Coed **Affiliation:** Lutheran **Scores:** 100% SAT V 400+; 100% SAT M 400+; 11% ACT 18-23; 46% ACT 24-29 **% Accepted:** 57 **Admission Plans:** Early Decision Plan; Deferred Admission **Application Deadline:** January 15 **Application Fee:** $40.00 **H.S. Requirements:** High school diploma required; GED accepted **Costs Per Year:** Application fee: $40. Comprehensive fee: $43,700 includes full-time tuition ($35,500) and college room and board ($8200). College room only: $3800. Full-time tuition varies according to course load. Room and board charges vary according to board plan and housing facility. Part-time tuition: $1110 per credit hour. Part-time tuition varies according to course load. **Scholarships:** Available **Calendar System:** 4-1-4, Summer Session Available **Enrollment:** FT 3,028, PT 71 **Faculty:** FT 207, PT 120 **Student-Faculty Ratio:** 12:1 **Exams:** SAT I or ACT. **% Receiving Financial Aid:** 66 **% Residing in College-Owned, -Operated, or -Affiliated Housing:** 96 **Final Year or Final Semester Residency Requirement:** Yes **Library Holdings:** 751,464 **Regional Accreditation:** North Central Association of Colleges and Schools **Credit Hours For Degree:** 35 courses, Bachelors **Professional Accreditation:** AACN, AAFCS, CSWE, NASD, NASM, NAST, NCATE, NLN **Intercollegiate Athletics:** Baseball M; Basketball M & W; Cross-Country Running M & W; Football M; Golf M & W; Ice Hockey M & W; Skiing (Cross-Country) M & W; Skiing (Downhill) M & W; Soccer M & W; Softball W; Swimming and Diving M & W; Tennis M & W; Track and Field M & W; Volleyball W; Wrestling M

SAINT PAUL COLLEGE—A COMMUNITY & TECHNICAL COLLEGE

235 Marshall Ave.
St. Paul, MN 55102-1800
Tel: (651)846-1600; Free: 800-227-6029
Fax: (651)221-1416
E-mail: admissions@saintpaul.edu
Web Site: http://www.saintpaul.edu/
President/CEO: Donovan Schwichtenberg
Admissions: Sarah Carrico
Type: Two-Year College **Sex:** Coed **Affiliation:** Minnesota State Colleges and Universities System **% Accepted:** 100 **Admission Plans:** Open Admission; Early Admission **Application Deadline:** Rolling **Application Fee:** $20.00 **H.S. Requirements:** High school diploma required; GED accepted **Scholarships:** Available **Calendar System:** Semester, Summer Session Available **Enrollment:** FT 2,454, PT 3,474 **Faculty:** FT 107, PT 209 **Student-Faculty Ratio:** 18:1 **Exams:** Other. **Library Holdings:** 12,000 **Regional Accreditation:** North Central Association of Colleges and Schools **Credit Hours For Degree:** 64 semester credits, Associates **Professional Accreditation:** ACF, CARC, NAACLS, NLN

SOUTH CENTRAL COLLEGE

1920 Lee Blvd.
North Mankato, MN 56003
Tel: (507)389-7200
Admissions: (507)389-7334
Web Site: http://southcentral.edu/
President/CEO: Keith Stover
Admissions: Beverly Herda
Type: Two-Year College **Sex:** Coed **Affiliation:** Minnesota State Colleges and Universities System **Admission Plans:** Open Admission **Application Deadline:** August 1 **Application Fee:** $20.00 **H.S. Requirements:** High school diploma required; GED accepted **Costs Per Year:** Application fee: $20. State resident tuition: $3342 full-time, $139.25 per credit part-time. Nonresident tuition: $3342 full-time, $139.25 per credit part-time. Mandatory fees: $415 full-time, $17.31 per credit part-time. **Calendar System:** Semester **Student-Faculty Ratio:** 12:1 **Regional Accreditation:** North Central Association of Colleges and Schools **Credit Hours For Degree:** 72 credits, Associates **Professional Accreditation:** ADA, NAACLS

SOUTHWEST MINNESOTA STATE UNIVERSITY

1501 State St.
Marshall, MN 56258
Tel: (507)537-7021; Free: 800-642-0684
Admissions: (507)537-6286
Fax: (507)537-7154
E-mail: leann.thooft@smsu.edu
Web Site: http://www.smsu.edu/
President/CEO: Dr. David C. Danahar
Admissions: LeAnn Thooft
Financial Aid: David Vikander
Type: Comprehensive **Sex:** Coed **Affiliation:** Minnesota State Colleges and Universities System **Scores:** 62% ACT 18-23; 24% ACT 24-29 **% Accepted:** 65 **Admission Plans:** Early Admission; Deferred Admission **Application Deadline:** August 13 **Application Fee:** $20.00 **H.S. Requirements:** High school diploma required; GED accepted **Costs Per Year:** Application fee: $20. One-time mandatory fee: $20. State resident tuition: $6250 full-time, $201 per credit hour part-time. Nonresident tuition: $6250 full-time, $201 per credit hour part-time. Mandatory fees: $979 full-time, $38 per credit hour

part-time, $38. Full-time tuition and fees vary according to course load, location, program, and reciprocity agreements. Part-time tuition and fees vary according to location, program, and reciprocity agreements. College room and board: $6846. College room only: $3927. Room and board charges vary according to board plan and housing facility. **Scholarships:** Available **Calendar System:** Semester, Summer Session Available **Enrollment:** FT 2,388, PT 3,833, Grad FT 345, Grad PT 174 **Faculty:** FT 122, PT 63 **Student-Faculty Ratio:** 20:1 **Exams:** ACT, SAT I or ACT. ACT essay not being used. **% Receiving Financial Aid:** 65 **% Residing in College-Owned, -Operated, or -Affiliated Housing:** 37 **Final Year or Final Semester Residency Requirement:** No **Library Holdings:** 402,933 **Regional Accreditation:** North Central Association of Colleges and Schools **Credit Hours For Degree:** 64 credit hours, Associates; 128 credit hours, Bachelors **Professional Accreditation:** CSWE, NASM **Intercollegiate Athletics:** Baseball M; Basketball M & W; Football M; Golf W; Soccer W; Softball W; Tennis W; Volleyball W; Wrestling M

UNIVERSITY OF MINNESOTA, CROOKSTON
2900 University Ave.
Crookston, MN 56716-5001
Tel: (218)281-6510; Free: 800-862-6466
Admissions: (218)281-8569
Fax: (218)281-8050
E-mail: umcinfo@umn.edu
Web Site: http://www.umcrookston.edu/
President/CEO: Dr. Charles H. Casey, DVM
Admissions: Amber Evans-Dailey
Financial Aid: Melissa Dingmann
Type: Four-Year College **Sex:** Coed **Affiliation:** University of Minnesota System **Scores:** 81% SAT V 400+; 86% SAT M 400+; 63% ACT 18-23; 22% ACT 24-29 **% Accepted:** 83 **Admission Plans:** Deferred Admission **Application Deadline:** Rolling **Application Fee:** $30.00 **H.S. Requirements:** High school diploma required; GED accepted **Costs Per Year:** Application fee: $30. State resident tuition: $7956 full-time, $306 per semester hour part-time. Nonresident tuition: $7956 full-time, $306 per semester hour part-time. Mandatory fees: $2691 full-time, $306 per semester hour part-time, $306. Full-time tuition and fees vary according to course load and reciprocity agreements. Part-time tuition and fees vary according to course load and reciprocity agreements. College room and board: $6563. College room only: $3087. Room and board charges vary according to board plan and housing facility. Tuition guaranteed not to increase for student's term of enrollment. **Scholarships:** Available **Calendar System:** Semester, Summer Session Available **Enrollment:** FT 1,152, PT 1,127 **Faculty:** FT 55, PT 46 **Student-Faculty Ratio:** 17:1 **Exams:** ACT, SAT I or ACT. ACT essay not being used. SAT essay not being used. **% Receiving Financial Aid:** 68 **% Residing in College-Owned, -Operated, or -Affiliated Housing:** 41 **Final Year or Final Semester Residency Requirement:** No **Library Holdings:** 55,303 **Regional Accreditation:** North Central Association of Colleges and Schools **Credit Hours For Degree:** 120 semester hours, Bachelors **ROTC:** Air Force **Intercollegiate Athletics:** Baseball M; Basketball M & W; Equestrian Sports W; Football M; Golf M & W; Soccer W; Softball W; Tennis W; Volleyball W

UNIVERSITY OF MINNESOTA, DULUTH
10 University Dr.
Duluth, MN 55812-2496
Tel: (218)726-8000; Free: 800-232-1339
Admissions: (218)726-7171
Fax: (218)726-6394
E-mail: umdadmis@d.umn.edu
Web Site: http://www.d.umn.edu/
President/CEO: Kathryn A. Martin
Financial Aid: Brenda Herzig
Type: Comprehensive **Sex:** Coed **Affiliation:** University of Minnesota System **Scores:** 91% SAT V 400+; 94% SAT M 400+; 49% ACT 18-23; 46% ACT 24-29 **% Accepted:** 71 **Application Deadline:** December 15 **Application Fee:** $35.00 **H.S. Requirements:** High school diploma required; GED accepted **Costs Per Year:** Application fee: $35. State resident tuition: $8830 full-time, $339.61 per credit part-time. Nonresident tuition: $10,830 full-time, $416.53 per credit part-time. Mandatory fees: $2174 full-time, $60 per credit part-time. Full-time tuition and fees vary according to class time, course load, degree level, program, and reciprocity agreements. Part-time tuition and fees vary according to class time, course load, degree level, program, and reciprocity agreements. College room and board: $6176. Room and board charges vary according to board plan and housing facility. **Scholarships:** Available **Calendar System:** Semester, Summer Session Available **Enrollment:** FT 9,212, PT 1,294, Grad FT 611, Grad PT 547 **Faculty:** FT 463, PT 88 **Student-Faculty Ratio:** 21:1 **Exams:** SAT I or ACT. ACT essay used for advising. ACT essay used for placement. **% Receiving Financial Aid:** 58 **% Residing in College-Owned, -Operated, or -Affiliated Housing:** 29 **Final Year or Final Semester Residency Requirement:** No **Library Holdings:** 757,341 **Regional Accreditation:** North Central Association of Colleges and Schools **Credit Hours For Degree:** 120 credits, Bachelors **ROTC:** Air Force **Professional Accreditation:** AACSB, ABET, ACA, ASLHA, CSWE, LCMEAMA, NASM, NCATE **Intercollegiate Athletics:** Baseball M; Basketball M & W; Cheerleading W; Crew M & W; Cross-Country Running M & W; Football M; Ice Hockey M & W; Lacrosse M & W; Rock Climbing M & W; Rugby M & W; Skiing (Cross-Country) M & W; Skiing (Downhill) M & W; Soccer M & W; Softball W; Swimming and Diving M & W; Tennis W; Track and Field M & W; Ultimate Frisbee M & W; Volleyball M & W

UNIVERSITY OF MINNESOTA, MORRIS
600 East 4th St.
Morris, MN 56267-2134
Tel: (320)589-2211; Free: 800-992-8863
Admissions: (320)539-6035
Fax: (320)589-6399
E-mail: admissions@morris.umn.edu
Web Site: http://www.mrs.umn.edu/
President/CEO: Jaqueline R. Johnson
Financial Aid: Jill Beauregard
Type: Four-Year College **Sex:** Coed **Affiliation:** University of Minnesota System **Scores:** 98% SAT V 400+; 96% SAT M 400+; 40% ACT 18-23; 45% ACT 24-29 **% Accepted:** 71 **Admission Plans:** Early Admission; Early Action; Deferred Admission **Application Deadline:** March 15 **Application Fee:** $35.00 **H.S. Requirements:** High school diploma required; GED accepted **Costs Per Year:** Application fee: $35. State resident tuition: $8830 full-time. Nonresident tuition: $8830 full-time. Mandatory fees: $1886 full-time. Full-time tuition and fees vary according to reciprocity agreements. College room and board: $7050. College room only: $3290. Room and board charges vary according to board plan and housing facility. **Scholarships:** Available **Calendar System:** Semester, Summer Session Available **Enrollment:** FT 1,489, PT 118 **Faculty:** FT 105, PT 48 **Student-Faculty Ratio:** 13:1 **Exams:** SAT I or ACT. **% Receiving Financial Aid:** 66 **Regional Accreditation:** North Central Association of Colleges and Schools **Credit Hours For Degree:** 120 credits, Bachelors **Professional Accreditation:** NCATE **Intercollegiate Athletics:** Baseball M; Basketball M & W; Cross-Country Running M & W; Football M; Golf M & W; Soccer M & W; Softball W; Swimming and Diving W; Tennis M & W; Track and Field M & W; Volleyball W

UNIVERSITY OF MINNESOTA, TWIN CITIES CAMPUS
100 Church St., SE
Minneapolis, MN 55455-0213
Tel: (612)625-5000; Free: 800-752-1000
Admissions: (612)625-2008
Fax: (612)626-1693
E-mail: admissions@tc.umn.edu
Web Site: http://www.umn.edu/tc/
President/CEO: Robert Bruininks
Admissions: Rachelle Hernandez
Financial Aid: Judy Swanson
Type: Comprehensive **Sex:** Coed **Affiliation:** University of Minnesota System **Scores:** 97.19% SAT V 400+; 99.63% SAT M 400+; 18.61% ACT 18-23; 56.41% ACT 24-29 **% Accepted:** 50 **Admission Plans:** Early Admission; Deferred Admission **Application Deadline:** Rolling **Application Fee:** $45.00 **H.S. Requirements:** High school diploma required; GED accepted **Costs Per Year:** Application fee: $45. State resident tuition: $9120 full-time, $350.76 per credit part-time. Nonresident tuition: $13,120 full-time, $504.61 per credit part-time. Mandatory fees: $1897 full-time. Full-time tuition and fees vary according to program and reciprocity agreements. Part-time tuition varies according to course load, program, and reciprocity agreements. College room and board: $7534. College room only: $4294. Room and board charges vary according to board plan, housing facility, and location. **Scholarships:** Available **Calendar System:** Semester, Summer Session Available **Enrollment:** FT 28,539, PT 4,697, Grad FT 9,555, Grad PT 8,868 **Faculty:** FT 1,834, PT 937 **Student-Faculty Ratio:** 21:1 **Exams:** SAT I or

ACT. **% Receiving Financial Aid:** 53 **% Residing in College-Owned, -Operated, or -Affiliated Housing:** 21 **Library Holdings:** 5,700,000 **Regional Accreditation:** North Central Association of Colleges and Schools **Credit Hours For Degree:** 120 semester credits, Bachelors **ROTC:** Army, Navy, Air Force **Professional Accreditation:** AACSB, ABET, ACPhE, ACEJMC, AAMFT, AACN, AANA, ABA, ABFSE, ACNM, ADA, ADtA, ACSP, AOTA, APTA, APA, ASLA, ASLHA, AVMA, ACIPE AALS, ACEHSA, FIDER, CEPH, CSWE, LCMEAMA, NAACLS, NAAB, NASD, NASM, NASPAA, NAST, NCATE, NLN, NRPA, SAF **Intercollegiate Athletics:** Baseball M; Basketball M & W; Cross-Country Running M & W; Football M; Golf M & W; Gymnastics M & W; Ice Hockey M & W; Soccer W; Softball W; Swimming and Diving M & W; Tennis M & W; Track and Field M & W; Volleyball W; Wrestling M

UNIVERSITY OF PHOENIX—MINNEAPOLIS/ST. LOUIS PARK CAMPUS
435 Ford Rd. Ste. No. 1000
St. Louis Park, MN 55426
Tel: (952)487-7226
Web Site: http://www.phoenix.edu/
President/CEO: William Pepicello, PhD
Type: Comprehensive **Sex:** Coed **Regional Accreditation:** North Central Association of Colleges and Schools

UNIVERSITY OF ST. THOMAS
2115 Summit Ave.
St. Paul, MN 55105-1096
Tel: (651)962-5000; Free: 800-328-6819
Fax: (651)962-6160
E-mail: admissions@stthomas.edu
Web Site: http://www.stthomas.edu/
President/CEO: Dennis Dease
Admissions: Marla Friederichs
Financial Aid: Ginny Reese
Type: University **Sex:** Coed **Affiliation:** Roman Catholic **Scores:** 99% SAT V 400+; 100% SAT M 400+; 29% ACT 18-23; 59% ACT 24-29 **% Accepted:** 87 **Admission Plans:** Deferred Admission **Application Deadline:** Rolling **Application Fee:** $0.00 **H.S. Requirements:** High school diploma required; GED accepted **Costs Per Year:** Application fee: $0. Comprehensive fee: $37,509 includes full-time tuition ($28,944), mandatory fees ($523), and college room and board ($8042). College room only: $5104. Part-time tuition: $904.50 per credit hour. **Scholarships:** Available **Calendar System:** 4-1-4, Summer Session Available **Enrollment:** FT 5,796, PT 350, Grad FT 1,224, Grad PT 3,481 **Student-Faculty Ratio:** 15:1 **Exams:** SAT I or ACT. **% Receiving Financial Aid:** 58 **% Residing in College-Owned, -Operated, or -Affiliated Housing:** 43 **Regional Accreditation:** North Central Association of Colleges and Schools **Credit Hours For Degree:** 132 credits, Bachelors **ROTC:** Army, Navy, Air Force **Professional Accreditation:** ABET, ABA, APA, ACIPE, ATS, ACEHSA, CSWE, NASM, NCATE **Intercollegiate Athletics:** Baseball M; Basketball M & W; Crew M & W; Cross-Country Running M & W; Football M; Golf M & W; Ice Hockey M & W; Lacrosse M & W; Skiing (Downhill) M & W; Soccer M & W; Softball W; Swimming and Diving M & W; Tennis M & W; Track and Field M & W; Volleyball W

VERMILION COMMUNITY COLLEGE
1900 East Camp St.
Ely, MN 55731-1996
Tel: (218)365-7200; Free: 800-657-3608
Admissions: (218)235-2100
Web Site: http://www.vcc.edu/
President/CEO: Dr. Mary DuBois
Admissions: Todd Heiman
Type: Two-Year College **Sex:** Coed **Affiliation:** Minnesota State Colleges and Universities System **% Accepted:** 57 **Admission Plans:** Open Admission; Early Admission; Deferred Admission **Application Deadline:** Rolling **Application Fee:** $20.00 **H.S. Requirements:** High school diploma required; GED accepted **Scholarships:** Available **Calendar System:** Semester, Summer Session Available **Enrollment:** FT 533, PT 212 **Faculty:** FT 25, PT 60 **Student-Faculty Ratio:** 13:1 **% Residing in College-Owned, -Operated, or -Affiliated Housing:** 50 **Library Holdings:** 19,500 **Regional Accreditation:** North Central Association of Colleges and Schools **Intercollegiate Athletics:** Baseball M; Basketball M & W; Football M; Softball W; Volleyball W

WALDEN UNIVERSITY
155 Fifth Ave. South
Minneapolis, MN 55401
Tel: (612)338-7224; Free: (866)492-5336
Admissions: 800-925-3368
E-mail: request@waldenu.edu
Web Site: http://www.waldenu.edu/
President/CEO: Jonathan A. Kaplan, JD
Type: Two-Year Upper Division **Sex:** Coed **Affiliation:** Laureate International Universities Network **Application Deadline:** Rolling **Application Fee:** $50.00 **H.S. Requirements:** High school diploma required; GED accepted **Costs Per Year:** Application fee: $50. Tuition: $9000 full-time, $255 per credit part-time. Mandatory fees: $105 full-time, $35 per term part-time. Full-time tuition and fees vary according to course level, course load, and program. Part-time tuition and fees vary according to course level, course load, and program. **Calendar System:** Miscellaneous **Enrollment:** FT 630, PT 4,726, Grad FT 29,231, Grad PT 6,127 **Faculty:** FT 146, PT 1,708 **Final Year or Final Semester Residency Requirement:** Yes **Library Holdings:** 31,644 **Regional Accreditation:** North Central Association of Colleges and Schools **Credit Hours For Degree:** 181 units, Bachelors **Professional Accreditation:** AACN

WINONA STATE UNIVERSITY
170 West Sanborn
PO Box 5838
Winona, MN 55987-5838
Tel: (507)457-5000; Free: 800-DIAL WSU
Admissions: (507)457-5100
Fax: (507)457-5620
E-mail: admissions@winona.edu
Web Site: http://www.winona.edu/
President/CEO: Judith A. Ramaley
Admissions: Carl Stange
Financial Aid: Cindy Groth
Type: Comprehensive **Sex:** Coed **Affiliation:** Minnesota State Colleges and Universities System **Scores:** 96% SAT V 400+; 96% SAT M 400+; 63% ACT 18-23; 34% ACT 24-29 **% Accepted:** 79 **Admission Plans:** Early Admission; Early Action; Deferred Admission **Application Deadline:** March 5 **Application Fee:** $20.00 **H.S. Requirements:** High school diploma required; GED accepted **Costs Per Year:** Application fee: $20. State resident tuition: $6056 full-time. Nonresident tuition: $10,890 full-time. Mandatory fees: $1860 full-time. Full-time tuition and fees vary according to location and reciprocity agreements. College room and board: $6556. Room and board charges vary according to board plan, housing facility, and location. **Scholarships:** Available **Calendar System:** Semester, Summer Session Available **Enrollment:** FT 7,471, PT 573, Grad FT 282, Grad PT 280 **Faculty:** FT 345, PT 135 **Student-Faculty Ratio:** 21:1 **Exams:** SAT I or ACT. **% Receiving Financial Aid:** 52 **% Residing in College-Owned, -Operated, or -Affiliated Housing:** 28 **Final Year or Final Semester Residency Requirement:** Yes **Library Holdings:** 350,000 **Regional Accreditation:** North Central Association of Colleges and Schools **Credit Hours For Degree:** 60 semester hours, Associates; 120 semester hours, Bachelors **ROTC:** Army **Professional Accreditation:** ABET, AACN, ACA, CSWE, JRCEPAT, NASM, NAST, NCATE, NLN **Intercollegiate Athletics:** Baseball M; Basketball M & W; Bowling M & W; Cross-Country Running M & W; Fencing M & W; Football M; Golf M & W; Gymnastics W; Rugby M & W; Skiing (Downhill) M & W; Soccer M & W; Softball W; Tennis W; Track and Field W; Ultimate Frisbee M & W; Volleyball M & W; Wrestling M

ALCORN STATE UNIVERSITY
1000 ASU Dr.
Alcorn State, MS 39096-7500
Tel: (601)877-6100; Free: 800-222-6790
Admissions: (601)877-6147
Fax: (601)877-6347
E-mail: ebarnes@alcorn.edu
Web Site: http://www.alcorn.edu/
President/CEO: Dr. George E. Ross
Admissions: Emanuel Barnes
Financial Aid: Juanita M. Russell
Type: Comprehensive **Sex:** Coed **Affiliation:** Mississippi Institutions of Higher Learning **Scores:** 68% SAT V 400+; 80% SAT M 400+; 41% ACT 18-23; 6% ACT 24-29 **% Accepted:** 40 **Admission Plans:** Early Admission; Deferred Admission **Application Deadline:** Rolling **Application Fee:** $0.00 **H.S. Requirements:** High school diploma required; GED accepted **Costs Per Year:** Application fee: $0. State resident tuition: $4488 full-time. Nonresident tuition: $11,054 full-time. Full-time tuition varies according to course load. College room and board: $5384. **Scholarships:** Available **Calendar System:** Semester, Summer Session Available **Enrollment:** FT 2,436, PT 264, Grad FT 205, Grad PT 429 **Faculty:** FT 183, PT 37 **Student-Faculty Ratio:** 15:1 **Exams:** SAT I or ACT. **% Receiving Financial Aid:** 91 **% Residing in College-Owned, -Operated, or -Affiliated Housing:** 51 **Library Holdings:** 335,252 **Regional Accreditation:** Southern Association of Colleges and Schools **ROTC:** Army **Professional Accreditation:** AAFCS, ADtA, NASM, NCATE, NLN, NAIT **Intercollegiate Athletics:** Baseball M; Basketball M & W; Cross-Country Running M & W; Football M; Golf M & W; Soccer W; Softball W; Tennis M & W; Track and Field M & W; Volleyball W

ANTONELLI COLLEGE (HATTIESBURG)
1500 North 31st Ave.
Hattiesburg, MS 39401
Tel: (601)583-4100
Fax: (601)583-0839
E-mail: admissionsh@antonellicollege.edu
Web Site: http://antonellicollege.edu/
President/CEO: Mary Ann Davis
Admissions: Karen Gautreau
Type: Two-Year College **Sex:** Coed **Application Fee:** $75.00 **Calendar System:** Quarter **Professional Accreditation:** ACCSCT

ANTONELLI COLLEGE (JACKSON)
2323 Lakeland Dr.
Jackson, MS 39232
Tel: (601)362-9991
Fax: (601)362-2333
E-mail: admissions.jackson@antonellicollege.edu
Web Site: http://www.antonellicollege.edu/
President/CEO: Mary Ann Davis
Admissions: Rafael Anderson, AIA
Type: Two-Year College **Sex:** Coed **Admission Plans:** Open Admission **Application Fee:** $75.00 **Scholarships:** Available **Calendar System:** Quarter **Professional Accreditation:** ACCSCT

BELHAVEN UNIVERSITY
1500 Peachtree St.
Jackson, MS 39202-1789
Tel: (601)968-5928; Free: 800-960-5940
Admissions: (601)968-5940
Fax: (601)968-9998
E-mail: admission@belhaven.edu
Web Site: http://www.belhaven.edu/
President/CEO: Dr. Roger Parrott
Admissions: Suzanne T. Sullivan
Financial Aid: Linda Phillips
Type: Comprehensive **Sex:** Coed **Affiliation:** Presbyterian **Scores:** 96% SAT V 400+; 90% SAT M 400+; 66% ACT 18-23; 24% ACT 24-29 **% Accepted:** 52 **Admission Plans:** Early Admission; Deferred Admission **Application Deadline:** Rolling **Application Fee:** $25.00 **H.S. Requirements:** High school diploma required; GED accepted **Costs Per Year:** Application fee: $25. Comprehensive fee: $24,200 includes full-time tuition ($17,700) and college room and board ($6500). Part-time tuition: $350 per semester hour. **Scholarships:** Available **Calendar System:** Semester, Summer Session Available **Enrollment:** FT 2,190, PT 140, Grad FT 144, Grad PT 112 **Faculty:** FT 63, PT 84 **Student-Faculty Ratio:** 10:1 **Exams:** SAT I or ACT. **% Receiving Financial Aid:** 72 **% Residing in College-Owned, -Operated, or -Affiliated Housing:** 86 **Library Holdings:** 13,201 **Regional Accreditation:** Southern Association of Colleges and Schools **Credit Hours For Degree:** 62 semester hours, Associates; 124 semester hours, Bachelors **ROTC:** Army, Air Force **Professional Accreditation:** NASAD, NASM **Intercollegiate Athletics:** Baseball M; Basketball M & W; Cross-Country Running M & W; Football M; Golf M & W; Soccer M & W; Softball W; Tennis M & W; Volleyball W

BLUE MOUNTAIN COLLEGE
PO Box 160
Blue Mountain, MS 38610-9509
Tel: (662)685-4771; Free: 800-235-0136
Fax: (662)685-4776
E-mail: mteel@bmc.edu
Web Site: http://www.bmc.edu/
President/CEO: Dr. Bettye R. Coward
Admissions: Maria Teel
Financial Aid: Michelle L. Hall
Type: Comprehensive **Sex:** Coed **Affiliation:** Southern Baptist **Scores:** 51% ACT 18-23; 29% ACT 24-29 **% Accepted:** 44 **Admission Plans:** Early Admission **Application Deadline:** Rolling **Application Fee:** $10.00 **H.S. Requirements:** High school diploma required; GED accepted **Costs Per Year:** Application fee: $10. Comprehensive fee: $12,420 includes full-time tuition ($7650), mandatory fees ($920), and college room and board ($3850). Full-time tuition and fees vary according to course load and degree level. Room and board charges vary according to board plan. Part-time tuition: $255 per credit hour. Part-time tuition varies according to course load and degree level. **Scholarships:** Available **Calendar System:** Semester, Summer Session Available **Enrollment:** FT 422, PT 72, Grad FT 8, Grad PT 3 **Faculty:** FT 27, PT 17 **Student-Faculty Ratio:** 14:1 **Exams:** SAT I or ACT. ACT essay not being used. SAT essay not being used. **% Receiving Financial Aid:** 57 **% Residing in College-Owned, -Operated, or -Affiliated Housing:** 38 **Final Year or Final Semester Residency Requirement:** Yes **Library Holdings:** 77,557 **Regional Accreditation:** Southern

Association of Colleges and Schools **Credit Hours For Degree:** 120 semester hours, Bachelors **Intercollegiate Athletics:** Baseball M; Basketball M & W; Cross-Country Running M & W; Golf M; Softball W

COAHOMA COMMUNITY COLLEGE
3240 Friars Point Rd.
Clarksdale, MS 38614-9799
Tel: (662)627-2571
Admissions: (662)621-4205
Web Site: http://www.ccc.cc.ms.us/
President/CEO: Dr. Vivian M. Presley
Admissions: Wanda Holmes
Type: Two-Year College **Sex:** Coed **Affiliation:** Mississippi State Board for Community and Junior Colleges **Admission Plans:** Open Admission **Application Deadline:** Rolling **Application Fee:** $0.00 **H.S. Requirements:** High school diploma required; GED accepted **Scholarships:** Available **Calendar System:** Semester **Enrollment:** FT 1,962, PT 254 **Faculty:** FT 53, PT 64 **Student-Faculty Ratio:** 19:1 **% Residing in College-Owned, -Operated, or -Affiliated Housing:** 22 **Regional Accreditation:** Southern Association of Colleges and Schools **Credit Hours For Degree:** 65 credit hours, Associates **Intercollegiate Athletics:** Baseball M; Basketball M & W; Cheerleading W; Football M; Softball W

COPIAH-LINCOLN COMMUNITY COLLEGE
PO Box 649
Wesson, MS 39191
Tel: (601)643-5101
Admissions: (601)643-8619
Fax: (601)643-8212
E-mail: julia.parker@colin.edu
Web Site: http://www.colin.edu/
President/CEO: Dr. Ronnie Nettles
Admissions: Julia Parker
Type: Two-Year College **Sex:** Coed **Affiliation:** Mississippi State Board for Community and Junior Colleges **Admission Plans:** Open Admission; Preferred Admission; Early Admission **Application Deadline:** Rolling **Application Fee:** $0.00 **H.S. Requirements:** High school diploma required; GED accepted **Costs Per Year:** Application fee: $0. State resident tuition: $1800 full-time, $105 per hour part-time. Nonresident tuition: $3700 full-time, $180 per hour part-time. College room and board: $3050. College room only: $1150. Room and board charges vary according to board plan. **Scholarships:** Available **Calendar System:** Semester, Summer Session Available **Faculty:** FT 82, PT 45 **Student-Faculty Ratio:** 20:1 **% Residing in College-Owned, -Operated, or -Affiliated Housing:** 30 **Library Holdings:** 38,900 **Regional Accreditation:** Southern Association of Colleges and Schools **Credit Hours For Degree:** 64 semester hours, Associates **Professional Accreditation:** JRCERT, NAACLS, NLN **Intercollegiate Athletics:** Baseball M; Basketball M & W; Football M; Golf M & W; Softball W; Tennis M & W; Track and Field M

COPIAH-LINCOLN COMMUNITY COLLEGE—NATCHEZ CAMPUS
11 Co-Lin Circle
Natchez, MS 39120-8446
Tel: (601)442-9111
Fax: (601)446-9967
E-mail: gwen.mccalip@colin.edu
Web Site: http://www.colin.edu/
President/CEO: Dr. Ronnie Nettles
Admissions: Gwen S. McCalip
Type: Two-Year College **Sex:** Coed **Affiliation:** Mississippi State Board for Community and Junior Colleges **Admission Plans:** Open Admission; Early Admission **Application Deadline:** Rolling **Application Fee:** $0.00 **H.S. Requirements:** High school diploma required; GED accepted. For welding program: High school diploma or equivalent not required **Scholarships:** Available **Calendar System:** Semester, Summer Session Available **Enrollment:** FT 663, PT 187 **Faculty:** FT 24, PT 33 **Student-Faculty Ratio:** 22:1 **Library Holdings:** 19,000 **Regional Accreditation:** Southern Association of Colleges and Schools **Credit Hours For Degree:** 64 semester hours, Associates **Professional Accreditation:** CARC

DELTA STATE UNIVERSITY
Hwy. 8 West
Cleveland, MS 38733-0001
Tel: (662)846-3000; Free: 800-468-6378
Admissions: (662)846-4655
Fax: (662)846-4016
E-mail: dheslep@deltastate.edu
Web Site: http://www.deltastate.edu/
President/CEO: Dr. John M. Hilpert
Admissions: Dr. Debbie Heslep
Financial Aid: Ann Margaret Mullins
Type: Comprehensive **Sex:** Coed **Affiliation:** Mississippi Institutions of Higher Learning **Scores:** 59.51% ACT 18-23; 15.02% ACT 24-29 **% Accepted:** 24 **Admission Plans:** Deferred Admission **Application Deadline:** Rolling **Application Fee:** $25.00 **H.S. Requirements:** High school diploma required; GED accepted **Costs Per Year:** Application fee: $25. State resident tuition: $4450 full-time, $185 per credit hour part-time. Nonresident tuition: $11,520 full-time, $480 per credit hour part-time. Part-time tuition varies according to course load. College room and board: $5714. Room and board charges vary according to housing facility. **Scholarships:** Available **Calendar System:** Semester, Summer Session Available **Enrollment:** FT 2,495, PT 620, Grad FT 286, Grad PT 630 **Faculty:** FT 193, PT 66 **Student-Faculty Ratio:** 15:1 **Exams:** ACT, SAT I or ACT. ACT essay not being used. SAT essay not being used. **% Receiving Financial Aid:** 62 **% Residing in College-Owned, -Operated, or -Affiliated Housing:** 30 **Final Year or Final Semester Residency Requirement:** No **Library Holdings:** 430,857 **Regional Accreditation:** Southern Association of Colleges and Schools **Credit Hours For Degree:** 124 semester hours, Bachelors **ROTC:** Army **Professional Accreditation:** AACN, AAFCS, ACA, ADtA, ACBSP, ATS, CSWE, NASAD, NASM, NCATE, NLN **Intercollegiate Athletics:** Baseball M; Basketball M & W; Cheerleading M & W; Cross-Country Running W; Football M; Golf M; Soccer M & W; Softball W; Swimming and Diving M & W; Tennis M & W

EAST CENTRAL COMMUNITY COLLEGE
PO Box 129
Decatur, MS 39327-0129
Tel: (601)635-2111; Free: 877-462-3222
Fax: (601)635-2150
Web Site: http://www.eccc.cc.ms.us/
President/CEO: Phil Sutphin
Admissions: Donna Luke
Type: Two-Year College **Sex:** Coed **Affiliation:** Mississippi State Board for Community and Junior Colleges **Admission Plans:** Open Admission; Early Admission **Application Deadline:** Rolling **Application Fee:** $0.00 **H.S. Requirements:** High school diploma required; GED accepted **Scholarships:** Available **Calendar System:** Semester, Summer Session Available **Regional Accreditation:** Southern Association of Colleges and Schools **Credit Hours For Degree:** 64 semester hours, Associates **Professional Accreditation:** ARCEST, NLN **Intercollegiate Athletics:** Baseball M; Basketball M & W; Football M; Golf M & W; Soccer M & W; Softball W; Tennis M & W

EAST MISSISSIPPI COMMUNITY COLLEGE
PO Box 158
Scooba, MS 39358-0158
Tel: (662)476-8442
Admissions: (662)476-5000
Web Site: http://www.eastms.edu/
President/CEO: Rick Young
Admissions: Melinda Sciple
Type: Two-Year College **Sex:** Coed **Affiliation:** Mississippi State Board for Community and Junior Colleges **Admission Plans:** Open Admission; Deferred Admission **Application Deadline:** Rolling **Application Fee:** $0.00 **H.S. Requirements:** High school diploma required; GED accepted **Scholarships:** Available **Calendar System:** Semester, Summer Session Available **Library Holdings:** 27,840 **Regional Accreditation:** Southern Association of Colleges and Schools **Credit Hours For Degree:** 64 semester hours, Associates **Professional Accreditation:** ABFSE **Intercollegiate Athletics:** Baseball M; Basketball M & W; Cheerleading W; Football M; Golf M; Soccer M & W; Softball W

HINDS COMMUNITY COLLEGE
PO Box 1100
Raymond, MS 39154-1100
Tel: (601)857-5261
Web Site: http://www.hindscc.edu/
President/CEO: Dr. V. Clyde Muse

Admissions: Ginger Turner
Type: Two-Year College **Sex:** Coed **Affiliation:** Mississippi State Board for Community and Junior Colleges **Admission Plans:** Open Admission; Early Admission **Application Deadline:** Rolling **Application Fee:** $0.00 **H.S. Requirements:** High school diploma required; GED accepted **Scholarships:** Available **Calendar System:** Semester, Summer Session Available **Exams:** SAT I and SAT II or ACT. **Library Holdings:** 165,260 **Regional Accreditation:** Southern Association of Colleges and Schools **Credit Hours For Degree:** 64 semester hours, Associates **ROTC:** Army **Professional Accreditation:** AAMAE, ADA, AHIMA, APTA, CARC, JRCERT, NAACLS, NLN **Intercollegiate Athletics:** Baseball M; Basketball M & W; Cross-Country Running M; Football M; Golf M; Soccer M & W; Softball W; Tennis M & W; Track and Field M & W

HOLMES COMMUNITY COLLEGE
PO Box 369
Goodman, MS 39079-0369
Tel: (662)472-2312
Fax: (662)472-9156
Web Site: http://www.holmescc.edu/
President/CEO: Dr. Glenn F. Boyce
Admissions: Dr. Lynn Wright
Type: Two-Year College **Sex:** Coed **Affiliation:** Mississippi State Board for Community and Junior Colleges **Admission Plans:** Open Admission; Early Admission **Application Deadline:** Rolling **Application Fee:** $0.00 **H.S. Requirements:** High school diploma required; GED accepted **Costs Per Year:** Application fee: $0. State resident tuition: $1300 full-time, $75 per semester hour part-time. Nonresident tuition: $3250 full-time, $85 per semester hour part-time. Mandatory fees: $360 full-time, $12 per semester hour part-time. Full-time tuition and fees vary according to course load. Part-time tuition and fees vary according to course load. College room and board: $2180. Room and board charges vary according to housing facility. **Scholarships:** Available **Calendar System:** Semester, Summer Session Available **Library Holdings:** 53,000 **Regional Accreditation:** Southern Association of Colleges and Schools **Credit Hours For Degree:** 64 semester hours, Associates **Professional Accreditation:** ARCEST, AOTA, JRCEMT, NLN **Intercollegiate Athletics:** Baseball M; Basketball M & W; Football M; Golf M; Soccer M; Softball W; Tennis W

ITAWAMBA COMMUNITY COLLEGE
602 West Hill St.
Fulton, MS 38843
Tel: (662)862-8000
Admissions: (601)862-8252
Fax: (662)862-8036
E-mail: laboggs@iccms.edu
Web Site: http://www.icc.cc.ms.us/
President/CEO: Dr. David C. Cole
Admissions: Larry Boggs
Type: Two-Year College **Sex:** Coed **Affiliation:** Mississippi State Board for Community and Junior Colleges **Admission Plans:** Open Admission; Early Admission **Application Deadline:** Rolling **Application Fee:** $0.00 **H.S. Requirements:** High school diploma required; GED accepted **Scholarships:** Available **Calendar System:** Semester, Summer Session Available **Enrollment:** FT 3,649, PT 1,564 **Faculty:** FT 85, PT 125 **Student-Faculty Ratio:** 24:1 **Library Holdings:** 36,816 **Regional Accreditation:** Southern Association of Colleges and Schools **Credit Hours For Degree:** 63 semester hours, Associates **ROTC:** Army **Professional Accreditation:** ARCEST, AHIMA, APTA, CARC, JRCERT, NLN **Intercollegiate Athletics:** Basketball M & W; Football M; Golf M; Tennis M & W; Track and Field M

ITT TECHNICAL INSTITUTE
382 Galleria Parkway
Ste. 100
Madison, MS 39110
Tel: (601)607-4500; Free: 800-209-2521
Web Site: http://www.itt-tech.edu/
President/CEO: Eric Stewart
Type: Four-Year College **Sex:** Coed **Affiliation:** ITT Educational Services, Inc. **Calendar System:** Quarter **Professional Accreditation:** ACICS

JACKSON STATE UNIVERSITY
1400 John R Lynch St.
Jackson, MS 39217
Tel: (601)979-2121; Free: 800-848-6817
Admissions: (601)979-2911
Fax: (601)979-2358
E-mail: schatman@ccaix.jsums.edu
Web Site: http://www.jsums.edu/
President/CEO: Dr. Ronald Mason, Jr.
Admissions: Linda Rush
Financial Aid: B. J. Moncure
Type: University **Sex:** Coed **Affiliation:** Mississippi Institutions of Higher Learning **Scores:** 51% ACT 18-23; 9% ACT 24-29 **% Accepted:** 54 **Admission Plans:** Early Admission; Deferred Admission **Application Deadline:** August 1 **Application Fee:** $0.00 **H.S. Requirements:** High school diploma required; GED accepted **Scholarships:** Available **Calendar System:** Semester, Summer Session Available **Enrollment:** FT 5,835, PT 970, Grad FT 800, Grad PT 1,178 **Faculty:** FT 406, PT 119 **Student-Faculty Ratio:** 16:1 **Exams:** SAT I or ACT. **% Residing in College-Owned, -Operated, or -Affiliated Housing:** 25 **Final Year or Final Semester Residency Requirement:** Yes **Library Holdings:** 749,089 **Regional Accreditation:** Southern Association of Colleges and Schools **Credit Hours For Degree:** 128 credit hours, Bachelors **ROTC:** Army, Air Force **Professional Accreditation:** AACSB, ABET, ACEJMC, ACA, ACSP, APA, ASLHA, CORE, CSWE, NASAD, NASM, NASPAA, NCATE, NAIT **Intercollegiate Athletics:** Baseball M; Basketball M & W; Bowling W; Cross-Country Running M & W; Football M; Golf M & W; Soccer W; Softball W; Tennis M & W; Track and Field M & W; Volleyball W

JONES COUNTY JUNIOR COLLEGE
900 South Ct. St.
Ellisville, MS 39437-3901
Tel: (601)477-4000
Fax: (601)477-4017
Web Site: http://www.jcjc.edu/
President/CEO: Jesse Smith
Admissions: Dianne Speed
Type: Two-Year College **Sex:** Coed **Affiliation:** Mississippi State Board for Community and Junior Colleges **Admission Plans:** Open Admission; Preferred Admission; Early Admission **Application Deadline:** August 26 **Application Fee:** $0.00 **H.S. Requirements:** High school diploma required; GED accepted **Scholarships:** Available **Calendar System:** Semester, Summer Session Available **Faculty:** FT 170, PT 5 **Student-Faculty Ratio:** 25:1 **Exams:** SAT I or ACT. **% Residing in College-Owned, -Operated, or -Affiliated Housing:** 20 **Library Holdings:** 62,349 **Regional Accreditation:** Southern Association of Colleges and Schools **Credit Hours For Degree:** 64 semester hours, Associates **ROTC:** Army, Air Force **Professional Accreditation:** ACBSP, JRCERT, JRCEMT, NLN **Intercollegiate Athletics:** Baseball M; Basketball M & W; Football M; Golf M; Soccer M & W; Softball W; Tennis M & W; Track and Field M

MERIDIAN COMMUNITY COLLEGE
910 Hwy. 19 North
Meridian, MS 39307
Tel: (601)483-8241
Admissions: (601)484-8357
E-mail: apayne@meridiancc.edu
Web Site: http://www.meridiancc.edu/
President/CEO: Dr. Scott D. Elliott, EdD
Admissions: Angela Payne
Type: Two-Year College **Sex:** Coed **Affiliation:** Mississippi State Board for Community and Junior Colleges **Admission Plans:** Open Admission; Early Admission **Application Deadline:** Rolling **Application Fee:** $0.00 **H.S. Requirements:** High school diploma required; GED accepted **Costs Per Year:** Application fee: $0. State resident tuition: $1600 full-time, $90 per semester hour part-time. Nonresident tuition: $2980 full-time, $147 per semester hour part-time. Mandatory fees: $160 full-time, $25 per credit hour part-time. Full-time tuition and fees vary according to course load and program. Part-time tuition and fees vary according to course load and program. College room and board: $3050. Room and board charges vary according to board plan. **Scholarships:** Available **Calendar System:** Semester, Summer Session Available **Enrollment:** FT 2,651, PT 963 **Faculty:** FT 154, PT 55 **Student-Faculty Ratio:** 18:1 **Exams:** ACT, Other. **% Residing in College-Owned, -Operated, or -Affiliated Housing:** 12 **Final Year or Final Semester Residency Requirement:** Yes **Library Holdings:** 50,000 **Regional Accreditation:** Southern Association of Colleges and Schools **Credit Hours For Degree:** 64 semester hours, Associates

Professional Accreditation: ADA, AHIMA, APTA, JRCERT, NAACLS, NLN **Intercollegiate Athletics:** Baseball M; Basketball M & W; Cheerleading W; Cross-Country Running M & W; Golf M; Soccer M; Softball W; Tennis M & W; Track and Field M & W

MILLSAPS COLLEGE
1701 North State St.
Jackson, MS 39210-0001
Tel: (601)974-1000; Free: 800-352-1050
Admissions: (601)974-1050
Fax: (601)974-1059
E-mail: admissions@millsaps.edu
Web Site: http://www.millsaps.edu/
President/CEO: Dr. Robert W. Pearigen, PhD
Admissions: Michael Thorp
Financial Aid: Patrick James
Type: Comprehensive **Sex:** Coed **Affiliation:** United Methodist **Scores:** 100% SAT V 400+; 99.04% SAT M 400+; 35.83% ACT 18-23; 44.88% ACT 24-29 **% Accepted:** 74 **Admission Plans:** Early Action; Deferred Admission **Application Deadline:** Rolling **Application Fee:** $0.00 **H.S. Requirements:** High school diploma required; GED accepted **Costs Per Year:** Application fee: $0. Comprehensive fee: $35,492 includes full-time tuition ($24,608), mandatory fees ($1632), and college room and board ($9252). College room only: $5216. Full-time tuition and fees vary according to reciprocity agreements. Room and board charges vary according to housing facility. Part-time tuition: $764 per credit hour. Part-time mandatory fees: $32 per credit hour. Part-time tuition and fees vary according to course load. **Scholarships:** Available **Calendar System:** Semester, Summer Session Available **Enrollment:** FT 998, PT 19, Grad FT 45, Grad PT 55 **Faculty:** FT 96, PT 20 **Student-Faculty Ratio:** 10:1 **Exams:** SAT I or ACT. **% Receiving Financial Aid:** 58 **% Residing in College-Owned, -Operated, or -Affiliated Housing:** 86 **Library Holdings:** 196,277 **Regional Accreditation:** Southern Association of Colleges and Schools **Credit Hours For Degree:** 128 semester hours, Bachelors **ROTC:** Army **Professional Accreditation:** AACSB, NCATE **Intercollegiate Athletics:** Baseball M; Basketball M & W; Cross-Country Running M & W; Football M; Golf M & W; Lacrosse M & W; Soccer M & W; Softball W; Tennis M & W; Track and Field M & W; Volleyball W

MISSISSIPPI COLLEGE
200 South Capitol St.
Clinton, MS 39058
Tel: (601)925-3000; Free: 800-738-1236
Admissions: (601)925-3800
Fax: (601)925-3804
E-mail: enrollment-services@mc.edu
Web Site: http://www.mc.edu/
President/CEO: Dr. Lee G. Royce
Admissions: Chad Phillips
Financial Aid: Karon McMillan
Type: Comprehensive **Sex:** Coed **Affiliation:** Southern Baptist **Scores:** 88% SAT V 400+; 96% SAT M 400+; 48% ACT 18-23; 36% ACT 24-29 **% Accepted:** 61 **Admission Plans:** Early Admission; Early Decision Plan; Deferred Admission **Application Deadline:** Rolling **Application Fee:** $0.00 **H.S. Requirements:** High school diploma required; GED accepted **Costs Per Year:** Application fee: $0. Comprehensive fee: $19,700 includes full-time tuition ($12,900), mandatory fees ($650), and college room and board ($6150). Full-time tuition and fees vary according to course load, location, and program. Room and board charges vary according to housing facility. Part-time tuition: $405 per credit hour. Part-time mandatory fees: $170 per term. Part-time tuition and fees vary according to course load, location, and program. **Scholarships:** Available **Calendar System:** Semester, Summer Session Available **Enrollment:** FT 2,686, PT 406, Grad FT 890, Grad PT 790 **Faculty:** FT 180, PT 244 **Student-Faculty Ratio:** 16:1 **Exams:** SAT I or ACT. ACT essay used for admission. SAT essay used for admission. ACT essay used for advising. SAT essay used for advising. **% Receiving Financial Aid:** 62 **% Residing in College-Owned, -Operated, or -Affiliated Housing:** 55 **Final Year or Final Semester Residency Requirement:** No **Library Holdings:** 382,586 **Regional Accreditation:** Southern Association of Colleges and Schools **Credit Hours For Degree:** 130 credit hours, Bachelors **ROTC:** Army, Air Force **Professional Accreditation:** AAFCS, ABA, ACA, AALS, ACBSP, CSWE, NASM, NCATE, NLN **Intercollegiate Athletics:** Baseball M; Basketball M & W; Cheerleading W; Cross-Country Running M & W; Equestrian Sports W; Football M; Golf M; Soccer M & W; Softball W; Table Tennis M & W; Tennis M & W; Track and Field M & W; Volleyball W

MISSISSIPPI DELTA COMMUNITY COLLEGE
PO Box 668
Hwy. 3 and Cherry St.
Moorhead, MS 38761-0668
Tel: (662)246-6322
Web Site: http://www.msdelta.edu/
President/CEO: Dr. Larry G. Bailey
Admissions: Joseph F. Ray, Jr.
Type: Two-Year College **Sex:** Coed **Affiliation:** Mississippi State Board for Community and Junior Colleges **% Accepted:** 100 **Admission Plans:** Preferred Admission; Deferred Admission **Application Deadline:** July 27 **Application Fee:** $0.00 **H.S. Requirements:** High school diploma required; GED accepted **Scholarships:** Available **Calendar System:** Semester, Summer Session Available **Exams:** ACT. **% Residing in College-Owned, -Operated, or -Affiliated Housing:** 25 **Library Holdings:** 33,020 **Regional Accreditation:** Southern Association of Colleges and Schools **Credit Hours For Degree:** 64 semester hours, Associates **Professional Accreditation:** ADA, JRCERT, NAACLS, NLN **Intercollegiate Athletics:** Baseball M; Basketball M & W; Football M; Golf M; Soccer M; Tennis M & W; Track and Field M

MISSISSIPPI GULF COAST COMMUNITY COLLEGE
PO Box 609
Perkinston, MS 39573
Tel: (601)928-5211
Fax: (601)928-6299
E-mail: ladd.taylor@mgccc.edu
Web Site: http://www.mgccc.edu/
President/CEO: Willis Lott
Admissions: Ladd Taylor
Type: Two-Year College **Sex:** Coed **Affiliation:** Mississippi State Board for Community and Junior Colleges **% Accepted:** 100 **Admission Plans:** Open Admission; Preferred Admission; Early Admission **Application Deadline:** Rolling **Application Fee:** $0.00 **H.S. Requirements:** High school diploma required; GED accepted **Costs Per Year:** Application fee: $0. State resident tuition: $1800 full-time, $90 per semester hour part-time. Nonresident tuition: $3646 full-time, $167 per semester hour part-time. Mandatory fees: $382 full-time, $3 per semester hour part-time, $110 per term part-time. College room and board: $3770. College room only: $2100. Room and board charges vary according to board plan and housing facility. **Scholarships:** Available **Calendar System:** Semester, Summer Session Available **Enrollment:** FT 5,551, PT 3,271 **Faculty:** FT 387, PT 237 **Student-Faculty Ratio:** 26:1 **% Residing in College-Owned, -Operated, or -Affiliated Housing:** 7 **Library Holdings:** 100,472 **Regional Accreditation:** Southern Association of Colleges and Schools **Credit Hours For Degree:** 64 semester hours, Associates **Professional Accreditation:** ABFSE, CARC, JRCERT, JRCEMT, NAACLS, NLN **Intercollegiate Athletics:** Baseball M; Basketball M & W; Football M; Golf M; Soccer M & W; Softball W; Tennis M & W; Track and Field M

MISSISSIPPI STATE UNIVERSITY
Mississippi State, MS 39762
Tel: (662)325-2323
Admissions: (662)325-2224
Fax: (662)325-3299
E-mail: admit@msstate.edu
Web Site: http://www.msstate.edu/
President/CEO: Dr. Mark E. Keenum
Admissions: Cheryl Dill
Financial Aid: Bruce Crain
Type: University **Sex:** Coed **Affiliation:** Mississippi Institutions of Higher Learning **Scores:** 93.5% SAT V 400+; 94.55% SAT M 400+; 43.57% ACT 18-23; 38.42% ACT 24-29 **% Accepted:** 65 **Application Deadline:** August 1 **Application Fee:** $35.00 **H.S. Requirements:** High school diploma required; GED accepted **Costs Per Year:** Application fee: $35. State resident tuition: $5151 full-time, $214.75 per credit hour part-time. Nonresident tuition: $13,021 full-time, $542.75 per credit hour part-time. Part-time tuition varies according to course load. College room and board: $7520. College room only: $4285. Room and board charges vary according to board plan, housing facility, and student level. **Scholarships:** Available **Calendar System:** Semester, Summer Session Available **Enrollment:** FT 13,206, PT 1,396, Grad FT 1,981, Grad PT 2,018 **Faculty:** FT 844, PT 124 **Student-Faculty Ratio:** 18:1 **Exams:** SAT I or ACT. **% Receiving Financial Aid:** 53 **% Residing in College-Owned, -Operated, or -Affiliated Hous-**

ing: 26 **Final Year or Final Semester Residency Requirement:** Yes **Library Holdings:** 2,190,629 **Regional Accreditation:** Southern Association of Colleges and Schools **Credit Hours For Degree:** 128 credit hours, Bachelors **ROTC:** Army, Air Force **Professional Accreditation:** AACSB, ABET, AAFCS, ACA, ADtA, APA, ASLA, AVMA, FIDER, CORE, CSWE, NAAB, NASAD, NASM, NASPAA, NCATE, SAF **Intercollegiate Athletics:** Baseball M; Basketball M & W; Cheerleading M & W; Cross-Country Running M & W; Football M; Golf M & W; Soccer W; Softball W; Tennis M & W; Track and Field M & W; Volleyball W

MISSISSIPPI UNIVERSITY FOR WOMEN
1100 College St., MUW-1600
Columbus, MS 39701-9998
Tel: (662)329-4750; Free: 877-GO 2 THE W
Admissions: (601)329-7106
Fax: (662)329-7297
E-mail: cderden@admissions.muw.edu
Web Site: http://www.muw.edu/
President/CEO: Dr. Claudia A Limbert
Admissions: Cassie Derden
Financial Aid: Dan Miller
Type: Comprehensive **Sex:** Coed **Affiliation:** Mississippi Institutions of Higher Learning **Scores:** 55% ACT 18-23; 25% ACT 24-29 **% Accepted:** 42 **Admission Plans:** Early Admission **Application Deadline:** Rolling **Application Fee:** $0.00 **H.S. Requirements:** High school diploma required; GED accepted **Costs Per Year:** Application fee: $0. State resident tuition: $4423 full-time, $184.25 per credit hour part-time. Nonresident tuition: $12,051 full-time, $502.05 per credit hour part-time. Part-time tuition varies according to course load. College room and board: $5164. College room only: $3014. Room and board charges vary according to housing facility. **Scholarships:** Available **Calendar System:** Semester, Summer Session Available **Enrollment:** FT 1,758, PT 514, Grad FT 97, Grad PT 107 **Faculty:** FT 134, PT 51 **Student-Faculty Ratio:** 13:1 **Exams:** SAT I or ACT. ACT essay not being used. SAT essay not being used. **% Receiving Financial Aid:** 74 **% Residing in College-Owned, -Operated, or -Affiliated Housing:** 32 **Final Year or Final Semester Residency Requirement:** No **Library Holdings:** 21,859 **Regional Accreditation:** Southern Association of Colleges and Schools **Credit Hours For Degree:** 71 semester hours, Associates; 124 semester hours, Bachelors **ROTC:** Army, Air Force **Professional Accreditation:** AACN, ASLHA, ACBSP, NASAD, NASM, NCATE, NLN

MISSISSIPPI VALLEY STATE UNIVERSITY
14000 Hwy. 82 West
Itta Bena, MS 38941-1400
Tel: (662)254-9041
Admissions: (662)254-3344
Fax: (662)254-7900
E-mail: nbtaylor@mvsu.edu
Web Site: http://www.mvsu.edu/
President/CEO: Dr. Donna H. Oliver
Admissions: Nora Taylor
Financial Aid: Lloyd E. Dixon
Type: Comprehensive **Sex:** Coed **Affiliation:** Mississippi Institutions of Higher Learning **Scores:** 36% ACT 18-23; 4% ACT 24-29 **% Accepted:** 30 **Admission Plans:** Deferred Admission **Application Deadline:** Rolling **Application Fee:** $0.00 **H.S. Requirements:** High school diploma required; GED accepted **Costs Per Year:** Application fee: $0. One-time mandatory fee: $50. State resident tuition: $190.62 per credit hour part-time. Nonresident tuition: $284.81 per credit hour part-time. **Scholarships:** Available **Calendar System:** Semester, Summer Session Available **Enrollment:** FT 2,194, PT 240, Grad FT 114, Grad PT 302 **Faculty:** FT 133, PT 46 **Student-Faculty Ratio:** 16:1 **Exams:** SAT I or ACT. **% Residing in College-Owned, -Operated, or -Affiliated Housing:** 36 **Final Year or Final Semester Residency Requirement:** No **Library Holdings:** 118,496 **Regional Accreditation:** Southern Association of Colleges and Schools **Credit Hours For Degree:** 124 semester hours, Bachelors **ROTC:** Army **Professional Accreditation:** ACBSP, CSWE, NASAD, NASM, NCATE **Intercollegiate Athletics:** Baseball M; Basketball M & W; Bowling W; Cross-Country Running M & W; Football M; Golf M & W; Softball W; Tennis M & W; Track and Field M & W

NORTHEAST MISSISSIPPI COMMUNITY COLLEGE
101 Cunningham Blvd.
Booneville, MS 38829
Tel: (662)728-7751; Free: 800-555-2154
Fax: (662)728-1165
E-mail: admitme@nemcc.edu
Web Site: http://www.nemcc.edu/
President/CEO: Johnny Allen
Type: Two-Year College **Sex:** Coed **Affiliation:** Mississippi State Board for Community and Junior Colleges **Admission Plans:** Open Admission; Early Admission **Application Deadline:** Rolling **Application Fee:** $0.00 **H.S. Requirements:** High school diploma required; GED accepted **Calendar System:** Semester, Summer Session Available **Exams:** SAT I or ACT. **Library Holdings:** 29,879 **Regional Accreditation:** Southern Association of Colleges and Schools **Credit Hours For Degree:** 63 semester hours, Associates **Professional Accreditation:** AAMAE, ADA, CARC, JRCERT, NAACLS, NLN **Intercollegiate Athletics:** Baseball M; Basketball M & W; Football M; Golf M; Softball W; Tennis M & W

NORTHWEST MISSISSIPPI COMMUNITY COLLEGE
4975 Hwy. 51 North
Senatobia, MS 38668-1701
Tel: (662)562-3200
Fax: (662)562-3911
Web Site: http://www.northwestms.edu/
President/CEO: Gary Spears
Admissions: Deanna Ferguson
Type: Two-Year College **Sex:** Coed **Affiliation:** Mississippi State Board for Community and Junior Colleges **% Accepted:** 100 **Admission Plans:** Open Admission; Early Admission; Deferred Admission **Application Deadline:** September 7 **Application Fee:** $0.00 **H.S. Requirements:** High school diploma required; GED accepted **Scholarships:** Available **Calendar System:** Semester, Summer Session Available **Student-Faculty Ratio:** 20:1 **Library Holdings:** 38,000 **Regional Accreditation:** Southern Association of Colleges and Schools **Credit Hours For Degree:** 66 semester hours, Associates **ROTC:** Air Force **Professional Accreditation:** ABFSE, CARC, NLN **Intercollegiate Athletics:** Baseball M; Basketball M & W; Equestrian Sports M & W; Football M; Golf M; Softball W; Tennis M & W

PEARL RIVER COMMUNITY COLLEGE
101 Hwy. 11 North
Poplarville, MS 39470
Tel: (601)403-1000; Free: 877-772-2338
Fax: (601)403-1135
E-mail: dford@prcc.edu
Web Site: http://www.prcc.edu/
President/CEO: William Lewis
Admissions: J. Dow Ford
Type: Two-Year College **Sex:** Coed **Affiliation:** Mississippi State Board for Community and Junior Colleges **Admission Plans:** Open Admission; Preferred Admission; Early Admission; Deferred Admission **Application Deadline:** Rolling **Application Fee:** $0.00 **H.S. Requirements:** High school diploma required; GED accepted **Scholarships:** Available **Calendar System:** Semester, Summer Session Available **Faculty:** FT 160, PT 65 **% Residing in College-Owned, -Operated, or -Affiliated Housing:** 20 **Library Holdings:** 40,000 **Regional Accreditation:** Southern Association of Colleges and Schools **Credit Hours For Degree:** 64 semester hours, Associates **Professional Accreditation:** ARCEST, ADA, AOTA, APTA, CARC, JRCERT, NAACLS, NLN **Intercollegiate Athletics:** Baseball M; Basketball M & W; Football M; Golf M & W; Soccer M & W; Softball W; Tennis M & W

RUST COLLEGE
150 Rust Ave.
Holly Springs, MS 38635-2328
Tel: (662)252-8000; Free: 888-886-8492
Admissions: (601)252-8000
Fax: (662)252-6107
E-mail: admissions@rustcollege.edu
Web Site: http://www.rustcollege.edu/
President/CEO: Dr. David L. Beckley
Admissions: Johnny McDonald
Financial Aid: Helen L. Street
Type: Four-Year College **Sex:** Coed **Affiliation:** United Methodist **Scores:** 25% ACT 18-23; 1% ACT 24-29 **% Accepted:** 40 **Admission Plans:** Deferred Admission **Application Deadline:** July 15 **Application Fee:** $10.00 **H.S. Requirements:** High school diploma required; GED accepted **Costs Per Year:** Application fee: $10. Comprehensive fee: $10,530 includes

full-time tuition ($7410) and college room and board ($3120). Room and board charges vary according to board plan. Part-time tuition: $198 per credit hour. Part-time tuition varies according to class time and course load. **Scholarships:** Available **Calendar System:** Semester, Summer Session Available **Enrollment:** FT 800, PT 179 **Faculty:** FT 42, PT 2 **Student-Faculty Ratio:** 20:1 **Exams:** ACT. **% Receiving Financial Aid:** 96 **% Residing in College-Owned, -Operated, or -Affiliated Housing:** 69 **Library Holdings:** 123,055 **Regional Accreditation:** Southern Association of Colleges and Schools **Credit Hours For Degree:** 66 credits, Associates; 124 credits, Bachelors **Professional Accreditation:** CSWE **Intercollegiate Athletics:** Baseball M; Basketball M & W; Cheerleading M & W; Cross-Country Running M & W; Tennis M & W; Track and Field M & W

SOUTHEASTERN BAPTIST COLLEGE
4229 Hwy. 15 North
Laurel, MS 39440-1096
Tel: (601)426-6346
President/CEO: Medrick Savell
Admissions: Emma Bond
Type: Four-Year College **Sex:** Coed **Affiliation:** Baptist **% Accepted:** 100 **Admission Plans:** Open Admission; Early Admission; Deferred Admission **Application Deadline:** Rolling **Application Fee:** $25.00 **H.S. Requirements:** High school diploma required; GED accepted **Calendar System:** Semester, Summer Session Available **Faculty:** FT 9 **% Residing in College-Owned, -Operated, or -Affiliated Housing:** 31 **Library Holdings:** 24,119 **Credit Hours For Degree:** 66 semester hours, Associates; 129 semester hours, Bachelors **Professional Accreditation:** ABHE

SOUTHWEST MISSISSIPPI COMMUNITY COLLEGE
1156 College Dr.
Summit, MS 39666
Tel: (601)276-2000
Admissions: (601)276-2001
Fax: (601)276-3888
E-mail: mattc@smcc.edu
Web Site: http://www.smcc.cc.ms.us/
President/CEO: Dr. Oliver Young
Admissions: Matthew Calhoun
Type: Two-Year College **Sex:** Coed **Affiliation:** Mississippi State Board for Community and Junior Colleges **Admission Plans:** Open Admission **Application Deadline:** August 1 **Application Fee:** $0.00 **H.S. Requirements:** High school diploma required; GED accepted **Costs Per Year:** Application fee: $0. State resident tuition: $1700 full-time, $85 per credit hour part-time. Nonresident tuition: $4400 full-time, $180 per credit hour part-time. Mandatory fees: $100 full-time, $50 per term part-time. Full-time tuition and fees vary according to class time. Part-time tuition and fees vary according to class time and course load. College room and board: $2530. College room only: $1130. Room and board charges vary according to board plan. **Scholarships:** Available **Calendar System:** Semester, Summer Session Available **Enrollment:** FT 1,822, PT 297 **Faculty:** FT 71, PT 19 **Student-Faculty Ratio:** 24:1 **% Residing in College-Owned, -Operated, or -Affiliated Housing:** 35 **Library Holdings:** 34,000 **Regional Accreditation:** Southern Association of Colleges and Schools **Credit Hours For Degree:** 64 semester hours, Associates **Professional Accreditation:** NLN **Intercollegiate Athletics:** Baseball M; Basketball M & W; Football M; Soccer M & W; Softball W; Tennis M & W; Track and Field M & W

TOUGALOO COLLEGE
500 West County Line Rd.
Tougaloo, MS 39174
Tel: (601)977-7700; Free: 888-42GALOO
Admissions: (601)977-7765
Fax: (601)977-7739
E-mail: jjacobs@tougaloo.edu
Web Site: http://www.tougaloo.edu/
President/CEO: Dr. Beverly W. Hogan
Admissions: Juno Jacobs
Type: Four-Year College **Sex:** Coed **Affiliation:** United Church of Christ **Scores:** 50% ACT 18-23; 8% ACT 24-29 **% Accepted:** 99 **Admission Plans:** Early Admission **Application Deadline:** Rolling **Application Fee:** $25.00 **H.S. Requirements:** High school diploma required; GED accepted **Scholarships:** Available **Calendar System:** Semester, Summer Session Not available **Enrollment:** FT 816, PT 40 **Faculty:** FT 70, PT 33 **Student-Faculty Ratio:** 13:1 **Exams:** SAT I or ACT. **Library Holdings:** 231,106 **Regional Accreditation:** Southern Association of Colleges and Schools **Credit Hours For Degree:** 64 hours, Associates; 124 hours, Bachelors **ROTC:** Army **Intercollegiate Athletics:** Basketball M & W; Cross-Country Running M & W; Golf M; Softball W

UNIVERSITY OF MISSISSIPPI
University, MS 38677
Tel: (662)915-7211
Admissions: (662)915-7226
Fax: (662)915-5869
E-mail: admissions@olemiss.edu
Web Site: http://www.olemiss.edu/
President/CEO: Dr. Daniel W. Jones
Admissions: Jody Lowe
Financial Aid: Laura Diven-Brown
Type: University **Sex:** Coed **Affiliation:** Mississippi Institutions of Higher Learning **Scores:** 96% SAT V 400+; 94% SAT M 400+; 50% ACT 18-23; 34% ACT 24-29 **% Accepted:** 79 **Admission Plans:** Early Admission; Deferred Admission **Application Deadline:** Rolling **Application Fee:** $50.00 **H.S. Requirements:** High school diploma required; GED accepted **Scholarships:** Available **Calendar System:** Semester, Summer Session Available **Enrollment:** FT 12,109, PT 1,095, Grad FT 1,860, Grad PT 868 **Faculty:** FT 729, PT 148 **Student-Faculty Ratio:** 17:1 **Exams:** SAT I or ACT. ACT essay not being used. SAT essay not being used. **% Receiving Financial Aid:** 44 **% Residing in College-Owned, -Operated, or -Affiliated Housing:** 27 **Final Year or Final Semester Residency Requirement:** No **Library Holdings:** 2,026,321 **Regional Accreditation:** Southern Association of Colleges and Schools **Credit Hours For Degree:** 126 semester hours, Bachelors **ROTC:** Army, Navy, Air Force **Professional Accreditation:** AACSB, ABET, ACPhE, ACEJMC, AAFCS, ABA, ACA, APA, ASLHA, AALS, CSWE, NASAD, NASM, NAST, NCATE, NRPA **Intercollegiate Athletics:** Baseball M; Basketball M & W; Cheerleading M & W; Cross-Country Running M & W; Fencing M & W; Football M; Golf M & W; Ice Hockey M; Lacrosse M & W; Riflery W; Rugby M; Soccer M & W; Softball W; Tennis M & W; Track and Field M & W; Volleyball M & W

UNIVERSITY OF MISSISSIPPI MEDICAL CENTER
2500 North State St.
Jackson, MS 39216-4505
Tel: (601)984-1000
Fax: (601)984-1080
Web Site: http://www.umc.edu/
President/CEO: Dr. James Keeton
Admissions: Barbara Westerfield
Financial Aid: Minetta Veazey
Type: Two-Year Upper Division **Sex:** Coed **Affiliation:** University of Mississippi **Admission Plans:** Preferred Admission **Application Fee:** $10.00 **H.S. Requirements:** High school diploma required; GED accepted **Scholarships:** Available **Calendar System:** Semester, Summer Session Not available **Enrollment:** FT 383, PT 129 **Faculty:** FT 698, PT 138 **Student-Faculty Ratio:** 2:1 **% Receiving Financial Aid:** 41 **Library Holdings:** 310,016 **Regional Accreditation:** Southern Association of Colleges and Schools **Credit Hours For Degree:** 133 semester hours, Bachelors **Professional Accreditation:** AACN, ADA, AHIMA, AOTA, APTA, APA, ASC, LCMEAMA, NAACLS, NLN

UNIVERSITY OF SOUTHERN MISSISSIPPI
118 College Dr.
Hattiesburg, MS 39406-0001
Tel: (601)266-7011
Admissions: (601)266-5000
E-mail: admissions@usm.edu
Web Site: http://www.usm.edu/
President/CEO: Dr. Martha Saunders
Admissions: Jason Beverly
Financial Aid: David Williamson
Type: University **Sex:** Coed **Affiliation:** Mississippi Institutions of Higher Learning **Scores:** 92% SAT V 400+; 95% SAT M 400+; 55% ACT 18-23; 26% ACT 24-29 **% Accepted:** 68 **Admission Plans:** Early Admission **Application Deadline:** July 1 **Application Fee:** $35.00 **H.S. Requirements:** High school diploma required; GED accepted **Costs Per Year:** Application fee: $35. State resident tuition: $5096 full-time, $213 per credit hour part-time. Nonresident tuition: $12,746 full-time, $545 per credit hour part-time. Part-time tuition varies according to course load and degree level. College

room and board: $6200. College room only: $3762. Room and board charges vary according to board plan and housing facility. **Scholarships:** Available **Calendar System:** Semester, Summer Session Available **Enrollment:** FT 10,664, PT 1,719, Grad FT 1,486, Grad PT 1,424 **Faculty:** FT 758, PT 185 **Student-Faculty Ratio:** 16:1 **Exams:** SAT I or ACT. **% Receiving Financial Aid:** 64 **% Residing in College-Owned, -Operated, or -Affiliated Housing:** 45 **Library Holdings:** 1,223,466 **Regional Accreditation:** Southern Association of Colleges and Schools **Credit Hours For Degree:** 128 semester hours, Bachelors **ROTC:** Army, Air Force **Professional Accreditation:** AACSB, ABET, ACEJMC, AAMFT, AACN, AAFCS, ACCE, ACA, ADtA, ALA, APA, ASLHA, CAEPK, FIDER, CEPH, CSWE, JRCEPAT, NAACLS, NASAD, NASD NASM, NAST, NCATE, NLN, NRPA **Intercollegiate Athletics:** Baseball M; Basketball M & W; Cheerleading M & W; Cross-Country Running W; Football M & W; Golf M & W; Soccer W; Softball W; Tennis M & W; Track and Field M & W; Volleyball W

VIRGINIA COLLEGE AT JACKSON
5360 I-55 North
Jackson, MS 39211
Tel: (601)977-0960; Free: (866)623-6765
Fax: (601)956-4325
Web Site: http://www.vc.edu/
President/CEO: Jeff Massien
Type: Two-Year College **Sex:** Coed **Scholarships:** Available **Calendar System:** Quarter **Student-Faculty Ratio:** 24:1 **Exams:** Other. **Professional Accreditation:** ACICS

WILLIAM CAREY UNIVERSITY
498 Tuscan Ave.
Hattiesburg, MS 39401-5499
Tel: (601)318-6051
Fax: (601)318-6454
E-mail: admissions@wmcarey.edu
Web Site: http://www.wmcarey.edu/
President/CEO: Tommy King
Admissions: William N. Curry
Financial Aid: Brenda Pittman
Type: Comprehensive **Sex:** Coed **Affiliation:** Southern Baptist **Scores:** 100% SAT V 400+; 100% SAT M 400+; 64% ACT 18-23; 27% ACT 24-29 **% Accepted:** 92 **Admission Plans:** Early Admission; Deferred Admission **Application Deadline:** Rolling **Application Fee:** $20.00 **H.S. Requirements:** High school diploma required; GED accepted **Costs Per Year:** Application fee: $20. Comprehensive fee: $14,565 includes full-time tuition ($9300), mandatory fees ($450), and college room and board ($4815). College room only: $2640. Full-time tuition and fees vary according to degree level and location. Room and board charges vary according to board plan, housing facility, and location. Part-time tuition: $310 per credit hour. Part-time mandatory fees: $310 per semester hour, $150 per term. Part-time tuition and fees vary according to degree level and location. **Scholarships:** Available **Calendar System:** Trimester, Summer Session Available **Enrollment:** FT 1,429, PT 224 **Faculty:** FT 93, PT 117 **Student-Faculty Ratio:** 15:1 **Exams:** SAT I or ACT. **% Residing in College-Owned, -Operated, or -Affiliated Housing:** 23 **Library Holdings:** 92,290 **Regional Accreditation:** Southern Association of Colleges and Schools **Credit Hours For Degree:** 128 credit hours, Bachelors **ROTC:** Army, Air Force **Professional Accreditation:** AACN, NASM, NLN **Intercollegiate Athletics:** Baseball M; Basketball M & W; Cheerleading M & W; Golf M; Soccer M & W; Softball W

ALLIED COLLEGE
13723 Riverport Dr.
Ste. 103
Maryland Heights, MO 63043
Tel: (314)595-3400; Free: (866)501-1291
Fax: (314)739-5133
Web Site: http://www.hightechinstitute.edu/
President/CEO: Heidi Wind
Type: Two-Year College **Sex:** Coed **Application Fee:** $50.00 **Professional Accreditation:** ABHES

AMERICAN COLLEGE OF TECHNOLOGY
2921 North Belt Hwy.
St. Joseph, MO 64506
Tel: 800-908-9329
Fax: 888-890-8190
Web Site: http://www.acot.edu/
Type: Two-Year College **Sex:** Coed **Professional Accreditation:** DETC

AVIATION INSTITUTE OF MAINTENANCE—KANSAS CITY
3130 Terrace St.
Kansas City, MO 64111
Tel: (816)753-9920; Free: 877-538-5627
Fax: (816)753-9941
E-mail: directoramk@tidetech.com
Web Site: http://www.aviationmaintenance.edu/aviation-kansascity.asp
President/CEO: David Meierotto
Type: Two-Year College **Sex:** Coed **Calendar System:** Quarter **Professional Accreditation:** ACCSCT

AVILA UNIVERSITY
11901 Wornall Rd.
Kansas City, MO 64145-1698
Tel: (816)942-8400; Free: 800-GO-AVILA
Admissions: (816)501-2400
Fax: (816)942-3362
E-mail: patti.harper@avila.edu
Web Site: http://www.avila.edu/
President/CEO: Dr. Ronald A. Slepitza
Admissions: Patricia Harper
Financial Aid: Nancy Merz
Type: Comprehensive **Sex:** Coed **Affiliation:** Roman Catholic; The Sisters of St. Joseph of Carondelet, St. Louis Province **Scores:** 100% SAT V 400+; 100% SAT M 400+; 55% ACT 18-23; 37% ACT 24-29 **% Accepted:** 43 **Admission Plans:** Early Admission **Application Deadline:** August 15 **Application Fee:** $25.00 **H.S. Requirements:** High school diploma required; GED accepted **Costs Per Year:** Application fee: $25. Comprehensive fee: $28,150 includes full-time tuition ($21,050), mandatory fees ($750), and college room and board ($6350). College room only: $3150. Full-time tuition and fees vary according to course load and program. Room and board charges vary according to board plan and housing facility. Part-time tuition: $535 per credit hour. Part-time mandatory fees: $25 per credit hour. Part-time tuition and fees vary according to course load and program. Tuition guaranteed not to increase for student's term of enrollment. **Scholarships:** Available **Calendar System:** Semester, Summer Session Available **Enrollment:** FT 950, PT 201, Grad FT 523, Grad PT 219 **Faculty:** FT 65, PT 149 **Student-Faculty Ratio:** 14:1 **Exams:** SAT I or ACT. **% Receiving Financial Aid:** 93 **% Residing in College-Owned, -Operated, or -Affiliated Housing:** 28 **Library Holdings:** 80,845 **Regional Accreditation:** North Central Association of Colleges and Schools **Credit Hours For Degree:** 128 credit hours, Bachelors **ROTC:** Army **Professional Accreditation:** AACN, CSWE, JRCERT **Intercollegiate Athletics:** Baseball M; Basketball M & W; Cheerleading W; Cross-Country Running M & W; Football M; Golf M & W; Soccer M & W; Softball W; Volleyball W

BAPTIST BIBLE COLLEGE
628 East Kearney St.
Springfield, MO 65803-3498
Tel: (417)268-6000
Fax: (417)831-8029
Web Site: http://www.gobbc.edu/
President/CEO: Jim Edge
Admissions: Terry Allcorn
Financial Aid: Bob Kotulski
Type: Comprehensive **Sex:** Coed **Affiliation:** Baptist **% Accepted:** 76 **Admission Plans:** Preferred Admission; Early Admission; Deferred Admission **Application Deadline:** Rolling **Application Fee:** $40.00 **H.S. Requirements:** High school diploma required; GED accepted **Scholarships:** Available **Calendar System:** Semester, Summer Session Available **Enrollment:** FT 444, PT 100 **Faculty:** FT 26, PT 27 **Exams:** SAT I or ACT. **% Residing in College-Owned, -Operated, or -Affiliated Housing:** 61 **Library Holdings:** 64,236 **Regional Accreditation:** North Central Association of Colleges and Schools **Credit Hours For Degree:** 71 hours, Associates; 131 hours, Bachelors **ROTC:** Army **Professional Accreditation:** ABHE **Intercollegiate Athletics:** Basketball M & W; Soccer M; Volleyball W

BROWN MACKIE COLLEGE—ST. LOUIS
No. 2 Soccer Park Rd.
Fenton, MO 63026
Tel: (636)651-3290
Admissions: (636)651-3290
Web Site: http://www.brownmackie.edu/st-louis/
Type: Two-Year College **Sex:** Coed

CALVARY BIBLE COLLEGE AND THEOLOGICAL SEMINARY
15800 Calvary Rd.
Kansas City, MO 64147-1341
Tel: (816)322-0110; Free: 800-326-3960
E-mail: admissions@calvary.edu
Web Site: http://www.calvary.edu/
President/CEO: Dr. James Clark
Admissions: Bob Crank
Type: Comprehensive **Sex:** Coed **Affiliation:** nondenominational **Scores:** 100% SAT V 400+; 100% SAT M 400+; 64% ACT 18-23; 32% ACT 24-29 **% Accepted:** 80 **Admission Plans:** Early Admission; Deferred Admission **Application Deadline:** July 15 **Application Fee:** $25.00 **H.S. Requirements:** High school diploma required; GED accepted **Costs Per Year:** Application fee: $25. Comprehensive fee: $14,448 includes full-time tuition ($9280), mandatory fees ($768), and college room and board ($4400). College room only: $2200. Room and board charges vary according to housing facility.

Part-time tuition: $280 per credit hour. Tuition guaranteed not to increase for student's term of enrollment. **Scholarships:** Available **Calendar System:** Semester, Summer Session Available **Enrollment:** FT 145, PT 73, Grad FT 20, Grad PT 38 **Faculty:** FT 12, PT 14 **Student-Faculty Ratio:** 10:1 **Exams:** SAT I or ACT. **Final Year or Final Semester Residency Requirement:** No **Library Holdings:** 62,435 **Regional Accreditation:** North Central Association of Colleges and Schools **Credit Hours For Degree:** 64 semester hours, Associates; 131 semester hours, Bachelors **ROTC:** Army **Professional Accreditation:** ABHE **Intercollegiate Athletics:** Basketball M & W; Soccer M; Volleyball W

CENTRAL BIBLE COLLEGE
3000 North Grant Ave.
Springfield, MO 65803-1096
Tel: (417)833-2551; Free: 800-831-4222
Fax: (417)833-5141
E-mail: jbell@cbcag.edu
Web Site: http://netcom.cbcag.edu/
President/CEO: Gary A. Denbow
Admissions: James Bell
Financial Aid: Rick Woolverton
Type: Four-Year College **Sex:** Coed **Affiliation:** Assemblies of God **Admission Plans:** Preferred Admission; Early Admission; Deferred Admission **Application Deadline:** Rolling **Application Fee:** $25.00 **H.S. Requirements:** High school diploma required; GED accepted **Scholarships:** Available **Calendar System:** Semester, Summer Session Available **% Receiving Financial Aid:** 69 **Library Holdings:** 107,023 **Regional Accreditation:** North Central Association of Colleges and Schools **Credit Hours For Degree:** 64 semester hours, Associates; 126 semester hours, Bachelors **Professional Accreditation:** ABHE

CENTRAL CHRISTIAN COLLEGE OF THE BIBLE
911 Urbandale Dr. East
Moberly, MO 65270-1997
Tel: (660)263-3900
Fax: (660)263-3936
E-mail: iwant2be@cccb.edu
Web Site: http://www.cccb.edu/
President/CEO: Ronald L. Oakes
Admissions: Jason Rodenbeck
Financial Aid: Rhonda J. Dunham
Type: Four-Year College **Sex:** Coed **Affiliation:** Christian Churches and Churches of Christ **Admission Plans:** Preferred Admission; Early Admission; Deferred Admission **Application Deadline:** Rolling **Application Fee:** $25.00 **H.S. Requirements:** High school diploma required; GED accepted **Scholarships:** Available **Calendar System:** Semester, Summer Session Not available **Enrollment:** FT 523, PT 8 **Faculty:** FT 16, PT 14 **Student-Faculty Ratio:** 31:1 **Exams:** SAT I or ACT. **% Receiving Financial Aid:** 92 **% Residing in College-Owned, -Operated, or -Affiliated Housing:** 75 **Library Holdings:** 35,000 **Credit Hours For Degree:** 64 credits, Associates; 134 credits, Bachelors **Professional Accreditation:** ABHE **Intercollegiate Athletics:** Basketball M & W; Golf M & W; Tennis M & W; Volleyball W

CENTRAL METHODIST UNIVERSITY
411 Central Methodist Square
Fayette, MO 65248-1198
Tel: (660)248-3391
Admissions: (660)248-6247
Fax: (660)248-2287
E-mail: admissions@centralmethodist.edu
Web Site: http://www.centralmethodist.edu/
President/CEO: Marianne E. Inman
Admissions: Larry Anderson
Financial Aid: Linda Mackey
Type: Comprehensive **Sex:** Coed **Affiliation:** Methodist **Scores:** 67.7% ACT 18-23; 23.37% ACT 24-29 **% Accepted:** 66 **Admission Plans:** Deferred Admission **Application Deadline:** Rolling **Application Fee:** $20.00 **H.S. Requirements:** High school diploma required; GED accepted **Costs Per Year:** Application fee: $20. One-time mandatory fee: $100. Comprehensive fee: $24,910 includes full-time tuition ($17,940), mandatory fees ($730), and college room and board ($6240). College room only: $3080. Full-time tuition and fees vary according to location. Room and board charges vary according to board plan and housing facility. Part-time tuition: $180 per semester hour. Part-time mandatory fees: $32.25 per credit hour. Part-time tuition and fees vary according to course load and location. **Scholarships:** Available **Calendar System:** Semester, Summer Session Not available **Enrollment:** FT 996, PT 35 **Faculty:** FT 59, PT 29 **Student-Faculty Ratio:** 14:1 **Exams:** ACT, SAT I or ACT. **% Receiving Financial Aid:** 68 **% Residing in College-Owned, -Operated, or -Affiliated Housing:** 60 **Library Holdings:** 97,793 **Regional Accreditation:** North Central Association of Colleges and Schools **Credit Hours For Degree:** 62 credit hours, Associates; 124 credit hours, Bachelors **ROTC:** Army, Air Force **Professional Accreditation:** JRCEPAT, NASM **Intercollegiate Athletics:** Baseball M; Basketball M & W; Cross-Country Running M & W; Football M; Soccer M & W; Softball W; Track and Field M & W; Volleyball W

CHAMBERLAIN COLLEGE OF NURSING
6150 Oakland Ave.
St. Louis, MO 63139-3215
Tel: (314)768-3044; Free: 800-942-4310
Admissions: (630)953-3690
Fax: (314)768-5673
E-mail: info@chamberlain.edu
Web Site: http://www.chamberlain.edu/
President/CEO: Susan Groenwald
Admissions: Larry Veeneman
Type: Four-Year College **Sex:** Coed **Affiliation:** DeVry Inc. **Admission Plans:** Early Admission; Deferred Admission **Application Deadline:** Rolling **Application Fee:** $50.00 **H.S. Requirements:** High school diploma required; GED accepted **Scholarships:** Available **Calendar System:** Semester, Summer Session Available **Exams:** SAT I or ACT. **Library Holdings:** 8,700 **Regional Accreditation:** North Central Association of Colleges and Schools **Credit Hours For Degree:** 68 credits, Associates; 128 credits, Bachelors **ROTC:** Army **Professional Accreditation:** NLN

CITY VISION COLLEGE
PO Box 413188
Kansas City, MO 64141-3188
Tel: (816)960-2008
Fax: (816)569-0223
Web Site: http://www.cityvision.edu/
Type: Two-Year Upper Division **Sex:** Coed **Professional Accreditation:** DETC

COLLEGE OF THE OZARKS
PO Box 17
Point Lookout, MO 65726
Tel: (417)334-6411; Free: 800-222-0525
Admissions: (417)690-2637
Fax: (417)335-2618
E-mail: admiss4@cofo.edu
Web Site: http://www.cofo.edu/
President/CEO: Dr. Jerry C. Davis
Admissions: Gayle Groves
Financial Aid: Kyla R. McCarty
Type: Four-Year College **Sex:** Coed **Affiliation:** Presbyterian **Scores:** 64% ACT 18-23; 30% ACT 24-29 **% Accepted:** 9 **Admission Plans:** Preferred Admission **Application Deadline:** February 15 **Application Fee:** $0.00 **H.S. Requirements:** High school diploma required; GED accepted **Costs Per Year:** Application fee: $0. Comprehensive fee: $5710 includes full-time tuition ($0), mandatory fees ($410), and college room and board ($5300). College room only: $2600. Part-time tuition: $295 per credit hour. Part-time tuition varies according to course load. the college guarantees to meet all of the tuition cost for each full-time student by using earnings from its endowment, operation of its own mandatory student work program, accepting student aid grants, gifts and other sources. In effect, each full-time student's Cost of Education (tuition) is met 100 percent by participating in the work program and a combination of private, institutional and federal/state student aid. **Scholarships:** Available **Calendar System:** Semester, Summer Session Not available **Enrollment:** FT 1,334, PT 22 **Faculty:** FT 95, PT 35 **Student-Faculty Ratio:** 13:1 **Exams:** SAT I or ACT. **% Receiving Financial Aid:** 90 **% Residing in College-Owned, -Operated, or -Affiliated Housing:** 82 **Final Year or Final Semester Residency Requirement:** No **Library Holdings:** 112,550 **Regional Accreditation:** North Central Association of Colleges and Schools **Credit Hours For Degree:** 125 semester hours, Bachelors **ROTC:** Army **Intercollegiate Athletics:** Baseball M; Basketball M & W; Cheerleading M & W; Volleyball W

COLORADO TECHNICAL UNIVERSITY NORTH KANSAS CITY
520 East 19th Ave.
North Kansas City, MO 64116
Tel: (816)472-7400
Admissions: 888-404-7555
Fax: (816)472-0688
E-mail: avietti@kc.coloradotech.edu
Web Site: http://kc.coloradotech.edu/
President/CEO: Dr. Wallace Pond
Admissions: Angela Vietti
Type: Four-Year College **Sex:** Coed **Affiliation:** Colorado Technical University **Admission Plans:** Deferred Admission **Application Deadline:** Rolling **Application Fee:** $50.00 **H.S. Requirements:** High school diploma required; GED accepted **Costs Per Year:** Application fee: $50. **Calendar System:** Quarter **Enrollment:** FT 338, PT 341 **Credit Hours For Degree:** 92 quarter hours, Associates **Professional Accreditation:** ABHES, ACICS, JRCERT

COLUMBIA COLLEGE
1001 Rogers St.
Columbia, MO 65216-0002
Tel: (573)875-8700; Free: 800-231-2391
Admissions: (573)875-7358
Fax: (573)875-7506
E-mail: admissions@ccis.edu
Web Site: http://www.ccis.edu/
President/CEO: Dr. Gerald T. Brouder
Admissions: Daniel Kruse
Financial Aid: Sharon Abernathy
Type: Comprehensive **Sex:** Coed **Affiliation:** Christian Church (Disciples of Christ) **Scores:** 87% SAT V 400+; 100% SAT M 400+; 43% ACT 18-23; 44% ACT 24-29 **% Accepted:** 47 **Admission Plans:** Deferred Admission **Application Deadline:** August 14 **Application Fee:** $35.00 **H.S. Requirements:** High school diploma required; GED accepted **Costs Per Year:** Application fee: $35. Comprehensive fee: $21,670 includes full-time tuition ($15,596) and college room and board ($6074). College room only: $3780. Full-time tuition varies according to class time and course load. Room and board charges vary according to board plan. Part-time tuition: $312 per semester hour. Part-time tuition varies according to class time, course load, and location. **Scholarships:** Available **Calendar System:** Semester, Summer Session Available **Enrollment:** FT 848, PT 234, Grad FT 201, Grad PT 59 **Faculty:** FT 66, PT 45 **Student-Faculty Ratio:** 14:1 **Exams:** SAT I or ACT. ACT essay not being used. SAT essay not being used. **% Receiving Financial Aid:** 54 **% Residing in College-Owned, -Operated, or -Affiliated Housing:** 33 **Final Year or Final Semester Residency Requirement:** Yes **Library Holdings:** 73,388 **Regional Accreditation:** North Central Association of Colleges and Schools **Credit Hours For Degree:** 60 semester hours, Associates; 120 semester hours, Bachelors **ROTC:** Army, Navy, Air Force **Professional Accreditation:** CSWE, NLN **Intercollegiate Athletics:** Basketball M & W; Soccer M; Softball W; Volleyball W

CONCEPTION SEMINARY COLLEGE
PO Box 502
Conception, MO 64433-0502
Tel: (660)944-3105
Fax: (660)944-2829
E-mail: vocations@conception.edu
Web Site: http://www.conceptionabbey.org/
President/CEO: Samuel Russell
Admissions: Fr. Pachomius Meade, OSB
Financial Aid: Br. Justin Hernandez, PhD
Type: Four-Year College **Sex:** Men **Affiliation:** Roman Catholic **Scores:** 59% ACT 18-23; 18% ACT 24-29 **% Accepted:** 87 **Admission Plans:** Preferred Admission **Application Deadline:** July 31 **Application Fee:** $0.00 **H.S. Requirements:** High school diploma required; GED accepted **Scholarships:** Available **Calendar System:** Semester, Summer Session Not available **Enrollment:** FT 74, PT 11 **Faculty:** FT 24, PT 2 **Student-Faculty Ratio:** 3:1 **Exams:** ACT. **% Receiving Financial Aid:** 34 **% Residing in College-Owned, -Operated, or -Affiliated Housing:** 100 **Library Holdings:** 115,000 **Regional Accreditation:** North Central Association of Colleges and Schools **Credit Hours For Degree:** 126 credits, Bachelors

CONCORDE CAREER INSTITUTE
3239 Broadway
Kansas City, MO 64111-2407
Tel: (816)531-5223
Fax: (816)756-3231
Web Site: http://www.concordecareercolleges.com/
President/CEO: Deborah Crow
Type: Two-Year College **Sex:** Coed **% Accepted:** 100 **Professional Accreditation:** ACCSCT, ADA, CARC

COTTEY COLLEGE
1000 West Austin
Nevada, MO 64772
Tel: (417)667-8181; Free: 888-526-8839
Fax: (417)667-8103
E-mail: enrollmgt@cottey.edu
Web Site: http://www.cottey.edu/
President/CEO: Dr. Judy Rogers
Admissions: Judi Steege
Financial Aid: Sherry Pennington
Type: Two-Year College **Sex:** Women **Scores:** 94% SAT V 400+; 90% SAT M 400+; 48% ACT 18-23; 40% ACT 24-29 **% Accepted:** 63 **Admission Plans:** Early Admission; Deferred Admission **Application Deadline:** Rolling **Application Fee:** $20.00 **H.S. Requirements:** High school diploma required; GED accepted **Costs Per Year:** Application fee: $20. Comprehensive fee: $20,300 includes full-time tuition ($13,800), mandatory fees ($700), and college room and board ($5800). Part-time tuition: $150 per credit hour. Part-time mandatory fees: $11 per credit hour. **Scholarships:** Available **Calendar System:** Semester, Summer Session Not available **Enrollment:** FT 331 **Faculty:** FT 34, PT 8 **Student-Faculty Ratio:** 9:1 **Exams:** SAT I or ACT. **% Residing in College-Owned, -Operated, or -Affiliated Housing:** 98 **Library Holdings:** 54,200 **Regional Accreditation:** North Central Association of Colleges and Schools **Credit Hours For Degree:** 62 credit hours, Associates **Professional Accreditation:** NASM **Intercollegiate Athletics:** Basketball W; Softball W; Volleyball W

COX COLLEGE OF NURSING AND HEALTH SCIENCES
1423 North Jefferson
Springfield, MO 65802
Tel: (417)269-3401
E-mail: admissions@coxcollege.edu
Web Site: http://www.coxcollege.edu/
President/CEO: Dr. Anne Brett
Admissions: Stacy Danaher
Financial Aid: Leesa Taylor
Type: Four-Year College **Sex:** Coed **Affiliation:** Cox Health Systems **Admission Plans:** Early Decision Plan **Application Deadline:** February 1 **Application Fee:** $30.00 **H.S. Requirements:** High school diploma required; GED accepted **Scholarships:** Available **Calendar System:** Semester, Summer Session Available **Enrollment:** FT 279, PT 313 **Faculty:** FT 21, PT 26 **Student-Faculty Ratio:** 13:1 **Exams:** SAT I or ACT. **% Residing in College-Owned, -Operated, or -Affiliated Housing:** 15 **Regional Accreditation:** North Central Association of Colleges and Schools **Credit Hours For Degree:** 66 credit hours, Associates; 122 credit hours, Bachelors **Professional Accreditation:** AACN, NLN

CROWDER COLLEGE
601 Laclede Ave.
Neosho, MO 64850-9160
Tel: (417)451-3223; Free: (866)238-7788
Fax: (417)451-4280
E-mail: jriggs@crowder.edu
Web Site: http://www.crowder.edu/
President/CEO: Dr. Alan Marble
Admissions: Jim Riggs
Type: Two-Year College **Sex:** Coed **Affiliation:** Missouri Coordinating Board for Higher Education **% Accepted:** 100 **Admission Plans:** Open Admission **Application Deadline:** Rolling **Application Fee:** $25.00 **H.S. Requirements:** High school diploma required; GED accepted **Costs Per Year:** Application fee: $25. Area resident tuition: $2040 full-time, $68 per credit hour part-time. State resident tuition: $2850 full-time, $95 per credit hour part-time. Nonresident tuition: $3690 full-time, $123 per credit hour part-time. Mandatory fees: $340 full-time. College room and board: $3870. **Scholarships:** Available **Calendar System:** Semester, Summer Session Available **Enrollment:** FT 2,111, PT 2,371 **Faculty:** FT 68, PT 236 **Student-Faculty Ratio:** 19:1 **% Residing in College-Owned, -Operated, or -Affiliated Housing:** 10 **Library Holdings:** 37,452 **Regional Accreditation:** North

Central Association of Colleges and Schools **Credit Hours For Degree:** 60 semester hours, Associates **Professional Accreditation:** NAIT **Intercollegiate Athletics:** Baseball M; Basketball W; Soccer M

CULINARY INSTITUTE OF ST. LOUIS AT HICKEY COLLEGE
940 West Port Plaza
St. Louis, MO 63146
Tel: (314)434-2212
Web Site: http://ci-stl.com/
Type: Two-Year College **Sex:** Coed

CULVER-STOCKTON COLLEGE
1 College Hill
Canton, MO 63435-1299
Tel: (217)231-6000; Free: 800-537-1883
Admissions: (573)288-6456
Fax: (217)231-6611
E-mail: dtabb@culver.edu
Web Site: http://www.culver.edu/
President/CEO: Richard D. Valentine
Admissions: Richard (Dick) Tabb
Financial Aid: Tina M. Wiseman
Type: Four-Year College **Sex:** Coed **Affiliation:** Christian Church (Disciples of Christ) **Scores:** 87.5% SAT V 400+; 100% SAT M 400+; 66% ACT 18-23; 25% ACT 24-29 **% Accepted:** 60 **Admission Plans:** Deferred Admission **Application Deadline:** Rolling **Application Fee:** $0.00 **H.S. Requirements:** High school diploma required; GED accepted **Costs Per Year:** Application fee: $0. One-time mandatory fee: $200. Comprehensive fee: $29,950 includes full-time tuition ($22,250), mandatory fees ($300), and college room and board ($7400). College room only: $3300. Full-time tuition and fees vary according to course level. Room and board charges vary according to board plan. Part-time tuition: $515 per credit hour. Part-time mandatory fees: $12.50 per credit hour. Part-time tuition and fees vary according to course level. **Scholarships:** Available **Calendar System:** Semester, Summer Session Available **Enrollment:** FT 699, PT 55 **Faculty:** FT 45, PT 39 **Student-Faculty Ratio:** 13:1 **Exams:** SAT I or ACT. ACT essay not being used. SAT essay not being used. **% Receiving Financial Aid:** 87 **% Residing in College-Owned, -Operated, or -Affiliated Housing:** 73 **Regional Accreditation:** North Central Association of Colleges and Schools **Credit Hours For Degree:** 120 hours, Bachelors **Professional Accreditation:** NASM, NLN **Intercollegiate Athletics:** Baseball M; Basketball M & W; Cheerleading M & W; Cross-Country Running M & W; Football M; Golf M & W; Soccer M & W; Softball W; Track and Field M & W; Volleyball W

DEVRY UNIVERSITY (KANSAS CITY)
City Center Square
1100 Main St., Ste. 118
Kansas City, MO 64105-2112
Tel: (816)221-1300
Fax: (816)474-0318
Web Site: http://www.devry.edu/
Type: Comprehensive **Sex:** Coed **Calendar System:** Semester **Regional Accreditation:** North Central Association of Colleges and Schools

DEVRY UNIVERSITY (KANSAS CITY)
11224 Holmes Rd.
Kansas City, MO 64131
Tel: (816)941-0430
Fax: (816)941-0896
Web Site: http://www.devry.edu/
President/CEO: Shane Smeed
Financial Aid: Maureen Kelly
Type: Comprehensive **Sex:** Coed **Affiliation:** DeVry University **Admission Plans:** Deferred Admission **Application Deadline:** Rolling **Application Fee:** $50.00 **H.S. Requirements:** High school diploma required; GED accepted **Costs Per Year:** Application fee: $50. Tuition: $14,080 full-time, $550 per credit hour part-time. **Scholarships:** Available **Calendar System:** Semester, Summer Session Available **Enrollment:** FT 573, PT 480, Grad FT 13, Grad PT 203 **Faculty:** FT 28, PT 53 **Student-Faculty Ratio:** 18:1 **Exams:** ACT essay used for admission. SAT essay used for admission. ACT essay used for placement. SAT essay used for placement. **% Receiving Financial Aid:** 77 **Regional Accreditation:** North Central Association of Colleges and Schools **Credit Hours For Degree:** 67 credit hours, Associates; 122 credit hours, Bachelors **Professional Accreditation:** ABET

DEVRY UNIVERSITY (ST. LOUIS)
1801 Park 270 Dr., Ste. 260
St. Louis, MO 63146-4020
Tel: (314)542-4222
Fax: (314)542-4004
Web Site: http://www.devry.edu/
Type: Comprehensive **Sex:** Coed **Calendar System:** Semester **Regional Accreditation:** North Central Association of Colleges and Schools

DRURY UNIVERSITY
900 North Benton Ave.
Springfield, MO 65802
Tel: (417)873-7879; Free: 800-922-2274
Admissions: (417)873-7205
Fax: (417)873-7529
E-mail: druryad@drury.edu
Web Site: http://www.drury.edu/
President/CEO: Todd Parnell
Admissions: Chip Parker
Financial Aid: Annette Avery
Type: Comprehensive **Sex:** Coed **Scores:** 40% ACT 18-23; 48% ACT 24-29 **% Accepted:** 70 **Admission Plans:** Deferred Admission **Application Deadline:** August 1 **Application Fee:** $25.00 **H.S. Requirements:** High school diploma required; GED accepted **Costs Per Year:** Application fee: $25. One-time mandatory fee: $145. Comprehensive fee: $26,825 includes full-time tuition ($19,325), mandatory fees ($529), and college room and board ($6971). Full-time tuition and fees vary according to class time. Room and board charges vary according to board plan and housing facility. **Scholarships:** Available **Calendar System:** Semester, Summer Session Available **Enrollment:** FT 1,518, PT 32, Grad FT 281, Grad PT 245 **Faculty:** FT 131, PT 48 **Student-Faculty Ratio:** 12:1 **Exams:** SAT I or ACT. **% Receiving Financial Aid:** 95 **% Residing in College-Owned, -Operated, or -Affiliated Housing:** 56 **Final Year or Final Semester Residency Requirement:** Yes **Library Holdings:** 189,895 **Regional Accreditation:** North Central Association of Colleges and Schools **Credit Hours For Degree:** 124 semester hours, Bachelors **ROTC:** Army **Professional Accreditation:** ACBSP, NAAB, NASM, NCATE **Intercollegiate Athletics:** Baseball M; Basketball M & W; Cheerleading M & W; Cross-Country Running M & W; Golf M & W; Soccer M & W; Softball W; Swimming and Diving M & W; Tennis M & W; Track and Field M & W; Volleyball W

EAST CENTRAL COLLEGE
1964 Prairie Dell Rd.
Union, MO 63084
Tel: (636)583-5193
Admissions: (636)584-6564
Fax: (636)583-1897
E-mail: poynterm@eastcentral.edu
Web Site: http://www.eastcentral.edu/
President/CEO: Dr. Edward Jackson
Admissions: Megen Poynter
Type: Two-Year College **Sex:** Coed **Scores:** 57% ACT 18-23; 20% ACT 24-29 **Admission Plans:** Open Admission; Early Admission; Deferred Admission **Application Deadline:** Rolling **Application Fee:** $0.00 **H.S. Requirements:** High school diploma required; GED accepted **Costs Per Year:** Application fee: $0. Area resident tuition: $1464 full-time, $61 per credit hour part-time. State resident tuition: $2088 full-time, $87 per credit hour part-time. Nonresident tuition: $3144 full-time, $131 per credit hour part-time. Mandatory fees: $240 full-time, $10 per credit hour part-time. Full-time tuition and fees vary according to program. Part-time tuition and fees vary according to program. **Scholarships:** Available **Calendar System:** Semester, Summer Session Available **Enrollment:** FT 2,137, PT 2,066 **Faculty:** FT 72, PT 169 **Student-Faculty Ratio:** 22:1 **Regional Accreditation:** North Central Association of Colleges and Schools **Credit Hours For Degree:** 64 semester hours, Associates **Intercollegiate Athletics:** Soccer M; Softball W; Volleyball W

EVANGEL UNIVERSITY
1111 North Glenstone
Springfield, MO 65802
Tel: (417)865-2811
Fax: (417)865-9599
E-mail: admissions@evangel.edu
Web Site: http://www.evangel.edu/

President/CEO: Dr. Robert H. Spence
Financial Aid: Dorynda Carpenter
Type: Comprehensive **Sex:** Coed **Affiliation:** Assemblies of God **Scores:** 90% SAT V 400+; 89% SAT M 400+; 52% ACT 18-23; 32% ACT 24-29 **% Accepted:** 74 **Admission Plans:** Deferred Admission **Application Deadline:** Rolling **Application Fee:** $25.00 **H.S. Requirements:** High school diploma required; GED accepted **Costs Per Year:** Application fee: $25. Comprehensive fee: $21,950 includes full-time tuition ($15,950) and college room and board ($6000). College room only: $3100. Full-time tuition varies according to course load. Room and board charges vary according to board plan. **Scholarships:** Available **Calendar System:** Semester, Summer Session Available **Enrollment:** FT 1,624, PT 111, Grad FT 84, Grad PT 136 **Faculty:** FT 93, PT 32 **Student-Faculty Ratio:** 18:1 **Exams:** SAT I or ACT. ACT essay used for placement. SAT essay used for placement. **% Receiving Financial Aid:** 83 **% Residing in College-Owned, -Operated, or -Affiliated Housing:** 75 **Regional Accreditation:** North Central Association of Colleges and Schools **Credit Hours For Degree:** 60 credit hours, Associates; 124 credit hours, Bachelors **ROTC:** Army **Professional Accreditation:** CSWE, NASM, NCATE **Intercollegiate Athletics:** Baseball M; Basketball M & W; Cross-Country Running M & W; Football M; Golf M & W; Softball W; Tennis M & W; Track and Field M & W; Volleyball W

EVEREST COLLEGE
1010 West Sunshine
Springfield, MO 65807-2488
Tel: (417)864-7220
Fax: (417)865-5697
Web Site: http://www.everest.edu/campus/springfield/
President/CEO: Gary L. Myers
Type: Two-Year College **Sex:** Coed **Affiliation:** Corinthian Colleges, Inc. **Application Deadline:** Rolling **Application Fee:** $25.00 **H.S. Requirements:** High school diploma required; GED accepted **Scholarships:** Available **Calendar System:** Quarter, Summer Session Available **Exams:** Other. **Credit Hours For Degree:** 96 credits, Associates **Professional Accreditation:** ACICS, AAMAE

FONTBONNE UNIVERSITY
6800 Wydown Blvd.
St. Louis, MO 63105-3098
Tel: (314)862-3456
Admissions: (314)889-1400
Fax: (314)719-8021
E-mail: pmusen@fontbonne.edu
Web Site: http://www.fontbonne.edu/
President/CEO: Dr. Dennis C. Golden
Admissions: Peggy Musen
Type: Comprehensive **Sex:** Coed **Affiliation:** Roman Catholic **% Accepted:** 85 **Admission Plans:** Early Admission; Deferred Admission **Application Deadline:** Rolling **Application Fee:** $25.00 **H.S. Requirements:** High school diploma required; GED accepted **Costs Per Year:** Application fee: $25. Comprehensive fee: $28,180 includes full-time tuition ($20,060), mandatory fees ($320), and college room and board ($7800). College room only: $4374. Full-time tuition and fees vary according to program. Room and board charges vary according to board plan and housing facility. Part-time tuition: $537 per credit hour. Part-time mandatory fees: $16 per credit hour. Part-time tuition and fees vary according to program. **Scholarships:** Available **Calendar System:** Semester, Summer Session Available **Enrollment:** FT 1,465, PT 603, Grad FT 398, Grad PT 536 **Faculty:** FT 75, PT 256 **Student-Faculty Ratio:** 13:1 **Exams:** SAT I or ACT. **% Residing in College-Owned, -Operated, or -Affiliated Housing:** 14 **Library Holdings:** 88,063 **Regional Accreditation:** North Central Association of Colleges and Schools **Credit Hours For Degree:** 128 credits, Bachelors **ROTC:** Army, Air Force **Professional Accreditation:** AAFCS, ASLHA, ACBSP, NCATE **Intercollegiate Athletics:** Baseball M; Basketball M & W; Bowling W; Cheerleading W; Cross-Country Running M & W; Field Hockey W; Golf M & W; Lacrosse M & W; Soccer M & W; Softball W; Tennis M & W; Track and Field M & W; Volleyball M & W

GLOBAL UNIVERSITY
1211 South Glenstone Ave.
Springfield, MO 65804
Tel: (417)862-9533; Free: 800-443-1083
Fax: (417)862-5318
E-mail: twaggoner@globaluniversity.edu
Web Site: http://www.globaluniversity.edu/
President/CEO: Dr. George Flattery
Admissions: Rev. Todd Waggoner
Type: Comprehensive **Sex:** Coed **Affiliation:** Assemblies of God **Admission Plans:** Open Admission **Application Deadline:** Rolling **Application Fee:** $40.00 **H.S. Requirements:** High school diploma required; GED accepted **Calendar System:** Continuous, Summer Session Not available **Enrollment:** FT 381, PT 3,795, Grad FT 60, Grad PT 315 **Faculty:** FT 81, PT 552 **Student-Faculty Ratio:** 11:1 **Regional Accreditation:** North Central Association of Colleges and Schools **Credit Hours For Degree:** 64 credits, Associates; 128 credits, Bachelors **Professional Accreditation:** DETC

GOLDFARB SCHOOL OF NURSING AT BARNES-JEWISH COLLEGE
4483 Duncan Ave.
St. Louis, MO 63110
Tel: (314)454-7055
Admissions: (314)362-9155
Fax: (314)454-5239
E-mail: mward@bjc.org
Web Site: http://www.barnesjewishcollege.edu/
President/CEO: Dr. Michael Evans, RN
Admissions: Dr. Michael D. Ward
Financial Aid: Regina Blackshear
Type: Comprehensive **Sex:** Coed **Affiliation:** Barnes Jewish Hospital **Admission Plans:** Deferred Admission **Application Fee:** $50.00 **H.S. Requirements:** High school diploma required; GED accepted **Costs Per Year:** Application fee: $50. Tuition: $16,440 full-time, $548 per credit hour part-time. Mandatory fees: $580 full-time. Full-time tuition and fees vary according to course load. Part-time tuition varies according to course load. **Scholarships:** Available **Calendar System:** Trimester, Summer Session Available **Enrollment:** FT 367, PT 150, Grad FT 61, Grad PT 56 **Faculty:** FT 35, PT 0 **Student-Faculty Ratio:** 11:1 **% Receiving Financial Aid:** 50 **Final Year or Final Semester Residency Requirement:** No **Library Holdings:** 1,100 **Regional Accreditation:** North Central Association of Colleges and Schools **Credit Hours For Degree:** 120 credit hours, Bachelors **Professional Accreditation:** AACN, AANA, ADtA, ASC, JRCERT, NAACLS, NLN

GRACELAND UNIVERSITY
1401 West Truman Rd.
Independence, MO 64050-3434
Tel: (816)833-0524
E-mail: gic@graceland.edu
Web Site: http://www.graceland.edu/
Type: Comprehensive **Sex:** Coed **Affiliation:** Community of Christ **Calendar System:** 4-1-4 **Regional Accreditation:** North Central Association of Colleges and Schools

GRANTHAM UNIVERSITY
7200 Northwest 86th St., Ste. M
Kansas City, MO 64153
Free: 800-955-2527
Fax: (816)595-5757
E-mail: admissions@grantham.edu
Web Site: http://www.grantham.edu/
President/CEO: Dr. John LaNear
Admissions: Matthew Hawes
Type: Comprehensive **Sex:** Coed **Admission Plans:** Open Admission **Application Deadline:** Rolling **Application Fee:** $30.00 **H.S. Requirements:** High school diploma required; GED accepted **Costs Per Year:** Application fee: $30. One-time mandatory fee: $30. Tuition: $7950 full-time, $265 per credit hour part-time. Tuition guaranteed not to increase for student's term of enrollment. **Calendar System:** Continuous, Summer Session Not available **Faculty:** FT 17, PT 166 **Library Holdings:** 2,044 **Credit Hours For Degree:** 60 credits, Associates; 125 credits, Bachelors **Professional Accreditation:** DETC

HANNIBAL-LAGRANGE COLLEGE
2800 Palmyra Rd.
Hannibal, MO 63401-1999
Tel: (573)221-3675; Free: 800-HLG-1119
Admissions: (573)629-2278
Fax: (573)221-6594
E-mail: admissio@hlg.edu

Web Site: http://www.hlg.edu/
President/CEO: Dr. Woodrow Burt
Admissions: Dr. Raymond Carty
Financial Aid: Brice Baumgardner
Type: Comprehensive **Sex:** Coed **Affiliation:** Southern Baptist **% Accepted:** 94 **Admission Plans:** Early Admission; Deferred Admission **Application Deadline:** September 10 **Application Fee:** $25.00 **H.S. Requirements:** High school diploma required; GED accepted **Costs Per Year:** Application fee: $25. One-time mandatory fee: $100. Comprehensive fee: $21,380 includes full-time tuition ($14,820), mandatory fees ($560), and college room and board ($6000). Full-time tuition and fees vary according to class time, course load, degree level, program, and reciprocity agreements. Room and board charges vary according to housing facility. Part-time tuition: $494 per credit hour. Part-time mandatory fees: $560 per year, $100 per year. Part-time tuition and fees vary according to class time, course load, degree level, program, and reciprocity agreements. **Scholarships:** Available **Calendar System:** Semester, Summer Session Available **Enrollment:** FT 845, PT 112, Grad FT 6, Grad PT 17 **Faculty:** FT 63, PT 83 **Student-Faculty Ratio:** 14:1 **Exams:** SAT I or ACT. ACT essay not being used. SAT essay not being used. **% Receiving Financial Aid:** 67 **% Residing in College-Owned, -Operated, or -Affiliated Housing:** 56 **Final Year or Final Semester Residency Requirement:** Yes **Library Holdings:** 112,378 **Regional Accreditation:** North Central Association of Colleges and Schools **Credit Hours For Degree:** 64 credit hours, Associates; 124 credit hours, Bachelors **Professional Accreditation:** CARC, NLN **Intercollegiate Athletics:** Baseball M; Basketball M & W; Cheerleading M & W; Cross-Country Running M & W; Golf M & W; Soccer M & W; Softball W; Swimming and Diving M & W; Track and Field M & W; Volleyball M & W; Wrestling M

HARRIS-STOWE STATE UNIVERSITY
3026 Laclede Ave.
St. Louis, MO 63103-2136
Tel: (314)340-3366
Admissions: (314)340-3300
Fax: (314)340-3322
E-mail: admissions@hssu.edu
Web Site: http://www.hssu.edu/
President/CEO: Dr. Henry Givens, Jr.
Admissions: Meghan Sprung
Financial Aid: Regina Blackshear
Type: Four-Year College **Sex:** Coed **Affiliation:** Missouri Coordinating Board for Higher Education **Scores:** 24% ACT 18-23; 1% ACT 24-29 **% Accepted:** 94 **Admission Plans:** Open Admission; Early Admission; Deferred Admission **Application Deadline:** Rolling **Application Fee:** $15.00 **H.S. Requirements:** High school diploma required; GED accepted **Costs Per Year:** Application fee: $15. State resident tuition: $4920 full-time, $164 per credit hour part-time. Nonresident tuition: $9692 full-time, $323.08 per credit hour part-time. Mandatory fees: $400 full-time, $200 per term part-time. Full-time tuition and fees vary according to course load. Part-time tuition and fees vary according to course load. College room and board: $7861. Room and board charges vary according to board plan. **Scholarships:** Available **Calendar System:** Semester, Summer Session Available **Enrollment:** FT 1,408, PT 478 **Faculty:** FT 56, PT 134 **Student-Faculty Ratio:** 30:1 **Exams:** Other, SAT I or ACT. ACT essay not being used. SAT essay not being used. **% Receiving Financial Aid:** 89 **% Residing in College-Owned, -Operated, or -Affiliated Housing:** 12 **Library Holdings:** 60,000 **Regional Accreditation:** North Central Association of Colleges and Schools **Credit Hours For Degree:** 120 credit hours, Bachelors **ROTC:** Army, Air Force **Professional Accreditation:** ACBSP, NCATE **Intercollegiate Athletics:** Baseball M; Basketball M & W; Cheerleading M & W; Soccer M & W; Softball W; Volleyball W

HERITAGE COLLEGE
1200 East 104th St.
Ste. 300
Kansas City, MO 64131
Tel: (816)942-5474; Free: 888-334-7339
Fax: (816)942-5405
E-mail: info@heritage-education.com
Web Site: http://www.heritage-education.com/
President/CEO: Larry Cartmill
Type: Two-Year College **Sex:** Coed **Admission Plans:** Open Admission **Student-Faculty Ratio:** 31:1 **Professional Accreditation:** ACCSCT

HICKEY COLLEGE
940 West Port Plaza
Ste. 101
St. Louis, MO 63146
Tel: (314)434-2212; Free: 800-777-1544
Fax: (314)434-1974
Web Site: http://www.hickeycollege.edu/
President/CEO: Christopher A. Gearin
Type: Four-Year College **Sex:** Coed **% Accepted:** 74 **H.S. Requirements:** High school diploma required; GED accepted **Calendar System:** Semester, Summer Session Not available **Enrollment:** FT 359 **% Residing in College-Owned, -Operated, or -Affiliated Housing:** 20 **Library Holdings:** 10,000 **Professional Accreditation:** ACICS

HIGH-TECH INSTITUTE
9001 State Line Rd.
Kansas City, MO 64114
Tel: (816)444-4300; Free: (866)296-2110
Fax: (816)444-4494
Web Site: http://www.high-techinstitute.com/
President/CEO: Marilyn Knight
Type: Two-Year College **Sex:** Coed **Application Fee:** $50.00 **Calendar System:** Semester **Professional Accreditation:** ACCSCT

IHM HEALTH STUDIES CENTER
2500 Abbott Place
St. Louis, MO 63143
Tel: (314)768-1234
Fax: (314)768-1595
E-mail: info@ihmhealthstudies.edu
Web Site: http://www.ihmhealthstudies.com/
Type: Two-Year College **Sex:** Coed **Calendar System:** Trimester

ITT TECHNICAL INSTITUTE (ARNOLD)
1930 Meyer Drury Dr.
Arnold, MO 63010
Tel: (636)464-6600; Free: 888-488-1082
Web Site: http://www.itt-tech.edu/
President/CEO: David Heckeler
Type: Two-Year College **Sex:** Coed **Affiliation:** ITT Educational Services, Inc. **H.S. Requirements:** High school diploma required; GED accepted **Scholarships:** Available **Calendar System:** Quarter, Summer Session Not available **Professional Accreditation:** ACICS

ITT TECHNICAL INSTITUTE (EARTH CITY)
3640 Corporate Trail Dr.
Earth City, MO 63045
Tel: (314)298-7800; Free: 800-235-5488
Fax: (314)298-0559
Web Site: http://www.itt-tech.edu/
President/CEO: John Eichkorn
Financial Aid: Robert Zellers
Type: Two-Year College **Sex:** Coed **Affiliation:** ITT Educational Services, Inc. **H.S. Requirements:** High school diploma required; GED accepted **Scholarships:** Available **Calendar System:** Quarter, Summer Session Not available **Credit Hours For Degree:** 96 credit hours, Associates; 180 credit hours, Bachelors **Professional Accreditation:** ACICS

ITT TECHNICAL INSTITUTE (KANSAS CITY)
9150 East 41st Terrace
Kansas City, MO 64133
Tel: (816)276-1400; Free: 877-488-1442
Web Site: http://www.itt-tech.edu/
President/CEO: David Roustio
Type: Two-Year College **Sex:** Coed **Affiliation:** ITT Educational Services, Inc. **Calendar System:** Quarter **Professional Accreditation:** ACICS

ITT TECHNICAL INSTITUTE (SPRINGFIELD)
3216 South National Ave.
Springfield, MO 65807
Tel: (417)877-4800; Free: 877-219-4387
Web Site: http://www.itt-tech.edu/
President/CEO: Schon Nielson

Type: Four-Year College **Sex:** Coed **Affiliation:** ITT Educational Services, Inc. **Calendar System:** Quarter

JEFFERSON COLLEGE
1000 Viking Dr.
Hillsboro, MO 63050-2441
Tel: (636)797-3000
Fax: (636)789-4012
E-mail: admissions@jeffco.edu
Web Site: http://www.jeffco.edu/
President/CEO: Dr. Raymond Cummiskey
Admissions: Julie Fraser
Financial Aid: Julie Fraser
Type: Two-Year College **Sex:** Coed **Admission Plans:** Open Admission; Early Admission **Application Deadline:** Rolling **Application Fee:** $25.00 **H.S. Requirements:** High school diploma required; GED accepted **Costs Per Year:** Application fee: $25. Area resident tuition: $2550 full-time, $85 per credit hour part-time. State resident tuition: $3840 full-time, $128 per credit hour part-time. Nonresident tuition: $5100 full-time, $170 per credit hour part-time. Full-time tuition varies according to program. Part-time tuition varies according to program. **Scholarships:** Available **Calendar System:** Semester, Summer Session Available **Enrollment:** FT 3,179, PT 2,609 **Faculty:** FT 94, PT 193 **Library Holdings:** 70,402 **Regional Accreditation:** North Central Association of Colleges and Schools **Credit Hours For Degree:** 62 semester hours, Associates **Intercollegiate Athletics:** Baseball M; Basketball W; Cheerleading M & W; Soccer M; Softball W; Volleyball W

KANSAS CITY ART INSTITUTE
4415 Warwick Blvd.
Kansas City, MO 64111-1874
Tel: (816)472-4852; Free: 800-522-5224
Admissions: (816)474-5224
Fax: (816)531-6296
E-mail: admiss@kcai.edu
Web Site: http://www.kcai.edu/
President/CEO: Kathleen Collins
Admissions: Gerald Valet
Financial Aid: Kimberly Warren
Type: Four-Year College **Sex:** Coed **Scores:** 97% SAT V 400+; 94% SAT M 400+; 51% ACT 18-23; 40% ACT 24-29 **% Accepted:** 63 **Admission Plans:** Deferred Admission **Application Deadline:** Rolling **Application Fee:** $35.00 **H.S. Requirements:** High school diploma required; GED accepted **Costs Per Year:** Application fee: $35. Comprehensive fee: $37,290 includes full-time tuition ($28,580) and college room and board ($8710). Full-time tuition varies according to program. Room and board charges vary according to board plan and housing facility. Part-time tuition: $1190 per credit hour. Part-time tuition varies according to program. **Scholarships:** Available **Calendar System:** Semester, Summer Session Available **Enrollment:** FT 669, PT 7 **Faculty:** FT 51, PT 53 **Student-Faculty Ratio:** 12:1 **Exams:** SAT I or ACT. **% Receiving Financial Aid:** 93 **% Residing in College-Owned, -Operated, or -Affiliated Housing:** 25 **Regional Accreditation:** North Central Association of Colleges and Schools **Credit Hours For Degree:** 129 credit hours, Bachelors **Professional Accreditation:** NASAD

LINCOLN UNIVERSITY
820 Chestnut St.
Jefferson City, MO 65102
Tel: (573)681-5000; Free: 800-521-5052
Admissions: (573)681-5599
Fax: (573)681-6074
E-mail: enroll@lincolnu.edu
Web Site: http://www.lincolnu.edu/
President/CEO: Dr. Carolyn R. Mahoney
Admissions: Mike Kosher
Financial Aid: Alfred Robinson
Type: Comprehensive **Sex:** Coed **Affiliation:** Missouri Coordinating Board for Higher Education **Scores:** 35.68% ACT 18-23; 6.22% ACT 24-29 **% Accepted:** 68 **Admission Plans:** Open Admission **Application Deadline:** July 15 **Application Fee:** $20.00 **H.S. Requirements:** High school diploma required; GED accepted **Costs Per Year:** Application fee: $20. State resident tuition: $5685 full-time, $189.50 per credit hour part-time. Nonresident tuition: $10,395 full-time, $346.50 per credit hour part-time. Mandatory fees: $15 per credit hour part-time, $20 per term part-time. Full-time tuition varies according to location and reciprocity agreements. Part-time tuition and fees vary according to location and reciprocity agreements. **Scholarships:** Available **Calendar System:** Semester, Summer Session Available **Enrollment:** FT 2,120, PT 996, Grad FT 52, Grad PT 146 **Faculty:** FT 139, PT 109 **Student-Faculty Ratio:** 15:1 **% Receiving Financial Aid:** 77 **% Residing in College-Owned, -Operated, or -Affiliated Housing:** 33 **Library Holdings:** 204,948 **Regional Accreditation:** North Central Association of Colleges and Schools **Credit Hours For Degree:** 62 credit hours, Associates; 121 credit hours, Bachelors **ROTC:** Army, Navy, Air Force **Professional Accreditation:** ACBSP, NASM, NCATE, NLN **Intercollegiate Athletics:** Baseball M; Basketball M & W; Cross-Country Running W; Football M; Golf M & W; Softball W; Tennis W; Track and Field M & W

LINDENWOOD UNIVERSITY
209 South Kingshighway
St. Charles, MO 63301-1695
Tel: (636)949-2000
Admissions: (636)949-4949
Fax: (636)949-4910
E-mail: jparisi@lindenwood.edu
Web Site: http://www.lindenwood.edu/
President/CEO: Dr. James D. Evans
Admissions: Joseph Parisi
Financial Aid: Lori Bode
Type: Comprehensive **Sex:** Coed **Affiliation:** Presbyterian **Scores:** 89% SAT V 400+; 92% SAT M 400+; 69% ACT 18-23; 24% ACT 24-29 **% Accepted:** 57 **Admission Plans:** Deferred Admission **Application Deadline:** Rolling **Application Fee:** $30.00 **H.S. Requirements:** High school diploma required; GED accepted **Costs Per Year:** Application fee: $30. Comprehensive fee: $20,810 includes full-time tuition ($13,260), mandatory fees ($340), and college room and board ($7210). College room only: $3980. Full-time tuition and fees vary according to program. Part-time tuition: $380 per credit hour. Part-time tuition varies according to course load. **Scholarships:** Available **Calendar System:** 4-1-4, Summer Session Available **Enrollment:** FT 6,153, PT 636, Grad FT 1,416, Grad PT 2,208 **Faculty:** FT 210, PT 310 **Student-Faculty Ratio:** 20:1 **Exams:** SAT I or ACT. **% Receiving Financial Aid:** 64 **% Residing in College-Owned, -Operated, or -Affiliated Housing:** 57 **Library Holdings:** 172,629 **Regional Accreditation:** North Central Association of Colleges and Schools **Credit Hours For Degree:** 128 credit hours, Bachelors **ROTC:** Army **Professional Accreditation:** ACBSP, TEAC **Intercollegiate Athletics:** Baseball M; Basketball M & W; Bowling M & W; Cheerleading M & W; Cross-Country Running M & W; Field Hockey W; Football M; Golf M & W; Ice Hockey M & W; Lacrosse M & W; Riflery M & W; Soccer M & W; Softball W; Swimming and Diving M & W; Table Tennis M & W; Tennis M & W; Track and Field M & W; Volleyball M & W; Water Polo M & W; Weight Lifting M & W; Wrestling M & W

LINN STATE TECHNICAL COLLEGE
One Technology Dr.
Linn, MO 65051-9606
Tel: (573)897-5000; Free: 800-743-TECH
Admissions: (573)897-5196
E-mail: becky.dunn@linnstate.edu
Web Site: http://www.linnstate.edu/
President/CEO: Dr. Donald Claycomb
Admissions: Becky Dunn
Type: Two-Year College **Sex:** Coed **Scores:** 56% ACT 18-23; 13% ACT 24-29 **% Accepted:** 57 **Admission Plans:** Open Admission **Application Deadline:** Rolling **Application Fee:** $0.00 **H.S. Requirements:** High school diploma required; GED accepted **Costs Per Year:** Application fee: $0. State resident tuition: $4380 full-time, $146 per credit hour part-time. Nonresident tuition: $8760 full-time, $292 per credit hour part-time. Mandatory fees: $990 full-time, $33 per credit hour part-time. College room and board: $4120. College room only: $3120. Room and board charges vary according to board plan. **Scholarships:** Available **Calendar System:** Semester, Summer Session Available **Enrollment:** FT 961, PT 181 **Faculty:** FT 82, PT 2 **Student-Faculty Ratio:** 13:1 **Exams:** ACT, Other. ACT essay not being used. SAT essay not being used. **% Residing in College-Owned, -Operated, or -Affiliated Housing:** 15 **Final Year or Final Semester Residency Requirement:** No **Library Holdings:** 14,984 **Regional Accreditation:** North Central Association of Colleges and Schools **Credit Hours For Degree:** 64 credit hours, Associates **ROTC:** Army **Professional Accreditation:** NAIT

LOGAN UNIVERSITY—COLLEGE OF CHIROPRACTIC
1851 Schoettler Rd., Box 1065
Chesterfield, MO 63006-1065

Tel: (636)227-2100; Free: 800-533-9210
Fax: (636)227-9338
E-mail: loganadm@logan.edu
Web Site: http://www.logan.edu/
President/CEO: Dr. George A. Goodman, DC
Financial Aid: Linda K. Haman
Type: Two-Year Upper Division **Sex:** Coed **Admission Plans:** Preferred Admission; Deferred Admission **Application Fee:** $50.00 **H.S. Requirements:** High school diploma required; GED accepted **Costs Per Year:** Application fee: $50. Tuition: $5400 full-time, $150 per credit hour part-time. Mandatory fees: $330 full-time. Full-time tuition and fees vary according to program. Part-time tuition varies according to program. **Scholarships:** Available **Calendar System:** Trimester, Summer Session Not available **Enrollment:** FT 48, PT 28, Grad FT 864, Grad PT 114 **Faculty:** FT 52, PT 52 **% Receiving Financial Aid:** 95 **Library Holdings:** 14,281 **Regional Accreditation:** North Central Association of Colleges and Schools **Credit Hours For Degree:** 133 credit hours, Bachelors **Professional Accreditation:** CCE **Intercollegiate Athletics:** Basketball M & W; Golf M; Soccer M; Tennis M

MARYVILLE UNIVERSITY OF SAINT LOUIS
650 Maryville University Dr.
St. Louis, MO 63141-7299
Tel: (314)529-9300; Free: 800-627-9855
Admissions: (314)529-9350
Fax: (314)529-9927
E-mail: admissions@maryville.edu
Web Site: http://www.maryville.edu/
President/CEO: Dr. Mark Lombardi
Admissions: Shani Lenore-Jenkins
Financial Aid: Martha Harbaugh
Type: Comprehensive **Sex:** Coed **Scores:** 41% ACT 18-23; 51% ACT 24-29 **% Accepted:** 66 **Admission Plans:** Deferred Admission **Application Deadline:** August 15 **Application Fee:** $30.00 **H.S. Requirements:** High school diploma required; GED accepted **Costs Per Year:** Application fee: $30. Comprehensive fee: $29,204 includes full-time tuition ($20,384), mandatory fees ($610), and college room and board ($8210). Full-time tuition and fees vary according to course load. Room and board charges vary according to housing facility. Part-time tuition: $612 per credit hour. Part-time mandatory fees: $152.50 per term. Part-time tuition and fees vary according to class time. **Scholarships:** Available **Calendar System:** Semester, Summer Session Available **Enrollment:** FT 1,669, PT 1,265, Grad FT 134, Grad PT 466 **Faculty:** FT 111, PT 282 **Student-Faculty Ratio:** 12:1 **Exams:** SAT I or ACT. **% Receiving Financial Aid:** 78 **% Residing in College-Owned, -Operated, or -Affiliated Housing:** 21 **Final Year or Final Semester Residency Requirement:** No **Library Holdings:** 158,930 **Regional Accreditation:** North Central Association of Colleges and Schools **Credit Hours For Degree:** 128 credit hours, Bachelors **ROTC:** Army **Professional Accreditation:** AACN, AOTA, APTA, ACBSP, FIDER, CORE, NASAD, NASM, NCATE, NLN **Intercollegiate Athletics:** Baseball M; Basketball M & W; Cross-Country Running M & W; Golf M & W; Soccer M & W; Softball W; Tennis M & W; Track and Field M & W; Volleyball W

MESSENGER COLLEGE
300 East 50th St.
Joplin, MO 64804
Tel: (417)624-7070
Fax: (417)624-5070
E-mail: info@messengercollege.edu
Web Site: http://www.messengercollege.edu/
President/CEO: Charles Scott
Admissions: Ron Cannon
Financial Aid: Susan Aleckson
Type: Four-Year College **Sex:** Coed **Affiliation:** Pentecostal **Scores:** 36% ACT 18-23; 21% ACT 24-29 **% Accepted:** 77 **Application Deadline:** August 14 **Application Fee:** $35.00 **H.S. Requirements:** High school diploma required; GED accepted **Scholarships:** Available **Calendar System:** Semester, Summer Session Not available **Enrollment:** FT 58, PT 12 **Faculty:** FT 6, PT 8 **Exams:** SAT I or ACT. **% Receiving Financial Aid:** 75 **Library Holdings:** 36,278 **Credit Hours For Degree:** 64 credits, Associates; 128 credits, Bachelors **Professional Accreditation:** TACCS

METRO BUSINESS COLLEGE (CAPE GIRARDEAU)
1732 North Kingshighway
Cape Girardeau, MO 63701
Tel: (573)334-9181
Fax: (573)334-0617
Web Site: http://www.metrobusinesscollege.edu/
President/CEO: George Holske
Admissions: Kyla Evans
Type: Two-Year College **Sex:** Coed **Application Fee:** $25.00 **Scholarships:** Available **Calendar System:** Quarter **Professional Accreditation:** ACICS

METRO BUSINESS COLLEGE (JEFFERSON CITY)
1407 Southwest Blvd.
Jefferson City, MO 65109
Tel: (573)635-6600; Free: 800-467-0786
Fax: (573)635-6999
E-mail: cheri@metrobusinesscollege.edu
Web Site: http://www.metrobusinesscollege.edu/
Admissions: Cheri Chockley
Type: Two-Year College **Sex:** Coed **% Accepted:** 75 **Application Deadline:** Rolling **Application Fee:** $25.00 **Costs Per Year:** Application fee: $25. Tuition: $9375 full-time. Mandatory fees: $125 full-time. Full-time tuition and fees vary according to class time, course load, location, and program. Tuition guaranteed not to increase for student's term of enrollment. **Calendar System:** Quarter **Enrollment:** FT 140, PT 15 **Faculty:** FT 8, PT 3 **Student-Faculty Ratio:** 14:1 **Exams:** Other. **Professional Accreditation:** ACICS

METRO BUSINESS COLLEGE (ROLLA)
1202 East Hwy. 72
Rolla, MO 65401
Tel: (573)364-8464; Free: 888-43-METRO
Fax: (573)364-8077
E-mail: inforolla@metrobusinesscollege.edu
Web Site: http://www.metrobusinesscollege.edu/
Type: Two-Year College **Sex:** Coed **Application Fee:** $25.00 **Calendar System:** Quarter **Professional Accreditation:** ACICS

METROPOLITAN COMMUNITY COLLEGE—BLUE RIVER
20301 East 78 Hwy.
Independence, MO 64015
Tel: (816)220-6500
Admissions: (816)604-6118
Fax: (816)655-6014
Web Site: http://www.mcckc.edu/
President/CEO: Dr. Joseph Seabrooks
Admissions: Dr. Jon Burke
Type: Two-Year College **Sex:** Coed **Affiliation:** Metropolitan Community Colleges System **% Accepted:** 100 **Admission Plans:** Open Admission; Early Admission; Deferred Admission **Application Deadline:** Rolling **Application Fee:** $0.00 **H.S. Requirements:** High school diploma required; GED accepted **Costs Per Year:** Application fee: $0. Area resident tuition: $2310 full-time, $77 per credit hour part-time. State resident tuition: $4230 full-time, $141 per credit hour part-time. Nonresident tuition: $5700 full-time, $190 per credit hour part-time. Mandatory fees: $150 full-time, $5 per credit hour part-time. **Scholarships:** Available **Calendar System:** Semester **Enrollment:** FT 1,481, PT 1,650 **Faculty:** FT 41, PT 349 **Student-Faculty Ratio:** 13:1 **Library Holdings:** 10,312 **Regional Accreditation:** North Central Association of Colleges and Schools **Credit Hours For Degree:** 62 credit hours, Associates **Intercollegiate Athletics:** Soccer M & W

METROPOLITAN COMMUNITY COLLEGE—BUSINESS & TECHNOLOGY CAMPUS
1775 Universal Ave.
Kansas City, MO 64120
Tel: (816)482-5210; Free: 800-841-7158
Admissions: (816)604-1090
Web Site: http://www.mcckc.edu/
President/CEO: Debbie Goodall
Admissions: Tom Wheeler
Type: Two-Year College **Sex:** Coed **Affiliation:** Metropolitan Community Colleges System **% Accepted:** 100 **Application Deadline:** Rolling **H.S. Requirements:** High school diploma required; GED accepted **Costs Per Year:** Area resident tuition: $2310 full-time. State resident tuition: $4230 full-time. Nonresident tuition: $5700 full-time. Mandatory fees: $150 full-time.

Calendar System: Semester **Enrollment:** FT 232, PT 475 **Faculty:** FT 13, PT 133 **Student-Faculty Ratio:** 7:1 **Regional Accreditation:** North Central Association of Colleges and Schools

METROPOLITAN COMMUNITY COLLEGE—LONGVIEW
500 Southwest Longview Rd.
Lee's Summit, MO 64081-2105
Tel: (816)604-2000
Admissions: (816)604-2249
E-mail: janet.cline@mcckc.edu
Web Site: http://www.mcckc.edu/
President/CEO: Fred Grogan
Admissions: Janet Cline
Type: Two-Year College **Sex:** Coed **Affiliation:** Metropolitan Community Colleges System **% Accepted:** 100 **Admission Plans:** Open Admission; Early Admission; Deferred Admission **Application Deadline:** Rolling **Application Fee:** $0.00 **H.S. Requirements:** High school diploma required; GED accepted **Costs Per Year:** Application fee: $0. Area resident tuition: $2310 full-time, $77 per credit hour part-time. State resident tuition: $4230 full-time, $141 per credit hour part-time. Nonresident tuition: $5700 full-time, $190 per credit hour part-time. Mandatory fees: $150 full-time, $5 per credit hour part-time. **Scholarships:** Available **Calendar System:** Semester **Enrollment:** FT 2,917, PT 3,375 **Faculty:** FT 85, PT 350 **Student-Faculty Ratio:** 21:1 **Library Holdings:** 56,266 **Regional Accreditation:** North Central Association of Colleges and Schools **Credit Hours For Degree:** 62 credit hours, Associates **Intercollegiate Athletics:** Baseball M; Cross-Country Running W; Volleyball W

METROPOLITAN COMMUNITY COLLEGE—MAPLE WOODS
2601 Northeast Barry Rd.
Kansas City, MO 64156-1299
Tel: (816)437-3000
Admissions: (816)604-3175
Web Site: http://www.mcckc.edu/
President/CEO: Merna Saliman
Admissions: Shelli Allen
Type: Two-Year College **Sex:** Coed **Affiliation:** Metropolitan Community Colleges System **% Accepted:** 100 **Admission Plans:** Open Admission; Early Admission; Deferred Admission **Application Deadline:** Rolling **Application Fee:** $0.00 **H.S. Requirements:** High school diploma required; GED accepted **Costs Per Year:** Application fee: $0. Area resident tuition: $2310 full-time, $77 per credit hour part-time. State resident tuition: $4230 full-time, $141 per credit hour part-time. Nonresident tuition: $5700 full-time, $190 per credit hour part-time. Mandatory fees: $150 full-time, $5 per credit hour part-time. **Scholarships:** Available **Calendar System:** Semester, Summer Session Available **Enrollment:** FT 2,138, PT 2,742 **Faculty:** FT 52, PT 271 **Student-Faculty Ratio:** 19:1 **Library Holdings:** 32,906 **Regional Accreditation:** North Central Association of Colleges and Schools **Credit Hours For Degree:** 62 credit hours, Associates **Intercollegiate Athletics:** Baseball M; Soccer M & W; Softball W

METROPOLITAN COMMUNITY COLLEGE—PENN VALLEY
3201 Southwest Trafficway
Kansas City, MO 64111
Tel: (816)759-4000
Admissions: (816)604-4101
Web Site: http://www.mcckc.edu/
President/CEO: Dr. Bernard Franklin
Admissions: Lisa Minis
Type: Two-Year College **Sex:** Coed **Affiliation:** Metropolitan Community Colleges System **% Accepted:** 100 **Admission Plans:** Open Admission; Early Admission **Application Deadline:** Rolling **Application Fee:** $0.00 **H.S. Requirements:** High school diploma required; GED accepted **Costs Per Year:** Application fee: $0. Area resident tuition: $2310 full-time, $77 per credit hour part-time. State resident tuition: $4230 full-time, $141 per credit hour part-time. Nonresident tuition: $5700 full-time, $190 per credit hour part-time. Mandatory fees: $150 full-time, $5 per credit hour part-time. **Scholarships:** Available **Calendar System:** Semester **Enrollment:** FT 1,541, PT 3,115 **Faculty:** FT 103, PT 329 **Student-Faculty Ratio:** 12:1 **Library Holdings:** 91,428 **Regional Accreditation:** North Central Association of Colleges and Schools **Credit Hours For Degree:** 62 credit hours, Associates **Professional Accreditation:** ADA, AHIMA, AOTA, APTA, JRCERT, NLN **Intercollegiate Athletics:** Basketball M & W

MIDWEST INSTITUTE (EARTH CITY)
4260 Shoreline Dr.
Earth City, MO 63045
Tel: (314)344-4440
Fax: (314)344-0495
Web Site: http://www.midwestinstitute.com/
Type: Two-Year College **Sex:** Coed **Professional Accreditation:** ABHES

MIDWEST INSTITUTE (KIRKWOOD)
10910 Manchester Rd.
Kirkwood, MO 63122
Tel: (314)965-8363
Fax: (314)965-1558
Web Site: http://www.midwestinstitute.com/
President/CEO: Christine Shreffler
Type: Two-Year College **Sex:** Coed **% Accepted:** 99

MIDWEST UNIVERSITY
PO Box 365, 851 Parr Rd.
Wentzville, MO 63385
Tel: (636)327-4645
Fax: (636)327-4715
E-mail: usa@midwest.edu
Web Site: http://www.midwest.edu/
President/CEO: James Song, PhD
Admissions: Jeoung H. Ham
Type: University **Sex:** Coed **Affiliation:** interdenominational **Application Fee:** $100.00 **Costs Per Year:** Application fee: $100. **Calendar System:** Semester **Student-Faculty Ratio:** 24:1 **Professional Accreditation:** TACCS

MINERAL AREA COLLEGE
PO Box 1000
Park Hills, MO 63601-1000
Tel: (573)431-4593
E-mail: lhuffman@mineralarea.edu
Web Site: http://www.mineralarea.edu/
President/CEO: Dr. Steven Kurtz
Admissions: Linda Huffman
Type: Two-Year College **Sex:** Coed **Affiliation:** Missouri Coordinating Board for Higher Education **Admission Plans:** Open Admission; Early Admission **Application Deadline:** Rolling **Application Fee:** $15.00 **H.S. Requirements:** High school diploma or equivalent not required. For allied health programs, law enforcement programs: High school diploma required; GED accepted **Scholarships:** Available **Calendar System:** Semester, Summer Session Available **Library Holdings:** 32,228 **Regional Accreditation:** North Central Association of Colleges and Schools **Credit Hours For Degree:** 62 credit hours, Associates **Intercollegiate Athletics:** Baseball M; Basketball M & W; Volleyball W

MISSOURI BAPTIST UNIVERSITY
One College Park Dr.
St. Louis, MO 63141-8660
Tel: (314)434-1115; Free: 877-434-1115
Fax: (314)434-7596
E-mail: admissions@mobap.edu
Web Site: http://www.mobap.edu/
President/CEO: R. Alton Lacey
Admissions: Terry Dale Cruse
Financial Aid: Laurie Wallace
Type: Comprehensive **Sex:** Coed **Affiliation:** Southern Baptist **% Accepted:** 59 **Application Deadline:** Rolling **Application Fee:** $30.00 **H.S. Requirements:** High school diploma required; GED accepted **Costs Per Year:** Application fee: $30. Comprehensive fee: $24,950 includes full-time tuition ($16,980), mandatory fees ($880), and college room and board ($7090). Full-time tuition and fees vary according to course load, degree level, and location. Room and board charges vary according to housing facility. Part-time tuition: $590 per credit hour. Part-time mandatory fees: $14 per credit hour, $30 per term. Part-time tuition and fees vary according to course load, degree level, and location. **Scholarships:** Available **Calendar System:** Semester, Summer Session Available **Enrollment:** FT 1,291, PT 2,122, Grad FT 436, Grad PT 987 **Faculty:** FT 70, PT 176 **Student-Faculty Ratio:** 18:1 **Exams:** SAT I or ACT. **% Receiving Financial Aid:** 88 **% Residing in College-Owned, -Operated, or -Affiliated Housing:** 14 **Library**

Holdings: 63,626 **Regional Accreditation:** North Central Association of Colleges and Schools **Credit Hours For Degree:** 64 credit hours, Associates; 128 credit hours, Bachelors **ROTC:** Army **Professional Accreditation:** NASM **Intercollegiate Athletics:** Baseball M; Basketball M & W; Bowling M & W; Cross-Country Running M & W; Golf M & W; Lacrosse M & W; Soccer M & W; Softball W; Tennis M & W; Track and Field M & W; Volleyball M & W; Wrestling M

MISSOURI COLLEGE
10121 Manchester Rd.
St. Louis, MO 63122-1583
Tel: (314)821-7700
Admissions: (314)768-7800
Web Site: http://www.mocollege.com/
President/CEO: Karl Petersen
Admissions: Doug Brinker
Type: Two-Year College **Sex:** Coed **Admission Plans:** Open Admission **Application Deadline:** Rolling **Application Fee:** $35.00 **H.S. Requirements:** High school diploma required; GED accepted **Scholarships:** Available **Professional Accreditation:** ACCSCT, ADA

MISSOURI SOUTHERN STATE UNIVERSITY
3950 East Newman Rd.
Joplin, MO 64801-1595
Tel: (417)625-9300; Free: (866)818-MSSU
Admissions: (417)625-9537
Fax: (417)659-4429
E-mail: admissions@mssu.edu
Web Site: http://www.mssu.edu/
President/CEO: Dr. Bruce Speck
Admissions: Derek Skaggs
Financial Aid: Kathy Feith
Type: Comprehensive **Sex:** Coed **Scores:** 54.6% ACT 18-23; 25.1% ACT 24-29 **% Accepted:** 95 **Admission Plans:** Deferred Admission **Application Deadline:** August 1 **Application Fee:** $15.00 **H.S. Requirements:** High school diploma required; GED accepted **Costs Per Year:** Application fee: $15. State resident tuition: $4290 full-time, $143 per credit hour part-time. Nonresident tuition: $8580 full-time, $286 per credit hour part-time. Full-time tuition varies according to course load. College room and board: $5500. Room and board charges vary according to board plan and housing facility. **Scholarships:** Available **Calendar System:** Semester, Summer Session Available **Enrollment:** FT 4,110, PT 1,529, Grad FT 5, Grad PT 57 **Faculty:** FT 208, PT 87 **Student-Faculty Ratio:** 19:1 **Exams:** ACT, Other, SAT I or ACT, SAT I and SAT II or ACT. ACT essay used for admission. ACT essay used for advising. ACT essay used for placement. ACT essay not being used. **% Receiving Financial Aid:** 74 **% Residing in College-Owned, -Operated, or -Affiliated Housing:** 30 **Regional Accreditation:** North Central Association of Colleges and Schools **Credit Hours For Degree:** 64 credits, Associates; 124 credits, Bachelors **Professional Accreditation:** ABET, ADA, ACBSP, CARC, JRCERT, NCATE, NLN **Intercollegiate Athletics:** Baseball M; Basketball M & W; Cross-Country Running M & W; Football M; Golf M; Soccer M & W; Softball W; Tennis W; Track and Field M & W; Volleyball W

MISSOURI STATE UNIVERSITY
901 South National
Springfield, MO 65897
Tel: (417)836-5000; Free: 800-492-7900
Admissions: (417)836-5517
Fax: (417)836-6334
E-mail: info@missouristate.edu
Web Site: http://www.missouristate.edu/
President/CEO: Dr. Michael T. Nietzel
Admissions: Jill Duncan
Financial Aid: Vicki Mattocks
Type: Comprehensive **Sex:** Coed **Scores:** 47.84% ACT 18-23; 39.91% ACT 24-29 **% Accepted:** 83 **Admission Plans:** Deferred Admission **Application Deadline:** July 20 **Application Fee:** $35.00 **H.S. Requirements:** High school diploma required; GED accepted **Costs Per Year:** Application fee: $35. State resident tuition: $6276 full-time, $186 per credit hour part-time. Nonresident tuition: $11,556 full-time, $362 per credit hour part-time. Mandatory fees: $696 full-time. Full-time tuition and fees vary according to course level, location, and program. Part-time tuition varies according to course level, course load, location, and program. College room and board: $5925. Room and board charges vary according to board plan and housing facility. **Scholarships:** Available **Calendar System:** Semester, Summer Session Available **Enrollment:** FT 13,319, PT 3,705, Grad FT 1,560, Grad PT 1,787 **Faculty:** FT 721, PT 306 **Student-Faculty Ratio:** 21:1 **Exams:** SAT I or ACT. **% Receiving Financial Aid:** 60 **% Residing in College-Owned, -Operated, or -Affiliated Housing:** 26 **Final Year or Final Semester Residency Requirement:** No **Library Holdings:** 1,830,434 **Regional Accreditation:** North Central Association of Colleges and Schools **Credit Hours For Degree:** 125 credit hours, Bachelors **ROTC:** Army **Professional Accreditation:** AACSB, ABET, AACN, AAFCS, AANA, ACSP, APTA, ASLHA, CSWE, JRCEPAT, NASM, NASPAA, NAST, NCATE, NLN, NRPA, NAIT **Intercollegiate Athletics:** Baseball M; Basketball M & W; Bowling M & W; Cross-Country Running W; Equestrian Sports M & W; Field Hockey W; Football M; Golf M & W; Ice Hockey M; Lacrosse M; Racquetball M & W; Soccer M & W; Softball W; Swimming and Diving M & W; Track and Field W; Ultimate Frisbee M & W; Volleyball M & W; Wrestling M

MISSOURI STATE UNIVERSITY—WEST PLAINS
128 Garfield
West Plains, MO 65775
Tel: (417)255-7255
Admissions: (417)255-7955
E-mail: melissajett@missouristate.edu
Web Site: http://wp.missouristate.edu/
President/CEO: Dr. Drew A Bennett
Admissions: Melissa Jett
Type: Two-Year College **Sex:** Coed **Affiliation:** Missouri State University **Scores:** 45% ACT 18-23; 15% ACT 24-29 **% Accepted:** 100 **Admission Plans:** Open Admission **Application Deadline:** August 20 **Application Fee:** $15.00 **H.S. Requirements:** High school diploma required; GED accepted **Costs Per Year:** Application fee: $15. State resident tuition: $102 per credit hour part-time. Nonresident tuition: $204 per credit hour part-time. Part-time tuition varies according to course load and location. **Scholarships:** Available **Calendar System:** Semester, Summer Session Available **Enrollment:** FT 1,260, PT 902 **Faculty:** FT 33, PT 78 **Student-Faculty Ratio:** 26:1 **% Residing in College-Owned, -Operated, or -Affiliated Housing:** 6 **Final Year or Final Semester Residency Requirement:** No **Library Holdings:** 50,717 **Regional Accreditation:** North Central Association of Colleges and Schools **Credit Hours For Degree:** 62 credit hours, Associates **Intercollegiate Athletics:** Basketball M; Volleyball W

MISSOURI TECH
1167 Corporate Lake Dr.
St. Louis, MO 63132-1716
Tel: (314)569-3600
Fax: (314)569-1167
Web Site: http://www.motech.edu/
President/CEO: Paul Dodge
Admissions: Bob Honaker
Type: Four-Year College **Sex:** Coed **Application Deadline:** Rolling **H.S. Requirements:** High school diploma required; GED accepted **Scholarships:** Available **Calendar System:** Semester, Summer Session Available **Exams:** ACT. **Credit Hours For Degree:** 94 credit hours, Associates; 172 credit hours, Bachelors **Professional Accreditation:** ACCSCT

MISSOURI UNIVERSITY OF SCIENCE AND TECHNOLOGY
1870 Miner Circle
Rolla, MO 65409
Tel: (573)341-4111; Free: 800-522-0938
Admissions: (573)341-4165
E-mail: admissions@mst.edu
Web Site: http://www.mst.edu/
President/CEO: Dr. John F. Carney
Financial Aid: Lynn K. Stichnote
Type: University **Sex:** Coed **Affiliation:** University of Missouri System **Scores:** 100% SAT V 400+; 100.01% SAT M 400+; 12.83% ACT 18-23; 51.59% ACT 24-29 **% Accepted:** 93 **Admission Plans:** Early Admission; Deferred Admission **Application Deadline:** July 1 **Application Fee:** $45.00 **H.S. Requirements:** High school diploma required; GED accepted **Costs Per Year:** Application fee: $45. State resident tuition: $7368 full-time, $246 per credit hour part-time. Nonresident tuition: $18,459 full-time, $615 per credit hour part-time. Mandatory fees: $1120 full-time, $120.52 per credit hour part-time. Full-time tuition and fees vary according to course load, degree level, and program. Part-time tuition and fees vary according to

course load, degree level, and program. College room and board: $7595. College room only: $4670. Room and board charges vary according to board plan, housing facility, and location. **Scholarships:** Available **Calendar System:** Semester, Summer Session Available **Enrollment:** FT 4,885, PT 321, Grad FT 975, Grad PT 634 **Faculty:** FT 360, PT 96 **Student-Faculty Ratio:** 16:1 **Exams:** ACT, SAT I or ACT. ACT essay not being used. SAT essay not being used. **% Receiving Financial Aid:** 76 **% Residing in College-Owned, -Operated, or -Affiliated Housing:** 51 **Final Year or Final Semester Residency Requirement:** Yes **Library Holdings:** 477,201 **Regional Accreditation:** North Central Association of Colleges and Schools **Credit Hours For Degree:** 120 credit hours, Bachelors **ROTC:** Army, Navy, Air Force **Professional Accreditation:** ABET **Intercollegiate Athletics:** Baseball M; Basketball M & W; Cross-Country Running M & W; Football M; Soccer M & W; Softball W; Swimming and Diving M; Track and Field M & W; Volleyball W

MISSOURI VALLEY COLLEGE
500 East College
Marshall, MO 65340-3197
Tel: (660)831-4000
Admissions: (660)831-4125
Fax: (660)831-4039
E-mail: admissions@moval.edu
Web Site: http://www.moval.edu/
President/CEO: Dr. Bonnie Humphrey
Admissions: Debi Bultmann
Financial Aid: Charles Richard Mayfield, Jr.
Type: Four-Year College **Sex:** Coed **Affiliation:** Presbyterian Church **Scores:** 71% SAT V 400+; 59% ACT 18-23; 8% ACT 24-29 **% Accepted:** 57 **Admission Plans:** Early Admission; Deferred Admission **Application Deadline:** Rolling **Application Fee:** $15.00 **H.S. Requirements:** High school diploma required; GED accepted **Scholarships:** Available **Calendar System:** Semester, Summer Session Available **Enrollment:** FT 1,394, PT 245 **Faculty:** FT 59, PT 31 **Student-Faculty Ratio:** 18:1 **Exams:** SAT I or ACT. **% Receiving Financial Aid:** 72 **% Residing in College-Owned, -Operated, or -Affiliated Housing:** 73 **Library Holdings:** 71,203 **Regional Accreditation:** North Central Association of Colleges and Schools **Credit Hours For Degree:** 64 credit hours, Associates; 128 credit hours, Bachelors **ROTC:** Army **Intercollegiate Athletics:** Baseball M; Basketball M & W; Cheerleading M & W; Cross-Country Running M & W; Football M; Golf M & W; Soccer M & W; Softball W; Tennis M & W; Track and Field M & W; Volleyball M & W; Wrestling M & W

MISSOURI WESTERN STATE UNIVERSITY
4525 Downs Dr.
St. Joseph, MO 64507-2294
Tel: (816)271-4200; Free: 800-662-7041
Admissions: (816)271-4267
Fax: (816)271-5833
E-mail: admission@missouriwestern.edu
Web Site: http://www.missouriwestern.edu/
President/CEO: Dr. Robert Vartabedian
Admissions: Howard McCauley
Financial Aid: Angela Beam
Type: Comprehensive **Sex:** Coed **Scores:** 47% ACT 18-23; 21% ACT 24-29 **% Accepted:** 100 **Admission Plans:** Open Admission; Early Admission **Application Deadline:** May 1 **Application Fee:** $15.00 **H.S. Requirements:** High school diploma required; GED accepted **Costs Per Year:** Application fee: $15. State resident tuition: $4992 full-time, $166.40 per credit hour part-time. Nonresident tuition: $9120 full-time, $304 per credit hour part-time. Mandatory fees: $568 full-time, $19.10 per credit hour part-time, $30 per term part-time. College room and board: $6600. Room and board charges vary according to board plan and housing facility. **Scholarships:** Available **Calendar System:** Semester, Summer Session Available **Enrollment:** FT 4,072, PT 1,562, Grad FT 16, Grad PT 53 **Faculty:** FT 192, PT 156 **Student-Faculty Ratio:** 19:1 **% Receiving Financial Aid:** 67 **% Residing in College-Owned, -Operated, or -Affiliated Housing:** 28 **Library Holdings:** 147,509 **Regional Accreditation:** North Central Association of Colleges and Schools **Credit Hours For Degree:** 62 credit hours, Associates; 124 credit hours, Bachelors **ROTC:** Army **Professional Accreditation:** ABET, AACN, AHIMA, APTA, CSWE, NASM, NCATE, NLN **Intercollegiate Athletics:** Baseball M; Basketball M & W; Football M; Golf M & W; Soccer W; Softball W; Tennis W; Volleyball W

MOBERLY AREA COMMUNITY COLLEGE
101 College Ave.
Moberly, MO 65270-1304
Tel: (660)263-4110; Free: 800-622-2070
Fax: (660)263-6252
E-mail: info@macc.edu
Web Site: http://www.macc.edu/
President/CEO: Evelyn Jorgenson
Admissions: Dr. James Grant
Type: Two-Year College **Sex:** Coed **Scores:** 58% ACT 18-23; 14% ACT 24-29 **Admission Plans:** Open Admission **Application Deadline:** Rolling **Application Fee:** $0.00 **H.S. Requirements:** High school diploma required; GED accepted **Scholarships:** Available **Calendar System:** Semester, Summer Session Available **Enrollment:** FT 2,023, PT 1,986 **Faculty:** FT 67, PT 166 **Student-Faculty Ratio:** 21:1 **Exams:** ACT, Other. **% Residing in College-Owned, -Operated, or -Affiliated Housing:** 1 **Library Holdings:** 23,027 **Regional Accreditation:** North Central Association of Colleges and Schools **Credit Hours For Degree:** 64 credit hours, Associates **Professional Accreditation:** NAIT **Intercollegiate Athletics:** Basketball M & W; Cheerleading M & W

NATIONAL AMERICAN UNIVERSITY
7490 Northwest 87th St.
Kansas City, MO 64153
Tel: (816)412-5500
Admissions: (816)412-7700
E-mail: zradmissions@national.edu
Web Site: http://www.national.edu/
President/CEO: Dr. Jerry Gallentine
Financial Aid: Mary Anderson
Type: Four-Year College **Sex:** Coed **Affiliation:** National College **Admission Plans:** Open Admission; Early Admission; Deferred Admission **Application Deadline:** Rolling **Application Fee:** $25.00 **H.S. Requirements:** High school diploma required; GED accepted **Scholarships:** Available **Calendar System:** Quarter, Summer Session Available **Library Holdings:** 1,500 **Regional Accreditation:** North Central Association of Colleges and Schools **Credit Hours For Degree:** 98 credits, Associates; 194 credits, Bachelors

NORTH CENTRAL MISSOURI COLLEGE
1301 Main St.
Trenton, MO 64683-1824
Tel: (660)359-3948; Free: 800-880-6180
E-mail: megoodin@mail.ncmissouri.edu
Web Site: http://www.ncmissouri.edu/
President/CEO: Dr. Neil Nuttall
Admissions: Megan Goodin
Type: Two-Year College **Sex:** Coed **% Accepted:** 88 **Admission Plans:** Open Admission **Application Deadline:** Rolling **Application Fee:** $15.00 **H.S. Requirements:** High school diploma required; GED accepted **Costs Per Year:** Application fee: $15. Area resident tuition: $1950 full-time. State resident tuition: $2910 full-time. Nonresident tuition: $4050 full-time. Mandatory fees: $600 full-time. Full-time tuition and fees vary according to course load and location. College room and board: $4796. Room and board charges vary according to board plan. **Scholarships:** Available **Calendar System:** Semester, Summer Session Available **Enrollment:** FT 796, PT 709 **Faculty:** FT 33, PT 61 **Student-Faculty Ratio:** 16:1 **Exams:** Other, SAT I or ACT. **Library Holdings:** 34,748 **Regional Accreditation:** North Central Association of Colleges and Schools **Credit Hours For Degree:** 60 credit hours, Associates **Intercollegiate Athletics:** Baseball M; Basketball M & W; Softball W

NORTHWEST MISSOURI STATE UNIVERSITY
800 University Dr.
Maryville, MO 64468-6001
Tel: (660)562-1212; Free: 800-633-1175
Admissions: (660)562-1146
Fax: (660)562-1121
E-mail: admissions@nwmissouri.edu
Web Site: http://www.nwmissouri.edu/
President/CEO: Dr. John Jasinski
Admissions: Tammi Grow
Financial Aid: Del Morley
Type: Comprehensive **Sex:** Coed **Affiliation:** Missouri Coordinating Board

for Higher Education **Scores:** 86.21% SAT V 400+; 96.55% SAT M 400+ **% Accepted:** 70 **Admission Plans:** Preferred Admission; Deferred Admission **Application Deadline:** Rolling **Application Fee:** $25.00 **H.S. Requirements:** High school diploma required; GED accepted **Costs Per Year:** Application fee: $25. One-time mandatory fee: $100. State resident tuition: $7032 full-time, $235 per credit hour part-time. Nonresident tuition: $11,753 full-time, $392 per credit hour part-time. Full-time tuition varies according to course load and reciprocity agreements. Part-time tuition varies according to course load. College room and board: $7408. College room only: $4584. Room and board charges vary according to board plan and housing facility. **Scholarships:** Available **Calendar System:** Trimester, Summer Session Available **Enrollment:** FT 5,467, PT 584, Grad FT 326, Grad PT 699 **Faculty:** FT 256, PT 78 **Student-Faculty Ratio:** 21:1 **Exams:** SAT I or ACT. ACT essay not being used. SAT essay not being used. **% Receiving Financial Aid:** 62 **% Residing in College-Owned, -Operated, or -Affiliated Housing:** 40 **Final Year or Final Semester Residency Requirement:** No **Library Holdings:** 386,196 **Regional Accreditation:** North Central Association of Colleges and Schools **Credit Hours For Degree:** 124 semester hours, Bachelors **ROTC:** Army **Professional Accreditation:** AAFCS, ACBSP, NASM, NCATE **Intercollegiate Athletics:** Baseball M; Basketball M & W; Cheerleading M & W; Cross-Country Running M & W; Football M; Golf W; Soccer W; Softball W; Tennis M & W; Track and Field M & W; Volleyball W

OZARK CHRISTIAN COLLEGE
1111 North Main St.
Joplin, MO 64801-4804
Tel: (417)624-2518; Free: 800-299-4622
Fax: (417)624-0090
E-mail: occadmin@occ.edu
Web Site: http://www.occ.edu/
President/CEO: Matt Proctor
Admissions: Troy B. Nelson
Financial Aid: Jill Kaminsky
Type: Four-Year College **Sex:** Coed **Affiliation:** Christian **Application Deadline:** August 5 **Application Fee:** $30.00 **H.S. Requirements:** High school diploma required; GED accepted **Scholarships:** Available **Calendar System:** Semester, Summer Session Available **Faculty:** FT 30, PT 30 **Student-Faculty Ratio:** 19:1 **Exams:** SAT I or ACT. **% Residing in College-Owned, -Operated, or -Affiliated Housing:** 63 **Library Holdings:** 59,808 **Credit Hours For Degree:** 96 credits, Associates; 128 credits, Bachelors **Professional Accreditation:** ABHE **Intercollegiate Athletics:** Basketball M & W; Cheerleading M & W; Soccer M; Volleyball W

OZARKS TECHNICAL COMMUNITY COLLEGE
PO Box 5958
1001 East Chestnut Expressway
Springfield, MO 65801
Tel: (417)447-7500
Fax: (417)895-7161
Web Site: http://www.otc.edu/
President/CEO: Hal Higdon
Admissions: Jeff Jochems
Type: Two-Year College **Sex:** Coed **Affiliation:** Missouri Coordinating Board for Higher Education **Admission Plans:** Open Admission; Early Admission **Application Fee:** $0.00 **H.S. Requirements:** High school diploma required; GED accepted **Scholarships:** Available **Calendar System:** Semester, Summer Session Available **Enrollment:** FT 4,232, PT 4,256 **Faculty:** FT 127, PT 266 **Library Holdings:** 6,000 **Regional Accreditation:** North Central Association of Colleges and Schools **Credit Hours For Degree:** 62 credit hours, Associates **Professional Accreditation:** ADA, AHIMA, AOTA, APTA, CARC, NAIT

PARK UNIVERSITY
8700 Northwest River Park Dr.
Parkville, MO 64152-3795
Tel: (816)741-2000; Free: 800-745-7275
Admissions: (816)584-6728
Fax: (816)741-4462
E-mail: admissions@mail.park.edu
Web Site: http://www.park.edu/
President/CEO: Dr. Beverley Byers-Pevitts
Admissions: Cathy Colapietro
Financial Aid: Carla Boren
Type: Comprehensive **Sex:** Coed **Scores:** 48% ACT 18-23; 40% ACT 24-29 **% Accepted:** 70 **Admission Plans:** Early Admission; Deferred Admission **Application Deadline:** August 1 **Application Fee:** $25.00 **H.S. Requirements:** High school diploma required; GED accepted **Costs Per Year:** Application fee: $25. Comprehensive fee: $16,478 includes full-time tuition ($8848), mandatory fees ($50), and college room and board ($7580). **Scholarships:** Available **Calendar System:** Semester, Summer Session Available **Enrollment:** FT 1,321, PT 10,740, Grad FT 15, Grad PT 699 **Student-Faculty Ratio:** 12:1 **Exams:** SAT I or ACT. **% Residing in College-Owned, -Operated, or -Affiliated Housing:** 1 **Library Holdings:** 150,503 **Regional Accreditation:** North Central Association of Colleges and Schools **Credit Hours For Degree:** 60 credit hours, Associates; 120 credit hours, Bachelors **ROTC:** Army **Professional Accreditation:** JRCEPAT, NLN **Intercollegiate Athletics:** Baseball M; Basketball M & W; Cross-Country Running M & W; Golf W; Soccer M & W; Softball W; Track and Field M & W; Volleyball M & W

PATRICIA STEVENS COLLEGE
330 North Fourth St.
Ste. 306
St. Louis, MO 63102
Tel: (314)421-0949; Free: 800-871-0949
Fax: (314)421-0304
E-mail: admission@patriciastevenscollege.com
Web Site: http://www.patriciastevenscollege.edu/
President/CEO: Cynthia Musterman
Admissions: John Willmon
Type: Four-Year College **Sex:** Coed **% Accepted:** 75 **Application Deadline:** Rolling **Application Fee:** $15.00 **H.S. Requirements:** High school diploma required; GED accepted **Scholarships:** Available **Calendar System:** Quarter, Summer Session Available **Enrollment:** FT 134, PT 66 **Faculty:** FT 7, PT 15 **Student-Faculty Ratio:** 10:1 **Exams:** SAT I or ACT. **Final Year or Final Semester Residency Requirement:** No **Credit Hours For Degree:** 114 quarter hours, Associates; 197 quarter hours, Bachelors **Professional Accreditation:** ACICS

PINNACLE CAREER INSTITUTE
1001 East 101st Terrace
Ste. 325
Kansas City, MO 64131
Tel: (816)331-5700; Free: 800-614-0900
Web Site: http://www.pcitraining.edu/
President/CEO: Monte Schaich
Admissions: Ruth Matous
Type: Two-Year College **Sex:** Coed **Application Deadline:** June 1 **Application Fee:** $50.00 **Scholarships:** Available **Professional Accreditation:** ACCSCT

RANKEN TECHNICAL COLLEGE
4431 Finney Ave.
St. Louis, MO 63113
Tel: (314)371-0233; Free: (866)4RA-NKEN
Admissions: (314)371-0236
Fax: (314)371-0241
Web Site: http://www.ranken.edu/
President/CEO: Stan Shoun
Admissions: Elizabeth Keserauskis
Type: Two-Year College **Sex:** Coed **Application Deadline:** Rolling **Application Fee:** $25.00 **H.S. Requirements:** High school diploma required; GED accepted **Costs Per Year:** Application fee: $25. Comprehensive fee: $20,418 includes full-time tuition ($12,348), mandatory fees ($570), and college room and board ($7500). College room only: $5120. Full-time tuition and fees vary according to class time, course load, degree level, and program. Room and board charges vary according to board plan. Part-time tuition: $4944 per year. Part-time tuition varies according to class time, course load, and program. **Scholarships:** Available **Calendar System:** Semester, Summer Session Available **Library Holdings:** 11,000 **Regional Accreditation:** North Central Association of Colleges and Schools **Credit Hours For Degree:** 96 semester hours, Associates; 136 semester hours, Bachelors

RESEARCH COLLEGE OF NURSING
2252 East Meyer Blvd.
Kansas City, MO 64132

Tel: (816)995-2800; Free: 800-842-6776
Admissions: (816)995-2820
Fax: (816)276-3526
E-mail: leslie.mendenhall@researchcollege.edu
Web Site: http://www.researchcollege.edu/
President/CEO: Dr. Nancy O. DeBasio
Admissions: Leslie A. Mendenhall
Financial Aid: Stacie Withers
Type: Comprehensive **Sex:** Coed **Affiliation:** Rockhurst University **% Accepted:** 68 **Admission Plans:** Deferred Admission **Application Deadline:** June 30 **Application Fee:** $20.00 **H.S. Requirements:** High school diploma required; GED accepted **Costs Per Year:** Application fee: $20. One-time mandatory fee: $210. Comprehensive fee: $32,980 includes full-time tuition ($24,960), mandatory fees ($740), and college room and board ($7280). College room only: $4180. Room and board charges vary according to board plan, housing facility, and location. Part-time tuition: $832 per credit hour. Part-time tuition varies according to class time. **Scholarships:** Available **Calendar System:** Semester, Summer Session Available **Enrollment:** FT 299, PT 3 **Faculty:** FT 26, PT 3 **Student-Faculty Ratio:** 7:1 **Exams:** SAT I or ACT. **% Receiving Financial Aid:** 55 **Library Holdings:** 150,000 **Regional Accreditation:** North Central Association of Colleges and Schools **Credit Hours For Degree:** 128 credit hours, Bachelors **ROTC:** Army **Professional Accreditation:** AACN, NLN **Intercollegiate Athletics:** Baseball M; Basketball M & W; Golf M & W; Soccer M & W; Softball W; Tennis M & W; Volleyball W

ROCKHURST UNIVERSITY
1100 Rockhurst Rd.
Kansas City, MO 64110-2561
Tel: (816)501-4000; Free: 800-842-6776
Admissions: (816)501-4100
Fax: (816)501-4241
E-mail: admission@rockhurst.edu
Web Site: http://www.rockhurst.edu/
President/CEO: Thomas B. Curran, OSFS
Admissions: Lane Ramey
Financial Aid: Angela Karlin
Type: Comprehensive **Sex:** Coed **Affiliation:** Roman Catholic (Jesuit) **Scores:** 100% SAT V 400+; 100% SAT M 400+; 39% ACT 18-23; 47% ACT 24-29 **% Accepted:** 76 **Admission Plans:** Deferred Admission **Application Deadline:** June 30 **Application Fee:** $25.00 **H.S. Requirements:** High school diploma required; GED accepted **Costs Per Year:** Application fee: $25. Comprehensive fee: $32,970 includes full-time tuition ($24,950), mandatory fees ($940), and college room and board ($7080). College room only: $4180. Full-time tuition and fees vary according to class time and course load. Room and board charges vary according to board plan and housing facility. Part-time tuition: $832 per credit hour. Part-time tuition varies according to class time and course load. **Scholarships:** Available **Calendar System:** Semester, Summer Session Available **Enrollment:** FT 1,409, PT 711, Grad FT 530, Grad PT 379 **Faculty:** FT 127, PT 101 **Student-Faculty Ratio:** 10:1 **Exams:** SAT I or ACT. **% Receiving Financial Aid:** 77 **% Residing in College-Owned, -Operated, or -Affiliated Housing:** 53 **Library Holdings:** 189,527 **Regional Accreditation:** North Central Association of Colleges and Schools **Credit Hours For Degree:** 128 semester hours, Bachelors **ROTC:** Army **Professional Accreditation:** AACSB, AOTA, APTA, ASLHA, NLN, TEAC **Intercollegiate Athletics:** Baseball M; Basketball M & W; Golf M & W; Soccer M & W; Softball W; Tennis M & W; Volleyball W

SAINT CHARLES COMMUNITY COLLEGE
4601 Mid Rivers Mall Dr.
Cottleville, MO 63376
Tel: (636)922-8000
Admissions: (636)922-8229
Fax: (636)922-8236
E-mail: regist@stchas.edu
Web Site: http://www.stchas.edu/
President/CEO: Dr. John M. McGuire
Admissions: Kathy Brockgreitens-Gober
Financial Aid: Karen Vossenkemper
Type: Two-Year College **Sex:** Coed **Affiliation:** Missouri Coordinating Board for Higher Education **% Accepted:** 100 **Admission Plans:** Open Admission; Early Admission; Deferred Admission **Application Deadline:** Rolling **Application Fee:** $0.00 **H.S. Requirements:** High school diploma required; GED accepted **Costs Per Year:** Application fee: $0. Area resident tuition: $1920 full-time, $80 per credit hour part-time. State resident tuition: $2832 full-time, $118 per credit hour part-time. Nonresident tuition: $4200 full-time, $175 per credit hour part-time. **Scholarships:** Available **Calendar System:** Semester, Summer Session Available **Enrollment:** FT 4,067, PT 3,747 **Faculty:** FT 93, PT 352 **Student-Faculty Ratio:** 24:1 **Exams:** ACT essay used for placement. **Final Year or Final Semester Residency Requirement:** No **Library Holdings:** 93,332 **Regional Accreditation:** North Central Association of Colleges and Schools **Credit Hours For Degree:** 64 semester hours, Associates **Professional Accreditation:** AHIMA, AOTA, NLN **Intercollegiate Athletics:** Baseball M; Soccer M & W; Softball W

ST. LOUIS CHRISTIAN COLLEGE
1360 Grandview Dr.
Florissant, MO 63033-6499
Tel: (314)837-6777; Free: 800-887-SLCC
Fax: (314)837-8291
E-mail: cchapman@slcconline.edu
Web Site: http://www.slcconline.edu/
President/CEO: Dr. Guthrie Veech
Admissions: Carrie Chapman
Financial Aid: Catherine Wilhoit
Type: Four-Year College **Sex:** Coed **Affiliation:** Christian **Scores:** 46% ACT 18-23; 28% ACT 24-29 **% Accepted:** 43 **Admission Plans:** Early Admission **Application Deadline:** August 7 **Application Fee:** $25.00 **H.S. Requirements:** High school diploma required; GED accepted **Costs Per Year:** Application fee: $25. Comprehensive fee: $14,600 includes full-time tuition ($10,350), mandatory fees ($650), and college room and board ($3600). Room and board charges vary according to housing facility. Part-time tuition: $345 per credit hour. **Scholarships:** Available **Calendar System:** Semester, Summer Session Available **Enrollment:** FT 292, PT 44 **Faculty:** FT 12, PT 24 **Student-Faculty Ratio:** 15:1 **Exams:** ACT. **% Receiving Financial Aid:** 77 **% Residing in College-Owned, -Operated, or -Affiliated Housing:** 60 **Final Year or Final Semester Residency Requirement:** No **Library Holdings:** 39,728 **Credit Hours For Degree:** 65 credit hours, Associates; 131 credit hours, Bachelors **Professional Accreditation:** ABHE **Intercollegiate Athletics:** Baseball M; Basketball M & W; Cross-Country Running W; Ultimate Frisbee M & W; Volleyball W

ST. LOUIS COLLEGE OF HEALTH CAREERS
909 South Taylor Ave.
St. Louis, MO 63110-1511
Tel: (314)652-0300; Free: (866)529-7380
Fax: (314)652-4825
Web Site: http://www.slchc.com/
President/CEO: Dr. Rush L. Robinson, PhD
Type: Two-Year College **Sex:** Coed **Application Fee:** $35.00

ST. LOUIS COLLEGE OF PHARMACY
4588 Parkview Place
St. Louis, MO 63110-1088
Tel: (314)367-8700
Admissions: (314)446-8328
Fax: (314)367-2784
E-mail: chorrall@stlcop.edu
Web Site: http://www.stlcop.edu/
President/CEO: Dr. Thomas F. Patton
Admissions: Connie Horrall
Financial Aid: David Rice
Type: Comprehensive **Sex:** Coed **Scores:** 75% ACT 24-29 **% Accepted:** 45 **Admission Plans:** Early Decision Plan **Application Deadline:** February 1 **Application Fee:** $50.00 **H.S. Requirements:** High school diploma required; GED accepted **Costs Per Year:** Application fee: $50. Comprehensive fee: $31,570 includes full-time tuition ($22,600), mandatory fees ($410), and college room and board ($8560). College room only: $4829. Full-time tuition and fees vary according to student level. Room and board charges vary according to housing facility. Part-time tuition: $800 per credit hour. **Scholarships:** Available **Calendar System:** Semester, Summer Session Available **Enrollment:** FT 664, PT 1, Grad FT 564, Grad PT 4 **Faculty:** FT 79, PT 34 **Student-Faculty Ratio:** 20:1 **Exams:** SAT I or ACT. **% Receiving Financial Aid:** 77 **% Residing in College-Owned, -Operated, or -Affiliated Housing:** 40 **Final Year or Final Semester Residency Requirement:** Yes **Library Holdings:** 69,820 **Regional Accreditation:** North Central Association of Colleges and Schools **ROTC:** Army, Navy, Air Force

Professional Accreditation: ACPhE **Intercollegiate Athletics:** Basketball M & W; Cross-Country Running M & W; Volleyball W

ST. LOUIS COMMUNITY COLLEGE AT FLORISSANT VALLEY

3400 Pershall Rd.
St. Louis, MO 63135-1499
Tel: (314)513-4200
Fax: (314)513-2224
Web Site: http://www.stlcc.edu/
President/CEO: Marcia Pfeiffer
Admissions: Brenda Davenport

Type: Two-Year College **Sex:** Coed **Affiliation:** St. Louis Community College System **Admission Plans:** Open Admission; Early Admission **Application Deadline:** August 19 **Application Fee:** $0.00 **H.S. Requirements:** High school diploma required; GED accepted **Scholarships:** Available **Calendar System:** Semester, Summer Session Available **Library Holdings:** 90,021 **Regional Accreditation:** North Central Association of Colleges and Schools **Credit Hours For Degree:** 64 credit hours, Associates **ROTC:** Army **Professional Accreditation:** NASAD, NLN **Intercollegiate Athletics:** Baseball M; Basketball M & W; Cross-Country Running M & W; Soccer M & W; Softball W; Track and Field M & W; Volleyball W

ST. LOUIS COMMUNITY COLLEGE AT FOREST PARK

5600 Oakland Ave.
St. Louis, MO 63110-1316
Tel: (314)644-9100
Admissions: (314)644-9129
E-mail: fp_admissions@stlcc.edu
Web Site: http://www.stlcc.edu/
President/CEO: Zernie Campbell

Type: Two-Year College **Sex:** Coed **Affiliation:** St. Louis Community College System **Admission Plans:** Open Admission; Preferred Admission; Early Admission **Application Deadline:** August 22 **Application Fee:** $0.00 **H.S. Requirements:** High school diploma required; GED accepted **Costs Per Year:** Application fee: $0. Area resident tuition: $1992 full-time, $83 per credit hour part-time. State resident tuition: $2952 full-time, $123 per credit hour part-time. Nonresident tuition: $3792 full-time, $158 per credit hour part-time. **Calendar System:** Semester, Summer Session Available **Student-Faculty Ratio:** 13:1 **Regional Accreditation:** North Central Association of Colleges and Schools **Credit Hours For Degree:** 64 credit hours, Associates **Professional Accreditation:** ABFSE, ADA, CARC, JRCERT, NAACLS, NLN **Intercollegiate Athletics:** Basketball M & W; Soccer M & W; Softball W

ST. LOUIS COMMUNITY COLLEGE AT MERAMEC

11333 Big Bend Blvd.
Kirkwood, MO 63122-5720
Tel: (314)984-7500
Admissions: (314)984-7601
Fax: (314)984-7117
E-mail: mc-admissions@stlcc.edu
Web Site: http://www.stlcc.edu/
President/CEO: Paul Pai

Type: Two-Year College **Sex:** Coed **Affiliation:** St. Louis Community College System **Admission Plans:** Open Admission **Application Deadline:** Rolling **Application Fee:** $0.00 **H.S. Requirements:** High school diploma required; GED accepted **Costs Per Year:** Application fee: $0. Area resident tuition: $1992 full-time, $83 per credit hour part-time. State resident tuition: $2952 full-time, $123 per credit hour part-time. Nonresident tuition: $3792 full-time, $158 per credit hour part-time. **Scholarships:** Available **Calendar System:** Semester, Summer Session Available **Student-Faculty Ratio:** 17:1 **Regional Accreditation:** North Central Association of Colleges and Schools **Credit Hours For Degree:** 64 credit hours, Associates **ROTC:** Army, Air Force **Professional Accreditation:** AOTA, APTA, NASAD, NLN **Intercollegiate Athletics:** Baseball M; Basketball M & W; Soccer M & W; Softball W; Volleyball W; Wrestling M

SAINT LOUIS UNIVERSITY

221 North Grand Blvd.
St. Louis, MO 63103-2097
Tel: (314)977-2222; Free: 800-758-3678
Admissions: (314)977-2500
Fax: (314)977-7136
E-mail: admitme@slu.edu
Web Site: http://www.slu.edu/
President/CEO: Lawrence H. Biondi, SJ
Financial Aid: Cari S. Wickliffe

Type: University **Sex:** Coed **Affiliation:** Roman Catholic (Jesuit) **Scores:** 98.04% SAT V 400+; 99.13% SAT M 400+; 17.17% ACT 18-23; 51.01% ACT 24-29 **% Accepted:** 71 **Admission Plans:** Deferred Admission **Application Deadline:** August 1 **Application Fee:** $25.00 **H.S. Requirements:** High school diploma required; GED accepted **Costs Per Year:** Application fee: $25. Comprehensive fee: $40,242 includes full-time tuition ($30,940), mandatory fees ($402), and college room and board ($8900). College room only: $5000. Full-time tuition and fees vary according to location and program. Room and board charges vary according to board plan, housing facility, and location. Part-time tuition: $1080 per credit hour. Part-time mandatory fees: $120. Part-time tuition and fees vary according to location and program. **Scholarships:** Available **Calendar System:** Semester, Summer Session Available **Enrollment:** FT 7,307, PT 812, Grad FT 3,172, Grad PT 2,022 **Faculty:** FT 639, PT 437 **Student-Faculty Ratio:** 13:1 **Exams:** SAT I or ACT. **% Receiving Financial Aid:** 54 **% Residing in College-Owned, -Operated, or -Affiliated Housing:** 53 **Library Holdings:** 1,832,105 **Regional Accreditation:** North Central Association of Colleges and Schools **Credit Hours For Degree:** 120 credit hours, Bachelors **ROTC:** Army, Air Force **Professional Accreditation:** AACSB, ABET, AACN, ABA, ADtA, AHIMA, AOTA, APTA, APA, ASLHA, ACIPE, AALS, CAA, ACEHSA, CEPH, CSWE, JRCNMT, LCMEAMA, NAACLS, NASPAA NCATE, NLN **Intercollegiate Athletics:** Badminton M & W; Baseball M; Basketball M & W; Bowling M & W; Crew M & W; Cross-Country Running M & W; Equestrian Sports M & W; Fencing M & W; Field Hockey W; Golf M & W; Ice Hockey M; Lacrosse M & W; Racquetball M & W; Rugby M & W; Soccer M & W; Softball W; Swimming and Diving M & W; Table Tennis M & W; Tennis M & W; Track and Field M & W; Ultimate Frisbee M & W; Volleyball M & W; Water Polo M

SAINT LUKE'S COLLEGE

8320 Ward Parkway, Ste. 300
Kansas City, MO 64114
Tel: (816)932-2233
Admissions: (816)932-3372
Web Site: http://www.saintlukescollege.edu/
President/CEO: Dr. Kathryn Ballou
Financial Aid: Marcia Shaw

Type: Two-Year Upper Division **Sex:** Coed **Affiliation:** Episcopal; Saint Luke's Hospital **Admission Plans:** Early Admission; Early Decision Plan **Application Fee:** $35.00 **H.S. Requirements:** High school diploma required; GED accepted **Costs Per Year:** Application fee: $35. Tuition: $8850 full-time. Mandatory fees: $670 full-time. **Scholarships:** Available **Calendar System:** Semester, Summer Session Available **Enrollment:** FT 101, PT 12 **Faculty:** FT 15, PT 0 **Student-Faculty Ratio:** 8:1 **% Receiving Financial Aid:** 72 **Regional Accreditation:** North Central Association of Colleges and Schools **Credit Hours For Degree:** 124 credit hours, Bachelors **Professional Accreditation:** AACN **Intercollegiate Athletics:** Ultimate Frisbee M & W; Volleyball M & W

SANFORD-BROWN COLLEGE (FENTON)

1203 Smizer Mill Rd.
Fenton, MO 63026
Tel: (636)349-4900; Free: 800-456-7222
Admissions: (636)651-1600
Fax: (636)349-9170
Web Site: http://www.sanford-brown.edu/
President/CEO: Melissa Mangold
Admissions: Judy Wilga

Type: Two-Year College **Sex:** Coed **Admission Plans:** Open Admission; Deferred Admission **Application Fee:** $25.00 **H.S. Requirements:** High school diploma required; GED accepted **Scholarships:** Available **Calendar System:** Quarter **Exams:** Other. **Credit Hours For Degree:** 91 credits, Associates **Professional Accreditation:** ACICS, CARC, JRCERT

SANFORD-BROWN COLLEGE (HAZELWOOD)

75 Village Square
Hazelwood, MO 63042
Tel: (314)731-1101
Admissions: (314)687-2900
Web Site: http://www.sanford-brown.edu/
President/CEO: Phyllis Forney
Admissions: Sherri Bremer

Type: Two-Year College **Sex:** Coed **Admission Plans:** Deferred Admission **Application Deadline:** Rolling **Application Fee:** $25.00 **H.S. Requirements:** High school diploma required; GED accepted **Scholarships:** Available **Calendar System:** Quarter **Credit Hours For Degree:** 91 credits, Associates **Professional Accreditation:** ABHES, ACICS

SANFORD-BROWN COLLEGE (ST. PETERS)
100 Richmond Center Blvd.
St. Peters, MO 63376
Tel: (636)696-2300
E-mail: karl.peterson@wix.net
Web Site: http://www.sanford-brown.edu/
President/CEO: Lisa Mancini
Admissions: Karl J. Petersen
Type: Two-Year College **Sex:** Coed **Admission Plans:** Deferred Admission **Application Deadline:** Rolling **Application Fee:** $25.00 **H.S. Requirements:** High school diploma required; GED accepted **Calendar System:** Quarter, Summer Session Available **Exams:** Other. **Library Holdings:** 1,350 **Credit Hours For Degree:** 91 credits, Associates **Professional Accreditation:** ACICS

SOUTHEAST MISSOURI HOSPITAL COLLEGE OF NURSING AND HEALTH SCIENCES
2001 William St.
Cape Girardeau, MO 63701
Tel: (573)334-6825
Admissions: (534)334-6825
Fax: (573)339-7805
E-mail: tbuttry@sehosp.org
Web Site: http://www.southeastmissourihospitalcollege.edu/
President/CEO: Dr. Tonya Buttry
Admissions: Tonya L. Buttry
Type: Two-Year College **Sex:** Coed **Scores:** 75% ACT 18-23; 24% ACT 24-29 **Application Deadline:** Rolling **Application Fee:** $40.00 **Costs Per Year:** Application fee: $40. Tuition: $11,500 full-time, $300 per credit hour part-time. Full-time tuition varies according to course load and program. Part-time tuition varies according to course load and program. **Calendar System:** Miscellaneous **Enrollment:** FT 170, PT 56 **Exams:** Other, SAT I or ACT. **Regional Accreditation:** North Central Association of Colleges and Schools

SOUTHEAST MISSOURI STATE UNIVERSITY
One University Plaza
Cape Girardeau, MO 63701-4799
Tel: (573)651-2000
Admissions: (573)651-2590
E-mail: dbelow@semo.edu
Web Site: http://www.semo.edu/
President/CEO: Dr. Kenneth Dobbins
Admissions: Dr. Deborah Below
Financial Aid: Kerri Saylor
Type: Comprehensive **Sex:** Coed **Affiliation:** Missouri Coordinating Board for Higher Education **Scores:** 90.19% SAT V 400+; 94.12% SAT M 400+; 55.83% ACT 18-23; 33.75% ACT 24-29 **% Accepted:** 92 **Application Deadline:** July 1 **Application Fee:** $25.00 **H.S. Requirements:** High school diploma required; GED accepted **Costs Per Year:** Application fee: $25. State resident tuition: $5544 full-time, $184.80 per credit hour part-time. Nonresident tuition: $10,179 full-time, $339.30 per credit hour part-time. Mandatory fees: $711 full-time, $23.70 per credit hour part-time. Full-time tuition and fees vary according to course load and location. Part-time tuition and fees vary according to course load and location. College room and board: $6358. College room only: $3960. Room and board charges vary according to board plan and housing facility. **Scholarships:** Available **Calendar System:** Semester, Summer Session Available **Enrollment:** FT 7,281, PT 2,307, Grad FT 248, Grad PT 1,023 **Faculty:** FT 419, PT 172 **Student-Faculty Ratio:** 18:1 **Exams:** SAT I or ACT. ACT essay not being used. SAT essay not being used. **% Receiving Financial Aid:** 54 **% Residing in College-Owned, -Operated, or -Affiliated Housing:** 29 **Final Year or Final Semester Residency Requirement:** Yes **Library Holdings:** 432,199 **Regional Accreditation:** North Central Association of Colleges and Schools **Credit Hours For Degree:** 64 credit hours, Associates; 120 credit hours, Bachelors **ROTC:** Air Force **Professional Accreditation:** AACSB, ABET, AACN, ACA, ADtA, ASLHA, CSWE, JRCEPAT, NASM, NCATE, NRPA, NAIT **Intercollegiate Athletics:** Baseball M; Basketball M & W; Cheerleading M & W; Cross-Country Running M & W; Football M; Gymnastics W; Soccer W; Softball W; Tennis W; Track and Field M & W; Volleyball W

SOUTHWEST BAPTIST UNIVERSITY
1600 University Ave.
Bolivar, MO 65613-2597
Tel: (417)326-5281; Free: 800-526-5859
Admissions: (417)328-1817
Fax: (417)328-1514
E-mail: dcrowder@sbuniv.edu
Web Site: http://www.sbuniv.edu/
President/CEO: Dr. C. Pat Taylor
Admissions: Darren Crowder
Financial Aid: Brad Gamble
Type: Comprehensive **Sex:** Coed **Affiliation:** Southern Baptist **Scores:** 88% SAT V 400+; 90% SAT M 400+ **% Accepted:** 92 **Application Deadline:** Rolling **Application Fee:** $30.00 **H.S. Requirements:** High school diploma required; GED accepted **Costs Per Year:** Application fee: $30. Comprehensive fee: $23,000 includes full-time tuition ($16,500), mandatory fees ($780), and college room and board ($5720). College room only: $2860. Full-time tuition and fees vary according to course load. Room and board charges vary according to board plan and housing facility. **Scholarships:** Available **Calendar System:** 4-1-4, Summer Session Available **Enrollment:** FT 2,007, PT 917, Grad FT 203, Grad PT 589 **Faculty:** FT 116, PT 144 **Student-Faculty Ratio:** 13:1 **Exams:** SAT I or ACT. ACT essay not being used. SAT essay not being used. **% Receiving Financial Aid:** 77 **% Residing in College-Owned, -Operated, or -Affiliated Housing:** 65 **Final Year or Final Semester Residency Requirement:** No **Library Holdings:** 208,233 **Regional Accreditation:** North Central Association of Colleges and Schools **Credit Hours For Degree:** 64 credit hours, Associates; 128 credit hours, Bachelors **ROTC:** Army **Professional Accreditation:** APTA, ACBSP, NASM, NLN **Intercollegiate Athletics:** Baseball M; Basketball M & W; Cheerleading M & W; Cross-Country Running M & W; Football M; Golf M; Soccer M & W; Softball W; Tennis M & W; Track and Field M & W; Volleyball W

STATE FAIR COMMUNITY COLLEGE
3201 West 16th St.
Sedalia, MO 65301-2199
Tel: (660)530-5800; Free: 877-311-7322
Admissions: (660)596-7221
Fax: (660)530-5820
E-mail: mcarter@sfccmo.edu
Web Site: http://www.sfccmo.edu/
President/CEO: Dr. Marsha Drennon
Admissions: Mark Carter
Financial Aid: Lina Mahnken
Type: Two-Year College **Sex:** Coed **Affiliation:** Missouri Coordinating Board for Higher Education **Admission Plans:** Open Admission **Application Deadline:** Rolling **Application Fee:** $25.00 **H.S. Requirements:** High school diploma required; GED accepted **Costs Per Year:** Application fee: $25. Area resident tuition: $2040 full-time, $68 per credit hour part-time. State resident tuition: $2880 full-time, $96 per credit hour part-time. Nonresident tuition: $4560 full-time, $152 per credit hour part-time. Mandatory fees: $540 full-time, $18 per credit hour part-time. Full-time tuition and fees vary according to location and program. Part-time tuition and fees vary according to location and program. College room and board: $4350. **Scholarships:** Available **Calendar System:** Semester, Summer Session Available **Enrollment:** FT 2,455, PT 1,808 **Faculty:** FT 67, PT 235 **Student-Faculty Ratio:** 21:1 **% Residing in College-Owned, -Operated, or -Affiliated Housing:** 2 **Final Year or Final Semester Residency Requirement:** No **Library Holdings:** 41,258 **Regional Accreditation:** North Central Association of Colleges and Schools **Credit Hours For Degree:** 64 semester hours, Associates **ROTC:** Army **Professional Accreditation:** ADA, NAIT **Intercollegiate Athletics:** Basketball M & W

STEPHENS COLLEGE
1200 East Broadway
Columbia, MO 65215-0002
Tel: (573)442-2211; Free: 800-876-7207
Admissions: (573)876-7207
Fax: (573)876-7237
E-mail: apply@stephens.edu

Web Site: http://www.stephens.edu/
President/CEO: Dr. Dianne Lynch
Admissions: Chris Collier
Financial Aid: Rachel Touchatt
Type: Comprehensive **Sex:** Coed **Scores:** 99% SAT V 400+; 93% SAT M 400+ **% Accepted:** 72 **Admission Plans:** Deferred Admission **Application Fee:** $25.00 **H.S. Requirements:** High school diploma required; GED accepted **Costs Per Year:** Application fee: $25. Comprehensive fee: $32,570 includes full-time tuition ($25,400) and college room and board ($7170). College room only: $4770. Full-time tuition varies according to degree level, program, and reciprocity agreements. Room and board charges vary according to board plan and housing facility. Part-time tuition: $700 per credit hour. Part-time tuition varies according to degree level and program. **Scholarships:** Available **Calendar System:** Semester, Summer Session Available **Enrollment:** FT 785, PT 197, Grad FT 208, Grad PT 48 **Faculty:** FT 60, PT 53 **Student-Faculty Ratio:** 12:1 **Exams:** SAT I or ACT. ACT essay not being used. SAT essay not being used. **% Receiving Financial Aid:** 77 **% Residing in College-Owned, -Operated, or -Affiliated Housing:** 66 **Final Year or Final Semester Residency Requirement:** No **Library Holdings:** 135,389 **Regional Accreditation:** North Central Association of Colleges and Schools **Credit Hours For Degree:** 120 credits, Associates; 60 credits, Bachelors **ROTC:** Army, Navy, Air Force **Professional Accreditation:** AHIMA **Intercollegiate Athletics:** Basketball W; Cross-Country Running W; Softball W; Swimming and Diving W; Tennis W; Volleyball W

THREE RIVERS COMMUNITY COLLEGE
2080 Three Rivers Blvd.
Poplar Bluff, MO 63901-2393
Tel: (573)840-9600; Free: 877-TRY-TRCC
Admissions: (573)840-9675
E-mail: trytrcc@trcc.edu
Web Site: http://www.trcc.edu/
President/CEO: Joseph T. Rozman, Jr.
Admissions: Marcia Fields
Type: Two-Year College **Sex:** Coed **Affiliation:** Missouri Coordinating Board for Higher Education **% Accepted:** 100 **Admission Plans:** Open Admission; Early Admission **Application Fee:** $20.00 **H.S. Requirements:** High school diploma required; GED accepted **Costs Per Year:** Application fee: $20. Area resident tuition: $2010 full-time, $67 per credit hour part-time. State resident tuition: $3210 full-time, $107 per credit hour part-time. Nonresident tuition: $4020 full-time, $134 per credit hour part-time. Mandatory fees: $605 full-time, $13.50 per credit hour part-time. College room only: $3324. **Scholarships:** Available **Calendar System:** Semester, Summer Session Available **Enrollment:** FT 1,942, PT 1,243 **Faculty:** FT 60, PT 129 **Student-Faculty Ratio:** 23:1 **% Residing in College-Owned, -Operated, or -Affiliated Housing:** 5 **Library Holdings:** 33,289 **Regional Accreditation:** North Central Association of Colleges and Schools **Credit Hours For Degree:** 64 credits, Associates **Professional Accreditation:** ACBSP, NAACLS, NLN **Intercollegiate Athletics:** Baseball M; Basketball M & W; Cheerleading M & W; Softball W

TRUMAN STATE UNIVERSITY
100 East Normal St.
Kirksville, MO 63501-4221
Tel: (660)785-4000
Admissions: (660)785-4114
Fax: (660)785-7456
E-mail: admissions@truman.edu
Web Site: http://www.truman.edu/
President/CEO: Dr. Darrell W. Krueger
Admissions: Melody Chambers
Financial Aid: Kathy Elsea
Type: Comprehensive **Sex:** Coed **Scores:** 99.29% SAT V 400+; 100% SAT M 400+; 16.54% ACT 18-23; 52.55% ACT 24-29 **% Accepted:** 72 **Admission Plans:** Preferred Admission; Deferred Admission **Application Deadline:** Rolling **Application Fee:** $0.00 **H.S. Requirements:** High school diploma required; GED accepted **Costs Per Year:** Application fee: $0. One-time mandatory fee: $305. State resident tuition: $6458 full-time, $269 per credit part-time. Nonresident tuition: $11,309 full-time, $471 per credit part-time. Mandatory fees: $234 full-time. Part-time tuition varies according to course load. College room and board: $6854. Room and board charges vary according to housing facility. **Scholarships:** Available **Calendar System:** Semester, Summer Session Available **Enrollment:** FT 5,359, PT 109, Grad FT 236, Grad PT 43 **Faculty:** FT 345, PT 27 **Student-Faculty Ratio:** 16:1 **Exams:** ACT, SAT I or ACT. ACT essay not being used. SAT essay not being used. **% Receiving Financial Aid:** 41 **% Residing in College-Owned, -Operated, or -Affiliated Housing:** 48 **Library Holdings:** 498,273 **Regional Accreditation:** North Central Association of Colleges and Schools **Credit Hours For Degree:** 124 credits, Bachelors **ROTC:** Army **Professional Accreditation:** AACSB, AACN, ACA, ASLHA, JRCEPAT, NASM, NCATE, NLN **Intercollegiate Athletics:** Baseball M; Basketball M & W; Cheerleading M & W; Cross-Country Running M & W; Equestrian Sports M & W; Football M; Golf M & W; Lacrosse W; Rugby M & W; Soccer M & W; Softball W; Swimming and Diving M & W; Tennis M & W; Track and Field M & W; Ultimate Frisbee M & W; Volleyball M & W; Weight Lifting M & W; Wrestling M

UNIVERSITY OF CENTRAL MISSOURI
Warrensburg, MO 64093
Tel: (660)543-4111
Admissions: (660)543-4170
Fax: (660)543-8517
E-mail: admit@ucmo.edu
Web Site: http://www.ucmo.edu/
President/CEO: Dr. Aaron Podolefsky
Admissions: Ann Nordyke
Financial Aid: Phil Shreves
Type: Comprehensive **Sex:** Coed **Scores:** 59.4% ACT 18-23; 28.1% ACT 24-29 **% Accepted:** 85 **Admission Plans:** Deferred Admission **Application Deadline:** Rolling **Application Fee:** $30.00 **H.S. Requirements:** High school diploma required; GED accepted **Costs Per Year:** Application fee: $30. State resident tuition: $6585 full-time, $219.50 per credit hour part-time. Nonresident tuition: $12,444 full-time, $414.80 per credit hour part-time. Mandatory fees: $726 full-time, $24.20 per credit hour part-time. Full-time tuition and fees vary according to course load and location. Part-time tuition and fees vary according to course load and location. College room and board: $6320. College room only: $4120. Room and board charges vary according to board plan and housing facility. **Scholarships:** Available **Calendar System:** Semester, Summer Session Available **Enrollment:** FT 7,565, PT 1,523, Grad FT 550, Grad PT 1,553 **Faculty:** FT 445, PT 114 **Student-Faculty Ratio:** 17:1 **Exams:** ACT. **% Receiving Financial Aid:** 34 **% Residing in College-Owned, -Operated, or -Affiliated Housing:** 28 **Library Holdings:** 1,290,831 **Regional Accreditation:** North Central Association of Colleges and Schools **Credit Hours For Degree:** 60 credit hours, Associates; 124 credit hours, Bachelors **ROTC:** Army, Air Force **Professional Accreditation:** AACSB, ABET, AACN, AAFCS, ACCE, ASLHA, CAA, CSWE, NASAD, NASM, NCATE, NLN, NAIT **Intercollegiate Athletics:** Baseball M; Basketball M & W; Bowling M & W; Cross-Country Running M & W; Football M; Golf M; Rock Climbing M & W; Soccer M & W; Softball W; Track and Field M & W; Volleyball W; Wrestling M

UNIVERSITY OF MISSOURI
Columbia, MO 65211
Tel: (573)882-2121
Admissions: (573)882-7786
Fax: (573)882-7887
E-mail: mu4u@missouri.edu
Web Site: http://www.missouri.edu/
President/CEO: Dr. Brady Deaton
Admissions: Barbara Rupp
Financial Aid: James Brooks
Type: University **Sex:** Coed **Affiliation:** University of Missouri System **Scores:** 98.56% SAT V 400+; 99.37% SAT M 400+; 29.99% ACT 18-23; 54.24% ACT 24-29 **% Accepted:** 83 **Admission Plans:** Deferred Admission **Application Deadline:** Rolling **Application Fee:** $45.00 **H.S. Requirements:** High school diploma required; GED accepted **Costs Per Year:** Application fee: $45. State resident tuition: $7368 full-time, $245.60 per credit hour part-time. Nonresident tuition: $18,459 full-time, $615.30 per credit hour part-time. Mandatory fees: $1133 full-time. Full-time tuition and fees vary according to course load, program, and reciprocity agreements. Part-time tuition varies according to course load, program, and reciprocity agreements. College room and board: $8100. Room and board charges vary according to board plan and housing facility. **Scholarships:** Available **Calendar System:** Semester, Summer Session Available **Enrollment:** FT 22,382, PT 1,487, Grad FT 4,184, Grad PT 3,261 **Faculty:** FT 1,266, PT 75 **Student-Faculty Ratio:** 19:1 **Exams:** ACT, SAT I or ACT. **% Receiving Financial Aid:** 47 **% Residing in College-Owned, -Operated, or -Affiliated Housing:** 30 **Library Holdings:** 3,523,795 **Regional Accreditation:** North Central As-

sociation of Colleges and Schools **ROTC:** Army, Navy, Air Force **Professional Accreditation:** AACSB, ABET, ACEJMC, AACN, AAFCS, ABA, ADtA, ALA, AOTA, APTA, APA, ASLHA, AVMA, AALS, ACEHSA, CARC, FIDER, CORE, CSWE, JRCERT JRCNMT, LCMEAMA, NASM, NASPAA, NCATE, NRPA, SAF, TEAC **Intercollegiate Athletics:** Baseball M; Basketball M & W; Cheerleading M & W; Cross-Country Running M & W; Football M; Golf M & W; Gymnastics W; Soccer W; Softball W; Swimming and Diving M & W; Tennis W; Track and Field M & W; Volleyball W; Wrestling M

UNIVERSITY OF MISSOURI—KANSAS CITY
5100 Rockhill Rd.
Kansas City, MO 64110-2499
Tel: (816)235-1000; Free: 800-775-8652
Admissions: (816)235-1111
Fax: (816)235-1717
E-mail: admit@umkc.edu
Web Site: http://www.umkc.edu/
President/CEO: Leo E. Morton
Admissions: Tammy Cloutier
Financial Aid: Jan Brandow
Type: University **Sex:** Coed **Affiliation:** University of Missouri System **Scores:** 97% SAT V 400+; 99% SAT M 400+; 40% ACT 18-23; 38% ACT 24-29 **% Accepted:** 62 **Admission Plans:** Deferred Admission **Application Deadline:** Rolling **Application Fee:** $45.00 **H.S. Requirements:** High school diploma required; GED accepted **Costs Per Year:** Application fee: $45. State resident tuition: $7368 full-time, $245.60 per credit hour part-time. Nonresident tuition: $18,459 full-time, $615.30 per credit hour part-time. Mandatory fees: $905 full-time, $30.15 per credit hour part-time, $30 per term part-time. Full-time tuition and fees vary according to course load and program. Part-time tuition and fees vary according to course load and program. College room and board: $10,467. Room and board charges vary according to board plan and housing facility. **Scholarships:** Available **Calendar System:** Semester, Summer Session Available **Enrollment:** FT 6,264, PT 3,134, Grad FT 2,865, Grad PT 2,555 **Faculty:** FT 721, PT 416 **Student-Faculty Ratio:** 13:1 **Exams:** SAT I or ACT. ACT essay not being used. SAT essay not being used. **% Receiving Financial Aid:** 65 **% Residing in College-Owned, -Operated, or -Affiliated Housing:** 16 **Final Year or Final Semester Residency Requirement:** Yes **Library Holdings:** 1,827,162 **Regional Accreditation:** North Central Association of Colleges and Schools **Credit Hours For Degree:** 120 credit hours, Bachelors **ROTC:** Army, Air Force **Professional Accreditation:** AACSB, ACPhE, AACN, AANA, ABA, ADA, APA, AALS, CSWE, LCMEAMA, NASM, NASPAA, NAST, NCATE **Intercollegiate Athletics:** Basketball M & W; Cheerleading W; Cross-Country Running M & W; Golf M & W; Riflery M & W; Soccer M; Softball W; Tennis M & W; Track and Field M & W; Volleyball W

UNIVERSITY OF MISSOURI—ST. LOUIS
One University Blvd.
St. Louis, MO 63121
Tel: (314)516-5000
Admissions: (314)516-6941
Fax: (314)516-5310
E-mail: askdrew@umsl.edu
Web Site: http://www.umsl.edu/
President/CEO: Dr. Thomas F. George
Admissions: Andrew L. Griffin
Financial Aid: Samantha M. Matchefts
Type: University **Sex:** Coed **Affiliation:** University of Missouri System **Scores:** 96% SAT M 400+; 49% ACT 18-23; 35% ACT 24-29 **% Accepted:** 79 **Application Deadline:** August 23 **Application Fee:** $35.00 **H.S. Requirements:** High school diploma required; GED accepted **Costs Per Year:** Application fee: $35. State resident tuition: $7368 full-time, $245.60 per credit hour part-time. Nonresident tuition: $18,459 full-time, $615.30 per credit hour part-time. Mandatory fees: $1227 full-time, $47.09 per credit hour part-time. Full-time tuition and fees vary according to course load, program, and reciprocity agreements. Part-time tuition and fees vary according to course load, program, and reciprocity agreements. College room and board: $8164. College room only: $4449. Room and board charges vary according to board plan and housing facility. **Scholarships:** Available **Calendar System:** Semester, Summer Session Available **Enrollment:** FT 6,029, PT 6,953, Grad FT 971, Grad PT 2,595 **Faculty:** FT 480, PT 378 **Student-Faculty Ratio:** 17:1 **Exams:** SAT I or ACT. **% Receiving Financial Aid:** 67 **% Residing in College-Owned, -Operated, or -Affiliated Housing:** 8 **Final Year or Final Semester Residency Requirement:** Yes **Library Holdings:** 1,212,610 **Regional Accreditation:** North Central Association of Colleges and Schools **Credit Hours For Degree:** 120 credit hours, Bachelors **ROTC:** Army, Air Force **Professional Accreditation:** AACSB, ABET, AACN, ACA, AOA, APA, CSWE, NASM, NASPAA, NCATE **Intercollegiate Athletics:** Baseball M; Basketball M & W; Cheerleading W; Golf M & W; Ice Hockey M; Soccer M & W; Softball W; Table Tennis M & W; Tennis M & W; Volleyball W

UNIVERSITY OF PHOENIX—KANSAS CITY CAMPUS
901 East 104th St., Ste. 200
Kansas City, MO 64131-4517
Tel: (816)943-9600; Free: 800-228-7240
Admissions: (480)557-6151
Fax: (816)943-6675
E-mail: audra.mcquarie@phoenix.edu
Web Site: http://www.phoenix.edu/
President/CEO: William Pepicello
Admissions: Audra McQuarie
Type: Comprehensive **Sex:** Coed **Admission Plans:** Open Admission; Deferred Admission **Application Deadline:** Rolling **Application Fee:** $0.00 **H.S. Requirements:** High school diploma required; GED accepted **Costs Per Year:** Application fee: $0. Tuition: $12,525 full-time. Full-time tuition varies according to course level and course load. **Scholarships:** Available **Calendar System:** Continuous, Summer Session Not available **Enrollment:** FT 617 **Faculty:** FT 8, PT 116 **Regional Accreditation:** North Central Association of Colleges and Schools **Credit Hours For Degree:** 60 credits, Associates; 120 credits, Bachelors

UNIVERSITY OF PHOENIX—ST. LOUIS CAMPUS
Riverport Lakes West
13801 Riverport Dr., Ste. 102
St. Louis, MO 63043-4828
Tel: (314)298-9755; Free: 800-228-7240
Admissions: (480)557-6151
Fax: (314)291-2901
E-mail: audra.mcquarie@phoenix.edu
Web Site: http://www.phoenix.edu/
President/CEO: William Pepicello
Admissions: Audra McQuarie
Type: Comprehensive **Sex:** Coed **Admission Plans:** Open Admission; Deferred Admission **Application Deadline:** Rolling **Application Fee:** $0.00 **H.S. Requirements:** High school diploma required; GED accepted **Costs Per Year:** Application fee: $0. Tuition: $13,200 full-time. Full-time tuition varies according to course level and course load. **Scholarships:** Available **Calendar System:** Continuous, Summer Session Not available **Enrollment:** FT 401 **Faculty:** FT 7, PT 97 **Regional Accreditation:** North Central Association of Colleges and Schools **Credit Hours For Degree:** 60 credits, Associates; 120 credits, Bachelors

UNIVERSITY OF PHOENIX—SPRINGFIELD CAMPUS
1343 East Kingsley St.
Springfield, MO 65804-7211
Tel: (480)557-6151; Free: 800-228-7240
Admissions: (480)557-6151
E-mail: audra.mcquarie@phoenix.edu
Web Site: http://www.phoenix.edu/
President/CEO: William Pepicello
Admissions: Audra McQuarie
Type: Comprehensive **Sex:** Coed **Admission Plans:** Open Admission; Deferred Admission **Application Deadline:** Rolling **Application Fee:** $45.00 **H.S. Requirements:** High school diploma required; GED accepted **Costs Per Year:** Application fee: $45. Tuition: $11,025 full-time. Full-time tuition varies according to course level and course load. **Scholarships:** Available **Enrollment:** FT 104 **Faculty:** FT 5, PT 34 **Student-Faculty Ratio:** 9:1 **Regional Accreditation:** North Central Association of Colleges and Schools **Credit Hours For Degree:** 60 credits, Associates; 120 credits, Bachelors

VATTEROTT COLLEGE (KANSAS CITY)
8955 East 38th Terrace
Kansas City, MO 64129
Tel: (816)861-1000; Free: (866)314-6454
Fax: (816)861-1400
Web Site: http://www.vatterott-college.edu/
President/CEO: Wayne Major

Type: Two-Year College **Sex:** Coed **% Accepted:** 84 **Calendar System:** Semester **Professional Accreditation:** ACCSCT

VATTEROTT COLLEGE (O'FALLON)
927 East Terra Ln.
O'Fallon, MO 63366
Tel: (636)978-7488; Free: 888-766-3601
Fax: (636)978-5121
E-mail: ofallon@vatterott-college.edu
Web Site: http://www.vatterott-college.edu/
President/CEO: Robert Donnell
Admissions: Gertrude Bogan-Jones
Type: Two-Year College **Sex:** Coed

VATTEROTT COLLEGE (ST. ANN)
3925 Industrial Dr.
St. Ann, MO 63074-1807
Tel: (314)428-5900; Free: (866)314-6454
Admissions: (314)264-1000
Web Site: http://www.vatterott-college.edu/
President/CEO: Robert Donnell
Admissions: Ann Farajallah
Type: Two-Year College **Sex:** Coed **H.S. Requirements:** High school diploma required; GED accepted **Scholarships:** Available **Calendar System:** Continuous, Summer Session Not available **Credit Hours For Degree:** 72 credit hours, Associates **Professional Accreditation:** ACCSCT

VATTEROTT COLLEGE (ST. JOSEPH)
3131 Frederick Ave.
St. Joseph, MO 64506
Tel: (816)364-5399; Free: 800-282-5327
Fax: (816)364-1593
Web Site: http://www.vatterott-college.edu/
President/CEO: Andy Stufflebean
Type: Two-Year College **Sex:** Coed **Admission Plans:** Open Admission **Calendar System:** Semester **Student-Faculty Ratio:** 22:1 **Professional Accreditation:** ACCSCT

VATTEROTT COLLEGE (ST. LOUIS)
12970 Maurer Industrial Dr.
St. Louis, MO 63127
Tel: (314)843-4200
Fax: (314)843-1709
Web Site: http://www.vatterott-college.edu/
President/CEO: Jamie Orf
Type: Two-Year College **Sex:** Coed **Admission Plans:** Open Admission **Calendar System:** Semester **Student-Faculty Ratio:** 21:1 **Professional Accreditation:** ACCSCT

VATTEROTT COLLEGE (SPRINGFIELD)
1258 East Trafficway St.
Springfield, MO 65802
Tel: (417)831-8116; Free: 800-766-5829
Fax: (417)831-5099
E-mail: springfield@vatterott-college.edu
Web Site: http://www.vatterott-college.edu/
President/CEO: Pam Bell
Admissions: Scott Lester
Type: Two-Year College **Sex:** Coed **H.S. Requirements:** High school diploma required; GED accepted **Calendar System:** Quarter **Faculty:** FT 14, PT 9 **Student-Faculty Ratio:** 30:1 **Credit Hours For Degree:** 108 quarter credit hours, Associates **Professional Accreditation:** ACCSCT

VET TECH INSTITUTE AT HICKEY COLLEGE
2780 North Lindbergh Blvd.
St. Louis, MO 63114
Tel: (314)434-2212
Admissions: 888-884-1459
Web Site: http://www.vettechinstitute.edu/
Type: Two-Year College **Sex:** Coed **% Accepted:** 55 **Professional Accreditation:** AVMA

WASHINGTON UNIVERSITY IN ST. LOUIS
One Brookings Dr.
St. Louis, MO 63130-4899
Tel: (314)935-5000; Free: 800-638-0700
Fax: (314)935-4290
E-mail: admissions@wustl.edu
Web Site: http://www.wustl.edu/
President/CEO: Mark Wrighton
Admissions: Julie Shimabukuro
Financial Aid: William Witbrodt
Type: University **Sex:** Coed **Scores:** 100% SAT V 400+; 100% SAT M 400+; 6% ACT 24-29 **% Accepted:** 22 **Admission Plans:** Early Admission; Early Decision Plan; Deferred Admission **Application Deadline:** January 15 **Application Fee:** $55.00 **H.S. Requirements:** High school diploma required; GED accepted **Costs Per Year:** Application fee: $55. Comprehensive fee: $53,315 includes full-time tuition ($39,400), mandatory fees ($974), and college room and board ($12,941). College room only: $8405. Room and board charges vary according to board plan and housing facility. **Scholarships:** Available **Calendar System:** Semester, Summer Session Available **Enrollment:** FT 6,135, PT 911, Grad FT 5,287, Grad PT 1,242 **Faculty:** FT 916, PT 176 **Student-Faculty Ratio:** 7:1 **Exams:** SAT I or ACT. ACT essay used for admission. SAT essay used for admission. **% Receiving Financial Aid:** 42 **% Residing in College-Owned, -Operated, or -Affiliated Housing:** 75 **Library Holdings:** 2,984,769 **Regional Accreditation:** North Central Association of Colleges and Schools **Credit Hours For Degree:** 120 semester hours, Bachelors **ROTC:** Army, Air Force **Professional Accreditation:** AACSB, ABET, ABA, AOTA, APTA, APA, ASLHA, ACIPE, AALS, ACEHSA, CSWE, LCMEAMA, NAAB, NASAD, NCATE **Intercollegiate Athletics:** Baseball M; Basketball M & W; Crew M & W; Cross-Country Running M & W; Equestrian Sports M & W; Fencing M & W; Field Hockey W; Football M; Golf M & W; Gymnastics M & W; Ice Hockey M; Lacrosse M & W; Rugby M & W; Sailing M & W; Soccer M & W; Softball W; Swimming and Diving M & W; Table Tennis M & W; Tennis M & W; Track and Field M & W; Ultimate Frisbee M & W; Volleyball M & W; Water Polo M & W

WEBSTER UNIVERSITY
470 East Lockwood Ave.
St. Louis, MO 63119-3194
Tel: (314)968-6900; Free: 800-75-ENROL
Admissions: (314)961-2660
Fax: (314)968-7115
E-mail: admit@webster.edu
Web Site: http://www.webster.edu/
President/CEO: Dr. Elizabeth (Beth) J. Stroble
Admissions: Andrew Laue
Financial Aid: Marilynn Shelton
Type: Comprehensive **Sex:** Coed **Scores:** 40% ACT 18-23; 42% ACT 24-29 **% Accepted:** 52 **Admission Plans:** Early Admission; Deferred Admission **Application Deadline:** June 1 **Application Fee:** $35.00 **H.S. Requirements:** High school diploma required; GED accepted **Costs Per Year:** Application fee: $35. Comprehensive fee: $30,126 includes full-time tuition ($21,056) and college room and board ($9070). College room only: $4830. Full-time tuition varies according to program. Room and board charges vary according to board plan and housing facility. Part-time tuition: $550 per credit hour. Part-time tuition varies according to location. **Scholarships:** Available **Calendar System:** Semester, Summer Session Available **Enrollment:** FT 2,638, PT 926, Grad FT 785, Grad PT 3,892 **Faculty:** FT 187, PT 718 **Student-Faculty Ratio:** 12:1 **Exams:** SAT I or ACT. ACT essay used for admission. SAT essay used for admission. **% Receiving Financial Aid:** 68 **% Residing in College-Owned, -Operated, or -Affiliated Housing:** 15 **Library Holdings:** 279,928 **Regional Accreditation:** North Central Association of Colleges and Schools **Credit Hours For Degree:** 128 credit hours, Bachelors **ROTC:** Army, Air Force **Professional Accreditation:** AANA, NASM, NCATE, NLN **Intercollegiate Athletics:** Baseball M; Basketball M & W; Cross-Country Running M & W; Golf M; Soccer M & W; Softball W; Swimming and Diving M & W; Tennis M & W; Track and Field M & W; Volleyball W

WENTWORTH MILITARY ACADEMY AND COLLEGE
1880 Washington Ave.
Lexington, MO 64067
Tel: (660)259-2221
Admissions: 800-962-7682
Fax: (660)259-2677

E-mail: admissions@wma1880.org
Web Site: http://www.wma1880.org/
President/CEO: William Sellers
Admissions: Dr. Roger Hamilton
Financial Aid: Cindy Dawn Howard
Type: Two-Year College **Sex:** Coed **Scores:** 80% SAT V 400+; 93% SAT M 400+ **% Accepted:** 100 **Application Deadline:** September 11 **Application Fee:** $100.00 **H.S. Requirements:** High school diploma required; GED accepted **Costs Per Year:** Application fee: $100. Comprehensive fee: $22,300 includes full-time tuition ($15,500) and college room and board ($6800). College room only: $3300. Full-time tuition varies according to student level. Part-time tuition: $175 per credit hour. **Scholarships:** Available **Calendar System:** Semester, Summer Session Available **Enrollment:** FT 234, PT 327 **Faculty:** FT 19, PT 44 **Student-Faculty Ratio:** 10:1 **Exams:** SAT I or ACT. **Library Holdings:** 18,890 **Regional Accreditation:** North Central Association of Colleges and Schools **Credit Hours For Degree:** 64 semester hours, Associates **ROTC:** Army **Intercollegiate Athletics:** Cross-Country Running M; Track and Field M & W; Wrestling M

WESTMINSTER COLLEGE
501 Westminster Ave.
Fulton, MO 65251-1299
Tel: (573)642-3361; Free: 800-475-3361
Admissions: (573)592-5251
Fax: (573)592-5227
E-mail: admissions@westminster-mo.edu
Web Site: http://www.westminster-mo.edu/
President/CEO: Dr. Barney Forsythe
Admissions: George Wolf
Financial Aid: Aimee Bristow
Type: Four-Year College **Sex:** Coed **Affiliation:** Presbyterian Church **Scores:** 90% SAT V 400+; 95% SAT M 400+; 43% ACT 18-23; 43% ACT 24-29 **% Accepted:** 78 **Admission Plans:** Early Admission; Deferred Admission **Application Fee:** $0.00 **H.S. Requirements:** High school diploma required; GED accepted **Costs Per Year:** Application fee: $0. Comprehensive fee: $25,110 includes full-time tuition ($17,990) and college room and board ($7120). College room only: $3700. Room and board charges vary according to board plan and housing facility. Part-time tuition: $750 per credit hour. **Scholarships:** Available **Calendar System:** Semester, Summer Session Available **Enrollment:** FT 1,076, PT 11 **Faculty:** FT 61, PT 30 **Student-Faculty Ratio:** 15:1 **Exams:** SAT I or ACT. **% Receiving Financial Aid:** 57 **% Residing in College-Owned, -Operated, or -Affiliated Housing:** 87 **Library Holdings:** 130,112 **Regional Accreditation:** North Central Association of Colleges and Schools **Credit Hours For Degree:** 122 credit hours, Bachelors **ROTC:** Army, Air Force **Intercollegiate Athletics:** Baseball M; Basketball M & W; Cross-Country Running M & W; Football M; Golf M & W; Soccer M & W; Softball M & W; Tennis M & W; Track and Field M & W; Volleyball W

WILLIAM JEWELL COLLEGE
500 College Hill
Liberty, MO 64068-1843
Tel: (816)781-7700; Free: 888-2JEWELL
Admissions: (816)415-7511
Fax: (816)415-5027
E-mail: gramblingb@william.jewell.edu
Web Site: http://www.jewell.edu/
President/CEO: Dr. David L. Sallee
Admissions: Bridget Gramling
Financial Aid: Sue Karnes
Type: Four-Year College **Sex:** Coed **Affiliation:** Baptist **Scores:** 96% SAT V 400+; 99% SAT M 400+; 30% ACT 18-23; 50% ACT 24-29 **% Accepted:** 55 **Admission Plans:** Deferred Admission **Application Deadline:** August 15 **Application Fee:** $25.00 **H.S. Requirements:** High school diploma required; GED accepted **Costs Per Year:** Application fee: $25. Comprehensive fee: $35,950 includes full-time tuition ($28,450), mandatory fees ($300), and college room and board ($7200). Full-time tuition and fees vary according to class time, course load, program, and student level. Room and board charges vary according to board plan and housing facility. Part-time tuition: $825 per credit hour. **Scholarships:** Available **Calendar System:** Semester, Summer Session Available **Enrollment:** FT 1,030, PT 53 **Faculty:** FT 70, PT 77 **Student-Faculty Ratio:** 11:1 **Exams:** SAT I or ACT. ACT essay used for advising. ACT essay used as a validity check on application essay. **% Receiving Financial Aid:** 71 **% Residing in College-Owned, -Operated, or -Affiliated Housing:** 75 **Final Year or Final Semester Residency Requirement:** Yes **Library Holdings:** 191,798 **Regional Accreditation:** North Central Association of Colleges and Schools **Credit Hours For Degree:** 124 semester hours, Bachelors **ROTC:** Army **Professional Accreditation:** AACN, NASM **Intercollegiate Athletics:** Baseball M; Basketball M & W; Cheerleading M & W; Cross-Country Running M & W; Football M; Golf M & W; Soccer M & W; Softball W; Tennis M & W; Track and Field M & W; Volleyball W

WILLIAM WOODS UNIVERSITY
One University Ave.
Fulton, MO 65251-1098
Tel: (573)642-2251; Free: 800-995-3159
Admissions: (573)592-4221
Fax: (573)592-1146
E-mail: admissions@williamwoods.edu
Web Site: http://www.williamwoods.edu/
President/CEO: Dr. Jahnae Barnett
Admissions: Sharon Horn
Financial Aid: Deana Ready
Type: Comprehensive **Sex:** Coed **Affiliation:** Christian Church (Disciples of Christ) **Scores:** 97.7% SAT V 400+; 83.7% SAT M 400+; 55.6% ACT 18-23; 29.2% ACT 24-29 **% Accepted:** 85 **Admission Plans:** Deferred Admission **Application Deadline:** Rolling **Application Fee:** $25.00 **H.S. Requirements:** High school diploma required; GED accepted **Costs Per Year:** Application fee: $25. Comprehensive fee: $24,260 includes full-time tuition ($16,850), mandatory fees ($460), and college room and board ($6950). Full-time tuition and fees vary according to degree level and program. Room and board charges vary according to board plan and housing facility. Part-time tuition: $560 per credit hour. Part-time mandatory fees: $205 per term. Part-time tuition and fees vary according to course load, degree level, and program. **Scholarships:** Available **Calendar System:** Semester, Summer Session Available **Enrollment:** FT 786, PT 189 **Faculty:** FT 55, PT 194 **Student-Faculty Ratio:** 14:1 **Exams:** SAT I or ACT. **% Receiving Financial Aid:** 63 **% Residing in College-Owned, -Operated, or -Affiliated Housing:** 80 **Library Holdings:** 139,986 **Regional Accreditation:** North Central Association of Colleges and Schools **Credit Hours For Degree:** 67 credit hours, Associates; 122 credit hours, Bachelors **ROTC:** Army, Navy, Air Force **Professional Accreditation:** CSWE **Intercollegiate Athletics:** Baseball M; Basketball M & W; Cross-Country Running M & W; Golf M & W; Soccer M & W; Softball W; Track and Field M & W; Volleyball M & W

BLACKFEET COMMUNITY COLLEGE
PO Box 819
Browning, MT 59417-0819
Tel: (406)338-5441; Free: 800-549-7457
Fax: (406)338-3272
Web Site: http://www.bfcc.org/
President/CEO: John E. Salois
Admissions: Deana M. McNabb
Type: Two-Year College **Sex:** Coed **Admission Plans:** Open Admission; Early Admission **Application Deadline:** August 29 **Application Fee:** $15.00 **H.S. Requirements:** High school diploma required; GED accepted **Costs Per Year:** Application fee: $15. Tuition: $1650 full-time, $75 per credit hour part-time. Mandatory fees: $350 full-time, $75 per credit hour part-time, $100 per term part-time. Full-time tuition and fees vary according to course load. Part-time tuition and fees vary according to course load. **Scholarships:** Available **Calendar System:** Semester, Summer Session Not available **Library Holdings:** 10,000 **Credit Hours For Degree:** 60 credit hours, Associates **Professional Accreditation:** NCCU

CARROLL COLLEGE
1601 North Benton Ave.
Helena, MT 59625-0002
Tel: (406)447-4300; Free: 800-992-3648
Fax: (406)447-4533
Web Site: http://www.carroll.edu/
President/CEO: Dr. Thomas Trebon
Admissions: Cynthia Thornquist
Financial Aid: Janet Riis
Type: Four-Year College **Sex:** Coed **Affiliation:** Roman Catholic **Scores:** 98% SAT V 400+; 99% SAT M 400+; 45% ACT 18-23; 45% ACT 24-29 **% Accepted:** 76 **Admission Plans:** Deferred Admission **Application Deadline:** June 1 **Application Fee:** $35.00 **H.S. Requirements:** High school diploma required; GED accepted **Costs Per Year:** Application fee: $35. Comprehensive fee: $29,710 includes full-time tuition ($22,252), mandatory fees ($340), and college room and board ($7118). **Scholarships:** Available **Calendar System:** Semester, Summer Session Available **Enrollment:** FT 1,225, PT 184 **Faculty:** FT 84, PT 73 **Exams:** SAT I or ACT, SAT II. **% Receiving Financial Aid:** 61 **% Residing in College-Owned, -Operated, or -Affiliated Housing:** 65 **Library Holdings:** 89,003 **Credit Hours For Degree:** 60 semester hours, Associates; 122 semester hours, Bachelors **ROTC:** Army **Professional Accreditation:** ABET, AACN, NLN, NCCU **Intercollegiate Athletics:** Basketball M & W; Cheerleading M & W; Cross-Country Running M & W; Football M; Golf M & W; Soccer W; Volleyball W

CHIEF DULL KNIFE COLLEGE
PO Box 98
1 College Dr.
Lame Deer, MT 59043-0098
Tel: (406)477-6215
Fax: (406)477-6219
Web Site: http://www.cdkc.edu/
President/CEO: Richard Littlebear
Admissions: William L. Wertman
Type: Two-Year College **Sex:** Coed **Admission Plans:** Open Admission; Early Admission **Application Deadline:** Rolling **Application Fee:** $0.00 **H.S. Requirements:** High school diploma required; GED accepted **Scholarships:** Available **Calendar System:** Semester, Summer Session Available **Faculty:** FT 8, PT 22 **Library Holdings:** 10,000 **Credit Hours For Degree:** 60 credit hours, Associates **Professional Accreditation:** NCCU

DAWSON COMMUNITY COLLEGE
Box 421
Glendive, MT 59330-0421
Tel: (406)377-3396; Free: 800-821-8320
Fax: (406)377-8132
Web Site: http://www.dawson.edu/
President/CEO: Jim Cargill
Admissions: Jolene Myers
Financial Aid: Jolene Myers
Type: Two-Year College **Sex:** Coed **Affiliation:** Montana University System **Admission Plans:** Open Admission; Deferred Admission **Application Deadline:** Rolling **Application Fee:** $30.00 **H.S. Requirements:** High school diploma required; GED accepted **Costs Per Year:** Application fee: $30. Area resident tuition: $1566 full-time, $52.20 per credit part-time. State resident tuition: $2673 full-time, $89.10 per credit part-time. Nonresident tuition: $7329 full-time, $244.30 per credit part-time. Mandatory fees: $1170 full-time, $39 per credit part-time. College room and board: $3300. **Scholarships:** Available **Calendar System:** Semester, Summer Session Available **Library Holdings:** 18,870 **Credit Hours For Degree:** 60 semester hours, Associates **Professional Accreditation:** NCCU **Intercollegiate Athletics:** Baseball M; Basketball M & W; Equestrian Sports M & W; Softball W

FLATHEAD VALLEY COMMUNITY COLLEGE
777 Grandview Dr.
Kalispell, MT 59901-2622
Tel: (406)756-3822; Free: 800-313-3822
Admissions: (406)756-3846
Fax: (406)756-3815
E-mail: mstoltz@fvcc.cc.mt.us
Web Site: http://www.fvcc.edu/
President/CEO: Dr. Jane A. Karas
Admissions: Marlene C. Stoltz
Financial Aid: Cynthia Kiefer
Type: Two-Year College **Sex:** Coed **Affiliation:** Montana University System **Admission Plans:** Open Admission; Early Admission; Deferred Admission **Application Deadline:** Rolling **Application Fee:** $15.00 **H.S. Requirements:** High school diploma required; GED accepted **Costs Per Year:** Application fee: $15. Area resident tuition: $2604 full-time, $93 per credit part-time. State resident tuition: $3976 full-time, $142 per credit part-time. Nonresident tuition: $9744 full-time, $348 per credit part-time. Mandatory fees: $892 full-time, $31.90 per credit part-time. Part-time tuition and fees vary according to course load. **Scholarships:** Available **Calendar System:** Semester, Summer Session Available **Enrollment:** FT 1,430, PT 1,071 **Faculty:** FT 43, PT 161 **Student-Faculty Ratio:** 18:1 **Final Year or Final Semester Residency Requirement:** No **Library Holdings:** 35,000 **Credit Hours For Degree:** 60 semester hours, Associates **Professional Accreditation:** AAMAE, NCCU **Intercollegiate Athletics:** Cross-Country Running M & W; Soccer M & W

FORT BELKNAP COLLEGE
PO Box 159
Harlem, MT 59526-0159
Tel: (406)353-2607
Fax: (406)353-2898
Web Site: http://www.fbcc.edu/
President/CEO: Carole Falcon-Chandler
Admissions: Dixie Brockie
Type: Two-Year College **Sex:** Coed **Admission Plans:** Open Admission; Early Admission; Deferred Admission **Application Deadline:** Rolling **Application Fee:** $10.00 **H.S. Requirements:** High school diploma required; GED accepted **Scholarships:** Available **Calendar System:** Quarter, Summer Session Not available **Enrollment:** FT 117, PT 41 **Faculty:** FT 8, PT 20 **Library Holdings:** 16,000 **Credit Hours For Degree:** 92 credits, Associates **Professional Accreditation:** NCCU **Intercollegiate Athletics:** Basketball M & W; Cross-Country Running M & W; Volleyball M & W

FORT PECK COMMUNITY COLLEGE
PO Box 398
Poplar, MT 59255-0398
Tel: (406)768-5551
Admissions: (406)768-6300
Web Site: http://www.fpcc.edu/
President/CEO: James E. Shanley
Admissions: Robert McAnally
Type: Two-Year College **Sex:** Coed **Admission Plans:** Open Admission; Early Admission **Application Deadline:** Rolling **Application Fee:** $15.00 **Scholarships:** Available **Calendar System:** Semester, Summer Session Available **Credit Hours For Degree:** 60 credit hours, Associates **Professional Accreditation:** NCCU

LITTLE BIG HORN COLLEGE
Box 370
1 Forest Ln.
Crow Agency, MT 59022-0370
Tel: (406)638-3104
Admissions: (406)638-3100
Web Site: http://www.lbhc.cc.mt.us/
President/CEO: Dr. David Yarlott, Jr.
Admissions: Ann Bullis
Type: Two-Year College **Sex:** Coed **Admission Plans:** Open Admission **Application Deadline:** Rolling **H.S. Requirements:** High school diploma or equivalent not required **Calendar System:** Quarter **Faculty:** FT 11, PT 1 **Student-Faculty Ratio:** 25:1 **Credit Hours For Degree:** 92 quarter hours, Associates **Professional Accreditation:** NCCU **Intercollegiate Athletics:** Basketball M & W

MILES COMMUNITY COLLEGE
2715 Dickinson
Miles City, MT 59301-4799
Tel: (406)874-6100; Free: 800-541-9281
Admissions: (406)874-6178
Fax: (406)874-6282
E-mail: samuelsonj@milescc.edu
Web Site: http://www.milescc.edu/
President/CEO: Dr. Stefani Gray Hicswa
Admissions: Jake Samuelson
Type: Two-Year College **Sex:** Coed **Affiliation:** Montana University System **% Accepted:** 100 **Admission Plans:** Open Admission; Early Admission; Deferred Admission **Application Deadline:** Rolling **Application Fee:** $30.00 **H.S. Requirements:** High school diploma required; GED accepted **Costs Per Year:** Application fee: $30. Area resident tuition: $2130 full-time, $71 per credit hour part-time. State resident tuition: $3000 full-time, $100 per credit hour part-time. Nonresident tuition: $5790 full-time, $193 per credit hour part-time. Mandatory fees: $1290 full-time, $43 per credit hour part-time. Full-time tuition and fees vary according to reciprocity agreements. Part-time tuition and fees vary according to reciprocity agreements. College room and board: $4200. College room only: $2250. Room and board charges vary according to board plan and housing facility. **Scholarships:** Available **Calendar System:** Semester, Summer Session Available **Enrollment:** FT 376, PT 124 **Faculty:** FT 26, PT 26 **Student-Faculty Ratio:** 14:1 **Exams:** ACT essay not being used. SAT essay not being used. **% Residing in College-Owned, -Operated, or -Affiliated Housing:** 32 **Final Year or Final Semester Residency Requirement:** No **Library Holdings:** 17,563 **Credit Hours For Degree:** 62 semester hours, Associates **Professional Accreditation:** NLN, NCCU **Intercollegiate Athletics:** Baseball M; Basketball M & W; Golf M & W

MONTANA STATE UNIVERSITY
Bozeman, MT 59717
Tel: (406)994-0211; Free: 888-MSU-CATS
Admissions: (406)994-2452
E-mail: admissions@montana.edu
Web Site: http://www.montana.edu/
President/CEO: Dr. Waded Cruzado
Admissions: Ronda Russell
Financial Aid: Brandi Payne
Type: University **Sex:** Coed **Affiliation:** Montana University System **Scores:** 96% SAT V 400+; 97% SAT M 400+; 42% ACT 18-23; 40% ACT 24-29 **% Accepted:** 64 **Admission Plans:** Early Admission; Deferred Admission **Application Deadline:** Rolling **Application Fee:** $30.00 **H.S. Requirements:** High school diploma required; GED accepted **Costs Per Year:** Application fee: $30. State resident tuition: $5988 full-time. Nonresident tuition: $17,651 full-time. Full-time tuition varies according to course load and degree level. **Scholarships:** Available **Calendar System:** Semester, Summer Session Available **Enrollment:** FT 8,962, PT 1,878, Grad FT 556, Grad PT 1,368 **Faculty:** FT 569, PT 239 **Student-Faculty Ratio:** 16:1 **Exams:** SAT I or ACT. ACT essay used for admission. SAT essay used for admission. ACT essay used for advising. SAT essay used for advising. ACT essay used for placement. SAT essay used for placement. **% Receiving Financial Aid:** 48 **% Residing in College-Owned, -Operated, or -Affiliated Housing:** 25 **Library Holdings:** 744,989 **Credit Hours For Degree:** 120 credits, Bachelors **ROTC:** Army, Air Force **Professional Accreditation:** AACSB, ABET, AACN, AAFCS, ACA, APA, NAAB, NASAD, NASM, NCATE, NCCU, TEAC **Intercollegiate Athletics:** Basketball M & W; Cheerleading M & W; Cross-Country Running M & W; Football M; Golf W; Skiing (Cross-Country) M & W; Skiing (Downhill) M & W; Tennis M & W; Track and Field M & W; Volleyball W

MONTANA STATE UNIVERSITY BILLINGS
1500 University Dr.
Billings, MT 59101-0298
Tel: (406)657-2011; Free: 800-565-6782
Admissions: (406)657-2158
Fax: (406)657-2302
E-mail: sandersen@msubillings.edu
Web Site: http://www.msubillings.edu/
President/CEO: Dr. Ronald P. Sexton
Admissions: Shelly Andersen
Financial Aid: Judy Chapman
Type: Comprehensive **Sex:** Coed **Affiliation:** Montana University System **Scores:** 99% SAT V 400+; 98% SAT M 400+ **% Accepted:** 100 **Admission Plans:** Early Admission; Deferred Admission **Application Deadline:** July 1 **Application Fee:** $30.00 **H.S. Requirements:** High school diploma required; GED accepted **Costs Per Year:** Application fee: $30. State resident tuition: $3988 full-time, $144 per credit hour part-time. Nonresident tuition: $14,648 full-time, $407 per credit hour part-time. Mandatory fees: $1219 full-time. Full-time tuition and fees vary according to course load, degree level, and location. Part-time tuition varies according to course load, degree level, and location. College room and board: $5460. Room and board charges vary according to board plan and housing facility. **Scholarships:** Available **Calendar System:** Semester, Summer Session Available **Faculty:** FT 154, PT 136 **Student-Faculty Ratio:** 20:1 **Exams:** SAT I or ACT. **% Receiving Financial Aid:** 59 **% Residing in College-Owned, -Operated, or -Affiliated Housing:** 12 **Library Holdings:** 365,212 **Credit Hours For Degree:** 64 credit hours, Associates; 120 credit hours, Bachelors **ROTC:** Army **Professional Accreditation:** CORE, NASAD, NASM, NCATE, NCCU **Intercollegiate Athletics:** Baseball M; Basketball M & W; Cross-Country Running M & W; Golf M & W; Soccer M & W; Softball W; Tennis M & W; Volleyball W

MONTANA STATE UNIVERSITY—GREAT FALLS COLLEGE OF TECHNOLOGY
2100 16th Ave., South
Great Falls, MT 59405
Tel: (406)771-4300
Fax: (406)771-4317
E-mail: dfreshly@msugf.edu

Web Site: http://www.msugf.edu/
President/CEO: Joseph Schaffer
Admissions: Dana Freshly
Type: Two-Year College **Sex:** Coed **Affiliation:** Montana University System **% Accepted:** 98 **Admission Plans:** Open Admission; Early Admission **Application Deadline:** Rolling **Application Fee:** $30.00 **H.S. Requirements:** High school diploma required; GED accepted **Costs Per Year:** Application fee: $30. State resident tuition: $2496 full-time, $104 per credit hour part-time. Nonresident tuition: $8748 full-time, $364.48 per credit hour part-time. Mandatory fees: $529 full-time, $67.35 per credit hour part-time. Full-time tuition and fees vary according to course load and program. Part-time tuition and fees vary according to course load and program. **Scholarships:** Available **Calendar System:** Semester, Summer Session Available **Enrollment:** FT 907, PT 1,544 **Faculty:** FT 46, PT 96 **Final Year or Final Semester Residency Requirement:** No **Library Holdings:** 8,783 **Credit Hours For Degree:** 60 credits, Associates **Professional Accreditation:** AAMAE, ADA, AHIMA, CARC, NCCU

MONTANA STATE UNIVERSITY—NORTHERN
PO Box 7751
Havre, MT 59501-7751
Tel: (406)265-3700
Fax: (406)265-3777
Web Site: http://www.msun.edu/
President/CEO: Frank Trocki
Admissions: Rosalie Spinler
Financial Aid: Cindy Small
Type: Comprehensive **Sex:** Coed **Affiliation:** Montana University System **% Accepted:** 100 **Admission Plans:** Early Admission; Deferred Admission **Application Deadline:** Rolling **Application Fee:** $30.00 **H.S. Requirements:** High school diploma required; GED accepted **Scholarships:** Available **Calendar System:** Semester, Summer Session Available **% Receiving Financial Aid:** 75 **Library Holdings:** 128,000 **Credit Hours For Degree:** 64 credits, Associates; 128 credits, Bachelors **Professional Accreditation:** ABET, NCATE, NLN, NCCU **Intercollegiate Athletics:** Basketball M & W; Football M; Golf W; Volleyball W; Wrestling M

MONTANA TECH OF THE UNIVERSITY OF MONTANA
1300 West Park St.
Butte, MT 59701-8997
Tel: (406)496-4101; Free: 800-445-TECH
Admissions: (406)496-4256
Fax: (406)496-4710
E-mail: tcampeau@mtech.edu
Web Site: http://www.mtech.edu/
President/CEO: Frank Gilmore
Admissions: Tony Campeau
Financial Aid: Mike Richardson
Type: Comprehensive **Sex:** Coed **Affiliation:** Montana University System **Scores:** 92% SAT V 400+; 98% SAT M 400+; 50% ACT 18-23; 37% ACT 24-29 **% Accepted:** 91 **Admission Plans:** Open Admission; Deferred Admission **Application Deadline:** Rolling **Application Fee:** $30.00 **H.S. Requirements:** High school diploma required; GED accepted **Costs Per Year:** Application fee: $30. State resident tuition: $4696 full-time, $195.65 per credit part-time. Nonresident tuition: $15,510 full-time, $646.25 per credit part-time. Mandatory fees: $1311 full-time. Full-time tuition and fees vary according to course load, degree level, location, and program. Part-time tuition varies according to course load, degree level, location, and program. College room and board: $6602. College room only: $2788. Room and board charges vary according to board plan. **Scholarships:** Available **Calendar System:** Semester, Summer Session Available **Enrollment:** FT 2,169, PT 391, Grad FT 63, Grad PT 71 **Faculty:** FT 127, PT 74 **Student-Faculty Ratio:** 15:1 **Exams:** SAT I or ACT. **% Receiving Financial Aid:** 54 **% Residing in College-Owned, -Operated, or -Affiliated Housing:** 15 **Library Holdings:** 174,528 **Credit Hours For Degree:** 60 credit hours, Associates; 120 credit hours, Bachelors **Professional Accreditation:** ABET, NCCU **Intercollegiate Athletics:** Basketball M & W; Football M; Golf M & W; Volleyball W

ROCKY MOUNTAIN COLLEGE
1511 Poly Dr.
Billings, MT 59102-1796
Tel: (406)657-1000; Free: 800-877-6259
Admissions: (406)657-1026
Fax: (406)259-9751
E-mail: admissions@rocky.edu
Web Site: http://www.rocky.edu/
President/CEO: Michael Mace
Admissions: Kelly Edwards
Financial Aid: Jessica Francischetti
Type: Comprehensive **Sex:** Coed **Affiliation:** interdenominational **Scores:** 88% SAT V 400+; 94% SAT M 400+; 53% ACT 18-23; 34% ACT 24-29 **% Accepted:** 63 **Admission Plans:** Early Admission; Early Action; Deferred Admission **Application Deadline:** Rolling **Application Fee:** $35.00 **H.S. Requirements:** High school diploma required; GED accepted **Costs Per Year:** Application fee: $35. Comprehensive fee: $27,680 includes full-time tuition ($20,650), mandatory fees ($450), and college room and board ($6580). Full-time tuition and fees vary according to course load, degree level, and program. Room and board charges vary according to board plan and housing facility. Part-time tuition: $860 per credit. Part-time tuition varies according to course load, degree level, and program. **Scholarships:** Available **Calendar System:** Semester, Summer Session Available **Enrollment:** FT 781, PT 33, Grad FT 65, Grad PT 1 **Faculty:** FT 65, PT 48 **Student-Faculty Ratio:** 10:1 **Exams:** SAT I or ACT. **% Receiving Financial Aid:** 73 **% Residing in College-Owned, -Operated, or -Affiliated Housing:** 55 **Final Year or Final Semester Residency Requirement:** No **Library Holdings:** 101,020 **Credit Hours For Degree:** 62 semester hours, Associates; 124 semester hours, Bachelors **ROTC:** Army **Professional Accreditation:** NCCU **Intercollegiate Athletics:** Basketball M & W; Cheerleading W; Cross-Country Running M & W; Equestrian Sports M & W; Football M; Golf M & W; Skiing (Downhill) M & W; Soccer M & W; Volleyball W

SALISH KOOTENAI COLLEGE
PO Box 70
Pablo, MT 59855-0117
Tel: (406)275-4800
Fax: (406)275-4801
E-mail: jackie_moran@skc.edu
Web Site: http://www.skc.edu/
President/CEO: Joseph F. McDonald
Admissions: Jackie Moran
Financial Aid: Chastity Wagner
Type: Two-Year College **Sex:** Coed **% Accepted:** 64 **Admission Plans:** Open Admission; Preferred Admission; Deferred Admission **Application Deadline:** Rolling **H.S. Requirements:** High school diploma required; GED accepted **Scholarships:** Available **Calendar System:** Quarter, Summer Session Available **Enrollment:** FT 585, PT 503 **Faculty:** FT 45, PT 35 **Library Holdings:** 24,000 **Credit Hours For Degree:** 92 credits, Associates; 180 credits, Bachelors **Professional Accreditation:** ADA, NLN, NCCU

STONE CHILD COLLEGE
RR1, Box 1082
Box Elder, MT 59521
Tel: (406)395-4313
Fax: (406)395-4836
E-mail: uanet337@quest.ocsc.montana.edu
Web Site: http://www.stonechild.edu/
President/CEO: Melody Henry
Admissions: Ted Whitford
Type: Two-Year College **Sex:** Coed **% Accepted:** 100 **Admission Plans:** Open Admission **Application Fee:** $10.00 **H.S. Requirements:** High school diploma required; GED accepted **Scholarships:** Available **Calendar System:** Semester **Faculty:** FT 10, PT 12 **Credit Hours For Degree:** 64 semester hours, Associates **Professional Accreditation:** NCCU

UNIVERSITY OF GREAT FALLS
1301 Twentieth St. South
Great Falls, MT 59405
Tel: (406)761-8210; Free: 800-856-9544
Admissions: (406)791-5202
Fax: (406)791-5209
E-mail: enroll@ugf.edu
Web Site: http://www.ugf.edu/
President/CEO: Dr. Eugene J. McAllister, PhD
Admissions: Kelly Braun
Financial Aid: Sandra Bauman
Type: Comprehensive **Sex:** Coed **Affiliation:** Roman Catholic; Providence Services **Scores:** 91.7% SAT V 400+; 92.7% SAT M 400+; 56.4% ACT 18-

23; 20% ACT 24-29 **Admission Plans:** Open Admission; Early Admission; Deferred Admission **Application Deadline:** August 1 **Application Fee:** $0.00 **H.S. Requirements:** High school diploma required; GED accepted. For home school students: High school diploma or equivalent not required **Costs Per Year:** Application fee: $0. Comprehensive fee: $25,568 includes full-time tuition ($17,856), mandatory fees ($1000), and college room and board ($6712). College room only: $3512. Full-time tuition and fees vary according to course load. Room and board charges vary according to housing facility. Part-time tuition: $566 per credit hour. Part-time tuition varies according to course load, location, and program. **Scholarships:** Available **Calendar System:** Semester, Summer Session Available **Enrollment:** FT 588, PT 194, Grad FT 25, Grad PT 51 **Faculty:** FT 41, PT 72 **Student-Faculty Ratio:** 12:1 **Exams:** SAT I or ACT. **% Receiving Financial Aid:** 73 **% Residing in College-Owned, -Operated, or -Affiliated Housing:** 58 **Library Holdings:** 108,926 **Credit Hours For Degree:** 64 credits, Associates; 128 credits, Bachelors **Professional Accreditation:** NCCU **Intercollegiate Athletics:** Basketball M & W; Cheerleading M & W; Cross-Country Running M & W; Equestrian Sports M & W; Golf M & W; Soccer M & W; Softball W; Track and Field M & W; Volleyball W; Wrestling M

THE UNIVERSITY OF MONTANA
Missoula, MT 59812-0002
Tel: (406)243-0211; Free: 800-462-8636
Admissions: (406)243-6266
Fax: (406)243-5711
E-mail: admiss@umontana.edu
Web Site: http://www.umt.edu/
President/CEO: Dr. George M. Dennison
Admissions: Juana Alcala
Financial Aid: Mick Hanson
Type: University **Sex:** Coed **Affiliation:** Montana University System **Scores:** 95% SAT V 400+; 95% SAT M 400+; 50% ACT 18-23; 38% ACT 24-29 **% Accepted:** 96 **Admission Plans:** Early Admission; Deferred Admission **Application Deadline:** Rolling **Application Fee:** $30.00 **H.S. Requirements:** High school diploma required; GED accepted. For home schooled applicants: High school diploma or equivalent not required **Costs Per Year:** Application fee: $30. State resident tuition: $4054 full-time, $169 per credit hour part-time. Nonresident tuition: $16,894 full-time, $704 per credit hour part-time. Mandatory fees: $1479 full-time, $98 per credit hour part-time. Full-time tuition and fees vary according to degree level, location, program, reciprocity agreements, and student level. Part-time tuition and fees vary according to course load, degree level, location, and student level. College room and board: $6611. College room only: $2989. Room and board charges vary according to board plan and housing facility. **Scholarships:** Available **Calendar System:** Semester, Summer Session Available **Enrollment:** FT 10,136, PT 2,060 **Faculty:** FT 564, PT 236 **Student-Faculty Ratio:** 19:1 **Exams:** SAT I or ACT. **% Receiving Financial Aid:** 57 **% Residing in College-Owned, -Operated, or -Affiliated Housing:** 29 **Library Holdings:** 1,145,726 **Credit Hours For Degree:** 65 credits, Associates; 120 credits, Bachelors **ROTC:** Army **Professional Accreditation:** AACSB, ABET, ACPhE, ACEJMC, ABA, ACA, ACF, APTA, APA, AALS, CARC, CSWE, JRCEPAT, NASAD, NASM, NAST, NCATE, NRPA, NCCU, SAF **Intercollegiate Athletics:** Baseball M; Basketball M & W; Crew M & W; Cross-Country Running M & W; Equestrian Sports M & W; Fencing M & W; Field Hockey W; Football M; Golf W; Gymnastics W; Ice Hockey M & W; Lacrosse M & W; Rugby M & W; Skiing (Downhill) M & W; Soccer W; Tennis M & W; Track and Field M & W; Ultimate Frisbee M & W; Volleyball W

THE UNIVERSITY OF MONTANA WESTERN
710 South Atlantic
Dillon, MT 59725-3598
Tel: (406)683-7011; Free: 877-683-7493
Admissions: (406)683-7331
Fax: (406)683-7493
E-mail: admissions@umwestern.edu
Web Site: http://www.umwestern.edu/
President/CEO: Dr. Richard Storey
Financial Aid: Erica L. Jones
Type: Four-Year College **Sex:** Coed **Affiliation:** Montana University System **Scores:** 79% SAT V 400+; 77% SAT M 400+; 58% ACT 18-23; 15% ACT 24-29 **% Accepted:** 70 **Admission Plans:** Early Admission; Deferred Admission **Application Deadline:** Rolling **Application Fee:** $30.00 **H.S. Requirements:** High school diploma required; GED accepted **Costs Per Year:** Application fee: $30. State resident tuition: $3355 full-time, $139.77 per credit hour part-time. Nonresident tuition: $12,035 full-time, $501.45 per credit hour part-time. Mandatory fees: $924 full-time. Full-time tuition and fees vary according to program and student level. Part-time tuition varies according to program and student level. College room and board: $6420. College room only: $2180. Room and board charges vary according to housing facility. **Scholarships:** Available **Calendar System:** Semester, Summer Session Available **Enrollment:** FT 1,041, PT 214 **Faculty:** FT 61, PT 28 **Student-Faculty Ratio:** 14:1 **Exams:** SAT I or ACT. ACT essay used for admission. SAT essay used for admission. **% Receiving Financial Aid:** 75 **% Residing in College-Owned, -Operated, or -Affiliated Housing:** 35 **Library Holdings:** 138,671 **Credit Hours For Degree:** 64 credits, Associates; 120 credits, Bachelors **Professional Accreditation:** NCATE, NCCU **Intercollegiate Athletics:** Basketball M & W; Equestrian Sports M & W; Football M; Golf M & W; Volleyball W

THE UNIVERSITY OF MONTANA—HELENA COLLEGE OF TECHNOLOGY
1115 North Roberts St.
Helena, MT 59601
Tel: (406)444-6800
Admissions: (406)444-5436
Fax: (406)444-6892
E-mail: kendall.may@umhelena.edu
Web Site: http://www.umhelena.edu/
President/CEO: Dr. Daniel Bingham
Admissions: Kendall May
Type: Two-Year College **Sex:** Coed **Affiliation:** Montana University System **% Accepted:** 74 **Admission Plans:** Open Admission; Early Admission; Deferred Admission **Application Deadline:** Rolling **Application Fee:** $30.00 **H.S. Requirements:** High school diploma required; GED accepted **Costs Per Year:** Application fee: $30. State resident tuition: $3041 full-time, $98.25 per credit hour part-time. Nonresident tuition: $8066 full-time. Full-time tuition varies according to course load and reciprocity agreements. Part-time tuition varies according to course load and reciprocity agreements. **Scholarships:** Available **Calendar System:** Semester, Summer Session Available **Enrollment:** FT 732, PT 648 **Faculty:** FT 55, PT 35 **Student-Faculty Ratio:** 14:1 **Final Year or Final Semester Residency Requirement:** No **Library Holdings:** 60,281 **Credit Hours For Degree:** 60 credit hours, Associates **Professional Accreditation:** NCCU

BELLEVUE UNIVERSITY
1000 Galvin Rd. South
Bellevue, NE 68005-3098
Tel: (402)291-8100; Free: 800-756-7920
Fax: (402)293-2020
E-mail: michelle.eppler@bellevue.edu
Web Site: http://www.bellevue.edu/
President/CEO: Mary Hawkins
Admissions: Michelle Eppler
Financial Aid: Jon Dotterer
Type: Comprehensive **Sex:** Coed **% Accepted:** 100 **Admission Plans:** Open Admission; Deferred Admission **Application Deadline:** Rolling **Application Fee:** $50.00 **H.S. Requirements:** High school diploma required; GED accepted **Scholarships:** Available **Calendar System:** Semester, Summer Session Available **Enrollment:** FT 3,404, PT 1,496 **Faculty:** FT 76, PT 294 **Student-Faculty Ratio:** 18:1 **% Receiving Financial Aid:** 87 **Library Holdings:** 100,904 **Regional Accreditation:** North Central Association of Colleges and Schools **Credit Hours For Degree:** 127 credit hours, Bachelors **ROTC:** Army, Air Force **Intercollegiate Athletics:** Baseball M; Basketball M; Soccer M & W; Softball W; Volleyball W

CENTRAL COMMUNITY COLLEGE—COLUMBUS CAMPUS
4500 63rd St., PO Box 1027
Columbus, NE 68602-1027
Tel: (402)564-7132
Admissions: (402)562-1296
Fax: (402)562-1201
E-mail: myoung@cccneb.edu
Web Site: http://www.cccneb.edu/
President/CEO: Dr. Matt Gotschall
Admissions: Mary Young
Type: Two-Year College **Sex:** Coed **Affiliation:** Central Community College **Admission Plans:** Open Admission; Early Admission **Application Deadline:** Rolling **Application Fee:** $0.00 **H.S. Requirements:** High school diploma required; GED accepted. For nursing program: High school diploma required; GED not accepted **Costs Per Year:** Application fee: $0. State resident tuition: $1776 full-time, $74 per credit part-time. Nonresident tuition: $2664 full-time, $111 per credit part-time. Mandatory fees: $168 full-time, $7 per credit part-time. College room and board: $5120. Room and board charges vary according to board plan. **Scholarships:** Available **Calendar System:** Semester, Summer Session Available **Enrollment:** FT 481, PT 2,120 **Faculty:** FT 40, PT 48 **% Residing in College-Owned, -Operated, or -Affiliated Housing:** 17 **Final Year or Final Semester Residency Requirement:** No **Library Holdings:** 22,000 **Regional Accreditation:** North Central Association of Colleges and Schools **Credit Hours For Degree:** 60 credits, Associates **Intercollegiate Athletics:** Basketball M; Golf M; Softball W; Volleyball W

CENTRAL COMMUNITY COLLEGE—GRAND ISLAND CAMPUS
PO Box 4903
Grand Island, NE 68802-4903
Tel: (308)398-4222
Admissions: (308)398-7406
Fax: (308)398-7398
E-mail: msvoboda@cccneb.edu
Web Site: http://www.cccneb.edu/
President/CEO: Dr. Lynn C. Black
Admissions: Michelle Svoboda
Financial Aid: Steve Millnitz
Type: Two-Year College **Sex:** Coed **Affiliation:** Central Community College **Admission Plans:** Open Admission; Early Admission **Application Deadline:** Rolling **Application Fee:** $0.00 **H.S. Requirements:** High school diploma required; GED accepted. For nursing program: High school diploma required; GED not accepted **Costs Per Year:** Application fee: $0. State resident tuition: $1776 full-time, $74 per credit part-time. Nonresident tuition: $2664 full-time, $111 per credit part-time. Mandatory fees: $168 full-time. **Scholarships:** Available **Calendar System:** Semester, Summer Session Available **Enrollment:** FT 456, PT 2,807 **Faculty:** FT 46, PT 66 **Student-Faculty Ratio:** 15:1 **% Residing in College-Owned, -Operated, or -Affiliated Housing:** 10 **Final Year or Final Semester Residency Requirement:** No **Library Holdings:** 5,700 **Regional Accreditation:** North Central Association of Colleges and Schools **Credit Hours For Degree:** 60 credits, Associates **Professional Accreditation:** ADA, NLN

CENTRAL COMMUNITY COLLEGE—HASTINGS CAMPUS
PO Box 1024
Hastings, NE 68902-1024
Tel: (402)463-9811
Admissions: (402)461-2428
E-mail: rglenn@ccneb.edu
Web Site: http://www.cccneb.edu/
President/CEO: Bill Hitesman
Admissions: Robert Glenn
Type: Two-Year College **Sex:** Coed **Affiliation:** Central Community College **Admission Plans:** Open Admission; Early Admission **Application Deadline:** Rolling **Application Fee:** $0.00 **H.S. Requirements:** High school diploma required; GED accepted. For nursing, dental hygiene, truck driving, medical laboratory technology programs: High school diploma required; GED not accepted **Costs Per Year:** Application fee: $0. State resident tuition: $1776 full-time, $74 per credit hour part-time. Nonresident tuition: $2664 full-time, $111 per credit hour part-time. Mandatory fees: $168 full-time, $7 per credit hour part-time. College room and board: $5120. Room and board charges vary according to board plan. **Scholarships:** Available **Calendar System:** Semester, Summer Session Available **Enrollment:** FT 1,083, PT 1,775 **Faculty:** FT 63, PT 28 **% Residing in College-Owned, -Operated, or -Affiliated Housing:** 26 **Final Year or Final Semester Residency Requirement:** No **Library Holdings:** 4,025 **Regional Accreditation:** North Central Association of Colleges and Schools **Credit Hours For Degree:** 60 credits, Associates **Professional Accreditation:** AAMAE, ADA, AHIMA, NAACLS

CHADRON STATE COLLEGE
1000 Main St.
Chadron, NE 69337
Tel: (308)432-6000
Fax: (308)432-6229
E-mail: inquire@csc1.csc.edu
Web Site: http://www.csc.edu/
President/CEO: Janie Park, Phd
Admissions: Tena Cook Gould

Financial Aid: Sherry Douglas
Type: Comprehensive **Sex:** Coed **Affiliation:** Nebraska State College System **Scores:** 53% ACT 18-23; 28% ACT 24-29 **Admission Plans:** Open Admission; Early Admission **Application Deadline:** Rolling **Application Fee:** $15.00 **H.S. Requirements:** High school diploma required; GED accepted **Scholarships:** Available **Calendar System:** Semester, Summer Session Available **Enrollment:** FT 1,634, PT 682 **Faculty:** FT 101, PT 9 **Student-Faculty Ratio:** 19:1 **% Receiving Financial Aid:** 97 **% Residing in College-Owned, -Operated, or -Affiliated Housing:** 65 **Library Holdings:** 593,140 **Regional Accreditation:** North Central Association of Colleges and Schools **Credit Hours For Degree:** 125 semester hours, Bachelors **Professional Accreditation:** AAFCS, ACBSP, CSWE, NCATE **Intercollegiate Athletics:** Basketball M & W; Equestrian Sports M & W; Football M; Golf W; Track and Field M & W; Volleyball W; Wrestling M

CLARKSON COLLEGE
101 South 42nd St.
Omaha, NE 68131-2739
Tel: (402)552-3100; Free: 800-647-5500
Fax: (402)552-6057
E-mail: workdenise@clarksoncollege.edu
Web Site: http://www.clarksoncollege.edu/
President/CEO: Dr. Louis Burgher
Admissions: Denise Work
Financial Aid: Pam Shelton
Type: Comprehensive **Sex:** Coed **Scores:** 61% ACT 18-23; 30% ACT 24-29 **% Accepted:** 55 **Admission Plans:** Deferred Admission **Application Deadline:** Rolling **Application Fee:** $35.00 **H.S. Requirements:** High school diploma required; GED accepted **Costs Per Year:** Application fee: $35. One-time mandatory fee: $100. Tuition: $10,660 full-time, $410 per credit hour part-time. Mandatory fees: $650 full-time. College room only: $6200. **Scholarships:** Available **Calendar System:** Semester, Summer Session Available **Enrollment:** FT 658 **Faculty:** FT 48, PT 53 **Student-Faculty Ratio:** 8:1 **Exams:** SAT I or ACT. **% Receiving Financial Aid:** 75 **% Residing in College-Owned, -Operated, or -Affiliated Housing:** 14 **Library Holdings:** 8,807 **Regional Accreditation:** North Central Association of Colleges and Schools **Credit Hours For Degree:** 70 credits, Associates; 128 credits, Bachelors **ROTC:** Army, Air Force **Professional Accreditation:** APTA, JRCERT, NLN

COLLEGE OF SAINT MARY
7000 Mercy Rd.
Omaha, NE 68106
Tel: (402)399-2400; Free: 800-926-5534
Admissions: (402)399-2406
Fax: (402)399-2412
E-mail: enroll@csm.edu
Web Site: http://www.csm.edu/
President/CEO: Dr. Maryanne Stevens, RSM
Admissions: Erika Pritchard
Financial Aid: Beth Sisk
Type: Comprehensive **Sex:** Women **Affiliation:** Roman Catholic **Scores:** 72% ACT 18-23; 14% ACT 24-29 **% Accepted:** 42 **Application Deadline:** Rolling **Application Fee:** $30.00 **H.S. Requirements:** High school diploma required; GED accepted **Costs Per Year:** Application fee: $30. Comprehensive fee: $29,530 includes full-time tuition ($22,650), mandatory fees ($480), and college room and board ($6400). Full-time tuition and fees vary according to location. Part-time tuition: $750 per credit. Part-time mandatory fees: $16 per credit. Part-time tuition and fees vary according to class time and location. **Scholarships:** Available **Calendar System:** Semester, Summer Session Available **Enrollment:** FT 687, PT 168, Grad FT 181, Grad PT 84 **Faculty:** FT 54, PT 134 **Student-Faculty Ratio:** 14:1 **Exams:** SAT I or ACT. ACT essay not being used. SAT essay not being used. **% Receiving Financial Aid:** 93 **% Residing in College-Owned, -Operated, or -Affiliated Housing:** 19 **Final Year or Final Semester Residency Requirement:** No **Library Holdings:** 89,216 **Regional Accreditation:** North Central Association of Colleges and Schools **Credit Hours For Degree:** 64 credit hours, Associates; 128 credit hours, Bachelors **ROTC:** Army, Air Force **Professional Accreditation:** AHIMA, AOTA, NLN **Intercollegiate Athletics:** Basketball W; Cross-Country Running W; Soccer W; Softball W; Swimming and Diving W; Volleyball W

CONCORDIA UNIVERSITY, NEBRASKA
800 North Columbia Ave.
Seward, NE 68434-1599
Tel: (402)643-3651; Free: 800-535-5494
Fax: (402)643-4073
E-mail: admiss@cune.edu
Web Site: http://www.cune.edu/
President/CEO: Rev. Brian L. Friedrich
Admissions: Aaron W. Roberts
Financial Aid: Aaron W. Roberts
Type: Comprehensive **Sex:** Coed **Affiliation:** Lutheran Church–Missouri Synod **Scores:** 87% SAT V 400+; 85% SAT M 400+; 37% ACT 18-23; 43% ACT 24-29 **% Accepted:** 75 **Admission Plans:** Deferred Admission **Application Deadline:** August 1 **Application Fee:** $0.00 **H.S. Requirements:** High school diploma required; GED accepted **Costs Per Year:** Application fee: $0. Comprehensive fee: $27,935 includes full-time tuition ($21,940), mandatory fees ($175), and college room and board ($5820). College room only: $2470. Room and board charges vary according to board plan and housing facility. Part-time tuition: $685 per credit hour. **Scholarships:** Available **Calendar System:** Miscellaneous, Summer Session Available **Enrollment:** FT 1,062, PT 195, Grad FT 364, Grad PT 96 **Faculty:** FT 55, PT 88 **Student-Faculty Ratio:** 13:1 **Exams:** SAT I or ACT. ACT essay not being used. SAT essay not being used. **% Receiving Financial Aid:** 77 **% Residing in College-Owned, -Operated, or -Affiliated Housing:** 76 **Final Year or Final Semester Residency Requirement:** No **Library Holdings:** 170,000 **Regional Accreditation:** North Central Association of Colleges and Schools **Credit Hours For Degree:** 128 credit hours, Bachelors **ROTC:** Army, Air Force **Professional Accreditation:** NASM, NCATE **Intercollegiate Athletics:** Baseball M; Basketball M & W; Cross-Country Running M & W; Football M; Golf M & W; Soccer M & W; Softball W; Tennis M & W; Track and Field M & W; Volleyball W; Wrestling M

CREATIVE CENTER
10850 Emmet St.
Omaha, NE 68164
Tel: (402)898-1000; Free: 888-898-1789
Fax: (402)898-1301
E-mail: admission@creativecenter.edu
Web Site: http://www.creativecenter.edu/
President/CEO: Ray Dotzler
Type: Two-Year College **Sex:** Coed **Application Fee:** $100.00 **H.S. Requirements:** High school diploma required; GED accepted **Calendar System:** Semester, Summer Session Not available **Student-Faculty Ratio:** 26:1 **Professional Accreditation:** ACCSCT

CREIGHTON UNIVERSITY
2500 California Plaza
Omaha, NE 68178-0001
Tel: (402)280-2700; Free: 800-282-5835
Admissions: (402)280-3105
Fax: (402)280-2685
E-mail: admissions@creighton.edu
Web Site: http://www.creighton.edu/
President/CEO: John P. Schlegel
Admissions: Mary Chase
Financial Aid: Sarah Sell
Type: University **Sex:** Coed **Affiliation:** Roman Catholic (Jesuit) **Scores:** 97.9% SAT V 400+; 98.3% SAT M 400+; 21.2% ACT 18-23; 53.9% ACT 24-29 **% Accepted:** 82 **Admission Plans:** Deferred Admission **Application Deadline:** February 15 **Application Fee:** $40.00 **H.S. Requirements:** High school diploma required; GED accepted **Costs Per Year:** Application fee: $40. Comprehensive fee: $30,932 includes full-time tuition ($20,812), mandatory fees ($1306), and college room and board ($8814). College room only: $4984. Full-time tuition and fees vary according to degree level and location. Room and board charges vary according to board plan and housing facility. Part-time tuition: $882 per semester hour. Part-time mandatory fees: $252 per year. Part-time tuition and fees vary according to degree level. **Scholarships:** Available **Calendar System:** Semester, Summer Session Available **Enrollment:** FT 3,869, PT 264, Grad FT 2,610, Grad PT 642 **Faculty:** FT 532, PT 203 **Student-Faculty Ratio:** 11:1 **Exams:** SAT I or ACT. **% Receiving Financial Aid:** 50 **% Residing in College-Owned, -Operated, or -Affiliated Housing:** 60 **Final Year or Final Semester Residency Requirement:** Yes **Library Holdings:** 816,843 **Regional Accreditation:** North Central Association of Colleges and Schools **Credit Hours For Degree:** 64 credits, Associates; 128 credits, Bachelors **ROTC:** Army, Air Force **Professional Accreditation:** AACSB, ACPhE, AACN, ABA, ADA, AOTA, APTA, AALS, CSWE, JRCEMT, LCMEAMA, NCATE **Intercol-**

legiate Athletics: Baseball M; Basketball M & W; Crew W; Cross-Country Running M & W; Golf M & W; Soccer M & W; Softball W; Tennis M & W; Volleyball W

DANA COLLEGE
2848 College Dr.
Blair, NE 68008-1099
Tel: (402)426-9000; Free: 800-444-3262
Admissions: (402)426-7220
Fax: (402)426-7386
E-mail: admissions@dana.edu
Web Site: http://www.dana.edu/
President/CEO: Janet Philipp
Admissions: Tina Blair
Financial Aid: Rita McManigal
Type: Four-Year College **Sex:** Coed **Affiliation:** Evangelical Lutheran Church in America **Scores:** 75% SAT V 400+; 93.75% SAT M 400+; 63. 64% ACT 18-23; 30.3% ACT 24-29 **% Accepted:** 66 **Admission Plans:** Deferred Admission **Application Deadline:** Rolling **Application Fee:** $0.00 **H.S. Requirements:** High school diploma required; GED accepted **Costs Per Year:** Application fee: $0. Comprehensive fee: $27,320 includes full-time tuition ($20,300), mandatory fees ($800), and college room and board ($6220). College room only: $2440. Room and board charges vary according to board plan and housing facility. Part-time tuition: $570 per credit hour. Part-time mandatory fees: $60 per year. Part-time tuition and fees vary according to course load. **Scholarships:** Available **Calendar System:** 4-1-4, Summer Session Available **Enrollment:** FT 576, PT 20 **Faculty:** FT 32, PT 26 **Student-Faculty Ratio:** 14:1 **Exams:** ACT, SAT I or ACT. ACT essay not being used. SAT essay not being used. **% Receiving Financial Aid:** 78 **% Residing in College-Owned, -Operated, or -Affiliated Housing:** 65 **Final Year or Final Semester Residency Requirement:** No **Library Holdings:** 158,752 **Regional Accreditation:** North Central Association of Colleges and Schools **Credit Hours For Degree:** 128 semester hours, Bachelors **ROTC:** Army, Air Force **Professional Accreditation:** ACBSP, CSWE, NCATE **Intercollegiate Athletics:** Baseball M; Basketball M & W; Cross-Country Running M & W; Football M; Golf W; Soccer M & W; Softball W; Track and Field M & W; Volleyball W; Wrestling M

DOANE COLLEGE
1014 Boswell Ave.
Crete, NE 68333-2430
Tel: (402)826-2161; Free: 800-333-6263
Fax: (402)826-8600
E-mail: joel.weyand@doane.edu
Web Site: http://www.doane.edu/
President/CEO: Jonathan M. Brand, Esq.
Admissions: Joel M. Weyand
Financial Aid: Peggy Tvrdy
Type: Comprehensive **Sex:** Coed **Affiliation:** United Church of Christ **Scores:** 50% ACT 18-23; 36% ACT 24-29 **% Accepted:** 76 **Admission Plans:** Early Admission; Deferred Admission **Application Deadline:** Rolling **Application Fee:** $0.00 **H.S. Requirements:** High school diploma required; GED accepted **Costs Per Year:** Application fee: $0. Comprehensive fee: $27,010 includes full-time tuition ($20,540), mandatory fees ($500), and college room and board ($5970). College room only: $2270. Full-time tuition and fees vary according to location. Room and board charges vary according to board plan, housing facility, and location. Part-time tuition: $680 per credit hour. Part-time tuition varies according to course load and location. **Scholarships:** Available **Calendar System:** 4-1-4, Summer Session Available **Enrollment:** FT 963, PT 6 **Faculty:** FT 70, PT 49 **Student-Faculty Ratio:** 11:1 **Exams:** SAT I or ACT. **% Receiving Financial Aid:** 79 **% Residing in College-Owned, -Operated, or -Affiliated Housing:** 82 **Library Holdings:** 332,788 **Regional Accreditation:** North Central Association of Colleges and Schools **Credit Hours For Degree:** 132 credit hours, Bachelors **ROTC:** Army, Air Force **Professional Accreditation:** ACBSP, NCATE **Intercollegiate Athletics:** Baseball M; Basketball M & W; Cross-Country Running M & W; Football M; Golf M & W; Soccer M & W; Softball W; Tennis M & W; Track and Field M & W; Volleyball W

GRACE UNIVERSITY
1311 South Ninth St.
Omaha, NE 68108
Tel: (402)449-2800; Free: 800-383-1422
Admissions: (402)449-2831
Fax: (402)341-9587
E-mail: admissions@graceuniversity.com
Web Site: http://www.graceuniversity.edu/
President/CEO: Dr. James P. Eckman
Admissions: Angela Wayman
Financial Aid: Marcy Pierce
Type: Comprehensive **Sex:** Coed **Affiliation:** interdenominational **% Accepted:** 64 **Admission Plans:** Early Admission; Deferred Admission **Application Deadline:** Rolling **Application Fee:** $20.00 **H.S. Requirements:** High school diploma required; GED accepted **Costs Per Year:** Application fee: $20. Comprehensive fee: $20,030 includes full-time tuition ($13,900), mandatory fees ($390), and college room and board ($5740). College room only: $2550. Part-time tuition: $390 per credit hour. Part-time mandatory fees: $165 per term. **Scholarships:** Available **Calendar System:** Semester, Summer Session Available **Enrollment:** FT 287, PT 79 **Faculty:** FT 25, PT 25 **Student-Faculty Ratio:** 18:1 **Exams:** SAT I or ACT. **% Receiving Financial Aid:** 74 **% Residing in College-Owned, -Operated, or -Affiliated Housing:** 60 **Library Holdings:** 46,736 **Regional Accreditation:** North Central Association of Colleges and Schools **Credit Hours For Degree:** 64 credit hours, Associates; 128 credit hours, Bachelors **ROTC:** Army, Air Force **Professional Accreditation:** ABHE **Intercollegiate Athletics:** Basketball M & W; Soccer M; Volleyball W

HASTINGS COLLEGE
800 North Turner Ave.
Hastings, NE 68901-7696
Tel: (402)463-2402; Free: 800-532-7642
Admissions: (402)461-7320
Fax: (402)463-3002
E-mail: mmolliconi@hastings.edu
Web Site: http://www.hastings.edu/
President/CEO: Dr. Phillip Dudley
Admissions: Mary Molliconi
Financial Aid: Ian Roberts
Type: Comprehensive **Sex:** Coed **Affiliation:** Presbyterian **Scores:** 97% SAT V 400+; 97% SAT M 400+; 54% ACT 18-23; 35% ACT 24-29 **% Accepted:** 78 **Application Deadline:** August 1 **Application Fee:** $20.00 **H.S. Requirements:** High school diploma required; GED accepted **Scholarships:** Available **Calendar System:** 4-1-4, Summer Session Available **Enrollment:** FT 1,068, PT 23 **Faculty:** FT 87, PT 36 **Student-Faculty Ratio:** 12:1 **Exams:** SAT I or ACT. **% Receiving Financial Aid:** 71 **% Residing in College-Owned, -Operated, or -Affiliated Housing:** 67 **Library Holdings:** 113,318 **Regional Accreditation:** North Central Association of Colleges and Schools **Credit Hours For Degree:** 127 semester hours, Bachelors **Professional Accreditation:** NASM, NCATE **Intercollegiate Athletics:** Baseball M; Basketball M & W; Cheerleading W; Cross-Country Running M & W; Football M; Golf M & W; Soccer M & W; Softball W; Tennis M & W; Track and Field M & W; Volleyball W

ITT TECHNICAL INSTITUTE
9814 M St.
Omaha, NE 68127-2056
Tel: (402)331-2900; Free: 800-677-9260
Fax: (402)331-9495
Web Site: http://www.itt-tech.edu/
President/CEO: Steve Kollar
Type: Two-Year College **Sex:** Coed **Affiliation:** ITT Educational Services, Inc. **H.S. Requirements:** High school diploma required; GED accepted **Scholarships:** Available **Calendar System:** Quarter, Summer Session Not available **Credit Hours For Degree:** 96 credit hours, Associates **Professional Accreditation:** ACICS

KAPLAN UNIVERSITY, LINCOLN
1821 K St.
Lincoln, NE 68501-2826
Tel: (402)474-5315
Fax: (402)474-5302
Web Site: http://www.lincoln.kaplanuniversity.edu/
President/CEO: Dr. Sandra J. Muskopf
Type: Two-Year College **Sex:** Coed **H.S. Requirements:** High school diploma required; GED accepted **Scholarships:** Available **Calendar System:** Quarter **Professional Accreditation:** ACICS, AAMAE

KAPLAN UNIVERSITY, OMAHA
5425 North 103rd St.
Omaha, NE 68134
Tel: (402)572-8500; Free: 800-642-1456
Fax: (402)573-1341
Web Site: http://www.omaha.kaplanuniversity.edu/
President/CEO: Jeremy Brunssen
Type: Two-Year College **Sex:** Coed **H.S. Requirements:** High school diploma required; GED accepted **Calendar System:** Quarter **Credit Hours For Degree:** 113 credit hours, Associates **Professional Accreditation:** ACICS, AAMAE

LITTLE PRIEST TRIBAL COLLEGE
PO Box 270
Winnebago, NE 68071
Tel: (402)878-2380
Fax: (402)878-2355
Web Site: http://www.lptc.bia.edu/
President/CEO: Darla LaPointe
Admissions: Karen Kemling
Type: Two-Year College **Sex:** Coed **Admission Plans:** Open Admission **Application Fee:** $10.00 **Costs Per Year:** Application fee: $10. Tuition: $2400 full-time, $80 per credit hour part-time. Mandatory fees: $575 full-time, $18.50 per credit hour part-time, $10 per term part-time. **Scholarships:** Available **Regional Accreditation:** North Central Association of Colleges and Schools

METROPOLITAN COMMUNITY COLLEGE
PO Box 3777
Omaha, NE 68103-0777
Tel: (402)457-2400; Free: 800-228-9553
Admissions: (402)457-2430
Fax: (402)457-2564
E-mail: mvazquez@mccneb.edu
Web Site: http://www.mccneb.edu/
President/CEO: Randy Schmailzl
Admissions: Maria Vazquez
Type: Two-Year College **Sex:** Coed **Affiliation:** Nebraska Coordinating Commission for Postsecondary Education **% Accepted:** 100 **Admission Plans:** Open Admission; Early Admission **Application Deadline:** Rolling **Application Fee:** $0.00 **H.S. Requirements:** High school diploma or equivalent not required. For allied health programs, pre-professional associate of science: High school diploma required; GED accepted **Costs Per Year:** Application fee: $0. State resident tuition: $2115 full-time, $47 per credit hour part-time. Nonresident tuition: $3,172 full-time, $70.50 per credit hour part-time. Mandatory fees: $225 full-time, $5 per credit hour part-time. Full-time tuition and fees vary according to course load. Part-time tuition and fees vary according to course load. College room and board: $4740. **Scholarships:** Available **Calendar System:** Quarter, Summer Session Available **Enrollment:** FT 7,095, PT 9,908 **Faculty:** FT 198, PT 679 **Student-Faculty Ratio:** 16:1 **Library Holdings:** 43,788 **Regional Accreditation:** North Central Association of Colleges and Schools **Credit Hours For Degree:** 96 quarter hours, Associates **ROTC:** Army **Professional Accreditation:** ACF, ADA, ACBSP, CARC, NLN

MID-PLAINS COMMUNITY COLLEGE
601 West State Farm Rd.
North Platte, NE 69101
Tel: (308)535-3600; Free: 800-658-4348
Admissions: (308)535-3710
Fax: (308)532-8590
E-mail: mihels@mpcc.edu
Web Site: http://www.mpcc.edu/
President/CEO: Dr. Michael Chipps
Admissions: Sherry Mihel
Type: Two-Year College **Sex:** Coed **Scores:** 56% ACT 18-23; 17.2% ACT 24-29 **% Accepted:** 100 **Admission Plans:** Open Admission **Application Deadline:** Rolling **Application Fee:** $0.00 **H.S. Requirements:** High school diploma required; GED accepted **Costs Per Year:** Application fee: $0. State resident tuition: $2010 full-time, $67 per credit hour part-time. Nonresident tuition: $2610 full-time, $87 per credit hour part-time. Mandatory fees: $420 full-time, $14 per credit hour part-time. College room and board: $4900. Room and board charges vary according to board plan, housing facility, and location. **Calendar System:** Semester, Summer Session Available **Enrollment:** FT 1,086, PT 1,679 **Faculty:** FT 67, PT 246 **Student-Faculty Ratio:** 9:1 **Exams:** ACT, Other. **% Residing in College-Owned, -Operated, or -Affiliated Housing:** 8 **Library Holdings:** 65,352 **Regional Accreditation:** North Central Association of Colleges and Schools **Credit Hours For Degree:** 60 semester hours, Associates **Professional Accreditation:** ADA, NAACLS **Intercollegiate Athletics:** Baseball M; Basketball M & W; Golf M; Softball W; Volleyball W

MIDLAND LUTHERAN COLLEGE
900 North Clarkson St.
Fremont, NE 68025-4200
Tel: (402)721-5480; Free: 800-642-8382
Admissions: (402)941-6504
Fax: (402)721-0250
E-mail: admissions@mlc.edu
Web Site: http://www.mlc.edu/
President/CEO: Dr. Stephen Fritz
Admissions: Todd Hansen
Financial Aid: Penny James
Type: Four-Year College **Sex:** Coed **Affiliation:** Lutheran **% Accepted:** 88 **Admission Plans:** Early Admission **Application Deadline:** Rolling **Application Fee:** $30.00 **H.S. Requirements:** High school diploma required; GED accepted **Scholarships:** Available **Calendar System:** 4-1-4, Summer Session Available **Enrollment:** FT 808, PT 19 **Faculty:** FT 54, PT 27 **Student-Faculty Ratio:** 14:1 **Exams:** SAT I or ACT. **% Receiving Financial Aid:** 81 **% Residing in College-Owned, -Operated, or -Affiliated Housing:** 62 **Library Holdings:** 110,000 **Regional Accreditation:** North Central Association of Colleges and Schools **Credit Hours For Degree:** 64 credit hours, Associates; 128 credit hours, Bachelors **Professional Accreditation:** NLN **Intercollegiate Athletics:** Baseball M; Basketball M & W; Cross-Country Running M & W; Football M; Golf M & W; Soccer M & W; Softball W; Tennis M & W; Track and Field M & W; Volleyball W

MYOTHERAPY INSTITUTE
6020 South 58th St.
Lincoln, NE 68516
Tel: (402)421-7410; Free: 800-896-3363
Fax: (402)421-6736
Web Site: http://www.myotherapy.edu/
President/CEO: Sue A. Kozisek
Type: Two-Year College **Sex:** Coed **Application Fee:** $75.00 **Professional Accreditation:** ACCSCT

NEBRASKA CHRISTIAN COLLEGE
12550 South 114th Steet
Papillion, NE 68046
Tel: (402)379-5000
Admissions: (402)935-9400
Web Site: http://www.nechristian.edu/
President/CEO: Richard D. Milliken
Admissions: Alisha Livengood
Financial Aid: Tina Larsen
Type: Four-Year College **Sex:** Coed **Affiliation:** Christian Churches and Churches of Christ **Application Deadline:** Rolling **Application Fee:** $25.00 **H.S. Requirements:** High school diploma required; GED accepted **Scholarships:** Available **Calendar System:** Semester, Summer Session Not available **Enrollment:** FT 140, PT 6 **Student-Faculty Ratio:** 7:1 **Exams:** ACT. **% Receiving Financial Aid:** 88 **% Residing in College-Owned, -Operated, or -Affiliated Housing:** 90 **Library Holdings:** 250,000 **Credit Hours For Degree:** 64 semester hours, Associates; 130 semester hours, Bachelors **Professional Accreditation:** ABHE **Intercollegiate Athletics:** Basketball M & W; Soccer M; Volleyball W

NEBRASKA COLLEGE OF TECHNICAL AGRICULTURE
RR3, Box 23A
Curtis, NE 69025-9205
Tel: (308)367-4124; Free: 800-3CU-RTIS
Fax: (308)367-5203
Web Site: http://www.ncta.unl.edu/
President/CEO: Dr. Weldon Sleight
Admissions: Kevin Martin
Type: Two-Year College **Sex:** Coed **Affiliation:** University of Nebraska System **Admission Plans:** Open Admission; Early Admission **Application Deadline:** Rolling **Application Fee:** $25.00 **H.S. Requirements:** High

school diploma required; GED accepted **Costs Per Year:** Application fee: $25. State resident tuition: $3015 full-time. Nonresident tuition: $6023 full-time. Mandatory fees: $628 full-time. College room and board: $4580. College room only: $2100. Room and board charges vary according to board plan. **Scholarships:** Available **Calendar System:** Miscellaneous, Summer Session Not available **Enrollment:** FT 246, PT 179 **Faculty:** FT 13, PT 8 **Student-Faculty Ratio:** 13:1 **Exams:** ACT. **% Residing in College-Owned, -Operated, or -Affiliated Housing:** 45 **Library Holdings:** 6,000 **Regional Accreditation:** North Central Association of Colleges and Schools **Credit Hours For Degree:** 64 semester hours, Associates **Intercollegiate Athletics:** Basketball M & W; Golf M

NEBRASKA INDIAN COMMUNITY COLLEGE
PO Box 428
Macy, NE 68039-0428
Tel: (402)837-5078; Free: 888-843-6432
Admissions: (402)494-2311
Fax: (402)878-2522
Web Site: http://www.thenicc.edu/
President/CEO: Michael Oltrogge
Admissions: Theresa Henry
Type: Two-Year College **Sex:** Coed **Admission Plans:** Open Admission; Early Admission; Deferred Admission **Application Deadline:** Rolling **Application Fee:** $50.00 **H.S. Requirements:** High school diploma required; GED accepted **Scholarships:** Available **Calendar System:** Semester **Enrollment:** FT 55, PT 60 **Faculty:** FT 5, PT 7 **Regional Accreditation:** North Central Association of Colleges and Schools **Credit Hours For Degree:** 90 quarter hours, Associates

NEBRASKA METHODIST COLLEGE
720 North 87th St.
Omaha, NE 68114
Tel: (402)354-7000; Free: 800-335-5510
Admissions: (402)354-7111
Fax: (402)354-4819
E-mail: sara.bonney@methodistcollege.edu
Web Site: http://www.methodistcollege.edu/
President/CEO: Dr. Dennis Joslin
Admissions: Sara Bonney
Financial Aid: Penny James
Type: Comprehensive **Sex:** Coed **Affiliation:** United Methodist Church **Scores:** 54% ACT 18-23; 37% ACT 24-29 **% Accepted:** 38 **Admission Plans:** Deferred Admission **Application Deadline:** Rolling **Application Fee:** $25.00 **H.S. Requirements:** High school diploma required; GED accepted **Costs Per Year:** Application fee: $25. One-time mandatory fee: $60. Tuition: $13,950 full-time, $465 per credit hour part-time. Mandatory fees: $650 full-time, $20 per credit hour part-time. College room only: $5770. Room charges vary according to housing facility. **Scholarships:** Available **Calendar System:** Semester, Summer Session Available **Enrollment:** FT 432, PT 158, Grad FT 56, Grad PT 26 **Faculty:** FT 49, PT 11 **Student-Faculty Ratio:** 9:1 **Exams:** SAT I or ACT. ACT essay not being used. SAT essay not being used. **% Receiving Financial Aid:** 62 **% Residing in College-Owned, -Operated, or -Affiliated Housing:** 16 **Final Year or Final Semester Residency Requirement:** No **Library Holdings:** 10,300 **Regional Accreditation:** North Central Association of Colleges and Schools **Credit Hours For Degree:** 82 credit hours, Associates; 127 credit hours, Bachelors **ROTC:** Army, Air Force **Professional Accreditation:** AACN, CARC, JRCEDMS, NLN

NEBRASKA WESLEYAN UNIVERSITY
5000 Saint Paul Ave.
Lincoln, NE 68504-2796
Tel: (402)466-2371; Free: 800-541-3818
Admissions: (402)465-2144
Fax: (402)465-2179
E-mail: admissions@nebrwesleyan.edu
Web Site: http://www.nebrwesleyan.edu/
President/CEO: Dr. Frederik Ohles
Admissions: David Duzik
Financial Aid: Thomas J. Ochsner
Type: Comprehensive **Sex:** Coed **Affiliation:** United Methodist **Scores:** 34% ACT 18-23; 54% ACT 24-29 **% Accepted:** 82 **Admission Plans:** Early Action; Deferred Admission **Application Deadline:** August 15 **Application Fee:** $20.00 **H.S. Requirements:** High school diploma required; GED accepted **Costs Per Year:** Application fee: $20. One-time mandatory fee: $120. Comprehensive fee: $28,662 includes full-time tuition ($21,980), mandatory fees ($452), and college room and board ($6230). Room and board charges vary according to board plan. Part-time tuition: $828 per credit hour. **Scholarships:** Available **Calendar System:** Semester, Summer Session Available **Enrollment:** FT 1,622, PT 230, Grad FT 57, Grad PT 184 **Faculty:** FT 103, PT 65 **Student-Faculty Ratio:** 13:1 **Exams:** SAT I or ACT. **% Receiving Financial Aid:** 71 **% Residing in College-Owned, -Operated, or -Affiliated Housing:** 60 **Final Year or Final Semester Residency Requirement:** Yes **Library Holdings:** 221,084 **Regional Accreditation:** North Central Association of Colleges and Schools **Credit Hours For Degree:** 126 semester credits, Bachelors **ROTC:** Army, Air Force **Professional Accreditation:** ACBSP, NASM, NCATE, NLN **Intercollegiate Athletics:** Baseball M; Basketball M & W; Cheerleading W; Cross-Country Running M & W; Football M; Golf M & W; Soccer M & W; Softball W; Tennis M & W; Track and Field M & W; Volleyball W

NORTHEAST COMMUNITY COLLEGE
801 East Benjamin Ave, PO Box 469
Norfolk, NE 68702-0469
Tel: (402)371-2020
Admissions: (402)844-7258
Fax: (402)644-0650
E-mail: admission@northeast.edu
Web Site: http://www.northeast.edu/
President/CEO: Dr. Bill Path
Admissions: Maureen Baker
Financial Aid: Stacy Dieckman
Type: Two-Year College **Sex:** Coed **Affiliation:** Nebraska Coordinating Commission for Postsecondary Education **Admission Plans:** Open Admission; Early Admission **Application Deadline:** Rolling **Application Fee:** $0.00 **H.S. Requirements:** High school diploma or equivalent not required **Costs Per Year:** Application fee: $0. State resident tuition: $2010 full-time. Nonresident tuition: $2513 full-time. Mandatory fees: $420 full-time. College room and board: $4980. College room only: $2820. Room and board charges vary according to board plan and housing facility. **Scholarships:** Available **Calendar System:** Semester, Summer Session Available **Enrollment:** FT 2,268, PT 2,937 **Faculty:** FT 113, PT 249 **Student-Faculty Ratio:** 16:1 **% Residing in College-Owned, -Operated, or -Affiliated Housing:** 16 **Library Holdings:** 64,122 **Regional Accreditation:** North Central Association of Colleges and Schools **Credit Hours For Degree:** 60 semester hours, Associates **Professional Accreditation:** APTA, NLN **Intercollegiate Athletics:** Basketball M & W; Cheerleading W

PERU STATE COLLEGE
PO Box 10
Peru, NE 68421
Tel: (402)872-3815
Admissions: (402)872-2221
E-mail: mwillis@peru.edu
Web Site: http://www.peru.edu/
President/CEO: Daniel H. Hanson, PhD
Admissions: Micki Willis
Financial Aid: Diana Lind
Type: Comprehensive **Sex:** Coed **Affiliation:** Nebraska State College System **Scores:** 48% ACT 18-23; 23% ACT 24-29 **% Accepted:** 48 **Admission Plans:** Open Admission **Application Deadline:** Rolling **Application Fee:** $0.00 **H.S. Requirements:** High school diploma required; GED accepted **Costs Per Year:** Application fee: $0. State resident tuition: $3855 full-time, $128.50 per credit hour part-time. Nonresident tuition: $129.50 per credit hour part-time. Mandatory fees: $908 full-time. Full-time tuition and fees vary according to course level, course load, and location. Part-time tuition varies according to course level, course load, and location. College room and board: $4962. Room and board charges vary according to housing facility. **Scholarships:** Available **Calendar System:** Semester, Summer Session Available **Enrollment:** FT 1,245, PT 897, Grad FT 96, Grad PT 272 **Student-Faculty Ratio:** 20:1 **Exams:** SAT I or ACT. **% Residing in College-Owned, -Operated, or -Affiliated Housing:** 30 **Library Holdings:** 177,373 **Regional Accreditation:** North Central Association of Colleges and Schools **Credit Hours For Degree:** 125 semester hours, Bachelors **ROTC:** Army, Air Force **Professional Accreditation:** NCATE **Intercollegiate Athletics:** Baseball M; Basketball M & W; Cheerleading M & W; Cross-Country Running W; Football M; Golf W; Softball W; Volleyball W

ST. GREGORY THE GREAT SEMINARY
800 Fletcher Rd.
Seward, NE 68434-8145
Tel: (402)643-4052
Fax: (402)643-6964
Web Site: http://www.stgregoryseminary.edu/
Type: Four-Year College **Sex:** Men **Regional Accreditation:** North Central Association of Colleges and Schools

SOUTHEAST COMMUNITY COLLEGE, BEATRICE CAMPUS
4771 West Scott Rd.
Beatrice, NE 68310
Tel: (402)228-3468; Free: 800-233-5027
Fax: (402)228-2218
Web Site: http://www.southeast.edu/
Type: Two-Year College **Sex:** Coed **Affiliation:** Southeast Community College System **Admission Plans:** Open Admission; Early Admission; Deferred Admission **Application Deadline:** Rolling **H.S. Requirements:** High school diploma required; GED accepted **Costs Per Year:** State resident tuition: $1128 full-time, $47 per credit hour part-time. Nonresident tuition: $1380 full-time, $57.50 per credit hour part-time. Mandatory fees: $24 full-time, $1 per credit hour part-time. College room only: $1920. **Scholarships:** Available **Calendar System:** Semester, Summer Session Available **Exams:** Other, SAT I or ACT. **Regional Accreditation:** North Central Association of Colleges and Schools **Credit Hours For Degree:** 60 credit hours, Associates **Professional Accreditation:** ACBSP, NLN **Intercollegiate Athletics:** Basketball M & W; Golf M; Volleyball W

SOUTHEAST COMMUNITY COLLEGE, LINCOLN CAMPUS
8800 O St.
Lincoln, NE 68520-1299
Tel: (402)471-3333; Free: 800-642-4075
Web Site: http://www.southeast.edu/
Type: Two-Year College **Sex:** Coed **Affiliation:** Southeast Community College System **Admission Plans:** Open Admission; Early Admission; Deferred Admission **Application Deadline:** Rolling **H.S. Requirements:** High school diploma required; GED accepted **Costs Per Year:** State resident tuition: $1128 full-time, $47 per credit hour part-time. Nonresident tuition: $1380 full-time, $57.50 per credit hour part-time. Mandatory fees: $24 full-time, $1 per credit hour part-time. **Scholarships:** Available **Calendar System:** Quarter, Summer Session Available **Regional Accreditation:** North Central Association of Colleges and Schools **Credit Hours For Degree:** 90 quarter credits, Associates **Professional Accreditation:** ARCEST, ACF, ADA, ACBSP, CARC, JRCERT, NAACLS, NLN

SOUTHEAST COMMUNITY COLLEGE, MILFORD CAMPUS
600 State St.
Milford, NE 68405
Tel: (402)761-2131; Free: 800-933-7223
Web Site: http://www.southeast.edu/
Type: Two-Year College **Sex:** Coed **Affiliation:** Southeast Community College System **Admission Plans:** Open Admission **Application Deadline:** Rolling **H.S. Requirements:** High school diploma required; GED accepted **Costs Per Year:** State resident tuition: $1128 full-time, $47 per credit hour part-time. Nonresident tuition: $1380 full-time, $57.50 per credit hour part-time. Mandatory fees: $24 full-time, $1 per credit hour part-time. College room and board: $2612. **Scholarships:** Available **Calendar System:** Quarter, Summer Session Not available **Exams:** ACT, SAT I. **Regional Accreditation:** North Central Association of Colleges and Schools **Credit Hours For Degree:** 108 credits, Associates **Professional Accreditation:** ACBSP

UNION COLLEGE
3800 South 48th St.
Lincoln, NE 68506-4300
Tel: (402)486-2600; Free: 800-228-4600
Fax: (402)486-2895
E-mail: ucenroll@ucollege.edu
Web Site: http://www.ucollege.edu/
President/CEO: David Smith
Admissions: Jennifer Enos
Financial Aid: John C. Burdick, IV
Type: Comprehensive **Sex:** Coed **Affiliation:** Seventh-day Adventist **Scores:** 49% ACT 18-23; 35% ACT 24-29 **% Accepted:** 41 **Application Deadline:** Rolling **Application Fee:** $0.00 **H.S. Requirements:** High school diploma required; GED accepted **Costs Per Year:** Application fee: $0. Comprehensive fee: $24,050 includes full-time tuition ($17,600), mandatory fees ($550), and college room and board ($5900). College room only: $3350. Full-time tuition and fees vary according to course load and degree level. Room and board charges vary according to housing facility. Part-time tuition: $735 per credit hour. **Calendar System:** Semester, Summer Session Available **Enrollment:** FT 664, PT 149, Grad FT 70 **Faculty:** FT 56, PT 35 **Student-Faculty Ratio:** 13:1 **Exams:** SAT I or ACT. **% Residing in College-Owned, -Operated, or -Affiliated Housing:** 62 **Library Holdings:** 147,813 **Regional Accreditation:** North Central Association of Colleges and Schools **Credit Hours For Degree:** 64 semester hours, Associates; 128 semester hours, Bachelors **Professional Accreditation:** AACN, NCATE **Intercollegiate Athletics:** Basketball M & W; Volleyball W

UNIVERSITY OF NEBRASKA AT KEARNEY
905 West 25th St.
Kearney, NE 68849-0001
Tel: (308)865-8441; Free: 800-532-7639
Admissions: (308)865-8702
Fax: (308)865-8987
E-mail: admissionsug@unk.edu
Web Site: http://www.unk.edu/
President/CEO: Douglas Kristensen
Admissions: Dusty Newton
Type: Comprehensive **Sex:** Coed **Affiliation:** University of Nebraska System **Scores:** 53% ACT 18-23; 35% ACT 24-29 **% Accepted:** 77 **Application Deadline:** Rolling **Application Fee:** $45.00 **H.S. Requirements:** High school diploma required; GED accepted **Costs Per Year:** Application fee: $45. State resident tuition: $4537 full-time, $151.25 per hour part-time. Nonresident tuition: $9300 full-time, $310 per hour part-time. Mandatory fees: $1097 full-time, $22.25 per hour part-time, $75 per term part-time. Full-time tuition and fees vary according to course level, course load, degree level, and location. Part-time tuition and fees vary according to course level, course load, degree level, and location. College room and board: $6830. College room only: $3450. Room and board charges vary according to board plan and housing facility. **Scholarships:** Available **Calendar System:** Semester, Summer Session Available **Enrollment:** FT 4,522, PT 509, Grad FT 500, Grad PT 1,119 **Faculty:** FT 305, PT 101 **Student-Faculty Ratio:** 16:1 **Exams:** SAT I and SAT II or ACT. ACT essay not being used. SAT essay not being used. **% Receiving Financial Aid:** 60 **% Residing in College-Owned, -Operated, or -Affiliated Housing:** 37 **Final Year or Final Semester Residency Requirement:** No **Library Holdings:** 464,532 **Regional Accreditation:** North Central Association of Colleges and Schools **Credit Hours For Degree:** 125 semester hours, Bachelors **ROTC:** Army **Professional Accreditation:** AACSB, AAFCS, ACA, ASLHA, CSWE, JRCEPAT, NASM, NCATE, NAIT **Intercollegiate Athletics:** Baseball M; Basketball M & W; Cross-Country Running M & W; Football M; Golf M & W; Soccer W; Softball W; Swimming and Diving W; Tennis M & W; Track and Field M & W; Volleyball W; Wrestling M

UNIVERSITY OF NEBRASKA MEDICAL CENTER
Nebraska Medical Center
Omaha, NE 68198
Tel: (402)559-4000; Free: 800-626-8431
Admissions: (402)559-6468
Fax: (402)559-6796
E-mail: ttonjes@unmc.edu
Web Site: http://www.unmc.edu/
President/CEO: Dr. Harold M. Maurer
Admissions: Tymaree Tonjes
Financial Aid: Judy D. Walker
Type: Two-Year Upper Division **Sex:** Coed **Affiliation:** University of Nebraska System **Admission Plans:** Preferred Admission; Deferred Admission **Application Fee:** $45.00 **H.S. Requirements:** High school diploma required; GED accepted **Scholarships:** Available **Calendar System:** Semester, Summer Session Available **Enrollment:** FT 720, PT 91, Grad FT 2,025, Grad PT 372 **Faculty:** FT 989, PT 201 **Student-Faculty Ratio:** 3:1 **% Receiving Financial Aid:** 70 **Final Year or Final Semester Residency Requirement:** Yes **Library Holdings:** 238,074 **Regional Accreditation:** North Central Association of Colleges and Schools **Credit Hours For Degree:** 131 semester hours, Bachelors **ROTC:** Army, Air Force **Professional Accreditation:** ACPE, ACPhE, AACN, ADA, ADtA, APTA, CEPH, JRCEDMS, JRCERT, JRCNMT, LCMEAMA, NAACLS

UNIVERSITY OF NEBRASKA AT OMAHA
6001 Dodge St.
Omaha, NE 68182
Tel: (402)554-2200
Admissions: (402)554-2416
Fax: (402)554-3472
E-mail: jadams@mail.unomaha.edu
Web Site: http://www.unomaha.edu/
President/CEO: John E. Christensen
Admissions: Jolene Adams
Type: University **Sex:** Coed **Affiliation:** University of Nebraska System **Scores:** 50% ACT 18-23; 32% ACT 24-29 **% Accepted:** 80 **Admission Plans:** Deferred Admission **Application Deadline:** August 1 **Application Fee:** $45.00 **H.S. Requirements:** High school diploma required; GED accepted **Costs Per Year:** Application fee: $45. State resident tuition: $5115 full-time, $170.50 per credit hour part-time. Nonresident tuition: $15,075 full-time, $502.50 per credit hour part-time. Mandatory fees: $1114 full-time. Full-time tuition and fees vary according to course load and reciprocity agreements. Part-time tuition varies according to course load and reciprocity agreements. College room and board: $7230. Room and board charges vary according to board plan and housing facility. **Scholarships:** Available **Calendar System:** Semester, Summer Session Available **Enrollment:** FT 9,064, PT 2,490, Grad FT 789, Grad PT 2,277 **Faculty:** FT 483, PT 392 **Student-Faculty Ratio:** 19:1 **Exams:** SAT I or ACT. **% Receiving Financial Aid:** 45 **% Residing in College-Owned, -Operated, or -Affiliated Housing:** 11 **Library Holdings:** 1,442,970 **Regional Accreditation:** North Central Association of Colleges and Schools **Credit Hours For Degree:** 125 semester hours, Bachelors **ROTC:** Army, Air Force **Professional Accreditation:** AACSB, ABET, ACA, ASLHA, CAA, CEPH, CSWE, JRCEPAT, NASAD, NASM, NASPAA, NCATE **Intercollegiate Athletics:** Baseball M; Basketball M & W; Cross-Country Running W; Football M; Golf W; Ice Hockey M; Soccer W; Softball W; Swimming and Diving W; Tennis W; Volleyball W; Wrestling M

UNIVERSITY OF NEBRASKA—LINCOLN
14th and R Sts.
Lincoln, NE 68588
Tel: (402)472-7211; Free: 800-742-8800
Admissions: (402)472-2023
Fax: (402)472-0670
E-mail: admissions@unl.edu
Web Site: http://www.unl.edu/
President/CEO: Harvey Perlman
Admissions: Pat McBride
Financial Aid: Jo Tederman
Type: University **Sex:** Coed **Affiliation:** University of Nebraska System **Scores:** 97% SAT V 400+; 98% SAT M 400+; 35% ACT 18-23; 45% ACT 24-29 **% Accepted:** 63 **Application Deadline:** May 1 **Application Fee:** $45.00 **H.S. Requirements:** High school diploma required; GED accepted **Costs Per Year:** Application fee: $45. State resident tuition: $5610 full-time, $187 per semester hour part-time. Nonresident tuition: $16,650 full-time, $555 per semester hour part-time. Mandatory fees: $1247 full-time, $10.35 per semester hour part-time, $272.70 per term part-time. Full-time tuition and fees vary according to course load, program, and reciprocity agreements. Part-time tuition and fees vary according to course load, program, and reciprocity agreements. College room and board: $7260. College room only: $3828. Room and board charges vary according to board plan and housing facility. **Scholarships:** Available **Calendar System:** Semester, Summer Session Available **Enrollment:** FT 17,737, PT 1,218, Grad FT 2,965, Grad PT 2,180 **Faculty:** FT 1,102, PT 9 **Student-Faculty Ratio:** 20:1 **Exams:** ACT, SAT I or ACT. ACT essay not being used. SAT essay not being used. **% Receiving Financial Aid:** 44 **% Residing in College-Owned, -Operated, or -Affiliated Housing:** 39 **Final Year or Final Semester Residency Requirement:** Yes **Library Holdings:** 3,487,244 **Regional Accreditation:** North Central Association of Colleges and Schools **Credit Hours For Degree:** 71 credit hours, Associates; 125 credit hours, Bachelors **ROTC:** Army, Navy, Air Force **Professional Accreditation:** AACSB, ABET, ACEJMC, AAMFT, AAFCS, ABA, ACCE, ADA, ADtA, ACSP, APA, ASLHA, AALS, FIDER, NAAB, NASAD, NASM, NAST, NCATE, TEAC **Intercollegiate Athletics:** Baseball M; Basketball M & W; Bowling W; Crew M & W; Cross-Country Running M & W; Fencing M & W; Football M; Golf M & W; Gymnastics M & W; Riflery W; Soccer W; Softball W; Swimming and Diving W; Tennis M & W; Track and Field M & W; Volleyball W; Wrestling M

UNIVERSITY OF PHOENIX—OMAHA CAMPUS
13321 California St., Ste. 200
Omaha, NE 68154-5240
Tel: (402)334-4936
Web Site: http://www.phoenix.edu/
Type: Comprehensive **Sex:** Coed **Regional Accreditation:** North Central Association of Colleges and Schools

VATTEROTT COLLEGE
5318 South 136th St.
Omaha, NE 68137
Tel: (402)891-9411
Fax: (402)891-9413
Web Site: http://www.vatterott-college.edu/
Type: Two-Year College **Sex:** Coed **Admission Plans:** Open Admission **Calendar System:** Semester **Student-Faculty Ratio:** 12:1 **Professional Accreditation:** ACCSCT

WAYNE STATE COLLEGE
1111 Main St.
Wayne, NE 68787
Tel: (402)375-7000
Admissions: (402)375-7234
Fax: (402)375-7204
E-mail: admit1@wsc.edu
Web Site: http://www.wsc.edu/
President/CEO: Dr. Richard Collings
Admissions: Tammy Young
Financial Aid: Kyle M. Rose
Type: Comprehensive **Sex:** Coed **Affiliation:** Nebraska State College System **Scores:** 51% ACT 18-23; 27% ACT 24-29 **% Accepted:** 100 **Admission Plans:** Open Admission; Deferred Admission **Application Deadline:** Rolling **Application Fee:** $30.00 **H.S. Requirements:** High school diploma required; GED accepted **Costs Per Year:** Application fee: $30. State resident tuition: $3675 full-time, $122.50 per credit hour part-time. Nonresident tuition: $7350 full-time, $245 per credit hour part-time. Mandatory fees: $1130 full-time, $44.50 per credit hour part-time. Full-time tuition and fees vary according to course level and course load. Part-time tuition and fees vary according to course level and course load. College room and board: $5280. College room only: $2510. Room and board charges vary according to board plan and housing facility. **Scholarships:** Available **Calendar System:** Semester, Summer Session Available **Enrollment:** FT 2,696, PT 243, Grad FT 84, Grad PT 608 **Faculty:** FT 122, PT 98 **Student-Faculty Ratio:** 20:1 **% Receiving Financial Aid:** 67 **% Residing in College-Owned, -Operated, or -Affiliated Housing:** 46 **Library Holdings:** 249,110 **Regional Accreditation:** North Central Association of Colleges and Schools **Credit Hours For Degree:** 125 semester hours, Bachelors **ROTC:** Army **Professional Accreditation:** AAFCS, NCATE, TEAC **Intercollegiate Athletics:** Baseball M; Basketball M & W; Cheerleading M & W; Cross-Country Running M & W; Football M; Golf M & W; Rugby M & W; Soccer M & W; Softball W; Track and Field M & W; Volleyball W; Wrestling M

WESTERN NEBRASKA COMMUNITY COLLEGE
371 College Dr.
Sidney, NE 69162
Tel: (308)254-5450; Free: 800-348-4435
Admissions: (308)635-3606
Fax: (308)254-7444
E-mail: rhovey@wncc.net
Web Site: http://www.wncc.net/
President/CEO: Eileen E. Ely
Admissions: Troy Archuleta
Type: Two-Year College **Sex:** Coed **Affiliation:** Western Community College Area System **% Accepted:** 100 **Admission Plans:** Open Admission **Application Deadline:** Rolling **Application Fee:** $0.00 **H.S. Requirements:** High school diploma required; GED accepted **Costs Per Year:** Application fee: $0. State resident tuition: $2040 full-time, $68 per credit hour part-time. Nonresident tuition: $2400 full-time, $80 per credit hour part-time. Mandatory fees: $390 full-time, $13 per credit hour part-time. Full-time tuition and fees vary according to course load. Part-time tuition and fees vary according to course load. College room and board: $4600. College room only: $1650. Room and board charges vary according to board plan, housing facility, and location. **Scholarships:** Available **Calendar System:** Semester, Summer Session Available **Faculty:** FT 66, PT 292 **Student-Faculty Ratio:** 15:1 **%**

Residing in College-Owned, -Operated, or -Affiliated Housing: 5 **Library Holdings:** 34,539 **Regional Accreditation:** North Central Association of Colleges and Schools **Credit Hours For Degree:** 60 semester hours, Associates **Professional Accreditation:** AHIMA **Intercollegiate Athletics:** Baseball M; Basketball M & W; Soccer M & W; Softball W; Volleyball W

YORK COLLEGE

1125 East 8th St.
York, NE 68467
Tel: (402)363-5600; Free: 800-950-9675
Admissions: (402)363-5627
Fax: (402)363-5666
E-mail: enroll@york.edu
Web Site: http://www.york.edu/
President/CEO: Steve Eckman
Admissions: Janae Parsons
Financial Aid: Brien Alley

Type: Four-Year College **Sex:** Coed **Affiliation:** Church of Christ **Scores:** 90% SAT V 400+; 80% SAT M 400+; 40% ACT 18-23; 27% ACT 24-29 **% Accepted:** 60 **Admission Plans:** Early Admission; Deferred Admission **Application Deadline:** Rolling **Application Fee:** $20.00 **H.S. Requirements:** High school diploma required; GED accepted **Costs Per Year:** Application fee: $20. Comprehensive fee: $20,678 includes full-time tuition ($13,158), mandatory fees ($1840), and college room and board ($5680). Full-time tuition and fees vary according to course load. Room and board charges vary according to board plan and housing facility. Part-time tuition: $460 per credit hour. Part-time mandatory fees: $220 per credit hour. Part-time tuition and fees vary according to course load. **Scholarships:** Available **Calendar System:** Semester, Summer Session Available **Enrollment:** FT 416, PT 14 **Faculty:** FT 22, PT 16 **Student-Faculty Ratio:** 11:1 **Exams:** SAT I or ACT. **% Receiving Financial Aid:** 85 **% Residing in College-Owned, -Operated, or -Affiliated Housing:** 80 **Library Holdings:** 134,738 **Regional Accreditation:** North Central Association of Colleges and Schools **Credit Hours For Degree:** 64 credit hours, Associates; 128 credit hours, Bachelors **ROTC:** Army, Navy, Air Force **Intercollegiate Athletics:** Baseball M; Basketball M & W; Cross-Country Running M & W; Soccer M & W; Softball W; Track and Field M & W; Volleyball W; Wrestling M

THE ART INSTITUTE OF LAS VEGAS
2350 Corporate Circle Dr.
Henderson, NV 89074
Tel: (702)369-9944
Fax: (702)992-8558
Web Site: http://www.artinstitutes.edu/lasvegas/
President/CEO: Steven E. Brooks
Type: Four-Year College **Sex:** Coed **Affiliation:** Education Management Corporation **Calendar System:** Quarter **Professional Accreditation:** ACCSCT

CAREER COLLEGE OF NORTHERN NEVADA
1421 Pullman Dr.
Sparks, NV 89434
Tel: (775)856-2266
E-mail: lgoldhammer@ccnn4u.com
Web Site: http://www.ccnn.edu/
President/CEO: L. Nathan Clark
Admissions: Laura Goldhammer
Type: Two-Year College **Sex:** Coed **% Accepted:** 100 **Admission Plans:** Open Admission **Application Deadline:** Rolling **Application Fee:** $25.00 **H.S. Requirements:** High school diploma required; GED accepted **Scholarships:** Available **Calendar System:** Quarter, Summer Session Available **Enrollment:** FT 363 **Faculty:** FT 11, PT 12 **Student-Faculty Ratio:** 20:1 **Library Holdings:** 380 **Credit Hours For Degree:** 99.5 units, Associates **Professional Accreditation:** ACCSCT

COLLEGE OF SOUTHERN NEVADA
3200 East Cheyenne Ave.
North Las Vegas, NV 89030-4296
Tel: (702)651-4000; Free: 800-492-5728
Admissions: (702)651-5000
Fax: (702)643-6243
E-mail: stops@ccmail.ccsn.nevada.edu
Web Site: http://www.csn.edu/
President/CEO: Dr. Michael Richards
Admissions: Arlie J. Stops
Type: Two-Year College **Sex:** Coed **Affiliation:** University and Community College System of Nevada **Admission Plans:** Open Admission; Early Admission **Application Deadline:** Rolling **Application Fee:** $5.00 **H.S. Requirements:** High school diploma or equivalent not required. For allied health programs: High school diploma required; GED accepted **Scholarships:** Available **Calendar System:** Semester, Summer Session Available **Enrollment:** FT 7,850, PT 26,354 **Faculty:** FT 390, PT 1,890 **Library Holdings:** 100,000 **Credit Hours For Degree:** 60 credit hours, Associates **ROTC:** Army **Professional Accreditation:** ACF, ADA, AHIMA, AOTA, APTA, COptA, CARC, JRCEDMS, NAACLS, NLN, NCCU **Intercollegiate Athletics:** Baseball M

DEVRY UNIVERSITY
2490 Paseo Verde Parkway
Henderson, NV 89074-7120
Tel: (702)933-9700
Fax: (702)933-9717
Web Site: http://www.devry.edu/
President/CEO: Maria Dezenberg
Type: Comprehensive **Sex:** Coed **Affiliation:** DeVry University **Admission Plans:** Deferred Admission **Application Deadline:** Rolling **Application Fee:** $50.00 **H.S. Requirements:** High school diploma required; GED accepted **Costs Per Year:** Application fee: $50. Tuition: $14,080 full-time, $550 per credit hour part-time. **Scholarships:** Available **Calendar System:** Semester, Summer Session Available **Enrollment:** FT 139, PT 144, Grad FT 11, Grad PT 79 **Faculty:** FT 2, PT 27 **Student-Faculty Ratio:** 20:1 **Exams:** ACT essay used for admission. SAT essay used for admission. ACT essay used for placement. SAT essay used for placement. **% Receiving Financial Aid:** 74 **Regional Accreditation:** North Central Association of Colleges and Schools

EVEREST COLLEGE
170 North Stephanie St., 1st Floor
Henderson, NV 89074
Tel: (702)567-1920
Web Site: http://www.everest.edu/campus/henderson/
Type: Two-Year College **Sex:** Coed

GREAT BASIN COLLEGE
1500 College Parkway
Elko, NV 89801-3348
Tel: (775)738-8493
E-mail: stdsvc@gbcnv.edu
Web Site: http://www.gbcnv.edu/
President/CEO: Carl Diekhans
Admissions: Julie Byrnes
Type: Two-Year College **Sex:** Coed **Affiliation:** University and Community College System of Nevada **Admission Plans:** Open Admission; Early Admission; Deferred Admission **Application Deadline:** Rolling **Application Fee:** $5.00 **H.S. Requirements:** High school diploma or equivalent not required. For nursing program: High school diploma required; GED accepted **Scholarships:** Available **Calendar System:** Semester, Summer Session Available **Enrollment:** FT 822, PT 2,527 **Faculty:** FT 67, PT 143 **Library Holdings:** 38,765 **Credit Hours For Degree:** 60 semester hours, Associates **Professional Accreditation:** NLN, NCCU

HIGH-TECH INSTITUTE
2320 South Rancho Dr.
Las Vegas, NV 89102
Tel: (702)385-6700; Free: (866)385-6700
Fax: (702)388-4463
Web Site: http://www.high-techinstitute.com/
President/CEO: Rose Frank
Type: Two-Year College **Sex:** Coed **Application Fee:** $50.00 **Calendar System:** Semester **Professional Accreditation:** ACCSCT

ITT TECHNICAL INSTITUTE
168 North Gibson Rd.
Henderson, NV 89014
Tel: (702)558-5404
Web Site: http://www.itt-tech.edu/
President/CEO: Donn Nimmer
Type: Two-Year College **Sex:** Coed **Affiliation:** ITT Educational Services, Inc. **H.S. Requirements:** High school diploma required; GED accepted

Scholarships: Available **Credit Hours For Degree:** 96 credit hours, Associates; 180 credit hours, Bachelors **Professional Accreditation:** ACICS

KAPLAN COLLEGE—LAS VEGAS CAMPUS
3535 West Sahara Ave.
Las Vegas, NV 89102
Tel: (702)368-2338; Free: 888-727-7863
Fax: (702)638-3853
Web Site: http://las-vegas.kaplancollege.com/
President/CEO: Rob Dillman
Type: Two-Year College **Sex:** Coed **Application Fee:** $20.00 **Professional Accreditation:** ACCSCT

LE CORDON BLEU COLLEGE OF CULINARY ARTS, LAS VEGAS
1451 Center Crossing Rd.
Las Vegas, NV 89144
Tel: (702)365-7690; Free: 888-551-8222
Admissions: (702)851-5380
Fax: (702)365-7911
Web Site: http://www.vegasculinary.com/
President/CEO: Shaun A. Elder
Type: Two-Year College **Sex:** Coed **Application Fee:** $50.00 **Professional Accreditation:** ACCSCT

MORRISON UNIVERSITY
10315 Professional Circle
Reno, NV 89521
Tel: (775)850-0700; Free: 800-369-6144
Admissions: (775)335-3500
Fax: (775)850-0711
E-mail: ctiminsky@morrison.neumont.edu
Web Site: http://www.morrison.neumont.edu/
President/CEO: R. David Wyckoff
Admissions: Charles Timinsky
Financial Aid: Kim Droniak
Type: Comprehensive **Sex:** Coed **Admission Plans:** Open Admission; Early Admission; Deferred Admission **Application Fee:** $25.00 **H.S. Requirements:** High school diploma required; GED accepted **Scholarships:** Available **Calendar System:** Miscellaneous, Summer Session Available **Enrollment:** FT 52, PT 62 **Faculty:** FT 15, PT 10 **Exams:** Other. **Library Holdings:** 6,000 **Credit Hours For Degree:** 90 credits, Associates; 180 credits, Bachelors **Professional Accreditation:** ACICS

NEVADA STATE COLLEGE AT HENDERSON
1125 Nevada State Dr.
Henderson, NV 89015
Tel: (702)992-2000
Admissions: (702)992-2114
Fax: (702)992-2226
E-mail: admissions@nsc.nevada.edu
Web Site: http://www.nsc.nevada.edu/
President/CEO: Dr. Fred Maryankski
Admissions: Patricia Ring
Type: Four-Year College **Sex:** Coed **Affiliation:** Nevada System of Higher Education **Scores:** 75% SAT V 400+; 70.45% SAT M 400+; 45.95% ACT 18-23; 24.32% ACT 24-29 **% Accepted:** 72 **Application Deadline:** August 20 **Application Fee:** $30.00 **H.S. Requirements:** High school diploma required; GED accepted **Costs Per Year:** Application fee: $30. One-time mandatory fee: $20. State resident tuition: $3563 full-time, $113.25 per credit hour part-time. Nonresident tuition: $13,381 full-time. **Calendar System:** Semester, Summer Session Available **Enrollment:** FT 999, PT 1,517 **Faculty:** FT 44, PT 99 **Student-Faculty Ratio:** 20:1 **Exams:** ACT essay used for advising. SAT essay used for advising. ACT essay used for placement. SAT essay used for placement. ACT essay not being used. SAT essay not being used. **Final Year or Final Semester Residency Requirement:** No **Library Holdings:** 12,905 **Credit Hours For Degree:** 124 units, Bachelors **ROTC:** Army **Professional Accreditation:** NCCU

PIMA MEDICAL INSTITUTE
3333 East Flamingo Rd.
Las Vegas, NV 89121
Tel: (702)458-9650; Free: 800-477-PIMA
Web Site: http://www.pmi.edu/
President/CEO: Sam Gentile
Type: Two-Year College **Sex:** Coed **Affiliation:** Vocational Training Institutes, Inc. **H.S. Requirements:** High school diploma required; GED accepted. For some certificate programs: High school diploma or equivalent not required **Calendar System:** Miscellaneous, Summer Session Not available **Exams:** Other. **Professional Accreditation:** ABHES

SIERRA NEVADA COLLEGE
999 Tahoe Blvd.
Incline Village, NV 89451
Tel: (775)831-1314
Fax: (775)831-1347
E-mail: admissions@sierranevada.edu
Web Site: http://www.sierranevada.edu/
President/CEO: Robert C. Maxson
Admissions: Matt Delekta, James McMaster
Financial Aid: Dorothy Caruso
Type: Comprehensive **Sex:** Coed **Scores:** 98% SAT V 400+; 97% SAT M 400+ **% Accepted:** 68 **Admission Plans:** Early Admission; Deferred Admission **Application Deadline:** Rolling **Application Fee:** $0.00 **H.S. Requirements:** High school diploma required; GED accepted **Costs Per Year:** Application fee: $0. Comprehensive fee: $32,242 includes full-time tuition ($22,768), mandatory fees ($300), and college room and board ($9174). Full-time tuition and fees vary according to class time, course level, course load, degree level, location, and program. Tuition guaranteed not to increase for student's term of enrollment. **Scholarships:** Available **Calendar System:** Semester, Summer Session Available **Enrollment:** FT 302 **Faculty:** FT 19, PT 56 **Student-Faculty Ratio:** 10:1 **Exams:** SAT I or ACT. **% Receiving Financial Aid:** 70 **% Residing in College-Owned, -Operated, or -Affiliated Housing:** 45 **Library Holdings:** 35,000 **Credit Hours For Degree:** 120 semester hours, Bachelors **ROTC:** Army **Professional Accreditation:** NCCU **Intercollegiate Athletics:** Equestrian Sports M & W; Skiing (Downhill) M & W

TRUCKEE MEADOWS COMMUNITY COLLEGE
7000 Dandini Blvd.
Reno, NV 89512-3901
Tel: (775)673-7000
Admissions: (775)674-7623
Fax: (775)673-7028
E-mail: dharbeck@tmcc.edu
Web Site: http://www.tmcc.edu/
President/CEO: Maria Sheehan
Admissions: Dave Harbeck
Type: Two-Year College **Sex:** Coed **Affiliation:** University and Community College System of Nevada **Admission Plans:** Open Admission; Early Admission; Deferred Admission **Application Deadline:** Rolling **Application Fee:** $10.00 **H.S. Requirements:** High school diploma or equivalent not required. For applicants under 18, allied health programs: High school diploma required; GED accepted **Costs Per Year:** Application fee: $10. State resident tuition: $1644 full-time, $68.50 per credit hour part-time. Nonresident tuition: $4738 full-time, $134.50 per credit hour part-time. Full-time tuition varies according to course load and reciprocity agreements. Part-time tuition varies according to course load and reciprocity agreements. **Scholarships:** Available **Calendar System:** Semester, Summer Session Available **Student-Faculty Ratio:** 22:1 **Credit Hours For Degree:** 60 credits, Associates **ROTC:** Army **Professional Accreditation:** ACF, ADA, JRCERT, NLN, NCCU

UNIVERSITY OF NEVADA, LAS VEGAS
4505 South Maryland Parkway
PO Box 451021
Las Vegas, NV 89154
Tel: (702)895-3011
Admissions: (702)774-8010
Fax: (702)895-1118
E-mail: admissions@unlv.edu
Web Site: http://www.unlv.edu/
President/CEO: Dr. Neil Smatresk
Admissions: Carrie Trentham
Type: University **Sex:** Coed **Affiliation:** Nevada System of Higher Education **Scores:** 91.8% SAT V 400+; 91.2% SAT M 400+; 54.8% ACT 18-23; 28.4% ACT 24-29 **% Accepted:** 78 **Admission Plans:** Early Admission; Deferred Admission **Application Deadline:** Rolling **Application Fee:** $60.00 **H.S. Requirements:** High school diploma required; GED accepted **Costs Per**

Year: Application fee: $60. State resident tuition: $4913 full-time, $156.75 per credit hour part-time. Nonresident tuition: $18,203 full-time, $313.75 per credit hour part-time. Mandatory fees: $612 full-time. Full-time tuition and fees vary according to course level and reciprocity agreements. Part-time tuition varies according to course level and reciprocity agreements. College room and board: $10,454. College room only: $6544. Room and board charges vary according to board plan. **Scholarships:** Available **Calendar System:** Semester, Summer Session Available **Enrollment:** FT 16,391, PT 6,317, Grad FT 2,837, Grad PT 3,541 **Faculty:** FT 897, PT 490 **Student-Faculty Ratio:** 21:1 **Exams:** SAT I or ACT. ACT essay not being used. SAT essay not being used. **% Receiving Financial Aid:** 48 **% Residing in College-Owned, -Operated, or -Affiliated Housing:** 5 **Final Year or Final Semester Residency Requirement:** No **Library Holdings:** 1,511,496 **Credit Hours For Degree:** 124 credit hours, Bachelors **ROTC:** Army, Air Force **Professional Accreditation:** AACSB, ABET, AAMFT, AACN, ABA, ACCE, ACA, ADA, APTA, ASLA, AALS, FIDER, CSWE, JRCEPAT, JRCNMT, NAACLS, NAAB, NASAD, NASM, NASPAA NAST, NCATE, NLN, NCCU **Intercollegiate Athletics:** Baseball M; Basketball M & W; Cheerleading M & W; Cross-Country Running W; Football M; Golf M; Soccer M & W; Softball W; Swimming and Diving M & W; Tennis M & W; Track and Field W; Volleyball W

UNIVERSITY OF NEVADA, RENO
Reno, NV 89557
Tel: (775)784-1110; Free: (866)263-8232
Admissions: (775)784-4700
E-mail: asknevada@unr.edu
Web Site: http://www.unr.edu/
President/CEO: Dr. Milton D. Glick
Admissions: Dr. Steve Maples
Financial Aid: Sandy Guidry
Type: University **Sex:** Coed **Affiliation:** Nevada System of Higher Education **Scores:** 94% SAT V 400+; 94% SAT M 400+; 47% ACT 18-23; 38% ACT 24-29 **% Accepted:** 88 **Admission Plans:** Early Admission; Deferred Admission **Application Deadline:** Rolling **Application Fee:** $60.00 **H.S. Requirements:** High school diploma required; GED not accepted **Costs Per Year:** Application fee: $60. One-time mandatory fee: $106. State resident tuition: $4635 full-time, $154.50 per credit part-time. Nonresident tuition: $16,975 full-time, $304 per credit part-time. Mandatory fees: $416 full-time. Full-time tuition and fees vary according to course load. Part-time tuition varies according to course load. College room and board: $10,595. College room only: $6100. Room and board charges vary according to board plan and housing facility. **Scholarships:** Available **Calendar System:** Semester, Summer Session Available **Faculty:** FT 585, PT 19 **Student-Faculty Ratio:** 23:1 **Exams:** SAT I or ACT. ACT essay not being used. SAT essay not being used. **% Receiving Financial Aid:** 34 **% Residing in College-Owned, -Operated, or -Affiliated Housing:** 14 **Credit Hours For Degree:** 124 credits, Bachelors **ROTC:** Army **Professional Accreditation:** AACSB, ABET, ACEJMC, AACN, ACA, ADtA, APA, ASLHA, CSWE, LCMEAMA, NASM, NCATE, NCCU **Intercollegiate Athletics:** Baseball M; Basketball M & W; Cheerleading M & W; Cross-Country Running W; Football M; Golf M & W; Riflery M & W; Skiing (Cross-Country) M & W; Skiing (Downhill) M & W; Soccer W; Softball W; Swimming and Diving W; Tennis M & W; Track and Field W; Volleyball W

UNIVERSITY OF PHOENIX—LAS VEGAS CAMPUS
7455 Washington Ave.
Ste. 317
Las Vegas, NV 89128
Tel: (702)638-7279; Free: 800-228-7240
Admissions: (480)557-6151
Fax: (702)638-8035
E-mail: audra.mcquarie@phoenix.edu
Web Site: http://www.phoenix.edu/
President/CEO: William Pepicello
Admissions: Audra McQuarie
Type: Comprehensive **Sex:** Coed **Admission Plans:** Open Admission; Deferred Admission **Application Deadline:** Rolling **Application Fee:** $0.00 **H.S. Requirements:** High school diploma required; GED accepted **Costs Per Year:** Application fee: $0. Tuition: $11,438 full-time. Full-time tuition varies according to course level and course load. **Scholarships:** Available **Calendar System:** Continuous, Summer Session Not available **Enrollment:** FT 2,301 **Faculty:** FT 35, PT 244 **Regional Accreditation:** North Central Association of Colleges and Schools **Credit Hours For Degree:** 60 credits, Associates; 120 credits, Bachelors

UNIVERSITY OF PHOENIX—NORTHERN NEVADA CAMPUS
10345 Professional Circle
Ste. 200
Reno, NV 89521-5862
Tel: (775)828-7999
Admissions: (480)557-6151
E-mail: audra.mcquarie@phoenix.edu
Web Site: http://www.phoenix.edu/
President/CEO: William Pepicello
Admissions: Audra McQuarie
Type: Comprehensive **Sex:** Coed **Admission Plans:** Open Admission **Application Fee:** $45.00 **H.S. Requirements:** High school diploma required; GED accepted **Costs Per Year:** Application fee: $45. Tuition: $11,438 full-time. Full-time tuition varies according to course level and course load. **Enrollment:** FT 401 **Faculty:** FT 24, PT 106 **Regional Accreditation:** North Central Association of Colleges and Schools

WESTERN NEVADA COLLEGE
2201 West College Parkway
Carson City, NV 89703-7316
Tel: (775)445-3000
Fax: (775)887-3141
E-mail: wncc_aro@wncc.edu
Web Site: http://www.wnc.edu/
President/CEO: Dr. Carol Lucey
Type: Two-Year College **Sex:** Coed **Affiliation:** Nevada System of Higher Education **% Accepted:** 100 **Admission Plans:** Open Admission; Early Admission **Application Deadline:** Rolling **Application Fee:** $15.00 **H.S. Requirements:** High school diploma required; GED accepted **Scholarships:** Available **Calendar System:** Semester, Summer Session Available **Enrollment:** FT 993, PT 4,538 **Faculty:** FT 79, PT 307 **Student-Faculty Ratio:** 15:1 **Library Holdings:** 50,612 **Credit Hours For Degree:** 60 credits, Associates **Professional Accreditation:** NLN, NCCU **Intercollegiate Athletics:** Baseball M; Equestrian Sports M & W; Soccer W

CHESTER COLLEGE OF NEW ENGLAND
40 Chester St.
Chester, NH 03036-4331
Tel: (603)887-4401; Free: 800-974-6372
E-mail: admissions@chestercollege.edu
Web Site: http://www.chestercollege.edu/
President/CEO: Robert Baines
Admissions: Sarah Vogell
Financial Aid: Jason Graves
Type: Four-Year College **Sex:** Coed **Scores:** 90.9% SAT V 400+; 81.7% SAT M 400+; 65% ACT 18-23 **% Accepted:** 50 **Admission Plans:** Deferred Admission **Application Deadline:** Rolling **Application Fee:** $35.00 **H.S. Requirements:** High school diploma required; GED accepted **Scholarships:** Available **Calendar System:** Semester, Summer Session Available **Enrollment:** FT 196, PT 9 **Faculty:** FT 18, PT 30 **Student-Faculty Ratio:** 12:1 **% Receiving Financial Aid:** 55 **% Residing in College-Owned, -Operated, or -Affiliated Housing:** 52 **Library Holdings:** 27,000 **Regional Accreditation:** New England Association of Schools and Colleges **Credit Hours For Degree:** 60 credits, Associates; 120 credits, Bachelors

COLBY-SAWYER COLLEGE
541 Main St.
New London, NH 03257
Tel: (603)526-3000; Free: 800-272-1015
Admissions: (603)526-3700
Fax: (603)526-3452
E-mail: admissions@colby-sawyer.edu
Web Site: http://www.colby-sawyer.edu/
President/CEO: Thomas Galligan, JD
Type: Four-Year College **Sex:** Coed **Scores:** 94% SAT V 400+; 90% SAT M 400+; 62% ACT 18-23; 16% ACT 24-29 **% Accepted:** 87 **Admission Plans:** Early Admission; Early Decision Plan; Deferred Admission **Application Deadline:** April 1 **Application Fee:** $45.00 **H.S. Requirements:** High school diploma required; GED accepted **Costs Per Year:** Application fee: $45. Comprehensive fee: $41,950. Part-time tuition: $1040 per credit hour. Part-time tuition varies according to course load. Tuition: $1040 per credit hour part-time. Part-time tuition varies according to course load. **Scholarships:** Available **Calendar System:** Semester, Summer Session Not available **Enrollment:** FT 928, PT 20 **Faculty:** FT 60, PT 67 **Student-Faculty Ratio:** 11:1 **Exams:** SAT I or ACT. **% Receiving Financial Aid:** 81 **% Residing in College-Owned, -Operated, or -Affiliated Housing:** 90 **Library Holdings:** 93,696 **Regional Accreditation:** New England Association of Schools and Colleges **Credit Hours For Degree:** 60 credit hours, Associates; 120 credit hours, Bachelors **ROTC:** Army, Air Force **Professional Accreditation:** AACN, JRCEPAT **Intercollegiate Athletics:** Baseball M; Basketball M & W; Cross-Country Running M & W; Equestrian Sports M & W; Field Hockey W; Golf M & W; Ice Hockey M & W; Lacrosse W; Rugby M & W; Skiing (Downhill) M & W; Soccer M & W; Softball W; Swimming and Diving M & W; Tennis M & W; Track and Field M & W; Volleyball W

DANIEL WEBSTER COLLEGE
20 University Dr.
Nashua, NH 03063-1300
Tel: (603)577-6000; Free: 800-325-6876
Admissions: (603)577-6600
Fax: (603)577-6001
E-mail: monahan@dwc.edu
Web Site: http://www.dwc.edu/
President/CEO: Dr. Robert E. Myers
Admissions: Daniel Monahan
Type: Comprehensive **Sex:** Coed **Scores:** 90% SAT V 400+; 90% SAT M 400+; 57% ACT 18-23; 16% ACT 24-29 **% Accepted:** 74 **Admission Plans:** Early Admission; Early Decision Plan; Deferred Admission **Application Deadline:** Rolling **Application Fee:** $35.00 **H.S. Requirements:** High school diploma required; GED accepted **Costs Per Year:** Application fee: $35. Comprehensive fee: $38,562 includes full-time tuition ($27,939), mandatory fees ($925), and college room and board ($9698). College room only: $4761. Full-time tuition and fees vary according to class time and course load. Room and board charges vary according to housing facility. Part-time tuition: $1050 per credit. Part-time mandatory fees: $275 per credit. Part-time tuition and fees vary according to class time and course load. **Scholarships:** Available **Calendar System:** Semester, Summer Session Available **Enrollment:** FT 797, PT 88 **Faculty:** FT 35, PT 27 **Student-Faculty Ratio:** 14:1 **Exams:** SAT I or ACT. **% Receiving Financial Aid:** 94 **% Residing in College-Owned, -Operated, or -Affiliated Housing:** 80 **Regional Accreditation:** New England Association of Schools and Colleges **Credit Hours For Degree:** 60 credits, Associates; 120 credits, Bachelors **ROTC:** Army, Air Force **Professional Accreditation:** CAA **Intercollegiate Athletics:** Baseball M; Basketball M & W; Cross-Country Running M & W; Field Hockey W; Golf M & W; Ice Hockey M & W; Lacrosse M & W; Soccer M & W; Softball W; Volleyball M & W

DANIEL WEBSTER COLLEGE—PORTSMOUTH CAMPUS
119 International Dr.
Pease International Tradeport
Portsmouth, NH 03801
Tel: (603)430-4077; Free: 800-794-6188
Fax: (603)766-6595
Web Site: http://www.dwc.edu/gcde/portsmouth/
Type: Comprehensive **Sex:** Coed **Regional Accreditation:** New England Association of Schools and Colleges

DARTMOUTH COLLEGE
Hanover, NH 03755
Tel: (603)646-1110
Admissions: (603)646-2875
Fax: (603)646-1216
E-mail: admissions.office@dartmouth.edu
Web Site: http://www.dartmouth.edu/
President/CEO: James Yong Kim
Admissions: Maria Laskaris
Financial Aid: Virginia S. Hazen
Type: University **Sex:** Coed **Scores:** 99% SAT V 400+; 99% SAT M 400+ **% Accepted:** 13 **Admission Plans:** Early Admission; Early Decision Plan; Deferred Admission **Application Deadline:** January 1 **Application Fee:** $70.00 **H.S. Requirements:** High school diploma required; GED not accepted **Costs Per Year:** Application fee: $70. Comprehensive fee: $49,974 includes full-time tuition ($38,445), mandatory fees ($234), and college room and board ($11,295). College room only: $6750. Room and board charges vary according to board plan. **Scholarships:** Available **Calendar System:**

Quarter, Summer Session Available **Enrollment:** FT 4,145, PT 51, Grad FT 1,668, Grad PT 123 **Faculty:** FT 492, PT 155 **Student-Faculty Ratio:** 8:1 **Exams:** SAT I or ACT, SAT II. ACT essay used for admission. SAT essay used for admission. ACT essay used for advising. SAT essay used for advising. ACT essay used for placement. SAT essay used for placement. **% Receiving Financial Aid:** 55 **% Residing in College-Owned, -Operated, or -Affiliated Housing:** 87 **Final Year or Final Semester Residency Requirement:** Yes **Regional Accreditation:** New England Association of Schools and Colleges **Credit Hours For Degree:** 35 courses, Bachelors **ROTC:** Army **Professional Accreditation:** AACSB, ABET, APA, CEPH, LCMEAMA, NAST **Intercollegiate Athletics:** Badminton M & W; Baseball M; Basketball M & W; Cheerleading M & W; Crew M & W; Cross-Country Running M & W; Equestrian Sports M & W; Fencing M & W; Field Hockey W; Football M; Golf M & W; Gymnastics M & W; Ice Hockey M & W; Lacrosse M & W; Rugby M & W; Sailing M & W; Skiing (Cross-Country) M & W; Skiing (Downhill) M & W; Soccer M & W; Softball W; Squash M & W; Swimming and Diving M & W; Table Tennis M & W; Tennis M & W; Track and Field M & W; Ultimate Frisbee M & W; Volleyball M & W; Water Polo M & W; Wrestling M

FRANKLIN PIERCE UNIVERSITY
40 University Dr.
Rindge, NH 03461-0060
Tel: (603)899-4000; Free: 800-437-0048
Admissions: (603)899-4050
Fax: (603)899-4372
E-mail: admissions@fpc.edu
Web Site: http://www.franklinpierce.edu/
President/CEO: James Birge
Financial Aid: Kenneth Ferreira
Type: University **Sex:** Coed **Scores:** 92.5% SAT V 400+; 91.7% SAT M 400+; 64.1% ACT 18-23; 7.7% ACT 24-29 **% Accepted:** 81 **Admission Plans:** Early Admission; Deferred Admission **Application Deadline:** Rolling **Application Fee:** $40.00 **H.S. Requirements:** High school diploma required; GED accepted. For early entrance program: High school diploma or equivalent not required **Costs Per Year:** Application fee: $40. Comprehensive fee: $38,500 includes full-time tuition ($27,700), mandatory fees ($1000), and college room and board ($9800). College room only: $5600. Full-time tuition and fees vary according to course load and location. Room and board charges vary according to board plan, housing facility, and student level. Part-time tuition: $923 per credit hour. **Scholarships:** Available **Calendar System:** Miscellaneous, Summer Session Available **Enrollment:** FT 1,600, PT 292, Grad FT 296, Grad PT 249 **Faculty:** FT 110, PT 141 **Student-Faculty Ratio:** 14:1 **Exams:** SAT I or ACT. ACT essay used for admission. SAT essay used for admission. ACT essay used for advising. SAT essay used for advising. ACT essay used for placement. SAT essay used for placement. **% Receiving Financial Aid:** 74 **% Residing in College-Owned, -Operated, or -Affiliated Housing:** 84 **Library Holdings:** 137,458 **Regional Accreditation:** New England Association of Schools and Colleges **Credit Hours For Degree:** 120 credits, Bachelors **ROTC:** Army, Air Force **Professional Accreditation:** APTA **Intercollegiate Athletics:** Baseball M; Basketball M & W; Crew M & W; Cross-Country Running M & W; Field Hockey W; Golf M; Ice Hockey M; Lacrosse M & W; Soccer M & W; Softball W; Tennis M & W; Volleyball W

GRANITE STATE COLLEGE
8 Old Suncook Rd.
Concord, NH 03301
Tel: (603)228-3000
Admissions: (603)513-1308
Fax: (603)229-0964
E-mail: tessa.mcdonnell@granite.edu
Web Site: http://www.granite.edu/
President/CEO: Dr. Karol A. LaCroix
Admissions: Tessa McDonnell
Type: Four-Year College **Sex:** Coed **Affiliation:** University System of New Hampshire **% Accepted:** 100 **Admission Plans:** Open Admission **Application Deadline:** Rolling **Application Fee:** $45.00 **H.S. Requirements:** High school diploma required; GED accepted **Costs Per Year:** Application fee: $45. State resident tuition: $6000 full-time, $250 per credit part-time. Nonresident tuition: $6360 full-time, $265 per credit part-time. Mandatory fees: $195 full-time, $65 per term part-time. **Calendar System:** Trimester, Summer Session Available **Enrollment:** FT 687, PT 831, Grad FT 21, Grad PT 195 **Faculty:** FT 0, PT 166 **Student-Faculty Ratio:** 10:1 **Final Year or Final Semester Residency Requirement:** No **Regional Accreditation:** New England Association of Schools and Colleges **Credit Hours For Degree:** 64 semester hours, Associates; 124 semester hours, Bachelors **ROTC:** Army

GREAT BAY COMMUNITY COLLEGE
320 Corporate Dr.
Portsmouth, NH 03801
Tel: (603)427-7600
Web Site: http://www.greatbay.edu/
President/CEO: Wildolfo Arvelo
Type: Two-Year College **Sex:** Coed **Regional Accreditation:** New England Association of Schools and Colleges

HESSER COLLEGE, CONCORD
25 Hall St., Ste. 104
Concord, NH 03301
Tel: (603)225-9200
Web Site: http://www.concord.hesser.edu/
Type: Two-Year College **Sex:** Coed **Regional Accreditation:** New England Association of Schools and Colleges

HESSER COLLEGE, MANCHESTER
3 Sundial Ave.
Manchester, NH 03103
Tel: (603)668-6660
Web Site: http://www.manchester.hesser.edu/
President/CEO: Dr. Harold Griffin
Type: Two-Year College **Sex:** Coed **H.S. Requirements:** High school diploma required; GED accepted **Scholarships:** Available **Calendar System:** Semester **Regional Accreditation:** New England Association of Schools and Colleges **Credit Hours For Degree:** 60 credits, Associates; 120 credits, Bachelors **Professional Accreditation:** AAMAE, APTA

HESSER COLLEGE, NASHUA
410 Amherst St.
Nashua, NH 03063
Tel: (603)883-0404
Web Site: http://www.nashua.hesser.edu/
Type: Two-Year College **Sex:** Coed **Regional Accreditation:** New England Association of Schools and Colleges

HESSER COLLEGE, PORTSMOUTH
170 Commerce Way
Portsmouth, NH 03801
Tel: (603)436-5300
Web Site: http://www.portsmouth.hesser.edu/
Type: Two-Year College **Sex:** Coed **H.S. Requirements:** High school diploma required; GED accepted **Regional Accreditation:** New England Association of Schools and Colleges

HESSER COLLEGE, SALEM
11 Manor Parkway
Salem, NH 03079
Tel: (603)898-3480
Web Site: http://www.salem.hesser.edu/
Type: Two-Year College **Sex:** Coed **H.S. Requirements:** High school diploma required; GED accepted **Regional Accreditation:** New England Association of Schools and Colleges

KEENE STATE COLLEGE
229 Main St.
Keene, NH 03435
Tel: (603)352-1909; Free: 800-KSC-1909
Admissions: (603)358-2273
Fax: (603)358-2767
E-mail: admissions@keene.edu
Web Site: http://www.keene.edu/
President/CEO: Dr. Helen Giles-Gee
Admissions: Margaret Richmond
Financial Aid: Patricia Blodgett
Type: Comprehensive **Sex:** Coed **Affiliation:** University System of New Hampshire **Scores:** 92.64% SAT V 400+; 92.8% SAT M 400+ **% Accepted:** 71 **Admission Plans:** Deferred Admission **Application Deadline:** April 1 **Application Fee:** $40.00 **H.S. Requirements:** High school diploma

required; GED accepted **Costs Per Year:** Application fee: $40. State resident tuition: $7000 full-time, $292 per credit part-time. Nonresident tuition: $15,170 full-time, $632 per credit part-time. Mandatory fees: $2334 full-time, $92 per credit part-time. Part-time tuition and fees vary according to course load. College room and board: $8444. College room only: $5520. Room and board charges vary according to board plan and housing facility. **Scholarships:** Available **Calendar System:** Semester, Summer Session Available **Enrollment:** FT 4,890, PT 345, Grad FT 8, Grad PT 113 **Faculty:** FT 194, PT 265 **Student-Faculty Ratio:** 18:1 **Exams:** SAT I or ACT. ACT essay used for admission. SAT essay used for admission. **% Receiving Financial Aid:** 52 **% Residing in College-Owned, -Operated, or -Affiliated Housing:** 55 **Final Year or Final Semester Residency Requirement:** No **Library Holdings:** 330,017 **Regional Accreditation:** New England Association of Schools and Colleges **Credit Hours For Degree:** 60 credits, Associates; 120 credits, Bachelors **ROTC:** Air Force **Professional Accreditation:** ADtA, JRCEPAT, NASM, NCATE **Intercollegiate Athletics:** Baseball M; Basketball M & W; Cross-Country Running M & W; Field Hockey W; Lacrosse M & W; Rock Climbing M & W; Skiing (Downhill) M & W; Soccer M & W; Softball W; Swimming and Diving M & W; Track and Field M & W; Volleyball W

LAKES REGION COMMUNITY COLLEGE
379 Belmont Rd.
Laconia, NH 03246
Tel: (603)524-3207
Fax: (603)524-8084
Web Site: http://www.lrcc.edu/
President/CEO: Mark Edelstein, PhD
Type: Two-Year College **Sex:** Coed **Regional Accreditation:** New England Association of Schools and Colleges

MAGDALEN COLLEGE
511 Kearsarge Mountain Rd.
Warner, NH 03278
Tel: (603)456-2656; Free: 877-498-1723
Fax: (603)456-2660
E-mail: admissions@magdalen.edu
Web Site: http://www.magdalen.edu/
President/CEO: Jeffrey Karls
Admissions: Justin Fout
Financial Aid: Bobbie Anne Abson
Type: Four-Year College **Sex:** Coed **Affiliation:** Roman Catholic **Scores:** 94% SAT V 400+; 87% SAT M 400+; 62% ACT 18-23; 38% ACT 24-29 **% Accepted:** 78 **Admission Plans:** Early Admission; Early Decision Plan **Application Deadline:** May 1 **Application Fee:** $35.00 **H.S. Requirements:** High school diploma required; GED accepted **Scholarships:** Available **Calendar System:** Semester, Summer Session Not available **Enrollment:** FT 72, PT 1 **Faculty:** FT 7, PT 2 **Student-Faculty Ratio:** 8:1 **Exams:** SAT I or ACT. **% Receiving Financial Aid:** 39 **% Residing in College-Owned, -Operated, or -Affiliated Housing:** 100 **Library Holdings:** 26,000 **Credit Hours For Degree:** 60 credit hours, Associates; 120 credit hours, Bachelors **Professional Accreditation:** AALE

MANCHESTER COMMUNITY COLLEGE
1066 Front St.
Manchester, NH 03102-8518
Tel: (603)668-6706
E-mail: jpoirier@nhctc.edu
Web Site: http://www.manchestercommunitycollege.edu/
President/CEO: Ronald Rioux
Admissions: Jacquie Poirier
Type: Two-Year College **Sex:** Coed **Affiliation:** New Hampshire Community Technical College System **Admission Plans:** Early Admission; Deferred Admission **Application Deadline:** Rolling **Application Fee:** $10.00 **H.S. Requirements:** High school diploma required; GED accepted **Scholarships:** Available **Calendar System:** Semester, Summer Session Available **Faculty:** FT 52, PT 150 **Student-Faculty Ratio:** 14:1 **Library Holdings:** 18,000 **Regional Accreditation:** New England Association of Schools and Colleges **Credit Hours For Degree:** 64 credit hours, Associates **Professional Accreditation:** ARCEST, AAMAE, ACBSP, NLN **Intercollegiate Athletics:** Basketball M; Skiing (Downhill) M & W; Soccer M & W; Volleyball M & W

NASHUA COMMUNITY COLLEGE
505 Amherst St.
Nashua, NH 03063-1026
Tel: (603)882-6923
Fax: (603)882-8690
E-mail: nashua@nhctc.edu
Web Site: http://www.nashuacc.edu/
President/CEO: Lucille A. Jordan
Admissions: Patricia Goodman
Type: Two-Year College **Sex:** Coed **Affiliation:** New Hampshire Community Technical College System **Admission Plans:** Deferred Admission **Application Deadline:** Rolling **Application Fee:** $10.00 **H.S. Requirements:** High school diploma required; GED accepted **Costs Per Year:** Application fee: $10. State resident tuition: $4392 full-time, $183 per credit hour part-time. Nonresident tuition: $10,032 full-time, $418 per credit hour part-time. Mandatory fees: $384 full-time, $16 per credit hour part-time. **Scholarships:** Available **Calendar System:** Semester, Summer Session Available **Enrollment:** FT 638, PT 1,087 **Faculty:** FT 42, PT 66 **Library Holdings:** 22,000 **Regional Accreditation:** New England Association of Schools and Colleges **Credit Hours For Degree:** 64 credits, Associates **Professional Accreditation:** ABET, AHIMA, AOTA, CARC, NAACLS, NLN **Intercollegiate Athletics:** Soccer M & W

NEW ENGLAND COLLEGE
15 Main St.
Henniker, NH 03242-3293
Tel: (603)428-2211; Free: 800-521-7642
Admissions: (603)428-2223
E-mail: admission@nec.edu
Web Site: http://www.nec.edu/
President/CEO: Dr. Michele D. Perkins
Admissions: Diane Raymond
Financial Aid: Kristen Blase
Type: Comprehensive **Sex:** Coed **Scores:** 70.74% SAT V 400+; 66.12% SAT M 400+; 40.91% ACT 18-23; 13.64% ACT 24-29 **% Accepted:** 81 **Admission Plans:** Deferred Admission **Application Deadline:** September 7 **Application Fee:** $30.00 **H.S. Requirements:** High school diploma required; GED accepted **Costs Per Year:** Application fee: $30. Comprehensive fee: $37,076 includes full-time tuition ($27,200), mandatory fees ($250), and college room and board ($9626). College room only: $5000. Full-time tuition and fees vary according to class time, course load, degree level, location, program, and reciprocity agreements. Room and board charges vary according to board plan and housing facility. Part-time tuition: $1300 per credit. Part-time tuition varies according to class time, course load, degree level, location, and program. **Scholarships:** Available **Calendar System:** Semester, Summer Session Available **Enrollment:** FT 939, PT 75, Grad FT 214, Grad PT 688 **Faculty:** FT 65, PT 115 **Student-Faculty Ratio:** 12:1 **% Receiving Financial Aid:** 71 **% Residing in College-Owned, -Operated, or -Affiliated Housing:** 65 **Final Year or Final Semester Residency Requirement:** Yes **Library Holdings:** 106,100 **Regional Accreditation:** New England Association of Schools and Colleges **ROTC:** Army, Air Force **Intercollegiate Athletics:** Baseball M; Basketball M & W; Cross-Country Running M & W; Field Hockey W; Ice Hockey M & W; Lacrosse M & W; Soccer M & W; Softball W

NEW HAMPSHIRE INSTITUTE OF ART
148 Concord St.
Manchester, NH 03104
Tel: (603)623-0313
Admissions: (866)241-4918
Fax: (603)641-1832
E-mail: aabbott@nhia.edu
Web Site: http://www.nhia.edu/
President/CEO: Roger Williams
Admissions: Amanda Abbott
Financial Aid: Linda Lavallee
Type: Four-Year College **Sex:** Coed **Scores:** 84% SAT V 400+; 87% SAT M 400+ **% Accepted:** 54 **Admission Plans:** Early Action; Deferred Admission **Application Deadline:** Rolling **Application Fee:** $25.00 **H.S. Requirements:** High school diploma required; GED accepted **Costs Per Year:** Application fee: $25. Tuition: $17,740 full-time, $1695 per course part-time. Mandatory fees: $1820 full-time, $233 per course part-time, $165 per term part-time. Part-time tuition and fees vary according to course load. College room only: $7000. Room charges vary according to housing facility.

Scholarships: Available **Calendar System:** Semester, Summer Session Available **Enrollment:** FT 389, PT 56 **Faculty:** FT 16, PT 63 **Student-Faculty Ratio:** 11:1 **Exams:** SAT I and SAT II or ACT. ACT essay not being used. SAT essay not being used. **% Residing in College-Owned, -Operated, or -Affiliated Housing:** 46 **Final Year or Final Semester Residency Requirement:** No **Library Holdings:** 14,183 **Regional Accreditation:** New England Association of Schools and Colleges **Credit Hours For Degree:** 120 credits, Bachelors **Professional Accreditation:** NASAD

NHTI, CONCORD'S COMMUNITY COLLEGE
31 College Dr.
Concord, NH 03301-7412
Tel: (603)271-6484; Free: 800-247-0179
Admissions: (603)271-7131
Fax: (603)271-7734
E-mail: fmeyer@nhctc.edu
Web Site: http://www.nhti.edu/
President/CEO: Lynn Kilchenstein
Admissions: Francis P. Meyer
Type: Two-Year College **Sex:** Coed **Affiliation:** Community College System of New Hampshire **Admission Plans:** Preferred Admission **Application Deadline:** Rolling **Application Fee:** $10.00 **H.S. Requirements:** High school diploma required; GED accepted **Costs Per Year:** Application fee: $10. State resident tuition: $4392 full-time, $183 per credit part-time. Nonresident tuition: $10,032 full-time, $418 per credit part-time. Mandatory fees: $480 full-time, $20 per credit part-time. Full-time tuition and fees vary according to course load. Part-time tuition and fees vary according to course load. College room and board: $7852. **Scholarships:** Available **Calendar System:** Semester, Summer Session Available **Student-Faculty Ratio:** 15:1 **Exams:** Other, SAT I or ACT. **% Residing in College-Owned, -Operated, or -Affiliated Housing:** 23 **Library Holdings:** 32,000 **Regional Accreditation:** New England Association of Schools and Colleges **Credit Hours For Degree:** 64 credit hours, Associates **Professional Accreditation:** ABET, ADA, JRCERT, JRCEMT, NLN **Intercollegiate Athletics:** Baseball M; Basketball M & W; Gymnastics M & W; Soccer M & W; Softball W; Volleyball M & W

PLYMOUTH STATE UNIVERSITY
17 High St.
Plymouth, NH 03264-1595
Tel: (603)535-5000; Free: 800-842-6900
Fax: (603)535-2714
E-mail: plymouthadmit@plymouth.edu
Web Site: http://www.plymouth.edu/
President/CEO: Sara Jayne Steen
Admissions: Eugene Fahey
Financial Aid: June Louise Schlabach
Type: Comprehensive **Sex:** Coed **Affiliation:** University System of New Hampshire **Scores:** 87% SAT V 400+; 88% SAT M 400+; 64% ACT 18-23; 12% ACT 24-29 **% Accepted:** 70 **Admission Plans:** Deferred Admission **Application Deadline:** April 1 **Application Fee:** $40.00 **H.S. Requirements:** High school diploma required; GED accepted **Costs Per Year:** Application fee: $40. State resident tuition: $7000 full-time, $292 per credit hour part-time. Nonresident tuition: $15,170 full-time, $632 per credit hour part-time. Mandatory fees: $1944 full-time, $84 per credit hour part-time. Full-time tuition and fees vary according to reciprocity agreements. Part-time tuition and fees vary according to course load and reciprocity agreements. College room and board: $8594. College room only: $5996. Room and board charges vary according to board plan and housing facility. **Scholarships:** Available **Calendar System:** Semester, Summer Session Available **Enrollment:** FT 4,025, PT 236, Grad FT 586, Grad PT 1,398 **Faculty:** FT 186, PT 230 **Student-Faculty Ratio:** 16:1 **Exams:** SAT I or ACT. **% Receiving Financial Aid:** 60 **% Residing in College-Owned, -Operated, or -Affiliated Housing:** 57 **Final Year or Final Semester Residency Requirement:** No **Library Holdings:** 349,390 **Regional Accreditation:** New England Association of Schools and Colleges **Credit Hours For Degree:** 120 semester credit hours, Bachelors **ROTC:** Army, Air Force **Professional Accreditation:** ACA, ACBSP, CSWE, JRCEPAT, NCATE **Intercollegiate Athletics:** Baseball M; Basketball M & W; Cheerleading M & W; Field Hockey W; Football M; Ice Hockey M & W; Lacrosse M & W; Skiing (Downhill) M & W; Soccer M & W; Softball W; Swimming and Diving W; Tennis W; Volleyball M & W; Wrestling M

RIVER VALLEY COMMUNITY COLLEGE
1 College Dr.
Claremont, NH 03743
Tel: (603)542-7744
Fax: (603)543-1844
Web Site: http://www.rivervalley.edu/
President/CEO: Steven Budd
Type: Two-Year College **Sex:** Coed **Regional Accreditation:** New England Association of Schools and Colleges

RIVIER COLLEGE
420 South Main St.
Nashua, NH 03060
Tel: (603)888-1311; Free: 800-44RIVIER
Admissions: (603)897-8507
Fax: (603)891-1799
E-mail: rivadmit@rivier.edu
Web Site: http://www.rivier.edu/
President/CEO: Dr. William Farrell
Admissions: David Boisvert
Financial Aid: Valerie Patnaude
Type: Comprehensive **Sex:** Coed **Affiliation:** Roman Catholic **Scores:** 87.3% SAT V 400+ **% Accepted:** 81 **Admission Plans:** Early Action; Deferred Admission **Application Deadline:** Rolling **Application Fee:** $25.00 **H.S. Requirements:** High school diploma required; GED accepted **Costs Per Year:** Application fee: $25. One-time mandatory fee: $175. Comprehensive fee: $34,478 includes full-time tuition ($24,450), mandatory fees ($600), and college room and board ($9428). Full-time tuition and fees vary according to degree level and program. Room and board charges vary according to board plan and housing facility. Part-time tuition: $815 per credit. Part-time mandatory fees: $25 per year. Part-time tuition and fees vary according to class time, course level, course load, degree level, and program. **Scholarships:** Available **Calendar System:** Semester, Summer Session Not available **Enrollment:** FT 967, PT 519, Grad FT 156, Grad PT 614 **Faculty:** FT 71, PT 122 **Student-Faculty Ratio:** 15:1 **Exams:** Other, SAT I or ACT. **% Receiving Financial Aid:** 82 **% Residing in College-Owned, -Operated, or -Affiliated Housing:** 31 **Regional Accreditation:** New England Association of Schools and Colleges **Credit Hours For Degree:** 60 credits, Associates; 120 credits, Bachelors **ROTC:** Air Force **Professional Accreditation:** ACBSP, NLN **Intercollegiate Athletics:** Baseball M; Basketball M & W; Cheerleading M & W; Cross-Country Running M & W; Golf M & W; Soccer M & W; Softball W; Volleyball M & W

SAINT ANSELM COLLEGE
100 Saint Anselm Dr.
Manchester, NH 03102-1310
Tel: (603)641-7000; Free: 888-4ANSELM
Admissions: (603)641-7500
Fax: (603)641-7550
E-mail: admission@anselm.edu
Web Site: http://www.anselm.edu/
President/CEO: Fr. Jonathan DeFelice
Admissions: Nancy Davis Griffin
Financial Aid: Elizabeth Keuffel
Type: Four-Year College **Sex:** Coed **Affiliation:** Roman Catholic **Scores:** 100% SAT V 400+; 100% SAT M 400+; 52% ACT 18-23; 32% ACT 24-29 **% Accepted:** 77 **Admission Plans:** Early Action; Early Decision Plan; Deferred Admission **Application Deadline:** March 1 **Application Fee:** $55.00 **H.S. Requirements:** High school diploma required; GED accepted **Costs Per Year:** Application fee: $55. Comprehensive fee: $42,065 includes full-time tuition ($29,720), mandatory fees ($795), and college room and board ($11,550). **Scholarships:** Available **Calendar System:** Semester, Summer Session Available **Enrollment:** FT 1,879, PT 36 **Faculty:** FT 144, PT 64 **Student-Faculty Ratio:** 11:1 **Exams:** SAT I or ACT. ACT essay used for admission. SAT essay used for admission. **% Receiving Financial Aid:** 72 **% Residing in College-Owned, -Operated, or -Affiliated Housing:** 91 **Final Year or Final Semester Residency Requirement:** No **Library Holdings:** 222,000 **Regional Accreditation:** New England Association of Schools and Colleges **Credit Hours For Degree:** 40 courses, Bachelors **ROTC:** Army, Air Force **Professional Accreditation:** AACN **Intercollegiate Athletics:** Baseball M; Basketball M & W; Cheerleading W; Cross-Country Running M & W; Field Hockey W; Football M; Golf M; Ice Hockey M & W; Lacrosse M & W; Skiing (Downhill) M & W; Soccer M & W; Softball W; Tennis M & W; Volleyball W

SOUTHERN NEW HAMPSHIRE UNIVERSITY
2500 North River Rd.
Manchester, NH 03106-1045
Tel: (603)668-2211; Free: 800-642-4968
Admissions: (603)645-9611
Fax: (603)645-9693
E-mail: admission@snhu.edu
Web Site: http://www.snhu.edu/
President/CEO: Dr. Paul J. LeBlanc
Admissions: Steve Soba
Type: Comprehensive **Sex:** Coed **Scores:** 92.39% SAT V 400+; 91.13% SAT M 400+; 64.52% ACT 18-23; 12.9% ACT 24-29 **% Accepted:** 86 **Admission Plans:** Early Action; Deferred Admission **Application Deadline:** Rolling **Application Fee:** $40.00 **H.S. Requirements:** High school diploma required; GED accepted **Costs Per Year:** Application fee: $40. Comprehensive fee: $36,618 includes full-time tuition ($26,112), mandatory fees ($330), and college room and board ($10,176). College room only: $7276. Full-time tuition and fees vary according to class time. Room and board charges vary according to board plan and housing facility. Part-time tuition: $1088 per credit. Part-time tuition varies according to class time. **Scholarships:** Available **Calendar System:** Semester, Summer Session Available **Enrollment:** FT 1,995, PT 42 **Faculty:** FT 132, PT 256 **Student-Faculty Ratio:** 16:1 **Exams:** SAT I or ACT. **% Receiving Financial Aid:** 72 **% Residing in College-Owned, -Operated, or -Affiliated Housing:** 78 **Library Holdings:** 94,580 **Regional Accreditation:** New England Association of Schools and Colleges **Credit Hours For Degree:** 60 credits, Associates; 120 credits, Bachelors **ROTC:** Army, Air Force **Professional Accreditation:** ACF, ACBSP **Intercollegiate Athletics:** Baseball M; Basketball M & W; Cheerleading M & W; Cross-Country Running M & W; Golf M; Ice Hockey M; Lacrosse M & W; Soccer M & W; Softball W; Tennis M & W; Volleyball W

THOMAS MORE COLLEGE OF LIBERAL ARTS
6 Manchester St.
Merrimack, NH 03054-4818
Tel: (603)880-8308; Free: 800-880-8308
Fax: (603)880-9280
E-mail: admissions@thomasmorecollege.edu
Web Site: http://www.thomasmorecollege.edu/
President/CEO: William E. Fahey
Admissions: Teddy Sifert
Financial Aid: Clinton A. Hanson, Jr.
Type: Four-Year College **Sex:** Coed **Affiliation:** Roman Catholic Church **Scores:** 95.45% SAT V 400+; 100% SAT M 400+; 100% ACT 24-29 **% Accepted:** 70 **Application Deadline:** Rolling **Application Fee:** $0.00 **H.S. Requirements:** High school diploma required; GED accepted **Scholarships:** Available **Calendar System:** Semester, Summer Session Not available **Enrollment:** FT 99 **Student-Faculty Ratio:** 12:1 **Exams:** SAT I or ACT. **% Receiving Financial Aid:** 69 **% Residing in College-Owned, -Operated, or -Affiliated Housing:** 97 **Library Holdings:** 45,000 **Regional Accreditation:** New England Association of Schools and Colleges **Credit Hours For Degree:** 120 credits, Bachelors **Professional Accreditation:** AALE

UNIVERSITY OF NEW HAMPSHIRE
Durham, NH 03824
Tel: (603)862-1234
Admissions: (603)862-0077
E-mail: admissions@unh.edu
Web Site: http://www.unh.edu/
President/CEO: Dr. Mark Huddleston
Financial Aid: Susan K. Allen
Type: University **Sex:** Coed **Affiliation:** University System of New Hampshire **Scores:** 99% SAT V 400+; 99% SAT M 400+; 38% ACT 18-23; 51% ACT 24-29 **% Accepted:** 72 **Admission Plans:** Preferred Admission; Early Action; Deferred Admission **Application Deadline:** February 1 **Application Fee:** $50.00 **H.S. Requirements:** High school diploma required; GED accepted **Costs Per Year:** Application fee: $50. State resident tuition: $10,080 full-time, $420 per credit hour part-time. Nonresident tuition: $24,050 full-time, $1002 per credit hour part-time. Mandatory fees: $2663 full-time, $665.75 per term part-time. Full-time tuition and fees vary according to degree level. Part-time tuition and fees vary according to degree level. College room and board: $8874. College room only: $5420. Room and board charges vary according to board plan and housing facility. **Scholarships:** Available **Calendar System:** Semester, Summer Session Available **Enrollment:** FT 12,035, PT 556, Grad FT 1,251, Grad PT 1,469 **Faculty:** FT 618, PT 358 **Student-Faculty Ratio:** 19:1 **Exams:** SAT I or ACT. ACT essay not being used. SAT essay not being used. **% Receiving Financial Aid:** 59 **% Residing in College-Owned, -Operated, or -Affiliated Housing:** 59 **Library Holdings:** 2,151,758 **Regional Accreditation:** New England Association of Schools and Colleges **Credit Hours For Degree:** 64 credits, Associates; 128 credits, Bachelors **ROTC:** Army, Air Force **Professional Accreditation:** AACSB, ABET, AAMFT, AACN, ADtA, AOTA, APA, ASLHA, CSWE, JRCEPAT, NAACLS, NASM, NRPA, SAF, TEAC **Intercollegiate Athletics:** Archery M & W; Badminton M & W; Baseball M; Basketball M & W; Crew M & W; Cross-Country Running M & W; Fencing M & W; Field Hockey W; Football M; Golf M & W; Gymnastics W; Ice Hockey M & W; Lacrosse M & W; Riflery M & W; Rock Climbing M & W; Rugby M & W; Sailing M & W; Skiing (Cross-Country) M & W; Skiing (Downhill) M & W; Soccer M & W; Softball W; Swimming and Diving W; Tennis M & W; Track and Field M & W; Ultimate Frisbee M & W; Volleyball M & W; Wrestling M

UNIVERSITY OF NEW HAMPSHIRE AT MANCHESTER
400 Commercial St.
Manchester, NH 03101-1113
Tel: (603)641-4321
Admissions: (603)641-4150
Fax: (603)641-4125
E-mail: unhm@unh.edu
Web Site: http://www.unhm.unh.edu/
President/CEO: Kristin Woolever
Admissions: Donna Lukasiak
Financial Aid: Jodi Abad
Type: Comprehensive **Sex:** Coed **Affiliation:** University System of New Hampshire **% Accepted:** 80 **Admission Plans:** Deferred Admission **Application Deadline:** June 15 **Application Fee:** $45.00 **H.S. Requirements:** High school diploma required; GED accepted **Costs Per Year:** Application fee: $45. State resident tuition: $9780 full-time, $408 per credit hour part-time. Nonresident tuition: $24,050 full-time, $1002 per credit hour part-time. Mandatory fees: $1346 full-time. Full-time tuition and fees vary according to course load and program. Part-time tuition varies according to course load and program. **Scholarships:** Available **Calendar System:** Semester, Summer Session Available **Enrollment:** FT 684, PT 161 **Faculty:** FT 36, PT 62 **Student-Faculty Ratio:** 12:1 **Exams:** SAT I or ACT. **% Receiving Financial Aid:** 49 **Final Year or Final Semester Residency Requirement:** Yes **Library Holdings:** 31,147 **Regional Accreditation:** New England Association of Schools and Colleges **Credit Hours For Degree:** 64 credits, Associates; 128 credits, Bachelors **ROTC:** Army, Air Force

WHITE MOUNTAINS COMMUNITY COLLEGE
2020 Riverside Dr.
Berlin, NH 03570
Tel: (603)752-1113; Free: 800-445-4525
Fax: (603)752-6335
E-mail: jrivard@ccsnh.edu
Web Site: http://www.wmcc.edu/
President/CEO: Katharine Eneguess
Admissions: Jamie Rivard
Type: Two-Year College **Sex:** Coed **Affiliation:** Community College System of New Hampshire **Application Deadline:** Rolling **Application Fee:** $10.00 **H.S. Requirements:** High school diploma required; GED accepted **Costs Per Year:** Application fee: $10. State resident tuition: $5490 full-time, $183 per credit part-time. Nonresident tuition: $12,540 full-time, $418 per credit part-time. Mandatory fees: $510 full-time, $17 per credit part-time. **Scholarships:** Available **Calendar System:** Semester, Summer Session Available **Enrollment:** FT 381, PT 604 **Faculty:** FT 29, PT 224 **Exams:** Other. **Library Holdings:** 18,000 **Regional Accreditation:** New England Association of Schools and Colleges **Credit Hours For Degree:** 64 credits, Associates **Intercollegiate Athletics:** Basketball M & W; Ice Hockey M & W; Soccer M & W

ASSUMPTION COLLEGE FOR SISTERS
350 Bernardsville Rd.
Mendham, NJ 07945-0800
Tel: (973)543-6528
Fax: (973)543-9459
E-mail: srgeraldine@scceat.org
Web Site: http://www.acs350.org/
President/CEO: Joseph Spring
Admissions: Sr. Gerardine Tantsits
Type: Two-Year College **Sex:** Women **Affiliation:** Roman Catholic **Scores:** 100% SAT V 400+; 100% SAT M 400+ **% Accepted:** 100 **Application Fee:** $0.00 **H.S. Requirements:** High school diploma required; GED accepted **Calendar System:** Semester, Summer Session Available **Enrollment:** FT 30, PT 7 **Faculty:** FT 1, PT 16 **Student-Faculty Ratio:** 5:1 **Library Holdings:** 25,000 **Regional Accreditation:** Middle State Association of Colleges and Schools **Credit Hours For Degree:** 66 credits, Associates

ATLANTIC CAPE COMMUNITY COLLEGE
5100 Black Horse Pike
Mays Landing, NJ 08330-2699
Tel: (609)625-1111; Free: 800-645-CHIEF
Fax: (609)343-4921
E-mail: accadmit@atlantic.edu
Web Site: http://www.atlantic.edu/
President/CEO: Dr. Peter L. Mora
Admissions: Linda McLeod
Type: Two-Year College **Sex:** Coed **Admission Plans:** Open Admission; Early Admission; Deferred Admission **Application Deadline:** July 1 **Application Fee:** $35.00 **H.S. Requirements:** High school diploma or equivalent not required **Scholarships:** Available **Calendar System:** Semester, Summer Session Available **Enrollment:** FT 3,074, PT 3,771 **Faculty:** FT 86, PT 292 **Student-Faculty Ratio:** 24:1 **Library Holdings:** 78,000 **Regional Accreditation:** Middle State Association of Colleges and Schools **Credit Hours For Degree:** 64 credits, Associates **Professional Accreditation:** AOTA, APTA, NLN **Intercollegiate Athletics:** Archery M & W; Basketball M

BERGEN COMMUNITY COLLEGE
400 Paramus Rd.
Paramus, NJ 07652-1595
Tel: (201)447-7100
Admissions: (201)447-7200
Fax: (201)444-7036
E-mail: admsoffice@bergen.edu
Web Site: http://www.bergen.edu/
President/CEO: G. Jeremiah Ryan
Type: Two-Year College **Sex:** Coed **Admission Plans:** Open Admission; Preferred Admission **H.S. Requirements:** High school diploma required; GED accepted **Scholarships:** Available **Calendar System:** Semester, Summer Session Available **Faculty:** FT 340, PT 459 **Student-Faculty Ratio:** 22:1 **Regional Accreditation:** Middle State Association of Colleges and Schools **Credit Hours For Degree:** 64 credits, Associates **Professional Accreditation:** AAMAE, ADA, APTA, CARC, JRCEDMS, JRCERT, NAACLS, NLN **Intercollegiate Athletics:** Baseball M; Basketball M & W; Cross-Country Running M & W; Golf M; Soccer M & W; Softball W; Tennis M & W; Track and Field M & W; Volleyball W; Wrestling M

BERKELEY COLLEGE
44 Rifle Camp Rd.
Woodland Park, NJ 07424-3353
Tel: (973)278-5400; Free: 800-446-5400
Fax: (973)278-2242
E-mail: info@berkeleycollege.edu
Web Site: http://www.berkeleycollege.edu/
President/CEO: Dr. Dario Cortes
Admissions: David Bertone
Type: Two-Year College **Sex:** Coed **Admission Plans:** Deferred Admission **Application Deadline:** Rolling **Application Fee:** $50.00 **H.S. Requirements:** High school diploma required; GED accepted **Costs Per Year:** Application fee: $50. Comprehensive fee: $31,650 includes full-time tuition ($19,050), mandatory fees ($900), and college room and board ($11,700). Full-time tuition and fees vary according to course load. Room and board charges vary according to housing facility. Part-time tuition: $450 per quarter hour. Part-time mandatory fees: $200 per term. Part-time tuition and fees vary according to course load. Tuition guaranteed not to increase for student's term of enrollment. **Scholarships:** Available **Calendar System:** Quarter, Summer Session Available **Enrollment:** FT 2,325, PT 404 **Faculty:** FT 51, PT 93 **Student-Faculty Ratio:** 22:1 **Exams:** SAT I or ACT. **% Residing in College-Owned, -Operated, or -Affiliated Housing:** 5 **Library Holdings:** 49,584 **Regional Accreditation:** Middle State Association of Colleges and Schools **Credit Hours For Degree:** 90 quarter hours, Associates; 180 quarter hours, Bachelors **Professional Accreditation:** ACBSP

BETH MEDRASH GOVOHA
617 Sixth St.
Lakewood, NJ 08701-2797
Tel: (732)367-1060
President/CEO: Rabbi Aaron Kotler
Type: Comprehensive **Sex:** Men **Affiliation:** Jewish **Application Fee:** $125.00 **H.S. Requirements:** High school diploma required; GED accepted **Calendar System:** Semester **Credit Hours For Degree:** 150 credits, Bachelors **Professional Accreditation:** AARTS

BLOOMFIELD COLLEGE
467 Franklin St.
Bloomfield, NJ 07003-9981
Tel: (973)748-9000; Free: 800-848-4555
Fax: (973)748-0916
E-mail: admission@bloomfield.edu
Web Site: http://www.bloomfield.edu/
President/CEO: Richard A. Levao
Admissions: Adam Castro
Financial Aid: Stacy Salinas
Type: Four-Year College **Sex:** Coed **Affiliation:** Presbyterian Church (U.S.A.) **Scores:** 56% SAT V 400+; 60% SAT M 400+ **% Accepted:** 52 **Admission Plans:** Early Action; Deferred Admission **Application Deadline:** August 1 **Application Fee:** $40.00 **H.S. Requirements:** High school diploma required; GED accepted **Costs Per Year:** Application fee: $40. Comprehensive fee: $31,300 includes full-time tuition ($20,000), mandatory

fees ($1000), and college room and board ($10,300). College room only: $5150. Full-time tuition and fees vary according to class time. Room and board charges vary according to housing facility. Part-time tuition: $2040 per course. Part-time mandatory fees: $125 per term. Part-time tuition and fees vary according to class time and course load. **Scholarships:** Available **Calendar System:** Semester, Summer Session Available **Enrollment:** FT 1,731, PT 411 **Faculty:** FT 68, PT 170 **Student-Faculty Ratio:** 15:1 **Exams:** SAT I or ACT. ACT essay not being used. SAT essay not being used. **% Receiving Financial Aid:** 88 **% Residing in College-Owned, -Operated, or -Affiliated Housing:** 24 **Final Year or Final Semester Residency Requirement:** No **Library Holdings:** 65,000 **Regional Accreditation:** Middle State Association of Colleges and Schools **Credit Hours For Degree:** 33 courses, Bachelors **ROTC:** Army **Professional Accreditation:** AACN **Intercollegiate Athletics:** Baseball M; Basketball M & W; Cross-Country Running M & W; Soccer M & W; Softball W; Tennis M; Volleyball W

BROOKDALE COMMUNITY COLLEGE
765 Newman Springs Rd.
Lincroft, NJ 07738-1597
Tel: (732)842-1900
Admissions: (732)224-2345
Fax: (732)576-1643
Web Site: http://www.brookdalecc.edu/
President/CEO: Peter F. Burnham
Admissions: Kim Toomey
Type: Two-Year College **Sex:** Coed **Affiliation:** New Jersey Commission on Higher Education **Admission Plans:** Open Admission; Preferred Admission; Early Admission; Deferred Admission **Application Deadline:** Rolling **Application Fee:** $25.00 **H.S. Requirements:** High school diploma required; GED accepted **Scholarships:** Available **Calendar System:** Semester, Summer Session Available **Library Holdings:** 150,000 **Regional Accreditation:** Middle State Association of Colleges and Schools **Credit Hours For Degree:** 60 credits, Associates **ROTC:** Army, Air Force **Professional Accreditation:** CARC, JRCERT, NLN **Intercollegiate Athletics:** Baseball M; Basketball M & W; Golf M; Soccer M & W; Softball W; Tennis M & W

BURLINGTON COUNTY COLLEGE
601 Pemberton Browns Mills Rd.
Pemberton, NJ 08068
Tel: (609)894-9311
Fax: (609)894-0183
E-mail: kgasioro@bcc.edu
Web Site: http://www.bcc.edu/
President/CEO: Dr. Robert Messina
Admissions: Kimberly Gasiorowski
Type: Two-Year College **Sex:** Coed **% Accepted:** 100 **Admission Plans:** Open Admission; Early Admission; Deferred Admission **Application Deadline:** Rolling **Application Fee:** $20.00 **H.S. Requirements:** High school diploma required; GED accepted **Costs Per Year:** Application fee: $20. Area resident tuition: $2760 full-time, $92 per credit part-time. State resident tuition: $3240 full-time, $108 per credit part-time. Nonresident tuition: $5190 full-time, $173 per credit part-time. Mandatory fees: $855 full-time, $28.50 per credit part-time. Full-time tuition and fees vary according to course load. Part-time tuition and fees vary according to course load. **Scholarships:** Available **Calendar System:** Semester, Summer Session Available **Enrollment:** FT 5,445, PT 4,248 **Faculty:** FT 52, PT 539 **Student-Faculty Ratio:** 30:1 **Final Year or Final Semester Residency Requirement:** No **Library Holdings:** 92,400 **Regional Accreditation:** Middle State Association of Colleges and Schools **Credit Hours For Degree:** 64 credit hours, Associates **Professional Accreditation:** ABET, AHIMA, NLN **Intercollegiate Athletics:** Baseball M; Basketball M & W; Golf M & W; Soccer M & W; Softball W

CALDWELL COLLEGE
9 Ryerson Ave.
Caldwell, NJ 07006-6195
Tel: (973)618-3000; Free: 888-864-9516
E-mail: admissions@caldwell.edu
Web Site: http://www.caldwell.edu/
President/CEO: Nancy H. Blattner, PhD
Admissions: Stephen Quinn
Financial Aid: Vincent Zelizo
Type: Comprehensive **Sex:** Coed **Affiliation:** Roman Catholic **Scores:** 82% SAT V 400+; 83% SAT M 400+ **% Accepted:** 66 **Admission Plans:** Early Admission; Early Action; Deferred Admission **Application Deadline:** April 1 **Application Fee:** $40.00 **H.S. Requirements:** High school diploma required; GED accepted **Scholarships:** Available **Calendar System:** Semester, Summer Session Available **Enrollment:** FT 1,093, PT 598 **Faculty:** FT 80, PT 104 **Student-Faculty Ratio:** 12:1 **Exams:** SAT I or ACT. **% Receiving Financial Aid:** 74 **% Residing in College-Owned, -Operated, or -Affiliated Housing:** 38 **Library Holdings:** 146,353 **Regional Accreditation:** Middle State Association of Colleges and Schools **Credit Hours For Degree:** 122 credits, Bachelors **ROTC:** Army **Professional Accreditation:** ACBSP, TEAC **Intercollegiate Athletics:** Baseball M; Basketball M & W; Cross-Country Running W; Golf M; Soccer M & W; Softball W; Tennis M & W

CAMDEN COUNTY COLLEGE
PO Box 200
Blackwood, NJ 08012-0200
Tel: (856)227-7200; Free: 888-228-2466
E-mail: ddelaney@camdencc.edu
Web Site: http://www.camdencc.edu/
President/CEO: Dr. Raymond A. Yannuzzi
Admissions: Donald Delaney
Type: Two-Year College **Sex:** Coed **Affiliation:** New Jersey Commission on Higher Education **Admission Plans:** Open Admission; Early Admission **Application Deadline:** Rolling **Application Fee:** $0.00 **H.S. Requirements:** High school diploma required; GED accepted **Costs Per Year:** Application fee: $0. Area resident tuition: $93 per credit part-time. State resident tuition: $97 per credit part-time. Nonresident tuition: $97 per credit part-time. Mandatory fees: $27 per credit part-time, $3 per term part-time. **Scholarships:** Available **Calendar System:** Semester, Summer Session Available **Enrollment:** FT 8,529, PT 7,141 **Faculty:** FT 139, PT 590 **Library Holdings:** 91,366 **Regional Accreditation:** Middle State Association of Colleges and Schools **Credit Hours For Degree:** 64 credits, Associates **Professional Accreditation:** ADA, COptA, NAACLS **Intercollegiate Athletics:** Baseball M; Basketball M & W; Golf M; Soccer M & W; Softball W

CENTENARY COLLEGE
400 Jefferson St.
Hackettstown, NJ 07840-2100
Tel: (908)852-1400; Free: 800-236-8679
Fax: (908)852-3454
Web Site: http://www.centenarycollege.edu/
President/CEO: Dr. Barbara Jayne Lewthwaite
Admissions: Diane Finnan
Financial Aid: Michelle Burwell
Type: Comprehensive **Sex:** Coed **Affiliation:** United Methodist Church **Scores:** 85% SAT V 400+; 83% SAT M 400+; 37% ACT 18-23; 21% ACT 24-29 **% Accepted:** 89 **Admission Plans:** Early Action; Deferred Admission **Application Deadline:** Rolling **Application Fee:** $30.00 **H.S. Requirements:** High school diploma required; GED accepted **Costs Per Year:** Application fee: $30. Tuition: $490 per credit part-time. Mandatory fees: $30 per term part-time. Part-time tuition and fees vary according to program. **Scholarships:** Available **Calendar System:** Semester, Summer Session Available **Enrollment:** FT 1,963, PT 177, Grad FT 395, Grad PT 404 **Faculty:** FT 69, PT 270 **Student-Faculty Ratio:** 16:1 **Exams:** SAT I or ACT. **% Receiving Financial Aid:** 69 **% Residing in College-Owned, -Operated, or -Affiliated Housing:** 53 **Library Holdings:** 72,129 **Regional Accreditation:** Middle State Association of Colleges and Schools **Professional Accreditation:** TEAC **Intercollegiate Athletics:** Baseball M; Basketball M & W; Cheerleading W; Cross-Country Running M & W; Equestrian Sports M & W; Golf M; Lacrosse M & W; Soccer M & W; Softball W; Volleyball W; Wrestling M

THE COLLEGE OF NEW JERSEY
PO Box 7718
Ewing, NJ 08628
Tel: (609)771-1855; Free: 800-624-0967
Admissions: (609)771-2131
E-mail: admiss@tcnj.edu
Web Site: http://www.tcnj.edu/
President/CEO: Dr. R. Barbara Gitenstein
Admissions: Lisa Angeloni
Financial Aid: Jamie Hightower
Type: Comprehensive **Sex:** Coed **Scores:** 101% SAT V 400+; 101% SAT M 400+ **% Accepted:** 46 **Admission Plans:** Early Admission; Early Decision Plan; Deferred Admission **Application Deadline:** January 15 **Application**

Fee: $70.00 **H.S. Requirements:** High school diploma required; GED accepted **Costs Per Year:** Application fee: $70. State resident tuition: $8980 full-time, $318.25 per credit hour part-time. Nonresident tuition: $17,666 full-time, $625.25 per credit hour part-time. Mandatory fees: $3742 full-time, $149.60 per credit hour part-time. Part-time tuition and fees vary according to course load. College room and board: $9996. College room only: $7238. Room and board charges vary according to board plan. **Scholarships:** Available **Calendar System:** Semester, Summer Session Available **Enrollment:** FT 6,080, PT 157, Grad FT 246, Grad PT 497 **Faculty:** FT 348, PT 402 **Student-Faculty Ratio:** 13:1 **Exams:** SAT I or ACT. SAT essay used for advising. SAT essay used as a validity check on application essay. **% Receiving Financial Aid:** 47 **% Residing in College-Owned, -Operated, or -Affiliated Housing:** 58 **Final Year or Final Semester Residency Requirement:** No **Library Holdings:** 561,250 **Regional Accreditation:** Middle State Association of Colleges and Schools **Credit Hours For Degree:** 120 semester hours, Bachelors **ROTC:** Army, Air Force **Professional Accreditation:** AACSB, ABET, AACN, ACA, ASLHA, NASM, NCATE, NLN **Intercollegiate Athletics:** Baseball M; Basketball M & W; Cross-Country Running M & W; Field Hockey W; Football M; Lacrosse W; Soccer M & W; Softball W; Swimming and Diving M & W; Tennis M & W; Track and Field M & W; Wrestling M

COLLEGE OF SAINT ELIZABETH
2 Convent Rd.
Morristown, NJ 07960-6989
Tel: (973)290-4000; Free: 800-210-7900
Admissions: (973)290-4700
Fax: (973)290-4710
E-mail: apply@csa.edu
Web Site: http://www.cse.edu/
President/CEO: Sr. Francis Raftery
Admissions: Donna Tatarka
Financial Aid: Debra Wulff
Type: Comprehensive **Affiliation:** Roman Catholic **Scores:** 71% SAT V 400+; 68% SAT M 400+ **% Accepted:** 83 **Admission Plans:** Early Admission; Deferred Admission **Application Deadline:** August 15 **Application Fee:** $35.00 **H.S. Requirements:** High school diploma required; GED accepted **Costs Per Year:** Application fee: $35. Comprehensive fee: $35,962 includes full-time tuition ($23,642), mandatory fees ($1416), and college room and board ($10,904). Part-time tuition: $623 per credit. Part-time mandatory fees: $65 per credit. Part-time tuition and fees vary according to course load and location. **Scholarships:** Available **Calendar System:** Semester, Summer Session Available **Enrollment:** FT 678, PT 603, Grad FT 194, Grad PT 682 **Faculty:** FT 72, PT 138 **Student-Faculty Ratio:** 11:1 **Exams:** SAT I or ACT. SAT essay used for admission. **% Receiving Financial Aid:** 75 **% Residing in College-Owned, -Operated, or -Affiliated Housing:** 67 **Library Holdings:** 119,438 **Regional Accreditation:** Middle State Association of Colleges and Schools **Credit Hours For Degree:** 128 semester hours, Bachelors **Professional Accreditation:** AAFCS, ADtA, NLN **Intercollegiate Athletics:** Basketball W; Equestrian Sports W; Soccer W; Softball W; Swimming and Diving W; Tennis W; Volleyball W

COUNTY COLLEGE OF MORRIS
214 Center Grove Rd.
Randolph, NJ 07869-2086
Tel: (973)328-5000; Free: 888-226-8001
Fax: (973)328-1282
E-mail: admiss@ccm.edu
Web Site: http://www.ccm.edu/
President/CEO: Edward Yaw
Type: Two-Year College **Sex:** Coed **Affiliation:** New Jersey Commission on Higher Education **Admission Plans:** Open Admission **Application Fee:** $30.00 **H.S. Requirements:** High school diploma or equivalent not required **Costs Per Year:** Application fee: $30. Area resident tuition: $3300 full-time, $110 per credit part-time. State resident tuition: $6600 full-time, $220 per credit part-time. Nonresident tuition: $9330 full-time, $311 per credit part-time. Mandatory fees: $645 full-time, $16.50 per credit part-time, $15. **Scholarships:** Available **Calendar System:** Semester **Enrollment:** FT 5,076, PT 3,662 **Regional Accreditation:** Middle State Association of Colleges and Schools **Professional Accreditation:** ABET, ACBSP, JRCERT, NLN **Intercollegiate Athletics:** Baseball M; Basketball M & W; Golf M; Ice Hockey M; Soccer M & W; Softball W; Tennis M

CUMBERLAND COUNTY COLLEGE
PO Box 1500, College Dr.
Vineland, NJ 08362
Tel: (856)691-8600
Fax: (856)691-6157
Web Site: http://www.cccnj.edu/
President/CEO: Thomas A. Isekenegbe
Admissions: Anne Daly-Eimer
Type: Two-Year College **Sex:** Coed **Affiliation:** New Jersey Commission on Higher Education **Admission Plans:** Open Admission; Early Admission; Deferred Admission **Application Deadline:** Rolling **Application Fee:** $25.00 **H.S. Requirements:** High school diploma required; GED accepted **Costs Per Year:** Application fee: $25. Area resident tuition: $2970 full-time, $99 per credit hour part-time. State resident tuition: $5940 full-time, $188 per credit hour part-time. Nonresident tuition: $11,880 full-time, $376 per credit hour part-time. Mandatory fees: $870 full-time, $29 per credit hour part-time. **Scholarships:** Available **Calendar System:** Semester, Summer Session Available **Enrollment:** FT 2,365, PT 1,649 **Faculty:** FT 47, PT 243 **Student-Faculty Ratio:** 14:1 **Library Holdings:** 51,000 **Regional Accreditation:** Middle State Association of Colleges and Schools **Credit Hours For Degree:** 64 credits, Associates **Professional Accreditation:** JRCERT, NLN **Intercollegiate Athletics:** Baseball M; Basketball M & W; Softball W; Track and Field M

DEVRY UNIVERSITY (NORTH BRUNSWICK)
630 US Hwy. 1
North Brunswick, NJ 08902-3362
Tel: (732)435-4880
Admissions: (732)729-3532
Web Site: http://www.devry.edu/
President/CEO: Chris Grevesen
Financial Aid: Albert Cama
Type: Comprehensive **Sex:** Coed **Affiliation:** DeVry University **Admission Plans:** Deferred Admission **Application Deadline:** Rolling **Application Fee:** $50.00 **H.S. Requirements:** High school diploma required; GED accepted **Costs Per Year:** Application fee: $50. Tuition: $14,720 full-time, $575 per credit hour part-time. **Scholarships:** Available **Calendar System:** Semester, Summer Session Available **Enrollment:** FT 836, PT 604 **Faculty:** FT 37, PT 118 **Student-Faculty Ratio:** 14:1 **Exams:** ACT essay used for admission. SAT essay used for admission. ACT essay used for placement. SAT essay used for placement. **% Receiving Financial Aid:** 74 **Regional Accreditation:** North Central Association of Colleges and Schools **Credit Hours For Degree:** 65 credit hours, Associates; 126 credit hours, Bachelors **Professional Accreditation:** ABET

DEVRY UNIVERSITY (PARAMUS)
35 Plaza, 81 East State Route 4
Ste. 102
Paramus, NJ 07652
Tel: (201)556-2840
Web Site: http://www.devry.edu/
Type: Comprehensive **Sex:** Coed

DREW UNIVERSITY
36 Madison Ave.
Madison, NJ 07940-1493
Tel: (973)408-3000
Admissions: (973)408-3250
Fax: (973)408-3939
E-mail: cadm@drew.edu
Web Site: http://www.drew.edu/
President/CEO: Dr. Robert Weisbuch
Admissions: Alyssa McCloud
Financial Aid: Renee Volak
Type: University **Sex:** Coed **Affiliation:** United Methodist Church **Scores:** 96.97% SAT V 400+; 96.72% SAT M 400+; 37.18% ACT 18-23; 46.15% ACT 24-29 **% Accepted:** 74 **Admission Plans:** Early Admission; Early Decision Plan; Deferred Admission **Application Deadline:** February 15 **Application Fee:** $50.00 **H.S. Requirements:** High school diploma required; GED not accepted **Costs Per Year:** Application fee: $50. Comprehensive fee: $48,385 includes full-time tuition ($37,310), mandatory fees ($707), and college room and board ($10,368). College room only: $6702. Full-time tuition and fees vary according to course load. Room and board charges vary according to board plan and housing facility. Part-time tuition: $1554 per credit.

Part-time tuition varies according to course load. **Scholarships:** Available **Calendar System:** Semester, Summer Session Available **Enrollment:** FT 1,679, PT 60, Grad FT 437, Grad PT 491 **Faculty:** FT 159, PT 99 **Student-Faculty Ratio:** 11:1 **Exams:** Other. ACT essay used for admission. SAT essay used for admission. **% Receiving Financial Aid:** 52 **% Residing in College-Owned, -Operated, or -Affiliated Housing:** 83 **Library Holdings:** 615,500 **Regional Accreditation:** Middle State Association of Colleges and Schools **Credit Hours For Degree:** 128 credits, Bachelors **Professional Accreditation:** ACIPE, ATS **Intercollegiate Athletics:** Baseball M; Basketball M & W; Cross-Country Running M & W; Equestrian Sports M & W; Fencing M & W; Field Hockey W; Lacrosse M & W; Rugby M & W; Soccer M & W; Softball W; Swimming and Diving M & W; Tennis M & W

ESSEX COUNTY COLLEGE
303 University Ave.
Newark, NJ 07102-1798
Tel: (973)877-3000
Admissions: (973)877-3119
Fax: (973)623-6449
Web Site: http://www.essex.edu/
President/CEO: A. Zachary Yamba
Admissions: Marva Mack
Type: Two-Year College **Sex:** Coed **Affiliation:** New Jersey Commission on Higher Education **% Accepted:** 100 **Admission Plans:** Open Admission; Deferred Admission **Application Deadline:** August 15 **Application Fee:** $25.00 **H.S. Requirements:** High school diploma or equivalent not required **Costs Per Year:** Application fee: $25. Area resident tuition: $3105 full-time, $103.50 per credit hour part-time. State resident tuition: $6210 full-time, $207 per credit hour part-time. Nonresident tuition: $6210 full-time, $207 per credit hour part-time. Mandatory fees: $915 full-time, $32.50 per credit hour part-time. **Scholarships:** Available **Calendar System:** Semester, Summer Session Available **Enrollment:** FT 7,915, PT 5,399 **Faculty:** FT 118, PT 483 **Student-Faculty Ratio:** 29:1 **Library Holdings:** 91,000 **Regional Accreditation:** Middle State Association of Colleges and Schools **Credit Hours For Degree:** 63 credit hours, Associates **ROTC:** Army **Professional Accreditation:** APTA, COptA, JRCERT, NLN **Intercollegiate Athletics:** Basketball M & W; Cross-Country Running M & W; Soccer M; Track and Field M & W

FAIRLEIGH DICKINSON UNIVERSITY, COLLEGE AT FLORHAM
285 Madison Ave.
Madison, NJ 07940-1099
Tel: (973)443-8500; Free: 800-338-8803
E-mail: globaleducation@fdu.edu
Web Site: http://www.fdu.edu/
President/CEO: Dr. J. Michael Adams
Admissions: Jonathan Wexler
Type: Comprehensive **Sex:** Coed **Scores:** 95.9% SAT V 400+; 95.5% SAT M 400+ **% Accepted:** 67 **Admission Plans:** Early Admission; Deferred Admission **Application Deadline:** Rolling **Application Fee:** $40.00 **H.S. Requirements:** High school diploma required; GED accepted **Costs Per Year:** Application fee: $40. Comprehensive fee: $42,322 includes full-time tuition ($30,392), mandatory fees ($872), and college room and board ($11,058). College room only: $6934. Room and board charges vary according to board plan and housing facility. Part-time tuition: $837 per credit. **Scholarships:** Available **Calendar System:** Semester, Summer Session Available **Enrollment:** FT 2,281, PT 199, Grad FT 390, Grad PT 639 **Student-Faculty Ratio:** 15:1 **Exams:** SAT I or ACT. **% Receiving Financial Aid:** 68 **% Residing in College-Owned, -Operated, or -Affiliated Housing:** 60 **Library Holdings:** 149,850 **Regional Accreditation:** Middle State Association of Colleges and Schools **Credit Hours For Degree:** 128 credits, Bachelors **ROTC:** Army, Air Force **Professional Accreditation:** AACSB **Intercollegiate Athletics:** Baseball M; Basketball M & W; Cross-Country Running M & W; Field Hockey W; Football M; Golf M; Lacrosse M & W; Soccer M & W; Softball W; Swimming and Diving M & W; Tennis M & W; Volleyball W

FAIRLEIGH DICKINSON UNIVERSITY, METROPOLITAN CAMPUS
1000 River Rd.
Teaneck, NJ 07666-1914
Tel: (201)692-2000; Free: 800-338-8803
E-mail: globaleducation@fdu.edu
Web Site: http://www.fdu.edu/
President/CEO: Dr. J. Michael Adams
Admissions: Jonathan Wexler
Type: Comprehensive **Sex:** Coed **Scores:** 92.4% SAT V 400+; 95.8% SAT M 400+ **% Accepted:** 57 **Admission Plans:** Early Admission; Deferred Admission **Application Deadline:** Rolling **Application Fee:** $40.00 **H.S. Requirements:** High school diploma required; GED accepted **Costs Per Year:** Application fee: $40. Comprehensive fee: $40,434 includes full-time tuition ($28,194), mandatory fees ($872), and college room and board ($11,368). College room only: $7244. Room and board charges vary according to board plan and housing facility. Part-time tuition: $837 per credit. **Scholarships:** Available **Calendar System:** Semester, Summer Session Available **Enrollment:** FT 2,471, PT 3,573, Grad FT 1,039, Grad PT 1,721 **Student-Faculty Ratio:** 16:1 **Exams:** SAT I or ACT. **% Receiving Financial Aid:** 69 **% Residing in College-Owned, -Operated, or -Affiliated Housing:** 21 **Library Holdings:** 196,703 **Regional Accreditation:** Middle State Association of Colleges and Schools **Credit Hours For Degree:** 128 credits, Bachelors **ROTC:** Army, Air Force **Professional Accreditation:** AACSB, ABET, AACN, APA, TEAC **Intercollegiate Athletics:** Baseball M; Basketball M & W; Bowling W; Cross-Country Running M & W; Fencing W; Golf M & W; Soccer M & W; Softball W; Tennis M & W; Track and Field M & W; Volleyball W

FELICIAN COLLEGE
262 South Main St.
Lodi, NJ 07644-2117
Tel: (201)559-6000
Admissions: (201)559-6131
Fax: (973)778-4111
E-mail: admissions@felician.edu
Web Site: http://www.felician.edu/
President/CEO: Sr. Theresa Mary Martin
Financial Aid: Janet Mariano Merli
Type: Comprehensive **Sex:** Coed **Affiliation:** Roman Catholic **Scores:** 64.9% SAT V 400+; 67.4% SAT M 400+ **% Accepted:** 84 **Admission Plans:** Deferred Admission **Application Deadline:** Rolling **Application Fee:** $30.00 **H.S. Requirements:** High school diploma required; GED accepted. For nursing, elementary education programs: High school diploma required; GED not accepted **Costs Per Year:** Application fee: $30. Comprehensive fee: $34,750 includes full-time tuition ($23,650), mandatory fees ($1400), and college room and board ($9700). Part-time tuition: $780 per credit. **Scholarships:** Available **Calendar System:** Semester, Summer Session Available **Enrollment:** FT 1,351, PT 407, Grad FT 18, Grad PT 335 **Faculty:** FT 102, PT 89 **Student-Faculty Ratio:** 12:1 **Exams:** ACT, SAT I or ACT, SAT II. **% Receiving Financial Aid:** 78 **Library Holdings:** 105,000 **Regional Accreditation:** Middle State Association of Colleges and Schools **Credit Hours For Degree:** 68 semester hours, Associates; 120 semester hours, Bachelors **Professional Accreditation:** AACN, NAACLS, NLN, TEAC **Intercollegiate Athletics:** Baseball M; Basketball M & W; Cross-Country Running M & W; Soccer M & W; Softball W; Track and Field M & W

GEORGIAN COURT UNIVERSITY
900 Lakewood Ave.
Lakewood, NJ 08701-2697
Tel: (732)987-2760; Free: 800-458-8422
Fax: (732)987-2000
E-mail: admissions@georgian.edu
Web Site: http://www.georgian.edu/
President/CEO: Sr. Rosemary E. Jeffries, PhD
Admissions: Kathie Gallant
Financial Aid: Larry Sharp
Type: Comprehensive **Sex:** Coed **Affiliation:** Roman Catholic **% Accepted:** 62 **Admission Plans:** Early Action; Deferred Admission **Application Deadline:** August 1 **Application Fee:** $40.00 **H.S. Requirements:** High school diploma required; GED accepted **Costs Per Year:** Application fee: $40. Comprehensive fee: $33,876 includes full-time tuition ($23,246), mandatory fees ($1244), and college room and board ($9386). Part-time tuition: $570 per credit. Part-time mandatory fees: $311 per term. Part-time tuition and fees vary according to location. **Scholarships:** Available **Calendar System:** Semester, Summer Session Available **Enrollment:** FT 1,516, PT 454, Grad FT 282, Grad PT 771 **Faculty:** FT 103, PT 186 **Student-Faculty Ratio:** 15:1 **Exams:** SAT I or ACT. ACT essay used for placement. SAT essay used for placement. **% Receiving Financial Aid:** 86 **% Residing in College-Owned, -Operated, or -Affiliated Housing:** 28 **Final Year or Final Semester Residency Requirement:** No **Library Holdings:** 148,026 **Regional Accreditation:** Middle State Association of Col-

leges and Schools **Credit Hours For Degree:** 120 credits, Bachelors **Professional Accreditation:** ACBSP, CSWE, TEAC **Intercollegiate Athletics:** Basketball W; Cross-Country Running W; Lacrosse W; Soccer W; Softball W; Tennis W; Track and Field W; Volleyball W

GLOUCESTER COUNTY COLLEGE
1400 Tanyard Rd.
Sewell, NJ 08080
Tel: (856)468-5000
Fax: (856)468-8498
E-mail: japkinso@gccnj.edu
Web Site: http://www.gccnj.edu/
President/CEO: Russell A. Davis
Admissions: Judy Apkinson
Financial Aid: Jeff Williams
Type: Two-Year College **Sex:** Coed **Affiliation:** New Jersey Commission on Higher Education **% Accepted:** 100 **Admission Plans:** Open Admission; Deferred Admission **Application Deadline:** Rolling **Application Fee:** $10.00 **H.S. Requirements:** High school diploma required; GED accepted. For those granted qualified admission: High school diploma or equivalent not required **Costs Per Year:** Application fee: $10. Area resident tuition: $2656 full-time, $83 per credit hour part-time. State resident tuition: $2880 full-time, $90 per credit hour part-time. Nonresident tuition: $5760 full-time, $180 per credit hour part-time. Mandatory fees: $672 full-time, $21 per credit hour part-time. Full-time tuition and fees vary according to course level and program. Part-time tuition and fees vary according to course level and program. **Scholarships:** Available **Calendar System:** Semester, Summer Session Available **Faculty:** FT 64, PT 228 **Student-Faculty Ratio:** 33:1 **Exams:** SAT I or ACT. **Library Holdings:** 55,710 **Regional Accreditation:** Middle State Association of Colleges and Schools **Credit Hours For Degree:** 63 credit hours, Associates **Professional Accreditation:** CARC, JRCEDMS, JRCNMT, NLN **Intercollegiate Athletics:** Baseball M; Basketball M & W; Cross-Country Running M & W; Soccer M & W; Softball W; Tennis M & W; Track and Field M & W; Wrestling M

HUDSON COUNTY COMMUNITY COLLEGE
25 Journal Square
Jersey City, NJ 07306
Tel: (201)656-2020
Admissions: (201)714-7100
Fax: (201)714-2136
E-mail: martin@hccc.edu
Web Site: http://www.hccc.edu/
President/CEO: Glen Gabert, PhD
Admissions: Robert Martin
Type: Two-Year College **Sex:** Coed **Affiliation:** New Jersey Commission on Higher Education **Admission Plans:** Open Admission; Preferred Admission **Application Deadline:** September 1 **Application Fee:** $15.00 **H.S. Requirements:** High school diploma or equivalent not required. For applicants under 18: High school diploma required; GED accepted **Costs Per Year:** Application fee: $15. Area resident tuition: $2887 full-time, $96.25 per credit part-time. State resident tuition: $5775 full-time, $192.50 per credit part-time. Nonresident tuition: $8662 full-time, $288.75 per credit part-time. Mandatory fees: $1162 full-time, $38.75 per credit part-time, $20 per term part-time. Full-time tuition and fees vary according to course load. Part-time tuition and fees vary according to course load. **Scholarships:** Available **Calendar System:** Semester, Summer Session Available **Library Holdings:** 32,000 **Regional Accreditation:** Middle State Association of Colleges and Schools **Credit Hours For Degree:** 66 credits, Associates **Professional Accreditation:** ABET, AAMAE, ACF, AHIMA

KEAN UNIVERSITY
1000 Morris Ave.
Union, NJ 07083
Tel: (908)737-KEAN
Admissions: (908)737-7100
Fax: (908)737-3415
E-mail: admitme@kean.edu
Web Site: http://www.kean.edu/
President/CEO: Dr. Dawood Farahi
Admissions: Valerie Winslow
Financial Aid: Sharon Audet
Type: Comprehensive **Sex:** Coed **Affiliation:** New Jersey State College System **Scores:** 79% SAT V 400+; 84.6% SAT M 400+ **% Accepted:** 62 **Application Deadline:** May 31 **Application Fee:** $50.00 **H.S. Requirements:** High school diploma required; GED accepted **Costs Per Year:** Application fee: $50. State resident tuition: $6165 full-time, $205.50 per credit hour part-time. Nonresident tuition: $10,800 full-time, $360 per credit hour part-time. Mandatory fees: $3281 full-time, $110.10 per credit hour part-time. Part-time tuition and fees vary according to course load. College room and board: $12,264. College room only: $9400. Room and board charges vary according to board plan and housing facility. **Scholarships:** Available **Calendar System:** Semester, Summer Session Available **Enrollment:** FT 9,355, PT 2,717, Grad FT 726, Grad PT 2,253 **Faculty:** FT 352, PT 977 **Student-Faculty Ratio:** 17:1 **Exams:** SAT I or ACT. ACT essay used for advising. SAT essay used for advising. ACT essay used for placement. SAT essay used for placement. **% Receiving Financial Aid:** 62 **% Residing in College-Owned, -Operated, or -Affiliated Housing:** 15 **Final Year or Final Semester Residency Requirement:** No **Library Holdings:** 375,186 **Regional Accreditation:** Middle State Association of Colleges and Schools **Credit Hours For Degree:** 124 semester hours, Bachelors **ROTC:** Army, Air Force **Professional Accreditation:** ACA, AHIMA, AOTA, ASLHA, FIDER, CSWE, JRCEPAT, NASAD, NASM, NASPAA, NAST, NCATE, NLN, NAIT **Intercollegiate Athletics:** Baseball M; Basketball M & W; Field Hockey W; Football M; Lacrosse M & W; Soccer M & W; Softball W; Tennis W; Track and Field M & W; Volleyball W

MERCER COUNTY COMMUNITY COLLEGE
1200 Old Trenton Rd., PO Box B
Trenton, NJ 08690-1004
Tel: (609)586-4800; Free: 800-392-MCCC
Fax: (609)586-6944
E-mail: admiss@mccc.edu
Web Site: http://www.mccc.edu/
President/CEO: Dr. Patricia Donohue
Admissions: Dr. L. Campbell
Type: Two-Year College **Sex:** Coed **Admission Plans:** Open Admission; Preferred Admission; Deferred Admission **Application Deadline:** Rolling **Application Fee:** $0.00 **H.S. Requirements:** High school diploma or equivalent not required **Costs Per Year:** Application fee: $0. Area resident tuition: $2316 full-time, $119 per credit hour part-time. State resident tuition: $3276 full-time, $159 per credit hour part-time. Nonresident tuition: $5196 full-time, $239 per credit hour part-time. Mandatory fees: $540 full-time, $22.50 per credit hour part-time. **Scholarships:** Available **Calendar System:** Semester, Summer Session Available **Enrollment:** FT 4,372, PT 5,249 **Faculty:** FT 131, PT 452 **Student-Faculty Ratio:** 22:1 **Library Holdings:** 57,317 **Regional Accreditation:** Middle State Association of Colleges and Schools **Credit Hours For Degree:** 60 credits, Associates **ROTC:** Army, Air Force **Professional Accreditation:** ABFSE, APTA, CAA, JRCERT, NAACLS, NLN **Intercollegiate Athletics:** Baseball M; Basketball M & W; Golf M & W; Soccer M & W; Softball W; Tennis M & W; Track and Field M & W

MIDDLESEX COUNTY COLLEGE
2600 Woodbridge Ave., PO Box 3050
Edison, NJ 08818-3050
Tel: (732)548-6000
Web Site: http://www.middlesexcc.edu/
President/CEO: Dr. Joann La Perla-Morales
Admissions: Peter W. Rice
Type: Two-Year College **Sex:** Coed **% Accepted:** 69 **Admission Plans:** Open Admission; Preferred Admission; Early Admission; Deferred Admission **Application Deadline:** Rolling **Application Fee:** $25.00 **H.S. Requirements:** High school diploma required; GED accepted **Scholarships:** Available **Calendar System:** Semester, Summer Session Available **Faculty:** FT 206, PT 346 **Student-Faculty Ratio:** 21:1 **Exams:** Other. **Library Holdings:** 85,160 **Regional Accreditation:** Middle State Association of Colleges and Schools **Credit Hours For Degree:** 64 credits, Associates **ROTC:** Army **Professional Accreditation:** ABET, ADA, JRCERT, NAACLS, NLN **Intercollegiate Athletics:** Baseball M; Basketball M & W; Cross-Country Running M & W; Field Hockey W; Golf M & W; Soccer M & W; Softball W; Tennis M & W; Track and Field M & W; Wrestling M

MONMOUTH UNIVERSITY
400 Cedar Ave.
West Long Branch, NJ 07764-1898
Tel: (732)571-3400; Free: 800-543-9671
Admissions: (732)571-3456

Fax: (732)263-5166
E-mail: admission@monmouth.edu
Web Site: http://www.monmouth.edu/
President/CEO: Paul G. Gaffney, II
Admissions: Victoria Bobik
Financial Aid: Claire Alasio
Type: Comprehensive **Sex:** Coed **Scores:** 100% SAT V 400+; 100% SAT M 400+; 54% ACT 18-23; 43% ACT 24-29 **% Accepted:** 62 **Admission Plans:** Early Action; Deferred Admission **Application Deadline:** March 1 **Application Fee:** $50.00 **H.S. Requirements:** High school diploma required; GED accepted **Costs Per Year:** Application fee: $50. One-time mandatory fee: $200. Comprehensive fee: $34,567 includes full-time tuition ($24,385), mandatory fees ($628), and college room and board ($9554). College room only: $5436. Room and board charges vary according to board plan and housing facility. Part-time tuition: $706 per credit hour. Part-time mandatory fees: $157 per term. **Scholarships:** Available **Calendar System:** Semester, Summer Session Available **Enrollment:** FT 4,306, PT 375, Grad FT 632, Grad PT 1,186 **Faculty:** FT 248, PT 326 **Student-Faculty Ratio:** 15:1 **Exams:** SAT I or ACT. **% Receiving Financial Aid:** 65 **% Residing in College-Owned, -Operated, or -Affiliated Housing:** 44 **Library Holdings:** 263,000 **Regional Accreditation:** Middle State Association of Colleges and Schools **Credit Hours For Degree:** 63 credits, Associates; 128 credits, Bachelors **ROTC:** Air Force **Professional Accreditation:** AACSB, AACN, ACA, CSWE, NCATE **Intercollegiate Athletics:** Baseball M; Basketball M & W; Bowling M & W; Cross-Country Running M & W; Field Hockey W; Football M; Golf M & W; Ice Hockey M; Lacrosse W; Sailing M & W; Soccer M & W; Softball W; Tennis M & W; Track and Field M & W; Wrestling M

MONTCLAIR STATE UNIVERSITY
1 Normal Ave.
Montclair, NJ 07043-1624
Tel: (973)655-4000; Free: 800-331-9205
Admissions: (973)655-5116
Fax: (973)893-5455
E-mail: undergraduate.admissions@montclair.edu
Web Site: http://www.montclair.edu/
President/CEO: Dr. Susan A. Cole
Admissions: Jason Langdon
Financial Aid: James T. Anderson
Type: Comprehensive **Sex:** Coed **Scores:** 92.94% SAT V 400+; 96% SAT M 400+ **% Accepted:** 47 **Admission Plans:** Deferred Admission **Application Deadline:** March 1 **Application Fee:** $60.00 **H.S. Requirements:** High school diploma required; GED accepted **Costs Per Year:** Application fee: $60. State resident tuition: $7042 full-time, $234.73 per credit part-time. **Scholarships:** Available **Calendar System:** Semester, Summer Session Available **Enrollment:** FT 12,113, PT 2,026, Grad FT 1,079, Grad PT 2,953 **Faculty:** FT 553, PT 936 **Student-Faculty Ratio:** 17:1 **Exams:** SAT I or ACT. SAT essay used for admission. SAT essay used for advising. SAT essay used for placement. **% Receiving Financial Aid:** 63 **% Residing in College-Owned, -Operated, or -Affiliated Housing:** 26 **Library Holdings:** 495,462 **Regional Accreditation:** Middle State Association of Colleges and Schools **Credit Hours For Degree:** 120 semester hours, Bachelors **ROTC:** Army, Navy, Air Force **Professional Accreditation:** AACSB, ABET, AAFCS, ADtA, ASLHA, NASAD, NASD, NASM, NAST, NCATE, NRPA **Intercollegiate Athletics:** Baseball M; Basketball M & W; Field Hockey W; Football M; Golf M & W; Lacrosse M & W; Soccer M & W; Softball W; Swimming and Diving M & W; Track and Field M & W; Volleyball W

NEW JERSEY CITY UNIVERSITY
2039 Kennedy Blvd.
Jersey City, NJ 07305-1597
Tel: (201)200-2000; Free: 888-441-NJCU
Admissions: (201)200-3234
Fax: (201)200-2044
E-mail: admissions@nicu.edu
Web Site: http://www.njcu.edu/
President/CEO: Dr. Carlos Hernandez, PhD
Admissions: Jose Balda
Financial Aid: Carmen Panlilio
Type: Comprehensive **Sex:** Coed **Scores:** 89% SAT V 400+; 90% SAT M 400+ **% Accepted:** 35 **Admission Plans:** Early Admission; Deferred Admission **Application Deadline:** April 1 **Application Fee:** $35.00 **H.S. Requirements:** High school diploma required; GED accepted **Costs Per Year:** Application fee: $35. State resident tuition: $6542 full-time, $218 per credit hour part-time. Nonresident tuition: $13,820 full-time, $461 per credit hour part-time. Mandatory fees: $2446 full-time, $79.40 per credit hour part-time. Part-time tuition and fees vary according to course load. College room and board: $9043. College room only: $5788. **Scholarships:** Available **Calendar System:** Semester, Summer Session Available **Enrollment:** FT 4,695, PT 1,672, Grad FT 457, Grad PT 1,575 **Faculty:** FT 246, PT 469 **Student-Faculty Ratio:** 13:1 **Exams:** SAT I or ACT. SAT essay used for admission. **% Receiving Financial Aid:** 72 **% Residing in College-Owned, -Operated, or -Affiliated Housing:** 4 **Library Holdings:** 319,360 **Regional Accreditation:** Middle State Association of Colleges and Schools **Credit Hours For Degree:** 128 credits, Bachelors **Professional Accreditation:** ACBSP, NASAD, NASM, NCATE, NLN, TEAC **Intercollegiate Athletics:** Baseball M; Basketball M & W; Bowling W; Cross-Country Running W; Soccer M & W; Softball W; Track and Field M & W; Volleyball M & W

NEW JERSEY INSTITUTE OF TECHNOLOGY
University Heights
Newark, NJ 07102
Tel: (973)596-3000; Free: 800-925-NJIT
Admissions: (973)596-3306
Fax: (973)802-1854
E-mail: admissions@njit.edu
Web Site: http://www.njit.edu/
President/CEO: Dr. Robert A. Altenkirch
Admissions: Stephen M. Eck
Financial Aid: Ivon Nunez
Type: University **Sex:** Coed **Scores:** 98.55% SAT V 400+; 100% SAT M 400+ **% Accepted:** 67 **Admission Plans:** Preferred Admission; Early Admission; Deferred Admission **Application Deadline:** April 1 **Application Fee:** $50.00 **H.S. Requirements:** High school diploma required; GED accepted **Costs Per Year:** Application fee: $50. State resident tuition: $10,816 full-time, $412 per credit part-time. Nonresident tuition: $20,560 full-time, $879 per credit part-time. Mandatory fees: $2040 full-time, $100 per credit part-time, $102 per term part-time. Full-time tuition and fees vary according to course load and degree level. Part-time tuition and fees vary according to course load and degree level. College room and board: $9806. College room only: $6890. Room and board charges vary according to board plan and housing facility. **Scholarships:** Available **Calendar System:** Semester, Summer Session Available **Enrollment:** FT 4,790, PT 1,134, Grad FT 1,630, Grad PT 1,286 **Faculty:** FT 403, PT 237 **Student-Faculty Ratio:** 15:1 **Exams:** SAT I or ACT. SAT essay used for admission. SAT essay used for placement. **% Receiving Financial Aid:** 50 **% Residing in College-Owned, -Operated, or -Affiliated Housing:** 27 **Library Holdings:** 160,000 **Regional Accreditation:** Middle State Association of Colleges and Schools **Credit Hours For Degree:** 124 credits, Bachelors **ROTC:** Army, Air Force **Professional Accreditation:** AACSB, ABET, CEPH, NAAB **Intercollegiate Athletics:** Baseball M; Basketball M & W; Bowling M; Cross-Country Running M & W; Fencing M & W; Ice Hockey M; Soccer M & W; Swimming and Diving M & W; Tennis M & W; Track and Field M & W; Volleyball M & W

OCEAN COUNTY COLLEGE
College Dr., PO Box 2001
Toms River, NJ 08754-2001
Tel: (732)255-0400
Admissions: (732)255-0304
E-mail: mfennessy@ocean.edu
Web Site: http://www.ocean.edu/
President/CEO: Dr. Jon H. Larson
Admissions: Mary Fennessey
Type: Two-Year College **Sex:** Coed **Affiliation:** New Jersey Commission on Higher Education **Admission Plans:** Open Admission; Preferred Admission; Early Admission; Deferred Admission **Application Deadline:** Rolling **Application Fee:** $20.00 **H.S. Requirements:** High school diploma or equivalent not required. For nursing program: High school diploma required; GED accepted **Costs Per Year:** Application fee: $20. Area resident tuition: $2256 full-time, $94 per credit part-time. State resident tuition: $3072 full-time, $128 per credit part-time. Nonresident tuition: $4990 full-time, $208 per credit part-time. Mandatory fees: $890 full-time, $28 per credit part-time, $20 per term part-time. Full-time tuition and fees vary according to program. Part-time tuition and fees vary according to program. **Scholarships:** Available **Calendar System:** Semester, Summer Session Available **Enrollment:** FT 5,907, PT 4,508 **Faculty:** FT 113, PT 412 **Student-Faculty Ratio:** 30:1 **Final Year or Final Semester Residency Requirement:** No **Library Holdings:** 74,215 **Regional Accreditation:** Middle State Association of Colleges

and Schools **Credit Hours For Degree:** 64 semester hours, Associates **Professional Accreditation:** NLN **Intercollegiate Athletics:** Baseball M; Basketball M & W; Cross-Country Running M & W; Golf M & W; Soccer M & W; Softball W; Swimming and Diving M & W; Tennis M & W

PASSAIC COUNTY COMMUNITY COLLEGE
One College Blvd.
Paterson, NJ 07505-1179
Tel: (973)684-6800
Web Site: http://www.pccc.cc.nj.us/
President/CEO: Steven M. Rose, EdD
Admissions: Patrick Noonan
Type: Two-Year College **Sex:** Coed **% Accepted:** 100 **Admission Plans:** Open Admission; Preferred Admission; Early Admission; Deferred Admission **Application Deadline:** Rolling **H.S. Requirements:** High school diploma or equivalent not required **Scholarships:** Available **Calendar System:** Semester, Summer Session Available **Faculty:** FT 78, PT 279 **Library Holdings:** 90,000 **Regional Accreditation:** Middle State Association of Colleges and Schools **Credit Hours For Degree:** 64 credits, Associates **ROTC:** Army **Professional Accreditation:** AHIMA, CARC, JRCERT, NLN **Intercollegiate Athletics:** Basketball M & W; Soccer M; Volleyball W

PRINCETON UNIVERSITY
Princeton, NJ 08544-1019
Tel: (609)258-3000
Admissions: (609)258-3060
E-mail: uaoffice@princeton.edu
Web Site: http://www.princeton.edu/
President/CEO: Dr. Shirley M. Tilghman
Admissions: Janet Rapelye
Financial Aid: Robin Moscato
Type: University **Sex:** Coed **Scores:** 100% SAT V 400+; 100% SAT M 400+; 11% ACT 24-29 **% Accepted:** 10 **Admission Plans:** Deferred Admission **Application Deadline:** January 1 **Application Fee:** $65.00 **H.S. Requirements:** High school diploma or equivalent not required **Costs Per Year:** Application fee: $65. Comprehensive fee: $48,580 includes full-time tuition ($36,640) and college room and board ($11,940). Room and board charges vary according to board plan. **Scholarships:** Available **Calendar System:** Semester, Summer Session Not available **Enrollment:** FT 5,044, PT 69, Grad FT 2,479 **Faculty:** FT 846, PT 212 **Student-Faculty Ratio:** 6:1 **Exams:** SAT I or ACT, SAT II. ACT essay used for admission. SAT essay used for admission. ACT essay used for advising. SAT essay used for advising. ACT essay used as a validity check on application essay. SAT essay used as a validity check on application essay. ACT essay used for placement. SAT essay used for placement. **% Receiving Financial Aid:** 56 **% Residing in College-Owned, -Operated, or -Affiliated Housing:** 98 **Library Holdings:** 6,941,254 **Regional Accreditation:** Middle State Association of Colleges and Schools **Credit Hours For Degree:** 31 courses, Bachelors **ROTC:** Army, Navy **Professional Accreditation:** ABET, NAAB **Intercollegiate Athletics:** Baseball M; Basketball M & W; Crew M & W; Cross-Country Running M & W; Fencing M & W; Field Hockey W; Football M; Golf M & W; Ice Hockey M & W; Lacrosse M & W; Soccer M & W; Softball W; Squash M & W; Swimming and Diving M & W; Tennis M & W; Track and Field M & W; Volleyball M & W; Water Polo M & W; Wrestling M

RABBI JACOB JOSEPH SCHOOL
One Plainfield Ave
Edison, NJ 08817
Tel: (908)985-6533
Admissions: (732)985-6533
President/CEO: Rabbi Joseph Eichenstein
Type: Four-Year College **Sex:** Men **Affiliation:** Jewish **% Accepted:** 100 **Professional Accreditation:** AARTS

RABBINICAL COLLEGE OF AMERICA
226 Sussex Ave., PO Box 1996
Morristown, NJ 07962-1996
Tel: (973)267-9404
Fax: (973)267-5208
E-mail: rca079@aol.com
President/CEO: Rabbi Moshe Herson
Admissions: Sharon Miller
Type: Four-Year College **Sex:** Men **Affiliation:** Jewish **% Accepted:** 100 **Application Deadline:** Rolling **Application Fee:** $150.00 **H.S. Requirements:** High school diploma required; GED accepted **Calendar System:** Semester, Summer Session Available **Faculty:** FT 16 **Student-Faculty Ratio:** 12:1 **Library Holdings:** 10,000 **Credit Hours For Degree:** 120 credits, Bachelors **Professional Accreditation:** AARTS **Intercollegiate Athletics:** Ultimate Frisbee M; Volleyball M

RAMAPO COLLEGE OF NEW JERSEY
505 Ramapo Valley Rd.
Mahwah, NJ 07430-1680
Tel: (201)684-7500
Admissions: (201)684-7300
Fax: (201)684-7508
E-mail: admissions@ramapo.edu
Web Site: http://www.ramapo.edu/
President/CEO: Dr. Peter P. Mercer
Admissions: Michael DiBartolomeo
Financial Aid: Bernice Mulch
Type: Comprehensive **Sex:** Coed **Affiliation:** New Jersey State College System **Scores:** 100% SAT V 400+; 100% SAT M 400+ **% Accepted:** 51 **Admission Plans:** Early Admission; Early Action; Deferred Admission **Application Deadline:** March 1 **Application Fee:** $60.00 **H.S. Requirements:** High school diploma required; GED accepted **Costs Per Year:** Application fee: $60. State resident tuition: $7683 full-time, $240.10 per credit part-time. Nonresident tuition: $15,366 full-time, $480.20 per credit part-time. Mandatory fees: $3733 full-time, $116.65 per credit part-time. Full-time tuition and fees vary according to degree level and reciprocity agreements. Part-time tuition and fees vary according to degree level and reciprocity agreements. College room and board: $11,290. College room only: $8200. Room and board charges vary according to board plan and housing facility. **Scholarships:** Available **Calendar System:** Semester, Summer Session Available **Enrollment:** FT 5,224, PT 552, Grad FT 6, Grad PT 244 **Faculty:** FT 213, PT 195 **Student-Faculty Ratio:** 18:1 **Exams:** ACT, SAT I. ACT essay not being used. SAT essay not being used. **% Receiving Financial Aid:** 45 **% Residing in College-Owned, -Operated, or -Affiliated Housing:** 53 **Library Holdings:** 280,588 **Regional Accreditation:** Middle State Association of Colleges and Schools **Credit Hours For Degree:** 128 credits, Bachelors **ROTC:** Air Force **Professional Accreditation:** CSWE, NLN **Intercollegiate Athletics:** Baseball M; Basketball M & W; Cross-Country Running M & W; Field Hockey W; Lacrosse W; Soccer M & W; Softball W; Swimming and Diving M & W; Tennis M & W; Track and Field M & W; Volleyball M & W

RARITAN VALLEY COMMUNITY COLLEGE
118 Lamington Rd.
Branchburg, NJ 08876
Tel: (908)526-1200
Fax: (908)704-3442
E-mail: dpalubni@raritanval.edu
Web Site: http://www.raritanval.edu/
President/CEO: Casey Crabill
Admissions: Daniel Palubniak
Financial Aid: Lenny Mesonas
Type: Two-Year College **Sex:** Coed **Admission Plans:** Open Admission; Early Admission **Application Deadline:** Rolling **Application Fee:** $25.00 **H.S. Requirements:** High school diploma required; GED accepted **Costs Per Year:** Application fee: $25. State resident tuition: $106 per credit part-time. Nonresident tuition: $106 per credit part-time. Mandatory fees: $22 per credit part-time, $80. Part-time tuition and fees vary according to course load. **Scholarships:** Available **Calendar System:** Semester, Summer Session Available **Enrollment:** FT 4,086, PT 3,802 **Faculty:** FT 115, PT 343 **Student-Faculty Ratio:** 23:1 **Final Year or Final Semester Residency Requirement:** No **Library Holdings:** 69,634 **Regional Accreditation:** Middle State Association of Colleges and Schools **Credit Hours For Degree:** 60 credits, Associates **ROTC:** Army, Air Force **Professional Accreditation:** COptA, NLN **Intercollegiate Athletics:** Baseball M; Basketball M & W; Soccer M; Softball W

THE RICHARD STOCKTON COLLEGE OF NEW JERSEY
PO Box 195, Jimmie Leeds Rd.
Pomona, NJ 08240-0195
Tel: (609)652-1776
Admissions: (609)652-4261
Fax: (609)748-5541
E-mail: admissions@stockton.edu

Web Site: http://www.stockton.edu/
President/CEO: Dr. Herman Saatkamp
Admissions: John Iacovelli
Financial Aid: Jeanne S. Lewis
Type: Comprehensive **Sex:** Coed **Affiliation:** New Jersey State College System **Scores:** 97% SAT V 400+; 98% SAT M 400+; 71% ACT 18-23; 19% ACT 24-29 **% Accepted:** 61 **Admission Plans:** Early Admission **Application Deadline:** May 1 **Application Fee:** $50.00 **H.S. Requirements:** High school diploma required; GED accepted **Costs Per Year:** Application fee: $50. State resident tuition: $7067 full-time, $235.55 per credit hour part-time. Nonresident tuition: $12,750 full-time, $425.01 per credit hour part-time. Mandatory fees: $3974 full-time, $129.12 per credit hour part-time, $50 per term part-time. Full-time tuition and fees vary according to degree level. Part-time tuition and fees vary according to course load and degree level. College room and board: $10,189. Room and board charges vary according to board plan and housing facility. **Scholarships:** Available **Calendar System:** Semester, Summer Session Available **Enrollment:** FT 6,068, PT 745, Grad FT 187, Grad PT 559 **Faculty:** FT 264, PT 255 **Student-Faculty Ratio:** 19:1 **Exams:** SAT I or ACT. ACT essay used for advising. SAT essay used for advising. ACT essay used for placement. SAT essay used for placement. **% Receiving Financial Aid:** 66 **% Residing in College-Owned, -Operated, or -Affiliated Housing:** 37 **Final Year or Final Semester Residency Requirement:** Yes **Library Holdings:** 281,155 **Regional Accreditation:** Middle State Association of Colleges and Schools **Credit Hours For Degree:** 128 credit hours, Bachelors **Professional Accreditation:** AACN, AOTA, APTA, CSWE, NLN **Intercollegiate Athletics:** Baseball M; Basketball M & W; Cheerleading M & W; Crew W; Cross-Country Running M & W; Field Hockey W; Lacrosse M; Soccer M & W; Softball W; Tennis W; Track and Field M & W; Volleyball W

RIDER UNIVERSITY
2083 Lawrenceville Rd.
Lawrenceville, NJ 08648-3001
Tel: (609)896-5000; Free: 800-257-9026
Fax: (609)895-6645
E-mail: wlarrousse@rider.edu
Web Site: http://www.rider.edu/
President/CEO: Mordechai Rozanski
Admissions: William Larrousse
Financial Aid: Dr. Dennis Levy
Type: Comprehensive **Sex:** Coed **Scores:** 96% SAT V 400+; 97% SAT M 400+; 60% ACT 18-23; 28% ACT 24-29 **% Accepted:** 75 **Admission Plans:** Early Admission; Early Action; Early Decision Plan; Deferred Admission **Application Deadline:** Rolling **Application Fee:** $50.00 **H.S. Requirements:** High school diploma required; GED accepted **Costs Per Year:** Application fee: $50. Comprehensive fee: $39,780 includes full-time tuition ($28,470), mandatory fees ($590), and college room and board ($10,720). College room only: $6420. Full-time tuition and fees vary according to course load and program. Room and board charges vary according to board plan, housing facility, and location. Part-time tuition: $508 per credit. Part-time mandatory fees: $35 per course. Part-time tuition and fees vary according to course load and program. **Scholarships:** Available **Calendar System:** Semester, Summer Session Available **Enrollment:** FT 4,074, PT 817, Grad FT 312, Grad PT 870 **Faculty:** FT 243, PT 383 **Student-Faculty Ratio:** 13:1 **Exams:** SAT I or ACT. **% Receiving Financial Aid:** 70 **% Residing in College-Owned, -Operated, or -Affiliated Housing:** 56 **Final Year or Final Semester Residency Requirement:** No **Library Holdings:** 481,958 **Regional Accreditation:** Middle State Association of Colleges and Schools **Credit Hours For Degree:** 60 semester hours, Associates; 120 semester hours, Bachelors **ROTC:** Army **Professional Accreditation:** AACSB, ACA, NASM, NCATE **Intercollegiate Athletics:** Baseball M; Basketball M & W; Cheerleading M & W; Cross-Country Running M & W; Field Hockey W; Golf M; Soccer M & W; Softball W; Swimming and Diving M & W; Tennis M & W; Track and Field M & W; Volleyball W; Wrestling M

ROWAN UNIVERSITY
201 Mullica Hill Rd.
Glassboro, NJ 08028-1701
Tel: (856)256-4500
Admissions: (856)256-4200
E-mail: admissions@rowan.edu
Web Site: http://www.rowan.edu/
President/CEO: Dr. Donald Farish
Admissions: Albert Betts
Financial Aid: Luis Tavarez
Type: Comprehensive **Sex:** Coed **Affiliation:** New Jersey State College System **Scores:** 94.7% SAT V 400+; 95.22% SAT M 400+ **% Accepted:** 68 **Admission Plans:** Early Admission; Deferred Admission **Application Deadline:** March 1 **Application Fee:** $50.00 **H.S. Requirements:** High school diploma required; GED accepted **Costs Per Year:** Application fee: $50. State resident tuition: $8074 full-time, $311 per credit hour part-time. Nonresident tuition: $15,148 full-time, $584 per credit hour part-time. Mandatory fees: $3160 full-time, $135 per credit hour part-time. Full-time tuition and fees vary according to course load, degree level, and program. Part-time tuition and fees vary according to degree level and program. College room and board: $9958. College room only: $6248. Room and board charges vary according to board plan and housing facility. **Scholarships:** Available **Calendar System:** Semester, Summer Session Available **Enrollment:** FT 8,335, PT 1,330, Grad FT 315, Grad PT 1,026 **Faculty:** FT 400, PT 616 **Student-Faculty Ratio:** 15:1 **Exams:** SAT I or ACT. ACT essay used for placement. SAT essay used for placement. **% Receiving Financial Aid:** 56 **% Residing in College-Owned, -Operated, or -Affiliated Housing:** 34 **Final Year or Final Semester Residency Requirement:** No **Library Holdings:** 435,205 **Regional Accreditation:** Middle State Association of Colleges and Schools **Credit Hours For Degree:** 120 credits, Bachelors **ROTC:** Army **Professional Accreditation:** AACSB, ABET, JRCEPAT, NASAD, NASM, NAST, NCATE **Intercollegiate Athletics:** Baseball M; Basketball M & W; Cross-Country Running M & W; Field Hockey W; Football M; Lacrosse W; Soccer M & W; Softball W; Swimming and Diving M & W; Tennis M & W; Track and Field M & W; Volleyball W

RUTGERS, THE STATE UNIVERSITY OF NEW JERSEY, CAMDEN
406 Penn St.
Camden, NJ 08102-1401
Tel: (856)225-1766
Admissions: (856)225-6104
E-mail: bowles@ugadm.rutgers.edu
Web Site: http://www.rutgers.edu/
President/CEO: Dr. Richard L. McCormick
Admissions: Dr. Deborah Bowles
Financial Aid: Willie L. Williams
Type: University **Sex:** Coed **Affiliation:** Rutgers, The State University of New Jersey **Scores:** 100% SAT V 400+; 100% SAT M 400+ **% Accepted:** 49 **Admission Plans:** Preferred Admission **Application Deadline:** December 1 **Application Fee:** $65.00 **H.S. Requirements:** High school diploma required; GED accepted **Costs Per Year:** Application fee: $65. State resident tuition: $9546 full-time, $307 per credit hour part-time. Nonresident tuition: $20,178 full-time, $654 per credit hour part-time. Mandatory fees: $2152 full-time. Part-time tuition varies according to course level. College room and board: $9788. College room only: $7048. Room and board charges vary according to board plan and housing facility. **Scholarships:** Available **Calendar System:** Semester, Summer Session Available **Enrollment:** FT 3,342, PT 779, Grad FT 908, Grad PT 752 **Faculty:** FT 252, PT 182 **Student-Faculty Ratio:** 12:1 **Exams:** SAT I or ACT. **% Receiving Financial Aid:** 72 **% Residing in College-Owned, -Operated, or -Affiliated Housing:** 11 **Library Holdings:** 729,987 **Regional Accreditation:** Middle State Association of Colleges and Schools **Credit Hours For Degree:** 120 credit hours, Bachelors **ROTC:** Army, Air Force **Professional Accreditation:** AACSB, AACN, ABA, APTA, AALS, CSWE, NASPAA **Intercollegiate Athletics:** Baseball M; Basketball M & W; Crew M & W; Cross-Country Running W; Golf M; Lacrosse W; Soccer M & W; Softball W; Track and Field M & W; Volleyball W

RUTGERS, THE STATE UNIVERSITY OF NEW JERSEY, NEW BRUNSWICK
65 Davidson Rd.
Room 202
Piscataway, NJ 08854-8097
Tel: (732)932-4636
Admissions: (732)445-4636
Web Site: http://www.rutgers.edu/
President/CEO: Dr. Richard L. McCormick
Admissions: Diane Williams Harris
Financial Aid: William Williams
Type: University **Sex:** Coed **Affiliation:** Rutgers, The State University of New Jersey **Scores:** 99.6% SAT V 400+; 99.9% SAT M 400+ **% Accepted:** 61 **Admission Plans:** Preferred Admission **Application Deadline:** December 1 **Application Fee:** $65.00 **H.S. Requirements:** High school

diploma required; GED accepted **Costs Per Year:** Application fee: $65. State resident tuition: $9546 full-time, $307 per credit hour part-time. Nonresident tuition: $20,178 full-time, $654 per credit hour part-time. Mandatory fees: $2340 full-time. Part-time tuition varies according to course level. College room and board: $10,676. College room only: $6526. Room and board charges vary according to board plan and housing facility. **Scholarships:** Available **Calendar System:** Semester **Enrollment:** FT 27,588, PT 1,507, Grad FT 4,557, Grad PT 3,712 **Faculty:** FT 1,678, PT 867 **Student-Faculty Ratio:** 14:1 **Exams:** SAT I or ACT. **% Receiving Financial Aid:** 56 **% Residing in College-Owned, -Operated, or -Affiliated Housing:** 49 **Library Holdings:** 5,080,676 **Regional Accreditation:** Middle State Association of Colleges and Schools **Credit Hours For Degree:** 120 credit hours, Bachelors **ROTC:** Army, Air Force **Professional Accreditation:** ABET, ACPhE, ACSP, ALA, APA, ASLA, CSWE, NASD, NASM, TEAC **Intercollegiate Athletics:** Baseball M; Basketball M & W; Crew M & W; Cross-Country Running M & W; Fencing M & W; Football M; Golf M & W; Gymnastics W; Lacrosse M & W; Soccer M & W; Softball W; Swimming and Diving M & W; Tennis M & W; Track and Field M & W; Volleyball W; Wrestling M

RUTGERS, THE STATE UNIVERSITY OF NEW JERSEY, NEWARK
249 University Ave.
Newark, NJ 07102
Tel: (973)353-1766
Admissions: (973)353-5205
Fax: (973)353-1048
E-mail: admissions@ugadm.rutgers.edu
Web Site: http://www.rutgers.edu/
President/CEO: Dr. Richard L. McCormick
Admissions: Jason Hand
Financial Aid: Willie L. Williams
Type: University **Sex:** Coed **Affiliation:** Rutgers, The State University of New Jersey **Scores:** 99.4% SAT V 400+; 100% SAT M 400+ **% Accepted:** 60 **Admission Plans:** Preferred Admission **Application Deadline:** December 1 **Application Fee:** $65.00 **H.S. Requirements:** High school diploma required; GED accepted **Costs Per Year:** Application fee: $65. State resident tuition: $9546 full-time, $307 per credit hour part-time. Nonresident tuition: $20,178 full-time, $654 per credit hour part-time. Mandatory fees: $1868 full-time. College room and board: $11,155. College room only: $6965. Room and board charges vary according to board plan and housing facility. **Scholarships:** Available **Calendar System:** Semester, Summer Session Available **Enrollment:** FT 5,754, PT 1,553, Grad FT 1,718, Grad PT 2,475 **Faculty:** FT 447, PT 257 **Student-Faculty Ratio:** 12:1 **Exams:** SAT I or ACT. **% Receiving Financial Aid:** 68 **% Residing in College-Owned, -Operated, or -Affiliated Housing:** 17 **Library Holdings:** 1,042,620 **Regional Accreditation:** Middle State Association of Colleges and Schools **Credit Hours For Degree:** 124 credit hours, Bachelors **ROTC:** Army, Air Force **Professional Accreditation:** AACSB, AACN, ABA, AALS, CSWE, NASPAA, NLN **Intercollegiate Athletics:** Baseball M; Basketball M & W; Cross-Country Running M & W; Soccer M & W; Tennis M & W; Track and Field M; Volleyball M & W

SAINT PETER'S COLLEGE
2641 Kennedy Blvd.
Jersey City, NJ 07306-5997
Tel: (201)761-6000; Free: 888-SPC-9933
Admissions: (201)761-7106
Fax: (201)432-5860
E-mail: admissions@spc.edu
Web Site: http://www.spc.edu/
President/CEO: Dr. Eugene Cornacchia
Admissions: Joe Giglio
Financial Aid: Jennifer Ragsdale
Type: Comprehensive **Sex:** Coed **Affiliation:** Roman Catholic (Jesuit) **Scores:** 90% SAT V 400+; 86% SAT M 400+; 25% ACT 18-23; 24% ACT 24-29 **% Accepted:** 54 **Admission Plans:** Early Admission; Deferred Admission **Application Deadline:** Rolling **Application Fee:** $0.00 **H.S. Requirements:** High school diploma required; GED accepted **Scholarships:** Available **Calendar System:** Semester, Summer Session Available **Enrollment:** FT 1,997, PT 369 **Student-Faculty Ratio:** 16:1 **Exams:** SAT I or ACT. **% Receiving Financial Aid:** 83 **% Residing in College-Owned, -Operated, or -Affiliated Housing:** 40 **Library Holdings:** 178,587 **Regional Accreditation:** Middle State Association of Colleges and Schools **Credit Hours For Degree:** 69 credits, Associates; 129 credits, Bachelors **ROTC:** Army, Air Force **Professional Accreditation:** AACN, NLN, TEAC **Intercollegiate Athletics:** Baseball M; Basketball M & W; Bowling M & W; Cross-Country Running M & W; Golf M; Soccer M & W; Softball W; Swimming and Diving M & W; Tennis M & W; Track and Field M & W; Volleyball W

SALEM COMMUNITY COLLEGE
460 Hollywood Ave.
Carneys Point, NJ 08069-2799
Tel: (856)299-2100
Fax: (856)299-9193
E-mail: info@salemcc.edu
Web Site: http://www.salemcc.edu/
President/CEO: Peter B. Contini
Admissions: Dr. Reva Curry
Type: Two-Year College **Sex:** Coed **Affiliation:** New Jersey Commission on Higher Education **Admission Plans:** Open Admission; Early Admission; Deferred Admission **Application Deadline:** Rolling **Application Fee:** $25.00 **H.S. Requirements:** High school diploma required; GED accepted **Costs Per Year:** Application fee: $25. Area resident tuition: $2790 full-time, $93 per credit hour part-time. State resident tuition: $3090 full-time, $103 per credit hour part-time. Nonresident tuition: $3090 full-time, $103 per credit hour part-time. Mandatory fees: $920 full-time, $31 per credit hour part-time, $27 per term part-time. Full-time tuition and fees vary according to course load and program. Part-time tuition and fees vary according to course load and program. **Scholarships:** Available **Calendar System:** Semester, Summer Session Available **Enrollment:** FT 686, PT 649 **Faculty:** FT 24, PT 61 **Student-Faculty Ratio:** 21:1 **Library Holdings:** 28,951 **Regional Accreditation:** Middle State Association of Colleges and Schools **Credit Hours For Degree:** 64 credits, Associates **Intercollegiate Athletics:** Baseball M; Basketball M & W; Softball W; Tennis M & W

SETON HALL UNIVERSITY
400 South Orange Ave.
South Orange, NJ 07079-2697
Tel: (973)761-9000; Free: 800-THE HALL
Admissions: (973)275-2498
Fax: (973)761-9452
E-mail: thehall@shu.edu
Web Site: http://www.shu.edu/
President/CEO: Msgr. Robert Sheeran
Admissions: Peter Nacy
Type: University **Sex:** Coed **Affiliation:** Roman Catholic **Scores:** 97% SAT V 400+; 95% SAT M 400+; 50% ACT 18-23; 38% ACT 24-29 **% Accepted:** 79 **Admission Plans:** Early Action; Deferred Admission **Application Deadline:** Rolling **Application Fee:** $55.00 **H.S. Requirements:** High school diploma required; GED accepted **Costs Per Year:** Application fee: $55. One-time mandatory fee: $300. Comprehensive fee: $43,940 includes full-time tuition ($29,940), mandatory fees ($1950), and college room and board ($12,050). College room only: $7774. Full-time tuition and fees vary according to course load. Room and board charges vary according to board plan and housing facility. Part-time tuition: $912 per credit hour. Part-time mandatory fees: $185 per term. Part-time tuition and fees vary according to course load. **Scholarships:** Available **Calendar System:** Semester, Summer Session Available **Enrollment:** FT 4,671, PT 542, Grad FT 1,904, Grad PT 2,499 **Faculty:** FT 460, PT 419 **Student-Faculty Ratio:** 14:1 **Exams:** SAT I or ACT. SAT essay used for admission. **% Receiving Financial Aid:** 62 **% Residing in College-Owned, -Operated, or -Affiliated Housing:** 43 **Final Year or Final Semester Residency Requirement:** No **Library Holdings:** 506,042 **Regional Accreditation:** Middle State Association of Colleges and Schools **Credit Hours For Degree:** 120 credits, Bachelors **ROTC:** Army **Professional Accreditation:** AACSB, AAMFT, AACN, ABA, AOTA, APTA, APA, ASLHA, ACIPE, AALS, ATS, CSWE, NASPAA, NCATE, NLN **Intercollegiate Athletics:** Baseball M; Basketball M & W; Golf M & W; Ice Hockey M; Rugby M; Soccer M & W; Softball W; Swimming and Diving M & W; Tennis W; Volleyball M & W

SOMERSET CHRISTIAN COLLEGE
10 College Way
PO Box 9035
Zarephath, NJ 08890-9035
Tel: (732)356-1595; Free: 800-234-9305
Fax: (732)356-4846
E-mail: info@somerset.edu
Web Site: http://www.somerset.edu/

President/CEO: David Schroeder
Admissions: Linda Aarni
Type: Four-Year College **Sex:** Coed **Affiliation:** Pillar of Fire International **% Accepted:** 48 **Admission Plans:** Deferred Admission **Application Deadline:** Rolling **Application Fee:** $35.00 **H.S. Requirements:** High school diploma required; GED accepted **Costs Per Year:** Application fee: $35. Tuition: $10,944 full-time, $456 per credit part-time. Mandatory fees: $350 full-time, $175. Full-time tuition and fees vary according to program. Part-time tuition and fees vary according to course load and program. **Calendar System:** Semester, Summer Session Available **Enrollment:** FT 174, PT 66 **Student-Faculty Ratio:** 15:1 **Exams:** SAT I or ACT. **Final Year or Final Semester Residency Requirement:** No **Library Holdings:** 60,000 **Regional Accreditation:** Middle State Association of Colleges and Schools **Credit Hours For Degree:** 60 credits, Associates; 120 credits, Bachelors **Professional Accreditation:** ABHE

STEVENS INSTITUTE OF TECHNOLOGY
Castle Point on Hudson
Hoboken, NJ 07030
Tel: (201)216-5000; Free: 800-458-5323
Admissions: (201)216-5197
Fax: (201)216-8348
E-mail: admissions@stevens.edu
Web Site: http://www.stevens.edu/
President/CEO: Dr. Harold J. Raveche
Admissions: Daniel Gallagher
Financial Aid: Adrienne Hynek
Type: University **Sex:** Coed **Scores:** 100% SAT V 400+; 100% SAT M 400+; 18% ACT 18-23; 58% ACT 24-29 **% Accepted:** 51 **Admission Plans:** Early Admission; Early Decision Plan; Deferred Admission **Application Deadline:** February 1 **Application Fee:** $55.00 **H.S. Requirements:** High school diploma required; GED not accepted **Costs Per Year:** Application fee: $55. Comprehensive fee: $50,130 includes full-time tuition ($36,600), mandatory fees ($1380), and college room and board ($12,150). Room and board charges vary according to board plan and housing facility. Part-time tuition: $1220 per credit. Part-time mandatory fees: $600 per term. **Scholarships:** Available **Calendar System:** Semester, Summer Session Available **Enrollment:** FT 2,233, PT 1, Grad FT 1,304, Grad PT 2,324 **Faculty:** FT 251, PT 187 **Student-Faculty Ratio:** 7:1 **Exams:** SAT I or ACT, SAT II. ACT essay not being used. SAT essay not being used. **% Receiving Financial Aid:** 68 **% Residing in College-Owned, -Operated, or -Affiliated Housing:** 85 **Final Year or Final Semester Residency Requirement:** No **Library Holdings:** 123,063 **Regional Accreditation:** Middle State Association of Colleges and Schools **Credit Hours For Degree:** 136 credits, Bachelors **ROTC:** Army, Air Force **Professional Accreditation:** ABET **Intercollegiate Athletics:** Baseball M; Basketball M & W; Cross-Country Running M & W; Equestrian Sports W; Fencing M & W; Field Hockey W; Golf M; Lacrosse M & W; Soccer M & W; Softball W; Swimming and Diving M & W; Tennis M & W; Track and Field M & W; Volleyball M & W; Wrestling M

STRAYER UNIVERSITY - CHERRY HILL CAMPUS
2201 Route 38
Ste. 100
Cherry Hill, NJ 08002
Tel: (856)482-4200
Fax: (856)482-4230
Web Site: http://www.strayer.edu/cherry_hill/
Type: Comprehensive **Sex:** Coed **Application Fee:** $50.00 **Costs Per Year:** Application fee: $50. **Regional Accreditation:** Middle State Association of Colleges and Schools

STRAYER UNIVERSITY - LAWRENCEVILLE CAMPUS
3150 Brunswick Pike
Ste. 100
Lawrenceville, NJ 08648
Tel: (609)406-7600
Fax: (609)771-8636
Web Site: http://www.strayer.edu/lawrenceville
Type: Comprehensive **Sex:** Coed **Application Fee:** $50.00 **Costs Per Year:** Application fee: $50. **Regional Accreditation:** Middle State Association of Colleges and Schools

STRAYER UNIVERSITY - PISCATAWAY CAMPUS
242 Old New Brunswick Rd.
Ste. 220
Piscataway, NJ 08854
Tel: (732)743-3800
Fax: (732)562-1780
Web Site: http://www.strayer.edu/piscataway
Type: Comprehensive **Sex:** Coed **Application Fee:** $50.00 **Costs Per Year:** Application fee: $50. **Regional Accreditation:** Middle State Association of Colleges and Schools

STRAYER UNIVERSITY - WILLINGBORO CAMPUS
300 Willingboro Parkway
Willingboro Town Center, Ste. 125
Willingboro, NJ 08046
Tel: (609)835-6000
Fax: (609)835-6030
Web Site: http://www.strayer.edu/willingboro/
Type: Comprehensive **Sex:** Coed **Application Fee:** $50.00 **Costs Per Year:** Application fee: $50. **Regional Accreditation:** Middle State Association of Colleges and Schools

SUSSEX COUNTY COMMUNITY COLLEGE
1 College Hill
Newton, NJ 07860
Tel: (973)300-2100
Admissions: (973)300-2219
E-mail: jdonohue@sussex.edu
Web Site: http://www.sussex.edu/
President/CEO: Dr. Constance Mierendorf
Admissions: James Donohue
Type: Two-Year College **Sex:** Coed **Affiliation:** New Jersey Commission on Higher Education **Admission Plans:** Open Admission **Application Deadline:** Rolling **Application Fee:** $15.00 **H.S. Requirements:** High school diploma or equivalent not required **Scholarships:** Available **Calendar System:** 4-1-4, Summer Session Available **Enrollment:** FT 2,059, PT 1,673 **Faculty:** FT 43, PT 233 **Student-Faculty Ratio:** 21:1 **Library Holdings:** 34,346 **Regional Accreditation:** Middle State Association of Colleges and Schools **Credit Hours For Degree:** 60 credits, Associates **Intercollegiate Athletics:** Baseball M; Basketball M; Soccer M & W; Softball W

TALMUDICAL ACADEMY OF NEW JERSEY
868 Route 524
Adelphia, NJ 07710
Tel: (732)431-1600
President/CEO: Mordecai Gottlieb
Type: Comprehensive **Sex:** Men **Affiliation:** Jewish **% Accepted:** 100 **H.S. Requirements:** High school diploma required; GED accepted **Calendar System:** Semester **Professional Accreditation:** AARTS

THOMAS EDISON STATE COLLEGE
101 West State St.
Trenton, NJ 08608-1176
Tel: (609)984-1100; Free: 888-442-8372
Fax: (609)292-9000
E-mail: admissions@tesc.edu
Web Site: http://www.tesc.edu/
President/CEO: Dr. George A. Pruitt
Admissions: David Hoftiezer
Type: Comprehensive **Sex:** Coed **Admission Plans:** Open Admission **Application Deadline:** Rolling **Application Fee:** $75.00 **H.S. Requirements:** High school diploma required; GED accepted **Costs Per Year:** Application fee: $75. State resident tuition: $4695 full-time, $136 per credit hour part-time. Nonresident tuition: $6720 full-time, $180 per credit hour part-time. Mandatory fees: $103 per year part-time. Part-time tuition and fees vary according to program and student level. students may choose either the Comprehensive Tuition Plan: $4,695 per year (state residents and military personnel), $6,720 (out-of-state), which covers up to 36 credits per year for all credit-earning options, or the Enrolled Options Plan: $1,390 per year (state residents and military personnel), $2,520 (out-of-state) and $3,440 (international) for annual enrollment tuition and a technology services fee ($103); tests, portfolios, courses and other fees at additional cost. Please visit www.tesc.edu for more details. **Scholarships:** Available **Calendar System:** Continuous, Summer Session Available **Enrollment:** , PT 17,320, Grad PT 886 **Final Year or Final Semester Residency Requirement:** No **Regional Accreditation:** Middle State Association of Colleges and Schools

Credit Hours For Degree: 60 credits, Associates; 120 credits, Bachelors **Professional Accreditation:** AACN, NLN

UNION COUNTY COLLEGE
1033 Springfield Ave.
Cranford, NJ 07016
Tel: (908)709-7000
Admissions: (908)709-7127
Fax: (908)709-0527
E-mail: Davis@ucc.edu
Web Site: http://www.ucc.edu/
President/CEO: Dr. John R. Farrell, Jr.
Admissions: Jo Ann Davis-Wayne
Type: Two-Year College **Sex:** Coed **Affiliation:** New Jersey Commission on Higher Education **% Accepted:** 84 **Admission Plans:** Open Admission; Early Admission; Deferred Admission **Application Deadline:** Rolling **Application Fee:** $35.00 **H.S. Requirements:** High school diploma required; GED accepted **Costs Per Year:** Application fee: $35. Area resident tuition: $2400 full-time, $100 per credit part-time. State resident tuition: $4800 full-time, $200 per credit part-time. Nonresident tuition: $4800 full-time, $200 per credit part-time. Mandatory fees: $810 full-time, $27 per credit part-time. Full-time tuition and fees vary according to course load. Part-time tuition and fees vary according to course load. **Scholarships:** Available **Calendar System:** Semester, Summer Session Available **Enrollment:** FT 6,338, PT 6,413 **Faculty:** FT 180, PT 281 **Student-Faculty Ratio:** 30:1 **Library Holdings:** 137,731 **Regional Accreditation:** Middle State Association of Colleges and Schools **Credit Hours For Degree:** 62 credits, Associates **ROTC:** Air Force **Professional Accreditation:** APTA, CARC, NLN **Intercollegiate Athletics:** Baseball M; Basketball M & W; Golf M & W; Soccer M; Volleyball W

UNIVERSITY OF PHOENIX—JERSEY CITY CAMPUS
100 Town Square Place
Jersey City, NJ 07310
Tel: (201)610-1408
Web Site: http://www.phoenix.edu/
President/CEO: William Pepicello, PhD
Type: Comprehensive **Sex:** Coed **Regional Accreditation:** North Central Association of Colleges and Schools

WARREN COUNTY COMMUNITY COLLEGE
475 Route 57 West
Washington, NJ 07882-4343
Tel: (908)835-9222
Web Site: http://www.warren.edu/
President/CEO: Dr. William Austin
Type: Two-Year College **Sex:** Coed **Affiliation:** New Jersey Commission on Higher Education **% Accepted:** 100 **Admission Plans:** Open Admission; Early Admission; Deferred Admission **Application Deadline:** Rolling **Application Fee:** $15.00 **H.S. Requirements:** High school diploma or equivalent not required **Scholarships:** Available **Calendar System:** Semester, Summer Session Available **Faculty:** FT 30, PT 40 **Student-Faculty Ratio:** 13:1 **Library Holdings:** 23,143 **Regional Accreditation:** Middle State Association of Colleges and Schools **Credit Hours For Degree:** 64 credits, Associates

WILLIAM PATERSON UNIVERSITY OF NEW JERSEY
300 Pompton Rd.
Wayne, NJ 07470-8420
Tel: (973)720-2000
Fax: (973)720-2910
E-mail: admissions@wpunj.edu
Web Site: http://www.wpunj.edu/
President/CEO: Arnold Speert
Admissions: Anthony Leckey
Financial Aid: Elizabeth Riquez
Type: Comprehensive **Sex:** Coed **Affiliation:** New Jersey State College System **Scores:** 93.7% SAT V 400+; 95.9% SAT M 400+ **% Accepted:** 65 **Admission Plans:** Early Admission; Early Decision Plan; Deferred Admission **Application Deadline:** May 1 **Application Fee:** $50.00 **H.S. Requirements:** High school diploma required; GED accepted **Costs Per Year:** Application fee: $50. State resident tuition: $6567 full-time, $210.47 per credit part-time. Nonresident tuition: $13,321 full-time, $431.47 per credit part-time. Mandatory fees: $4271 full-time, $137.53 per credit part-time. Full-time tuition and fees vary according to program. Part-time tuition and fees vary according to course load and program. College room and board: $10,280. College room only: $6800. Room and board charges vary according to board plan and housing facility. **Scholarships:** Available **Calendar System:** Semester, Summer Session Available **Enrollment:** FT 7,768, PT 1,411, Grad FT 307, Grad PT 1,333 **Faculty:** FT 371, PT 571 **Student-Faculty Ratio:** 15:1 **Exams:** SAT I or ACT. ACT essay not being used. SAT essay not being used. **% Receiving Financial Aid:** 65 **% Residing in College-Owned, -Operated, or -Affiliated Housing:** 23 **Final Year or Final Semester Residency Requirement:** Yes **Library Holdings:** 338,573 **Regional Accreditation:** Middle State Association of Colleges and Schools **Credit Hours For Degree:** 120 credits, Bachelors **ROTC:** Air Force **Professional Accreditation:** AACSB, AACN, ACA, ASLHA, JRCEPAT, NASAD, NASM, NCATE **Intercollegiate Athletics:** Baseball M; Basketball M & W; Bowling M & W; Cheerleading M & W; Field Hockey W; Football M; Golf M; Ice Hockey M; Skiing (Downhill) M & W; Soccer M & W; Softball W; Swimming and Diving M & W; Volleyball W

BROOKLINE COLLEGE
4201 Central Ave. NW
Ste. J
Albuquerque, NM 87105-1649
Tel: (505)880-2877; Free: 888-660-2428
Fax: (505)352-0199
E-mail: awebb@brooklinecollege.edu
Web Site: http://brooklinecollege.edu/
President/CEO: Andrew Webb
Admissions: Andrew Webb
Type: Four-Year College **Sex:** Coed **Admission Plans:** Open Admission **Application Deadline:** Rolling **Application Fee:** $0.00 **H.S. Requirements:** High school diploma required; GED accepted **Costs Per Year:** Application fee: $0. Tuition: $14,000 full-time. Full-time tuition varies according to degree level and program. Tuition guaranteed not to increase for student's term of enrollment. **Calendar System:** Continuous **Enrollment:** FT 472 **Faculty:** FT 15, PT 12 **Professional Accreditation:** ACICS

BROWN MACKIE COLLEGE—ALBUQUERQUE
10500 Cooper Ave. NE
Albuquerque, NM 87123
Tel: (505)559-5200; Free: 877-271-3488
Fax: (505)559-5222
Web Site: http://www.brownmackie.edu/
Type: Two-Year College **Sex:** Coed

CENTRAL NEW MEXICO COMMUNITY COLLEGE
525 Buena Vista, SE
Albuquerque, NM 87106-4096
Tel: (505)224-3000
Admissions: (505)224-3160
Fax: (505)224-4740
Web Site: http://www.cnm.edu/
President/CEO: Katharine W. Winograd
Admissions: Jane Campbell
Type: Two-Year College **Sex:** Coed **% Accepted:** 100 **Admission Plans:** Open Admission **Application Deadline:** Rolling **Application Fee:** $0.00 **H.S. Requirements:** High school diploma or equivalent not required **Costs Per Year:** Application fee: $0. Area resident tuition: $1476 full-time, $41 per credit hour part-time. State resident tuition: $1836 full-time, $51 per credit hour part-time. Nonresident tuition: $7200 full-time, $200 per credit hour part-time. Mandatory fees: $120 full-time, $43 per term part-time. Full-time tuition and fees vary according to course load. Part-time tuition and fees vary according to course load. **Scholarships:** Available **Calendar System:** Trimester, Summer Session Available **Enrollment:** FT 8,980, PT 18,958 **Faculty:** FT 327, PT 771 **Student-Faculty Ratio:** 26:1 **Library Holdings:** 75,167 **Regional Accreditation:** North Central Association of Colleges and Schools **Credit Hours For Degree:** 60 credit hours, Associates **ROTC:** Army, Navy, Air Force **Professional Accreditation:** ABET, ACCE, ACF, ADA, ACBSP, CARC, NAACLS, NLN

CLOVIS COMMUNITY COLLEGE
417 Schepps Blvd.
Clovis, NM 88101-8381
Tel: (575)769-2811
Admissions: (575)769-4962
E-mail: admissions@clovis.edu
Web Site: http://www.clovis.edu/
President/CEO: Dr. John Neibling
Admissions: Rosie Corrie
Type: Two-Year College **Sex:** Coed **% Accepted:** 100 **Admission Plans:** Open Admission **Application Deadline:** Rolling **Application Fee:** $0.00 **H.S. Requirements:** High school diploma required; GED accepted **Costs Per Year:** Application fee: $0. Area resident tuition: $30 per credit hour part-time. State resident tuition: $32 per credit hour part-time. Nonresident tuition: $65 per credit hour part-time. Mandatory fees: $20 per term part-time. Part-time tuition and fees vary according to course load and program. **Scholarships:** Available **Calendar System:** Semester, Summer Session Available **Enrollment:** FT 582, PT 3,124 **Faculty:** FT 47, PT 128 **Student-Faculty Ratio:** 15:1 **Library Holdings:** 52,000 **Regional Accreditation:** North Central Association of Colleges and Schools **Credit Hours For Degree:** 64 credit hours, Associates **Professional Accreditation:** JRCERT, NLN

COLLEGE OF SANTA FE
1600 Saint Michael's Dr.
Santa Fe, NM 87505-7634
Tel: (505)473-6011; Free: 800-456-2673
Admissions: (505)473-6133
Fax: (505)473-6127
E-mail: admissions@csf.edu
Web Site: http://www.csf.edu/
President/CEO: Larry Hinz
Admissions: Jackie Donohoe
Financial Aid: Jill Robertson
Type: Comprehensive **Sex:** Coed **Scores:** 99% SAT V 400+; 92% SAT M 400+; 43% ACT 18-23; 48% ACT 24-29 **% Accepted:** 83 **Admission Plans:** Early Admission; Early Decision Plan; Deferred Admission **Application Deadline:** Rolling **Application Fee:** $35.00 **H.S. Requirements:** High school diploma required; GED accepted **Costs Per Year:** Application fee: $35. Comprehensive fee: $36,598 includes full-time tuition ($27,358), mandatory fees ($1146), and college room and board ($8094). Room and board charges vary according to board plan and housing facility. **Scholarships:** Available **Calendar System:** Semester, Summer Session Available **Enrollment:** FT 611, PT 61 **Faculty:** FT 73, PT 105 **Student-Faculty Ratio:** 12:1 **Exams:** SAT I or ACT. **% Residing in College-Owned, -Operated, or -Affiliated Housing:** 63 **Final Year or Final Semester Residency Requirement:** Yes **Regional Accreditation:** North Central Association of Colleges and Schools **Credit Hours For Degree:** 64 semester hours, Associates; 128 semester hours, Bachelors

DOÑA ANA BRANCH COMMUNITY COLLEGE
MSC-3DA, Box 30001
3400 South Espina St.
Las Cruces, NM 88003-8001
Tel: (505)527-7500
Admissions: (575)527-7683
Fax: (505)527-7515
Web Site: http://dabcc-www.nmsu.edu/
President/CEO: Dr. Margie Huerta
Admissions: Ricci Montes

Type: Two-Year College **Sex:** Coed **Affiliation:** New Mexico State University System **Admission Plans:** Open Admission; Deferred Admission **Application Deadline:** Rolling **Application Fee:** $15.00 **H.S. Requirements:** High school diploma required; GED accepted **Costs Per Year:** Application fee: $15. Area resident tuition: $1272 full-time, $53 per credit hour part-time. State resident tuition: $1512 full-time, $63 per credit hour part-time. Nonresident tuition: $3984 full-time, $166 per credit hour part-time. Full-time tuition varies according to course load and program. Part-time tuition varies according to course load and program. College room and board: $8924. College room only: $5739. Room and board charges vary according to board plan and housing facility. **Scholarships:** Available **Calendar System:** Semester, Summer Session Available **Enrollment:** FT 2,552, PT 5,251 **Student-Faculty Ratio:** 21:1 **Exams:** Other. **Library Holdings:** 17,140 **Regional Accreditation:** North Central Association of Colleges and Schools **Credit Hours For Degree:** 66 credits, Associates **ROTC:** Army, Air Force **Professional Accreditation:** ADA, ACBSP, CARC, JRCERT, JRCEMT, NLN

EASTERN NEW MEXICO UNIVERSITY
1200 West University
Portales, NM 88130
Tel: (575)562-1011; Free: 800-367-3668
Admissions: (575)562-2178
Fax: (575)562-2118
E-mail: donna.kittrell@enmu.edu
Web Site: http://www.enmu.edu/
President/CEO: Dr. Steven Gamble
Admissions: Donna Kittrell
Financial Aid: Brent Small
Type: Comprehensive **Sex:** Coed **Affiliation:** Eastern New Mexico University System **Scores:** 81% SAT V 400+; 86% SAT M 400+; 53% ACT 18-23; 18% ACT 24-29 **% Accepted:** 65 **Admission Plans:** Early Admission; Deferred Admission **Application Deadline:** Rolling **Application Fee:** $0.00 **H.S. Requirements:** High school diploma required; GED accepted **Costs Per Year:** Application fee: $0. State resident tuition: $2514 full-time, $104.75 per credit hour part-time. Nonresident tuition: $8064 full-time, $336 per credit hour part-time. Mandatory fees: $1038 full-time, $43.25 per credit hour part-time. Full-time tuition and fees vary according to course load and reciprocity agreements. College room and board: $5374. College room only: $2542. Room and board charges vary according to housing facility. **Scholarships:** Available **Calendar System:** Semester, Summer Session Available **Enrollment:** FT 2,524, PT 1,310, Grad FT 222, Grad PT 623 **Faculty:** FT 148, PT 173 **Student-Faculty Ratio:** 17:1 **Exams:** SAT I or ACT. ACT essay not being used. SAT essay not being used. **% Receiving Financial Aid:** 61 **% Residing in College-Owned, -Operated, or -Affiliated Housing:** 72 **Library Holdings:** 782,076 **Regional Accreditation:** North Central Association of Colleges and Schools **Credit Hours For Degree:** 64 credit hours, Associates; 128 credit hours, Bachelors **Professional Accreditation:** AAFCS, ASLHA, ACBSP, NASM, NCATE, NLN **Intercollegiate Athletics:** Baseball M; Basketball M & W; Cross-Country Running M & W; Football M; Soccer W; Softball W; Track and Field M & W; Volleyball W

EASTERN NEW MEXICO UNIVERSITY—ROSWELL
PO Box 6000
Roswell, NM 88202-6000
Tel: (505)624-7000
Admissions: (575)624-7000
Fax: (505)624-7119
Web Site: http://www.enmu.edu/
President/CEO: Dr. John Madden
Admissions: James Mares
Financial Aid: Jessie Sjue
Type: Two-Year College **Sex:** Coed **Affiliation:** Eastern New Mexico University System **% Accepted:** 55 **Admission Plans:** Open Admission; Early Admission **Application Deadline:** Rolling **Application Fee:** $0.00 **H.S. Requirements:** High school diploma required; GED accepted **Scholarships:** Available **Calendar System:** Semester, Summer Session Available **Faculty:** FT 63, PT 207 **Student-Faculty Ratio:** 16:1 **Exams:** ACT. **% Residing in College-Owned, -Operated, or -Affiliated Housing:** 5 **Regional Accreditation:** North Central Association of Colleges and Schools **Credit Hours For Degree:** 64 credit hours, Associates **ROTC:** Army, Navy, Air Force **Professional Accreditation:** AAMAE, AOTA, CARC, JRCEMT, NLN

INSTITUTE OF AMERICAN INDIAN ARTS
83 Avan Nu Po Rd.
Santa Fe, NM 87508
Tel: (505)424-2300
Admissions: (505)424-2328
Fax: (505)424-0505
Web Site: http://www.iaia.edu/
Admissions: Myra Garro
Financial Aid: Lala M. Gallegos
Type: Two-Year College **Sex:** Coed **Admission Plans:** Deferred Admission **Application Deadline:** April 15 **Application Fee:** $5.00 **H.S. Requirements:** High school diploma required; GED accepted **Scholarships:** Available **Calendar System:** Semester, Summer Session Not available **Library Holdings:** 15,200 **Regional Accreditation:** North Central Association of Colleges and Schools **Credit Hours For Degree:** 65 credits, Associates **Professional Accreditation:** NASAD

ITT TECHNICAL INSTITUTE
5100 Masthead, NE
Albuquerque, NM 87109-4366
Tel: (505)828-1114
Fax: (505)828-1849
Web Site: http://www.itt-tech.edu/
President/CEO: Michael Roane
Type: Two-Year College **Sex:** Coed **Affiliation:** ITT Educational Services, Inc. **H.S. Requirements:** High school diploma required; GED accepted **Scholarships:** Available **Calendar System:** Quarter, Summer Session Not available **Professional Accreditation:** ACICS

LUNA COMMUNITY COLLEGE
PO Box 1510
Las Vegas, NM 87701
Tel: (505)454-2500; Free: 800-588-7232
E-mail: hgriego@luna.cc.nm.us
Web Site: http://www.luna.edu/
President/CEO: Dr. Pete Campos
Admissions: Henrietta Griego
Type: Two-Year College **Sex:** Coed **Admission Plans:** Open Admission **H.S. Requirements:** High school diploma required; GED accepted **Scholarships:** Available **Calendar System:** Semester **Enrollment:** FT 544, PT 1,245 **Library Holdings:** 37,343 **Regional Accreditation:** North Central Association of Colleges and Schools **Credit Hours For Degree:** 66 credit hours, Associates

MESALANDS COMMUNITY COLLEGE
911 South Tenth St.
Tucumcari, NM 88401
Tel: (505)461-4413
Admissions: (575)461-4413
Fax: (505)461-1901
Web Site: http://www.mesalands.edu/
President/CEO: Phillip Barry
Admissions: Ken Brashear
Type: Two-Year College **Sex:** Coed **Application Deadline:** Rolling **Calendar System:** Semester **Regional Accreditation:** North Central Association of Colleges and Schools

NATIONAL AMERICAN UNIVERSITY (ALBUQUERQUE)
4775 Indian School, NE, Ste. 200
Albuquerque, NM 87110
Tel: (505)265-7517; Free: 800-843-8892
Admissions: (505)348-3700
Fax: (505)265-7542
E-mail: albadmissions@national.edu
Web Site: http://www.national.edu/
President/CEO: Dr. Jerry Gallentine
Type: Four-Year College **Sex:** Coed **Admission Plans:** Open Admission **Application Deadline:** Rolling **Application Fee:** $25.00 **H.S. Requirements:** High school diploma required; GED accepted **Scholarships:** Available **Calendar System:** Quarter, Summer Session Available **Regional Accreditation:** North Central Association of Colleges and Schools **Credit Hours For Degree:** 192 credits, Bachelors

NATIONAL AMERICAN UNIVERSITY (RIO RANCHO)
1601 Rio Rancho
Ste. 200
Rio Rancho, NM 87124

Tel: (505)348-3750
Web Site: http://www.national.edu/
President/CEO: Dr. Jerry Gallentine
Type: Two-Year College **Sex:** Coed **Application Fee:** $25.00 **Regional Accreditation:** North Central Association of Colleges and Schools

NATIONAL COLLEGE OF MIDWIFERY
209 State Rd. 240
Taos, NM 87571
Tel: (505)758-8914
Fax: (505)758-0302
E-mail: info@midwiferycollege.org
Web Site: http://www.midwiferycollege.org/
Admissions: Beth Enson
Type: Comprehensive **Sex:** Women **Calendar System:** Trimester **Professional Accreditation:** MEAC

NAVAJO TECHNICAL COLLEGE
PO Box 849
Crownpoint, NM 87313
Tel: (505)786-4100
Fax: (505)786-5644
Web Site: http://www.navajotech.edu/
President/CEO: Dr. Elmer Guy
Type: Two-Year College **Sex:** Coed **Admission Plans:** Open Admission **Costs Per Year:** Tuition: $960 full-time, $40 per credit hour part-time. Mandatory fees: $120 full-time. Tuition is $860 year, $40 per credit hour for enrolled tribal members; $1920 year, $80 per credit for students not members of federally recognized tribes. **Calendar System:** Semester **Regional Accreditation:** North Central Association of Colleges and Schools

NEW MEXICO HIGHLANDS UNIVERSITY
PO Box 9000
Las Vegas, NM 87701
Tel: (505)454-3000; Free: 800-338-6648
Admissions: (505)454-3566
Fax: (505)454-3311
E-mail: judycordova@nmhu.edu
Web Site: http://www.nmhu.edu/
President/CEO: Dr. James Fries
Admissions: Judy Cordova
Financial Aid: Eileen Sedillo
Type: Comprehensive **Sex:** Coed **Scores:** 47% ACT 18-23; 5% ACT 24-29 **% Accepted:** 56 **Admission Plans:** Open Admission; Early Admission; Deferred Admission **Application Deadline:** Rolling **Application Fee:** $15.00 **H.S. Requirements:** High school diploma required; GED accepted **Costs Per Year:** Application fee: $15. State resident tuition: $2741 full-time, $114 per credit hour part-time. Nonresident tuition: $4308 full-time, $180 per credit hour part-time. Full-time tuition varies according to course load and location. Part-time tuition varies according to course load and location. College room and board: $5967. College room only: $2612. Room and board charges vary according to board plan and housing facility. **Scholarships:** Available **Calendar System:** Semester, Summer Session Available **Enrollment:** FT 1,634, PT 624, Grad FT 591, Grad PT 935 **Faculty:** FT 146 **Student-Faculty Ratio:** 15:1 **Exams:** Other, SAT I or ACT. ACT essay used for advising. ACT essay used for placement. **% Receiving Financial Aid:** 66 **% Residing in College-Owned, -Operated, or -Affiliated Housing:** 16 **Library Holdings:** 436,742 **Regional Accreditation:** North Central Association of Colleges and Schools **Credit Hours For Degree:** 64 semester hours, Associates; 128 semester hours, Bachelors **Professional Accreditation:** ACBSP, CSWE, NCATE **Intercollegiate Athletics:** Baseball M; Basketball M & W; Cross-Country Running M & W; Football M; Soccer W; Softball W; Track and Field M & W; Volleyball W

NEW MEXICO INSTITUTE OF MINING AND TECHNOLOGY
801 Leroy Place
Socorro, NM 87801
Tel: (505)835-5011; Free: 800-428-TECH
Admissions: (575)835-5424
Fax: (505)835-5989
E-mail: admission@admin.nmt.edu
Web Site: http://www.nmt.edu/
President/CEO: Dr. Daniel H. Lopez
Admissions: Mike Kloeppel
Financial Aid: Annette Kaus
Type: University **Sex:** Coed **Scores:** 99% SAT V 400+; 100% SAT M 400+; 32% ACT 18-23; 53% ACT 24-29 **% Accepted:** 79 **Admission Plans:** Deferred Admission **Application Deadline:** August 1 **Application Fee:** $15.00 **H.S. Requirements:** High school diploma required; GED accepted **Costs Per Year:** Application fee: $15. State resident tuition: $3980 full-time, $166 per credit hour part-time. Nonresident tuition: $12,941 full-time, $539 per credit hour part-time. Mandatory fees: $627 full-time. Part-time tuition varies according to course load. College room and board: $5702. Room and board charges vary according to board plan and housing facility. **Scholarships:** Available **Calendar System:** Semester, Summer Session Available **Enrollment:** FT 1,095, PT 227, Grad FT 267, Grad PT 308 **Faculty:** FT 124, PT 29 **Student-Faculty Ratio:** 11:1 **Exams:** ACT, SAT I or ACT. ACT essay not being used. SAT essay not being used. **% Receiving Financial Aid:** 44 **% Residing in College-Owned, -Operated, or -Affiliated Housing:** 49 **Final Year or Final Semester Residency Requirement:** Yes **Library Holdings:** 321,829 **Regional Accreditation:** North Central Association of Colleges and Schools **Credit Hours For Degree:** 65 credit hours, Associates; 130 credit hours, Bachelors **Professional Accreditation:** ABET **Intercollegiate Athletics:** Golf M & W; Rugby M & W; Soccer M & W

NEW MEXICO JUNIOR COLLEGE
5317 Lovington Hwy.
Hobbs, NM 88240-9123
Tel: (505)392-4510
Admissions: (505)492-2787
Fax: (505)392-2527
Web Site: http://www.nmjc.edu/
President/CEO: Steve McCleery
Admissions: Robert Bensing
Type: Two-Year College **Sex:** Coed **Affiliation:** New Mexico Commission on Higher Education **Admission Plans:** Open Admission; Early Admission; Deferred Admission **Application Deadline:** Rolling **Application Fee:** $0.00 **H.S. Requirements:** High school diploma or equivalent not required. For automotive technology, medical laboratory technology, nursing programs: High school diploma required; GED accepted **Costs Per Year:** Application fee: $0. Area resident tuition: $696 full-time, $29 per credit hour part-time. State resident tuition: $1128 full-time, $47 per credit hour part-time. Nonresident tuition: $1248 full-time, $52 per credit hour part-time. Mandatory fees: $360 full-time, $15 per credit hour part-time. Full-time tuition and fees vary according to course load and program. Part-time tuition and fees vary according to course load and program. College room and board: $4800. College room only: $2400. Room and board charges vary according to board plan and housing facility. **Scholarships:** Available **Calendar System:** Semester, Summer Session Available **Faculty:** FT 65, PT 55 **Student-Faculty Ratio:** 19:1 **% Residing in College-Owned, -Operated, or -Affiliated Housing:** 15 **Library Holdings:** 118,500 **Regional Accreditation:** North Central Association of Colleges and Schools **Credit Hours For Degree:** 64 semester hours, Associates **Professional Accreditation:** NLN **Intercollegiate Athletics:** Baseball M; Basketball M & W; Golf M

NEW MEXICO MILITARY INSTITUTE
101 West College Blvd.
Roswell, NM 88201-5173
Tel: (505)622-6250; Free: 800-421-5376
Fax: (505)624-8067
E-mail: admissions@nmmi.edu
Web Site: http://www.nmmi.edu/
President/CEO: MG Jerry Grizzle
Financial Aid: Sonya Rodriguez
Type: Two-Year College **Sex:** Coed **Affiliation:** New Mexico Commission on Higher Education **% Accepted:** 62 **Admission Plans:** Preferred Admission; Early Admission; Deferred Admission **Application Deadline:** August 1 **Application Fee:** $60.00 **H.S. Requirements:** High school diploma required; GED accepted **Scholarships:** Available **Calendar System:** Semester, Summer Session Available **Enrollment:** FT 480 **Faculty:** FT 65, PT 0 **Student-Faculty Ratio:** 17:1 **Exams:** SAT I or ACT. **% Residing in College-Owned, -Operated, or -Affiliated Housing:** 100 **Library Holdings:** 65,000 **Regional Accreditation:** North Central Association of Colleges and Schools **Credit Hours For Degree:** 68 hours, Associates **ROTC:** Army **Intercollegiate Athletics:** Baseball M; Basketball M; Fencing M & W; Football M; Golf M; Riflery M & W; Tennis M & W; Track and Field M; Volleyball W

NEW MEXICO STATE UNIVERSITY
PO Box 30001
Las Cruces, NM 88003-8001

Tel: (575)646-0111; Free: 800-662-6678
Admissions: (575)646-3121
E-mail: admssions@nmsu.edu
Web Site: http://www.nmsu.edu/
President/CEO: Dr. Barbara Couture
Admissions: Valerie Pickett
Financial Aid: Michael Zimmerman
Type: University **Sex:** Coed **Affiliation:** New Mexico State University System **Scores:** 84% SAT V 400+; 85% SAT M 400+; 51% ACT 18-23; 22% ACT 24-29 **% Accepted:** 96 **Admission Plans:** Early Admission; Deferred Admission **Application Deadline:** August 19 **Application Fee:** $20.00 **H.S. Requirements:** High school diploma required; GED accepted **Costs Per Year:** Application fee: $20. State resident tuition: $3720 full-time, $208.25 per credit hour part-time. Nonresident tuition: $13,872 full-time, $631.25 per credit hour part-time. Mandatory fees: $1278 full-time. College room and board: $6338. College room only: $3628. Room and board charges vary according to board plan and housing facility. **Scholarships:** Available **Calendar System:** Semester, Summer Session Available **Enrollment:** FT 12,621, PT 2,077, Grad FT 2,047, Grad PT 1,752 **Faculty:** FT 699, PT 324 **Student-Faculty Ratio:** 20:1 **Exams:** SAT I or ACT. **% Receiving Financial Aid:** 56 **% Residing in College-Owned, -Operated, or -Affiliated Housing:** 18 **Library Holdings:** 1,799,043 **Regional Accreditation:** North Central Association of Colleges and Schools **Credit Hours For Degree:** 66 credits, Associates; 128 credits, Bachelors **ROTC:** Army, Air Force **Professional Accreditation:** AACSB, ABET, ACEJMC, AACN, AAFCS, ACA, APA, ASLHA, CEPH, CSWE, JRCEPAT, NASM, NASPAA, NCATE **Intercollegiate Athletics:** Baseball M; Basketball M & W; Cross-Country Running M & W; Equestrian Sports M & W; Football M; Golf M & W; Softball W; Swimming and Diving W; Tennis M & W; Track and Field W; Volleyball W

NEW MEXICO STATE UNIVERSITY—ALAMOGORDO

2400 North Scenic Dr.
Alamogordo, NM 88311-0477
Tel: (505)439-3600
Admissions: (505)439-3700
E-mail: advisor@nmsua.nmsu.edu
Web Site: http://nmsua.edu/
President/CEO: Dr. Cheri Jimeno
Admissions: Kathy Fuller
Type: Two-Year College **Sex:** Coed **Affiliation:** New Mexico State University System **Admission Plans:** Open Admission; Early Admission; Deferred Admission **Application Deadline:** Rolling **Application Fee:** $15.00 **H.S. Requirements:** High school diploma required; GED accepted **Costs Per Year:** Application fee: $15. Area resident tuition: $1512 full-time, $63 per credit hour part-time. State resident tuition: $1728 full-time, $72 per credit hour part-time. Nonresident tuition: $4176 full-time, $174 per credit hour part-time. Mandatory fees: $48 full-time, $2 per credit hour part-time. **Scholarships:** Available **Calendar System:** Semester, Summer Session Available **Enrollment:** FT 801, PT 2,436 **Faculty:** FT 51, PT 49 **Student-Faculty Ratio:** 29:1 **Library Holdings:** 39,000 **Regional Accreditation:** North Central Association of Colleges and Schools **Credit Hours For Degree:** 66 credits, Associates **Professional Accreditation:** NAACLS, NLN

NEW MEXICO STATE UNIVERSITY—CARLSBAD

1500 University Dr.
Carlsbad, NM 88220-3509
Tel: (575)234-9200
Admissions: (575)234-9222
E-mail: eshannon@nmsu.edu
Web Site: http://www.cavern.nmsu.edu/
President/CEO: Russell Hardy
Admissions: Everal Shannon
Type: Two-Year College **Sex:** Coed **Affiliation:** New Mexico State University System **Scores:** 41% ACT 18-23; 2% ACT 24-29 **% Accepted:** 100 **Admission Plans:** Open Admission; Early Admission **Application Deadline:** Rolling **Application Fee:** $20.00 **H.S. Requirements:** High school diploma required; GED accepted **Costs Per Year:** Application fee: $20. One-time mandatory fee: $15. Area resident tuition: $864 full-time, $36 per credit hour part-time. State resident tuition: $1320 full-time, $55 per credit hour part-time. Nonresident tuition: $2712 full-time, $113 per credit hour part-time. Mandatory fees: $100 full-time. **Scholarships:** Available **Calendar System:** Semester, Summer Session Available **Enrollment:** FT 583, PT 1,415 **Faculty:** FT 41, PT 50 **Library Holdings:** 25,890 **Regional Accreditation:** North Central Association of Colleges and Schools **Credit Hours For Degree:** 66 credit hours, Associates **Professional Accreditation:** NLN

NEW MEXICO STATE UNIVERSITY—GRANTS

1500 3rd St.
Grants, NM 87020-2025
Tel: (505)287-7981
Web Site: http://grants.nmsu.edu/
President/CEO: Felicia Casados
Admissions: Irene Lutz
Type: Two-Year College **Sex:** Coed **Affiliation:** New Mexico State University System **Admission Plans:** Open Admission; Early Admission **Application Deadline:** July 30 **Application Fee:** $15.00 **H.S. Requirements:** High school diploma required; GED accepted **Scholarships:** Available **Calendar System:** Semester, Summer Session Available **Exams:** Other. **Library Holdings:** 30,000 **Regional Accreditation:** North Central Association of Colleges and Schools **Credit Hours For Degree:** 66 credits, Associates

NORTHERN NEW MEXICO COLLEGE

921 Paseo de Oñate
Española, NM 87532
Tel: (505)747-2100
Admissions: (505)747-2193
E-mail: dms@nnmc.edu
Web Site: http://www.nnmc.edu/
President/CEO: Dr. Jose Griego
Admissions: Mike L. Costello
Type: Two-Year College **Sex:** Coed **% Accepted:** 100 **Admission Plans:** Open Admission; Early Admission; Deferred Admission **Application Deadline:** Rolling **Application Fee:** $0.00 **H.S. Requirements:** High school diploma required; GED accepted **Scholarships:** Available **Calendar System:** Semester, Summer Session Available **Faculty:** FT 45, PT 208 **% Residing in College-Owned, -Operated, or -Affiliated Housing:** 1 **Library Holdings:** 18,065 **Regional Accreditation:** North Central Association of Colleges and Schools **Credit Hours For Degree:** 64 credits, Associates **Professional Accreditation:** ACBSP, JRCERT

PIMA MEDICAL INSTITUTE

2201 San Pedro NE
Bldg. 3, Ste. 100
Albuquerque, NM 87110
Tel: (505)881-1234; Free: 888-898-9048
Fax: (505)884-8371
Web Site: http://www.pmi.edu/
President/CEO: Holly Woelber
Type: Two-Year College **Sex:** Coed **Affiliation:** Vocational Training Institutes, Inc. **Admission Plans:** Early Admission **Application Fee:** $0.00 **H.S. Requirements:** High school diploma required; GED accepted **Scholarships:** Available **Calendar System:** Miscellaneous, Summer Session Not available **Exams:** Other. **Credit Hours For Degree:** 88.5 credits, Associates **Professional Accreditation:** ABHES, JRCERT

ST. JOHN'S COLLEGE

1160 Camino Cruz Blanca
Santa Fe, NM 87505
Tel: (505)984-6000; Free: 800-331-5232
Admissions: (505)984-6060
E-mail: admissions@sjcsf.edu
Web Site: http://www.stjohnscollege.edu/
President/CEO: Michael P. Peters
Admissions: Larry Clendenin
Financial Aid: Michael Rodriguez
Type: Comprehensive **Sex:** Coed **Affiliation:** St. John's College (MD) **Scores:** 100% SAT V 400+; 100% SAT M 400+; 20% ACT 18-23; 51% ACT 24-29 **% Accepted:** 81 **Admission Plans:** Early Admission; Deferred Admission **Application Deadline:** Rolling **Application Fee:** $0.00 **H.S. Requirements:** High school diploma required; GED accepted **Costs Per Year:** Application fee: $0. Comprehensive fee: $49,954 includes full-time tuition ($39,992), mandatory fees ($400), and college room and board ($9562). College room only: $4781. **Scholarships:** Available **Calendar System:** Semester, Summer Session Available **Enrollment:** FT 428, PT 3 **Faculty:** FT 68, PT 1 **Student-Faculty Ratio:** 7:1 **Exams:** SAT I. **% Receiving Financial Aid:** 64 **% Residing in College-Owned, -Operated, or -Affiliated Housing:** 72 **Library Holdings:** 65,104 **Regional Accreditation:**

North Central Association of Colleges and Schools **Credit Hours For Degree:** 132 credits, Bachelors **Intercollegiate Athletics:** Fencing M & W

SAN JUAN COLLEGE
4601 College Blvd.
Farmington, NM 87402-4699
Tel: (505)326-3311
Admissions: (505)566-3300
Fax: (505)599-3385
E-mail: mastons@sanjuancollege.edu
Web Site: http://www.sanjuancollege.edu/
President/CEO: Dr. Carol J. Spencer
Admissions: Skylar Maston
Type: Two-Year College **Sex:** Coed **Affiliation:** New Mexico Higher Education Department **% Accepted:** 100 **Admission Plans:** Open Admission; Early Admission; Deferred Admission **Application Deadline:** Rolling **Application Fee:** $0.00 **H.S. Requirements:** High school diploma required; GED accepted **Costs Per Year:** Application fee: $0. State resident tuition: $1110 full-time, $37 per credit hour part-time. Nonresident tuition: $2730 full-time, $91 per credit hour part-time. Mandatory fees: $180 full-time, $6 per credit hour part-time. Full-time tuition and fees vary according to reciprocity agreements. **Scholarships:** Available **Calendar System:** Semester, Summer Session Available **Enrollment:** FT 3,028, PT 5,962 **Faculty:** FT 145, PT 304 **Student-Faculty Ratio:** 24:1 **Library Holdings:** 81,116 **Regional Accreditation:** North Central Association of Colleges and Schools **Credit Hours For Degree:** 63 credits, Associates **Professional Accreditation:** ABET, ADA, AHIMA, APTA, ACBSP, NLN

SANTA FE COMMUNITY COLLEGE
6401 Richards Ave.
Santa Fe, NM 87508
Tel: (505)428-1000
Admissions: (505)428-1604
Fax: (505)428-1237
E-mail: restrada@sfccnm.edu
Web Site: http://www.sfccnm.edu/
President/CEO: Dr. Sheila Ortego
Admissions: Rebecca Estrada
Type: Two-Year College **Sex:** Coed **Admission Plans:** Open Admission; Early Admission; Deferred Admission **Application Deadline:** Rolling **Application Fee:** $0.00 **H.S. Requirements:** High school diploma required; GED accepted **Costs Per Year:** Application fee: $0. Area resident tuition: $969 full-time, $32.30 per credit part-time. State resident tuition: $1290 full-time, $43 per credit part-time. Nonresident tuition: $2325 full-time, $77.50 per credit part-time. Mandatory fees: $144 full-time, $4.80 per credit part-time. **Scholarships:** Available **Calendar System:** Semester, Summer Session Available **Enrollment:** FT 889, PT 3,085 **Faculty:** FT 59, PT 257 **Student-Faculty Ratio:** 13:1 **Library Holdings:** 38,226 **Regional Accreditation:** North Central Association of Colleges and Schools **Credit Hours For Degree:** 64 credits, Associates **Professional Accreditation:** ADA, NLN

SOUTHWESTERN INDIAN POLYTECHNIC INSTITUTE
9169 Coors, NW, Box 10146
Albuquerque, NM 87184-0146
Tel: (505)346-2347
Admissions: (505)346-2324
Fax: (505)346-2343
E-mail: jcarpio@sipi.bia.edu
Web Site: http://www.sipi.edu/
President/CEO: Dr. Sherry R. Allison
Admissions: Joseph M. Carpio
Type: Two-Year College **Sex:** Coed **Admission Plans:** Preferred Admission **Application Deadline:** July 30 **Application Fee:** $0.00 **H.S. Requirements:** High school diploma required; GED accepted **Costs Per Year:** Application fee: $0. State resident tuition: $675 full-time. Nonresident tuition: $675 full-time. Mandatory fees: $150 per term part-time. Part-time fees vary according to course load. College room and board: $165. Students attending SIPI are required to be registered member of federally recognized Indian Tribes. **Scholarships:** Available **Calendar System:** Trimester, Summer Session Available **Enrollment:** FT 502, PT 133 **Faculty:** FT 17, PT 31 **Student-Faculty Ratio:** 15:1 **% Residing in College-Owned, -Operated, or -Affiliated Housing:** 60 **Final Year or Final Semester Residency Requirement:** No **Library Holdings:** 26,000 **Regional Accreditation:** North Central Association of Colleges and Schools **Credit Hours For Degree:** 64 credit hours, Associates **Professional Accreditation:** COptA

UNIVERSITY OF NEW MEXICO
Albuquerque, NM 87131-2039
Tel: (505)277-0111
Admissions: (505)277-8900
Fax: (505)277-6686
E-mail: apply@unm.edu
Web Site: http://www.unm.edu/
President/CEO: Dr. David J. Schmidly
Admissions: Kathleen Roberts
Type: University **Sex:** Coed **Scores:** 94% SAT V 400+; 95% SAT M 400+; 51% ACT 18-23; 30% ACT 24-29 **% Accepted:** 62 **Admission Plans:** Early Admission; Deferred Admission **Application Deadline:** Rolling **Application Fee:** $20.00 **H.S. Requirements:** High school diploma required; GED accepted **Costs Per Year:** Application fee: $20. State resident tuition: $5101 full-time, $212.55 per credit hour part-time. Nonresident tuition: $17,253 full-time, $718.90 per credit hour part-time. Part-time tuition varies according to course load. College room and board: $7778. College room only: $4554. Room and board charges vary according to board plan and housing facility. **Scholarships:** Available **Calendar System:** Semester, Summer Session Available **Enrollment:** FT 16,050, PT 5,282, Grad FT 3,388, Grad PT 2,521 **Faculty:** FT 957, PT 524 **Student-Faculty Ratio:** 19:1 **Exams:** SAT I or ACT. **% Receiving Financial Aid:** 48 **Library Holdings:** 3,117,590 **Regional Accreditation:** North Central Association of Colleges and Schools **Credit Hours For Degree:** 60 semester hours, Associates; 128 semester hours, Bachelors **ROTC:** Army, Navy, Air Force **Professional Accreditation:** AACSB, ABET, ACPhE, AACN, AAFCS, ABA, ACNM, ACCE, ACA, ADA, ADtA, ACSP, AOTA, APTA, APA, ASLA, ASLHA, AALS, CEPH, JRCEMT JRCEPAT, LCMEAMA, NAACLS, NAAB, NASD, NASM, NASPAA, NAST, NCATE **Intercollegiate Athletics:** Baseball M; Basketball M & W; Cross-Country Running M & W; Football M; Golf M & W; Skiing (Cross-Country) M & W; Skiing (Downhill) M & W; Soccer M & W; Softball W; Swimming and Diving W; Tennis M & W; Track and Field M & W; Volleyball W

UNIVERSITY OF NEW MEXICO—GALLUP
200 College Rd.
Gallup, NM 87301-5603
Tel: (505)863-7500
Fax: (505)863-7532
Web Site: http://www.gallup.unm.edu/
President/CEO: Dr. Sylvia Rodriquez-Andrew
Admissions: Pearl A. Morris
Type: Two-Year College **Sex:** Coed **Affiliation:** New Mexico Commission on Higher Education **Admission Plans:** Open Admission; Early Admission **Application Deadline:** Rolling **Application Fee:** $15.00 **H.S. Requirements:** High school diploma required; GED accepted **Costs Per Year:** Application fee: $15. State resident tuition: $60.90 per credit hour part-time. Nonresident tuition: $133.90 per credit hour part-time. Part-time tuition varies according to course load, degree level, and location. **Scholarships:** Available **Calendar System:** Semester, Summer Session Available **Faculty:** FT 75, PT 84 **Student-Faculty Ratio:** 25:1 **Exams:** ACT, SAT I. **Library Holdings:** 36,172 **Regional Accreditation:** North Central Association of Colleges and Schools **Credit Hours For Degree:** 60 credit hours, Associates; 136 credit hours, Bachelors **Professional Accreditation:** ADA, AHIMA, NAACLS, NLN

UNIVERSITY OF NEW MEXICO—LOS ALAMOS BRANCH
4000 University Dr.
Los Alamos, NM 87544-2233
Tel: (505)662-5919
E-mail: aapodaca@la.unm.edu
Web Site: http://www.la.unm.edu/
President/CEO: Cedric D. Page
Admissions: Anna Mae Apodaca
Type: Two-Year College **Sex:** Coed **Affiliation:** New Mexico Commission on Higher Education **% Accepted:** 100 **Admission Plans:** Open Admission; Early Admission; Deferred Admission **Application Deadline:** August 12 **Application Fee:** $15.00 **H.S. Requirements:** High school diploma required; GED accepted **Costs Per Year:** Application fee: $15. State resident tuition: $49 per credit hour part-time. Nonresident tuition: $141 per credit hour part-time. Mandatory fees: $54 per term part-time. Part-time tuition and fees vary according to course load. College room and board: $2786. College room only: $1913. Room and board charges vary according to housing facility.

Scholarships: Available **Calendar System:** Semester, Summer Session Available **Faculty:** FT 0, PT 96 **Library Holdings:** 10,000 **Regional Accreditation:** North Central Association of Colleges and Schools **Credit Hours For Degree:** 64 semester hours, Associates

UNIVERSITY OF NEW MEXICO—TAOS
115 Civic Plaza Dr.
Taos, NM 87571
Tel: (575)737-6200
Web Site: http://taos.unm.edu/
President/CEO: Dr. Catherine M. O'Neill
Type: Two-Year College **Sex:** Coed **Application Fee:** $15.00 **Calendar System:** Semester **Regional Accreditation:** North Central Association of Colleges and Schools

UNIVERSITY OF NEW MEXICO—VALENCIA CAMPUS
280 La Entrada
Los Lunas, NM 87031-7633
Tel: (505)925-8580
Admissions: (505)925-8500
Fax: (505)925-8563
Web Site: http://www.unm.edu/~unmvc/
President/CEO: Alice V. Letteney, PhD
Admissions: Lucy Sanchez
Type: Two-Year College **Sex:** Coed **Affiliation:** New Mexico Commission on Higher Education **Admission Plans:** Open Admission; Early Admission; Deferred Admission **Application Deadline:** Rolling **Application Fee:** $15.00 **H.S. Requirements:** High school diploma required; GED accepted **Scholarships:** Available **Calendar System:** Semester, Summer Session Available **Faculty:** FT 19, PT 74 **Library Holdings:** 9,500 **Regional Accreditation:** North Central Association of Colleges and Schools **Credit Hours For Degree:** 60 credit hours, Associates

UNIVERSITY OF PHOENIX—NEW MEXICO CAMPUS
5700 Pasadena NE
Albuquerque, NM 87113-1570
Tel: (505)821-4800; Free: 800-228-7240
Admissions: (480)557-6151
E-mail: audra.mcquarie@phoenix.edu
Web Site: http://www.phoenix.edu/
President/CEO: William Pepicello
Admissions: Audra McQuarie
Type: Comprehensive **Sex:** Coed **Admission Plans:** Open Admission; Deferred Admission **Application Deadline:** Rolling **Application Fee:** $0.00 **H.S. Requirements:** High school diploma required; GED accepted **Costs Per Year:** Application fee: $0. Tuition: $10,950 full-time. Full-time tuition varies according to course level and course load. **Scholarships:** Available **Calendar System:** Continuous, Summer Session Not available **Enrollment:** FT 3,452 **Faculty:** FT 45, PT 382 **Regional Accreditation:** North Central Association of Colleges and Schools **Credit Hours For Degree:** 60 credits, Associates; 120 credits, Bachelors **Professional Accreditation:** NLN

UNIVERSITY OF THE SOUTHWEST
6610 Lovington Hwy.
Hobbs, NM 88240-9129
Tel: (575)392-6561; Free: 800-530-4400
Admissions: (575)392-6563
E-mail: ataylor@usw.edu
Web Site: http://www.usw.edu/
President/CEO: Dr. Gary A. Dill
Admissions: Ashley Taylor
Financial Aid: Kerrie Mitchell
Type: Comprehensive **Sex:** Coed **Scores:** 81% SAT V 400+; 91% SAT M 400+; 54% ACT 18-23; 9% ACT 24-29 **% Accepted:** 91 **Admission Plans:** Early Admission; Deferred Admission **Application Deadline:** Rolling **Application Fee:** $25.00 **H.S. Requirements:** High school diploma required; GED accepted **Costs Per Year:** Application fee: $25. Tuition: $11,664 full-time, $486 per semester hour part-time. Full-time tuition varies according to course load. Part-time tuition varies according to course load. College room only: $3370. Room charges vary according to housing facility. **Scholarships:** Available **Calendar System:** Semester, Summer Session Available **Enrollment:** FT 266, PT 51, Grad FT 112, Grad PT 99 **Faculty:** FT 15, PT 43 **Student-Faculty Ratio:** 10:1 **Exams:** SAT I or ACT. **% Receiving Financial Aid:** 86 **% Residing in College-Owned, -Operated, or -Affiliated Housing:** 48 **Library Holdings:** 76,869 **Regional Accreditation:** North Central Association of Colleges and Schools **Credit Hours For Degree:** 120 semester hours, Bachelors **Intercollegiate Athletics:** Baseball M; Basketball M & W; Cross-Country Running M & W; Golf M & W; Soccer M & W; Softball W; Tennis M & W; Track and Field M & W

WESTERN NEW MEXICO UNIVERSITY
PO Box 680
Silver City, NM 88062-0680
Tel: (505)538-6336
Admissions: (505)538-6106
Fax: (505)538-6155
E-mail: tresslerd@wnmu.edu
Web Site: http://www.wnmu.edu/
President/CEO: Dr. John E. Counts
Admissions: Dan Tressler
Financial Aid: Debra Reyes
Type: Comprehensive **Sex:** Coed **Scores:** 43% ACT 18-23; 5% ACT 24-29 **% Accepted:** 100 **Admission Plans:** Open Admission; Early Admission; Deferred Admission **Application Deadline:** August 1 **Application Fee:** $0.00 **H.S. Requirements:** High school diploma required; GED accepted **Costs Per Year:** Application fee: $0. State resident tuition: $2616 full-time. Nonresident tuition: $11,832 full-time. Mandatory fees: $973 full-time. Full-time tuition and fees vary according to course load, location, and reciprocity agreements. College room and board: $5200. College room only: $2000. Room and board charges vary according to board plan and housing facility. **Scholarships:** Available **Calendar System:** Semester, Summer Session Available **Enrollment:** FT 1,363, PT 856 **Faculty:** FT 128, PT 131 **Student-Faculty Ratio:** 17:1 **Exams:** ACT. **% Receiving Financial Aid:** 76 **Library Holdings:** 245,146 **Regional Accreditation:** North Central Association of Colleges and Schools **Credit Hours For Degree:** 64 credit hours, Associates; 128 credit hours, Bachelors **Professional Accreditation:** AOTA, ACBSP, CSWE, NCATE, NLN **Intercollegiate Athletics:** Basketball M & W; Cheerleading M & W; Cross-Country Running M & W; Football M; Golf M & W; Rock Climbing M & W; Softball W; Tennis M & W; Volleyball W

ADELPHI UNIVERSITY
One South Ave.
PO Box 701
Garden City, NY 11530-0701
Tel: (516)877-3000; Free: 800-ADE-LPHI
Admissions: (516)877-3050
Fax: (516)877-3039
E-mail: admissions@adelphi.edu
Web Site: http://www.adelphi.edu/
President/CEO: Dr. Robert A. Scott
Admissions: Christine Murphy
Financial Aid: Sheryl Mihopulos
Type: University **Sex:** Coed **Scores:** 99.48% SAT V 400+; 99% SAT M 400+; 53.64% ACT 18-23; 41.72% ACT 24-29 **% Accepted:** 70 **Admission Plans:** Early Action; Deferred Admission **Application Deadline:** Rolling **Application Fee:** $35.00 **H.S. Requirements:** High school diploma required; GED accepted **Costs Per Year:** Application fee: $35. Tuition: $780 per credit hour part-time. Part-time tuition varies according to course level, location, and program. **Scholarships:** Available **Calendar System:** Semester, Summer Session Available **Enrollment:** FT 4,300, PT 654, Grad FT 981, Grad PT 2,016 **Faculty:** FT 308, PT 585 **Student-Faculty Ratio:** 9:1 **Exams:** SAT I or ACT. ACT essay used for admission. SAT essay used for admission. **% Receiving Financial Aid:** 61 **% Residing in College-Owned, -Operated, or -Affiliated Housing:** 23 **Library Holdings:** 593,920 **Regional Accreditation:** Middle State Association of Colleges and Schools **Credit Hours For Degree:** 120 credits, Bachelors **ROTC:** Army, Air Force **Professional Accreditation:** AACSB, AACN, APA, ASLHA, CSWE, NCATE, NLN **Intercollegiate Athletics:** Baseball M; Basketball M & W; Bowling W; Cross-Country Running M & W; Field Hockey W; Golf M; Lacrosse M & W; Soccer M & W; Softball W; Swimming and Diving M & W; Tennis M & W; Track and Field M & W; Volleyball W

ADIRONDACK COMMUNITY COLLEGE
640 Bay Rd.
Queensbury, NY 12804
Tel: (518)743-2200
Fax: (518)745-1433
Web Site: http://www.sunyacc.edu/
President/CEO: Dr. Ronald C. Heacock
Type: Two-Year College **Sex:** Coed **Affiliation:** State University of New York System **Admission Plans:** Open Admission **Application Fee:** $40.00 **H.S. Requirements:** High school diploma required; GED accepted **Costs Per Year:** Application fee: $40. State resident tuition: $3256 full-time, $136 per credit hour part-time. Nonresident tuition: $6512 full-time, $272 per credit hour part-time. Mandatory fees: $254 full-time, $8.75 per credit hour part-time. Full-time tuition and fees vary according to course load. Part-time tuition and fees vary according to course load. **Scholarships:** Available **Calendar System:** Semester, Summer Session Available **Library Holdings:** 65,000 **Regional Accreditation:** Middle State Association of Colleges and Schools **Credit Hours For Degree:** 64 credit hours, Associates **Professional Accreditation:** AHIMA, NLN **Intercollegiate Athletics:** Baseball M; Basketball M & W; Bowling M; Golf M; Soccer M; Softball W; Tennis M; Volleyball W

ALBANY COLLEGE OF PHARMACY AND HEALTH SCIENCES
106 New Scotland Ave.
Albany, NY 12208
Tel: (518)445-7200; Free: 888-203-8010
Admissions: (518)694-7221
Fax: (518)445-7202
E-mail: admissions@acphs.edu
Web Site: http://www.acphs.edu/
President/CEO: James Gozzo, PhD
Admissions: Matthew Stever
Financial Aid: Tiffany M. Gutierrez
Type: Comprehensive **Sex:** Coed **Scores:** 100% SAT V 400+; 100% SAT M 400+; 12% ACT 18-23; 70% ACT 24-29 **% Accepted:** 66 **Admission Plans:** Early Decision Plan; Deferred Admission **Application Deadline:** February 1 **Application Fee:** $75.00 **H.S. Requirements:** High school diploma required; GED accepted **Costs Per Year:** Application fee: $75. Comprehensive fee: $32,160 includes full-time tuition ($23,260), mandatory fees ($600), and college room and board ($8300). College room only: $6100. Full-time tuition and fees vary according to location. Room and board charges vary according to board plan and housing facility. Part-time tuition: $775 per credit hour. Part-time tuition varies according to course load and location. **Scholarships:** Available **Calendar System:** Semester, Summer Session Available **Enrollment:** FT 1,097, PT 17, Grad FT 452 **Faculty:** FT 94, PT 28 **Student-Faculty Ratio:** 15:1 **Exams:** SAT I or ACT. ACT essay used for admission. SAT essay used for admission. **% Receiving Financial Aid:** 85 **% Residing in College-Owned, -Operated, or -Affiliated Housing:** 65 **Library Holdings:** 17,166 **Regional Accreditation:** Middle State Association of Colleges and Schools **Credit Hours For Degree:** 131 semester hours, Bachelors **ROTC:** Army, Navy, Air Force **Professional Accreditation:** ACPhE, ASC **Intercollegiate Athletics:** Basketball M & W; Soccer M & W

ALFRED UNIVERSITY
One Saxon Dr.
Alfred, NY 14802-1205
Tel: (607)871-2111; Free: 800-541-9229
Admissions: (607)871-2115
Fax: (607)871-2198
E-mail: admissions@alfred.edu
Web Site: http://www.alfred.edu/
President/CEO: Dr. Charles M. Edmondson
Admissions: Jeremy C. Spencer
Financial Aid: Earl Pierce
Type: University **Sex:** Coed **Scores:** 97.5% SAT V 400+; 98.1% SAT M 400+; 42.5% ACT 18-23; 42.5% ACT 24-29 **% Accepted:** 70 **Admission Plans:** Early Admission; Early Decision Plan; Deferred Admission **Application Deadline:** February 1 **Application Fee:** $50.00 **H.S. Requirements:** High school diploma required; GED accepted **Costs Per Year:** Application fee: $50. Comprehensive fee: $37,340 includes full-time tuition ($25,096), mandatory fees ($880), and college room and board ($11,364). College room only: $5766. Full-time tuition and fees vary according to program. Room and board charges vary according to board plan and housing facility. Part-time tuition: $814 per credit hour. Part-time mandatory fees: $72 per term. Part-time tuition and fees vary according to course load. **Scholarships:** Available **Calendar System:** Semester, Summer Session Available **Enrollment:** FT 1,827, PT 82, Grad FT 168, Grad PT 242 **Faculty:** FT 165, PT 34 **Student-Faculty Ratio:** 12:1 **Exams:** SAT I or ACT. ACT essay used in place of application essay. SAT essay used in place of application essay. **% Receiving Financial Aid:** 77 **% Residing in College-Owned, -Operated, or -Affiliated Housing:** 77 **Final Year or Final Semester Residency**

Requirement: No **Library Holdings:** 297,996 **Regional Accreditation:** Middle State Association of Colleges and Schools **Credit Hours For Degree:** 124 credits, Bachelors **ROTC:** Army **Professional Accreditation:** AACSB, ABET, APA, NASAD, TEAC **Intercollegiate Athletics:** Basketball M & W; Cross-Country Running M & W; Equestrian Sports M & W; Football M; Lacrosse M & W; Skiing (Downhill) M & W; Soccer M & W; Softball W; Swimming and Diving M & W; Tennis M & W; Track and Field M & W; Volleyball W

AMERICAN ACADEMY OF DRAMATIC ARTS
120 Madison Ave.
New York, NY 10016-7004
Tel: (212)686-9244; Free: 800-463-8990
E-mail: admissions-ny@aada.org
Web Site: http://www.aada.org/
President/CEO: Roger Croucher
Admissions: Karen Higginbotham
Financial Aid: Roberto Lopez
Type: Two-Year College **Sex:** Coed **% Accepted:** 52 **Admission Plans:** Deferred Admission **Application Deadline:** Rolling **Application Fee:** $50.00 **H.S. Requirements:** High school diploma required; GED accepted **Costs Per Year:** Application fee: $50. Tuition: $28,620 full-time. Mandatory fees: $600 full-time. **Scholarships:** Available **Calendar System:** Continuous, Summer Session Not available **Enrollment:** FT 228 **Faculty:** FT 7, PT 19 **Student-Faculty Ratio:** 14:1 **Library Holdings:** 7,467 **Regional Accreditation:** Middle State Association of Colleges and Schools **Credit Hours For Degree:** 70 units, Associates **Professional Accreditation:** NAST, NYSBR

AMERICAN ACADEMY MCALLISTER INSTITUTE OF FUNERAL SERVICE
619 West 54th St.
New York, NY 10019-3602
Tel: (212)757-1190; Free: (866)932-2264
Fax: (212)765-5923
Web Site: http://www.funeraleducation.org/
President/CEO: Meg Dunn
Admissions: Norman Provost
Type: Two-Year College **Sex:** Coed **Admission Plans:** Open Admission; Early Admission; Deferred Admission **Application Deadline:** Rolling **Application Fee:** $35.00 **H.S. Requirements:** High school diploma required; GED accepted **Scholarships:** Available **Calendar System:** Semester, Summer Session Not available **Enrollment:** FT 130 **Faculty:** FT 2, PT 18 **Student-Faculty Ratio:** 25:1 **Library Holdings:** 1,672 **Credit Hours For Degree:** 74 credits, Associates **Professional Accreditation:** ABFSE

THE ART INSTITUTE OF NEW YORK CITY
11 Beach St.
New York, NY 10013
Tel: (212)226-5500; Free: 800-654-2433
Fax: (212)226-5644
Web Site: http://www.artinstitutes.edu/newyork/
President/CEO: Dr. David Warren
Type: Two-Year College **Sex:** Coed **Affiliation:** Education Management Corporation **Calendar System:** Quarter **Professional Accreditation:** ACICS, ACF

ASA INSTITUTE, THE COLLEGE OF ADVANCED TECHNOLOGY
151 Lawrence St., 2nd Floor
Brooklyn, NY 11201
Tel: (718)522-9073
Fax: (718)834-0835
Web Site: http://www.asa.edu/
President/CEO: Alex Shchegol
Type: Two-Year College **Sex:** Coed **Application Fee:** $25.00 **Calendar System:** Semester **Regional Accreditation:** Middle State Association of Colleges and Schools **Professional Accreditation:** ACICS, AAMAE

BARD COLLEGE
PO Box 5000
Annandale-on-Hudson, NY 12504
Tel: (845)758-6822
Admissions: (845)758-7472
E-mail: admission@bard.edu
Web Site: http://www.bard.edu/
President/CEO: Dr. Leon Botstein
Admissions: Mary Backlund
Financial Aid: Denise Ann Ackerman
Type: Comprehensive **Sex:** Coed **Scores:** 100% SAT M 400+ **% Accepted:** 33 **Admission Plans:** Early Admission; Early Action; Deferred Admission **Application Deadline:** January 15 **Application Fee:** $50.00 **H.S. Requirements:** High school diploma required; GED accepted **Costs Per Year:** Application fee: $50. One-time mandatory fee: $890. Comprehensive fee: $51,180 includes full-time tuition ($39,080), mandatory fees ($800), and college room and board ($11,300). Part-time tuition: $1222 per credit. **Scholarships:** Available **Calendar System:** Semester, Summer Session Not available **Enrollment:** FT 1,866, PT 73, Grad FT 271, Grad PT 24 **Faculty:** FT 145, PT 92 **Student-Faculty Ratio:** 10:1 **% Receiving Financial Aid:** 62 **% Residing in College-Owned, -Operated, or -Affiliated Housing:** 64 **Library Holdings:** 351,163 **Regional Accreditation:** Middle State Association of Colleges and Schools **Credit Hours For Degree:** 60 credits, Associates; 124 credits, Bachelors **Professional Accreditation:** TEAC **Intercollegiate Athletics:** Basketball M & W; Cross-Country Running M & W; Soccer M & W; Squash M; Tennis M & W; Track and Field M & W; Volleyball M & W

BARNARD COLLEGE
3009 Broadway
New York, NY 10027-6598
Tel: (212)854-5262
Admissions: (212)854-2014
Fax: (212)854-6220
E-mail: admissions@barnard.edu
Web Site: http://www.barnard.edu/
President/CEO: Dr. Judith R. Shapiro
Admissions: Jennifer Gill Fondiller
Financial Aid: Nanette DiLauro
Type: Four-Year College **Sex:** Women **Affiliation:** Columbia University **Scores:** 101% SAT V 400+; 100% SAT M 400+; 4% ACT 18-23; 40% ACT 24-29 **% Accepted:** 31 **Admission Plans:** Early Admission; Early Decision Plan; Deferred Admission **Application Deadline:** January 1 **Application Fee:** $55.00 **H.S. Requirements:** High school diploma required; GED not accepted **Costs Per Year:** Application fee: $55. Comprehensive fee: $50,969 includes full-time tuition ($37,051), mandatory fees ($1599), and college room and board ($12,319). College room only: $7577. Room and board charges vary according to board plan and housing facility. Part-time tuition: $1235 per credit. **Scholarships:** Available **Calendar System:** Semester, Summer Session Not available **Enrollment:** FT 2,356, PT 61 **Faculty:** FT 208, PT 141 **Student-Faculty Ratio:** 9:1 **Exams:** Other. ACT essay used for admission. SAT essay used for admission. **% Receiving Financial Aid:** 44 **% Residing in College-Owned, -Operated, or -Affiliated Housing:** 90 **Library Holdings:** 205,920 **Regional Accreditation:** Middle State Association of Colleges and Schools **Credit Hours For Degree:** 122 credits, Bachelors **Professional Accreditation:** NASD **Intercollegiate Athletics:** Archery W; Basketball W; Crew W; Cross-Country Running W; Equestrian Sports W; Fencing W; Field Hockey W; Golf W; Ice Hockey W; Lacrosse W; Rugby W; Sailing W; Skiing (Downhill) W; Soccer W; Softball W; Squash W; Swimming and Diving W; Tennis W; Track and Field W; Volleyball W

BEIS MEDRASH HEICHAL DOVID
257 Beach 17th St.
Far Rockaway, NY 11691
Tel: (718)868-2300
Fax: (718)868-0517
President/CEO: Rabbi Yakov Bender
Type: Comprehensive **Sex:** Men **Application Fee:** $100.00 **Professional Accreditation:** AARTS

BERKELEY COLLEGE—NEW YORK CITY CAMPUS
3 East 43rd St.
New York, NY 10017-4604
Tel: (212)986-4343; Free: 800-446-5400
Fax: (212)697-3371
E-mail: info@berkeleycollege.edu
Web Site: http://www.berkeleycollege.edu/
Admissions: Linda Pinsky
Type: Two-Year College **Sex:** Coed **Affiliation:** Berkeley College **% Accepted:** 73 **Admission Plans:** Deferred Admission **Application Deadline:** Rolling **Application Fee:** $50.00 **H.S. Requirements:** High school diploma

required; GED accepted **Costs Per Year:** Application fee: $50. Tuition: $19,050 full-time, $450 per quarter hour part-time. Mandatory fees: $900 full-time, $200 per term part-time. Full-time tuition and fees vary according to course load. Part-time tuition and fees vary according to course load. Tuition guaranteed not to increase for student's term of enrollment. **Scholarships:** Available **Calendar System:** Quarter, Summer Session Available **Enrollment:** FT 2,202, PT 210 **Faculty:** FT 40, PT 100 **Student-Faculty Ratio:** 26:1 **Exams:** SAT I or ACT. **Library Holdings:** 13,164 **Regional Accreditation:** Middle State Association of Colleges and Schools **Credit Hours For Degree:** 90 quarter hour, Associates; 180 quarter hours, Bachelors

BERKELEY COLLEGE—WESTCHESTER CAMPUS
99 Church St.
White Plains, NY 10601
Tel: (914)694-1122; Free: 800-446-5400
Fax: (914)694-5832
E-mail: info@berkeleycollege.edu
Web Site: http://www.berkeleycollege.edu/
Admissions: John Wool
Type: Two-Year College **Sex:** Coed **Admission Plans:** Deferred Admission **Application Deadline:** Rolling **Application Fee:** $50.00 **H.S. Requirements:** High school diploma required; GED accepted **Costs Per Year:** Application fee: $50. Tuition: $19,050 full-time, $450 per quarter hour part-time. Mandatory fees: $900 full-time, $200 per term part-time. Full-time tuition and fees vary according to course load. Part-time tuition and fees vary according to course load. College room only: $7800. Tuition guaranteed not to increase for student's term of enrollment. **Scholarships:** Available **Calendar System:** Quarter, Summer Session Available **Enrollment:** FT 591, PT 49 **Faculty:** FT 17, PT 25 **Student-Faculty Ratio:** 22:1 **Exams:** SAT I or ACT. **% Residing in College-Owned, -Operated, or -Affiliated Housing:** 10 **Library Holdings:** 9,526 **Regional Accreditation:** Middle State Association of Colleges and Schools **Credit Hours For Degree:** 90 quarter hours, Associates; 180 quarter hours, Bachelors

BERNARD M. BARUCH COLLEGE OF THE CITY UNIVERSITY OF NEW YORK
1 Bernard Baruch Way
New York, NY 10010-5585
Tel: (646)312-1000
Admissions: (646)312-1400
E-mail: jimmy.jung@baruch.cuny.edu
Web Site: http://www.baruch.cuny.edu/
President/CEO: Dr. Stan Altman
Admissions: Jimmy Jung
Type: Comprehensive **Sex:** Coed **Affiliation:** City University of New York System **Scores:** 98% SAT V 400+; 100% SAT M 400+ **% Accepted:** 23 **Admission Plans:** Early Admission; Early Decision Plan; Deferred Admission **Application Deadline:** February 1 **Application Fee:** $65.00 **H.S. Requirements:** High school diploma required; GED accepted **Costs Per Year:** Application fee: $65. State resident tuition: $4600 full-time. Nonresident tuition: $12,450 full-time. Full-time tuition varies according to course load. **Scholarships:** Available **Calendar System:** Semester, Summer Session Available **Enrollment:** FT 9,473, PT 2,859, Grad FT 906, Grad PT 2,957 **Faculty:** FT 498, PT 668 **Student-Faculty Ratio:** 17:1 **Exams:** SAT I or ACT. **% Receiving Financial Aid:** 65 **Final Year or Final Semester Residency Requirement:** No **Library Holdings:** 566,509 **Regional Accreditation:** Middle State Association of Colleges and Schools **Credit Hours For Degree:** 124 credits, Bachelors **ROTC:** Army **Professional Accreditation:** AACSB, ACEHSA, NASPAA **Intercollegiate Athletics:** Baseball M; Basketball M & W; Cheerleading M & W; Cross-Country Running M & W; Soccer M; Softball W; Swimming and Diving M & W; Tennis M & W; Volleyball M & W

BETH HAMEDRASH SHAAREI YOSHER INSTITUTE
4102-10 Sixteenth Ave.
Brooklyn, NY 11204
Tel: (718)854-2290
President/CEO: Yosef Mayer
Type: Comprehensive **Sex:** Men **Affiliation:** Jewish **% Accepted:** 100 **H.S. Requirements:** High school diploma required; GED accepted **Calendar System:** Semester **Professional Accreditation:** AARTS

BETH HATALMUD RABBINICAL COLLEGE
2127 Eighty-second St.
Brooklyn, NY 11214
Tel: (718)259-2525
President/CEO: Mendel Bromberg
Type: Comprehensive **Sex:** Men **Affiliation:** Jewish **% Accepted:** 100 **H.S. Requirements:** High school diploma required; GED accepted **Calendar System:** Semester **Professional Accreditation:** AARTS

BORICUA COLLEGE
3755 Broadway
New York, NY 10032-1560
Tel: (212)694-1000
Admissions: (718)782-2200
E-mail: mpfeffer@boricuacollege.edu
Web Site: http://www.boricuacollege.edu/
President/CEO: Dr. Victor G. Alicea
Admissions: Miriam Pfeffer
Financial Aid: Rosalia Cruz
Type: Comprehensive **Sex:** Coed **% Accepted:** 40 **Admission Plans:** Deferred Admission **Application Deadline:** Rolling **Application Fee:** $25.00 **H.S. Requirements:** High school diploma required; GED accepted **Costs Per Year:** Application fee: $25. One-time mandatory fee: $25. Tuition: $9000 full-time. **Scholarships:** Available **Calendar System:** Miscellaneous, Summer Session Available **Enrollment:** FT 1,004 **Faculty:** FT 57, PT 76 **Student-Faculty Ratio:** 20:1 **Exams:** Other. **% Receiving Financial Aid:** 94 **Library Holdings:** 112,600 **Regional Accreditation:** Middle State Association of Colleges and Schools **Credit Hours For Degree:** 60 credits, Associates; 124 credits, Bachelors

BOROUGH OF MANHATTAN COMMUNITY COLLEGE OF THE CITY UNIVERSITY OF NEW YORK
199 Chambers St.
New York, NY 10007-1097
Tel: (212)346-8000
Admissions: (212)220-8000
Fax: (212)346-8816
E-mail: admissions@bmcc.cuny.edu
Web Site: http://www.bmcc.cuny.edu/
President/CEO: Antonio Perez
Admissions: Eugenio Barrios
Type: Two-Year College **Sex:** Coed **Affiliation:** City University of New York System **Scores:** 47% SAT V 400+; 48% SAT M 400+ **% Accepted:** 89 **Admission Plans:** Open Admission; Preferred Admission; Deferred Admission **Application Deadline:** Rolling **Application Fee:** $65.00 **H.S. Requirements:** High school diploma required; GED accepted. For applicants 21 or over who are on the 24 College Credit Plan: High school diploma or equivalent not required **Scholarships:** Available **Calendar System:** Semester, Summer Session Available **Enrollment:** FT 10,809, PT 7,967 **Faculty:** FT 378, PT 697 **Student-Faculty Ratio:** 22:1 **Library Holdings:** 101,869 **Regional Accreditation:** Middle State Association of Colleges and Schools **Credit Hours For Degree:** 60 credits, Associates **Professional Accreditation:** AHIMA, CARC, JRCEMT, NLN **Intercollegiate Athletics:** Baseball M; Basketball M & W; Soccer M

BRAMSON ORT COLLEGE
69-30 Austin St.
Forest Hills, NY 11375-4239
Tel: (718)261-5800
E-mail: admission@bramsonort.edu
Web Site: http://www.bramsonort.edu/
President/CEO: Ephraim Buhks
Type: Two-Year College **Sex:** Coed **Admission Plans:** Open Admission; Early Admission; Deferred Admission **Application Deadline:** Rolling **Application Fee:** $50.00 **H.S. Requirements:** High school diploma required; GED accepted **Costs Per Year:** Application fee: $50. One-time mandatory fee: $30. Tuition: $10,080 full-time, $420 per credit part-time. Mandatory fees: $330 full-time, $330 per year part-time. Full-time tuition and fees vary according to course load. Part-time tuition and fees vary according to course load. Tuition guaranteed not to increase for student's term of enrollment. **Scholarships:** Available **Calendar System:** Semester, Summer Session Available **Faculty:** FT 32, PT 48 **Library Holdings:** 8,000 **Credit Hours For Degree:** 62 credits, Associates **Professional Accreditation:** NYSBR

BRIARCLIFFE COLLEGE
1055 Stewart Ave.
Bethpage, NY 11714

Tel: (516)918-3600
Fax: (516)470-6020
E-mail: info@bcl.edu
Web Site: http://www.bcl.edu/
President/CEO: Dr. George Santiago, Jr.
Admissions: Theresa Donohue
Financial Aid: Johanna Kelly
Type: Four-Year College **Sex:** Coed **Affiliation:** Career Education Corporation **Admission Plans:** Deferred Admission **Application Deadline:** Rolling **Application Fee:** $35.00 **H.S. Requirements:** High school diploma required; GED accepted **Scholarships:** Available **Calendar System:** Semester, Summer Session Available **Enrollment:** FT 1,561, PT 782 **Faculty:** FT 50, PT 197 **Regional Accreditation:** Middle State Association of Colleges and Schools **Credit Hours For Degree:** 60 credits, Associates; 120 credits, Bachelors **Intercollegiate Athletics:** Baseball M; Bowling M & W; Lacrosse M; Soccer W; Softball W; Track and Field M & W

BRONX COMMUNITY COLLEGE OF THE CITY UNIVERSITY OF NEW YORK
2155 University Ave.
Bronx, NY 10453
Tel: (718)289-5100
Admissions: (718)289-5888
E-mail: admission@bcc.cuny.edu
Web Site: http://www.bcc.cuny.edu/
President/CEO: Dr. Carolyn Grubbs Williams, PhD
Admissions: Alba N. Cancetty
Type: Two-Year College **Sex:** Coed **Affiliation:** City University of New York System **Admission Plans:** Open Admission; Early Admission **Application Deadline:** July 1 **Application Fee:** $65.00 **H.S. Requirements:** High school diploma required; GED accepted **Costs Per Year:** Application fee: $65. State resident tuition: $3150 full-time, $135 per credit hour part-time. Nonresident tuition: $5040 full-time, $210 per credit hour part-time. Mandatory fees: $354 full-time. Full-time tuition and fees vary according to course load. Part-time tuition varies according to course load. **Calendar System:** Semester, Summer Session Available **Enrollment:** FT 6,013, PT 4,118 **Faculty:** FT 260, PT 103 **Student-Faculty Ratio:** 28:1 **Exams:** SAT I or ACT. ACT essay used for placement. SAT essay used for placement. **Final Year or Final Semester Residency Requirement:** No **Library Holdings:** 75,000 **Regional Accreditation:** Middle State Association of Colleges and Schools **Credit Hours For Degree:** 60 credits, Associates **Professional Accreditation:** ABET, ACBSP, JRCERT, JRCNMT, NLN **Intercollegiate Athletics:** Baseball M; Basketball M; Cross-Country Running M & W; Soccer M; Track and Field M & W; Volleyball W

BROOKLYN COLLEGE OF THE CITY UNIVERSITY OF NEW YORK
2900 Bedford Ave.
Brooklyn, NY 11210-2889
Tel: (718)951-5000
Admissions: (718)951-5001
E-mail: adminqry@brooklyn.cuny.edu
Web Site: http://www.brooklyn.cuny.edu/
President/CEO: Dean Karen L. Gould
Admissions: Duane Lee
Financial Aid: Sherwood Johnson
Type: Comprehensive **Sex:** Coed **Affiliation:** City University of New York System **Scores:** 93.7% SAT V 400+; 99% SAT M 400+ **% Accepted:** 28 **Admission Plans:** Early Admission **Application Deadline:** February 1 **Application Fee:** $65.00 **H.S. Requirements:** High school diploma required; GED accepted **Costs Per Year:** Application fee: $65. State resident tuition: $4600 full-time, $195 per credit part-time. Nonresident tuition: $12,450 full-time, $415 per credit part-time. Mandatory fees: $451 full-time, $351.10 per year part-time. **Scholarships:** Available **Calendar System:** Semester, Summer Session Available **Enrollment:** FT 9,268, PT 3,801, Grad FT 607, Grad PT 3,418 **Faculty:** FT 557, PT 844 **Student-Faculty Ratio:** 15:1 **Exams:** SAT I or ACT. ACT essay not being used. SAT essay not being used. **% Receiving Financial Aid:** 74 **Final Year or Final Semester Residency Requirement:** No **Library Holdings:** 1,305,602 **Regional Accreditation:** Middle State Association of Colleges and Schools **Credit Hours For Degree:** 120 credits, Bachelors **Professional Accreditation:** ADtA, ASLHA, CEPH, NCATE **Intercollegiate Athletics:** Basketball M & W; Cross-Country Running M & W; Soccer M; Softball W; Swimming and Diving M & W; Tennis M & W; Track and Field M & W; Volleyball M & W

BROOME COMMUNITY COLLEGE
PO Box 1017
Binghamton, NY 13902-1017
Tel: (607)778-5000
Admissions: (607)778-5001
E-mail: admissions@sunybroome.edu
Web Site: http://www.sunybroome.edu/
President/CEO: Dr. Kevin E. Drumm
Admissions: Jenae Norris
Type: Two-Year College **Sex:** Coed **Affiliation:** State University of New York System **Admission Plans:** Open Admission; Preferred Admission; Early Admission **Application Deadline:** Rolling **Application Fee:** $0.00 **H.S. Requirements:** High school diploma required; GED accepted **Costs Per Year:** Application fee: $0. One-time mandatory fee: $70. State resident tuition: $3276 full-time, $137 per credit hour part-time. Nonresident tuition: $6552 full-time, $274 per credit hour part-time. Mandatory fees: $325 full-time, $7 per credit hour part-time, $228 per year part-time. Full-time tuition and fees vary according to course load. Part-time tuition and fees vary according to course load. **Scholarships:** Available **Calendar System:** Semester, Summer Session Available **Enrollment:** FT 4,655, PT 2,222 **Faculty:** FT 141, PT 265 **Regional Accreditation:** Middle State Association of Colleges and Schools **Credit Hours For Degree:** 62 credit hours, Associates **Professional Accreditation:** ABET, AAMAE, ADA, AHIMA, APTA, JRCERT, NAACLS, NLN **Intercollegiate Athletics:** Baseball M; Basketball M & W; Cross-Country Running M & W; Golf M; Ice Hockey M; Lacrosse M; Soccer M & W; Softball W; Tennis M & W; Volleyball W

BRYANT & STRATTON COLLEGE - ALBANY CAMPUS
1259 Central Ave.
Albany, NY 12205-5230
Tel: (518)437-1802
Fax: (518)437-1048
Web Site: http://www.bryantstratton.edu/
President/CEO: Michael A. Gutierrez
Admissions: Robert Ferrell
Type: Two-Year College **Sex:** Coed **Affiliation:** Bryant and Stratton College, Inc. **Admission Plans:** Deferred Admission **Application Deadline:** Rolling **H.S. Requirements:** High school diploma required; GED accepted **Scholarships:** Available **Calendar System:** Semester, Summer Session Available **Enrollment:** FT 354, PT 116 **Faculty:** FT 12, PT 33 **Exams:** Other, SAT I or ACT. **Library Holdings:** 3,500 **Regional Accreditation:** Middle State Association of Colleges and Schools **Credit Hours For Degree:** 60 credit hours, Associates **Professional Accreditation:** AAMAE

BRYANT & STRATTON COLLEGE - AMHERST CAMPUS
Audubon Business Center, 40 Hazelwood Dr.
Amherst, NY 14228
Tel: (716)691-0012
Fax: (716)691-6716
E-mail: bkdioguardi@bryantstratton.edu
Web Site: http://www.bryantstratton.edu/
President/CEO: Marvel Ross Jones, PhD
Admissions: Brian K. Dioguardi
Type: Two-Year College **Sex:** Coed **Admission Plans:** Early Admission **Application Deadline:** Rolling **H.S. Requirements:** High school diploma or equivalent not required **Scholarships:** Available **Calendar System:** Trimester, Summer Session Available **Enrollment:** FT 277, PT 197 **Faculty:** FT 9, PT 58 **Exams:** Other, SAT I or ACT. **Library Holdings:** 4,500 **Regional Accreditation:** Middle State Association of Colleges and Schools **Credit Hours For Degree:** 60 credits, Associates; 120 credits, Bachelors

BRYANT & STRATTON COLLEGE - BUFFALO CAMPUS
465 Main St.
Ste. 400
Buffalo, NY 14203
Tel: (716)884-9120
E-mail: pjstruebel@bryantstratton.edu
Web Site: http://www.bryantstratton.edu/
President/CEO: Jeff Tredo
Admissions: Philip J. Struebel
Type: Two-Year College **Sex:** Coed **% Accepted:** 75 **Admission Plans:** Early Admission **Application Deadline:** Rolling **H.S. Requirements:** High school diploma or equivalent not required **Scholarships:** Available **Calendar System:** Trimester, Summer Session Available **Enrollment:** FT

473, PT 220 **Faculty:** FT 11, PT 42 **Exams:** Other, SAT I or ACT. **Library Holdings:** 30,000 **Regional Accreditation:** Middle State Association of Colleges and Schools **Credit Hours For Degree:** 60 credits, Associates; 120 credits, Bachelors **Professional Accreditation:** AAMAE

BRYANT & STRATTON COLLEGE - GREECE CAMPUS
150 Bellwood Dr.
Rochester, NY 14606
Tel: (585)720-0660
Fax: (585)720-9226
Web Site: http://www.bryantstratton.edu/
President/CEO: Marc Ambrosi
Admissions: John Schifano
Type: Two-Year College **Sex:** Coed **Affiliation:** Bryant and Stratton College, Inc. **Admission Plans:** Deferred Admission **Application Deadline:** Rolling **H.S. Requirements:** High school diploma required; GED accepted. For applicants 19 or over who meet entrance testing requirements: High school diploma required; GED not accepted **Costs Per Year:** Tuition: $14,670 full-time, $489 per credit hour part-time. Mandatory fees: $35 full-time, $35. **Scholarships:** Available **Calendar System:** Semester, Summer Session Available **Enrollment:** FT 192, PT 87 **Faculty:** FT 8, PT 41 **Student-Faculty Ratio:** 10:1 **Exams:** Other, SAT I or ACT. **Library Holdings:** 2,824 **Regional Accreditation:** Middle State Association of Colleges and Schools **Credit Hours For Degree:** 60 semester hours, Associates **Professional Accreditation:** AAMAE

BRYANT & STRATTON COLLEGE - HENRIETTA CAMPUS
1225 Jefferson Rd.
Rochester, NY 14623-3136
Tel: (585)292-5627
Fax: (585)292-6015
E-mail: djprofita@bryantstratton.edu
Web Site: http://www.bryantstratton.edu/
President/CEO: Jeffery Moore
Admissions: David Profita
Type: Two-Year College **Sex:** Coed **Affiliation:** Bryant and Stratton College, Inc. **% Accepted:** 78 **Admission Plans:** Deferred Admission **Application Deadline:** Rolling **H.S. Requirements:** High school diploma required; GED accepted. For applicants 19 or over who meet entrance testing requirements: High school diploma required; GED not accepted **Costs Per Year:** Tuition: $14,670 full-time, $489 per credit hour part-time. Mandatory fees: $35 full-time, $35. **Scholarships:** Available **Calendar System:** Semester, Summer Session Available **Enrollment:** FT 288, PT 119 **Faculty:** FT 17, PT 47 **Student-Faculty Ratio:** 10:1 **Exams:** Other, SAT I or ACT. **Library Holdings:** 4,056 **Regional Accreditation:** Middle State Association of Colleges and Schools **Credit Hours For Degree:** 60 semester hours, Associates **Professional Accreditation:** AAMAE

BRYANT & STRATTON COLLEGE - NORTH CAMPUS
8687 Carling Rd.
Liverpool, NY 13090-1315
Tel: (315)652-6500
Web Site: http://www.bryantstratton.edu/
President/CEO: Stephanie Laterra
Admissions: Heather Macnik
Type: Two-Year College **Sex:** Coed **Affiliation:** Bryant and Stratton Business Institute, Inc. **Admission Plans:** Open Admission; Deferred Admission **Application Deadline:** Rolling **Application Fee:** $25.00 **H.S. Requirements:** High school diploma required; GED accepted. For applicants 19 or over who meet entrance testing requirements: High school diploma required; GED not accepted **Scholarships:** Available **Calendar System:** Semester, Summer Session Available **Enrollment:** FT 333, PT 164 **Faculty:** FT 16, PT 41 **Student-Faculty Ratio:** 9:1 **Exams:** Other. **Library Holdings:** 1,936 **Regional Accreditation:** Middle State Association of Colleges and Schools **Credit Hours For Degree:** 64 semester hours, Associates

BRYANT & STRATTON COLLEGE - SOUTHTOWNS CAMPUS
200 Redtail
Orchard Park, NY 14127
Tel: (716)821-9331
Admissions: (716)677-9500
E-mail: tdominiak@bryantstratton.edu
Web Site: http://www.bryantstratton.edu/
President/CEO: Paul C. Bahr
Admissions: Tracy Dominiak
Type: Two-Year College **Sex:** Coed **Admission Plans:** Early Admission **Application Deadline:** Rolling **H.S. Requirements:** High school diploma or equivalent not required **Scholarships:** Available **Calendar System:** Trimester, Summer Session Available **Enrollment:** FT 663, PT 543 **Faculty:** FT 23, PT 52 **Exams:** Other, SAT I or ACT. **Library Holdings:** 1,402 **Regional Accreditation:** Middle State Association of Colleges and Schools **Credit Hours For Degree:** 60 credits, Associates; 120 credits, Bachelors

BRYANT & STRATTON COLLEGE - SYRACUSE CAMPUS
953 James St.
Syracuse, NY 13203-2502
Tel: (315)472-6603
Fax: (315)474-4383
Web Site: http://www.bryantstratton.edu/
President/CEO: Michael Sattler
Admissions: Dawn Rajkowski
Type: Two-Year College **Sex:** Coed **Affiliation:** Bryant and Stratton Business Institute, Inc. **% Accepted:** 94 **Application Deadline:** Rolling **H.S. Requirements:** High school diploma required; GED accepted. For applicants 19 or over who meet entrance testing requirements: High school diploma required; GED not accepted **Scholarships:** Available **Calendar System:** Semester, Summer Session Available **Enrollment:** FT 494, PT 221 **Faculty:** FT 21, PT 34 **Student-Faculty Ratio:** 13:1 **Exams:** Other, SAT I or ACT. **% Residing in College-Owned, -Operated, or -Affiliated Housing:** 12 **Library Holdings:** 1,325 **Regional Accreditation:** Middle State Association of Colleges and Schools **Credit Hours For Degree:** 60 semester hours, Associates **Professional Accreditation:** AAMAE **Intercollegiate Athletics:** Soccer M & W

BUFFALO STATE COLLEGE, STATE UNIVERSITY OF NEW YORK
1300 Elmwood Ave.
Buffalo, NY 14222-1095
Tel: (716)878-4000
Admissions: (716)878-4017
Fax: (716)878-6100
E-mail: admissions@buffalostate.edu
Web Site: http://www.buffalostate.edu/
President/CEO: Dennis Ponton
Admissions: Carmella Thompson
Financial Aid: Kent McGowan
Type: Comprehensive **Sex:** Coed **Affiliation:** State University of New York System **Scores:** 91.1% SAT V 400+; 92.07% SAT M 400+ **% Accepted:** 43 **Admission Plans:** Early Admission; Early Decision Plan; Deferred Admission **Application Deadline:** Rolling **Application Fee:** $40.00 **H.S. Requirements:** High school diploma required; GED accepted **Costs Per Year:** Application fee: $40. State resident tuition: $4970 full-time, $207 per credit hour part-time. Nonresident tuition: $12,870 full-time, $536 per credit hour part-time. Mandatory fees: $1037 full-time, $42.80 per credit hour part-time. Part-time tuition and fees vary according to course load. College room and board: $9748. College room only: $5770. Room and board charges vary according to board plan, housing facility, and student level. **Scholarships:** Available **Calendar System:** Semester, Summer Session Available **Enrollment:** FT 8,780, PT 1,042, Grad FT 630, Grad PT 1,262 **Faculty:** FT 425, PT 453 **Student-Faculty Ratio:** 17:1 **Exams:** SAT I and SAT II or ACT, SAT I. **% Residing in College-Owned, -Operated, or -Affiliated Housing:** 25 **Library Holdings:** 618,429 **Regional Accreditation:** Middle State Association of Colleges and Schools **Credit Hours For Degree:** 123 semester hours, Bachelors **ROTC:** Army **Professional Accreditation:** ABET, ADtA, ASLHA, FIDER, CSWE, NASAD, NCATE **Intercollegiate Athletics:** Baseball M; Basketball M & W; Bowling M & W; Cheerleading W; Cross-Country Running M & W; Fencing M; Football M; Ice Hockey M & W; Lacrosse M & W; Rugby M & W; Skiing (Cross-Country) M & W; Skiing (Downhill) M & W; Soccer M & W; Softball W; Swimming and Diving M & W; Tennis W; Track and Field M & W; Volleyball M & W

BUSINESS INFORMATICS CENTER, INC.
134 South Central Ave.
Valley Stream, NY 11580-5431
Tel: (516)561-0050
Fax: (516)561-0074
Web Site: http://www.thecollegeforbusiness.com/
President/CEO: Constance Brown

Type: Two-Year College **Sex:** Coed **% Accepted:** 78 **Application Fee:** $50.00 **Exams:** Other. **Professional Accreditation:** ACCSCT

CANISIUS COLLEGE
2001 Main St.
Buffalo, NY 14208-1098
Tel: (716)883-7000; Free: 800-843-1517
Admissions: (716)888-2200
Fax: (716)888-2377
E-mail: admissions@canisius.edu
Web Site: http://www.canisius.edu/
President/CEO: Fr. Vincent M. Cooke, SJ
Admissions: Ann Marie Moscovic
Financial Aid: Curtis Gaume
Type: Comprehensive **Sex:** Coed **Affiliation:** Roman Catholic (Jesuit) **Scores:** 98.1% SAT V 400+; 98.7% SAT M 400+; 23.2% ACT 18-23; 55.8% ACT 24-29 **% Accepted:** 77 **Admission Plans:** Early Admission; Deferred Admission **Application Deadline:** May 1 **Application Fee:** $40.00 **H.S. Requirements:** High school diploma required; GED accepted **Costs Per Year:** Application fee: $40. Comprehensive fee: $40,068 includes full-time tuition ($28,455), mandatory fees ($1057), and college room and board ($10,556). College room only: $6230. Full-time tuition and fees vary according to course load. Room and board charges vary according to board plan and housing facility. Part-time tuition: $812 per credit hour. Part-time mandatory fees: $20.50 per credit hour, $33 per term. Part-time tuition and fees vary according to course load. **Scholarships:** Available **Calendar System:** Semester, Summer Session Available **Enrollment:** FT 3,050, PT 146, Grad FT 799, Grad PT 779 **Faculty:** FT 230, PT 233 **Student-Faculty Ratio:** 11:1 **Exams:** SAT I or ACT. ACT essay used for advising. SAT essay used for advising. ACT essay used for placement. SAT essay used for placement. **% Receiving Financial Aid:** 76 **% Residing in College-Owned, -Operated, or -Affiliated Housing:** 46 **Library Holdings:** 379,498 **Regional Accreditation:** Middle State Association of Colleges and Schools **Credit Hours For Degree:** 120 credit hours, Bachelors **ROTC:** Army **Professional Accreditation:** AACSB, ACA, JRCEPAT, NCATE **Intercollegiate Athletics:** Baseball M; Basketball M & W; Cross-Country Running M & W; Golf M; Ice Hockey M; Lacrosse M & W; Rugby M; Soccer M & W; Softball W; Swimming and Diving M & W; Volleyball M & W

CAYUGA COUNTY COMMUNITY COLLEGE
197 Franklin St.
Auburn, NY 13021-3099
Tel: (315)255-1743
Web Site: http://www.cayuga-cc.edu/
President/CEO: Daniel Paul Larson, DMA
Admissions: Bruce M. Blodgett
Type: Two-Year College **Sex:** Coed **Affiliation:** State University of New York System **Admission Plans:** Open Admission; Deferred Admission **Application Deadline:** Rolling **Application Fee:** $0.00 **H.S. Requirements:** High school diploma required; GED accepted. For applicants 19 or over: High school diploma or equivalent not required **Scholarships:** Available **Calendar System:** Semester, Summer Session Available **Library Holdings:** 82,205 **Regional Accreditation:** Middle State Association of Colleges and Schools **Credit Hours For Degree:** 60 credit hours, Associates **Professional Accreditation:** NLN **Intercollegiate Athletics:** Basketball M & W; Lacrosse M & W; Soccer M & W

CAZENOVIA COLLEGE
22 Sullivan St.
Cazenovia, NY 13035-1084
Tel: (315)655-7000; Free: 800-654-3210
Admissions: (315)655-7208
Fax: (315)655-2190
E-mail: admission@cazenovia.edu
Web Site: http://www.cazenovia.edu/
President/CEO: Mark J. Tierno
Financial Aid: Christine L. Mandel
Type: Four-Year College **Sex:** Coed **Scores:** 89% SAT V 400+; 89% SAT M 400+; 45% ACT 18-23; 29% ACT 24-29 **% Accepted:** 74 **Admission Plans:** Deferred Admission **Application Deadline:** Rolling **Application Fee:** $30.00 **H.S. Requirements:** High school diploma required; GED accepted **Costs Per Year:** Application fee: $30. Comprehensive fee: $34,374 includes full-time tuition ($23,752), mandatory fees ($400), and college room and board ($10,222). Full-time tuition and fees vary according to class time, course load, and program. Room and board charges vary according to board plan and housing facility. Part-time tuition: $504 per credit hour. Part-time tuition varies according to class time and course load. **Scholarships:** Available **Calendar System:** Semester, Summer Session Available **Enrollment:** FT 966, PT 153 **Faculty:** FT 56, PT 90 **Student-Faculty Ratio:** 12:1 **Exams:** SAT I or ACT. **% Receiving Financial Aid:** 85 **% Residing in College-Owned, -Operated, or -Affiliated Housing:** 90 **Final Year or Final Semester Residency Requirement:** No **Library Holdings:** 83,340 **Regional Accreditation:** Middle State Association of Colleges and Schools **Credit Hours For Degree:** 60 credits, Associates; 120 credits, Bachelors **ROTC:** Army, Air Force **Intercollegiate Athletics:** Basketball M & W; Cheerleading M & W; Crew M & W; Cross-Country Running M; Equestrian Sports M & W; Golf M; Lacrosse M & W; Soccer M & W; Softball W; Volleyball W

CENTRAL YESHIVA TOMCHEI TMIMIM-LUBAVITCH
841-853 Ocean Parkway
Brooklyn, NY 11230
Tel: (718)434-0784
President/CEO: Abraham Rosenfeld
Financial Aid: Rabbi Moshe M. Gluckowsky
Type: Comprehensive **Sex:** Men **Affiliation:** Jewish **% Accepted:** 100 **H.S. Requirements:** High school diploma required; GED accepted **Calendar System:** Semester **Professional Accreditation:** AARTS

CITY COLLEGE OF THE CITY UNIVERSITY OF NEW YORK
160 Convent Ave.
New York, NY 10031-9198
Tel: (212)650-7000
Admissions: (212)650-6977
Fax: (212)650-6417
E-mail: admissions@ccny.cuny.edu
Web Site: http://www.ccny.cuny.edu/
President/CEO: Robert E. Paaswell
Admissions: Joseph Fantozzi
Financial Aid: Thelma Mason
Type: Comprehensive **Sex:** Coed **Affiliation:** City University of New York System **Scores:** 90% SAT V 400+; 97% SAT M 400+ **% Accepted:** 38 **Admission Plans:** Early Admission; Deferred Admission **Application Deadline:** February 1 **Application Fee:** $65.00 **H.S. Requirements:** High school diploma required; GED accepted **Costs Per Year:** Application fee: $65. State resident tuition: $4600 full-time. Nonresident tuition: $9960 full-time. Mandatory fees: $329 full-time. Full-time tuition and fees vary according to course load and program. **Scholarships:** Available **Calendar System:** Semester, Summer Session Available **Enrollment:** FT 9,641, PT 3,319, Grad FT 373, Grad PT 2,975 **Faculty:** FT 519, PT 610 **Student-Faculty Ratio:** 13:1 **Exams:** SAT I or ACT. **% Receiving Financial Aid:** 89 **% Residing in College-Owned, -Operated, or -Affiliated Housing:** 1 **Regional Accreditation:** Middle State Association of Colleges and Schools **Credit Hours For Degree:** 120 credits, Bachelors **ROTC:** Army, Air Force **Professional Accreditation:** ABET, APA, ASLA, NAAB, NCATE **Intercollegiate Athletics:** Baseball M; Basketball M & W; Cross-Country Running M & W; Fencing W; Lacrosse M; Soccer M & W; Softball W; Tennis M & W; Track and Field M & W; Volleyball W

CLARKSON UNIVERSITY
Potsdam, NY 13699
Tel: (315)268-6400; Free: 800-527-6577
Admissions: (315)268-6480
Fax: (315)268-7647
E-mail: admission@clarkson.edu
Web Site: http://www.clarkson.edu/
President/CEO: Dr. Anthony G. Collins
Admissions: Brian T. Grant
Financial Aid: Pamela A. Nichols
Type: University **Sex:** Coed **Scores:** 98% SAT V 400+; 100% SAT M 400+; 32% ACT 18-23; 56% ACT 24-29 **% Accepted:** 73 **Admission Plans:** Early Admission; Early Decision Plan; Deferred Admission **Application Deadline:** January 15 **Application Fee:** $50.00 **H.S. Requirements:** High school diploma required; GED accepted **Costs Per Year:** Application fee: $50. Comprehensive fee: $46,324 includes full-time tuition ($34,070), mandatory fees ($690), and college room and board ($11,564). College room only: $6126. Full-time tuition and fees vary according to course load. Room and board charges vary according to board plan and housing facility. Part-time

tuition: $1136 per credit. Part-time tuition varies according to course load. **Scholarships:** Available **Calendar System:** Semester, Summer Session Available **Enrollment:** FT 2,735, PT 11, Grad FT 394, Grad PT 47 **Faculty:** FT 204, PT 22 **Student-Faculty Ratio:** 15:1 **Exams:** SAT I or ACT, SAT II. SAT essay used for admission. **% Receiving Financial Aid:** 81 **% Residing in College-Owned, -Operated, or -Affiliated Housing:** 80 **Final Year or Final Semester Residency Requirement:** No **Library Holdings:** 338,321 **Regional Accreditation:** Middle State Association of Colleges and Schools **Credit Hours For Degree:** 120 credit hours, Bachelors **ROTC:** Army, Air Force **Professional Accreditation:** AACSB, ABET, APTA **Intercollegiate Athletics:** Baseball M; Basketball M & W; Cross-Country Running M & W; Golf M; Ice Hockey M & W; Lacrosse M & W; Skiing (Cross-Country) M & W; Skiing (Downhill) M & W; Soccer M & W; Swimming and Diving M & W; Volleyball W

CLINTON COMMUNITY COLLEGE
136 Clinton Point Dr.
Plattsburgh, NY 12901-9573
Tel: (518)562-4200; Free: 800-552-1160
Admissions: (518)562-4170
Fax: (518)562-8621
Web Site: http://clintoncc.suny.edu/
President/CEO: Frederick Woodward
Admissions: Karen L. Burnam
Type: Two-Year College **Sex:** Coed **Affiliation:** State University of New York System **Admission Plans:** Open Admission; Preferred Admission; Deferred Admission **Application Deadline:** August 26 **Application Fee:** $0.00 **H.S. Requirements:** High school diploma required; GED accepted **Scholarships:** Available **Calendar System:** Semester, Summer Session Available **Enrollment:** FT 1,259, PT 933 **Faculty:** FT 49, PT 93 **Student-Faculty Ratio:** 18:1 **Library Holdings:** 33,862 **Regional Accreditation:** Middle State Association of Colleges and Schools **Credit Hours For Degree:** 60 credits, Associates **Professional Accreditation:** NAACLS, NLN **Intercollegiate Athletics:** Baseball M; Basketball M & W; Soccer M & W; Softball W

COCHRAN SCHOOL OF NURSING
967 North Broadway
Yonkers, NY 10701
Tel: (914)964-4283
Admissions: (914)964-4606
E-mail: kvitola@riversidehealth.org
Web Site: http://www.cochranschoolofnursing.us/
President/CEO: Dr. Kathleen Dirshel
Admissions: Kathleen Vitola
Type: Two-Year College **Sex:** Coed **Affiliation:** Mercy College, International Academic Alliance (NIT) **Admission Plans:** Deferred Admission **Application Deadline:** April 15 **Application Fee:** $35.00 **H.S. Requirements:** High school diploma required; GED accepted **Costs Per Year:** Application fee: $35. Tuition: $8704 full-time, $512 per credit part-time. Mandatory fees: $1511 full-time, $559 per term part-time. Full-time tuition and fees vary according to course load and student level. Part-time tuition and fees vary according to course load and student level. **Scholarships:** Available **Calendar System:** Semester, Summer Session Not available **Faculty:** FT 24, PT 0 **Student-Faculty Ratio:** 10:1 **Exams:** Other, SAT I. **Library Holdings:** 4,314 **Credit Hours For Degree:** 72 credits, Associates

COLGATE UNIVERSITY
13 Oak Dr.
Hamilton, NY 13346-1386
Tel: (315)228-1000
Admissions: (315)228-7401
Fax: (315)228-7798
E-mail: admission@mail.colgate.edu
Web Site: http://www.colgate.edu/
President/CEO: Lyle Roelofs
Admissions: Gary L. Ross
Type: Comprehensive **Sex:** Coed **Scores:** 100% SAT V 400+; 100% SAT M 400+; 3% ACT 18-23; 26% ACT 24-29 **% Accepted:** 32 **Admission Plans:** Early Decision Plan; Deferred Admission **Application Deadline:** January 15 **Application Fee:** $55.00 **H.S. Requirements:** High school diploma required; GED accepted **Costs Per Year:** Application fee: $55. One-time mandatory fee: $50. Comprehensive fee: $50,940 includes full-time tuition ($40,690), mandatory fees ($280), and college room and board ($9970). College room only: $4815. Full-time tuition and fees vary according to course load. Room and board charges vary according to board plan and housing facility. Part-time tuition: $5,086.25 per course. Part-time tuition varies according to course load. **Scholarships:** Available **Calendar System:** Semester, Summer Session Not available **Enrollment:** FT 2,800, PT 25, Grad FT 7, Grad PT 5 **Faculty:** FT 266, PT 49 **Student-Faculty Ratio:** 10:1 **Exams:** SAT I or ACT. **% Receiving Financial Aid:** 35 **% Residing in College-Owned, -Operated, or -Affiliated Housing:** 91 **Library Holdings:** 1,172,551 **Regional Accreditation:** Middle State Association of Colleges and Schools **Credit Hours For Degree:** 32 courses, Bachelors **ROTC:** Army **Professional Accreditation:** TEAC **Intercollegiate Athletics:** Baseball M; Basketball M & W; Cheerleading M & W; Crew M & W; Cross-Country Running M & W; Equestrian Sports M & W; Fencing M & W; Field Hockey W; Football M; Golf M & W; Ice Hockey M & W; Lacrosse M & W; Rugby M & W; Sailing M & W; Skiing (Downhill) M & W; Soccer M & W; Softball W; Squash M & W; Swimming and Diving M & W; Table Tennis M & W; Tennis M & W; Track and Field M & W; Volleyball M & W; Water Polo M & W; Wrestling M & W

THE COLLEGE AT BROCKPORT, STATE UNIVERSITY OF NEW YORK
350 New Campus Dr.
Brockport, NY 14420-2997
Tel: (585)395-2211
Admissions: (585)395-2751
Fax: (585)395-5452
E-mail: admit@brockport.edu
Web Site: http://www.brockport.edu/
President/CEO: Dr. John R. Halstead
Admissions: Bernard Valento
Financial Aid: J. Scott Atkinson
Type: Comprehensive **Sex:** Coed **Affiliation:** State University of New York System **Scores:** 96.6% SAT V 400+; 98% SAT M 400+; 51.6% ACT 18-23; 42% ACT 24-29 **% Accepted:** 45 **Admission Plans:** Preferred Admission; Deferred Admission **Application Deadline:** Rolling **Application Fee:** $40.00 **H.S. Requirements:** High school diploma required; GED accepted **Costs Per Year:** Application fee: $40. State resident tuition: $4970 full-time. Nonresident tuition: $12,870 full-time. Mandatory fees: $1138 full-time. College room and board: $9200. College room only: $6040. Room and board charges vary according to board plan and housing facility. **Scholarships:** Available **Calendar System:** Semester, Summer Session Available **Enrollment:** FT 6,474, PT 645, Grad FT 371, Grad PT 1,000 **Faculty:** FT 328, PT 269 **Student-Faculty Ratio:** 18:1 **Exams:** SAT I or ACT. ACT essay not being used. SAT essay not being used. **% Receiving Financial Aid:** 70 **Regional Accreditation:** Middle State Association of Colleges and Schools **Credit Hours For Degree:** 120 credit hours, Bachelors **ROTC:** Army, Navy, Air Force **Professional Accreditation:** AACSB, ABET, AACN, ACA, CSWE, JRCEPAT, NASD, NASPAA, NCATE, NRPA **Intercollegiate Athletics:** Baseball M; Basketball M & W; Cross-Country Running M & W; Field Hockey W; Football M; Gymnastics W; Ice Hockey M; Lacrosse M & W; Soccer M & W; Softball W; Swimming and Diving M & W; Tennis W; Track and Field M & W; Volleyball W; Wrestling M

COLLEGE OF MOUNT SAINT VINCENT
6301 Riverdale Ave.
Riverdale, NY 10471-1093
Tel: (718)405-3200; Free: 800-665-CMSV
Fax: (718)549-7945
E-mail: roland.pinzon@mountsaintvincent.edu
Web Site: http://www.mountsaintvincent.edu/
President/CEO: Charles L. Flynn, Jr.
Admissions: Roland Pinzon
Financial Aid: Monica Simotas
Type: Comprehensive **Sex:** Coed **Scores:** 83% SAT V 400+; 79% SAT M 400+ **% Accepted:** 72 **Admission Plans:** Early Admission; Early Action; Deferred Admission **Application Deadline:** Rolling **Application Fee:** $35.00 **H.S. Requirements:** High school diploma required; GED accepted **Costs Per Year:** Application fee: $35. Comprehensive fee: $37,290 includes full-time tuition ($25,600), mandatory fees ($1310), and college room and board ($10,380). Room and board charges vary according to housing facility. Part-time tuition: $760 per credit. Part-time mandatory fees: $500 per term. **Scholarships:** Available **Calendar System:** Semester, Summer Session Available **Enrollment:** FT 1,350, PT 205, Grad FT 43, Grad PT 298 **Faculty:** FT 73, PT 123 **Student-Faculty Ratio:** 12:1 **Exams:** SAT I or ACT. **% Receiving Financial Aid:** 71 **% Residing in College-Owned, -Operated,**

or -Affiliated Housing: 51 **Final Year or Final Semester Residency Requirement:** No **Library Holdings:** 104,158 **Regional Accreditation:** Middle State Association of Colleges and Schools **Credit Hours For Degree:** 62 credits, Associates; 120 credits, Bachelors **ROTC:** Air Force **Professional Accreditation:** AACN, ACBSP, TEAC **Intercollegiate Athletics:** Baseball M; Basketball M & W; Cheerleading W; Cross-Country Running M & W; Lacrosse M & W; Soccer M & W; Softball W; Swimming and Diving W; Tennis M & W; Track and Field W; Volleyball M & W

THE COLLEGE OF NEW ROCHELLE
29 Castle Place
New Rochelle, NY 10805-2308
Tel: (914)654-5000; Free: 800-933-5923
Admissions: (914)654-5452
Fax: (914)654-5554
E-mail: admission@cnr.edu
Web Site: http://www.cnr.edu/
President/CEO: Dr. Stephen J. Sweeny
Admissions: Bridget Kennedy
Financial Aid: Anne Pelak
Type: Comprehensive **Sex:** Coed **Scores:** 98.1% SAT V 400+; 100% SAT M 400+ **% Accepted:** 30 **Admission Plans:** Early Admission; Early Decision Plan; Deferred Admission **Application Deadline:** Rolling **Application Fee:** $20.00 **H.S. Requirements:** High school diploma required; GED accepted **Costs Per Year:** Application fee: $20. Comprehensive fee: $36,026 includes full-time tuition ($25,576), mandatory fees ($850), and college room and board ($9600). Full-time tuition and fees vary according to course load and program. Room and board charges vary according to housing facility. Part-time tuition: $861 per credit. Part-time mandatory fees: $225 per term. Part-time tuition and fees vary according to course load. **Scholarships:** Available **Calendar System:** Semester, Summer Session Available **Enrollment:** FT 552, PT 299, Grad FT 212, Grad PT 757 **Faculty:** FT 90, PT 127 **Student-Faculty Ratio:** 11:1 **Exams:** SAT I or ACT. **% Receiving Financial Aid:** 89 **% Residing in College-Owned, -Operated, or -Affiliated Housing:** 37 **Library Holdings:** 220,000 **Regional Accreditation:** Middle State Association of Colleges and Schools **Credit Hours For Degree:** 120 credits, Bachelors **Professional Accreditation:** AACN, CSWE, NLN **Intercollegiate Athletics:** Basketball W; Cross-Country Running W; Softball W; Swimming and Diving W; Tennis W; Volleyball W

THE COLLEGE OF SAINT ROSE
432 Western Ave.
Albany, NY 12203-1419
Tel: (518)454-5111; Free: 800-637-8556
Admissions: (518)454-5154
Fax: (518)451-2013
E-mail: admit@strose.edu
Web Site: http://www.strose.edu/
President/CEO: Dr. R. Mark Sullivan
Admissions: Jeremy Bogan
Financial Aid: Steven Dwire
Type: Comprehensive **Sex:** Coed **Scores:** 97% SAT V 400+; 96% SAT M 400+; 58% ACT 18-23; 28% ACT 24-29 **% Accepted:** 72 **Admission Plans:** Early Admission; Early Action; Deferred Admission **Application Deadline:** May 1 **Application Fee:** $40.00 **H.S. Requirements:** High school diploma required; GED accepted **Costs Per Year:** Application fee: $40. Comprehensive fee: $34,015 includes full-time tuition ($23,329), mandatory fees ($806), and college room and board ($9880). College room only: $4859. Full-time tuition and fees vary according to class time and course load. Room and board charges vary according to board plan and housing facility. Part-time tuition: $776 per credit. Part-time tuition varies according to class time and course load. **Scholarships:** Available **Calendar System:** Semester, Summer Session Available **Enrollment:** FT 2,844, PT 192, Grad FT 853, Grad PT 1,269 **Faculty:** FT 213, PT 228 **Student-Faculty Ratio:** 14:1 **Exams:** SAT I or ACT. **% Receiving Financial Aid:** 97 **% Residing in College-Owned, -Operated, or -Affiliated Housing:** 38 **Final Year or Final Semester Residency Requirement:** No **Library Holdings:** 223,218 **Regional Accreditation:** Middle State Association of Colleges and Schools **Credit Hours For Degree:** 122 credit hours, Bachelors **ROTC:** Army, Navy, Air Force **Professional Accreditation:** ASLHA, ACBSP, CSWE, NASAD, NASM, NCATE **Intercollegiate Athletics:** Baseball M; Basketball M & W; Cross-Country Running M & W; Golf M; Soccer M & W; Softball W; Swimming and Diving M & W; Tennis W; Track and Field M & W; Volleyball W

COLLEGE OF STATEN ISLAND OF THE CITY UNIVERSITY OF NEW YORK
2800 Victory Blvd.
Staten Island, NY 10314-6600
Tel: (718)982-2000
Admissions: (718)982-2010
Fax: (718)982-2500
E-mail: admissions@mail.cuny.csi.edu
Web Site: http://www.csi.cuny.edu/
President/CEO: Dr. Tomas D. Morales
Admissions: Emmanuel Esperance, Jr.
Financial Aid: Philippe Marius
Type: Comprehensive **Sex:** Coed **Affiliation:** City University of New York System **Scores:** 94.52% SAT V 400+; 97.19% SAT M 400+ **% Accepted:** 100 **Admission Plans:** Open Admission; Deferred Admission **Application Deadline:** Rolling **Application Fee:** $65.00 **H.S. Requirements:** High school diploma required; GED accepted **Costs Per Year:** Application fee: $65. State resident tuition: $4600 full-time, $195 per credit part-time. Nonresident tuition: $9960 full-time, $415 per credit part-time. Mandatory fees: $378 full-time, $113 per term part-time. Full-time tuition and fees vary according to course load. Part-time tuition and fees vary according to course load. **Scholarships:** Available **Calendar System:** Semester, Summer Session Available **Enrollment:** FT 9,231, PT 3,655, Grad FT 95, Grad PT 877 **Faculty:** FT 319, PT 703 **Student-Faculty Ratio:** 18:1 **Exams:** SAT I or ACT. ACT essay used for advising. SAT essay used for advising. ACT essay used for placement. SAT essay used for placement. **% Receiving Financial Aid:** 57 **Library Holdings:** 250,000 **Regional Accreditation:** Middle State Association of Colleges and Schools **Credit Hours For Degree:** 60 credits, Associates; 120 credits, Bachelors **Professional Accreditation:** ABET, APTA, NCATE, NLN **Intercollegiate Athletics:** Baseball M; Basketball M & W; Cheerleading M & W; Cross-Country Running M & W; Soccer M & W; Softball W; Swimming and Diving M & W; Tennis M & W; Volleyball W

THE COLLEGE OF WESTCHESTER
325 Central Ave., PO Box 710
White Plains, NY 10602
Tel: (914)948-4442; Free: 800-333-4924
Fax: (914)948-5441
E-mail: admissions@cw.edu
Web Site: http://www.cw.edu/
President/CEO: Karen J. Smith
Admissions: Dale T. Smith
Type: Two-Year College **Sex:** Coed **Admission Plans:** Deferred Admission **Application Deadline:** Rolling **Application Fee:** $40.00 **H.S. Requirements:** High school diploma required; GED accepted **Costs Per Year:** Application fee: $40. Tuition: $21,100 full-time, $655 per credit hour part-time. Mandatory fees: $1000 full-time, $200 per term part-time. Full-time tuition and fees vary according to course load. Part-time tuition and fees vary according to course load. **Scholarships:** Available **Calendar System:** Quarter, Summer Session Available **Enrollment:** FT 829, PT 210 **Faculty:** FT 25, PT 57 **Student-Faculty Ratio:** 15:1 **Exams:** SAT I. **Regional Accreditation:** Middle State Association of Colleges and Schools **Credit Hours For Degree:** 60 credits, Associates

COLUMBIA-GREENE COMMUNITY COLLEGE
4400 Route 23
Hudson, NY 12534-0327
Tel: (518)828-4181
Fax: (518)828-8543
E-mail: info@mycommunitycollege.com
Web Site: http://www.sunycgcc.edu/
President/CEO: James R. Campion
Type: Two-Year College **Sex:** Coed **Affiliation:** State University of New York System **% Accepted:** 99 **Admission Plans:** Open Admission; Preferred Admission; Early Admission; Deferred Admission **Application Deadline:** Rolling **Application Fee:** $40.00 **H.S. Requirements:** High school diploma or equivalent not required **Scholarships:** Available **Calendar System:** Semester, Summer Session Available **Enrollment:** FT 1,001, PT 770 **Faculty:** FT 50, PT 60 **Student-Faculty Ratio:** 17:1 **Library Holdings:** 62,694 **Regional Accreditation:** Middle State Association of Colleges and Schools **Credit Hours For Degree:** 62 credits, Associates **Professional Accreditation:** NLN **Intercollegiate Athletics:** Baseball M; Basketball M; Soccer M & W; Softball W

COLUMBIA UNIVERSITY
116th St. and Broadway
New York, NY 10027
Tel: (212)854-1754
Admissions: (212)854-1222
Web Site: http://www.columbia.edu/
President/CEO: Lee Bollinger
Admissions: Jessica Marinaccio
Financial Aid: Daniel T. Barkowitz
Type: University **Sex:** Coed **Scores:** 100% SAT V 400+; 100% SAT M 400+ **% Accepted:** 10 **Admission Plans:** Early Admission; Early Decision Plan; Deferred Admission **Application Deadline:** January 2 **Application Fee:** $75.00 **H.S. Requirements:** High school diploma required; GED accepted **Costs Per Year:** Application fee: $75. Comprehensive fee: $49,524 includes full-time tuition ($39,296) and college room and board ($10,228). **Scholarships:** Available **Calendar System:** Semester **Enrollment:** FT 5,766 **Faculty:** FT 1,444, PT 352 **Student-Faculty Ratio:** 6:1 **Exams:** SAT I and SAT II or ACT. **% Receiving Financial Aid:** 50 **% Residing in College-Owned, -Operated, or -Affiliated Housing:** 95 **Library Holdings:** 9,500,000 **Regional Accreditation:** Middle State Association of Colleges and Schools **Professional Accreditation:** AACSB, ACEJMC, AACN, AANA, ABA, ACNM, ADA, ACSP, AOTA, APTA, AALS, ACEHSA, CEPH, CSWE, LCMEAMA, NAAB, NLN **Intercollegiate Athletics:** Archery M & W; Badminton M & W; Baseball M; Basketball M & W; Crew M & W; Cross-Country Running M & W; Fencing M & W; Field Hockey W; Football M; Golf M; Ice Hockey W; Lacrosse M & W; Racquetball M & W; Riflery M & W; Rugby M & W; Skiing (Cross-Country) M & W; Skiing (Downhill) M & W; Soccer M & W; Softball W; Squash M & W; Swimming and Diving M & W; Table Tennis M & W; Tennis M & W; Track and Field M & W; Ultimate Frisbee M & W; Volleyball M & W; Water Polo M & W; Wrestling M

COLUMBIA UNIVERSITY, SCHOOL OF GENERAL STUDIES
2970 Broadway
408 Lewisohn Hall, MC 4101
New York, NY 10027-6939
Tel: (212)854-2772; Free: 800-895-1169
E-mail: gs-admit@columbia.edu
Web Site: http://www.gs.columbia.edu/
President/CEO: Lee C. Bollinger
Admissions: Curtis M. Rodgers
Financial Aid: Skip Bailey
Type: Four-Year College **Sex:** Coed **Affiliation:** Columbia University **% Accepted:** 37 **Admission Plans:** Early Action; Deferred Admission **Application Deadline:** June 1 **Application Fee:** $65.00 **H.S. Requirements:** High school diploma required; GED accepted **Costs Per Year:** Application fee: $65. Comprehensive fee: $51,930 includes full-time tuition ($38,100), mandatory fees ($1810), and college room and board ($12,020). College room only: $8550. Full-time tuition and fees vary according to course load. Room and board charges vary according to board plan and housing facility. Part-time tuition: $1270 per credit hour. Part-time tuition varies according to course load. **Scholarships:** Available **Calendar System:** Semester, Summer Session Available **Enrollment:** FT 812, PT 539 **Faculty:** FT 777, PT 247 **Student-Faculty Ratio:** 7:1 **Exams:** Other, SAT I or ACT, SAT I and SAT II or ACT. **% Residing in College-Owned, -Operated, or -Affiliated Housing:** 28 **Library Holdings:** 9,500,000 **Regional Accreditation:** Middle State Association of Colleges and Schools **Credit Hours For Degree:** 124 credits, Bachelors **ROTC:** Army, Air Force **Intercollegiate Athletics:** Archery W; Badminton M & W; Baseball M; Basketball M & W; Crew M & W; Cross-Country Running M & W; Equestrian Sports W; Fencing M & W; Field Hockey W; Football M; Golf M; Gymnastics W; Ice Hockey M & W; Lacrosse M; Racquetball M & W; Rugby M & W; Sailing M & W; Skiing (Downhill) M & W; Soccer M & W; Squash M & W; Swimming and Diving M & W; Table Tennis M & W; Tennis M & W; Track and Field M & W; Volleyball W; Water Polo M & W; Wrestling M

CONCORDIA COLLEGE—NEW YORK
171 White Plains Rd.
Bronxville, NY 10708-1998
Tel: (914)337-9300; Free: 800-YES-COLLEGE
Fax: (914)395-4500
E-mail: admission@concordia-ny.edu
Web Site: http://www.concordia-ny.edu/
President/CEO: Dr. Viji D. George
Admissions: Donna J. Hoyt
Financial Aid: Janice Spikereit
Type: Four-Year College **Sex:** Coed **Affiliation:** Lutheran; Concordia University System **Scores:** 85.62% SAT V 400+; 83.35% SAT M 400+; 44.83% ACT 18-23; 17.24% ACT 24-29 **% Accepted:** 67 **Admission Plans:** Early Admission; Early Action; Deferred Admission **Application Deadline:** March 15 **Application Fee:** $50.00 **H.S. Requirements:** High school diploma required; GED accepted **Scholarships:** Available **Calendar System:** Semester, Summer Session Not available **Enrollment:** FT 643, PT 105 **Faculty:** FT 33, PT 44 **Student-Faculty Ratio:** 12:1 **Exams:** SAT I or ACT. **% Receiving Financial Aid:** 70 **% Residing in College-Owned, -Operated, or -Affiliated Housing:** 68 **Library Holdings:** 71,500 **Regional Accreditation:** Middle State Association of Colleges and Schools **Credit Hours For Degree:** 62 credit hours, Associates; 122 credit hours, Bachelors **Professional Accreditation:** CSWE **Intercollegiate Athletics:** Baseball M; Basketball M & W; Cross-Country Running M & W; Soccer M & W; Softball W; Tennis M & W; Volleyball W

COOPER UNION FOR THE ADVANCEMENT OF SCIENCE AND ART
30 Cooper Square
New York, NY 10003-7120
Tel: (212)353-4100
Admissions: (212)353-4120
Fax: (212)353-4343
E-mail: admissions@cooper.edu
Web Site: http://www.cooper.edu/
President/CEO: Dr. George Campbell
Admissions: Mitchell L. Lipton
Financial Aid: Mary Ruokonen
Type: Comprehensive **Sex:** Coed **Scores:** 100% SAT V 400+; 98% SAT M 400+ **% Accepted:** 7 **Admission Plans:** Early Admission; Early Decision Plan; Deferred Admission **Application Deadline:** January 1 **Application Fee:** $65.00 **H.S. Requirements:** High school diploma required; GED accepted **Costs Per Year:** Application fee: $65. Comprehensive fee: $50,350 includes full-time tuition ($35,000), mandatory fees ($1650), and college room and board ($13,700). College room only: $9700. Room and board charges vary according to board plan and housing facility. **Scholarships:** Available **Calendar System:** Semester, Summer Session Available **Enrollment:** FT 895, PT 2, Grad FT 73, Grad PT 20 **Faculty:** FT 55, PT 173 **Student-Faculty Ratio:** 9:1 **Exams:** SAT I or ACT, SAT I and SAT II or ACT. **% Receiving Financial Aid:** 28 **% Residing in College-Owned, -Operated, or -Affiliated Housing:** 20 **Final Year or Final Semester Residency Requirement:** Yes **Regional Accreditation:** Middle State Association of Colleges and Schools **Credit Hours For Degree:** 128 credits, Bachelors **Professional Accreditation:** ABET, NAAB, NASAD **Intercollegiate Athletics:** Badminton M & W; Basketball M & W; Cross-Country Running M & W; Football M; Soccer M & W; Tennis M & W; Volleyball M & W

CORNELL UNIVERSITY
Ithaca, NY 14853-0001
Tel: (607)255-2000
Admissions: (607)255-1446
Fax: (607)255-0659
E-mail: admissions@cornell.edu
Web Site: http://www.cornell.edu/
President/CEO: David Skorton
Admissions: Jason Locke
Financial Aid: Thomas Keane
Type: University **Sex:** Coed **Scores:** 100% SAT V 400+; 100% SAT M 400+; 2% ACT 18-23; 27% ACT 24-29 **% Accepted:** 19 **Admission Plans:** Early Admission; Early Decision Plan; Deferred Admission **Application Deadline:** January 2 **Application Fee:** $70.00 **H.S. Requirements:** High school diploma or equivalent not required **Costs Per Year:** Application fee: $70. Comprehensive fee: $50,114 includes full-time tuition ($37,750), mandatory fees ($204), and college room and board ($12,160). College room only: $7210. Full-time tuition and fees vary according to degree level and program. Room and board charges vary according to board plan and housing facility. **Scholarships:** Available **Calendar System:** Semester, Summer Session Available **Enrollment:** FT 13,931, Grad FT 6,702 **Faculty:** FT 1,685, PT 163 **Student-Faculty Ratio:** 9:1 **Exams:** SAT I or ACT, SAT II. ACT essay not being used. SAT essay not being used. **% Receiving Financial Aid:** 46 **% Residing in College-Owned, -Operated, or -Affiliated Housing:** 56 **Library Holdings:** 8,036,029 **Regional Accreditation:** Middle State Association of Colleges and Schools **Credit Hours For Degree:** 120 credit hours, Bachelors **ROTC:** Army, Navy, Air Force **Profes-**

sional Accreditation: AACSB, ABET, AAFCS, ABA, ADtA, ACSP, ASLA, AVMA, AALS, ACEHSA, FIDER, NAAB **Intercollegiate Athletics:** Baseball M; Basketball M & W; Crew M & W; Cross-Country Running M & W; Equestrian Sports W; Fencing W; Field Hockey W; Football M; Golf M; Gymnastics W; Ice Hockey M & W; Lacrosse M & W; Soccer M & W; Softball W; Squash M & W; Swimming and Diving M & W; Tennis M & W; Track and Field M & W; Volleyball W; Wrestling M

CORNING COMMUNITY COLLEGE
One Academic Dr.
Corning, NY 14830-3297
Tel: (607)962-9CCC
Admissions: (607)962-9427
Fax: (607)962-9456
E-mail: admissions@corning-cc.edu
Web Site: http://www.corning-cc.edu/
President/CEO: Dr. Floyd F. Amann
Admissions: Karen Brown
Type: Two-Year College **Sex:** Coed **Affiliation:** State University of New York System **Admission Plans:** Open Admission; Preferred Admission; Early Admission **Application Deadline:** Rolling **Application Fee:** $25.00 **H.S. Requirements:** High school diploma required; GED accepted. Applicants without a high school diploma or GED are required to take and pass an Ability to Benefit Test. **Costs Per Year:** Application fee: $25. State resident tuition: $3570 full-time, $149 per credit part-time. Nonresident tuition: $7140 full-time, $298 per credit part-time. Mandatory fees: $408 full-time, $8 per credit part-time. **Scholarships:** Available **Calendar System:** Semester, Summer Session Available **Enrollment:** FT 2,558, PT 3,113 **Faculty:** FT 97, PT 167 **Student-Faculty Ratio:** 26:1 **Library Holdings:** 53,438 **Regional Accreditation:** Middle State Association of Colleges and Schools **Credit Hours For Degree:** 62 credit hours, Associates **ROTC:** Army, Navy, Air Force **Professional Accreditation:** NLN **Intercollegiate Athletics:** Baseball M; Basketball M & W; Golf M & W; Soccer M & W; Softball W; Volleyball W

CROUSE HOSPITAL SCHOOL OF NURSING
736 Irving Ave.
Syracuse, NY 13210
Tel: (315)470-7481
E-mail: amygraham@crouse.org
Web Site: http://www.crouse.org/nursing/
President/CEO: Ann Sedore
Admissions: Amy Graham
Financial Aid: F. Peter Bullock
Type: Two-Year College **Sex:** Coed **Admission Plans:** Deferred Admission **Application Deadline:** February 1 **Application Fee:** $30.00 **H.S. Requirements:** High school diploma required; GED accepted **Costs Per Year:** Application fee: $30. Tuition: $8136 full-time, $245 per credit hour part-time. Mandatory fees: $850 full-time, $990 per term part-time. Full-time tuition and fees vary according to course load. Part-time tuition and fees vary according to course load. College room only: $3500. **Scholarships:** Available **Calendar System:** Semester, Summer Session Not available **Exams:** SAT I or ACT. **Library Holdings:** 5,000 **Credit Hours For Degree:** 70 credits, Associates

THE CULINARY INSTITUTE OF AMERICA
1946 Campus Dr.
Hyde Park, NY 12538-1499
Tel: (845)452-9600; Free: 800-CULINARY
Admissions: (845)451-1459
Fax: (845)452-8629
E-mail: admissions@culinary.edu
Web Site: http://www.ciachef.edu/
President/CEO: Dr. L. Timothy Ryan
Admissions: Rachel Birchwood
Financial Aid: Patricia A. Arcuri
Type: Four-Year College **Sex:** Coed **% Accepted:** 87 **Admission Plans:** Preferred Admission; Deferred Admission **Application Deadline:** Rolling **Application Fee:** $50.00 **H.S. Requirements:** High school diploma required; GED accepted **Costs Per Year:** Application fee: $50. Comprehensive fee: $32,660 includes full-time tuition ($23,380), mandatory fees ($1170), and college room and board ($8110). College room only: $5660. Full-time tuition and fees vary according to degree level. Room and board charges vary according to housing facility. **Scholarships:** Available **Calendar System:** Semester **Enrollment:** FT 2,914 **Faculty:** FT 155, PT 43 **Student-Faculty Ratio:** 18:1 **Exams:** SAT I or ACT. **% Receiving Financial Aid:** 83 **% Residing in College-Owned, -Operated, or -Affiliated Housing:** 84 **Library Holdings:** 76,000 **Regional Accreditation:** Middle State Association of Colleges and Schools **Credit Hours For Degree:** 69 credits, Associates; 132 credits, Bachelors **Professional Accreditation:** ACCSCT **Intercollegiate Athletics:** Basketball M & W; Soccer M & W; Tennis M & W

DAEMEN COLLEGE
4380 Main St.
Amherst, NY 14226-3592
Tel: (716)839-3600; Free: 800-462-7652
Admissions: (716)839-8225
Fax: (716)839-8516
E-mail: admissions@daemen.edu
Web Site: http://www.daemen.edu/
President/CEO: Dr. Martin J. Anisman
Admissions: Frank Williams
Financial Aid: Jeffrey Pagano
Type: Comprehensive **Sex:** Coed **Scores:** 90.2% SAT V 400+; 90.5% SAT M 400+; 51.2% ACT 18-23; 35.8% ACT 24-29 **% Accepted:** 62 **Admission Plans:** Early Admission; Deferred Admission **Application Deadline:** Rolling **Application Fee:** $25.00 **H.S. Requirements:** High school diploma required; GED accepted **Costs Per Year:** Application fee: $25. Comprehensive fee: $30,170 includes full-time tuition ($20,250), mandatory fees ($470), and college room and board ($9450). Full-time tuition and fees vary according to course load. Room and board charges vary according to board plan and housing facility. Part-time tuition: $675 per credit hour. Part-time mandatory fees: $4 per credit hour, $70 per term. Part-time tuition and fees vary according to course load. **Scholarships:** Available **Calendar System:** Semester, Summer Session Available **Enrollment:** FT 1,502, PT 537, Grad FT 513, Grad PT 369 **Faculty:** FT 100, PT 158 **Student-Faculty Ratio:** 15:1 **Exams:** SAT I or ACT. **% Receiving Financial Aid:** 90 **Final Year or Final Semester Residency Requirement:** Yes **Library Holdings:** 136,883 **Regional Accreditation:** Middle State Association of Colleges and Schools **Credit Hours For Degree:** 120 credits, Bachelors **ROTC:** Army **Professional Accreditation:** APTA, CSWE, NLN **Intercollegiate Athletics:** Basketball M & W; Cross-Country Running M & W; Golf M; Soccer M & W; Volleyball W

DARKEI NOAM RABBINICAL COLLEGE
2822 Ave. J
Brooklyn, NY 11210
Tel: (718)338-6464
Admissions: (718)338-9444
President/CEO: Pinchus Horowitz
Admissions: Rabbi Pinchas Horowitz
Financial Aid: Rivi Horowitz
Type: Comprehensive **Sex:** Men **Affiliation:** Jewish **% Accepted:** 100 **Calendar System:** Semester **Library Holdings:** 53,000 **Credit Hours For Degree:** 75 credits, Bachelors **Professional Accreditation:** AARTS

DAVIS COLLEGE
400 Riverside Dr.
Johnson City, NY 13790
Tel: (607)729-1581; Free: 800-331-4137
Fax: (607)729-2962
E-mail: admissions@davisny.edu
Web Site: http://www.davisny.edu/
President/CEO: Dr. Dino Pedrone
Financial Aid: Stephanie D. Baker
Type: Four-Year College **Sex:** Coed **Affiliation:** nondenominational **Scores:** 36% ACT 18-23; 21% ACT 24-29 **% Accepted:** 68 **Admission Plans:** Deferred Admission **Application Deadline:** Rolling **Application Fee:** $45.00 **H.S. Requirements:** High school diploma required; GED accepted **Costs Per Year:** Application fee: $45. Comprehensive fee: $18,600 includes full-time tuition ($11,700), mandatory fees ($900), and college room and board ($6000). Full-time tuition and fees vary according to course load. Room and board charges vary according to housing facility. Part-time tuition: $405 per credit hour. Part-time mandatory fees: $450 per year. Part-time tuition and fees vary according to course load. **Scholarships:** Available **Calendar System:** Semester, Summer Session Available **Enrollment:** FT 202, PT 121 **Faculty:** FT 7, PT 17 **Student-Faculty Ratio:** 14:1 **Exams:** SAT I or ACT. **% Receiving Financial Aid:** 62 **% Residing in College-Owned, -Operated,**

or -Affiliated Housing: 61 **Library Holdings:** 77,000 **Regional Accreditation:** Middle State Association of Colleges and Schools **Credit Hours For Degree:** 66 credits, Associates; 130 credits, Bachelors **Professional Accreditation:** ABHE **Intercollegiate Athletics:** Basketball M & W; Soccer M & W

DEVRY COLLEGE OF NEW YORK

30-20 Thomson Ave.
Long Island City, NY 11101
Tel: (718)472-2728
Web Site: http://www.devry.edu/
President/CEO: Carol Zajac
Financial Aid: Elvira Senese

Type: Comprehensive **Sex:** Coed **Affiliation:** DeVry University **Admission Plans:** Deferred Admission **Application Deadline:** Rolling **Application Fee:** $50.00 **H.S. Requirements:** High school diploma required; GED accepted **Costs Per Year:** Application fee: $50. Tuition: $14,720 full-time, $575 per credit hour part-time. **Scholarships:** Available **Calendar System:** Semester, Summer Session Available **Enrollment:** FT 911, PT 255, Grad FT 21, Grad PT 203 **Faculty:** FT 39, PT 71 **Student-Faculty Ratio:** 17:1 **Exams:** ACT essay used for admission. SAT essay used for admission. ACT essay used for placement. SAT essay used for placement. **% Receiving Financial Aid:** 84 **Regional Accreditation:** North Central Association of Colleges and Schools **Credit Hours For Degree:** 67 credit hours, Associates; 128 credit hours, Bachelors **Professional Accreditation:** ABET

DOMINICAN COLLEGE

470 Western Hwy.
Orangeburg, NY 10962-1210
Tel: (845)359-7800; Free: (866)432-4636
Admissions: (845)359-7900
Fax: (845)359-2313
E-mail: admissions@dc.edu
Web Site: http://www.dc.edu/
President/CEO: Sr. Mary Eileen O'Brien, PhD
Admissions: Joyce Elbe
Financial Aid: Eileen Felske

Type: Comprehensive **Sex:** Coed **Scores:** 78% SAT V 400+; 76% SAT M 400+; 58% ACT 18-23; 10% ACT 24-29 **% Accepted:** 73 **Admission Plans:** Deferred Admission **Application Deadline:** Rolling **Application Fee:** $35.00 **H.S. Requirements:** High school diploma required; GED accepted **Costs Per Year:** Application fee: $35. One-time mandatory fee: $35. Comprehensive fee: $31,270 includes full-time tuition ($20,420), mandatory fees ($700), and college room and board ($10,150). Room and board charges vary according to board plan and housing facility. Part-time tuition: $615 per credit hour. Part-time mandatory fees: $175 per term. Part-time tuition and fees vary according to program. **Scholarships:** Available **Calendar System:** Semester, Summer Session Available **Enrollment:** FT 1,363, PT 314, Grad FT 148, Grad PT 189 **Faculty:** FT 72, PT 163 **Student-Faculty Ratio:** 15:1 **Exams:** SAT I or ACT. ACT essay used for admission. SAT essay used for admission. ACT essay used for advising. SAT essay used for advising. ACT essay used for placement. SAT essay used for placement. **% Receiving Financial Aid:** 91 **% Residing in College-Owned, -Operated, or -Affiliated Housing:** 54 **Final Year or Final Semester Residency Requirement:** No **Library Holdings:** 125,000 **Regional Accreditation:** Middle State Association of Colleges and Schools **Credit Hours For Degree:** 60 credits, Associates; 120 credits, Bachelors **Professional Accreditation:** AACN, AOTA, APTA, CSWE, TEAC **Intercollegiate Athletics:** Baseball M; Basketball M & W; Cross-Country Running W; Golf M; Lacrosse M & W; Soccer M & W; Softball W; Track and Field W; Volleyball W

DOROTHEA HOPFER SCHOOL OF NURSING AT THE MOUNT VERNON HOSPITAL

53 Valentine St.
Mount Vernon, NY 10550
Tel: (914)664-8000
Admissions: (914)361-6537
Fax: (914)665-7047
Web Site: http://www.ssmc.org/
President/CEO: Maureen Pace

Type: Two-Year College **Sex:** Coed **% Accepted:** 33 **Application Fee:** $40.00

DOWLING COLLEGE

150 Idle Hour Blvd.
Oakdale, NY 11769-1999
Tel: (631)244-3000; Free: 800-DOW-LING
Admissions: (631)244-3357
Fax: (631)563-3827
Web Site: http://www.dowling.edu/
President/CEO: Robert J. Gaffney
Admissions: Glenn S. Berman
Financial Aid: Patricia Noren

Type: Comprehensive **Sex:** Coed **Scores:** 71.1% SAT V 400+; 80.8% SAT M 400+ **% Accepted:** 86 **Admission Plans:** Early Action; Deferred Admission **Application Deadline:** Rolling **Application Fee:** $35.00 **H.S. Requirements:** High school diploma required; GED accepted **Costs Per Year:** Application fee: $35. Comprehensive fee: $33,050 includes full-time tuition ($20,860), mandatory fees ($1990), and college room and board ($10,200). Full-time tuition and fees vary according to course load and degree level. Room and board charges vary according to housing facility and location. Part-time tuition: $698 per credit. Part-time mandatory fees: $500 per term. Part-time tuition and fees vary according to course load and degree level. **Scholarships:** Available **Calendar System:** Semester, Summer Session Available **Enrollment:** FT 2,133, PT 1,232, Grad FT 794, Grad PT 1,373 **Faculty:** FT 119, PT 339 **Student-Faculty Ratio:** 16:1 **Exams:** SAT I. SAT essay used for admission. SAT essay used for advising. SAT essay used for placement. **% Receiving Financial Aid:** 72 **% Residing in College-Owned, -Operated, or -Affiliated Housing:** 8 **Final Year or Final Semester Residency Requirement:** No **Library Holdings:** 154,031 **Regional Accreditation:** Middle State Association of Colleges and Schools **Credit Hours For Degree:** 122 credit hours, Bachelors **ROTC:** Army, Air Force **Professional Accreditation:** NCATE **Intercollegiate Athletics:** Baseball M; Basketball M & W; Crew M & W; Cross-Country Running M & W; Equestrian Sports M & W; Golf M; Lacrosse M & W; Soccer M & W; Softball W; Tennis M & W; Volleyball W

DUTCHESS COMMUNITY COLLEGE

53 Pendell Rd.
Poughkeepsie, NY 12601-1595
Tel: (845)431-8000
Admissions: (845)431-8010
E-mail: banner@sunydutchess.edu
Web Site: http://www.sunydutchess.edu/
President/CEO: Dr. David Conklin
Admissions: Rita Banner
Financial Aid: Susan L. Mead

Type: Two-Year College **Sex:** Coed **Affiliation:** State University of New York System **Admission Plans:** Open Admission; Preferred Admission; Early Admission; Deferred Admission **Application Deadline:** Rolling **H.S. Requirements:** High school diploma required; GED accepted **Costs Per Year:** State resident tuition: $2900 full-time, $121 per credit hour part-time. Nonresident tuition: $5800 full-time, $242 per credit hour part-time. Mandatory fees: $407 full-time, $10 per credit hour part-time, $13 per term part-time. **Scholarships:** Available **Calendar System:** Semester, Summer Session Available **Enrollment:** FT 4,206, PT 4,042 **Faculty:** FT 135, PT 282 **Library Holdings:** 103,272 **Regional Accreditation:** Middle State Association of Colleges and Schools **Credit Hours For Degree:** 64 credits, Associates **Professional Accreditation:** NAACLS, NLN **Intercollegiate Athletics:** Baseball M; Basketball M & W; Bowling M & W; Golf M; Soccer M & W; Softball W; Tennis M & W; Volleyball W

D'YOUVILLE COLLEGE

320 Porter Ave.
Buffalo, NY 14201-1084
Tel: (716)829-8000; Free: 800-777-3921
Admissions: (716)829-7600
Fax: (716)829-7790
Web Site: http://www.dyc.edu/
President/CEO: Sr. Denise A. Roche, GNSH
Admissions: Dr. Steve Smith
Financial Aid: Lorraine A. Metz

Type: Comprehensive **Sex:** Coed **Scores:** 98% SAT V 400+; 99% SAT M 400+; 55% ACT 18-23; 40% ACT 24-29 **% Accepted:** 83 **Admission Plans:** Deferred Admission **Application Deadline:** Rolling **Application Fee:** $25.00 **H.S. Requirements:** High school diploma required; GED accepted **Costs Per Year:** Application fee: $25. Comprehensive fee: $29,830 includes full-time tuition ($19,800), mandatory fees ($230), and college room and board ($9800). Full-time tuition and fees vary according to course load, degree level, and program. Room and board charges vary according to board plan and housing facility. Part-time tuition: $575 per credit hour. Part-time mandatory fees: $2 per credit hour, $40 per term. Part-time tuition and fees vary according to course load, degree level, and program. **Scholarships:** Available **Calendar System:** Semester, Summer Session Available **Enrollment:** FT 1,467, PT 399, Grad FT 798, Grad PT 307 **Faculty:** FT 144, PT 178 **Student-Faculty Ratio:** 12:1 **Exams:** SAT I or ACT. **% Receiving Financial Aid:** 83 **% Residing in College-Owned, -Operated, or -Affiliated Housing:** 13 **Library Holdings:** 116,237 **Regional Accreditation:** Middle State Association of Colleges and Schools **Credit Hours For Degree:** 120 credit hours, Bachelors **ROTC:** Army **Professional Accreditation:** AACN, ADtA, AOTA, APTA, CCE **Intercollegiate Athletics:** Baseball M; Basketball M & W; Cheerleading W; Cross-Country Running M & W; Golf M & W; Soccer M & W; Softball W; Tennis M & W; Volleyball M & W

ELLIS HOSPITAL SCHOOL OF NURSING
1101 Nott St.
Schenectady, NY 12308
Tel: (518)243-4471
Web Site: http://www.ehson.org/
President/CEO: Marilyn Stapleton, PhD,RN
Admissions: Mary Lee Pollard
Type: Two-Year College **Sex:** Coed **% Accepted:** 50 **Application Deadline:** Rolling **Application Fee:** $30.00 **Scholarships:** Available **Enrollment:** FT 35, PT 34 **Faculty:** FT 9, PT 0 **Student-Faculty Ratio:** 8:1 **Exams:** SAT I.

ELMIRA BUSINESS INSTITUTE
303 North Main St.
Elmira, NY 14901
Tel: (607)733-7177; Free: 800-843-1812
Fax: (607)733-7178
E-mail: lroan@ebi-college.com
Web Site: http://www.ebi-college.com/
President/CEO: Brad C. Phillips
Admissions: Lisa Roan
Type: Two-Year College **Sex:** Coed **% Accepted:** 62 **Admission Plans:** Open Admission **Application Deadline:** Rolling **Application Fee:** $0.00 **H.S. Requirements:** High school diploma required; GED accepted **Scholarships:** Available **Calendar System:** Semester, Summer Session Not available **Enrollment:** FT 192, PT 88 **Faculty:** FT 6, PT 21 **Student-Faculty Ratio:** 11:1 **Library Holdings:** 800 **Credit Hours For Degree:** 61 credits, Associates **Professional Accreditation:** ACICS

ELMIRA COLLEGE
One Park Place
Elmira, NY 14901
Tel: (607)735-1800; Free: 800-935-6472
Admissions: (607)735-1724
Fax: (607)735-1718
E-mail: admissions@elmira.edu
Web Site: http://www.elmira.edu/
President/CEO: Dr. Thomas K. Meier
Admissions: Brett Moore
Financial Aid: Kathleen L. Cohen
Type: Comprehensive **Sex:** Coed **Scores:** 100% SAT V 400+; 60% ACT 18-23; 36% ACT 24-29 **% Accepted:** 79 **Admission Plans:** Early Decision Plan; Deferred Admission **Application Deadline:** March 31 **Application Fee:** $50.00 **H.S. Requirements:** High school diploma required; GED not accepted **Costs Per Year:** Application fee: $50. Comprehensive fee: $45,600 includes full-time tuition ($33,500), mandatory fees ($1300), and college room and board ($10,800). Room and board charges vary according to housing facility. **Scholarships:** Available **Calendar System:** Miscellaneous, Summer Session Available **Enrollment:** FT 1,125, PT 234, Grad FT 34, Grad PT 264 **Faculty:** FT 82, PT 119 **Student-Faculty Ratio:** 12:1 **Exams:** SAT I or ACT. **% Receiving Financial Aid:** 78 **% Residing in College-Owned, -Operated, or -Affiliated Housing:** 93 **Library Holdings:** 203,343 **Regional Accreditation:** Middle State Association of Colleges and Schools **Credit Hours For Degree:** 120 credits, Bachelors **ROTC:** Army, Air Force **Professional Accreditation:** NLN **Intercollegiate Athletics:** Basketball M & W; Cheerleading W; Field Hockey W; Golf M & W; Ice Hockey M & W; Lacrosse M & W; Soccer M & W; Softball W; Tennis M & W; Volleyball M & W

ERIE COMMUNITY COLLEGE
121 Ellicott St.
Buffalo, NY 14203-2698
Tel: (716)851-1001
Admissions: (716)851-1155
Fax: (716)842-1972
Web Site: http://www.ecc.edu/
President/CEO: Jack F. Quinn, Jr.
Financial Aid: Scott Weltjen
Type: Two-Year College **Sex:** Coed **Affiliation:** State University of New York System **Admission Plans:** Open Admission **Application Deadline:** Rolling **Application Fee:** $25.00 **H.S. Requirements:** High school diploma required; GED accepted **Costs Per Year:** Application fee: $25. One-time mandatory fee: $50. Area resident tuition: $3300 full-time, $138 per credit hour part-time. State resident tuition: $6600 full-time, $276 per credit hour part-time. Nonresident tuition: $6600 full-time, $276 per credit hour part-time. Mandatory fees: $340 full-time, $5 per credit hour part-time, $50 per term part-time. **Scholarships:** Available **Calendar System:** Semester, Summer Session Available **Enrollment:** FT 2,646, PT 953 **Faculty:** FT 90, PT 283 **Student-Faculty Ratio:** 18:1 **Library Holdings:** 26,269 **Regional Accreditation:** Middle State Association of Colleges and Schools **Credit Hours For Degree:** 60 credit hours, Associates **ROTC:** Army **Professional Accreditation:** ABET, AAMAE, ACBSP, COptA, JRCERT, NLN **Intercollegiate Athletics:** Baseball M; Basketball M & W; Bowling M & W; Cheerleading W; Cross-Country Running M & W; Football M; Golf M & W; Ice Hockey M; Lacrosse W; Soccer M & W; Softball W; Swimming and Diving M & W; Track and Field M & W; Volleyball W

ERIE COMMUNITY COLLEGE, NORTH CAMPUS
6205 Main St.
Williamsville, NY 14221-7095
Tel: (716)851-1002
Admissions: (716)851-1455
Fax: (716)634-3802
Web Site: http://www.ecc.edu/
President/CEO: Jack F. Quinn, Jr.
Financial Aid: Scott Weltjen
Type: Two-Year College **Sex:** Coed **Affiliation:** State University of New York System **Admission Plans:** Open Admission **Application Deadline:** Rolling **Application Fee:** $25.00 **H.S. Requirements:** High school diploma required; GED accepted **Costs Per Year:** Application fee: $25. One-time mandatory fee: $50. Area resident tuition: $3300 full-time, $138 per credit hour part-time. State resident tuition: $6600 full-time, $276 per credit hour part-time. Nonresident tuition: $6600 full-time, $276 per credit hour part-time. Mandatory fees: $340 full-time, $5 per credit hour part-time, $50 per term part-time. **Scholarships:** Available **Calendar System:** Semester, Summer Session Available **Enrollment:** FT 4,502, PT 2,239 **Faculty:** FT 171, PT 393 **Student-Faculty Ratio:** 18:1 **Library Holdings:** 54,438 **Regional Accreditation:** Middle State Association of Colleges and Schools **Credit Hours For Degree:** 60 credit hours, Associates **ROTC:** Army **Professional Accreditation:** ADA, AHIMA, AOTA, CARC, NAACLS, NLN **Intercollegiate Athletics:** Baseball M; Basketball M & W; Bowling M & W; Cheerleading W; Cross-Country Running M & W; Football M; Golf M & W; Ice Hockey M; Lacrosse W; Soccer M & W; Softball W; Swimming and Diving M & W; Track and Field M & W; Volleyball W

ERIE COMMUNITY COLLEGE, SOUTH CAMPUS
4041 Southwestern Blvd.
Orchard Park, NY 14127-2199
Tel: (716)851-1003
Admissions: (716)851-1655
Fax: (716)648-9953
Web Site: http://www.ecc.edu/
President/CEO: Jack F. Quinn, Jr.
Financial Aid: Scott Weltjen
Type: Two-Year College **Sex:** Coed **Affiliation:** State University of New York System **Admission Plans:** Open Admission **Application Deadline:** Rolling **Application Fee:** $25.00 **H.S. Requirements:** High school diploma required; GED accepted **Costs Per Year:** Application fee: $25. One-time mandatory fee: $50. Area resident tuition: $3300 full-time, $138 per credit hour part-time. State resident tuition: $6600 full-time, $276 per credit hour part-time. Nonresident tuition: $6600 full-time, $276 per credit hour part-time. Mandatory fees: $340 full-time, $5 per credit hour part-time, $50 per term part-time. **Scholarships:** Available **Calendar System:** Semester, Summer

Session Available **Enrollment:** FT 2,801, PT 1,682 **Faculty:** FT 109, PT 432 **Student-Faculty Ratio:** 18:1 **Library Holdings:** 45,501 **Regional Accreditation:** Middle State Association of Colleges and Schools **Credit Hours For Degree:** 60 credit hours, Associates **ROTC:** Army **Professional Accreditation:** ADA **Intercollegiate Athletics:** Baseball M; Basketball M & W; Bowling M & W; Cheerleading W; Cross-Country Running M & W; Football M; Golf M & W; Ice Hockey M; Lacrosse W; Soccer M & W; Softball W; Swimming and Diving M & W; Track and Field M & W; Volleyball W

EUGENE LANG COLLEGE THE NEW SCHOOL FOR LIBERAL ARTS

65 West 11th St.
New York, NY 10011-8601
Tel: (212)229-5600; Free: 877-528-3321
Admissions: (212)229-5665
Fax: (212)229-5355
E-mail: lang@newschool.edu
Web Site: http://www.lang.edu/
President/CEO: Bob Kerrey
Admissions: Karen Williams

Type: Four-Year College **Sex:** Coed **Affiliation:** The New School **Scores:** 97% SAT V 400+; 93% SAT M 400+; 39% ACT 18-23; 55% ACT 24-29 **% Accepted:** 68 **Admission Plans:** Early Decision Plan; Deferred Admission **Application Deadline:** February 1 **Application Fee:** $50.00 **H.S. Requirements:** High school diploma required; GED accepted **Costs Per Year:** Application fee: $50. Comprehensive fee: $49,810 includes full-time tuition ($33,810), mandatory fees ($740), and college room and board ($15,260). College room only: $12,260. Room and board charges vary according to board plan and housing facility. Part-time tuition: $1150 per credit. Part-time tuition varies according to course load. **Scholarships:** Available **Calendar System:** Semester, Summer Session Available **Enrollment:** FT 1,353, PT 86 **Faculty:** FT 70, PT 73 **Student-Faculty Ratio:** 15:1 **Exams:** SAT I or ACT. **% Receiving Financial Aid:** 55 **% Residing in College-Owned, -Operated, or -Affiliated Housing:** 30 **Library Holdings:** 1,906,046 **Regional Accreditation:** Middle State Association of Colleges and Schools **Credit Hours For Degree:** 120 credits, Bachelors

EUGENIO MARÍA DE HOSTOS COMMUNITY COLLEGE OF THE CITY UNIVERSITY OF NEW YORK

500 Grand Concourse
Bronx, NY 10451
Tel: (718)518-4444
Fax: (718)518-4256
E-mail: admissions2@hostos.cuny.edu
Web Site: http://www.hostos.cuny.edu/
President/CEO: Félix V. Matos Rodríguez
Admissions: Roland Velez

Type: Two-Year College **Sex:** Coed **Affiliation:** City University of New York System **% Accepted:** 100 **Admission Plans:** Open Admission **Application Deadline:** Rolling **Application Fee:** $65.00 **H.S. Requirements:** High school diploma required; GED accepted **Scholarships:** Available **Calendar System:** Semester, Summer Session Available **Faculty:** FT 161, PT 163 **Student-Faculty Ratio:** 14:1 **Library Holdings:** 56,100 **Regional Accreditation:** Middle State Association of Colleges and Schools **Credit Hours For Degree:** 60 credits, Associates **Professional Accreditation:** ADA, JRCERT **Intercollegiate Athletics:** Baseball M; Basketball M & W; Volleyball W

EVEREST INSTITUTE

1630 Portland Ave.
Rochester, NY 14621
Tel: (585)266-0430
Web Site: http://www.everest.edu/campus/rochester/
President/CEO: Carl A. Silvio
Admissions: Deanna Pfluke

Type: Two-Year College **Sex:** Coed **Affiliation:** Corinthian Colleges, Inc. **Admission Plans:** Early Admission; Deferred Admission **Application Deadline:** Rolling **H.S. Requirements:** High school diploma or equivalent not required **Scholarships:** Available **Calendar System:** Quarter, Summer Session Available **Student-Faculty Ratio:** 16:1 **Exams:** Other. **Credit Hours For Degree:** 96 quarter hours, Associates **Professional Accreditation:** ACICS

EXCELSIOR COLLEGE

7 Columbia Circle
Albany, NY 12203-5159
Tel: (518)464-8500; Free: 888-647-2388
Fax: (518)464-8777
E-mail: admissions@excelsior.edu
Web Site: http://www.excelsior.edu/
President/CEO: John F. Ebersole
Financial Aid: Donna L. Cooper

Type: Comprehensive **Sex:** Coed **Admission Plans:** Open Admission **Application Deadline:** Rolling **Application Fee:** $75.00 **H.S. Requirements:** High school diploma required; GED accepted **Costs Per Year:** Application fee: $75. Tuition: $315 per credit hour part-time. Mandatory fees: $440 per year part-time. **Scholarships:** Available **Calendar System:** Continuous **Enrollment:** , PT 30,780, Grad PT 1,144 **Faculty:** FT 35, PT 369 **Student-Faculty Ratio:** 79:1 **Final Year or Final Semester Residency Requirement:** No **Regional Accreditation:** Middle State Association of Colleges and Schools **Credit Hours For Degree:** 60 credits, Associates; 120 credits, Bachelors **Professional Accreditation:** ABET, NLN

FARMINGDALE STATE COLLEGE

2350 Broadhollow Rd.
Farmingdale, NY 11735
Tel: (631)420-2000; Free: 877-4-FARMINGDALE
Admissions: (631)420-2457
Fax: (631)420-2633
Web Site: http://www.farmingdale.edu/
President/CEO: Dr. Hubert Keen
Admissions: Jim Hall
Financial Aid: Dionne Walker-Belgrave

Type: Four-Year College **Sex:** Coed **Affiliation:** State University of New York System **Scores:** 93% SAT V 400+; 95% SAT M 400+ **% Accepted:** 40 **Admission Plans:** Early Admission **Application Deadline:** Rolling **Application Fee:** $40.00 **H.S. Requirements:** High school diploma required; GED accepted **Costs Per Year:** Application fee: $40. State resident tuition: $4970 full-time, $207 per credit part-time. Nonresident tuition: $12,870 full-time, $536 per credit part-time. Mandatory fees: $1030 full-time, $.85 per credit part-time. College room and board: $11,618. College room only: $6850. Room and board charges vary according to board plan and location. **Scholarships:** Available **Calendar System:** Semester, Summer Session Available **Enrollment:** FT 5,019, PT 1,969 **Faculty:** FT 191, PT 364 **Student-Faculty Ratio:** 18:1 **Exams:** SAT I or ACT. **% Receiving Financial Aid:** 44 **% Residing in College-Owned, -Operated, or -Affiliated Housing:** 10 **Final Year or Final Semester Residency Requirement:** No **Library Holdings:** 125,000 **Regional Accreditation:** Middle State Association of Colleges and Schools **Credit Hours For Degree:** 60 credits, Associates; 122 credits, Bachelors **Professional Accreditation:** ABET, ADA, NAACLS, NLN **Intercollegiate Athletics:** Baseball M; Basketball M & W; Cross-Country Running M & W; Golf M; Ice Hockey M; Lacrosse M & W; Soccer M & W; Softball W; Tennis M & W; Track and Field M & W; Volleyball W

FASHION INSTITUTE OF TECHNOLOGY

Seventh Ave. at 27th St.
New York, NY 10001-5992
Tel: (212)217-7999; Free: 800-GOT-OFIT
Admissions: (212)217-3760
Fax: (212)217-7481
E-mail: fitinfo@fitnyc.edu
Web Site: http://www.fitnyc.edu/
President/CEO: Dr. Joyce F. Brown
Admissions: Yamiley Saintvil

Type: Comprehensive **Sex:** Coed **Affiliation:** State University of New York System **% Accepted:** 40 **Application Deadline:** January 15 **Application Fee:** $40.00 **H.S. Requirements:** High school diploma required; GED accepted **Costs Per Year:** Application fee: $40. State resident tuition: $5168 full-time, $215 per credit hour part-time. Nonresident tuition: $12,604 full-time, $525 per credit hour part-time. Mandatory fees: $450 full-time, $70 per year part-time. Full-time tuition and fees vary according to degree level. Part-time tuition and fees vary according to degree level. College room and board: $11,248. Room and board charges vary according to board plan and housing facility. **Scholarships:** Available **Calendar System:** Semester, Summer Session Available **Enrollment:** FT 7,163, PT 3,044, Grad FT 127, Grad PT 79 **Faculty:** FT 253, PT 754 **Student-Faculty Ratio:** 17:1 **% Receiving Financial Aid:** 47 **% Residing in College-Owned, -Operated, or -Affiliated Housing:** 25 **Final Year or Final Semester Residency Requirement:** No **Regional Accreditation:** Middle State Association of Colleges and Schools **Credit Hours For Degree:** 60 credits, Associates; 120 credits, Bachelors **Professional Accreditation:** FIDER, NASAD **Intercollegiate Athletics:** Basketball M; Cheerleading W; Cross-Country Running M & W; Swimming and Diving M & W; Table Tennis M & W; Tennis W; Volleyball W

FINGER LAKES COMMUNITY COLLEGE
3325 Marvin Sands Dr.
Canandaigua, NY 14424-8395
Tel: (585)394-3500
Fax: (585)394-5005
E-mail: admissions@flcc.edu
Web Site: http://www.flcc.edu/
President/CEO: Dr. Barbara Risser
Admissions: Bonnie B. Ritts
Type: Two-Year College **Sex:** Coed **Affiliation:** State University of New York System **% Accepted:** 81 **Admission Plans:** Open Admission; Preferred Admission; Early Admission; Deferred Admission **Application Deadline:** Rolling **Application Fee:** $0.00 **H.S. Requirements:** High school diploma required; GED accepted **Costs Per Year:** Application fee: $0. State resident tuition: $3296 full-time, $126 per credit hour part-time. Nonresident tuition: $6592 full-time, $252 per credit hour part-time. Mandatory fees: $410 full-time, $12 per credit hour part-time. Full-time tuition and fees vary according to course load. Part-time tuition and fees vary according to course load. **Scholarships:** Available **Calendar System:** Semester, Summer Session Available **Enrollment:** FT 3,750, PT 2,949 **Faculty:** FT 112, PT 230 **Student-Faculty Ratio:** 20:1 **Library Holdings:** 75,610 **Regional Accreditation:** Middle State Association of Colleges and Schools **Credit Hours For Degree:** 64 credit hours, Associates **ROTC:** Army **Professional Accreditation:** NLN **Intercollegiate Athletics:** Baseball M; Basketball M & W; Cross-Country Running M & W; Lacrosse M; Soccer M & W; Softball W; Track and Field M & W; Volleyball W

FIORELLO H. LAGUARDIA COMMUNITY COLLEGE OF THE CITY UNIVERSITY OF NEW YORK
31-10 Thomson Ave.
Long Island City, NY 11101-3071
Tel: (718)482-7200
Admissions: (718)482-5114
Fax: (718)482-5599
E-mail: admissions@lagcc.cuny.edu
Web Site: http://www.lagcc.cuny.edu/
President/CEO: Dr. Gail O. Mellow
Admissions: LaVora Desvigne
Type: Two-Year College **Sex:** Coed **Affiliation:** City University of New York System **% Accepted:** 100 **Admission Plans:** Open Admission; Early Admission; Deferred Admission **Application Deadline:** Rolling **Application Fee:** $65.00 **H.S. Requirements:** High school diploma required; GED accepted **Costs Per Year:** Application fee: $65. State resident tuition: $3150 full-time, $135 per credit hour part-time. Nonresident tuition: $5040 full-time, $210 per credit hour part-time. Mandatory fees: $342 full-time, $85.85 per term part-time. **Scholarships:** Available **Calendar System:** Miscellaneous, Summer Session Available **Enrollment:** FT 9,324, PT 7,639 **Faculty:** FT 304, PT 741 **Library Holdings:** 211,914 **Regional Accreditation:** Middle State Association of Colleges and Schools **Credit Hours For Degree:** 60 units, Associates **Professional Accreditation:** AOTA, APTA, NLN

FIVE TOWNS COLLEGE
305 North Service Rd.
Dix Hills, NY 11746-6055
Tel: (631)424-7000
Fax: (631)656-2172
E-mail: jcohen@ftc.edu
Web Site: http://www.ftc.edu/
President/CEO: Dr. Stanley G. Cohen
Admissions: Jerry Cohen
Financial Aid: Mary Venezia
Type: Comprehensive **Sex:** Coed **% Accepted:** 53 **Admission Plans:** Early Decision Plan; Deferred Admission **Application Deadline:** Rolling **Application Fee:** $35.00 **H.S. Requirements:** High school diploma required; GED accepted **Costs Per Year:** Application fee: $35. One-time mandatory fee: $500. Comprehensive fee: $30,050 includes full-time tuition ($17,400), mandatory fees ($350), and college room and board ($12,300). College room only: $7800. Full-time tuition and fees vary according to course load, degree level, and program. Room and board charges vary according to board plan. Part-time tuition: $725 per credit hour. Part-time mandatory fees: $60 per term. Part-time tuition and fees vary according to course load, degree level, and program. **Scholarships:** Available **Calendar System:** Semester, Summer Session Available **Enrollment:** FT 1,230, PT 32, Grad FT 130, Grad PT 55 **Faculty:** FT 33, PT 96 **Student-Faculty Ratio:** 13:1 **Exams:** SAT I or ACT. ACT essay used for admission. SAT essay used for admission. ACT essay used for advising. SAT essay used for advising. **% Receiving Financial Aid:** 74 **% Residing in College-Owned, -Operated, or -Affiliated Housing:** 20 **Library Holdings:** 40,000 **Regional Accreditation:** Middle State Association of Colleges and Schools **Credit Hours For Degree:** 60 credits, Associates; 120 credits, Bachelors **Professional Accreditation:** NCATE

FORDHAM UNIVERSITY
441 East Fordham Rd.
New York, NY 10458
Tel: (718)817-1000; Free: 800-FOR-DHAM
Admissions: (718)817-4000
Fax: (718)367-9404
E-mail: enroll@fordham.edu
Web Site: http://www.fordham.edu/
President/CEO: Fr. Joseph M. McShane, SJ
Admissions: Peter Farrell
Financial Aid: Angela Van Dekker
Type: University **Sex:** Coed **Affiliation:** Roman Catholic (Jesuit) **Scores:** 99.81% SAT V 400+; 99.82% SAT M 400+; 10.32% ACT 18-23; 63.6% ACT 24-29 **% Accepted:** 50 **Admission Plans:** Early Admission; Early Action; Deferred Admission **Application Deadline:** January 15 **Application Fee:** $50.00 **H.S. Requirements:** High school diploma required; GED accepted **Scholarships:** Available **Calendar System:** Semester, Summer Session Available **Enrollment:** FT 7,370, PT 580, Grad FT 3,538, Grad PT 3,056 **Faculty:** FT 723, PT 663 **Student-Faculty Ratio:** 13:1 **Exams:** SAT I or ACT, SAT II. **% Receiving Financial Aid:** 63 **% Residing in College-Owned, -Operated, or -Affiliated Housing:** 55 **Library Holdings:** 2,421,980 **Regional Accreditation:** Middle State Association of Colleges and Schools **Credit Hours For Degree:** 124 credits, Bachelors **ROTC:** Army, Navy, Air Force **Professional Accreditation:** AACSB, ABA, APA, AALS, CSWE, NASD, NCATE **Intercollegiate Athletics:** Baseball M; Basketball M & W; Cheerleading M & W; Crew M & W; Cross-Country Running M & W; Football M; Golf M; Ice Hockey M; Lacrosse M & W; Rugby M & W; Sailing M & W; Soccer M & W; Softball W; Squash M; Swimming and Diving M & W; Tennis M & W; Track and Field M & W; Ultimate Frisbee M & W; Volleyball W; Water Polo M

FULTON-MONTGOMERY COMMUNITY COLLEGE
2805 State Hwy. 67
Johnstown, NY 12095-3790
Tel: (518)762-4651
Fax: (518)762-6518
E-mail: llaporte@fmcc.suny.edu
Web Site: http://www.fmcc.suny.edu/
President/CEO: Dr. Dustin Swanger
Admissions: Laura LaPorte
Type: Two-Year College **Sex:** Coed **Affiliation:** State University of New York System **Admission Plans:** Open Admission; Early Admission; Deferred Admission **Application Deadline:** September 10 **Application Fee:** $0.00 **H.S. Requirements:** High school diploma or equivalent not required. For nursing and radiological technology programs: High school diploma required; GED accepted **Costs Per Year:** Application fee: $0. State resident tuition: $3194 full-time, $133 per credit hour part-time. Nonresident tuition: $6388 full-time, $266 per credit hour part-time. Mandatory fees: $534 full-time. Part-time tuition varies according to course load. College room and board: $8290. College room only: $5660. **Scholarships:** Available **Calendar System:** Semester, Summer Session Available **Enrollment:** FT 1,784, PT 948 **Faculty:** FT 53, PT 87 **Student-Faculty Ratio:** 24:1 **Library Holdings:** 51,642 **Regional Accreditation:** Middle State Association of Colleges and Schools **Credit Hours For Degree:** 62 credits, Associates **Intercollegiate Athletics:** Baseball M; Basketball M & W; Soccer M & W; Softball W; Volleyball W

GAMLA COLLEGE
1213 Elm Ave.
Brooklyn, NY 11230

Tel: (718)339-4747
Fax: (718)998-5766
Type: Two-Year College **Sex:** Coed **Calendar System:** Semester

GENESEE COMMUNITY COLLEGE

1 College Rd.
Batavia, NY 14020-9704
Tel: (585)343-0055; Free: 800-CALL GCC
Fax: (585)345-4541
E-mail: tmlanemartin@genesee.edu
Web Site: http://www.genesee.edu/
President/CEO: Dr. Stuart Steiner
Admissions: Tanya Lane-Martin
Type: Two-Year College **Sex:** Coed **Affiliation:** State University of New York System **Admission Plans:** Open Admission **Application Deadline:** Rolling **Application Fee:** $0.00 **H.S. Requirements:** High school diploma required; GED accepted **Costs Per Year:** Application fee: $0. State resident tuition: $3720 full-time, $140 per credit hour part-time. Nonresident tuition: $4320 full-time, $160 per credit hour part-time. Mandatory fees: $320 full-time, $24 per credit hour part-time. Full-time tuition and fees vary according to course load. Part-time tuition and fees vary according to course load. College room only: $5300. Room charges vary according to housing facility. **Scholarships:** Available **Calendar System:** Semester, Summer Session Available **Enrollment:** FT 3,452, PT 3,756 **Faculty:** FT 76, PT 240 **Student-Faculty Ratio:** 18:1 **Exams:** ACT. **Final Year or Final Semester Residency Requirement:** Yes **Library Holdings:** 80,000 **Regional Accreditation:** Middle State Association of Colleges and Schools **Credit Hours For Degree:** 62 credit hours, Associates **Professional Accreditation:** AOTA, APTA, CARC, NLN **Intercollegiate Athletics:** Baseball M; Basketball M & W; Cross-Country Running M & W; Golf M & W; Lacrosse M; Soccer M & W; Softball W; Swimming and Diving M & W; Volleyball M & W

GLOBAL COLLEGE OF LONG ISLAND UNIVERSITY

9 Hanover Place, 4th Floor
Brooklyn, NY 11201
Tel: (631)287-8474
Admissions: (718)780-4320
Fax: (631)287-8463
E-mail: amy.greenstein@liu.edu
Web Site: http://www.liu.edu/globalcollege/
President/CEO: Dr. David Steinberg
Admissions: Amy Greenstein
Type: Four-Year College **Sex:** Coed **Affiliation:** Long Island University **% Accepted:** 73 **Admission Plans:** Open Admission; Early Admission; Deferred Admission **Application Deadline:** Rolling **Application Fee:** $30.00 **H.S. Requirements:** High school diploma required; GED accepted **Calendar System:** Semester, Summer Session Not available **Enrollment:** FT 98 **Student-Faculty Ratio:** 4:1 **Library Holdings:** 115,380 **Regional Accreditation:** Middle State Association of Colleges and Schools **Credit Hours For Degree:** 120 credits, Bachelors

GLOBE INSTITUTE OF TECHNOLOGY

500 7th Ave.
New York, NY 10018
Tel: (212)349-4330; Free: 877-394-5623
Fax: (212)227-5920
E-mail: admissions@globe.edu
Web Site: http://www.globe.edu/
President/CEO: Martin Oliner
Admissions: Michael Scalice
Type: Four-Year College **Sex:** Coed **Admission Plans:** Open Admission **Application Deadline:** Rolling **Application Fee:** $50.00 **H.S. Requirements:** High school diploma required; GED accepted **Scholarships:** Available **Calendar System:** Semester, Summer Session Available **Exams:** SAT I or ACT. **Library Holdings:** 20,000 **Credit Hours For Degree:** 60 credits, Associates; 120 credits, Bachelors **Professional Accreditation:** ACICS, NYSBR **Intercollegiate Athletics:** Baseball M; Basketball M & W; Cross-Country Running M & W; Soccer M; Track and Field M & W; Volleyball W

HAMILTON COLLEGE

198 College Hill Rd.
Clinton, NY 13323-1296
Tel: (315)859-4011; Free: 800-843-2655
Fax: (315)859-4124
E-mail: admission@hamilton.edu
Web Site: http://www.hamilton.edu/
President/CEO: Dr. Joan Hinde Stewart
Admissions: Monica Inzer
Type: Four-Year College **Sex:** Coed **Scores:** 100% SAT V 400+; 100% SAT M 400+; 6.45% ACT 18-23; 37.1% ACT 24-29 **% Accepted:** 30 **Admission Plans:** Early Decision Plan; Deferred Admission **Application Deadline:** January 1 **Application Fee:** $75.00 **H.S. Requirements:** High school diploma required; GED accepted **Costs Per Year:** Application fee: $75. Comprehensive fee: $49,860 includes full-time tuition ($39,370), mandatory fees ($390), and college room and board ($10,100). College room only: $5520. Room and board charges vary according to board plan. Part-time tuition: $4921 per course. **Scholarships:** Available **Calendar System:** Semester, Summer Session Not available **Enrollment:** FT 1,851, PT 31 **Faculty:** FT 177, PT 42 **Student-Faculty Ratio:** 10:1 **Exams:** SAT I and SAT II or ACT. ACT essay used for admission. SAT essay used for admission. **% Receiving Financial Aid:** 41 **% Residing in College-Owned, -Operated, or -Affiliated Housing:** 97 **Library Holdings:** 634,831 **Regional Accreditation:** Middle State Association of Colleges and Schools **Credit Hours For Degree:** 32 courses, Bachelors **ROTC:** Army, Air Force **Intercollegiate Athletics:** Baseball M; Basketball M & W; Crew M & W; Cross-Country Running M & W; Field Hockey W; Football M; Golf M & W; Ice Hockey M & W; Lacrosse M & W; Soccer M & W; Softball W; Squash M & W; Swimming and Diving M & W; Tennis M & W; Track and Field M & W; Volleyball M & W; Water Polo M & W

HARTWICK COLLEGE

One Hartwick Dr.
Oneonta, NY 13820-4020
Tel: (607)431-4200; Free: 888-HARTWICK
Admissions: (607)431-4150
Fax: (607)431-4138
E-mail: admissions@hartwick.edu
Web Site: http://www.hartwick.edu/
President/CEO: Dr. Margaret L. Drugovich
Financial Aid: Melissa Allen
Type: Four-Year College **Sex:** Coed **Scores:** 98% SAT V 400+; 99% SAT M 400+; 42% ACT 18-23; 49% ACT 24-29 **% Accepted:** 91 **Admission Plans:** Early Admission; Early Decision Plan; Deferred Admission **Application Deadline:** February 15 **Application Fee:** $35.00 **H.S. Requirements:** High school diploma required; GED accepted **Costs Per Year:** Application fee: $35. One-time mandatory fee: $300. Comprehensive fee: $42,405 includes full-time tuition ($32,550), mandatory fees ($780), and college room and board ($9075). College room only: $4700. Full-time tuition and fees vary according to student level. Room and board charges vary according to board plan and housing facility. Part-time tuition: $1030 per credit hour. **Scholarships:** Available **Calendar System:** 4-1-4, Summer Session Not available **Enrollment:** FT 1,427, PT 46 **Faculty:** FT 103, PT 92 **Student-Faculty Ratio:** 11:1 **Exams:** SAT I. **% Receiving Financial Aid:** 74 **% Residing in College-Owned, -Operated, or -Affiliated Housing:** 86 **Final Year or Final Semester Residency Requirement:** No **Library Holdings:** 311,063 **Regional Accreditation:** Middle State Association of Colleges and Schools **Credit Hours For Degree:** 36 courses, Bachelors **Professional Accreditation:** AACN, NASAD, NASM, NLN **Intercollegiate Athletics:** Basketball M & W; Cheerleading W; Cross-Country Running M & W; Equestrian Sports W; Field Hockey W; Football M; Ice Hockey M; Lacrosse M & W; Rugby M; Soccer M & W; Swimming and Diving M & W; Tennis M & W; Volleyball W; Water Polo M & W

HELENE FULD COLLEGE OF NURSING OF NORTH GENERAL HOSPITAL

1879 Madison Ave.
New York, NY 10035-2709
Tel: (212)423-2700
Admissions: (212)616-7200
Web Site: http://www.helenefuld.edu/
President/CEO: Margaret Wines
Admissions: Gladys Pineda
Type: Two-Year College **Sex:** Coed **% Accepted:** 100 **Admission Plans:** Preferred Admission; Deferred Admission **Application Deadline:** Rolling **Application Fee:** $50.00 **H.S. Requirements:** High school diploma required; GED accepted **Scholarships:** Available **Calendar System:** Quarter, Summer Session Available **Faculty:** FT 10, PT 16 **Student-Faculty Ratio:** 13:1 **Exams:** Other. **Library Holdings:** 6,200 **Regional Accredita-**

tion: Middle State Association of Colleges and Schools **Credit Hours For Degree:** 70 credits, Associates **Professional Accreditation:** NLN

HERKIMER COUNTY COMMUNITY COLLEGE
Reservoir Rd.
Herkimer, NY 13350
Tel: (315)866-0300
Fax: (315)866-7253
Web Site: http://www.herkimer.edu/
President/CEO: Ann Marie Murray
Admissions: Scott J. Hughes
Type: Two-Year College **Sex:** Coed **Affiliation:** State University of New York System **Admission Plans:** Open Admission; Preferred Admission; Early Admission **Application Deadline:** August 20 **Application Fee:** $0.00 **H.S. Requirements:** High school diploma required; GED accepted **Scholarships:** Available **Calendar System:** Semester, Summer Session Available **Library Holdings:** 70,000 **Regional Accreditation:** Middle State Association of Colleges and Schools **Credit Hours For Degree:** 63 credit hours, Associates **Professional Accreditation:** AOTA, APTA **Intercollegiate Athletics:** Baseball M; Basketball M & W; Bowling M & W; Cross-Country Running M & W; Lacrosse M & W; Soccer M & W; Softball W; Swimming and Diving M & W; Tennis M & W; Track and Field M & W; Volleyball W

HILBERT COLLEGE
5200 South Park Ave.
Hamburg, NY 14075-1597
Tel: (716)649-7900
Fax: (716)649-0702
E-mail: tlee@hilbert.edu
Web Site: http://www.hilbert.edu/
President/CEO: Cynthia Zane
Admissions: Timothy Lee
Financial Aid: Beverly Chudy
Type: Four-Year College **Sex:** Coed **Scores:** 84% SAT V 400+; 85% SAT M 400+; 53% ACT 18-23; 18% ACT 24-29 **% Accepted:** 85 **Admission Plans:** Early Admission; Deferred Admission **Application Deadline:** September 1 **Application Fee:** $20.00 **H.S. Requirements:** High school diploma required; GED accepted **Costs Per Year:** Application fee: $20. Comprehensive fee: $26,480 includes full-time tuition ($17,890), mandatory fees ($600), and college room and board ($7990). College room only: $4050. Full-time tuition and fees vary according to course load. Room and board charges vary according to board plan and housing facility. Part-time tuition: $450 per credit hour. Part-time tuition varies according to course load. **Scholarships:** Available **Calendar System:** Semester, Summer Session Available **Enrollment:** FT 798, PT 248 **Faculty:** FT 48, PT 67 **Student-Faculty Ratio:** 12:1 **Exams:** SAT I or ACT. **% Receiving Financial Aid:** 87 **% Residing in College-Owned, -Operated, or -Affiliated Housing:** 25 **Library Holdings:** 41,322 **Regional Accreditation:** Middle State Association of Colleges and Schools **Credit Hours For Degree:** 60 credit hours, Associates; 120 credit hours, Bachelors **ROTC:** Army **Intercollegiate Athletics:** Baseball M; Basketball M & W; Cross-Country Running M & W; Golf M & W; Soccer M & W; Softball W; Volleyball M & W

HOBART AND WILLIAM SMITH COLLEGES
Geneva, NY 14456-3397
Tel: (315)781-3000; Free: 800-245-0100
Admissions: (315)781-3622
Fax: (315)781-5471
E-mail: emmons@hws.edu
Web Site: http://www.hws.edu/
President/CEO: Mark D. Gearan
Admissions: Don W. Emmons
Financial Aid: Beth Turner
Type: Comprehensive **Sex:** Coed **Scores:** 100% SAT V 400+; 99% SAT M 400+ **% Accepted:** 55 **Admission Plans:** Early Admission; Early Decision Plan; Deferred Admission **Application Deadline:** February 1 **Application Fee:** $45.00 **H.S. Requirements:** High school diploma required; GED accepted **Scholarships:** Available **Calendar System:** Semester, Summer Session Not available **Enrollment:** FT 1,998, PT 3 **Faculty:** FT 183, PT 29 **Student-Faculty Ratio:** 11:1 **Exams:** SAT I or ACT. **% Receiving Financial Aid:** 75 **% Residing in College-Owned, -Operated, or -Affiliated Housing:** 90 **Library Holdings:** 380,419 **Regional Accreditation:** Middle State Association of Colleges and Schools **Credit Hours For Degree:** 32 courses, Bachelors **Intercollegiate Athletics:** Basketball M & W; Crew M & W; Cross-Country Running M & W; Equestrian Sports M & W; Field Hockey W; Football M; Golf M & W; Ice Hockey M & W; Lacrosse M & W; Rock Climbing M & W; Rugby M & W; Sailing M & W; Skiing (Downhill) M & W; Soccer M & W; Squash M & W; Swimming and Diving W; Tennis M & W; Ultimate Frisbee M & W

HOFSTRA UNIVERSITY
100 Hofstra University
Hempstead, NY 11549
Tel: (516)463-6600; Free: 800-HOF-STRA
Admissions: (516)463-6700
Fax: (516)560-7660
E-mail: admission@hofstra.edu
Web Site: http://www.hofstra.edu/
President/CEO: Stuart Rabinowitz, JD
Admissions: Sunil Samuel
Financial Aid: Sandra Filbry
Type: University **Sex:** Coed **Scores:** 100% SAT V 400+; 100% SAT M 400+; 23% ACT 18-23; 65% ACT 24-29 **% Accepted:** 57 **Admission Plans:** Early Admission; Early Action; Deferred Admission **Application Deadline:** Rolling **Application Fee:** $70.00 **H.S. Requirements:** High school diploma required; GED accepted **Costs Per Year:** Application fee: $70. Comprehensive fee: $41,460 includes full-time tuition ($29,080), mandatory fees ($1050), and college room and board ($11,330). College room only: $7600. Full-time tuition and fees vary according to course load and program. Room and board charges vary according to board plan and housing facility. Part-time tuition: $890 per term. Part-time mandatory fees: $155 per term. Part-time tuition and fees vary according to course load and program. **Scholarships:** Available **Calendar System:** 4-1-4, Summer Session Available **Enrollment:** FT 7,327, PT 592, Grad FT 2,457, Grad PT 1,692 **Faculty:** FT 544, PT 636 **Student-Faculty Ratio:** 14:1 **Exams:** SAT I or ACT, SAT II. ACT essay used as a validity check on application essay. SAT essay used as a validity check on application essay. **% Receiving Financial Aid:** 61 **% Residing in College-Owned, -Operated, or -Affiliated Housing:** 49 **Final Year or Final Semester Residency Requirement:** Yes **Library Holdings:** 1,200,000 **Regional Accreditation:** Middle State Association of Colleges and Schools **Credit Hours For Degree:** 124 semester hours, Bachelors **ROTC:** Army **Professional Accreditation:** AACSB, ABET, ACEJMC, ABA, APA, ASLHA, AALS, CORE, JRCEPAT, NCATE, TEAC **Intercollegiate Athletics:** Baseball M; Basketball M & W; Cross-Country Running M & W; Field Hockey W; Golf M & W; Lacrosse M & W; Soccer M & W; Softball W; Tennis M & W; Volleyball W; Wrestling M

HOLY TRINITY ORTHODOX SEMINARY
PO Box 36
Jordanville, NY 13361
Tel: (315)858-0945
Fax: (315)858-0945
E-mail: info@hts.edu
Web Site: http://www.hts.edu/
President/CEO: Rev. Archimandrite Luke Murianka
Admissions: Fr. Vladimir Tsurikov
Type: Five-Year College **Sex:** Men **Affiliation:** Russian Orthodox **% Accepted:** 80 **Application Deadline:** May 1 **Application Fee:** $0.00 **H.S. Requirements:** High school diploma required; GED accepted **Costs Per Year:** Application fee: $0. Comprehensive fee: $5525 includes full-time tuition ($3000), mandatory fees ($25), and college room and board ($2500). Part-time tuition: $300 per course. **Calendar System:** Semester, Summer Session Not available **Enrollment:** FT 25, PT 3 **Faculty:** FT 10, PT 5 **Student-Faculty Ratio:** 2:1 **% Residing in College-Owned, -Operated, or -Affiliated Housing:** 100 **Library Holdings:** 25,000 **Credit Hours For Degree:** 162 credit hours, Bachelors **Professional Accreditation:** NYSBR

HOUGHTON COLLEGE
One Willard Ave.
Houghton, NY 14744
Tel: (585)567-9200; Free: 800-777-2556
Admissions: (585)567-9353
Fax: (585)567-9522
E-mail: admission@houghton.edu
Web Site: http://www.houghton.edu/
President/CEO: Dr. Shirley Mullen
Admissions: Matthew Reitnour
Financial Aid: Troy Martin

Type: Comprehensive **Sex:** Coed **Affiliation:** Wesleyan **Scores:** 99% SAT V 400+; 98% SAT M 400+; 36% ACT 18-23; 42% ACT 24-29 **% Accepted:** 82 **Admission Plans:** Deferred Admission **Application Deadline:** Rolling **Application Fee:** $40.00 **H.S. Requirements:** High school diploma required; GED accepted **Costs Per Year:** Application fee: $40. Comprehensive fee: $31,440 includes full-time tuition ($24,440) and college room and board ($7000). College room only: $3780. Room and board charges vary according to board plan and housing facility. Part-time tuition: $1025 per credit hour. **Scholarships:** Available **Calendar System:** Semester, Summer Session Available **Enrollment:** FT 1,252, PT 59, Grad FT 8, Grad PT 17 **Faculty:** FT 88, PT 56 **Student-Faculty Ratio:** 12:1 **Exams:** SAT I or ACT. SAT essay used for placement. **% Receiving Financial Aid:** 82 **% Residing in College-Owned, -Operated, or -Affiliated Housing:** 89 **Final Year or Final Semester Residency Requirement:** Yes **Library Holdings:** 230,070 **Regional Accreditation:** Middle State Association of Colleges and Schools **Credit Hours For Degree:** 62 credit hours, Associates; 124 credit hours, Bachelors **ROTC:** Army **Professional Accreditation:** NASM **Intercollegiate Athletics:** Basketball M & W; Cross-Country Running M & W; Field Hockey W; Soccer M & W; Track and Field M & W; Volleyball W

HUDSON VALLEY COMMUNITY COLLEGE
80 Vandenburgh Ave.
Troy, NY 12180-6096
Tel: (518)629-4822
E-mail: panzajul@hvcc.edu
Web Site: http://www.hvcc.edu/
President/CEO: Andrew J. Matonak
Admissions: MaryClaire Bauer
Type: Two-Year College **Sex:** Coed **Affiliation:** State University of New York System **% Accepted:** 90 **Admission Plans:** Open Admission; Early Admission; Deferred Admission **Application Deadline:** Rolling **Application Fee:** $30.00 **H.S. Requirements:** High school diploma required; GED accepted **Scholarships:** Available **Calendar System:** Semester, Summer Session Available **Faculty:** FT 215, PT 359 **Student-Faculty Ratio:** 19:1 **Library Holdings:** 148,189 **Regional Accreditation:** Middle State Association of Colleges and Schools **Credit Hours For Degree:** 60 credits, Associates **ROTC:** Army, Air Force **Professional Accreditation:** ABET, ABFSE, ACCE, ADA, CARC, JRCERT, JRCEMT, NLN **Intercollegiate Athletics:** Basketball M & W; Bowling M & W; Cross-Country Running M & W; Football M; Golf M & W; Lacrosse M; Soccer M; Tennis M & W; Track and Field M & W; Volleyball W

HUNTER COLLEGE OF THE CITY UNIVERSITY OF NEW YORK
695 Park Ave.
New York, NY 10021-5085
Tel: (212)772-4000
Admissions: (212)772-4490
E-mail: bill.zlata@hunter.cuny.edu
Web Site: http://www.hunter.cuny.edu/
President/CEO: Dr. Jennifer J. Raab
Admissions: William Zlata
Financial Aid: Aristalia Cortorreal Diaz
Type: Comprehensive **Sex:** Coed **Affiliation:** City University of New York System **Scores:** 100% SAT V 400+; 100% SAT M 400+ **% Accepted:** 26 **Admission Plans:** Early Admission **Application Deadline:** March 15 **Application Fee:** $65.00 **H.S. Requirements:** High school diploma required; GED accepted **Costs Per Year:** Application fee: $65. State resident tuition: $4600 full-time, $195 per term part-time. Nonresident tuition: $12,450 full-time, $415 per term part-time. Mandatory fees: $399 full-time, $183.50 per term part-time. Full-time tuition and fees vary according to degree level and program. Part-time tuition and fees vary according to degree level and program. College room only: $5500. **Scholarships:** Available **Calendar System:** Semester, Summer Session Available **Enrollment:** FT 11,171, PT 4,713 **Faculty:** FT 694, PT 1,086 **Student-Faculty Ratio:** 15:1 **Exams:** SAT I or ACT. **% Receiving Financial Aid:** 57 **% Residing in College-Owned, -Operated, or -Affiliated Housing:** 1 **Library Holdings:** 815,668 **Regional Accreditation:** Middle State Association of Colleges and Schools **Credit Hours For Degree:** 120 credits, Bachelors **Professional Accreditation:** ABET, AACN, ADtA, ACSP, APTA, ASLHA, CEPH, CORE, CSWE, NCATE **Intercollegiate Athletics:** Basketball M & W; Cross-Country Running M & W; Fencing M & W; Gymnastics W; Soccer M; Swimming and Diving W; Tennis M & W; Track and Field M & W; Volleyball M & W; Wrestling M

INSTITUTE OF DESIGN AND CONSTRUCTION
141 Willoughby St.
Brooklyn, NY 11201-5317
Tel: (718)855-3661
Fax: (718)852-5889
Web Site: http://www.idcbrooklyn.org/
President/CEO: Vincent C. Battista
Admissions: Kevin Giannetti
Type: Two-Year College **Sex:** Coed **% Accepted:** 86 **Application Deadline:** Rolling **Application Fee:** $30.00 **H.S. Requirements:** High school diploma required; GED accepted **Scholarships:** Available **Calendar System:** Semester, Summer Session Available **Faculty:** FT 0, PT 32 **Credit Hours For Degree:** 72 credits, Associates **Professional Accreditation:** NYSBR

IONA COLLEGE
715 North Ave.
New Rochelle, NY 10801-1890
Tel: (914)633-2000
Admissions: (914)633-2502
Fax: (914)633-2096
E-mail: icad@iona.edu
Web Site: http://www.iona.edu/
President/CEO: Br. James A. Liguori, CFC
Admissions: Kevin Cavanagh
Financial Aid: Mary Grant
Type: Comprehensive **Sex:** Coed **Affiliation:** Roman Catholic Church **Scores:** 98% SAT V 400+; 97% SAT M 400+ **% Accepted:** 58 **Admission Plans:** Early Action; Deferred Admission **Application Deadline:** February 15 **Application Fee:** $50.00 **H.S. Requirements:** High school diploma required; GED accepted **Costs Per Year:** Application fee: $50. Comprehensive fee: $40,650 includes full-time tuition ($26,850), mandatory fees ($2000), and college room and board ($11,800). Full-time tuition and fees vary according to class time. Room and board charges vary according to housing facility. Part-time tuition: $892 per credit. Part-time tuition varies according to class time and course load. **Scholarships:** Available **Calendar System:** Semester, Summer Session Available **Enrollment:** FT 3,245, PT 99, Grad FT 261, Grad PT 643 **Faculty:** FT 183, PT 207 **Student-Faculty Ratio:** 13:1 **Exams:** SAT I or ACT, SAT II. ACT essay used for advising. SAT essay used for advising. ACT essay used for placement. SAT essay used for placement. **% Receiving Financial Aid:** 75 **% Residing in College-Owned, -Operated, or -Affiliated Housing:** 31 **Final Year or Final Semester Residency Requirement:** No **Library Holdings:** 272,014 **Regional Accreditation:** Middle State Association of Colleges and Schools **Credit Hours For Degree:** 120 credits, Bachelors **ROTC:** Army, Air Force **Professional Accreditation:** AACSB, ACEJMC, AAMFT, CSWE, NCATE **Intercollegiate Athletics:** Baseball M; Basketball M & W; Crew M & W; Cross-Country Running M & W; Golf M; Lacrosse W; Soccer M & W; Softball W; Swimming and Diving M & W; Track and Field M & W; Volleyball W; Water Polo M & W

ISLAND DRAFTING AND TECHNICAL INSTITUTE
128 Broadway
Amityville, NY 11701
Tel: (631)691-8733
Fax: (631)691-8738
E-mail: info@idti.edu
Web Site: http://www.idti.edu/
President/CEO: James Di Liberto
Admissions: Jaimie Laudicina
Type: Two-Year College **Sex:** Coed **% Accepted:** 93 **Admission Plans:** Open Admission; Early Admission **Application Fee:** $25.00 **H.S. Requirements:** High school diploma required; GED accepted **Costs Per Year:** Application fee: $25. Tuition: $14,250 full-time, $475 per credit hour part-time. Mandatory fees: $350 full-time. Tuition guaranteed not to increase for student's term of enrollment. **Scholarships:** Available **Calendar System:** Semester, Summer Session Available **Enrollment:** FT 131 **Faculty:** FT 5, PT 6 **Student-Faculty Ratio:** 15:1 **Credit Hours For Degree:** 60 credits, Associates **Professional Accreditation:** ACCSCT

ITHACA COLLEGE
953 Danby Rd.
Ithaca, NY 14850
Tel: (607)274-3011; Free: 800-429-4274
Admissions: (607)274-3124
Fax: (607)274-1900
E-mail: admission@ithaca.edu
Web Site: http://www.ithaca.edu/

President/CEO: Thomas R. Rochon
Admissions: Gerard Turbide
Financial Aid: Larry Chambers
Type: Comprehensive **Sex:** Coed **Scores:** 99.6% SAT V 400+; 99.4% SAT M 400+ **% Accepted:** 79 **Admission Plans:** Early Admission; Early Decision Plan; Deferred Admission **Application Deadline:** February 1 **Application Fee:** $60.00 **H.S. Requirements:** High school diploma required; GED accepted **Costs Per Year:** Application fee: $60. Comprehensive fee: $43,840 includes full-time tuition ($32,060) and college room and board ($11,780). College room only: $6238. Room and board charges vary according to board plan. Part-time tuition: $1067 per credit hour. **Scholarships:** Available **Calendar System:** Semester, Summer Session Available **Enrollment:** FT 6,370, PT 70, Grad FT 413, Grad PT 41 **Faculty:** FT 461, PT 241 **Student-Faculty Ratio:** 12:1 **Exams:** SAT I or ACT. **% Receiving Financial Aid:** 69 **% Residing in College-Owned, -Operated, or -Affiliated Housing:** 76 **Final Year or Final Semester Residency Requirement:** No **Library Holdings:** 348,515 **Regional Accreditation:** Middle State Association of Colleges and Schools **Credit Hours For Degree:** 120 credit hours, Bachelors **ROTC:** Army, Air Force **Professional Accreditation:** AACSB, AOTA, APTA, ASLHA, JRCEPAT, NASM, NAST, NRPA **Intercollegiate Athletics:** Baseball M; Basketball M & W; Crew M & W; Cross-Country Running M & W; Field Hockey W; Football M; Golf W; Gymnastics W; Lacrosse M & W; Soccer M & W; Softball W; Swimming and Diving M & W; Tennis M & W; Track and Field M & W; Volleyball W; Wrestling M

ITT TECHNICAL INSTITUTE (ALBANY)
13 Airline Dr.
Albany, NY 12205
Tel: (518)452-9300
Web Site: http://www.itt-tech.edu/
President/CEO: Michael Mariani
Type: Two-Year College **Sex:** Coed **Affiliation:** ITT Educational Services, Inc. **H.S. Requirements:** High school diploma required; GED accepted **Scholarships:** Available **Calendar System:** Quarter, Summer Session Not available **Credit Hours For Degree:** 96 credit hours, Associates **Professional Accreditation:** ACICS

ITT TECHNICAL INSTITUTE (GETZVILLE)
2295 Millersport Hwy.
PO Box 327
Getzville, NY 14068
Tel: (716)689-2200
Web Site: http://www.itt-tech.edu/
President/CEO: Lester Burgess
Type: Two-Year College **Sex:** Coed **Affiliation:** ITT Educational Services, Inc. **H.S. Requirements:** High school diploma required; GED accepted **Scholarships:** Available **Professional Accreditation:** ACICS

ITT TECHNICAL INSTITUTE (LIVERPOOL)
235 Greenfield Parkway
Liverpool, NY 13088
Tel: (315)461-8000
Web Site: http://www.itt-tech.edu/
President/CEO: Jennifer Hill
Type: Two-Year College **Sex:** Coed **Affiliation:** ITT Educational Services, Inc. **H.S. Requirements:** High school diploma required; GED accepted **Scholarships:** Available **Calendar System:** Semester, Summer Session Not available **Credit Hours For Degree:** 96 credit hours, Associates **Professional Accreditation:** ACICS

JAMESTOWN BUSINESS COLLEGE
7 Fairmount Ave., Box 429
Jamestown, NY 14702-0429
Tel: (716)664-5100
Fax: (716)664-3144
E-mail: admissions@jbcny.org
Web Site: http://www.jbcny.org/
President/CEO: David Conklin
Admissions: Brenda Salemme
Type: Two-Year College **Sex:** Coed **% Accepted:** 91 **Application Deadline:** Rolling **Application Fee:** $25.00 **H.S. Requirements:** High school diploma required; GED accepted **Costs Per Year:** Application fee: $25. One-time mandatory fee: $25. Tuition: $10,200 full-time, $283 per credit hour part-time. Mandatory fees: $900 full-time, $150 per term part-time. **Scholarships:** Available **Calendar System:** Quarter, Summer Session Available **Enrollment:** FT 311, PT 18 **Faculty:** FT 8, PT 14 **Student-Faculty Ratio:** 25:1 **Library Holdings:** 279,270 **Regional Accreditation:** Middle State Association of Colleges and Schools **Credit Hours For Degree:** 90 quarter hours, Associates

JAMESTOWN COMMUNITY COLLEGE
525 Falconer St.
Jamestown, NY 14701-1999
Tel: (716)338-1000
Admissions: (716)338-1001
E-mail: admissions@mail.sunyjcc.edu
Web Site: http://www.sunyjcc.edu/
President/CEO: Dr. Gregory T. DeCinque
Admissions: Wendy Present
Type: Two-Year College **Sex:** Coed **Affiliation:** State University of New York System **% Accepted:** 91 **Admission Plans:** Open Admission; Deferred Admission **Application Deadline:** Rolling **H.S. Requirements:** High school diploma required; GED accepted **Costs Per Year:** State resident tuition: $3640 full-time, $151 per credit hour part-time. Nonresident tuition: $7280 full-time, $272 per credit hour part-time. Mandatory fees: $500 full-time. Full-time tuition and fees vary according to course load and program. Part-time tuition varies according to course load and program. College room and board: $7850. Room and board charges vary according to board plan. **Scholarships:** Available **Calendar System:** Semester, Summer Session Available **Enrollment:** FT 2,807, PT 1,124 **Faculty:** FT 81, PT 297 **Student-Faculty Ratio:** 18:1 **Library Holdings:** 66,808 **Regional Accreditation:** Middle State Association of Colleges and Schools **Credit Hours For Degree:** 60 semester hours, Associates **Professional Accreditation:** AOTA, NLN **Intercollegiate Athletics:** Baseball M; Basketball M & W; Cheerleading W; Cross-Country Running M & W; Golf M; Soccer M & W; Softball W; Swimming and Diving M & W; Volleyball W; Wrestling M

JEFFERSON COMMUNITY COLLEGE
1220 Coffeen St.
Watertown, NY 13601
Tel: (315)786-2200
Admissions: (315)786-2277
Fax: (315)786-0158
E-mail: admissions@sunyjefferson.edu
Web Site: http://www.sunyjefferson.edu/
President/CEO: Dr. Carole A. McCoy
Admissions: Rosanne N. Weir
Type: Two-Year College **Sex:** Coed **Affiliation:** State University of New York System **Admission Plans:** Preferred Admission; Early Admission; Deferred Admission **Application Deadline:** September 6 **Application Fee:** $0.00 **H.S. Requirements:** High school diploma required; GED accepted **Costs Per Year:** Application fee: $0. State resident tuition: $3312 full-time, $138 per credit hour part-time. Nonresident tuition: $5160 full-time, $215 per credit hour part-time. Mandatory fees: $382 full-time, $15 per credit hour part-time. Full-time tuition and fees vary according to course load and reciprocity agreements. Part-time tuition and fees vary according to course load and reciprocity agreements. **Scholarships:** Available **Calendar System:** Semester, Summer Session Available **Enrollment:** FT 2,024, PT 1,290 **Faculty:** FT 77, PT 114 **Student-Faculty Ratio:** 18:1 **Exams:** SAT I or ACT. **Final Year or Final Semester Residency Requirement:** No **Library Holdings:** 68,664 **Regional Accreditation:** Middle State Association of Colleges and Schools **Credit Hours For Degree:** 62 credit hours, Associates **Professional Accreditation:** NLN **Intercollegiate Athletics:** Baseball M; Basketball M & W; Lacrosse M & W; Soccer M & W; Softball W; Volleyball W

THE JEWISH THEOLOGICAL SEMINARY
3080 Broadway
New York, NY 10027-4649
Tel: (212)678-8000
Admissions: (212)678-8820
Fax: (212)678-8947
E-mail: lcadmissions@jtsa.edu
Web Site: http://www.jtsa.edu/
President/CEO: Dr. Arnold Eisen
Admissions: Sergio Lineberge
Financial Aid: Linda Levine
Type: University **Sex:** Coed **Affiliation:** Jewish **Scores:** 100% SAT V 400+; 100% SAT M 400+; 39% ACT 24-29 **% Accepted:** 60 **Admission Plans:**

fees vary according to course load. Room and board charges vary according to board plan and housing facility. **Scholarships:** Available **Calendar System:** Semester, Summer Session Not available **Enrollment:** FT 388, PT 4, Grad FT 527, Grad PT 11 **Faculty:** FT 84, PT 285 **Student-Faculty Ratio:** 6:1 **Exams:** SAT I or ACT. ACT essay not being used. SAT essay not being used. **% Receiving Financial Aid:** 60 **% Residing in College-Owned, -Operated, or -Affiliated Housing:** 67 **Library Holdings:** 13,189 **Regional Accreditation:** Middle State Association of Colleges and Schools **Credit Hours For Degree:** 120 credits, Bachelors

MANHATTANVILLE COLLEGE
2900 Purchase St.
Purchase, NY 10577-2132
Tel: (914)694-2200; Free: 800-328-4553
Admissions: (914)323-5129
Fax: (914)694-1732
E-mail: admissions@mville.edu
Web Site: http://www.manhattanville.edu/
President/CEO: Dr. Molly Easo Smith
Admissions: Erica Padilla
Financial Aid: Maria A. Barlaam
Type: Comprehensive **Sex:** Coed **% Accepted:** 53 **Admission Plans:** Early Admission; Deferred Admission **Application Deadline:** March 1 **Application Fee:** $70.00 **H.S. Requirements:** High school diploma required; GED accepted **Costs Per Year:** Application fee: $70. Comprehensive fee: $48,270 includes full-time tuition ($33,030), mandatory fees ($1320), and college room and board ($13,920). College room only: $8250. Room and board charges vary according to board plan. Part-time tuition: $765 per credit. Part-time mandatory fees: $60 per term. Part-time tuition and fees vary according to program. **Scholarships:** Available **Calendar System:** Semester, Summer Session Available **Enrollment:** FT 1,717, PT 118, Grad FT 382, Grad PT 673 **Faculty:** FT 101, PT 231 **Student-Faculty Ratio:** 13:1 **% Receiving Financial Aid:** 66 **% Residing in College-Owned, -Operated, or -Affiliated Housing:** 78 **Final Year or Final Semester Residency Requirement:** No **Library Holdings:** 250,209 **Regional Accreditation:** Middle State Association of Colleges and Schools **Credit Hours For Degree:** 120 credits, Bachelors **Professional Accreditation:** NCATE **Intercollegiate Athletics:** Baseball M; Basketball M & W; Field Hockey W; Golf M; Ice Hockey M & W; Lacrosse M & W; Soccer M & W; Softball W; Swimming and Diving W; Tennis M & W; Volleyball W

MANNES COLLEGE THE NEW SCHOOL FOR MUSIC
150 West 85th St.
New York, NY 10024-4402
Tel: (212)580-0210; Free: 800-292-3040
Fax: (212)580-1738
E-mail: mannesadmissions@newschool.edu
Web Site: http://www.mannes.edu/
President/CEO: Bob Kerrey
Admissions: Georgia Schmitt
Type: Comprehensive **Sex:** Coed **Affiliation:** The New School **% Accepted:** 35 **Application Deadline:** December 1 **Application Fee:** $100.00 **H.S. Requirements:** High school diploma required; GED accepted **Costs Per Year:** Application fee: $100. Comprehensive fee: $48,860 includes full-time tuition ($32,860), mandatory fees ($740), and college room and board ($15,260). College room only: $12,260. Room and board charges vary according to board plan and housing facility. Part-time tuition: $1076 per credit. Part-time tuition varies according to course load. **Scholarships:** Available **Calendar System:** Semester, Summer Session Available **Enrollment:** FT 190, PT 20, Grad FT 173, Grad PT 1 **Faculty:** FT 6, PT 138 **Student-Faculty Ratio:** 7:1 **% Receiving Financial Aid:** 30 **% Residing in College-Owned, -Operated, or -Affiliated Housing:** 16 **Library Holdings:** 1,906,046 **Regional Accreditation:** Middle State Association of Colleges and Schools

MARIA COLLEGE
700 New Scotland Ave.
Albany, NY 12208-1798
Tel: (518)438-3111
E-mail: admissions@mariacollege.edu
Web Site: http://www.mariacollege.edu/
President/CEO: Sr. Laureen Fitzgerald
Admissions: Laurie A. Gilmore
Type: Four-Year College **Sex:** Coed **% Accepted:** 46 **Admission Plans:** Early Admission **Application Deadline:** August 25 **Application Fee:** $35.00 **H.S. Requirements:** High school diploma required; GED accepted **Costs Per Year:** Application fee: $35. Tuition: $9000 full-time, $375 per credit hour part-time. Mandatory fees: $320 full-time, $80 per term part-time. Full-time tuition and fees vary according to degree level and program. Part-time tuition and fees vary according to degree level and program. **Scholarships:** Available **Calendar System:** Semester, Summer Session Available **Enrollment:** FT 251, PT 600 **Faculty:** FT 30, PT 59 **Student-Faculty Ratio:** 14:1 **Exams:** SAT I or ACT. **Final Year or Final Semester Residency Requirement:** No **Library Holdings:** 56,746 **Regional Accreditation:** Middle State Association of Colleges and Schools **Credit Hours For Degree:** 64 credits, Associates; 120 credits, Bachelors **ROTC:** Air Force **Professional Accreditation:** AOTA, NLN

MARIST COLLEGE
3399 North Rd.
Poughkeepsie, NY 12601-1387
Tel: (845)575-3000; Free: 800-436-5483
Admissions: (845)575-3226
Fax: (845)471-6213
E-mail: admission@marist.edu
Web Site: http://www.marist.edu/
President/CEO: Dr. Dennis Murray
Admissions: Kenton Rinehart
Financial Aid: Joseph R. Weglarz
Type: Comprehensive **Sex:** Coed **Scores:** 99.3% SAT V 400+; 99.6% SAT M 400+; 26.4% ACT 18-23; 62.4% ACT 24-29 **% Accepted:** 36 **Admission Plans:** Early Admission; Early Action; Early Decision Plan; Deferred Admission **Application Deadline:** February 15 **Application Fee:** $50.00 **H.S. Requirements:** High school diploma required; GED accepted **Costs Per Year:** Application fee: $50. Comprehensive fee: $37,829 includes full-time tuition ($26,104), mandatory fees ($500), and college room and board ($11,225). College room only: $7235. Room and board charges vary according to board plan and housing facility. Part-time tuition: $610 per credit. Part-time mandatory fees: $40 per term. **Scholarships:** Available **Calendar System:** Semester, Summer Session Available **Enrollment:** FT 4,542, PT 788, Grad FT 366, Grad PT 483 **Faculty:** FT 220, PT 377 **Student-Faculty Ratio:** 15:1 **Exams:** SAT I or ACT. ACT essay used for placement. SAT essay used for placement. **% Receiving Financial Aid:** 61 **% Residing in College-Owned, -Operated, or -Affiliated Housing:** 74 **Final Year or Final Semester Residency Requirement:** No **Library Holdings:** 207,000 **Regional Accreditation:** Middle State Association of Colleges and Schools **Credit Hours For Degree:** 120 credits, Bachelors **ROTC:** Army **Professional Accreditation:** AACSB, CSWE, NAACLS **Intercollegiate Athletics:** Baseball M; Basketball M & W; Bowling M & W; Cheerleading M & W; Crew M & W; Cross-Country Running M & W; Equestrian Sports M & W; Fencing M & W; Football M; Ice Hockey M; Lacrosse M & W; Rugby M & W; Skiing (Downhill) M & W; Soccer M & W; Softball W; Swimming and Diving M & W; Tennis M & W; Track and Field M & W; Volleyball M & W; Water Polo W

MARYMOUNT MANHATTAN COLLEGE
221 East 71st St.
New York, NY 10021-4597
Tel: (212)517-0400; Free: 800-MARYMOUNT
Admissions: (212)517-0430
E-mail: admissions@mmm.edu
Web Site: http://www.mmm.edu/
President/CEO: Judson R. Shaver
Admissions: James Rogers
Type: Four-Year College **Sex:** Coed **Scores:** 97% SAT V 400+; 94% SAT M 400+; 50% ACT 18-23; 41% ACT 24-29 **% Accepted:** 70 **Admission Plans:** Deferred Admission **Application Deadline:** Rolling **Application Fee:** $60.00 **H.S. Requirements:** High school diploma required; GED accepted **Costs Per Year:** Application fee: $60. Comprehensive fee: $35,530 includes full-time tuition ($21,578), mandatory fees ($1078), and college room and board ($12,874). College room only: $10,874. Part-time tuition: $689 per credit hour. Part-time mandatory fees: $367 per term. **Scholarships:** Available **Calendar System:** Semester, Summer Session Available **Enrollment:** FT 1,751, PT 289 **Faculty:** FT 96, PT 214 **Student-Faculty Ratio:** 11:1 **Exams:** SAT I or ACT. **% Receiving Financial Aid:** 62 **% Residing in College-Owned, -Operated, or -Affiliated Housing:** 36 **Regional Accreditation:** Middle State Association of Colleges and Schools **Credit Hours For Degree:** 120 credits, Bachelors

Early Admission; Early Decision Plan; Deferred Admission **Application Deadline:** February 15 **Application Fee:** $65.00 **H.S. Requirements:** High school diploma required; GED accepted **Costs Per Year:** Application fee: $65. Tuition: $14,200 full-time, $750 per credit part-time. Mandatory fees: $800 full-time. Full-time tuition and fees vary according to program. Part-time tuition varies according to program. College room only: $9200. Room charges vary according to housing facility. **Scholarships:** Available **Calendar System:** Semester, Summer Session Available **Enrollment:** FT 182, PT 8 **Faculty:** FT 63, PT 67 **Student-Faculty Ratio:** 5:1 **Exams:** SAT I or ACT. **% Receiving Financial Aid:** 43 **% Residing in College-Owned, -Operated, or -Affiliated Housing:** 75 **Library Holdings:** 380,000 **Regional Accreditation:** Middle State Association of Colleges and Schools **Credit Hours For Degree:** 156 credits (96 in residence), Bachelors **ROTC:** Army, Navy, Air Force **Professional Accreditation:** ACIPE

JOHN JAY COLLEGE OF CRIMINAL JUSTICE OF THE CITY UNIVERSITY OF NEW YORK
899 Tenth Ave.
New York, NY 10019-1093
Tel: (212)237-8000; Free: 877-JOHNJAY
Admissions: (212)237-8878
E-mail: spalleja@jjay.cuny.edu
Web Site: http://www.jjay.cuny.edu/
President/CEO: Jeremy Travis
Admissions: Sandra Palleja
Financial Aid: Sylvia Lopez-Crespo
Type: Comprehensive **Sex:** Coed **Affiliation:** City University of New York System **Scores:** 78.3% SAT V 400+; 83% SAT M 400+ **% Accepted:** 63 **Application Deadline:** May 31 **Application Fee:** $65.00 **H.S. Requirements:** High school diploma required; GED accepted **Costs Per Year:** Application fee: $65. State resident tuition: $4600 full-time, $195 per credit part-time. Nonresident tuition: $12,450 full-time, $415 per credit part-time. Mandatory fees: $139.85. **Scholarships:** Available **Calendar System:** Semester, Summer Session Available **Enrollment:** FT 10,383, PT 2,963, Grad FT 442, Grad PT 1,542 **Faculty:** FT 439, PT 662 **Student-Faculty Ratio:** 19:1 **Exams:** SAT I or ACT. SAT essay used for admission. SAT essay used for advising. ACT essay used for placement. SAT essay used for placement. **% Receiving Financial Aid:** 77 **Final Year or Final Semester Residency Requirement:** No **Library Holdings:** 335,000 **Regional Accreditation:** Middle State Association of Colleges and Schools **Credit Hours For Degree:** 60 credits, Associates; 120 credits, Bachelors **ROTC:** Air Force **Professional Accreditation:** NASPAA **Intercollegiate Athletics:** Baseball M; Basketball M & W; Cross-Country Running M & W; Soccer M & W; Softball W; Swimming and Diving W; Tennis M & W; Volleyball W

THE JUILLIARD SCHOOL
60 Lincoln Center Plaza
New York, NY 10023-6588
Tel: (212)799-5000
Fax: (212)724-0263
E-mail: admissions@julliard.edu
Web Site: http://www.juilliard.edu/
President/CEO: Joseph W. Polisi
Admissions: Lee Cioppa
Financial Aid: Lee Cioppa
Type: Comprehensive **Sex:** Coed **% Accepted:** 7 **Application Deadline:** December 1 **Application Fee:** $100.00 **H.S. Requirements:** High school diploma required; GED accepted **Costs Per Year:** Application fee: $100. Comprehensive fee: $42,310 includes full-time tuition ($30,500) and college room and board ($11,810). Room and board charges vary according to housing facility. **Scholarships:** Available **Calendar System:** Semester, Summer Session Not available **Enrollment:** FT 489, Grad FT 304, Grad PT 40 **Faculty:** FT 116, PT 176 **Student-Faculty Ratio:** 3:1 **% Receiving Financial Aid:** 81 **% Residing in College-Owned, -Operated, or -Affiliated Housing:** 50 **Regional Accreditation:** Middle State Association of Colleges and Schools **Credit Hours For Degree:** 140 credits, Bachelors

KEHILATH YAKOV RABBINICAL SEMINARY
340 Illington Rd.
Ossining, NY 10562
Tel: (718)963-1212
Fax: (718)387-8586
President/CEO: Joseph Weber
Type: Comprehensive **Sex:** Men **Affiliation:** Jewish **Calendar System:** Semester **Professional Accreditation:** AARTS

KEUKA COLLEGE
Keuka Park, NY 14478-0098
Tel: (315)279-5000; Free: 800-33-KEUKA
Admissions: (315)279-5254
Fax: (315)279-5216
E-mail: admissions@mail.keuka.edu
Web Site: http://www.keuka.edu/
President/CEO: Dr. Joseph G. Burke
Admissions: Fred Hoyle
Financial Aid: Jennifer Bates
Type: Comprehensive **Sex:** Coed **Affiliation:** American Baptist Churches in the U.S.A. **Scores:** 78% SAT V 400+; 84% SAT M 400+; 48% ACT 18-23; 23% ACT 24-29 **% Accepted:** 77 **Admission Plans:** Early Admission; Deferred Admission **Application Deadline:** Rolling **Application Fee:** $30.00 **H.S. Requirements:** High school diploma required; GED accepted **Costs Per Year:** Application fee: $30. Comprehensive fee: $31,840 includes full-time tuition ($22,040), mandatory fees ($640), and college room and board ($9160). College room only: $4350. Full-time tuition and fees vary according to program. Room and board charges vary according to board plan and housing facility. Part-time tuition: $735 per credit hour. Part-time tuition varies according to program. **Scholarships:** Available **Calendar System:** 4-1-4, Summer Session Available **Enrollment:** FT 1,223, PT 299, Grad FT 100, Grad PT 54 **Faculty:** FT 74, PT 101 **Student-Faculty Ratio:** 14:1 **Exams:** SAT I or ACT. ACT essay used for advising. SAT essay used for advising. **% Receiving Financial Aid:** 90 **% Residing in College-Owned, -Operated, or -Affiliated Housing:** 81 **Library Holdings:** 112,541 **Regional Accreditation:** Middle State Association of Colleges and Schools **Credit Hours For Degree:** 120 credit hours, Bachelors **Professional Accreditation:** AOTA, CSWE, NLN **Intercollegiate Athletics:** Baseball M; Basketball M & W; Cross-Country Running M & W; Golf W; Lacrosse M; Soccer M & W; Softball W; Swimming and Diving W; Track and Field M; Volleyball W

THE KING'S COLLEGE
350 Fifth Ave.
15th Floor Empire State Bldg.
New York, NY 10118
Tel: (212)659-7200; Free: 888-969-7200
Admissions: (212)659-7217
E-mail: bparker@tkc.edu
Web Site: http://www.tkc.edu/
President/CEO: Andy Mills
Admissions: Brian Parker
Financial Aid: Anna Peters
Type: Four-Year College **Sex:** Coed **Affiliation:** nondenominational **Scores:** 100% SAT V 400+; 100% SAT M 400+; 18.2% ACT 18-23; 72.7% ACT 24-29 **% Accepted:** 74 **Admission Plans:** Early Action; Deferred Admission **Application Deadline:** Rolling **Application Fee:** $30.00 **H.S. Requirements:** High school diploma required; GED accepted **Costs Per Year:** Application fee: $30. Tuition: $27,000 full-time, $1125 per credit hour part-time. Mandatory fees: $350 full-time. Full-time tuition and fees vary according to course load. Part-time tuition varies according to course load. College room only: $10,500. **Scholarships:** Available **Calendar System:** Semester, Summer Session Available **Enrollment:** FT 289, PT 13 **Faculty:** FT 16, PT 16 **Student-Faculty Ratio:** 14:1 **Exams:** SAT I or ACT. ACT essay not being used. SAT essay not being used. **% Receiving Financial Aid:** 70 **% Residing in College-Owned, -Operated, or -Affiliated Housing:** 85 **Library Holdings:** 16,000 **Regional Accreditation:** Middle State Association of Colleges and Schools **Credit Hours For Degree:** 120 credits, Bachelors **Professional Accreditation:** NYSBR

KINGSBOROUGH COMMUNITY COLLEGE OF THE CITY UNIVERSITY OF NEW YORK
2001 Oriental Blvd, Manhattan Beach
Brooklyn, NY 11235
Tel: (718)368-5000
Admissions: (718)368-4600
E-mail: info@kbcc.cuny.edu
Web Site: http://www.kbcc.cuny.edu/
President/CEO: Dr. Regina Peruggi
Admissions: Robert Ingenito

Type: Two-Year College **Sex:** Coed **Affiliation:** City University of New York System **Admission Plans:** Open Admission **Application Deadline:** August 15 **Application Fee:** $65.00 **H.S. Requirements:** High school diploma required; GED accepted **Costs Per Year:** Application fee: $65. State resident tuition: $3150 full-time. Nonresident tuition: $6300 full-time. **Scholarships:** Available **Calendar System:** Semester, Summer Session Available **Enrollment:** FT 10,382, PT 7,411 **Faculty:** FT 311, PT 547 **Student-Faculty Ratio:** 23:1 **Library Holdings:** 185,912 **Regional Accreditation:** Middle State Association of Colleges and Schools **Credit Hours For Degree:** 60 credits, Associates **Professional Accreditation:** APTA, NLN **Intercollegiate Athletics:** Baseball M; Basketball M & W; Soccer M; Softball W; Tennis M & W; Track and Field M & W; Volleyball W

KOL YAAKOV TORAH CENTER
29 West Maple Ave.
Monsey, NY 10952-2954
Tel: (914)425-3863
Admissions: (845)425-3863
E-mail: horizonss@aol.com
Web Site: http://horizons.edu/
President/CEO: Leib Tropper
Type: Comprehensive **Sex:** Men **Affiliation:** Jewish **% Accepted:** 100 **Admission Plans:** Early Admission **Application Deadline:** Rolling **H.S. Requirements:** High school diploma or equivalent not required **Calendar System:** Semester, Summer Session Available **Library Holdings:** 2,000 **Credit Hours For Degree:** 130 credits, Bachelors **Professional Accreditation:** AARTS

LE MOYNE COLLEGE
1419 Salt Springs Rd.
Syracuse, NY 13214
Tel: (315)445-4100; Free: 800-333-4733
Admissions: (315)445-4300
Fax: (315)445-4711
E-mail: admission@lemoyne.edu
Web Site: http://www.lemoyne.edu/
President/CEO: Fred P. Pestello, PhD
Admissions: Dennis J. Nicholson
Financial Aid: William C. Cheetham
Type: Comprehensive **Sex:** Coed **Affiliation:** Roman Catholic (Jesuit) **Scores:** 97% SAT V 400+; 98% SAT M 400+; 55% ACT 18-23; 36% ACT 24-29 **% Accepted:** 67 **Admission Plans:** Early Admission; Early Decision Plan; Deferred Admission **Application Deadline:** February 1 **Application Fee:** $35.00 **H.S. Requirements:** High school diploma required; GED accepted **Costs Per Year:** Application fee: $35. Comprehensive fee: $35,820 includes full-time tuition ($25,110), mandatory fees ($720), and college room and board ($9990). College room only: $6340. Room and board charges vary according to board plan and housing facility. Part-time tuition: $526 per credit hour. Part-time tuition varies according to class time. **Scholarships:** Available **Calendar System:** Semester, Summer Session Available **Enrollment:** FT 2,332, PT 452, Grad FT 137, Grad PT 603 **Faculty:** FT 158, PT 167 **Student-Faculty Ratio:** 13:1 **Exams:** SAT I or ACT. ACT essay not being used. SAT essay not being used. **% Receiving Financial Aid:** 82 **% Residing in College-Owned, -Operated, or -Affiliated Housing:** 60 **Final Year or Final Semester Residency Requirement:** Yes **Library Holdings:** 270,763 **Regional Accreditation:** Middle State Association of Colleges and Schools **Credit Hours For Degree:** 120 credit hours, Bachelors **ROTC:** Army, Air Force **Professional Accreditation:** AACSB, AACN, TEAC **Intercollegiate Athletics:** Baseball M; Basketball M & W; Cross-Country Running M & W; Golf M & W; Lacrosse M & W; Soccer M & W; Softball W; Swimming and Diving M & W; Tennis M & W; Volleyball W

LEHMAN COLLEGE OF THE CITY UNIVERSITY OF NEW YORK
250 Bedford Park Blvd. West
Bronx, NY 10468-1589
Tel: (718)960-8000; Free: 877-Lehman1
Admissions: (718)960-8713
Fax: (718)960-8712
E-mail: enroll@lehman.cuny.edu
Web Site: http://www.lehman.cuny.edu/
President/CEO: Dr. Ricardo R. Fernandez
Admissions: Clarence Wilkes
Financial Aid: David Martinez
Type: Comprehensive **Sex:** Coed **Affiliation:** City University of New York System **Scores:** 96% SAT V 400+; 97% SAT M 400+ **% Accepted:** 26 **Admission Plans:** Deferred Admission **Application Deadline:** Rolling **Application Fee:** $65.00 **H.S. Requirements:** High school diploma required; GED accepted **Costs Per Year:** Application fee: $65. State resident tuition: $4600 full-time, $195 per credit part-time. Nonresident tuition: $9960 full-time, $415 per credit part-time. Mandatory fees: $340 full-time. Full-time tuition and fees vary according to program. Part-time tuition varies according to program. College room and board: $12,569. College room only: $9612. **Scholarships:** Available **Calendar System:** Semester, Summer Session Available **Enrollment:** FT 5,984, PT 3,734, Grad FT 271, Grad PT 2,199 **Faculty:** FT 371, PT 401 **Student-Faculty Ratio:** 14:1 **Exams:** SAT I or ACT. ACT essay used for admission. SAT essay used for admission. **% Receiving Financial Aid:** 81 **Library Holdings:** 595,952 **Regional Accreditation:** Middle State Association of Colleges and Schools **Credit Hours For Degree:** 120 credits, Bachelors **ROTC:** Army **Professional Accreditation:** AACN, ACA, ADtA, ASLHA, CSWE, NCATE, NLN **Intercollegiate Athletics:** Baseball M; Basketball M & W; Cross-Country Running M & W; Racquetball M & W; Soccer M & W; Softball W; Swimming and Diving M & W; Table Tennis M & W; Tennis M & W; Track and Field M & W; Volleyball M & W; Water Polo M; Wrestling M

LIM COLLEGE
12 East 53rd St.
New York, NY 10022-5268
Tel: (212)752-1530; Free: 800-677-1323
Fax: (212)832-6708
E-mail: admissions@limcollege.edu
Web Site: http://www.limcollege.edu/
President/CEO: Elizabeth S. Marcuse
Admissions: Kristina Ortiz
Financial Aid: Christopher Barto
Type: Comprehensive **Sex:** Coed **Scores:** 94% SAT V 400+; 90% SAT M 400+ **% Accepted:** 65 **Admission Plans:** Early Action; Deferred Admission **Application Deadline:** Rolling **Application Fee:** $40.00 **H.S. Requirements:** High school diploma required; GED accepted **Costs Per Year:** Application fee: $40. Comprehensive fee: $41,325 includes full-time tuition ($20,900), mandatory fees ($550), and college room and board ($19,875). College room only: $15,875. Room and board charges vary according to board plan. Part-time tuition: $695 per credit hour. Part-time mandatory fees: $125 per term. **Scholarships:** Available **Calendar System:** Semester, Summer Session Available **Enrollment:** FT 1,285, PT 61, Grad FT 30, Grad PT 12 **Faculty:** FT 25, PT 145 **Student-Faculty Ratio:** 18:1 **Exams:** SAT I or ACT. **% Receiving Financial Aid:** 56 **% Residing in College-Owned, -Operated, or -Affiliated Housing:** 24 **Final Year or Final Semester Residency Requirement:** Yes **Library Holdings:** 25,000 **Regional Accreditation:** Middle State Association of Colleges and Schools **Credit Hours For Degree:** 64 credits, Associates; 126 credits, Bachelors **Professional Accreditation:** ACBSP

LONG ISLAND BUSINESS INSTITUTE
6500 Jericho Turnpike
Commack, NY 11725
Tel: (631)499-7100
Admissions: (718)939-5100
Fax: (631)499-7114
E-mail: rnazar@libi.edu
Web Site: http://www.libi.edu/
President/CEO: Monica W. Foote
Admissions: Robert Nazar
Type: Two-Year College **Sex:** Coed **Affiliation:** Long Island Business Institute in Flushing, NY **% Accepted:** 81 **Application Deadline:** Rolling **Application Fee:** $50.00 **H.S. Requirements:** High school diploma required; GED accepted **Costs Per Year:** Application fee: $50. Tuition: $11,250 full-time, $375 per credit hour part-time. Mandatory fees: $700 full-time. **Calendar System:** Semester, Summer Session Available **Enrollment:** FT 412, PT 241 **Faculty:** FT 23, PT 71 **Student-Faculty Ratio:** 15:1 **Exams:** Other. **Library Holdings:** 4,400 **Credit Hours For Degree:** 61 credits, Associates **Professional Accreditation:** ACICS

LONG ISLAND COLLEGE HOSPITAL SCHOOL OF NURSING
350 Henry St.
7th Floor
Brooklyn, NY 11201
Tel: (718)780-1953

Admissions: (718)780-1071
Fax: (718)780-1936
E-mail: bevans@chpnet.org
Web Site: http://www.futurenurselich.org/
President/CEO: Nancy DiMauro, MA, RN
Admissions: Barbara Evans
Type: Two-Year College **Sex:** Coed **% Accepted:** 14 **Application Deadline:** April 21 **Application Fee:** $50.00 **H.S. Requirements:** High school diploma required; GED accepted **Scholarships:** Available **Calendar System:** Semester, Summer Session Available **Enrollment:** FT 70, PT 103 **Faculty:** FT 7, PT 11 **Student-Faculty Ratio:** 18:1 **Library Holdings:** 16,000 **Credit Hours For Degree:** 67 credits, Associates **Professional Accreditation:** NLN

LONG ISLAND UNIVERSITY, BRENTWOOD CAMPUS
100 Second Ave.
Brentwood, NY 11717
Tel: (631)273-5112
Fax: (631)952-0809
Web Site: http://www.liu.edu/
President/CEO: Dr. David J. Steinberg
Admissions: John P. Metcalfe
Type: Two-Year Upper Division **Sex:** Coed **Affiliation:** Long Island University **Application Fee:** $30.00 **Calendar System:** Semester, Summer Session Available **Student-Faculty Ratio:** 8:1 **Regional Accreditation:** Middle State Association of Colleges and Schools **Credit Hours For Degree:** 128 credits, Bachelors

LONG ISLAND UNIVERSITY, BROOKLYN CAMPUS
One University Plaza
Brooklyn, NY 11201-8423
Tel: (718)488-1000; Free: 800-LIU-PLAN
Admissions: (718)488-1011
E-mail: admissions@brooklyn.liu.edu
Web Site: http://www.liu.edu/
President/CEO: Dr. David J. Steinberg
Admissions: Elizabeth Storinge
Financial Aid: Rose Iannicelli
Type: University **Sex:** Coed **Affiliation:** Long Island University **Scores:** 79% SAT V 400+; 78% SAT M 400+; 46% ACT 18-23; 13% ACT 24-29 **% Accepted:** 80 **Admission Plans:** Deferred Admission **Application Deadline:** Rolling **Application Fee:** $30.00 **H.S. Requirements:** High school diploma required; GED accepted **Scholarships:** Available **Calendar System:** Semester, Summer Session Available **Enrollment:** FT 3,160, PT 785 **Faculty:** FT 304, PT 414 **Student-Faculty Ratio:** 14:1 **Exams:** SAT I or ACT. **% Receiving Financial Aid:** 82 **Library Holdings:** 314,565 **Regional Accreditation:** Middle State Association of Colleges and Schools **Credit Hours For Degree:** 64 credits, Associates; 128 credits, Bachelors **Professional Accreditation:** ACPhE, AACN, AOTA, APTA, APA, ASLHA, CARC, CSWE, NASPAA, TEAC **Intercollegiate Athletics:** Baseball M; Basketball M & W; Cross-Country Running M & W; Golf M & W; Lacrosse W; Soccer M & W; Softball W; Tennis W; Track and Field M & W; Volleyball W

LONG ISLAND UNIVERSITY, C.W. POST CAMPUS
720 Northern Blvd.
Brookville, NY 11548-1300
Tel: (516)299-2000; Free: 800-LIU-PLAN
Admissions: (516)299-2900
E-mail: enroll@cwpost.liu.edu
Web Site: http://www.liu.edu/
President/CEO: Dr. David J. Steinberg
Admissions: Joanne Graziano
Financial Aid: Karen Urdahl
Type: Comprehensive **Sex:** Coed **Affiliation:** Long Island University **Scores:** 93% SAT V 400+; 89% SAT M 400+; 60% ACT 18-23; 24% ACT 24-29 **% Accepted:** 82 **Admission Plans:** Deferred Admission **Application Deadline:** Rolling **Application Fee:** $30.00 **H.S. Requirements:** High school diploma required; GED accepted **Scholarships:** Available **Calendar System:** Semester, Summer Session Available **Enrollment:** FT 4,115, PT 4,353, Grad FT 1,404, Grad PT 1,877 **Faculty:** FT 324, PT 565 **Student-Faculty Ratio:** 13:1 **Exams:** SAT I or ACT. SAT essay used for advising. SAT essay used for placement. **% Receiving Financial Aid:** 66 **% Residing in College-Owned, -Operated, or -Affiliated Housing:** 33 **Library Holdings:** 177,108 **Regional Accreditation:** Middle State Association of Colleges and Schools **Credit Hours For Degree:** 64 credits, Associates; 129 credits, Bachelors **ROTC:** Army, Air Force **Professional Accreditation:** AACSB, AACN, ACA, ADtA, AHIMA, ALA, APA, ASLHA, CSWE, JRCERT, NAACLS, NASPAA, NLN, TEAC **Intercollegiate Athletics:** Baseball M; Basketball M & W; Crew M & W; Cross-Country Running M & W; Equestrian Sports M & W; Field Hockey W; Football M; Lacrosse M & W; Soccer M & W; Softball W; Swimming and Diving W; Tennis W; Volleyball W

MACHZIKEI HADATH RABBINICAL COLLEGE
5407 Sixteenth Ave.
Brooklyn, NY 11204-1805
Tel: (718)854-8777
Admissions: (718)854-8791
President/CEO: Rabbi Yisroel Aurbach
Admissions: Rabbi Abraham M. Lezerowitz
Financial Aid: Rabbi Baruch Rozmarin
Type: Comprehensive **Sex:** Men **Affiliation:** Jewish **Application Deadline:** Rolling **H.S. Requirements:** High school diploma required; GED not accepted **Calendar System:** Semester **Library Holdings:** 20,000 **Credit Hours For Degree:** 120 credits, Bachelors **Professional Accreditation:** AARTS

MANHATTAN COLLEGE
4513 Manhattan College Parkway
Riverdale, NY 10471
Tel: (718)862-8000
Admissions: (718)862-7200
Fax: (718)862-8019
E-mail: admit@manhattan.edu
Web Site: http://www.manhattan.edu/
President/CEO: Dr. Brennan O'Donnell
Admissions: William Bisset
Financial Aid: Edward Keough
Type: Comprehensive **Sex:** Coed **Affiliation:** Roman Catholic Church **Scores:** 98% SAT V 400+; 99% SAT M 400+ **% Accepted:** 65 **Admission Plans:** Early Admission; Early Decision Plan; Deferred Admission **Application Deadline:** April 15 **Application Fee:** $60.00 **H.S. Requirements:** High school diploma required; GED accepted **Costs Per Year:** Application fee: $60. Comprehensive fee: $38,125 includes full-time tuition ($25,520), mandatory fees ($1935), and college room and board ($10,670). Full-time tuition and fees vary according to course load and program. Room and board charges vary according to board plan. Part-time tuition: $689 per credit hour. Part-time tuition varies according to course load and program. **Scholarships:** Available **Calendar System:** Semester, Summer Session Available **Enrollment:** FT 2,962, PT 90, Grad FT 132, Grad PT 277 **Faculty:** FT 192, PT 188 **Student-Faculty Ratio:** 12:1 **Exams:** SAT I or ACT. **% Receiving Financial Aid:** 64 **% Residing in College-Owned, -Operated, or -Affiliated Housing:** 60 **Final Year or Final Semester Residency Requirement:** No **Library Holdings:** 289,255 **Regional Accreditation:** Middle State Association of Colleges and Schools **Credit Hours For Degree:** 120 credit hours, Bachelors **ROTC:** Army, Air Force **Professional Accreditation:** AACSB, ABET, TEAC **Intercollegiate Athletics:** Baseball M; Basketball M & W; Cheerleading M & W; Crew M & W; Cross-Country Running M & W; Golf M; Lacrosse M & W; Rugby M; Soccer M & W; Softball W; Swimming and Diving W; Tennis M & W; Track and Field M & W; Volleyball M & W

MANHATTAN SCHOOL OF MUSIC
120 Claremont Ave.
New York, NY 10027-4698
Tel: (212)749-2802
Admissions: (917)493-4501
Fax: (212)749-5471
E-mail: admission@msmnyc.edu
Web Site: http://www.msmnyc.edu/
President/CEO: Dr. Robert Sirota
Admissions: Amy Anderson
Financial Aid: Amy Anderson
Type: Comprehensive **Sex:** Coed **% Accepted:** 35 **Admission Plans:** Deferred Admission **Application Deadline:** December 1 **Application Fee:** $100.00 **H.S. Requirements:** High school diploma required; GED accepted **Costs Per Year:** Application fee: $100. Comprehensive fee: $49,450 includes full-time tuition ($32,000), mandatory fees ($2800), and college room and board ($14,650). College room only: $9150. Full-time tuition and

MEDAILLE COLLEGE
18 Agassiz Circle
Buffalo, NY 14214-2695
Tel: (716)884-3281
Admissions: (716)880-2200
Fax: (716)884-0291
E-mail: admissionsug@medaille.edu
Web Site: http://www.medaille.edu/
President/CEO: Richard T. Jurasek, PhD
Admissions: Greg Florczak
Financial Aid: Catherine Buzanski
Type: Comprehensive **Sex:** Coed **Scores:** 79% SAT V 400+; 82% SAT M 400+ **% Accepted:** 72 **Admission Plans:** Early Admission; Deferred Admission **Application Deadline:** August 1 **Application Fee:** $25.00 **H.S. Requirements:** High school diploma required; GED not accepted **Costs Per Year:** Application fee: $25. Comprehensive fee: $28,878 includes full-time tuition ($19,590) and college room and board ($9288). Full-time tuition varies according to location. Room and board charges vary according to housing facility. Part-time tuition: $677 per credit hour. Part-time tuition varies according to course load. **Scholarships:** Available **Calendar System:** Semester, Summer Session Available **Enrollment:** FT 1,711, PT 100, Grad FT 1,053, Grad PT 59 **Faculty:** FT 84, PT 238 **Student-Faculty Ratio:** 17:1 **Exams:** SAT I or ACT, SAT I. **% Receiving Financial Aid:** 96 **% Residing in College-Owned, -Operated, or -Affiliated Housing:** 24 **Library Holdings:** 100,313 **Regional Accreditation:** Middle State Association of Colleges and Schools **Credit Hours For Degree:** 60 credit hours, Associates; 120 credit hours, Bachelors **ROTC:** Army **Professional Accreditation:** TEAC **Intercollegiate Athletics:** Baseball M; Basketball M & W; Bowling W; Cross-Country Running M & W; Golf M; Lacrosse M & W; Soccer M & W; Softball W; Volleyball M & W

MEDGAR EVERS COLLEGE OF THE CITY UNIVERSITY OF NEW YORK
1650 Bedford St.
Brooklyn, NY 11225-2298
Tel: (718)270-4900
Admissions: (718)270-6021
E-mail: jaugustin@mec.cuny.edu
Web Site: http://www.mec.cuny.edu/
President/CEO: Dr. William L. Pollard
Admissions: Julie M. Augustin
Financial Aid: Conley James
Type: Four-Year College **Sex:** Coed **Affiliation:** City University of New York System **Scores:** 42% SAT V 400+; 41.2% SAT M 400+ **% Accepted:** 100 **Admission Plans:** Open Admission; Preferred Admission; Deferred Admission **Application Deadline:** Rolling **Application Fee:** $65.00 **H.S. Requirements:** High school diploma required; GED accepted **Costs Per Year:** Application fee: $65. State resident tuition: $4600 full-time, $195 per credit hour part-time. Nonresident tuition: $9960 full-time, $415 per credit hour part-time. Mandatory fees: $302 full-time, $150.85 per term part-time. Full-time tuition and fees vary according to course load. Part-time tuition and fees vary according to course load. **Scholarships:** Available **Calendar System:** Semester, Summer Session Available **Enrollment:** FT 4,652, PT 2,429 **Faculty:** FT 189, PT 308 **Student-Faculty Ratio:** 19:1 **Exams:** SAT I and SAT II or ACT. SAT essay used for placement. **% Receiving Financial Aid:** 83 **Final Year or Final Semester Residency Requirement:** No **Library Holdings:** 120,000 **Regional Accreditation:** Middle State Association of Colleges and Schools **Credit Hours For Degree:** 64 credits, Associates; 120 credits, Bachelors **Professional Accreditation:** ACBSP, NLN **Intercollegiate Athletics:** Basketball M & W; Cross-Country Running M & W; Soccer M & W; Tennis W; Track and Field M & W; Volleyball M & W

MEMORIAL HOSPITAL SCHOOL OF NURSING
600 Northern Blvd.
Albany, NY 12204
Tel: (518)471-3260
Fax: (518)447-3559
Web Site: http://www.nehealth.com/son/
President/CEO: Linda D'Arcangelis
Type: Two-Year College **Sex:** Coed **Calendar System:** Semester

MERCY COLLEGE
555 Broadway
Dobbs Ferry, NY 10522-1189
Tel: (914)693-4500; Free: 800-MERCY-NY
Admissions: (914)674-7762
Fax: (914)674-7382
E-mail: admissions@mercy.edu
Web Site: http://www.mercy.edu/
President/CEO: Dr. Kimberly R. Cline
Admissions: Tara Fay-Reilly
Type: Comprehensive **Sex:** Coed **% Accepted:** 59 **Admission Plans:** Deferred Admission **Application Deadline:** Rolling **Application Fee:** $40.00 **H.S. Requirements:** High school diploma required; GED accepted **Costs Per Year:** Application fee: $40. Tuition: $16,490 full-time. Mandatory fees: $520 full-time. Full-time tuition and fees vary according to program and reciprocity agreements. **Scholarships:** Available **Calendar System:** Semester, Summer Session Available **Enrollment:** FT 4,103, PT 1,816, Grad FT 1,283, Grad PT 2,471 **Faculty:** FT 193, PT 635 **Student-Faculty Ratio:** 17:1 **Exams:** SAT I or ACT, SAT I and SAT II or ACT, SAT II. ACT essay used for admission. SAT essay used for admission. ACT essay used for advising. SAT essay used for advising. ACT essay used for placement. SAT essay used for placement. **% Residing in College-Owned, -Operated, or -Affiliated Housing:** 3 **Final Year or Final Semester Residency Requirement:** No **Library Holdings:** 401,714 **Regional Accreditation:** Middle State Association of Colleges and Schools **Credit Hours For Degree:** 60 credits, Associates; 120 credits, Bachelors **ROTC:** Army, Air Force **Professional Accreditation:** NACSCAO, AACN, AOTA, APTA, ASLHA, ACBSP, CSWE **Intercollegiate Athletics:** Baseball M; Basketball M & W; Cross-Country Running M & W; Lacrosse M & W; Soccer M & W; Softball W; Tennis M; Track and Field M & W; Volleyball W

MESIVTA OF EASTERN PARKWAY—YESHIVA ZICHRON MEILECH
510 Dahill Rd.
Brooklyn, NY 11218-5559
Tel: (718)438-1002
President/CEO: Ira Liberman
Admissions: Rabbi Joseph Halberstadt
Financial Aid: Rabbi Joseph Halberstadt
Type: Comprehensive **Sex:** Men **Affiliation:** Jewish **% Accepted:** 100 **Application Deadline:** Rolling **Calendar System:** Semester, Summer Session Not available **Library Holdings:** 7,500 **Professional Accreditation:** AARTS

MESIVTA TIFERETH JERUSALEM OF AMERICA
145 East Broadway
New York, NY 10002-6301
Tel: (212)964-2830
President/CEO: Yisrael H. Eidelman
Type: Comprehensive **Sex:** Men **Affiliation:** Jewish **% Accepted:** 100 **Calendar System:** Semester **Professional Accreditation:** AARTS

MESIVTA TORAH VODAATH RABBINICAL SEMINARY
425 East Ninth St.
Brooklyn, NY 11218-5299
Tel: (718)941-8000
Fax: (718)941-8032
President/CEO: Chaim Leshkowitz
Admissions: Rabbi Issac Braun
Financial Aid: Kayla Goldring
Type: Comprehensive **Sex:** Men **Affiliation:** Jewish **Admission Plans:** Preferred Admission; Early Admission; Deferred Admission **Application Deadline:** Rolling **Application Fee:** $200.00 **H.S. Requirements:** High school diploma required; GED accepted **Calendar System:** Semester, Summer Session Available **Library Holdings:** 40,000 **Credit Hours For Degree:** 128 credits, Bachelors **Professional Accreditation:** AARTS

METROPOLITAN COLLEGE OF NEW YORK
431 Canal St.
New York, NY 10013
Tel: (212)343-1234
Fax: (212)343-8470
Web Site: http://www.metropolitan.edu/
President/CEO: Dr. Vinton Thompson
Financial Aid: Rosibel Gomez
Type: Comprehensive **Sex:** Coed **% Accepted:** 51 **Admission Plans:** Deferred Admission **Application Deadline:** August 15 **Application Fee:** $30.00 **H.S. Requirements:** High school diploma required; GED accepted **Costs Per Year:** Application fee: $30. Tuition: $16,350 full-time, $545 per

credit part-time. Mandatory fees: $400 full-time, $200 per term part-time. Full-time tuition and fees vary according to degree level and program. Part-time tuition and fees vary according to degree level and program. Tuition guaranteed not to increase for student's term of enrollment. **Scholarships:** Available **Calendar System:** Miscellaneous, Summer Session Available **Enrollment:** FT 631, PT 45, Grad FT 372, Grad PT 36 **Faculty:** FT 26, PT 157 **Student-Faculty Ratio:** 11:1 **Exams:** Other, SAT I or ACT. **% Receiving Financial Aid:** 83 **Library Holdings:** 39,217 **Regional Accreditation:** Middle State Association of Colleges and Schools **Credit Hours For Degree:** 64 credits, Associates; 128 credits, Bachelors **Professional Accreditation:** NCATE

MILDRED ELLEY SCHOOL
855 Central Ave.
Albany, NY 12206
Tel: (518)786-0855; Free: 800-622-6327
Fax: (518)786-0898
Web Site: http://www.mildred-elley.edu/
President/CEO: Faith Ann Takes
Admissions: Michael Cahalan
Type: Two-Year College **Sex:** Coed **Application Fee:** $25.00 **Scholarships:** Available **Exams:** Other. **Professional Accreditation:** ACICS

MIRRER YESHIVA
1795 Ocean Parkway
Brooklyn, NY 11223-2010
Tel: (718)645-0536
President/CEO: Osher Kalmanowitz
Type: Comprehensive **Sex:** Men **Affiliation:** Jewish **% Accepted:** 100 **H.S. Requirements:** High school diploma or equivalent not required **Calendar System:** Semester **Professional Accreditation:** AARTS

MOHAWK VALLEY COMMUNITY COLLEGE
1101 Sherman Dr.
Utica, NY 13501-5394
Tel: (315)792-5400
Admissions: (315)792-5640
Fax: (315)792-5527
E-mail: sfiebiger@mvcc.edu
Web Site: http://www.mvcc.edu/
President/CEO: Dr. Randall VanWagoner
Admissions: Sandra Fiebiger
Type: Two-Year College **Sex:** Coed **Affiliation:** State University of New York System **% Accepted:** 81 **Admission Plans:** Open Admission; Early Decision Plan; Deferred Admission **Application Deadline:** Rolling **Application Fee:** $0.00 **H.S. Requirements:** High school diploma or equivalent not required **Costs Per Year:** Application fee: $0. State resident tuition: $3350 full-time, $120 per credit hour part-time. Nonresident tuition: $6700 full-time, $240 per credit hour part-time. Mandatory fees: $424 full-time, $5 per credit hour part-time, $35. College room and board: $7500. College room only: $4550. **Scholarships:** Available **Calendar System:** Semester, Summer Session Available **Enrollment:** FT 4,403, PT 2,298 **Faculty:** FT 137, PT 219 **Student-Faculty Ratio:** 23:1 **% Residing in College-Owned, -Operated, or -Affiliated Housing:** 9 **Final Year or Final Semester Residency Requirement:** No **Library Holdings:** 98,317 **Regional Accreditation:** Middle State Association of Colleges and Schools **Credit Hours For Degree:** 63 credits, Associates **ROTC:** Army **Professional Accreditation:** ABET, AHIMA, CARC, NLN **Intercollegiate Athletics:** Baseball M; Basketball M & W; Bowling M & W; Cross-Country Running M & W; Golf M & W; Ice Hockey M; Lacrosse M; Soccer M & W; Softball W; Tennis M & W; Track and Field M & W; Volleyball W

MOLLOY COLLEGE
1000 Hempstead Ave.
Rockville Centre, NY 11571-5002
Tel: (516)678-5000; Free: 888-4MOLLOY
E-mail: admissions@molloy.edu
Web Site: http://www.molloy.edu/
President/CEO: Drew Bogner, PhD
Admissions: Marguerite Lane
Financial Aid: Ana C. Lockward
Type: Comprehensive **Sex:** Coed **Scores:** 100% SAT V 400+; 98% SAT M 400+; 33% ACT 18-23; 50% ACT 24-29 **% Accepted:** 59 **Admission Plans:** Early Admission; Early Action; Deferred Admission **Application Deadline:** Rolling **Application Fee:** $30.00 **H.S. Requirements:** High school diploma required; GED accepted **Costs Per Year:** Application fee: $30. One-time mandatory fee: $150. Tuition: $19,970 full-time, $660 per credit part-time. Mandatory fees: $990 full-time. **Scholarships:** Available **Calendar System:** 4-1-4, Summer Session Available **Enrollment:** FT 2,308, PT 729, Grad FT 192, Grad PT 796 **Faculty:** FT 169, PT 350 **Student-Faculty Ratio:** 10:1 **Exams:** SAT I or ACT. ACT essay used for placement. SAT essay used for placement. **% Receiving Financial Aid:** 86 **Library Holdings:** 110,000 **Regional Accreditation:** Middle State Association of Colleges and Schools **Credit Hours For Degree:** 64 credits, Associates; 128 credits, Bachelors **ROTC:** Army, Navy, Air Force **Professional Accreditation:** AACN, AHIMA, CARC, CSWE, JRCNMT **Intercollegiate Athletics:** Baseball M; Basketball M & W; Cross-Country Running M & W; Equestrian Sports W; Lacrosse M & W; Rugby M & W; Soccer M & W; Softball W; Tennis W; Track and Field M & W; Volleyball W

MONROE COLLEGE (BRONX)
Monroe College Way
Bronx, NY 10468-5407
Tel: (718)933-6700; Free: 800-55MONROE
Web Site: http://www.monroecollege.edu/
President/CEO: Stephen Jerome
Admissions: Evan Jerome
Financial Aid: Howard Leslie
Type: Comprehensive **Sex:** Coed **% Accepted:** 61 **Admission Plans:** Early Admission; Early Action; Early Decision Plan; Deferred Admission **Application Deadline:** August 26 **Application Fee:** $35.00 **H.S. Requirements:** High school diploma or equivalent not required **Costs Per Year:** Application fee: $35. Comprehensive fee: $20,484 includes full-time tuition ($11,744), mandatory fees ($800), and college room and board ($7940). Full-time tuition and fees vary according to degree level and program. Room and board charges vary according to board plan. **Scholarships:** Available **Calendar System:** Trimester, Summer Session Available **Enrollment:** FT 3,471, PT 1,334, Grad FT 143, Grad PT 120 **Faculty:** FT 61, PT 190 **Student-Faculty Ratio:** 32:1 **Exams:** SAT I or ACT. **% Receiving Financial Aid:** 98 **% Residing in College-Owned, -Operated, or -Affiliated Housing:** 1 **Library Holdings:** 28,000 **Regional Accreditation:** Middle State Association of Colleges and Schools **Credit Hours For Degree:** 20 courses, Associates; 40 courses, Bachelors **Professional Accreditation:** AHIMA **Intercollegiate Athletics:** Baseball M; Basketball M & W; Soccer M; Softball W; Track and Field M & W; Volleyball W

MONROE COLLEGE (NEW ROCHELLE)
434 Main St.
New Rochelle, NY 10801
Tel: (914)632-5400; Free: 800-55MONROE
Admissions: (914)654-3200
Fax: (914)632-5462
E-mail: lscorca@monroecollege.edu
Web Site: http://www.monroecollege.edu/
President/CEO: Marc M. Jerome
Admissions: Lisa Scorca
Financial Aid: James Gathard
Type: Comprehensive **Sex:** Coed **% Accepted:** 60 **Admission Plans:** Early Admission; Deferred Admission **Application Deadline:** August 26 **Application Fee:** $35.00 **H.S. Requirements:** High school diploma or equivalent not required. For criminal justice and medical assisting: High school diploma required; GED accepted **Costs Per Year:** Application fee: $35. Comprehensive fee: $19,684 includes full-time tuition ($10,944), mandatory fees ($800), and college room and board ($7940). Full-time tuition and fees vary according to degree level and program. Room and board charges vary according to board plan. Part-time tuition: $456 per credit. Part-time mandatory fees: $200 per term. Part-time tuition and fees vary according to degree level and program. **Scholarships:** Available **Calendar System:** Trimester, Summer Session Available **Enrollment:** FT 1,713, PT 306, Grad FT 134, Grad PT 69 **Faculty:** FT 24, PT 69 **Student-Faculty Ratio:** 38:1 **% Receiving Financial Aid:** 92 **% Residing in College-Owned, -Operated, or -Affiliated Housing:** 20 **Library Holdings:** 8,400 **Credit Hours For Degree:** 20 courses, Associates; 40 courses, Bachelors **Intercollegiate Athletics:** Baseball M; Basketball M & W; Soccer M; Softball W; Volleyball W

MONROE COMMUNITY COLLEGE
1000 East Henrietta Rd.
Rochester, NY 14623-5780

Tel: (585)292-2000
Fax: (585)427-2749
E-mail: admissions@monroecc.edu
Web Site: http://www.monroecc.edu/
President/CEO: Anne M. Kress
Admissions: Andrew Freeman
Type: Two-Year College **Sex:** Coed **Affiliation:** State University of New York System **Admission Plans:** Open Admission; Preferred Admission; Early Admission **Application Deadline:** Rolling **Application Fee:** $20.00 **H.S. Requirements:** High school diploma required; GED accepted **Scholarships:** Available **Calendar System:** Semester, Summer Session Available **Enrollment:** FT 10,432, PT 7,050 **Faculty:** FT 308, PT 560 **Student-Faculty Ratio:** 26:1 **Library Holdings:** 110,748 **Regional Accreditation:** Middle State Association of Colleges and Schools **Credit Hours For Degree:** 62 credits, Associates **ROTC:** Army, Air Force **Professional Accreditation:** ABET, ADA, AHIMA, JRCERT, JRCEMT, NLN **Intercollegiate Athletics:** Baseball M; Basketball M & W; Golf M; Ice Hockey M; Lacrosse M; Soccer M & W; Softball W; Swimming and Diving M & W; Tennis M & W; Volleyball W

MOUNT SAINT MARY COLLEGE
330 Powell Ave.
Newburgh, NY 12550-3494
Tel: (845)561-0800; Free: 888-937-6762
Admissions: (845)569-3248
Fax: (845)562-6762
E-mail: admissions@msmc.edu
Web Site: http://www.msmc.edu/
President/CEO: Fr. Kevin Mackin
Admissions: Rodney Morrison
Financial Aid: Michelle Taylor
Type: Comprehensive **Sex:** Coed **Scores:** 95% SAT V 400+; 94% SAT M 400+; 65% ACT 18-23; 20% ACT 24-29 **% Accepted:** 72 **Admission Plans:** Early Admission; Deferred Admission **Application Deadline:** August 15 **Application Fee:** $45.00 **H.S. Requirements:** High school diploma required; GED accepted **Costs Per Year:** Application fee: $45. Comprehensive fee: $35,200 includes full-time tuition ($22,350), mandatory fees ($950), and college room and board ($11,900). College room only: $6900. Full-time tuition and fees vary according to class time, degree level, and location. Room and board charges vary according to board plan and housing facility. Part-time tuition: $745 per credit hour. Part-time mandatory fees: $70. Part-time tuition and fees vary according to class time, degree level, and location. **Scholarships:** Available **Calendar System:** Semester, Summer Session Available **Enrollment:** FT 1,867, PT 378, Grad FT 107, Grad PT 365 **Faculty:** FT 81, PT 138 **Student-Faculty Ratio:** 17:1 **Exams:** SAT I or ACT. ACT essay used for admission. SAT essay used for admission. **% Receiving Financial Aid:** 77 **% Residing in College-Owned, -Operated, or -Affiliated Housing:** 39 **Final Year or Final Semester Residency Requirement:** No **Library Holdings:** 105,999 **Regional Accreditation:** Middle State Association of Colleges and Schools **Credit Hours For Degree:** 120 credit hours, Bachelors **ROTC:** Army **Professional Accreditation:** AACN, NCATE **Intercollegiate Athletics:** Baseball M; Basketball M & W; Cross-Country Running M & W; Lacrosse M & W; Soccer M & W; Softball W; Swimming and Diving M & W; Tennis M & W; Volleyball W

NASSAU COMMUNITY COLLEGE
1 Education Dr.
Garden City, NY 11530-6793
Tel: (516)572-7500
Admissions: (516)572-7345
E-mail: admissions@sunynassau.edu
Web Site: http://www.ncc.edu/
President/CEO: Dr. Sean A Fanelli
Admissions: Craig Wright
Financial Aid: Dr. Evangeline Manjares
Type: Two-Year College **Sex:** Coed **Affiliation:** State University of New York System **Admission Plans:** Open Admission; Deferred Admission **Application Deadline:** August 7 **Application Fee:** $40.00 **H.S. Requirements:** High school diploma required; GED accepted **Scholarships:** Available **Calendar System:** Semester, Summer Session Available **Enrollment:** FT 14,702, PT 7,250 **Faculty:** FT 555, PT 934 **Student-Faculty Ratio:** 18:1 **Exams:** SAT I or ACT. **Library Holdings:** 186,782 **Regional Accreditation:** Middle State Association of Colleges and Schools **Credit Hours For Degree:** 64 credits, Associates **Professional Accreditation:** ABET, ARCEST, ABFSE, APTA, CARC, JRCERT, NASM, NLN **Intercollegiate Athletics:** Baseball M; Basketball M & W; Bowling M & W; Cheerleading M & W; Cross-Country Running M & W; Equestrian Sports M & W; Football M; Golf M & W; Lacrosse M & W; Soccer M & W; Softball W; Tennis M & W; Track and Field M & W; Volleyball W; Wrestling M

NAZARETH COLLEGE OF ROCHESTER
4245 East Ave.
Rochester, NY 14618-3790
Tel: (585)389-2525
Admissions: (585)389-2860
Fax: (585)389-2826
E-mail: admissions@naz.edu
Web Site: http://www.naz.edu/
President/CEO: Daan Braveman
Admissions: Thomas DaRin
Financial Aid: Samantha Veeder
Type: Comprehensive **Sex:** Coed **Scores:** 99% SAT V 400+; 98% SAT M 400+ **% Accepted:** 77 **Admission Plans:** Early Admission; Early Action; Early Decision Plan; Deferred Admission **Application Deadline:** February 15 **Application Fee:** $40.00 **H.S. Requirements:** High school diploma required; GED accepted **Costs Per Year:** Application fee: $40. Comprehensive fee: $36,856 includes full-time tuition ($25,044), mandatory fees ($1096), and college room and board ($10,716). Room and board charges vary according to board plan and housing facility. **Scholarships:** Available **Calendar System:** Semester, Summer Session Available **Enrollment:** FT 2,070, PT 157, Grad FT 485, Grad PT 595 **Faculty:** FT 156, PT 258 **Student-Faculty Ratio:** 12:1 **% Receiving Financial Aid:** 82 **% Residing in College-Owned, -Operated, or -Affiliated Housing:** 53 **Final Year or Final Semester Residency Requirement:** No **Library Holdings:** 283,248 **Regional Accreditation:** Middle State Association of Colleges and Schools **Credit Hours For Degree:** 120 credit hours, Bachelors **ROTC:** Army, Air Force **Professional Accreditation:** AACN, APTA, ASLHA, CSWE, NASM, TEAC **Intercollegiate Athletics:** Basketball M & W; Cross-Country Running M & W; Equestrian Sports M & W; Field Hockey W; Golf M & W; Lacrosse M & W; Soccer M & W; Softball W; Swimming and Diving M & W; Tennis M & W; Track and Field M & W; Volleyball M & W

THE NEW SCHOOL FOR GENERAL STUDIES
66 West 12th St.
New York, NY 10011-8603
Tel: (212)229-5600; Free: 800-862-5039
Admissions: (212)229-5630
Fax: (212)645-0661
E-mail: nsadmissions@newschool.edu
Web Site: http://www.newschool.edu/generalstudies/
President/CEO: Bob Kerrey
Admissions: Cory Meyers
Type: Two-Year Upper Division **Sex:** Coed **Affiliation:** The New School **% Accepted:** 56 **Admission Plans:** Deferred Admission **Application Deadline:** June 1 **Application Fee:** $50.00 **H.S. Requirements:** High school diploma required; GED accepted **Costs Per Year:** Application fee: $50. Comprehensive fee: $39,548 includes full-time tuition ($24,288) and college room and board ($15,260). College room only: $12,260. Room and board charges vary according to board plan and housing facility. Part-time tuition: $1012 per credit. Part-time tuition varies according to course load. **Scholarships:** Available **Calendar System:** Semester, Summer Session Available **Enrollment:** FT 337, PT 363, Grad FT 707, Grad PT 464 **Faculty:** FT 44, PT 316 **Student-Faculty Ratio:** 9:1 **% Receiving Financial Aid:** 43 **% Residing in College-Owned, -Operated, or -Affiliated Housing:** 3 **Library Holdings:** 1,906,046 **Regional Accreditation:** Middle State Association of Colleges and Schools **Credit Hours For Degree:** 120 credits, Bachelors

THE NEW SCHOOL FOR JAZZ AND CONTEMPORARY MUSIC
55 West 13th St., 5th Floor
New York, NY 10011
Tel: (212)229-5896
E-mail: jazzadm@newschool.edu
Web Site: http://www.jazz.newschool.edu/
President/CEO: Bob Kerrey
Admissions: Terri Lucas
Financial Aid: Eileen F. Doyle
Type: Four-Year College **Sex:** Coed **Affiliation:** The New School **% Ac-**

cepted: 71 **Admission Plans:** Deferred Admission **Application Deadline:** January 1 **Application Fee:** $75.00 **H.S. Requirements:** High school diploma required; GED accepted **Costs Per Year:** Application fee: $75. Comprehensive fee: $48,860 includes full-time tuition ($32,860), mandatory fees ($740), and college room and board ($15,260). College room only: $12,260. Room and board charges vary according to board plan and housing facility. Part-time tuition: $1076 per credit. Part-time tuition varies according to course load and program. **Scholarships:** Available **Calendar System:** Semester **Enrollment:** FT 239, PT 14 **Faculty:** FT 2, PT 64 **Student-Faculty Ratio:** 11:1 **Exams:** SAT I or ACT. **% Receiving Financial Aid:** 43 **% Residing in College-Owned, -Operated, or -Affiliated Housing:** 25 **Library Holdings:** 1,906,046 **Regional Accreditation:** Middle State Association of Colleges and Schools

NEW YORK CAREER INSTITUTE

11 Park Place- 4th Floor
New York, NY 10007
Tel: (212)962-0002
Fax: (212)385-7574
E-mail: cmcmahon@nyci.edu
Web Site: http://www.nyci.com/
President/CEO: Ivan Londa
Admissions: Cindy McMahon

Type: Two-Year College **Sex:** Coed **Application Deadline:** September 21 **Application Fee:** $50.00 **H.S. Requirements:** High school diploma required; GED accepted **Scholarships:** Available **Calendar System:** Trimester, Summer Session Available **Enrollment:** FT 498, PT 66 **Faculty:** FT 4, PT 24 **Exams:** Other. **Library Holdings:** 5,010 **Credit Hours For Degree:** 60 credits, Associates **Professional Accreditation:** NYSBR

NEW YORK CITY COLLEGE OF TECHNOLOGY OF THE CITY UNIVERSITY OF NEW YORK

300 Jay St.
Brooklyn, NY 11201-2983
Tel: (718)260-5000
Admissions: (718)260-5500
Fax: (718)260-5198
E-mail: achaconis@citytech.cuny.edu
Web Site: http://www.citytech.cuny.edu/
President/CEO: Dr. Russell K. Hotzler
Admissions: Alexis Chaconis
Financial Aid: Sandra Higgins

Type: Four-Year College **Sex:** Coed **Affiliation:** City University of New York System **% Accepted:** 84 **Admission Plans:** Open Admission **Application Deadline:** March 15 **Application Fee:** $65.00 **H.S. Requirements:** High school diploma required; GED accepted **Costs Per Year:** Application fee: $65. State resident tuition: $4600 full-time, $195 per credit part-time. Nonresident tuition: $12,450 full-time, $415 per credit part-time. Mandatory fees: $339 full-time, $85.20 per term part-time. College room and board: $1500. **Scholarships:** Available **Calendar System:** Semester, Summer Session Available **Enrollment:** FT 9,130, PT 6,274 **Faculty:** FT 411, PT 790 **Student-Faculty Ratio:** 17:1 **Exams:** SAT I or ACT. **% Receiving Financial Aid:** 77 **Library Holdings:** 179,062 **Regional Accreditation:** Middle State Association of Colleges and Schools **Credit Hours For Degree:** 60 credits, Associates; 120 credits, Bachelors **ROTC:** Air Force **Professional Accreditation:** ABET, ADA, COptA, JRCERT, NLN **Intercollegiate Athletics:** Basketball M & W; Cross-Country Running M & W; Soccer M; Softball W; Tennis M & W; Track and Field M & W; Volleyball M & W

NEW YORK COLLEGE OF HEALTH PROFESSIONS

6801 Jericho Turnpike
Syosset, NY 11791-4413
Tel: (516)364-0808; Free: 800-922-7337
Fax: (516)364-0989
E-mail: rdodas@nycollege.edu
Web Site: http://www.nycollege.edu/
President/CEO: Lisa Pamintuan
Admissions: Mary Rodas

Type: Two-Year College **Sex:** Coed **Admission Plans:** Deferred Admission **Application Deadline:** Rolling **Application Fee:** $85.00 **H.S. Requirements:** High school diploma required; GED accepted **Scholarships:** Available **Calendar System:** Trimester, Summer Session Available **Enrollment:** FT 332, PT 469 **Faculty:** FT 17, PT 76 **Student-Faculty Ratio:** 19:1 **Library Holdings:** 5,500 **Regional Accreditation:** Western Association of Schools and Colleges **Credit Hours For Degree:** 72 credits, Associates **Professional Accreditation:** NACSCAO

NEW YORK INSTITUTE OF TECHNOLOGY

PO Box 8000
Old Westbury, NY 11568-8000
Tel: (516)686-7516; Free: 800-345-NYIT
Admissions: (516)686-1083
Fax: (516)686-7613
E-mail: admissions@nyit.edu
Web Site: http://www.nyit.edu/
President/CEO: Dr. Edward Guiliano
Admissions: Doreen Meyer
Financial Aid: Doreen Meyer

Type: University **Sex:** Coed **Scores:** 98% SAT V 400+; 100% SAT M 400+; 58% ACT 18-23; 24% ACT 24-29 **% Accepted:** 74 **Admission Plans:** Deferred Admission **Application Deadline:** Rolling **Application Fee:** $50.00 **H.S. Requirements:** High school diploma required; GED accepted **Costs Per Year:** Application fee: $50. Comprehensive fee: $34,660 includes full-time tuition ($23,380), mandatory fees ($760), and college room and board ($10,520). Full-time tuition and fees vary according to course load and program. Room and board charges vary according to board plan, housing facility, and location. Part-time tuition: $790 per credit hour. Part-time mandatory fees: $330 per term. Part-time tuition and fees vary according to course load. **Scholarships:** Available **Calendar System:** Semester, Summer Session Available **Enrollment:** FT 5,950, PT 1,501, Grad FT 2,703, Grad PT 1,541 **Faculty:** FT 273, PT 944 **Student-Faculty Ratio:** 14:1 **Exams:** SAT I or ACT. **% Receiving Financial Aid:** 51 **% Residing in College-Owned, -Operated, or -Affiliated Housing:** 9 **Library Holdings:** 157,763 **Regional Accreditation:** Middle State Association of Colleges and Schools **Credit Hours For Degree:** 68 credits, Associates; 120 credits, Bachelors **ROTC:** Army, Air Force **Professional Accreditation:** ABET, ACF, ADtA, AOTA, AOsA, APTA, FIDER, NAAB, NCATE **Intercollegiate Athletics:** Baseball M; Basketball M & W; Cross-Country Running M & W; Lacrosse M; Soccer M & W; Softball W; Volleyball W

NEW YORK SCHOOL OF INTERIOR DESIGN

170 East 70th St.
New York, NY 10021-5110
Tel: (212)472-1500; Free: 800-336-9743
Fax: (212)472-1867
E-mail: admissions@nysid.edu
Web Site: http://www.nysid.edu/
President/CEO: Christopher Cyphers
Admissions: Cassandra Ramirez
Financial Aid: Rashmi H. Wadhvani

Type: Comprehensive **Sex:** Coed **Scores:** 75% SAT V 400+; 85% SAT M 400+ **% Accepted:** 52 **Admission Plans:** Deferred Admission **Application Deadline:** March 1 **Application Fee:** $50.00 **H.S. Requirements:** High school diploma required; GED accepted **Costs Per Year:** Application fee: $50. Tuition: $22,605 full-time, $765 per credit part-time. Mandatory fees: $290 full-time, $195 per term part-time. Full-time tuition and fees vary according to course load. Part-time tuition and fees vary according to course load. College room only: $15,600. **Scholarships:** Available **Calendar System:** Semester, Summer Session Available **Enrollment:** FT 200, PT 456, Grad FT 58 **Faculty:** FT 8, PT 72 **Student-Faculty Ratio:** 9:1 **Exams:** SAT I or ACT. **% Receiving Financial Aid:** 27 **% Residing in College-Owned, -Operated, or -Affiliated Housing:** 4 **Final Year or Final Semester Residency Requirement:** No **Credit Hours For Degree:** 66 credits, Associates; 132 credits, Bachelors **Professional Accreditation:** FIDER, NASAD

NEW YORK UNIVERSITY

70 Washington Square South
New York, NY 10012-1019
Tel: (212)998-1212
Admissions: (212)998-4500
Fax: (212)995-4902
E-mail: nyuadmit@uccvm.nyu.edu
Web Site: http://www.nyu.edu/
President/CEO: Dr. John E. Sexton

Type: University **Sex:** Coed **Scores:** 100% SAT V 400+; 101% SAT M 400+; 2% ACT 18-23; 50% ACT 24-29 **% Accepted:** 38 **Admission Plans:**

Early Decision Plan; Deferred Admission **Application Deadline:** January 1 **Application Fee:** $65.00 **H.S. Requirements:** High school diploma required; GED accepted **Costs Per Year:** Application fee: $65. Comprehensive fee: $51,993 includes full-time tuition ($36,586), mandatory fees ($2179), and college room and board ($13,228). Full-time tuition and fees vary according to course load and program. Room and board charges vary according to board plan and housing facility. Part-time tuition: $1078 per credit. Part-time mandatory fees: $59 per credit, $403 per term. Part-time tuition and fees vary according to program. Tuition guaranteed not to increase for student's term of enrollment. **Scholarships:** Available **Calendar System:** Semester, Summer Session Available **Enrollment:** FT 20,281, PT 1,357, Grad FT 12,860, Grad PT 8,906 **Faculty:** FT 2,315, PT 2,845 **Student-Faculty Ratio:** 11:1 **Exams:** Other, SAT I and SAT II or ACT. ACT essay used for admission. SAT essay used for admission. **% Receiving Financial Aid:** 51 **% Residing in College-Owned, -Operated, or -Affiliated Housing:** 51 **Final Year or Final Semester Residency Requirement:** No **Library Holdings:** 5,770,100 **Regional Accreditation:** Middle State Association of Colleges and Schools **Credit Hours For Degree:** 60 credits, Associates; 128 credits, Bachelors **ROTC:** Army, Navy, Air Force **Professional Accreditation:** AACSB, ACEJMC, AACN, ABA, ACNM, ADA, ADtA, ACSP, AOTA, APTA, APA, ASLHA, ACIPE, AALS, ACEHSA, CEPH, CORE, CSWE, JRCEDMS, LCMEAMA MACTE, NASPAA, NLN, TEAC **Intercollegiate Athletics:** Baseball M; Basketball M & W; Cheerleading M & W; Crew M & W; Cross-Country Running M & W; Equestrian Sports M & W; Fencing M & W; Golf M & W; Ice Hockey M; Lacrosse M & W; Soccer M & W; Softball W; Swimming and Diving M & W; Tennis M & W; Track and Field M & W; Ultimate Frisbee M & W; Volleyball M & W; Wrestling M

NIAGARA COUNTY COMMUNITY COLLEGE
3111 Saunders Settlement Rd.
Sanborn, NY 14132-9460
Tel: (716)614-6222
Admissions: (716)614-6200
Fax: (716)731-4053
E-mail: admissions@niagaracc.suny.edu
Web Site: http://www.niagaracc.suny.edu/
President/CEO: Dr. James P. Klyczek
Admissions: Kathy Saunders
Financial Aid: Jim Trimboli
Type: Two-Year College **Sex:** Coed **Affiliation:** State University of New York System **% Accepted:** 100 **Admission Plans:** Open Admission; Early Admission **Application Fee:** $0.00 **H.S. Requirements:** High school diploma required; GED accepted **Costs Per Year:** Application fee: $0. State resident tuition: $3408 full-time, $142 per credit hour part-time. Nonresident tuition: $6816 full-time, $284 per credit hour part-time. Mandatory fees: $342 full-time, $84 per term part-time. Full-time tuition and fees vary according to course load and program. Part-time tuition and fees vary according to course load and program. College room only: $4900. **Scholarships:** Available **Calendar System:** Semester, Summer Session Available **Enrollment:** FT 4,647, PT 2,632 **Faculty:** FT 114, PT 295 **Student-Faculty Ratio:** 17:1 **Library Holdings:** 94,782 **Regional Accreditation:** Middle State Association of Colleges and Schools **Credit Hours For Degree:** 62 credit hours, Associates **ROTC:** Army **Professional Accreditation:** ARCEST, AAMAE, APTA, JRCEET, JRCERT, NLN **Intercollegiate Athletics:** Baseball M; Basketball M & W; Golf M & W; Lacrosse M & W; Soccer M & W; Softball W; Volleyball W; Wrestling M

NIAGARA UNIVERSITY
Niagara University, NY 14109
Tel: (716)285-1212; Free: 800-462-2111
Admissions: (716)286-8700
Fax: (716)286-8355
E-mail: admissions@niagara.edu
Web Site: http://www.niagara.edu/
President/CEO: Rev. Joseph L. Levesque, CM
Admissions: Christine M. McDermott
Financial Aid: Maureen E. Salfi
Type: Comprehensive **Sex:** Coed **Affiliation:** Roman Catholic Church **Scores:** 98% SAT V 400+; 98% SAT M 400+; 61% ACT 18-23; 26% ACT 24-29 **% Accepted:** 74 **Admission Plans:** Early Admission; Deferred Admission **Application Deadline:** August 1 **Application Fee:** $30.00 **H.S. Requirements:** High school diploma required; GED accepted **Costs Per Year:** Application fee: $30. Comprehensive fee: $34,950 includes full-time tuition ($23,700), mandatory fees ($1000), and college room and board ($10,250). Part-time tuition: $790 per credit. **Scholarships:** Available **Calendar System:** Semester, Summer Session Available **Enrollment:** FT 3,031, PT 295 **Faculty:** FT 150, PT 225 **Student-Faculty Ratio:** 14:1 **Exams:** SAT I or ACT. **% Receiving Financial Aid:** 71 **% Residing in College-Owned, -Operated, or -Affiliated Housing:** 52 **Library Holdings:** 297,813 **Regional Accreditation:** Middle State Association of Colleges and Schools **Credit Hours For Degree:** 60 credit hours, Associates; 120 credit hours, Bachelors **ROTC:** Army **Professional Accreditation:** AACSB, CSWE, NCATE **Intercollegiate Athletics:** Baseball M; Basketball M & W; Cross-Country Running M & W; Golf M & W; Ice Hockey M & W; Lacrosse M & W; Soccer M & W; Softball W; Swimming and Diving M & W; Tennis M & W; Volleyball W

NORTH COUNTRY COMMUNITY COLLEGE
23 Santanoni Ave., PO Box 89
Saranac Lake, NY 12983-0089
Tel: (518)891-2915; Free: 888-TRY-NCCC
Fax: (518)891-2915
E-mail: info@nccc.edu
Web Site: http://www.nccc.edu/
President/CEO: Fred Smith
Financial Aid: Edwin A. Trathen
Type: Two-Year College **Sex:** Coed **Affiliation:** State University of New York System **Admission Plans:** Open Admission; Preferred Admission; Early Admission; Early Decision Plan; Deferred Admission **Application Deadline:** Rolling **Application Fee:** $0.00 **H.S. Requirements:** High school diploma required; GED accepted **Scholarships:** Available **Calendar System:** Semester, Summer Session Available **Enrollment:** FT 956, PT 795 **Faculty:** FT 46, PT 105 **Student-Faculty Ratio:** 15:1 **Exams:** SAT I or ACT. **% Residing in College-Owned, -Operated, or -Affiliated Housing:** 7 **Library Holdings:** 58,556 **Regional Accreditation:** Middle State Association of Colleges and Schools **Credit Hours For Degree:** 62 semester hours, Associates **Professional Accreditation:** JRCERT **Intercollegiate Athletics:** Basketball M & W; Ice Hockey M; Soccer M & W; Softball W; Volleyball W

NYACK COLLEGE
One South Blvd.
Nyack, NY 10960-3698
Tel: (845)358-1710; Free: 800-33-NYACK
Admissions: (845)675-4414
Fax: (845)358-3047
E-mail: admissions@nyack.edu
Web Site: http://www.nyack.edu/
President/CEO: Dr. Michael G. Scales
Admissions: Andrea Hennessey, JD
Financial Aid: Steve Phillips
Type: Comprehensive **Sex:** Coed **Affiliation:** The Christian and Missionary Alliance **Scores:** 76% SAT V 400+; 71% SAT M 400+; 44% ACT 18-23; 32% ACT 24-29 **% Accepted:** 99 **Admission Plans:** Deferred Admission **Application Deadline:** Rolling **Application Fee:** $25.00 **H.S. Requirements:** High school diploma required; GED accepted. For home schooled students provide a transcript/record of courses and grades: High school diploma required; GED accepted **Costs Per Year:** Application fee: $25. Comprehensive fee: $28,700 includes full-time tuition ($19,500), mandatory fees ($1000), and college room and board ($8200). Full-time tuition and fees vary according to course load, location, and program. Room and board charges vary according to board plan. Part-time tuition: $812 per credit hour. Part-time tuition varies according to course load, location, and program. **Scholarships:** Available **Calendar System:** Semester, Summer Session Available **Enrollment:** FT 1,634, PT 380, Grad FT 333, Grad PT 804 **Faculty:** FT 148, PT 190 **Student-Faculty Ratio:** 20:1 **Exams:** SAT I or ACT. ACT essay not being used. SAT essay not being used. **% Receiving Financial Aid:** 85 **% Residing in College-Owned, -Operated, or -Affiliated Housing:** 80 **Library Holdings:** 177,701 **Regional Accreditation:** Middle State Association of Colleges and Schools **Credit Hours For Degree:** 63 credit hours, Associates; 126 credit hours, Bachelors **Professional Accreditation:** NASM

OHR HAMEIR THEOLOGICAL SEMINARY
141 Furnace Woods Rd.
Cortlandt Manor, NY 10567
Tel: (914)736-1500
President/CEO: Eli Kanarek
Type: Comprehensive **Sex:** Men **Affiliation:** Jewish **% Accepted:** 100 **H.S.**

Requirements: High school diploma required; GED accepted **Calendar System:** Semester **Professional Accreditation:** AARTS

OHR SOMAYACH/JOSEPH TANENBAUM EDUCATIONAL CENTER
PO Box 334, 244 Route 306
Monsey, NY 10952-0334
Tel: (845)425-1370
E-mail: ohr@os.edu
Web Site: http://ohr.edu/
President/CEO: Rabbi Avrohom Braun
Admissions: Rabbi Avrohom Braun
Type: Comprehensive **Sex:** Men **Affiliation:** Jewish **% Accepted:** 65 **Admission Plans:** Early Admission **Application Deadline:** Rolling **H.S. Requirements:** High school diploma required; GED accepted **Calendar System:** Semester, Summer Session Available **Enrollment:** FT 78, PT 1, Grad FT 10 **Faculty:** FT 8, PT 10 **Library Holdings:** 2,300 **Credit Hours For Degree:** 132 credit hours, Bachelors **Professional Accreditation:** AARTS

OLEAN BUSINESS INSTITUTE
301 North Union St.
Olean, NY 14760-2691
Tel: (716)372-7978
Fax: (716)372-2120
Web Site: http://www.obi.edu/
President/CEO: Jennifer Madison
Admissions: Lori Kincaid
Financial Aid: Valerie Goodwin
Type: Two-Year College **Sex:** Coed **Application Deadline:** August 31 **Application Fee:** $25.00 **H.S. Requirements:** High school diploma required; GED accepted **Scholarships:** Available **Calendar System:** Semester, Summer Session Available **Library Holdings:** 1,800 **Credit Hours For Degree:** 68 credit hours, Associates **Professional Accreditation:** ACICS

ONONDAGA COMMUNITY COLLEGE
4585 West Seneca Turnpike
Syracuse, NY 13215
Tel: (315)498-2622
Admissions: (315)488-2602
Fax: (315)469-2107
E-mail: admissions@sunyocc.edu
Web Site: http://www.sunyocc.edu/
President/CEO: Dr. Debbie L. Sydow
Admissions: Katherine Perry
Type: Two-Year College **Sex:** Coed **Affiliation:** State University of New York System **Admission Plans:** Open Admission; Preferred Admission **Application Deadline:** August 26 **Application Fee:** $0.00 **H.S. Requirements:** High school diploma required; GED accepted. For those who demonstrate ability to benefit from program: High school diploma or equivalent not required **Scholarships:** Available **Calendar System:** Semester, Summer Session Available **Enrollment:** FT 5,644, PT 4,993 **Faculty:** FT 163, PT 407 **Student-Faculty Ratio:** 20:1 **Library Holdings:** 96,611 **Regional Accreditation:** Middle State Association of Colleges and Schools **Credit Hours For Degree:** 62 credits, Associates **ROTC:** Air Force **Professional Accreditation:** ABET, ADA, AHIMA, APTA, CARC, NLN **Intercollegiate Athletics:** Baseball M; Basketball M & W; Lacrosse M & W; Softball W; Tennis M & W; Volleyball W

ORANGE COUNTY COMMUNITY COLLEGE
115 South St.
Middletown, NY 10940-6437
Tel: (845)344-6222
Fax: (845)343-1228
E-mail: admssns@sunyorange.edu
Web Site: http://www.orange.cc.ny.us/
President/CEO: William Richards
Admissions: Margot St. Lawrence
Type: Two-Year College **Sex:** Coed **Affiliation:** State University of New York System **% Accepted:** 100 **Admission Plans:** Open Admission; Preferred Admission; Early Admission; Deferred Admission **Application Deadline:** August 1 **Application Fee:** $30.00 **H.S. Requirements:** High school diploma required; GED accepted. For 24 credit hour guideline program: High school diploma or equivalent not required **Scholarships:** Available **Calendar System:** Semester, Summer Session Available **Enrollment:** FT 3,344, PT 3,097 **Faculty:** FT 137, PT 245 **Student-Faculty Ratio:** 16:1 **Library Holdings:** 101,342 **Regional Accreditation:** Middle State Association of Colleges and Schools **Credit Hours For Degree:** 62 credits, Associates **Professional Accreditation:** ADA, AOTA, APTA, ACBSP, NAACLS, NLN **Intercollegiate Athletics:** Baseball M; Basketball M & W; Golf M & W; Soccer M & W; Softball W; Tennis M & W; Volleyball W

PACE UNIVERSITY
One Pace Plaza
New York, NY 10038
Tel: (212)346-1200; Free: 800-874-7223
Admissions: (212)346-1794
Fax: (212)346-1040
E-mail: dhoyt@pace.edu
Web Site: http://www.pace.edu/
President/CEO: Stephen J. Friedman
Admissions: Donna J. Hoyt
Financial Aid: Mark Stephens
Type: University **Sex:** Coed **Scores:** 99% SAT M 400+; 37% ACT 18-23; 59% ACT 24-29 **% Accepted:** 78 **Admission Plans:** Early Action; Deferred Admission **Application Deadline:** February 15 **Application Fee:** $50.00 **H.S. Requirements:** High school diploma required; GED accepted **Costs Per Year:** Application fee: $50. Comprehensive fee: $45,782 includes full-time tuition ($32,476), mandatory fees ($1066), and college room and board ($12,240). Room and board charges vary according to board plan and housing facility. Part-time tuition: $937 per credit hour. Part-time tuition varies according to course load. **Scholarships:** Available **Calendar System:** Semester, Summer Session Available **Enrollment:** FT 6,498, PT 1,473, Grad FT 1,734, Grad PT 3,001 **Faculty:** FT 452, PT 666 **Student-Faculty Ratio:** 15:1 **Exams:** SAT I or ACT. ACT essay not being used. SAT essay not being used. **% Receiving Financial Aid:** 74 **% Residing in College-Owned, -Operated, or -Affiliated Housing:** 45 **Library Holdings:** 808,429 **Regional Accreditation:** Middle State Association of Colleges and Schools **Credit Hours For Degree:** 64 credits, Associates; 128 credits, Bachelors **ROTC:** Army, Air Force **Professional Accreditation:** AACSB, ABET, AACN, ABA, APA, AALS, NCATE **Intercollegiate Athletics:** Baseball M; Basketball M & W; Cross-Country Running M & W; Equestrian Sports W; Football M; Golf M; Lacrosse M; Soccer W; Softball W; Swimming and Diving M & W; Tennis M & W; Track and Field M & W; Volleyball W

PARSONS THE NEW SCHOOL FOR DESIGN
65 Fifth Ave.
New York, NY 10011-8878
Tel: (212)229-8900; Free: 877-528-3321
Admissions: (212)229-8989
Fax: (212)229-8975
E-mail: parsadm@newschool.edu
Web Site: http://www.parsons.edu/
President/CEO: Bob Kerrey
Type: Comprehensive **Sex:** Coed **Affiliation:** The New School **Scores:** 96% SAT V 400+; 96% SAT M 400+; 45% ACT 18-23; 46% ACT 24-29 **% Accepted:** 62 **Admission Plans:** Deferred Admission **Application Deadline:** February 1 **Application Fee:** $50.00 **H.S. Requirements:** High school diploma required; GED accepted **Costs Per Year:** Application fee: $50. Comprehensive fee: $51,270 includes full-time tuition ($35,220), mandatory fees ($790), and college room and board ($15,260). College room only: $12,260. Room and board charges vary according to board plan and housing facility. Part-time tuition: $1202 per credit. Part-time tuition varies according to course load. **Scholarships:** Available **Calendar System:** Semester, Summer Session Available **Enrollment:** FT 3,677, PT 430, Grad FT 413, Grad PT 78 **Faculty:** FT 148, PT 917 **Student-Faculty Ratio:** 9:1 **Exams:** SAT I or ACT. ACT essay not being used. SAT essay not being used. **% Receiving Financial Aid:** 46 **% Residing in College-Owned, -Operated, or -Affiliated Housing:** 22 **Library Holdings:** 1,906,046 **Regional Accreditation:** Middle State Association of Colleges and Schools **Credit Hours For Degree:** 65 credits, Associates; 134 credits, Bachelors **Professional Accreditation:** NAAB, NASAD

PAUL SMITH'S COLLEGE
PO Box 265
Paul Smiths, NY 12970-0265
Tel: (518)327-6000; Free: 800-421-2605
Fax: (518)327-6060
E-mail: admissions@paulsmiths.edu

Web Site: http://www.paulsmiths.edu/
President/CEO: Dr. John Mills
Financial Aid: Mary Ellen Chamberlain
Type: Four-Year College **Sex:** Coed **Scores:** 81% SAT V 400+; 85% SAT M 400+; 51% ACT 18-23; 16% ACT 24-29 **% Accepted:** 86 **Admission Plans:** Deferred Admission **Application Deadline:** Rolling **Application Fee:** $30.00 **H.S. Requirements:** High school diploma required; GED accepted **Scholarships:** Available **Calendar System:** Semester, Summer Session Available **Faculty:** FT 57, PT 26 **Student-Faculty Ratio:** 14:1 **Exams:** SAT I or ACT. **% Receiving Financial Aid:** 85 **% Residing in College-Owned, -Operated, or -Affiliated Housing:** 85 **Library Holdings:** 56,000 **Regional Accreditation:** Middle State Association of Colleges and Schools **Credit Hours For Degree:** 60 credit hours, Associates; 120 credit hours, Bachelors **Professional Accreditation:** ABET, ACF **Intercollegiate Athletics:** Basketball M & W; Cross-Country Running M & W; Skiing (Cross-Country) M & W; Soccer M & W; Volleyball W

PHILLIPS BETH ISRAEL SCHOOL OF NURSING
776 6th Ave.
New York, NY 10001
Tel: (212)614-6110
Fax: (212)614-6109
E-mail: bstern@bethisraelny.org
Web Site: http://www.futurenursebi.org/
President/CEO: Janet Mackin
Admissions: Bernice Pass-Stern
Type: Two-Year College **Sex:** Coed **Scores:** 100% SAT V 400+; 100% SAT M 400+ **% Accepted:** 17 **Admission Plans:** Deferred Admission **Application Deadline:** April 1 **Application Fee:** $50.00 **H.S. Requirements:** High school diploma required; GED accepted **Costs Per Year:** Application fee: $50. Tuition: $15,580 full-time, $380 per credit part-time. Mandatory fees: $2590 full-time. Full-time tuition and fees vary according to course load. Part-time tuition varies according to course load. **Scholarships:** Available **Calendar System:** Semester, Summer Session Available **Enrollment:** FT 26, PT 230 **Faculty:** FT 10, PT 15 **Student-Faculty Ratio:** 10:1 **Exams:** Other, SAT I. **Library Holdings:** 12,000 **Credit Hours For Degree:** 68 credits, Associates **Professional Accreditation:** NLN

PLAZA COLLEGE
7409 37th Ave.
Jackson Heights, NY 11372-6300
Tel: (718)779-1430
Fax: (718)779-1456
E-mail: info@plazacollege.edu
Web Site: http://www.plazacollege.edu/
President/CEO: Charles Callahan
Admissions: Dean Rose Ann Black
Type: Two-Year College **Sex:** Coed **Application Deadline:** Rolling **Application Fee:** $100.00 **H.S. Requirements:** High school diploma required; GED accepted. For adult education program: High school diploma or equivalent not required **Costs Per Year:** Application fee: $100. One-time mandatory fee: $100. Tuition: $9900 full-time. Mandatory fees: $1450 full-time. Full-time tuition and fees vary according to program. **Scholarships:** Available **Calendar System:** Semester, Summer Session Available **Exams:** Other. **Regional Accreditation:** Middle State Association of Colleges and Schools **Credit Hours For Degree:** 60 credits, Associates; 120 credits, Bachelors

POLYTECHNIC INSTITUTE OF NYU
Six Metrotech Center
Brooklyn, NY 11201-2990
Tel: (718)260-3600; Free: 800-POLYTECH
Admissions: (718)260-5917
Fax: (718)260-3136
E-mail: uadmit@poly.edu
Web Site: http://www.poly.edu/
President/CEO: Jerry Hultin
Admissions: Joy Colelli
Financial Aid: Christine Falzerano
Type: University **Sex:** Coed **Affiliation:** New York University **Scores:** 99% SAT V 400+; 99% SAT M 400+ **% Accepted:** 55 **Admission Plans:** Early Admission; Deferred Admission **Application Deadline:** February 1 **Application Fee:** $50.00 **H.S. Requirements:** High school diploma required; GED accepted **Costs Per Year:** Application fee: $50. Comprehensive fee: $43,420 includes full-time tuition ($33,274), mandatory fees ($1146), and college room and board ($9000). College room only: $6961. Full-time tuition and fees vary according to course load. Room and board charges vary according to housing facility. Part-time tuition: $1058 per credit hour. Part-time mandatory fees: $418 per year. Part-time tuition and fees vary according to course load. Tuition guaranteed not to increase for student's term of enrollment. **Scholarships:** Available **Calendar System:** Semester, Summer Session Available **Enrollment:** FT 1,665, PT 67, Grad FT 1,673, Grad PT 1,109 **Faculty:** FT 152, PT 189 **Student-Faculty Ratio:** 15:1 **Exams:** SAT I or ACT, SAT II. **% Receiving Financial Aid:** 72 **% Residing in College-Owned, -Operated, or -Affiliated Housing:** 26 **Final Year or Final Semester Residency Requirement:** No **Library Holdings:** 140,000 **Regional Accreditation:** Middle State Association of Colleges and Schools **Credit Hours For Degree:** 124 credits, Bachelors **ROTC:** Army, Air Force **Professional Accreditation:** ABET **Intercollegiate Athletics:** Baseball M; Basketball M & W; Cross-Country Running M & W; Soccer M & W; Softball W; Tennis M & W; Track and Field M & W; Volleyball M & W

PRATT INSTITUTE
200 Willoughby Ave.
Brooklyn, NY 11205-3899
Tel: (718)636-3600; Free: 800-331-0834
Fax: (718)636-3670
E-mail: visit@pratt.edu
Web Site: http://www.pratt.edu/
President/CEO: Thomas Schutte
Admissions: Olga Burger
Financial Aid: Fiona Approo
Type: Comprehensive **Sex:** Coed **Scores:** 97% SAT V 400+; 98% SAT M 400+; 30% ACT 18-23; 60% ACT 24-29 **% Accepted:** 41 **Admission Plans:** Early Action; Deferred Admission **Application Deadline:** January 5 **Application Fee:** $50.00 **H.S. Requirements:** High school diploma required; GED accepted **Costs Per Year:** Application fee: $50. Comprehensive fee: $46,810 includes full-time tuition ($35,410), mandatory fees ($1380), and college room and board ($10,020). College room only: $6340. Part-time tuition: $1142 per credit. **Scholarships:** Available **Calendar System:** Semester, Summer Session Available **Enrollment:** FT 2,837, PT 161, Grad FT 1,408, Grad PT 301 **Faculty:** FT 120, PT 877 **Student-Faculty Ratio:** 11:1 **Exams:** SAT I or ACT, SAT II. ACT essay used for admission. SAT essay used for admission. ACT essay used as a validity check on application essay. SAT essay used as a validity check on application essay. **% Receiving Financial Aid:** 69 **% Residing in College-Owned, -Operated, or -Affiliated Housing:** 49 **Regional Accreditation:** Middle State Association of Colleges and Schools **Credit Hours For Degree:** 66 credits, Associates; 132 credits, Bachelors **Professional Accreditation:** ACSP, ALA, FIDER, NAAB, NASAD **Intercollegiate Athletics:** Basketball M; Cross-Country Running M & W; Soccer M & W; Tennis M & W; Track and Field M & W; Volleyball W

PURCHASE COLLEGE, STATE UNIVERSITY OF NEW YORK
735 Anderson Hill Rd.
Purchase, NY 10577-1400
Tel: (914)251-6000
Admissions: (914)251-6300
E-mail: admission@purchase.edu
Web Site: http://www.purchase.edu/
President/CEO: Thomas Schwarz
Admissions: Stephanie McCaine
Financial Aid: Corey York
Type: Comprehensive **Sex:** Coed **Affiliation:** State University of New York System **Scores:** 100% SAT V 400+; 97% SAT M 400+; 52% ACT 18-23; 44% ACT 24-29 **% Accepted:** 27 **Admission Plans:** Early Admission; Early Decision Plan; Deferred Admission **Application Deadline:** July 15 **Application Fee:** $40.00 **H.S. Requirements:** High school diploma required; GED accepted **Costs Per Year:** Application fee: $40. One-time mandatory fee: $200. State resident tuition: $4970 full-time, $207 per credit hour part-time. Nonresident tuition: $12,870 full-time, $536 per credit hour part-time. Mandatory fees: $1461 full-time, $.85 per credit hour part-time. Full-time tuition and fees vary according to program. Part-time tuition and fees vary according to course load and program. College room and board: $9908. College room only: $6240. Room and board charges vary according to board plan and housing facility. **Scholarships:** Available **Calendar System:** Semester, Summer Session Available **Enrollment:** FT 3,698, PT 379, Grad FT 116, Grad PT 11 **Faculty:** FT 150, PT 234 **Student-Faculty Ratio:** 16:1 **Exams:** SAT I or ACT, SAT I. **% Receiving Financial Aid:** 56 **% Residing in**

College-Owned, -Operated, or -Affiliated Housing: 68 **Library Holdings:** 241,984 **Regional Accreditation:** Middle State Association of Colleges and Schools **Credit Hours For Degree:** 120 credits, Bachelors **Professional Accreditation:** NASAD, NASM **Intercollegiate Athletics:** Baseball M & W; Basketball M & W; Cross-Country Running M & W; Golf M; Soccer M & W; Softball M & W; Swimming and Diving W; Volleyball M & W

QUEENS COLLEGE OF THE CITY UNIVERSITY OF NEW YORK
65-30 Kissena Blvd.
Flushing, NY 11367-1597
Tel: (718)997-5000
Admissions: (718)997-5600
Fax: (718)997-5617
E-mail: vincent.angrisani@qc.cuny.edu
Web Site: http://www.qc.cuny.edu/
President/CEO: Dr. James L. Muyskens
Admissions: Vincent Angrisani
Financial Aid: Rena Smith-Kiawu
Type: Comprehensive **Sex:** Coed **Affiliation:** City University of New York System **Scores:** 100% SAT V 400+; 100% SAT M 400+ **% Accepted:** 33 **Admission Plans:** Deferred Admission **Application Deadline:** May 15 **Application Fee:** $65.00 **H.S. Requirements:** High school diploma required; GED accepted **Costs Per Year:** Application fee: $65. State resident tuition: $4600 full-time, $195 per credit part-time. Nonresident tuition: $9960 full-time, $415 per credit part-time. Mandatory fees: $447 full-time, $140.75 per term part-time. College room and board: $11,125. Room and board charges vary according to housing facility. **Scholarships:** Available **Calendar System:** Semester, Summer Session Available **Enrollment:** FT 11,762, PT 4,297, Grad FT 510, Grad PT 4,142 **Faculty:** FT 636, PT 766 **Student-Faculty Ratio:** 16:1 **Exams:** SAT I or ACT, SAT II. **% Receiving Financial Aid:** 78 **% Residing in College-Owned, -Operated, or -Affiliated Housing:** 3 **Library Holdings:** 1,075,178 **Regional Accreditation:** Middle State Association of Colleges and Schools **Credit Hours For Degree:** 120 credits, Bachelors **ROTC:** Army, Navy **Professional Accreditation:** AAFCS, ADtA, ALA, ASLHA, NCATE **Intercollegiate Athletics:** Baseball M; Basketball M & W; Cross-Country Running M & W; Fencing W; Golf M; Lacrosse W; Soccer M & W; Softball W; Swimming and Diving M & W; Table Tennis M & W; Tennis M & W; Track and Field M & W; Volleyball W; Water Polo M

QUEENSBOROUGH COMMUNITY COLLEGE OF THE CITY UNIVERSITY OF NEW YORK
222-05 56th Ave.
Bayside, NY 11364
Tel: (718)631-6262
Fax: (718)281-5189
Web Site: http://www.qcc.cuny.edu/
President/CEO: Eduardo J. Marti
Admissions: Ann Tullio
Type: Two-Year College **Sex:** Coed **Affiliation:** City University of New York System **Scores:** 33.3% SAT V 400+; 47.6% SAT M 400+ **% Accepted:** 100 **Admission Plans:** Open Admission; Deferred Admission **Application Deadline:** Rolling **Application Fee:** $40.00 **H.S. Requirements:** High school diploma required; GED accepted **Costs Per Year:** Application fee: $40. State resident tuition: $3150 full-time. Nonresident tuition: $5040 full-time. Mandatory fees: $308 full-time. Full-time tuition and fees vary according to course load. **Scholarships:** Available **Calendar System:** Semester, Summer Session Available **Faculty:** FT 291, PT 445 **Student-Faculty Ratio:** 21:1 **Library Holdings:** 140,000 **Regional Accreditation:** Middle State Association of Colleges and Schools **Credit Hours For Degree:** 60 credits, Associates **ROTC:** Army **Professional Accreditation:** ABET, ACBSP, NLN **Intercollegiate Athletics:** Baseball M; Basketball M & W; Cross-Country Running M & W; Soccer M; Softball W; Tennis M & W; Track and Field M & W; Volleyball M & W

RABBINICAL ACADEMY MESIVTA RABBI CHAIM BERLIN
1605 Coney Island Ave.
Brooklyn, NY 11230-4715
Tel: (718)377-0777
President/CEO: Abraham Fruchthandler
Type: Comprehensive **Sex:** Men **Affiliation:** Jewish **% Accepted:** 100 **Calendar System:** Semester **Credit Hours For Degree:** 150 credits, Bachelors **Professional Accreditation:** AARTS

RABBINICAL COLLEGE BETH SHRAGA
28 Saddle River Rd.
Monsey, NY 10952-3035
Tel: (914)356-1980
Admissions: (845)356-1980
President/CEO: Sydney Schiff
Admissions: Rabbi Sydney Schiff
Type: Comprehensive **Sex:** Men **Affiliation:** Jewish **% Accepted:** 100 **Calendar System:** Semester **Professional Accreditation:** AARTS

RABBINICAL COLLEGE BOBOVER YESHIVA B'NEI ZION
1577 Forty-eighth St.
Brooklyn, NY 11219
Tel: (718)438-2018
President/CEO: Mordechai Z. Geller
Type: Comprehensive **Sex:** Men **Affiliation:** Jewish **Calendar System:** Semester **Professional Accreditation:** AARTS

RABBINICAL COLLEGE CH'SAN SOFER
1876 Fiftieth St.
Brooklyn, NY 11204
Tel: (718)236-1171
President/CEO: William Greenwald
Type: Comprehensive **Sex:** Men **Affiliation:** Jewish **Calendar System:** Semester **Professional Accreditation:** AARTS

RABBINICAL COLLEGE OF LONG ISLAND
205 West Beech St.
Long Beach, NY 11561-3305
Tel: (516)431-7414
President/CEO: Yitzchok Feigelstock
Type: Comprehensive **Sex:** Men **Affiliation:** Jewish **% Accepted:** 100 **H.S. Requirements:** High school diploma required; GED accepted **Calendar System:** Semester **Professional Accreditation:** AARTS

RABBINICAL COLLEGE OF OHR SHIMON YISROEL
215-217 Hewes St.
Brooklyn, NY 11211
Tel: (718)855-4092
President/CEO: Rosa Friedman
Type: Four-Year College **Sex:** Men **Affiliation:** Jewish **Professional Accreditation:** AARTS

RABBINICAL SEMINARY ADAS YEREIM
185 Wilson St.
Brooklyn, NY 11211-7206
Tel: (718)388-1751
Admissions: (212)388-1751
President/CEO: Heshy Greenzweig
Financial Aid: Israel Weingarten
Type: Comprehensive **Sex:** Men **Affiliation:** Jewish **Calendar System:** Semester **Professional Accreditation:** AARTS

RABBINICAL SEMINARY OF AMERICA
76-01 147th St.
Flushing, NY 11367
Tel: (718)268-4700
President/CEO: H. Schwartz
Admissions: Rabbi Abraham Semmel
Financial Aid: Leah Eisenstein
Type: Comprehensive **Sex:** Men **Affiliation:** Jewish **Admission Plans:** Early Admission **Application Deadline:** December 1 **Application Fee:** $0.00 **H.S. Requirements:** High school diploma required; GED accepted **Calendar System:** Semester **% Residing in College-Owned, -Operated, or -Affiliated Housing:** 90 **Library Holdings:** 30,000 **Credit Hours For Degree:** 150 credits, Bachelors **Professional Accreditation:** AARTS

RABBINICAL SEMINARY M'KOR CHAIM
1571 Fifty-fifth St.
Brooklyn, NY 11219
Tel: (718)851-0183
President/CEO: Tzvi Davidowitz
Type: Four-Year College **Sex:** Men **Affiliation:** Jewish **% Accepted:** 100 **Calendar System:** Semester **Professional Accreditation:** AARTS

RENSSELAER POLYTECHNIC INSTITUTE
110 8th St.
Troy, NY 12180-3590
Tel: (518)276-6000; Free: 800-448-6562
Admissions: (518)276-6216
Fax: (518)276-4072
E-mail: admissions@rpi.edu
Web Site: http://www.rpi.edu/
President/CEO: Dr. Shirley Ann Jackson
Admissions: Paul Marthers
Financial Aid: Lynnette E. Koch
Type: University **Sex:** Coed **Scores:** 100% SAT V 400+; 100% SAT M 400+; 13% ACT 18-23; 60% ACT 24-29 **% Accepted:** 43 **Admission Plans:** Early Admission; Early Decision Plan; Deferred Admission **Application Deadline:** January 15 **Application Fee:** $70.00 **H.S. Requirements:** High school diploma required; GED accepted **Costs Per Year:** Application fee: $70. Comprehensive fee: $50,310 includes full-time tuition ($38,100), mandatory fees ($1065), and college room and board ($11,145). College room only: $6300. Room and board charges vary according to board plan and location. Part-time tuition: $1155 per credit hour. **Scholarships:** Available **Calendar System:** Semester, Summer Session Available **Enrollment:** FT 5,601, PT 58, Grad FT 1,103, Grad PT 894 **Faculty:** FT 386, PT 89 **Student-Faculty Ratio:** 16:1 **Exams:** SAT I or ACT, SAT I and SAT II or ACT. ACT essay used for admission. SAT essay used for admission. **% Receiving Financial Aid:** 65 **% Residing in College-Owned, -Operated, or -Affiliated Housing:** 59 **Library Holdings:** 438,802 **Regional Accreditation:** Middle State Association of Colleges and Schools **Credit Hours For Degree:** 124 credit hours, Bachelors **ROTC:** Army, Navy, Air Force **Professional Accreditation:** AACSB, ABET, NAAB **Intercollegiate Athletics:** Archery M & W; Badminton M & W; Baseball M & W; Basketball M & W; Crew M & W; Cross-Country Running M & W; Equestrian Sports M & W; Fencing M & W; Field Hockey W; Golf M; Ice Hockey M & W; Lacrosse M & W; Racquetball M & W; Riflery M & W; Rugby M & W; Sailing M & W; Skiing (Cross-Country) M & W; Soccer M & W; Softball W; Squash M & W; Swimming and Diving M & W; Table Tennis M & W; Tennis M & W; Track and Field M & W; Ultimate Frisbee M & W; Volleyball M & W; Water Polo M & W; Weight Lifting M & W

ROBERTS WESLEYAN COLLEGE
2301 Westside Dr.
Rochester, NY 14624-1997
Tel: (585)594-6000; Free: 800-777-4RWC
Admissions: (585)594-6400
Fax: (585)594-6371
E-mail: admissions@roberts.edu
Web Site: http://www.roberts.edu/
President/CEO: Dr. John A. Martin
Admissions: Linda Kurtz Hoffman
Type: Comprehensive **Sex:** Coed **Affiliation:** Free Methodist Church of North America **Scores:** 97% SAT V 400+; 95% SAT M 400+; 50% ACT 18-23; 35% ACT 24-29 **% Accepted:** 65 **Admission Plans:** Early Admission; Deferred Admission **Application Deadline:** February 1 **Application Fee:** $35.00 **H.S. Requirements:** High school diploma required; GED accepted **Costs Per Year:** Application fee: $35. Comprehensive fee: $32,300 includes full-time tuition ($22,580), mandatory fees ($1200), and college room and board ($8520). College room only: $5816. Room and board charges vary according to board plan and housing facility. Part-time tuition: $493 per credit. Part-time tuition varies according to course load. **Scholarships:** Available **Calendar System:** Semester, Summer Session Available **Enrollment:** FT 1,265, PT 123, Grad FT 350, Grad PT 190 **Faculty:** FT 102, PT 146 **Student-Faculty Ratio:** 11:1 **Exams:** SAT I or ACT. **% Receiving Financial Aid:** 89 **% Residing in College-Owned, -Operated, or -Affiliated Housing:** 65 **Final Year or Final Semester Residency Requirement:** Yes **Library Holdings:** 134,798 **Regional Accreditation:** Middle State Association of Colleges and Schools **Credit Hours For Degree:** 62 semester hours, Associates; 124 semester hours, Bachelors **ROTC:** Army, Air Force **Professional Accreditation:** AACN, CSWE, NASAD, NASM, NLN **Intercollegiate Athletics:** Basketball M & W; Cross-Country Running M & W; Golf M & W; Soccer M & W; Tennis M & W; Track and Field M & W; Volleyball W

ROCHESTER INSTITUTE OF TECHNOLOGY
One Lomb Memorial Dr.
Rochester, NY 14623-5603
Tel: (585)475-2411
Admissions: (585)475-6631
Fax: (585)475-7424
E-mail: admissions@rit.edu
Web Site: http://www.rit.edu/
President/CEO: Dr. William Destler
Admissions: Dr. Daniel Shelley
Financial Aid: Verna Hazen
Type: Comprehensive **Sex:** Coed **Scores:** 100% SAT V 400+; 100% SAT M 400+; 18% ACT 18-23; 53% ACT 24-29 **% Accepted:** 61 **Admission Plans:** Early Admission; Early Decision Plan; Deferred Admission **Application Deadline:** February 1 **Application Fee:** $50.00 **H.S. Requirements:** High school diploma required; GED accepted **Costs Per Year:** Application fee: $50. Comprehensive fee: $38,925 includes full-time tuition ($28,866), mandatory fees ($417), and college room and board ($9642). College room only: $5583. Full-time tuition and fees vary according to course load. Room and board charges vary according to board plan and housing facility. Part-time tuition: $641 per quarter hour. Part-time mandatory fees: $35 per term. Part-time tuition and fees vary according to class time and course load. **Scholarships:** Available **Calendar System:** Quarter, Summer Session Available **Enrollment:** FT 12,367, PT 1,678, Grad FT 1,451, Grad PT 1,277 **Faculty:** FT 945, PT 481 **Student-Faculty Ratio:** 13:1 **Exams:** SAT I or ACT. **% Receiving Financial Aid:** 72 **% Residing in College-Owned, -Operated, or -Affiliated Housing:** 68 **Library Holdings:** 452,355 **Regional Accreditation:** Middle State Association of Colleges and Schools **Credit Hours For Degree:** 90 credit hours, Associates; 180 credit hours, Bachelors **ROTC:** Army, Navy, Air Force **Professional Accreditation:** AACSB, ABET, FIDER, CSWE, JRCEDMS, JRCNMT, NASAD, TEAC **Intercollegiate Athletics:** Baseball M; Basketball M & W; Bowling M & W; Cheerleading M & W; Crew M & W; Cross-Country Running M & W; Equestrian Sports M & W; Fencing M & W; Field Hockey W; Ice Hockey M & W; Lacrosse M & W; Skiing (Downhill) M & W; Soccer M & W; Softball W; Swimming and Diving M & W; Tennis M & W; Track and Field M & W; Ultimate Frisbee M & W; Volleyball M & W; Water Polo M & W; Wrestling M

ROCKLAND COMMUNITY COLLEGE
145 College Rd.
Suffern, NY 10901-3699
Tel: (845)574-4000; Free: 800-722-7666
Admissions: (845)574-4237
E-mail: lglynn@sunyrockland.edu
Web Site: http://www.sunyrockland.edu/
President/CEO: Cliff L. Wood
Admissions: Lorraine Glynn
Financial Aid: Debra Bouabidi
Type: Two-Year College **Sex:** Coed **Affiliation:** State University of New York System **Admission Plans:** Open Admission; Early Admission; Deferred Admission **Application Deadline:** Rolling **H.S. Requirements:** High school diploma required; GED accepted **Scholarships:** Available **Calendar System:** Semester, Summer Session Available **Enrollment:** FT 4,314, PT 2,670 **Regional Accreditation:** Middle State Association of Colleges and Schools **Credit Hours For Degree:** 60 credits, Associates **Professional Accreditation:** AHIMA, AOTA, NLN **Intercollegiate Athletics:** Baseball M; Basketball M & W; Bowling M & W; Golf M; Soccer M & W; Softball W; Tennis M & W; Volleyball W

RUSSELL SAGE COLLEGE
45 Ferry St.
Troy, NY 12180-4115
Tel: (518)244-2000; Free: 888-VERY SAGE
Admissions: (518)244-2444
Fax: (518)244-6880
E-mail: ruschk@sage.edu
Web Site: http://www.sage.edu/rsc/
President/CEO: Dr. Susan Scrimshaw, PhD
Admissions: Kathy Rusch
Financial Aid: James K. Dease
Type: Four-Year College **Sex:** Women **Affiliation:** The Sage Colleges **Scores:** 95% SAT V 400+; 95% SAT M 400+; 36% ACT 18-23; 52% ACT 24-29 **% Accepted:** 76 **Admission Plans:** Early Admission; Early Action; Deferred Admission **Application Deadline:** Rolling **Application Fee:** $30.00 **H.S. Requirements:** High school diploma required; GED accepted **Costs Per Year:** Application fee: $30. Comprehensive fee: $37,460 includes full-time tuition ($27,000), mandatory fees ($790), and college room and board

($9670). College room only: $4940. Room and board charges vary according to board plan. Part-time tuition: $900 per credit hour. **Scholarships:** Available **Calendar System:** Semester, Summer Session Available **Enrollment:** FT 692, PT 57 **Faculty:** FT 56, PT 18 **Student-Faculty Ratio:** 11:1 **Exams:** SAT I or ACT. **% Receiving Financial Aid:** 89 **% Residing in College-Owned, -Operated, or -Affiliated Housing:** 51 **Final Year or Final Semester Residency Requirement:** No **Library Holdings:** 256,905 **Regional Accreditation:** Middle State Association of Colleges and Schools **Credit Hours For Degree:** 120 credits, Bachelors **ROTC:** Army, Air Force **Professional Accreditation:** AOTA, NASAD, NCATE, NLN **Intercollegiate Athletics:** Basketball W; Lacrosse W; Soccer W; Softball W; Tennis W; Volleyball W

SAGE COLLEGE OF ALBANY
140 New Scotland Ave.
Albany, NY 12208-3425
Tel: (518)292-1730; Free: 888-VERY-SAGE
Fax: (518)292-1912
E-mail: scaadm@sage.edu
Web Site: http://www.sage.edu/
President/CEO: Dr. Susan Scrimshaw, PhD
Admissions: Andrew Palumbo
Financial Aid: James K. Dease
Type: Four-Year College **Sex:** Coed **Affiliation:** The Sage Colleges **Scores:** 85% SAT V 400+; 86% SAT M 400+ **% Accepted:** 65 **Admission Plans:** Deferred Admission **Application Deadline:** Rolling **Application Fee:** $30.00 **H.S. Requirements:** High school diploma required; GED accepted **Costs Per Year:** Application fee: $30. Comprehensive fee: $37,620 includes full-time tuition ($27,000), mandatory fees ($790), and college room and board ($9830). College room only: $5100. Room and board charges vary according to board plan. Part-time tuition: $900 per credit hour. **Scholarships:** Available **Calendar System:** Semester, Summer Session Available **Enrollment:** FT 557, PT 291 **Faculty:** FT 40, PT 60 **Student-Faculty Ratio:** 12:1 **Exams:** SAT I or ACT. **% Receiving Financial Aid:** 93 **% Residing in College-Owned, -Operated, or -Affiliated Housing:** 37 **Final Year or Final Semester Residency Requirement:** No **Library Holdings:** 256,905 **Regional Accreditation:** Middle State Association of Colleges and Schools **Credit Hours For Degree:** 60 credits, Associates; 120 credits, Bachelors **ROTC:** Army, Air Force **Professional Accreditation:** NASAD **Intercollegiate Athletics:** Basketball M & W; Golf M; Lacrosse W; Soccer M & W; Softball W; Tennis M & W; Volleyball M & W

ST. BONAVENTURE UNIVERSITY
Route 417
St. Bonaventure, NY 14778-2284
Tel: (716)375-2000; Free: 800-462-5050
Admissions: (716)375-2400
Fax: (716)375-2005
E-mail: memery@sbu.edu
Web Site: http://www.sbu.edu/
President/CEO: Sr. Margaret Carney
Admissions: Monica Emery
Financial Aid: Elisabeth T. Rankin
Type: Comprehensive **Sex:** Coed **Affiliation:** Roman Catholic Church **Scores:** 96% SAT V 400+; 94% SAT M 400+; 53% ACT 18-23; 29% ACT 24-29 **% Accepted:** 84 **Admission Plans:** Deferred Admission **Application Deadline:** July 15 **Application Fee:** $30.00 **H.S. Requirements:** High school diploma required; GED accepted **Costs Per Year:** Application fee: $30. Comprehensive fee: $35,966 includes full-time tuition ($25,930), mandatory fees ($965), and college room and board ($9071). College room only: $4441. Room and board charges vary according to board plan and housing facility. Part-time tuition: $775 per credit hour. **Scholarships:** Available **Calendar System:** Semester, Summer Session Available **Enrollment:** FT 1,865, PT 102, Grad FT 289, Grad PT 216 **Faculty:** FT 154, PT 83 **Student-Faculty Ratio:** 14:1 **Exams:** SAT I or ACT, SAT II. **% Receiving Financial Aid:** 76 **% Residing in College-Owned, -Operated, or -Affiliated Housing:** 80 **Library Holdings:** 331,219 **Regional Accreditation:** Middle State Association of Colleges and Schools **Credit Hours For Degree:** 120 credit hours, Bachelors **ROTC:** Army **Professional Accreditation:** AACSB, ACA, NCATE **Intercollegiate Athletics:** Baseball M; Basketball M & W; Cheerleading M & W; Cross-Country Running M & W; Field Hockey W; Golf M; Lacrosse M & W; Rugby M & W; Soccer M & W; Softball W; Swimming and Diving M & W; Tennis M & W

ST. ELIZABETH COLLEGE OF NURSING
2215 Genesee St.
Utica, NY 13501
Tel: (315)798-8144
E-mail: mmonahan@stemc.org
Web Site: http://www.secon.edu/
President/CEO: Marianne Monahan
Admissions: Marian Kovatchitch, MS, RN
Type: Two-Year College **Sex:** Coed **Affiliation:** St. Elizabeth Medical Center **Scores:** 94% SAT V 400+; 94% SAT M 400+; 100% ACT 18-23 **% Accepted:** 45 **Admission Plans:** Open Admission **Application Deadline:** Rolling **Application Fee:** $65.00 **H.S. Requirements:** High school diploma required; GED accepted **Costs Per Year:** Application fee: $65. Tuition: $11,530 full-time, $325 per credit hour part-time. Mandatory fees: $950 full-time, $475 per term part-time. Full-time tuition and fees vary according to course load, program, and student level. Part-time tuition and fees vary according to course load, program, and student level. **Calendar System:** Semester, Summer Session Available **Enrollment:** FT 157, PT 82 **Faculty:** FT 17, PT 4 **Student-Faculty Ratio:** 10:1 **Exams:** SAT I or ACT. ACT essay not being used. SAT essay not being used. **Regional Accreditation:** Middle State Association of Colleges and Schools **Credit Hours For Degree:** 68 credits, Associates

ST. FRANCIS COLLEGE
180 Remsen St.
Brooklyn Heights, NY 11201-4398
Tel: (718)522-2300
Admissions: (718)489-5226
Fax: (718)522-1274
E-mail: mmichalski@stfranciscollege.edu
Web Site: http://www.stfranciscollege.edu/
President/CEO: Brendan J. Dugan
Admissions: Monica Michalski
Financial Aid: Joseph Cummings
Type: Comprehensive **Sex:** Coed **Affiliation:** Roman Catholic **Scores:** 85% SAT V 400+; 80% SAT M 400+ **% Accepted:** 78 **Admission Plans:** Deferred Admission **Application Deadline:** Rolling **Application Fee:** $35.00 **H.S. Requirements:** High school diploma required; GED accepted **Costs Per Year:** Application fee: $35. Comprehensive fee: $31,350 includes full-time tuition ($16,480), mandatory fees ($520), and college room and board ($14,350). Full-time tuition and fees vary according to course level, course load, and degree level. Part-time tuition: $485 per credit. Part-time mandatory fees: $140 per term. Part-time tuition and fees vary according to course level, course load, and degree level. **Scholarships:** Available **Calendar System:** Semester, Summer Session Available **Enrollment:** FT 2,204, PT 277, Grad FT 27, Grad PT 3 **Faculty:** FT 80, PT 163 **Student-Faculty Ratio:** 18:1 **Exams:** SAT I. SAT essay not being used. **% Receiving Financial Aid:** 87 **% Residing in College-Owned, -Operated, or -Affiliated Housing:** 1 **Final Year or Final Semester Residency Requirement:** No **Library Holdings:** 116,716 **Regional Accreditation:** Middle State Association of Colleges and Schools **Credit Hours For Degree:** 64 credits, Associates; 128 credits, Bachelors **ROTC:** Army, Air Force **Intercollegiate Athletics:** Basketball M & W; Cross-Country Running M & W; Golf M & W; Soccer M; Swimming and Diving M & W; Tennis M & W; Track and Field M & W; Volleyball W; Water Polo M & W

ST. JOHN FISHER COLLEGE
3690 East Ave.
Rochester, NY 14618-3597
Tel: (585)385-8000; Free: 800-444-4640
Admissions: (585)385-8064
Fax: (585)385-8129
E-mail: admissions@sjfc.edu
Web Site: http://www.sjfc.edu/
President/CEO: Dr. Donald Bain
Admissions: Stacy A. Ledermann
Financial Aid: Angela Monnat
Type: Comprehensive **Sex:** Coed **Affiliation:** Roman Catholic Church **Scores:** 99% SAT V 400+; 100% SAT M 400+; 48% ACT 18-23; 50% ACT 24-29 **% Accepted:** 65 **Admission Plans:** Early Admission; Early Decision Plan; Deferred Admission **Application Deadline:** Rolling **Application Fee:** $30.00 **H.S. Requirements:** High school diploma required; GED not accepted **Costs Per Year:** Application fee: $30. Comprehensive fee: $34,410 includes full-time tuition ($23,850), mandatory fees ($470), and college room

and board ($10,090). College room only: $6550. Room and board charges vary according to board plan. Part-time tuition: $650 per credit. Part-time mandatory fees: $25 per term. Part-time tuition and fees vary according to course load. **Scholarships:** Available **Calendar System:** Semester, Summer Session Available **Enrollment:** FT 2,628, PT 204, Grad FT 574, Grad PT 507 **Faculty:** FT 201, PT 174 **Student-Faculty Ratio:** 14:1 **Exams:** SAT I or ACT. **% Receiving Financial Aid:** 82 **% Residing in College-Owned, -Operated, or -Affiliated Housing:** 49 **Final Year or Final Semester Residency Requirement:** No **Library Holdings:** 214,834 **Regional Accreditation:** Middle State Association of Colleges and Schools **Credit Hours For Degree:** 120 credit hours, Bachelors **ROTC:** Army, Navy, Air Force **Professional Accreditation:** AACSB, ACPhE, AACN, ACA, NCATE **Intercollegiate Athletics:** Baseball M; Basketball M & W; Football M; Golf M & W; Lacrosse M & W; Soccer M & W; Softball W; Tennis M & W; Volleyball W

ST. JOHN'S UNIVERSITY
8000 Utopia Parkway
Queens, NY 11439
Tel: (718)990-6161; Free: 888-9STJOHNS
Admissions: (718)990-2000
E-mail: admhelp@stjohns.edu
Web Site: http://www.stjohns.edu/
President/CEO: Rev. Donald J. Harrington, CM
Admissions: Karen Vahey
Financial Aid: Jorge Rodriguez
Type: University **Sex:** Coed **Affiliation:** Roman Catholic Church **Scores:** 99% SAT V 400+; 99% SAT M 400+ **% Accepted:** 43 **Admission Plans:** Early Admission; Deferred Admission **Application Deadline:** Rolling **Application Fee:** $50.00 **H.S. Requirements:** High school diploma required; GED accepted **Costs Per Year:** Application fee: $50. Comprehensive fee: $43,180 includes full-time tuition ($29,350), mandatory fees ($690), and college room and board ($13,140). College room only: $8250. Full-time tuition and fees vary according to class time, course load, program, and student level. Room and board charges vary according to board plan, housing facility, and location. Part-time tuition: $978 per credit. Part-time mandatory fees: $247.50 per term. Part-time tuition and fees vary according to class time, course load, program, and student level. **Scholarships:** Available **Calendar System:** Semester, Summer Session Available **Enrollment:** FT 11,824, PT 2,984, Grad FT 3,000, Grad PT 2,544 **Faculty:** FT 669, PT 771 **Student-Faculty Ratio:** 19:1 **Exams:** SAT I or ACT. **% Receiving Financial Aid:** 80 **% Residing in College-Owned, -Operated, or -Affiliated Housing:** 30 **Library Holdings:** 1,176,743 **Regional Accreditation:** Middle State Association of Colleges and Schools **Credit Hours For Degree:** 60 credits, Associates; 126 credits, Bachelors **ROTC:** Army **Professional Accreditation:** AACSB, ACPhE, ABA, ACA, ALA, APA, ASLHA, ACIPE, AALS, CORE, TEAC **Intercollegiate Athletics:** Baseball M; Basketball M & W; Cross-Country Running W; Fencing M & W; Golf M & W; Lacrosse M; Soccer M & W; Softball W; Tennis M & W; Track and Field W; Volleyball W

ST. JOSEPH'S COLLEGE, LONG ISLAND CAMPUS
155 West Roe Blvd.
Patchogue, NY 11772-2399
Tel: (631)447-3200
Admissions: (631)447-3216
Fax: (631)447-1734
E-mail: glamens@sjcny.edu
Web Site: http://www.sjcny.edu/
President/CEO: Sr. Elizabeth A. Hill, JD
Admissions: Gigi Lamens
Financial Aid: Amy Thompson
Type: Comprehensive **Sex:** Coed **Scores:** 100% SAT V 400+; 99% SAT M 400+ **% Accepted:** 74 **Admission Plans:** Early Admission; Deferred Admission **Application Deadline:** August 15 **Application Fee:** $25.00 **H.S. Requirements:** High school diploma required; GED accepted **Costs Per Year:** Application fee: $25. Tuition: $16,200 full-time, $530 per credit hour part-time. Mandatory fees: $565 full-time. **Scholarships:** Available **Calendar System:** 4-1-4, Summer Session Available **Enrollment:** FT 3,127, PT 758, Grad FT 18, Grad PT 455 **Faculty:** FT 115, PT 291 **Student-Faculty Ratio:** 17:1 **Exams:** SAT I or ACT. **% Receiving Financial Aid:** 62 **Library Holdings:** 107,466 **Regional Accreditation:** Middle State Association of Colleges and Schools **Credit Hours For Degree:** 128 credits, Bachelors **ROTC:** Army, Air Force **Intercollegiate Athletics:** Basketball M & W; Cross-Country Running M & W; Softball W; Volleyball M & W

ST. JOSEPH'S COLLEGE, NEW YORK
245 Clinton Ave.
Brooklyn, NY 11205-3688
Tel: (718)636-6800
Admissions: (718)636-6868
Fax: (718)636-7242
E-mail: asinfob@sjcny.edu
Web Site: http://www.sjcny.edu/
President/CEO: Sr. Elizabeth A. Hill, JD
Admissions: Theresa LaRocca Meyer
Financial Aid: Amy Thompson
Type: Comprehensive **Sex:** Coed **Scores:** 94% SAT V 400+; 90% SAT M 400+ **% Accepted:** 73 **Admission Plans:** Early Admission; Deferred Admission **Application Deadline:** August 15 **Application Fee:** $25.00 **H.S. Requirements:** High school diploma required; GED accepted **Costs Per Year:** Application fee: $25. Tuition: $16,200 full-time, $530 per credit hour part-time. Mandatory fees: $565 full-time. **Scholarships:** Available **Calendar System:** Semester, Summer Session Available **Enrollment:** FT 827, PT 323, Grad FT 12, Grad PT 196 **Faculty:** FT 52, PT 87 **Student-Faculty Ratio:** 13:1 **Exams:** SAT I or ACT. **% Receiving Financial Aid:** 77 **Library Holdings:** 156,570 **Regional Accreditation:** Middle State Association of Colleges and Schools **Credit Hours For Degree:** 128 credits, Bachelors **Professional Accreditation:** NLN **Intercollegiate Athletics:** Basketball M & W; Cross-Country Running M & W; Softball W; Volleyball M & W

ST. JOSEPH'S COLLEGE OF NURSING
206 Prospect Ave.
Syracuse, NY 13203
Tel: (315)448-5040
Fax: (315)448-5745
E-mail: collegeofnursing@sjhsyr.org
Web Site: http://www.sjhsyr.org/nursing/
President/CEO: Marianne Markowitz
Admissions: Rhonda Reader
Type: Two-Year College **Sex:** Coed **Scores:** 100% SAT V 400+; 100% SAT M 400+; 99% ACT 18-23; 1% ACT 24-29 **% Accepted:** 55 **Admission Plans:** Deferred Admission **Application Fee:** $50.00 **H.S. Requirements:** High school diploma required; GED accepted **Costs Per Year:** Application fee: $50. Tuition: $330 per credit hour part-time. Part-time tuition varies according to course load. **Scholarships:** Available **Calendar System:** Semester **Faculty:** FT 16, PT 13 **Student-Faculty Ratio:** 9:1 **Exams:** SAT I or ACT. **% Residing in College-Owned, -Operated, or -Affiliated Housing:** 25 **Library Holdings:** 4,500 **Credit Hours For Degree:** 66 credit hours, Associates

ST. LAWRENCE UNIVERSITY
Canton, NY 13617-1455
Tel: (315)229-5011; Free: 800-285-1856
Admissions: (315)229-5261
Fax: (315)229-5502
E-mail: tcowdrey@stlawu.edu
Web Site: http://www.stlawu.edu/
President/CEO: William L. Fox
Admissions: Terry Cowdrey
Financial Aid: Patricia J. B. Farmer
Type: Comprehensive **Sex:** Coed **Scores:** 99.7% SAT V 400+; 99.4% SAT M 400+; 6.5% ACT 18-23; 70.9% ACT 24-29 **% Accepted:** 39 **Admission Plans:** Early Admission; Early Decision Plan; Deferred Admission **Application Deadline:** February 1 **Application Fee:** $60.00 **H.S. Requirements:** High school diploma required; GED accepted **Costs Per Year:** Application fee: $60. Comprehensive fee: $49,925 includes full-time tuition ($39,520), mandatory fees ($245), and college room and board ($10,160). College room only: $5460. Room and board charges vary according to board plan. **Scholarships:** Available **Calendar System:** Semester, Summer Session Available **Enrollment:** FT 2,274, PT 21, Grad FT 23, Grad PT 83 **Faculty:** FT 170, PT 29 **Student-Faculty Ratio:** 11:1 **Exams:** ACT essay used for admission. SAT essay used for admission. **% Receiving Financial Aid:** 62 **% Residing in College-Owned, -Operated, or -Affiliated Housing:** 98 **Final Year or Final Semester Residency Requirement:** No **Library Holdings:** 594,276 **Regional Accreditation:** Middle State Association of Colleges and Schools **Credit Hours For Degree:** 33.5 units, Bachelors **ROTC:** Army, Air Force **Professional Accreditation:** TEAC **Intercollegiate Athletics:** Baseball M; Basketball M & W; Crew M & W; Cross-Country Running M

& W; Equestrian Sports M & W; Field Hockey W; Football M; Golf M & W; Ice Hockey M & W; Lacrosse M & W; Skiing (Cross-Country) M & W; Skiing (Downhill) M & W; Soccer M & W; Softball W; Squash M & W; Swimming and Diving M & W; Tennis M & W; Track and Field M & W; Volleyball W

ST. PAUL'S SCHOOL OF NURSING
30-50 Whitestone Expressway
Ste. 400
Flushing, NY 11354
Tel: (718)357-0500
Fax: (718)357-4683
E-mail: nwolinski@svcmcny.org
Web Site: http://www.stpaulsschoolofnursing.com/
President/CEO: Genevieve M. Jensen
Admissions: Nancy Wolinski
Type: Two-Year College **Sex:** Coed **% Accepted:** 9 **Admission Plans:** Deferred Admission **Application Deadline:** April 1 **Application Fee:** $45.00 **H.S. Requirements:** High school diploma required; GED accepted **Scholarships:** Available **Calendar System:** Semester, Summer Session Not available **Enrollment:** FT 106 **Faculty:** FT 8, PT 2 **Student-Faculty Ratio:** 10:1 **Exams:** Other. **Credit Hours For Degree:** 64 credits, Associates

ST. THOMAS AQUINAS COLLEGE
125 Route 340
Sparkill, NY 10976
Tel: (845)398-4000; Free: 800-999-STAC
Admissions: (845)398-4100
E-mail: dmackay@stac.edu
Web Site: http://www.stac.edu/
President/CEO: Dr. Margaret M. Fitzpatrick, SC
Admissions: Danielle Mac Kay
Financial Aid: Margaret McGrail
Type: Comprehensive **Sex:** Coed **Scores:** 83% SAT V 400+; 87% SAT M 400+; 45% ACT 18-23; 28% ACT 24-29 **% Accepted:** 84 **Admission Plans:** Early Action; Early Decision Plan; Deferred Admission **Application Deadline:** Rolling **Application Fee:** $30.00 **H.S. Requirements:** High school diploma required; GED accepted **Costs Per Year:** Application fee: $30. Comprehensive fee: $32,710 includes full-time tuition ($21,910), mandatory fees ($500), and college room and board ($10,300). Room and board charges vary according to board plan and housing facility. Part-time tuition: $705 per credit hour. Part-time mandatory fees: $125 per term. **Scholarships:** Available **Calendar System:** Semester, Summer Session Available **Enrollment:** FT 1,338, PT 584, Grad FT 96, Grad PT 114 **Faculty:** FT 66, PT 74 **Student-Faculty Ratio:** 16:1 **Exams:** SAT I or ACT. ACT essay used for placement. SAT essay used for placement. **% Residing in College-Owned, -Operated, or -Affiliated Housing:** 42 **Library Holdings:** 93,478 **Regional Accreditation:** Middle State Association of Colleges and Schools **Credit Hours For Degree:** 120 credits, Bachelors **ROTC:** Air Force **Professional Accreditation:** NCATE **Intercollegiate Athletics:** Baseball M; Basketball M & W; Cross-Country Running M & W; Golf M & W; Lacrosse W; Soccer M & W; Softball W; Tennis M & W; Volleyball W

SAMARITAN HOSPITAL SCHOOL OF NURSING
2215 Burdett Ave.
Troy, NY 12180
Tel: (518)271-3285
Admissions: (518)271-3734
Fax: (518)271-3303
E-mail: marronej@nehealth.com
Web Site: http://www.nehealth.com/
President/CEO: Susan Birkhead, MPH,RN
Admissions: Jennifer Marrone
Type: Two-Year College **Sex:** Coed **Affiliation:** Samaritan Hospital (Troy, NY) **Application Deadline:** Rolling **H.S. Requirements:** High school diploma required; GED accepted **Scholarships:** Available **Enrollment:** FT 36, PT 83 **Faculty:** FT 5, PT 4 **Exams:** Other, SAT I or ACT.

SARAH LAWRENCE COLLEGE
1 Mead Way
Bronxville, NY 10708-5999
Tel: (914)337-0700; Free: 800-888-2858
Admissions: (914)395-2510
Fax: (914)395-2668
E-mail: slcadmit@sarahlawrence.edu
Web Site: http://www.sarahlawrence.edu/
President/CEO: Dr. Karen R. Lawrence
Admissions: Stephen M. Schierloh
Financial Aid: Heather McDonnell
Type: Comprehensive **Sex:** Coed **% Accepted:** 59 **Admission Plans:** Early Admission; Early Decision Plan; Deferred Admission **Application Deadline:** January 1 **Application Fee:** $60.00 **H.S. Requirements:** High school diploma required; GED accepted **Scholarships:** Available **Calendar System:** Semester, Summer Session Not available **Enrollment:** FT 1,318, PT 49, Grad FT 259, Grad PT 75 **Faculty:** FT 107, PT 203 **Student-Faculty Ratio:** 9:1 **% Receiving Financial Aid:** 60 **% Residing in College-Owned, -Operated, or -Affiliated Housing:** 83 **Final Year or Final Semester Residency Requirement:** No **Library Holdings:** 298,611 **Regional Accreditation:** Middle State Association of Colleges and Schools **Credit Hours For Degree:** 120 credits, Bachelors **Intercollegiate Athletics:** Basketball M; Crew M & W; Cross-Country Running M & W; Equestrian Sports M & W; Soccer M; Softball W; Swimming and Diving W; Tennis M & W; Volleyball W

SCHENECTADY COUNTY COMMUNITY COLLEGE
78 Washington Ave.
Schenectady, NY 12305-2294
Tel: (518)381-1200
E-mail: sampsodg@gw.sunysccc.edu
Web Site: http://www.sunysccc.edu/
President/CEO: Quintin Bullock
Admissions: David Sampson
Financial Aid: Brian McGarvey
Type: Two-Year College **Sex:** Coed **Affiliation:** State University of New York System **Admission Plans:** Open Admission; Preferred Admission; Early Admission; Deferred Admission **Application Deadline:** Rolling **Application Fee:** $0.00 **H.S. Requirements:** High school diploma required; GED accepted **Scholarships:** Available **Calendar System:** Semester, Summer Session Available **Library Holdings:** 85,000 **Regional Accreditation:** Middle State Association of Colleges and Schools **Credit Hours For Degree:** 60 credit hours, Associates **Professional Accreditation:** ACF, ACBSP, NASM **Intercollegiate Athletics:** Baseball M; Basketball M & W; Bowling M & W; Softball W

SCHOOL OF VISUAL ARTS
209 East 23rd St.
New York, NY 10010-3994
Tel: (212)592-2000; Free: 800-436-4204
Admissions: (212)592-2100
Fax: (212)592-2116
E-mail: admissions@sva.edu
Web Site: http://www.sva.edu/
President/CEO: David Rhodes
Type: Comprehensive **Sex:** Coed **Scores:** 92% SAT V 400+; 91% SAT M 400+; 51% ACT 18-23; 30% ACT 24-29 **% Accepted:** 69 **Admission Plans:** Early Action; Deferred Admission **Application Deadline:** Rolling **Application Fee:** $50.00 **H.S. Requirements:** High school diploma required; GED accepted **Scholarships:** Available **Calendar System:** Semester, Summer Session Available **Faculty:** FT 138, PT 811 **Student-Faculty Ratio:** 9:1 **Exams:** SAT I or ACT. **% Receiving Financial Aid:** 55 **% Residing in College-Owned, -Operated, or -Affiliated Housing:** 29 **Regional Accreditation:** Middle State Association of Colleges and Schools **Credit Hours For Degree:** 120 credits, Bachelors **Professional Accreditation:** FIDER, NASAD

SH'OR YOSHUV RABBINICAL COLLEGE
1 Cedarlawn Ave.
Lawrence, NY 11559-1714
Tel: (718)327-2048
Admissions: (516)239-9002
E-mail: mrubin@shoryoshuv.org
Web Site: http://www.shoryoshuv.org/
President/CEO: Rabbi Naftali Jaeger
Admissions: Rabbi Moshe Rubin
Type: Comprehensive **Sex:** Men **Affiliation:** Jewish **Application Deadline:** September 20 **H.S. Requirements:** High school diploma or equivalent not required **Calendar System:** Semester, Summer Session Available **Enroll-**

ment: FT 217 **Faculty:** FT 17 **Student-Faculty Ratio:** 15:1 **% Residing in College-Owned, -Operated, or -Affiliated Housing:** 84 **Professional Accreditation:** AARTS

SIENA COLLEGE
515 Loudon Rd.
Loudonville, NY 12211-1462
Tel: (518)783-2300; Free: 888-AT-SIENA
Admissions: (518)783-2426
Fax: (518)783-4293
E-mail: admit@siena.edu
Web Site: http://www.siena.edu/
President/CEO: Fr. Kevin J. Mullen, OFM
Admissions: Heather Renault
Financial Aid: Mary K. Lawyer
Type: Comprehensive **Sex:** Coed **Affiliation:** Roman Catholic **Scores:** 97.5% SAT V 400+; 98.6% SAT M 400+; 29.4% ACT 18-23; 59.3% ACT 24-29 **% Accepted:** 53 **Admission Plans:** Early Admission; Early Action; Early Decision Plan; Deferred Admission **Application Deadline:** March 1 **Application Fee:** $50.00 **H.S. Requirements:** High school diploma required; GED accepted **Costs Per Year:** Application fee: $50. One-time mandatory fee: $280. Comprehensive fee: $35,215 includes full-time tuition ($25,060), mandatory fees ($225), and college room and board ($9930). Full-time tuition and fees vary according to program. Room and board charges vary according to board plan and housing facility. Part-time tuition: $450 per credit hour. Part-time mandatory fees: $160 per term. Part-time tuition and fees vary according to program. **Scholarships:** Available **Calendar System:** Semester, Summer Session Available **Enrollment:** FT 3,101, PT 184, Grad FT 20 **Faculty:** FT 194, PT 136 **Student-Faculty Ratio:** 13:1 **Exams:** SAT I or ACT. ACT essay not being used. SAT essay not being used. **% Receiving Financial Aid:** 66 **% Residing in College-Owned, -Operated, or -Affiliated Housing:** 76 **Library Holdings:** 354,963 **Regional Accreditation:** Middle State Association of Colleges and Schools **Credit Hours For Degree:** 120 credit hours, Bachelors **ROTC:** Army, Navy, Air Force **Professional Accreditation:** CSWE **Intercollegiate Athletics:** Baseball M; Basketball M & W; Cheerleading W; Cross-Country Running M & W; Equestrian Sports M & W; Field Hockey W; Golf M & W; Ice Hockey M; Lacrosse M & W; Rugby M & W; Soccer M & W; Softball W; Swimming and Diving W; Tennis M & W; Track and Field M & W; Volleyball M & W; Water Polo W

SIMMONS INSTITUTE OF FUNERAL SERVICE
1828 South Ave.
Syracuse, NY 13207
Tel: (315)475-5142; Free: 800-727-3536
Fax: (315)477-3817
E-mail: admissions@simmonsinstitute.com
Web Site: http://www.simmonsinstitute.com/
President/CEO: Maurice C. Wightman
Admissions: Vera Wightman
Type: Two-Year College **Sex:** Coed **Admission Plans:** Open Admission **Application Deadline:** June 30 **Application Fee:** $50.00 **H.S. Requirements:** High school diploma required; GED accepted **Costs Per Year:** Application fee: $50. Tuition: $10,300 full-time, $430 per credit hour part-time. **Scholarships:** Available **Calendar System:** Semester **Student-Faculty Ratio:** 11:1 **Credit Hours For Degree:** 64 semester hours, Associates **Professional Accreditation:** ABFSE

SKIDMORE COLLEGE
815 North Broadway
Saratoga Springs, NY 12866
Tel: (518)580-5000; Free: 800-867-6007
Admissions: (518)580-5570
Fax: (518)581-7462
E-mail: admissions@skidmore.edu
Web Site: http://www.skidmore.edu/
President/CEO: Dr. Philip A. Glotzbach
Admissions: Mary Lou Bates
Financial Aid: Beth A. Post-Lundquist
Type: Comprehensive **Sex:** Coed **Scores:** 99.5% SAT V 400+; 99.8% SAT M 400+; 7.8% ACT 18-23; 60.7% ACT 24-29 **% Accepted:** 42 **Admission Plans:** Early Admission; Early Decision Plan; Deferred Admission **Application Deadline:** January 15 **Application Fee:** $60.00 **H.S. Requirements:** High school diploma required; GED accepted **Costs Per Year:** Application fee: $60. Comprehensive fee: $51,196 includes full-time tuition ($39,600), mandatory fees ($820), and college room and board ($10,776). College room only: $6376. Full-time tuition and fees vary according to course load. Room and board charges vary according to board plan and housing facility. Part-time tuition: $1320 per credit hour. Part-time mandatory fees: $25 per term. Part-time tuition and fees vary according to course load. **Scholarships:** Available **Calendar System:** Semester, Summer Session Available **Enrollment:** FT 2,591, PT 83, Grad PT 46 **Faculty:** FT 248, PT 89 **Student-Faculty Ratio:** 9:1 **Exams:** SAT I or ACT, SAT II. ACT essay not being used. SAT essay not being used. **% Receiving Financial Aid:** 44 **% Residing in College-Owned, -Operated, or -Affiliated Housing:** 85 **Regional Accreditation:** Middle State Association of Colleges and Schools **Credit Hours For Degree:** 120 semester hours, Bachelors **ROTC:** Army, Air Force **Professional Accreditation:** CSWE, NASAD **Intercollegiate Athletics:** Baseball M; Basketball M & W; Crew M & W; Equestrian Sports W; Field Hockey W; Golf M; Ice Hockey M; Lacrosse M & W; Soccer M & W; Softball W; Swimming and Diving M & W; Tennis M & W; Volleyball W

STATE UNIVERSITY OF NEW YORK AT BINGHAMTON
PO Box 6000
Binghamton, NY 13902-6000
Tel: (607)777-2000
Admissions: (607)777-2171
E-mail: admit@binghamton.edu
Web Site: http://www.binghamton.edu/
President/CEO: Lois B. DeFleur
Admissions: Cheryl S. Brown
Financial Aid: Dennis Chavez
Type: University **Sex:** Coed **Affiliation:** State University of New York System **Scores:** 99.7% SAT V 400+; 100% SAT M 400+; 6.1% ACT 18-23; 56.4% ACT 24-29 **% Accepted:** 33 **Admission Plans:** Early Admission; Early Action; Deferred Admission **Application Deadline:** January 15 **Application Fee:** $40.00 **H.S. Requirements:** High school diploma required; GED accepted **Costs Per Year:** Application fee: $40. State resident tuition: $4970 full-time, $207 per credit hour part-time. Nonresident tuition: $12,870 full-time, $536 per credit hour part-time. Mandatory fees: $1791 full-time, $65.75 per credit hour part-time, $105.50 per term part-time. Part-time tuition and fees vary according to course load. College room and board: $10,614. College room only: $6546. Room and board charges vary according to board plan and housing facility. **Scholarships:** Available **Calendar System:** Semester, Summer Session Available **Enrollment:** FT 11,279, PT 425, Grad FT 1,665, Grad PT 1,342 **Faculty:** FT 596, PT 275 **Student-Faculty Ratio:** 20:1 **Exams:** SAT I or ACT. ACT essay used for admission. SAT essay used for admission. **% Receiving Financial Aid:** 46 **% Residing in College-Owned, -Operated, or -Affiliated Housing:** 61 **Final Year or Final Semester Residency Requirement:** No **Library Holdings:** 2,380,358 **Regional Accreditation:** Middle State Association of Colleges and Schools **ROTC:** Army, Air Force **Professional Accreditation:** AACSB, ABET, AACN, APA, CSWE, NASM, NASPAA, TEAC **Intercollegiate Athletics:** Baseball M; Basketball M & W; Cheerleading M & W; Cross-Country Running M & W; Golf M; Lacrosse M & W; Soccer M & W; Softball W; Swimming and Diving M & W; Tennis M & W; Track and Field M & W; Volleyball W; Wrestling M

STATE UNIVERSITY OF NEW YORK COLLEGE OF AGRICULTURE AND TECHNOLOGY AT COBLESKILL
Cobleskill, NY 12043
Tel: (518)255-5011; Free: 800-295-8988
Admissions: (518)255-5525
Fax: (518)255-5333
E-mail: admissions@cobleskill.edu
Web Site: http://www.cobleskill.edu/
President/CEO: Dr. Donald Zingale
Admissions: Christopher Tacea
Financial Aid: Brian Smith
Type: Four-Year College **Sex:** Coed **Affiliation:** State University of New York System **Scores:** 55.6% ACT 18-23; 8% ACT 24-29 **% Accepted:** 79 **Admission Plans:** Early Admission; Deferred Admission **Application Deadline:** Rolling **Application Fee:** $40.00 **H.S. Requirements:** High school diploma required; GED accepted. For home schooled students: High school diploma or equivalent not required **Costs Per Year:** Application fee: $40. State resident tuition: $4970 full-time, $207 per credit hour part-time. Nonresident tuition: $12,870 full-time, $536 per credit hour part-time. Mandatory fees: $1341 full-time, $64.75 per credit hour part-time. Full-time tuition and fees vary according to degree level. Part-time tuition and fees vary ac-

cording to degree level. College room and board: $9460. College room only: $5690. Room and board charges vary according to board plan. **Scholarships:** Available **Calendar System:** Semester, Summer Session Available **Enrollment:** FT 2,498, PT 121 **Faculty:** FT 101, PT 74 **Student-Faculty Ratio:** 17:1 **Exams:** SAT I or ACT. **% Receiving Financial Aid:** 61 **% Residing in College-Owned, -Operated, or -Affiliated Housing:** 76 **Library Holdings:** 75,155 **Regional Accreditation:** Middle State Association of Colleges and Schools **Credit Hours For Degree:** 66 credit hours, Associates; 126 credit hours, Bachelors **Professional Accreditation:** ACF, NAACLS **Intercollegiate Athletics:** Baseball M; Basketball M & W; Cheerleading M & W; Cross-Country Running M & W; Golf M & W; Lacrosse M; Soccer M & W; Softball W; Swimming and Diving M & W; Tennis M & W; Track and Field M & W; Volleyball W

STATE UNIVERSITY OF NEW YORK COLLEGE OF AGRICULTURE AND TECHNOLOGY AT MORRISVILLE
PO Box 901
Morrisville, NY 13408-0901
Tel: (315)684-6000
Admissions: 800-258-0111
Fax: (315)684-6116
E-mail: admissions@morrisville.edu
Web Site: http://www.morrisville.edu/
President/CEO: Dr. Raymond W. Cross
Admissions: Thomas VerDow
Type: Four-Year College **Sex:** Coed **Affiliation:** State University of New York System **Scores:** 92% SAT V 400+; 95% SAT M 400+ **% Accepted:** 75 **Admission Plans:** Early Admission; Deferred Admission **Application Deadline:** Rolling **Application Fee:** $40.00 **H.S. Requirements:** High school diploma required; GED accepted **Scholarships:** Available **Calendar System:** Semester, Summer Session Available **Enrollment:** FT 2,802, PT 630 **Faculty:** FT 132, PT 129 **Student-Faculty Ratio:** 13:1 **Exams:** Other, SAT I or ACT, SAT I. **% Receiving Financial Aid:** 84 **% Residing in College-Owned, -Operated, or -Affiliated Housing:** 73 **Library Holdings:** 100,000 **Regional Accreditation:** Middle State Association of Colleges and Schools **Credit Hours For Degree:** 64 credits, Associates; 128 credits, Bachelors **ROTC:** Army **Professional Accreditation:** ABET, ACBSP, NLN **Intercollegiate Athletics:** Basketball M & W; Equestrian Sports M & W; Field Hockey W; Football M; Ice Hockey M; Lacrosse M & W; Soccer M & W; Softball W; Swimming and Diving M & W; Tennis W; Track and Field M & W; Volleyball W; Wrestling M

STATE UNIVERSITY OF NEW YORK COLLEGE AT CORTLAND
PO Box 2000
Cortland, NY 13045
Tel: (607)753-2011
Admissions: (607)753-4711
Fax: (607)753-5999
E-mail: admissions@cortland.edu
Web Site: http://www.cortland.edu/
President/CEO: Dr. Erik J. Bitterbaum
Admissions: Mark Yacavone
Financial Aid: Karen Gallagher
Type: Comprehensive **Sex:** Coed **Affiliation:** State University of New York System **Scores:** 99% SAT V 400+; 99% SAT M 400+ **% Accepted:** 39 **Admission Plans:** Early Admission; Early Decision Plan; Deferred Admission **Application Deadline:** Rolling **Application Fee:** $40.00 **H.S. Requirements:** High school diploma required; GED accepted **Scholarships:** Available **Calendar System:** Semester, Summer Session Available **Enrollment:** FT 6,053, PT 205, Grad FT 384, Grad PT 680 **Faculty:** FT 336, PT 261 **Student-Faculty Ratio:** 16:1 **Exams:** SAT I or ACT. **% Receiving Financial Aid:** 59 **% Residing in College-Owned, -Operated, or -Affiliated Housing:** 50 **Regional Accreditation:** Middle State Association of Colleges and Schools **Credit Hours For Degree:** 124 credits, Bachelors **ROTC:** Army, Air Force **Professional Accreditation:** JRCEPAT, NCATE, NRPA **Intercollegiate Athletics:** Baseball M; Basketball M & W; Cross-Country Running M & W; Field Hockey W; Football M & W; Golf W; Gymnastics W; Ice Hockey M & W; Lacrosse M & W; Racquetball M & W; Rugby M & W; Soccer M & W; Softball W; Swimming and Diving M & W; Tennis W; Track and Field M & W; Volleyball M & W; Wrestling M

STATE UNIVERSITY OF NEW YORK COLLEGE OF ENVIRONMENTAL SCIENCE AND FORESTRY
1 Forestry Dr.
Syracuse, NY 13210-2779
Tel: (315)470-6500; Free: 800-777-7373
Admissions: (315)470-6600
Fax: (315)470-6933
E-mail: esfinfo@esf.edu
Web Site: http://www.esf.edu/
President/CEO: Dr. Cornelius B. Murphy, Jr.
Admissions: Susan Sanford
Financial Aid: John E. View
Type: University **Sex:** Coed **Affiliation:** State University of New York System **Scores:** 100% SAT M 400+; 20% ACT 18-23; 67% ACT 24-29 **% Accepted:** 43 **Admission Plans:** Early Admission; Early Action; Deferred Admission **Application Deadline:** Rolling **Application Fee:** $40.00 **H.S. Requirements:** High school diploma required; GED accepted **Costs Per Year:** Application fee: $40. State resident tuition: $4970 full-time, $207 per credit hour part-time. Nonresident tuition: $12,870 full-time, $536 per credit hour part-time. Mandatory fees: $921 full-time. Full-time tuition and fees vary according to location. Part-time tuition varies according to course load and location. College room and board: $12,460. College room only: $6250. Room and board charges vary according to board plan, housing facility, and location. **Scholarships:** Available **Calendar System:** Semester, Summer Session Not available **Enrollment:** FT 1,525, PT 45, Grad FT 333, Grad PT 296 **Faculty:** FT 146, PT 27 **Student-Faculty Ratio:** 12:1 **Exams:** SAT I or ACT. **% Receiving Financial Aid:** 60 **% Residing in College-Owned, -Operated, or -Affiliated Housing:** 40 **Final Year or Final Semester Residency Requirement:** No **Library Holdings:** 135,258 **Regional Accreditation:** Middle State Association of Colleges and Schools **Credit Hours For Degree:** 78 credit hours, Associates; 121 credit hours, Bachelors **ROTC:** Army, Air Force **Professional Accreditation:** ABET, ASLA, SAF **Intercollegiate Athletics:** Cross-Country Running M & W; Golf M & W; Soccer M & W

STATE UNIVERSITY OF NEW YORK COLLEGE OF ENVIRONMENTAL SCIENCE & FORESTRY, RANGER SCHOOL
PO Box 48, 257 Ranger School Rd.
Wanakena, NY 13695
Tel: (315)848-2566; Free: 800-777-7373
Admissions: (315)470-6600
Fax: (315)470-6933
E-mail: esfinfo@esf.edu
Web Site: http://www.esf.edu/
Admissions: Susan Sanford
Financial Aid: John View
Type: Two-Year College **Sex:** Coed **Affiliation:** State University of New York System **% Accepted:** 76 **Admission Plans:** Deferred Admission **Application Deadline:** Rolling **Application Fee:** $40.00 **H.S. Requirements:** High school diploma required; GED not accepted **Costs Per Year:** Application fee: $40. State resident tuition: $4970 full-time, $207 per credit hour part-time. Nonresident tuition: $12,870 full-time, $536 per credit hour part-time. Mandatory fees: $1388 full-time. Full-time tuition and fees vary according to location. Part-time tuition varies according to location. College room and board: $9640. College room only: $2620. Room and board charges vary according to housing facility. **Scholarships:** Available **Calendar System:** Semester, Summer Session Not available **Enrollment:** FT 43 **Faculty:** FT 6, PT 0 **Student-Faculty Ratio:** 7:1 **Exams:** SAT I or ACT. **% Residing in College-Owned, -Operated, or -Affiliated Housing:** 100 **Library Holdings:** 5,000 **Regional Accreditation:** Middle State Association of Colleges and Schools **Credit Hours For Degree:** 75 credit hours, Associates **Professional Accreditation:** ABET, SAF

STATE UNIVERSITY OF NEW YORK COLLEGE AT GENESEO
1 College Circle
Geneseo, NY 14454-1401
Tel: (585)245-5211; Free: (866)245-5211
Admissions: (585)245-5571
Fax: (585)245-5005
E-mail: admissions@geneseo.edu
Web Site: http://www.geneseo.edu/
President/CEO: Dr. Christopher C. Dahl
Admissions: Kris Shay
Financial Aid: Archie Cureton
Type: Comprehensive **Sex:** Coed **Affiliation:** State University of New York System **Scores:** 99.2% SAT V 400+; 100% SAT M 400+; 2.9% ACT 18-23; 58.4% ACT 24-29 **% Accepted:** 35 **Admission Plans:** Early Admission; Early Decision Plan; Deferred Admission **Application Deadline:** January 1

Application Fee: $40.00 **H.S. Requirements:** High school diploma required; GED accepted **Costs Per Year:** Application fee: $40. State resident tuition: $4970 full-time, $207 per credit hour part-time. Nonresident tuition: $12,870 full-time, $536 per credit hour part-time. Mandatory fees: $1356 full-time, $56.32 per credit hour part-time. Part-time tuition and fees vary according to course load. College room and board: $9550. Room and board charges vary according to board plan and housing facility. **Scholarships:** Available **Calendar System:** Semester, Summer Session Available **Enrollment:** FT 5,395, PT 100, Grad FT 59, Grad PT 106 **Faculty:** FT 251, PT 102 **Student-Faculty Ratio:** 19:1 **Exams:** SAT I or ACT. **% Receiving Financial Aid:** 44 **% Residing in College-Owned, -Operated, or -Affiliated Housing:** 55 **Final Year or Final Semester Residency Requirement:** Yes **Library Holdings:** 677,184 **Regional Accreditation:** Middle State Association of Colleges and Schools **Credit Hours For Degree:** 120 semester hours, Bachelors **ROTC:** Army, Air Force **Professional Accreditation:** AACSB, ASLHA, NCATE **Intercollegiate Athletics:** Baseball M & W; Basketball M & W; Cheerleading M & W; Crew M & W; Cross-Country Running M & W; Equestrian Sports W; Fencing M & W; Field Hockey W; Ice Hockey M & W; Lacrosse M & W; Rugby M & W; Skiing (Downhill) M & W; Soccer M & W; Softball W; Swimming and Diving M & W; Tennis M & W; Track and Field M & W; Ultimate Frisbee M & W; Volleyball M & W; Water Polo M & W

STATE UNIVERSITY OF NEW YORK COLLEGE AT OLD WESTBURY
PO Box 210
Old Westbury, NY 11568-0210
Tel: (516)876-3000
Admissions: (516)876-3073
Fax: (516)876-3307
E-mail: enroll@oldwestbury.edu
Web Site: http://www.oldwestbury.edu/
President/CEO: Dr. Calvin O. Butts, III
Financial Aid: Dee Darrell
Type: Comprehensive **Sex:** Coed **Affiliation:** State University of New York System **Scores:** 95% SAT V 400+; 98% SAT M 400+; 82% ACT 18-23; 12% ACT 24-29 **% Accepted:** 51 **Admission Plans:** Early Admission; Early Decision Plan; Deferred Admission **Application Deadline:** Rolling **Application Fee:** $40.00 **H.S. Requirements:** High school diploma required; GED accepted **Costs Per Year:** Application fee: $40. State resident tuition: $4970 full-time, $207 per credit hour part-time. Nonresident tuition: $12,870 full-time, $536 per credit hour part-time. Mandatory fees: $827 full-time, $18.35 per credit hour part-time, $105.50 per term part-time. Part-time tuition and fees vary according to course load. College room and board: $9390. College room only: $6440. Room and board charges vary according to board plan and housing facility. **Scholarships:** Available **Calendar System:** Semester, Summer Session Available **Enrollment:** FT 3,205, PT 608, Grad FT 40, Grad PT 44 **Faculty:** FT 131, PT 120 **Student-Faculty Ratio:** 20:1 **Exams:** SAT I or ACT. **% Receiving Financial Aid:** 61 **% Residing in College-Owned, -Operated, or -Affiliated Housing:** 26 **Library Holdings:** 195,254 **Regional Accreditation:** Middle State Association of Colleges and Schools **Credit Hours For Degree:** 120 credits, Bachelors **ROTC:** Army, Air Force **Intercollegiate Athletics:** Baseball M; Basketball M & W; Cross-Country Running M & W; Golf M; Soccer M; Softball W; Swimming and Diving M & W; Volleyball M & W

STATE UNIVERSITY OF NEW YORK COLLEGE AT ONEONTA
Ravine Parkway
Oneonta, NY 13820-4015
Tel: (607)436-3500; Free: 800-SUNY-123
Admissions: (607)436-2524
Fax: (607)436-3074
E-mail: admissions@oneonta.edu
Web Site: http://www.oneonta.edu/
President/CEO: Dr. Nancy Kleniewski
Admissions: Karen Brown
Financial Aid: Bill Goodhue
Type: Comprehensive **Sex:** Coed **Affiliation:** State University of New York System **Scores:** 100% SAT V 400+; 100% SAT M 400+; 29% ACT 18-23; 66% ACT 24-29 **% Accepted:** 39 **Admission Plans:** Early Admission; Early Action; Deferred Admission **Application Deadline:** Rolling **Application Fee:** $40.00 **H.S. Requirements:** High school diploma required; GED accepted **Costs Per Year:** Application fee: $40. State resident tuition: $4970 full-time, $207 per semester hour part-time. Nonresident tuition: $12,870 full-time, $536 per semester hour part-time. Mandatory fees: $1215 full-time, $40.53 per semester hour part-time. Part-time tuition and fees vary according to course load. College room and board: $8900. College room only: $5200. Room and board charges vary according to board plan and housing facility. **Scholarships:** Available **Calendar System:** Semester, Summer Session Available **Enrollment:** FT 5,580, PT 131, Grad FT 80, Grad PT 102 **Faculty:** FT 261, PT 238 **Student-Faculty Ratio:** 17:1 **Exams:** SAT I or ACT. ACT essay not being used. SAT essay not being used. **% Receiving Financial Aid:** 56 **% Residing in College-Owned, -Operated, or -Affiliated Housing:** 58 **Library Holdings:** 525,850 **Regional Accreditation:** Middle State Association of Colleges and Schools **Credit Hours For Degree:** 122 semester hours, Bachelors **Professional Accreditation:** AAFCS, ADtA, NCATE **Intercollegiate Athletics:** Baseball M; Basketball M & W; Cheerleading W; Cross-Country Running M & W; Fencing M & W; Field Hockey W; Ice Hockey M; Lacrosse M & W; Rugby M & W; Soccer M & W; Softball W; Swimming and Diving M & W; Tennis M & W; Track and Field M & W; Volleyball W; Wrestling M

STATE UNIVERSITY OF NEW YORK COLLEGE AT POTSDAM
44 Pierrepont Ave.
Potsdam, NY 13676
Tel: (315)267-2000; Free: 877-POTSDAM
Admissions: (315)267-2180
Fax: (315)267-2163
E-mail: admissions@potsdam.edu
Web Site: http://www.potsdam.edu/
President/CEO: Dr. John F. Schwaller
Admissions: Thomas Nesbitt
Financial Aid: Susan C. Aldrich
Type: Comprehensive **Sex:** Coed **Affiliation:** State University of New York System **Scores:** 97% SAT V 400+; 96% SAT M 400+; 58% ACT 18-23; 31% ACT 24-29 **% Accepted:** 66 **Admission Plans:** Early Admission; Deferred Admission **Application Deadline:** Rolling **Application Fee:** $40.00 **H.S. Requirements:** High school diploma required; GED accepted **Costs Per Year:** Application fee: $40. State resident tuition: $4970 full-time, $207 per credit hour part-time. Nonresident tuition: $12,870 full-time, $536 per credit hour part-time. Mandatory fees: $1154 full-time, $52.20 per credit hour part-time. College room and board: $9270. College room only: $5370. Room and board charges vary according to board plan and housing facility. **Scholarships:** Available **Calendar System:** Semester, Summer Session Available **Enrollment:** FT 3,631, PT 103, Grad FT 381, Grad PT 183 **Faculty:** FT 262, PT 100 **Student-Faculty Ratio:** 13:1 **Exams:** SAT I or ACT. ACT essay not being used. SAT essay not being used. **% Receiving Financial Aid:** 65 **% Residing in College-Owned, -Operated, or -Affiliated Housing:** 40 **Library Holdings:** 467,382 **Regional Accreditation:** Middle State Association of Colleges and Schools **Credit Hours For Degree:** 120 credit hours, Bachelors **ROTC:** Army, Air Force **Professional Accreditation:** NASM, NCATE **Intercollegiate Athletics:** Basketball M & W; Cross-Country Running M & W; Equestrian Sports M & W; Golf M; Ice Hockey M & W; Lacrosse M & W; Rugby W; Soccer M & W; Softball W; Swimming and Diving M & W; Tennis W; Track and Field M & W; Volleyball W

STATE UNIVERSITY OF NEW YORK COLLEGE OF TECHNOLOGY AT ALFRED
10 Upper College Dr.
Alfred, NY 14802
Tel: (607)587-4111; Free: 800-4-ALFRED
Admissions: (607)587-4215
Fax: (607)587-4299
E-mail: admissions@alfredstate.edu
Web Site: http://www.alfredstate.edu/
President/CEO: Dr. John Anderson
Admissions: Deborah Goodrich
Financial Aid: Christian Vernam
Type: Two-Year College **Sex:** Coed **Affiliation:** The State University of New York System **% Accepted:** 61 **Application Deadline:** Rolling **Application Fee:** $40.00 **H.S. Requirements:** High school diploma required; GED accepted **Costs Per Year:** Application fee: $40. Area resident tuition: $207 per credit hour part-time. State resident tuition: $4970 full-time. Nonresident tuition: $8750 full-time, $365 per credit hour part-time. Mandatory fees: $1192 full-time. Full-time tuition and fees vary according to degree level. Part-time tuition varies according to degree level. College room and board: $9190. Room and board charges vary according to board plan and housing facility. **Scholarships:** Available **Calendar System:** Semester, Summer

Session Available **Enrollment:** FT 3,184, PT 355 **Faculty:** FT 158, PT 43 **Student-Faculty Ratio:** 18:1 **Exams:** SAT I or ACT. **% Residing in College-Owned, -Operated, or -Affiliated Housing:** 67 **Library Holdings:** 64,151 **Regional Accreditation:** Middle State Association of Colleges and Schools **Credit Hours For Degree:** 60 credit hours, Associates; 120 credit hours, Bachelors **ROTC:** Army **Professional Accreditation:** ABET, ACCE, AHIMA, NLN **Intercollegiate Athletics:** Baseball M; Basketball M & W; Cross-Country Running M & W; Football M; Lacrosse M; Soccer M & W; Softball W; Swimming and Diving M & W; Track and Field M & W; Volleyball W; Wrestling M

STATE UNIVERSITY OF NEW YORK COLLEGE OF TECHNOLOGY AT CANTON

Cornell Dr.
Canton, NY 13617
Tel: (315)386-7011; Free: 800-388-7123
Admissions: (315)386-7123
Fax: (315)386-7930
E-mail: admissions@canton.edu
Web Site: http://www.canton.edu/
President/CEO: Dr. Joseph L. Kennedy
Admissions: Randy B. Sieminski
Financial Aid: Kerrie Cooper

Type: Four-Year College **Sex:** Coed **Affiliation:** State University of New York System **Scores:** 75% SAT V 400+; 72% SAT M 400+; 53% ACT 18-23; 11% ACT 24-29 **% Accepted:** 87 **Admission Plans:** Early Admission; Deferred Admission **Application Deadline:** Rolling **Application Fee:** $40.00 **H.S. Requirements:** High school diploma required; GED accepted **Costs Per Year:** Application fee: $40. One-time mandatory fee: $90. State resident tuition: $4970 full-time, $207 per credit hour part-time. Nonresident tuition: $8750 full-time, $536 per credit hour part-time. Mandatory fees: $1309 full-time, $49 per credit hour part-time, $5 per term part-time. Full-time tuition and fees vary according to degree level, location, and program. Part-time tuition and fees vary according to degree level, location, and program. College room and board: $9320. College room only: $5400. Room and board charges vary according to housing facility. **Scholarships:** Available **Calendar System:** Semester, Summer Session Available **Enrollment:** FT 2,572, PT 748 **Faculty:** FT 117, PT 83 **Student-Faculty Ratio:** 19:1 **Exams:** SAT I or ACT. ACT essay not being used. SAT essay not being used. **% Residing in College-Owned, -Operated, or -Affiliated Housing:** 32 **Final Year or Final Semester Residency Requirement:** No **Library Holdings:** 55,000 **Regional Accreditation:** Middle State Association of Colleges and Schools **Credit Hours For Degree:** 60 credit hours, Associates; 120 credit hours, Bachelors **ROTC:** Army, Air Force **Professional Accreditation:** ABET, ABFSE, AOTA, APTA, NLN **Intercollegiate Athletics:** Baseball M; Basketball M & W; Cross-Country Running M & W; Ice Hockey M; Soccer M & W; Softball W

STATE UNIVERSITY OF NEW YORK COLLEGE OF TECHNOLOGY AT DELHI

Main St.
Delhi, NY 13753
Tel: (607)746-4000; Free: 800-96-DELHI
Admissions: (607)746-4550
Fax: (607)746-4104
E-mail: wesleycs@delhi.edu
Web Site: http://www.delhi.edu/
President/CEO: Dr. Candace Vancko
Admissions: Craig Wesley

Type: Four-Year College **Sex:** Coed **Affiliation:** State University of New York System **% Accepted:** 52 **Admission Plans:** Early Admission; Deferred Admission **Application Deadline:** Rolling **Application Fee:** $40.00 **H.S. Requirements:** High school diploma required; GED accepted **Costs Per Year:** Application fee: $40. State resident tuition: $4970 full-time, $207 per credit hour part-time. Nonresident tuition: $12,870 full-time, $536 per credit hour part-time. Mandatory fees: $1390 full-time, $57.10 per credit hour part-time, $695 per term part-time. Full-time tuition and fees vary according to degree level. Part-time tuition and fees vary according to degree level. College room and board: $9300. College room only: $5400. Room and board charges vary according to board plan and location. **Scholarships:** Available **Calendar System:** Semester, Summer Session Available **Enrollment:** FT 2,494, PT 477 **Faculty:** FT 116, PT 71 **Student-Faculty Ratio:** 16:1 **Exams:** SAT I or ACT. **% Receiving Financial Aid:** 90 **Regional Accreditation:** Middle State Association of Colleges and Schools **Credit Hours For Degree:** 60 credit hours, Associates; 126 credit hours, Bachelors **Professional Accreditation:** ACCE, NLN **Intercollegiate Athletics:** Basketball M & W; Cross-Country Running M & W; Golf M & W; Lacrosse M; Soccer M & W; Softball W; Swimming and Diving M & W; Tennis M & W; Track and Field M & W; Volleyball W; Wrestling M

STATE UNIVERSITY OF NEW YORK DOWNSTATE MEDICAL CENTER

450 Clarkson Ave.
Brooklyn, NY 11203-2098
Tel: (718)270-1000
Admissions: (718)270-2446
Fax: (718)270-7592
E-mail: admissions@downstate.edu
Web Site: http://www.downstate.edu/
President/CEO: Dr. John C. La Rosa

Type: Two-Year Upper Division **Sex:** Coed **Affiliation:** State University of New York System **% Accepted:** 14 **Admission Plans:** Preferred Admission **Application Fee:** $30.00 **H.S. Requirements:** High school diploma required; GED accepted **Scholarships:** Available **Calendar System:** Semester, Summer Session Available **Enrollment:** FT 187, PT 142, Grad FT 974, Grad PT 357 **Faculty:** FT 838, PT 143 **Regional Accreditation:** Middle State Association of Colleges and Schools **Credit Hours For Degree:** 125 credits, Bachelors **Professional Accreditation:** AACN, AANA, ACNM, AOTA, APTA, JRCEDMS, LCMEAMA, NLN

STATE UNIVERSITY OF NEW YORK EMPIRE STATE COLLEGE

1 Union Ave.
Saratoga Springs, NY 12866-4391
Tel: (518)587-2100; Free: 800-847-3000
Fax: (518)587-2100
E-mail: admissions@esc.edu
Web Site: http://www.esc.edu/
President/CEO: Dr. Alan Davis
Admissions: Jennifer D'Agostino

Type: Comprehensive **Sex:** Coed **Affiliation:** State University of New York System **% Accepted:** 78 **Admission Plans:** Early Admission **Application Deadline:** Rolling **Application Fee:** $0.00 **H.S. Requirements:** High school diploma required; GED accepted **Costs Per Year:** Application fee: $0. One-time mandatory fee: $350. State resident tuition: $4970 full-time, $207 per credit hour part-time. Nonresident tuition: $12,870 full-time, $536 per credit hour part-time. Mandatory fees: $225 full-time, $7.10 per credit hour part-time, $75 per term part-time. Full-time tuition and fees vary according to course level, location, and program. Part-time tuition and fees vary according to course level, location, and program. **Calendar System:** Continuous **Enrollment:** FT 4,876, PT 8,523, Grad FT 57, Grad PT 869 **Faculty:** FT 181, PT 1,266 **Student-Faculty Ratio:** 10:1 **Final Year or Final Semester Residency Requirement:** No **Library Holdings:** 70,000 **Regional Accreditation:** Middle State Association of Colleges and Schools **Credit Hours For Degree:** 64 credits, Associates; 128 credits, Bachelors **Professional Accreditation:** TEAC

STATE UNIVERSITY OF NEW YORK AT FREDONIA

Fredonia, NY 14063-1136
Tel: (716)673-3111; Free: 800-252-1212
Admissions: (716)673-3251
Fax: (716)673-3249
E-mail: admissions@fredonia.edu
Web Site: http://www.fredonia.edu/
President/CEO: Dr. Dennis Hefner
Financial Aid: Jeremy Corrente

Type: Comprehensive **Sex:** Coed **Affiliation:** State University of New York System **Scores:** 99% SAT V 400+; 100% SAT M 400+; 46% ACT 18-23; 40% ACT 24-29 **% Accepted:** 49 **Admission Plans:** Early Admission; Early Decision Plan; Deferred Admission **Application Deadline:** Rolling **Application Fee:** $40.00 **H.S. Requirements:** High school diploma required; GED accepted **Costs Per Year:** Application fee: $40. State resident tuition: $5020 full-time, $207 per credit hour part-time. Nonresident tuition: $12,920 full-time, $536 per credit hour part-time. Mandatory fees: $1288 full-time, $51.40 per credit hour part-time. Full-time tuition and fees vary according to program. Part-time tuition and fees vary according to program. College room and board: $9330. College room only: $5650. Room and board charges vary according to board plan and housing facility. **Scholarships:** Available **Calendar System:** Semester, Summer Session Available **Enrollment:** FT

5,209, PT 166, Grad FT 207, Grad PT 194 **Faculty:** FT 258, PT 186 **Student-Faculty Ratio:** 16:1 **Exams:** SAT I or ACT. **% Receiving Financial Aid:** 66 **% Residing in College-Owned, -Operated, or -Affiliated Housing:** 53 **Regional Accreditation:** Middle State Association of Colleges and Schools **Credit Hours For Degree:** 120 credit hours, Bachelors **ROTC:** Army **Professional Accreditation:** ASLHA, CSWE, NASM, NAST, NCATE **Intercollegiate Athletics:** Baseball M; Basketball M & W; Cheerleading M & W; Cross-Country Running M & W; Field Hockey M & W; Ice Hockey M; Lacrosse W; Soccer M & W; Softball W; Swimming and Diving M & W; Tennis M & W; Track and Field M & W; Volleyball M & W

STATE UNIVERSITY OF NEW YORK INSTITUTE OF TECHNOLOGY

PO Box 3050
Utica, NY 13504-3050
Tel: (315)792-7100; Free: 800-SUN-YTEC
Admissions: (315)792-7500
Fax: (315)792-7837
E-mail: admissions@sunyit.edu
Web Site: http://www.sunyit.edu/
President/CEO: Dr. Peter A. Spina
Admissions: Amy Stokes
Type: Comprehensive **Sex:** Coed **Affiliation:** State University of New York System **Scores:** 99% SAT V 400+; 100% SAT M 400+; 56% ACT 18-23; 44% ACT 24-29 **% Accepted:** 39 **Admission Plans:** Early Admission; Early Decision Plan; Deferred Admission **Application Deadline:** Rolling **Application Fee:** $40.00 **H.S. Requirements:** High school diploma required; GED not accepted **Scholarships:** Available **Calendar System:** Semester, Summer Session Available **Enrollment:** FT 1,412, PT 798 **Faculty:** FT 88, PT 95 **Student-Faculty Ratio:** 19:1 **Exams:** SAT I or ACT. **% Receiving Financial Aid:** 69 **% Residing in College-Owned, -Operated, or -Affiliated Housing:** 21 **Library Holdings:** 200,730 **Regional Accreditation:** Middle State Association of Colleges and Schools **Credit Hours For Degree:** 124 semester hours, Bachelors **ROTC:** Army, Air Force **Professional Accreditation:** AACSB, ABET, AACN, AHIMA, NLN **Intercollegiate Athletics:** Baseball M; Basketball M & W; Bowling M & W; Cross-Country Running W; Golf M & W; Lacrosse M; Soccer M & W; Softball W; Volleyball W

STATE UNIVERSITY OF NEW YORK MARITIME COLLEGE

6 Pennyfield Ave.
Throggs Neck, NY 10465-4198
Tel: (718)409-7200; Free: 800-642-1874
Admissions: (718)409-7222
Fax: (718)409-7392
E-mail: jwhite@sunymaritime.edu
Web Site: http://www.sunymaritime.edu/
President/CEO: Vice Adm. John W. Craine
Admissions: Jonathan White
Financial Aid: Madeline Aponte
Type: Comprehensive **Sex:** Coed **Affiliation:** State University of New York System **Scores:** 97% SAT V 400+; 99% SAT M 400+; 71% ACT 18-23; 21% ACT 24-29 **% Accepted:** 63 **Admission Plans:** Deferred Admission **Application Deadline:** Rolling **Application Fee:** $40.00 **H.S. Requirements:** High school diploma required; GED accepted **Costs Per Year:** Application fee: $40. State resident tuition: $4970 full-time, $207 per credit part-time. Nonresident tuition: $12,870 full-time, $536 per credit part-time. Mandatory fees: $1120 full-time, $46.65 per credit part-time. Full-time tuition and fees vary according to degree level and program. Part-time tuition and fees vary according to course load, degree level, and program. College room and board: $9930. College room only: $6180. Room and board charges vary according to board plan and housing facility. **Scholarships:** Available **Calendar System:** Semester, Summer Session Available **Enrollment:** FT 1,463, PT 112, Grad FT 114, Grad PT 68 **Faculty:** FT 70, PT 59 **Student-Faculty Ratio:** 17:1 **Exams:** SAT I or ACT. ACT essay not being used. SAT essay not being used. **% Residing in College-Owned, -Operated, or -Affiliated Housing:** 80 **Library Holdings:** 66,316 **Regional Accreditation:** Middle State Association of Colleges and Schools **Credit Hours For Degree:** 80 credits, Associates; 156 credits, Bachelors **ROTC:** Army, Navy **Professional Accreditation:** ABET **Intercollegiate Athletics:** Baseball M; Basketball M & W; Crew W; Cross-Country Running M & W; Football M; Ice Hockey M; Lacrosse M & W; Riflery M & W; Soccer M & W; Softball W; Swimming and Diving M & W; Volleyball W

STATE UNIVERSITY OF NEW YORK AT NEW PALTZ

1 Hawk Dr.
New Paltz, NY 12561
Tel: (845)257-2121
Admissions: (845)257-3200
Fax: (845)257-3209
E-mail: admissions@newpaltz.edu
Web Site: http://www.newpaltz.edu/
President/CEO: Steven Poskanzer
Admissions: Kimberly A. Strano
Financial Aid: Daniel Sistarenik
Type: Comprehensive **Sex:** Coed **Affiliation:** State University of New York System **Scores:** 97% SAT V 400+; 98% SAT M 400+; 31% ACT 18-23; 64% ACT 24-29 **% Accepted:** 34 **Admission Plans:** Early Admission; Early Action **Application Deadline:** April 1 **Application Fee:** $40.00 **H.S. Requirements:** High school diploma required; GED accepted **Costs Per Year:** Application fee: $40. State resident tuition: $4970 full-time, $207 per credit part-time. Nonresident tuition: $12,870 full-time, $536 per credit part-time. Mandatory fees: $1111 full-time, $32.45 per credit part-time, $165 per term part-time. College room and board: $9202. College room only: $6020. Room and board charges vary according to board plan. **Scholarships:** Available **Calendar System:** Semester, Summer Session Available **Enrollment:** FT 5,935, PT 619, Grad FT 519, Grad PT 884 **Faculty:** FT 325, PT 343 **Student-Faculty Ratio:** 16:1 **Exams:** SAT I or ACT. ACT essay used for advising. SAT essay used for advising. ACT essay used for placement. SAT essay used for placement. **% Receiving Financial Aid:** 51 **Library Holdings:** 527,000 **Regional Accreditation:** Middle State Association of Colleges and Schools **Credit Hours For Degree:** 120 credits, Bachelors **Professional Accreditation:** ABET, AACN, ASLHA, NASAD, NASM, NAST, NCATE **Intercollegiate Athletics:** Baseball M; Basketball M & W; Cross-Country Running M & W; Equestrian Sports W; Fencing M & W; Field Hockey W; Ice Hockey M; Lacrosse M & W; Racquetball M & W; Rugby M & W; Skiing (Cross-Country) M & W; Soccer M & W; Softball W; Squash W; Swimming and Diving M & W; Tennis M & W; Track and Field M & W; Ultimate Frisbee M & W; Volleyball M & W

STATE UNIVERSITY OF NEW YORK AT OSWEGO

7060 Route 104
Oswego, NY 13126
Tel: (315)312-2500
Admissions: (315)312-2250
Fax: (315)312-5799
E-mail: admiss@oswego.edu
Web Site: http://www.oswego.edu/
President/CEO: Dr. Deborah Stanley
Admissions: Dr. Joseph Grant
Financial Aid: Mark C. Humbert
Type: Comprehensive **Sex:** Coed **Affiliation:** State University of New York System **Scores:** 100% SAT V 400+; 100% SAT M 400+; 58% ACT 18-23; 38% ACT 24-29 **% Accepted:** 47 **Admission Plans:** Early Admission; Early Decision Plan; Deferred Admission **Application Deadline:** Rolling **Application Fee:** $40.00 **H.S. Requirements:** High school diploma required; GED accepted **Costs Per Year:** Application fee: $40. State resident tuition: $4970 full-time, $207 per credit hour part-time. Nonresident tuition: $12,870 full-time, $536 per credit hour part-time. Mandatory fees: $1286 full-time, $49.21 per credit hour part-time. Full-time tuition and fees vary according to degree level. Part-time tuition and fees vary according to course load and degree level. College room and board: $10,870. College room only: $6890. Room and board charges vary according to board plan and housing facility. **Scholarships:** Available **Calendar System:** Semester, Summer Session Available **Enrollment:** FT 6,766, PT 434, Grad FT 399, Grad PT 520 **Faculty:** FT 312, PT 201 **Student-Faculty Ratio:** 18:1 **Exams:** SAT I or ACT. ACT essay not being used. SAT essay not being used. **% Receiving Financial Aid:** 64 **% Residing in College-Owned, -Operated, or -Affiliated Housing:** 58 **Library Holdings:** 579,889 **Regional Accreditation:** Middle State Association of Colleges and Schools **Credit Hours For Degree:** 122 credit hours, Bachelors **ROTC:** Army **Professional Accreditation:** AACSB, NASAD, NASM, NCATE **Intercollegiate Athletics:** Baseball M; Basketball M & W; Crew M & W; Cross-Country Running M & W; Field Hockey W; Golf M & W; Ice Hockey M; Lacrosse M & W; Soccer M & W; Softball W; Swimming and Diving M & W; Tennis M & W; Track and Field M & W; Volleyball W; Wrestling M

STATE UNIVERSITY OF NEW YORK AT PLATTSBURGH

101 Broad Steet
Plattsburgh, NY 12901-2681
Tel: (518)564-2000

Admissions: 888-673-0012
Fax: (518)564-2045
E-mail: carrie.woodward@plattsburgh.edu
Web Site: http://www.plattsburgh.edu/
President/CEO: Dr. John Ettling
Admissions: Carrie Woodward
Financial Aid: Todd Moravec
Type: Comprehensive **Sex:** Coed **Affiliation:** State University of New York System **Scores:** 99.1% SAT V 400+; 99.5% SAT M 400+; 67.8% ACT 18-23; 26.5% ACT 24-29 **% Accepted:** 48 **Admission Plans:** Early Admission; Early Decision Plan; Deferred Admission **Application Fee:** $40.00 **H.S. Requirements:** High school diploma required; GED accepted **Costs Per Year:** Application fee: $40. State resident tuition: $4970 full-time, $207 per credit hour part-time. Nonresident tuition: $12,870 full-time, $536 per credit hour part-time. Mandatory fees: $1130 full-time, $45.67 per credit hour part-time. College room and board: $8600. College room only: $5500. Room and board charges vary according to board plan. **Scholarships:** Available **Calendar System:** Semester, Summer Session Available **Enrollment:** FT 5,563, PT 343, Grad FT 284, Grad PT 263 **Faculty:** FT 281, PT 226 **Student-Faculty Ratio:** 17:1 **Exams:** SAT I or ACT. **% Receiving Financial Aid:** 59 **% Residing in College-Owned, -Operated, or -Affiliated Housing:** 47 **Library Holdings:** 592,543 **Regional Accreditation:** Middle State Association of Colleges and Schools **ROTC:** Army **Professional Accreditation:** AACSB, AACN, ACA, ASLHA, CSWE, NLN, TEAC **Intercollegiate Athletics:** Baseball M; Basketball M & W; Cross-Country Running M & W; Ice Hockey M & W; Lacrosse M; Soccer M & W; Softball W; Tennis W; Track and Field M & W; Volleyball W

STATE UNIVERSITY OF NEW YORK UPSTATE MEDICAL UNIVERSITY

766 Irving Ave.
Syracuse, NY 13210-2334
Tel: (315)464-5540; Free: 800-736-2171
Admissions: (315)464-4570
Fax: (315)464-8823
E-mail: admiss@upstate.edu
Web Site: http://www.upstate.edu/
President/CEO: Dr. David R. Smith
Admissions: Donna L. Vavonese
Financial Aid: Michael Pede
Type: Two-Year Upper Division **Sex:** Coed **Affiliation:** State University of New York System **% Accepted:** 31 **Admission Plans:** Preferred Admission; Early Admission; Deferred Admission **Application Fee:** $40.00 **H.S. Requirements:** High school diploma required; GED accepted **Costs Per Year:** Application fee: $40. State resident tuition: $4970 full-time, $207 per credit part-time. Nonresident tuition: $12,870 full-time, $536 per credit part-time. Mandatory fees: $580 full-time, $32 per credit part-time. Full-time tuition and fees vary according to course load and program. Part-time tuition and fees vary according to course load and program. College room and board: $10,422. College room only: $6525. Room and board charges vary according to housing facility. **Scholarships:** Available **Calendar System:** Semester, Summer Session Available **Enrollment:** FT 150, PT 148, Grad FT 876, Grad PT 269 **Faculty:** FT 44, PT 37 **% Receiving Financial Aid:** 77 **% Residing in College-Owned, -Operated, or -Affiliated Housing:** 50 **Library Holdings:** 226,060 **Regional Accreditation:** Middle State Association of Colleges and Schools **Credit Hours For Degree:** 120 credits, Bachelors **ROTC:** Army **Professional Accreditation:** ACPE, AACN, APTA, APA, ASC, CARC, JRCERT, LCMEAMA, NAACLS, NLN

STONY BROOK UNIVERSITY, STATE UNIVERSITY OF NEW YORK

Nicolls Rd.
Stony Brook, NY 11794
Tel: (631)632-6000; Free: 800-872-7869
Admissions: (631)632-6868
E-mail: enroll@stonybrook.edu
Web Site: http://www.sunysb.edu/
President/CEO: Dr. Samuel L. Stanley, Jr.
Admissions: Judith Burke-Berhanan
Type: University **Sex:** Coed **Affiliation:** State University of New York System **Scores:** 98% SAT V 400+; 100% SAT M 400+; 19% ACT 18-23; 64% ACT 24-29 **% Accepted:** 40 **Admission Plans:** Early Action; Deferred Admission **Application Deadline:** March 1 **Application Fee:** $40.00 **H.S. Requirements:** High school diploma required; GED accepted **Costs Per Year:** Application fee: $40. State resident tuition: $4970 full-time, $207 per credit part-time. Nonresident tuition: $12,870 full-time, $536 per credit part-time. Mandatory fees: $1519 full-time, $74 per credit hour part-time. College room and board: $9590. College room only: $6112. Room and board charges vary according to board plan and housing facility. **Scholarships:** Available **Calendar System:** Semester, Summer Session Available **Enrollment:** FT 15,124, PT 1,271, Grad FT 4,789, Grad PT 3,508 **Faculty:** FT 972, PT 510 **Student-Faculty Ratio:** 19:1 **Exams:** SAT I or ACT, SAT II. ACT essay used for placement. SAT essay used for placement. **% Receiving Financial Aid:** 55 **% Residing in College-Owned, -Operated, or -Affiliated Housing:** 51 **Library Holdings:** 2,531,924 **Regional Accreditation:** Middle State Association of Colleges and Schools **Credit Hours For Degree:** 120 credits, Bachelors **ROTC:** Army, Air Force **Professional Accreditation:** ABET, AACN, ACNM, ADA, ADtA, AOTA, APTA, APA, ASC, CARC, CSWE, LCMEAMA, NAACLS, NCATE **Intercollegiate Athletics:** Baseball M; Basketball M & W; Cross-Country Running M & W; Football M; Lacrosse M & W; Soccer M & W; Softball W; Swimming and Diving M & W; Tennis M & W; Track and Field M & W; Volleyball W

SUFFOLK COUNTY COMMUNITY COLLEGE

533 College Rd.
Selden, NY 11784-2899
Tel: (631)451-4110
Admissions: (631)451-4000
Web Site: http://www.sunysuffolk.edu/
President/CEO: Dr. Shaun McKay, AIA
Admissions: Dr. Kate B. Rowe
Type: Two-Year College **Sex:** Coed **Affiliation:** State University of New York System **Scores:** 77% SAT V 400+; 80% SAT M 400+; 26.11% ACT 18-23; 4.08% ACT 24-29 **Admission Plans:** Open Admission; Preferred Admission; Deferred Admission **Application Deadline:** Rolling **Application Fee:** $35.00 **H.S. Requirements:** High school diploma required; GED accepted. For applicants with extenuating circumstances: High school diploma or equivalent not required **Costs Per Year:** Application fee: $35. Area resident tuition: $4196 full-time, $158 per credit hour part-time. State resident tuition: $8392 full-time, $316 per credit hour part-time. Nonresident tuition: $8392 full-time, $316 per credit hour part-time. **Scholarships:** Available **Calendar System:** Semester, Summer Session Available **Enrollment:** FT 12,200, PT 12,360 **Faculty:** FT 308, PT 854 **Student-Faculty Ratio:** 18:1 **Final Year or Final Semester Residency Requirement:** No **Regional Accreditation:** Middle State Association of Colleges and Schools **Credit Hours For Degree:** 66 credits, Associates **ROTC:** Army **Professional Accreditation:** AAMAE, AHIMA, AOTA, APTA, NLN **Intercollegiate Athletics:** Baseball M; Basketball M & W; Bowling M & W; Cross-Country Running M & W; Golf M & W; Lacrosse M; Soccer M; Softball W; Swimming and Diving M & W; Tennis M & W; Track and Field M & W; Volleyball W

SULLIVAN COUNTY COMMUNITY COLLEGE

112 College Rd.
Loch Sheldrake, NY 12759
Tel: (845)434-5750
Fax: (845)434-4806
E-mail: sarir@sullivan.suny.edu
Web Site: http://www.sullivan.suny.edu/
President/CEO: Dr. Mamie Howard Golladay
Admissions: Sari Rosenheck
Financial Aid: James M. Winderl
Type: Two-Year College **Sex:** Coed **Affiliation:** State University of New York System **% Accepted:** 71 **Admission Plans:** Open Admission; Early Admission; Deferred Admission **Application Deadline:** Rolling **Application Fee:** $0.00 **H.S. Requirements:** High school diploma required; GED accepted **Scholarships:** Available **Calendar System:** 4-1-4, Summer Session Available **Enrollment:** FT 1,067, PT 617 **Faculty:** FT 49, PT 65 **Student-Faculty Ratio:** 18:1 **Library Holdings:** 65,699 **Regional Accreditation:** Middle State Association of Colleges and Schools **Credit Hours For Degree:** 63 credits, Associates **Professional Accreditation:** ACF, ACBSP, NLN **Intercollegiate Athletics:** Basketball M & W; Cheerleading W; Cross-Country Running M & W; Golf M; Softball W; Volleyball W

SWEDISH INSTITUTE, COLLEGE OF HEALTH SCIENCES

226 West 26th St.
New York, NY 10001-6700
Tel: (212)924-5900
Fax: (212)924-7600
E-mail: admissions@swedishinstitute.edu

Web Site: http://www.swedishinstitute.org/
President/CEO: Trey Gilbert
Type: Comprehensive **Sex:** Coed **% Accepted:** 95 **Application Deadline:** November 9 **Application Fee:** $50.00 **Calendar System:** Trimester **Enrollment:** FT 304, PT 137 **Faculty:** FT 17, PT 33 **Student-Faculty Ratio:** 11:1 **Exams:** Other. **Library Holdings:** 2,700 **Professional Accreditation:** NACSCAO, ACCSCT

SYRACUSE UNIVERSITY
Syracuse, NY 13244
Tel: (315)443-1870
Admissions: (315)443-3611
E-mail: orange@syr.edu
Web Site: http://www.syracuse.edu/
President/CEO: Dr. Nancy Cantor
Financial Aid: Youlanda Copeland-Morgan
Type: University **Sex:** Coed **Scores:** 97.8% SAT V 400+; 98.8% SAT M 400+; 27% ACT 18-23; 56% ACT 24-29 **% Accepted:** 60 **Admission Plans:** Early Admission; Early Decision Plan; Deferred Admission **Application Deadline:** January 1 **Application Fee:** $70.00 **H.S. Requirements:** High school diploma required; GED accepted **Costs Per Year:** Application fee: $70. Comprehensive fee: $47,300 includes full-time tuition ($33,630), mandatory fees ($1296), and college room and board ($12,374). College room only: $6560. Room and board charges vary according to board plan and housing facility. Part-time tuition: $1646 per credit hour. **Scholarships:** Available **Calendar System:** Semester, Summer Session Available **Enrollment:** FT 13,040, PT 696, Grad FT 4,034, Grad PT 1,868 **Faculty:** FT 962, PT 545 **Student-Faculty Ratio:** 15:1 **Exams:** SAT I or ACT. ACT essay not being used. SAT essay not being used. **% Receiving Financial Aid:** 59 **% Residing in College-Owned, -Operated, or -Affiliated Housing:** 75 **Library Holdings:** 3,201,031 **Regional Accreditation:** Middle State Association of Colleges and Schools **Credit Hours For Degree:** 120 credit hours, Bachelors **ROTC:** Army, Air Force **Professional Accreditation:** AACSB, ABET, ACEJMC, AAMFT, ABA, ACA, ADtA, ALA, APA, ASLHA, AALS, FIDER, CORE, CSWE, NAAB, NASAD, NASM, NASPAA, NCATE, NLN **Intercollegiate Athletics:** Badminton M & W; Baseball M & W; Basketball M & W; Bowling M & W; Cheerleading M & W; Crew M & W; Cross-Country Running M & W; Equestrian Sports M & W; Field Hockey W; Football M; Gymnastics M & W; Ice Hockey M & W; Lacrosse M & W; Riflery M & W; Rugby M & W; Sailing M & W; Skiing (Downhill) M & W; Soccer M & W; Softball M & W; Squash M & W; Swimming and Diving M & W; Tennis M & W; Track and Field M & W; Volleyball M & W; Water Polo M & W; Wrestling M

TALMUDICAL INSTITUTE OF UPSTATE NEW YORK
769 Park Ave.
Rochester, NY 14607-3046
Tel: (716)473-2810
Fax: (716)442-0417
E-mail: yeshiva@tiuny.org
Web Site: http://www.tiuny.org/
President/CEO: Menachem Davidowitz
Admissions: Rabbi Menachem Davidowitz
Financial Aid: Ella Berenstein
Type: Five-Year College **Sex:** Men **Affiliation:** Jewish **% Accepted:** 100 **Admission Plans:** Early Admission **Application Deadline:** Rolling **Application Fee:** $0.00 **H.S. Requirements:** High school diploma required; GED accepted **Scholarships:** Available **Calendar System:** Semester **Library Holdings:** 3,000 **Credit Hours For Degree:** 150 credits, Bachelors **Professional Accreditation:** AARTS

TALMUDICAL SEMINARY OHOLEI TORAH
667 Eastern Parkway
Brooklyn, NY 11213-3310
Tel: (718)774-5050
E-mail: info@oholeitorah.com
President/CEO: Rabbi Moshe Susskind
Admissions: Rabbi Yisroel Friedman
Type: Four-Year College **Sex:** Men **Affiliation:** Jewish **% Accepted:** 100 **Admission Plans:** Deferred Admission **Application Deadline:** September 1 **H.S. Requirements:** High school diploma required; GED accepted **Calendar System:** Semester, Summer Session Not available **Credit Hours For Degree:** 128 credits, Bachelors **Professional Accreditation:** AARTS

TAYLOR BUSINESS INSTITUTE
23 West 17th St.
7th floor
New York, NY 10011
Tel: (212)229-1963
Fax: (212)229-2187
Web Site: http://www.tbiglobal.com/
Admissions: Christopher Carbowell
Type: Two-Year College **Sex:** Coed **Affiliation:** Phillips Colleges, Inc. **Admission Plans:** Deferred Admission **Application Deadline:** Rolling **Application Fee:** $0.00 **H.S. Requirements:** High school diploma required; GED accepted **Calendar System:** Quarter, Summer Session Available **Exams:** Other. **Library Holdings:** 2,873 **Credit Hours For Degree:** 97 credits, Associates **Professional Accreditation:** ACICS

TCI—THE COLLEGE OF TECHNOLOGY
320 West 31st St.
New York, NY 10001-2705
Tel: (212)594-4000; Free: 800-878-8246
Fax: (212)629-3937
E-mail: admissions@tcicollege.edu
Web Site: http://www.tciedu.com/
President/CEO: Dr. James Melville
Type: Two-Year College **Sex:** Coed **Admission Plans:** Open Admission **Application Deadline:** Rolling **H.S. Requirements:** High school diploma required; GED accepted **Costs Per Year:** One-time mandatory fee: $100. Tuition: $11,520 full-time, $470 per credit hour part-time. Mandatory fees: $530 full-time, $265 per term part-time. **Scholarships:** Available **Calendar System:** Semester, Summer Session Available **Student-Faculty Ratio:** 34:1 **Regional Accreditation:** Middle State Association of Colleges and Schools **Credit Hours For Degree:** 65 credits, Associates **Professional Accreditation:** ABET, NYSBR **Intercollegiate Athletics:** Basketball M & W

TOMPKINS CORTLAND COMMUNITY COLLEGE
170 North St., PO Box 139
Dryden, NY 13053-0139
Tel: (607)844-8211
Fax: (607)844-6538
E-mail: admissions@tc3.edu
Web Site: http://www.TC3.edu/
President/CEO: Carl E. Haynes, PhD
Admissions: Sandy Drumluk
Type: Two-Year College **Sex:** Coed **Affiliation:** State University of New York System **Admission Plans:** Open Admission; Early Admission; Deferred Admission **Application Deadline:** Rolling **Application Fee:** $15.00 **H.S. Requirements:** High school diploma required; GED accepted. For nursing program: High school diploma required; GED not accepted **Costs Per Year:** Application fee: $15. State resident tuition: $3580 full-time, $135 per credit hour part-time. Nonresident tuition: $7460 full-time, $280 per credit hour part-time. Mandatory fees: $626 full-time, $35.30 per credit hour part-time. Part-time tuition and fees vary according to course load. College room and board: $7500. Room and board charges vary according to board plan and housing facility. **Scholarships:** Available **Calendar System:** Semester, Summer Session Available **Enrollment:** FT 2,874, PT 825 **Faculty:** FT 76, PT 236 **Student-Faculty Ratio:** 19:1 **% Residing in College-Owned, -Operated, or -Affiliated Housing:** 22 **Library Holdings:** 51,700 **Regional Accreditation:** Middle State Association of Colleges and Schools **Credit Hours For Degree:** 62 credits, Associates **Professional Accreditation:** NLN **Intercollegiate Athletics:** Baseball M; Basketball M & W; Golf M & W; Lacrosse M; Soccer M & W; Softball W; Volleyball W

TORAH TEMIMAH TALMUDICAL SEMINARY
507 Ocean Parkway
Brooklyn, NY 11218-5913
Tel: (718)853-8500
President/CEO: Yaakov Applegrad
Type: Four-Year College **Sex:** Men **Affiliation:** Jewish **% Accepted:** 100 **Calendar System:** Semester **Professional Accreditation:** AARTS

TOURO COLLEGE
27-33 West 23rd St.
New York, NY 10010
Tel: (212)463-0400
Fax: (212)779-2344

Web Site: http://www.touro.edu/
President/CEO: Bernard Lander
Admissions: Andre Baron
Type: Comprehensive **Sex:** Coed **Admission Plans:** Open Admission; Early Admission; Deferred Admission **Application Deadline:** Rolling **Application Fee:** $50.00 **H.S. Requirements:** High school diploma required; GED accepted **Costs Per Year:** Application fee: $50. Tuition: $15,000 full-time, $550 per credit hour part-time. Mandatory fees: $300 full-time. Full-time tuition and fees vary according to degree level and program. Part-time tuition varies according to degree level and program. College room only: $6600. Room charges vary according to housing facility. **Scholarships:** Available **Calendar System:** Semester, Summer Session Available **Exams:** SAT I or ACT. **% Receiving Financial Aid:** 100 **Library Holdings:** 302,700 **Regional Accreditation:** Middle State Association of Colleges and Schools **Credit Hours For Degree:** 60 credits, Associates; 120 credits, Bachelors **Professional Accreditation:** ABA, AOTA, APTA, ASLHA, AALS

TROCAIRE COLLEGE
360 Choate Ave.
Buffalo, NY 14220-2094
Tel: (716)826-1200
Fax: (716)826-4704
E-mail: info@trocaire.edu
Web Site: http://www.trocaire.edu/
President/CEO: Paul B. Hurley, Jr.
Admissions: Theresa Horner
Type: Two-Year College **Sex:** Coed **Scores:** 88% SAT V 400+; 76% SAT M 400+; 67% ACT 18-23 **% Accepted:** 93 **Admission Plans:** Deferred Admission **Application Deadline:** Rolling **Application Fee:** $25.00 **H.S. Requirements:** High school diploma required; GED accepted **Costs Per Year:** Application fee: $25. Tuition: $12,292 full-time, $484 per credit hour part-time. Full-time tuition varies according to course load, program, and reciprocity agreements. Part-time tuition varies according to course load, program, and reciprocity agreements. **Scholarships:** Available **Calendar System:** Semester, Summer Session Available **Faculty:** FT 38, PT 75 **Student-Faculty Ratio:** 15:1 **Exams:** SAT I or ACT. **Library Holdings:** 15,403 **Regional Accreditation:** Middle State Association of Colleges and Schools **Credit Hours For Degree:** 60 credit hours, Associates **Professional Accreditation:** ARCEST, AAMAE, AHIMA, JRCERT, NLN

ULSTER COUNTY COMMUNITY COLLEGE
491 Cottekill Rd.
Stone Ridge, NY 12484
Tel: (845)687-5000; Free: 800-724-0833
Admissions: (845)687-5022
E-mail: admissionsoffice@sunyulster.edu
Web Site: http://www.sunyulster.edu/
President/CEO: Dr. Donald C. Katt
Type: Two-Year College **Sex:** Coed **Affiliation:** State University of New York System **% Accepted:** 100 **Admission Plans:** Open Admission; Early Admission; Deferred Admission **Application Deadline:** Rolling **Application Fee:** $0.00 **H.S. Requirements:** High school diploma required; GED accepted **Costs Per Year:** Application fee: $0. State resident tuition: $3620 full-time, $135 per credit part-time. Nonresident tuition: $7240 full-time, $270 per credit part-time. Mandatory fees: $500 full-time, $45 per course part-time, $22. **Scholarships:** Available **Calendar System:** Semester, Summer Session Available **Enrollment:** FT 1,759, PT 1,781 **Faculty:** FT 66, PT 123 **Student-Faculty Ratio:** 19:1 **Final Year or Final Semester Residency Requirement:** No **Library Holdings:** 86,597 **Regional Accreditation:** Middle State Association of Colleges and Schools **Credit Hours For Degree:** 60 credit hours, Associates **Professional Accreditation:** NLN **Intercollegiate Athletics:** Baseball M; Basketball M & W; Golf M; Soccer M; Softball W; Tennis M; Volleyball W

UNION COLLEGE
807 Union St.
Schenectady, NY 12308-2311
Tel: (518)388-6000
Admissions: (518)388-6112
Fax: (518)388-6986
E-mail: admissions@union.edu
Web Site: http://www.union.edu/
President/CEO: Dr. Stephen C. Ainlay
Financial Aid: Linda Parker
Type: Four-Year College **Sex:** Coed **Scores:** 100% SAT V 400+; 100% SAT M 400+; 6.2% ACT 18-23; 59.29% ACT 24-29 **% Accepted:** 41 **Admission Plans:** Early Admission; Early Decision Plan; Deferred Admission **Application Deadline:** January 15 **Application Fee:** $50.00 **H.S. Requirements:** High school diploma required; GED not accepted **Costs Per Year:** Application fee: $50. Comprehensive fee: $50,439. **Scholarships:** Available **Calendar System:** Trimester, Summer Session Available **Enrollment:** FT 2,157, PT 37 **Faculty:** FT 199, PT 29 **Student-Faculty Ratio:** 10:1 **Exams:** SAT I and SAT II or ACT. ACT essay used for admission. SAT essay used for admission. **% Receiving Financial Aid:** 47 **% Residing in College-Owned, -Operated, or -Affiliated Housing:** 87 **Final Year or Final Semester Residency Requirement:** Yes **Library Holdings:** 634,183 **Regional Accreditation:** Middle State Association of Colleges and Schools **Credit Hours For Degree:** 36 courses, Bachelors **ROTC:** Army, Navy, Air Force **Professional Accreditation:** ABET **Intercollegiate Athletics:** Baseball M; Basketball M & W; Cheerleading M & W; Crew M & W; Cross-Country Running M & W; Fencing M & W; Field Hockey W; Football M; Golf M & W; Ice Hockey M & W; Lacrosse M & W; Rugby M & W; Soccer M & W; Softball W; Swimming and Diving M & W; Tennis M & W; Track and Field M & W; Ultimate Frisbee M & W; Volleyball W

UNITED STATES MERCHANT MARINE ACADEMY
300 Steamboat Rd.
Kings Point, NY 11024-1699
Tel: (516)773-5000; Free: (866)546-4778
Admissions: (516)773-5391
Fax: (516)773-5390
E-mail: admissions@usmma.edu
Web Site: http://www.usmma.edu/
President/CEO: Rear Adm. Allen Worley
Admissions: Capt. Robert E. Johnson
Type: Comprehensive **Sex:** Coed **Scores:** 100% SAT V 400+; 100% SAT M 400+; 2% ACT 18-23; 89% ACT 24-29 **% Accepted:** 18 **Admission Plans:** Early Decision Plan **Application Deadline:** March 1 **Application Fee:** $0.00 **H.S. Requirements:** High school diploma required; GED accepted **Calendar System:** Trimester, Summer Session Not available **Enrollment:** FT 985 **Faculty:** FT 95 **Student-Faculty Ratio:** 11:1 **Exams:** SAT I or ACT. **% Residing in College-Owned, -Operated, or -Affiliated Housing:** 100 **Library Holdings:** 187,191 **Regional Accreditation:** Middle State Association of Colleges and Schools **Credit Hours For Degree:** 216 quarter hours, Bachelors **Professional Accreditation:** ABET **Intercollegiate Athletics:** Baseball M; Basketball M & W; Crew M & W; Cross-Country Running M & W; Football M; Golf M & W; Ice Hockey M; Lacrosse M; Rugby M; Sailing M & W; Soccer M; Softball W; Swimming and Diving M & W; Tennis M & W; Track and Field M & W; Volleyball W; Wrestling M

UNITED STATES MILITARY ACADEMY
600 Thayer Rd.
West Point, NY 10996
Tel: (845)938-4011
Admissions: (845)938-4041
Fax: (845)938-3021
E-mail: 8dad@sunams.usma.army.mil
Web Site: http://www.usma.edu/
President/CEO: Lt. Gen. Franklin L. Hagenbeck
Admissions: Col. Deborah J. McDonald
Type: Four-Year College **Sex:** Coed **Scores:** 100% SAT V 400+; 100% SAT M 400+; 13% ACT 18-23; 59% ACT 24-29 **% Accepted:** 14 **Application Deadline:** February 28 **H.S. Requirements:** High school diploma required; GED accepted **Costs Per Year:** Comprehensive fee: $0. Tuition is covered by a full scholarship for all students who attend West Point. All students are on Active Duty Status as members of the U.S. Army and receive an annual salary of approximately $10,150. Room and board, medical and dental care are provided for by the U.S. Army; however, a one-time deposit of $2,000 is required upon admission in order to defray the initial cost of uniforms, books, supplies, equipment and fees. A cadet's salary pays for uniforms, activities, services, books, sundries, and other personal services they are permitted.. **Calendar System:** Semester, Summer Session Available **Enrollment:** FT 4,621 **Faculty:** FT 625, PT 0 **Student-Faculty Ratio:** 7:1 **Exams:** SAT I or ACT. **% Residing in College-Owned, -Operated, or -Affiliated Housing:** 100 **Library Holdings:** 507,775 **Regional Accreditation:** Middle State Association of Colleges and Schools **Credit Hours For Degree:** 40 courses, Bachelors **Professional Accreditation:** ABET **Intercollegiate Athletics:** Baseball M; Basketball M & W; Bowling M; Cheerleading M & W; Crew M &

W; Cross-Country Running M & W; Equestrian Sports M & W; Fencing M & W; Football M; Golf M; Gymnastics M; Ice Hockey M; Lacrosse M & W; Riflery M & W; Rock Climbing M & W; Rugby M & W; Sailing M & W; Skiing (Cross-Country) M & W; Skiing (Downhill) M & W; Soccer M & W; Softball W; Swimming and Diving M & W; Tennis M & W; Track and Field M & W; Volleyball M & W; Water Polo M; Weight Lifting M & W; Wrestling M

UNITED TALMUDICAL SEMINARY
191 Rodney St.
Brooklyn, NY 11211
Tel: (718)963-9260
Admissions: (718)963-9770
Type: Comprehensive **Sex:** Men **Affiliation:** Jewish **Admission Plans:** Open Admission **H.S. Requirements:** High school diploma required; GED accepted **Calendar System:** Semester **Professional Accreditation:** AARTS

UNIVERSITY AT ALBANY, STATE UNIVERSITY OF NEW YORK
1400 Washington Ave.
Albany, NY 12222-0001
Tel: (518)442-3300
Admissions: (518)442-5435
E-mail: ugadmissions@albany.edu
Web Site: http://www.albany.edu/
President/CEO: George M. Philip, Esq.
Admissions: Robert Andrea
Financial Aid: Diane Corbett
Type: University **Sex:** Coed **Affiliation:** State University of New York System **Scores:** 100% SAT V 400+; 100% SAT M 400+ **% Accepted:** 47 **Admission Plans:** Early Admission; Early Action; Deferred Admission **Application Deadline:** March 1 **Application Fee:** $50.00 **H.S. Requirements:** High school diploma required; GED accepted **Costs Per Year:** Application fee: $50. State resident tuition: $4970 full-time, $207 per credit part-time. Nonresident tuition: $12,870 full-time, $536 per credit part-time. Mandatory fees: $1778 full-time. Part-time tuition varies according to course load. College room and board: $10,238. College room only: $6324. Room and board charges vary according to board plan and housing facility. **Scholarships:** Available **Calendar System:** Semester, Summer Session Available **Enrollment:** FT 12,319, PT 795, Grad FT 2,374, Grad PT 2,532 **Faculty:** FT 637, PT 631 **Student-Faculty Ratio:** 19:1 **Exams:** SAT I or ACT. **% Receiving Financial Aid:** 58 **% Residing in College-Owned, -Operated, or -Affiliated Housing:** 57 **Library Holdings:** 2,186,337 **Regional Accreditation:** Middle State Association of Colleges and Schools **Credit Hours For Degree:** 120 credits, Bachelors **ROTC:** Army, Air Force **Professional Accreditation:** AACSB, ACSP, ALA, APA, CEPH, CORE, CSWE, NASPAA, TEAC **Intercollegiate Athletics:** Baseball M; Basketball M & W; Crew M & W; Cross-Country Running M & W; Field Hockey W; Football M; Golf W; Lacrosse M & W; Rock Climbing M & W; Soccer M & W; Softball W; Tennis W; Track and Field M & W; Volleyball W

UNIVERSITY AT BUFFALO, THE STATE UNIVERSITY OF NEW YORK
Capen Hall
Buffalo, NY 14260
Tel: (716)645-2000; Free: 888-UB-ADMIT
Admissions: (716)645-6900
Fax: (716)645-6411
E-mail: ub-admissions@buffalo.edu
Web Site: http://www.buffalo.edu/
President/CEO: Dr. John B. Simpson
Admissions: Patricia Armstrong
Financial Aid: Joseph V. Alongi
Type: University **Sex:** Coed **Affiliation:** State University of New York System **Scores:** 100% SAT V 400+; 100% SAT M 400+; 29% ACT 18-23; 58% ACT 24-29 **% Accepted:** 52 **Admission Plans:** Early Admission; Early Decision Plan **Application Fee:** $40.00 **H.S. Requirements:** High school diploma required; GED accepted **Costs Per Year:** Application fee: $40. State resident tuition: $4970 full-time, $207 per credit hour part-time. Nonresident tuition: $12,870 full-time, $536 per credit hour part-time. Mandatory fees: $2043 full-time, $90 per credit hour part-time. Part-time tuition and fees vary according to course load. College room and board: $9648. College room only: $5748. Room and board charges vary according to board plan and housing facility. **Scholarships:** Available **Calendar System:** Semester, Summer Session Available **Enrollment:** FT 17,966, PT 1,402, Grad FT 6,135, Grad PT 3,378 **Faculty:** FT 1,209, PT 528 **Student-Faculty Ratio:** 16:1 **Exams:** SAT I or ACT. ACT essay not being used. SAT essay not being used. **% Receiving Financial Aid:** 51 **% Residing in College-Owned, -Operated, or -Affiliated Housing:** 34 **Final Year or Final Semester Residency Requirement:** No **Library Holdings:** 3,852,074 **Regional Accreditation:** Middle State Association of Colleges and Schools **Credit Hours For Degree:** 120 credit hours, Bachelors **ROTC:** Army **Professional Accreditation:** AACSB, ABET, ACPhE, AACN, AANA, ABA, ADA, ADtA, ACSP, ALA, AOTA, APTA, APA, ASLHA, AALS, CORE, CSWE, JRCNMT, LCMEAMA, NAACLS NAAB, NASAD, TEAC, NAIT **Intercollegiate Athletics:** Baseball M; Basketball M & W; Crew W; Cross-Country Running M & W; Football M; Soccer M & W; Softball W; Swimming and Diving M & W; Tennis M & W; Track and Field M & W; Volleyball W; Wrestling M

UNIVERSITY OF ROCHESTER
Wilson Blvd.
Rochester, NY 14627
Tel: (585)275-2121; Free: 888-822-2256
Admissions: (585)275-3221
Fax: (585)273-1118
E-mail: admit@admissions.rochester.edu
Web Site: http://www.rochester.edu/
President/CEO: Joel Seligman
Financial Aid: Charles W. Puls
Type: University **Sex:** Coed **Scores:** 100% SAT V 400+; 100% SAT M 400+; 4% ACT 18-23; 44% ACT 24-29 **% Accepted:** 39 **Admission Plans:** Early Admission; Early Decision Plan; Deferred Admission **Application Deadline:** January 1 **Application Fee:** $60.00 **H.S. Requirements:** High school diploma required; GED accepted **Costs Per Year:** Application fee: $60. Comprehensive fee: $49,890 includes full-time tuition ($37,870), mandatory fees ($820), and college room and board ($11,200). College room only: $6750. Room and board charges vary according to board plan. Part-time tuition: $1183 per credit hour. Part-time tuition varies according to course load. **Scholarships:** Available **Calendar System:** Semester, Summer Session Available **Enrollment:** FT 5,193, PT 254, Grad FT 3,175, Grad PT 1,354 **Faculty:** FT 524, PT 280 **Student-Faculty Ratio:** 9:1 **Exams:** SAT I or ACT, SAT I and SAT II or ACT, SAT II. ACT essay used as a validity check on application essay. SAT essay used as a validity check on application essay. **% Receiving Financial Aid:** 57 **% Residing in College-Owned, -Operated, or -Affiliated Housing:** 83 **Library Holdings:** 3,672,976 **Regional Accreditation:** Middle State Association of Colleges and Schools **Credit Hours For Degree:** 128 credit hours, Bachelors **ROTC:** Army, Navy, Air Force **Professional Accreditation:** AACSB, ABET, AAMFT, AACN, ACA, APA, ACIPE, CEPH, LCMEAMA, NASM, NCATE, NLN **Intercollegiate Athletics:** Badminton M & W; Baseball M; Basketball M & W; Crew M & W; Cross-Country Running M & W; Equestrian Sports M & W; Field Hockey W; Football M; Golf M; Ice Hockey M & W; Lacrosse M & W; Rugby M & W; Skiing (Downhill) M & W; Soccer M & W; Softball W; Squash M; Swimming and Diving M & W; Tennis M & W; Track and Field M & W; Ultimate Frisbee M & W; Volleyball M & W; Water Polo M & W

U.T.A. MESIVTA OF KIRYAS JOEL
9 Nickelsburg Rd., Unit 312
Monroe, NY 10950
Tel: (845)873-9901
Admissions: (845)783-9901
Fax: (845)782-3620
President/CEO: David Schwartz
Type: Four-Year College **Sex:** Men **Affiliation:** Jewish **Admission Plans:** Open Admission **Professional Accreditation:** AARTS

UTICA COLLEGE
1600 Burrstone Rd.
Utica, NY 13502-4892
Tel: (315)792-3111; Free: 800-782-8884
Admissions: (315)792-3006
Fax: (315)792-3003
Web Site: http://www.utica.edu/
President/CEO: Dr. Todd S. Hutton
Admissions: Patrick Quinn
Financial Aid: Laura Bedford
Type: Comprehensive **Sex:** Coed **Scores:** 80.96% SAT V 400+; 84.39% SAT M 400+; 51.9% ACT 18-23; 22% ACT 24-29 **% Accepted:** 78 **Admission Plans:** Early Admission; Deferred Admission **Application Deadline:** Rolling **Application Fee:** $40.00 **H.S. Requirements:** High school diploma

required; GED accepted **Costs Per Year:** Application fee: $40. Comprehensive fee: $38,134 includes full-time tuition ($26,764), mandatory fees ($520), and college room and board ($10,850). Full-time tuition and fees vary according to class time and course load. Room and board charges vary according to board plan and housing facility. Part-time tuition: $905 per credit hour. Part-time tuition varies according to class time and course load. **Scholarships:** Available **Calendar System:** Semester, Summer Session Available **Enrollment:** FT 2,064, PT 473, Grad FT 194, Grad PT 542 **Faculty:** FT 131, PT 212 **Student-Faculty Ratio:** 11:1 **Exams:** SAT I or ACT. **% Receiving Financial Aid:** 91 **% Residing in College-Owned, -Operated, or -Affiliated Housing:** 50 **Library Holdings:** 17,884 **Regional Accreditation:** Middle State Association of Colleges and Schools **Credit Hours For Degree:** 120 credit hours, Bachelors **ROTC:** Army, Air Force **Professional Accreditation:** AOTA, APTA, NLN, TEAC **Intercollegiate Athletics:** Baseball M; Basketball M & W; Field Hockey W; Football M; Golf M & W; Ice Hockey M & W; Lacrosse M & W; Soccer M & W; Softball W; Swimming and Diving M & W; Tennis M & W; Volleyball W; Water Polo W

UTICA SCHOOL OF COMMERCE
201 Bleecker St.
Utica, NY 13501-2280
Tel: (315)733-2307; Free: 800-321-4USC
Fax: (315)733-9281
Web Site: http://www.uscny.edu/
President/CEO: Philip Williams
Type: Two-Year College **Sex:** Coed **% Accepted:** 100 **Application Deadline:** Rolling **H.S. Requirements:** High school diploma required; GED accepted **Costs Per Year:** Tuition: $11,340 full-time, $99 per credit hour part-time. Mandatory fees: $420 full-time. Full-time tuition and fees vary according to program. Part-time tuition varies according to program. **Scholarships:** Available **Calendar System:** Quarter, Summer Session Available **Student-Faculty Ratio:** 14:1 **Credit Hours For Degree:** 90 quarter hours, Associates **Professional Accreditation:** NYSBR

VASSAR COLLEGE
124 Raymond Ave.
Poughkeepsie, NY 12604
Tel: (845)437-7000; Free: 800-827-7270
Admissions: (845)437-7300
Fax: (845)437-7063
E-mail: admissions@vassar.edu
Web Site: http://www.vassar.edu/
President/CEO: Catherine B. Hill
Admissions: Dr. David M. Borus
Financial Aid: Michael Fraher
Type: Comprehensive **Sex:** Coed **Scores:** 100% SAT V 400+; 100% SAT M 400+; 24% ACT 24-29 **% Accepted:** 25 **Admission Plans:** Early Decision Plan; Deferred Admission **Application Deadline:** January 1 **Application Fee:** $60.00 **H.S. Requirements:** High school diploma required; GED accepted **Costs Per Year:** Application fee: $60. Comprehensive fee: $51,300 includes full-time tuition ($41,335), mandatory fees ($595), and college room and board ($9370). College room only: $5090. Room and board charges vary according to board plan and housing facility. Part-time tuition: $4890 per course. Part-time tuition varies according to course load. **Scholarships:** Available **Calendar System:** Semester, Summer Session Not available **Enrollment:** FT 2,394, PT 58, Grad PT 1 **Faculty:** FT 296, PT 32 **Student-Faculty Ratio:** 8:1 **Exams:** SAT I and SAT II or ACT. ACT essay used for admission. SAT essay used for admission. ACT essay used as a validity check on application essay. SAT essay used as a validity check on application essay. **% Receiving Financial Aid:** 56 **% Residing in College-Owned, -Operated, or -Affiliated Housing:** 95 **Final Year or Final Semester Residency Requirement:** Yes **Library Holdings:** 967,820 **Regional Accreditation:** Middle State Association of Colleges and Schools **Credit Hours For Degree:** 34 units, Bachelors **Intercollegiate Athletics:** Baseball M; Basketball M & W; Crew M & W; Cross-Country Running M & W; Fencing M & W; Field Hockey W; Golf W; Lacrosse M & W; Rugby M & W; Soccer M & W; Squash M & W; Swimming and Diving M & W; Tennis M & W; Track and Field M & W; Ultimate Frisbee M & W; Volleyball M & W

VAUGHN COLLEGE OF AERONAUTICS AND TECHNOLOGY
86-01 23rd Ave.
Flushing, NY 11369
Tel: (718)429-6600
Fax: (718)429-0256
E-mail: ernie.shepelsky@vaughn.edu
Web Site: http://www.vaughn.edu/
President/CEO: Dr. John C. Fitzpatrick
Admissions: Ernie Shepelsky
Financial Aid: Dorothy Martin
Type: Comprehensive **Sex:** Coed **Admission Plans:** Open Admission **Application Deadline:** Rolling **Application Fee:** $40.00 **H.S. Requirements:** High school diploma required; GED accepted. For for bachelor degree applicants: High school diploma required; GED accepted **Costs Per Year:** Application fee: $40. Comprehensive fee: $27,980 includes full-time tuition ($16,300), mandatory fees ($400), and college room and board ($11,280). Full-time tuition and fees vary according to course load. Room and board charges vary according to board plan and housing facility. Part-time tuition: $550 per credit hour. Part-time tuition varies according to course load. **Scholarships:** Available **Calendar System:** Semester, Summer Session Available **Enrollment:** FT 935, PT 359, Grad FT 2, Grad PT 14 **Student-Faculty Ratio:** 14:1 **Exams:** SAT I and SAT II or ACT. ACT essay used for admission. SAT essay used for admission. **% Receiving Financial Aid:** 83 **% Residing in College-Owned, -Operated, or -Affiliated Housing:** 10 **Final Year or Final Semester Residency Requirement:** No **Library Holdings:** 42,000 **Regional Accreditation:** Middle State Association of Colleges and Schools **Credit Hours For Degree:** 60 credits, Associates; 120 credits, Bachelors **ROTC:** Army, Air Force **Professional Accreditation:** ABET

VILLA MARIA COLLEGE OF BUFFALO
240 Pine Ridge Rd.
Buffalo, NY 14225-3999
Tel: (716)896-0700
Fax: (716)896-0705
E-mail: admissions@villa.edu
Web Site: http://www.villa.edu/
President/CEO: Sr. Marcella Marie Garus
Admissions: Kevin Donovan
Financial Aid: Christina Horner
Type: Four-Year College **Sex:** Coed **Affiliation:** Roman Catholic Church **Scores:** 76% SAT M 400+; 67% ACT 18-23; 17% ACT 24-29 **% Accepted:** 71 **Admission Plans:** Deferred Admission **Application Deadline:** Rolling **H.S. Requirements:** High school diploma required; GED accepted **Costs Per Year:** Tuition: $14,380 full-time, $485 per credit part-time. Mandatory fees: $125 per term part-time. Full-time tuition varies according to course level, course load, degree level, program, and student level. Part-time tuition and fees vary according to course level, course load, degree level, program, and student level. **Scholarships:** Available **Calendar System:** Semester, Summer Session Available **Enrollment:** FT 419, PT 84 **Faculty:** FT 31, PT 46 **Student-Faculty Ratio:** 10:1 **% Receiving Financial Aid:** 73 **Library Holdings:** 37,000 **Regional Accreditation:** Middle State Association of Colleges and Schools **Credit Hours For Degree:** 61 credits, Associates; 120 credits, Bachelors **Professional Accreditation:** APTA

WAGNER COLLEGE
1 Campus Rd.
Staten Island, NY 10301-4495
Tel: (718)390-3100; Free: 800-221-1010
Admissions: (718)420-4242
Fax: (718)390-3105
E-mail: leigh-ann.nowicki@wagner.edu
Web Site: http://www.wagner.edu/
President/CEO: Dr. Richard Guarasci
Admissions: Leigh-Ann Nowicki
Financial Aid: Angelo Araimo
Type: Comprehensive **Sex:** Coed **Scores:** 99% SAT V 400+; 100% SAT M 400+; 10% ACT 18-23; 81% ACT 24-29 **% Accepted:** 70 **Admission Plans:** Early Decision Plan; Deferred Admission **Application Deadline:** February 15 **Application Fee:** $50.00 **H.S. Requirements:** High school diploma required; GED accepted **Costs Per Year:** Application fee: $50. Comprehensive fee: $42,280 includes full-time tuition ($32,430), mandatory fees ($150), and college room and board ($9700). Full-time tuition and fees vary according to course load. Part-time tuition: $4054 per unit. Part-time tuition varies according to course load. **Scholarships:** Available **Calendar System:** Semester, Summer Session Available **Enrollment:** FT 1,799, PT 71, Grad FT 219, Grad PT 176 **Faculty:** FT 99, PT 139 **Student-Faculty Ratio:** 13:1 **Exams:** SAT I or ACT. ACT essay used as a validity check on application essay. SAT essay used as a validity check on application essay. **% Receiving Financial Aid:** 59 **% Residing in College-Owned, -Operated, or**

-**Affiliated Housing:** 68 **Final Year or Final Semester Residency Requirement:** No **Library Holdings:** 175,344 **Regional Accreditation:** Middle State Association of Colleges and Schools **Credit Hours For Degree:** 36 units, Bachelors **ROTC:** Army **Professional Accreditation:** ACBSP, NCATE, NLN **Intercollegiate Athletics:** Baseball M; Basketball M & W; Cross-Country Running M & W; Football M; Golf M & W; Ice Hockey M; Lacrosse M & W; Soccer W; Softball W; Swimming and Diving W; Tennis M & W; Track and Field M & W; Water Polo W

WEBB INSTITUTE
Crescent Beach Rd.
Glen Cove, NY 11542-1398
Tel: (516)671-2213
Fax: (516)674-9838
E-mail: admissions@webb-institute.edu
Web Site: http://www.webb-institute.edu/
President/CEO: Robert C. Olsen
Financial Aid: William G. Murray
Type: Four-Year College **Sex:** Coed **Scores:** 100% SAT V 400+; 100% SAT M 400+ **% Accepted:** 35 **Admission Plans:** Early Decision Plan **Application Deadline:** February 15 **Application Fee:** $25.00 **H.S. Requirements:** High school diploma required; GED not accepted **Costs Per Year:** Application fee: $25. Comprehensive fee: $10,200 includes full-time tuition ($0) and college room and board ($10,200). all students are awarded full tuition scholarships. **Scholarships:** Available **Calendar System:** Semester, Summer Session Not available **Enrollment:** FT 89 **Faculty:** FT 11, PT 3 **Student-Faculty Ratio:** 7:1 **Exams:** SAT I, SAT II. **% Receiving Financial Aid:** 21 **% Residing in College-Owned, -Operated, or -Affiliated Housing:** 100 **Library Holdings:** 53,319 **Regional Accreditation:** Middle State Association of Colleges and Schools **Credit Hours For Degree:** 146 credits, Bachelors **Professional Accreditation:** ABET **Intercollegiate Athletics:** Basketball M & W; Cross-Country Running M & W; Sailing M & W; Soccer M & W; Tennis M & W; Volleyball M & W

WELLS COLLEGE
170 Main St.
Aurora, NY 13026
Tel: (315)364-3266; Free: 800-952-9355
Admissions: (315)364-3264
Fax: (315)364-3227
E-mail: admissions@wells.edu
Web Site: http://www.wells.edu/
President/CEO: Lisa Marsh Ryerson
Admissions: Susan Raith Sloan
Financial Aid: Cathleen A. Patella
Type: Four-Year College **Sex:** Coed **Scores:** 96% SAT V 400+; 96% SAT M 400+; 41% ACT 18-23; 45% ACT 24-29 **% Accepted:** 64 **Admission Plans:** Early Admission; Early Action; Early Decision Plan; Deferred Admission **Application Deadline:** March 1 **Application Fee:** $40.00 **H.S. Requirements:** High school diploma required; GED accepted **Costs Per Year:** Application fee: $40. Comprehensive fee: $38,680 includes full-time tuition ($28,180), mandatory fees ($1500), and college room and board ($9000). Part-time tuition: $790 per credit hour. **Scholarships:** Available **Calendar System:** Semester, Summer Session Not available **Enrollment:** FT 557, PT 11 **Faculty:** FT 44, PT 44 **Student-Faculty Ratio:** 9:1 **Exams:** SAT I or ACT. **% Receiving Financial Aid:** 83 **% Residing in College-Owned, -Operated, or -Affiliated Housing:** 87 **Library Holdings:** 218,000 **Regional Accreditation:** Middle State Association of Colleges and Schools **Credit Hours For Degree:** 120 credits, Bachelors **ROTC:** Army, Air Force **Intercollegiate Athletics:** Basketball M & W; Cross-Country Running M & W; Field Hockey W; Golf M & W; Lacrosse M & W; Soccer M & W; Softball W; Swimming and Diving M & W; Tennis W

WESTCHESTER COMMUNITY COLLEGE
75 Grasslands Rd.
Valhalla, NY 10595-1698
Tel: (914)785-6600
Admissions: (914)606-6735
E-mail: admissions@sunywcc.edu
Web Site: http://www.sunywcc.edu/
President/CEO: Dr. Joseph N. Hankin
Admissions: Gloria Leon
Type: Two-Year College **Sex:** Coed **Affiliation:** State University of New York System **% Accepted:** 100 **Admission Plans:** Open Admission; Early Admission **Application Deadline:** Rolling **Application Fee:** $25.00 **H.S. Requirements:** High school diploma required; GED accepted **Costs Per Year:** Application fee: $25. State resident tuition: $3650 full-time, $153 per credit part-time. Nonresident tuition: $9126 full-time, $383 per credit part-time. Mandatory fees: $363 full-time, $83 per term part-time. **Scholarships:** Available **Calendar System:** Semester, Summer Session Available **Enrollment:** FT 7,789, PT 6,358 **Faculty:** FT 170, PT 309 **Student-Faculty Ratio:** 18:1 **Library Holdings:** 190,772 **Regional Accreditation:** Middle State Association of Colleges and Schools **Credit Hours For Degree:** 64 credits, Associates **Professional Accreditation:** CARC, JRCERT **Intercollegiate Athletics:** Baseball M; Basketball M & W; Bowling M & W; Golf M; Soccer M; Softball W; Volleyball W

WOOD TOBE—COBURN SCHOOL
8 East 40th St.
New York, NY 10016
Tel: (212)686-9040; Free: 800-394-9663
Fax: (212)686-9171
Web Site: http://www.woodtobecoburn.edu/
President/CEO: Sandi Gruninger
Type: Two-Year College **Sex:** Coed **Affiliation:** Bradford Schools, Inc. **% Accepted:** 84 **H.S. Requirements:** High school diploma required; GED accepted **Scholarships:** Available **Calendar System:** Semester, Summer Session Not available **Credit Hours For Degree:** 60 credits, Associates **Professional Accreditation:** NYSBR

YESHIVA DERECH CHAIM
1573 39th St.
Brooklyn, NY 11218
Tel: (718)438-3070
Admissions: (718)438-5476
President/CEO: Mordechai Rennert
Type: Comprehensive **Sex:** Men **Affiliation:** Jewish **% Accepted:** 100 **H.S. Requirements:** High school diploma required; GED not accepted **Calendar System:** Semester **Professional Accreditation:** AARTS

YESHIVA D'MONSEY RABBINICAL COLLEGE
2 Roman Blvd.
Monsey, NY 10952
Tel: (914)352-5852
Admissions: (845)352-5852
Fax: (914)362-3453
President/CEO: Rabbi Aron Berger
Type: Four-Year College **Sex:** Men **Affiliation:** Jewish **% Accepted:** 100 **Professional Accreditation:** AARTS

YESHIVA GEDOLAH IMREI YOSEF D'SPINKA
1466 56th St.
Brooklyn, NY 11219
Tel: (718)851-8721
President/CEO: Yehuda Kornreich
Type: Four-Year College **Sex:** Men **Affiliation:** Jewish **Admission Plans:** Open Admission **Professional Accreditation:** AARTS

YESHIVA KARLIN STOLIN RABBINICAL INSTITUTE
1818 Fifty-fourth St.
Brooklyn, NY 11204
Tel: (718)232-7800
Fax: (718)331-4833
President/CEO: Mayer Pilchick
Financial Aid: Daniel Ross
Type: Comprehensive **Sex:** Men **Affiliation:** Jewish **% Accepted:** 100 **Admission Plans:** Preferred Admission **Application Deadline:** Rolling **H.S. Requirements:** High school diploma required; GED accepted **Scholarships:** Available **Calendar System:** Semester, Summer Session Not available **Library Holdings:** 6,000 **Credit Hours For Degree:** 130 credits, Bachelors **Professional Accreditation:** AARTS

YESHIVA AND KOLEL BAIS MEDRASH ELYON
73 Main St.
Monsey, NY 10952
Tel: (845)356-7064
President/CEO: Rabbi Rachmiel Ungarischer

Type: Four-Year College **Sex:** Men **Affiliation:** Jewish **% Accepted:** 100 **Professional Accreditation:** AARTS

YESHIVA AND KOLLEL HARBOTZAS TORAH
1049 East 15th St.
Brooklyn, NY 11230
Tel: (718)692-0208
President/CEO: Yekusiel Bittersfeld
Type: Four-Year College **Sex:** Men **Affiliation:** Jewish **Professional Accreditation:** AARTS

YESHIVA OF NITRA RABBINICAL COLLEGE
Pines Bridge Rd.
Mount Kisco, NY 10549
Tel: (718)384-5460
President/CEO: Alexander Fischer
Financial Aid: Yosef Rosen
Type: Comprehensive **Sex:** Men **Affiliation:** Jewish **H.S. Requirements:** High school diploma required; GED accepted **Calendar System:** Semester **Professional Accreditation:** AARTS

YESHIVA SHAAR HATORAH TALMUDIC RESEARCH INSTITUTE
117-06 84th Ave.
Kew Gardens, NY 11418-1469
Tel: (718)846-1940
President/CEO: Rabbi Yankelewitz
Financial Aid: Yoel Yankelewitz
Type: Comprehensive **Sex:** Men **Affiliation:** Jewish **Application Fee:** $100.00 **Scholarships:** Available **Calendar System:** Semester **Professional Accreditation:** AARTS

YESHIVA SHAAREI TORAH OF ROCKLAND
91 West Carlton Rd.
Suffern, NY 10901
Tel: (845)352-3431
Type: Four-Year College **Sex:** Men **Affiliation:** Jewish **Application Fee:** $250.00 **Professional Accreditation:** AARTS

YESHIVA OF THE TELSHE ALUMNI
4904 Independence Ave.
Riverdale, NY 10471
Tel: (718)601-3523
President/CEO: Noson Joseph
Type: Four-Year College **Sex:** Men **Affiliation:** Jewish **% Accepted:** 100 **Application Fee:** $50.00 **Professional Accreditation:** AARTS

YESHIVA UNIVERSITY
500 West 185th St.
New York, NY 10033-3201
Tel: (212)960-5400
Admissions: (212)960-5277
Fax: (212)960-0086
Web Site: http://www.yu.edu/
President/CEO: Richard Joel, JD
Admissions: Michael Kranzler
Financial Aid: Jean Belmont
Type: University **Sex:** Coed **Scores:** 99.58% SAT V 400+; 99.58% SAT M 400+; 35.64% ACT 18-23; 47.52% ACT 24-29 **% Accepted:** 63 **Admission Plans:** Early Admission; Deferred Admission **Application Deadline:** February 1 **Application Fee:** $65.00 **H.S. Requirements:** High school diploma required; GED accepted **Costs Per Year:** Application fee: $65. Comprehensive fee: $42,474 includes full-time tuition ($31,594), mandatory fees ($500), and college room and board ($10,380). College room only: $7510. Part-time tuition: $1075 per credit. **Scholarships:** Available **Calendar System:** Semester, Summer Session Available **Enrollment:** FT 2,782, PT 89, Grad FT 2,761, Grad PT 614 **Student-Faculty Ratio:** 7:1 **Exams:** SAT I or ACT. **% Receiving Financial Aid:** 41 **% Residing in College-Owned, -Operated, or -Affiliated Housing:** 78 **Regional Accreditation:** Middle State Association of Colleges and Schools **Credit Hours For Degree:** 128 credits, Bachelors **Professional Accreditation:** ABA, APA, AALS, CSWE, LCMEAMA **Intercollegiate Athletics:** Baseball M; Basketball M & W; Cross-Country Running M & W; Fencing M & W; Golf M; Soccer M & W; Tennis M & W; Volleyball M; Wrestling M

YESHIVAS NOVOMINSK
1569 47th St.
Brooklyn, NY 11219
Tel: (718)438-2727
President/CEO: Lipa Brennan
Type: Four-Year College **Sex:** Men **Affiliation:** Jewish **% Accepted:** 100 **Application Fee:** $100.00 **Professional Accreditation:** AARTS

YESHIVAT MIKDASH MELECH
1326 Ocean Parkway
Brooklyn, NY 11230-5601
Tel: (718)339-1090
E-mail: mikdashmelech@verizon.net
President/CEO: Haim Benoliel
Admissions: Rabbi S. Beyda
Type: Four-Year College **Sex:** Men **Affiliation:** Jewish **% Accepted:** 100 **Application Deadline:** Rolling **Calendar System:** Continuous **Professional Accreditation:** AARTS

YESHIVATH VIZNITZ
25 Phyllis Terrace
Monsey, NY 10952
Tel: (914)356-1010
President/CEO: R. Gershon Neiman
Type: Comprehensive **Sex:** Men **Affiliation:** Jewish **% Accepted:** 100 **Calendar System:** Semester **Professional Accreditation:** AARTS

YESHIVATH ZICHRON MOSHE
Laurel Park Rd.
South Fallsburg, NY 12779
Tel: (914)434-5240
Admissions: Rabbi Abba Gorelick
Financial Aid: Miryom R. Miller
Type: Comprehensive **Sex:** Men **Affiliation:** Jewish **% Accepted:** 100 **Calendar System:** Semester **Professional Accreditation:** AARTS

YORK COLLEGE OF THE CITY UNIVERSITY OF NEW YORK
94-20 Guy R Brewer Blvd.
Jamaica, NY 11451-0001
Tel: (718)262-2000
Admissions: (718)262-2188
E-mail: warmsley@york.cuny.edu
Web Site: http://www.york.cuny.edu/
President/CEO: Dr. Marcia Keizs
Admissions: Diane Warmsley
Financial Aid: Cathy Tsiapanos
Type: Comprehensive **Sex:** Coed **Affiliation:** City University of New York System **Scores:** 76.05% SAT V 400+; 82.6% SAT M 400+ **Admission Plans:** Early Admission; Deferred Admission **Application Deadline:** Rolling **Application Fee:** $65.00 **H.S. Requirements:** High school diploma required; GED accepted **Costs Per Year:** Application fee: $65. State resident tuition: $4600 full-time, $195 per credit part-time. Nonresident tuition: $9960 full-time, $415 per credit part-time. Mandatory fees: $312 full-time. Tuition guaranteed not to increase for student's term of enrollment. **Scholarships:** Available **Calendar System:** Semester, Summer Session Available **Enrollment:** FT 4,886, PT 2,846, Grad FT 44, Grad PT 4 **Faculty:** FT 220, PT 304 **Student-Faculty Ratio:** 17:1 **Exams:** SAT I or ACT. ACT essay not being used. SAT essay not being used. **% Receiving Financial Aid:** 69 **Library Holdings:** 424,049 **Regional Accreditation:** Middle State Association of Colleges and Schools **Credit Hours For Degree:** 120 credits, Bachelors **ROTC:** Army, Air Force **Professional Accreditation:** AOTA, CSWE, NLN **Intercollegiate Athletics:** Baseball M & W; Basketball M & W; Cross-Country Running M & W; Soccer M; Softball W; Swimming and Diving M & W; Tennis M; Track and Field M & W; Volleyball M & W

ALAMANCE COMMUNITY COLLEGE
PO Box 8000
Graham, NC 27253-8000
Tel: (336)578-2002
Admissions: (336)506-4120
Fax: (336)578-1987
E-mail: brehlere@alamancecc.edu
Web Site: http://www.alamancecc.edu/
President/CEO: Dr. Martin Nadelman
Admissions: Elizabeth Brehler
Financial Aid: Elizabeth Solazzo
Type: Two-Year College **Sex:** Coed **Affiliation:** North Carolina Community College System **% Accepted:** 100 **Admission Plans:** Open Admission **Application Deadline:** Rolling **Application Fee:** $0.00 **H.S. Requirements:** High school diploma required; GED accepted **Costs Per Year:** Application fee: $0. State resident tuition: $1600 full-time, $50 per credit hour part-time. Nonresident tuition: $7720 full-time, $241.30 per credit hour part-time. Mandatory fees: $30 full-time, $5 per term part-time. Full-time tuition and fees vary according to course load. Part-time tuition and fees vary according to course load. **Scholarships:** Available **Calendar System:** Semester, Summer Session Available **Enrollment:** FT 2,717, PT 2,766 **Faculty:** FT 102, PT 284 **Student-Faculty Ratio:** 12:1 **Library Holdings:** 22,114 **Regional Accreditation:** Southern Association of Colleges and Schools **Credit Hours For Degree:** 64 semester hours, Associates **Professional Accreditation:** ADA, NAACLS

APEX SCHOOL OF THEOLOGY
2945 South Miami Blvd., Ste. 114
Durham, NC 27703
Tel: (919)572-1625
Fax: (919)572-1762
E-mail: registrar@apexsot.edu
Web Site: http://www.apexsot.edu/
President/CEO: Dr. Joseph Perkins
Admissions: Dr. Henry D. Wells, Jr.
Type: Comprehensive **Sex:** Coed **Affiliation:** interdenominational **% Accepted:** 100 **Admission Plans:** Open Admission **Application Fee:** $0.00 **H.S. Requirements:** High school diploma required; GED accepted **Calendar System:** Semester **Enrollment:** FT 166, PT 21, Grad FT 91, Grad PT 16 **Faculty:** FT 3, PT 12 **Professional Accreditation:** TACCS

APPALACHIAN STATE UNIVERSITY
Boone, NC 28608
Tel: (828)262-2000
Admissions: (828)262-2120
Fax: (828)262-3296
E-mail: admissions@appstate.edu
Web Site: http://www.appstate.edu/
President/CEO: Dr. Kenneth Peacock
Admissions: Misti Reese
Financial Aid: Esther Manogin
Type: Comprehensive **Sex:** Coed **Affiliation:** University of North Carolina System **Scores:** 99.25% SAT V 400+; 99.77% SAT M 400+; 41.06% ACT 18-23; 49.92% ACT 24-29 **% Accepted:** 63 **Admission Plans:** Deferred Admission **Application Fee:** $50.00 **H.S. Requirements:** High school diploma required; GED not accepted **Costs Per Year:** Application fee: $50. State resident tuition: $2341 full-time, $79 per semester hour part-time. Nonresident tuition: $12,962 full-time, $437.75 per semester hour part-time. Mandatory fees: $2084 full-time, $12.25 per semester hour part-time. Part-time tuition and fees vary according to course load. College room and board: $6400. College room only: $3500. Room and board charges vary according to board plan and housing facility. **Scholarships:** Available **Calendar System:** Semester, Summer Session Available **Enrollment:** FT 14,116, PT 756, Grad FT 807, Grad PT 1,289 **Faculty:** FT 824, PT 320 **Student-Faculty Ratio:** 17:1 **Exams:** SAT I or ACT. ACT essay used for admission. SAT essay used for admission. ACT essay used for placement. SAT essay used for placement. **% Receiving Financial Aid:** 41 **% Residing in College-Owned, -Operated, or -Affiliated Housing:** 33 **Final Year or Final Semester Residency Requirement:** No **Library Holdings:** 955,717 **Regional Accreditation:** Southern Association of Colleges and Schools **Credit Hours For Degree:** 122 semester hours, Bachelors **ROTC:** Army **Professional Accreditation:** AACSB, ABET, AAMFT, AAFCS, ACA, ADtA, APA, ASLHA, CSWE, JRCEPAT, NASAD, NASM, NASPAA, NAST, NCATE, NRPA **Intercollegiate Athletics:** Baseball M; Basketball M & W; Cross-Country Running M & W; Field Hockey W; Football M; Golf M & W; Soccer M & W; Softball W; Tennis M & W; Track and Field M & W; Volleyball W; Wrestling M

THE ART INSTITUTE OF CHARLOTTE
Three LakePointe Plaza
2110 Water Ridge Parkway
Charlotte, NC 28217
Tel: (704)357-8020; Free: 800-872-4417
Fax: (704)357-1133
Web Site: http://www.artinstitutes.edu/charlotte/
President/CEO: Stacey Sweeney
Type: Four-Year College **Sex:** Coed **Affiliation:** Education Management Corporation **Calendar System:** Quarter, Summer Session Available **Professional Accreditation:** ACICS

THE ART INSTITUTE OF RALEIGH-DURHAM
410 Blackwell St.
Ste. 200
Durham, NC 27701
Free: 888-245-9593
Web Site: http://www.artinstitutes.edu/raleigh-durham
President/CEO: Mike DePrisco
Type: Four-Year College **Sex:** Coed **Affiliation:** Education Management Corporation

ASHEVILLE-BUNCOMBE TECHNICAL COMMUNITY COLLEGE
340 Victoria Rd.
Asheville, NC 28801-4897
Tel: (828)254-1921
Fax: (828)251-6355
E-mail: lbush@abtech.edu
Web Site: http://www.abtech.edu/
President/CEO: Richard Mauney
Admissions: Lisa Bush
Type: Two-Year College **Sex:** Coed **Affiliation:** North Carolina Community

College System **% Accepted:** 100 **Admission Plans:** Open Admission; Deferred Admission **Application Deadline:** Rolling **Application Fee:** $0.00 **H.S. Requirements:** High school diploma required; GED accepted **Scholarships:** Available **Calendar System:** Semester, Summer Session Available **Student-Faculty Ratio:** 17:1 **Library Holdings:** 37,439 **Regional Accreditation:** Southern Association of Colleges and Schools **Credit Hours For Degree:** 64 semester hours, Associates **Professional Accreditation:** ADA, JRCERT, NAACLS

BARTON COLLEGE
PO Box 5000
Wilson, NC 27893-7000
Tel: (252)399-6300; Free: 800-345-4973
Fax: (252)237-4957
E-mail: ahmetts@barton.edu
Web Site: http://www.barton.edu/
President/CEO: Dr. Norval C. Kneten
Admissions: Amanda Metts
Financial Aid: Bridget Ellis
Type: Four-Year College **Sex:** Coed **Affiliation:** Christian Church (Disciples of Christ) **Scores:** 89% SAT V 400+; 90% SAT M 400+; 60% ACT 18-23; 6% ACT 24-29 **% Accepted:** 51 **Admission Plans:** Deferred Admission **Application Deadline:** Rolling **Application Fee:** $25.00 **H.S. Requirements:** High school diploma required; GED accepted **Costs Per Year:** Application fee: $25. Comprehensive fee: $27,660 includes full-time tuition ($19,100), mandatory fees ($1548), and college room and board ($7012). College room only: $3782. Full-time tuition and fees vary according to class time, course load, and program. Room and board charges vary according to housing facility. Part-time tuition: $810 per credit hour. Part-time tuition varies according to class time, course load, and program. **Scholarships:** Available **Calendar System:** 4-1-4, Summer Session Available **Enrollment:** FT 875, PT 275 **Faculty:** FT 68, PT 49 **Student-Faculty Ratio:** 12:1 **Exams:** SAT I or ACT. **% Receiving Financial Aid:** 84 **% Residing in College-Owned, -Operated, or -Affiliated Housing:** 48 **Regional Accreditation:** Southern Association of Colleges and Schools **Credit Hours For Degree:** 126 semester hours, Bachelors **Professional Accreditation:** CSWE, NCATE, NLN **Intercollegiate Athletics:** Baseball M; Basketball M & W; Cross-Country Running M & W; Golf M; Soccer M & W; Softball W; Tennis M & W; Volleyball W

BEAUFORT COUNTY COMMUNITY COLLEGE
PO Box 1069
Washington, NC 27889-1069
Tel: (252)946-6194
Admissions: (252)940-6233
Fax: (252)946-0271
E-mail: garyb@beaufortccc.edu
Web Site: http://www.beaufortccc.edu/
President/CEO: Dr. David McLawhorn
Admissions: Gary Burbage
Financial Aid: Karen Toler
Type: Two-Year College **Sex:** Coed **Affiliation:** North Carolina Community College System **% Accepted:** 100 **Admission Plans:** Open Admission **Application Deadline:** Rolling **Application Fee:** $0.00 **H.S. Requirements:** High school diploma required; GED accepted. **Costs Per Year:** Application fee: $0. State resident tuition: $1600 full-time, $50 per credit hour part-time. Nonresident tuition: $7722 full-time, $241 per credit hour part-time. Mandatory fees: $64 full-time, $2 per credit hour part-time. Part-time tuition and fees vary according to course load. **Scholarships:** Available **Calendar System:** Semester, Summer Session Available **Exams:** Other, SAT I or ACT. **Library Holdings:** 25,734 **Regional Accreditation:** Southern Association of Colleges and Schools **Professional Accreditation:** NAACLS

BELMONT ABBEY COLLEGE
100 Belmont-Mt. Holly Rd.
Belmont, NC 28012-1802
Tel: (704)825-6700; Free: 888-BAC-0110
Admissions: (704)461-6668
Fax: (704)825-6670
E-mail: danielleblanchard@bac.edu
Web Site: http://www.belmontabbeycollege.edu/
President/CEO: Dr. William Thierfelder
Admissions: Danielle Blanchard
Financial Aid: Julie Hodge
Type: Four-Year College **Sex:** Coed **Affiliation:** Roman Catholic **Scores:** 94% SAT V 400+; 95% SAT M 400+ **% Accepted:** 63 **Admission Plans:** Deferred Admission **Application Deadline:** August 1 **Application Fee:** $35.00 **H.S. Requirements:** High school diploma required; GED accepted **Costs Per Year:** Application fee: $35. One-time mandatory fee: $1006. Comprehensive fee: $31,454 includes full-time tuition ($20,356), mandatory fees ($1150), and college room and board ($9948). College room only: $5766. Full-time tuition and fees vary according to class time, course level, course load, location, program, and reciprocity agreements. Room and board charges vary according to board plan, housing facility, and location. Part-time tuition: $678 per credit hour. Part-time mandatory fees: $38 per credit hour. Part-time tuition and fees vary according to class time, course level, course load, location, and reciprocity agreements. **Scholarships:** Available **Calendar System:** Semester, Summer Session Available **Enrollment:** FT 1,520, PT 118 **Faculty:** FT 69, PT 63 **Student-Faculty Ratio:** 18:1 **Exams:** SAT I or ACT. **% Receiving Financial Aid:** 79 **% Residing in College-Owned, -Operated, or -Affiliated Housing:** 48 **Library Holdings:** 118,827 **Regional Accreditation:** Southern Association of Colleges and Schools **Credit Hours For Degree:** 120 credit hours, Bachelors **ROTC:** Army, Air Force **Professional Accreditation:** NCATE **Intercollegiate Athletics:** Baseball M; Basketball M & W; Cheerleading M & W; Cross-Country Running M & W; Golf M & W; Lacrosse M & W; Soccer M & W; Softball W; Tennis M & W; Track and Field M & W; Volleyball W; Wrestling M

BENNETT COLLEGE FOR WOMEN
900 East Washington St.
Greensboro, NC 27401-3239
Tel: (336)273-4431
Admissions: (336)517-2167
E-mail: jbiggs@bennett.edu
Web Site: http://www.bennett.edu/
President/CEO: Dr. Julianne Malveaux
Admissions: Jocelyn Biggs
Financial Aid: Monty K. Hickman
Type: Four-Year College **Sex:** Women **Affiliation:** United Methodist **Scores:** 52% SAT V 400+; 35% SAT M 400+ **% Accepted:** 54 **Admission Plans:** Deferred Admission **Application Deadline:** Rolling **Application Fee:** $30.00 **H.S. Requirements:** High school diploma required; GED accepted **Scholarships:** Available **Calendar System:** Semester, Summer Session Available **Enrollment:** FT 709, PT 57 **Faculty:** FT 56, PT 26 **Student-Faculty Ratio:** 11:1 **Exams:** SAT I or ACT. **% Receiving Financial Aid:** 85 **% Residing in College-Owned, -Operated, or -Affiliated Housing:** 62 **Final Year or Final Semester Residency Requirement:** No **Library Holdings:** 90,161 **Regional Accreditation:** Southern Association of Colleges and Schools **Credit Hours For Degree:** 124 semester hours, Bachelors **ROTC:** Army, Air Force **Professional Accreditation:** CSWE, NCATE **Intercollegiate Athletics:** Basketball W

BLADEN COMMUNITY COLLEGE
PO Box 266
Dublin, NC 28332-0266
Tel: (910)879-5500
Admissions: (910)879-5593
Fax: (910)879-5508
E-mail: acarterfisher@bladencc.edu
Web Site: http://www.bladen.cc.nc.us/
President/CEO: Dr. William Findt
Admissions: Andrea Fisher
Type: Two-Year College **Sex:** Coed **Affiliation:** North Carolina Community College System **Admission Plans:** Open Admission; Deferred Admission **Application Deadline:** August 1 **Application Fee:** $0.00 **H.S. Requirements:** High school diploma required; GED accepted **Costs Per Year:** Application fee: $0. State resident tuition: $1200 full-time. Nonresident tuition: $5791 full-time. Mandatory fees: $83 full-time. Full-time tuition and fees vary according to course load. **Scholarships:** Available **Calendar System:** Semester, Summer Session Available **Faculty:** FT 35, PT 50 **Exams:** Other, SAT I or ACT. **Library Holdings:** 19,881 **Regional Accreditation:** Southern Association of Colleges and Schools **Credit Hours For Degree:** 64 semester hours, Associates

BLUE RIDGE COMMUNITY COLLEGE
180 West Campus Dr.
Flat Rock, NC 28731
Tel: (828)694-1700

Fax: (828)694-1690
E-mail: kirstenb@blueridge.edu
Web Site: http://www.blueridge.edu/
President/CEO: Molly A. Parkhill
Admissions: Kirsten Bunch
Type: Two-Year College **Sex:** Coed **Affiliation:** North Carolina Community College System **Admission Plans:** Open Admission; Early Admission **Application Deadline:** Rolling **H.S. Requirements:** High school diploma required; GED accepted **Scholarships:** Available **Calendar System:** Semester, Summer Session Available **Enrollment:** FT 766, PT 1,722 **Library Holdings:** 47,655 **Regional Accreditation:** Southern Association of Colleges and Schools **Credit Hours For Degree:** 64 credit hours, Associates **Intercollegiate Athletics:** Baseball M; Volleyball W

BREVARD COLLEGE
1 Brevard College Dr.
Brevard, NC 28712-3306
Tel: (828)883-8292; Free: 800-527-9090
Admissions: (828)884-8378
Fax: (828)884-3790
E-mail: admissions@brevard.edu
Web Site: http://www.brevard.edu/
President/CEO: Dr. Drew L. Van Horn
Admissions: Karen Atkins
Financial Aid: Lisanne J. Masterson
Type: Four-Year College **Sex:** Coed **Affiliation:** United Methodist **Scores:** 90% SAT V 400+; 82% SAT M 400+; 60% ACT 18-23; 10% ACT 24-29 **% Accepted:** 54 **Admission Plans:** Deferred Admission **Application Deadline:** Rolling **Application Fee:** $30.00 **H.S. Requirements:** High school diploma required; GED accepted **Costs Per Year:** Application fee: $30. Comprehensive fee: $28,750 includes full-time tuition ($20,900) and college room and board ($7850). Full-time tuition varies according to course load. Room and board charges vary according to board plan and housing facility. Part-time tuition: $770 per contact hour. Part-time tuition varies according to course load. **Scholarships:** Available **Calendar System:** Semester, Summer Session Not available **Enrollment:** FT 642, PT 16 **Faculty:** FT 55, PT 35 **Student-Faculty Ratio:** 10:1 **Exams:** SAT I or ACT. ACT essay not being used. SAT essay not being used. **% Receiving Financial Aid:** 72 **% Residing in College-Owned, -Operated, or -Affiliated Housing:** 74 **Library Holdings:** 181,963 **Regional Accreditation:** Southern Association of Colleges and Schools **Credit Hours For Degree:** 124 semester hours, Bachelors **Professional Accreditation:** NASM **Intercollegiate Athletics:** Baseball M; Basketball M & W; Cheerleading W; Cross-Country Running M & W; Football M; Golf M & W; Soccer M & W; Softball W; Tennis M & W; Track and Field M & W; Volleyball W

BRUNSWICK COMMUNITY COLLEGE
50 College Rd.
PO Box 30
Supply, NC 28462-0030
Tel: (910)755-7300; Free: 800-754-1050
Fax: (910)754-9609
E-mail: olsenj@brunswickcc.edu
Web Site: http://www.brunswickcc.edu/
President/CEO: Stephen G. Greiner
Admissions: Julie Olsen
Type: Two-Year College **Sex:** Coed **Affiliation:** North Carolina Community College System **Admission Plans:** Open Admission **Application Deadline:** Rolling **Application Fee:** $0.00 **H.S. Requirements:** High school diploma required; GED accepted **Scholarships:** Available **Calendar System:** Semester, Summer Session Available **Enrollment:** FT 433, PT 578 **Faculty:** FT 32, PT 73 **Student-Faculty Ratio:** 11:1 **Library Holdings:** 20,032 **Regional Accreditation:** Southern Association of Colleges and Schools **Credit Hours For Degree:** 64 semester hours, Associates **Professional Accreditation:** AHIMA **Intercollegiate Athletics:** Basketball M & W; Golf M; Softball W

CABARRUS COLLEGE OF HEALTH SCIENCES
401 Medical Park Dr.
Concord, NC 28025
Tel: (704)783-1555
Admissions: (704)403-1616
Fax: (704)783-1764
E-mail: mellison@cabarruscollege.edu
Web Site: http://www.cabarruscollege.edu/
President/CEO: Dianne Snyder
Admissions: Mark Ellison
Financial Aid: Valerie Richard
Type: Four-Year College **Sex:** Coed **Scores:** 95% SAT V 400+; 90% SAT M 400+; 70% ACT 18-23; 21% ACT 24-29 **% Accepted:** 43 **Application Deadline:** March 1 **Application Fee:** $35.00 **H.S. Requirements:** High school diploma required; GED accepted **Costs Per Year:** Application fee: $35. Tuition: $9660 full-time, $300 per semester hour part-time. Mandatory fees: $290 full-time. **Scholarships:** Available **Calendar System:** Semester, Summer Session Not available **Enrollment:** FT 226, PT 146 **Faculty:** FT 25, PT 26 **Student-Faculty Ratio:** 7:1 **Exams:** SAT I or ACT. **Regional Accreditation:** Southern Association of Colleges and Schools **Credit Hours For Degree:** 61 semester hours, Associates; 120 semester hours, Bachelors **Professional Accreditation:** ARCEST, AACN, AOTA, NLN

CALDWELL COMMUNITY COLLEGE AND TECHNICAL INSTITUTE
2855 Hickory Blvd.
Hudson, NC 28638-2397
Tel: (828)726-2200
Admissions: (828)726-2703
Fax: (828)726-2490
E-mail: cwoodard@cccti.edu
Web Site: http://www.cccti.edu/
President/CEO: Dr. Kenneth A. Boham
Admissions: Carolyn Woodard
Type: Two-Year College **Sex:** Coed **Affiliation:** North Carolina Community College System **Admission Plans:** Open Admission; Early Admission **Application Deadline:** Rolling **Application Fee:** $0.00 **H.S. Requirements:** High school diploma required; GED accepted **Costs Per Year:** Application fee: $0. One-time mandatory fee: $28. State resident tuition: $1600 full-time, $50 per credit hour part-time. Nonresident tuition: $7800 full-time, $241.30 per credit hour part-time. Mandatory fees: $7. Full-time tuition varies according to course load and program. Part-time tuition and fees vary according to course load and program. **Scholarships:** Available **Calendar System:** Semester, Summer Session Available **Enrollment:** FT 1,388, PT 2,340 **Faculty:** FT 130, PT 290 **Library Holdings:** 50,770 **Regional Accreditation:** Southern Association of Colleges and Schools **Credit Hours For Degree:** 65 semester hours, Associates **Professional Accreditation:** JRCEDMS, JRCERT, JRCNMT **Intercollegiate Athletics:** Basketball M & W; Golf M; Volleyball W

CAMPBELL UNIVERSITY
450 Leslie Campbell Ave.
Buies Creek, NC 27506
Tel: (910)893-1200; Free: 800-334-4111
Admissions: (910)893-1290
Fax: (910)893-1288
E-mail: adm@mailcenter.campbell.edu
Web Site: http://www.campbell.edu/
President/CEO: Dr. Jerry M. Wallace
Admissions: Peggy Mason
Type: University **Sex:** Coed **Affiliation:** North Carolina Baptist State Convention **Scores:** 92% SAT V 400+; 92% SAT M 400+ **% Accepted:** 60 **Admission Plans:** Early Admission; Deferred Admission **Application Deadline:** Rolling **Application Fee:** $35.00 **H.S. Requirements:** High school diploma required; GED accepted **Scholarships:** Available **Calendar System:** Semester, Summer Session Available **Enrollment:** FT 2,731, PT 203 **Faculty:** FT 196, PT 109 **Student-Faculty Ratio:** 14:1 **Exams:** SAT I or ACT. **% Receiving Financial Aid:** 79 **% Residing in College-Owned, -Operated, or -Affiliated Housing:** 62 **Library Holdings:** 231,298 **Regional Accreditation:** Southern Association of Colleges and Schools **Credit Hours For Degree:** 64 semester hours, Associates; 128 semester hours, Bachelors **ROTC:** Army **Professional Accreditation:** ACPhE, ABA, ACBSP, ATS, CSWE, JRCEPAT, NCATE **Intercollegiate Athletics:** Baseball M; Basketball M & W; Cheerleading W; Cross-Country Running M & W; Golf M & W; Soccer M & W; Softball W; Swimming and Diving W; Tennis M & W; Track and Field M & W; Volleyball W; Wrestling M

CAPE FEAR COMMUNITY COLLEGE
411 North Front St.
Wilmington, NC 28401-3993
Tel: (910)362-7000
Admissions: (910)362-7054

E-mail: admissions@cfcc.edu
Web Site: http://www.cfcc.edu/
President/CEO: Dr. Eric B. McKeithan
Admissions: Linda Kasyan
Financial Aid: Jo-Ann Craig
Type: Two-Year College **Sex:** Coed **Affiliation:** North Carolina Community College System **Admission Plans:** Open Admission; Early Admission **Application Deadline:** August 15 **Application Fee:** $0.00 **H.S. Requirements:** High school diploma required; GED accepted **Costs Per Year:** Application fee: $0. State resident tuition: $1600 full-time, $50 per credit part-time. Nonresident tuition: $7722 full-time, $241.30 per credit part-time. Mandatory fees: $137 full-time. Full-time tuition and fees vary according to course load. Part-time tuition varies according to course load. **Scholarships:** Available **Calendar System:** Semester, Summer Session Available **Enrollment:** FT 3,984, PT 5,005 **Faculty:** FT 258, PT 237 **Student-Faculty Ratio:** 15:1 **Library Holdings:** 47,352 **Regional Accreditation:** Southern Association of Colleges and Schools **Credit Hours For Degree:** 64 semester hours, Associates **Professional Accreditation:** ADA, AOTA, NLN **Intercollegiate Athletics:** Basketball M; Cheerleading M & W; Golf M & W; Soccer M & W; Volleyball M & W

CAROLINA CHRISTIAN COLLEGE
4209 Indiana Ave.
PO Box 777
Winston-Salem, NC 27102-0777
Tel: (336)744-0900
Fax: (336)744-0901
E-mail: info@wsbc.edu
Web Site: http://www.carolina.edu/
President/CEO: Donald Young, PhD
Financial Aid: LaTanya V. Lucas
Type: Four-Year College **Sex:** Coed **Affiliation:** nondenominational **Admission Plans:** Open Admission **Application Deadline:** Rolling **Application Fee:** $50.00 **H.S. Requirements:** High school diploma required; GED accepted **Costs Per Year:** Application fee: $50. Tuition: $6200 full-time, $875 per course part-time. **Scholarships:** Available **Calendar System:** Semester **Enrollment:** FT 20, PT 3 **Faculty:** FT 1, PT 8 **Student-Faculty Ratio:** 40:1 **% Receiving Financial Aid:** 90 **Final Year or Final Semester Residency Requirement:** No **Library Holdings:** 30,000 **Professional Accreditation:** ABHE

CAROLINAS COLLEGE OF HEALTH SCIENCES
PO Box 32861, 1200 Blythe Blvd.
Charlotte, NC 28232-2861
Tel: (704)355-5043
Fax: (704)355-5967
E-mail: cchsinformation@carolinashealthcare.org
Web Site: http://www.carolinascollege.edu/
President/CEO: Dr. Ellen Sheppard
Admissions: Nicki Sabourin
Financial Aid: Jill Powell
Type: Two-Year College **Sex:** Coed **% Accepted:** 25 **Admission Plans:** Preferred Admission **Application Deadline:** February 5 **Application Fee:** $50.00 **H.S. Requirements:** High school diploma required; GED accepted **Costs Per Year:** Application fee: $50. Tuition: $7848 full-time, $218 per credit hour part-time. Mandatory fees: $215 full-time, $110 per term part-time. Full-time tuition and fees vary according to course load and program. Part-time tuition and fees vary according to course load and program. **Scholarships:** Available **Calendar System:** Semester, Summer Session Available **Enrollment:** FT 101, PT 409 **Faculty:** FT 26, PT 45 **Student-Faculty Ratio:** 7:1 **Exams:** SAT I or ACT. ACT essay not being used. SAT essay not being used. **Final Year or Final Semester Residency Requirement:** Yes **Library Holdings:** 9,810 **Regional Accreditation:** Southern Association of Colleges and Schools **Credit Hours For Degree:** 60 credit hours, Associates **Professional Accreditation:** NAACLS, NLN

CARTERET COMMUNITY COLLEGE
3505 Arendell St.
Morehead City, NC 28557-2989
Tel: (252)222-6000
Admissions: (252)222-6155
Fax: (252)222-6274
E-mail: admissions@carteret.edu
Web Site: http://www.carteret.edu/
President/CEO: Dr. Kerry L. Youngblood
Admissions: Margie Ward
Financial Aid: Brenda J. Long
Type: Two-Year College **Sex:** Coed **Affiliation:** North Carolina Community College System **% Accepted:** 91 **Admission Plans:** Open Admission **Application Deadline:** Rolling **Application Fee:** $0.00 **H.S. Requirements:** High school diploma required; GED accepted **Costs Per Year:** Application fee: $0. State resident tuition: $1263 full-time, $50 per credit hour part-time. Nonresident tuition: $5854 full-time, $241.30 per credit hour part-time. Mandatory fees: $51 full-time, $19.25 per term part-time. Full-time tuition and fees vary according to course load and program. **Scholarships:** Available **Calendar System:** Semester, Summer Session Available **Enrollment:** FT 804, PT 1,068 **Faculty:** FT 66, PT 187 **Student-Faculty Ratio:** 9:1 **Exams:** SAT I or ACT. **Library Holdings:** 22,000 **Regional Accreditation:** Southern Association of Colleges and Schools **Credit Hours For Degree:** 65 semester hours, Associates **Professional Accreditation:** CARC, JRCERT

CATAWBA COLLEGE
2300 West Innes St.
Salisbury, NC 28144-2488
Tel: (704)637-4111; Free: 800-CAT-AWBA
Admissions: (704)637-4414
E-mail: admissions@catawba.edu
Web Site: http://www.catawba.edu/
President/CEO: Dr. W. Craig Turner
Admissions: Lois Williams
Financial Aid: Melanie McCulloh
Type: Comprehensive **Sex:** Coed **Affiliation:** United Church of Christ **Scores:** 95% SAT V 400+; 97% SAT M 400+; 42% ACT 18-23; 36% ACT 24-29 **% Accepted:** 70 **Admission Plans:** Early Admission; Deferred Admission **Application Deadline:** Rolling **Application Fee:** $25.00 **H.S. Requirements:** High school diploma required; GED accepted **Costs Per Year:** Application fee: $25. Comprehensive fee: $31,940 includes full-time tuition ($23,740) and college room and board ($8200). Part-time tuition: $620 per credit hour. **Scholarships:** Available **Calendar System:** Semester, Summer Session Available **Enrollment:** FT 1,269, PT 55, Grad PT 34 **Faculty:** FT 71, PT 35 **Student-Faculty Ratio:** 16:1 **Exams:** SAT I or ACT. **% Receiving Financial Aid:** 74 **% Residing in College-Owned, -Operated, or -Affiliated Housing:** 72 **Final Year or Final Semester Residency Requirement:** Yes **Library Holdings:** 204,645 **Regional Accreditation:** Southern Association of Colleges and Schools **Credit Hours For Degree:** 124 semester hours, Bachelors **ROTC:** Army **Professional Accreditation:** JRCEPAT, NCATE **Intercollegiate Athletics:** Baseball M; Basketball M & W; Cheerleading M & W; Cross-Country Running M & W; Football M; Golf M & W; Lacrosse M; Soccer M & W; Softball W; Swimming and Diving M & W; Tennis M & W; Volleyball W

CATAWBA VALLEY COMMUNITY COLLEGE
2550 Hwy. 70 SE
Hickory, NC 28602-9699
Tel: (828)327-7000
Fax: (828)327-7000
E-mail: lwegner@cvcc.edu
Web Site: http://www.cvcc.edu/
President/CEO: Dr. Garrett Hinshaw
Admissions: Laurie Wegner
Type: Two-Year College **Sex:** Coed **Affiliation:** North Carolina Community College System **% Accepted:** 100 **Admission Plans:** Open Admission; Early Admission; Deferred Admission **Application Deadline:** Rolling **Application Fee:** $0.00 **H.S. Requirements:** High school diploma required; GED accepted. For some vocational programs: High school diploma required; GED not accepted **Costs Per Year:** Application fee: $0. State resident tuition: $1600 full-time, $50 per credit hour part-time. Nonresident tuition: $7723 full-time, $241 per credit hour part-time. Mandatory fees: $87 full-time, $43.50 per term part-time. Part-time tuition and fees vary according to course load. **Scholarships:** Available **Calendar System:** Semester, Summer Session Available **Enrollment:** FT 2,135, PT 3,393 **Faculty:** FT 144, PT 339 **Student-Faculty Ratio:** 11:1 **Final Year or Final Semester Residency Requirement:** No **Library Holdings:** 25,000 **Regional Accreditation:** Southern Association of Colleges and Schools **Credit Hours For Degree:** 65 semester hours, Associates **Professional Accreditation:** ADA, AHIMA, ACBSP, CARC, JRCEMT, NLN **Intercollegiate Athletics:** Baseball M; Basketball M & W; Volleyball W

CENTRAL CAROLINA COMMUNITY COLLEGE
1105 Kelly Dr.
Sanford, NC 27330-9000
Tel: (919)775-5401
Admissions: (919)718-7239
Fax: (919)775-1221
Web Site: http://www.cccc.edu/
President/CEO: Dr. T. Eston "Bud" Marchant
Admissions: Michelle Wheeler
Type: Two-Year College **Sex:** Coed **Affiliation:** North Carolina Community College System **Admission Plans:** Open Admission; Preferred Admission; Early Admission; Deferred Admission **Application Deadline:** Rolling **Application Fee:** $0.00 **H.S. Requirements:** High school diploma required; GED accepted **Costs Per Year:** Application fee: $0. State resident tuition: $1594 full-time. Nonresident tuition: $7329 full-time. Full-time tuition varies according to course load. **Scholarships:** Available **Calendar System:** Semester, Summer Session Available **Enrollment:** FT 5,411 **Faculty:** FT 352, PT 148 **Student-Faculty Ratio:** 10:1 **Library Holdings:** 50,479 **Regional Accreditation:** Southern Association of Colleges and Schools **Credit Hours For Degree:** 64 semester hours, Associates **Intercollegiate Athletics:** Basketball M & W; Golf M & W; Softball W; Volleyball W

CENTRAL PIEDMONT COMMUNITY COLLEGE
PO Box 35009
Charlotte, NC 28235-5009
Tel: (704)330-2722
Admissions: (704)330-6784
Web Site: http://www.cpcc.edu/
President/CEO: Dr. P. Anthony Zeiss
Admissions: Linda McComb
Type: Two-Year College **Sex:** Coed **Affiliation:** North Carolina Community College System **% Accepted:** 100 **Admission Plans:** Open Admission **Application Deadline:** Rolling **Application Fee:** $0.00 **H.S. Requirements:** High school diploma required; GED accepted. For welding program: High school diploma required; GED not accepted **Costs Per Year:** Application fee: $0. State resident tuition: $1500 full-time, $50 per semester hour part-time. Nonresident tuition: $7722 full-time, $241.30 per semester hour part-time. Mandatory fees: $218 full-time, $1 per credit hour part-time, $60 per term part-time. **Scholarships:** Available **Calendar System:** Semester, Summer Session Available **Enrollment:** FT 7,630, PT 11,734 **Faculty:** FT 337, PT 1,404 **Library Holdings:** 102,649 **Regional Accreditation:** Southern Association of Colleges and Schools **Credit Hours For Degree:** 64 semester hours, Associates **Professional Accreditation:** ABET, AAMAE, ADA, AHIMA, APTA, CARC, NAACLS

CHOWAN UNIVERSITY
One University Place
Murfreesboro, NC 27855
Tel: (252)398-6500; Free: 888-4-Chowan
Admissions: (252)398-6298
Fax: (252)398-1190
E-mail: holtc@chowan.edu
Web Site: http://www.chowan.edu/
President/CEO: Dr. M Christopher White
Admissions: Chad Holt
Financial Aid: Sharon W. Rose
Type: Four-Year College **Sex:** Coed **Affiliation:** Baptist **% Accepted:** 53 **Application Deadline:** Rolling **Application Fee:** $20.00 **H.S. Requirements:** High school diploma required; GED accepted **Costs Per Year:** Application fee: $20. One-time mandatory fee: $145. Comprehensive fee: $26,160 includes full-time tuition ($18,850) and college room and board ($7310). College room only: $3460. Room and board charges vary according to board plan. Part-time tuition: $325 per credit hour. **Scholarships:** Available **Calendar System:** Semester, Summer Session Available **Enrollment:** FT 1,080 **Faculty:** FT 53, PT 7 **Student-Faculty Ratio:** 16:1 **Exams:** SAT I or ACT. **% Receiving Financial Aid:** 94 **% Residing in College-Owned, -Operated, or -Affiliated Housing:** 78 **Final Year or Final Semester Residency Requirement:** No **Library Holdings:** 93,676 **Regional Accreditation:** Southern Association of Colleges and Schools **Credit Hours For Degree:** 61 semester hours, Associates; 120 semester hours, Bachelors **Professional Accreditation:** NASM, NCATE **Intercollegiate Athletics:** Baseball M; Basketball M & W; Bowling W; Cheerleading M & W; Football M; Golf M; Soccer M & W; Softball W; Tennis M & W; Volleyball W

CLEVELAND COMMUNITY COLLEGE
137 South Post Rd.
Shelby, NC 28152
Tel: (704)484-4000
E-mail: price@cleveland.cc.nc.us
Web Site: http://www.clevelandcommunitycollege.edu/
President/CEO: L. Steve Thornburg
Admissions: Alan Price
Type: Two-Year College **Sex:** Coed **Affiliation:** North Carolina Community College System **Admission Plans:** Open Admission; Deferred Admission **Application Deadline:** Rolling **Application Fee:** $0.00 **H.S. Requirements:** High school diploma required; GED accepted **Scholarships:** Available **Calendar System:** Semester, Summer Session Available **Enrollment:** FT 1,379, PT 1,962 **Faculty:** FT 83, PT 308 **Student-Faculty Ratio:** 9:1 **Library Holdings:** 34,000 **Regional Accreditation:** Southern Association of Colleges and Schools **Credit Hours For Degree:** 64 semester hours, Associates **Professional Accreditation:** JRCERT

COASTAL CAROLINA COMMUNITY COLLEGE
444 Western Blvd.
Jacksonville, NC 28546-6899
Tel: (910)455-1221
Admissions: (910)938-6241
Fax: (910)455-2767
E-mail: calihanh@coastal.cc.nc.us
Web Site: http://www.coastalcarolina.edu/
President/CEO: Dr. Ronald K. Lingle
Admissions: Heather Calihan
Type: Two-Year College **Sex:** Coed **Affiliation:** North Carolina Community College System **% Accepted:** 62 **Admission Plans:** Open Admission; Deferred Admission **Application Deadline:** Rolling **Application Fee:** $0.00 **H.S. Requirements:** High school diploma required; GED accepted **Scholarships:** Available **Calendar System:** Semester, Summer Session Available **Enrollment:** FT 1,476, PT 2,873 **Faculty:** FT 140, PT 329 **Student-Faculty Ratio:** 17:1 **Library Holdings:** 44,062 **Regional Accreditation:** Southern Association of Colleges and Schools **Credit Hours For Degree:** 64 semester hours, Associates **Professional Accreditation:** ARCEST, ADA, NAACLS

COLLEGE OF THE ALBEMARLE
PO Box 2327
Elizabeth City, NC 27906-2327
Tel: (252)335-0821
Fax: (252)335-2011
E-mail: kkrentz@albemarle.edu
Web Site: http://www.albemarle.edu/
President/CEO: Lynne M. Bunch
Admissions: Kenny Krentz
Type: Two-Year College **Sex:** Coed **Affiliation:** North Carolina Community College System **Scores:** 52% SAT V 400+; 64% SAT M 400+ **Admission Plans:** Open Admission; Early Admission; Deferred Admission **Application Deadline:** Rolling **Application Fee:** $0.00 **H.S. Requirements:** High school diploma required; GED accepted **Costs Per Year:** Application fee: $0. One-time mandatory fee: $25. State resident tuition: $1600 full-time, $50 per hour part-time. Nonresident tuition: $7722 full-time, $241.30 per hour part-time. Full-time tuition varies according to course load and program. **Scholarships:** Available **Calendar System:** Semester, Summer Session Available **Enrollment:** FT 854, PT 1,217 **Faculty:** FT 60, PT 62 **Library Holdings:** 48,400 **Regional Accreditation:** Southern Association of Colleges and Schools **Credit Hours For Degree:** 65 semester hours, Associates **Professional Accreditation:** NLN **Intercollegiate Athletics:** Soccer M

CRAVEN COMMUNITY COLLEGE
800 College Ct.
New Bern, NC 28562-4984
Tel: (252)638-4131
Admissions: (252)638-7200
Fax: (252)638-4649
Web Site: http://www.craven.cc.nc.us/
President/CEO: Catherine Chew
Admissions: Millicent Fulford
Type: Two-Year College **Sex:** Coed **Affiliation:** North Carolina Community College System **Admission Plans:** Open Admission **Application Deadline:** Rolling **Application Fee:** $0.00 **H.S. Requirements:** High school diploma

required; GED accepted **Costs Per Year:** Application fee: $0. State resident tuition: $1600 full-time, $50 per credit hour part-time. Nonresident tuition: $7722 full-time, $241.50 per credit hour part-time. Mandatory fees: $60 full-time. Full-time tuition and fees vary according to course load. Part-time tuition varies according to course load. **Scholarships:** Available **Calendar System:** Semester, Summer Session Available **Library Holdings:** 21,000 **Regional Accreditation:** Southern Association of Colleges and Schools **Credit Hours For Degree:** 64 semester hours, Associates

DAVIDSON COLLEGE
Davidson, NC 28035
Tel: (704)894-2000; Free: 800-768-0380
Admissions: (704)894-2230
Fax: (704)894-2016
E-mail: admission@davidson.edu
Web Site: http://www.davidson.edu/
President/CEO: Thomas W. Ross
Admissions: Christopher J. Gruber
Financial Aid: David R. Gelinas
Type: Four-Year College **Sex:** Coed **Affiliation:** Presbyterian **Scores:** 100% SAT V 400+; 99% SAT M 400+; 2% ACT 18-23; 36% ACT 24-29 **% Accepted:** 26 **Admission Plans:** Early Admission; Early Decision Plan; Deferred Admission **Application Deadline:** January 2 **Application Fee:** $50.00 **H.S. Requirements:** High school diploma required; GED not accepted **Costs Per Year:** Application fee: $50. Comprehensive fee: $45,030 includes full-time tuition ($34,776), mandatory fees ($348), and college room and board ($9906). College room only: $5231. **Scholarships:** Available **Calendar System:** Semester, Summer Session Not available **Enrollment:** FT 1,743 **Faculty:** FT 164, PT 5 **Student-Faculty Ratio:** 11:1 **Exams:** SAT I or ACT, SAT II. **% Receiving Financial Aid:** 43 **% Residing in College-Owned, -Operated, or -Affiliated Housing:** 93 **Library Holdings:** 577,604 **Regional Accreditation:** Southern Association of Colleges and Schools **Credit Hours For Degree:** 32 courses, Bachelors **ROTC:** Army, Air Force **Professional Accreditation:** NCATE **Intercollegiate Athletics:** Baseball M; Basketball M & W; Crew M & W; Cross-Country Running M & W; Fencing M & W; Field Hockey W; Football M; Golf M; Lacrosse W; Rugby M; Sailing M & W; Soccer M & W; Swimming and Diving M & W; Tennis M & W; Track and Field M & W; Ultimate Frisbee M & W; Volleyball W; Weight Lifting M & W; Wrestling M

DAVIDSON COUNTY COMMUNITY COLLEGE
PO Box 1287
Lexington, NC 27293-1287
Tel: (336)249-8186
Fax: (336)249-0379
E-mail: admissions@davidsonccc.edu
Web Site: http://www.davidsonccc.edu/
President/CEO: Mary E. Rittling
Type: Two-Year College **Sex:** Coed **Affiliation:** North Carolina Community College System **% Accepted:** 100 **Admission Plans:** Open Admission; Early Admission; Deferred Admission **Application Deadline:** Rolling **Application Fee:** $0.00 **H.S. Requirements:** High school diploma or equivalent not required **Scholarships:** Available **Calendar System:** Semester, Summer Session Available **Enrollment:** FT 829, PT 1,474 **Faculty:** FT 72, PT 140 **Student-Faculty Ratio:** 11:1 **Library Holdings:** 56,445 **Regional Accreditation:** Southern Association of Colleges and Schools **Credit Hours For Degree:** 64 semester hours, Associates **Professional Accreditation:** ABET, AHIMA, NAACLS, NLN

DEVRY UNIVERSITY
2015 Ayrsley Town Blvd., Ste. 109
Charlotte, NC 28273-4068
Tel: (704)362-2345
Fax: (704)362-2668
Web Site: http://www.devry.edu/
President/CEO: Regina Campbell
Type: Comprehensive **Sex:** Coed **Affiliation:** DeVry University **Admission Plans:** Deferred Admission **Application Deadline:** Rolling **Application Fee:** $50.00 **H.S. Requirements:** High school diploma required; GED accepted **Costs Per Year:** Application fee: $50. Tuition: $14,080 full-time, $550 per credit hour part-time. **Scholarships:** Available **Calendar System:** Semester, Summer Session Available **Enrollment:** FT 144, PT 106, Grad FT 14, Grad PT 129 **Faculty:** FT 2, PT 5 **Student-Faculty Ratio:** 64:1 **Exams:** ACT essay used for admission. SAT essay used for admission. ACT essay used for placement. SAT essay used for placement. **% Receiving Financial Aid:** 78 **Regional Accreditation:** North Central Association of Colleges and Schools **Credit Hours For Degree:** 122 credits, Bachelors

DUKE UNIVERSITY
Durham, NC 27708-0586
Tel: (919)684-8111
Admissions: (919)684-3214
Fax: (919)681-8941
E-mail: askduke@admiss.duke.edu
Web Site: http://www.duke.edu/
President/CEO: Dr. Richard Brodhead
Admissions: Christoph Guttentag
Financial Aid: Alison Rabil
Type: University **Sex:** Coed **Affiliation:** United Methodist Church **Scores:** 100% SAT V 400+; 100% SAT M 400+; 2% ACT 18-23; 21% ACT 24-29 **% Accepted:** 19 **Admission Plans:** Preferred Admission; Early Admission; Early Decision Plan; Deferred Admission **Application Deadline:** January 2 **Application Fee:** $75.00 **H.S. Requirements:** High school diploma required; GED not accepted **Costs Per Year:** Application fee: $75. Comprehensive fee: $51,865 includes full-time tuition ($38,985), mandatory fees ($1258), and college room and board ($11,622). College room only: $6502. Room and board charges vary according to board plan and housing facility. Part-time tuition: $4872 per course. Part-time tuition varies according to course load. **Scholarships:** Available **Calendar System:** Semester, Summer Session Available **Enrollment:** FT 6,550, PT 28, Grad FT 7,320, Grad PT 452 **Faculty:** FT 1,038, PT 117 **Student-Faculty Ratio:** 8:1 **Exams:** SAT I and SAT II or ACT. ACT essay used for admission. SAT essay used for admission. **% Receiving Financial Aid:** 42 **% Residing in College-Owned, -Operated, or -Affiliated Housing:** 84 **Final Year or Final Semester Residency Requirement:** No **Library Holdings:** 5,950,442 **Regional Accreditation:** Southern Association of Colleges and Schools **Credit Hours For Degree:** 34 courses, Bachelors **ROTC:** Army, Navy, Air Force **Professional Accreditation:** AACSB, ABET, AACN, AANA, ABA, APTA, APA, ACIPE, AALS, ATS, ACEHSA, LCMEAMA, NCATE, NLN, SAF **Intercollegiate Athletics:** Badminton M & W; Baseball M; Basketball M & W; Crew M & W; Cross-Country Running M & W; Equestrian Sports M & W; Fencing M & W; Field Hockey M & W; Football M & W; Golf M & W; Ice Hockey M & W; Lacrosse M & W; Racquetball M & W; Rugby M & W; Sailing M & W; Skiing (Cross-Country) M & W; Skiing (Downhill) M & W; Soccer M & W; Softball M & W; Squash M & W; Swimming and Diving M & W; Table Tennis M & W; Tennis M & W; Track and Field M & W; Ultimate Frisbee M & W; Volleyball M & W; Water Polo M & W; Wrestling M

DURHAM TECHNICAL COMMUNITY COLLEGE
1637 Lawson St.
Durham, NC 27703-5023
Tel: (919)686-3300
Admissions: (919)536-7200
Web Site: http://www.durhamtech.edu/
President/CEO: William G. Ingram
Admissions: Penny Augustine
Type: Two-Year College **Sex:** Coed **Affiliation:** North Carolina Community College System **Admission Plans:** Open Admission; Deferred Admission **Application Deadline:** Rolling **Application Fee:** $0.00 **H.S. Requirements:** High school diploma required; GED accepted **Scholarships:** Available **Calendar System:** Semester, Summer Session Available **Library Holdings:** 36,388 **Regional Accreditation:** Southern Association of Colleges and Schools **Credit Hours For Degree:** 64 credit hours, Associates **Professional Accreditation:** ADA, AOTA, COptA, CARC

EAST CAROLINA UNIVERSITY
East 5th St.
Greenville, NC 27858-4353
Tel: (252)328-6131
Fax: (252)328-6495
E-mail: admis@ecu.edu
Web Site: http://www.ecu.edu/
President/CEO: Dr. Steven C. Ballard
Admissions: Anthony C. Britt
Financial Aid: Julie Poorman
Type: University **Sex:** Coed **Affiliation:** University of North Carolina System **Scores:** 97.77% SAT V 400+; 99.12% SAT M 400+; 72.36% ACT 18-23; 19.24% ACT 24-29 **% Accepted:** 67 **Admission Plans:** Preferred Admis-

sion; Early Admission; Deferred Admission **Application Deadline:** March 15 **Application Fee:** $60.00 **H.S. Requirements:** High school diploma required; GED accepted **Costs Per Year:** Application fee: $60. State resident tuition: $2491 full-time. Nonresident tuition: $13,325 full-time. Mandatory fees: $1986 full-time. College room and board: $7480. College room only: $4350. Room and board charges vary according to board plan and housing facility. **Scholarships:** Available **Calendar System:** Semester, Summer Session Available **Enrollment:** FT 18,392, PT 3,066, Grad FT 2,550, Grad PT 3,646 **Faculty:** FT 1,234, PT 240 **Student-Faculty Ratio:** 18:1 **Exams:** SAT I or ACT. ACT essay used for admission. SAT essay used for admission. ACT essay used for advising. SAT essay used for advising. ACT essay used for placement. SAT essay used for placement. **% Receiving Financial Aid:** 50 **Regional Accreditation:** Southern Association of Colleges and Schools **Credit Hours For Degree:** 120 semester hours, Bachelors **ROTC:** Army, Air Force **Professional Accreditation:** AACSB, AAMFT, AAFCS, AANA, ACNM, ACCE, ADtA, AHIMA, ACSP, AOTA, APTA, ASLHA, FIDER, CORE, CSWE, JRCEPAT, LCMEAMA, NAACLS, NASAD, NASM NASPAA, NCATE, NLN, NRPA, NAIT **Intercollegiate Athletics:** Baseball M; Basketball M & W; Cross-Country Running M & W; Football M; Golf M & W; Soccer M & W; Softball W; Swimming and Diving M & W; Tennis M & W; Track and Field M & W; Volleyball W

ECPI TECHNICAL COLLEGE
4101 Doie Cope Rd.
Raleigh, NC 27613
Tel: (919)571-0057; Free: 800-986-1200
Fax: (919)571-0780
E-mail: swells@ecpi.edu
Web Site: http://www.ecpi.edu/
Admissions: Susan Wells
Type: Two-Year College **Sex:** Coed **Application Deadline:** Rolling **H.S. Requirements:** High school diploma required; GED accepted **Calendar System:** Trimester, Summer Session Not available **Student-Faculty Ratio:** 13:1 **Exams:** SAT I or ACT, SAT I, SAT II. **Credit Hours For Degree:** 65 credits, Associates **Professional Accreditation:** ACCSCT

EDGECOMBE COMMUNITY COLLEGE
2009 West Wilson St.
Tarboro, NC 27886-9399
Tel: (252)823-5166
Fax: (252)823-6817
Web Site: http://www.edgecombe.edu/
President/CEO: Deborah L. Lamm
Admissions: Jackie Heath
Type: Two-Year College **Sex:** Coed **Affiliation:** North Carolina Community College System **Admission Plans:** Open Admission **Application Deadline:** Rolling **Application Fee:** $0.00 **H.S. Requirements:** High school diploma required; GED accepted **Scholarships:** Available **Calendar System:** Semester, Summer Session Available **Library Holdings:** 42,460 **Regional Accreditation:** Southern Association of Colleges and Schools **Credit Hours For Degree:** 64 semester hours, Associates **Professional Accreditation:** AHIMA, CARC, JRCERT

ELIZABETH CITY STATE UNIVERSITY
1704 Weeksville Rd.
Elizabeth City, NC 27909-7806
Tel: (252)335-3400; Free: 800-347-3278
Fax: (252)335-3731
Web Site: http://www.ecsu.edu/
President/CEO: Willie J. Gilchrist
Admissions: Harold Murrill
Type: Comprehensive **Sex:** Coed **Affiliation:** University of North Carolina System **Scores:** 52.46% SAT V 400+; 59.35% SAT M 400+; 20.88% ACT 18-23; 5.49% ACT 24-29 **% Accepted:** 47 **Admission Plans:** Preferred Admission; Deferred Admission **Application Deadline:** May 8 **Application Fee:** $30.00 **H.S. Requirements:** High school diploma required; GED accepted **Costs Per Year:** Application fee: $30. State resident tuition: $1681 full-time. Nonresident tuition: $10,730 full-time. College room and board: $5495. College room only: $3267. **Scholarships:** Available **Calendar System:** Semester, Summer Session Available **Enrollment:** FT 2,871, PT 337, Grad FT 5, Grad PT 51 **Faculty:** FT 165, PT 77 **Student-Faculty Ratio:** 20:1 **Exams:** SAT I or ACT, SAT I. ACT essay used for admission. **% Receiving Financial Aid:** 98 **% Residing in College-Owned, -Operated, or -Affiliated Housing:** 56 **Library Holdings:** 200,226 **Regional Accreditation:** Southern Association of Colleges and Schools **Credit Hours For Degree:** 124 semester hours, Bachelors **ROTC:** Army **Professional Accreditation:** NCATE, NAIT **Intercollegiate Athletics:** Baseball M; Basketball M & W; Bowling W; Cheerleading W; Cross-Country Running M & W; Football M; Golf M; Softball W; Tennis W; Volleyball W

ELON UNIVERSITY
2700 Campus Box
Elon, NC 27244-2010
Tel: (336)278-2000; Free: 800-334-8448
Admissions: (336)278-3566
Fax: (336)538-3986
E-mail: admissions@elon.edu
Web Site: http://www.elon.edu/
President/CEO: Dr. Leo M. Lambert
Admissions: Melinda Wood
Financial Aid: Patrick Murphy
Type: Comprehensive **Sex:** Coed **Affiliation:** United Church of Christ **Scores:** 100% SAT V 400+; 100% SAT M 400+; 16% ACT 18-23; 65% ACT 24-29 **% Accepted:** 48 **Admission Plans:** Early Admission; Early Action; Early Decision Plan; Deferred Admission **Application Deadline:** January 10 **Application Fee:** $50.00 **H.S. Requirements:** High school diploma required; GED accepted **Costs Per Year:** Application fee: $50. Comprehensive fee: $33,725 includes full-time tuition ($25,159), mandatory fees ($330), and college room and board ($8236). College room only: $3992. Room and board charges vary according to board plan and housing facility. Part-time tuition: $790 per hour. Part-time tuition varies according to course load. **Scholarships:** Available **Calendar System:** Semester, Summer Session Available **Enrollment:** FT 4,873, PT 122, Grad FT 530, Grad PT 141 **Faculty:** FT 343, PT 143 **Student-Faculty Ratio:** 13:1 **Exams:** SAT I or ACT. **% Receiving Financial Aid:** 34 **% Residing in College-Owned, -Operated, or -Affiliated Housing:** 58 **Library Holdings:** 302,630 **Regional Accreditation:** Southern Association of Colleges and Schools **Credit Hours For Degree:** 132 semester hours, Bachelors **ROTC:** Army, Air Force **Professional Accreditation:** AACSB, ABA, APTA, JRCEPAT, NCATE **Intercollegiate Athletics:** Baseball M; Basketball M & W; Cheerleading M & W; Cross-Country Running M & W; Equestrian Sports M & W; Field Hockey W; Football M; Golf M & W; Lacrosse M & W; Rugby M & W; Soccer M & W; Softball W; Swimming and Diving M & W; Tennis M & W; Track and Field W; Ultimate Frisbee M & W; Volleyball W

FAYETTEVILLE STATE UNIVERSITY
1200 Murchison Rd.
Fayetteville, NC 28301-4298
Tel: (910)672-1111; Free: 800-222-2594
Admissions: (910)672-1371
Fax: (910)672-1769
E-mail: admissions@uncfsu.edu
Web Site: http://www.uncfsu.edu/
President/CEO: Dr. James A. Anderson
Admissions: Ulisa E. Bowles
Financial Aid: Lois L. McKoy
Type: Comprehensive **Sex:** Coed **Affiliation:** University of North Carolina System **% Accepted:** 69 **Admission Plans:** Early Admission; Early Action; Early Decision Plan; Deferred Admission **Application Deadline:** June 30 **Application Fee:** $35.00 **H.S. Requirements:** High school diploma required; GED accepted **Scholarships:** Available **Calendar System:** Semester, Summer Session Available **Enrollment:** FT 4,246, PT 1,340 **Faculty:** FT 287, PT 34 **Student-Faculty Ratio:** 20:1 **Exams:** SAT I or ACT. **% Receiving Financial Aid:** 83 **% Residing in College-Owned, -Operated, or -Affiliated Housing:** 25 **Library Holdings:** 317,412 **Regional Accreditation:** Southern Association of Colleges and Schools **Credit Hours For Degree:** 60 credit hours, Associates; 120 credit hours, Bachelors **ROTC:** Army, Air Force **Professional Accreditation:** AACSB, AACN, CSWE, NCATE **Intercollegiate Athletics:** Basketball M; Bowling W; Cheerleading M & W; Cross-Country Running M & W; Football M & W; Golf M; Softball W; Tennis W; Volleyball W

FAYETTEVILLE TECHNICAL COMMUNITY COLLEGE
PO Box 35236
Fayetteville, NC 28303-0236
Tel: (910)678-8400
Admissions: (910)678-8473
Fax: (910)678-8407

E-mail: castanov@faytechcc.edu
Web Site: http://www.faytechcc.edu/
President/CEO: Dr. J. Larry Keen
Admissions: Dr. Vincent Castano
Type: Two-Year College **Sex:** Coed **Affiliation:** North Carolina Community College System **% Accepted:** 100 **Admission Plans:** Open Admission **Application Deadline:** Rolling **Application Fee:** $0.00 **H.S. Requirements:** High school diploma required; GED accepted **Costs Per Year:** Application fee: $0. One-time mandatory fee: $25. State resident tuition: $1600 full-time, $50 per credit hour part-time. Nonresident tuition: $7722 full-time, $242 per credit hour part-time. Mandatory fees: $60 full-time, $30 per term part-time. Full-time tuition and fees vary according to course load. Part-time tuition and fees vary according to course load. **Scholarships:** Available **Calendar System:** Semester, Summer Session Available **Enrollment:** FT 3,496, PT 7,707 **Faculty:** FT 303, PT 469 **Student-Faculty Ratio:** 13:1 **Exams:** Other. ACT essay not being used. SAT essay not being used. **Final Year or Final Semester Residency Requirement:** No **Library Holdings:** 68,604 **Regional Accreditation:** Southern Association of Colleges and Schools **Credit Hours For Degree:** 65 semester hours, Associates **Professional Accreditation:** ABET, ABFSE, ADA, APTA, CARC, JRCERT, NLN

FORSYTH TECHNICAL COMMUNITY COLLEGE
2100 Silas Creek Parkway
Winston-Salem, NC 27103-5197
Tel: (336)723-0371
Fax: (336)761-2098
E-mail: admissions@forsythtech.edu
Web Site: http://www.forsythtech.edu/
President/CEO: Dr. Gary Green
Admissions: Patrice Mitchell
Type: Two-Year College **Sex:** Coed **Affiliation:** North Carolina Community College System **% Accepted:** 100 **Admission Plans:** Open Admission **Application Deadline:** August 25 **H.S. Requirements:** High school diploma required; GED accepted **Costs Per Year:** State resident tuition: $1600 full-time, $50 per credit hour part-time. Nonresident tuition: $7722 full-time, $241.30 per credit hour part-time. **Scholarships:** Available **Calendar System:** Semester, Summer Session Available **Enrollment:** FT 2,509, PT 4,469 **Faculty:** FT 175, PT 311 **Student-Faculty Ratio:** 14:1 **Exams:** Other, SAT I or ACT. **Library Holdings:** 41,606 **Regional Accreditation:** Southern Association of Colleges and Schools **Professional Accreditation:** ABET, AAMAE, ADA, CARC, JRCEDMS, JRCERT, JRCNMT

GARDNER-WEBB UNIVERSITY
PO Box 997
Boiling Springs, NC 28017
Tel: (704)406-2361; Free: 800-253-6472
Admissions: (704)406-4491
Fax: (704)434-4488
E-mail: admissions@gardner-webb.edu
Web Site: http://www.gardner-webb.edu/
President/CEO: Dr. A. Frank Bonner
Admissions: Nathan Alexander
Financial Aid: Summer Nance
Type: Comprehensive **Sex:** Coed **Affiliation:** Baptist **Scores:** 90% SAT V 400+; 82% SAT M 400+ **% Accepted:** 62 **Application Deadline:** Rolling **Application Fee:** $40.00 **H.S. Requirements:** High school diploma required; GED accepted **Costs Per Year:** Application fee: $40. One-time mandatory fee: $100. Comprehensive fee: $29,250 includes full-time tuition ($22,050), mandatory fees ($390), and college room and board ($6810). College room only: $3490. Full-time tuition and fees vary according to degree level and program. Room and board charges vary according to board plan and housing facility. Part-time tuition: $345 per credit hour. Part-time tuition varies according to course load. **Scholarships:** Available **Calendar System:** Semester, Summer Session Available **Enrollment:** FT 2,256, PT 384, Grad FT 203, Grad PT 1,012 **Faculty:** FT 140 **Student-Faculty Ratio:** 13:1 **Exams:** SAT I or ACT. SAT essay used for advising. SAT essay used for placement. **% Receiving Financial Aid:** 52 **% Residing in College-Owned, -Operated, or -Affiliated Housing:** 50 **Final Year or Final Semester Residency Requirement:** No **Library Holdings:** 238,861 **Regional Accreditation:** Southern Association of Colleges and Schools **Credit Hours For Degree:** 72 semester hours, Associates; 120 semester hours, Bachelors **ROTC:** Army, Air Force **Professional Accreditation:** ACA, ACIPE, ACBSP, ATS, NASM, NCATE, NLN **Intercollegiate Athletics:** Baseball M; Basketball M & W; Cheerleading M & W; Cross-Country Running M & W; Football M; Golf M & W; Soccer M & W; Softball W; Swimming and Diving M & W; Tennis M & W; Track and Field M & W; Volleyball W; Wrestling M

GASTON COLLEGE
201 Hwy. 321 South
Dallas, NC 28034-1499
Tel: (704)922-6200
Web Site: http://www.gaston.edu/
President/CEO: Patricia Skinner
Admissions: Alice D. Hopper
Type: Two-Year College **Sex:** Coed **Affiliation:** North Carolina Community College System **% Accepted:** 100 **Admission Plans:** Open Admission **Application Deadline:** Rolling **Application Fee:** $0.00 **H.S. Requirements:** High school diploma required; GED accepted. For vocational programs: High school diploma or equivalent not required **Costs Per Year:** Application fee: $0. State resident tuition: $1600 full-time, $50 per credit hour part-time. Nonresident tuition: $7721 full-time, $241 per credit hour part-time. Mandatory fees: $176 full-time, $88 per term part-time. Full-time tuition and fees vary according to course load and program. Part-time tuition and fees vary according to course load and program. **Scholarships:** Available **Calendar System:** Semester, Summer Session Available **Enrollment:** FT 1,807, PT 2,966 **Faculty:** FT 124, PT 328 **Student-Faculty Ratio:** 14:1 **Exams:** Other, SAT I and SAT II or ACT. **Library Holdings:** 50,910 **Regional Accreditation:** Southern Association of Colleges and Schools **Credit Hours For Degree:** 64 semester hours, Associates **Professional Accreditation:** ABET, AAMAE

GREENSBORO COLLEGE
815 West Market St.
Greensboro, NC 27401-1875
Tel: (336)272-7102; Free: 800-346-8226
Fax: (336)271-6634
E-mail: admissions@greensborocollege.edu
Web Site: http://www.greensborocollege.edu/index.cfm/
President/CEO: Dr. Larry D. Czarda
Admissions: Timothy L. Jackson
Financial Aid: Dawn VanArsdale Young
Type: Comprehensive **Sex:** Coed **Affiliation:** United Methodist **Scores:** 89% SAT V 400+; 88% SAT M 400+; 46% ACT 18-23; 15% ACT 24-29 **% Accepted:** 55 **Admission Plans:** Early Admission; Early Action; Deferred Admission **Application Deadline:** Rolling **Application Fee:** $35.00 **H.S. Requirements:** High school diploma required; GED accepted **Costs Per Year:** Application fee: $35. Comprehensive fee: $32,337 includes full-time tuition ($23,346), mandatory fees ($270), and college room and board ($8721). College room only: $4500. Full-time tuition and fees vary according to course load, degree level, and program. Room and board charges vary according to housing facility. Part-time tuition: $635 per credit hour. Part-time tuition varies according to course load, degree level, and program. **Scholarships:** Available **Calendar System:** Semester, Summer Session Available **Faculty:** FT 62, PT 34 **Student-Faculty Ratio:** 11:1 **Exams:** SAT I or ACT. **% Residing in College-Owned, -Operated, or -Affiliated Housing:** 65 **Library Holdings:** 108,350 **Regional Accreditation:** Southern Association of Colleges and Schools **Credit Hours For Degree:** 124 semester hours, Bachelors **ROTC:** Army, Air Force **Professional Accreditation:** NASM, NCATE **Intercollegiate Athletics:** Baseball M; Basketball M & W; Cheerleading M & W; Cross-Country Running M & W; Football M; Golf M; Lacrosse M & W; Soccer M & W; Softball W; Swimming and Diving W; Tennis M & W; Volleyball W

GUILFORD COLLEGE
5800 West Friendly Ave.
Greensboro, NC 27410-4173
Tel: (336)316-2000; Free: 800-992-7759
Admissions: (336)316-2100
Fax: (336)316-2954
E-mail: admission@guilford.edu
Web Site: http://www.guilford.edu/
President/CEO: Dr. Kent John Chabotar
Admissions: Tania Johnson
Financial Aid: Paul J. Coscia
Type: Four-Year College **Sex:** Coed **Affiliation:** Society of Friends **Scores:** 91% SAT V 400+; 95% SAT M 400+; 46% ACT 18-23; 40% ACT 24-29 **% Accepted:** 62 **Admission Plans:** Preferred Admission; Early Admission;

Early Action; Deferred Admission **Application Deadline:** February 15 **Application Fee:** $25.00 **H.S. Requirements:** High school diploma required; GED accepted **Costs Per Year:** Application fee: $25. Comprehensive fee: $35,010 includes full-time tuition ($27,120), mandatory fees ($330), and college room and board ($7560). Room and board charges vary according to board plan and housing facility. Part-time tuition: $840 per credit hour. Part-time mandatory fees: $285 per credit hour. Part-time tuition and fees vary according to course load. **Scholarships:** Available **Calendar System:** Semester, Summer Session Available **Enrollment:** FT 2,312, PT 521 **Faculty:** FT 126, PT 118 **Student-Faculty Ratio:** 15:1 **Exams:** SAT I or ACT. **% Receiving Financial Aid:** 73 **% Residing in College-Owned, -Operated, or -Affiliated Housing:** 70 **Library Holdings:** 253,041 **Regional Accreditation:** Southern Association of Colleges and Schools **Credit Hours For Degree:** 128 credits, Bachelors **ROTC:** Army, Navy, Air Force **Professional Accreditation:** NCATE **Intercollegiate Athletics:** Baseball M; Basketball M & W; Cross-Country Running M & W; Football M; Golf M; Lacrosse M & W; Rugby M & W; Soccer M & W; Softball W; Swimming and Diving W; Tennis M & W; Volleyball W

GUILFORD TECHNICAL COMMUNITY COLLEGE
PO Box 309
Jamestown, NC 27282-0309
Tel: (336)334-4822
E-mail: jlcross@gtcc.edu
Web Site: http://www.gtcc.edu/
President/CEO: Dr. Donald W. Cameron
Admissions: Jesse L. Cross
Type: Two-Year College **Sex:** Coed **Affiliation:** North Carolina Community College System **% Accepted:** 60 **Admission Plans:** Open Admission; Early Admission; Deferred Admission **Application Deadline:** Rolling **Application Fee:** $0.00 **H.S. Requirements:** High school diploma required; GED accepted **Costs Per Year:** Application fee: $0. State resident tuition: $1600 full-time, $50 per credit hour part-time. Nonresident tuition: $7722 full-time, $241 per credit hour part-time. Mandatory fees: $173 full-time, $45 per term part-time. Full-time tuition and fees vary according to course load and program. Part-time tuition and fees vary according to course load and program. **Scholarships:** Available **Calendar System:** Semester, Summer Session Available **Enrollment:** FT 9,930, PT 3,602 **Faculty:** FT 292, PT 728 **Student-Faculty Ratio:** 21:1 **Final Year or Final Semester Residency Requirement:** Yes **Library Holdings:** 117,599 **Regional Accreditation:** Southern Association of Colleges and Schools **Credit Hours For Degree:** 64 semester hours, Associates **ROTC:** Army, Air Force **Professional Accreditation:** AAMAE, ACF, ADA, APTA **Intercollegiate Athletics:** Baseball M; Basketball M & W; Volleyball W

HALIFAX COMMUNITY COLLEGE
PO Drawer 809
Weldon, NC 27890-0809
Tel: (252)536-4221
Admissions: (252)536-7242
Fax: (252)536-4144
Web Site: http://www.hcc.cc.nc.us/
President/CEO: Dr. Ervin Griffin
Admissions: Scottie Dickens
Type: Two-Year College **Sex:** Coed **Affiliation:** North Carolina Community College System **Admission Plans:** Open Admission; Deferred Admission **Application Deadline:** Rolling **Application Fee:** $0.00 **H.S. Requirements:** High school diploma required; GED accepted **Scholarships:** Available **Calendar System:** Semester, Summer Session Available **Library Holdings:** 26,527 **Regional Accreditation:** Southern Association of Colleges and Schools **Credit Hours For Degree:** 65 semester hours, Associates **Professional Accreditation:** ADA, NAACLS

HAYWOOD COMMUNITY COLLEGE
185 Freedlander Dr.
Clyde, NC 28721-9453
Tel: (828)627-2821
Fax: (828)627-4513
Web Site: http://www.haywood.edu/
President/CEO: Dr. Rose Johnson
Admissions: Debbie Rowland
Type: Two-Year College **Sex:** Coed **Affiliation:** North Carolina Community College System **Admission Plans:** Open Admission **Application Deadline:** Rolling **Application Fee:** $0.00 **H.S. Requirements:** High school diploma required; GED accepted **Scholarships:** Available **Calendar System:** Semester, Summer Session Not available **Library Holdings:** 26,788 **Regional Accreditation:** Southern Association of Colleges and Schools **Credit Hours For Degree:** 65 semester hours, Associates **Professional Accreditation:** AAMAE

HERITAGE BIBLE COLLEGE
PO Box 1628
Dunn, NC 28335-1628
Tel: (910)892-3178; Free: 800-297-6351
Fax: (910)892-1809
E-mail: tnewton@heritagebiblecollege.edu
Web Site: http://www.heritagebiblecollege.edu/
President/CEO: Dr. Elvin Butts
Admissions: Traci Newton
Financial Aid: Laurie Minard
Type: Four-Year College **Sex:** Coed **Affiliation:** Pentecostal Free Will Baptist **Admission Plans:** Open Admission **Application Deadline:** Rolling **Application Fee:** $25.00 **H.S. Requirements:** High school diploma required; GED accepted **Costs Per Year:** Application fee: $25. Comprehensive fee: $10,290 includes full-time tuition ($6240), mandatory fees ($600), and college room and board ($3450). Room and board charges vary according to board plan and housing facility. Part-time tuition: $260 per credit hour. Part-time mandatory fees: $25 per credit hour. **Scholarships:** Available **Calendar System:** Semester, Summer Session Available **Enrollment:** FT 34, PT 35 **Faculty:** FT 4, PT 14 **Student-Faculty Ratio:** 20:1 **% Receiving Financial Aid:** 75 **% Residing in College-Owned, -Operated, or -Affiliated Housing:** 12 **Final Year or Final Semester Residency Requirement:** No **Credit Hours For Degree:** 69 credit hours, Associates; 129 credit hours, Bachelors **Professional Accreditation:** TACCS

HIGH POINT UNIVERSITY
University Station, Montlieu Ave.
High Point, NC 27262-3598
Tel: (336)841-9000; Free: 800-345-6993
Admissions: (336)841-9148
Fax: (336)841-5123
E-mail: jmcilrat@highpoint.edu
Web Site: http://www.highpoint.edu/
President/CEO: Dr. Nido Qubein
Admissions: Beth McCarthy
Financial Aid: Julie Setzer
Type: Comprehensive **Sex:** Coed **Affiliation:** United Methodist **Scores:** 98% SAT V 400+; 98% SAT M 400+; 59% ACT 18-23; 32% ACT 24-29 **% Accepted:** 71 **Admission Plans:** Early Action; Early Decision Plan; Deferred Admission **Application Deadline:** August 15 **Application Fee:** $40.00 **H.S. Requirements:** High school diploma required; GED accepted **Costs Per Year:** Application fee: $40. Comprehensive fee: $35,900. Part-time tuition: $749 per credit hour. Part-time tuition varies according to class time, course load, and reciprocity agreements. Tuition: $749 per credit hour part-time. Part-time tuition varies according to class time, course load, and reciprocity agreements. **Scholarships:** Available **Calendar System:** Semester, Summer Session Available **Enrollment:** FT 3,149, PT 128, Grad FT 21, Grad PT 305 **Faculty:** FT 159, PT 133 **Student-Faculty Ratio:** 16:1 **Exams:** SAT I or ACT, SAT II. **% Receiving Financial Aid:** 66 **% Residing in College-Owned, -Operated, or -Affiliated Housing:** 93 **Final Year or Final Semester Residency Requirement:** No **Library Holdings:** 163,075 **Regional Accreditation:** Southern Association of Colleges and Schools **Credit Hours For Degree:** 124 semester hours, Bachelors **ROTC:** Army, Air Force **Professional Accreditation:** ACBSP, JRCEPAT, NCATE **Intercollegiate Athletics:** Baseball M; Basketball M & W; Cross-Country Running M & W; Golf M; Soccer M & W; Tennis M & W; Track and Field M & W; Volleyball W

ISOTHERMAL COMMUNITY COLLEGE
PO Box 804
Spindale, NC 28160-0804
Tel: (828)286-3636
Fax: (828)286-8109
E-mail: vsearcy@isothermal.edu
Web Site: http://www.isothermal.edu/
President/CEO: Myra B. Johnson
Admissions: Vickie Searcy
Type: Two-Year College **Sex:** Coed **Affiliation:** North Carolina Community

College System **Admission Plans:** Open Admission; Early Admission; Deferred Admission **Application Deadline:** Rolling **Application Fee:** $0.00 **H.S. Requirements:** High school diploma required; GED accepted **Scholarships:** Available **Calendar System:** Semester, Summer Session Available **Enrollment:** FT 988, PT 1,017 **Faculty:** FT 60, PT 54 **Student-Faculty Ratio:** 17:1 **Library Holdings:** 35,200 **Regional Accreditation:** Southern Association of Colleges and Schools **Credit Hours For Degree:** 64 semester hours, Associates

ITT TECHNICAL INSTITUTE (CHARLOTTE)
10926 David Taylor Dr.
Ste. 100
Charlotte, NC 28262
Tel: (704)548-2300; Free: 877-243-7685
Web Site: http://www.itt-tech.edu/
President/CEO: Paul Wehrum
Type: Four-Year College **Sex:** Coed **Affiliation:** ITT Educational Services, Inc. **Calendar System:** Quarter **Professional Accreditation:** ACICS

ITT TECHNICAL INSTITUTE (CHARLOTTE)
4135 Southstream Blvd.
Ste. 200
Charlotte, NC 28217
Tel: (704)423-3100; Free: 800-488-0173
Web Site: http://www.itt-tech.edu/
President/CEO: Tina Daley-Ball
Type: Two-Year College **Sex:** Coed

ITT TECHNICAL INSTITUTE (HIGH POINT)
4050 Piedmont Parkway
Ste. 110
High Point, NC 27265
Tel: (336)819-5900; Free: 877-536-5231
Web Site: http://www.itt-tech.edu/
President/CEO: Tenika Glenn
Type: Two-Year College **Sex:** Coed **Affiliation:** ITT Educational Services, Inc. **Calendar System:** Quarter

ITT TECHNICAL INSTITUTE (MORRISVILLE)
3200 Gateway Centre Blvd., Ste. 105
Morrisville, NC 27560
Tel: (919)463-5800; Free: 877-203-5533
Admissions: (919)463-5800
Web Site: http://www.itt-tech.edu/
President/CEO: Coleman Walker
Type: Two-Year College **Sex:** Coed **Affiliation:** ITT Educational Services, Inc.

JAMES SPRUNT COMMUNITY COLLEGE
PO Box 398
Kenansville, NC 28349-0398
Tel: (910)296-2400
Admissions: (910)296-6078
Fax: (910)296-1222
E-mail: lgrady@jamessprunt.edu
Web Site: http://www.jamessprunt.com/
President/CEO: Dr. Lawrence Rouse
Admissions: Lea Grady
Type: Two-Year College **Sex:** Coed **Affiliation:** North Carolina Community College System **% Accepted:** 61 **Admission Plans:** Open Admission **Application Deadline:** Rolling **Application Fee:** $0.00 **H.S. Requirements:** High school diploma required; GED accepted **Costs Per Year:** Application fee: $0. State resident tuition: $1600 full-time, $50 per semester hour part-time. Nonresident tuition: $7722 full-time, $241.30 per semester hour part-time. Mandatory fees: $70 full-time, $35 per term part-time. Full-time tuition and fees vary according to course load. Part-time tuition and fees vary according to course load. **Scholarships:** Available **Calendar System:** Semester, Summer Session Available **Enrollment:** FT 724, PT 810 **Faculty:** FT 61, PT 82 **Library Holdings:** 27,471 **Regional Accreditation:** Southern Association of Colleges and Schools **Credit Hours For Degree:** 64 semester hours, Associates **Professional Accreditation:** AAMAE **Intercollegiate Athletics:** Softball M & W; Volleyball M & W

JOHN WESLEY COLLEGE
2314 North Centennial St.
High Point, NC 27265-3197
Tel: (336)889-2262
E-mail: admissions@johnwesley.edu
Web Site: http://www.johnwesley.edu/
President/CEO: Joel Key
Admissions: Jeremy Reese
Financial Aid: Shirley Carter
Type: Four-Year College **Sex:** Coed **Affiliation:** interdenominational **% Accepted:** 68 **Admission Plans:** Early Admission; Deferred Admission **Application Deadline:** August 1 **Application Fee:** $35.00 **H.S. Requirements:** High school diploma required; GED accepted **Costs Per Year:** Application fee: $35. Tuition: $10,000 full-time, $375 per semester hour part-time. Mandatory fees: $730 full-time, $365 per term part-time. Full-time tuition and fees vary according to course load. Part-time tuition and fees vary according to course load. College room only: $2344. Room charges vary according to housing facility. **Scholarships:** Available **Calendar System:** Semester, Summer Session Available **Enrollment:** FT 67, PT 28 **Faculty:** FT 3, PT 34 **Student-Faculty Ratio:** 7:1 **Exams:** Other. **% Receiving Financial Aid:** 72 **Library Holdings:** 37,905 **Credit Hours For Degree:** 66 semester hours, Associates; 128 semester hours, Bachelors **Professional Accreditation:** ABHE

JOHNSON C. SMITH UNIVERSITY
100 Beatties Ford Rd.
Charlotte, NC 28216-5398
Tel: (704)378-1000; Free: 800-782-7303
Admissions: (704)378-3500
E-mail: kwilliams@jcsu.edu
Web Site: http://www.jcsu.edu/
President/CEO: Dr. Ronald L. Carter
Admissions: Dr. Kevin Williams
Financial Aid: Keisha Ramey
Type: Four-Year College **Sex:** Coed **Scores:** 79.5% SAT V 400+; 75.5% SAT M 400+; 39% ACT 18-23; 2% ACT 24-29 **% Accepted:** 30 **Admission Plans:** Early Admission; Deferred Admission **Application Deadline:** March 15 **Application Fee:** $25.00 **H.S. Requirements:** High school diploma required; GED accepted **Costs Per Year:** Application fee: $25. Comprehensive fee: $21,886 includes full-time tuition ($13,361), mandatory fees ($2393), and college room and board ($6132). College room only: $3529. Full-time tuition and fees vary according to course load. Room and board charges vary according to board plan and housing facility. Part-time tuition: $361 per credit hour. Part-time mandatory fees: $252.50 per term. Part-time tuition and fees vary according to course load. **Scholarships:** Available **Calendar System:** Semester, Summer Session Available **Enrollment:** FT 1,538, PT 33 **Faculty:** FT 100, PT 31 **Student-Faculty Ratio:** 13:1 **Exams:** SAT I or ACT. ACT essay not being used. SAT essay not being used. **% Receiving Financial Aid:** 92 **% Residing in College-Owned, -Operated, or -Affiliated Housing:** 64 **Final Year or Final Semester Residency Requirement:** No **Library Holdings:** 105,249 **Regional Accreditation:** Southern Association of Colleges and Schools **Credit Hours For Degree:** 122 semester hours, Bachelors **ROTC:** Army, Air Force **Professional Accreditation:** ACBSP, CSWE, NCATE **Intercollegiate Athletics:** Basketball M & W; Cheerleading W; Cross-Country Running M & W; Football M; Golf M & W; Softball W; Tennis M & W; Track and Field M & W; Volleyball W

JOHNSON & WALES UNIVERSITY - CHARLOTTE CAMPUS
801 West Trade St.
Charlotte, NC 28202
Tel: (980)598-1000; Free: (866)598-2427
E-mail: admissions.clt@jwu.edu
Web Site: http://www.jwu.edu/charlotte/
President/CEO: Arthur J. Gallagher
Financial Aid: Lynn Robinson
Type: Four-Year College **Sex:** Coed **Scores:** 78.7% SAT V 400+; 80.6% SAT M 400+ **% Accepted:** 62 **Admission Plans:** Early Admission; Deferred Admission **Application Deadline:** Rolling **Application Fee:** $0.00 **H.S. Requirements:** High school diploma required; GED accepted **Costs Per Year:** Application fee: $0. Comprehensive fee: $34,347 includes full-time tuition ($23,034), mandatory fees ($1395), and college room and board ($9918). Room and board charges vary according to board plan, housing facility, and location. **Scholarships:** Available **Calendar System:** Quarter **Enrollment:** FT 2,428, PT 24 **Faculty:** FT 83, PT 19 **Student-Faculty**

Ratio: 27:1 **Exams:** SAT I or ACT. **% Receiving Financial Aid:** 80 **% Residing in College-Owned, -Operated, or -Affiliated Housing:** 52 **Regional Accreditation:** New England Association of Schools and Colleges

JOHNSTON COMMUNITY COLLEGE
PO Box 2350
Smithfield, NC 27577-2350
Tel: (919)934-3051
Admissions: (919)209-2048
Fax: (919)934-2150
E-mail: pjharrell@johnstoncc.edu
Web Site: http://www.johnstoncc.edu/
President/CEO: Dr. David N. Johnson
Admissions: Dr. Pamela J. Harrell
Type: Two-Year College **Sex:** Coed **Affiliation:** North Carolina Community College System **Admission Plans:** Open Admission **Application Deadline:** Rolling **Application Fee:** $0.00 **H.S. Requirements:** High school diploma required; GED accepted **Costs Per Year:** Application fee: $0. State resident tuition: $1600 full-time, $50 per credit hour part-time. Nonresident tuition: $7722 full-time, $241.30 per credit hour part-time. Mandatory fees: $97 full-time. Full-time tuition and fees vary according to course load. Part-time tuition varies according to course load. **Scholarships:** Available **Calendar System:** Semester, Summer Session Available **Enrollment:** FT 2,283, PT 2,127 **Faculty:** FT 144, PT 241 **Student-Faculty Ratio:** 14:1 **Exams:** Other, SAT I or ACT. **Library Holdings:** 33,094 **Regional Accreditation:** Southern Association of Colleges and Schools **Credit Hours For Degree:** 64 credit hours, Associates **Professional Accreditation:** JRCERT **Intercollegiate Athletics:** Golf M & W; Softball M & W; Volleyball M & W

KING'S COLLEGE
322 Lamar Ave.
Charlotte, NC 28204-2436
Tel: (704)372-0266; Free: 800-768-2255
Fax: (704)348-2029
Web Site: http://www.kingscollegecharlotte.edu/
President/CEO: Barbara Rockecharlie
Type: Two-Year College **Sex:** Coed **% Accepted:** 82 **Calendar System:** Quarter **Professional Accreditation:** ACICS

LEES-MCRAE COLLEGE
PO Box 128
Banner Elk, NC 28604
Tel: (828)898-5241; Free: 800-280-4562
Fax: (828)898-8814
E-mail: admissions@lmc.edu
Web Site: http://www.lmc.edu/
President/CEO: Scott Colley
Admissions: Bill Sliwa
Financial Aid: Cathy Shell
Type: Four-Year College **Sex:** Coed **Affiliation:** Presbyterian Church (U.S.A.) **Scores:** 90% SAT V 400+; 88% SAT M 400+; 47% ACT 18-23; 16% ACT 24-29 **% Accepted:** 53 **Application Deadline:** Rolling **Application Fee:** $0.00 **H.S. Requirements:** High school diploma required; GED accepted **Scholarships:** Available **Calendar System:** Semester, Summer Session Available **Enrollment:** FT 896, PT 10 **Faculty:** FT 52, PT 2 **Student-Faculty Ratio:** 16:1 **Exams:** SAT I or ACT. ACT essay not being used. SAT essay not being used. **% Receiving Financial Aid:** 72 **% Residing in College-Owned, -Operated, or -Affiliated Housing:** 68 **Regional Accreditation:** Southern Association of Colleges and Schools **Credit Hours For Degree:** 124 credit hours, Bachelors **Professional Accreditation:** AACN, NCATE **Intercollegiate Athletics:** Basketball M & W; Cross-Country Running M & W; Golf M; Lacrosse M & W; Soccer M & W; Softball W; Tennis M & W; Track and Field M & W; Volleyball M & W

LENOIR COMMUNITY COLLEGE
PO Box 188
Kinston, NC 28502-0188
Tel: (252)527-6223
E-mail: tbuck@lenoircc.edu
Web Site: http://www.lenoircc.edu/
President/CEO: Brantley Briley
Admissions: Tammy Buck
Type: Two-Year College **Sex:** Coed **Affiliation:** North Carolina Community College System **Admission Plans:** Open Admission; Early Admission **Application Deadline:** Rolling **H.S. Requirements:** High school diploma required; GED accepted **Scholarships:** Available **Calendar System:** Semester, Summer Session Available **Faculty:** FT 95, PT 250 **Library Holdings:** 55,053 **Regional Accreditation:** Southern Association of Colleges and Schools **Credit Hours For Degree:** 64 semester hours, Associates **Professional Accreditation:** AAMAE **Intercollegiate Athletics:** Baseball M; Basketball M; Volleyball M & W

LENOIR-RHYNE UNIVERSITY
625 7th Ave. NE
Hickory, NC 28601
Tel: (828)328-1741; Free: 800-277-5721
Admissions: (828)328-7300
Fax: (828)328-7338
E-mail: admission@lr.edu
Web Site: http://www.lr.edu/
President/CEO: Dr. Wayne B. Powell
Admissions: Karen Feezor
Financial Aid: Eric Brandon
Type: Comprehensive **Sex:** Coed **Affiliation:** Lutheran **Scores:** 92% SAT V 400+; 95.9% SAT M 400+ **% Accepted:** 81 **Admission Plans:** Early Admission; Early Action; Deferred Admission **Application Deadline:** August 15 **Application Fee:** $35.00 **H.S. Requirements:** High school diploma required; GED accepted **Scholarships:** Available **Calendar System:** Semester, Summer Session Available **Enrollment:** FT 1,277, PT 104 **Faculty:** FT 93, PT 82 **Student-Faculty Ratio:** 13:1 **Exams:** SAT I or ACT. **% Receiving Financial Aid:** 74 **% Residing in College-Owned, -Operated, or -Affiliated Housing:** 54 **Library Holdings:** 275,961 **Regional Accreditation:** Southern Association of Colleges and Schools **Credit Hours For Degree:** 128 credit hours, Bachelors **ROTC:** Army **Professional Accreditation:** AOTA, ACBSP, JRCEPAT, NCATE, NLN **Intercollegiate Athletics:** Baseball M; Basketball M & W; Cheerleading M & W; Cross-Country Running M & W; Football M; Golf M & W; Soccer M & W; Softball W; Swimming and Diving W; Tennis M & W; Track and Field M & W; Volleyball W

LIVINGSTONE COLLEGE
701 West Monroe St.
Salisbury, NC 28144-5298
Tel: (704)216-6000; Free: 800-835-3435
Admissions: (704)216-6001
Fax: (704)216-6217
E-mail: admissions@livingstone.edu
Web Site: http://www.livingstone.edu/
President/CEO: Dr. Jimmy R. Jenkins, Jr.
Financial Aid: Terry Jefferies
Type: Four-Year College **Sex:** Coed **Affiliation:** African Methodist Episcopal Zion Church **Scores:** 53.63% SAT M 400+; 17.24% ACT 18-23; 3.45% ACT 24-29 **% Accepted:** 98 **Admission Plans:** Deferred Admission **Application Deadline:** Rolling **Application Fee:** $25.00 **H.S. Requirements:** High school diploma required; GED accepted **Costs Per Year:** Application fee: $25. Comprehensive fee: $20,000 includes full-time tuition ($11,354), mandatory fees ($2304), and college room and board ($6342). College room only: $3045. Part-time tuition: $586 per credit hour. Part-time mandatory fees: $120 per credit hour. **Scholarships:** Available **Calendar System:** Semester, Summer Session Not available **Enrollment:** FT 947, PT 13 **Faculty:** FT 51, PT 22 **Student-Faculty Ratio:** 16:1 **Exams:** SAT I or ACT. **% Residing in College-Owned, -Operated, or -Affiliated Housing:** 60 **Library Holdings:** 75,000 **Regional Accreditation:** Southern Association of Colleges and Schools **Credit Hours For Degree:** 125 semester hours, Bachelors **ROTC:** Army **Professional Accreditation:** CSWE, NCATE **Intercollegiate Athletics:** Basketball M & W; Bowling W; Cross-Country Running M & W; Football M; Softball W; Tennis W; Track and Field M & W; Volleyball W

LOUISBURG COLLEGE
501 North Main St.
Louisburg, NC 27549-2399
Tel: (919)496-2521; Free: 800-775-0208
Fax: (919)496-1788
E-mail: admissions@louisburg.edu
Web Site: http://www.louisburg.edu/
President/CEO: Mark D. LaBranche
Admissions: Jim Schlimmer
Type: Two-Year College **Sex:** Coed **Affiliation:** United Methodist **Scores:**

47% SAT V 400+; 54% SAT M 400+; 12% ACT 18-23; 1% ACT 24-29 **% Accepted:** 62 **Admission Plans:** Deferred Admission **Application Deadline:** Rolling **Application Fee:** $25.00 **H.S. Requirements:** High school diploma required; GED accepted **Costs Per Year:** Application fee: $25. Comprehensive fee: $22,547 includes full-time tuition ($12,125), mandatory fees ($1790), and college room and board ($8632). College room only: $5289. Full-time tuition and fees vary according to course load. **Scholarships:** Available **Calendar System:** Semester, Summer Session Not available **Enrollment:** FT 717, PT 13 **Faculty:** FT 45, PT 38 **Student-Faculty Ratio:** 13:1 **Exams:** SAT I or ACT. **% Residing in College-Owned, -Operated, or -Affiliated Housing:** 90 **Library Holdings:** 60,000 **Regional Accreditation:** Southern Association of Colleges and Schools **Credit Hours For Degree:** 64 semester hours, Associates **Intercollegiate Athletics:** Baseball M; Basketball M & W; Golf M & W; Soccer M & W; Softball W; Volleyball M & W

MARS HILL COLLEGE
PO Box 370
Mars Hill, NC 28754
Tel: (828)689-1307; Free: (866)MHC-4-YOU
Admissions: (828)689-1201
Fax: (828)689-1474
E-mail: ehoffmeyer@mhc.edu
Web Site: http://www.mhc.edu/
President/CEO: Dr. Dan Lunsford
Admissions: Ed Hoffmeyer
Financial Aid: Amanda Randolph Willis
Type: Four-Year College **Sex:** Coed **Affiliation:** Baptist **Scores:** 88% SAT V 400+; 92% SAT M 400+; 42% ACT 18-23; 27% ACT 24-29 **% Accepted:** 57 **Admission Plans:** Early Admission; Deferred Admission **Application Deadline:** Rolling **Application Fee:** $25.00 **H.S. Requirements:** High school diploma required; GED accepted **Costs Per Year:** Application fee: $25. One-time mandatory fee: $100. Comprehensive fee: $28,134 includes full-time tuition ($20,849) and college room and board ($7285). Room and board charges vary according to board plan and housing facility. Part-time tuition: $690 per credit hour. Part-time mandatory fees: $85 per credit hour. **Scholarships:** Available **Calendar System:** Semester, Summer Session Available **Enrollment:** FT 1,147, PT 90 **Faculty:** FT 70, PT 86 **Student-Faculty Ratio:** 12:1 **Exams:** SAT I or ACT. **% Receiving Financial Aid:** 87 **% Residing in College-Owned, -Operated, or -Affiliated Housing:** 61 **Library Holdings:** 98,150 **Regional Accreditation:** Southern Association of Colleges and Schools **Credit Hours For Degree:** 128 credits, Bachelors **Professional Accreditation:** CSWE, JRCEPAT, NASM, NAST, NCATE **Intercollegiate Athletics:** Baseball M; Basketball M & W; Cheerleading M & W; Cross-Country Running M & W; Football M; Golf M & W; Lacrosse M; Soccer M & W; Softball W; Swimming and Diving M & W; Tennis M & W; Track and Field M & W; Volleyball W

MARTIN COMMUNITY COLLEGE
1161 Kehukee Park Rd.
Williamston, NC 27892
Tel: (252)792-1521
Fax: (252)792-4425
Web Site: http://www.martin.cc.nc.us/
President/CEO: Dr. Ann R. Britt
Admissions: Sonya C. Atkinson
Type: Two-Year College **Sex:** Coed **Affiliation:** North Carolina Community College System **% Accepted:** 100 **Admission Plans:** Open Admission **Application Deadline:** Rolling **Application Fee:** $0.00 **H.S. Requirements:** High school diploma required; GED accepted **Scholarships:** Available **Calendar System:** Semester, Summer Session Available **Enrollment:** FT 281, PT 553 **Faculty:** FT 28, PT 31 **Student-Faculty Ratio:** 14:1 **Library Holdings:** 36,443 **Regional Accreditation:** Southern Association of Colleges and Schools **Credit Hours For Degree:** 64 semester hours, Associates **Professional Accreditation:** AAMAE, ADA, APTA

MAYLAND COMMUNITY COLLEGE
PO Box 547
Spruce Pine, NC 28777-0547
Tel: (828)765-7351
Fax: (828)765-0728
Web Site: http://www.mayland.edu/
President/CEO: Dr. Suzanne Y. Owens
Admissions: Cathy Morrison
Type: Two-Year College **Sex:** Coed **Affiliation:** North Carolina Community College System **Admission Plans:** Open Admission; Deferred Admission **Application Deadline:** Rolling **Application Fee:** $0.00 **H.S. Requirements:** High school diploma required; GED accepted **Scholarships:** Available **Calendar System:** Semester, Summer Session Available **Exams:** Other. **Library Holdings:** 19,041 **Regional Accreditation:** Southern Association of Colleges and Schools **Credit Hours For Degree:** 65 credits, Associates **Intercollegiate Athletics:** Basketball M; Volleyball W

MCDOWELL TECHNICAL COMMUNITY COLLEGE
54 College Dr.
Marion, NC 28752-9724
Tel: (828)652-6021
Fax: (828)652-1014
E-mail: rickw@mcdowelltech.edu
Web Site: http://www.mcdowelltech.edu/
President/CEO: Dr. Bryan Wilson
Admissions: Rick L. Wilson
Type: Two-Year College **Sex:** Coed **Affiliation:** North Carolina Community College System **Admission Plans:** Open Admission; Early Admission; Deferred Admission **Application Deadline:** Rolling **Application Fee:** $0.00 **H.S. Requirements:** High school diploma required; GED accepted **Costs Per Year:** Application fee: $0. State resident tuition: $1600 full-time, $50 per credit hour part-time. Nonresident tuition: $7722 full-time, $242.30 per credit hour part-time. Mandatory fees: $50 full-time, $1 per credit hour part-time, $5 per term part-time. **Scholarships:** Available **Calendar System:** Semester, Summer Session Available **Faculty:** FT 40, PT 18 **Library Holdings:** 18,055 **Regional Accreditation:** Southern Association of Colleges and Schools **Credit Hours For Degree:** 64 credit hours, Associates **Intercollegiate Athletics:** Tennis M

MEREDITH COLLEGE
3800 Hillsborough St.
Raleigh, NC 27607-5298
Tel: (919)760-8600; Free: 800-MEREDITH
Admissions: (919)760-8581
Fax: (919)829-2348
E-mail: admissions@meredith.edu
Web Site: http://www.meredith.edu/
President/CEO: Dr. Maureen A. Hartford
Admissions: Christan Trahey Harris
Financial Aid: Kevin Michaelsen
Type: Comprehensive **Scores:** 96% SAT V 400+; 95% SAT M 400+; 48% ACT 18-23; 29% ACT 24-29 **% Accepted:** 65 **Admission Plans:** Early Admission; Early Decision Plan; Deferred Admission **Application Deadline:** February 15 **Application Fee:** $40.00 **H.S. Requirements:** High school diploma required; GED not accepted **Scholarships:** Available **Calendar System:** Semester, Summer Session Available **Enrollment:** FT 1,766, PT 201, Grad FT 79, Grad PT 216 **Faculty:** FT 138, PT 142 **Student-Faculty Ratio:** 10:1 **Exams:** SAT I or ACT, SAT II. **% Receiving Financial Aid:** 71 **% Residing in College-Owned, -Operated, or -Affiliated Housing:** 60 **Final Year or Final Semester Residency Requirement:** No **Library Holdings:** 155,165 **Regional Accreditation:** Southern Association of Colleges and Schools **Credit Hours For Degree:** 124 semester hours, Bachelors **ROTC:** Army, Air Force **Professional Accreditation:** AAFCS, ADtA, FIDER, CSWE, NASM, NCATE **Intercollegiate Athletics:** Basketball W; Cross-Country Running W; Soccer W; Softball W; Tennis W; Volleyball W

METHODIST UNIVERSITY
5400 Ramsey St.
Fayetteville, NC 28311-1498
Tel: (910)630-7000; Free: 800-488-7110
Admissions: (910)630-7027
Fax: (910)630-7317
E-mail: admissions@methodist.edu
Web Site: http://www.methodist.edu/
President/CEO: Dr. M. Elton Hendricks
Admissions: Jamie Legg
Financial Aid: Bonnie Adamson
Type: Comprehensive **Sex:** Coed **Affiliation:** United Methodist **Scores:** 89% SAT V 400+; 94% SAT M 400+; 62% ACT 18-23; 18% ACT 24-29 **% Accepted:** 63 **Admission Plans:** Deferred Admission **Application Deadline:** Rolling **Application Fee:** $25.00 **H.S. Requirements:** High school diploma required; GED accepted **Costs Per Year:** Application fee:

$25. Comprehensive fee: $32,620 includes full-time tuition ($23,780), mandatory fees ($440), and college room and board ($8400). Full-time tuition and fees vary according to class time. Room and board charges vary according to housing facility. **Scholarships:** Available **Calendar System:** Semester, Summer Session Available **Enrollment:** FT 1,728, PT 273, Grad FT 124, Grad PT 58 **Faculty:** FT 127, PT 86 **Student-Faculty Ratio:** 12:1 **Exams:** SAT I or ACT. **% Receiving Financial Aid:** 87 **% Residing in College-Owned, -Operated, or -Affiliated Housing:** 57 **Library Holdings:** 86,259 **Regional Accreditation:** Southern Association of Colleges and Schools **Credit Hours For Degree:** 62 semester hours, Associates; 124 semester hours, Bachelors **ROTC:** Army, Air Force **Professional Accreditation:** ACBSP, CSWE, JRCEPAT, NCATE **Intercollegiate Athletics:** Baseball M; Basketball M & W; Cheerleading M & W; Cross-Country Running M & W; Football M; Golf M & W; Ice Hockey M; Lacrosse M & W; Soccer M & W; Softball W; Tennis M & W; Track and Field M & W; Volleyball W

MID-ATLANTIC CHRISTIAN UNIVERSITY
715 North Poindexter St.
Elizabeth City, NC 27909-4054
Tel: (252)334-2070; Free: 800-RBC-8980
Admissions: (252)334-2028
Fax: (252)334-2071
E-mail: julie.fields@macuniversity.edu
Web Site: http://www.macuniversity.edu/
President/CEO: Dr. D. Clay Perkins
Admissions: Julie A. Fields
Financial Aid: Lisa W. Pipkin
Type: Four-Year College **Sex:** Coed **Affiliation:** Christian **Scores:** 95% SAT V 400+; 91% SAT M 400+; 57% ACT 18-23; 14% ACT 24-29 **% Accepted:** 40 **Admission Plans:** Early Admission; Deferred Admission **Application Deadline:** August 1 **Application Fee:** $50.00 **H.S. Requirements:** High school diploma required; GED accepted **Costs Per Year:** Application fee: $50. Comprehensive fee: $17,110 includes full-time tuition ($9920), mandatory fees ($400), and college room and board ($6790). College room only: $3590. Room and board charges vary according to housing facility. Part-time tuition: $310 per credit hour. Part-time mandatory fees: $21 per credit hour. **Scholarships:** Available **Calendar System:** Semester, Summer Session Not available **Enrollment:** FT 131, PT 34 **Faculty:** FT 8, PT 23 **Student-Faculty Ratio:** 12:1 **Exams:** SAT I or ACT. ACT essay not being used. SAT essay not being used. **% Receiving Financial Aid:** 92 **% Residing in College-Owned, -Operated, or -Affiliated Housing:** 60 **Final Year or Final Semester Residency Requirement:** No **Library Holdings:** 29,192 **Regional Accreditation:** Southern Association of Colleges and Schools **Credit Hours For Degree:** 64 semester hours, Associates; 128 semester hours, Bachelors **ROTC:** Army **Professional Accreditation:** ABHE **Intercollegiate Athletics:** Basketball M & W; Volleyball W

MITCHELL COMMUNITY COLLEGE
500 West Broad
Statesville, NC 28677-5293
Tel: (704)878-3200
Fax: (704)878-0872
Web Site: http://www.mitchellcc.edu/
President/CEO: Douglas Eason
Admissions: Doug Rhoney
Type: Two-Year College **Sex:** Coed **Affiliation:** North Carolina Community College System **Admission Plans:** Open Admission **Application Deadline:** Rolling **Application Fee:** $0.00 **H.S. Requirements:** High school diploma required; GED accepted **Scholarships:** Available **Calendar System:** Semester, Summer Session Available **Library Holdings:** 37,760 **Regional Accreditation:** Southern Association of Colleges and Schools **Credit Hours For Degree:** 64 semester hours, Associates **ROTC:** Army **Professional Accreditation:** AAMAE

MONTGOMERY COMMUNITY COLLEGE
1011 Page St.
Troy, NC 27371
Tel: (910)576-6222; Free: 800-839-6222
E-mail: fryek@montgomery.edu
Web Site: http://www.montgomery.edu/
President/CEO: Dr. Mary K. Kirk
Admissions: Karen Frye
Type: Two-Year College **Sex:** Coed **Affiliation:** North Carolina Community College System **Admission Plans:** Open Admission; Preferred Admission; Early Admission; Deferred Admission **Application Deadline:** Rolling **Application Fee:** $0.00 **H.S. Requirements:** High school diploma required; GED accepted **Costs Per Year:** Application fee: $0. State resident tuition: $1600 full-time, $50 per credit hour part-time. Nonresident tuition: $7722 full-time, $241.30 per credit hour part-time. Mandatory fees: $65 full-time, $32.60 per term part-time. Full-time tuition and fees vary according to course load. Part-time tuition and fees vary according to course load. **Scholarships:** Available **Calendar System:** Semester, Summer Session Available **Enrollment:** FT 346, PT 693 **Faculty:** FT 36, PT 40 **Library Holdings:** 19,850 **Regional Accreditation:** Southern Association of Colleges and Schools **Credit Hours For Degree:** 64 semester hours, Associates **Professional Accreditation:** AAMAE

MONTREAT COLLEGE
PO Box 1267
Montreat, NC 28757-1267
Tel: (828)669-8012
Fax: (828)669-0120
E-mail: admissions@montreat.edu
Web Site: http://www.montreat.edu/
President/CEO: Dr. Dan Struble
Admissions: Kate Rogers
Financial Aid: Beth Pocock
Type: Comprehensive **Sex:** Coed **Affiliation:** Presbyterian Church (U.S.A.) **Scores:** 85% SAT V 400+; 88% SAT M 400+; 68% ACT 18-23; 14% ACT 24-29 **% Accepted:** 62 **Admission Plans:** Early Admission; Deferred Admission **Application Deadline:** August 1 **Application Fee:** $30.00 **H.S. Requirements:** High school diploma required; GED accepted **Scholarships:** Available **Calendar System:** Semester, Summer Session Not available **Enrollment:** FT 938, PT 21 **Faculty:** FT 46, PT 40 **Student-Faculty Ratio:** 17:1 **Exams:** SAT I or ACT. **% Receiving Financial Aid:** 87 **% Residing in College-Owned, -Operated, or -Affiliated Housing:** 34 **Library Holdings:** 68,100 **Regional Accreditation:** Southern Association of Colleges and Schools **Credit Hours For Degree:** 60 semester hours, Associates; 126 semester hours, Bachelors **Professional Accreditation:** NCATE **Intercollegiate Athletics:** Baseball M; Basketball M & W; Cross-Country Running M & W; Golf M; Soccer M & W; Softball W; Tennis M & W; Volleyball W

MOUNT OLIVE COLLEGE
634 Henderson St.
Mount Olive, NC 28365
Tel: (919)658-2502
Fax: (919)658-8934
E-mail: admissions@moc.edu
Web Site: http://www.moc.edu/
President/CEO: Philip P. Kerstetter
Admissions: Tim Woodard
Financial Aid: Katrina K. Lee
Type: Four-Year College **Sex:** Coed **Affiliation:** Free Will Baptist **Scores:** 78.86% SAT V 400+; 49% ACT 18-23; 3% ACT 24-29 **% Accepted:** 50 **Admission Plans:** Open Admission; Deferred Admission **Application Deadline:** August 18 **Application Fee:** $20.00 **H.S. Requirements:** High school diploma required; GED accepted **Costs Per Year:** Application fee: $20. Comprehensive fee: $19,316 includes full-time tuition ($13,776) and college room and board ($5540). College room only: $2300. Part-time tuition: $310 per credit hour. **Scholarships:** Available **Calendar System:** Miscellaneous, Summer Session Available **Enrollment:** FT 2,812, PT 757 **Faculty:** FT 80, PT 111 **Student-Faculty Ratio:** 26:1 **Exams:** Other. **% Receiving Financial Aid:** 82 **% Residing in College-Owned, -Operated, or -Affiliated Housing:** 10 **Regional Accreditation:** Southern Association of Colleges and Schools **Credit Hours For Degree:** 64 semester hours, Associates; 126 semester hours, Bachelors **ROTC:** Air Force **Intercollegiate Athletics:** Baseball M; Basketball M & W; Cheerleading W; Cross-Country Running M & W; Golf M; Soccer M & W; Softball W; Tennis M & W; Volleyball M & W

NASH COMMUNITY COLLEGE
522 North Old Carriage Rd.
Rocky Mount, NC 27804
Tel: (252)443-4011
Fax: (252)443-0828
E-mail: dgardner@nashcc.edu
Web Site: http://www.nash.cc.nc.us/

President/CEO: William S. Carver, II
Admissions: Dorothy Gardner
Type: Two-Year College **Sex:** Coed **Affiliation:** North Carolina Community College System **Admission Plans:** Open Admission; Deferred Admission **Application Deadline:** Rolling **Application Fee:** $0.00 **H.S. Requirements:** High school diploma required; GED accepted **Scholarships:** Available **Calendar System:** Semester, Summer Session Available **Exams:** Other, SAT I or ACT, SAT I and SAT II or ACT. **Library Holdings:** 34,000 **Regional Accreditation:** Southern Association of Colleges and Schools **Credit Hours For Degree:** 65 semester hours, Associates **Professional Accreditation:** APTA

NEW LIFE THEOLOGICAL SEMINARY
PO Box 790106
Charlotte, NC 28206-7901
Tel: (704)334-6882
Fax: (704)334-6885
Web Site: http://www.nlts.org/
President/CEO: Dean Eddie G. Grigg
Admissions: Paula Emrich
Type: Comprehensive **Sex:** Coed **% Accepted:** 100 **Admission Plans:** Open Admission **Application Fee:** $40.00 **H.S. Requirements:** High school diploma required; GED accepted **Costs Per Year:** Application fee: $40. Tuition: $6450 full-time, $280 per credit hour part-time. Mandatory fees: $120 per term part-time. Full-time tuition varies according to program. Part-time tuition and fees vary according to program. **Calendar System:** Quarter, Summer Session Available **Enrollment:** FT 48, PT 30, Grad FT 8, Grad PT 12 **Faculty:** FT 6, PT 26 **Student-Faculty Ratio:** 6:1 **Final Year or Final Semester Residency Requirement:** No **Credit Hours For Degree:** 66 credit hours, Associates; 128 credit hours, Bachelors **Professional Accreditation:** TACCS

NORTH CAROLINA AGRICULTURAL AND TECHNICAL STATE UNIVERSITY
1601 East Market St.
Greensboro, NC 27411
Tel: (336)334-7500
Admissions: (336)334-7946
Fax: (336)334-7082
E-mail: uadmit@ncat.edu
Web Site: http://www.ncat.edu/
President/CEO: Dr. Harold L. Martin
Admissions: Dr. Yvette Young, PhD
Financial Aid: Sherri Avent
Type: University **Sex:** Coed **Affiliation:** University of North Carolina System **Scores:** 69% SAT V 400+; 77% SAT M 400+; 47.38% ACT 18-23; 12.67% ACT 24-29 **% Accepted:** 65 **Admission Plans:** Early Admission; Deferred Admission **Application Deadline:** Rolling **Application Fee:** $45.00 **H.S. Requirements:** High school diploma required; GED accepted. For Department-Specific (i.e., Engineering): High school diploma required; GED not accepted **Costs Per Year:** Application fee: $45. One-time mandatory fee: $140. State resident tuition: $2104 full-time. Nonresident tuition: $11,546 full-time. Mandatory fees: $1795 full-time. Full-time tuition and fees vary according to course load. College room and board: $5839. College room only: $3359. Room and board charges vary according to board plan. **Scholarships:** Available **Calendar System:** Semester, Summer Session Available **Enrollment:** FT 8,039, PT 916, Grad FT 783, Grad PT 876 **Student-Faculty Ratio:** 16:1 **Exams:** SAT I or ACT, SAT I and SAT II or ACT. **% Receiving Financial Aid:** 74 **% Residing in College-Owned, -Operated, or -Affiliated Housing:** 20 **Library Holdings:** 597,093 **Regional Accreditation:** Southern Association of Colleges and Schools **Credit Hours For Degree:** 124 semester hours, Bachelors **ROTC:** Army, Air Force **Professional Accreditation:** AACSB, ABET, AAFCS, ACCE, ACA, ASLA, CSWE, NASM, NAST, NCATE, NLN, NAIT **Intercollegiate Athletics:** Baseball M; Basketball M & W; Cross-Country Running M & W; Football M; Softball W; Swimming and Diving W; Tennis M & W; Track and Field M & W; Volleyball W

NORTH CAROLINA CENTRAL UNIVERSITY
1801 Fayetteville St.
Durham, NC 27707-3129
Tel: (919)560-6100; Free: 877-667-7533
Admissions: (919)530-6298
E-mail: admissions@nccu.edu
Web Site: http://www.nccu.edu/
President/CEO: Dr. Charlie Nelms
Admissions: Anthony Brooks
Financial Aid: Sharon J. Oliver
Type: Comprehensive **Sex:** Coed **Affiliation:** University of North Carolina System **Scores:** 68% SAT M 400+; 28% ACT 18-23; 2% ACT 24-29 **% Accepted:** 81 **Admission Plans:** Preferred Admission; Deferred Admission **Application Deadline:** July 1 **Application Fee:** $40.00 **H.S. Requirements:** High school diploma required; GED accepted **Scholarships:** Available **Calendar System:** Semester, Summer Session Available **Enrollment:** FT 5,326, PT 1,115, Grad FT 1,253, Grad PT 893 **Faculty:** FT 409, PT 199 **Student-Faculty Ratio:** 15:1 **Exams:** SAT I or ACT. **% Receiving Financial Aid:** 80 **% Residing in College-Owned, -Operated, or -Affiliated Housing:** 38 **Final Year or Final Semester Residency Requirement:** No **Regional Accreditation:** Southern Association of Colleges and Schools **Credit Hours For Degree:** 124 semester hours, Bachelors **ROTC:** Army, Air Force **Professional Accreditation:** AACSB, AAFCS, ABA, ACA, ADtA, ALA, ASLHA, ACBSP, CSWE, NAST, NCATE, NLN, NRPA **Intercollegiate Athletics:** Baseball M; Basketball M & W; Bowling M & W; Cross-Country Running M & W; Football M; Golf M & W; Softball W; Tennis M & W; Track and Field M & W; Volleyball W

NORTH CAROLINA STATE UNIVERSITY
Raleigh, NC 27695
Tel: (919)515-2011
Admissions: (919)515-2434
Fax: (919)515-5039
E-mail: undergrad_admissions@ncsu.edu
Web Site: http://www.ncsu.edu/
President/CEO: Dr. Randy Woodson
Admissions: Thomas Griffin
Financial Aid: Julia Rice Mallette
Type: University **Sex:** Coed **Affiliation:** University of North Carolina System **Scores:** 99% SAT V 400+; 100% SAT M 400+; 30% ACT 18-23; 55% ACT 24-29 **% Accepted:** 55 **Admission Plans:** Preferred Admission; Early Action; Deferred Admission **Application Deadline:** February 1 **Application Fee:** $70.00 **H.S. Requirements:** High school diploma or equivalent not required **Costs Per Year:** Application fee: $70. State resident tuition: $3953 full-time. Nonresident tuition: $16,438 full-time. Mandatory fees: $1521 full-time. Full-time tuition and fees vary according to degree level and program. College room and board: $7966. College room only: $4798. Room and board charges vary according to board plan and housing facility. **Scholarships:** Available **Calendar System:** Semester, Summer Session Available **Enrollment:** FT 22,018, PT 3,237, Grad FT 4,718, Grad PT 3,846 **Faculty:** FT 1,773, PT 172 **Student-Faculty Ratio:** 17:1 **Exams:** SAT I or ACT, SAT II. SAT essay used for admission. **% Receiving Financial Aid:** 44 **% Residing in College-Owned, -Operated, or -Affiliated Housing:** 35 **Library Holdings:** 4,000,000 **Regional Accreditation:** Southern Association of Colleges and Schools **Credit Hours For Degree:** 64 credit hours, Associates; 120 credit hours, Bachelors **ROTC:** Army, Navy, Air Force **Professional Accreditation:** AACSB, ABET, ACA, APA, ASLA, AVMA, CSWE, NAAB, NASAD, NASPAA, NCATE, NRPA, SAF **Intercollegiate Athletics:** Badminton M & W; Baseball M; Basketball M & W; Bowling M & W; Cheerleading M & W; Crew M & W; Cross-Country Running M & W; Equestrian Sports M & W; Fencing M & W; Field Hockey M & W; Football M; Golf M & W; Gymnastics W; Ice Hockey M & W; Lacrosse M & W; Racquetball M & W; Riflery M & W; Rugby M & W; Sailing M & W; Skiing (Downhill) M & W; Soccer M & W; Softball W; Swimming and Diving M & W; Table Tennis M & W; Tennis M & W; Track and Field M & W; Ultimate Frisbee M & W; Volleyball M & W; Water Polo M & W; Wrestling M

NORTH CAROLINA WESLEYAN COLLEGE
3400 North Wesleyan Blvd.
Rocky Mount, NC 27804-8677
Tel: (252)985-5100; Free: 800-488-6292
Admissions: (252)985-5200
Fax: (252)985-5325
E-mail: adm@ncwc.edu
Web Site: http://www.ncwc.edu/
President/CEO: Dr. Stanley Caine
Admissions: Cecelia Summers
Financial Aid: Deana M. Summerlin
Type: Four-Year College **Sex:** Coed **Affiliation:** United Methodist Church **Scores:** 66% SAT V 400+; 82% SAT M 400+ **% Accepted:** 63 **Application**

Deadline: Rolling **Application Fee:** $25.00 **H.S. Requirements:** High school diploma required; GED accepted **Scholarships:** Available **Calendar System:** Semester, Summer Session Available **Enrollment:** FT 1,160, PT 350 **Faculty:** FT 56, PT 113 **Student-Faculty Ratio:** 18:1 **Exams:** SAT I or ACT. **% Receiving Financial Aid:** 74 **% Residing in College-Owned, -Operated, or -Affiliated Housing:** 32 **Library Holdings:** 95,608 **Regional Accreditation:** Southern Association of Colleges and Schools **Credit Hours For Degree:** 124 semester hours, Bachelors **Professional Accreditation:** NCATE **Intercollegiate Athletics:** Baseball M; Basketball M & W; Football M; Golf M; Soccer M & W; Softball W; Tennis M & W; Volleyball W

PAMLICO COMMUNITY COLLEGE
PO Box 185
Grantsboro, NC 28529-0185
Tel: (252)249-1851
Fax: (252)249-2377
Web Site: http://www.pamlico.cc.nc.us/
President/CEO: Cleve H. Cox, EdD
Admissions: Floyd H. Hardison
Type: Two-Year College **Sex:** Coed **Affiliation:** North Carolina Community College System **Admission Plans:** Open Admission; Early Admission; Deferred Admission **Application Deadline:** Rolling **Application Fee:** $0.00 **H.S. Requirements:** High school diploma required; GED accepted **Scholarships:** Available **Calendar System:** Semester, Summer Session Available **Faculty:** FT 6, PT 4 **Library Holdings:** 19,500 **Regional Accreditation:** Southern Association of Colleges and Schools **Professional Accreditation:** AAMAE

PEACE COLLEGE
15 East Peace St.
Raleigh, NC 27604-1194
Tel: (919)508-2000; Free: 800-PEACE-47
Admissions: (919)509-2000
Fax: (919)508-2328
E-mail: mtgreen@peace.edu
Web Site: http://www.peace.edu/
President/CEO: Laura Carpenter Bingham
Admissions: Matt Green
Financial Aid: Angela J. Kirkley
Type: Four-Year College **Sex:** Women **Affiliation:** Presbyterian Church (U. S.A.) **Scores:** 81.4% SAT V 400+; 77% SAT M 400+; 40% ACT 18-23; 3% ACT 24-29 **% Accepted:** 64 **Application Deadline:** Rolling **Application Fee:** $25.00 **H.S. Requirements:** High school diploma required; GED accepted **Costs Per Year:** Application fee: $25. Comprehensive fee: $32,558 includes full-time tuition ($23,958), mandatory fees ($350), and college room and board ($8250). Full-time tuition and fees vary according to course load. Room and board charges vary according to board plan and housing facility. Part-time tuition: $360 per semester hour. Part-time tuition varies according to course load. **Scholarships:** Available **Calendar System:** Semester, Summer Session Available **Enrollment:** FT 659, PT 34 **Faculty:** FT 44, PT 33 **Student-Faculty Ratio:** 14:1 **Exams:** SAT I or ACT, SAT I and SAT II or ACT, SAT II. ACT essay not being used. SAT essay not being used. **% Receiving Financial Aid:** 81 **% Residing in College-Owned, -Operated, or -Affiliated Housing:** 25 **Final Year or Final Semester Residency Requirement:** Yes **Library Holdings:** 51,118 **Regional Accreditation:** Southern Association of Colleges and Schools **Credit Hours For Degree:** 125 semester hours, Bachelors **ROTC:** Army, Navy, Air Force **Intercollegiate Athletics:** Basketball W; Cross-Country Running W; Soccer W; Softball W; Tennis W; Volleyball W

PFEIFFER UNIVERSITY
PO Box 960
Misenheimer, NC 28109-0960
Tel: (704)463-1360; Free: 800-338-2060
Admissions: (704)463-3052
Fax: (704)463-1363
E-mail: admiss@pfeiffer.edu
Web Site: http://www.pfeiffer.edu/
President/CEO: Dr. Charles M. Ambrose
Admissions: Diane Martin
Financial Aid: Amy Brown
Type: Comprehensive **Sex:** Coed **Affiliation:** United Methodist **Scores:** 85% SAT V 400+; 91% SAT M 400+ **% Accepted:** 71 **Admission Plans:** Early Admission; Deferred Admission **Application Deadline:** Rolling **Application Fee:** $25.00 **H.S. Requirements:** High school diploma required; GED accepted **Costs Per Year:** Application fee: $25. Comprehensive fee: $26,838 includes full-time tuition ($19,040) and college room and board ($7798). College room only: $4658. Full-time tuition varies according to course load. Room and board charges vary according to housing facility. Part-time tuition: $435 per credit hour. Part-time tuition varies according to course load. **Scholarships:** Available **Calendar System:** Semester, Summer Session Available **Faculty:** FT 76, PT 74 **Student-Faculty Ratio:** 14:1 **Exams:** SAT I or ACT. **% Residing in College-Owned, -Operated, or -Affiliated Housing:** 65 **Library Holdings:** 125,972 **Regional Accreditation:** Southern Association of Colleges and Schools **Credit Hours For Degree:** 124 semester hours, Bachelors **ROTC:** Army **Professional Accreditation:** NASM, NCATE **Intercollegiate Athletics:** Baseball M; Basketball M & W; Cheerleading M & W; Cross-Country Running M & W; Golf M & W; Lacrosse M & W; Soccer M & W; Softball W; Swimming and Diving M & W; Tennis M & W; Volleyball W

PIEDMONT BAPTIST COLLEGE AND GRADUATE SCHOOL
420 South Broad St.
Winston-Salem, NC 27101-5197
Tel: (336)725-8344; Free: 800-937-5097
Fax: (336)725-5522
E-mail: admissions@pbc.edu
Web Site: http://www.pbc.edu/
President/CEO: Charles W. Petitt
Admissions: Angela Hoover
Financial Aid: Sherry Melton
Type: Comprehensive **Sex:** Coed **Affiliation:** Baptist **% Accepted:** 48 **Admission Plans:** Open Admission; Early Admission; Early Action; Deferred Admission **Application Deadline:** Rolling **Application Fee:** $50.00 **H.S. Requirements:** High school diploma required; GED accepted **Costs Per Year:** Application fee: $50. Comprehensive fee: $16,930 includes full-time tuition ($10,380), mandatory fees ($790), and college room and board ($5760). Full-time tuition and fees vary according to course load, degree level, location, and program. Part-time tuition: $450 per credit hour. Part-time mandatory fees: $220 per term. Part-time tuition and fees vary according to course load, degree level, location, and program. **Scholarships:** Available **Calendar System:** Semester, Summer Session Available **Exams:** ACT. **Library Holdings:** 50,000 **Credit Hours For Degree:** 69 credit hours, Associates; 135 credit hours, Bachelors **Professional Accreditation:** TACCS **Intercollegiate Athletics:** Basketball M & W; Soccer M; Volleyball W

PIEDMONT COMMUNITY COLLEGE
PO Box 1197
Roxboro, NC 27573-1197
Tel: (336)599-1181
Fax: (336)597-3817
Web Site: http://www.piedmont.cc.nc.us/
President/CEO: Dr. Walter C. Bartlett
Admissions: Shelia Williamson
Type: Two-Year College **Sex:** Coed **Affiliation:** North Carolina Community College System **Admission Plans:** Open Admission; Early Admission; Deferred Admission **Application Deadline:** Rolling **H.S. Requirements:** High school diploma required; GED accepted **Costs Per Year:** State resident tuition: $1549 full-time, $51.25 per credit hour part-time. Nonresident tuition: $7288 full-time, $241.30 per credit hour part-time. Mandatory fees: $49 full-time, $21.25 per term part-time. **Scholarships:** Available **Calendar System:** Semester, Summer Session Available **Enrollment:** FT 1,251, PT 1,623 **Library Holdings:** 24,166 **Regional Accreditation:** Southern Association of Colleges and Schools **Credit Hours For Degree:** 74 semester hours, Associates

PITT COMMUNITY COLLEGE
Hwy. 11 South, PO Drawer 7007
Greenville, NC 27835-7007
Tel: (252)321-4200
Admissions: (252)493-7217
Fax: (252)321-4401
E-mail: pittadm@pcc.pitt.cc.nc.us
Web Site: http://www.pittcc.edu/
President/CEO: Dr. G. Dennis Massey
Admissions: Bev Webster
Financial Aid: Lisa Reichstein
Type: Two-Year College **Sex:** Coed **Affiliation:** North Carolina Community

College System **Admission Plans:** Open Admission; Deferred Admission **Application Deadline:** Rolling **Application Fee:** $0.00 **H.S. Requirements:** High school diploma required; GED accepted **Costs Per Year:** Application fee: $0. State resident tuition: $1600 full-time, $50 per credit hour part-time. Nonresident tuition: $7722 full-time, $241.30 per credit hour part-time. Mandatory fees: $86 full-time, $43 per term part-time. Part-time tuition and fees vary according to course level. **Scholarships:** Available **Calendar System:** Semester, Summer Session Available **Enrollment:** FT 3,822, PT 3,254 **Library Holdings:** 43,302 **Regional Accreditation:** Southern Association of Colleges and Schools **Credit Hours For Degree:** 65 semester hours, Associates **ROTC:** Army **Professional Accreditation:** AAMAE, AHIMA, AOTA, CARC, JRCEDMS, JRCERT **Intercollegiate Athletics:** Baseball M; Basketball M; Golf M; Softball W; Volleyball W

QUEENS UNIVERSITY OF CHARLOTTE
1900 Selwyn Ave.
Charlotte, NC 28274-0002
Tel: (704)337-2200; Free: 800-849-0202
Admissions: (704)337-2212
Fax: (704)337-2403
E-mail: admissions@queens.edu
Web Site: http://www.queens.edu/
President/CEO: Pamela Davies, PhD
Financial Aid: Lauren H. Mack
Type: Comprehensive **Sex:** Coed **Affiliation:** Presbyterian **Scores:** 96.3% SAT V 400+; 95% SAT M 400+; 53.8% ACT 18-23; 35.9% ACT 24-29 **% Accepted:** 76 **Admission Plans:** Deferred Admission **Application Deadline:** Rolling **Application Fee:** $40.00 **H.S. Requirements:** High school diploma required; GED accepted **Costs Per Year:** Application fee: $40. One-time mandatory fee: $395. Comprehensive fee: $30,966 includes full-time tuition ($22,730) and college room and board ($8236). Room and board charges vary according to board plan. Part-time tuition: $395 per credit hour. **Scholarships:** Available **Calendar System:** Semester, Summer Session Available **Enrollment:** FT 1,312, PT 600, Grad FT 237, Grad PT 419 **Faculty:** FT 109, PT 107 **Student-Faculty Ratio:** 12:1 **Exams:** SAT I or ACT. ACT essay used for admission. SAT essay used for admission. ACT essay used in place of application essay. SAT essay used in place of application essay. ACT essay used as a validity check on application essay. SAT essay used as a validity check on application essay. **% Receiving Financial Aid:** 55 **% Residing in College-Owned, -Operated, or -Affiliated Housing:** 72 **Library Holdings:** 126,242 **Regional Accreditation:** Southern Association of Colleges and Schools **Credit Hours For Degree:** 122 credit hours, Bachelors **ROTC:** Army, Air Force **Professional Accreditation:** AACSB, AACN, ACBSP, NASM, NCATE **Intercollegiate Athletics:** Basketball M & W; Cheerleading M; Cross-Country Running M & W; Golf M & W; Lacrosse M & W; Soccer M & W; Softball W; Tennis M & W; Volleyball W

RANDOLPH COMMUNITY COLLEGE
PO Box 1009
Asheboro, NC 27204-1009
Tel: (336)633-0200
Admissions: (336)633-0213
Fax: (336)629-4695
E-mail: bhagerman@randolph.edu
Web Site: http://www.randolph.edu/
President/CEO: Dr. Robert S. Shackleford, Jr.
Admissions: Brandi F. Hagerman
Type: Two-Year College **Sex:** Coed **Affiliation:** North Carolina Community College System **% Accepted:** 100 **Admission Plans:** Open Admission; Deferred Admission **Application Deadline:** Rolling **Application Fee:** $0.00 **H.S. Requirements:** High school diploma required; GED accepted **Costs Per Year:** Application fee: $0. State resident tuition: $1600 full-time, $50 per credit hour part-time. Nonresident tuition: $7722 full-time, $241.30 per credit hour part-time. Mandatory fees: $88 full-time, $2.75 per credit hour part-time. **Scholarships:** Available **Calendar System:** Semester, Summer Session Available **Enrollment:** FT 1,366, PT 1,681 **Faculty:** FT 60, PT 255 **Student-Faculty Ratio:** 13:1 **Library Holdings:** 41,000 **Regional Accreditation:** Southern Association of Colleges and Schools **Credit Hours For Degree:** 64 semester hours, Associates **Professional Accreditation:** NLN

RICHMOND COMMUNITY COLLEGE
PO Box 1189
Hamlet, NC 28345-1189
Tel: (910)582-7000
Admissions: (910)410-1700
Fax: (910)582-7102
Web Site: http://www.richmondcc.edu/
President/CEO: Dr. Sharon Morrissey
Admissions: Wanda Watts
Type: Two-Year College **Sex:** Coed **Affiliation:** North Carolina Community College System **Admission Plans:** Open Admission; Deferred Admission **Application Deadline:** Rolling **Application Fee:** $0.00 **H.S. Requirements:** High school diploma required; GED accepted **Scholarships:** Available **Calendar System:** Semester, Summer Session Available **Enrollment:** FT 691, PT 781 **Faculty:** FT 51, PT 9 **Student-Faculty Ratio:** 29:1 **Library Holdings:** 26,381 **Regional Accreditation:** Southern Association of Colleges and Schools **Credit Hours For Degree:** 64 semester hours, Associates

ROANOKE-CHOWAN COMMUNITY COLLEGE
109 Community College Rd.
Ahoskie, NC 27910
Tel: (252)862-1200
Fax: (252)862-1353
Web Site: http://www.roanokechowan.edu/
President/CEO: Dr. Ralph G. Soney
Admissions: Sandra Copeland
Type: Two-Year College **Sex:** Coed **Affiliation:** North Carolina Community College System **Admission Plans:** Open Admission; Early Admission **Application Deadline:** Rolling **H.S. Requirements:** High school diploma required; GED accepted **Scholarships:** Available **Calendar System:** Semester, Summer Session Available **Library Holdings:** 29,268 **Regional Accreditation:** Southern Association of Colleges and Schools

ROBESON COMMUNITY COLLEGE
PO Box 1420
5160 Fayetteville Rd.
Lumberton, NC 28359-1420
Tel: (910)272-3700
Fax: (910)272-3328
Web Site: http://www.robeson.cc.nc.us/
President/CEO: Dr. Charles V. Chrestman
Admissions: Judy Revels
Type: Two-Year College **Sex:** Coed **Affiliation:** North Carolina Community College System **Admission Plans:** Open Admission; Early Admission **Application Deadline:** Rolling **H.S. Requirements:** High school diploma required; GED accepted **Calendar System:** Semester **Faculty:** FT 44, PT 70 **Library Holdings:** 39,000 **Regional Accreditation:** Southern Association of Colleges and Schools **Credit Hours For Degree:** 65 semester hours, Associates **Professional Accreditation:** CARC

ROCKINGHAM COMMUNITY COLLEGE
PO Box 38
Wentworth, NC 27375-0038
Tel: (336)342-4261
E-mail: admissions@rockinghamcc.edu
Web Site: http://www.rockinghamcc.edu/
President/CEO: Dr. Robert C. Keys
Admissions: Leigh Tysor
Type: Two-Year College **Sex:** Coed **Affiliation:** North Carolina Community College System **Admission Plans:** Open Admission; Early Admission; Deferred Admission **Application Deadline:** Rolling **Application Fee:** $0.00 **H.S. Requirements:** High school diploma required; GED accepted **Costs Per Year:** Application fee: $0. State resident tuition: $1600 full-time, $50 per credit hour part-time. Nonresident tuition: $7722 full-time, $241.30 per credit hour part-time. Mandatory fees: $96 full-time. Full-time tuition and fees vary according to course load. Part-time tuition varies according to course load. **Scholarships:** Available **Calendar System:** Semester, Summer Session Available **Enrollment:** FT 1,160, PT 1,476 **Faculty:** FT 66, PT 45 **Student-Faculty Ratio:** 18:1 **Library Holdings:** 43,044 **Regional Accreditation:** Southern Association of Colleges and Schools **Intercollegiate Athletics:** Baseball M; Basketball M; Golf M & W; Softball W; Volleyball W

ROWAN-CABARRUS COMMUNITY COLLEGE
PO Box 1595
Salisbury, NC 28145-1595
Tel: (704)637-0760

Admissions: (704)216-3602
Fax: (704)633-6804
Web Site: http://www.rowancabarrus.edu/
President/CEO: Dr. Carol Spalding
Admissions: Gail Cummins
Type: Two-Year College **Sex:** Coed **Affiliation:** North Carolina Community College System **Admission Plans:** Open Admission **Application Deadline:** Rolling **Application Fee:** $0.00 **H.S. Requirements:** High school diploma required; GED accepted **Scholarships:** Available **Calendar System:** Semester, Summer Session Available **Library Holdings:** 23,005 **Regional Accreditation:** Southern Association of Colleges and Schools **Credit Hours For Degree:** 64 semester hours, Associates **Professional Accreditation:** ADA, JRCERT, NLN

ST. ANDREWS PRESBYTERIAN COLLEGE
1700 Dogwood Mile
Laurinburg, NC 28352-5598
Tel: (910)277-5000; Free: 800-763-0198
Admissions: (910)277-5555
Fax: (910)277-5087
E-mail: admission@sapc.edu
Web Site: http://www.sapc.edu/
President/CEO: Paul Baldasare
Admissions: Kristen Simmons
Financial Aid: Kimberly Driggers
Type: Four-Year College **Sex:** Coed **Affiliation:** Presbyterian **Scores:** 84% SAT V 400+; 94% SAT M 400+; 56% ACT 18-23; 11% ACT 24-29 **% Accepted:** 76 **Admission Plans:** Early Decision Plan; Deferred Admission **Application Deadline:** Rolling **Application Fee:** $30.00 **H.S. Requirements:** High school diploma required; GED accepted **Costs Per Year:** Application fee: $30. One-time mandatory fee: $150. Comprehensive fee: $29,862 includes full-time tuition ($21,190) and college room and board ($8672). Full-time tuition varies according to course load and location. Room and board charges vary according to housing facility. **Scholarships:** Available **Calendar System:** Semester, Summer Session Available **Enrollment:** FT 559, PT 41 **Faculty:** FT 34, PT 41 **Student-Faculty Ratio:** 10:1 **Exams:** SAT I or ACT. **% Receiving Financial Aid:** 75 **% Residing in College-Owned, -Operated, or -Affiliated Housing:** 83 **Library Holdings:** 170,073 **Regional Accreditation:** Southern Association of Colleges and Schools **Credit Hours For Degree:** 120 credits, Bachelors **Professional Accreditation:** NCATE **Intercollegiate Athletics:** Baseball M; Basketball M & W; Cross-Country Running M & W; Equestrian Sports M & W; Golf M & W; Lacrosse M & W; Rugby M & W; Soccer M & W; Softball W; Tennis M & W; Volleyball W; Wrestling M

SAINT AUGUSTINE'S COLLEGE
1315 Oakwood Ave.
Raleigh, NC 27610-2298
Tel: (919)516-4000; Free: 800-948-1126
Admissions: (919)516-4012
Fax: (919)516-4415
E-mail: jesousa@st-aug.edu
Web Site: http://www.st-aug.edu/
President/CEO: Dr. Dianne Boardley Suber
Admissions: Jorge E. Sousa
Financial Aid: Wanda C. White
Type: Four-Year College **Sex:** Coed **Affiliation:** Episcopal **Scores:** 38.5% SAT M 400+; 18.1% ACT 18-23 **% Accepted:** 98 **Admission Plans:** Deferred Admission **Application Deadline:** Rolling **Application Fee:** $25.00 **H.S. Requirements:** High school diploma required; GED accepted **Costs Per Year:** Application fee: $25. Comprehensive fee: $24,286 includes full-time tuition ($12,364), mandatory fees ($4796), and college room and board ($7126). College room only: $2948. Full-time tuition and fees vary according to course load and program. Room and board charges vary according to housing facility. Part-time tuition: $515 per semester hour. Part-time mandatory fees: $200 per credit hour. Part-time tuition and fees vary according to course load and program. **Scholarships:** Available **Calendar System:** Semester, Summer Session Available **Enrollment:** FT 1,478, PT 51 **Faculty:** FT 79, PT 55 **Student-Faculty Ratio:** 16:1 **Exams:** SAT I or ACT. ACT essay used for placement. SAT essay used for placement. **% Receiving Financial Aid:** 81 **% Residing in College-Owned, -Operated, or -Affiliated Housing:** 79 **Final Year or Final Semester Residency Requirement:** Yes **Library Holdings:** 125,000 **Regional Accreditation:** Southern Association of Colleges and Schools **Credit Hours For Degree:** 120 semester hours, Bachelors **ROTC:** Army, Air Force **Professional Accreditation:** NCATE **Intercollegiate Athletics:** Baseball M; Basketball M & W; Bowling W; Cross-Country Running M & W; Football M; Golf M; Softball W; Tennis M & W; Track and Field M & W; Volleyball W

SALEM COLLEGE
601 South Church St.
Winston-Salem, NC 27101
Tel: (336)721-2600; Free: 800-327-2536
Admissions: (336)721-2621
Fax: (336)724-7102
E-mail: admissions@salem.edu
Web Site: http://www.salem.edu/
President/CEO: Susan Pauly
Admissions: Dean Katherine Knapp Watts
Financial Aid: Lori A. Lewis
Type: Comprehensive **Sex:** Coed **Scores:** 95% SAT V 400+; 95% SAT M 400+; 34% ACT 18-23; 55% ACT 24-29 **% Accepted:** 60 **Admission Plans:** Early Admission; Deferred Admission **Application Deadline:** Rolling **Application Fee:** $30.00 **H.S. Requirements:** High school diploma required; GED accepted **Costs Per Year:** Application fee: $30. Comprehensive fee: $33,485 includes full-time tuition ($21,610), mandatory fees ($355), and college room and board ($11,520). Part-time tuition: $1074 per course. Part-time tuition varies according to course load. **Scholarships:** Available **Calendar System:** 4-1-4, Summer Session Available **Enrollment:** FT 612, PT 152, Grad FT 17, Grad PT 204 **Faculty:** FT 59, PT 40 **Student-Faculty Ratio:** 11:1 **Exams:** SAT I or ACT. **% Receiving Financial Aid:** 70 **% Residing in College-Owned, -Operated, or -Affiliated Housing:** 86 **Final Year or Final Semester Residency Requirement:** Yes **Library Holdings:** 152,000 **Regional Accreditation:** Southern Association of Colleges and Schools **Credit Hours For Degree:** 36 courses, Bachelors **ROTC:** Army, Air Force **Professional Accreditation:** NASM, NCATE **Intercollegiate Athletics:** Basketball W; Cross-Country Running W; Field Hockey W; Soccer W; Swimming and Diving W; Tennis W; Volleyball W

SAMPSON COMMUNITY COLLEGE
PO Box 318
1801 Sunset Ave.
Hwy. 24 West
Clinton, NC 28329-0318
Tel: (910)592-8081
Fax: (910)592-8048
Web Site: http://www.sampsoncc.edu/
President/CEO: William Aiken
Admissions: William R. Jordan
Type: Two-Year College **Sex:** Coed **Affiliation:** North Carolina Community College System **% Accepted:** 100 **Admission Plans:** Open Admission; Deferred Admission **Application Deadline:** Rolling **Application Fee:** $0.00 **H.S. Requirements:** High school diploma required; GED accepted **Scholarships:** Available **Calendar System:** Semester, Summer Session Available **Enrollment:** FT 679, PT 900 **Faculty:** FT 45, PT 50 **Student-Faculty Ratio:** 20:1 **Library Holdings:** 25,000 **Regional Accreditation:** Southern Association of Colleges and Schools **Credit Hours For Degree:** 65 credits, Associates

SANDHILLS COMMUNITY COLLEGE
3395 Airport Rd.
Pinehurst, NC 28374-8299
Tel: (910)692-6185
Fax: (910)695-1823
E-mail: robledoi@sandhills.edu
Web Site: http://www.sandhills.edu/
President/CEO: John Dempsey
Admissions: Isai Robledo
Type: Two-Year College **Sex:** Coed **Affiliation:** North Carolina Community College System **Admission Plans:** Open Admission; Deferred Admission **Application Deadline:** Rolling **Application Fee:** $0.00 **H.S. Requirements:** High school diploma required; GED accepted **Scholarships:** Available **Calendar System:** Semester, Summer Session Available **Faculty:** FT 118, PT 60 **Student-Faculty Ratio:** 18:1 **Library Holdings:** 76,080 **Regional Accreditation:** Southern Association of Colleges and Schools **Credit Hours For Degree:** 64 semester hours, Associates **Professional Accreditation:** CARC, JRCERT, NAACLS **Intercollegiate Athletics:** Basketball M; Golf M & W; Volleyball W

SCHOOL OF COMMUNICATION ARTS
3000 Wakefield Crossing Dr.
Raleigh, NC 27614
Tel: (919)488-8500; Free: 800-288-7442
Admissions: (919)488-5912
E-mail: wmoseley@hdigi.com
Web Site: http://www.higherdigital.com/
President/CEO: Debra A. Hooper
Admissions: Wayne Moseley
Type: Two-Year College **Sex:** Coed **% Accepted:** 100 **Admission Plans:** Early Admission; Early Action; Early Decision Plan; Deferred Admission **Application Fee:** $25.00 **H.S. Requirements:** High school diploma required; GED accepted **Calendar System:** Quarter **Enrollment:** FT 325 **Faculty:** FT 19, PT 11 **Student-Faculty Ratio:** 11:1 **Exams:** Other. **Professional Accreditation:** COE

SHAW UNIVERSITY
118 East South St.
Raleigh, NC 27601-2399
Tel: (919)546-8200; Free: 800-214-6683
Admissions: (919)546-8275
Fax: (919)546-8271
E-mail: sclifton@shawu.edu
Web Site: http://www.shawu.edu/
President/CEO: Dr. Clarence G. Newsome
Admissions: Sandy Clifton
Financial Aid: Rochelle King
Type: Comprehensive **Sex:** Coed **Affiliation:** Baptist **Scores:** 41% SAT V 400+; 36% SAT M 400+; 17% ACT 18-23; 1% ACT 24-29 **% Accepted:** 44 **Admission Plans:** Early Admission; Deferred Admission **Application Deadline:** July 30 **Application Fee:** $25.00 **H.S. Requirements:** High school diploma required; GED accepted **Scholarships:** Available **Calendar System:** Semester, Summer Session Available **Enrollment:** FT 2,135, PT 207, Grad FT 148, Grad PT 48 **Faculty:** FT 105, PT 131 **Student-Faculty Ratio:** 16:1 **Exams:** SAT I or ACT. **% Receiving Financial Aid:** 92 **% Residing in College-Owned, -Operated, or -Affiliated Housing:** 31 **Regional Accreditation:** Southern Association of Colleges and Schools **Credit Hours For Degree:** 60 credit hours, Associates; 120 credit hours, Bachelors **ROTC:** Army, Air Force **Professional Accreditation:** ATS, CAEPK, NCATE **Intercollegiate Athletics:** Baseball M; Basketball M & W; Bowling W; Cross-Country Running M & W; Football M; Golf M; Softball W; Tennis M & W; Track and Field M & W; Volleyball W

SOUTH COLLEGE—ASHEVILLE
1567 Patton Ave.
Asheville, NC 28806
Tel: (828)252-2486
Admissions: (828)277-5521
Web Site: http://www.southcollegenc.com/
President/CEO: Robert A. Davis
Type: Two-Year College **Sex:** Coed **Admission Plans:** Open Admission; Deferred Admission **Application Deadline:** Rolling **Application Fee:** $50.00 **H.S. Requirements:** High school diploma required; GED accepted **Scholarships:** Available **Calendar System:** Quarter, Summer Session Available **Student-Faculty Ratio:** 8:1 **Exams:** Other. **Credit Hours For Degree:** 102 credits, Associates **Professional Accreditation:** ACICS

SOUTH PIEDMONT COMMUNITY COLLEGE
PO Box 126
Polkton, NC 28135-0126
Tel: (704)272-7635; Free: 800-766-0319
Admissions: (704)272-5300
E-mail: abaucom@vnet.net
Web Site: http://www.spcc.edu/
President/CEO: Dr. John McKay
Admissions: Jeania Martin
Type: Two-Year College **Sex:** Coed **Affiliation:** North Carolina Community College System **% Accepted:** 84 **Admission Plans:** Open Admission; Early Admission; Deferred Admission **Application Deadline:** Rolling **Application Fee:** $0.00 **H.S. Requirements:** High school diploma required; GED accepted **Scholarships:** Available **Calendar System:** Semester, Summer Session Available **Student-Faculty Ratio:** 17:1 **Library Holdings:** 18,917 **Regional Accreditation:** Southern Association of Colleges and Schools **Credit Hours For Degree:** 64 semester hours, Associates **Professional Accreditation:** AAMAE, AHIMA

SOUTHEASTERN BAPTIST THEOLOGICAL SEMINARY
PO Box 1889
Wake Forest, NC 27588-1889
Tel: (919)556-3101; Free: 800-284-6317
Web Site: http://www.sebts.edu/
President/CEO: Dr. Bruce Riley Ashford
Admissions: Penny Keathley
Type: Comprehensive **Sex:** Coed **Affiliation:** Southern Baptist **% Accepted:** 96 **Admission Plans:** Open Admission **Application Deadline:** July 20 **Application Fee:** $25.00 **H.S. Requirements:** High school diploma required; GED accepted **Scholarships:** Available **Calendar System:** Semester, Summer Session Available **Enrollment:** FT 228, PT 163 **Faculty:** FT 61, PT 22 **Student-Faculty Ratio:** 17:1 **Exams:** SAT I or ACT. **Regional Accreditation:** Southern Association of Colleges and Schools **Credit Hours For Degree:** 64 credits, Associates; 128 credits, Bachelors **Professional Accreditation:** ACIPE, ATS

SOUTHEASTERN COMMUNITY COLLEGE
PO Box 151
Whiteville, NC 28472-0151
Tel: (910)642-7141
E-mail: start@sccnc.edu
Web Site: http://www.sccnc.edu/
President/CEO: Kathy Matlock
Admissions: Sylvia Tart
Type: Two-Year College **Sex:** Coed **Affiliation:** North Carolina Community College System **% Accepted:** 100 **Admission Plans:** Open Admission; Early Admission; Deferred Admission **Application Deadline:** Rolling **Application Fee:** $0.00 **H.S. Requirements:** High school diploma required; GED accepted **Costs Per Year:** Application fee: $0. State resident tuition: $1200 full-time, $50 per semester hour part-time. Nonresident tuition: $5791 full-time, $241.30 per semester hour part-time. Mandatory fees: $100 full-time, $49.50. **Scholarships:** Available **Calendar System:** Semester, Summer Session Available **Enrollment:** FT 1,780, PT 169 **Faculty:** FT 75, PT 16 **Student-Faculty Ratio:** 20:1 **Library Holdings:** 50,297 **Regional Accreditation:** Southern Association of Colleges and Schools **Credit Hours For Degree:** 65 semester hours, Associates **Professional Accreditation:** NAACLS **Intercollegiate Athletics:** Baseball M; Softball W; Squash W; Volleyball W

SOUTHWESTERN COMMUNITY COLLEGE
447 College Dr.
Sylva, NC 28779
Tel: (828)586-4091
Fax: (828)586-4093
E-mail: delos@southwesterncc.edu
Web Site: http://www.southwesterncc.edu/
President/CEO: Cecil L. Groves
Admissions: Delos Monteith
Type: Two-Year College **Sex:** Coed **Affiliation:** North Carolina Community College System **Scores:** 65% SAT V 400+; 65% SAT M 400+; 20% ACT 18-23 **Admission Plans:** Open Admission; Early Admission; Deferred Admission **Application Deadline:** Rolling **Application Fee:** $0.00 **H.S. Requirements:** High school diploma required; GED accepted **Scholarships:** Available **Calendar System:** Semester, Summer Session Available **Enrollment:** FT 841, PT 1,224 **Faculty:** FT 72, PT 188 **Student-Faculty Ratio:** 11:1 **Exams:** SAT I or ACT. **Library Holdings:** 37,860 **Regional Accreditation:** Southern Association of Colleges and Schools **Credit Hours For Degree:** 64 semester hours, Associates **Professional Accreditation:** AHIMA, APTA, CARC, JRCEET, JRCERT, NAACLS

STANLY COMMUNITY COLLEGE
141 College Dr.
Albemarle, NC 28001-7458
Tel: (704)982-0121
Fax: (704)982-0819
E-mail: dross7926@stanly.edu
Web Site: http://www.stanly.edu/
President/CEO: Michael R. Taylor
Admissions: Denise B. Ross

Type: Two-Year College **Sex:** Coed **Affiliation:** North Carolina Community College System **% Accepted:** 100 **Admission Plans:** Open Admission; Early Admission; Deferred Admission **Application Deadline:** Rolling **H.S. Requirements:** High school diploma required; GED accepted **Scholarships:** Available **Calendar System:** Semester, Summer Session Available **Faculty:** FT 53, PT 53 **Student-Faculty Ratio:** 9:1 **Exams:** ACT essay not being used. SAT essay not being used. **Library Holdings:** 23,966 **Regional Accreditation:** Southern Association of Colleges and Schools **Credit Hours For Degree:** 65 semester hours, Associates **Professional Accreditation:** AAMAE, CARC **Intercollegiate Athletics:** Baseball M; Softball W

STRAYER UNIVERSITY - GARNER CAMPUS
1812 Garner Station Blvd.
Raleigh, NC 27603
Tel: (919)890-7500
Fax: (919)890-7530
Web Site: http://www.strayer.edu/garner/
Type: Comprehensive **Sex:** Coed **Application Fee:** $50.00 **Costs Per Year:** Application fee: $50. **Regional Accreditation:** Middle State Association of Colleges and Schools

STRAYER UNIVERSITY - GREENSBORO CAMPUS
4900 Koger Blvd., Ste. 400
Greensboro, NC 27407
Tel: (336)315-7800
Fax: (336)315-7830
Web Site: http://www.strayer.edu/greensboro
Type: Comprehensive **Sex:** Coed **Application Fee:** $50.00 **Costs Per Year:** Application fee: $50. **Regional Accreditation:** Middle State Association of Colleges and Schools

STRAYER UNIVERSITY - HUNTERSVILLE CAMPUS
13620 Reese Blvd.
Ste. 130
Huntersville, NC 28078
Tel: (704)379-6800
Fax: (704)379-6830
Web Site: http://www.strayer.edu/huntersville/
Type: Comprehensive **Sex:** Coed **Application Fee:** $50.00 **Costs Per Year:** Application fee: $50. **Regional Accreditation:** Middle State Association of Colleges and Schools

STRAYER UNIVERSITY - NORTH CHARLOTTE CAMPUS
8335 IBM Dr.
Ste. 150
Charlotte, NC 28262
Tel: (704)717-4000
Fax: (704)503-0686
Web Site: http://www.strayer.edu/north_charlotte
Type: Comprehensive **Sex:** Coed **Application Fee:** $50.00 **Costs Per Year:** Application fee: $50. **Regional Accreditation:** Middle State Association of Colleges and Schools

STRAYER UNIVERSITY - NORTH RALEIGH CAMPUS
3200 Spring Forest Rd., Ste. 214
Raleigh, NC 27616
Tel: (919)878-9900
Fax: (919)878-6625
Web Site: http://www.strayer.edu/north_raleigh
Type: Comprehensive **Sex:** Coed **Application Fee:** $50.00 **Costs Per Year:** Application fee: $50. **Regional Accreditation:** Middle State Association of Colleges and Schools

STRAYER UNIVERSITY - RTP CAMPUS
4 Copley Parkway
Morrisville, NC 27560
Tel: (919)466-4400
Fax: (919)466-4430
Web Site: http://www.strayer.edu/rtp_campus/
Type: Comprehensive **Sex:** Coed **Application Fee:** $50.00 **Costs Per Year:** Application fee: $50. **Regional Accreditation:** Middle State Association of Colleges and Schools

STRAYER UNIVERSITY - SOUTH CHARLOTTE CAMPUS
9101 Kings Parade Blvd.
Ste. 200
Charlotte, NC 28273
Tel: (704)499-9200
Fax: (704)499-9230
Web Site: http://www.strayer.edu/south_charlotte
Type: Comprehensive **Sex:** Coed **Application Fee:** $50.00 **Costs Per Year:** Application fee: $50. **Regional Accreditation:** Middle State Association of Colleges and Schools

SURRY COMMUNITY COLLEGE
630 South Main St.
PO Box 304
Dobson, NC 27017
Tel: (336)386-8121
Fax: (336)386-8951
E-mail: hazelwoodr@surry.edu
Web Site: http://www.surry.edu/
President/CEO: Dr. Deborah Friedman
Admissions: Renita Hazelwood
Type: Two-Year College **Sex:** Coed **Affiliation:** North Carolina Community College System **Admission Plans:** Open Admission; Early Admission; Deferred Admission **Application Fee:** $0.00 **H.S. Requirements:** High school diploma required; GED accepted **Scholarships:** Available **Calendar System:** Semester, Summer Session Available **Faculty:** FT 150, PT 300 **Student-Faculty Ratio:** 27:1 **Exams:** Other. **Library Holdings:** 47,526 **Regional Accreditation:** Southern Association of Colleges and Schools **Credit Hours For Degree:** 65 semester hours, Associates **Intercollegiate Athletics:** Baseball M; Basketball M; Volleyball W

TRI-COUNTY COMMUNITY COLLEGE
21 Campus Circle
Murphy, NC 28906-7919
Tel: (828)837-6810
Fax: (828)837-3266
E-mail: jchambers@tricountycc.edu
Web Site: http://www.tricountycc.edu/
President/CEO: Dr. Donna Tipton-Rogers
Admissions: Dr. Jason Chambers
Type: Two-Year College **Sex:** Coed **Affiliation:** North Carolina Community College System **Admission Plans:** Open Admission; Preferred Admission **Application Deadline:** Rolling **Application Fee:** $0.00 **H.S. Requirements:** High school diploma required; GED accepted **Costs Per Year:** Application fee: $0. State resident tuition: $1200 full-time. Nonresident tuition: $5791 full-time. Mandatory fees: $29 full-time. **Scholarships:** Available **Calendar System:** Semester, Summer Session Available **Faculty:** FT 46, PT 34 **Student-Faculty Ratio:** 21:1 **Library Holdings:** 16,224 **Regional Accreditation:** Southern Association of Colleges and Schools

THE UNIVERSITY OF NORTH CAROLINA AT ASHEVILLE
One University Heights
Asheville, NC 28804-3299
Tel: (828)251-6600; Free: 800-531-9842
Admissions: (828)251-6481
Fax: (828)251-6385
E-mail: admissions@unca.edu
Web Site: http://www.unca.edu/
President/CEO: Anne Ponder
Admissions: Leigh McBride
Financial Aid: Elizabeth D. Bartlett
Type: Comprehensive **Sex:** Coed **Affiliation:** University of North Carolina System **Scores:** 100% SAT V 400+; 99.8% SAT M 400+; 35.8% ACT 18-23; 55.2% ACT 24-29 **% Accepted:** 77 **Admission Plans:** Early Action; Deferred Admission **Application Deadline:** February 15 **Application Fee:** $50.00 **H.S. Requirements:** High school diploma required; GED not accepted **Costs Per Year:** Application fee: $50. State resident tuition: $2389 full-time. Nonresident tuition: $14,106 full-time. Mandatory fees: $2022 full-time. Full-time tuition and fees vary according to course load. College room and board: $6890. College room only: $3890. Room and board charges vary according to housing facility. **Scholarships:** Available **Calendar System:** Semester, Summer Session Available **Enrollment:** FT 3,132, PT 713, Grad FT 3, Grad PT 49 **Faculty:** FT 208, PT 92 **Student-Faculty Ratio:** 14:1 **Exams:** SAT I or ACT. **% Receiving Financial Aid:** 47 **% Residing in**

College-Owned, -Operated, or -Affiliated Housing: 35 **Library Holdings:** 271,741 **Regional Accreditation:** Southern Association of Colleges and Schools **Credit Hours For Degree:** 120 semester hours, Bachelors **Professional Accreditation:** NCATE **Intercollegiate Athletics:** Baseball M; Basketball M & W; Cheerleading M & W; Cross-Country Running M & W; Soccer M & W; Tennis M & W; Track and Field M & W; Volleyball W

THE UNIVERSITY OF NORTH CAROLINA AT CHAPEL HILL

Chapel Hill, NC 27599
Tel: (919)962-2211
Admissions: (919)966-3621
E-mail: uadm@email.unc.edu
Web Site: http://www.unc.edu/
President/CEO: Dr. H. Holden Thorp
Admissions: Stephen Farmer
Financial Aid: Shirley A. Ort

Type: University **Sex:** Coed **Affiliation:** University of North Carolina System **Scores:** 99.82% SAT V 400+; 99.82% SAT M 400+; 9.15% ACT 18-23; 45.69% ACT 24-29 **% Accepted:** 32 **Admission Plans:** Preferred Admission; Early Action; Deferred Admission **Application Deadline:** January 15 **Application Fee:** $70.00 **H.S. Requirements:** High school diploma required; GED not accepted **Costs Per Year:** Application fee: $70. State resident tuition: $3865 full-time. Nonresident tuition: $21,753 full-time. Mandatory fees: $1761 full-time. Full-time tuition and fees vary according to program. College room and board: $8670. College room only: $5250. Room and board charges vary according to board plan, housing facility, and location. **Scholarships:** Available **Calendar System:** Semester, Summer Session Available **Enrollment:** FT 17,275, PT 706, Grad FT 6,871, Grad PT 4,064 **Faculty:** FT 1,628, PT 136 **Student-Faculty Ratio:** 14:1 **Exams:** SAT I or ACT. ACT essay used for admission. SAT essay used for admission. ACT essay used for advising. SAT essay used for advising. ACT essay used for placement. SAT essay used for placement. **% Receiving Financial Aid:** 32 **% Residing in College-Owned, -Operated, or -Affiliated Housing:** 47 **Final Year or Final Semester Residency Requirement:** No **Library Holdings:** 6,735,325 **Regional Accreditation:** Southern Association of Colleges and Schools **Credit Hours For Degree:** 120 credit hours, Bachelors **ROTC:** Army, Navy, Air Force **Professional Accreditation:** AACSB, ABET, ACPhE, ACEJMC, AACN, ABA, ACA, ADA, ADtA, ACSP, ALA, AOTA, APTA, APA, ASLHA, ACIPE, AALS, ACEHSA, CEPH, CORE CSWE, JRCERT, JRCEPAT, LCMEAMA, NAACLS, NASPAA, NCATE, NLN, NRPA **Intercollegiate Athletics:** Baseball M; Basketball M & W; Crew W; Cross-Country Running M & W; Fencing M & W; Field Hockey W; Football M; Golf M & W; Gymnastics W; Lacrosse M & W; Racquetball M & W; Soccer M & W; Softball W; Swimming and Diving M & W; Tennis M & W; Track and Field M & W; Ultimate Frisbee M & W; Volleyball M & W; Water Polo M & W; Wrestling M

THE UNIVERSITY OF NORTH CAROLINA AT CHARLOTTE

9201 University City Blvd.
Charlotte, NC 28223-0001
Tel: (704)687-2000
Admissions: (704)687-2213
Fax: (704)510-6483
E-mail: unccadm@uncc.edu
Web Site: http://www.uncc.edu/
President/CEO: Dr. Philip L. Dubois
Admissions: Tina McEntire
Financial Aid: Anthony D. Carter

Type: University **Sex:** Coed **Affiliation:** University of North Carolina System **Scores:** 98% SAT V 400+; 99% SAT M 400+; 64% ACT 18-23; 26% ACT 24-29 **% Accepted:** 76 **Admission Plans:** Preferred Admission; Early Admission; Early Action **Application Deadline:** July 1 **Application Fee:** $50.00 **H.S. Requirements:** High school diploma required; GED accepted **Costs Per Year:** Application fee: $50. State resident tuition: $2516 full-time. Nonresident tuition: $13,128 full-time. Mandatory fees: $1911 full-time. Full-time tuition and fees vary according to course load. College room and board: $6796. College room only: $3466. Room and board charges vary according to board plan and housing facility. **Scholarships:** Available **Calendar System:** Semester, Summer Session Available **Enrollment:** FT 16,494, PT 2,925, Grad FT 1,885, Grad PT 3,397 **Faculty:** FT 981, PT 344 **Student-Faculty Ratio:** 19:1 **Exams:** SAT I or ACT. ACT essay used for admission. SAT essay used for admission. **% Receiving Financial Aid:** 55 **% Residing in College-Owned, -Operated, or -Affiliated Housing:** 25 **Library Holdings:** 1,073,727 **Regional Accreditation:** Southern Association of Colleges and Schools **Credit Hours For Degree:** 120 semester hours, Bachelors **ROTC:** Army, Air Force **Professional Accreditation:** AACSB, ABET, AACN, AANA, ACA, APA, ACEHSA, CSWE, NAAB, NASPAA, NCATE **Intercollegiate Athletics:** Baseball M; Basketball M & W; Cheerleading M & W; Cross-Country Running M & W; Golf M; Soccer M & W; Softball W; Tennis M & W; Track and Field M & W; Volleyball W

THE UNIVERSITY OF NORTH CAROLINA AT GREENSBORO

1400 Spring Garden St.
Greensboro, NC 27412-5001
Tel: (336)334-5000
Admissions: (336)334-5243
Fax: (336)334-4180
E-mail: admissions@uncg.edu
Web Site: http://www.uncg.edu/
President/CEO: Linda P. Brady
Financial Aid: Bruce Cabiness

Type: University **Sex:** Coed **Affiliation:** University of North Carolina System **Scores:** 97.79% SAT V 400+; 98.2% SAT M 400+ **% Accepted:** 73 **Admission Plans:** Early Admission; Early Action; Deferred Admission **Application Deadline:** March 1 **Application Fee:** $45.00 **H.S. Requirements:** High school diploma required; GED not accepted **Costs Per Year:** Application fee: $45. State resident tuition: $2590 full-time, $324 per course part-time. Nonresident tuition: $14,351 full-time, $1794 per course part-time. Mandatory fees: $1644 full-time, $59.09 per credit hour part-time. Part-time tuition and fees vary according to course load. College room and board: $6506. College room only: $3706. Room and board charges vary according to board plan and housing facility. **Scholarships:** Available **Calendar System:** Semester, Summer Session Available **Enrollment:** FT 12,855, PT 1,783, Grad FT 1,365, Grad PT 2,430 **Faculty:** FT 788, PT 467 **Student-Faculty Ratio:** 17:1 **Exams:** SAT I or ACT. ACT essay used for admission. SAT essay used for admission. **% Receiving Financial Aid:** 75 **% Residing in College-Owned, -Operated, or -Affiliated Housing:** 30 **Library Holdings:** 2,000,000 **Regional Accreditation:** Southern Association of Colleges and Schools **Credit Hours For Degree:** 122 semester hours, Bachelors **ROTC:** Army, Air Force **Professional Accreditation:** AACSB, ABET, AACN, AAFCS, AANA, ACA, ADtA, ALA, APA, ASLHA, FIDER, CEPH, CSWE, NASD, NASM, NASPAA, NAST, NCATE, NLN, NRPA **Intercollegiate Athletics:** Baseball M; Basketball M & W; Cross-Country Running M & W; Golf M & W; Soccer M & W; Softball W; Tennis M & W; Volleyball W; Wrestling M

THE UNIVERSITY OF NORTH CAROLINA AT PEMBROKE

One University Dr., PO Box 1510
Pembroke, NC 28372-1510
Tel: (910)521-6000; Free: 800-949-UNCP
Admissions: (910)521-6507
E-mail: jennifer.mcneill@uncp.edu
Web Site: http://www.uncp.edu/
President/CEO: Dr. Charles R. Jenkins
Admissions: Jennifer McNeil
Financial Aid: Mildred Weber

Type: Comprehensive **Sex:** Coed **Affiliation:** University of North Carolina System **% Accepted:** 79 **Admission Plans:** Deferred Admission **Application Deadline:** Rolling **Application Fee:** $40.00 **H.S. Requirements:** High school diploma required; GED accepted **Costs Per Year:** Application fee: $40. State resident tuition: $2173 full-time, $145.86 per credit hour part-time. Nonresident tuition: $11,380 full-time, $146.91 per credit hour part-time. Mandatory fees: $1717 full-time, $56.61 per unit part-time, $56.61. College room and board: $5990. College room only: $5040. Room and board charges vary according to board plan and housing facility. **Scholarships:** Available **Calendar System:** Semester, Summer Session Available **Enrollment:** FT 4,700, PT 1,210, Grad FT 118, Grad PT 633 **Faculty:** FT 323, PT 111 **Student-Faculty Ratio:** 15:1 **Exams:** SAT I or ACT. **% Receiving Financial Aid:** 73 **% Residing in College-Owned, -Operated, or -Affiliated Housing:** 27 **Library Holdings:** 367,565 **Regional Accreditation:** Southern Association of Colleges and Schools **Credit Hours For Degree:** 120 semester hours, Bachelors **ROTC:** Army, Air Force **Professional Accreditation:** AACN, CSWE, NASM, NCATE **Intercollegiate Athletics:** Baseball M; Basketball M & W; Cheerleading M & W; Cross-Country Running M & W; Football M; Golf M & W; Soccer M & W; Softball W; Tennis W; Track and Field M & W; Volleyball W; Wrestling M

UNIVERSITY OF NORTH CAROLINA SCHOOL OF THE ARTS

1533 South Main St.
PO Box 12189

Winston-Salem, NC 27127-2188
Tel: (336)770-3399
Admissions: (336)770-3290
Fax: (336)770-3370
E-mail: admissions@uncsa.edu
Web Site: http://www.uncsa.edu/
President/CEO: John Mauceri
Admissions: Sheeler Lawson
Financial Aid: Jane C. Kamiab
Type: Comprehensive **Sex:** Coed **Affiliation:** University of North Carolina System **% Accepted:** 45 **Application Deadline:** March 1 **Application Fee:** $60.00 **H.S. Requirements:** High school diploma required; GED accepted **Costs Per Year:** Application fee: $60. State resident tuition: $3357 full-time. Nonresident tuition: $15,303 full-time. Mandatory fees: $1942 full-time. Full-time tuition and fees vary according to program. College room and board: $7256. College room only: $3625. Room and board charges vary according to board plan and housing facility. **Scholarships:** Available **Calendar System:** Trimester, Summer Session Not available **Enrollment:** FT 739, PT 9, Grad FT 119, Grad PT 6 **Faculty:** FT 144, PT 35 **Student-Faculty Ratio:** 8:1 **Exams:** SAT I or ACT. **% Receiving Financial Aid:** 53 **% Residing in College-Owned, -Operated, or -Affiliated Housing:** 55 **Final Year or Final Semester Residency Requirement:** Yes **Library Holdings:** 87,917 **Regional Accreditation:** Southern Association of Colleges and Schools **Credit Hours For Degree:** 142 credits, Bachelors

THE UNIVERSITY OF NORTH CAROLINA WILMINGTON

601 South College Rd.
Wilmington, NC 28403-3297
Tel: (910)962-3000; Free: 800-228-5571
Admissions: (910)962-3876
Fax: (910)962-3038
E-mail: admissions@uncw.edu
Web Site: http://www.uncw.edu/
President/CEO: Dr. Rosemary DePaolo
Admissions: Dr. Terrence M. Curran
Financial Aid: Emily Bliss
Type: Comprehensive **Sex:** Coed **Affiliation:** University of North Carolina System **Scores:** 100% SAT V 400+; 99% SAT M 400+; 39% ACT 18-23; 54% ACT 24-29 **% Accepted:** 58 **Admission Plans:** Early Admission; Early Action; Deferred Admission **Application Deadline:** February 1 **Application Fee:** $60.00 **H.S. Requirements:** High school diploma required; GED accepted **Costs Per Year:** Application fee: $60. State resident tuition: $2565 full-time. Nonresident tuition: $13,447 full-time. Mandatory fees: $2308 full-time. Full-time tuition and fees vary according to course load. College room and board: $7798. College room only: $4648. Room and board charges vary according to board plan and housing facility. **Scholarships:** Available **Calendar System:** Semester, Summer Session Available **Enrollment:** FT 10,152, PT 1,045, Grad FT 515, Grad PT 701 **Faculty:** FT 592, PT 282 **Student-Faculty Ratio:** 17:1 **Exams:** SAT I or ACT. ACT essay used for admission. SAT essay used for admission. **% Receiving Financial Aid:** 45 **% Residing in College-Owned, -Operated, or -Affiliated Housing:** 38 **Library Holdings:** 1,071,435 **Regional Accreditation:** Southern Association of Colleges and Schools **Credit Hours For Degree:** 124 semester hours, Bachelors **Professional Accreditation:** AACSB, AACN, CSWE, NASM, NASPAA, NCATE, NLN, NRPA **Intercollegiate Athletics:** Baseball M; Basketball M & W; Cheerleading M & W; Cross-Country Running M & W; Golf M & W; Soccer M & W; Softball W; Swimming and Diving M & W; Tennis M & W; Track and Field M & W; Volleyball W

UNIVERSITY OF PHOENIX—CHARLOTTE CAMPUS

3800 Arco Corporate Dr., Ste. 100
Charlotte, NC 28273-3409
Tel: (704)504-5409; Free: 800-228-7240
Admissions: (480)557-6151
E-mail: audra.mcquarie@phoenix.edu
Web Site: http://www.phoenix.edu/
President/CEO: William Pepicello
Admissions: Audra McQuarie
Type: Comprehensive **Sex:** Coed **Admission Plans:** Open Admission; Deferred Admission **Application Deadline:** Rolling **Application Fee:** $45.00 **H.S. Requirements:** High school diploma required; GED accepted **Costs Per Year:** Application fee: $45. Tuition: $11,300 full-time. Full-time tuition varies according to course level and course load. **Scholarships:** Available **Calendar System:** Continuous, Summer Session Not available **Enrollment:** FT 866 **Faculty:** FT 18, PT 123 **Regional Accreditation:** North Central Association of Colleges and Schools **Credit Hours For Degree:** 60 credits, Associates; 120 credits, Bachelors

UNIVERSITY OF PHOENIX—RALEIGH CAMPUS

5511 Capital Center Dr.
Ste. 390
Raleigh, NC 27606
Tel: (480)557-6151; Free: 800-228-7240
Admissions: (480)557-6151
E-mail: audra.mcquarie@phoenix.edu
Web Site: http://www.phoenix.edu/
President/CEO: William Pepicello
Admissions: Audra McQuarie
Type: Comprehensive **Sex:** Coed **Admission Plans:** Open Admission; Deferred Admission **Application Deadline:** Rolling **Application Fee:** $45.00 **H.S. Requirements:** High school diploma required; GED accepted **Costs Per Year:** Application fee: $45. Tuition: $11,775 full-time. Full-time tuition varies according to course level and course load. **Scholarships:** Available **Enrollment:** FT 372 **Faculty:** FT 14, PT 88 **Regional Accreditation:** North Central Association of Colleges and Schools **Credit Hours For Degree:** 60 credits, Associates; 120 credits, Bachelors

VANCE-GRANVILLE COMMUNITY COLLEGE

PO Box 917
Henderson, NC 27536-0917
Tel: (252)492-2061
Fax: (252)430-0460
Web Site: http://www.vgcc.edu/
President/CEO: Randy Parker
Admissions: Kathy Kutl
Type: Two-Year College **Sex:** Coed **Affiliation:** North Carolina Community College System **% Accepted:** 100 **Admission Plans:** Open Admission; Preferred Admission; Early Admission; Deferred Admission **Application Deadline:** Rolling **Application Fee:** $0.00 **H.S. Requirements:** High school diploma required; GED accepted. For vocational programs: High school diploma or equivalent not required **Scholarships:** Available **Calendar System:** Semester, Summer Session Available **Enrollment:** FT 1,718, PT 2,339 **Faculty:** FT 141, PT 212 **Student-Faculty Ratio:** 9:1 **Library Holdings:** 38,720 **Regional Accreditation:** Southern Association of Colleges and Schools **Credit Hours For Degree:** 65 semester hours, Associates **Professional Accreditation:** JRCERT

WAKE FOREST UNIVERSITY

PO Box 7373
Reynolda Station
Winston-Salem, NC 27109
Tel: (336)758-5000
Admissions: (336)758-5201
Fax: (336)758-6074
Web Site: http://www.wfu.edu/
President/CEO: Dr. Nathan O. Hatch
Admissions: Martha Allman
Financial Aid: Adam Holyfield
Type: University **Sex:** Coed **Scores:** 99.5% SAT V 400+; 100% SAT M 400+; 8.9% ACT 18-23; 45.9% ACT 24-29 **% Accepted:** 38 **Admission Plans:** Early Admission; Early Action; Early Decision Plan **Application Deadline:** January 1 **Application Fee:** $50.00 **H.S. Requirements:** High school diploma required; GED accepted **Costs Per Year:** Application fee: $50. Comprehensive fee: $50,980 includes full-time tuition ($39,544), mandatory fees ($426), and college room and board ($11,010). College room only: $7150. Part-time tuition: $1640 per semester hour. **Scholarships:** Available **Calendar System:** Semester, Summer Session Available **Enrollment:** FT 4,514, PT 55, Grad FT 2,395, Grad PT 115 **Faculty:** FT 476, PT 149 **Student-Faculty Ratio:** 11:1 **% Receiving Financial Aid:** 38 **% Residing in College-Owned, -Operated, or -Affiliated Housing:** 70 **Regional Accreditation:** Southern Association of Colleges and Schools **Credit Hours For Degree:** 120 hours, Bachelors **ROTC:** Army **Professional Accreditation:** AACSB, AANA, ABA, ACA, ACIPE, AALS, ATS, LCMEAMA, NAACLS, NCATE **Intercollegiate Athletics:** Baseball M; Basketball M & W; Cross-Country Running M & W; Field Hockey W; Football M; Golf M & W; Soccer M & W; Tennis M & W; Track and Field M & W; Volleyball W

WAKE TECHNICAL COMMUNITY COLLEGE
9101 Fayetteville Rd.
Raleigh, NC 27603-5696
Tel: (919)662-3400
Admissions: (919)866-5452
Fax: (919)662-3529
E-mail: srbloomfield@waketech.edu
Web Site: http://www.waketech.edu/
President/CEO: Dr. Stephen Scott
Admissions: Susan Bloomfield
Type: Two-Year College **Sex:** Coed **Affiliation:** North Carolina Community College System **Admission Plans:** Open Admission; Early Admission **Application Deadline:** Rolling **Application Fee:** $0.00 **H.S. Requirements:** High school diploma required; GED accepted **Costs Per Year:** Application fee: $0. State resident tuition: $1600 full-time, $50 per credit hour part-time. Nonresident tuition: $7722 full-time, $241.30 per credit hour part-time. Mandatory fees: $82 full-time, $1 per credit hour part-time, $25 per term part-time. **Scholarships:** Available **Calendar System:** Semester, Summer Session Available **Student-Faculty Ratio:** 11:1 **Regional Accreditation:** Southern Association of Colleges and Schools **Credit Hours For Degree:** 64 semester hours, Associates **Professional Accreditation:** ABET, ADA, JRCERT, NAACLS

WARREN WILSON COLLEGE
PO Box 9000
Asheville, NC 28815-9000
Tel: (828)298-3325; Free: 800-934-3536
Admissions: (828)771-2073
Fax: (828)298-1440
E-mail: admit@warren-wilson.edu
Web Site: http://www.warren-wilson.edu/
President/CEO: Dr. William Sanborn Pfeiffer
Admissions: Richard Blomgren
Type: Comprehensive **Sex:** Coed **Affiliation:** Presbyterian Church (U.S.A.) **Scores:** 98% SAT V 400+; 96% SAT M 400+; 24% ACT 18-23; 65% ACT 24-29 **% Accepted:** 76 **Admission Plans:** Early Admission; Early Decision Plan; Deferred Admission **Application Deadline:** March 15 **Application Fee:** $0.00 **H.S. Requirements:** High school diploma required; GED accepted **Costs Per Year:** Application fee: $0. Comprehensive fee: $31,966 includes full-time tuition ($23,896), mandatory fees ($300), and college room and board ($7770). Part-time tuition: $996 per credit. **Scholarships:** Available **Calendar System:** Semester, Summer Session Not available **Enrollment:** FT 918, PT 9 **Faculty:** FT 65, PT 19 **Student-Faculty Ratio:** 13:1 **Exams:** SAT I or ACT. **% Receiving Financial Aid:** 63 **% Residing in College-Owned, -Operated, or -Affiliated Housing:** 89 **Library Holdings:** 106,837 **Regional Accreditation:** Southern Association of Colleges and Schools **Credit Hours For Degree:** 128 semester hours, Bachelors **Professional Accreditation:** CSWE, NCATE **Intercollegiate Athletics:** Basketball M & W; Cross-Country Running M & W; Soccer M & W; Swimming and Diving M & W

WAYNE COMMUNITY COLLEGE
PO Box 8002
Goldsboro, NC 27533-8002
Tel: (919)735-5151
Fax: (919)736-3204
E-mail: jbparker@waynecc.edu
Web Site: http://www.waynecc.edu/
President/CEO: Dr. Kay H. Albertson, EdD
Admissions: Jennifer Parker
Type: Two-Year College **Sex:** Coed **Affiliation:** North Carolina Community College System **% Accepted:** 56 **Admission Plans:** Open Admission; Deferred Admission **Application Deadline:** Rolling **Application Fee:** $0.00 **H.S. Requirements:** High school diploma required; GED accepted **Costs Per Year:** Application fee: $0. State resident tuition: $1600 full-time, $50 per credit hour part-time. Nonresident tuition: $7722 full-time, $241.30 per credit hour part-time. **Scholarships:** Available **Calendar System:** Semester, Summer Session Available **Enrollment:** FT 2,008, PT 1,577 **Faculty:** FT 124, PT 178 **Student-Faculty Ratio:** 20:1 **Exams:** ACT essay not being used. SAT essay not being used. **Final Year or Final Semester Residency Requirement:** No **Library Holdings:** 35,000 **Regional Accreditation:** Southern Association of Colleges and Schools **Credit Hours For Degree:** 64 credit hours, Associates **Professional Accreditation:** AAMAE, ADA

WESTERN CAROLINA UNIVERSITY
Cullowhee, NC 28723
Tel: (828)227-7211; Free: 877-WCU4YOU
Admissions: (828)227-7317
E-mail: admiss@email.wcu.edu
Web Site: http://www.wcu.edu/
President/CEO: Dr. John W. Bardo
Admissions: Chris Parrish
Financial Aid: Trina F. Orr
Type: Comprehensive **Sex:** Coed **Affiliation:** University of North Carolina System **Scores:** 97% SAT V 400+; 98% SAT M 400+; 65% ACT 18-23; 18% ACT 24-29 **% Accepted:** 44 **Admission Plans:** Early Admission; Early Action **Application Deadline:** March 1 **Application Fee:** $45.00 **H.S. Requirements:** High school diploma required; GED accepted **Costs Per Year:** Application fee: $45. State resident tuition: $2106 full-time. Nonresident tuition: $11,703 full-time. Mandatory fees: $2224 full-time. Full-time tuition and fees vary according to degree level. College room and board: $5912. College room only: $3062. Room and board charges vary according to board plan and housing facility. **Scholarships:** Available **Calendar System:** Semester, Summer Session Available **Enrollment:** FT 6,175, PT 1,275, Grad FT 677, Grad PT 1,302 **Faculty:** FT 473, PT 166 **Student-Faculty Ratio:** 15:1 **Exams:** SAT I or ACT, SAT I. ACT essay used for admission. SAT essay used for admission. **% Receiving Financial Aid:** 56 **% Residing in College-Owned, -Operated, or -Affiliated Housing:** 48 **Library Holdings:** 625,730 **Regional Accreditation:** Southern Association of Colleges and Schools **Credit Hours For Degree:** 120 credit hours, Bachelors **Professional Accreditation:** AACSB, ABET, AACN, AAFCS, AANA, ACA, ADtA, AHIMA, APTA, ASLHA, FIDER, CSWE, JRCEMT, NAACLS, NASM, NCATE **Intercollegiate Athletics:** Baseball M; Basketball M & W; Cross-Country Running M & W; Equestrian Sports M & W; Fencing M & W; Football M; Golf M & W; Rock Climbing M & W; Rugby M; Soccer W; Softball W; Swimming and Diving M & W; Tennis M & W; Track and Field M & W; Ultimate Frisbee M & W; Volleyball W; Wrestling M

WESTERN PIEDMONT COMMUNITY COLLEGE
1001 Burkemont Ave.
Morganton, NC 28655-4511
Tel: (828)438-6000
Fax: (828)438-6015
E-mail: swilliams@wpcc.edu
Web Site: http://www.wpcc.edu/
President/CEO: Jim Burnett
Admissions: Susan Williams
Financial Aid: Keith Conley
Type: Two-Year College **Sex:** Coed **Affiliation:** North Carolina Community College System **% Accepted:** 100 **Admission Plans:** Open Admission **Application Deadline:** Rolling **H.S. Requirements:** High school diploma required; GED accepted **Scholarships:** Available **Calendar System:** Semester, Summer Session Available **Faculty:** FT 60, PT 73 **Library Holdings:** 31,195 **Regional Accreditation:** Southern Association of Colleges and Schools **Credit Hours For Degree:** 64 semester hours, Associates **Professional Accreditation:** AAMAE, ADA, NAACLS, NLN

WILKES COMMUNITY COLLEGE
1328 Collegiate Dr., PO Box 120
Wilkesboro, NC 28697
Tel: (336)838-6100
Fax: (336)838-6277
E-mail: mac.warren@wilkescc.edu
Web Site: http://www.wilkescc.edu/
President/CEO: Gordon Burns
Admissions: Mac Warren
Type: Two-Year College **Sex:** Coed **Affiliation:** North Carolina Community College System **% Accepted:** 100 **Admission Plans:** Open Admission; Deferred Admission **Application Deadline:** Rolling **Application Fee:** $0.00 **H.S. Requirements:** High school diploma required; GED accepted **Costs Per Year:** Application fee: $0. State resident tuition: $1600 full-time, $50 per semester hour part-time. Nonresident tuition: $7722 full-time, $241.30 per semester hour part-time. Mandatory fees: $120 full-time, $5.25 per semester hour part-time, $11.25 per term part-time. **Scholarships:** Available **Calendar System:** Semester, Summer Session Available **Enrollment:** FT 1,347, PT 1,270 **Faculty:** FT 73, PT 289 **Student-Faculty Ratio:** 10:1 **Library Holdings:** 56,142 **Regional Accreditation:** Southern Association of

Colleges and Schools **Credit Hours For Degree:** 64 credit hours, Associates **Professional Accreditation:** ADA **Intercollegiate Athletics:** Baseball M; Basketball M & W; Volleyball W

WILSON COMMUNITY COLLEGE
902 Herring Ave., PO Box 4305
Wilson, NC 27893-3310
Tel: (252)291-1195
Fax: (252)243-7148
E-mail: mwilliams@wilsoncc.edu
Web Site: http://www.wilsoncc.edu/
President/CEO: Rusty Stephens
Admissions: Maegan Williams
Type: Two-Year College **Sex:** Coed **Affiliation:** North Carolina Community College System **Admission Plans:** Open Admission; Deferred Admission **Application Deadline:** Rolling **Application Fee:** $0.00 **H.S. Requirements:** High school diploma required; GED accepted **Costs Per Year:** Application fee: $0. State resident tuition: $1600 full-time, $50 per credit hour part-time. Nonresident tuition: $7722 full-time, $241.30 per credit hour part-time. Mandatory fees: $87 full-time, $1.35 per credit hour part-time, $22 per term part-time. **Scholarships:** Available **Calendar System:** Semester, Summer Session Available **Enrollment:** FT 984, PT 1,135 **Faculty:** FT 51, PT 53 **Student-Faculty Ratio:** 20:1 **Library Holdings:** 38,466 **Regional Accreditation:** Southern Association of Colleges and Schools **Credit Hours For Degree:** 65 credit hours, Associates

WINGATE UNIVERSITY
PO Box 159
Wingate, NC 28174-0159
Tel: (704)233-8000; Free: 800-755-5550
E-mail: admit@wingate.edu
Web Site: http://www.wingate.edu/
President/CEO: Dr. Jerry McGee
Admissions: Lindsay Kreis
Financial Aid: Teresa G. Williams
Type: Comprehensive **Sex:** Coed **Affiliation:** Baptist **Scores:** 92% SAT V 400+; 96% SAT M 400+; 52% ACT 18-23; 31% ACT 24-29 **% Accepted:** 52 **Admission Plans:** Early Admission; Deferred Admission **Application Deadline:** Rolling **Application Fee:** $30.00 **H.S. Requirements:** High school diploma required; GED accepted **Costs Per Year:** Application fee: $30. Comprehensive fee: $29,490 includes full-time tuition ($19,990), mandatory fees ($1150), and college room and board ($8350). Room and board charges vary according to board plan. Part-time tuition: $666 per semester hour. Part-time tuition varies according to course load. **Scholarships:** Available **Calendar System:** Semester, Summer Session Available **Enrollment:** FT 1,372, PT 45, Grad FT 341, Grad PT 401 **Faculty:** FT 119, PT 73 **Student-Faculty Ratio:** 13:1 **Exams:** SAT I or ACT. **% Receiving Financial Aid:** 63 **% Residing in College-Owned, -Operated, or -Affiliated Housing:** 80 **Library Holdings:** 102,542 **Regional Accreditation:** Southern Association of Colleges and Schools **Credit Hours For Degree:** 125 credit hours, Bachelors **ROTC:** Army, Air Force **Professional Accreditation:** ACPhE, AAMAE, ACBSP, JRCEPAT, NASM, NCATE **Intercollegiate Athletics:** Baseball M; Basketball M & W; Cross-Country Running M & W; Football M; Golf M & W; Lacrosse M; Soccer M & W; Softball W; Swimming and Diving M & W; Tennis M & W; Volleyball W

WINSTON-SALEM STATE UNIVERSITY
601 Martin Luther King Jr Dr.
Winston-Salem, NC 27110-0003
Tel: (336)750-2000; Free: 800-257-4052
Admissions: (336)750-2070
Fax: (336)750-2079
E-mail: Legrandet@wssu.edu
Web Site: http://www.wssu.edu/
President/CEO: Dr. Donald Julian Reaves
Admissions: Tomikia LeGrande
Financial Aid: Raymond Solomon
Type: Comprehensive **Sex:** Coed **Affiliation:** University of North Carolina System **Scores:** 76% SAT V 400+; 78% SAT M 400+; 39.62% ACT 18-23; 3.14% ACT 24-29 **% Accepted:** 54 **Admission Plans:** Deferred Admission **Application Deadline:** February 15 **Application Fee:** $40.00 **H.S. Requirements:** High school diploma required; GED accepted **Costs Per Year:** Application fee: $40. State resident tuition: $1769 full-time. Nonresident tuition: $10,755 full-time. Mandatory fees: $1753 full-time. Full-time tuition and fees vary according to location. College room and board: $6954. College room only: $4500. Room and board charges vary according to board plan and housing facility. **Scholarships:** Available **Calendar System:** Semester, Summer Session Available **Enrollment:** FT 5,327, PT 633, Grad FT 261, Grad PT 206 **Faculty:** FT 334, PT 2 **Student-Faculty Ratio:** 19:1 **Exams:** SAT I or ACT. **% Receiving Financial Aid:** 76 **% Residing in College-Owned, -Operated, or -Affiliated Housing:** 36 **Regional Accreditation:** Southern Association of Colleges and Schools **Credit Hours For Degree:** 120 semester hours, Bachelors **ROTC:** Army, Air Force **Professional Accreditation:** AACSB, ABET, AACN, AOTA, APTA, CORE, NAACLS, NASM, NCATE, NLN, NRPA **Intercollegiate Athletics:** Basketball M & W; Bowling M & W; Cheerleading M; Cross-Country Running M & W; Football M; Golf M; Softball M & W; Tennis M & W; Volleyball W

BISMARCK STATE COLLEGE
PO Box 5587
Bismarck, ND 58506-5587
Tel: (701)224-5400; Free: 800-445-5073
Fax: (701)224-5643
E-mail: karla.gabriel@bsc.nodak.edu
Web Site: http://www.bismarckstate.edu/
President/CEO: Larry C. Skogen
Admissions: Karla Gabriel
Financial Aid: Jeff Jacobs
Type: Two-Year College **Sex:** Coed **Affiliation:** North Dakota University System **Admission Plans:** Open Admission **Application Deadline:** Rolling **Application Fee:** $35.00 **H.S. Requirements:** High school diploma required; GED accepted **Scholarships:** Available **Calendar System:** Semester **Enrollment:** FT 2,192, PT 1,285 **Faculty:** FT 107, PT 144 **Student-Faculty Ratio:** 17:1 **Exams:** SAT I or ACT. **% Residing in College-Owned, -Operated, or -Affiliated Housing:** 8 **Library Holdings:** 69,142 **Regional Accreditation:** North Central Association of Colleges and Schools **Credit Hours For Degree:** 60 credits, Associates **ROTC:** Army, Air Force **Professional Accreditation:** ARCEST, JRCEMT, NAACLS **Intercollegiate Athletics:** Baseball M; Basketball M & W; Golf M & W; Tennis M & W; Volleyball W

CANKDESKA CIKANA COMMUNITY COLLEGE
PO Box 269
Fort Totten, ND 58335-0269
Tel: (701)766-4415
Fax: (701)766-4077
Web Site: http://www.littlehoop.edu/
President/CEO: Cynthia Lindquist
Admissions: Ermen Brown, Jr.
Type: Two-Year College **Sex:** Coed **Admission Plans:** Open Admission; Early Admission; Deferred Admission **Application Deadline:** August 22 **H.S. Requirements:** High school diploma required; GED accepted **Calendar System:** Semester, Summer Session Available **Faculty:** FT 5, PT 10 **Student-Faculty Ratio:** 12:1 **Library Holdings:** 7,500 **Regional Accreditation:** North Central Association of Colleges and Schools **Credit Hours For Degree:** 61 credits, Associates

DAKOTA COLLEGE AT BOTTINEAU
105 Simrall Blvd.
Bottineau, ND 58318-1198
Tel: (701)228-2277; Free: 800-542-6866
Admissions: (701)228-5494
Fax: (701)228-5499
E-mail: jancy.brisson@dakotacollege.edu
Web Site: http://www.dakotacollege.edu/
President/CEO: Dr. Ken Gross
Admissions: Jancy Brisson
Type: Two-Year College **Sex:** Coed **Affiliation:** North Dakota University System **Admission Plans:** Open Admission; Early Admission; Deferred Admission **Application Deadline:** Rolling **Application Fee:** $35.00 **H.S. Requirements:** High school diploma required; GED accepted **Costs Per Year:** Application fee: $35. State resident tuition: $3837 full-time. Nonresident tuition: $5397 full-time. Mandatory fees: $182.50 per credit hour part-time. Full-time tuition varies according to location and reciprocity agreements. Part-time fees vary according to course load, location, and reciprocity agreements. College room and board: $4328. Room and board charges vary according to gender, housing facility, and location. **Scholarships:** Available **Calendar System:** Semester, Summer Session Available **Enrollment:** FT 348, PT 400 **Faculty:** FT 25, PT 51 **Student-Faculty Ratio:** 17:1 **Exams:** ACT. ACT essay not being used. **Final Year or Final Semester Residency Requirement:** Yes **Library Holdings:** 46,294 **Regional Accreditation:** North Central Association of Colleges and Schools **Credit Hours For Degree:** 61 credits, Associates **Intercollegiate Athletics:** Baseball M; Basketball M & W; Football M; Ice Hockey M; Softball W; Volleyball W

DICKINSON STATE UNIVERSITY
291 Campus Dr.
Dickinson, ND 58601-4896
Tel: (701)483-2507; Free: 800-279-4295
Admissions: (701)483-2175
Fax: (701)483-2006
E-mail: dsu.hawks@dsu.nodak.edu
Web Site: http://www.dsu.nodak.edu/
President/CEO: Dr. Richard J. McCallum
Admissions: Norman Coley
Financial Aid: Sandy Klein
Type: Four-Year College **Sex:** Coed **Affiliation:** North Dakota University System **Scores:** 75% SAT V 400+; 57% ACT 18-23; 20% ACT 24-29 **% Accepted:** 96 **Admission Plans:** Open Admission; Early Admission; Deferred Admission **Application Deadline:** Rolling **Application Fee:** $35.00 **H.S. Requirements:** High school diploma required; GED accepted **Costs Per Year:** Application fee: $35. State resident tuition: $4160 full-time. Nonresident tuition: $11,106 full-time. Mandatory fees: $1089 full-time. College room and board: $4262. College room only: $1610. Room and board charges vary according to board plan. **Scholarships:** Available **Calendar System:** Semester, Summer Session Available **Enrollment:** FT 1,797, PT 970 **Faculty:** FT 96, PT 265 **Student-Faculty Ratio:** 15:1 **Exams:** SAT I or ACT. ACT essay used for advising. ACT essay used as a validity check on application essay. **% Receiving Financial Aid:** 46 **% Residing in College-Owned, -Operated, or -Affiliated Housing:** 33 **Final Year or Final Semester Residency Requirement:** No **Library Holdings:** 105,713 **Regional Accreditation:** North Central Association of Colleges and Schools **Credit Hours For Degree:** 64 semester hours, Associates; 128 semester hours, Bachelors **Professional Accreditation:** NCATE, NLN **Intercollegiate Athletics:** Badminton M & W; Baseball M; Basketball M & W; Cheerleading M & W; Cross-Country Running M & W; Football M; Golf M & W; Softball W; Track and Field M & W; Volleyball W; Wrestling M

FORT BERTHOLD COMMUNITY COLLEGE
PO Box 490
220 8th Ave. North
New Town, ND 58763-0490
Tel: (701)627-4738
Fax: (701)627-3609
E-mail: taulau@fbcc.bia.edu
President/CEO: Russell Mason, Jr.
Admissions: Twila Aulaumea
Type: Two-Year College **Sex:** Coed **Admission Plans:** Open Admission;

Deferred Admission **Application Deadline:** Rolling **Application Fee:** $10.00 **H.S. Requirements:** High school diploma required; GED accepted. For those who demonstrate ability to benefit from program: High school diploma or equivalent not required **Scholarships:** Available **Calendar System:** Semester, Summer Session Available **Faculty:** FT 12, PT 30 **Library Holdings:** 10,000 **Regional Accreditation:** North Central Association of Colleges and Schools **Credit Hours For Degree:** 64 semester hours, Associates **Intercollegiate Athletics:** Basketball M & W; Cross-Country Running M & W

JAMESTOWN COLLEGE
6000 College Ln.
Jamestown, ND 58405
Tel: (701)252-3467; Free: 800-336-2554
Fax: (701)253-4318
E-mail: admissions@jc.edu
Web Site: http://www.jc.edu/
President/CEO: Robert S. Badal
Admissions: Tena Lawrence
Financial Aid: Margery Michael
Type: Four-Year College **Sex:** Coed **Affiliation:** Presbyterian **Scores:** 56% ACT 18-23; 36% ACT 24-29 **% Accepted:** 67 **Admission Plans:** Deferred Admission **Application Deadline:** Rolling **Application Fee:** $35.00 **H.S. Requirements:** High school diploma required; GED accepted **Costs Per Year:** Application fee: $35. Comprehensive fee: $22,316 includes full-time tuition ($16,360), mandatory fees ($420), and college room and board ($5536). College room only: $2456. Room and board charges vary according to board plan. Part-time tuition: $400 per credit hour. Part-time tuition varies according to course load. **Scholarships:** Available **Calendar System:** Semester, Summer Session Available **Enrollment:** FT 933, PT 71 **Faculty:** FT 57, PT 22 **Student-Faculty Ratio:** 15:1 **Exams:** SAT I or ACT. **% Receiving Financial Aid:** 67 **% Residing in College-Owned, -Operated, or -Affiliated Housing:** 60 **Library Holdings:** 107,732 **Regional Accreditation:** North Central Association of Colleges and Schools **Credit Hours For Degree:** 128 semester hours, Bachelors **Professional Accreditation:** NLN **Intercollegiate Athletics:** Baseball M; Basketball M & W; Cross-Country Running M & W; Football M; Golf M & W; Soccer M & W; Softball W; Track and Field M & W; Volleyball W; Wrestling M & W

LAKE REGION STATE COLLEGE
1801 College Dr. North
Devils Lake, ND 58301-1598
Tel: (701)662-1600; Free: 800-443-1313
Admissions: (701)662-1514
Fax: (701)662-1570
E-mail: diane.knodel@lrsc.edu
Web Site: http://www.lrsc.edu/
President/CEO: Dr. Mike Bower
Admissions: Diane Knodel
Financial Aid: Katie Nettell
Type: Two-Year College **Sex:** Coed **Affiliation:** North Dakota University System **% Accepted:** 99 **Admission Plans:** Open Admission **Application Deadline:** Rolling **Application Fee:** $35.00 **H.S. Requirements:** High school diploma required; GED accepted **Costs Per Year:** Application fee: $35. State resident tuition: $3065 full-time, $127.71 per credit hour part-time. Nonresident tuition: $3065 full-time, $127.71 per credit hour part-time. College room and board: $5230. College room only: $1820. Room and board charges vary according to board plan and housing facility. **Scholarships:** Available **Calendar System:** Semester, Summer Session Available **Enrollment:** FT 490, PT 1,212 **Faculty:** FT 35, PT 106 **Student-Faculty Ratio:** 13:1 **Exams:** Other, SAT I or ACT. **% Residing in College-Owned, -Operated, or -Affiliated Housing:** 30 **Final Year or Final Semester Residency Requirement:** No **Library Holdings:** 60,000 **Regional Accreditation:** North Central Association of Colleges and Schools **Credit Hours For Degree:** 60 semester hours, Associates **Intercollegiate Athletics:** Basketball M & W

MAYVILLE STATE UNIVERSITY
330 3rd St., NE
Mayville, ND 58257-1299
Tel: (701)786-2301; Free: 800-437-4104
Admissions: (701)788-4842
Fax: (701)786-4748
E-mail: james.morowski@mayvillestate.edu
Web Site: http://www.mayvillestate.edu/
President/CEO: Dr. Gary Hagen
Admissions: Jim Morowski
Financial Aid: Shirley Hanson
Type: Four-Year College **Sex:** Coed **Affiliation:** North Dakota University System **Scores:** 47% ACT 18-23; 14% ACT 24-29 **% Accepted:** 57 **Admission Plans:** Open Admission; Deferred Admission **Application Deadline:** Rolling **Application Fee:** $35.00 **H.S. Requirements:** High school diploma required; GED accepted **Costs Per Year:** Application fee: $35. State resident tuition: $4124 full-time, $172 per credit hour part-time. Nonresident tuition: $6180 full-time, $257 per credit hour part-time. Mandatory fees: $1669 full-time, $70 per credit hour part-time. Full-time tuition and fees vary according to course load and reciprocity agreements. Part-time tuition and fees vary according to course load and reciprocity agreements. College room and board: $4488. College room only: $1818. Room and board charges vary according to board plan and housing facility. **Scholarships:** Available **Calendar System:** Semester, Summer Session Available **Enrollment:** FT 544, PT 343 **Faculty:** FT 36, PT 35 **Student-Faculty Ratio:** 14:1 **Exams:** SAT I or ACT. ACT essay not being used. SAT essay not being used. **% Receiving Financial Aid:** 83 **% Residing in College-Owned, -Operated, or -Affiliated Housing:** 24 **Final Year or Final Semester Residency Requirement:** No **Library Holdings:** 93,684 **Regional Accreditation:** North Central Association of Colleges and Schools **Credit Hours For Degree:** 64 semester hours, Associates; 120 semester hours, Bachelors **ROTC:** Army, Air Force **Professional Accreditation:** NCATE **Intercollegiate Athletics:** Baseball M; Basketball M & W; Football M; Softball W; Volleyball W

MEDCENTER ONE COLLEGE OF NURSING
512 North 7th St.
Bismarck, ND 58501-4494
Tel: (701)323-6271
E-mail: msmith@mohs.org
Web Site: http://www.medcenterone.com/collegeofnursing/index.asp
President/CEO: Karen Latham
Admissions: Mary Smith
Financial Aid: Janell Thomas
Type: Two-Year Upper Division **Sex:** Coed **Affiliation:** Medcenter One Health Systems **% Accepted:** 58 **Admission Plans:** Preferred Admission; Early Admission **Application Fee:** $40.00 **H.S. Requirements:** High school diploma required; GED accepted **Costs Per Year:** Application fee: $40. Tuition: $10,012 full-time. **Scholarships:** Available **Calendar System:** Semester, Summer Session Not available **Enrollment:** FT 89 **Faculty:** FT 10, PT 2 **Student-Faculty Ratio:** 8:1 **% Receiving Financial Aid:** 76 **Library Holdings:** 26,078 **Regional Accreditation:** North Central Association of Colleges and Schools **Credit Hours For Degree:** 128 credits, Bachelors **Professional Accreditation:** NLN

MINOT STATE UNIVERSITY
500 University Ave. West
Minot, ND 58707-0002
Tel: (701)858-3000; Free: 800-777-0750
Admissions: (701)858-3126
Fax: (701)839-6933
E-mail: askmsu@minotstateu.edu
Web Site: http://www.minotstateu.edu/
President/CEO: Dr. David Fuller
Admissions: Kevin Harmon
Financial Aid: Dale Gehring
Type: Comprehensive **Sex:** Coed **Affiliation:** North Dakota University System **% Accepted:** 82 **Admission Plans:** Deferred Admission **Application Deadline:** Rolling **Application Fee:** $35.00 **H.S. Requirements:** High school diploma required; GED accepted **Costs Per Year:** Application fee: $35. State resident tuition: $5389 full-time, $224.57 per credit hour part-time. Nonresident tuition: $5389 full-time, $224.57 per credit hour part-time. Full-time tuition varies according to class time, course load, degree level, location, program, and reciprocity agreements. Part-time tuition varies according to class time, degree level, location, program, and reciprocity agreements. College room and board: $4602. Room and board charges vary according to board plan and housing facility. **Scholarships:** Available **Calendar System:** Semester, Summer Session Available **Enrollment:** FT 2,300, PT 1,045, Grad FT 232, Grad PT 188 **Faculty:** FT 179, PT 112 **Student-Faculty Ratio:** 13:1 **Exams:** SAT I or ACT. **% Receiving Financial Aid:** 83 **% Residing in College-Owned, -Operated, or -Affiliated Housing:** 16 **Regional**

Accreditation: North Central Association of Colleges and Schools **Credit Hours For Degree:** 128 semester hours, Bachelors **Professional Accreditation:** ASLHA, CSWE, NASM, NCATE, NLN **Intercollegiate Athletics:** Baseball M; Basketball M & W; Cheerleading W; Cross-Country Running M & W; Football M; Golf M & W; Ice Hockey W; Softball W; Track and Field M & W; Volleyball W

NORTH DAKOTA STATE COLLEGE OF SCIENCE

800 North Sixth St.
Wahpeton, ND 58076
Tel: (701)671-2401; Free: 800-342-4325
Admissions: (701)671-2189
Fax: (701)671-2332
Web Site: http://www.ndscs.nodak.edu/
President/CEO: Dr. John Richman
Admissions: Karen Reilly
Financial Aid: Shelley Blome
Type: Two-Year College **Sex:** Coed **Affiliation:** North Dakota University System **Admission Plans:** Open Admission; Early Admission **Application Deadline:** Rolling **Application Fee:** $35.00 **H.S. Requirements:** High school diploma required; GED accepted **Scholarships:** Available **Calendar System:** Semester, Summer Session Available **Enrollment:** FT 902, PT 315 **Student-Faculty Ratio:** 18:1 **% Residing in College-Owned, -Operated, or -Affiliated Housing:** 38 **Library Holdings:** 78,876 **Regional Accreditation:** North Central Association of Colleges and Schools **Credit Hours For Degree:** 64 credits, Associates **Professional Accreditation:** ADA, AHIMA, AOTA, NLN **Intercollegiate Athletics:** Basketball M & W; Football M; Softball W; Volleyball W

NORTH DAKOTA STATE UNIVERSITY

1301 North University Ave.
Fargo, ND 58108
Tel: (701)231-8011; Free: 800-488-NDSU
Admissions: (701)231-8643
Fax: (701)231-8802
E-mail: ndsu.admission@ndsu.edu
Web Site: http://www.ndsu.edu/
President/CEO: Richard Hanson
Admissions: Jobey Lichtblau
Financial Aid: Jeanne Enebo
Type: University **Sex:** Coed **Affiliation:** North Dakota University System **Scores:** 94.5% SAT V 400+; 97.9% SAT M 400+; 49.1% ACT 18-23; 37.9% ACT 24-29 **% Accepted:** 79 **Application Deadline:** August 15 **Application Fee:** $35.00 **H.S. Requirements:** High school diploma required; GED accepted **Costs Per Year:** Application fee: $35. One-time mandatory fee: $45. State resident tuition: $5448 full-time, $227.02 per credit part-time. Nonresident tuition: $14,547 full-time, $606.12 per credit part-time. Mandatory fees: $962 full-time, $40.09 per credit part-time. Full-time tuition and fees vary according to reciprocity agreements. Part-time tuition and fees vary according to course load and reciprocity agreements. College room and board: $6568. College room only: $2868. Room and board charges vary according to board plan and housing facility. **Scholarships:** Available **Calendar System:** Semester, Summer Session Available **Enrollment:** FT 10,658, PT 1,075, Grad FT 1,021, Grad PT 1,435 **Faculty:** FT 647, PT 134 **Student-Faculty Ratio:** 18:1 **Exams:** SAT I or ACT. ACT essay not being used. SAT essay not being used. **% Receiving Financial Aid:** 57 **% Residing in College-Owned, -Operated, or -Affiliated Housing:** 35 **Final Year or Final Semester Residency Requirement:** Yes **Regional Accreditation:** North Central Association of Colleges and Schools **Credit Hours For Degree:** 122 credits, Bachelors **ROTC:** Army, Air Force **Professional Accreditation:** AACSB, ABET, ACPhE, AAMFT, AACN, AAFCS, ACCE, ACA, ADtA, ASLA, CARC, FIDER, JRCEPAT, NAAB, NASAD, NASM, NAST, NCATE, NLN **Intercollegiate Athletics:** Archery M & W; Baseball M; Basketball M & W; Bowling M & W; Cheerleading M & W; Cross-Country Running M & W; Football M; Golf M & W; Ice Hockey M; Lacrosse M; Riflery M & W; Rugby M & W; Soccer M & W; Softball W; Track and Field M & W; Volleyball M & W; Wrestling M

RASMUSSEN COLLEGE BISMARCK

1701 East Century Ave.
Bismarck, ND 58503
Tel: (701)530-9600; Free: 877-530-9600
Fax: (701)530-9604
Web Site: http://www.rasmussen.edu/
President/CEO: Brian Bowker
Type: Two-Year College **Sex:** Coed **Costs Per Year:** Tuition: $365 per credit part-time. Part-time tuition varies according to course level and program. **Regional Accreditation:** North Central Association of Colleges and Schools

RASMUSSEN COLLEGE FARGO

4012 19th Ave., SW
Fargo, ND 58103
Tel: (701)277-3889; Free: 800-817-0009
Fax: (701)277-5604
Web Site: http://www.rasmussen.edu/
President/CEO: Elizabeth Largent
Admissions: Elizabeth Largent
Type: Two-Year College **Sex:** Coed **Application Deadline:** October 1 **Application Fee:** $60.00 **Costs Per Year:** Application fee: $60. Tuition: $365 per credit part-time. Part-time tuition varies according to course level, course load, and program. **Calendar System:** Quarter **Enrollment:** FT 282, PT 361 **Faculty:** FT 6, PT 25 **Student-Faculty Ratio:** 13:1 **Professional Accreditation:** ACICS

SITTING BULL COLLEGE

1341 92nd St.
Fort Yates, ND 58538-9701
Tel: (701)854-8000
Fax: (701)854-3403
E-mail: melodys@sbcl.edu
Web Site: http://www.sittingbull.edu/
President/CEO: Laurel Vermillion
Admissions: Melody Silk
Type: Two-Year College **Sex:** Coed **% Accepted:** 100 **Admission Plans:** Open Admission; Early Admission **Application Deadline:** September 6 **Application Fee:** $10.00 **H.S. Requirements:** High school diploma required; GED accepted **Scholarships:** Available **Calendar System:** Semester, Summer Session Not available **Faculty:** FT 16, PT 16 **Student-Faculty Ratio:** 6:1 **Library Holdings:** 10,000 **Regional Accreditation:** North Central Association of Colleges and Schools **Credit Hours For Degree:** 67 credit hours, Associates **Intercollegiate Athletics:** Basketball M & W

TRINITY BIBLE COLLEGE

50 South 6th Ave.
Ellendale, ND 58436-7150
Tel: (701)349-3621; Free: 888-TBC-2DAY
Admissions: 888-822-2329
Fax: (701)349-5443
Web Site: http://www.trinitybiblecollege.edu/
President/CEO: Garnett Strom
Admissions: Rev. Steve Tvedt
Financial Aid: Susan Healy
Type: Four-Year College **Sex:** Coed **Affiliation:** Assemblies of God **Admission Plans:** Open Admission; Deferred Admission **Application Deadline:** Rolling **Application Fee:** $25.00 **H.S. Requirements:** High school diploma required; GED accepted **Scholarships:** Available **Calendar System:** Semester, Summer Session Available **Exams:** ACT, SAT I. **Library Holdings:** 67,868 **Regional Accreditation:** North Central Association of Colleges and Schools **Credit Hours For Degree:** 64 credits, Associates; 128 credits, Bachelors **Professional Accreditation:** ABHE **Intercollegiate Athletics:** Baseball M; Basketball M & W; Football M; Golf M; Track and Field M & W; Volleyball W; Wrestling M

TURTLE MOUNTAIN COMMUNITY COLLEGE

Box 340
Belcourt, ND 58316-0340
Tel: (701)477-7862
Fax: (701)477-7807
E-mail: jlafontaine@tm.edu
Web Site: http://www.turtle-mountain.cc.nd.us/
President/CEO: Dr. James Davis
Admissions: Joni LaFontaine
Type: Two-Year College **Sex:** Coed **% Accepted:** 100 **Admission Plans:** Open Admission; Early Admission; Deferred Admission **Application Deadline:** Rolling **H.S. Requirements:** High school diploma required; GED accepted **Scholarships:** Available **Calendar System:** Semester, Summer Session Not available **Enrollment:** FT 378, PT 201 **Faculty:** FT 21, PT 21

Exams: ACT. **Library Holdings:** 20,500 **Regional Accreditation:** North Central Association of Colleges and Schools **Credit Hours For Degree:** 62 semester hours, Associates

UNITED TRIBES TECHNICAL COLLEGE
3315 University Dr.
Bismarck, ND 58504-7596
Tel: (701)255-3285
E-mail: vgillette@uttc.edu
Web Site: http://www.uttc.edu/
President/CEO: Dr. David Gipp
Admissions: Vivian Gillette
Type: Two-Year College **Sex:** Coed **% Accepted:** 84 **Admission Plans:** Open Admission **Application Deadline:** Rolling **Application Fee:** $0.00 **H.S. Requirements:** High school diploma required; GED accepted **Costs Per Year:** Application fee: $0. State resident tuition: $2800 full-time, $87.50 per credit part-time. Mandatory fees: $630 full-time. College room and board: $5210. College room only: $3000. Room and board charges vary according to housing facility and location. **Scholarships:** Available **Calendar System:** Semester, Summer Session Available **Enrollment:** FT 552, PT 52 **Faculty:** FT 49, PT 14 **Student-Faculty Ratio:** 8:1 **Library Holdings:** 6,000 **Regional Accreditation:** North Central Association of Colleges and Schools **Credit Hours For Degree:** 60 credit hours, Associates **Professional Accreditation:** AHIMA **Intercollegiate Athletics:** Basketball M; Cross-Country Running M & W

UNIVERSITY OF MARY
7500 University Dr.
Bismarck, ND 58504-9652
Tel: (701)255-7500; Free: 800-288-6279
Admissions: (701)355-8390
Fax: (701)255-7687
E-mail: phelm@umary.edu
Web Site: http://www.umary.edu/
President/CEO: Fr. James Patrick Shea
Admissions: Pam Helm
Financial Aid: Brenda Zastoupil
Type: Comprehensive **Sex:** Coed **Affiliation:** Roman Catholic **Scores:** 59% ACT 18-23; 31% ACT 24-29 **% Accepted:** 78 **Admission Plans:** Early Admission; Deferred Admission **Application Deadline:** Rolling **Application Fee:** $25.00 **H.S. Requirements:** High school diploma required; GED accepted **Costs Per Year:** Application fee: $25. Comprehensive fee: $18,276 includes full-time tuition ($12,800), mandatory fees ($326), and college room and board ($5150). College room only: $2350. Full-time tuition and fees vary according to course load, degree level, and program. Room and board charges vary according to board plan and housing facility. Part-time tuition: $400 per credit hour. Part-time tuition varies according to course load, degree level, and program. **Scholarships:** Available **Calendar System:** Miscellaneous, Summer Session Available **Enrollment:** FT 1,603, PT 424, Grad FT 479, Grad PT 343 **Faculty:** FT 93, PT 180 **Student-Faculty Ratio:** 15:1 **Exams:** SAT I or ACT. ACT essay not being used. **% Residing in College-Owned, -Operated, or -Affiliated Housing:** 31 **Final Year or Final Semester Residency Requirement:** No **Library Holdings:** 64,524 **Regional Accreditation:** North Central Association of Colleges and Schools **Credit Hours For Degree:** 64 credit hours, Associates; 128 credit hours, Bachelors **Professional Accreditation:** AACN, AOTA, APTA, CARC, CSWE, JRCEPAT, NLN **Intercollegiate Athletics:** Baseball M; Basketball M & W; Cross-Country Running M & W; Football M; Golf M & W; Soccer M & W; Softball W; Tennis M & W; Track and Field M & W; Volleyball W; Wrestling M

UNIVERSITY OF NORTH DAKOTA
264 Centennial Dr.
Grand Forks, ND 58202
Tel: (701)777-2011; Free: 800-CAL-LUND
Admissions: (701)777-3821
Fax: (701)777-3650
E-mail: enrollmentservices@mail.und.nodak.edu
Web Site: http://www.und.nodak.edu/
President/CEO: Robert O. Kelley
Admissions: Deborah Melby
Financial Aid: Robin Holden
Type: University **Sex:** Coed **Affiliation:** North Dakota University System **Scores:** 50% ACT 18-23; 40% ACT 24-29 **% Accepted:** 73 **Admission Plans:** Deferred Admission **Application Fee:** $35.00 **H.S. Requirements:** High school diploma required; GED accepted **Costs Per Year:** Application fee: $35. State resident tuition: $5461 full-time, $227 per credit hour part-time. Nonresident tuition: $14,580 full-time, $607 per credit hour part-time. Mandatory fees: $1266 full-time. Full-time tuition and fees vary according to degree level, program, and reciprocity agreements. Part-time tuition varies according to course load, degree level, program, and reciprocity agreements. College room and board: $5702. College room only: $2289. Room and board charges vary according to board plan and housing facility. **Scholarships:** Available **Calendar System:** Semester, Summer Session Available **Enrollment:** FT 8,739, PT 1,701, Grad FT 1,476, Grad PT 1,256 **Faculty:** FT 594, PT 70 **Student-Faculty Ratio:** 18:1 **Exams:** ACT, SAT I or ACT. **% Receiving Financial Aid:** 73 **% Residing in College-Owned, -Operated, or -Affiliated Housing:** 32 **Library Holdings:** 1,083,215 **Regional Accreditation:** North Central Association of Colleges and Schools **Credit Hours For Degree:** 125 credit hours, Bachelors **ROTC:** Army, Air Force **Professional Accreditation:** AACSB, ABET, AACN, AANA, ABA, ADtA, AOTA, APTA, APA, ASC, ASLHA, AALS, CAA, CSWE, JRCEPAT, LCMEAMA, NAACLS, NASAD, NASM, NASPAA NAST, NCATE, NAIT **Intercollegiate Athletics:** Baseball M; Basketball M & W; Cross-Country Running M & W; Football M; Golf M & W; Ice Hockey M & W; Soccer W; Softball W; Swimming and Diving M & W; Tennis W; Track and Field M & W; Volleyball W

VALLEY CITY STATE UNIVERSITY
101 College St., SW
Valley City, ND 58072
Tel: (701)845-7990; Free: 800-532-8641
Admissions: (701)845-7204
Fax: (701)845-7245
E-mail: alison.kasowski@vcsu.edu
Web Site: http://www.vcsu.edu/
President/CEO: Dr. Steven Shirley
Admissions: Alison Kasowski
Financial Aid: Betty Kuss Schumacher
Type: Comprehensive **Sex:** Coed **Affiliation:** North Dakota University System **Scores:** 85% SAT V 400+; 93% SAT M 400+; 56% ACT 18-23; 21% ACT 24-29 **% Accepted:** 90 **Admission Plans:** Open Admission; Early Admission; Deferred Admission **Application Deadline:** Rolling **Application Fee:** $35.00 **H.S. Requirements:** High school diploma required; GED accepted **Costs Per Year:** Application fee: $35. State resident tuition: $4433 full-time, $147.76 per semester hour part-time. Nonresident tuition: $11,835 full-time, $394.50 per semester hour part-time. Mandatory fees: $1642 full-time, $68.45 per semester hour part-time. Full-time tuition and fees vary according to course load, location, program, and reciprocity agreements. Part-time tuition and fees vary according to course load, location, program, and reciprocity agreements. College room and board: $4528. College room only: $1812. Room and board charges vary according to board plan and housing facility. **Scholarships:** Available **Calendar System:** Semester, Summer Session Available **Enrollment:** FT 688, PT 273, Grad FT 7, Grad PT 115 **Faculty:** FT 58, PT 37 **Student-Faculty Ratio:** 12:1 **Exams:** SAT I or ACT. ACT essay not being used. SAT essay not being used. **% Receiving Financial Aid:** 66 **% Residing in College-Owned, -Operated, or -Affiliated Housing:** 40 **Final Year or Final Semester Residency Requirement:** No **Library Holdings:** 149,822 **Regional Accreditation:** North Central Association of Colleges and Schools **Credit Hours For Degree:** 128 semester hours, Bachelors **Professional Accreditation:** NASM, NCATE **Intercollegiate Athletics:** Baseball M; Basketball M & W; Football M; Softball W; Tennis M & W; Track and Field M & W; Volleyball W

WILLISTON STATE COLLEGE
Box 1326
Williston, ND 58802-1326
Tel: (701)774-4200; Free: 888-863-9455
Fax: (701)774-4211
E-mail: wsc.admission@wsc.nodak.edu
Web Site: http://www.wsc.nodak.edu/
President/CEO: Dr. Raymond Nadolny
Admissions: Jan Solem
Type: Two-Year College **Sex:** Coed **Affiliation:** North Dakota University System **% Accepted:** 98 **Admission Plans:** Open Admission **Application Deadline:** Rolling **Application Fee:** $35.00 **H.S. Requirements:** High school diploma required; GED accepted **Costs Per Year:** Application fee: $35. One-time mandatory fee: $35. State resident tuition: $100.68 per credit

hour part-time. Nonresident tuition: $151.02 per credit hour part-time. Mandatory fees: $29.76 per credit hour part-time. Part-time tuition and fees vary according to course load, location, program, and reciprocity agreements. College room and board: $3032. College room only: $1390. Room and board charges vary according to housing facility. **Scholarships:** Available **Calendar System:** Semester, Summer Session Available **Enrollment:** FT 557, PT 390 **Faculty:** FT 26, PT 67 **Student-Faculty Ratio:** 14:1 **% Residing in College-Owned, -Operated, or -Affiliated Housing:** 13 **Library Holdings:** 16,218 **Regional Accreditation:** North Central Association of Colleges and Schools **Credit Hours For Degree:** 62 credit hours, Associates **Professional Accreditation:** APTA **Intercollegiate Athletics:** Baseball M; Basketball M & W; Volleyball W

ACADEMY OF COURT REPORTING (AKRON)
2930 West Market St.
Akron, OH 44333
Tel: (330)867-4030; Free: (866)323-0540
E-mail: careeradvocate@miamijacobs.edu
Web Site: http://www.acr.edu/
President/CEO: Lynn Mizanin
Type: Two-Year College **Sex:** Coed **Admission Plans:** Open Admission **Application Fee:** $25.00

ACADEMY OF COURT REPORTING (CLEVELAND)
2044 Euclid Ave.
Cleveland, OH 44115
Tel: (216)861-3222
Fax: (216)861-4517
E-mail: admissionaocr@hotmail.com
Web Site: http://www.acr.edu/
President/CEO: Lynn M. Mizanin, CPE
Admissions: Sheila Woods
Type: Two-Year College **Sex:** Coed **Application Fee:** $100.00 **Professional Accreditation:** ACICS

ALLEGHENY WESLEYAN COLLEGE
2161 Woodsdale Rd.
Salem, OH 44460
Tel: (330)337-6403; Free: 800-292-3153
Fax: (330)337-6255
E-mail: college@awc.edu
Web Site: http://www.awc.edu/
President/CEO: Robert E. England, Sr.
Financial Aid: Esther Phelps
Type: Four-Year College **Sex:** Coed **Admission Plans:** Open Admission **Application Fee:** $35.00 **Calendar System:** Semester **Professional Accreditation:** ABHE

ANTIOCH UNIVERSITY MCGREGOR
900 Dayton St.
Yellow Springs, OH 45387-1609
Tel: (937)769-1800
Admissions: (937)769-1823
Fax: (937)769-1805
E-mail: orobinson@antioch.edu
Web Site: http://www.mcgregor.edu/
President/CEO: Dr. Michael Fishbein
Admissions: Oscar Robinson
Financial Aid: Kathy John
Type: Two-Year Upper Division **Sex:** Coed **Affiliation:** Antioch University **Admission Plans:** Deferred Admission **Application Fee:** $45.00 **H.S. Requirements:** High school diploma required; GED accepted **Costs Per Year:** Application fee: $45. Tuition: $20,160 full-time, $315 per credit hour part-time. Mandatory fees: $600 full-time. **Scholarships:** Available **Calendar System:** Quarter, Summer Session Available **Enrollment:** FT 88, PT 88, Grad FT 365, Grad PT 157 **Faculty:** FT 20, PT 46 **Student-Faculty Ratio:** 10:1 **% Receiving Financial Aid:** 78 **Final Year or Final Semester Residency Requirement:** No **Library Holdings:** 521,562 **Regional Accreditation:** North Central Association of Colleges and Schools **Credit Hours For Degree:** 180 credit hours, Bachelors **Professional Accreditation:** NCATE

ANTONELLI COLLEGE
124 East Seventh St.
Cincinnati, OH 45202
Tel: (513)241-4338; Free: 800-505-4338
Fax: (513)241-9396
E-mail: admissions.cincinnati@antonellicollege.edu
Web Site: http://www.antonellicollege.edu/
President/CEO: Mary Ann Davis
Admissions: Rashawn Jones
Type: Two-Year College **Sex:** Coed **Admission Plans:** Open Admission; Early Admission; Deferred Admission **Application Deadline:** Rolling **Application Fee:** $100.00 **H.S. Requirements:** High school diploma required; GED accepted **Scholarships:** Available **Calendar System:** Quarter, Summer Session Available **Library Holdings:** 2,000 **Credit Hours For Degree:** 95 credit hours, Associates **Professional Accreditation:** ACCSCT

ART ACADEMY OF CINCINNATI
1212 Jackson St.
Cincinnati, OH 45202
Tel: (513)562-6262
Admissions: (513)562-8744
Fax: (513)562-8778
E-mail: admissions@artacademy.edu
Web Site: http://www.artacademy.edu/
President/CEO: Gregory Allgire Smith
Admissions: John J. Wadell
Financial Aid: Karen Geiger
Type: Comprehensive **Sex:** Coed **Scores:** 96% SAT V 400+; 93% SAT M 400+; 58% ACT 18-23; 21% ACT 24-29 **% Accepted:** 21 **Admission Plans:** Deferred Admission **Application Deadline:** June 30 **Application Fee:** $0.00 **H.S. Requirements:** High school diploma required; GED accepted **Costs Per Year:** Application fee: $0. Tuition: $21,500 full-time, $900 per hour part-time. Mandatory fees: $380 full-time, $190 per term part-time. College room only: $6000. **Scholarships:** Available **Calendar System:** Semester, Summer Session Available **Enrollment:** FT 153, PT 11 **Faculty:** FT 14, PT 30 **Student-Faculty Ratio:** 10:1 **Exams:** SAT I or ACT. **% Receiving Financial Aid:** 77 **% Residing in College-Owned, -Operated, or -Affiliated Housing:** 18 **Regional Accreditation:** North Central Association of Colleges and Schools **Credit Hours For Degree:** 65 credit hours, Associates; 132 credit hours, Bachelors **Professional Accreditation:** NASAD

THE ART INSTITUTE OF CINCINNATI
1171 East Kemper Rd.
Cincinnati, OH 45246
Tel: (513)751-1206
Fax: (513)751-1209
Web Site: http://www.theartinstituteofcincinnati.com/
President/CEO: Sean M. Mendell
Type: Two-Year College **Sex:** Coed **Application Fee:** $100.00 **Student-Faculty Ratio:** 7:1 **Credit Hours For Degree:** 120 credits, Associates **Professional Accreditation:** ACCSCT

THE ART INSTITUTE OF OHIO—CINCINNATI
8845 Governors Hill Dr.
Cincinnati, OH 45249-3317
Tel: (513)833-2400; Free: (866)613-5184
Fax: 877-477-8486
Web Site: http://www.artinstitutes.edu/cincinnati/
President/CEO: Maurice Lee
Type: Two-Year College **Sex:** Coed **Affiliation:** Education Management Corporation **Calendar System:** Continuous **Regional Accreditation:** North Central Association of Colleges and Schools

ASHLAND UNIVERSITY
401 College Ave.
Ashland, OH 44805-3702
Tel: (419)289-4142; Free: 800-882-1548
Admissions: (419)289-5052
Fax: (419)289-5999
E-mail: enrollme@ashland.edu
Web Site: http://www.exploreashland.com/
President/CEO: Dr. Frederick Finks
Admissions: Thomas Mansperger
Financial Aid: Stephen C. Howell
Type: Comprehensive **Sex:** Coed **Affiliation:** Brethren Church **Scores:** 89% SAT V 400+; 91% SAT M 400+; 57% ACT 18-23; 31% ACT 24-29 **% Accepted:** 82 **Admission Plans:** Deferred Admission **Application Deadline:** Rolling **Application Fee:** $0.00 **H.S. Requirements:** High school diploma required; GED accepted **Costs Per Year:** Application fee: $0. Comprehensive fee: $34,992 includes full-time tuition ($24,828), mandatory fees ($812), and college room and board ($9352). College room only: $5022. Full-time tuition and fees vary according to degree level, location, and reciprocity agreements. Room and board charges vary according to board plan and housing facility. Part-time tuition: $762 per credit. Part-time mandatory fees: $18 per credit. Part-time tuition and fees vary according to course load, degree level, location, and program. **Scholarships:** Available **Calendar System:** Semester, Summer Session Available **Enrollment:** FT 2,364, PT 290 **Faculty:** FT 234, PT 347 **Student-Faculty Ratio:** 16:1 **Exams:** SAT I or ACT. **% Receiving Financial Aid:** 82 **% Residing in College-Owned, -Operated, or -Affiliated Housing:** 72 **Library Holdings:** 205,200 **Regional Accreditation:** North Central Association of Colleges and Schools **Credit Hours For Degree:** 64 credit hours, Associates; 128 credit hours, Bachelors **Professional Accreditation:** AACN, AAFCS, ACBSP, ATS, CSWE, NASM, NCATE **Intercollegiate Athletics:** Baseball M; Basketball M & W; Cross-Country Running M & W; Football M; Golf M & W; Soccer M & W; Softball M & W; Swimming and Diving M & W; Tennis M & W; Track and Field M & W; Volleyball W; Wrestling M

ATS INSTITUTE OF TECHNOLOGY
325 Alpha Park
Highland Heights, OH 44143
Tel: (440)449-1700
Fax: (440)449-1389
E-mail: info@atsinstitute.com
Web Site: http://www.atsinstitute.edu/
President/CEO: Yelena Bykov
Type: Two-Year College **Sex:** Coed **Admission Plans:** Open Admission **Application Fee:** $30.00 **H.S. Requirements:** High school diploma required; GED accepted **Costs Per Year:** Application fee: $30. Tuition: $497 per credit hour part-time. Part-time tuition varies according to course load and program. **Exams:** Other. **Credit Hours For Degree:** 80.5 credits, Associates **Professional Accreditation:** ACICS

BALDWIN-WALLACE COLLEGE
275 Eastland Rd.
Berea, OH 44017-2088
Tel: (440)826-2900
Admissions: (440)826-2222
Fax: (440)826-3830
E-mail: admission@bw.edu
Web Site: http://www.bw.edu/
President/CEO: Richard Durst
Admissions: Patricia Skrha
Financial Aid: Dr. George L. Rolleston
Type: Comprehensive **Sex:** Coed **Affiliation:** Methodist **Scores:** 94.97% SAT V 400+; 95.09% SAT M 400+; 41.8% ACT 18-23; 43% ACT 24-29 **% Accepted:** 67 **Admission Plans:** Deferred Admission **Application Deadline:** March 1 **Application Fee:** $25.00 **H.S. Requirements:** High school diploma required; GED accepted **Costs Per Year:** Application fee: $25. Comprehensive fee: $32,190 includes full-time tuition ($24,230) and college room and board ($7960). College room only: $3888. Full-time tuition varies according to class time and course load. Part-time tuition: $770 per semester hour. Part-time tuition varies according to class time and course load. **Scholarships:** Available **Calendar System:** Semester, Summer Session Available **Enrollment:** FT 3,180, PT 504, Grad FT 380, Grad PT 333 **Faculty:** FT 167, PT 251 **Student-Faculty Ratio:** 15:1 **Exams:** SAT I or ACT. ACT essay not being used. **% Receiving Financial Aid:** 80 **% Residing in College-Owned, -Operated, or -Affiliated Housing:** 61 **Library Holdings:** 200,000 **Regional Accreditation:** North Central Association of Colleges and Schools **Credit Hours For Degree:** 124 semester hours, Bachelors **ROTC:** Army, Air Force **Professional Accreditation:** NASM, NCATE **Intercollegiate Athletics:** Baseball M; Basketball M & W; Cross-Country Running M & W; Football M; Golf M & W; Soccer M & W; Softball W; Swimming and Diving M & W; Tennis M & W; Track and Field M & W; Volleyball W; Wrestling M

BELMONT TECHNICAL COLLEGE
120 Fox Shannon Place
St. Clairsville, OH 43950-9735
Tel: (740)695-9500
Fax: (740)695-2247
E-mail: msterling@btc.edu
Web Site: http://www.btc.edu/
President/CEO: Joseph E. Bukowski
Admissions: Michael Sterling
Type: Two-Year College **Sex:** Coed **Affiliation:** Ohio Board of Regents **Admission Plans:** Open Admission; Early Admission **Application Deadline:** Rolling **H.S. Requirements:** High school diploma required; GED accepted **Scholarships:** Available **Calendar System:** Quarter, Summer Session Available **Library Holdings:** 5,612 **Regional Accreditation:** North Central Association of Colleges and Schools **Credit Hours For Degree:** 90 credits, Associates **Professional Accreditation:** AAMAE

BLUFFTON UNIVERSITY
1 University Dr.
Bluffton, OH 45817
Tel: (419)358-3000; Free: 800-488-3257
Admissions: (419)358-3254
Fax: (419)358-3232
E-mail: admissions@bluffton.edu
Web Site: http://www.bluffton.edu/
President/CEO: Dr. James M. Harder
Admissions: Chris Jebsen
Financial Aid: Lawrence Matthews
Type: Comprehensive **Sex:** Coed **Affiliation:** Mennonite **Scores:** 82% SAT V 400+; 84% SAT M 400+; 56% ACT 18-23; 27% ACT 24-29 **% Accepted:** 66 **Admission Plans:** Deferred Admission **Application Deadline:** August 15 **Application Fee:** $20.00 **H.S. Requirements:** High school diploma required; GED accepted **Costs Per Year:** Application fee: $20. Comprehensive fee: $33,278 includes full-time tuition ($24,480), mandatory fees ($450), and college room and board ($8348). College room only: $4102. Full-time tuition and fees vary according to course load. Room and board charges vary according to board plan and housing facility. Part-time tuition: $1020 per credit hour. Part-time mandatory fees: $113 per term. Part-time tuition and fees vary according to course load. **Scholarships:** Available **Calendar System:** Semester, Summer Session Available **Enrollment:** FT 911, PT 94, Grad FT 105, Grad PT 17 **Faculty:** FT 62, PT 47 **Student-Faculty Ratio:** 13:1 **Exams:** SAT I or ACT. ACT essay not being used. SAT essay not being used. **% Receiving Financial Aid:** 88 **% Residing in College-Owned, -Operated, or -Affiliated Housing:** 82 **Final Year or Final Semester Residency Requirement:** Yes **Library Holdings:** 161,372 **Regional Accreditation:** North Central Association of Colleges and Schools **Credit Hours For Degree:** 124 semester hours, Bachelors **Professional Accreditation:** CSWE, NASM, NCATE **Intercollegiate Athletics:** Baseball M; Basketball M & W; Cross-Country Running M & W; Football M; Soccer M & W; Softball W; Track and Field M & W; Volleyball W

BOWLING GREEN STATE UNIVERSITY
Bowling Green, OH 43403
Tel: (419)372-2531

Admissions: (419)372-BGSU
E-mail: choosebgsu@bgsu.edu
Web Site: http://www.bgsu.edu/
President/CEO: Dr. Carol A. Cartwright
Admissions: Gary Swegan
Financial Aid: Eric Bucks
Type: University **Sex:** Coed **Scores:** 92% SAT V 400+; 91% SAT M 400+; 57% ACT 18-23; 29% ACT 24-29 **% Accepted:** 89 **Admission Plans:** Deferred Admission **Application Deadline:** July 15 **Application Fee:** $40.00 **H.S. Requirements:** High school diploma required; GED accepted **Costs Per Year:** Application fee: $40. State resident tuition: $7778 full-time, $324 per credit hour part-time. Nonresident tuition: $15,086 full-time, $629 per credit hour part-time. Mandatory fees: $1282 full-time, $53 per credit hour part-time. Full-time tuition and fees vary according to course load and location. Part-time tuition and fees vary according to course load and location. College room and board: $7670. Room and board charges vary according to board plan and housing facility. **Scholarships:** Available **Calendar System:** Semester, Summer Session Available **Enrollment:** FT 13,162, PT 1,157, Grad FT 1,531, Grad PT 1,459 **Faculty:** FT 795, PT 157 **Student-Faculty Ratio:** 18:1 **Exams:** SAT I or ACT. **% Receiving Financial Aid:** 62 **% Residing in College-Owned, -Operated, or -Affiliated Housing:** 40 **Final Year or Final Semester Residency Requirement:** No **Library Holdings:** 2,312,426 **Regional Accreditation:** North Central Association of Colleges and Schools **Credit Hours For Degree:** 122 credit hours, Bachelors **ROTC:** Army, Air Force **Professional Accreditation:** AACSB, ACEJMC, AAFCS, ACCE, ADtA, APTA, APA, ASLHA, CARC, CEPH, CORE, CSWE, NAACLS, NASAD, NASM, NAST, NCATE, NRPA, NAIT **Intercollegiate Athletics:** Baseball M; Basketball M & W; Cross-Country Running M & W; Football M; Golf M & W; Gymnastics W; Ice Hockey M; Soccer M & W; Softball W; Swimming and Diving W; Tennis W; Track and Field W; Volleyball W

BOWLING GREEN STATE UNIVERSITY—FIRELANDS COLLEGE
One University Dr.
Huron, OH 44839-9791
Tel: (419)433-5560
E-mail: divers@bgsu.edu
Web Site: http://www.firelands.bgsu.edu/
President/CEO: Dr. William K. Balzer
Admissions: Debralee Divers
Type: Two-Year College **Sex:** Coed **Affiliation:** Bowling Green State University System **Admission Plans:** Open Admission; Early Admission; Deferred Admission **Application Deadline:** August 6 **Application Fee:** $40.00 **H.S. Requirements:** High school diploma required; GED accepted **Costs Per Year:** Application fee: $40. State resident tuition: $4022 full-time, $2352 per year part-time. Nonresident tuition: $11,300 full-time, $6012 per year part-time. Mandatory fees: $206 full-time, $136 per year part-time. Full-time tuition and fees vary according to course load and location. Part-time tuition and fees vary according to course load and location. **Calendar System:** Semester, Summer Session Available **Enrollment:** FT 1,352, PT 1,103, Grad PT 1 **Faculty:** FT 51, PT 93 **Student-Faculty Ratio:** 18:1 **Library Holdings:** 61,019 **Regional Accreditation:** North Central Association of Colleges and Schools **Credit Hours For Degree:** 62 credit hours, Associates **ROTC:** Army, Air Force **Professional Accreditation:** AHIMA

BRADFORD SCHOOL
2469 Stelzer Rd.
Columbus, OH 43219
Tel: (614)416-6200; Free: 800-678-7981
Web Site: http://www.bradfordschoolcolumbus.edu/
President/CEO: Dennis Bartels
Type: Two-Year College **Sex:** Coed **% Accepted:** 54 **H.S. Requirements:** High school diploma required; GED accepted **Scholarships:** Available **Calendar System:** Semester, Summer Session Not available **Professional Accreditation:** ACICS

BROWN MACKIE COLLEGE—AKRON
755 White Pond Dr.
Ste. 101
Akron, OH 44320
Tel: (330)869-3600
Fax: (330)733-5853
Web Site: http://www.brownmackie.edu/akron/
President/CEO: Tod Gibbs
Type: Two-Year College **Sex:** Coed **Affiliation:** Education Management Corporation **Calendar System:** Quarter **Professional Accreditation:** ACICS, AAMAE

BROWN MACKIE COLLEGE—CINCINNATI
1011 Glendale-Milford Rd.
Cincinnati, OH 45215
Tel: (513)771-2424; Free: 800-888-1445
Web Site: http://www.brownmackie.edu/cincinnati/
President/CEO: Robin Krout
Type: Two-Year College **Sex:** Coed **Affiliation:** Education Management Corporation **Calendar System:** Quarter **Professional Accreditation:** ACICS, AAMAE

BROWN MACKIE COLLEGE—FINDLAY
1700 Fostoria Ave.
Ste. 100
Findlay, OH 45840
Tel: (419)423-2211; Free: 800-842-3687
Fax: (419)423-0725
Web Site: http://www.brownmackie.edu/findlay/
President/CEO: Wayne Korpics
Type: Two-Year College **Sex:** Coed **Affiliation:** Education Management Corporation **Calendar System:** Continuous **Professional Accreditation:** ACICS

BROWN MACKIE COLLEGE—NORTH CANTON
4300 Munson St. NW
Canton, OH 44718-3674
Tel: (330)494-1214
Web Site: http://www.brownmackie.edu/northcanton/
President/CEO: Peter J. Perkowski
Type: Two-Year College **Sex:** Coed **Affiliation:** Education Management Corporation **Calendar System:** Quarter **Professional Accreditation:** ACICS

BRYANT & STRATTON COLLEGE (CLEVELAND)
1700 East 13th St.
Cleveland, OH 44114-3203
Tel: (216)771-1700
Fax: (216)771-1700
Web Site: http://www.bryantstratton.edu/
President/CEO: James Ploskonka, PhD
Financial Aid: Bill Davenport
Type: Four-Year College **Sex:** Coed **Affiliation:** Bryant and Stratton College, Inc. **Admission Plans:** Deferred Admission **Application Deadline:** Rolling **H.S. Requirements:** High school diploma required; GED accepted **Scholarships:** Available **Calendar System:** Semester, Summer Session Available **Enrollment:** FT 376, PT 148 **Faculty:** FT 13, PT 24 **Student-Faculty Ratio:** 10:1 **Exams:** Other, SAT I or ACT. **% Receiving Financial Aid:** 87 **% Residing in College-Owned, -Operated, or -Affiliated Housing:** 10 **Library Holdings:** 4,466 **Regional Accreditation:** Middle State Association of Colleges and Schools **Credit Hours For Degree:** 64 semester credit hours, Associates; 136 semester credit hours, Bachelors

BRYANT & STRATTON COLLEGE (EASTLAKE)
35350 Curtis Blvd.
Eastlake, OH 44095
Tel: (440)510-1112
Web Site: http://www.bryantstratton.edu/
President/CEO: Dr. Ted Hansen
Admissions: Melanie Pettit
Type: Two-Year College **Sex:** Coed **Affiliation:** Bryant and Stratton College, Inc. **Admission Plans:** Deferred Admission **Application Deadline:** Rolling **Application Fee:** $35.00 **H.S. Requirements:** High school diploma required; GED accepted. For applicants 19 or over who meet entrance testing requirements: High school diploma required; GED not accepted **Scholarships:** Available **Calendar System:** Semester, Summer Session Available **Enrollment:** FT 490, PT 272 **Faculty:** FT 24, PT 39 **Student-Faculty Ratio:** 12:1 **Exams:** Other, SAT I or ACT. **Library Holdings:** 1,500 **Regional Accreditation:** Middle State Association of Colleges and Schools **Credit Hours For Degree:** 68 semester hours, Associates

BRYANT & STRATTON COLLEGE (PARMA)
12955 Snow Rd.
Parma, OH 44130-1013
Tel: (216)265-3151
Fax: (216)265-0325
E-mail: atinman@bryantstratton.edu
Web Site: http://www.bryantstratton.edu/
President/CEO: Lisa Mason
Admissions: Andrea Inman
Type: Two-Year College **Sex:** Coed **Affiliation:** Bryant and Stratton College, Inc. **Admission Plans:** Deferred Admission **Application Deadline:** Rolling **H.S. Requirements:** High school diploma required; GED accepted. For applicants 19 or over who meet entrance testing requirements: High school diploma required; GED not accepted **Scholarships:** Available **Calendar System:** Semester, Summer Session Available **Enrollment:** FT 288, PT 240 **Faculty:** FT 16, PT 41 **Student-Faculty Ratio:** 12:1 **Exams:** Other, SAT I or ACT. **Library Holdings:** 1,500 **Regional Accreditation:** Middle State Association of Colleges and Schools **Credit Hours For Degree:** 68 semester hours, Associates

CAPITAL UNIVERSITY
1 College and Main
Columbus, OH 43209-2394
Tel: (614)236-6011; Free: 800-289-6289
Admissions: (614)236-6574
Fax: (614)236-6820
E-mail: asteiner@capital.edu
Web Site: http://www.capital.edu/
President/CEO: Dr. Denvy Bowman
Admissions: Amanda Steiner
Financial Aid: Pamela Varda
Type: Comprehensive **Sex:** Coed **Affiliation:** Evangelical Lutheran Church in America **Scores:** 97% SAT V 400+; 96% SAT M 400+; 45% ACT 18-23; 43% ACT 24-29 **% Accepted:** 75 **Admission Plans:** Deferred Admission **Application Deadline:** May 1 **Application Fee:** $25.00 **H.S. Requirements:** High school diploma required; GED accepted **Costs Per Year:** Application fee: $25. Comprehensive fee: $35,990 includes full-time tuition ($28,480) and college room and board ($7510). Full-time tuition varies according to course load, degree level, program, and student level. Room and board charges vary according to board plan and housing facility. Part-time tuition: $950 per credit hour. Part-time tuition varies according to course load, degree level, program, and student level. **Scholarships:** Available **Calendar System:** Semester, Summer Session Available **Enrollment:** FT 2,359, PT 271, Grad FT 554, Grad PT 356 **Faculty:** FT 203, PT 189 **Student-Faculty Ratio:** 11:1 **Exams:** SAT I or ACT. ACT essay not being used. SAT essay not being used. **% Receiving Financial Aid:** 78 **% Residing in College-Owned, -Operated, or -Affiliated Housing:** 47 **Final Year or Final Semester Residency Requirement:** No **Library Holdings:** 209,524 **Regional Accreditation:** North Central Association of Colleges and Schools **Credit Hours For Degree:** 124 semester hours, Bachelors **ROTC:** Army, Air Force **Professional Accreditation:** AACN, ABA, AALS, ACBSP, CSWE, JRCEPAT, NASM, NCATE **Intercollegiate Athletics:** Baseball M; Basketball M & W; Cross-Country Running M & W; Football M; Golf M & W; Soccer M & W; Softball W; Tennis M & W; Track and Field M & W; Volleyball W

CASE WESTERN RESERVE UNIVERSITY
10900 Euclid Ave.
Cleveland, OH 44106
Tel: (216)368-2000
Admissions: (216)368-4450
Fax: (216)368-5111
E-mail: admission@case.edu
Web Site: http://www.case.edu/
President/CEO: Barbara R. Snyder
Admissions: Robert McCullough
Financial Aid: Venus M. Puliafico
Type: University **Sex:** Coed **Scores:** 99.7% SAT V 400+; 99.9% SAT M 400+; 2.5% ACT 18-23; 38.5% ACT 24-29 **% Accepted:** 70 **Admission Plans:** Early Admission; Early Action; Deferred Admission **Application Deadline:** January 15 **Application Fee:** $0.00 **H.S. Requirements:** High school diploma required; GED accepted **Costs Per Year:** Application fee: $0. One-time mandatory fee: $370. Comprehensive fee: $47,128 includes full-time tuition ($35,900), mandatory fees ($338), and college room and board ($10,890). College room only: $6270. Room and board charges vary according to board plan, housing facility, and student level. Part-time tuition: $1496 per credit hour. Part-time tuition varies according to course load. **Scholarships:** Available **Calendar System:** Semester, Summer Session Available **Enrollment:** FT 4,095, PT 133, Grad FT 4,360, Grad PT 1,150 **Faculty:** FT 746, PT 171 **Student-Faculty Ratio:** 9:1 **Exams:** SAT I or ACT. **% Receiving Financial Aid:** 65 **% Residing in College-Owned, -Operated, or -Affiliated Housing:** 78 **Library Holdings:** 2,777,529 **Regional Accreditation:** North Central Association of Colleges and Schools **Credit Hours For Degree:** 120 credits, Bachelors **ROTC:** Army, Air Force **Professional Accreditation:** AACSB, ABET, ARCAA, AANA, ABA, ACNM, ADA, ADtA, APA, ASLHA, AALS, CSWE, LCMEAMA, NASM, NLN, TEAC **Intercollegiate Athletics:** Archery M & W; Baseball M; Basketball M & W; Cheerleading M & W; Crew M & W; Cross-Country Running M & W; Fencing M & W; Football M; Ice Hockey M & W; Soccer M & W; Softball W; Swimming and Diving M & W; Tennis M & W; Track and Field M & W; Ultimate Frisbee M & W; Volleyball M & W; Wrestling M

CEDARVILLE UNIVERSITY
251 North Main St.
Cedarville, OH 45314-0601
Tel: (937)766-2211; Free: 800-CEDARVILLE
Admissions: (937)766-7700
Fax: (937)766-7575
E-mail: admiss@cedarville.edu
Web Site: http://www.cedarville.edu/
President/CEO: Dr. Bill Brown
Admissions: Mark Weinstein
Financial Aid: Fred Merritt
Type: Comprehensive **Sex:** Coed **Affiliation:** Baptist **Scores:** 95% SAT V 400+; 99% SAT M 400+; 28% ACT 18-23; 53% ACT 24-29 **% Accepted:** 76 **Admission Plans:** Early Admission; Deferred Admission **Application Deadline:** Rolling **Application Fee:** $30.00 **H.S. Requirements:** High school diploma required; GED accepted **Costs Per Year:** Application fee: $30. One-time mandatory fee: $130. Comprehensive fee: $28,586 includes full-time tuition ($23,500) and college room and board ($5086). College room only: $2820. Room and board charges vary according to board plan. **Scholarships:** Available **Calendar System:** Semester, Summer Session Available **Enrollment:** FT 2,841, PT 188, Grad FT 1, Grad PT 64 **Faculty:** FT 195, PT 97 **Student-Faculty Ratio:** 15:1 **Exams:** SAT I or ACT, SAT I and SAT II or ACT. **% Receiving Financial Aid:** 62 **% Residing in College-Owned, -Operated, or -Affiliated Housing:** 98 **Library Holdings:** 184,296 **Regional Accreditation:** North Central Association of Colleges and Schools **Credit Hours For Degree:** 128 semester hours, Bachelors **ROTC:** Army, Air Force **Professional Accreditation:** ABET, AACN, CSWE **Intercollegiate Athletics:** Baseball M; Basketball M & W; Cross-Country Running M & W; Golf M; Soccer M & W; Softball W; Tennis M & W; Track and Field M & W; Volleyball W

CENTRAL OHIO TECHNICAL COLLEGE
1179 University Dr.
Newark, OH 43055-1767
Tel: (740)366-1351
Admissions: (740)366-9222
Fax: (740)366-5047
E-mail: jmerrin@cotc.edu
Web Site: http://www.cotc.edu/
President/CEO: Dr. Bonnie L. Coe
Admissions: John K. Merrin
Type: Two-Year College **Sex:** Coed **Affiliation:** Ohio Board of Regents **% Accepted:** 100 **Admission Plans:** Open Admission; Early Admission; Deferred Admission **Application Deadline:** Rolling **Application Fee:** $20.00 **H.S. Requirements:** High school diploma required; GED accepted **Costs Per Year:** Application fee: $20. State resident tuition: $3726 full-time, $103.50 per credit hour part-time. Nonresident tuition: $6426 full-time, $178.50 per credit hour part-time. **Scholarships:** Available **Calendar System:** Quarter, Summer Session Available **Enrollment:** FT 2,213, PT 2,137 **Faculty:** FT 58, PT 273 **Student-Faculty Ratio:** 22:1 **Final Year or Final Semester Residency Requirement:** Yes **Library Holdings:** 45,000 **Regional Accreditation:** North Central Association of Colleges and Schools **Credit Hours For Degree:** 90 quarter credit hours, Associates **Professional Accreditation:** ARCEST, JRCEDMS, JRCERT, NLN **Intercollegiate Athletics:** Baseball M; Basketball M & W; Softball W; Volleyball M & W

CENTRAL STATE UNIVERSITY
1400 Brush Row Rd.
PO Box 1004
Wilberforce, OH 45384
Tel: (937)376-6011
Admissions: (937)376-6580
Fax: (937)376-6648
E-mail: admissions@centralstate.edu
Web Site: http://www.centralstate.edu/
President/CEO: John W. Garland
Admissions: Robin Rucker
Financial Aid: Jean Hurst
Type: Comprehensive **Sex:** Coed **Affiliation:** Ohio Board of Regents **Scores:** 48% SAT V 400+; 37% SAT M 400+; 20% ACT 18-23; 1% ACT 24-29 **% Accepted:** 39 **Admission Plans:** Open Admission **Application Deadline:** June 15 **Application Fee:** $20.00 **H.S. Requirements:** High school diploma required; GED accepted **Costs Per Year:** Application fee: $20. State resident tuition: $5294 full-time, $218 per credit hour part-time. Nonresident tuition: $11,806 full-time, $511 per credit hour part-time. Full-time tuition varies according to course load. Part-time tuition varies according to course load. College room and board: $7920. College room only: $4256. Room and board charges vary according to board plan. **Scholarships:** Available **Calendar System:** Semester, Summer Session Available **Enrollment:** FT 2,230, PT 170, Grad FT 6, Grad PT 30 **Faculty:** FT 113, PT 81 **Student-Faculty Ratio:** 16:1 **Exams:** ACT, SAT I or ACT. **% Receiving Financial Aid:** 91 **% Residing in College-Owned, -Operated, or -Affiliated Housing:** 57 **Library Holdings:** 223,745 **Regional Accreditation:** North Central Association of Colleges and Schools **Credit Hours For Degree:** 124 semester hours, Bachelors **ROTC:** Army **Professional Accreditation:** ABET, NASM, NCATE **Intercollegiate Athletics:** Basketball M & W; Cheerleading M & W; Cross-Country Running M & W; Golf M & W; Tennis M & W; Track and Field M & W; Volleyball W

CHANCELLOR UNIVERSITY
3921 Chester Ave.
Cleveland, OH 44114-4624
Tel: (216)391-6937; Free: 877-366-9377
Fax: (216)426-9296
E-mail: admissions@myers.edu
Web Site: http://www.chancelloru.edu/
President/CEO: George Kidd
Financial Aid: Eric Damon
Type: Comprehensive **Sex:** Coed **Admission Plans:** Early Admission; Deferred Admission **Application Deadline:** Rolling **Application Fee:** $25.00 **H.S. Requirements:** High school diploma required; GED accepted **Scholarships:** Available **Calendar System:** Semester, Summer Session Available **Exams:** SAT I or ACT. **% Receiving Financial Aid:** 87 **Library Holdings:** 15,027 **Regional Accreditation:** North Central Association of Colleges and Schools **Credit Hours For Degree:** 60 credits, Associates; 120 credits, Bachelors

CHATFIELD COLLEGE
20918 State Route 251
St. Martin, OH 45118-9705
Tel: (513)875-3344
Fax: (513)875-3912
E-mail: chatfield@chatfield.edu
Web Site: http://www.chatfield.edu/
President/CEO: John P. Tafaro, JD
Admissions: Anna Jones
Financial Aid: Zana Smith
Type: Two-Year College **Sex:** Coed **Affiliation:** Roman Catholic Church **% Accepted:** 100 **Admission Plans:** Open Admission; Early Admission; Deferred Admission **Application Deadline:** Rolling **Application Fee:** $10.00 **H.S. Requirements:** High school diploma required; GED accepted **Scholarships:** Available **Calendar System:** Semester, Summer Session Available **Faculty:** FT 3, PT 40 **Student-Faculty Ratio:** 12:1 **Library Holdings:** 15,000 **Regional Accreditation:** North Central Association of Colleges and Schools **Credit Hours For Degree:** 62 semester hours, Associates

THE CHRIST COLLEGE OF NURSING AND HEALTH SCIENCES
2139 Auburn Ave.
Cincinnati, OH 45219
Tel: (513)585-2401
Admissions: (513)585-2498
Fax: (513)585-3540
Web Site: http://www.thechristcollege.edu/
President/CEO: Susan Croushore
Type: Two-Year College **Sex:** Coed **Regional Accreditation:** North Central Association of Colleges and Schools

CINCINNATI CHRISTIAN UNIVERSITY
2700 Glenway Ave.
PO Box 04320
Cincinnati, OH 45204-3200
Tel: (513)244-8100
Fax: (513)244-8140
Web Site: http://www.ccuniversity.edu/
President/CEO: Dr. David Faust
Admissions: Paul Presta
Financial Aid: Michael R. Gibboney, Jr.
Type: Comprehensive **Sex:** Coed **Affiliation:** Church of Christ **Scores:** 96.8% SAT V 400+; 93.5% SAT M 400+; 54.74% ACT 18-23; 20% ACT 24-29 **% Accepted:** 99 **Admission Plans:** Early Admission; Deferred Admission **Application Deadline:** July 1 **Application Fee:** $40.00 **H.S. Requirements:** High school diploma required; GED accepted. For nontraditional students: High school diploma or equivalent not required **Costs Per Year:** Application fee: $40. Comprehensive fee: $19,050 includes full-time tuition ($12,380), mandatory fees ($200), and college room and board ($6470). College room only: $3210. Full-time tuition and fees vary according to course load and student level. Room and board charges vary according to board plan, housing facility, and student level. Part-time tuition: $399 per credit hour. Part-time tuition varies according to course load and student level. **Scholarships:** Available **Calendar System:** Semester, Summer Session Available **Enrollment:** FT 685, PT 97, Grad FT 131, Grad PT 107 **Faculty:** FT 34, PT 44 **Student-Faculty Ratio:** 20:1 **Exams:** SAT I or ACT. ACT essay not being used. SAT essay not being used. **% Receiving Financial Aid:** 56 **% Residing in College-Owned, -Operated, or -Affiliated Housing:** 36 **Regional Accreditation:** North Central Association of Colleges and Schools **Credit Hours For Degree:** 66 semester hours, Associates; 132 semester hours, Bachelors **Professional Accreditation:** ABHE, ATS **Intercollegiate Athletics:** Baseball M; Basketball M & W; Cross-Country Running M & W; Golf M; Soccer M & W; Volleyball W

CINCINNATI COLLEGE OF MORTUARY SCIENCE
645 West North Bend Rd.
Cincinnati, OH 45224-1462
Tel: (513)761-2020
Fax: (513)761-3333
Web Site: http://www.ccms.edu/
President/CEO: Karen Giles
Financial Aid: Pat Leon
Type: Four-Year College **Sex:** Coed **Admission Plans:** Open Admission; Deferred Admission **Application Deadline:** Rolling **Application Fee:** $40.00 **H.S. Requirements:** High school diploma required; GED accepted **Costs Per Year:** Application fee: $40. Tuition: $20,250 full-time. Full-time tuition varies according to course load, degree level, and program. Tuition guaranteed not to increase for student's term of enrollment. **Scholarships:** Available **Calendar System:** Quarter, Summer Session Available **Enrollment:** FT 117 **Faculty:** FT 9, PT 5 **Student-Faculty Ratio:** 5:1 **Exams:** SAT I or ACT. ACT essay used for admission. **Final Year or Final Semester Residency Requirement:** No **Library Holdings:** 5,000 **Regional Accreditation:** North Central Association of Colleges and Schools **Credit Hours For Degree:** 104 quarter hours, Associates; 180 quarter hours, Bachelors **Professional Accreditation:** ABFSE

CINCINNATI STATE TECHNICAL AND COMMUNITY COLLEGE
3520 Central Parkway
Cincinnati, OH 45223-2690
Tel: (513)569-1500
Admissions: (513)569-1550
Fax: (513)569-1562
E-mail: adm@cincinnatistate.edu
Web Site: http://www.cincinnatistate.edu/
President/CEO: Dr. John Henderson
Admissions: Gabriele Boeckermann
Type: Two-Year College **Sex:** Coed **Affiliation:** Ohio Board of Regents **Admission Plans:** Open Admission **Application Deadline:** Rolling **Ap-**

plication Fee: $0.00 **H.S. Requirements:** High school diploma required; GED accepted **Costs Per Year:** Application fee: $0. One-time mandatory fee: $10. State resident tuition: $4675 full-time, $83 per credit hour part-time. Nonresident tuition: $9350 full-time, $166 per credit hour part-time. Mandatory fees: $258 full-time, $6 per credit hour part-time, $31 per term part-time. **Scholarships:** Available **Calendar System:** Miscellaneous, Summer Session Available **Enrollment:** FT 4,065, PT 6,100 **Faculty:** FT 173, PT 444 **Student-Faculty Ratio:** 15:1 **Library Holdings:** 39,802 **Regional Accreditation:** North Central Association of Colleges and Schools **Credit Hours For Degree:** 102 credit hours, Associates **Professional Accreditation:** ABET, ARCEST, AAMAE, ACCE, ACF, AHIMA, AOTA, CARC, NAACLS, NLN **Intercollegiate Athletics:** Basketball M & W; Golf M & W; Soccer M & W

CLARK STATE COMMUNITY COLLEGE
570 East Leffel Ln., PO Box 570
Springfield, OH 45501-0570
Tel: (937)325-0691
E-mail: admissions@clarkstate.edu
Web Site: http://www.clarkstate.edu/
President/CEO: Karen E. Rafinski, PhD
Type: Two-Year College **Sex:** Coed **Affiliation:** Ohio Board of Regents **Admission Plans:** Open Admission; Early Admission; Deferred Admission **Application Deadline:** Rolling **Application Fee:** $15.00 **H.S. Requirements:** High school diploma or equivalent not required **Scholarships:** Available **Calendar System:** Quarter, Summer Session Available **Faculty:** FT 61, PT 371 **Student-Faculty Ratio:** 13:1 **Library Holdings:** 31,988 **Regional Accreditation:** North Central Association of Colleges and Schools **Credit Hours For Degree:** 90 credit hours, Associates **ROTC:** Army **Professional Accreditation:** APTA, NAACLS, NLN **Intercollegiate Athletics:** Basketball M & W; Softball W; Volleyball W

THE CLEVELAND INSTITUTE OF ART
11141 East Blvd.
Cleveland, OH 44106-1700
Tel: (216)421-7000; Free: 800-223-4700
Admissions: (216)421-7418
Fax: (216)421-7438
E-mail: admissions@cia.edu
Web Site: http://www.cia.edu/
President/CEO: David Deming
Financial Aid: Karen Kopp
Type: Four-Year College **Sex:** Coed **Scores:** 93% SAT V 400+; 85% SAT M 400+; 46% ACT 18-23; 39% ACT 24-29 **% Accepted:** 79 **Admission Plans:** Early Action; Deferred Admission **Application Deadline:** Rolling **Application Fee:** $30.00 **H.S. Requirements:** High school diploma required; GED accepted **Costs Per Year:** Application fee: $30. Comprehensive fee: $42,440 includes full-time tuition ($29,870), mandatory fees ($2034), and college room and board ($10,536). College room only: $6126. Full-time tuition and fees vary according to program. Room and board charges vary according to board plan. Part-time tuition: $1250 per credit hour. Part-time mandatory fees: $140 per credit hour. Part-time tuition and fees vary according to course load and program. **Scholarships:** Available **Calendar System:** Semester, Summer Session Not available **Enrollment:** FT 493, PT 14 **Faculty:** FT 47, PT 36 **Student-Faculty Ratio:** 8:1 **Exams:** SAT I or ACT. **% Receiving Financial Aid:** 88 **% Residing in College-Owned, -Operated, or -Affiliated Housing:** 21 **Library Holdings:** 45,000 **Regional Accreditation:** North Central Association of Colleges and Schools **Professional Accreditation:** NASAD

CLEVELAND INSTITUTE OF ELECTRONICS
1776 East Seventeenth St.
Cleveland, OH 44114-3636
Tel: (216)781-9400; Free: 800-243-6446
E-mail: instruct@cie-wc.edu
Web Site: http://www.cie-wc.edu/
President/CEO: John R. Drinko
Admissions: Scott Katzenmeyer
Type: Two-Year College **Sex:** Coed **Admission Plans:** Open Admission; Early Admission **Application Deadline:** Rolling **H.S. Requirements:** High school diploma required; GED accepted **Costs Per Year:** Tuition: $1885 per term part-time. Tuition guaranteed not to increase for student's term of enrollment. **Calendar System:** Continuous, Summer Session Not available **Enrollment:** , PT 2,146 **Faculty:** FT 4, PT 4 **Library Holdings:** 5,000 **Credit Hours For Degree:** 96 quarter hours, Associates **Professional Accreditation:** DETC

CLEVELAND INSTITUTE OF MUSIC
11021 East Blvd.
Cleveland, OH 44106-1776
Tel: (216)791-5000
Fax: (216)791-1530
E-mail: cimadmission@po.cwru.edu
Web Site: http://www.cim.edu/
President/CEO: Joel Smirnoff
Admissions: William Fay
Financial Aid: Kristie Gripp
Type: Comprehensive **Sex:** Coed **% Accepted:** 38 **Admission Plans:** Early Admission; Deferred Admission **Application Deadline:** December 1 **Application Fee:** $100.00 **H.S. Requirements:** High school diploma required; GED accepted **Costs Per Year:** Application fee: $100. Comprehensive fee: $45,642 includes full-time tuition ($33,750), mandatory fees ($2840), and college room and board ($9052). Room and board charges vary according to board plan. Part-time tuition: $1406 per credit hour. **Scholarships:** Available **Calendar System:** Semester, Summer Session Available **Enrollment:** FT 233, PT 1 **Faculty:** FT 42, PT 63 **Student-Faculty Ratio:** 7:1 **Exams:** SAT I or ACT. **% Receiving Financial Aid:** 62 **% Residing in College-Owned, -Operated, or -Affiliated Housing:** 40 **Library Holdings:** 50,924 **Regional Accreditation:** North Central Association of Colleges and Schools **Credit Hours For Degree:** 124 credits, Bachelors **ROTC:** Army, Air Force **Professional Accreditation:** NASM

CLEVELAND STATE UNIVERSITY
2121 Euclid Ave.
Cleveland, OH 44115
Tel: (216)687-2000; Free: 888-CSU-OHIO
Admissions: (216)687-2100
Fax: (216)687-9366
E-mail: admissions@csuohio.edu
Web Site: http://www.csuohio.edu/
President/CEO: Dr. Ronald Berkman
Type: University **Sex:** Coed **Affiliation:** University System of Ohio **Scores:** 82.05% SAT V 400+; 86.42% SAT M 400+; 53.43% ACT 18-23; 19.7% ACT 24-29 **% Accepted:** 64 **Admission Plans:** Early Action; Deferred Admission **Application Deadline:** Rolling **Application Fee:** $30.00 **H.S. Requirements:** High school diploma required; GED accepted **Costs Per Year:** Application fee: $30. State resident tuition: $8196 full-time, $341.50 per credit hour part-time. Nonresident tuition: $11,026 full-time, $459.40 per credit hour part-time. Full-time tuition varies according to course load and program. Part-time tuition varies according to course load and program. College room and board: $10,250. College room only: $6700. Room and board charges vary according to board plan and housing facility. **Scholarships:** Available **Calendar System:** Semester, Summer Session Available **Enrollment:** FT 7,563, PT 2,868, Grad FT 2,116, Grad PT 3,584 **Faculty:** FT 537, PT 487 **Student-Faculty Ratio:** 18:1 **Exams:** SAT I or ACT. **% Receiving Financial Aid:** 76 **% Residing in College-Owned, -Operated, or -Affiliated Housing:** 8 **Final Year or Final Semester Residency Requirement:** No **Regional Accreditation:** North Central Association of Colleges and Schools **Credit Hours For Degree:** 120 semester hours, Bachelors **ROTC:** Army, Air Force **Professional Accreditation:** AACSB, ABET, AACN, ABA, ACA, ACSP, AOTA, APTA, ASLHA, AALS, CEPH, CSWE, NASM, NASPAA, NCATE, NLN **Intercollegiate Athletics:** Baseball M; Basketball M & W; Cheerleading M & W; Cross-Country Running W; Fencing M & W; Golf M & W; Soccer M & W; Softball W; Swimming and Diving M & W; Tennis M & W; Track and Field W; Volleyball W; Wrestling M

COLLEGE OF MOUNT ST. JOSEPH
5701 Delhi Rd.
Cincinnati, OH 45233-1670
Tel: (513)244-4200; Free: 800-654-9314
Admissions: (513)244-4531
Fax: (513)244-4629
E-mail: admissions@mail.msj.edu
Web Site: http://www.msj.edu/
President/CEO: Tony Aretz, PhD
Admissions: Peggy Minnich
Financial Aid: Kathryn Kelly

Type: Comprehensive **Sex:** Coed **Affiliation:** Roman Catholic **Scores:** 90% SAT V 400+; 86% SAT M 400+; 59% ACT 18-23; 29% ACT 24-29 **% Accepted:** 70 **Admission Plans:** Deferred Admission **Application Deadline:** August 15 **Application Fee:** $25.00 **H.S. Requirements:** High school diploma required; GED accepted **Costs Per Year:** Application fee: $25. One-time mandatory fee: $150. Comprehensive fee: $29,800 includes full-time tuition ($22,000), mandatory fees ($800), and college room and board ($7000). College room only: $3500. Full-time tuition and fees vary according to course load, program, and reciprocity agreements. Room and board charges vary according to board plan and housing facility. Part-time tuition: $465 per credit hour. Part-time mandatory fees: $400 per year. Part-time tuition and fees vary according to course load, location, program, and reciprocity agreements. **Scholarships:** Available **Calendar System:** Semester, Summer Session Available **Enrollment:** FT 1,347, PT 556, Grad FT 205, Grad PT 216 **Faculty:** FT 117, PT 119 **Student-Faculty Ratio:** 12:1 **Exams:** SAT I or ACT. **% Receiving Financial Aid:** 82 **% Residing in College-Owned, -Operated, or -Affiliated Housing:** 24 **Library Holdings:** 97,165 **Regional Accreditation:** North Central Association of Colleges and Schools **Credit Hours For Degree:** 64 semester hours, Associates; 128 semester hours, Bachelors **ROTC:** Army, Air Force **Professional Accreditation:** AACN, APTA, CSWE, NASM, NLN, TEAC **Intercollegiate Athletics:** Baseball M; Basketball M & W; Cheerleading W; Cross-Country Running M & W; Football M; Golf M & W; Lacrosse M & W; Soccer M & W; Softball W; Tennis M & W; Track and Field M & W; Volleyball M & W; Wrestling M

THE COLLEGE OF WOOSTER

1189 Beall Ave.
Wooster, OH 44691-2363
Tel: (330)263-2000; Free: 800-877-9905
Admissions: (330)263-2270
Fax: (330)263-2621
E-mail: admissions@wooster.edu
Web Site: http://www.wooster.edu/
President/CEO: Dr. Grant H. Cornwell
Admissions: Mary Karen Vellines
Financial Aid: Dr. David Miller

Type: Four-Year College **Sex:** Coed **Affiliation:** Presbyterian Church (U.S.A.) **Scores:** 100% SAT V 400+; 98% SAT M 400+; 23% ACT 18-23; 52% ACT 24-29 **% Accepted:** 59 **Admission Plans:** Early Admission; Early Action; Early Decision Plan; Deferred Admission **Application Deadline:** February 15 **Application Fee:** $40.00 **H.S. Requirements:** High school diploma required; GED accepted **Costs Per Year:** Application fee: $40. Comprehensive fee: $45,668 includes full-time tuition ($36,320), mandatory fees ($278), and college room and board ($9070). College room only: $4110. Full-time tuition and fees vary according to course load. Room and board charges vary according to board plan and housing facility. **Scholarships:** Available **Calendar System:** Semester, Summer Session Not available **Enrollment:** FT 1,807, PT 47 **Faculty:** FT 131, PT 29 **Student-Faculty Ratio:** 11:1 **Exams:** SAT I or ACT. ACT essay used for advising. SAT essay used for advising. ACT essay used for placement. SAT essay used for placement. **% Receiving Financial Aid:** 60 **% Residing in College-Owned, -Operated, or -Affiliated Housing:** 96 **Library Holdings:** 645,818 **Regional Accreditation:** North Central Association of Colleges and Schools **Credit Hours For Degree:** 32 courses, Bachelors **Professional Accreditation:** NASM **Intercollegiate Athletics:** Badminton M & W; Baseball M; Basketball M & W; Cheerleading W; Cross-Country Running M & W; Equestrian Sports W; Field Hockey W; Football M; Golf M & W; Lacrosse M & W; Rugby M & W; Soccer M & W; Softball W; Swimming and Diving M & W; Tennis M & W; Track and Field M & W; Ultimate Frisbee M & W; Volleyball M & W

COLUMBUS COLLEGE OF ART & DESIGN

60 Cleveland Ave.
Columbus, OH 43215-1758
Tel: (614)224-9101; Free: 877-997-2223
E-mail: admissions@ccad.edu
Web Site: http://www.ccad.edu/
President/CEO: Dennison W. Griffith
Financial Aid: Anna Marie Schofield

Type: Four-Year College **Sex:** Coed **Scores:** 92% SAT V 400+; 82% SAT M 400+; 59% ACT 18-23; 23% ACT 24-29 **% Accepted:** 72 **Admission Plans:** Deferred Admission **Application Deadline:** Rolling **Application Fee:** $30.00 **H.S. Requirements:** High school diploma required; GED accepted **Costs Per Year:** Application fee: $30. Comprehensive fee: $33,278 includes full-time tuition ($23,688), mandatory fees ($960), and college room and board ($8630). Full-time tuition and fees vary according to course load. Room and board charges vary according to housing facility and student level. Part-time tuition: $987 per credit hour. Part-time mandatory fees: $180 per term. Part-time tuition and fees vary according to course load. **Scholarships:** Available **Calendar System:** Semester, Summer Session Available **Enrollment:** FT 1,240, PT 253 **Faculty:** FT 77, PT 107 **Student-Faculty Ratio:** 12:1 **Exams:** SAT I or ACT. ACT essay not being used. SAT essay not being used. **% Receiving Financial Aid:** 81 **% Residing in College-Owned, -Operated, or -Affiliated Housing:** 29 **Library Holdings:** 62,561 **Regional Accreditation:** North Central Association of Colleges and Schools **Credit Hours For Degree:** 120 semester hours, Bachelors **Professional Accreditation:** FIDER, NASAD

COLUMBUS CULINARY INSTITUTE AT BRADFORD SCHOOL

2435 Stelzer Rd.
Columbus, OH 43219
Tel: (614)944-4200; Free: 800-678-7981
Admissions: (614)944-4200
Web Site: http://www.columbusculinary.com/

Type: Two-Year College **Sex:** Coed **% Accepted:** 55 **Calendar System:** Semester

COLUMBUS STATE COMMUNITY COLLEGE

Box 1609
Columbus, OH 43216-1609
Tel: (614)287-2400; Free: 800-621-6407
Admissions: (614)287-5353
Fax: (614)287-5117
E-mail: tblaney@cscc.edu
Web Site: http://www.cscc.edu/
President/CEO: M. Valeriana Moeller
Admissions: Tari Blaney

Type: Two-Year College **Sex:** Coed **Affiliation:** Ohio Board of Regents **Admission Plans:** Open Admission; Early Admission; Deferred Admission **Application Deadline:** Rolling **Application Fee:** $50.00 **H.S. Requirements:** High school diploma or equivalent not required. For most technology programs, gerontology, health information management,interpreting, chef's apprentice, nursing, radiology: High school diploma required; GED accepted. **Scholarships:** Available **Calendar System:** Quarter, Summer Session Available **Library Holdings:** 38,192 **Regional Accreditation:** North Central Association of Colleges and Schools **Credit Hours For Degree:** 92 quarter hours, Associates **ROTC:** Army, Air Force **Professional Accreditation:** ABET, ARCEST, AAMAE, ACCE, ACF, ADA, AHIMA, ACBSP, CARC, JRCERT, JRCEMT, NAACLS, NLN **Intercollegiate Athletics:** Baseball M; Basketball M & W; Cross-Country Running M & W; Golf M; Soccer M; Softball W; Track and Field M & W; Volleyball W

CUYAHOGA COMMUNITY COLLEGE

700 Carnegie Ave.
Cleveland, OH 44115-2878
Tel: (216)987-6000; Free: 800-954-8742
Admissions: (216)987-4030
Fax: (216)987-5050
Web Site: http://www.tri-c.edu/
President/CEO: Dr. Jerry Sue Thornton
Admissions: Kevin McDaniel

Type: Two-Year College **Sex:** Coed **% Accepted:** 100 **Admission Plans:** Open Admission; Early Admission; Deferred Admission **Application Deadline:** Rolling **Application Fee:** $0.00 **H.S. Requirements:** High school diploma or equivalent not required **Costs Per Year:** Application fee: $0. Area resident tuition: $2537 full-time, $84.56 per credit hour part-time. State resident tuition: $3354 full-time, $111.79 per credit hour part-time. Nonresident tuition: $6868 full-time, $228.94 per credit hour part-time. **Scholarships:** Available **Calendar System:** Semester, Summer Session Available **Enrollment:** FT 12,120, PT 18,205 **Faculty:** FT 334, PT 1,274 **Student-Faculty Ratio:** 18:1 **Library Holdings:** 177,767 **Regional Accreditation:** North Central Association of Colleges and Schools **Credit Hours For Degree:** 64 credit hours, Associates **Professional Accreditation:** ARCEST, ACF, ADA, AHIMA, AOTA, APTA, ACBSP, CARC, JRCEDMS, JRCERT, JRCNMT, NLN **Intercollegiate Athletics:** Baseball M; Basketball M; Cross-Country Running M & W; Soccer M; Softball W

DAVIS COLLEGE

4747 Monroe St.
Toledo, OH 43623-4307

Tel: (419)473-2700; Free: 800-477-7021
E-mail: dstern@daviscollege.edu
Web Site: http://daviscollege.edu/
President/CEO: Diane Brunner
Admissions: Dana Stern
Type: Two-Year College **Sex:** Coed **% Accepted:** 100 **Admission Plans:** Early Admission; Deferred Admission **Application Deadline:** Rolling **Application Fee:** $30.00 **H.S. Requirements:** High school diploma required; GED accepted **Costs Per Year:** Application fee: $30. Comprehensive fee: $18,021 includes full-time tuition ($8748), mandatory fees ($480), and college room and board ($8793). Part-time tuition: $243 per credit hour. **Scholarships:** Available **Calendar System:** Quarter, Summer Session Available **Enrollment:** FT 207, PT 320 **Faculty:** FT 15, PT 18 **Student-Faculty Ratio:** 15:1 **Exams:** Other. **Library Holdings:** 3,400 **Regional Accreditation:** North Central Association of Colleges and Schools **Credit Hours For Degree:** 94 credit hours, Associates **Professional Accreditation:** AAMAE

DAYMAR COLLEGE (CHILLICOTHE)
1410 Industrial Dr.
Chillicothe, OH 45601
Tel: (740)774-6300; Free: 877-258-7796
Fax: (740)774-2071
Web Site: http://www.daymarcollege.edu/
President/CEO: Debi O'Dea
Type: Two-Year College **Sex:** Coed **Admission Plans:** Open Admission **Application Fee:** $125.00 **Scholarships:** Available **Calendar System:** Quarter **Professional Accreditation:** ACICS

DAYMAR COLLEGE (JACKSON)
504 McCarty Ln.
Jackson, OH 45640
Tel: (740)286-1554
Fax: (740)286-4476
E-mail: todd_sbc@yahoo.com
Web Site: http://www.daymarcollege.edu/
President/CEO: Heather Morris
Admissions: Todd A. Riegel
Type: Two-Year College **Sex:** Coed **Application Fee:** $15.00 **Calendar System:** Quarter **Professional Accreditation:** ACICS

DAYMAR COLLEGE (LANCASTER)
1579 Victor Rd., NW
Lancaster, OH 43130
Tel: (740)687-6126
Fax: (740)687-0431
E-mail: rp_sbc@yahoo.com
Web Site: http://www.daymarcollege.edu/
President/CEO: Heather Morris
Admissions: Ray Predmore
Type: Two-Year College **Sex:** Coed **Application Fee:** $15.00 **Calendar System:** Quarter **Professional Accreditation:** ACICS

DAYMAR COLLEGE (NEW BOSTON)
3879 Rhodes Ave.
New Boston, OH 45662
Tel: (740)456-4124
Web Site: http://www.daymarcollege.edu/
President/CEO: Heather Morris
Type: Two-Year College **Sex:** Coed **Application Fee:** $15.00

DEFIANCE COLLEGE
701 North Clinton St.
Defiance, OH 43512-1610
Tel: (419)784-4010; Free: 800-520-4632
Admissions: (419)783-2365
Fax: (419)783-2468
E-mail: bharsha@defiance.edu
Web Site: http://www.defiance.edu/
President/CEO: Mark Gordon
Admissions: Brad Harsha
Financial Aid: Amy Francis
Type: Comprehensive **Sex:** Coed **Affiliation:** United Church of Christ **Scores:** 88% SAT V 400+; 58% ACT 18-23; 28% ACT 24-29 **% Accepted:** 74 **Admission Plans:** Deferred Admission **Application Deadline:** August 15 **Application Fee:** $25.00 **H.S. Requirements:** High school diploma required; GED accepted **Costs Per Year:** Application fee: $25. One-time mandatory fee: $75. Comprehensive fee: $32,450 includes full-time tuition ($23,800), mandatory fees ($530), and college room and board ($8120). College room only: $4460. Full-time tuition and fees vary according to program. Room and board charges vary according to board plan and housing facility. Part-time tuition: $385 per credit hour. Part-time mandatory fees: $75 per term. Part-time tuition and fees vary according to course load. **Scholarships:** Available **Calendar System:** Semester, Summer Session Available **Enrollment:** FT 755, PT 202, Grad FT 8, Grad PT 105 **Faculty:** FT 45, PT 50 **Student-Faculty Ratio:** 13:1 **Exams:** SAT I or ACT. ACT essay not being used. SAT essay not being used. **% Receiving Financial Aid:** 93 **% Residing in College-Owned, -Operated, or -Affiliated Housing:** 60 **Library Holdings:** 146,344 **Regional Accreditation:** North Central Association of Colleges and Schools **Credit Hours For Degree:** 60 semester hours, Associates; 120 semester hours, Bachelors **Professional Accreditation:** CSWE, NCATE **Intercollegiate Athletics:** Baseball M; Basketball M & W; Cross-Country Running M & W; Football M; Golf M & W; Soccer M & W; Softball W; Tennis M & W; Track and Field M & W; Volleyball W

DENISON UNIVERSITY
Granville, OH 43023
Tel: (740)587-0810; Free: 800-DEN-ISON
Admissions: (740)587-6276
Fax: (740)587-6306
E-mail: admissions@denison.edu
Web Site: http://www.denison.edu/
President/CEO: Dr. Dale T. Knobel
Admissions: Perry Robinson
Financial Aid: Nancy Hoover
Type: Four-Year College **Sex:** Coed **Scores:** 100% SAT V 400+; 100% SAT M 400+; 2% ACT 18-23; 59% ACT 24-29 **% Accepted:** 50 **Admission Plans:** Early Admission; Early Decision Plan; Deferred Admission **Application Deadline:** January 15 **Application Fee:** $40.00 **H.S. Requirements:** High school diploma required; GED accepted **Costs Per Year:** Application fee: $40. Comprehensive fee: $45,490 includes full-time tuition ($35,650), mandatory fees ($910), and college room and board ($8930). College room only: $5040. Room and board charges vary according to housing facility. Part-time tuition: $1115 per semester hour. Part-time mandatory fees: $1115 per semester hour, $455 per term. Part-time tuition and fees vary according to course load. **Scholarships:** Available **Calendar System:** Semester, Summer Session Not available **Enrollment:** FT 2,237, PT 30 **Faculty:** FT 197, PT 20 **Student-Faculty Ratio:** 10:1 **Exams:** SAT I or ACT. ACT essay not being used. SAT essay not being used. **% Receiving Financial Aid:** 46 **% Residing in College-Owned, -Operated, or -Affiliated Housing:** 98 **Regional Accreditation:** North Central Association of Colleges and Schools **Credit Hours For Degree:** 127 credit hours, Bachelors **ROTC:** Army **Intercollegiate Athletics:** Baseball M; Basketball M & W; Crew M; Cross-Country Running M & W; Equestrian Sports M & W; Field Hockey W; Football M; Golf M; Ice Hockey M; Lacrosse M & W; Riflery M & W; Rugby M & W; Sailing M & W; Skiing (Downhill) M & W; Soccer M & W; Softball W; Squash M & W; Swimming and Diving M & W; Tennis M & W; Track and Field M & W; Volleyball W

DEVRY UNIVERSITY (COLUMBUS)
8800 Lyra Dr.
Columbus, OH 43240
Tel: (614)854-7500
Web Site: http://www.devry.edu/
Type: Comprehensive **Sex:** Coed

DEVRY UNIVERSITY (COLUMBUS)
1350 Alum Creek Dr.
Columbus, OH 43209-2705
Tel: (614)253-7291
Admissions: (630)706-2172
Web Site: http://www.devry.edu/
President/CEO: Galen Graham
Financial Aid: Cynthia Price
Type: Comprehensive **Sex:** Coed **Affiliation:** DeVry University **Admission Plans:** Deferred Admission **Application Deadline:** Rolling **Application Fee:** $50.00 **H.S. Requirements:** High school diploma required; GED accepted **Costs Per Year:** Application fee: $50. Tuition: $14,080 full-time, $550 per

credit hour part-time. **Scholarships:** Available **Calendar System:** Semester, Summer Session Available **Enrollment:** FT 1,432, PT 1,272, Grad FT 25, Grad PT 282 **Faculty:** FT 44, PT 198 **Student-Faculty Ratio:** 18:1 **Exams:** ACT essay used for admission. SAT essay used for admission. ACT essay used for placement. SAT essay used for placement. **% Receiving Financial Aid:** 85 **Regional Accreditation:** North Central Association of Colleges and Schools **ROTC:** Army **Professional Accreditation:** ABET

DEVRY UNIVERSITY (SEVEN HILLS)
The Genesis Bldg.
6000 Lombardo Center, Ste. 200
Seven Hills, OH 44131
Tel: (216)328-8754; Free: (866)453-3879
Fax: (216)328-8764
Web Site: http://www.devry.edu/
Type: Comprehensive **Sex:** Coed **Scholarships:** Available **Calendar System:** Semester **% Receiving Financial Aid:** 80 **Regional Accreditation:** North Central Association of Colleges and Schools

EASTERN GATEWAY COMMUNITY COLLEGE
4000 Sunset Blvd.
Steubenville, OH 43952-3598
Tel: (740)264-5591
Fax: (740)266-2706
E-mail: cmascellino@jcc.edu
Web Site: http://www.easterngatewaycc.com/
President/CEO: Laura M. Meeks
Admissions: Kristen Taylor
Type: Two-Year College **Sex:** Coed **Affiliation:** Ohio Board of Regents **% Accepted:** 100 **Admission Plans:** Open Admission; Early Admission; Deferred Admission **Application Deadline:** August 20 **Application Fee:** $20.00 **H.S. Requirements:** High school diploma required; GED accepted **Costs Per Year:** Application fee: $20. Area resident tuition: $2700 full-time, $90 per credit part-time. State resident tuition: $2880 full-time, $96 per credit part-time. Nonresident tuition: $3680 full-time, $123 per credit part-time. Full-time tuition varies according to reciprocity agreements. Part-time tuition varies according to reciprocity agreements. **Scholarships:** Available **Calendar System:** Semester, Summer Session Available **Enrollment:** FT 927, PT 673 **Faculty:** FT 35, PT 89 **Student-Faculty Ratio:** 16:1 **Exams:** SAT I or ACT. **Library Holdings:** 12,500 **Regional Accreditation:** North Central Association of Colleges and Schools **Credit Hours For Degree:** 60 semester hours, Associates **Professional Accreditation:** AAMAE, ADA, CARC, JRCERT, NAACLS **Intercollegiate Athletics:** Basketball M & W

EDISON STATE COMMUNITY COLLEGE
1973 Edison Dr.
Piqua, OH 45356-9253
Tel: (937)778-8600
Admissions: (937)778-7852
Fax: (937)778-1920
E-mail: chare@edisonohio.edu
Web Site: http://www.edisonohio.edu/
President/CEO: Dr. Kenneth A. Yowell
Admissions: Chip Hare
Type: Two-Year College **Sex:** Coed **Affiliation:** Ohio Board of Regents **Scores:** 65% ACT 18-23; 10% ACT 24-29 **% Accepted:** 100 **Admission Plans:** Open Admission **Application Deadline:** Rolling **Application Fee:** $20.00 **H.S. Requirements:** High school diploma required; GED accepted **Costs Per Year:** Application fee: $20. State resident tuition: $3570 full-time, $119 per credit hour part-time. Nonresident tuition: $6660 full-time, $222 per credit hour part-time. Mandatory fees: $15 full-time. Full-time tuition and fees vary according to course load, program, and reciprocity agreements. Part-time tuition varies according to course load, program, and reciprocity agreements. **Calendar System:** Semester, Summer Session Available **Enrollment:** FT 1,357, PT 2,100 **Faculty:** FT 53, PT 158 **Student-Faculty Ratio:** 19:1 **Exams:** Other. **Final Year or Final Semester Residency Requirement:** No **Library Holdings:** 29,851 **Regional Accreditation:** North Central Association of Colleges and Schools **Credit Hours For Degree:** 60 credit hours, Associates **Professional Accreditation:** NLN **Intercollegiate Athletics:** Basketball M & W; Volleyball W

ETI TECHNICAL COLLEGE OF NILES
2076 Youngstown-Warren Rd.
Niles, OH 44446-4398
Tel: (330)652-9919
Fax: (330)652-4399
Web Site: http://www.eti-college.com/
President/CEO: Renee Zuzolo
Admissions: Diane Marsteller
Financial Aid: Kay E. Madigan
Type: Two-Year College **Sex:** Coed **% Accepted:** 100 **Admission Plans:** Early Admission; Deferred Admission **Application Deadline:** Rolling **Application Fee:** $50.00 **H.S. Requirements:** High school diploma required; GED accepted **Costs Per Year:** Application fee: $50. Tuition: $7715 full-time, $261 per credit hour part-time. Mandatory fees: $375 full-time, $150 per term part-time. Full-time tuition and fees vary according to course load and program. Part-time tuition and fees vary according to course load and program. **Scholarships:** Available **Calendar System:** Semester, Summer Session Not available **Faculty:** FT 6, PT 13 **Student-Faculty Ratio:** 22:1 **Exams:** ACT, SAT I. **Credit Hours For Degree:** 72 credits, Associates **Professional Accreditation:** ACCSCT

EVEREST INSTITUTE
2545 Bailey Rd.
Cuyahoga Falls, OH 44221
Tel: (330)923-9959; Free: 888-519-4689
Fax: (330)923-0886
Web Site: http://www.everest.edu/
President/CEO: Carson Burke
Type: Two-Year College **Sex:** Coed **Application Fee:** $55.00 **Professional Accreditation:** ACCSCT

FORTIS COLLEGE
555 East Alex Bell Rd.
Centerville, OH 45459
Tel: (937)433-3410; Free: 800-837-7387
Fax: (937)435-6516
E-mail: twallace@retstechcenter.com
Web Site: http://www.retstechcenter.com/
President/CEO: Dr. Richard S. Rucker, PhD
Admissions: Tony Wallace
Type: Two-Year College **Sex:** Coed **Admission Plans:** Early Admission; Deferred Admission **Application Deadline:** Rolling **Application Fee:** $100.00 **H.S. Requirements:** High school diploma required; GED accepted **Costs Per Year:** Application fee: $100. Tuition: $9721 full-time. Mandatory fees: $598 full-time. Full-time tuition and fees vary according to class time, course load, degree level, and program. **Scholarships:** Available **Calendar System:** Semester, Summer Session Available **Enrollment:** FT 533 **Faculty:** FT 41, PT 81 **Student-Faculty Ratio:** 18:1 **Library Holdings:** 2,200 **Professional Accreditation:** ACCSCT, AAMAE

FORTIS COLLEGE—RAVENNA
653 Enterprise Parkway
Ravenna, OH 44266
Tel: (330)297-7319
Fax: (330)297-7315
Web Site: http://www.fortis.edu/
President/CEO: Trudy Diehl
Type: Two-Year College **Sex:** Coed **Application Fee:** $60.00 **Scholarships:** Available **Professional Accreditation:** ACICS

FRANCISCAN UNIVERSITY OF STEUBENVILLE
1235 University Blvd.
Steubenville, OH 43952-1763
Tel: (740)283-3771; Free: 800-783-6220
Admissions: (740)283-6226
Fax: (740)283-6472
E-mail: admissions@franciscan.edu
Web Site: http://www.franciscan.edu/
President/CEO: Rev. Terence Henry, TOR
Admissions: Margaret Weber
Financial Aid: John Herrmann
Type: Comprehensive **Sex:** Coed **Affiliation:** Roman Catholic **Scores:** 100% SAT V 400+; 99.22% SAT M 400+; 33.5% ACT 18-23; 47.72% ACT 24-29 **% Accepted:** 72 **Admission Plans:** Deferred Admission **Application Deadline:** Rolling **Application Fee:** $20.00 **H.S. Requirements:** High school diploma required; GED accepted **Costs Per Year:** Application fee: $20. One-time mandatory fee: $150. Comprehensive fee: $27,220 includes

full-time tuition ($19,900), mandatory fees ($420), and college room and board ($6900). Full-time tuition and fees vary according to degree level. Room and board charges vary according to board plan. Part-time tuition: $665 per credit hour. Part-time mandatory fees: $15 per credit hour. Part-time tuition and fees vary according to class time, course load, and degree level. **Scholarships:** Available **Calendar System:** Semester, Summer Session Available **Enrollment:** FT 1,948, PT 133, Grad FT 183, Grad PT 461 **Faculty:** FT 112, PT 111 **Student-Faculty Ratio:** 15:1 **Exams:** SAT I or ACT. ACT essay not being used. SAT essay not being used. **% Receiving Financial Aid:** 68 **% Residing in College-Owned, -Operated, or -Affiliated Housing:** 74 **Final Year or Final Semester Residency Requirement:** Yes **Regional Accreditation:** North Central Association of Colleges and Schools **Credit Hours For Degree:** 60 credits, Associates; 124 credits, Bachelors **ROTC:** Army, Air Force **Professional Accreditation:** NCATE, NLN **Intercollegiate Athletics:** Baseball M; Basketball M & W; Cross-Country Running M & W; Rugby M; Soccer M & W; Softball W; Tennis M & W; Track and Field M & W; Volleyball W

FRANKLIN UNIVERSITY
201 South Grant Ave.
Columbus, OH 43215-5399
Tel: (614)797-4700; Free: 877-341-6300
Fax: (614)224-8027
Web Site: http://www.franklin.edu/
President/CEO: Dr. David R. Decker
Financial Aid: Marlowe Collier
Type: Comprehensive **Sex:** Coed **Admission Plans:** Open Admission; Deferred Admission **Application Deadline:** Rolling **Application Fee:** $0.00 **H.S. Requirements:** High school diploma required; GED accepted **Costs Per Year:** Application fee: $0. Tuition: $10,728 full-time, $298 per credit hour part-time. Full-time tuition varies according to program. Part-time tuition varies according to program. **Scholarships:** Available **Calendar System:** Trimester, Summer Session Available **Enrollment:** FT 2,625, PT 4,430, Grad FT 718, Grad PT 169 **Faculty:** FT 59, PT 628 **Student-Faculty Ratio:** 12:1 **% Receiving Financial Aid:** 57 **Final Year or Final Semester Residency Requirement:** No **Library Holdings:** 27,547 **Regional Accreditation:** North Central Association of Colleges and Schools **Credit Hours For Degree:** 64 credit hours, Associates; 124 credit hours, Bachelors **ROTC:** Army, Air Force

GALLIPOLIS CAREER COLLEGE
1176 Jackson Pike
Ste. 312
Gallipolis, OH 45631
Tel: (740)446-4367; Free: 800-214-0452
Fax: (740)446-4124
E-mail: admissions@gallipoliscareercollege.com
Web Site: http://www.gallipoliscareercollege.com/
President/CEO: Robert L. Shirey
Admissions: Jack Henson
Type: Two-Year College **Sex:** Coed **Application Deadline:** Rolling **Application Fee:** $50.00 **H.S. Requirements:** High school diploma required; GED accepted **Costs Per Year:** Application fee: $50. Tuition: $9600 full-time, $200 per credit hour part-time. Mandatory fees: $100 full-time, $100 per year part-time. Tuition guaranteed not to increase for student's term of enrollment. **Calendar System:** Quarter, Summer Session Available **Enrollment:** FT 145, PT 9 **Faculty:** FT 2, PT 14 **Student-Faculty Ratio:** 22:1 **Exams:** Other. **Credit Hours For Degree:** 100 quarter hours, Associates **Professional Accreditation:** ACICS

GOD'S BIBLE SCHOOL AND COLLEGE
1810 Young St.
Cincinnati, OH 45202-6838
Tel: (513)721-7944; Free: 800-486-4637
Fax: (513)721-3971
E-mail: lprofitt@gbs.edu
Web Site: http://www.gbs.edu/
President/CEO: Michael Avery
Admissions: Lisa Profitt
Financial Aid: Lori Waggoner
Type: Four-Year College **Sex:** Coed **Affiliation:** interdenominational **% Accepted:** 88 **Application Deadline:** August 18 **Application Fee:** $25.00 **H.S. Requirements:** High school diploma required; GED accepted **Scholarships:** Available **Calendar System:** Semester, Summer Session Available **Enrollment:** FT 207, PT 65 **Faculty:** FT 12, PT 17 **Student-Faculty Ratio:** 13:1 **Exams:** SAT I or ACT, SAT I. **% Residing in College-Owned, -Operated, or -Affiliated Housing:** 63 **Library Holdings:** 41,756 **Regional Accreditation:** North Central Association of Colleges and Schools **Credit Hours For Degree:** 65 semester hours, Associates; 130 semester hours, Bachelors **Professional Accreditation:** ABHE

GOOD SAMARITAN COLLEGE OF NURSING AND HEALTH SCIENCE
375 Dixmyth Ave.
Cincinnati, OH 45220
Tel: (513)862-2743
Admissions: (513)862-2631
Fax: (513)862-3572
Web Site: http://www.gscollege.edu/
President/CEO: Morris Cohen
Type: Two-Year College **Sex:** Coed **Regional Accreditation:** North Central Association of Colleges and Schools

HARRISON COLLEGE
3880 Jackpot Rd.
Grove City, OH 43123
Tel: (614)539-8800; Free: 888-544-4422
E-mail: mark.jones@harrison.edu
Web Site: http://www.harrison.edu/
President/CEO: Goldean Gibbs
Admissions: Mark Jones
Type: Two-Year College **Sex:** Coed **Application Deadline:** Rolling **Application Fee:** $50.00 **H.S. Requirements:** High school diploma required; GED accepted **Costs Per Year:** Application fee: $50. **Calendar System:** Quarter **Exams:** Other. **Professional Accreditation:** ACICS

HEIDELBERG UNIVERSITY
310 East Market St.
Tiffin, OH 44883-2462
Tel: (419)448-2000; Free: 800-434-3352
Admissions: (419)448-2330
Fax: (419)448-2334
E-mail: adminfo@heidelberg.edu
Web Site: http://www.heidelberg.edu/
President/CEO: Dr. Robert Huntington
Admissions: Lindsay Sooy
Financial Aid: Juli L. Weininger
Type: Comprehensive **Sex:** Coed **Affiliation:** United Church of Christ **Scores:** 84% SAT V 400+; 57.9% ACT 18-23; 24.4% ACT 24-29 **% Accepted:** 69 **Admission Plans:** Deferred Admission **Application Deadline:** August 15 **Application Fee:** $25.00 **H.S. Requirements:** High school diploma required; GED accepted **Costs Per Year:** Application fee: $25. Comprehensive fee: $31,597 includes full-time tuition ($22,424), mandatory fees ($538), and college room and board ($8635). College room only: $4087. Full-time tuition and fees vary according to course load, degree level, and location. Room and board charges vary according to housing facility and location. **Scholarships:** Available **Calendar System:** Semester, Summer Session Available **Enrollment:** FT 1,214, PT 233, Grad FT 21, Grad PT 188 **Faculty:** FT 70, PT 93 **Student-Faculty Ratio:** 13:1 **Exams:** SAT I or ACT. **% Receiving Financial Aid:** 71 **% Residing in College-Owned, -Operated, or -Affiliated Housing:** 85 **Regional Accreditation:** North Central Association of Colleges and Schools **Credit Hours For Degree:** 124 semester hours, Bachelors **ROTC:** Army, Air Force **Professional Accreditation:** NASM, NCATE **Intercollegiate Athletics:** Baseball M; Basketball M & W; Cross-Country Running M & W; Football M; Golf M & W; Soccer M & W; Softball W; Tennis M & W; Track and Field M & W; Volleyball M & W; Wrestling M

HIRAM COLLEGE
Box 67
Hiram, OH 44234-0067
Tel: (330)569-3211; Free: 800-362-5280
Admissions: (330)569-5169
Fax: (330)569-5944
E-mail: admission@hiram.edu
Web Site: http://www.hiram.edu/
President/CEO: Thomas V. Chema
Admissions: Sherman C. Dean, II

Financial Aid: Ann Marie Gruber
Type: Comprehensive **Sex:** Coed **Affiliation:** Christian Church (Disciples of Christ) **Scores:** 93% SAT V 400+; 89% SAT M 400+; 55% ACT 18-23; 35% ACT 24-29 **% Accepted:** 88 **Admission Plans:** Early Admission; Deferred Admission **Application Deadline:** April 1 **Application Fee:** $0.00 **H.S. Requirements:** High school diploma required; GED accepted **Costs Per Year:** Application fee: $0. Comprehensive fee: $36,145 includes full-time tuition ($26,435), mandatory fees ($700), and college room and board ($9010). Full-time tuition and fees vary according to student level. Room and board charges vary according to housing facility. Tuition guaranteed not to increase for student's term of enrollment. **Scholarships:** Available **Calendar System:** Semester, Summer Session Available **Enrollment:** FT 1,189, PT 178, Grad PT 28 **Faculty:** FT 79, PT 60 **Student-Faculty Ratio:** 13:1 **Exams:** SAT I or ACT. **% Receiving Financial Aid:** 78 **% Residing in College-Owned, -Operated, or -Affiliated Housing:** 82 **Library Holdings:** 506,792 **Regional Accreditation:** North Central Association of Colleges and Schools **Credit Hours For Degree:** 120 credit hours, Bachelors **ROTC:** Army **Professional Accreditation:** NASM **Intercollegiate Athletics:** Baseball M; Basketball M & W; Cheerleading M & W; Cross-Country Running M & W; Equestrian Sports M & W; Football M; Golf M & W; Rugby M & W; Sailing M & W; Soccer M & W; Softball W; Swimming and Diving M & W; Table Tennis M & W; Tennis M & W; Track and Field M & W; Ultimate Frisbee M & W; Volleyball M & W

HOCKING COLLEGE
3301 Hocking Parkway
Nelsonville, OH 45764-9588
Tel: (740)753-3591; Free: 877-462-5464
Fax: (740)753-7065
E-mail: hull_lyn@hocking.edu
Web Site: http://www.hocking.edu/
President/CEO: Ron Erickson
Admissions: Lyn Hull
Type: Two-Year College **Sex:** Coed **Affiliation:** Ohio Board of Regents **Admission Plans:** Open Admission **Application Deadline:** Rolling **Application Fee:** $15.00 **H.S. Requirements:** High school diploma required; GED accepted **Scholarships:** Available **Calendar System:** Quarter, Summer Session Available **Faculty:** FT 182, PT 54 **% Residing in College-Owned, -Operated, or -Affiliated Housing:** 9 **Library Holdings:** 19,663 **Regional Accreditation:** North Central Association of Colleges and Schools **Credit Hours For Degree:** 90 credit hours, Associates **ROTC:** Army **Professional Accreditation:** ABET, AAMAE, ACF, AHIMA, APTA, ACBSP, NLN

HONDROS COLLEGE
4140 Executive Parkway
Westerville, OH 43081-3855
Tel: (614)508-7277; Free: 800-783-0095
Admissions: 888-466-3767
Fax: (614)508-7279
Web Site: http://www.hondroscollege.com/
President/CEO: Linda Schwan Hondros
Admissions: Carol Thomas
Type: Two-Year College **Sex:** Coed **Admission Plans:** Open Admission **Application Fee:** $25.00 **Calendar System:** Quarter **Professional Accreditation:** ACICS

INTERNATIONAL COLLEGE OF BROADCASTING
6 South Smithville Rd.
Dayton, OH 45431-1833
Tel: (937)258-8251
Web Site: http://www.icbcollege.com/
President/CEO: Michael A. Lemaster
Admissions: Aan McIntosh
Type: Two-Year College **Sex:** Coed **Application Fee:** $100.00 **Scholarships:** Available **Calendar System:** Semester **Professional Accreditation:** ACCSCT

ITT TECHNICAL INSTITUTE (AKRON)
3428 West Market St.
Akron, OH 44333
Tel: (330)865-8600; Free: 877-818-0154
Web Site: http://www.itt-tech.edu/
Type: Two-Year College **Sex:** Coed **Professional Accreditation:** ACICS

ITT TECHNICAL INSTITUTE (COLUMBUS)
4717 Hilton Corporate Dr.
Columbus, OH 43232
Tel: (614)868-2000
Web Site: http://www.itt-tech.edu/
President/CEO: Thomas Flemming
Type: Two-Year College **Sex:** Coed **Affiliation:** ITT Educational Services, Inc. **Calendar System:** Quarter

ITT TECHNICAL INSTITUTE (DAYTON)
3325 Stop 8 Rd.
Dayton, OH 45414-3425
Tel: (937)264-7700
Web Site: http://www.itt-tech.edu/
President/CEO: Bradford Johnston
Type: Two-Year College **Sex:** Coed **Affiliation:** ITT Educational Services, Inc. **H.S. Requirements:** High school diploma required; GED accepted **Scholarships:** Available **Calendar System:** Quarter, Summer Session Not available **Credit Hours For Degree:** 96 credit hours, Associates **Professional Accreditation:** ACICS

ITT TECHNICAL INSTITUTE (HILLIARD)
3781 Park Mill Run Dr.
Hilliard, OH 43026
Tel: (614)771-4888; Free: 888-483-4888
Fax: (614)921-4179
Web Site: http://www.itt-tech.edu/
Type: Two-Year College **Sex:** Coed **Affiliation:** ITT Educational Services, Inc. **Calendar System:** Quarter **Professional Accreditation:** ACICS

ITT TECHNICAL INSTITUTE (MAUMEE)
1656 Henthorne Dr.
Ste. B
Maumee, OH 43537
Tel: (419)861-6500; Free: 877-205-4639
Web Site: http://www.itt-tech.edu/
President/CEO: James Unger
Type: Two-Year College **Sex:** Coed

ITT TECHNICAL INSTITUTE (NORWOOD)
4750 Wesley Ave.
Norwood, OH 45212
Tel: (513)531-8300; Free: 800-314-8324
Web Site: http://www.itt-tech.edu/
President/CEO: Robert Elmore
Type: Two-Year College **Sex:** Coed **Affiliation:** ITT Educational Services, Inc. **H.S. Requirements:** High school diploma required; GED accepted **Scholarships:** Available **Calendar System:** Quarter, Summer Session Not available **Professional Accreditation:** ACICS

ITT TECHNICAL INSTITUTE (STRONGSVILLE)
14955 Sprague Rd.
Strongsville, OH 44136
Tel: (440)234-9091; Free: 800-331-1488
Web Site: http://www.itt-tech.edu/
President/CEO: Kimberly Ames
Type: Two-Year College **Sex:** Coed **Affiliation:** ITT Educational Services, Inc. **H.S. Requirements:** High school diploma required; GED accepted **Scholarships:** Available **Calendar System:** Quarter, Summer Session Not available **Credit Hours For Degree:** 96 credit hours, Associates **Professional Accreditation:** ACICS

ITT TECHNICAL INSTITUTE (WARRENSVILLE HEIGHTS)
4700 Richmond Rd.
Warrensville Heights, OH 44128
Tel: (216)896-6500
Admissions: (216)896-6500
Web Site: http://www.itt-tech.edu/
President/CEO: Gerald Kraatz
Type: Two-Year College **Sex:** Coed **Calendar System:** Quarter

ITT TECHNICAL INSTITUTE (YOUNGSTOWN)
1030 North Meridian Rd.
Youngstown, OH 44509-4098

Tel: (330)270-1600; Free: 800-832-5001
Fax: (330)270-8333
Web Site: http://www.itt-tech.edu/
President/CEO: Frank Quartini
Type: Two-Year College **Sex:** Coed **Affiliation:** ITT Educational Services, Inc. **H.S. Requirements:** High school diploma required; GED accepted **Scholarships:** Available **Calendar System:** Quarter, Summer Session Not available **Credit Hours For Degree:** 96 credit hours, Associates **Professional Accreditation:** ACICS

JAMES A. RHODES STATE COLLEGE
4240 Campus Dr.
Lima, OH 45804-3597
Tel: (419)995-8000
Admissions: (419)221-1112
Fax: (419)995-8098
E-mail: peterl@ltc.tec.oh.us
Web Site: http://www.rhodesstate.edu/
President/CEO: Debra L. McCurdy
Admissions: Scot Lingrell
Type: Two-Year College **Sex:** Coed **Admission Plans:** Open Admission; Early Admission; Deferred Admission **Application Deadline:** Rolling **Application Fee:** $25.00 **H.S. Requirements:** High school diploma required; GED accepted **Costs Per Year:** Application fee: $25. One-time mandatory fee: $25. State resident tuition: $4154 full-time, $92.30 per credit hour part-time. Nonresident tuition: $8307 full-time, $184.60 per credit hour part-time. Mandatory fees: $75 full-time, $25 per term part-time. Full-time tuition and fees vary according to program. Part-time tuition and fees vary according to program. **Scholarships:** Available **Calendar System:** Quarter, Summer Session Available **Library Holdings:** 80,000 **Regional Accreditation:** North Central Association of Colleges and Schools **Credit Hours For Degree:** 106 credit hours, Associates **Professional Accreditation:** ABET, AAMAE, ADA, AOTA, APTA, ACBSP, CARC, JRCERT, NLN **Intercollegiate Athletics:** Baseball M; Basketball M & W; Golf M

JOHN CARROLL UNIVERSITY
20700 North Park Blvd.
University Heights, OH 44118-4581
Tel: (216)397-1886
Admissions: (216)397-4294
Fax: (216)397-3098
E-mail: svitatoe@jcu.edu
Web Site: http://www.jcu.edu/
President/CEO: Fr. Robert Niehoff
Admissions: Steven P. Vitatoe
Type: Comprehensive **Sex:** Coed **Affiliation:** Roman Catholic (Jesuit) **Scores:** 97.1% SAT V 400+; 95.6% SAT M 400+; 50% ACT 18-23; 41% ACT 24-29 **% Accepted:** 81 **Admission Plans:** Deferred Admission **Application Deadline:** February 1 **Application Fee:** $0.00 **H.S. Requirements:** High school diploma required; GED accepted **Costs Per Year:** Application fee: $0. One-time mandatory fee: $325. Comprehensive fee: $39,000 includes full-time tuition ($29,250), mandatory fees ($1000), and college room and board ($8750). College room only: $4640. Room and board charges vary according to board plan and housing facility. Part-time tuition: $890 per credit hour. Part-time tuition varies according to course load. **Scholarships:** Available **Calendar System:** Semester, Summer Session Available **Enrollment:** FT 2,906, PT 81, Grad FT 242, Grad PT 485 **Faculty:** FT 212, PT 153 **Student-Faculty Ratio:** 15:1 **Exams:** SAT I or ACT. ACT essay used for admission. SAT essay used for admission. ACT essay used for advising. SAT essay used for advising. ACT essay used for placement. SAT essay used for placement. **% Receiving Financial Aid:** 55 **% Residing in College-Owned, -Operated, or -Affiliated Housing:** 65 **Final Year or Final Semester Residency Requirement:** Yes **Library Holdings:** 620,000 **Regional Accreditation:** North Central Association of Colleges and Schools **Credit Hours For Degree:** 128 credit hours, Bachelors **ROTC:** Army **Professional Accreditation:** AACSB, ACA, NCATE **Intercollegiate Athletics:** Baseball M; Basketball M & W; Cheerleading W; Crew M & W; Cross-Country Running M & W; Field Hockey W; Football M; Golf M & W; Ice Hockey M; Lacrosse M & W; Rugby M & W; Sailing M & W; Skiing (Cross-Country) M & W; Skiing (Downhill) M & W; Soccer M & W; Softball W; Swimming and Diving M & W; Tennis M & W; Track and Field M & W; Ultimate Frisbee M; Volleyball M & W; Wrestling M

KAPLAN COLLEGE, CINCINNATI CAMPUS
801 Linn St.
Cincinnati, OH 45203
Tel: (513)421-9900
Web Site: http://www.kc-cincy.com/
Type: Two-Year College **Sex:** Coed **H.S. Requirements:** High school diploma required; GED accepted **Professional Accreditation:** ACCSCT

KAPLAN COLLEGE, COLUMBUS CAMPUS
2745 Winchester Pike
Columbus, OH 43232
Tel: (614)456-4600
Web Site: http://www.kc-columbus.com/
President/CEO: Ann Contiguglia
Type: Two-Year College **Sex:** Coed **H.S. Requirements:** High school diploma required; GED accepted **Professional Accreditation:** ACCSCT

KAPLAN COLLEGE, DAYTON CAMPUS
2800 East River Rd.
Dayton, OH 45439
Tel: (937)294-6155; Free: 800-932-9698
Fax: (937)294-2259
Web Site: http://www.kc-dayton.com/
President/CEO: Karen Larson-Reuter
Type: Two-Year College **Sex:** Coed **H.S. Requirements:** High school diploma required; GED accepted **Scholarships:** Available **Calendar System:** Quarter **Professional Accreditation:** ACCSCT

KENT STATE UNIVERSITY
PO Box 5190
Kent, OH 44242-0001
Tel: (330)672-3000; Free: 800-988-KENT
Admissions: (330)672-2444
Fax: (330)672-2499
E-mail: admissions@kent.edu
Web Site: http://www.kent.edu/
President/CEO: Dr. Lester A. Lefton
Admissions: Christopher Buttenschon
Financial Aid: Mark A. Evans
Type: University **Sex:** Coed **Affiliation:** Kent State University System **Scores:** 95% SAT V 400+; 93% SAT M 400+; 59% ACT 18-23; 30% ACT 24-29 **% Accepted:** 72 **Admission Plans:** Early Admission **Application Deadline:** Rolling **Application Fee:** $40.00 **H.S. Requirements:** High school diploma required; GED accepted **Costs Per Year:** Application fee: $40. State resident tuition: $8726 full-time, $397 per credit hour part-time. Nonresident tuition: $16,418 full-time, $747 per credit hour part-time. Full-time tuition varies according to course level, course load, degree level, program, and reciprocity agreements. Part-time tuition varies according to course level, course load, degree level, program, and reciprocity agreements. College room and board: $7940. College room only: $4850. Room and board charges vary according to board plan and housing facility. **Scholarships:** Available **Calendar System:** Semester, Summer Session Available **Enrollment:** FT 17,550, PT 2,171, Grad FT 2,676, Grad PT 2,533 **Faculty:** FT 888, PT 652 **Student-Faculty Ratio:** 20:1 **Exams:** SAT I or ACT. **% Receiving Financial Aid:** 62 **% Residing in College-Owned, -Operated, or -Affiliated Housing:** 34 **Library Holdings:** 2,300,000 **Regional Accreditation:** North Central Association of Colleges and Schools **Credit Hours For Degree:** 60 semester hours, Associates; 120 semester hours, Bachelors **ROTC:** Army, Air Force **Professional Accreditation:** AACSB, ACEJMC, AACN, ACA, ADtA, ALA, APA, ASLHA, FIDER, CEPH, CORE, NAAB, NASAD, NASD, NASM, NASPAA, NAST, NCATE, NRPA **Intercollegiate Athletics:** Baseball M; Basketball M & W; Cross-Country Running M & W; Field Hockey W; Football M; Golf M & W; Gymnastics W; Soccer W; Softball W; Track and Field M & W; Volleyball W; Wrestling M

KENT STATE UNIVERSITY AT ASHTABULA
3300 Lake Rd. West
Ashtabula, OH 44004-2299
Tel: (440)964-3322
Fax: (440)964-4269
E-mail: sanford@ashtabula.kent.edu
Web Site: http://www.ashtabula.kent.edu/
President/CEO: Dr. Susan Stocker
Admissions: Kelly Sanford

Financial Aid: Lisa Jackson
Type: Two-Year College **Sex:** Coed **Affiliation:** Kent State University System **Scores:** 100% SAT V 400+; 100% SAT M 400+; 52.2% ACT 18-23; 14.71% ACT 24-29 **% Accepted:** 79 **Admission Plans:** Open Admission; Early Admission; Deferred Admission **Application Deadline:** August 1 **Application Fee:** $30.00 **H.S. Requirements:** High school diploma required; GED accepted **Costs Per Year:** Application fee: $30. State resident tuition: $4938 full-time, $225 per credit hour part-time. Nonresident tuition: $12,630 full-time, $575 per credit hour part-time. Full-time tuition varies according to course level and course load. Part-time tuition varies according to course level and course load. **Scholarships:** Available **Calendar System:** Semester, Summer Session Available **Enrollment:** FT 1,161, PT 1,026, Grad FT 1, Grad PT 4 **Faculty:** FT 49, PT 58 **Student-Faculty Ratio:** 22:1 **Exams:** SAT I or ACT. ACT essay not being used. SAT essay not being used. **Library Holdings:** 51,884 **Regional Accreditation:** North Central Association of Colleges and Schools **Credit Hours For Degree:** 66 semester hours, Associates **ROTC:** Army **Professional Accreditation:** APTA, ACBSP, NLN

KENT STATE UNIVERSITY AT EAST LIVERPOOL
400 East 4th St.
East Liverpool, OH 43920-3497
Tel: (330)385-3805
Admissions: (330)382-7400
Fax: (330)385-6348
E-mail: admissions@eliv.kent.edu
Web Site: http://www.eliv.kent.edu/
President/CEO: Dr. Jeffrey Nolte
Admissions: Anthony M. Underwood
Type: Two-Year College **Sex:** Coed **Affiliation:** Kent State University System **Scores:** 100% SAT V 400+; 100% SAT M 400+; 52.5% ACT 18-23; 12.5% ACT 24-29 **% Accepted:** 76 **Admission Plans:** Open Admission; Early Admission; Deferred Admission **Application Deadline:** Rolling **Application Fee:** $30.00 **H.S. Requirements:** High school diploma required; GED accepted **Scholarships:** Available **Calendar System:** Semester, Summer Session Available **Enrollment:** FT 706, PT 529 **Faculty:** FT 26, PT 40 **Student-Faculty Ratio:** 22:1 **Exams:** SAT I. **Library Holdings:** 31,320 **Regional Accreditation:** North Central Association of Colleges and Schools **Credit Hours For Degree:** 65 semester hours, Associates **ROTC:** Navy, Air Force **Professional Accreditation:** AOTA, APTA, ACBSP, NLN

KENT STATE UNIVERSITY AT GEAUGA
14111 Claridon-Troy Rd.
Burton, OH 44021-9500
Tel: (440)834-4187
Fax: (440)834-0919
E-mail: thoiles@kent.edu
Web Site: http://www.geauga.kent.edu/
President/CEO: Dr. David Mohan
Admissions: Thomas Hoiles
Financial Aid: Donna Holcomb
Type: Two-Year College **Sex:** Coed **Affiliation:** Kent State University System **Scores:** 82.3% SAT M 400+ **Admission Plans:** Deferred Admission **Application Deadline:** Rolling **Application Fee:** $30.00 **H.S. Requirements:** High school diploma required; GED accepted **Scholarships:** Available **Calendar System:** Semester, Summer Session Available **Enrollment:** FT 1,116, PT 750, Grad FT 3, Grad PT 6 **Faculty:** FT 25, PT 68 **Student-Faculty Ratio:** 29:1 **Exams:** SAT I or ACT. ACT essay not being used. SAT essay not being used. **Library Holdings:** 8,300 **Regional Accreditation:** North Central Association of Colleges and Schools **Credit Hours For Degree:** 65 semester hours, Associates; 120 semester hours, Bachelors **ROTC:** Army, Air Force **Professional Accreditation:** ACBSP

KENT STATE UNIVERSITY AT SALEM
2491 State Route 45 South
Salem, OH 44460-9412
Tel: (330)332-0361
Fax: (330)332-9256
E-mail: ask-us@salem.kent.edu
Web Site: http://www.salem.kent.edu/
President/CEO: Dr. Jeffrey Nolte
Admissions: Judy Heisler
Type: Two-Year College **Sex:** Coed **Affiliation:** Kent State University System **Scores:** 100% SAT M 400+; 56.59% ACT 18-23; 10.85% ACT 24-29 **% Accepted:** 62 **Admission Plans:** Open Admission; Early Admission; Deferred Admission **Application Deadline:** Rolling **Application Fee:** $30.00 **H.S. Requirements:** High school diploma required; GED accepted **Scholarships:** Available **Calendar System:** Semester, Summer Session Available **Enrollment:** FT 1,132, PT 445, Grad FT 1, Grad PT 2 **Faculty:** FT 41, PT 58 **Student-Faculty Ratio:** 21:1 **Exams:** SAT I or ACT. ACT essay not being used. SAT essay not being used. **Library Holdings:** 19,000 **Regional Accreditation:** North Central Association of Colleges and Schools **Credit Hours For Degree:** 65 semester hours, Associates **ROTC:** Army, Air Force **Professional Accreditation:** ACBSP, JRCERT, JRCNMT

KENT STATE UNIVERSITY AT STARK
6000 Frank Ave., NW
Canton, OH 44720-7599
Tel: (330)499-9600
Fax: (330)494-6121
E-mail: admit@stark.kent.edu
Web Site: http://www.stark.kent.edu/
President/CEO: Dr. Ruth Capasso
Admissions: Deborah Ann Speck
Financial Aid: Gail Pukys
Type: Comprehensive **Sex:** Coed **Affiliation:** Kent State University System **Scores:** 94% SAT V 400+; 88% SAT M 400+; 58% ACT 18-23; 16% ACT 24-29 **% Accepted:** 73 **Admission Plans:** Open Admission; Early Admission; Deferred Admission **Application Deadline:** Rolling **Application Fee:** $30.00 **H.S. Requirements:** High school diploma required; GED accepted **Costs Per Year:** Application fee: $30. State resident tuition: $4938 full-time, $225 per credit hour part-time. Nonresident tuition: $12,630 full-time, $575 per credit hour part-time. Full-time tuition varies according to course level, course load, and location. Part-time tuition varies according to course level, course load, and location. **Scholarships:** Available **Calendar System:** Semester, Summer Session Available **Enrollment:** FT 2,910, PT 1,376, Grad FT 8, Grad PT 69 **Faculty:** FT 102, PT 104 **Student-Faculty Ratio:** 25:1 **Exams:** SAT I or ACT. ACT essay not being used. SAT essay not being used. **% Receiving Financial Aid:** 62 **Library Holdings:** 81,962 **Regional Accreditation:** North Central Association of Colleges and Schools **Credit Hours For Degree:** 65 semester hours, Associates; 121 semester hours, Bachelors **ROTC:** Army, Air Force

KENT STATE UNIVERSITY AT TRUMBULL
4314 Mahoning Ave., NW
Warren, OH 44483-1998
Tel: (330)847-0571
Admissions: (330)675-8935
E-mail: lppetril@kent.edu
Web Site: http://www.trumbull.kent.edu/
President/CEO: Dr. Wanda Thomas
Admissions: Linda Petrilla
Financial Aid: Sarah Helmick
Type: Two-Year College **Sex:** Coed **Affiliation:** Kent State University System **Scores:** 71.43% SAT V 400+; 100% SAT M 400+; 53.33% ACT 18-23; 10% ACT 24-29 **% Accepted:** 79 **Admission Plans:** Open Admission; Deferred Admission **Application Deadline:** Rolling **Application Fee:** $30.00 **H.S. Requirements:** High school diploma required; GED accepted **Scholarships:** Available **Calendar System:** Semester, Summer Session Available **Enrollment:** FT 1,637, PT 970, Grad PT 5 **Faculty:** FT 58, PT 56 **Student-Faculty Ratio:** 25:1 **Exams:** SAT I or ACT. **Library Holdings:** 65,951 **Regional Accreditation:** North Central Association of Colleges and Schools **Credit Hours For Degree:** 65 credit hours, Associates **ROTC:** Army, Air Force **Professional Accreditation:** ACBSP

KENT STATE UNIVERSITY AT TUSCARAWAS
330 University Dr., NE
New Philadelphia, OH 44663-9403
Tel: (330)339-3391
Fax: (330)339-3321
E-mail: ldonley@kent.edu
Web Site: http://www.tusc.kent.edu/
President/CEO: Dr. Gregg Andrews
Admissions: Laurie R. Donley
Financial Aid: Dawn Plug
Type: Two-Year College **Sex:** Coed **Affiliation:** Kent State University System **Scores:** 100% SAT V 400+; 64.14% ACT 18-23; 14.35% ACT 24-29 **% Accepted:** 82 **Admission Plans:** Open Admission; Early Admission;

Deferred Admission **Application Deadline:** September 1 **Application Fee:** $30.00 **H.S. Requirements:** High school diploma required; GED accepted **Costs Per Year:** Application fee: $30. State resident tuition: $4938 full-time, $225 per credit hour part-time. Nonresident tuition: $12,630 full-time, $575 per credit hour part-time. Full-time tuition varies according to course level, location, and program. Part-time tuition varies according to course level, location, and program. **Scholarships:** Available **Calendar System:** Semester, Summer Session Available **Enrollment:** FT 1,424, PT 960 **Faculty:** FT 49, PT 67 **Student-Faculty Ratio:** 24:1 **Exams:** SAT I or ACT. ACT essay not being used. SAT essay not being used. **Final Year or Final Semester Residency Requirement:** No **Library Holdings:** 63,880 **Regional Accreditation:** North Central Association of Colleges and Schools **Credit Hours For Degree:** 61 semester hours, Associates; 121 semester hours, Bachelors **ROTC:** Army, Air Force **Professional Accreditation:** ABET, ACBSP, NLN

KENYON COLLEGE
Gambier, OH 43022-9623
Tel: (740)427-5000; Free: 800-848-2468
Admissions: (740)427-5776
Fax: (740)427-2634
E-mail: admissions@kenyon.edu
Web Site: http://www.kenyon.edu/
President/CEO: S. Georgia Nugent
Admissions: Jennifer Delahunty
Financial Aid: Craig Daugherty
Type: Four-Year College **Sex:** Coed **Scores:** 100% SAT V 400+; 100% SAT M 400+; 4.3% ACT 18-23; 34.6% ACT 24-29 **% Accepted:** 39 **Admission Plans:** Early Admission; Early Decision Plan; Deferred Admission **Application Deadline:** January 15 **Application Fee:** $45.00 **H.S. Requirements:** High school diploma required; GED accepted **Costs Per Year:** Application fee: $45. Comprehensive fee: $50,400 includes full-time tuition ($39,420), mandatory fees ($1480), and college room and board ($9500). **Scholarships:** Available **Calendar System:** Semester, Summer Session Not available **Enrollment:** FT 1,618, PT 15 **Faculty:** FT 156, PT 46 **Student-Faculty Ratio:** 10:1 **Exams:** SAT I or ACT. ACT essay not being used. SAT essay not being used. **% Receiving Financial Aid:** 42 **% Residing in College-Owned, -Operated, or -Affiliated Housing:** 98 **Library Holdings:** 889,142 **Regional Accreditation:** North Central Association of Colleges and Schools **Credit Hours For Degree:** 16 units, Bachelors **Intercollegiate Athletics:** Archery M & W; Baseball M; Basketball M & W; Cross-Country Running M & W; Equestrian Sports M & W; Fencing M & W; Field Hockey W; Football M; Golf M; Lacrosse M & W; Rugby M & W; Sailing M & W; Soccer M & W; Softball W; Squash M & W; Swimming and Diving M & W; Tennis M & W; Track and Field M & W; Ultimate Frisbee M & W; Volleyball W

KETTERING COLLEGE OF MEDICAL ARTS
3737 Southern Blvd.
Kettering, OH 45429-1299
Tel: (937)395-8601; Free: 800-433-5262
Admissions: (937)395-8628
Fax: (937)395-8333
Web Site: http://www.kcma.edu/
President/CEO: Charles Scriven
Admissions: Becky McDonald
Type: Comprehensive **Sex:** Coed **Affiliation:** Seventh-day Adventist; Kettering Health Network **Scores:** 74% ACT 18-23; 26% ACT 24-29 **% Accepted:** 50 **Admission Plans:** Early Admission **Application Deadline:** Rolling **Application Fee:** $25.00 **H.S. Requirements:** High school diploma required; GED accepted **Costs Per Year:** Application fee: $25. Comprehensive fee: $16,710 includes full-time tuition ($10,050), mandatory fees ($560), and college room and board ($6100). College room only: $5560. Full-time tuition and fees vary according to course load, degree level, and program. Part-time tuition: $335 per credit hour. Part-time mandatory fees: $120 per term. Part-time tuition and fees vary according to course load, degree level, and program. **Scholarships:** Available **Calendar System:** Semester, Summer Session Available **Enrollment:** FT 394, PT 347 **Faculty:** FT 55, PT 15 **Student-Faculty Ratio:** 10:1 **Exams:** ACT, SAT I. **% Residing in College-Owned, -Operated, or -Affiliated Housing:** 15 **Library Holdings:** 29,390 **Regional Accreditation:** North Central Association of Colleges and Schools **Credit Hours For Degree:** 64 semester hours, Associates; 126 semester hours, Bachelors **Professional Accreditation:** CARC, JRCEDMS, JRCERT, NLN

LAKE ERIE COLLEGE
391 West Washington St.
Painesville, OH 44077-3389
Tel: (440)296-1856; Free: 800-916-0904
Admissions: (440)375-7050
Fax: (440)352-3533
E-mail: admissions@lec.edu
Web Site: http://www.lec.edu/
President/CEO: Michael T. Victor
Admissions: Eric Felver
Financial Aid: Patricia Pangonis
Type: Comprehensive **Sex:** Coed **Scores:** 90.5% SAT V 400+; 88% SAT M 400+; 57% ACT 18-23; 19% ACT 24-29 **% Accepted:** 56 **Admission Plans:** Deferred Admission **Application Deadline:** August 1 **Application Fee:** $30.00 **H.S. Requirements:** High school diploma required; GED accepted **Costs Per Year:** Application fee: $30. One-time mandatory fee: $200. Comprehensive fee: $33,866 includes full-time tuition ($24,308), mandatory fees ($1366), and college room and board ($8192). College room only: $4057. Full-time tuition and fees vary according to course load and program. Room and board charges vary according to board plan. Part-time tuition: $665 per credit hour. Part-time mandatory fees: $51 per credit hour. Part-time tuition and fees vary according to course load and program. **Scholarships:** Available **Calendar System:** Semester, Summer Session Available **Enrollment:** FT 854, PT 49, Grad FT 46, Grad PT 182 **Student-Faculty Ratio:** 15:1 **Exams:** SAT I or ACT. **% Receiving Financial Aid:** 91 **% Residing in College-Owned, -Operated, or -Affiliated Housing:** 47 **Final Year or Final Semester Residency Requirement:** Yes **Library Holdings:** 80,000 **Regional Accreditation:** North Central Association of Colleges and Schools **Credit Hours For Degree:** 128 semester hours, Bachelors **Intercollegiate Athletics:** Baseball M; Basketball M & W; Cross-Country Running M & W; Football M; Golf M & W; Lacrosse M & W; Soccer M & W; Softball W; Tennis M & W; Track and Field M & W; Volleyball W

LAKELAND COMMUNITY COLLEGE
7700 Clocktower Dr.
Kirtland, OH 44094-5198
Tel: (440)525-7000
Admissions: (440)525-7230
Fax: (440)525-4330
Web Site: http://www.lakeland.cc.oh.us/
President/CEO: Dr. Morris W. Beverage
Admissions: Tracey Cooper
Financial Aid: Lynn Axten
Type: Two-Year College **Sex:** Coed **Affiliation:** Ohio Board of Regents **Admission Plans:** Open Admission; Early Admission; Deferred Admission **Application Deadline:** September 1 **Application Fee:** $15.00 **H.S. Requirements:** High school diploma required; GED accepted **Costs Per Year:** Application fee: $15. Area resident tuition: $2888 full-time, $96.25 per credit hour part-time. State resident tuition: $3537 full-time, $117.90 per credit hour part-time. Nonresident tuition: $7569 full-time, $252.30 per credit hour part-time. Mandatory fees: $14.25 per term part-time. Full-time tuition varies according to course load. Part-time tuition and fees vary according to course load. **Scholarships:** Available **Calendar System:** Semester, Summer Session Available **Enrollment:** FT 4,151, PT 5,255 **Faculty:** FT 117, PT 513 **Student-Faculty Ratio:** 20:1 **Library Holdings:** 65,814 **Regional Accreditation:** North Central Association of Colleges and Schools **Credit Hours For Degree:** 64 semester hours, Associates **Professional Accreditation:** ABET, ARCEST, ADA, CARC, JCAHPO, JRCERT, NAACLS, NLN **Intercollegiate Athletics:** Baseball M; Basketball M & W; Golf M; Soccer M; Softball W; Volleyball W

LAURA AND ALVIN SIEGAL COLLEGE OF JUDAIC STUDIES
26500 Shaker Blvd.
Beachwood, OH 44122-7116
Tel: (216)464-4050; Free: 888-336-2257
Fax: (216)464-5827
E-mail: admissions@siegalcollege.edu
Web Site: http://www.siegalcollege.edu/
President/CEO: Brian Amkraut
Admissions: Ruth Kronick
Financial Aid: Ruth Kronick
Type: Comprehensive **Sex:** Coed **% Accepted:** 100 **Admission Plans:** Open Admission; Deferred Admission **Application Deadline:** Rolling **Application Fee:** $50.00 **H.S. Requirements:** High school diploma required;

GED accepted **Costs Per Year:** Application fee: $50. Tuition: $12,600 full-time, $525 per credit hour part-time. Mandatory fees: $25 per term part-time. **Scholarships:** Available **Calendar System:** Semester, Summer Session Available **Enrollment:** , PT 16, Grad FT 1, Grad PT 88 **% Receiving Financial Aid:** 100 **Final Year or Final Semester Residency Requirement:** No **Library Holdings:** 28,000 **Regional Accreditation:** North Central Association of Colleges and Schools **Credit Hours For Degree:** 120 credits, Bachelors

LORAIN COUNTY COMMUNITY COLLEGE
1005 Abbe Rd., North
Elyria, OH 44035
Tel: (440)365-5222; Free: 800-995-5222
Admissions: (440)366-5222
Fax: (440)365-6519
Web Site: http://www.lorainccc.edu/
President/CEO: Dr. Roy Church
Admissions: Thalia Fountain
Financial Aid: Karen Tijanich
Type: Two-Year College **Sex:** Coed **Affiliation:** Ohio Board of Regents **% Accepted:** 100 **Admission Plans:** Open Admission; Early Admission; Deferred Admission **Application Deadline:** Rolling **Application Fee:** $0.00 **H.S. Requirements:** High school diploma required; GED accepted **Scholarships:** Available **Calendar System:** Semester, Summer Session Available **Enrollment:** FT 4,089, PT 6,432 **Faculty:** FT 126, PT 653 **Student-Faculty Ratio:** 18:1 **Library Holdings:** 198,984 **Regional Accreditation:** North Central Association of Colleges and Schools **Credit Hours For Degree:** 63 semester hours, Associates **Professional Accreditation:** ARCEST, AAMAE, ADA, APTA, JRCEDMS, JRCERT, NAACLS, NLN

LOURDES COLLEGE
6832 Convent Blvd.
Sylvania, OH 43560-2898
Tel: (419)885-3211; Free: 800-878-3210
Admissions: (419)885-5291
Fax: (419)882-3987
E-mail: lcadmits@lourdes.edu
Web Site: http://www.lourdes.edu/
President/CEO: Dr. Robert Helmer
Admissions: Amy Mergen
Financial Aid: Denise McClusky
Type: Comprehensive **Sex:** Coed **Affiliation:** Roman Catholic **Scores:** 66% SAT V 400+; 54% ACT 18-23; 12% ACT 24-29 **% Accepted:** 80 **Admission Plans:** Early Admission; Deferred Admission **Application Deadline:** Rolling **Application Fee:** $25.00 **H.S. Requirements:** High school diploma required; GED accepted **Costs Per Year:** Application fee: $25. Tuition: $13,440 full-time, $448 per credit hour part-time. Mandatory fees: $1860 full-time, $62 per credit hour part-time. Full-time tuition and fees vary according to course load and location. Part-time tuition and fees vary according to course load and location. **Scholarships:** Available **Calendar System:** Semester, Summer Session Available **Enrollment:** FT 1,025, PT 928, Grad FT 187, Grad PT 80 **Faculty:** FT 80, PT 153 **Student-Faculty Ratio:** 11:1 **% Receiving Financial Aid:** 85 **Final Year or Final Semester Residency Requirement:** No **Library Holdings:** 66,068 **Regional Accreditation:** North Central Association of Colleges and Schools **Credit Hours For Degree:** 60 semester hours, Associates; 120 semester hours, Bachelors **ROTC:** Army, Air Force **Professional Accreditation:** AACN, CSWE, NLN, TEAC **Intercollegiate Athletics:** Basketball M; Golf M & W; Volleyball W

MALONE UNIVERSITY
2600 Cleveland Ave., NW
Canton, OH 44709
Tel: (330)471-8100; Free: 800-521-1146
Admissions: (330)471-8145
Fax: (330)454-6977
E-mail: admissions@malone.edu
Web Site: http://www3.malone.edu/
President/CEO: Dr. Gary W. Streit
Financial Aid: Pamela Pustay
Type: Comprehensive **Sex:** Coed **Affiliation:** Evangelical Friends Church–Eastern Region **Scores:** 96.7% SAT V 400+; 89.2% SAT M 400+; 51.5% ACT 18-23; 39.4% ACT 24-29 **% Accepted:** 71 **Admission Plans:** Early Admission; Deferred Admission **Application Deadline:** July 1 **Application Fee:** $20.00 **H.S. Requirements:** High school diploma required; GED accepted **Costs Per Year:** Application fee: $20. Comprehensive fee: $29,992 includes full-time tuition ($21,954), mandatory fees ($490), and college room and board ($7548). College room only: $3848. Room and board charges vary according to board plan. Part-time tuition: $425 per credit hour. Part-time mandatory fees: $122.50 per term. Part-time tuition and fees vary according to course load. **Scholarships:** Available **Calendar System:** Semester, Summer Session Available **Enrollment:** FT 1,857, PT 334, Grad FT 44, Grad PT 385 **Faculty:** FT 110, PT 108 **Student-Faculty Ratio:** 15:1 **Exams:** SAT I or ACT. ACT essay used for advising. SAT essay used for advising. **% Receiving Financial Aid:** 79 **% Residing in College-Owned, -Operated, or -Affiliated Housing:** 52 **Final Year or Final Semester Residency Requirement:** Yes **Library Holdings:** 181,420 **Regional Accreditation:** North Central Association of Colleges and Schools **Credit Hours For Degree:** 124 credit hours, Bachelors **ROTC:** Army, Air Force **Professional Accreditation:** AACN, CSWE, NCATE, NLN **Intercollegiate Athletics:** Baseball M; Basketball M & W; Cheerleading M & W; Cross-Country Running M & W; Football M; Golf M & W; Soccer M & W; Softball W; Swimming and Diving M & W; Tennis M & W; Track and Field M & W; Volleyball W

MARIETTA COLLEGE
215 Fifth St.
Marietta, OH 45750-4000
Tel: (740)376-4000; Free: 800-331-7896
Admissions: (740)376-4600
Fax: (740)376-4896
E-mail: admit@marietta.edu
Web Site: http://www.marietta.edu/
President/CEO: Dr. Jean A. Scott
Admissions: Jason Turley
Financial Aid: Kevin Lamb
Type: Comprehensive **Sex:** Coed **Scores:** 99% SAT V 400+; 98% SAT M 400+; 47% ACT 18-23; 40% ACT 24-29 **% Accepted:** 76 **Admission Plans:** Early Admission; Deferred Admission **Application Deadline:** May 1 **Application Fee:** $25.00 **H.S. Requirements:** High school diploma required; GED accepted **Costs Per Year:** Application fee: $25. Comprehensive fee: $35,112 includes full-time tuition ($26,386), mandatory fees ($680), and college room and board ($8046). College room only: $4400. Full-time tuition and fees vary according to course load and degree level. Room and board charges vary according to housing facility. Part-time tuition: $875 per credit hour. Part-time tuition varies according to course load and degree level. **Scholarships:** Available **Calendar System:** Semester, Summer Session Available **Enrollment:** FT 1,428, PT 78, Grad FT 75, Grad PT 7 **Faculty:** FT 105, PT 41 **Student-Faculty Ratio:** 12:1 **Exams:** SAT I or ACT, SAT II. **% Receiving Financial Aid:** 77 **% Residing in College-Owned, -Operated, or -Affiliated Housing:** 81 **Library Holdings:** 281,750 **Regional Accreditation:** North Central Association of Colleges and Schools **Credit Hours For Degree:** 61 credit hours, Associates; 120 credit hours, Bachelors **Professional Accreditation:** ABET, JRCEPAT, NCATE **Intercollegiate Athletics:** Baseball M; Basketball M & W; Cheerleading W; Crew M & W; Cross-Country Running M & W; Football M; Lacrosse M; Soccer M & W; Softball W; Tennis M & W; Track and Field M & W; Volleyball W; Wrestling M & W

MARION TECHNICAL COLLEGE
1467 Mount Vernon Ave.
Marion, OH 43302-5694
Tel: (740)389-4636
Fax: (740)389-6136
E-mail: enroll@mtc.edu
Web Site: http://www.mtc.edu/
President/CEO: Dr. Richard Bryson
Admissions: Joel Liles
Type: Two-Year College **Sex:** Coed **Affiliation:** Ohio Board of Regents **Admission Plans:** Open Admission; Early Admission; Deferred Admission **Application Deadline:** Rolling **Application Fee:** $20.00 **H.S. Requirements:** High school diploma required; GED accepted **Costs Per Year:** Application fee: $20. State resident tuition: $3636 full-time, $101 per credit hour part-time. Nonresident tuition: $5544 full-time, $154 per credit hour part-time. Mandatory fees: $150 full-time. **Scholarships:** Available **Calendar System:** Quarter, Summer Session Available **Enrollment:** FT 1,369, PT 1,290 **Faculty:** FT 35, PT 150 **Student-Faculty Ratio:** 18:1 **Exams:** ACT, Other. **Library Holdings:** 52,000 **Regional Accreditation:** North Central Association of Colleges and Schools **Credit Hours For Degree:** 100 quarter hours,

Associates **Professional Accreditation:** APTA, JRCERT, NAACLS, NLN **Intercollegiate Athletics:** Basketball M & W; Golf M & W; Rugby M; Softball W; Volleyball W

MERCY COLLEGE OF NORTHWEST OHIO
2221 Madison Ave.
Toledo, OH 43604
Tel: (419)251-1313; Free: 888-80-Mercy
Fax: (419)251-4116
E-mail: admissions@mercycollege.edu
Web Site: http://www.mercycollege.edu/
President/CEO: John Hayward, JD
Financial Aid: Julie Leslie
Type: Four-Year College **Sex:** Coed **Affiliation:** Roman Catholic Church; Mercy Health Partners **Application Deadline:** Rolling **Application Fee:** $25.00 **H.S. Requirements:** High school diploma required; GED accepted **Costs Per Year:** Application fee: $25. One-time mandatory fee: $15. Tuition: $9440 full-time, $326 per credit hour part-time. Mandatory fees: $650 full-time, $5 per credit hour part-time. Full-time tuition and fees vary according to course load. Part-time tuition and fees vary according to course load. **Scholarships:** Available **Calendar System:** Semester, Summer Session Available **Enrollment:** FT 544, PT 504 **Faculty:** FT 60, PT 63 **Student-Faculty Ratio:** 11:1 **Exams:** SAT I or ACT. **% Receiving Financial Aid:** 73 **% Residing in College-Owned, -Operated, or -Affiliated Housing:** 5 **Library Holdings:** 6,000 **Regional Accreditation:** North Central Association of Colleges and Schools **Credit Hours For Degree:** 60 semester hours, Associates; 120 semester hours, Bachelors **Professional Accreditation:** AHIMA, JRCERT, NAACLS, NLN

MIAMI UNIVERSITY
Oxford, OH 45056
Tel: (513)529-1809
Admissions: (513)529-2531
Fax: (513)529-1550
E-mail: admission@muohio.edu
Web Site: http://www.muohio.edu/
President/CEO: Dr. David Hodge
Financial Aid: Chuck Knepfle
Type: University **Sex:** Coed **Affiliation:** Miami University System **Scores:** 99% SAT V 400+; 100% SAT M 400+; 23% ACT 18-23; 58% ACT 24-29 **% Accepted:** 79 **Admission Plans:** Early Action; Early Decision Plan; Deferred Admission **Application Deadline:** February 1 **Application Fee:** $50.00 **H.S. Requirements:** High school diploma required; GED accepted **Costs Per Year:** Application fee: $50. State resident tuition: $11,442 full-time. Nonresident tuition: $26,202 full-time. Mandatory fees: $2070 full-time. Full-time tuition and fees vary according to location and program. College room and board: $9458. College room only: $4786. Room and board charges vary according to board plan and housing facility. **Scholarships:** Available **Calendar System:** Semester, Summer Session Available **Enrollment:** FT 14,457, PT 214, Grad FT 1,030, Grad PT 1,183 **Faculty:** FT 827, PT 361 **Student-Faculty Ratio:** 17:1 **Exams:** SAT I or ACT. ACT essay not being used. SAT essay not being used. **% Receiving Financial Aid:** 43 **% Residing in College-Owned, -Operated, or -Affiliated Housing:** 50 **Final Year or Final Semester Residency Requirement:** No **Library Holdings:** 3,718,214 **Regional Accreditation:** North Central Association of Colleges and Schools **Credit Hours For Degree:** 64 credit hours, Associates; 128 credit hours, Bachelors **ROTC:** Army, Navy, Air Force **Professional Accreditation:** AACSB, ABET, APA, ASLHA, FIDER, CSWE, JRCEPAT, NAAB, NASAD, NASM, NAST, NCATE, NLN **Intercollegiate Athletics:** Baseball M & W; Basketball M & W; Cross-Country Running M & W; Equestrian Sports M & W; Fencing M & W; Field Hockey M & W; Football M; Golf M; Gymnastics M & W; Ice Hockey M & W; Lacrosse M & W; Rugby M & W; Sailing M & W; Soccer M & W; Softball M & W; Swimming and Diving M & W; Tennis M & W; Track and Field M & W; Ultimate Frisbee M & W; Volleyball M & W; Water Polo M & W; Weight Lifting M & W; Wrestling M & W

MIAMI UNIVERSITY HAMILTON
1601 Peck Blvd.
Hamilton, OH 45011-3399
Tel: (513)785-3000
Admissions: (513)785-3111
E-mail: nelsona3@muohio.edu
Web Site: http://www.ham.muohio.edu/
President/CEO: Daniel E. Hall
Admissions: Archie Nelson
Type: Comprehensive **Sex:** Coed **Affiliation:** Miami University System **Admission Plans:** Open Admission **Application Deadline:** Rolling **Application Fee:** $35.00 **H.S. Requirements:** High school diploma required; GED accepted **Costs Per Year:** Application fee: $35. State resident tuition: $3948 full-time. Nonresident tuition: $15,948 full-time. Mandatory fees: $402 full-time. **Scholarships:** Available **Calendar System:** Semester, Summer Session Available **Enrollment:** FT 3,280, PT 902, Grad FT 7, Grad PT 5 **Faculty:** FT 84, PT 140 **Student-Faculty Ratio:** 21:1 **Library Holdings:** 68,000 **Regional Accreditation:** North Central Association of Colleges and Schools **Credit Hours For Degree:** 64 credits, Associates; 128 credits, Bachelors **ROTC:** Navy, Air Force **Professional Accreditation:** NLN **Intercollegiate Athletics:** Baseball M; Basketball M & W; Cheerleading W; Golf M; Softball W; Tennis M & W; Volleyball W

MIAMI UNIVERSITY—MIDDLETOWN CAMPUS
4200 East University Blvd.
Middletown, OH 45042-3497
Tel: (513)727-3200; Free: (866)426-4643
Admissions: (513)727-3346
Fax: (513)727-3223
E-mail: cantondm@muohio.edu
Web Site: http://www.mid.muohio.edu/
President/CEO: Kelly Cowan
Admissions: Diane Cantonwine
Type: Two-Year College **Sex:** Coed **Affiliation:** Miami University System **Admission Plans:** Open Admission; Early Admission; Deferred Admission **Application Deadline:** Rolling **Application Fee:** $35.00 **H.S. Requirements:** High school diploma required; GED accepted **Scholarships:** Available **Calendar System:** Semester, Summer Session Available **Faculty:** FT 79, PT 130 **Student-Faculty Ratio:** 13:1 **Regional Accreditation:** North Central Association of Colleges and Schools **Credit Hours For Degree:** 64 semester hours, Associates; 128 semester hours, Bachelors **ROTC:** Air Force **Professional Accreditation:** NLN **Intercollegiate Athletics:** Baseball M; Basketball M & W; Golf M & W; Softball W; Tennis M & W; Volleyball W

MIAMI—JACOBS COLLEGE
PO Box 1433
Dayton, OH 45401-1433
Tel: (937)461-5174
Fax: (937)461-3384
Web Site: http://www.miamijacobs.edu/
President/CEO: Darlene R. Waite
Admissions: Mary Percell
Type: Two-Year College **Sex:** Coed **Admission Plans:** Early Admission; Deferred Admission **Application Deadline:** August 15 **Application Fee:** $20.00 **H.S. Requirements:** High school diploma required; GED accepted **Scholarships:** Available **Calendar System:** Quarter, Summer Session Available **Exams:** ACT, Other, SAT I or ACT. **Credit Hours For Degree:** 91 credits, Associates **Professional Accreditation:** ACICS, AAMAE

MOUNT CARMEL COLLEGE OF NURSING
127 South Davis Ave.
Columbus, OH 43222
Tel: (614)234-5800
Admissions: (614)234-1085
Web Site: http://www.mccn.edu/
President/CEO: Dr. Ann E. Schiele
Financial Aid: Carol Graham
Type: Comprehensive **Sex:** Coed **Scores:** 74.26% ACT 18-23; 21.78% ACT 24-29 **% Accepted:** 86 **Application Deadline:** April 1 **Application Fee:** $30.00 **H.S. Requirements:** High school diploma required; GED accepted **Costs Per Year:** Application fee: $30. One-time mandatory fee: $225. Tuition: $14,749 full-time, $314 per semester hour part-time. Mandatory fees: $312 full-time, $312 per year part-time. Full-time tuition and fees vary according to course load and student level. Part-time tuition and fees vary according to course load and student level. College room only: $4500. **Scholarships:** Available **Calendar System:** Semester **Enrollment:** FT 595, PT 127, Grad FT 6, Grad PT 54 **Faculty:** FT 35, PT 46 **Exams:** SAT I or ACT. **% Receiving Financial Aid:** 93 **% Residing in College-Owned, -Operated, or -Affiliated Housing:** 12 **Regional Accreditation:** North Central Association of Colleges and Schools **ROTC:** Army, Air Force **Professional Accreditation:** AACN, ADtA, NLN

MOUNT VERNON NAZARENE UNIVERSITY
800 Martinsburg Rd.
Mount Vernon, OH 43050-9500
Tel: (740)392-6868; Free: (866)462-6868
E-mail: admissions@mvnu.edu
Web Site: http://www.mvnu.edu/
President/CEO: Dr. Daniel J. Martin
Admissions: James Smith
Type: Comprehensive **Sex:** Coed **Affiliation:** Nazarene **Scores:** 90% SAT V 400+; 96% SAT M 400+; 53% ACT 18-23; 31% ACT 24-29 **% Accepted:** 72 **Admission Plans:** Deferred Admission **Application Deadline:** July 15 **Application Fee:** $25.00 **H.S. Requirements:** High school diploma required; GED accepted **Costs Per Year:** Application fee: $25. Comprehensive fee: $27,510 includes full-time tuition ($20,700), mandatory fees ($630), and college room and board ($6180). College room only: $3450. Full-time tuition and fees vary according to course load, program, and reciprocity agreements. Part-time tuition: $739 per credit hour. Part-time mandatory fees: $21 per credit hour. Part-time tuition and fees vary according to course load, program, and reciprocity agreements. **Scholarships:** Available **Calendar System:** 4-1-4, Summer Session Available **Enrollment:** FT 1,736, PT 338, Grad FT 487, Grad PT 61 **Faculty:** FT 108, PT 159 **Student-Faculty Ratio:** 14:1 **Exams:** SAT I or ACT. ACT essay not being used. SAT essay not being used. **% Receiving Financial Aid:** 70 **% Residing in College-Owned, -Operated, or -Affiliated Housing:** 73 **Library Holdings:** 162,643 **Regional Accreditation:** North Central Association of Colleges and Schools **Credit Hours For Degree:** 64 credit hours, Associates; 124 credit hours, Bachelors **Professional Accreditation:** ACBSP, NCATE **Intercollegiate Athletics:** Baseball M; Basketball M & W; Cross-Country Running M & W; Golf M; Soccer M & W; Softball W; Volleyball W

MUSKINGUM UNIVERSITY
163 Stormont St.
New Concord, OH 43762
Tel: (740)826-8211; Free: 800-752-6082
Fax: (740)826-8404
E-mail: adminfo@muskingum.edu
Web Site: http://www.muskingum.edu/
President/CEO: Anne C. Steele
Admissions: Beth DaLonzo
Financial Aid: Jeff Zellers
Type: Comprehensive **Sex:** Coed **Affiliation:** Presbyterian Church (U.S.A.) **Admission Plans:** Early Admission; Deferred Admission **Application Deadline:** June 1 **Application Fee:** $0.00 **H.S. Requirements:** High school diploma required; GED accepted **Scholarships:** Available **Calendar System:** Semester, Summer Session Available **Exams:** SAT I or ACT. **% Receiving Financial Aid:** 82 **Library Holdings:** 233,000 **Regional Accreditation:** North Central Association of Colleges and Schools **Credit Hours For Degree:** 124 credits, Bachelors **Professional Accreditation:** NASM, NCATE **Intercollegiate Athletics:** Baseball M; Basketball M & W; Cross-Country Running M & W; Football M; Golf M & W; Soccer M & W; Softball W; Tennis M & W; Track and Field M & W; Volleyball W; Wrestling M

NORTH CENTRAL STATE COLLEGE
2441 Kenwood Circle, PO Box 698
Mansfield, OH 44901-0698
Tel: (419)755-4800
Fax: (419)755-4750
E-mail: nfletcher@ncstatecollege.edu
Web Site: http://www.ncstatecollege.edu/
President/CEO: Donald L. Plotts
Admissions: Nikia L. Fletcher
Type: Two-Year College **Sex:** Coed **Affiliation:** Ohio Board of Regents **Admission Plans:** Open Admission; Early Admission; Deferred Admission **Application Deadline:** Rolling **H.S. Requirements:** High school diploma required; GED accepted **Scholarships:** Available **Calendar System:** Quarter, Summer Session Available **Library Holdings:** 52,700 **Regional Accreditation:** North Central Association of Colleges and Schools **Credit Hours For Degree:** 100 quarter hours, Associates **Professional Accreditation:** APTA, ACBSP, CARC, JRCERT, NLN

NORTHWEST STATE COMMUNITY COLLEGE
22-600 State Route 34
Archbold, OH 43502-9542
Tel: (419)267-5511
Fax: (419)267-3688
Web Site: http://www.northweststate.edu/
President/CEO: Thomas Stuckey
Admissions: Jeffrey Ferezan
Type: Two-Year College **Sex:** Coed **Affiliation:** Ohio Board of Regents **Admission Plans:** Open Admission; Early Admission; Deferred Admission **Application Deadline:** Rolling **Application Fee:** $20.00 **H.S. Requirements:** High school diploma required; GED accepted **Costs Per Year:** Application fee: $20. State resident tuition: $3930 full-time, $131 per credit part-time. Nonresident tuition: $7680 full-time, $256 per credit part-time. Mandatory fees: $60 full-time, $30 per term part-time. Full-time tuition and fees vary according to course load. Part-time tuition and fees vary according to course load. **Scholarships:** Available **Calendar System:** Semester, Summer Session Available **Library Holdings:** 15,321 **Regional Accreditation:** North Central Association of Colleges and Schools **Credit Hours For Degree:** 62 semester hours, Associates **Professional Accreditation:** ABET, ACBSP, NLN

NOTRE DAME COLLEGE
4545 College Rd.
South Euclid, OH 44121-4293
Tel: (216)381-1680; Free: 800-632-1680
Fax: (216)381-3802
E-mail: admissinos@ndc.edu
Web Site: http://www.notredamecollege.edu/
President/CEO: Andrew P. Roth, PhD
Admissions: David Armstrong
Financial Aid: Dianna Roberts
Type: Comprehensive **Sex:** Coed **Affiliation:** Roman Catholic **Scores:** 87% SAT V 400+; 84% SAT M 400+; 68% ACT 18-23; 9% ACT 24-29 **% Accepted:** 52 **Admission Plans:** Deferred Admission **Application Deadline:** Rolling **Application Fee:** $30.00 **H.S. Requirements:** High school diploma required; GED accepted **Costs Per Year:** Application fee: $30. Comprehensive fee: $30,334 includes full-time tuition ($22,192), mandatory fees ($550), and college room and board ($7592). Full-time tuition and fees vary according to course load and degree level. Room and board charges vary according to board plan and housing facility. Part-time tuition: $460 per credit. Part-time tuition varies according to course load and degree level. **Scholarships:** Available **Calendar System:** Semester, Summer Session Available **Enrollment:** FT 793, PT 447 **Faculty:** FT 34, PT 84 **Student-Faculty Ratio:** 13:1 **Exams:** SAT I or ACT. **% Residing in College-Owned, -Operated, or -Affiliated Housing:** 44 **Regional Accreditation:** North Central Association of Colleges and Schools **Credit Hours For Degree:** 64 semester hours, Associates; 128 semester hours, Bachelors **Intercollegiate Athletics:** Baseball M; Basketball M & W; Cross-Country Running M & W; Field Hockey W; Golf M & W; Soccer M & W; Softball W; Tennis M; Track and Field M & W; Volleyball W

OBERLIN COLLEGE
173 West Lorain St.
Oberlin, OH 44074
Tel: (440)775-8121; Free: 800-622-OBIE
Admissions: (440)775-8411
Fax: (440)775-8886
E-mail: college.admissions@oberlin.edu
Web Site: http://www.oberlin.edu/
President/CEO: Marvin Krislov
Admissions: Debra Chermonte
Financial Aid: Robert Reddy, Jr.
Type: Comprehensive **Sex:** Coed **Scores:** 100% SAT V 400+; 100% SAT M 400+; 6% ACT 18-23; 34% ACT 24-29 **% Accepted:** 34 **Admission Plans:** Early Admission; Early Decision Plan; Deferred Admission **Application Deadline:** January 15 **Application Fee:** $35.00 **H.S. Requirements:** High school diploma required; GED accepted **Costs Per Year:** Application fee: $35. Comprehensive fee: $50,484 includes full-time tuition ($39,686), mandatory fees ($318), and college room and board ($10,480). College room only: $5450. Room and board charges vary according to board plan and housing facility. Part-time tuition: $1654 per credit hour. **Scholarships:** Available **Calendar System:** 4-1-4, Summer Session Not available **Enrollment:** FT 2,842, PT 46 **Student-Faculty Ratio:** 9:1 **Exams:** SAT I or ACT, SAT II. ACT essay used for admission. SAT essay used for admission. ACT essay used for advising. SAT essay used for advising. **% Receiving Financial Aid:** 55 **% Residing in College-Owned, -Operated, or -Affiliated Housing:** 86 **Library Holdings:** 1,427,793 **Regional Accredita-**

tion: North Central Association of Colleges and Schools **Credit Hours For Degree:** 112 credit hours, Bachelors **Professional Accreditation:** NASM, TEAC **Intercollegiate Athletics:** Baseball M; Basketball M & W; Cheerleading W; Cross-Country Running M & W; Equestrian Sports M & W; Fencing M & W; Field Hockey W; Football M; Golf M & W; Ice Hockey M & W; Lacrosse M & W; Rugby M & W; Soccer M & W; Softball W; Swimming and Diving M & W; Tennis M & W; Track and Field M & W; Ultimate Frisbee M & W; Volleyball M & W; Water Polo M & W

OHIO BUSINESS COLLEGE (LORAIN)
1907 North Ridge Rd.
Lorain, OH 44055
Tel: (440)277-0021; Free: 888-514-3126
Admissions: (440)934-3101
Fax: (440)277-7989
Web Site: http://www.ohiobusinesscollege.com/
President/CEO: Rosanne Catella
Admissions: Jim Unger
Type: Two-Year College **Sex:** Coed **Affiliation:** Tri State Educational Systems **Admission Plans:** Open Admission **Application Deadline:** Rolling **Application Fee:** $25.00 **H.S. Requirements:** High school diploma required; GED accepted **Scholarships:** Available **Calendar System:** Quarter, Summer Session Available **Library Holdings:** 850 **Professional Accreditation:** ACICS

OHIO BUSINESS COLLEGE (SANDUSKY)
5202 Timber Commons Dr.
Sandusky, OH 44870
Tel: (419)627-8345; Free: 888-627-8345
Fax: (419)627-1958
E-mail: rpickering@ohiobusinesscollege.edu
Web Site: http://www.ohiobusinesscollege.com/
President/CEO: Theresa M. Fisher
Admissions: Rohnda Pickering
Type: Two-Year College **Sex:** Coed **% Accepted:** 100 **Application Fee:** $25.00 **Costs Per Year:** Application fee: $25. Tuition: $23,220 full-time, $3870 per year part-time. Mandatory fees: $1980 full-time, $215 per credit part-time. Full-time tuition and fees vary according to course load. Part-time tuition and fees vary according to course load. Tuition guaranteed not to increase for student's term of enrollment. **Calendar System:** Quarter **Enrollment:** FT 157, PT 35 **Faculty:** PT 30 **Student-Faculty Ratio:** 10:1 **Professional Accreditation:** ACICS

OHIO CHRISTIAN UNIVERSITY
1476 Lancaster Pike, PO Box 458
Circleville, OH 43113-9487
Tel: (740)474-8896; Free: 800-701-0222
Fax: (740)477-7755
E-mail: enroll@ohiochristian.edu
Web Site: http://www.ohiochristian.edu/
President/CEO: Dr. Mark A. Smith
Admissions: Mike Egenreider
Financial Aid: Michael Fracassa
Type: Four-Year College **Sex:** Coed **Affiliation:** Churches of Christ in Christian Union **Admission Plans:** Early Admission **Application Deadline:** Rolling **Application Fee:** $25.00 **H.S. Requirements:** High school diploma required; GED accepted **Scholarships:** Available **Calendar System:** Semester, Summer Session Available **Exams:** ACT, SAT I. **% Receiving Financial Aid:** 83 **Library Holdings:** 37,521 **Regional Accreditation:** North Central Association of Colleges and Schools **Credit Hours For Degree:** 62 semester hours, Associates; 124 semester hours, Bachelors **Professional Accreditation:** ABHE **Intercollegiate Athletics:** Baseball M; Basketball M & W; Golf M; Soccer M; Softball W; Volleyball W

OHIO COLLEGE OF MASSOTHERAPY
225 Heritage Woods Dr.
Akron, OH 44321
Tel: (330)665-1084; Free: 888-888-4325
Fax: (330)665-5021
E-mail: johna@ocm.edu
Web Site: http://www.ocm.edu/
President/CEO: Jeffrey S. Morrow
Admissions: John Atkins
Type: Two-Year College **Sex:** Coed **Application Fee:** $25.00 **Calendar System:** Semester **Professional Accreditation:** ACCSCT

OHIO DOMINICAN UNIVERSITY
1216 Sunbury Rd.
Columbus, OH 43219-2099
Tel: (614)253-2741; Free: 800-854-2670
Admissions: (614)251-4500
Fax: (614)252-0776
E-mail: admissions@ohiodominican.edu
Web Site: http://www.ohiodominican.edu/
President/CEO: Ronald J. Seiffert
Admissions: Nicole A. Evans
Financial Aid: Cynthia A. Hahn
Type: Comprehensive **Sex:** Coed **Affiliation:** Roman Catholic **Scores:** 67% ACT 18-23; 24% ACT 24-29 **% Accepted:** 59 **Admission Plans:** Deferred Admission **Application Deadline:** Rolling **Application Fee:** $25.00 **H.S. Requirements:** High school diploma required; GED accepted **Costs Per Year:** Application fee: $25. Comprehensive fee: $32,716 includes full-time tuition ($24,116), mandatory fees ($500), and college room and board ($8100). Room and board charges vary according to board plan and housing facility. Part-time tuition: $488 per credit hour. Part-time mandatory fees: $135. **Scholarships:** Available **Calendar System:** Semester, Summer Session Available **Enrollment:** FT 1,547, PT 733, Grad FT 681, Grad PT 91 **Faculty:** FT 75, PT 95 **Student-Faculty Ratio:** 14:1 **Exams:** SAT I or ACT. **% Residing in College-Owned, -Operated, or -Affiliated Housing:** 76 **Library Holdings:** 128,788 **Regional Accreditation:** North Central Association of Colleges and Schools **Credit Hours For Degree:** 62 credit hours, Associates; 124 credit hours, Bachelors **ROTC:** Army **Professional Accreditation:** ACBSP, NCATE **Intercollegiate Athletics:** Baseball M; Basketball M & W; Cheerleading M & W; Cross-Country Running M & W; Football M; Golf M & W; Soccer M & W; Softball W; Tennis M & W; Volleyball W

OHIO NORTHERN UNIVERSITY
525 South Main
Ada, OH 45810-1599
Tel: (419)772-2000; Free: 888-408-4ONU
Admissions: (419)772-2260
Fax: (419)772-2313
E-mail: admissions-ug@onu.edu
Web Site: http://www.onu.edu/
President/CEO: Dr. Kendall Baker
Admissions: Deborah Miller
Financial Aid: Melanie Weaver
Type: Comprehensive **Sex:** Coed **Affiliation:** United Methodist Church **Scores:** 98% SAT V 400+; 100% SAT M 400+; 26% ACT 18-23; 53% ACT 24-29 **% Accepted:** 89 **Admission Plans:** Deferred Admission **Application Deadline:** August 15 **Application Fee:** $30.00 **H.S. Requirements:** High school diploma required; GED accepted **Costs Per Year:** Application fee: $30. Comprehensive fee: $40,146 includes full-time tuition ($31,626), mandatory fees ($240), and college room and board ($8280). College room only: $4140. Full-time tuition and fees vary according to course load, degree level, program, and student level. Room and board charges vary according to board plan and housing facility. Part-time tuition: $880 per quarter hour. Part-time mandatory fees: $30 per term. Part-time tuition and fees vary according to course load, degree level, program, and student level. **Scholarships:** Available **Calendar System:** Quarter, Summer Session Available **Enrollment:** FT 2,423, PT 256, Grad FT 941, Grad PT 31 **Faculty:** FT 242, PT 72 **Student-Faculty Ratio:** 12:1 **Exams:** SAT I or ACT. **% Receiving Financial Aid:** 78 **% Residing in College-Owned, -Operated, or -Affiliated Housing:** 68 **Regional Accreditation:** North Central Association of Colleges and Schools **Credit Hours For Degree:** 182 credit hours, Bachelors **ROTC:** Army, Air Force **Professional Accreditation:** AACSB, ABET, ACPhE, ABA, AALS, JRCEPAT, NASM, NCATE **Intercollegiate Athletics:** Baseball M; Basketball M & W; Cross-Country Running M & W; Football M; Golf M & W; Soccer M & W; Softball W; Swimming and Diving M & W; Tennis M & W; Track and Field M & W; Volleyball M & W; Wrestling M

THE OHIO STATE UNIVERSITY
Enarson Hall, 154 West 12th Ave.
Columbus, OH 43210
Tel: (614)292-6446
Admissions: (614)292-3980

Fax: (614)292-4818
E-mail: askabuckeye@osu.edu
Web Site: http://www.osu.edu/
President/CEO: Dr. E. Gordon Gee
Admissions: Dr. Mabel Freeman
Financial Aid: Diane Stemper
Type: University **Sex:** Coed **Affiliation:** Ohio State University System **Scores:** 99% SAT V 400+; 100% SAT M 400+; 9% ACT 18-23; 64% ACT 24-29 **% Accepted:** 76 **Application Deadline:** February 1 **Application Fee:** $40.00 **H.S. Requirements:** High school diploma required; GED accepted **Costs Per Year:** Application fee: $40. State resident tuition: $8406 full-time. Nonresident tuition: $21,978 full-time. Mandatory fees: $300 full-time. Full-time tuition and fees vary according to course load, program, and reciprocity agreements. College room and board: $8409. Room and board charges vary according to board plan and housing facility. **Scholarships:** Available **Calendar System:** Quarter, Summer Session Available **Enrollment:** FT 37,864, PT 3,484, Grad FT 9,265, Grad PT 4,401 **Faculty:** FT 3,310, PT 1,158 **Student-Faculty Ratio:** 12:1 **Exams:** SAT I or ACT. ACT essay used for admission. SAT essay used for admission. **% Receiving Financial Aid:** 55 **% Residing in College-Owned, -Operated, or -Affiliated Housing:** 24 **Library Holdings:** 6,206,643 **Regional Accreditation:** North Central Association of Colleges and Schools **Credit Hours For Degree:** 181 quarter hours, Bachelors **ROTC:** Army, Navy, Air Force **Professional Accreditation:** AACSB, ABET, ACPE, ACPhE, AAMFT, AACN, AAFCS, ABA, ACNM, ADA, ADtA, AHIMA, ACSP, AOTA, AOA, APTA, APA, ASLA, ASLHA, AVMA ACIPE, AALS, ACEHSA, CARC, FIDER, CEPH, CORE, CSWE, LCMEAMA, NAACLS, NAAB, NASAD, NASD, NASM, NASPAA, NAST, NCATE, SAF **Intercollegiate Athletics:** Baseball M; Basketball M & W; Cheerleading M & W; Cross-Country Running M & W; Fencing M & W; Field Hockey W; Football M; Golf M & W; Gymnastics M & W; Ice Hockey M & W; Lacrosse M & W; Riflery M & W; Soccer M & W; Softball W; Swimming and Diving M & W; Tennis M & W; Track and Field M & W; Volleyball M & W; Wrestling M

THE OHIO STATE UNIVERSITY AGRICULTURAL TECHNICAL INSTITUTE

1328 Dover Rd.
Wooster, OH 44691
Tel: (330)264-3911
Admissions: (330)287-1228
E-mail: elvey.3@osu.edu
Web Site: http://www.ati.osu.edu/
President/CEO: Dr. Stephen G.P. Nameth
Admissions: Sarah Elvey
Type: Two-Year College **Sex:** Coed **Affiliation:** Ohio State University System **Scores:** 46% ACT 18-23; 11% ACT 24-29 **% Accepted:** 95 **Admission Plans:** Open Admission **Application Deadline:** July 1 **Application Fee:** $40.00 **H.S. Requirements:** High school diploma required; GED accepted **Costs Per Year:** Application fee: $40. State resident tuition: $5859 full-time. Nonresident tuition: $19,431 full-time. Full-time tuition varies according to course load. College room and board: $6765. College room only: $5655. Room and board charges vary according to board plan. **Calendar System:** Quarter, Summer Session Available **Enrollment:** FT 747 **Faculty:** FT 33, PT 37 **Student-Faculty Ratio:** 16:1 **Exams:** SAT I or ACT. ACT essay not being used. SAT essay not being used. **Final Year or Final Semester Residency Requirement:** No **Library Holdings:** 9,000 **Regional Accreditation:** North Central Association of Colleges and Schools **Credit Hours For Degree:** 100 quarter hours, Associates **ROTC:** Army, Navy, Air Force

THE OHIO STATE UNIVERSITY AT LIMA

4240 Campus Dr.
Lima, OH 45804
Tel: (419)995-8600
Admissions: (419)995-8434
Fax: (419)995-8483
E-mail: admissions@lima.ohio-state.edu
Web Site: http://www.lima.ohio-state.edu/
President/CEO: Dr. E. Gordon Gee
Admissions: Garlene Smithson
Type: Comprehensive **Sex:** Coed **Affiliation:** Ohio State University System **Scores:** 95% SAT V 400+; 100% SAT M 400+; 62% ACT 18-23; 27% ACT 24-29 **% Accepted:** 98 **Admission Plans:** Open Admission **Application Deadline:** July 1 **Application Fee:** $40.00 **H.S. Requirements:** High school diploma required; GED accepted **Costs Per Year:** Application fee: $40. State resident tuition: $5661 full-time. Nonresident tuition: $19,233 full-time. Full-time tuition varies according to course load. **Calendar System:** Quarter, Summer Session Available **Enrollment:** FT 1,203, PT 199, Grad FT 23, Grad PT 83 **Faculty:** FT 39, PT 48 **Student-Faculty Ratio:** 17:1 **Exams:** SAT I or ACT. ACT essay used for admission. SAT essay used for admission. **Final Year or Final Semester Residency Requirement:** No **Library Holdings:** 6,206,443 **Regional Accreditation:** North Central Association of Colleges and Schools **Credit Hours For Degree:** 90 quarter hours, Associates; 181 quarter hours, Bachelors **ROTC:** Army, Navy, Air Force **Intercollegiate Athletics:** Baseball M; Basketball M & W; Volleyball M & W

THE OHIO STATE UNIVERSITY AT MARION

1465 Mount Vernon Ave.
Marion, OH 43302-5695
Tel: (740)389-6786
Admissions: (740)725-6337
E-mail: moreau.1@osu.edu
Web Site: http://www.marion.ohio-state.edu/
President/CEO: Dr. Gregory S. Rose
Admissions: Matthew Moreau
Type: Comprehensive **Sex:** Coed **Affiliation:** Ohio State University System **Scores:** 92% SAT V 400+; 92% SAT M 400+; 59% ACT 18-23; 27% ACT 24-29 **% Accepted:** 98 **Admission Plans:** Open Admission **Application Deadline:** July 1 **Application Fee:** $40.00 **H.S. Requirements:** High school diploma required; GED accepted **Costs Per Year:** Application fee: $40. State resident tuition: $5661 full-time. Nonresident tuition: $19,233 full-time. Full-time tuition varies according to course load. **Calendar System:** Quarter, Summer Session Available **Enrollment:** FT 1,484, PT 261, Grad FT 49, Grad PT 34 **Faculty:** FT 38, PT 79 **Student-Faculty Ratio:** 16:1 **Exams:** SAT I or ACT. ACT essay used for admission. SAT essay used for admission. **Final Year or Final Semester Residency Requirement:** No **Regional Accreditation:** North Central Association of Colleges and Schools **Credit Hours For Degree:** 90 quarter hours, Associates; 181 quarter hours, Bachelors **ROTC:** Army, Navy, Air Force **Intercollegiate Athletics:** Basketball M; Cheerleading W; Soccer M; Softball M & W; Volleyball W

THE OHIO STATE UNIVERSITY—MANSFIELD CAMPUS

1680 University Dr.
Mansfield, OH 44906-1599
Tel: (419)755-4011
Admissions: (419)755-4225
E-mail: admissions@mansfield.ohio-state.edu
Web Site: http://www.mansfield.osu.edu/
President/CEO: Dr. Evelyn B. Freeman
Admissions: Henry D. Thomas
Type: Comprehensive **Sex:** Coed **Affiliation:** Ohio State University System **Scores:** 92% SAT V 400+; 96% SAT M 400+; 56% ACT 18-23; 33% ACT 24-29 **% Accepted:** 99 **Admission Plans:** Open Admission; Early Admission **Application Deadline:** July 1 **Application Fee:** $40.00 **H.S. Requirements:** High school diploma required; GED accepted **Costs Per Year:** Application fee: $40. State resident tuition: $5661 full-time. Nonresident tuition: $19,233 full-time. Full-time tuition varies according to course load. College room only: $5205. Room charges vary according to housing facility. **Calendar System:** Quarter, Summer Session Available **Enrollment:** FT 1,156, PT 428, Grad FT 31, Grad PT 32 **Faculty:** FT 46, PT 47 **Student-Faculty Ratio:** 12:1 **Exams:** SAT I or ACT. ACT essay used for admission. SAT essay used for admission. **% Residing in College-Owned, -Operated, or -Affiliated Housing:** 15 **Final Year or Final Semester Residency Requirement:** No **Regional Accreditation:** North Central Association of Colleges and Schools **Credit Hours For Degree:** 90 quarter hours, Associates; 181 quarter hours, Bachelors **ROTC:** Army, Navy, Air Force **Intercollegiate Athletics:** Soccer M & W

THE OHIO STATE UNIVERSITY—NEWARK CAMPUS

1179 University Dr.
Newark, OH 43055-1797
Tel: (740)366-3321
Admissions: (740)366-9333
E-mail: barclay.3@osu.edu
Web Site: http://www.newark.osu.edu/
President/CEO: Dr. Willilam L. MacDonald
Admissions: Ann Donahue
Type: Comprehensive **Sex:** Coed **Affiliation:** Ohio State University System **Scores:** 91% SAT V 400+; 90% SAT M 400+; 61% ACT 18-23; 22% ACT

24-29 **% Accepted:** 99 **Admission Plans:** Open Admission **Application Deadline:** July 1 **Application Fee:** $40.00 **H.S. Requirements:** High school diploma required; GED accepted **Costs Per Year:** Application fee: $40. State resident tuition: $5661 full-time. Nonresident tuition: $19,233 full-time. Full-time tuition varies according to course load. **Calendar System:** Quarter, Summer Session Available **Enrollment:** FT 2,073, PT 338, Grad FT 40, Grad PT 64 **Faculty:** FT 53, PT 83 **Student-Faculty Ratio:** 19:1 **Exams:** SAT I or ACT. ACT essay used for admission. SAT essay used for admission. **% Residing in College-Owned, -Operated, or -Affiliated Housing:** 8 **Final Year or Final Semester Residency Requirement:** No **Library Holdings:** 6,206,443 **Regional Accreditation:** North Central Association of Colleges and Schools **Credit Hours For Degree:** 90 quarter hours, Associates; 181 quarter hours, Bachelors **ROTC:** Army, Navy, Air Force

OHIO TECHNICAL COLLEGE
1374 East 51st St.
Cleveland, OH 44103
Tel: (216)881-1700; Free: 800-322-7000
Fax: (216)881-9145
E-mail: ohioauto@aol.com
Web Site: http://www.ohiotechnicalcollege.com/
President/CEO: Marc L. Brenner
Admissions: Marc Brenner
Type: Two-Year College **Sex:** Coed **Application Fee:** $100.00 **Professional Accreditation:** ACCSCT

OHIO UNIVERSITY
Athens, OH 45701-2979
Tel: (740)593-1000
Admissions: (740)593-4100
Fax: (740)593-4229
E-mail: admissions@ohio.edu
Web Site: http://www.ohio.edu/
President/CEO: Dr. Roderick J. McDavis
Financial Aid: Sondra Williams
Type: University **Sex:** Coed **Affiliation:** Ohio Board of Regents, University System of Ohio **Scores:** 97% SAT V 400+; 97% SAT M 400+; 50% ACT 18-23; 40% ACT 24-29 **% Accepted:** 82 **Admission Plans:** Early Admission; Deferred Admission **Application Deadline:** February 1 **Application Fee:** $45.00 **H.S. Requirements:** High school diploma required; GED accepted **Costs Per Year:** Application fee: $45. State resident tuition: $8973 full-time, $305 per quarter hour part-time. Nonresident tuition: $17,937 full-time, $600 per quarter hour part-time. Full-time tuition varies according to course load, degree level, location, and program. Part-time tuition varies according to course load, degree level, location, and program. College room and board: $9408. College room only: $5196. Room and board charges vary according to board plan. **Scholarships:** Available **Calendar System:** Quarter, Summer Session Available **Enrollment:** FT 16,523, PT 2,066, Grad FT 2,969, Grad PT 1,089 **Faculty:** FT 907, PT 294 **Student-Faculty Ratio:** 19:1 **Exams:** SAT I or ACT. **% Receiving Financial Aid:** 55 **% Residing in College-Owned, -Operated, or -Affiliated Housing:** 40 **Final Year or Final Semester Residency Requirement:** Yes **Library Holdings:** 2,958,684 **Regional Accreditation:** North Central Association of Colleges and Schools **Credit Hours For Degree:** 96 quarter hours, Associates; 192 quarter hours, Bachelors **ROTC:** Army, Air Force **Professional Accreditation:** AACSB, ABET, ACEJMC, AACN, AAFCS, ACA, AOsA, APTA, APA, ASLHA, FIDER, CORE, CSWE, JRCEPAT, NASAD, NASD, NASM, NAST, NCATE, NLN NRPA **Intercollegiate Athletics:** Baseball M; Basketball M & W; Cheerleading M & W; Cross-Country Running M & W; Field Hockey W; Football M; Golf M & W; Ice Hockey M; Soccer W; Softball W; Swimming and Diving W; Track and Field W; Volleyball W; Wrestling M

OHIO UNIVERSITY—CHILLICOTHE
101 University Dr.
Chillicothe, OH 45601
Tel: (740)774-7200
Fax: (740)774-7295
Web Site: http://www.chillicothe.ohiou.edu/
President/CEO: Dr. Richard Bebee
Admissions: TJ Eveland
Financial Aid: Sondra Williams
Type: Comprehensive **Sex:** Coed **Affiliation:** Ohio Board of Regents **Admission Plans:** Open Admission; Early Admission **Application Deadline:** September 1 **Application Fee:** $20.00 **H.S. Requirements:** High school diploma required; GED accepted **Scholarships:** Available **Calendar System:** Quarter, Summer Session Available **% Receiving Financial Aid:** 84 **Library Holdings:** 47,900 **Regional Accreditation:** North Central Association of Colleges and Schools **Credit Hours For Degree:** 96 credit hours, Associates; 192 credit hours, Bachelors **ROTC:** Army, Air Force **Professional Accreditation:** NLN

OHIO UNIVERSITY—EASTERN
45425 National Rd.
St. Clairsville, OH 43950-9724
Tel: (740)695-1720
E-mail: howardn@ohio.edu
Web Site: http://www.eastern.ohiou.edu/
President/CEO: Dr. Richard Greenlee
Admissions: N. Kip Howard
Financial Aid: Sondra Williams
Type: Comprehensive **Sex:** Coed **Affiliation:** Ohio Board of Regents **Admission Plans:** Open Admission; Early Admission; Deferred Admission **Application Deadline:** Rolling **Application Fee:** $20.00 **H.S. Requirements:** High school diploma required; GED accepted **Scholarships:** Available **Calendar System:** Quarter, Summer Session Available **% Receiving Financial Aid:** 78 **Library Holdings:** 50,000 **Regional Accreditation:** North Central Association of Colleges and Schools **Credit Hours For Degree:** 96 quarter hours, Associates; 192 quarter hours, Bachelors **Intercollegiate Athletics:** Basketball M & W; Volleyball W

OHIO UNIVERSITY—LANCASTER
1570 Granville Pike
Lancaster, OH 43130-1097
Tel: (740)654-6711; Free: 888-446-4468
Fax: (740)687-9497
E-mail: fox@ohio.edu
Web Site: http://www.ohiou.edu/lancaster/
President/CEO: Dr. John Furlow
Admissions: Pat Fox
Financial Aid: Sondra Williams
Type: Comprehensive **Sex:** Coed **Affiliation:** Ohio Board of Regents **Admission Plans:** Open Admission; Early Admission; Deferred Admission **Application Deadline:** Rolling **Application Fee:** $20.00 **H.S. Requirements:** High school diploma required; GED accepted **Scholarships:** Available **Calendar System:** Quarter, Summer Session Available **% Receiving Financial Aid:** 82 **Library Holdings:** 94,688 **Regional Accreditation:** North Central Association of Colleges and Schools **Credit Hours For Degree:** 96 quarter hours, Associates; 192 quarter hours, Bachelors **ROTC:** Army, Air Force **Professional Accreditation:** AAMAE

OHIO UNIVERSITY—SOUTHERN CAMPUS
1804 Liberty Ave.
Ironton, OH 45638-2214
Tel: (740)533-4600; Free: 800-626-0513
Fax: (740)533-4632
E-mail: harlow@ohio.edu
Web Site: http://www.ohiou.edu/
President/CEO: Dr. William Willan
Admissions: Linda Harlow
Financial Aid: Sondra Williams
Type: Comprehensive **Sex:** Coed **Affiliation:** Ohio Board of Regents **% Accepted:** 100 **Admission Plans:** Open Admission; Early Admission; Deferred Admission **Application Deadline:** Rolling **Application Fee:** $20.00 **H.S. Requirements:** High school diploma required; GED accepted **Scholarships:** Available **Calendar System:** Quarter, Summer Session Available **Enrollment:** FT 850, PT 849 **Exams:** ACT. **% Receiving Financial Aid:** 92 **Library Holdings:** 26,000 **Regional Accreditation:** North Central Association of Colleges and Schools **Credit Hours For Degree:** 96 quarter hours, Associates; 192 quarter hours, Bachelors

OHIO UNIVERSITY—ZANESVILLE
1425 Newark Rd.
Zanesville, OH 43701-2695
Tel: (740)453-0762
Admissions: (740)588-1440
Fax: (740)453-6161
E-mail: ouzservices@ohio.edu
Web Site: http://www.zanesville.ohiou.edu/

President/CEO: James Fonseca
Admissions: Karen Ragsdale
Financial Aid: Sondra Williams
Type: Comprehensive **Sex:** Coed **Affiliation:** Ohio Board of Regents **Scores:** 53% ACT 18-23; 21% ACT 24-29 **% Accepted:** 91 **Admission Plans:** Open Admission **Application Deadline:** Rolling **Application Fee:** $20.00 **H.S. Requirements:** High school diploma required; GED accepted **Costs Per Year:** Application fee: $20. State resident tuition: $4662 full-time, $137 per credit hour part-time. Nonresident tuition: $8985 full-time, $268 per credit hour part-time. Mandatory fees: $5 per term part-time. Full-time tuition varies according to student level. Part-time tuition and fees vary according to student level. **Scholarships:** Available **Calendar System:** Quarter, Summer Session Available **Enrollment:** FT 1,163, PT 822 **Faculty:** FT 31, PT 99 **Student-Faculty Ratio:** 23:1 **Exams:** SAT I or ACT. **% Receiving Financial Aid:** 83 **Library Holdings:** 64,227 **Regional Accreditation:** North Central Association of Colleges and Schools **Credit Hours For Degree:** 96 quarter hours, Associates; 192 quarter hours, Bachelors **Professional Accreditation:** NLN **Intercollegiate Athletics:** Baseball M; Basketball M & W; Golf M & W; Softball W; Tennis M & W; Ultimate Frisbee M & W; Volleyball M & W

OHIO VALLEY COLLEGE OF TECHNOLOGY

16808 St. Clair Ave., PO Box 7000
East Liverpool, OH 43920
Tel: (330)385-1070
Web Site: http://www.ovct.edu/
President/CEO: Scott S. Rogers
Admissions: Scott S. Rogers
Type: Two-Year College **Sex:** Coed **Application Deadline:** Rolling **Application Fee:** $0.00 **H.S. Requirements:** High school diploma required; GED accepted **Scholarships:** Available **Calendar System:** Semester, Summer Session Available **Enrollment:** FT 132, PT 15 **Faculty:** FT 4, PT 8 **Student-Faculty Ratio:** 18:1 **Exams:** Other. **Credit Hours For Degree:** 64 credits, Associates **Professional Accreditation:** ACICS, AAMAE

OHIO WESLEYAN UNIVERSITY

61 South Sandusky St.
Delaware, OH 43015
Tel: (740)368-2000; Free: 800-922-8953
Admissions: (740)368-3059
Fax: (740)368-3314
E-mail: cjdelpro@owu.edu
Web Site: http://www.owu.edu/
President/CEO: Dr. David O. Robbins
Admissions: Carol DelPropost
Financial Aid: John L. Harrell, Jr.
Type: Four-Year College **Sex:** Coed **Affiliation:** United Methodist **Scores:** 99.39% SAT V 400+; 98.18% SAT M 400+; 29.22% ACT 18-23; 45.18% ACT 24-29 **% Accepted:** 64 **Admission Plans:** Early Admission; Early Action; Early Decision Plan; Deferred Admission **Application Deadline:** March 1 **Application Fee:** $35.00 **H.S. Requirements:** High school diploma required; GED accepted **Costs Per Year:** Application fee: $35. Comprehensive fee: $44,254 includes full-time tuition ($34,570), mandatory fees ($460), and college room and board ($9224). College room only: $4490. Room and board charges vary according to board plan. Part-time tuition: $3770 per course. **Scholarships:** Available **Calendar System:** Semester, Summer Session Available **Enrollment:** FT 1,869, PT 24 **Faculty:** FT 138, PT 76 **Student-Faculty Ratio:** 11:1 **Exams:** SAT I or ACT. **% Receiving Financial Aid:** 58 **% Residing in College-Owned, -Operated, or -Affiliated Housing:** 81 **Regional Accreditation:** North Central Association of Colleges and Schools **Credit Hours For Degree:** 34 units, Bachelors **Professional Accreditation:** NASM **Intercollegiate Athletics:** Baseball M; Basketball M & W; Cross-Country Running M & W; Equestrian Sports M & W; Field Hockey W; Football M; Golf M; Ice Hockey M & W; Lacrosse M & W; Rugby M & W; Sailing M & W; Soccer M & W; Softball W; Swimming and Diving M & W; Tennis M & W; Track and Field M & W; Ultimate Frisbee M & W; Volleyball M & W

OTTERBEIN UNIVERSITY

1 South Grove St.
Westerville, OH 43081
Tel: (614)890-3000; Free: 800-488-8144
Admissions: (614)823-1500
Fax: (614)823-1200
E-mail: uotterb@otterbein.edu
Web Site: http://www.otterbein.edu/
President/CEO: Dr. C. Brent DeVore
Admissions: Dr. Cass Johnson
Financial Aid: Thomas V. Yarnell
Type: Comprehensive **Sex:** Coed **Affiliation:** United Methodist **Scores:** 90% SAT V 400+; 100% SAT M 400+; 49% ACT 18-23; 40% ACT 24-29 **% Accepted:** 82 **Admission Plans:** Deferred Admission **Application Deadline:** March 1 **Application Fee:** $25.00 **H.S. Requirements:** High school diploma required; GED accepted **Scholarships:** Available **Calendar System:** Quarter, Summer Session Available **Enrollment:** FT 2,326, PT 420 **Faculty:** FT 161, PT 119 **Student-Faculty Ratio:** 12:1 **Exams:** SAT I or ACT. **% Receiving Financial Aid:** 77 **% Residing in College-Owned, -Operated, or -Affiliated Housing:** 53 **Library Holdings:** 182,629 **Regional Accreditation:** North Central Association of Colleges and Schools **Credit Hours For Degree:** 180 credit hours, Bachelors **ROTC:** Army, Air Force **Professional Accreditation:** AACN, JRCEPAT, NASM, NAST, NCATE, NLN **Intercollegiate Athletics:** Baseball M; Basketball M & W; Cheerleading M & W; Cross-Country Running M & W; Equestrian Sports M & W; Football M; Golf M & W; Ice Hockey W; Lacrosse M; Soccer M & W; Softball W; Tennis M & W; Track and Field M & W; Volleyball W

OWENS COMMUNITY COLLEGE

PO Box 10000
Toledo, OH 43699-1947
Tel: (419)661-7000; Free: 800-GO-OWENS
Admissions: (567)661-7225
E-mail: jennifer_irelan@owens.edu
Web Site: http://www.owens.edu/
President/CEO: Dr. Larry McDougle
Admissions: Jennifer Irelan
Type: Two-Year College **Sex:** Coed **Scores:** 86% SAT V 400+; 70% SAT M 400+; 50% ACT 18-23; 9% ACT 24-29 **% Accepted:** 100 **Admission Plans:** Open Admission; Early Admission **Application Deadline:** Rolling **Application Fee:** $0.00 **H.S. Requirements:** High school diploma or equivalent not required **Costs Per Year:** Application fee: $0. State resident tuition: $2683 full-time, $127.50 per credit hour part-time. Nonresident tuition: $5366 full-time, $255 per credit hour part-time. Mandatory fees: $432 full-time. Full-time tuition and fees vary according to reciprocity agreements. Part-time tuition varies according to reciprocity agreements. **Scholarships:** Available **Calendar System:** Semester, Summer Session Available **Enrollment:** FT 9,100, PT 14,461 **Faculty:** FT 203, PT 1,481 **Student-Faculty Ratio:** 20:1 **Exams:** ACT essay used for advising. SAT essay used for advising. ACT essay used for placement. SAT essay used for placement. **Final Year or Final Semester Residency Requirement:** No **Library Holdings:** 55,708 **Regional Accreditation:** North Central Association of Colleges and Schools **Credit Hours For Degree:** 65 semester hours, Associates **ROTC:** Army, Air Force **Professional Accreditation:** ABET, ARCEST, ADA, AOTA, APTA, ACBSP, JRCEDMS, JRCERT, NLN **Intercollegiate Athletics:** Baseball M; Basketball M & W; Soccer M; Softball W; Volleyball W

PONTIFICAL COLLEGE JOSEPHINUM

7625 North High St.
Columbus, OH 43235
Tel: (614)885-5585; Free: 888-252-5812
Admissions: (614)985-2241
E-mail: acrawford@pcj.edu
Web Site: http://www.pcj.edu/
President/CEO: Msgr. Paul J. Langsfeld
Admissions: Arminda Crawford
Financial Aid: Marky Leichtnam
Type: Comprehensive **Sex:** Men **Affiliation:** Roman Catholic **Scores:** 50% SAT V 400+; 50% SAT M 400+; 50% ACT 18-23; 25% ACT 24-29 **% Accepted:** 75 **Admission Plans:** Preferred Admission **Application Deadline:** July 31 **Application Fee:** $25.00 **H.S. Requirements:** High school diploma required; GED accepted **Scholarships:** Available **Calendar System:** Semester, Summer Session Not available **Enrollment:** FT 78, Grad FT 41 **Faculty:** FT 13, PT 9 **Student-Faculty Ratio:** 7:1 **Exams:** SAT I or ACT. **% Receiving Financial Aid:** 52 **% Residing in College-Owned, -Operated, or -Affiliated Housing:** 100 **Final Year or Final Semester Residency Requirement:** Yes **Library Holdings:** 137,883 **Regional Accreditation:** North Central Association of Colleges and Schools **Credit Hours For Degree:** 132 credit hours, Bachelors **Professional Accreditation:** ATS

PROFESSIONAL SKILLS INSTITUTE

20 Arco Dr.
Toledo, OH 43607

Tel: (419)531-9610
Admissions: (419)720-6670
Fax: (419)531-4732
Web Site: http://www.proskills.com/
President/CEO: Daniel A. Finch
Admissions: Hope Finch
Type: Two-Year College **Sex:** Coed **Application Fee:** $25.00 **H.S. Requirements:** High school diploma required; GED accepted **Scholarships:** Available **Calendar System:** Quarter, Summer Session Not available **Exams:** Other. **Library Holdings:** 2,200 **Credit Hours For Degree:** 119 quarter hours, Associates **Professional Accreditation:** ABHES, APTA

RABBINICAL COLLEGE OF TELSHE
28400 Euclid Ave.
Wickliffe, OH 44092-2523
Tel: (216)943-5300
Admissions: (440)943-5300
President/CEO: Rabbi Zalman Gifter
Type: Comprehensive **Sex:** Men **Affiliation:** Jewish **Admission Plans:** Open Admission **Application Fee:** $100.00 **Student-Faculty Ratio:** 3:1 **Professional Accreditation:** AARTS

REMINGTON COLLEGE—CLEVELAND CAMPUS
14445 Broadway Ave.
Cleveland, OH 44125
Tel: (216)475-7520
Fax: (216)475-6055
Web Site: http://www.remingtoncollege.edu/
President/CEO: Charles Dull
Type: Two-Year College **Sex:** Coed **H.S. Requirements:** High school diploma required; GED accepted **Calendar System:** Continuous **Credit Hours For Degree:** 96 quarter credit hours, Associates **Professional Accreditation:** ACCSCT

REMINGTON COLLEGE—CLEVELAND WEST CAMPUS
26350 Brookpark Rd.
North Olmsted, OH 44070
Tel: (440)777-2560
Fax: (440)777-3238
E-mail: james.malley@remingtoncollege.edu
Web Site: http://www.remingtoncollege.edu/
President/CEO: Gary Azotea
Admissions: James Malley, Jr.
Type: Two-Year College **Sex:** Coed **Calendar System:** Quarter

ROSEDALE BIBLE COLLEGE
2270 Rosedale Rd.
Irwin, OH 43029-9501
Tel: (740)857-1311
Fax: 877-857-1312
E-mail: pweber@rosedale.edu
Web Site: http://www.rosedalebible.org/
President/CEO: Christopher Jones
Admissions: John Showalter
Type: Two-Year College **Sex:** Coed **Affiliation:** Mennonite **% Accepted:** 94 **Application Fee:** $50.00 **Calendar System:** Miscellaneous **Exams:** SAT I or ACT. **Professional Accreditation:** ABHE

SCHOOL OF ADVERTISING ART
1725 East David Rd.
Kettering, OH 45440
Tel: (937)294-0592; Free: 877-300-9866
Fax: (937)294-5869
E-mail: nathan@saacollege.com
Web Site: http://www.saacollege.com/
President/CEO: Jessica Graves
Admissions: Nathan Summers
Type: Two-Year College **Sex:** Coed **Application Fee:** $0.00 **H.S. Requirements:** High school diploma required; GED accepted **Costs Per Year:** Application fee: $0. One-time mandatory fee: $100. Tuition: $21,350 full-time. Mandatory fees: $2638 full-time. **Calendar System:** Trimester **Enrollment:** FT 150 **Faculty:** FT 10, PT 7 **Student-Faculty Ratio:** 12:1 **Professional Accreditation:** ACCSCT

SHAWNEE STATE UNIVERSITY
940 Second St.
Portsmouth, OH 45662-4344
Tel: (740)354-3205; Free: 800-959-2SSU
Admissions: (740)351-3610
Fax: (740)355-2470
E-mail: admsn@shawnee.edu
Web Site: http://www.shawnee.edu/
President/CEO: Dr. Rita Rice Morris
Admissions: Bob Trusz
Financial Aid: Barbara Bradbury
Type: Comprehensive **Sex:** Coed **Affiliation:** University System of Ohio **Scores:** 42% ACT 18-23; 18% ACT 24-29 **% Accepted:** 84 **Admission Plans:** Open Admission; Deferred Admission **Application Deadline:** Rolling **Application Fee:** $0.00 **H.S. Requirements:** High school diploma required; GED accepted **Costs Per Year:** Application fee: $0. State resident tuition: $5184 full-time, $216 per credit hour part-time. Nonresident tuition: $9528 full-time, $397 per credit hour part-time. Mandatory fees: $948 full-time, $39.50 per credit hour part-time. Full-time tuition and fees vary according to course load, reciprocity agreements, and student level. Part-time tuition and fees vary according to course load, reciprocity agreements, and student level. College room and board: $7944. College room only: $4984. Room and board charges vary according to board plan and housing facility. **Scholarships:** Available **Calendar System:** Semester, Summer Session Available **Enrollment:** FT 3,533, PT 687, Grad FT 40, Grad PT 40 **Faculty:** FT 151, PT 171 **Student-Faculty Ratio:** 18:1 **Exams:** ACT. ACT essay not being used. SAT essay not being used. **% Receiving Financial Aid:** 67 **% Residing in College-Owned, -Operated, or -Affiliated Housing:** 21 **Final Year or Final Semester Residency Requirement:** No **Library Holdings:** 144,595 **Regional Accreditation:** North Central Association of Colleges and Schools **Credit Hours For Degree:** 60 semester hours, Associates; 124 semester hours, Bachelors **Professional Accreditation:** ADA, AOTA, APTA, ACBSP, CARC, JRCERT, NAACLS, NCATE, NLN **Intercollegiate Athletics:** Baseball M; Basketball M & W; Cross-Country Running M & W; Golf M; Soccer M & W; Softball W; Tennis W; Volleyball W

SINCLAIR COMMUNITY COLLEGE
444 West Third St.
Dayton, OH 45402-1460
Tel: (937)512-2500
Admissions: (937)512-3000
E-mail: ssmith@sinclair.edu
Web Site: http://www.sinclair.edu/
President/CEO: Dr. Steven Lee Johnson
Admissions: Sara Smith
Type: Two-Year College **Sex:** Coed **Affiliation:** Ohio Board of Regents **% Accepted:** 100 **Admission Plans:** Open Admission; Early Admission; Deferred Admission **Application Deadline:** Rolling **Application Fee:** $10.00 **H.S. Requirements:** High school diploma or equivalent not required. For allied health programs: High school diploma required; GED accepted **Scholarships:** Available **Calendar System:** Quarter, Summer Session Available **Enrollment:** FT 7,550, PT 12,013 **Faculty:** FT 466, PT 651 **Student-Faculty Ratio:** 19:1 **Library Holdings:** 147,613 **Regional Accreditation:** North Central Association of Colleges and Schools **Credit Hours For Degree:** 90 quarter hours, Associates **ROTC:** Army, Air Force **Professional Accreditation:** ABET, ARCEST, AAMAE, ACF, ADA, AHIMA, AOTA, APTA, ACBSP, CARC, JRCERT, NASAD, NASM, NLN, NAIT **Intercollegiate Athletics:** Baseball M; Basketball M & W; Golf M; Tennis M & W; Volleyball W

SOUTHERN STATE COMMUNITY COLLEGE
100 Hobart Dr.
Hillsboro, OH 45133-9487
Tel: (937)393-3431
Fax: (937)393-9370
E-mail: wjohnson@sscc.edu
Web Site: http://www.sscc.edu/
President/CEO: Dr. Kevin Boys
Admissions: Wendy Johnson
Financial Aid: Janeen S. Deatley
Type: Two-Year College **Sex:** Coed **% Accepted:** 100 **Admission Plans:** Open Admission; Early Admission; Deferred Admission **Application Deadline:** Rolling **Application Fee:** $0.00 **H.S. Requirements:** High school diploma required; GED accepted. For applicants who will attend part-time:

High school diploma required; GED not accepted **Costs Per Year:** Application fee: $0. State resident tuition: $3390 full-time, $87 per quarter hour part-time. Nonresident tuition: $6528 full-time, $168 per quarter hour part-time. Full-time tuition varies according to course load. Part-time tuition varies according to course load. **Scholarships:** Available **Calendar System:** Quarter, Summer Session Available **Enrollment:** FT 2,084, PT 1,279 **Faculty:** FT 58, PT 120 **Student-Faculty Ratio:** 26:1 **Library Holdings:** 50,550 **Regional Accreditation:** North Central Association of Colleges and Schools **Credit Hours For Degree:** 90 quarter hours, Associates **Professional Accreditation:** AAMAE, NLN **Intercollegiate Athletics:** Baseball M; Basketball M & W; Soccer M; Softball W; Volleyball W

SOUTHWESTERN COLLEGE OF BUSINESS (CINCINNATI)
632 Vine St.
Ste. 200
Cincinnati, OH 45202-4304
Tel: (513)421-3212
Web Site: http://www.swcollege.net/
Type: Two-Year College **Sex:** Coed **Admission Plans:** Open Admission **Application Deadline:** Rolling **Application Fee:** $100.00 **H.S. Requirements:** High school diploma required; GED accepted **Calendar System:** Quarter, Summer Session Available **Exams:** Other. **Credit Hours For Degree:** 99 credit hours, Associates **Professional Accreditation:** ACICS

SOUTHWESTERN COLLEGE OF BUSINESS (CINCINNATI)
149 Northland Blvd.
Cincinnati, OH 45246-1122
Tel: (513)874-0432
Web Site: http://www.swcollege.net/
President/CEO: David Caldwell
Type: Two-Year College **Sex:** Coed **Admission Plans:** Open Admission **Application Deadline:** Rolling **Application Fee:** $100.00 **H.S. Requirements:** High school diploma required; GED accepted **Calendar System:** Quarter, Summer Session Available **Exams:** Other. **Credit Hours For Degree:** 96 credits, Associates **Professional Accreditation:** ACICS

SOUTHWESTERN COLLEGE OF BUSINESS (DAYTON)
111 West First St.
Dayton, OH 45402-3003
Tel: (937)224-0061
Fax: (937)224-0065
Web Site: http://www.swcollege.net/
President/CEO: James A. Smolinski
Admissions: William Furlong
Type: Two-Year College **Sex:** Coed **Admission Plans:** Open Admission **Application Deadline:** Rolling **Application Fee:** $0.00 **H.S. Requirements:** High school diploma required; GED accepted **Calendar System:** Quarter, Summer Session Available **Student-Faculty Ratio:** 28:1 **Credit Hours For Degree:** 96 credits, Associates **Professional Accreditation:** ACICS

SOUTHWESTERN COLLEGE OF BUSINESS (FRANKLIN)
201 East Second St.
Franklin, OH 45005
Tel: (937)746-6633
Web Site: http://www.swcollege.net/
President/CEO: Ronald L. Mills, Jr.
Type: Two-Year College **Sex:** Coed **Admission Plans:** Open Admission **Application Deadline:** Rolling **H.S. Requirements:** High school diploma required; GED accepted **Calendar System:** Quarter **Credit Hours For Degree:** 99 credit hours, Associates **Professional Accreditation:** ACICS

STARK STATE COLLEGE OF TECHNOLOGY
6200 Frank Ave., NW
North Canton, OH 44720-7299
Tel: (330)494-6170; Free: 800-797-8275
Admissions: (330)966-5450
Fax: (330)497-6313
E-mail: info@starkstate.edu
Web Site: http://www.starkstate.edu/
President/CEO: Dr. John O'Donnell
Admissions: Wallace Hoffer
Type: Two-Year College **Sex:** Coed **Affiliation:** Ohio Board of Regents **Scores:** 50% ACT 18-23; 13% ACT 24-29 **Admission Plans:** Open Admission; Early Admission; Deferred Admission **Application Deadline:** Rolling **Application Fee:** $65.00 **H.S. Requirements:** High school diploma required; GED accepted **Costs Per Year:** Application fee: $65. State resident tuition: $3810 full-time, $127 per credit hour part-time. Nonresident tuition: $5610 full-time, $187 per credit hour part-time. **Scholarships:** Available **Calendar System:** Semester, Summer Session Available **Faculty:** FT 154, PT 565 **Student-Faculty Ratio:** 17:1 **Exams:** SAT I or ACT. **Library Holdings:** 81,962 **Regional Accreditation:** North Central Association of Colleges and Schools **Credit Hours For Degree:** 70 semester hours, Associates **Professional Accreditation:** ABET, AAMAE, ADA, AHIMA, AOTA, APTA, CARC, NAACLS, NLN

STAUTZENBERGER COLLEGE
1796 Indian Wood Circle
Maumee, OH 43537
Tel: (419)866-0261; Free: 800-552-5099
Fax: (419)867-9821
E-mail: klfitzgerald@stautzenberger.com
Web Site: http://www.stautzen.com/
President/CEO: George Simon
Admissions: Karen Fitzgerald
Financial Aid: Angela Lewis
Type: Two-Year College **Sex:** Coed **Admission Plans:** Open Admission **Application Fee:** $25.00 **Scholarships:** Available **Calendar System:** Quarter **Student-Faculty Ratio:** 26:1 **Professional Accreditation:** ACICS, AAMAE

STRAYER UNIVERSITY - AKRON CAMPUS
51 Park West Blvd.
Akron, OH 44320
Tel: (330)734-6700
Fax: (330)835-9060
Web Site: http://strayer.edu/akron
Type: Comprehensive **Sex:** Coed **Application Fee:** $50.00 **Costs Per Year:** Application fee: $50. **Regional Accreditation:** Middle State Association of Colleges and Schools

STRAYER UNIVERSITY - COLUMBUS CAMPUS
8425 Pulsar Place
Ste. 400
Columbus, OH 43240
Tel: (614)310-6700
Fax: (614)430-9716
Web Site: http://www.strayer.edu/columbus/
Type: Comprehensive **Sex:** Coed **Application Fee:** $50.00 **Costs Per Year:** Application fee: $50. **Regional Accreditation:** Middle State Association of Colleges and Schools

STRAYER UNIVERSITY - FAIRVIEW PARK CAMPUS
22730 Fairview Center Dr.
Ste. 150
Fairview Park, OH 44126-3616
Tel: (440)471-6400
Fax: (440)716-8050
Web Site: http://strayer.edu/fairview_park
Type: Comprehensive **Sex:** Coed **Application Fee:** $50.00 **Costs Per Year:** Application fee: $50. **Regional Accreditation:** Middle State Association of Colleges and Schools

STRAYER UNIVERSITY - MASON CAMPUS
4605 Duke Dr.
Ste. 700
Mason, OH 45040
Tel: (513)234-6450
Fax: (513)204-6920
Web Site: http://www.strayer.edu/mason/
Type: Comprehensive **Sex:** Coed **Application Fee:** $50.00 **Costs Per Year:** Application fee: $50. **Regional Accreditation:** Middle State Association of Colleges and Schools

TEMPLE BAPTIST COLLEGE
11965 Kenn Rd.
Cincinnati, OH 45240
Tel: (513)851-3800
Fax: (513)851-3800
Web Site: http://www.templebaptistcollege.com/

President/CEO: Dr. Joseph Paturi
Type: Four-Year College **Sex:** Coed **Affiliation:** Baptist **Application Fee:** $50.00 **Calendar System:** Quarter **Professional Accreditation:** TACCS **Intercollegiate Athletics:** Basketball M & W

TERRA STATE COMMUNITY COLLEGE
2830 Napoleon Rd.
Fremont, OH 43420-9670
Tel: (419)334-8400
Admissions: (419)559-2350
Fax: (419)334-9035
E-mail: hmartin01@terra.edu
Web Site: http://www.terra.edu/
President/CEO: Dr. Marsha Bordner
Admissions: Heath Martin
Type: Two-Year College **Sex:** Coed **Affiliation:** Ohio Board of Regents **Admission Plans:** Open Admission; Early Admission; Deferred Admission **Application Deadline:** Rolling **Application Fee:** $0.00 **H.S. Requirements:** High school diploma required; GED accepted. For post secondary options, tech prep students: High school diploma or equivalent not required **Costs Per Year:** Application fee: $0. State resident tuition: $2769 full-time, $115.37 per semester hour part-time. Nonresident tuition: $4523 full-time, $188.46 per semester hour part-time. Mandatory fees: $307 full-time, $12.80 per semester hour part-time. Full-time tuition and fees vary according to course load. Part-time tuition and fees vary according to course load. **Scholarships:** Available **Calendar System:** Semester, Summer Session Available **Enrollment:** FT 1,459, PT 1,693 **Faculty:** FT 40, PT 164 **Student-Faculty Ratio:** 21:1 **Final Year or Final Semester Residency Requirement:** No **Library Holdings:** 22,675 **Regional Accreditation:** North Central Association of Colleges and Schools **Credit Hours For Degree:** 60 semester hours, Associates

TIFFIN UNIVERSITY
155 Miami St.
Tiffin, OH 44883-2161
Tel: (419)447-6442; Free: 800-968-6446
Admissions: (419)448-3301
Fax: (419)447-9605
E-mail: marinisjj@tiffin.edu
Web Site: http://www.tiffin.edu/
President/CEO: Dr. Paul Marion
Admissions: Jeremy Marinis
Financial Aid: Cindy Little
Type: Comprehensive **Sex:** Coed **Scores:** 90.5% SAT V 400+; 86.5% SAT M 400+; 61.4% ACT 18-23; 21.4% ACT 24-29 **% Accepted:** 60 **Application Deadline:** Rolling **Application Fee:** $20.00 **H.S. Requirements:** High school diploma required; GED accepted **Costs Per Year:** Application fee: $20. Comprehensive fee: $26,730 includes full-time tuition ($18,390) and college room and board ($8340). College room only: $4310. Full-time tuition varies according to course load. Room and board charges vary according to board plan and housing facility. Part-time tuition: $613 per credit hour. **Scholarships:** Available **Calendar System:** Semester, Summer Session Available **Enrollment:** FT 1,853, PT 522, Grad FT 351, Grad PT 703 **Faculty:** FT 66, PT 226 **Student-Faculty Ratio:** 19:1 **Exams:** SAT I or ACT. **% Receiving Financial Aid:** 90 **% Residing in College-Owned, -Operated, or -Affiliated Housing:** 38 **Final Year or Final Semester Residency Requirement:** No **Library Holdings:** 40,003 **Regional Accreditation:** North Central Association of Colleges and Schools **Credit Hours For Degree:** 60 semester hours, Associates; 121 semester hours, Bachelors **ROTC:** Army, Air Force **Professional Accreditation:** ACBSP **Intercollegiate Athletics:** Baseball M; Basketball M & W; Cheerleading M & W; Cross-Country Running M & W; Equestrian Sports M & W; Football M; Golf M & W; Lacrosse W; Soccer M & W; Softball W; Tennis M & W; Track and Field M & W; Volleyball W

TRI-STATE BIBLE COLLEGE
506 Margaret St.
PO Box 445
South Point, OH 45680-8402
Tel: (740)377-2520
Fax: (740)377-0001
E-mail: recruitment@tsbc.edu
Web Site: http://www.tsbc.edu/
President/CEO: Jack Finch
Type: Four-Year College **Sex:** Coed **Affiliation:** nondenominational **Admission Plans:** Open Admission **Application Fee:** $25.00 **Calendar System:** Semester **Professional Accreditation:** ABHE

TRUMBULL BUSINESS COLLEGE
3200 Ridge Rd.
Warren, OH 44484
Tel: (330)369-3200
Fax: (330)369-6792
E-mail: admissions@tbc-trumbullbusiness.com
Web Site: http://www.tbc-trumbullbusiness.com/
President/CEO: Dennis R. Griffith
Type: Two-Year College **Sex:** Coed **% Accepted:** 100 **Application Deadline:** Rolling **Application Fee:** $75.00 **Scholarships:** Available **Calendar System:** Quarter **Enrollment:** FT 292, PT 29 **Faculty:** FT 9, PT 4 **Student-Faculty Ratio:** 28:1 **Professional Accreditation:** ACICS

UNION INSTITUTE & UNIVERSITY
440 East McMillan St.
Cincinnati, OH 45206-1925
Tel: (513)861-6400; Free: 800-486-3116
Admissions: (513)487-1173
Fax: (513)861-0779
Web Site: http://www.tui.edu/
President/CEO: Dr. Roger H. Sublett, PhD
Admissions: Dr. Gregory Stewart
Financial Aid: Rebecca Zackerman
Type: University **Sex:** Coed **Admission Plans:** Deferred Admission **Application Deadline:** Rolling **Application Fee:** $35.00 **H.S. Requirements:** High school diploma required; GED accepted **Scholarships:** Available **Calendar System:** Trimester, Summer Session Available **Enrollment:** FT 653, PT 310, Grad FT 329, Grad PT 231 **Faculty:** FT 35, PT 280 **% Receiving Financial Aid:** 76 **Final Year or Final Semester Residency Requirement:** No **Library Holdings:** 86,751 **Regional Accreditation:** North Central Association of Colleges and Schools **Credit Hours For Degree:** 120 credits, Bachelors

THE UNIVERSITY OF AKRON
302 Buchtel Common
Akron, OH 44325
Tel: (330)972-7111; Free: 800-655-4884
Admissions: (330)972-7100
Fax: (330)972-7676
E-mail: admissions@uakron.edu
Web Site: http://www.uakron.edu/
President/CEO: Dr. Luis M. Proenza
Admissions: Diane Raybuck
Financial Aid: Michelle Ellis
Type: University **Sex:** Coed **Scores:** 86.4% SAT V 400+; 83.5% SAT M 400+; 48.1% ACT 18-23; 24.3% ACT 24-29 **% Accepted:** 76 **Admission Plans:** Open Admission; Early Action; Deferred Admission **Application Deadline:** August 11 **Application Fee:** $30.00 **H.S. Requirements:** High school diploma required; GED accepted **Costs Per Year:** Application fee: $30. State resident tuition: $7345 full-time, $306 per credit hour part-time. Nonresident tuition: $16,593 full-time, $614 per credit hour part-time. Mandatory fees: $1407 full-time, $49 per credit hour part-time. Full-time tuition and fees vary according to course load, degree level, and location. Part-time tuition and fees vary according to course load, degree level, and location. College room and board: $8697. College room only: $5499. Room and board charges vary according to board plan and housing facility. **Scholarships:** Available **Calendar System:** Semester, Summer Session Available **Enrollment:** FT 16,632, PT 4,695, Grad FT 2,293, Grad PT 2,339 **Faculty:** FT 768, PT 924 **Student-Faculty Ratio:** 21:1 **Exams:** SAT I or ACT. **% Receiving Financial Aid:** 70 **% Residing in College-Owned, -Operated, or -Affiliated Housing:** 16 **Library Holdings:** 1,273,967 **Regional Accreditation:** North Central Association of Colleges and Schools **Credit Hours For Degree:** 64 credits, Associates; 128 credits, Bachelors **ROTC:** Army, Air Force **Professional Accreditation:** AACSB, ABET, ARCEST, AAMFT, AACN, AAFCS, AAMAE, AANA, ABA, ACA, ADtA, APA, ASC, ASLHA, AALS, CARC, FIDER, CEPH, CSWE, NASAD NASD, NASM, NASPAA, NCATE, NLN **Intercollegiate Athletics:** Baseball M; Basketball M & W; Cheerleading M & W; Cross-Country Running M & W; Football M; Golf M & W; Riflery M & W; Soccer M & W; Softball W; Swimming and Diving W; Tennis W; Track and Field M & W; Volleyball W

THE UNIVERSITY OF AKRON—WAYNE COLLEGE
1901 Smucker Rd.
Orrville, OH 44667-9192
Tel: (330)683-2010
Admissions: 800-221-8308
Fax: (330)684-8989
E-mail: wayneadmissions@uakron.edu
Web Site: http://www.wayne.uakron.edu/
President/CEO: Dr. John P. Kristofco
Admissions: Alicia Broadus
Type: Two-Year College **Sex:** Coed **Affiliation:** The University of Akron **Scores:** 54.7% ACT 18-23; 17% ACT 24-29 **% Accepted:** 90 **Admission Plans:** Open Admission; Early Admission; Deferred Admission **Application Deadline:** August 30 **Application Fee:** $30.00 **H.S. Requirements:** High school diploma required; GED accepted **Costs Per Year:** Application fee: $30. State resident tuition: $5177 full-time, $215.69 per credit hour part-time. Nonresident tuition: $12,700 full-time, $466.48 per credit hour part-time. Mandatory fees: $154 full-time, $6.43 per credit hour part-time, $12. Full-time tuition and fees vary according to course load and location. Part-time tuition and fees vary according to course load and location. **Scholarships:** Available **Calendar System:** Semester, Summer Session Available **Enrollment:** FT 1,040, PT 815 **Faculty:** FT 26, PT 113 **Student-Faculty Ratio:** 21:1 **Exams:** Other, SAT I or ACT. **Library Holdings:** 23,450 **Regional Accreditation:** North Central Association of Colleges and Schools **Credit Hours For Degree:** 64 credits, Associates **ROTC:** Army, Air Force **Professional Accreditation:** ACBSP **Intercollegiate Athletics:** Basketball M & W; Cheerleading W; Golf M; Volleyball W

UNIVERSITY OF CINCINNATI
PO Box 210063
Cincinnati, OH 45221
Tel: (513)556-6000
Admissions: (513)556-1100
E-mail: admissions@uc.edu
Web Site: http://www.uc.edu/
President/CEO: Dr. Gregory H. Williams
Admissions: Thomas Canepa
Financial Aid: Dana Pawlowicz
Type: University **Sex:** Coed **Affiliation:** University System of Ohio **Scores:** 98.44% SAT V 400+; 99.22% SAT M 400+; 40.18% ACT 18-23; 48.53% ACT 24-29 **% Accepted:** 67 **Admission Plans:** Deferred Admission **Application Deadline:** September 1 **Application Fee:** $40.00 **H.S. Requirements:** High school diploma required; GED accepted **Costs Per Year:** Application fee: $40. State resident tuition: $7896 full-time, $262 per credit hour part-time. Nonresident tuition: $23,922 full-time, $665 per credit hour part-time. Mandatory fees: $1503 full-time, $42 per credit hour part-time. Full-time tuition and fees vary according to course load, degree level, location, program, and reciprocity agreements. Part-time tuition and fees vary according to course load, degree level, location, program, and reciprocity agreements. College room and board: $9702. College room only: $5799. Room and board charges vary according to board plan and housing facility. **Scholarships:** Available **Calendar System:** Quarter, Summer Session Available **Enrollment:** FT 18,247, PT 3,637, Grad FT 5,561, Grad PT 3,689 **Faculty:** FT 1,187, PT 38 **Student-Faculty Ratio:** 16:1 **Exams:** SAT I or ACT. **% Receiving Financial Aid:** 57 **% Residing in College-Owned, -Operated, or -Affiliated Housing:** 20 **Final Year or Final Semester Residency Requirement:** No **Library Holdings:** 3,715,957 **Regional Accreditation:** North Central Association of Colleges and Schools **Credit Hours For Degree:** 90 credit hours, Associates; 185 credit hours, Bachelors **ROTC:** Army, Air Force **Professional Accreditation:** AACSB, ABET, ACPhE, AABB, AACN, AANA, ABA, ACNM, ACCE, ACA, ADtA, ACSP, APTA, APA, ASLHA, AALS, FIDER, CSWE, JRCEPAT, JRCNMT LCMEAMA, NAACLS, NAAB, NASAD, NASD, NASM, NAST, NCATE **Intercollegiate Athletics:** Baseball M; Basketball M & W; Cheerleading M & W; Cross-Country Running M & W; Football M; Golf M & W; Lacrosse W; Soccer M & W; Swimming and Diving M & W; Tennis W; Track and Field M & W; Volleyball W

UNIVERSITY OF CINCINNATI CLERMONT COLLEGE
4200 Clermont College Dr.
Batavia, OH 45103-1785
Tel: (513)732-5200
Admissions: (513)732-5294
E-mail: jamie.adkins@uc.edu
Web Site: http://www.ucclermont.edu/
President/CEO: Robert M. McLaughlin
Admissions: Jamie Adkins
Type: Two-Year College **Sex:** Coed **Affiliation:** University of Cincinnati System **% Accepted:** 79 **Admission Plans:** Open Admission; Deferred Admission **Application Deadline:** Rolling **Application Fee:** $50.00 **H.S. Requirements:** High school diploma required; GED accepted **Costs Per Year:** Application fee: $50. State resident tuition: $3861 full-time, $107 per credit hour part-time. Nonresident tuition: $10,713 full-time, $297 per credit hour part-time. Mandatory fees: $681 full-time, $20 per credit hour part-time. Full-time tuition and fees vary according to course load, program, and reciprocity agreements. Part-time tuition and fees vary according to course load, program, and reciprocity agreements. **Scholarships:** Available **Calendar System:** Quarter, Summer Session Available **Enrollment:** FT 2,391, PT 1,322 **Faculty:** FT 77, PT 259 **Student-Faculty Ratio:** 20:1 **Final Year or Final Semester Residency Requirement:** No **Regional Accreditation:** North Central Association of Colleges and Schools **Credit Hours For Degree:** 93 quarter hours, Associates **ROTC:** Air Force **Intercollegiate Athletics:** Baseball M; Basketball M & W; Golf M; Softball W; Volleyball W

UNIVERSITY OF CINCINNATI RAYMOND WALTERS COLLEGE
9555 Plainfield Rd.
Cincinnati, OH 45236-1007
Tel: (513)745-5600
Fax: (513)745-5780
Web Site: http://www.rwc.uc.edu/
President/CEO: Dolores Straker
Admissions: Leigh Schlegal
Type: Two-Year College **Sex:** Coed **Affiliation:** University of Cincinnati System **Admission Plans:** Open Admission; Deferred Admission **Application Deadline:** Rolling **Application Fee:** $40.00 **H.S. Requirements:** High school diploma required; GED accepted **Costs Per Year:** Application fee: $40. State resident tuition: $5232 full-time, $146 per credit hour part-time. Nonresident tuition: $13,566 full-time, $377 per credit hour part-time. **Scholarships:** Available **Calendar System:** Quarter, Summer Session Available **Student-Faculty Ratio:** 14:1 **Regional Accreditation:** North Central Association of Colleges and Schools **Credit Hours For Degree:** 90 credit hours, Associates **ROTC:** Army, Air Force **Professional Accreditation:** ADA, JRCERT, NLN

UNIVERSITY OF DAYTON
300 College Park
Dayton, OH 45469-1300
Tel: (937)229-1000; Free: 800-837-7433
Admissions: (937)229-4411
Fax: (937)229-4545
E-mail: admission@udayton.edu
Web Site: http://www.udayton.edu/
President/CEO: Dr. Daniel J. Curran
Admissions: Robert Durkle
Financial Aid: Kathy Harmon
Type: University **Sex:** Coed **Affiliation:** Roman Catholic **Scores:** 99.25% SAT V 400+; 99.04% SAT M 400+; 24.73% ACT 18-23; 56.79% ACT 24-29 **% Accepted:** 73 **Admission Plans:** Deferred Admission **Application Deadline:** Rolling **Application Fee:** $50.00 **H.S. Requirements:** High school diploma required; GED accepted **Costs Per Year:** Application fee: $50. Comprehensive fee: $39,330 includes full-time tuition ($28,700), mandatory fees ($1230), and college room and board ($9400). College room only: $5940. Full-time tuition and fees vary according to degree level and program. Room and board charges vary according to board plan, housing facility, and student level. Part-time tuition: $917 per credit hour. Part-time tuition varies according to course load, degree level, and program. **Scholarships:** Available **Calendar System:** Semester, Summer Session Available **Enrollment:** FT 6,900, PT 506, Grad FT 1,999, Grad PT 1,503 **Faculty:** FT 475, PT 462 **Student-Faculty Ratio:** 15:1 **Exams:** SAT I or ACT. ACT essay not being used. SAT essay not being used. **% Receiving Financial Aid:** 54 **% Residing in College-Owned, -Operated, or -Affiliated Housing:** 75 **Library Holdings:** 929,704 **Regional Accreditation:** North Central Association of Colleges and Schools **Credit Hours For Degree:** 120 semester hours, Bachelors **ROTC:** Army, Air Force **Professional Accreditation:** AACSB, ABET, ABA, AALS, NASM, NASPAA, NCATE **Intercollegiate Athletics:** Baseball M; Basketball M & W; Cheerleading M & W; Crew W;

Cross-Country Running M & W; Football M; Golf M & W; Soccer M & W; Softball W; Tennis M & W; Track and Field W; Volleyball W

THE UNIVERSITY OF FINDLAY

1000 North Main St.
Findlay, OH 45840-3653
Tel: (419)422-8313; Free: 800-548-0932
Admissions: (419)434-4540
Fax: (419)424-4822
E-mail: admissions@findlay.edu
Web Site: http://www.findlay.edu/
President/CEO: Dr. DeBow Freed, PhD
Admissions: Donna Gruber
Financial Aid: Arman Habegger

Type: Comprehensive **Sex:** Coed **Affiliation:** Church of God **Scores:** 94.8% SAT V 400+; 95.9% SAT M 400+ **% Accepted:** 68 **Admission Plans:** Deferred Admission **Application Deadline:** Rolling **Application Fee:** $0.00 **H.S. Requirements:** High school diploma required; GED accepted **Costs Per Year:** Application fee: $0. Comprehensive fee: $34,328 includes full-time tuition ($25,016), mandatory fees ($758), and college room and board ($8554). College room only: $4268. Full-time tuition and fees vary according to course load and program. Part-time tuition: $552 per semester hour. Part-time mandatory fees: $722 per term. Part-time tuition and fees vary according to course load and program. **Scholarships:** Available **Calendar System:** Semester, Summer Session Available **Enrollment:** FT 2,632, PT 379, Grad FT 475, Grad PT 792 **Faculty:** FT 195, PT 125 **Student-Faculty Ratio:** 17:1 **Exams:** SAT I or ACT. **% Receiving Financial Aid:** 71 **% Residing in College-Owned, -Operated, or -Affiliated Housing:** 40 **Final Year or Final Semester Residency Requirement:** Yes **Library Holdings:** 145,948 **Regional Accreditation:** North Central Association of Colleges and Schools **Credit Hours For Degree:** 62 semester hours, Associates; 124 semester hours, Bachelors **ROTC:** Army, Air Force **Professional Accreditation:** ACPhE, AOTA, APTA, CSWE, JRCNMT, NCATE, TEAC **Intercollegiate Athletics:** Baseball M; Basketball M & W; Cheerleading M & W; Cross-Country Running M & W; Equestrian Sports W; Football M; Golf M & W; Soccer M & W; Softball W; Swimming and Diving M & W; Tennis M & W; Track and Field M & W; Volleyball W; Water Polo M & W; Wrestling M

UNIVERSITY OF MOUNT UNION

1972 Clark Ave.
Alliance, OH 44601-3993
Tel: (330)821-5320; Free: 800-992-6682
Admissions: (330)823-2590
Fax: (330)821-0425
E-mail: admission@muc.edu
Web Site: http://www.mountunion.edu/
President/CEO: Dr. Richard F. Giese
Admissions: Vincent Heslop
Financial Aid: Emily Swain

Type: Comprehensive **Sex:** Coed **Affiliation:** United Methodist **Scores:** 89% SAT V 400+; 89% SAT M 400+; 57% ACT 18-23; 31% ACT 24-29 **% Accepted:** 75 **Admission Plans:** Early Admission; Deferred Admission **Application Deadline:** Rolling **Application Fee:** $0.00 **H.S. Requirements:** High school diploma required; GED accepted **Costs Per Year:** Application fee: $0. Comprehensive fee: $31,300 includes full-time tuition ($23,630), mandatory fees ($250), and college room and board ($7420). Room and board charges vary according to board plan and housing facility. Part-time tuition: $995 per credit hour. **Scholarships:** Available **Calendar System:** Semester, Summer Session Available **Enrollment:** FT 2,148, PT 45, Grad FT 19 **Faculty:** FT 121, PT 104 **Student-Faculty Ratio:** 14:1 **Exams:** SAT I or ACT. **% Receiving Financial Aid:** 81 **% Residing in College-Owned, -Operated, or -Affiliated Housing:** 74 **Library Holdings:** 295,690 **Regional Accreditation:** North Central Association of Colleges and Schools **Credit Hours For Degree:** 120 credits, Bachelors **ROTC:** Army, Air Force **Professional Accreditation:** JRCEPAT, NASM **Intercollegiate Athletics:** Baseball M; Basketball M & W; Cheerleading W; Cross-Country Running M & W; Football M; Golf M & W; Soccer M & W; Softball W; Swimming and Diving M & W; Tennis M & W; Track and Field M & W; Volleyball W; Wrestling M

UNIVERSITY OF NORTHWESTERN OHIO

1441 North Cable Rd.
Lima, OH 45805-1498
Tel: (419)227-3141
Admissions: (419)998-3140
Fax: (419)229-6926
E-mail: klopp_d@unoh.edu
Web Site: http://www.unoh.edu/
President/CEO: Jeffrey Jarvis
Admissions: Dan Klopp

Type: Two-Year College **Sex:** Coed **% Accepted:** 98 **Admission Plans:** Open Admission; Early Admission; Deferred Admission **Application Deadline:** Rolling **Application Fee:** $50.00 **H.S. Requirements:** High school diploma required; GED accepted **Scholarships:** Available **Calendar System:** Quarter, Summer Session Available **Enrollment:** FT 3,223, PT 212 **Faculty:** FT 93, PT 34 **Student-Faculty Ratio:** 20:1 **Exams:** SAT I. **% Residing in College-Owned, -Operated, or -Affiliated Housing:** 33 **Library Holdings:** 4,553 **Regional Accreditation:** North Central Association of Colleges and Schools **Credit Hours For Degree:** 108 credits, Associates; 180 credits, Bachelors **Professional Accreditation:** AAMAE, ACBSP

UNIVERSITY OF PHOENIX—CINCINNATI CAMPUS

9050 Centre Pointe Dr., Ste. 250
West Chester, OH 45069-4875
Tel: (513)772-9600; Free: 800-228-7240
Admissions: (480)557-6151
E-mail: audra.mcquarie@phoenix.edu
Web Site: http://www.phoenix.edu/
President/CEO: William Pepicello
Admissions: Audra McQuarie

Type: Comprehensive **Sex:** Coed **Admission Plans:** Open Admission; Deferred Admission **Application Deadline:** Rolling **Application Fee:** $45.00 **H.S. Requirements:** High school diploma required; GED accepted **Costs Per Year:** Application fee: $45. Tuition: $11,925 full-time. Full-time tuition varies according to course level and course load. **Scholarships:** Available **Calendar System:** Continuous, Summer Session Not available **Enrollment:** FT 70 **Faculty:** FT 6, PT 41 **Regional Accreditation:** North Central Association of Colleges and Schools **Credit Hours For Degree:** 60 credits, Associates; 120 credits, Bachelors

UNIVERSITY OF PHOENIX—CLEVELAND CAMPUS

5005 Rockside Rd., Ste. 130
Independence, OH 44131-2194
Tel: (216)447-8807; Free: 800-228-7240
Admissions: (480)557-6151
E-mail: audra.mcquarie@phoenix.edu
Web Site: http://www.phoenix.edu/
President/CEO: William Pepicello
Admissions: Audra McQuarie

Type: Comprehensive **Sex:** Coed **Admission Plans:** Open Admission; Deferred Admission **Application Deadline:** Rolling **Application Fee:** $0.00 **H.S. Requirements:** High school diploma required; GED accepted **Costs Per Year:** Application fee: $0. Tuition: $13,200 full-time. Full-time tuition varies according to course level and course load. **Scholarships:** Available **Calendar System:** Continuous, Summer Session Not available **Enrollment:** FT 394 **Faculty:** FT 10, PT 113 **Regional Accreditation:** North Central Association of Colleges and Schools **Credit Hours For Degree:** 60 credits, Associates; 120 credits, Bachelors

UNIVERSITY OF PHOENIX—COLUMBUS OHIO CAMPUS

8415 Pulsar Place
Columbus, OH 43240-4032
Tel: (614)433-0095; Free: 800-228-7240
Admissions: (480)557-6151
E-mail: audra.mcquarie@phoenix.edu
Web Site: http://www.phoenix.edu/
President/CEO: William Pepicello
Admissions: Audra McQuarie

Type: Comprehensive **Sex:** Coed **Admission Plans:** Open Admission; Deferred Admission **Application Deadline:** Rolling **Application Fee:** $45.00 **H.S. Requirements:** High school diploma required; GED accepted **Costs Per Year:** Application fee: $45. Tuition: $13,200 full-time. Full-time tuition varies according to course level and course load. **Scholarships:** Available **Calendar System:** Continuous, Summer Session Not available **Enrollment:** FT 128 **Faculty:** FT 4, PT 61 **Regional Accreditation:** North Central Association of Colleges and Schools **Credit Hours For Degree:** 60 credits, Associates; 120 credits, Bachelors

UNIVERSITY OF RIO GRANDE
218 North College Ave.
Rio Grande, OH 45674
Tel: (740)245-5353
Admissions: (740)245-7425
Fax: (740)245-9220
E-mail: admissions@rio.edu
Web Site: http://www.rio.edu/
President/CEO: Paul Harrison
Admissions: Rebecca Long
Financial Aid: Dr. John Hill
Type: Comprehensive **Sex:** Coed **Scores:** 57% ACT 18-23; 10% ACT 24-29 **% Accepted:** 76 **Admission Plans:** Open Admission **Application Deadline:** Rolling **Application Fee:** $25.00 **H.S. Requirements:** High school diploma required; GED accepted **Costs Per Year:** Application fee: $25. Comprehensive fee: $26,360 includes full-time tuition ($18,260), mandatory fees ($500), and college room and board ($7600). Full-time tuition and fees vary according to course level, course load, degree level, program, reciprocity agreements, and student level. Room and board charges vary according to board plan, housing facility, and student level. Part-time tuition: $765 per credit hour. Part-time tuition varies according to course level, course load, degree level, program, reciprocity agreements, and student level. **Scholarships:** Available **Calendar System:** Semester, Summer Session Available **Enrollment:** FT 1,618, PT 420, Grad FT 26, Grad PT 78 **Faculty:** FT 92, PT 92 **Student-Faculty Ratio:** 15:1 **Exams:** ACT. **% Receiving Financial Aid:** 72 **% Residing in College-Owned, -Operated, or -Affiliated Housing:** 32 **Library Holdings:** 96,731 **Regional Accreditation:** North Central Association of Colleges and Schools **Credit Hours For Degree:** 62 semester hours, Associates; 124 semester hours, Bachelors **ROTC:** Army **Professional Accreditation:** CSWE, NAACLS, NCATE, NLN **Intercollegiate Athletics:** Archery M; Baseball M; Basketball M & W; Cross-Country Running M & W; Soccer M & W; Softball W; Track and Field M & W; Volleyball W

THE UNIVERSITY OF TOLEDO
2801 West Bancroft
Toledo, OH 43606-3390
Tel: (419)530-4636
Admissions: (419)530-5705
Fax: (419)530-4940
E-mail: william.pierce@utoledo.edu
Web Site: http://www.utoledo.edu/
President/CEO: Dr. Lloyd A. Jacobs
Admissions: William Pierce
Financial Aid: Carolyn Baumgartner
Type: University **Sex:** Coed **Scores:** 49.38% ACT 18-23; 25.71% ACT 24-29 **% Accepted:** 90 **Admission Plans:** Open Admission; Deferred Admission **Application Deadline:** Rolling **Application Fee:** $40.00 **H.S. Requirements:** High school diploma required; GED accepted **Costs Per Year:** Application fee: $40. State resident tuition: $6935 full-time, $294 per semester hour part-time. Nonresident tuition: $15,746 full-time, $661 per semester hour part-time. Mandatory fees: $1131 full-time, $47.92 per semester hour part-time. Full-time tuition and fees vary according to course load, program, and reciprocity agreements. Part-time tuition and fees vary according to course load, program, and reciprocity agreements. College room and board: $9478. College room only: $6348. Room and board charges vary according to board plan and housing facility. **Scholarships:** Available **Calendar System:** Semester, Summer Session Available **Enrollment:** FT 14,968, PT 3,172, Grad FT 3,307, Grad PT 1,617 **Faculty:** FT 809, PT 461 **Student-Faculty Ratio:** 19:1 **Exams:** SAT I or ACT. **% Receiving Financial Aid:** 67 **% Residing in College-Owned, -Operated, or -Affiliated Housing:** 23 **Final Year or Final Semester Residency Requirement:** No **Library Holdings:** 2,090,789 **Regional Accreditation:** North Central Association of Colleges and Schools **Credit Hours For Degree:** 60 semester hours, Associates; 124 semester hours, Bachelors **ROTC:** Army, Air Force **Professional Accreditation:** AACSB, ABET, ACPhE, AACN, AAMAE, ABA, ACA, AOTA, APTA, APA, ASLHA, AALS, CARC, CAEPK, CEPH, CSWE, JRCECT, JRCEPAT, LCMEAMA, NASAD NASM, NASPAA, NCATE, NLN, NRPA **Intercollegiate Athletics:** Baseball M; Basketball M & W; Cross-Country Running M & W; Football M; Golf M & W; Soccer W; Softball W; Swimming and Diving W; Tennis M & W; Track and Field W; Volleyball W

URBANA UNIVERSITY
579 College Way
Urbana, OH 43078-2091
Tel: (937)484-1400; Free: 800-7-URBANA
Admissions: (937)484-1301
Fax: (937)484-1389
E-mail: admiss@urbana.edu
Web Site: http://www.urbana.edu/
President/CEO: Stephen B. Jones
Admissions: Paula Brown
Financial Aid: Amy M. Barnhart
Type: Comprehensive **Sex:** Coed **Affiliation:** Church of the New Jerusalem **% Accepted:** 65 **Admission Plans:** Deferred Admission **Application Deadline:** Rolling **Application Fee:** $25.00 **H.S. Requirements:** High school diploma required; GED accepted **Scholarships:** Available **Calendar System:** Semester, Summer Session Available **Enrollment:** FT 904, PT 557 **Faculty:** FT 55, PT 65 **Student-Faculty Ratio:** 16:1 **Exams:** SAT I or ACT. **% Receiving Financial Aid:** 88 **Library Holdings:** 61,600 **Regional Accreditation:** North Central Association of Colleges and Schools **Credit Hours For Degree:** 63 credit hours, Associates; 126 credit hours, Bachelors **Intercollegiate Athletics:** Baseball M; Basketball M & W; Football M; Golf M & W; Soccer M & W; Softball W; Volleyball W

URSULINE COLLEGE
2550 Lander Rd.
Pepper Pike, OH 44124-4398
Tel: (440)449-4200; Free: 888-URSULINE
Admissions: (440)449-4203
Fax: (440)449-2235
E-mail: admission@ursuline.edu
Web Site: http://www.ursuline.edu/
President/CEO: Diana Stano
Admissions: Kimberly Shepherd
Financial Aid: Mary Lynn Perri
Type: Comprehensive **Sex:** Coed **Affiliation:** Roman Catholic **Scores:** 82% SAT V 400+; 82% SAT M 400+; 73% ACT 18-23; 18% ACT 24-29 **% Accepted:** 90 **Admission Plans:** Early Action; Deferred Admission **Application Deadline:** Rolling **Application Fee:** $25.00 **H.S. Requirements:** High school diploma required; GED accepted **Costs Per Year:** Application fee: $25. Comprehensive fee: $30,664 includes full-time tuition ($22,770), mandatory fees ($230), and college room and board ($7664). College room only: $3916. Full-time tuition and fees vary according to location. Room and board charges vary according to board plan and housing facility. Part-time tuition: $759 per credit hour. Part-time tuition varies according to location. **Scholarships:** Available **Calendar System:** Semester, Summer Session Available **Enrollment:** FT 690, PT 387, Grad FT 102, Grad PT 336 **Faculty:** FT 70, PT 118 **Student-Faculty Ratio:** 9:1 **Exams:** SAT I or ACT. ACT essay not being used. SAT essay not being used. **% Receiving Financial Aid:** 86 **% Residing in College-Owned, -Operated, or -Affiliated Housing:** 16 **Final Year or Final Semester Residency Requirement:** Yes **Library Holdings:** 136,684 **Regional Accreditation:** North Central Association of Colleges and Schools **Credit Hours For Degree:** 128 semester hours, Bachelors **ROTC:** Army **Professional Accreditation:** AACN, CSWE, NCATE **Intercollegiate Athletics:** Basketball W; Bowling W; Cross-Country Running W; Golf W; Soccer W; Softball W; Swimming and Diving W; Tennis W; Track and Field W; Volleyball W

VATTEROTT COLLEGE
5025 East Royalton Rd.
Broadview Heights, OH 44147
Tel: (440)526-1660; Free: (866)314-6454
Fax: (440)526-1933
Web Site: http://www.vatterott-college.edu/
President/CEO: Kate Spies
Admissions: Jack Chalk
Type: Two-Year College **Sex:** Coed **% Accepted:** 93 **Calendar System:** Semester **Professional Accreditation:** ACCSCT

VET TECH INSTITUTE AT BRADFORD SCHOOL
2469 Stelzer Rd.
Columbus, OH 43219
Tel: (614)416-6200; Free: 800-678-7981
Fax: (614)416-5197
Web Site: http://www.vettechinstitute.edu/
Type: Two-Year College **Sex:** Coed **% Accepted:** 36 **Professional Accreditation:** AVMA

VIRGINIA MARTI COLLEGE OF ART AND DESIGN
11724 Detroit Ave., PO Box 580
Lakewood, OH 44107-3002
Tel: (216)221-8584
E-mail: qmarti@vmcad.edu
Web Site: http://www.vmcad.edu/
President/CEO: Dennis Marti
Admissions: Quinn Marti
Type: Two-Year College **Sex:** Coed **Admission Plans:** Early Admission; Deferred Admission **Application Deadline:** Rolling **Application Fee:** $50.00 **H.S. Requirements:** High school diploma required; GED accepted **Calendar System:** Quarter, Summer Session Available **Student-Faculty Ratio:** 12:1 **Exams:** Other. **Credit Hours For Degree:** 110 quarter hours, Associates **Professional Accreditation:** ACCSCT

WALSH UNIVERSITY
2020 East Maple St., NW
North Canton, OH 44720-3396
Tel: (330)499-7090; Free: 800-362-8846
Admissions: (330)490-7171
Fax: (330)490-7165
E-mail: admissions@walsh.edu
Web Site: http://www.walsh.edu/
President/CEO: Richard Jusseaume
Admissions: Brett Freshour
Financial Aid: Holly Van Gilder
Type: Comprehensive **Sex:** Coed **Affiliation:** Roman Catholic **Scores:** 93% SAT V 400+; 95% SAT M 400+; 61% ACT 18-23; 31% ACT 24-29 **% Accepted:** 81 **Admission Plans:** Early Admission; Deferred Admission **Application Deadline:** Rolling **Application Fee:** $25.00 **H.S. Requirements:** High school diploma required; GED accepted **Costs Per Year:** Application fee: $25. One-time mandatory fee: $215. Comprehensive fee: $30,640 includes full-time tuition ($21,380), mandatory fees ($900), and college room and board ($8360). College room only: $4420. Full-time tuition and fees vary according to location. Room and board charges vary according to board plan and housing facility. Part-time tuition: $710 per semester hour. Part-time mandatory fees: $30 per semester hour. Part-time tuition and fees vary according to course load and location. **Scholarships:** Available **Calendar System:** Semester, Summer Session Available **Faculty:** FT 108, PT 158 **Student-Faculty Ratio:** 14:1 **Exams:** SAT I or ACT. **% Receiving Financial Aid:** 74 **% Residing in College-Owned, -Operated, or -Affiliated Housing:** 54 **Library Holdings:** 389,094 **Regional Accreditation:** North Central Association of Colleges and Schools **Credit Hours For Degree:** 60 credit hours, Associates; 125 credit hours, Bachelors **Professional Accreditation:** ACA, APTA, NCATE, NLN **Intercollegiate Athletics:** Baseball M; Basketball M & W; Cheerleading W; Cross-Country Running M & W; Football M; Golf M & W; Soccer M & W; Softball W; Tennis M & W; Track and Field M & W; Volleyball W

WASHINGTON STATE COMMUNITY COLLEGE
710 Colegate Dr.
Marietta, OH 45750-9225
Tel: (740)374-8716
Fax: (740)376-0257
E-mail: rperoni@wscc.edu
Web Site: http://www.wscc.edu/
President/CEO: Charlotte Hatfield
Admissions: Rebecca Peroni
Type: Two-Year College **Sex:** Coed **Affiliation:** Ohio Board of Regents **Admission Plans:** Open Admission; Early Admission; Deferred Admission **Application Deadline:** Rolling **H.S. Requirements:** High school diploma or equivalent not required. For medical laboratory technology, nursing programs: High school diploma required; GED accepted **Scholarships:** Available **Calendar System:** Quarter, Summer Session Available **Enrollment:** FT 1,174, PT 912 **Faculty:** FT 57, PT 87 **Student-Faculty Ratio:** 14:1 **Library Holdings:** 15,000 **Regional Accreditation:** North Central Association of Colleges and Schools **Credit Hours For Degree:** 90 credit hours, Associates **Professional Accreditation:** APTA, CARC, NAACLS

WILBERFORCE UNIVERSITY
1055 North Bickett Rd.
Wilberforce, OH 45384
Tel: (937)376-2911; Free: 800-367-8568
Fax: (937)376-4751
E-mail: kmesser@wilberforce.edu
Web Site: http://www.wilberforce.edu/
President/CEO: Patricia L. Hardaway, MPW,JD
Admissions: Kenya LeNoir Messer
Type: Comprehensive **Sex:** Coed **Affiliation:** African Methodist Episcopal Church **Admission Plans:** Early Admission; Early Decision Plan; Deferred Admission **Application Deadline:** July 1 **Application Fee:** $25.00 **H.S. Requirements:** High school diploma required; GED accepted **Scholarships:** Available **Calendar System:** Semester, Summer Session Not available **Exams:** SAT I or ACT. **Library Holdings:** 63,000 **Regional Accreditation:** North Central Association of Colleges and Schools **Credit Hours For Degree:** 128 credit hours, Bachelors **ROTC:** Army, Air Force **Intercollegiate Athletics:** Basketball M & W; Cross-Country Running M & W

WILMINGTON COLLEGE
1870 Quaker Way
Wilmington, OH 45177
Tel: (937)382-6661; Free: 800-341-9318
Fax: (937)382-7077
E-mail: admissions@wilmington.edu
Web Site: http://www.wilmington.edu/
President/CEO: Daniel A. Dibiasio
Admissions: Tina Garland
Financial Aid: Donna Barton
Type: Comprehensive **Sex:** Coed **Affiliation:** Friends **Scores:** 86.03% SAT V 400+; 84.95% SAT M 400+; 54.39% ACT 18-23; 18.95% ACT 24-29 **% Accepted:** 93 **Admission Plans:** Deferred Admission **Application Deadline:** August 1 **Application Fee:** $25.00 **H.S. Requirements:** High school diploma required; GED accepted **Costs Per Year:** Application fee: $25. Comprehensive fee: $32,558 includes full-time tuition ($23,786), mandatory fees ($500), and college room and board ($8272). Room and board charges vary according to board plan and housing facility. **Scholarships:** Available **Calendar System:** Semester, Summer Session Available **Enrollment:** FT 1,267, PT 288, Grad FT 24, Grad PT 24 **Faculty:** FT 68, PT 45 **Student-Faculty Ratio:** 14:1 **Exams:** SAT I or ACT. ACT essay not being used. SAT essay not being used. **% Receiving Financial Aid:** 88 **% Residing in College-Owned, -Operated, or -Affiliated Housing:** 75 **Regional Accreditation:** North Central Association of Colleges and Schools **Credit Hours For Degree:** 124 credit hours, Bachelors **Professional Accreditation:** JRCEPAT, TEAC **Intercollegiate Athletics:** Baseball M; Basketball M & W; Cross-Country Running M & W; Football M; Golf M & W; Soccer M & W; Softball W; Swimming and Diving M & W; Tennis M & W; Track and Field M & W; Volleyball W; Wrestling M

WITTENBERG UNIVERSITY
PO Box 720
Springfield, OH 45501-0720
Tel: (937)327-6231; Free: 800-677-7558
Admissions: 877-206-0332
Fax: (937)327-6379
E-mail: admission@wittenberg.edu
Web Site: http://www.wittenberg.edu/
President/CEO: Dr. Mark H. Erickson
Admissions: Karen Hunt
Financial Aid: J. Randy Green
Type: Comprehensive **Sex:** Coed **Affiliation:** Evangelical Lutheran Church **Scores:** 96% SAT V 400+; 95% SAT M 400+; 32% ACT 18-23; 50% ACT 24-29 **% Accepted:** 72 **Admission Plans:** Preferred Admission; Early Admission; Early Action; Early Decision Plan; Deferred Admission **Application Fee:** $40.00 **H.S. Requirements:** High school diploma required; GED accepted **Costs Per Year:** Application fee: $40. Comprehensive fee: $42,962 includes full-time tuition ($33,890), mandatory fees ($300), and college room and board ($8772). College room only: $4554. Room and board charges vary according to board plan and housing facility. Part-time tuition: $1130 per credit hour. Part-time tuition varies according to course load. **Scholarships:** Available **Calendar System:** Semester, Summer Session Available **Enrollment:** FT 1,801, PT 98, Grad PT 35 **Faculty:** FT 140, PT 57 **Student-Faculty Ratio:** 12:1 **Exams:** Other. ACT essay not being used. SAT essay not being used. **% Receiving Financial Aid:** 73 **% Residing in College-Owned, -Operated, or -Affiliated Housing:** 89 **Final Year or Final Semester Residency Requirement:** No **Library Holdings:** 423,930 **Regional Accreditation:** North Central Association of Colleges and Schools **Credit Hours For Degree:** 130 credits, Bachelors **ROTC:** Army, Air Force **Professional Accreditation:** NASM, NCATE **Intercollegiate Athletics:**

Baseball M; Basketball M & W; Crew M & W; Cross-Country Running M & W; Field Hockey W; Football M; Golf M & W; Lacrosse M & W; Rugby M & W; Soccer M & W; Softball W; Swimming and Diving M & W; Tennis M & W; Track and Field M & W; Volleyball M & W

WRIGHT STATE UNIVERSITY
3640 Colonel Glenn Hwy.
Dayton, OH 45435
Tel: (937)775-3333; Free: 800-247-1770
Admissions: (937)775-5700
Fax: (937)775-5795
E-mail: admissions@wright.edu
Web Site: http://www.wright.edu/
President/CEO: Dr. David Hopkins
Admissions: Cathy Davis
Financial Aid: Jennifer L. Penick
Type: University **Sex:** Coed **Affiliation:** University System of Ohio **Scores:** 88% SAT V 400+; 87% SAT M 400+; 52% ACT 18-23; 23% ACT 24-29 **% Accepted:** 84 **Admission Plans:** Early Admission; Deferred Admission **Application Deadline:** Rolling **Application Fee:** $30.00 **H.S. Requirements:** High school diploma required; GED accepted **Costs Per Year:** Application fee: $30. State resident tuition: $7797 full-time, $235 per credit hour part-time. Nonresident tuition: $15,213 full-time, $462 per credit hour part-time. **Scholarships:** Available **Calendar System:** Quarter, Summer Session Available **Enrollment:** FT 11,299, PT 2,205, Grad FT 2,451, Grad PT 1,603 **Faculty:** FT 853, PT 27 **Student-Faculty Ratio:** 17:1 **Exams:** SAT I or ACT. ACT essay not being used. SAT essay not being used. **% Receiving Financial Aid:** 68 **% Residing in College-Owned, -Operated, or -Affiliated Housing:** 22 **Library Holdings:** 703,000 **Regional Accreditation:** North Central Association of Colleges and Schools **Credit Hours For Degree:** 96 credit hours, Associates; 187 credit hours, Bachelors **ROTC:** Army, Air Force **Professional Accreditation:** AACSB, ABET, AACN, ACA, APA, CORE, CSWE, JRCEPAT, LCMEAMA, NAACLS, NASM, NASPAA, NCATE, NLN **Intercollegiate Athletics:** Baseball M; Basketball M & W; Cross-Country Running M & W; Golf M; Soccer M & W; Softball W; Swimming and Diving M & W; Tennis M & W; Track and Field W; Volleyball W

WRIGHT STATE UNIVERSITY, LAKE CAMPUS
7600 State Route 703
Celina, OH 45822-2921
Tel: (419)586-0300
Fax: (419)586-0358
Web Site: http://www.wright.edu/lake/
President/CEO: Jim Sayer
Admissions: Sandra Gilbert
Type: Two-Year College **Sex:** Coed **Affiliation:** Ohio Board of Regents **% Accepted:** 99 **Admission Plans:** Open Admission; Early Admission; Deferred Admission **Application Deadline:** Rolling **Application Fee:** $40.00 **H.S. Requirements:** High school diploma required; GED accepted **Calendar System:** Quarter, Summer Session Available **Faculty:** FT 18, PT 30 **Student-Faculty Ratio:** 15:1 **Library Holdings:** 26,000 **Regional Accreditation:** North Central Association of Colleges and Schools **Credit Hours For Degree:** 94 credit hours, Associates **Intercollegiate Athletics:** Basketball M & W

XAVIER UNIVERSITY
3800 Victory Parkway
Cincinnati, OH 45207
Tel: (513)745-3000; Free: 800-344-4698
Fax: (513)745-4319
E-mail: xuadmit@xavier.edu
Web Site: http://www.xu.edu/
President/CEO: Rev. Michael J. Graham, SJ
Type: Comprehensive **Sex:** Coed **Affiliation:** Roman Catholic **Scores:** 100% SAT V 400+; 99% SAT M 400+; 35% ACT 18-23; 50% ACT 24-29 **% Accepted:** 73 **Admission Plans:** Deferred Admission **Application Deadline:** February 1 **Application Fee:** $35.00 **H.S. Requirements:** High school diploma required; GED accepted **Costs Per Year:** Application fee: $35. One-time mandatory fee: $190. Comprehensive fee: $38,100 includes full-time tuition ($27,900), mandatory fees ($670), and college room and board ($9530). College room only: $5250. Full-time tuition and fees vary according to course load and program. Room and board charges vary according to board plan and housing facility. Part-time tuition: $550 per credit hour. Part-time tuition varies according to course load and location. **Scholarships:** Available **Calendar System:** Semester, Summer Session Available **Enrollment:** FT 3,729, PT 499, Grad FT 795, Grad PT 1,943 **Faculty:** FT 317, PT 308 **Student-Faculty Ratio:** 13:1 **Exams:** SAT I or ACT. **% Receiving Financial Aid:** 60 **% Residing in College-Owned, -Operated, or -Affiliated Housing:** 48 **Final Year or Final Semester Residency Requirement:** No **Library Holdings:** 363,140 **Regional Accreditation:** North Central Association of Colleges and Schools **Credit Hours For Degree:** 60 semester hours, Associates; 120 semester hours, Bachelors **ROTC:** Army, Air Force **Professional Accreditation:** AACSB, AACN, ACA, AOTA, APA, ACEHSA, CSWE, JRCERT, JRCEPAT, MACTE, TEAC **Intercollegiate Athletics:** Baseball M; Basketball M & W; Cheerleading M & W; Crew M & W; Cross-Country Running M & W; Equestrian Sports M & W; Fencing M & W; Field Hockey M & W; Football M; Golf M & W; Gymnastics M & W; Ice Hockey M & W; Lacrosse M & W; Racquetball M & W; Rugby M & W; Soccer M & W; Softball M & W; Swimming and Diving M & W; Tennis M & W; Track and Field M & W; Ultimate Frisbee M & W; Volleyball M & W; Water Polo M & W

YOUNGSTOWN STATE UNIVERSITY
One University Plaza
Youngstown, OH 44555-0001
Tel: (330)941-3000; Free: 877-468-6978
Admissions: (330)941-2000
Fax: (330)941-1998
E-mail: enroll@ysu.edu
Web Site: http://www.ysu.edu/
President/CEO: Dr. David Sweet
Admissions: Sue Davis
Financial Aid: Beth Bartlett
Type: Comprehensive **Sex:** Coed **Scores:** 78% SAT V 400+; 76% SAT M 400+; 52% ACT 18-23; 17% ACT 24-29 **% Accepted:** 89 **Admission Plans:** Open Admission; Early Admission; Early Decision Plan; Deferred Admission **Application Deadline:** August 15 **Application Fee:** $30.00 **H.S. Requirements:** High school diploma required; GED accepted **Costs Per Year:** Application fee: $30. State resident tuition: $6727 full-time, $290 per credit part-time. Nonresident tuition: $12,400 full-time, $526 per credit part-time. Mandatory fees: $229 full-time, $10 per credit part-time. Full-time tuition and fees vary according to course load. Part-time tuition and fees vary according to course load. College room and board: $7400. Room and board charges vary according to board plan and housing facility. **Scholarships:** Available **Calendar System:** Semester, Summer Session Available **Enrollment:** FT 10,443, PT 2,926, Grad FT 498, Grad PT 805 **Faculty:** FT 447, PT 564 **Student-Faculty Ratio:** 19:1 **Exams:** SAT I or ACT. ACT essay not being used. SAT essay not being used. **% Receiving Financial Aid:** 62 **% Residing in College-Owned, -Operated, or -Affiliated Housing:** 10 **Final Year or Final Semester Residency Requirement:** Yes **Regional Accreditation:** North Central Association of Colleges and Schools **Credit Hours For Degree:** 64credits, Associates; 124 credits, Bachelors **ROTC:** Army, Air Force **Professional Accreditation:** AACSB, ABET, AAFCS, AAMAE, AANA, ACA, ADA, ADtA, APTA, CARC, CEPH, CSWE, JRCEMT, NAACLS, NASAD, NASM, NAST, NCATE, NLN **Intercollegiate Athletics:** Baseball M; Basketball M & W; Cross-Country Running M & W; Football M; Golf M & W; Soccer W; Softball W; Swimming and Diving W; Tennis M & W; Track and Field M & W; Volleyball W

ZANE STATE COLLEGE
1555 Newark Rd.
Zanesville, OH 43701-2626
Tel: (740)454-2501
Web Site: http://www.zanestate.edu/
President/CEO: Paul Brown
Admissions: Paul Young
Type: Two-Year College **Sex:** Coed **% Accepted:** 82 **Admission Plans:** Open Admission; Early Admission **Application Deadline:** Rolling **Application Fee:** $20.00 **H.S. Requirements:** High school diploma required; GED accepted **Scholarships:** Available **Calendar System:** Quarter, Summer Session Available **Faculty:** FT 50, PT 66 **Student-Faculty Ratio:** 18:1 **Exams:** Other, SAT I or ACT. **Regional Accreditation:** North Central Association of Colleges and Schools **Credit Hours For Degree:** 110 credits, Associates **Professional Accreditation:** ABET, AAMAE, ACF, AOTA, APTA, JRCERT, NAACLS **Intercollegiate Athletics:** Baseball M; Basketball M & W; Golf M & W

BACONE COLLEGE
2299 Old Bacone Rd.
Muskogee, OK 74403-1597
Tel: (918)683-4581; Free: 888-682-5514
Fax: (918)682-5514
Web Site: http://www.bacone.edu/
President/CEO: Rev. Robert J. Duncan, Jr.
Financial Aid: Kathye Watson
Type: Four-Year College **Sex:** Coed **Affiliation:** American Baptist Churches in the U.S.A. **Admission Plans:** Early Admission; Deferred Admission **Application Deadline:** Rolling **Application Fee:** $25.00 **H.S. Requirements:** High school diploma required; GED accepted **Scholarships:** Available **Calendar System:** Semester, Summer Session Available **Exams:** ACT, SAT I or ACT. **Library Holdings:** 34,564 **Regional Accreditation:** North Central Association of Colleges and Schools **Credit Hours For Degree:** 62 semester hours, Associates; 124 semester hours, Bachelors **Professional Accreditation:** JRCERT, NLN

BROWN MACKIE COLLEGE—TULSA
4608 South Garnett
Ste. 110
Tulsa, OK 74146
Tel: (918)628-3700; Free: 888-794-8411
Fax: (918)828-9083
Web Site: http://www.brownmackie.edu/tulsa/
President/CEO: Denise Choquette
Type: Two-Year College **Sex:** Coed

CAMERON UNIVERSITY
2800 West Gore Blvd.
Lawton, OK 73505-6377
Tel: (580)581-2200; Free: 888-454-7600
Admissions: (580)581-5496
Fax: (580)581-5514
E-mail: admissions@cameron.edu
Web Site: http://www.cameron.edu/
President/CEO: Dr. Cindy Ross
Admissions: Frank Myers
Financial Aid: Carol Claiborne
Type: Comprehensive **Sex:** Coed **Affiliation:** Oklahoma State Regents for Higher Education **Scores:** 49.9% ACT 18-23; 15.4% ACT 24-29 **% Accepted:** 100 **Admission Plans:** Open Admission; Deferred Admission **Application Deadline:** Rolling **Application Fee:** $15.00 **H.S. Requirements:** High school diploma required; GED accepted **Costs Per Year:** Application fee: $15. State resident tuition: $4110 full-time, $93.50 per credit hour part-time. Nonresident tuition: $9974 full-time, $289 per credit hour part-time. Mandatory fees: $1305 full-time, $43.50 per credit hour part-time. Full-time tuition and fees vary according to course load. Part-time tuition and fees vary according to course load. College room and board: $3589. College room only: $2586. Room and board charges vary according to board plan. **Scholarships:** Available **Calendar System:** Semester, Summer Session Available **Enrollment:** FT 3,816, PT 1,874, Grad FT 177, Grad PT 264 **Faculty:** FT 183, PT 146 **Student-Faculty Ratio:** 20:1 **Exams:** SAT I or ACT. ACT essay not being used. **% Receiving Financial Aid:** 53 **% Residing in College-Owned, -Operated, or -Affiliated Housing:** 9 **Final Year or Final Semester Residency Requirement:** No **Library Holdings:** 189,872 **Regional Accreditation:** North Central Association of Colleges and Schools **Credit Hours For Degree:** 64 semester hours, Associates; 128 semester hours, Bachelors **ROTC:** Army **Professional Accreditation:** ACBSP, NASM, NCATE **Intercollegiate Athletics:** Baseball M; Basketball M & W; Cross-Country Running M; Golf M & W; Softball W; Tennis M & W; Volleyball W

CARL ALBERT STATE COLLEGE
1507 South McKenna
Poteau, OK 74953-5208
Tel: (918)647-1200
Admissions: (918)647-1300
Fax: (918)647-1306
E-mail: dwebster@carlalbert.edu
Web Site: http://www.carlalbert.edu/
President/CEO: Dr. Brandon Webb
Admissions: Dawn Webster
Financial Aid: Crystle Wiles
Type: Two-Year College **Sex:** Coed **Affiliation:** Oklahoma State Regents for Higher Education **Admission Plans:** Open Admission **Application Deadline:** August 13 **Application Fee:** $0.00 **H.S. Requirements:** High school diploma or equivalent not required. For nursing, physical therapy assistant programs: High school diploma required; GED accepted **Costs Per Year:** Application fee: $0. State resident tuition: $1800 full-time, $75 per credit hour part-time. Nonresident tuition: $4176 full-time, $174 per credit hour part-time. Mandatory fees: $4 full-time. Full-time tuition and fees vary according to course load. Part-time tuition varies according to course load. College room and board: $2900. College room only: $1300. Room and board charges vary according to board plan. **Scholarships:** Available **Calendar System:** Semester **Enrollment:** FT 1,369, PT 994 **Faculty:** FT 51, PT 103 **Student-Faculty Ratio:** 16:1 **Library Holdings:** 27,200 **Regional Accreditation:** North Central Association of Colleges and Schools **Credit Hours For Degree:** 62 credit hours, Associates **Professional Accreditation:** APTA, NLN **Intercollegiate Athletics:** Baseball M; Basketball M & W; Softball M

CLARY SAGE COLLEGE
3131 South Sheridan
Tulsa, OK 74145
Tel: (918)298-8200
Admissions: (918)610-0027
Fax: (918)298-0099
E-mail: tknox@clarysagecollege.com
Web Site: http://www.clarysagecollege.com/
President/CEO: Dr. Kevin Kirk
Admissions: Teresa Knox
Type: Two-Year College **Sex:** Coed **Affiliation:** Dental Directions, Inc. **Admission Plans:** Open Admission; Deferred Admission **Application Deadline:** Rolling **Application Fee:** $100.00 **H.S. Requirements:** High school diploma required; GED accepted **Costs Per Year:** Application fee: $100. Tuition: $9,733 full-time. Mandatory fees: $2000 full-time. Full-time tuition and fees vary according to program. **Enrollment:** FT 118 **Faculty:** FT 13, PT 2 **Student-Faculty Ratio:** 15:1

COMMUNITY CARE COLLEGE
4242 South Sheridan Rd.
Tulsa, OK 74145
Tel: (918)610-0027
Fax: (918)610-0029
E-mail: tknox@communitycarecollege.com
Web Site: http://www.communitycarecollege.edu/
President/CEO: Dr. Kevin L. Kirk
Admissions: Teresa Knox
Type: Two-Year College **Sex:** Coed **Affiliation:** Dental Directions, Inc. **Admission Plans:** Open Admission **Application Deadline:** Rolling **Application Fee:** $100.00 **H.S. Requirements:** High school diploma required; GED accepted **Costs Per Year:** Application fee: $100. Tuition: $15,000 full-time. Mandatory fees: $1900 full-time. Full-time tuition and fees vary according to course load, degree level, and program. Tuition guaranteed not to increase for student's term of enrollment. **Calendar System:** Continuous **Enrollment:** FT 286 **Faculty:** FT 26, PT 0 **Student-Faculty Ratio:** 20:1 **Professional Accreditation:** ABHES

CONNORS STATE COLLEGE
Route 1 Box 1000
Warner, OK 74469-9700
Tel: (918)463-2931
Web Site: http://www.connorsstate.edu/
President/CEO: Dr. Donnie L. Nero
Admissions: Sonya Baker
Type: Two-Year College **Sex:** Coed **Affiliation:** Oklahoma State Regents for Higher Education **Admission Plans:** Open Admission; Early Admission; Deferred Admission **Application Deadline:** Rolling **Application Fee:** $0.00 **H.S. Requirements:** High school diploma or equivalent not required **Scholarships:** Available **Calendar System:** Semester, Summer Session Available **Library Holdings:** 63,728 **Regional Accreditation:** North Central Association of Colleges and Schools **Credit Hours For Degree:** 60 semester hours, Associates **Professional Accreditation:** NLN **Intercollegiate Athletics:** Baseball M; Basketball M & W; Softball W

DEVRY UNIVERSITY
Lakepointe Towers
4013 Northwest Expressway St., Ste. 100
Oklahoma City, OK 73116
Tel: (405)767-9516
Web Site: http://www.devry.edu/
President/CEO: Anthony Spano
Type: Comprehensive **Sex:** Coed **Admission Plans:** Deferred Admission **Application Deadline:** Rolling **Application Fee:** $50.00 **H.S. Requirements:** High school diploma required; GED accepted **Costs Per Year:** Application fee: $50. Tuition: $14,080 full-time, $550 per credit hour part-time. **Scholarships:** Available **Enrollment:** FT 53, PT 58, Grad FT 3, Grad PT 41 **Faculty:** FT 0, PT 10 **Student-Faculty Ratio:** 27:1 **Exams:** ACT essay used for admission. SAT essay used for admission. ACT essay used for placement. SAT essay used for placement. **% Receiving Financial Aid:** 83 **Regional Accreditation:** North Central Association of Colleges and Schools

EAST CENTRAL UNIVERSITY
1100 East 14th St.
Ada, OK 74820-6899
Tel: (580)332-8000
Admissions: (580)310-5233
Fax: (580)436-5495
E-mail: pdenny@ecok.edu
Web Site: http://www.ecok.edu/
President/CEO: Dr. John R. Hargrave
Admissions: Pam Denny
Financial Aid: Marcia Carter
Type: Comprehensive **Sex:** Coed **Affiliation:** Oklahoma State Regents for Higher Education **Scores:** 84% SAT V 400+; 89% SAT M 400+; 55% ACT 18-23; 21% ACT 24-29 **% Accepted:** 93 **Admission Plans:** Early Admission **Application Fee:** $20.00 **H.S. Requirements:** High school diploma required; GED accepted **Costs Per Year:** Application fee: $20. State resident tuition: $2410 full-time, $100.40 per semester hour part-time. Nonresident tuition: $7222 full-time, $300.90 per semester hour part-time. Mandatory fees: $1026 full-time, $38.80 per semester hour part-time, $47.50 per term part-time. College room and board: $4100. College room only: $1696. Room and board charges vary according to board plan and housing facility. Tuition guaranteed not to increase for student's term of enrollment. **Scholarships:** Available **Calendar System:** Semester, Summer Session Available **Enrollment:** FT 3,014, PT 716, Grad FT 239, Grad PT 643 **Faculty:** FT 168, PT 110 **Student-Faculty Ratio:** 18:1 **Exams:** ACT, SAT I or ACT. **% Receiving Financial Aid:** 67 **% Residing in College-Owned, -Operated, or -Affiliated Housing:** 25 **Library Holdings:** 251,780 **Regional Accreditation:** North Central Association of Colleges and Schools **Credit Hours For Degree:** 124 semester hours, Bachelors **Professional Accreditation:** AHIMA, ACBSP, CORE, CSWE, NASM, NCATE, NLN **Intercollegiate Athletics:** Baseball M; Basketball M & W; Cheerleading M & W; Cross-Country Running M & W; Football M; Golf M & W; Soccer W; Softball W; Tennis M & W; Track and Field M & W; Volleyball W

EASTERN OKLAHOMA STATE COLLEGE
1301 West Main
Wilburton, OK 74578-4999
Tel: (918)465-2361
Fax: (918)465-2431
E-mail: lmiller@eosc.edu
Web Site: http://www.eosc.edu/
President/CEO: Dr. Steve Smith
Admissions: Leah McLaughlin
Type: Two-Year College **Sex:** Coed **Affiliation:** Oklahoma State Regents for Higher Education **Admission Plans:** Open Admission; Early Admission; Deferred Admission **Application Deadline:** Rolling **Application Fee:** $10.00 **H.S. Requirements:** High school diploma required; GED accepted. For state residents 18 or over: High school diploma or equivalent not required **Scholarships:** Available **Calendar System:** Semester, Summer Session Available **Library Holdings:** 41,639 **Regional Accreditation:** North Central Association of Colleges and Schools **Credit Hours For Degree:** 64 semester hours, Associates **Professional Accreditation:** NLN **Intercollegiate Athletics:** Baseball M; Basketball M & W; Equestrian Sports M & W; Softball W

HERITAGE COLLEGE
7100 I-35 Services Rd.
Ste. 7118
Oklahoma City, OK 73149
Tel: (405)631-3399; Free: 888-334-7339
Fax: (405)631-6711
E-mail: info@heritage-education.com
Web Site: http://www.heritage-education.com/campus_oklahoma.htm
President/CEO: Cheryl Morris
Type: Two-Year College **Sex:** Coed **Admission Plans:** Open Admission **Student-Faculty Ratio:** 33:1 **Professional Accreditation:** ACCSCT

HILLSDALE FREE WILL BAPTIST COLLEGE
3701 South I-35 Service Rd.
PO Box 7208
Moore, OK 73160-1208
Tel: (405)912-9000
Admissions: (405)912-9007
Fax: (405)912-9050
E-mail: recruitment@hc.edu
Web Site: http://www.hc.edu/
President/CEO: Timothy W. Eaton
Financial Aid: Denise Conklin
Type: Comprehensive **Sex:** Coed **Affiliation:** Free Will Baptist **Scores:** 53.8% ACT 18-23; 10% ACT 24-29 **Admission Plans:** Early Admission; Deferred Admission **Application Fee:** $20.00 **H.S. Requirements:** High school diploma required; GED accepted **Costs Per Year:** Application fee: $20. One-time mandatory fee: $20. Comprehensive fee: $14,850 includes full-time tuition ($8100), mandatory fees ($1550), and college room and board ($5200). College room only: $2200. Full-time tuition and fees vary according to course load. Room and board charges vary according to board plan and housing facility. Part-time tuition: $340 per credit hour. Part-time mandatory fees: $20 per credit hour, $210 per term. Part-time tuition and fees vary according to course load. **Scholarships:** Available **Calendar System:** Semester, Summer Session Available **Enrollment:** FT 210, PT 21, Grad FT 2, Grad PT 8 **Exams:** SAT I or ACT. **% Receiving Financial Aid:** 66 **Library Holdings:** 28,000 **Credit Hours For Degree:** 64 credit hours, Associates; 128 credit hours, Bachelors **Professional Accreditation:** TACCS **Intercollegiate Athletics:** Baseball M; Basketball M & W; Soccer M; Softball W; Volleyball W

ITT TECHNICAL INSTITUTE (OKLAHOMA CITY)
50 Penn Place Office Tower
1900 Northwest Expressway, Ste. 305R
Oklahoma City, OK 73118
Tel: (405)810-4100; Free: 800-518-1612
Web Site: http://www.itt-tech.edu/
President/CEO: Terri Lowery
Type: Four-Year College **Sex:** Coed **Affiliation:** ITT Educational Services, Inc. **Calendar System:** Quarter

ITT TECHNICAL INSTITUTE (TULSA)
8421 East 61st St.
Ste. U
Tulsa, OK 74133
Tel: (918)615-3900
Admissions: (918)615-3900
Web Site: http://www.itt-tech.edu/
President/CEO: Karen J. Selby
Type: Two-Year College **Sex:** Coed **Calendar System:** Quarter

LANGSTON UNIVERSITY
PO Box 907
Langston, OK 73050
Tel: (405)466-2231
Admissions: (405)466-3428
Fax: (405)466-3381
Web Site: http://www.lunet.edu/
President/CEO: Dr. Joann W. Haysbert
Admissions: Maurice Osborne
Financial Aid: Linda Morris
Type: Comprehensive **Sex:** Coed **Affiliation:** Oklahoma State Regents for Higher Education **% Accepted:** 37 **Admission Plans:** Open Admission **Application Deadline:** Rolling **H.S. Requirements:** High school diploma required; GED accepted **Scholarships:** Available **Calendar System:** Semester, Summer Session Available **Student-Faculty Ratio:** 30:1 **Exams:** SAT I or ACT. **% Receiving Financial Aid:** 73 **Library Holdings:** 97,565 **Regional Accreditation:** North Central Association of Colleges and Schools **Credit Hours For Degree:** 62 credit hours, Associates; 124 credit hours, Bachelors **ROTC:** Army **Professional Accreditation:** APTA, ACBSP, CORE, NCATE, NLN **Intercollegiate Athletics:** Basketball M & W; Football M; Track and Field M & W

MID-AMERICA CHRISTIAN UNIVERSITY
3500 Southwest 119th St.
Oklahoma City, OK 73170-4504
Tel: (405)691-3800
Fax: (405)692-5165
E-mail: info@macu.edu
Web Site: http://www.macu.edu/
President/CEO: Dr. John Fozard
Admissions: Jason Duda
Financial Aid: Todd Martin
Type: Comprehensive **Sex:** Coed **Affiliation:** Church of God **Admission Plans:** Open Admission; Early Admission **Application Deadline:** Rolling **Application Fee:** $25.00 **H.S. Requirements:** High school diploma required; GED accepted **Costs Per Year:** Application fee: $25. Comprehensive fee: $18,515 includes full-time tuition ($12,480), mandatory fees ($475), and college room and board ($5560). College room only: $2900. Full-time tuition and fees vary according to course load. Part-time tuition: $520 per credit hour. Part-time mandatory fees: $415. Part-time tuition and fees vary according to course load. **Scholarships:** Available **Calendar System:** Semester, Summer Session Available **% Receiving Financial Aid:** 86 **Library Holdings:** 60,000 **Regional Accreditation:** North Central Association of Colleges and Schools **Credit Hours For Degree:** 64 semester hours, Associates; 124 semester hours, Bachelors **Intercollegiate Athletics:** Baseball M; Basketball M & W; Golf M; Soccer M & W; Softball W; Volleyball W

MURRAY STATE COLLEGE
One Murray Campus
Tishomingo, OK 73460-3130
Tel: (580)371-2371
Fax: (580)371-9844
E-mail: gmarten@mscok.edu
Web Site: http://www.mscok.edu/
President/CEO: Dr. Noble Jobe
Admissions: Genna Marten
Type: Two-Year College **Sex:** Coed **Affiliation:** Oklahoma State Regents for Higher Education **Admission Plans:** Open Admission; Early Admission **Application Deadline:** Rolling **H.S. Requirements:** High school diploma required; GED accepted **Scholarships:** Available **Calendar System:** Semester, Summer Session Available **Enrollment:** FT 1,291, PT 1,206 **Faculty:** FT 43, PT 30 **Student-Faculty Ratio:** 27:1 **Exams:** SAT I or ACT. **% Residing in College-Owned, -Operated, or -Affiliated Housing:** 6 **Library Holdings:** 20,000 **Regional Accreditation:** North Central Association of Colleges and Schools **Credit Hours For Degree:** 63 credit hours, Associates **Professional Accreditation:** APTA, NLN **Intercollegiate Athletics:** Baseball M; Basketball M & W; Softball W

NORTHEASTERN OKLAHOMA AGRICULTURAL AND MECHANICAL COLLEGE
200 I St., NE
Miami, OK 74354-6434
Tel: (918)542-8441
Admissions: (918)540-6212
Fax: (918)542-9759
E-mail: neoadmission@neo.edu
Web Site: http://www.neo.edu/
President/CEO: Dr. Glenn E. Mayle
Admissions: Amy Ishmael
Financial Aid: Aimee McMain
Type: Two-Year College **Sex:** Coed **Affiliation:** Oklahoma State Regents for Higher Education **Admission Plans:** Open Admission **Application Deadline:** Rolling **Application Fee:** $0.00 **H.S. Requirements:** High school diploma required; GED accepted **Costs Per Year:** Application fee: $0. State resident tuition: $1737 full-time, $57.90 per credit hour part-time. Nonresident tuition: $5558 full-time, $185.25 per credit hour part-time. Mandatory fees: $890 full-time, $29.65 per credit hour part-time. College room and board: $4006. Room and board charges vary according to board plan. **Scholarships:** Available **Calendar System:** Semester, Summer Session Available **Enrollment:** FT 1,396, PT 503 **Faculty:** FT 77, PT 33 **Student-Faculty Ratio:** 17:1 **Library Holdings:** 74,000 **Regional Accreditation:** North Central Association of Colleges and Schools **Credit Hours For Degree:** 60 credit hours, Associates **Professional Accreditation:** APTA, NAACLS, NLN **Intercollegiate Athletics:** Baseball M; Basketball M & W; Cheerleading M & W; Football M; Golf M; Soccer M & W; Softball W; Volleyball W

NORTHEASTERN STATE UNIVERSITY
600 North Grand
Tahlequah, OK 74464-2399
Tel: (918)456-5511
Admissions: (918)444-2211
Fax: (918)458-2342
E-mail: cain@nsuok.edu
Web Site: http://www.nsuok.edu/
President/CEO: Dr. Don Betz
Admissions: Dawn Cain
Financial Aid: Dr. Teri Cochran
Type: Comprehensive **Sex:** Coed **Affiliation:** Regional University System of Oklahoma **Scores:** 57% ACT 18-23; 16.9% ACT 24-29 **% Accepted:** 72 **Admission Plans:** Deferred Admission **Application Deadline:** August 1 **Application Fee:** $0.00 **H.S. Requirements:** High school diploma required; GED accepted **Costs Per Year:** Application fee: $0. State resident tuition: $3210 full-time, $107 per credit hour part-time. Nonresident tuition: $9300 full-time, $310 per credit hour part-time. Mandatory fees: $945 full-time, $31.50 per credit hour part-time. Full-time tuition and fees vary according to course load and program. Part-time tuition and fees vary according to course load and program. College room and board: $4826. Room and board charges vary according to board plan and housing facility. **Scholarships:** Available **Calendar System:** Semester, Summer Session Available **Enrollment:** FT 5,873, PT 2,227, Grad FT 424, Grad PT 794 **Faculty:** FT 299, PT 171 **Student-Faculty Ratio:** 22:1 **Exams:** ACT. ACT essay not being used. **% Receiving Financial Aid:** 57 **% Residing in College-Owned, -Operated, or -Affiliated Housing:** 17 **Library Holdings:** 418,643 **Regional Accreditation:** North Central Association of Colleges and Schools **Credit Hours For Degree:** 124 semester hours, Bachelors **ROTC:** Army **Professional Accreditation:** AOA, ASLHA, ACBSP, CSWE, NASM, NCATE, NLN **Intercol-**

legiate Athletics: Baseball M; Basketball M & W; Football M; Golf M & W; Rock Climbing M & W; Soccer M & W; Softball W; Tennis W

NORTHERN OKLAHOMA COLLEGE
1220 East Grand Ave., PO Box 310
Tonkawa, OK 74653-0310
Tel: (580)628-6200; Free: 800-429-5715
Fax: (580)628-6371
Web Site: http://www.north-ok.edu/
President/CEO: Roger Stacy
Admissions: Sheri Snyder
Type: Two-Year College **Sex:** Coed **Affiliation:** Oklahoma State Regents for Higher Education **Admission Plans:** Open Admission; Early Admission **Application Deadline:** Rolling **Application Fee:** $25.00 **H.S. Requirements:** High school diploma required; GED accepted. For applicants 24 or over: High school diploma or equivalent not required **Scholarships:** Available **Calendar System:** Semester, Summer Session Available **Faculty:** FT 45, PT 35 **Student-Faculty Ratio:** 35:1 **% Residing in College-Owned, -Operated, or -Affiliated Housing:** 20 **Library Holdings:** 34,458 **Regional Accreditation:** North Central Association of Colleges and Schools **Credit Hours For Degree:** 60 credit hours, Associates **Professional Accreditation:** ACBSP, NLN **Intercollegiate Athletics:** Baseball M; Basketball M & W; Soccer M & W; Softball W; Volleyball M & W

NORTHWESTERN OKLAHOMA STATE UNIVERSITY
709 Oklahoma Blvd.
Alva, OK 73717-2799
Tel: (580)327-1700
Admissions: (580)327-8545
Fax: (580)327-1881
E-mail: wmadair@nwosu.edu
Web Site: http://www.nwosu.edu/
President/CEO: Dr. Janet Cunningham
Admissions: Matt Adair
Financial Aid: Calleb N. Mosburg
Type: Comprehensive **Sex:** Coed **Affiliation:** Oklahoma State Regents for Higher Education **Scores:** 42% ACT 18-23; 21% ACT 24-29 **% Accepted:** 100 **Admission Plans:** Early Admission **Application Deadline:** Rolling **Application Fee:** $15.00 **H.S. Requirements:** High school diploma required; GED accepted **Scholarships:** Available **Calendar System:** Semester, Summer Session Available **Enrollment:** FT 1,372, PT 619, Grad FT 69, Grad PT 172 **Faculty:** FT 72, PT 95 **Student-Faculty Ratio:** 16:1 **Exams:** SAT I or ACT. ACT essay not being used. SAT essay not being used. **% Residing in College-Owned, -Operated, or -Affiliated Housing:** 25 **Final Year or Final Semester Residency Requirement:** Yes **Library Holdings:** 266,731 **Regional Accreditation:** North Central Association of Colleges and Schools **Credit Hours For Degree:** 124 semester hours, Bachelors **Professional Accreditation:** NCATE, NLN **Intercollegiate Athletics:** Baseball M; Basketball M & W; Cheerleading M & W; Cross-Country Running M & W; Football M; Golf M & W; Soccer W; Softball W

OKLAHOMA BAPTIST UNIVERSITY
500 West University
Shawnee, OK 74804
Tel: (405)275-2850; Free: 800-654-3285
Admissions: (405)878-2033
Fax: (405)878-2046
E-mail: admissions@mail.okbu.edu
Web Site: http://www.okbu.edu/
President/CEO: Dr. David W. Whitlock
Admissions: Bruce Perkins
Financial Aid: Jonna Raney
Type: Comprehensive **Sex:** Coed **Affiliation:** Southern Baptist **Scores:** 97% SAT V 400+; 100% SAT M 400+; 48% ACT 18-23; 38% ACT 24-29 **% Accepted:** 66 **Admission Plans:** Early Admission; Deferred Admission **Application Deadline:** Rolling **H.S. Requirements:** High school diploma required; GED accepted **Costs Per Year:** One-time mandatory fee: $50. Comprehensive fee: $24,300 includes full-time tuition ($17,220), mandatory fees ($1450), and college room and board ($5630). Full-time tuition and fees vary according to course load. Room and board charges vary according to housing facility. Part-time tuition: $560 per credit hour. Part-time tuition varies according to course load. **Scholarships:** Available **Calendar System:** 4-1-4, Summer Session Available **Enrollment:** FT 1,442, PT 267, Grad FT 48, Grad PT 7 **Faculty:** FT 107, PT 56 **Student-Faculty Ratio:** 11:1 **Exams:** SAT I or ACT. ACT essay not being used. SAT essay not being used. **% Receiving Financial Aid:** 67 **% Residing in College-Owned, -Operated, or -Affiliated Housing:** 80 **Final Year or Final Semester Residency Requirement:** No **Library Holdings:** 230,000 **Regional Accreditation:** North Central Association of Colleges and Schools **Credit Hours For Degree:** 64 semester credit hours, Associates; 128 credit hours, Bachelors **ROTC:** Air Force **Professional Accreditation:** ACBSP, NASM, NCATE, NLN **Intercollegiate Athletics:** Baseball M; Basketball M & W; Cross-Country Running M & W; Golf M & W; Soccer M & W; Softball W; Tennis M & W; Track and Field M & W

OKLAHOMA CHRISTIAN UNIVERSITY
PO Box 11000
Oklahoma City, OK 73136-1100
Tel: (405)425-5000
Admissions: (405)425-5050
Fax: (405)425-5208
E-mail: info@oc.edu
Web Site: http://www.oc.edu/
President/CEO: Dr. Mike O'Neal
Admissions: Risa Forrester
Financial Aid: Clint LaRue
Type: Comprehensive **Sex:** Coed **Affiliation:** Church of Christ **Scores:** 92% SAT V 400+; 94% SAT M 400+; 34% ACT 18-23; 40% ACT 24-29 **% Accepted:** 56 **Admission Plans:** Early Admission; Deferred Admission **Application Deadline:** Rolling **Application Fee:** $25.00 **H.S. Requirements:** High school diploma required; GED accepted **Costs Per Year:** Application fee: $25. Comprehensive fee: $23,306 includes full-time tuition ($15,600), mandatory fees ($1856), and college room and board ($5850). College room only: $2700. Full-time tuition and fees vary according to course load. Room and board charges vary according to board plan and housing facility. Part-time tuition: $650 per credit hour. Part-time mandatory fees: $915 per term. Part-time tuition and fees vary according to course load. **Scholarships:** Available **Calendar System:** Semester, Summer Session Available **Enrollment:** FT 1,865, PT 53, Grad FT 254 **Faculty:** FT 106, PT 68 **Student-Faculty Ratio:** 15:1 **Exams:** SAT I or ACT. **% Receiving Financial Aid:** 65 **% Residing in College-Owned, -Operated, or -Affiliated Housing:** 79 **Library Holdings:** 141,377 **Regional Accreditation:** North Central Association of Colleges and Schools **Credit Hours For Degree:** 126 semester hours, Bachelors **ROTC:** Army, Air Force **Professional Accreditation:** ABET, ACBSP, NASM, NCATE **Intercollegiate Athletics:** Baseball M; Basketball M & W; Cross-Country Running M & W; Golf M; Soccer M & W; Softball W; Tennis M & W; Track and Field M & W

OKLAHOMA CITY COMMUNITY COLLEGE
7777 South May Ave.
Oklahoma City, OK 73159-4419
Tel: (405)682-1611
Admissions: (405)682-7515
E-mail: jhorinek@occc.edu
Web Site: http://www.occc.edu/
President/CEO: Dr. Paul W. Sechrist
Admissions: Jon Horinek
Financial Aid: Meghan Morgan
Type: Two-Year College **Sex:** Coed **Affiliation:** Oklahoma State Regents for Higher Education **Scores:** 54% ACT 18-23; 16% ACT 24-29 **Admission Plans:** Open Admission **Application Deadline:** Rolling **Application Fee:** $25.00 **H.S. Requirements:** High school diploma or equivalent not required. For applicants whose HS class has not graduated, nursing, occupational therapy, physical therapy programs: High school diploma required; GED accepted. **Costs Per Year:** Application fee: $25. One-time mandatory fee: $25. State resident tuition: $1454 full-time, $60.55 per credit hour part-time. Nonresident tuition: $4814 full-time, $200.55 per credit hour part-time. Mandatory fees: $562 full-time, $23.45 per credit hour part-time. Full-time tuition and fees vary according to class time and course level. Part-time tuition and fees vary according to class time and course level. **Scholarships:** Available **Calendar System:** Semester, Summer Session Available **Enrollment:** FT 5,705, PT 8,454 **Faculty:** FT 147, PT 393 **Student-Faculty Ratio:** 26:1 **Exams:** Other. **Final Year or Final Semester Residency Requirement:** No **Library Holdings:** 93,808 **Regional Accreditation:** North Central Association of Colleges and Schools **Credit Hours For Degree:** 61 credit hours, Associates **Professional Accreditation:** AOTA, APTA, CARC, JRCEMT, NLN

OKLAHOMA CITY UNIVERSITY
2501 North Blackwelder
Oklahoma City, OK 73106-1402
Tel: (405)208-5000; Free: 800-633-7242
Admissions: (405)208-5340
E-mail: mlockhart@okcu.edu
Web Site: http://www.okcu.edu/
President/CEO: Dr. Thomas J. McDaniel
Admissions: Michelle Lockhart
Financial Aid: Denise Flis
Type: Comprehensive **Sex:** Coed **Affiliation:** United Methodist **Scores:** 100% SAT V 400+; 100% SAT M 400+; 30% ACT 18-23; 57% ACT 24-29 **% Accepted:** 79 **Admission Plans:** Deferred Admission **Application Deadline:** August 21 **Application Fee:** $40.00 **H.S. Requirements:** High school diploma required; GED accepted **Costs Per Year:** Application fee: $40. Comprehensive fee: $30,600 includes full-time tuition ($22,250) and college room and board ($8350). College room only: $4650. Full-time tuition varies according to program. Room and board charges vary according to board plan and housing facility. Part-time tuition: $760 per credit hour. Part-time mandatory fees: $60. Part-time tuition and fees vary according to program. **Scholarships:** Available **Calendar System:** Semester, Summer Session Available **Enrollment:** FT 1,886, PT 397, Grad FT 1,135, Grad PT 392 **Faculty:** FT 198, PT 141 **Student-Faculty Ratio:** 11:1 **Exams:** SAT I or ACT. ACT essay not being used. **% Receiving Financial Aid:** 56 **% Residing in College-Owned, -Operated, or -Affiliated Housing:** 69 **Final Year or Final Semester Residency Requirement:** Yes **Library Holdings:** 520,953 **Regional Accreditation:** North Central Association of Colleges and Schools **Credit Hours For Degree:** 124 semester hours, Bachelors **ROTC:** Army, Air Force **Professional Accreditation:** ABA, AALS, ACBSP, MACTE, NASM, NLN **Intercollegiate Athletics:** Baseball M; Basketball M & W; Cheerleading M & W; Crew M & W; Golf M & W; Soccer M & W; Softball W; Track and Field M & W; Wrestling M & W

OKLAHOMA PANHANDLE STATE UNIVERSITY
PO Box 430
Goodwell, OK 73939-0430
Tel: (580)349-2611; Free: 800-664-6778
Admissions: (580)349-1376
Fax: (580)349-2302
E-mail: opsu@opsu.edu
Web Site: http://www.opsu.edu/
President/CEO: David Bryant
Admissions: Bobby Jenkins
Financial Aid: Mary Ellen Riley
Type: Four-Year College **Sex:** Coed **Affiliation:** Oklahoma State Regents for Higher Education **Scores:** 56% SAT V 400+; 78% SAT M 400+; 49% ACT 18-23; 13% ACT 24-29 **% Accepted:** 100 **Application Deadline:** Rolling **Application Fee:** $0.00 **H.S. Requirements:** High school diploma required; GED accepted **Costs Per Year:** Application fee: $0. State resident tuition: $2738 full-time, $91.25 per credit hour part-time. Nonresident tuition: $8077 full-time, $269.25 per credit hour part-time. Mandatory fees: $1504 full-time. Full-time tuition and fees vary according to course level, program, and student level. Part-time tuition varies according to course level and student level. College room and board: $3320. College room only: $900. Room and board charges vary according to board plan and housing facility. Tuition guaranteed not to increase for student's term of enrollment. **Scholarships:** Available **Calendar System:** Semester, Summer Session Available **Enrollment:** FT 1,041, PT 227 **Faculty:** FT 67, PT 35 **Student-Faculty Ratio:** 12:1 **Exams:** SAT I or ACT. **% Receiving Financial Aid:** 96 **% Residing in College-Owned, -Operated, or -Affiliated Housing:** 46 **Regional Accreditation:** North Central Association of Colleges and Schools **Credit Hours For Degree:** 64 credit hours, Associates; 124 credit hours, Bachelors **Professional Accreditation:** NCATE, NLN **Intercollegiate Athletics:** Baseball M; Basketball M & W; Cheerleading W; Cross-Country Running M & W; Equestrian Sports W; Football M; Golf M & W; Soccer M & W; Softball W; Volleyball W

OKLAHOMA STATE UNIVERSITY
Stillwater, OK 74078
Tel: (405)744-5000; Free: 800-852-1255
Admissions: (405)744-3087
Fax: (405)744-5285
E-mail: christine.crenshaw@okstate.edu
Web Site: http://www.okstate.edu/
President/CEO: Burns Hargis
Admissions: Christine Crenshaw
Type: University **Sex:** Coed **Affiliation:** Oklahoma State University **Scores:** 95.64% SAT V 400+; 96.59% SAT M 400+; 37.47% ACT 18-23; 45.41% ACT 24-29 **% Accepted:** 86 **Admission Plans:** Deferred Admission **Application Deadline:** Rolling **Application Fee:** $40.00 **H.S. Requirements:** High school diploma required; GED accepted **Costs Per Year:** Application fee: $40. One-time mandatory fee: $95. State resident tuition: $3941 full-time, $131.35 per credit hour part-time. Nonresident tuition: $14,295 full-time, $476.50 per credit hour part-time. Mandatory fees: $2261 full-time, $75.35 per credit hour part-time. Full-time tuition and fees vary according to program and student level. Part-time tuition and fees vary according to program and student level. College room and board: $6402. College room only: $3402. Room and board charges vary according to board plan and housing facility. **Scholarships:** Available **Calendar System:** Semester, Summer Session Available **Enrollment:** FT 15,296, PT 2,553, Grad FT 2,019, Grad PT 2,977 **Faculty:** FT 999, PT 274 **Student-Faculty Ratio:** 18:1 **Exams:** SAT I or ACT. ACT essay not being used. SAT essay not being used. **% Receiving Financial Aid:** 50 **% Residing in College-Owned, -Operated, or -Affiliated Housing:** 39 **Final Year or Final Semester Residency Requirement:** No **Regional Accreditation:** North Central Association of Colleges and Schools **Credit Hours For Degree:** 120 credit hours, Bachelors **ROTC:** Army, Air Force **Professional Accreditation:** AACSB, ABET, ACEJMC, AAMFT, ADtA, APA, ASLA, ASLHA, AVMA, FIDER, JRCEPAT, NAAB, NASM, NAST, NCATE, NRPA, SAF

OKLAHOMA STATE UNIVERSITY INSTITUTE OF TECHNOLOGY
1801 East Fourth St.
Okmulgee, OK 74447-3901
Tel: (918)293-4678; Free: 800-722-4471
E-mail: mary.r.graves@okstate.edu
Web Site: http://www.osuit.edu/
President/CEO: Robert Klabenes
Admissions: Mary Graves
Type: Two-Year College **Sex:** Coed **Affiliation:** Oklahoma State University **Admission Plans:** Open Admission; Deferred Admission **Application Deadline:** Rolling **Application Fee:** $15.00 **H.S. Requirements:** High school diploma or equivalent not required **Costs Per Year:** Application fee: $15. One-time mandatory fee: $50. State resident tuition: $5940 full-time. Nonresident tuition: $13,905 full-time. Full-time tuition varies according to course load, program, and reciprocity agreements. College room and board: $7533. College room only: $4770. Room and board charges vary according to housing facility. Tuition guaranteed not to increase for student's term of enrollment. **Scholarships:** Available **Calendar System:** Trimester, Summer Session Available **Enrollment:** FT 1,717, PT 612 **Faculty:** FT 129 **% Residing in College-Owned, -Operated, or -Affiliated Housing:** 25 **Library Holdings:** 9,965 **Regional Accreditation:** North Central Association of Colleges and Schools **Credit Hours For Degree:** 84 credit hours, Associates

OKLAHOMA STATE UNIVERSITY, OKLAHOMA CITY
900 North Portland
Oklahoma City, OK 73107-6120
Tel: (405)947-4421
Admissions: (405)945-9152
Fax: (405)945-3277
E-mail: wilkylw@osuokc.edu
Web Site: http://www.osuokc.edu/
President/CEO: Dr. Jerry Carroll
Admissions: Kyle Williams
Financial Aid: Joyce Murphy
Type: Two-Year College **Sex:** Coed **Affiliation:** Oklahoma State University **% Accepted:** 100 **Admission Plans:** Open Admission; Early Admission **Application Deadline:** Rolling **Application Fee:** $0.00 **H.S. Requirements:** High school diploma required; GED accepted **Costs Per Year:** Application fee: $0. State resident tuition: $2889 full-time, $96.30 per credit hour part-time. Nonresident tuition: $7749 full-time, $258.30 per credit hour part-time. Mandatory fees: $30 full-time, $10.50 per credit hour part-time. Full-time tuition and fees vary according to course level, degree level, and program. Part-time tuition and fees vary according to course level, degree level, and program. Tuition guaranteed not to increase for student's term of enrollment. **Scholarships:** Available **Calendar System:** Semester, Summer Session Available **Faculty:** FT 81, PT 259 **Student-Faculty Ratio:** 20:1 **Library Holdings:** 11,973 **Regional Accreditation:** North Central Association of

Colleges and Schools **Credit Hours For Degree:** 60 semester hours, Associates **Professional Accreditation:** NLN

OKLAHOMA TECHNICAL COLLEGE
4444 South Sheridan
Tulsa, OK 74145
Tel: (918)895-7500
Admissions: (918)610-0027
E-mail: tknox@communitycarecollege.com
Web Site: http://www.oklahomatechnicalcollege.com/
President/CEO: Dr. Kevin Kirk
Admissions: Teresa Knox
Type: Two-Year College **Sex:** Coed **Affiliation:** Dental Directions, Inc. **Admission Plans:** Open Admission **Application Deadline:** Rolling **H.S. Requirements:** High school diploma required; GED accepted **Costs Per Year:** Tuition: $14,000 full-time. Full-time tuition varies according to program. **Faculty:** FT 6 **Student-Faculty Ratio:** 13:1

OKLAHOMA WESLEYAN UNIVERSITY
2201 Silver Lake Rd.
Bartlesville, OK 74006-6299
Tel: (918)335-6200
Admissions: (866)222-8226
Fax: (918)335-6229
E-mail: admissions@okwu.edu
Web Site: http://www.okwu.edu/
President/CEO: Dr. Everett Piper
Admissions: Jennifer Weaver
Financial Aid: Lee Kanakis
Type: Comprehensive **Sex:** Coed **Affiliation:** Wesleyan Church **Scores:** 82% SAT V 400+; 58% ACT 18-23; 31% ACT 24-29 **% Accepted:** 14 **Admission Plans:** Open Admission **Application Deadline:** Rolling **Application Fee:** $25.00 **H.S. Requirements:** High school diploma required; GED accepted **Costs Per Year:** Application fee: $25. Comprehensive fee: $24,258 includes full-time tuition ($16,870), mandatory fees ($1100), and college room and board ($6288). College room only: $3288. Full-time tuition and fees vary according to course load. Room and board charges vary according to board plan and housing facility. Part-time tuition: $700 per credit hour. Part-time mandatory fees: $55 per credit hour. **Scholarships:** Available **Calendar System:** Semester, Summer Session Available **Enrollment:** FT 456, PT 585, Grad PT 59 **Faculty:** FT 29, PT 39 **Student-Faculty Ratio:** 14:1 **Exams:** SAT I or ACT. **% Receiving Financial Aid:** 77 **% Residing in College-Owned, -Operated, or -Affiliated Housing:** 27 **Final Year or Final Semester Residency Requirement:** Yes **Library Holdings:** 83,859 **Regional Accreditation:** North Central Association of Colleges and Schools **Credit Hours For Degree:** 64 semester hours, Associates; 126 semester hours, Bachelors **Professional Accreditation:** AACN, NCATE **Intercollegiate Athletics:** Baseball M; Basketball M & W; Cross-Country Running M & W; Golf M; Soccer M & W; Tennis M & W; Track and Field M & W; Volleyball W

ORAL ROBERTS UNIVERSITY
7777 South Lewis Ave.
Tulsa, OK 74171
Tel: (918)495-6161; Free: 800-678-8876
Admissions: (333)495-6161
Fax: (918)495-6222
E-mail: admissions@oru.edu
Web Site: http://www.oru.edu/
President/CEO: Mark Rutland
Type: Comprehensive **Sex:** Coed **Affiliation:** interdenominational **Scores:** 94.8% SAT V 400+; 90.48% SAT M 400+; 50.91% ACT 18-23; 33.64% ACT 24-29 **% Accepted:** 74 **Admission Plans:** Early Action; Deferred Admission **Application Deadline:** Rolling **Application Fee:** $35.00 **H.S. Requirements:** High school diploma required; GED accepted **Costs Per Year:** Application fee: $35. Comprehensive fee: $26,832 includes full-time tuition ($18,476), mandatory fees ($440), and college room and board ($7916). College room only: $3860. Full-time tuition and fees vary according to degree level. Room and board charges vary according to board plan and housing facility. Part-time tuition: $772 per credit hour. Part-time tuition varies according to degree level. **Scholarships:** Available **Calendar System:** Semester, Summer Session Available **Enrollment:** FT 2,317, PT 241, Grad FT 150, Grad PT 215 **Faculty:** FT 186, PT 105 **Student-Faculty Ratio:** 12:1 **Exams:** SAT I or ACT. ACT essay not being used. SAT essay not being used. **% Receiving Financial Aid:** 69 **% Residing in College-Owned, -Operated, or -Affiliated Housing:** 75 **Regional Accreditation:** North Central Association of Colleges and Schools **Credit Hours For Degree:** 128 credit hours, Bachelors **ROTC:** Air Force **Professional Accreditation:** ABET, ACBSP, ATS, CSWE, NASM, NCATE, NLN **Intercollegiate Athletics:** Baseball M; Basketball M & W; Cross-Country Running M & W; Golf M & W; Soccer M & W; Tennis M & W; Track and Field M & W; Volleyball W; Wrestling M

PLATT COLLEGE (MOORE)
201 North Eastern Ave.
Moore, OK 73160
Tel: (405)912-3260
Fax: (405)912-4360
Web Site: http://plattcollege.org/campuses/moore-campus/
President/CEO: Michael A. Pugliese
Type: Two-Year College **Sex:** Coed **% Accepted:** 100 **Application Fee:** $100.00 **Professional Accreditation:** ACCSCT

PLATT COLLEGE (OKLAHOMA CITY)
309 South Ann Arbor Ave.
Oklahoma City, OK 73128
Tel: (405)946-7799
Fax: (405)943-2150
E-mail: janen@plattcollege.org
Web Site: http://www.plattcollege.org/
President/CEO: Jane Nowlin
Admissions: Jane Nowlin
Type: Two-Year College **Sex:** Coed **Admission Plans:** Open Admission **Application Fee:** $100.00 **Calendar System:** Continuous **Student-Faculty Ratio:** 16:1 **Professional Accreditation:** ACCSCT

PLATT COLLEGE (TULSA)
3801 South Sheridan Rd.
Tulsa, OK 74145-1111
Tel: (918)663-9000
Fax: (918)622-1240
E-mail: susanr@plattcollege.org
Web Site: http://www.plattcollege.org/
President/CEO: Mike Pugliese
Admissions: Susan Rone
Type: Two-Year College **Sex:** Coed **Application Fee:** $100.00 **Calendar System:** Continuous **Professional Accreditation:** ACCSCT

REDLANDS COMMUNITY COLLEGE
1300 South Country Club Rd.
El Reno, OK 73036-5304
Tel: (405)262-2552; Free: (866)415-6367
E-mail: hobsont@redlandscc.edu
Web Site: http://www.redlandscc.edu/
President/CEO: Dr. Larry F. Devane
Admissions: Tricia Hobson
Type: Two-Year College **Sex:** Coed **Affiliation:** Oklahoma State Regents for Higher Education **Admission Plans:** Open Admission; Early Admission; Deferred Admission **Application Deadline:** Rolling **Application Fee:** $25.00 **H.S. Requirements:** High school diploma required; GED accepted **Costs Per Year:** Application fee: $25. State resident tuition: $2903 full-time, $96.75 per credit hour part-time. Nonresident tuition: $5153 full-time, $171.75 per credit hour part-time. Mandatory fees: $600 full-time, $20 per credit hour part-time. Full-time tuition and fees vary according to location, program, and reciprocity agreements. Part-time tuition and fees vary according to location, program, and reciprocity agreements. College room only: $4050. Room charges vary according to housing facility. **Scholarships:** Available **Calendar System:** Semester, Summer Session Available **Enrollment:** FT 881, PT 1,582 **Faculty:** FT 35, PT 75 **Student-Faculty Ratio:** 18:1 **Exams:** ACT. **Library Holdings:** 14,810 **Regional Accreditation:** North Central Association of Colleges and Schools **Credit Hours For Degree:** 64 semester hours, Associates **Professional Accreditation:** NLN **Intercollegiate Athletics:** Baseball M; Basketball M & W; Gymnastics W; Volleyball W

ROGERS STATE UNIVERSITY
1701 West Will Rogers Blvd.
Claremore, OK 74017-3252
Tel: (918)343-7777; Free: 800-256-7511

Admissions: (918)343-7545
Fax: (918)343-7898
E-mail: info@rsu.edu
Web Site: http://www.rsu.edu/
President/CEO: Dr. Larry Rice
Admissions: Julie Rampey
Financial Aid: David Barron
Type: Four-Year College **Sex:** Coed **Affiliation:** Oklahoma State Regents for Higher Education **Scores:** 57% ACT 18-23; 17% ACT 24-29 **% Accepted:** 58 **Admission Plans:** Open Admission **Application Deadline:** Rolling **Application Fee:** $0.00 **H.S. Requirements:** High school diploma required; GED accepted **Costs Per Year:** Application fee: $0. State resident tuition: $2729 full-time, $90.95 per credit hour part-time. Nonresident tuition: $8186 full-time, $272.85 per credit hour part-time. Mandatory fees: $1548 full-time, $51 per credit hour part-time, $15 per term part-time. Full-time tuition and fees vary according to course load, location, and program. Part-time tuition and fees vary according to course load, location, and program. College room only: $4505. Room charges vary according to housing facility. **Scholarships:** Available **Calendar System:** Semester, Summer Session Available **Enrollment:** FT 2,613, PT 1,541 **Faculty:** FT 104, PT 141 **Student-Faculty Ratio:** 21:1 **Exams:** ACT, Other, SAT I or ACT. **% Receiving Financial Aid:** 66 **% Residing in College-Owned, -Operated, or -Affiliated Housing:** 6 **Final Year or Final Semester Residency Requirement:** No **Library Holdings:** 77,650 **Regional Accreditation:** North Central Association of Colleges and Schools **Credit Hours For Degree:** 60 credit hours, Associates; 120 credit hours, Bachelors **Professional Accreditation:** NLN **Intercollegiate Athletics:** Baseball M; Basketball M & W; Cheerleading M & W; Golf M & W; Soccer M & W; Softball W

ROSE STATE COLLEGE
6420 Southeast 15th St.
Midwest City, OK 73110-2799
Tel: (405)733-7673; Free: (866)621-0987
Admissions: (405)733-7311
Fax: (405)733-7399
E-mail: maitson@ms.rose.cc.ok.us
Web Site: http://www.rose.edu/
President/CEO: Terry D. Britton
Admissions: Mechelle Aitson-Roessler
Type: Two-Year College **Sex:** Coed **Affiliation:** Oklahoma State Regents for Higher Education **Admission Plans:** Open Admission; Early Admission; Deferred Admission **Application Deadline:** Rolling **Application Fee:** $15.00 **H.S. Requirements:** High school diploma required; GED accepted **Scholarships:** Available **Calendar System:** Semester, Summer Session Available **Faculty:** FT 143, PT 269 **Library Holdings:** 90,000 **Regional Accreditation:** North Central Association of Colleges and Schools **Credit Hours For Degree:** 62 credit hours, Associates **ROTC:** Army, Air Force **Professional Accreditation:** ADA, AHIMA, CARC, JRCERT, NAACLS, NLN **Intercollegiate Athletics:** Baseball M; Basketball M & W; Soccer W

ST. GREGORY'S UNIVERSITY
1900 West MacArthur Dr.
Shawnee, OK 74804-2499
Tel: (405)878-5100; Free: 888-STGREGS
Admissions: (405)878-5447
Fax: (405)878-5198
E-mail: admissions@stgregorys.edu
Web Site: http://www.stgregorys.edu/
President/CEO: Dr. David A. Wagie
Financial Aid: Matt McCoin
Type: Comprehensive **Sex:** Coed **Affiliation:** Roman Catholic **Scores:** 80% SAT V 400+; 50% SAT M 400+; 63% ACT 18-23; 11% ACT 24-29 **% Accepted:** 97 **Admission Plans:** Deferred Admission **Application Deadline:** Rolling **Application Fee:** $25.00 **H.S. Requirements:** High school diploma required; GED accepted **Costs Per Year:** Application fee: $25. Comprehensive fee: $22,490 includes full-time tuition ($15,394), mandatory fees ($900), and college room and board ($6196). College room only: $3400. Room and board charges vary according to board plan. Part-time tuition: $515 per hour. Part-time mandatory fees: $37.50 per hour. Part-time tuition and fees vary according to course load and reciprocity agreements. **Scholarships:** Available **Calendar System:** Semester, Summer Session Available **Enrollment:** FT 293, PT 406 **Faculty:** FT 32, PT 64 **Student-Faculty Ratio:** 9:1 **Exams:** SAT I or ACT. **% Receiving Financial Aid:** 72 **% Residing in College-Owned, -Operated, or -Affiliated Housing:** 65 **Library Holdings:** 85,622 **Regional Accreditation:** North Central Association of Colleges and Schools **Credit Hours For Degree:** 64 credit hours, Associates; 128 credit hours, Bachelors **ROTC:** Air Force **Intercollegiate Athletics:** Baseball M; Basketball M & W; Cheerleading M & W; Soccer M & W; Softball W; Volleyball W

SEMINOLE STATE COLLEGE
PO Box 351
Seminole, OK 74818-0351
Tel: (405)382-9950
E-mail: lindley_c@ssc.cc.ok.us
Web Site: http://www.ssc.cc.ok.us/
President/CEO: Dr. Jim Utterback
Admissions: Chris Lindley
Type: Two-Year College **Sex:** Coed **Affiliation:** Oklahoma State Regents for Higher Education **Scores:** 50% ACT 18-23; 6% ACT 24-29 **Admission Plans:** Open Admission; Early Admission; Deferred Admission **Application Deadline:** Rolling **Application Fee:** $15.00 **H.S. Requirements:** High school diploma or equivalent not required. For applicants under 18, nursing, medical laboratory technology programs: High school diploma required; GED accepted **Scholarships:** Available **Calendar System:** Semester, Summer Session Available **Faculty:** FT 46, PT 55 **Student-Faculty Ratio:** 25:1 **Exams:** ACT. **% Residing in College-Owned, -Operated, or -Affiliated Housing:** 8 **Library Holdings:** 27,507 **Regional Accreditation:** North Central Association of Colleges and Schools **Credit Hours For Degree:** 62 credit hours, Associates **Professional Accreditation:** NAACLS, NLN **Intercollegiate Athletics:** Baseball M; Basketball M & W; Golf M & W; Softball W; Volleyball W

SOUTHEASTERN OKLAHOMA STATE UNIVERSITY
1405 North 4th Ave.
Durant, OK 74701-0609
Tel: (580)745-2000; Free: 800-435-1327
Admissions: (580)745-2060
Fax: (580)745-7490
E-mail: kluke@se.edu
Web Site: http://www.se.edu/
President/CEO: Dr. Larry Minks
Admissions: Kristie Luke
Financial Aid: Sherry Hudson
Type: Comprehensive **Sex:** Coed **Affiliation:** Oklahoma State Regents for Higher Education **Scores:** 64.3% ACT 18-23; 14.6% ACT 24-29 **Admission Plans:** Open Admission **Application Deadline:** Rolling **Application Fee:** $20.00 **H.S. Requirements:** High school diploma required; GED accepted **Costs Per Year:** Application fee: $20. State resident tuition: $3639 full-time, $121.30 per credit hour part-time. Nonresident tuition: $10,009 full-time, $333.65 per credit hour part-time. Mandatory fees: $677 full-time, $22.55 per credit hour part-time. Full-time tuition and fees vary according to course level. Part-time tuition and fees vary according to course level and course load. College room and board: $4290. College room only: $1850. Room and board charges vary according to board plan and housing facility. **Scholarships:** Available **Calendar System:** Semester, Summer Session Available **Enrollment:** FT 2,954, PT 819, Grad FT 156, Grad PT 299 **Faculty:** FT 143, PT 104 **Student-Faculty Ratio:** 18:1 **Exams:** SAT I or ACT. **% Receiving Financial Aid:** 65 **% Residing in College-Owned, -Operated, or -Affiliated Housing:** 18 **Library Holdings:** 308,095 **Regional Accreditation:** North Central Association of Colleges and Schools **Credit Hours For Degree:** 124 credit hours, Bachelors **Professional Accreditation:** AACSB, ACBSP, NASM, NCATE **Intercollegiate Athletics:** Baseball M; Basketball M & W; Cross-Country Running W; Football M; Softball W; Tennis M & W; Volleyball W

SOUTHERN NAZARENE UNIVERSITY
6729 Northwest 39th Expressway
Bethany, OK 73008
Tel: (405)789-6400; Free: 800-648-9899
Admissions: (405)491-6324
Fax: (405)491-6381
E-mail: admiss@snu.edu
Web Site: http://www.snu.edu/
President/CEO: Dr. Loren P. Gresham
Admissions: Warren W. Rogers, III
Financial Aid: Diana Lee
Type: Comprehensive **Sex:** Coed **Affiliation:** Nazarene **Scores:** 40% ACT

18-23; 37% ACT 24-29 **% Accepted:** 100 **Admission Plans:** Open Admission; Deferred Admission **Application Deadline:** August 15 **Application Fee:** $35.00 **H.S. Requirements:** High school diploma required; GED accepted **Costs Per Year:** Application fee: $35. Comprehensive fee: $24,154 includes full-time tuition ($17,040), mandatory fees ($624), and college room and board ($6490). College room only: $3200. Part-time tuition: $568 per credit hour. Part-time mandatory fees: $23 per credit hour. **Scholarships:** Available **Calendar System:** Semester, Summer Session Available **Enrollment:** FT 1,567, PT 61 **Faculty:** FT 74, PT 124 **Student-Faculty Ratio:** 15:1 **Exams:** ACT, SAT I or ACT. **% Receiving Financial Aid:** 80 **% Residing in College-Owned, -Operated, or -Affiliated Housing:** 67 **Library Holdings:** 95,535 **Regional Accreditation:** North Central Association of Colleges and Schools **Credit Hours For Degree:** 62 credit hours, Associates; 124 credit hours, Bachelors **ROTC:** Army, Air Force **Professional Accreditation:** AACN, ACBSP, NASM, NCATE **Intercollegiate Athletics:** Baseball M; Basketball M & W; Cheerleading M & W; Cross-Country Running M & W; Football M; Golf M & W; Soccer M & W; Softball W; Tennis M & W; Track and Field M & W; Volleyball W

SOUTHWESTERN CHRISTIAN UNIVERSITY

PO Box 340
Bethany, OK 73008-0340
Tel: (405)789-7661
E-mail: admissions@swcu.edu
Web Site: http://www.swcu.edu/
President/CEO: J. Dwight Burchett
Admissions: Jason Vaughn
Financial Aid: Billie Stewart

Type: Comprehensive **Sex:** Coed **Affiliation:** Pentecostal Holiness Church **Admission Plans:** Early Admission; Deferred Admission **Application Deadline:** Rolling **H.S. Requirements:** High school diploma required; GED accepted **Scholarships:** Available **Calendar System:** Semester, Summer Session Available **Exams:** ACT. **% Receiving Financial Aid:** 89 **Library Holdings:** 38,900 **Regional Accreditation:** North Central Association of Colleges and Schools **Credit Hours For Degree:** 64 credits, Associates; 128 credits, Bachelors **Intercollegiate Athletics:** Basketball M; Golf M; Soccer M; Track and Field M & W; Volleyball W

SOUTHWESTERN OKLAHOMA STATE UNIVERSITY

100 Campus Dr.
Weatherford, OK 73096-3098
Tel: (580)772-6611
Fax: (580)774-3795
E-mail: ropers@swosu.edu
Web Site: http://www.swosu.edu/
President/CEO: John M. Hays
Admissions: Connie Phillips
Financial Aid: Jerome Wichert

Type: Comprehensive **Sex:** Coed **Affiliation:** Southwestern Oklahoma State University **Scores:** 53% ACT 18-23; 23% ACT 24-29 **% Accepted:** 92 **Admission Plans:** Preferred Admission; Deferred Admission **Application Deadline:** Rolling **Application Fee:** $15.00 **H.S. Requirements:** High school diploma required; GED accepted **Scholarships:** Available **Calendar System:** Semester, Summer Session Available **Enrollment:** FT 3,635, PT 703, Grad FT 464, Grad PT 244 **Faculty:** FT 215, PT 15 **Student-Faculty Ratio:** 20:1 **Exams:** SAT I or ACT. ACT essay not being used. **% Receiving Financial Aid:** 61 **% Residing in College-Owned, -Operated, or -Affiliated Housing:** 25 **Regional Accreditation:** North Central Association of Colleges and Schools **Credit Hours For Degree:** 124 credit hours, Bachelors **Professional Accreditation:** ABET, ACPhE, AHIMA, APTA, ACBSP, CSWE, NASM, NCATE, NLN **Intercollegiate Athletics:** Baseball M; Basketball M & W; Cheerleading M & W; Cross-Country Running W; Equestrian Sports M & W; Football M; Golf M & W; Soccer W; Softball W

SOUTHWESTERN OKLAHOMA STATE UNIVERSITY AT SAYRE

409 East Mississippi St.
Sayre, OK 73662-1236
Tel: (580)928-5533
E-mail: kim.seymour@swosu.edu
Web Site: http://www.swosu.edu/sayre/
President/CEO: John Hays
Admissions: Kim Seymour

Type: Two-Year College **Sex:** Coed **Affiliation:** Southwestern Oklahoma State University **Admission Plans:** Open Admission **Application Deadline:** Rolling **Application Fee:** $15.00 **H.S. Requirements:** High school diploma required; GED accepted. For applicants 18 or over: High school diploma or equivalent not required **Scholarships:** Available **Calendar System:** Semester, Summer Session Available **Enrollment:** FT 237, PT 288 **Faculty:** FT 14 **Student-Faculty Ratio:** 18:1 **Exams:** ACT. **Library Holdings:** 9,975 **Regional Accreditation:** North Central Association of Colleges and Schools **Credit Hours For Degree:** 64 credit hours, Associates **Professional Accreditation:** ABHES, AOTA, JRCERT

SPARTAN COLLEGE OF AERONAUTICS AND TECHNOLOGY

8820 East Pine St., PO Box 582833
Tulsa, OK 74158-2833
Tel: (918)836-6886; Free: 800-331--124
Web Site: http://www.spartan.edu/
President/CEO: Jeremy Gibson
Admissions: Mark Fowler

Type: Two-Year College **Sex:** Men **Application Deadline:** Rolling **Application Fee:** $100.00 **H.S. Requirements:** High school diploma required; GED accepted **Scholarships:** Available **Calendar System:** Miscellaneous, Summer Session Not available **Enrollment:** FT 1,438 **Student-Faculty Ratio:** 14:1 **Credit Hours For Degree:** 42 credit hours, Associates **Professional Accreditation:** ACCSCT

TULSA COMMUNITY COLLEGE

6111 East Skelly Dr.
Tulsa, OK 74135-6198
Tel: (918)595-7000
Fax: (918)595-7910
E-mail: lbrewer@tulsacc.edu
Web Site: http://www.tulsacc.edu/
President/CEO: Tom McKeon
Admissions: Leanne Brewer

Type: Two-Year College **Sex:** Coed **Affiliation:** Oklahoma State Regents for Higher Education **Scores:** 53.3% ACT 18-23; 15.3% ACT 24-29 **% Accepted:** 100 **Admission Plans:** Open Admission; Early Admission **Application Deadline:** Rolling **Application Fee:** $20.00 **H.S. Requirements:** High school diploma required; GED accepted. For adult students: High school diploma or equivalent not required **Scholarships:** Available **Calendar System:** Semester, Summer Session Available **Enrollment:** FT 5,947, PT 10,685 **Faculty:** FT 291, PT 710 **Student-Faculty Ratio:** 20:1 **Library Holdings:** 124,000 **Regional Accreditation:** North Central Association of Colleges and Schools **Credit Hours For Degree:** 60 credit hours, Associates **Professional Accreditation:** AAMAE, ADA, AHIMA, AOTA, APTA, CARC, JRCERT, NAACLS, NLN

TULSA WELDING SCHOOL

2545 East 11th St.
Tulsa, OK 74104-3909
Tel: (918)587-6789; Free: 800-WELD-PRO
Fax: (918)295-6821
E-mail: dburke@twsweld.com
Web Site: http://www.weldingschool.com/
President/CEO: Debbie Burke
Admissions: Debbie Renee Burke

Type: Two-Year College **Sex:** Coed **Affiliation:** Tulsa Welding School, Jacksonville Branch **H.S. Requirements:** High school diploma required; GED accepted **Calendar System:** Continuous **Enrollment:** FT 604 **Faculty:** FT 17, PT 0 **Student-Faculty Ratio:** 18:1 **Library Holdings:** 403 **Credit Hours For Degree:** 62 credits, Associates **Professional Accreditation:** ACCSCT

UNIVERSITY OF CENTRAL OKLAHOMA

100 North University Dr.
Edmond, OK 73034-5209
Tel: (405)974-2000; Free: 800-254-4215
Admissions: (405)974-2338
Fax: (405)974-4964
E-mail: admituco@uco.edu
Web Site: http://www.uco.edu/
President/CEO: Dr. W. Roger Webb
Admissions: Linda Lofton
Financial Aid: Becky Garrett

Type: Comprehensive **Sex:** Coed **Affiliation:** Oklahoma State Regents for Higher Education **Scores:** 62.71% ACT 18-23; 22.45% ACT 24-29 **% Ac-**

cepted: 75 **Admission Plans:** Deferred Admission **Application Deadline:** Rolling **Application Fee:** $25.00 **H.S. Requirements:** High school diploma required; GED accepted **Costs Per Year:** Application fee: $25. State resident tuition: $3681 full-time, $122.70 per credit hour part-time. Nonresident tuition: $10,110 full-time, $337 per credit hour part-time. Mandatory fees: $542 full-time, $18.50 per credit hour part-time. Full-time tuition and fees vary according to course load, degree level, and program. Part-time tuition and fees vary according to course load, degree level, and program. College room and board: $7776. College room only: $4716. Room and board charges vary according to board plan and housing facility. Tuition guaranteed not to increase for student's term of enrollment. **Scholarships:** Available **Calendar System:** Semester, Summer Session Available **Enrollment:** FT 9,875, PT 4,538, Grad FT 639, Grad PT 1,040 **Faculty:** FT 449, PT 411 **Student-Faculty Ratio:** 19:1 **Exams:** ACT, SAT I or ACT, SAT I and SAT II or ACT, SAT I. ACT essay not being used. SAT essay not being used. **% Receiving Financial Aid:** 49 **% Residing in College-Owned, -Operated, or -Affiliated Housing:** 11 **Regional Accreditation:** North Central Association of Colleges and Schools **Credit Hours For Degree:** 124 credit hours, Bachelors **ROTC:** Army **Professional Accreditation:** ABFSE, ADtA, ASLHA, ACBSP, FIDER, NASM, NCATE, NLN **Intercollegiate Athletics:** Baseball M; Basketball M & W; Cross-Country Running M & W; Football M; Golf M & W; Soccer W; Softball W; Tennis M & W; Volleyball W; Wrestling M

UNIVERSITY OF OKLAHOMA
660 Parrington Oval
Norman, OK 73019-0390
Tel: (405)325-0311; Free: 800-234-6868
Admissions: (405)325-2151
Fax: (405)325-7478
E-mail: ou-pss@ou.edu
Web Site: http://www.ou.edu/
President/CEO: David L. Boren
Admissions: Craig Hayes
Type: University **Sex:** Coed **Scores:** 98.6% SAT V 400+; 99.26% SAT M 400+; 25.47% ACT 18-23; 44.29% ACT 24-29 **% Accepted:** 93 **Application Deadline:** April 1 **Application Fee:** $40.00 **H.S. Requirements:** High school diploma required; GED accepted **Costs Per Year:** Application fee: $40. State resident tuition: $2830 full-time, $117.90 per credit hour part-time. Nonresident tuition: $10,814 full-time, $450.60 per credit hour part-time. Mandatory fees: $2415 full-time, $90.10 per credit hour part-time, $126.50 per term part-time. Full-time tuition and fees vary according to course load, location, program, and reciprocity agreements. Part-time tuition and fees vary according to course load, location, program, and reciprocity agreements. College room and board: $7598. College room only: $4160. Room and board charges vary according to board plan and housing facility. Tuition guaranteed not to increase for student's term of enrollment. **Scholarships:** Available **Calendar System:** Semester, Summer Session Available **Enrollment:** FT 17,022, PT 2,816, Grad FT 3,574, Grad PT 3,226 **Faculty:** FT 1,142, PT 233 **Student-Faculty Ratio:** 19:1 **Exams:** SAT I or ACT. ACT essay not being used. SAT essay not being used. **% Receiving Financial Aid:** 52 **% Residing in College-Owned, -Operated, or -Affiliated Housing:** 34 **Library Holdings:** 5,103,980 **Regional Accreditation:** North Central Association of Colleges and Schools **Credit Hours For Degree:** 124 credit hours, Bachelors **ROTC:** Army, Navy, Air Force **Professional Accreditation:** AACSB, ABET, ACEJMC, ABA, ACCE, ACSP, ALA, APA, ASLA, AALS, FIDER, CSWE, NAAB, NASM, NAST, NCATE **Intercollegiate Athletics:** Baseball M; Basketball M & W; Crew W; Cross-Country Running M & W; Football M; Golf M & W; Gymnastics M & W; Soccer W; Softball W; Tennis M & W; Track and Field M & W; Volleyball W; Wrestling M

UNIVERSITY OF OKLAHOMA HEALTH SCIENCES CENTER
PO Box 26901
Oklahoma City, OK 73190
Tel: (405)271-4000
Admissions: (405)271-2359
Fax: (405)271-2480
E-mail: scott-boeh@ouhsc.edu
Web Site: http://www.ouhsc.edu/
President/CEO: David Boren
Admissions: Scott Boeh
Type: Two-Year Upper Division **Sex:** Coed **Affiliation:** University of Oklahoma **% Accepted:** 36 **Admission Plans:** Preferred Admission; Deferred Admission **H.S. Requirements:** High school diploma required; GED accepted **Costs Per Year:** State resident tuition: $3537 full-time, $117.90 per credit hour part-time. Nonresident tuition: $13,518 full-time, $450.60 per credit hour part-time. Mandatory fees: $2020 full-time, $52.45 per credit hour part-time, $223.25 per term part-time. Full-time tuition and fees vary according to course load, degree level, program, and student level. Part-time tuition and fees vary according to course load, degree level, program, and student level. **Calendar System:** Semester, Summer Session Available **Enrollment:** FT 1,146, PT 89, Grad FT 2,326, Grad PT 403 **Faculty:** FT 303, PT 160 **Student-Faculty Ratio:** 9:1 **Library Holdings:** 329,056 **Regional Accreditation:** North Central Association of Colleges and Schools **Credit Hours For Degree:** 124 credit hours, Bachelors **ROTC:** Army, Air Force **Professional Accreditation:** ABET, ACPhE, ADA, ADtA, AOTA, APTA, APA, ASLHA, ACIPE, ACEHSA, CEPH, JRCEDMS, JRCERT, JRCNMT, LCMEAMA, NLN

UNIVERSITY OF PHOENIX—OKLAHOMA CITY CAMPUS
6501 North Broadway, Ste. 100
Oklahoma City, OK 73116-8244
Tel: (405)842-8007; Free: 800-228-7240
Admissions: (480)557-3303
E-mail: audra.mcquarie@phoenix.edu
Web Site: http://www.phoenix.edu/
President/CEO: William Pepicello
Admissions: Audra McQuarie
Type: Comprehensive **Sex:** Coed **% Accepted:** 100 **Admission Plans:** Open Admission; Deferred Admission **Application Deadline:** Rolling **Application Fee:** $0.00 **H.S. Requirements:** High school diploma required; GED accepted **Costs Per Year:** Application fee: $0. Tuition: $11,025 full-time. Full-time tuition varies according to course level and course load. **Scholarships:** Available **Calendar System:** Continuous, Summer Session Not available **Enrollment:** FT 732 **Faculty:** FT 16, PT 119 **Student-Faculty Ratio:** 13:1 **Regional Accreditation:** North Central Association of Colleges and Schools **Credit Hours For Degree:** 60 credits, Associates; 120 credits, Bachelors

UNIVERSITY OF PHOENIX—TULSA CAMPUS
14002 East 21st St.
Ste. 1000
Tulsa, OK 74134-1412
Tel: (918)622-4877; Free: 800-228-7240
Admissions: (480)557-3303
E-mail: evelyn.gaskin@phoenix.edu
Web Site: http://www.phoenix.edu/
President/CEO: William Pepicello
Admissions: Evelyn Gaskin
Type: Comprehensive **Sex:** Coed **Admission Plans:** Open Admission; Deferred Admission **Application Deadline:** Rolling **Application Fee:** $45.00 **H.S. Requirements:** High school diploma required; GED accepted **Costs Per Year:** Application fee: $45. Tuition: $11,025 full-time. Full-time tuition varies according to course level and course load. **Scholarships:** Available **Calendar System:** Continuous, Summer Session Not available **Enrollment:** FT 703 **Faculty:** FT 16, PT 139 **Regional Accreditation:** North Central Association of Colleges and Schools **Credit Hours For Degree:** 60 credits, Associates; 120 credits, Bachelors

UNIVERSITY OF SCIENCE AND ARTS OF OKLAHOMA
1727 West Alabama
Chickasha, OK 73018
Tel: (405)224-3140; Free: 800-933-8726
Admissions: (405)574-1357
Fax: (405)574-1220
E-mail: usao-admissions@usao.edu
Web Site: http://www.usao.edu/
President/CEO: Dr. John Feaver
Admissions: Kellee Johnson
Financial Aid: Nancy Moats
Type: Four-Year College **Sex:** Coed **Affiliation:** Oklahoma State Regents for Higher Education **Scores:** 50% SAT V 400+; 100% SAT M 400+; 48.4% ACT 18-23; 32% ACT 24-29 **% Accepted:** 74 **Admission Plans:** Deferred Admission **Application Deadline:** September 1 **Application Fee:** $25.00 **H.S. Requirements:** High school diploma required; GED accepted **Costs Per Year:** Application fee: $25. State resident tuition: $3270 full-time, $109 per credit hour part-time. Nonresident tuition: $9390 full-time, $313 per credit hour part-time. Mandatory fees: $1170 full-time, $39 per credit hour part-time. College room and board: $4850. College room only: $2530. Room and

board charges vary according to board plan and housing facility. Tuition guaranteed not to increase for student's term of enrollment. **Scholarships:** Available **Calendar System:** Trimester, Summer Session Available **Enrollment:** FT 927, PT 160 **Faculty:** FT 55, PT 33 **Student-Faculty Ratio:** 15:1 **Exams:** SAT I or ACT. ACT essay not being used. SAT essay not being used. **% Receiving Financial Aid:** 61 **% Residing in College-Owned, -Operated, or -Affiliated Housing:** 47 **Final Year or Final Semester Residency Requirement:** No **Library Holdings:** 73,748 **Regional Accreditation:** North Central Association of Colleges and Schools **Credit Hours For Degree:** 124 hours, Bachelors **Professional Accreditation:** NASM, NCATE **Intercollegiate Athletics:** Baseball M; Basketball M & W; Cheerleading M & W; Soccer M & W; Softball W

UNIVERSITY OF TULSA
800 South Tucker Dr.
Tulsa, OK 74104-3189
Tel: (918)631-2000; Free: 800-331-3050
Admissions: (918)631-2307
Fax: (918)631-2247
E-mail: admission@utulsa.edu
Web Site: http://www.utulsa.edu/
President/CEO: Dr. Steadman Upham
Admissions: Earl Johnson
Financial Aid: Vicki Hendrickson
Type: University **Sex:** Coed **Affiliation:** Presbyterian Church (U.S.A.) **Scores:** 100% SAT V 400+; 100% SAT M 400+; 18% ACT 18-23; 49% ACT 24-29 **% Accepted:** 46 **Admission Plans:** Early Admission; Deferred Admission **Application Deadline:** Rolling **Application Fee:** $35.00 **H.S. Requirements:** High school diploma required; GED accepted **Costs Per Year:** Application fee: $35. One-time mandatory fee: $425. Comprehensive fee: $33,688 includes full-time tuition ($25,054), mandatory fees ($90), and college room and board ($8544). College room only: $4724. Room and board charges vary according to board plan and housing facility. Part-time tuition: $899 per credit. **Scholarships:** Available **Calendar System:** Semester, Summer Session Available **Enrollment:** FT 2,870, PT 179 **Faculty:** FT 317, PT 80 **Student-Faculty Ratio:** 10:1 **Exams:** SAT I or ACT. **% Receiving Financial Aid:** 42 **% Residing in College-Owned, -Operated, or -Affiliated Housing:** 70 **Library Holdings:** 1,124,126 **Regional Accreditation:** North Central Association of Colleges and Schools **Credit Hours For Degree:** 126 credit hours, Bachelors **ROTC:** Air Force **Professional Accreditation:** AACSB, ABET, ABA, APA, ASLHA, AALS, JRCEPAT, NASM, NCATE, NLN, TEAC **Intercollegiate Athletics:** Basketball M & W; Crew W; Cross-Country Running M & W; Football M; Golf M & W; Soccer M & W; Softball W; Tennis M & W; Track and Field M & W; Volleyball W

VATTEROTT COLLEGE (OKLAHOMA CITY)
4629 Northwest 23rd St.
Oklahoma City, OK 73127
Tel: (405)945-0088; Free: 888-948-0088
Fax: (405)945-0788
E-mail: mark.hybers@vatterott-college.edu
Web Site: http://www.vatterott-college.edu/
President/CEO: Terry Dubberly
Admissions: Mark Hybers
Type: Two-Year College **Sex:** Coed **% Accepted:** 57 **Calendar System:** Semester **Enrollment:** FT 367 **Faculty:** FT 15, PT 21 **Student-Faculty Ratio:** 11:1 **Professional Accreditation:** ACCSCT

VATTEROTT COLLEGE (TULSA)
555 South Memorial Dr.
Tulsa, OK 74112
Tel: (918)835-8288; Free: 888-857-4016
Admissions: (918)836-6656
Fax: (918)836-9698
E-mail: tulsa@vatterott-college.edu
Web Site: http://www.vatterott-college.edu/
President/CEO: Pamela Bell
Admissions: Terry Queeno
Type: Two-Year College **Sex:** Coed **Affiliation:** Vatterott Educational Centers, Inc. **Application Fee:** $0.00 **H.S. Requirements:** High school diploma required; GED accepted **Calendar System:** Semester **Enrollment:** FT 146 **Faculty:** FT 10, PT 11 **Student-Faculty Ratio:** 12:1 **Professional Accreditation:** ACCSCT

WESTERN OKLAHOMA STATE COLLEGE
2801 North Main St.
Altus, OK 73521-1397
Tel: (580)477-2000
Fax: (580)477-7723
E-mail: larry.paxton@wosc.edu
Web Site: http://www.wosc.edu/
President/CEO: Randy Cumby
Admissions: Dr. Larry W. Paxton
Type: Two-Year College **Sex:** Coed **Affiliation:** Oklahoma State Regents for Higher Education **% Accepted:** 100 **Admission Plans:** Open Admission; Early Admission **Application Deadline:** Rolling **Application Fee:** $15.00 **H.S. Requirements:** High school diploma required; GED accepted **Scholarships:** Available **Calendar System:** Semester, Summer Session Available **Enrollment:** FT 859, PT 1,202 **Faculty:** FT 37, PT 63 **Student-Faculty Ratio:** 20:1 **Exams:** ACT. **Library Holdings:** 33,000 **Regional Accreditation:** North Central Association of Colleges and Schools **Credit Hours For Degree:** 64 credits, Associates **Professional Accreditation:** JRCERT, NLN **Intercollegiate Athletics:** Baseball M; Basketball M & W; Equestrian Sports M & W; Golf M & W; Softball W

AMERICAN COLLEGE OF HEALTHCARE SCIENCES
5940 Southwest Hood Ave.
Portland, OR 97239-3719
Tel: (503)244-0726; Free: 800-487-8839
Fax: (503)244-0727
E-mail: admissions@achs.edu
Web Site: http://www.achs.edu/
President/CEO: Dorene Petersen
Type: Two-Year College **Sex:** Coed **Application Deadline:** Rolling **H.S. Requirements:** High school diploma required; GED accepted **Costs Per Year:** Tuition: $255 per credit part-time.

APOLLO COLLEGE—PORTLAND
2600 SE 98th Ave.
Portland, OR 97266
Tel: (602)433-1333; Free: 877-205-1458
Admissions: (503)761-6100
Fax: (503)761-3351
Web Site: http://www.apollocollege.edu/
President/CEO: Chuck Ericson
Type: Two-Year College **Sex:** Coed **Application Fee:** $95.00

THE ART INSTITUTE OF PORTLAND
1122 NW Davis St.
Portland, OR 97209
Tel: (503)228-6528; Free: 888-228-6528
Fax: (503)228-4227
Web Site: http://www.artinstitutes.edu/portland/
President/CEO: Steven Goldman
Type: Four-Year College **Sex:** Coed **Affiliation:** Education Management Corporation **Calendar System:** Quarter **Professional Accreditation:** NCCU

BIRTHINGWAY COLLEGE OF MIDWIFERY
12113 SE Foster Rd.
Portland, OR 97299
Tel: (503)760-3131
E-mail: info@birthingway.edu
Web Site: http://www.birthingway.edu/
President/CEO: Holly Scholles
Type: Two-Year Upper Division **Sex:** Coed **Application Fee:** $50.00 **Costs Per Year:** Application fee: $50. **Calendar System:** Miscellaneous **Student-Faculty Ratio:** 9:1 **Professional Accreditation:** MEAC

BLUE MOUNTAIN COMMUNITY COLLEGE
2411 Northwest Carden Ave.
PO Box 100
Pendleton, OR 97801-1000
Tel: (541)276-1260
Fax: (541)278-5886
E-mail: tbosworth@bluecc.edu
Web Site: http://www.bluecc.edu/
President/CEO: John Turner
Admissions: Theresa Bosworth
Type: Two-Year College **Sex:** Coed **Admission Plans:** Open Admission **Application Deadline:** Rolling **H.S. Requirements:** High school diploma or equivalent not required **Costs Per Year:** State resident tuition: $3235 full-time, $68 per credit hour part-time. Nonresident tuition: $9705 full-time, $204 per credit hour part-time. Mandatory fees: $175 full-time, $3.50 per credit hour part-time, $18 per term part-time. Full-time tuition and fees vary according to course load, program, and reciprocity agreements. Part-time tuition and fees vary according to course load, program, and reciprocity agreements. **Scholarships:** Available **Calendar System:** Quarter, Summer Session Available **Library Holdings:** 39,026 **Credit Hours For Degree:** 90 credit hours, Associates **Professional Accreditation:** ABET, ADA, NCCU **Intercollegiate Athletics:** Baseball M; Basketball M & W; Softball W; Volleyball W

CENTRAL OREGON COMMUNITY COLLEGE
2600 Northwest College Way
Bend, OR 97701-5998
Tel: (541)383-7700
Admissions: (541)383-7500
Fax: (541)383-7506
E-mail: welcome@metolius.cocc.edu
Web Site: http://www.cocc.edu/
President/CEO: Dr. Jim Middleton
Admissions: Aimee Metcalf
Type: Two-Year College **Sex:** Coed **Affiliation:** Oregon Community College Association **% Accepted:** 100 **Admission Plans:** Open Admission; Preferred Admission **Application Deadline:** Rolling **Application Fee:** $25.00 **H.S. Requirements:** High school diploma required; GED accepted **Costs Per Year:** Application fee: $25. Area resident tuition: $2970 full-time. State resident tuition: $4095 full-time. Nonresident tuition: $8370 full-time. Mandatory fees: $123 full-time. College room and board: $7326. **Scholarships:** Available **Calendar System:** Quarter, Summer Session Available **Enrollment:** FT 2,876, PT 3,385 **Faculty:** FT 100, PT 141 **Student-Faculty Ratio:** 27:1 **% Residing in College-Owned, -Operated, or -Affiliated Housing:** 1 **Library Holdings:** 76,421 **Credit Hours For Degree:** 93 credits, Associates **ROTC:** Army **Professional Accreditation:** ACF, ADA, AHIMA, NCCU **Intercollegiate Athletics:** Golf M & W

CHEMEKETA COMMUNITY COLLEGE
4000 Lancaster Dr. NE
P.O. Box 14007
Salem, OR 97309
Tel: (503)399-5000
Fax: (503)399-3918
E-mail: registrar@chemeketa.edu
Web Site: http://www.chemeketa.edu/
President/CEO: Cheryl Roberts
Type: Two-Year College **Sex:** Coed **Admission Plans:** Open Admission; Deferred Admission **Application Deadline:** Rolling **Application Fee:** $0.00 **H.S. Requirements:** High school diploma or equivalent not required. For nursing, fire science, allied health, emergency medical technology programs: High school diploma required; GED accepted **Scholarships:** Available **Calendar System:** Quarter, Summer Session Available **Credit Hours For Degree:** 90 credit hours, Associates **Professional Accreditation:** ADA, JRCEMT, NLN, NCCU **Intercollegiate Athletics:** Baseball M; Basketball M & W; Cross-Country Running M & W; Track and Field M & W; Volleyball W

CLACKAMAS COMMUNITY COLLEGE
19600 Molalla Ave.
Oregon City, OR 97045-7998
Tel: (503)657-6958
Fax: (503)650-6654
E-mail: pattyw@clackamas.edu
Web Site: http://www.clackamas.edu/
President/CEO: Joanne Truesdell
Admissions: Tara Sprehe
Type: Two-Year College **Sex:** Coed **Admission Plans:** Open Admission; Early Admission **Application Deadline:** Rolling **Application Fee:** $0.00 **H.S. Requirements:** High school diploma or equivalent not required **Costs Per Year:** Application fee: $0. State resident tuition: $3465 full-time. Nonresident tuition: $9585 full-time. Mandatory fees: $225 full-time. **Scholarships:** Available **Calendar System:** Quarter, Summer Session Available **Enrollment:** FT 3,205, PT 4,939 **Faculty:** FT 148, PT 429 **Student-Faculty Ratio:** 14:1 **Library Holdings:** 41,263 **Credit Hours For Degree:** 93 credit hours, Associates **Professional Accreditation:** NLN, NCCU **Intercollegiate Athletics:** Baseball M; Basketball M & W; Cross-Country Running M & W; Soccer W; Softball W; Track and Field M & W; Volleyball W; Wrestling M

CLATSOP COMMUNITY COLLEGE
1653 Jerome
Astoria, OR 97103-3698
Tel: (503)325-0910
Admissions: (503)338-2326
Fax: (503)325-5738
E-mail: admissions@clatsopcc.edu
Web Site: http://www.clatsopcc.edu/
President/CEO: Dr. Greg Hamann
Admissions: Kristen Lee
Type: Two-Year College **Sex:** Coed **% Accepted:** 81 **Admission Plans:** Open Admission **Application Deadline:** Rolling **Application Fee:** $15.00 **H.S. Requirements:** High school diploma or equivalent not required **Scholarships:** Available **Calendar System:** Quarter, Summer Session Available **Enrollment:** FT 363, PT 899 **Faculty:** FT 47, PT 72 **Student-Faculty Ratio:** 10:1 **Library Holdings:** 48,517 **Credit Hours For Degree:** 90 credits, Associates **Professional Accreditation:** NCCU

COLUMBIA GORGE COMMUNITY COLLEGE
400 East Scenic Dr.
The Dalles, OR 97058
Tel: (541)296-6182
Admissions: (541)506-6000
Fax: (541)298-3104
E-mail: kcarter@cgcc.cc.or.us
Web Site: http://www.cgcc.cc.or.us/
President/CEO: Dr. Frank K. Toda
Admissions: Karen Carter
Type: Two-Year College **Sex:** Coed **Admission Plans:** Open Admission **Costs Per Year:** State resident tuition: $2240 full-time, $70 per credit hour part-time. **Calendar System:** Quarter **Professional Accreditation:** NCCU

CONCORDIA UNIVERSITY
2811 Northeast Holman
Portland, OR 97211-6099
Tel: (503)288-9371; Free: 800-321-9371
Admissions: (503)493-6526
Fax: (503)280-8531
E-mail: admissions@cu-portland.edu
Web Site: http://www.cu-portland.edu/
President/CEO: Dr. Charles E. Schlimpert
Admissions: Bobi Swan
Financial Aid: James W. Cullen
Type: Comprehensive **Sex:** Coed **Affiliation:** Lutheran Church–Missouri Synod; Concordia University System **Scores:** 91.5% SAT V 400+; 86% SAT M 400+ **% Accepted:** 60 **Admission Plans:** Deferred Admission **Application Deadline:** Rolling **Application Fee:** $20.00 **H.S. Requirements:** High school diploma required; GED accepted **Costs Per Year:** Application fee: $20. Comprehensive fee: $30,200 includes full-time tuition ($22,900), mandatory fees ($500), and college room and board ($6800). College room only: $3250. Full-time tuition and fees vary according to program. Room and board charges vary according to board plan and housing facility. Part-time tuition: $715 per credit. Part-time tuition varies according to course load and program. **Scholarships:** Available **Calendar System:** Semester, Summer Session Available **Enrollment:** FT 882, PT 183 **Faculty:** FT 49, PT 123 **Student-Faculty Ratio:** 16:1 **Exams:** SAT I or ACT. **% Receiving Financial Aid:** 76 **% Residing in College-Owned, -Operated, or -Affiliated Housing:** 40 **Library Holdings:** 88,103 **Credit Hours For Degree:** 62 semester hours, Associates; 124 semester hours, Bachelors **ROTC:** Air Force **Professional Accreditation:** NCCU **Intercollegiate Athletics:** Baseball M; Basketball M & W; Cross-Country Running M & W; Golf M & W; Soccer M & W; Softball W; Track and Field M & W; Volleyball W

CORBAN UNIVERSITY
5000 Deer Park Dr., SE
Salem, OR 97301-9392
Tel: (503)581-8600; Free: 800-845-3005
Admissions: (503)375-7115
Fax: (503)585-4316
E-mail: admissions@corban.edu
Web Site: http://www.corban.edu/
President/CEO: Dr. Reno Hoff
Admissions: Heidi Stowman
Financial Aid: Nathan Warthan
Type: Comprehensive **Sex:** Coed **Scores:** 96.5% SAT V 400+; 94.5% SAT M 400+; 43.5% ACT 18-23; 39.5% ACT 24-29 **% Accepted:** 57 **Application Deadline:** August 1 **Application Fee:** $35.00 **H.S. Requirements:** High school diploma required; GED accepted **Costs Per Year:** Application fee: $35. One-time mandatory fee: $100. Comprehensive fee: $31,872 includes full-time tuition ($23,950), mandatory fees ($280), and college room and board ($7642). Room and board charges vary according to board plan. Part-time tuition: $997.92 per credit hour. Part-time tuition varies according to course load. **Scholarships:** Available **Calendar System:** Semester, Summer Session Available **Enrollment:** FT 758, PT 130, Grad FT 100, Grad PT 112 **Faculty:** FT 45, PT 62 **Student-Faculty Ratio:** 14:1 **Exams:** SAT I or ACT. ACT essay used for advising. SAT essay used for advising. **% Receiving Financial Aid:** 83 **% Residing in College-Owned, -Operated, or -Affiliated Housing:** 43 **Final Year or Final Semester Residency Requirement:** Yes **Library Holdings:** 105,000 **Credit Hours For Degree:** 64 credit hours, Associates; 128 credit hours, Bachelors **ROTC:** Army, Air Force **Professional Accreditation:** NCCU **Intercollegiate Athletics:** Baseball M; Basketball M & W; Cross-Country Running M & W; Golf M & W; Soccer M & W; Softball W; Track and Field M & W; Volleyball W

DEVRY UNIVERSITY
9755 Southwest Barnes Rd.
Ste. 150
Portland, OR 97225-6651
Tel: (503)296-7468
Web Site: http://www.devry.edu/
President/CEO: Ron Karsten
Type: Comprehensive **Sex:** Coed **Affiliation:** DeVry University **Admission Plans:** Deferred Admission **Application Deadline:** Rolling **Application Fee:** $50.00 **H.S. Requirements:** High school diploma required; GED accepted **Costs Per Year:** Application fee: $50. Tuition: $14,080 full-time, $550 per credit hour part-time. **Scholarships:** Available **Calendar System:** Semester, Summer Session Available **Enrollment:** FT 65, PT 66, Grad FT 8, Grad PT 79 **Faculty:** FT 0, PT 32 **Student-Faculty Ratio:** 11:1 **Exams:** ACT essay used for admission. SAT essay used for admission. ACT essay used for placement. SAT essay used for placement. **% Receiving Financial Aid:** 74 **Regional Accreditation:** North Central Association of Colleges and Schools **Credit Hours For Degree:** 122 credits, Bachelors

EASTERN OREGON UNIVERSITY
1 University Blvd.
La Grande, OR 97850-2899
Tel: (541)962-3672; Free: 800-452-3393
Admissions: (541)962-3085
Fax: (541)962-3418
E-mail: admissions@eou.edu
Web Site: http://www.eou.edu/
President/CEO: Dixie Lund
Admissions: Tyler Dubsky
Financial Aid: Sam Collie
Type: Comprehensive **Sex:** Coed **Affiliation:** Oregon University System **Scores:** 83.4% SAT V 400+; 81.4% SAT M 400+; 50.9% ACT 18-23; 14.5%

ACT 24-29 **% Accepted:** 78 **Admission Plans:** Early Action; Deferred Admission **Application Deadline:** September 1 **Application Fee:** $50.00 **H.S. Requirements:** High school diploma required; GED accepted **Costs Per Year:** Application fee: $50. State resident tuition: $5109 full-time, $115 per credit hour part-time. Nonresident tuition: $5109 full-time, $115 per credit hour part-time. Mandatory fees: $1347 full-time. Full-time tuition and fees vary according to course load. Part-time tuition varies according to course load. College room and board: $7870. College room only: $4335. Room and board charges vary according to board plan and housing facility. **Scholarships:** Available **Calendar System:** Quarter, Summer Session Available **Enrollment:** FT 2,098, PT 1,391, Grad FT 136, Grad PT 332 **Faculty:** FT 115, PT 12 **Student-Faculty Ratio:** 24:1 **Exams:** SAT I or ACT. SAT essay used for admission. **% Receiving Financial Aid:** 74 **% Residing in College-Owned, -Operated, or -Affiliated Housing:** 4 **Credit Hours For Degree:** 186 credit hours, Bachelors **ROTC:** Army **Professional Accreditation:** NCCU **Intercollegiate Athletics:** Basketball M & W; Cross-Country Running M & W; Football M; Skiing (Cross-Country) M & W; Skiing (Downhill) M & W; Soccer W; Track and Field M & W; Volleyball W

EUGENE BIBLE COLLEGE
2155 Bailey Hill Rd.
Eugene, OR 97405
Tel: (541)485-1780; Free: 800-322-2638
Fax: (541)343-5801
E-mail: admissions@ebc.edu
Web Site: http://www.ebc.edu/
President/CEO: David L. Cole
Admissions: Sarah Maestas
Financial Aid: Rulena Mellor
Type: Four-Year College **Sex:** Coed **Affiliation:** Open Bible Standard Churches **% Accepted:** 100 **Admission Plans:** Deferred Admission **Application Deadline:** August 1 **Application Fee:** $30.00 **H.S. Requirements:** High school diploma required; GED accepted **Costs Per Year:** Application fee: $30. Comprehensive fee: $18,440 includes full-time tuition ($11,280), mandatory fees ($1150), and college room and board ($6010). College room only: $2250. Room and board charges vary according to housing facility. Part-time tuition: $470 per hour. Part-time tuition varies according to class time and course load. **Scholarships:** Available **Calendar System:** Semester, Summer Session Available **Enrollment:** FT 89, PT 12 **Faculty:** FT 6, PT 14 **Student-Faculty Ratio:** 7:1 **% Receiving Financial Aid:** 98 **% Residing in College-Owned, -Operated, or -Affiliated Housing:** 71 **Professional Accreditation:** ABHE, NCCU **Intercollegiate Athletics:** Basketball M; Soccer M & W; Volleyball M & W

EVEREST COLLEGE
425 Southwest Washington St.
Portland, OR 97204
Tel: (503)222-3225
Fax: (503)228-6926
E-mail: mzea@cci.edu
Web Site: http://www.everest.edu/
President/CEO: Mickey Sieracki
Admissions: Melanie Zea
Type: Two-Year College **Sex:** Coed **% Accepted:** 100 **Scholarships:** Available **Calendar System:** Quarter **Professional Accreditation:** ACICS

GEORGE FOX UNIVERSITY
414 North Meridian
Newberg, OR 97132-2697
Tel: (503)538-8383; Free: 800-765-4369
Admissions: (503)554-2240
Fax: (503)554-3830
E-mail: admissions@georgefox.edu
Web Site: http://www.georgefox.edu/
President/CEO: Dr. Robin Baker
Admissions: Ryan Dougherty
Financial Aid: James Oshiro
Type: University **Sex:** Coed **Affiliation:** Friends **Scores:** 97.03% SAT V 400+; 93.79% SAT M 400+; 53.73% ACT 18-23; 32.84% ACT 24-29 **% Accepted:** 69 **Admission Plans:** Early Action; Deferred Admission **Application Deadline:** Rolling **Application Fee:** $40.00 **H.S. Requirements:** High school diploma required; GED accepted **Costs Per Year:** Application fee: $40. Comprehensive fee: $34,500 includes full-time tuition ($25,860), mandatory fees ($320), and college room and board ($8320). College room only: $4680. Room and board charges vary according to board plan. Part-time tuition: $780 per semester hour. Part-time tuition varies according to course load. **Scholarships:** Available **Calendar System:** Semester, Summer Session Available **Enrollment:** FT 1,679, PT 288, Grad FT 418, Grad PT 1,003 **Faculty:** FT 165, PT 199 **Student-Faculty Ratio:** 11:1 **Exams:** SAT I or ACT. **% Receiving Financial Aid:** 74 **% Residing in College-Owned, -Operated, or -Affiliated Housing:** 67 **Final Year or Final Semester Residency Requirement:** No **Library Holdings:** 218,240 **Credit Hours For Degree:** 126 semester hours, Bachelors **ROTC:** Air Force **Professional Accreditation:** APA, ACIPE, ACBSP, ATS, JRCEPAT, NASM, NCATE, NCCU **Intercollegiate Athletics:** Baseball M; Basketball M & W; Cross-Country Running M & W; Golf M & W; Soccer M & W; Softball W; Tennis M & W; Track and Field M & W; Volleyball W

GUTENBERG COLLEGE
1883 University St.
Eugene, OR 97403
Tel: (541)683-5141
Admissions: (541)736-9071
Fax: (541)683-6997
E-mail: tstollar@gutenberg.edu
Web Site: http://www.gutenberg.edu/
President/CEO: Dr. David Crabtree
Admissions: Terry Stollar
Type: Four-Year College **Sex:** Coed **Scores:** 100% SAT V 400+; 86% SAT M 400+ **% Accepted:** 64 **Application Deadline:** March 1 **Application Fee:** $40.00 **H.S. Requirements:** High school diploma required; GED accepted **Costs Per Year:** Application fee: $40. Comprehensive fee: $16,852 includes full-time tuition ($11,202), mandatory fees ($650), and college room and board ($5000). Full-time tuition and fees vary according to student level. Room and board charges vary according to housing facility. **Enrollment:** FT 38 **Faculty:** FT 8, PT 2 **Student-Faculty Ratio:** 6:1 **Exams:** SAT I. **% Residing in College-Owned, -Operated, or -Affiliated Housing:** 75 **Professional Accreditation:** TACCS

HEALD COLLEGE—PORTLAND
625 SW Broadway, 4th Floor
Portland, OR 97205
Tel: (503)229-0492
Admissions: (503)505-5492
Fax: (503)229-0498
E-mail: info@heald.edu
Web Site: http://www.heald.edu/
President/CEO: Jason Ferguson
Type: Two-Year College **Sex:** Coed **Admission Plans:** Open Admission; Early Admission; Deferred Admission **Application Deadline:** Rolling **Application Fee:** $40.00 **H.S. Requirements:** High school diploma required; GED accepted **Scholarships:** Available **Calendar System:** Quarter, Summer Session Available **Enrollment:** FT 149, PT 57 **Faculty:** FT 15, PT 6 **Student-Faculty Ratio:** 10:1 **Exams:** Other. **Regional Accreditation:** Western Association of Schools and Colleges

ITT TECHNICAL INSTITUTE
9500 Northeast Cascades Parkway
Portland, OR 97220
Tel: (503)255-6500; Free: 800-234-5488
Fax: (503)255-6135
Web Site: http://www.itt-tech.edu/
President/CEO: Wayne Matulich
Type: Two-Year College **Sex:** Coed **Affiliation:** ITT Educational Services, Inc. **H.S. Requirements:** High school diploma required; GED accepted **Scholarships:** Available **Calendar System:** Quarter, Summer Session Not available **Professional Accreditation:** ACICS

KLAMATH COMMUNITY COLLEGE
7390 South 6th St.
Klamath Falls, OR 97603
Tel: (541)882-3521
Web Site: http://www.klamathcc.edu/
President/CEO: Gerald Hamilton
Type: Two-Year College **Sex:** Coed **Costs Per Year:** State resident tuition: $2340 full-time, $65 per credit part-time. Nonresident tuition: $5148 full-time, $143 per credit part-time. **Calendar System:** Quarter **Professional Accreditation:** NCCU

LANE COMMUNITY COLLEGE
4000 East 30th Ave.
Eugene, OR 97405-0640
Tel: (541)747-4501
Admissions: (541)463-3000
Fax: (541)744-3995
Web Site: http://www.lanecc.edu/
President/CEO: Mary Spilde
Admissions: Helen Garrett
Type: Two-Year College **Sex:** Coed **Admission Plans:** Open Admission; Preferred Admission; Early Admission **Application Deadline:** Rolling **H.S. Requirements:** High school diploma or equivalent not required. For applicants under 18 admitted with a high school release to attend credit classes: High school diploma required; GED accepted **Scholarships:** Available **Calendar System:** Quarter, Summer Session Available **Library Holdings:** 67,051 **Credit Hours For Degree:** 93 credit hours, Associates **Professional Accreditation:** ADA, CARC, NLN, NCCU **Intercollegiate Athletics:** Baseball M; Basketball M & W; Cross-Country Running M & W; Soccer W; Track and Field M & W

LEWIS & CLARK COLLEGE
0615 Southwest Palatine Hill Rd.
Portland, OR 97219-7899
Tel: (503)768-7000; Free: 800-444-4111
Admissions: (503)768-7040
Fax: (503)768-7055
E-mail: admissions@lclark.edu
Web Site: http://www.lclark.edu/
President/CEO: Dr. Jane Atkinson
Admissions: Erica Johnson
Financial Aid: Glendi Gaddis
Type: Comprehensive **Sex:** Coed **Scores:** 99.9% SAT V 400+; 100.1% SAT M 400+; 5% ACT 18-23; 58.7% ACT 24-29 **% Accepted:** 65 **Admission Plans:** Early Action; Deferred Admission **Application Deadline:** February 1 **Application Fee:** $50.00 **H.S. Requirements:** High school diploma required; GED accepted **Costs Per Year:** Application fee: $50. Comprehensive fee: $44,239 includes full-time tuition ($34,995), mandatory fees ($238), and college room and board ($9006). College room only: $4886. Room and board charges vary according to board plan and housing facility. Part-time tuition: $1762 per credit hour. **Scholarships:** Available **Calendar System:** Semester, Summer Session Available **Enrollment:** FT 1,956, PT 21, Grad FT 946, Grad PT 600 **Faculty:** FT 231, PT 149 **Student-Faculty Ratio:** 12:1 **Exams:** Other, SAT I or ACT. ACT essay not being used. SAT essay not being used. **% Receiving Financial Aid:** 55 **% Residing in College-Owned, -Operated, or -Affiliated Housing:** 67 **Library Holdings:** 311,100 **Credit Hours For Degree:** 128 semester hours, Bachelors **Professional Accreditation:** ABA, AALS, NCATE, NCCU **Intercollegiate Athletics:** Baseball M; Basketball M & W; Crew M & W; Cross-Country Running M & W; Football M; Golf M & W; Lacrosse M & W; Soccer M & W; Softball W; Swimming and Diving M & W; Tennis M & W; Track and Field M & W; Volleyball W

LINFIELD COLLEGE
900 SE Baker St.
McMinnville, OR 97128-6894
Tel: (503)883-2200; Free: 800-640-2287
Admissions: (503)883-2213
Fax: (503)883-2472
E-mail: admission@linfield.edu
Web Site: http://www.linfield.edu/
President/CEO: Dr. Thomas L. Hellie
Admissions: Lisa Knodle-Bragiel
Financial Aid: Crisanne Werner
Type: Four-Year College **Sex:** Coed **Affiliation:** American Baptist Churches in the USA **Scores:** 99% SAT V 400+; 99% SAT M 400+; 43% ACT 18-23; 41% ACT 24-29 **% Accepted:** 82 **Admission Plans:** Early Action; Deferred Admission **Application Deadline:** February 15 **Application Fee:** $40.00 **H.S. Requirements:** High school diploma required; GED accepted **Costs Per Year:** Application fee: $40. Comprehensive fee: $37,314 includes full-time tuition ($28,760), mandatory fees ($274), and college room and board ($8280). College room only: $4480. Full-time tuition and fees vary according to location. Room and board charges vary according to board plan, housing facility, and location. Part-time tuition: $895 per semester hour. Part-time tuition varies according to course load and location. **Scholarships:** Available **Calendar System:** 4-1-4, Summer Session Available **Enrollment:** FT 1,627, PT 50 **Faculty:** FT 108, PT 74 **Student-Faculty Ratio:** 12:1 **Exams:** SAT I or ACT. ACT essay used for advising. SAT essay used for advising. ACT essay used as a validity check on application essay. SAT essay used as a validity check on application essay. **% Receiving Financial Aid:** 69 **% Residing in College-Owned, -Operated, or -Affiliated Housing:** 77 **Library Holdings:** 185,842 **Credit Hours For Degree:** 125 credit hours, Bachelors **ROTC:** Air Force **Professional Accreditation:** JRCEPAT, NASM, NLN, NCCU **Intercollegiate Athletics:** Baseball M; Basketball M & W; Cross-Country Running M & W; Football M; Golf M & W; Lacrosse W; Soccer M & W; Softball W; Swimming and Diving M & W; Tennis M & W; Track and Field M & W; Volleyball W

LINN-BENTON COMMUNITY COLLEGE
6500 Southwest Pacific Blvd.
Albany, OR 97321
Tel: (541)917-4999
Admissions: (541)917-4813
Fax: (541)917-4838
E-mail: admissions@linnbenton.edu
Web Site: http://www.linnbenton.edu/
President/CEO: Dr. Rita Cavin
Admissions: Christine Baker
Type: Two-Year College **Sex:** Coed **Admission Plans:** Open Admission; Preferred Admission; Deferred Admission **Application Deadline:** Rolling **Application Fee:** $30.00 **H.S. Requirements:** High school diploma or equivalent not required. For nursing, dental assistant, public safety dispatcher, radiological technology, pharmacy technician, phlebotomy: High school diploma required; GED accepted. **Costs Per Year:** Application fee: $30. State resident tuition: $3092 full-time. Nonresident tuition: $7637 full-time. Mandatory fees: $238 full-time. **Scholarships:** Available **Calendar System:** Quarter, Summer Session Available **Enrollment:** FT 3,551, PT 2,988 **Faculty:** FT 166, PT 347 **Library Holdings:** 42,561 **Credit Hours For Degree:** 90 quarter hours, Associates **ROTC:** Army, Air Force **Professional Accreditation:** AAMAE, ADA, NLN, NCCU **Intercollegiate Athletics:** Baseball M; Basketball M & W; Volleyball W

MARYLHURST UNIVERSITY
17600 Pacific Hwy., PO Box 261
Marylhurst, OR 97036-0261
Tel: (503)636-8141; Free: 800-634-9982
Fax: (503)636-9526
E-mail: admissions@marylhurst.edu
Web Site: http://www.marylhurst.edu/
President/CEO: Judith Johansen
Admissions: Gretchen Potter
Financial Aid: Tracy Reisinger
Type: Comprehensive **Sex:** Coed **Affiliation:** Roman Catholic **% Accepted:** 61 **Admission Plans:** Deferred Admission **Application Deadline:** Rolling **Application Fee:** $40.00 **H.S. Requirements:** High school diploma required; GED accepted. For transfer students with at least 45 credits: High school diploma or equivalent not required **Costs Per Year:** Application fee: $40. Tuition: $16,920 full-time, $376 per credit part-time. Full-time tuition varies according to course load, degree level, and program. Part-time tuition varies according to course load, degree level, and program. **Scholarships:** Available **Calendar System:** Quarter, Summer Session Available **Enrollment:** FT 277, PT 692, Grad FT 161, Grad PT 772 **Faculty:** FT 52, PT 201 **Student-Faculty Ratio:** 6:1 **% Receiving Financial Aid:** 84 **Final Year or Final Semester Residency Requirement:** No **Library Holdings:** 109,963 **Credit Hours For Degree:** 180 quarter hours, Bachelors **Professional Accreditation:** NASM, NCCU

MOUNT ANGEL SEMINARY
St. Benedict, OR 97373
Tel: (503)845-3951
E-mail: seminary@mountangelabbey.org
Web Site: http://www.mountangelabbey.org/seminary/
President/CEO: Very Rev. Richard Paperini
Financial Aid: Dorene Preis
Type: Comprehensive **Affiliation:** Roman Catholic **% Accepted:** 100 **Admission Plans:** Preferred Admission **Application Deadline:** July 15 **Application Fee:** $27.00 **H.S. Requirements:** High school diploma required; GED accepted **Scholarships:** Available **Calendar System:** Semester, Sum-

mer Session Not available **Exams:** SAT I. **Library Holdings:** 240,000 **Credit Hours For Degree:** 124 credit hours, Bachelors **Professional Accreditation:** ACIPE, ATS, NCCU

MT. HOOD COMMUNITY COLLEGE
26000 Southeast Stark St.
Gresham, OR 97030-3300
Tel: (503)491-6422
Fax: (503)491-7388
Web Site: http://www.mhcc.cc.or.us/
President/CEO: John J. Sygielski
Admissions: Dr. Craig Kolins
Type: Two-Year College **Sex:** Coed **Admission Plans:** Open Admission; Preferred Admission; Early Admission; Deferred Admission **Application Deadline:** Rolling **Application Fee:** $25.00 **H.S. Requirements:** High school diploma or equivalent not required. For allied health, some professional-technical programs: High school diploma required; GED accepted **Scholarships:** Available **Calendar System:** Quarter, Summer Session Available **Enrollment:** FT 3,178, PT 5,593 **Faculty:** FT 173, PT 465 **Student-Faculty Ratio:** 25:1 **Library Holdings:** 64,000 **Credit Hours For Degree:** 90 credits, Associates **Professional Accreditation:** ARCEST, AAMAE, ABFSE, ADA, APTA, CARC, NLN, NCCU **Intercollegiate Athletics:** Baseball M; Basketball M & W; Cross-Country Running M & W; Softball W; Track and Field M & W; Volleyball W

MULTNOMAH UNIVERSITY
8435 Northeast Glisan St.
Portland, OR 97220-5898
Tel: (503)255-0332; Free: 800-275-4672
Fax: (503)254-1268
E-mail: admiss@multnomah.edu
Web Site: http://www.multnomah.edu/
President/CEO: Dr. Daniel R. Lockwood
Admissions: Nancy Gerecz
Financial Aid: Mary J. McGlothlan
Type: Comprehensive **Sex:** Coed **Affiliation:** interdenominational **Scores:** 96.5% SAT V 400+; 92.9% SAT M 400+; 33.4% ACT 18-23; 60% ACT 24-29 **% Accepted:** 87 **Admission Plans:** Deferred Admission **Application Deadline:** July 15 **Application Fee:** $40.00 **H.S. Requirements:** High school diploma required; GED accepted **Costs Per Year:** Application fee: $40. Tuition: $510 per credit hour part-time. Part-time tuition varies according to course load, location, and program. **Scholarships:** Available **Calendar System:** Semester, Summer Session Available **Enrollment:** FT 468, PT 98, Grad FT 173, Grad PT 102 **Faculty:** FT 27, PT 35 **Student-Faculty Ratio:** 13:1 **Exams:** SAT I or ACT. **% Receiving Financial Aid:** 84 **% Residing in College-Owned, -Operated, or -Affiliated Housing:** 45 **Final Year or Final Semester Residency Requirement:** Yes **Library Holdings:** 105,827 **Credit Hours For Degree:** 128 semester hours, Bachelors **Professional Accreditation:** ABHE, ATS, NCCU **Intercollegiate Athletics:** Basketball M; Volleyball W

NORTHWEST CHRISTIAN UNIVERSITY
828 East 11th Ave.
Eugene, OR 97401-3745
Tel: (541)343-1641; Free: 877-463-6622
Admissions: (541)684-7201
Fax: (541)684-7317
E-mail: admissions@northwestchristian.edu
Web Site: http://www.northwestchristian.edu/
President/CEO: Dr. David W. Wilson
Admissions: Jennifer Samples
Financial Aid: David Haggard
Type: Comprehensive **Sex:** Coed **Affiliation:** Christian **% Accepted:** 95 **Admission Plans:** Deferred Admission **Application Deadline:** Rolling **Application Fee:** $0.00 **H.S. Requirements:** High school diploma required; GED accepted **Costs Per Year:** Application fee: $0. Comprehensive fee: $29,700 includes full-time tuition ($22,900) and college room and board ($6800). Full-time tuition varies according to course load. Room and board charges vary according to board plan and housing facility. Part-time tuition: $770 per credit. Part-time tuition varies according to course load. **Scholarships:** Available **Calendar System:** Quarter, Summer Session Available **Enrollment:** FT 366, PT 79, Grad FT 93, Grad PT 19 **Faculty:** FT 22, PT 4 **Student-Faculty Ratio:** 21:1 **Exams:** SAT I or ACT. ACT essay used for admission. SAT essay used for admission. ACT essay used for placement. SAT essay used for placement. **% Receiving Financial Aid:** 74 **Final Year or Final Semester Residency Requirement:** No **Library Holdings:** 70,025 **Credit Hours For Degree:** 60 semester hours, Associates; 124 semester hours, Bachelors **Professional Accreditation:** NCCU **Intercollegiate Athletics:** Basketball M & W; Cross-Country Running M & W; Golf M & W; Soccer M & W; Softball W; Track and Field M & W; Volleyball W

OREGON COAST COMMUNITY COLLEGE
400 Southeast College Way
Newport, OR 97366
Tel: (541)265-2283
E-mail: webinfo@occc.cc.or.us
Web Site: http://www.occc.cc.or.us/
President/CEO: Dr. Patrick O'Connor
Type: Two-Year College **Sex:** Coed **Affiliation:** Chemeketa Community College **Admission Plans:** Open Admission **H.S. Requirements:** High school diploma or equivalent not required. For nursing and aquarium science programs: High school diploma required; GED accepted **Costs Per Year:** State resident tuition: $2664 full-time, $74 per credit part-time. Nonresident tuition: $6192 full-time, $172 per credit part-time. Mandatory fees: $110 full-time, $11 per course part-time. Full-time tuition and fees vary according to program. Part-time tuition and fees vary according to program. **Calendar System:** Quarter, Summer Session Available **Enrollment:** FT 178, PT 474 **Faculty:** FT 8, PT 42 **Student-Faculty Ratio:** 15:1 **Exams:** Other. **Library Holdings:** 10,455 **Credit Hours For Degree:** 90 credits, Associates

OREGON COLLEGE OF ART & CRAFT
8245 Southwest Barnes Rd.
Portland, OR 97225
Tel: (503)297-5544; Free: 800-390-0632
Fax: (503)297-3155
E-mail: admissions@ocac.edu
Web Site: http://www.ocac.edu/
President/CEO: Bonnie Laing-Malcolmson
Admissions: Devon Simpson
Financial Aid: Lisa Newman
Type: Four-Year College **Sex:** Coed **Scores:** 96% SAT M 400+; 60% ACT 18-23; 40% ACT 24-29 **% Accepted:** 91 **Admission Plans:** Deferred Admission **Application Deadline:** Rolling **Application Fee:** $35.00 **H.S. Requirements:** High school diploma required; GED accepted **Costs Per Year:** Application fee: $35. Comprehensive fee: $28,818 includes full-time tuition ($20,938), mandatory fees ($1670), and college room and board ($6210). Part-time tuition: $914 per credit hour. **Scholarships:** Available **Calendar System:** Semester, Summer Session Not available **Enrollment:** FT 99, PT 54, Grad FT 3, Grad PT 13 **Faculty:** FT 10, PT 13 **Student-Faculty Ratio:** 9:1 **Exams:** ACT, SAT I. ACT essay not being used. SAT essay not being used. **% Receiving Financial Aid:** 88 **% Residing in College-Owned, -Operated, or -Affiliated Housing:** 3 **Library Holdings:** 9,000 **Credit Hours For Degree:** 120 credits, Bachelors **Professional Accreditation:** NASAD, NCCU

OREGON HEALTH & SCIENCE UNIVERSITY
3181 Southwest Sam Jackson Park Rd.
Portland, OR 97239-3098
Tel: (503)494-8311
Admissions: (503)494-0647
Fax: (503)494-5738
E-mail: andersje@ohsu.edu
Web Site: http://www.ohsu.edu/
President/CEO: Joseph Robertson, MD,MBA
Admissions: Jennifer Anderson
Financial Aid: Debbie Cox
Type: Two-Year Upper Division **Sex:** Coed **Admission Plans:** Preferred Admission **Application Fee:** $125.00 **H.S. Requirements:** High school diploma required; GED accepted **Costs Per Year:** Application fee: $125. State resident tuition: $10,692 full-time, $297 per credit part-time. Nonresident tuition: $19,692 full-time, $547 per credit part-time. Mandatory fees: $5359 full-time. Full-time tuition and fees vary according to course level, degree level, location, program, reciprocity agreements, and student level. Part-time tuition varies according to course level, course load, degree level, location, program, reciprocity agreements, and student level. **Scholarships:** Available **Calendar System:** Quarter, Summer Session Available **Enrollment:** FT 176, PT 532, Grad FT 1,426, Grad PT 449 **% Receiving Financial Aid:** 86 **Library Holdings:** 272,853 **Credit Hours For Degree:**

186 quarter hours, Bachelors **ROTC:** Army **Professional Accreditation:** AACN, AANA, ACNM, ADA, ADtA, APA, CEPH, JRCERT, LCMEAMA, NAACLS, NLN, NCCU

OREGON INSTITUTE OF TECHNOLOGY
3201 Campus Dr.
Klamath Falls, OR 97601-8801
Tel: (541)885-1000; Free: 800-343-6653
Admissions: (541)885-1151
Fax: (541)885-1115
E-mail: oit@oit.edu
Web Site: http://www.oit.edu/
President/CEO: Dr. Chris Maples
Admissions: Ginny Garner
Financial Aid: Tracey Lehman
Type: Comprehensive **Sex:** Coed **Affiliation:** Oregon University System **Scores:** 93.34% SAT V 400+; 92.67% SAT M 400+; 43.37% ACT 18-23; 33.73% ACT 24-29 **% Accepted:** 93 **Admission Plans:** Deferred Admission **Application Deadline:** October 1 **Application Fee:** $50.00 **H.S. Requirements:** High school diploma required; GED accepted **Costs Per Year:** Application fee: $50. State resident tuition: $5199 full-time, $108 per credit part-time. Nonresident tuition: $16,629 full-time, $108 per credit part-time. Mandatory fees: $1566 full-time. Full-time tuition and fees vary according to course level, course load, degree level, location, program, and reciprocity agreements. Part-time tuition varies according to course level, course load, degree level, location, program, and reciprocity agreements. College room and board: $8615. College room only: $5330. Room and board charges vary according to board plan and housing facility. **Scholarships:** Available **Calendar System:** Quarter, Summer Session Available **Enrollment:** FT 2,078, PT 1,817, Grad FT 9, Grad PT 11 **Faculty:** FT 134, PT 113 **Student-Faculty Ratio:** 20:1 **Exams:** SAT I or ACT. **% Receiving Financial Aid:** 84 **% Residing in College-Owned, -Operated, or -Affiliated Housing:** 13 **Credit Hours For Degree:** 90 credit hours, Associates; 180 credit hours, Bachelors **ROTC:** Army **Professional Accreditation:** ABET, ADA, JRCERT, NAACLS, NCCU **Intercollegiate Athletics:** Baseball M; Basketball M & W; Cross-Country Running M & W; Soccer W; Softball W; Track and Field M & W; Volleyball W

OREGON STATE UNIVERSITY
Corvallis, OR 97331
Tel: (541)737-1000
Admissions: (541)737-4411
Fax: (541)737-6157
E-mail: osuadmit@ccmail.orst.edu
Web Site: http://www.oregonstate.edu/
President/CEO: Dr. Edward Ray
Admissions: Michele Sandlin
Financial Aid: Doug Severs
Type: University **Sex:** Coed **Affiliation:** Oregon University System **Scores:** 94% SAT V 400+; 95% SAT M 400+; 44% ACT 18-23; 40% ACT 24-29 **% Accepted:** 83 **Admission Plans:** Early Action; Deferred Admission **Application Deadline:** September 1 **Application Fee:** $50.00 **H.S. Requirements:** High school diploma required; GED accepted **Costs Per Year:** Application fee: $50. State resident tuition: $5436 full-time, $151 per credit hour part-time. Nonresident tuition: $18,360 full-time, $510 per credit hour part-time. Mandatory fees: $1291 full-time. Full-time tuition and fees vary according to course load. Part-time tuition varies according to course load. College room and board: $8352. Room and board charges vary according to board plan and housing facility. **Scholarships:** Available **Calendar System:** Quarter, Summer Session Available **Enrollment:** FT 15,213, PT 2,854, Grad FT 2,648, Grad PT 1,254 **Faculty:** FT 861, PT 334 **Student-Faculty Ratio:** 20:1 **Exams:** SAT I or ACT, SAT II. **% Receiving Financial Aid:** 53 **% Residing in College-Owned, -Operated, or -Affiliated Housing:** 21 **Final Year or Final Semester Residency Requirement:** No **Library Holdings:** 1,594,918 **Credit Hours For Degree:** 180 quarter hours, Bachelors **ROTC:** Army, Navy, Air Force **Professional Accreditation:** AACSB, ABET, ACPhE, AAFCS, ACCE, ACA, AVMA, CEPH, JRCEPAT, NCATE, NCCU, SAF **Intercollegiate Athletics:** Baseball M; Basketball M & W; Crew M & W; Football M; Golf M & W; Gymnastics W; Soccer M & W; Softball W; Swimming and Diving W; Volleyball W; Wrestling M

OREGON STATE UNIVERSITY—CASCADES
2600 Northwest College Way
Bend, OR 97701
Tel: (541)322-3100
E-mail: cascadeadmit@osucascades.edu
Web Site: http://www.osucascades.edu/
President/CEO: Jay Casbon
Type: Comprehensive **Sex:** Coed **Affiliation:** Oregon University System **Application Deadline:** Rolling **Application Fee:** $50.00 **Costs Per Year:** Application fee: $50. State resident tuition: $5256 full-time, $146 per credit hour part-time. Nonresident tuition: $18,360 full-time, $510 per credit hour part-time. Mandatory fees: $540 full-time. Full-time tuition and fees vary according to program. Part-time tuition varies according to program. **Calendar System:** Quarter, Summer Session Available **Student-Faculty Ratio:** 15:1 **Professional Accreditation:** NCCU

PACIFIC NORTHWEST COLLEGE OF ART
1241 NW Johnson St.
Portland, OR 97209
Tel: (503)226-4391
Admissions: (503)821-8972
Fax: (503)226-3587
E-mail: admissions@pnca.edu
Web Site: http://www.pnca.edu/
President/CEO: Dr. Thomas Manley
Admissions: Chris Sweet, Jr.
Financial Aid: Peggy Burgus
Type: Comprehensive **Sex:** Coed **% Accepted:** 51 **Admission Plans:** Deferred Admission **Application Fee:** $35.00 **H.S. Requirements:** High school diploma required; GED accepted **Costs Per Year:** Application fee: $35. Comprehensive fee: $31,288 includes full-time tuition ($22,320), mandatory fees ($964), and college room and board ($8004). Full-time tuition and fees vary according to course load. Room and board charges vary according to housing facility. Part-time tuition: $930 per credit hour. Part-time mandatory fees: $38 per semester hour. Part-time tuition and fees vary according to course load. **Scholarships:** Available **Calendar System:** Semester, Summer Session Not available **Enrollment:** FT 441, PT 36 **Faculty:** FT 22, PT 89 **Student-Faculty Ratio:** 9:1 **% Receiving Financial Aid:** 81 **Library Holdings:** 14,650 **Credit Hours For Degree:** 120 semester hours, Bachelors **Professional Accreditation:** NASAD, NCCU

PACIFIC UNIVERSITY
2043 College Way
Forest Grove, OR 97116-1797
Tel: (503)357-6151; Free: 877-722-8648
Admissions: (503)352-2218
Fax: (503)352-3191
E-mail: admissions@pacificu.edu
Web Site: http://www.pacificu.edu/
President/CEO: Dr. Phillip D. Creighton
Admissions: Karen Dunston
Type: Comprehensive **Sex:** Coed **Scores:** 97% SAT V 400+; 97% SAT M 400+; 42% ACT 18-23; 48% ACT 24-29 **% Accepted:** 78 **Admission Plans:** Deferred Admission **Application Deadline:** August 15 **Application Fee:** $40.00 **H.S. Requirements:** High school diploma required; GED accepted **Costs Per Year:** Application fee: $40. Comprehensive fee: $38,084 includes full-time tuition ($29,290), mandatory fees ($676), and college room and board ($8118). College room only: $4094. Room and board charges vary according to board plan and housing facility. Part-time tuition: $1219 per credit hour. Part-time tuition varies according to course load. **Scholarships:** Available **Calendar System:** 4-1-4, Summer Session Available **Enrollment:** FT 1,403, PT 78 **Faculty:** FT 205, PT 148 **Student-Faculty Ratio:** 11:1 **Exams:** SAT I or ACT. **% Receiving Financial Aid:** 80 **% Residing in College-Owned, -Operated, or -Affiliated Housing:** 62 **Library Holdings:** 206,198 **Credit Hours For Degree:** 124 semester hours, Bachelors **ROTC:** Army, Air Force **Professional Accreditation:** ACPhE, AOTA, AOA, APTA, APA, NASM, NCATE, NCCU **Intercollegiate Athletics:** Baseball M; Basketball M & W; Cross-Country Running M & W; Golf M & W; Lacrosse W; Soccer M & W; Softball W; Swimming and Diving M & W; Tennis M & W; Track and Field M & W; Volleyball W; Wrestling M & W

PIONEER PACIFIC COLLEGE (CLACKAMAS)
8800 SE Sunnyside Rd.
Clackamas, OR 97015
Tel: (503)654-8000; Free: (866)772-4636
Admissions: (503)654-8000
E-mail: inquiries@pioneerpacific.edu

Web Site: http://www.pioneerpacific.edu/
Type: Four-Year College **Sex:** Coed **H.S. Requirements:** High school diploma required; GED accepted **Exams:** Other.

PIONEER PACIFIC COLLEGE (WILSONVILLE)
27501 Southwest Parkway Ave.
Wilsonville, OR 97070
Tel: (503)682-3903
Fax: (503)682-1514
E-mail: inquiries@pioneerpacific.edu
Web Site: http://www.pioneerpacific.edu/
President/CEO: Don Moutos
Admissions: Kristin Lynn
Type: Four-Year College **Sex:** Coed **Admission Plans:** Open Admission **Application Deadline:** Rolling **H.S. Requirements:** High school diploma required; GED accepted **Scholarships:** Available **Calendar System:** Continuous, Summer Session Not available **Faculty:** FT 49, PT 70 **Student-Faculty Ratio:** 15:1 **Exams:** Other. **Library Holdings:** 2,500 **Credit Hours For Degree:** 90 credit hours, Associates; 182.5 credit hours, Bachelors **Professional Accreditation:** ACICS

PIONEER PACIFIC COLLEGE—EUGENE/SPRINGFIELD BRANCH
3800 Sports Way
Springfield, OR 97477
Tel: (541)684-4644; Free: (866)772-4636
Admissions: (541)684-4644
E-mail: inquiries@pioneerpacific.edu
Web Site: http://www.pioneerpacific.edu/
Type: Four-Year College **Sex:** Coed **H.S. Requirements:** High school diploma required; GED accepted **Exams:** Other.

PORTLAND COMMUNITY COLLEGE
PO Box 19000
Portland, OR 97280-0990
Tel: (503)244-6111
Fax: (503)452-4988
Web Site: http://www.pcc.edu/
President/CEO: Preston Pulliams
Type: Two-Year College **Sex:** Coed **Admission Plans:** Open Admission **Application Deadline:** Rolling **Application Fee:** $25.00 **H.S. Requirements:** High school diploma or equivalent not required. For career and technical programs: High school diploma required; GED not accepted **Scholarships:** Available **Calendar System:** Quarter, Summer Session Available **Library Holdings:** 91,472 **Credit Hours For Degree:** 90 credit hours, Associates **Professional Accreditation:** ADA, AHIMA, JCAHPO, JRCERT, NAACLS, NLN, NCCU **Intercollegiate Athletics:** Basketball M & W

PORTLAND STATE UNIVERSITY
PO Box 751
Portland, OR 97207-0751
Tel: (503)725-3000; Free: 800-547-8887
Admissions: (503)725-5502
Fax: (503)725-5525
E-mail: askadm@ofa.pdx.edu
Web Site: http://www.pdx.edu/
President/CEO: Wim Wiewel
Admissions: Agnes A. Hoffman
Financial Aid: Phillip Rodgers
Type: University **Sex:** Coed **Affiliation:** Oregon University System **Scores:** 93% SAT V 400+; 94% SAT M 400+; 49% ACT 18-23; 30% ACT 24-29 **% Accepted:** 90 **Admission Plans:** Early Admission; Deferred Admission **Application Deadline:** Rolling **Application Fee:** $50.00 **H.S. Requirements:** High school diploma required; GED accepted **Costs Per Year:** Application fee: $50. One-time mandatory fee: $265. State resident tuition: $5321 full-time, $118.25 per credit hour part-time. Nonresident tuition: $19,755 full-time, $439 per credit hour part-time. Mandatory fees: $1443 full-time, $17 per credit hour part-time, $95 per term part-time. Full-time tuition and fees vary according to program and reciprocity agreements. Part-time tuition and fees vary according to course level. College room and board: $9774. College room only: $6891. Room and board charges vary according to board plan and housing facility. **Scholarships:** Available **Calendar System:** Quarter, Summer Session Available **Enrollment:** FT 12,709, PT 7,621, Grad FT 2,491, Grad PT 3,561 **Faculty:** FT 800, PT 665 **Student-Faculty Ratio:** 20:1 **Exams:** SAT I or ACT. **% Receiving Financial Aid:** 61 **% Residing in College-Owned, -Operated, or -Affiliated Housing:** 12 **Credit Hours For Degree:** 180 credit hours, Bachelors **ROTC:** Army, Air Force **Professional Accreditation:** AACSB, ABET, ACA, ACSP, ASLHA, CEPH, CORE, CSWE, NASAD, NASM, NASPAA, NAST, NCATE, NCCU **Intercollegiate Athletics:** Baseball M; Basketball M & W; Cross-Country Running M & W; Football M; Golf M & W; Soccer W; Softball W; Tennis M & W; Track and Field M & W; Volleyball W; Wrestling M

REED COLLEGE
3203 Southeast Woodstock Blvd.
Portland, OR 97202-8199
Tel: (503)771-1112; Free: 800-547-4750
Admissions: (503)777-7511
Fax: (503)777-7553
E-mail: admission@reed.edu
Web Site: http://www.reed.edu/
President/CEO: Colin S. Diver
Admissions: Keith Todd
Financial Aid: Leslie Limper
Type: Comprehensive **Sex:** Coed **Scores:** 100% SAT V 400+; 100% SAT M 400+; 2% ACT 18-23; 27% ACT 24-29 **% Accepted:** 41 **Admission Plans:** Early Admission; Early Decision Plan; Deferred Admission **Application Deadline:** January 15 **Application Fee:** $50.00 **H.S. Requirements:** High school diploma required; GED accepted **Costs Per Year:** Application fee: $50. Comprehensive fee: $49,950 includes full-time tuition ($39,440), mandatory fees ($260), and college room and board ($10,250). College room only: $5350. Room and board charges vary according to board plan and housing facility. Part-time tuition: $1675 per semester hour. Part-time tuition varies according to course load. **Scholarships:** Available **Calendar System:** Semester, Summer Session Not available **Enrollment:** FT 1,406, PT 46, Grad PT 29 **Faculty:** FT 121, PT 12 **Student-Faculty Ratio:** 10:1 **Exams:** SAT I or ACT, SAT II. ACT essay used for admission. SAT essay used for admission. ACT essay used as a validity check on application essay. SAT essay used as a validity check on application essay. **% Receiving Financial Aid:** 52 **% Residing in College-Owned, -Operated, or -Affiliated Housing:** 65 **Final Year or Final Semester Residency Requirement:** No **Library Holdings:** 592,335 **Credit Hours For Degree:** 120 semester hours, Bachelors **Professional Accreditation:** NCCU **Intercollegiate Athletics:** Basketball M; Fencing M & W; Rugby M & W; Soccer M & W; Squash M & W

ROGUE COMMUNITY COLLEGE
3345 Redwood Hwy.
Grants Pass, OR 97527-9298
Tel: (541)956-7500
Admissions: (541)956-7176
E-mail: csullivan@roguecc.edu
Web Site: http://www.roguecc.edu/
President/CEO: Dr. Peter Angstadt
Admissions: Claudia Sullivan
Type: Two-Year College **Sex:** Coed **Admission Plans:** Open Admission; Preferred Admission; Early Admission **Application Deadline:** Rolling **Application Fee:** $0.00 **H.S. Requirements:** High school diploma or equivalent not required. For respiratory therapy, nursing, human services, emergency medical technology, mental health technician programs: High school diploma required; GED not accepted. **Costs Per Year:** Application fee: $0. State resident tuition: $2628 full-time, $73 per credit hour part-time. Nonresident tuition: $3204 full-time, $89 per credit hour part-time. Mandatory fees: $330 full-time, $110 per term part-time. **Scholarships:** Available **Calendar System:** Quarter, Summer Session Available **Enrollment:** FT 2,490, PT 2,951 **Faculty:** FT 78, PT 260 **Student-Faculty Ratio:** 21:1 **Final Year or Final Semester Residency Requirement:** No **Library Holdings:** 33,000 **Credit Hours For Degree:** 90 credits, Associates **Professional Accreditation:** CARC, NLN, NCCU

SOUTHERN OREGON UNIVERSITY
1250 Siskiyou Blvd.
Ashland, OR 97520
Tel: (541)552-7672
Admissions: (541)552-6411
Fax: (541)552-6329
E-mail: admissions@sou.edu
Web Site: http://www.sou.edu/
President/CEO: Dr. Mary Cullinan

Admissions: Mark Bottorff
Type: Comprehensive **Sex:** Coed **Affiliation:** Oregon University System **Scores:** 89.4% SAT V 400+; 89.7% SAT M 400+; 50.8% ACT 18-23; 29.4% ACT 24-29 **% Accepted:** 89 **Admission Plans:** Early Admission; Deferred Admission **Application Deadline:** Rolling **Application Fee:** $50.00 **H.S. Requirements:** High school diploma required; GED accepted **Scholarships:** Available **Calendar System:** Quarter, Summer Session Available **Enrollment:** FT 3,365, PT 1,061, Grad FT 220, Grad PT 457 **Faculty:** FT 181, PT 109 **Student-Faculty Ratio:** 18:1 **Exams:** SAT I or ACT, SAT II. **% Receiving Financial Aid:** 64 **% Residing in College-Owned, -Operated, or -Affiliated Housing:** 24 **Library Holdings:** 315,000 **Credit Hours For Degree:** 180 credits, Bachelors **Professional Accreditation:** NASM, NCCU **Intercollegiate Athletics:** Basketball M & W; Cross-Country Running M & W; Football M; Skiing (Downhill) M & W; Soccer W; Softball W; Tennis W; Track and Field M & W; Volleyball W; Wrestling M

SOUTHWESTERN OREGON COMMUNITY COLLEGE
1988 Newmark Ave.
Coos Bay, OR 97420-2912
Tel: (541)888-2525
E-mail: lwells@socc.edu
Web Site: http://www.socc.edu/
President/CEO: Patty M. Scott, EdD
Admissions: Lela Wells
Type: Two-Year College **Sex:** Coed **% Accepted:** 100 **Admission Plans:** Open Admission; Early Admission **Application Deadline:** Rolling **Application Fee:** $30.00 **H.S. Requirements:** High school diploma or equivalent not required. For nursing program: High school diploma required; GED accepted **Costs Per Year:** Application fee: $30. State resident tuition: $2484 full-time, $69 per credit hour part-time. Nonresident tuition: $2484 full-time, $69 per credit hour part-time. Mandatory fees: $912 full-time, $17 per credit hour part-time, $25. College room and board: $6605. Room and board charges vary according to board plan. $15 per online course fee, $3000 Nursing program fee, $23,000 comprehensive fee for Culinary Arts program and $23,000 comprehensive fee for Baking and Pastry program. **Scholarships:** Available **Calendar System:** Quarter, Summer Session Available **Enrollment:** FT 976, PT 1,004 **Faculty:** FT 66, PT 153 **Student-Faculty Ratio:** 10:1 **Library Holdings:** 40,505 **Credit Hours For Degree:** 93 credit hours, Associates **Professional Accreditation:** NCCU **Intercollegiate Athletics:** Baseball M; Basketball M & W; Cheerleading M & W; Cross-Country Running M & W; Golf M & W; Soccer M & W; Softball W; Track and Field M & W; Volleyball W; Wrestling M

TILLAMOOK BAY COMMUNITY COLLEGE
4301 Third St.
Tillamook, OR 97141
Tel: (503)842-8222
Fax: (503)842-2214
E-mail: gates@tillamookbay.cc
Web Site: http://www.tbcc.cc.or.us/
President/CEO: Jon Carnahan
Admissions: Lori Gates
Type: Two-Year College **Sex:** Coed **Affiliation:** Portland Community College **% Accepted:** 100 **Application Fee:** $0.00 **Calendar System:** Quarter **Enrollment:** FT 73, PT 226 **Faculty:** FT 6, PT 30 **Student-Faculty Ratio:** 8:1 **Professional Accreditation:** NCCU

TREASURE VALLEY COMMUNITY COLLEGE
650 College Blvd.
Ontario, OR 97914-3423
Tel: (541)889-6493
Admissions: (541)881-8822
Fax: (541)881-2721
E-mail: clbell@tvcc.cc
Web Site: http://www.tvcc.cc.or.us/
President/CEO: Dr. James E. Sorensen
Admissions: Candace Bell
Type: Two-Year College **Sex:** Coed **% Accepted:** 100 **Admission Plans:** Open Admission; Early Admission; Deferred Admission **Application Deadline:** Rolling **Application Fee:** $0.00 **H.S. Requirements:** High school diploma or equivalent not required. For nursing program: High school diploma required; GED accepted **Scholarships:** Available **Calendar System:** Quarter, Summer Session Available **Enrollment:** FT 997, PT 1,013 **Faculty:** FT 48, PT 92 **Student-Faculty Ratio:** 11:1 **% Residing in College-Owned, -Operated, or -Affiliated Housing:** 6 **Library Holdings:** 28,000 **Credit Hours For Degree:** 90 credits, Associates **ROTC:** Army **Professional Accreditation:** NCCU **Intercollegiate Athletics:** Baseball M; Basketball M & W; Cross-Country Running M & W; Soccer M & W; Softball M & W; Tennis M & W; Track and Field M & W; Volleyball W

UMPQUA COMMUNITY COLLEGE
PO Box 967
Roseburg, OR 97470-0226
Tel: (541)440-4600
Fax: (541)440-4612
E-mail: Ted.Swagerty@umpqua.edu
Web Site: http://www.umpqua.edu/
President/CEO: Dr. Blaine Nisson
Admissions: Ted Swagerty
Type: Two-Year College **Sex:** Coed **% Accepted:** 100 **Admission Plans:** Open Admission; Early Admission; Deferred Admission **Application Deadline:** Rolling **Application Fee:** $25.00 **H.S. Requirements:** High school diploma or equivalent not required. For nursing, emergency medical technology program: High school diploma required; GED accepted **Costs Per Year:** Application fee: $25. State resident tuition: $3585 full-time, $65 per credit hour part-time. Nonresident tuition: $8865 full-time, $192 per credit hour part-time. Mandatory fees: $300 full-time, $7 per credit hour part-time, $15 per term part-time. **Scholarships:** Available **Calendar System:** Quarter, Summer Session Available **Enrollment:** FT 1,376, PT 1,210 **Faculty:** FT 62, PT 109 **Student-Faculty Ratio:** 23:1 **Library Holdings:** 41,000 **Credit Hours For Degree:** 93 credits, Associates **Professional Accreditation:** NLN, NCCU **Intercollegiate Athletics:** Basketball M & W; Volleyball W

UNIVERSITY OF OREGON
Eugene, OR 97403
Tel: (541)346-3111
Admissions: (541)346-3201
Fax: (541)346-5815
E-mail: uoadmit@uoregon.edu
Web Site: http://www.uoregon.edu/
President/CEO: Richard Lariviere
Admissions: Brian Henley
Financial Aid: Elizabeth Bickford
Type: University **Sex:** Coed **Affiliation:** Oregon University System **Scores:** 97% SAT V 400+; 97% SAT M 400+ **% Accepted:** 80 **Admission Plans:** Early Action **Application Deadline:** January 15 **Application Fee:** $50.00 **H.S. Requirements:** High school diploma required; GED accepted **Costs Per Year:** Application fee: $50. One-time mandatory fee: $300. State resident tuition: $6180 full-time, $130 per credit hour part-time. Nonresident tuition: $22,470 full-time, $485 per credit hour part-time. Mandatory fees: $1248 full-time. Full-time tuition and fees vary according to course load, degree level, and program. Part-time tuition varies according to course load, degree level, and program. College room and board: $8620. Room and board charges vary according to board plan and housing facility. **Scholarships:** Available **Calendar System:** Quarter, Summer Session Available **Enrollment:** FT 16,971, PT 1,538, Grad FT 3,098, Grad PT 728 **Faculty:** FT 892, PT 382 **Student-Faculty Ratio:** 20:1 **Exams:** SAT I or ACT, SAT I and SAT II or ACT. **% Receiving Financial Aid:** 41 **% Residing in College-Owned, -Operated, or -Affiliated Housing:** 20 **Library Holdings:** 3,083,407 **Credit Hours For Degree:** 180 credit hours, Bachelors **ROTC:** Army, Air Force **Professional Accreditation:** AACSB, ACEJMC, ABA, ACSP, APA, ASLA, ASLHA, AALS, FIDER, NAAB, NASAD, NASM, NASPAA, NCCU **Intercollegiate Athletics:** Baseball M; Basketball M & W; Cross-Country Running M & W; Football M; Golf M & W; Gymnastics W; Lacrosse W; Soccer W; Softball W; Tennis M & W; Track and Field M & W; Volleyball W

UNIVERSITY OF PHOENIX—OREGON CAMPUS
13221 SW 68th Parkway, Ste. 500
Tigard, OR 97223
Tel: (503)670-0590; Free: 800-228-7240
Admissions: (480)557-6151
Fax: (503)670-0614
E-mail: audra.mcquarie@phoenix.edu
Web Site: http://www.phoenix.edu/
President/CEO: William Pepicello
Admissions: Audra McQuarie

Type: Comprehensive **Sex:** Coed **Admission Plans:** Open Admission; Deferred Admission **Application Deadline:** Rolling **Application Fee:** $0.00 **H.S. Requirements:** High school diploma required; GED accepted **Costs Per Year:** Application fee: $0. Tuition: $12,225 full-time. Full-time tuition varies according to course level and course load. **Scholarships:** Available **Calendar System:** Continuous, Summer Session Not available **Enrollment:** FT 1,042 **Faculty:** FT 31, PT 222 **Regional Accreditation:** North Central Association of Colleges and Schools **Credit Hours For Degree:** 60 credits, Associates; 120 credits, Bachelors

UNIVERSITY OF PORTLAND
5000 North Willamette Blvd.
Portland, OR 97203-5798
Tel: (503)943-7911; Free: 888-627-5601
Admissions: (503)943-7147
Fax: (503)943-7399
E-mail: admissions@up.edu
Web Site: http://www.up.edu/
President/CEO: Fr. William Beauchamp, CSC
Admissions: Jason McDonald
Financial Aid: Janet Turner
Type: Comprehensive **Sex:** Coed **Affiliation:** Roman Catholic **Scores:** 100% SAT M 400+ **% Accepted:** 56 **Admission Plans:** Deferred Admission **Application Deadline:** June 1 **Application Fee:** $50.00 **H.S. Requirements:** High school diploma required; GED accepted **Costs Per Year:** Application fee: $50. Comprehensive fee: $41,131 includes full-time tuition ($30,800), mandatory fees ($1196), and college room and board ($9135). College room only: $4245. Full-time tuition and fees vary according to program. Room and board charges vary according to board plan and housing facility. Part-time tuition: $970 per credit hour. Part-time tuition varies according to course load and program. **Scholarships:** Available **Calendar System:** Semester, Summer Session Available **Enrollment:** FT 3,038, PT 68, Grad FT 189, Grad PT 411 **Faculty:** FT 207, PT 108 **Student-Faculty Ratio:** 13:1 **Exams:** SAT I or ACT. SAT essay not being used. **% Receiving Financial Aid:** 63 **% Residing in College-Owned, -Operated, or -Affiliated Housing:** 54 **Final Year or Final Semester Residency Requirement:** No **Library Holdings:** 350,000 **Credit Hours For Degree:** 120 semester hours, Bachelors **ROTC:** Army, Air Force **Professional Accreditation:** AACSB, ABET, AACN, NASM, NAST, NCATE, NLN, NCCU **Intercollegiate Athletics:** Baseball M; Basketball M & W; Cross-Country Running M & W; Golf M & W; Rugby M; Soccer M & W; Tennis M & W; Track and Field M & W; Volleyball W

WARNER PACIFIC COLLEGE
2219 Southeast 68th Ave.
Portland, OR 97215-4099
Tel: (503)517-1000; Free: 800-804-1510
Admissions: (503)517-1020
Fax: (503)788-7425
E-mail: admiss@warnerpacific.edu
Web Site: http://www.warnerpacific.edu/
President/CEO: Dr. Andrea Cook
Admissions: Shannon Mackey
Financial Aid: Bryan Cook
Type: Comprehensive **Sex:** Coed **Affiliation:** Church of God **Scores:** 90.8% SAT V 400+; 87.3% SAT M 400+ **% Accepted:** 61 **Application Deadline:** Rolling **Application Fee:** $50.00 **H.S. Requirements:** High school diploma required; GED accepted **Costs Per Year:** Application fee: $50. Comprehensive fee: $23,756 includes full-time tuition ($16,480), mandatory fees ($630), and college room and board ($6646). Full-time tuition and fees vary according to course load, degree level, location, reciprocity agreements, and student level. Room and board charges vary according to board plan and housing facility. Part-time tuition: $750 per credit. Part-time mandatory fees: $475 per credit. Part-time tuition and fees vary according to course load, degree level, location, and reciprocity agreements. **Scholarships:** Available **Calendar System:** Semester, Summer Session Available **Enrollment:** FT 1,166, PT 15, Grad FT 147, Grad PT 5 **Faculty:** FT 24, PT 92 **Student-Faculty Ratio:** 22:1 **Exams:** SAT I or ACT, SAT II. ACT essay used for advising. SAT essay used for advising. **% Receiving Financial Aid:** 90 **% Residing in College-Owned, -Operated, or -Affiliated Housing:** 19 **Credit Hours For Degree:** 62 semester hours, Associates; 124 semester hours, Bachelors **ROTC:** Air Force **Professional Accreditation:** NCCU **Intercollegiate Athletics:** Basketball M & W; Cross-Country Running M & W; Golf M & W; Soccer M & W; Track and Field M & W; Volleyball W

WESTERN CULINARY INSTITUTE
921 Southwest Morrison St.
Ste. 400
Portland, OR 97205
Tel: (503)223-2245; Free: 888-891-6222
Fax: (503)223-0126
Web Site: http://www.wci.edu/
President/CEO: Jon Alberts
Type: Two-Year College **Sex:** Coed **Calendar System:** Continuous **Professional Accreditation:** ACCSCT, ACF

WESTERN OREGON UNIVERSITY
345 North Monmouth Ave.
Monmouth, OR 97361-1394
Tel: (503)838-8000; Free: 877-877-1593
Admissions: (503)838-8211
Fax: (503)838-8067
E-mail: wolfgram@wou.edu
Web Site: http://www.wou.edu/
President/CEO: Dr. John P. Minahan
Admissions: Rob Findtner
Financial Aid: Donna Fossum
Type: Comprehensive **Sex:** Coed **Affiliation:** Oregon University System **Scores:** 85% SAT V 400+; 87% SAT M 400+; 55% ACT 18-23; 17% ACT 24-29 **% Accepted:** 89 **Admission Plans:** Deferred Admission **Application Deadline:** Rolling **Application Fee:** $50.00 **H.S. Requirements:** High school diploma required; GED accepted **Costs Per Year:** Application fee: $50. One-time mandatory fee: $171. State resident tuition: $6285 full-time, $130 per credit hour part-time. Nonresident tuition: $17,376 full-time, $371 per credit hour part-time. Mandatory fees: $1173 full-time. Full-time tuition and fees vary according to course level, course load, degree level, and reciprocity agreements. Part-time tuition varies according to course level, course load, degree level, and reciprocity agreements. College room and board: $8208. Room and board charges vary according to board plan and housing facility. Tuition guaranteed not to increase for student's term of enrollment. **Scholarships:** Available **Calendar System:** Quarter, Summer Session Available **Enrollment:** FT 4,274, PT 601, Grad FT 238, Grad PT 541 **Faculty:** FT 209, PT 150 **Student-Faculty Ratio:** 25:1 **Exams:** SAT I or ACT. **% Receiving Financial Aid:** 75 **Final Year or Final Semester Residency Requirement:** No **Library Holdings:** 227,707 **Credit Hours For Degree:** 93 credit hours, Associates; 180 credit hours, Bachelors **ROTC:** Army, Air Force **Professional Accreditation:** CORE, NASM, NCATE, NCCU **Intercollegiate Athletics:** Baseball M; Basketball M & W; Cross-Country Running M & W; Football M; Soccer W; Softball W; Track and Field M & W; Volleyball W

WILLAMETTE UNIVERSITY
900 State St.
Salem, OR 97301-3931
Tel: (503)370-6300; Free: 877-542-2787
Fax: (503)375-5363
E-mail: libarts@willamette.edu
Web Site: http://www.willamette.edu/
President/CEO: Dr. M. Lee Pelton
Admissions: Susan Rauch
Financial Aid: Patty Hoban
Type: Comprehensive **Sex:** Coed **Affiliation:** United Methodist **Scores:** 100% SAT V 400+; 100% SAT M 400+; 10% ACT 18-23; 64% ACT 24-29 **% Accepted:** 60 **Admission Plans:** Early Action; Deferred Admission **Application Deadline:** February 1 **Application Fee:** $50.00 **H.S. Requirements:** High school diploma required; GED accepted **Costs Per Year:** Application fee: $50. Comprehensive fee: $43,960 includes full-time tuition ($35,400), mandatory fees ($210), and college room and board ($8350). Full-time tuition and fees vary according to course load. Room and board charges vary according to board plan and housing facility. Part-time tuition: $4425 per course. Part-time tuition varies according to course load. **Scholarships:** Available **Calendar System:** Semester, Summer Session Not available **Enrollment:** FT 1,856, PT 141, Grad FT 762, Grad PT 127 **Faculty:** FT 213, PT 83 **Student-Faculty Ratio:** 10:1 **Exams:** SAT I or ACT. ACT essay used for advising. SAT essay used for advising. ACT essay used for placement. SAT essay used for placement. **% Receiving Financial Aid:** 63 **% Residing in College-Owned, -Operated, or -Affiliated Housing:** 71 **Library Holdings:** 317,000 **Credit Hours For Degree:** 124 semester hours, Bachelors **ROTC:** Army, Air Force **Professional Accreditation:** AACSB, ABA, AALS,

NASM, NASPAA, NCATE, NCCU **Intercollegiate Athletics:** Baseball M; Basketball M & W; Crew M & W; Cross-Country Running M & W; Football M; Golf M & W; Lacrosse M; Soccer M & W; Softball W; Swimming and Diving M & W; Tennis M & W; Track and Field M & W; Volleyball W

ALBRIGHT COLLEGE
13th and Bern Sts., PO Box 15234
Reading, PA 19612-5234
Tel: (610)921-2381; Free: 800-252-1856
Admissions: (610)921-7260
Fax: (610)921-7530
E-mail: admission@albright.edu
Web Site: http://www.albright.edu/
President/CEO: Dr. Lex O. McMillan
Admissions: Gregory Eichhorn
Financial Aid: Mary Ellen Duffy
Type: Comprehensive **Sex:** Coed **Affiliation:** United Methodist Church **Scores:** 99% SAT V 400+; 99% SAT M 400+ **% Accepted:** 56 **Admission Plans:** Early Admission; Deferred Admission **Application Deadline:** Rolling **Application Fee:** $25.00 **H.S. Requirements:** High school diploma required; GED accepted **Costs Per Year:** Application fee: $25. Comprehensive fee: $41,598 includes full-time tuition ($31,940), mandatory fees ($800), and college room and board ($8858). College room only: $4919. Full-time tuition and fees vary according to course load. Room and board charges vary according to board plan and housing facility. **Scholarships:** Available **Calendar System:** 4-1-4, Summer Session Available **Enrollment:** FT 2,253, PT 29, Grad PT 76 **Faculty:** FT 114, PT 47 **Student-Faculty Ratio:** 13:1 **Exams:** Other. **% Receiving Financial Aid:** 82 **% Residing in College-Owned, -Operated, or -Affiliated Housing:** 69 **Final Year or Final Semester Residency Requirement:** Yes **Library Holdings:** 228,700 **Regional Accreditation:** Middle State Association of Colleges and Schools **Credit Hours For Degree:** 32 courses, Bachelors **Intercollegiate Athletics:** Badminton W; Baseball M; Basketball M & W; Cheerleading M & W; Cross-Country Running M & W; Field Hockey W; Football M; Golf M; Lacrosse M & W; Rugby M & W; Soccer M & W; Softball W; Swimming and Diving M & W; Tennis M & W; Track and Field M & W; Volleyball W

ALLEGHENY COLLEGE
520 North Main St.
Meadville, PA 16335
Tel: (814)332-3100; Free: 800-521-5293
Admissions: (814)332-4351
Fax: (814)337-0431
E-mail: admissions@allegheny.edu
Web Site: http://www.allegheny.edu/
President/CEO: Dr. James H. Mullen, Jr.
Admissions: Jennifer Winge
Financial Aid: Sheryle Proper
Type: Four-Year College **Sex:** Coed **Scores:** 99% SAT V 400+; 100% SAT M 400+; 31% ACT 18-23; 46% ACT 24-29 **% Accepted:** 66 **Admission Plans:** Early Admission; Early Decision Plan; Deferred Admission **Application Deadline:** February 15 **Application Fee:** $35.00 **H.S. Requirements:** High school diploma required; GED accepted **Costs Per Year:** Application fee: $35. Comprehensive fee: $43,600 includes full-time tuition ($34,490), mandatory fees ($320), and college room and board ($8790). College room only: $4620. Room and board charges vary according to board plan and housing facility. Part-time tuition: $1437 per credit hour. Part-time mandatory fees: $160 per term. Part-time tuition and fees vary according to course load. **Scholarships:** Available **Calendar System:** Semester, Summer Session Not available **Enrollment:** FT 2,094, PT 38 **Faculty:** FT 152, PT 33 **Student-Faculty Ratio:** 13:1 **Exams:** SAT I or ACT. **% Receiving Financial Aid:** 69 **% Residing in College-Owned, -Operated, or -Affiliated Housing:** 78 **Final Year or Final Semester Residency Requirement:** Yes **Library Holdings:** 305,767 **Regional Accreditation:** Middle State Association of Colleges and Schools **Credit Hours For Degree:** 128 credit hours, Bachelors **Intercollegiate Athletics:** Baseball M; Basketball M & W; Cheerleading M & W; Crew M & W; Cross-Country Running M & W; Equestrian Sports M & W; Fencing M & W; Football M; Golf M & W; Ice Hockey M; Lacrosse W; Rugby M & W; Soccer M & W; Softball W; Swimming and Diving M & W; Table Tennis M & W; Tennis M & W; Track and Field M & W; Ultimate Frisbee M & W; Volleyball M & W

ALVERNIA UNIVERSITY
400 Saint Bernardine St.
Reading, PA 19607-1799
Tel: (610)796-8200
Admissions: (610)796-8269
Fax: (610)796-8336
E-mail: admissions@alvernia.edu
Web Site: http://www.alvernia.edu/
President/CEO: Dr. Tom Flynn
Admissions: Jeff Dittman
Financial Aid: Rachel Gordon
Type: Comprehensive **Sex:** Coed **Affiliation:** Roman Catholic **Scores:** 91% SAT V 400+; 90% SAT M 400+; 60% ACT 18-23; 11% ACT 24-29 **% Accepted:** 78 **Admission Plans:** Deferred Admission **Application Deadline:** Rolling **Application Fee:** $25.00 **H.S. Requirements:** High school diploma required; GED accepted **Costs Per Year:** Application fee: $25. Comprehensive fee: $33,562 includes full-time tuition ($23,900), mandatory fees ($450), and college room and board ($9212). Full-time tuition and fees vary according to class time and reciprocity agreements. Room and board charges vary according to board plan and housing facility. **Scholarships:** Available **Calendar System:** Semester, Summer Session Available **Enrollment:** FT 1,612, PT 464, Grad FT 180, Grad PT 600 **Faculty:** FT 85, PT 212 **Student-Faculty Ratio:** 14:1 **Exams:** SAT I or ACT. ACT essay not being used. SAT essay not being used. **% Receiving Financial Aid:** 70 **% Residing in College-Owned, -Operated, or -Affiliated Housing:** 49 **Library Holdings:** 85,823 **Regional Accreditation:** Middle State Association of Colleges and Schools **Credit Hours For Degree:** 65 credits, Associates; 123 credits, Bachelors **ROTC:** Army **Professional Accreditation:** AACN, AOTA, ACBSP, CSWE, JRCEPAT, NLN **Intercollegiate Athletics:** Baseball M; Basketball M & W; Cross-Country Running M & W; Field Hockey W; Golf M & W; Lacrosse M & W; Soccer M & W; Softball W; Tennis M & W; Track and Field M & W; Volleyball W

ANTONELLI INSTITUTE
300 Montgomery Ave.
Erdenheim, PA 19038
Tel: (215)836-2222; Free: 800-722-7871
Fax: (215)836-2794
Web Site: http://www.antonelli.edu/
President/CEO: Dr. Thomas D. Treacy
Admissions: Anthony Detore
Type: Two-Year College **Sex:** Coed **% Accepted:** 65 **Admission Plans:** Open Admission; Deferred Admission **Application Deadline:** September 1 **Application Fee:** $25.00 **H.S. Requirements:** High school diploma

required; GED accepted **Scholarships:** Available **Calendar System:** Semester, Summer Session Not available **Enrollment:** FT 183, PT 6 **Faculty:** FT 14, PT 2 **Student-Faculty Ratio:** 13:1 **% Residing in College-Owned, -Operated, or -Affiliated Housing:** 40 **Library Holdings:** 4,000 **Credit Hours For Degree:** 60 credit hours, Associates **Professional Accreditation:** ACCSCT

ARCADIA UNIVERSITY
450 South Easton Rd.
Glenside, PA 19038-3295
Tel: (215)572-2900; Free: 877-ARCADIA
Admissions: (215)572-2910
Fax: (215)572-4049
E-mail: admiss@arcadia.edu
Web Site: http://www.arcadia.edu/
President/CEO: Dr. Jerry M. Greiner
Admissions: Mark Lapreziosa
Financial Aid: Holly Kirkpatrick
Type: Comprehensive **Sex:** Coed **Affiliation:** Presbyterian Church (U.S.A.) **Scores:** 99% SAT V 400+; 99% SAT M 400+; 49% ACT 18-23; 40% ACT 24-29 **% Accepted:** 61 **Admission Plans:** Deferred Admission **Application Deadline:** March 1 **Application Fee:** $30.00 **H.S. Requirements:** High school diploma required; GED accepted **Costs Per Year:** Application fee: $30. One-time mandatory fee: $100. Comprehensive fee: $41,940 includes full-time tuition ($30,780), mandatory fees ($480), and college room and board ($10,680). College room only: $7620. Full-time tuition and fees vary according to course load, degree level, and program. Room and board charges vary according to board plan. Part-time tuition: $515 per credit. **Scholarships:** Available **Calendar System:** Semester, Summer Session Available **Enrollment:** FT 2,022, PT 231, Grad FT 631, Grad PT 1,137 **Faculty:** FT 107, PT 308 **Student-Faculty Ratio:** 15:1 **Exams:** SAT I or ACT. **% Receiving Financial Aid:** 88 **% Residing in College-Owned, -Operated, or -Affiliated Housing:** 55 **Library Holdings:** 157,438 **Regional Accreditation:** Middle State Association of Colleges and Schools **Credit Hours For Degree:** 128 credits, Bachelors **Professional Accreditation:** APTA, ACBSP, NASAD **Intercollegiate Athletics:** Baseball M; Basketball M & W; Equestrian Sports M & W; Field Hockey W; Golf M & W; Lacrosse W; Soccer M & W; Softball W; Swimming and Diving M & W; Tennis M & W; Volleyball W

THE ART INSTITUTE OF PHILADELPHIA
1622 Chestnut St.
Philadelphia, PA 19103
Tel: (215)567-7080; Free: 800-275-2474
Web Site: http://www.artinstitutes.edu/philadelphia/
President/CEO: Dr. William Larkin
Type: Four-Year College **Sex:** Coed **Affiliation:** Education Management Corporation **Calendar System:** Quarter **Regional Accreditation:** Middle State Association of Colleges and Schools **Professional Accreditation:** ACICS, ACF

THE ART INSTITUTE OF PITTSBURGH
420 Blvd. of the Allies
Pittsburgh, PA 15219
Tel: (412)263-6600; Free: 800-275-2470
Admissions: (412)291-6200
Fax: (412)263-6667
Web Site: http://www.artinstitutes.edu/pittsburgh/
President/CEO: George L. Pry
Type: Four-Year College **Sex:** Coed **Affiliation:** Education Management Corporation **Calendar System:** Quarter **Regional Accreditation:** Middle State Association of Colleges and Schools **Professional Accreditation:** ACICS

THE ART INSTITUTE OF YORK—PENNSYLVANIA
1409 Williams Rd.
York, PA 17402-9012
Tel: (717)755-2300; Free: 800-864-7725
Fax: (717)840-1951
Web Site: http://www.artinstitutes.edu/york/
President/CEO: Tim Howard
Type: Two-Year College **Sex:** Coed **Affiliation:** Education Management Corporation **Calendar System:** Quarter **Professional Accreditation:** ACCSCT

BAPTIST BIBLE COLLEGE OF PENNSYLVANIA
538 Venard Rd.
Clarks Summit, PA 18411-1297
Tel: (570)586-2400; Free: 800-451-7664
Fax: (570)585-9400
E-mail: admissions@bbc.edu
Web Site: http://www.bbc.edu/
President/CEO: Dr. Jim Jeffery
Admissions: Summer Kinder
Financial Aid: Charis Henson
Type: Comprehensive **Sex:** Coed **Affiliation:** Baptist **Scores:** 91% SAT V 400+; 86% SAT M 400+; 50% ACT 18-23; 32% ACT 24-29 **% Accepted:** 64 **Admission Plans:** Early Admission; Deferred Admission **Application Deadline:** August 15 **Application Fee:** $30.00 **H.S. Requirements:** High school diploma required; GED accepted **Costs Per Year:** Application fee: $30. Comprehensive fee: $23,690 includes full-time tuition ($16,200), mandatory fees ($1140), and college room and board ($6350). College room only: $2300. Room and board charges vary according to board plan. Part-time tuition: $540 per credit. Part-time tuition varies according to course load. **Scholarships:** Available **Calendar System:** Semester, Summer Session Available **Enrollment:** FT 524, PT 48, Grad FT 180, Grad PT 247 **Faculty:** FT 38, PT 29 **Student-Faculty Ratio:** 14:1 **Exams:** SAT I or ACT. **% Receiving Financial Aid:** 77 **% Residing in College-Owned, -Operated, or -Affiliated Housing:** 91 **Final Year or Final Semester Residency Requirement:** No **Library Holdings:** 95,266 **Regional Accreditation:** Middle State Association of Colleges and Schools **Credit Hours For Degree:** 64 semester hours, Associates; 124 semester hours, Bachelors **ROTC:** Army, Navy, Air Force **Professional Accreditation:** ABHE **Intercollegiate Athletics:** Baseball M; Basketball M & W; Cheerleading W; Cross-Country Running M & W; Golf M; Soccer M & W; Softball W; Tennis W; Track and Field M & W; Volleyball W

BERKS TECHNICAL INSTITUTE
2205 Ridgewood Rd.
Wyomissing, PA 19610-1168
Tel: (610)372-1722; Free: 800-821-4662
Fax: (610)376-4684
E-mail: abrussolo@berks.edu
Web Site: http://www.berkstech.com/
President/CEO: Joseph F. Reichard
Admissions: Allan Brussolo
Type: Two-Year College **Sex:** Coed **Affiliation:** Delta Career Education Corporation **Admission Plans:** Early Admission **Application Fee:** $50.00 **H.S. Requirements:** High school diploma required; GED accepted **Scholarships:** Available **Calendar System:** Semester, Summer Session Not available **Enrollment:** FT 490, PT 119 **Faculty:** FT 37, PT 17 **Exams:** Other. **Library Holdings:** 3,000 **Professional Accreditation:** ACCSCT, AAMAE

BIDWELL TRAINING CENTER
1815 Metropolitan St.
Pittsburgh, PA 15233
Tel: (412)323-4000
Fax: (412)321-2120
E-mail: admissions@mcg-btc.org
Web Site: http://www.bidwell-training.org/
President/CEO: William E. Strickland, Jr.
Type: Two-Year College **Sex:** Coed **Professional Accreditation:** ACCSCT

BLOOMSBURG UNIVERSITY OF PENNSYLVANIA
400 East Second St.
Bloomsburg, PA 17815-1301
Tel: (570)389-4000
Admissions: (570)389-4316
E-mail: buadmiss@bloomu.edu
Web Site: http://www.bloomu.edu/
President/CEO: Dr. David Soltz
Admissions: Christopher Keller
Financial Aid: Thomas M. Lyons
Type: Comprehensive **Sex:** Coed **Affiliation:** Pennsylvania State System of Higher Education **Scores:** 92.1% SAT V 400+; 92.8% SAT M 400+ **% Accepted:** 64 **Admission Plans:** Preferred Admission; Early Admission; Early Action; Deferred Admission **Application Deadline:** Rolling **Application Fee:** $30.00 **H.S. Requirements:** High school diploma required; GED accepted **Costs Per Year:** Application fee: $30. State resident tuition: $5554 full-time,

$231 per credit part-time. Nonresident tuition: $13,886 full-time, $579 per credit part-time. Mandatory fees: $1556 full-time, $44.50 per credit part-time, $100 per term part-time. Full-time tuition and fees vary according to course load. Part-time tuition and fees vary according to course load. College room and board: $6488. College room only: $3882. Room and board charges vary according to board plan and housing facility. **Scholarships:** Available **Calendar System:** Semester, Summer Session Available **Enrollment:** FT 8,105, PT 500, Grad FT 447, Grad PT 460 **Faculty:** FT 400, PT 91 **Student-Faculty Ratio:** 21:1 **Exams:** SAT I or ACT. ACT essay not being used. SAT essay not being used. **% Receiving Financial Aid:** 80 **% Residing in College-Owned, -Operated, or -Affiliated Housing:** 49 **Final Year or Final Semester Residency Requirement:** No **Library Holdings:** 489,636 **Regional Accreditation:** Middle State Association of Colleges and Schools **Credit Hours For Degree:** 60 credits, Associates; 120 credits, Bachelors **ROTC:** Army, Air Force **Professional Accreditation:** AACSB, AACN, AANA, ASLHA, CSWE, NCATE **Intercollegiate Athletics:** Baseball M; Basketball M & W; Cheerleading M & W; Cross-Country Running M & W; Equestrian Sports M & W; Field Hockey W; Football M; Ice Hockey M; Lacrosse W; Soccer M & W; Softball W; Swimming and Diving M & W; Tennis M & W; Track and Field M & W; Volleyball M & W; Wrestling M

BRADFORD SCHOOL
125 West Station Square Dr.
Ste. 129
Pittsburgh, PA 15219
Tel: (412)391-6710; Free: 800-391-6810
Fax: (412)471-6714
Web Site: http://www.bradfordpittsburgh.edu/
President/CEO: Vincent S. Graziano
Type: Two-Year College **Sex:** Coed **% Accepted:** 86 **Scholarships:** Available **Professional Accreditation:** ACICS

BRYN ATHYN COLLEGE OF THE NEW CHURCH
2965 College Dr.
PO Box 717
Bryn Athyn, PA 19009-0717
Tel: (267)502-2543
Admissions: (267)502-6000
Fax: (267)502-2658
E-mail: admissions@brynathyn.edu
Web Site: http://www.brynathyn.edu/
President/CEO: Dr. Chris M. Clark
Financial Aid: Wendy Cooper
Type: Comprehensive **Sex:** Coed **Affiliation:** Church of the New Jerusalem; Christian; The Academy of the New Church **Scores:** 95% SAT V 400+; 93% SAT M 400+; 77% ACT 18-23; 15% ACT 24-29 **% Accepted:** 92 **Admission Plans:** Deferred Admission **Application Deadline:** July 1 **Application Fee:** $0.00 **H.S. Requirements:** High school diploma required; GED accepted **Costs Per Year:** Application fee: $0. Comprehensive fee: $23,541 includes full-time tuition ($13,188), mandatory fees ($1812), and college room and board ($8541). College room only: $3801. Room and board charges vary according to housing facility. Part-time tuition: $355 per credit. Part-time mandatory fees: $74 per credit. **Scholarships:** Available **Calendar System:** Trimester, Summer Session Not available **Enrollment:** FT 181, PT 7, Grad FT 15, Grad PT 8 **Faculty:** FT 24, PT 26 **Student-Faculty Ratio:** 6:1 **Exams:** SAT I or ACT. ACT essay not being used. SAT essay not being used. **% Receiving Financial Aid:** 49 **% Residing in College-Owned, -Operated, or -Affiliated Housing:** 68 **Final Year or Final Semester Residency Requirement:** No **Library Holdings:** 125,575 **Regional Accreditation:** Middle State Association of Colleges and Schools **Credit Hours For Degree:** 68 credits, Associates; 136 credits, Bachelors **ROTC:** Army, Air Force **Intercollegiate Athletics:** Badminton M & W; Ice Hockey M; Lacrosse M; Soccer M; Volleyball W

BRYN MAWR COLLEGE
101 North Merion Ave.
Bryn Mawr, PA 19010-2899
Tel: (610)526-5000; Free: 800-BMC-1885
Admissions: (610)526-5152
Fax: (610)526-7471
E-mail: admissions@brynmawr.edu
Web Site: http://www.brynmawr.edu/
President/CEO: Dr. Jane McAuliffe
Admissions: Marjorie Torchon
Financial Aid: Ethel M. Desmarais
Type: University **Scores:** 100.01% SAT V 400+; 100% SAT M 400+; 4.96% ACT 18-23; 61.98% ACT 24-29 **% Accepted:** 49 **Admission Plans:** Early Admission; Early Decision Plan; Deferred Admission **Application Deadline:** January 15 **Application Fee:** $50.00 **H.S. Requirements:** High school diploma required; GED accepted **Costs Per Year:** Application fee: $50. Comprehensive fee: $51,780 includes full-time tuition ($38,420), mandatory fees ($940), and college room and board ($12,420). College room only: $7100. Part-time tuition: $4800 per course. **Scholarships:** Available **Calendar System:** Semester, Summer Session Available **Faculty:** FT 158, PT 53 **Student-Faculty Ratio:** 8:1 **Exams:** SAT I and SAT II or ACT. **% Receiving Financial Aid:** 57 **% Residing in College-Owned, -Operated, or -Affiliated Housing:** 95 **Regional Accreditation:** Middle State Association of Colleges and Schools **Credit Hours For Degree:** 32 courses, Bachelors **ROTC:** Air Force **Professional Accreditation:** CSWE **Intercollegiate Athletics:** Badminton W; Basketball W; Crew W; Cross-Country Running W; Field Hockey W; Lacrosse W; Soccer W; Swimming and Diving W; Tennis W; Track and Field W; Volleyball W

BUCKNELL UNIVERSITY
701 Moore Ave.
Lewisburg, PA 17837
Tel: (570)577-2000
Admissions: (570)577-1101
Fax: (570)577-3760
E-mail: admissions@bucknell.edu
Web Site: http://www.bucknell.edu/
President/CEO: Dr. Brian C. Mitchell
Admissions: Dean Robert Springall
Financial Aid: Andrea Leithner Stauffer
Type: Comprehensive **Sex:** Coed **Scores:** 100% SAT V 400+; 100% SAT M 400+; 5% ACT 18-23; 52% ACT 24-29 **% Accepted:** 30 **Admission Plans:** Preferred Admission; Early Decision Plan; Deferred Admission **Application Deadline:** January 15 **Application Fee:** $60.00 **H.S. Requirements:** High school diploma required; GED accepted **Costs Per Year:** Application fee: $60. Comprehensive fee: $52,280 includes full-time tuition ($42,112), mandatory fees ($230), and college room and board ($9938). College room only: $5768. Room and board charges vary according to board plan and housing facility. **Scholarships:** Available **Calendar System:** Semester, Summer Session Available **Enrollment:** FT 3,523, PT 20, Grad FT 80, Grad PT 50 **Faculty:** FT 345, PT 22 **Student-Faculty Ratio:** 10:1 **Exams:** SAT I or ACT. **% Receiving Financial Aid:** 46 **% Residing in College-Owned, -Operated, or -Affiliated Housing:** 87 **Final Year or Final Semester Residency Requirement:** Yes **Library Holdings:** 917,328 **Regional Accreditation:** Middle State Association of Colleges and Schools **Credit Hours For Degree:** 32 courses, Bachelors **ROTC:** Army **Professional Accreditation:** ABET, NASM **Intercollegiate Athletics:** Baseball M; Basketball M & W; Cheerleading M & W; Crew M & W; Cross-Country Running M & W; Equestrian Sports M & W; Field Hockey W; Football M; Golf M & W; Ice Hockey M; Lacrosse M & W; Rock Climbing M & W; Rugby M & W; Skiing (Downhill) M & W; Soccer M & W; Softball W; Swimming and Diving M & W; Tennis M & W; Track and Field M & W; Ultimate Frisbee M & W; Volleyball M & W; Water Polo M & W; Weight Lifting M & W; Wrestling M

BUCKS COUNTY COMMUNITY COLLEGE
275 Swamp Rd.
Newtown, PA 18940-1525
Tel: (215)968-8000
Fax: (215)968-8110
E-mail: wilsona@bucks.edu
Web Site: http://www.bucks.edu/
President/CEO: James J. Linksz
Admissions: Marlene Barlow
Financial Aid: Donna M. Wilkoski
Type: Two-Year College **Sex:** Coed **Admission Plans:** Open Admission; Early Admission **Application Fee:** $0.00 **H.S. Requirements:** High school diploma required; GED accepted **Costs Per Year:** Application fee: $0. Area resident tuition: $2970 full-time, $99 per credit hour part-time. State resident tuition: $5940 full-time, $198 per credit hour part-time. Nonresident tuition: $8910 full-time, $297 per credit hour part-time. Mandatory fees: $824 full-time. Full-time tuition and fees vary according to course load and reciprocity agreements. Part-time tuition varies according to course load and reciprocity agreements. **Scholarships:** Available **Calendar System:** Semester, Summer Session Available **Enrollment:** FT 5,209, PT 5,800 **Faculty:** FT 163, PT

474 **Student-Faculty Ratio:** 22:1 **Library Holdings:** 155,779 **Regional Accreditation:** Middle State Association of Colleges and Schools **Credit Hours For Degree:** 60 credits, Associates **Professional Accreditation:** AAMAE, ACBSP, NASAD, NASM, NLN **Intercollegiate Athletics:** Baseball M; Basketball M; Equestrian Sports M & W; Golf M & W; Soccer M & W; Tennis M & W; Volleyball W

BUTLER COUNTY COMMUNITY COLLEGE
107 College Dr.
Butler, PA 16003-1203
Tel: (724)287-8711; Free: 888-826-2829
Fax: (724)285-6047
E-mail: pattie.bajoszik@bc3.edu
Web Site: http://www.bc3.edu/
President/CEO: Dr. Nicholas Neupauer
Admissions: Patricia Bajuszik
Type: Two-Year College **Sex:** Coed **Admission Plans:** Open Admission **Application Deadline:** August 15 **Application Fee:** $25.00 **H.S. Requirements:** High school diploma required; GED accepted **Scholarships:** Available **Calendar System:** Semester, Summer Session Available **Enrollment:** FT 1,967, PT 1,689 **Faculty:** FT 64, PT 271 **Student-Faculty Ratio:** 20:1 **Library Holdings:** 70,000 **Regional Accreditation:** Middle State Association of Colleges and Schools **Credit Hours For Degree:** 63 credits, Associates **Professional Accreditation:** APTA, ACBSP, NLN, NAIT **Intercollegiate Athletics:** Baseball M; Basketball M; Golf M & W; Softball W; Volleyball W

CABRINI COLLEGE
610 King of Prussia Rd.
Radnor, PA 19087-3698
Tel: (610)902-8100; Free: 800-848-1003
Admissions: (610)902-8557
Fax: (610)902-8309
E-mail: admit@cabrini.edu
Web Site: http://www.cabrini.edu/
President/CEO: Dr. Marie George
Admissions: Stephen Colfer
Financial Aid: Mike Colahan
Type: Comprehensive **Sex:** Coed **Affiliation:** Roman Catholic **Scores:** 91% SAT V 400+; 88% SAT M 400+ **% Accepted:** 75 **Admission Plans:** Deferred Admission **Application Deadline:** Rolling **Application Fee:** $35.00 **H.S. Requirements:** High school diploma required; GED accepted. For transfer students with 30 or more credits: High school diploma or equivalent not required **Costs Per Year:** Application fee: $35. Comprehensive fee: $42,430 includes full-time tuition ($30,120), mandatory fees ($910), and college room and board ($11,400). Room and board charges vary according to board plan and housing facility. Part-time tuition: $455 per credit hour. Part-time mandatory fees: $45 per term. Part-time tuition and fees vary according to course load. **Scholarships:** Available **Calendar System:** Semester, Summer Session Available **Enrollment:** FT 1,452, PT 102, Grad FT 135, Grad PT 1,825 **Faculty:** FT 70, PT 254 **Student-Faculty Ratio:** 14:1 **Exams:** SAT I or ACT. **% Receiving Financial Aid:** 73 **% Residing in College-Owned, -Operated, or -Affiliated Housing:** 56 **Final Year or Final Semester Residency Requirement:** Yes **Library Holdings:** 112,749 **Regional Accreditation:** Middle State Association of Colleges and Schools **Credit Hours For Degree:** 123 credits, Bachelors **ROTC:** Army, Air Force **Professional Accreditation:** CSWE **Intercollegiate Athletics:** Basketball M & W; Cross-Country Running M & W; Field Hockey W; Golf M; Lacrosse M & W; Soccer M & W; Softball W; Swimming and Diving M & W; Tennis M & W; Track and Field M & W; Volleyball W

CALIFORNIA UNIVERSITY OF PENNSYLVANIA
250 University Ave.
California, PA 15419-1394
Tel: (724)938-4000
Admissions: (724)938-4400
Fax: (724)938-4138
E-mail: inquiry@cup.edu
Web Site: http://www.cup.edu/
President/CEO: Angelo Armenti, Jr.
Admissions: William Edmonds
Type: Comprehensive **Sex:** Coed **Affiliation:** Pennsylvania State System of Higher Education **Scores:** 99% SAT V 400+; 99% SAT M 400+; 100% ACT 18-23 **% Accepted:** 68 **Admission Plans:** Early Admission; Deferred Admission **Application Deadline:** May 1 **Application Fee:** $25.00 **H.S. Requirements:** High school diploma required; GED accepted **Scholarships:** Available **Calendar System:** Semester, Summer Session Available **Enrollment:** FT 5,615, PT 684 **Faculty:** FT 298, PT 104 **Student-Faculty Ratio:** 20:1 **Exams:** SAT I or ACT. **% Receiving Financial Aid:** 67 **% Residing in College-Owned, -Operated, or -Affiliated Housing:** 29 **Library Holdings:** 437,160 **Regional Accreditation:** Middle State Association of Colleges and Schools **Credit Hours For Degree:** 60 credits, Associates; 120 credits, Bachelors **ROTC:** Army **Professional Accreditation:** AACN, ACA, APTA, ASLHA, CSWE, JRCEPAT, NCATE, NLN **Intercollegiate Athletics:** Baseball M; Basketball M & W; Cheerleading M & W; Cross-Country Running M & W; Fencing M & W; Football M; Golf M & W; Soccer M & W; Softball W; Swimming and Diving W; Tennis W; Track and Field M & W; Volleyball M & W

CAMBRIA-ROWE BUSINESS COLLEGE (INDIANA)
422 South 13th St.
Indiana, PA 15701
Tel: (724)463-0222
Admissions: (724)483-0222
Fax: (724)463-7246
E-mail: sbell-leger@crbc.net
Web Site: http://www.crbc.net/
President/CEO: Jeffrey Allen
Admissions: Stacey Bell-Leger
Type: Two-Year College **Sex:** Coed **% Accepted:** 78 **Costs Per Year:** Tuition: $9300 full-time, $255 per credit part-time. Mandatory fees: $990 full-time, $690 per term part-time. Full-time tuition and fees vary according to course load and program. Part-time tuition and fees vary according to course load and program. **Calendar System:** Quarter **Enrollment:** FT 98, PT 3 **Faculty:** FT 8, PT 0 **Student-Faculty Ratio:** 13:1 **Professional Accreditation:** ACICS

CAMBRIA-ROWE BUSINESS COLLEGE (JOHNSTOWN)
221 Central Ave.
Johnstown, PA 15902-2494
Tel: (814)536-5168
Fax: (814)536-5160
E-mail: admissions@crbc.net
Web Site: http://www.crbc.net/
President/CEO: Jeffrey Allen
Admissions: Amanda Artim
Type: Two-Year College **Sex:** Coed **Admission Plans:** Early Admission **Application Deadline:** Rolling **Application Fee:** $15.00 **H.S. Requirements:** High school diploma required; GED accepted **Costs Per Year:** Application fee: $15. Tuition: $9150 full-time, $255 per credit part-time. Mandatory fees: $990 full-time, $290 per term part-time. Part-time tuition and fees vary according to course load. **Scholarships:** Available **Calendar System:** Quarter, Summer Session Available **Enrollment:** FT 230 **Faculty:** FT 11, PT 0 **Student-Faculty Ratio:** 20:1 **Credit Hours For Degree:** 90 quarter credits, Associates **Professional Accreditation:** ACICS

CAREER TRAINING ACADEMY (MONROEVILLE)
4314 Old William Penn Hwy.
Ste. 103
Monroeville, PA 15146
Tel: (412)372-3900
Fax: (412)373-4262
E-mail: admissions@careerta.edu
Web Site: http://www.careerta.edu/
President/CEO: John M. Reddy
Admissions: Cassandra Dehnel
Type: Two-Year College **Sex:** Coed **Application Fee:** $30.00 **H.S. Requirements:** High school diploma required; GED accepted **Calendar System:** Quarter **Professional Accreditation:** ACCSCT, AAMAE

CAREER TRAINING ACADEMY (NEW KENSINGTON)
950 Fifth Ave.
New Kensington, PA 15068-6301
Tel: (724)337-1000
Fax: (724)335-7140
E-mail: admissions@careeta.edu
Web Site: http://www.careeta.com/
President/CEO: John M. Reddy

Admissions: Tyna Pitignano
Type: Two-Year College **Sex:** Coed **Application Deadline:** Rolling **Application Fee:** $30.00 **H.S. Requirements:** High school diploma required; GED accepted **Calendar System:** Quarter **Faculty:** FT 14, PT 8 **Student-Faculty Ratio:** 20:1 **Professional Accreditation:** ACCSCT, AAMAE

CAREER TRAINING ACADEMY (PITTSBURGH)
1500 Northway Mall
Ste. 200
Pittsburgh, PA 15237
Tel: (412)367-4000
E-mail: admission3@careerta.edu
Web Site: http://www.careerta.edu/
President/CEO: Carla Ryba
Admissions: Jamie Vignone
Type: Two-Year College **Sex:** Coed **Application Deadline:** Rolling **Application Fee:** $30.00 **H.S. Requirements:** High school diploma required; GED accepted **Calendar System:** Continuous **Enrollment:** FT 85 **Faculty:** FT 8, PT 3 **Student-Faculty Ratio:** 11:1 **Credit Hours For Degree:** 90 credits, Associates **Professional Accreditation:** ACCSCT

CARLOW UNIVERSITY
3333 Fifth Ave.
Pittsburgh, PA 15213-3165
Tel: (412)578-6000; Free: 800-333-CARLOW
Admissions: (412)578-6059
Fax: (412)578-6668
E-mail: admissions@carlow.edu
Web Site: http://www.carlow.edu/
President/CEO: Dr. Mary E. Hines
Admissions: Susan Winstel
Financial Aid: Natalie Wilson
Type: Comprehensive **Sex:** Coed **Affiliation:** Roman Catholic **Scores:** 93.8% SAT V 400+; 88.9% SAT M 400+; 59.5% ACT 18-23; 20.3% ACT 24-29 **% Accepted:** 70 **Admission Plans:** Early Admission; Early Action; Deferred Admission **Application Deadline:** Rolling **Application Fee:** $20.00 **H.S. Requirements:** High school diploma required; GED accepted **Costs Per Year:** Application fee: $20. Comprehensive fee: $30,272 includes full-time tuition ($20,854), mandatory fees ($866), and college room and board ($8552). College room only: $4370. Full-time tuition and fees vary according to course load, degree level, program, and reciprocity agreements. Room and board charges vary according to board plan. Part-time tuition: $682 per credit. Part-time tuition varies according to course load, degree level, program, and reciprocity agreements. **Scholarships:** Available **Calendar System:** Semester, Summer Session Available **Enrollment:** FT 1,113, PT 698, Grad FT 221, Grad PT 501 **Faculty:** FT 96, PT 182 **Student-Faculty Ratio:** 10:1 **Exams:** SAT I or ACT. ACT essay not being used. SAT essay not being used. **% Residing in College-Owned, -Operated, or -Affiliated Housing:** 24 **Final Year or Final Semester Residency Requirement:** No **Library Holdings:** 133,864 **Regional Accreditation:** Middle State Association of Colleges and Schools **Credit Hours For Degree:** 120 credits, Bachelors **ROTC:** Army, Navy, Air Force **Professional Accreditation:** AACN, CSWE **Intercollegiate Athletics:** Basketball W; Crew W; Soccer W; Softball W; Tennis W; Volleyball W

CARNEGIE MELLON UNIVERSITY
5000 Forbes Ave.
Pittsburgh, PA 15213-3891
Tel: (412)268-2000
Admissions: (412)268-2082
Fax: (412)268-7838
E-mail: undergraduate-admissions@andrew.cmu.edu
Web Site: http://www.cmu.edu/
President/CEO: Dr. Jared L. Cohon
Admissions: Michael Steidel
Financial Aid: Linda M. Anderson
Type: University **Sex:** Coed **Scores:** 100% SAT V 400+; 100% SAT M 400+; 2% ACT 18-23; 28% ACT 24-29 **% Accepted:** 36 **Admission Plans:** Early Admission; Early Decision Plan; Deferred Admission **Application Deadline:** January 1 **Application Fee:** $70.00 **H.S. Requirements:** High school diploma required; GED accepted **Costs Per Year:** Application fee: $70. One-time mandatory fee: $192. Comprehensive fee: $51,568 includes full-time tuition ($40,300), mandatory fees ($428), and college room and board ($10,840). College room only: $6060. Room and board charges vary according to board plan and housing facility. Part-time tuition: $547 per unit. **Scholarships:** Available **Calendar System:** Semester, Summer Session Available **Enrollment:** FT 5,862, PT 161, Grad FT 4,174, Grad PT 1,246 **Faculty:** FT 883, PT 80 **Student-Faculty Ratio:** 12:1 **Exams:** SAT I or ACT, SAT II. ACT essay used for admission. SAT essay used for admission. **% Receiving Financial Aid:** 49 **% Residing in College-Owned, -Operated, or -Affiliated Housing:** 64 **Library Holdings:** 1,129,808 **Regional Accreditation:** Middle State Association of Colleges and Schools **Credit Hours For Degree:** 360 units, Bachelors **ROTC:** Army, Navy, Air Force **Professional Accreditation:** AACSB, ABET, NAAB, NASAD, NASM, NASPAA **Intercollegiate Athletics:** Badminton W; Baseball M; Basketball M & W; Cheerleading M & W; Crew M & W; Cross-Country Running M & W; Fencing M & W; Football M; Golf M; Ice Hockey M & W; Lacrosse M & W; Racquetball M & W; Rugby M & W; Soccer M & W; Softball W; Squash M & W; Swimming and Diving M & W; Tennis M & W; Track and Field M & W; Ultimate Frisbee M & W; Volleyball M & W; Water Polo M & W

CEDAR CREST COLLEGE
100 College Dr.
Allentown, PA 18104-6196
Tel: (610)437-4471; Free: 800-360-1222
Admissions: (610)606-4666
Fax: (610)606-4647
E-mail: astewart@cedarcrest.edu
Web Site: http://www.cedarcrest.edu/
President/CEO: Carmen Twillie Ambar
Admissions: Andrea Stewart
Financial Aid: Lori Williams
Type: Comprehensive **Sex:** Women **Affiliation:** United Church of Christ **Scores:** 98% SAT M 400+; 47% ACT 18-23; 51% ACT 24-29 **% Accepted:** 63 **Admission Plans:** Early Admission; Deferred Admission **Application Deadline:** Rolling **Application Fee:** $30.00 **H.S. Requirements:** High school diploma required; GED accepted **Costs Per Year:** Application fee: $30. Comprehensive fee: $37,456 includes full-time tuition ($27,735), mandatory fees ($400), and college room and board ($9321). College room only: $4912. Full-time tuition and fees vary according to class time, course load, degree level, and program. Room and board charges vary according to board plan and housing facility. Part-time tuition: $772 per credit hour. Part-time mandatory fees: $125 per term. Part-time tuition and fees vary according to class time, course load, degree level, and program. **Scholarships:** Available **Calendar System:** Semester, Summer Session Available **Enrollment:** FT 967, PT 718, Grad FT 56, Grad PT 146 **Faculty:** FT 92, PT 81 **Student-Faculty Ratio:** 11:1 **Exams:** SAT I or ACT. ACT essay used for admission. SAT essay used for admission. ACT essay used for advising. SAT essay used for advising. **% Receiving Financial Aid:** 90 **% Residing in College-Owned, -Operated, or -Affiliated Housing:** 61 **Final Year or Final Semester Residency Requirement:** No **Library Holdings:** 144,037 **Regional Accreditation:** Middle State Association of Colleges and Schools **Credit Hours For Degree:** 120 credit hours, Bachelors **ROTC:** Army **Professional Accreditation:** CSWE, JRCNMT, NLN **Intercollegiate Athletics:** Basketball W; Cross-Country Running W; Equestrian Sports W; Field Hockey W; Lacrosse W; Soccer W; Softball W; Tennis W; Track and Field W; Volleyball W

CENTRAL PENNSYLVANIA COLLEGE
College Hill & Valley Roads
Summerdale, PA 17093-0309
Tel: (717)732-0702; Free: 800-759-2727
Admissions: (717)728-2531
Fax: (717)732-5254
E-mail: stacyscott@centralpenn.edu
Web Site: http://www.centralpenn.edu/
President/CEO: Todd A. Milano
Admissions: Stacy Scott
Financial Aid: Kathy Shepard
Type: Four-Year College **Sex:** Coed **% Accepted:** 51 **Application Deadline:** Rolling **Application Fee:** $0.00 **H.S. Requirements:** High school diploma required; GED accepted **Costs Per Year:** Application fee: $0. Comprehensive fee: $20,130 includes full-time tuition ($13,140), mandatory fees ($705), and college room and board ($6285). College room only: $4665. Full-time tuition and fees vary according to program. Room and board charges vary according to board plan and housing facility. Part-time tuition: $365 per credit hour. Part-time mandatory fees: $235 per term. Part-time tuition and fees vary according to program. **Scholarships:** Available

Calendar System: Quarter, Summer Session Available **Enrollment:** FT 674, PT 542 **Faculty:** FT 24, PT 98 **Student-Faculty Ratio:** 15:1 **Exams:** SAT I or ACT. **Final Year or Final Semester Residency Requirement:** No **Library Holdings:** 22,637 **Regional Accreditation:** Middle State Association of Colleges and Schools **Credit Hours For Degree:** 62 credits, Associates; 125 credits, Bachelors **Professional Accreditation:** AAMAE, APTA **Intercollegiate Athletics:** Basketball M & W; Bowling M & W; Golf M & W

CHATHAM UNIVERSITY
Woodland Rd.
Pittsburgh, PA 15232-2826
Tel: (412)365-1100; Free: 800-837-1290
Admissions: (412)365-1672
Fax: (412)365-1609
E-mail: lmeyers@chatham.edu
Web Site: http://www.chatham.edu/
President/CEO: Dr. Esther L. Barazzone
Admissions: Lisa D. Meyers
Financial Aid: Jennifer Burns
Type: University **Scores:** 95.9% SAT V 400+; 90.8% SAT M 400+; 25% ACT 18-23; 50% ACT 24-29 **% Accepted:** 68 **Admission Plans:** Early Admission; Deferred Admission **Application Deadline:** August 1 **Application Fee:** $35.00 **H.S. Requirements:** High school diploma required; GED accepted **Costs Per Year:** Application fee: $35. Tuition: $662 per credit hour part-time. Part-time tuition varies according to course load. **Scholarships:** Available **Calendar System:** Miscellaneous, Summer Session Available **Enrollment:** FT 683, PT 393, Grad FT 717, Grad PT 426 **Faculty:** FT 88, PT 180 **Student-Faculty Ratio:** 10:1 **Exams:** ACT essay not being used. SAT essay not being used. **% Receiving Financial Aid:** 76 **% Residing in College-Owned, -Operated, or -Affiliated Housing:** 54 **Library Holdings:** 90,780 **Regional Accreditation:** Middle State Association of Colleges and Schools **Credit Hours For Degree:** 120 credit hours, Bachelors **ROTC:** Army, Navy, Air Force **Professional Accreditation:** AACN, AOTA, APTA, ASLA, CSWE **Intercollegiate Athletics:** Basketball W; Crew W; Cross-Country Running W; Ice Hockey W; Soccer W; Softball W; Swimming and Diving W; Tennis W; Volleyball W; Water Polo W

CHESTNUT HILL COLLEGE
9601 Germantown Ave.
Philadelphia, PA 19118-2693
Tel: (215)248-7000; Free: 800-248-0052
Admissions: (215)248-7001
Fax: (215)248-7056
Web Site: http://www.chc.edu/
President/CEO: Dr. Carol Jean Vale, SSJ
Financial Aid: Nicholas Flocco
Type: Comprehensive **Sex:** Coed **Affiliation:** Roman Catholic **Scores:** 93% SAT V 400+; 90% SAT M 400+; 86% ACT 18-23; 14% ACT 24-29 **% Accepted:** 72 **Admission Plans:** Open Admission; Early Admission; Early Decision Plan; Deferred Admission **Application Deadline:** Rolling **Application Fee:** $35.00 **H.S. Requirements:** High school diploma required; GED accepted **Costs Per Year:** Application fee: $35. Comprehensive fee: $35,900 includes full-time tuition ($27,000), mandatory fees ($100), and college room and board ($8800). Room and board charges vary according to housing facility. Part-time tuition: $575 per credit. **Scholarships:** Available **Calendar System:** Semester, Summer Session Available **Enrollment:** FT 1,019, PT 310 **Faculty:** FT 76, PT 223 **Student-Faculty Ratio:** 10:1 **Exams:** SAT I or ACT. **% Receiving Financial Aid:** 77 **% Residing in College-Owned, -Operated, or -Affiliated Housing:** 63 **Library Holdings:** 132,434 **Regional Accreditation:** Middle State Association of Colleges and Schools **Credit Hours For Degree:** 60 semester hours, Associates; 120 semester hours, Bachelors **Professional Accreditation:** MACTE **Intercollegiate Athletics:** Baseball M; Basketball M & W; Cross-Country Running M & W; Golf M & W; Lacrosse M & W; Soccer M & W; Softball W; Tennis M & W; Volleyball W

CHEYNEY UNIVERSITY OF PENNSYLVANIA
1837 University Circle, PO Box 200
Cheyney, PA 19319
Tel: (610)399-2000; Free: 800-CHE-YNEY
Admissions: (610)399-2275
Fax: (610)399-2099
E-mail: abrown@cheyney.edu
Web Site: http://www.cheyney.edu/
President/CEO: Dr. Michelle Howard-Vital
Admissions: Angela Brown
Financial Aid: James Brown
Type: Comprehensive **Sex:** Coed **Affiliation:** Pennsylvania State System of Higher Education **Scores:** 35% SAT V 400+; 34% SAT M 400+; 42% ACT 18-23 **% Accepted:** 50 **Admission Plans:** Preferred Admission; Deferred Admission **Application Deadline:** March 31 **Application Fee:** $20.00 **H.S. Requirements:** High school diploma required; GED accepted **Costs Per Year:** Application fee: $20. One-time mandatory fee: $100. State resident tuition: $5554 full-time, $231 per credit part-time. Nonresident tuition: $13,886 full-time, $579 per credit part-time. Mandatory fees: $1806 full-time. College room and board: $7746. College room only: $4500. Room and board charges vary according to board plan. **Scholarships:** Available **Calendar System:** Semester, Summer Session Available **Enrollment:** FT 1,262, PT 140, Grad FT 38, Grad PT 48 **Faculty:** FT 75, PT 24 **Student-Faculty Ratio:** 15:1 **Exams:** ACT, SAT I and SAT II or ACT, SAT I. **% Receiving Financial Aid:** 94 **% Residing in College-Owned, -Operated, or -Affiliated Housing:** 74 **Regional Accreditation:** Middle State Association of Colleges and Schools **Credit Hours For Degree:** 120 credit hours, Bachelors **ROTC:** Army **Professional Accreditation:** NCATE **Intercollegiate Athletics:** Basketball M & W; Bowling W; Cross-Country Running M & W; Football M; Track and Field M & W; Volleyball W

CHI INSTITUTE, BROOMALL CAMPUS
1991 Sproul Rd.
Ste. 42
Broomall, PA 19008
Tel: (610)353-7630
Web Site: http://www.chitraining.com/
President/CEO: Dale Wintemberg
Type: Two-Year College **Sex:** Coed **H.S. Requirements:** High school diploma required; GED accepted **Scholarships:** Available **Calendar System:** Quarter **Professional Accreditation:** ACCSCT

CHI INSTITUTE, FRANKLIN MILLS CAMPUS
177 Franklin Mills Blvd.
Philadelphia, PA 19154
Tel: (215)612-6600; Free: 800-336-7696
Web Site: http://www.chitraining.com/
President/CEO: Eric Heller
Type: Two-Year College **Sex:** Coed **Application Fee:** $0.00 **H.S. Requirements:** High school diploma required; GED accepted **Scholarships:** Available **Calendar System:** Quarter **Professional Accreditation:** ACCSCT

CLARION UNIVERSITY OF PENNSYLVANIA
890 Wood St.
Clarion, PA 16214
Tel: (814)393-2000; Free: 800-672-7171
Admissions: (814)393-2306
Fax: (814)393-2030
E-mail: wbailey@clarion.edu
Web Site: http://www.clarion.edu/
President/CEO: Dr. Joseph P. Grunenwald
Admissions: William Bailey
Financial Aid: Dr. Kenneth Grugel
Type: Comprehensive **Sex:** Coed **Affiliation:** Pennsylvania State System of Higher Education **Scores:** 82.9% SAT V 400+; 84.7% SAT M 400+ **% Accepted:** 68 **Admission Plans:** Deferred Admission **Application Deadline:** Rolling **Application Fee:** $30.00 **H.S. Requirements:** High school diploma required; GED accepted **Costs Per Year:** Application fee: $30. One-time mandatory fee: $30. State resident tuition: $5554 full-time, $231 per credit hour part-time. Nonresident tuition: $11,108 full-time, $463 per credit hour part-time. Mandatory fees: $1827 full-time, $54 per credit hour part-time, $54. Full-time tuition and fees vary according to course load. Part-time tuition and fees vary according to course load. College room and board: $6884. College room only: $4348. Room and board charges vary according to board plan. **Scholarships:** Available **Calendar System:** Semester, Summer Session Available **Enrollment:** FT 5,258, PT 965, Grad FT 215, Grad PT 908 **Faculty:** FT 256, PT 120 **Student-Faculty Ratio:** 19:1 **Exams:** SAT I or ACT. **% Receiving Financial Aid:** 69 **% Residing in College-Owned, -Operated, or -Affiliated Housing:** 33 **Library Holdings:** 442,871 **Regional Accreditation:** Middle State Association of Colleges and Schools **Credit Hours For Degree:** 62 credits, Associates; 128 credits, Bachelors **ROTC:** Army **Professional Accreditation:** AACSB, ALA, ASLHA, NASAD,

NASM, NCATE, NLN **Intercollegiate Athletics:** Baseball M; Basketball M & W; Cross-Country Running W; Football M; Golf M; Softball W; Swimming and Diving M & W; Tennis W; Track and Field W; Volleyball W; Wrestling M

COMMONWEALTH TECHNICAL INSTITUTE
727 Goucher St.
Johnstown, PA 15905-3092
Tel: (814)255-8200
E-mail: rhalza@state.pa.us
Web Site: http://www.hgac.org/
President/CEO: Jack B. Demuth
Admissions: Rebecca Halza
Financial Aid: Jason Gies
Type: Two-Year College **Sex:** Coed **% Accepted:** 89 **Admission Plans:** Open Admission; Preferred Admission **Application Deadline:** Rolling **Application Fee:** $0.00 **H.S. Requirements:** High school diploma required; GED accepted **Scholarships:** Available **Calendar System:** Trimester **Enrollment:** FT 275 **Faculty:** FT 33 **Student-Faculty Ratio:** 10:1 **Library Holdings:** 4,294 **Professional Accreditation:** ACCSCT

COMMUNITY COLLEGE OF ALLEGHENY COUNTY
800 Allegheny Ave.
Pittsburgh, PA 15233-1894
Tel: (412)323-2323
Web Site: http://www.ccac.edu/
President/CEO: Alex Johnson, PhD
Financial Aid: Margaret Barton
Type: Two-Year College **Sex:** Coed **Admission Plans:** Open Admission **Application Deadline:** Rolling **Application Fee:** $0.00 **H.S. Requirements:** High school diploma required; GED accepted **Scholarships:** Available **Calendar System:** Semester, Summer Session Available **Enrollment:** FT 8,525, PT 11,995 **Faculty:** FT 273, PT 1,352 **Student-Faculty Ratio:** 17:1 **Regional Accreditation:** Middle State Association of Colleges and Schools **Credit Hours For Degree:** 60 credits, Associates **Professional Accreditation:** ARCEST, AAMAE, AHIMA, AOTA, APTA, CARC, JRCEDMS, JRCERT, JRCNMT, NAACLS, NLN **Intercollegiate Athletics:** Baseball M; Basketball M & W; Bowling M & W; Golf M & W; Ice Hockey M; Softball W; Table Tennis M & W; Tennis M & W; Volleyball W

COMMUNITY COLLEGE OF BEAVER COUNTY
One Campus Dr.
Monaca, PA 15061-2588
Tel: (724)775-8561; Free: 800-335-0222
Fax: (724)728-7599
E-mail: mike.macon@ccbc.edu
Web Site: http://www.ccbc.edu/
President/CEO: Joe D. Forrester
Admissions: Michael Macon
Type: Two-Year College **Sex:** Coed **% Accepted:** 100 **Admission Plans:** Open Admission; Early Admission **Application Deadline:** Rolling **Application Fee:** $25.00 **H.S. Requirements:** High school diploma or equivalent not required. For nursing, medical laboratory technology programs: High school diploma required; GED accepted **Costs Per Year:** Application fee: $25. Area resident tuition: $3404 full-time, $89.50 per credit hour part-time. State resident tuition: $6540 full-time, $179 per credit hour part-time. Nonresident tuition: $9675 full-time, $268.50 per credit hour part-time. Mandatory fees: $24 per credit hour part-time. Full-time tuition varies according to program. Part-time tuition and fees vary according to program. **Scholarships:** Available **Calendar System:** Semester, Summer Session Available **Faculty:** FT 48, PT 92 **Student-Faculty Ratio:** 13:1 **Library Holdings:** 52,857 **Regional Accreditation:** Middle State Association of Colleges and Schools **Credit Hours For Degree:** 60 credits, Associates **Professional Accreditation:** NLN **Intercollegiate Athletics:** Baseball M; Basketball M; Softball W; Tennis M & W; Volleyball W

COMMUNITY COLLEGE OF PHILADELPHIA
1700 Spring Garden St.
Philadelphia, PA 19130-3991
Tel: (215)751-8010
E-mail: admissions@ccp.edu
Web Site: http://www.ccp.edu/
President/CEO: Dr. Stephen M. Curtis
Admissions: Luke Kasim
Type: Two-Year College **Sex:** Coed **Admission Plans:** Open Admission; Preferred Admission; Early Admission; Deferred Admission **Application Deadline:** Rolling **Application Fee:** $20.00 **H.S. Requirements:** High school diploma required; GED accepted **Costs Per Year:** Application fee: $20. Area resident tuition: $4410 full-time. State resident tuition: $8160 full-time. Nonresident tuition: $11,910 full-time. **Calendar System:** Semester, Summer Session Available **Faculty:** FT 409, PT 674 **Library Holdings:** 110,000 **Regional Accreditation:** Middle State Association of Colleges and Schools **Credit Hours For Degree:** 60 credit hours, Associates **ROTC:** Army **Professional Accreditation:** AAMAE, ADA, AHIMA, CARC, JRCERT, NAACLS, NLN **Intercollegiate Athletics:** Baseball M; Basketball M & W; Cheerleading W; Cross-Country Running M & W; Soccer M; Softball W; Tennis M & W; Track and Field M & W; Volleyball M & W

CONSOLIDATED SCHOOL OF BUSINESS (LANCASTER)
2124 Ambassador Circle
Lancaster, PA 17603
Tel: (717)394-6211
Fax: (717)394-6213
E-mail: lpaul@csb.edu
Web Site: http://www.csb.edu/
President/CEO: Patricia Marcus
Admissions: Libby Paul
Type: Two-Year College **Sex:** Coed **Admission Plans:** Open Admission **Application Deadline:** Rolling **H.S. Requirements:** High school diploma required; GED accepted **Costs Per Year:** Tuition: $26,500 full-time, $350 per credit hour part-time. Mandatory fees: $3750 full-time. Full-time tuition and fees vary according to course load and program. Part-time tuition varies according to course load and program. Tuition guaranteed not to increase for student's term of enrollment. **Scholarships:** Available **Calendar System:** Continuous, Summer Session Not available **Enrollment:** FT 179, PT 3 **Faculty:** FT 24, PT 1 **Student-Faculty Ratio:** 15:1 **Credit Hours For Degree:** 81 credit hours, Associates **Professional Accreditation:** ACICS

CONSOLIDATED SCHOOL OF BUSINESS (YORK)
1605 Clugston Rd.
York, PA 17404
Tel: (717)764-9550; Free: 800-520-0691
Fax: (717)764-9469
E-mail: sswanger@csb.edu
Web Site: http://www.csb.edu/
President/CEO: Patricia R. Marcus
Admissions: Sandra Swanger
Type: Two-Year College **Sex:** Coed **Application Deadline:** Rolling **Application Fee:** $25.00 **H.S. Requirements:** High school diploma required; GED accepted **Costs Per Year:** Application fee: $25. Tuition: $11,850 full-time. Full-time tuition varies according to program. Tuition guaranteed not to increase for student's term of enrollment. **Scholarships:** Available **Calendar System:** Continuous, Summer Session Not available **Enrollment:** FT 176 **Faculty:** FT 18, PT 3 **Student-Faculty Ratio:** 15:1 **Credit Hours For Degree:** 72 credit hours, Associates **Professional Accreditation:** ACICS

CURTIS INSTITUTE OF MUSIC
1726 Locust St.
Philadelphia, PA 19103-6107
Tel: (215)893-5252
Admissions: (215)893-5262
Fax: (215)893-7900
E-mail: chris.hodges@curtis.edu
Web Site: http://www.curtis.edu/
President/CEO: Roberto Diaz
Admissions: Christopher Hodges
Financial Aid: Richard Woodland
Type: Comprehensive **Sex:** Coed **Admission Plans:** Early Admission **Application Deadline:** December 11 **Application Fee:** $150.00 **H.S. Requirements:** High school diploma required; GED not accepted **Costs Per Year:** Application fee: $150. Tuition: $0 full-time. Mandatory fees: $2290 full-time. The Curtis Institute of Music provides merit-based full-tuition scholarships to students. **Scholarships:** Available **Calendar System:** Semester, Summer Session Not available **Library Holdings:** 70,000 **Regional Accreditation:** Middle State Association of Colleges and Schools **Credit Hours For Degree:** 124 semester hours, Bachelors **Professional Accreditation:** NASM

DEAN INSTITUTE OF TECHNOLOGY
1501 West Liberty Ave.
Pittsburgh, PA 15226-1103
Tel: (412)531-4433
Fax: (412)531-4435
Web Site: http://www.deantech.edu/
President/CEO: James Dean
Admissions: Richard D. Ali
Type: Two-Year College **Sex:** Coed **Admission Plans:** Open Admission; Early Admission; Deferred Admission **Application Deadline:** Rolling **Application Fee:** $50.00 **H.S. Requirements:** High school diploma required; GED accepted **Scholarships:** Available **Calendar System:** Quarter, Summer Session Not available **Library Holdings:** 2,500 **Credit Hours For Degree:** 30 courses, Associates **Professional Accreditation:** ACCSCT

DELAWARE COUNTY COMMUNITY COLLEGE
901 South Media Line Rd.
Media, PA 19063-1094
Tel: (610)359-5000; Free: 800-543-0146
E-mail: admiss@dccc.edu
Web Site: http://www.dccc.edu/
President/CEO: Jerome S. Parker
Admissions: Hope Diehl
Type: Two-Year College **Sex:** Coed **% Accepted:** 100 **Admission Plans:** Open Admission; Preferred Admission; Early Admission **Application Deadline:** Rolling **Application Fee:** $25.00 **H.S. Requirements:** High school diploma required; GED accepted. For applicants 19 and over who demonstrate equivalent life experience: High school diploma or equivalent not required **Costs Per Year:** Application fee: $25. One-time mandatory fee: $50. Area resident tuition: $2232 full-time, $93 per credit hour part-time. State resident tuition: $4464 full-time, $186 per credit hour part-time. Nonresident tuition: $6696 full-time, $279 per credit hour part-time. Mandatory fees: $928 full-time, $37 per credit hour part-time, $20 per term part-time. Full-time tuition and fees vary according to course load. Part-time tuition and fees vary according to course load. **Scholarships:** Available **Calendar System:** Semester, Summer Session Available **Enrollment:** FT 5,557, PT 6,680 **Faculty:** FT 143, PT 659 **Student-Faculty Ratio:** 24:1 **Final Year or Final Semester Residency Requirement:** No **Library Holdings:** 55,779 **Regional Accreditation:** Middle State Association of Colleges and Schools **Credit Hours For Degree:** 60 credit hours, Associates **Professional Accreditation:** ARCEST, AAMAE, CARC, NLN **Intercollegiate Athletics:** Baseball M; Basketball M & W; Golf M & W; Soccer M; Softball W; Tennis M & W; Volleyball W

DELAWARE VALLEY COLLEGE
700 East Butler Ave.
Doylestown, PA 18901-2697
Tel: (215)345-1500
Admissions: (215)489-2211
Fax: (215)345-5277
E-mail: admitme@devalcol.edu
Web Site: http://www.delval.edu/
President/CEO: Dr. Joseph Brosnan
Admissions: Stephen Zenko
Financial Aid: Joan Hock
Type: Comprehensive **Sex:** Coed **Scores:** 93.2% SAT V 400+; 95.47% SAT M 400+; 54.17% ACT 18-23; 39.58% ACT 24-29 **% Accepted:** 72 **Admission Plans:** Deferred Admission **Application Deadline:** May 1 **Application Fee:** $50.00 **H.S. Requirements:** High school diploma required; GED accepted **Costs Per Year:** Application fee: $50. Comprehensive fee: $39,610 includes full-time tuition ($27,234), mandatory fees ($2050), and college room and board ($10,326). College room only: $4682. Part-time tuition: $750 per credit. **Scholarships:** Available **Calendar System:** Semester, Summer Session Available **Enrollment:** FT 1,660, PT 328, Grad FT 29, Grad PT 231 **Faculty:** FT 82, PT 118 **Student-Faculty Ratio:** 15:1 **Exams:** SAT I or ACT. ACT essay used for advising. SAT essay used for advising. ACT essay used for placement. SAT essay used for placement. **% Receiving Financial Aid:** 79 **% Residing in College-Owned, -Operated, or -Affiliated Housing:** 67 **Regional Accreditation:** Middle State Association of Colleges and Schools **Credit Hours For Degree:** 65 credits, Associates; 126 credits, Bachelors **Intercollegiate Athletics:** Baseball M; Basketball M & W; Cheerleading W; Cross-Country Running M & W; Equestrian Sports M & W; Field Hockey W; Football M; Golf M; Soccer M & W; Softball W; Track and Field M & W; Volleyball W; Wrestling M

DESALES UNIVERSITY
2755 Station Ave.
Center Valley, PA 18034-9568
Tel: (610)282-1100; Free: 877-4DESALES
Fax: (610)282-2254
E-mail: derrick.wetzell@desales.edu
Web Site: http://www.desales.edu/
President/CEO: Very Rev. Bernard F. O'Connor, OSFS
Admissions: Derrick Wetzell
Financial Aid: Joyce Farmer
Type: Comprehensive **Sex:** Coed **Affiliation:** Roman Catholic **Scores:** 99% SAT V 400+; 97% SAT M 400+; 69% ACT 18-23; 25% ACT 24-29 **% Accepted:** 73 **Application Deadline:** August 1 **Application Fee:** $30.00 **H.S. Requirements:** High school diploma required; GED accepted **Costs Per Year:** Application fee: $30. One-time mandatory fee: $200. Comprehensive fee: $36,950 includes full-time tuition ($26,000), mandatory fees ($1200), and college room and board ($9750). Full-time tuition and fees vary according to class time and degree level. Room and board charges vary according to board plan. Part-time tuition: $1085 per credit hour. Part-time tuition varies according to class time and degree level. **Scholarships:** Available **Calendar System:** Semester, Summer Session Available **Enrollment:** FT 1,729, PT 604, Grad FT 61, Grad PT 756 **Faculty:** FT 104, PT 184 **Student-Faculty Ratio:** 12:1 **Exams:** SAT I or ACT. **% Receiving Financial Aid:** 74 **% Residing in College-Owned, -Operated, or -Affiliated Housing:** 65 **Final Year or Final Semester Residency Requirement:** No **Library Holdings:** 154,960 **Regional Accreditation:** Middle State Association of Colleges and Schools **Credit Hours For Degree:** 120 credits, Bachelors **ROTC:** Army **Professional Accreditation:** ACBSP, NLN **Intercollegiate Athletics:** Baseball M; Basketball M & W; Cross-Country Running M & W; Field Hockey W; Golf M; Lacrosse M & W; Soccer M & W; Softball W; Tennis M & W; Track and Field M & W; Volleyball W

DEVRY UNIVERSITY (FORT WASHINGTON)
1140 Virginia Dr.
Fort Washington, PA 19034
Tel: (215)591-5700
Web Site: http://www.devry.edu/
President/CEO: Darryl Field
Type: Comprehensive **Sex:** Coed **Affiliation:** DeVry University **Admission Plans:** Deferred Admission **Application Deadline:** Rolling **Application Fee:** $50.00 **H.S. Requirements:** High school diploma required; GED accepted **Costs Per Year:** Application fee: $50. Tuition: $14,720 full-time, $575 per credit hour part-time. **Scholarships:** Available **Calendar System:** Semester, Summer Session Available **Enrollment:** FT 441, PT 450, Grad FT 11, Grad PT 147 **Faculty:** FT 24, PT 131 **Student-Faculty Ratio:** 10:1 **Exams:** ACT essay used for admission. SAT essay used for admission. ACT essay used for placement. SAT essay used for placement. **% Receiving Financial Aid:** 81 **Regional Accreditation:** North Central Association of Colleges and Schools

DEVRY UNIVERSITY (KING OF PRUSSIA)
150 Allendale Rd., Buillding 3, Ste. 3201
King of Prussia, PA 19406-2926
Tel: (610)205-3130
Web Site: http://www.devry.edu/
Type: Comprehensive **Sex:** Coed **Calendar System:** Semester **Regional Accreditation:** North Central Association of Colleges and Schools

DEVRY UNIVERSITY (PHILADELPHIA)
Philadelphia Downtown Center
1800 JFK Blvd., Ste. 104
Philadelphia, PA 19103-7421
Web Site: http://www.devry.edu/
Type: Comprehensive **Sex:** Coed **Regional Accreditation:** North Central Association of Colleges and Schools

DEVRY UNIVERSITY (PITTSBURGH)
FreeMarkets Center
210 Sixth Ave., Ste. 200
Pittsburgh, PA 15222-2606
Tel: (412)642-9072; Free: (866)77D-EVRY
Web Site: http://www.devry.edu/
Type: Comprehensive **Sex:** Coed **Calendar System:** Semester **Regional Accreditation:** North Central Association of Colleges and Schools

DICKINSON COLLEGE
PO Box 1773
Carlisle, PA 17013-2896
Tel: (717)243-5121; Free: 800-644-1773
Admissions: (717)245-1231
Fax: (717)245-1442
E-mail: admit@dickinson.edu
Web Site: http://www.dickinson.edu/
President/CEO: William G. Durden
Admissions: Stephanie Balmer
Financial Aid: Judith B. Carter
Type: Four-Year College **Sex:** Coed **Scores:** 99.7% SAT V 400+; 100% SAT M 400+; 5.4% ACT 18-23; 63.8% ACT 24-29 **% Accepted:** 49 **Admission Plans:** Early Action; Early Decision Plan; Deferred Admission **Application Deadline:** February 1 **Application Fee:** $65.00 **H.S. Requirements:** High school diploma required; GED accepted **Costs Per Year:** Application fee: $65. One-time mandatory fee: $25. Comprehensive fee: $50,194 includes full-time tuition ($39,780), mandatory fees ($334), and college room and board ($10,080). College room only: $5200. Room and board charges vary according to board plan and housing facility. Part-time tuition: $4975 per course. Part-time mandatory fees: $42 per course. **Scholarships:** Available **Calendar System:** Semester, Summer Session Available **Enrollment:** FT 2,340, PT 36 **Faculty:** FT 193, PT 44 **Student-Faculty Ratio:** 10:1 **Exams:** SAT I or ACT. ACT essay not being used. SAT essay not being used. **% Receiving Financial Aid:** 52 **% Residing in College-Owned, -Operated, or -Affiliated Housing:** 94 **Final Year or Final Semester Residency Requirement:** No **Library Holdings:** 501,043 **Regional Accreditation:** Middle State Association of Colleges and Schools **Credit Hours For Degree:** 32 courses, Bachelors **ROTC:** Army **Intercollegiate Athletics:** Baseball M; Basketball M & W; Cheerleading M & W; Cross-Country Running M & W; Equestrian Sports M & W; Fencing M & W; Field Hockey W; Football M; Golf M & W; Ice Hockey M; Lacrosse M & W; Skiing (Downhill) M & W; Soccer M & W; Softball W; Squash M & W; Swimming and Diving M & W; Tennis M & W; Track and Field M & W; Ultimate Frisbee M & W; Volleyball M & W; Wrestling M

DOUGLAS EDUCATION CENTER
130 Seventh St.
Monessen, PA 15062
Tel: (724)684-3684
Fax: (724)684-7463
Web Site: http://www.dec.edu/
President/CEO: Jeffrey D. Imbrescia
Admissions: Sherry Lee Walters
Type: Two-Year College **Sex:** Coed **Admission Plans:** Open Admission **Application Deadline:** Rolling **Application Fee:** $50.00 **H.S. Requirements:** High school diploma required; GED accepted **Scholarships:** Available **Enrollment:** FT 354 **Student-Faculty Ratio:** 10:1 **Exams:** Other. **Professional Accreditation:** ACICS

DREXEL UNIVERSITY
3141 Chestnut St.
Philadelphia, PA 19104-2875
Tel: (215)895-2000; Free: 800-2-DREXEL
Admissions: (215)895-2400
Fax: (215)895-5939
E-mail: enroll@drexel.edu
Web Site: http://www.drexel.edu/
President/CEO: C.R. Pennoni
Admissions: Margaret Sparzani
Financial Aid: Helen Gourousis
Type: University **Sex:** Coed **Scores:** 100% SAT V 400+; 100% SAT M 400+ **% Accepted:** 55 **Admission Plans:** Deferred Admission **Application Deadline:** March 1 **Application Fee:** $75.00 **H.S. Requirements:** High school diploma required; GED accepted **Costs Per Year:** Application fee: $75. Comprehensive fee: $46,130 includes full-time tuition ($30,900), mandatory fees ($2105), and college room and board ($13,125). College room only: $7875. Full-time tuition and fees vary according to course load, program, and student level. Room and board charges vary according to board plan and housing facility. Part-time tuition: $850 per credit hour. Part-time tuition varies according to course load and program. **Scholarships:** Available **Calendar System:** Quarter, Summer Session Available **Enrollment:** FT 10,817, PT 2,667, Grad FT 4,564, Grad PT 4,445 **Faculty:** FT 928, PT 571 **Student-Faculty Ratio:** 9:1 **Exams:** SAT I or ACT, SAT I. ACT essay not being used. SAT essay not being used. **% Receiving Financial Aid:** 65 **% Residing in College-Owned, -Operated, or -Affiliated Housing:** 34 **Library Holdings:** 643,869 **Regional Accreditation:** Middle State Association of Colleges and Schools **Credit Hours For Degree:** 180 credit hours, Bachelors **ROTC:** Army, Navy, Air Force **Professional Accreditation:** AACSB, ABET, ACPE, AAMFT, AACN, AANA, ALA, APTA, APA, FIDER, CEPH, LCMEAMA, NAAB, NASAD, NLN **Intercollegiate Athletics:** Basketball M & W; Crew M & W; Field Hockey W; Golf M; Lacrosse M & W; Soccer M & W; Softball W; Swimming and Diving M & W; Tennis M & W; Wrestling M

DUBOIS BUSINESS COLLEGE
1 Beaver Dr.
DuBois, PA 15801-2401
Tel: (814)371-6920
E-mail: dotylj@dbcollege.com
Web Site: http://www.dbcollege.com/
President/CEO: Jackie Diehl Syktich
Admissions: Lisa Doty
Type: Two-Year College **Sex:** Coed **Admission Plans:** Deferred Admission **Application Deadline:** Rolling **Application Fee:** $25.00 **H.S. Requirements:** High school diploma required; GED accepted **Scholarships:** Available **Calendar System:** Quarter, Summer Session Available **Library Holdings:** 2,100 **Credit Hours For Degree:** 90 credits, Associates **Professional Accreditation:** ACICS

DUQUESNE UNIVERSITY
600 Forbes Ave.
Pittsburgh, PA 15282-0001
Tel: (412)396-6000; Free: 800-456-0590
Admissions: (412)396-5002
Fax: (412)396-5779
E-mail: admissions@duq.edu
Web Site: http://www.duq.edu/
President/CEO: Dr. Charles J. Dougherty
Admissions: Paul-James Cukanna
Financial Aid: Richard C. Esposito
Type: University **Sex:** Coed **Affiliation:** Roman Catholic **Scores:** 100% SAT V 400+; 100% SAT M 400+; 29% ACT 18-23; 60% ACT 24-29 **% Accepted:** 76 **Admission Plans:** Early Admission; Early Action; Early Decision Plan; Deferred Admission **Application Deadline:** July 1 **Application Fee:** $50.00 **H.S. Requirements:** High school diploma required; GED accepted **Costs Per Year:** Application fee: $50. Comprehensive fee: $35,668 includes full-time tuition ($24,385), mandatory fees ($2083), and college room and board ($9200). College room only: $5018. Full-time tuition and fees vary according to program. Room and board charges vary according to board plan and housing facility. Part-time tuition: $795 per credit. Part-time mandatory fees: $81 per credit. Part-time tuition and fees vary according to program. **Scholarships:** Available **Calendar System:** Semester, Summer Session Available **Enrollment:** FT 5,545, PT 222, Grad FT 3,466, Grad PT 1,037 **Faculty:** FT 472, PT 511 **Student-Faculty Ratio:** 14:1 **Exams:** SAT I or ACT. ACT essay used for admission. SAT essay used for admission. **% Receiving Financial Aid:** 69 **% Residing in College-Owned, -Operated, or -Affiliated Housing:** 58 **Final Year or Final Semester Residency Requirement:** No **Library Holdings:** 715,518 **Regional Accreditation:** Middle State Association of Colleges and Schools **Credit Hours For Degree:** 120 credits, Bachelors **ROTC:** Army, Navy, Air Force **Professional Accreditation:** AACSB, ACPhE, AACN, ABA, ACA, AHIMA, AOTA, APTA, APA, ASLHA, AALS, JRCEPAT, NASM, NCATE **Intercollegiate Athletics:** Basketball M & W; Cheerleading M & W; Crew M & W; Cross-Country Running M & W; Football M; Ice Hockey M; Lacrosse W; Soccer M & W; Swimming and Diving W; Tennis M & W; Track and Field M & W; Volleyball W

EAST STROUDSBURG UNIVERSITY OF PENNSYLVANIA
200 Prospect St.
East Stroudsburg, PA 18301-2999
Tel: (570)422-3211; Free: 877-230-5547
Admissions: (570)422-3542
Fax: (570)422-3933
E-mail: undergrads@po-box.esu.edu
Web Site: http://www4.esu.edu/
President/CEO: Dr. Robert J. Dillman
Admissions: Jeff Jones
Financial Aid: Kizzy Morris

Type: Comprehensive **Sex:** Coed **Affiliation:** Pennsylvania State System of Higher Education **Scores:** 94.51% SAT V 400+; 96.2% SAT M 400+ **% Accepted:** 69 **Admission Plans:** Preferred Admission **Application Deadline:** April 1 **Application Fee:** $35.00 **H.S. Requirements:** High school diploma required; GED accepted **Costs Per Year:** Application fee: $35. State resident tuition: $5554 full-time, $231 per credit part-time. Nonresident tuition: $13,886 full-time, $579 per credit part-time. Mandatory fees: $1840 full-time, $66 per credit hour part-time. Full-time tuition and fees vary according to course load. Part-time tuition and fees vary according to course load. College room and board: $6418. College room only: $4272. Room and board charges vary according to board plan and housing facility. **Scholarships:** Available **Calendar System:** Semester, Summer Session Available **Enrollment:** FT 5,837, PT 554, Grad FT 414, Grad PT 771 **Faculty:** FT 311, PT 55 **Student-Faculty Ratio:** 18:1 **Exams:** SAT I or ACT. ACT essay used for advising. SAT essay used for advising. ACT essay used for placement. SAT essay used for placement. **% Receiving Financial Aid:** 43 **% Residing in College-Owned, -Operated, or -Affiliated Housing:** 43 **Library Holdings:** 557,505 **Regional Accreditation:** Middle State Association of Colleges and Schools **Credit Hours For Degree:** 60 credits, Associates; 120 credits, Bachelors **ROTC:** Army, Air Force **Professional Accreditation:** ASLHA, CEPH, JRCEPAT, NCATE, NLN, NRPA **Intercollegiate Athletics:** Baseball M; Basketball M & W; Cross-Country Running M & W; Field Hockey W; Football M; Golf W; Lacrosse W; Soccer M & W; Softball W; Swimming and Diving W; Tennis M & W; Track and Field M & W; Volleyball W; Wrestling M

EASTERN UNIVERSITY
1300 Eagle Rd.
St. Davids, PA 19087-3696
Tel: (610)341-5800; Free: 800-452-0996
Fax: (610)341-1723
E-mail: ugadm@eastern.edu
Web Site: http://www.eastern.edu/
President/CEO: David R. Black
Admissions: Michael Dziedziak
Type: Comprehensive **Sex:** Coed **Affiliation:** American Baptist Churches in the USA **Scores:** 97% SAT V 400+; 94% SAT M 400+; 56% ACT 18-23; 25% ACT 24-29 **% Accepted:** 77 **Admission Plans:** Early Admission; Deferred Admission **Application Deadline:** Rolling **Application Fee:** $25.00 **H.S. Requirements:** High school diploma required; GED accepted **Costs Per Year:** Application fee: $25. One-time mandatory fee: $50. Comprehensive fee: $32,640 includes full-time tuition ($23,770) and college room and board ($8870). College room only: $4830. Full-time tuition varies according to course load, degree level, and program. Room and board charges vary according to board plan, housing facility, and location. Part-time tuition: $500 per credit hour. Part-time tuition varies according to degree level and program. **Scholarships:** Available **Calendar System:** Semester, Summer Session Available **Enrollment:** FT 2,192, PT 190 **Faculty:** FT 82, PT 261 **Student-Faculty Ratio:** 13:1 **Exams:** SAT I or ACT. **% Receiving Financial Aid:** 69 **% Residing in College-Owned, -Operated, or -Affiliated Housing:** 65 **Library Holdings:** 143,815 **Regional Accreditation:** Middle State Association of Colleges and Schools **Credit Hours For Degree:** 60 credits, Associates; 127 credits, Bachelors **ROTC:** Army, Air Force **Professional Accreditation:** AACN, ACIPE, ATS, CSWE **Intercollegiate Athletics:** Baseball M; Basketball M & W; Field Hockey W; Golf M; Lacrosse M & W; Soccer M & W; Softball W; Volleyball W

EDINBORO UNIVERSITY OF PENNSYLVANIA
Edinboro, PA 16444
Tel: (814)732-2000; Free: 800-626-2203
Admissions: (814)732-2761
Fax: (814)732-2420
E-mail: eup_admissions@edinboro.edu
Web Site: http://www.edinboro.edu/
President/CEO: Dr. Jeremy D. Brown
Admissions: J. P. Cooney
Financial Aid: Dorothy Body
Type: Comprehensive **Sex:** Coed **Affiliation:** Pennsylvania State System of Higher Education **Scores:** 84.3% SAT V 400+; 80.3% SAT M 400+; 54% ACT 18-23; 14.7% ACT 24-29 **% Accepted:** 73 **Admission Plans:** Deferred Admission **Application Fee:** $30.00 **H.S. Requirements:** High school diploma required; GED accepted **Costs Per Year:** Application fee: $30. State resident tuition: $5554 full-time, $231 per credit hour part-time. Nonresident tuition: $8332 full-time, $347 per credit hour part-time. Mandatory fees: $1762 full-time, $65.03 per credit hour part-time. Part-time tuition and fees vary according to course load. College room and board: $7430. College room only: $4780. Room and board charges vary according to board plan. **Scholarships:** Available **Calendar System:** Semester, Summer Session Available **Enrollment:** FT 5,731, PT 741, Grad FT 521, Grad PT 440 **Faculty:** FT 346, PT 63 **Exams:** SAT I or ACT. ACT essay used for advising. SAT essay used for advising. ACT essay used for placement. SAT essay used for placement. **% Receiving Financial Aid:** 75 **% Residing in College-Owned, -Operated, or -Affiliated Housing:** 29 **Library Holdings:** 496,628 **Regional Accreditation:** Middle State Association of Colleges and Schools **Credit Hours For Degree:** 60 credits, Associates; 120 credits, Bachelors **ROTC:** Army **Professional Accreditation:** AACN, ACA, ADtA, ASLHA, ACBSP, CORE, CSWE, NASAD, NASM, NCATE, NLN **Intercollegiate Athletics:** Basketball M & W; Cross-Country Running M & W; Football M; Ice Hockey M; Lacrosse W; Soccer W; Softball W; Swimming and Diving M & W; Track and Field M & W; Volleyball W; Wrestling M

ELIZABETHTOWN COLLEGE
1 Alpha Dr.
Elizabethtown, PA 17022-2298
Tel: (717)361-1000
Admissions: (717)361-1400
E-mail: admissions@etown.edu
Web Site: http://www.etown.edu/
President/CEO: Dr. Theodore E. Long
Admissions: Debra Murray
Financial Aid: Elizabeth K. McCloud
Type: Comprehensive **Sex:** Coed **Affiliation:** Church of the Brethren **Scores:** 98% SAT V 400+; 99% SAT M 400+; 42% ACT 18-23; 38% ACT 24-29 **% Accepted:** 75 **Admission Plans:** Deferred Admission **Application Deadline:** March 1 **Application Fee:** $30.00 **H.S. Requirements:** High school diploma required; GED accepted **Costs Per Year:** Application fee: $30. Comprehensive fee: $41,750 includes full-time tuition ($33,250) and college room and board ($8500). College room only: $4250. Full-time tuition varies according to course load. Room and board charges vary according to board plan and housing facility. Part-time tuition: $805 per credit hour. Part-time tuition varies according to class time and course load. **Scholarships:** Available **Calendar System:** Semester, Summer Session Available **Enrollment:** FT 1,886, PT 436, Grad FT 33, Grad PT 12 **Faculty:** FT 125, PT 149 **Student-Faculty Ratio:** 12:1 **Exams:** SAT I or ACT. ACT essay not being used. SAT essay not being used. **% Receiving Financial Aid:** 73 **% Residing in College-Owned, -Operated, or -Affiliated Housing:** 83 **Library Holdings:** 254,318 **Regional Accreditation:** Middle State Association of Colleges and Schools **Credit Hours For Degree:** 125 credits, Bachelors **Professional Accreditation:** AOTA, ACBSP, CSWE, NASM **Intercollegiate Athletics:** Baseball M; Basketball M & W; Cheerleading M & W; Cross-Country Running M & W; Field Hockey W; Golf M; Lacrosse M & W; Soccer M & W; Softball W; Swimming and Diving M & W; Tennis M & W; Track and Field M & W; Volleyball M & W; Wrestling M

ERIE BUSINESS CENTER, MAIN
246 West Ninth St.
Erie, PA 16501-1392
Tel: (814)456-7504; Free: 800-352-3743
Fax: (814)456-4882
E-mail: mellor@eriebc.com
Web Site: http://www.eriebc.edu/
President/CEO: Sam McCaughtry
Admissions: Rose Mello
Type: Two-Year College **Sex:** Coed **% Accepted:** 90 **Admission Plans:** Deferred Admission **Application Deadline:** Rolling **Application Fee:** $25.00 **H.S. Requirements:** High school diploma required; GED accepted **Scholarships:** Available **Calendar System:** Trimester, Summer Session Available **Enrollment:** FT 279, PT 114 **Faculty:** FT 12, PT 34 **Student-Faculty Ratio:** 14:1 **Exams:** Other. **% Residing in College-Owned, -Operated, or -Affiliated Housing:** 1 **Library Holdings:** 3,035 **Credit Hours For Degree:** 78 credits, Associates **Professional Accreditation:** ACICS

ERIE BUSINESS CENTER, SOUTH
170 Cascade Galleria
New Castle, PA 16101-3950
Tel: (724)658-9066
Fax: (724)658-3083
E-mail: admissions@eriebcs.com

Web Site: http://www.eriebc.edu/
President/CEO: Steven O'Rourke
Type: Two-Year College **Sex:** Coed **Affiliation:** Erie Business Center - Main Campus **% Accepted:** 87 **Admission Plans:** Deferred Admission **Application Deadline:** Rolling **Application Fee:** $25.00 **H.S. Requirements:** High school diploma required; GED accepted **Costs Per Year:** Application fee: $25. Tuition: $6624 full-time, $184 per credit part-time. Mandatory fees: $300 full-time, $145 per term part-time. **Scholarships:** Available **Calendar System:** Quarter **Enrollment:** FT 100 **Faculty:** FT 2, PT 2 **Exams:** Other, SAT I or ACT, SAT I and SAT II or ACT. **Library Holdings:** 1,725 **Credit Hours For Degree:** 78 credits, Associates **Professional Accreditation:** ACICS

ERIE INSTITUTE OF TECHNOLOGY
940 Millcreek Mall
Erie, PA 16565
Tel: (814)868-9900; Free: (866)868-3743
Fax: (814)868-9977
E-mail: info@erieit.edu
Web Site: http://www.erieit.edu/
Admissions: Barb Bolt
Type: Two-Year College **Sex:** Coed **Admission Plans:** Open Admission **Application Fee:** $25.00 **Calendar System:** Semester **Student-Faculty Ratio:** 10:1

EVEREST INSTITUTE
100 Forbes Ave.
Ste. 1200
Pittsburgh, PA 15222
Tel: (412)261-4520; Free: 888-279-3314
Fax: (412)261-4546
Web Site: http://www.everest.edu/
President/CEO: James P. Callahan
Type: Two-Year College **Sex:** Coed **Admission Plans:** Deferred Admission **Application Deadline:** Rolling **H.S. Requirements:** High school diploma required; GED accepted **Scholarships:** Available **Calendar System:** Quarter, Summer Session Available **Exams:** Other. **Credit Hours For Degree:** 103 credits, Associates **Professional Accreditation:** ACICS

FORTIS INSTITUTE
166 Slocum St.
Forty Fort, PA 18704
Tel: (570)288-8400
Fax: (717)287-7936
Web Site: http://www.fortis.edu/
President/CEO: Ruth L. Brumagin
Type: Two-Year College **Sex:** Coed **Application Fee:** $50.00 **Professional Accreditation:** ACCSCT

FRANKLIN & MARSHALL COLLEGE
PO Box 3003
Lancaster, PA 17604-3003
Tel: (717)291-3911
Admissions: (717)291-3953
Fax: (717)291-4389
E-mail: sara.harbersob@fandm.edu
Web Site: http://www.fandm.edu/
President/CEO: John Anderson Fry
Admissions: Sara Shapiro Harberson
Financial Aid: Clarke Paine
Type: Four-Year College **Sex:** Coed **Scores:** 99% SAT V 400+; 100% SAT M 400+; 1.4% ACT 18-23; 49.3% ACT 24-29 **% Accepted:** 48 **Admission Plans:** Early Admission; Early Decision Plan; Deferred Admission **Application Deadline:** February 1 **Application Fee:** $60.00 **H.S. Requirements:** High school diploma required; GED accepted **Costs Per Year:** Application fee: $60. Comprehensive fee: $50,420 includes full-time tuition ($39,930), mandatory fees ($60), and college room and board ($10,430). College room only: $6575. Room and board charges vary according to board plan and housing facility. Part-time tuition: $4991 per course. **Scholarships:** Available **Calendar System:** Semester, Summer Session Available **Enrollment:** FT 2,132, PT 47 **Faculty:** FT 201, PT 49 **Student-Faculty Ratio:** 10:1 **% Receiving Financial Aid:** 44 **% Residing in College-Owned, -Operated, or -Affiliated Housing:** 96 **Final Year or Final Semester Residency Requirement:** Yes **Library Holdings:** 523,323 **Regional Accreditation:** Middle State Association of Colleges and Schools **Credit Hours For Degree:** 32 credits, Bachelors **Intercollegiate Athletics:** Baseball M; Basketball M & W; Crew M & W; Cross-Country Running M & W; Equestrian Sports W; Field Hockey W; Football M; Golf M & W; Ice Hockey M; Lacrosse M & W; Rugby M & W; Soccer M & W; Softball W; Squash M & W; Swimming and Diving M & W; Tennis M & W; Track and Field M & W; Ultimate Frisbee M & W; Volleyball M & W; Wrestling M

GANNON UNIVERSITY
109 University Square
Erie, PA 16541-0001
Tel: (814)871-7000; Free: 800-GAN-NONU
Admissions: (814)871-7240
Fax: (814)871-5803
E-mail: admissions@gannon.edu
Web Site: http://www.gannon.edu/
President/CEO: Dr. Antoine M. Garibaldi
Financial Aid: Sharon Krahe
Type: University **Sex:** Coed **Affiliation:** Roman Catholic **Scores:** 90% SAT V 400+; 91% SAT M 400+; 42% ACT 18-23; 36.4% ACT 24-29 **% Accepted:** 84 **Admission Plans:** Early Admission; Deferred Admission **Application Deadline:** Rolling **Application Fee:** $25.00 **H.S. Requirements:** High school diploma required; GED accepted **Costs Per Year:** Application fee: $25. Comprehensive fee: $32,904 includes full-time tuition ($23,050), mandatory fees ($524), and college room and board ($9330). College room only: $4850. Full-time tuition and fees vary according to class time and program. Room and board charges vary according to board plan and housing facility. Part-time tuition: $715 per credit hour. Part-time mandatory fees: $17 per credit hour. Part-time tuition and fees vary according to class time and program. **Scholarships:** Available **Calendar System:** Semester, Summer Session Available **Enrollment:** FT 2,444, PT 534, Grad FT 492, Grad PT 768 **Faculty:** FT 200, PT 155 **Student-Faculty Ratio:** 13:1 **Exams:** SAT I or ACT. ACT essay not being used. SAT essay not being used. **% Receiving Financial Aid:** 85 **% Residing in College-Owned, -Operated, or -Affiliated Housing:** 46 **Final Year or Final Semester Residency Requirement:** Yes **Library Holdings:** 263,600 **Regional Accreditation:** Middle State Association of Colleges and Schools **Credit Hours For Degree:** 64 credits, Associates; 128 credits, Bachelors **ROTC:** Army **Professional Accreditation:** ABET, AACN, AANA, ACA, ADtA, AOTA, APTA, ACBSP, CARC, CSWE, JRCERT, NLN **Intercollegiate Athletics:** Baseball M; Basketball M & W; Cheerleading M & W; Cross-Country Running M & W; Football M; Golf M & W; Lacrosse W; Soccer M & W; Softball W; Swimming and Diving M & W; Volleyball W; Water Polo M & W; Wrestling M

GENEVA COLLEGE
3200 College Ave.
Beaver Falls, PA 15010-3599
Tel: (724)846-5100; Free: 800-847-8255
Admissions: (724)847-6500
Fax: (724)847-6687
E-mail: admissions@geneva.edu
Web Site: http://www.geneva.edu/
President/CEO: Dr. Kenneth A. Smith
Admissions: David Layton
Financial Aid: Steve Bell
Type: Comprehensive **Sex:** Coed **Affiliation:** Reformed Presbyterian Church of North America **Scores:** 96% SAT V 400+; 96% SAT M 400+; 54% ACT 18-23; 32% ACT 24-29 **% Accepted:** 80 **Admission Plans:** Early Admission; Early Action; Deferred Admission **Application Deadline:** Rolling **Application Fee:** $40.00 **H.S. Requirements:** High school diploma required; GED accepted **Costs Per Year:** Application fee: $40. Comprehensive fee: $30,236 includes full-time tuition ($22,236) and college room and board ($8000). Full-time tuition varies according to course load. Room and board charges vary according to board plan. Part-time tuition: $745 per credit. Part-time tuition varies according to course load. **Scholarships:** Available **Calendar System:** Semester, Summer Session Available **Enrollment:** FT 1,293, PT 24, Grad FT 169, Grad PT 94 **Faculty:** FT 74, PT 97 **Student-Faculty Ratio:** 13:1 **Exams:** SAT I or ACT. **% Receiving Financial Aid:** 84 **% Residing in College-Owned, -Operated, or -Affiliated Housing:** 70 **Final Year or Final Semester Residency Requirement:** Yes **Library Holdings:** 165,314 **Regional Accreditation:** Middle State Association of Colleges and Schools **Credit Hours For Degree:** 63 credits, Associates; 126 credits, Bachelors **ROTC:** Army **Professional Accreditation:** ABET, ACA, ACBSP, JRCECT **Intercollegiate Athletics:** Baseball M;

Basketball M & W; Cross-Country Running M & W; Football M; Soccer M & W; Softball W; Tennis W; Track and Field M & W; Volleyball M & W

GETTYSBURG COLLEGE
300 North Washington St.
Gettysburg, PA 17325-1483
Tel: (717)337-6000; Free: 800-431-0803
Admissions: (717)337-6100
Fax: (717)337-6008
E-mail: admiss@gettysburg.edu
Web Site: http://www.gettysburg.edu/
President/CEO: Dr. Janet Morgan Riggs
Admissions: Gail Sweezey
Financial Aid: Christina Gormley
Type: Four-Year College **Sex:** Coed **Affiliation:** Evangelical Lutheran Church in America **Scores:** 100% SAT V 400+; 100% SAT M 400+ **% Accepted:** 40 **Admission Plans:** Early Admission; Early Decision Plan; Deferred Admission **Application Deadline:** February 1 **Application Fee:** $55.00 **H.S. Requirements:** High school diploma required; GED accepted **Scholarships:** Available **Calendar System:** Semester, Summer Session Not available **Enrollment:** FT 2,498, PT 18 **Faculty:** FT 209, PT 77 **Student-Faculty Ratio:** 11:1 **Exams:** SAT I or ACT, SAT II. ACT essay not being used. SAT essay not being used. **% Receiving Financial Aid:** 53 **% Residing in College-Owned, -Operated, or -Affiliated Housing:** 94 **Library Holdings:** 408,120 **Regional Accreditation:** Middle State Association of Colleges and Schools **Credit Hours For Degree:** 32 courses, Bachelors **ROTC:** Army **Intercollegiate Athletics:** Baseball M; Basketball M & W; Cheerleading M & W; Cross-Country Running M & W; Equestrian Sports M & W; Field Hockey W; Football M; Golf M & W; Ice Hockey M; Lacrosse M & W; Rugby M & W; Soccer M & W; Softball W; Swimming and Diving M & W; Tennis M & W; Track and Field M & W; Volleyball W; Wrestling M

GRATZ COLLEGE
7605 Old York Rd.
Melrose Park, PA 19027
Tel: (215)635-7300; Free: 800-475-4635
Fax: (215)635-7320
E-mail: admissions@gratz.edu
Web Site: http://www.gratzcollege.edu/
President/CEO: Joy Goldstein
Admissions: Ruthann Crosby
Financial Aid: Karen West
Type: Comprehensive **Sex:** Coed **Affiliation:** Jewish **% Accepted:** 100 **Admission Plans:** Early Admission; Deferred Admission **Application Deadline:** Rolling **Application Fee:** $50.00 **H.S. Requirements:** High school diploma required; GED accepted **Scholarships:** Available **Calendar System:** Semester, Summer Session Available **Enrollment:** FT 6, PT 7 **Faculty:** FT 8, PT 7 **% Receiving Financial Aid:** 80 **Library Holdings:** 100,000 **Regional Accreditation:** Middle State Association of Colleges and Schools **Credit Hours For Degree:** 120 credits, Bachelors

GROVE CITY COLLEGE
100 Campus Dr.
Grove City, PA 16127-2104
Tel: (724)458-2000
Admissions: (724)458-2100
Fax: (724)458-3395
E-mail: admissions@gcc.edu
Web Site: http://www.gcc.edu/
President/CEO: Dr. Richard G. Jewell
Admissions: Jeffrey Mincey
Financial Aid: Thomas G. Ball
Type: Four-Year College **Sex:** Coed **Affiliation:** Presbyterian **Scores:** 100% SAT V 400+; 100% SAT M 400+; 11% ACT 18-23; 60% ACT 24-29 **% Accepted:** 64 **Admission Plans:** Preferred Admission; Early Admission; Early Decision Plan; Deferred Admission **Application Deadline:** February 1 **Application Fee:** $50.00 **H.S. Requirements:** High school diploma required; GED accepted. For home schooled applicants: High school diploma or equivalent not required **Costs Per Year:** Application fee: $50. Comprehensive fee: $19,414 includes full-time tuition ($12,590) and college room and board ($6824). Full-time tuition varies according to course load. Room and board charges vary according to housing facility. Part-time tuition: $395 per credit. **Scholarships:** Available **Calendar System:** Semester, Summer Session Not available **Enrollment:** FT 2,499, PT 31 **Faculty:** FT 128, PT 86 **Student-Faculty Ratio:** 16:1 **Exams:** SAT I or ACT. ACT essay not being used. SAT essay not being used. **% Receiving Financial Aid:** 38 **% Residing in College-Owned, -Operated, or -Affiliated Housing:** 93 **Library Holdings:** 135,100 **Regional Accreditation:** Middle State Association of Colleges and Schools **Credit Hours For Degree:** 128 credit hours, Bachelors **ROTC:** Army **Professional Accreditation:** ABET **Intercollegiate Athletics:** Baseball M; Basketball M & W; Cheerleading W; Cross-Country Running M & W; Football M; Golf M & W; Soccer M & W; Softball W; Swimming and Diving M & W; Tennis M & W; Track and Field M & W; Volleyball W; Water Polo W

GWYNEDD-MERCY COLLEGE
Sumneytown Pike
PO Box 901
Gwynedd Valley, PA 19437-0901
Tel: (215)646-7300
Fax: (215)641-5556
E-mail: admissions@gmc.edu
Web Site: http://www.gmc.edu/
President/CEO: Dr. Kathleen Owens
Admissions: Michelle Diehl
Financial Aid: Sr. Barbara A. Kaufmann
Type: Comprehensive **Sex:** Coed **Affiliation:** Roman Catholic **Scores:** 92% SAT V 400+; 88% SAT M 400+ **% Accepted:** 67 **Admission Plans:** Deferred Admission **Application Deadline:** Rolling **Application Fee:** $25.00 **H.S. Requirements:** High school diploma required; GED accepted **Costs Per Year:** Application fee: $25. Comprehensive fee: $35,370 includes full-time tuition ($25,160), mandatory fees ($450), and college room and board ($9760). Full-time tuition and fees vary according to program. Room and board charges vary according to board plan and housing facility. Part-time tuition: $515 per credit hour. Part-time mandatory fees: $10 per credit. Part-time tuition and fees vary according to program. **Scholarships:** Available **Calendar System:** Semester, Summer Session Available **Enrollment:** FT 1,500, PT 703, Grad FT 137, Grad PT 296 **Faculty:** FT 75, PT 206 **Student-Faculty Ratio:** 13:1 **Exams:** SAT I or ACT. **% Receiving Financial Aid:** 74 **% Residing in College-Owned, -Operated, or -Affiliated Housing:** 31 **Library Holdings:** 105,070 **Regional Accreditation:** Middle State Association of Colleges and Schools **Credit Hours For Degree:** 62 credits, Associates; 125 credits, Bachelors **Professional Accreditation:** AHIMA, CARC, JRCECT, JRCERT, NLN **Intercollegiate Athletics:** Baseball M; Basketball M & W; Cheerleading W; Cross-Country Running M & W; Field Hockey W; Golf M; Lacrosse M & W; Soccer M & W; Softball W; Tennis M & W; Track and Field M & W; Volleyball W

HARCUM COLLEGE
750 Montgomery Ave.
Bryn Mawr, PA 19010-3476
Tel: (610)525-4100; Free: 800-345-2600
Admissions: (610)526-6050
Fax: (610)526-6147
E-mail: enroll@harcum.edu
Web Site: http://www.harcum.edu/
President/CEO: Dr. Jon Jay DeTemple
Financial Aid: Eli Moinester
Type: Two-Year College **Sex:** Coed **% Accepted:** 65 **Admission Plans:** Deferred Admission **Application Deadline:** Rolling **Application Fee:** $50.00 **H.S. Requirements:** High school diploma required; GED accepted **Scholarships:** Available **Calendar System:** Semester, Summer Session Available **Faculty:** FT 36, PT 154 **Student-Faculty Ratio:** 12:1 **Exams:** SAT I or ACT. **% Residing in College-Owned, -Operated, or -Affiliated Housing:** 20 **Final Year or Final Semester Residency Requirement:** No **Library Holdings:** 39,994 **Regional Accreditation:** Middle State Association of Colleges and Schools **Credit Hours For Degree:** 62 credits, Associates **Professional Accreditation:** ADA, APTA, NAACLS **Intercollegiate Athletics:** Basketball M & W; Track and Field M & W; Volleyball W

HARRISBURG AREA COMMUNITY COLLEGE
1 HACC Dr.
Harrisburg, PA 17110-2999
Tel: (717)780-2300
Admissions: (717)780-2406
Fax: (717)231-7674
E-mail: admit@hacc.edu

Web Site: http://www.hacc.edu/
President/CEO: Edna V. Baehre
Admissions: Vanita L. Cowan
Type: Two-Year College **Sex:** Coed **% Accepted:** 97 **Admission Plans:** Open Admission; Early Admission; Deferred Admission **Application Deadline:** Rolling **Application Fee:** $35.00 **H.S. Requirements:** High school diploma or equivalent not required. For allied health programs: High school diploma required; GED accepted **Costs Per Year:** Application fee: $35. One-time mandatory fee: $35. Area resident tuition: $2955 full-time, $98.50 per credit hour part-time. State resident tuition: $5460 full-time, $182 per credit hour part-time. Nonresident tuition: $8265 full-time, $275.50 per credit hour part-time. Mandatory fees: $525 full-time, $17.50 per credit hour part-time. Full-time tuition and fees vary according to program. Part-time tuition and fees vary according to program. **Scholarships:** Available **Calendar System:** Semester, Summer Session Available **Enrollment:** FT 8,838, PT 13,691 **Faculty:** FT 352, PT 816 **Student-Faculty Ratio:** 21:1 **Library Holdings:** 174,523 **Regional Accreditation:** Middle State Association of Colleges and Schools **Credit Hours For Degree:** 61 credit hours, Associates **ROTC:** Army **Professional Accreditation:** ADA, ACBSP, CARC, JRCEMT, NAACLS, NLN **Intercollegiate Athletics:** Basketball M & W; Soccer M; Tennis M & W

HARRISBURG UNIVERSITY OF SCIENCE AND TECHNOLOGY
326 Market St.
Harrisburg, PA 17101
Tel: (717)901-5100; Free: (866)HBG-UNIV
Admissions: (717)901-5158
Fax: (717)901-5150
E-mail: tdawson@harrisburgu.edu
Web Site: http://www.HarrisburgU.edu/
President/CEO: Dr. Melvyn D. Schiavelli
Admissions: Timothy Dawson
Financial Aid: Vince P. Frank
Type: Comprehensive **Sex:** Coed **% Accepted:** 55 **Application Deadline:** Rolling **Application Fee:** $0.00 **H.S. Requirements:** High school diploma required; GED accepted **Costs Per Year:** Application fee: $0. Tuition: $19,500 full-time, $800 per semester hour part-time. Part-time tuition varies according to course load. **Scholarships:** Available **Calendar System:** Semester, Summer Session Available **Faculty:** FT 10, PT 17 **Student-Faculty Ratio:** 5:1 **Exams:** SAT I or ACT. **Library Holdings:** 40,000 **Regional Accreditation:** Middle State Association of Colleges and Schools **Credit Hours For Degree:** 120 semester credit hours, Bachelors

HAVERFORD COLLEGE
370 Lancaster Ave.
Haverford, PA 19041-1392
Tel: (610)896-1000
Admissions: (610)896-1350
Fax: (610)896-1338
E-mail: admitme@haverford.edu
Web Site: http://www.haverford.edu/
President/CEO: Stephen G. Emerson, MD
Admissions: Jess Lord
Financial Aid: David J. Hoy
Type: Four-Year College **Sex:** Coed **Scores:** 99% SAT V 400+; 100% SAT M 400+ **% Accepted:** 25 **Admission Plans:** Preferred Admission; Early Admission; Early Decision Plan; Deferred Admission **Application Deadline:** January 15 **Application Fee:** $60.00 **H.S. Requirements:** High school diploma or equivalent not required **Costs Per Year:** Application fee: $60. One-time mandatory fee: $190. Comprehensive fee: $50,975 includes full-time tuition ($38,735), mandatory fees ($350), and college room and board ($11,890). College room only: $6750. **Scholarships:** Available **Calendar System:** Semester, Summer Session Not available **Enrollment:** FT 1,190 **Faculty:** FT 121, PT 17 **Student-Faculty Ratio:** 8:1 **Exams:** Other. ACT essay used for admission. SAT essay used for admission. **% Receiving Financial Aid:** 48 **% Residing in College-Owned, -Operated, or -Affiliated Housing:** 99 **Library Holdings:** 773,401 **Regional Accreditation:** Middle State Association of Colleges and Schools **Credit Hours For Degree:** 32 courses, Bachelors **Intercollegiate Athletics:** Badminton W; Baseball M; Basketball M & W; Crew M & W; Cross-Country Running M & W; Fencing M & W; Field Hockey W; Golf M & W; Lacrosse M & W; Rugby M; Soccer M & W; Softball W; Squash M & W; Tennis M & W; Track and Field M & W; Ultimate Frisbee M & W; Volleyball M & W; Wrestling M

HOLY FAMILY UNIVERSITY
9801 Frankford Ave.
Philadelphia, PA 19114
Tel: (215)637-7700; Free: 800-637-1191
Admissions: (215)637-3050
Fax: (215)281-1022
E-mail: admissions@holyfamily.edu
Web Site: http://www.holyfamily.edu/
President/CEO: Sr. Francesca Onley, PhD
Admissions: Lauren McDermott-Campbell
Type: Comprehensive **Sex:** Coed **Affiliation:** Roman Catholic **Scores:** 90% SAT V 400+; 84.9% SAT M 400+; 86% ACT 18-23 **% Accepted:** 74 **Admission Plans:** Deferred Admission **Application Deadline:** Rolling **Application Fee:** $25.00 **H.S. Requirements:** High school diploma required; GED accepted **Costs Per Year:** Application fee: $25. Comprehensive fee: $33,920 includes full-time tuition ($22,870), mandatory fees ($650), and college room and board ($10,400). College room only: $6200. Full-time tuition and fees vary according to course load and program. Room and board charges vary according to board plan and housing facility. Part-time tuition: $490 per credit hour. Part-time mandatory fees: $60 per term. Part-time tuition and fees vary according to course load and program. **Scholarships:** Available **Calendar System:** Semester, Summer Session Available **Enrollment:** FT 1,556, PT 701, Grad FT 111, Grad PT 977 **Faculty:** FT 94, PT 260 **Student-Faculty Ratio:** 12:1 **Exams:** SAT I or ACT. ACT essay used for advising. SAT essay used for advising. ACT essay used for placement. SAT essay used for placement. **% Receiving Financial Aid:** 82 **% Residing in College-Owned, -Operated, or -Affiliated Housing:** 17 **Final Year or Final Semester Residency Requirement:** No **Library Holdings:** 142,800 **Regional Accreditation:** Middle State Association of Colleges and Schools **Credit Hours For Degree:** 74 credits, Associates; 120 credits, Bachelors **Professional Accreditation:** AACN, ACBSP, JRCERT, NLN, TEAC **Intercollegiate Athletics:** Basketball M & W; Cheerleading W; Cross-Country Running M & W; Golf M; Lacrosse W; Soccer M & W; Softball W; Tennis W; Track and Field M & W; Volleyball W

HUSSIAN SCHOOL OF ART
The Bourse - Ste. 300
111 South Independence Mall East
Philadelphia, PA 19106
Tel: (215)981-0900
Admissions: (215)574-9600
Fax: (215)864-9115
E-mail: lwartman@hussianart.edu
Web Site: http://www.hussianart.edu/
President/CEO: Ronald Dove
Admissions: Lynne Wartman
Type: Two-Year College **Sex:** Coed **% Accepted:** 97 **Admission Plans:** Deferred Admission **Application Deadline:** Rolling **Application Fee:** $25.00 **H.S. Requirements:** High school diploma required; GED accepted **Costs Per Year:** Application fee: $25. Tuition: $12,000 full-time. Mandatory fees: $550 full-time. **Scholarships:** Available **Calendar System:** Semester, Summer Session Not available **Enrollment:** FT 136 **Faculty:** FT 3, PT 23 **Credit Hours For Degree:** 120 credits, Associates **Professional Accreditation:** ACCSCT

IMMACULATA UNIVERSITY
1145 King Rd.
Immaculata, PA 19345
Tel: (610)647-4400; Free: 877-428-6329
Fax: (610)251-1668
E-mail: admiss@immaculata.edu
Web Site: http://www.immaculata.edu/
President/CEO: Sr. R. Patricia Fadden
Admissions: Rebecca Bowlby
Financial Aid: Peter Lysionek
Type: Comprehensive **Sex:** Coed **Affiliation:** Roman Catholic **Scores:** 88. 88% SAT V 400+; 80.5% SAT M 400+; 58% ACT 18-23; 13% ACT 24-29 **% Accepted:** 80 **Admission Plans:** Early Admission; Deferred Admission **Application Deadline:** Rolling **Application Fee:** $35.00 **H.S. Requirements:** High school diploma required; GED accepted. For continuing education applicants 25 or over: High school diploma or equivalent not required **Costs Per Year:** Application fee: $35. Comprehensive fee: $39,330 includes full-time tuition ($27,870) and college room and board ($11,460). College room only: $6160. Full-time tuition varies according to student level. Room and

board charges vary according to board plan and housing facility. Part-time tuition: $440 per credit hour. Tuition guaranteed not to increase for student's term of enrollment. **Scholarships:** Available **Calendar System:** Semester, Summer Session Available **Enrollment:** FT 1,062, PT 2,009, Grad FT 175, Grad PT 1,056 **Faculty:** FT 103, PT 308 **Student-Faculty Ratio:** 11:1 **Exams:** SAT I or ACT. ACT essay used for advising. SAT essay used for advising. ACT essay used for placement. SAT essay used for placement. **% Receiving Financial Aid:** 68 **% Residing in College-Owned, -Operated, or -Affiliated Housing:** 58 **Regional Accreditation:** Middle State Association of Colleges and Schools **Credit Hours For Degree:** 63 credits, Associates; 128 credits, Bachelors **ROTC:** Army **Professional Accreditation:** AACN, ADtA, APA, NASM, NLN **Intercollegiate Athletics:** Basketball W; Cross-Country Running W; Field Hockey W; Lacrosse W; Soccer W; Softball W; Tennis W; Volleyball W

INDIANA UNIVERSITY OF PENNSYLVANIA
Indiana, PA 15705-1087
Tel: (724)357-2100; Free: 800-442-6830
Admissions: (724)357-2230
Fax: (724)357-2685
E-mail: admissions-inquiry@iup.edu
Web Site: http://www.iup.edu/
President/CEO: Dr. Tony Atwater
Financial Aid: Patricia C. McCarthy
Type: University **Sex:** Coed **Affiliation:** Pennsylvania State System of Higher Education **Scores:** 95% SAT V 400+; 95.5% SAT M 400+ **% Accepted:** 60 **Admission Plans:** Early Admission; Deferred Admission **Application Deadline:** Rolling **Application Fee:** $35.00 **H.S. Requirements:** High school diploma required; GED accepted **Costs Per Year:** Application fee: $35. State resident tuition: $5554 full-time, $231 per credit hour part-time. Nonresident tuition: $13,886 full-time, $579 per credit hour part-time. Mandatory fees: $1655 full-time, $23.10 per credit hour part-time, $238.50. Full-time tuition and fees vary according to course load and reciprocity agreements. Part-time tuition and fees vary according to course load and reciprocity agreements. College room and board: $8558. Room and board charges vary according to board plan, housing facility, and location. **Scholarships:** Available **Calendar System:** Semester, Summer Session Available **Enrollment:** FT 11,361, PT 930, Grad FT 1,061, Grad PT 1,286 **Faculty:** FT 611, PT 62 **Student-Faculty Ratio:** 18:1 **Exams:** SAT I or ACT. **% Receiving Financial Aid:** 66 **Library Holdings:** 875,888 **Regional Accreditation:** Middle State Association of Colleges and Schools **Credit Hours For Degree:** 60 semester hours, Associates; 124 semester hours, Bachelors **ROTC:** Army **Professional Accreditation:** AACSB, ABET, AACN, AAFCS, ACA, ACF, ADtA, APA, ASLHA, CARC, JRCEPAT, NASAD, NASM, NAST, NCATE **Intercollegiate Athletics:** Baseball M; Basketball M & W; Cross-Country Running M & W; Field Hockey W; Football M; Golf M; Lacrosse W; Soccer W; Softball W; Swimming and Diving M & W; Tennis W; Track and Field M & W; Volleyball W

ITT TECHNICAL INSTITUTE (BENSALEM)
3330 Tillman Dr.
Bensalem, PA 19020
Tel: (215)244-8871
Web Site: http://www.itt-tech.edu/
President/CEO: Ray Joll
Type: Two-Year College **Sex:** Coed **Affiliation:** ITT Educational Services, Inc. **H.S. Requirements:** High school diploma required; GED accepted **Scholarships:** Available **Calendar System:** Quarter, Summer Session Not available **Professional Accreditation:** ACICS

ITT TECHNICAL INSTITUTE (DUNMORE)
1000 Meade St.
Dunmore, PA 18512
Tel: (570)330-0600; Free: 800-774-9791
Web Site: http://www.itt-tech.edu/
President/CEO: Chad Muse
Type: Two-Year College **Sex:** Coed **Affiliation:** ITT Educational Services, Inc. **Calendar System:** Quarter

ITT TECHNICAL INSTITUTE (HARRISBURG)
449 Eisenhower Blvd., Ste. 100
Harrisburg, PA 17111
Tel: (717)565-1700
Admissions: (717)565-1700
Web Site: http://www.itt-tech.edu/
President/CEO: Dana Melvin
Type: Two-Year College **Sex:** Coed **Affiliation:** ITT Educational Services, Inc.

ITT TECHNICAL INSTITUTE (KING OF PRUSSIA)
760 Moore Rd.
Ste. 150
King of Prussia, PA 19406-1212
Tel: (610)491-8004; Free: (866)902-8324
Web Site: http://www.itt-tech.edu/
President/CEO: Jude Nix
Type: Two-Year College **Sex:** Coed **Affiliation:** ITT Educational Services, Inc. **Calendar System:** Quarter **Professional Accreditation:** ACICS

ITT TECHNICAL INSTITUTE (PITTSBURGH)
10 Parkway Center
Pittsburgh, PA 15220-3801
Tel: (412)937-9150; Free: 800-353-8324
Web Site: http://www.itt-tech.edu/
President/CEO: Douglas Nelson
Type: Two-Year College **Sex:** Coed **Affiliation:** ITT Educational Services, Inc. **Scholarships:** Available **Calendar System:** Quarter, Summer Session Not available **Credit Hours For Degree:** 96 credit hours, Associates **Professional Accreditation:** ACICS

ITT TECHNICAL INSTITUTE (TARENTUM)
100 Pittsburgh Mills Circle
Tarentum, PA 15084
Tel: (724)274-1400
Admissions: (412)856-5920
Web Site: http://www.itt-tech.edu/
President/CEO: Linda Richert
Type: Two-Year College **Sex:** Coed **Affiliation:** ITT Educational Services, Inc. **H.S. Requirements:** High school diploma required; GED accepted **Scholarships:** Available **Calendar System:** Quarter, Summer Session Not available **Professional Accreditation:** ACICS

JNA INSTITUTE OF CULINARY ARTS
1212 South Broad St.
Philadelphia, PA 19146
Tel: (215)468-8800
Fax: (215)468-8838
Web Site: http://www.culinaryarts.com/
President/CEO: Joseph Digironimo
Type: Two-Year College **Sex:** Coed **Costs Per Year:** Tuition: $10,000 full-time, $325 per credit hour part-time. Tuition guaranteed not to increase for student's term of enrollment. **Calendar System:** Continuous **Professional Accreditation:** ACCSCT

JOHNSON COLLEGE
3427 North Main Ave.
Scranton, PA 18508-1495
Tel: (570)342-6404; Free: 800-2-WE-WORK
Admissions: (570)702-8910
Fax: (570)348-2181
E-mail: admit@johnson.edu
Web Site: http://www.johnson.edu/
President/CEO: Dr. Ann Pipinski
Admissions: Melissa Ide
Type: Two-Year College **Sex:** Coed **Admission Plans:** Deferred Admission **Application Deadline:** May 1 **Application Fee:** $30.00 **H.S. Requirements:** High school diploma required; GED accepted **Scholarships:** Available **Calendar System:** Semester, Summer Session Available **Enrollment:** FT 363, PT 13 **Faculty:** FT 21, PT 2 **Student-Faculty Ratio:** 17:1 **Exams:** SAT I. **Library Holdings:** 4,473 **Credit Hours For Degree:** 74 credits, Associates **Professional Accreditation:** ACCSCT **Intercollegiate Athletics:** Basketball M & W; Bowling M & W; Cross-Country Running M & W; Golf M & W

JUNIATA COLLEGE
1700 Moore St.
Huntingdon, PA 16652-2119
Tel: (814)641-3000; Free: 877-JUNIATA

Admissions: (814)641-3424
Fax: (814)641-3100
E-mail: admissions@juniata.edu
Web Site: http://www.juniata.edu/
President/CEO: Thomas Kepple, Jr.
Admissions: Terry Bollman-Dalansky
Financial Aid: Valerie Rennell
Type: Four-Year College **Sex:** Coed **Affiliation:** Church of the Brethren **Scores:** 99.7% SAT V 400+; 100% SAT M 400+ **% Accepted:** 72 **Admission Plans:** Early Admission; Early Action; Early Decision Plan; Deferred Admission **Application Deadline:** March 15 **Application Fee:** $30.00 **H.S. Requirements:** High school diploma required; GED accepted **Costs Per Year:** Application fee: $30. Comprehensive fee: $41,800 includes full-time tuition ($32,120), mandatory fees ($700), and college room and board ($8980). College room only: $4730. Room and board charges vary according to board plan. **Scholarships:** Available **Calendar System:** Semester, Summer Session Available **Enrollment:** FT 1,400, PT 68 **Faculty:** FT 100, PT 40 **Student-Faculty Ratio:** 12:1 **Exams:** SAT I or ACT. **% Receiving Financial Aid:** 71 **% Residing in College-Owned, -Operated, or -Affiliated Housing:** 82 **Library Holdings:** 350,000 **Regional Accreditation:** Middle State Association of Colleges and Schools **Credit Hours For Degree:** 120 semester hours, Bachelors **Professional Accreditation:** CSWE **Intercollegiate Athletics:** Baseball M; Basketball M & W; Cross-Country Running M & W; Equestrian Sports M & W; Field Hockey W; Football M; Golf M & W; Lacrosse M; Rugby M & W; Soccer M & W; Softball W; Swimming and Diving W; Tennis M & W; Track and Field M & W; Ultimate Frisbee M & W; Volleyball M & W

KAPLAN CAREER INSTITUTE, HARRISBURG
5650 Derry St.
Harrisburg, PA 17111-3518
Tel: (717)558-1300; Free: 800-431-1995
Admissions: (717)564-4112
Fax: (717)564-3779
Web Site: http://harrisburg.kaplancareerinstitute.com/
President/CEO: Sherry Rosenberg
Type: Two-Year College **Sex:** Coed **H.S. Requirements:** High school diploma required; GED accepted **Scholarships:** Available **Calendar System:** Quarter **Professional Accreditation:** ACICS

KAPLAN CAREER INSTITUTE, ICM CAMPUS
10 Wood St.
Pittsburgh, PA 15222-1977
Tel: (412)261-2647; Free: 800-441-5222
Web Site: http://www.kci-pittsburgh.com/
President/CEO: Hunter Hopkins
Type: Two-Year College **Sex:** Coed **H.S. Requirements:** High school diploma required; GED accepted **Scholarships:** Available **Calendar System:** Continuous **Credit Hours For Degree:** 1500 hours, Associates **Professional Accreditation:** ACICS, AOTA

KEYSTONE COLLEGE
One College Green
La Plume, PA 18440
Tel: (570)945-5141; Free: 877-4COLLEGE
Admissions: (570)945-8111
E-mail: admissions@keystone.edu
Web Site: http://www.keystone.edu/
President/CEO: Dr. Edward G. Boehm, Jr.
Admissions: Jessica Lopez
Financial Aid: Ginger Kline
Type: Four-Year College **Sex:** Coed **Scores:** 72.5% SAT V 400+; 68.5% SAT M 400+; 42% ACT 18-23 **% Accepted:** 95 **Admission Plans:** Early Admission; Deferred Admission **Application Deadline:** July 15 **Application Fee:** $30.00 **H.S. Requirements:** High school diploma required; GED accepted **Costs Per Year:** Application fee: $30. One-time mandatory fee: $200. Comprehensive fee: $28,370 includes full-time tuition ($18,170), mandatory fees ($950), and college room and board ($9250). College room only: $4500. Full-time tuition and fees vary according to course load. Room and board charges vary according to board plan and housing facility. Part-time tuition: $390 per credit. Part-time mandatory fees: $200 per term. Part-time tuition and fees vary according to course load. **Scholarships:** Available **Calendar System:** Semester, Summer Session Available **Enrollment:** FT 1,278, PT 363, Grad FT 17, Grad PT 33 **Faculty:** FT 71, PT 206 **Student-Faculty Ratio:** 10:1 **Exams:** SAT I or ACT. ACT essay used for advising. SAT essay used for advising. ACT essay used as a validity check on application essay. SAT essay used as a validity check on application essay. ACT essay used for placement. SAT essay used for placement. **% Receiving Financial Aid:** 86 **% Residing in College-Owned, -Operated, or -Affiliated Housing:** 23 **Final Year or Final Semester Residency Requirement:** No **Library Holdings:** 42,473 **Regional Accreditation:** Middle State Association of Colleges and Schools **Credit Hours For Degree:** 61 credit hours, Associates; 120 credit hours, Bachelors **ROTC:** Army, Air Force **Intercollegiate Athletics:** Baseball M; Basketball M & W; Cross-Country Running M & W; Field Hockey W; Golf M; Soccer M & W; Softball W; Tennis M & W; Track and Field M & W; Volleyball W

KEYSTONE TECHNICAL INSTITUTE
2301 Academy Dr.
Harrisburg, PA 17112
Tel: (717)545-4747
Fax: (717)901-9090
E-mail: info@acadcampus.com
Web Site: http://www.acadcampus.com/
President/CEO: David W. Snyder
Admissions: Tom Bogush
Type: Two-Year College **Sex:** Coed **Admission Plans:** Open Admission **Application Deadline:** Rolling **Application Fee:** $20.00 **H.S. Requirements:** High school diploma required; GED accepted **Scholarships:** Available **Calendar System:** Continuous, Summer Session Not available **Library Holdings:** 1,620 **Credit Hours For Degree:** 64 credit hours, Associates **Professional Accreditation:** ACCSCT

KING'S COLLEGE
133 North River St.
Wilkes-Barre, PA 18711-0801
Tel: (570)208-5900; Free: 888-KINGSPA
Admissions: (570)208-5858
Fax: (570)208-5971
E-mail: admissions@kings.edu
Web Site: http://www.kings.edu/
President/CEO: Rev. Thomas J. O'Hara, CSC
Admissions: Michelle Lawrence-Schmude
Financial Aid: Donna Cerza
Type: Comprehensive **Sex:** Coed **Affiliation:** Roman Catholic **Scores:** 89% SAT V 400+; 86% SAT M 400+ **% Accepted:** 75 **Admission Plans:** Deferred Admission **Application Deadline:** Rolling **Application Fee:** $30.00 **H.S. Requirements:** High school diploma required; GED accepted **Costs Per Year:** Application fee: $30. Comprehensive fee: $35,482 includes full-time tuition ($25,644) and college room and board ($9838). College room only: $4578. Room and board charges vary according to board plan. Part-time tuition: $495 per credit hour. **Scholarships:** Available **Calendar System:** Semester, Summer Session Available **Enrollment:** FT 1,966, PT 330, Grad FT 56, Grad PT 293 **Faculty:** FT 124, PT 87 **Student-Faculty Ratio:** 13:1 **Exams:** SAT I or ACT. ACT essay used for advising. SAT essay used for advising. SAT essay used as a validity check on application essay. **% Receiving Financial Aid:** 80 **% Residing in College-Owned, -Operated, or -Affiliated Housing:** 52 **Library Holdings:** 180,042 **Regional Accreditation:** Middle State Association of Colleges and Schools **Credit Hours For Degree:** 60 credit hours, Associates; 120 credit hours, Bachelors **ROTC:** Army, Air Force **Professional Accreditation:** AACSB, ACEHSA, JRCEPAT, NCATE **Intercollegiate Athletics:** Baseball M; Basketball M & W; Cheerleading M & W; Cross-Country Running M & W; Field Hockey W; Football M; Golf M; Lacrosse M & W; Soccer M & W; Softball W; Swimming and Diving M & W; Tennis M & W; Volleyball W; Wrestling M

KUTZTOWN UNIVERSITY OF PENNSYLVANIA
15200 Kutztown Rd.
Kutztown, PA 19530-0730
Tel: (610)683-4000; Free: 877-628-1915
Admissions: (610)683-4060
Fax: (610)683-1375
E-mail: admission@kutztown.edu
Web Site: http://www.kutztown.edu/
President/CEO: Dr. F. Javier Cevallos
Admissions: Dr. William Stahler
Financial Aid: Bernard McCree
Type: Comprehensive **Sex:** Coed **Affiliation:** Pennsylvania State System of

Higher Education **Scores:** 93.5% SAT V 400+; 92.8% SAT M 400+; 60.1% ACT 18-23; 11.5% ACT 24-29 **% Accepted:** 66 **Admission Plans:** Early Admission; Deferred Admission **Application Deadline:** Rolling **Application Fee:** $35.00 **H.S. Requirements:** High school diploma required; GED accepted **Costs Per Year:** Application fee: $35. State resident tuition: $5554 full-time, $231 per credit hour part-time. Nonresident tuition: $13,886 full-time, $579 per credit hour part-time. Mandatory fees: $1843 full-time, $68 per credit hour part-time, $60 per term part-time. College room and board: $7698. College room only: $4768. Room and board charges vary according to board plan and housing facility. **Scholarships:** Available **Calendar System:** Semester, Summer Session Available **Enrollment:** FT 8,734, PT 880, Grad FT 359, Grad PT 661 **Faculty:** FT 461, PT 43 **Student-Faculty Ratio:** 19:1 **Exams:** SAT I or ACT, SAT II. **% Receiving Financial Aid:** 57 **% Residing in College-Owned, -Operated, or -Affiliated Housing:** 48 **Library Holdings:** 555,934 **Regional Accreditation:** Middle State Association of Colleges and Schools **Credit Hours For Degree:** 120 credits, Bachelors **ROTC:** Army **Professional Accreditation:** CSWE, NASAD, NASM, NCATE, NLN **Intercollegiate Athletics:** Baseball M; Basketball M & W; Bowling W; Cheerleading W; Cross-Country Running M & W; Equestrian Sports M & W; Field Hockey W; Football M; Golf W; Ice Hockey M; Lacrosse M & W; Rugby M & W; Skiing (Downhill) M & W; Soccer M & W; Softball W; Swimming and Diving W; Tennis M & W; Track and Field M & W; Ultimate Frisbee M & W; Volleyball M & W; Wrestling M

LA ROCHE COLLEGE
9000 Babcock Blvd.
Pittsburgh, PA 15237-5898
Tel: (412)367-9300; Free: 800-838-4LRC
Admissions: (412)536-1275
Fax: (412)536-1075
E-mail: admissions@laroche.edu
Web Site: http://www.laroche.edu/
President/CEO: Sr. Candace Introcaso, PhD
Admissions: David McFarland
Financial Aid: Sharon Platt
Type: Comprehensive **Sex:** Coed **Affiliation:** Roman Catholic Church **Scores:** 71% SAT V 400+; 73% SAT M 400+; 55% ACT 18-23; 15% ACT 24-29 **% Accepted:** 68 **Admission Plans:** Early Admission; Deferred Admission **Application Deadline:** Rolling **Application Fee:** $50.00 **H.S. Requirements:** High school diploma required; GED accepted **Costs Per Year:** Application fee: $50. Comprehensive fee: $30,394 includes full-time tuition ($20,938), mandatory fees ($700), and college room and board ($8756). College room only: $5484. Full-time tuition and fees vary according to program. Room and board charges vary according to board plan. Part-time tuition: $525 per credit hour. Part-time tuition varies according to program. **Scholarships:** Available **Calendar System:** Semester, Summer Session Available **Enrollment:** FT 984, PT 246, Grad FT 60, Grad PT 66 **Faculty:** FT 63, PT 110 **Student-Faculty Ratio:** 12:1 **Exams:** SAT I or ACT. **% Receiving Financial Aid:** 71 **% Residing in College-Owned, -Operated, or -Affiliated Housing:** 37 **Final Year or Final Semester Residency Requirement:** Yes **Library Holdings:** 122,642 **Regional Accreditation:** Middle State Association of Colleges and Schools **Credit Hours For Degree:** 67 credit hours, Associates; 120 credit hours, Bachelors **ROTC:** Army, Air Force **Professional Accreditation:** AANA, ACBSP, FIDER, NASAD, NLN **Intercollegiate Athletics:** Baseball M; Basketball M & W; Cross-Country Running M & W; Golf M; Lacrosse M; Soccer M & W; Softball W; Tennis W; Volleyball W

LA SALLE UNIVERSITY
1900 West Olney Ave.
Philadelphia, PA 19141-1199
Tel: (215)951-1000; Free: 800-328-1910
Admissions: (215)951-1500
Fax: (215)951-1656
E-mail: admiss@lasalle.edu
Web Site: http://www.lasalle.edu/
President/CEO: Br. Michael J. McGinniss, FSC
Admissions: James Plunkett
Financial Aid: Robert G. Voss
Type: Comprehensive **Sex:** Coed **Affiliation:** Roman Catholic **Scores:** 94% SAT V 400+; 94% SAT M 400+ **% Accepted:** 66 **Admission Plans:** Early Admission; Early Action; Early Decision Plan; Deferred Admission **Application Fee:** $35.00 **H.S. Requirements:** High school diploma required; GED accepted **Costs Per Year:** Application fee: $35. One-time mandatory fee: $150. Comprehensive fee: $44,930 includes full-time tuition ($33,500), mandatory fees ($200), and college room and board ($11,230). College room only: $5910. Full-time tuition and fees vary according to course load and program. Room and board charges vary according to board plan and housing facility. Part-time tuition: $460 per credit hour. Part-time tuition varies according to course load and program. **Scholarships:** Available **Calendar System:** Semester, Summer Session Available **Enrollment:** FT 3,320, PT 1,127, Grad FT 401, Grad PT 1,622 **Faculty:** FT 231, PT 165 **Student-Faculty Ratio:** 13:1 **Exams:** SAT I or ACT. **% Receiving Financial Aid:** 74 **% Residing in College-Owned, -Operated, or -Affiliated Housing:** 61 **Library Holdings:** 400,000 **Regional Accreditation:** Middle State Association of Colleges and Schools **Credit Hours For Degree:** 60 credit hours, Associates; 120 credit hours, Bachelors **ROTC:** Army, Air Force **Professional Accreditation:** AACSB, AACN, AANA, ADtA, APA, ASLHA, CSWE, NLN **Intercollegiate Athletics:** Baseball M; Basketball M & W; Crew M & W; Cross-Country Running M & W; Field Hockey W; Golf M & W; Lacrosse W; Soccer M & W; Softball W; Swimming and Diving M & W; Tennis M & W; Track and Field M & W; Volleyball W

LACKAWANNA COLLEGE
501 Vine St.
Scranton, PA 18509
Tel: (570)961-7810
Admissions: (570)961-7868
Fax: (570)961-7858
E-mail: muchals@lackawanna.edu
Web Site: http://www.lackawanna.edu/
President/CEO: Raymond Angeli
Admissions: Stacey Muchal
Financial Aid: Barbara Hapeman
Type: Two-Year College **Sex:** Coed **Scores:** 65% SAT V 400+; 62% SAT M 400+ **% Accepted:** 64 **Admission Plans:** Open Admission; Early Admission; Deferred Admission **Application Deadline:** Rolling **Application Fee:** $30.00 **H.S. Requirements:** High school diploma required; GED accepted **Costs Per Year:** Application fee: $30. Comprehensive fee: $18,160 includes full-time tuition ($11,000), mandatory fees ($160), and college room and board ($7000). Full-time tuition and fees vary according to course load. Part-time tuition: $370 per credit hour. Part-time mandatory fees: $55 per term. Part-time tuition and fees vary according to course load. **Scholarships:** Available **Calendar System:** Semester, Summer Session Available **Enrollment:** FT 999, PT 388 **Faculty:** FT 32, PT 183 **Student-Faculty Ratio:** 13:1 **Exams:** ACT, SAT I or ACT, SAT I. **% Residing in College-Owned, -Operated, or -Affiliated Housing:** 17 **Library Holdings:** 17,068 **Regional Accreditation:** Middle State Association of Colleges and Schools **Credit Hours For Degree:** 60 credits, Associates **ROTC:** Army, Air Force **Intercollegiate Athletics:** Baseball M; Basketball M & W; Cheerleading W; Cross-Country Running M & W; Football M; Golf M & W; Soccer W; Softball W; Volleyball W

LAFAYETTE COLLEGE
Easton, PA 18042-1798
Tel: (610)330-5000
Admissions: (610)330-5100
Fax: (610)330-5127
E-mail: admissions@lafayette.edu
Web Site: http://www.lafayette.edu/
President/CEO: Dr. Daniel Weiss
Admissions: Carol Rowlands
Financial Aid: Arlinda DeNardo
Type: Four-Year College **Sex:** Coed **Affiliation:** Presbyterian Church (U.S.A.) **Scores:** 100% SAT V 400+; 100% SAT M 400+; 8.46% ACT 18-23; 59.7% ACT 24-29 **% Accepted:** 42 **Admission Plans:** Early Admission; Early Decision Plan; Deferred Admission **Application Deadline:** January 1 **Application Fee:** $60.00 **H.S. Requirements:** High school diploma or equivalent not required **Costs Per Year:** Application fee: $60. One-time mandatory fee: $675. Comprehensive fee: $49,614 includes full-time tuition ($37,520), mandatory fees ($295), and college room and board ($11,799). College room only: $7105. Room and board charges vary according to board plan. Part-time tuition: $1682 per course. **Scholarships:** Available **Calendar System:** Semester, Summer Session Available **Enrollment:** FT 2,365, PT 41 **Faculty:** FT 199, PT 35 **Student-Faculty Ratio:** 11:1 **Exams:** SAT I or ACT, SAT II. **% Receiving Financial Aid:** 46 **Regional Accreditation:** Middle State Association of Colleges and Schools **Credit Hours For Degree:** 120 credits, Bachelors **ROTC:** Army **Professional Accreditation:**

ABET **Intercollegiate Athletics:** Baseball M; Basketball M & W; Crew M & W; Cross-Country Running M & W; Equestrian Sports M & W; Fencing M & W; Field Hockey W; Football M; Golf M; Ice Hockey M; Lacrosse M & W; Rugby M & W; Skiing (Downhill) M & W; Soccer M & W; Softball W; Squash M; Swimming and Diving M & W; Tennis M & W; Track and Field M & W; Volleyball W; Weight Lifting M & W; Wrestling M

LANCASTER BIBLE COLLEGE & GRADUATE SCHOOL
901 Eden Rd.
Lancaster, PA 17601
Tel: (717)569-7071; Free: (866)LBC-4YOU
Fax: (717)560-8213
E-mail: admissions@lbc.edu
Web Site: http://www.lbc.edu/
President/CEO: Peter W. Teague
Admissions: Joanne M. Roper
Financial Aid: Karen Fox
Type: Comprehensive **Sex:** Coed **Affiliation:** nondenominational **Scores:** 98% SAT V 400+; 92% SAT M 400+; 52% ACT 18-23; 19% ACT 24-29 **% Accepted:** 57 **Admission Plans:** Early Admission; Deferred Admission **Application Deadline:** Rolling **Application Fee:** $25.00 **H.S. Requirements:** High school diploma required; GED accepted **Costs Per Year:** Application fee: $25. Comprehensive fee: $22,620 includes full-time tuition ($15,240), mandatory fees ($600), and college room and board ($6780). College room only: $2990. Room and board charges vary according to board plan. Part-time tuition: $513 per credit hour. Part-time mandatory fees: $25 per credit hour. Part-time tuition and fees vary according to course load. **Scholarships:** Available **Calendar System:** Semester, Summer Session Available **Enrollment:** FT 560, PT 226 **Faculty:** FT 44, PT 42 **Student-Faculty Ratio:** 15:1 **Exams:** SAT I or ACT. **% Receiving Financial Aid:** 91 **% Residing in College-Owned, -Operated, or -Affiliated Housing:** 54 **Library Holdings:** 132,599 **Regional Accreditation:** Middle State Association of Colleges and Schools **Credit Hours For Degree:** 62 credit hours, Associates; 120 credit hours, Bachelors **Professional Accreditation:** ABHE **Intercollegiate Athletics:** Baseball M; Basketball M & W; Lacrosse W; Soccer M & W; Volleyball M & W

LANCASTER GENERAL COLLEGE OF NURSING & HEALTH SCIENCES
410 North Lime St.
Lancaster, PA 17602
Tel: (717)544-4912
Fax: (717)290-5970
Web Site: http://www.lancastergeneralcollege.edu/content/
President/CEO: Dr. Mary Grace Simcox
Type: Two-Year College **Sex:** Coed **Application Fee:** $50.00 **Exams:** SAT I or ACT. **Regional Accreditation:** Middle State Association of Colleges and Schools

LANSDALE SCHOOL OF BUSINESS
201 Church Rd.
North Wales, PA 19454-4148
Tel: (215)699-5700
Fax: (215)699-8770
E-mail: mjohnson@lsb.edu
Web Site: http://www.lsbonline.com/
President/CEO: Marlon Keller
Admissions: Marianne H. Johnson
Type: Two-Year College **Sex:** Coed **Application Deadline:** Rolling **Application Fee:** $30.00 **H.S. Requirements:** High school diploma required; GED accepted **Scholarships:** Available **Calendar System:** Semester, Summer Session Available **Library Holdings:** 2,000 **Credit Hours For Degree:** 68 credits, Associates **Professional Accreditation:** ACICS

LAUREL BUSINESS INSTITUTE
11-15 Penn St.
Uniontown, PA 15401
Tel: (724)439-4900
Fax: (724)439-3607
E-mail: ldolan@laurel.edu
Web Site: http://www.laurel.edu/
President/CEO: Nancy Decker
Admissions: Lisa Dolan
Type: Two-Year College **Sex:** Coed **% Accepted:** 59 **Admission Plans:** Open Admission; Deferred Admission **Application Deadline:** Rolling **Application Fee:** $55.00 **H.S. Requirements:** High school diploma required; GED accepted **Costs Per Year:** Application fee: $55. One-time mandatory fee: $75. Tuition: $11,400 full-time, $250 per credit part-time. Mandatory fees: $1350 full-time, $250 per credit part-time, $450 per term part-time. Full-time tuition and fees vary according to course load and program. Part-time tuition and fees vary according to course load and program. **Scholarships:** Available **Calendar System:** Trimester **Enrollment:** FT 305 **Faculty:** FT 16, PT 9 **Student-Faculty Ratio:** 16:1 **Exams:** Other. **Library Holdings:** 1,537 **Professional Accreditation:** ACICS, AAMAE

LAUREL TECHNICAL INSTITUTE (MEADVILLE)
628 Arch St., Ste. B105
Meadville, PA 16335
Tel: (814)724-0700
Fax: (814)724-2777
E-mail: info@biop.edu
Web Site: http://www.laurel.edu/lti/
Admissions: Cheryl Mever
Type: Two-Year College **Sex:** Coed **% Accepted:** 82 **Application Fee:** $50.00 **Calendar System:** Quarter **Enrollment:** FT 68 **Faculty:** FT 3, PT 3 **Student-Faculty Ratio:** 17:1 **Exams:** Other. **Professional Accreditation:** ACICS

LAUREL TECHNICAL INSTITUTE (SHARON)
335 Boyd Dr.
Sharon, PA 16146
Tel: (724)983-0700; Free: 800-289-2069
Fax: (724)983-8355
E-mail: info@biop.edu
Web Site: http://www.laurel.edu/lti/
President/CEO: Edward Petrunak
Admissions: Irene Lewis
Type: Two-Year College **Sex:** Coed **% Accepted:** 80 **H.S. Requirements:** High school diploma required; GED accepted **Scholarships:** Available **Calendar System:** Quarter **Enrollment:** FT 98, PT 8 **Faculty:** FT 5, PT 4 **Student-Faculty Ratio:** 16:1 **Exams:** ACT. **Professional Accreditation:** ACICS

LEBANON VALLEY COLLEGE
101 North College Ave.
Annville, PA 17003-1400
Tel: (717)867-6100; Free: (866)LVC-4ADM
Admissions: (717)867-6181
Fax: (717)867-6124
E-mail: admission@lvc.edu
Web Site: http://www.lvc.edu/
President/CEO: Dr. Stephen C. MacDonald
Admissions: Susan Jones
Financial Aid: Kendra M. Feigert
Type: Comprehensive **Sex:** Coed **Affiliation:** United Methodist **Scores:** 94.2% SAT V 400+; 96.1% SAT M 400+; 51% ACT 18-23; 39.2% ACT 24-29 **% Accepted:** 81 **Application Deadline:** Rolling **Application Fee:** $30.00 **H.S. Requirements:** High school diploma required; GED accepted **Costs Per Year:** Application fee: $30. Comprehensive fee: $38,570 includes full-time tuition ($29,780), mandatory fees ($710), and college room and board ($8080). College room only: $3960. Room and board charges vary according to board plan and housing facility. Part-time tuition: $500 per credit. Part-time tuition varies according to class time and degree level. **Scholarships:** Available **Calendar System:** Semester, Summer Session Available **Enrollment:** FT 1,582, PT 165, Grad FT 62, Grad PT 236 **Faculty:** FT 100, PT 98 **Student-Faculty Ratio:** 13:1 **Exams:** ACT essay not being used. SAT essay not being used. **% Receiving Financial Aid:** 81 **% Residing in College-Owned, -Operated, or -Affiliated Housing:** 74 **Final Year or Final Semester Residency Requirement:** Yes **Library Holdings:** 197,177 **Regional Accreditation:** Middle State Association of Colleges and Schools **Credit Hours For Degree:** 60 credits, Associates; 120 credits, Bachelors **ROTC:** Army **Professional Accreditation:** APTA, ACBSP, NASM **Intercollegiate Athletics:** Baseball M; Basketball M & W; Cross-Country Running M & W; Field Hockey W; Football M; Golf M; Ice Hockey M; Lacrosse M & W; Soccer M & W; Softball W; Swimming and Diving M & W; Tennis M & W; Track and Field M & W; Volleyball W

LEHIGH CARBON COMMUNITY COLLEGE
4525 Education Park Dr.
Schnecksville, PA 18078-2598
Tel: (610)799-2121
Admissions: (610)799-1575
Fax: (610)799-1527
E-mail: tellme@lccc.edu
Web Site: http://www.lccc.edu/
President/CEO: Donald W. Snyder
Admissions: Mary Theresa Taglang
Type: Two-Year College **Sex:** Coed **% Accepted:** 100 **Admission Plans:** Open Admission **Application Deadline:** Rolling **Application Fee:** $30.00 **H.S. Requirements:** High school diploma or equivalent not required. For allied health, aviation, veterinary technician programs: High school diploma required; GED accepted **Costs Per Year:** Application fee: $30. Area resident tuition: $2640 full-time, $88 per credit part-time. State resident tuition: $5550 full-time, $185 per credit part-time. Nonresident tuition: $8460 full-time, $282 per credit part-time. Mandatory fees: $480 full-time, $16 per credit part-time. **Scholarships:** Available **Calendar System:** Semester, Summer Session Available **Enrollment:** FT 3,421, PT 4,706 **Faculty:** FT 107, PT 381 **Student-Faculty Ratio:** 18:1 **Exams:** Other. **Final Year or Final Semester Residency Requirement:** No **Library Holdings:** 88,426 **Regional Accreditation:** Middle State Association of Colleges and Schools **Credit Hours For Degree:** 60 credits, Associates **ROTC:** Army **Professional Accreditation:** AAMAE, AHIMA, AOTA, APTA, ACBSP, NLN **Intercollegiate Athletics:** Baseball M; Basketball M & W; Golf M & W; Soccer M; Softball W; Volleyball W

LEHIGH UNIVERSITY
27 Memorial Dr. West
Bethlehem, PA 18015-3094
Tel: (610)758-3000
Admissions: (610)758-3100
Fax: (610)758-4361
E-mail: admissions@lehigh.edu
Web Site: http://www.lehigh.edu/
President/CEO: Dr. Alice P. Gast
Admissions: J. Bruce Gardiner
Financial Aid: Linda F. Bell
Type: University **Sex:** Coed **Scores:** 100% SAT V 400+; 100% SAT M 400+ **% Accepted:** 33 **Admission Plans:** Early Admission; Early Decision Plan; Deferred Admission **Application Deadline:** January 1 **Application Fee:** $70.00 **H.S. Requirements:** High school diploma or equivalent not required **Costs Per Year:** Application fee: $70. Comprehensive fee: $48,830 includes full-time tuition ($38,330), mandatory fees ($300), and college room and board ($10,200). College room only: $5910. Room and board charges vary according to board plan. Part-time tuition: $1600 per credit hour. **Scholarships:** Available **Calendar System:** Semester, Summer Session Available **Enrollment:** FT 4,755, PT 54, Grad FT 1,033, Grad PT 1,154 **Faculty:** FT 464, PT 208 **Student-Faculty Ratio:** 10:1 **Exams:** SAT I or ACT. **% Receiving Financial Aid:** 45 **% Residing in College-Owned, -Operated, or -Affiliated Housing:** 68 **Library Holdings:** 1,191,785 **Regional Accreditation:** Middle State Association of Colleges and Schools **Credit Hours For Degree:** 120 credit hours, Bachelors **ROTC:** Army **Professional Accreditation:** AACSB, ABET, APA, NAST **Intercollegiate Athletics:** Baseball M; Basketball M & W; Cheerleading M & W; Crew M & W; Cross-Country Running M & W; Equestrian Sports M & W; Fencing M & W; Field Hockey W; Football M; Golf M & W; Ice Hockey M; Lacrosse M & W; Rugby M & W; Skiing (Downhill) M & W; Soccer M & W; Softball W; Swimming and Diving M & W; Tennis M & W; Track and Field M & W; Volleyball M & W; Wrestling M

LINCOLN TECHNICAL INSTITUTE (ALLENTOWN)
5151 Tilghman St.
Allentown, PA 18104-3298
Tel: (610)398-5300
Web Site: http://www.lincolnedu.com/
President/CEO: Lisa Kuntz
Type: Two-Year College **Sex:** Coed **Affiliation:** Lincoln Technical Institute, Inc **Admission Plans:** Open Admission; Early Admission **Application Deadline:** Rolling **Application Fee:** $25.00 **H.S. Requirements:** High school diploma required; GED accepted **Scholarships:** Available **Calendar System:** Semester, Summer Session Available **Credit Hours For Degree:** 97 credits, Associates **Professional Accreditation:** ACCSCT

LINCOLN TECHNICAL INSTITUTE (PHILADELPHIA)
9191 Torresdale Ave.
Philadelphia, PA 19136-1595
Tel: (215)335-0800; Free: 800-238-8381
Fax: (215)335-1443
E-mail: jkuntz@lincolntech.com
Web Site: http://www.lincolnedu.com/
President/CEO: Mark Bohen
Admissions: James Kuntz
Type: Two-Year College **Sex:** Coed **Affiliation:** Lincoln Technical Institute, Inc **Admission Plans:** Open Admission; Deferred Admission **Application Deadline:** Rolling **Application Fee:** $25.00 **H.S. Requirements:** High school diploma required; GED accepted **Scholarships:** Available **Calendar System:** Miscellaneous, Summer Session Not available **Credit Hours For Degree:** 76 credits, Associates **Professional Accreditation:** ACCSCT

LINCOLN TECHNICAL INSTITUTE (PLYMOUTH MEETING)
1 Plymouth Meeting
No. 300
Plymouth Meeting, PA 19462-1326
Tel: (610)941-0319
Web Site: http://www.lincolnedu.com/
Type: Two-Year College **Sex:** Coed **Application Fee:** $125.00

LINCOLN UNIVERSITY
PO Box 179
Lincoln University, PA 19352
Tel: (484)365-8000; Free: 800-790-0191
Admissions: (484)365-7218
E-mail: admiss@lincoln.edu
Web Site: http://www.lincoln.edu/
President/CEO: Dr. Ivory V. Nelson
Admissions: Germel Eaton-Clarke
Financial Aid: Thelma Ross
Type: Comprehensive **Sex:** Coed **Scores:** 55% SAT V 400+; 47% SAT M 400+; 35% ACT 18-23; 5% ACT 24-29 **% Accepted:** 31 **Admission Plans:** Preferred Admission; Early Admission; Deferred Admission **Application Deadline:** Rolling **Application Fee:** $20.00 **H.S. Requirements:** High school diploma required; GED accepted **Costs Per Year:** Application fee: $20. State resident tuition: $5862 full-time, $246 per credit hour part-time. Nonresident tuition: $9976 full-time, $417 per credit hour part-time. Mandatory fees: $2360 full-time, $102 per credit hour part-time. Part-time tuition and fees vary according to course load. College room and board: $7770. College room only: $4218. Room and board charges vary according to board plan and housing facility. **Scholarships:** Available **Calendar System:** Semester, Summer Session Available **Enrollment:** FT 2,001, PT 34, Grad FT 440, Grad PT 174 **Faculty:** FT 101, PT 93 **Student-Faculty Ratio:** 19:1 **Exams:** SAT I or ACT. **% Receiving Financial Aid:** 87 **Final Year or Final Semester Residency Requirement:** No **Library Holdings:** 185,306 **Regional Accreditation:** Middle State Association of Colleges and Schools **Credit Hours For Degree:** 120 credit hours, Bachelors **ROTC:** Army, Air Force **Professional Accreditation:** NRPA **Intercollegiate Athletics:** Baseball M; Basketball M & W; Bowling W; Cross-Country Running M & W; Football M; Soccer M & W; Softball W; Tennis M & W; Track and Field M & W; Volleyball W

LOCK HAVEN UNIVERSITY OF PENNSYLVANIA
401 North Fairview St.
Lock Haven, PA 17745-2390
Tel: (570)893-2011; Free: 800-233-8978
Admissions: (570)484-2027
Fax: (570)893-2201
E-mail: admissions@lhup.edu
Web Site: http://www.lhup.edu/
President/CEO: Dr. Keith T. Miller
Admissions: Steven Lee
Financial Aid: James Theeuwes
Type: Comprehensive **Sex:** Coed **Affiliation:** Pennsylvania State System of Higher Education **Scores:** 85.92% SAT V 400+; 86.1% SAT M 400+; 53. 17% ACT 18-23; 7.94% ACT 24-29 **% Accepted:** 76 **Admission Plans:** Deferred Admission **Application Deadline:** Rolling **Application Fee:** $25.00 **H.S. Requirements:** High school diploma required; GED accepted **Costs Per Year:** Application fee: $25. One-time mandatory fee: $25. State resident tuition: $5554 full-time, $231 per credit hour part-time. Nonresident tuition:

$11,886 full-time, $495 per credit hour part-time. Mandatory fees: $1647 full-time, $44.35 per credit hour part-time, $119 per term part-time. Full-time tuition and fees vary according to course load and location. Part-time tuition and fees vary according to course load and location. College room and board: $6736. College room only: $3648. Room and board charges vary according to board plan and housing facility. **Scholarships:** Available **Calendar System:** Semester, Summer Session Available **Enrollment:** FT 4,669, PT 375, Grad FT 100, Grad PT 185 **Faculty:** FT 231, PT 12 **Student-Faculty Ratio:** 21:1 **Exams:** SAT I or ACT. **% Receiving Financial Aid:** 72 **% Residing in College-Owned, -Operated, or -Affiliated Housing:** 36 **Regional Accreditation:** Middle State Association of Colleges and Schools **Credit Hours For Degree:** 60 semester hours, Associates; 120 semester hours, Bachelors **ROTC:** Army **Professional Accreditation:** CSWE, JRCEPAT, NCATE, NLN **Intercollegiate Athletics:** Baseball M; Basketball M & W; Cross-Country Running M & W; Field Hockey W; Football M; Lacrosse W; Soccer M & W; Softball W; Swimming and Diving W; Track and Field M & W; Volleyball W; Wrestling M

LUZERNE COUNTY COMMUNITY COLLEGE
1333 South Prospect St.
Nanticoke, PA 18634-9804
Tel: (570)740-0300
Admissions: (570)740-0337
E-mail: admissions@luzerne.edu
Web Site: http://www.luzerne.edu/
President/CEO: Thomas P. Leary
Admissions: Francis Curry
Type: Two-Year College **Sex:** Coed **Admission Plans:** Open Admission; Early Admission; Deferred Admission **Application Deadline:** Rolling **Application Fee:** $40.00 **H.S. Requirements:** High school diploma required; GED accepted. For those who demonstrate ability to benefit from program: High school diploma or equivalent not required **Scholarships:** Available **Calendar System:** Semester, Summer Session Available **Enrollment:** FT 2,940, PT 3,230 **Faculty:** FT 104, PT 371 **Student-Faculty Ratio:** 19:1 **Library Holdings:** 60,000 **Regional Accreditation:** Middle State Association of Colleges and Schools **Credit Hours For Degree:** 60 semester hours, Associates **ROTC:** Air Force **Professional Accreditation:** ARCEST, ADA, NLN **Intercollegiate Athletics:** Baseball M; Basketball M & W; Cross-Country Running M & W; Golf M & W; Soccer M & W; Softball W; Volleyball W

LYCOMING COLLEGE
700 College Place
Williamsport, PA 17701-5192
Tel: (570)321-4000; Free: 800-345-3920
Admissions: (570)321-4026
Fax: (570)321-4337
E-mail: admissions@lycoming.edu
Web Site: http://www.lycoming.edu/
President/CEO: Dr. James E. Douthat
Admissions: James Spencer
Financial Aid: James S. Lakis
Type: Four-Year College **Sex:** Coed **Affiliation:** United Methodist **Scores:** 98% SAT V 400+; 95% SAT M 400+; 41% ACT 18-23; 45% ACT 24-29 **% Accepted:** 68 **Admission Plans:** Deferred Admission **Application Deadline:** May 1 **Application Fee:** $35.00 **H.S. Requirements:** High school diploma required; GED accepted **Costs Per Year:** Application fee: $35. Comprehensive fee: $38,028 includes full-time tuition ($29,344), mandatory fees ($550), and college room and board ($8134). College room only: $4150. Room and board charges vary according to board plan and housing facility. Part-time tuition: $917 per credit hour. Part-time tuition varies according to course load. **Scholarships:** Available **Calendar System:** Semester, Summer Session Available **Enrollment:** FT 1,347, PT 26 **Faculty:** FT 89, PT 37 **Student-Faculty Ratio:** 13:1 **Exams:** SAT I or ACT. **% Receiving Financial Aid:** 85 **% Residing in College-Owned, -Operated, or -Affiliated Housing:** 85 **Library Holdings:** 205,663 **Regional Accreditation:** Middle State Association of Colleges and Schools **Credit Hours For Degree:** 128 credits, Bachelors **ROTC:** Army **Professional Accreditation:** ACBSP **Intercollegiate Athletics:** Basketball M & W; Cheerleading M & W; Crew M & W; Cross-Country Running M & W; Equestrian Sports M & W; Fencing M & W; Football M; Golf M & W; Lacrosse M & W; Soccer M & W; Softball W; Swimming and Diving M & W; Tennis M & W; Ultimate Frisbee M & W; Volleyball W; Water Polo M & W; Wrestling M

MANOR COLLEGE
700 Fox Chase Rd.
Jenkintown, PA 19046
Tel: (215)885-2360
E-mail: ftadmiss@manor.edu
Web Site: http://www.manor.edu/
President/CEO: Sr. Mary Cecilia Jurasinski, OSBM
Admissions: I. Jerry Czenstuch
Financial Aid: Natalie Stusyk
Type: Two-Year College **Sex:** Coed **Affiliation:** Byzantine Catholic **Scores:** 73% SAT V 400+; 62% SAT M 400+ **% Accepted:** 50 **Admission Plans:** Deferred Admission **Application Deadline:** Rolling **Application Fee:** $20.00 **H.S. Requirements:** High school diploma required; GED accepted **Scholarships:** Available **Calendar System:** Semester, Summer Session Available **Enrollment:** FT 433, PT 432 **Faculty:** FT 24, PT 87 **Student-Faculty Ratio:** 14:1 **Exams:** SAT I or ACT. **Library Holdings:** 42,000 **Regional Accreditation:** Middle State Association of Colleges and Schools **Credit Hours For Degree:** 60 credit hours, Associates **Professional Accreditation:** ADA **Intercollegiate Athletics:** Basketball M & W; Soccer M & W; Volleyball W

MANSFIELD UNIVERSITY OF PENNSYLVANIA
Academy St.
Mansfield, PA 16933
Tel: (570)662-4000; Free: 800-577-6826
Admissions: (570)662-4813
Fax: (570)662-4121
E-mail: admissions@mnsfld.edu
Web Site: http://www.mansfield.edu/
President/CEO: Dr. Maravene S. Loeschke
Admissions: Brian Barden
Financial Aid: Barbara Schmitt
Type: Comprehensive **Sex:** Coed **Affiliation:** Pennsylvania State System of Higher Education **Scores:** 88.2% SAT V 400+; 87.1% SAT M 400+ **% Accepted:** 75 **Admission Plans:** Early Admission; Deferred Admission **Application Deadline:** Rolling **Application Fee:** $25.00 **H.S. Requirements:** High school diploma required; GED accepted **Scholarships:** Available **Calendar System:** Semester, Summer Session Available **Enrollment:** FT 2,838, PT 230, Grad FT 81, Grad PT 420 **Faculty:** FT 156, PT 67 **Student-Faculty Ratio:** 16:1 **Exams:** SAT I or ACT. ACT essay used for advising. SAT essay used for advising. ACT essay used for placement. SAT essay used for placement. ACT essay not being used. SAT essay not being used. **% Receiving Financial Aid:** 85 **% Residing in College-Owned, -Operated, or -Affiliated Housing:** 50 **Library Holdings:** 249,874 **Regional Accreditation:** Middle State Association of Colleges and Schools **Credit Hours For Degree:** 61 credits, Associates; 120 credits, Bachelors **ROTC:** Army **Professional Accreditation:** CARC, CSWE, JRCERT, NASM, NCATE, NLN **Intercollegiate Athletics:** Baseball M; Basketball M & W; Cross-Country Running M & W; Field Hockey W; Football M; Soccer W; Softball W; Swimming and Diving W; Track and Field M & W

MARYWOOD UNIVERSITY
2300 Adams Ave.
Scranton, PA 18509-1598
Tel: (570)348-6211; Free: (866)279-9663
Admissions: (570)348-6234
Fax: (570)961-4763
E-mail: yourfuture@marywood.edu
Web Site: http://www.marywood.edu/
President/CEO: Sr. Anne Munley, PhD
Admissions: Christian DiGregorio
Financial Aid: Stanley F. Skrutski
Type: Comprehensive **Sex:** Coed **Affiliation:** Roman Catholic **Scores:** 99.5% SAT V 400+; 99% SAT M 400+ **% Accepted:** 72 **Admission Plans:** Early Admission; Deferred Admission **Application Deadline:** Rolling **Application Fee:** $35.00 **H.S. Requirements:** High school diploma required; GED accepted **Costs Per Year:** Application fee: $35. One-time mandatory fee: $1120. Comprehensive fee: $37,768 includes full-time tuition ($25,150), mandatory fees ($1120), and college room and board ($11,498). College room only: $6566. Full-time tuition and fees vary according to course load. Room and board charges vary according to board plan and housing facility. Part-time tuition: $575 per credit. Part-time mandatory fees: $200 per term. Part-time tuition and fees vary according to course load. **Scholarships:** Available **Calendar System:** Semester, Summer Session Available **Enrollment:** FT 2,053, PT 131, Grad FT 538, Grad PT 749 **Faculty:** FT 142, PT

240 **Student-Faculty Ratio:** 13:1 **Exams:** SAT I or ACT. ACT essay used for admission. SAT essay used for admission. **% Receiving Financial Aid:** 85 **% Residing in College-Owned, -Operated, or -Affiliated Housing:** 45 **Final Year or Final Semester Residency Requirement:** No **Library Holdings:** 220,998 **Regional Accreditation:** Middle State Association of Colleges and Schools **Credit Hours For Degree:** 126 credits, Bachelors **ROTC:** Army, Air Force **Professional Accreditation:** AAFCS, ACA, ADtA, ASLHA, ACBSP, CSWE, NASAD, NASM, NCATE, NLN **Intercollegiate Athletics:** Baseball M; Basketball M & W; Cheerleading M & W; Cross-Country Running M & W; Field Hockey W; Golf M & W; Lacrosse M & W; Skiing (Cross-Country) M & W; Soccer M & W; Softball W; Swimming and Diving M & W; Tennis M & W; Track and Field M & W; Volleyball W

MCCANN SCHOOL OF BUSINESS & TECHNOLOGY
2650 Woodglen Rd.
Pottsville, PA 17901
Tel: (570)622-7622
Fax: (570)622-7770
Web Site: http://www.mccannschool.com/
Admissions: Linda Walinsky
Type: Two-Year College **Sex:** Coed **Admission Plans:** Open Admission **Application Deadline:** Rolling **Application Fee:** $40.00 **H.S. Requirements:** High school diploma required; GED accepted **Scholarships:** Available **Calendar System:** Quarter, Summer Session Available **Exams:** Other. **Library Holdings:** 1,850 **Credit Hours For Degree:** 90 credits, Associates **Professional Accreditation:** ACICS

MERCYHURST COLLEGE
501 East 38th St.
Erie, PA 16546
Tel: (814)824-2000; Free: 800-825-1926
Admissions: (814)824-2202
Fax: (814)824-2071
E-mail: ccoons@mercyhurst.edu
Web Site: http://www.mercyhurst.edu/
President/CEO: Dr. Thomas Gamble
Admissions: Christopher Coons
Financial Aid: Carrie Newman
Type: Comprehensive **Sex:** Coed **Affiliation:** Roman Catholic **Scores:** 97% SAT V 400+; 96% SAT M 400+; 53% ACT 18-23; 36% ACT 24-29 **% Accepted:** 74 **Admission Plans:** Deferred Admission **Application Deadline:** Rolling **Application Fee:** $30.00 **H.S. Requirements:** High school diploma required; GED accepted **Costs Per Year:** Application fee: $30. Comprehensive fee: $35,541 includes full-time tuition ($24,648), mandatory fees ($1698), and college room and board ($9195). College room only: $4542. Full-time tuition and fees vary according to program. Room and board charges vary according to board plan and housing facility. Part-time tuition: $822 per credit hour. Part-time tuition varies according to class time, course load, degree level, and location. **Scholarships:** Available **Calendar System:** Miscellaneous, Summer Session Available **Enrollment:** FT 2,650, PT 214, Grad FT 194, Grad PT 159 **Faculty:** FT 145, PT 62 **Student-Faculty Ratio:** 16:1 **Exams:** SAT I or ACT, SAT II. **% Receiving Financial Aid:** 71 **% Residing in College-Owned, -Operated, or -Affiliated Housing:** 73 **Final Year or Final Semester Residency Requirement:** No **Library Holdings:** 140,000 **Regional Accreditation:** Middle State Association of Colleges and Schools **Credit Hours For Degree:** 60 credits, Associates; 121 credits, Bachelors **ROTC:** Army, Air Force **Professional Accreditation:** AAFCS, ADtA, APTA, CSWE, JRCEPAT, NASM, NLN **Intercollegiate Athletics:** Baseball M; Basketball M & W; Crew M & W; Cross-Country Running M & W; Field Hockey W; Football M; Golf M & W; Ice Hockey M & W; Lacrosse M & W; Soccer M & W; Softball W; Tennis M & W; Volleyball W; Water Polo M & W; Wrestling M

MERCYHURST NORTH EAST
16 West Division St.
North East, PA 16428
Tel: (717)725-6100; Free: (866)846-6042
Admissions: (814)725-6217
E-mail: neadmiss@mercyhurst.edu
Web Site: http://northeast.mercyhurst.edu/
President/CEO: Dr. Thomas J. Gamble
Admissions: Travis Lindahl
Type: Two-Year College **Sex:** Coed **Affiliation:** Roman Catholic **Calendar System:** Miscellaneous **Regional Accreditation:** Middle State Association of Colleges and Schools

MESSIAH COLLEGE
One College Ave.
Grantham, PA 17027
Tel: (717)766-2511; Free: 800-233-4220
Admissions: (717)691-6000
Fax: (717)796-5374
E-mail: admiss@messiah.edu
Web Site: http://www.messiah.edu/
President/CEO: Dr. Kim S. Phipps
Admissions: John Chopka
Financial Aid: Michael Strite
Type: Comprehensive **Sex:** Coed **Affiliation:** interdenominational **Scores:** 99.41% SAT V 400+; 99.4% SAT M 400+; 26.85% ACT 18-23; 51.01% ACT 24-29 **% Accepted:** 69 **Admission Plans:** Deferred Admission **Application Deadline:** Rolling **Application Fee:** $30.00 **H.S. Requirements:** High school diploma required; GED accepted **Costs Per Year:** Application fee: $30. Comprehensive fee: $35,640 includes full-time tuition ($26,680), mandatory fees ($800), and college room and board ($8160). College room only: $4320. Room and board charges vary according to board plan, housing facility, and location. Part-time tuition: $1112 per credit. **Scholarships:** Available **Calendar System:** Semester, Summer Session Available **Enrollment:** FT 2,712, PT 54, Grad FT 20, Grad PT 15 **Faculty:** FT 170, PT 109 **Student-Faculty Ratio:** 13:1 **Exams:** SAT I or ACT. SAT essay used for placement. ACT essay not being used. **% Receiving Financial Aid:** 72 **% Residing in College-Owned, -Operated, or -Affiliated Housing:** 87 **Library Holdings:** 289,053 **Regional Accreditation:** Middle State Association of Colleges and Schools **Credit Hours For Degree:** 126 credits, Bachelors **Professional Accreditation:** ABET, AACN, JRCEPAT, NASAD, NASM **Intercollegiate Athletics:** Baseball M; Basketball M & W; Cross-Country Running M & W; Field Hockey W; Golf M; Lacrosse M & W; Soccer M & W; Softball W; Swimming and Diving M & W; Tennis M & W; Track and Field M & W; Volleyball W; Wrestling M

METROPOLITAN CAREER CENTER
100 South Broad St.
Ste. 830
Philadelphia, PA 19110
Tel: (215)568-9215
Fax: (215)568-3511
Web Site: http://www.careersinit.org/
President/CEO: Amy Miller
Type: Two-Year College **Sex:** Coed **Calendar System:** Semester **Student-Faculty Ratio:** 15:1 **Professional Accreditation:** ACCSCT

MILLERSVILLE UNIVERSITY OF PENNSYLVANIA
PO Box 1002
Millersville, PA 17551-0302
Tel: (717)872-3011; Free: 800-MU-ADMIT
Admissions: (717)872-3371
E-mail: admissions@millersville.edu
Web Site: http://www.millersville.edu/
President/CEO: Dr. Francine G. McNairy
Admissions: Dr. Douglas Zander
Financial Aid: Dwight G. Horsey
Type: Comprehensive **Sex:** Coed **Affiliation:** Pennsylvania State System of Higher Education **Scores:** 96.21% SAT V 400+; 96.68% SAT M 400+; 60% ACT 18-23; 23.87% ACT 24-29 **% Accepted:** 53 **Admission Plans:** Early Admission; Deferred Admission **Application Deadline:** Rolling **Application Fee:** $50.00 **H.S. Requirements:** High school diploma required; GED accepted **Costs Per Year:** Application fee: $50. State resident tuition: $5554 full-time, $231 per credit part-time. Nonresident tuition: $13,886 full-time, $579 per credit part-time. Mandatory fees: $1593 full-time, $57.75 per credit part-time, $60. Full-time tuition and fees vary according to degree level. Part-time tuition and fees vary according to course load and degree level. College room and board: $7766. College room only: $4608. Room and board charges vary according to board plan and housing facility. **Scholarships:** Available **Calendar System:** 4-1-4, Summer Session Available **Enrollment:** FT 6,689, PT 670, Grad FT 281, Grad PT 787 **Faculty:** FT 304, PT 133 **Student-Faculty Ratio:** 21:1 **Exams:** SAT I or ACT. ACT essay not being used. SAT essay not being used. **% Receiving Financial Aid:** 57 **% Resid-**

ing in College-Owned, -Operated, or -Affiliated Housing: 31 **Final Year or Final Semester Residency Requirement:** No **Library Holdings:** 603,224 **Regional Accreditation:** Middle State Association of Colleges and Schools **Credit Hours For Degree:** 60 credits, Associates; 120 credits, Bachelors **ROTC:** Army **Professional Accreditation:** ABET, ACBSP, CARC, CSWE, NASAD, NASM, NCATE, NLN, NAIT **Intercollegiate Athletics:** Baseball M; Basketball M & W; Cheerleading W; Cross-Country Running M & W; Field Hockey W; Football M; Golf M; Lacrosse W; Soccer M & W; Softball W; Swimming and Diving W; Tennis M & W; Track and Field M & W; Volleyball W; Wrestling M

MISERICORDIA UNIVERSITY
301 Lake St.
Dallas, PA 18612-1098
Tel: (570)674-6400; Free: (866)262-6363
Admissions: (570)675-6264
Fax: (570)675-2441
E-mail: admiss@misericordia.edu
Web Site: http://www.misericordia.edu/
President/CEO: Dr. Michael A. MacDowell
Admissions: Glenn Bozinski
Financial Aid: Jane Dessoye
Type: Comprehensive **Sex:** Coed **Affiliation:** Roman Catholic **Scores:** 98% SAT V 400+; 96% SAT M 400+; 53% ACT 18-23; 40% ACT 24-29 **% Accepted:** 69 **Admission Plans:** Early Admission; Deferred Admission **Application Deadline:** Rolling **Application Fee:** $25.00 **H.S. Requirements:** High school diploma required; GED accepted **Costs Per Year:** Application fee: $25. Comprehensive fee: $34,100 includes full-time tuition ($22,850), mandatory fees ($1200), and college room and board ($10,050). College room only: $5830. Room and board charges vary according to board plan and housing facility. Part-time tuition: $450 per credit. Part-time tuition varies according to class time and location. **Scholarships:** Available **Calendar System:** Semester, Summer Session Available **Enrollment:** FT 1,665, PT 703, Grad PT 368 **Faculty:** FT 96, PT 179 **Student-Faculty Ratio:** 13:1 **Exams:** SAT I or ACT. ACT essay not being used. SAT essay not being used. **% Receiving Financial Aid:** 83 **% Residing in College-Owned, -Operated, or -Affiliated Housing:** 37 **Library Holdings:** 79,503 **Regional Accreditation:** Middle State Association of Colleges and Schools **Credit Hours For Degree:** 120 credits, Bachelors **ROTC:** Army, Air Force **Professional Accreditation:** AACN, AOTA, APTA, ASLHA, CSWE, JRCERT, NLN, TEAC **Intercollegiate Athletics:** Baseball M; Basketball M & W; Cheerleading W; Cross-Country Running M & W; Field Hockey W; Golf M; Lacrosse M & W; Soccer M & W; Softball W; Swimming and Diving M & W; Tennis M & W; Track and Field M & W; Volleyball W

MONTGOMERY COUNTY COMMUNITY COLLEGE
340 DeKalb Pike
Blue Bell, PA 19422-0796
Tel: (215)641-6300
Admissions: (215)641-6551
Fax: (215)653-0585
E-mail: admrec@admin.mc3.edu
Web Site: http://www.mc3.edu/
President/CEO: Dr. Karen A. Stout
Admissions: Penny Sawyer
Type: Two-Year College **Sex:** Coed **% Accepted:** 100 **Admission Plans:** Open Admission; Preferred Admission; Early Admission; Deferred Admission **Application Fee:** $25.00 **H.S. Requirements:** High school diploma required; GED accepted. For early admissions program: High school diploma or equivalent not required **Costs Per Year:** Application fee: $25. Area resident tuition: $2700 full-time, $90 per credit hour part-time. State resident tuition: $5700 full-time, $180 per credit hour part-time. Nonresident tuition: $8700 full-time, $270 per credit hour part-time. Mandatory fees: $570 full-time, $19 per credit hour part-time. **Scholarships:** Available **Calendar System:** Semester, Summer Session Available **Enrollment:** FT 6,288, PT 7,022 **Faculty:** FT 194, PT 560 **Student-Faculty Ratio:** 23:1 **Library Holdings:** 92,850 **Regional Accreditation:** Middle State Association of Colleges and Schools **Credit Hours For Degree:** 60 credits, Associates **Professional Accreditation:** ADA, NAACLS, NLN **Intercollegiate Athletics:** Baseball M; Basketball M & W; Soccer M & W; Softball W

MOORE COLLEGE OF ART & DESIGN
20th and the Parkway
Philadelphia, PA 19103
Tel: (215)568-4515; Free: 800-523-2025
Admissions: (215)965-4014
Fax: (215)568-3547
E-mail: enroll@moore.edu
Web Site: http://www.moore.edu/
President/CEO: Happy C. Fernandez
Admissions: Heesung Lee
Financial Aid: Kristina Fripps
Type: Comprehensive **Sex:** Women **Scores:** 96% SAT V 400+; 82% SAT M 400+; 50% ACT 18-23; 34% ACT 24-29 **% Accepted:** 64 **Admission Plans:** Deferred Admission **Application Deadline:** August 15 **Application Fee:** $40.00 **H.S. Requirements:** High school diploma required; GED accepted **Costs Per Year:** Application fee: $40. Comprehensive fee: $41,776 includes full-time tuition ($29,265), mandatory fees ($1144), and college room and board ($11,367). Room and board charges vary according to board plan and housing facility. Part-time tuition: $1221 per credit. Part-time tuition varies according to course load and program. **Scholarships:** Available **Calendar System:** Semester, Summer Session Available **Enrollment:** FT 493, PT 34, Grad FT 21, Grad PT 34 **Faculty:** FT 24, PT 105 **Student-Faculty Ratio:** 9:1 **Exams:** SAT I or ACT. **% Receiving Financial Aid:** 78 **Regional Accreditation:** Middle State Association of Colleges and Schools **Credit Hours For Degree:** 125.5 credits, Bachelors **Professional Accreditation:** FIDER, NASAD

MORAVIAN COLLEGE
1200 Main St.
Bethlehem, PA 18018-6650
Tel: (610)861-1300; Free: 800-441-3191
Admissions: (610)861-1320
Fax: (610)861-3956
E-mail: admissions@moravian.edu
Web Site: http://www.moravian.edu/
President/CEO: Christopher Thomforde
Admissions: James Mackin
Financial Aid: Stephen C. Cassel
Type: Comprehensive **Sex:** Coed **Affiliation:** Moravian Church **Scores:** 100% SAT V 400+; 100% SAT M 400+ **% Accepted:** 75 **Admission Plans:** Early Admission; Early Decision Plan; Deferred Admission **Application Deadline:** March 1 **Application Fee:** $40.00 **H.S. Requirements:** High school diploma required; GED accepted **Costs Per Year:** Application fee: $40. Comprehensive fee: $41,341 includes full-time tuition ($31,662), mandatory fees ($515), and college room and board ($9164). College room only: $5149. Room and board charges vary according to board plan and housing facility. Part-time tuition: $853.75 per credit hour. Part-time tuition varies according to class time. **Scholarships:** Available **Calendar System:** Semester, Summer Session Available **Enrollment:** FT 1,558, PT 237, Grad FT 27, Grad PT 235 **Faculty:** FT 120, PT 79 **Student-Faculty Ratio:** 10:1 **Exams:** SAT I or ACT. ACT essay used for admission. SAT essay used for admission. ACT essay used for advising. SAT essay used for advising. ACT essay used for placement. SAT essay used for placement. **% Receiving Financial Aid:** 79 **% Residing in College-Owned, -Operated, or -Affiliated Housing:** 71 **Library Holdings:** 249,308 **Regional Accreditation:** Middle State Association of Colleges and Schools **Credit Hours For Degree:** 128 credits, Bachelors **ROTC:** Army **Professional Accreditation:** AACN, NASM **Intercollegiate Athletics:** Baseball M; Basketball M & W; Cheerleading W; Cross-Country Running M & W; Equestrian Sports M & W; Field Hockey W; Football M; Golf M & W; Ice Hockey M & W; Lacrosse M & W; Soccer M & W; Softball W; Tennis M & W; Track and Field M & W; Volleyball W

MOUNT ALOYSIUS COLLEGE
7373 Admiral Peary Hwy.
Cresson, PA 16630-1999
Tel: (814)886-4131; Free: 888-823-2220
Admissions: (814)886-6383
Fax: (814)886-2978
E-mail: admissions@mtaloy.edu
Web Site: http://www.mtaloy.edu/
President/CEO: Sr. Mary Ann Dillon, PhD
Admissions: Frank C. Crouse, Jr.
Financial Aid: Stacy L. Schenk
Type: Comprehensive **Sex:** Coed **Affiliation:** Roman Catholic **Scores:** 83% SAT V 400+; 82% SAT M 400+; 57% ACT 18-23; 7% ACT 24-29 **% Accepted:** 80 **Admission Plans:** Early Admission; Deferred Admission **Ap-**

plication Deadline: Rolling **Application Fee:** $30.00 **H.S. Requirements:** High school diploma required; GED accepted **Costs Per Year:** Application fee: $30. Comprehensive fee: $24,580 includes full-time tuition ($16,580), mandatory fees ($700), and college room and board ($7300). College room only: $3750. Part-time tuition: $480 per credit. Part-time mandatory fees: $185 per term. **Scholarships:** Available **Calendar System:** Semester, Summer Session Available **Enrollment:** FT 1,165, PT 412, Grad FT 17, Grad PT 10 **Faculty:** FT 62, PT 129 **Student-Faculty Ratio:** 14:1 **Exams:** SAT I or ACT. **% Receiving Financial Aid:** 97 **Regional Accreditation:** Middle State Association of Colleges and Schools **Professional Accreditation:** ARCEST, AAMAE, AOTA, APTA, NLN **Intercollegiate Athletics:** Baseball M; Basketball M & W; Cross-Country Running M & W; Golf M & W; Soccer M & W; Softball W; Volleyball W

MUHLENBERG COLLEGE
2400 Chew St.
Allentown, PA 18104-5586
Tel: (484)664-3100
Admissions: (484)664-3245
Fax: (484)664-3234
E-mail: adm@muhlenberg.edu
Web Site: http://www.muhlenberg.edu/
President/CEO: Dr. Peyton R. Helm
Admissions: Christopher Hooker-Haring
Financial Aid: Greg Mitton
Type: Four-Year College **Sex:** Coed **Affiliation:** Lutheran Church **Scores:** 99.8% SAT V 400+; 99.5% SAT M 400+; 10.3% ACT 18-23; 66.8% ACT 24-29 **% Accepted:** 45 **Admission Plans:** Early Admission; Early Decision Plan; Deferred Admission **Application Deadline:** February 15 **Application Fee:** $50.00 **H.S. Requirements:** High school diploma required; GED accepted **Costs Per Year:** Application fee: $50. Comprehensive fee: $45,430 includes full-time tuition ($36,730), mandatory fees ($260), and college room and board ($8440). College room only: $4985. Room and board charges vary according to board plan, housing facility, and location. Part-time tuition: $4320 per course. Part-time tuition varies according to program. **Scholarships:** Available **Calendar System:** Semester, Summer Session Available **Enrollment:** FT 2,352, PT 165 **Faculty:** FT 166, PT 94 **Student-Faculty Ratio:** 12:1 **Exams:** SAT I or ACT. **% Receiving Financial Aid:** 44 **% Residing in College-Owned, -Operated, or -Affiliated Housing:** 92 **Library Holdings:** 409,798 **Regional Accreditation:** Middle State Association of Colleges and Schools **Credit Hours For Degree:** 34 courses, Bachelors **ROTC:** Army **Intercollegiate Athletics:** Baseball M; Basketball M & W; Cheerleading M & W; Cross-Country Running M & W; Field Hockey W; Football M; Golf M & W; Lacrosse M & W; Soccer M & W; Softball W; Tennis M & W; Track and Field M & W; Volleyball W; Wrestling M

NEUMANN UNIVERSITY
One Neumann Dr.
Aston, PA 19014-1298
Tel: (610)459-0905; Free: 800-963-8626
Admissions: (610)361-2448
E-mail: neumann@neumann.edu
Web Site: http://www.neumann.edu/
President/CEO: Dr. Rosalie Mirenda
Admissions: Dennis J. Murphy
Financial Aid: Katherine Markert
Type: Comprehensive **Sex:** Coed **Affiliation:** Roman Catholic **Scores:** 79% SAT V 400+; 68% SAT M 400+ **% Accepted:** 94 **Application Deadline:** April 1 **Application Fee:** $35.00 **H.S. Requirements:** High school diploma required; GED accepted **Costs Per Year:** Application fee: $35. Comprehensive fee: $31,078 includes full-time tuition ($20,580), mandatory fees ($780), and college room and board ($9718). College room only: $5732. Room and board charges vary according to board plan. Part-time tuition: $470 per credit hour. **Scholarships:** Available **Calendar System:** Semester, Summer Session Available **Enrollment:** FT 2,012, PT 489, Grad FT 139, Grad PT 459 **Faculty:** FT 91, PT 195 **Student-Faculty Ratio:** 14:1 **Exams:** SAT I or ACT. **% Receiving Financial Aid:** 90 **% Residing in College-Owned, -Operated, or -Affiliated Housing:** 40 **Library Holdings:** 75,000 **Regional Accreditation:** Middle State Association of Colleges and Schools **Credit Hours For Degree:** 60 credits, Associates; 120 credits, Bachelors **ROTC:** Army **Professional Accreditation:** APTA, NAACLS, NLN **Intercollegiate Athletics:** Baseball M; Basketball M & W; Cross-Country Running M & W; Field Hockey W; Golf M; Ice Hockey M & W; Lacrosse M & W; Soccer M & W; Softball W; Tennis M & W; Volleyball W

NEW CASTLE SCHOOL OF TRADES
New Castle Youngstown Rd., Route 422 RD1
Pulaski, PA 16143-9721
Tel: (724)964-8811; Free: 800-837-8299
Web Site: http://www.ncstrades.com/
President/CEO: Jim Buttermore
Admissions: James Catheline
Type: Two-Year College **Sex:** Coed **Affiliation:** Educational Enterprises Incorporated **% Accepted:** 100 **Application Fee:** $25.00 **Scholarships:** Available **Calendar System:** Quarter **Exams:** Other. **Professional Accreditation:** ACCSCT

NEWPORT BUSINESS INSTITUTE (LOWER BURRELL)
945 Greensburg Rd.
Lower Burrell, PA 15068-3929
Tel: (724)339-7542; Free: 800-752-7695
Admissions: (724)339-0455
Fax: (724)339-2950
Web Site: http://www.nbi.edu/
President/CEO: Raymond Wroblewski
Admissions: Melissa Beck
Type: Two-Year College **Sex:** Coed **% Accepted:** 100 **Admission Plans:** Open Admission; Early Admission **Application Deadline:** Rolling **Application Fee:** $25.00 **H.S. Requirements:** High school diploma required; GED accepted **Scholarships:** Available **Calendar System:** Quarter, Summer Session Not available **Enrollment:** FT 79 **Faculty:** FT 6 **Student-Faculty Ratio:** 14:1 **Library Holdings:** 962 **Credit Hours For Degree:** 90 quarter hours, Associates **Professional Accreditation:** ACICS

NEWPORT BUSINESS INSTITUTE (WILLIAMSPORT)
941 West Third St.
Williamsport, PA 17701-5855
Tel: (570)326-2869; Free: 800-962-6971
Fax: (570)326-2136
E-mail: admissions_NBI@suscom.net
Web Site: http://www.nbi.edu/
President/CEO: Mary O. Weaver
Admissions: David Andrus
Type: Two-Year College **Sex:** Coed **% Accepted:** 100 **Admission Plans:** Deferred Admission **Application Deadline:** Rolling **Application Fee:** $25.00 **H.S. Requirements:** High school diploma required; GED accepted **Scholarships:** Available **Calendar System:** Quarter, Summer Session Available **Enrollment:** FT 124 **Faculty:** FT 6, PT 9 **Student-Faculty Ratio:** 14:1 **Credit Hours For Degree:** 90 quarter hours, Associates **Professional Accreditation:** ACICS

NORTH CENTRAL INDUSTRIAL TECHNICAL EDUCATION CENTER
653 Montmorenci Ave.
Ridgway, PA 15853
Tel: (814)772-1012; Free: 800-242-5872
Fax: (814)772-1554
E-mail: linzana@ncentral.com
Web Site: http://web2.ncentral.com/itec/
Admissions: Lugene Inzana
Type: Two-Year College **Sex:** Coed **Application Fee:** $50.00 **Calendar System:** Trimester **Professional Accreditation:** ACCSCT

NORTHAMPTON COMMUNITY COLLEGE
3835 Green Pond Rd.
Bethlehem, PA 18020-7599
Tel: (610)861-5300
Admissions: (610)861-5506
E-mail: jrmccarthy@northampton.edu
Web Site: http://www.northampton.edu/
President/CEO: Dr. Arthur L. Scott
Admissions: James McCarthy
Financial Aid: Cindy King
Type: Two-Year College **Sex:** Coed **% Accepted:** 100 **Admission Plans:** Open Admission; Deferred Admission **Application Deadline:** Rolling **Application Fee:** $25.00 **H.S. Requirements:** High school diploma required; GED accepted **Costs Per Year:** Application fee: $25. Area resident tuition: $2310 full-time, $77 per credit hour part-time. State resident tuition: $4620 full-time, $154 per credit hour part-time. Nonresident tuition: $6930 full-time, $231 per credit hour part-time. Mandatory fees: $870 full-time, $29 per credit

hour part-time. Full-time tuition and fees vary according to course load. Part-time tuition and fees vary according to course load. College room and board: $6862. College room only: $3944. Room and board charges vary according to board plan and housing facility. **Scholarships:** Available **Calendar System:** Semester, Summer Session Available **Enrollment:** FT 5,427, PT 5,791 **Faculty:** FT 123, PT 565 **Student-Faculty Ratio:** 24:1 **% Residing in College-Owned, -Operated, or -Affiliated Housing:** 2 **Final Year or Final Semester Residency Requirement:** No **Library Holdings:** 90,642 **Regional Accreditation:** Middle State Association of Colleges and Schools **Credit Hours For Degree:** 60 credit hours, Associates **Professional Accreditation:** ABFSE, ADA, ACBSP, JRCERT, NLN **Intercollegiate Athletics:** Baseball M; Basketball M & W; Golf M & W; Soccer M; Softball W; Tennis M & W; Volleyball M & W

OAKBRIDGE ACADEMY OF ARTS
1250 Greensburg Rd.
Lower Burrell, PA 15068
Tel: (724)335-5336; Free: 800-734-5601
Fax: (724)335-3367
Web Site: http://www.akvalley.com/oakbridge/
President/CEO: J. Bryant Mullen
Admissions: Melissa Beck
Type: Two-Year College **Sex:** Coed **Application Deadline:** August 31 **Application Fee:** $50.00 **H.S. Requirements:** High school diploma required; GED accepted **Scholarships:** Available **Calendar System:** Quarter **Enrollment:** FT 66 **Faculty:** FT 3, PT 2 **Student-Faculty Ratio:** 16:1 **Library Holdings:** 3,000 **Credit Hours For Degree:** 90 quarter hours, Associates **Professional Accreditation:** ACCSCT

ORLEANS TECHNICAL INSTITUTE
2770 Red Lion Rd.
Philadelphia, PA 19114
Tel: (215)728-4700
Admissions: (215)854-1853
Fax: (215)745-1689
Web Site: http://www.orleanstech.edu/
Admissions: Gary Bello
Type: Two-Year College **Sex:** Coed **Admission Plans:** Open Admission **Application Deadline:** Rolling **Application Fee:** $100.00 **H.S. Requirements:** High school diploma required; GED accepted **Scholarships:** Available **Calendar System:** Trimester, Summer Session Available **Exams:** Other. **Library Holdings:** 625 **Credit Hours For Degree:** 82 credits, Associates **Professional Accreditation:** ACCSCT

PACE INSTITUTE
606 Ct. St.
Reading, PA 19601
Tel: (610)375-1212
Fax: (610)375-1924
Web Site: http://www.paceinstitute.com/
President/CEO: Rhoda E. Dersh
Admissions: Ed Levandowski
Type: Two-Year College **Sex:** Coed **Application Fee:** $10.00 **Scholarships:** Available **Enrollment:** FT 201, PT 73 **Faculty:** FT 6, PT 8 **Student-Faculty Ratio:** 18:1 **Professional Accreditation:** ACICS

PEIRCE COLLEGE
1420 Pine St.
Philadelphia, PA 19102-4699
Tel: (215)545-6400; Free: 888-467-3472
Admissions: (215)670-9214
Fax: (215)546-5996
E-mail: info@peirce.edu
Web Site: http://www.peirce.edu/
President/CEO: James J. Mergiotti
Admissions: Paul Ballentine
Financial Aid: Lisa A. Gargiulo
Type: Four-Year College **Sex:** Coed **Admission Plans:** Open Admission **Application Deadline:** Rolling **Application Fee:** $50.00 **H.S. Requirements:** High school diploma required; GED accepted **Costs Per Year:** Application fee: $50. Tuition: $13,800 full-time, $460 per credit part-time. Mandatory fees: $1050 full-time, $105 per course part-time. Full-time tuition and fees vary according to course load. Part-time tuition and fees vary according to course load. **Scholarships:** Available **Calendar System:** Semester, Summer Session Available **Enrollment:** FT 831, PT 1,252 **Faculty:** FT 30, PT 129 **Student-Faculty Ratio:** 17:1 **% Receiving Financial Aid:** 59 **Final Year or Final Semester Residency Requirement:** No **Library Holdings:** 50,191 **Regional Accreditation:** Middle State Association of Colleges and Schools **Credit Hours For Degree:** 61 credits, Associates; 121 credits, Bachelors **Professional Accreditation:** ACBSP

PENN COMMERCIAL BUSINESS AND TECHNICAL SCHOOL
242 Oak Spring Rd.
Washington, PA 15301
Tel: (724)222-5330
Fax: (724)222-4722
E-mail: mjoyce@penn-commercial.com
Web Site: http://www.penncommercial.net/
President/CEO: Robert S. Bazant
Admissions: Michael John Joyce
Type: Two-Year College **Sex:** Coed **Admission Plans:** Open Admission; Early Admission; Deferred Admission **Application Deadline:** Rolling **Application Fee:** $100.00 **H.S. Requirements:** High school diploma required; GED accepted **Scholarships:** Available **Calendar System:** Quarter, Summer Session Available **Library Holdings:** 400 **Credit Hours For Degree:** 1500 hours, Associates **Professional Accreditation:** ACICS, AAMAE

PENN FOSTER CAREER SCHOOL
925 Oak St.
Scranton, PA 18515
Tel: (570)342-7701; Free: 800-233-4191
Web Site: http://www.pennfoster.edu/
Admissions: Connie Dempsey
Type: Two-Year College **Sex:** Coed **% Accepted:** 99 **Admission Plans:** Open Admission **Application Deadline:** Rolling **H.S. Requirements:** High school diploma required; GED accepted **Calendar System:** Semester, Summer Session Available **Faculty:** FT 17, PT 26 **Exams:** Other. **Credit Hours For Degree:** 62 credits, Associates **Professional Accreditation:** DETC

PENN STATE ABINGTON
1600 Woodland Rd.
Abington, PA 19001
Tel: (215)881-7300
Admissions: (814)865-4700
E-mail: admissions@psu.edu
Web Site: http://www.abington.psu.edu/
President/CEO: Dr. Graham Spanier
Admissions: Anne L. Rohrbach
Financial Aid: Debbie Meditz
Type: Four-Year College **Sex:** Coed **Affiliation:** Pennsylvania State University **Scores:** 81.21% SAT V 400+; 85.11% SAT M 400+ **% Accepted:** 84 **Admission Plans:** Early Admission; Deferred Admission **Application Deadline:** Rolling **Application Fee:** $50.00 **H.S. Requirements:** High school diploma required; GED accepted **Costs Per Year:** Application fee: $50. State resident tuition: $11,442 full-time, $463 per credit hour part-time. Nonresident tuition: $17,460 full-time, $728 per credit hour part-time. Mandatory fees: $808 full-time. **Scholarships:** Available **Calendar System:** Semester, Summer Session Available **Enrollment:** FT 2,698, PT 699, Grad PT 27 **Faculty:** FT 105, PT 132 **Student-Faculty Ratio:** 20:1 **Exams:** SAT I or ACT. ACT essay not being used. SAT essay not being used. **% Receiving Financial Aid:** 64 **Regional Accreditation:** Middle State Association of Colleges and Schools **Credit Hours For Degree:** 60 credits, Associates; 120 credits, Bachelors **ROTC:** Army, Air Force **Intercollegiate Athletics:** Baseball M; Basketball M & W; Golf M; Soccer M & W; Softball W; Tennis M & W; Volleyball W

PENN STATE ALTOONA
3000 Ivyside Park
Altoona, PA 16601-3760
Tel: (814)949-5000; Free: 800-848-9843
Admissions: (814)865-4700
Fax: (814)949-5011
E-mail: admissions@psu.edu
Web Site: http://www.aa.psu.edu/
President/CEO: Dr. Graham Spanier
Admissions: Anne L. Rohrbach
Financial Aid: David Pearlman
Type: Four-Year College **Sex:** Coed **Affiliation:** Pennsylvania State

University **Scores:** 91.75% SAT V 400+; 92.49% SAT M 400+ **% Accepted:** 87 **Admission Plans:** Early Admission; Deferred Admission **Application Deadline:** Rolling **Application Fee:** $50.00 **H.S. Requirements:** High school diploma required; GED accepted **Costs Per Year:** Application fee: $50. State resident tuition: $11,942 full-time, $498 per credit hour part-time. Nonresident tuition: $18,270 full-time, $761 per credit hour part-time. Mandatory fees: $808 full-time. Full-time tuition and fees vary according to course level, location, program, and student level. Part-time tuition varies according to course level, course load, location, program, and student level. College room and board: $8170. College room only: $4430. Room and board charges vary according to board plan, housing facility, and location. **Scholarships:** Available **Calendar System:** Semester, Summer Session Available **Enrollment:** FT 3,924, PT 223, Grad PT 35 **Faculty:** FT 184, PT 141 **Student-Faculty Ratio:** 17:1 **Exams:** SAT I or ACT. ACT essay not being used. SAT essay not being used. **% Receiving Financial Aid:** 65 **% Residing in College-Owned, -Operated, or -Affiliated Housing:** 22 **Regional Accreditation:** Middle State Association of Colleges and Schools **Credit Hours For Degree:** 60 credits, Associates; 120 credits, Bachelors **ROTC:** Army, Air Force **Professional Accreditation:** ABET **Intercollegiate Athletics:** Baseball M; Basketball M & W; Cross-Country Running M & W; Golf M & W; Soccer M & W; Softball W; Swimming and Diving M & W; Tennis M & W

PENN STATE BEAVER
100 University Dr.
Monaca, PA 15061
Tel: (724)773-3800
Fax: (724)773-3557
E-mail: br-admissions@psu.edu
Web Site: http://www.br.psu.edu/
President/CEO: Gary B. Keefer
Admissions: Randall C. Deike
Financial Aid: Gail Gray
Type: Two-Year College **Sex:** Coed **Affiliation:** Pennsylvania State University **Scores:** 79.4% SAT V 400+; 84.97% SAT M 400+ **% Accepted:** 93 **Admission Plans:** Early Admission; Deferred Admission **Application Deadline:** Rolling **Application Fee:** $50.00 **H.S. Requirements:** High school diploma required; GED accepted **Costs Per Year:** Application fee: $50. State resident tuition: $11,442 full-time, $463 per credit hour part-time. Nonresident tuition: $17,460 full-time, $728 per credit hour part-time. Mandatory fees: $808 full-time. Full-time tuition and fees vary according to course level, location, and program. Part-time tuition varies according to course level, location, and program. College room and board: $8170. College room only: $4430. Room and board charges vary according to board plan, housing facility, and location. **Scholarships:** Available **Calendar System:** Semester, Summer Session Available **Enrollment:** FT 658, PT 193, Grad PT 4 **Faculty:** FT 33, PT 25 **Student-Faculty Ratio:** 18:1 **Exams:** SAT I or ACT. ACT essay not being used. SAT essay not being used. **% Residing in College-Owned, -Operated, or -Affiliated Housing:** 21 **Regional Accreditation:** Middle State Association of Colleges and Schools **Credit Hours For Degree:** 60 credits, Associates **Professional Accreditation:** ABET **Intercollegiate Athletics:** Baseball M; Basketball M; Softball M & W; Volleyball W

PENN STATE BERKS
Tulpehocken Rd., PO Box 7009
Reading, PA 19610-6009
Tel: (610)396-6000
Admissions: (814)865-4700
E-mail: admissions@psu.edu
Web Site: http://www.bk.psu.edu/
President/CEO: Dr. Graham Spanier
Admissions: Anne L. Rohrbach
Financial Aid: Maryann Hubick
Type: Four-Year College **Sex:** Coed **Affiliation:** Pennsylvania State University **Scores:** 90.52% SAT V 400+; 89.42% SAT M 400+ **% Accepted:** 83 **Admission Plans:** Early Admission; Deferred Admission **Application Deadline:** Rolling **Application Fee:** $50.00 **H.S. Requirements:** High school diploma required; GED accepted **Costs Per Year:** Application fee: $50. State resident tuition: $11,942 full-time, $498 per credit hour part-time. Nonresident tuition: $18,270 full-time, $761 per credit hour part-time. Mandatory fees: $808 full-time. Full-time tuition and fees vary according to course level, location, program, and student level. Part-time tuition varies according to course level, course load, location, program, and student level. College room and board: $8940. College room only: $5200. Room and board charges vary according to board plan, housing facility, and location. **Scholarships:** Available **Calendar System:** Semester, Summer Session Available **Enrollment:** FT 2,361, PT 286, Grad PT 112 **Faculty:** FT 113, PT 87 **Student-Faculty Ratio:** 18:1 **Exams:** SAT I or ACT. ACT essay not being used. SAT essay not being used. **% Receiving Financial Aid:** 59 **% Residing in College-Owned, -Operated, or -Affiliated Housing:** 31 **Regional Accreditation:** Middle State Association of Colleges and Schools **Credit Hours For Degree:** 60 credits, Associates; 120 credits, Bachelors **ROTC:** Army **Professional Accreditation:** ABET, AOTA **Intercollegiate Athletics:** Baseball M; Basketball M & W; Cheerleading M & W; Cross-Country Running M & W; Golf M; Soccer M & W; Softball W; Tennis M & W; Volleyball W

PENN STATE BRANDYWINE
25 Yearsley Mill Rd.
Media, PA 19063-5596
Tel: (610)892-1200
E-mail: bwadmissions@psu.edu
Web Site: http://www.brandywine.psu.edu/
President/CEO: Sophia T. Wisniewska
Admissions: Randall C. Deike
Type: Two-Year College **Sex:** Coed **Affiliation:** Pennsylvania State University **Scores:** 82.8% SAT V 400+; 87.57% SAT M 400+ **% Accepted:** 85 **Admission Plans:** Early Admission; Deferred Admission **Application Deadline:** Rolling **Application Fee:** $50.00 **H.S. Requirements:** High school diploma required; GED accepted **Costs Per Year:** Application fee: $50. State resident tuition: $11,442 full-time, $463 per credit hour part-time. Nonresident tuition: $17,460 full-time, $728 per credit hour part-time. Mandatory fees: $708 full-time. Full-time tuition and fees vary according to course level, location, program, and student level. Part-time tuition varies according to course level, course load, location, program, and student level. **Scholarships:** Available **Calendar System:** Semester, Summer Session Available **Enrollment:** FT 1,383, PT 224, Grad PT 1 **Faculty:** FT 59, PT 74 **Student-Faculty Ratio:** 17:1 **Exams:** SAT I or ACT. ACT essay not being used. SAT essay not being used. **Regional Accreditation:** Middle State Association of Colleges and Schools **Credit Hours For Degree:** 60 credits, Associates; 120 credits, Bachelors **ROTC:** Army, Air Force **Intercollegiate Athletics:** Baseball M; Basketball M & W; Soccer M & W; Tennis M & W; Volleyball W

PENN STATE DUBOIS
College Place
DuBois, PA 15801-3199
Tel: (814)375-4700; Free: 800-346-7627
E-mail: duboisinfo@psu.edu
Web Site: http://www.ds.psu.edu/
President/CEO: Anita D. McDonald
Admissions: Randall C. Deike
Type: Two-Year College **Sex:** Coed **Affiliation:** Pennsylvania State University **Scores:** 81.08% SAT M 400+ **% Accepted:** 92 **Admission Plans:** Early Admission; Deferred Admission **Application Deadline:** Rolling **Application Fee:** $50.00 **H.S. Requirements:** High school diploma required; GED accepted **Costs Per Year:** Application fee: $50. State resident tuition: $11,442 full-time, $463 per credit hour part-time. Nonresident tuition: $17,460 full-time, $728 per credit hour part-time. Mandatory fees: $688 full-time. Full-time tuition and fees vary according to course level, location, program, and student level. Part-time tuition varies according to course level, course load, location, program, and student level. **Scholarships:** Available **Calendar System:** Semester, Summer Session Available **Enrollment:** FT 763, PT 174, Grad PT 1 **Faculty:** FT 46, PT 48 **Student-Faculty Ratio:** 13:1 **Exams:** SAT I or ACT. ACT essay not being used. SAT essay not being used. **Regional Accreditation:** Middle State Association of Colleges and Schools **Credit Hours For Degree:** 60 credits, Associates **Professional Accreditation:** ABET, AOTA, APTA **Intercollegiate Athletics:** Basketball M; Cross-Country Running M & W; Golf M & W; Volleyball W

PENN STATE ERIE, THE BEHREND COLLEGE
5091 Station Rd.
Erie, PA 16563-0001
Tel: (814)898-6000; Free: (866)374-3378
Admissions: (814)865-4700
E-mail: admissions@psu.edu
Web Site: http://www.pserie.psu.edu/
President/CEO: Dr. Graham Spanier
Admissions: Anne L. Rohrbach

Financial Aid: Jane Brady
Type: Comprehensive **Sex:** Coed **Affiliation:** Pennsylvania State University **Scores:** 93.02% SAT V 400+; 96.19% SAT M 400+ **% Accepted:** 87 **Admission Plans:** Early Admission; Deferred Admission **Application Deadline:** Rolling **Application Fee:** $50.00 **H.S. Requirements:** High school diploma required; GED accepted **Costs Per Year:** Application fee: $50. State resident tuition: $11,942 full-time, $498 per credit hour part-time. Nonresident tuition: $18,270 full-time, $761 per credit hour part-time. Mandatory fees: $808 full-time. Full-time tuition and fees vary according to course level, location, program, and student level. Part-time tuition varies according to course level, course load, location, program, and student level. College room and board: $8170. College room only: $4430. Room and board charges vary according to board plan, housing facility, and location. **Scholarships:** Available **Calendar System:** Semester, Summer Session Available **Enrollment:** FT 3,988, PT 302, Grad FT 43, Grad PT 67 **Faculty:** FT 222, PT 66 **Student-Faculty Ratio:** 17:1 **Exams:** SAT I or ACT. ACT essay not being used. SAT essay not being used. **% Receiving Financial Aid:** 71 **% Residing in College-Owned, -Operated, or -Affiliated Housing:** 39 **Regional Accreditation:** Middle State Association of Colleges and Schools **Credit Hours For Degree:** 60 credits, Associates; 124 credits, Bachelors **ROTC:** Army **Professional Accreditation:** AACSB, ABET **Intercollegiate Athletics:** Baseball M; Basketball M & W; Cheerleading M & W; Cross-Country Running M & W; Golf M & W; Ice Hockey M; Lacrosse M; Skiing (Downhill) M & W; Soccer M & W; Softball W; Swimming and Diving M & W; Tennis M & W; Track and Field M & W; Volleyball M & W; Water Polo M & W

PENN STATE FAYETTE, THE EBERLY CAMPUS
1 University Dr., PO Box 519
Uniontown, PA 15401-0519
Tel: (724)430-4100; Free: 877-568-4130
Fax: (724)430-4184
E-mail: feadm@psu.edu
Web Site: http://www.fe.psu.edu/
President/CEO: Emmanuel I. Osagie
Admissions: Randall C. Deike
Financial Aid: Al Thompson
Type: Two-Year College **Sex:** Coed **Affiliation:** Pennsylvania State University **Scores:** 75.96% SAT M 400+ **% Accepted:** 93 **Admission Plans:** Early Admission; Deferred Admission **Application Deadline:** Rolling **Application Fee:** $50.00 **H.S. Requirements:** High school diploma required; GED accepted **Costs Per Year:** Application fee: $50. State resident tuition: $11,442 full-time, $463 per credit hour part-time. Nonresident tuition: $17,460 full-time, $728 per credit hour part-time. Mandatory fees: $708 full-time. Full-time tuition and fees vary according to course level, location, program, and student level. Part-time tuition varies according to course level, course load, location, program, and student level. **Scholarships:** Available **Calendar System:** Semester, Summer Session Available **Enrollment:** FT 807, PT 288 **Faculty:** FT 54, PT 40 **Student-Faculty Ratio:** 13:1 **Exams:** SAT I or ACT. ACT essay not being used. SAT essay not being used. **Regional Accreditation:** Middle State Association of Colleges and Schools **Credit Hours For Degree:** 60 credits, Associates **Professional Accreditation:** ABET **Intercollegiate Athletics:** Baseball M; Basketball M; Softball W; Volleyball W

PENN STATE GREATER ALLEGHENY
4000 University Dr.
McKeesport, PA 15132-7698
Tel: (412)675-9000
E-mail: psumk@psu.edu
Web Site: http://www.mk.psu.edu/
President/CEO: Curtiss E. Porter
Admissions: Randall C. Deike
Financial Aid: Robert Heyl
Type: Two-Year College **Sex:** Coed **Affiliation:** Pennsylvania State University **Scores:** 72.61% SAT V 400+; 75.1% SAT M 400+ **% Accepted:** 86 **Admission Plans:** Early Admission; Deferred Admission **Application Deadline:** Rolling **Application Fee:** $50.00 **H.S. Requirements:** High school diploma required; GED accepted **Costs Per Year:** Application fee: $50. State resident tuition: $11,442 full-time, $463 per credit hour part-time. Nonresident tuition: $17,460 full-time, $728 per credit hour part-time. Mandatory fees: $808 full-time. Full-time tuition and fees vary according to course level, location, program, and student level. Part-time tuition varies according to course level, course load, location, program, and student level. College room and board: $8170. College room only: $4430. Room and board charges vary according to board plan, housing facility, and location. **Scholarships:** Available **Calendar System:** Semester, Summer Session Available **Enrollment:** FT 645, PT 105 **Faculty:** FT 36, PT 25 **Student-Faculty Ratio:** 15:1 **Exams:** SAT I or ACT. ACT essay not being used. SAT essay not being used. **% Residing in College-Owned, -Operated, or -Affiliated Housing:** 28 **Regional Accreditation:** Middle State Association of Colleges and Schools **Credit Hours For Degree:** 60 credits, Associates **Intercollegiate Athletics:** Baseball M; Basketball M; Softball W; Volleyball W

PENN STATE HARRISBURG
777 West Harrisburg Pike
Middletown, PA 17057-4898
Tel: (717)948-6000; Free: 800-222-2056
Admissions: (814)865-4700
E-mail: admissions@psu.edu
Web Site: http://www.hbg.psu.edu/
President/CEO: Dr. Graham Spanier
Admissions: Anne L. Rohrbach
Financial Aid: Carolyn Julian
Type: Comprehensive **Sex:** Coed **Affiliation:** Pennsylvania State University **Scores:** 91.31% SAT V 400+; 95.31% SAT M 400+ **% Accepted:** 86 **Admission Plans:** Early Admission; Deferred Admission **Application Deadline:** Rolling **Application Fee:** $50.00 **H.S. Requirements:** High school diploma required; GED accepted **Costs Per Year:** Application fee: $50. State resident tuition: $11,942 full-time, $498 per credit hour part-time. Nonresident tuition: $18,270 full-time, $761 per credit hour part-time. Mandatory fees: $808 full-time. Full-time tuition and fees vary according to course level, location, program, and student level. Part-time tuition varies according to course level, course load, location, program, and student level. College room and board: $9350. College room only: $5610. Room and board charges vary according to board plan, housing facility, and location. **Scholarships:** Available **Calendar System:** Semester, Summer Session Available **Enrollment:** FT 2,226, PT 482, Grad FT 190, Grad PT 1,114 **Faculty:** FT 200, PT 97 **Student-Faculty Ratio:** 13:1 **Exams:** SAT I or ACT. ACT essay not being used. SAT essay not being used. **% Receiving Financial Aid:** 62 **% Residing in College-Owned, -Operated, or -Affiliated Housing:** 12 **Regional Accreditation:** Middle State Association of Colleges and Schools **Credit Hours For Degree:** 60 credits, Associates; 120 credits, Bachelors **ROTC:** Army **Professional Accreditation:** AACSB, ABET, NASPAA **Intercollegiate Athletics:** Baseball M; Basketball M & W; Cross-Country Running M & W; Golf M & W; Soccer M & W; Softball W; Tennis M & W; Volleyball W

PENN STATE HAZLETON
Hazleton, PA 18202-1291
Tel: (570)450-3000; Free: 800-279-8495
E-mail: admissions-hn@psu.edu
Web Site: http://www.hn.psu.edu/
President/CEO: Gary M. Lawler
Admissions: Randall C. Deike
Financial Aid: Sarah Walton
Type: Two-Year College **Sex:** Coed **Affiliation:** Pennsylvania State University **Scores:** 78.8% SAT V 400+; 80.3% SAT M 400+ **% Accepted:** 92 **Admission Plans:** Early Admission; Deferred Admission **Application Deadline:** Rolling **Application Fee:** $50.00 **H.S. Requirements:** High school diploma required; GED accepted **Costs Per Year:** Application fee: $50. State resident tuition: $11,442 full-time, $463 per credit hour part-time. Nonresident tuition: $17,460 full-time, $728 per credit hour part-time. Mandatory fees: $758 full-time. Full-time tuition and fees vary according to course level, location, program, and student level. Part-time tuition varies according to course level, course load, location, program, and student level. College room and board: $8170. College room only: $4430. Room and board charges vary according to board plan, housing facility, and location. **Scholarships:** Available **Calendar System:** Semester, Summer Session Available **Enrollment:** FT 1,191, PT 54 **Faculty:** FT 54, PT 31 **Student-Faculty Ratio:** 19:1 **Exams:** SAT I or ACT. ACT essay not being used. SAT essay not being used. **% Residing in College-Owned, -Operated, or -Affiliated Housing:** 38 **Regional Accreditation:** Middle State Association of Colleges and Schools **Credit Hours For Degree:** 60 credits, Associates **ROTC:** Army, Air Force **Professional Accreditation:** ABET, APTA, NAACLS **Intercollegiate Athletics:** Baseball M; Basketball M & W; Cheerleading M & W; Soccer M; Softball W; Tennis M & W; Volleyball M & W

PENN STATE LEHIGH VALLEY
8380 Mohr Ln.
Fogelsville, PA 18051-9999
Tel: (610)285-5000
E-mail: admissions-lv@psu.edu
Web Site: http://www.lv.psu.edu/
President/CEO: Ann M. Williams
Admissions: Randall C. Deike
Financial Aid: Maryann Hubick
Type: Two-Year College **Sex:** Coed **Affiliation:** Pennsylvania State University **Scores:** 86.3% SAT V 400+; 84.93% SAT M 400+ **% Accepted:** 94 **Admission Plans:** Early Admission; Deferred Admission **Application Deadline:** Rolling **Application Fee:** $50.00 **H.S. Requirements:** High school diploma required; GED accepted **Costs Per Year:** Application fee: $50. State resident tuition: $11,442 full-time, $463 per credit hour part-time. Nonresident tuition: $17,460 full-time, $728 per credit hour part-time. Mandatory fees: $808 full-time. Full-time tuition and fees vary according to course level, location, program, and student level. Part-time tuition varies according to course level, course load, location, program, and student level. **Scholarships:** Available **Calendar System:** Semester, Summer Session Available **Enrollment:** FT 612, PT 212, Grad FT 1, Grad PT 15 **Faculty:** FT 35, PT 60 **Student-Faculty Ratio:** 13:1 **Exams:** SAT I or ACT. ACT essay not being used. SAT essay not being used. **Regional Accreditation:** Middle State Association of Colleges and Schools **Credit Hours For Degree:** 60 credits, Associates; 120 credits, Bachelors **ROTC:** Army **Intercollegiate Athletics:** Baseball M; Basketball M & W; Bowling M & W; Cheerleading M & W; Cross-Country Running M & W; Football M; Golf M & W; Ice Hockey M & W; Skiing (Downhill) M & W; Soccer M & W; Tennis M & W; Volleyball M & W

PENN STATE MONT ALTO
1 Campus Dr.
Mont Alto, PA 17237-9703
Tel: (717)749-6000; Free: 800-392-6173
E-mail: psuma@psu.edu
Web Site: http://www.ma.psu.edu/
President/CEO: David C. Gnage
Admissions: Randall C. Deike
Type: Two-Year College **Sex:** Coed **Affiliation:** Pennsylvania State University **Scores:** 79.57% SAT V 400+; 80.9% SAT M 400+ **% Accepted:** 90 **Admission Plans:** Early Admission; Deferred Admission **Application Deadline:** Rolling **Application Fee:** $50.00 **H.S. Requirements:** High school diploma required; GED accepted **Costs Per Year:** Application fee: $50. State resident tuition: $11,442 full-time, $463 per credit hour part-time. Nonresident tuition: $17,460 full-time, $728 per credit hour part-time. Mandatory fees: $808 full-time. Full-time tuition and fees vary according to course level, location, program, and student level. Part-time tuition varies according to course level, course load, location, program, and student level. College room and board: $8170. College room only: $4430. Room and board charges vary according to board plan, housing facility, and location. **Scholarships:** Available **Calendar System:** Semester, Summer Session Available **Enrollment:** FT 885, PT 289, Grad PT 8 **Faculty:** FT 58, PT 59 **Student-Faculty Ratio:** 13:1 **Exams:** SAT I or ACT. ACT essay not being used. SAT essay not being used. **% Residing in College-Owned, -Operated, or -Affiliated Housing:** 37 **Regional Accreditation:** Middle State Association of Colleges and Schools **Credit Hours For Degree:** 60 credits, Associates **ROTC:** Army **Professional Accreditation:** AOTA, APTA **Intercollegiate Athletics:** Basketball M & W; Cheerleading M & W; Cross-Country Running M & W; Golf M & W; Soccer M & W; Softball W; Tennis M & W; Volleyball W

PENN STATE NEW KENSINGTON
3550 Seventh St. Rd.
New Kensington, PA 15068
Tel: (724)334-5466; Free: 888-968-7297
Fax: (724)334-6111
E-mail: nkadmissions@psu.edu
Web Site: http://www.nk.psu.edu/
President/CEO: Kevin J.G. Snider
Admissions: Randall C. Deike
Type: Two-Year College **Sex:** Coed **Affiliation:** Pennsylvania State University **Scores:** 80.35% SAT V 400+; 87.5% SAT M 400+ **% Accepted:** 89 **Admission Plans:** Early Admission; Deferred Admission **Application Deadline:** Rolling **Application Fee:** $50.00 **H.S. Requirements:** High school diploma required; GED accepted **Costs Per Year:** Application fee: $50. State resident tuition: $11,442 full-time, $463 per credit hour part-time. Nonresident tuition: $17,460 full-time, $728 per credit hour part-time. Mandatory fees: $758 full-time. Full-time tuition and fees vary according to course level, location, program, and student level. Part-time tuition varies according to course level, course load, location, program, and student level. **Scholarships:** Available **Calendar System:** Semester, Summer Session Available **Enrollment:** FT 617, PT 202, Grad PT 1 **Faculty:** FT 39, PT 35 **Student-Faculty Ratio:** 14:1 **Exams:** SAT I or ACT. ACT essay not being used. SAT essay not being used. **Regional Accreditation:** Middle State Association of Colleges and Schools **Credit Hours For Degree:** 60 credits, Associates **ROTC:** Air Force **Professional Accreditation:** ABET, JRCERT, NAACLS **Intercollegiate Athletics:** Baseball M; Basketball M & W; Cheerleading M & W; Golf M & W; Softball W; Volleyball W

PENN STATE SCHUYLKILL
200 University Dr.
Schuylkill Haven, PA 17972-2208
Tel: (570)385-6000
E-mail: sl-admissions@psu.edu
Web Site: http://www.sl.psu.edu/
President/CEO: R. Keith Hillkirk
Admissions: Randall C. Deike
Financial Aid: Tracy Miller
Type: Two-Year College **Sex:** Coed **Affiliation:** Pennsylvania State University **Scores:** 66.35% SAT V 400+; 63.52% SAT M 400+ **% Accepted:** 86 **Admission Plans:** Early Admission; Deferred Admission **Application Deadline:** Rolling **Application Fee:** $50.00 **H.S. Requirements:** High school diploma required; GED accepted **Costs Per Year:** Application fee: $50. State resident tuition: $11,442 full-time, $463 per credit hour part-time. Nonresident tuition: $17,460 full-time, $728 per credit hour part-time. Mandatory fees: $708 full-time. Full-time tuition and fees vary according to course level, location, program, and student level. Part-time tuition varies according to course level, course load, location, program, and student level. **Scholarships:** Available **Calendar System:** Semester, Summer Session Available **Enrollment:** FT 859, PT 148, Grad PT 3 **Faculty:** FT 43, PT 34 **Student-Faculty Ratio:** 17:1 **Exams:** SAT I or ACT. ACT essay not being used. SAT essay not being used. **% Residing in College-Owned, -Operated, or -Affiliated Housing:** 25 **Regional Accreditation:** Middle State Association of Colleges and Schools **Credit Hours For Degree:** 60 credits, Associates; 120 credits, Bachelors **Professional Accreditation:** ABET, JRCERT **Intercollegiate Athletics:** Basketball M; Cross-Country Running M & W; Golf M; Soccer M; Softball W; Volleyball W

PENN STATE SHENANGO
147 Shenango Ave.
Sharon, PA 16146-1537
Tel: (724)983-2803
Fax: (724)983-2820
E-mail: psushenango@psu.edu
Web Site: http://www.shenango.psu.edu/
President/CEO: Fredric M. Leeds
Admissions: Randall C. Deike
Financial Aid: Shawn O'Neill
Type: Two-Year College **Sex:** Coed **Affiliation:** Pennsylvania State University **Scores:** 79.78% SAT V 400+; 84.27% SAT M 400+ **% Accepted:** 77 **Admission Plans:** Early Admission; Deferred Admission **Application Deadline:** Rolling **Application Fee:** $50.00 **H.S. Requirements:** High school diploma required; GED accepted **Costs Per Year:** Application fee: $50. State resident tuition: $11,442 full-time, $463 per credit hour part-time. Nonresident tuition: $17,460 full-time, $728 per credit hour part-time. Mandatory fees: $608 full-time. Full-time tuition and fees vary according to course level, location, program, and student level. Part-time tuition varies according to course level, course load, location, program, and student level. **Scholarships:** Available **Calendar System:** Semester, Summer Session Available **Enrollment:** FT 493, PT 323 **Faculty:** FT 31, PT 42 **Student-Faculty Ratio:** 13:1 **Exams:** SAT I or ACT. ACT essay not being used. SAT essay not being used. **Regional Accreditation:** Middle State Association of Colleges and Schools **Credit Hours For Degree:** 60 credits, Associates **Professional Accreditation:** ABET, APTA

PENN STATE UNIVERSITY PARK
201 Old Main
University Park, PA 16802-1503
Tel: (814)865-4700

E-mail: admissions@psu.edu
Web Site: http://www.psu.edu/
President/CEO: Dr. Graham B. Spanier
Admissions: Anne L. Rohrbach
Financial Aid: Anna Griswold
Type: University **Sex:** Coed **Affiliation:** Pennsylvania State University **Scores:** 98.6% SAT V 400+; 98.86% SAT M 400+ **% Accepted:** 52 **Admission Plans:** Early Admission; Deferred Admission **Application Deadline:** Rolling **Application Fee:** $50.00 **H.S. Requirements:** High school diploma required; GED accepted **Costs Per Year:** Application fee: $50. State resident tuition: $13,604 full-time, $567 per credit hour part-time. Nonresident tuition: $25,134 full-time, $1047 per credit hour part-time. Mandatory fees: $812 full-time. Full-time tuition and fees vary according to course level, degree level, location, program, and student level. Part-time tuition varies according to course level, course load, degree level, location, program, and student level. College room and board: $8170. College room only: $4430. Room and board charges vary according to board plan, housing facility, and location. **Scholarships:** Available **Calendar System:** Semester, Summer Session Available **Enrollment:** FT 37,485, PT 1,145, Grad FT 5,580, Grad PT 975 **Faculty:** FT 2,432, PT 365 **Student-Faculty Ratio:** 17:1 **Exams:** SAT I or ACT. ACT essay not being used. SAT essay not being used. **% Receiving Financial Aid:** 49 **% Residing in College-Owned, -Operated, or -Affiliated Housing:** 36 **Final Year or Final Semester Residency Requirement:** No **Library Holdings:** 5,354,645 **Regional Accreditation:** Middle State Association of Colleges and Schools **Credit Hours For Degree:** 60 credits, Associates; 120 credits, Bachelors **ROTC:** Army, Navy, Air Force **Professional Accreditation:** AACSB, ABET, ACEJMC, AACN, ACA, ADtA, APA, ASLA, ASLHA, ACEHSA, CORE, JRCEPAT, NAAB, NASAD, NASM, NAST, NCATE, NLN, SAF **Intercollegiate Athletics:** Archery M & W; Badminton M & W; Baseball M; Basketball M & W; Bowling M; Cheerleading M & W; Cross-Country Running M & W; Equestrian Sports M & W; Fencing M & W; Field Hockey W; Football M; Golf M & W; Gymnastics M & W; Ice Hockey M & W; Lacrosse M & W; Rugby M & W; Skiing (Downhill) M & W; Soccer M & W; Softball W; Swimming and Diving M & W; Table Tennis M; Tennis M & W; Track and Field M & W; Volleyball M & W; Water Polo M & W; Weight Lifting M & W; Wrestling M

PENN STATE WILKES-BARRE
PO PSU
Lehman, PA 18627-0217
Tel: (570)675-2171; Free: 800-966-6613
E-mail: wbadmissions@psu.edu
Web Site: http://www.wb.psu.edu/
President/CEO: Charles H. Davis
Admissions: Randall C. Deike
Financial Aid: Stacey Zelinka
Type: Two-Year College **Sex:** Coed **Affiliation:** Pennsylvania State University **Scores:** 86.91% SAT V 400+; 85.34% SAT M 400+ **% Accepted:** 91 **Admission Plans:** Early Admission; Deferred Admission **Application Deadline:** Rolling **Application Fee:** $50.00 **H.S. Requirements:** High school diploma required; GED accepted **Costs Per Year:** Application fee: $50. State resident tuition: $11,442 full-time, $463 per credit hour part-time. Nonresident tuition: $17,460 full-time, $728 per credit hour part-time. Mandatory fees: $708 full-time. Full-time tuition and fees vary according to course level, location, program, and student level. Part-time tuition varies according to course level, course load, location, program, and student level. **Scholarships:** Available **Calendar System:** Semester, Summer Session Available **Enrollment:** FT 578, PT 94, Grad PT 39 **Faculty:** FT 36, PT 20 **Student-Faculty Ratio:** 15:1 **Exams:** SAT I or ACT. ACT essay not being used. SAT essay not being used. **Regional Accreditation:** Middle State Association of Colleges and Schools **Credit Hours For Degree:** 60 credits, Associates **ROTC:** Army, Air Force **Professional Accreditation:** ABET **Intercollegiate Athletics:** Baseball M; Basketball M; Cross-Country Running M & W; Golf M & W; Soccer M & W; Volleyball W

PENN STATE WORTHINGTON SCRANTON
120 Ridge View Dr.
Dunmore, PA 18512-1699
Tel: (570)963-2500
Fax: (570)963-2535
E-mail: wsadmissions@psu.edu
Web Site: http://www.sn.psu.edu/
President/CEO: Mary-Beth Krogh-Jespersen
Admissions: Randall C. Deike
Financial Aid: Mary Beth Dougherty
Type: Two-Year College **Sex:** Coed **Affiliation:** Pennsylvania State University **Scores:** 78.88% SAT V 400+; 76.71% SAT M 400+ **% Accepted:** 89 **Admission Plans:** Early Admission; Deferred Admission **Application Deadline:** Rolling **Application Fee:** $50.00 **H.S. Requirements:** High school diploma required; GED accepted **Costs Per Year:** Application fee: $50. State resident tuition: $11,442 full-time, $463 per credit hour part-time. Nonresident tuition: $17,460 full-time, $728 per credit hour part-time. Mandatory fees: $668 full-time. Full-time tuition and fees vary according to course level, location, program, and student level. Part-time tuition varies according to course level, course load, location, program, and student level. **Scholarships:** Available **Calendar System:** Semester, Summer Session Available **Enrollment:** FT 1,084, PT 304 **Faculty:** FT 57, PT 46 **Student-Faculty Ratio:** 16:1 **Exams:** SAT I or ACT. ACT essay not being used. SAT essay not being used. **Regional Accreditation:** Middle State Association of Colleges and Schools **Credit Hours For Degree:** 60 credits, Associates **ROTC:** Army, Air Force **Professional Accreditation:** ABET **Intercollegiate Athletics:** Baseball M; Basketball M & W; Cheerleading M & W; Cross-Country Running M & W; Soccer M; Softball W; Volleyball W

PENN STATE YORK
1031 Edgecomb Ave.
York, PA 17403-3398
Tel: (717)771-4000; Free: 800-778-6227
Fax: (717)771-4062
E-mail: ykadmission@psu.edu
Web Site: http://www.yk.psu.edu/
President/CEO: Joel M. Rodney
Admissions: Randall C. Deike
Financial Aid: Yolanda Beattie
Type: Two-Year College **Sex:** Coed **Affiliation:** Pennsylvania State University **Scores:** 85.29% SAT V 400+; 87.14% SAT M 400+ **% Accepted:** 87 **Admission Plans:** Early Admission; Deferred Admission **Application Deadline:** Rolling **Application Fee:** $50.00 **H.S. Requirements:** High school diploma required; GED accepted **Costs Per Year:** Application fee: $50. State resident tuition: $11,442 full-time, $463 per credit hour part-time. Nonresident tuition: $17,460 full-time, $728 per credit hour part-time. Mandatory fees: $668 full-time. Full-time tuition and fees vary according to course level, location, program, and student level. Part-time tuition varies according to course level, course load, location, program, and student level. **Scholarships:** Available **Calendar System:** Semester, Summer Session Available **Enrollment:** FT 973, PT 466, Grad PT 66 **Faculty:** FT 58, PT 50 **Student-Faculty Ratio:** 15:1 **Exams:** SAT I or ACT. ACT essay not being used. SAT essay not being used. **Regional Accreditation:** Middle State Association of Colleges and Schools **Credit Hours For Degree:** 60 credits, Associates **Professional Accreditation:** ABET

PENNCO TECH
3815 Otter St.
Bristol, PA 19007-3696
Tel: (215)824-3200
Admissions: (215)785-0111
E-mail: admissions@penncotech.com
Web Site: http://www.penncotech.com/
President/CEO: Alfred William Parcells, Jr.
Admissions: Glenn Slater
Type: Two-Year College **Sex:** Coed **Affiliation:** Pennco Institutes, Inc. **Application Deadline:** Rolling **Application Fee:** $100.00 **H.S. Requirements:** High school diploma required; GED accepted. For applicants who demonstrate ability to benefit from college: High school diploma or equivalent not required **Scholarships:** Available **Calendar System:** Miscellaneous, Summer Session Not available **Enrollment:** FT 245, PT 155 **Faculty:** FT 23, PT 5 **Student-Faculty Ratio:** 14:1 **Exams:** Other, SAT I and SAT II or ACT. **% Residing in College-Owned, -Operated, or -Affiliated Housing:** 2 **Library Holdings:** 6,000 **Credit Hours For Degree:** 2100 clock hours, Associates **Professional Accreditation:** ACCSCT

PENNSYLVANIA COLLEGE OF ART & DESIGN
204 North Prince St., PO Box 59
Lancaster, PA 17608-0059
Tel: (717)396-7833
Fax: (717)396-1339
E-mail: admissions@pcad.edu
Web Site: http://www.pcad.edu/

President/CEO: Mary Colleen Heil
Financial Aid: J. David Hershey
Type: Four-Year College **Sex:** Coed **% Accepted:** 42 **Admission Plans:** Deferred Admission **Application Deadline:** Rolling **Application Fee:** $40.00 **H.S. Requirements:** High school diploma required; GED accepted **Costs Per Year:** Application fee: $40. Tuition: $16,500 full-time, $688 per credit part-time. Mandatory fees: $780 full-time, $300 per credit part-time. Part-time tuition and fees vary according to course load. **Scholarships:** Available **Calendar System:** Semester, Summer Session Not available **Enrollment:** FT 252, PT 26 **Faculty:** FT 14, PT 33 **Student-Faculty Ratio:** 9:1 **Library Holdings:** 19,573 **Regional Accreditation:** Middle State Association of Colleges and Schools **Credit Hours For Degree:** 120 credits, Bachelors **Professional Accreditation:** NASAD

PENNSYLVANIA COLLEGE OF TECHNOLOGY
One College Ave.
Williamsport, PA 17701-5778
Tel: (570)326-3761
Admissions: (570)327-4761
Fax: (570)321-5551
E-mail: dcorrell@pct.edu
Web Site: http://www.pct.edu/
President/CEO: Dr. Davie Jane Gilmour
Admissions: Dennis Correll
Financial Aid: Candace Baran
Type: Four-Year College **Sex:** Coed **Affiliation:** Pennsylvania State University **% Accepted:** 88 **Admission Plans:** Open Admission; Early Admission; Deferred Admission **Application Deadline:** July 1 **Application Fee:** $50.00 **H.S. Requirements:** High school diploma required; GED accepted **Costs Per Year:** Application fee: $50. State resident tuition: $10,500 full-time, $416 per credit hour part-time. Nonresident tuition: $13,650 full-time, $521 per credit hour part-time. Mandatory fees: $1980 full-time. Full-time tuition and fees vary according to course load and program. Part-time tuition varies according to course load and program. College room and board: $8350. College room only: $5350. Room and board charges vary according to board plan, housing facility, and location. **Scholarships:** Available **Calendar System:** Semester, Summer Session Available **Enrollment:** FT 5,469, PT 940 **Faculty:** FT 296, PT 188 **Student-Faculty Ratio:** 18:1 **Exams:** SAT I. **% Receiving Financial Aid:** 92 **% Residing in College-Owned, -Operated, or -Affiliated Housing:** 23 **Library Holdings:** 127,995 **Regional Accreditation:** Middle State Association of Colleges and Schools **Credit Hours For Degree:** 60 credits, Associates; 120 credits, Bachelors **ROTC:** Army **Professional Accreditation:** ABET, ACF, ADA, AOTA, JRCERT, JRCEMT, NLN **Intercollegiate Athletics:** Archery M & W; Baseball M; Basketball M & W; Bowling M & W; Cross-Country Running M & W; Golf M & W; Soccer M & W; Softball W; Tennis M & W; Volleyball M & W

PENNSYLVANIA CULINARY INSTITUTE
717 Liberty Ave.
Pittsburgh, PA 15222-3500
Tel: (412)566-2433; Free: 800-432-2433
Fax: (412)566-2434
Web Site: http://www.paculinary.com/
Admissions: Juliette Mariani
Type: Two-Year College **Sex:** Coed **Application Fee:** $50.00 **H.S. Requirements:** High school diploma required; GED accepted **Scholarships:** Available **Calendar System:** Semester, Summer Session Not available **Library Holdings:** 5,000 **Professional Accreditation:** ACCSCT, ACF

PENNSYLVANIA HIGHLANDS COMMUNITY COLLEGE
101 Community College Way
Johnstown, PA 15904
Tel: (814)262-6400
Admissions: (814)262-6431
E-mail: jmaul@pennhighlands.edu
Web Site: http://www.pennhighlands.edu/
President/CEO: Dr. Walter Asonevich
Admissions: Jeff Maul
Type: Two-Year College **Sex:** Coed **Admission Plans:** Open Admission **Application Fee:** $20.00 **H.S. Requirements:** High school diploma or equivalent not required **Scholarships:** Available **Calendar System:** Semester **Enrollment:** FT 923, PT 845 **Student-Faculty Ratio:** 13:1 **Regional Accreditation:** Middle State Association of Colleges and Schools **Credit Hours For Degree:** 61 credits, Associates

PENNSYLVANIA INSTITUTE OF TECHNOLOGY
800 Manchester Ave.
Media, PA 19063
Tel: (610)892-1500; Free: 800-422-0025
Admissions: (610)565-7900
Fax: (610)892-1510
E-mail: info@pit.edu
Web Site: http://www.pit.edu/
President/CEO: John C. Strayer
Admissions: Angela Cassetta
Type: Two-Year College **Sex:** Coed **Admission Plans:** Deferred Admission **Application Deadline:** September 19 **Application Fee:** $25.00 **H.S. Requirements:** High school diploma required; GED accepted **Costs Per Year:** Application fee: $25. Tuition: $9900 full-time, $330 per credit part-time. Mandatory fees: $900 full-time, $30 per credit part-time. Full-time tuition and fees vary according to course load, degree level, and program. Part-time tuition and fees vary according to course load, degree level, and program. **Scholarships:** Available **Calendar System:** Semester, Summer Session Available **Enrollment:** FT 923, PT 123 **Faculty:** FT 24, PT 62 **Student-Faculty Ratio:** 22:1 **Library Holdings:** 16,500 **Regional Accreditation:** Middle State Association of Colleges and Schools **Credit Hours For Degree:** 60 credits, Associates

PENNSYLVANIA SCHOOL OF BUSINESS
406 West Hamilton St.
Allentown, PA 18101
Tel: (610)841-3333
E-mail: wbarber@pennschoolofbusiness.edu
Web Site: http://www.psb.edu/
President/CEO: Michael O'Brien
Admissions: Bill Barber
Type: Two-Year College **Sex:** Coed **Admission Plans:** Open Admission **Professional Accreditation:** ACCSCT

PHILADELPHIA BIBLICAL UNIVERSITY
200 Manor Ave.
Langhorne, PA 19047-2990
Tel: (215)752-5800; Free: 800-366-0049
Admissions: (215)702-4550
Fax: (215)752-5812
E-mail: admissions@pbu.edu
Web Site: http://www.pbu.edu/
President/CEO: Dr. Todd J. Williams
Admissions: Lisa Yoder
Financial Aid: Raye Thompson
Type: Comprehensive **Sex:** Coed **Affiliation:** nondenominational **Scores:** 96.1% SAT V 400+; 92.2% SAT M 400+; 50% ACT 18-23; 38% ACT 24-29 **% Accepted:** 94 **Admission Plans:** Early Admission; Deferred Admission **Application Deadline:** Rolling **Application Fee:** $25.00 **H.S. Requirements:** High school diploma required; GED accepted **Costs Per Year:** Application fee: $25. Comprehensive fee: $28,047 includes full-time tuition ($19,797), mandatory fees ($200), and college room and board ($8050). College room only: $4300. Full-time tuition and fees vary according to course load, location, and program. Room and board charges vary according to board plan, housing facility, and location. Part-time tuition: $587 per credit hour. Part-time tuition varies according to course load, location, and program. **Scholarships:** Available **Calendar System:** Semester, Summer Session Available **Enrollment:** FT 987, PT 74 **Faculty:** FT 55, PT 74 **Student-Faculty Ratio:** 14:1 **Exams:** SAT I or ACT. **% Receiving Financial Aid:** 84 **% Residing in College-Owned, -Operated, or -Affiliated Housing:** 65 **Library Holdings:** 109,085 **Regional Accreditation:** Middle State Association of Colleges and Schools **Credit Hours For Degree:** 60 credits, Associates; 126 credits, Bachelors **ROTC:** Air Force **Professional Accreditation:** ABHE, CSWE, NASM **Intercollegiate Athletics:** Baseball M; Basketball M & W; Golf M; Soccer M & W; Softball W; Tennis W; Volleyball M & W

PHILADELPHIA UNIVERSITY
School House Ln. and Henry Ave.
Philadelphia, PA 19144
Tel: (215)951-2700
Admissions: (215)951-2800
Fax: (215)951-2907
E-mail: admissions@philau.edu

Web Site: http://www.philau.edu/
President/CEO: Dr. Stephen Spinelli Spinelli, Jr.
Admissions: Christine Greb
Financial Aid: Lisa J. Cooper
Type: Comprehensive **Sex:** Coed **Scores:** 99.9% SAT V 400+; 99.8% SAT M 400+ **% Accepted:** 71 **Admission Plans:** Deferred Admission **Application Deadline:** Rolling **Application Fee:** $40.00 **H.S. Requirements:** High school diploma required; GED accepted **Costs Per Year:** Application fee: $40. Comprehensive fee: $36,680 includes full-time tuition ($27,428), mandatory fees ($70), and college room and board ($9182). College room only: $4540. Full-time tuition and fees vary according to degree level and program. Room and board charges vary according to board plan and housing facility. Part-time tuition: $486 per credit hour. Part-time tuition varies according to class time, course load, degree level, and program. **Scholarships:** Available **Calendar System:** Semester, Summer Session Available **Enrollment:** FT 2,675, PT 217, Grad FT 350, Grad PT 255 **Faculty:** FT 110, PT 328 **Student-Faculty Ratio:** 15:1 **Exams:** SAT I or ACT. **% Receiving Financial Aid:** 73 **% Residing in College-Owned, -Operated, or -Affiliated Housing:** 49 **Regional Accreditation:** Middle State Association of Colleges and Schools **Credit Hours For Degree:** 124 credits, Bachelors **Professional Accreditation:** ABET, ACNM, AOTA, FIDER, NAAB, NASAD **Intercollegiate Athletics:** Baseball M; Basketball M & W; Field Hockey W; Golf M; Lacrosse W; Soccer M & W; Softball W; Tennis M & W; Volleyball W

PITTSBURGH INSTITUTE OF AERONAUTICS
PO Box 10897
Pittsburgh, PA 15236-0897
Tel: (412)462-9011; Free: 800-444-1440
Admissions: (412)346-2100
Fax: (412)466-0513
E-mail: admissions@pia.edu
Web Site: http://www.pia.edu/
President/CEO: John Graham, III
Admissions: Vincent J. Mezza
Type: Two-Year College **Sex:** Coed **% Accepted:** 100 **Admission Plans:** Open Admission; Deferred Admission **Application Deadline:** Rolling **Application Fee:** $150.00 **H.S. Requirements:** High school diploma required; GED accepted **Calendar System:** Quarter **Enrollment:** FT 571 **Faculty:** FT 31, PT 6 **Student-Faculty Ratio:** 17:1 **Library Holdings:** 15,000 **Credit Hours For Degree:** 2520 hours, Associates **Professional Accreditation:** ACCSCT

PITTSBURGH INSTITUTE OF MORTUARY SCIENCE, INCORPORATED
5808 Baum Blvd.
Pittsburgh, PA 15206-3706
Tel: (412)362-8500; Free: 800-933-5808
Fax: (412)362-1684
E-mail: pims5808@aol.com
Web Site: http://www.pims.edu/
President/CEO: Eugene Ogrodnik
Admissions: Karen Rocco
Financial Aid: Karen Rocco
Type: Two-Year College **Sex:** Coed **Admission Plans:** Open Admission **Application Deadline:** Rolling **Application Fee:** $40.00 **H.S. Requirements:** High school diploma required; GED accepted **Costs Per Year:** Application fee: $40. Tuition: $9200 full-time, $265 per semester hour part-time. Mandatory fees: $1700 full-time. **Scholarships:** Available **Calendar System:** Trimester **Enrollment:** FT 85, PT 108 **Faculty:** FT 2, PT 22 **Student-Faculty Ratio:** 13:1 **Library Holdings:** 2,547 **Credit Hours For Degree:** 96 credits, Associates **Professional Accreditation:** ABFSE

PITTSBURGH TECHNICAL INSTITUTE
1111 McKee Rd.
Oakdale, PA 15071
Tel: (412)809-5100; Free: 800-784-9675
Fax: (412)809-5388
E-mail: goodlin.nancy@pti.edu
Web Site: http://www.pti.edu/
President/CEO: Greg DeFeo
Admissions: Nancy Goodlin
Type: Two-Year College **Sex:** Coed **% Accepted:** 88 **Admission Plans:** Open Admission; Deferred Admission **Application Deadline:** Rolling **Application Fee:** $0.00 **H.S. Requirements:** High school diploma required; GED accepted **Calendar System:** Quarter **Enrollment:** FT 2,073 **Faculty:** FT 74, PT 47 **% Residing in College-Owned, -Operated, or -Affiliated Housing:** 40 **Library Holdings:** 6,763 **Regional Accreditation:** Middle State Association of Colleges and Schools

THE PJA SCHOOL
7900 West Chester Pike
Upper Darby, PA 19082-1926
Tel: (610)789-6700; Free: 800-RING-PJA
E-mail: dgentile@pjaschool.com
Web Site: http://www.pjaschool.com/
President/CEO: Patricia Fleming
Admissions: Dina Gentile
Type: Two-Year College **Sex:** Coed **Affiliation:** Prism Education Group **H.S. Requirements:** High school diploma required; GED accepted **Enrollment:** FT 244 **Faculty:** FT 5, PT 23 **Student-Faculty Ratio:** 19:1 **Exams:** Other. **Library Holdings:** 2,350 **Professional Accreditation:** ACCSCT

POINT PARK UNIVERSITY
201 Wood St.
Pittsburgh, PA 15222-1984
Tel: (412)391-4100; Free: 800-321-0129
Admissions: (412)392-3430
Fax: (412)391-1980
E-mail: enroll@pointpark.edu
Web Site: http://www.pointpark.edu/
President/CEO: Dr. Paul Hennigan
Admissions: Joell Minford
Financial Aid: Sandra M. Cronin
Type: Comprehensive **Sex:** Coed **Scores:** 94% SAT V 400+; 91% SAT M 400+; 59% ACT 18-23; 29% ACT 24-29 **% Accepted:** 72 **Admission Plans:** Early Admission; Deferred Admission **Application Deadline:** Rolling **Application Fee:** $40.00 **H.S. Requirements:** High school diploma required; GED accepted **Costs Per Year:** Application fee: $40. Comprehensive fee: $30,354 includes full-time tuition ($20,720), mandatory fees ($614), and college room and board ($9020). College room only: $4300. Full-time tuition and fees vary according to program. Room and board charges vary according to board plan and housing facility. Part-time tuition: $574 per credit. Part-time mandatory fees: $22 per credit. Part-time tuition and fees vary according to program. **Scholarships:** Available **Calendar System:** Semester, Summer Session Available **Enrollment:** FT 2,602, PT 805, Grad FT 233, Grad PT 346 **Faculty:** FT 122, PT 310 **Student-Faculty Ratio:** 14:1 **Exams:** SAT I or ACT. **% Receiving Financial Aid:** 81 **% Residing in College-Owned, -Operated, or -Affiliated Housing:** 25 **Library Holdings:** 125,000 **Regional Accreditation:** Middle State Association of Colleges and Schools **Credit Hours For Degree:** 60 credits, Associates; 120 credits, Bachelors **ROTC:** Army, Air Force **Professional Accreditation:** ABET, NASD **Intercollegiate Athletics:** Baseball M; Basketball M & W; Cross-Country Running M & W; Golf M & W; Soccer M; Softball W; Volleyball W

READING AREA COMMUNITY COLLEGE
PO Box 1706
Reading, PA 19603-1706
Tel: (610)372-4721
Admissions: (610)607-6224
Fax: (610)375-8255
E-mail: mmitchell@racc.edu
Web Site: http://www.racc.edu/
President/CEO: Dr. Anna Weitz
Admissions: Maria Mitchell
Type: Two-Year College **Sex:** Coed **% Accepted:** 100 **Admission Plans:** Open Admission; Early Admission; Deferred Admission **Application Deadline:** Rolling **Application Fee:** $0.00 **H.S. Requirements:** High school diploma required; GED accepted **Costs Per Year:** Application fee: $0. Area resident tuition: $2002 full-time, $77 per credit part-time. State resident tuition: $4004 full-time, $154 per quarter hour part-time. Nonresident tuition: $6006 full-time, $231 per credit part-time. Mandatory fees: $1196 full-time, $46 per credit part-time. Full-time tuition and fees vary according to program. Part-time tuition and fees vary according to program. **Scholarships:** Available **Calendar System:** Quarter, Summer Session Available **Enrollment:** FT 2,009, PT 2,673 **Faculty:** FT 68, PT 160 **Student-Faculty Ratio:** 24:1 **Exams:** Other. **Library Holdings:** 25,541 **Regional Accreditation:** Middle State Association of Colleges and Schools **Credit Hours For Degree:** 60

credits, Associates **Professional Accreditation:** CARC, NAACLS, NLN **Intercollegiate Athletics:** Basketball M & W; Soccer M & W

THE RESTAURANT SCHOOL AT WALNUT HILL COLLEGE
4207 Walnut St.
Philadelphia, PA 19104-3518
Tel: (215)222-4200; Free: 877-925-6884
Admissions: (267)295-2373
Fax: (215)222-4219
E-mail: kbecker@walnuthillcollege.edu
Web Site: http://www.walnuthillcollege.edu/
President/CEO: Daniel Literatoscioli
Admissions: Karl D. Becker
Type: Two-Year College **Sex:** Coed **Admission Plans:** Open Admission; Early Admission; Early Decision Plan; Deferred Admission **Application Deadline:** Rolling **Application Fee:** $50.00 **H.S. Requirements:** High school diploma required; GED accepted **Scholarships:** Available **Calendar System:** Quarter, Summer Session Not available **Student-Faculty Ratio:** 29:1 **Exams:** SAT I or ACT. **Professional Accreditation:** ACCSCT

ROBERT MORRIS UNIVERSITY
6001 University Blvd.
Moon Township, PA 15108-1189
Tel: (412)262-8200; Free: 800-762-0097
Admissions: (412)397-5200
Fax: (412)262-8619
E-mail: admissionsoffice@rmu.edu
Web Site: http://www.rmu.edu/
President/CEO: Dr. Gregory G. Dell'Omo
Financial Aid: Stephanie Hendershot
Type: University **Sex:** Coed **Scores:** 92.9% SAT V 400+; 94.2% SAT M 400+; 49.5% ACT 18-23; 37.6% ACT 24-29 **% Accepted:** 92 **Admission Plans:** Deferred Admission **Application Deadline:** July 1 **Application Fee:** $30.00 **H.S. Requirements:** High school diploma required; GED accepted **Costs Per Year:** Application fee: $30. Comprehensive fee: $30,930 includes full-time tuition ($19,950), mandatory fees ($610), and college room and board ($10,370). College room only: $5010. Full-time tuition and fees vary according to degree level and program. Room and board charges vary according to board plan and housing facility. Part-time tuition: $665 per credit hour. Part-time mandatory fees: $30 per credit hour. Part-time tuition and fees vary according to course load, degree level, and program. **Scholarships:** Available **Calendar System:** Semester, Summer Session Available **Enrollment:** FT 3,106, PT 551, Grad PT 1,126 **Faculty:** FT 177, PT 202 **Student-Faculty Ratio:** 15:1 **Exams:** SAT I or ACT. **% Receiving Financial Aid:** 77 **% Residing in College-Owned, -Operated, or -Affiliated Housing:** 33 **Final Year or Final Semester Residency Requirement:** No **Library Holdings:** 125,121 **Regional Accreditation:** Middle State Association of Colleges and Schools **Credit Hours For Degree:** 126 credits, Bachelors **ROTC:** Army, Air Force **Professional Accreditation:** AACSB, ABET, AACN, JRCERT, TEAC **Intercollegiate Athletics:** Baseball M; Basketball M & W; Cheerleading M & W; Crew W; Field Hockey W; Football M; Golf M & W; Ice Hockey M & W; Lacrosse M & W; Soccer M & W; Softball W; Tennis M & W; Track and Field M & W; Volleyball W

ROSEDALE TECHNICAL INSTITUTE
215 Beecham Dr.
Ste. 2
Pittsburgh, PA 15205-9791
Tel: (412)521-6200; Free: 800-521-6262
Fax: (412)521-9277
E-mail: admissions@rosedaletech.org
Web Site: http://www.rosedaletech.org/
President/CEO: Dennis Wilke
Admissions: Debbie Bier
Type: Two-Year College **Sex:** Coed **% Accepted:** 65 **Calendar System:** Semester **Enrollment:** FT 200 **Faculty:** FT 14, PT 4 **Student-Faculty Ratio:** 13:1 **Professional Accreditation:** ACCSCT

ROSEMONT COLLEGE
1400 Montgomery Ave.
Rosemont, PA 19010-1699
Tel: (610)527-0200; Free: 800-331-0708
Fax: (610)527-1041
E-mail: admissions@rosemont.edu
Web Site: http://www.rosemont.edu/
President/CEO: Sharon Latchaw Hirsh, PhD
Admissions: Chuck Walz
Financial Aid: Chuck Walz
Type: Comprehensive **Sex:** Coed **Affiliation:** Roman Catholic **Scores:** 78% SAT V 400+; 80% SAT M 400+; 100% ACT 18-23 **% Accepted:** 54 **Admission Plans:** Early Admission; Deferred Admission **Application Deadline:** Rolling **Application Fee:** $35.00 **H.S. Requirements:** High school diploma required; GED accepted **Costs Per Year:** Application fee: $35. Comprehensive fee: $36,830 includes full-time tuition ($25,000), mandatory fees ($1250), and college room and board ($10,580). Room and board charges vary according to housing facility. Part-time tuition: $950 per credit hour. Part-time mandatory fees: $330 per term. **Scholarships:** Available **Calendar System:** Semester, Summer Session Available **Enrollment:** FT 434, PT 122, Grad FT 90, Grad PT 294 **Faculty:** FT 29, PT 108 **Student-Faculty Ratio:** 9:1 **Exams:** SAT I or ACT. ACT essay used for admission. SAT essay used for admission. **% Receiving Financial Aid:** 93 **% Residing in College-Owned, -Operated, or -Affiliated Housing:** 70 **Final Year or Final Semester Residency Requirement:** No **Library Holdings:** 165,000 **Regional Accreditation:** Middle State Association of Colleges and Schools **Credit Hours For Degree:** 120 credits, Bachelors **ROTC:** Army **Intercollegiate Athletics:** Basketball M & W; Cross-Country Running M & W; Field Hockey W; Golf M; Lacrosse M & W; Soccer M; Softball W; Tennis M & W; Volleyball W

ST. CHARLES BORROMEO SEMINARY, OVERBROOK
100 East Wynnewood Rd.
Wynnewood, PA 19096
Tel: (610)667-3394
Admissions: (610)785-6271
E-mail: cao@adphila.org
Web Site: http://www.scs.edu/
President/CEO: Msgr. Joseph G. Prior
Admissions: Rev. Msgr. David E. Diamond
Financial Aid: Nora M. Downey
Type: Comprehensive **Sex:** Coed **Affiliation:** Roman Catholic **% Accepted:** 100 **Admission Plans:** Deferred Admission **Application Deadline:** July 15 **Application Fee:** $0.00 **H.S. Requirements:** High school diploma required; GED accepted **Costs Per Year:** Application fee: $0. Comprehensive fee: $24,750 includes full-time tuition ($14,240), mandatory fees ($950), and college room and board ($9560). Room and board charges vary according to board plan. Part-time tuition: $777 per course. **Scholarships:** Available **Calendar System:** Semester, Summer Session Available **Enrollment:** FT 89, PT 51, Grad FT 64, Grad PT 41 **Faculty:** FT 17, PT 18 **Student-Faculty Ratio:** 8:1 **Exams:** SAT I or ACT. ACT essay not being used. SAT essay not being used. **% Receiving Financial Aid:** 27 **% Residing in College-Owned, -Operated, or -Affiliated Housing:** 94 **Library Holdings:** 128,738 **Regional Accreditation:** Middle State Association of Colleges and Schools **Credit Hours For Degree:** 125 credits, Bachelors **Professional Accreditation:** ATS

SAINT FRANCIS UNIVERSITY
PO Box 600, 117 Evergreen Dr.
Loretto, PA 15940-0600
Tel: (814)472-3000; Free: 800-342-5732
Admissions: (814)472-3100
Fax: (814)472-3044
E-mail: rbeener@francis.edu
Web Site: http://www.francis.edu/
President/CEO: Fr. Gabriel Zeis
Admissions: Robert Beener
Financial Aid: Shane Himes
Type: Comprehensive **Sex:** Coed **Affiliation:** Roman Catholic **Scores:** 95% SAT V 400+; 93% SAT M 400+; 32% ACT 18-23; 55% ACT 24-29 **% Accepted:** 77 **Admission Plans:** Deferred Admission **Application Deadline:** Rolling **Application Fee:** $30.00 **H.S. Requirements:** High school diploma required; GED accepted **Costs Per Year:** Application fee: $30. Comprehensive fee: $34,270 includes full-time tuition ($24,504), mandatory fees ($1050), and college room and board ($8716). College room only: $4380. Full-time tuition and fees vary according to course load and program. Room and board charges vary according to board plan and housing facility. Part-time tuition: $765 per credit hour. Part-time mandatory fees: $362 per credit hour. Part-time tuition and fees vary according to class time. **Scholarships:** Available **Calendar System:** Semester, Summer Session Available **Enroll-**

ment: FT 1,566, PT 113, Grad FT 203, Grad PT 418 **Faculty:** FT 110, PT 115 **Student-Faculty Ratio:** 14:1 **Exams:** SAT I or ACT. ACT essay used for advising. SAT essay used for advising. **% Receiving Financial Aid:** 85 **% Residing in College-Owned, -Operated, or -Affiliated Housing:** 80 **Final Year or Final Semester Residency Requirement:** No **Library Holdings:** 126,167 **Regional Accreditation:** Middle State Association of Colleges and Schools **Credit Hours For Degree:** 63 credits, Associates; 128 credits, Bachelors **ROTC:** Army **Professional Accreditation:** AACN, AOTA, APTA, CSWE, TEAC **Intercollegiate Athletics:** Basketball M & W; Bowling W; Cross-Country Running M & W; Field Hockey W; Football M; Golf M & W; Lacrosse W; Soccer M & W; Softball W; Swimming and Diving M & W; Tennis M & W; Track and Field M & W; Volleyball M & W

SAINT JOSEPH'S UNIVERSITY
5600 City Ave.
Philadelphia, PA 19131-1395
Tel: (610)660-1000
Admissions: (610)660-1300
E-mail: admit@sju.edu
Web Site: http://www.sju.edu/
President/CEO: Rev. Timothy R. Lannon, SJ
Financial Aid: Eileen M. Tucker
Type: Comprehensive **Sex:** Coed **Affiliation:** Roman Catholic (Jesuit) **Scores:** 99% SAT V 400+; 100% SAT M 400+; 49% ACT 18-23; 42% ACT 24-29 **% Accepted:** 82 **Admission Plans:** Early Action; Deferred Admission **Application Deadline:** February 1 **Application Fee:** $60.00 **H.S. Requirements:** High school diploma required; GED not accepted. The College of Professional and Liberal Studies and the university's adult undergraduate program accepts either a HS diploma or GED. **Costs Per Year:** Application fee: $60. One-time mandatory fee: $225. Comprehensive fee: $45,665 includes full-time tuition ($33,940), mandatory fees ($150), and college room and board ($11,575). College room only: $7320. Full-time tuition and fees vary according to course load. Room and board charges vary according to board plan and housing facility. Part-time tuition: $456 per credit. evening college, continuing education student tuition: $456 per credit. **Scholarships:** Available **Calendar System:** Semester, Summer Session Available **Enrollment:** FT 4,526, PT 877, Grad FT 546, Grad PT 2,388 **Faculty:** FT 284, PT 372 **Student-Faculty Ratio:** 14:1 **Exams:** SAT I or ACT. ACT essay not being used. SAT essay not being used. **% Receiving Financial Aid:** 50 **% Residing in College-Owned, -Operated, or -Affiliated Housing:** 59 **Library Holdings:** 355,000 **Regional Accreditation:** Middle State Association of Colleges and Schools **Credit Hours For Degree:** 60 credit hours, Associates; 120 credit hours, Bachelors **ROTC:** Army, Navy, Air Force **Professional Accreditation:** AACSB, AANA **Intercollegiate Athletics:** Baseball M; Basketball M & W; Cheerleading M & W; Crew M & W; Cross-Country Running M & W; Field Hockey W; Golf M; Lacrosse M & W; Soccer M & W; Softball W; Tennis M & W; Track and Field M & W

SAINT VINCENT COLLEGE
300 Fraser Purchase Rd.
Latrobe, PA 15650-2690
Tel: (724)532-6600; Free: 800-782-5549
Fax: (724)537-4554
E-mail: admission@stvincent.edu
Web Site: http://www.stvincent.edu/
President/CEO: H. James Towey
Admissions: David Collins
Financial Aid: Kimberly Woodley
Type: Comprehensive **Sex:** Coed **Affiliation:** Roman Catholic **Scores:** 97.2% SAT V 400+; 97.8% SAT M 400+ **% Accepted:** 67 **Admission Plans:** Early Admission; Deferred Admission **Application Deadline:** April 1 **Application Fee:** $25.00 **H.S. Requirements:** High school diploma required; GED accepted **Costs Per Year:** Application fee: $25. Comprehensive fee: $36,238 includes full-time tuition ($26,350), mandatory fees ($840), and college room and board ($9048). College room only: $4896. Room and board charges vary according to board plan and housing facility. Part-time tuition: $824 per credit. **Scholarships:** Available **Calendar System:** Semester, Summer Session Available **Enrollment:** FT 1,645, PT 96, Grad FT 128, Grad PT 115 **Faculty:** FT 104, PT 83 **Student-Faculty Ratio:** 13:1 **Exams:** SAT I or ACT. **% Receiving Financial Aid:** 77 **% Residing in College-Owned, -Operated, or -Affiliated Housing:** 70 **Library Holdings:** 379,857 **Regional Accreditation:** Middle State Association of Colleges and Schools **Credit Hours For Degree:** 124 credits, Bachelors **ROTC:** Army, Air Force **Professional Accreditation:** ACBSP **Intercollegiate Athletics:** Baseball M; Basketball M & W; Cheerleading M & W; Cross-Country Running M & W; Equestrian Sports M & W; Fencing M & W; Field Hockey W; Golf M & W; Ice Hockey M; Lacrosse M & W; Soccer M & W; Softball W; Swimming and Diving M & W; Tennis M & W; Track and Field M; Volleyball W

SANFORD-BROWN INSTITUTE—MONROEVILLE
Penn Center East
777 Penn Center Blvd., Bldg. 7
Pittsburgh, PA 15235
Tel: (412)373-6400; Free: 888-381-2433
Fax: (412)373-2544
Web Site: http://www.monroeville.sanfordbrown.edu/
President/CEO: R. Thomas Contrella
Admissions: Timothy Babyok
Type: Two-Year College **Sex:** Coed **Application Fee:** $25.00 **Calendar System:** Continuous **Professional Accreditation:** ACCSCT

SANFORD-BROWN INSTITUTE—PITTSBURGH
421 Seventh Ave.
Pittsburgh, PA 15219-1907
Tel: (412)281-2600; Free: 800-333-6607
Fax: (412)281-0319
Web Site: http://www.sanfordbrown.edu/
President/CEO: Patti Yakshe
Admissions: Bruce E. Jones
Type: Two-Year College **Sex:** Coed **Admission Plans:** Early Admission; Deferred Admission **Application Fee:** $25.00 **H.S. Requirements:** High school diploma required; GED accepted **Scholarships:** Available **Calendar System:** Continuous, Summer Session Not available **Exams:** SAT I or ACT, SAT II. **Library Holdings:** 1,687 **Credit Hours For Degree:** 65 credits, Associates **Professional Accreditation:** ACCSCT, CARC, JRCEDMS, JRCERT

SETON HILL UNIVERSITY
Seton Hill Dr.
Greensburg, PA 15601
Tel: (724)834-2200; Free: 800-826-6234
Admissions: (724)838-4255
Fax: (724)830-4611
E-mail: admit@setonhill.edu
Web Site: http://www.setonhill.edu/
President/CEO: Dr. JoAnne W. Boyle
Admissions: Sherri Bett
Financial Aid: Maryann Dudas
Type: Comprehensive **Sex:** Coed **Affiliation:** Roman Catholic **% Accepted:** 66 **Admission Plans:** Early Admission; Deferred Admission **Application Deadline:** August 15 **Application Fee:** $35.00 **H.S. Requirements:** High school diploma required; GED accepted **Costs Per Year:** Application fee: $35. Comprehensive fee: $35,432 includes full-time tuition ($26,322), mandatory fees ($300), and college room and board ($8810). Room and board charges vary according to board plan and housing facility. Part-time tuition: $705 per credit. Part-time mandatory fees: $150 per term. Part-time tuition and fees vary according to course load. **Scholarships:** Available **Calendar System:** Semester, Summer Session Available **Enrollment:** FT 1,376, PT 356, Grad FT 201, Grad PT 212 **Faculty:** FT 78, PT 107 **Student-Faculty Ratio:** 15:1 **Exams:** SAT I or ACT. ACT essay used for placement. SAT essay used for placement. **% Receiving Financial Aid:** 83 **% Residing in College-Owned, -Operated, or -Affiliated Housing:** 56 **Final Year or Final Semester Residency Requirement:** Yes **Library Holdings:** 119,381 **Regional Accreditation:** Middle State Association of Colleges and Schools **Credit Hours For Degree:** 120 credits, Bachelors **ROTC:** Army, Air Force **Professional Accreditation:** AAMFT, AAFCS, ADtA, CSWE, NASM, TEAC **Intercollegiate Athletics:** Baseball M; Basketball M & W; Cross-Country Running M & W; Equestrian Sports M & W; Field Hockey W; Football M; Golf W; Lacrosse M & W; Soccer M & W; Softball W; Tennis W; Track and Field M & W; Volleyball W; Wrestling M

SHIPPENSBURG UNIVERSITY OF PENNSYLVANIA
1871 Old Main Dr.
Shippensburg, PA 17257-2299
Tel: (717)477-7447
Admissions: (717)477-1231
Fax: (717)477-1273

E-mail: admiss@ship.edu
Web Site: http://www.ship.edu/
President/CEO: Dr. William N. Ruud
Admissions: Dr. Thomas Speakman
Financial Aid: Trina Snyder
Type: Comprehensive **Sex:** Coed **Affiliation:** Pennsylvania State System of Higher Education **Scores:** 95% SAT V 400+; 94.2% SAT M 400+; 64.7% ACT 18-23; 16.8% ACT 24-29 **% Accepted:** 72 **Admission Plans:** Early Admission; Early Action; Deferred Admission **Application Deadline:** Rolling **Application Fee:** $30.00 **H.S. Requirements:** High school diploma required; GED accepted **Costs Per Year:** Application fee: $30. State resident tuition: $5554 full-time, $231 per credit hour part-time. Nonresident tuition: $13,886 full-time, $579 per credit hour part-time. Mandatory fees: $1890 full-time, $186 per course part-time, $60 per term part-time. College room and board: $7086. College room only: $3750. Room and board charges vary according to board plan and housing facility. **Scholarships:** Available **Calendar System:** Semester, Summer Session Available **Enrollment:** FT 6,636, PT 306, Grad FT 284, Grad PT 1,027 **Faculty:** FT 329, PT 73 **Student-Faculty Ratio:** 20:1 **Exams:** SAT I or ACT. ACT essay used for advising. SAT essay used for advising. ACT essay used for placement. SAT essay used for placement. **% Receiving Financial Aid:** 55 **% Residing in College-Owned, -Operated, or -Affiliated Housing:** 36 **Final Year or Final Semester Residency Requirement:** No **Library Holdings:** 377,847 **Regional Accreditation:** Middle State Association of Colleges and Schools **Credit Hours For Degree:** 120 credit hours, Bachelors **ROTC:** Army **Professional Accreditation:** AACSB, ACA, CSWE, NCATE **Intercollegiate Athletics:** Baseball M; Basketball M & W; Cross-Country Running M & W; Field Hockey W; Football M; Lacrosse W; Soccer M & W; Softball W; Swimming and Diving M & W; Tennis W; Track and Field M & W; Volleyball W; Wrestling M

SLIPPERY ROCK UNIVERSITY OF PENNSYLVANIA
1 Morrow Way
Slippery Rock, PA 16057-1383
Tel: (724)738-9000; Free: 800-SRU-9111
Admissions: (724)738-2015
Fax: (724)738-2098
E-mail: asktherock@sru.edu
Web Site: http://www.sru.edu/
President/CEO: Dr. Robert Smith
Admissions: Mimi Campbell
Financial Aid: Patty A. Hladio
Type: Comprehensive **Sex:** Coed **Affiliation:** Pennsylvania State System of Higher Education **Scores:** 97.56% SAT V 400+; 97.41% SAT M 400+; 64. 46% ACT 18-23; 25.46% ACT 24-29 **% Accepted:** 63 **Admission Plans:** Deferred Admission **Application Fee:** $30.00 **H.S. Requirements:** High school diploma required; GED accepted **Costs Per Year:** Application fee: $30. State resident tuition: $5554 full-time, $231 per credit hour part-time. Nonresident tuition: $8331 full-time, $463 per credit hour part-time. Mandatory fees: $1681 full-time, $82 per credit hour part-time, $60 per term part-time. Full-time tuition and fees vary according to course load and degree level. Part-time tuition and fees vary according to course load and degree level. College room and board: $8454. College room only: $5846. Room and board charges vary according to board plan and housing facility. **Scholarships:** Available **Calendar System:** Semester, Summer Session Available **Enrollment:** FT 7,250, PT 575, Grad FT 401, Grad PT 422 **Faculty:** FT 348, PT 61 **Student-Faculty Ratio:** 20:1 **Exams:** SAT I or ACT. SAT essay used for placement. ACT essay not being used. **% Receiving Financial Aid:** 67 **% Residing in College-Owned, -Operated, or -Affiliated Housing:** 36 **Library Holdings:** 515,095 **Regional Accreditation:** Middle State Association of Colleges and Schools **Credit Hours For Degree:** 120 credits, Bachelors **ROTC:** Army **Professional Accreditation:** ACA, APTA, ACBSP, CSWE, JRCEPAT, NASD, NASM, NCATE, NLN, NRPA **Intercollegiate Athletics:** Baseball M; Basketball M & W; Cheerleading M & W; Cross-Country Running M & W; Equestrian Sports M & W; Field Hockey W; Football M; Golf M & W; Gymnastics W; Ice Hockey M & W; Lacrosse M & W; Racquetball M & W; Rugby M & W; Skiing (Downhill) M & W; Soccer M & W; Softball W; Swimming and Diving M & W; Tennis M & W; Track and Field M & W; Ultimate Frisbee M & W; Volleyball M & W; Water Polo M; Wrestling M & W

SOUTH HILLS SCHOOL OF BUSINESS & TECHNOLOGY (ALTOONA)
508 58th St.
Altoona, PA 16602
Tel: (814)944-6134
Fax: (814)944-4684
E-mail: hemerick@southhills.edu
Web Site: http://www.southhills.edu/
President/CEO: S. Paul Mazza
Admissions: Holly J. Emerick
Type: Two-Year College **Sex:** Coed **% Accepted:** 60 **Application Deadline:** September 1 **Application Fee:** $25.00 **H.S. Requirements:** High school diploma required; GED accepted **Scholarships:** Available **Calendar System:** Trimester, Summer Session Available **Enrollment:** FT 189 **Faculty:** FT 10, PT 1 **Student-Faculty Ratio:** 13:1 **Exams:** Other. **Credit Hours For Degree:** 90 credits, Associates **Professional Accreditation:** ACICS

SOUTH HILLS SCHOOL OF BUSINESS & TECHNOLOGY (STATE COLLEGE)
480 Waupelani Dr.
State College, PA 16801-4516
Tel: (814)234-7755; Free: 888-282-7427
Fax: (814)234-0926
E-mail: admissions@southhills.edu
Web Site: http://www.southhills.edu/
President/CEO: Mark Maggs
Admissions: Diane M. Brown
Type: Two-Year College **Sex:** Coed **% Accepted:** 77 **Application Deadline:** September 2 **Application Fee:** $25.00 **H.S. Requirements:** High school diploma required; GED accepted **Scholarships:** Available **Calendar System:** Quarter **Enrollment:** FT 611, PT 52 **Faculty:** FT 37, PT 23 **Student-Faculty Ratio:** 15:1 **Exams:** Other. **Credit Hours For Degree:** 90 credits, Associates **Professional Accreditation:** ACICS, AHIMA

STRAYER UNIVERSITY - ALLENTOWN CAMPUS
3800 Sierra Circle
Ste. 300
Center Valley, PA 18034
Tel: (484)809-7770
Fax: (610)791-0210
Web Site: http://www.strayer.edu/allentown/
Type: Comprehensive **Sex:** Coed **Application Fee:** $50.00 **Costs Per Year:** Application fee: $50. **Regional Accreditation:** Middle State Association of Colleges and Schools

STRAYER UNIVERSITY - CENTER CITY CAMPUS
1601 Cherry St., Ste. 100
Philadelphia, PA 19102
Tel: (267)256-0200
Fax: (267)256-0230
Web Site: http://www.strayer.edu/center_city
Type: Comprehensive **Sex:** Coed **Application Fee:** $50.00 **Costs Per Year:** Application fee: $50. **Regional Accreditation:** Middle State Association of Colleges and Schools

STRAYER UNIVERSITY - CRANBERRY WOODS CAMPUS
Regional Learning Alliance
850 Cranberry Woods Dr., Ste. 2241
Cranberry Township, PA 16066
Tel: (724)741-1064
Fax: (724)741-1050
Web Site: http://www.strayer.edu/cranberry_woods
Type: Comprehensive **Sex:** Coed **Application Fee:** $50.00 **Costs Per Year:** Application fee: $50. **Regional Accreditation:** Middle State Association of Colleges and Schools

STRAYER UNIVERSITY - DELAWARE COUNTY CAMPUS
760 West Sproul Rd., Ste. 200
Springfield, PA 19064-1215
Tel: (610)604-7700
Fax: (610)543-6599
Web Site: http://www.strayer.edu/delaware_county
Type: Comprehensive **Sex:** Coed **Application Fee:** $50.00 **Costs Per Year:** Application fee: $50. **Regional Accreditation:** Middle State Association of Colleges and Schools

STRAYER UNIVERSITY - KING OF PRUSSIA CAMPUS
234 Mall Blvd.
Ste. G-50
King of Prussia, PA 19406
Tel: (610)992-1700
Fax: (610)992-9777
Web Site: http://www.strayer.edu/king_of_prussia
Type: Comprehensive **Sex:** Coed **Application Fee:** $50.00 **Costs Per Year:** Application fee: $50. **Regional Accreditation:** Middle State Association of Colleges and Schools

STRAYER UNIVERSITY - LOWER BUCKS COUNTY CAMPUS
3600 Horizon Blvd., Ste. 100
Trevose, PA 19053
Tel: (215)953-5999
Fax: (215)953-9464
Web Site: http://www.strayer.edu/lower_bucks_county/
Type: Comprehensive **Sex:** Coed **Application Fee:** $50.00 **Costs Per Year:** Application fee: $50. **Regional Accreditation:** Middle State Association of Colleges and Schools

STRAYER UNIVERSITY - PENN CENTER WEST CAMPUS
One Penn Center West, Ste. 320
Pittsburgh, PA 15276
Tel: (412)747-7800
Fax: (412)747-7830
Web Site: http://www.strayer.edu/penn_center_west/
Type: Comprehensive **Sex:** Coed **Application Fee:** $50.00 **Costs Per Year:** Application fee: $50. **Regional Accreditation:** Middle State Association of Colleges and Schools

SUSQUEHANNA UNIVERSITY
514 University Ave.
Selinsgrove, PA 17870
Tel: (570)374-0101; Free: 800-326-9672
Admissions: (570)372-4260
Fax: (570)372-2722
E-mail: suadmiss@susqu.edu
Web Site: http://www.susqu.edu/
President/CEO: L. Jay Lemons
Admissions: Chris Markle
Financial Aid: Helen S. Nunn
Type: Four-Year College **Sex:** Coed **Affiliation:** Evangelical Lutheran Church in America **Scores:** 98.9% SAT V 400+; 99.7% SAT M 400+; 32.2% ACT 18-23; 61% ACT 24-29 **% Accepted:** 75 **Admission Plans:** Early Admission; Early Decision Plan; Deferred Admission **Application Deadline:** March 1 **Application Fee:** $35.00 **H.S. Requirements:** High school diploma required; GED accepted **Costs Per Year:** Application fee: $35. Comprehensive fee: $41,650 includes full-time tuition ($32,450), mandatory fees ($400), and college room and board ($8800). College room only: $4600. Room and board charges vary according to board plan and housing facility. **Scholarships:** Available **Calendar System:** Semester, Summer Session Available **Enrollment:** FT 2,187, PT 44 **Faculty:** FT 133, PT 104 **Student-Faculty Ratio:** 13:1 **Exams:** SAT I or ACT. **% Receiving Financial Aid:** 68 **% Residing in College-Owned, -Operated, or -Affiliated Housing:** 74 **Library Holdings:** 258,263 **Regional Accreditation:** Middle State Association of Colleges and Schools **Credit Hours For Degree:** 130 semester hours, Bachelors **ROTC:** Army **Professional Accreditation:** AACSB, NASM **Intercollegiate Athletics:** Baseball M; Basketball M & W; Cheerleading M & W; Crew M & W; Cross-Country Running M & W; Equestrian Sports M & W; Field Hockey W; Football M; Golf M & W; Lacrosse M & W; Rugby M & W; Soccer M & W; Softball W; Swimming and Diving M & W; Tennis M & W; Track and Field M & W; Volleyball M & W

SWARTHMORE COLLEGE
500 College Ave.
Swarthmore, PA 19081-1397
Tel: (610)328-8000; Free: 800-667-3110
Admissions: (610)328-8300
Fax: (610)328-8673
E-mail: admissions@swarthmore.edu
Web Site: http://www.swarthmore.edu/
President/CEO: Rebecca S. Chopp
Admissions: Jim Bock
Financial Aid: Laura Talbot
Type: Four-Year College **Sex:** Coed **Scores:** 100.1% SAT V 400+; 100% SAT M 400+; 1.6% ACT 18-23; 23.4% ACT 24-29 **% Accepted:** 17 **Admission Plans:** Early Admission; Early Decision Plan; Deferred Admission **Application Deadline:** January 2 **Application Fee:** $60.00 **H.S. Requirements:** High school diploma or equivalent not required **Costs Per Year:** Application fee: $60. Comprehensive fee: $49,600 includes full-time tuition ($37,510), mandatory fees ($350), and college room and board ($11,740). College room only: $6018. Room and board charges vary according to board plan. **Scholarships:** Available **Calendar System:** Semester, Summer Session Not available **Enrollment:** FT 1,510, PT 15 **Faculty:** FT 171, PT 40 **Student-Faculty Ratio:** 8:1 **Exams:** SAT I and SAT II or ACT. **% Receiving Financial Aid:** 49 **% Residing in College-Owned, -Operated, or -Affiliated Housing:** 95 **Library Holdings:** 842,722 **Regional Accreditation:** Middle State Association of Colleges and Schools **Credit Hours For Degree:** 32 courses, Bachelors **ROTC:** Army, Navy, Air Force **Professional Accreditation:** ABET **Intercollegiate Athletics:** Badminton M & W; Baseball M; Basketball M & W; Cross-Country Running M & W; Fencing M & W; Field Hockey W; Golf M; Ice Hockey M & W; Lacrosse M & W; Rugby M & W; Soccer M & W; Softball W; Squash M & W; Swimming and Diving M & W; Tennis M & W; Track and Field M & W; Ultimate Frisbee M & W; Volleyball M & W; Water Polo M & W

TALMUDICAL YESHIVA OF PHILADELPHIA
6063 Drexel Rd.
Philadelphia, PA 19131-1296
Tel: (215)473-1212
Fax: (215)477-5065
President/CEO: Rabbi Shmuel Kamenetsky
Admissions: Rabbi Shmuel Kamenetsky
Type: Four-Year College **Sex:** Men **Affiliation:** Jewish **Admission Plans:** Early Admission; Deferred Admission **Application Deadline:** July 15 **H.S. Requirements:** High school diploma required; GED accepted **Scholarships:** Available **Calendar System:** Trimester, Summer Session Not available **% Receiving Financial Aid:** 63 **Library Holdings:** 4,800 **Credit Hours For Degree:** 170 credit hours, Bachelors **Professional Accreditation:** AARTS

TEMPLE UNIVERSITY
1801 North Broad St.
Philadelphia, PA 19122-6096
Tel: (215)204-7000; Free: 888-340-2222
Admissions: (215)204-7200
Fax: (215)204-5694
E-mail: tuadm@temple.edu
Web Site: http://www.temple.edu/
President/CEO: Dr. Ann Weaver Hart
Admissions: Karin Mormando
Financial Aid: Dr. John F. Morris
Type: University **Sex:** Coed **Scores:** 98% SAT V 400+; 98% SAT M 400+; 45% ACT 18-23; 41% ACT 24-29 **% Accepted:** 61 **Admission Plans:** Early Admission; Deferred Admission **Application Deadline:** March 1 **Application Fee:** $50.00 **H.S. Requirements:** High school diploma required; GED accepted **Costs Per Year:** Application fee: $50. State resident tuition: $11,174 full-time, $432 per credit part-time. Nonresident tuition: $20,454 full-time, $728 per credit part-time. Mandatory fees: $590 full-time, $220 per year part-time. Full-time tuition and fees vary according to course load, program, and reciprocity agreements. Part-time tuition and fees vary according to course load, program, and reciprocity agreements. College room and board: $9198. College room only: $6126. Room and board charges vary according to board plan and housing facility. **Scholarships:** Available **Calendar System:** Semester, Summer Session Available **Enrollment:** FT 24,112, PT 2,933, Grad FT 6,182, Grad PT 3,278 **Faculty:** FT 1,384, PT 1,506 **Student-Faculty Ratio:** 17:1 **Exams:** SAT I or ACT. SAT essay used for admission. **% Receiving Financial Aid:** 64 **% Residing in College-Owned, -Operated, or -Affiliated Housing:** 19 **Final Year or Final Semester Residency Requirement:** No **Regional Accreditation:** Middle State Association of Colleges and Schools **Credit Hours For Degree:** 64 semester hours, Associates; 124 semester hours, Bachelors **ROTC:** Army, Navy, Air Force **Professional Accreditation:** AACSB, ABET, ACPhE, ACEJMC, AACN, ABA, ADA, AHIMA, AOTA, APTA, APMA, APA, ASLA, ASLHA, AALS, ACEHSA, CEPH, CSWE, JRCEPAT, LCMEAMA NAAB, NASAD, NASD, NASM, NAST, NCATE, NRPA, TEAC **Intercollegiate Athletics:** Baseball M; Basketball M & W; Cheerleading M & W; Crew M &

W; Cross-Country Running M & W; Fencing W; Field Hockey W; Football M; Golf M; Gymnastics M & W; Lacrosse W; Soccer M & W; Softball W; Tennis M & W; Track and Field M & W; Volleyball W

THADDEUS STEVENS COLLEGE OF TECHNOLOGY
750 East King St.
Lancaster, PA 17602-3198
Tel: (717)299-7730
Fax: (717)391-6929
Web Site: http://www.stevenscollege.edu/
President/CEO: William E. Griscom
Admissions: Erin Kate Nelsen
Type: Two-Year College **Sex:** Coed **Admission Plans:** Preferred Admission; Deferred Admission **Application Deadline:** June 30 **Application Fee:** $25.00 **H.S. Requirements:** High school diploma required; GED accepted **Costs Per Year:** Application fee: $25. State resident tuition: $6220 full-time, $259 per credit part-time. College room and board: $7400. **Scholarships:** Available **Calendar System:** Semester, Summer Session Not available **Student-Faculty Ratio:** 13:1 **Exams:** Other. **Regional Accreditation:** Middle State Association of Colleges and Schools **Credit Hours For Degree:** 60 credits, Associates **Intercollegiate Athletics:** Basketball M; Cross-Country Running M; Football M; Track and Field M; Wrestling M

THIEL COLLEGE
75 College Ave.
Greenville, PA 16125-2181
Tel: (724)589-2000; Free: 800-248-4435
Admissions: (724)589-2182
Fax: (724)589-2013
E-mail: admissions@thiel.edu
Web Site: http://www.thiel.edu/
President/CEO: Dr. Troy VanAken
Admissions: Amy Becker
Financial Aid: Cynthia H. Farrell
Type: Four-Year College **Sex:** Coed **Affiliation:** Evangelical Lutheran Church in America **Scores:** 84.8% SAT V 400+; 80.3% SAT M 400+; 53.7% ACT 18-23; 17.4% ACT 24-29 **% Accepted:** 72 **Admission Plans:** Deferred Admission **Application Deadline:** Rolling **Application Fee:** $0.00 **H.S. Requirements:** High school diploma required; GED accepted **Costs Per Year:** Application fee: $0. Comprehensive fee: $29,788 includes full-time tuition ($20,998) and college room and board ($8790). College room only: $4400. Room and board charges vary according to board plan and housing facility. Part-time tuition: $670 per credit hour. Part-time mandatory fees: $50 per credit hour. Part-time tuition and fees vary according to course load. **Scholarships:** Available **Calendar System:** Semester, Summer Session Available **Enrollment:** FT 942, PT 57 **Faculty:** FT 61, PT 50 **Student-Faculty Ratio:** 13:1 **Exams:** SAT I or ACT. **% Receiving Financial Aid:** 80 **% Residing in College-Owned, -Operated, or -Affiliated Housing:** 80 **Final Year or Final Semester Residency Requirement:** Yes **Library Holdings:** 186,643 **Regional Accreditation:** Middle State Association of Colleges and Schools **Credit Hours For Degree:** 64 credit hours, Associates; 124 credit hours, Bachelors **Intercollegiate Athletics:** Baseball M; Basketball M & W; Cheerleading M & W; Cross-Country Running M & W; Football M; Golf M & W; Lacrosse M & W; Soccer M & W; Softball W; Track and Field M & W; Volleyball M & W; Wrestling M

THOMAS JEFFERSON UNIVERSITY
Eleventh and Walnut Sts.
Philadelphia, PA 19107
Tel: (215)955-6000; Free: 877-533-3247
Fax: (215)503-7241
E-mail: chpadmissions@mail.tju.edu
Web Site: http://www.jefferson.edu/
President/CEO: Robert L. Barchi, MD
Admissions: Karen Jacobs
Financial Aid: Susan McFadden
Type: University **Sex:** Coed **% Accepted:** 51 **Admission Plans:** Deferred Admission **Application Deadline:** Rolling **Application Fee:** $50.00 **H.S. Requirements:** High school diploma required; GED accepted **Scholarships:** Available **Calendar System:** Semester, Summer Session Not available **Enrollment:** FT 688, PT 369 **Faculty:** FT 76, PT 190 **Student-Faculty Ratio:** 10:1 **Exams:** Other, SAT I or ACT. **% Residing in College-Owned, -Operated, or -Affiliated Housing:** 30 **Library Holdings:** 170,000 **Regional Accreditation:** Middle State Association of Colleges and Schools **Credit Hours For Degree:** 126 credits, Bachelors **ROTC:** Air Force **Professional Accreditation:** ACPhE, AACN, AANA, AOTA, APTA, ASC, ACIPE, JRCEDMS, JRCERT, LCMEAMA, NAACLS **Intercollegiate Athletics:** Rugby M

TRI-STATE BUSINESS INSTITUTE
5757 West 26th St.
Erie, PA 16506
Tel: (814)838-7673
Fax: (814)838-8642
E-mail: geuliano@tsbi.org
Web Site: http://www.tsbi.edu/
President/CEO: Guy M. Euliano
Admissions: Guy M. Euliano
Type: Two-Year College **Sex:** Coed **% Accepted:** 68 **Application Fee:** $50.00 **Professional Accreditation:** ACICS

TRIANGLE TECH INC—BETHLEHEM
Lehigh Valley Industrial Park IV
31 South Commerce Way
Bethlehem, PA 18017
Tel: (610)691-1300
Web Site: http://www.triangle-tech.edu/
President/CEO: Michael Biechy
Type: Two-Year College **Sex:** Coed **% Accepted:** 99 **Admission Plans:** Open Admission **Application Fee:** $0.00 **H.S. Requirements:** High school diploma required; GED accepted **Costs Per Year:** Application fee: $0. **Enrollment:** FT 140 **Faculty:** FT 8, PT 2 **Student-Faculty Ratio:** 15:1 **Exams:** Other. **Credit Hours For Degree:** 72 credits, Associates **Professional Accreditation:** ACCSCT

TRIANGLE TECH, INC.—DUBOIS SCHOOL
PO Box 551
DuBois, PA 15801-0551
Tel: (814)371-2090; Free: 800-874-8324
Admissions: (412)359-1000
Fax: (814)371-9227
E-mail: info@triangle-tech.com
Web Site: http://www.triangle-tech.edu/
President/CEO: Stephanie Craig
Admissions: Jason Vallozzi
Type: Two-Year College **Sex:** Coed **Affiliation:** Triangle Tech Group, Inc. **% Accepted:** 100 **Admission Plans:** Deferred Admission **Application Deadline:** Rolling **Application Fee:** $0.00 **H.S. Requirements:** High school diploma required; GED accepted **Costs Per Year:** Application fee: $0. Tuition: $13,864 full-time. Mandatory fees: $447 full-time. **Scholarships:** Available **Calendar System:** Semester, Summer Session Not available **Enrollment:** FT 331 **Faculty:** FT 21, PT 0 **Student-Faculty Ratio:** 15:1 **Library Holdings:** 1,200 **Credit Hours For Degree:** 72 credits, Associates **Professional Accreditation:** ACCSCT

TRIANGLE TECH, INC.—ERIE SCHOOL
2000 Liberty St.
Erie, PA 16502-2594
Tel: (814)453-6016; Free: 800-TRI-TECH
Fax: (814)454-2818
Web Site: http://www.triangle-tech.com/
President/CEO: Timothy J. McMahon
Type: Two-Year College **Sex:** Coed **Affiliation:** Triangle Tech Group, Inc. **% Accepted:** 100 **Admission Plans:** Deferred Admission **Application Deadline:** Rolling **Application Fee:** $75.00 **H.S. Requirements:** High school diploma required; GED accepted **Scholarships:** Available **Calendar System:** Semester **Enrollment:** FT 176 **Faculty:** FT 14, PT 2 **Student-Faculty Ratio:** 12:1 **Library Holdings:** 1,000 **Credit Hours For Degree:** 72 credits, Associates **Professional Accreditation:** ACCSCT

TRIANGLE TECH, INC.—PITTSBURGH SCHOOL
1940 Perrysville Ave.
Pittsburgh, PA 15214-3897
Tel: (412)359-1000; Free: 800-874-8324
Fax: (412)359-1012
E-mail: info@triangle-tech.edu
Web Site: http://www.triangle-tech.edu/
President/CEO: Paul Beadle

Type: Two-Year College **Sex:** Coed **Affiliation:** Triangle Tech Group, Inc. **Application Deadline:** Rolling **H.S. Requirements:** High school diploma required; GED accepted **Scholarships:** Available **Calendar System:** Semester, Summer Session Not available **Student-Faculty Ratio:** 12:1 **Credit Hours For Degree:** 72 credits, Associates **Professional Accreditation:** ACCSCT

TRIANGLE TECH, INC.—SUNBURY SCHOOL
191 Performance Rd.
Sunbury, PA 17801
Tel: (570)988-0700
Admissions: (412)359-1000
Web Site: http://www.triangle-tech.edu/
President/CEO: Joseph Drumm
Admissions: John Mazzarese
Type: Two-Year College **Sex:** Coed **% Accepted:** 100 **H.S. Requirements:** High school diploma required; GED accepted **Calendar System:** Semester, Summer Session Not available **Enrollment:** FT 170 **Faculty:** FT 14, PT 1 **Student-Faculty Ratio:** 12:1 **Library Holdings:** 300 **Credit Hours For Degree:** 72 credits, Associates **Professional Accreditation:** ACCSCT

TRIANGLE TECH—GREENSBURG SCHOOL
222 East Pittsburgh St.
Ste. A
Greensburg, PA 15601-3304
Tel: (724)832-1050; Free: 800-874-8324
Admissions: (412)359-1000
Web Site: http://www.triangle-tech.com/
President/CEO: Timothy J. McMahon
Admissions: John Mazzarese
Type: Two-Year College **Sex:** Coed **Affiliation:** Triangle Tech Group, Inc. **% Accepted:** 100 **Admission Plans:** Deferred Admission **Application Deadline:** Rolling **Application Fee:** $75.00 **H.S. Requirements:** High school diploma required; GED accepted **Costs Per Year:** Application fee: $75. Tuition: $14,557 full-time. Mandatory fees: $348 full-time. **Scholarships:** Available **Calendar System:** Semester, Summer Session Available **Enrollment:** FT 260 **Faculty:** FT 21, PT 0 **Student-Faculty Ratio:** 12:1 **Library Holdings:** 550 **Credit Hours For Degree:** 72 credits, Associates **Professional Accreditation:** ACCSCT

THE UNIVERSITY OF THE ARTS
320 South Broad St.
Philadelphia, PA 19102-4944
Tel: (215)717-6000; Free: 800-616-ARTS
Admissions: (215)717-6030
Fax: (215)717-6045
E-mail: admissions@uarts.edu
Web Site: http://www.uarts.edu/
President/CEO: Sean T. Buffington
Admissions: Susan Gandy
Type: Comprehensive **Sex:** Coed **Scores:** 93% SAT V 400+; 89.5% SAT M 400+; 49% ACT 18-23; 33% ACT 24-29 **% Accepted:** 52 **Admission Plans:** Early Admission; Deferred Admission **Application Deadline:** Rolling **Application Fee:** $60.00 **H.S. Requirements:** High school diploma required; GED accepted **Costs Per Year:** Application fee: $60. Tuition: $30,700 full-time, $1280 per credit hour part-time. Mandatory fees: $300 full-time. College room only: $7200. Room charges vary according to housing facility. **Scholarships:** Available **Calendar System:** Semester, Summer Session Not available **Enrollment:** FT 2,136, PT 47 **Faculty:** FT 118, PT 376 **Student-Faculty Ratio:** 10:1 **Exams:** SAT I or ACT. **% Residing in College-Owned, -Operated, or -Affiliated Housing:** 35 **Regional Accreditation:** Middle State Association of Colleges and Schools **Credit Hours For Degree:** 123 credits, Bachelors **Professional Accreditation:** NASAD, NASM

UNIVERSITY OF PENNSYLVANIA
3451 Walnut St.
Philadelphia, PA 19104
Tel: (215)898-5000
E-mail: info@admissions.ugao.upenn.edu
Web Site: http://www.upenn.edu/
President/CEO: Amy Gutmann
Financial Aid: William Schilling
Type: University **Sex:** Coed **Scores:** 100% SAT V 400+; 101% SAT M 400+; 21% ACT 24-29 **% Accepted:** 18 **Admission Plans:** Early Admission; Early Decision Plan; Deferred Admission **Application Deadline:** January 1 **Application Fee:** $75.00 **H.S. Requirements:** High school diploma or equivalent not required **Costs Per Year:** Application fee: $75. Comprehensive fee: $51,944 includes full-time tuition ($36,208), mandatory fees ($4306), and college room and board ($11,430). College room only: $7248. Room and board charges vary according to board plan. **Scholarships:** Available **Calendar System:** Semester, Summer Session Available **Enrollment:** FT 9,490, PT 278, Grad FT 8,136, Grad PT 1,407 **Faculty:** FT 1,411, PT 789 **Student-Faculty Ratio:** 6:1 **Exams:** SAT I and SAT II or ACT. ACT essay used for admission. SAT essay used for admission. ACT essay used as a validity check on application essay. SAT essay used as a validity check on application essay. **% Receiving Financial Aid:** 43 **% Residing in College-Owned, -Operated, or -Affiliated Housing:** 62 **Library Holdings:** 5,842,099 **Regional Accreditation:** Middle State Association of Colleges and Schools **Credit Hours For Degree:** 16 course units, Bachelors **ROTC:** Army, Navy, Air Force **Professional Accreditation:** AACSB, ABET, AACN, AANA, ABA, ACNM, ADA, ACSP, APA, ASLA, AVMA, ACIPE, AALS, ACEHSA, CSWE, LCMEAMA, NAAB, NLN **Intercollegiate Athletics:** Baseball M; Basketball M & W; Crew M & W; Cross-Country Running M & W; Fencing M & W; Field Hockey W; Football M; Golf M & W; Gymnastics W; Lacrosse M & W; Soccer M & W; Softball W; Squash M & W; Swimming and Diving M & W; Tennis M & W; Track and Field M & W; Volleyball W; Wrestling M

UNIVERSITY OF PHOENIX—HARRISBURG CAMPUS
4050 Crums Mill Rd.
Harrisburg, PA 17112
Tel: (717)540-3300
Web Site: http://www.phoenix.edu/
President/CEO: William Pepicello, PhD
Type: Comprehensive **Sex:** Coed **Regional Accreditation:** North Central Association of Colleges and Schools

UNIVERSITY OF PHOENIX—PHILADELPHIA CAMPUS
170 South Warner Rd.
Ste. 200
Wayne, PA 19087-2121
Tel: (610)989-0880; Free: 800-228-7240
Admissions: (480)557-6151
Fax: (610)989-0881
E-mail: audra.mcquarie@phoenix.edu
Web Site: http://www.phoenix.edu/
President/CEO: William Pepicello
Admissions: Audra McQuarie
Type: Comprehensive **Sex:** Coed **Admission Plans:** Open Admission; Deferred Admission **Application Deadline:** Rolling **Application Fee:** $0.00 **H.S. Requirements:** High school diploma required; GED accepted **Costs Per Year:** Application fee: $0. Tuition: $13,875 full-time. Full-time tuition varies according to course level and course load. **Scholarships:** Available **Calendar System:** Continuous, Summer Session Not available **Enrollment:** FT 778 **Faculty:** FT 24, PT 153 **Regional Accreditation:** North Central Association of Colleges and Schools **Credit Hours For Degree:** 60 credits, Associates; 120 credits, Bachelors

UNIVERSITY OF PHOENIX—PITTSBURGH CAMPUS
Penn Center West Six
Ste. 100
Pittsburgh, PA 15276
Tel: (412)747-9000; Free: 800-228-7240
Admissions: (480)557-6151
Fax: (412)747-0676
E-mail: audra.mcquarie@phoenix.edu
Web Site: http://www.phoenix.edu/
President/CEO: William Pepicello
Admissions: Audra McQuarie
Type: Comprehensive **Sex:** Coed **% Accepted:** 100 **Admission Plans:** Open Admission; Deferred Admission **Application Deadline:** Rolling **Application Fee:** $0.00 **H.S. Requirements:** High school diploma required; GED accepted **Costs Per Year:** Application fee: $0. Tuition: $13,875 full-time. Full-time tuition varies according to course level and course load. **Scholarships:** Available **Calendar System:** Continuous, Summer Session Not available **Enrollment:** FT 82 **Faculty:** FT 8, PT 71 **Regional Accredita-**

tion: North Central Association of Colleges and Schools **Credit Hours For Degree:** 60 credits, Associates; 120 credits, Bachelors

UNIVERSITY OF PITTSBURGH
4200 Fifth Ave.
Pittsburgh, PA 15260
Tel: (412)624-4141
Admissions: (412)624-7488
Fax: (412)648-8815
E-mail: oafa@pitt.edu
Web Site: http://www.pitt.edu/
President/CEO: Mark A. Nordenberg
Admissions: Dr. Betsy A. Porter
Financial Aid: Dr. Betsy A. Porter
Type: University **Sex:** Coed **Affiliation:** Commonwealth System of Higher Education **Scores:** 100% SAT V 400+; 100% SAT M 400+; 12% ACT 18-23; 57% ACT 24-29 **% Accepted:** 59 **Admission Plans:** Early Admission **Application Deadline:** Rolling **Application Fee:** $45.00 **H.S. Requirements:** High school diploma required; GED not accepted **Costs Per Year:** Application fee: $45. State resident tuition: $13,344 full-time, $556 per credit part-time. Nonresident tuition: $23,042 full-time, $960 per credit part-time. Mandatory fees: $810 full-time, $189 per term part-time. Full-time tuition and fees vary according to program. Part-time tuition and fees vary according to program. College room and board: $8900. College room only: $5300. Room and board charges vary according to board plan and housing facility. **Scholarships:** Available **Calendar System:** Semester, Summer Session Available **Enrollment:** FT 16,719, PT 1,312, Grad FT 7,358, Grad PT 2,939 **Faculty:** FT 1,642, PT 623 **Student-Faculty Ratio:** 15:1 **Exams:** SAT I or ACT. ACT essay not being used. SAT essay not being used. **% Receiving Financial Aid:** 55 **% Residing in College-Owned, -Operated, or -Affiliated Housing:** 45 **Library Holdings:** 5,505,919 **Regional Accreditation:** Middle State Association of Colleges and Schools **Credit Hours For Degree:** 120 credits, Bachelors **ROTC:** Army, Navy, Air Force **Professional Accreditation:** AACSB, ABET, ACPhE, AACN, AANA, ABA, ACA, ADA, ADtA, AHIMA, ALA, AOTA, APTA, APA, ASLHA, AALS, ACEHSA, CEPH, CORE, CSWE JRCEMT, JRCEPAT, LCMEAMA, NASPAA, NAST, TEAC **Intercollegiate Athletics:** Baseball M; Basketball M & W; Cross-Country Running M & W; Football M; Gymnastics W; Soccer M & W; Softball W; Swimming and Diving M & W; Tennis W; Track and Field M & W; Volleyball W; Wrestling M

UNIVERSITY OF PITTSBURGH AT BRADFORD
300 Campus Dr.
Bradford, PA 16701-2812
Tel: (814)362-7500; Free: 800-872-1787
Admissions: (814)362-7552
Fax: (814)362-7578
E-mail: monti@pitt.edu
Web Site: http://www.upb.pitt.edu/
President/CEO: Dr. Livingston Alexander
Admissions: Vicky Pingie
Financial Aid: Melissa Ibanez
Type: Four-Year College **Sex:** Coed **Affiliation:** University of Pittsburgh System **Scores:** 90.21% SAT V 400+; 93.65% SAT M 400+; 73.33% ACT 18-23; 21.67% ACT 24-29 **% Accepted:** 48 **Admission Plans:** Deferred Admission **Application Deadline:** Rolling **Application Fee:** $45.00 **H.S. Requirements:** High school diploma required; GED accepted **Costs Per Year:** Application fee: $45. State resident tuition: $11,012 full-time, $458 per credit hour part-time. Nonresident tuition: $20,572 full-time, $857 per credit hour part-time. Mandatory fees: $710 full-time, $105 per term part-time. Full-time tuition and fees vary according to course load and program. Part-time tuition and fees vary according to course load and program. College room and board: $7480. College room only: $4540. Room and board charges vary according to board plan and housing facility. **Scholarships:** Available **Calendar System:** Semester, Summer Session Available **Enrollment:** FT 1,453, PT 199 **Faculty:** FT 72, PT 76 **Student-Faculty Ratio:** 18:1 **Exams:** SAT I or ACT. ACT essay not being used. SAT essay not being used. **% Receiving Financial Aid:** 89 **% Residing in College-Owned, -Operated, or -Affiliated Housing:** 55 **Library Holdings:** 97,963 **Regional Accreditation:** Middle State Association of Colleges and Schools **Credit Hours For Degree:** 60 credits, Associates; 120 credits, Bachelors **ROTC:** Army **Professional Accreditation:** NLN **Intercollegiate Athletics:** Baseball M; Basketball M & W; Cross-Country Running M & W; Golf M & W; Soccer M & W; Softball W; Swimming and Diving M & W; Tennis M & W; Volleyball W

UNIVERSITY OF PITTSBURGH AT GREENSBURG
150 Finoli Dr.
Greensburg, PA 15601-5860
Tel: (724)837-7040
Admissions: (724)836-9880
Fax: (724)836-9901
E-mail: upgadmit@pitt.edu
Web Site: http://www.greensburg.pitt.edu/
President/CEO: Dr. Sharon P. Smith
Admissions: Heather Kabala
Financial Aid: Brandi S. Darr
Type: Four-Year College **Sex:** Coed **Affiliation:** University of Pittsburgh System **Scores:** 95.2% SAT V 400+; 94.73% SAT M 400+; 71.67% ACT 18-23; 16.67% ACT 24-29 **% Accepted:** 74 **Admission Plans:** Early Admission; Deferred Admission **Application Deadline:** August 1 **Application Fee:** $45.00 **H.S. Requirements:** High school diploma required; GED accepted **Costs Per Year:** Application fee: $45. State resident tuition: $11,012 full-time, $458 per credit hour part-time. Nonresident tuition: $20,572 full-time, $857 per credit hour part-time. Mandatory fees: $840 full-time. College room and board: $7840. Room and board charges vary according to board plan and housing facility. **Scholarships:** Available **Calendar System:** Semester, Summer Session Available **Enrollment:** FT 1,676, PT 132 **Faculty:** FT 73, PT 60 **Student-Faculty Ratio:** 18:1 **Exams:** SAT I or ACT. **% Receiving Financial Aid:** 71 **% Residing in College-Owned, -Operated, or -Affiliated Housing:** 35 **Final Year or Final Semester Residency Requirement:** No **Library Holdings:** 75,000 **Regional Accreditation:** Middle State Association of Colleges and Schools **Credit Hours For Degree:** 120 credits, Bachelors **ROTC:** Army, Air Force **Intercollegiate Athletics:** Baseball M; Basketball M & W; Cross-Country Running M & W; Golf M & W; Soccer M & W; Softball W; Tennis M; Volleyball W

UNIVERSITY OF PITTSBURGH AT JOHNSTOWN
450 Schoolhouse Rd.
Johnstown, PA 15904-2990
Tel: (814)269-7000; Free: 800-765-4875
Admissions: (814)269-7050
Fax: (814)269-7044
E-mail: upjadmit@pitt.edu
Web Site: http://www.upj.pitt.edu/
President/CEO: Dr. Jem Spectar
Financial Aid: Jeanine M. Lawn
Type: Four-Year College **Sex:** Coed **Affiliation:** University of Pittsburgh System **Scores:** 93.92% SAT V 400+; 93.68% SAT M 400+; 60.5% ACT 18-23; 20.17% ACT 24-29 **% Accepted:** 85 **Admission Plans:** Early Admission; Deferred Admission **Application Deadline:** Rolling **Application Fee:** $45.00 **H.S. Requirements:** High school diploma required; GED accepted **Costs Per Year:** Application fee: $45. State resident tuition: $11,012 full-time, $458 per credit part-time. Nonresident tuition: $20,572 full-time, $857 per credit hour part-time. Mandatory fees: $742 full-time, $87 per term part-time. Full-time tuition and fees vary according to program. Part-time tuition and fees vary according to program. College room and board: $7290. College room only: $4570. Room and board charges vary according to board plan and housing facility. **Scholarships:** Available **Calendar System:** Semester, Summer Session Available **Enrollment:** FT 2,925, PT 132 **Student-Faculty Ratio:** 18:1 **Exams:** SAT I or ACT. ACT essay used for advising. SAT essay used for advising. **% Receiving Financial Aid:** 73 **% Residing in College-Owned, -Operated, or -Affiliated Housing:** 76 **Final Year or Final Semester Residency Requirement:** No **Library Holdings:** 145,547 **Regional Accreditation:** Middle State Association of Colleges and Schools **Credit Hours For Degree:** 65 credits, Associates; 120 credits, Bachelors **Professional Accreditation:** ABET, CARC **Intercollegiate Athletics:** Baseball M; Basketball M & W; Cheerleading W; Cross-Country Running W; Golf M & W; Soccer M & W; Track and Field W; Volleyball W; Wrestling M

UNIVERSITY OF PITTSBURGH AT TITUSVILLE
PO Box 287
Titusville, PA 16354
Tel: (814)827-4400; Free: 888-878-0462
Admissions: (814)827-4409
Fax: (814)827-4448
E-mail: uptadm@pitt.edu
Web Site: http://www.upt.pitt.edu/
President/CEO: Dr. William A. Shields

Admissions: John R. Mumford
Financial Aid: Sue A. Bloom
Type: Two-Year College **Sex:** Coed **Affiliation:** University of Pittsburgh System **Scores:** 76.02% SAT V 400+; 70.76% SAT M 400+; 48.28% ACT 18-23; 10.34% ACT 24-29 **Admission Plans:** Early Admission; Deferred Admission **Application Deadline:** Rolling **Application Fee:** $45.00 **H.S. Requirements:** High school diploma required; GED accepted **Costs Per Year:** Application fee: $45. State resident tuition: $9700 full-time, $404 per credit part-time. Nonresident tuition: $18,320 full-time, $763 per credit part-time. Mandatory fees: $800 full-time, $113 per term part-time. Full-time tuition and fees vary according to program. Part-time tuition and fees vary according to program. College room and board: $8156. Room and board charges vary according to board plan. **Scholarships:** Available **Calendar System:** Semester, Summer Session Available **Enrollment:** FT 466, PT 78 **Exams:** SAT I or ACT, SAT I. **% Residing in College-Owned, -Operated, or -Affiliated Housing:** 48 **Library Holdings:** 49,256 **Regional Accreditation:** Middle State Association of Colleges and Schools **Credit Hours For Degree:** 60 credits, Associates **Professional Accreditation:** APTA **Intercollegiate Athletics:** Basketball M & W

UNIVERSITY OF THE SCIENCES IN PHILADELPHIA
600 South 43rd St.
Philadelphia, PA 19104-4495
Tel: (215)596-8800
Admissions: (215)596-8815
Fax: (215)895-1100
E-mail: admit@usp.edu
Web Site: http://www.usip.edu/
President/CEO: Dr. Philip P. Gerbino
Admissions: Dianna Collins
Financial Aid: Paula Lehrberger
Type: University **Sex:** Coed **Scores:** 100% SAT V 400+; 100% SAT M 400+; 29% ACT 18-23; 65% ACT 24-29 **% Accepted:** 62 **Admission Plans:** Deferred Admission **Application Deadline:** Rolling **Application Fee:** $45.00 **H.S. Requirements:** High school diploma required; GED accepted **Costs Per Year:** Application fee: $45. Comprehensive fee: $41,212 includes full-time tuition ($28,190), mandatory fees ($1440), and college room and board ($11,582). College room only: $7076. Full-time tuition and fees vary according to degree level and program. Room and board charges vary according to board plan. Part-time tuition: $1175 per credit hour. Part-time mandatory fees: $45 per credit hour. Part-time tuition and fees vary according to course load and degree level. **Scholarships:** Available **Calendar System:** Semester, Summer Session Available **Enrollment:** FT 2,570, PT 50, Grad FT 134, Grad PT 230 **Faculty:** FT 166, PT 110 **Student-Faculty Ratio:** 14:1 **Exams:** SAT I or ACT, SAT I. ACT essay used for admission. SAT essay used for admission. ACT essay used for placement. SAT essay used for placement. **% Receiving Financial Aid:** 81 **% Residing in College-Owned, -Operated, or -Affiliated Housing:** 34 **Final Year or Final Semester Residency Requirement:** Yes **Library Holdings:** 87,125 **Regional Accreditation:** Middle State Association of Colleges and Schools **Credit Hours For Degree:** 120 credits, Bachelors **ROTC:** Army, Air Force **Professional Accreditation:** ACPhE, AOTA, APTA **Intercollegiate Athletics:** Baseball M; Basketball M & W; Cross-Country Running M & W; Golf M & W; Riflery M & W; Softball W; Tennis M & W; Volleyball W

THE UNIVERSITY OF SCRANTON
800 Linden St.
Scranton, PA 18510
Tel: (570)941-7400; Free: 888-SCRANTON
Admissions: (570)941-7540
Fax: (570)941-5928
E-mail: admissions@scranton.edu
Web Site: http://www.scranton.edu/
President/CEO: Rev. Scott R. Pilarz, SJ
Admissions: Joseph Roback
Financial Aid: William R. Burke
Type: Comprehensive **Sex:** Coed **Affiliation:** Roman Catholic (Jesuit) **Scores:** 100% SAT V 400+; 99.7% SAT M 400+ **% Accepted:** 70 **Admission Plans:** Early Admission; Early Action; Deferred Admission **Application Deadline:** March 1 **Application Fee:** $0.00 **H.S. Requirements:** High school diploma required; GED accepted **Costs Per Year:** Application fee: $0. Comprehensive fee: $46,398 includes full-time tuition ($34,236), mandatory fees ($300), and college room and board ($11,862). College room only: $7002. Room and board charges vary according to board plan and housing facility. Part-time tuition: $882 per credit hour. **Scholarships:** Available **Calendar System:** 4-1-4, Summer Session Available **Enrollment:** FT 3,952, PT 202, Grad FT 887, Grad PT 770 **Faculty:** FT 267, PT 235 **Student-Faculty Ratio:** 12:1 **Exams:** SAT I or ACT. ACT essay not being used. SAT essay not being used. **% Receiving Financial Aid:** 68 **% Residing in College-Owned, -Operated, or -Affiliated Housing:** 53 **Final Year or Final Semester Residency Requirement:** No **Library Holdings:** 389,832 **Regional Accreditation:** Middle State Association of Colleges and Schools **Credit Hours For Degree:** 60 credit hours, Associates; 130 credit hours, Bachelors **ROTC:** Army, Air Force **Professional Accreditation:** AACSB, ABET, AACN, AANA, ACA, AOTA, APTA, ACEHSA, CORE, NCATE **Intercollegiate Athletics:** Baseball M; Basketball M & W; Bowling M & W; Crew M & W; Cross-Country Running M & W; Equestrian Sports M & W; Field Hockey W; Golf M; Ice Hockey M; Lacrosse M & W; Rugby M & W; Skiing (Downhill) M & W; Soccer M & W; Softball W; Swimming and Diving M & W; Tennis M & W; Track and Field M & W; Volleyball M & W; Wrestling M

URSINUS COLLEGE
Box 1000, Main St.
Collegeville, PA 19426-1000
Tel: (610)409-3000
Admissions: (610)409-3200
Fax: (610)489-0627
E-mail: admissions@ursinus.edu
Web Site: http://www.ursinus.edu/
President/CEO: Dr. John Strassburger
Admissions: Richard Floyd
Financial Aid: Suzanne B. Sparrow
Type: Four-Year College **Sex:** Coed **Scores:** 100% SAT V 400+; 100% SAT M 400+; 19% ACT 18-23; 61% ACT 24-29 **% Accepted:** 57 **Admission Plans:** Early Admission; Early Action; Early Decision Plan; Deferred Admission **Application Deadline:** February 15 **Application Fee:** $0.00 **H.S. Requirements:** High school diploma required; GED accepted **Costs Per Year:** Application fee: $0. Comprehensive fee: $49,870 includes full-time tuition ($39,950), mandatory fees ($170), and college room and board ($9750). College room only: $4875. Part-time tuition: $1249 per credit hour. Part-time mandatory fees: $170 per year. **Scholarships:** Available **Calendar System:** Semester, Summer Session Not available **Enrollment:** FT 1,718, PT 24 **Faculty:** FT 125, PT 69 **Student-Faculty Ratio:** 12:1 **Exams:** SAT I or ACT. ACT essay not being used. SAT essay not being used. **% Receiving Financial Aid:** 70 **% Residing in College-Owned, -Operated, or -Affiliated Housing:** 95 **Final Year or Final Semester Residency Requirement:** No **Library Holdings:** 420,000 **Regional Accreditation:** Middle State Association of Colleges and Schools **Credit Hours For Degree:** 128 semester hours, Bachelors **Intercollegiate Athletics:** Baseball M; Basketball M & W; Cross-Country Running M & W; Field Hockey W; Football M; Golf M & W; Gymnastics W; Lacrosse M & W; Rugby M & W; Soccer M & W; Softball W; Swimming and Diving M & W; Tennis M & W; Track and Field M & W; Volleyball W; Wrestling M

VALLEY FORGE CHRISTIAN COLLEGE
1401 Charlestown Rd.
Phoenixville, PA 19460
Tel: (610)935-0450; Free: 800-432-8322
E-mail: admissions@vfcc.edu
Web Site: http://www.vfcc.edu/
President/CEO: Don Meyer, PhD
Admissions: Rev. William Chenco
Financial Aid: Linda Stein
Type: Comprehensive **Sex:** Coed **Affiliation:** Assemblies of God **Scores:** 100% SAT V 400+; 74.7% SAT M 400+; 43.8% ACT 18-23; 25% ACT 24-29 **% Accepted:** 73 **Admission Plans:** Open Admission; Early Admission; Deferred Admission **Application Deadline:** August 1 **Application Fee:** $25.00 **H.S. Requirements:** High school diploma required; GED accepted **Costs Per Year:** Application fee: $25. One-time mandatory fee: $75. Comprehensive fee: $23,806 includes full-time tuition ($14,600), mandatory fees ($1650), and college room and board ($7556). College room only: $3860. Part-time tuition: $564 per credit. Part-time mandatory fees: $250 per term. **Scholarships:** Available **Calendar System:** Semester, Summer Session Available **Enrollment:** FT 834, PT 316, Grad FT 1, Grad PT 14 **Faculty:** FT 31, PT 46 **Student-Faculty Ratio:** 19:1 **Exams:** SAT I or ACT. ACT essay used for placement. SAT essay used for placement. **% Receiving Financial Aid:** 73 **% Residing in College-Owned, -Operated, or -Affiliated Housing:** 84 **Final Year or Final Semester Residency Require-

ment: No **Library Holdings:** 74,386 **Regional Accreditation:** Middle State Association of Colleges and Schools **Credit Hours For Degree:** 60 credit hours, Associates; 126 credit hours, Bachelors **Intercollegiate Athletics:** Baseball M; Basketball M & W; Cross-Country Running M; Soccer M & W; Volleyball W

VALLEY FORGE MILITARY COLLEGE
1001 Eagle Rd.
Wayne, PA 19087-3695
Tel: (610)989-1200; Free: 800-234-8362
Admissions: (610)989-1203
Fax: (610)688-1545
E-mail: admissions@vfmac.edu
Web Site: http://www.vfmac.edu/
President/CEO: Tony McGeorge
Admissions: Maj. Greg Potts
Type: Two-Year College **Sex:** Coed **Scores:** 82% SAT V 400+ **% Accepted:** 89 **Admission Plans:** Early Admission; Deferred Admission **Application Deadline:** August 2 **Application Fee:** $25.00 **H.S. Requirements:** High school diploma required; GED accepted **Costs Per Year:** Application fee: $25. Comprehensive fee: $37,055. **Scholarships:** Available **Calendar System:** 4-1-4, Summer Session Not available **Faculty:** FT 16, PT 10 **Student-Faculty Ratio:** 10:1 **Exams:** SAT I or ACT. **% Residing in College-Owned, -Operated, or -Affiliated Housing:** 100 **Library Holdings:** 75,830 **Regional Accreditation:** Middle State Association of Colleges and Schools **Credit Hours For Degree:** 60 credits, Associates **ROTC:** Army, Air Force **Intercollegiate Athletics:** Basketball M; Cross-Country Running M; Equestrian Sports M; Football M; Golf M; Lacrosse M; Riflery M; Soccer M; Tennis M; Wrestling M

VET TECH INSTITUTE
125 7th St.
Pittsburgh, PA 15222-3400
Tel: (412)391-7021
Fax: (412)232-4348
Web Site: http://www.vettechinstitute.edu/
President/CEO: Jackie Flynn
Type: Two-Year College **Sex:** Coed **% Accepted:** 66 **H.S. Requirements:** High school diploma required; GED accepted **Scholarships:** Available **Calendar System:** Quarter, Summer Session Not available **Credit Hours For Degree:** 63 semester credits, Associates **Professional Accreditation:** ACCSCT, ADA

VILLANOVA UNIVERSITY
800 Lancaster Ave.
Villanova, PA 19085-1699
Tel: (610)519-4500
Admissions: (610)519-4000
Fax: (610)519-6450
E-mail: gotovu@villanova.edu
Web Site: http://www.villanova.edu/
President/CEO: Rev. Peter M. Donohue, OSA
Admissions: Michael Gaynor
Financial Aid: Bonnie Lee Behm
Type: Comprehensive **Sex:** Coed **Affiliation:** Roman Catholic **Scores:** 100% SAT V 400+; 100% SAT M 400+; 4% ACT 18-23; 39% ACT 24-29 **% Accepted:** 46 **Admission Plans:** Early Action; Deferred Admission **Application Deadline:** January 7 **Application Fee:** $75.00 **H.S. Requirements:** High school diploma required; GED accepted **Costs Per Year:** Application fee: $75. Comprehensive fee: $48,625 includes full-time tuition ($37,725), mandatory fees ($580), and college room and board ($10,320). College room only: $5460. Full-time tuition and fees vary according to class time, course level, program, and student level. Room and board charges vary according to board plan and housing facility. Part-time tuition: $1545 per course. Part-time tuition varies according to class time, course level, and program. **Scholarships:** Available **Calendar System:** Semester, Summer Session Available **Enrollment:** FT 6,604, PT 597, Grad FT 1,358, Grad PT 1,816 **Faculty:** FT 570, PT 339 **Student-Faculty Ratio:** 11:1 **Exams:** SAT I or ACT. **% Receiving Financial Aid:** 48 **% Residing in College-Owned, -Operated, or -Affiliated Housing:** 70 **Final Year or Final Semester Residency Requirement:** Yes **Library Holdings:** 730,000 **Regional Accreditation:** Middle State Association of Colleges and Schools **Credit Hours For Degree:** 60 credit hours, Associates; 122 credit hours, Bachelors **ROTC:** Army, Navy, Air Force **Professional Accreditation:** AACSB, ABET, AACN, AANA, ABA, AALS, NLN **Intercollegiate Athletics:** Baseball M; Basketball M & W; Cheerleading M & W; Crew M & W; Cross-Country Running M & W; Equestrian Sports W; Field Hockey W; Football M; Golf M; Ice Hockey M & W; Lacrosse M & W; Sailing M & W; Skiing (Downhill) M & W; Soccer M & W; Softball W; Swimming and Diving M & W; Tennis M & W; Track and Field M & W; Volleyball M & W; Water Polo M & W

WASHINGTON & JEFFERSON COLLEGE
60 South Lincoln St.
Washington, PA 15301
Tel: (724)222-4400; Free: 888-WANDJAY
Admissions: (724)223-6025
Fax: (724)223-5271
E-mail: admission@washjeff.edu
Web Site: http://www.washjeff.edu/
President/CEO: Dr. Tori Haring-Smith
Admissions: Alton E. Newell
Financial Aid: Michelle Anderson
Type: Four-Year College **Sex:** Coed **Scores:** 100% SAT V 400+; 100% SAT M 400+; 37% ACT 18-23; 50% ACT 24-29 **% Accepted:** 42 **Admission Plans:** Early Admission; Early Action; Early Decision Plan; Deferred Admission **Application Deadline:** March 1 **Application Fee:** $25.00 **H.S. Requirements:** High school diploma required; GED accepted **Costs Per Year:** Application fee: $25. Comprehensive fee: $41,820 includes full-time tuition ($32,495), mandatory fees ($400), and college room and board ($8925). College room only: $5256. Room and board charges vary according to board plan and housing facility. Part-time tuition: $815 per credit hour. Part-time tuition varies according to course load. **Scholarships:** Available **Calendar System:** 4-1-4, Summer Session Available **Enrollment:** FT 1,496, PT 18 **Faculty:** FT 116, PT 43 **Student-Faculty Ratio:** 12:1 **Exams:** ACT essay not being used. SAT essay not being used. **% Receiving Financial Aid:** 77 **% Residing in College-Owned, -Operated, or -Affiliated Housing:** 92 **Final Year or Final Semester Residency Requirement:** No **Library Holdings:** 163,148 **Regional Accreditation:** Middle State Association of Colleges and Schools **Credit Hours For Degree:** 34 courses, Bachelors **ROTC:** Army, Air Force **Intercollegiate Athletics:** Baseball M; Basketball M & W; Cheerleading M & W; Cross-Country Running M & W; Field Hockey W; Football M; Golf M & W; Lacrosse M & W; Soccer M & W; Softball W; Swimming and Diving M & W; Tennis M & W; Track and Field M & W; Volleyball W; Water Polo M & W; Wrestling M

WAYNESBURG UNIVERSITY
51 West College St.
Waynesburg, PA 15370-1222
Tel: (724)627-8191; Free: 800-225-7393
Admissions: (724)852-3333
Fax: (724)627-8124
E-mail: admissions@waynesburg.edu
Web Site: http://www.waynesburg.edu/
President/CEO: Timothy R. Thyreen
Admissions: Robin L. King
Financial Aid: Matthew C. Stokan
Type: Comprehensive **Sex:** Coed **Affiliation:** Presbyterian Church (U.S.A.) **% Accepted:** 71 **Admission Plans:** Early Admission **Application Deadline:** Rolling **Application Fee:** $20.00 **H.S. Requirements:** High school diploma required; GED accepted **Costs Per Year:** Application fee: $20. Comprehensive fee: $25,130 includes full-time tuition ($17,400), mandatory fees ($360), and college room and board ($7370). College room only: $3750. Full-time tuition and fees vary according to class time. Room and board charges vary according to board plan. Part-time tuition: $730 per credit hour. Part-time tuition varies according to class time, course load, and location. **Scholarships:** Available **Calendar System:** Semester, Summer Session Not available **Enrollment:** FT 1,547, PT 165, Grad FT 102, Grad PT 701 **Faculty:** FT 72, PT 154 **Student-Faculty Ratio:** 15:1 **Exams:** SAT I or ACT. ACT essay used for placement. SAT essay used for placement. **% Receiving Financial Aid:** 71 **% Residing in College-Owned, -Operated, or -Affiliated Housing:** 44 **Final Year or Final Semester Residency Requirement:** No **Library Holdings:** 100,000 **Regional Accreditation:** Middle State Association of Colleges and Schools **Credit Hours For Degree:** 60 credit hours, Associates; 124 credit hours, Bachelors **ROTC:** Army **Professional Accreditation:** AACN, JRCEPAT, NLN **Intercollegiate Athletics:** Baseball M; Basketball M & W; Cross-Country Running M & W; Football M; Golf M & W; Lacrosse W; Soccer M & W; Softball W; Tennis M & W; Track and Field M & W; Volleyball W; Wrestling M

WEST CHESTER UNIVERSITY OF PENNSYLVANIA
University Ave. and High St.
West Chester, PA 19383
Tel: (610)436-1000
Admissions: (610)436-3414
E-mail: ugadmiss@wcupa.edu
Web Site: http://www.wcupa.edu/
President/CEO: Dr. Greg R. Weisenstein
Admissions: Marsha Haug
Financial Aid: Dana Parker
Type: Comprehensive **Sex:** Coed **Affiliation:** Pennsylvania State System of Higher Education **Scores:** 96.9% SAT V 400+; 97.1% SAT M 400+ **% Accepted:** 49 **Admission Plans:** Early Admission; Deferred Admission **Application Deadline:** Rolling **Application Fee:** $35.00 **H.S. Requirements:** High school diploma required; GED accepted **Costs Per Year:** Application fee: $35. State resident tuition: $5554 full-time, $231 per credit part-time. Nonresident tuition: $13,886 full-time, $579 per credit part-time. Mandatory fees: $1657 full-time, $60.18 per credit part-time. Full-time tuition and fees vary according to course load. Part-time tuition and fees vary according to course load. College room and board: $7032. College room only: $4692. Room and board charges vary according to board plan and housing facility. **Scholarships:** Available **Calendar System:** Semester, Summer Session Available **Enrollment:** FT 10,844, PT 1,076, Grad FT 717, Grad PT 1,574 **Faculty:** FT 560, PT 265 **Student-Faculty Ratio:** 17:1 **Exams:** SAT I or ACT. SAT essay used for placement. **% Receiving Financial Aid:** 46 **% Residing in College-Owned, -Operated, or -Affiliated Housing:** 38 **Final Year or Final Semester Residency Requirement:** No **Library Holdings:** 1,337,040 **Regional Accreditation:** Middle State Association of Colleges and Schools **Credit Hours For Degree:** 120 credits, Bachelors **ROTC:** Army, Air Force **Professional Accreditation:** AACSB, AACN, ACA, ASLHA, CARC, CEPH, CSWE, JRCEPAT, NASM, NCATE, NLN **Intercollegiate Athletics:** Baseball M; Basketball M & W; Bowling M & W; Cheerleading W; Cross-Country Running M & W; Equestrian Sports M & W; Fencing M & W; Field Hockey W; Football M; Golf M & W; Gymnastics W; Ice Hockey M & W; Lacrosse M & W; Rugby M & W; Skiing (Downhill) M & W; Soccer M & W; Softball W; Swimming and Diving M & W; Tennis M & W; Track and Field M & W; Volleyball M & W; Water Polo W

WESTMINSTER COLLEGE
319 South Market St.
New Wilmington, PA 16172-0001
Tel: (724)946-8761
Fax: (724)946-7171
E-mail: tokarbp@westminster.edu
Web Site: http://www.westminster.edu/
President/CEO: Richard H. Dorman
Admissions: Bradley Tokar
Financial Aid: Cheryl A. Gerber
Type: Comprehensive **Sex:** Coed **Affiliation:** Presbyterian Church (U.S.A.) **Scores:** 96% SAT V 400+; 99% SAT M 400+; 57% ACT 18-23; 32% ACT 24-29 **% Accepted:** 77 **Admission Plans:** Deferred Admission **Application Deadline:** May 1 **Application Fee:** $35.00 **H.S. Requirements:** High school diploma required; GED accepted **Costs Per Year:** Application fee: $35. Comprehensive fee: $37,990 includes full-time tuition ($28,020), mandatory fees ($1130), and college room and board ($8840). College room only: $4770. **Scholarships:** Available **Calendar System:** Semester, Summer Session Available **Enrollment:** FT 1,410, PT 54 **Faculty:** FT 100, PT 49 **Student-Faculty Ratio:** 12:1 **Exams:** SAT I or ACT. **% Receiving Financial Aid:** 83 **Library Holdings:** 283,070 **Regional Accreditation:** Middle State Association of Colleges and Schools **ROTC:** Army **Professional Accreditation:** NASM **Intercollegiate Athletics:** Baseball M; Basketball M & W; Cross-Country Running M & W; Equestrian Sports M & W; Football M; Golf M & W; Soccer M & W; Softball W; Swimming and Diving M & W; Tennis M & W; Track and Field M & W; Volleyball W

WESTMORELAND COUNTY COMMUNITY COLLEGE
145 Pavilion Ln.
Youngwood, PA 15697
Tel: (724)925-4000
Admissions: (724)925-4064
Fax: (724)925-1150
E-mail: admission@wccc.edu
Web Site: http://www.wccc.edu/
President/CEO: Dr. Daniel J. Obara
Admissions: Andrew Colosimo
Type: Two-Year College **Sex:** Coed **% Accepted:** 100 **Admission Plans:** Open Admission; Early Admission **Application Deadline:** Rolling **Application Fee:** $10.00 **H.S. Requirements:** High school diploma or equivalent not required **Scholarships:** Available **Calendar System:** Semester, Summer Session Available **Enrollment:** FT 3,608, PT 3,481 **Faculty:** FT 89, PT 465 **Student-Faculty Ratio:** 19:1 **Library Holdings:** 64,000 **Regional Accreditation:** Middle State Association of Colleges and Schools **Credit Hours For Degree:** 60 credits, Associates **Professional Accreditation:** ACF, ADA **Intercollegiate Athletics:** Baseball M; Basketball M & W; Bowling M & W; Cross-Country Running M & W; Golf M & W; Softball W; Volleyball W

WIDENER UNIVERSITY
One University Place
Chester, PA 19013-5792
Tel: (610)499-4000; Free: 888-WIDENER
Admissions: (610)499-4126
Fax: (610)499-4676
E-mail: admissions.office@widener.edu
Web Site: http://www.widener.edu/
President/CEO: Dr. James T. Harris, III
Financial Aid: Thomas K. Malloy
Type: Comprehensive **Sex:** Coed **Scores:** 95% SAT V 400+; 96% SAT M 400+ **% Accepted:** 70 **Admission Plans:** Deferred Admission **Application Deadline:** Rolling **Application Fee:** $35.00 **H.S. Requirements:** High school diploma required; GED accepted **Costs Per Year:** Application fee: $35. Comprehensive fee: $43,110 includes full-time tuition ($31,340), mandatory fees ($500), and college room and board ($11,270). College room only: $5820. Full-time tuition and fees vary according to class time, course load, and program. Room and board charges vary according to board plan and housing facility. Part-time tuition: $1045 per credit hour. **Scholarships:** Available **Calendar System:** Semester, Summer Session Available **Enrollment:** FT 2,717, PT 695, Grad FT 2,102, Grad PT 1,035 **Faculty:** FT 310, PT 356 **Student-Faculty Ratio:** 12:1 **Exams:** SAT I or ACT. **% Receiving Financial Aid:** 80 **% Residing in College-Owned, -Operated, or -Affiliated Housing:** 47 **Final Year or Final Semester Residency Requirement:** Yes **Library Holdings:** 218,284 **Regional Accreditation:** Middle State Association of Colleges and Schools **Credit Hours For Degree:** 120 credits, Bachelors **ROTC:** Army, Navy, Air Force **Professional Accreditation:** AACSB, ABET, AACN, ABA, APTA, APA, AALS, ACEHSA, CSWE, NLN **Intercollegiate Athletics:** Baseball M; Basketball M & W; Cheerleading W; Cross-Country Running M & W; Field Hockey W; Football M; Golf M; Lacrosse M & W; Soccer M & W; Softball W; Swimming and Diving M & W; Tennis M & W; Track and Field M & W; Volleyball W

WILKES UNIVERSITY
84 West South St.
Wilkes-Barre, PA 18766-0002
Tel: (570)408-5000; Free: 800-945-5378
Admissions: (570)408-4400
Fax: (570)408-7820
E-mail: admissions@wilkes.edu
Web Site: http://www.wilkes.edu/
President/CEO: Dr. Joseph Gilmour
Admissions: Melanie Mickelson
Financial Aid: Melanie Mickelson
Type: Comprehensive **Sex:** Coed **Scores:** 94% SAT V 400+; 95% SAT M 400+ **% Accepted:** 76 **Admission Plans:** Early Admission; Deferred Admission **Application Deadline:** Rolling **Application Fee:** $40.00 **H.S. Requirements:** High school diploma required; GED accepted **Costs Per Year:** Application fee: $40. Comprehensive fee: $37,110 includes full-time tuition ($24,690), mandatory fees ($1320), and college room and board ($11,100). College room only: $6680. Room and board charges vary according to board plan and housing facility. Part-time tuition: $685 per credit hour. Part-time mandatory fees: $60 per credit hour. **Scholarships:** Available **Calendar System:** Semester, Summer Session Available **Enrollment:** FT 2,011, PT 229, Grad FT 582, Grad PT 3,417 **Faculty:** FT 149, PT 305 **Student-Faculty Ratio:** 15:1 **Exams:** SAT I or ACT. **% Receiving Financial Aid:** 83 **% Residing in College-Owned, -Operated, or -Affiliated Housing:** 40 **Regional Accreditation:** Middle State Association of Colleges and Schools **Credit Hours For Degree:** 120 credits, Bachelors **ROTC:** Army, Air Force **Professional Accreditation:** ABET, ACPhE, AACN, ACBSP **Intercollegiate Athletics:** Baseball M; Basketball M & W; Cross-Country Running M & W;

Field Hockey W; Football M; Golf M; Lacrosse W; Soccer M & W; Softball W; Tennis M & W; Volleyball W; Wrestling M

THE WILLIAMSON FREE SCHOOL OF MECHANICAL TRADES
106 South New Middletown Rd.
Media, PA 19063
Tel: (610)566-1776
Fax: (610)566-6502
E-mail: jmerillat@williamson.edu
Web Site: http://www.williamson.edu/
Admissions: Jay Merillat
Type: Two-Year College **Sex:** Men **% Accepted:** 23 **Admission Plans:** Preferred Admission **Application Deadline:** February 15 **H.S. Requirements:** High school diploma required; GED accepted **Costs Per Year:** Tuition: $0 full-time. Mandatory fees: $650 full-time. All Williamson students attend on full scholarships covering tuition, room, board, and textbooks. **Scholarships:** Available **Calendar System:** Semester **Enrollment:** FT 251 **Faculty:** FT 29 **Student-Faculty Ratio:** 12:1 **Exams:** Other. **% Residing in College-Owned, -Operated, or -Affiliated Housing:** 100 **Library Holdings:** 1,600 **Credit Hours For Degree:** 148 credit hours, Associates **Professional Accreditation:** ACCSCT **Intercollegiate Athletics:** Baseball M; Basketball M; Cross-Country Running M; Football M; Lacrosse M; Soccer M; Wrestling M

WILSON COLLEGE
1015 Philadelphia Ave.
Chambersburg, PA 17201-1285
Tel: (717)264-4141; Free: 800-421-8402
Admissions: (717)262-2002
Fax: (717)264-1578
E-mail: admissions@wilson.edu
Web Site: http://www.wilson.edu/
President/CEO: Dr. Lorna D. Edmundson
Admissions: Deborah Arthur
Financial Aid: Linda Brittain
Type: Comprehensive **Sex:** Coed **Affiliation:** Presbyterian Church (U.S.A.) **Scores:** 91% SAT V 400+; 84% SAT M 400+; 45% ACT 18-23; 20% ACT 24-29 **% Accepted:** 70 **Admission Plans:** Early Admission; Deferred Admission **Application Deadline:** Rolling **Application Fee:** $35.00 **H.S. Requirements:** High school diploma required; GED accepted **Costs Per Year:** Application fee: $35. Comprehensive fee: $37,650 includes full-time tuition ($27,640), mandatory fees ($580), and college room and board ($9430). College room only: $4910. Room and board charges vary according to board plan. Part-time tuition: $2765 per course. Part-time mandatory fees: $45 per course, $50 per term. Part-time tuition and fees vary according to course load. **Scholarships:** Available **Calendar System:** 4-1-4, Summer Session Available **Enrollment:** FT 375, PT 432, Grad PT 31 **Faculty:** FT 45, PT 34 **Student-Faculty Ratio:** 10:1 **Exams:** Other, SAT I or ACT. **% Receiving Financial Aid:** 84 **% Residing in College-Owned, -Operated, or -Affiliated Housing:** 48 **Final Year or Final Semester Residency Requirement:** Yes **Library Holdings:** 180,000 **Regional Accreditation:** Middle State Association of Colleges and Schools **Credit Hours For Degree:** 18 course credits, Associates; 36 course credits, Bachelors **ROTC:** Army **Intercollegiate Athletics:** Basketball W; Field Hockey W; Gymnastics W; Lacrosse W; Soccer W; Softball W; Tennis W

WYOTECH
500 Innovation Dr.
Blairsville, PA 15717
Tel: (724)459-9500; Free: 800-822-8253
Admissions: (724)459-2311
Fax: (724)459-6499
E-mail: tsmyers@wyotech.edu
Web Site: http://www.wyotech.com/
President/CEO: Stephen Whitson
Admissions: Tim Smyers
Type: Two-Year College **Sex:** Coed **Application Fee:** $100.00 **Calendar System:** Miscellaneous **Professional Accreditation:** ACCSCT

YESHIVA BETH MOSHE
930 Hickory St., PO Box 1141
Scranton, PA 18505-2124
Tel: (717)346-1747
Admissions: (570)346-1747
President/CEO: Avraham Pressman
Type: Comprehensive **Sex:** Men **Affiliation:** Jewish **Admission Plans:** Open Admission **H.S. Requirements:** High school diploma required; GED not accepted **Calendar System:** Semester **Professional Accreditation:** AARTS

YORK COLLEGE OF PENNSYLVANIA
York, PA 17405-7199
Tel: (717)846-7788; Free: 800-455-8018
Admissions: (717)849-1600
E-mail: admissions@ycp.edu
Web Site: http://www.ycp.edu/
President/CEO: Dr. George W. Waldner
Admissions: Nancy L. Spataro
Financial Aid: Calvin Williams
Type: Comprehensive **Sex:** Coed **Scores:** 100.01% SAT V 400+; 99.41% SAT M 400+; 57.89% ACT 18-23; 35.26% ACT 24-29 **% Accepted:** 56 **Admission Plans:** Deferred Admission **Application Deadline:** August 15 **Application Fee:** $30.00 **H.S. Requirements:** High school diploma required; GED accepted **Costs Per Year:** Application fee: $30. Comprehensive fee: $23,670 includes full-time tuition ($13,640), mandatory fees ($1500), and college room and board ($8530). College room only: $4750. Room and board charges vary according to housing facility. Part-time tuition: $425 per credit hour. Part-time mandatory fees: $330 per term. **Scholarships:** Available **Calendar System:** Semester, Summer Session Available **Enrollment:** FT 4,596, PT 685, Grad FT 47, Grad PT 236 **Faculty:** FT 156, PT 400 **Student-Faculty Ratio:** 17:1 **Exams:** SAT I or ACT. ACT essay not being used. SAT essay not being used. **% Receiving Financial Aid:** 61 **% Residing in College-Owned, -Operated, or -Affiliated Housing:** 45 **Final Year or Final Semester Residency Requirement:** No **Library Holdings:** 159,273 **Regional Accreditation:** Middle State Association of Colleges and Schools **Credit Hours For Degree:** 62 credit hours, Associates; 124 credit hours, Bachelors **ROTC:** Army **Professional Accreditation:** ABET, AACN, AANA, ACBSP, CARC, NLN, NRPA **Intercollegiate Athletics:** Baseball M; Basketball M & W; Cheerleading W; Cross-Country Running M & W; Field Hockey W; Golf M; Lacrosse M & W; Soccer M & W; Softball W; Swimming and Diving M & W; Tennis M & W; Track and Field M & W; Volleyball M & W; Wrestling M

YORKTOWNE BUSINESS INSTITUTE
West Seventh Ave.
York, PA 17404
Tel: (717)846-5000; Free: 800-840-1004
Fax: (717)848-4584
Web Site: http://www.ybi.edu/
President/CEO: James P. Murphy
Financial Aid: Daneen Collier
Type: Two-Year College **Sex:** Coed **Application Deadline:** Rolling **H.S. Requirements:** High school diploma required; GED accepted **Scholarships:** Available **Calendar System:** Semester **Student-Faculty Ratio:** 16:1 **Credit Hours For Degree:** 75 credit hours, Associates **Professional Accreditation:** ACICS

YTI CAREER INSTITUTE—YORK
1405 Williams Rd.
York, PA 17402-9017
Tel: (717)757-1100; Free: 800-227-9675
Fax: (717)757-4964
Web Site: http://www.yti.edu/
President/CEO: Harold Maley
Type: Two-Year College **Sex:** Coed **Admission Plans:** Open Admission **Application Fee:** $50.00 **H.S. Requirements:** High school diploma required; GED accepted **Scholarships:** Available **Calendar System:** Continuous **Enrollment:** FT 902 **Faculty:** FT 87 **Student-Faculty Ratio:** 25:1 **Exams:** Other. **Professional Accreditation:** ACCSCT

AMERICAN UNIVERSITY OF PUERTO RICO
PO Box 2037
Bayamón, PR 00960-2037
Tel: (787)620-2040
Fax: (787)785-7377
Web Site: http://www.aupr.edu/
President/CEO: Juan B. Nazario-Negron
Admissions: Margarita Cruz Santiago
Financial Aid: Yahaira Melendez
Type: Comprehensive **Sex:** Coed **Admission Plans:** Open Admission; Deferred Admission **Application Fee:** $25.00 **H.S. Requirements:** High school diploma required; GED accepted **Scholarships:** Available **Calendar System:** Semester, Summer Session Available **Faculty:** FT 101, PT 120 **Exams:** SAT I and SAT II or ACT, SAT I, SAT II. **% Receiving Financial Aid:** 99 **Library Holdings:** 100,000 **Regional Accreditation:** Middle State Association of Colleges and Schools **Credit Hours For Degree:** 60 credits, Associates; 133 credits, Bachelors **ROTC:** Army **Intercollegiate Athletics:** Basketball M & W; Swimming and Diving M & W; Track and Field M & W; Volleyball M & W; Weight Lifting M

ATLANTIC COLLEGE
PO Box 3918
Guaynabo, PR 00970
Tel: (787)720-1022
Fax: (787)720-1092
E-mail: admisiones@atlanticcollege.edu
Web Site: http://www.atlanticcollege.edu/
President/CEO: Teresa de Dios-Unanue
Admissions: Zaida Perez
Financial Aid: Velma Aponte
Type: Comprehensive **Sex:** Coed **Admission Plans:** Open Admission **Application Fee:** $30.00 **H.S. Requirements:** High school diploma required; GED accepted **Scholarships:** Available **Calendar System:** Semester, Summer Session Not available **% Receiving Financial Aid:** 86 **Library Holdings:** 8,663 **Credit Hours For Degree:** 78 credits, Associates; 138 credits, Bachelors **Professional Accreditation:** ACICS

BAYAMON CENTRAL UNIVERSITY
PO Box 1725
Bayamón, PR 00960-1725
Tel: (787)786-3030
Web Site: http://www.ucb.edu.pr/
President/CEO: Prof. Nilda Nadal Carreras
Admissions: Sra. Christine M. Hernandez
Type: Comprehensive **Sex:** Coed **Affiliation:** Roman Catholic **% Accepted:** 20 **Application Fee:** $15.00 **H.S. Requirements:** High school diploma required; GED accepted **Scholarships:** Available **Calendar System:** Semester, Summer Session Available **Exams:** Other. **Library Holdings:** 51,011 **Regional Accreditation:** Middle State Association of Colleges and Schools **Credit Hours For Degree:** 72 credits, Associates; 131 credits, Bachelors **ROTC:** Army, Air Force **Intercollegiate Athletics:** Basketball M; Bowling M & W; Cross-Country Running M & W; Swimming and Diving M & W; Track and Field M & W; Volleyball M & W; Weight Lifting M & W

CARIBBEAN UNIVERSITY
Box 493
Bayamón, PR 00960-0493
Tel: (787)780-0070
Fax: (787)785-0101
Web Site: http://www.caribbean.edu/
President/CEO: Dr. Ana E. Cucurella-Adorno
Admissions: Hector Gracia
Type: Comprehensive **Sex:** Coed **Admission Plans:** Open Admission; Deferred Admission **Application Deadline:** Rolling **Application Fee:** $25.00 **H.S. Requirements:** High school diploma required; GED accepted **Scholarships:** Available **Calendar System:** Trimester, Summer Session Available **Library Holdings:** 17,632 **Regional Accreditation:** Middle State Association of Colleges and Schools **Credit Hours For Degree:** 79 credit hours, Associates; 140 credit hours, Bachelors **ROTC:** Army **Intercollegiate Athletics:** Basketball M & W; Cross-Country Running M & W; Table Tennis M & W; Track and Field M & W; Volleyball M & W; Weight Lifting M & W

CARLOS ALBIZU UNIVERSITY
151 Tanca St.
San Juan, PR 00901
Tel: (787)725-6500
Fax: (787)721-7187
E-mail: crodriguez@albizu.edu
Web Site: http://www.albizu.edu/
President/CEO: Dr. Ileana Rodriguez
Admissions: Carlos Rodriguez
Financial Aid: Doris J. Quero
Type: University **Sex:** Coed **% Accepted:** 88 **Admission Plans:** Early Admission; Deferred Admission **Application Deadline:** July 16 **Application Fee:** $75.00 **H.S. Requirements:** High school diploma required; GED accepted **Costs Per Year:** Application fee: $75. Tuition: $5760 full-time, $160 per credit part-time. Mandatory fees: $979 full-time, $323 per term part-time. **Scholarships:** Available **Calendar System:** Semester, Summer Session Not available **Enrollment:** FT 96, PT 71, Grad FT 584, Grad PT 143 **Faculty:** FT 23, PT 5 **Student-Faculty Ratio:** 33:1 **Exams:** Other. **% Receiving Financial Aid:** 84 **Final Year or Final Semester Residency Requirement:** No **Library Holdings:** 17,048 **Regional Accreditation:** Middle State Association of Colleges and Schools **Credit Hours For Degree:** 126 credits, Bachelors **Professional Accreditation:** APA

CENTRO DE ESTUDIOS MULTIDISCIPLINARIOS
Calle 13 No. 1206
Ext. San Agustin
Rio Piedras, PR 00926
Tel: (787)765-4210
Web Site: http://www.cempr.edu/
President/CEO: Laura Delgado
Type: Two-Year College **Sex:** Coed **% Accepted:** 84 **Application Fee:** $30.00 **Professional Accreditation:** ACCSCT

COLEGIO PENTECOSTAL MIZPA
Bo Caimito Rd. 199
Apartado 20966
Río Piedras, PR 00928-0966

Tel: (787)720-4476
Fax: (787)720-2012
President/CEO: Daniel Cruz
Type: Four-Year College **Sex:** Coed **Affiliation:** Pentecostal Church **Admission Plans:** Open Admission **Application Fee:** $40.00 **Calendar System:** Semester **Professional Accreditation:** ABHE

COLEGIO UNIVERSITARIO DE SAN JUAN
180 Jose R Oliver St.
Tres Monjitas Industrial Park
San Juan, PR 00918
Tel: (787)250-7111
Fax: (787)250-7395
Web Site: http://www.cunisanjuan.edu/
President/CEO: Deborah Drahus-Capo
Admissions: Nilsa E. Rivera-Almenas
Type: Two-Year College **Sex:** Coed **% Accepted:** 83 **Application Fee:** $15.00 **H.S. Requirements:** High school diploma required; GED accepted **Scholarships:** Available **Calendar System:** Semester, Summer Session Available **Exams:** SAT I. **Library Holdings:** 14,298 **Regional Accreditation:** Middle State Association of Colleges and Schools **Credit Hours For Degree:** 69 credits, Associates **Professional Accreditation:** NLN

COLUMBIA COLLEGE (CAGUAS)
PO Box 8517
Caguas, PR 00726
Tel: (787)743-4041
Fax: (787)744-7931
E-mail: xsanchez@columbianco.edu
Web Site: http://www.columbiaco.edu/
President/CEO: Michelle Velez
Admissions: Xiomara Sanchez
Type: Comprehensive **Sex:** Coed **Application Deadline:** Rolling **Application Fee:** $50.00 **H.S. Requirements:** High school diploma required; GED accepted **Costs Per Year:** Application fee: $50. Tuition: $9000 full-time. Mandatory fees: $100 full-time, $100 per credit part-time. Full-time tuition and fees vary according to program. Part-time fees vary according to program. **Scholarships:** Available **Calendar System:** Semester, Summer Session Not available **Enrollment:** FT 699, PT 559, Grad FT 58, Grad PT 28 **Faculty:** FT 14, PT 79 **Student-Faculty Ratio:** 21:1 **% Receiving Financial Aid:** 84 **Final Year or Final Semester Residency Requirement:** No **Regional Accreditation:** Middle State Association of Colleges and Schools **Credit Hours For Degree:** 71 credits, Associates; 120 credits, Bachelors **Professional Accreditation:** ACICS

COLUMBIA COLLEGE (YAUCO)
Box 3062
Yauco, PR 00698
Tel: (787)856-0945
Admissions: (787)856-0845
Fax: (787)267-2335
E-mail: rpadilla@columbiaco.edu
Web Site: http://www.columbiaco.edu/
President/CEO: Alex De Jorge
Admissions: Rosario Padilla
Type: Four-Year College **Sex:** Coed **% Accepted:** 79 **Admission Plans:** Open Admission **Application Deadline:** Rolling **Application Fee:** $50.00 **H.S. Requirements:** High school diploma required; GED accepted **Calendar System:** Trimester **Enrollment:** FT 311, PT 255 **Faculty:** FT 12, PT 49 **Student-Faculty Ratio:** 9:1 **Library Holdings:** 3,111 **Professional Accreditation:** ACICS

CONSERVATORY OF MUSIC OF PUERTO RICO
350 Rafael Lamar St at FDR Ave
San Juan, PR 00918
Tel: (787)751-0160
E-mail: admisiones@cmpr.edu
Web Site: http://www.cmpr.edu/
President/CEO: Maria Del Carmen Gil
Admissions: Eutimia Santiago
Financial Aid: Jorge Medina
Type: Comprehensive **Sex:** Coed **Admission Plans:** Early Admission **Application Deadline:** March 6 **Application Fee:** $35.00 **H.S. Requirements:** High school diploma required; GED accepted **Scholarships:** Available **Calendar System:** Semester, Summer Session Available **Exams:** SAT I, SAT II. **% Receiving Financial Aid:** 53 **Library Holdings:** 24,865 **Regional Accreditation:** Middle State Association of Colleges and Schools **Credit Hours For Degree:** 142 credits, Bachelors **ROTC:** Army

EDP COLLEGE OF PUERTO RICO, INC.
560 Ave. Ponce de Leon
Hato Rey, PR 00918
Tel: (787)765-3560
E-mail: landino@edpcollege.edu
Web Site: http://www.edpcollege.edu/
President/CEO: Galdys Nieves Vazquez
Admissions: Leila M. Andino
Financial Aid: Marie Luz Pastrana Muriel
Type: Comprehensive **Sex:** Coed **% Accepted:** 86 **Admission Plans:** Deferred Admission **Application Deadline:** Rolling **Application Fee:** $15.00 **H.S. Requirements:** High school diploma required; GED accepted **Costs Per Year:** Application fee: $15. Tuition: $5400 full-time, $156 per credit part-time. Mandatory fees: $720 full-time, $156 per credit part-time, $360 per term part-time. Full-time tuition and fees vary according to course load and program. Part-time tuition and fees vary according to course load and program. **Scholarships:** Available **Calendar System:** Semester, Summer Session Available **Enrollment:** FT 614, PT 315, Grad FT 58, Grad PT 26 **Faculty:** FT 14, PT 70 **Student-Faculty Ratio:** 19:1 **Exams:** Other. **% Receiving Financial Aid:** 85 **Library Holdings:** 11,955 **Regional Accreditation:** Middle State Association of Colleges and Schools **Credit Hours For Degree:** 74 credits, Associates; 132 credits, Bachelors **ROTC:** Army, Air Force **Professional Accreditation:** ACICS

EDP COLLEGE OF PUERTO RICO—SAN SEBASTIAN
Ave. Betances No. 49
San Sebastian, PR 00685
Tel: (787)896-2137
Admissions: (787)896-2252
Fax: (787)896-0066
E-mail: zolavarria@edpcollege.edu
Web Site: http://www.edpcollege.edu/
President/CEO: Prof. Mayra Rivera de la Cruz
Admissions: Zenaida Olavarria Rodriguez
Type: Four-Year College **Sex:** Coed **Application Deadline:** Rolling **Application Fee:** $15.00 **H.S. Requirements:** High school diploma required; GED accepted **Costs Per Year:** Application fee: $15. Tuition: $5400 full-time, $156 per credit hour part-time. Mandatory fees: $720 full-time, $156 per credit hour part-time, $360 per term part-time. Full-time tuition and fees vary according to course load and program. Part-time tuition and fees vary according to course load and program. **Calendar System:** Semester **Faculty:** FT 19, PT 44 **Exams:** Other. **Library Holdings:** 11,031 **Professional Accreditation:** ACICS

ESCUELA DE ARTES PLASTICAS DE PUERTO RICO
PO Box 9021112
San Juan, PR 00902-1112
Tel: (787)725-8120
Admissions: (787)729-0007
E-mail: nadjac_eap@yahoo.com
Web Site: http://www.eap.edu/
President/CEO: Marimar Benitez
Admissions: Liza Layer
Financial Aid: Alfred Diaz Melendez
Type: Four-Year College **Sex:** Coed **Affiliation:** Instituto de Cultura de Puerto Rico **% Accepted:** 50 **Application Deadline:** March 6 **Application Fee:** $25.00 **H.S. Requirements:** High school diploma required; GED accepted **Scholarships:** Available **Calendar System:** Semester, Summer Session Not available **Enrollment:** FT 365, PT 165 **Faculty:** FT 16, PT 48 **Student-Faculty Ratio:** 13:1 **Exams:** SAT I. SAT essay not being used. **% Receiving Financial Aid:** 83 **Library Holdings:** 37,295 **Regional Accreditation:** Middle State Association of Colleges and Schools **Credit Hours For Degree:** 132 credit hours, Bachelors

HUERTAS JUNIOR COLLEGE
PO Box 8429
Caguas, PR 00726
Tel: (787)743-2156
Admissions: (787)746-1400

E-mail: huertas@huertas.org
Web Site: http://www.huertas.edu/
President/CEO: Edwin Ramos Rivera, Esq.
Admissions: Barbara Hassim López
Type: Two-Year College **Sex:** Coed **Admission Plans:** Open Admission; Deferred Admission **Application Deadline:** Rolling **Application Fee:** $25.00 **H.S. Requirements:** High school diploma required; GED accepted **Scholarships:** Available **Calendar System:** Trimester, Summer Session Not available **Library Holdings:** 5,524 **Regional Accreditation:** Middle State Association of Colleges and Schools **Credit Hours For Degree:** 76 credits, Associates **Professional Accreditation:** ACICS, AHIMA

HUMACAO COMMUNITY COLLEGE

PO Box 9139
Humacao, PR 00792
Tel: (787)852-1430
Fax: (787)850-1760
President/CEO: Jorge E. Mojica Rodriguez
Admissions: Xiomara Sanchez
Type: Two-Year College **Sex:** Coed **Admission Plans:** Open Admission; Early Admission **Application Fee:** $15.00 **H.S. Requirements:** High school diploma required; GED accepted **Scholarships:** Available **Calendar System:** Trimester **Professional Accreditation:** ACICS

INSTITUTO COMERCIAL DE PUERTO RICO JUNIOR COLLEGE

558 Munoz Rivera Ave., PO Box 190304
San Juan, PR 00919-0304
Tel: (787)753-6000
Fax: (787)763-7249
Web Site: http://www.icprjc.edu/
President/CEO: Olga Rivera
Type: Two-Year College **Sex:** Coed **Admission Plans:** Early Admission **Application Fee:** $25.00 **H.S. Requirements:** High school diploma required; GED accepted **Scholarships:** Available **Calendar System:** Trimester, Summer Session Not available **Faculty:** FT 34, PT 55 **Student-Faculty Ratio:** 17:1 **Library Holdings:** 40,858 **Regional Accreditation:** Middle State Association of Colleges and Schools **Credit Hours For Degree:** 73 credits, Associates **ROTC:** Army

INTER AMERICAN UNIVERSITY OF PUERTO RICO, AGUADILLA CAMPUS

Call Box 20000
Aguadilla, PR 00605
Tel: (787)891-0925
Web Site: http://www.aguadilla.inter.edu/
President/CEO: Dr. Elie Agesilas
Admissions: Doris Perez
Financial Aid: Juan Gonzalez
Type: Comprehensive **Sex:** Coed **Affiliation:** Inter American University of Puerto Rico **% Accepted:** 59 **Application Deadline:** Rolling **Application Fee:** $0.00 **H.S. Requirements:** High school diploma required; GED accepted **Costs Per Year:** Application fee: $0. Tuition: $5017 full-time. Mandatory fees: $478 full-time. Full-time tuition and fees vary according to program. **Calendar System:** Semester, Summer Session Available **Enrollment:** FT 3,507, PT 730, Grad FT 220, Grad PT 45 **Faculty:** FT 77, PT 154 **Student-Faculty Ratio:** 29:1 **Exams:** Other, SAT I or ACT. **Library Holdings:** 61,359 **Regional Accreditation:** Middle State Association of Colleges and Schools **Credit Hours For Degree:** 55 semester hours, Associates; 129 semester hours, Bachelors **ROTC:** Army, Air Force **Intercollegiate Athletics:** Baseball M; Basketball M & W; Cheerleading M & W; Cross-Country Running M & W; Soccer M; Softball M & W; Table Tennis M & W; Tennis M & W; Track and Field M & W; Volleyball M & W; Weight Lifting M & W

INTER AMERICAN UNIVERSITY OF PUERTO RICO, ARECIBO CAMPUS

PO Box 4050
Arecibo, PR 00614-4050
Tel: (787)878-5475
Fax: (787)880-1624
E-mail: pmontalvo@arecibo.inter.edu
Web Site: http://www.arecibo.inter.edu/
President/CEO: Dr. Rafael Ramirez
Admissions: Provi Montalvo
Financial Aid: Ramón O. de Jesús
Type: Comprehensive **Sex:** Coed **Affiliation:** Inter American University of Puerto Rico **Admission Plans:** Early Admission; Deferred Admission **Application Deadline:** Rolling **Application Fee:** $0.00 **H.S. Requirements:** High school diploma required; GED accepted **Scholarships:** Available **Calendar System:** Semester, Summer Session Available **Enrollment:** FT 3,789, PT 758, Grad FT 267, Grad PT 64 **Faculty:** FT 88, PT 210 **Student-Faculty Ratio:** 24:1 **Exams:** Other. **% Receiving Financial Aid:** 85 **Library Holdings:** 73,642 **Regional Accreditation:** Middle State Association of Colleges and Schools **Credit Hours For Degree:** 60 credit hours, Associates; 124 credit hours, Bachelors **ROTC:** Army **Professional Accreditation:** AANA, CSWE, NLN **Intercollegiate Athletics:** Baseball M; Basketball M & W; Cheerleading M & W; Track and Field M & W; Volleyball M & W

INTER AMERICAN UNIVERSITY OF PUERTO RICO, BARRANQUITAS CAMPUS

PO Box 517
Barranquitas, PR 00794
Tel: (787)857-3600
Fax: (787)857-2284
E-mail: acartagena@br.inter.edu
Web Site: http://www.br.inter.edu/
President/CEO: Manuel J. Fernos
Admissions: Aramilda Cartagena
Financial Aid: Eduardo Fontanez Colon
Type: Comprehensive **Sex:** Coed **Affiliation:** Inter American University of Puerto Rico **% Accepted:** 34 **Admission Plans:** Deferred Admission **Application Deadline:** May 15 **Application Fee:** $0.00 **H.S. Requirements:** High school diploma required; GED accepted **Scholarships:** Available **Calendar System:** Semester, Summer Session Available **Enrollment:** FT 1,699, PT 407 **Faculty:** FT 41, PT 94 **Student-Faculty Ratio:** 29:1 **Exams:** Other, SAT I or ACT. **Library Holdings:** 32,863 **Regional Accreditation:** Middle State Association of Colleges and Schools **Credit Hours For Degree:** 60 semester hours, Associates; 124 semester hours, Bachelors **ROTC:** Army **Intercollegiate Athletics:** Basketball M & W; Cross-Country Running M & W; Softball M & W; Table Tennis M & W; Tennis M & W; Track and Field M & W; Volleyball M & W; Weight Lifting M & W; Wrestling M & W

INTER AMERICAN UNIVERSITY OF PUERTO RICO, BAYAMON CAMPUS

500 Rd. 830
Bayamón, PR 00957
Tel: (787)279-1912
Fax: (787)279-2205
E-mail: calicea@bc.inter.edu
Web Site: http://www.bc.inter.edu/
President/CEO: Juan F. Martinez
Admissions: Carlos Alicea
Financial Aid: Carlos N. Alicea
Type: Comprehensive **Sex:** Coed **Affiliation:** Inter American University of Puerto Rico **Application Deadline:** July 30 **Application Fee:** $0.00 **H.S. Requirements:** High school diploma required; GED accepted **Costs Per Year:** Application fee: $0. Tuition: $4620 full-time. Mandatory fees: $516 full-time. **Scholarships:** Available **Calendar System:** Semester, Summer Session Available **Enrollment:** FT 4,376, PT 722, Grad PT 64 **Faculty:** FT 100, PT 249 **Student-Faculty Ratio:** 23:1 **Exams:** Other, SAT I. **% Receiving Financial Aid:** 57 **Library Holdings:** 40,920 **Regional Accreditation:** Middle State Association of Colleges and Schools **Credit Hours For Degree:** 70 semester hours, Associates; 120 semester hours, Bachelors **ROTC:** Army **Intercollegiate Athletics:** Baseball M; Basketball M & W; Cross-Country Running M & W; Softball M & W; Swimming and Diving M & W; Table Tennis M & W; Track and Field M & W; Volleyball M & W; Weight Lifting M

INTER AMERICAN UNIVERSITY OF PUERTO RICO, FAJARDO CAMPUS

Call Box 70003
Fajardo, PR 00738-7003
Tel: (787)863-2390
E-mail: jackeline.melendez@fajardo.inter.edu
Web Site: http://www.fajardo.inter.edu/
President/CEO: Dr. Ismael Suarez
Admissions: Jackeline Melèndez
Type: Comprehensive **Sex:** Coed **Affiliation:** Inter American University of Puerto Rico **% Accepted:** 39 **Admission Plans:** Early Admission; Deferred

Admission **Application Deadline:** Rolling **Application Fee:** $0.00 **H.S. Requirements:** High school diploma required; GED accepted **Costs Per Year:** Application fee: $0. Tuition: $163 per credit part-time. Part-time tuition varies according to degree level. **Calendar System:** Semester, Summer Session Available **Enrollment:** FT 1,702, PT 515, Grad PT 22 **Faculty:** FT 39, PT 107 **Student-Faculty Ratio:** 11:1 **Exams:** Other. **Library Holdings:** 39,951 **Regional Accreditation:** Middle State Association of Colleges and Schools **Credit Hours For Degree:** 60 semester hours, Associates; 124 semester hours, Bachelors **ROTC:** Army

INTER AMERICAN UNIVERSITY OF PUERTO RICO, GUAYAMA CAMPUS
Call Box 10004
Guayama, PR 00785
Tel: (787)864-2222
E-mail: lferrer@inter.edu
Web Site: http://www.guayama.inter.edu/
President/CEO: Prof. Carlos E. Colon
Admissions: Laura E. Ferrer
Financial Aid: Jose A. Vechini
Type: Comprehensive **Sex:** Coed **Affiliation:** Inter American University of Puerto Rico **Application Deadline:** August 1 **Application Fee:** $0.00 **H.S. Requirements:** High school diploma required; GED accepted **Costs Per Year:** Application fee: $0. Tuition: $4890 full-time. Mandatory fees: $478 full-time. **Scholarships:** Available **Calendar System:** Semester, Summer Session Available **Enrollment:** FT 1,881, PT 408, Grad FT 47, Grad PT 20 **Faculty:** FT 46, PT 146 **Student-Faculty Ratio:** 25:1 **Exams:** Other, SAT I. **% Receiving Financial Aid:** 81 **Regional Accreditation:** Middle State Association of Colleges and Schools **Credit Hours For Degree:** 52 academic credits, Associates; 110 academic credits, Bachelors **ROTC:** Army **Intercollegiate Athletics:** Baseball M; Basketball M & W; Cross-Country Running M & W; Swimming and Diving M

INTER AMERICAN UNIVERSITY OF PUERTO RICO, METROPOLITAN CAMPUS
PO Box 191293
San Juan, PR 00919-1293
Tel: (787)250-1912
E-mail: jbetancourt@metro.inter.edu
Web Site: http://metro.inter.edu/
President/CEO: Prof. Marilina Wayland
Admissions: Ida G. Betancourt
Financial Aid: Luz M. Medina
Type: Comprehensive **Sex:** Coed **Affiliation:** Inter American University of Puerto Rico **% Accepted:** 27 **Application Fee:** $0.00 **H.S. Requirements:** High school diploma required; GED accepted **Scholarships:** Available **Calendar System:** Semester, Summer Session Available **% Receiving Financial Aid:** 80 **Library Holdings:** 171,173 **Regional Accreditation:** Middle State Association of Colleges and Schools **Credit Hours For Degree:** 60 credits, Associates; 120 credits, Bachelors **ROTC:** Army, Navy, Air Force **Professional Accreditation:** ABA, CSWE, NAACLS, NLN

INTER AMERICAN UNIVERSITY OF PUERTO RICO, PONCE CAMPUS
104 Industrial Park Turpò RD 1
Mercedita, PR 00715-1602
Tel: (787)284-1912
E-mail: fidiaz@ponce.inter.edu
Web Site: http://www.ponce.inter.edu/
President/CEO: Dra. Vilma E. Colon
Admissions: Franco Diaz
Financial Aid: Juan Portalatin
Type: Comprehensive **Sex:** Coed **Affiliation:** Inter American University of Puerto Rico **% Accepted:** 97 **Admission Plans:** Deferred Admission **Application Deadline:** May 15 **Application Fee:** $0.00 **H.S. Requirements:** High school diploma required; GED accepted **Costs Per Year:** Application fee: $0. Tuition: $3912 full-time, $163 per credit part-time. Mandatory fees: $516 full-time, $422 per year part-time. Full-time tuition and fees vary according to course load and program. Part-time tuition and fees vary according to course load and program. **Scholarships:** Available **Calendar System:** Semester, Summer Session Available **Enrollment:** FT 4,911, PT 792, Grad FT 216, Grad PT 78 **Faculty:** FT 81, PT 176 **Exams:** Other, SAT I. **% Receiving Financial Aid:** 82 **Library Holdings:** 49,531 **Regional Accreditation:** Middle State Association of Colleges and Schools **Credit Hours For Degree:** 60 semester hours, Associates; 124 semester hours, Bachelors **Intercollegiate Athletics:** Baseball M & W; Cross-Country Running M & W; Softball M & W; Table Tennis M & W; Track and Field M & W; Volleyball M & W; Weight Lifting M & W

INTER AMERICAN UNIVERSITY OF PUERTO RICO, SAN GERMAN CAMPUS
PO Box 5100
San Germán, PR 00683-5008
Tel: (787)264-1912
Fax: (787)892-6350
E-mail: milcama@sg.inter.edu
Web Site: http://www.sg.inter.edu/
President/CEO: Prof. Agnes Mojica
Admissions: Prof. Mildred Camacho
Financial Aid: María I. Lugo
Type: University **Sex:** Coed **Affiliation:** Inter American University of Puerto Rico **% Accepted:** 84 **Admission Plans:** Early Admission **Application Deadline:** May 15 **Application Fee:** $0.00 **H.S. Requirements:** High school diploma required; GED accepted **Costs Per Year:** Application fee: $0. Tuition: $5100 full-time, $170 per credit part-time. Mandatory fees: $516 full-time, $170 per credit part-time, $258 per term part-time. **Scholarships:** Available **Calendar System:** Semester, Summer Session Available **Enrollment:** FT 4,147, PT 678, Grad FT 627, Grad PT 264 **Faculty:** FT 129, PT 178 **Student-Faculty Ratio:** 27:1 **Exams:** Other. **% Receiving Financial Aid:** 81 **% Residing in College-Owned, -Operated, or -Affiliated Housing:** 10 **Final Year or Final Semester Residency Requirement:** No **Library Holdings:** 158,290 **Regional Accreditation:** Middle State Association of Colleges and Schools **Credit Hours For Degree:** 60 credits, Associates; 124 credits, Bachelors **ROTC:** Army, Navy, Air Force **Professional Accreditation:** AHIMA, NAACLS **Intercollegiate Athletics:** Baseball M; Basketball M & W; Cross-Country Running M & W; Soccer M; Softball M & W; Swimming and Diving M & W; Table Tennis M & W; Tennis M & W; Track and Field M & W; Volleyball M & W; Weight Lifting M

NATIONAL UNIVERSITY COLLEGE
PO Box 2036
National College Plaza Bldg.
Bayamón, PR 00960
Tel: (787)780-5134; Free: 800-780-5134
Fax: (787)740-7360
E-mail: infobayamon@nationalcollegepr.edu
Web Site: http://www.nuc.edu/
President/CEO: Dra. Carmen Zoraida Claudio
Type: Four-Year College **Sex:** Coed **Application Deadline:** Rolling **Application Fee:** $25.00 **Scholarships:** Available **Professional Accreditation:** ACICS

POLYTECHNIC UNIVERSITY OF PUERTO RICO
377 Ponce de Leon Ave.
Hato Rey, PR 00919
Tel: (787)754-8000
E-mail: tcardona@pupr.edu
Web Site: http://www.pupr.edu/
President/CEO: Prof. Ernesto Vazquez-Barquet
Admissions: Teresa Cardona
Financial Aid: Sergio E. Villoldo
Type: Comprehensive **Sex:** Coed **% Accepted:** 94 **Admission Plans:** Early Admission; Deferred Admission **Application Deadline:** August 15 **Application Fee:** $30.00 **H.S. Requirements:** High school diploma required; GED accepted **Costs Per Year:** Application fee: $30. Comprehensive fee: $18,541 includes full-time tuition ($6192), mandatory fees ($645), and college room and board ($11,704). Full-time tuition and fees vary according to course load, degree level, and program. Part-time tuition: $173 per credit hour. Part-time tuition varies according to course load, degree level, and program. **Scholarships:** Available **Calendar System:** Trimester, Summer Session Available **Enrollment:** FT 2,557, PT 2,287, Grad FT 369, Grad PT 307 **Faculty:** FT 172, PT 107 **Student-Faculty Ratio:** 20:1 **% Receiving Financial Aid:** 68 **Library Holdings:** 111,422 **Regional Accreditation:** Middle State Association of Colleges and Schools **Credit Hours For Degree:** 132 credit hours, Bachelors **ROTC:** Army **Professional Accreditation:** ABET **Intercollegiate Athletics:** Basketball M & W; Cross-Country Running M & W; Soccer M; Softball M & W; Table Tennis M & W; Tennis M & W; Track and Field M & W; Volleyball M & W

PONTIFICAL CATHOLIC UNIVERSITY OF PUERTO RICO
2250 Las Americas Ave., Ste. 564
Ponce, PR 00717-0777
Tel: (787)841-2000; Free: 800-981-5040
Fax: (787)840-4295
E-mail: admissions@email.pucpr.edu
Web Site: http://www.pucpr.edu/
President/CEO: Dr. Jorge I. Velez
Admissions: Sra. Ana O. Bonilla
Financial Aid: Margaret Alustiza
Type: University **Sex:** Coed **Affiliation:** Roman Catholic **% Accepted:** 83 **Admission Plans:** Early Admission; Deferred Admission **Application Fee:** $15.00 **H.S. Requirements:** High school diploma required; GED accepted **Scholarships:** Available **Calendar System:** Semester, Summer Session Available **Enrollment:** FT 4,857, PT 514, Grad FT 1,608, Grad PT 703 **Faculty:** FT 191, PT 194 **Student-Faculty Ratio:** 23:1 **Exams:** Other, SAT I. **% Receiving Financial Aid:** 91 **Regional Accreditation:** Middle State Association of Colleges and Schools **Credit Hours For Degree:** 67 credits, Associates; 130 credits, Bachelors **ROTC:** Army, Air Force **Professional Accreditation:** ABA, ACBSP, CSWE, NAACLS, NLN **Intercollegiate Athletics:** Basketball M; Cross-Country Running M & W; Swimming and Diving M & W; Table Tennis M & W; Tennis M & W; Track and Field M & W; Volleyball M & W; Weight Lifting M & W; Wrestling M

PUERTO RICO TECHNICAL JUNIOR COLLEGE
703 Ponce De Leon Ave., Hato Rey
San Juan, PR 00917
Tel: (787)751-0133
Admissions: (787)754-3431
Fax: (787)754-3431
President/CEO: Hector M. Collazo
Type: Two-Year College **Sex:** Coed **Admission Plans:** Open Admission **Application Fee:** $25.00 **Professional Accreditation:** ACCSCT

RAMIREZ COLLEGE OF BUSINESS AND TECHNOLOGY
Ave. Ponce de Leon No. 70
San Juan, PR 00918
Tel: (787)763-3120
E-mail: ramirezcollege@prtc.net
Web Site: http://www.galeon.com/ramirezcollege/
President/CEO: Juan E. Feliciano
Admissions: Arnaldo Castro
Type: Two-Year College **Sex:** Coed **Admission Plans:** Open Admission **Application Deadline:** Rolling **Application Fee:** $25.00 **H.S. Requirements:** High school diploma required; GED accepted **Scholarships:** Available **Calendar System:** Trimester, Summer Session Not available **Library Holdings:** 9,000 **Credit Hours For Degree:** 75 credits, Associates **Professional Accreditation:** ACICS

UNIVERSIDAD ADVENTISTA DE LAS ANTILLAS
PO Box 118
Mayagüez, PR 00681-0118
Tel: (787)834-9595
Fax: (787)834-9597
E-mail: admissions@uaa.edu
Web Site: http://www.uaa.edu/
President/CEO: Dr. Myrna Costa, EdD
Admissions: Evelyn del Valle
Financial Aid: Awilda Matos
Type: Comprehensive **Sex:** Coed **Affiliation:** Seventh-day Adventist **% Accepted:** 44 **Admission Plans:** Early Admission **Application Fee:** $20.00 **H.S. Requirements:** High school diploma required; GED accepted **Costs Per Year:** Application fee: $20. Comprehensive fee: $9070 includes full-time tuition ($6170) and college room and board ($2900). College room only: $1100. Room and board charges vary according to board plan and housing facility. Part-time tuition: $155 per credit hour. Tuition guaranteed not to increase for student's term of enrollment. **Scholarships:** Available **Calendar System:** Semester, Summer Session Available **Enrollment:** FT 886, PT 69, Grad FT 46, Grad PT 18 **Faculty:** FT 43, PT 42 **Student-Faculty Ratio:** 17:1 **Exams:** Other, SAT I or ACT. ACT essay not being used. SAT essay not being used. **% Receiving Financial Aid:** 100 **% Residing in College-Owned, -Operated, or -Affiliated Housing:** 30 **Regional Accreditation:** Middle State Association of Colleges and Schools **Credit Hours For Degree:** 64 credits, Associates; 128 credits, Bachelors **Professional Accreditation:** AHIMA, CARC, NLN **Intercollegiate Athletics:** Softball M

UNIVERSIDAD CENTRAL DEL CARIBE
PO Box 60-327
Bayamón, PR 00960-6032
Tel: (787)798-3001
Web Site: http://www.uccaribe.edu/
President/CEO: Dr. José Ginel Rodríguez
Type: Two-Year College **Sex:** Coed **% Accepted:** 79 **Application Fee:** $25.00 **Calendar System:** Semester **Regional Accreditation:** Middle State Association of Colleges and Schools **Professional Accreditation:** JRCERT, LCMEAMA

UNIVERSIDAD DEL ESTE
PO Box 2010
Carolina, PR 00984
Tel: (787)257-7373
Fax: (787)257-7373
E-mail: ue_csantiago@suagm.edu
Web Site: http://www.suagm.edu/une/
President/CEO: Alberto Maldonado
Admissions: Clotilde Santiago
Financial Aid: Clotilde Santiago
Type: Comprehensive **Sex:** Coed **Affiliation:** Ana G. Méndez University System **Admission Plans:** Deferred Admission **Application Fee:** $15.00 **H.S. Requirements:** High school diploma required; GED accepted **Calendar System:** Semester, Summer Session Available **Regional Accreditation:** Middle State Association of Colleges and Schools **Credit Hours For Degree:** 62 credits, Associates **Professional Accreditation:** AHIMA

UNIVERSIDAD METROPOLITANA
Apartado 21150
San Juan, PR 00928-1150
Tel: (787)766-1717; Free: 800-747-8362
Fax: (787)759-7663
E-mail: um_frivera@suagm1.suagm.edu
Web Site: http://www.suagm.edu/umet/
President/CEO: Dr. Federico M. Matheu
Admissions: Julio Rodriguez Soiza
Type: Comprehensive **Sex:** Coed **Affiliation:** Ana G. Méndez University System **% Accepted:** 62 **Admission Plans:** Early Admission **Application Deadline:** July 30 **Application Fee:** $15.00 **Calendar System:** Semester, Summer Session Available **Enrollment:** FT 7,796, PT 2,000 **Faculty:** FT 107, PT 796 **Regional Accreditation:** Middle State Association of Colleges and Schools **Credit Hours For Degree:** 72 credits, Associates; 128 credits, Bachelors **Professional Accreditation:** NLN **Intercollegiate Athletics:** Softball M & W; Table Tennis M & W; Tennis M & W; Track and Field M & W; Volleyball M & W; Weight Lifting M & W

UNIVERSIDAD TEOLOGICA DEL CARIBE
PO Box 901
St. Just, PR 00978-0901
Tel: (787)761-0640
E-mail: registraduriautc@yahoo.com
Web Site: http://www.cbp.edu/
President/CEO: Francisco Ortiz
Admissions: Carolyn Figueroa
Financial Aid: Luz Y. Luciano
Type: Four-Year College **Sex:** Coed **Affiliation:** Pentecostal **% Accepted:** 82 **Admission Plans:** Early Admission **Application Fee:** $25.00 **Costs Per Year:** Application fee: $25. One-time mandatory fee: $8. Comprehensive fee: $5920 includes full-time tuition ($3140), mandatory fees ($380), and college room and board ($2400). College room only: $1200. Room and board charges vary according to board plan. Part-time tuition: $18 per credit. Part-time mandatory fees: $115 per credit, $2450 per term. **Scholarships:** Available **Calendar System:** Semester, Summer Session Available **Enrollment:** FT 90, PT 161 **Faculty:** FT 6, PT 19 **Student-Faculty Ratio:** 15:1 **% Receiving Financial Aid:** 92 **% Residing in College-Owned, -Operated, or -Affiliated Housing:** 0 **Library Holdings:** 15,619 **Credit Hours For Degree:** 133 credits, Bachelors **Professional Accreditation:** ABHE

UNIVERSIDAD DEL TURABO
PO Box 3030
Gurabo, PR 00778-3030
Tel: (787)743-7979
E-mail: ut_crivera@suagm.edu
Web Site: http://www.suagm.edu/ut/
President/CEO: Dennis Alicea
Admissions: Carmen Rivera
Financial Aid: Ivette Vázquez Ríos
Type: University **Sex:** Coed **Affiliation:** Ana G. Méndez University System **Application Deadline:** Rolling **Application Fee:** $15.00 **H.S. Requirements:** High school diploma required; GED accepted **Calendar System:** Semester, Summer Session Available **Student-Faculty Ratio:** 38:1 **Regional Accreditation:** Middle State Association of Colleges and Schools **Credit Hours For Degree:** 64 credits, Associates; 126 credits, Bachelors **ROTC:** Army, Air Force **Professional Accreditation:** AACN

UNIVERSITY OF PHOENIX—PUERTO RICO CAMPUS
B7 Tabonuco St., Ste. 700 Santander Tower
PO Box 3870
Guaynabo, PR 00968
Tel: (787)731-5400; Free: 800-228-7240
Admissions: (480)557-6151
Fax: (787)731-1510
E-mail: audra.mcquarie@phoenix.edu
Web Site: http://www.phoenix.edu/
President/CEO: William Pepicello
Admissions: Audra McQuarie
Type: Comprehensive **Sex:** Coed **% Accepted:** 100 **Admission Plans:** Open Admission; Deferred Admission **Application Deadline:** Rolling **Application Fee:** $0.00 **H.S. Requirements:** High school diploma required; GED accepted **Costs Per Year:** Application fee: $0. Tuition: $6750 full-time. Full-time tuition varies according to course level and course load. **Scholarships:** Available **Calendar System:** Continuous, Summer Session Not available **Enrollment:** FT 1,117 **Faculty:** FT 22, PT 206 **Regional Accreditation:** North Central Association of Colleges and Schools **Credit Hours For Degree:** 60 credits, Associates; 120 credits, Bachelors

UNIVERSITY OF PUERTO RICO, AGUADILLA UNIVERSITY COLLEGE
PO Box 6150
Aguadilla, PR 00604
Tel: (787)890-2681
Web Site: http://www.uprag.edu/
President/CEO: Jose L. Arbona
Admissions: Melba Serrano Lugo
Type: Four-Year College **Sex:** Coed **Affiliation:** University of Puerto Rico System **% Accepted:** 85 **Admission Plans:** Early Admission; Deferred Admission **Application Fee:** $20.00 **H.S. Requirements:** High school diploma required; GED accepted **Calendar System:** Semester, Summer Session Available **Exams:** Other, SAT I, SAT II. **Library Holdings:** 31,420 **Regional Accreditation:** Middle State Association of Colleges and Schools **Credit Hours For Degree:** 66 credits, Associates; 129 credits, Bachelors **ROTC:** Army **Intercollegiate Athletics:** Baseball M; Basketball M; Cross-Country Running M & W; Softball W; Swimming and Diving M & W; Table Tennis M; Tennis W; Track and Field M & W; Weight Lifting M & W

UNIVERSITY OF PUERTO RICO AT ARECIBO
PO Box 4010
Arecibo, PR 00613
Tel: (787)878-2830
Admissions: (787)815-0000
E-mail: dbarrios@upra.edu
Web Site: http://www.upra.edu/
President/CEO: Ana J. Gomez
Admissions: Delma Barrios Colon
Financial Aid: Luis Rodriguez
Type: Four-Year College **Sex:** Coed **Affiliation:** University of Puerto Rico System **% Accepted:** 46 **Application Fee:** $20.00 **H.S. Requirements:** High school diploma required; GED accepted **Scholarships:** Available **Calendar System:** Semester, Summer Session Available **Exams:** Other, SAT II. **Library Holdings:** 65,000 **Regional Accreditation:** Middle State Association of Colleges and Schools **Credit Hours For Degree:** 68 credits, Associates; 132 credits, Bachelors **ROTC:** Army **Professional Accreditation:** NLN **Intercollegiate Athletics:** Baseball M; Basketball M & W; Cross-Country Running M & W; Softball W; Swimming and Diving M & W; Tennis M & W; Track and Field M & W; Volleyball M & W; Weight Lifting M & W; Wrestling M

UNIVERSITY OF PUERTO RICO AT BAYAMON
Industrial Minillas 170 Carr 174
Bayamón, PR 00959
Tel: (787)786-2885
Admissions: (787)993-8952
E-mail: cmontes@upr.edu
Web Site: http://www.uprb.edu/
President/CEO: Dr. Arturo Aviles-Gonzalez
Admissions: Carmen I. Montes
Financial Aid: Hector Cuadrado
Type: Four-Year College **Sex:** Coed **Affiliation:** University of Puerto Rico System **% Accepted:** 22 **Application Deadline:** December 15 **Application Fee:** $15.00 **H.S. Requirements:** High school diploma required; GED accepted **Costs Per Year:** Application fee: $15. Commonwealth resident tuition: $1734 full-time, $51 per credit part-time. Nonresident tuition: $4039 full-time. Mandatory fees: $342 full-time, $144 per term part-time. Full-time tuition and fees vary according to class time, course load, and program. Part-time tuition and fees vary according to class time, course load, and program. Tuition guaranteed not to increase for student's term of enrollment. **Scholarships:** Available **Calendar System:** Semester, Summer Session Available **Enrollment:** FT 4,417, PT 767 **Faculty:** FT 191, PT 133 **Student-Faculty Ratio:** 20:1 **Exams:** Other. **Library Holdings:** 65,000 **Regional Accreditation:** Middle State Association of Colleges and Schools **Credit Hours For Degree:** 72 credits, Associates; 130 credits, Bachelors **ROTC:** Army, Air Force **Intercollegiate Athletics:** Baseball M; Basketball M & W; Cheerleading M & W; Cross-Country Running M & W; Softball W; Swimming and Diving M & W; Table Tennis M & W; Tennis M & W; Track and Field M & W; Volleyball M & W; Weight Lifting M & W; Wrestling M

UNIVERSITY OF PUERTO RICO AT CAROLINA
PO Box 4800
Carolina, PR 00984-4800
Tel: (787)257-0000
Web Site: http://uprc.edu/
President/CEO: Dr. Victor Borrero Aldahondo
Admissions: Celia Mendez
Type: Two-Year College **Sex:** Coed **Affiliation:** University of Puerto Rico System **% Accepted:** 34 **Application Fee:** $20.00 **H.S. Requirements:** High school diploma required; GED accepted **Calendar System:** Quarter, Summer Session Not available **Faculty:** FT 125, PT 83 **Exams:** ACT, Other, SAT I, SAT II. **Library Holdings:** 37,958 **Regional Accreditation:** Middle State Association of Colleges and Schools **Credit Hours For Degree:** 68 credits, Associates; 137 credits, Bachelors **ROTC:** Army, Air Force **Intercollegiate Athletics:** Basketball M & W; Cross-Country Running M & W; Tennis M & W; Track and Field M & W; Volleyball M & W

UNIVERSITY OF PUERTO RICO, CAYEY UNIVERSITY COLLEGE
205 Ave. Antonio R. Barcelo
Cayey, PR 00736
Tel: (787)738-2161
E-mail: wilfredo.lopez3@upr.edu
Web Site: http://www.cayey.upr.edu/
President/CEO: Dr. Raul Castro
Admissions: Wilfredo Lopez
Financial Aid: Hector Maldonado Otero
Type: Four-Year College **Sex:** Coed **Affiliation:** University of Puerto Rico System **% Accepted:** 78 **Admission Plans:** Early Admission; Early Decision Plan **Application Fee:** $20.00 **H.S. Requirements:** High school diploma required; GED accepted **Costs Per Year:** Application fee: $20. Commonwealth resident tuition: $1973 full-time. Nonresident tuition: $4387 full-time. College room and board: $8180. **Scholarships:** Available **Calendar System:** Semester, Summer Session Available **Enrollment:** FT 3,458, PT 372 **Student-Faculty Ratio:** 21:1 **Exams:** Other, SAT I. **% Receiving Financial Aid:** 76 **Library Holdings:** 109,776 **Regional Accreditation:** Middle State Association of Colleges and Schools **Credit Hours For Degree:** 72 credits, Associates; 128 credits, Bachelors **ROTC:** Army **Intercollegiate Athletics:** Basketball M & W; Cross-Country Running M &

W; Soccer M; Softball M & W; Swimming and Diving M & W; Table Tennis M; Tennis M & W; Track and Field M & W; Volleyball M & W; Weight Lifting M & W; Wrestling M

UNIVERSITY OF PUERTO RICO AT HUMACAO
HUC Station 100, Rd. 908
Humacao, PR 00791
Tel: (787)850-0000
Admissions: (787)850-9301
Fax: (787)852-4638
E-mail: elizabeth.gerena@upr.edu
Web Site: http://www.uprh.edu/
President/CEO: Dr. Angel M. Gierbolini
Admissions: Elizabeth Gerena
Financial Aid: Larry Cruz
Type: Four-Year College **Sex:** Coed **Affiliation:** University of Puerto Rico System **% Accepted:** 37 **Admission Plans:** Deferred Admission **Application Deadline:** January 9 **Application Fee:** $20.00 **H.S. Requirements:** High school diploma required; GED accepted **Costs Per Year:** Application fee: $20. Area resident tuition: $49 per credit part-time. Commonwealth resident tuition: $1666 full-time. Nonresident tuition: $3596 full-time. Mandatory fees: $347 full-time, $347 per term part-time. Full-time tuition and fees vary according to class time, course load, and student level. Part-time tuition and fees vary according to class time, course load, and student level. Tuition guaranteed not to increase for student's term of enrollment. **Scholarships:** Available **Calendar System:** Semester, Summer Session Available **Enrollment:** FT 4,184, PT 492 **Faculty:** FT 285, PT 35 **Student-Faculty Ratio:** 15:1 **Exams:** Other, SAT I or ACT, SAT II. **% Receiving Financial Aid:** 82 **Library Holdings:** 74,732 **Regional Accreditation:** Middle State Association of Colleges and Schools **Credit Hours For Degree:** 65 credits, Associates; 128 credits, Bachelors **Professional Accreditation:** AOTA, APTA, CSWE, NLN **Intercollegiate Athletics:** Baseball M; Basketball M & W; Cheerleading M & W; Cross-Country Running M & W; Softball W; Swimming and Diving M & W; Tennis W; Track and Field M & W; Volleyball M & W; Weight Lifting M & W; Wrestling M

UNIVERSITY OF PUERTO RICO, MAYAGÜEZ CAMPUS
PO Box 9000
Mayagüez, PR 00681-9000
Tel: (787)832-4040
E-mail: smarty@uprm.edu
Web Site: http://www.uprm.edu/
President/CEO: Dr. Jorge Rivera Santos
Admissions: Sheila Marty-Rodriquez
Financial Aid: Ana I. Rodríguez
Type: University **Sex:** Coed **Affiliation:** University of Puerto Rico System **Scores:** 99.1% SAT V 400+; 99.5% SAT M 400+ **% Accepted:** 77 **Admission Plans:** Early Action **Application Fee:** $20.00 **H.S. Requirements:** High school diploma required; GED accepted **Scholarships:** Available **Calendar System:** Semester, Summer Session Available **Faculty:** FT 748, PT 18 **Student-Faculty Ratio:** 17:1 **Exams:** Other, SAT II. **% Receiving Financial Aid:** 54 **Library Holdings:** 921,392 **Regional Accreditation:** Middle State Association of Colleges and Schools **Credit Hours For Degree:** 134 credits, Bachelors **ROTC:** Army, Air Force **Professional Accreditation:** ABET, NCATE, NLN **Intercollegiate Athletics:** Baseball M; Basketball M & W; Cross-Country Running M & W; Soccer M; Softball W; Swimming and Diving M & W; Tennis M & W; Track and Field M & W; Volleyball M & W; Water Polo M; Wrestling M

UNIVERSITY OF PUERTO RICO, MEDICAL SCIENCES CAMPUS
PO Box 365067
San Juan, PR 00936-5067
Tel: (787)758-2525
Fax: (787)754-0474
E-mail: margarita.rivera4@upr.edu
Web Site: http://www.rcm.upr.edu/
President/CEO: Jose R. Carlo
Admissions: Margarita Rivera Rosario
Financial Aid: Zoraida Figueroa
Type: University **Sex:** Coed **Affiliation:** University of Puerto Rico System **Admission Plans:** Preferred Admission **Application Fee:** $20.00 **Scholarships:** Available **Calendar System:** Semester, Summer Session Available **% Receiving Financial Aid:** 69 **Regional Accreditation:** Middle State Association of Colleges and Schools **Credit Hours For Degree:** 91 credits, Bachelors **Professional Accreditation:** ACPhE, AACN, AANA, ACNM, ADA, ADtA, AHIMA, AOTA, APTA, ASLHA, ACEHSA, CEPH, JRCERT, JRCNMT, LCMEAMA, NAACLS, NLN

UNIVERSITY OF PUERTO RICO AT PONCE
PO Box 7186
Ponce, PR 00732-7186
Tel: (787)844-8181
Fax: (787)844-8679
E-mail: avelazquez@uprp.edu
Web Site: http://upr-ponce.upr.edu/
President/CEO: Prof. Jaime C. Marrero Vazquez
Admissions: Acmin Velazquez Rivera
Financial Aid: Carmelo Vega Montes
Type: Four-Year College **Sex:** Coed **Affiliation:** University of Puerto Rico System **Scores:** 97% SAT V 400+; 97% SAT M 400+ **% Accepted:** 37 **Admission Plans:** Early Admission **Application Deadline:** November 15 **Application Fee:** $20.00 **H.S. Requirements:** High school diploma required; GED accepted **Scholarships:** Available **Calendar System:** Semester, Summer Session Available **Enrollment:** FT 2,847, PT 385 **Faculty:** FT 158, PT 39 **Student-Faculty Ratio:** 16:1 **Exams:** SAT I and SAT II or ACT. **% Receiving Financial Aid:** 75 **Library Holdings:** 125,056 **Regional Accreditation:** Middle State Association of Colleges and Schools **Credit Hours For Degree:** 73 credits, Associates; 136 credits, Bachelors **ROTC:** Army **Professional Accreditation:** APTA **Intercollegiate Athletics:** Baseball M; Basketball M & W; Cross-Country Running M & W; Table Tennis M & W; Tennis M; Track and Field M & W; Volleyball M & W; Weight Lifting M & W

UNIVERSITY OF PUERTO RICO, RÍO PIEDRAS
PO Box 23300
San Juan, PR 00931-3300
Tel: (787)764-0000
Web Site: http://www.uprrp.edu/
President/CEO: Ana Guadalupe, PhD
Admissions: Cruz B. Valentìn
Financial Aid: Efraim Williams
Type: University **Sex:** Coed **Affiliation:** University of Puerto Rico System **% Accepted:** 36 **Application Deadline:** December 15 **Application Fee:** $20.00 **H.S. Requirements:** High school diploma required; GED accepted **Costs Per Year:** Application fee: $20. Commonwealth resident tuition: $1176 full-time, $49 per credit part-time. Nonresident tuition: $3883 full-time, $161.83 per credit part-time. Mandatory fees: $144 full-time, $72 per term part-time. Full-time tuition and fees vary according to degree level and reciprocity agreements. Part-time tuition and fees vary according to degree level and reciprocity agreements. College room and board: $8280. **Scholarships:** Available **Calendar System:** Semester, Summer Session Available **Faculty:** FT 749, PT 335 **Student-Faculty Ratio:** 16:1 **Exams:** Other, SAT I. **Library Holdings:** 1,804,010 **Regional Accreditation:** Middle State Association of Colleges and Schools **Credit Hours For Degree:** 120 credits, Bachelors **ROTC:** Army, Air Force **Professional Accreditation:** ABA, ACSP, ALA, AALS, CORE, CSWE, NAAB, NCATE **Intercollegiate Athletics:** Baseball M; Basketball M & W; Cross-Country Running M & W; Soccer M; Softball M & W; Swimming and Diving M & W; Table Tennis M & W; Tennis M & W; Track and Field M & W; Volleyball M & W; Water Polo M & W; Weight Lifting M & W; Wrestling M & W

UNIVERSITY OF PUERTO RICO AT UTUADO
PO Box 2500
Utuado, PR 00641-2500
Tel: (787)894-2828
Web Site: http://www.uprutuado.edu/
President/CEO: Cesar Cordero Montalvo
Admissions: Maria Robles Serrano
Financial Aid: Edgar Salvá
Type: Four-Year College **Sex:** Coed **Affiliation:** University of Puerto Rico System **% Accepted:** 45 **Admission Plans:** Early Admission; Deferred Admission **Application Deadline:** Rolling **Application Fee:** $20.00 **H.S. Requirements:** High school diploma required; GED accepted **Scholarships:** Available **Calendar System:** Semester, Summer Session Available **Enrollment:** FT 1,448, PT 175 **Faculty:** FT 74, PT 33 **Student-Faculty Ratio:** 18:1 **Exams:** Other, SAT II. **Regional Accreditation:** Middle State Association of Colleges and Schools **Credit Hours For Degree:** 60 credits, Associates; 137 credits, Bachelors **Intercollegiate Athletics:** Basketball M

& W; Cross-Country Running M & W; Softball M & W; Table Tennis M & W; Track and Field M & W; Volleyball M & W; Weight Lifting M & W

UNIVERSITY OF THE SACRED HEART
PO Box 12383
San Juan, PR 00914-0383
Tel: (787)728-1515
Web Site: http://www.sagrado.edu/
President/CEO: Dr. Jose J. Rivera
Admissions: Luis Heviquez
Financial Aid: Maria Torres
Type: Comprehensive **Sex:** Coed **Affiliation:** Roman Catholic **% Accepted:** 35 **Admission Plans:** Early Admission **Application Deadline:** June 30 **Application Fee:** $15.00 **H.S. Requirements:** High school diploma required; GED accepted **Costs Per Year:** Application fee: $15. Tuition: $5100 full-time, $170 per credit part-time. Mandatory fees: $770 full-time. College room only: $2500. **Scholarships:** Available **Calendar System:** Semester, Summer Session Available **Enrollment:** FT 3,765, PT 870 **Faculty:** FT 122, PT 245 **Student-Faculty Ratio:** 20:1 **Regional Accreditation:** Middle State Association of Colleges and Schools **Credit Hours For Degree:** 67 credits, Associates; 133 credits, Bachelors **Professional Accreditation:** CSWE, NAACLS, NLN **Intercollegiate Athletics:** Basketball M & W; Swimming and Diving M & W; Tennis M & W; Track and Field M & W; Ultimate Frisbee M & W; Volleyball M & W; Weight Lifting M & W

BROWN UNIVERSITY
One Prospect St.
Providence, RI 02912
Tel: (401)863-1000
Admissions: (401)863-2378
Fax: (401)863-9300
E-mail: admission_undergraduate@brown.edu
Web Site: http://www.brown.edu/
President/CEO: Ruth J. Simmons
Admissions: James Miller
Type: University **Sex:** Coed **Scores:** 100% SAT V 400+; 100% SAT M 400+; 2% ACT 18-23; 28% ACT 24-29 **% Accepted:** 11 **Admission Plans:** Early Decision Plan; Deferred Admission **Application Deadline:** January 1 **Application Fee:** $75.00 **H.S. Requirements:** High school diploma required; GED not accepted **Scholarships:** Available **Calendar System:** Semester, Summer Session Available **Enrollment:** FT 6,002, PT 242, Grad FT 2,167, Grad PT 163 **Faculty:** FT 792, PT 184 **Student-Faculty Ratio:** 9:1 **Exams:** SAT I and SAT II or ACT. ACT essay used for admission. SAT essay used for admission. **% Receiving Financial Aid:** 44 **% Residing in College-Owned, -Operated, or -Affiliated Housing:** 79 **Regional Accreditation:** New England Association of Schools and Colleges **Credit Hours For Degree:** 30 courses, Bachelors **ROTC:** Army **Professional Accreditation:** ABET, APA, CEPH, LCMEAMA **Intercollegiate Athletics:** Baseball M; Basketball M & W; Crew M & W; Cross-Country Running M & W; Equestrian Sports W; Fencing M & W; Field Hockey W; Football M; Golf M & W; Gymnastics W; Ice Hockey M & W; Lacrosse M & W; Rugby M & W; Sailing M & W; Skiing (Downhill) M & W; Soccer M & W; Softball W; Squash M & W; Swimming and Diving M & W; Tennis M & W; Track and Field M & W; Volleyball M & W; Water Polo M & W; Wrestling M

BRYANT UNIVERSITY
1150 Douglas Pike
Smithfield, RI 02917
Tel: (401)232-6000; Free: 800-622-7001
Admissions: (401)232-6100
Fax: (401)232-6741
E-mail: admission@bryant.edu
Web Site: http://www.bryant.edu/
President/CEO: Ronald K. Machtley
Admissions: Michelle Beauregard
Financial Aid: John B. Canning
Type: Comprehensive **Sex:** Coed **Scores:** 99.47% SAT V 400+; 100% SAT M 400+; 34.97% ACT 18-23; 61.35% ACT 24-29 **% Accepted:** 53 **Admission Plans:** Early Action; Early Decision Plan; Deferred Admission **Application Deadline:** February 1 **Application Fee:** $50.00 **H.S. Requirements:** High school diploma required; GED accepted **Costs Per Year:** Application fee: $50. Comprehensive fee: $43,863 includes full-time tuition ($31,794), mandatory fees ($312), and college room and board ($11,757). College room only: $7038. Room and board charges vary according to board plan and housing facility. Part-time tuition: $1347 per course. Part-time tuition varies according to course load. **Scholarships:** Available **Calendar System:** Semester, Summer Session Available **Enrollment:** FT 3,254, PT 132, Grad FT 59, Grad PT 187 **Faculty:** FT 158, PT 98 **Student-Faculty Ratio:** 18:1 **Exams:** SAT I or ACT. **% Receiving Financial Aid:** 67 **% Residing in College-Owned, -Operated, or -Affiliated Housing:** 83 **Final Year or Final Semester Residency Requirement:** No **Library Holdings:** 150,000 **Regional Accreditation:** New England Association of Schools and Colleges **Credit Hours For Degree:** 123 credits, Bachelors **ROTC:** Army **Professional Accreditation:** AACSB **Intercollegiate Athletics:** Badminton M & W; Baseball M; Basketball M & W; Bowling M & W; Cheerleading M & W; Cross-Country Running M & W; Field Hockey W; Football M; Golf M; Ice Hockey M; Lacrosse M & W; Racquetball M & W; Rugby M & W; Soccer M & W; Softball W; Squash M & W; Swimming and Diving M & W; Table Tennis M & W; Tennis M & W; Track and Field M & W; Ultimate Frisbee M & W; Volleyball M & W; Wrestling M

COMMUNITY COLLEGE OF RHODE ISLAND
400 East Ave.
Warwick, RI 02886-1807
Tel: (401)825-1000
Admissions: (401)333-7490
Fax: (401)825-2418
E-mail: webadmission@ccri.edu/
Web Site: http://www.ccri.edu/
President/CEO: Raymond M. DiPasquale
Type: Two-Year College **Sex:** Coed **% Accepted:** 99 **Admission Plans:** Open Admission; Preferred Admission; Deferred Admission **Application Deadline:** Rolling **Application Fee:** $20.00 **H.S. Requirements:** High school diploma required; GED accepted. For nursing, dental, allied health programs: High school diploma required; GED not accepted **Costs Per Year:** Application fee: $20. State resident tuition: $3356 full-time, $153 per credit hour part-time. Nonresident tuition: $9496 full-time, $454 per credit hour part-time. Mandatory fees: $11 per credit hour part-time, $17 per term part-time. Part-time tuition and fees vary according to course load. **Scholarships:** Available **Calendar System:** Semester, Summer Session Available **Enrollment:** FT 6,663, PT 11,097 **Faculty:** FT 325, PT 474 **Student-Faculty Ratio:** 22:1 **Regional Accreditation:** New England Association of Schools and Colleges **Credit Hours For Degree:** 60 credits, Associates **ROTC:** Army **Professional Accreditation:** ADA, AOTA, APTA, ACBSP, CARC, JRCERT, NAACLS, NLN **Intercollegiate Athletics:** Baseball M; Basketball M & W; Cross-Country Running M & W; Golf M & W; Soccer M & W; Softball W; Tennis M & W; Track and Field M & W; Volleyball W

JOHNSON & WALES UNIVERSITY
8 Abbott Park Place
Providence, RI 02903-3703
Tel: (401)598-1000; Free: 800-342-5598
Admissions: (401)598-2310
Fax: (401)598-1835
E-mail: admissions.pvd@jwu.edu
Web Site: http://www.jwu.edu/
President/CEO: Dr. Irving Schneider
Admissions: Maureen Dumas
Financial Aid: Lynn Robinson
Type: Comprehensive **Sex:** Coed **Scores:** 83.3% SAT V 400+; 84.5% SAT M 400+ **% Accepted:** 72 **Admission Plans:** Early Admission; Deferred Admission **Application Deadline:** Rolling **Application Fee:** $0.00 **H.S. Requirements:** High school diploma required; GED accepted **Costs Per Year:** Application fee: $0. One-time mandatory fee: $288. Tuition: $23,034 full-time. Mandatory fees: $1107 full-time. **Scholarships:** Available **Calendar System:** Quarter, Summer Session Available **Enrollment:** FT

8,707, PT 788, Grad FT 851, Grad PT 363 **Faculty:** FT 292, PT 182 **Student-Faculty Ratio:** 31:1 **Exams:** SAT I or ACT. **% Receiving Financial Aid:** 68 **% Residing in College-Owned, -Operated, or -Affiliated Housing:** 40 **Regional Accreditation:** New England Association of Schools and Colleges **Credit Hours For Degree:** 90 credit hours, Associates; 180 credit hours, Bachelors **ROTC:** Army **Intercollegiate Athletics:** Baseball M; Basketball M & W; Cross-Country Running M & W; Equestrian Sports M & W; Golf M & W; Ice Hockey M; Sailing M & W; Soccer M & W; Softball W; Tennis M & W; Volleyball M & W; Wrestling M

MATER ECCLESIAE COLLEGE
60 Austin Ave.
Greenville, RI 02828
Tel: (401)949-2820
Web Site: http://www.materecclesiae.net/
Type: Four-Year College **Sex:** Women **Regional Accreditation:** New England Association of Schools and Colleges

NEW ENGLAND INSTITUTE OF TECHNOLOGY
2500 Post Rd.
Warwick, RI 02886-2244
Tel: (401)739-5000
Admissions: (401)467-7744
E-mail: neit@ids.net
Web Site: http://www.neit.edu/
President/CEO: Richard Gouse
Admissions: Michael Kwiatkowski
Type: Two-Year College **Sex:** Coed **Admission Plans:** Open Admission; Early Admission; Deferred Admission **Application Deadline:** Rolling **Application Fee:** $25.00 **H.S. Requirements:** High school diploma required; GED accepted **Costs Per Year:** Application fee: $25. Tuition: $16,800 full-time, $400 per credit hour part-time. Mandatory fees: $1340 full-time. Full-time tuition and fees vary according to program. Part-time tuition varies according to program. Tuition guaranteed not to increase for student's term of enrollment. **Scholarships:** Available **Calendar System:** Quarter, Summer Session Available **Enrollment:** FT 2,614, PT 395 **Faculty:** FT 100, PT 130 **Library Holdings:** 48,701 **Regional Accreditation:** New England Association of Schools and Colleges **Credit Hours For Degree:** 90 credits, Associates; 180 credits, Bachelors **Professional Accreditation:** ABET, ARCEST, AOTA

PROVIDENCE COLLEGE
1 Cunningham Square
Providence, RI 02918
Tel: (401)865-1000; Free: 800-721-6444
Admissions: (401)865-2535
Fax: (401)865-2826
E-mail: pcadmiss@providence.edu
Web Site: http://www.providence.edu/
President/CEO: Rev. Brian Shanley, OP
Admissions: Christopher Lydon
Financial Aid: Sandra J. Oliveira
Type: Comprehensive **Sex:** Coed **Affiliation:** Roman Catholic **Scores:** 98% SAT V 400+; 99% SAT M 400+; 27% ACT 18-23; 58% ACT 24-29 **% Accepted:** 60 **Admission Plans:** Early Admission; Early Action; Deferred Admission **Application Deadline:** January 15 **Application Fee:** $55.00 **H.S. Requirements:** High school diploma required; GED not accepted **Costs Per Year:** Application fee: $55. Comprehensive fee: $51,125 includes full-time tuition ($38,610), mandatory fees ($825), and college room and board ($11,690). College room only: $6790. Full-time tuition and fees vary according to degree level and student level. Room and board charges vary according to board plan and housing facility. Part-time tuition: $1120 per credit hour. Part-time tuition varies according to degree level. **Scholarships:** Available **Calendar System:** Semester, Summer Session Available **Enrollment:** FT 3,831, PT 6, Grad FT 187, Grad PT 476 **Faculty:** FT 297, PT 103 **Student-Faculty Ratio:** 13:1 **Exams:** ACT essay used for admission. SAT essay used for admission. ACT essay used for advising. SAT essay used for advising. ACT essay used for placement. SAT essay used for placement. **% Receiving Financial Aid:** 55 **% Residing in College-Owned, -Operated, or -Affiliated Housing:** 76 **Library Holdings:** 636,909 **Regional Accreditation:** New England Association of Schools and Colleges **Credit Hours For Degree:** 60 credits, Associates; 116 credits, Bachelors **ROTC:** Army **Professional Accreditation:** CSWE **Intercollegiate Athletics:** Basketball M & W; Cheerleading W; Cross-Country Running M & W; Field Hockey W; Golf M & W; Ice Hockey M & W; Lacrosse M; Racquetball M & W; Rugby M & W; Sailing M & W; Soccer M & W; Softball W; Swimming and Diving M & W; Tennis W; Track and Field M & W; Volleyball M & W

RHODE ISLAND COLLEGE
600 Mount Pleasant Ave.
Providence, RI 02908-1991
Tel: (401)456-8000; Free: 800-669-5760
Admissions: (401)456-8234
Fax: (401)456-8379
E-mail: admissions@ric.edu
Web Site: http://www.ric.edu/
President/CEO: Dr. Nancy Carriuolo
Admissions: Deborah Johnson
Financial Aid: James T. Hanbury
Type: Comprehensive **Sex:** Coed **Scores:** 83.8% SAT V 400+; 81.9% SAT M 400+; 51.3% ACT 18-23; 11.5% ACT 24-29 **% Accepted:** 77 **Admission Plans:** Early Admission **Application Deadline:** March 15 **Application Fee:** $50.00 **H.S. Requirements:** High school diploma required; GED accepted **Costs Per Year:** Application fee: $50. State resident tuition: $5988 full-time, $250 per credit part-time. Nonresident tuition: $15,880 full-time, $604 per credit part-time. Mandatory fees: $988 full-time, $28 per credit part-time, $72 per term part-time. Part-time tuition and fees vary according to course load. College room and board: $9270. College room only: $5266. Room and board charges vary according to board plan and housing facility. **Scholarships:** Available **Calendar System:** Semester, Summer Session Available **Enrollment:** FT 5,842, PT 2,041, Grad FT 269, Grad PT 1,108 **Faculty:** FT 311, PT 450 **Student-Faculty Ratio:** 16:1 **Exams:** SAT I or ACT. ACT essay used for advising. SAT essay used for advising. ACT essay not being used. SAT essay not being used. **% Receiving Financial Aid:** 56 **% Residing in College-Owned, -Operated, or -Affiliated Housing:** 16 **Final Year or Final Semester Residency Requirement:** No **Library Holdings:** 694,541 **Regional Accreditation:** New England Association of Schools and Colleges **Credit Hours For Degree:** 120 semester hours, Bachelors **ROTC:** Army **Professional Accreditation:** AACN, CSWE, NASAD, NASM, NCATE, NLN **Intercollegiate Athletics:** Baseball M; Basketball M & W; Cross-Country Running M & W; Golf M; Gymnastics W; Lacrosse W; Soccer M & W; Softball W; Tennis M & W; Track and Field M & W; Volleyball W; Wrestling M

RHODE ISLAND SCHOOL OF DESIGN
2 College St.
Providence, RI 02903-2784
Tel: (401)454-6100; Free: 800-364-7473
Fax: (401)454-6309
E-mail: admissions@risd.edu
Web Site: http://www.risd.edu/
President/CEO: John Maeda
Admissions: Edward Newhall
Type: Comprehensive **Sex:** Coed **Scores:** 97.9% SAT V 400+; 99.3% SAT M 400+ **% Accepted:** 33 **Admission Plans:** Early Admission; Early Action; Deferred Admission **Application Deadline:** February 15 **Application Fee:** $50.00 **H.S. Requirements:** High school diploma required; GED accepted **Costs Per Year:** Application fee: $50. Comprehensive fee: $47,505 includes full-time tuition ($36,364), mandatory fees ($295), and college room and board ($10,846). College room only: $6120. Room and board charges vary according to board plan and housing facility. Part-time tuition: $1205 per credit. **Scholarships:** Available **Calendar System:** 4-1-4, Summer Session Not available **Enrollment:** FT 1,863 **Faculty:** FT 146, PT 357 **Student-Faculty Ratio:** 9:1 **Exams:** SAT I or ACT. **% Receiving Financial Aid:** 48 **% Residing in College-Owned, -Operated, or -Affiliated Housing:** 52 **Library Holdings:** 130,000 **Regional Accreditation:** New England Association of Schools and Colleges **Credit Hours For Degree:** 126 credits, Bachelors **Professional Accreditation:** ASLA, NAAB, NASAD

ROGER WILLIAMS UNIVERSITY
1 Old Ferry Rd.
Bristol, RI 02809
Tel: (401)253-1040; Free: 800-458-7144
Admissions: (401)254-3500
Fax: (401)254-3557
E-mail: admit@rwu.edu
Web Site: http://www.rwu.edu/
President/CEO: Dr. Roy J. Nirschel, PhD
Admissions: Didier Bouvet

Financial Aid: Greg Rogers
Type: Comprehensive **Sex:** Coed **Scores:** 99.3% SAT V 400+; 99.23% SAT M 400+; 54.6% ACT 18-23; 40.8% ACT 24-29 **% Accepted:** 61 **Admission Plans:** Deferred Admission **Application Deadline:** February 1 **Application Fee:** $50.00 **H.S. Requirements:** High school diploma required; GED accepted **Scholarships:** Available **Calendar System:** Semester, Summer Session Available **Enrollment:** FT 3,771, PT 574 **Faculty:** FT 210, PT 374 **Student-Faculty Ratio:** 12:1 **Exams:** SAT I or ACT. **% Receiving Financial Aid:** 57 **% Residing in College-Owned, -Operated, or -Affiliated Housing:** 63 **Library Holdings:** 224,278 **Regional Accreditation:** New England Association of Schools and Colleges **Credit Hours For Degree:** 60 credits, Associates; 120 credits, Bachelors **ROTC:** Army **Professional Accreditation:** ABET, ABA, ACCE, NAAB **Intercollegiate Athletics:** Baseball M; Basketball M & W; Cheerleading W; Crew M & W; Cross-Country Running M & W; Equestrian Sports M & W; Lacrosse M & W; Rugby M; Sailing M & W; Soccer M & W; Softball W; Swimming and Diving M & W; Tennis M & W; Track and Field M & W; Volleyball M & W; Wrestling M

SALVE REGINA UNIVERSITY
100 Ochre Point Ave.
Newport, RI 02840-4192
Tel: (401)847-6650; Free: 888-GO SALVE
Admissions: (401)341-2908
Fax: (401)848-2823
E-mail: sruadmis@salve.edu
Web Site: http://www.salve.edu/
President/CEO: Sr. Jane Gerety
Admissions: Colleen Emerson
Financial Aid: Aida Mirante
Type: Comprehensive **Sex:** Coed **Affiliation:** Roman Catholic **Scores:** 100% SAT V 400+; 100% SAT M 400+; 41% ACT 18-23; 58% ACT 24-29 **% Accepted:** 64 **Admission Plans:** Early Action; Deferred Admission **Application Deadline:** February 1 **Application Fee:** $50.00 **H.S. Requirements:** High school diploma required; GED accepted **Costs Per Year:** Application fee: $50. One-time mandatory fee: $2350. Comprehensive fee: $40,950 includes full-time tuition ($29,800), mandatory fees ($200), and college room and board ($10,950). Room and board charges vary according to board plan and housing facility. Part-time tuition: $993 per credit hour. Part-time mandatory fees: $40 per term. Part-time tuition and fees vary according to course load. **Scholarships:** Available **Calendar System:** Semester, Summer Session Available **Enrollment:** FT 1,889, PT 95, Grad FT 135, Grad PT 459 **Faculty:** FT 117, PT 131 **Student-Faculty Ratio:** 14:1 **Exams:** SAT I or ACT. SAT essay used for advising. SAT essay used for placement. **% Receiving Financial Aid:** 71 **% Residing in College-Owned, -Operated, or -Affiliated Housing:** 63 **Final Year or Final Semester Residency Requirement:** No **Regional Accreditation:** New England Association of Schools and Colleges **Credit Hours For Degree:** 64 credit hours, Associates; 120 credit hours, Bachelors **ROTC:** Army **Professional Accreditation:** CORE, CSWE, NASAD, NLN **Intercollegiate Athletics:** Baseball M; Basketball M & W; Cross-Country Running M & W; Equestrian Sports M & W; Field Hockey W; Football M; Ice Hockey M & W; Lacrosse M & W; Rugby M; Sailing M & W; Soccer M & W; Softball W; Tennis M & W; Track and Field W; Volleyball W

UNIVERSITY OF RHODE ISLAND
Kingston, RI 02881
Tel: (401)874-1000
Admissions: (401)874-7110
Fax: (401)874-5523
E-mail: lynch@uri.edu
Web Site: http://www.uri.edu/
President/CEO: Dr. David M. Dooley
Admissions: Joanne Lynch
Financial Aid: Horace J. Amaral, Jr.
Type: University **Sex:** Coed **Affiliation:** Rhode Island Board of Governors for Higher Education **Scores:** 98.91% SAT V 400+; 99.14% SAT M 400+; 50.62% ACT 18-23; 39.26% ACT 24-29 **% Accepted:** 84 **Admission Plans:** Preferred Admission; Early Admission; Early Action; Deferred Admission **Application Deadline:** February 1 **Application Fee:** $65.00 **H.S. Requirements:** High school diploma required; GED accepted **Costs Per Year:** Application fee: $65. State resident tuition: $8238 full-time, $343 per credit hour part-time. Nonresident tuition: $24,736 full-time, $1031 per credit hour part-time. Mandatory fees: $1290 full-time, $27 per credit hour part-time, $49 per term part-time. Full-time tuition and fees vary according to course load, location, and reciprocity agreements. Part-time tuition and fees vary according to course load, location, and reciprocity agreements. College room and board: $9892. College room only: $6182. Room and board charges vary according to board plan and housing facility. **Scholarships:** Available **Calendar System:** Semester, Summer Session Available **Enrollment:** FT 11,776, PT 1,458, Grad FT 1,665, Grad PT 1,493 **Faculty:** FT 662, PT 600 **Student-Faculty Ratio:** 15:1 **Exams:** SAT I or ACT. **% Receiving Financial Aid:** 60 **% Residing in College-Owned, -Operated, or -Affiliated Housing:** 45 **Library Holdings:** 1,396,958 **Regional Accreditation:** New England Association of Schools and Colleges **Credit Hours For Degree:** 120 credits, Bachelors **ROTC:** Army **Professional Accreditation:** AACSB, ABET, ACPhE, AAMFT, AACN, ACNM, ADtA, ACSP, ALA, APTA, APA, ASLA, ASLHA, NASM, NCATE **Intercollegiate Athletics:** Baseball M; Basketball M & W; Cheerleading M & W; Crew M & W; Cross-Country Running M & W; Equestrian Sports M & W; Football M; Golf M; Ice Hockey M & W; Lacrosse M & W; Rugby M & W; Sailing M & W; Skiing (Downhill) M & W; Soccer M & W; Softball W; Swimming and Diving W; Tennis W; Track and Field M & W; Ultimate Frisbee M; Volleyball M & W; Wrestling M

AIKEN TECHNICAL COLLEGE
PO Drawer 696
Aiken, SC 29802-0696
Tel: (803)593-9231
E-mail: pridepae@atc.edu
Web Site: http://www.aik.tec.sc.us/
President/CEO: Susan A. Winsor
Admissions: Evelyn Pride Patterson
Type: Two-Year College **Sex:** Coed **Affiliation:** South Carolina State Board for Technical and Comprehensive Education **% Accepted:** 65 **Admission Plans:** Open Admission; Deferred Admission **Application Deadline:** Rolling **Application Fee:** $0.00 **H.S. Requirements:** High school diploma required; GED accepted **Scholarships:** Available **Calendar System:** Semester, Summer Session Available **Enrollment:** FT 1,397, PT 1,119 **Faculty:** FT 55, PT 109 **Library Holdings:** 32,118 **Regional Accreditation:** Southern Association of Colleges and Schools **Credit Hours For Degree:** 64 semester hours, Associates **Professional Accreditation:** ABET, ADA, ACBSP **Intercollegiate Athletics:** Basketball M

ALLEN UNIVERSITY
1530 Harden St.
Columbia, SC 29204
Tel: (803)254-4165
Admissions: (803)376-5733
Fax: (803)376-5731
E-mail: tparker@allenuniversity.edu
Web Site: http://www.allenuniversity.edu/
President/CEO: Charles E. Young
Admissions: Terri Parker
Financial Aid: Donna Foster
Type: Four-Year College **Sex:** Coed **Affiliation:** African Methodist Episcopal **Scores:** 44% SAT V 400+; 44% SAT M 400+ **% Accepted:** 72 **Admission Plans:** Open Admission **Application Deadline:** July 31 **Application Fee:** $20.00 **H.S. Requirements:** High school diploma required; GED accepted **Costs Per Year:** Application fee: $20. Tuition: $10,881 full-time, $450 per credit hour part-time. **Scholarships:** Available **Calendar System:** Semester, Summer Session Available **Enrollment:** FT 804, PT 23 **Faculty:** FT 29, PT 12 **Exams:** SAT I or ACT. **% Receiving Financial Aid:** 80 **Library Holdings:** 50,000 **Regional Accreditation:** Southern Association of Colleges and Schools **Credit Hours For Degree:** 125 credit hours, Bachelors **ROTC:** Army **Intercollegiate Athletics:** Basketball M & W; Cross-Country Running M & W; Golf M & W; Track and Field M & W; Volleyball W

ANDERSON UNIVERSITY
316 Blvd.
Anderson, SC 29621-4035
Tel: (864)231-2000; Free: 800-542-3594
Admissions: (864)231-2030
Fax: (864)231-2004
E-mail: admissions@andersonuniversity.edu
Web Site: http://www.andersonuniversity.edu/
President/CEO: Dr. Evans P. Whitaker
Admissions: Pam Bryant
Financial Aid: Becky Pressley
Type: Comprehensive **Sex:** Coed **Affiliation:** Baptist **Scores:** 90% SAT V 400+; 92% SAT M 400+; 55% ACT 18-23; 25% ACT 24-29 **% Accepted:** 78 **Admission Plans:** Deferred Admission **Application Deadline:** July 1 **Application Fee:** $25.00 **H.S. Requirements:** High school diploma required; GED accepted **Costs Per Year:** Application fee: $25. Comprehensive fee: $26,462 includes full-time tuition ($17,876), mandatory fees ($1336), and college room and board ($7250). College room only: $3700. Full-time tuition and fees vary according to course load and program. Room and board charges vary according to board plan and housing facility. Part-time tuition: $450 per credit hour. Part-time tuition varies according to program. **Scholarships:** Available **Calendar System:** Semester, Summer Session Available **Enrollment:** FT 1,508, PT 469 **Faculty:** FT 74, PT 94 **Student-Faculty Ratio:** 17:1 **Exams:** SAT I or ACT. **% Residing in College-Owned, -Operated, or -Affiliated Housing:** 85 **Library Holdings:** 69,069 **Regional Accreditation:** Southern Association of Colleges and Schools **Credit Hours For Degree:** 128 semester hours, Bachelors **ROTC:** Army, Air Force **Professional Accreditation:** ACBSP, NASM, NCATE **Intercollegiate Athletics:** Baseball M; Basketball M & W; Cheerleading W; Cross-Country Running M & W; Golf M & W; Soccer M & W; Softball W; Tennis M & W; Track and Field M & W; Volleyball W; Wrestling M

THE ART INSTITUTE OF CHARLESTON
24 North Market St.
Charleston, SC 29401
Tel: (843)727-3500; Free: (866)211-0107
Fax: (843)727-3440
Web Site: http://www.artinstitutes.edu/charleston/
President/CEO: Rick Jerue
Type: Four-Year College **Sex:** Coed **Affiliation:** Education Management Corporation **Calendar System:** Quarter **Regional Accreditation:** Southern Association of Colleges and Schools

BENEDICT COLLEGE
1600 Harden St.
Columbia, SC 29204
Tel: (803)256-4220
Fax: (803)253-5167
E-mail: thompsop@benedict.edu
Web Site: http://www.benedict.edu/
President/CEO: David H. Swinton
Admissions: Phyllis Thompson
Financial Aid: Bichevia Green
Type: Four-Year College **Sex:** Coed **Affiliation:** Baptist **Admission Plans:** Open Admission; Early Admission; Deferred Admission **Application Deadline:** Rolling **Application Fee:** $25.00 **H.S. Requirements:** High school diploma required; GED accepted **Scholarships:** Available **Calendar System:** Semester, Summer Session Available **Library Holdings:** 114,770 **Regional Accreditation:** Southern Association of Colleges and Schools **Credit Hours For Degree:** 125 semester hours, Bachelors **ROTC:** Army, Air Force **Professional Accreditation:** CSWE, NCATE **Intercollegiate Athletics:** Baseball M; Basketball M & W; Cheerleading W; Football M; Golf M; Softball W; Tennis M; Track and Field M; Volleyball W

BOB JONES UNIVERSITY
1700 Wade Hampton Blvd.
Greenville, SC 29614

Tel: (864)242-5100; Free: 800-BJA-NDME
E-mail: admissions@bju.edu
Web Site: http://www.bju.edu/
President/CEO: Dr. Stephen Jones
Admissions: Gary Deedrick
Type: University **Sex:** Coed **Scores:** 40.47% ACT 18-23; 41.71% ACT 24-29 **% Accepted:** 75 **Application Deadline:** August 1 **Application Fee:** $45.00 **H.S. Requirements:** High school diploma required; GED accepted **Costs Per Year:** Application fee: $45. One-time mandatory fee: $610. Comprehensive fee: $17,020 includes full-time tuition ($11,920) and college room and board ($5100). Part-time tuition: $576 per unit. **Scholarships:** Available **Calendar System:** Semester, Summer Session Available **Enrollment:** FT 3,355, PT 102, Grad FT 346, Grad PT 153 **Faculty:** FT 228, PT 67 **Student-Faculty Ratio:** 13:1 **Exams:** ACT. ACT essay used for advising. ACT essay used for placement. **% Residing in College-Owned, -Operated, or -Affiliated Housing:** 77 **Final Year or Final Semester Residency Requirement:** Yes **Library Holdings:** 332,117 **Credit Hours For Degree:** 90 credits, Associates; 128 credits, Bachelors

BROWN MACKIE COLLEGE—GREENVILLE
Two Liberty Square
75 Beattie Place, Ste. 100
Greenville, SC 29601
Tel: (864)239-5300; Free: 877-479-8465
Fax: (864)232-4094
Web Site: http://www.brownmackie.edu/greenville/
President/CEO: Karen Burgess
Type: Two-Year College **Sex:** Coed

CENTRAL CAROLINA TECHNICAL COLLEGE
506 North Guignard Dr.
Sumter, SC 29150-2499
Tel: (803)778-1961; Free: 800-221-8711
Fax: (803)773-4859
E-mail: brackenlm@cctech.edu
Web Site: http://www.cctech.edu/
President/CEO: Blon Tim Hardee, EdD
Admissions: Barbara Wright
Financial Aid: Diana Reardon
Type: Two-Year College **Sex:** Coed **Affiliation:** South Carolina State Board for Technical and Comprehensive Education **Admission Plans:** Open Admission **Application Deadline:** Rolling **Application Fee:** $0.00 **H.S. Requirements:** High school diploma required; GED accepted. For nursing programs: High school diploma required; GED not accepted **Costs Per Year:** Application fee: $0. Area resident tuition: $3300 full-time, $138 per credit hour part-time. State resident tuition: $3388 full-time, $162 per credit hour part-time. Nonresident tuition: $5888 full-time, $245 per credit hour part-time. Mandatory fees: $20 full-time. **Scholarships:** Available **Calendar System:** Semester, Summer Session Available **Enrollment:** FT 1,438, PT 2,699 **Faculty:** FT 88, PT 140 **Student-Faculty Ratio:** 19:1 **Exams:** ACT, Other, SAT I or ACT, SAT I. **Final Year or Final Semester Residency Requirement:** No **Library Holdings:** 20,356 **Regional Accreditation:** Southern Association of Colleges and Schools **Credit Hours For Degree:** 60 semester hours, Associates **Professional Accreditation:** ABET, ACBSP, NLN

CHARLESTON SOUTHERN UNIVERSITY
PO Box 118087
Charleston, SC 29423-8087
Tel: (843)863-7000; Free: 800-947-7474
Admissions: (843)863-7050
E-mail: enroll@csuniv.edu
Web Site: http://www.charlestonsouthern.edu/
President/CEO: Dr. Jairy C. Hunter, Jr.
Admissions: Jim Rhoden
Financial Aid: Jim Rhoden
Type: Comprehensive **Sex:** Coed **Affiliation:** Baptist **Scores:** 92.94% SAT V 400+; 92.37% SAT M 400+; 60.94% ACT 18-23; 14.7% ACT 24-29 **Application Deadline:** Rolling **Application Fee:** $30.00 **H.S. Requirements:** High school diploma required; GED accepted **Costs Per Year:** Application fee: $30. Comprehensive fee: $26,662 includes full-time tuition ($19,238), mandatory fees ($30), and college room and board ($7394). Part-time tuition: $400 per semester hour. Part-time mandatory fees: $30 per year. Part-time tuition and fees vary according to program. **Scholarships:** Available **Calendar System:** Miscellaneous, Summer Session Available **Enrollment:** FT 2,444, PT 391 **Faculty:** FT 115, PT 95 **Student-Faculty Ratio:** 18:1 **Exams:** SAT I or ACT. **% Receiving Financial Aid:** 82 **% Residing in College-Owned, -Operated, or -Affiliated Housing:** 49 **Library Holdings:** 192,600 **Regional Accreditation:** Southern Association of Colleges and Schools **Credit Hours For Degree:** 62 credit hours, Associates; 125 credit hours, Bachelors **ROTC:** Air Force **Professional Accreditation:** NASM, NCATE, NLN **Intercollegiate Athletics:** Baseball M; Basketball M & W; Cheerleading M & W; Cross-Country Running M & W; Football M; Golf M & W; Soccer W; Softball W; Tennis M & W; Track and Field M & W; Volleyball W

THE CITADEL, THE MILITARY COLLEGE OF SOUTH CAROLINA
171 Moultrie St.
Charleston, SC 29409
Tel: (843)953-5000; Free: 800-868-1842
Admissions: (843)953-5230
Fax: (843)953-7084
E-mail: john.powell@citadel.edu
Web Site: http://www.citadel.edu/
President/CEO: Lt. Gen. John W. Rosa
Admissions: Lt. Col. John W. Powell, Jr.
Financial Aid: Lt. Col. Hank M. Fuller
Type: Comprehensive **Sex:** Coed **Scores:** 99% SAT V 400+; 100% SAT M 400+; 76% ACT 18-23; 22% ACT 24-29 **% Accepted:** 79 **Admission Plans:** Preferred Admission; Early Decision Plan **Application Deadline:** Rolling **Application Fee:** $40.00 **H.S. Requirements:** High school diploma required; GED accepted **Costs Per Year:** Application fee: $40. State resident tuition: $8735 full-time, $341 per credit part-time. Nonresident tuition: $22,545 full-time, $598 per credit part-time. Mandatory fees: $1089 full-time, $15 per term part-time. College room and board: $5965. **Scholarships:** Available **Calendar System:** Semester, Summer Session Available **Enrollment:** FT 2,238, PT 128, Grad FT 193, Grad PT 780 **Faculty:** FT 172, PT 66 **Student-Faculty Ratio:** 16:1 **Exams:** SAT I or ACT. ACT essay not being used. SAT essay not being used. **% Receiving Financial Aid:** 52 **% Residing in College-Owned, -Operated, or -Affiliated Housing:** 100 **Final Year or Final Semester Residency Requirement:** No **Library Holdings:** 207,950 **Regional Accreditation:** Southern Association of Colleges and Schools **ROTC:** Army, Navy, Air Force **Professional Accreditation:** AACSB, ABET, ACA, NCATE **Intercollegiate Athletics:** Baseball M; Basketball M; Cross-Country Running M & W; Football M; Golf W; Ice Hockey M & W; Lacrosse M & W; Riflery M & W; Rugby M & W; Skiing (Downhill) M & W; Tennis M; Track and Field M & W; Volleyball W; Wrestling M

CLAFLIN UNIVERSITY
400 Magnolia St.
Orangeburg, SC 29115
Tel: (803)535-5097
Fax: (803)531-2860
Web Site: http://www.claflin.edu/
President/CEO: Dr. Henry N. Tisdale
Financial Aid: Yolanda Frazier
Type: Comprehensive **Sex:** Coed **Affiliation:** United Methodist **Scores:** 80% SAT V 400+; 72% SAT M 400+ **% Accepted:** 35 **Admission Plans:** Deferred Admission **Application Deadline:** Rolling **Application Fee:** $20.00 **H.S. Requirements:** High school diploma required; GED accepted **Costs Per Year:** Application fee: $20. Comprehensive fee: $19,472 includes full-time tuition ($10,628), mandatory fees ($2038), and college room and board ($6806). College room only: $3034. Full-time tuition and fees vary according to class time. Room and board charges vary according to housing facility. Part-time tuition: $443 per credit hour. Part-time mandatory fees: $73 per credit hour. Part-time tuition and fees vary according to class time. **Scholarships:** Available **Calendar System:** Semester, Summer Session Available **Enrollment:** FT 1,710, PT 69, Grad FT 62, Grad PT 19 **Faculty:** FT 109, PT 26 **Student-Faculty Ratio:** 14:1 **Exams:** SAT I or ACT, SAT II. **% Receiving Financial Aid:** 92 **Library Holdings:** 162,316 **Regional Accreditation:** Southern Association of Colleges and Schools **Credit Hours For Degree:** 124 semester hours, Bachelors **ROTC:** Army **Professional Accreditation:** ACBSP, NCATE **Intercollegiate Athletics:** Baseball M & W; Basketball M & W; Cross-Country Running M & W; Softball W; Track and Field M & W; Volleyball W

CLEMSON UNIVERSITY
Clemson, SC 29634
Tel: (864)656-3311

Admissions: (864)656-2287
Fax: (864)656-2464
E-mail: cuadmissions@clemson.edu
Web Site: http://www.clemson.edu/
President/CEO: Dr. James F. Barker
Admissions: Audrey R. Bodell
Financial Aid: Marvin G. Carmichael
Type: University **Sex:** Coed **Scores:** 100% SAT V 400+; 100% SAT M 400+; 13% ACT 18-23; 59% ACT 24-29 **% Accepted:** 63 **Admission Plans:** Preferred Admission **Application Deadline:** May 1 **Application Fee:** $50.00 **H.S. Requirements:** High school diploma required; GED accepted **Costs Per Year:** Application fee: $50. One-time mandatory fee: $1250. State resident tuition: $11,487 full-time. Nonresident tuition: $25,788 full-time. Mandatory fees: $122 full-time. Full-time tuition and fees vary according to course load, location, and program. College room and board: $6774. College room only: $4132. Room and board charges vary according to board plan, housing facility, and location. **Scholarships:** Available **Calendar System:** Semester, Summer Session Available **Enrollment:** FT 13,780, PT 933 **Faculty:** FT 1,106, PT 171 **Student-Faculty Ratio:** 14:1 **Exams:** SAT I or ACT. **% Receiving Financial Aid:** 43 **% Residing in College-Owned, -Operated, or -Affiliated Housing:** 41 **Library Holdings:** 1,233,478 **Regional Accreditation:** Southern Association of Colleges and Schools **Credit Hours For Degree:** 128 hours, Bachelors **ROTC:** Army, Air Force **Professional Accreditation:** AACSB, ABET, AACN, ACCE, ACA, ADtA, ACSP, ASLA, NAAB, NASAD, NCATE, NLN, NRPA, SAF **Intercollegiate Athletics:** Baseball M; Basketball M & W; Bowling M & W; Cheerleading M & W; Crew M & W; Cross-Country Running M & W; Equestrian Sports M & W; Fencing M & W; Field Hockey M & W; Football M; Golf M; Ice Hockey M & W; Lacrosse M & W; Riflery M & W; Rugby M & W; Sailing M & W; Soccer M & W; Softball W; Swimming and Diving M & W; Tennis M & W; Track and Field M & W; Ultimate Frisbee M & W; Volleyball M & W; Weight Lifting M & W; Wrestling M

CLINTON JUNIOR COLLEGE
PO Box 968, 1029 Crawford Rd.
Rock Hill, SC 29730
Tel: (803)327-7402
Fax: (803)327-3261
E-mail: ecopeland@clintonjrcollege.org
Web Site: http://www.clintonjuniorcollege.edu/
President/CEO: Dr. Elaine Johnson Copeland
Admissions: Dr. Janis Pen
Type: Two-Year College **Sex:** Coed **Affiliation:** African Methodist Episcopal Zion Church **Application Fee:** $25.00 **Calendar System:** Semester **Professional Accreditation:** TACCS

COASTAL CAROLINA UNIVERSITY
PO Box 261954
Conway, SC 29528-6054
Tel: (843)347-3161; Free: 800-277-7000
Admissions: (843)349-2037
Fax: (843)349-2127
E-mail: admissions@coastal.edu
Web Site: http://www.coastal.edu/
President/CEO: Dr. David DeCenzo
Admissions: Dr. Judy Vogt
Financial Aid: Dawn Hitchcock
Type: Comprehensive **Sex:** Coed **Scores:** 97.57% SAT V 400+; 98.38% SAT M 400+; 79.48% ACT 18-23; 12.57% ACT 24-29 **% Accepted:** 74 **Admission Plans:** Preferred Admission; Deferred Admission **Application Deadline:** August 15 **Application Fee:** $45.00 **H.S. Requirements:** High school diploma required; GED accepted **Costs Per Year:** Application fee: $45. State resident tuition: $8870 full-time, $373 per credit hour part-time. Nonresident tuition: $18,690 full-time, $782 per credit hour part-time. Mandatory fees: $80 full-time. Full-time tuition and fees vary according to course load. Part-time tuition varies according to course load. College room and board: $7200. College room only: $4650. Room and board charges vary according to board plan and housing facility. **Scholarships:** Available **Calendar System:** Semester, Summer Session Available **Enrollment:** FT 7,138, PT 782, Grad FT 116, Grad PT 324 **Faculty:** FT 315, PT 242 **Student-Faculty Ratio:** 18:1 **Exams:** SAT I or ACT. **% Receiving Financial Aid:** 58 **% Residing in College-Owned, -Operated, or -Affiliated Housing:** 28 **Library Holdings:** 190,564 **Regional Accreditation:** Southern Association of Colleges and Schools **Credit Hours For Degree:** 120 semester hours, Bachelors **ROTC:** Army **Professional Accreditation:** AACSB, ABET, NASAD, NCATE **Intercollegiate Athletics:** Baseball M; Basketball M & W; Cheerleading M & W; Cross-Country Running M & W; Football M; Golf M & W; Soccer M & W; Softball W; Tennis M & W; Track and Field M & W; Volleyball W

COKER COLLEGE
300 East College Ave.
Hartsville, SC 29550
Tel: (843)383-8000; Free: 800-950-1908
Admissions: (843)383-8050
Fax: (843)383-8056
E-mail: admissions@coker.edu
Web Site: http://www.coker.edu/
President/CEO: Dr. Robert Wyatt
Admissions: Perry Wilson
Financial Aid: Betty Williams
Type: Four-Year College **Sex:** Coed **Scores:** 92% SAT V 400+; 93% SAT M 400+; 20% ACT 18-23; 80% ACT 24-29 **% Accepted:** 56 **Admission Plans:** Early Admission; Deferred Admission **Application Deadline:** August 1 **Application Fee:** $15.00 **H.S. Requirements:** High school diploma required; GED accepted **Costs Per Year:** Application fee: $15. Comprehensive fee: $26,098 includes full-time tuition ($19,368), mandatory fees ($490), and college room and board ($6240). College room only: $3070. Part-time tuition: $807 per semester hour. **Scholarships:** Available **Calendar System:** Semester, Summer Session Available **Enrollment:** FT 645, PT 13 **Faculty:** FT 58, PT 22 **Student-Faculty Ratio:** 10:1 **Exams:** SAT I or ACT. **% Receiving Financial Aid:** 86 **Regional Accreditation:** Southern Association of Colleges and Schools **Credit Hours For Degree:** 120 semester hours, Bachelors **Professional Accreditation:** NASM **Intercollegiate Athletics:** Baseball M; Basketball M & W; Cross-Country Running M & W; Golf M; Soccer M & W; Softball W; Tennis M & W; Volleyball W

COLLEGE OF CHARLESTON
66 George St.
Charleston, SC 29424-0001
Tel: (843)953-5507
Admissions: (843)953-5670
E-mail: admissions@cofc.edu
Web Site: http://www.cofc.edu/
President/CEO: P. George Benson
Admissions: Suzette Stille
Financial Aid: Don Griggs
Type: Comprehensive **Sex:** Coed **Scores:** 100% SAT V 400+; 99.9% SAT M 400+; 34.5% ACT 18-23; 59.1% ACT 24-29 **% Accepted:** 70 **Admission Plans:** Early Action; Deferred Admission **Application Deadline:** April 1 **Application Fee:** $50.00 **H.S. Requirements:** High school diploma required; GED accepted **Costs Per Year:** Application fee: $50. State resident tuition: $8988 full-time, $375 per semester hour part-time. Nonresident tuition: $21,846 full-time, $910 per semester hour part-time. Full-time tuition varies according to degree level. Part-time tuition varies according to course load and degree level. College room and board: $9411. College room only: $6421. Room and board charges vary according to board plan and housing facility. **Scholarships:** Available **Calendar System:** Semester, Summer Session Available **Enrollment:** FT 9,334, PT 813, Grad FT 319, Grad PT 1,306 **Faculty:** FT 523, PT 370 **Student-Faculty Ratio:** 16:1 **Exams:** SAT I or ACT. **% Receiving Financial Aid:** 42 **% Residing in College-Owned, -Operated, or -Affiliated Housing:** 33 **Library Holdings:** 779,942 **Regional Accreditation:** Southern Association of Colleges and Schools **Credit Hours For Degree:** 122 semester hours, Bachelors **ROTC:** Air Force **Professional Accreditation:** AACSB, ABET, JRCEPAT, NASM, NASPAA, NCATE **Intercollegiate Athletics:** Baseball M; Basketball M & W; Cheerleading M & W; Cross-Country Running M & W; Equestrian Sports W; Golf M & W; Sailing M & W; Soccer M & W; Softball W; Swimming and Diving M & W; Tennis M & W; Track and Field W; Volleyball W

COLUMBIA COLLEGE
1301 Columbia College Dr.
Columbia, SC 29203-5998
Tel: (803)786-3012; Free: 800-277-1301
Admissions: (803)786-3765
Fax: (803)786-3674
E-mail: admissions@colacoll.edu
Web Site: http://www.columbiacollegesc.edu/

President/CEO: Dr. Caroline Whitson
Admissions: Julie King
Financial Aid: Anita Kaminer Elliott
Type: Comprehensive **Affiliation:** United Methodist **Scores:** 93% SAT V 400+; 95% SAT M 400+ **% Accepted:** 74 **Application Deadline:** August 1 **Application Fee:** $25.00 **H.S. Requirements:** High school diploma required; GED accepted **Costs Per Year:** Application fee: $25. Comprehensive fee: $29,930 includes full-time tuition ($23,030), mandatory fees ($450), and college room and board ($6450). Full-time tuition and fees vary according to class time. Room and board charges vary according to board plan and housing facility. Part-time tuition: $620 per semester hour. Part-time tuition varies according to course load. **Scholarships:** Available **Calendar System:** Semester, Summer Session Available **Enrollment:** FT 964, PT 225, Grad FT 175, Grad PT 81 **Faculty:** FT 78, PT 65 **Student-Faculty Ratio:** 10:1 **Exams:** SAT I or ACT. **% Receiving Financial Aid:** 78 **% Residing in College-Owned, -Operated, or -Affiliated Housing:** 44 **Library Holdings:** 146,135 **Regional Accreditation:** Southern Association of Colleges and Schools **Credit Hours For Degree:** 127 credits, Bachelors **ROTC:** Army, Navy, Air Force **Professional Accreditation:** CSWE, NASAD, NASD, NASM, NCATE **Intercollegiate Athletics:** Basketball W; Soccer W; Softball W; Tennis W; Volleyball W

COLUMBIA INTERNATIONAL UNIVERSITY
PO Box 3122
Columbia, SC 29230-3122
Tel: (803)754-4100; Free: 800-777-2227
Admissions: (803)807-5024
Fax: (803)786-4209
E-mail: yesciu@ciu.edu
Web Site: http://www.ciu.edu/
President/CEO: Dr. Bill Jones
Financial Aid: Nicole Mathison
Type: University **Sex:** Coed **Affiliation:** nondenominational **Scores:** 100% SAT V 400+; 97% SAT M 400+; 57% ACT 18-23; 35% ACT 24-29 **% Accepted:** 82 **Admission Plans:** Deferred Admission **Application Deadline:** Rolling **Application Fee:** $45.00 **H.S. Requirements:** High school diploma required; GED accepted **Costs Per Year:** Application fee: $45. Comprehensive fee: $23,805 includes full-time tuition ($16,850), mandatory fees ($545), and college room and board ($6410). Full-time tuition and fees vary according to course load. Room and board charges vary according to board plan. Part-time tuition: $695 per credit. Part-time tuition varies according to course load. **Scholarships:** Available **Calendar System:** Semester, Summer Session Available **Enrollment:** FT 503, PT 87, Grad FT 247, Grad PT 302 **Faculty:** FT 44, PT 9 **Student-Faculty Ratio:** 20:1 **Exams:** SAT I or ACT. **% Receiving Financial Aid:** 56 **Regional Accreditation:** Southern Association of Colleges and Schools **Credit Hours For Degree:** 63 semester hours, Associates; 128 semester hours, Bachelors **Professional Accreditation:** ABHE, ATS

CONVERSE COLLEGE
580 East Main St.
Spartanburg, SC 29302-0006
Tel: (864)596-9000; Free: 800-766-1125
Admissions: (864)596-9040
Fax: (864)596-9158
E-mail: admissions@converse.edu
Web Site: http://www.converse.edu/
President/CEO: Dr. Elizabeth Fleming
Admissions: April Lewis
Financial Aid: Margaret P. Collins
Type: Comprehensive **Scores:** 96% SAT V 400+; 97% SAT M 400+; 51% ACT 18-23; 41% ACT 24-29 **% Accepted:** 68 **Admission Plans:** Early Admission; Deferred Admission **Application Deadline:** Rolling **Application Fee:** $0.00 **H.S. Requirements:** High school diploma required; GED accepted **Costs Per Year:** Application fee: $0. One-time mandatory fee: $100. Comprehensive fee: $34,170 includes full-time tuition ($26,138) and college room and board ($8032). Full-time tuition varies according to reciprocity agreements. Room and board charges vary according to housing facility. **Scholarships:** Available **Calendar System:** Miscellaneous, Summer Session Available **Enrollment:** FT 621, PT 108, Grad FT 184, Grad PT 807 **Faculty:** FT 78, PT 10 **Student-Faculty Ratio:** 9:1 **Exams:** SAT I or ACT. ACT essay not being used. SAT essay not being used. **% Receiving Financial Aid:** 83 **% Residing in College-Owned, -Operated, or -Affiliated Housing:** 90 **Final Year or Final Semester Residency Requirement:** No **Library Holdings:** 155,731 **Regional Accreditation:** Southern Association of Colleges and Schools **Credit Hours For Degree:** 120 credit hours, Bachelors **ROTC:** Army **Professional Accreditation:** AAMFT, NASM, NCATE **Intercollegiate Athletics:** Basketball W; Cheerleading W; Cross-Country Running W; Lacrosse W; Soccer W; Swimming and Diving W; Tennis W; Volleyball W

DENMARK TECHNICAL COLLEGE
Solomon Blatt Blvd., Box 327
Denmark, SC 29042-0327
Tel: (803)793-5100
Admissions: (803)793-5182
Fax: (803)793-5942
E-mail: thomast@denmarktech.edu
Web Site: http://www.denmarktech.edu/
President/CEO: Dr. Walter M. Townsend, Sr.
Admissions: Tonya Thomas
Type: Two-Year College **Sex:** Coed **Affiliation:** South Carolina State Board for Technical and Comprehensive Education **Admission Plans:** Open Admission; Early Admission; Deferred Admission **Application Deadline:** Rolling **Application Fee:** $10.00 **H.S. Requirements:** High school diploma required; GED accepted **Costs Per Year:** Application fee: $10. State resident tuition: $2492 full-time, $91 per credit hour part-time. Nonresident tuition: $4676 full-time, $182 per credit hour part-time. College room and board: $3432. College room only: $1696. Tuition guaranteed not to increase for student's term of enrollment. **Scholarships:** Available **Calendar System:** Semester, Summer Session Available **Enrollment:** FT 896, PT 209 **Faculty:** FT 33, PT 19 **Student-Faculty Ratio:** 25:1 **Exams:** Other, SAT I or ACT. **Library Holdings:** 18,727 **Regional Accreditation:** Southern Association of Colleges and Schools **Credit Hours For Degree:** 60 credit hours, Associates **Professional Accreditation:** ABET, ACBSP **Intercollegiate Athletics:** Basketball M & W; Cheerleading W

ERSKINE COLLEGE
2 Washington St.
PO Box 338
Due West, SC 29639
Tel: (864)379-2131; Free: 800-241-8721
Admissions: (864)379-8838
Fax: (864)379-8759
E-mail: ocain@erskine.edu
Web Site: http://www.erskine.edu/
President/CEO: Dr. Randall T. Ruble
Admissions: Woody O'Cain
Financial Aid: Becky Pressley
Type: Comprehensive **Sex:** Coed **Affiliation:** Associate Reformed Presbyterian Church; Erskine Theological Seminary **Scores:** 95% SAT V 400+; 97% SAT M 400+; 31% ACT 18-23; 56% ACT 24-29 **% Accepted:** 70 **Admission Plans:** Preferred Admission; Early Admission; Early Action; Deferred Admission **Application Deadline:** Rolling **Application Fee:** $25.00 **H.S. Requirements:** High school diploma required; GED accepted **Costs Per Year:** Application fee: $25. Comprehensive fee: $32,970 includes full-time tuition ($23,000), mandatory fees ($1645), and college room and board ($8325). Part-time tuition: $852 per semester hour. **Scholarships:** Available **Calendar System:** 4-1-4, Summer Session Available **Enrollment:** FT 567, PT 15, Grad FT 69, Grad PT 223 **Faculty:** FT 42, PT 25 **Student-Faculty Ratio:** 11:1 **Exams:** SAT I or ACT. **% Receiving Financial Aid:** 69 **% Residing in College-Owned, -Operated, or -Affiliated Housing:** 90 **Library Holdings:** 268,645 **Regional Accreditation:** Southern Association of Colleges and Schools **Credit Hours For Degree:** 124 semester hours, Bachelors **Intercollegiate Athletics:** Baseball M; Basketball M & W; Cross-Country Running M & W; Equestrian Sports W; Golf M & W; Lacrosse W; Soccer M & W; Softball W; Tennis M & W; Volleyball W

FLORENCE-DARLINGTON TECHNICAL COLLEGE
2715 West Lucas St.
PO Box 100548
Florence, SC 29501-0548
Tel: (843)661-8324; Free: 800-228-5745
Fax: (843)661-8306
E-mail: kirvenp@flo.tec.sc.us
Web Site: http://www.fdtc.edu/
President/CEO: Charles W. Gould
Admissions: Kevin Qualls

Financial Aid: Joseph M. DuRant
Type: Two-Year College **Sex:** Coed **Affiliation:** South Carolina State Board for Technical and Comprehensive Education **Admission Plans:** Open Admission; Deferred Admission **Application Deadline:** August 1 **Application Fee:** $15.00 **H.S. Requirements:** High school diploma or equivalent not required. For nursing, dental services, chemical engineering technology, surgical technology, health information management, medical laboratory technology programs: High school diploma required; GED accepted **Scholarships:** Available **Calendar System:** Semester, Summer Session Available **Enrollment:** FT 2,147, PT 1,894 **Faculty:** FT 110, PT 202 **Student-Faculty Ratio:** 17:1 **Exams:** Other, SAT I or ACT. **Library Holdings:** 34,814 **Regional Accreditation:** Southern Association of Colleges and Schools **Credit Hours For Degree:** 61 credit hours, Associates **ROTC:** Army **Professional Accreditation:** ABET, ADA, AHIMA, ACBSP, CARC, JRCERT, NAACLS, NLN

FORREST JUNIOR COLLEGE
601 East River St.
Anderson, SC 29624
Tel: (864)225-7653
Fax: (864)261-7471
E-mail: janieturmon@forrestcollege.com
Web Site: http://www.forrestcollege.edu/
President/CEO: Rod Kruse
Admissions: Janie Turmon
Type: Two-Year College **Sex:** Coed **% Accepted:** 71 **Admission Plans:** Deferred Admission **Application Deadline:** Rolling **Application Fee:** $50.00 **H.S. Requirements:** High school diploma required; GED accepted **Costs Per Year:** Application fee: $50. Tuition: $8820 full-time, $245 per credit hour part-time. Mandatory fees: $150 full-time, $245 per credit hour part-time. **Scholarships:** Available **Calendar System:** Quarter, Summer Session Available **Enrollment:** FT 56, PT 38 **Faculty:** FT 2, PT 18 **Student-Faculty Ratio:** 5:1 **Exams:** Other. **Final Year or Final Semester Residency Requirement:** No **Library Holdings:** 40,000 **Credit Hours For Degree:** 90 quarter hours, Associates **Professional Accreditation:** ACICS

FRANCIS MARION UNIVERSITY
PO Box 100547
Florence, SC 29502-0547
Tel: (843)661-1362; Free: 800-368-7551
Admissions: (843)661-1231
Fax: (843)661-4635
E-mail: admission@fmarion.edu
Web Site: http://www.fmarion.edu/
President/CEO: Dr. Fred Carter
Admissions: James Schlimmer
Financial Aid: Kim Ellisor
Type: Comprehensive **Sex:** Coed **Scores:** 90.6% SAT V 400+; 92.9% SAT M 400+; 65% ACT 18-23; 14.1% ACT 24-29 **% Accepted:** 56 **Admission Plans:** Early Admission; Deferred Admission **Application Deadline:** Rolling **Application Fee:** $30.00 **H.S. Requirements:** High school diploma required; GED accepted **Costs Per Year:** Application fee: $30. State resident tuition: $8145 full-time, $407.25 per credit hour part-time. Nonresident tuition: $16,290 full-time, $814.50 per credit hour part-time. Mandatory fees: $335 full-time, $12.25 per credit hour part-time, $30 per term part-time. Part-time tuition and fees vary according to course load. College room and board: $6380. College room only: $3600. Room and board charges vary according to board plan and housing facility. **Scholarships:** Available **Calendar System:** Semester, Summer Session Available **Enrollment:** FT 3,302, PT 327, Grad FT 27, Grad PT 301 **Faculty:** FT 200, PT 54 **Student-Faculty Ratio:** 15:1 **Exams:** SAT I or ACT. **% Receiving Financial Aid:** 75 **% Residing in College-Owned, -Operated, or -Affiliated Housing:** 41 **Library Holdings:** 343,220 **Regional Accreditation:** Southern Association of Colleges and Schools **Credit Hours For Degree:** 120 semester hours, Bachelors **Professional Accreditation:** AACSB, NASAD, NAST, NCATE **Intercollegiate Athletics:** Baseball M; Basketball M & W; Cross-Country Running M & W; Golf M; Soccer M & W; Softball W; Tennis M & W; Track and Field M & W; Volleyball W

FURMAN UNIVERSITY
3300 Poinsett Hwy.
Greenville, SC 29613
Tel: (864)294-2000
Admissions: (864)294-2034
Fax: (864)294-3127
E-mail: admissions@furman.edu
Web Site: http://www.furman.edu/
President/CEO: Dr. David E. Shi
Admissions: Brad Pochard
Financial Aid: Forrest Stuart
Type: Comprehensive **Sex:** Coed **Scores:** 100% SAT V 400+; 100% SAT M 400+; 11.5% ACT 18-23; 54.6% ACT 24-29 **% Accepted:** 68 **Admission Plans:** Preferred Admission; Early Admission; Early Decision Plan **Application Deadline:** January 15 **Application Fee:** $50.00 **H.S. Requirements:** High school diploma required; GED accepted **Costs Per Year:** Application fee: $50. Comprehensive fee: $45,826 includes full-time tuition ($36,296), mandatory fees ($360), and college room and board ($9170). College room only: $4928. Room and board charges vary according to board plan and housing facility. Part-time tuition: $1134 per credit hour. Part-time tuition varies according to course load. **Scholarships:** Available **Calendar System:** Miscellaneous, Summer Session Available **Enrollment:** FT 2,622, PT 132, Grad FT 52, Grad PT 158 **Faculty:** FT 234, PT 36 **Student-Faculty Ratio:** 11:1 **Exams:** SAT I or ACT. **% Receiving Financial Aid:** 47 **% Residing in College-Owned, -Operated, or -Affiliated Housing:** 96 **Library Holdings:** 526,690 **Regional Accreditation:** Southern Association of Colleges and Schools **Credit Hours For Degree:** 128 credits, Bachelors **ROTC:** Army **Professional Accreditation:** NASM, NCATE **Intercollegiate Athletics:** Baseball M; Basketball M & W; Cheerleading M & W; Crew M & W; Cross-Country Running M & W; Equestrian Sports W; Fencing M & W; Football M; Golf M & W; Ice Hockey M; Lacrosse M & W; Rugby M & W; Soccer M & W; Softball W; Swimming and Diving M & W; Tennis M & W; Track and Field M & W; Ultimate Frisbee M & W; Volleyball W; Weight Lifting M & W; Wrestling M

GREENVILLE TECHNICAL COLLEGE
PO Box 5616
Greenville, SC 29606-5616
Tel: (864)250-8111; Free: 800-723-0673
Fax: (864)250-8534
Web Site: http://www.greenvilletech.com/
President/CEO: Keith Miller, PhD
Admissions: Martha S. White
Financial Aid: Carol Parker
Type: Two-Year College **Sex:** Coed **Affiliation:** South Carolina State Board for Technical and Comprehensive Education **Admission Plans:** Open Admission; Early Admission; Deferred Admission **Application Deadline:** Rolling **Application Fee:** $25.00 **H.S. Requirements:** High school diploma required; GED accepted **Scholarships:** Available **Calendar System:** Semester, Summer Session Available **Faculty:** FT 248, PT 230 **Exams:** Other. **Library Holdings:** 49,500 **Regional Accreditation:** Southern Association of Colleges and Schools **Credit Hours For Degree:** 60 semester hours, Associates **Professional Accreditation:** ABET, ACF, ADA, AHIMA, AOTA, APTA, ACBSP, CARC, JRCERT, JRCEMT, NAACLS, NLN

HORRY-GEORGETOWN TECHNICAL COLLEGE
2050 Hwy. 501, PO Box 261966
Conway, SC 29528-6066
Tel: (843)347-3186
Admissions: (843)349-5277
Fax: (843)347-4207
E-mail: george.swindoll@hgtc.edu
Web Site: http://www.hgtc.edu/
President/CEO: Neyle Wilson
Admissions: George Swindoll
Type: Two-Year College **Sex:** Coed **Affiliation:** South Carolina State Board for Technical and Comprehensive Education **Admission Plans:** Open Admission; Early Admission **Application Deadline:** Rolling **Application Fee:** $25.00 **H.S. Requirements:** High school diploma or equivalent not required. For health science programs: High school diploma required; GED accepted **Costs Per Year:** Application fee: $25. Area resident tuition: $3000 full-time, $126 per credit hour part-time. State resident tuition: $3832 full-time, $160 per credit hour part-time. Nonresident tuition: $4840 full-time, $202 per credit hour part-time. Mandatory fees: $211 full-time, $1.50 per credit hour part-time, $80 per term part-time. Part-time tuition and fees vary according to course load. **Scholarships:** Available **Calendar System:** Semester, Summer Session Available **Faculty:** FT 134, PT 283 **Student-Faculty Ratio:** 16:1 **Regional Accreditation:** Southern Association of Col-

leges and Schools **Credit Hours For Degree:** 63 semester hours, Associates **Professional Accreditation:** ABET, ACF, ADA, ACBSP, JRCERT, NLN

ITT TECHNICAL INSTITUTE (COLUMBIA)
720 Gracern Rd.
Ste. 120
Columbia, SC 29210
Tel: (803)216-6000; Free: 800-242-5158
Admissions: (803)216-6600
Web Site: http://www.itt-tech.edu/
President/CEO: John Shrader
Type: Two-Year College **Sex:** Coed **Affiliation:** ITT Educational Services, Inc.

ITT TECHNICAL INSTITUTE (GREENVILLE)
6 Independence Pointe
Greenville, SC 29615
Tel: (864)288-0777
Fax: (864)297-0053
Web Site: http://www.itt-tech.edu/
President/CEO: Josh Brown
Type: Two-Year College **Sex:** Coed **Affiliation:** ITT Educational Services, Inc. **H.S. Requirements:** High school diploma required; GED accepted **Scholarships:** Available **Calendar System:** Quarter, Summer Session Not available **Professional Accreditation:** ACICS

LANDER UNIVERSITY
320 Stanley Ave.
Greenwood, SC 29649-2099
Tel: (864)388-8000; Free: 888-452-6337
Admissions: (864)388-8307
Fax: (864)388-8125
E-mail: admissions@lander.edu
Web Site: http://www.lander.edu/
President/CEO: Dr. Daniel W. Ball
Admissions: Dr. Bettie R. Horne
Type: Comprehensive **Sex:** Coed **Affiliation:** South Carolina Commission on Higher Education **Scores:** 82.9% SAT V 400+; 89.3% SAT M 400+; 62.5% ACT 18-23; 13% ACT 24-29 **% Accepted:** 47 **Admission Plans:** Early Admission; Deferred Admission **Application Deadline:** August 1 **Application Fee:** $35.00 **H.S. Requirements:** High school diploma required; GED accepted **Costs Per Year:** Application fee: $35. State resident tuition: $8760 full-time, $365 per semester hour part-time. Nonresident tuition: $16,560 full-time, $690 per semester hour part-time. Mandatory fees: $780 full-time. Full-time tuition and fees vary according to course load, degree level, and program. Part-time tuition varies according to course load, degree level, and program. College room and board: $6400. College room only: $3846. Room and board charges vary according to board plan and housing facility. **Scholarships:** Available **Calendar System:** Semester, Summer Session Available **Enrollment:** FT 2,277, PT 278 **Faculty:** FT 137, PT 85 **Student-Faculty Ratio:** 14:1 **Exams:** SAT I or ACT. **% Receiving Financial Aid:** 39 **% Residing in College-Owned, -Operated, or -Affiliated Housing:** 33 **Library Holdings:** 186,690 **Regional Accreditation:** Southern Association of Colleges and Schools **Credit Hours For Degree:** 125 semester hours, Bachelors **ROTC:** Army **Professional Accreditation:** AACSB, MACTE, NASAD, NASM, NAST, NCATE, NLN **Intercollegiate Athletics:** Baseball M; Basketball M & W; Cross-Country Running W; Golf M; Soccer M & W; Softball W; Tennis M & W; Volleyball W

LIMESTONE COLLEGE
1115 College Dr.
Gaffney, SC 29340-3799
Tel: (864)489-7151; Free: 800-795-7151
Admissions: (864)488-4554
Fax: (864)487-8706
E-mail: cphenicie@limestone.edu
Web Site: http://www.limestone.edu/
President/CEO: Dr. Walt Griffin
Admissions: Sharon Chery
Financial Aid: Bobby Greer
Type: Four-Year College **Sex:** Coed **Scores:** 81% SAT V 400+; 87% SAT M 400+; 39% ACT 18-23; 24% ACT 24-29 **% Accepted:** 71 **Application Deadline:** Rolling **Application Fee:** $25.00 **H.S. Requirements:** High school diploma required; GED accepted **Costs Per Year:** Application fee: $25. Comprehensive fee: $26,200 includes full-time tuition ($19,200) and college room and board ($7000). College room only: $3500. Full-time tuition varies according to class time and location. Room and board charges vary according to housing facility. Part-time tuition: $800 per semester hour. Part-time tuition varies according to class time and location. **Scholarships:** Available **Calendar System:** Semester, Summer Session Available **Enrollment:** FT 795, PT 13 **Faculty:** FT 63, PT 16 **Student-Faculty Ratio:** 12:1 **Exams:** SAT I or ACT. **% Receiving Financial Aid:** 81 **% Residing in College-Owned, -Operated, or -Affiliated Housing:** 43 **Final Year or Final Semester Residency Requirement:** No **Library Holdings:** 132,203 **Regional Accreditation:** Southern Association of Colleges and Schools **Credit Hours For Degree:** 62 semester hours, Associates; 123 semester hours, Bachelors **ROTC:** Army **Professional Accreditation:** CSWE, NASM **Intercollegiate Athletics:** Baseball M; Basketball M & W; Cross-Country Running M & W; Field Hockey W; Golf M & W; Lacrosse M & W; Soccer M & W; Softball W; Swimming and Diving M & W; Tennis M & W; Track and Field M & W; Volleyball M & W; Wrestling M

MEDICAL UNIVERSITY OF SOUTH CAROLINA
179 Ashley Ave.
Charleston, SC 29425
Tel: (843)792-2300
Admissions: (843)792-7408
Fax: (843)792-3764
E-mail: hudsonly@musc.edu
Web Site: http://www.musc.edu/
President/CEO: Dr. Raymond S. Greenberg
Admissions: Lyla E. Hudson
Financial Aid: Cecile Kamath, PhD
Type: Two-Year Upper Division **Sex:** Coed **Admission Plans:** Preferred Admission; Early Decision Plan; Deferred Admission **Application Fee:** $85.00 **H.S. Requirements:** High school diploma required; GED accepted **Costs Per Year:** Application fee: $85. One-time mandatory fee: $440. State resident tuition: $12,658 full-time, $573 per semester hour part-time. Nonresident tuition: $22,266 full-time, $1030 per semester hour part-time. Mandatory fees: $1110 full-time, $860 per term part-time. Full-time tuition and fees vary according to program. Part-time tuition and fees vary according to course load and program. **Scholarships:** Available **Calendar System:** Semester, Summer Session Not available **Enrollment:** FT 218, PT 49, Grad FT 2,069, Grad PT 178 **Faculty:** FT 133, PT 67 **Student-Faculty Ratio:** 8:1 **Exams:** SAT I or ACT. **% Receiving Financial Aid:** 73 **Library Holdings:** 193,599 **Regional Accreditation:** Southern Association of Colleges and Schools **ROTC:** Air Force **Professional Accreditation:** ACPE, ACPhE, AACN, AANA, ACNM, ADA, ADtA, AOTA, APTA, APA, ASC, ASLHA, ACEHSA, LCMEAMA, NLN

MIDLANDS TECHNICAL COLLEGE
PO Box 2408
Columbia, SC 29202-2408
Tel: (803)738-1400
Admissions: (803)738-8324
Fax: (803)738-7784
E-mail: admissions@midlandstech.edu
Web Site: http://www.midlandstech.edu/
President/CEO: Dr. Marshall White, Jr.
Admissions: Sylvia Littlejohn
Type: Two-Year College **Sex:** Coed **Affiliation:** South Carolina State Board for Technical and Comprehensive Education **% Accepted:** 65 **Admission Plans:** Open Admission; Early Admission; Deferred Admission **Application Deadline:** Rolling **Application Fee:** $35.00 **H.S. Requirements:** High school diploma or equivalent not required **Costs Per Year:** Application fee: $35. One-time mandatory fee: $25. Area resident tuition: $3408 full-time, $142 per credit hour part-time. State resident tuition: $4272 full-time, $178 per credit hour part-time. Nonresident tuition: $10,224 full-time, $426 per credit hour part-time. Mandatory fees: $200 full-time, $100 per term part-time. Full-time tuition and fees vary according to course load. Part-time tuition and fees vary according to course load. **Scholarships:** Available **Calendar System:** Semester, Summer Session Available **Enrollment:** FT 5,564, PT 6,326 **Faculty:** FT 216, PT 517 **Student-Faculty Ratio:** 20:1 **Exams:** Other, SAT I or ACT. **Library Holdings:** 98,507 **Regional Accreditation:** Southern Association of Colleges and Schools **Credit Hours For Degree:** 60 semester hours, Associates **Professional Accreditation:** ABET, ADA, AHIMA, APTA, ACBSP, CARC, JRCERT, NAACLS, NLN

MILLER-MOTTE TECHNICAL COLLEGE
8085 Rivers Ave.
Ste. E
Charleston, SC 29406
Tel: (843)574-0101; Free: 877-617-4740
Fax: (843)266-3434
E-mail: juliasc@miller-mott.net
Web Site: http://www.miller-motte.com/
President/CEO: Elaine Cue
Admissions: Elaine Cue
Type: Two-Year College **Sex:** Coed **Affiliation:** Delta Career Education Corporation **Admission Plans:** Open Admission **Application Fee:** $35.00 **H.S. Requirements:** High school diploma required; GED accepted **Costs Per Year:** Application fee: $35. Tuition: $11,750 full-time. Mandatory fees: $575 full-time. Full-time tuition and fees vary according to course load and program. Tuition guaranteed not to increase for student's term of enrollment. **Calendar System:** Quarter **Exams:** Other. **Credit Hours For Degree:** 96 quarter credits, Associates **Professional Accreditation:** ACICS

MORRIS COLLEGE
100 West College St.
Sumter, SC 29150-3599
Tel: (803)934-3200; Free: (866)853-1345
Admissions: (803)934-3225
Fax: (803)773-3687
E-mail: dcalhoun@morris.edu
Web Site: http://www.morris.edu/
President/CEO: Dr. Luns C. Richardson
Admissions: Deborah C. Calhoun
Financial Aid: Sandra S. Gibson
Type: Four-Year College **Sex:** Coed **Affiliation:** Baptist Educational and Missionary Convention of South Carolina **% Accepted:** 91 **Admission Plans:** Open Admission; Deferred Admission **Application Deadline:** Rolling **Application Fee:** $20.00 **H.S. Requirements:** High school diploma required; GED accepted **Costs Per Year:** Application fee: $20. Comprehensive fee: $14,287 includes full-time tuition ($9630), mandatory fees ($271), and college room and board ($4386). Part-time tuition: $401 per credit hour. Part-time mandatory fees: $61 per term. **Scholarships:** Available **Calendar System:** Semester, Summer Session Available **Enrollment:** FT 952, PT 14 **Faculty:** FT 48, PT 17 **Student-Faculty Ratio:** 18:1 **% Receiving Financial Aid:** 96 **% Residing in College-Owned, -Operated, or -Affiliated Housing:** 76 **Library Holdings:** 82,156 **Regional Accreditation:** Southern Association of Colleges and Schools **Credit Hours For Degree:** 124 credit hours, Bachelors **ROTC:** Army **Intercollegiate Athletics:** Baseball M; Basketball M & W; Cross-Country Running M & W; Golf M; Softball W; Tennis M & W; Track and Field M & W; Volleyball W

NEWBERRY COLLEGE
2100 College St.
Newberry, SC 29108-2197
Tel: (803)276-5010; Free: 800-845-4955
Admissions: (803)321-5129
E-mail: admissions@newberry.edu
Web Site: http://www.newberry.edu/
President/CEO: Dr. John H. Hudgens
Admissions: Amanda Richardson
Financial Aid: Melissa A. Lutz
Type: Four-Year College **Sex:** Coed **Affiliation:** Evangelical Lutheran **% Accepted:** 69 **Admission Plans:** Early Admission; Deferred Admission **Application Deadline:** Rolling **Application Fee:** $30.00 **H.S. Requirements:** High school diploma required; GED accepted **Costs Per Year:** Application fee: $30. Comprehensive fee: $30,220 includes full-time tuition ($20,500), mandatory fees ($1970), and college room and board ($7750). College room only: $3800. Full-time tuition and fees vary according to class time, course load, and student level. Room and board charges vary according to housing facility. Part-time tuition: $500 per credit hour. Part-time mandatory fees: $100 per term. Part-time tuition and fees vary according to class time, course load, and student level. **Scholarships:** Available **Calendar System:** Semester, Summer Session Available **Enrollment:** FT 1,083, PT 20 **Faculty:** FT 52, PT 36 **Student-Faculty Ratio:** 17:1 **Exams:** SAT I or ACT. **% Residing in College-Owned, -Operated, or -Affiliated Housing:** 84 **Library Holdings:** 84,874 **Regional Accreditation:** Southern Association of Colleges and Schools **Credit Hours For Degree:** 126 semester hours, Bachelors **ROTC:** Army **Professional Accreditation:** NASM, NCATE **Intercollegiate Athletics:** Baseball M; Basketball M & W; Cheerleading W; Cross-Country Running M & W; Football M; Golf M & W; Soccer M & W; Softball W; Tennis M & W; Volleyball W; Wrestling M

NORTH GREENVILLE UNIVERSITY
PO Box 1892
Tigerville, SC 29688-1892
Tel: (864)977-7000; Free: 800-468-6642
Admissions: (864)977-7052
Fax: (864)977-7177
E-mail: ksewell@ngu.edu
Web Site: http://www.ngu.edu/
President/CEO: Dr. James B. Epting
Admissions: Keli Sewell
Financial Aid: Mike Jordan
Type: Comprehensive **Sex:** Coed **Affiliation:** Southern Baptist **Scores:** 93% SAT V 400+; 92% SAT M 400+; 53% ACT 18-23; 24% ACT 24-29 **% Accepted:** 55 **Admission Plans:** Preferred Admission; Early Admission; Deferred Admission **Application Deadline:** August 18 **Application Fee:** $25.00 **H.S. Requirements:** High school diploma required; GED accepted **Costs Per Year:** Application fee: $25. Comprehensive fee: $19,320 includes full-time tuition ($12,264) and college room and board ($7056). College room only: $3192. Full-time tuition varies according to course load. Room and board charges vary according to housing facility. Part-time tuition: $210 per credit hour. **Scholarships:** Available **Calendar System:** Semester, Summer Session Available **Enrollment:** FT 1,894, PT 238, Grad PT 129 **Faculty:** FT 124, PT 43 **Student-Faculty Ratio:** 15:1 **Exams:** Other, SAT I or ACT. **% Receiving Financial Aid:** 94 **% Residing in College-Owned, -Operated, or -Affiliated Housing:** 70 **Library Holdings:** 50,000 **Regional Accreditation:** Southern Association of Colleges and Schools **Credit Hours For Degree:** 64 semester hours, Associates; 121 semester hours, Bachelors **ROTC:** Army **Intercollegiate Athletics:** Baseball M; Basketball M & W; Cheerleading M & W; Cross-Country Running M & W; Football M; Golf M & W; Soccer M & W; Softball W; Tennis M & W; Volleyball W

NORTHEASTERN TECHNICAL COLLEGE
PO Drawer 1007
Cheraw, SC 29520-1007
Tel: (843)921-6900
Admissions: (843)921-6935
Fax: (843)537-6148
E-mail: mpace@netc.edu
Web Site: http://www.netc.edu/
President/CEO: Dr. Ron Bartley
Admissions: Mary K. Newton
Type: Two-Year College **Sex:** Coed **Affiliation:** South Carolina State Board for Technical and Comprehensive Education **% Accepted:** 100 **Admission Plans:** Open Admission; Early Admission **Application Deadline:** August 4 **Application Fee:** $25.00 **H.S. Requirements:** High school diploma required; GED accepted **Scholarships:** Available **Calendar System:** Semester **Enrollment:** FT 446, PT 530 **Student-Faculty Ratio:** 25:1 **Exams:** Other, SAT I. **Library Holdings:** 24,129 **Regional Accreditation:** Southern Association of Colleges and Schools **Credit Hours For Degree:** 60 semester hours, Associates

ORANGEBURG-CALHOUN TECHNICAL COLLEGE
3250 St Matthews Rd., NE
Orangeburg, SC 29118-8299
Tel: (803)536-0311
Admissions: (803)535-1219
Fax: (803)535-1388
Web Site: http://www.octech.edu/
President/CEO: Dr. Anne Crook
Admissions: Dana Rickards
Type: Two-Year College **Sex:** Coed **Affiliation:** State Board for Technical and Comprehensive Education, South Carolina **Admission Plans:** Open Admission **Application Deadline:** Rolling **Application Fee:** $15.00 **H.S. Requirements:** High school diploma required; GED accepted **Scholarships:** Available **Calendar System:** Semester, Summer Session Available **Enrollment:** FT 1,538, PT 1,681 **Faculty:** FT 75, PT 88 **Student-Faculty Ratio:** 20:1 **Library Holdings:** 43,500 **Regional Accreditation:** Southern Association of Colleges and Schools **Credit Hours For Degree:** 60 semester hours, Associates **Professional Accreditation:** ABET, ACBSP, JRCERT, NAACLS, NLN

PIEDMONT TECHNICAL COLLEGE
620 North Emerald Rd.
PO Box 1467
Greenwood, SC 29648-1467
Tel: (864)941-8324
Fax: (864)941-8555
Web Site: http://www.ptc.edu/
President/CEO: Ray Brooks
Admissions: Steve Coleman
Type: Two-Year College **Sex:** Coed **Affiliation:** South Carolina State Board for Technical and Comprehensive Education **% Accepted:** 100 **Admission Plans:** Open Admission; Early Admission; Deferred Admission **Application Deadline:** Rolling **Application Fee:** $25.00 **H.S. Requirements:** High school diploma required; GED accepted **Scholarships:** Available **Calendar System:** Semester, Summer Session Available **Faculty:** FT 103, PT 130 **Student-Faculty Ratio:** 18:1 **Library Holdings:** 27,497 **Regional Accreditation:** Southern Association of Colleges and Schools **Credit Hours For Degree:** 60 credits, Associates **Professional Accreditation:** ABET, ABFSE, ACBSP, CARC, JRCERT, NLN

PRESBYTERIAN COLLEGE
503 South Broad St.
Clinton, SC 29325
Tel: (864)833-2820; Free: 800-476-7272
Admissions: (864)833-8229
Fax: (864)833-8481
E-mail: lpatters@presby.edu
Web Site: http://www.presby.edu/
President/CEO: Dr. John V. Griffith
Admissions: Leni N. Patterson
Financial Aid: Jeff Holliday
Type: Four-Year College **Sex:** Coed **Affiliation:** Presbyterian Church (U.S.A.) **Scores:** 99% SAT V 400+; 99% SAT M 400+; 41% ACT 18-23; 48% ACT 24-29 **% Accepted:** 70 **Admission Plans:** Early Admission; Early Action; Early Decision Plan; Deferred Admission **Application Deadline:** February 1 **Application Fee:** $40.00 **H.S. Requirements:** High school diploma required; GED accepted **Costs Per Year:** Application fee: $40. One-time mandatory fee: $406. Comprehensive fee: $37,225 includes full-time tuition ($26,436), mandatory fees ($2444), and college room and board ($8345). Full-time tuition and fees vary according to course level, program, and reciprocity agreements. Room and board charges vary according to board plan and housing facility. Part-time tuition: $1102 per credit hour. Part-time mandatory fees: $17 per credit hour, $22 per term. Part-time tuition and fees vary according to course level, course load, and program. **Scholarships:** Available **Calendar System:** Semester, Summer Session Available **Enrollment:** FT 1,198, PT 23 **Faculty:** FT 87, PT 61 **Student-Faculty Ratio:** 12:1 **Exams:** SAT I or ACT. ACT essay not being used. SAT essay not being used. **% Receiving Financial Aid:** 68 **% Residing in College-Owned, -Operated, or -Affiliated Housing:** 96 **Final Year or Final Semester Residency Requirement:** Yes **Library Holdings:** 140,467 **Regional Accreditation:** Southern Association of Colleges and Schools **Credit Hours For Degree:** 122 semester hours, Bachelors **ROTC:** Army **Professional Accreditation:** ACBSP, NCATE **Intercollegiate Athletics:** Baseball M; Basketball M & W; Cheerleading M & W; Cross-Country Running M & W; Football M; Golf M & W; Lacrosse M & W; Soccer M & W; Softball W; Tennis M & W; Volleyball W

SOUTH CAROLINA STATE UNIVERSITY
300 College St. Northeast
Orangeburg, SC 29117-0001
Tel: (803)536-7000; Free: 800-260-5956
Admissions: (803)536-7186
Fax: (803)536-8990
E-mail: admissions@scsu.edu
Web Site: http://www.scsu.edu/
President/CEO: Dr. George M. Cooper
Admissions: Antonio Boyle
Financial Aid: Sandra S. Davis
Type: Comprehensive **Sex:** Coed **Affiliation:** South Carolina Commission on Higher Education **Scores:** 66% SAT V 400+; 72% SAT M 400+; 31% ACT 18-23; 6% ACT 24-29 **% Accepted:** 78 **Admission Plans:** Deferred Admission **Application Deadline:** July 31 **Application Fee:** $25.00 **H.S. Requirements:** High school diploma required; GED accepted **Costs Per Year:** Application fee: $25. State resident tuition: $8462 full-time, $353 per credit hour part-time. Nonresident tuition: $16,626 full-time, $693 per credit hour part-time. College room and board: $8862. College room only: $6000. Room and board charges vary according to housing facility. **Scholarships:** Available **Calendar System:** Semester, Summer Session Available **Enrollment:** FT 3,567, PT 307, Grad FT 284, Grad PT 380 **Faculty:** FT 228, PT 61 **Student-Faculty Ratio:** 16:1 **Exams:** SAT I or ACT, SAT II. **% Residing in College-Owned, -Operated, or -Affiliated Housing:** 60 **Library Holdings:** 313,329 **Regional Accreditation:** Southern Association of Colleges and Schools **Credit Hours For Degree:** 120 semester hours, Bachelors **ROTC:** Army, Air Force **Professional Accreditation:** AACSB, ABET, AAFCS, ACA, ASLHA, CORE, CSWE, NASM, NCATE **Intercollegiate Athletics:** Basketball M & W; Bowling W; Cross-Country Running M & W; Football M; Golf M & W; Soccer W; Softball W; Tennis M & W; Track and Field M & W; Volleyball W

SOUTH UNIVERSITY
9 Science Ct.
Columbia, SC 29203
Tel: (803)799-9082; Free: (866)629-3031
Fax: (803)799-9038
Web Site: http://www.southuniversity.edu/columbia/
President/CEO: Brad C. Kauffman
Type: Comprehensive **Sex:** Coed **Affiliation:** Education Management Corporation **Calendar System:** Quarter **Professional Accreditation:** ACBSP

SOUTHERN METHODIST COLLEGE
541 Broughton St., PO Box 1027
Orangeburg, SC 29115
Tel: (803)534-7826; Free: 800-360-1503
E-mail: jwebb@smcollege.edu
Web Site: http://www.smcollege.edu/
President/CEO: Gary K. Briden
Admissions: Juanta Webb
Type: Four-Year College **Sex:** Coed **% Accepted:** 100 **Admission Plans:** Early Admission; Early Action; Deferred Admission **Application Deadline:** July 15 **Application Fee:** $35.00 **H.S. Requirements:** High school diploma required; GED accepted **Scholarships:** Available **Exams:** SAT I or ACT. **Library Holdings:** 21,743 **Credit Hours For Degree:** 63 credits, Associates; 124 credits, Bachelors **Professional Accreditation:** TACCS

SOUTHERN WESLEYAN UNIVERSITY
907 Wesleyan Dr., PO Box 1020
Central, SC 29630-1020
Tel: (864)644-5000; Free: 800-289-1292
Admissions: (864)644-5149
Fax: (864)644-5900
E-mail: broe@swu.edu
Web Site: http://www.swu.edu/
President/CEO: Dr. David J. Spittal
Admissions: Beth Roe
Financial Aid: Sherri Peters
Type: Comprehensive **Sex:** Coed **Affiliation:** Wesleyan Church **Scores:** 87% SAT V 400+; 91% SAT M 400+; 59% ACT 18-23; 21% ACT 24-29 **% Accepted:** 95 **Admission Plans:** Deferred Admission **Application Deadline:** August 1 **Application Fee:** $25.00 **H.S. Requirements:** High school diploma required; GED accepted **Costs Per Year:** Application fee: $25. Comprehensive fee: $26,700 includes full-time tuition ($19,000), mandatory fees ($500), and college room and board ($7200). College room only: $2600. Full-time tuition and fees vary according to class time, course load, location, and program. Room and board charges vary according to board plan and housing facility. Part-time tuition: $775 per credit hour. Part-time tuition varies according to class time, course load, location, and program. **Scholarships:** Available **Calendar System:** Semester, Summer Session Available **Enrollment:** FT 1,649, PT 28, Grad FT 705 **Faculty:** FT 50, PT 169 **Student-Faculty Ratio:** 23:1 **Exams:** SAT I or ACT. **% Receiving Financial Aid:** 80 **% Residing in College-Owned, -Operated, or -Affiliated Housing:** 58 **Final Year or Final Semester Residency Requirement:** Yes **Library Holdings:** 116,200 **Regional Accreditation:** Southern Association of Colleges and Schools **Credit Hours For Degree:** 64 hours, Associates; 120 hours, Bachelors **ROTC:** Army, Air Force **Professional Accreditation:** NCATE **Intercollegiate Athletics:** Baseball M; Basketball M & W; Cheerleading M & W; Cross-Country Running M & W; Golf M; Soccer M & W; Softball W; Volleyball W

SPARTANBURG COMMUNITY COLLEGE
Business I-85 & New Cut Rd.
PO Box 4386
Spartanburg, SC 29305-4386
Tel: (864)592-4600
Admissions: (864)592-4815
E-mail: admissions@stcsc.edu
Web Site: http://www.sccsc.edu/
President/CEO: Dr. Para M. Jones
Admissions: Kathy Jo Lancaster
Financial Aid: Nancy T. Garmroth
Type: Two-Year College **Sex:** Coed **Affiliation:** South Carolina State Board for Technical and Comprehensive Education **% Accepted:** 57 **Admission Plans:** Open Admission; Early Admission **Application Deadline:** Rolling **Application Fee:** $0.00 **H.S. Requirements:** High school diploma required; GED accepted. For industrial technology programs: High school diploma required; GED accepted **Costs Per Year:** Application fee: $0. Area resident tuition: $3434 full-time, $142 per credit hour part-time. State resident tuition: $4282 full-time, $177 per credit hour part-time. Nonresident tuition: $7196 full-time, $299 per credit hour part-time. Mandatory fees: $20 per term part-time. **Scholarships:** Available **Calendar System:** Semester, Summer Session Available **Enrollment:** FT 3,076, PT 2,637 **Faculty:** FT 111, PT 254 **Student-Faculty Ratio:** 16:1 **Exams:** SAT I or ACT. **Library Holdings:** 40,078 **Regional Accreditation:** Southern Association of Colleges and Schools **Credit Hours For Degree:** 60 semester hours, Associates **Professional Accreditation:** ABET, ADA, ACBSP, CARC, JRCERT, NAACLS

SPARTANBURG METHODIST COLLEGE
1000 Powell Mill Rd.
Spartanburg, SC 29301
Tel: (864)587-4000; Free: 800-772-7286
Admissions: (864)587-4223
Fax: (864)587-4355
E-mail: admiss@smcsc.edu
Web Site: http://www.smcsc.edu/
President/CEO: Dr. Colleen P. Keith
Admissions: Daniel L. Philbeck
Type: Two-Year College **Sex:** Coed **Affiliation:** Methodist **Scores:** 71.7% SAT V 400+; 76% SAT M 400+ **% Accepted:** 70 **Admission Plans:** Deferred Admission **Application Deadline:** Rolling **Application Fee:** $20.00 **H.S. Requirements:** High school diploma required; GED accepted **Costs Per Year:** Application fee: $20. One-time mandatory fee: $150. Comprehensive fee: $20,363 includes full-time tuition ($12,723), mandatory fees ($225), and college room and board ($7415). Part-time tuition: $334 per semester hour. **Scholarships:** Available **Calendar System:** Semester, Summer Session Available **Enrollment:** FT 775, PT 33 **Faculty:** FT 32, PT 36 **Student-Faculty Ratio:** 18:1 **Exams:** SAT I or ACT. **% Residing in College-Owned, -Operated, or -Affiliated Housing:** 68 **Library Holdings:** 75,000 **Regional Accreditation:** Southern Association of Colleges and Schools **Credit Hours For Degree:** 64 semester hours, Associates **Intercollegiate Athletics:** Baseball M; Basketball M & W; Cross-Country Running M & W; Golf M & W; Soccer M & W; Softball W; Tennis M & W; Volleyball W; Wrestling M

STRAYER UNIVERSITY - CHARLESTON CAMPUS
5010 Wetland Crossing
North Charleston, SC 29418
Tel: (843)746-5100
Fax: (843)746-5130
Web Site: http://www.strayer.edu/charleston/
Type: Comprehensive **Sex:** Coed **Application Fee:** $50.00 **Costs Per Year:** Application fee: $50. **Regional Accreditation:** Middle State Association of Colleges and Schools

STRAYER UNIVERSITY - COLUMBIA CAMPUS
200 Center Point Circle, Ste. 300
Columbia, SC 29210
Tel: (803)750-2500
Fax: (803)750-2530
Web Site: http://www.strayer.edu/columbia
Type: Comprehensive **Sex:** Coed **Application Fee:** $50.00 **Costs Per Year:** Application fee: $50. **Regional Accreditation:** Middle State Association of Colleges and Schools

STRAYER UNIVERSITY - GREENVILLE CAMPUS
555 North Pleasantburg Dr.
Ste. 300
Greenville, SC 29607
Tel: (864)250-7000
Fax: (864)232-3611
Web Site: http://www.strayer.edu/greenville
Type: Comprehensive **Sex:** Coed **Application Fee:** $50.00 **Costs Per Year:** Application fee: $50. **Regional Accreditation:** Middle State Association of Colleges and Schools

TECHNICAL COLLEGE OF THE LOWCOUNTRY
921 Ribaut Rd., PO Box 1288
Beaufort, SC 29901-1288
Tel: (843)525-8324
Admissions: (843)525-8229
E-mail: rcole@tcl.edu
Web Site: http://www.tclonline.org/
President/CEO: Thomas Leitzel
Admissions: Rhonda Cole
Type: Two-Year College **Sex:** Coed **Affiliation:** South Carolina Technical and Comprehensive Education System **Admission Plans:** Early Admission; Deferred Admission **Application Deadline:** Rolling **Application Fee:** $25.00 **H.S. Requirements:** High school diploma required; GED accepted **Costs Per Year:** Application fee: $25. Area resident tuition: $3232 full-time, $135 per credit hour part-time. State resident tuition: $7286 full-time, $304 per credit hour part-time. Nonresident tuition: $8032 full-time, $335 per credit hour part-time. Mandatory fees: $150 full-time, $5 per credit hour part-time, $25 per term part-time. **Scholarships:** Available **Calendar System:** Semester, Summer Session Available **Student-Faculty Ratio:** 15:1 **Exams:** Other, SAT I and SAT II or ACT. **Regional Accreditation:** Southern Association of Colleges and Schools **Credit Hours For Degree:** 64 credit hours, Associates **Professional Accreditation:** ACBSP, NLN

TRI-COUNTY TECHNICAL COLLEGE
PO Box 587, 7900 Hwy. 76
Pendleton, SC 29670-0587
Tel: (864)646-8361
Admissions: (864)646-1550
E-mail: infocent@tctc.edu
Web Site: http://www.tctc.edu/
President/CEO: Dr. Ronnie Booth
Admissions: Renae Frazier
Type: Two-Year College **Sex:** Coed **Affiliation:** South Carolina State Board for Technical and Comprehensive Education **Admission Plans:** Open Admission; Early Admission **Application Deadline:** Rolling **Application Fee:** $30.00 **H.S. Requirements:** High school diploma required; GED accepted. For welding, industrial mechanics programs: High school diploma or equivalent not required **Costs Per Year:** Application fee: $30. Area resident tuition: $3024 full-time, $126 per credit hour part-time. State resident tuition: $3360 full-time, $140 per credit hour part-time. Nonresident tuition: $6888 full-time, $287 per credit hour part-time. Mandatory fees: $144 full-time, $6 per credit hour part-time. **Scholarships:** Available **Calendar System:** Semester, Summer Session Available **Student-Faculty Ratio:** 21:1 **Regional Accreditation:** Southern Association of Colleges and Schools **Credit Hours For Degree:** 60 credits, Associates **ROTC:** Army, Air Force **Professional Accreditation:** ABET, ADA, ACBSP, NAACLS, NLN **Intercollegiate Athletics:** Golf M; Soccer M

TRIDENT TECHNICAL COLLEGE
PO Box 118067
Charleston, SC 29423-8067
Tel: (843)574-6111
Admissions: (843)574-6626
Fax: (843)574-6109
E-mail: Clara.Martin@tridenttech.edu
Web Site: http://www.tridenttech.edu/
President/CEO: Dr. Mary Thornley
Admissions: Clara Martin
Financial Aid: Ellen Green
Type: Two-Year College **Sex:** Coed **Affiliation:** South Carolina State Board for Technical and Comprehensive Education **Admission Plans:** Open Admission; Early Admission **Application Deadline:** August 9 **Application Fee:** $30.00 **H.S. Requirements:** High school diploma required; GED ac-

cepted **Costs Per Year:** Application fee: $30. Area resident tuition: $3450 full-time. State resident tuition: $3828 full-time. Nonresident tuition: $6532 full-time. Full-time tuition varies according to course load. **Scholarships:** Available **Calendar System:** Semester, Summer Session Available **Enrollment:** FT 6,856, PT 7,978 **Faculty:** FT 306, PT 393 **Student-Faculty Ratio:** 20:1 **Library Holdings:** 135,345 **Regional Accreditation:** Southern Association of Colleges and Schools **Credit Hours For Degree:** 60 credit hours, Associates **Professional Accreditation:** ABET, ACF, ADA, AOTA, APTA, ACBSP, CARC, JRCERT, NAACLS, NLN

UNIVERSITY OF PHOENIX—COLUMBIA CAMPUS
1001 Pinnacle Point Dr., Ste. 200
Columbia, SC 29223
Tel: (803)699-5096
Web Site: http://www.phoenix.edu/
President/CEO: William Pepicello, PhD
Type: Comprehensive **Sex:** Coed **Regional Accreditation:** North Central Association of Colleges and Schools

UNIVERSITY OF SOUTH CAROLINA
Columbia, SC 29208
Tel: (803)777-7000
Admissions: (803)777-7700
E-mail: admissions-ugrad@sc.edu
Web Site: http://www.sc.edu/
President/CEO: Dr. Harris Pastides
Admissions: Dr. Mary Wagner
Financial Aid: Dr. Ed Miller
Type: University **Sex:** Coed **Affiliation:** University of South Carolina System **Scores:** 99.68% SAT V 400+; 99.92% SAT M 400+; 21.84% ACT 18-23; 60.02% ACT 24-29 **% Accepted:** 64 **Admission Plans:** Early Action **Application Deadline:** December 1 **Application Fee:** $50.00 **H.S. Requirements:** High school diploma required; GED accepted **Costs Per Year:** Application fee: $50. State resident tuition: $8756 full-time, $410 per credit hour part-time. Nonresident tuition: $23,332 full-time, $1065 per credit hour part-time. Mandatory fees: $400 full-time, $17 per credit hour part-time. Full-time tuition and fees vary according to course load, program, and reciprocity agreements. Part-time tuition and fees vary according to course load and program. College room and board: $7328. College room only: $4677. Room and board charges vary according to board plan, housing facility, and location. **Scholarships:** Available **Calendar System:** Semester, Summer Session Available **Enrollment:** FT 18,979, PT 1,515, Grad FT 4,989, Grad PT 2,998 **Faculty:** FT 1,142, PT 518 **Student-Faculty Ratio:** 18:1 **Exams:** SAT I or ACT. **% Receiving Financial Aid:** 45 **% Residing in College-Owned, -Operated, or -Affiliated Housing:** 33 **Final Year or Final Semester Residency Requirement:** Yes **Library Holdings:** 3,320,392 **Regional Accreditation:** Southern Association of Colleges and Schools **Credit Hours For Degree:** 60 credit hours, Associates; 120 credit hours, Bachelors **ROTC:** Army, Navy, Air Force **Professional Accreditation:** AACSB, ABET, ACPhE, ACEJMC, AACN, AANA, ABA, ACA, ALA, APTA, APA, ASLHA, AALS, ACEHSA, CEPH, CORE, CSWE, JRCEPAT, LCMEAMA, NASAD NASM, NASPAA, NAST, NCATE **Intercollegiate Athletics:** Baseball M; Basketball M & W; Cross-Country Running W; Equestrian Sports W; Football M; Golf M & W; Soccer M & W; Softball W; Swimming and Diving M & W; Tennis M & W; Track and Field M & W; Volleyball W

UNIVERSITY OF SOUTH CAROLINA AIKEN
471 University Parkway
Aiken, SC 29801-6309
Tel: (803)648-6851; Free: 888-WOW-USCA
Fax: (803)641-3727
E-mail: admit@usca.edu
Web Site: http://www.usca.edu/
President/CEO: Dr. Thomas L. Hallman
Admissions: Andrew Hendrix
Financial Aid: Glenn Shumpert
Type: Comprehensive **Sex:** Coed **Affiliation:** University of South Carolina System **Scores:** 92% SAT V 400+; 95% SAT M 400+; 64% ACT 18-23; 18% ACT 24-29 **% Accepted:** 38 **Admission Plans:** Early Admission; Deferred Admission **Application Deadline:** August 1 **Application Fee:** $45.00 **H.S. Requirements:** High school diploma required; GED accepted **Scholarships:** Available **Calendar System:** Semester, Summer Session Available **Enrollment:** FT 2,459, PT 743, Grad FT 17, Grad PT 50 **Faculty:** FT 150, PT 83 **Student-Faculty Ratio:** 15:1 **Exams:** SAT I or ACT. **% Receiving Financial Aid:** 58 **% Residing in College-Owned, -Operated, or -Affiliated Housing:** 27 **Regional Accreditation:** Southern Association of Colleges and Schools **Credit Hours For Degree:** 120 semester hours, Bachelors **Professional Accreditation:** AACSB, NCATE, NLN **Intercollegiate Athletics:** Baseball M; Basketball M & W; Cheerleading M & W; Cross-Country Running W; Golf M; Soccer M & W; Softball W; Tennis M & W; Volleyball W

UNIVERSITY OF SOUTH CAROLINA BEAUFORT
One University Blvd.
Bluffton, SC 29909
Tel: (843)208-8000
Admissions: (843)208-8112
E-mail: mrwilli5@uscb.edu
Web Site: http://www.uscb.edu/
President/CEO: Dr. Jane T. Upshaw
Admissions: Monica Williams
Financial Aid: Tina Wells
Type: Four-Year College **Sex:** Coed **Affiliation:** University of South Carolina System **% Accepted:** 73 **Admission Plans:** Deferred Admission **Application Deadline:** Rolling **Application Fee:** $40.00 **H.S. Requirements:** High school diploma required; GED accepted **Costs Per Year:** Application fee: $40. State resident tuition: $6914 full-time. Nonresident tuition: $14,764 full-time. Mandatory fees: $416 full-time. Full-time tuition and fees vary according to reciprocity agreements. College room and board: $6100. Room and board charges vary according to housing facility. **Scholarships:** Available **Calendar System:** Semester, Summer Session Available **Enrollment:** FT 1,260, PT 424 **Faculty:** FT 62, PT 91 **Student-Faculty Ratio:** 16:1 **Exams:** SAT I or ACT. **% Residing in College-Owned, -Operated, or -Affiliated Housing:** 18 **Library Holdings:** 84,865 **Regional Accreditation:** Southern Association of Colleges and Schools **Credit Hours For Degree:** 60 semester hours, Associates; 120 semester hours, Bachelors **Intercollegiate Athletics:** Baseball M; Cross-Country Running M & W; Golf M & W; Track and Field M & W

UNIVERSITY OF SOUTH CAROLINA LANCASTER
PO Box 889
Lancaster, SC 29721-0889
Tel: (803)313-7000
Fax: (803)313-7106
E-mail: vinsons@mailbox.sc.edu
Web Site: http://usclancaster.sc.edu/
President/CEO: Dr. John Catalano
Admissions: Susan Vinson
Financial Aid: Kenneth Tobey Cole
Type: Two-Year College **Sex:** Coed **Affiliation:** University of South Carolina System **% Accepted:** 100 **Admission Plans:** Open Admission; Early Admission **Application Deadline:** Rolling **Application Fee:** $40.00 **H.S. Requirements:** High school diploma required; GED accepted **Costs Per Year:** Application fee: $40. One-time mandatory fee: $50. State resident tuition: $5136 full-time, $214 per credit hour part-time. Nonresident tuition: $12,912 full-time, $538 per credit hour part-time. Mandatory fees: $462 full-time, $15 per credit hour part-time. Full-time tuition and fees vary according to student level. Part-time tuition and fees vary according to student level. **Scholarships:** Available **Calendar System:** Semester, Summer Session Not available **Enrollment:** FT 794, PT 799 **Faculty:** FT 63, PT 42 **Student-Faculty Ratio:** 14:1 **Exams:** SAT I or ACT. ACT essay not being used. SAT essay not being used. **Final Year or Final Semester Residency Requirement:** Yes **Library Holdings:** 82,000 **Regional Accreditation:** Southern Association of Colleges and Schools **Credit Hours For Degree:** 60 semester hours, Associates **Professional Accreditation:** ACBSP, NLN **Intercollegiate Athletics:** Baseball M; Golf M; Soccer W; Tennis M & W

UNIVERSITY OF SOUTH CAROLINA SALKEHATCHIE
PO Box 617
Allendale, SC 29810-0617
Tel: (803)584-3446
Admissions: 800-922-5500
E-mail: cdbrown@mailbox.sc.edu
Web Site: http://uscsalkehatchie.sc.edu/
President/CEO: Ann C. Carmichael
Admissions: Carmen Brown
Financial Aid: Julie Hadwin
Type: Two-Year College **Sex:** Coed **Affiliation:** University of South Carolina

System **Application Deadline:** Rolling **Application Fee:** $40.00 **H.S. Requirements:** High school diploma required; GED accepted **Scholarships:** Available **Calendar System:** Semester, Summer Session Available **Student-Faculty Ratio:** 16:1 **Exams:** SAT I or ACT. ACT essay not being used. SAT essay not being used. **Regional Accreditation:** Southern Association of Colleges and Schools **Credit Hours For Degree:** 60 semester hours, Associates **Intercollegiate Athletics:** Baseball M; Basketball M; Soccer M & W; Softball W; Volleyball W

UNIVERSITY OF SOUTH CAROLINA SUMTER
200 Miller Rd.
Sumter, SC 29150-2498
Tel: (803)775-8727
E-mail: kbritton@usc.sumter.edu
Web Site: http://www.uscsumter.edu/
President/CEO: C. Leslie Carpenter
Admissions: Keith Britton
Financial Aid: Sue Sims
Type: Two-Year College **Sex:** Coed **Affiliation:** University of South Carolina System **Scores:** 85.2% SAT V 400+; 85.2% SAT M 400+; 57.4% ACT 18-23; 3.7% ACT 24-29 **% Accepted:** 62 **Application Deadline:** August 8 **Application Fee:** $40.00 **H.S. Requirements:** High school diploma required; GED accepted **Scholarships:** Available **Calendar System:** Semester, Summer Session Available **Enrollment:** FT 575, PT 513 **Faculty:** FT 41, PT 25 **Student-Faculty Ratio:** 19:1 **Exams:** SAT I or ACT. **Library Holdings:** 81,114 **Regional Accreditation:** Southern Association of Colleges and Schools **Credit Hours For Degree:** 60 semester hours, Associates **ROTC:** Army, Air Force

UNIVERSITY OF SOUTH CAROLINA UNION
PO Drawer 729
Union, SC 29379-0729
Tel: (864)427-3681
Admissions: (864)429-8728
E-mail: tyoung@gwm.sc.edu
Web Site: http://uscunion.sc.edu/
President/CEO: Hugh C. Rowland
Admissions: Terry Young
Type: Two-Year College **Sex:** Coed **Affiliation:** University of South Carolina System **Application Deadline:** Rolling **Application Fee:** $40.00 **H.S. Requirements:** High school diploma required; GED accepted **Costs Per Year:** Application fee: $40. State resident tuition: $2784 full-time, $229 per credit hour part-time. Nonresident tuition: $3850 full-time, $349 per credit hour part-time. Full-time tuition varies according to course load, degree level, and student level. Part-time tuition varies according to student level. **Scholarships:** Available **Calendar System:** Semester **Enrollment:** FT 182, PT 216 **Faculty:** FT 12, PT 13 **Student-Faculty Ratio:** 14:1 **Exams:** SAT I or ACT. **Regional Accreditation:** Southern Association of Colleges and Schools **Credit Hours For Degree:** 60 semester hours, Associates

UNIVERSITY OF SOUTH CAROLINA UPSTATE
800 University Way
Spartanburg, SC 29303-4999
Tel: (864)503-5000; Free: 800-277-8727
Admissions: (864)503-5280
Fax: (864)503-5201
E-mail: dstewart@uscupstate.edu
Web Site: http://www.uscupstate.edu/
President/CEO: Dr. John C. Stockwell
Admissions: Donette Stewart
Financial Aid: Kim Jenerette
Type: Comprehensive **Sex:** Coed **Affiliation:** University of South Carolina System **Scores:** 90.67% SAT V 400+; 93.72% SAT M 400+; 66.08% ACT 18-23; 14.19% ACT 24-29 **% Accepted:** 78 **Admission Plans:** Deferred Admission **Application Fee:** $40.00 **H.S. Requirements:** High school diploma required; GED accepted **Costs Per Year:** Application fee: $40. State resident tuition: $8362 full-time, $357 per semester hour part-time. Nonresident tuition: $17,004 full-time, $723 per semester hour part-time. Mandatory fees: $500 full-time. Full-time tuition and fees vary according to course load and program. Part-time tuition varies according to course load and program. College room and board: $6300. College room only: $3600. Room and board charges vary according to board plan and housing facility. **Scholarships:** Available **Calendar System:** Semester, Summer Session Available **Enrollment:** FT 4,157, PT 1,134, Grad FT 5, Grad PT 107 **Faculty:** FT 206, PT 176 **Student-Faculty Ratio:** 17:1 **Exams:** SAT I or ACT. **% Receiving Financial Aid:** 67 **% Residing in College-Owned, -Operated, or -Affiliated Housing:** 17 **Library Holdings:** 201,237 **Regional Accreditation:** Southern Association of Colleges and Schools **Credit Hours For Degree:** 71 semester hours, Associates; 120 semester hours, Bachelors **ROTC:** Army **Professional Accreditation:** AACSB, ABET, NCATE, NLN **Intercollegiate Athletics:** Baseball M; Basketball M & W; Cross-Country Running M & W; Golf M & W; Soccer M & W; Softball W; Tennis M & W; Track and Field M & W; Volleyball W

VOORHEES COLLEGE
213 Wiggins Dr.
PO Box 678
Denmark, SC 29042
Tel: (803)780-1234; Free: (866)685-9904
Admissions: (803)703-1049
Fax: (803)793-5773
E-mail: williej@voorhees.edu
Web Site: http://www.voorhees.edu/
President/CEO: Dr. Cleveland Sellers
Admissions: Dr. Willie Jefferson
Financial Aid: Augusta L. Kitchen
Type: Four-Year College **Sex:** Coed **Affiliation:** Episcopal **% Accepted:** 70 **Admission Plans:** Deferred Admission **Application Deadline:** Rolling **Application Fee:** $25.00 **H.S. Requirements:** High school diploma required; GED accepted **Costs Per Year:** Application fee: $25. Comprehensive fee: $16,478 includes full-time tuition ($9664), mandatory fees ($500), and college room and board ($6314). **Scholarships:** Available **Calendar System:** Semester, Summer Session Available **Enrollment:** FT 671, PT 30 **Faculty:** FT 38, PT 18 **Student-Faculty Ratio:** 16:1 **Exams:** SAT I or ACT. **% Receiving Financial Aid:** 91 **% Residing in College-Owned, -Operated, or -Affiliated Housing:** 74 **Library Holdings:** 107,260 **Regional Accreditation:** Southern Association of Colleges and Schools **Credit Hours For Degree:** 124 credit hours, Bachelors **ROTC:** Army **Professional Accreditation:** ACBSP **Intercollegiate Athletics:** Baseball M; Basketball M & W; Cross-Country Running M & W; Softball W; Track and Field M & W; Volleyball W

WILLIAMSBURG TECHNICAL COLLEGE
601 Martin Luther King, Jr Ave.
Kingstree, SC 29556-4197
Tel: (843)355-4110; Free: 800-768-2021
Admissions: (843)355-4162
Fax: (843)355-4296
E-mail: wrighta@wiltech.edu
Web Site: http://www.wiltech.edu/
President/CEO: Cheryl Cox
Admissions: Alexis Wright
Type: Two-Year College **Sex:** Coed **Affiliation:** South Carolina State Board for Technical and Comprehensive Education **Admission Plans:** Open Admission; Early Admission; Deferred Admission **Application Deadline:** Rolling **Application Fee:** $10.00 **H.S. Requirements:** High school diploma required; GED accepted **Costs Per Year:** Application fee: $10. Area resident tuition: $3000 full-time, $125 per credit hour part-time. State resident tuition: $3120 full-time, $130 per credit hour part-time. Nonresident tuition: $5808 full-time, $242 per credit hour part-time. Mandatory fees: $42 full-time, $1.75 per credit hour part-time. Full-time tuition and fees vary according to course load. Part-time tuition and fees vary according to course load. **Scholarships:** Available **Calendar System:** Semester, Summer Session Available **Student-Faculty Ratio:** 11:1 **Regional Accreditation:** Southern Association of Colleges and Schools **Credit Hours For Degree:** 62 semester hours, Associates **Professional Accreditation:** ACBSP

WINTHROP UNIVERSITY
701 Oakland Ave.
Rock Hill, SC 29733
Tel: (803)323-2211; Free: 800-763-0230
Admissions: (803)323-2191
Fax: (803)323-2137
E-mail: admissions@winthrop.edu
Web Site: http://www.winthrop.edu/
President/CEO: Dr. Anthony J. DiGiorgio
Admissions: Deborah Barber
Financial Aid: Leah Sturgis

Type: Comprehensive **Sex:** Coed **Affiliation:** South Carolina Commission on Higher Education **Scores:** 99% SAT V 400+; 100% SAT M 400+; 63% ACT 18-23; 32% ACT 24-29 **% Accepted:** 65 **Admission Plans:** Deferred Admission **Application Deadline:** May 1 **Application Fee:** $40.00 **H.S. Requirements:** High school diploma required; GED accepted **Costs Per Year:** Application fee: $40. State resident tuition: $11,606 full-time, $484 per semester hour part-time. Nonresident tuition: $21,596 full-time, $900 per semester hour part-time. Full-time tuition varies according to degree level. Part-time tuition varies according to degree level. College room and board: $6530. College room only: $4130. Room and board charges vary according to board plan and housing facility. **Scholarships:** Available **Calendar System:** Semester, Summer Session Available **Enrollment:** FT 4,473, PT 624, Grad FT 464, Grad PT 680 **Faculty:** FT 276, PT 276 **Student-Faculty Ratio:** 15:1 **Exams:** SAT I or ACT. ACT essay used for admission. SAT essay used for admission. **% Receiving Financial Aid:** 68 **% Residing in College-Owned, -Operated, or -Affiliated Housing:** 44 **Final Year or Final Semester Residency Requirement:** No **Library Holdings:** 499,697 **Regional Accreditation:** Southern Association of Colleges and Schools **Credit Hours For Degree:** 124 semester hours, Bachelors **ROTC:** Army **Professional Accreditation:** AACSB, ABET, ACEJMC, ACA, ADtA, FIDER, CSWE, NASAD, NASD, NASM, NAST, NCATE **Intercollegiate Athletics:** Baseball M; Basketball M & W; Cheerleading M & W; Cross-Country Running M & W; Fencing M & W; Golf M & W; Lacrosse M & W; Rugby M; Soccer M; Softball W; Tennis M & W; Track and Field M & W; Volleyball W

WOFFORD COLLEGE
429 North Church St.
Spartanburg, SC 29303-3663
Tel: (864)597-4000
Admissions: (864)597-4130
Fax: (864)597-4149
E-mail: admission@wofford.edu
Web Site: http://www.wofford.edu/
President/CEO: Dr. Benjamin B. Dunlap
Admissions: S. Wells Shepard
Financial Aid: Kay C. Walton
Type: Four-Year College **Sex:** Coed **Affiliation:** United Methodist Church **Scores:** 100% SAT V 400+; 100% SAT M 400+; 33% ACT 18-23; 47% ACT 24-29 **% Accepted:** 58 **Admission Plans:** Early Admission; Early Decision Plan; Deferred Admission **Application Deadline:** February 1 **Application Fee:** $35.00 **H.S. Requirements:** High school diploma required; GED accepted **Costs Per Year:** Application fee: $35. Comprehensive fee: $38,760 includes full-time tuition ($30,280) and college room and board ($8480). Part-time tuition: $1195 per credit hour. **Scholarships:** Available **Calendar System:** 4-1-4, Summer Session Available **Enrollment:** FT 1,420, PT 19 **Faculty:** FT 117, PT 30 **Student-Faculty Ratio:** 11:1 **Exams:** SAT I or ACT. **% Receiving Financial Aid:** 56 **% Residing in College-Owned, -Operated, or -Affiliated Housing:** 94 **Library Holdings:** 267,870 **Regional Accreditation:** Southern Association of Colleges and Schools **Credit Hours For Degree:** 124 semester hours, Bachelors **ROTC:** Army **Intercollegiate Athletics:** Baseball M; Basketball M & W; Cheerleading W; Cross-Country Running M & W; Football M; Golf M & W; Riflery M & W; Soccer M & W; Tennis M & W; Track and Field M & W; Volleyball W

YORK TECHNICAL COLLEGE
452 South Anderson Rd.
Rock Hill, SC 29730-3395
Tel: (803)327-8000
Admissions: (803)327-8008
Fax: (803)327-8059
E-mail: kaldridge@yorktech.com
Web Site: http://www.yorktech.com/
President/CEO: Dr. Greg Rutherford
Admissions: Kenny Aldridge
Financial Aid: Ottalee Frazier-Darden
Type: Two-Year College **Sex:** Coed **Affiliation:** South Carolina State Board for Technical and Comprehensive Education **Admission Plans:** Open Admission **Application Deadline:** Rolling **Application Fee:** $0.00 **H.S. Requirements:** High school diploma or equivalent not required. For health and human services program applicants: High school diploma required; GED accepted **Scholarships:** Available **Calendar System:** Semester, Summer Session Available **Enrollment:** FT 2,279, PT 2,452 **Faculty:** FT 128, PT 139 **Student-Faculty Ratio:** 16:1 **Exams:** Other. **Library Holdings:** 26,947 **Regional Accreditation:** Southern Association of Colleges and Schools **Credit Hours For Degree:** 62 semester hours, Associates **Professional Accreditation:** ABET, ADA, ACBSP, JRCERT, NAACLS, NLN

AUGUSTANA COLLEGE
2001 South Summit Ave.
Sioux Falls, SD 57197
Tel: (605)274-0770; Free: 800-727-2844
Admissions: (605)274-5516
Fax: (605)274-5518
E-mail: admission@augie.edu
Web Site: http://www.augie.edu/
President/CEO: Robert C. Oliver
Admissions: Nancy Davidson
Financial Aid: Brenda L. Murtha
Type: Comprehensive **Sex:** Coed **Affiliation:** Evangelical Lutheran Church in America **Scores:** 32.78% ACT 18-23; 53.59% ACT 24-29 **% Accepted:** 81 **Admission Plans:** Deferred Admission **Application Deadline:** August 1 **Application Fee:** $0.00 **H.S. Requirements:** High school diploma required; GED accepted **Costs Per Year:** Application fee: $0. Comprehensive fee: $29,738 includes full-time tuition ($23,276), mandatory fees ($274), and college room and board ($6188). College room only: $2976. Full-time tuition and fees vary according to course load and degree level. Room and board charges vary according to board plan and housing facility. Part-time tuition: $352 per credit hour. Part-time tuition varies according to course load and degree level. **Scholarships:** Available **Calendar System:** 4-1-4, Summer Session Available **Enrollment:** FT 1,666, PT 105, Grad FT 1, Grad PT 21 **Faculty:** FT 125, PT 56 **Student-Faculty Ratio:** 12:1 **Exams:** Other, SAT I or ACT. ACT essay not being used. SAT essay not being used. **% Receiving Financial Aid:** 69 **% Residing in College-Owned, -Operated, or -Affiliated Housing:** 73 **Library Holdings:** 258,451 **Regional Accreditation:** North Central Association of Colleges and Schools **Credit Hours For Degree:** 130 credit hours, Bachelors **ROTC:** Army, Air Force **Professional Accreditation:** AACN, CSWE, JRCEPAT, NASM, NCATE **Intercollegiate Athletics:** Baseball M; Basketball M & W; Cheerleading W; Cross-Country Running M & W; Football M; Golf M & W; Rugby W; Soccer M & W; Softball W; Tennis M & W; Track and Field M & W; Volleyball W; Wrestling M

BLACK HILLS STATE UNIVERSITY
1200 University St.
Spearfish, SD 57799
Tel: (605)642-6011; Free: 800-255-2478
Admissions: (605)642-6343
E-mail: admissions@bhsu.edu
Web Site: http://www.bhsu.edu/
President/CEO: Dr. Kay Schallenkamp
Financial Aid: Deb Henriksen
Type: Comprehensive **Sex:** Coed **Affiliation:** South Dakota State University System **Scores:** 63.3% ACT 18-23; 20.9% ACT 24-29 **% Accepted:** 93 **Application Deadline:** July 18 **Application Fee:** $20.00 **H.S. Requirements:** High school diploma required; GED accepted **Costs Per Year:** Application fee: $20. State resident tuition: $2751 full-time, $91.70 per credit hour part-time. Nonresident tuition: $4124 full-time, $137.45 per credit hour part-time. Mandatory fees: $3476 full-time. Full-time tuition and fees vary according to course load and reciprocity agreements. Part-time tuition varies according to course load and reciprocity agreements. College room and board: $5523. College room only: $2701. Room and board charges vary according to board plan and housing facility. **Scholarships:** Available **Calendar System:** Semester, Summer Session Available **Enrollment:** FT 2,549, PT 1,220, Grad FT 14, Grad PT 293 **Faculty:** FT 136, PT 105 **Student-Faculty Ratio:** 19:1 **Exams:** SAT I or ACT. **% Residing in College-Owned, -Operated, or -Affiliated Housing:** 21 **Regional Accreditation:** North Central Association of Colleges and Schools **Credit Hours For Degree:** 64 credits, Associates; 128 credits, Bachelors **ROTC:** Army **Professional Accreditation:** NASM, NCATE **Intercollegiate Athletics:** Basketball M & W; Cross-Country Running M & W; Football M; Golf W; Track and Field M & W; Volleyball W

COLORADO TECHNICAL UNIVERSITY SIOUX FALLS
3901 West 59th St.
Sioux Falls, SD 57108
Tel: (605)361-0200
Fax: (605)361-5954
Web Site: http://www.ctu-siouxfalls.com/
President/CEO: Dr. Wallace Pond
Financial Aid: Vikki Van Hull
Type: Comprehensive **Sex:** Coed **Affiliation:** Colorado Technical University **Admission Plans:** Deferred Admission **Application Deadline:** Rolling **Application Fee:** $50.00 **H.S. Requirements:** High school diploma required; GED accepted **Costs Per Year:** Application fee: $50. **Scholarships:** Available **Calendar System:** Quarter, Summer Session Available **Enrollment:** FT 490, PT 326 **% Receiving Financial Aid:** 92 **Regional Accreditation:** North Central Association of Colleges and Schools **Credit Hours For Degree:** 87 credit hours, Associates; 178 credit hours, Bachelors **ROTC:** Army **Professional Accreditation:** AAMAE

DAKOTA STATE UNIVERSITY
820 North Washington
Madison, SD 57042-1799
Tel: (605)256-5111; Free: 888-DSU-9988
Admissions: (605)256-5139
Fax: (605)256-5316
E-mail: yourfuture@dsu.edu
Web Site: http://www.dsu.edu/
President/CEO: Dr. Douglas Knowlton
Admissions: Dana Hoff
Financial Aid: Denise Grayson
Type: Comprehensive **Sex:** Coed **Affiliation:** South Dakota Board of Regents **Scores:** 52.96% ACT 18-23; 30% ACT 24-29 **% Accepted:** 94 **Admission Plans:** Deferred Admission **Application Deadline:** Rolling **Application Fee:** $20.00 **H.S. Requirements:** High school diploma required; GED accepted **Costs Per Year:** Application fee: $20. State resident tuition: $2751 full-time, $92 per credit hour part-time. Nonresident tuition: $4124 full-time, $137 per credit hour part-time. Mandatory fees: $4121 full-time, $114 per credit hour part-time. Full-time tuition and fees vary according to location and reciprocity agreements. Part-time tuition and fees vary according to location and reciprocity agreements. College room and board: $4818. College room only: $2640. Room and board charges vary according to board plan and housing facility. **Scholarships:** Available **Calendar System:** Semester, Summer Session Available **Enrollment:** FT 1,143, PT 1,449, Grad FT 53, Grad PT 182 **Faculty:** FT 94, PT 28 **Student-Faculty Ratio:** 17:1 **Exams:** SAT I or ACT. **% Receiving Financial Aid:** 64 **% Residing in College-Owned, -Operated, or -Affiliated Housing:** 37 **Final Year or Final Semester Residency Requirement:** No **Library Holdings:** 96,833 **Regional Accreditation:** North Central Association of Colleges and Schools **Credit Hours For Degree:** 64 credit hours, Associates; 128 credit hours,

Bachelors **ROTC:** Air Force **Professional Accreditation:** AHIMA, ACBSP, CARC, NCATE **Intercollegiate Athletics:** Baseball M; Basketball M & W; Cheerleading M & W; Cross-Country Running M & W; Football M; Softball W; Track and Field M & W; Volleyball W

DAKOTA WESLEYAN UNIVERSITY
1200 West University Ave.
Mitchell, SD 57301-4398
Tel: (605)995-2600; Free: 800-333-8506
Fax: (605)995-2699
E-mail: admissions@dwu.edu
Web Site: http://www.dwu.edu/
President/CEO: Dr. Robert G. Duffett
Admissions: Melissa Herr-Valburg
Financial Aid: Kristy O'Kief
Type: Comprehensive **Sex:** Coed **Affiliation:** United Methodist **Scores:** 85% SAT V 400+; 67% ACT 18-23; 24% ACT 24-29 **% Accepted:** 81 **Application Deadline:** August 27 **Application Fee:** $25.00 **H.S. Requirements:** High school diploma required; GED accepted **Costs Per Year:** Application fee: $25. Tuition: $19,850 full-time. **Scholarships:** Available **Calendar System:** Semester, Summer Session Available **Enrollment:** FT 677, PT 59, Grad FT 5, Grad PT 23 **Faculty:** FT 45, PT 32 **Student-Faculty Ratio:** 13:1 **Exams:** SAT I or ACT. **% Receiving Financial Aid:** 86 **% Residing in College-Owned, -Operated, or -Affiliated Housing:** 45 **Final Year or Final Semester Residency Requirement:** No **Library Holdings:** 78,928 **Regional Accreditation:** North Central Association of Colleges and Schools **Credit Hours For Degree:** 62 semester hours, Associates; 125 semester hours, Bachelors **ROTC:** Army **Professional Accreditation:** JRCEPAT, NLN **Intercollegiate Athletics:** Baseball M; Basketball M & W; Cheerleading M & W; Cross-Country Running M & W; Football M; Golf M & W; Softball W; Track and Field M & W; Volleyball W; Wrestling M

GLOBE UNIVERSITY
5101 South Broadband Ln.
Sioux Falls, SD 57108-2208
Tel: (605)977-0705; Free: (866)437-0705
Fax: (605)977-0784
Web Site: http://www.globeuniversity.edu/
Type: Four-Year College **Sex:** Coed

KILIAN COMMUNITY COLLEGE
300 East 6th St.
Sioux Falls, SD 57104-6014
Tel: (605)221-3100; Free: 800-888-1147
Fax: (605)336-2606
E-mail: info@killian.edu
Web Site: http://www.kilian.edu/
President/CEO: Mark Millage
Admissions: Mary Klockman
Financial Aid: Patti Ann Klinkhammer
Type: Two-Year College **Sex:** Coed **Admission Plans:** Open Admission; Deferred Admission **Application Deadline:** Rolling **Application Fee:** $25.00 **H.S. Requirements:** High school diploma required; GED accepted **Costs Per Year:** Application fee: $25. Tuition: $8820 full-time, $245 per credit hour part-time. Mandatory fees: $255 full-time, $85. **Scholarships:** Available **Calendar System:** Trimester, Summer Session Available **Enrollment:** FT 64, PT 272 **Faculty:** FT 6, PT 26 **Student-Faculty Ratio:** 5:1 **Final Year or Final Semester Residency Requirement:** No **Library Holdings:** 78,000 **Regional Accreditation:** North Central Association of Colleges and Schools **Credit Hours For Degree:** 60 credit hours, Associates

LAKE AREA TECHNICAL INSTITUTE
230 11th St., NE
Watertown, SD 57201
Tel: (605)882-5284; Free: 800-657-4344
E-mail: latiinfo@lati.tec.sd.us
Web Site: http://www.lakeareatech.edu/
President/CEO: Debra Shephard
Admissions: Debra Shephard
Type: Two-Year College **Sex:** Coed **Application Fee:** $20.00 **H.S. Requirements:** High school diploma required; GED accepted **Costs Per Year:** Application fee: $20. One-time mandatory fee: $20. State resident tuition: $3024 full-time. Nonresident tuition: $3024 full-time. Mandatory fees: $1958 full-time. Full-time tuition and fees vary according to program. **Scholarships:** Available **Calendar System:** Semester, Summer Session Not available **Exams:** ACT. **Library Holdings:** 5,000 **Regional Accreditation:** North Central Association of Colleges and Schools **Credit Hours For Degree:** 70 credits, Associates **Professional Accreditation:** AAMAE, ADA, AOTA, APTA, NAACLS

MITCHELL TECHNICAL INSTITUTE
821 North Capital
Mitchell, SD 57301
Tel: (605)995-3024; Free: 800-952-0042
Admissions: (605)995-3025
Fax: (605)996-3299
E-mail: clayton.deuter@mitchelltech.edu
Web Site: http://www.mitchelltech.edu/
President/CEO: Greg Von Wald
Admissions: Clayton Deuter
Financial Aid: Grant Uecker
Type: Two-Year College **Sex:** Coed **% Accepted:** 48 **Admission Plans:** Open Admission **Application Deadline:** Rolling **Application Fee:** $25.00 **H.S. Requirements:** High school diploma required; GED accepted **Costs Per Year:** Application fee: $25. State resident tuition: $3240 full-time, $90 per credit hour part-time. Nonresident tuition: $3240 full-time, $90 per credit hour part-time. Mandatory fees: $3000 full-time, $49 per credit hour part-time, $49. Full-time tuition and fees vary according to program. Part-time tuition and fees vary according to program. **Scholarships:** Available **Calendar System:** Semester, Summer Session Available **Enrollment:** FT 882, PT 121 **Faculty:** FT 53, PT 8 **Student-Faculty Ratio:** 16:1 **Exams:** ACT, Other. ACT essay not being used. **Final Year or Final Semester Residency Requirement:** No **Regional Accreditation:** North Central Association of Colleges and Schools **Credit Hours For Degree:** 67 credits, Associates **Professional Accreditation:** AAMAE, NAACLS **Intercollegiate Athletics:** Equestrian Sports M & W

MOUNT MARTY COLLEGE
1105 West 8th St.
Yankton, SD 57078-3724
Tel: (605)668-1011; Free: 800-658-4552
Admissions: (605)668-1545
Fax: (605)668-1607
E-mail: brandi.defries@mtmc.edu
Web Site: http://www.mtmc.edu/
President/CEO: Dr. James T. Barry
Admissions: Brandi DeFries
Financial Aid: Ken Kocer
Type: Comprehensive **Sex:** Coed **Affiliation:** Roman Catholic **Scores:** 60% ACT 18-23; 28% ACT 24-29 **% Accepted:** 78 **Admission Plans:** Early Admission; Deferred Admission **Application Deadline:** Rolling **Application Fee:** $35.00 **H.S. Requirements:** High school diploma required; GED accepted **Costs Per Year:** Application fee: $35. Comprehensive fee: $24,274 includes full-time tuition ($17,078), mandatory fees ($1830), and college room and board ($5366). Full-time tuition and fees vary according to location. Room and board charges vary according to board plan. Part-time tuition: $199 per credit hour. Part-time mandatory fees: $25 per credit hour. Part-time tuition and fees vary according to course load and location. **Scholarships:** Available **Calendar System:** Semester, Summer Session Available **Enrollment:** FT 588, PT 493, Grad FT 133 **Faculty:** FT 43, PT 57 **Student-Faculty Ratio:** 13:1 **Exams:** SAT I or ACT. **% Receiving Financial Aid:** 90 **% Residing in College-Owned, -Operated, or -Affiliated Housing:** 60 **Library Holdings:** 76,571 **Regional Accreditation:** North Central Association of Colleges and Schools **Credit Hours For Degree:** 64 credit hours, Associates; 128 credit hours, Bachelors **ROTC:** Army **Professional Accreditation:** AANA, ADtA, NLN **Intercollegiate Athletics:** Baseball M; Basketball M & W; Cross-Country Running M & W; Golf M & W; Soccer M & W; Softball W; Track and Field M & W; Volleyball W

NATIONAL AMERICAN UNIVERSITY (ELLSWORTH AFB)
1000 Ellsworth St.
Ste. 2400B
Ellsworth AFB, SD 57706
Tel: (605)718-6550
Web Site: http://www.national.edu/
President/CEO: Dr. Jerry Gallentine
Type: Two-Year College **Sex:** Coed **Application Fee:** $25.00 **Regional Accreditation:** North Central Association of Colleges and Schools

NATIONAL AMERICAN UNIVERSITY (RAPID CITY)
321 Kansas City St.
Rapid City, SD 57701
Tel: (605)394-4800; Free: 800-843-8892
Fax: (605)394-4871
E-mail: abeck@national.edu
Web Site: http://www.national.edu/Locations/RapidCity/
President/CEO: Dr. Jerry Gallentine
Type: Comprehensive **Sex:** Coed **Affiliation:** National College **Admission Plans:** Open Admission; Early Admission; Deferred Admission **Application Deadline:** Rolling **Application Fee:** $25.00 **H.S. Requirements:** High school diploma required; GED accepted **Scholarships:** Available **Calendar System:** Quarter, Summer Session Available **Enrollment:** FT 350, PT 131 **Faculty:** FT 13, PT 34 **Student-Faculty Ratio:** 26:1 **Exams:** ACT. **% Residing in College-Owned, -Operated, or -Affiliated Housing:** 21 **Library Holdings:** 31,018 **Regional Accreditation:** North Central Association of Colleges and Schools **Credit Hours For Degree:** 97 credit hours, Associates; 193 credit hours, Bachelors **ROTC:** Army **Professional Accreditation:** AAMAE **Intercollegiate Athletics:** Equestrian Sports M & W; Ultimate Frisbee M & W; Volleyball M & W

NATIONAL AMERICAN UNIVERSITY—SIOUX FALLS BRANCH
2801 South Kiwanis Ave.
Ste. 100
Sioux Falls, SD 57105-4293
Tel: (605)334-5430; Free: 800-388-5430
Admissions: (605)336-4600
E-mail: lhoutsma@national.edu
Web Site: http://www.national.edu/
President/CEO: Dr. Jerry Gallentine
Admissions: Lisa Houtsma
Financial Aid: Rhonda Kohnen
Type: Comprehensive **Sex:** Coed **Affiliation:** National College **% Accepted:** 100 **Admission Plans:** Open Admission; Deferred Admission **Application Deadline:** Rolling **Application Fee:** $25.00 **H.S. Requirements:** High school diploma required; GED accepted **Scholarships:** Available **Calendar System:** Quarter, Summer Session Available **Faculty:** FT 0, PT 35 **Library Holdings:** 1,580 **Regional Accreditation:** North Central Association of Colleges and Schools **Credit Hours For Degree:** 91 credit hours, Associates; 184 credit hours, Bachelors

NORTHERN STATE UNIVERSITY
1200 South Jay St.
Aberdeen, SD 57401-7198
Tel: (605)626-3011; Free: 800-678-5330
Admissions: (605)626-2544
Fax: (605)626-3022
E-mail: admission2@northern.edu
Web Site: http://www.northern.edu/
President/CEO: Dr. James Smith
Admissions: Allan Vogel
Financial Aid: Sharon Kienow
Type: Comprehensive **Sex:** Coed **Affiliation:** South Dakota Board of Regents **Scores:** 55.15% ACT 18-23; 32.12% ACT 24-29 **% Accepted:** 93 **Admission Plans:** Early Admission; Deferred Admission **Application Fee:** $20.00 **H.S. Requirements:** High school diploma required; GED accepted **Costs Per Year:** Application fee: $20. State resident tuition: $2751 full-time, $91.70 per credit hour part-time. Nonresident tuition: $8827 full-time, $294.25 per credit hour part-time. Mandatory fees: $3312 full-time, $110.40 per credit hour part-time. Full-time tuition and fees vary according to course level, course load, and reciprocity agreements. Part-time tuition and fees vary according to course level, course load, and reciprocity agreements. College room and board: $4874. College room only: $2575. Room and board charges vary according to board plan. **Scholarships:** Available **Calendar System:** Semester, Summer Session Available **Enrollment:** FT 1,539, PT 761, Grad FT 44, Grad PT 281 **Student-Faculty Ratio:** 17:1 **Exams:** SAT I or ACT. **% Receiving Financial Aid:** 64 **Library Holdings:** 192,007 **Regional Accreditation:** North Central Association of Colleges and Schools **Credit Hours For Degree:** 64 credit hours, Associates; 128 credit hours, Bachelors **Professional Accreditation:** NASM, NCATE **Intercollegiate Athletics:** Baseball M; Basketball M & W; Cross-Country Running M & W; Football M; Golf M & W; Soccer W; Softball W; Swimming and Diving W; Tennis M & W; Track and Field M & W; Volleyball W; Wrestling M

OGLALA LAKOTA COLLEGE
490 Piya Wiconi Rd.
Kyle, SD 57752-0490
Tel: (605)455-6000
Fax: (605)455-2787
E-mail: lmeseteth@olc.edu
Web Site: http://www.olc.edu/
President/CEO: Thomas Shortbull
Type: Comprehensive **Sex:** Coed **Admission Plans:** Open Admission; Preferred Admission; Early Admission **Application Fee:** $0.00 **H.S. Requirements:** High school diploma required; GED accepted **Scholarships:** Available **Calendar System:** Semester, Summer Session Available **Library Holdings:** 15,000 **Regional Accreditation:** North Central Association of Colleges and Schools **Credit Hours For Degree:** 65 credit hours, Associates; 128 credit hours, Bachelors

PRESENTATION COLLEGE
1500 North Main St.
Aberdeen, SD 57401-1299
Tel: (605)225-1634; Free: 800-437-6060
Admissions: (605)229-8492
Fax: (605)229-8518
E-mail: admit@presentation.edu
Web Site: http://www.presentation.edu/
President/CEO: Dr. Lorraine M. Hale, PBVM
Admissions: Jo Ellen Lindner
Financial Aid: Janel Wagner
Type: Four-Year College **Sex:** Coed **Affiliation:** Roman Catholic **Scores:** 59% ACT 18-23; 22% ACT 24-29 **% Accepted:** 76 **Admission Plans:** Open Admission **Application Deadline:** Rolling **Application Fee:** $25.00 **H.S. Requirements:** High school diploma required; GED accepted **Costs Per Year:** Application fee: $25. Comprehensive fee: $19,750 includes full-time tuition ($14,250) and college room and board ($5500). College room only: $4100. Full-time tuition varies according to course load, location, and program. Room and board charges vary according to board plan, housing facility, and student level. Part-time tuition: $525 per credit. Part-time tuition varies according to course load, location, and program. **Scholarships:** Available **Calendar System:** Semester, Summer Session Available **Enrollment:** FT 441, PT 259 **Faculty:** FT 39, PT 30 **Student-Faculty Ratio:** 10:1 **Exams:** SAT I or ACT. ACT essay not being used. SAT essay not being used. **% Receiving Financial Aid:** 95 **% Residing in College-Owned, -Operated, or -Affiliated Housing:** 26 **Final Year or Final Semester Residency Requirement:** No **Library Holdings:** 40,000 **Regional Accreditation:** North Central Association of Colleges and Schools **Credit Hours For Degree:** 60 credit hours, Associates; 120 credit hours, Bachelors **Professional Accreditation:** ARCEST, AAMAE, CSWE, JRCERT, NAACLS, NLN **Intercollegiate Athletics:** Baseball M; Basketball M & W; Cross-Country Running M & W; Golf M & W; Soccer M & W; Softball W; Volleyball W

SINTE GLESKA UNIVERSITY
101 Antelope Lake Circle
PO Box 105
Mission, SD 57555
Tel: (605)856-8100
Fax: (605)747-2098
Web Site: http://www.sintegleska.edu/
President/CEO: Lionel R. Bordeaux
Admissions: Jack Herman
Type: Comprehensive **Sex:** Coed **Admission Plans:** Open Admission **Application Deadline:** August 20 **Application Fee:** $20.00 **H.S. Requirements:** High school diploma required; GED accepted **Scholarships:** Available **Calendar System:** Semester, Summer Session Available **Library Holdings:** 25,000 **Regional Accreditation:** North Central Association of Colleges and Schools **Credit Hours For Degree:** 68 credits, Associates; 128 credits, Bachelors

SISSETON-WAHPETON COMMUNITY COLLEGE
Old Agency Box 689
Sisseton, SD 57262
Tel: (605)698-3966
E-mail: DRedday@swc.tc
Web Site: http://www.swc.tc/
President/CEO: Diana Canku

Admissions: Darlene Redday
Type: Two-Year College **Sex:** Coed **% Accepted:** 94 **Admission Plans:** Open Admission **Application Deadline:** Rolling **Application Fee:** $0.00 **H.S. Requirements:** High school diploma required; GED accepted **Costs Per Year:** Application fee: $0. State resident tuition: $3300 full-time, $110 per credit hour part-time. Nonresident tuition: $3300 full-time, $110 per credit hour part-time. Full-time tuition varies according to course load and program. Part-time tuition varies according to course load and program. College room and board: $6000. Tuition guaranteed not to increase for student's term of enrollment. **Scholarships:** Available **Calendar System:** Semester, Summer Session Available **Enrollment:** FT 181, PT 56 **Faculty:** FT 10, PT 20 **Student-Faculty Ratio:** 10:1 **Exams:** Other. **Library Holdings:** 15,481 **Regional Accreditation:** North Central Association of Colleges and Schools **Credit Hours For Degree:** 64 semester hours, Associates

SOUTH DAKOTA SCHOOL OF MINES AND TECHNOLOGY

501 East Saint Joseph
Rapid City, SD 57701-3995
Tel: (605)394-2511; Free: 800-544-8162
Admissions: (605)394-2414
Fax: (605)394-2914
E-mail: admissions@sdsmt.edu
Web Site: http://www.sdsmt.edu/
President/CEO: Dr. Robert Wharton
Admissions: Genene Sigler
Financial Aid: David W. Martin
Type: University **Sex:** Coed **Affiliation:** South Dakota State Board of Regents University System **Scores:** 94.5% SAT V 400+; 100% SAT M 400+; 20.8% ACT 18-23; 62% ACT 24-29 **% Accepted:** 82 **Application Deadline:** Rolling **Application Fee:** $20.00 **H.S. Requirements:** High school diploma required; GED accepted **Costs Per Year:** Application fee: $20. State resident tuition: $2750 full-time, $91.70 per credit hour part-time. Nonresident tuition: $4130 full-time, $137.45 per credit hour part-time. Mandatory fees: $4080 full-time, $141.95 per credit hour part-time. Full-time tuition and fees vary according to course load, location, program, and reciprocity agreements. Part-time tuition and fees vary according to course load, location, program, and reciprocity agreements. College room and board: $5080. College room only: $2640. Room and board charges vary according to board plan and housing facility. **Scholarships:** Available **Calendar System:** Semester, Summer Session Available **Enrollment:** FT 1,507, PT 406, Grad FT 182, Grad PT 82 **Faculty:** FT 121, PT 14 **Student-Faculty Ratio:** 14:1 **Exams:** SAT I or ACT. **% Receiving Financial Aid:** 54 **% Residing in College-Owned, -Operated, or -Affiliated Housing:** 33 **Final Year or Final Semester Residency Requirement:** No **Library Holdings:** 252,260 **Regional Accreditation:** North Central Association of Colleges and Schools **Credit Hours For Degree:** 64 semester hours, Associates; 128 semester hours, Bachelors **ROTC:** Army **Professional Accreditation:** ABET **Intercollegiate Athletics:** Basketball M & W; Cross-Country Running M & W; Football M; Golf M & W; Tennis M; Track and Field M & W; Volleyball W

SOUTH DAKOTA STATE UNIVERSITY

PO Box 2201
Brookings, SD 57007
Tel: (605)688-4151; Free: 800-952-3541
Admissions: (605)688-4121
Fax: (605)688-6384
E-mail: sdsu.admissions@sdstate.edu
Web Site: http://www.sdstate.edu/
President/CEO: David L. Chicoine
Admissions: Michelle Kuebler
Financial Aid: Jay Larsen
Type: University **Sex:** Coed **Affiliation:** South Dakota Board of Regents **Scores:** 47% ACT 18-23; 41% ACT 24-29 **% Accepted:** 93 **Admission Plans:** Deferred Admission **Application Deadline:** Rolling **Application Fee:** $20.00 **H.S. Requirements:** High school diploma required; GED accepted **Costs Per Year:** Application fee: $20. State resident tuition: $2751 full-time, $91.70 per credit hour part-time. Nonresident tuition: $4124 full-time, $137.45 per credit hour part-time. Mandatory fees: $3404 full-time, $113.45 per credit hour part-time. Full-time tuition and fees vary according to course level, course load, location, program, and reciprocity agreements. Part-time tuition and fees vary according to course level, course load, location, program, and reciprocity agreements. College room and board: $5668. College room only: $2540. Room and board charges vary according to board plan and housing facility. **Scholarships:** Available **Calendar System:** Semester, Summer Session Available **Enrollment:** FT 8,579, PT 2,215, Grad FT 505, Grad PT 1,077 **Faculty:** FT 476, PT 203 **Student-Faculty Ratio:** 18:1 **Exams:** SAT I or ACT. ACT essay not being used. SAT essay not being used. **% Receiving Financial Aid:** 76 **% Residing in College-Owned, -Operated, or -Affiliated Housing:** 34 **Library Holdings:** 926,000 **Regional Accreditation:** North Central Association of Colleges and Schools **Credit Hours For Degree:** 64 credits, Associates; 128 credits, Bachelors **ROTC:** Army, Air Force **Professional Accreditation:** ABET, ACPhE, ACEJMC, AACN, AAFCS, ACA, JRCEPAT, NASM, NCATE **Intercollegiate Athletics:** Baseball M; Basketball M & W; Bowling M & W; Cheerleading M & W; Cross-Country Running M & W; Equestrian Sports W; Football M; Golf M & W; Ice Hockey M & W; Rugby M & W; Soccer M & W; Softball W; Swimming and Diving M & W; Tennis M & W; Track and Field M & W; Volleyball W; Wrestling M

SOUTHEAST TECHNICAL INSTITUTE

2320 North Career Ave.
Sioux Falls, SD 57107-1301
Tel: (605)367-7624
Admissions: (605)367-4458
E-mail: scott.dorman@southeasttech.edu
Web Site: http://www.southeasttech.edu/
President/CEO: Jeff Holcomb
Admissions: Scott Dorman
Type: Two-Year College **Sex:** Coed **% Accepted:** 49 **Application Deadline:** Rolling **Application Fee:** $0.00 **H.S. Requirements:** High school diploma required; GED accepted **Costs Per Year:** Application fee: $0. State resident tuition: $2520 full-time, $84 per credit hour part-time. Nonresident tuition: $2520 full-time, $84 per credit hour part-time. Mandatory fees: $1717 full-time, $57.25 per credit hour part-time. College room only: $4600. **Scholarships:** Available **Calendar System:** Semester, Summer Session Available **Enrollment:** FT 1,967, PT 522 **Faculty:** FT 80, PT 56 **Student-Faculty Ratio:** 16:1 **Exams:** ACT. **% Residing in College-Owned, -Operated, or -Affiliated Housing:** 7 **Final Year or Final Semester Residency Requirement:** No **Library Holdings:** 10,643 **Regional Accreditation:** North Central Association of Colleges and Schools **Credit Hours For Degree:** 63 credits, Associates **Professional Accreditation:** JRCECT, JRCNMT

UNIVERSITY OF SIOUX FALLS

1101 West 22nd St.
Sioux Falls, SD 57105-1699
Tel: (605)331-5000; Free: 800-888-1047
Admissions: (605)331-6600
Fax: (605)331-6615
E-mail: admissions@usiouxfalls.edu
Web Site: http://www.usiouxfalls.edu/
President/CEO: Dr. Mark Benedetto
Admissions: Amanda Anderson
Financial Aid: Rachel Gunn
Type: Comprehensive **Sex:** Coed **Affiliation:** American Baptist Churches in the USA **Scores:** 89% SAT V 400+; 89% SAT M 400+; 51% ACT 18-23; 36% ACT 24-29 **% Accepted:** 97 **Admission Plans:** Early Admission; Deferred Admission **Application Deadline:** Rolling **Application Fee:** $25.00 **H.S. Requirements:** High school diploma required; GED accepted **Costs Per Year:** Application fee: $25. Comprehensive fee: $26,190 includes full-time tuition ($19,870), mandatory fees ($400), and college room and board ($5920). College room only: $2770. Full-time tuition and fees vary according to course load, degree level, and program. Room and board charges vary according to board plan and housing facility. Part-time tuition: $280 per semester hour. Part-time mandatory fees: $150 per year. Part-time tuition and fees vary according to course load, degree level, and program. **Scholarships:** Available **Calendar System:** 4-1-4, Summer Session Available **Enrollment:** FT 1,011, PT 232 **Faculty:** FT 60, PT 80 **Student-Faculty Ratio:** 15:1 **Exams:** SAT I or ACT. **% Residing in College-Owned, -Operated, or -Affiliated Housing:** 53 **Library Holdings:** 85,713 **Regional Accreditation:** North Central Association of Colleges and Schools **Credit Hours For Degree:** 64 semester hours, Associates; 128 semester hours, Bachelors **Professional Accreditation:** CSWE, NCATE **Intercollegiate Athletics:** Baseball M; Basketball M & W; Cheerleading W; Cross-Country Running M & W; Football M; Golf M & W; Soccer M & W; Softball W; Tennis M & W; Track and Field M & W; Volleyball W

THE UNIVERSITY OF SOUTH DAKOTA

414 East Clark St.
Vermillion, SD 57069-2390

Tel: (605)677-5011; Free: 877-269-6837
Admissions: (605)677-5434
Fax: (605)677-6753
E-mail: admiss@usd.edu
Web Site: http://www.usd.edu/
President/CEO: James W. Abbott
Admissions: Stephanie Moser
Financial Aid: Julie Pier

Type: University **Sex:** Coed **Scores:** 85% SAT V 400+; 89% SAT M 400+; 50% ACT 18-23; 37% ACT 24-29 **% Accepted:** 87 **Admission Plans:** Early Admission; Deferred Admission **Application Deadline:** Rolling **Application Fee:** $20.00 **H.S. Requirements:** High school diploma required; GED accepted **Costs Per Year:** Application fee: $20. State resident tuition: $2751 full-time, $92 per credit hour part-time. Nonresident tuition: $4124 full-time, $138 per credit hour part-time. Mandatory fees: $3717 full-time, $124 per credit hour part-time. Full-time tuition and fees vary according to course load and reciprocity agreements. Part-time tuition and fees vary according to course load and reciprocity agreements. College room and board: $5787. College room only: $2858. Room and board charges vary according to board plan and housing facility. **Scholarships:** Available **Calendar System:** Semester, Summer Session Available **Enrollment:** FT 4,385, PT 2,713, Grad FT 1,213, Grad PT 1,306 **Faculty:** FT 395, PT 146 **Student-Faculty Ratio:** 15:1 **Exams:** SAT I or ACT. **% Receiving Financial Aid:** 56 **% Residing in College-Owned, -Operated, or -Affiliated Housing:** 30 **Library Holdings:** 716,915 **Regional Accreditation:** North Central Association of Colleges and Schools **Credit Hours For Degree:** 66 credit hours, Associates; 128 credit hours, Bachelors **ROTC:** Army **Professional Accreditation:** AACSB, ACEJMC, ABA, ACA, ADA, ADtA, AOTA, APTA, APA, ASLHA, AALS, CSWE, LCMEAMA, NASAD, NASM, NASPAA, NAST, NCATE, NLN **Intercollegiate Athletics:** Basketball M & W; Cross-Country Running M & W; Football M; Golf M & W; Soccer W; Softball W; Swimming and Diving M & W; Tennis W; Track and Field M & W; Volleyball W

WESTERN DAKOTA TECHNICAL INSTITUTE

800 Mickelson Dr.
Rapid City, SD 57703
Tel: (605)394-4034; Free: 800-544-8765
Admissions: (605)718-2411
E-mail: jill.elder@wdt.edu
Web Site: http://www.westerndakotatech.org/
President/CEO: Dr. Craig Bailey
Admissions: Jill Elder

Type: Two-Year College **Sex:** Coed **Application Deadline:** August 1 **Application Fee:** $20.00 **H.S. Requirements:** High school diploma or equivalent not required **Costs Per Year:** Application fee: $20. One-time mandatory fee: $100. State resident tuition: $3024 full-time, $84 per credit hour part-time. Nonresident tuition: $3024 full-time, $84 per credit hour part-time. Mandatory fees: $2160 full-time, $60 per credit hour part-time. Full-time tuition and fees vary according to course load and program. Part-time tuition and fees vary according to course load. **Scholarships:** Available **Calendar System:** Semester, Summer Session Available **Student-Faculty Ratio:** 13:1 **Regional Accreditation:** North Central Association of Colleges and Schools **Credit Hours For Degree:** 71 credits, Associates

AMERICAN BAPTIST COLLEGE OF AMERICAN BAPTIST THEOLOGICAL SEMINARY
1800 Baptist World Center Dr.
Nashville, TN 37207
Tel: (615)256-1463
Admissions: (615)687-6896
E-mail: mlockhart@abcnash.edu
Web Site: http://www.abcnash.edu/
President/CEO: Dr. Forrest E. Harris, Sr.
Admissions: Marcella Lockhart
Financial Aid: Marcella Lockhart
Type: Four-Year College **Sex:** Coed **Affiliation:** Baptist **% Accepted:** 77 **Admission Plans:** Open Admission; Deferred Admission **Application Deadline:** July 12 **Application Fee:** $20.00 **H.S. Requirements:** High school diploma required; GED accepted **Costs Per Year:** Application fee: $20. Comprehensive fee: $7400 includes full-time tuition ($4560), mandatory fees ($240), and college room and board ($2600). College room only: $1800. Room and board charges vary according to board plan and housing facility. Part-time tuition: $190 per credit hour. Part-time mandatory fees: $240 per term. **Scholarships:** Available **Calendar System:** Semester, Summer Session Available **Enrollment:** FT 56, PT 28 **Faculty:** FT 2, PT 11 **Student-Faculty Ratio:** 14:1 **% Receiving Financial Aid:** 100 **% Residing in College-Owned, -Operated, or -Affiliated Housing:** 20 **Final Year or Final Semester Residency Requirement:** No **Library Holdings:** 33,676 **Credit Hours For Degree:** 63 credit hours, Associates; 120 credit hours, Bachelors **Professional Accreditation:** ABHE

AQUINAS COLLEGE
4210 Harding Rd.
Nashville, TN 37205-2005
Tel: (615)297-7545; Free: 800-649-9956
Fax: (615)297-7970
E-mail: hansomc@aquinascollege.edu
Web Site: http://www.aquinascollege.edu/
President/CEO: Sr. Mary Peter Muehlenkamp, OP
Admissions: Connie Hansom
Financial Aid: Kylie Pruitt
Type: Four-Year College **Sex:** Coed **Affiliation:** Roman Catholic; The Dominican Sisters of the Saint Cecilia Congregation **% Accepted:** 16 **Admission Plans:** Open Admission; Deferred Admission **Application Deadline:** Rolling **Application Fee:** $25.00 **H.S. Requirements:** High school diploma required; GED accepted **Costs Per Year:** Application fee: $25. Tuition: $17,180 full-time. Full-time tuition varies according to course load and program. **Scholarships:** Available **Calendar System:** Semester, Summer Session Available **Faculty:** FT 36, PT 62 **Student-Faculty Ratio:** 14:1 **Exams:** SAT I or ACT. **Final Year or Final Semester Residency Requirement:** No **Library Holdings:** 71,339 **Regional Accreditation:** Southern Association of Colleges and Schools **Credit Hours For Degree:** 64 semester hours, Associates; 126 semester hours, Bachelors **Professional Accreditation:** NLN

ARGOSY UNIVERSITY, NASHVILLE
100 Centerview Dr., Ste. 225
Nashville, TN 37214
Tel: (615)525-2800; Free: (866)833-6598
Fax: (615)369-0601
Web Site: http://www.argosy.edu/nashville/
President/CEO: Sandra Wise
Type: University **Sex:** Coed **Calendar System:** Semester **Regional Accreditation:** North Central Association of Colleges and Schools

THE ART INSTITUTE OF TENNESSEE—NASHVILLE
100 Centerview Dr., Ste. 250
Nashville, TN 37214
Tel: (615)874-1067; Free: (866)747-5770
Web Site: http://www.artinstitutes.edu/nashville/
President/CEO: Carol Menck
Type: Four-Year College **Sex:** Coed **Affiliation:** Education Management Corporation **Regional Accreditation:** Southern Association of Colleges and Schools

AUSTIN PEAY STATE UNIVERSITY
601 College St.
Clarksville, TN 37044
Tel: (931)221-7011; Free: 800-844-2778
Admissions: (931)221-7661
Fax: (931)221-5994
E-mail: admissions@apsu.edu
Web Site: http://www.apsu.edu/
President/CEO: Timothy Hall
Admissions: Ryan Forsythe
Financial Aid: Donna Price
Type: Comprehensive **Sex:** Coed **Affiliation:** Tennessee Board of Regents **Scores:** 90% SAT V 400+; 87% SAT M 400+; 64% ACT 18-23; 23% ACT 24-29 **% Accepted:** 90 **Admission Plans:** Early Admission; Deferred Admission **Application Deadline:** July 25 **Application Fee:** $15.00 **H.S. Requirements:** High school diploma required; GED accepted **Costs Per Year:** Application fee: $15. State resident tuition: $4584 full-time, $191 per credit hour part-time. Nonresident tuition: $16,512 full-time, $688 per credit hour part-time. Mandatory fees: $1224 full-time, $61.20 per credit hour part-time. Full-time tuition and fees vary according to location and program. Part-time tuition and fees vary according to location and program. College room and board: $6120. College room only: $3750. Room and board charges vary according to board plan and housing facility. **Scholarships:** Available **Calendar System:** Semester, Summer Session Available **Enrollment:** FT 6,975, PT 2,321, Grad FT 289, Grad PT 603 **Faculty:** FT 310, PT 240 **Student-Faculty Ratio:** 21:1 **Exams:** SAT I or ACT. **% Receiving Financial Aid:** 72 **% Residing in College-Owned, -Operated, or -Affiliated Housing:** 14 **Library Holdings:** 416,874 **Regional Accreditation:** Southern Association of Colleges and Schools **Credit Hours For Degree:** 64 semester hours, Associates; 128 semester hours, Bachelors **ROTC:** Army, Air Force **Professional Accreditation:** CSWE, NAACLS, NASAD, NASM, NCATE, NLN **Intercollegiate Athletics:** Baseball M; Basketball M & W; Cheerleading M & W; Cross-Country Running M & W; Football M; Golf M & W; Riflery W; Soccer W; Softball W; Tennis M & W; Track and Field W; Volleyball W

BAPTIST COLLEGE OF HEALTH SCIENCES
1003 Monroe Ave.
Memphis, TN 38104
Tel: (901)227-4330; Free: (866)575-2247

Admissions: (901)572-2441
E-mail: Lissa.Morgan@bchs.edu
Web Site: http://www.bchs.edu/
President/CEO: Dr. Betty Sue McGarvey
Admissions: Lissa Morgan
Financial Aid: Leanne Smith
Type: Four-Year College **Sex:** Coed **Affiliation:** Southern Baptist; Baptist Memorial Health Care Corporation **Scores:** 85% ACT 18-23; 14% ACT 24-29 **% Accepted:** 15 **Admission Plans:** Early Admission **Application Deadline:** May 1 **Application Fee:** $25.00 **H.S. Requirements:** High school diploma required; GED not accepted **Costs Per Year:** Application fee: $25. Tuition: $8880 full-time, $296 per credit hour part-time. Mandatory fees: $850 full-time, $25 per credit hour part-time, $50 per term part-time. **Scholarships:** Available **Calendar System:** Trimester, Summer Session Available **Enrollment:** FT 556, PT 465 **Faculty:** FT 60, PT 46 **Student-Faculty Ratio:** 14:1 **Exams:** ACT, Other. **% Residing in College-Owned, -Operated, or -Affiliated Housing:** 10 **Library Holdings:** 14,547 **Regional Accreditation:** Southern Association of Colleges and Schools **Credit Hours For Degree:** 128 credits, Bachelors **Professional Accreditation:** AACN, CARC, JRCEDMS, JRCNMT

BELHAVEN UNIVERSITY
5100 Poplar Ave., Ste. 200
Memphis, TN 38137
Tel: (901)888-3343
Fax: (901)888-0771
E-mail: memphisadmission@belhaven.edu
Web Site: http://www.belhaven.edu/
Type: Comprehensive **Sex:** Coed **Affiliation:** Presbyterian **Application Fee:** $25.00 **Costs Per Year:** Application fee: $25. Tuition: $9840 full-time, $410 per credit hour part-time. **Calendar System:** Semester **Regional Accreditation:** Southern Association of Colleges and Schools

BELMONT UNIVERSITY
1900 Belmont Blvd.
Nashville, TN 37212-3757
Tel: (615)460-6000; Free: 800-56E-NROL
Admissions: (615)460-6785
E-mail: buadmission@belmont.edu
Web Site: http://www.belmont.edu/
President/CEO: Dr. Robert C. Fisher
Financial Aid: Pat Smedley
Type: Comprehensive **Sex:** Coed **Affiliation:** Christian **Scores:** 101% SAT V 400+; 100% SAT M 400+; 13.3% ACT 18-23; 59.1% ACT 24-29 **% Accepted:** 77 **Admission Plans:** Early Admission; Deferred Admission **Application Deadline:** August 1 **Application Fee:** $50.00 **H.S. Requirements:** High school diploma required; GED accepted **Costs Per Year:** Application fee: $50. Comprehensive fee: $32,360 includes full-time tuition ($21,270), mandatory fees ($1090), and college room and board ($10,000). College room only: $6300. Full-time tuition and fees vary according to class time and course load. Room and board charges vary according to board plan, housing facility, and location. Part-time tuition: $820 per credit hour. Part-time mandatory fees: $365 per term. Part-time tuition and fees vary according to course load. **Scholarships:** Available **Calendar System:** Semester, Summer Session Available **Enrollment:** FT 4,035, PT 343, Grad FT 505, Grad PT 541 **Faculty:** FT 269, PT 336 **Student-Faculty Ratio:** 12:1 **Exams:** SAT I or ACT. **% Receiving Financial Aid:** 52 **% Residing in College-Owned, -Operated, or -Affiliated Housing:** 45 **Library Holdings:** 220,637 **Regional Accreditation:** Southern Association of Colleges and Schools **Credit Hours For Degree:** 128 semester hours, Bachelors **ROTC:** Army, Navy, Air Force **Professional Accreditation:** AACSB, ACPhE, AACN, AOTA, APTA, CSWE, NASM, NCATE **Intercollegiate Athletics:** Baseball M; Basketball M & W; Cross-Country Running M & W; Golf M & W; Soccer M & W; Softball W; Tennis M & W; Track and Field M & W; Volleyball W

BETHEL UNIVERSITY
325 Cherry Ave.
McKenzie, TN 38201
Tel: (731)352-4000
Admissions: (731)352-4030
Fax: (731)352-4069
E-mail: hodgest@bethelu.edu
Web Site: http://www.bethel-college.edu/
President/CEO: Dr. Robert Prosser
Admissions: Tina Hodges
Financial Aid: Laura Bateman
Type: Comprehensive **Sex:** Coed **Affiliation:** Cumberland Presbyterian **% Accepted:** 54 **Admission Plans:** Open Admission; Early Admission; Deferred Admission **Application Deadline:** Rolling **Application Fee:** $30.00 **H.S. Requirements:** High school diploma required; GED accepted **Costs Per Year:** Application fee: $30. Comprehensive fee: $19,168 includes full-time tuition ($11,592), mandatory fees ($650), and college room and board ($6926). Full-time tuition and fees vary according to program. Part-time tuition: $358 per credit hour. Part-time mandatory fees: $13 per credit hour, $80 per term. Part-time tuition and fees vary according to course load and program. **Scholarships:** Available **Calendar System:** Semester, Summer Session Available **Enrollment:** FT 2,515, PT 35, Grad FT 102, Grad PT 489 **Faculty:** FT 97, PT 194 **Student-Faculty Ratio:** 19:1 **Exams:** SAT I or ACT. **% Residing in College-Owned, -Operated, or -Affiliated Housing:** 29 **Library Holdings:** 45,000 **Regional Accreditation:** Southern Association of Colleges and Schools **Credit Hours For Degree:** 128 semester hours, Bachelors **Intercollegiate Athletics:** Baseball M; Basketball M & W; Bowling M & W; Cheerleading M & W; Cross-Country Running M & W; Football M; Golf M & W; Riflery M & W; Soccer M & W; Softball W; Tennis M & W; Track and Field M & W; Volleyball W

BRYAN COLLEGE
PO Box 7000
Dayton, TN 37321-7000
Tel: (423)775-2041; Free: 800-277-9522
Fax: (423)775-7330
E-mail: admissions@bryan.edu
Web Site: http://www.bryan.edu/
President/CEO: Dr. Stephen D. Livesay
Admissions: Michael Sapienza
Financial Aid: Rick Taphorn
Type: Comprehensive **Sex:** Coed **Affiliation:** interdenominational **Scores:** 99% SAT V 400+; 96% SAT M 400+; 33% ACT 18-23; 46% ACT 24-29 **% Accepted:** 75 **Admission Plans:** Early Action; Deferred Admission **Application Deadline:** Rolling **Application Fee:** $35.00 **H.S. Requirements:** High school diploma required; GED accepted **Costs Per Year:** Application fee: $35. Comprehensive fee: $24,194 includes full-time tuition ($18,620), mandatory fees ($120), and college room and board ($5454). Room and board charges vary according to board plan and housing facility. Part-time tuition: $775 per credit. **Scholarships:** Available **Calendar System:** Semester, Summer Session Available **Enrollment:** FT 974, PT 126, Grad FT 58, Grad PT 2 **Faculty:** FT 43, PT 23 **Student-Faculty Ratio:** 17:1 **Exams:** SAT I or ACT. ACT essay used for placement. SAT essay used for placement. **% Receiving Financial Aid:** 75 **% Residing in College-Owned, -Operated, or -Affiliated Housing:** 82 **Regional Accreditation:** Southern Association of Colleges and Schools **Credit Hours For Degree:** 60 semester hours, Associates; 124 semester hours, Bachelors **Intercollegiate Athletics:** Baseball M; Basketball M & W; Cross-Country Running M & W; Soccer M & W; Track and Field M & W; Volleyball W

CARSON-NEWMAN COLLEGE
1646 Russell Ave., PO Box 557
Jefferson City, TN 37760
Tel: (865)471-2000; Free: 800-678-9061
Admissions: (865)471-3223
Fax: (865)471-3502
E-mail: cnadmiss@cn.edu
Web Site: http://www.cn.edu/
President/CEO: Dr. Randall O'Brien
Admissions: Melanie Redding
Financial Aid: Danette Seale
Type: Comprehensive **Sex:** Coed **Affiliation:** Southern Baptist **Scores:** 58% ACT 18-23; 31% ACT 24-29 **% Accepted:** 74 **Admission Plans:** Deferred Admission **Application Deadline:** August 1 **Application Fee:** $25.00 **H.S. Requirements:** High school diploma required; GED accepted **Costs Per Year:** Application fee: $25. Comprehensive fee: $26,480 includes full-time tuition ($19,628), mandatory fees ($934), and college room and board ($5918). Full-time tuition and fees vary according to class time and course load. Room and board charges vary according to board plan, gender, and housing facility. Part-time tuition: $818 per semester hour. **Scholarships:** Available **Calendar System:** Semester, Summer Session Available **Enrollment:** FT 1,772, PT 128, Grad FT 133, Grad PT 115 **Faculty:** FT 124, PT 58 **Student-Faculty Ratio:** 12:1 **Exams:** SAT I or ACT. **% Receiving**

Financial Aid: 79 **% Residing in College-Owned, -Operated, or -Affiliated Housing:** 51 **Library Holdings:** 218,371 **Regional Accreditation:** Southern Association of Colleges and Schools **Credit Hours For Degree:** 128 semester hours, Bachelors **ROTC:** Army, Air Force **Professional Accreditation:** AACN, AAFCS, NASAD, NASM, NCATE, NLN **Intercollegiate Athletics:** Baseball M; Basketball M & W; Cross-Country Running M & W; Football M; Golf M; Soccer M & W; Softball W; Tennis M & W; Track and Field M & W; Volleyball W; Wrestling M

CHATTANOOGA COLLEGE—MEDICAL, DENTAL AND TECHNICAL CAREERS

3805 Brainerd Rd.
Chattanooga, TN 37411-3798
Tel: (423)624-0077
Web Site: http://www.ecpconline.com/
President/CEO: William G. Faour
Admissions: Toney McFadden

Type: Two-Year College **Sex:** Coed **Admission Plans:** Open Admission **Application Fee:** $75.00 **Scholarships:** Available **Professional Accreditation:** ACCSCT

CHATTANOOGA STATE COMMUNITY COLLEGE

4501 Amnicola Hwy.
Chattanooga, TN 37406-1097
Tel: (423)697-4400
Admissions: (423)697-4401
Fax: (423)697-4709
E-mail: diane.norris@chattanoogastate.edu
Web Site: http://www.chattanoogastate.edu/
President/CEO: Dr. James Catanzaro
Admissions: Diane Norris

Type: Two-Year College **Sex:** Coed **Affiliation:** Tennessee Board of Regents **% Accepted:** 100 **Admission Plans:** Open Admission; Early Admission; Deferred Admission **Application Deadline:** Rolling **Application Fee:** $15.00 **H.S. Requirements:** High school diploma required; GED accepted **Costs Per Year:** Application fee: $15. State resident tuition: $2955 full-time, $111 per credit hour part-time. Nonresident tuition: $11,331 full-time, $349 per credit hour part-time. Mandatory fees: $291 full-time. **Scholarships:** Available **Calendar System:** Semester, Summer Session Available **Enrollment:** FT 4,412, PT 5,019 **Faculty:** FT 214, PT 414 **Student-Faculty Ratio:** 19:1 **Final Year or Final Semester Residency Requirement:** Yes **Library Holdings:** 161,086 **Regional Accreditation:** Southern Association of Colleges and Schools **Credit Hours For Degree:** 60 semester hours, Associates **Professional Accreditation:** ABET, ADA, AHIMA, APTA, CARC, NLN **Intercollegiate Athletics:** Baseball M; Basketball M & W; Softball W

CHRISTIAN BROTHERS UNIVERSITY

650 East Parkway South
Memphis, TN 38104-5581
Tel: (901)321-3000; Free: 800-288-7576
Admissions: (901)321-3205
Fax: (901)321-3202
E-mail: admissions@cbu.edu
Web Site: http://www.cbu.edu/
President/CEO: Dr. John Smarrelli, Jr.
Admissions: Dr. Anne Kenworthy
Financial Aid: Jim Shannon

Type: Comprehensive **Sex:** Coed **Affiliation:** Roman Catholic **Scores:** 50% ACT 18-23; 41% ACT 24-29 **% Accepted:** 49 **Admission Plans:** Early Admission; Deferred Admission **Application Deadline:** August 1 **Application Fee:** $25.00 **H.S. Requirements:** High school diploma required; GED accepted **Costs Per Year:** Application fee: $25. Comprehensive fee: $29,870 includes full-time tuition ($23,180), mandatory fees ($550), and college room and board ($6140). College room only: $2800. Full-time tuition and fees vary according to class time and course load. Room and board charges vary according to board plan and housing facility. Part-time tuition: $740 per credit hour. Part-time tuition varies according to class time. **Scholarships:** Available **Calendar System:** Semester, Summer Session Available **Enrollment:** FT 1,257, PT 168, Grad FT 69, Grad PT 432 **Faculty:** FT 99, PT 60 **Student-Faculty Ratio:** 13:1 **Exams:** SAT I or ACT. **% Receiving Financial Aid:** 75 **% Residing in College-Owned, -Operated, or -Affiliated Housing:** 40 **Library Holdings:** 165,204 **Regional Accreditation:** Southern Association of Colleges and Schools **Credit Hours For Degree:** 122 semester hours, Bachelors **ROTC:** Army, Navy, Air Force **Professional Accreditation:** ABET **Intercollegiate Athletics:** Baseball M; Basketball M & W; Cross-Country Running M & W; Golf M & W; Soccer M & W; Softball W; Tennis M & W; Volleyball W

CLEVELAND STATE COMMUNITY COLLEGE

PO Box 3570
Cleveland, TN 37320-3570
Tel: (423)472-7141
Fax: (423)478-6255
E-mail: mburnette@clevelandstatecc.edu
Web Site: http://www.clevelandstatecc.edu/
President/CEO: Dr. Carl Hite
Admissions: Midge Burnette

Type: Two-Year College **Sex:** Coed **Affiliation:** Tennessee Board of Regents **Scores:** 62% ACT 18-23; 11% ACT 24-29 **Admission Plans:** Open Admission; Early Admission; Deferred Admission **Application Deadline:** Rolling **Application Fee:** $10.00 **H.S. Requirements:** High school diploma required; GED accepted **Costs Per Year:** Application fee: $10. State resident tuition: $3039 full-time, $111 per credit hour part-time. Nonresident tuition: $11,487 full-time, $460 per credit hour part-time. Mandatory fees: $269 full-time, $14.25 per credit hour part-time. Full-time tuition and fees vary according to course load. **Scholarships:** Available **Calendar System:** Semester, Summer Session Available **Enrollment:** FT 2,032, PT 1,583 **Faculty:** FT 69, PT 118 **Student-Faculty Ratio:** 14:1 **Exams:** SAT I or ACT. **Library Holdings:** 147,405 **Regional Accreditation:** Southern Association of Colleges and Schools **Credit Hours For Degree:** 64 semester hours, Associates **Professional Accreditation:** AAMAE, NLN, NAIT **Intercollegiate Athletics:** Baseball M; Basketball M & W; Softball W

COLUMBIA STATE COMMUNITY COLLEGE

PO Box 1315
Columbia, TN 38402-1315
Tel: (931)540-2722
Fax: (931)540-2535
E-mail: scruggs@coscc.cc.tn.us
Web Site: http://www.columbiastate.edu/
President/CEO: Janet F. Smith
Admissions: Joey Scruggs
Financial Aid: Paulette Burns

Type: Two-Year College **Sex:** Coed **% Accepted:** 100 **Admission Plans:** Early Admission **Application Deadline:** Rolling **Application Fee:** $10.00 **H.S. Requirements:** High school diploma required; GED accepted **Costs Per Year:** Application fee: $10. State resident tuition: $2664 full-time, $111 per semester hour part-time. Nonresident tuition: $11,040 full-time, $460 per semester hour part-time. Mandatory fees: $241 full-time, $10 per credit hour part-time, $8 per term part-time. Full-time tuition and fees vary according to course load. Part-time tuition and fees vary according to course load. **Scholarships:** Available **Calendar System:** Semester, Summer Session Available **Library Holdings:** 61,200 **Regional Accreditation:** Southern Association of Colleges and Schools **Credit Hours For Degree:** 66 semester hours, Associates **Professional Accreditation:** CARC, JRCERT, JRCEMT, NLN **Intercollegiate Athletics:** Baseball M; Basketball M & W; Softball W

CONCORDE CAREER COLLEGE

5100 Poplar Ave.
Ste. 132
Memphis, TN 38137
Tel: (901)761-9494
Fax: (901)761-3293
Web Site: http://www.concordecareercolleges.com/
President/CEO: Tommy Stewart

Type: Two-Year College **Sex:** Coed **% Accepted:** 100 **Professional Accreditation:** COE

CUMBERLAND UNIVERSITY

One Cumberland Square
Lebanon, TN 37087
Tel: (615)444-2562; Free: 800-467-0562
Admissions: (615)547-1244
Fax: (615)444-2569
E-mail: admissions@cumberland.edu
Web Site: http://www.cumberland.edu/
President/CEO: Dr. Harvill C. Eaton

Admissions: Beatrice LaChance
Financial Aid: Beatrice LaChance
Type: Comprehensive **Sex:** Coed **Scores:** 93% SAT V 400+; 66% ACT 18-23; 22% ACT 24-29 **% Accepted:** 57 **Admission Plans:** Deferred Admission **Application Deadline:** Rolling **Application Fee:** $25.00 **H.S. Requirements:** High school diploma required; GED accepted **Costs Per Year:** Application fee: $25. Comprehensive fee: $25,016 includes full-time tuition ($17,356), mandatory fees ($900), and college room and board ($6760). Full-time tuition and fees vary according to degree level. Part-time tuition: $723 per credit hour. Part-time mandatory fees: $450 per term. Part-time tuition and fees vary according to course load and degree level. **Scholarships:** Available **Calendar System:** Semester, Summer Session Available **Enrollment:** FT 903, PT 138, Grad FT 80, Grad PT 234 **Faculty:** FT 39, PT 71 **Student-Faculty Ratio:** 16:1 **Exams:** SAT I or ACT, SAT I. **% Receiving Financial Aid:** 79 **% Residing in College-Owned, -Operated, or -Affiliated Housing:** 25 **Library Holdings:** 75,000 **Regional Accreditation:** Southern Association of Colleges and Schools **Credit Hours For Degree:** 64 semester hours, Associates; 120 semester hours, Bachelors **ROTC:** Army **Professional Accreditation:** ACBSP, NCATE, NLN **Intercollegiate Athletics:** Baseball M; Basketball M & W; Bowling M & W; Cheerleading M & W; Football M; Golf M & W; Soccer M & W; Softball W; Tennis M & W; Volleyball W; Wrestling M

DAYMAR INSTITUTE (CLARKSVILLE)
1860 Wilma Rudolph Blvd.
Clarksville, TN 37040
Tel: (931)552-7600
Fax: (931)552-3624
E-mail: aprather@daymarinstitute.edu
Web Site: http://www.daymarinstitute.edu/
President/CEO: Katharine Purnell
Admissions: Alphonse Prather
Type: Four-Year College **Sex:** Coed **Admission Plans:** Open Admission **Application Deadline:** Rolling **Application Fee:** $0.00 **H.S. Requirements:** High school diploma required; GED accepted **Costs Per Year:** Application fee: $0. One-time mandatory fee: $180. Tuition: $13,440 full-time, $270 per quarter hour part-time. Mandatory fees: $960 full-time, $80. Full-time tuition and fees vary according to course load, location, and program. Part-time tuition and fees vary according to course load, location, and program. **Scholarships:** Available **Calendar System:** Quarter **Enrollment:** FT 381, PT 151 **Faculty:** FT 20, PT 19 **Student-Faculty Ratio:** 7:1 **Final Year or Final Semester Residency Requirement:** No **Credit Hours For Degree:** 96 quarter credits, Associates; 180 quarter credits, Bachelors **Professional Accreditation:** ACICS

DAYMAR INSTITUTE (NASHVILLE)
340 Plus Park Blvd.
Nashville, TN 37217
Tel: (615)361-7555
Web Site: http://www.daymarinstitute.edu/
President/CEO: Mark A. Gabis
Type: Two-Year College **Sex:** Coed **Admission Plans:** Open Admission; Deferred Admission **Application Deadline:** Rolling **H.S. Requirements:** High school diploma required; GED accepted **Scholarships:** Available **Calendar System:** Semester, Summer Session Available **Library Holdings:** 3,250 **Credit Hours For Degree:** 60 semester hours, Associates **Professional Accreditation:** ACICS

DEVRY UNIVERSITY (MEMPHIS)
6401 Poplar Ave., Ste. 600
Memphis, TN 38119
Tel: (901)537-2560; Free: 888-563-3879
Fax: (901)682-1326
Web Site: http://www.devry.edu/
President/CEO: Sheila Kell
Type: Comprehensive **Sex:** Coed **Admission Plans:** Deferred Admission **Application Deadline:** Rolling **Application Fee:** $50.00 **H.S. Requirements:** High school diploma required; GED accepted **Costs Per Year:** Application fee: $50. Tuition: $14,080 full-time, $550 per credit hour part-time. **Scholarships:** Available **Enrollment:** FT 44, PT 43, Grad FT 13, Grad PT 72 **Exams:** ACT essay used for admission. SAT essay used for admission. ACT essay used for placement. SAT essay used for placement. **% Receiving Financial Aid:** 75 **Regional Accreditation:** North Central Association of Colleges and Schools

DEVRY UNIVERSITY (NASHVILLE)
3343 Perimeter Hill Dr., Ste. 200
Nashville, TN 37211-4147
Tel: (615)445-3456
Web Site: http://www.devry.edu/
Type: Comprehensive **Sex:** Coed

DYERSBURG STATE COMMUNITY COLLEGE
1510 Lake Rd.
Dyersburg, TN 38024
Tel: (731)286-3200
Fax: (731)286-3325
E-mail: gulett@dscc.edu
Web Site: http://www.dscc.edu/
President/CEO: Karen Bowyer
Admissions: Ron Coffman
Type: Two-Year College **Sex:** Coed **Affiliation:** Tennessee Board of Regents **Scores:** 49.3% ACT 18-23; 5.4% ACT 24-29 **% Accepted:** 99 **Admission Plans:** Open Admission; Early Admission **Application Deadline:** Rolling **Application Fee:** $10.00 **H.S. Requirements:** High school diploma required; GED accepted. For adult students: High school diploma or equivalent not required **Scholarships:** Available **Calendar System:** Semester, Summer Session Available **Enrollment:** FT 1,315, PT 1,271 **Faculty:** FT 57, PT 148 **Student-Faculty Ratio:** 17:1 **Exams:** SAT I or ACT. **Library Holdings:** 44,355 **Regional Accreditation:** Southern Association of Colleges and Schools **Credit Hours For Degree:** 60 semester hours, Associates **Professional Accreditation:** NLN **Intercollegiate Athletics:** Baseball M; Basketball M & W; Cheerleading W; Softball W

EAST TENNESSEE STATE UNIVERSITY
807 University Parkway
Johnson City, TN 37614
Tel: (423)439-1000; Free: 800-462-3878
Admissions: (423)439-4213
Fax: (423)439-5770
E-mail: go2etsu@etsu.edu
Web Site: http://www.etsu.edu/
President/CEO: Dr. Paul E. Stanton, Jr.
Admissions: Mike Pitts
Financial Aid: Cindy A. Johnson
Type: University **Sex:** Coed **Affiliation:** State University and Community College System of Tennessee **Scores:** 85.5% SAT V 400+; 87.45% SAT M 400+; 53.27% ACT 18-23; 31.25% ACT 24-29 **% Accepted:** 85 **Admission Plans:** Early Admission **Application Deadline:** Rolling **Application Fee:** $15.00 **H.S. Requirements:** High school diploma required; GED accepted **Costs Per Year:** Application fee: $15. State resident tuition: $4584 full-time, $191 per credit hour part-time. Nonresident tuition: $16,512 full-time, $688 per credit hour part-time. Mandatory fees: $949 full-time, $59 per credit hour part-time. Full-time tuition and fees vary according to course load and program. Part-time tuition and fees vary according to course load and program. College room and board: $5500. College room only: $2770. Room and board charges vary according to board plan and housing facility. **Scholarships:** Available **Calendar System:** Semester, Summer Session Available **Enrollment:** FT 9,855, PT 1,793, Grad FT 1,787, Grad PT 986 **Faculty:** FT 532, PT 309 **Student-Faculty Ratio:** 19:1 **Exams:** SAT I or ACT. ACT essay not being used. SAT essay not being used. **% Receiving Financial Aid:** 58 **% Residing in College-Owned, -Operated, or -Affiliated Housing:** 20 **Final Year or Final Semester Residency Requirement:** Yes **Library Holdings:** 1,073,382 **Regional Accreditation:** Southern Association of Colleges and Schools **Credit Hours For Degree:** 120 semester hours, Bachelors **ROTC:** Army **Professional Accreditation:** AACSB, ABET, ACEJMC, AACN, AAFCS, AAMAE, ACA, ADA, ADtA, APTA, ASLHA, CARC, CEPH, CSWE, JRCERT, LCMEAMA, NAACLS, NASAD, NASM, NCATE NLN **Intercollegiate Athletics:** Baseball M; Basketball M & W; Cross-Country Running M & W; Golf M & W; Soccer M & W; Softball W; Tennis M & W; Track and Field M & W; Volleyball W

FISK UNIVERSITY
1000 17th Ave. North
Nashville, TN 37208-3051
Tel: (615)329-8500; Free: 800-443-FISK
Admissions: (615)329-8665
Fax: (615)329-8576
E-mail: admit@fisk.edu

Web Site: http://www.fisk.edu/
President/CEO: Hazel R. O'Leary
Financial Aid: Russelle Keese
Type: Comprehensive **Sex:** Coed **Affiliation:** United Church of Christ **% Accepted:** 65 **Application Deadline:** March 1 **Application Fee:** $50.00 **H.S. Requirements:** High school diploma required; GED accepted **Costs Per Year:** Application fee: $50. Comprehensive fee: $26,930 includes full-time tuition ($16,835), mandatory fees ($1510), and college room and board ($8585). College room only: $4975. Full-time tuition and fees vary according to course load. Room and board charges vary according to board plan. **Scholarships:** Available **Calendar System:** Semester, Summer Session Not available **Enrollment:** FT 560, PT 34, Grad FT 27, Grad PT 14 **Faculty:** FT 59, PT 21 **Student-Faculty Ratio:** 9:1 **Exams:** SAT I or ACT. ACT essay used for advising. SAT essay used for advising. **% Receiving Financial Aid:** 95 **% Residing in College-Owned, -Operated, or -Affiliated Housing:** 68 **Library Holdings:** 127,070 **Regional Accreditation:** Southern Association of Colleges and Schools **Credit Hours For Degree:** 120 credit hours, Bachelors **ROTC:** Army, Navy **Professional Accreditation:** ACBSP, NASM **Intercollegiate Athletics:** Basketball M & W

FOUNTAINHEAD COLLEGE OF TECHNOLOGY

3203 Tazewell Pike
Knoxville, TN 37918-2530
Tel: (865)688-9422; Free: 888-218-7335
Fax: (865)688-2419
Web Site: http://www.fountainheadcollege.edu/
President/CEO: Richard W. Rackley
Admissions: Todd Hill
Type: Two-Year College **Sex:** Coed **Admission Plans:** Open Admission **Application Deadline:** Rolling **Application Fee:** $100.00 **H.S. Requirements:** High school diploma required; GED accepted **Scholarships:** Available **Calendar System:** Semester, Summer Session Available **Faculty:** FT 9, PT 1 **Student-Faculty Ratio:** 13:1 **Library Holdings:** 1,200 **Credit Hours For Degree:** 75 credits, Associates; 120 credits, Bachelors **Professional Accreditation:** ACCSCT

FREE WILL BAPTIST BIBLE COLLEGE

3606 West End Ave.
Nashville, TN 37205-2498
Tel: (615)844-5000; Free: 800-763-9222
Admissions: (615)844-5197
Fax: (615)269-6028
E-mail: hhubbard@fwbbc.edu
Web Site: http://www.fwbbc.edu/
President/CEO: Dr. J. Matthew Pinson
Admissions: Heath Hubbard
Financial Aid: Jeff Caudill
Type: Four-Year College **Sex:** Coed **Affiliation:** Free Will Baptist **Scores:** 48% ACT 18-23; 21% ACT 24-29 **% Accepted:** 75 **Admission Plans:** Preferred Admission; Early Admission; Deferred Admission **Application Deadline:** Rolling **Application Fee:** $35.00 **H.S. Requirements:** High school diploma required; GED accepted **Costs Per Year:** Application fee: $35. Comprehensive fee: $19,234 includes full-time tuition ($12,690), mandatory fees ($844), and college room and board ($5700). Room and board charges vary according to board plan. Part-time tuition: $423 per semester hour. **Scholarships:** Available **Calendar System:** Semester, Summer Session Available **Enrollment:** FT 229, PT 74 **Faculty:** FT 21, PT 28 **Student-Faculty Ratio:** 11:1 **Exams:** ACT. **% Receiving Financial Aid:** 72 **% Residing in College-Owned, -Operated, or -Affiliated Housing:** 57 **Library Holdings:** 131,200 **Regional Accreditation:** Southern Association of Colleges and Schools **Credit Hours For Degree:** 66 semester hours, Associates; 124 semester hours, Bachelors **ROTC:** Army, Air Force **Professional Accreditation:** ABHE **Intercollegiate Athletics:** Baseball M; Basketball M & W

FREED-HARDEMAN UNIVERSITY

158 East Main St.
Henderson, TN 38340-2399
Tel: (731)989-6000; Free: 800-630-3480
Admissions: (731)989-6651
Fax: (731)989-6047
E-mail: admissions@fhu.edu
Web Site: http://www.fhu.edu/
President/CEO: Joe Wiley
Admissions: Dr. Belinda Anderson
Financial Aid: Molly Risley
Type: Comprehensive **Sex:** Coed **Affiliation:** Church of Christ **Scores:** 90% SAT V 400+; 92% SAT M 400+; 45% ACT 18-23; 36% ACT 24-29 **% Accepted:** 56 **Admission Plans:** Early Admission; Deferred Admission **Application Deadline:** Rolling **Application Fee:** $0.00 **H.S. Requirements:** High school diploma required; GED accepted **Costs Per Year:** Application fee: $0. Comprehensive fee: $22,088 includes full-time tuition ($12,060), mandatory fees ($2938), and college room and board ($7090). College room only: $3980. Full-time tuition and fees vary according to course load and degree level. Room and board charges vary according to board plan and housing facility. Part-time tuition: $402 per semester hour. Part-time tuition varies according to course load and degree level. **Scholarships:** Available **Calendar System:** Semester, Summer Session Available **Enrollment:** FT 1,410, PT 124 **Faculty:** FT 106, PT 45 **Student-Faculty Ratio:** 14:1 **Exams:** SAT I or ACT. **% Receiving Financial Aid:** 79 **Library Holdings:** 147,821 **Regional Accreditation:** Southern Association of Colleges and Schools **Credit Hours For Degree:** 132 semester hours, Bachelors **Professional Accreditation:** ACBSP, CSWE, NCATE **Intercollegiate Athletics:** Baseball M; Basketball M & W; Cheerleading M & W; Soccer M & W; Softball W; Volleyball W

HIGH-TECH INSTITUTE (MEMPHIS)

5865 Shelby Oaks Circle
Ste. 100
Memphis, TN 38134
Tel: (901)432-3800; Free: (866)269-7251
Fax: (901)387-1181
Web Site: http://www.high-techinstitute.com/
President/CEO: Catherine McClarin
Type: Two-Year College **Sex:** Coed **Application Fee:** $50.00 **Calendar System:** Semester **Professional Accreditation:** ACCSCT

HIGH-TECH INSTITUTE (NASHVILLE)

560 Royal Parkway
Nashville, TN 37214
Tel: (615)232-3700; Free: 888-616-6549
Fax: (615)902-9766
Web Site: http://www.high-techinstitute.com/
President/CEO: Brenda Nash
Type: Two-Year College **Sex:** Coed **Application Fee:** $50.00 **Calendar System:** Semester **Professional Accreditation:** ACCSCT

HUNTINGTON COLLEGE OF HEALTH SCIENCES

1204 -D Kenesaw, Sequoyah Hills Center
Knoxville, TN 37919-7736
Tel: (865)524-8079; Free: 800-290-4226
Fax: (865)524-8339
E-mail: cfreeman@hchs.edu
Web Site: http://www.hchs.edu/
President/CEO: Dr. Arthur Presser
Admissions: Cheryl Freeman
Type: Comprehensive **Sex:** Coed **% Accepted:** 100 **Admission Plans:** Open Admission; Deferred Admission **Application Deadline:** Rolling **H.S. Requirements:** High school diploma required; GED accepted **Calendar System:** Continuous, Summer Session Available **Enrollment:** FT 400 **Faculty:** FT 3, PT 17 **Student-Faculty Ratio:** 29:1 **Credit Hours For Degree:** 60 credit hours, Associates **Professional Accreditation:** DETC

ITT TECHNICAL INSTITUTE (CHATTANOOGA)

5600 Brainerd Rd., Ste. G-1
Chattanooga, TN 37411
Tel: (423)510-6800; Free: 877-474-8312
Admissions: (423)510-6800
Web Site: http://www.itt-tech.edu/
President/CEO: Chad Jaynes
Type: Two-Year College **Sex:** Coed **Affiliation:** ITT Educational Services, Inc.

ITT TECHNICAL INSTITUTE (CORDOVA)

7260 Goodlett Farms Parkway
Cordova, TN 38016
Tel: (901)381-0200
Web Site: http://www.itt-tech.edu/

President/CEO: Steven Temple
Type: Two-Year College **Sex:** Coed **Affiliation:** ITT Educational Services, Inc. **H.S. Requirements:** High school diploma required; GED accepted **Scholarships:** Available **Calendar System:** Quarter, Summer Session Not available **Professional Accreditation:** ACICS

ITT TECHNICAL INSTITUTE (JOHNSON CITY)
4721 Lake Park Dr.
Ste. 100
Johnson City, TN 37615
Tel: (423)952-4400; Free: 877-301-9691
Web Site: http://www.itt-tech.edu/
Type: Two-Year College **Sex:** Coed **Professional Accreditation:** ACICS

ITT TECHNICAL INSTITUTE (KNOXVILLE)
10208 Technology Dr.
Knoxville, TN 37932
Tel: (865)671-2800
Fax: (865)691-0337
Web Site: http://www.itt-tech.edu/
President/CEO: Jamie Carpenter
Type: Two-Year College **Sex:** Coed **Affiliation:** ITT Educational Services, Inc. **H.S. Requirements:** High school diploma required; GED accepted **Scholarships:** Available **Calendar System:** Quarter, Summer Session Not available **Professional Accreditation:** ACICS

ITT TECHNICAL INSTITUTE (NASHVILLE)
2845 Elm Hill Pike
Nashville, TN 37214
Tel: (615)889-8700
Fax: (615)872-7209
Web Site: http://www.itt-tech.edu/
President/CEO: James R. Coakley
Type: Two-Year College **Sex:** Coed **Affiliation:** ITT Educational Services, Inc. **H.S. Requirements:** High school diploma required; GED accepted **Scholarships:** Available **Calendar System:** Quarter, Summer Session Not available **Professional Accreditation:** ACICS

JACKSON STATE COMMUNITY COLLEGE
2046 North Parkway
Jackson, TN 38301-3797
Tel: (731)424-3520
Admissions: (731)425-8844
Fax: (731)425-2647
E-mail: awinchester@jscc.edu
Web Site: http://www.jscc.edu/
President/CEO: Dr. Bruce Blanding
Admissions: Andrea Winchester
Financial Aid: Lori Thorne
Type: Two-Year College **Sex:** Coed **Affiliation:** Tennessee Board of Regents **Admission Plans:** Open Admission; Preferred Admission **Application Deadline:** August 23 **Application Fee:** $10.00 **H.S. Requirements:** High school diploma required; GED accepted **Costs Per Year:** Application fee: $10. One-time mandatory fee: $10. State resident tuition: $2953 full-time, $111 per credit hour part-time. Nonresident tuition: $11,184 full-time, $349 per credit hour part-time. Mandatory fees: $253 full-time, $9 per credit hour part-time, $14 per term part-time. Full-time tuition and fees vary according to course load. Part-time tuition and fees vary according to course load. **Scholarships:** Available **Calendar System:** Semester, Summer Session Available **Faculty:** FT 98, PT 208 **Student-Faculty Ratio:** 21:1 **Exams:** ACT, Other, SAT I or ACT. **Final Year or Final Semester Residency Requirement:** Yes **Library Holdings:** 56,024 **Regional Accreditation:** Southern Association of Colleges and Schools **Credit Hours For Degree:** 60 semester hours, Associates **ROTC:** Army **Professional Accreditation:** APTA, ACBSP, CARC, JRCERT, JRCEMT, NAACLS, NLN, NAIT **Intercollegiate Athletics:** Baseball M; Basketball M & W; Softball W

JOHN A. GUPTON COLLEGE
1616 Church St.
Nashville, TN 37203-2920
Tel: (615)327-3927
Fax: (615)321-4518
Web Site: http://www.guptoncollege.edu/
President/CEO: B. Steven Spann
Admissions: Lisa Bolin
Type: Two-Year College **Sex:** Coed **% Accepted:** 55 **Admission Plans:** Deferred Admission **Application Deadline:** Rolling **Application Fee:** $20.00 **H.S. Requirements:** High school diploma required; GED accepted **Scholarships:** Available **Calendar System:** Semester **Enrollment:** FT 91, PT 6 **Faculty:** FT 2, PT 16 **Student-Faculty Ratio:** 13:1 **Exams:** ACT. **Library Holdings:** 4,000 **Regional Accreditation:** Southern Association of Colleges and Schools **Credit Hours For Degree:** 65 semester hours, Associates **Professional Accreditation:** ABFSE

JOHNSON BIBLE COLLEGE
7900 Johnson Dr.
Knoxville, TN 37998-1001
Tel: (865)573-4517; Free: 800-827-2122
Admissions: (865)251-2346
Fax: (865)251-2337
E-mail: twingfield@jbc.edu
Web Site: http://www.jbc.edu/
President/CEO: Gary Weedman
Admissions: Tim Wingfield
Financial Aid: Lawrence Rector, CPA
Type: Comprehensive **Sex:** Coed **Affiliation:** Christian Churches and Churches of Christ **Scores:** 97.5% SAT V 400+; 94.8% SAT M 400+; 44.7% ACT 18-23; 40.8% ACT 24-29 **% Accepted:** 72 **Admission Plans:** Deferred Admission **Application Deadline:** July 1 **Application Fee:** $0.00 **H.S. Requirements:** High school diploma required; GED accepted **Costs Per Year:** Application fee: $0. Comprehensive fee: $14,200 includes full-time tuition ($8300), mandatory fees ($800), and college room and board ($5100). College room only: $2400. Room and board charges vary according to board plan and housing facility. Part-time tuition: $332 per credit hour. Part-time mandatory fees: $35 per credit hour. Part-time tuition and fees vary according to course load. **Scholarships:** Available **Calendar System:** Semester, Summer Session Available **Enrollment:** FT 645, PT 31, Grad FT 28, Grad PT 75 **Faculty:** FT 30, PT 23 **Student-Faculty Ratio:** 15:1 **Exams:** ACT, SAT I or ACT. **% Receiving Financial Aid:** 90 **% Residing in College-Owned, -Operated, or -Affiliated Housing:** 88 **Final Year or Final Semester Residency Requirement:** No **Library Holdings:** 108,126 **Regional Accreditation:** Southern Association of Colleges and Schools **Credit Hours For Degree:** 62 semester hours, Associates; 124 semester hours, Bachelors **Professional Accreditation:** ABHE **Intercollegiate Athletics:** Baseball M; Basketball M & W; Cheerleading M & W; Cross-Country Running M & W; Soccer M & W; Volleyball W

KAPLAN CAREER INSTITUTE, NASHVILLE CAMPUS
750 Envious Ln.
Nashville, TN 37217
Tel: (615)279-8300; Free: 800-336-4457
Fax: (615)297-6678
Web Site: http://www.kci-nashville.com/
President/CEO: Adam Butler
Type: Two-Year College **Sex:** Coed **H.S. Requirements:** High school diploma required; GED accepted **Professional Accreditation:** COE

KING COLLEGE
1350 King College Rd.
Bristol, TN 37620-2699
Tel: (423)968-1187; Free: 800-362-0014
Admissions: (423)652-4861
Fax: (423)968-4456
E-mail: admissions@king.edu
Web Site: http://www.king.edu/
President/CEO: Dr. Gregory D. Jordan
Admissions: Greg King
Financial Aid: Nancy M. Beverly
Type: Comprehensive **Sex:** Coed **Affiliation:** Presbyterian Church (U.S.A.) **Scores:** 84.62% SAT V 400+; 91.34% SAT M 400+; 56.99% ACT 18-23; 32.64% ACT 24-29 **% Accepted:** 62 **Admission Plans:** Early Admission; Deferred Admission **Application Deadline:** Rolling **Application Fee:** $20.00 **H.S. Requirements:** High school diploma required; GED accepted **Costs Per Year:** Application fee: $20. Comprehensive fee: $29,298 includes full-time tuition ($20,592), mandatory fees ($1288), and college room and board ($7418). College room only: $3726. Full-time tuition and fees vary according to course load and program. Room and board charges vary according to board plan. Part-time tuition: $600 per credit hour. Part-time mandatory fees:

$120 per term. Part-time tuition and fees vary according to course load and program. **Scholarships:** Available **Calendar System:** Semester, Summer Session Available **Enrollment:** FT 1,342, PT 177, Grad FT 205, Grad PT 80 **Faculty:** FT 81, PT 71 **Student-Faculty Ratio:** 14:1 **Exams:** SAT I or ACT. ACT essay not being used. SAT essay not being used. **% Receiving Financial Aid:** 81 **% Residing in College-Owned, -Operated, or -Affiliated Housing:** 27 **Library Holdings:** 97,836 **Regional Accreditation:** Southern Association of Colleges and Schools **Credit Hours For Degree:** 124 semester hours, Bachelors **ROTC:** Army **Professional Accreditation:** AACN **Intercollegiate Athletics:** Baseball M; Basketball M & W; Cheerleading M & W; Cross-Country Running M & W; Golf M & W; Soccer M & W; Softball W; Swimming and Diving M & W; Tennis M & W; Track and Field M & W; Volleyball W; Wrestling M

LAMBUTH UNIVERSITY
705 Lambuth Blvd.
Jackson, TN 38301
Tel: (731)425-2500; Free: 800-526-2884
Admissions: (731)425-3332
Fax: (731)988-4600
E-mail: myers-k@lambuth.edu
Web Site: http://www.lambuth.edu/
President/CEO: Dr. Jerry Israel
Admissions: Karen Myers
Financial Aid: Karen Myers
Type: Four-Year College **Sex:** Coed **Affiliation:** United Methodist **Scores:** 94% SAT V 400+; 100% SAT M 400+; 55% ACT 18-23; 33% ACT 24-29 **% Accepted:** 62 **Admission Plans:** Early Admission; Deferred Admission **Application Deadline:** Rolling **Application Fee:** $25.00 **H.S. Requirements:** High school diploma required; GED accepted **Costs Per Year:** Application fee: $25. Comprehensive fee: $26,585 includes full-time tuition ($18,020), mandatory fees ($550), and college room and board ($8015). College room only: $3615. Room and board charges vary according to housing facility. Part-time tuition: $750 per credit hour. Part-time mandatory fees: $225 per term. Part-time tuition and fees vary according to course load. **Scholarships:** Available **Calendar System:** Semester, Summer Session Available **Enrollment:** FT 748, PT 67 **Faculty:** FT 51, PT 47 **Student-Faculty Ratio:** 12:1 **Exams:** SAT I or ACT. **% Receiving Financial Aid:** 81 **% Residing in College-Owned, -Operated, or -Affiliated Housing:** 54 **Library Holdings:** 292,361 **Regional Accreditation:** Southern Association of Colleges and Schools **Credit Hours For Degree:** 128 credit hours, Bachelors **Professional Accreditation:** ACBSP **Intercollegiate Athletics:** Baseball M; Basketball M & W; Football M; Golf M; Soccer M & W; Softball W; Tennis M & W

LANE COLLEGE
545 Ln. Ave.
Jackson, TN 38301-4598
Tel: (731)426-7500; Free: 800-960-7533
Admissions: (731)426-7533
Fax: (731)426-7559
E-mail: kboyd@lanecollege.edu
Web Site: http://www.lanecollege.edu/
President/CEO: Dr. Wesley Cornelious McClure
Admissions: Kelly Boyd
Financial Aid: Tony Calhoun
Type: Four-Year College **Sex:** Coed **Affiliation:** Christian Methodist Episcopal Church **Scores:** 17% ACT 18-23; 1% ACT 24-29 **% Accepted:** 37 **Admission Plans:** Deferred Admission **Application Deadline:** Rolling **Application Fee:** $0.00 **H.S. Requirements:** High school diploma required; GED accepted **Costs Per Year:** Application fee: $0. Comprehensive fee: $13,520 includes full-time tuition ($7330), mandatory fees ($670), and college room and board ($5520). Full-time tuition and fees vary according to course load. Part-time tuition: $310 per hour. Part-time mandatory fees: $670 per year. Part-time tuition and fees vary according to course load. **Scholarships:** Available **Calendar System:** Semester, Summer Session Available **Enrollment:** FT 2,121, PT 25 **Faculty:** FT 94, PT 8 **Student-Faculty Ratio:** 21:1 **Exams:** SAT I or ACT. **% Receiving Financial Aid:** 95 **% Residing in College-Owned, -Operated, or -Affiliated Housing:** 61 **Library Holdings:** 144,191 **Regional Accreditation:** Southern Association of Colleges and Schools **Credit Hours For Degree:** 124 semester hours, Bachelors **Intercollegiate Athletics:** Baseball M; Basketball M & W; Cheerleading W; Cross-Country Running M & W; Football M; Softball W; Tennis M & W; Track and Field M & W; Volleyball W

LEE UNIVERSITY
PO Box 3450
Cleveland, TN 37320-3450
Tel: (423)614-8000; Free: 800-533-9930
Admissions: (423)614-8500
Fax: (423)614-8533
E-mail: admissions@leeuniversity.edu
Web Site: http://www.leeuniversity.edu/
President/CEO: Dr. C. Paul Conn
Admissions: Phillip Cook
Financial Aid: Michael Ellis
Type: Comprehensive **Sex:** Coed **Affiliation:** Church of God **Scores:** 95.55% SAT V 400+; 88.88% SAT M 400+; 35.1% ACT 18-23; 40.09% ACT 24-29 **% Accepted:** 65 **Admission Plans:** Early Admission; Deferred Admission **Application Deadline:** September 1 **Application Fee:** $25.00 **H.S. Requirements:** High school diploma required; GED accepted **Costs Per Year:** Application fee: $25. Comprehensive fee: $17,260 includes full-time tuition ($11,100), mandatory fees ($510), and college room and board ($5650). College room only: $2720. Full-time tuition and fees vary according to course load. Room and board charges vary according to board plan and housing facility. Part-time tuition: $463 per credit hour. Part-time tuition varies according to course load. **Scholarships:** Available **Calendar System:** Semester, Summer Session Available **Enrollment:** FT 3,431, PT 472, Grad FT 155, Grad PT 204 **Faculty:** FT 149, PT 179 **Student-Faculty Ratio:** 18:1 **Exams:** SAT I or ACT. ACT essay not being used. SAT essay not being used. **% Receiving Financial Aid:** 64 **% Residing in College-Owned, -Operated, or -Affiliated Housing:** 46 **Final Year or Final Semester Residency Requirement:** Yes **Library Holdings:** 147,863 **Regional Accreditation:** Southern Association of Colleges and Schools **Credit Hours For Degree:** 130 semester hours, Bachelors **Professional Accreditation:** NASM, NCATE, TEAC **Intercollegiate Athletics:** Baseball M; Basketball M & W; Cheerleading M & W; Cross-Country Running M & W; Golf M; Rugby M & W; Soccer M & W; Softball W; Tennis M & W; Volleyball W

LEMOYNE-OWEN COLLEGE
807 Walker Ave.
Memphis, TN 38126-6595
Tel: (901)774-9090
Admissions: (901)435-1500
Fax: (901)942-6272
E-mail: samuel_king@loc.edu
Web Site: http://www.loc.edu/
President/CEO: Johnnie B. Watson
Admissions: Samuel King
Financial Aid: Phyllis Nettles Torry
Type: Four-Year College **Sex:** Coed **Affiliation:** United Church of Christ **Scores:** 12% ACT 18-23; 3% ACT 24-29 **% Accepted:** 51 **Admission Plans:** Open Admission **Application Deadline:** April 1 **Application Fee:** $25.00 **H.S. Requirements:** High school diploma required; GED accepted **Costs Per Year:** Application fee: $25. Comprehensive fee: $15,170 includes full-time tuition ($10,098), mandatory fees ($220), and college room and board ($4852). Part-time tuition: $421 per credit hour. **Scholarships:** Available **Calendar System:** Semester, Summer Session Available **Enrollment:** FT 501, PT 91 **Faculty:** FT 55, PT 33 **Student-Faculty Ratio:** 10:1 **Exams:** SAT I or ACT. **% Receiving Financial Aid:** 96 **% Residing in College-Owned, -Operated, or -Affiliated Housing:** 25 **Regional Accreditation:** Southern Association of Colleges and Schools **Credit Hours For Degree:** 120 credit hours, Bachelors **ROTC:** Army, Air Force **Professional Accreditation:** NCATE **Intercollegiate Athletics:** Baseball M; Basketball M & W; Cross-Country Running M & W; Golf M & W; Softball W; Tennis M & W; Volleyball W

LINCOLN MEMORIAL UNIVERSITY
6965 Cumberland Gap Parkway
Harrogate, TN 37752-1901
Tel: (423)869-3611; Free: 800-325-0900
Admissions: (423)869-6280
Fax: (423)869-6250
E-mail: admissions@lmunet.edu
Web Site: http://www.lmunet.edu/
President/CEO: Dr. C Warren Neel
Admissions: Cindy Skaruppa
Financial Aid: Bryan Erslan
Type: Comprehensive **Sex:** Coed **Scores:** 94% SAT V 400+; 88% SAT M

400+; 64.2% ACT 18-23; 18.3% ACT 24-29 **% Accepted:** 78 **Application Deadline:** Rolling **Application Fee:** $25.00 **H.S. Requirements:** High school diploma required; GED accepted **Costs Per Year:** Application fee: $25. Comprehensive fee: $21,380 includes full-time tuition ($15,120), mandatory fees ($580), and college room and board ($5680). College room only: $2540. Room and board charges vary according to board plan and housing facility. Part-time tuition: $630 per credit. Part-time mandatory fees: $630 per credit hour, $290 per term. **Scholarships:** Available **Calendar System:** Semester, Summer Session Available **Enrollment:** FT 1,283, PT 277, Grad FT 899, Grad PT 1,489 **Faculty:** FT 170, PT 56 **Student-Faculty Ratio:** 12:1 **Exams:** SAT I or ACT. ACT essay not being used. SAT essay not being used. **% Receiving Financial Aid:** 86 **% Residing in College-Owned, -Operated, or -Affiliated Housing:** 36 **Library Holdings:** 199,892 **Regional Accreditation:** Southern Association of Colleges and Schools **Credit Hours For Degree:** 64 semester hours, Associates; 128 semester hours, Bachelors **Professional Accreditation:** AANA, AOsA, ACBSP, CSWE, JRCEPAT, NAACLS, NLN **Intercollegiate Athletics:** Baseball M; Basketball M & W; Cross-Country Running M & W; Golf M & W; Soccer M & W; Softball W; Tennis M & W; Volleyball W

LIPSCOMB UNIVERSITY
One University Park Dr.
Nashville, TN 37204-3951
Tel: (615)966-1000; Free: 877-582-4766
Admissions: (615)966-1776
Fax: (615)966-1804
E-mail: admissions@lipscomb.edu
Web Site: http://www.lipscomb.edu/
President/CEO: L. Randolph Lowry, III
Financial Aid: Karita McCaleb Waters
Type: Comprehensive **Sex:** Coed **Affiliation:** Church of Christ **Scores:** 95.54% SAT V 400+; 94.91% SAT M 400+; 46.57% ACT 18-23; 36.82% ACT 24-29 **% Accepted:** 66 **Admission Plans:** Early Admission; Deferred Admission **Application Deadline:** Rolling **Application Fee:** $25.00 **H.S. Requirements:** High school diploma required; GED accepted **Costs Per Year:** Application fee: $25. Comprehensive fee: $28,240 includes full-time tuition ($19,330), mandatory fees ($1060), and college room and board ($7850). College room only: $4720. Full-time tuition and fees vary according to class time, course load, and degree level. Room and board charges vary according to board plan and housing facility. Part-time tuition: $775 per hour. Part-time mandatory fees: $45 per credit hour. Part-time tuition and fees vary according to class time, course load, and degree level. **Scholarships:** Available **Calendar System:** Semester, Summer Session Available **Enrollment:** FT 2,311, PT 207, Grad FT 462, Grad PT 438 **Faculty:** FT 130, PT 205 **Student-Faculty Ratio:** 16:1 **Exams:** SAT I or ACT. **% Receiving Financial Aid:** 62 **% Residing in College-Owned, -Operated, or -Affiliated Housing:** 63 **Library Holdings:** 253,398 **Regional Accreditation:** Southern Association of Colleges and Schools **Credit Hours For Degree:** 132 semester hours, Bachelors **ROTC:** Army, Air Force **Professional Accreditation:** ACPhE, ADtA, ACBSP, ATS, CSWE, JRCEPAT, NASM, NCATE **Intercollegiate Athletics:** Baseball M; Basketball M & W; Cross-Country Running M & W; Golf M & W; Soccer M & W; Softball W; Tennis M & W; Volleyball W

MARTIN METHODIST COLLEGE
433 West Madison St.
Pulaski, TN 38478-2716
Tel: (931)363-9868; Free: 800-467-1273
Admissions: (931)363-9800
Fax: (931)363-9818
E-mail: admit@martinmethodist.edu
Web Site: http://www.martinmethodist.edu/
President/CEO: Ted Brown
Admissions: Lisa Smith
Financial Aid: Anita Beecham
Type: Four-Year College **Sex:** Coed **Affiliation:** United Methodist **Admission Plans:** Early Admission; Deferred Admission **Application Deadline:** August 26 **Application Fee:** $25.00 **H.S. Requirements:** High school diploma required; GED accepted **Scholarships:** Available **Calendar System:** Semester, Summer Session Available **Exams:** SAT I or ACT. **% Receiving Financial Aid:** 54 **Library Holdings:** 84,000 **Regional Accreditation:** Southern Association of Colleges and Schools **Credit Hours For Degree:** 63 hours, Associates; 120 hours, Bachelors **Intercollegiate Athletics:** Baseball M; Basketball M & W; Bowling M & W; Cheerleading W; Golf M & W; Soccer M & W; Softball W; Tennis M & W; Volleyball W

MARYVILLE COLLEGE
502 East Lamar Alexander Parkway
Maryville, TN 37804-5907
Tel: (865)981-8000; Free: 800-597-2687
Admissions: (865)981-8092
Fax: (865)983-0581
E-mail: admissions@maryvillecollege.edu
Web Site: http://www.maryvillecollege.edu/
President/CEO: Dr. Gerald W. Gibson
Admissions: Linda L. Moore
Financial Aid: Richard Brand
Type: Four-Year College **Sex:** Coed **Affiliation:** Presbyterian **Scores:** 97% SAT V 400+; 96% SAT M 400+; 40% ACT 18-23; 47% ACT 24-29 **% Accepted:** 73 **Admission Plans:** Early Admission; Early Action; Early Decision Plan; Deferred Admission **Application Deadline:** March 1 **Application Fee:** $0.00 **H.S. Requirements:** High school diploma required; GED accepted **Costs Per Year:** Application fee: $0. Comprehensive fee: $38,505 includes full-time tuition ($28,798), mandatory fees ($675), and college room and board ($9032). College room only: $4516. Full-time tuition and fees vary according to course load. Room and board charges vary according to board plan and housing facility. Part-time tuition: $1199 per credit hour. Part-time mandatory fees: $15 per credit hour. Part-time tuition and fees vary according to course load. **Scholarships:** Available **Calendar System:** 4-1-4, Summer Session Available **Enrollment:** FT 1,092, PT 11 **Student-Faculty Ratio:** 11:1 **Exams:** SAT I or ACT. ACT essay used for admission. SAT essay used for admission. ACT essay used for advising. SAT essay used for advising. **% Receiving Financial Aid:** 83 **% Residing in College-Owned, -Operated, or -Affiliated Housing:** 71 **Final Year or Final Semester Residency Requirement:** Yes **Library Holdings:** 249,723 **Regional Accreditation:** Southern Association of Colleges and Schools **Credit Hours For Degree:** 128 semester hours, Bachelors **Professional Accreditation:** NASM **Intercollegiate Athletics:** Baseball M; Basketball M & W; Cheerleading M & W; Cross-Country Running M & W; Equestrian Sports M & W; Football M; Golf M & W; Soccer M & W; Softball W; Swimming and Diving M & W; Tennis M & W; Ultimate Frisbee M & W; Volleyball W

MEDVANCE INSTITUTE
1025 Hwy. 111
Cookeville, TN 38501
Tel: (931)526-3660; Free: 800-256-9085
Fax: (931)372-2603
Web Site: http://www.medvance.edu/
President/CEO: John Hopkins
Admissions: Sharon Mellott
Type: Two-Year College **Sex:** Coed **Application Deadline:** Rolling **Application Fee:** $25.00 **H.S. Requirements:** High school diploma required; GED accepted **Scholarships:** Available **Calendar System:** Quarter, Summer Session Not available **Exams:** Other. **Credit Hours For Degree:** 96 quarter hours, Associates **Professional Accreditation:** COE, NAACLS

MEMPHIS COLLEGE OF ART
Overton Park, 1930 Poplar Ave.
Memphis, TN 38104-2764
Tel: (901)272-5100; Free: 800-727-1088
Admissions: (901)272-5153
Fax: (901)272-5104
E-mail: amoore@mca.edu
Web Site: http://www.mca.edu/
President/CEO: Jeffrey Nesin
Admissions: Annette Moore
Financial Aid: Lynn Holladay
Type: Comprehensive **Sex:** Coed **Scores:** 49% ACT 18-23; 39% ACT 24-29 **% Accepted:** 47 **Admission Plans:** Deferred Admission **Application Deadline:** Rolling **Application Fee:** $25.00 **H.S. Requirements:** High school diploma required; GED accepted **Costs Per Year:** Application fee: $25. Comprehensive fee: $31,950 includes full-time tuition ($23,300), mandatory fees ($650), and college room and board ($8000). College room only: $6000. Room and board charges vary according to housing facility. Part-time tuition: $1012 per credit hour. **Scholarships:** Available **Calendar System:** Semester, Summer Session Available **Enrollment:** FT 338, PT 21, Grad FT 19, Grad PT 71 **Faculty:** FT 25, PT 41 **Student-Faculty Ratio:** 10:1 **Exams:** SAT I or ACT. **% Receiving Financial Aid:** 82 **% Residing in College-Owned, -Operated, or -Affiliated Housing:** 44 **Final Year or Final Semester Residency Requirement:** Yes **Regional Accreditation:**

Southern Association of Colleges and Schools **Credit Hours For Degree:** 120 credit hours, Bachelors **Professional Accreditation:** NASAD

MID-AMERICA BAPTIST THEOLOGICAL SEMINARY
2095 Appling Rd.
Cordova, TN 38016
Tel: (901)751-8453; Free: 800-968-4508
Fax: (901)751-8454
E-mail: info@mabts.edu
Web Site: http://www.mabts.edu/
Admissions: Duffy Guyton
Type: Two-Year College **Sex:** Men **Affiliation:** Southern Baptist **Admission Plans:** Open Admission **Application Deadline:** August 4 **Application Fee:** $25.00 **H.S. Requirements:** High school diploma required; GED accepted **Calendar System:** Semester, Summer Session Available **Enrollment:** FT 29, PT 22 **Faculty:** FT 27, PT 0 **Student-Faculty Ratio:** 15:1 **Library Holdings:** 119,000 **Regional Accreditation:** Southern Association of Colleges and Schools **Credit Hours For Degree:** 64 semester hours, Associates

MIDDLE TENNESSEE STATE UNIVERSITY
1301 East Main St.
Murfreesboro, TN 37132
Tel: (615)898-2300
E-mail: admissions@mtsu.edu
Web Site: http://www.mtsu.edu/
President/CEO: Dr. Sidney A. McPhee
Admissions: Lynn Palmer
Financial Aid: David Hutton
Type: University **Sex:** Coed **Affiliation:** Tennessee Board of Regents **Scores:** 92% SAT V 400+; 92% SAT M 400+; 59% ACT 18-23; 29% ACT 24-29 **% Accepted:** 70 **Application Fee:** $25.00 **H.S. Requirements:** High school diploma required; GED accepted **Costs Per Year:** Application fee: $25. State resident tuition: $4584 full-time, $191 per semester hour part-time. Nonresident tuition: $16,512 full-time, $688 per semester hour part-time. Mandatory fees: $1404 full-time, $59 per semester hour part-time. Full-time tuition and fees vary according to course load. Part-time tuition and fees vary according to course load. College room and board: $6514. College room only: $4050. Room and board charges vary according to board plan and housing facility. **Scholarships:** Available **Calendar System:** Semester, Summer Session Available **Enrollment:** FT 18,912, PT 3,387, Grad FT 295, Grad PT 2,594 **Student-Faculty Ratio:** 20:1 **Exams:** SAT I or ACT. ACT essay not being used. SAT essay not being used. **% Receiving Financial Aid:** 49 **% Residing in College-Owned, -Operated, or -Affiliated Housing:** 12 **Regional Accreditation:** Southern Association of Colleges and Schools **Credit Hours For Degree:** 65 semester hours, Associates; 120 semester hours, Bachelors **ROTC:** Army, Air Force **Professional Accreditation:** AACSB, ABET, ACEJMC, AACN, AAFCS, ACA, CAA, FIDER, CSWE, NASM, NCATE, NLN, NRPA, NAIT **Intercollegiate Athletics:** Baseball M; Basketball M & W; Cheerleading M & W; Cross-Country Running M & W; Equestrian Sports M & W; Football M; Golf M; Soccer W; Softball W; Tennis M & W; Track and Field M & W; Volleyball W

MILLER-MOTTE TECHNICAL COLLEGE
1820 Business Park Dr.
Clarksville, TN 37040
Tel: (931)553-0071
Fax: (931)552-2916
E-mail: lisateague@hotmail.com
Web Site: http://www.miller-motte.com/
President/CEO: Gina Castleberry
Admissions: Lisa Teague
Type: Two-Year College **Sex:** Coed **Scholarships:** Available **Calendar System:** Quarter **Professional Accreditation:** ACICS, AAMAE

MILLIGAN COLLEGE
PO Box 500
Milligan College, TN 37682
Tel: (423)461-8700
Admissions: (423)461-8730
Fax: (423)461-8960
E-mail: admissions@milligan.edu
Web Site: http://www.milligan.edu/
President/CEO: Dr. Donald R. Jeanes
Admissions: Tracy Brinn
Financial Aid: Diane Keasling
Type: Comprehensive **Sex:** Coed **Affiliation:** Christian **Scores:** 96% SAT V 400+; 93% SAT M 400+; 50% ACT 18-23; 39% ACT 24-29 **% Accepted:** 68 **Admission Plans:** Deferred Admission **Application Deadline:** August 1 **Application Fee:** $30.00 **H.S. Requirements:** High school diploma required; GED accepted **Costs Per Year:** Application fee: $30. One-time mandatory fee: $75. Comprehensive fee: $29,110 includes full-time tuition ($22,600), mandatory fees ($860), and college room and board ($5650). College room only: $2650. Full-time tuition and fees vary according to course load. Room and board charges vary according to housing facility. Part-time tuition: $360 per credit hour. Part-time tuition varies according to course load. **Scholarships:** Available **Calendar System:** Semester, Summer Session Available **Enrollment:** FT 811, PT 92, Grad FT 63, Grad PT 30 **Faculty:** FT 67, PT 50 **Student-Faculty Ratio:** 13:1 **Exams:** SAT I or ACT. **% Receiving Financial Aid:** 79 **% Residing in College-Owned, -Operated, or -Affiliated Housing:** 74 **Final Year or Final Semester Residency Requirement:** Yes **Library Holdings:** 145,605 **Regional Accreditation:** Southern Association of Colleges and Schools **Credit Hours For Degree:** 128 semester hours, Bachelors **ROTC:** Army **Professional Accreditation:** AACN, AOTA, NCATE **Intercollegiate Athletics:** Baseball M; Basketball M & W; Cross-Country Running M & W; Golf M; Soccer M & W; Softball W; Swimming and Diving M & W; Tennis M & W; Volleyball W

MOTLOW STATE COMMUNITY COLLEGE
PO Box 8500
Lynchburg, TN 37352-8500
Tel: (931)393-1500
Admissions: (931)393-1764
Fax: (931)393-1681
E-mail: lmonks@mscc.edu
Web Site: http://www.mscc.cc.tn.us/
President/CEO: Dr. Mary Lou Apple
Admissions: Laura Monks
Type: Two-Year College **Sex:** Coed **Affiliation:** Tennessee Board of Regents **Admission Plans:** Open Admission; Early Admission; Deferred Admission **Application Deadline:** August 13 **Application Fee:** $10.00 **H.S. Requirements:** High school diploma required; GED accepted **Costs Per Year:** Application fee: $10. State resident tuition: $2664 full-time, $111 per credit hour part-time. Nonresident tuition: $8376 full-time, $349 per credit hour part-time. Mandatory fees: $259 full-time. **Scholarships:** Available **Calendar System:** Semester, Summer Session Available **Enrollment:** FT 2,216, PT 1,897 **Faculty:** FT 81, PT 155 **Student-Faculty Ratio:** 21:1 **Library Holdings:** 116,049 **Regional Accreditation:** Southern Association of Colleges and Schools **Credit Hours For Degree:** 60 semester hours, Associates **Professional Accreditation:** ACBSP, NLN **Intercollegiate Athletics:** Baseball M; Basketball M & W; Softball W

NASHVILLE AUTO DIESEL COLLEGE
1524 Gallatin Rd.
Nashville, TN 37206-3298
Tel: (615)226-3990; Free: 800-228-NADC
Fax: (615)262-8488
E-mail: wpruitt@nadcedu.com
Web Site: http://www.nadcedu.com/
President/CEO: Lisa Bacon
Admissions: Peggie Werrbach
Type: Two-Year College **Sex:** Coed **% Accepted:** 89 **Admission Plans:** Deferred Admission **Application Deadline:** Rolling **Application Fee:** $100.00 **H.S. Requirements:** High school diploma required; GED accepted **Scholarships:** Available **Calendar System:** Continuous, Summer Session Not available **Enrollment:** FT 1,306 **Faculty:** FT 73, PT 4 **Student-Faculty Ratio:** 30:1 **Exams:** SAT I or ACT. **% Residing in College-Owned, -Operated, or -Affiliated Housing:** 21 **Library Holdings:** 1,309 **Professional Accreditation:** ACCSCT

NASHVILLE STATE TECHNICAL COMMUNITY COLLEGE
120 White Bridge Rd.
Nashville, TN 37209-4515
Tel: (615)353-3333; Free: 800-272-7363
Admissions: (615)353-3214
Fax: (615)353-3243
E-mail: beth.mahan@nscc.edu
Web Site: http://www.nscc.edu/
President/CEO: Dr. George H. Van Allen

Admissions: Beth Mahan
Type: Two-Year College **Sex:** Coed **Affiliation:** Tennessee Board of Regents **Admission Plans:** Open Admission; Preferred Admission; Deferred Admission **Application Deadline:** Rolling **Application Fee:** $5.00 **H.S. Requirements:** High school diploma required; GED accepted **Costs Per Year:** Application fee: $5. State resident tuition: $3510 full-time, $121 per credit hour part-time. Nonresident tuition: $14,520 full-time, $470 per credit hour part-time. Mandatory fees: $225 full-time. Part-time tuition varies according to course load. **Scholarships:** Available **Calendar System:** Semester, Summer Session Available **Enrollment:** FT 2,556, PT 4,521 **Faculty:** FT 136, PT 267 **Student-Faculty Ratio:** 18:1 **Exams:** SAT I or ACT. **Library Holdings:** 38,502 **Regional Accreditation:** Southern Association of Colleges and Schools **Credit Hours For Degree:** 64 semester hours, Associates **Professional Accreditation:** ABET, AOTA, ACBSP

NATIONAL COLLEGE (BRISTOL)
1328 Hwy. 11 West
Bristol, TN 37620
Tel: (423)878-4440
Web Site: http://www.national-college.edu/
Admissions: Patrick DeMesa
Type: Two-Year College **Sex:** Coed **Affiliation:** National College of Business and Technology **Admission Plans:** Open Admission **Application Deadline:** Rolling **H.S. Requirements:** High school diploma required; GED accepted **Scholarships:** Available **Calendar System:** Quarter, Summer Session Available **Credit Hours For Degree:** 96 quarter hours, Associates **Professional Accreditation:** ACICS, AAMAE

NATIONAL COLLEGE (KNOXVILLE)
8415 Kingston Pike
Knoxville, TN 37919
Tel: (865)539-2011; Free: 800-664-1886
Fax: (865)539-2049
Web Site: http://www.national-college.edu/
Admissions: Frank Alvey
Type: Two-Year College **Sex:** Coed **Affiliation:** National College of Business and Technology **Calendar System:** Quarter

NATIONAL COLLEGE (NASHVILLE)
5042 Linbar Dr.
Ste. 200
Nashville, TN 37211
Tel: (615)333-3344; Free: 800-664-1886
Web Site: http://www.national-college.edu/
President/CEO: Frank Longaker
Admissions: Jerry Lafferty
Type: Two-Year College **Sex:** Coed **Affiliation:** National College of Business and Technology **Admission Plans:** Open Admission **Application Deadline:** Rolling **H.S. Requirements:** High school diploma required; GED accepted **Scholarships:** Available **Calendar System:** Quarter, Summer Session Available **Credit Hours For Degree:** 96 credit hours, Associates **Professional Accreditation:** ACICS, AAMAE

NORTH CENTRAL INSTITUTE
168 Jack Miller Blvd.
Clarksville, TN 37042
Tel: (931)431-9700
Fax: (931)431-9771
E-mail: admissions@nci.edu
Web Site: http://www.nci.edu/
President/CEO: John D. McCurdy
Admissions: Sheri Nash-Kutch
Type: Two-Year College **Sex:** Coed **% Accepted:** 100 **Admission Plans:** Open Admission; Early Admission **Application Deadline:** Rolling **Application Fee:** $35.00 **H.S. Requirements:** High school diploma required; GED accepted **Scholarships:** Available **Calendar System:** Continuous, Summer Session Available **Enrollment:** FT 52, PT 78 **Faculty:** FT 6, PT 11 **Student-Faculty Ratio:** 8:1 **Library Holdings:** 200 **Credit Hours For Degree:** 62 credits, Associates **Professional Accreditation:** COE

NORTHEAST STATE TECHNICAL COMMUNITY COLLEGE
PO Box 246
Blountville, TN 37617-0246
Tel: (423)323-3191
Fax: (423)323-0215
E-mail: jpharr@northeaststate.edu
Web Site: http://www.northeaststate.edu/
President/CEO: William W. Locke
Admissions: Dr. Jon P. Harr
Type: Two-Year College **Sex:** Coed **Affiliation:** Tennessee Board of Regents **Scores:** 48.6% ACT 18-23; 7.1% ACT 24-29 **% Accepted:** 100 **Admission Plans:** Open Admission; Preferred Admission **Application Deadline:** Rolling **Application Fee:** $10.00 **H.S. Requirements:** High school diploma required; GED accepted **Scholarships:** Available **Calendar System:** Semester, Summer Session Available **Enrollment:** FT 2,927, PT 2,543 **Faculty:** FT 107, PT 161 **Student-Faculty Ratio:** 11:1 **Library Holdings:** 50,553 **Regional Accreditation:** Southern Association of Colleges and Schools **Credit Hours For Degree:** 60 semester hours, Associates **Professional Accreditation:** AAMAE, ADA, ACBSP, NAACLS, NAIT

NOSSI COLLEGE OF ART
907 Rivergate Parkway
Goodlettsville, TN 37072
Tel: (615)851-1088; Free: 877-860-1601
Fax: (615)851-1087
E-mail: admissions@nossi.com
Web Site: http://www.nossi.com/
President/CEO: Nossi Vatandoost
Admissions: Mary Alexander
Financial Aid: Mary P. Kidd
Type: Two-Year College **Sex:** Coed **% Accepted:** 64 **Application Fee:** $100.00 **H.S. Requirements:** High school diploma required; GED accepted **Scholarships:** Available **Calendar System:** Semester **Enrollment:** FT 250 **Faculty:** FT 4, PT 25 **Student-Faculty Ratio:** 17:1 **Professional Accreditation:** ACCSCT

O'MORE COLLEGE OF DESIGN
423 South Margin St.
Franklin, TN 37064-2816
Tel: (615)794-4254
Fax: (615)790-1662
E-mail: clee@omorecollege.edu
Web Site: http://www.omorecollege.edu/
President/CEO: Dr. K. Mark Hilliard
Admissions: Chris Lee
Type: Four-Year College **Sex:** Coed **Scores:** 65.2% ACT 18-23; 26% ACT 24-29 **Admission Plans:** Deferred Admission **Application Deadline:** August 1 **Application Fee:** $50.00 **H.S. Requirements:** High school diploma required; GED accepted **Scholarships:** Available **Calendar System:** Semester, Summer Session Available **Enrollment:** FT 190, PT 32 **Faculty:** FT 11, PT 36 **Student-Faculty Ratio:** 8:1 **Exams:** SAT I or ACT. ACT essay not being used. SAT essay not being used. **Library Holdings:** 7,000 **Credit Hours For Degree:** 121 semester hours, Bachelors **Professional Accreditation:** ACCSCT, FIDER

PELLISSIPPI STATE TECHNICAL COMMUNITY COLLEGE
PO Box 22990
Knoxville, TN 37933-0990
Tel: (865)694-6400
E-mail: latouzeau@pstcc.cc.tn.us
Web Site: http://www.pstcc.edu/
President/CEO: Dr. Allen G. Edwards
Admissions: Leigh Anne Touzeau
Type: Two-Year College **Sex:** Coed **Affiliation:** Tennessee Board of Regents **Scores:** 55.4% ACT 18-23; 12.3% ACT 24-29 **Admission Plans:** Open Admission; Early Admission; Deferred Admission **Application Deadline:** Rolling **Application Fee:** $5.00 **H.S. Requirements:** High school diploma required; GED accepted. For non-degree seeking applicants 21 or over: High school diploma or equivalent not required **Scholarships:** Available **Calendar System:** Semester, Summer Session Available **Enrollment:** FT 3,882, PT 3,804 **Faculty:** FT 169, PT 243 **Student-Faculty Ratio:** 21:1 **Library Holdings:** 43,000 **Regional Accreditation:** Southern Association of Colleges and Schools **Credit Hours For Degree:** 64 semester hours, Associates **Professional Accreditation:** ABET, ACBSP

REMINGTON COLLEGE—MEMPHIS CAMPUS
2731 Nonconnah Blvd.
Memphis, TN 38132-2131

Tel: (901)291-4200
Admissions: (901)345-1000
Fax: (901)396-8310
E-mail: randal.hayes@remingtoncollege.edu
Web Site: http://www.remingtoncollege.edu/
President/CEO: Lori May
Admissions: Randal Hayes
Type: Two-Year College **Sex:** Coed **Scholarships:** Available **Calendar System:** Quarter **Professional Accreditation:** ACCSCT

REMINGTON COLLEGE—NASHVILLE CAMPUS
441 Donelson Pike
Ste. 150
Nashville, TN 37214
Tel: (615)889-5520
Fax: (615)889-5528
E-mail: frank.vivelo@remingtoncollege.edu
Web Site: http://www.remingtoncollege.edu/
President/CEO: Larry Collins
Admissions: Frank Vivelo
Type: Two-Year College **Sex:** Coed **Calendar System:** Quarter

RHODES COLLEGE
2000 North Parkway
Memphis, TN 38112-1690
Tel: (901)843-3000; Free: 800-844-5969
Admissions: (901)843-3700
Fax: (901)843-3719
E-mail: adminfo@rhodes.edu
Web Site: http://www.rhodes.edu/
President/CEO: Dr. William E. Troutt
Admissions: David J. Wottle
Financial Aid: Art Weeden
Type: Comprehensive **Sex:** Coed **Affiliation:** Presbyterian **Scores:** 100.01% SAT V 400+; 100% SAT M 400+; 5.05% ACT 18-23; 61.51% ACT 24-29 **% Accepted:** 42 **Admission Plans:** Early Admission; Early Decision Plan; Deferred Admission **Application Deadline:** January 15 **Application Fee:** $45.00 **H.S. Requirements:** High school diploma required; GED accepted **Costs Per Year:** Application fee: $45. Comprehensive fee: $42,024 includes full-time tuition ($33,400), mandatory fees ($310), and college room and board ($8314). Room and board charges vary according to board plan and housing facility. Part-time tuition: $1350 per credit hour. **Scholarships:** Available **Calendar System:** Semester, Summer Session Not available **Enrollment:** FT 1,661, PT 14, Grad FT 10 **Faculty:** FT 161, PT 32 **Student-Faculty Ratio:** 10:1 **Exams:** SAT I or ACT. ACT essay not being used. SAT essay not being used. **% Receiving Financial Aid:** 47 **% Residing in College-Owned, -Operated, or -Affiliated Housing:** 76 **Regional Accreditation:** Southern Association of Colleges and Schools **Credit Hours For Degree:** 112 credit hours, Bachelors **ROTC:** Army, Air Force **Intercollegiate Athletics:** Baseball M; Basketball M & W; Cheerleading W; Cross-Country Running M & W; Field Hockey W; Football M; Golf M & W; Lacrosse M & W; Rugby M; Soccer M & W; Softball W; Swimming and Diving M & W; Tennis M & W; Track and Field M & W; Volleyball W

ROANE STATE COMMUNITY COLLEGE
276 Patton Ln.
Harriman, TN 37748-5011
Tel: (865)354-3000
Fax: (865)882-4562
E-mail: admissions@roanestate.edu
Web Site: http://www.roanestate.edu/
President/CEO: Gary Goff
Financial Aid: Sandy Brock
Type: Two-Year College **Sex:** Coed **Affiliation:** Tennessee Board of Regents **Scores:** 57.3% ACT 18-23; 12.4% ACT 24-29 **% Accepted:** 100 **Admission Plans:** Open Admission; Preferred Admission; Early Admission; Deferred Admission **Application Deadline:** Rolling **Application Fee:** $10.00 **H.S. Requirements:** High school diploma required; GED accepted **Scholarships:** Available **Calendar System:** Semester, Summer Session Available **Enrollment:** FT 2,987, PT 2,366 **Faculty:** FT 136, PT 223 **Student-Faculty Ratio:** 18:1 **Library Holdings:** 103,404 **Regional Accreditation:** Southern Association of Colleges and Schools **Credit Hours For Degree:** 60 semester hours, Associates **ROTC:** Army, Air Force **Professional Accreditation:** ADA, AHIMA, AOTA, APTA, COptA, CARC, JRCERT, NLN **Intercollegiate Athletics:** Baseball M; Basketball M & W; Cheerleading W; Softball W

SEWANEE: THE UNIVERSITY OF THE SOUTH
735 University Ave.
Sewanee, TN 37383-1000
Tel: (931)598-1000; Free: 800-522-2234
Admissions: (931)598-1238
Fax: (931)598-1145
E-mail: admiss@sewanee.edu
Web Site: http://www.sewanee.edu/
President/CEO: Dr. Joel Cunningham
Admissions: Jay Fisher
Financial Aid: Beth A. Cragar
Type: Comprehensive **Sex:** Coed **Affiliation:** Episcopal **Scores:** 100% SAT V 400+; 100% SAT M 400+; 9.4% ACT 18-23; 57.3% ACT 24-29 **% Accepted:** 68 **Admission Plans:** Early Admission; Early Decision Plan; Deferred Admission **Application Deadline:** February 1 **Application Fee:** $45.00 **H.S. Requirements:** High school diploma required; GED not accepted **Costs Per Year:** Application fee: $45. Comprehensive fee: $46,112 includes full-time tuition ($35,590), mandatory fees ($272), and college room and board ($10,250). College room only: $5330. Part-time mandatory fees: $1230 per credit hour. **Scholarships:** Available **Calendar System:** Semester, Summer Session Available **Enrollment:** FT 1,455, PT 14, Grad FT 67, Grad PT 7 **Faculty:** FT 134, PT 38 **Student-Faculty Ratio:** 11:1 **Exams:** Other, SAT I or ACT. ACT essay used for admission. SAT essay used for admission. ACT essay used for advising. SAT essay used for advising. ACT essay used as a validity check on application essay. SAT essay used as a validity check on application essay. **% Receiving Financial Aid:** 49 **% Residing in College-Owned, -Operated, or -Affiliated Housing:** 96 **Library Holdings:** 914,901 **Regional Accreditation:** Southern Association of Colleges and Schools **Credit Hours For Degree:** 130 semester hours, Bachelors **Professional Accreditation:** ACIPE, ATS **Intercollegiate Athletics:** Baseball M; Basketball M & W; Crew M & W; Cross-Country Running M & W; Equestrian Sports M & W; Fencing M & W; Field Hockey W; Football M; Golf M & W; Lacrosse M & W; Rugby M; Soccer M & W; Softball W; Swimming and Diving M & W; Tennis M & W; Track and Field M & W; Volleyball W

SOUTH COLLEGE
720 North Fifth Ave.
Knoxville, TN 37917
Tel: (865)524-3043
Fax: (865)673-8019
E-mail: whosea@southcollegetn.edu
Web Site: http://www.southcollegetn.edu/
President/CEO: Stephen A. South
Admissions: Walter Hosea
Type: Comprehensive **Sex:** Coed **% Accepted:** 100 **Admission Plans:** Early Admission; Deferred Admission **Application Deadline:** October 1 **Application Fee:** $50.00 **H.S. Requirements:** High school diploma required; GED accepted **Scholarships:** Available **Calendar System:** Quarter, Summer Session Available **Student-Faculty Ratio:** 16:1 **Regional Accreditation:** Southern Association of Colleges and Schools **Credit Hours For Degree:** 94 quarter hours, Associates **Professional Accreditation:** AAMAE, AOTA, APTA

SOUTHERN ADVENTIST UNIVERSITY
PO Box 370
Collegedale, TN 37315-0370
Tel: (423)236-2000; Free: 800-768-8437
Admissions: (423)236-2844
Fax: (423)236-1000
E-mail: admissions@southern.edu
Web Site: http://www.southern.edu/
President/CEO: Gordon Bietz
Admissions: Marc Grundy
Financial Aid: Marc Grundy
Type: Comprehensive **Sex:** Coed **Affiliation:** Seventh-day Adventist **Scores:** 93% SAT V 400+; 90% SAT M 400+; 51% ACT 18-23; 34% ACT 24-29 **% Accepted:** 71 **Admission Plans:** Deferred Admission **Application Deadline:** Rolling **Application Fee:** $25.00 **H.S. Requirements:** High school diploma required; GED accepted **Costs Per Year:** Application fee:

$25. Comprehensive fee: $22,886 includes full-time tuition ($16,942), mandatory fees ($770), and college room and board ($5174). College room only: $3174. Room and board charges vary according to housing facility. **Scholarships:** Available **Calendar System:** Semester, Summer Session Available **Enrollment:** FT 2,195, PT 452, Grad FT 78, Grad PT 166 **Faculty:** FT 139, PT 118 **Student-Faculty Ratio:** 15:1 **Exams:** SAT I or ACT. ACT essay used for advising. SAT essay used for advising. **% Receiving Financial Aid:** 46 **% Residing in College-Owned, -Operated, or -Affiliated Housing:** 61 **Final Year or Final Semester Residency Requirement:** Yes **Library Holdings:** 166,905 **Regional Accreditation:** Southern Association of Colleges and Schools **Credit Hours For Degree:** 64 semester hours, Associates; 124 semester hours, Bachelors **Professional Accreditation:** CSWE, NASM, NCATE, NLN

SOUTHWEST TENNESSEE COMMUNITY COLLEGE

PO Box 780
Memphis, TN 38101-0780
Tel: (901)333-5000; Free: 877-717-STCC
Admissions: (901)333-4195
Fax: (901)333-4273
E-mail: cmeziere@southwest.tn.edu
Web Site: http://www.southwest.tn.edu/
Admissions: Cindy Meziere

Type: Two-Year College **Sex:** Coed **Affiliation:** Tennessee Board of Regents **Scores:** 35% ACT 18-23; 3% ACT 24-29 **% Accepted:** 100 **Admission Plans:** Open Admission; Early Admission; Deferred Admission **Application Deadline:** September 1 **Application Fee:** $5.00 **H.S. Requirements:** High school diploma required; GED accepted **Scholarships:** Available **Calendar System:** Semester, Summer Session Available **Enrollment:** FT 5,656, PT 5,900 **Faculty:** FT 252, PT 314 **Library Holdings:** 87,280 **Regional Accreditation:** Southern Association of Colleges and Schools **Credit Hours For Degree:** 64 semester hours, Associates **ROTC:** Army, Air Force **Professional Accreditation:** ABET, APTA, ACBSP, JRCERT, NAACLS, NLN

STRAYER UNIVERSITY - KNOXVILLE CAMPUS

10118 Parkside Dr.
Ste. 200
Knoxville, TN 37922
Tel: (865)288-6000
Fax: (865)288-6030
Web Site: http://www.strayer.edu/knoxville/

Type: Comprehensive **Sex:** Coed **Application Fee:** $50.00 **Costs Per Year:** Application fee: $50. **Regional Accreditation:** Middle State Association of Colleges and Schools

STRAYER UNIVERSITY - NASHVILLE CAMPUS

1809 Dabbs Ave.
Nashville, TN 37210
Tel: (615)871-2260
Fax: (615)391-5330
Web Site: http://www.strayer.edu/nashville

Type: Comprehensive **Sex:** Coed **Application Fee:** $50.00 **Costs Per Year:** Application fee: $50. **Regional Accreditation:** Middle State Association of Colleges and Schools

STRAYER UNIVERSITY - SHELBY OAKS CAMPUS

6211 Shelby Oaks Dr.
Ste. 100
Memphis, TN 38134
Tel: (901)383-6750
Fax: (901)373-8700
Web Site: http://www.strayer.edu/shelby_oaks/

Type: Comprehensive **Sex:** Coed **Application Fee:** $50.00 **Costs Per Year:** Application fee: $50. **Regional Accreditation:** Middle State Association of Colleges and Schools

STRAYER UNIVERSITY - THOUSAND OAKS CAMPUS

2620 Thousand Oaks Blvd.
Ste. 1100
Memphis, TN 38118
Tel: (901)369-0835
Fax: (901)565-9400
Web Site: http://www.strayer.edu/thousand_oaks_campus/

Type: Comprehensive **Sex:** Coed **Application Fee:** $50.00 **Costs Per Year:** Application fee: $50. **Regional Accreditation:** Middle State Association of Colleges and Schools

TENNESSEE STATE UNIVERSITY

3500 John A Merritt Blvd.
Nashville, TN 37209-1561
Tel: (615)963-5000
Admissions: (615)963-5104
Fax: (615)963-5108
E-mail: vsmith@tnstate.edu
Web Site: http://www.tnstate.edu/
President/CEO: Dr. Melvin N. Johnson
Admissions: Vernella Smith
Financial Aid: Mary Chambliss

Type: Comprehensive **Sex:** Coed **Affiliation:** Tennessee Board of Regents **% Accepted:** 91 **Admission Plans:** Preferred Admission **Application Deadline:** August 1 **Application Fee:** $25.00 **H.S. Requirements:** High school diploma required; GED accepted **Scholarships:** Available **Calendar System:** Semester, Summer Session Available **Enrollment:** FT 5,139, PT 1,292 **Faculty:** FT 434, PT 169 **Student-Faculty Ratio:** 15:1 **Exams:** SAT I or ACT. **% Receiving Financial Aid:** 74 **% Residing in College-Owned, -Operated, or -Affiliated Housing:** 39 **Library Holdings:** 630,890 **Regional Accreditation:** Southern Association of Colleges and Schools **Credit Hours For Degree:** 65 semester hours, Associates; 132 semester hours, Bachelors **ROTC:** Army, Navy, Air Force **Professional Accreditation:** AACSB, ABET, AAFCS, ADA, AHIMA, AOTA, APTA, APA, ASLHA, CARC, CSWE, NAACLS, NASAD, NASM, NASPAA, NCATE, NLN **Intercollegiate Athletics:** Basketball M & W; Cross-Country Running M & W; Football M; Golf M; Softball W; Tennis M & W; Track and Field M & W; Volleyball W

TENNESSEE TECHNOLOGICAL UNIVERSITY

North Dixie Ave.
Cookeville, TN 38505
Tel: (931)372-3101; Free: 800-255-8881
Admissions: (931)372-3888
Fax: (931)372-6250
E-mail: admissions@tntech.edu
Web Site: http://www.tntech.edu/
President/CEO: Dr. Robert Bell
Admissions: Vanessa Palmer
Financial Aid: Lester McKenzie

Type: University **Sex:** Coed **Affiliation:** Tennessee Board of Regents **Scores:** 93% SAT V 400+; 96% SAT M 400+; 55% ACT 18-23; 36% ACT 24-29 **% Accepted:** 84 **Admission Plans:** Preferred Admission; Early Admission; Deferred Admission **Application Deadline:** August 1 **Application Fee:** $15.00 **H.S. Requirements:** High school diploma required; GED accepted **Costs Per Year:** Application fee: $15. State resident tuition: $5498 full-time, $254 per hour part-time. Nonresident tuition: $17,454 full-time, $751 per hour part-time. Full-time tuition varies according to course load. Part-time tuition varies according to course load. College room and board: $7124. College room only: $3560. Room and board charges vary according to board plan and housing facility. **Scholarships:** Available **Calendar System:** Semester, Summer Session Available **Enrollment:** FT 8,017, PT 901, Grad FT 662, Grad PT 1,267 **Faculty:** FT 385, PT 248 **Student-Faculty Ratio:** 19:1 **Exams:** ACT, SAT I or ACT. **% Receiving Financial Aid:** 53 **% Residing in College-Owned, -Operated, or -Affiliated Housing:** 30 **Library Holdings:** 693,169 **Regional Accreditation:** Southern Association of Colleges and Schools **Credit Hours For Degree:** 120 semester hours, Bachelors **ROTC:** Army, Air Force **Professional Accreditation:** AACSB, ABET, AACN, AAFCS, NASAD, NASM, NCATE, NLN, NAIT **Intercollegiate Athletics:** Baseball M; Basketball M & W; Cheerleading M & W; Cross-Country Running M & W; Football M; Golf M & W; Riflery M & W; Soccer W; Softball W; Tennis M & W; Track and Field W; Volleyball W

TENNESSEE TEMPLE UNIVERSITY

1815 Union Ave.
Chattanooga, TN 37404-3587
Tel: (423)493-4100; Free: 800-553-4050
Fax: (423)493-4497
E-mail: eric.lovett@tntemple.edu
Web Site: http://www.tntemple.edu/
President/CEO: Dr. J. Daniel Lovett

Admissions: Eric Lovett
Type: Comprehensive **Sex:** Coed **Affiliation:** Baptist **Admission Plans:** Deferred Admission **Application Deadline:** August 20 **Application Fee:** $30.00 **H.S. Requirements:** High school diploma required; GED accepted **Costs Per Year:** Application fee: $30. One-time mandatory fee: $35. Comprehensive fee: $16,980 includes full-time tuition ($10,500), mandatory fees ($450), and college room and board ($6030). College room only: $2458. Full-time tuition and fees vary according to course load, degree level, and program. Room and board charges vary according to board plan. Part-time tuition: $375 per semester hour. Part-time mandatory fees: $450 per term. Part-time tuition and fees vary according to course load, degree level, and program. **Scholarships:** Available **Calendar System:** Semester, Summer Session Available **Exams:** SAT I or ACT. **Library Holdings:** 150,711 **Credit Hours For Degree:** 64 credit hours, Associates; 128 credit hours, Bachelors **Professional Accreditation:** TACCS **Intercollegiate Athletics:** Baseball M; Basketball M & W; Soccer M; Volleyball W

TENNESSEE WESLEYAN COLLEGE
PO Box 40
Athens, TN 37371-0040
Tel: (423)745-7504; Free: 800-PICK-TWC
Admissions: (423)746-7504
Fax: (423)744-9968
E-mail: sharrison@twcnet.edu
Web Site: http://www.twcnet.edu/
President/CEO: Dr. Stephen Condon
Admissions: Stan Harrison
Financial Aid: Bob Perry
Type: Four-Year College **Sex:** Coed **Affiliation:** United Methodist **Scores:** 83% SAT V 400+; 78% SAT M 400+; 59% ACT 18-23; 27% ACT 24-29 **% Accepted:** 84 **Admission Plans:** Deferred Admission **Application Fee:** $25.00 **H.S. Requirements:** High school diploma required; GED accepted **Costs Per Year:** Application fee: $25. Comprehensive fee: $24,700 includes full-time tuition ($18,000), mandatory fees ($600), and college room and board ($6100). Full-time tuition and fees vary according to location. Room and board charges vary according to housing facility. Part-time tuition: $495 per credit hour. Part-time mandatory fees: $10 per credit hour. Part-time tuition and fees vary according to class time and location. **Scholarships:** Available **Calendar System:** Semester, Summer Session Available **Enrollment:** FT 935, PT 135 **Faculty:** FT 53, PT 34 **Student-Faculty Ratio:** 15:1 **Exams:** SAT I or ACT. **% Receiving Financial Aid:** 78 **% Residing in College-Owned, -Operated, or -Affiliated Housing:** 32 **Regional Accreditation:** Southern Association of Colleges and Schools **Credit Hours For Degree:** 128 semester hours, Bachelors **ROTC:** Army, Navy, Air Force **Professional Accreditation:** AACN **Intercollegiate Athletics:** Baseball M; Basketball M & W; Cheerleading M & W; Cross-Country Running M & W; Golf M & W; Lacrosse M; Soccer M & W; Softball W; Tennis M & W; Volleyball W

TREVECCA NAZARENE UNIVERSITY
333 Murfreesboro Rd.
Nashville, TN 37210-2877
Tel: (615)248-1200; Free: 888-210-4TNU
Admissions: (615)248-1320
Fax: (615)248-7728
E-mail: admissions_und@trevecca.edu
Web Site: http://www.trevecca.edu/
President/CEO: Dr. Dan Boone
Admissions: Dr. Michael Cantrell
Financial Aid: Eddie White
Type: Comprehensive **Sex:** Coed **Affiliation:** Nazarene **Scores:** 90% SAT V 400+; 83% SAT M 400+; 51% ACT 18-23; 29% ACT 24-29 **% Accepted:** 69 **Admission Plans:** Early Admission; Deferred Admission **Application Deadline:** August 1 **Application Fee:** $25.00 **H.S. Requirements:** High school diploma required; GED accepted **Costs Per Year:** Application fee: $25. Comprehensive fee: $26,052 includes full-time tuition ($18,318) and college room and board ($7734). College room only: $3582. Full-time tuition varies according to course load. Room and board charges vary according to board plan. **Scholarships:** Available **Calendar System:** Semester, Summer Session Available **Enrollment:** FT 1,153, PT 145, Grad FT 997, Grad PT 181 **Faculty:** FT 87, PT 135 **Student-Faculty Ratio:** 12:1 **Exams:** SAT I or ACT. ACT essay used as a validity check on application essay. SAT essay used as a validity check on application essay. **% Residing in College-Owned, -Operated, or -Affiliated Housing:** 61 **Library Holdings:** 85,792 **Regional Accreditation:** Southern Association of Colleges and Schools **Credit Hours For Degree:** 60 semester hours, Associates; 120 semester hours, Bachelors **ROTC:** Army **Professional Accreditation:** NASM, NCATE **Intercollegiate Athletics:** Baseball M; Basketball M & W; Golf M & W; Soccer M & W; Softball W; Volleyball W

TUSCULUM COLLEGE
60 Shiloh Rd.
Greeneville, TN 37743-9997
Tel: (423)636-7300; Free: 800-729-0256
Fax: (423)638-7166
E-mail: admissions@tusculum.edu
Web Site: http://www.tusculum.edu/
President/CEO: Dr. Russell Nichols
Admissions: Melissa Ripley
Financial Aid: Melena Verity
Type: Comprehensive **Sex:** Coed **Affiliation:** Presbyterian **Scores:** 85% SAT V 400+; 90% SAT M 400+; 61% ACT 18-23; 27% ACT 24-29 **% Accepted:** 75 **Admission Plans:** Early Admission; Deferred Admission **Application Deadline:** Rolling **Application Fee:** $0.00 **H.S. Requirements:** High school diploma required; GED accepted **Costs Per Year:** Application fee: $0. Comprehensive fee: $27,265 includes full-time tuition ($19,530) and college room and board ($7735). Full-time tuition varies according to degree level and reciprocity agreements. Part-time tuition: $825 per semester hour. Part-time tuition varies according to degree level and reciprocity agreements. **Scholarships:** Available **Calendar System:** Semester, Summer Session Available **Enrollment:** FT 1,962, PT 57, Grad FT 182, Grad PT 2 **Faculty:** FT 77, PT 147 **Student-Faculty Ratio:** 16:1 **Exams:** SAT I or ACT. **% Receiving Financial Aid:** 71 **% Residing in College-Owned, -Operated, or -Affiliated Housing:** 65 **Final Year or Final Semester Residency Requirement:** No **Library Holdings:** 49,905 **Regional Accreditation:** Southern Association of Colleges and Schools **Credit Hours For Degree:** 128 credit hours, Bachelors **Intercollegiate Athletics:** Baseball M; Basketball M & W; Cheerleading W; Cross-Country Running M & W; Football M; Golf M & W; Soccer M & W; Softball W; Tennis M & W; Volleyball W

UNION UNIVERSITY
1050 Union University Dr.
Jackson, TN 38305-3697
Tel: (731)668-1818; Free: 800-33-UNION
Admissions: (731)661-5590
Fax: (731)661-5187
E-mail: rgraves@uu.edu
Web Site: http://www.uu.edu/
President/CEO: Dr. David S. Dockery
Admissions: Robbie Graves
Financial Aid: John Thomas Brandt
Type: Comprehensive **Sex:** Coed **Affiliation:** Southern Baptist **Scores:** 95% SAT V 400+; 97% SAT M 400+; 34% ACT 18-23; 46% ACT 24-29 **% Accepted:** 84 **Admission Plans:** Early Admission; Early Action; Deferred Admission **Application Deadline:** Rolling **Application Fee:** $35.00 **H.S. Requirements:** High school diploma required; GED accepted **Costs Per Year:** Application fee: $35. Comprehensive fee: $27,870 includes full-time tuition ($20,280), mandatory fees ($660), and college room and board ($6930). Full-time tuition and fees vary according to course load. Room and board charges vary according to board plan and housing facility. Part-time tuition: $690 per credit hour. Part-time mandatory fees: $210 per term. **Scholarships:** Available **Calendar System:** 4-1-4, Summer Session Available **Enrollment:** FT 2,186, PT 594, Grad FT 784, Grad PT 358 **Faculty:** FT 210, PT 5 **Student-Faculty Ratio:** 12:1 **Exams:** SAT I or ACT, SAT II. **% Receiving Financial Aid:** 72 **% Residing in College-Owned, -Operated, or -Affiliated Housing:** 55 **Library Holdings:** 155,500 **Regional Accreditation:** Southern Association of Colleges and Schools **Credit Hours For Degree:** 66 semester hours, Associates; 128 semester hours, Bachelors **Professional Accreditation:** AACN, AANA, CSWE, NASAD, NASM, NCATE **Intercollegiate Athletics:** Baseball M; Basketball M & W; Cheerleading W; Cross-Country Running M & W; Golf M; Soccer M & W; Softball W; Track and Field M & W; Volleyball W

UNIVERSITY OF MEMPHIS
Memphis, TN 38152
Tel: (901)678-2000; Free: 800-669-2678
Admissions: (901)678-2111
Fax: (901)678-3053

E-mail: bmeredith@memphis.edu
Web Site: http://www.memphis.edu/
President/CEO: Dr. Shirley Raines
Admissions: Dr. Brian Meredith
Financial Aid: Richard Ritzman
Type: University **Sex:** Coed **Affiliation:** Tennessee Board of Regents **Scores:** 54% ACT 18-23; 26.5% ACT 24-29 **% Accepted:** 67 **Admission Plans:** Early Admission **Application Deadline:** July 1 **Application Fee:** $25.00 **H.S. Requirements:** High school diploma required; GED accepted **Costs Per Year:** Application fee: $25. State resident tuition: $5304 full-time, $221 per credit part-time. Nonresident tuition: $18,024 full-time, $751 per credit part-time. Mandatory fees: $1154 full-time, $78 per credit part-time. Full-time tuition and fees vary according to course load, degree level, program, and reciprocity agreements. Part-time tuition and fees vary according to course load, degree level, and program. College room and board: $5950. College room only: $3690. Room and board charges vary according to board plan and housing facility. **Scholarships:** Available **Calendar System:** Semester, Summer Session Available **Enrollment:** FT 12,519, PT 4,200, Grad FT 2,181, Grad PT 2,524 **Faculty:** FT 840, PT 495 **Student-Faculty Ratio:** 15:1 **Exams:** SAT I or ACT. **% Receiving Financial Aid:** 63 **% Residing in College-Owned, -Operated, or -Affiliated Housing:** 13 **Library Holdings:** 1,840,413 **Regional Accreditation:** Southern Association of Colleges and Schools **Credit Hours For Degree:** 120 semester hours, Bachelors **ROTC:** Army, Navy, Air Force **Professional Accreditation:** AACSB, ABET, ACEJMC, AACN, AAFCS, ABA, ACA, ADtA, ACSP, APA, ASLHA, AALS, ACEHSA, FIDER, CORE, CSWE, NASAD, NASM, NASPAA, NAST NCATE, NLN **Intercollegiate Athletics:** Baseball M; Basketball M & W; Cheerleading M & W; Cross-Country Running M & W; Football M; Golf M & W; Racquetball M & W; Riflery M & W; Soccer M & W; Softball W; Swimming and Diving M & W; Tennis M & W; Track and Field M & W; Volleyball W

UNIVERSITY OF PHOENIX—CHATTANOOGA CAMPUS
1208 Pointe Centre Dr.
Chattanooga, TN 37421-3707
Tel: (423)499-2500
Web Site: http://www.phoenix.edu/
Type: Comprehensive **Sex:** Coed **Regional Accreditation:** North Central Association of Colleges and Schools

UNIVERSITY OF PHOENIX—MEMPHIS CAMPUS
65 Germantown Ct.
Cordova, TN 38018
Tel: (901)751-1086
Web Site: http://www.phoenix.edu/
President/CEO: William Pepicello, PhD
Type: Comprehensive **Sex:** Coed **Regional Accreditation:** North Central Association of Colleges and Schools

UNIVERSITY OF PHOENIX—NASHVILLE CAMPUS
616 Marriott Dr., Ste. 150
Nashville, TN 37214-5048
Tel: (615)872-0188; Free: 800-228-7240
Admissions: (480)557-6151
E-mail: audra.mcquarie@phoenix.edu
Web Site: http://www.phoenix.edu/
President/CEO: William Pepicello
Admissions: Audra McQuarie
Type: Comprehensive **Sex:** Coed **Admission Plans:** Open Admission; Deferred Admission **Application Deadline:** Rolling **Application Fee:** $45.00 **H.S. Requirements:** High school diploma required; GED accepted **Costs Per Year:** Application fee: $45. Tuition: $11,421 full-time. Full-time tuition varies according to course level and course load. **Scholarships:** Available **Calendar System:** Continuous, Summer Session Not available **Enrollment:** FT 751 **Faculty:** FT 16, PT 113 **Regional Accreditation:** North Central Association of Colleges and Schools **Credit Hours For Degree:** 60 credits, Associates; 120 credits, Bachelors

THE UNIVERSITY OF TENNESSEE
Knoxville, TN 37996
Tel: (865)974-1000
Admissions: (865)974-2184
E-mail: admissions@tennessee.edu
Web Site: http://www.tennessee.edu/
President/CEO: Dr. Jan Simek
Admissions: Norma Harrington
Type: University **Sex:** Coed **Affiliation:** University of Tennessee System **Scores:** 98.48% SAT V 400+; 98.87% SAT M 400+; 19.5% ACT 18-23; 59.33% ACT 24-29 **% Accepted:** 73 **Admission Plans:** Early Admission **Application Deadline:** December 1 **Application Fee:** $30.00 **H.S. Requirements:** High school diploma required; GED accepted. For engineering: High school diploma required; GED not accepted **Costs Per Year:** Application fee: $30. State resident tuition: $6850 full-time, $248 per hour part-time. Nonresident tuition: $20,946 full-time, $823 per hour part-time. Mandatory fees: $36 per hour part-time. Full-time tuition varies according to location and program. Part-time tuition and fees vary according to location and program. College room and board: $7254. Room and board charges vary according to board plan and housing facility. **Scholarships:** Available **Calendar System:** Semester, Summer Session Available **Enrollment:** FT 19,774, PT 1,408, Grad FT 6,534, Grad PT 2,218 **Faculty:** FT 1,536, PT 84 **Student-Faculty Ratio:** 16:1 **Exams:** SAT I or ACT. ACT essay not being used. SAT essay not being used. **% Receiving Financial Aid:** 50 **% Residing in College-Owned, -Operated, or -Affiliated Housing:** 26 **Library Holdings:** 3,041,145 **Regional Accreditation:** Southern Association of Colleges and Schools **Credit Hours For Degree:** 120 semester hours, Bachelors **ROTC:** Army, Air Force **Professional Accreditation:** AACSB, ABET, ACEJMC, AACN, AAFCS, AANA, ABA, ACA, ADtA, ACSP, ALA, APA, ASLHA, AVMA, ACIPE, AALS, FIDER, CEPH, CORE, CSWE JRCNMT, NAACLS, NAAB, NASAD, NASM, NASPAA, NCATE, NLN, NRPA, SAF **Intercollegiate Athletics:** Badminton M & W; Baseball M; Basketball M & W; Bowling M & W; Cheerleading M & W; Crew M & W; Cross-Country Running M & W; Equestrian Sports M & W; Fencing M & W; Field Hockey W; Football M; Golf M & W; Gymnastics M & W; Ice Hockey M; Lacrosse M & W; Rugby M & W; Sailing M & W; Skiing (Downhill) M & W; Soccer M & W; Softball W; Swimming and Diving M & W; Tennis M & W; Track and Field M & W; Ultimate Frisbee M & W; Volleyball M & W; Water Polo M & W

THE UNIVERSITY OF TENNESSEE AT CHATTANOOGA
615 McCallie Ave.
Chattanooga, TN 37403-2598
Tel: (423)425-4111
Admissions: (423)425-4662
Fax: (423)425-4157
E-mail: yancy-freeman@utc.edu
Web Site: http://www.utc.edu/
President/CEO: Dr. Roger Brown
Admissions: Yancy Freeman
Financial Aid: Dianne Cox
Type: Comprehensive **Sex:** Coed **Affiliation:** University of Tennessee System **Scores:** 99% SAT V 400+; 97.2% SAT M 400+; 60.47% ACT 18-23; 31.16% ACT 24-29 **% Accepted:** 79 **Admission Plans:** Deferred Admission **Application Deadline:** August 1 **Application Fee:** $30.00 **H.S. Requirements:** High school diploma required; GED accepted **Costs Per Year:** Application fee: $30. State resident tuition: $4506 full-time, $188 per credit hour part-time. Nonresident tuition: $15,804 full-time, $471 per credit hour part-time. Mandatory fees: $1150 full-time, $33 per credit hour part-time, $85 per term part-time. College room and board: $8056. College room only: $5200. Room and board charges vary according to board plan and housing facility. **Scholarships:** Available **Calendar System:** Semester, Summer Session Available **Enrollment:** FT 8,009, PT 1,030, Grad FT 642, Grad PT 845 **Faculty:** FT 411, PT 285 **Student-Faculty Ratio:** 18:1 **Exams:** SAT I or ACT. ACT essay not being used. SAT essay not being used. **% Receiving Financial Aid:** 59 **% Residing in College-Owned, -Operated, or -Affiliated Housing:** 34 **Final Year or Final Semester Residency Requirement:** No **Library Holdings:** 596,000 **Regional Accreditation:** Southern Association of Colleges and Schools **Credit Hours For Degree:** 120 semester hours, Bachelors **ROTC:** Army **Professional Accreditation:** AACSB, ABET, ACEJMC, AACN, AANA, ACA, APTA, FIDER, CSWE, NASAD, NASM, NASPAA, NCATE **Intercollegiate Athletics:** Basketball M & W; Cross-Country Running M & W; Football M; Golf M & W; Soccer W; Softball W; Tennis M & W; Track and Field M & W; Volleyball W; Wrestling M

THE UNIVERSITY OF TENNESSEE AT MARTIN
University St.
Martin, TN 38238-1000
Tel: (731)881-7000; Free: 800-829-8861
Admissions: (731)881-7032
Fax: (731)881-7029

E-mail: jrayburn@utm.edu
Web Site: http://www.utm.edu/
President/CEO: Dr. Thomas A. Rakes
Admissions: Judy Rayburn
Financial Aid: Sheryl L. Frazier
Type: Comprehensive **Sex:** Coed **Affiliation:** University of Tennessee System **Scores:** 63.67% ACT 18-23; 29.37% ACT 24-29 **% Accepted:** 75 **Admission Plans:** Early Admission; Deferred Admission **Application Deadline:** Rolling **Application Fee:** $30.00 **H.S. Requirements:** High school diploma required; GED accepted **Costs Per Year:** Application fee: $30. State resident tuition: $4708 full-time, $197 per credit hour part-time. Nonresident tuition: $16,094 full-time, $672 per credit hour part-time. Mandatory fees: $1061 full-time, $44 per credit hour part-time. Part-time tuition and fees vary according to course load. College room and board: $4914. College room only: $2390. Room and board charges vary according to board plan and housing facility. **Scholarships:** Available **Calendar System:** Semester, Summer Session Available **Enrollment:** FT 5,856, PT 1,730, Grad FT 101, Grad PT 414 **Faculty:** FT 270, PT 263 **Student-Faculty Ratio:** 19:1 **Exams:** SAT I or ACT. **% Receiving Financial Aid:** 70 **% Residing in College-Owned, -Operated, or -Affiliated Housing:** 30 **Final Year or Final Semester Residency Requirement:** Yes **Library Holdings:** 534,802 **Regional Accreditation:** Southern Association of Colleges and Schools **Credit Hours For Degree:** 120 semester hours, Bachelors **ROTC:** Army **Professional Accreditation:** AACSB, ABET, ACEJMC, AAFCS, ADtA, CSWE, NASM, NCATE, NLN **Intercollegiate Athletics:** Baseball M; Basketball M & W; Cheerleading W; Cross-Country Running M & W; Equestrian Sports W; Football M; Golf M; Riflery M & W; Soccer W; Softball W; Tennis W; Volleyball W

VANDERBILT UNIVERSITY
Nashville, TN 37240-1001
Tel: (615)322-7311; Free: 800-288-0432
Admissions: (615)936-2811
Fax: (615)343-7765
E-mail: admissions@vanderbilt.edu
Web Site: http://www.vanderbilt.edu/
President/CEO: Nicholas S. Zeppos
Admissions: John O. Gaines
Financial Aid: David Mohning
Type: University **Sex:** Coed **Scores:** 99.9% SAT V 400+; 100% SAT M 400+; 1% ACT 18-23; 16.5% ACT 24-29 **% Accepted:** 20 **Admission Plans:** Early Admission; Early Decision Plan; Deferred Admission **Application Deadline:** January 3 **Application Fee:** $50.00 **H.S. Requirements:** High school diploma required; GED accepted **Costs Per Year:** Application fee: $50. One-time mandatory fee: $620. Comprehensive fee: $51,228 includes full-time tuition ($37,632), mandatory fees ($946), and college room and board ($12,650). College room only: $8200. Room and board charges vary according to board plan. Part-time tuition: $1568 per credit hour. **Scholarships:** Available **Calendar System:** Semester, Summer Session Available **Enrollment:** FT 6,738, PT 56, Grad FT 4,953, Grad PT 759 **Faculty:** FT 866 **Student-Faculty Ratio:** 8:1 **Exams:** SAT I or ACT. ACT essay used as a validity check on application essay. SAT essay used as a validity check on application essay. **% Receiving Financial Aid:** 43 **% Residing in College-Owned, -Operated, or -Affiliated Housing:** 89 **Library Holdings:** 1,812,869 **Regional Accreditation:** Southern Association of Colleges and Schools **Credit Hours For Degree:** 120 semester hours, Bachelors **ROTC:** Army, Navy, Air Force **Professional Accreditation:** AACSB, ABET, ABA, ACNM, ACA, ADtA, APA, ASLHA, ACIPE, AALS, ATS, JRCNMT, LCMEAMA, NAACLS, NASM, NCATE, NLN **Intercollegiate Athletics:** Baseball M; Basketball M & W; Bowling W; Cross-Country Running M & W; Football M; Golf M & W; Lacrosse W; Soccer W; Tennis M & W; Track and Field W

VATTEROTT COLLEGE
2655 Dividend Dr.
Memphis, TN 38132
Tel: (901)761-5730; Free: (866)314-6454
Fax: (901)763-2897
Web Site: http://www.vatterott-college.edu/
President/CEO: Almeta Slater Rogers
Type: Two-Year College **Sex:** Coed **% Accepted:** 45 **Calendar System:** Semester **Professional Accreditation:** ACCSCT

VICTORY UNIVERSITY
255 North Highland St.
Memphis, TN 38111
Tel: (901)320-9700; Free: 800-960-9777
Admissions: (901)320-9777
Fax: (901)320-9709
E-mail: admissions@crichton.edu
Web Site: http://www.victory.edu/
President/CEO: Dr. John M. Borek, Jr.
Admissions: Shelley Dunn
Financial Aid: LaTonya Branch
Type: Four-Year College **Sex:** Coed **Affiliation:** nondenominational **Scores:** 33.33% ACT 18-23 **Admission Plans:** Deferred Admission **Application Deadline:** Rolling **Application Fee:** $25.00 **H.S. Requirements:** High school diploma required; GED accepted **Costs Per Year:** Application fee: $25. Tuition: $9750 full-time, $325 per credit hour part-time. Mandatory fees: $570 full-time. Full-time tuition and fees vary according to course load. Part-time tuition varies according to course load. **Scholarships:** Available **Calendar System:** Semester, Summer Session Available **Enrollment:** FT 487, PT 188, Grad FT 9, Grad PT 33 **Faculty:** FT 23, PT 35 **Student-Faculty Ratio:** 18:1 **Exams:** SAT I or ACT. **% Receiving Financial Aid:** 88 **Final Year or Final Semester Residency Requirement:** No **Library Holdings:** 46,623 **Regional Accreditation:** Southern Association of Colleges and Schools **Credit Hours For Degree:** 60 semester hours, Associates; 120 semester hours, Bachelors

VOLUNTEER STATE COMMUNITY COLLEGE
1480 Nashville Pike
Gallatin, TN 37066-3188
Tel: (615)452-8600; Free: 888-335-8722
Fax: (615)230-3577
E-mail: admissions@volstate.edu
Web Site: http://www.volstate.edu/
President/CEO: Dr. Warren Nichols
Admissions: Tim Amyx
Financial Aid: Sue Pedigo
Type: Two-Year College **Sex:** Coed **Affiliation:** Tennessee Board of Regents **Scores:** 55% ACT 18-23; 10% ACT 24-29 **% Accepted:** 100 **Admission Plans:** Open Admission; Early Admission; Deferred Admission **Application Deadline:** August 28 **Application Fee:** $10.00 **H.S. Requirements:** High school diploma required; GED accepted **Costs Per Year:** Application fee: $10. State resident tuition: $2664 full-time, $110 per credit hour part-time. Nonresident tuition: $11,040 full-time, $460 per credit hour part-time. Mandatory fees: $265 full-time, $9 per credit hour part-time, $18. Full-time tuition and fees vary according to course load. Part-time tuition and fees vary according to course load. **Scholarships:** Available **Calendar System:** Semester, Summer Session Available **Enrollment:** FT 4,348, PT 4,082 **Faculty:** FT 148, PT 249 **Student-Faculty Ratio:** 25:1 **Exams:** SAT I or ACT. **Library Holdings:** 53,000 **Regional Accreditation:** Southern Association of Colleges and Schools **Credit Hours For Degree:** 60 semester hours, Associates **Professional Accreditation:** ADA, AHIMA, APTA, ACBSP, CARC, JRCERT, JRCEMT **Intercollegiate Athletics:** Baseball M; Basketball M & W; Softball W

WALTERS STATE COMMUNITY COLLEGE
500 South Davy Crockett Parkway
Morristown, TN 37813-6899
Tel: (423)585-2600
Admissions: (423)585-2682
E-mail: mike.campbell@ws.edu
Web Site: http://www.ws.edu/
President/CEO: Dean Wade B. McCamey
Admissions: Michael Campbell
Type: Two-Year College **Sex:** Coed **Affiliation:** Tennessee Board of Regents **Scores:** 80% SAT V 400+; 80% SAT M 400+; 34% ACT 18-23; 20% ACT 24-29 **% Accepted:** 100 **Admission Plans:** Open Admission; Early Admission **Application Deadline:** Rolling **Application Fee:** $10.00 **H.S. Requirements:** High school diploma required; GED accepted **Costs Per Year:** Application fee: $10. State resident tuition: $2664 full-time, $111 per semester hour part-time. Nonresident tuition: $11,400 full-time, $460 per semester hour part-time. Mandatory fees: $269 full-time, $16 per semester hour part-time, $16. **Scholarships:** Available **Calendar System:** Semester, Summer Session Available **Enrollment:** FT 3,591, PT 3,262 **Faculty:** FT 141, PT 247 **Student-Faculty Ratio:** 22:1 **Exams:** SAT I or ACT. **Final Year or Final Semester Residency Requirement:** No **Library Holdings:** 154,995 **Regional Accreditation:** Southern Association of Colleges and Schools **Credit Hours For Degree:** 60 semester hours, Associates **ROTC:**

Army **Professional Accreditation:** ACF, APTA, ACBSP, CARC, NLN, NAIT **Intercollegiate Athletics:** Baseball M; Basketball M & W; Golf M; Softball W

WATKINS COLLEGE OF ART, DESIGN, & FILM
2298 Rosa L. Parks Blvd.
Nashville, TN 37228
Tel: (615)383-4848
Fax: (615)383-4849
E-mail: admissions@watkins.edu
Web Site: http://www.watkins.edu/
President/CEO: Ellen L. Meyer
Admissions: Linda E. Schwab
Financial Aid: Lyle Jones
Type: Four-Year College **Sex:** Coed **% Accepted:** 75 **Admission Plans:** Early Admission; Deferred Admission **Application Deadline:** July 15 **Application Fee:** $50.00 **H.S. Requirements:** High school diploma required; GED accepted **Costs Per Year:** Application fee: $50. Tuition: $17,250 full-time, $575 per credit part-time. Mandatory fees: $1350 full-time, $45 per credit part-time. College room only: $6000. **Scholarships:** Available **Calendar System:** Semester, Summer Session Available **Enrollment:** FT 262, PT 117 **Faculty:** FT 20, PT 24 **Student-Faculty Ratio:** 8:1 **Exams:** SAT I or ACT. ACT essay not being used. SAT essay not being used. **% Receiving Financial Aid:** 79 **% Residing in College-Owned, -Operated, or -Affiliated Housing:** 24 **Final Year or Final Semester Residency Requirement:** Yes **Library Holdings:** 19,409 **Credit Hours For Degree:** 120 credit hours, Bachelors **Professional Accreditation:** FIDER, NASAD

WILLIAMSON CHRISTIAN COLLEGE
200 Seaboard Ln.
Franklin, TN 37067
Tel: (615)771-7821
Fax: (615)771-7810
E-mail: mary@williamsoncc.edu
Web Site: http://www.williamsoncc.edu/
President/CEO: Dr. Kenneth W. Oosting
Admissions: Mary Newby
Financial Aid: Jeanie Maguire
Type: Four-Year College **Sex:** Coed **Affiliation:** interdenominational **Admission Plans:** Early Admission; Deferred Admission **Application Deadline:** September 1 **Application Fee:** $25.00 **H.S. Requirements:** High school diploma required; GED accepted **Scholarships:** Available **Calendar System:** Semester, Summer Session Not available **Enrollment:** FT 55, PT 9 **Faculty:** FT 5, PT 12 **Student-Faculty Ratio:** 5:1 **Exams:** SAT I or ACT. **% Receiving Financial Aid:** 18 **Library Holdings:** 14,384 **Credit Hours For Degree:** 60 credits, Associates; 124 credits, Bachelors **Professional Accreditation:** ABHE, TACCS

ABILENE CHRISTIAN UNIVERSITY
ACU Box 29100
Abilene, TX 79699-9100
Tel: (325)674-2000
Admissions: (325)674-2650
E-mail: info@admissions.acu.edu
Web Site: http://www.acu.edu/
President/CEO: Dr. Royce Money
Financial Aid: Barrett Bell
Type: Comprehensive **Sex:** Coed **Affiliation:** Church of Christ **Scores:** 97% SAT V 400+; 98.3% SAT M 400+; 43.85% ACT 18-23; 39.82% ACT 24-29 **% Accepted:** 49 **Admission Plans:** Early Admission **Application Deadline:** February 15 **Application Fee:** $50.00 **H.S. Requirements:** High school diploma required; GED accepted **Costs Per Year:** Application fee: $50. Comprehensive fee: $27,800 includes full-time tuition ($19,200), mandatory fees ($1090), and college room and board ($7510). College room only: $3260. Full-time tuition and fees vary according to course load. Room and board charges vary according to board plan and student level. Part-time tuition: $640 per semester hour. Part-time mandatory fees: $53.50 per semester hour, $10 per term. Part-time tuition and fees vary according to course load. **Scholarships:** Available **Calendar System:** Semester, Summer Session Available **Enrollment:** FT 3,591, PT 325, Grad FT 356, Grad PT 541 **Faculty:** FT 236, PT 135 **Student-Faculty Ratio:** 15:1 **Exams:** SAT I or ACT. **% Receiving Financial Aid:** 67 **% Residing in College-Owned, -Operated, or -Affiliated Housing:** 42 **Final Year or Final Semester Residency Requirement:** Yes **Library Holdings:** 530,254 **Regional Accreditation:** Southern Association of Colleges and Schools **Credit Hours For Degree:** 64 semester hours, Associates; 128 semester hours, Bachelors **Professional Accreditation:** AACSB, ACEJMC, AAMFT, AACN, AAFCS, ASLHA, ACBSP, ATS, CSWE, NASM **Intercollegiate Athletics:** Baseball M; Basketball M & W; Cross-Country Running M & W; Football M; Golf M; Soccer W; Softball W; Tennis M & W; Track and Field M & W; Volleyball W.

THE ACADEMY OF HEALTH CARE PROFESSIONS
1900 North Loop West
Ste. 100
Houston, TX 77018
Tel: (713)862-2633; Free: 800-487-6728
Admissions: (713)425-3100
Fax: (713)746-5466
Web Site: http://www.academyofhealth.com/
President/CEO: A. John Emerald
Type: Two-Year College **Sex:** Coed **% Accepted:** 100 **Application Fee:** $100.00 **Calendar System:** Semester **Student-Faculty Ratio:** 17:1 **Professional Accreditation:** ABHES

ALVIN COMMUNITY COLLEGE
3110 Mustang Rd.
Alvin, TX 77511-4898
Tel: (281)756-3500
Fax: (281)756-3854
E-mail: info@alvincollege.edu
Web Site: http://www.alvincollege.edu/
President/CEO: A. Rodney Allbright
Admissions: Stephanie Stockstill
Type: Two-Year College **Sex:** Coed **Admission Plans:** Open Admission **Application Deadline:** Rolling **Application Fee:** $0.00 **H.S. Requirements:** High school diploma required; GED accepted **Costs Per Year:** Application fee: $0. Area resident tuition: $960 full-time, $32 per credit hour part-time. State resident tuition: $1950 full-time, $65 per credit hour part-time. Nonresident tuition: $3300 full-time, $110 per credit hour part-time. Mandatory fees: $376 full-time. Full-time tuition and fees vary according to program. Part-time tuition varies according to program. **Scholarships:** Available **Calendar System:** Semester, Summer Session Available **Enrollment:** FT 1,325, PT 3,075 **Faculty:** FT 98, PT 164 **Student-Faculty Ratio:** 17:1 **Regional Accreditation:** Southern Association of Colleges and Schools **Credit Hours For Degree:** 62 credits, Associates **Professional Accreditation:** CARC, NLN **Intercollegiate Athletics:** Baseball M; Softball W

AMARILLO COLLEGE
PO Box 447
Amarillo, TX 79178-0001
Tel: (806)371-5000
Fax: (806)371-5370
E-mail: askac@actx.edu
Web Site: http://www.actx.edu/
President/CEO: Dr. Paul Matney
Type: Two-Year College **Sex:** Coed **Admission Plans:** Open Admission; Early Admission; Deferred Admission **Application Fee:** $0.00 **H.S. Requirements:** High school diploma or equivalent not required **Costs Per Year:** Application fee: $0. Area resident tuition: $1763 full-time, $75.75 per semester hour part-time. State resident tuition: $2273 full-time, $92.75 per semester hour part-time. Nonresident tuition: $3353 full-time, $243.25 per semester hour part-time. Full-time tuition varies according to course load. Part-time tuition varies according to course load. **Scholarships:** Available **Calendar System:** Semester, Summer Session Available **Enrollment:** FT 3,610, PT 7,679 **Faculty:** FT 202, PT 226 **Library Holdings:** 116,000 **Regional Accreditation:** Southern Association of Colleges and Schools **Credit Hours For Degree:** 62 semester hours, Associates **Professional Accreditation:** ABET, ARCEST, ABFSE, ADA, AOTA, APTA, CARC, JRCERT, JRCNMT, NAACLS, NASM, NLN

AMBERTON UNIVERSITY
1700 Eastgate Dr.
Garland, TX 75041-5595
Tel: (972)279-6511
Fax: (972)279-9773
E-mail: advisor@amberton.edu
Web Site: http://www.amberton.edu/
President/CEO: Dr. Melinda Reagan
Admissions: Dr. Don Hebbard
Type: Two-Year Upper Division **Sex:** Coed **Affiliation:** nondenominational **Admission Plans:** Deferred Admission **Application Fee:** $0.00 **Costs Per Year:** Application fee: $0. Tuition: $5400 full-time, $675 per course part-time. **Calendar System:** Miscellaneous, Summer Session Available **Enrollment:** FT 221, PT 168, Grad FT 411, Grad PT 733 **Faculty:** FT 15, PT 25 **Student-Faculty Ratio:** 25:1 **Library Holdings:** 21,000 **Regional Accreditation:** Southern Association of Colleges and Schools **Credit Hours For Degree:** 126 semester hours, Bachelors

AMERICAN INTERCONTINENTAL UNIVERSITY
9999 Richmond Ave.
Houston, TX 77042
Tel: (832)242-5788; Free: 888-607-9888
Admissions: 877-564-6248
Fax: (832)242-5775
Web Site: http://www.aiuniv.edu/
President/CEO: Stephen J. Tober
Type: Comprehensive **Sex:** Coed **Affiliation:** American InterContinental University **Admission Plans:** Deferred Admission **Application Deadline:** Rolling **Application Fee:** $50.00 **H.S. Requirements:** High school diploma required; GED accepted **Costs Per Year:** Application fee: $50. **Calendar System:** Miscellaneous **Enrollment:** FT 330, PT 85 **Regional Accreditation:** North Central Association of Colleges and Schools

ANGELINA COLLEGE
PO Box 1768
Lufkin, TX 75902-1768
Tel: (936)639-1301
Fax: (936)639-4299
Web Site: http://www.angelina.cc.tx.us/
President/CEO: Larry M. Phillips
Admissions: Judith Cutting
Type: Two-Year College **Sex:** Coed **Admission Plans:** Open Admission; Early Admission; Deferred Admission **Application Deadline:** Rolling **Application Fee:** $0.00 **H.S. Requirements:** High school diploma required; GED accepted **Costs Per Year:** Application fee: $0. Area resident tuition: $840 full-time, $35 per semester hour part-time. State resident tuition: $1368 full-time, $57 per semester hour part-time. Nonresident tuition: $2016 full-time, $84 per semester hour part-time. Mandatory fees: $270 full-time, $9 per semester hour part-time. Full-time tuition and fees vary according to course load and program. Part-time tuition and fees vary according to course load and program. **Scholarships:** Available **Calendar System:** Semester, Summer Session Available **% Residing in College-Owned, -Operated, or -Affiliated Housing:** 1 **Library Holdings:** 37,000 **Regional Accreditation:** Southern Association of Colleges and Schools **Credit Hours For Degree:** 70 semester hours, Associates **ROTC:** Army **Professional Accreditation:** CARC, JRCERT **Intercollegiate Athletics:** Baseball M; Basketball M & W

ANGELO STATE UNIVERSITY
2601 West Ave. N
San Angelo, TX 76909
Tel: (325)942-2555
Admissions: (325)942-2259
Fax: (325)942-2038
E-mail: admissions@angelo.edu
Web Site: http://www.angelo.edu/
President/CEO: Dr. Joseph C. Rallo
Admissions: Megan Wheeler
Financial Aid: Michelle Bennett
Type: Comprehensive **Sex:** Coed **Affiliation:** Texas Tech University System **Scores:** 83.35% SAT V 400+; 89.53% SAT M 400+; 56.75% ACT 18-23; 19.5% ACT 24-29 **% Accepted:** 92 **Admission Plans:** Early Admission; Deferred Admission **Application Deadline:** Rolling **Application Fee:** $25.00 **H.S. Requirements:** High school diploma required; GED accepted **Costs Per Year:** Application fee: $25. State resident tuition: $4245 full-time, $141.50 per hour part-time. Nonresident tuition: $12,675 full-time, $422.50 per hour part-time. Mandatory fees: $1893 full-time, $366 per term part-time. College room and board: $6612. College room only: $4112. Room and board charges vary according to board plan and housing facility. **Scholarships:** Available **Calendar System:** Semester, Summer Session Available **Enrollment:** FT 4,899, PT 960, Grad FT 219, Grad PT 309 **Faculty:** FT 246, PT 86 **Student-Faculty Ratio:** 19:1 **Exams:** SAT I or ACT. **% Receiving Financial Aid:** 62 **% Residing in College-Owned, -Operated, or -Affiliated Housing:** 35 **Library Holdings:** 650,000 **Regional Accreditation:** Southern Association of Colleges and Schools **Credit Hours For Degree:** 68 semester hours, Associates; 120 semester hours, Bachelors **ROTC:** Air Force **Professional Accreditation:** APTA, ACBSP, NASM, NCATE, NLN **Intercollegiate Athletics:** Baseball M; Basketball M & W; Cross-Country Running M & W; Football M; Soccer W; Softball W; Track and Field M & W; Volleyball W

ARGOSY UNIVERSITY, DALLAS
5001 Lyndon B. Johnson Freeway
Heritage Square
Farmers Branch, TX 75244
Tel: (214)890-9900; Free: (866)954-9900
Fax: (214)656-3900
Web Site: http://www.argosy.edu/dallas/
President/CEO: Ronald Hyson
Type: University **Sex:** Coed **Affiliation:** Education Management Corporation **Calendar System:** Semester **Regional Accreditation:** North Central Association of Colleges and Schools

ARLINGTON BAPTIST COLLEGE
3001 West Division
Arlington, TX 76012-3425
Tel: (817)461-8741
Fax: (817)274-1138
E-mail: jhall@abconline.org
Web Site: http://www.abconline.edu/
President/CEO: Dr. David Bryant
Admissions: Janie Taylor
Financial Aid: David B. Clogston, Jr.
Type: Four-Year College **Sex:** Coed **Affiliation:** Baptist **% Accepted:** 100 **Admission Plans:** Preferred Admission; Early Admission; Deferred Admission **Application Deadline:** Rolling **Application Fee:** $15.00 **H.S. Requirements:** High school diploma required; GED accepted **Costs Per Year:** Application fee: $15. Comprehensive fee: $10,940 includes full-time tuition ($6000), mandatory fees ($740), and college room and board ($4200). Full-time tuition and fees vary according to course load. Part-time tuition: $220 per credit hour. Part-time mandatory fees: $700 per year. Part-time tuition and fees vary according to course load. **Scholarships:** Available **Calendar System:** Semester, Summer Session Available **Enrollment:** FT 107, PT 31 **Faculty:** FT 8, PT 10 **Student-Faculty Ratio:** 7:1 **% Receiving Financial Aid:** 67 **% Residing in College-Owned, -Operated, or -Affiliated Housing:** 31 **Credit Hours For Degree:** 128 semester hours, Bachelors **Professional Accreditation:** ABHE

THE ART INSTITUTE OF AUSTIN
101 W. Louis Henna Blvd.
Ste. 100
Austin, TX 78728
Tel: (512)691-1707; Free: (866)583-7952
Web Site: http://www.artinstitutes.edu/austin
President/CEO: Newton Myvett
Type: Four-Year College **Sex:** Coed **Affiliation:** Education Management Corporation **Regional Accreditation:** Southern Association of Colleges and Schools

THE ART INSTITUTE OF DALLAS
8080 Park Ln.
Ste. 100
Dallas, TX 75231-5993
Tel: (214)692-8080; Free: 800-275-4243
Fax: (214)750-9460
Web Site: http://www.artinstitutes.edu/dallas/
President/CEO: Thomas Newsom
Type: Four-Year College **Sex:** Coed **Affiliation:** Education Management Corporation **Calendar System:** Quarter **Regional Accreditation:** Southern Association of Colleges and Schools **Professional Accreditation:** ACF, FIDER

THE ART INSTITUTE OF FORT WORTH
7000 Calmont Ave.
Ste. 150
Fort Worth, TX 76116
Tel: (817)210-0808; Free: 888-422-9686
Fax: (817)210-0901
Web Site: http://www.artinstitutes.edu/fort-worth/
Type: Four-Year College **Sex:** Coed

THE ART INSTITUTE OF HOUSTON
1900 Yorktown St.
Houston, TX 77056
Tel: (713)623-2040; Free: 800-275-4244
Fax: (713)966-2797
Web Site: http://www.artinstitutes.edu/houston/
President/CEO: Larry Horn

Type: Four-Year College **Sex:** Coed **Affiliation:** Education Management Corporation **Calendar System:** Quarter **Regional Accreditation:** Southern Association of Colleges and Schools **Professional Accreditation:** ACF

THE ART INSTITUTE OF HOUSTON - NORTH
10740 North Gessner Dr.
Ste. 190
Houston, TX 77064
Tel: (281)671-3381; Free: (866)830-4450
Admissions: (281)671-3381
Web Site: http://www.artinstitutes.edu/houston-north
Type: Four-Year College **Sex:** Coed **Regional Accreditation:** Southern Association of Colleges and Schools

THE ART INSTITUTE OF SAN ANTONIO
1000 IH-10 West, Ste. 200
San Antonio, TX 78230
Tel: (210)338-7320; Free: 888-222-0040
Fax: (210)338-7321
Web Site: http://www.artinstitutes.edu/san-antonio/
Type: Four-Year College **Sex:** Coed

ATI TECHNICAL TRAINING CENTER
6627 Maple Ave.
Dallas, TX 75235
Tel: (214)263-4284
Admissions: (214)902-8191
Fax: (214)358-7500
Web Site: http://www.aticareertraining.edu/
President/CEO: Anthony DeVore
Type: Two-Year College **Sex:** Coed **Admission Plans:** Open Admission **Application Fee:** $100.00 **Calendar System:** Quarter **Professional Accreditation:** ACCSCT

AUSTIN COLLEGE
900 North Grand Ave.
Sherman, TX 75090-4400
Tel: (903)813-2000; Free: 800-442-5363
Admissions: (903)813-3000
Fax: (903)813-3198
E-mail: admission@austincollege.edu
Web Site: http://www.austincollege.edu/
President/CEO: Dr. Marjorie Hass
Admissions: Nan Davis
Financial Aid: Laurie Coulter
Type: Comprehensive **Sex:** Coed **Affiliation:** Presbyterian **Scores:** 98.9% SAT V 400+; 99.87% SAT M 400+; 24.3% ACT 18-23; 55.9% ACT 24-29 **% Accepted:** 80 **Admission Plans:** Early Admission; Deferred Admission **Application Deadline:** May 1 **Application Fee:** $35.00 **H.S. Requirements:** High school diploma required; GED accepted **Costs Per Year:** Application fee: $35. Comprehensive fee: $38,784 includes full-time tuition ($29,075), mandatory fees ($160), and college room and board ($9549). Full-time tuition and fees vary according to student level. Room and board charges vary according to board plan. Part-time tuition: $4216 per course. **Scholarships:** Available **Calendar System:** 4-1-4, Summer Session Available **Enrollment:** FT 1,325, PT 10, Grad FT 29 **Faculty:** FT 91, PT 28 **Student-Faculty Ratio:** 14:1 **Exams:** SAT I or ACT. **% Receiving Financial Aid:** 61 **% Residing in College-Owned, -Operated, or -Affiliated Housing:** 70 **Library Holdings:** 230,222 **Regional Accreditation:** Southern Association of Colleges and Schools **Credit Hours For Degree:** 34 courses, Bachelors **Intercollegiate Athletics:** Baseball M; Basketball M & W; Cheerleading M & W; Football M; Soccer M & W; Softball W; Swimming and Diving M & W; Tennis M & W; Volleyball W

AUSTIN COMMUNITY COLLEGE
5930 Middle Fiskville Rd.
Austin, TX 78752-4390
Tel: (512)223-7000
Admissions: (512)223-7503
Fax: (512)223-7665
E-mail: admission@austincc.edu
Web Site: http://www.austincc.edu/
President/CEO: Dr. Stephen B. Kinslow
Admissions: Linda Kluck
Type: Two-Year College **Sex:** Coed **Admission Plans:** Open Admission **Application Deadline:** Rolling **Application Fee:** $0.00 **H.S. Requirements:** High school diploma required; GED accepted **Costs Per Year:** Application fee: $0. Area resident tuition: $1170 full-time, $39 per credit hour part-time. State resident tuition: $3810 full-time, $127 per credit hour part-time. Nonresident tuition: $8550 full-time, $285 per credit hour part-time. Mandatory fees: $438 full-time, $15 per credit hour part-time. Full-time tuition and fees vary according to course load. Part-time tuition and fees vary according to course load. **Scholarships:** Available **Calendar System:** Semester, Summer Session Available **Enrollment:** FT 10,815, PT 29,433 **Faculty:** FT 559, PT 1,403 **Student-Faculty Ratio:** 20:1 **Final Year or Final Semester Residency Requirement:** No **Library Holdings:** 172,938 **Regional Accreditation:** Southern Association of Colleges and Schools **Credit Hours For Degree:** 62 semester hours, Associates **ROTC:** Army, Air Force **Professional Accreditation:** ARCEST, ACF, ADA, AOTA, APTA, JRCEDMS, JRCERT, JRCEMT, NAACLS, NLN

AUSTIN GRADUATE SCHOOL OF THEOLOGY
7640 Guadalupe St.
Austin, TX 78752
Tel: (512)476-2772; Free: (866)AUS-GRAD
Fax: (512)476-3919
E-mail: registrar@austingrad.edu
Web Site: http://www.austingrad.edu/
President/CEO: Stanley G. Reid
Admissions: Celeste Scarbrough
Financial Aid: David Arthur
Type: Two-Year Upper Division **Sex:** Coed **Affiliation:** Church of Christ **% Accepted:** 100 **Application Fee:** $0.00 **H.S. Requirements:** High school diploma required; GED accepted **Costs Per Year:** Application fee: $0. Tuition: $7000 full-time, $275 per semester hour part-time. Mandatory fees: $100 full-time, $50 per term part-time. Full-time tuition and fees vary according to course load. Part-time tuition and fees vary according to course load. **Scholarships:** Available **Calendar System:** Semester, Summer Session Available **Enrollment:** FT 6, PT 24, Grad FT 11, Grad PT 19 **Faculty:** FT 4, PT 6 **Library Holdings:** 29,728 **Regional Accreditation:** Southern Association of Colleges and Schools **Credit Hours For Degree:** 120 semester hours, Bachelors

BAPTIST MISSIONARY ASSOCIATION THEOLOGICAL SEMINARY
1530 East Pine St.
Jacksonville, TX 75766-5407
Tel: (903)586-2501
E-mail: attebery@bmats.edu
Web Site: http://www.bmats.edu/
President/CEO: Charley Holmes
Admissions: Dr. Philip Attebery
Financial Aid: Dr. Philip Attebery
Type: Comprehensive **Sex:** Coed **Affiliation:** Baptist **Admission Plans:** Open Admission **Application Deadline:** July 25 **Application Fee:** $35.00 **H.S. Requirements:** High school diploma required; GED accepted. For applicants to the associate's degree program 30 or over: High school diploma or equivalent not required **Scholarships:** Available **Calendar System:** Semester, Summer Session Available **% Receiving Financial Aid:** 67 **Library Holdings:** 63,603 **Regional Accreditation:** Southern Association of Colleges and Schools **Credit Hours For Degree:** 66 semester hours, Associates; 130 semester hours, Bachelors **Professional Accreditation:** ATS

BAPTIST UNIVERSITY OF THE AMERICAS
8019 South Pan Am Expressway
San Antonio, TX 78224-2701
Tel: (210)924-4338; Free: 800-721-1396
Fax: (210)924-2701
E-mail: agarcia@bua.edu
Web Site: http://www.bua.edu/
President/CEO: Rene Maciel
Admissions: Abraham Garcia
Financial Aid: Araceli G. Acosta
Type: Four-Year College **Sex:** Coed **Affiliation:** Baptist **% Accepted:** 50 **Application Deadline:** February 15 **Application Fee:** $25.00 **Scholarships:** Available **Calendar System:** Semester **Enrollment:** FT 131, PT 40 **Faculty:** FT 7, PT 9 **Student-Faculty Ratio:** 14:1 **Exams:** Other. **Professional Accreditation:** ABHE

BAYLOR UNIVERSITY
Waco, TX 76798
Tel: (254)710-1011; Free: 800-BAY-LORU
Admissions: (254)710-3435
E-mail: admissions@baylor.edu
Web Site: http://www.baylor.edu/
President/CEO: Dr. David Garland
Admissions: Jessica King Gereghty
Type: University **Sex:** Coed **Affiliation:** Baptist **Scores:** 99% SAT V 400+; 100% SAT M 400+; 28% ACT 18-23; 53% ACT 24-29 **% Accepted:** 50 **Admission Plans:** Early Admission; Early Action **Application Deadline:** February 1 **Application Fee:** $50.00 **H.S. Requirements:** High school diploma required; GED accepted **Costs Per Year:** Application fee: $50. Comprehensive fee: $38,085 includes full-time tuition ($26,996), mandatory fees ($2758), and college room and board ($8331). College room only: $4494. Room and board charges vary according to board plan and housing facility. Part-time tuition: $1124 per semester hour. **Scholarships:** Available **Calendar System:** Semester, Summer Session Available **Enrollment:** FT 11,905, PT 244, Grad FT 2,088, Grad PT 377 **Faculty:** FT 859, PT 287 **Student-Faculty Ratio:** 15:1 **Exams:** Other, SAT I or ACT. ACT essay used in place of application essay. SAT essay used in place of application essay. **% Receiving Financial Aid:** 55 **% Residing in College-Owned, -Operated, or -Affiliated Housing:** 39 **Final Year or Final Semester Residency Requirement:** Yes **Library Holdings:** 2,252,780 **Regional Accreditation:** Southern Association of Colleges and Schools **Credit Hours For Degree:** 124 semester hours, Bachelors **ROTC:** Army, Air Force **Professional Accreditation:** AACSB, ABET, ACEJMC, AALE, AACN, AAFCS, ABA, ADtA, APTA, APA, ASLHA, ACIPE, AALS, ATS, ACEHSA, CSWE, NASM, NAST, NCATE **Intercollegiate Athletics:** Badminton M & W; Baseball M; Basketball M & W; Crew M & W; Cross-Country Running M & W; Equestrian Sports W; Fencing M & W; Football M; Golf M & W; Gymnastics M & W; Ice Hockey M; Lacrosse M & W; Racquetball M & W; Rugby M & W; Sailing M & W; Soccer M & W; Softball W; Tennis M & W; Track and Field M & W; Volleyball M & W; Water Polo M & W; Wrestling M

BLINN COLLEGE
902 College Ave.
Brenham, TX 77833-4049
Tel: (979)830-4000
E-mail: recruit@blinn.edu
Web Site: http://www.blinn.edu/
President/CEO: Dr. Daniel J. Holt
Admissions: Stephanie Wehring
Type: Two-Year College **Sex:** Coed **% Accepted:** 100 **Admission Plans:** Open Admission; Early Admission; Deferred Admission **Application Deadline:** Rolling **Application Fee:** $0.00 **H.S. Requirements:** High school diploma required; GED accepted **Scholarships:** Available **Calendar System:** Semester, Summer Session Available **Enrollment:** FT 7,505, PT 6,511 **Faculty:** FT 215, PT 360 **Student-Faculty Ratio:** 24:1 **% Residing in College-Owned, -Operated, or -Affiliated Housing:** 9 **Library Holdings:** 130,000 **Regional Accreditation:** Southern Association of Colleges and Schools **Credit Hours For Degree:** 63 credit hours, Associates **Professional Accreditation:** ADA, APTA, JRCERT, NLN **Intercollegiate Athletics:** Baseball M; Basketball M & W; Cheerleading M & W; Football M; Softball W; Volleyball W

BRAZOSPORT COLLEGE
500 College Dr.
Lake Jackson, TX 77566-3199
Tel: (979)230-3000
Fax: (979)230-3443
E-mail: pleyende@brazosport.edu
Web Site: http://www.brazosport.edu/
President/CEO: Millicent M. Valek
Admissions: Patricia S. Leyendecker
Type: Two-Year College **Sex:** Coed **Admission Plans:** Open Admission; Early Admission; Deferred Admission **Application Deadline:** August 15 **Application Fee:** $0.00 **H.S. Requirements:** High school diploma required; GED accepted **Costs Per Year:** Application fee: $0. Area resident tuition: $864 full-time, $36 per credit hour part-time. State resident tuition: $1368 full-time, $57 per credit hour part-time. Nonresident tuition: $2496 full-time, $104 per credit hour part-time. Mandatory fees: $378 full-time. Full-time tuition and fees vary according to course level, course load, degree level, and student level. Part-time tuition varies according to course level, course load, degree level, and student level. **Scholarships:** Available **Calendar System:** Semester, Summer Session Available **Enrollment:** FT 1,670, PT 1,833 **Faculty:** FT 72, PT 94 **Student-Faculty Ratio:** 18:1 **Library Holdings:** 85,425 **Regional Accreditation:** Southern Association of Colleges and Schools **Credit Hours For Degree:** 62 semester hours, Associates

BROOKHAVEN COLLEGE
3939 Valley View Ln.
Farmers Branch, TX 75244-4997
Tel: (972)860-4700
Fax: (972)860-4897
E-mail: bhcinfo@dcccd.edu
Web Site: http://www.brookhavencollege.edu/
President/CEO: Dr. Richard McCrary
Type: Two-Year College **Sex:** Coed **Affiliation:** Dallas County Community College District System **% Accepted:** 100 **Admission Plans:** Open Admission; Early Admission; Deferred Admission **Application Deadline:** Rolling **Application Fee:** $0.00 **H.S. Requirements:** High school diploma or equivalent not required **Costs Per Year:** Application fee: $0. Area resident tuition: $984 full-time, $41 per credit hour part-time. State resident tuition: $1824 full-time, $76 per credit hour part-time. Nonresident tuition: $2904 full-time, $121 per credit hour part-time. Full-time tuition varies according to course load. Part-time tuition varies according to course load. **Calendar System:** Semester, Summer Session Available **Enrollment:** FT 931, PT 9,338 **Faculty:** FT 123, PT 579 **Student-Faculty Ratio:** 20:1 **Exams:** Other. **Library Holdings:** 58,225 **Regional Accreditation:** Southern Association of Colleges and Schools **Credit Hours For Degree:** 60 semester hours, Associates **ROTC:** Army **Intercollegiate Athletics:** Tennis M & W; Volleyball W

CEDAR VALLEY COLLEGE
3030 North Dallas Ave.
Lancaster, TX 75134-3799
Tel: (972)860-8201
Admissions: (972)860-8258
E-mail: cboswell-ward@dcccd.edu
Web Site: http://www.cedarvalleycollege.edu/
President/CEO: Dr. Jennifer Wimbish
Admissions: Carolyn Ward
Type: Two-Year College **Sex:** Coed **Affiliation:** Dallas County Community College District System **% Accepted:** 100 **Admission Plans:** Open Admission; Early Admission **Application Deadline:** Rolling **Application Fee:** $0.00 **H.S. Requirements:** High school diploma required; GED accepted **Scholarships:** Available **Calendar System:** Semester, Summer Session Available **Enrollment:** FT 1,472, PT 3,032 **Faculty:** FT 64, PT 110 **Student-Faculty Ratio:** 26:1 **Exams:** Other, SAT I or ACT. **Library Holdings:** 43,788 **Regional Accreditation:** Southern Association of Colleges and Schools **Credit Hours For Degree:** 61 semester hours, Associates **ROTC:** Army **Intercollegiate Athletics:** Baseball M; Basketball M; Soccer W; Volleyball W

CENTER FOR ADVANCED LEGAL STUDIES
3910 Kirby Dr.
Ste. 200
Houston, TX 77098-4151
Tel: (713)529-2778
Fax: (713)523-2715
E-mail: james.scheffer@paralegal.edu
Web Site: http://www.paralegal.edu/
President/CEO: Doyle Happe
Admissions: James Scheffer
Type: Two-Year College **Sex:** Coed **Application Deadline:** Rolling **Application Fee:** $100.00 **H.S. Requirements:** High school diploma required; GED accepted **Enrollment:** FT 176 **Faculty:** FT 2, PT 23 **Student-Faculty Ratio:** 17:1 **Exams:** Other. **Professional Accreditation:** COE

CENTRAL TEXAS COLLEGE
PO Box 1800
Killeen, TX 76540-1800
Tel: (254)526-7161; Free: 800-792-3348
Admissions: (254)526-1696
E-mail: admrec@ctcd.edu
Web Site: http://www.ctcd.edu/
President/CEO: Dr. James R. Anderson
Type: Two-Year College **Sex:** Coed **Admission Plans:** Open Admission;

Early Admission; Deferred Admission **Application Deadline:** Rolling **Application Fee:** $0.00 **H.S. Requirements:** High school diploma required; GED accepted **Costs Per Year:** Application fee: $0. Area resident tuition: $1200 full-time. State resident tuition: $1500 full-time. Nonresident tuition: $3900 full-time. Mandatory fees: $390 full-time. College room and board: $4550. **Scholarships:** Available **Calendar System:** Semester, Summer Session Available **Enrollment:** FT 4,163, PT 20,335 **Faculty:** FT 252, PT 2,161 **Student-Faculty Ratio:** 11:1 **% Residing in College-Owned, -Operated, or -Affiliated Housing:** 1 **Library Holdings:** 80,381 **Regional Accreditation:** Southern Association of Colleges and Schools **Credit Hours For Degree:** 64 semester hours, Associates **ROTC:** Army **Professional Accreditation:** NAACLS, NLN

CISCO COLLEGE
101 College Heights
Cisco, TX 76437-9321
Tel: (254)442-5000
Fax: (254)442-5100
E-mail: oodom@cjc.edu
Web Site: http://www.cisco.edu/
President/CEO: Colleen Smith
Admissions: Olin O. Odom, III
Type: Two-Year College **Sex:** Coed **% Accepted:** 100 **Admission Plans:** Open Admission; Early Admission **Application Deadline:** Rolling **Application Fee:** $0.00 **H.S. Requirements:** High school diploma required; GED accepted **Scholarships:** Available **Calendar System:** Semester, Summer Session Available **Enrollment:** FT 1,601, PT 2,421 **Student-Faculty Ratio:** 18:1 **Exams:** ACT, SAT I. **% Residing in College-Owned, -Operated, or -Affiliated Housing:** 12 **Library Holdings:** 34,000 **Regional Accreditation:** Southern Association of Colleges and Schools **Credit Hours For Degree:** 63 credit hours, Associates **ROTC:** Army **Professional Accreditation:** AAMAE, NLN **Intercollegiate Athletics:** Baseball M; Basketball W; Cheerleading M & W; Football M; Soccer M; Softball W; Volleyball W

CLARENDON COLLEGE
PO Box 968
Clarendon, TX 79226-0968
Tel: (806)874-3571
E-mail: martha.smith@clarendoncollege.edu
Web Site: http://www.clarendoncollege.edu/
President/CEO: Dr. William Auvenshine
Admissions: Martha Smith
Financial Aid: Reagan Silva
Type: Two-Year College **Sex:** Coed **% Accepted:** 100 **Admission Plans:** Open Admission; Early Admission; Deferred Admission **Application Deadline:** Rolling **Application Fee:** $0.00 **H.S. Requirements:** High school diploma required; GED accepted **Costs Per Year:** Application fee: $0. Area resident tuition: $1140 full-time. State resident tuition: $1710 full-time, $38 per credit hour part-time. Nonresident tuition: $2280 full-time, $57 per credit hour part-time. Mandatory fees: $1230 full-time, $41 per credit hour part-time. College room and board: $3500. College room only: $1200. **Scholarships:** Available **Calendar System:** Semester, Summer Session Available **Enrollment:** FT 371, PT 743 **Faculty:** FT 33, PT 48 **Student-Faculty Ratio:** 18:1 **% Residing in College-Owned, -Operated, or -Affiliated Housing:** 21 **Final Year or Final Semester Residency Requirement:** No **Library Holdings:** 21,027 **Regional Accreditation:** Southern Association of Colleges and Schools **Credit Hours For Degree:** 62 semester hours, Associates **Intercollegiate Athletics:** Baseball M; Basketball M & W; Cheerleading M & W; Cross-Country Running M & W; Softball W; Volleyball W

COASTAL BEND COLLEGE
3800 Charco Rd.
Beeville, TX 78102-2197
Tel: (361)358-2838
Admissions: (361)354-2245
Fax: (361)354-2254
E-mail: register@coastalbend.edu
Web Site: http://www.coastalbend.edu/
President/CEO: Dr. Thomas Baynum
Admissions: Alicia Ulloa
Type: Two-Year College **Sex:** Coed **% Accepted:** 100 **Admission Plans:** Open Admission; Deferred Admission **Application Deadline:** Rolling **Application Fee:** $0.00 **H.S. Requirements:** High school diploma required; GED accepted **Scholarships:** Available **Calendar System:** Semester, Summer Session Available **Enrollment:** FT 1,186, PT 1,956 **Faculty:** FT 85, PT 66 **Student-Faculty Ratio:** 14:1 **% Residing in College-Owned, -Operated, or -Affiliated Housing:** 5 **Library Holdings:** 43,004 **Regional Accreditation:** Southern Association of Colleges and Schools **Credit Hours For Degree:** 62 semester hours, Associates **Professional Accreditation:** ADA, AHIMA **Intercollegiate Athletics:** Basketball M; Volleyball W

COLLEGE OF BIBLICAL STUDIES—HOUSTON
7000 Regency Square Blvd.
Houston, TX 77036
Tel: (713)785-5995
Admissions: (832)252-3377
Fax: (713)785-5998
E-mail: admissions@cbshouston.edu
Web Site: http://www.cbshouston.edu/
President/CEO: Dr. Jay A Quine
Type: Comprehensive **Sex:** Coed **Affiliation:** nondenominational **Admission Plans:** Open Admission **Application Fee:** $40.00 **H.S. Requirements:** High school diploma required; GED accepted **Costs Per Year:** Application fee: $40. Tuition: $4320 full-time, $180 per credit hour part-time. Mandatory fees: $240 full-time, $120 per term part-time. Full-time tuition and fees vary according to course level, course load, degree level, and student level. Part-time tuition and fees vary according to course level, course load, degree level, and student level. **Calendar System:** Trimester, Summer Session Available **Final Year or Final Semester Residency Requirement:** No **Library Holdings:** 40,000 **Credit Hours For Degree:** 64 credits, Associates; 120 credits, Bachelors **Professional Accreditation:** ABHE

COLLEGE OF THE MAINLAND
1200 Amburn Rd.
Texas City, TX 77591-2499
Tel: (409)938-1211
Fax: (409)938-1306
E-mail: sem@com.edu
Web Site: http://www.com.edu/
President/CEO: Dr. Michael Elam
Admissions: Kelly Musick
Financial Aid: Rebecca Miles
Type: Two-Year College **Sex:** Coed **Admission Plans:** Open Admission; Early Admission; Deferred Admission **Application Deadline:** Rolling **Application Fee:** $0.00 **H.S. Requirements:** High school diploma required; GED accepted **Costs Per Year:** Application fee: $0. Area resident tuition: $792 full-time, $33 per credit hour part-time. State resident tuition: $1560 full-time, $65 per credit hour part-time. Nonresident tuition: $2544 full-time, $106 per credit hour part-time. Mandatory fees: $167 full-time. **Scholarships:** Available **Calendar System:** Semester, Summer Session Available **Enrollment:** FT 1,093, PT 2,468 **Faculty:** FT 100, PT 105 **Student-Faculty Ratio:** 14:1 **Exams:** SAT I or ACT. **Library Holdings:** 84,128 **Regional Accreditation:** Southern Association of Colleges and Schools **Credit Hours For Degree:** 60 credit hours, Associates **Professional Accreditation:** NLN

THE COLLEGE OF SAINT THOMAS MORE
3020 Lubbock St.
Fort Worth, TX 76109-2323
Tel: (817)923-8459; Free: 800-583-6489
Fax: (817)924-3206
E-mail: more-info@cstm.edu
Web Site: http://www.cstm.edu/
President/CEO: Dr. James Patrick
Admissions: Dr. James A. Patrick
Financial Aid: Mary E. Swanson
Type: Four-Year College **Sex:** Coed **Affiliation:** Roman Catholic Church **% Accepted:** 83 **Admission Plans:** Early Admission; Deferred Admission **Application Deadline:** Rolling **Application Fee:** $35.00 **H.S. Requirements:** High school diploma required; GED accepted **Scholarships:** Available **Calendar System:** Semester, Summer Session Available **Enrollment:** FT 21, PT 32 **Faculty:** FT 3, PT 6 **Student-Faculty Ratio:** 5:1 **% Receiving Financial Aid:** 63 **% Residing in College-Owned, -Operated, or -Affiliated Housing:** 51 **Library Holdings:** 13,739 **Regional Accreditation:** Southern Association of Colleges and Schools **Credit Hours For Degree:** 69 credit hours, Associates; 120 credit hours, Bachelors **ROTC:** Army

COLLIN COUNTY COMMUNITY COLLEGE DISTRICT
3452 Spur 399
McKinney, TX 75069

Tel: (972)599-3100
Admissions: (972)881-5174
Fax: (972)758-5468
E-mail: tfields@collin.edu
Web Site: http://www.collin.edu/
President/CEO: Dr. Cary A. Israel
Admissions: Todd Fields
Type: Two-Year College **Sex:** Coed **Admission Plans:** Open Admission **Application Deadline:** Rolling **Application Fee:** $0.00 **H.S. Requirements:** High school diploma required; GED accepted **Costs Per Year:** Application fee: $0. Area resident tuition: $810 full-time, $27 per semester hour part-time. State resident tuition: $1575 full-time, $54 per semester hour part-time. Nonresident tuition: $3225 full-time, $109 per semester hour part-time. Mandatory fees: $255 full-time, $7 per semester hour part-time. **Scholarships:** Available **Calendar System:** Semester, Summer Session Available **Enrollment:** FT 9,675, PT 15,197 **Faculty:** FT 326, PT 692 **Student-Faculty Ratio:** 27:1 **Exams:** Other. **Library Holdings:** 178,212 **Regional Accreditation:** Southern Association of Colleges and Schools **Credit Hours For Degree:** 60 credit hours, Associates **ROTC:** Air Force **Professional Accreditation:** ADA, CARC, NLN **Intercollegiate Athletics:** Basketball M & W; Tennis M & W; Volleyball W

COMMONWEALTH INSTITUTE OF FUNERAL SERVICE
415 Barren Springs Dr.
Houston, TX 77090
Tel: (281)873-0262; Free: 800-628-1580
Fax: (281)873-5232
E-mail: p.moreno@commonwealth.edu
Web Site: http://www.commonwealth.edu/
President/CEO: Jason Altieri
Admissions: Patricia Moreno
Type: Two-Year College **Sex:** Coed **% Accepted:** 100 **Application Deadline:** Rolling **Application Fee:** $50.00 **H.S. Requirements:** High school diploma required; GED accepted **Costs Per Year:** Application fee: $50. One-time mandatory fee: $100. Comprehensive fee: $22,800 includes full-time tuition ($12,800), mandatory fees ($100), and college room and board ($9900). Full-time tuition and fees vary according to course load and program. **Scholarships:** Available **Calendar System:** Quarter, Summer Session Not available **Exams:** Other, SAT I or ACT. **Library Holdings:** 1,500 **Credit Hours For Degree:** 97 quarter hours, Associates **Professional Accreditation:** ABFSE

COMPUTER CAREER CENTER
6101 Montana Ave.
El Paso, TX 79925
Tel: (915)779-8031
Web Site: http://www.computercareercenter.com/
President/CEO: Jim Tolbert
Admissions: Sarah Hernandez
Type: Two-Year College **Sex:** Coed **Admission Plans:** Open Admission **Application Fee:** $100.00 **H.S. Requirements:** High school diploma required; GED accepted **Scholarships:** Available **Calendar System:** Miscellaneous **Credit Hours For Degree:** 68 units, Associates **Professional Accreditation:** COE

CONCORDIA UNIVERSITY TEXAS
11400 Concordia University Dr.
Austin, TX 78726
Tel: (512)486-2000; Free: 800-865-4282
Admissions: (512)313-3000
Fax: (512)459-8517
E-mail: ctxadmis@crf.cuis.edu
Web Site: http://www.concordia.edu/
President/CEO: Thomas E. Cedel
Admissions: Kristi Kirk
Financial Aid: Cathy L. Schryer
Type: Comprehensive **Sex:** Coed **Affiliation:** Lutheran Church–Missouri Synod; Concordia University System **Scores:** 95.03% SAT V 400+; 95.03% SAT M 400+; 57% ACT 18-23; 27.13% ACT 24-29 **% Accepted:** 53 **Admission Plans:** Early Admission; Deferred Admission **Application Deadline:** Rolling **Application Fee:** $25.00 **H.S. Requirements:** High school diploma required; GED accepted **Costs Per Year:** Application fee: $25. Comprehensive fee: $29,200 includes full-time tuition ($20,800), mandatory fees ($400), and college room and board ($8000). College room only: $4700. Full-time tuition and fees vary according to course load, degree level, location, and program. Room and board charges vary according to board plan. Part-time tuition: $700 per hour. Part-time mandatory fees: $18 per credit hour, $200 per term. Part-time tuition and fees vary according to course load, degree level, location, and program. **Scholarships:** Available **Calendar System:** Semester, Summer Session Available **Enrollment:** FT 861, PT 249, Grad FT 46, Grad PT 1,029 **Faculty:** FT 55, PT 226 **Student-Faculty Ratio:** 10:1 **Exams:** SAT I or ACT. ACT essay used for admission. SAT essay used for admission. **% Receiving Financial Aid:** 24 **% Residing in College-Owned, -Operated, or -Affiliated Housing:** 15 **Regional Accreditation:** Southern Association of Colleges and Schools **Credit Hours For Degree:** 64 semester hours, Associates; 128 semester hours, Bachelors **ROTC:** Army, Air Force **Intercollegiate Athletics:** Baseball M; Basketball M & W; Cross-Country Running M & W; Golf M & W; Soccer M & W; Softball W; Tennis M & W; Volleyball W

COURT REPORTING INSTITUTE OF DALLAS
8585 North Stemmons Freeway, Ste. 200 North
Dallas, TX 75247
Tel: (214)350-9722; Free: 800-880-9722
Fax: (214)631-0143
Web Site: http://www.crid.com/
President/CEO: Joe P. Mehlmann
Admissions: Debra Smith-Armstrong
Type: Two-Year College **Sex:** Coed **Admission Plans:** Open Admission; Early Decision Plan **Application Fee:** $100.00 **Scholarships:** Available **Calendar System:** Quarter **Professional Accreditation:** ACICS

COURT REPORTING INSTITUTE OF HOUSTON
13101 Northwest Freeway, Ste. 100
Houston, TX 77040
Tel: (713)996-8300; Free: (866)996-8300
Web Site: http://www.crid.com/
Type: Two-Year College **Sex:** Coed **Costs Per Year:** One-time mandatory fee: $100. Tuition: $9600 full-time. Mandatory fees: $600 full-time. **Calendar System:** Quarter **Professional Accreditation:** ACICS

THE CRISWELL COLLEGE
4010 Gaston Ave.
Dallas, TX 75246-1537
Tel: (214)821-5433; Free: 800-899-0012
Fax: (214)818-1310
Web Site: http://www.criswell.edu/
President/CEO: Dr. Lamar E. Cooper, Sr.
Financial Aid: Ester Waggoner
Type: Comprehensive **Sex:** Coed **Affiliation:** Southern Baptist Convention **Application Fee:** $35.00 **H.S. Requirements:** High school diploma required; GED accepted **Costs Per Year:** Application fee: $35. Tuition: $5952 full-time, $248 per credit hour part-time. Mandatory fees: $580 full-time, $290 per term part-time. **Scholarships:** Available **Calendar System:** Semester, Summer Session Available **Regional Accreditation:** Southern Association of Colleges and Schools **Credit Hours For Degree:** 63 semester hours, Associates; 129 semester hours, Bachelors

CULINARY INSTITUTE ALAIN & MARIE LENOTRE
7070 Allensby
Houston, TX 77022-4322
Tel: (713)692-0077
Fax: (713)692-7399
Web Site: http://www.ciaml.com/
President/CEO: Alain Lenotre
Type: Two-Year College **Sex:** Coed **Application Fee:** $50.00 **Professional Accreditation:** ACCSCT

DALLAS BAPTIST UNIVERSITY
3000 Mountain Creek Parkway
Dallas, TX 75211-9299
Tel: (214)333-7100; Free: 800-460-1328
Admissions: (214)333-5360
Fax: (214)333-5447
E-mail: admiss@dbu.edu
Web Site: http://www.dbu.edu/
President/CEO: Dr. Gary R. Cook
Admissions: Erin Dennis

Financial Aid: Donald G. Zackary
Type: Comprehensive **Sex:** Coed **Affiliation:** Baptist General Convention of Texas **Scores:** 99% SAT V 400+; 99% SAT M 400+; 72% ACT 18-23; 22% ACT 24-29 **% Accepted:** 46 **Admission Plans:** Early Admission; Deferred Admission **Application Deadline:** Rolling **Application Fee:** $25.00 **H.S. Requirements:** High school diploma required; GED accepted **Costs Per Year:** Application fee: $25. Comprehensive fee: $23,126 includes full-time tuition ($17,490) and college room and board ($5636). College room only: $2236. Room and board charges vary according to board plan and housing facility. Part-time tuition: $583 per credit hour. **Scholarships:** Available **Calendar System:** 4-1-4, Summer Session Available **Enrollment:** FT 2,214, PT 1,319, Grad FT 587, Grad PT 1,280 **Faculty:** FT 123, PT 409 **Student-Faculty Ratio:** 14:1 **Exams:** SAT I or ACT. **% Receiving Financial Aid:** 61 **% Residing in College-Owned, -Operated, or -Affiliated Housing:** 42 **Final Year or Final Semester Residency Requirement:** No **Library Holdings:** 315,195 **Regional Accreditation:** Southern Association of Colleges and Schools **Credit Hours For Degree:** 65 credit hours, Associates; 126 credit hours, Bachelors **ROTC:** Army, Air Force **Professional Accreditation:** ACBSP, NASM **Intercollegiate Athletics:** Baseball M; Basketball M; Cross-Country Running M & W; Football W; Golf M & W; Soccer W; Tennis M & W; Track and Field M & W; Volleyball W

DALLAS CHRISTIAN COLLEGE
2700 Christian Parkway
Dallas, TX 75234-7299
Tel: (972)241-3371
Fax: (972)241-8021
E-mail: kboggs@dallas.edu
Web Site: http://www.dallas.edu/
President/CEO: Dustin D. Rubeck
Admissions: Kristi Boggs
Financial Aid: Robin L. Walker
Type: Four-Year College **Sex:** Coed **Affiliation:** Christian Churches and Churches of Christ **% Accepted:** 18 **Admission Plans:** Preferred Admission; Deferred Admission **Application Deadline:** Rolling **Application Fee:** $40.00 **H.S. Requirements:** High school diploma required; GED accepted **Costs Per Year:** Application fee: $40. Comprehensive fee: $17,270 includes full-time tuition ($10,170), mandatory fees ($600), and college room and board ($6500). Part-time tuition: $329 per hour. **Scholarships:** Available **Calendar System:** Semester, Summer Session Available **Enrollment:** FT 203, PT 112 **Faculty:** FT 9, PT 48 **Student-Faculty Ratio:** 16:1 **Exams:** SAT I or ACT. **% Residing in College-Owned, -Operated, or -Affiliated Housing:** 41 **Credit Hours For Degree:** 130 semester hours, Bachelors **Professional Accreditation:** ABHE **Intercollegiate Athletics:** Basketball M & W; Soccer M & W; Volleyball W

DALLAS INSTITUTE OF FUNERAL SERVICE
3909 South Buckner Blvd.
Dallas, TX 75227
Tel: (214)388-5466; Free: 800-235-5444
Fax: (214)388-0316
E-mail: difs@dallasinstitute.edu
Web Site: http://www.dallasinstitute.edu/
President/CEO: James M. Shoemake
Admissions: Terry Parrish
Type: Two-Year College **Sex:** Coed **Admission Plans:** Open Admission **Application Fee:** $50.00 **H.S. Requirements:** High school diploma required; GED accepted **Scholarships:** Available **Calendar System:** Quarter **Enrollment:** FT 247 **Faculty:** FT 6, PT 4 **Student-Faculty Ratio:** 32:1 **Credit Hours For Degree:** 101 quarter hours, Associates **Professional Accreditation:** ABFSE

DEL MAR COLLEGE
101 Baldwin Blvd.
Corpus Christi, TX 78404-3897
Tel: (361)698-1200
Admissions: (361)698-1255
Fax: (361)698-1559
E-mail: fjordan@delmar.edu
Web Site: http://www.delmar.edu/
President/CEO: Dr. Mark Escamilla
Admissions: Frances P. Jordan
Type: Two-Year College **Sex:** Coed **Admission Plans:** Open Admission; Early Admission; Deferred Admission **Application Deadline:** Rolling **Application Fee:** $0.00 **H.S. Requirements:** High school diploma required; GED accepted **Costs Per Year:** Application fee: $0. Area resident tuition: $38 per credit hour part-time. State resident tuition: $88 per credit hour part-time. Nonresident tuition: $125 per credit hour part-time. Mandatory fees: $30 per credit hour part-time, $57 per term part-time. Part-time tuition and fees vary according to course load. **Scholarships:** Available **Calendar System:** Semester, Summer Session Available **Enrollment:** FT 3,722, PT 8,285 **Faculty:** FT 267, PT 293 **Student-Faculty Ratio:** 18:1 **Final Year or Final Semester Residency Requirement:** No **Library Holdings:** 127,717 **Regional Accreditation:** Southern Association of Colleges and Schools **Credit Hours For Degree:** 62 semester hours, Associates **ROTC:** Army **Professional Accreditation:** ABET, ARCEST, ACF, ADA, AHIMA, AOTA, APTA, CARC, JRCEDMS, JRCERT, NAACLS, NASAD, NASM, NAST, NLN

DEVRY UNIVERSITY (HOUSTON)
11125 Equity Dr.
Houston, TX 77041
Tel: (713)850-0888; Free: (866)703-3879
Fax: (713)850-0858
Web Site: http://www.devry.edu/
Type: Comprehensive **Sex:** Coed **Admission Plans:** Deferred Admission **Application Deadline:** Rolling **Application Fee:** $50.00 **H.S. Requirements:** High school diploma required; GED accepted **Costs Per Year:** Application fee: $50. Tuition: $14,080 full-time, $550 per credit hour part-time. **Scholarships:** Available **Calendar System:** Semester, Summer Session Available **Enrollment:** FT 801, PT 643, Grad FT 42, Grad PT 208 **Faculty:** FT 24, PT 151 **Student-Faculty Ratio:** 15:1 **Exams:** ACT essay used for admission. SAT essay used for admission. ACT essay used for placement. SAT essay used for placement. **% Receiving Financial Aid:** 83 **Regional Accreditation:** North Central Association of Colleges and Schools

DEVRY UNIVERSITY (IRVING)
4800 Regent Blvd.
Irving, TX 75063-2439
Tel: (972)929-6777
Web Site: http://www.devry.edu/
President/CEO: Simon Lumley
Financial Aid: Tommy Sims
Type: Comprehensive **Sex:** Coed **Affiliation:** DeVry University **Admission Plans:** Deferred Admission **Application Deadline:** Rolling **Application Fee:** $50.00 **H.S. Requirements:** High school diploma required; GED accepted **Costs Per Year:** Application fee: $50. Tuition: $14,080 full-time, $550 per credit hour part-time. **Scholarships:** Available **Calendar System:** Semester, Summer Session Available **Enrollment:** FT 819, PT 898, Grad FT 26, Grad PT 276 **Faculty:** FT 47, PT 86 **Student-Faculty Ratio:** 16:1 **Exams:** ACT essay used for admission. SAT essay used for admission. ACT essay used for placement. SAT essay used for placement. **% Receiving Financial Aid:** 79 **Regional Accreditation:** North Central Association of Colleges and Schools **Credit Hours For Degree:** 66 credit hours, Associates; 122 credit hours, Bachelors **Professional Accreditation:** ABET

DEVRY UNIVERSITY (RICHARDSON)
Richardson Center
2201 North Central Expressway
Richardson, TX 75080
Tel: (972)792-7450
Fax: (972)437-6892
Web Site: http://www.devry.edu/
Type: Comprehensive **Sex:** Coed **Calendar System:** Semester **Regional Accreditation:** North Central Association of Colleges and Schools

EAST TEXAS BAPTIST UNIVERSITY
1209 North Grove
Marshall, TX 75670-1498
Tel: (903)935-7963; Free: 800-804-ETBU
Admissions: (903)923-2000
Fax: (903)938-1705
E-mail: admissions@etbu.edu
Web Site: http://www.etbu.edu/
President/CEO: Dr. Samuel W. Oliver
Admissions: Melissa Fitts
Financial Aid: Tommy Young
Type: Four-Year College **Sex:** Coed **Affiliation:** Baptist **Scores:** 88% SAT V 400+; 94% SAT M 400+; 64% ACT 18-23; 23% ACT 24-29 **% Accepted:** 53

Application Deadline: August 16 **Application Fee:** $25.00 **H.S. Requirements:** High school diploma required; GED accepted **Costs Per Year:** Application fee: $25. Comprehensive fee: $24,986 includes full-time tuition ($18,750), mandatory fees ($800), and college room and board ($5436). College room only: $2340. Room and board charges vary according to board plan and housing facility. Part-time tuition: $625 per credit hour. Part-time mandatory fees: $20 per credit hour. **Scholarships:** Available **Calendar System:** Semester, Summer Session Available **Enrollment:** FT 1,082, PT 97 **Faculty:** FT 64, PT 36 **Student-Faculty Ratio:** 15:1 **Exams:** SAT I or ACT. ACT essay not being used. SAT essay not being used. **% Receiving Financial Aid:** 80 **% Residing in College-Owned, -Operated, or -Affiliated Housing:** 81 **Final Year or Final Semester Residency Requirement:** No **Library Holdings:** 245,374 **Regional Accreditation:** Southern Association of Colleges and Schools **Credit Hours For Degree:** 120 semester hours, Bachelors **Professional Accreditation:** AACN, NASM **Intercollegiate Athletics:** Baseball M; Basketball M & W; Cross-Country Running M & W; Football M; Soccer M & W; Softball W; Volleyball W

EASTFIELD COLLEGE
3737 Motley Dr.
Mesquite, TX 75150-2099
Tel: (972)860-7100
Admissions: (972)860-7010
Fax: (972)860-8373
E-mail: efc@dcccd.edu
Web Site: http://www.efc.dcccd.edu/
President/CEO: Dr. Jean Conway
Admissions: Glynis Miller
Type: Two-Year College **Sex:** Coed **Affiliation:** Dallas County Community College District System **% Accepted:** 100 **Admission Plans:** Open Admission; Early Admission; Deferred Admission **Application Deadline:** Rolling **Application Fee:** $0.00 **H.S. Requirements:** High school diploma required; GED accepted **Costs Per Year:** Application fee: $0. Area resident tuition: $1230 full-time, $41 per credit part-time. State resident tuition: $2280 full-time, $76 per credit part-time. Nonresident tuition: $3630 full-time, $121 per credit part-time. Full-time tuition varies according to course load. Part-time tuition varies according to course load. **Scholarships:** Available **Calendar System:** Semester, Summer Session Available **Enrollment:** FT 3,140, PT 8,804 **Faculty:** FT 117, PT 280 **Student-Faculty Ratio:** 29:1 **Library Holdings:** 66,988 **Regional Accreditation:** Southern Association of Colleges and Schools **Credit Hours For Degree:** 61 credit hours, Associates **Intercollegiate Athletics:** Baseball M; Basketball M; Golf M; Soccer W; Tennis M & W; Volleyball M & W

EL CENTRO COLLEGE
801 Main St.
Dallas, TX 75202-3604
Tel: (214)860-2037
Admissions: (214)860-2618
Fax: (214)860-2335
E-mail: rgarza@dcccd.edu
Web Site: http://www.ecc.dcccd.edu/
President/CEO: Paul McCarthy
Admissions: Rebecca Garza
Type: Two-Year College **Sex:** Coed **Affiliation:** Dallas County Community College District System **% Accepted:** 100 **Admission Plans:** Open Admission; Early Admission **Application Deadline:** Rolling **Application Fee:** $0.00 **H.S. Requirements:** High school diploma required; GED accepted. For applicants 18 or over who graduated from unaccredited high schools: High school diploma required; GED not accepted **Costs Per Year:** Application fee: $0. Area resident tuition: $984 full-time, $41 per credit hour part-time. State resident tuition: $1824 full-time, $76 per credit hour part-time. Nonresident tuition: $2904 full-time, $121 per credit hour part-time. Full-time tuition varies according to class time and program. Part-time tuition varies according to class time and program. **Scholarships:** Available **Calendar System:** Semester, Summer Session Available **Enrollment:** FT 1,733, PT 6,780 **Faculty:** FT 130, PT 330 **Student-Faculty Ratio:** 16:1 **Library Holdings:** 77,902 **Regional Accreditation:** Southern Association of Colleges and Schools **Credit Hours For Degree:** 61 credit hours, Associates **ROTC:** Army **Professional Accreditation:** CARC, FIDER, JRCECT, JRCEDMS, JRCERT, NAACLS, NLN

EL PASO COMMUNITY COLLEGE
PO Box 20500
El Paso, TX 79998-0500
Tel: (915)831-2000
Fax: (915)831-6145
E-mail: daryleh@epcc.edu
Web Site: http://www.epcc.edu/
President/CEO: Dr. Richard Rhodes
Admissions: Daryle Hendry
Type: Two-Year College **Sex:** Coed **Admission Plans:** Open Admission; Early Admission; Deferred Admission **Application Deadline:** August 3 **Application Fee:** $10.00 **H.S. Requirements:** High school diploma required; GED accepted **Costs Per Year:** Application fee: $10. State resident tuition: $1428 full-time, $59.50 per hour part-time. Nonresident tuition: $1980 full-time, $82.50 per hour part-time. Mandatory fees: $240 full-time. Full-time tuition and fees vary according to course load. Part-time tuition varies according to course load. **Scholarships:** Available **Calendar System:** Semester, Summer Session Available **Enrollment:** FT 10,943, PT 17,225 **Faculty:** FT 408, PT 1,003 **Library Holdings:** 442,879 **Regional Accreditation:** Southern Association of Colleges and Schools **Credit Hours For Degree:** 60 credit hours, Associates **ROTC:** Army **Professional Accreditation:** ARCEST, AAMAE, ADA, AHIMA, APTA, COptA, CARC, NAACLS, NLN **Intercollegiate Athletics:** Baseball M; Softball W; Track and Field M & W

EVEREST COLLEGE (ARLINGTON)
2801 East Division St.
Ste. 250
Arlington, TX 76011
Tel: (817)652-7790
Fax: (817)649-6033
Web Site: http://www.everest.edu/
President/CEO: Kendra Williams
Type: Two-Year College **Sex:** Coed **% Accepted:** 100 **Application Fee:** $25.00 **Calendar System:** Miscellaneous **Professional Accreditation:** ACICS

EVEREST COLLEGE (DALLAS)
6060 North Central Expressway
Ste. 101
Dallas, TX 75206-5209
Tel: (214)234-4850
Fax: (214)696-6208
Web Site: http://www.everest.edu/
President/CEO: Stacy Pniewski
Type: Two-Year College **Sex:** Coed **% Accepted:** 88 **Calendar System:** Miscellaneous **Professional Accreditation:** ACICS

EVEREST COLLEGE (FORT WORTH)
5237 North Riverside Dr.
Ste. 100
Fort Worth, TX 76137
Tel: (817)838-3000
Fax: (817)838-2040
Web Site: http://www.everest.edu/
President/CEO: Marilyn Long
Type: Two-Year College **Sex:** Coed **% Accepted:** 100 **Application Fee:** $25.00

FRANK PHILLIPS COLLEGE
Box 5118
Borger, TX 79008-5118
Tel: (806)274-5311; Free: 800-687-2056
Admissions: (806)457-4200
Fax: (806)274-6835
E-mail: braper@fpctx.edu
Web Site: http://www.fpctx.edu/
President/CEO: Dr. Herbert J. Swender
Admissions: Beth Raper
Type: Two-Year College **Sex:** Coed **% Accepted:** 100 **Admission Plans:** Open Admission; Early Admission; Deferred Admission **Application Deadline:** August 25 **Application Fee:** $0.00 **H.S. Requirements:** High school diploma required; GED accepted **Costs Per Year:** Application fee: $0. Area resident tuition: $768 full-time, $32 per hour part-time. State resident tuition: $1272 full-time, $53 per hour part-time. Nonresident tuition: $1460 full-time, $60 per hour part-time. Mandatory fees: $1162 full-time, $44 per hour part-time, $53. Part-time tuition and fees vary according to course load. College room and board: $3950. Room and board charges vary ac-

cording to housing facility. **Scholarships:** Available **Calendar System:** Semester, Summer Session Available **Enrollment:** FT 585, PT 663 **Faculty:** FT 30, PT 67 **Student-Faculty Ratio:** 16:1 **% Residing in College-Owned, -Operated, or -Affiliated Housing:** 20 **Library Holdings:** 35,700 **Regional Accreditation:** Southern Association of Colleges and Schools **Credit Hours For Degree:** 64 credit hours, Associates **Intercollegiate Athletics:** Baseball M; Basketball M & W; Golf M; Softball W; Volleyball W

GALVESTON COLLEGE
4015 Ave. Q
Galveston, TX 77550-7496
Tel: (409)763-6551
Admissions: (409)944-1234
Fax: (409)762-9367
E-mail: calcala@gc.edu
Web Site: http://www.gc.edu/
President/CEO: Dr. W. Myles Shelton, EdD
Admissions: Cynthia Alcala
Type: Two-Year College **Sex:** Coed **Admission Plans:** Open Admission **Application Deadline:** Rolling **Application Fee:** $0.00 **H.S. Requirements:** High school diploma required; GED accepted **Costs Per Year:** Application fee: $0. State resident tuition: $900 full-time, $30 per semester hour part-time. Nonresident tuition: $1800 full-time, $60 per semester hour part-time. Mandatory fees: $514 full-time, $13 per credit hour part-time, $62 per term part-time. **Scholarships:** Available **Calendar System:** Semester, Summer Session Available **Enrollment:** FT 851, PT 1,379 **Faculty:** FT 55, PT 46 **Student-Faculty Ratio:** 11:1 **Library Holdings:** 45,193 **Regional Accreditation:** Southern Association of Colleges and Schools **Credit Hours For Degree:** 60 credit hours, Associates **Professional Accreditation:** JRCERT, JRCEMT, JRCNMT, NLN **Intercollegiate Athletics:** Baseball M; Softball W; Volleyball W

GRAYSON COUNTY COLLEGE
6101 Grayson Dr.
Denison, TX 75020-8299
Tel: (903)465-6030
Fax: (903)463-5284
Web Site: http://www.grayson.edu/
President/CEO: Dr. Alan Scheibmeir
Admissions: Dr. Debbie Plyler
Type: Two-Year College **Sex:** Coed **% Accepted:** 100 **Admission Plans:** Open Admission; Early Admission; Deferred Admission **Application Deadline:** August 31 **Application Fee:** $0.00 **H.S. Requirements:** High school diploma required; GED accepted **Scholarships:** Available **Calendar System:** Semester, Summer Session Available **Enrollment:** FT 1,697, PT 1,647 **Faculty:** FT 94, PT 125 **Student-Faculty Ratio:** 16:1 **Library Holdings:** 51,500 **Regional Accreditation:** Southern Association of Colleges and Schools **Credit Hours For Degree:** 62 semester hours, Associates **Professional Accreditation:** ADA, NAACLS, NLN **Intercollegiate Athletics:** Baseball M; Basketball M & W; Softball W

HALLMARK COLLEGE OF TECHNOLOGY
10401 IH 10 West
San Antonio, TX 78230
Tel: (210)690-9000; Free: 800-880-6600
Fax: (210)697-8225
E-mail: sross@hallmarkcollege.edu
Web Site: http://www.hallmarkcollege.edu/
President/CEO: Joe Fisher
Admissions: Sonia Ross
Type: Two-Year College **Sex:** Coed **Application Deadline:** Rolling **Application Fee:** $110.00 **H.S. Requirements:** High school diploma required; GED accepted **Costs Per Year:** Application fee: $110. **Scholarships:** Available **Calendar System:** Continuous **Enrollment:** FT 294 **Faculty:** FT 18, PT 11 **Student-Faculty Ratio:** 10:1 **Exams:** Other. **Credit Hours For Degree:** 72 credit hours, Associates **Professional Accreditation:** ACCSCT

HALLMARK INSTITUTE OF AERONAUTICS
8901 Wetmore Rd.
San Antonio, TX 78216
Tel: (210)826-1000; Free: 888-656-9300
Fax: (210)826-3707
E-mail: sross@hallmarkcollege.edu
Web Site: http://www.hallmarkcollege.edu/programs-school-of-aeronautics.aspx/
President/CEO: Bret Johnson
Admissions: Sal Ross
Type: Two-Year College **Sex:** Coed **Affiliation:** Hallmark College of Technology **Application Deadline:** Rolling **Application Fee:** $110.00 **H.S. Requirements:** High school diploma required; GED accepted **Scholarships:** Available **Calendar System:** Continuous **Enrollment:** FT 218 **Student-Faculty Ratio:** 17:1 **Credit Hours For Degree:** 72 units, Associates **Professional Accreditation:** ACCSCT

HARDIN-SIMMONS UNIVERSITY
2200 Hickory St.
Abilene, TX 79698-0001
Tel: (325)670-1000; Free: 877-464-7889
Admissions: (325)670-5890
Fax: (325)677-8351
E-mail: breynolds@hsutx.edu
Web Site: http://www.hsutx.edu/
President/CEO: Dr. Lanny Hall
Admissions: Brynn Reynolds
Financial Aid: Jim Jones
Type: Comprehensive **Sex:** Coed **Affiliation:** Baptist **Scores:** 94.18% SAT V 400+; 97.41% SAT M 400+; 57.39% ACT 18-23; 32.65% ACT 24-29 **% Accepted:** 38 **Admission Plans:** Deferred Admission **Application Deadline:** Rolling **Application Fee:** $50.00 **H.S. Requirements:** High school diploma required; GED accepted **Costs Per Year:** Application fee: $50. Comprehensive fee: $27,272 includes full-time tuition ($19,950), mandatory fees ($1040), and college room and board ($6282). College room only: $3123. Full-time tuition and fees vary according to program. Room and board charges vary according to board plan and housing facility. Part-time tuition: $665 per credit hour. Part-time mandatory fees: $150 per term. Part-time tuition and fees vary according to course load and program. Tuition guaranteed not to increase for student's term of enrollment. **Scholarships:** Available **Calendar System:** Semester, Summer Session Available **Enrollment:** FT 1,730, PT 176, Grad FT 216, Grad PT 183 **Faculty:** FT 136, PT 72 **Student-Faculty Ratio:** 13:1 **Exams:** SAT I or ACT. ACT essay used for admission. SAT essay used for admission. ACT essay used for advising. SAT essay used for advising. ACT essay used for placement. SAT essay used for placement. **% Receiving Financial Aid:** 71 **% Residing in College-Owned, -Operated, or -Affiliated Housing:** 44 **Final Year or Final Semester Residency Requirement:** Yes **Library Holdings:** 279,976 **Regional Accreditation:** Southern Association of Colleges and Schools **Credit Hours For Degree:** 124 semester hours, Bachelors **Professional Accreditation:** AACN, APTA, ACBSP, ATS, CSWE, NASM **Intercollegiate Athletics:** Baseball M; Basketball M & W; Cheerleading M & W; Cross-Country Running M & W; Football M; Golf M & W; Soccer M & W; Softball W; Tennis M & W; Track and Field M & W; Volleyball W

HILL COLLEGE OF THE HILL JUNIOR COLLEGE DISTRICT
112 Lamar Dr.
Hillsboro, TX 76645
Tel: (254)582-2555
Admissions: (254)659-7500
E-mail: diharvey@hill-college.cc.tx.us
Web Site: http://www.hillcollege.edu/
President/CEO: Dr. Sheryl Smith Kappus
Admissions: Diane Harvey
Type: Two-Year College **Sex:** Coed **Admission Plans:** Open Admission; Early Admission; Deferred Admission **Application Deadline:** Rolling **Application Fee:** $0.00 **H.S. Requirements:** High school diploma required; GED accepted **Scholarships:** Available **Calendar System:** Semester, Summer Session Available **Library Holdings:** 40,000 **Regional Accreditation:** Southern Association of Colleges and Schools **Credit Hours For Degree:** 62 credit hours, Associates **Intercollegiate Athletics:** Baseball M; Basketball M & W; Golf M; Soccer M & W; Softball W; Volleyball W

HOUSTON BAPTIST UNIVERSITY
7502 Fondren Rd.
Houston, TX 77074-3298
Tel: (281)649-3000; Free: 800-696-3210
Admissions: (281)649-3299
Fax: (281)649-3209
E-mail: eborges@hbu.edu

Web Site: http://www.hbu.edu/
President/CEO: Dr. Robert B. Sloan, Jr.
Admissions: Eduardo Borges
Financial Aid: Sherry Byrd
Type: Comprehensive **Sex:** Coed **Affiliation:** Baptist **Scores:** 98.2% SAT V 400+; 98.9% SAT M 400+; 66.3% ACT 18-23; 30.6% ACT 24-29 **% Accepted:** 42 **Admission Plans:** Early Admission **Application Deadline:** Rolling **Application Fee:** $0.00 **H.S. Requirements:** High school diploma required; GED accepted **Costs Per Year:** Application fee: $0. Comprehensive fee: $30,155 includes full-time tuition ($21,970), mandatory fees ($1210), and college room and board ($6975). Room and board charges vary according to board plan and housing facility. Part-time tuition: $750 per semester hour. Part-time tuition varies according to course load. **Scholarships:** Available **Calendar System:** Semester, Summer Session Available **Enrollment:** FT 2,005, PT 328, Grad FT 132, Grad PT 245 **Faculty:** FT 115, PT 131 **Student-Faculty Ratio:** 15:1 **Exams:** SAT I or ACT. **% Receiving Financial Aid:** 68 **% Residing in College-Owned, -Operated, or -Affiliated Housing:** 34 **Final Year or Final Semester Residency Requirement:** Yes **Library Holdings:** 235,973 **Regional Accreditation:** Southern Association of Colleges and Schools **Credit Hours For Degree:** 72 credit hours, Associates; 130 credit hours, Bachelors **ROTC:** Army, Navy, Air Force **Professional Accreditation:** ACBSP, NLN **Intercollegiate Athletics:** Baseball M; Basketball M & W; Cheerleading M & W; Cross-Country Running M & W; Golf M & W; Soccer M & W; Softball W; Track and Field M & W; Volleyball W

HOUSTON COMMUNITY COLLEGE SYSTEM
3100 Main St.
PO Box 667517
Houston, TX 77266-7517
Tel: (713)718-2000
Admissions: (713)718-8500
Fax: (713)718-2111
Web Site: http://www.hccs.edu/
President/CEO: Dr. Mary Spangler
Admissions: Mary Lemburg
Type: Two-Year College **Sex:** Coed **Admission Plans:** Open Admission **Application Deadline:** Rolling **H.S. Requirements:** High school diploma or equivalent not required **Costs Per Year:** Area resident tuition: $1392 full-time, $57.50 per credit hour part-time. State resident tuition: $2688 full-time, $111.50 per credit hour part-time. Nonresident tuition: $3168 full-time, $131.50 per credit hour part-time. Mandatory fees: $6 per term part-time. Full-time tuition varies according to course load. Part-time tuition and fees vary according to course load. **Scholarships:** Available **Calendar System:** Semester, Summer Session Available **Enrollment:** FT 16,821, PT 38,121 **Faculty:** FT 813, PT 2,139 **Regional Accreditation:** Southern Association of Colleges and Schools **Credit Hours For Degree:** 60 semester hours, Associates **ROTC:** Army, Air Force **Professional Accreditation:** ABET, ADA, AHIMA, AOTA, APTA, CARC, JRCERT, JRCEMT, JRCNMT, NAACLS

HOWARD COLLEGE
1001 Birdwell Ln.
Big Spring, TX 79720
Tel: (915)264-5000; Free: (866)HC-HAWKS
Admissions: (432)264-5105
Fax: (915)264-5082
E-mail: trichardson@howardcollege.edu
Web Site: http://www.howardcollege.edu/
President/CEO: Dr. Cheryl T. Sparks
Admissions: TaNeal Richardson
Type: Two-Year College **Sex:** Coed **Affiliation:** Howard County Junior College District System **Admission Plans:** Open Admission; Early Admission **Application Deadline:** Rolling **Application Fee:** $0.00 **H.S. Requirements:** High school diploma required; GED accepted **Costs Per Year:** Application fee: $0. Area resident tuition: $1500 full-time, $40 per hour part-time. State resident tuition: $1920 full-time, $52 per hour part-time. Nonresident tuition: $2620 full-time, $74 per hour part-time. Mandatory fees: $212 full-time, $176 per term part-time. Full-time tuition and fees vary according to course load and location. Part-time tuition and fees vary according to course load and location. College room and board: $3984. Room and board charges vary according to housing facility and location. **Scholarships:** Available **Calendar System:** Semester, Summer Session Available **Enrollment:** FT 1,636, PT 2,467 **Faculty:** FT 144, PT 99 **Student-Faculty Ratio:** 14:1 **Exams:** ACT essay used for advising. SAT essay used for advising. ACT essay used for placement. SAT essay used for placement. **% Residing in College-Owned, -Operated, or -Affiliated Housing:** 8 **Library Holdings:** 30,921 **Regional Accreditation:** Southern Association of Colleges and Schools **Credit Hours For Degree:** 62 credit hours, Associates **Professional Accreditation:** ADA, AHIMA, NLN **Intercollegiate Athletics:** Baseball M; Basketball M & W; Cheerleading M & W; Softball W

HOWARD PAYNE UNIVERSITY
1000 Fisk St.
Brownwood, TX 76801-2715
Tel: (325)646-2502; Free: 800-880-4478
Admissions: (325)649-8027
Fax: (325)649-8905
E-mail: enroll@hputx.edu
Web Site: http://www.hputx.edu/
President/CEO: Dr. William N. Ellis
Admissions: Cheryl Mangrum
Financial Aid: Glenda Huff
Type: Comprehensive **Sex:** Coed **Affiliation:** Baptist General Convention of Texas **Scores:** 82% SAT V 400+; 89% SAT M 400+; 47% ACT 18-23; 27% ACT 24-29 **% Accepted:** 59 **Application Deadline:** Rolling **Application Fee:** $0.00 **H.S. Requirements:** High school diploma required; GED accepted **Costs Per Year:** Application fee: $0. Comprehensive fee: $25,644 includes full-time tuition ($18,850), mandatory fees ($1100), and college room and board ($5694). College room only: $2280. Full-time tuition and fees vary according to location and program. Room and board charges vary according to board plan and housing facility. Part-time tuition: $575 per credit hour. Part-time tuition varies according to location and program. Tuition guaranteed not to increase for student's term of enrollment. **Scholarships:** Available **Calendar System:** Semester, Summer Session Available **Enrollment:** FT 939, PT 278, Grad FT 3, Grad PT 12 **Faculty:** FT 78, PT 66 **Student-Faculty Ratio:** 10:1 **Exams:** Other, SAT I or ACT. ACT essay not being used. SAT essay not being used. **% Receiving Financial Aid:** 78 **% Residing in College-Owned, -Operated, or -Affiliated Housing:** 60 **Final Year or Final Semester Residency Requirement:** No **Library Holdings:** 129,902 **Regional Accreditation:** Southern Association of Colleges and Schools **Credit Hours For Degree:** 64 semester hours, Associates; 128 semester hours, Bachelors **Professional Accreditation:** CSWE, NASM **Intercollegiate Athletics:** Baseball M; Basketball M & W; Cross-Country Running M & W; Football M; Soccer M & W; Softball W; Tennis M & W; Volleyball W

HUSTON-TILLOTSON UNIVERSITY
900 Chicon St.
Austin, TX 78702-2795
Tel: (512)505-3000
Admissions: (512)505-3029
Fax: (512)505-3190
E-mail: slstinson@htu.edu
Web Site: http://www.htu.edu/
President/CEO: Dr. Larry L. Earvin, PhD
Admissions: Shakitha Stinson
Financial Aid: Antonio Holloway
Type: Four-Year College **Sex:** Coed **Affiliation:** interdenominational **Scores:** 52% SAT V 400+; 54% SAT M 400+; 28% ACT 18-23; 3% ACT 24-29 **% Accepted:** 48 **Admission Plans:** Deferred Admission **Application Deadline:** July 1 **Application Fee:** $25.00 **H.S. Requirements:** High school diploma required; GED accepted **Costs Per Year:** Application fee: $25. Comprehensive fee: $18,124 includes full-time tuition ($9450), mandatory fees ($1984), and college room and board ($6690). College room only: $2880. Full-time tuition and fees vary according to course load. Room and board charges vary according to housing facility. Part-time tuition: $315 per credit hour. Part-time mandatory fees: $138 per credit hour. Part-time tuition and fees vary according to course load. **Scholarships:** Available **Calendar System:** Semester, Summer Session Available **Enrollment:** FT 808, PT 36, Grad PT 38 **Faculty:** FT 40, PT 40 **Student-Faculty Ratio:** 16:1 **Exams:** SAT I or ACT. ACT essay not being used. SAT essay not being used. **% Receiving Financial Aid:** 87 **% Residing in College-Owned, -Operated, or -Affiliated Housing:** 41 **Library Holdings:** 93,034 **Regional Accreditation:** Southern Association of Colleges and Schools **Credit Hours For Degree:** 120 credit hours, Bachelors **ROTC:** Army, Navy **Intercollegiate Athletics:** Baseball M; Basketball M & W; Cross-Country Running W; Soccer M & W; Softball W; Track and Field M & W; Volleyball W

ITT TECHNICAL INSTITUTE (ARLINGTON)
551 Ryan Plaza Dr.
Arlington, TX 76011
Tel: (817)794-5100
Fax: (817)275-8446
Web Site: http://www.itt-tech.edu/
President/CEO: Kim Horn
Type: Two-Year College **Sex:** Coed **Affiliation:** ITT Educational Services, Inc. **H.S. Requirements:** High school diploma required; GED accepted **Scholarships:** Available **Calendar System:** Quarter, Summer Session Not available **Credit Hours For Degree:** 96 credit hours, Associates **Professional Accreditation:** ACICS

ITT TECHNICAL INSTITUTE (AUSTIN)
6330 East Hwy. 290, Ste. 150
Austin, TX 78723-1061
Tel: (512)467-6800; Free: 800-431-0677
Web Site: http://www.itt-tech.edu/
President/CEO: Doug Howard
Type: Two-Year College **Sex:** Coed **Affiliation:** ITT Educational Services, Inc. **H.S. Requirements:** High school diploma required; GED accepted **Scholarships:** Available **Calendar System:** Quarter, Summer Session Not available **Professional Accreditation:** ACICS

ITT TECHNICAL INSTITUTE (DESOTO)
921 West Belt Line Rd.
Ste. 181
DeSoto, TX 75115
Tel: (972)274-8600; Free: 877-854-5728
Web Site: http://www.itt-tech.edu/
Type: Two-Year College **Sex:** Coed **Professional Accreditation:** ACICS

ITT TECHNICAL INSTITUTE (HOUSTON)
2950 South Gessner
Houston, TX 77063-3751
Tel: (713)952-2294
Web Site: http://www.itt-tech.edu/
President/CEO: Cathy Clark
Type: Two-Year College **Sex:** Coed **Affiliation:** ITT Educational Services, Inc. **H.S. Requirements:** High school diploma required; GED accepted **Scholarships:** Available **Calendar System:** Quarter, Summer Session Not available **Professional Accreditation:** ACICS

ITT TECHNICAL INSTITUTE (HOUSTON)
15621 North Freeway
Houston, TX 77090
Tel: (281)873-0512
Fax: (281)873-0518
Web Site: http://www.itt-tech.edu/
President/CEO: Kathy Shearer
Type: Two-Year College **Sex:** Coed **Affiliation:** ITT Educational Services, Inc. **H.S. Requirements:** High school diploma required; GED accepted **Scholarships:** Available **Calendar System:** Quarter, Summer Session Not available **Credit Hours For Degree:** 96 credit hours, Associates **Professional Accreditation:** ACICS

ITT TECHNICAL INSTITUTE (RICHARDSON)
2101 Waterview Parkway
Richardson, TX 75080
Tel: (972)690-9100; Free: 888-488-5761
Web Site: http://www.itt-tech.edu/
President/CEO: Donna Clarkin
Type: Two-Year College **Sex:** Coed **Affiliation:** ITT Educational Services, Inc. **H.S. Requirements:** High school diploma required; GED accepted **Scholarships:** Available **Calendar System:** Quarter, Summer Session Not available **Credit Hours For Degree:** 96 credit hours, Associates **Professional Accreditation:** ACICS

ITT TECHNICAL INSTITUTE (SAN ANTONIO)
5700 Northwest Parkway
San Antonio, TX 78249-3303
Tel: (210)694-4612; Free: 800-880-0570
Fax: (210)694-4651
Web Site: http://www.itt-tech.edu/
President/CEO: Kathryn Barrera
Type: Two-Year College **Sex:** Coed **Affiliation:** ITT Educational Services, Inc. **H.S. Requirements:** High school diploma required; GED accepted **Scholarships:** Available **Calendar System:** Quarter, Summer Session Not available **Credit Hours For Degree:** 96 credit hours, Associates **Professional Accreditation:** ACICS

ITT TECHNICAL INSTITUTE (WEBSTER)
1001 Magnolia Ave.
Webster, TX 77598
Tel: (281)316-4700
Web Site: http://www.itt-tech.edu/
President/CEO: Aaron Armendariz
Type: Two-Year College **Sex:** Coed **Affiliation:** ITT Educational Services, Inc. **H.S. Requirements:** High school diploma required; GED accepted **Scholarships:** Available **Calendar System:** Quarter, Summer Session Not available **Professional Accreditation:** ACICS

JACKSONVILLE COLLEGE
105 B J Albritton Dr.
Jacksonville, TX 75766-4759
Tel: (903)586-2518; Free: 800-256-8522
E-mail: admissions@jacksonville-college.org
Web Site: http://www.jacksonville-college.edu/
President/CEO: Edwin Crank
Admissions: Melissa Walles
Financial Aid: Paul Galyean
Type: Two-Year College **Sex:** Coed **Affiliation:** Baptist **% Accepted:** 41 **Admission Plans:** Open Admission; Early Admission **Application Deadline:** August 15 **Application Fee:** $15.00 **H.S. Requirements:** High school diploma required; GED accepted **Scholarships:** Available **Calendar System:** Semester, Summer Session Available **Enrollment:** FT 220, PT 80 **Faculty:** FT 10, PT 14 **Student-Faculty Ratio:** 16:1 **Exams:** ACT, Other, SAT I. **% Residing in College-Owned, -Operated, or -Affiliated Housing:** 39 **Library Holdings:** 22,000 **Regional Accreditation:** Southern Association of Colleges and Schools **Credit Hours For Degree:** 64 semester hours, Associates **Intercollegiate Athletics:** Basketball M & W; Volleyball W

JARVIS CHRISTIAN COLLEGE
PO Box 1470
Hawkins, TX 75765-1470
Tel: (903)769-5700
Admissions: (903)769-5734
Fax: (903)769-4842
E-mail: robert.harper@jarvis.edu
Web Site: http://www.jarvis.edu/
President/CEO: Dr. Cornell Thomas
Admissions: Robert Harper
Financial Aid: Alice Copeland
Type: Four-Year College **Sex:** Coed **Affiliation:** Christian Church (Disciples of Christ) **Scores:** 28% SAT V 400+; 22% SAT M 400+; 13% ACT 18-23 **% Accepted:** 23 **Admission Plans:** Open Admission **Application Deadline:** August 1 **Application Fee:** $50.00 **H.S. Requirements:** High school diploma required; GED accepted **Costs Per Year:** Application fee: $50. One-time mandatory fee: $25. Comprehensive fee: $16,315 includes full-time tuition ($8520), mandatory fees ($1080), and college room and board ($6715). College room only: $2997. Room and board charges vary according to housing facility. Part-time tuition: $355 per semester hour. Part-time mandatory fees: $1080 per term. Part-time tuition and fees vary according to course load. **Scholarships:** Available **Calendar System:** Semester, Summer Session Available **Enrollment:** FT 614, PT 14 **Faculty:** FT 27, PT 22 **Student-Faculty Ratio:** 13:1 **Exams:** SAT I or ACT. **% Receiving Financial Aid:** 100 **% Residing in College-Owned, -Operated, or -Affiliated Housing:** 98 **Library Holdings:** 56,894 **Regional Accreditation:** Southern Association of Colleges and Schools **Credit Hours For Degree:** 124 semester hours, Bachelors **Professional Accreditation:** ACBSP **Intercollegiate Athletics:** Baseball M; Basketball M & W; Cheerleading W; Volleyball W

KAPLAN COLLEGE, ARLINGTON
2241 South Watson Rd.
Arlington, TX 76010
Free: (866)249-2074
Web Site: http://www.kc-arlington.com/

Type: Two-Year College **Sex:** Coed **H.S. Requirements:** High school diploma required; GED accepted **Professional Accreditation:** COE

KAPLAN COLLEGE, DALLAS
12005 Ford Rd.
Ste. 100
Dallas, TX 75234
Tel: (972)385-1446; Free: 800-525-1446
Fax: (972)385-0641
Web Site: http://www.kc-dallas.com/
President/CEO: Michelle Taylor
Type: Two-Year College **Sex:** Coed **H.S. Requirements:** High school diploma required; GED accepted **Professional Accreditation:** COE

KD STUDIO
2600 Stemmons Freeway, No. 117
Dallas, TX 75207
Tel: (214)638-0484
Fax: (214)630-5140
E-mail: tataylor@kdstudio.com
Web Site: http://www.kdstudio.com/
President/CEO: Kathy Tyner
Admissions: T. A. Taylor
Type: Two-Year College **Sex:** Coed **Admission Plans:** Open Admission; Deferred Admission **Application Deadline:** Rolling **Application Fee:** $100.00 **H.S. Requirements:** High school diploma required; GED accepted **Scholarships:** Available **Calendar System:** Semester, Summer Session Not available **Enrollment:** FT 102 **Faculty:** FT 21 **Student-Faculty Ratio:** 5:1 **Library Holdings:** 800 **Credit Hours For Degree:** 70 credits, Associates **Professional Accreditation:** NAST

KILGORE COLLEGE
1100 Broadway Blvd.
Kilgore, TX 75662-3299
Tel: (903)984-8531
Fax: (903)983-8607
E-mail: register@kilgore.cc.tx.us
Web Site: http://www.kilgore.edu/
President/CEO: William M. Holda
Admissions: Jeanna Centers
Type: Two-Year College **Sex:** Coed **Admission Plans:** Open Admission; Early Admission **Application Deadline:** Rolling **Application Fee:** $0.00 **H.S. Requirements:** High school diploma required; GED accepted **Costs Per Year:** Application fee: $0. Area resident tuition: $552 full-time, $23 per semester hour part-time. State resident tuition: $1776 full-time, $74 per semester hour part-time. Nonresident tuition: $2640 full-time, $110 per semester hour part-time. Mandatory fees: $528 full-time, $22 per semester hour part-time. College room and board: $3980. **Scholarships:** Available **Calendar System:** Semester, Summer Session Available **Enrollment:** FT 2,977, PT 3,398 **Faculty:** FT 139, PT 142 **Student-Faculty Ratio:** 22:1 **% Residing in College-Owned, -Operated, or -Affiliated Housing:** 7 **Final Year or Final Semester Residency Requirement:** No **Library Holdings:** 65,000 **Regional Accreditation:** Southern Association of Colleges and Schools **Credit Hours For Degree:** 62 credits, Associates **Professional Accreditation:** ARCEST, AAMAE, APTA, JRCERT, NAACLS, NLN **Intercollegiate Athletics:** Basketball M & W; Cheerleading M & W; Football M

LAMAR INSTITUTE OF TECHNOLOGY
855 East Lavaca
Beaumont, TX 77705
Tel: (409)880-8321; Free: 800-950-6989
Web Site: http://www.lit.edu/
President/CEO: Dr. Paul Szuch
Type: Two-Year College **Sex:** Coed **Costs Per Year:** One-time mandatory fee: $10. State resident tuition: $2640 full-time, $88 per credit hour part-time. Nonresident tuition: $11,010 full-time, $367 per credit hour part-time. Mandatory fees: $1340 full-time, $165 per credit hour part-time, $426 per term part-time. Full-time tuition and fees vary according to course load. Part-time tuition and fees vary according to course load. College room and board: $6290. College room only: $4190. **Scholarships:** Available **Calendar System:** Semester **Regional Accreditation:** Southern Association of Colleges and Schools **Professional Accreditation:** ADA, AHIMA, CARC

LAMAR STATE COLLEGE—ORANGE
410 Front St.
Orange, TX 77630
Tel: (409)883-7750
Admissions: (409)882-3362
Fax: (409)882-3374
Web Site: http://www.lsco.edu/
President/CEO: Dr. Michael Shahan
Admissions: Kerry Olson
Type: Two-Year College **Sex:** Coed **Affiliation:** Texas State University System **Admission Plans:** Open Admission **Application Deadline:** Rolling **Application Fee:** $0.00 **H.S. Requirements:** High school diploma required; GED accepted **Scholarships:** Available **Calendar System:** Semester, Summer Session Available **Enrollment:** FT 929, PT 1,076 **Faculty:** FT 50, PT 46 **Student-Faculty Ratio:** 19:1 **Library Holdings:** 71,092 **Regional Accreditation:** Southern Association of Colleges and Schools **Credit Hours For Degree:** 62 credit hours, Associates **Professional Accreditation:** ADA, NAACLS

LAMAR STATE COLLEGE—PORT ARTHUR
PO Box 310
Port Arthur, TX 77641-0310
Tel: (409)983-4921; Free: 800-477-5872
Admissions: (409)984-6342
Fax: (409)984-6032
E-mail: connie.nicholas@lamarpa.edu
Web Site: http://www.lamarpa.edu/
President/CEO: W. Sam Monroe
Admissions: Connie Nicholas
Financial Aid: Diane Hargett
Type: Two-Year College **Sex:** Coed **Affiliation:** Texas State University System **% Accepted:** 61 **Admission Plans:** Open Admission; Early Admission; Deferred Admission **Application Deadline:** Rolling **Application Fee:** $0.00 **H.S. Requirements:** High school diploma or equivalent not required **Scholarships:** Available **Calendar System:** Semester, Summer Session Available **Enrollment:** FT 980, PT 1,550 **Faculty:** FT 64, PT 61 **Student-Faculty Ratio:** 13:1 **Library Holdings:** 43,726 **Regional Accreditation:** Southern Association of Colleges and Schools **Credit Hours For Degree:** 64 credit hours, Associates **ROTC:** Army **Professional Accreditation:** ARCEST, ACBSP

LAMAR UNIVERSITY
4400 Martin Luther King Parkway
Beaumont, TX 77710
Tel: (409)880-7011
Admissions: (409)880-8888
Fax: (409)880-8463
E-mail: admissions@lamar.edu
Web Site: http://www.lamar.edu/
President/CEO: Dr. James M. Simmons
Admissions: Melissa Chesser
Type: University **Sex:** Coed **Affiliation:** Texas State University System **Scores:** 79.92% SAT V 400+; 84.64% SAT M 400+; 49.68% ACT 18-23; 11.83% ACT 24-29 **% Accepted:** 59 **Admission Plans:** Early Admission **Application Deadline:** August 1 **Application Fee:** $0.00 **H.S. Requirements:** High school diploma required; GED accepted **Costs Per Year:** Application fee: $0. State resident tuition: $4740 full-time, $158 per credit hour part-time. Nonresident tuition: $14,040 full-time, $468 per credit hour part-time. Mandatory fees: $2204 full-time. College room and board: $6900. College room only: $4500. **Scholarships:** Available **Calendar System:** Semester, Summer Session Available **Enrollment:** FT 6,864, PT 2,741, Grad FT 744, Grad PT 3,643 **Faculty:** FT 404, PT 179 **Student-Faculty Ratio:** 20:1 **Exams:** SAT I or ACT, SAT II. **% Receiving Financial Aid:** 54 **Library Holdings:** 526,180 **Regional Accreditation:** Southern Association of Colleges and Schools **Credit Hours For Degree:** 60 semester hours, Associates; 124 semester hours, Bachelors **Professional Accreditation:** AACSB, ABET, AAFCS, ACF, ADtA, ASLHA, CSWE, JRCERT, NASM, NCATE, NLN **Intercollegiate Athletics:** Baseball M; Basketball M & W; Cheerleading M & W; Cross-Country Running M & W; Football M; Golf M & W; Soccer W; Tennis M & W; Track and Field M & W; Volleyball W

LAREDO COMMUNITY COLLEGE
West End Washington St.
Laredo, TX 78040-4395

Tel: (956)722-0521
Admissions: (956)721-5394
Fax: (956)721-5493
Web Site: http://www.laredo.edu/
President/CEO: Juan L. Maldonado
Admissions: Josie Soliz
Type: Two-Year College **Sex:** Coed **% Accepted:** 100 **Admission Plans:** Open Admission; Early Admission; Deferred Admission **Application Deadline:** Rolling **Application Fee:** $0.00 **Scholarships:** Available **Calendar System:** Semester, Summer Session Available **Enrollment:** FT 3,044, PT 5,108 **Faculty:** FT 203, PT 140 **Student-Faculty Ratio:** 18:1 **Exams:** ACT, SAT I. **Library Holdings:** 88,006 **Regional Accreditation:** Southern Association of Colleges and Schools **Credit Hours For Degree:** 60 credit hours, Associates **Professional Accreditation:** AOTA, APTA, JRCERT, NAACLS, NLN **Intercollegiate Athletics:** Baseball M; Tennis M & W; Volleyball W

LEE COLLEGE
PO Box 818
Baytown, TX 77522-0818
Tel: (281)427-5611; Free: 800-621-8724
Fax: (281)425-6831
E-mail: bgriffit@lee.edu
Web Site: http://www.lee.edu/
President/CEO: Dr. Michael Murphy
Admissions: Becki Griffith
Type: Two-Year College **Sex:** Coed **Admission Plans:** Open Admission; Early Admission; Deferred Admission **Application Deadline:** Rolling **Application Fee:** $0.00 **H.S. Requirements:** High school diploma or equivalent not required **Scholarships:** Available **Calendar System:** Semester, Summer Session Available **Enrollment:** FT 1,795, PT 3,552 **Faculty:** FT 185, PT 214 **Student-Faculty Ratio:** 14:1 **Library Holdings:** 100,000 **Regional Accreditation:** Southern Association of Colleges and Schools **Credit Hours For Degree:** 60 credit hours, Associates **ROTC:** Army **Professional Accreditation:** AHIMA, JRCEMT, NLN **Intercollegiate Athletics:** Basketball M; Tennis W; Volleyball W

LETOURNEAU UNIVERSITY
PO Box 7001
Longview, TX 75607-7001
Tel: (903)233-3000; Free: 800-759-8811
Admissions: (903)233-3400
Fax: (903)233-3411
E-mail: admissions@letu.edu
Web Site: http://www.letu.edu/
President/CEO: Dr. Dale A Lunsford
Admissions: James Townsend
Financial Aid: Lindy Hall
Type: Comprehensive **Sex:** Coed **Affiliation:** nondenominational **Scores:** 96.93% SAT V 400+; 100% SAT M 400+; 30% ACT 18-23; 45.56% ACT 24-29 **% Accepted:** 70 **Admission Plans:** Deferred Admission **Application Deadline:** Rolling **Application Fee:** $25.00 **H.S. Requirements:** High school diploma required; GED accepted **Costs Per Year:** Application fee: $25. Comprehensive fee: $30,370 includes full-time tuition ($21,510), mandatory fees ($470), and college room and board ($8390). Room and board charges vary according to board plan. Part-time tuition: $858 per credit hour. Part-time tuition varies according to course load. **Scholarships:** Available **Calendar System:** Semester, Summer Session Available **Enrollment:** FT 2,899, PT 199, Grad FT 288 **Faculty:** FT 70, PT 184 **Student-Faculty Ratio:** 23:1 **Exams:** SAT I or ACT. ACT essay used for placement. SAT essay used for placement. **% Receiving Financial Aid:** 77 **% Residing in College-Owned, -Operated, or -Affiliated Housing:** 75 **Regional Accreditation:** Southern Association of Colleges and Schools **Credit Hours For Degree:** 63 semester hours, Associates; 124 semester hours, Bachelors **Professional Accreditation:** ABET **Intercollegiate Athletics:** Baseball M; Basketball M & W; Cross-Country Running M & W; Golf M & W; Soccer M & W; Softball W; Tennis M & W; Volleyball W

LON MORRIS COLLEGE
800 College Ave.
Jacksonville, TX 75766
Tel: (903)589-4000; Free: 800-259-5753
Admissions: (903)589-4059
Fax: (903)586-8562
Web Site: http://www.lonmorris.edu/
President/CEO: Dr. Miles McCall
Admissions: Rafael Gonzalez
Type: Two-Year College **Sex:** Coed **Affiliation:** United Methodist **Scores:** 61% SAT V 400+; 66% SAT M 400+; 34% ACT 18-23; 4% ACT 24-29 **Admission Plans:** Deferred Admission **Application Deadline:** Rolling **Application Fee:** $35.00 **H.S. Requirements:** High school diploma required; GED accepted **Scholarships:** Available **Calendar System:** Semester, Summer Session Available **Enrollment:** FT 747, PT 68 **Faculty:** FT 42, PT 30 **Student-Faculty Ratio:** 15:1 **Exams:** ACT, SAT I or ACT, SAT I. ACT essay used for admission. SAT essay used for admission. ACT essay used for advising. SAT essay used for advising. ACT essay used for placement. SAT essay used for placement. **% Residing in College-Owned, -Operated, or -Affiliated Housing:** 75 **Library Holdings:** 26,000 **Regional Accreditation:** Southern Association of Colleges and Schools **Credit Hours For Degree:** 62 credits, Associates **Intercollegiate Athletics:** Baseball M; Basketball M & W; Cheerleading M & W; Cross-Country Running M & W; Football M; Golf M & W; Soccer M & W; Softball W

LONESTAR COLLEGE—CY-FAIR
9191 Barker Cypress Rd.
Cypress, TX 77433-1383
Tel: (281)290-3200
E-mail: cfc.info@lonestar.edu
Web Site: http://www.lonestar.edu/cyfair
President/CEO: Dr. Audre Levy
Type: Two-Year College **Sex:** Coed **Affiliation:** Lone Star College System **% Accepted:** 100 **Admission Plans:** Open Admission; Early Admission **Application Fee:** $0.00 **H.S. Requirements:** High school diploma required; GED accepted **Costs Per Year:** Application fee: $0. Area resident tuition: $912 full-time, $38 per credit hour part-time. State resident tuition: $2592 full-time, $108 per credit hour part-time. Nonresident tuition: $2952 full-time, $123 per credit hour part-time. Mandatory fees: $288 full-time, $11 per credit hour part-time, $12 per term part-time. Full-time tuition and fees vary according to course load. Part-time tuition and fees vary according to course load. **Calendar System:** Semester, Summer Session Available **Enrollment:** FT 4,208, PT 10,967 **Faculty:** FT 636, PT 1,157 **Final Year or Final Semester Residency Requirement:** No **Regional Accreditation:** Southern Association of Colleges and Schools **Credit Hours For Degree:** 62 credit hours, Associates

LONESTAR COLLEGE—KINGWOOD
20000 Kingwood Dr.
Kingwood, TX 77339-3801
Tel: (281)312-1600
Admissions: (281)312-1525
Fax: (281)312-1477
E-mail: kingwoodadvising@lonestar.edu
Web Site: http://www.lonestar.edu/kingwood.htm
President/CEO: Dr. Katherine Persson
Financial Aid: Shannon Infante
Type: Two-Year College **Sex:** Coed **Affiliation:** Lone Star College System **% Accepted:** 100 **Admission Plans:** Open Admission; Early Admission **Application Deadline:** Rolling **Application Fee:** $0.00 **H.S. Requirements:** High school diploma required; GED accepted **Costs Per Year:** Application fee: $0. One-time mandatory fee: $24. Area resident tuition: $1200 full-time. State resident tuition: $2880 full-time. Nonresident tuition: $3240 full-time. Mandatory fees: $528 full-time. Full-time tuition and fees vary according to program. **Scholarships:** Available **Calendar System:** Semester, Summer Session Available **Enrollment:** FT 2,364, PT 6,929 **Faculty:** FT 499, PT 755 **Final Year or Final Semester Residency Requirement:** No **Regional Accreditation:** Southern Association of Colleges and Schools **Credit Hours For Degree:** 62 credit hours, Associates **Professional Accreditation:** ADA, AOTA, CARC

LONESTAR COLLEGE—MONTGOMERY
3200 College Park Dr.
Conroe, TX 77384
Tel: (936)273-7000
Admissions: (936)273-7236
Fax: (936)273-7234
E-mail: mc.advising@lonestar.edu
Web Site: http://www.lonestar.edu/montgomery
President/CEO: Dr. Austin Lane

Type: Two-Year College **Sex:** Coed **Affiliation:** Lone Star College System **% Accepted:** 100 **Admission Plans:** Open Admission; Early Admission **Application Deadline:** Rolling **H.S. Requirements:** High school diploma required; GED accepted **Costs Per Year:** Area resident tuition: $912 full-time, $38 per credit hour part-time. State resident tuition: $2592 full-time, $108 per credit hour part-time. Nonresident tuition: $2952 full-time, $123 per credit hour part-time. Mandatory fees: $288 full-time, $11 per credit hour part-time, $12 per term part-time. Full-time tuition and fees vary according to course load. Part-time tuition and fees vary according to course load. **Scholarships:** Available **Calendar System:** Semester, Summer Session Available **Enrollment:** FT 3,113, PT 7,849 **Faculty:** FT 525, PT 797 **Regional Accreditation:** Southern Association of Colleges and Schools **Credit Hours For Degree:** 62 credit hours, Associates **Professional Accreditation:** APTA

LONESTAR COLLEGE—NORTH HARRIS

2700 W. W. Thorne Dr.
Houston, TX 77073-3499
Tel: (281)618-5400
Admissions: (281)618-5410
E-mail: nhcounselor@lonestar.edu
Web Site: http://www.lonestar.edu/northharris
President/CEO: Dr. Stephen C. Head

Type: Two-Year College **Sex:** Coed **Affiliation:** Lone Star College System **% Accepted:** 100 **Admission Plans:** Open Admission; Early Admission **Application Deadline:** Rolling **Application Fee:** $0.00 **H.S. Requirements:** High school diploma required; GED accepted **Costs Per Year:** Application fee: $0. Area resident tuition: $912 full-time, $38 per credit hour part-time. State resident tuition: $2592 full-time, $108 per credit hour part-time. Nonresident tuition: $2952 full-time, $123 per credit hour part-time. Mandatory fees: $11 per credit hour part-time, $12 per term part-time. Full-time tuition varies according to course load. Part-time tuition and fees vary according to course load. **Scholarships:** Available **Calendar System:** Semester, Summer Session Available **Enrollment:** FT 2,714, PT 10,835 **Faculty:** FT 748, PT 861 **Regional Accreditation:** Southern Association of Colleges and Schools **Credit Hours For Degree:** 62 credits, Associates **Professional Accreditation:** AHIMA, MACTE, NLN

LONESTAR COLLEGE—TOMBALL

30555 Tomball Parkway
Tomball, TX 77375-4036
Tel: (281)351-3300
Admissions: (281)351-3310
Fax: (281)351-3384
E-mail: tcinfo@lonestar.edu
Web Site: http://www.lonestar.edu/tomball
President/CEO: Dr. Susan Karr

Type: Two-Year College **Sex:** Coed **Affiliation:** Lone Star College System **% Accepted:** 100 **Admission Plans:** Open Admission; Early Admission **Application Deadline:** Rolling **Application Fee:** $0.00 **H.S. Requirements:** High school diploma required; GED accepted **Costs Per Year:** Application fee: $0. Area resident tuition: $912 full-time, $38 per credit hour part-time. State resident tuition: $2592 full-time, $108 per credit hour part-time. Nonresident tuition: $2952 full-time, $123 per credit hour part-time. Mandatory fees: $288 full-time, $11 per credit hour part-time, $12 per term part-time. Full-time tuition and fees vary according to class time and program. Part-time tuition and fees vary according to class time and program. **Scholarships:** Available **Calendar System:** Semester, Summer Session Available **Enrollment:** FT 2,137, PT 7,728 **Faculty:** FT 470, PT 558 **Regional Accreditation:** Southern Association of Colleges and Schools **Credit Hours For Degree:** 62 credit hours, Associates **Professional Accreditation:** AOTA

LUBBOCK CHRISTIAN UNIVERSITY

5601 19th St.
Lubbock, TX 79407-2099
Tel: (806)796-8800; Free: 800-933-7601
Admissions: (806)720-7156
Fax: (806)796-8917
E-mail: admissions@lcu.edu
Web Site: http://www.lcu.edu/
President/CEO: Dr. L. Ken Jones
Admissions: Charles Webb
Financial Aid: Amy Hardesty

Type: Comprehensive **Sex:** Coed **Affiliation:** Church of Christ **Scores:** 88.64% SAT V 400+; 54.64% ACT 18-23; 24.6% ACT 24-29 **% Accepted:** 66 **Application Deadline:** August 1 **Application Fee:** $25.00 **H.S. Requirements:** High school diploma required; GED accepted **Costs Per Year:** Application fee: $25. Comprehensive fee: $21,302 includes full-time tuition ($14,100), mandatory fees ($1020), and college room and board ($6182). Full-time tuition and fees vary according to degree level and program. Room and board charges vary according to board plan and housing facility. Part-time tuition: $455 per semester hour. Part-time mandatory fees: $445 per term. Part-time tuition and fees vary according to course load, degree level, and program. **Scholarships:** Available **Calendar System:** Semester, Summer Session Available **Enrollment:** FT 1,278, PT 263, Grad FT 87, Grad PT 278 **Faculty:** FT 85, PT 86 **Student-Faculty Ratio:** 12:1 **Exams:** SAT I or ACT. ACT essay used for advising. SAT essay used for advising. ACT essay used for placement. SAT essay used for placement. **% Receiving Financial Aid:** 73 **% Residing in College-Owned, -Operated, or -Affiliated Housing:** 28 **Final Year or Final Semester Residency Requirement:** No **Library Holdings:** 172,464 **Regional Accreditation:** Southern Association of Colleges and Schools **Credit Hours For Degree:** 126 semester hours, Bachelors **ROTC:** Army, Air Force **Professional Accreditation:** CSWE, NLN **Intercollegiate Athletics:** Baseball M; Basketball M & W; Cheerleading M & W; Cross-Country Running M & W; Golf M & W; Softball W; Track and Field M & W; Volleyball W

MCLENNAN COMMUNITY COLLEGE

1400 College Dr.
Waco, TX 76708-1499
Tel: (254)299-8622
Admissions: (254)299-8000
E-mail: vjefferson@mclennan.edu
Web Site: http://www.mclennan.edu/
President/CEO: Johnette McKown
Admissions: Dr. Vivian G. Jefferson

Type: Two-Year College **Sex:** Coed **% Accepted:** 100 **Admission Plans:** Open Admission; Early Admission **Application Deadline:** Rolling **Application Fee:** $0.00 **H.S. Requirements:** High school diploma required; GED accepted **Costs Per Year:** Application fee: $0. Area resident tuition: $1608 full-time, $67 per credit hour part-time. State resident tuition: $1896 full-time, $79 per credit hour part-time. Nonresident tuition: $3048 full-time, $127 per credit hour part-time. Mandatory fees: $216 full-time, $9 per credit hour part-time. Full-time tuition and fees vary according to location. Part-time tuition and fees vary according to location. **Scholarships:** Available **Calendar System:** Semester, Summer Session Available **Enrollment:** FT 3,467, PT 4,327 **Exams:** Other. **Library Holdings:** 93,000 **Regional Accreditation:** Southern Association of Colleges and Schools **Credit Hours For Degree:** 60 semester hours, Associates **ROTC:** Air Force **Professional Accreditation:** AHIMA, APTA, CARC, JRCERT, NAACLS, NLN **Intercollegiate Athletics:** Baseball M; Basketball M & W; Golf M & W; Softball W

MCMURRY UNIVERSITY

South 14th and Sayles
Abilene, TX 79697
Tel: (325)793-3800; Free: 800-477-0077
Admissions: (325)793-4700
Fax: (325)691-6599
E-mail: admissions@mcm.edu
Web Site: http://www.mcm.edu/
President/CEO: Dr. John H. Russell
Financial Aid: Rachel Atkins

Type: Four-Year College **Sex:** Coed **Affiliation:** United Methodist **Scores:** 83% SAT V 400+; 86% SAT M 400+; 46% ACT 18-23; 25% ACT 24-29 **% Accepted:** 57 **Admission Plans:** Deferred Admission **Application Deadline:** August 15 **Application Fee:** $20.00 **H.S. Requirements:** High school diploma required; GED accepted **Costs Per Year:** Application fee: $20. One-time mandatory fee: $150. Comprehensive fee: $25,962 includes full-time tuition ($18,345), mandatory fees ($860), and college room and board ($6757). College room only: $3264. Full-time tuition and fees vary according to course load. Room and board charges vary according to board plan and housing facility. Part-time tuition: $570 per semester hour. Part-time tuition varies according to course load. **Scholarships:** Available **Calendar System:** Semester, Summer Session Available **Enrollment:** FT 1,216, PT 293 **Faculty:** FT 77, PT 68 **Student-Faculty Ratio:** 14:1 **Exams:** SAT I or ACT. **% Receiving Financial Aid:** 84 **% Residing in College-Owned, -Operated, or -Affiliated Housing:** 48 **Final Year or Final Semester**

Residency Requirement: Yes **Library Holdings:** 179,583 **Regional Accreditation:** Southern Association of Colleges and Schools **Credit Hours For Degree:** 120 semester hours, Bachelors **Professional Accreditation:** AACN **Intercollegiate Athletics:** Baseball M; Basketball M & W; Cross-Country Running M & W; Football M; Golf M & W; Soccer M & W; Swimming and Diving M & W; Tennis M & W; Track and Field M & W; Volleyball W

MIDLAND COLLEGE
3600 North Garfield
Midland, TX 79705-6399
Tel: (432)685-4500
Admissions: (432)685-5502
Fax: (432)685-4714
E-mail: rgibbs@midland.edu
Web Site: http://www.midland.edu/
President/CEO: Dr. Stephen Thomas
Admissions: Ryan Gibbs
Financial Aid: Latisha Williams
Type: Four-Year College **Sex:** Coed **Admission Plans:** Open Admission **Application Deadline:** Rolling **Application Fee:** $0.00 **H.S. Requirements:** High school diploma or equivalent not required. For nursing, respiratory therapy, radiological technology programs: High school diploma required; GED accepted **Costs Per Year:** Application fee: $0. Area resident tuition: $1800 full-time, $102 per credit hour part-time. State resident tuition: $2460 full-time, $124 per credit hour part-time. Nonresident tuition: $3450 full-time, $157 per credit hour part-time. Mandatory fees: $392 full-time, $65 per credit hour part-time. Full-time tuition and fees vary according to course load, program, and reciprocity agreements. Part-time tuition and fees vary according to course load. College room and board: $3900. **Scholarships:** Available **Calendar System:** Semester, Summer Session Not available **Enrollment:** FT 1,756, PT 3,983 **Faculty:** FT 128, PT 141 **Student-Faculty Ratio:** 18:1 **Library Holdings:** 65,760 **Regional Accreditation:** Southern Association of Colleges and Schools **Credit Hours For Degree:** 62 semester hours, Associates; 127 semester hours, Bachelors **Professional Accreditation:** AHIMA, CARC, JRCERT, NLN

MIDWESTERN STATE UNIVERSITY
3410 Taft Blvd.
Wichita Falls, TX 76308
Tel: (940)397-4000; Free: 800-842-1922
Admissions: (940)397-4334
Fax: (940)397-4302
E-mail: admissions@mwsu.edu
Web Site: http://www.mwsu.edu/
President/CEO: Dr. Jesse Rogers
Admissions: Barbara Merkle
Financial Aid: Kathy Pennartz
Type: Comprehensive **Sex:** Coed **Scores:** 93.5% SAT V 400+; 96.93% SAT M 400+; 62.16% ACT 18-23; 22.31% ACT 24-29 **% Accepted:** 88 **Admission Plans:** Early Action **Application Deadline:** August 7 **Application Fee:** $25.00 **H.S. Requirements:** High school diploma required; GED accepted **Costs Per Year:** Application fee: $25. State resident tuition: $1500 full-time, $50 per credit hour part-time. Nonresident tuition: $2400 full-time, $80 per credit hour part-time. Mandatory fees: $4726 full-time, $145.60 per credit hour part-time, $179 per term part-time. Full-time tuition and fees vary according to course load, location, and program. Part-time tuition and fees vary according to course load, location, and program. College room and board: $5560. College room only: $2990. Room and board charges vary according to board plan and housing facility. **Scholarships:** Available **Calendar System:** Semester, Summer Session Available **Enrollment:** FT 4,169, PT 1,437, Grad FT 214, Grad PT 521 **Faculty:** FT 241, PT 94 **Student-Faculty Ratio:** 18:1 **Exams:** SAT I or ACT. ACT essay used for admission. SAT essay used for admission. ACT essay used for advising. SAT essay used for advising. ACT essay used for placement. SAT essay used for placement. **% Receiving Financial Aid:** 51 **% Residing in College-Owned, -Operated, or -Affiliated Housing:** 22 **Final Year or Final Semester Residency Requirement:** No **Library Holdings:** 515,252 **Regional Accreditation:** Southern Association of Colleges and Schools **Credit Hours For Degree:** 72 semester hours, Associates; 120 semester hours, Bachelors **ROTC:** Air Force **Professional Accreditation:** ABET, AACN, ADA, ACBSP, CARC, CSWE, NASM, NLN **Intercollegiate Athletics:** Basketball M & W; Cheerleading M & W; Cross-Country Running W; Fencing M & W; Football M; Golf M & W; Soccer M & W; Softball W; Tennis M & W; Volleyball W

MOUNTAIN VIEW COLLEGE
4849 West Illinois Ave.
Dallas, TX 75211-6599
Tel: (214)860-8600
Admissions: (214)860-8680
Fax: (214)860-8570
E-mail: ghall@dcccd.edu
Web Site: http://www.mvc.dcccd.edu/
President/CEO: Felix Zamora
Admissions: Glenda Hall
Type: Two-Year College **Sex:** Coed **Affiliation:** Dallas County Community College District System **Admission Plans:** Open Admission; Early Admission; Deferred Admission **Application Deadline:** Rolling **Application Fee:** $0.00 **H.S. Requirements:** High school diploma required; GED accepted **Scholarships:** Available **Calendar System:** Semester, Summer Session Available **Enrollment:** FT 6,496 **Faculty:** FT 80, PT 230 **Regional Accreditation:** Southern Association of Colleges and Schools **Credit Hours For Degree:** 61 credit hours, Associates **ROTC:** Army **Professional Accreditation:** AHIMA

NAVARRO COLLEGE
3200 West 7th Ave.
Corsicana, TX 75110-4899
Tel: (903)874-6501; Free: 800-628-2776
E-mail: david.edwards@navarrocollege.edu
Web Site: http://www.navarrocollege.edu/
President/CEO: Dr. Richard M. Sanchez
Admissions: David Edwards
Financial Aid: Ed Ephlin
Type: Two-Year College **Sex:** Coed **% Accepted:** 100 **Admission Plans:** Open Admission; Early Admission **H.S. Requirements:** High school diploma required; GED accepted **Scholarships:** Available **Calendar System:** Semester, Summer Session Available **Enrollment:** FT 2,516, PT 1,895 **Faculty:** FT 99, PT 281 **% Residing in College-Owned, -Operated, or -Affiliated Housing:** 25 **Library Holdings:** 40,000 **Regional Accreditation:** Southern Association of Colleges and Schools **Credit Hours For Degree:** 63 semester hours, Associates **Professional Accreditation:** AOTA, NAACLS, NLN **Intercollegiate Athletics:** Baseball M; Basketball M; Football M; Soccer W; Softball W; Volleyball W

NORTH CENTRAL TEXAS COLLEGE
1525 West California St.
Gainesville, TX 76240-4699
Tel: (940)668-7731
Fax: (940)668-6049
E-mail: mcarroll@nctc.edu
Web Site: http://www.nctc.edu/
President/CEO: Eddie Hadlock
Admissions: Melinda Carroll
Financial Aid: Stephanie Martin
Type: Two-Year College **Sex:** Coed **% Accepted:** 100 **Admission Plans:** Open Admission; Early Admission **Application Deadline:** Rolling **H.S. Requirements:** High school diploma required; GED accepted. For some adult applicants: High school diploma or equivalent not required **Costs Per Year:** Area resident tuition: $36 per credit hour part-time. State resident tuition: $70 per credit hour part-time. Nonresident tuition: $116 per credit hour part-time. Mandatory fees: $10 per credit hour part-time. **Scholarships:** Available **Calendar System:** Semester, Summer Session Available **Faculty:** FT 123, PT 272 **Student-Faculty Ratio:** 25:1 **% Residing in College-Owned, -Operated, or -Affiliated Housing:** 1 **Library Holdings:** 44,861 **Regional Accreditation:** Southern Association of Colleges and Schools **Credit Hours For Degree:** 62 credit hours, Associates **ROTC:** Army **Professional Accreditation:** NLN **Intercollegiate Athletics:** Baseball M; Equestrian Sports M & W; Tennis W; Volleyball W

NORTH LAKE COLLEGE
5001 North MacArthur Blvd.
Irving, TX 75038-3899
Tel: (972)273-3000
Admissions: (972)273-3183
Web Site: http://www.northlakecollege.edu/
President/CEO: Dr. Herlinda Glasscock
Type: Two-Year College **Sex:** Coed **Affiliation:** Dallas County Community College District System **Admission Plans:** Open Admission; Early Admis-

sion **Application Deadline:** Rolling **Application Fee:** $0.00 **H.S. Requirements:** High school diploma required; GED accepted **Costs Per Year:** Application fee: $0. Area resident tuition: $41 per credit hour part-time. State resident tuition: $76 per credit hour part-time. Nonresident tuition: $121 per credit hour part-time. **Scholarships:** Available **Calendar System:** Semester, Summer Session Available **Enrollment:** FT 3,171, PT 7,003 **Faculty:** FT 95, PT 409 **Student-Faculty Ratio:** 21:1 **Library Holdings:** 35,000 **Regional Accreditation:** Southern Association of Colleges and Schools **Credit Hours For Degree:** 62 semester hours, Associates **Professional Accreditation:** ACCE **Intercollegiate Athletics:** Baseball M; Basketball M; Cheerleading W; Swimming and Diving M & W; Volleyball W

NORTHEAST TEXAS COMMUNITY COLLEGE

PO Box 1307
Mount Pleasant, TX 75456-1307
Tel: (903)572-1911
Admissions: (903)434-8100
Fax: (903)572-6712
Web Site: http://www.ntcc.edu/
President/CEO: Bradley Johnson
Admissions: Sherry Keys
Financial Aid: Pat Durst
Type: Two-Year College **Sex:** Coed **Admission Plans:** Open Admission; Early Admission **Application Deadline:** Rolling **H.S. Requirements:** High school diploma required; GED accepted **Scholarships:** Available **Calendar System:** Semester, Summer Session Available **Library Holdings:** 24,501 **Regional Accreditation:** Southern Association of Colleges and Schools **Credit Hours For Degree:** 62 credit hours, Associates **Intercollegiate Athletics:** Baseball M; Softball W

NORTHWEST VISTA COLLEGE

3535 North Ellison Dr.
San Antonio, TX 78251
Tel: (210)348-2000
Admissions: (210)486-4000
E-mail: elang@accd.edu
Web Site: http://www.alamo.edu/nvc/
President/CEO: Dr. Jacqueline E. Claunch
Admissions: Dr. Elaine Lang
Type: Two-Year College **Sex:** Coed **Affiliation:** Alamo Community College District System **Application Fee:** $0.00 **Calendar System:** Semester, Summer Session Available **Faculty:** FT 83, PT 414 **Student-Faculty Ratio:** 12:1 **Regional Accreditation:** Southern Association of Colleges and Schools

NORTHWOOD UNIVERSITY, TEXAS CAMPUS

1114 West FM 1382
Cedar Hill, TX 75104-1204
Tel: (972)291-1541; Free: 800-927-9663
Admissions: (972)293-5400
Fax: (972)291-3824
E-mail: txadmit@northwood.edu
Web Site: http://www.northwood.edu/
President/CEO: Keith A Pretty, JD
Admissions: Sylvia Correa
Financial Aid: Shana Thompson
Type: Four-Year College **Sex:** Coed **Affiliation:** Northwood University (MI) **Scores:** 83% SAT V 400+; 88% SAT M 400+; 62% ACT 18-23; 15% ACT 24-29 **% Accepted:** 55 **Admission Plans:** Early Admission; Deferred Admission **Application Deadline:** Rolling **Application Fee:** $25.00 **H.S. Requirements:** High school diploma required; GED accepted **Costs Per Year:** Application fee: $25. One-time mandatory fee: $125. Comprehensive fee: $25,998 includes full-time tuition ($17,430), mandatory fees ($978), and college room and board ($7590). Full-time tuition and fees vary according to class time. Room and board charges vary according to board plan and housing facility. Part-time tuition: $363 per quarter hour. Part-time tuition varies according to class time. **Scholarships:** Available **Calendar System:** Quarter, Summer Session Available **Enrollment:** FT 436, PT 25 **Faculty:** FT 23, PT 18 **Student-Faculty Ratio:** 15:1 **Exams:** SAT I or ACT. **% Receiving Financial Aid:** 70 **% Residing in College-Owned, -Operated, or -Affiliated Housing:** 27 **Regional Accreditation:** North Central Association of Colleges and Schools **Credit Hours For Degree:** 90 credit hours, Associates; 180 credit hours, Bachelors **Intercollegiate Athletics:** Baseball M; Cross-Country Running M & W; Golf M & W; Soccer M & W; Softball W; Track and Field M & W

ODESSA COLLEGE

201 West University Ave.
Odessa, TX 79764-7127
Tel: (432)335-6400
Admissions: (432)335-6816
Fax: (432)335-6860
E-mail: thilliard@odessa.edu
Web Site: http://www.odessa.edu/
President/CEO: Dr. Gregory Williams
Admissions: Tracy Hilliard
Financial Aid: Dee Nesmith
Type: Two-Year College **Sex:** Coed **% Accepted:** 100 **Admission Plans:** Open Admission; Early Admission; Deferred Admission **Application Deadline:** Rolling **Application Fee:** $0.00 **H.S. Requirements:** High school diploma required; GED accepted. For applicants with extenuating circumstances: High school diploma required; GED not accepted **Costs Per Year:** Application fee: $0. Area resident tuition: $1410 full-time, $141 per course part-time. State resident tuition: $2010 full-time, $201 per course part-time. Nonresident tuition: $2910 full-time, $411 per course part-time. Mandatory fees: $330 full-time, $33 per course part-time. **Scholarships:** Available **Calendar System:** Semester, Summer Session Available **Enrollment:** FT 1,475, PT 3,657 **Faculty:** FT 118, PT 118 **Student-Faculty Ratio:** 19:1 **% Residing in College-Owned, -Operated, or -Affiliated Housing:** 4 **Library Holdings:** 123,000 **Regional Accreditation:** Southern Association of Colleges and Schools **Credit Hours For Degree:** 62 semester hours, Associates **Professional Accreditation:** ARCEST, APTA, CARC, JRCERT, NAACLS, NASM, NLN **Intercollegiate Athletics:** Baseball M; Basketball M & W; Cross-Country Running M & W; Golf M; Softball W

OUR LADY OF THE LAKE UNIVERSITY OF SAN ANTONIO

411 Southwest 24th St.
San Antonio, TX 78207-4689
Tel: (210)434-6711; Free: 800-436-6558
Fax: (210)436-0824
E-mail: admission@lake.ollusa.edu
Web Site: http://www.ollusa.edu/
President/CEO: Tessa Martinez Pollock, PhD
Admissions: Gilberto Becerra
Financial Aid: Michael Fuller
Type: Comprehensive **Sex:** Coed **Affiliation:** Roman Catholic **Scores:** 70% SAT V 400+; 79% SAT M 400+; 45% ACT 18-23; 11% ACT 24-29 **% Accepted:** 63 **Admission Plans:** Deferred Admission **Application Deadline:** Rolling **Application Fee:** $25.00 **H.S. Requirements:** High school diploma required; GED accepted **Costs Per Year:** Application fee: $25. Comprehensive fee: $28,738 includes full-time tuition ($21,400), mandatory fees ($500), and college room and board ($6838). College room only: $3988. Full-time tuition and fees vary according to degree level and location. Room and board charges vary according to board plan. Part-time tuition: $690 per credit hour. Part-time mandatory fees: $12 per credit hour, $58. Part-time tuition and fees vary according to degree level and location. **Scholarships:** Available **Calendar System:** Semester, Summer Session Available **Enrollment:** FT 1,180, PT 415, Grad FT 254, Grad PT 811 **Faculty:** FT 108, PT 120 **Student-Faculty Ratio:** 11:1 **Exams:** SAT I or ACT. **% Residing in College-Owned, -Operated, or -Affiliated Housing:** 41 **Final Year or Final Semester Residency Requirement:** No **Library Holdings:** 93,551 **Regional Accreditation:** Southern Association of Colleges and Schools **Credit Hours For Degree:** 128 credit hours, Bachelors **ROTC:** Army, Air Force **Professional Accreditation:** APA, ASLHA, ACBSP, CSWE **Intercollegiate Athletics:** Baseball M & W; Cross-Country Running M & W; Golf M & W; Soccer M & W; Tennis M & W; Volleyball W

PALO ALTO COLLEGE

1400 West Villaret
San Antonio, TX 78224-2499
Tel: (210)921-5000
Admissions: (210)921-5279
E-mail: pacar@accd.edu
Web Site: http://www.alamo.edu/pac/
President/CEO: Dr. Ana M. Guzman
Admissions: Rachel Montejano
Type: Two-Year College **Sex:** Coed **Affiliation:** Alamo Community College District System **% Accepted:** 100 **Admission Plans:** Open Admission; Early Admission **Application Deadline:** Rolling **Application Fee:** $0.00 **H.S. Requirements:** High school diploma required; GED accepted **Scholar-**

ships: Available **Calendar System:** Semester, Summer Session Available **Faculty:** FT 197, PT 278 **Student-Faculty Ratio:** 19:1 **Regional Accreditation:** Southern Association of Colleges and Schools **Credit Hours For Degree:** 60 semester hours, Associates **Intercollegiate Athletics:** Cross-Country Running M & W; Swimming and Diving M & W; Track and Field M & W

PANOLA COLLEGE
1109 West Panola St.
Carthage, TX 75633-2397
Tel: (903)693-2000
Admissions: (903)693-2009
E-mail: bsimpson@panola.edu
Web Site: http://www.panola.edu/
President/CEO: Dr. Gregory Powell
Admissions: Jeremy Dorman
Financial Aid: Denise Welch
Type: Two-Year College **Sex:** Coed **Admission Plans:** Open Admission; Early Admission **Application Deadline:** Rolling **H.S. Requirements:** High school diploma required; GED accepted **Costs Per Year:** Area resident tuition: $56 per credit hour part-time. State resident tuition: $87 per credit hour part-time. Nonresident tuition: $113 per credit hour part-time. **Scholarships:** Available **Calendar System:** Semester, Summer Session Available **Enrollment:** FT 949, PT 1,175 **Faculty:** FT 65, PT 57 **Student-Faculty Ratio:** 16:1 **% Residing in College-Owned, -Operated, or -Affiliated Housing:** 9 **Library Holdings:** 81,337 **Regional Accreditation:** Southern Association of Colleges and Schools **Credit Hours For Degree:** 60 credits, Associates **Professional Accreditation:** AHIMA, AOTA **Intercollegiate Athletics:** Baseball M; Basketball M & W; Volleyball W

PARIS JUNIOR COLLEGE
2400 Clarksville St.
Paris, TX 75460-6298
Tel: (903)785-7661; Free: 800-232-5804
Admissions: (903)782-0425
E-mail: sreece@parisjc.edu
Web Site: http://www.parisjc.edu/
President/CEO: Dr. Pamela Anglin
Admissions: Sheila Reece
Type: Two-Year College **Sex:** Coed **% Accepted:** 100 **Admission Plans:** Open Admission; Early Admission **Application Deadline:** Rolling **Application Fee:** $0.00 **H.S. Requirements:** High school diploma required; GED accepted **Costs Per Year:** Application fee: $0. Area resident tuition: $936 full-time, $39 per credit hour part-time. State resident tuition: $1680 full-time, $70 per credit hour part-time. Nonresident tuition: $2664 full-time, $111 per credit hour part-time. Mandatory fees: $228 full-time. Full-time tuition and fees vary according to course load. Part-time tuition varies according to course load. College room and board: $3400. Room and board charges vary according to board plan. **Scholarships:** Available **Calendar System:** Semester, Summer Session Available **Enrollment:** FT 2,649, PT 2,931 **Faculty:** FT 99, PT 130 **Student-Faculty Ratio:** 25:1 **% Residing in College-Owned, -Operated, or -Affiliated Housing:** 4 **Library Holdings:** 38,150 **Regional Accreditation:** Southern Association of Colleges and Schools **Credit Hours For Degree:** 63 semester hours, Associates **Professional Accreditation:** NLN **Intercollegiate Athletics:** Baseball M; Basketball M & W; Golf M; Softball W; Volleyball W

PAUL QUINN COLLEGE
3837 Simpson-Stuart Rd.
Dallas, TX 75241-4331
Tel: (214)376-1000; Free: 800-237-2648
Admissions: (214)302-3575
Fax: (214)302-3559
Web Site: http://www.pqc.edu/
President/CEO: Michael J. Sorrell
Admissions: Nena Taylor-Richey
Financial Aid: Khaleelah Ali
Type: Four-Year College **Sex:** Coed **Affiliation:** African Methodist Episcopal **Scores:** 43% SAT V 400+; 37% SAT M 400+; 6% ACT 18-23 **% Accepted:** 9 **Application Deadline:** June 1 **Application Fee:** $35.00 **H.S. Requirements:** High school diploma required; GED accepted **Scholarships:** Available **Calendar System:** Semester, Summer Session Available **Enrollment:** FT 482, PT 85 **Faculty:** FT 26, PT 43 **Student-Faculty Ratio:** 5:1 **Exams:** SAT I or ACT. **% Receiving Financial Aid:** 98 **% Residing in College-Owned, -Operated, or -Affiliated Housing:** 35 **Library Holdings:** 87,000 **Regional Accreditation:** Southern Association of Colleges and Schools **Credit Hours For Degree:** 124 semester hours, Bachelors **Intercollegiate Athletics:** Baseball M; Basketball M & W; Soccer M & W; Track and Field M & W

PRAIRIE VIEW A&M UNIVERSITY
PO Box 519
Prairie View, TX 77446-0519
Tel: (936)857-3311
Admissions: (936)261-1066
Fax: (936)857-2699
E-mail: megooch@pvamu.edu
Web Site: http://www.pvamu.edu/
President/CEO: Dr. George C. Wright
Admissions: Mary Gooch
Financial Aid: A. D. James, Jr.
Type: University **Sex:** Coed **Affiliation:** Texas A&M University System **Scores:** 61% SAT V 400+; 67% SAT M 400+; 37% ACT 18-23; 4% ACT 24-29 **% Accepted:** 86 **Admission Plans:** Deferred Admission **Application Deadline:** June 1 **Application Fee:** $25.00 **H.S. Requirements:** High school diploma required; GED accepted **Costs Per Year:** Application fee: $25. State resident tuition: $4884 full-time, $193 per credit hour part-time. Nonresident tuition: $13,194 full-time, $472 per credit hour part-time. Mandatory fees: $1780 full-time, $59.33 per credit hour part-time, $118.67. Full-time tuition and fees vary according to program. Part-time tuition and fees vary according to program. College room and board: $6738. College room only: $4544. Room and board charges vary according to board plan, housing facility, and student level. Tuition guaranteed not to increase for student's term of enrollment. **Scholarships:** Available **Calendar System:** Semester, Summer Session Available **Enrollment:** FT 6,080, PT 645, Grad FT 585, Grad PT 1,298 **Faculty:** FT 352, PT 104 **Student-Faculty Ratio:** 18:1 **Exams:** SAT I or ACT. ACT essay not being used. SAT essay not being used. **% Receiving Financial Aid:** 91 **% Residing in College-Owned, -Operated, or -Affiliated Housing:** 67 **Library Holdings:** 1,174,860 **Regional Accreditation:** Southern Association of Colleges and Schools **Credit Hours For Degree:** 120 credit hours, Bachelors **ROTC:** Army, Navy **Professional Accreditation:** AACSB, ABET, AACN, ADtA, CSWE, NCATE, NLN **Intercollegiate Athletics:** Baseball M; Basketball M & W; Cross-Country Running M & W; Football M; Golf M & W; Soccer W; Softball W; Tennis M & W; Track and Field M & W; Volleyball W

RANGER COLLEGE
1100 College Circle
Ranger, TX 76470
Tel: (254)647-3234
Web Site: http://www.ranger.cc.tx.us/
President/CEO: Dr. William J. Campion
Admissions: Dr. Jim Davis
Financial Aid: Sharon King
Type: Two-Year College **Sex:** Coed **Admission Plans:** Open Admission; Early Admission **Application Deadline:** Rolling **H.S. Requirements:** High school diploma required; GED accepted **Scholarships:** Available **Calendar System:** Semester, Summer Session Available **Faculty:** FT 28, PT 23 **% Residing in College-Owned, -Operated, or -Affiliated Housing:** 45 **Library Holdings:** 24,211 **Regional Accreditation:** Southern Association of Colleges and Schools **Credit Hours For Degree:** 62 semester hours, Associates **Intercollegiate Athletics:** Baseball M; Basketball M & W; Cross-Country Running M & W; Football M; Golf M; Softball W; Track and Field M & W

REMINGTON COLLEGE—DALLAS CAMPUS
1800 Eastgate Dr.
Garland, TX 75041
Tel: (972)686-7878
Fax: (972)686-5116
E-mail: shonda.wisenhunt@remingtoncollege.edu
Web Site: http://www.remingtoncollege.edu/
President/CEO: Skip Walls
Admissions: Shonda Wisenhunt
Type: Two-Year College **Sex:** Coed **Professional Accreditation:** ACICS

REMINGTON COLLEGE—FORT WORTH CAMPUS
300 East Loop 820
Fort Worth, TX 76112

Tel: (817)451-0017; Free: 800-336-6668
Fax: (817)496-1257
E-mail: marcia.kline@remingtoncollege.edu
Web Site: http://www.remingtoncollege.edu/
President/CEO: Gregg Falcon
Admissions: Marcia Kline
Type: Two-Year College **Sex:** Coed **Professional Accreditation:** ACCSCT

REMINGTON COLLEGE—HOUSTON CAMPUS
3110 Hayes Rd.
Ste. 380
Houston, TX 77082
Tel: (281)899-1240
Fax: (281)597-8466
E-mail: kevin.wilkinson@remingtoncollege.edu
Web Site: http://www.remingtoncollege.edu/houston/
President/CEO: Hiram Nall
Admissions: Kevin Wilkinson
Type: Two-Year College **Sex:** Coed **Professional Accreditation:** ACCSCT

REMINGTON COLLEGE—HOUSTON SOUTHEAST
20985 Interstate 45 South
Webster, TX 77598
Tel: (281)554-1700
Admissions: (281)554-1700
E-mail: lori.minor@remingtoncollege.edu
Web Site: http://www.remingtoncollege.edu/houstonsoutheast/
President/CEO: Bob Doty
Admissions: Lori Minor
Type: Two-Year College **Sex:** Coed **Professional Accreditation:** ACCSCT

REMINGTON COLLEGE—NORTH HOUSTON CAMPUS
11310 Greens Crossing Blvd.
Ste. 300
Houston, TX 77067
Tel: (281)885-4450
Admissions: (281)885-4450
E-mail: edmund.flores@remingtoncollege.edu
Web Site: http://www.remingtoncollege.edu/
President/CEO: Andrew Bossaller
Admissions: Edmund Flores
Type: Two-Year College **Sex:** Coed **Professional Accreditation:** ACCSCT

RICE UNIVERSITY
6100 Main St.
PO Box 1892
Houston, TX 77251-1892
Tel: (713)348-0000; Free: 800-527-OWLS
Admissions: (713)348-RICE
Fax: (713)348-5323
E-mail: admi@rice.edu
Web Site: http://www.rice.edu/
President/CEO: David W. Leebron
Financial Aid: Anne Walker
Type: University **Sex:** Coed **Scores:** 99.9% SAT V 400+; 100% SAT M 400+; 3.3% ACT 18-23; 19.7% ACT 24-29 **% Accepted:** 22 **Admission Plans:** Early Decision Plan; Deferred Admission **Application Deadline:** January 2 **Application Fee:** $65.00 **H.S. Requirements:** High school diploma or equivalent not required **Costs Per Year:** Application fee: $65. Comprehensive fee: $43,335 includes full-time tuition ($31,430), mandatory fees ($675), and college room and board ($11,230). College room only: $7510. Full-time tuition and fees vary according to student level. Room and board charges vary according to board plan. Part-time tuition: $1310 per credit hour. Part-time tuition varies according to course load. **Scholarships:** Available **Calendar System:** Semester, Summer Session Available **Enrollment:** FT 3,262, PT 57, Grad FT 2,190, Grad PT 154 **Faculty:** FT 619, PT 136 **Student-Faculty Ratio:** 5:1 **Exams:** SAT I and SAT II or ACT. ACT essay used for admission. SAT essay used for admission. **% Receiving Financial Aid:** 37 **% Residing in College-Owned, -Operated, or -Affiliated Housing:** 70 **Library Holdings:** 2,620,342 **Regional Accreditation:** Southern Association of Colleges and Schools **Credit Hours For Degree:** 120 semester hours, Bachelors **ROTC:** Army, Navy, Air Force **Professional Accreditation:** AACSB, ABET, NAAB, TEAC **Intercollegiate Athletics:** Badminton M & W; Baseball M; Basketball M & W; Cheerleading M & W; Crew M & W; Cross-Country Running M & W; Equestrian Sports M & W; Fencing M & W; Field Hockey W; Football M; Golf M; Lacrosse M & W; Riflery M & W; Rugby M & W; Sailing M & W; Soccer M & W; Softball W; Swimming and Diving W; Tennis M & W; Track and Field M & W; Ultimate Frisbee M & W; Volleyball M & W; Water Polo M & W

RICHLAND COLLEGE
12800 Abrams Rd.
Dallas, TX 75243-2199
Tel: (972)238-6106
Fax: (972)238-6957
Web Site: http://www.rlc.dcccd.edu/
President/CEO: Dr. Kay Eggleston
Admissions: Carol McKinney
Type: Two-Year College **Sex:** Coed **Affiliation:** Dallas County Community College District System **Admission Plans:** Open Admission; Early Admission **Application Deadline:** Rolling **Application Fee:** $0.00 **H.S. Requirements:** High school diploma or equivalent not required **Scholarships:** Available **Calendar System:** Semester, Summer Session Available **Faculty:** FT 165, PT 500 **Library Holdings:** 63,000 **Regional Accreditation:** Southern Association of Colleges and Schools **Credit Hours For Degree:** 61 credits, Associates **Intercollegiate Athletics:** Baseball M; Basketball M; Soccer M & W; Volleyball W

RIO GRANDE BIBLE INSTITUTE
4300 S US Hwy 281
Edinburg, TX 78539
Tel: (956)380-8100
Fax: (956)380-8256
Web Site: http://www.riogrande.edu/
Type: Four-Year College **Sex:** Coed **Professional Accreditation:** ABHE

ST. EDWARD'S UNIVERSITY
3001 South Congress Ave.
Austin, TX 78704
Tel: (512)448-8400; Free: 800-555-0164
Admissions: (512)448-8580
Fax: (512)448-8492
E-mail: seu.admit@stedwards.edu
Web Site: http://www.gotostedwards.com/
President/CEO: Dr. George E. Martin
Admissions: Karen Gregg
Type: Comprehensive **Sex:** Coed **Affiliation:** Roman Catholic **Scores:** 99% SAT V 400+; 100% SAT M 400+; 39% ACT 18-23; 56% ACT 24-29 **% Accepted:** 66 **Admission Plans:** Deferred Admission **Application Deadline:** May 1 **Application Fee:** $45.00 **H.S. Requirements:** High school diploma required; GED accepted **Costs Per Year:** Application fee: $45. Comprehensive fee: $35,520 includes full-time tuition ($26,084), mandatory fees ($400), and college room and board ($9036). College room only: $5036. Full-time tuition and fees vary according to course load and degree level. Room and board charges vary according to board plan and housing facility. Part-time tuition: $870 per credit hour. Part-time mandatory fees: $50 per term. Part-time tuition and fees vary according to course load and degree level. **Scholarships:** Available **Calendar System:** Semester, Summer Session Available **Enrollment:** FT 3,463, PT 905, Grad FT 149, Grad PT 776 **Faculty:** FT 184, PT 295 **Student-Faculty Ratio:** 15:1 **Exams:** SAT I or ACT. ACT essay used for admission. SAT essay used for admission. ACT essay used as a validity check on application essay. SAT essay used as a validity check on application essay. **% Receiving Financial Aid:** 64 **% Residing in College-Owned, -Operated, or -Affiliated Housing:** 38 **Final Year or Final Semester Residency Requirement:** No **Library Holdings:** 201,930 **Regional Accreditation:** Southern Association of Colleges and Schools **Credit Hours For Degree:** 120 credit hours, Bachelors **ROTC:** Army, Air Force **Professional Accreditation:** CSWE **Intercollegiate Athletics:** Baseball M; Basketball M & W; Golf M & W; Soccer M & W; Softball W; Tennis M & W; Volleyball W

ST. MARY'S UNIVERSITY
1 Camino Santa Maria
San Antonio, TX 78228-8507
Tel: (210)436-3011; Free: 800-FOR-STMU
Admissions: (210)436-3126
Fax: (210)431-6742
E-mail: uadm@stmarytx.edu

Web Site: http://www.stmarytx.edu/
President/CEO: Dr. Charles L. Cotrell
Admissions: Chadd J. Bridwell
Financial Aid: David R. Krause
Type: Comprehensive **Sex:** Coed **Affiliation:** Roman Catholic **Scores:** 97.8% SAT V 400+; 97.36% SAT M 400+; 60.1% ACT 18-23; 29.06% ACT 24-29 **% Accepted:** 76 **Admission Plans:** Deferred Admission **Application Deadline:** Rolling **Application Fee:** $30.00 **H.S. Requirements:** High school diploma required; GED accepted **Costs Per Year:** Application fee: $30. Comprehensive fee: $30,106 includes full-time tuition ($21,980), mandatory fees ($576), and college room and board ($7550). College room only: $4750. Room and board charges vary according to board plan and housing facility. Part-time tuition: $660 per credit hour. Part-time mandatory fees: $163 per term. **Scholarships:** Available **Calendar System:** Semester, Summer Session Available **Enrollment:** FT 2,212, PT 160, Grad FT 1,059, Grad PT 462 **Faculty:** FT 197, PT 143 **Student-Faculty Ratio:** 13:1 **Exams:** SAT I or ACT. **% Receiving Financial Aid:** 79 **% Residing in College-Owned, -Operated, or -Affiliated Housing:** 55 **Final Year or Final Semester Residency Requirement:** Yes **Library Holdings:** 601,478 **Regional Accreditation:** Southern Association of Colleges and Schools **Credit Hours For Degree:** 128 semester hours, Bachelors **ROTC:** Army, Air Force **Professional Accreditation:** AACSB, ABET, AAMFT, ABA, ACA, AALS, NASM **Intercollegiate Athletics:** Baseball M; Basketball M & W; Cheerleading M & W; Cross-Country Running W; Golf M & W; Rugby M; Soccer M & W; Softball W; Tennis M & W; Volleyball W

ST. PHILIP'S COLLEGE
1801 Martin Luther King Dr.
San Antonio, TX 78203-2098
Tel: (210)486-2000
Admissions: (210)486-2283
Fax: (210)531-4831
E-mail: pvelasco@alamo.edu
Web Site: http://www.alamo.edu/spc/
President/CEO: Dr. Adena Williams Loston
Admissions: Penelope Velasco
Type: Two-Year College **Sex:** Coed **Affiliation:** Alamo Community College District System **Admission Plans:** Open Admission; Early Admission **Application Deadline:** Rolling **Application Fee:** $0.00 **H.S. Requirements:** High school diploma required; GED accepted **Costs Per Year:** Application fee: $0. Area resident tuition: $1605 full-time, $53.50 per semester hour part-time. State resident tuition: $3105 full-time, $103.50 per semester hour part-time. Nonresident tuition: $6090 full-time, $203.50 per semester hour part-time. Mandatory fees: $284 full-time, $142. **Scholarships:** Available **Calendar System:** Semester, Summer Session Available **Enrollment:** FT 3,465, PT 7,543 **Faculty:** FT 232, PT 301 **Student-Faculty Ratio:** 18:1 **Library Holdings:** 125,966 **Regional Accreditation:** Southern Association of Colleges and Schools **Credit Hours For Degree:** 60 credits, Associates **ROTC:** Army **Professional Accreditation:** ACF, AHIMA, AOTA, APTA, CARC, JRCERT, NAACLS, NLN

SAM HOUSTON STATE UNIVERSITY
Huntsville, TX 77341
Tel: (936)294-1111; Free: (866)232-7528
Admissions: (936)294-1828
E-mail: admissions@shsu.edu
Web Site: http://www.shsu.edu/
President/CEO: Dr. James F. Gaertner
Admissions: Trevor B. Thorn
Financial Aid: Lisa Tatom
Type: University **Sex:** Coed **Affiliation:** Texas State University System **Scores:** 91.5% SAT V 400+; 95.7% SAT M 400+; 66% ACT 18-23; 15.7% ACT 24-29 **% Accepted:** 72 **Application Deadline:** August 1 **Application Fee:** $40.00 **H.S. Requirements:** High school diploma required; GED accepted **Costs Per Year:** Application fee: $40. State resident tuition: $4890 full-time, $163 per credit hour part-time. Nonresident tuition: $14,190 full-time, $473 per credit hour part-time. Mandatory fees: $2110 full-time. Full-time tuition and fees vary according to course level, course load, degree level, location, program, and student level. Part-time tuition varies according to course level, course load, degree level, location, program, and student level. College room and board: $7022. College room only: $3914. Room and board charges vary according to board plan and housing facility. **Scholarships:** Available **Calendar System:** Semester, Summer Session Available **Enrollment:** FT 12,223, PT 2,346, Grad FT 566, Grad PT 1,637 **Faculty:** FT 532, PT 16 **Exams:** SAT I or ACT. **% Receiving Financial Aid:** 26 **% Residing in College-Owned, -Operated, or -Affiliated Housing:** 22 **Library Holdings:** 1,296,696 **Regional Accreditation:** Southern Association of Colleges and Schools **Credit Hours For Degree:** 128 semester hours, Bachelors **ROTC:** Army **Professional Accreditation:** AACSB, AAFCS, ADtA, NASM, NCATE **Intercollegiate Athletics:** Baseball M; Basketball M & W; Cross-Country Running M & W; Equestrian Sports M & W; Football M; Golf M & W; Lacrosse M; Riflery M & W; Rugby M; Soccer M & W; Softball M & W; Tennis M & W; Track and Field M & W; Volleyball W

SAN ANTONIO COLLEGE
1300 San Pedro Ave.
San Antonio, TX 78212-4299
Tel: (210)733-2000; Free: 800-944-7575
Admissions: (210)486-0000
Fax: (210)733-2200
Web Site: http://www.alamo.edu/sac/sacmain/sac.htm
President/CEO: Robert Zeigler
Admissions: J. Martin Ortega
Type: Two-Year College **Sex:** Coed **Affiliation:** Alamo Community College District System **Admission Plans:** Open Admission; Early Admission **Application Deadline:** Rolling **Application Fee:** $0.00 **H.S. Requirements:** High school diploma required; GED accepted **Calendar System:** Semester, Summer Session Available **Enrollment:** FT 8,375, PT 13,425 **Faculty:** FT 407, PT 593 **Student-Faculty Ratio:** 22:1 **Exams:** Other. **Library Holdings:** 233,714 **Regional Accreditation:** Southern Association of Colleges and Schools **Credit Hours For Degree:** 60 credits, Associates **ROTC:** Army, Air Force **Professional Accreditation:** AAMAE, ABFSE, ADA, NLN

SAN JACINTO COLLEGE DISTRICT
4624 Fairmont Parkway
Pasadena, TX 77504-3323
Tel: (281)998-6150
E-mail: Wanda.Munson@sjcd.edu
Web Site: http://www.sanjac.edu/
President/CEO: Dr. Brenda Hellyer, EdD
Admissions: Dr. Wanda Munson, EdD
Type: Two-Year College **Sex:** Coed **% Accepted:** 100 **Admission Plans:** Open Admission; Early Admission **H.S. Requirements:** High school diploma required; GED accepted **Costs Per Year:** Area resident tuition: $1376 full-time, $33 per credit hour part-time. State resident tuition: $2176 full-time, $58 per credit hour part-time. Nonresident tuition: $3776 full-time, $108 per credit hour part-time. Mandatory fees: $260 full-time, $130 per term part-time. Full-time tuition and fees vary according to course load. Part-time tuition and fees vary according to course load. **Calendar System:** Semester, Summer Session Available **Enrollment:** FT 9,689, PT 17,322 **Faculty:** FT 458, PT 675 **Student-Faculty Ratio:** 24:1 **Final Year or Final Semester Residency Requirement:** No **Library Holdings:** 280,000 **Regional Accreditation:** Southern Association of Colleges and Schools **Credit Hours For Degree:** 61 credits, Associates **ROTC:** Army, Air Force **Intercollegiate Athletics:** Baseball M; Basketball M; Cheerleading M; Golf M; Soccer M & W; Softball W; Tennis M & W; Volleyball W

SCHREINER UNIVERSITY
2100 Memorial Blvd.
Kerrville, TX 78028-5697
Tel: (830)896-5411; Free: 800-343-4919
Fax: (830)792-7226
E-mail: admissions@schreiner.edu
Web Site: http://www.schreiner.edu/
President/CEO: Dr. Tim Summerlin
Admissions: Sandy Speed
Financial Aid: Toni Bryant
Type: Comprehensive **Sex:** Coed **Affiliation:** Presbyterian **Scores:** 89.91% SAT V 400+ **% Accepted:** 62 **Admission Plans:** Deferred Admission **Application Deadline:** May 1 **Application Fee:** $25.00 **H.S. Requirements:** High school diploma required; GED accepted **Costs Per Year:** Application fee: $25. Comprehensive fee: $27,457 includes full-time tuition ($18,131), mandatory fees ($600), and college room and board ($8726). College room only: $5050. Room and board charges vary according to board plan and housing facility. Part-time tuition: $774 per credit hour. Part-time mandatory fees: $75 per term. **Scholarships:** Available **Calendar System:** Semester, Summer Session Available **Enrollment:** FT 977, PT 51, Grad FT 21 **Faculty:** FT 61, PT 31 **Student-Faculty Ratio:** 14:1 **Exams:** SAT I or ACT.

% Receiving Financial Aid: 76 **% Residing in College-Owned, -Operated, or -Affiliated Housing:** 87 **Library Holdings:** 110,300 **Regional Accreditation:** Southern Association of Colleges and Schools **Credit Hours For Degree:** 64 credit hours, Associates; 120 credit hours, Bachelors **Intercollegiate Athletics:** Baseball M; Basketball M & W; Cross-Country Running M & W; Golf M & W; Soccer M & W; Softball W; Tennis M & W; Volleyball W

SOUTH PLAINS COLLEGE
1401 South College Ave.
Levelland, TX 79336-6595
Tel: (806)894-9611
Fax: (806)897-3167
E-mail: arangel@southplainscollege.edu
Web Site: http://www.southplainscollege.edu/
President/CEO: Dr. Kelvin Sharp, EdD
Admissions: Andrea Rangel
Type: Two-Year College **Sex:** Coed **% Accepted:** 100 **Admission Plans:** Open Admission; Early Admission **Application Deadline:** Rolling **Application Fee:** $0.00 **H.S. Requirements:** High school diploma required; GED accepted. For some applicants 18 or over: High school diploma required; GED not accepted **Costs Per Year:** Application fee: $0. Area resident tuition: $1484 full-time, $26 per credit hour part-time. State resident tuition: $2012 full-time, $48 per credit hour part-time. Nonresident tuition: $2396 full-time, $64 per credit hour part-time. Mandatory fees: $1142 full-time, $580 per credit hour part-time, $69 per term part-time. Full-time tuition and fees vary according to class time, course load, location, and program. Part-time tuition and fees vary according to class time, course load, location, and program. College room and board: $3100. Room and board charges vary according to housing facility. **Scholarships:** Available **Calendar System:** Semester, Summer Session Available **Enrollment:** FT 4,704, PT 5,324 **Faculty:** FT 271, PT 183 **Student-Faculty Ratio:** 20:1 **Exams:** ACT, SAT II. **% Residing in College-Owned, -Operated, or -Affiliated Housing:** 10 **Library Holdings:** 70,000 **Regional Accreditation:** Southern Association of Colleges and Schools **Credit Hours For Degree:** 62 semester hours, Associates **ROTC:** Army, Air Force **Professional Accreditation:** AHIMA, CARC, JRCERT, NLN **Intercollegiate Athletics:** Basketball M & W; Cross-Country Running M & W; Equestrian Sports M & W; Track and Field M & W

SOUTH TEXAS COLLEGE
3201 West Pecan
McAllen, TX 78501
Tel: (956)618-8323; Free: 800-742-7822
Admissions: (956)872-2147
Fax: (956)928-4445
E-mail: mshebbar@southtexascollege.edu
Web Site: http://www.southtexascollege.edu/
President/CEO: Dr. Shirley A. Reed
Admissions: Matthew Hebbard
Type: Two-Year College **Sex:** Coed **Admission Plans:** Open Admission; Early Admission; Deferred Admission **Application Deadline:** Rolling **Application Fee:** $0.00 **H.S. Requirements:** High school diploma required; GED accepted **Costs Per Year:** Application fee: $0. Area resident tuition: $1512 full-time, $64 per credit hour part-time. State resident tuition: $1826 full-time, $77.40 per credit hour part-time. Nonresident tuition: $4848 full-time, $202 per credit hour part-time. Mandatory fees: $636 full-time, $12 per credit hour part-time, $7. Full-time tuition and fees vary according to course load, degree level, location, and program. Part-time tuition and fees vary according to course load, degree level, location, and program. **Scholarships:** Available **Calendar System:** Semester, Summer Session Available **Enrollment:** FT 7,027, PT 12,800 **Faculty:** FT 434, PT 195 **Student-Faculty Ratio:** 25:1 **Exams:** Other. **Library Holdings:** 15,811 **Regional Accreditation:** Southern Association of Colleges and Schools **Credit Hours For Degree:** 60 semester hours, Associates **ROTC:** Army **Professional Accreditation:** AHIMA, AOTA

SOUTHERN METHODIST UNIVERSITY
6425 Boaz
Dallas, TX 75275
Tel: (214)768-2000; Free: 800-323-0672
Admissions: (214)768-2058
E-mail: ugadmission@smu.edu
Web Site: http://www.smu.edu/
President/CEO: Dr. R. Gerald Turner
Admissions: Dr. Ron W. Moss
Financial Aid: Marc Peterson
Type: University **Sex:** Coed **Affiliation:** United Methodist Church **Scores:** 99.47% SAT V 400+; 99.9% SAT M 400+; 11.81% ACT 18-23; 59.58% ACT 24-29 **% Accepted:** 50 **Admission Plans:** Early Admission; Early Action; Deferred Admission **Application Deadline:** January 15 **Application Fee:** $60.00 **H.S. Requirements:** High school diploma required; GED not accepted **Costs Per Year:** Application fee: $60. Comprehensive fee: $47,605 includes full-time tuition ($31,200), mandatory fees ($3960), and college room and board ($12,445). Full-time tuition and fees vary according to class time. Room and board charges vary according to board plan and housing facility. Part-time tuition: $1304 per credit hour. Part-time mandatory fees: $166 per credit hour. Part-time tuition and fees vary according to class time and course load. **Scholarships:** Available **Calendar System:** Semester, Summer Session Available **Enrollment:** FT 5,921, PT 307, Grad FT 2,200, Grad PT 2,463 **Faculty:** FT 656, PT 378 **Student-Faculty Ratio:** 12:1 **Exams:** SAT I or ACT, SAT II. **% Receiving Financial Aid:** 36 **% Residing in College-Owned, -Operated, or -Affiliated Housing:** 38 **Library Holdings:** 2,848,971 **Regional Accreditation:** Southern Association of Colleges and Schools **Credit Hours For Degree:** 122 credit hours, Bachelors **ROTC:** Army, Air Force **Professional Accreditation:** AACSB, ABET, ABA, ACIPE, AALS, ATS, NASAD, NASD, NASM, NAST **Intercollegiate Athletics:** Baseball M; Basketball M & W; Cheerleading M & W; Crew W; Cross-Country Running W; Equestrian Sports W; Fencing M & W; Football M; Golf M & W; Ice Hockey M; Lacrosse M; Rugby M & W; Soccer M & W; Swimming and Diving M & W; Tennis M & W; Track and Field W; Volleyball W; Wrestling M

SOUTHWEST INSTITUTE OF TECHNOLOGY
5424 Hwy. 290 West, Ste. 200
Austin, TX 78735-8800
Tel: (512)892-2640
Fax: (512)892-1045
Web Site: http://www.swse.net/
President/CEO: Howard Roose
Type: Two-Year College **Sex:** Coed **Admission Plans:** Open Admission **Application Fee:** $100.00 **Scholarships:** Available **Calendar System:** Continuous **Student-Faculty Ratio:** 7:1 **Professional Accreditation:** ACCSCT

SOUTHWEST TEXAS JUNIOR COLLEGE
2401 Garner Field Rd.
Uvalde, TX 78801-6297
Tel: (830)278-4401
Web Site: http://www.swtjc.net/
President/CEO: Ismael Sosa, Jr.
Admissions: Joe C. Barker
Type: Two-Year College **Sex:** Coed **Admission Plans:** Open Admission; Preferred Admission; Early Admission; Deferred Admission **Application Deadline:** Rolling **H.S. Requirements:** High school diploma required; GED accepted **Scholarships:** Available **Calendar System:** Semester, Summer Session Available **Faculty:** FT 66, PT 100 **% Residing in College-Owned, -Operated, or -Affiliated Housing:** 9 **Library Holdings:** 30,890 **Regional Accreditation:** Southern Association of Colleges and Schools **Credit Hours For Degree:** 62 semester hours, Associates **Intercollegiate Athletics:** Basketball M & W; Equestrian Sports M & W

SOUTHWESTERN ADVENTIST UNIVERSITY
100 Hillcrest Dr.
Keene, TX 76059
Tel: (817)645-3921; Free: 800-433-2240
Admissions: (817)202-6252
Fax: (817)556-4744
E-mail: ddennis@swau.edu
Web Site: http://www.swau.edu/
President/CEO: Dr. Eric Anderson
Admissions: Diem Dennis
Type: Comprehensive **Sex:** Coed **Affiliation:** Seventh-day Adventist **Scores:** 77% SAT V 400+; 79% SAT M 400+; 61% ACT 18-23; 16% ACT 24-29 **% Accepted:** 56 **Admission Plans:** Deferred Admission **Application Deadline:** August 31 **Application Fee:** $0.00 **H.S. Requirements:** High school diploma required; GED accepted **Costs Per Year:** Application fee: $0. Comprehensive fee: $23,364 includes full-time tuition ($15,836), mandatory fees ($380), and college room and board ($7148). College room only: $3128. Full-time tuition and fees vary according to course load and program.

Room and board charges vary according to board plan. Part-time tuition: $644 per credit hour. Part-time mandatory fees: $180 per term. Part-time tuition and fees vary according to course load and program. **Scholarships:** Available **Calendar System:** Semester, Summer Session Available **Enrollment:** FT 674, PT 111, Grad FT 9, Grad PT 21 **Faculty:** FT 55, PT 15 **Student-Faculty Ratio:** 12:1 **Exams:** SAT I or ACT. ACT essay not being used. SAT essay not being used. **% Residing in College-Owned, -Operated, or -Affiliated Housing:** 40 **Final Year or Final Semester Residency Requirement:** Yes **Library Holdings:** 135,774 **Regional Accreditation:** Southern Association of Colleges and Schools **Credit Hours For Degree:** 64 semester hours, Associates; 128 semester hours, Bachelors **Professional Accreditation:** CSWE, NLN

SOUTHWESTERN ASSEMBLIES OF GOD UNIVERSITY
1200 Sycamore St.
Waxahachie, TX 75165-5735
Tel: (972)937-4010; Free: 888-937-7248
Admissions: 888-937-4010
E-mail: edavis@sagu.edu
Web Site: http://www.sagu.edu/
President/CEO: Kermit Bridges
Admissions: Eddie M. Davis
Type: Comprehensive **Sex:** Coed **Affiliation:** Assemblies of God **Admission Plans:** Early Admission; Deferred Admission **Application Deadline:** Rolling **Application Fee:** $35.00 **H.S. Requirements:** High school diploma required; GED accepted **Costs Per Year:** Application fee: $35. Comprehensive fee: $18,892 includes full-time tuition ($12,900), mandatory fees ($880), and college room and board ($5112). College room only: $2190. Room and board charges vary according to housing facility. Part-time tuition: $430 per credit hour. **Scholarships:** Available **Calendar System:** Semester, Summer Session Available **Enrollment:** FT 1,402, PT 306, Grad FT 87, Grad PT 223 **Faculty:** FT 69, PT 73 **Student-Faculty Ratio:** 16:1 **Exams:** SAT I or ACT. SAT essay used for admission. SAT essay used for placement. **% Receiving Financial Aid:** 70 **% Residing in College-Owned, -Operated, or -Affiliated Housing:** 80 **Final Year or Final Semester Residency Requirement:** Yes **Library Holdings:** 107,563 **Regional Accreditation:** Southern Association of Colleges and Schools **Credit Hours For Degree:** 62 credit hours, Associates; 120 credit hours, Bachelors **ROTC:** Air Force **Intercollegiate Athletics:** Baseball M; Basketball M & W; Football M; Soccer M & W; Volleyball W

SOUTHWESTERN CHRISTIAN COLLEGE
Box 10
200 Bowser St.
Terrell, TX 75160
Tel: (972)524-3341
Web Site: http://www.swcc.edu/
President/CEO: Jack Evans
Type: Four-Year College **Sex:** Coed **Affiliation:** Church of Christ **Admission Plans:** Open Admission; Early Admission; Deferred Admission **Application Deadline:** August 1 **Application Fee:** $20.00 **H.S. Requirements:** High school diploma required; GED accepted **Scholarships:** Available **Calendar System:** Semester, Summer Session Not available **% Residing in College-Owned, -Operated, or -Affiliated Housing:** 80 **Library Holdings:** 25,687 **Regional Accreditation:** Southern Association of Colleges and Schools **Credit Hours For Degree:** 62 credit hours, Associates; 124 credit hours, Bachelors **Intercollegiate Athletics:** Basketball M & W; Track and Field M & W

SOUTHWESTERN UNIVERSITY
1001 East University Ave.
Georgetown, TX 78626
Tel: (512)863-6511; Free: 800-252-3166
Admissions: (512)863-1200
Fax: (512)863-6511
E-mail: admission@southwestern.edu
Web Site: http://www.southwestern.edu/
President/CEO: Jake Schrum
Admissions: Tom Oliver
Financial Aid: James P. Gaeta
Type: Four-Year College **Sex:** Coed **Affiliation:** Methodist **Scores:** 99.41% SAT V 400+; 99.71% SAT M 400+; 16.67% ACT 18-23; 52.31% ACT 24-29 **% Accepted:** 63 **Admission Plans:** Early Action; Early Decision Plan; Deferred Admission **Application Deadline:** Rolling **Application Fee:** $40.00 **H.S. Requirements:** High school diploma required; GED accepted **Costs Per Year:** Application fee: $40. Comprehensive fee: $39,350 includes full-time tuition ($30,220) and college room and board ($9130). College room only: $4860. Room and board charges vary according to board plan and housing facility. Part-time tuition: $1255 per semester hour. Part-time tuition varies according to course load. **Scholarships:** Available **Calendar System:** Semester, Summer Session Available **Enrollment:** FT 1,280, PT 21 **Faculty:** FT 122, PT 44 **Student-Faculty Ratio:** 10:1 **Exams:** SAT I and SAT II or ACT, SAT I. **% Receiving Financial Aid:** 57 **% Residing in College-Owned, -Operated, or -Affiliated Housing:** 82 **Library Holdings:** 378,865 **Regional Accreditation:** Southern Association of Colleges and Schools **Credit Hours For Degree:** 121 semester hours, Bachelors **Professional Accreditation:** JRCEPAT, NASM **Intercollegiate Athletics:** Baseball M; Basketball M & W; Cross-Country Running M & W; Golf M & W; Lacrosse M; Soccer M & W; Softball W; Swimming and Diving M & W; Tennis M & W; Volleyball W

STEPHEN F. AUSTIN STATE UNIVERSITY
1936 North St.
Nacogdoches, TX 75962
Tel: (936)468-2011; Free: 800-731-2902
Admissions: (936)468-2504
Fax: (936)468-3849
E-mail: admissions@sfasu.edu
Web Site: http://www.sfasu.edu/
President/CEO: Dr. Baker Pattillo
Admissions: Beth Smith
Type: Comprehensive **Sex:** Coed **Scores:** 87.25% SAT V 400+; 91.57% SAT M 400+; 57.02% ACT 18-23; 19.51% ACT 24-29 **% Accepted:** 73 **Application Deadline:** Rolling **Application Fee:** $35.00 **H.S. Requirements:** High school diploma required; GED accepted **Costs Per Year:** Application fee: $35. State resident tuition: $4830 full-time, $161 per credit hour part-time. Nonresident tuition: $13,140 full-time, $438 per credit hour part-time. Mandatory fees: $1902 full-time, $147 per credit hour part-time. Full-time tuition and fees vary according to course load, degree level, and location. Part-time tuition and fees vary according to course load, degree level, and location. College room and board: $7377. Room and board charges vary according to board plan and housing facility. **Scholarships:** Available **Calendar System:** Semester, Summer Session Available **Enrollment:** FT 9,663, PT 1,481, Grad FT 644, Grad PT 1,057 **Faculty:** FT 485, PT 172 **Student-Faculty Ratio:** 21:1 **Exams:** SAT I or ACT. **% Receiving Financial Aid:** 58 **% Residing in College-Owned, -Operated, or -Affiliated Housing:** 44 **Library Holdings:** 735,445 **Regional Accreditation:** Southern Association of Colleges and Schools **Credit Hours For Degree:** 120 semester hours, Bachelors **ROTC:** Army **Professional Accreditation:** AACSB, ABET, AAFCS, ACA, ADtA, ASLHA, FIDER, CORE, CSWE, NASAD, NASM, NAST, NCATE, NLN, SAF **Intercollegiate Athletics:** Baseball M; Basketball M & W; Bowling W; Cross-Country Running M & W; Equestrian Sports W; Football M; Golf M & W; Soccer W; Softball W; Tennis W; Track and Field M & W; Volleyball W

STRAYER UNIVERSITY - NORTH AUSTIN CAMPUS
8501 North Mopac Expressway
Ste. 100
Austin, TX 78759
Tel: (512)568-3300
Fax: (512)340-9130
E-mail: centralaustin@strayer.edu
Web Site: http://www.strayer.edu/north_austin
Type: Comprehensive **Sex:** Coed **Application Fee:** $50.00 **Costs Per Year:** Application fee: $50. **Regional Accreditation:** Middle State Association of Colleges and Schools

SUL ROSS STATE UNIVERSITY
East Hwy. 90
Alpine, TX 79832
Tel: (432)837-8011; Free: 888-722-7778
Admissions: (432)837-8432
Fax: (432)837-8334
E-mail: gschwab@sulross.edu
Web Site: http://www.sulross.edu/
President/CEO: Dr. Ricardo Maestas
Admissions: Gregory Schwab
Financial Aid: Rena Gallego

Type: Comprehensive **Sex:** Coed **Affiliation:** Texas State University System **Scores:** 67% SAT V 400+; 64% SAT M 400+; 37% ACT 18-23; 6% ACT 24-29 **% Accepted:** 73 **Admission Plans:** Deferred Admission **Application Deadline:** Rolling **Application Fee:** $25.00 **H.S. Requirements:** High school diploma required; GED accepted **Costs Per Year:** Application fee: $25. State resident tuition: $2928 full-time. Nonresident tuition: $9576 full-time. College room and board: $6370. College room only: $3820. **Scholarships:** Available **Calendar System:** Semester, Summer Session Available **Enrollment:** FT 1,285, PT 693 **Faculty:** FT 128, PT 31 **Student-Faculty Ratio:** 14:1 **Exams:** SAT I or ACT. **% Receiving Financial Aid:** 57 **Regional Accreditation:** Southern Association of Colleges and Schools **Credit Hours For Degree:** 67 semester hours, Associates; 130 semester hours, Bachelors **Professional Accreditation:** ACBSP **Intercollegiate Athletics:** Baseball M; Basketball M & W; Cheerleading M & W; Cross-Country Running W; Football M; Softball W; Tennis M & W; Track and Field M & W; Volleyball W

TARLETON STATE UNIVERSITY
Box T-0001
Tarleton Station
Stephenville, TX 76402
Tel: (254)968-9000
Admissions: (254)968-9123
Fax: (254)968-9920
E-mail: uadm@tarleton.edu
Web Site: http://www.tarleton.edu/
President/CEO: Dr. F. Dominic Dottavio
Admissions: Cindy Hess
Financial Aid: Betty Murray
Type: Comprehensive **Sex:** Coed **Affiliation:** Texas A&M University System **Scores:** 86.55% SAT V 400+; 94% SAT M 400+; 64.23% ACT 18-23; 17.45% ACT 24-29 **% Accepted:** 56 **Admission Plans:** Early Action **Application Deadline:** August 1 **Application Fee:** $30.00 **H.S. Requirements:** High school diploma required; GED accepted **Costs Per Year:** Application fee: $30. State resident tuition: $5565 full-time, $138.50 per credit hour part-time. Nonresident tuition: $13,995 full-time, $415.50 per credit hour part-time. Mandatory fees: $1585 full-time. Full-time tuition and fees vary according to course load. Part-time tuition varies according to course load. College room and board: $6591. College room only: $3291. Room and board charges vary according to board plan and housing facility. **Scholarships:** Available **Calendar System:** Semester, Summer Session Available **Enrollment:** FT 6,233, PT 2,293, Grad FT 346, Grad PT 1,552 **Faculty:** FT 335, PT 272 **Student-Faculty Ratio:** 18:1 **Exams:** SAT I or ACT. **% Residing in College-Owned, -Operated, or -Affiliated Housing:** 21 **Library Holdings:** 400,000 **Regional Accreditation:** Southern Association of Colleges and Schools **Credit Hours For Degree:** 69 credit hours, Associates; 120 semester hours, Bachelors **ROTC:** Army **Professional Accreditation:** AACN, AAFCS, ACBSP, CSWE, NAACLS, NASM **Intercollegiate Athletics:** Baseball M; Basketball M & W; Cheerleading M & W; Cross-Country Running M & W; Football M; Golf W; Softball W; Tennis W; Track and Field M & W; Volleyball W

TARRANT COUNTY COLLEGE DISTRICT
1500 Houston St.
Fort Worth, TX 76102-6599
Tel: (817)515-5100
Fax: (817)515-5295
E-mail: billy.roessler@tccd.edu
Web Site: http://www.tccd.edu/
President/CEO: Erma Johnson Hadley
Admissions: Dr. Billy Roessler
Financial Aid: David Ximenez
Type: Two-Year College **Sex:** Coed **Admission Plans:** Open Admission; Early Admission **Application Deadline:** Rolling **Application Fee:** $0.00 **H.S. Requirements:** High school diploma or equivalent not required. For dental assisting, nursing programs: High school diploma required; GED accepted **Costs Per Year:** Application fee: $0. Area resident tuition: $1200 full-time, $50 per credit hour part-time. State resident tuition: $1752 full-time, $73 per credit hour part-time. Nonresident tuition: $3960 full-time, $165 per credit hour part-time. **Scholarships:** Available **Calendar System:** Semester, Summer Session Available **Enrollment:** FT 13,623, PT 25,973 **Faculty:** FT 593 **Student-Faculty Ratio:** 23:1 **Library Holdings:** 197,352 **Regional Accreditation:** Southern Association of Colleges and Schools **Credit Hours For Degree:** 64 semester hours, Associates **ROTC:** Army, Air Force **Professional Accreditation:** ADA, AHIMA, APTA, CARC, JRCERT, NLN

TEMPLE COLLEGE
2600 South First St.
Temple, TX 76504-7435
Tel: (254)298-8282
Admissions: (254)298-8303
E-mail: carey.rose@templejc.edu
Web Site: http://www.templejc.edu/
President/CEO: Dr. Glenda O. Barron
Admissions: Carey Rose
Financial Aid: Federico Pena, Jr.
Type: Two-Year College **Sex:** Coed **% Accepted:** 100 **Admission Plans:** Open Admission; Early Admission **Application Deadline:** Rolling **Application Fee:** $0.00 **H.S. Requirements:** High school diploma required; GED accepted **Costs Per Year:** Application fee: $0. Area resident tuition: $2250 full-time, $75 per semester hour part-time. State resident tuition: $3600 full-time, $120 per semester hour part-time. Nonresident tuition: $5700 full-time, $310 per semester hour part-time. Mandatory fees: $150 full-time, $24 per course part-time, $25 per term part-time. College room and board: $7309. Allied health courses cost an additional $15 per semester hour. **Scholarships:** Available **Calendar System:** Semester, Summer Session Available **Enrollment:** FT 2,250, PT 3,409 **Faculty:** FT 126, PT 158 **Student-Faculty Ratio:** 19:1 **Exams:** Other. **Final Year or Final Semester Residency Requirement:** Yes **Library Holdings:** 58,907 **Regional Accreditation:** Southern Association of Colleges and Schools **Credit Hours For Degree:** 64 semester hours, Associates **Professional Accreditation:** ADA, CARC, NAACLS, NLN **Intercollegiate Athletics:** Baseball M; Basketball M & W; Softball W; Tennis M & W; Volleyball W

TEXARKANA COLLEGE
2500 North Robison Rd.
Texarkana, TX 75599-0001
Tel: (903)838-4541
Fax: (903)832-5030
E-mail: vmiller@texarkanacollege.edu
Web Site: http://www.texarkanacollege.edu/
President/CEO: Frank Coleman
Admissions: Van Miller
Type: Two-Year College **Sex:** Coed **Admission Plans:** Open Admission; Early Admission **Application Deadline:** Rolling **Application Fee:** $0.00 **H.S. Requirements:** High school diploma required; GED accepted **Scholarships:** Available **Calendar System:** Semester, Summer Session Available **Enrollment:** FT 1,795, PT 2,644 **Faculty:** FT 107, PT 113 **Student-Faculty Ratio:** 19:1 **% Residing in College-Owned, -Operated, or -Affiliated Housing:** 2 **Library Holdings:** 46,700 **Regional Accreditation:** Southern Association of Colleges and Schools **Credit Hours For Degree:** 62 semester hours, Associates **Professional Accreditation:** NLN **Intercollegiate Athletics:** Baseball M; Softball W

TEXAS A&M HEALTH SCIENCE CENTER
301 Tarrow St.
7th Floor
College Station, TX 77840
Tel: (979)458-7200
Admissions: (214)828-8232
Fax: (979)458-7202
Web Site: http://www.tamhsc.edu/
President/CEO: Dr. Nancy W. Dickey
Admissions: Dr. Jack L. Long
Type: Two-Year Upper Division **Sex:** Coed **Affiliation:** Texas A&M University System Health Science Center **Application Fee:** $35.00 **Calendar System:** Semester, Summer Session Not available **Enrollment:** FT 60 **Faculty:** FT 137, PT 118 **Regional Accreditation:** Southern Association of Colleges and Schools **Professional Accreditation:** ADA, CEPH, LCMEAMA

TEXAS A&M INTERNATIONAL UNIVERSITY
5201 University Blvd.
Laredo, TX 78041-1900
Tel: (956)326-2001; Free: 888-489-2648
Admissions: (956)326-2200
Fax: (956)326-2348
E-mail: adms@tamiu.edu
Web Site: http://www.tamiu.edu/
President/CEO: Dr. Ray M. Keck, III

Admissions: Rosa Dickinson
Financial Aid: Laura Elizondo
Type: Comprehensive **Sex:** Coed **Affiliation:** Texas A&M University System **Scores:** 71.85% SAT V 400+; 83.11% SAT M 400+; 45.52% ACT 18-23; 7.09% ACT 24-29 **% Accepted:** 53 **Admission Plans:** Early Admission; Deferred Admission **Application Deadline:** July 1 **Application Fee:** $0.00 **H.S. Requirements:** High school diploma required; GED accepted **Costs Per Year:** Application fee: $0. State resident tuition: $4055 full-time. Nonresident tuition: $12,365 full-time. Mandatory fees: $1662 full-time. Full-time tuition and fees vary according to course load. College room and board: $6918. College room only: $4842. Room and board charges vary according to board plan and housing facility. **Scholarships:** Available **Calendar System:** Semester, Summer Session Available **Enrollment:** FT 3,349, PT 1,966, Grad FT 169, Grad PT 935 **Faculty:** FT 162, PT 141 **Student-Faculty Ratio:** 20:1 **Exams:** SAT I or ACT. ACT essay not being used. SAT essay not being used. **% Receiving Financial Aid:** 70 **% Residing in College-Owned, -Operated, or -Affiliated Housing:** 13 **Library Holdings:** 368,166 **Regional Accreditation:** Southern Association of Colleges and Schools **Credit Hours For Degree:** 124 semester hours, Bachelors **ROTC:** Army **Professional Accreditation:** AACSB, NLN **Intercollegiate Athletics:** Baseball M & W; Basketball M & W; Cross-Country Running M & W; Golf M & W; Soccer M & W; Softball M & W; Volleyball W

TEXAS A&M UNIVERSITY

College Station, TX 77843
Tel: (979)845-3211
Admissions: (979)845-3741
E-mail: admissions@tamu.edu
Web Site: http://www.tamu.edu/
President/CEO: Dr. Bowen Loftin
Admissions: Scott McDonald
Type: University **Sex:** Coed **Affiliation:** Texas A&M University System **Scores:** 98% SAT V 400+; 99% SAT M 400+; 20% ACT 18-23; 52% ACT 24-29 **% Accepted:** 67 **Admission Plans:** Preferred Admission **Application Deadline:** January 15 **Application Fee:** $60.00 **H.S. Requirements:** High school diploma required; GED accepted **Costs Per Year:** Application fee: $60. State resident tuition: $5152 full-time, $171.74 per credit hour part-time. Nonresident tuition: $19,582 full-time, $652.74 per credit hour part-time. Mandatory fees: $3024 full-time. College room and board: $8039. Room and board charges vary according to board plan, housing facility, and location. **Scholarships:** Available **Calendar System:** Semester, Summer Session Available **Enrollment:** FT 35,401, PT 3,409, Grad FT 7,938, Grad PT 1,955 **Faculty:** FT 2,317, PT 501 **Student-Faculty Ratio:** 19:1 **Exams:** SAT I or ACT. ACT essay used as a validity check on application essay. SAT essay used as a validity check on application essay. **% Receiving Financial Aid:** 37 **% Residing in College-Owned, -Operated, or -Affiliated Housing:** 24 **Final Year or Final Semester Residency Requirement:** No **Library Holdings:** 4,088,969 **Regional Accreditation:** Southern Association of Colleges and Schools **Credit Hours For Degree:** 128 semester hours, Bachelors **ROTC:** Army, Navy, Air Force **Professional Accreditation:** AACSB, ABET, ACEJMC, AAFCS, ACCE, ADtA, ACSP, APA, ASLA, AVMA, NAAB, NASPAA, NCATE, NRPA, SAF **Intercollegiate Athletics:** Archery W; Baseball M; Basketball M & W; Cross-Country Running M & W; Equestrian Sports W; Football M; Golf M & W; Soccer W; Softball W; Swimming and Diving M & W; Tennis M & W; Track and Field M & W; Volleyball W

TEXAS A&M UNIVERSITY AT GALVESTON

PO Box 1675
Galveston, TX 77553-1675
Tel: (409)740-4400
Admissions: (409)740-4448
Fax: (409)740-4709
E-mail: seaaggie@tamug.edu
Web Site: http://www.tamug.edu/
President/CEO: William Hearn
Admissions: Sarah Trombley
Financial Aid: Dennis Carlton
Type: Comprehensive **Sex:** Coed **Affiliation:** Texas A&M University System **Scores:** 99% SAT V 400+; 99% SAT M 400+; 54% ACT 18-23; 37% ACT 24-29 **% Accepted:** 77 **Admission Plans:** Early Admission; Deferred Admission **Application Deadline:** Rolling **Application Fee:** $45.00 **H.S. Requirements:** High school diploma required; GED accepted **Costs Per Year:** Application fee: $45. One-time mandatory fee: $75. State resident tuition: $5248 full-time, $175 per credit hour part-time. Nonresident tuition: $13,558 full-time, $452 per credit hour part-time. Mandatory fees: $1570 full-time, $640 per term part-time. Full-time tuition and fees vary according to course load and program. Part-time tuition and fees vary according to course load and program. College room and board: $5676. College room only: $2150. Room and board charges vary according to board plan and housing facility. **Scholarships:** Available **Calendar System:** Semester, Summer Session Available **Enrollment:** FT 1,591, PT 128, Grad FT 28, Grad PT 27 **Faculty:** FT 117, PT 53 **Student-Faculty Ratio:** 12:1 **Exams:** SAT I or ACT, SAT II. **% Receiving Financial Aid:** 46 **% Residing in College-Owned, -Operated, or -Affiliated Housing:** 37 **Library Holdings:** 56,589 **Regional Accreditation:** Southern Association of Colleges and Schools **Credit Hours For Degree:** 128 credit hours, Bachelors **ROTC:** Navy **Professional Accreditation:** ABET **Intercollegiate Athletics:** Crew M & W; Lacrosse M; Sailing M & W

TEXAS A&M UNIVERSITY—COMMERCE

PO Box 3011
Commerce, TX 75429-3011
Tel: (903)886-5081; Free: 800-331-3878
Admissions: (903)886-5103
Fax: (903)886-5888
E-mail: admissions@tamu-commerce.edu
Web Site: http://www.tamu-commerce.edu/
President/CEO: Keith D. McFarland, PhD
Admissions: Hope Young
Financial Aid: Maria Ramos
Type: University **Sex:** Coed **Affiliation:** Texas A&M University System **Scores:** 87.42% SAT V 400+; 90.1% SAT M 400+ **% Accepted:** 70 **Admission Plans:** Early Admission **Application Deadline:** August 11 **Application Fee:** $25.00 **H.S. Requirements:** High school diploma required; GED accepted **Costs Per Year:** Application fee: $25. State resident tuition: $5500 full-time. Nonresident tuition: $13,840 full-time. Full-time tuition varies according to course load. College room and board: $7090. Room and board charges vary according to board plan and housing facility. **Scholarships:** Available **Calendar System:** Semester, Summer Session Available **Enrollment:** FT 4,100, PT 1,250, Grad FT 219, Grad PT 3,601 **Faculty:** FT 361, PT 482 **Student-Faculty Ratio:** 17:1 **Exams:** SAT I or ACT. **% Receiving Financial Aid:** 69 **% Residing in College-Owned, -Operated, or -Affiliated Housing:** 24 **Library Holdings:** 1,098,728 **Regional Accreditation:** Southern Association of Colleges and Schools **Credit Hours For Degree:** 126 semester hours, Bachelors **Professional Accreditation:** AACSB, ACA, CSWE, NASM, NAIT **Intercollegiate Athletics:** Basketball M & W; Cheerleading M & W; Cross-Country Running M & W; Football M; Golf M & W; Soccer W; Track and Field M & W; Volleyball W

TEXAS A&M UNIVERSITY—CORPUS CHRISTI

6300 Ocean Dr.
Corpus Christi, TX 78412-5503
Tel: (361)825-5700; Free: 800-482-6822
Admissions: (361)825-2624
Fax: (361)825-5810
E-mail: monica.martinez@tamucc.edu
Web Site: http://www.tamucc.edu/
President/CEO: Dr. Flavius Killebrew
Admissions: Monica Martinez
Type: University **Sex:** Coed **Affiliation:** Texas A&M University System **Scores:** 87.19% SAT V 400+; 91.32% SAT M 400+; 58.56% ACT 18-23; 14.36% ACT 24-29 **% Accepted:** 85 **Application Deadline:** July 1 **Application Fee:** $25.00 **H.S. Requirements:** High school diploma required; GED accepted **Costs Per Year:** Application fee: $25. State resident tuition: $4456 full-time, $155.50 per credit hour part-time. Nonresident tuition: $13,016 full-time, $440.81 per credit hour part-time. Mandatory fees: $1765 full-time, $65.82 per credit hour part-time. Full-time tuition and fees vary according to course load, degree level, and student level. Part-time tuition and fees vary according to course load, degree level, and student level. College room and board: $9528. College room only: $6677. Room and board charges vary according to housing facility and location. **Scholarships:** Available **Calendar System:** Semester, Summer Session Available **Enrollment:** FT 5,826, PT 1,765, Grad FT 602, Grad PT 1,275 **Faculty:** FT 328, PT 200 **Student-Faculty Ratio:** 19:1 **Exams:** SAT I or ACT. ACT essay not being used. SAT essay not being used. **% Receiving Financial Aid:** 53 **% Residing in College-Owned, -Operated, or -Affiliated Housing:** 16 **Final Year or Final Semester Residency Requirement:** No **Library Holdings:** 731,586 **Regional Accreditation:** Southern Association of Colleges and Schools

Credit Hours For Degree: 124 semester hours, Bachelors **ROTC:** Army **Professional Accreditation:** AACSB, ABET, AACN, ACA, NAACLS, NASM **Intercollegiate Athletics:** Baseball M; Basketball M & W; Cross-Country Running M & W; Golf W; Softball W; Tennis M & W; Track and Field M & W; Volleyball W

TEXAS A&M UNIVERSITY—KINGSVILLE
West Santa Gertrudis
Kingsville, TX 78363
Tel: (361)593-2111; Free: 800-687-6000
Admissions: (361)593-2315
Web Site: http://www.tamuk.edu/
President/CEO: Dr. Steven H. Tallant
Admissions: William Carter
Financial Aid: Ralph Perri
Type: University **Sex:** Coed **Affiliation:** Texas A&M University System **% Accepted:** 91 **Admission Plans:** Open Admission; Early Admission; Deferred Admission **Application Deadline:** Rolling **Application Fee:** $15.00 **H.S. Requirements:** High school diploma required; GED accepted **Costs Per Year:** Application fee: $15. State resident tuition: $5882 full-time. Nonresident tuition: $14,192 full-time. Full-time tuition varies according to course load and degree level. College room and board: $5020. Room and board charges vary according to board plan and housing facility. **Scholarships:** Available **Calendar System:** Semester, Summer Session Available **Faculty:** FT 269, PT 290 **Student-Faculty Ratio:** 15:1 **Exams:** SAT I or ACT. **% Receiving Financial Aid:** 90 **Final Year or Final Semester Residency Requirement:** Yes **Regional Accreditation:** Southern Association of Colleges and Schools **Credit Hours For Degree:** 124 credits, Bachelors **ROTC:** Army **Professional Accreditation:** ABET, ADtA, ASLHA, ACBSP, CSWE, NASM, NAIT **Intercollegiate Athletics:** Baseball M; Basketball M & W; Cross-Country Running M & W; Equestrian Sports M & W; Football M; Softball W; Track and Field M & W; Volleyball W

TEXAS A&M UNIVERSITY—SAN ANTONIO
1450 Gillette Blvd.
San Antonio, TX 78224
Tel: (210)932-6299
Web Site: http://www.tamuk.edu/sanantonio/
Type: Comprehensive **Sex:** Coed

TEXAS A&M UNIVERSITY—TEXARKANA
PO Box 5518
Texarkana, TX 75505-5518
Tel: (903)223-3000
Fax: (903)832-8890
E-mail: admissions@tamut.edu
Web Site: http://www.tamut.edu/
President/CEO: Carlisle B. Rathburn, III
Admissions: Patricia Black
Financial Aid: Becky Ann Hejduk
Type: Two-Year Upper Division **Sex:** Coed **Affiliation:** Texas A&M University System **% Accepted:** 52 **Admission Plans:** Open Admission **Application Fee:** $0.00 **H.S. Requirements:** High school diploma required; GED accepted **Scholarships:** Available **Calendar System:** Semester, Summer Session Available **Enrollment:** FT 394, PT 612 **Student-Faculty Ratio:** 14:1 **% Receiving Financial Aid:** 64 **Library Holdings:** 132,065 **Regional Accreditation:** Southern Association of Colleges and Schools **Credit Hours For Degree:** 120 semester hours, Bachelors **Professional Accreditation:** AACN

TEXAS CHRISTIAN UNIVERSITY
2800 South University Dr.
Fort Worth, TX 76129-0002
Tel: (817)257-7000; Free: 800-828-3764
Admissions: (817)257-7490
E-mail: frogmail@tcu.edu
Web Site: http://www.tcu.edu/
President/CEO: Dr. Victor J. Boschini, Jr.
Admissions: Wes Waggoner
Financial Aid: Michael Scott
Type: University **Sex:** Coed **Affiliation:** Christian Church (Disciples of Christ) **% Accepted:** 59 **Admission Plans:** Early Action; Deferred Admission **Application Deadline:** February 15 **Application Fee:** $40.00 **H.S. Requirements:** High school diploma required; GED not accepted **Costs Per Year:** Application fee: $40. Comprehensive fee: $40,160 includes full-time tuition ($30,000), mandatory fees ($48), and college room and board ($10,112). College room only: $6370. Room and board charges vary according to board plan and housing facility. **Scholarships:** Available **Calendar System:** Semester, Summer Session Available **Enrollment:** FT 7,326, PT 314, Grad FT 503, Grad PT 710 **Faculty:** FT 523, PT 276 **Student-Faculty Ratio:** 13:1 **Exams:** SAT I or ACT. ACT essay used as a validity check on application essay. SAT essay used as a validity check on application essay. **% Receiving Financial Aid:** 42 **% Residing in College-Owned, -Operated, or -Affiliated Housing:** 46 **Library Holdings:** 1,429,817 **Regional Accreditation:** Southern Association of Colleges and Schools **Credit Hours For Degree:** 124 semester hours, Bachelors **ROTC:** Army, Air Force **Professional Accreditation:** AACSB, ABET, ACEJMC, AACN, AANA, ADtA, ASLHA, ACIPE, ATS, FIDER, CSWE, JRCEPAT, NASAD, NASM **Intercollegiate Athletics:** Baseball M; Basketball M & W; Cross-Country Running M & W; Equestrian Sports W; Football M; Golf M & W; Riflery W; Soccer W; Swimming and Diving M & W; Tennis M & W; Track and Field M & W; Volleyball W

TEXAS COLLEGE
2404 North Grand Ave.
PO Box 4500
Tyler, TX 75712-4500
Tel: (903)593-8311; Free: 800-306-6299
E-mail: jroberts@texascollege.edu
Web Site: http://www.texascollege.edu/
President/CEO: Dr. Dwight J. Fennell
Admissions: John Roberts
Financial Aid: Cecelia K. Jones
Type: Four-Year College **Sex:** Coed **Affiliation:** Christian Methodist Episcopal Church **Scores:** 30% ACT 18-23; 1% ACT 24-29 **Admission Plans:** Open Admission; Early Admission **Application Deadline:** Rolling **Application Fee:** $20.00 **H.S. Requirements:** High school diploma required; GED accepted **Costs Per Year:** Application fee: $20. One-time mandatory fee: $20. Comprehensive fee: $16,090 includes full-time tuition ($8000), mandatory fees ($1490), and college room and board ($6600). College room only: $3600. Part-time tuition: $333 per credit hour. Part-time mandatory fees: $745 per term. **Scholarships:** Available **Calendar System:** Semester, Summer Session Available **Enrollment:** FT 910, PT 26, Grad FT 24, Grad PT 4 **Faculty:** FT 34, PT 17 **Student-Faculty Ratio:** 24:1 **Exams:** SAT I or ACT. **% Receiving Financial Aid:** 84 **Final Year or Final Semester Residency Requirement:** Yes **Library Holdings:** 80,500 **Regional Accreditation:** Southern Association of Colleges and Schools **Credit Hours For Degree:** 66 credit hours, Associates; 124 credit hours, Bachelors **Intercollegiate Athletics:** Baseball M; Basketball M & W; Cheerleading M & W; Football M; Soccer M & W; Softball W; Track and Field M & W; Volleyball W

TEXAS CULINARY ACADEMY
3110 Esperanza Crossing
Ste. 100
Austin, TX 78758
Tel: (512)323-2511; Free: 888-553-2433
Admissions: (512)837-2665
Fax: (512)323-2126
E-mail: ppaulette@txca.com
Web Site: http://www.txca.com/
President/CEO: Julia Brooks
Admissions: Paula Paulette
Type: Two-Year College **Sex:** Coed **Admission Plans:** Open Admission **Application Deadline:** Rolling **Application Fee:** $100.00 **Scholarships:** Available **Calendar System:** Continuous **Student-Faculty Ratio:** 27:1 **Professional Accreditation:** COE

TEXAS LUTHERAN UNIVERSITY
1000 West Ct. St.
Seguin, TX 78155-5999
Tel: (830)372-8000; Free: 800-771-8521
Admissions: (830)372-8053
Fax: (830)372-8096
E-mail: njones@tlu.edu
Web Site: http://www.tlu.edu/
President/CEO: Rev. Ann Svennungsen
Admissions: Norm Jones

Financial Aid: Cathleen Wright
Type: Four-Year College **Sex:** Coed **Affiliation:** Evangelical Lutheran Church **Scores:** 92.1% SAT V 400+; 96.04% SAT M 400+; 59.39% ACT 18-23; 22.42% ACT 24-29 **% Accepted:** 66 **Admission Plans:** Deferred Admission **Application Deadline:** Rolling **Application Fee:** $25.00 **H.S. Requirements:** High school diploma required; GED accepted **Costs Per Year:** Application fee: $25. Comprehensive fee: $28,310 includes full-time tuition ($21,780), mandatory fees ($130), and college room and board ($6400). College room only: $3200. Full-time tuition and fees vary according to course load. Room and board charges vary according to board plan, housing facility, and location. Part-time tuition: $700 per semester hour. Part-time mandatory fees: $65 per term. Part-time tuition and fees vary according to course load. **Scholarships:** Available **Calendar System:** Semester, Summer Session Available **Enrollment:** FT 1,305, PT 82 **Faculty:** FT 68, PT 66 **Student-Faculty Ratio:** 15:1 **Exams:** SAT I or ACT. **% Receiving Financial Aid:** 73 **% Residing in College-Owned, -Operated, or -Affiliated Housing:** 61 **Final Year or Final Semester Residency Requirement:** No **Library Holdings:** 201,925 **Regional Accreditation:** Southern Association of Colleges and Schools **Credit Hours For Degree:** 124 credit hours, Bachelors **ROTC:** Army, Air Force **Professional Accreditation:** ACBSP **Intercollegiate Athletics:** Baseball M; Basketball M & W; Cross-Country Running W; Football M; Golf M & W; Soccer M & W; Softball W; Tennis M & W; Track and Field W; Volleyball W

TEXAS SOUTHERN UNIVERSITY
3100 Cleburne Ave.
Houston, TX 77004-4584
Tel: (713)313-7011
Admissions: (713)313-7071
Fax: (713)527-7842
E-mail: eservices@em.tsu.edu
Web Site: http://www.tsu.edu/
President/CEO: Dr. John Rudley
Type: University **Sex:** Coed **Affiliation:** Texas Higher Education Coordinating Board **Scores:** 50% SAT V 400+; 57% SAT M 400+; 32% ACT 18-23; 3% ACT 24-29 **% Accepted:** 26 **Admission Plans:** Open Admission **Application Deadline:** August 15 **Application Fee:** $42.00 **H.S. Requirements:** High school diploma required; GED accepted **Costs Per Year:** Application fee: $42. State resident tuition: $7080 full-time. Nonresident tuition: $15,390 full-time. Full-time tuition varies according to course level, course load, degree level, and program. College room and board: $11,620. Room and board charges vary according to board plan and housing facility. **Scholarships:** Available **Calendar System:** Semester, Summer Session Available **Enrollment:** FT 5,907, PT 1,351, Grad FT 1,419, Grad PT 717 **Faculty:** FT 337, PT 272 **Student-Faculty Ratio:** 19:1 **Exams:** SAT I or ACT. **% Receiving Financial Aid:** 52 **% Residing in College-Owned, -Operated, or -Affiliated Housing:** 15 **Library Holdings:** 264,254 **Regional Accreditation:** Southern Association of Colleges and Schools **Credit Hours For Degree:** 120 semester hours, Bachelors **ROTC:** Army, Navy **Professional Accreditation:** AACSB, ABET, ACPhE, ABA, AHIMA, ACSP, CARC, CSWE, NAACLS, NCATE, NAIT **Intercollegiate Athletics:** Baseball M; Basketball M & W; Bowling W; Cross-Country Running M & W; Football M; Golf M; Soccer M & W; Softball W; Tennis M & W; Track and Field M & W; Volleyball M & W

TEXAS SOUTHMOST COLLEGE
80 Fort Brown
Brownsville, TX 78520-4991
Tel: (956)882-8200; Free: 877-882-8721
Web Site: http://www.utb.edu/
President/CEO: Juliet Garcia
Type: Two-Year College **Sex:** Coed **Affiliation:** University of Texas System **Admission Plans:** Open Admission **Application Deadline:** August 1 **H.S. Requirements:** High school diploma required; GED accepted **Costs Per Year:** State resident tuition: $3180 full-time, $132.50 per credit hour part-time. Nonresident tuition: $9828 full-time, $409.50 per credit hour part-time. Mandatory fees: $1367 full-time, $36 per credit hour part-time, $251.30 per term part-time. Full-time tuition and fees vary according to class time, course level, course load, location, and program. Part-time tuition and fees vary according to class time, course level, course load, location, and program. College room and board: $5742. College room only: $2992. Room and board charges vary according to board plan. **Calendar System:** Semester, Summer Session Available **Regional Accreditation:** Southern Association of Colleges and Schools **Credit Hours For Degree:** 62 credits, Associates **Professional Accreditation:** CARC, JRCERT, NAACLS, NLN **Intercollegiate Athletics:** Baseball M; Golf M & W; Soccer M & W; Volleyball W

TEXAS STATE TECHNICAL COLLEGE HARLINGEN
1902 North Loop 499
Harlingen, TX 78550-3697
Tel: (956)364-4000
Admissions: (956)364-4100
Fax: (956)364-5140
E-mail: blanca.guerra@harlingen.tstc.edu
Web Site: http://www.harlingen.tstc.edu/
President/CEO: Dr. Gilbert Leal
Admissions: Blanca Guerra
Type: Two-Year College **Sex:** Coed **Affiliation:** Texas State Technical College System **Admission Plans:** Open Admission; Early Admission; Deferred Admission **Application Deadline:** Rolling **Application Fee:** $0.00 **H.S. Requirements:** High school diploma required; GED accepted **Scholarships:** Available **Calendar System:** Semester, Summer Session Available **Enrollment:** FT 1,729, PT 2,299 **Faculty:** FT 157, PT 22 **Student-Faculty Ratio:** 17:1 **Library Holdings:** 25,000 **Regional Accreditation:** Southern Association of Colleges and Schools **Credit Hours For Degree:** 72 semester hours, Associates **Professional Accreditation:** ADA, AHIMA

TEXAS STATE TECHNICAL COLLEGE WACO
3801 Campus Dr.
Waco, TX 76705-1695
Tel: (254)799-3611
Admissions: (254)867-2026
E-mail: marcus.balch@tstc.edu
Web Site: http://waco.tstc.edu/
President/CEO: Elton E. Stuckly, Jr.
Admissions: Marcus Balch
Financial Aid: Jackie Adler
Type: Two-Year College **Sex:** Coed **Affiliation:** Texas State Technical College System **Admission Plans:** Open Admission; Early Admission **Application Deadline:** Rolling **Application Fee:** $0.00 **H.S. Requirements:** High school diploma required; GED accepted **Costs Per Year:** Application fee: $0. State resident tuition: $2412 full-time, $67 per credit hour part-time. Nonresident tuition: $6768 full-time, $188 per credit hour part-time. Mandatory fees: $1224 full-time. College room and board: $4110. College room only: $3375. Room and board charges vary according to housing facility and location. **Scholarships:** Available **Calendar System:** Trimester, Summer Session Available **Enrollment:** FT 2,989, PT 1,463 **Faculty:** FT 243, PT 35 **Student-Faculty Ratio:** 16:1 **Exams:** Other. **Library Holdings:** 60,000 **Regional Accreditation:** Southern Association of Colleges and Schools **Credit Hours For Degree:** 72 semester credits, Associates **Professional Accreditation:** ADA

TEXAS STATE TECHNICAL COLLEGE WEST TEXAS
300 College Dr.
Sweetwater, TX 79556-4108
Tel: (915)235-7300; Free: 800-592-8784
Admissions: (325)235-7300
Fax: (915)235-7359
E-mail: maria.aquirre@sweetwater.tstc.edu
Web Site: http://www.westtexas.tstc.edu/
President/CEO: Michael Reeser
Admissions: Maria Aguirre-Acuna
Financial Aid: MaryLou Bledsoe
Type: Two-Year College **Sex:** Coed **Affiliation:** Texas State Technical College System **% Accepted:** 100 **Admission Plans:** Open Admission; Early Admission; Deferred Admission **Application Deadline:** Rolling **Application Fee:** $0.00 **H.S. Requirements:** High school diploma or equivalent not required. For skill development programs: High school diploma required; GED accepted **Costs Per Year:** Application fee: $0. State resident tuition: $2412 full-time, $67 per semester hour part-time. Nonresident tuition: $6768 full-time, $188 per semester hour part-time. Mandatory fees: $1224 full-time, $37 per semester hour part-time. College room and board: $6900. College room only: $3375. Room and board charges vary according to board plan and housing facility. **Scholarships:** Available **Calendar System:** Semester, Summer Session Available **Enrollment:** FT 299, PT 1,390 **Faculty:** FT 89, PT 27 **Student-Faculty Ratio:** 7:1 **Exams:** Other. **% Residing in College-Owned, -Operated, or -Affiliated Housing:** 14 **Final Year or Final Semester Residency Requirement:** No **Library Holdings:** 59,711

Regional Accreditation: Southern Association of Colleges and Schools **Credit Hours For Degree:** 60 credits, Associates

TEXAS STATE TECHNICAL COLLEGE—MARSHALL

2650 East End Blvd. South
Marshall, TX 75671
Tel: (903)935-1010
E-mail: Pat.Robbins@marshall.tstc.edu
Web Site: http://www.marshall.tstc.edu/
President/CEO: Randall Wooten
Admissions: Pat Robbins

Type: Two-Year College **Sex:** Coed **Affiliation:** Texas State Technical College System **Application Fee:** $0.00 **H.S. Requirements:** High school diploma required; GED accepted **Costs Per Year:** Application fee: $0. State resident tuition: $2412 full-time, $67 per credit hour part-time. Nonresident tuition: $6768 full-time, $188 per credit hour part-time. Mandatory fees: $1224 full-time, $34 per credit hour part-time. College room only: $3585. Room charges vary according to housing facility. **Calendar System:** Semester **Enrollment:** FT 322, PT 383 **Faculty:** FT 30, PT 11 **Student-Faculty Ratio:** 12:1 **Regional Accreditation:** Southern Association of Colleges and Schools

TEXAS STATE UNIVERSITY—SAN MARCOS

601 University Dr.
San Marcos, TX 78666
Tel: (512)245-2111
Admissions: (512)245-2364
Fax: (512)245-8044
E-mail: admissions@txstate.edu
Web Site: http://www.txstate.edu/
President/CEO: Dr. Denise M. Trauth
Admissions: Stephanie Anderson
Financial Aid: Chris Murr

Type: University **Sex:** Coed **Affiliation:** Texas State University System **Scores:** 97.1% SAT V 400+; 98.3% SAT M 400+; 56.6% ACT 18-23; 37.1% ACT 24-29 **% Accepted:** 76 **Admission Plans:** Early Admission; Deferred Admission **Application Deadline:** May 1 **Application Fee:** $60.00 **H.S. Requirements:** High school diploma required; GED accepted **Costs Per Year:** Application fee: $60. State resident tuition: $5460 full-time, $182 per credit hour part-time. Nonresident tuition: $13,770 full-time, $459 per credit hour part-time. Mandatory fees: $2022 full-time, $46 per credit hour part-time, $366 per term part-time. Full-time tuition and fees vary according to course load. Part-time tuition and fees vary according to course load. College room and board: $6392. College room only: $4180. Room and board charges vary according to board plan and housing facility. **Scholarships:** Available **Calendar System:** Semester, Summer Session Available **Enrollment:** FT 21,215, PT 4,787, Grad FT 2,159, Grad PT 2,642 **Faculty:** FT 963, PT 408 **Student-Faculty Ratio:** 22:1 **Exams:** SAT I or ACT. ACT essay used as a validity check on application essay. SAT essay used as a validity check on application essay. **% Receiving Financial Aid:** 52 **% Residing in College-Owned, -Operated, or -Affiliated Housing:** 24 **Library Holdings:** 1,513,583 **Regional Accreditation:** Southern Association of Colleges and Schools **Credit Hours For Degree:** 128 semester hours, Bachelors **ROTC:** Army, Air Force **Professional Accreditation:** AACSB, ABET, ACEJMC, AAFCS, ACA, ADtA, AHIMA, APTA, APA, ASLHA, ACEHSA, CARC, FIDER, CSWE, JRCERT, JRCEPAT, NAACLS, NASM, NASPAA, NRPA **Intercollegiate Athletics:** Baseball M; Basketball M & W; Cheerleading M & W; Cross-Country Running M & W; Equestrian Sports M & W; Fencing M & W; Football M; Golf M & W; Gymnastics M & W; Lacrosse M & W; Rugby M & W; Soccer M & W; Softball M & W; Tennis M & W; Track and Field M & W; Ultimate Frisbee M & W; Volleyball W; Water Polo M & W; Weight Lifting M & W; Wrestling M & W

TEXAS TECH UNIVERSITY

Lubbock, TX 79409
Tel: (806)742-2011
Admissions: (806)742-1480
Fax: (806)742-3055
Web Site: http://www.ttu.edu/
President/CEO: Guy Bailey
Admissions: Ethan Logan
Financial Aid: Becky Wilson

Type: University **Sex:** Coed **Affiliation:** Texas Tech University System **Scores:** 97.8% SAT V 400+; 99.4% SAT M 400+; 48.9% ACT 18-23; 40.9% ACT 24-29 **% Accepted:** 68 **Admission Plans:** Early Admission **Application Deadline:** May 1 **Application Fee:** $50.00 **H.S. Requirements:** High school diploma required; GED accepted **Costs Per Year:** Application fee: $50. State resident tuition: $4875 full-time, $162.50 per credit hour part-time. Nonresident tuition: $13,185 full-time, $439.50 per credit hour part-time. Mandatory fees: $2610 full-time, $50 per credit hour part-time, $555 per term part-time. Full-time tuition and fees vary according to course load, program, and reciprocity agreements. Part-time tuition and fees vary according to course load, program, and reciprocity agreements. College room and board: $7527. College room only: $4100. Room and board charges vary according to board plan and housing facility. **Scholarships:** Available **Calendar System:** Semester, Summer Session Available **Enrollment:** FT 22,061, PT 2,175, Grad FT 3,799, Grad PT 2,014 **Faculty:** FT 1,148, PT 168 **Student-Faculty Ratio:** 22:1 **Exams:** SAT I or ACT. **% Receiving Financial Aid:** 39 **% Residing in College-Owned, -Operated, or -Affiliated Housing:** 25 **Final Year or Final Semester Residency Requirement:** Yes **Library Holdings:** 2,450,322 **Regional Accreditation:** Southern Association of Colleges and Schools **Credit Hours For Degree:** 120 semester hours, Bachelors **ROTC:** Army, Air Force **Professional Accreditation:** AACSB, ABET, ACEJMC, AAMFT, AAFCS, ABA, ACA, ADtA, APA, ASLA, ASLHA, AALS, ACEHSA, FIDER, CSWE, JRCEMT, NAAB, NASAD, NASM, NASPAA NAST, NCATE **Intercollegiate Athletics:** Baseball M; Basketball M & W; Cross-Country Running M & W; Football M; Golf M & W; Soccer W; Softball W; Tennis M & W; Track and Field M & W; Volleyball W

TEXAS WESLEYAN UNIVERSITY

1201 Wesleyan St.
Fort Worth, TX 76105-1536
Tel: (817)531-4444
Admissions: (817)531-4422
Fax: (817)531-7515
E-mail: admission@txwes.edu
Web Site: http://www.txwes.edu/
President/CEO: Dr. Harold G. Jeffcoat

Type: Comprehensive **Sex:** Coed **Affiliation:** United Methodist **Scores:** 82% SAT V 400+; 88% SAT M 400+; 60% ACT 18-23; 19% ACT 24-29 **% Accepted:** 61 **Admission Plans:** Deferred Admission **Application Deadline:** Rolling **Application Fee:** $25.00 **H.S. Requirements:** High school diploma required; GED accepted **Costs Per Year:** Application fee: $25. Comprehensive fee: $24,416 includes full-time tuition ($16,120), mandatory fees ($1640), and college room and board ($6656). College room only: $3900. Full-time tuition and fees vary according to degree level and program. Room and board charges vary according to housing facility. Part-time tuition: $546 per credit hour. Part-time mandatory fees: $62 per credit hour. Part-time tuition and fees vary according to degree level and program. **Scholarships:** Available **Calendar System:** Semester, Summer Session Available **Enrollment:** FT 1,171, PT 631, Grad FT 1,018, Grad PT 513 **Faculty:** FT 165, PT 94 **Student-Faculty Ratio:** 12:1 **Exams:** SAT I or ACT. **% Receiving Financial Aid:** 82 **% Residing in College-Owned, -Operated, or -Affiliated Housing:** 19 **Final Year or Final Semester Residency Requirement:** No **Library Holdings:** 237,916 **Regional Accreditation:** Southern Association of Colleges and Schools **Credit Hours For Degree:** 124 credit hours, Bachelors **ROTC:** Army **Professional Accreditation:** AANA, ABA, ACBSP, NASM **Intercollegiate Athletics:** Baseball M; Basketball M & W; Golf M; Soccer M & W; Softball W; Table Tennis M; Volleyball W

TEXAS WOMAN'S UNIVERSITY

304 Administration Dr.
Denton, TX 76201
Tel: (940)898-2000; Free: (866)809-6130
Admissions: (940)898-3188
Fax: (940)898-3198
E-mail: admissions@twu.edu
Web Site: http://www.twu.edu/
President/CEO: Dr. Ann Stuart
Admissions: Erma Nieto-Brecht
Financial Aid: Governor Jackson

Type: University **Sex:** Coed **Scores:** 88% SAT V 400+; 92% SAT M 400+; 49% ACT 18-23; 29% ACT 24-29 **% Accepted:** 84 **Admission Plans:** Early Admission; Deferred Admission **Application Deadline:** July 1 **Application Fee:** $50.00 **H.S. Requirements:** High school diploma required; GED accepted **Costs Per Year:** Application fee: $50. State resident tuition: $4740 full-time, $158 per credit hour part-time. Nonresident tuition: $13,080 full-time, $435 per credit hour part-time. Mandatory fees: $1920 full-time. Full-time tuition and fees vary according to course load. Part-time tuition varies according to course load. College room and board: $5967. College room only: $3058. Room and board charges vary according to board plan and housing facility. **Scholarships:** Available **Calendar System:** Semester, Summer Session Available **Enrollment:** FT 5,327, PT 2,409, Grad FT 2,119, Grad PT 3,382 **Faculty:** FT 306, PT 443 **Student-Faculty Ratio:** 17:1 **Exams:** SAT I or ACT. ACT essay not being used. SAT essay not being used. **% Receiving Financial Aid:** 62 **% Residing in College-Owned, -Operated, or -Affiliated Housing:** 20 **Final Year or Final Semester Residency Requirement:** Yes **Library Holdings:** 643,323 **Regional Accreditation:** Southern Association of Colleges and Schools **Credit Hours For Degree:** 124 semester hours, Bachelors **ROTC:** Army, Air Force **Professional Accreditation:** AACN, AAFCS, ACA, ADA, ADtA, ALA, AOTA, APTA, APA, ASLHA, ACEHSA, CSWE, NASD, NASM, NLN **Intercollegiate Athletics:** Basketball W; Gymnastics W; Soccer W; Softball W; Volleyball W

TRINITY UNIVERSITY
One Trinity Place
San Antonio, TX 78212-7200
Tel: (210)999-7011; Free: 800-TRI-NITY
Admissions: (210)999-7207
Fax: (210)999-8164
E-mail: admissions@trinity.edu
Web Site: http://www.trinity.edu/
President/CEO: Dr. John R. Brazil
Admissions: Christopher Ellertson
Financial Aid: Sean Smith
Type: Comprehensive **Sex:** Coed **Affiliation:** Presbyterian Church **Scores:** 100% SAT V 400+; 100% SAT M 400+; 1% ACT 18-23; 53.7% ACT 24-29 **% Accepted:** 59 **Admission Plans:** Early Action; Early Decision Plan; Deferred Admission **Application Deadline:** February 1 **Application Fee:** $50.00 **H.S. Requirements:** High school diploma required; GED accepted **Costs Per Year:** Application fee: $50. Comprehensive fee: $38,212 includes full-time tuition ($28,272), mandatory fees ($1045), and college room and board ($8895). College room only: $5825. Full-time tuition and fees vary according to course load. Room and board charges vary according to board plan. Part-time tuition: $1178 per credit hour. Part-time tuition varies according to course load. **Scholarships:** Available **Calendar System:** Semester, Summer Session Available **Enrollment:** FT 2,435, PT 52, Grad FT 128, Grad PT 78 **Faculty:** FT 243, PT 83 **Student-Faculty Ratio:** 9:1 **Exams:** SAT I or ACT. **% Receiving Financial Aid:** 39 **% Residing in College-Owned, -Operated, or -Affiliated Housing:** 72 **Library Holdings:** 1,127,516 **Regional Accreditation:** Southern Association of Colleges and Schools **Credit Hours For Degree:** 124 semester hours, Bachelors **ROTC:** Air Force **Professional Accreditation:** AACSB, ABET, ACEHSA, NASM, NCATE **Intercollegiate Athletics:** Baseball M; Basketball M & W; Cross-Country Running M & W; Fencing M & W; Football M; Golf M & W; Lacrosse M & W; Riflery M & W; Soccer M & W; Softball W; Swimming and Diving M & W; Tennis M & W; Track and Field M & W; Volleyball M & W; Water Polo M & W

TRINITY VALLEY COMMUNITY COLLEGE
100 Cardinal Dr.
Athens, TX 75751-2765
Tel: (903)677-TVCC
Admissions: (903)675-6209
Web Site: http://www.tvcc.edu/
President/CEO: Dr. Glendon Forgey
Admissions: Dr. Colette Hilliard
Type: Two-Year College **Sex:** Coed **Admission Plans:** Open Admission; Early Admission **Application Deadline:** Rolling **H.S. Requirements:** High school diploma required; GED accepted **Costs Per Year:** Area resident tuition: $1200 full-time. State resident tuition: $1800 full-time. Nonresident tuition: $2400 full-time. College room and board: $3870. Room and board charges vary according to board plan. **Scholarships:** Available **Calendar System:** Semester, Summer Session Available **Enrollment:** FT 2,688, PT 4,050 **Faculty:** FT 138, PT 115 **Student-Faculty Ratio:** 22:1 **% Residing in College-Owned, -Operated, or -Affiliated Housing:** 12 **Library Holdings:** 54,940 **Regional Accreditation:** Southern Association of Colleges and Schools **Credit Hours For Degree:** 64 semester hours, Associates **Professional Accreditation:** ARCEST, NLN **Intercollegiate Athletics:** Basketball M & W; Cheerleading M & W; Football M; Volleyball W

TYLER JUNIOR COLLEGE
PO Box 9020
Tyler, TX 75711-9020
Tel: (903)510-2200; Free: 800-687-5680
Web Site: http://www.tjc.edu/
President/CEO: Mike Metke
Admissions: Janna Chancey
Type: Two-Year College **Sex:** Coed **Admission Plans:** Open Admission; Preferred Admission; Early Admission **Application Deadline:** Rolling **Application Fee:** $0.00 **H.S. Requirements:** High school diploma required; GED accepted. For allied health programs: High school diploma required; GED not accepted **Scholarships:** Available **Calendar System:** Semester, Summer Session Available **Faculty:** FT 234, PT 222 **Student-Faculty Ratio:** 21:1 **% Residing in College-Owned, -Operated, or -Affiliated Housing:** 8 **Regional Accreditation:** Southern Association of Colleges and Schools **Credit Hours For Degree:** 60 semester hours, Associates **Professional Accreditation:** ARCEST, ADA, AHIMA, COptA, CARC, JRCEDMS, JRCERT, NAACLS **Intercollegiate Athletics:** Baseball M; Basketball M & W; Football M; Golf M & W; Soccer M; Tennis M & W; Volleyball W

UNIVERSAL TECHNICAL INSTITUTE
721 Lockhaven Dr.
Houston, TX 77073-5598
Tel: (281)443-6262; Free: 800-325-0354
Web Site: http://www.uti.edu/
President/CEO: Ken Golaszewski
Type: Two-Year College **Sex:** Coed **Admission Plans:** Open Admission **Student-Faculty Ratio:** 22:1 **Professional Accreditation:** ACCSCT

UNIVERSITY OF DALLAS
1845 East Northgate Dr.
Irving, TX 75062-4736
Tel: (972)721-5000; Free: 800-628-6999
Admissions: (972)721-5266
Fax: (972)721-5017
E-mail: ugadmis@udallas.edu
Web Site: http://www.udallas.edu/
President/CEO: Thomas W. Keefe, JD
Admissions: Amanda Lively
Financial Aid: Laurie Rosenkrantz
Type: University **Sex:** Coed **Affiliation:** Roman Catholic **Scores:** 100% SAT V 400+; 98.8% SAT M 400+; 28.22% ACT 18-23; 45.4% ACT 24-29 **% Accepted:** 92 **Admission Plans:** Early Admission; Early Action; Deferred Admission **Application Deadline:** August 1 **Application Fee:** $40.00 **H.S. Requirements:** High school diploma required; GED accepted **Costs Per Year:** Application fee: $40. Comprehensive fee: $36,465 includes full-time tuition ($26,100), mandatory fees ($1715), and college room and board ($8650). College room only: $4820. Room and board charges vary according to board plan and housing facility. **Scholarships:** Available **Calendar System:** Semester, Summer Session Available **Enrollment:** FT 1,279, PT 23, Grad FT 445, Grad PT 1,136 **Faculty:** FT 125, PT 108 **Student-Faculty Ratio:** 13:1 **Exams:** SAT I or ACT. **% Receiving Financial Aid:** 61 **% Residing in College-Owned, -Operated, or -Affiliated Housing:** 57 **Library Holdings:** 245,228 **Regional Accreditation:** Southern Association of Colleges and Schools **Credit Hours For Degree:** 120 credits, Bachelors **ROTC:** Army, Air Force **Professional Accreditation:** AALE, ACBSP **Intercollegiate Athletics:** Baseball M; Basketball M & W; Cross-Country Running M & W; Golf M; Lacrosse M & W; Soccer M & W; Softball W; Track and Field M & W; Volleyball W

UNIVERSITY OF HOUSTON
4800 Calhoun Rd.
Houston, TX 77204
Tel: (713)743-1000
Admissions: (713)743-1010
Fax: (713)743-9633
E-mail: jdfuller@central.uh.edu
Web Site: http://www.uh.edu/
President/CEO: Dr. Renu Khator
Admissions: Jeff Fuller
Type: University **Sex:** Coed **Affiliation:** University of Houston System **Scores:** 94% SAT V 400+; 98% SAT M 400+; 54% ACT 18-23; 30% ACT 24-29 **% Accepted:** 70 **Application Deadline:** April 1 **Application Fee:** $50.00 **H.S. Requirements:** High school diploma required; GED accepted

Costs Per Year: Application fee: $50. State resident tuition: $5542 full-time, $185 per credit hour part-time. Nonresident tuition: $13,852 full-time, $462 per credit hour part-time. Mandatory fees: $2954 full-time. Full-time tuition and fees vary according to course level, course load, and program. Part-time tuition varies according to course level, course load, and program. College room and board: $7164. College room only: $4224. Room and board charges vary according to board plan and housing facility. **Scholarships:** Available **Calendar System:** Semester, Summer Session Available **Enrollment:** FT 21,096, PT 8,202, Grad FT 5,289, Grad PT 2,413 **Faculty:** FT 1,256, PT 524 **Student-Faculty Ratio:** 22:1 **Exams:** SAT I or ACT. ACT essay not being used. SAT essay not being used. **% Receiving Financial Aid:** 56 **% Residing in College-Owned, -Operated, or -Affiliated Housing:** 13 **Final Year or Final Semester Residency Requirement:** Yes **Library Holdings:** 2,666,072 **Regional Accreditation:** Southern Association of Colleges and Schools **Credit Hours For Degree:** 120 semester hours, Bachelors **ROTC:** Army, Navy, Air Force **Professional Accreditation:** AACSB, ABET, ACPhE, ABA, ADtA, AOA, APA, ASLHA, AALS, CSWE, NAAB, NASM, NCATE **Intercollegiate Athletics:** Baseball M; Basketball M & W; Cross-Country Running M & W; Football M & W; Golf M; Soccer W; Softball W; Swimming and Diving W; Tennis W; Track and Field M & W; Volleyball W

UNIVERSITY OF HOUSTON—CLEAR LAKE
2700 Bay Area Blvd.
Houston, TX 77058-1098
Tel: (281)283-7600
Admissions: (281)283-2518
Fax: (281)283-2530
E-mail: admissions@uhcl.edu
Web Site: http://www.uhcl.edu/
President/CEO: Dr. William Staples
Admissions: Rauchelle Jones
Financial Aid: Billy Satterfield

Type: Two-Year Upper Division **Sex:** Coed **Affiliation:** University of Houston System **Admission Plans:** Early Admission; Deferred Admission **Application Fee:** $35.00 **Costs Per Year:** Application fee: $35. State resident tuition: $4560 full-time, $152 per credit hour part-time. Nonresident tuition: $13,770 full-time, $459 per credit hour part-time. Mandatory fees: $1148 full-time, $436 per term part-time. Full-time tuition and fees vary according to course load, location, and program. Part-time tuition and fees vary according to course load, location, and program. College room only: $7896. Room charges vary according to housing facility. **Scholarships:** Available **Calendar System:** Semester, Summer Session Available **Enrollment:** FT 2,027, PT 2,200, Grad FT 1,277, Grad PT 2,158 **Faculty:** FT 220, PT 305 **Student-Faculty Ratio:** 10:1 **% Receiving Financial Aid:** 65 **% Residing in College-Owned, -Operated, or -Affiliated Housing:** 1 **Final Year or Final Semester Residency Requirement:** Yes **Regional Accreditation:** Southern Association of Colleges and Schools **Credit Hours For Degree:** 120 semester hours, Bachelors **Professional Accreditation:** AACSB, ABET, AAMFT, ACEHSA, NCATE

UNIVERSITY OF HOUSTON—DOWNTOWN
One Main St.
Houston, TX 77002
Tel: (713)221-8000
Admissions: (713)221-8522
Fax: (713)221-8157
E-mail: uhdadmit@uhd.edu
Web Site: http://www.uhd.edu/
President/CEO: Dr. William V. Flores
Admissions: Patricia Santos

Type: Comprehensive **Sex:** Coed **Affiliation:** University of Houston System **% Accepted:** 100 **Admission Plans:** Open Admission; Early Admission **Application Deadline:** June 1 **Application Fee:** $35.00 **H.S. Requirements:** High school diploma required; GED accepted **Costs Per Year:** Application fee: $35. One-time mandatory fee: $10. State resident tuition: $4200 full-time, $140 per credit hour part-time. Nonresident tuition: $12,510 full-time, $417 per credit hour part-time. Mandatory fees: $1032 full-time. Full-time tuition and fees vary according to course load. Part-time tuition varies according to course load. international students must also pay an international student service fee of $45 per semester. **Scholarships:** Available **Calendar System:** Semester, Summer Session Available **Enrollment:** FT 6,091, PT 6,488, Grad FT 11, Grad PT 152 **Faculty:** FT 316, PT 278 **Student-Faculty Ratio:** 20:1 **Exams:** ACT essay not being used. SAT essay not being used. **% Receiving Financial Aid:** 77 **Final Year or Final Semester Residency Requirement:** Yes **Library Holdings:** 322,786 **Regional Accreditation:** Southern Association of Colleges and Schools **Credit Hours For Degree:** 120 credit hours, Bachelors **ROTC:** Army, Air Force **Professional Accreditation:** AACSB, ABET

UNIVERSITY OF HOUSTON—VICTORIA
3007 North Ben Wilson St.
Victoria, TX 77901-4450
Tel: (361)570-4848; Free: 877-970-4848
Admissions: (361)570-4290
Fax: (361)572-9377
E-mail: worthamt@uhv.edu
Web Site: http://www.uhv.edu/
President/CEO: Dr. Tim Hudson
Admissions: Trudy Wortham
Financial Aid: Carolyn Mallory

Type: Two-Year Upper Division **Sex:** Coed **Affiliation:** University of Houston System **Application Deadline:** Rolling **Costs Per Year:** State resident tuition: $4290 full-time, $143 per credit hour part-time. Nonresident tuition: $12,600 full-time, $420 per credit hour part-time. Mandatory fees: $1110 full-time, $52 per credit hour part-time. Full-time tuition and fees vary according to course level and course load. Part-time tuition and fees vary according to course level and course load. **Scholarships:** Available **Calendar System:** Semester, Summer Session Available **Enrollment:** FT 673, PT 1,109, Grad FT 404, Grad PT 1,469 **Faculty:** FT 88, PT 88 **Student-Faculty Ratio:** 16:1 **% Receiving Financial Aid:** 55 **Library Holdings:** 50,000 **Regional Accreditation:** Southern Association of Colleges and Schools **Credit Hours For Degree:** 122 semester hours, Bachelors **Professional Accreditation:** AACSB, TEAC

UNIVERSITY OF THE INCARNATE WORD
4301 Broadway
San Antonio, TX 78209-6397
Tel: (210)829-6000; Free: 800-749-WORD
Admissions: (210)829-6005
Fax: (210)829-3921
E-mail: admis@uiwtx.edu
Web Site: http://www.uiw.edu/
President/CEO: Dr. Louis Agnese
Admissions: Andrea Cyterski-Acosta
Financial Aid: Amy Carcanagues

Type: Comprehensive **Sex:** Coed **Affiliation:** Roman Catholic **Scores:** 86.84% SAT V 400+; 90.2% SAT M 400+; 55.4% ACT 18-23; 21.6% ACT 24-29 **% Accepted:** 66 **Admission Plans:** Deferred Admission **Application Deadline:** Rolling **Application Fee:** $20.00 **H.S. Requirements:** High school diploma required; GED accepted **Costs Per Year:** Application fee: $20. Comprehensive fee: $31,110 includes full-time tuition ($21,000), mandatory fees ($890), and college room and board ($9220). College room only: $5540. Full-time tuition and fees vary according to course load, degree level, location, and reciprocity agreements. Room and board charges vary according to board plan and housing facility. Part-time tuition: $675 per semester hour. Part-time tuition varies according to course load, degree level, location, and reciprocity agreements. **Scholarships:** Available **Calendar System:** Semester, Summer Session Available **Enrollment:** FT 3,373, PT 1,846, Grad FT 640, Grad PT 897 **Faculty:** FT 219, PT 349 **Student-Faculty Ratio:** 15:1 **Exams:** SAT I or ACT. ACT essay used for placement. SAT essay used for placement. **% Receiving Financial Aid:** 87 **% Residing in College-Owned, -Operated, or -Affiliated Housing:** 13 **Library Holdings:** 271,657 **Regional Accreditation:** Southern Association of Colleges and Schools **Credit Hours For Degree:** 64 semester hours, Associates; 128 semester hours, Bachelors **ROTC:** Army, Air Force **Professional Accreditation:** ACPhE, AACN, ADtA, AOA, ACBSP, JRCNMT, NAST **Intercollegiate Athletics:** Baseball M; Basketball M & W; Cross-Country Running M & W; Football M; Golf M & W; Soccer M & W; Softball W; Swimming and Diving M & W; Tennis M & W; Track and Field M & W; Volleyball W

UNIVERSITY OF MARY HARDIN-BAYLOR
900 College St.
Belton, TX 76513
Tel: (254)295-8642; Free: 800-727-8642
Admissions: (254)295-4520
Fax: (254)295-4535
E-mail: admission@umhb.edu
Web Site: http://www.umhb.edu/

President/CEO: Randy O'Rear, PhD
Admissions: Brent Burks
Financial Aid: David Orsag
Type: Comprehensive **Sex:** Coed **Affiliation:** Southern Baptist **Scores:** 96% SAT V 400+; 97% SAT M 400+; 52% ACT 18-23; 37% ACT 24-29 **% Accepted:** 42 **Admission Plans:** Early Admission; Deferred Admission **Application Deadline:** Rolling **Application Fee:** $35.00 **H.S. Requirements:** High school diploma required; GED accepted **Costs Per Year:** Application fee: $35. Comprehensive fee: $26,000 includes full-time tuition ($18,300), mandatory fees ($2350), and college room and board ($5350). Full-time tuition and fees vary according to course load. Room and board charges vary according to board plan and housing facility. Part-time tuition: $610 per credit hour. Part-time mandatory fees: $75 per credit hour, $50 per term. Part-time tuition and fees vary according to course load. **Scholarships:** Available **Calendar System:** Semester, Summer Session Available **Enrollment:** FT 2,302, PT 245, Grad FT 124, Grad PT 97 **Faculty:** FT 143, PT 95 **Student-Faculty Ratio:** 14:1 **Exams:** SAT I or ACT. **% Receiving Financial Aid:** 83 **% Residing in College-Owned, -Operated, or -Affiliated Housing:** 48 **Final Year or Final Semester Residency Requirement:** No **Regional Accreditation:** Southern Association of Colleges and Schools **Credit Hours For Degree:** 124 semester hours, Bachelors **ROTC:** Army, Air Force **Professional Accreditation:** AACN, CSWE, NLN **Intercollegiate Athletics:** Baseball M; Basketball M & W; Football M; Golf M & W; Soccer M & W; Softball W; Tennis M & W; Volleyball W

UNIVERSITY OF NORTH TEXAS
1155 Union Circle No. 311425
Denton, TX 76203
Tel: (940)565-2000
Admissions: (940)565-3921
Fax: (940)565-2408
E-mail: undergradadm@unt.edu
Web Site: http://www.unt.edu/
President/CEO: Gretchen M. Bataille
Admissions: Dr. Rebecca Lothringer
Financial Aid: Carolyn Cunningham
Type: University **Sex:** Coed **Affiliation:** University of North Texas System **Scores:** 97.93% SAT V 400+; 98.49% SAT M 400+; 52.4% ACT 18-23; 35.8% ACT 24-29 **% Accepted:** 64 **Admission Plans:** Early Admission; Deferred Admission **Application Deadline:** August 1 **Application Fee:** $40.00 **H.S. Requirements:** High school diploma required; GED accepted **Costs Per Year:** Application fee: $40. State resident tuition: $5360 full-time, $178.67 per credit hour part-time. Nonresident tuition: $13,670 full-time, $455.67 per credit hour part-time. Mandatory fees: $1941 full-time, $267.10 per credit hour part-time. Full-time tuition and fees vary according to course load. Part-time tuition and fees vary according to course load. College room and board: $6534. Room and board charges vary according to board plan and housing facility. **Scholarships:** Available **Calendar System:** Semester, Summer Session Available **Enrollment:** FT 22,140, PT 6,334, Grad FT 2,932, Grad PT 4,717 **Faculty:** FT 1,018, PT 487 **Student-Faculty Ratio:** 23:1 **Exams:** SAT I or ACT. ACT essay used for admission. SAT essay used for admission. ACT essay used in place of application essay. SAT essay used in place of application essay. **% Receiving Financial Aid:** 50 **% Residing in College-Owned, -Operated, or -Affiliated Housing:** 16 **Library Holdings:** 2,526,168 **Regional Accreditation:** Southern Association of Colleges and Schools **Credit Hours For Degree:** 124 semester hours, Bachelors **ROTC:** Army, Air Force **Professional Accreditation:** AACSB, ABET, ACEJMC, AAFCS, ACA, ALA, APA, ASLHA, FIDER, CORE, CSWE, NASAD, NASM, NASPAA, NCATE, NRPA **Intercollegiate Athletics:** Baseball M; Basketball M & W; Bowling M & W; Cross-Country Running M & W; Fencing M & W; Football M; Golf M & W; Ice Hockey M; Lacrosse M & W; Racquetball M & W; Rock Climbing M; Sailing M & W; Soccer M & W; Softball M & W; Swimming and Diving M & W; Tennis M & W; Track and Field M & W; Ultimate Frisbee M & W; Volleyball W

UNIVERSITY OF PHOENIX—AUSTIN CAMPUS
10801 North Mopac
Austin, TX 78759
Tel: (512)344-1400
Web Site: http://www.phoenix.edu/
Type: Comprehensive **Sex:** Coed **Regional Accreditation:** North Central Association of Colleges and Schools

UNIVERSITY OF PHOENIX—DALLAS CAMPUS
Churchill Tower
12400 Coit Rd., Ste. 200
Dallas, TX 75251-2009
Tel: (972)385-1055; Free: 800-228-7240
Admissions: (480)557-6151
Fax: (972)385-1700
E-mail: audra.mcquarie@phoenix.edu
Web Site: http://www.phoenix.edu/
President/CEO: William Pepicello
Admissions: Audra McQuarie
Type: Comprehensive **Sex:** Coed **Admission Plans:** Open Admission; Deferred Admission **Application Deadline:** Rolling **Application Fee:** $0.00 **H.S. Requirements:** High school diploma required; GED accepted **Costs Per Year:** Application fee: $0. Tuition: $12,525 full-time. Full-time tuition varies according to course level and course load. **Scholarships:** Available **Calendar System:** Continuous, Summer Session Not available **Enrollment:** FT 1,075 **Faculty:** FT 15, PT 166 **Regional Accreditation:** North Central Association of Colleges and Schools **Credit Hours For Degree:** 60 credits, Associates; 120 credits, Bachelors

UNIVERSITY OF PHOENIX—HOUSTON CAMPUS
11451 Katy Freeway
Ste. 100
Houston, TX 77079-2004
Tel: (281)596-0363; Free: 800-228-7240
Admissions: (480)557-6151
Fax: (281)596-0336
E-mail: audra.mcquarie@phoenix.edu
Web Site: http://www.phoenix.edu/
President/CEO: William Pepicello, PhD
Admissions: Audra McQuarie
Type: Comprehensive **Sex:** Coed **Admission Plans:** Open Admission; Deferred Admission **Application Deadline:** Rolling **Application Fee:** $0.00 **H.S. Requirements:** High school diploma required; GED accepted **Costs Per Year:** Application fee: $0. Tuition: $12,525 full-time. Full-time tuition varies according to course level and course load. **Scholarships:** Available **Calendar System:** Continuous, Summer Session Not available **Enrollment:** FT 2,286 **Faculty:** FT 16, PT 309 **Regional Accreditation:** North Central Association of Colleges and Schools **Credit Hours For Degree:** 60 credits, Associates; 120 credits, Bachelors

UNIVERSITY OF PHOENIX—SAN ANTONIO CAMPUS
8200 IH-10 West, Ste. 900
San Antonio, TX 78230
Tel: (210)524-2100; Free: 800-697-8223
Web Site: http://www.phoenix.edu/
President/CEO: William Pepicello, PhD
Type: Comprehensive **Sex:** Coed **Regional Accreditation:** North Central Association of Colleges and Schools

UNIVERSITY OF ST. THOMAS
3800 Montrose Blvd.
Houston, TX 77006-4696
Tel: (713)522-7911; Free: 800-856-8565
Admissions: (713)525-3500
Fax: (713)525-3558
E-mail: admissions@stthom.edu
Web Site: http://www.stthom.edu/
President/CEO: Dr. Robert Ivany
Financial Aid: Lynda McKendree
Type: Comprehensive **Sex:** Coed **Affiliation:** Roman Catholic **Scores:** 99.53% SAT V 400+; 99.53% SAT M 400+; 36.36% ACT 18-23; 54.55% ACT 24-29 **% Accepted:** 80 **Admission Plans:** Early Action; Deferred Admission **Application Deadline:** May 1 **Application Fee:** $25.00 **H.S. Requirements:** High school diploma required; GED accepted **Costs Per Year:** Application fee: $25. Comprehensive fee: $29,230 includes full-time tuition ($21,510), mandatory fees ($320), and college room and board ($7400). College room only: $4400. Full-time tuition and fees vary according to course load. Room and board charges vary according to board plan and housing facility. Part-time tuition: $719 per credit hour. Part-time tuition varies according to course load. **Scholarships:** Available **Calendar System:** Semester, Summer Session Available **Enrollment:** FT 1,313, PT 479, Grad FT 259, Grad PT 1,183 **Faculty:** FT 125, PT 137 **Student-Faculty Ratio:** 12:1 **Exams:** SAT I or ACT. ACT essay used for admission. SAT essay used for admission. ACT essay used for placement. SAT essay used for placement. **% Receiving Financial Aid:** 59 **% Residing in College-Owned,**

-Operated, or -Affiliated Housing: 18 **Library Holdings:** 237,456 **Regional Accreditation:** Southern Association of Colleges and Schools **Credit Hours For Degree:** 126 credit hours, Bachelors **ROTC:** Army, Air Force **Professional Accreditation:** ACIPE, ACBSP, ATS, TEAC **Intercollegiate Athletics:** Baseball M; Basketball M; Cheerleading M & W; Fencing M & W; Rugby M; Soccer M & W; Tennis M & W; Ultimate Frisbee M & W; Volleyball W

THE UNIVERSITY OF TEXAS AT ARLINGTON

701 South Nedderman Dr.
Arlington, TX 76019
Tel: (817)272-2011
Admissions: (817)272-6287
Fax: (817)272-5656
E-mail: admissions@uta.edu
Web Site: http://www.uta.edu/
President/CEO: James D. Spaniolo
Admissions: Dr. Hans Gatterdam
Financial Aid: Karen Krause

Type: University **Sex:** Coed **Affiliation:** University of Texas System **Scores:** 93% SAT V 400+; 96% SAT M 400+; 49% ACT 18-23; 35% ACT 24-29 **% Accepted:** 69 **Admission Plans:** Deferred Admission **Application Deadline:** June 1 **Application Fee:** $35.00 **H.S. Requirements:** High school diploma required; GED not accepted **Costs Per Year:** Application fee: $35. State resident tuition: $8186 full-time. Nonresident tuition: $16,496 full-time. Full-time tuition varies according to course level, course load, and program. College room and board: $6658. College room only: $3493. Room and board charges vary according to board plan and housing facility. **Scholarships:** Available **Calendar System:** Semester, Summer Session Available **Enrollment:** FT 14,293, PT 7,077, Grad FT 3,158, Grad PT 3,557 **Faculty:** FT 823, PT 328 **Student-Faculty Ratio:** 23:1 **Exams:** SAT I or ACT. ACT essay used for admission. SAT essay used for admission. **% Receiving Financial Aid:** 64 **% Residing in College-Owned, -Operated, or -Affiliated Housing:** 16 **Library Holdings:** 1,434,932 **Regional Accreditation:** Southern Association of Colleges and Schools **Credit Hours For Degree:** 120 semester hours, Bachelors **ROTC:** Army, Air Force **Professional Accreditation:** AACSB, ABET, AACN, ACSP, ASLA, FIDER, CSWE, NAAB, NASAD, NASM, NASPAA, NCATE, NLN **Intercollegiate Athletics:** Baseball M; Basketball M & W; Cross-Country Running M & W; Golf M; Softball M; Tennis M & W; Track and Field M & W; Volleyball W

THE UNIVERSITY OF TEXAS AT AUSTIN

Austin, TX 78712-1111
Tel: (512)471-3434
Admissions: (512)475-7440
Fax: (512)475-7475
Web Site: http://www.utexas.edu/
President/CEO: William C. Powers, Jr.
Admissions: Kedra Ishop
Financial Aid: Tom Melecki, PhD

Type: University **Sex:** Coed **Affiliation:** University of Texas System **Scores:** 98.4% SAT V 400+; 99.5% SAT M 400+; 19% ACT 18-23; 44.8% ACT 24-29 **% Accepted:** 45 **Admission Plans:** Preferred Admission; Deferred Admission **Application Deadline:** December 1 **Application Fee:** $60.00 **H.S. Requirements:** High school diploma required; GED accepted **Costs Per Year:** Application fee: $60. State resident tuition: $8930 full-time. Nonresident tuition: $30,006 full-time. Full-time tuition varies according to course load and program. College room and board: $9602. Room and board charges vary according to housing facility. **Scholarships:** Available **Calendar System:** Semester, Summer Session Available **Enrollment:** FT 35,364, PT 2,804, Grad FT 11,199, Grad PT 1,628 **Faculty:** FT 2,770, PT 269 **Student-Faculty Ratio:** 17:1 **Exams:** SAT I or ACT, SAT II. ACT essay used for admission. SAT essay used for admission. **% Receiving Financial Aid:** 44 **% Residing in College-Owned, -Operated, or -Affiliated Housing:** 19 **Library Holdings:** 9,853,414 **Regional Accreditation:** Southern Association of Colleges and Schools **Credit Hours For Degree:** 120 semester hours, Bachelors **ROTC:** Army, Navy, Air Force **Professional Accreditation:** AACSB, ABET, ACPhE, ACEJMC, AACN, ABA, ADtA, ACSP, ALA, APA, ASLHA, AALS, FIDER, CORE, CSWE, NAAB, NASAD, NASD, NASM, NASPAA NAST **Intercollegiate Athletics:** Archery M & W; Badminton M & W; Baseball M; Basketball M & W; Crew M & W; Cross-Country Running M & W; Fencing M & W; Football M; Golf M & W; Gymnastics M & W; Ice Hockey M; Lacrosse M & W; Racquetball M & W; Rugby M & W; Sailing M & W; Soccer M & W; Softball W; Swimming and Diving M & W; Tennis M & W; Track and Field M & W; Volleyball M & W; Water Polo M & W; Weight Lifting M & W; Wrestling M & W

THE UNIVERSITY OF TEXAS AT BROWNSVILLE

80 Fort Brown
Brownsville, TX 78520-4991
Tel: (956)544-8200
Admissions: (956)882-8860
Fax: (956)544-8832
E-mail: admissions@utb.edu
Web Site: http://www.utb.edu/
President/CEO: Dr. Juliet V. Garcia
Admissions: Carlo Tamayo
Financial Aid: Georgiana M. Velarde

Type: Comprehensive **Sex:** Coed **Affiliation:** University of Texas System **% Accepted:** 100 **Admission Plans:** Open Admission; Early Admission **Application Deadline:** July 1 **Application Fee:** $0.00 **H.S. Requirements:** High school diploma required; GED not accepted **Costs Per Year:** Application fee: $0. State resident tuition: $3180 full-time, $132.50 per credit hour part-time. Nonresident tuition: $9828 full-time, $409.50 per credit hour part-time. Mandatory fees: $1367 full-time, $36 per credit hour part-time, $251.30 per term part-time. Full-time tuition and fees vary according to class time, course level, course load, location, and program. Part-time tuition and fees vary according to class time, course level, course load, location, and program. College room and board: $5742. College room only: $2992. Room and board charges vary according to board plan. **Scholarships:** Available **Calendar System:** Semester, Summer Session Available **Enrollment:** FT 5,694, PT 10,646 **Faculty:** FT 366, PT 335 **Student-Faculty Ratio:** 21:1 **% Receiving Financial Aid:** 81 **% Residing in College-Owned, -Operated, or -Affiliated Housing:** 2 **Library Holdings:** 174,660 **Regional Accreditation:** Southern Association of Colleges and Schools **Credit Hours For Degree:** 124 semester hours, Bachelors **Professional Accreditation:** JRCERT, NLN **Intercollegiate Athletics:** Baseball M; Golf M & W; Soccer M & W; Volleyball W

THE UNIVERSITY OF TEXAS AT DALLAS

800 West Campbell Rd.
Richardson, TX 75080
Tel: (972)883-2111; Free: 800-889-2443
Admissions: (972)883-2270
Fax: (972)883-6803
E-mail: interest@utdallas.edu
Web Site: http://www.utdallas.edu/
President/CEO: Dr. David E. Daniel
Financial Aid: Dr. Karen M. Jarrell

Type: University **Sex:** Coed **Affiliation:** University of Texas System **Scores:** 97% SAT V 400+; 100% SAT M 400+; 21% ACT 18-23; 48% ACT 24-29 **% Accepted:** 52 **Admission Plans:** Deferred Admission **Application Deadline:** July 1 **Application Fee:** $50.00 **H.S. Requirements:** High school diploma required; GED accepted **Costs Per Year:** Application fee: $50. State resident tuition: $10,340 full-time, $344.67 per credit hour part-time. Nonresident tuition: $23,730 full-time, $791 per credit hour part-time. Full-time tuition varies according to course load and degree level. Part-time tuition varies according to course load and degree level. College room and board: $7733. Room and board charges vary according to board plan and housing facility. Tuition guaranteed not to increase for student's term of enrollment. **Scholarships:** Available **Calendar System:** Semester, Summer Session Available **Enrollment:** FT 7,326, PT 2,475, Grad FT 3,116, Grad PT 2,866 **Faculty:** FT 533, PT 261 **Student-Faculty Ratio:** 20:1 **Exams:** Other, SAT I or ACT. **% Receiving Financial Aid:** 46 **% Residing in College-Owned, -Operated, or -Affiliated Housing:** 24 **Library Holdings:** 2,421,549 **Regional Accreditation:** Southern Association of Colleges and Schools **Credit Hours For Degree:** 120 semester hours, Bachelors **ROTC:** Army, Air Force **Professional Accreditation:** AACSB, ABET, ASLHA, NASPAA **Intercollegiate Athletics:** Baseball M; Basketball M & W; Cross-Country Running M & W; Golf M & W; Soccer M & W; Softball W; Tennis M & W; Volleyball W

THE UNIVERSITY OF TEXAS AT EL PASO

500 West University Ave.
El Paso, TX 79968-0001
Tel: (915)747-5000; Free: 877-746-4636
Admissions: (915)747-5588
Fax: (915)747-5122

E-mail: futureminer@utep.edu
Web Site: http://www.utep.edu/
President/CEO: Dr. Diana Natalicio
Financial Aid: Raul Lerma
Type: University **Sex:** Coed **Scores:** 71.7% SAT V 400+; 81% SAT M 400+; 42.3% ACT 18-23; 11.6% ACT 24-29 **% Accepted:** 99 **Admission Plans:** Deferred Admission **Application Deadline:** July 31 **Application Fee:** $0.00 **H.S. Requirements:** High school diploma required; GED accepted **Scholarships:** Available **Calendar System:** Semester, Summer Session Available **Enrollment:** FT 11,434, PT 5,771, Grad FT 1,253, Grad PT 2,553 **Faculty:** FT 695, PT 463 **Student-Faculty Ratio:** 20:1 **Exams:** SAT I or ACT. **Library Holdings:** 1,329,946 **Regional Accreditation:** Southern Association of Colleges and Schools **Credit Hours For Degree:** 123 semester hours, Bachelors **ROTC:** Army, Air Force **Professional Accreditation:** AACSB, ABET, AACN, ACNM, AOTA, APTA, ASLHA, CSWE, NAACLS, NASM, NASPAA **Intercollegiate Athletics:** Basketball M & W; Cross-Country Running M & W; Football M; Golf M; Riflery M & W; Tennis W; Track and Field M & W; Volleyball W

THE UNIVERSITY OF TEXAS HEALTH SCIENCE CENTER AT HOUSTON
PO Box 20036
Houston, TX 77225-0036
Tel: (713)500-3333
Admissions: (713)500-3361
Fax: (713)500-3026
E-mail: registrar@uth.tmc.edu
Web Site: http://www.uth.tmc.edu/
President/CEO: Larry R. Kaiser, MD
Admissions: Robert L. Jenkins
Financial Aid: Wanda Williams
Type: Two-Year Upper Division **Sex:** Coed **Affiliation:** University of Texas System **% Accepted:** 35 **Admission Plans:** Preferred Admission **Application Fee:** $30.00 **H.S. Requirements:** High school diploma required; GED accepted **Costs Per Year:** Application fee: $30. State resident tuition: $149 per credit hour part-time. Nonresident tuition: $623 per credit hour part-time. Mandatory fees: $157 per credit hour part-time. **Scholarships:** Available **Calendar System:** Semester, Summer Session Available **Enrollment:** FT 342, PT 120, Grad FT 2,419, Grad PT 1,088 **Faculty:** FT 37, PT 7 **Student-Faculty Ratio:** 11:1 **Exams:** Other. **% Receiving Financial Aid:** 53 **Library Holdings:** 364,744 **Regional Accreditation:** Southern Association of Colleges and Schools **Credit Hours For Degree:** 125 semester hours, Bachelors **ROTC:** Army **Professional Accreditation:** ABET, AACN, AANA, ADA, ADtA, APA, ASC, ACIPE, CEPH, JRCERT, LCMEAMA, NAACLS, NLN

THE UNIVERSITY OF TEXAS HEALTH SCIENCE CENTER AT SAN ANTONIO
7703 Floyd Curl Dr.
San Antonio, TX 78229-3900
Tel: (210)567-7000
Admissions: (210)567-2621
Fax: (210)567-2685
Web Site: http://www.uthscsa.edu/
President/CEO: William L. Henrich, MD
Financial Aid: Robert T. Lawson
Type: Two-Year Upper Division **Sex:** Coed **Affiliation:** University of Texas System **Application Fee:** $45.00 **H.S. Requirements:** High school diploma required; GED accepted **Scholarships:** Available **Calendar System:** Semester, Summer Session Available **Student-Faculty Ratio:** 3:1 **Regional Accreditation:** Southern Association of Colleges and Schools **Credit Hours For Degree:** 120 semester hours, Bachelors **ROTC:** Army, Air Force **Professional Accreditation:** AABB, AACN, ADA, AOTA, APTA, APA, CARC, JRCEMT, LCMEAMA, NAACLS

THE UNIVERSITY OF TEXAS MEDICAL BRANCH
301 University Blvd.
Galveston, TX 77555
Tel: (409)772-1011
Admissions: (409)772-1215
Fax: (409)772-5056
E-mail: enrollment.services@utmb.edu
Web Site: http://www.utmb.edu/
President/CEO: Dr. David L. Callender
Admissions: Vicki L. Brewer
Financial Aid: Carol A. Cromie
Type: Comprehensive **Sex:** Coed **Affiliation:** University of Texas System **Admission Plans:** Preferred Admission **Application Fee:** $30.00 **Costs Per Year:** Application fee: $30. State resident tuition: $4695 full-time, $156.50 per credit hour part-time. Nonresident tuition: $13,125 full-time, $437.50 per credit hour part-time. Mandatory fees: $807 full-time, $10.99 per credit hour part-time, $201.33 per term part-time. Full-time tuition and fees vary according to course load, degree level, and program. Part-time tuition and fees vary according to course load, degree level, and program. College room only: $4620. Room charges vary according to housing facility. **Scholarships:** Available **Calendar System:** Semester, Summer Session Available **Enrollment:** FT 315, PT 177, Grad FT 1,619, Grad PT 319 **% Receiving Financial Aid:** 59 **Regional Accreditation:** Southern Association of Colleges and Schools **Credit Hours For Degree:** 120 semester hours, Bachelors **Professional Accreditation:** AACN, ACNM, AOTA, APTA, APA, CARC, CEPH, LCMEAMA, NAACLS, NLN **Intercollegiate Athletics:** Ultimate Frisbee M & W; Volleyball M & W

THE UNIVERSITY OF TEXAS OF THE PERMIAN BASIN
4901 East University Blvd.
Odessa, TX 79762-0001
Tel: (432)552-2020; Free: (866)552-UTPB
Admissions: (432)552-2605
Fax: (432)552-2109
E-mail: admissions@utpb.edu
Web Site: http://www.utpb.edu/
President/CEO: Dr. David Watts
Admissions: Scott Smiley
Financial Aid: Robert L. Vasquez
Type: Comprehensive **Sex:** Coed **Affiliation:** University of Texas System **Scores:** 93.9% SAT V 400+; 95.3% SAT M 400+; 68.3% ACT 18-23; 20.3% ACT 24-29 **% Accepted:** 85 **Admission Plans:** Deferred Admission **Application Deadline:** July 15 **Application Fee:** $0.00 **H.S. Requirements:** High school diploma required; GED accepted **Costs Per Year:** Application fee: $0. State resident tuition: $4380 full-time, $146 per semester hour part-time. Nonresident tuition: $12,690 full-time, $423 per semester hour part-time. Mandatory fees: $998 full-time. Full-time tuition and fees vary according to course load and location. Part-time tuition varies according to course load and location. College room and board: $6445. College room only: $3744. Room and board charges vary according to board plan and housing facility. **Scholarships:** Available **Calendar System:** Semester, Summer Session Available **Enrollment:** FT 1,927, PT 812, Grad FT 181, Grad PT 626 **Faculty:** FT 119, PT 101 **Student-Faculty Ratio:** 17:1 **Exams:** SAT I or ACT. **% Receiving Financial Aid:** 57 **% Residing in College-Owned, -Operated, or -Affiliated Housing:** 19 **Final Year or Final Semester Residency Requirement:** No **Library Holdings:** 286,608 **Regional Accreditation:** Southern Association of Colleges and Schools **Credit Hours For Degree:** 120 semester hours, Bachelors **Professional Accreditation:** AACSB, NCATE **Intercollegiate Athletics:** Baseball M; Basketball M & W; Cheerleading M & W; Cross-Country Running M & W; Soccer M & W; Softball W; Swimming and Diving M & W; Volleyball W

THE UNIVERSITY OF TEXAS AT SAN ANTONIO
One UTSA Circle
San Antonio, TX 78249-0617
Tel: (210)458-4011; Free: 800-669-0919
Admissions: (210)458-4536
E-mail: prospects@utsa.edu
Web Site: http://www.utsa.edu/
President/CEO: Dr. Ricardo Romo
Admissions: Jennifer Ehlers
Financial Aid: Kim Canady
Type: University **Sex:** Coed **Affiliation:** University of Texas System **Scores:** 92.83% SAT V 400+; 95.64% SAT M 400+; 55.79% ACT 18-23; 29.3% ACT 24-29 **% Accepted:** 87 **Application Deadline:** July 1 **Application Fee:** $40.00 **H.S. Requirements:** High school diploma required; GED accepted. For concurrent enrollment of high school students: High school diploma or equivalent not required **Costs Per Year:** Application fee: $40. State resident tuition: $5126 full-time, $170.85 per hour part-time. Nonresident tuition: $13,436 full-time, $447.85 per hour part-time. Mandatory fees: $2401 full-time. Full-time tuition and fees vary according to course level, course load, and degree level. Part-time tuition varies according to course level, course load, and degree level. College room and board: $8937. College room only: $6075. Room and board charges vary according to board plan and housing

facility. **Scholarships:** Available **Calendar System:** Semester, Summer Session Available **Enrollment:** FT 19,773, PT 5,233, Grad FT 1,550, Grad PT 2,399 **Faculty:** FT 966, PT 255 **Student-Faculty Ratio:** 23:1 **Exams:** SAT I or ACT. **% Receiving Financial Aid:** 56 **% Residing in College-Owned, -Operated, or -Affiliated Housing:** 12 **Library Holdings:** 1,279,564 **Regional Accreditation:** Southern Association of Colleges and Schools **Credit Hours For Degree:** 120 semester hours, Bachelors **ROTC:** Army, Air Force **Professional Accreditation:** AACSB, ABET, AACN, FIDER, CSWE, NASAD, NASM, NASPAA **Intercollegiate Athletics:** Baseball M; Basketball M & W; Cross-Country Running M & W; Golf M; Softball W; Tennis M & W; Track and Field M & W; Volleyball W

THE UNIVERSITY OF TEXAS SOUTHWESTERN MEDICAL CENTER AT DALLAS
5323 Harry Hines Blvd.
Dallas, TX 75390
Tel: (214)648-3111
Admissions: (214)648-5617
Fax: (214)648-3289
E-mail: admissions@utsouthwestern.edu
Web Site: http://www.utsouthwestern.edu/
President/CEO: Daniel K. Podolsky, MD
Admissions: Anne Mclane
Financial Aid: Lisa J. McGaha
Type: Two-Year Upper Division **Sex:** Coed **Affiliation:** University of Texas System **% Accepted:** 28 **Admission Plans:** Preferred Admission **Application Fee:** $10.00 **Costs Per Year:** Application fee: $10. State resident tuition: $3658 full-time, $118 per credit hour part-time. Nonresident tuition: $12,369 full-time, $399 per credit hour part-time. Mandatory fees: $1220 full-time. Full-time tuition and fees vary according to course load and program. Part-time tuition varies according to course load and program. College room and board: $11,353. **Scholarships:** Available **Calendar System:** Semester, Summer Session Not available **Enrollment:** FT 77, PT 13, Grad FT 1,699, Grad PT 656 **% Receiving Financial Aid:** 91 **Library Holdings:** 257,782 **Regional Accreditation:** Southern Association of Colleges and Schools **Credit Hours For Degree:** 120 semester hours, Bachelors **Professional Accreditation:** ARCMI, ACNM, ADtA, APTA, APA, CORE, LCMEAMA, NAACLS, NANPWH, NCOPE

THE UNIVERSITY OF TEXAS AT TYLER
3900 University Blvd.
Tyler, TX 75799-0001
Tel: (903)566-7000
Admissions: (903)566-7057
Fax: (903)566-7068
E-mail: admissions@uttyler.edu
Web Site: http://www.uttyler.edu/
President/CEO: Dr. Rodney H. Mabry
Admissions: Sarah Bowdin
Financial Aid: Candice A. Lindsey
Type: Comprehensive **Sex:** Coed **Affiliation:** University of Texas System **Scores:** 95.04% SAT V 400+; 97.41% SAT M 400+; 58.81% ACT 18-23; 33.33% ACT 24-29 **% Accepted:** 86 **Admission Plans:** Deferred Admission **Application Deadline:** Rolling **Application Fee:** $25.00 **H.S. Requirements:** High school diploma required; GED accepted **Costs Per Year:** Application fee: $25. State resident tuition: $4650 full-time, $50 per semester hour part-time. Nonresident tuition: $13,080 full-time, $331 per semester hour part-time. Mandatory fees: $1392 full-time. Full-time tuition and fees vary according to course level, course load, and degree level. College room and board: $8016. College room only: $5102. Room and board charges vary according to board plan and housing facility. **Scholarships:** Available **Calendar System:** Semester, Summer Session Available **Enrollment:** FT 3,862, PT 1,189, Grad FT 299, Grad PT 813 **Faculty:** FT 261, PT 126 **Student-Faculty Ratio:** 16:1 **Exams:** SAT I or ACT. SAT essay used for admission. ACT essay not being used. **% Receiving Financial Aid:** 52 **Library Holdings:** 486,895 **Regional Accreditation:** Southern Association of Colleges and Schools **Credit Hours For Degree:** 124 semester hours, Bachelors **Professional Accreditation:** AACSB, ABET, AACN, NLN, TEAC, NAIT **Intercollegiate Athletics:** Baseball M; Basketball M & W; Cheerleading M & W; Cross-Country Running M & W; Golf M & W; Soccer M & W; Tennis M & W; Track and Field M & W; Volleyball W

THE UNIVERSITY OF TEXAS—PAN AMERICAN
1201 West University Dr.
Edinburg, TX 78539
Tel: (956)381-2011
Admissions: (956)381-2481
E-mail: recruitment@utpa.edu
Web Site: http://www.utpa.edu/
President/CEO: Dr. Blandina Cardenas
Admissions: Dr. Magdalena Hinojosa
Financial Aid: Elaine Rivera
Type: Comprehensive **Sex:** Coed **Affiliation:** University of Texas System **Scores:** 82% SAT V 400+; 90% SAT M 400+; 57% ACT 18-23; 7% ACT 24-29 **% Accepted:** 68 **Application Deadline:** August 11 **Application Fee:** $0.00 **H.S. Requirements:** High school diploma required; GED accepted **Costs Per Year:** Application fee: $0. State resident tuition: $3305 full-time, $137.70 per credit hour part-time. Nonresident tuition: $10,049 full-time, $418.70 per credit hour part-time. Mandatory fees: $999 full-time, $116.05 per credit hour part-time, $137.20 per term part-time. Full-time tuition and fees vary according to course load and location. Part-time tuition and fees vary according to course load and location. College room and board: $5294. College room only: $3200. Room and board charges vary according to board plan and housing facility. **Scholarships:** Available **Calendar System:** Semester, Summer Session Available **Enrollment:** FT 11,786, PT 4,161, Grad FT 773, Grad PT 1,617 **Faculty:** FT 644, PT 162 **Student-Faculty Ratio:** 21:1 **Exams:** SAT I or ACT. ACT essay not being used. SAT essay not being used. **% Receiving Financial Aid:** 78 **Regional Accreditation:** Southern Association of Colleges and Schools **Credit Hours For Degree:** 124 semester hours, Bachelors **ROTC:** Army **Professional Accreditation:** AACSB, ABET, AACN, ADtA, AOTA, ASLHA, CORE, CSWE, NAACLS, NAST **Intercollegiate Athletics:** Baseball M; Basketball M & W; Cross-Country Running M & W; Golf M & W; Tennis M & W; Track and Field M & W; Volleyball W

VERNON COLLEGE
4400 College Dr.
Vernon, TX 76384-4092
Tel: (940)552-6291
Fax: (940)553-1753
Web Site: http://www.vernoncollege.edu/
President/CEO: Dusty R. Johnston, EdD
Admissions: Joe Hite
Financial Aid: Melissa Elliott
Type: Two-Year College **Sex:** Coed **Admission Plans:** Open Admission; Early Admission **Application Deadline:** Rolling **Application Fee:** $10.00 **H.S. Requirements:** High school diploma required; GED accepted **Scholarships:** Available **Calendar System:** Semester, Summer Session Available **Faculty:** FT 57, PT 71 **Student-Faculty Ratio:** 17:1 **Library Holdings:** 29,000 **Regional Accreditation:** Southern Association of Colleges and Schools **Credit Hours For Degree:** 60 semester hours, Associates **Professional Accreditation:** AHIMA **Intercollegiate Athletics:** Baseball M; Equestrian Sports M & W; Softball W; Volleyball W

VET TECH INSTITUTE OF HOUSTON
4669 Southwest Freeway
No. 300
Houston, TX 77027
Tel: (713)629-1500
Fax: (713)629-0059
Web Site: http://www.vettechinstitute.edu/
President/CEO: Elbert Hamilton, Jr.
Type: Two-Year College **Sex:** Coed **% Accepted:** 57

VICTORIA COLLEGE
2200 East Red River
Victoria, TX 77901-4494
Tel: (361)573-3291; Free: 877-843-4369
Fax: (361)572-3850
E-mail: registrar@victoriacollege.edu
Web Site: http://www.victoriacollege.edu/
President/CEO: Dr. Jimmy Goodson
Admissions: Lavern Dentler
Type: Two-Year College **Sex:** Coed **Admission Plans:** Open Admission **Application Deadline:** Rolling **H.S. Requirements:** High school diploma required; GED accepted **Costs Per Year:** Area resident tuition: $1020 full-time, $34 per semester hour part-time. State resident tuition: $2370 full-time, $79 per semester hour part-time. Nonresident tuition: $3000 full-time, $100 per semester hour part-time. Mandatory fees: $1050 full-time, $35 per

semester hour part-time. Full-time tuition and fees vary according to course load and location. Part-time tuition and fees vary according to course load and location. **Scholarships:** Available **Calendar System:** Semester, Summer Session Available **Enrollment:** FT 1,362, PT 2,692 **Faculty:** FT 98, PT 88 **Student-Faculty Ratio:** 18:1 **Library Holdings:** 150,000 **Regional Accreditation:** Southern Association of Colleges and Schools **Credit Hours For Degree:** 62 semester hours, Associates **Professional Accreditation:** CARC, NAACLS, NLN

VIRGINIA COLLEGE AT AUSTIN
6301 East Hwy. 290
Austin, TX 78723
Tel: (512)371-3500; Free: (866)314-6324
Fax: (512)371-3502
Web Site: http://www.vc.edu/
President/CEO: Harvey Giblin
Type: Two-Year College **Sex:** Coed **% Accepted:** 69 **Application Fee:** $100.00 **Calendar System:** Quarter **Professional Accreditation:** ACICS

WADE COLLEGE
INFOMart, 1950 Stemmons Freeway
Ste. 2026, Box 562
Dallas, TX 75207
Tel: (214)637-3530; Free: 800-624-4850
Fax: (214)637-0827
E-mail: jandalman@wadecollege.edu
Web Site: http://www.wadecollege.edu/
President/CEO: Harry Davros
Admissions: Julia Andalman
Financial Aid: Lisa Hoover
Type: Two-Year College **Sex:** Coed **Admission Plans:** Open Admission **Application Deadline:** Rolling **H.S. Requirements:** High school diploma required; GED accepted **Scholarships:** Available **Calendar System:** Trimester, Summer Session Available **Faculty:** FT 9, PT 9 **Student-Faculty Ratio:** 15:1 **Final Year or Final Semester Residency Requirement:** No **Library Holdings:** 4,782 **Regional Accreditation:** Southern Association of Colleges and Schools **Credit Hours For Degree:** 63 credits, Associates

WAYLAND BAPTIST UNIVERSITY
1900 West Seventh St.
Plainview, TX 79072-6998
Tel: (806)291-1000; Free: 800-588-1928
Admissions: (806)291-3500
Fax: (806)291-1960
E-mail: admityou@wbu.edu
Web Site: http://www.wbu.edu/
President/CEO: Dr. Paul Armes
Admissions: Debbie Stennett
Financial Aid: Karen LaQuey
Type: Comprehensive **Sex:** Coed **Affiliation:** Baptist **Scores:** 85% SAT V 400+; 88% SAT M 400+; 53% ACT 18-23; 21% ACT 24-29 **% Accepted:** 99 **Application Deadline:** August 1 **Application Fee:** $35.00 **H.S. Requirements:** High school diploma required; GED accepted **Costs Per Year:** Application fee: $35. One-time mandatory fee: $270. Comprehensive fee: $16,334 includes full-time tuition ($11,850), mandatory fees ($620), and college room and board ($3864). College room only: $1328. Full-time tuition and fees vary according to course load and location. Room and board charges vary according to board plan and housing facility. Part-time tuition: $395 per credit hour. Part-time mandatory fees: $60 per term. Part-time tuition and fees vary according to course load and location. **Scholarships:** Available **Calendar System:** Semester, Summer Session Available **Enrollment:** FT 748, PT 227, Grad FT 12, Grad PT 273 **Faculty:** FT 92, PT 33 **Student-Faculty Ratio:** 10:1 **Exams:** SAT I or ACT. **% Receiving Financial Aid:** 71 **% Residing in College-Owned, -Operated, or -Affiliated Housing:** 53 **Library Holdings:** 129,082 **Regional Accreditation:** Southern Association of Colleges and Schools **Credit Hours For Degree:** 60 semester hours, Associates; 124 semester hours, Bachelors **ROTC:** Army, Air Force **Professional Accreditation:** NASM **Intercollegiate Athletics:** Baseball M; Basketball M & W; Cheerleading M & W; Cross-Country Running M & W; Golf M & W; Soccer M & W; Track and Field M & W; Volleyball W

WEATHERFORD COLLEGE
225 College Park Ave.
Weatherford, TX 76086-5699
Tel: (817)594-5471; Free: 800-287-5471
Admissions: (817)598-6248
Fax: (817)598-6205
E-mail: willingham@wc.edu
Web Site: http://www.wc.edu/
President/CEO: Dr. Joe Birmingham
Admissions: Ralph Willingham
Type: Two-Year College **Sex:** Coed **Admission Plans:** Open Admission; Early Admission **Application Deadline:** Rolling **Application Fee:** $0.00 **H.S. Requirements:** High school diploma required; GED accepted. For some adult applicants: High school diploma or equivalent not required **Costs Per Year:** Application fee: $0. Area resident tuition: $1830 full-time, $61 per semester hour part-time. State resident tuition: $2760 full-time, $92 per semester hour part-time. Nonresident tuition: $4140 full-time, $138 per semester hour part-time. Full-time tuition varies according to course load. Part-time tuition varies according to course load. College room and board: $6530. College room only: $4430. Room and board charges vary according to board plan. **Scholarships:** Available **Calendar System:** Semester, Summer Session Available **Faculty:** FT 95, PT 125 **Student-Faculty Ratio:** 22:1 **% Residing in College-Owned, -Operated, or -Affiliated Housing:** 7 **Library Holdings:** 59,499 **Regional Accreditation:** Southern Association of Colleges and Schools **Credit Hours For Degree:** 63 semester hours, Associates **ROTC:** Air Force **Professional Accreditation:** CARC **Intercollegiate Athletics:** Baseball M; Basketball M & W; Cheerleading M & W; Equestrian Sports M & W; Tennis W

WEST TEXAS A&M UNIVERSITY
2501 4th Ave.
Canyon, TX 79016-0001
Tel: (806)651-2000; Free: 800-99-WTAMU
Admissions: (806)651-2020
Fax: (806)651-2126
E-mail: sthomas@mail.wtamu.edu
Web Site: http://www.wtamu.edu/
President/CEO: Dr. Patrick O'Brien
Admissions: Shawn Thomas
Financial Aid: Jim Reed
Type: Comprehensive **Sex:** Coed **Affiliation:** Texas A&M University System **Scores:** 87.9% SAT V 400+; 92.95% SAT M 400+; 60.6% ACT 18-23; 18.1% ACT 24-29 **% Accepted:** 66 **Admission Plans:** Deferred Admission **Application Deadline:** Rolling **Application Fee:** $25.00 **H.S. Requirements:** High school diploma required; GED accepted **Scholarships:** Available **Calendar System:** Semester, Summer Session Available **Enrollment:** FT 4,674, PT 1,422 **Faculty:** FT 252, PT 90 **Student-Faculty Ratio:** 18:1 **Exams:** SAT I or ACT. **% Receiving Financial Aid:** 61 **% Residing in College-Owned, -Operated, or -Affiliated Housing:** 19 **Library Holdings:** 1,096,058 **Regional Accreditation:** Southern Association of Colleges and Schools **Credit Hours For Degree:** 127 semester hours, Bachelors **Professional Accreditation:** AACN, ASLHA, ACBSP, CSWE, NASM **Intercollegiate Athletics:** Baseball M; Basketball M & W; Bowling M & W; Cross-Country Running M & W; Equestrian Sports M & W; Football M; Golf M & W; Soccer M & W; Softball W; Volleyball W

WESTERN TECHNICAL COLLEGE (EL PASO)
9451 Diana
El Paso, TX 79930-2610
Tel: (915)566-9621; Free: 800-201-9232
E-mail: lpena@westerntech.edu
Web Site: http://www.westerntech.edu/
President/CEO: Allan Sharpe
Admissions: Laura Pena
Type: Two-Year College **Sex:** Coed **Application Fee:** $100.00 **Costs Per Year:** Application fee: $100. Tuition: $14.85 per hour part-time. Part-time tuition varies according to class time, course load, and program. Tuition guaranteed not to increase for student's term of enrollment. **Scholarships:** Available **Student-Faculty Ratio:** 12:1 **Professional Accreditation:** ACCSCT

WESTERN TECHNICAL COLLEGE (EL PASO)
9624 Plaza Circle
El Paso, TX 79927
Tel: (915)532-3737
E-mail: bterrell@wtc-ep.edu
Web Site: http://www.westerntech.edu/

President/CEO: Allan Sharpe
Admissions: Bill Terrell
Type: Two-Year College **Sex:** Coed **Admission Plans:** Open Admission; Early Admission; Deferred Admission **H.S. Requirements:** High school diploma required; GED accepted **Calendar System:** Continuous **Enrollment:** FT 600, PT 225 **Faculty:** FT 98, PT 32 **Student-Faculty Ratio:** 18:1 **Professional Accreditation:** ACCSCT

WESTERN TEXAS COLLEGE
6200 College Ave.
Snyder, TX 79549
Tel: (325)573-8511; Free: 888-GO-TO-WTC
E-mail: jclifton@wtc.cc.tx.us
Web Site: http://www.wtc.edu/
President/CEO: Mike Dreith
Admissions: Dr. Jim Clifton
Financial Aid: Kathy Hall
Type: Two-Year College **Sex:** Coed **% Accepted:** 95 **Admission Plans:** Open Admission; Early Admission; Deferred Admission **Application Deadline:** Rolling **H.S. Requirements:** High school diploma required; GED accepted **Scholarships:** Available **Calendar System:** Semester, Summer Session Available **Faculty:** FT 48, PT 16 **Student-Faculty Ratio:** 17:1 **% Residing in College-Owned, -Operated, or -Affiliated Housing:** 20 **Library Holdings:** 43,000 **Regional Accreditation:** Southern Association of Colleges and Schools **Credit Hours For Degree:** 62 semester hours, Associates **Intercollegiate Athletics:** Baseball M; Softball W

WESTWOOD COLLEGE—DALLAS
8390 LBJ Freeway
Executive Center 1, Ste. 100
Dallas, TX 75243
Tel: (214)570-0100; Free: 800-281-2978
Fax: (214)570-8502
Web Site: http://www.westwood.edu/
President/CEO: Paul Kepic
Type: Four-Year College **Sex:** Coed **Calendar System:** Continuous **Professional Accreditation:** ACICS

WESTWOOD COLLEGE—FORT WORTH
4232 North Freeway
Fort Worth, TX 76137
Tel: (817)605-8111
Admissions: (817)547-9600
Fax: (817)605-6972
Web Site: http://www.westwood.edu/
President/CEO: David F. Bostick
Type: Four-Year College **Sex:** Coed **Scholarships:** Available **Calendar System:** Continuous **Professional Accreditation:** ACICS

WESTWOOD COLLEGE—HOUSTON SOUTH CAMPUS
7322 Southwest Freeway No. 110
Houston, TX 77074
Tel: (713)777-4433; Free: 800-281-2978
Fax: (713)219-2088
Web Site: http://www.westwood.edu/
President/CEO: Rick Skinner
Type: Two-Year College **Sex:** Coed **Calendar System:** Continuous **Professional Accreditation:** ACCSCT

WHARTON COUNTY JUNIOR COLLEGE
911 Boling Hwy.
Wharton, TX 77488-3298
Tel: (979)532-4560
E-mail: albertb@wcjc.edu
Web Site: http://www.wcjc.edu/
President/CEO: Betty McCrohan
Admissions: Albert Barnes
Financial Aid: Richard Hyde
Type: Two-Year College **Sex:** Coed **Admission Plans:** Open Admission **Application Deadline:** August 14 **Application Fee:** $10.00 **H.S. Requirements:** High school diploma required; GED accepted **Scholarships:** Available **Calendar System:** Semester, Summer Session Available **Faculty:** FT 136, PT 121 **Student-Faculty Ratio:** 22:1 **% Residing in College-Owned, -Operated, or -Affiliated Housing:** 5 **Library Holdings:** 51,478 **Regional Accreditation:** Southern Association of Colleges and Schools **Credit Hours For Degree:** 62 semester hours, Associates **Professional Accreditation:** ADA, AHIMA, APTA, JRCERT **Intercollegiate Athletics:** Baseball M; Volleyball W

WILEY COLLEGE
711 Wiley Ave.
Marshall, TX 75670-5199
Tel: (903)927-3300; Free: 800-658-6889
Admissions: (903)927-3222
Fax: (903)938-8100
E-mail: ajones@wileyc.edu
Web Site: http://www.wileyc.edu/
President/CEO: Dr. Haywood L. Strickland
Admissions: Alvena Jones
Financial Aid: Cecelia Jones
Type: Four-Year College **Sex:** Coed **Affiliation:** United Methodist Church **Scores:** 25% SAT V 400+; 50% SAT M 400+ **% Accepted:** 40 **Admission Plans:** Open Admission; Early Admission; Deferred Admission **Application Deadline:** August 1 **Application Fee:** $10.00 **H.S. Requirements:** High school diploma required; GED accepted **Scholarships:** Available **Calendar System:** Semester, Summer Session Available **Enrollment:** FT 803, PT 122 **Faculty:** FT 51, PT 29 **Student-Faculty Ratio:** 15:1 **Exams:** Other, SAT I or ACT. **% Receiving Financial Aid:** 92 **% Residing in College-Owned, -Operated, or -Affiliated Housing:** 50 **Library Holdings:** 24,000 **Regional Accreditation:** Southern Association of Colleges and Schools **Credit Hours For Degree:** 65 credit hours, Associates; 124 credit hours, Bachelors **Intercollegiate Athletics:** Baseball M; Basketball M & W; Cheerleading M & W; Track and Field M & W; Volleyball W

UNIVERSITY OF THE VIRGIN ISLANDS
2 John Brewers Bay
St. Thomas, VI 00802-9990
Tel: (340)776-9200
Admissions: (340)693-1152
E-mail: jedwin@uvi.edu
Web Site: http://www.uvi.edu/
President/CEO: Dr. David Hall
Admissions: Dr. Judith Edwin
Financial Aid: Mavis M. Gilchrist
Type: Comprehensive **Sex:** Coed **Scores:** 53% SAT V 400+; 34% SAT M 400+; 28% ACT 18-23; 4% ACT 24-29 **% Accepted:** 70 **Admission Plans:** Early Admission; Deferred Admission **Application Deadline:** April 30 **Application Fee:** $30.00 **H.S. Requirements:** High school diploma required; GED accepted **Costs Per Year:** Application fee: $30. Territory resident tuition: $3600 full-time, $150 per credit part-time. Nonresident tuition: $10,800 full-time, $450 per credit part-time. Mandatory fees: $550 full-time, $500 per year part-time. Full-time tuition and fees vary according to reciprocity agreements. Part-time tuition and fees vary according to course load and reciprocity agreements. College room and board: $8570. College room only: $3220. Room and board charges vary according to board plan and housing facility. **Scholarships:** Available **Calendar System:** Semester, Summer Session Available **Enrollment:** FT 1,542, PT 889, Grad FT 38, Grad PT 133 **Faculty:** FT 110, PT 122 **Student-Faculty Ratio:** 16:1 **Exams:** SAT I or ACT. ACT essay not being used. SAT essay not being used. **% Receiving Financial Aid:** 83 **% Residing in College-Owned, -Operated, or -Affiliated Housing:** 12 **Library Holdings:** 106,361 **Regional Accreditation:** Middle State Association of Colleges and Schools **Credit Hours For Degree:** 62 credits, Associates; 120 credits, Bachelors **ROTC:** Army **Professional Accreditation:** ACBSP, NLN **Intercollegiate Athletics:** Basketball M & W; Cheerleading W; Cross-Country Running M & W; Swimming and Diving M & W; Table Tennis M & W; Track and Field M & W; Volleyball M

ARGOSY UNIVERSITY, SALT LAKE CITY
121 West Election Rd., Ste. 300
Draper, UT 84020
Tel: (801)601-5000; Free: 888-639-4756
Admissions: (801)601-5000
Web Site: http://www.argosy.edu/saltlakecity/
President/CEO: Julie Johnson
Type: University **Sex:** Coed **Regional Accreditation:** North Central Association of Colleges and Schools

THE ART INSTITUTE OF SALT LAKE CITY
121 West Election Rd.
Ste. 100
Draper, UT 84020-9492
Free: 800-978-0096
Web Site: http://www.artinstitutes.edu/SaltLakeCity/
President/CEO: Ronald Moss
Type: Four-Year College **Sex:** Coed **Affiliation:** Education Management Corporation **Professional Accreditation:** ACCSCT

BRIGHAM YOUNG UNIVERSITY
Provo, UT 84602-1001
Tel: (801)422-1211
Admissions: (801)422-2507
Fax: (801)422-5278
E-mail: admissions@byu.edu
Web Site: http://www.byu.edu/
President/CEO: Cecil O. Samuelson
Admissions: Tom Gourley
Financial Aid: Paul R. Conrad
Type: University **Sex:** Coed **Affiliation:** The Church of Jesus Christ of Latter-day Saints **Scores:** 100% SAT V 400+; 99% SAT M 400+; 10% ACT 18-23; 58% ACT 24-29 **% Accepted:** 69 **Admission Plans:** Early Admission; Deferred Admission **Application Deadline:** February 1 **Application Fee:** $30.00 **H.S. Requirements:** High school diploma required; GED accepted **Costs Per Year:** Application fee: $30. Comprehensive fee: $11,540 includes full-time tuition ($4420) and college room and board ($7120). Part-time tuition: $227 per credit hour. Part-time tuition varies according to course load. Latter Day Saints full-time student $4,420 per year, non-LDS full-time student $8,840. **Scholarships:** Available **Calendar System:** Semester, Summer Session Available **Enrollment:** FT 28,048, PT 2,697, Grad FT 2,061, Grad PT 1,324 **Faculty:** FT 1,283, PT 403 **Student-Faculty Ratio:** 21:1 **Exams:** SAT I or ACT. ACT essay used for placement. **% Receiving Financial Aid:** 36 **% Residing in College-Owned, -Operated, or -Affiliated Housing:** 5 **Final Year or Final Semester Residency Requirement:** No **Library Holdings:** 3,539,032 **Credit Hours For Degree:** 120 credits, Bachelors **ROTC:** Army, Air Force **Professional Accreditation:** AACSB, ABET, ACEJMC, AAMFT, AACN, ABA, ACCE, ACA, ADtA, APA, ASLHA, AALS, CSWE, JRCEPAT, NAACLS, NASAD, NASD, NASM, NASPAA, NAST NCATE, NLN, NRPA, NCCU, TEAC **Intercollegiate Athletics:** Baseball M; Basketball M & W; Cheerleading M & W; Cross-Country Running M & W; Football M; Golf M & W; Gymnastics W; Lacrosse M; Racquetball M & W; Rugby M; Soccer M & W; Softball W; Swimming and Diving M & W; Tennis M & W; Track and Field M & W; Volleyball M & W

DEVRY UNIVERSITY
9350 South 150 E, Ste. 420
Sandy, UT 84070
Tel: (801)565-5110
Fax: (801)561-1710
Web Site: http://www.devry.edu/
President/CEO: Michael Townsley
Type: Comprehensive **Sex:** Coed **Admission Plans:** Deferred Admission **Application Deadline:** Rolling **Application Fee:** $50.00 **H.S. Requirements:** High school diploma required; GED accepted **Costs Per Year:** Application fee: $50. Tuition: $14,080 full-time, $550 per credit part-time. **Scholarships:** Available **Enrollment:** FT 45, PT 53, Grad FT 3, Grad PT 46 **Faculty:** FT 0, PT 19 **Student-Faculty Ratio:** 13:1 **Exams:** ACT essay used for admission. SAT essay used for admission. ACT essay used for placement. SAT essay used for placement. **% Receiving Financial Aid:** 62 **Regional Accreditation:** North Central Association of Colleges and Schools

DIXIE STATE COLLEGE OF UTAH
225 South 700 East
St. George, UT 84770-3876
Tel: (435)652-7500; Free: 888-GO2DIXIE
Admissions: (435)652-7591
Fax: (435)656-4005
E-mail: bboulter@dixie.edu
Web Site: http://www.dixie.edu/
President/CEO: Dr. Stephen D. Nadauld
Admissions: Brandon Boulter
Financial Aid: J.D. Robertson
Type: Four-Year College **Sex:** Coed **Affiliation:** Utah System of Higher Education **Scores:** 55.91% ACT 18-23; 20.72% ACT 24-29 **% Accepted:** 66 **Admission Plans:** Open Admission; Deferred Admission **Application Deadline:** Rolling **Application Fee:** $35.00 **H.S. Requirements:** High school diploma required; GED accepted **Costs Per Year:** Application fee: $35. State resident tuition: $2640 full-time, $110 per credit part-time. Nonresident tuition: $10,392 full-time, $433 per credit part-time. Mandatory fees: $506 full-time. Full-time tuition and fees vary according to course load and program. Part-time tuition varies according to course load and program. College room and board: $3948. College room only: $1450. Room and board charges vary according to board plan and housing facility. **Scholarships:** Available **Calendar System:** Semester, Summer Session Available **Enrollment:** FT 4,520, PT 3,188 **Faculty:** FT 143, PT 357 **Student-Faculty Ratio:** 21:1 **Exams:** SAT I or ACT. **% Residing in College-Owned, -Operated, or -Affiliated Housing:** 4 **Library Holdings:** 153,051 **Credit Hours For Degree:** 63 credits, Associates; 121 credits, Bachelors **ROTC:** Army **Professional Accreditation:** ADA, JRCEMT, NCCU **Intercollegiate Athletics:** Baseball M; Basketball M & W; Football M; Golf M; Soccer M & W; Softball W; Tennis W; Volleyball W

EVEREST COLLEGE
3280 West 3500 South
West Valley City, UT 84119
Tel: (801)840-4800
Fax: (801)969-0828
Web Site: http://www.everest.edu/
President/CEO: Stephanie Byrd

Type: Two-Year College **Sex:** Coed **Affiliation:** Corinthian Colleges, Inc. **Admission Plans:** Deferred Admission **Application Deadline:** Rolling **H.S. Requirements:** High school diploma required; GED accepted **Scholarships:** Available **Calendar System:** Quarter, Summer Session Available **Student-Faculty Ratio:** 20:1 **Exams:** Other, SAT I or ACT. **Credit Hours For Degree:** 90 quarter hours, Associates **Professional Accreditation:** ACICS, AAMAE

INDEPENDENCE UNIVERSITY
5295 South Commerce Dr.
Salt Lake City, UT 84107
Tel: 800-221-7374; Free: 800-791-7353
Fax: (801)263-0345
Web Site: http://www.independence.edu/
Admissions: Deborah Hopkins
Type: Comprehensive **Sex:** Coed **Admission Plans:** Open Admission; Deferred Admission **Application Deadline:** Rolling **H.S. Requirements:** High school diploma required; GED accepted **Scholarships:** Available **Calendar System:** Continuous, Summer Session Not available **% Receiving Financial Aid:** 96 **Credit Hours For Degree:** 60 semester hours, Associates; 120 semester hours, Bachelors **Professional Accreditation:** ACCSCT, CARC, DETC

ITT TECHNICAL INSTITUTE
920 West Levoy Dr.
Murray, UT 84123-2500
Tel: (801)263-3313; Free: 800-365-2136
Web Site: http://www.itt-tech.edu/
President/CEO: Chris Bowcutt
Type: Two-Year College **Sex:** Coed **Affiliation:** ITT Educational Services, Inc. **H.S. Requirements:** High school diploma required; GED accepted **Scholarships:** Available **Calendar System:** Quarter, Summer Session Not available **Credit Hours For Degree:** 96 credit hours, Associates; 180 credit hours, Bachelors **Professional Accreditation:** ACICS

LDS BUSINESS COLLEGE
95 North 300 West
Salt Lake City, UT 84101-3503
Tel: (801)524-8100; Free: 800-999-5767
Fax: (801)524-1900
E-mail: DFellows@ldsbc.edu
Web Site: http://www.ldsbc.edu/
President/CEO: J. Lawrence Richards
Admissions: Dawn Fellows
Type: Two-Year College **Sex:** Coed **Affiliation:** The Church of Jesus Christ of Latter-day Saints **% Accepted:** 85 **Admission Plans:** Open Admission; Deferred Admission **Application Deadline:** Rolling **Application Fee:** $35.00 **H.S. Requirements:** High school diploma required; GED accepted **Costs Per Year:** Application fee: $35. Tuition: $2900 full-time, $121 per credit hour part-time. Full-time tuition varies according to course load. Part-time tuition varies according to course load. Students who are not members of the LDS Church pay $5,800 per year. **Scholarships:** Available **Calendar System:** Semester, Summer Session Available **Enrollment:** FT 1,218, PT 370 **Faculty:** FT 19, PT 81 **Student-Faculty Ratio:** 20:1 **Exams:** SAT I or ACT. ACT essay not being used. SAT essay not being used. **Final Year or Final Semester Residency Requirement:** No **Library Holdings:** 383,760 **Credit Hours For Degree:** 62 credit hours, Associates **ROTC:** Army, Air Force **Professional Accreditation:** AAMAE, NCCU

MIDWIVES COLLEGE OF UTAH
1174 East 2700 South, Ste. 2
Salt Lake City, UT 84106
Tel: (801)764-9068; Free: (866)764-9068
Admissions: (801)649-5230
Fax: (801)434-8704
E-mail: office@midwifery.edu
Web Site: http://www.midwifery.edu/
President/CEO: Kristy Ridd-Young
Admissions: Kristi Ridd-Young
Type: Comprehensive **Sex:** Women **Application Deadline:** July 29 **Application Fee:** $35.00 **H.S. Requirements:** High school diploma required; GED accepted **Calendar System:** Semester **Enrollment:** , PT 130 **Professional Accreditation:** MEAC **Intercollegiate Athletics:** Ultimate Frisbee M & W; Volleyball M & W

NEUMONT UNIVERSITY
10701 South River Front Parkway, Ste. 300
South Jordan, UT 84095
Tel: (801)438-1100; Free: (866)622-3448
Admissions: (801)302-2856
Fax: (801)438-1111
E-mail: charlie.parker@neumont.edu
Web Site: http://www.neumont.edu/
President/CEO: Edward H. Levine
Admissions: Charlie Parker
Type: Comprehensive **Sex:** Coed **Scores:** 45% ACT 18-23; 41% ACT 24-29 **% Accepted:** 94 **Application Deadline:** Rolling **Application Fee:** $35.00 **H.S. Requirements:** High school diploma required; GED accepted **Costs Per Year:** Application fee: $35. Tuition: $28,800 full-time, $495 per credit hour part-time. College room only: $5700. Tuition guaranteed not to increase for student's term of enrollment. **Calendar System:** Quarter **Enrollment:** FT 232, Grad FT 8 **Faculty:** FT 11, PT 25 **Student-Faculty Ratio:** 13:1 **Exams:** SAT I or ACT. **% Residing in College-Owned, -Operated, or -Affiliated Housing:** 50 **Final Year or Final Semester Residency Requirement:** No **Credit Hours For Degree:** 180 units, Bachelors **Professional Accreditation:** ACICS

PROVO COLLEGE
1450 West 820 North
Provo, UT 84601
Tel: (801)818-8900; Free: 877-777-5886
Fax: (801)375-9728
E-mail: gordonp@provocollege.org
Web Site: http://www.provocollege.edu/
President/CEO: Gordon C. Peters
Admissions: Gordon Peters
Type: Two-Year College **Sex:** Coed **Application Fee:** $25.00 **Professional Accreditation:** ACCSCT, ADA, APTA

SALT LAKE COMMUNITY COLLEGE
PO Box 30808
Salt Lake City, UT 84130-0808
Tel: (801)957-4111
Admissions: (801)957-4485
Fax: (801)957-4958
E-mail: kathy.thompson@slcc.edu
Web Site: http://www.slcc.edu/
President/CEO: Cynthia A. Bioteau, PhD
Admissions: Kathy Thompson
Type: Two-Year College **Sex:** Coed **Affiliation:** Utah System of Higher Education **% Accepted:** 100 **Admission Plans:** Open Admission; Early Admission **Application Deadline:** Rolling **Application Fee:** $40.00 **H.S. Requirements:** High school diploma or equivalent not required. For health science programs: High school diploma required; GED accepted **Costs Per Year:** Application fee: $40. State resident tuition: $2376 full-time, $102 per credit hour part-time. Nonresident tuition: $8316 full-time, $358 per credit hour part-time. Mandatory fees: $414 full-time, $23 per credit hour part-time. **Scholarships:** Available **Calendar System:** Semester, Summer Session Available **Enrollment:** FT 9,566, PT 23,265 **Faculty:** FT 333, PT 1,166 **Student-Faculty Ratio:** 20:1 **Library Holdings:** 152,537 **Credit Hours For Degree:** 60 credits, Associates **ROTC:** Army, Air Force **Professional Accreditation:** ACF, ADA, AOTA, APTA, ACBSP, JRCERT, NAACLS, NLN, NCCU **Intercollegiate Athletics:** Baseball M; Basketball M & W; Cheerleading M & W; Soccer M & W; Softball W; Volleyball W

SNOW COLLEGE
150 East College Ave.
Ephraim, UT 84627-1203
Tel: (435)283-7000
Admissions: (435)283-7144
Fax: (435)283-6879
E-mail: snowcollege@snow.edu
Web Site: http://www.snow.edu/
President/CEO: Scott L. Wyatt
Admissions: Lorie Parry
Type: Two-Year College **Sex:** Coed **Affiliation:** Utah System of Higher Education **Scores:** 51% ACT 18-23; 20% ACT 24-29 **% Accepted:** 100 **Admission Plans:** Open Admission; Early Admission **Application Deadline:** June 15 **Application Fee:** $30.00 **H.S. Requirements:** High

school diploma required; GED accepted **Costs Per Year:** Application fee: $30. State resident tuition: $2152 full-time, $140 per credit hour part-time. Nonresident tuition: $7848 full-time, $500 per credit hour part-time. Mandatory fees: $390 full-time, $25 per credit hour part-time. Full-time tuition and fees vary according to course load. Part-time tuition and fees vary according to course load. College room and board: $4000. Room and board charges vary according to board plan, housing facility, and location. **Scholarships:** Available **Calendar System:** Semester, Summer Session Available **Enrollment:** FT 2,666, PT 1,702 **Faculty:** FT 113, PT 145 **Student-Faculty Ratio:** 18:1 **Exams:** SAT I or ACT. **Library Holdings:** 31,911 **Credit Hours For Degree:** 63 semester credits, Associates **Professional Accreditation:** NASM, NCCU **Intercollegiate Athletics:** Basketball M & W; Football M; Softball W; Volleyball W

SOUTHERN UTAH UNIVERSITY
351 West University Blvd.
Cedar City, UT 84720-2498
Tel: (435)586-7700
Fax: (435)586-5475
E-mail: adminfo@suu.edu
Web Site: http://www.suu.edu/
President/CEO: Michael Benson
Admissions: Stephen Allen
Financial Aid: Jan Carey-McDonald
Type: Comprehensive **Sex:** Coed **Affiliation:** Utah System of Higher Education **Scores:** 88.37% SAT V 400+; 90.12% SAT M 400+; 51.05% ACT 18-23; 30.52% ACT 24-29 **% Accepted:** 81 **Admission Plans:** Early Admission; Early Action; Deferred Admission **Application Deadline:** August 1 **Application Fee:** $40.00 **H.S. Requirements:** High school diploma required; GED accepted **Costs Per Year:** Application fee: $40. State resident tuition: $3730 full-time, $182 per credit hour part-time. Nonresident tuition: $12,308 full-time, $600 per credit hour part-time. Mandatory fees: $539 full-time, $539 per year part-time. Part-time tuition and fees vary according to course load. College room only: $1950. Room charges vary according to housing facility. **Scholarships:** Available **Calendar System:** Semester, Summer Session Available **Enrollment:** FT 5,467, PT 1,762, Grad FT 168, Grad PT 669 **Faculty:** FT 216, PT 110 **Student-Faculty Ratio:** 26:1 **Exams:** SAT I or ACT. ACT essay not being used. SAT essay not being used. **% Receiving Financial Aid:** 59 **% Residing in College-Owned, -Operated, or -Affiliated Housing:** 13 **ROTC:** Army **Professional Accreditation:** AACSB, AAFCS, ACBSP, NASAD, NASM, NCATE, NCCU, TEAC **Intercollegiate Athletics:** Baseball M; Basketball M & W; Cross-Country Running M & W; Football M; Golf M; Gymnastics W; Softball W; Tennis W; Track and Field M & W

STEVENS-HENAGER COLLEGE
1890 South 1350 West
West Haven, UT 84401
Tel: (801)394-7791; Free: 800-622-2640
Fax: (801)393-1745
Web Site: http://www.stevenshenager.edu/
President/CEO: Vicky Dewsnup
Type: Comprehensive **Sex:** Coed **Admission Plans:** Open Admission; Early Admission; Deferred Admission **Application Deadline:** Rolling **H.S. Requirements:** High school diploma required; GED accepted **Scholarships:** Available **Calendar System:** Quarter, Summer Session Not available **Student-Faculty Ratio:** 18:1 **Exams:** Other, SAT I or ACT. **Professional Accreditation:** ARCEST, AAMAE

STRAYER UNIVERSITY - SALT LAKE CAMPUS
9815 South Monroe St.
Ste. 200
Sandy, UT 84070
Tel: (801)432-5000
Fax: (801)561-5700
Web Site: http://www.strayer.edu/salt_lake/
Type: Comprehensive **Sex:** Coed **Application Fee:** $50.00 **Costs Per Year:** Application fee: $50. **Regional Accreditation:** Middle State Association of Colleges and Schools

UNIVERSITY OF PHOENIX—UTAH CAMPUS
5373 South Green St.
Salt Lake City, UT 84123-4617
Tel: (801)263-1444; Free: 800-228-7240
Admissions: (480)557-3303
Fax: (801)269-9766
E-mail: evelyn.gaskin@phoenix.edu
Web Site: http://www.phoenix.edu/
President/CEO: William Pepicello
Admissions: Evelyn Gaskin
Type: Comprehensive **Sex:** Coed **% Accepted:** 100 **Admission Plans:** Open Admission; Deferred Admission **Application Deadline:** Rolling **H.S. Requirements:** High school diploma required; GED accepted **Costs Per Year:** Tuition: $11,500 full-time. Full-time tuition varies according to course level and course load. **Scholarships:** Available **Calendar System:** Continuous, Summer Session Not available **Enrollment:** FT 1,936 **Faculty:** FT 57, PT 349 **Regional Accreditation:** North Central Association of Colleges and Schools **Credit Hours For Degree:** 60 credits, Associates; 120 credits, Bachelors **Professional Accreditation:** ACA, NLN

UNIVERSITY OF UTAH
201 South University St.
Salt Lake City, UT 84112-1107
Tel: (801)581-7200; Free: 800-444-8638
Admissions: (801)581-8761
Fax: (801)585-3034
E-mail: mremsburg@sa.utah.edu
Web Site: http://www.utah.edu/
President/CEO: Dr. Michael K. Young, JD
Admissions: Mateo Remsburg
Financial Aid: Amy Capps
Type: University **Sex:** Coed **Affiliation:** Utah System of Higher Education **Scores:** 95% SAT V 400+; 97% SAT M 400+; 44% ACT 18-23; 41% ACT 24-29 **% Accepted:** 80 **Admission Plans:** Early Admission **Application Deadline:** April 1 **Application Fee:** $45.00 **H.S. Requirements:** High school diploma required; GED accepted **Costs Per Year:** Application fee: $45. State resident tuition: $4956 full-time, $139.22 per credit hour part-time. Nonresident tuition: $17,346 full-time, $478.66 per credit hour part-time. Mandatory fees: $790 full-time. Full-time tuition and fees vary according to course level, course load, degree level, program, and student level. Part-time tuition varies according to course level, course load, degree level, program, and student level. College room and board: $6240. College room only: $3096. Room and board charges vary according to board plan and housing facility. **Scholarships:** Available **Calendar System:** Semester, Summer Session Available **Enrollment:** FT 15,189, PT 6,960, Grad FT 5,345, Grad PT 1,790 **Faculty:** FT 1,269, PT 620 **Student-Faculty Ratio:** 15:1 **Exams:** ACT, SAT I or ACT. ACT essay not being used. SAT essay not being used. **% Receiving Financial Aid:** 36 **% Residing in College-Owned, -Operated, or -Affiliated Housing:** 12 **Library Holdings:** 4,092,976 **Credit Hours For Degree:** 122 credit hours, Bachelors **ROTC:** Army, Navy, Air Force **Professional Accreditation:** AACSB, ABET, ACPhE, ACEJMC, AACN, ABA, ACNM, ADtA, ACSP, AOTA, APTA, APA, ASC, ASLHA, AALS, CEPH, CSWE, JRCEPAT, LCMEAMA, NAACLS NAAB, NASD, NASM, NASPAA, NRPA, NCCU, TEAC **Intercollegiate Athletics:** Baseball M; Basketball M & W; Cheerleading M & W; Cross-Country Running W; Football M; Golf M; Gymnastics W; Rugby M; Skiing (Cross-Country) M & W; Skiing (Downhill) M & W; Soccer W; Softball W; Swimming and Diving M & W; Table Tennis M & W; Tennis M & W; Track and Field W; Volleyball W

UTAH CAREER COLLEGE
1902 West 7800 South
West Jordan, UT 84088
Tel: (801)304-4224; Free: (866)304-4224
Fax: (801)304-4229
E-mail: kcooper@utahcollege.edu
Web Site: http://www.utahcollege.edu/
President/CEO: Robert Salmon
Admissions: Karma Cooper
Type: Two-Year College **Sex:** Coed **% Accepted:** 100 **Application Deadline:** October 1 **Scholarships:** Available **Calendar System:** Quarter **Enrollment:** FT 152, PT 418 **Faculty:** FT 9, PT 33 **Student-Faculty Ratio:** 12:1 **Professional Accreditation:** ACCSCT, AAMAE

UTAH CAREER COLLEGE—LAYTON CAMPUS
869 West Hill Field Rd.
Layton, UT 84041
Tel: (801)660-6000

Web Site: http://www.utahcollege.edu/
President/CEO: James Cox
Type: Two-Year College **Sex:** Coed

UTAH STATE UNIVERSITY
Old Main Hill
Logan, UT 84322
Tel: (435)797-1000; Free: 800-488-8108
Admissions: (435)797-1079
Fax: (435)797-3900
E-mail: admit@usu.edu
Web Site: http://www.usu.edu/
President/CEO: Dr. Stan L. Albrecht
Admissions: Jenn Putnam
Financial Aid: Tamara Allen
Type: University **Sex:** Coed **Affiliation:** Utah System of Higher Education **Scores:** 93.8% SAT V 400+; 95.6% SAT M 400+; 45.3% ACT 18-23; 39.6% ACT 24-29 **% Accepted:** 98 **Admission Plans:** Early Admission; Deferred Admission **Application Deadline:** Rolling **Application Fee:** $40.00 **H.S. Requirements:** High school diploma required; GED accepted **Costs Per Year:** Application fee: $40. State resident tuition: $4043 full-time. Nonresident tuition: $13,017 full-time. Mandatory fees: $785 full-time. Full-time tuition and fees vary according to course load, program, reciprocity agreements, and student level. College room and board: $4900. College room only: $1650. Room and board charges vary according to board plan and housing facility. **Scholarships:** Available **Calendar System:** Semester, Summer Session Available **Enrollment:** FT 11,632, PT 2,177, Grad FT 952, Grad PT 851 **Faculty:** FT 708, PT 169 **Student-Faculty Ratio:** 18:1 **Exams:** SAT I or ACT. ACT essay not being used. SAT essay not being used. **% Receiving Financial Aid:** 51 **Library Holdings:** 1,647,042 **Credit Hours For Degree:** 60 credit hours, Associates; 120 credit hours, Bachelors **ROTC:** Army, Air Force **Professional Accreditation:** AACSB, ABET, AAMFT, ADtA, APA, ASLA, ASLHA, FIDER, CORE, CSWE, NASM, NCATE, NRPA, NCCU, SAF, TEAC **Intercollegiate Athletics:** Baseball M; Basketball M & W; Cross-Country Running M & W; Equestrian Sports M & W; Football M; Golf M; Gymnastics W; Ice Hockey M; Rugby M & W; Soccer M & W; Softball W; Tennis M & W; Track and Field M & W; Volleyball M & W

UTAH STATE UNIVERSITY—COLLEGE OF EASTERN UTAH
451 East 400 North
Price, UT 84501-2699
Tel: (435)637-2120
Admissions: (435)613-5217
Fax: (435)637-4102
E-mail: todd.olsen@ceu.edu
Web Site: http://www.ceu.edu/
President/CEO: Dr. Michael King
Admissions: Todd Olsen
Financial Aid: Kim Rasbold
Type: Two-Year College **Sex:** Coed **Affiliation:** Utah System of Higher Education **Admission Plans:** Open Admission; Early Admission **Application Deadline:** Rolling **Application Fee:** $25.00 **H.S. Requirements:** High school diploma required; GED accepted **Scholarships:** Available **Calendar System:** Semester, Summer Session Available **Enrollment:** FT 1,103, PT 982 **Faculty:** FT 86, PT 56 **Student-Faculty Ratio:** 15:1 **Exams:** ACT. **% Residing in College-Owned, -Operated, or -Affiliated Housing:** 15 **Library Holdings:** 44,490 **Credit Hours For Degree:** 63 credits, Associates **Professional Accreditation:** NLN, NCCU **Intercollegiate Athletics:** Baseball M; Basketball M & W; Volleyball W

UTAH VALLEY UNIVERSITY
800 West University Parkway
Orem, UT 84058-5999
Tel: (801)222-8000
Admissions: (801)863-8460
Fax: (801)225-4677
E-mail: info@uvsc.edu
Web Site: http://www.uvu.edu/
President/CEO: Matthew S. Holland
Admissions: Liz Childs
Financial Aid: Joanna McCormick
Type: Comprehensive **Sex:** Coed **Affiliation:** Advent Christian Church; Utah System of Higher Education **Scores:** 83.87% SAT V 400+; 83.91% SAT M 400+; 41.83% ACT 18-23; 23.69% ACT 24-29 **% Accepted:** 100 **Admission Plans:** Open Admission; Early Admission; Deferred Admission **Application Deadline:** Rolling **Application Fee:** $35.00 **H.S. Requirements:** High school diploma required; GED accepted **Costs Per Year:** Application fee: $35. State resident tuition: $3674 full-time, $144.33 per credit hour part-time. Nonresident tuition: $11,304 full-time, $471 per credit hour part-time. Mandatory fees: $584 full-time, $584 per term part-time. Full-time tuition and fees vary according to course load. Part-time tuition and fees vary according to course load. **Scholarships:** Available **Calendar System:** Semester, Summer Session Available **Enrollment:** FT 15,066, PT 13,652, Grad FT 6, Grad PT 41 **Faculty:** FT 476, PT 1,064 **Student-Faculty Ratio:** 24:1 **% Receiving Financial Aid:** 58 **Library Holdings:** 228,000 **Credit Hours For Degree:** 60 semester hours, Associates; 120 semester hours, Bachelors **ROTC:** Army, Air Force **Professional Accreditation:** ABET, ADA, NLN, NCCU, TEAC **Intercollegiate Athletics:** Baseball M; Basketball M & W; Cross-Country Running M & W; Golf M & W; Soccer W; Softball W; Track and Field M & W; Volleyball W; Wrestling M

WEBER STATE UNIVERSITY
1001 University Circle
Ogden, UT 84408-1001
Tel: (801)626-6000; Free: 800-848-7770
Admissions: (801)626-6047
Fax: (801)626-6747
E-mail: admissions@weber.edu
Web Site: http://www.weber.edu/
President/CEO: Ann Millner
Admissions: Mark Simpson
Financial Aid: Richard O. Effiong
Type: Comprehensive **Sex:** Coed **Affiliation:** Utah System of Higher Education **Scores:** 53% ACT 18-23; 27% ACT 24-29 **% Accepted:** 100 **Admission Plans:** Open Admission; Early Admission; Deferred Admission **Application Deadline:** August 22 **Application Fee:** $30.00 **H.S. Requirements:** High school diploma required; GED accepted **Costs Per Year:** Application fee: $30. State resident tuition: $3133 per term part-time. Nonresident tuition: $10,439 per term part-time. **Scholarships:** Available **Calendar System:** Semester, Summer Session Available **Enrollment:** FT 10,570, PT 11,811, Grad FT 268, Grad PT 352 **Faculty:** FT 481, PT 385 **Student-Faculty Ratio:** 22:1 **Exams:** Other, SAT I or ACT. **% Receiving Financial Aid:** 44 **% Residing in College-Owned, -Operated, or -Affiliated Housing:** 4 **Library Holdings:** 646,666 **Credit Hours For Degree:** 60 credit hours, Associates; 120 credit hours, Bachelors **ROTC:** Army, Navy, Air Force **Professional Accreditation:** AACSB, ABET, ADA, AHIMA, CARC, CSWE, JRCEMT, NAACLS, NASM, NCATE, NLN, NCCU **Intercollegiate Athletics:** Baseball M; Basketball M & W; Bowling M & W; Cheerleading M & W; Cross-Country Running M & W; Fencing M & W; Football M; Golf M & W; Ice Hockey M; Lacrosse M & W; Racquetball M & W; Rugby M & W; Skiing (Downhill) M & W; Soccer M & W; Softball W; Swimming and Diving M & W; Tennis M & W; Track and Field M & W; Volleyball W; Water Polo M & W

WESTERN GOVERNORS UNIVERSITY
4001 South 700 East, Ste. 700
Salt Lake City, UT 84107
Tel: (801)274-3280; Free: 877-435-7948
Fax: (801)274-3305
E-mail: admissions@wgu.edu
Web Site: http://www.wgu.edu/
President/CEO: Robert Mendenhall
Financial Aid: Jenny Allen Ryan
Type: Comprehensive **Sex:** Coed **Application Fee:** $65.00 **H.S. Requirements:** High school diploma required; GED accepted **Scholarships:** Available **Calendar System:** Continuous, Summer Session Not available **% Receiving Financial Aid:** 42 **Professional Accreditation:** DETC, NCATE, NCCU

WESTMINSTER COLLEGE
1840 South 1300 East
Salt Lake City, UT 84105-3697
Tel: (801)484-7651; Free: 800-748-4753
Admissions: (801)832-2200
Fax: (801)484-3252
E-mail: admission@westminstercollege.edu
Web Site: http://www.westminstercollege.edu/
President/CEO: Dr. Michael Bassis

Admissions: Louis Levy
Financial Aid: Elizabeth Key
Type: Comprehensive **Sex:** Coed **Scores:** 96% SAT V 400+; 97% SAT M 400+; 36% ACT 18-23; 50% ACT 24-29 **% Accepted:** 82 **Admission Plans:** Deferred Admission **Application Deadline:** Rolling **Application Fee:** $40.00 **H.S. Requirements:** High school diploma required; GED accepted **Costs Per Year:** Application fee: $40. Comprehensive fee: $32,002 includes full-time tuition ($24,576), mandatory fees ($420), and college room and board ($7006). Full-time tuition and fees vary according to course load. Room and board charges vary according to board plan. Part-time tuition: $1024 per credit hour. Part-time mandatory fees: $122 per term. Part-time tuition and fees vary according to course load. **Scholarships:** Available **Calendar System:** Miscellaneous, Summer Session Available **Enrollment:** FT 2,035, PT 137, Grad FT 416, Grad PT 449 **Faculty:** FT 136, PT 191 **Student-Faculty Ratio:** 10:1 **Exams:** SAT I or ACT. ACT essay used for admission. SAT essay used for admission. ACT essay used for advising. SAT essay used for advising. ACT essay used in place of application essay. SAT essay used in place of application essay. ACT essay used for placement. SAT essay used for placement. **% Receiving Financial Aid:** 60 **% Residing in College-Owned, -Operated, or -Affiliated Housing:** 28 **Final Year or Final Semester Residency Requirement:** No **Library Holdings:** 168,573 **Credit Hours For Degree:** 124 semester hours, Bachelors **ROTC:** Army, Navy, Air Force **Professional Accreditation:** AACN, AANA, ACBSP, NCCU, TEAC **Intercollegiate Athletics:** Basketball M & W; Cross-Country Running M & W; Golf M & W; Lacrosse M & W; Skiing (Downhill) M & W; Soccer M & W; Volleyball W

BENNINGTON COLLEGE
One College Dr.
Bennington, VT 05201
Tel: (802)442-5401; Free: 800-833-6845
Admissions: (802)440-4312
Fax: (802)447-4269
E-mail: admissions@bennington.edu
Web Site: http://www.bennington.edu/
President/CEO: Dr. Elizabeth Coleman
Admissions: Ken Himmelman
Financial Aid: Meg Woolmington
Type: Comprehensive **Sex:** Coed **Scores:** 100% SAT V 400+; 100% SAT M 400+; 3.33% ACT 18-23; 53.33% ACT 24-29 **% Accepted:** 66 **Admission Plans:** Early Admission; Early Decision Plan; Deferred Admission **Application Deadline:** January 3 **Application Fee:** $60.00 **H.S. Requirements:** High school diploma required; GED accepted **Costs Per Year:** Application fee: $60. Comprehensive fee: $50,860 includes full-time tuition ($38,730), mandatory fees ($1030), and college room and board ($11,100). College room only: $5950. Part-time tuition: $1290 per credit hour. **Scholarships:** Available **Calendar System:** Semester, Summer Session Not available **Enrollment:** FT 660, PT 4, Grad FT 127, Grad PT 17 **Faculty:** FT 62, PT 32 **Student-Faculty Ratio:** 9:1 **Exams:** SAT essay used for placement. **% Receiving Financial Aid:** 69 **% Residing in College-Owned, -Operated, or -Affiliated Housing:** 96 **Final Year or Final Semester Residency Requirement:** No **Library Holdings:** 126,463 **Regional Accreditation:** New England Association of Schools and Colleges **Credit Hours For Degree:** 128 credits, Bachelors **Intercollegiate Athletics:** Basketball M & W; Soccer M & W

BURLINGTON COLLEGE
95 North Ave.
Burlington, VT 05401-2998
Tel: (802)862-9616; Free: 800-862-9616
Fax: (802)658-0071
E-mail: admissions@burlington.edu
Web Site: http://www.burlington.edu/
President/CEO: Dr. Jane Sanders
Admissions: Gillian Homsted
Financial Aid: Lindy Walsh
Type: Four-Year College **Sex:** Coed **% Accepted:** 83 **Admission Plans:** Early Action; Deferred Admission **Application Deadline:** August 15 **Application Fee:** $50.00 **H.S. Requirements:** High school diploma required; GED accepted **Costs Per Year:** Application fee: $50. One-time mandatory fee: $200. Tuition: $20,424 full-time, $675 per credit hour part-time. Full-time tuition varies according to course load, program, and reciprocity agreements. Part-time tuition varies according to course load, program, and reciprocity agreements. College room only: $6750. Room charges vary according to housing facility. **Scholarships:** Available **Calendar System:** Semester, Summer Session Available **Enrollment:** FT 120, PT 55 **Faculty:** FT 6, PT 55 **Student-Faculty Ratio:** 6:1 **% Receiving Financial Aid:** 68 **% Residing in College-Owned, -Operated, or -Affiliated Housing:** 11 **Final Year or Final Semester Residency Requirement:** Yes **Library Holdings:** 14,591 **Regional Accreditation:** New England Association of Schools and Colleges **Credit Hours For Degree:** 60 credits, Associates; 120 credits, Bachelors

CASTLETON STATE COLLEGE
Castleton, VT 05735
Tel: (802)468-5611; Free: 800-639-8521
Admissions: (802)468-1213
Fax: (802)468-1476
E-mail: info@castleton.edu
Web Site: http://www.castleton.edu/
President/CEO: David Wolk
Admissions: Maurice Ouimet
Financial Aid: Kathleen O'Meara
Type: Comprehensive **Sex:** Coed **Affiliation:** Vermont State Colleges System **Scores:** 92% SAT V 400+; 91% SAT M 400+; 62% ACT 18-23; 11% ACT 24-29 **% Accepted:** 71 **Admission Plans:** Deferred Admission **Application Deadline:** Rolling **Application Fee:** $40.00 **H.S. Requirements:** High school diploma required; GED accepted **Costs Per Year:** Application fee: $40. One-time mandatory fee: $200. State resident tuition: $8232 full-time, $343 per credit part-time. Nonresident tuition: $18,792 full-time, $783 per credit part-time. Mandatory fees: $864 full-time. College room and board: $8120. **Scholarships:** Available **Calendar System:** Semester, Summer Session Available **Enrollment:** FT 1,813, PT 221, Grad FT 8, Grad PT 149 **Faculty:** FT 90, PT 132 **Student-Faculty Ratio:** 14:1 **Exams:** SAT I or ACT. **% Receiving Financial Aid:** 66 **% Residing in College-Owned, -Operated, or -Affiliated Housing:** 50 **Library Holdings:** 190,437 **Regional Accreditation:** New England Association of Schools and Colleges **Credit Hours For Degree:** 64 credits, Associates; 122 credits, Bachelors **ROTC:** Army **Professional Accreditation:** CSWE, JRCEPAT, NLN **Intercollegiate Athletics:** Baseball M; Basketball M & W; Cheerleading M & W; Cross-Country Running M & W; Equestrian Sports M & W; Field Hockey W; Football M; Golf M; Ice Hockey M & W; Lacrosse M & W; Rugby M & W; Skiing (Downhill) M & W; Soccer M & W; Softball W; Tennis M & W; Volleyball W

CHAMPLAIN COLLEGE
PO Box 670
Burlington, VT 05402-0670
Tel: (802)860-2700; Free: 800-570-5858
Admissions: (802)860-2727
Fax: (802)862-2772
E-mail: admission@champlain.edu
Web Site: http://www.champlain.edu/
President/CEO: Dr. David F. Finney
Admissions: Ian Mortimer
Financial Aid: David B. Myette
Type: Comprehensive **Sex:** Coed **Scores:** 99% SAT V 400+; 98% SAT M 400+; 53% ACT 18-23; 39% ACT 24-29 **% Accepted:** 78 **Admission Plans:** Early Decision Plan **Application Deadline:** January 31 **Application Fee:** $40.00 **H.S. Requirements:** High school diploma required; GED accepted **Costs Per Year:** Application fee: $40. Comprehensive fee: $37,620 includes full-time tuition ($25,850), mandatory fees ($100), and college room and board ($11,670). Full-time tuition and fees vary according to course load. Room and board charges vary according to housing facility. Part-time tuition: $1075 per credit hour. Part-time tuition varies according to course load. **Scholarships:** Available **Calendar System:** Semester, Summer Session Available **Enrollment:** FT 1,938, PT 53, Grad PT 277 **Faculty:** FT 90, PT 244 **Student-Faculty Ratio:** 14:1 **Exams:** SAT I or ACT, SAT II. **% Receiving Financial Aid:** 63 **% Residing in College-Owned, -Operated, or

-Affiliated Housing: 41 **Final Year or Final Semester Residency Requirement:** No **Library Holdings:** 94,008 **Regional Accreditation:** New England Association of Schools and Colleges **Credit Hours For Degree:** 120 credit hours, Bachelors **ROTC:** Army **Professional Accreditation:** CARC, JRCERT

COLLEGE OF ST. JOSEPH
71 Clement Rd.
Rutland, VT 05701-3899
Tel: (802)773-5900
E-mail: admissions@csj.edu
Web Site: http://www.csj.edu/
President/CEO: Dr. Frank G. Miglorie, Jr.
Admissions: Susan Englese
Financial Aid: Julie Rosmus
Type: Comprehensive **Sex:** Coed **Affiliation:** Roman Catholic **Scores:** 36.7% SAT M 400+; 60% ACT 18-23 **Admission Plans:** Early Admission; Deferred Admission **Application Deadline:** Rolling **Application Fee:** $25.00 **H.S. Requirements:** High school diploma required; GED accepted **Costs Per Year:** Application fee: $25. Comprehensive fee: $26,900 includes full-time tuition ($17,900), mandatory fees ($400), and college room and board ($8600). Full-time tuition and fees vary according to course load, degree level, and program. Room and board charges vary according to housing facility. Tuition guaranteed not to increase for student's term of enrollment. **Scholarships:** Available **Calendar System:** Semester, Summer Session Available **Enrollment:** FT 175, PT 67, Grad FT 48, Grad PT 132 **Faculty:** FT 13, PT 52 **Student-Faculty Ratio:** 10:1 **Exams:** SAT I or ACT. ACT essay used for admission. SAT essay used for admission. ACT essay used for advising. SAT essay used for advising. ACT essay used for placement. SAT essay used for placement. **% Receiving Financial Aid:** 91 **% Residing in College-Owned, -Operated, or -Affiliated Housing:** 41 **Final Year or Final Semester Residency Requirement:** No **Library Holdings:** 57,708 **Regional Accreditation:** New England Association of Schools and Colleges **Credit Hours For Degree:** 60 credits, Associates; 127 credits, Bachelors **Intercollegiate Athletics:** Basketball M & W; Cross-Country Running M & W; Soccer M & W

COMMUNITY COLLEGE OF VERMONT
PO Box 489
Montpelier, VT 05601
Tel: (802)828-2800
Admissions: (802)654-0505
Fax: (802)828-2805
E-mail: adam.warrington@ccv.edu
Web Site: http://www.ccv.edu/
President/CEO: Joyce Judy
Admissions: Adam G. Warrington
Type: Two-Year College **Sex:** Coed **Affiliation:** Vermont State Colleges System **% Accepted:** 100 **Admission Plans:** Open Admission **Application Deadline:** Rolling **Application Fee:** $0.00 **H.S. Requirements:** High school diploma required; GED accepted. For high school diploma/GED not required of non-degree students: High school diploma required; GED accepted **Costs Per Year:** Application fee: $0. State resident tuition: $6150 full-time, $205 per credit hour part-time. Nonresident tuition: $12,300 full-time, $410 per credit hour part-time. Mandatory fees: $150 full-time, $50 per term part-time. **Scholarships:** Available **Calendar System:** Semester, Summer Session Available **Enrollment:** FT 1,283, PT 5,016 **Faculty:** FT 0, PT 698 **Student-Faculty Ratio:** 13:1 **Exams:** ACT essay not being used. SAT essay not being used. **Library Holdings:** 57,000 **Regional Accreditation:** New England Association of Schools and Colleges **Credit Hours For Degree:** 60 credits, Associates

GODDARD COLLEGE
123 Pitkin Rd.
Plainfield, VT 05667-9432
Tel: (802)454-8311; Free: 800-906-8312
Fax: (802)454-1029
E-mail: admissions@goddard.edu
Web Site: http://www.goddard.edu/
President/CEO: Dr. Mark Schulman
Admissions: Erin Johnson
Financial Aid: Beverly Jene
Type: Comprehensive **Sex:** Coed **% Accepted:** 83 **Admission Plans:** Deferred Admission **Application Deadline:** Rolling **Application Fee:** $40.00 **H.S. Requirements:** High school diploma required; GED accepted **Costs Per Year:** Application fee: $40. One-time mandatory fee: $125. Comprehensive fee: $14,174 includes full-time tuition ($12,854), mandatory fees ($168), and college room and board ($1152). Full-time tuition and fees vary according to program. **Scholarships:** Available **Calendar System:** Semester, Summer Session Not available **Enrollment:** FT 275, Grad FT 492, Grad PT 1 **Faculty:** FT 6, PT 124 **Student-Faculty Ratio:** 12:1 **% Receiving Financial Aid:** 90 **Library Holdings:** 70,000 **Regional Accreditation:** New England Association of Schools and Colleges **Credit Hours For Degree:** 120 credit hours, Bachelors

GREEN MOUNTAIN COLLEGE
One Brennan Circle
Poultney, VT 05764-1199
Tel: (802)287-8000; Free: 800-776-6675
Admissions: (802)287-8207
Fax: (802)287-8099
E-mail: admiss@greenmtn.edu
Web Site: http://www.greenmtn.edu/
President/CEO: Dr. Paul J. Fonteyn, PhD
Admissions: Dr. Sandra Bartholomew
Financial Aid: Wendy J. Ellis
Type: Comprehensive **Sex:** Coed **% Accepted:** 72 **Admission Plans:** Deferred Admission **Application Deadline:** Rolling **Application Fee:** $30.00 **H.S. Requirements:** High school diploma required; GED accepted **Costs Per Year:** Application fee: $30. One-time mandatory fee: $225. Comprehensive fee: $36,580 includes full-time tuition ($25,910), mandatory fees ($1000), and college room and board ($9670). College room only: $5704. Full-time tuition and fees vary according to course load, location, and program. Room and board charges vary according to housing facility. Part-time tuition: $864 per credit. Part-time mandatory fees: $990. Part-time tuition and fees vary according to course load, location, and program. **Scholarships:** Available **Calendar System:** Semester, Summer Session Available **Enrollment:** FT 736, PT 25, Grad FT 97 **Faculty:** FT 49, PT 33 **Student-Faculty Ratio:** 14:1 **Exams:** SAT I or ACT. SAT essay used as a validity check on application essay. **% Receiving Financial Aid:** 79 **% Residing in College-Owned, -Operated, or -Affiliated Housing:** 80 **Library Holdings:** 112,000 **Regional Accreditation:** New England Association of Schools and Colleges **Credit Hours For Degree:** 120 credits, Bachelors **Professional Accreditation:** NRPA **Intercollegiate Athletics:** Basketball M & W; Cross-Country Running M & W; Golf M; Lacrosse M & W; Skiing (Downhill) M & W; Soccer M & W; Softball W; Tennis M; Volleyball W

JOHNSON STATE COLLEGE
337 College Hill
Johnson, VT 05656
Tel: (802)635-2356; Free: 800-635-2356
Admissions: (802)635-1219
Fax: (802)635-1230
E-mail: jscadmissions@jsc.edu
Web Site: http://www.jsc.edu/
President/CEO: Barbara Murphy
Admissions: Bethany Harrington
Financial Aid: Kimberly Goodell
Type: Comprehensive **Sex:** Coed **Affiliation:** Vermont State Colleges System **Scores:** 86% SAT V 400+; 84% SAT M 400+ **% Accepted:** 82 **Admission Plans:** Early Action; Deferred Admission **Application Deadline:** Rolling **Application Fee:** $39.00 **H.S. Requirements:** High school diploma required; GED accepted **Costs Per Year:** Application fee: $39. State resident tuition: $7992 full-time, $333 per credit part-time. Nonresident tuition: $17,232 full-time, $718 per credit part-time. Mandatory fees: $921 full-time. College room and board: $7808. College room only: $4650. **Scholarships:** Available **Calendar System:** Semester, Summer Session Available **Enrollment:** FT 1,202, PT 489, Grad FT 14, Grad PT 284 **Faculty:** FT 53, PT 88 **Student-Faculty Ratio:** 17:1 **Exams:** SAT I or ACT. SAT essay not being used. **% Residing in College-Owned, -Operated, or -Affiliated Housing:** 57 **Final Year or Final Semester Residency Requirement:** No **Library Holdings:** 100,053 **Regional Accreditation:** New England Association of Schools and Colleges **Credit Hours For Degree:** 60 credits, Associates; 120 credits, Bachelors **ROTC:** Army **Intercollegiate Athletics:** Basketball M & W; Cross-Country Running M & W; Golf M; Lacrosse W; Soccer M & W; Softball W; Tennis M & W; Volleyball W

LANDMARK COLLEGE
River Rd. South
Putney, VT 05346

Tel: (802)387-4767
Admissions: (802)387-6718
Fax: (802)387-4779
E-mail: admissions@landmark.edu
Web Site: http://www.landmark.edu/
President/CEO: Dr. Lynda J. Katz
Financial Aid: Cathy Mullins
Type: Two-Year College **Sex:** Coed **% Accepted:** 73 **Admission Plans:** Deferred Admission **Application Deadline:** Rolling **Application Fee:** $75.00 **H.S. Requirements:** High school diploma required; GED accepted **Costs Per Year:** Application fee: $75. Comprehensive fee: $56,500 includes full-time tuition ($47,500), mandatory fees ($500), and college room and board ($8500). Room and board charges vary according to board plan and housing facility. **Scholarships:** Available **Calendar System:** Semester, Summer Session Available **Enrollment:** FT 498 **Faculty:** FT 86, PT 2 **Student-Faculty Ratio:** 6:1 **Exams:** Other. **% Residing in College-Owned, -Operated, or -Affiliated Housing:** 95 **Final Year or Final Semester Residency Requirement:** No **Library Holdings:** 32,786 **Regional Accreditation:** New England Association of Schools and Colleges **Credit Hours For Degree:** 60 credits, Associates **Intercollegiate Athletics:** Baseball M; Basketball M & W; Cross-Country Running M & W; Equestrian Sports M & W; Rock Climbing M & W; Soccer M & W; Softball W

LYNDON STATE COLLEGE
PO Box 919
Lyndonville, VT 05851-0919
Tel: (802)626-6200; Free: 800-225-1998
Admissions: (802)626-6413
Fax: (802)626-6335
E-mail: admissions@lyndonstate.edu
Web Site: http://www.lyndonstate.edu/
President/CEO: Dr. Carol A. Moore
Admissions: Donna "Dee" Gile
Type: Comprehensive **Sex:** Coed **Affiliation:** Vermont State Colleges System **Scores:** 76.79% SAT V 400+; 73.5% SAT M 400+ **Admission Plans:** Early Admission; Deferred Admission **Application Deadline:** Rolling **Application Fee:** $36.00 **H.S. Requirements:** High school diploma required; GED accepted **Scholarships:** Available **Calendar System:** Semester, Summer Session Available **Faculty:** FT 58, PT 109 **Student-Faculty Ratio:** 15:1 **Exams:** SAT I or ACT. **% Residing in College-Owned, -Operated, or -Affiliated Housing:** 51 **Library Holdings:** 109,629 **Regional Accreditation:** New England Association of Schools and Colleges **Credit Hours For Degree:** 62 credit hours, Associates; 122 credit hours, Bachelors **ROTC:** Air Force **Professional Accreditation:** NRPA **Intercollegiate Athletics:** Baseball M; Basketball M & W; Cross-Country Running M & W; Lacrosse M; Soccer M & W; Softball W; Tennis M & W; Volleyball W

MARLBORO COLLEGE
PO Box A, South Rd.
Marlboro, VT 05344
Tel: (802)257-4333; Free: 800-343-0049
E-mail: admissions@marlboro.edu
Web Site: http://www.marlboro.edu/
President/CEO: Ellen McCulloch-Lovell
Admissions: Mark Crowther
Financial Aid: Cathy S. Fuller
Type: Comprehensive **Sex:** Coed **Scores:** 100% SAT V 400+; 99% SAT M 400+; 23% ACT 18-23; 65% ACT 24-29 **% Accepted:** 71 **Admission Plans:** Early Admission; Early Action; Early Decision Plan; Deferred Admission **Application Deadline:** March 1 **Application Fee:** $50.00 **H.S. Requirements:** High school diploma required; GED accepted. For home schooled applicants with curriculum documentation: High school diploma or equivalent not required **Costs Per Year:** Application fee: $50. Comprehensive fee: $42,880 includes full-time tuition ($32,550), mandatory fees ($1110), and college room and board ($9220). College room only: $5080. Full-time tuition and fees vary according to degree level, location, and program. Part-time tuition: $1085 per credit. Part-time tuition varies according to course load, degree level, location, and program. **Scholarships:** Available **Calendar System:** Semester, Summer Session Not available **Enrollment:** FT 308, PT 5 **Faculty:** FT 39, PT 7 **Student-Faculty Ratio:** 8:1 **% Receiving Financial Aid:** 74 **% Residing in College-Owned, -Operated, or -Affiliated Housing:** 82 **Regional Accreditation:** New England Association of Schools and Colleges **Credit Hours For Degree:** 120 credits, Bachelors **Intercollegiate Athletics:** Soccer M & W

MIDDLEBURY COLLEGE
Middlebury, VT 05753-6002
Tel: (802)443-5000
Admissions: (802)443-3000
Fax: (802)443-2056
E-mail: admissions@middlebury.edu
Web Site: http://www.middlebury.edu/
President/CEO: Dr. Ronald D. Liebowitz
Admissions: Robert Clagett
Financial Aid: Marguerite Corbin
Type: Comprehensive **Sex:** Coed **Scores:** 100% SAT V 400+; 100% SAT M 400+; 2% ACT 18-23; 20% ACT 24-29 **% Accepted:** 20 **Admission Plans:** Early Admission; Early Decision Plan; Deferred Admission **Application Deadline:** January 1 **Application Fee:** $65.00 **H.S. Requirements:** High school diploma or equivalent not required **Costs Per Year:** Application fee: $65. Comprehensive fee: $50,780. **Scholarships:** Available **Calendar System:** 4-1-4, Summer Session Available **Enrollment:** FT 2,456, PT 26 **Faculty:** FT 260, PT 51 **Student-Faculty Ratio:** 9:1 **Exams:** Other. **% Receiving Financial Aid:** 49 **% Residing in College-Owned, -Operated, or -Affiliated Housing:** 97 **Library Holdings:** 716,328 **Regional Accreditation:** New England Association of Schools and Colleges **Credit Hours For Degree:** 36 courses, Bachelors **ROTC:** Army **Intercollegiate Athletics:** Baseball M; Basketball M & W; Cross-Country Running M & W; Field Hockey W; Football M; Golf M & W; Ice Hockey M & W; Lacrosse M & W; Skiing (Cross-Country) M & W; Skiing (Downhill) M & W; Soccer M & W; Softball W; Squash W; Swimming and Diving M & W; Tennis M & W; Track and Field M & W; Volleyball W

NEW ENGLAND CULINARY INSTITUTE
56 College St.
Montpelier, VT 05602-9720
Tel: (802)223-6324; Free: 877-223-6324
Fax: (802)223-0634
E-mail: janknutsen@neci.edu
Web Site: http://www.neci.edu/
President/CEO: Francis Voigt
Admissions: Jan Knutsen
Type: Two-Year College **Sex:** Coed **% Accepted:** 92 **Admission Plans:** Early Admission; Deferred Admission **Application Deadline:** Rolling **Application Fee:** $0.00 **H.S. Requirements:** High school diploma required; GED accepted **Scholarships:** Available **Calendar System:** Quarter, Summer Session Not available **Enrollment:** FT 569 **Faculty:** FT 70, PT 15 **Student-Faculty Ratio:** 8:1 **% Residing in College-Owned, -Operated, or -Affiliated Housing:** 80 **Library Holdings:** 2,400 **Credit Hours For Degree:** 60 credits, Associates; 92 credits, Bachelors **Professional Accreditation:** ACCSCT

NEW ENGLAND CULINARY INSTITUTE AT ESSEX
48 1/2 Park St.
Essex Junction, VT 05452
Tel: (802)872-3400
Admissions: (802)223-6324
E-mail: sherrigilmore@neci.edu
Web Site: http://www.neci.edu/
President/CEO: Francis Voigt
Admissions: Sherri Gilmore
Type: Two-Year College **Sex:** Coed **% Accepted:** 78 **Application Fee:** $0.00 **Calendar System:** Quarter **Enrollment:** FT 501 **Faculty:** FT 65, PT 11 **Professional Accreditation:** ACCSCT

NORWICH UNIVERSITY
158 Harmon Dr.
Northfield, VT 05663
Tel: (802)485-2000; Free: 800-468-6679
Admissions: (802)485-2658
Fax: (802)485-2580
E-mail: nuadm@norwich.edu
Web Site: http://www.norwich.edu/
President/CEO: Richard Schneider
Admissions: Shelby Wallace
Type: Comprehensive **Sex:** Coed **% Accepted:** 59 **Application Deadline:** Rolling **Application Fee:** $35.00 **H.S. Requirements:** High school diploma required; GED accepted **Scholarships:** Available **Calendar System:** Semester, Summer Session Available **Enrollment:** FT 1,889, PT 69

Faculty: FT 122, PT 189 **Student-Faculty Ratio:** 14:1 **Exams:** SAT I or ACT. **% Residing in College-Owned, -Operated, or -Affiliated Housing:** 82 **Library Holdings:** 280,000 **Regional Accreditation:** New England Association of Schools and Colleges **Credit Hours For Degree:** 120 credit hours, Bachelors **ROTC:** Army, Navy, Air Force **Professional Accreditation:** ABET, AACN, ACBSP, NAAB, NLN **Intercollegiate Athletics:** Baseball M; Basketball M & W; Cross-Country Running M & W; Fencing M & W; Football M; Ice Hockey M & W; Lacrosse M; Riflery M & W; Rugby M & W; Sailing M & W; Skiing (Cross-Country) M & W; Skiing (Downhill) M & W; Soccer M & W; Softball W; Swimming and Diving M & W; Tennis M & W; Track and Field M & W; Volleyball M & W; Weight Lifting M & W; Wrestling M

SAINT MICHAEL'S COLLEGE
One Winooski Park
Colchester, VT 05439
Tel: (802)654-2000; Free: 800-762-8000
Admissions: (802)654-3000
Fax: (802)654-2242
E-mail: admission@smcvt.edu
Web Site: http://www.smcvt.edu/
President/CEO: Dr. John Neuhauser
Admissions: Jacqueline Murphy
Financial Aid: Nelberta B. Lunde
Type: Comprehensive **Sex:** Coed **Affiliation:** Roman Catholic **Scores:** 99% SAT V 400+; 99% SAT M 400+ **% Accepted:** 81 **Admission Plans:** Early Action; Deferred Admission **Application Deadline:** February 1 **Application Fee:** $50.00 **H.S. Requirements:** High school diploma required; GED accepted **Costs Per Year:** Application fee: $50. Comprehensive fee: $43,530 includes full-time tuition ($34,555), mandatory fees ($290), and college room and board ($8685). Room and board charges vary according to housing facility. Part-time tuition: $1155 per credit. **Scholarships:** Available **Calendar System:** Semester, Summer Session Available **Enrollment:** FT 1,900, PT 50, Grad FT 77, Grad PT 439 **Faculty:** FT 151, PT 63 **Student-Faculty Ratio:** 13:1 **Exams:** SAT I or ACT. ACT essay used for admission. SAT essay used for admission. ACT essay used as a validity check on application essay. SAT essay used as a validity check on application essay. **% Receiving Financial Aid:** 62 **% Residing in College-Owned, -Operated, or -Affiliated Housing:** 97 **Final Year or Final Semester Residency Requirement:** Yes **Library Holdings:** 267,650 **Regional Accreditation:** New England Association of Schools and Colleges **Credit Hours For Degree:** 124 semester hours, Bachelors **ROTC:** Army, Air Force **Intercollegiate Athletics:** Baseball M; Basketball M & W; Cheerleading M & W; Cross-Country Running M & W; Field Hockey W; Golf M; Ice Hockey M & W; Lacrosse M & W; Rugby M & W; Skiing (Cross-Country) M & W; Skiing (Downhill) M & W; Soccer M & W; Softball W; Swimming and Diving M & W; Tennis M & W; Volleyball W

SOUTHERN VERMONT COLLEGE
982 Mansion Dr.
Bennington, VT 05201
Tel: (802)442-5427; Free: 800-378-2782
Fax: (802)447-4695
E-mail: admis@svc.edu
Web Site: http://www.svc.edu/
President/CEO: Karen Gross, JD
Type: Four-Year College **Sex:** Coed **Scores:** 86.82% SAT V 400+; 72.54% SAT M 400+; 45.45% ACT 18-23 **% Accepted:** 85 **Admission Plans:** Early Admission; Deferred Admission **Application Deadline:** Rolling **Application Fee:** $30.00 **H.S. Requirements:** High school diploma required; GED accepted **Costs Per Year:** Application fee: $30. Tuition: $635 per credit hour part-time. Part-time tuition varies according to course load. **Scholarships:** Available **Calendar System:** Semester, Summer Session Available **Enrollment:** FT 428, PT 58 **Faculty:** FT 24, PT 32 **Student-Faculty Ratio:** 17:1 **Exams:** SAT I or ACT. **% Receiving Financial Aid:** 79 **% Residing in College-Owned, -Operated, or -Affiliated Housing:** 50 **Library Holdings:** 26,000 **Regional Accreditation:** New England Association of Schools and Colleges **Credit Hours For Degree:** 60 credits, Associates; 120 credits, Bachelors **Professional Accreditation:** NLN **Intercollegiate Athletics:** Baseball M; Basketball M & W; Cross-Country Running M & W; Rugby M & W; Soccer M & W; Softball W; Track and Field M & W; Volleyball M & W; Wrestling M

STERLING COLLEGE
PO Box 72
Craftsbury Common, VT 05827-0072
Tel: (802)586-7711; Free: 800-648-3591
E-mail: lbirdsall@sterlingcollege.edu
Web Site: http://www.sterlingcollege.edu/
President/CEO: Will Wootton
Admissions: Lynne A. Birdsall
Financial Aid: Barbara Stuart
Type: Four-Year College **Sex:** Coed **% Accepted:** 79 **Admission Plans:** Early Admission; Early Action; Deferred Admission **Application Deadline:** February 15 **Application Fee:** $35.00 **H.S. Requirements:** High school diploma required; GED accepted. For home schooled students may submit a portfolio of educational and life experiences: High school diploma or equivalent not required **Costs Per Year:** Application fee: $35. Comprehensive fee: $31,175 includes full-time tuition ($23,196), mandatory fees ($425), and college room and board ($7554). College room only: $3440. Full-time tuition and fees vary according to course load. Room and board charges vary according to board plan. Part-time tuition: $700 per credit hour. Part-time tuition varies according to course load. **Scholarships:** Available **Calendar System:** Semester, Summer Session Available **Enrollment:** FT 100, PT 8 **Faculty:** FT 9, PT 15 **Student-Faculty Ratio:** 7:1 **% Receiving Financial Aid:** 77 **% Residing in College-Owned, -Operated, or -Affiliated Housing:** 82 **Library Holdings:** 14,112 **Regional Accreditation:** New England Association of Schools and Colleges **Credit Hours For Degree:** 120 credits, Bachelors

UNIVERSITY OF VERMONT
Burlington, VT 05405
Tel: (802)656-3131
Admissions: (802)656-3370
E-mail: admissions@uvm.edu
Web Site: http://www.uvm.edu/
President/CEO: Dr. Daniel M. Fogel
Admissions: Beth A. Wiser, PhD
Type: University **Sex:** Coed **Scores:** 99% SAT V 400+; 100% SAT M 400+; 22% ACT 18-23; 62% ACT 24-29 **% Accepted:** 71 **Admission Plans:** Preferred Admission; Early Action; Deferred Admission **Application Deadline:** January 15 **Application Fee:** $55.00 **H.S. Requirements:** High school diploma required; GED accepted **Costs Per Year:** Application fee: $55. State resident tuition: $11,712 full-time, $488 per credit hour part-time. Nonresident tuition: $29,568 full-time, $1232 per credit hour part-time. Mandatory fees: $1812 full-time. Part-time tuition varies according to course load. College room and board: $9026. College room only: $5964. Room and board charges vary according to board plan and housing facility. **Scholarships:** Available **Calendar System:** Semester, Summer Session Available **Enrollment:** FT 10,212, PT 1,170, Grad FT 1,193, Grad PT 26 **Faculty:** FT 597, PT 155 **Student-Faculty Ratio:** 17:1 **Exams:** SAT I or ACT. ACT essay used for admission. SAT essay used for admission. **% Receiving Financial Aid:** 59 **% Residing in College-Owned, -Operated, or -Affiliated Housing:** 51 **Final Year or Final Semester Residency Requirement:** Yes **Library Holdings:** 2,642,058 **Regional Accreditation:** New England Association of Schools and Colleges **Credit Hours For Degree:** 122 credits, Bachelors **ROTC:** Army **Professional Accreditation:** AACSB, ABET, AACN, ACA, ADA, APTA, APA, ASC, ASLHA, CSWE, JRCEPAT, JRCNMT, LCMEAMA, NAACLS, NCATE, NLN, SAF **Intercollegiate Athletics:** Basketball M & W; Cheerleading M & W; Crew M & W; Cross-Country Running M & W; Equestrian Sports M & W; Fencing M & W; Field Hockey W; Gymnastics M & W; Ice Hockey M & W; Lacrosse M & W; Rugby M & W; Sailing M & W; Skiing (Cross-Country) M & W; Skiing (Downhill) M & W; Soccer M & W; Swimming and Diving W; Table Tennis M & W; Track and Field M & W; Ultimate Frisbee M & W; Volleyball M & W; Water Polo M & W

VERMONT TECHNICAL COLLEGE
PO Box 500
Randolph Center, VT 05061-0500
Tel: (802)728-1000; Free: 800-442-VTC1
Admissions: (802)728-1244
Fax: (802)728-1390
E-mail: admissions@vtc.edu
Web Site: http://www.vtc.edu/
President/CEO: Dr. Ty Handy
Admissions: Dwight A. Cross
Financial Aid: Catherine R. McCullough
Type: Four-Year College **Sex:** Coed **Affiliation:** Vermont State Colleges System **Scores:** 84% SAT V 400+; 92% SAT M 400+; 67% ACT 18-23; 15% ACT 24-29 **% Accepted:** 63 **Application Deadline:** Rolling **Applica-**

tion Fee: $38.00 **H.S. Requirements:** High school diploma required; GED accepted **Costs Per Year:** Application fee: $38. State resident tuition: $9960 full-time, $415 per credit part-time. Nonresident tuition: $19,008 full-time, $792 per credit part-time. Mandatory fees: $932 full-time. Full-time tuition and fees vary according to course load and program. Part-time tuition varies according to program. College room and board: $7808. Room and board charges vary according to board plan. **Scholarships:** Available **Calendar System:** Semester, Summer Session Available **Enrollment:** FT 1,264, PT 399 **Faculty:** FT 85, PT 111 **Student-Faculty Ratio:** 10:1 **Exams:** SAT I or ACT. **% Receiving Financial Aid:** 71 **% Residing in College-Owned, -Operated, or -Affiliated Housing:** 35 **Library Holdings:** 55,338 **Regional Accreditation:** New England Association of Schools and Colleges **Credit Hours For Degree:** 60 credit hours, Associates; 130 credit hours, Bachelors **ROTC:** Army **Professional Accreditation:** ABET, NLN **Intercollegiate Athletics:** Baseball M; Basketball M & W; Golf M & W; Soccer M & W; Softball W

ACT COLLEGE
1100 Wilson Blvd.
Arlington, VA 22209
Tel: (703)527-6660
Web Site: http://www.healthtraining.com/
President/CEO: Jeffrey S. Moore
Type: Two-Year College **Sex:** Coed **Application Fee:** $50.00

ADVANCED TECHNOLOGY INSTITUTE
5700 Southern Blvd.
Virginia Beach, VA 23462
Tel: (757)490-1241
Web Site: http://www.auto.edu/
President/CEO: Mark Dreyfus
Type: Two-Year College **Sex:** Coed **% Accepted:** 75 **Application Fee:** $50.00

ARGOSY UNIVERSITY, WASHINGTON DC
1550 Wilson Blvd., Ste. 600
Arlington, VA 22209
Tel: (703)526-5800; Free: (866)703-2777
Fax: (703)526-5850
Web Site: http://www.argosy.edu/washingtondc/
President/CEO: David Erekson
Type: University **Sex:** Coed **Affiliation:** Argosy Education Group **Calendar System:** Semester **Regional Accreditation:** North Central Association of Colleges and Schools **Professional Accreditation:** APA

THE ART INSTITUTE OF VIRGINIA BEACH
Two Columbus Center
4500 Main St., Ste. 100
Virginia Beach, VA 23462
Tel: (757)493-6700; Free: 877-437-4428
Fax: (757)493-6800
Web Site: http://www.artinstitutes.edu/virginia-beach/
Type: Four-Year College **Sex:** Coed

THE ART INSTITUTE OF WASHINGTON
1820 North Fort Meyer Dr.
Arlington, VA 22209
Tel: (703)358-9550; Free: 877-303-3771
Fax: (703)358-9759
Web Site: http://www.artinstitutes.edu/arlington/
President/CEO: George Sebolt
Type: Four-Year College **Sex:** Coed **Affiliation:** Education Management Corporation **Calendar System:** Quarter **Regional Accreditation:** Southern Association of Colleges and Schools

THE ART INSTITUTE OF WASHINGTON—NORTHERN VIRGINIA
The Corporate Office Park at Dulles Town Center
21000 Atlantic Blvd., Ste. 100
Sterling, VA 20166
Tel: (571)449-4400; Free: 888-627-5008
Fax: (571)449-4500
Web Site: http://www.artinstitutes.edu/northern-virginia/
President/CEO: Samuel Ortiz
Type: Four-Year College **Sex:** Coed

AVERETT UNIVERSITY
420 West Main St.
Danville, VA 24541-3692
Tel: (434)791-5600; Free: 800-AVE-RETT
Admissions: (434)791-5663
Fax: (434)791-5637
E-mail: joel.nester@averett.edu
Web Site: http://www.averett.edu/
President/CEO: Dr. Tiffany Franks
Admissions: Joel Nester
Financial Aid: Carl Bradsher
Type: Comprehensive **Sex:** Coed **Affiliation:** Baptist General Association of Virginia **Scores:** 84% SAT V 400+; 86.5% SAT M 400+; 47.27% ACT 18-23; 12.79% ACT 24-29 **% Accepted:** 91 **Admission Plans:** Deferred Admission **Application Deadline:** July 15 **Application Fee:** $0.00 **H.S. Requirements:** High school diploma required; GED accepted **Costs Per Year:** Application fee: $0. Comprehensive fee: $29,912 includes full-time tuition ($21,112), mandatory fees ($1000), and college room and board ($7800). College room only: $5280. Full-time tuition and fees vary according to course load, degree level, location, and program. Room and board charges vary according to board plan and housing facility. Part-time tuition: $360 per credit hour. Part-time tuition varies according to course load, degree level, location, and program. **Scholarships:** Available **Calendar System:** Semester, Summer Session Available **Enrollment:** FT 714, PT 73, Grad FT 6, Grad PT 35 **Faculty:** FT 52, PT 33 **Student-Faculty Ratio:** 12:1 **Exams:** SAT I or ACT. **% Receiving Financial Aid:** 85 **% Residing in College-Owned, -Operated, or -Affiliated Housing:** 62 **Regional Accreditation:** Southern Association of Colleges and Schools **Credit Hours For Degree:** 67 credit hours, Associates; 123 credit hours, Bachelors **Intercollegiate Athletics:** Baseball M; Basketball M & W; Cross-Country Running M & W; Equestrian Sports M & W; Football M; Golf M; Soccer M & W; Softball W; Tennis M & W; Volleyball W

AVIATION INSTITUTE OF MAINTENANCE—MANASSAS
9821 Godwin Dr.
Manassas, VA 20110
Tel: (703)257-5515; Free: 877-604-2121
Fax: (703)257-5523
E-mail: directoramm@tidetech.com
Web Site: http://www.aviationmaintenance.edu/aviation-washington-dc.asp
President/CEO: Keith Zobel
Type: Two-Year College **Sex:** Coed **Application Fee:** $25.00 **Calendar System:** Quarter **Professional Accreditation:** ACCSCT

AVIATION INSTITUTE OF MAINTENANCE—VIRGINIA BEACH
1429 Miller Store Rd.
Virginia Beach, VA 23455
Tel: (757)363-2121; Free: 888-349-5387
Admissions: (757)363-2121
E-mail: directoramn@tidetech.com
Web Site: http://www.aviationmaintenance.edu/aviation-norfolk.asp

President/CEO: Michael Huffman
Type: Two-Year College **Sex:** Coed **Application Fee:** $25.00 **Calendar System:** Quarter **Professional Accreditation:** ACCSCT

BLUE RIDGE COMMUNITY COLLEGE
PO Box 80
Weyers Cave, VA 24486-0080
Tel: (540)234-9261
E-mail: waylandm@brcc.edu
Web Site: http://www.brcc.edu/
President/CEO: John A. Downey
Admissions: Mary Wayland
Type: Two-Year College **Sex:** Coed **Affiliation:** Virginia Community College System **% Accepted:** 100 **Admission Plans:** Open Admission; Early Admission **Application Deadline:** Rolling **Application Fee:** $0.00 **H.S. Requirements:** High school diploma required; GED accepted **Scholarships:** Available **Calendar System:** Semester, Summer Session Available **Enrollment:** FT 1,513, PT 2,291 **Faculty:** FT 60, PT 126 **Student-Faculty Ratio:** 22:1 **Library Holdings:** 59,735 **Regional Accreditation:** Southern Association of Colleges and Schools **Credit Hours For Degree:** 63 semester hours, Associates **Professional Accreditation:** NLN

BLUEFIELD COLLEGE
3000 College Dr.
Bluefield, VA 24605-1799
Tel: (276)326-3682; Free: 800-872-0175
Admissions: (276)326-4340
Fax: (276)326-4288
E-mail: mhipes@bluefield.edu
Web Site: http://www.bluefield.edu/
President/CEO: Dr. David Olive
Admissions: Mark Hipes
Financial Aid: Sheila Nelson-Hensley
Type: Four-Year College **Sex:** Coed **Affiliation:** Southern Baptist **Scores:** 87% SAT V 400+; 89% SAT M 400+; 52% ACT 18-23; 10% ACT 24-29 **% Accepted:** 47 **Admission Plans:** Deferred Admission **Application Deadline:** Rolling **Application Fee:** $30.00 **H.S. Requirements:** High school diploma required; GED accepted **Costs Per Year:** Application fee: $30. Comprehensive fee: $26,150 includes full-time tuition ($17,990), mandatory fees ($810), and college room and board ($7350). Full-time tuition and fees vary according to program. Room and board charges vary according to housing facility. Part-time tuition: $750 per credit hour. Part-time mandatory fees: $240 per term. Part-time tuition and fees vary according to program. **Scholarships:** Available **Calendar System:** Semester, Summer Session Available **Enrollment:** FT 643, PT 95 **Faculty:** FT 36, PT 82 **Student-Faculty Ratio:** 11:1 **Exams:** SAT I or ACT. **% Receiving Financial Aid:** 85 **% Residing in College-Owned, -Operated, or -Affiliated Housing:** 65 **Final Year or Final Semester Residency Requirement:** No **Library Holdings:** 74,150 **Regional Accreditation:** Southern Association of Colleges and Schools **Credit Hours For Degree:** 126 semester hours, Bachelors **Intercollegiate Athletics:** Baseball M; Basketball M & W; Cross-Country Running M & W; Golf M; Soccer M & W; Softball W; Tennis M & W; Volleyball W

BRIDGEWATER COLLEGE
402 East College St.
Bridgewater, VA 22812-1599
Tel: (540)828-8000; Free: 800-759-8328
Admissions: (540)828-5375
Fax: (540)828-5481
E-mail: admissions@bridgewater.edu
Web Site: http://www.bridgewater.edu/
President/CEO: Dr. Phillip C. Stone
Admissions: Linda Stout
Financial Aid: Scott Morrison
Type: Four-Year College **Sex:** Coed **Affiliation:** Church of the Brethren **Scores:** 96.2% SAT V 400+; 95.3% SAT M 400+; 57.5% ACT 18-23; 21.9% ACT 24-29 **% Accepted:** 86 **Admission Plans:** Deferred Admission **Application Deadline:** Rolling **Application Fee:** $30.00 **H.S. Requirements:** High school diploma required; GED accepted **Costs Per Year:** Application fee: $30. Comprehensive fee: $35,850 includes full-time tuition ($25,500) and college room and board ($10,350). College room only: $5260. Room and board charges vary according to board plan and housing facility. Part-time tuition: $850 per credit hour. Part-time mandatory fees: $30 per term. **Scholarships:** Available **Calendar System:** 4-1-4, Summer Session Available **Enrollment:** FT 1,576, PT 14 **Faculty:** FT 101, PT 35 **Student-Faculty Ratio:** 14:1 **Exams:** SAT I or ACT. ACT essay not being used. SAT essay not being used. **% Receiving Financial Aid:** 76 **% Residing in College-Owned, -Operated, or -Affiliated Housing:** 84 **Final Year or Final Semester Residency Requirement:** Yes **Library Holdings:** 147,856 **Regional Accreditation:** Southern Association of Colleges and Schools **Credit Hours For Degree:** 123 credits, Bachelors **Intercollegiate Athletics:** Baseball M; Basketball M & W; Cheerleading M & W; Cross-Country Running M & W; Equestrian Sports M & W; Field Hockey W; Football M; Golf M; Lacrosse M & W; Soccer M & W; Softball W; Swimming and Diving W; Tennis M & W; Track and Field M & W; Volleyball W

BRYANT & STRATTON COLLEGE - RICHMOND CAMPUS
8141 Hull St. Rd.
Richmond, VA 23235-6411
Tel: (804)745-2444
Fax: (804)499-7799
E-mail: tlawson@bryanstratton.edu
Web Site: http://www.bryantstratton.edu/
President/CEO: Beth Murphy
Admissions: David K. Mayle
Type: Two-Year College **Sex:** Coed **Affiliation:** Bryant and Stratton Business Institute, Inc. **Admission Plans:** Deferred Admission **Application Deadline:** Rolling **H.S. Requirements:** High school diploma required; GED accepted. For applicants 19 or over who meet entrance testing requirements: High school diploma required; GED not accepted **Calendar System:** Semester, Summer Session Available **Enrollment:** FT 280, PT 292 **Faculty:** FT 14, PT 35 **Student-Faculty Ratio:** 10:1 **Exams:** Other, SAT I or ACT. **Library Holdings:** 3,176 **Regional Accreditation:** Middle State Association of Colleges and Schools **Credit Hours For Degree:** 68 per credit, Associates

BRYANT & STRATTON COLLEGE - VIRGINIA BEACH
301 Centre Pointe Dr.
Virginia Beach, VA 23462-4417
Tel: (757)499-7900
Fax: (757)499-7799
E-mail: dmsoutherland@bryantstratton.edu
Web Site: http://www.bryantstratton.edu/
President/CEO: Lee E. Hicklin
Admissions: Deana M. Southerland
Type: Two-Year College **Sex:** Coed **Affiliation:** Bryant and Stratton Business Institute, Inc. **% Accepted:** 88 **Admission Plans:** Open Admission **Application Deadline:** Rolling **Application Fee:** $35.00 **H.S. Requirements:** High school diploma required; GED accepted **Costs Per Year:** Application fee: $35. One-time mandatory fee: $135. Tuition: $14,670 full-time, $489 per credit hour part-time. **Scholarships:** Available **Calendar System:** Semester, Summer Session Available **Enrollment:** FT 267, PT 328 **Faculty:** FT 20, PT 40 **Student-Faculty Ratio:** 12:1 **Exams:** Other. **Final Year or Final Semester Residency Requirement:** No **Library Holdings:** 8,700 **Regional Accreditation:** Middle State Association of Colleges and Schools **Credit Hours For Degree:** 60 credit hours, Associates; 120 credit hours, Bachelors

CENTRAL VIRGINIA COMMUNITY COLLEGE
3506 Wards Rd.
Lynchburg, VA 24502-2498
Tel: (434)832-7600
Fax: (434)832-7626
Web Site: http://www.cvcc.vccs.edu/
President/CEO: Darrel Staat
Admissions: Judy Wilhelm
Type: Two-Year College **Sex:** Coed **Affiliation:** Virginia Community College System **Admission Plans:** Open Admission; Early Admission; Deferred Admission **Application Deadline:** Rolling **Application Fee:** $0.00 **H.S. Requirements:** High school diploma or equivalent not required. For allied health programs: High school diploma required; GED not accepted **Costs Per Year:** Application fee: $0. State resident tuition: $2616 full-time, $87.20 per credit hour part-time. Nonresident tuition: $7779 full-time, $259.30 per credit hour part-time. Mandatory fees: $270 full-time, $9 per credit hour part-time. **Scholarships:** Available **Calendar System:** Semester, Summer Session Available **Faculty:** FT 57, PT 116 **Library Holdings:** 37,000 **Regional**

Accreditation: Southern Association of Colleges and Schools **Credit Hours For Degree:** 62 semester hours, Associates **Professional Accreditation:** JRCERT, NAACLS

CENTURA COLLEGE (CHESAPEAKE)
932 Ventures Way
Chesapeake, VA 23320
Tel: (757)549-2121
Fax: (757)548-1196
Web Site: http://www.centuracollege.com/
President/CEO: Yvonna Santos
Type: Two-Year College **Sex:** Coed **Professional Accreditation:** ACCSCT

CENTURA COLLEGE (NEWPORT NEWS)
616 Denbigh Blvd.
Newport News, VA 23608
Tel: (757)874-2121
Fax: (757)874-3857
Web Site: http://www.centuracollege.edu/
President/CEO: James Luck
Type: Two-Year College **Sex:** Coed

CENTURA COLLEGE (NORFOLK)
7020 North Military Hwy.
Norfolk, VA 23518
Tel: (757)853-2121
Fax: (757)852-9017
Web Site: http://www.centuracollege.edu/
President/CEO: Chauntrell Artis
Type: Two-Year College **Sex:** Coed

CENTURA COLLEGE (RICHMOND)
7001 West Broad St.
Richmond, VA 23294
Tel: (804)672-2300
Fax: (804)672-3338
Web Site: http://www.centuracollege.edu/
President/CEO: Antoinette S. Bennett
Type: Two-Year College **Sex:** Coed **Professional Accreditation:** ACCSCT

CENTURA COLLEGE (RICHMOND)
7914 Midlothian Turnpike
Richmond, VA 23235-5230
Tel: (804)330-0111
Fax: (804)330-3809
E-mail: directorbtr@tidetech.com
Web Site: http://www.centuracollege.edu/
President/CEO: Zoe Thompson
Type: Two-Year College **Sex:** Coed **Application Fee:** $25.00 **Professional Accreditation:** ACCSCT

CENTURA COLLEGE (VIRGINIA BEACH)
2697 Dean Dr.
Ste. 100
Virginia Beach, VA 23452
Tel: (757)340-2121; Free: 877-604-2121
Fax: (757)340-9704
Web Site: http://www.centuracollege.edu/
President/CEO: Beth Hall
Type: Two-Year College **Sex:** Coed **Application Fee:** $25.00 **Professional Accreditation:** ACCSCT

CHRISTENDOM COLLEGE
134 Christendom Dr.
Front Royal, VA 22630-5103
Tel: (540)636-2900; Free: 800-877-5456
Fax: (540)636-1655
E-mail: tmcfadden@christendom.edu
Web Site: http://www.christendom.edu/
President/CEO: Dr. Timothy O'Donnell
Admissions: Tom McFadden
Financial Aid: Alisa Polk
Type: Comprehensive **Sex:** Coed **Affiliation:** Roman Catholic **Scores:** 100% SAT V 400+; 99% SAT M 400+ **% Accepted:** 86 **Admission Plans:** Early Admission; Early Action **Application Deadline:** March 1 **Application Fee:** $25.00 **H.S. Requirements:** High school diploma or equivalent not required **Costs Per Year:** Application fee: $25. Comprehensive fee: $27,174 includes full-time tuition ($19,118), mandatory fees ($550), and college room and board ($7506). **Scholarships:** Available **Calendar System:** Semester, Summer Session Available **Enrollment:** FT 385, PT 5, Grad FT 5, Grad PT 55 **Faculty:** FT 20, PT 21 **Student-Faculty Ratio:** 14:1 **Exams:** SAT I or ACT. SAT essay used for admission. ACT essay not being used. **% Receiving Financial Aid:** 47 **% Residing in College-Owned, -Operated, or -Affiliated Housing:** 95 **Final Year or Final Semester Residency Requirement:** No **Library Holdings:** 64,265 **Regional Accreditation:** Southern Association of Colleges and Schools **Credit Hours For Degree:** 84 credit hours, Associates; 126 credit hours, Bachelors **Intercollegiate Athletics:** Baseball M; Basketball M & W; Golf M & W; Soccer M & W; Volleyball W

CHRISTOPHER NEWPORT UNIVERSITY
1 University Place
Newport News, VA 23606-2998
Tel: (757)594-7000; Free: 800-333-4268
Admissions: (757)594-7015
Fax: (757)594-7333
E-mail: admit@cnu.edu
Web Site: http://www.cnu.edu/
President/CEO: Sen. Paul S. Trible, Jr.
Admissions: Curtis Davidson
Financial Aid: Mary L. Wigginton
Type: Comprehensive **Sex:** Coed **Scores:** 100% SAT V 400+; 100% SAT M 400+; 35% ACT 18-23; 55% ACT 24-29 **% Accepted:** 60 **Admission Plans:** Early Admission; Early Action; Deferred Admission **Application Deadline:** March 1 **Application Fee:** $45.00 **H.S. Requirements:** High school diploma required; GED accepted **Costs Per Year:** Application fee: $45. State resident tuition: $8050 full-time, $335 per credit hour part-time. Nonresident tuition: $15,992 full-time, $665 per credit hour part-time. Mandatory fees: $3670 full-time, $152 per credit hour part-time. Full-time tuition and fees vary according to course load and degree level. Part-time tuition and fees vary according to course load and degree level. College room and board: $9240. Room and board charges vary according to board plan and housing facility. **Scholarships:** Available **Calendar System:** Semester, Summer Session Available **Enrollment:** FT 4,620, PT 166, Grad FT 102, Grad PT 64 **Faculty:** FT 236, PT 93 **Student-Faculty Ratio:** 18:1 **Exams:** SAT I or ACT. ACT essay not being used. SAT essay not being used. **% Receiving Financial Aid:** 40 **% Residing in College-Owned, -Operated, or -Affiliated Housing:** 58 **Library Holdings:** 201,174 **Regional Accreditation:** Southern Association of Colleges and Schools **Credit Hours For Degree:** 120 semester hours, Bachelors **ROTC:** Army **Professional Accreditation:** ABET, AACN, CSWE, NASM **Intercollegiate Athletics:** Baseball M; Basketball M & W; Cheerleading M & W; Cross-Country Running M & W; Field Hockey W; Football M; Golf M; Lacrosse M & W; Sailing M & W; Soccer M & W; Softball W; Tennis M & W; Track and Field M & W; Volleyball W

THE COLLEGE OF WILLIAM AND MARY
PO Box 8795
Williamsburg, VA 23187-8795
Tel: (757)221-4000
Admissions: (757)221-4223
Fax: (757)221-1242
E-mail: admission@wm.edu
Web Site: http://www.wm.edu/
President/CEO: Taylor Reveley
Admissions: Henry Broaddus
Financial Aid: Edward P. Irish
Type: University **Sex:** Coed **Scores:** 100% SAT V 400+; 100% SAT M 400+; 6.2% ACT 18-23; 38.6% ACT 24-29 **% Accepted:** 34 **Admission Plans:** Preferred Admission; Early Admission; Early Decision Plan; Deferred Admission **Application Deadline:** January 1 **Application Fee:** $60.00 **H.S. Requirements:** High school diploma or equivalent not required **Costs Per Year:** Application fee: $60. One-time mandatory fee: $153. State resident tuition: $6388 full-time, $240 per credit hour part-time. Nonresident tuition: $26,180 full-time, $880 per credit hour part-time. Mandatory fees: $4412 full-time. College room and board: $8382. College room only: $4930. Room and board charges vary according to board plan and housing facility. **Scholarships:** Available **Calendar System:** Semester, Summer Session Available **Enrollment:** FT 5,760, PT 76, Grad FT 1,637, Grad PT 401 **Faculty:** FT 628, PT 173 **Student-Faculty Ratio:** 11:1 **Exams:** SAT I or ACT, SAT II. %

Receiving Financial Aid: 30 **% Residing in College-Owned, -Operated, or -Affiliated Housing:** 74 **Final Year or Final Semester Residency Requirement:** Yes **Library Holdings:** 2,227,720 **Regional Accreditation:** Southern Association of Colleges and Schools **Credit Hours For Degree:** 120 credit hours, Bachelors **ROTC:** Army **Professional Accreditation:** AACSB, ABA, ACA, APA, AALS, NCATE **Intercollegiate Athletics:** Baseball M; Basketball M & W; Cross-Country Running M & W; Field Hockey W; Football M; Golf M & W; Gymnastics M & W; Lacrosse W; Soccer M & W; Swimming and Diving M & W; Tennis M & W; Track and Field M & W; Volleyball W

CULINARY INSTITUTE OF VIRGINIA
2428 Almeda Ave., Ste. 316
Norfolk, VA 23513
Tel: (757)853-3508; Free: (866)619-CHEF
Admissions: (757)858-2433
Fax: (757)857-4869
E-mail: hsadmissions@chefva.com
Web Site: http://www.jwu.edu/
President/CEO: Dorothea A. Bovani
Financial Aid: Lynn Robinson
Type: Four-Year College **Sex:** Coed **Affiliation:** ECPI College of Technology **Application Deadline:** Rolling **Application Fee:** $100.00 **H.S. Requirements:** High school diploma required; GED accepted **Scholarships:** Available **Faculty:** FT 16, PT 3 **% Receiving Financial Aid:** 80 **Final Year or Final Semester Residency Requirement:** No **Regional Accreditation:** New England Association of Schools and Colleges **Credit Hours For Degree:** 83 semester credits, Associates; 121 semester credits, Bachelors

DABNEY S. LANCASTER COMMUNITY COLLEGE
1000 Dabney Dr., PO Box 1000
Clifton Forge, VA 24422
Tel: (540)863-2800
Admissions: (540)863-2815
Fax: (540)863-2915
E-mail: knicely@dslcc.edu
Web Site: http://www.dslcc.edu/
President/CEO: Dr. Richard R. Teaff
Admissions: Kathy Nicely
Financial Aid: Sandra J. Haverlack
Type: Two-Year College **Sex:** Coed **Affiliation:** Virginia Community College System **Admission Plans:** Open Admission; Early Admission; Deferred Admission **Application Deadline:** Rolling **Application Fee:** $0.00 **H.S. Requirements:** High school diploma required; GED accepted. For applicants 18 or over who demonstrate ability to benefit from a specific program: High school diploma required; GED not accepted **Costs Per Year:** Application fee: $0. State resident tuition: $2268 full-time, $94.50 per credit hour part-time. Nonresident tuition: $6398 full-time, $266.60 per credit hour part-time. Mandatory fees: $173 full-time. Full-time tuition and fees vary according to reciprocity agreements. Part-time tuition varies according to reciprocity agreements. **Scholarships:** Available **Calendar System:** Semester, Summer Session Available **Faculty:** FT 21, PT 74 **Student-Faculty Ratio:** 15:1 **Final Year or Final Semester Residency Requirement:** No **Library Holdings:** 37,716 **Regional Accreditation:** Southern Association of Colleges and Schools **Credit Hours For Degree:** 68 semester hours, Associates **Professional Accreditation:** NLN **Intercollegiate Athletics:** Basketball M

DANVILLE COMMUNITY COLLEGE
1008 South Main St.
Danville, VA 24541-4088
Tel: (434)797-2222; Free: 800-560-4291
Fax: (434)797-8541
Web Site: http://www.dcc.vccs.edu/
President/CEO: B. Carlyle Ramsey
Admissions: Peter Castiglione
Type: Two-Year College **Sex:** Coed **Affiliation:** Virginia Community College System **Admission Plans:** Open Admission; Preferred Admission; Early Admission; Deferred Admission **Application Deadline:** Rolling **Application Fee:** $0.00 **H.S. Requirements:** High school diploma required; GED accepted **Scholarships:** Available **Calendar System:** Semester, Summer Session Available **Faculty:** FT 53, PT 148 **Student-Faculty Ratio:** 19:1 **Library Holdings:** 41,600 **Regional Accreditation:** Southern Association of Colleges and Schools **Credit Hours For Degree:** 62 semester hours, Associates

DEVRY UNIVERSITY (ARLINGTON)
2450 Crystal Dr.
Arlington, VA 22202
Tel: (703)414-4000
Fax: (703)414-4040
Web Site: http://www.devry.edu/
President/CEO: Loretta Franklin
Financial Aid: Roberta McDevitt
Type: Comprehensive **Sex:** Coed **Affiliation:** DeVry University **Admission Plans:** Deferred Admission **Application Deadline:** Rolling **Application Fee:** $50.00 **H.S. Requirements:** High school diploma required; GED accepted **Costs Per Year:** Application fee: $50. Tuition: $14,080 full-time, $550 per credit hour part-time. **Scholarships:** Available **Calendar System:** Semester, Summer Session Available **Enrollment:** FT 410, PT 288, Grad FT 13, Grad PT 122 **Faculty:** FT 16, PT 125 **Student-Faculty Ratio:** 10:1 **Exams:** ACT essay used for admission. SAT essay used for admission. ACT essay used for placement. SAT essay used for placement. **% Receiving Financial Aid:** 75 **Regional Accreditation:** North Central Association of Colleges and Schools **Credit Hours For Degree:** 67 credit hours, Associates; 122 credit hours, Bachelors

DEVRY UNIVERSITY (CHESAPEAKE)
1317 Executive Blvd., Ste. 100
Chesapeake, VA 23320-3671
Tel: (757)382-5680
Web Site: http://www.devry.edu/
Type: Comprehensive **Sex:** Coed

DEVRY UNIVERSITY (MANASSAS)
10432 Balls Ford Rd., Ste. 130
Manassas, VA 20109-3173
Tel: (703)396-6611
Web Site: http://www.devry.edu/
Type: Comprehensive **Sex:** Coed **Calendar System:** Semester **Regional Accreditation:** North Central Association of Colleges and Schools

EASTERN MENNONITE UNIVERSITY
1200 Park Rd.
Harrisonburg, VA 22802-2462
Tel: (540)432-4000; Free: 800-368-2665
Admissions: (540)432-4118
Fax: (540)432-4444
E-mail: admiss@emu.edu
Web Site: http://www.emu.edu/
President/CEO: Dr. Loren E. Swartzendruber
Admissions: Stephanie C. Shafer
Financial Aid: Renee Leap
Type: Comprehensive **Sex:** Coed **Affiliation:** Mennonite **Scores:** 94.61% SAT M 400+; 32.35% ACT 18-23; 39.71% ACT 24-29 **% Accepted:** 41 **Admission Plans:** Deferred Admission **Application Deadline:** Rolling **Application Fee:** $25.00 **H.S. Requirements:** High school diploma required; GED accepted **Costs Per Year:** Application fee: $25. Comprehensive fee: $31,770 includes full-time tuition ($24,120) and college room and board ($7650). Room and board charges vary according to board plan, housing facility, and student level. Part-time tuition: $1010 per credit hour. Part-time tuition varies according to course load. **Scholarships:** Available **Calendar System:** Semester, Summer Session Available **Enrollment:** FT 846, PT 227, Grad FT 119, Grad PT 333 **Faculty:** FT 97, PT 91 **Student-Faculty Ratio:** 7:1 **Exams:** SAT I or ACT. **% Receiving Financial Aid:** 72 **% Residing in College-Owned, -Operated, or -Affiliated Housing:** 69 **Library Holdings:** 166,154 **Regional Accreditation:** Southern Association of Colleges and Schools **Credit Hours For Degree:** 64 semester hours, Associates; 128 semester hours, Bachelors **Professional Accreditation:** ACA, ACIPE, ATS, CSWE, NCATE **Intercollegiate Athletics:** Baseball M; Basketball M & W; Cross-Country Running M & W; Field Hockey W; Soccer M & W; Softball W; Track and Field M & W; Volleyball M & W

EASTERN SHORE COMMUNITY COLLEGE
29300 Lankford Hwy.
Melfa, VA 23410-3000

Tel: (757)789-1789; Free: 877-871-8455
Admissions: (757)789-1732
Fax: (757)789-1739
E-mail: bsmith@es.vccs.edu
Web Site: http://www.es.vccs.edu/
President/CEO: Dr. Linda Thomas-Glover, PhD
Admissions: P. Bryan Smith
Type: Two-Year College **Sex:** Coed **Affiliation:** Virginia Community College System **Admission Plans:** Open Admission; Preferred Admission **Application Deadline:** Rolling **Application Fee:** $0.00 **H.S. Requirements:** High school diploma required; GED accepted **Costs Per Year:** Application fee: $0. State resident tuition: $2468 full-time, $87.20 per credit hour part-time. Nonresident tuition: $7372 full-time, $259.30 per credit hour part-time. Mandatory fees: $225 full-time, $7.50 per credit hour part-time. Full-time tuition and fees vary according to course load. Part-time tuition and fees vary according to course load. **Scholarships:** Available **Calendar System:** Semester, Summer Session Available **Enrollment:** FT 229, PT 1,103 **Faculty:** FT 18, PT 39 **Student-Faculty Ratio:** 13:1 **Exams:** Other. **Library Holdings:** 25,000 **Regional Accreditation:** Southern Association of Colleges and Schools **Credit Hours For Degree:** 62 semester hours, Associates

ECPI COLLEGE OF TECHNOLOGY
5555 Greenwich Rd.
Virginia Beach, VA 23462
Tel: (757)671-7171; Free: 800-986-1200
E-mail: rballance@ecpi.edu
Web Site: http://www.ecpi.edu/
President/CEO: Mark Dreyfus
Admissions: Ronald Ballance
Financial Aid: Kathi Turner
Type: Four-Year College **Sex:** Coed **% Accepted:** 80 **Admission Plans:** Deferred Admission **Application Fee:** $100.00 **H.S. Requirements:** High school diploma required; GED accepted **Scholarships:** Available **Calendar System:** Continuous, Summer Session Available **Enrollment:** FT 12,669 **Faculty:** FT 326, PT 465 **Student-Faculty Ratio:** 16:1 **Exams:** ACT, SAT I or ACT, SAT I, SAT II. **Final Year or Final Semester Residency Requirement:** No **Library Holdings:** 107,640 **Regional Accreditation:** Southern Association of Colleges and Schools **Credit Hours For Degree:** 60 semester credit hours, Associates; 120 semester credit hours, Bachelors

ECPI TECHNICAL COLLEGE (RICHMOND)
800 Moorefield Park Dr.
Richmond, VA 23236
Tel: (804)330-5533; Free: 800-986-1200
E-mail: agerard@ecpi.edu
Web Site: http://www.ecpitech.edu/
President/CEO: Mark Dreyfus
Type: Two-Year College **Sex:** Coed **% Accepted:** 80 **Admission Plans:** Deferred Admission **Application Deadline:** Rolling **Application Fee:** $100.00 **H.S. Requirements:** High school diploma required; GED accepted **Scholarships:** Available **Calendar System:** Semester, Summer Session Available **Enrollment:** FT 865 **Faculty:** FT 20, PT 18 **Student-Faculty Ratio:** 18:1 **Exams:** SAT I, SAT II. **Library Holdings:** 3,165 **Credit Hours For Degree:** 60 semester hours, Associates **Professional Accreditation:** ACCSCT

ECPI TECHNICAL COLLEGE (ROANOKE)
5234 Airport Rd.
Roanoke, VA 24012
Tel: (540)563-8080; Free: 800-986-1200
Fax: (540)362-5400
E-mail: wmerchant@ecpi.edu
Web Site: http://www.ecpi.edu/
President/CEO: Mark Dreyfus
Admissions: Dr. Walter Merchant
Financial Aid: Amanda Little
Type: Four-Year College **Sex:** Coed **% Accepted:** 80 **Admission Plans:** Deferred Admission **Application Deadline:** Rolling **Application Fee:** $100.00 **H.S. Requirements:** High school diploma required; GED accepted **Scholarships:** Available **Calendar System:** Semester, Summer Session Available **Enrollment:** FT 461 **Faculty:** FT 17, PT 19 **Student-Faculty Ratio:** 13:1 **Exams:** ACT, SAT I, SAT II. **Final Year or Final Semester Residency Requirement:** No **Library Holdings:** 67,042 **Credit Hours For Degree:** 60 credit hours, Associates; 120 semester credit hours, Bachelors **Professional Accreditation:** ACCSCT

EMORY & HENRY COLLEGE
PO Box 947
Emory, VA 24327-0947
Tel: (276)944-4121; Free: 800-848-5493
Admissions: (276)944-6133
Fax: (276)944-6934
E-mail: ehadmiss@ehc.edu
Web Site: http://www.ehc.edu/
President/CEO: Dr. Rosalind Reichard
Admissions: David Hawsey
Financial Aid: Margaret L. Murphy
Type: Comprehensive **Sex:** Coed **Affiliation:** United Methodist **Scores:** 91.63% SAT V 400+; 94.42% SAT M 400+; 49% ACT 18-23; 29% ACT 24-29 **% Accepted:** 70 **Admission Plans:** Early Action; Deferred Admission **Application Deadline:** Rolling **Application Fee:** $30.00 **H.S. Requirements:** High school diploma required; GED accepted **Costs Per Year:** Application fee: $30. Comprehensive fee: $33,180 includes full-time tuition ($24,880) and college room and board ($8300). College room only: $4250. Full-time tuition varies according to course load and degree level. Room and board charges vary according to board plan. Part-time tuition: $995 per credit hour. Part-time tuition varies according to course load and degree level. **Scholarships:** Available **Calendar System:** Semester, Summer Session Available **Enrollment:** FT 899, PT 73, Grad FT 16, Grad PT 14 **Faculty:** FT 75, PT 56 **Student-Faculty Ratio:** 10:1 **Exams:** SAT I or ACT. **% Receiving Financial Aid:** 81 **% Residing in College-Owned, -Operated, or -Affiliated Housing:** 73 **Library Holdings:** 243,813 **Regional Accreditation:** Southern Association of Colleges and Schools **Credit Hours For Degree:** 116 semester hours, Bachelors **Professional Accreditation:** JRCEPAT **Intercollegiate Athletics:** Baseball M; Basketball M & W; Cross-Country Running M & W; Football M; Golf M; Soccer M & W; Softball W; Tennis M & W; Volleyball W

EVEREST COLLEGE
801 North Quincy St.
Ste. 501
Arlington, VA 22203
Tel: (703)248-8887
Fax: (703)351-2202
Web Site: http://www.everest.edu/
President/CEO: Troy Ralston
Type: Two-Year College **Sex:** Coed **Calendar System:** Quarter **Professional Accreditation:** ACICS

FERRUM COLLEGE
PO Box 1000
Ferrum, VA 24088
Tel: (540)365-2121; Free: 800-868-9797
Admissions: (540)365-4290
Fax: (540)365-4266
E-mail: admissions@ferrum.edu
Web Site: http://www.ferrum.edu/
President/CEO: Dr. Jennifer L. Braaten
Admissions: Gilda Q. Woods
Financial Aid: Heather Hollandsworth
Type: Four-Year College **Sex:** Coed **Affiliation:** United Methodist **Scores:** 75% SAT V 400+; 78% SAT M 400+; 45% ACT 18-23; 12% ACT 24-29 **% Accepted:** 80 **Admission Plans:** Early Admission; Deferred Admission **Application Deadline:** Rolling **Application Fee:** $25.00 **H.S. Requirements:** High school diploma required; GED accepted **Costs Per Year:** Application fee: $25. Comprehensive fee: $31,195 includes full-time tuition ($23,520), mandatory fees ($45), and college room and board ($7630). College room only: $3880. Full-time tuition and fees vary according to course load. Room and board charges vary according to housing facility. Part-time tuition: $470 per credit hour. Part-time tuition varies according to course load. **Scholarships:** Available **Calendar System:** Semester, Summer Session Available **Enrollment:** FT 1,388, PT 38 **Faculty:** FT 69, PT 40 **Student-Faculty Ratio:** 16:1 **Exams:** SAT I or ACT. **% Receiving Financial Aid:** 88 **Regional Accreditation:** Southern Association of Colleges and Schools **Credit Hours For Degree:** 127 credit hours, Bachelors **Professional Accreditation:** CSWE, NRPA **Intercollegiate Athletics:** Baseball M; Basketball M & W; Cheerleading M & W; Cross-Country Running M & W; Football M; Golf M; Lacrosse W; Soccer M & W; Softball W; Tennis M & W; Volleyball W

GEORGE MASON UNIVERSITY
4400 University Dr.
Fairfax, VA 22030
Tel: (703)993-1000
Admissions: (703)993-2398
E-mail: etallent@gmu.edu
Web Site: http://www.gmu.edu/
President/CEO: Dr. Alan G. Merten
Admissions: Eddie Tallent
Type: University **Sex:** Coed **Scores:** 99% SAT V 400+; 100% SAT M 400+; 33% ACT 18-23; 58% ACT 24-29 **% Accepted:** 63 **Admission Plans:** Early Admission; Early Action; Deferred Admission **Application Deadline:** January 15 **Application Fee:** $75.00 **H.S. Requirements:** High school diploma required; GED accepted **Costs Per Year:** Application fee: $75. State resident tuition: $5640 full-time, $235 per credit hour part-time. Nonresident tuition: $21,624 full-time, $901 per credit hour part-time. Mandatory fees: $2384 full-time, $91 per credit hour part-time. Full-time tuition and fees vary according to course load. Part-time tuition and fees vary according to course load. College room and board: $7700. College room only: $4500. Room and board charges vary according to board plan and housing facility. **Scholarships:** Available **Calendar System:** Semester, Summer Session Available **Enrollment:** FT 15,189, PT 4,513, Grad FT 2,807, Grad PT 9,558 **Faculty:** FT 1,128, PT 1,072 **Student-Faculty Ratio:** 16:1 **Exams:** SAT I or ACT, SAT I and SAT II or ACT. ACT essay not being used. SAT essay not being used. **% Receiving Financial Aid:** 45 **% Residing in College-Owned, -Operated, or -Affiliated Housing:** 26 **Final Year or Final Semester Residency Requirement:** No **Library Holdings:** 1,867,357 **Regional Accreditation:** Southern Association of Colleges and Schools **Credit Hours For Degree:** 120 credit hours, Bachelors **ROTC:** Army, Air Force **Professional Accreditation:** AACSB, ABET, AACN, ABA, APA, AALS, CSWE, NASM, NASPAA, NCATE, NLN **Intercollegiate Athletics:** Baseball M; Basketball M & W; Cheerleading M & W; Crew W; Cross-Country Running M & W; Golf M; Lacrosse W; Soccer M & W; Softball W; Swimming and Diving M & W; Tennis M & W; Track and Field M & W; Volleyball M & W; Wrestling M

GERMANNA COMMUNITY COLLEGE
2130 Germanna Hwy.
Locust Grove, VA 22508-2102
Tel: (540)727-3000
Admissions: (540)891-3020
Fax: (540)727-3207
Web Site: http://www.gcc.vccs.edu/
President/CEO: Dr. David A. Sam
Admissions: Rita Dunston
Type: Two-Year College **Sex:** Coed **Affiliation:** Virginia Community College System **% Accepted:** 100 **Admission Plans:** Open Admission; Early Admission **Application Deadline:** Rolling **Application Fee:** $0.00 **H.S. Requirements:** High school diploma or equivalent not required. For nursing program: High school diploma required; GED accepted **Costs Per Year:** Application fee: $0. State resident tuition: $2879 full-time, $94.95 per credit hour part-time. Nonresident tuition: $8312 full-time, $277.05 per credit hour part-time. Full-time tuition varies according to course load. Part-time tuition varies according to course load. **Scholarships:** Available **Calendar System:** Semester, Summer Session Available **Enrollment:** FT 2,296, PT 4,739 **Faculty:** FT 69, PT 303 **Student-Faculty Ratio:** 19:1 **Library Holdings:** 124,808 **Regional Accreditation:** Southern Association of Colleges and Schools **Credit Hours For Degree:** 61 semester hours, Associates **Professional Accreditation:** NLN

HAMPDEN-SYDNEY COLLEGE
PO Box 667
Hampden-Sydney, VA 23943
Tel: (434)223-6000; Free: 800-755-0733
Admissions: (434)223-6120
Fax: (434)223-6346
E-mail: hsapp@hsc.edu
Web Site: http://www.hsc.edu/
President/CEO: Christopher B. Howard
Admissions: Anita Garland
Financial Aid: Zita Marie Barree
Type: Four-Year College **Sex:** Men **Affiliation:** Presbyterian Church (U.S.A.) **Scores:** 97.96% SAT V 400+; 97.96% SAT M 400+ **% Accepted:** 56 **Admission Plans:** Early Admission; Early Action; Early Decision Plan **Application Deadline:** March 1 **Application Fee:** $30.00 **H.S. Requirements:** High school diploma required; GED accepted **Costs Per Year:** Application fee: $30. Comprehensive fee: $42,490 includes full-time tuition ($30,994), mandatory fees ($1370), and college room and board ($10,126). Room and board charges vary according to board plan and housing facility. **Scholarships:** Available **Calendar System:** Semester, Summer Session Available **Enrollment:** FT 1,068 **Faculty:** FT 98, PT 21 **Student-Faculty Ratio:** 9:1 **Exams:** SAT I or ACT, SAT II. **% Receiving Financial Aid:** 52 **% Residing in College-Owned, -Operated, or -Affiliated Housing:** 95 **Library Holdings:** 284,961 **Regional Accreditation:** Southern Association of Colleges and Schools **Credit Hours For Degree:** 120 semester hours, Bachelors **ROTC:** Army **Intercollegiate Athletics:** Baseball M; Basketball M; Crew M; Cross-Country Running M; Fencing M; Football M; Golf M; Lacrosse M; Riflery M; Rugby M; Soccer M; Tennis M; Ultimate Frisbee M

HAMPTON UNIVERSITY
Hampton, VA 23668
Tel: (757)727-5000; Free: 800-624-3328
Admissions: (757)727-5901
Fax: (757)727-5084
E-mail: patra.johnson@hamptonu.edu
Web Site: http://www.hamptonu.edu/
President/CEO: Dr. William Harvey
Admissions: Patra Johnson
Financial Aid: Martin Miles
Type: Comprehensive **Sex:** Coed **Scores:** 100% SAT V 400+; 99.8% SAT M 400+; 55% ACT 18-23; 20% ACT 24-29 **% Accepted:** 56 **Admission Plans:** Early Admission; Deferred Admission **Application Deadline:** March 1 **Application Fee:** $35.00 **H.S. Requirements:** High school diploma required; GED accepted **Costs Per Year:** Application fee: $35. Comprehensive fee: $24,876 includes full-time tuition ($15,464), mandatory fees ($1748), and college room and board ($7664). College room only: $3986. Full-time tuition and fees vary according to course load, degree level, and program. Room and board charges vary according to board plan and housing facility. Part-time tuition: $390 per credit hour. Part-time mandatory fees: $1748 per year. **Scholarships:** Available **Calendar System:** Semester, Summer Session Available **Enrollment:** FT 4,236, PT 329, Grad FT 553, Grad PT 284 **Faculty:** FT 358, PT 70 **Student-Faculty Ratio:** 13:1 **Exams:** SAT I or ACT. ACT essay not being used. SAT essay not being used. **% Receiving Financial Aid:** 41 **% Residing in College-Owned, -Operated, or -Affiliated Housing:** 59 **Library Holdings:** 526,154 **Regional Accreditation:** Southern Association of Colleges and Schools **Credit Hours For Degree:** 121 semester hours, Bachelors **ROTC:** Army, Navy **Professional Accreditation:** ABET, ACPhE, ACEJMC, AACN, APTA, ASLHA, CAA, NAAB, NASM, NCATE, NLN **Intercollegiate Athletics:** Basketball M & W; Bowling W; Cross-Country Running M & W; Football M; Golf M & W; Sailing M & W; Softball W; Tennis M & W; Track and Field M & W; Volleyball W

HOLLINS UNIVERSITY
PO Box 9603
Roanoke, VA 24020-1603
Tel: (540)362-6000; Free: 800-456-9595
Admissions: (540)362-6401
Fax: (540)362-6218
E-mail: huadm@hollins.edu
Web Site: http://www.hollins.edu/
President/CEO: Nancy Oliver Gray
Admissions: Rebecca Eckstein
Financial Aid: Amy Moore
Type: Comprehensive **Scores:** 100% SAT V 400+; 96.1% SAT M 400+; 35.7% ACT 18-23; 55.7% ACT 24-29 **% Accepted:** 90 **Admission Plans:** Early Admission; Early Decision Plan; Deferred Admission **Application Deadline:** Rolling **Application Fee:** $40.00 **H.S. Requirements:** High school diploma required; GED accepted **Costs Per Year:** Application fee: $40. Comprehensive fee: $38,155 includes full-time tuition ($27,550), mandatory fees ($565), and college room and board ($10,040). Part-time tuition: $860 per credit. Part-time mandatory fees: $143.75 per term. **Scholarships:** Available **Calendar System:** 4-1-4, Summer Session Not available **Enrollment:** FT 763, PT 33, Grad FT 81, Grad PT 180 **Faculty:** FT 72, PT 26 **Student-Faculty Ratio:** 11:1 **Exams:** SAT I or ACT. ACT essay used for admission. SAT essay used for admission. ACT essay used for advising. SAT essay used for advising. **% Receiving Financial Aid:** 79 **% Residing in College-Owned, -Operated, or -Affiliated Housing:** 78 **Final Year or Final Semester Residency Requirement:** No **Library Holdings:** 236,427 **Regional Accreditation:** Southern Association of Colleges and

Schools **Credit Hours For Degree:** 128 credits, Bachelors **Professional Accreditation:** TEAC **Intercollegiate Athletics:** Basketball W; Equestrian Sports W; Fencing W; Golf W; Lacrosse W; Soccer W; Softball W; Swimming and Diving W; Tennis W

ITT TECHNICAL INSTITUTE (CHANTILLY)
14420 Abermarle Point Place
Chantilly, VA 20151
Tel: (703)263-2541; Free: 888-895-8324
Web Site: http://www.itt-tech.edu/
President/CEO: Deborah Brent
Type: Two-Year College **Sex:** Coed **Affiliation:** ITT Educational Services, Inc. **H.S. Requirements:** High school diploma required; GED accepted **Scholarships:** Available **Calendar System:** Quarter, Summer Session Not available **Professional Accreditation:** ACICS

ITT TECHNICAL INSTITUTE (NORFOLK)
863 Glenrock Rd., Ste. 100
Norfolk, VA 23502-3701
Tel: (757)466-1260
Web Site: http://www.itt-tech.edu/
President/CEO: John Murray
Type: Two-Year College **Sex:** Coed **Affiliation:** ITT Educational Services, Inc. **H.S. Requirements:** High school diploma required; GED accepted **Scholarships:** Available **Calendar System:** Quarter, Summer Session Not available **Professional Accreditation:** ACICS

ITT TECHNICAL INSTITUTE (RICHMOND)
300 Gateway Centre Parkway
Richmond, VA 23235
Tel: (804)330-4992
Web Site: http://www.itt-tech.edu/
President/CEO: Elaine Bartoli
Type: Two-Year College **Sex:** Coed **Affiliation:** ITT Educational Services, Inc. **H.S. Requirements:** High school diploma required; GED accepted **Scholarships:** Available **Calendar System:** Quarter, Summer Session Not available **Professional Accreditation:** ACICS

ITT TECHNICAL INSTITUTE (SALEM)
2159 Apperson Dr.
Salem, VA 24153
Tel: (540)989-2500; Free: 877-208-6132
Web Site: http://www.itt-tech.edu/
Type: Two-Year College **Sex:** Coed **Professional Accreditation:** ACICS

ITT TECHNICAL INSTITUTE (SPRINGFIELD)
7300 Boston Blvd.
Springfield, VA 22153
Tel: (703)440-9535; Free: (866)817-8324
Fax: (703)440-9561
Web Site: http://www.itt-tech.edu/
President/CEO: Andrew Scoblionko
Type: Two-Year College **Sex:** Coed **Affiliation:** ITT Educational Services, Inc. **H.S. Requirements:** High school diploma required; GED accepted **Scholarships:** Available **Calendar System:** Quarter, Summer Session Not available **Credit Hours For Degree:** 96 credit hours, Associates **Professional Accreditation:** ACICS

J. SARGEANT REYNOLDS COMMUNITY COLLEGE
PO Box 85622
Richmond, VA 23285-5622
Tel: (804)371-3000
Fax: (804)371-3650
E-mail: kpettis-walden@reynolds.edu
Web Site: http://www.reynolds.edu/
President/CEO: Dr. Gary Rhodes
Admissions: Karen Pettis-Walden
Financial Aid: Kiesha Pope
Type: Two-Year College **Sex:** Coed **Affiliation:** Virginia Community College System **Admission Plans:** Open Admission **Application Deadline:** Rolling **Application Fee:** $0.00 **H.S. Requirements:** High school diploma required; GED accepted **Costs Per Year:** Application fee: $0. State resident tuition: $3000 full-time, $100 per credit hour part-time. Nonresident tuition: $8463 full-time, $282.10 per credit hour part-time. Full-time tuition varies according to course load. Part-time tuition varies according to course load. **Scholarships:** Available **Calendar System:** Semester, Summer Session Available **Library Holdings:** 101,858 **Regional Accreditation:** Southern Association of Colleges and Schools **Credit Hours For Degree:** 61 credit hours, Associates **Professional Accreditation:** ADA, COptA, CARC, NAACLS, NLN

JAMES MADISON UNIVERSITY
800 South Main St.
Harrisonburg, VA 22807
Tel: (540)568-6211
Admissions: (540)568-5681
Fax: (540)568-3332
E-mail: admissions@jmu.edu
Web Site: http://www.jmu.edu/
President/CEO: Dr. Linwood H. Rose
Admissions: Michael D. Walsh
Financial Aid: Lisa L. Tumer
Type: Comprehensive **Sex:** Coed **Scores:** 99.1% SAT V 400+; 99.5% SAT M 400+; 36% ACT 18-23; 56% ACT 24-29 **% Accepted:** 61 **Admission Plans:** Preferred Admission; Early Action; Deferred Admission **Application Deadline:** January 15 **Application Fee:** $50.00 **H.S. Requirements:** High school diploma required; GED accepted **Costs Per Year:** Application fee: $50. State resident tuition: $4182 full-time. Nonresident tuition: $16,946 full-time. Mandatory fees: $3678 full-time. College room and board: $8020. College room only: $4028. **Scholarships:** Available **Calendar System:** Semester, Summer Session Available **Enrollment:** FT 16,489, PT 792, Grad FT 973, Grad PT 717 **Faculty:** FT 906, PT 434 **Student-Faculty Ratio:** 16:1 **Exams:** SAT I or ACT. ACT essay not being used. SAT essay not being used. **% Receiving Financial Aid:** 34 **% Residing in College-Owned, -Operated, or -Affiliated Housing:** 37 **Final Year or Final Semester Residency Requirement:** No **Library Holdings:** 1,307,874 **Regional Accreditation:** Southern Association of Colleges and Schools **Credit Hours For Degree:** 120 credit hours, Bachelors **ROTC:** Army, Air Force **Professional Accreditation:** AACSB, AACN, ACA, ADtA, AOTA, APA, ASLHA, FIDER, CSWE, JRCEPAT, NASAD, NASD, NASM, NAST, NCATE **Intercollegiate Athletics:** Baseball M; Basketball M & W; Cheerleading M & W; Cross-Country Running W; Field Hockey W; Football M; Golf M & W; Lacrosse W; Soccer M & W; Softball W; Swimming and Diving W; Tennis M & W; Track and Field W; Volleyball W

JEFFERSON COLLEGE OF HEALTH SCIENCES
PO Box 13186
Roanoke, VA 24031-3186
Tel: (540)985-8483; Free: 888-985-8483
Admissions: (540)985-9083
Fax: (540)985-9773
E-mail: cijom1@jchs.edu
Web Site: http://www.jchs.edu/
President/CEO: Carol M. Seavor
Admissions: Judith McKeon
Financial Aid: Debra A. Johnson
Type: Comprehensive **Sex:** Coed **Scores:** 92% SAT V 400+; 89% SAT M 400+; 53% ACT 18-23; 5% ACT 24-29 **% Accepted:** 44 **Admission Plans:** Deferred Admission **Application Deadline:** Rolling **Application Fee:** $35.00 **H.S. Requirements:** High school diploma required; GED accepted **Costs Per Year:** Application fee: $35. Comprehensive fee: $24,750 includes full-time tuition ($17,740) and college room and board ($7010). Part-time tuition: $515 per credit hour. **Scholarships:** Available **Calendar System:** Semester, Summer Session Available **Enrollment:** FT 623, PT 270, Grad FT 134, Grad PT 14 **Faculty:** FT 71, PT 45 **Student-Faculty Ratio:** 10:1 **Exams:** SAT I or ACT, SAT I. **% Receiving Financial Aid:** 32 **% Residing in College-Owned, -Operated, or -Affiliated Housing:** 5 **Library Holdings:** 10,533 **Regional Accreditation:** Southern Association of Colleges and Schools **Credit Hours For Degree:** 60 credit hours, Associates; 120 credit hours, Bachelors **Professional Accreditation:** AACN, AOTA, APTA, CARC, JRCEMT, NLN **Intercollegiate Athletics:** Basketball M; Cross-Country Running M & W; Softball M & W; Tennis M & W; Volleyball M & W

JOHN TYLER COMMUNITY COLLEGE
13101 Jefferson Davis Hwy.
Chester, VA 23831-5316
Tel: (804)796-4000
Admissions: (804)796-4150
Fax: (804)796-4163

Web Site: http://www.jtcc.edu/
President/CEO: Dr. Marshall W. Smith
Admissions: Joy James
Type: Two-Year College **Sex:** Coed **Affiliation:** Virginia Community College System **% Accepted:** 100 **Admission Plans:** Open Admission; Preferred Admission; Early Admission; Deferred Admission **Application Deadline:** Rolling **Application Fee:** $0.00 **H.S. Requirements:** High school diploma or equivalent not required. For nursing, funeral services, physical therapist assistant programs: High school diploma required; GED accepted **Costs Per Year:** Application fee: $0. State resident tuition: $2225 full-time, $92.70 per credit hour part-time. Nonresident tuition: $6595 full-time, $274.80 per credit hour part-time. Mandatory fees: $50 full-time, $25 per term part-time. Full-time tuition and fees vary according to course load. Part-time tuition and fees vary according to course load. **Scholarships:** Available **Calendar System:** Semester, Summer Session Available **Enrollment:** FT 2,773, PT 6,919 **Faculty:** FT 77, PT 323 **Student-Faculty Ratio:** 20:1 **Library Holdings:** 49,393 **Regional Accreditation:** Southern Association of Colleges and Schools **Credit Hours For Degree:** 65 semester hours, Associates **ROTC:** Army **Professional Accreditation:** ABFSE, NLN

LIBERTY UNIVERSITY
1971 University Blvd.
Lynchburg, VA 24502
Tel: (434)582-2000; Free: 800-543-5317
Admissions: (434)592-3054
Fax: (434)582-2304
E-mail: admissions@liberty.edu
Web Site: http://www.liberty.edu/
President/CEO: Jerry Falwell, Jr.
Admissions: Tim Rees
Financial Aid: Robert Ritz
Type: Comprehensive **Sex:** Coed **Affiliation:** nondenominational **Scores:** 90.62% SAT V 400+; 87.29% SAT M 400+; 52.39% ACT 18-23; 25.61% ACT 24-29 **Admission Plans:** Early Admission; Deferred Admission **Application Deadline:** June 30 **Application Fee:** $40.00 **H.S. Requirements:** High school diploma required; GED accepted. For home schooled students provide records of academic work, grades and evaluations: High school diploma or equivalent not required **Costs Per Year:** Application fee: $40. Comprehensive fee: $23,198 includes full-time tuition ($15,992), mandatory fees ($1210), and college room and board ($5996). Full-time tuition and fees vary according to course load. Room and board charges vary according to housing facility. Part-time tuition: $550 per hour. Part-time tuition varies according to course load. **Scholarships:** Available **Calendar System:** Semester, Summer Session Available **Enrollment:** FT 18,617, PT 10,246, Grad FT 6,913, Grad PT 10,350 **Faculty:** FT 379, PT 1,040 **Exams:** SAT I or ACT. **% Residing in College-Owned, -Operated, or -Affiliated Housing:** 63 **Final Year or Final Semester Residency Requirement:** No **Library Holdings:** 495,255 **Regional Accreditation:** Southern Association of Colleges and Schools **Credit Hours For Degree:** 60 semester hours, Associates; 120 semester hours, Bachelors **ROTC:** Army, Air Force **Professional Accreditation:** AACN, AAFCS, ABA, ACIPE, NCATE, NLN, TACCS **Intercollegiate Athletics:** Baseball M; Basketball M & W; Cheerleading M & W; Cross-Country Running M & W; Equestrian Sports W; Field Hockey W; Football M; Golf M; Ice Hockey M; Lacrosse M; Soccer M & W; Softball W; Tennis M & W; Track and Field M & W; Volleyball W

LONGWOOD UNIVERSITY
201 High St.
Farmville, VA 23909
Tel: (434)395-2000; Free: 800-281-4677
Admissions: (434)395-2060
Fax: (434)395-2332
E-mail: admissions@longwood.edu
Web Site: http://www.longwood.edu/
President/CEO: Dr. Patricia P. Cormier
Admissions: Robert J. Chonko
Financial Aid: Caroline Gibbs
Type: Comprehensive **Sex:** Coed **Affiliation:** The State Council of Higher Education for Virginia **Scores:** 98.63% SAT V 400+; 99.32% SAT M 400+; 71.97% ACT 18-23; 25.75% ACT 24-29 **% Accepted:** 69 **Admission Plans:** Early Admission; Early Action; Deferred Admission **Application Deadline:** March 1 **Application Fee:** $40.00 **H.S. Requirements:** High school diploma required; GED accepted **Costs Per Year:** Application fee: $40. State resident tuition: $4680 full-time, $156 per credit hour part-time. Nonresident tuition: $13,590 full-time, $453 per credit hour part-time. Mandatory fees: $4245 full-time. Full-time tuition and fees vary according to course load. Part-time tuition varies according to course load. College room and board: $7596. College room only: $4910. Room and board charges vary according to board plan, housing facility, and location. **Scholarships:** Available **Calendar System:** Semester, Summer Session Available **Enrollment:** FT 3,868, PT 218, Grad FT 83, Grad PT 663 **Faculty:** FT 207, PT 72 **Student-Faculty Ratio:** 18:1 **Exams:** SAT I or ACT. ACT essay not being used. SAT essay not being used. **% Receiving Financial Aid:** 42 **% Residing in College-Owned, -Operated, or -Affiliated Housing:** 75 **Library Holdings:** 344,567 **Regional Accreditation:** Southern Association of Colleges and Schools **Credit Hours For Degree:** 120 credit hours, Bachelors **ROTC:** Army **Professional Accreditation:** AACSB, CSWE, JRCEPAT, NASM, NAST, NCATE, NRPA **Intercollegiate Athletics:** Baseball M; Basketball M & W; Cross-Country Running M & W; Equestrian Sports M & W; Field Hockey W; Golf M & W; Lacrosse W; Rugby M & W; Soccer M & W; Softball W; Swimming and Diving M & W; Tennis M & W; Track and Field M & W; Volleyball M & W; Wrestling M

LORD FAIRFAX COMMUNITY COLLEGE
173 Skirmisher Ln.
Middletown, VA 22645
Tel: (540)868-7000; Free: 800-906-5322
Fax: (540)868-7100
E-mail: lfsmitt@lfcc.edu
Web Site: http://www.lfcc.edu/
President/CEO: Cheryl Thompson-Stacy
Admissions: Cynthia Bambara
Type: Two-Year College **Sex:** Coed **Affiliation:** Virginia Community College System **Admission Plans:** Open Admission; Early Admission **Application Deadline:** Rolling **Application Fee:** $0.00 **H.S. Requirements:** High school diploma or equivalent not required **Costs Per Year:** Application fee: $0. State resident tuition: $2093 full-time, $87 per credit hour part-time. Nonresident tuition: $6223 full-time, $259 per credit hour part-time. Mandatory fees: $188 full-time, $6.65 per credit hour part-time, $14 per term part-time. Full-time tuition and fees vary according to course load. **Scholarships:** Available **Calendar System:** Semester, Summer Session Available **Enrollment:** FT 1,535, PT 3,957 **Faculty:** FT 57, PT 252 **Library Holdings:** 41,000 **Regional Accreditation:** Southern Association of Colleges and Schools **Credit Hours For Degree:** 62 semester hours, Associates

LYNCHBURG COLLEGE
1501 Lakeside Dr.
Lynchburg, VA 24501-3199
Tel: (434)544-8100; Free: 800-426-8101
Admissions: (434)544-8300
Fax: (434)544-8653
E-mail: admissions@lynchburg.edu
Web Site: http://www.lynchburg.edu/
President/CEO: Dr. Kenneth R. Garren
Admissions: Sharon Walters-Bower
Financial Aid: Michelle Davis
Type: Comprehensive **Sex:** Coed **Affiliation:** Christian Church (Disciples of Christ) **Scores:** 96% SAT V 400+; 92% SAT M 400+; 56% ACT 18-23; 27% ACT 24-29 **% Accepted:** 66 **Admission Plans:** Early Admission; Early Decision Plan; Deferred Admission **Application Deadline:** Rolling **Application Fee:** $30.00 **H.S. Requirements:** High school diploma required; GED accepted **Costs Per Year:** Application fee: $30. Comprehensive fee: $35,895 includes full-time tuition ($27,980), mandatory fees ($945), and college room and board ($6970). College room only: $3930. Room and board charges vary according to board plan and housing facility. Part-time tuition: $390 per credit hour. Part-time mandatory fees: $5.10 per credit hour. Part-time tuition and fees vary according to course load. **Scholarships:** Available **Calendar System:** Semester, Summer Session Available **Enrollment:** FT 2,110, PT 89, Grad FT 97, Grad PT 293 **Faculty:** FT 155, PT 104 **Student-Faculty Ratio:** 12:1 **Exams:** SAT I or ACT. ACT essay not being used. SAT essay not being used. **% Receiving Financial Aid:** 69 **% Residing in College-Owned, -Operated, or -Affiliated Housing:** 78 **Library Holdings:** 234,000 **Regional Accreditation:** Southern Association of Colleges and Schools **Credit Hours For Degree:** 124 semester hours, Bachelors **Professional Accreditation:** AACN, ACA, ACBSP, NLN **Intercollegiate Athletics:** Baseball M; Basketball M & W; Cheerleading M & W; Cross-Country Running M & W; Equestrian Sports W; Field Hockey W; Golf M; Lacrosse M & W; Soccer M & W; Softball W; Tennis M & W; Track and Field M & W; Volleyball W

MARY BALDWIN COLLEGE
201 East Frederick St.
Staunton, VA 24401-3610
Tel: (540)887-7000; Free: 800-468-2262
Admissions: (540)887-7260
Fax: (540)886-6634
E-mail: rpalmer@mbc.edu
Web Site: http://www.mbc.edu/
President/CEO: Dr. Pamela Fox
Admissions: Roberta Palmer
Financial Aid: Robin Dietrich
Type: Comprehensive **Sex:** Coed **Scores:** 96% SAT V 400+; 88% SAT M 400+; 55% ACT 18-23; 19% ACT 24-29 **% Accepted:** 62 **Admission Plans:** Early Admission; Early Decision Plan; Deferred Admission **Application Deadline:** Rolling **Application Fee:** $35.00 **H.S. Requirements:** High school diploma required; GED accepted **Costs Per Year:** Application fee: $35. One-time mandatory fee: $215. Comprehensive fee: $31,655 includes full-time tuition ($24,370), mandatory fees ($215), and college room and board ($7070). College room only: $4505. Full-time tuition and fees vary according to degree level. Room and board charges vary according to housing facility. Part-time tuition: $420 per semester hour. Part-time tuition varies according to degree level. **Scholarships:** Available **Calendar System:** 4-1-4, Summer Session Not available **Enrollment:** FT 1,062, PT 463, Grad FT 109, Grad PT 149 **Faculty:** FT 76, PT 60 **Student-Faculty Ratio:** 10:1 **Exams:** SAT I or ACT. **% Receiving Financial Aid:** 81 **% Residing in College-Owned, -Operated, or -Affiliated Housing:** 83 **Library Holdings:** 148,446 **Regional Accreditation:** Southern Association of Colleges and Schools **Credit Hours For Degree:** 132 semester hours, Bachelors **ROTC:** Army, Navy, Air Force **Professional Accreditation:** TEAC **Intercollegiate Athletics:** Basketball W; Cross-Country Running W; Field Hockey W; Soccer W; Softball W; Swimming and Diving W; Tennis W; Volleyball W

MARYMOUNT UNIVERSITY
2807 North Glebe Rd.
Arlington, VA 22207-4299
Tel: (703)522-5600; Free: 800-548-7638
Admissions: (703)284-1500
Fax: (703)522-0349
E-mail: admissions@marymount.edu
Web Site: http://www.marymount.edu/
President/CEO: Dr. James E. Bundschuh
Admissions: Mike Canfield
Financial Aid: Debbie A. Raines
Type: Comprehensive **Sex:** Coed **Affiliation:** Roman Catholic Church **Scores:** 92% SAT V 400+; 89% SAT M 400+; 63% ACT 18-23; 15% ACT 24-29 **% Accepted:** 83 **Admission Plans:** Deferred Admission **Application Deadline:** Rolling **Application Fee:** $40.00 **H.S. Requirements:** High school diploma required; GED accepted **Costs Per Year:** Application fee: $40. Comprehensive fee: $32,365 includes full-time tuition ($22,370), mandatory fees ($250), and college room and board ($9745). Part-time tuition: $725 per credit hour. Part-time mandatory fees: $7.50 per credit hour. **Scholarships:** Available **Calendar System:** Semester, Summer Session Available **Enrollment:** FT 1,899, PT 325, Grad FT 500, Grad PT 756 **Faculty:** FT 141, PT 178 **Student-Faculty Ratio:** 14:1 **Exams:** SAT I or ACT. **% Receiving Financial Aid:** 60 **% Residing in College-Owned, -Operated, or -Affiliated Housing:** 32 **Final Year or Final Semester Residency Requirement:** No **Library Holdings:** 236,315 **Regional Accreditation:** Southern Association of Colleges and Schools **Credit Hours For Degree:** 64 semester hours, Associates; 120 semester hours, Bachelors **ROTC:** Army **Professional Accreditation:** AACN, ACA, APTA, ACBSP, ACEHSA, FIDER, NCATE, NLN **Intercollegiate Athletics:** Basketball M & W; Cross-Country Running M & W; Golf M; Lacrosse M & W; Soccer M & W; Swimming and Diving M & W; Volleyball W

MEDICAL CAREERS INSTITUTE (NEWPORT NEWS)
1001 Omni Blvd.
Ste. 200
Newport News, VA 23606
Tel: (757)873-2423
Admissions: (804)521-0400
Fax: (757)873-2472
Web Site: http://www.medical.edu/
President/CEO: Mark Dreyfus
Type: Two-Year College **Sex:** Coed **% Accepted:** 64 **Application Fee:** $75.00 **Calendar System:** Semester **Professional Accreditation:** COE

MEDICAL CAREERS INSTITUTE (RICHMOND)
800 Moorefield Park Dr., Ste. 302
Richmond, VA 23236-3659
Tel: (804)521-0400
Fax: (804)521-0406
Web Site: http://www.careers.edu/
Type: Two-Year College **Sex:** Coed **Calendar System:** Semester **Professional Accreditation:** COE

MEDICAL CAREERS INSTITUTE (VIRGINIA BEACH)
5501 Greenwich Rd.
No. 100
Virginia Beach, VA 23462
Tel: (757)497-8400
Web Site: http://www.medical.edu/
Type: Two-Year College **Sex:** Coed **Calendar System:** Semester **Professional Accreditation:** COE

MOUNTAIN EMPIRE COMMUNITY COLLEGE
3441 Mountain Empire Rd.
Big Stone Gap, VA 24219
Tel: (276)523-2400
E-mail: khall@me.vccs.edu
Web Site: http://www.mecc.edu/
President/CEO: Dr. Terrance Suarez
Admissions: Kristy Hall
Type: Two-Year College **Sex:** Coed **Affiliation:** Virginia Community College System **Admission Plans:** Open Admission; Early Admission; Deferred Admission **Application Deadline:** Rolling **Application Fee:** $0.00 **H.S. Requirements:** High school diploma required; GED accepted **Costs Per Year:** Application fee: $0. State resident tuition: $2297 full-time, $95.70 per credit hour part-time. Nonresident tuition: $6667 full-time, $227.80 per credit hour part-time. **Scholarships:** Available **Calendar System:** Semester, Summer Session Available **Enrollment:** FT 1,471, PT 1,912 **Faculty:** FT 41, PT 148 **Library Holdings:** 43,674 **Regional Accreditation:** Southern Association of Colleges and Schools **Professional Accreditation:** CARC, NLN

NATIONAL COLLEGE (BLUEFIELD)
100 Logan St.
PO Box 629
Bluefield, VA 24605-1405
Tel: (276)326-3621; Free: 800-664-1886
Fax: (276)322-5731
Web Site: http://www.national-college.edu/
Admissions: Denver Riffe
Type: Two-Year College **Sex:** Coed **Affiliation:** National College of Business and Technology **Admission Plans:** Open Admission **Application Deadline:** Rolling **H.S. Requirements:** High school diploma required; GED accepted **Scholarships:** Available **Calendar System:** Quarter, Summer Session Available **Credit Hours For Degree:** 96 quarter hours, Associates **Professional Accreditation:** ACICS, AAMAE

NATIONAL COLLEGE (CHARLOTTESVILLE)
1819 Emmet St.
Charlottesville, VA 22901
Tel: (434)295-0136; Free: 800-664-1886
Fax: (434)986-1344
Web Site: http://www.national-college.edu/
Admissions: Kimberly Moore
Type: Two-Year College **Sex:** Coed **Affiliation:** National College of Business and Technology **Admission Plans:** Open Admission **Application Deadline:** Rolling **H.S. Requirements:** High school diploma required; GED accepted **Scholarships:** Available **Calendar System:** Quarter, Summer Session Available **Credit Hours For Degree:** 96 quarter hours, Associates **Professional Accreditation:** ACICS, AAMAE

NATIONAL COLLEGE (DANVILLE)
734 Main St.
Danville, VA 24541-1819
Tel: (434)793-6822; Free: 800-664-1886
Fax: (434)793-3634

Web Site: http://www.national-college.edu/
Type: Two-Year College **Sex:** Coed **Affiliation:** National College of Business and Technology **Admission Plans:** Open Admission **Application Deadline:** Rolling **H.S. Requirements:** High school diploma required; GED accepted **Scholarships:** Available **Calendar System:** Quarter, Summer Session Available **Credit Hours For Degree:** 96 quarter hours, Associates **Professional Accreditation:** ACICS, AAMAE

NATIONAL COLLEGE (HARRISONBURG)
51 B Burgess Rd.
Harrisonburg, VA 22801-9709
Tel: (540)432-0943; Free: 800-664-1886
Fax: (540)986-1344
Web Site: http://www.national-college.edu/
Admissions: Jack Evey
Type: Two-Year College **Sex:** Coed **Affiliation:** National College of Business and Technology **Admission Plans:** Open Admission **Application Deadline:** Rolling **H.S. Requirements:** High school diploma required; GED accepted **Scholarships:** Available **Calendar System:** Quarter, Summer Session Available **Credit Hours For Degree:** 96 credit hours, Associates **Professional Accreditation:** ACICS, AAMAE

NATIONAL COLLEGE (LYNCHBURG)
104 Candlewood Ct.
Lynchburg, VA 24502-2653
Tel: (434)239-3500; Free: 800-664-1886
Admissions: (804)239-3500
Fax: (434)986-1344
Web Site: http://www.national-college.edu/
Type: Two-Year College **Sex:** Coed **Affiliation:** National College of Business and Technology **Admission Plans:** Open Admission **Application Deadline:** Rolling **H.S. Requirements:** High school diploma required; GED accepted **Scholarships:** Available **Calendar System:** Quarter, Summer Session Available **Credit Hours For Degree:** 96 quarter hours, Associates **Professional Accreditation:** ACICS, AAMAE

NATIONAL COLLEGE (MARTINSVILLE)
10 Church St., PO Box 232
Martinsville, VA 24114
Tel: (276)632-5621; Free: 800-664-1866
Fax: (276)986-1344
Web Site: http://www.national-college.edu/
Admissions: John Scott
Type: Two-Year College **Sex:** Coed **Affiliation:** National College of Business and Technology **Admission Plans:** Open Admission **Application Deadline:** Rolling **H.S. Requirements:** High school diploma required; GED accepted **Scholarships:** Available **Calendar System:** Quarter, Summer Session Available **Credit Hours For Degree:** 96 quarter hours, Associates **Professional Accreditation:** ACICS

NATIONAL COLLEGE (SALEM)
1813 East Main St.
Salem, VA 24153
Tel: (540)986-1800; Free: 800-664-1886
Fax: (540)986-1344
Web Site: http://www.national-college.edu/
President/CEO: Frank Longaker
Type: Two-Year College **Sex:** Coed **Affiliation:** National College of Business and Technology **Admission Plans:** Open Admission **Application Deadline:** Rolling **H.S. Requirements:** High school diploma required; GED accepted **Scholarships:** Available **Calendar System:** Quarter, Summer Session Available **Credit Hours For Degree:** 96 quarter hours, Associates; 180 quarter hours, Bachelors **Professional Accreditation:** ACICS, AAMAE

NEW RIVER COMMUNITY COLLEGE
PO Box 1127
Dublin, VA 24084-1127
Tel: (540)674-3600
Fax: (540)674-3644
E-mail: nrtaylm@nr.edu
Web Site: http://www.nr.edu/
President/CEO: Jack M. Lewis
Admissions: Margaret G. Taylor
Type: Two-Year College **Sex:** Coed **Affiliation:** Virginia Community College System **Admission Plans:** Open Admission; Preferred Admission; Early Admission; Deferred Admission **Application Deadline:** Rolling **Application Fee:** $0.00 **H.S. Requirements:** High school diploma or equivalent not required. For applicants under 18: High school diploma required; GED accepted **Scholarships:** Available **Calendar System:** Semester, Summer Session Available **Enrollment:** FT 2,008, PT 2,337 **Faculty:** FT 51, PT 155 **Student-Faculty Ratio:** 22:1 **Library Holdings:** 33,993 **Regional Accreditation:** Southern Association of Colleges and Schools **Credit Hours For Degree:** 62 semester hours, Associates

NORFOLK STATE UNIVERSITY
700 Park Ave.
Norfolk, VA 23504
Tel: (757)823-8600
Admissions: (757)823-9222
Fax: (757)823-9435
E-mail: admissions@nsu.edu
Web Site: http://www.nsu.edu/
President/CEO: Dr. Carolyn W. Meyers
Admissions: Kevin M. Holmes
Financial Aid: Kevin Burns
Type: Comprehensive **Sex:** Coed **Affiliation:** State Council of Higher Education for Virginia **Scores:** 78.1% SAT V 400+; 78.3% SAT M 400+; 39.4% ACT 18-23; 6.3% ACT 24-29 **% Accepted:** 68 **Admission Plans:** Deferred Admission **Application Fee:** $35.00 **H.S. Requirements:** High school diploma required; GED accepted **Costs Per Year:** Application fee: $35. State resident tuition: $2652 full-time, $260.69 per credit hour part-time. Nonresident tuition: $14,411 full-time, $622.26 per credit hour part-time. Mandatory fees: $2486 full-time. Full-time tuition and fees vary according to course load. Part-time tuition varies according to course load. **Scholarships:** Available **Calendar System:** Semester **Enrollment:** FT 5,194, PT 956, Grad FT 485, Grad PT 358 **Student-Faculty Ratio:** 18:1 **Exams:** SAT I or ACT. ACT essay not being used. SAT essay not being used. **% Receiving Financial Aid:** 85 **% Residing in College-Owned, -Operated, or -Affiliated Housing:** 41 **Final Year or Final Semester Residency Requirement:** No **Library Holdings:** 348,953 **Regional Accreditation:** Southern Association of Colleges and Schools **Credit Hours For Degree:** 60 semester hours, Associates; 120 semester hours, Bachelors **ROTC:** Army, Navy **Professional Accreditation:** AACSB, ABET, ACEJMC, ABFSE, APA, CAEPK, CSWE, NAACLS, NASM, NCATE, NLN, NAIT **Intercollegiate Athletics:** Baseball M; Basketball M & W; Bowling W; Football M; Softball W; Tennis M & W; Track and Field M & W; Volleyball W

NORTHERN VIRGINIA COMMUNITY COLLEGE
4001 Wakefield Chapel Rd.
Annandale, VA 22003-3796
Tel: (703)323-3000
Web Site: http://www.nvcc.edu/
President/CEO: Robert G. Templin, Jr.
Admissions: Dr. Max L. Bassett
Type: Two-Year College **Sex:** Coed **Affiliation:** Virginia Community College System **Admission Plans:** Open Admission; Early Admission; Deferred Admission **Application Deadline:** Rolling **Application Fee:** $0.00 **H.S. Requirements:** High school diploma required; GED accepted. For veterinary technology, dental hygiene, other health-related programs: High school diploma required; GED not accepted **Scholarships:** Available **Calendar System:** Semester, Summer Session Available **Library Holdings:** 228,009 **Regional Accreditation:** Southern Association of Colleges and Schools **Credit Hours For Degree:** 60 credit hours, Associates **Professional Accreditation:** ADA, AHIMA, APTA, CARC, JRCEMT, NAACLS, NLN

OLD DOMINION UNIVERSITY
5115 Hampton Blvd.
Norfolk, VA 23529
Tel: (757)683-3000; Free: 800-348-7926
Admissions: (757)683-3648
Fax: (757)683-5357
E-mail: admit@odu.edu
Web Site: http://www.odu.edu/
President/CEO: John R. Broderick
Admissions: Barbara Boyce
Financial Aid: Veronica Finch
Type: University **Sex:** Coed **Scores:** 99% SAT V 400+; 100% SAT M 400+; 66% ACT 18-23; 18% ACT 24-29 **% Accepted:** 72 **Admission Plans:** Early

Admission; Early Action; Deferred Admission **Application Deadline:** February 1 **Application Fee:** $50.00 **H.S. Requirements:** High school diploma required; GED accepted **Costs Per Year:** Application fee: $50. State resident tuition: $7080 full-time, $236 per credit hour part-time. Nonresident tuition: $19,530 full-time, $651 per credit hour part-time. Mandatory fees: $238 full-time, $59 per term part-time. Full-time tuition and fees vary according to course level, course load, location, and student level. Part-time tuition and fees vary according to course level, course load, location, and student level. College room and board: $7868. College room only: $4552. Room and board charges vary according to board plan and housing facility. **Scholarships:** Available **Calendar System:** Semester, Summer Session Available **Enrollment:** FT 13,776, PT 4,477, Grad FT 1,867, Grad PT 3,893 **Faculty:** FT 696, PT 461 **Student-Faculty Ratio:** 18:1 **Exams:** SAT I or ACT. **% Receiving Financial Aid:** 54 **% Residing in College-Owned, -Operated, or -Affiliated Housing:** 25 **Final Year or Final Semester Residency Requirement:** No **Library Holdings:** 1,183,464 **Regional Accreditation:** Southern Association of Colleges and Schools **Credit Hours For Degree:** 120 semester hours, Bachelors **ROTC:** Army, Navy **Professional Accreditation:** AACSB, ABET, AACN, AANA, ACA, ADA, APTA, APA, ASC, ASLHA, CEPH, JCAHPO, JRCNMT, NAACLS, NASAD, NASM, NASPAA, NAST, NCATE, NRPA **Intercollegiate Athletics:** Baseball M; Basketball M & W; Crew M & W; Cross-Country Running M & W; Fencing M & W; Field Hockey W; Football M; Golf M & W; Ice Hockey M & W; Lacrosse M & W; Rock Climbing M & W; Rugby M; Sailing M & W; Soccer M & W; Softball W; Swimming and Diving M & W; Tennis M & W; Wrestling M

PATRICK HENRY COLLEGE
Ten Patrick Henry Circle
Purcellville, VA 20132
Tel: (540)338-1776
Fax: (540)338-8707
E-mail: admissions@phc.edu
Web Site: http://www.phc.edu/
President/CEO: Dr. Graham Walker
Financial Aid: William K. Kellaris, Jr.
Type: Four-Year College **Sex:** Coed **Affiliation:** nondenominational **Scores:** 100% SAT V 400+; 100% SAT M 400+; 7% ACT 18-23; 36% ACT 24-29 **Admission Plans:** Early Action; Deferred Admission **Application Deadline:** June 15 **Application Fee:** $40.00 **H.S. Requirements:** High school diploma required; GED accepted **Costs Per Year:** Application fee: $40. Comprehensive fee: $30,300 includes full-time tuition ($21,270), mandatory fees ($500), and college room and board ($8530). Full-time tuition and fees vary according to course load. Room and board charges vary according to board plan. Part-time tuition: $645 per credit hour. Part-time tuition varies according to course load. **Scholarships:** Available **Calendar System:** Semester **Enrollment:** FT 305, PT 99 **Faculty:** FT 21, PT 22 **Student-Faculty Ratio:** 11:1 **Exams:** SAT I or ACT. **% Residing in College-Owned, -Operated, or -Affiliated Housing:** 81 **Library Holdings:** 219,699 **Regional Accreditation:** Southern Association of Colleges and Schools **Professional Accreditation:** AALE, TACCS **Intercollegiate Athletics:** Basketball M & W; Soccer M & W

PATRICK HENRY COMMUNITY COLLEGE
PO Box 5311
Martinsville, VA 24115-5311
Tel: (276)638-8777
Admissions: (276)656-0311
Fax: (276)656-0247
Web Site: http://www.ph.vccs.edu/
President/CEO: Dr. Max Wingett
Admissions: Travis Tisdale
Type: Two-Year College **Sex:** Coed **Affiliation:** Virginia Community College System **Admission Plans:** Open Admission; Preferred Admission; Early Admission; Deferred Admission **Application Deadline:** Rolling **Application Fee:** $0.00 **H.S. Requirements:** High school diploma required; GED accepted **Scholarships:** Available **Calendar System:** Semester, Summer Session Available **Enrollment:** FT 3,501 **Faculty:** FT 49, PT 100 **Final Year or Final Semester Residency Requirement:** No **Library Holdings:** 26,160 **Regional Accreditation:** Southern Association of Colleges and Schools **Credit Hours For Degree:** 62 semester hours, Associates **Professional Accreditation:** NLN

PAUL D. CAMP COMMUNITY COLLEGE
PO Box 737, 100 North College Dr.
Franklin, VA 23851-0737
Tel: (757)569-6700
Admissions: (757)569-6744
E-mail: jedenfield@pc.vccs.edu
Web Site: http://www.pc.vccs.edu/
President/CEO: Dr. Douglas W. Boyce
Admissions: Joe Edenfield
Type: Two-Year College **Sex:** Coed **Affiliation:** Virginia Community College System **Scores:** 54% SAT V 400+; 54% SAT M 400+ **% Accepted:** 100 **Admission Plans:** Open Admission; Preferred Admission; Deferred Admission **Application Deadline:** Rolling **Application Fee:** $0.00 **H.S. Requirements:** High school diploma required; GED accepted **Scholarships:** Available **Calendar System:** Semester, Summer Session Available **Faculty:** FT 23, PT 90 **Student-Faculty Ratio:** 17:1 **Library Holdings:** 22,000 **Regional Accreditation:** Southern Association of Colleges and Schools **Credit Hours For Degree:** 61 semester hours, Associates **Professional Accreditation:** NLN

PIEDMONT VIRGINIA COMMUNITY COLLEGE
501 College Dr.
Charlottesville, VA 22902-7589
Tel: (434)977-3900
Admissions: (434)961-6540
Fax: (434)971-8232
E-mail: mwalsh@pvcc.edu
Web Site: http://www.pvcc.edu/
President/CEO: Dr. Frank Friedman
Admissions: Mary Lee Walsh
Type: Two-Year College **Sex:** Coed **Affiliation:** Virginia Community College System **Admission Plans:** Open Admission; Early Admission **Application Deadline:** Rolling **Application Fee:** $0.00 **H.S. Requirements:** High school diploma or equivalent not required **Costs Per Year:** Application fee: $0. State resident tuition: $2616 full-time, $87.20 per credit hour part-time. Nonresident tuition: $7779 full-time, $259.30 per credit hour part-time. Mandatory fees: $245 full-time, $8.15 per credit hour part-time. Full-time tuition and fees vary according to course load. Part-time tuition and fees vary according to course load. **Scholarships:** Available **Calendar System:** Semester, Summer Session Available **Enrollment:** FT 1,063, PT 3,611 **Faculty:** FT 67, PT 193 **Student-Faculty Ratio:** 17:1 **Library Holdings:** 39,117 **Regional Accreditation:** Southern Association of Colleges and Schools **Credit Hours For Degree:** 67 semester hours, Associates **ROTC:** Army **Professional Accreditation:** NLN

POTOMAC COLLEGE
1029 Herndon Parkway
Herndon, VA 20170
Tel: (703)709-5875
Admissions: (703)709-5875
E-mail: admissions@potomac.edu
Web Site: http://www.potomac.edu/
President/CEO: Jim Otten
Financial Aid: Melva Carty
Type: Four-Year College **Sex:** Coed **Application Fee:** $15.00 **Costs Per Year:** Application fee: $15. Tuition: $16,020 full-time, $495 per credit part-time. **Scholarships:** Available **Student-Faculty Ratio:** 27:1 **Regional Accreditation:** Middle State Association of Colleges and Schools

RADFORD UNIVERSITY
801 East Main St.
Radford, VA 24142
Tel: (540)831-5000; Free: 800-890-4265
Admissions: (540)831-5460
Fax: (540)831-5138
E-mail: ruadmiss@radford.edu
Web Site: http://www.radford.edu/
President/CEO: Penelope W. Kyle
Admissions: Dr. Steven Nape
Financial Aid: Barbara Porter
Type: Comprehensive **Sex:** Coed **Scores:** 99% SAT V 400+; 98% SAT M 400+; 79% ACT 18-23; 18% ACT 24-29 **% Accepted:** 71 **Admission Plans:** Early Admission; Early Action; Deferred Admission **Application Deadline:** February 1 **Application Fee:** $50.00 **H.S. Requirements:** High school diploma required; GED accepted **Costs Per Year:** Application fee: $50. State resident tuition: $4396 full-time, $183 per credit hour part-time. Nonresident tuition: $14,060 full-time, $586 per credit hour part-time. Manda-

tory fees: $2508 full-time, $105 per credit hour part-time. College room and board: $6970. College room only: $3698. Room and board charges vary according to board plan and housing facility. **Scholarships:** Available **Calendar System:** Semester, Summer Session Available **Enrollment:** FT 7,440, PT 333, Grad FT 487, Grad PT 618 **Faculty:** FT 387, PT 140 **Student-Faculty Ratio:** 19:1 **Exams:** SAT I or ACT. ACT essay used for advising. SAT essay used for advising. **% Receiving Financial Aid:** 44 **% Residing in College-Owned, -Operated, or -Affiliated Housing:** 37 **Final Year or Final Semester Residency Requirement:** Yes **Library Holdings:** 383,664 **Regional Accreditation:** Southern Association of Colleges and Schools **Credit Hours For Degree:** 120 semester hours, Bachelors **ROTC:** Army **Professional Accreditation:** AACSB, ABET, AACN, ACA, ADtA, ASLHA, CSWE, NASM, NAST, NCATE, NLN, NRPA **Intercollegiate Athletics:** Baseball M; Basketball M & W; Cross-Country Running M & W; Field Hockey W; Golf M & W; Soccer M & W; Softball W; Swimming and Diving W; Tennis M & W; Track and Field M & W; Volleyball W

RANDOLPH COLLEGE
2500 Rivermont Ave.
Lynchburg, VA 24503
Tel: (434)947-8000; Free: 800-745-7692
Admissions: (434)947-8100
Fax: (434)947-8996
E-mail: admissions@randolphcollege.edu
Web Site: http://www.randolphcollege.edu/
President/CEO: John E. Klein
Admissions: Margaret Blount
Financial Aid: Kay G. Mattox
Type: Comprehensive **Sex:** Coed **Affiliation:** Methodist **Scores:** 98% SAT V 400+; 96% SAT M 400+; 41% ACT 18-23; 26% ACT 24-29 **% Accepted:** 81 **Admission Plans:** Early Admission; Early Action; Deferred Admission **Application Deadline:** April 1 **Application Fee:** $50.00 **H.S. Requirements:** High school diploma required; GED accepted **Costs Per Year:** Application fee: $50. Comprehensive fee: $39,249 includes full-time tuition ($28,744), mandatory fees ($510), and college room and board ($9995). **Scholarships:** Available **Calendar System:** Semester, Summer Session Not available **Enrollment:** FT 548, PT 14, Grad FT 12 **Faculty:** FT 65, PT 21 **Student-Faculty Ratio:** 8:1 **Exams:** SAT I or ACT. ACT essay not being used. SAT essay not being used. **% Receiving Financial Aid:** 70 **% Residing in College-Owned, -Operated, or -Affiliated Housing:** 90 **Library Holdings:** 197,332 **Regional Accreditation:** Southern Association of Colleges and Schools **Credit Hours For Degree:** 124 semester hours, Bachelors **Intercollegiate Athletics:** Basketball M & W; Cross-Country Running M & W; Equestrian Sports M & W; Lacrosse M & W; Soccer M & W; Softball W; Tennis M & W; Volleyball W

RANDOLPH-MACON COLLEGE
PO Box 5005
Ashland, VA 23005-5505
Tel: (804)752-7200; Free: 800-888-1762
Admissions: (804)752-7305
Fax: (804)752-4707
E-mail: admissions@rmc.edu
Web Site: http://www.rmc.edu/
President/CEO: Robert Lindgren
Admissions: Anthony Ambrogi
Financial Aid: Mary Neal
Type: Four-Year College **Sex:** Coed **Affiliation:** United Methodist **Scores:** 101% SAT V 400+ **% Accepted:** 58 **Admission Plans:** Early Admission; Early Action; Deferred Admission **Application Deadline:** March 1 **Application Fee:** $30.00 **H.S. Requirements:** High school diploma required; GED accepted **Costs Per Year:** Application fee: $30. Comprehensive fee: $38,073 includes full-time tuition ($28,397), mandatory fees ($785), and college room and board ($8891). Full-time tuition and fees vary according to reciprocity agreements. Room and board charges vary according to housing facility. Part-time tuition: $3155 per course. Part-time mandatory fees: $785 per year. **Scholarships:** Available **Calendar System:** 4-1-4, Summer Session Available **Enrollment:** FT 1,218, PT 28 **Faculty:** FT 91, PT 52 **Student-Faculty Ratio:** 11:1 **Exams:** SAT I or ACT, SAT II. **% Receiving Financial Aid:** 65 **% Residing in College-Owned, -Operated, or -Affiliated Housing:** 82 **Library Holdings:** 220,161 **Regional Accreditation:** Southern Association of Colleges and Schools **Credit Hours For Degree:** 110 semester hours, Bachelors **ROTC:** Army **Intercollegiate Athletics:** Baseball M; Basketball M & W; Field Hockey W; Football M; Golf M; Lacrosse M & W; Soccer M & W; Softball W; Swimming and Diving W; Tennis M & W; Volleyball W

RAPPAHANNOCK COMMUNITY COLLEGE
12745 College Dr.
Glenns, VA 23149-2616
Tel: (804)758-6700
Fax: (804)758-3852
Web Site: http://www.rappahannock.edu/
President/CEO: Elizabeth H. Crowther
Admissions: Wilnet Willis
Type: Two-Year College **Sex:** Coed **Affiliation:** Virginia Community College System **Admission Plans:** Open Admission; Early Admission **Application Deadline:** Rolling **Application Fee:** $0.00 **H.S. Requirements:** High school diploma or equivalent not required **Scholarships:** Available **Calendar System:** Semester, Summer Session Available **Enrollment:** FT 837, PT 2,569 **Library Holdings:** 46,000 **Regional Accreditation:** Southern Association of Colleges and Schools **Credit Hours For Degree:** 60 semester hours, Associates

REGENT UNIVERSITY
1000 Regent University Dr.
Virginia Beach, VA 23464-9800
Tel: (757)226-4127; Free: 800-373-5504
Admissions: (757)352-4845
E-mail: kbaker@regent.edu
Web Site: http://www.regent.edu/
President/CEO: Dr. M.G. Robertson
Admissions: Ken Baker
Type: Comprehensive **Sex:** Coed **Scores:** 97% SAT V 400+; 88% SAT M 400+; 62% ACT 18-23; 10% ACT 24-29 **% Accepted:** 64 **Application Deadline:** August 1 **Application Fee:** $50.00 **H.S. Requirements:** High school diploma required; GED accepted **Costs Per Year:** Application fee: $50. Tuition: $13,950 full-time, $465 per credit hour part-time. Mandatory fees: $250 full-time. Full-time tuition and fees vary according to course level, course load, program, and student level. Part-time tuition varies according to course level, course load, program, and student level. College room only: $5175. Room charges vary according to housing facility. **Scholarships:** Available **Calendar System:** Trimester, Summer Session Available **Enrollment:** FT 1,050, PT 868, Grad FT 1,084, Grad PT 1,884 **Faculty:** FT 178, PT 378 **Student-Faculty Ratio:** 16:1 **Exams:** SAT I or ACT. **% Residing in College-Owned, -Operated, or -Affiliated Housing:** 20 **Final Year or Final Semester Residency Requirement:** No **Library Holdings:** 410,014 **Regional Accreditation:** Southern Association of Colleges and Schools **Credit Hours For Degree:** 64 credits, Associates; 120 credits, Bachelors **ROTC:** Army **Professional Accreditation:** ABA, ACA, APA, ACIPE, ATS

RICHARD BLAND COLLEGE OF THE COLLEGE OF WILLIAM AND MARY
11301 Johnson Rd.
Petersburg, VA 23805-7100
Tel: (804)862-6100
Admissions: (804)862-6249
Fax: (804)862-6189
Web Site: http://www.rbc.edu/
President/CEO: Dr. James B. McNeer
Type: Two-Year College **Sex:** Coed **Affiliation:** College of William and Mary **Scores:** 71% SAT V 400+ **% Accepted:** 89 **Application Deadline:** August 15 **Application Fee:** $20.00 **H.S. Requirements:** High school diploma required; GED accepted **Costs Per Year:** Application fee: $20. State resident tuition: $3102 full-time, $102 per credit hour part-time. Nonresident tuition: $11,830 full-time, $465 per credit hour part-time. Mandatory fees: $1010 full-time, $12 per credit hour part-time. Full-time tuition and fees vary according to program. Part-time tuition and fees vary according to program. College room only: $8240. Contact school for availability and cost of single, double, or quad occupancy rooms. **Scholarships:** Available **Calendar System:** Semester, Summer Session Available **Enrollment:** FT 1,038, PT 596 **Faculty:** FT 33, PT 38 **Student-Faculty Ratio:** 25:1 **Exams:** SAT I or ACT. **Library Holdings:** 126,242 **Regional Accreditation:** Southern Association of Colleges and Schools **Credit Hours For Degree:** 63 semester hours, Associates **ROTC:** Army

ROANOKE COLLEGE
221 College Ln.
Salem, VA 24153-3794
Tel: (540)375-2500; Free: 800-388-2276
Admissions: (540)375-2270
Fax: (540)375-2267
E-mail: admissions@roanoke.edu
Web Site: http://www.roanoke.edu/
President/CEO: Michael C. Maxey
Admissions: Brenda Poggendorf
Financial Aid: Thomas S. Blair, Jr.
Type: Four-Year College **Sex:** Coed **Affiliation:** Evangelical Lutheran Church in America **Scores:** 100% SAT V 400+; 99% SAT M 400+ **% Accepted:** 68 **Admission Plans:** Early Admission; Early Decision Plan; Deferred Admission **Application Deadline:** March 15 **Application Fee:** $33.00 **H.S. Requirements:** High school diploma required; GED accepted **Costs Per Year:** Application fee: $33. Comprehensive fee: $41,522 includes full-time tuition ($30,314), mandatory fees ($900), and college room and board ($10,308). College room only: $4788. Room and board charges vary according to board plan and housing facility. Part-time tuition: $1450 per course. Part-time tuition varies according to course load. **Scholarships:** Available **Calendar System:** Semester, Summer Session Available **Enrollment:** FT 1,934, PT 110 **Faculty:** FT 166, PT 42 **Student-Faculty Ratio:** 13:1 **Exams:** SAT I or ACT. **% Receiving Financial Aid:** 67 **% Residing in College-Owned, -Operated, or -Affiliated Housing:** 63 **Final Year or Final Semester Residency Requirement:** Yes **Library Holdings:** 205,296 **Regional Accreditation:** Southern Association of Colleges and Schools **Credit Hours For Degree:** 33.5 courses, Bachelors **Professional Accreditation:** ACBSP, JRCEPAT **Intercollegiate Athletics:** Baseball M; Basketball M & W; Cross-Country Running M & W; Field Hockey W; Golf M & W; Ice Hockey M; Lacrosse M & W; Soccer M & W; Softball W; Tennis M & W; Track and Field M & W; Volleyball M & W

SAINT PAUL'S COLLEGE
115 College Dr.
Lawrenceville, VA 23868-1202
Tel: (434)848-3111; Free: 800-678-7071
Admissions: (434)848-6493
Fax: (434)848-0403
E-mail: rlewis@saintpauls.edu
Web Site: http://www.saintpauls.edu/
President/CEO: Dr. Robert L. Satcher, Sr.
Admissions: Rosemary Lewis
Financial Aid: Joan Mayo
Type: Four-Year College **Sex:** Coed **Affiliation:** Episcopal **Scores:** 34% SAT M 400+; 1% ACT 18-23; 2.7% ACT 24-29 **% Accepted:** 99 **Admission Plans:** Deferred Admission **Application Deadline:** Rolling **Application Fee:** $20.00 **H.S. Requirements:** High school diploma required; GED accepted **Costs Per Year:** Application fee: $20. Comprehensive fee: $19,850 includes full-time tuition ($11,880), mandatory fees ($1330), and college room and board ($6640). College room only: $3140. Part-time tuition: $495 per credit hour. Part-time mandatory fees: $29 per credit hour. **Scholarships:** Available **Calendar System:** Semester, Summer Session Available **Enrollment:** FT 566, PT 18 **Faculty:** FT 28, PT 18 **Student-Faculty Ratio:** 17:1 **Exams:** SAT I or ACT. ACT essay not being used. **% Receiving Financial Aid:** 96 **% Residing in College-Owned, -Operated, or -Affiliated Housing:** 78 **Regional Accreditation:** Southern Association of Colleges and Schools **Credit Hours For Degree:** 120 credits, Bachelors **ROTC:** Army **Intercollegiate Athletics:** Baseball M; Basketball M & W; Cross-Country Running M & W; Football M; Golf M & W; Softball W; Tennis M & W; Track and Field M & W; Volleyball M & W

SHENANDOAH UNIVERSITY
1460 University Dr.
Winchester, VA 22601-5195
Tel: (540)665-4500; Free: 800-432-2266
Admissions: (540)665-4581
Fax: (540)665-4627
E-mail: admit@su.edu
Web Site: http://www.su.edu/
President/CEO: Tracy Fitzsimmons
Admissions: David Anthony
Financial Aid: Nancy Bragg
Type: Comprehensive **Sex:** Coed **Affiliation:** United Methodist **Scores:** 90.43% SAT V 400+; 91.62% SAT M 400+; 59% ACT 18-23; 20% ACT 24-29 **% Accepted:** 84 **Admission Plans:** Deferred Admission **Application Deadline:** Rolling **Application Fee:** $30.00 **H.S. Requirements:** High school diploma required; GED accepted **Costs Per Year:** Application fee: $30. Comprehensive fee: $33,950 includes full-time tuition ($24,780), mandatory fees ($300), and college room and board ($8870). Full-time tuition and fees vary according to course load and program. Room and board charges vary according to board plan and housing facility. Part-time tuition: $723 per credit hour. Part-time tuition varies according to course load and program. **Scholarships:** Available **Calendar System:** Semester, Summer Session Available **Enrollment:** FT 1,673, PT 94 **Faculty:** FT 216, PT 175 **Student-Faculty Ratio:** 9:1 **Exams:** SAT I or ACT. **% Receiving Financial Aid:** 68 **% Residing in College-Owned, -Operated, or -Affiliated Housing:** 49 **Library Holdings:** 202,815 **Regional Accreditation:** Southern Association of Colleges and Schools **Credit Hours For Degree:** 60 semester hours, Associates; 120 semester hours, Bachelors **Professional Accreditation:** AACSB, ACPhE, AACN, ACNM, AOTA, APTA, CARC, NASM, NLN, TEAC **Intercollegiate Athletics:** Baseball M; Basketball M & W; Cross-Country Running M & W; Field Hockey W; Football M; Golf M; Lacrosse M & W; Soccer M & W; Softball W; Tennis M & W; Volleyball W

SOUTH UNIVERSITY (GLEN ALLEN)
2151 Old Brick Rd.
Glen Allen, VA 23060
Tel: (804)727-6800; Free: 888-422-5076
Fax: (804)727-6790
Web Site: http://www.southuniversity.edu/richmond
Type: Comprehensive **Sex:** Coed

SOUTH UNIVERSITY (VIRGINIA BEACH)
301 Bendix Rd., Ste. 100
Virginia Beach, VA 23452
Tel: (757)493-6900; Free: 877-206-1845
Fax: (757)493-6990
Web Site: http://www.southuniversity.edu/virginia-beach
Type: Comprehensive **Sex:** Coed

SOUTHERN VIRGINIA UNIVERSITY
One College Hill Dr.
Buena Vista, VA 24416
Tel: (540)261-8400; Free: 800-229-8420
Fax: (540)261-8559
E-mail: admissions@southernvirginia.edu
Web Site: http://www.svu.edu/
President/CEO: Rodney K. Smith
Admissions: Tony Caputo
Financial Aid: Darin Hassell
Type: Four-Year College **Sex:** Coed **Affiliation:** Latter-day Saints **Scores:** 95.6% SAT V 400+; 95.2% SAT M 400+; 46.9% ACT 18-23; 39.4% ACT 24-29 **% Accepted:** 52 **Application Deadline:** July 31 **Application Fee:** $35.00 **H.S. Requirements:** High school diploma required; GED accepted **Costs Per Year:** Application fee: $35. Comprehensive fee: $23,000 includes full-time tuition ($17,000) and college room and board ($6000). College room only: $3100. Room and board charges vary according to board plan and student level. Part-time tuition: $600 per credit hour. Part-time tuition varies according to course load. **Scholarships:** Available **Calendar System:** Semester, Summer Session Available **Enrollment:** FT 714, PT 35 **Faculty:** FT 34, PT 35 **Student-Faculty Ratio:** 16:1 **Exams:** SAT I or ACT. **% Receiving Financial Aid:** 81 **% Residing in College-Owned, -Operated, or -Affiliated Housing:** 65 **Library Holdings:** 107,630 **Credit Hours For Degree:** 93 credits, Bachelors **ROTC:** Army **Professional Accreditation:** AALE **Intercollegiate Athletics:** Baseball M; Basketball M & W; Cheerleading M & W; Cross-Country Running M & W; Football M; Golf M & W; Lacrosse M & W; Soccer M & W; Softball W; Tennis M & W; Track and Field M & W; Volleyball W; Wrestling M

SOUTHSIDE VIRGINIA COMMUNITY COLLEGE
109 Campus Dr.
Alberta, VA 23821-9719
Tel: (434)949-1000
Admissions: (434)949-1012
Fax: (434)949-7863
E-mail: rhina.jones@sv.vccs.edu

Web Site: http://www.southside.edu/
President/CEO: Dr. John Cavan
Admissions: Brent Richey
Type: Two-Year College **Sex:** Coed **Affiliation:** Virginia Community College System **% Accepted:** 100 **Admission Plans:** Open Admission; Preferred Admission; Deferred Admission **Application Deadline:** Rolling **Application Fee:** $0.00 **H.S. Requirements:** High school diploma required; GED accepted. For applicants 18 or over who demonstrate ability to benefit from occupational program: High school diploma required; GED not accepted **Scholarships:** Available **Calendar System:** Semester, Summer Session Available **Enrollment:** FT 1,359, PT 3,327 **Faculty:** FT 70, PT 225 **Student-Faculty Ratio:** 17:1 **Library Holdings:** 27,691 **Regional Accreditation:** Southern Association of Colleges and Schools **Credit Hours For Degree:** 65 semester hours, Associates **ROTC:** Army

SOUTHWEST VIRGINIA COMMUNITY COLLEGE
PO Box SVCC
Richlands, VA 24641
Tel: (276)964-2555
Admissions: (276)964-7300
Fax: (276)964-9307
Web Site: http://www.sw.edu/
President/CEO: Dr. J. Mark Estepp
Admissions: Jim Farris
Type: Two-Year College **Sex:** Coed **Affiliation:** Virginia Community College System **Admission Plans:** Open Admission; Preferred Admission; Early Admission; Deferred Admission **Application Deadline:** Rolling **Application Fee:** $0.00 **H.S. Requirements:** High school diploma required; GED accepted **Costs Per Year:** Application fee: $0. State resident tuition: $2424 full-time, $103 per credit hour part-time. Nonresident tuition: $7226 full-time, $301.10 per credit hour part-time. Mandatory fees: $192 full-time, $7 per credit hour part-time. **Scholarships:** Available **Calendar System:** Semester, Summer Session Available **Enrollment:** FT 1,648, PT 2,207 **Faculty:** FT 54, PT 202 **Student-Faculty Ratio:** 20:1 **Exams:** Other. **Final Year or Final Semester Residency Requirement:** No **Library Holdings:** 110,000 **Regional Accreditation:** Southern Association of Colleges and Schools **Credit Hours For Degree:** 61 semester hours, Associates **Professional Accreditation:** CARC, JRCERT, NLN

STRATFORD UNIVERSITY (FALLS CHURCH)
7777 Leesburg Pike
Ste. 100 South
Falls Church, VA 22043
Tel: (703)821-8570; Free: 800-444-0804
Fax: (703)556-9892
E-mail: kmartin@stratford.edu
Web Site: http://www.stratford.edu/
President/CEO: Dr. Richard R. Shurtz, II
Admissions: Kelly Martin
Type: Comprehensive **Sex:** Coed **Admission Plans:** Early Decision Plan **Application Deadline:** July 30 **Application Fee:** $50.00 **H.S. Requirements:** High school diploma required; GED accepted **Calendar System:** Quarter **Enrollment:** FT 189, PT 256 **Faculty:** FT 20, PT 41 **Student-Faculty Ratio:** 20:1 **Exams:** SAT I. **Library Holdings:** 1,800 **Credit Hours For Degree:** 90 quarter credits, Associates; 180 quarter credits, Bachelors **Professional Accreditation:** ACICS, ACF, COE

STRATFORD UNIVERSITY (WOODBRIDGE)
14349 Gideon Dr.
Woodbridge, VA 22192
Tel: (703)897-1982; Free: 888-546-1250
Admissions: (703)897-1982
E-mail: admissions@stratford.edu
Web Site: http://www.stratford.edu/
Type: Comprehensive **Sex:** Coed **Admission Plans:** Open Admission **Application Deadline:** Rolling **Application Fee:** $50.00 **Costs Per Year:** Application fee: $50. One-time mandatory fee: $100. Tuition: $340 per credit hour part-time. **Final Year or Final Semester Residency Requirement:** No

STRAYER UNIVERSITY - ALEXANDRIA CAMPUS
2730 Eisenhower Ave.
Alexandria, VA 22314
Tel: (703)317-2626
Fax: (703)329-9602
Web Site: http://www.strayer.edu/alexandria
Type: Comprehensive **Sex:** Coed **Application Fee:** $50.00 **Costs Per Year:** Application fee: $50. **Regional Accreditation:** Middle State Association of Colleges and Schools

STRAYER UNIVERSITY - ARLINGTON CAMPUS
2121 15th St. North
Arlington, VA 22201
Tel: (703)892-5100
Fax: (703)769-2677
Web Site: http://www.strayer.edu/arlington
Type: Comprehensive **Sex:** Coed **Application Fee:** $50.00 **Costs Per Year:** Application fee: $50. **Regional Accreditation:** Middle State Association of Colleges and Schools

STRAYER UNIVERSITY - CHESAPEAKE CAMPUS
700 Independent Parkway, Ste. 400
Chesapeake, VA 23320
Tel: (757)382-9900
Fax: (757)547-6078
Web Site: http://www.strayer.edu/chesapeake/
Type: Comprehensive **Sex:** Coed **Application Fee:** $50.00 **Costs Per Year:** Application fee: $50. **Regional Accreditation:** Middle State Association of Colleges and Schools

STRAYER UNIVERSITY - CHESTERFIELD CAMPUS
2820 Waterford Lake Dr.
Ste. 100
Midlothian, VA 23112
Tel: (804)763-6300
Fax: (804)763-6304
Web Site: http://www.strayer.edu/chesterfield/
Type: Comprehensive **Sex:** Coed **Application Fee:** $50.00 **Costs Per Year:** Application fee: $50. **Regional Accreditation:** Middle State Association of Colleges and Schools

STRAYER UNIVERSITY - FREDERICKSBURG CAMPUS
150 Riverside Parkway
Ste. 100
Fredericksburg, VA 22406
Tel: (540)374-4300
Web Site: http://www.strayer.edu/fredericksburg
Type: Comprehensive **Sex:** Coed **Application Fee:** $50.00 **Costs Per Year:** Application fee: $50. **Regional Accreditation:** Middle State Association of Colleges and Schools

STRAYER UNIVERSITY - HENRICO CAMPUS
11501 Nuckols Rd.
Glen Allen, VA 23059
Tel: (804)527-1000
Fax: (804)527-6963
Web Site: http://www.strayer.edu/henrico
Type: Comprehensive **Sex:** Coed **Application Fee:** $50.00 **Costs Per Year:** Application fee: $50.

STRAYER UNIVERSITY - LOUDOUN CAMPUS
45150 Russell Branch Parkway
Ste. 200
Ashburn, VA 20147
Tel: (703)729-8800
Fax: (703)729-8820
Web Site: http://www.strayer.edu/loudoun
Type: Comprehensive **Sex:** Coed **Application Fee:** $50.00 **Costs Per Year:** Application fee: $50. **Regional Accreditation:** Middle State Association of Colleges and Schools

STRAYER UNIVERSITY - MANASSAS CAMPUS
9990 Battleview Parkway
Manassas, VA 20109
Tel: (703)330-8400
Fax: (703)330-8135
Web Site: http://www.strayer.edu/manassas

Type: Comprehensive **Sex:** Coed **Application Fee:** $50.00 **Costs Per Year:** Application fee: $50. **Regional Accreditation:** Middle State Association of Colleges and Schools

STRAYER UNIVERSITY - NEWPORT NEWS CAMPUS
813 Diligence Dr., Ste. 100
Newport News, VA 23606
Tel: (757)873-3100
Fax: (757)873-3131
Web Site: http://www.strayer.edu/newport_news
Type: Comprehensive **Sex:** Coed **Application Fee:** $50.00 **Costs Per Year:** Application fee: $50. **Regional Accreditation:** Middle State Association of Colleges and Schools

STRAYER UNIVERSITY - VIRGINIA BEACH CAMPUS
249 Central Park Ave., Ste. 350
Virginia Beach, VA 23462
Tel: (757)493-6000
Fax: (757)493-6030
Web Site: http://www.strayer.edu/virginia_beach
Type: Comprehensive **Sex:** Coed **Application Fee:** $50.00 **Costs Per Year:** Application fee: $50. **Regional Accreditation:** Middle State Association of Colleges and Schools

STRAYER UNIVERSITY - WOODBRIDGE CAMPUS
13385 Minnieville Rd.
Woodbridge, VA 22192
Tel: (703)878-2800
Fax: (703)878-2993
Web Site: http://www.strayer.edu/woodbridge
Type: Comprehensive **Sex:** Coed **Application Fee:** $50.00 **Costs Per Year:** Application fee: $50. **Regional Accreditation:** Middle State Association of Colleges and Schools

SWEET BRIAR COLLEGE
Sweet Briar, VA 24595
Tel: (434)381-6100; Free: 800-381-6142
Fax: (434)381-6173
E-mail: admissions@sbc.edu
Web Site: http://www.sbc.edu/
President/CEO: Dr. Jo Ellen J. Parker
Financial Aid: Bobbi Carpenter
Type: Comprehensive **Sex:** Women **Scores:** 97.16% SAT V 400+; 90.78% SAT M 400+; 50% ACT 18-23; 38.46% ACT 24-29 **% Accepted:** 82 **Admission Plans:** Early Admission; Deferred Admission **Application Deadline:** February 1 **Application Fee:** $40.00 **H.S. Requirements:** High school diploma required; GED accepted **Costs Per Year:** Application fee: $40. Comprehensive fee: $40,975 includes full-time tuition ($29,720), mandatory fees ($475), and college room and board ($10,780). Full-time tuition and fees vary according to program. Room and board charges vary according to board plan. Part-time tuition: $760 per credit hour. Part-time tuition varies according to program. **Scholarships:** Available **Calendar System:** Semester, Summer Session Available **Enrollment:** FT 709, PT 36, Grad FT 7, Grad PT 4 **Faculty:** FT 76, PT 31 **Student-Faculty Ratio:** 8:1 **Exams:** SAT I or ACT. **% Receiving Financial Aid:** 64 **% Residing in College-Owned, -Operated, or -Affiliated Housing:** 91 **Library Holdings:** 377,648 **Regional Accreditation:** Southern Association of Colleges and Schools **Credit Hours For Degree:** 120 semester hours, Bachelors **Professional Accreditation:** TEAC **Intercollegiate Athletics:** Equestrian Sports W; Fencing W; Field Hockey W; Lacrosse W; Soccer W; Softball W; Swimming and Diving W; Tennis W; Volleyball W

TESST COLLEGE OF TECHNOLOGY
6315 Bren Mar Dr.
Alexandria, VA 22312-6342
Tel: (703)354-1005; Free: 800-833-0209
Admissions: (703)548-4800
Fax: (703)354-3661
E-mail: tesstal@erols.com
Web Site: http://www.tesst.com/
Admissions: Bob Somers
Type: Two-Year College **Sex:** Coed **Calendar System:** Quarter **Professional Accreditation:** ACCSCT

THOMAS NELSON COMMUNITY COLLEGE
PO Box 9407
Hampton, VA 23670-0407
Tel: (757)825-2700
Admissions: (757)825-2800
E-mail: admissions@tncc.edu
Web Site: http://www.tncc.edu/
President/CEO: Dr. Alvin Schexnider
Admissions: Jerri Newson
Type: Two-Year College **Sex:** Coed **Affiliation:** Virginia Community College System **Admission Plans:** Open Admission; Preferred Admission; Early Admission; Deferred Admission **Application Deadline:** Rolling **Application Fee:** $0.00 **H.S. Requirements:** High school diploma or equivalent not required **Costs Per Year:** Application fee: $0. State resident tuition: $2616 full-time, $87.20 per credit hour part-time. Nonresident tuition: $7779 full-time, $259.30 per credit hour part-time. Mandatory fees: $186 full-time, $5.50 per credit hour part-time, $10.50 per term part-time. **Scholarships:** Available **Calendar System:** Semester, Summer Session Available **Student-Faculty Ratio:** 22:1 **Library Holdings:** 56,143 **Regional Accreditation:** Southern Association of Colleges and Schools **Credit Hours For Degree:** 60 semester hours, Associates **Professional Accreditation:** NAACLS, NLN

TIDEWATER COMMUNITY COLLEGE
121 College Place
Norfolk, VA 23510
Tel: (757)822-1122
Fax: (757)822-1060
E-mail: CentralRecords@tcc.edu
Web Site: http://www.tcc.edu/
President/CEO: Deborah M. Dicroce
Admissions: Kellie Sorey, PhD
Type: Two-Year College **Sex:** Coed **Affiliation:** Virginia Community College System **Admission Plans:** Open Admission; Early Admission; Deferred Admission **Application Deadline:** Rolling **Application Fee:** $0.00 **H.S. Requirements:** High school diploma or equivalent not required. For nursing, allied health programs: High school diploma required; GED accepted **Costs Per Year:** Application fee: $0. State resident tuition: $2268 full-time, $94.50 per credit hour part-time. Nonresident tuition: $6398 full-time, $266.60 per credit hour part-time. Mandatory fees: $510 full-time, $36 per credit hour part-time. **Scholarships:** Available **Calendar System:** Semester, Summer Session Available **Enrollment:** FT 12,101, PT 18,346 **Faculty:** FT 325, PT 894 **Student-Faculty Ratio:** 29:1 **Final Year or Final Semester Residency Requirement:** No **Library Holdings:** 147,126 **Regional Accreditation:** Southern Association of Colleges and Schools **Credit Hours For Degree:** 65 semester hours, Associates **Professional Accreditation:** AHIMA, AOTA, CARC, JRCERT, JRCEMT, MACTE, NLN

UNIVERSITY OF MANAGEMENT AND TECHNOLOGY
1901 North Fort Myers Dr.
Arlington, VA 22209
Tel: (703)516-0035
Fax: (703)516-0985
E-mail: admissions@umtweb.edu
Web Site: http://www.umtweb.edu/
President/CEO: Dr. Yanping Chen
Type: Comprehensive **Sex:** Coed **Calendar System:** Continuous **Professional Accreditation:** DETC

UNIVERSITY OF MARY WASHINGTON
1301 College Ave.
Fredericksburg, VA 22401-5358
Tel: (540)654-1000; Free: 800-468-5614
Admissions: (540)654-2000
Fax: (540)654-1073
E-mail: admit@umw.edu
Web Site: http://www.umw.edu/
President/CEO: Dr. Judy G. Hample
Admissions: Kimberly Johnston
Financial Aid: Debra J. Harber
Type: Comprehensive **Sex:** Coed **Scores:** 100% SAT V 400+; 100% SAT M 400+; 18% ACT 18-23; 72% ACT 24-29 **% Accepted:** 71 **Admission Plans:** Preferred Admission; Early Action; Deferred Admission **Application Deadline:** February 1 **Application Fee:** $50.00 **H.S. Requirements:** High

school diploma required; GED accepted **Costs Per Year:** Application fee: $50. One-time mandatory fee: $75. State resident tuition: $3900 full-time, $172 per credit hour part-time. Nonresident tuition: $16,810 full-time, $700 per credit hour part-time. Part-time tuition varies according to course load and location. College room and board: $8200. College room only: $4850. Room and board charges vary according to board plan and housing facility. **Scholarships:** Available **Calendar System:** Semester, Summer Session Available **Enrollment:** FT 3,602, PT 629 **Faculty:** FT 246, PT 131 **Student-Faculty Ratio:** 15:1 **Exams:** SAT I or ACT, SAT II. **% Receiving Financial Aid:** 29 **% Residing in College-Owned, -Operated, or -Affiliated Housing:** 59 **Library Holdings:** 418,240 **Regional Accreditation:** Southern Association of Colleges and Schools **Credit Hours For Degree:** 122 semester hours, Bachelors **Professional Accreditation:** NASM **Intercollegiate Athletics:** Baseball M; Basketball M & W; Cheerleading M & W; Crew M & W; Cross-Country Running M & W; Equestrian Sports M & W; Field Hockey W; Lacrosse M & W; Rugby M & W; Soccer M & W; Softball W; Swimming and Diving M & W; Tennis M & W; Track and Field M & W; Volleyball M & W

UNIVERSITY OF PHOENIX—NORTHERN VIRGINIA CAMPUS
11730 Plaza American Dr., Ste. 2000
Reston, VA 20190
Tel: (703)435-4402; Free: 800-228-7240
Admissions: (480)557-6151
E-mail: audra.mcquarie@phoenix.edu
Web Site: http://www.phoenix.edu/
President/CEO: William Pepicello
Admissions: Audra McQuarie
Type: Comprehensive **Sex:** Coed **Admission Plans:** Open Admission; Deferred Admission **Application Deadline:** Rolling **Application Fee:** $45.00 **H.S. Requirements:** High school diploma required; GED accepted **Costs Per Year:** Application fee: $45. Tuition: $12,250 full-time. Full-time tuition varies according to course level and course load. **Scholarships:** Available **Enrollment:** FT 309 **Faculty:** FT 12, PT 90 **Regional Accreditation:** North Central Association of Colleges and Schools **Credit Hours For Degree:** 60 credits, Associates; 120 credits, Bachelors

UNIVERSITY OF PHOENIX—RICHMOND CAMPUS
6600 West Broad St.
Richmond, VA 23230
Tel: (804)288-3390; Free: 800-228-7240
Admissions: (480)557-6151
E-mail: audra.mcquarie@phoenix.edu
Web Site: http://www.phoenix.edu/
President/CEO: William Pepicello
Admissions: Audra McQuarie
Type: Comprehensive **Sex:** Coed **Admission Plans:** Open Admission; Deferred Admission **Application Deadline:** Rolling **Application Fee:** $45.00 **H.S. Requirements:** High school diploma required; GED accepted **Costs Per Year:** Application fee: $45. Tuition: $13,200 full-time. Full-time tuition varies according to course level and course load. **Scholarships:** Available **Enrollment:** FT 89 **Faculty:** FT 8, PT 73 **Regional Accreditation:** North Central Association of Colleges and Schools **Credit Hours For Degree:** 60 credits, Associates; 120 credits, Bachelors

UNIVERSITY OF RICHMOND
28 Westhampton Way
University of Richmond, VA 23173
Tel: (804)289-8000; Free: 800-700-1662
Admissions: (804)289-8640
Fax: (804)287-6003
E-mail: admissions@richmond.edu
Web Site: http://www.richmond.edu/
President/CEO: Dr. Edward L. Ayers
Admissions: Pamela Spence
Type: Comprehensive **Sex:** Coed **Scores:** 99.99% SAT V 400+; 100% SAT M 400+; 9.4% ACT 18-23; 52.2% ACT 24-29 **% Accepted:** 39 **Admission Plans:** Early Admission; Early Decision Plan; Deferred Admission **Application Deadline:** January 15 **Application Fee:** $50.00 **H.S. Requirements:** High school diploma required; GED accepted **Costs Per Year:** Application fee: $50. Comprehensive fee: $50,420 includes full-time tuition ($41,610) and college room and board ($8810). College room only: $3970. Full-time tuition varies according to course load and student level. Room and board charges vary according to board plan and housing facility. **Scholarships:** Available **Calendar System:** Semester, Summer Session Available **Enrollment:** FT 2,872, PT 53, Grad FT 524, Grad PT 64 **Faculty:** FT 321, PT 102 **Student-Faculty Ratio:** 8:1 **Exams:** SAT I or ACT. ACT essay not being used. SAT essay not being used. **% Receiving Financial Aid:** 46 **% Residing in College-Owned, -Operated, or -Affiliated Housing:** 95 **Library Holdings:** 1,098,581 **Regional Accreditation:** Southern Association of Colleges and Schools **Credit Hours For Degree:** 60 semester hours, Associates; 120 semester hours, Bachelors **ROTC:** Army **Professional Accreditation:** AACSB, ABA, AALS, NASM **Intercollegiate Athletics:** Baseball M; Basketball M & W; Cheerleading W; Crew M & W; Cross-Country Running M & W; Equestrian Sports M & W; Fencing M & W; Field Hockey W; Football M; Golf M & W; Gymnastics M & W; Ice Hockey M; Lacrosse M & W; Rugby M & W; Soccer M & W; Squash M & W; Swimming and Diving M & W; Tennis M & W; Track and Field M & W; Ultimate Frisbee M & W; Volleyball M & W; Water Polo M & W

UNIVERSITY OF VIRGINIA
Charlottesville, VA 22903
Tel: (434)924-0311
Admissions: (434)982-3200
Fax: (434)924-3587
E-mail: undergrad-admission@virginia.edu
Web Site: http://www.virginia.edu/
President/CEO: Dr. John T. Casteen, III
Admissions: Gregory W. Roberts
Financial Aid: Yvonne B. Hubbard
Type: University **Sex:** Coed **Scores:** 100% SAT V 400+; 100% SAT M 400+; 6% ACT 18-23; 39% ACT 24-29 **% Accepted:** 32 **Admission Plans:** Preferred Admission; Deferred Admission **Application Deadline:** January 1 **Application Fee:** $60.00 **H.S. Requirements:** High school diploma required; GED accepted **Costs Per Year:** Application fee: $60. State resident tuition: $7496 full-time, $250 per credit hour part-time. Nonresident tuition: $29,054 full-time, $968 per credit hour part-time. Mandatory fees: $2176 full-time, $2176 per year part-time. College room and board: $8290. College room only: $4510. Room and board charges vary according to board plan and housing facility. **Scholarships:** Available **Calendar System:** Semester, Summer Session Available **Enrollment:** FT 14,695, PT 769, Grad FT 6,080, Grad PT 2,718 **Faculty:** FT 1,220, PT 104 **Student-Faculty Ratio:** 16:1 **Exams:** Other, SAT I or ACT, SAT II. SAT essay used for admission. SAT essay used for advising. ACT essay used for placement. SAT essay used for placement. **% Receiving Financial Aid:** 29 **% Residing in College-Owned, -Operated, or -Affiliated Housing:** 43 **Final Year or Final Semester Residency Requirement:** Yes **Library Holdings:** 5,605,891 **Regional Accreditation:** Southern Association of Colleges and Schools **Credit Hours For Degree:** 120 semester hours, Bachelors **ROTC:** Army, Navy, Air Force **Professional Accreditation:** AACSB, ABET, AACN, ABA, ACA, ADtA, ACSP, APA, ASLA, ASLHA, ACIPE, AALS, LCMEAMA, NAAB, NAST, NCATE, NLN, TEAC **Intercollegiate Athletics:** Baseball M; Basketball M & W; Crew W; Cross-Country Running M & W; Field Hockey W; Football M; Golf M & W; Lacrosse M & W; Soccer M & W; Softball W; Swimming and Diving M & W; Tennis M & W; Track and Field M & W; Volleyball W; Wrestling M

THE UNIVERSITY OF VIRGINIA'S COLLEGE AT WISE
1 College Ave.
Wise, VA 24293
Tel: (276)328-0100; Free: 888-282-9324
Admissions: (276)328-0322
Fax: (276)328-0251
E-mail: admissions@uvawise.edu
Web Site: http://www.uvawise.edu/
President/CEO: Dr. David J. Prior
Admissions: Russell D. Necessary
Financial Aid: Bill Wendle
Type: Four-Year College **Sex:** Coed **Affiliation:** University of Virginia **Scores:** 86% SAT V 400+; 87% SAT M 400+; 52% ACT 18-23; 12% ACT 24-29 **% Accepted:** 89 **Admission Plans:** Early Admission; Early Action **Application Deadline:** August 1 **Application Fee:** $25.00 **H.S. Requirements:** High school diploma required; GED accepted **Costs Per Year:** Application fee: $25. State resident tuition: $3586 full-time, $153 per semester hour part-time. Nonresident tuition: $15,714 full-time, $666 per semester hour part-time. Mandatory fees: $3162 full-time, $81.31 per semester hour part-time, $894.43 per term part-time. Part-time tuition and fees vary according to course load. College room and board: $7323. College room only: $3994. Room and board charges vary according to board plan and housing

facility. **Scholarships:** Available **Calendar System:** Semester, Summer Session Available **Enrollment:** FT 1,495, PT 520 **Faculty:** FT 93, PT 71 **Student-Faculty Ratio:** 14:1 **Exams:** SAT I or ACT. **% Receiving Financial Aid:** 75 **% Residing in College-Owned, -Operated, or -Affiliated Housing:** 36 **Library Holdings:** 157,706 **Regional Accreditation:** Southern Association of Colleges and Schools **Credit Hours For Degree:** 120 semester hours, Bachelors **ROTC:** Army **Professional Accreditation:** AACN **Intercollegiate Athletics:** Baseball M; Basketball M & W; Cross-Country Running M & W; Football M; Golf M & W; Softball W; Tennis M & W; Track and Field M & W; Volleyball W

VALLEY FORGE CHRISTIAN COLLEGE WOODBRIDGE CAMPUS
13909 Smoketown Rd.
Woodbridge, VA 22192
Tel: (703)580-4810
Fax: (703)580-4806
Web Site: http://www.vfcc.edu/woodbridge/
Financial Aid: Christiana Bruwaa-Frimpong
Type: Four-Year College **Sex:** Coed **Affiliation:** Assemblies of God; Valley Forge Christian College **Costs Per Year:** Tuition: $7150 full-time. **Scholarships:** Available **Regional Accreditation:** Middle State Association of Colleges and Schools

VIRGINIA COMMONWEALTH UNIVERSITY
901 West Franklin St.
Richmond, VA 23284-9005
Tel: (804)828-0100; Free: 800-841-3638
Admissions: (804)828-6125
Fax: (804)828-1899
E-mail: schallor@vcu.edu
Web Site: http://www.vcu.edu/
President/CEO: Dr. Michael Rao
Admissions: Sybil Halloran
Type: University **Sex:** Coed **Scores:** 98% SAT V 400+; 99% SAT M 400+; 55% ACT 18-23; 34% ACT 24-29 **% Accepted:** 59 **Admission Plans:** Early Admission; Deferred Admission **Application Fee:** $50.00 **H.S. Requirements:** High school diploma required; GED accepted **Costs Per Year:** Application fee: $50. State resident tuition: $5253 full-time, $221 per credit hour part-time. Nonresident tuition: $18,477 full-time, $772 per credit hour part-time. Mandatory fees: $1864 full-time, $73.20 per credit hour part-time. College room and board: $8335. College room only: $5059. Room and board charges vary according to board plan. **Scholarships:** Available **Calendar System:** Semester, Summer Session Available **Enrollment:** FT 19,181, PT 3,968, Grad FT 5,116, Grad PT 4,171 **Faculty:** FT 1,919, PT 1,128 **Student-Faculty Ratio:** 18:1 **Exams:** SAT I or ACT. **% Receiving Financial Aid:** 47 **% Residing in College-Owned, -Operated, or -Affiliated Housing:** 22 **Library Holdings:** 1,900,000 **Regional Accreditation:** Southern Association of Colleges and Schools **Credit Hours For Degree:** 120 credits, Bachelors **ROTC:** Army **Professional Accreditation:** AACSB, ABET, ACPhE, ACEJMC, AANA, ACA, ADA, ADtA, ACSP, AOTA, APTA, APA, ACIPE, ACEHSA, FIDER, CEPH, CORE, CSWE, JRCERT, JRCNMT LCMEAMA, NAACLS, NASAD, NASD, NASM, NASPAA, NAST, NCATE, NLN, NRPA **Intercollegiate Athletics:** Baseball M; Basketball M & W; Cross-Country Running M & W; Field Hockey W; Golf M; Soccer M & W; Tennis M & W; Track and Field M & W; Volleyball W

VIRGINIA HIGHLANDS COMMUNITY COLLEGE
PO Box 828
100 VHCC Dr. Abingdon
Abingdon, VA 24212
Tel: (276)739-2400; Free: 877-207-6115
Admissions: (276)739-2490
Fax: (276)739-2590
E-mail: kcheers@vhcc.edu
Web Site: http://www.vhcc.edu/
President/CEO: Dr. David Wilkin
Admissions: Karen Cheers
Type: Two-Year College **Sex:** Coed **Affiliation:** Virginia Community College System **Admission Plans:** Open Admission; Preferred Admission; Early Admission; Deferred Admission **Application Deadline:** Rolling **H.S. Requirements:** High school diploma or equivalent not required. For nursing program: High school diploma required; GED accepted **Scholarships:** Available **Calendar System:** Semester, Summer Session Available **Enrollment:** FT 1,001, PT 1,579 **Faculty:** FT 58, PT 39 **Library Holdings:** 29,683 **Regional Accreditation:** Southern Association of Colleges and Schools **Credit Hours For Degree:** 65 semester hours, Associates **Professional Accreditation:** JRCERT, NLN

VIRGINIA INTERMONT COLLEGE
1013 Moore St.
Bristol, VA 24201
Tel: (276)669-6101; Free: 800-451-1842
Admissions: (276)466-7856
Fax: (276)669-5763
E-mail: viadmit@vic.edu
Web Site: http://www.vic.edu/
President/CEO: Dr. Robert Rainwater
Admissions: Con Sauls
Financial Aid: Denise Posey
Type: Four-Year College **Sex:** Coed **Affiliation:** Baptist Church **Scores:** 81% SAT V 400+; 81% SAT M 400+ **% Accepted:** 46 **Admission Plans:** Early Admission; Deferred Admission **Application Deadline:** Rolling **Application Fee:** $25.00 **H.S. Requirements:** High school diploma required; GED accepted **Costs Per Year:** Application fee: $25. Comprehensive fee: $30,697 includes full-time tuition ($23,373) and college room and board ($7324). College room only: $3581. Full-time tuition varies according to class time, program, reciprocity agreements, and student level. Room and board charges vary according to housing facility. Part-time tuition: $240 per credit hour. Part-time tuition varies according to class time, course level, course load, program, reciprocity agreements, and student level. **Scholarships:** Available **Calendar System:** Semester, Summer Session Available **Enrollment:** FT 497, PT 92 **Faculty:** FT 41, PT 76 **Student-Faculty Ratio:** 9:1 **Exams:** SAT I or ACT. ACT essay not being used. SAT essay not being used. **% Receiving Financial Aid:** 85 **% Residing in College-Owned, -Operated, or -Affiliated Housing:** 41 **Library Holdings:** 166,729 **Regional Accreditation:** Southern Association of Colleges and Schools **Credit Hours For Degree:** 64 semester hours, Associates; 124 semester hours, Bachelors **Professional Accreditation:** CSWE **Intercollegiate Athletics:** Baseball M; Basketball M & W; Equestrian Sports M & W; Golf M; Soccer M; Softball W; Volleyball W

VIRGINIA INTERNATIONAL UNIVERSITY
11200 Waples Mill Rd.
Fairfax, VA 22030
Tel: (703)591-7042; Free: 800-514 6848
Fax: (703)591-7048
E-mail: admissions@viu.edu
Web Site: http://www.viu.edu/
Type: Comprehensive **Sex:** Coed **Costs Per Year:** Tuition: $9450 full-time, $327 per credit hour part-time. Mandatory fees: $220 full-time, $110 per term part-time.

VIRGINIA MILITARY INSTITUTE
Lexington, VA 24450
Tel: (540)464-7207; Free: 800-767-4207
Admissions: (540)464-7211
Fax: (540)464-7746
E-mail: admissions@vmi.edu
Web Site: http://www.vmi.edu/
President/CEO: Gen. J.H. Binford Peay, III
Admissions: Lt. Col. Tom Mortenson
Financial Aid: Col. Timothy P. Golden
Type: Four-Year College **Sex:** Coed **Scores:** 99.6% SAT V 400+; 100% SAT M 400+; 34.6% ACT 18-23; 53.8% ACT 24-29 **% Accepted:** 56 **Admission Plans:** Early Admission; Early Decision Plan **Application Deadline:** February 1 **Application Fee:** $40.00 **H.S. Requirements:** High school diploma required; GED not accepted **Costs Per Year:** Application fee: $40. One-time mandatory fee: $2368. State resident tuition: $5500 full-time. Nonresident tuition: $23,048 full-time. Mandatory fees: $5690 full-time. College room and board: $6792. **Scholarships:** Available **Calendar System:** Semester, Summer Session Available **Enrollment:** FT 1,500 **Faculty:** FT 122, PT 50 **Student-Faculty Ratio:** 11:1 **Exams:** SAT I or ACT. ACT essay not being used. SAT essay not being used. **% Receiving Financial Aid:** 43 **% Residing in College-Owned, -Operated, or -Affiliated Housing:** 100 **Regional Accreditation:** Southern Association of Colleges and Schools **Credit Hours For Degree:** 136 semester hours, Bachelors **ROTC:** Army, Navy, Air Force **Professional Accreditation:** ABET **Intercollegiate Athletics:** Baseball M; Basketball M; Cross-Country Running M & W; Football M;

Golf M; Lacrosse M; Riflery M & W; Soccer M; Swimming and Diving M; Tennis M; Track and Field M & W; Wrestling M

VIRGINIA POLYTECHNIC INSTITUTE AND STATE UNIVERSITY
Blacksburg, VA 24061
Tel: (540)231-6000
Admissions: (540)231-6267
Fax: (540)231-3242
E-mail: vtadmiss@vt.edu
Web Site: http://www.vt.edu/
President/CEO: Dr. Charles Steger
Admissions: Mildred R. Johnson
Financial Aid: Dr. Barry Simmons
Type: University **Sex:** Coed **Scores:** 97% SAT V 400+; 99% SAT M 400+ **% Accepted:** 61 **Admission Plans:** Early Admission; Early Decision Plan; Deferred Admission **Application Deadline:** January 15 **Application Fee:** $50.00 **H.S. Requirements:** High school diploma required; GED accepted **Scholarships:** Available **Calendar System:** Semester, Summer Session Available **Enrollment:** FT 23,104, PT 454, Grad FT 4,783, Grad PT 2,529 **Faculty:** FT 1,364, PT 224 **Student-Faculty Ratio:** 16:1 **Exams:** SAT I or ACT, SAT I and SAT II or ACT. **% Receiving Financial Aid:** 36 **% Residing in College-Owned, -Operated, or -Affiliated Housing:** 39 **Library Holdings:** 2,385,815 **Regional Accreditation:** Southern Association of Colleges and Schools **Credit Hours For Degree:** 72 credit hours, Associates; 126 credit hours, Bachelors **ROTC:** Army, Navy, Air Force **Professional Accreditation:** AACSB, ABET, AAMFT, AAFCS, ACCE, ACA, ADtA, ACSP, APA, ASLA, AVMA, FIDER, NAAB, NASAD, NASPAA, NAST, NCATE, SAF **Intercollegiate Athletics:** Baseball M; Basketball M; Cross-Country Running M & W; Football M; Golf M; Lacrosse W; Soccer M & W; Swimming and Diving M & W; Tennis M & W; Track and Field M & W; Ultimate Frisbee M & W; Volleyball W

VIRGINIA STATE UNIVERSITY
1 Hayden Dr.
Petersburg, VA 23806-0001
Tel: (804)524-5000; Free: 800-871-7611
Admissions: (804)524-5902
Fax: (804)524-5055
E-mail: ilogan@vsu.edu
Web Site: http://www.vsu.edu/
President/CEO: Eddie N. Moore, Jr.
Admissions: Irene Logan
Financial Aid: Henry DeBose
Type: Comprehensive **Sex:** Coed **Affiliation:** State Council of Higher Education for Virginia **Scores:** 76% SAT V 400+; 73% SAT M 400+ **% Accepted:** 67 **Application Deadline:** May 1 **Application Fee:** $25.00 **H.S. Requirements:** High school diploma required; GED accepted **Costs Per Year:** Application fee: $25. State resident tuition: $3584 full-time, $208 per credit hour part-time. Nonresident tuition: $11,646 full-time, $482 per credit hour part-time. Mandatory fees: $2590 full-time, $10 per credit hour part-time. Full-time tuition and fees vary according to course load. Part-time tuition and fees vary according to course load. College room and board: $8050. College room only: $4640. Room and board charges vary according to board plan and housing facility. **Scholarships:** Available **Calendar System:** Semester, Summer Session Available **Enrollment:** FT 4,547, PT 324, Grad FT 88, Grad PT 407 **Faculty:** FT 247, PT 103 **Student-Faculty Ratio:** 17:1 **Exams:** SAT I or ACT. **% Receiving Financial Aid:** 85 **% Residing in College-Owned, -Operated, or -Affiliated Housing:** 62 **Library Holdings:** 334,334 **Regional Accreditation:** Southern Association of Colleges and Schools **Credit Hours For Degree:** 120 credit hours, Bachelors **ROTC:** Army **Professional Accreditation:** ABET, ADtA, NASAD, NASM, NCATE **Intercollegiate Athletics:** Baseball M; Basketball M & W; Bowling W; Cheerleading M & W; Cross-Country Running M & W; Football M; Golf M & W; Softball W; Tennis M & W; Track and Field M & W; Volleyball W

VIRGINIA UNION UNIVERSITY
1500 North Lombardy St.
Richmond, VA 23220-1170
Tel: (804)257-5600; Free: 800-368-3227
Admissions: (804)257-5881
E-mail: gpowell@vuu.edu
Web Site: http://www.vuu.edu/
President/CEO: Dr. Claude G. Perkins
Admissions: Gil Powell
Financial Aid: Donna Mack-Tatum
Type: Comprehensive **Sex:** Coed **Affiliation:** Baptist **Scores:** 46.93% SAT V 400+; 39.88% SAT M 400+ **% Accepted:** 81 **Admission Plans:** Deferred Admission **Application Deadline:** Rolling **Application Fee:** $25.00 **H.S. Requirements:** High school diploma required; GED accepted **Costs Per Year:** Application fee: $25. Comprehensive fee: $21,460 includes full-time tuition ($13,314), mandatory fees ($1316), and college room and board ($6830). College room only: $3084. Full-time tuition and fees vary according to course level and course load. Room and board charges vary according to housing facility. Part-time tuition: $422 per credit hour. Part-time mandatory fees: $40 per credit hour. Part-time tuition and fees vary according to course level and course load. **Scholarships:** Available **Calendar System:** Semester, Summer Session Available **Enrollment:** FT 1,309, PT 35 **Faculty:** FT 84, PT 56 **Student-Faculty Ratio:** 15:1 **Exams:** SAT I or ACT. **% Receiving Financial Aid:** 84 **Library Holdings:** 147,611 **Regional Accreditation:** Southern Association of Colleges and Schools **Credit Hours For Degree:** 124 semester hours, Bachelors **ROTC:** Army **Professional Accreditation:** ACIPE, ACBSP, ATS, CSWE, NCATE **Intercollegiate Athletics:** Basketball M & W; Cross-Country Running M & W; Football M; Golf M; Softball W; Tennis M; Track and Field M & W; Volleyball W

VIRGINIA UNIVERSITY OF LYNCHBURG
2058 Garfield Ave.
Lynchburg, VA 24501-6417
Tel: (804)528-5276
Admissions: (434)528-5276
Fax: (804)528-4257
E-mail: cglass@vul.edu
Web Site: http://www.vul.edu/
President/CEO: Dr. Ralph Reavis
Admissions: Cheryl Glass
Financial Aid: Charlene P. Scruggs
Type: Comprehensive **Sex:** Coed **Admission Plans:** Open Admission **Application Deadline:** Rolling **Application Fee:** $25.00 **H.S. Requirements:** High school diploma required; GED accepted **Costs Per Year:** Application fee: $25. Comprehensive fee: $8900 includes full-time tuition ($5000), mandatory fees ($300), and college room and board ($3600). Full-time tuition and fees vary according to location and program. Part-time tuition: $167 per credit hour. Part-time tuition varies according to location and program. **Scholarships:** Available **Calendar System:** Semester, Summer Session Available **Enrollment:** FT 138, PT 95, Grad FT 72, Grad PT 22 **Faculty:** FT 22, PT 44 **Student-Faculty Ratio:** 9:1 **% Residing in College-Owned, -Operated, or -Affiliated Housing:** 14 **Final Year or Final Semester Residency Requirement:** No **Credit Hours For Degree:** 64 credits, Associates; 120 credits, Bachelors **Professional Accreditation:** TACCS **Intercollegiate Athletics:** Basketball M & W

VIRGINIA WESLEYAN COLLEGE
1584 Wesleyan Dr.
Norfolk, VA 23502-5599
Tel: (757)455-3200; Free: 800-737-8684
Admissions: (757)455-3208
Fax: (757)461-5238
E-mail: admissions@vwc.edu
Web Site: http://www.vwc.edu/
President/CEO: Dr. William T. Greer, Jr.
Admissions: Sara Gastler
Financial Aid: Angie T. Hawkins
Type: Four-Year College **Sex:** Coed **Affiliation:** United Methodist **Scores:** 95.1% SAT V 400+; 96.2% SAT M 400+; 61.9% ACT 18-23; 23.6% ACT 24-29 **% Accepted:** 75 **Application Deadline:** Rolling **Application Fee:** $40.00 **H.S. Requirements:** High school diploma required; GED accepted **Costs Per Year:** Application fee: $40. Comprehensive fee: $34,860 includes full-time tuition ($26,976), mandatory fees ($500), and college room and board ($7384). Room and board charges vary according to board plan and housing facility. Part-time tuition: $1124 per hour. **Scholarships:** Available **Calendar System:** 4-1-4, Summer Session Available **Enrollment:** FT 1,143, PT 193 **Student-Faculty Ratio:** 11:1 **Exams:** SAT I or ACT. ACT essay used for placement. SAT essay used for placement. **% Receiving Financial Aid:** 73 **% Residing in College-Owned, -Operated, or -Affiliated Housing:** 69 **Final Year or Final Semester Residency Requirement:** Yes **Library Holdings:** 175,200 **Regional Accreditation:** Southern Association of Colleges and Schools **Credit Hours For Degree:** 120 semester hours, Bachelors **ROTC:** Army **Professional Accreditation:** NRPA **Intercollegiate Athletics:**

Baseball M; Basketball M & W; Cheerleading W; Cross-Country Running M & W; Field Hockey W; Golf M; Lacrosse M & W; Soccer M & W; Softball W; Tennis M & W; Track and Field M & W; Volleyball W

VIRGINIA WESTERN COMMUNITY COLLEGE
PO Box 14007
Roanoke, VA 24038
Tel: (540)857-7311
Fax: (540)857-7204
Web Site: http://www.virginiawestern.edu/
President/CEO: Robert Sandel
Type: Two-Year College **Sex:** Coed **Affiliation:** Virginia Community College System **Admission Plans:** Open Admission; Preferred Admission; Early Admission; Deferred Admission **Application Deadline:** Rolling **Application Fee:** $0.00 **H.S. Requirements:** High school diploma required; GED accepted **Scholarships:** Available **Calendar System:** Semester, Summer Session Available **Enrollment:** FT 1,929, PT 5,707 **Faculty:** FT 87, PT 319 **Student-Faculty Ratio:** 25:1 **Library Holdings:** 67,129 **Regional Accreditation:** Southern Association of Colleges and Schools **Credit Hours For Degree:** 60 semester hours, Associates **Professional Accreditation:** ADA, ACBSP, JRCERT, NLN

WASHINGTON AND LEE UNIVERSITY
Lexington, VA 24450-0303
Tel: (540)458-8400
Admissions: (540)458-8710
Fax: (540)463-8062
E-mail: admissions@wlu.edu
Web Site: http://www.wlu.edu/
President/CEO: Dr. Kenneth P. Ruscio
Admissions: William M. Hartog
Financial Aid: John DeCourcy
Type: Comprehensive **Sex:** Coed **Scores:** 100% SAT V 400+; 100% SAT M 400+; 26% ACT 24-29 **% Accepted:** 19 **Admission Plans:** Early Decision Plan; Deferred Admission **Application Deadline:** January 15 **Application Fee:** $50.00 **H.S. Requirements:** High school diploma or equivalent not required **Costs Per Year:** Application fee: $50. Comprehensive fee: $47,287 includes full-time tuition ($37,990), mandatory fees ($887), and college room and board ($8410). College room only: $3285. Full-time tuition and fees vary according to degree level. Room and board charges vary according to board plan and housing facility. Part-time tuition: $1267 per credit hour. Part-time tuition varies according to degree level. **Scholarships:** Available **Calendar System:** Miscellaneous, Summer Session Not available **Enrollment:** FT 1,758, PT 1, Grad FT 394 **Faculty:** FT 225, PT 56 **Student-Faculty Ratio:** 9:1 **Exams:** Other, SAT I or ACT. SAT essay used for admission. SAT essay used as a validity check on application essay. **% Receiving Financial Aid:** 35 **% Residing in College-Owned, -Operated, or -Affiliated Housing:** 60 **Library Holdings:** 717,288 **Regional Accreditation:** Southern Association of Colleges and Schools **Credit Hours For Degree:** 113 credits, Bachelors **ROTC:** Army **Professional Accreditation:** AACSB, ACEJMC, ABA, AALS **Intercollegiate Athletics:** Baseball M; Basketball M & W; Cheerleading M & W; Cross-Country Running M & W; Equestrian Sports W; Fencing M & W; Field Hockey W; Football M; Golf M; Ice Hockey M & W; Lacrosse M & W; Rugby M; Skiing (Cross-Country) M & W; Soccer M & W; Softball W; Swimming and Diving M & W; Tennis M & W; Track and Field M & W; Ultimate Frisbee M & W; Volleyball M & W; Wrestling M

WESTWOOD COLLEGE—ANNANDALE CAMPUS
7611 Little River Turnpike, 5th Floor
Annandale, VA 22003
Tel: (706)642-3770; Free: 800-281-2978
Admissions: (703)642-3770
Web Site: http://www.westwood.edu/
President/CEO: Lauck Walton
Type: Four-Year College **Sex:** Coed **Affiliation:** Westwood Colleges, Inc.

WESTWOOD COLLEGE—ARLINGTON BALLSTON CAMPUS
4300 Wilson Blvd.
Ste. 200
Arlington, VA 22203
Tel: (703)243-3900
Web Site: http://www.westwood.edu/
President/CEO: Deborah Mahon
Type: Four-Year College **Sex:** Coed **Affiliation:** Westwood Colleges, Inc. **Professional Accreditation:** ACCSCT

WORLD COLLEGE
5193 Shore Dr., Ste. 105
Virginia Beach, VA 23455-2500
Tel: (757)464-4600; Free: 800-696-7532
E-mail: instruct@cie-wc.edu
Web Site: http://www.worldcollege.edu/
President/CEO: John R. Drinko
Admissions: Audre Piratsky
Type: Four-Year College **Sex:** Coed **Admission Plans:** Open Admission; Early Admission **Application Deadline:** Rolling **H.S. Requirements:** High school diploma required; GED accepted **Calendar System:** Semester **Faculty:** FT 4, PT 2 **Credit Hours For Degree:** 139 semester hours, Bachelors **Professional Accreditation:** DETC

WYTHEVILLE COMMUNITY COLLEGE
1000 East Main St.
Wytheville, VA 24382-3308
Tel: (276)223-4700
Fax: (276)223-4778
E-mail: wcdixxs@wcc.vccs.edu
Web Site: http://www.wcc.vccs.edu/
President/CEO: Charlie White
Admissions: Sabrina Terry
Type: Two-Year College **Sex:** Coed **Affiliation:** Virginia Community College System **% Accepted:** 100 **Admission Plans:** Open Admission; Preferred Admission; Early Admission **Application Deadline:** Rolling **Application Fee:** $0.00 **H.S. Requirements:** High school diploma or equivalent not required. For allied health programs: High school diploma required; GED accepted **Costs Per Year:** Application fee: $0. State resident tuition: $2100 full-time, $87.20 per credit hour part-time. Nonresident tuition: $6463 full-time, $269.30 per credit hour part-time. Mandatory fees: $156 full-time, $6.50 per credit hour part-time. Full-time tuition and fees vary according to course load, program, and reciprocity agreements. Part-time tuition and fees vary according to course load, program, and reciprocity agreements. **Scholarships:** Available **Calendar System:** Semester, Summer Session Available **Faculty:** FT 46 **Student-Faculty Ratio:** 16:1 **Library Holdings:** 29,000 **Regional Accreditation:** Southern Association of Colleges and Schools **Credit Hours For Degree:** 62 credit hours, Associates **Professional Accreditation:** ADA, APTA, NAACLS, NLN

ANTIOCH UNIVERSITY SEATTLE
2326 Sixth Ave.
Seattle, WA 98121-1814
Tel: (206)441-5352
Admissions: (206)268-4202
E-mail: admissions@antiochseattle.edu
Web Site: http://www.antiochsea.edu/
President/CEO: Cassandra Manuelito-Kerkvliet
Financial Aid: Katy Stahl
Type: University **Sex:** Coed **Affiliation:** Antioch University **Admission Plans:** Deferred Admission **Application Fee:** $75.00 **H.S. Requirements:** High school diploma required; GED accepted **Costs Per Year:** Application fee: $75. Tuition: $11,760 full-time, $490 per credit part-time. Mandatory fees: $270 full-time, $135 per term part-time. **Scholarships:** Available **Calendar System:** Quarter, Summer Session Available **Enrollment:** FT 52, PT 258, Grad FT 763, Grad PT 85 **Student-Faculty Ratio:** 8:1 **% Receiving Financial Aid:** 78 **Regional Accreditation:** North Central Association of Colleges and Schools **Credit Hours For Degree:** 180 credits, Bachelors

APOLLO COLLEGE
10102 East Knox
Ste. 200
Spokane, WA 99206
Tel: (509)532-8888
Fax: (509)533-5983
Web Site: http://www.apollocollege.com/
Admissions: Deanna Baker
Type: Two-Year College **Sex:** Coed **Professional Accreditation:** ABHES, JRCERT

ARGOSY UNIVERSITY, SEATTLE
2601-A Elliott Ave.
Seattle, WA 98121
Tel: (206)283-4500; Free: (866)283-2777
Fax: (206)393-3592
Web Site: http://www.argosy.edu/seattle/
President/CEO: Tom Dyer, EdD
Type: University **Sex:** Coed **Affiliation:** Education Management Corporation **Calendar System:** Semester **Regional Accreditation:** North Central Association of Colleges and Schools

THE ART INSTITUTE OF SEATTLE
2323 Elliott Ave.
Seattle, WA 98121-1642
Tel: (206)448-6600; Free: 800-275-2471
Admissions: (206)448-0900
Fax: (206)269-0275
Web Site: http://www.artinstitutes.edu/seattle/
President/CEO: Barbara Singer
Type: Two-Year College **Sex:** Coed **Affiliation:** Education Management Corporation **Calendar System:** Quarter **Professional Accreditation:** ACF, NCCU

BASTYR UNIVERSITY
14500 Juanita Dr., NE
Kenmore, WA 98028-4966
Tel: (425)823-1300
Admissions: (425)602-3101
Fax: (425)823-6222
E-mail: admissions@bastyr.edu
Web Site: http://www.bastyr.edu/
President/CEO: Dr. Daniel K. Church
Admissions: Ted Olsen
Financial Aid: Sheila Arisa
Type: Two-Year Upper Division **Sex:** Coed **Admission Plans:** Deferred Admission **Application Fee:** $60.00 **H.S. Requirements:** High school diploma required; GED accepted **Costs Per Year:** Application fee: $60. Tuition: $19,050 full-time. Full-time tuition varies according to course load and program. **Scholarships:** Available **Calendar System:** Quarter, Summer Session Available **Enrollment:** FT 144, PT 47, Grad FT 638, Grad PT 99 **Faculty:** FT 49, PT 95 **Student-Faculty Ratio:** 9:1 **% Receiving Financial Aid:** 85 **% Residing in College-Owned, -Operated, or -Affiliated Housing:** 7 **Library Holdings:** 24,000 **Credit Hours For Degree:** 180 credits, Bachelors **Professional Accreditation:** NACSCAO, ADtA, NCCU

BATES TECHNICAL COLLEGE
1101 South Yakima Ave.
Tacoma, WA 98405-4895
Tel: (253)596-1500
Admissions: (253)680-7000
E-mail: registration@bates.ctc.edu
Web Site: http://www.bates.ctc.edu/
President/CEO: Dr. David Borofsky
Type: Two-Year College **Sex:** Coed **Affiliation:** Washington State Board for Community and Technical Colleges **Admission Plans:** Open Admission **Application Deadline:** Rolling **Application Fee:** $56.00 **Scholarships:** Available **Calendar System:** Quarter **Professional Accreditation:** ADA, NCCU

BELLEVUE COLLEGE
3000 Landerholm Circle, SE
Bellevue, WA 98007-6484
Tel: (425)564-1000
Fax: (425)564-2261
Web Site: http://www.bcc.ctc.edu/
President/CEO: B. Jean Floten
Admissions: Morenika Jacobs
Type: Two-Year College **Sex:** Coed **Affiliation:** Washington State Board for Community and Technical Colleges **Admission Plans:** Open Admission **Application Deadline:** Rolling **Application Fee:** $28.00 **H.S. Requirements:** High school diploma or equivalent not required. For applicants under 18: High school diploma required; GED accepted **Scholarships:** Available **Calendar System:** Quarter, Summer Session Available **Library Holdings:** 42,000 **Credit Hours For Degree:** 90 quarter hours, Associates **Professional Accreditation:** JRCEDMS, JRCERT, NLN, NCCU **Intercollegiate Athletics:** Baseball M; Basketball M & W; Cross-Country Running M & W; Golf M; Soccer M; Softball W; Tennis W; Track and Field M & W; Volleyball W

BELLINGHAM TECHNICAL COLLEGE
3028 Lindbergh Ave.
Bellingham, WA 98225

Tel: (360)752-7000
Fax: (360)676-2798
E-mail: beltcadm@beltc.ctc.edu
Web Site: http://www.btc.ctc.edu/
President/CEO: Thomas Eckert
Admissions: Erin Runestrand
Type: Two-Year College **Sex:** Coed **% Accepted:** 88 **Admission Plans:** Open Admission; Early Admission; Deferred Admission **Application Deadline:** Rolling **Application Fee:** $33.17 **H.S. Requirements:** High school diploma or equivalent not required. For dental assisting (certificate): High school diploma required; GED accepted **Scholarships:** Available **Enrollment:** FT 968, PT 3,191 **Faculty:** FT 56, PT 111 **Student-Faculty Ratio:** 20:1 **Library Holdings:** 9,537 **Credit Hours For Degree:** 1800 clock hours, Associates **Professional Accreditation:** ACF, ADA, NCCU

BIG BEND COMMUNITY COLLEGE
7662 Chanute St., NE
Moses Lake, WA 98837-3299
Tel: (509)762-5351
Admissions: (509)793-2222
Fax: (509)762-6243
E-mail: admissions@bigbend.edu
Web Site: http://www.bigbend.edu/
President/CEO: William Bonaudi
Admissions: Candis Lacher
Type: Two-Year College **Sex:** Coed **% Accepted:** 100 **Admission Plans:** Open Admission; Early Admission; Deferred Admission **Application Deadline:** Rolling **Application Fee:** $30.00 **H.S. Requirements:** High school diploma or equivalent not required. For aviation, nursing programs: High school diploma required; GED accepted **Scholarships:** Available **Calendar System:** Quarter, Summer Session Available **Faculty:** FT 54, PT 78 **Student-Faculty Ratio:** 20:1 **% Residing in College-Owned, -Operated, or -Affiliated Housing:** 5 **Library Holdings:** 41,900 **Credit Hours For Degree:** 90 credit hours, Associates **Professional Accreditation:** NCCU **Intercollegiate Athletics:** Baseball M; Basketball M & W; Softball W; Volleyball W

CASCADIA COMMUNITY COLLEGE
18345 Campus Way, NE
Bothell, WA 98011
Tel: (425)352-8000
Fax: (425)398-5730
E-mail: admissions@cascadia.ctc.edu
Web Site: http://www.cascadia.edu/
President/CEO: Dr. William Christopher
Admissions: Erin Blakeney
Type: Two-Year College **Sex:** Coed **Admission Plans:** Open Admission **Application Deadline:** Rolling **Application Fee:** $0.00 **H.S. Requirements:** High school diploma or equivalent not required **Costs Per Year:** Application fee: $0. State resident tuition: $2925 full-time, $81 per credit hour part-time. Nonresident tuition: $8145 full-time, $253 per credit hour part-time. Mandatory fees: $150 full-time, $50 per term part-time. **Calendar System:** Quarter, Summer Session Available **Enrollment:** FT 1,467, PT 1,783 **Faculty:** FT 32, PT 91 **Student-Faculty Ratio:** 26:1 **Library Holdings:** 73,749 **Credit Hours For Degree:** 90 credits, Associates **Professional Accreditation:** NCCU

CENTRAL WASHINGTON UNIVERSITY
400 East University Way
Ellensburg, WA 98926
Tel: (509)963-1111; Free: (866)298-4968
Admissions: (509)963-1211
Fax: (509)963-3022
E-mail: cwuadmis@cwu.edu
Web Site: http://www.cwu.edu/
President/CEO: Dr. James L. Gaudino
Admissions: Lisa Garcia-Hanson
Financial Aid: Agnes Canedo
Type: Comprehensive **Sex:** Coed **Scores:** 89.5% SAT V 400+; 92.3% SAT M 400+; 55% ACT 18-23; 21.5% ACT 24-29 **% Accepted:** 79 **Application Deadline:** April 1 **Application Fee:** $50.00 **H.S. Requirements:** High school diploma required; GED accepted **Costs Per Year:** Application fee: $50. State resident tuition: $5517 full-time, $184 per credit part-time. Nonresident tuition: $16,860 full-time, $526 per credit part-time. Mandatory fees: $882 full-time. Part-time tuition varies according to course load. College room and board: $8460. Room and board charges vary according to board plan and housing facility. **Scholarships:** Available **Calendar System:** Quarter, Summer Session Available **Enrollment:** FT 8,728, PT 1,453 **Faculty:** FT 432, PT 169 **Student-Faculty Ratio:** 20:1 **Exams:** SAT I or ACT. **% Receiving Financial Aid:** 50 **% Residing in College-Owned, -Operated, or -Affiliated Housing:** 34 **Library Holdings:** 434,424 **Credit Hours For Degree:** 180 credits, Bachelors **ROTC:** Army, Air Force **Professional Accreditation:** ABET, ACCE, ACA, ADtA, JRCEMT, NASM, NCATE, NCCU **Intercollegiate Athletics:** Baseball M; Basketball M & W; Bowling M & W; Cheerleading M & W; Cross-Country Running M & W; Fencing M & W; Football M; Golf M & W; Ice Hockey M & W; Rugby M & W; Soccer M & W; Softball W; Track and Field M & W; Volleyball W; Water Polo M & W

CENTRALIA COLLEGE
600 Centralia College Blvd.
Centralia, WA 98531-4099
Tel: (360)736-9391
E-mail: admissions@centralia.edu
Web Site: http://www.centralia.edu/
President/CEO: James M. Walton
Admissions: Scott Copeland
Type: Two-Year College **Sex:** Coed **Affiliation:** Washington State Board for Community and Technical Colleges **% Accepted:** 100 **Admission Plans:** Open Admission **Application Deadline:** Rolling **Application Fee:** $0.00 **H.S. Requirements:** High school diploma required; GED accepted **Costs Per Year:** Application fee: $0. State resident tuition: $2925 full-time, $81 per credit part-time. Nonresident tuition: $3315 full-time, $253 per credit part-time. Mandatory fees: $4 per credit part-time, $5. Full-time tuition varies according to course load. Part-time tuition and fees vary according to course load. **Scholarships:** Available **Calendar System:** Quarter, Summer Session Available **Enrollment:** FT 1,827, PT 1,981 **Faculty:** FT 58, PT 182 **Student-Faculty Ratio:** 25:1 **Library Holdings:** 38,000 **Credit Hours For Degree:** 93 credits, Associates **Professional Accreditation:** NCCU **Intercollegiate Athletics:** Baseball M; Basketball M & W; Golf W; Softball W; Volleyball W

CITY UNIVERSITY OF SEATTLE
11900 Northeast First St.
Bellevue, WA 98005
Tel: (425)637-1010; Free: 888-42-CITYU
Admissions: 888-422-4898
Fax: (425)277-2437
E-mail: info@cityu.edu
Web Site: http://www.cityu.edu/
President/CEO: E. Lee Gorsuch, II
Financial Aid: Jean L. Roberts
Type: Comprehensive **Sex:** Coed **Admission Plans:** Open Admission; Deferred Admission **Application Deadline:** Rolling **Application Fee:** $50.00 **H.S. Requirements:** High school diploma required; GED accepted **Costs Per Year:** Application fee: $50. One-time mandatory fee: $50. Tuition: $15,615 full-time, $347 per credit hour part-time. Full-time tuition varies according to degree level and program. Part-time tuition varies according to degree level and program. **Scholarships:** Available **Calendar System:** Quarter, Summer Session Available **Enrollment:** FT 738, PT 582, Grad FT 1,015, Grad PT 550 **Faculty:** FT 62, PT 983 **Student-Faculty Ratio:** 13:1 **% Receiving Financial Aid:** 25 **Library Holdings:** 46,399 **Credit Hours For Degree:** 90 credits, Associates; 180 credits, Bachelors **Professional Accreditation:** NCCU

CLARK COLLEGE
1933 Fort Vancouver Way
Vancouver, WA 98663-3598
Tel: (360)992-2000
Admissions: (360)992-2308
E-mail: sanderson@clark.edu
Web Site: http://www.clark.edu/
President/CEO: Robert K. Knight
Admissions: Sheryl Anderson
Type: Two-Year College **Sex:** Coed **Affiliation:** Washington State Board for Community and Technical Colleges **Admission Plans:** Open Admission; Early Admission; Deferred Admission **Application Deadline:** July 30 **Application Fee:** $20.00 **H.S. Requirements:** High school diploma or equivalent not required **Costs Per Year:** Application fee: $20. State resident tuition: $3175 full-time, $87 per credit hour part-time. Nonresident tuition:

$8395 full-time, $259 per credit hour part-time. Full-time tuition varies according to course load and reciprocity agreements. Part-time tuition varies according to course load and reciprocity agreements. **Scholarships:** Available **Calendar System:** Quarter, Summer Session Available **Enrollment:** FT 6,181, PT 6,465 **Faculty:** FT 253, PT 525 **Student-Faculty Ratio:** 19:1 **Final Year or Final Semester Residency Requirement:** No **Library Holdings:** 67,991 **Credit Hours For Degree:** 90 quarter hours, Associates **ROTC:** Army, Air Force **Professional Accreditation:** AAMAE, ADA, NLN, NCCU **Intercollegiate Athletics:** Baseball M; Basketball M & W; Cross-Country Running M & W; Fencing M & W; Soccer M & W; Softball W; Track and Field M & W; Volleyball W

CLOVER PARK TECHNICAL COLLEGE
4500 Steilacoom Blvd., SW
Lakewood, WA 98499
Tel: (253)589-5678
Admissions: (253)589-5800
Web Site: http://www.cptc.edu/
President/CEO: John Walstrum
Admissions: Judy Richardson
Type: Two-Year College **Sex:** Coed **Affiliation:** Washington State Community and Technical College System **Admission Plans:** Open Admission **Application Deadline:** September 27 **Application Fee:** $41.00 **H.S. Requirements:** High school diploma required; GED accepted **Scholarships:** Available **Library Holdings:** 11,219 **Professional Accreditation:** ADA, NAACLS, NCCU

COLUMBIA BASIN COLLEGE
2600 North 20th Ave.
Pasco, WA 99301-3397
Tel: (509)547-0511
Fax: (509)546-0401
Web Site: http://www.columbiabasin.edu/
President/CEO: Richard Cummins
Admissions: Donna Korstad
Type: Two-Year College **Sex:** Coed **Affiliation:** Washington State Board for Community and Technical Colleges **Admission Plans:** Open Admission **Application Deadline:** Rolling **Application Fee:** $26.00 **H.S. Requirements:** High school diploma required; GED accepted **Scholarships:** Available **Calendar System:** Quarter, Summer Session Available **Enrollment:** FT 2,425, PT 3,412 **Faculty:** FT 114, PT 495 **Student-Faculty Ratio:** 10:1 **Library Holdings:** 54,331 **Credit Hours For Degree:** 90 quarter hours, Associates **Professional Accreditation:** ADA, JRCEMT, NLN, NCCU **Intercollegiate Athletics:** Baseball M; Basketball M & W; Golf M & W; Soccer M & W; Volleyball W

CORNISH COLLEGE OF THE ARTS
1000 Lenora St.
Seattle, WA 98102-4696
Tel: (206)726-5151; Free: 800-726-ARTS
Admissions: (206)726-5017
Fax: (206)720-1011
E-mail: admissions@cornish.edu
Web Site: http://www.cornish.edu/
President/CEO: Sergei Tschernisch
Admissions: Sharron Starling
Financial Aid: Sharron Starling
Type: Four-Year College **Sex:** Coed **% Accepted:** 67 **Admission Plans:** Deferred Admission **Application Deadline:** August 15 **Application Fee:** $35.00 **H.S. Requirements:** High school diploma required; GED accepted **Costs Per Year:** Application fee: $35. Comprehensive fee: $36,797 includes full-time tuition ($27,810), mandatory fees ($487), and college room and board ($8500). College room only: $5900. Room and board charges vary according to board plan. **Scholarships:** Available **Calendar System:** Semester, Summer Session Available **Enrollment:** FT 775, PT 19 **Faculty:** FT 55, PT 110 **Student-Faculty Ratio:** 8:1 **Exams:** SAT I or ACT. **% Receiving Financial Aid:** 74 **Library Holdings:** 26,629 **Credit Hours For Degree:** 130 credits, Bachelors **Professional Accreditation:** NASAD, NCCU

DEVRY UNIVERSITY (BELLEVUE)
600 108th Ave. NE, Ste. 230
Bellevue, WA 98004-5110
Tel: (425)455-2242
Fax: (425)455-2322
Web Site: http://www.devry.edu/
Type: Comprehensive **Sex:** Coed **Calendar System:** Semester **Regional Accreditation:** North Central Association of Colleges and Schools

DEVRY UNIVERSITY (FEDERAL WAY)
3600 South 344th Way
Federal Way, WA 98001
Tel: (253)943-2800
Web Site: http://www.devry.edu/
President/CEO: David Stewart
Financial Aid: Diane Rooney
Type: Comprehensive **Sex:** Coed **Affiliation:** DeVry University **Admission Plans:** Deferred Admission **Application Deadline:** Rolling **Application Fee:** $50.00 **H.S. Requirements:** High school diploma required; GED accepted **Costs Per Year:** Application fee: $50. Tuition: $14,720 full-time, $575 per credit hour part-time. **Scholarships:** Available **Calendar System:** Semester, Summer Session Available **Enrollment:** FT 426, PT 248, Grad FT 14, Grad PT 139 **Faculty:** FT 19, PT 60 **Student-Faculty Ratio:** 15:1 **Exams:** ACT essay used for admission. SAT essay used for admission. ACT essay used for placement. SAT essay used for placement. **% Receiving Financial Aid:** 90 **Regional Accreditation:** North Central Association of Colleges and Schools **Credit Hours For Degree:** 67 credit hours, Associates; 122 credit hours, Bachelors **ROTC:** Army

DIGIPEN INSTITUTE OF TECHNOLOGY
5001 150th Ave., NE
Redmond, WA 98052
Tel: (425)558-0299
Admissions: (425)895-4438
Fax: (425)558-0299
E-mail: admissions@digipen.edu
Web Site: http://www.digipen.edu/
President/CEO: Claude Comair
Admissions: Angela Kugler
Financial Aid: Kimberly King
Type: Comprehensive **Sex:** Coed **% Accepted:** 33 **Admission Plans:** Deferred Admission **Application Deadline:** Rolling **Application Fee:** $35.00 **H.S. Requirements:** High school diploma required; GED accepted **Costs Per Year:** Application fee: $35. One-time mandatory fee: $150. Tuition: $20,600 full-time, $515 per semester hour part-time. Mandatory fees: $160 full-time, $80 per term part-time. Full-time tuition and fees vary according to course load, location, and program. Part-time tuition and fees vary according to course load, location, and program. **Scholarships:** Available **Calendar System:** Semester, Summer Session Available **Faculty:** FT 43, PT 29 **Student-Faculty Ratio:** 12:1 **Exams:** SAT I or ACT. ACT essay used for admission. SAT essay used for admission. **Final Year or Final Semester Residency Requirement:** No **Library Holdings:** 7,044 **Credit Hours For Degree:** 142 semester credits, Bachelors **Professional Accreditation:** ACCSCT

EASTERN WASHINGTON UNIVERSITY
526 5th St.
Cheney, WA 99004-2431
Tel: (509)359-6200
Admissions: (509)359-6582
Fax: (509)359-4330
E-mail: admissions@mail.ewu.edu
Web Site: http://www.ewu.edu/
President/CEO: Dr. Rodolfo Arevalo
Admissions: Shannon Carr
Financial Aid: Bruce DeFrates
Type: Comprehensive **Sex:** Coed **Scores:** 82.3% SAT V 400+; 85.51% SAT M 400+; 53.24% ACT 18-23; 18.65% ACT 24-29 **% Accepted:** 82 **Admission Plans:** Deferred Admission **Application Deadline:** August 15 **Application Fee:** $50.00 **H.S. Requirements:** High school diploma or equivalent not required **Costs Per Year:** Application fee: $50. State resident tuition: $5340 full-time, $160 per credit hour part-time. Nonresident tuition: $14,058 full-time, $451 per credit hour part-time. Mandatory fees: $532 full-time, $532.14 per year part-time. Full-time tuition and fees vary according to course load and program. Part-time tuition and fees vary according to course load and program. College room and board: $7080. Room and board charges vary according to board plan and housing facility. **Scholarships:** Available **Calendar System:** Quarter, Summer Session Available **Enrollment:** FT 8,631, PT 1,288, Grad FT 904, Grad PT 479 **Faculty:** FT 412, PT 207

Student-Faculty Ratio: 21:1 **Exams:** SAT I or ACT. **% Receiving Financial Aid:** 55 **% Residing in College-Owned, -Operated, or -Affiliated Housing:** 16 **Credit Hours For Degree:** 180 quarter hours, Bachelors **ROTC:** Army **Professional Accreditation:** AACSB, ABET, AACN, ACA, ADA, ACSP, AOTA, APTA, ASLHA, CSWE, NASM, NCATE, NLN, NRPA, NCCU **Intercollegiate Athletics:** Basketball M & W; Cross-Country Running M & W; Football M; Golf W; Soccer W; Tennis M & W; Track and Field M & W; Volleyball W

EDMONDS COMMUNITY COLLEGE
20000 68th Ave. West
Lynnwood, WA 98036
Tel: (425)640-1500
Admissions: (425)640-1853
Fax: (425)640-1159
E-mail: nanci.froemming@edcc.edu
Web Site: http://www.edcc.edu/
President/CEO: Dr. Jack Oharah
Admissions: Nancy Froemming
Type: Two-Year College **Sex:** Coed **Affiliation:** Washington State Board for Community and Technical Colleges **% Accepted:** 100 **Admission Plans:** Open Admission; Early Admission; Deferred Admission **Application Deadline:** Rolling **Application Fee:** $18.00 **H.S. Requirements:** High school diploma or equivalent not required **Costs Per Year:** Application fee: $18. State resident tuition: $3128 full-time, $80.60 per credit hour part-time. Nonresident tuition: $8348 full-time, $252.60 per credit hour part-time. Full-time tuition varies according to course load. Part-time tuition varies according to course load. **Scholarships:** Available **Calendar System:** Quarter, Summer Session Available **Enrollment:** FT 3,656, PT 4,779 **Faculty:** FT 145, PT 335 **Student-Faculty Ratio:** 21:1 **Library Holdings:** 47,947 **Credit Hours For Degree:** 90 credits, Associates **Professional Accreditation:** NCCU **Intercollegiate Athletics:** Baseball M; Basketball M & W; Golf M & W; Soccer M & W; Softball W; Volleyball W

EVEREST COLLEGE
120 Northeast 136th Ave.
Ste. 130
Vancouver, WA 98684
Tel: (360)254-3282
E-mail: rschiffhauer@cci.edu
Web Site: http://www.everest.edu/
President/CEO: Edward Yakimchick
Admissions: Renee Schiffhauer
Type: Two-Year College **Sex:** Coed **Application Deadline:** Rolling **H.S. Requirements:** High school diploma required; GED accepted **Calendar System:** Quarter **Faculty:** FT 8, PT 17 **Student-Faculty Ratio:** 14:1 **Professional Accreditation:** ACICS

EVERETT COMMUNITY COLLEGE
2000 Tower St.
Everett, WA 98201-1327
Tel: (425)388-9100
Admissions: (425)388-9219
Fax: (425)388-9173
E-mail: admissions@everettcc.edu
Web Site: http://www.everettcc.edu/
President/CEO: Dr. David Beyer
Admissions: Linda Baca
Type: Two-Year College **Sex:** Coed **Affiliation:** Washington State Board for Community and Technical Colleges **Admission Plans:** Open Admission; Early Admission; Deferred Admission **Application Deadline:** Rolling **Application Fee:** $0.00 **H.S. Requirements:** High school diploma or equivalent not required. For cosmetology, nursing, criminal justice, and fire science programs: High school diploma required; GED accepted **Scholarships:** Available **Calendar System:** Quarter, Summer Session Available **Enrollment:** FT 3,707, PT 3,855 **Faculty:** FT 135, PT 234 **Student-Faculty Ratio:** 24:1 **Exams:** Other. **Credit Hours For Degree:** 90 quarter hours, Associates **Professional Accreditation:** NLN, NCCU **Intercollegiate Athletics:** Baseball M; Basketball M & W; Cross-Country Running M & W; Soccer M & W; Softball W; Volleyball W

THE EVERGREEN STATE COLLEGE
2700 Evergreen Parkway, NW
Olympia, WA 98505
Tel: (360)867-6000
Admissions: (360)867-6170
Fax: (360)867-6577
E-mail: admissions@evergreen.edu
Web Site: http://www.evergreen.edu/
President/CEO: Dr. Thomas Les Purce
Admissions: Doug P. Scrima
Type: Comprehensive **Sex:** Coed **Affiliation:** Washington State Public Baccalaureate Institution **Scores:** 97% SAT V 400+; 92% SAT M 400+; 37% ACT 18-23; 45% ACT 24-29 **% Accepted:** 95 **Admission Plans:** Preferred Admission; Deferred Admission **Application Deadline:** Rolling **Application Fee:** $50.00 **H.S. Requirements:** High school diploma required; GED accepted **Costs Per Year:** Application fee: $50. State resident tuition: $5412 full-time, $180.40 per credit hour part-time. Nonresident tuition: $16,440 full-time, $547.60 per credit hour part-time. Mandatory fees: $547 full-time, $7.85 per credit hour part-time, $61 per term part-time. Full-time tuition and fees vary according to location. Part-time tuition and fees vary according to course load and location. College room and board: $8052. College room only: $5454. Room and board charges vary according to board plan, housing facility, location, and student level. **Scholarships:** Available **Calendar System:** Quarter, Summer Session Available **Enrollment:** FT 4,119, PT 432, Grad FT 152, Grad PT 188 **Faculty:** FT 169, PT 74 **Student-Faculty Ratio:** 23:1 **Exams:** SAT I or ACT. ACT essay not being used. SAT essay not being used. **% Receiving Financial Aid:** 56 **% Residing in College-Owned, -Operated, or -Affiliated Housing:** 21 **Final Year or Final Semester Residency Requirement:** No **Library Holdings:** 480,716 **Credit Hours For Degree:** 180 quarter hours, Bachelors **Professional Accreditation:** NCCU **Intercollegiate Athletics:** Basketball M & W; Crew M & W; Cross-Country Running M & W; Soccer M & W; Track and Field M & W; Volleyball W

GONZAGA UNIVERSITY
502 East Boone Ave.
Spokane, WA 99258
Tel: (509)328-4220; Free: 800-322-2584
Admissions: (509)313-6591
Fax: (509)324-5780
E-mail: admissions@gonzaga.edu
Web Site: http://www.gonzaga.edu/
President/CEO: Dr. Thayne McCulloh
Admissions: Julie McCulloh
Financial Aid: James White
Type: Comprehensive **Sex:** Coed **Affiliation:** Roman Catholic **Scores:** 100% SAT V 400+; 99.51% SAT M 400+; 15.35% ACT 18-23; 65.84% ACT 24-29 **% Accepted:** 78 **Admission Plans:** Early Action; Deferred Admission **Application Deadline:** February 1 **Application Fee:** $50.00 **H.S. Requirements:** High school diploma required; GED not accepted **Scholarships:** Available **Calendar System:** Semester, Summer Session Available **Enrollment:** FT 4,604, PT 125, Grad FT 837, Grad PT 2,071 **Faculty:** FT 393, PT 334 **Student-Faculty Ratio:** 10:1 **Exams:** SAT I or ACT. **% Receiving Financial Aid:** 58 **% Residing in College-Owned, -Operated, or -Affiliated Housing:** 59 **Library Holdings:** 305,517 **Credit Hours For Degree:** 128 credit hours, Bachelors **ROTC:** Army **Professional Accreditation:** AACSB, ABET, AAMFT, AACN, AANA, ABA, ACA, ACIPE, AALS, ATS, NCATE, NCCU **Intercollegiate Athletics:** Baseball M; Basketball M & W; Crew M & W; Cross-Country Running M & W; Golf M & W; Skiing (Cross-Country) M & W; Skiing (Downhill) M & W; Soccer M & W; Tennis M & W; Track and Field M & W; Volleyball W

GRAYS HARBOR COLLEGE
1620 Edward P Smith Dr.
Aberdeen, WA 98520-7599
Tel: (360)532-9020
Fax: (360)538-4293
Web Site: http://www.ghc.ctc.edu/
President/CEO: Dr. Edward J. Brewster
Admissions: Brenda Dell
Financial Aid: Ben Beus
Type: Two-Year College **Sex:** Coed **Affiliation:** Washington State Board for Community and Technical Colleges **Admission Plans:** Open Admission; Early Admission **Application Deadline:** Rolling **Application Fee:** $0.00 **H.S. Requirements:** High school diploma required; GED accepted **Costs Per Year:** Application fee: $0. State resident tuition: $2913 full-time, $80.60 per credit hour part-time. Nonresident tuition: $8133 full-time, $252.60 per

credit hour part-time. Mandatory fees: $225 full-time, $5.50 per credit hour part-time. **Scholarships:** Available **Calendar System:** Quarter, Summer Session Available **Enrollment:** FT 1,183, PT 1,147 **Faculty:** FT 66, PT 90 **Student-Faculty Ratio:** 16:1 **Library Holdings:** 40,000 **Credit Hours For Degree:** 93 credits, Associates **Professional Accreditation:** NLN, NCCU **Intercollegiate Athletics:** Baseball M; Basketball M & W; Golf M & W; Softball W

GREEN RIVER COMMUNITY COLLEGE
12401 Southeast 320th St.
Auburn, WA 98092-3699
Tel: (253)833-9111
Fax: (253)288-3454
Web Site: http://www.greenriver.edu/
President/CEO: Richard A. Rutkowski
Admissions: Peggy Morgan
Type: Two-Year College **Sex:** Coed **Affiliation:** Washington State Board for Community and Technical Colleges **Admission Plans:** Open Admission; Early Admission; Deferred Admission **Application Deadline:** Rolling **Application Fee:** $0.00 **H.S. Requirements:** High school diploma required; GED accepted. For nursing, physical therapy, and occupational therapy programs: High school diploma required; GED not accepted **Costs Per Year:** Application fee: $0. State resident tuition: $2925 full-time, $81 per credit hour part-time. Nonresident tuition: $3345 full-time, $94 per credit hour part-time. Mandatory fees: $398 full-time, $12 per credit hour part-time, $120. Full-time tuition and fees vary according to course load. Part-time tuition and fees vary according to course load. **Scholarships:** Available **Calendar System:** Quarter, Summer Session Available **Enrollment:** FT 5,056, PT 3,149 **Faculty:** FT 134, PT 302 **Student-Faculty Ratio:** 23:1 **Final Year or Final Semester Residency Requirement:** No **Library Holdings:** 32,500 **Credit Hours For Degree:** 90 quarter hours, Associates **Professional Accreditation:** AOTA, NCCU **Intercollegiate Athletics:** Baseball M; Basketball M & W; Golf M & W; Soccer W; Softball W; Tennis M & W; Volleyball W

HERITAGE UNIVERSITY
3240 Fort Rd.
Toppenish, WA 98948-9599
Tel: (509)865-8500
Fax: (509)865-4469
E-mail: garcia_l@heritage.edu
Web Site: http://www.heritage.edu/
President/CEO: Kathleen Ross
Admissions: Leticia Garcia
Financial Aid: Norberto Espindola
Type: Comprehensive **Sex:** Coed **% Accepted:** 60 **Admission Plans:** Open Admission; Early Admission; Early Decision Plan; Deferred Admission **Application Deadline:** Rolling **Application Fee:** $0.00 **H.S. Requirements:** High school diploma required; GED accepted **Scholarships:** Available **Calendar System:** Semester, Summer Session Available **Enrollment:** FT 568, PT 238 **Faculty:** FT 47, PT 140 **Student-Faculty Ratio:** 11:1 **Exams:** SAT I or ACT. **% Receiving Financial Aid:** 54 **Library Holdings:** 47,500 **Credit Hours For Degree:** 60 semester hours, Associates; 126 semester hours, Bachelors **Professional Accreditation:** CSWE, NCCU

HIGHLINE COMMUNITY COLLEGE
2400 South 240th St.
Des Moines, WA 98198-9800
Tel: (206)878-3710
Fax: (206)870-3782
Web Site: http://www.highline.edu/
President/CEO: Dr. Jack Bermingham
Admissions: Laura Westergard
Type: Two-Year College **Sex:** Coed **Affiliation:** Washington State Board for Community and Technical Colleges **% Accepted:** 100 **Admission Plans:** Open Admission **Application Deadline:** Rolling **Application Fee:** $26.00 **H.S. Requirements:** High school diploma or equivalent not required. For nursing, allied health programs: High school diploma required; GED accepted **Costs Per Year:** Application fee: $26. Area resident tuition: $87 per credit part-time. State resident tuition: $3135 full-time, $105 per credit part-time. Nonresident tuition: $3771 full-time, $259 per credit part-time. Mandatory fees: $75 full-time. Full-time tuition and fees vary according to course load. Part-time tuition varies according to course load. **Scholarships:** Available **Calendar System:** Quarter, Summer Session Available **Enrollment:** FT 3,722, PT 3,003 **Faculty:** FT 144, PT 216 **Student-Faculty Ratio:** 22:1 **Final Year or Final Semester Residency Requirement:** No **Library Holdings:** 57,678 **Credit Hours For Degree:** 90 quarter hours, Associates **ROTC:** Army, Air Force **Professional Accreditation:** AAMAE, CARC, NLN, NCCU **Intercollegiate Athletics:** Basketball M & W; Cross-Country Running M & W; Soccer M & W; Softball W; Track and Field M & W; Volleyball W; Wrestling M

ITT TECHNICAL INSTITUTE (EVERETT)
1615 75th St. SW
Everett, WA 98203
Tel: (425)583-0200
Admissions: (425)583-0200
Web Site: http://www.itt-tech.edu/
President/CEO: Dean Kempter
Type: Two-Year College **Sex:** Coed **Affiliation:** ITT Educational Services, Inc. **Professional Accreditation:** ACICS

ITT TECHNICAL INSTITUTE (SEATTLE)
12720 Gateway Dr., Ste. 100
Seattle, WA 98168-3333
Tel: (206)244-3300; Free: 800-422-2029
Web Site: http://www.itt-tech.edu/
President/CEO: Patricia Corrales-Toy
Type: Two-Year College **Sex:** Coed **Affiliation:** ITT Educational Services, Inc. **H.S. Requirements:** High school diploma required; GED accepted **Scholarships:** Available **Calendar System:** Quarter, Summer Session Not available **Professional Accreditation:** ACICS

ITT TECHNICAL INSTITUTE (SPOKANE VALLEY)
13518 East Indiana Ave.
Spokane Valley, WA 99212-2682
Tel: (509)926-2900; Free: 800-777-8324
Web Site: http://www.itt-tech.edu/
President/CEO: William King
Financial Aid: Helen J. Horton
Type: Two-Year College **Sex:** Coed **Affiliation:** ITT Educational Services, Inc. **H.S. Requirements:** High school diploma required; GED accepted **Scholarships:** Available **Calendar System:** Quarter, Summer Session Not available **Credit Hours For Degree:** 96 credit hours, Associates; 180 credit hours, Bachelors **Professional Accreditation:** ACICS

LAKE WASHINGTON TECHNICAL COLLEGE
11605 132nd Ave. NE
Kirkland, WA 98034-8506
Tel: (425)739-8100
E-mail: info@lwtc.edu
Web Site: http://www.lwtc.edu/
President/CEO: Dr. Sharon McGavick
Admissions: Shawn Miller
Type: Two-Year College **Sex:** Coed **Affiliation:** Washington State Board for Community and Technical Colleges **Admission Plans:** Open Admission; Early Admission **Application Deadline:** Rolling **Application Fee:** $0.00 **H.S. Requirements:** High school diploma or equivalent not required. For nursing, dental hygiene, medical assistant, dental assistant programs: High school diploma required; GED accepted **Costs Per Year:** Application fee: $0. State resident tuition: $87.80 per credit part-time. Nonresident tuition: $259.80 per credit part-time. **Scholarships:** Available **Calendar System:** Quarter, Summer Session Available **Library Holdings:** 18,300 **Credit Hours For Degree:** 90 credits, Associates **Professional Accreditation:** AAMAE, ACF, ADA, NCCU

LOWER COLUMBIA COLLEGE
PO Box 3010
Longview, WA 98632-0310
Tel: (360)442-2000
Admissions: (360)442-2300
Fax: (360)442-2109
E-mail: registration@lowercolumbia.edu
Web Site: http://www.lcc.ctc.edu/
President/CEO: Dr. James L. McLaughlin
Admissions: Mary Harding
Type: Two-Year College **Sex:** Coed **Affiliation:** Washington State Board for Community and Technical Colleges **Admission Plans:** Open Admission **Ap-**

plication Deadline: Rolling **Application Fee:** $14.35 **H.S. Requirements:** High school diploma or equivalent not required **Costs Per Year:** Application fee: $14.35. One-time mandatory fee: $16. State resident tuition: $3145 full-time, $81 per credit part-time. Nonresident tuition: $3670 full-time, $104 per credit part-time. Mandatory fees: $290 full-time, $7.35 per credit part-time, $7.35. Full-time tuition and fees vary according to course load and reciprocity agreements. Part-time tuition and fees vary according to course load and reciprocity agreements. **Scholarships:** Available **Calendar System:** Quarter, Summer Session Available **Enrollment:** FT 2,012, PT 2,233 **Faculty:** FT 74, PT 139 **Student-Faculty Ratio:** 24:1 **Library Holdings:** 40,674 **Credit Hours For Degree:** 90 credits, Associates **Professional Accreditation:** AAMAE, NLN, NCCU **Intercollegiate Athletics:** Baseball M; Basketball M & W; Volleyball W

NORTH SEATTLE COMMUNITY COLLEGE
9600 College Way North
Seattle, WA 98103-3599
Tel: (206)527-3600
Admissions: (206)527-3663
Fax: (206)527-3635
E-mail: arrc@sccd.ctc.edu
Web Site: http://www.northseattle.edu/
President/CEO: Ronald H. LaFayette, EdD
Admissions: Betsy Abts
Type: Two-Year College **Sex:** Coed **Affiliation:** Seattle Community College District **% Accepted:** 100 **Admission Plans:** Open Admission; Early Admission; Deferred Admission **Application Deadline:** Rolling **Application Fee:** $0.00 **H.S. Requirements:** High school diploma or equivalent not required **Costs Per Year:** Application fee: $0. State resident tuition: $2925 full-time, $81 per credit part-time. Nonresident tuition: $8145 full-time, $253 per credit part-time. Mandatory fees: $285 full-time. Full-time tuition and fees vary according to course load. Part-time tuition varies according to course load. **Scholarships:** Available **Calendar System:** Quarter, Summer Session Available **Enrollment:** FT 1,823, PT 4,461 **Faculty:** FT 100, PT 203 **Student-Faculty Ratio:** 20:1 **Library Holdings:** 52,496 **Credit Hours For Degree:** 90 credits, Associates **ROTC:** Army **Professional Accreditation:** AAMAE, ACF, NCCU **Intercollegiate Athletics:** Basketball M & W

NORTHWEST AVIATION COLLEGE
506 23rd, NE
Auburn, WA 98002
Tel: (253)854-4960; Free: 800-246-4960
Fax: (253)931-0768
E-mail: spratt@afsmac.com
Web Site: http://www.afsnac.com/
Admissions: Shawn Pratt
Type: Two-Year College **Sex:** Coed **Application Deadline:** Rolling **Application Fee:** $50.00 **H.S. Requirements:** High school diploma required; GED accepted **Scholarships:** Available **Calendar System:** Quarter, Summer Session Available **Credit Hours For Degree:** 90 quarter hours, Associates **Professional Accreditation:** ACCSCT

NORTHWEST COLLEGE OF ART
16301 Creative Dr., NE
Poulsbo, WA 98370
Tel: (360)779-9993; Free: 800-769-ARTS
Fax: (360)779-9933
E-mail: mstoddard@nca.edu
Web Site: http://www.nca.edu/
President/CEO: Kim Perigard
Admissions: Mark Stoddard
Financial Aid: Kim Y. Perigard
Type: Four-Year College **Sex:** Coed **Admission Plans:** Deferred Admission **Application Deadline:** June 1 **Application Fee:** $50.00 **H.S. Requirements:** High school diploma required; GED accepted **Costs Per Year:** Application fee: $50. Tuition: $17,100 full-time, $775 per credit part-time. Mandatory fees: $100 full-time, $100 per term part-time. Full-time tuition and fees vary according to course load. Part-time tuition and fees vary according to course load. **Scholarships:** Available **Calendar System:** Semester, Summer Session Available **Credit Hours For Degree:** 120 credits, Bachelors **Professional Accreditation:** ACCSCT

NORTHWEST INDIAN COLLEGE
2522 Kwina Rd.
Bellingham, WA 98226
Tel: (360)676-2772
Fax: (360)738-0136
E-mail: cbogby@nwic.edu
Web Site: http://www.nwic.edu/
President/CEO: Cheryl Crazy Bull
Type: Two-Year College **Sex:** Coed **Admission Plans:** Open Admission; Preferred Admission **Application Fee:** $25.00 **Scholarships:** Available **Calendar System:** Quarter, Summer Session Available **Faculty:** FT 23, PT 40 **Credit Hours For Degree:** 92 credits, Associates **Professional Accreditation:** NCCU **Intercollegiate Athletics:** Basketball M & W

NORTHWEST SCHOOL OF WOODEN BOATBUILDING
42 North Water St.
Port Hadlock, WA 98339
Tel: (360)385-4948
Fax: (360)385-5089
E-mail: info@nwboatschool.org
Web Site: http://www.nwboatschool.org/
President/CEO: Bill Mahler
Type: Two-Year College **Sex:** Coed **Calendar System:** Semester **Professional Accreditation:** ACCSCT

NORTHWEST UNIVERSITY
5520 108th Ave. NE
Kirkland, WA 98033
Tel: (425)822-8266; Free: 800-669-3781
Admissions: (425)889-5212
Fax: (425)425-0148
E-mail: admissions@northwestu.edu
Web Site: http://www.northwestu.edu/
President/CEO: Joseph Castleberry, EdD
Admissions: Ben Thomas
Financial Aid: Lana J. Walter
Type: Comprehensive **Sex:** Coed **Affiliation:** Assemblies of God **Scores:** 93% SAT V 400+; 89% SAT M 400+; 45% ACT 18-23; 29% ACT 24-29 **% Accepted:** 74 **Admission Plans:** Early Action; Deferred Admission **Application Deadline:** July 15 **Application Fee:** $30.00 **H.S. Requirements:** High school diploma required; GED accepted. Transfer students with 30 semester or 45 quarter credits completed can have their HS transcript requirement waived. **Costs Per Year:** Application fee: $30. Comprehensive fee: $29,374 includes full-time tuition ($22,360), mandatory fees ($290), and college room and board ($6724). Full-time tuition and fees vary according to class time and program. Room and board charges vary according to board plan and housing facility. Part-time tuition: $930 per credit hour. Part-time tuition varies according to course load. **Scholarships:** Available **Calendar System:** Semester, Summer Session Available **Enrollment:** FT 972, PT 174, Grad FT 160, Grad PT 77 **Faculty:** FT 54, PT 54 **Student-Faculty Ratio:** 17:1 **Exams:** SAT I or ACT. **% Receiving Financial Aid:** 77 **% Residing in College-Owned, -Operated, or -Affiliated Housing:** 55 **Library Holdings:** 100,356 **Credit Hours For Degree:** 62 credit hours, Associates; 125 credit hours, Bachelors **ROTC:** Army **Professional Accreditation:** AACN, ACBSP, NCCU **Intercollegiate Athletics:** Basketball M & W; Cross-Country Running M & W; Soccer M & W; Track and Field M & W; Volleyball W

OLYMPIC COLLEGE
1600 Chester Ave.
Bremerton, WA 98337-1699
Tel: (360)792-6050; Free: 800-259-6718
Admissions: (360)475-7128
Fax: (360)792-2135
E-mail: jfyllingness@olympic.edu
Web Site: http://www.olympic.edu/
President/CEO: Dr. David Mitchell
Admissions: Jennifer Fyllingness
Type: Two-Year College **Sex:** Coed **Affiliation:** Washington State Board for Community and Technical Colleges **% Accepted:** 100 **Admission Plans:** Open Admission; Early Admission; Deferred Admission **Application Deadline:** Rolling **Application Fee:** $0.00 **H.S. Requirements:** High school diploma or equivalent not required. For nursing program, medical office assistant program: High school diploma or equivalent not required **Costs Per Year:** Application fee: $0. State resident tuition: $2925 full-time, $81 per quarter hour part-time. Nonresident tuition: $3315 full-time, $94 per credit part-time. Mandatory fees: $240 full-time, $4.50 per credit part-time, $60.50 per term part-time. Full-time tuition and fees vary according to course level,

course load, and degree level. Part-time tuition and fees vary according to course level, course load, and degree level. **Scholarships:** Available **Calendar System:** Quarter, Summer Session Available **Enrollment:** FT 3,930, PT 3,606 **Faculty:** FT 116, PT 382 **Student-Faculty Ratio:** 21:1 **Library Holdings:** 60,000 **Credit Hours For Degree:** 90 credits, Associates; 180 credits, Bachelors **Professional Accreditation:** NLN, NCCU **Intercollegiate Athletics:** Baseball M; Basketball M & W; Cross-Country Running M & W; Golf M & W; Soccer M & W; Softball W; Volleyball W

PACIFIC LUTHERAN UNIVERSITY
Tacoma, WA 98447
Tel: (253)531-6900; Free: 800-274-6758
Admissions: (253)535-7151
Fax: (253)536-5136
E-mail: admission@plu.edu
Web Site: http://www.plu.edu/
President/CEO: Dr. Loren J. Anderson
Admissions: Karl Stumo
Financial Aid: Katherine Walker Loffer
Type: Comprehensive **Sex:** Coed **Affiliation:** Evangelical Lutheran Church in America **Scores:** 98.52% SAT V 400+; 96.49% SAT M 400+; 26.25% ACT 18-23; 51.88% ACT 24-29 **% Accepted:** 78 **Admission Plans:** Early Admission; Deferred Admission **Application Deadline:** Rolling **Application Fee:** $40.00 **H.S. Requirements:** High school diploma required; GED accepted **Costs Per Year:** Application fee: $40. Comprehensive fee: $36,700 includes full-time tuition ($28,100) and college room and board ($8600). College room only: $4140. Room and board charges vary according to board plan and housing facility. Part-time tuition: $880 per credit hour. **Scholarships:** Available **Calendar System:** 4-1-4, Summer Session Available **Enrollment:** FT 3,139, PT 166, Grad FT 159, Grad PT 117 **Student-Faculty Ratio:** 14:1 **Exams:** SAT I or ACT. **% Receiving Financial Aid:** 71 **% Residing in College-Owned, -Operated, or -Affiliated Housing:** 49 **Credit Hours For Degree:** 128 semester hours, Bachelors **ROTC:** Army **Professional Accreditation:** AACSB, ABET, AAMFT, AACN, CSWE, NASM, NCATE, NLN, NCCU **Intercollegiate Athletics:** Baseball M; Basketball M & W; Cheerleading M & W; Crew M & W; Cross-Country Running M & W; Football M; Golf M & W; Lacrosse M & W; Soccer M & W; Softball W; Swimming and Diving M & W; Tennis M & W; Track and Field M & W; Ultimate Frisbee M & W; Volleyball M & W

PENINSULA COLLEGE
1502 East Lauridsen Blvd.
Port Angeles, WA 98362-2779
Tel: (360)452-9277
Admissions: (360)417-6596
Fax: (360)457-8100
E-mail: admissions@pcadmin.ctc.edu
Web Site: http://www.pc.ctc.edu/
President/CEO: Dr. Thomas Keegan
Admissions: Pauline Marvin
Type: Two-Year College **Sex:** Coed **Affiliation:** Washington State Community and Technical Colleges **Admission Plans:** Open Admission **Application Deadline:** Rolling **Application Fee:** $0.00 **H.S. Requirements:** High school diploma or equivalent not required **Costs Per Year:** Application fee: $0. State resident tuition: $3012 full-time, $81 per credit hour part-time. Nonresident tuition: $3402 full-time, $94 per credit hour part-time. Mandatory fees: $87 full-time, $87 per year part-time. Full-time tuition and fees vary according to course load. Part-time tuition and fees vary according to course load. **Scholarships:** Available **Calendar System:** Quarter, Summer Session Available **Enrollment:** FT 1,835, PT 1,941 **Faculty:** FT 62, PT 122 **Student-Faculty Ratio:** 18:1 **Library Holdings:** 33,736 **Credit Hours For Degree:** 90 credits, Associates **Professional Accreditation:** NCCU **Intercollegiate Athletics:** Basketball M & W; Soccer M; Softball W

PIERCE COLLEGE AT FORT STEILACOOM
9401 Farwest Dr. SW
Lakewood, WA 98498
Tel: (253)964-6500
Web Site: http://www.pierce.ctc.edu/
President/CEO: Denise Yochum
Type: Two-Year College **Sex:** Coed **Calendar System:** Quarter

PIERCE COLLEGE AT PUYALLUP
1601 39th Ave. Southeast
Puyallup, WA 98374-2222
Tel: (253)840-8400
Fax: (253)840-8423
Web Site: http://www.pierce.ctc.edu/
President/CEO: Tana Hasart
Admissions: Cindy Burbank
Type: Two-Year College **Sex:** Coed **Affiliation:** Washington State Board for Community and Technical Colleges **Admission Plans:** Open Admission; Early Admission **Application Deadline:** Rolling **Application Fee:** $0.00 **H.S. Requirements:** High school diploma or equivalent not required. For international students, veterinary technology, dental hygiene programs: High school diploma required; GED accepted **Costs Per Year:** Application fee: $0. State resident tuition: $2628 full-time, $81 per quarter hour part-time. Nonresident tuition: $7812 full-time, $253 per quarter hour part-time. Mandatory fees: $909 full-time, $303 per term part-time. Full-time tuition and fees vary according to course load and location. Part-time tuition and fees vary according to course load and location. **Scholarships:** Available **Calendar System:** Quarter, Summer Session Available **Faculty:** FT 240, PT 350 **Library Holdings:** 55,000 **Credit Hours For Degree:** 90 quarter hours, Associates **ROTC:** Army **Professional Accreditation:** ADA, NCCU **Intercollegiate Athletics:** Baseball M; Basketball M & W; Soccer M; Softball W; Volleyball W

PIMA MEDICAL INSTITUTE
9709 Third Ave. NE
Ste. 400
Seattle, WA 98115
Tel: (206)322-6100; Free: 888-898-9048
Fax: (206)324-1985
Web Site: http://www.pmi.edu/
President/CEO: Carey Hochman
Type: Two-Year College **Sex:** Coed **Affiliation:** Vocational Training Institutes, Inc. **Scholarships:** Available **Calendar System:** Miscellaneous **Exams:** Other. **Professional Accreditation:** ABHES, JRCERT

RENTON TECHNICAL COLLEGE
3000 NE Fourth St.
Renton, WA 98056
Tel: (425)235-2352
Fax: (425)235-7832
Web Site: http://www.rtc.edu/
President/CEO: Steve Hanson
Admissions: Becky Riverman
Financial Aid: Aubrey Durbin
Type: Two-Year College **Sex:** Coed **Affiliation:** Washington State Board for Community and Technical Colleges **Admission Plans:** Open Admission; Early Admission **Application Deadline:** Rolling **Application Fee:** $25.00 **H.S. Requirements:** High school diploma or equivalent not required **Scholarships:** Available **Calendar System:** Quarter, Summer Session Available **Enrollment:** FT 4,019, PT 5,282 **Faculty:** FT 84, PT 198 **Student-Faculty Ratio:** 15:1 **Library Holdings:** 12,876 **Credit Hours For Degree:** 100 quarter hours, Associates **Professional Accreditation:** ARCEST, ACF, ADA, NCCU

SAINT MARTIN'S UNIVERSITY
5300 Pacific Ave., SE
Lacey, WA 98503
Tel: (360)491-4700; Free: 800-368-8803
Admissions: (360)438-4596
Fax: (360)459-4124
E-mail: admissions@stmartin.edu
Web Site: http://www.stmartin.edu/
President/CEO: Dr. Roy F. Heynderickx
Admissions: Matt Gruhler
Financial Aid: Rachelle Shahan-Riehl
Type: Comprehensive **Sex:** Coed **Affiliation:** Roman Catholic **Scores:** 89% SAT V 400+; 86% SAT M 400+; 30% ACT 18-23; 22% ACT 24-29 **% Accepted:** 78 **Application Fee:** $35.00 **H.S. Requirements:** High school diploma required; GED accepted **Costs Per Year:** Application fee: $35. Comprehensive fee: $35,062 includes full-time tuition ($26,100), mandatory fees ($302), and college room and board ($8660). College room only: $4290. Full-time tuition and fees vary according to location. Room and board charges vary according to board plan. Part-time tuition: $870 per credit hour. Part-time tuition varies according to course load and location. **Scholarships:** Available **Calendar System:** Semester, Summer Session Available **Enroll-**

ment: FT 1,053, PT 306, Grad FT 216, Grad PT 112 **Faculty:** FT 78, PT 114 **Student-Faculty Ratio:** 12:1 **Exams:** SAT I or ACT. ACT essay used for admission. SAT essay used for admission. **% Receiving Financial Aid:** 81 **% Residing in College-Owned, -Operated, or -Affiliated Housing:** 31 **Final Year or Final Semester Residency Requirement:** Yes **Library Holdings:** 86,461 **Credit Hours For Degree:** 64 semester credits, Associates; 128 semester credits, Bachelors **ROTC:** Army, Air Force **Professional Accreditation:** ABET, NCCU, TEAC **Intercollegiate Athletics:** Baseball M; Basketball M & W; Cross-Country Running M & W; Golf M & W; Soccer M & W; Softball W; Track and Field M & W; Volleyball W

SEATTLE CENTRAL COMMUNITY COLLEGE
1701 Broadway
Seattle, WA 98122-2400
Tel: (206)587-3800
Web Site: http://www.seattlecentral.edu/
President/CEO: Mildred Ollee
Type: Two-Year College **Sex:** Coed **Affiliation:** Seattle Community College District System **Admission Plans:** Open Admission **Application Deadline:** Rolling **H.S. Requirements:** High school diploma or equivalent not required. For health programs: High school diploma required; GED accepted **Costs Per Year:** State resident tuition: $2628 full-time, $81 per credit part-time. Nonresident tuition: $7812 full-time, $253 per credit part-time. Mandatory fees: $145 full-time, $48 per term part-time. Part-time tuition and fees vary according to course load. College room and board: $8460. **Scholarships:** Available **Calendar System:** Quarter, Summer Session Available **Faculty:** FT 156, PT 282 **Library Holdings:** 56,338 **Credit Hours For Degree:** 90 credits, Associates **ROTC:** Army, Navy, Air Force **Professional Accreditation:** ACF, COptA, CARC, NLN, NCCU

SEATTLE PACIFIC UNIVERSITY
3307 Third Ave. West
Seattle, WA 98119-1997
Tel: (206)281-2000; Free: 800-366-3344
Admissions: (206)281-2021
E-mail: admissions@spu.edu
Web Site: http://www.spu.edu/
President/CEO: Philip Eaton
Admissions: Jobe Korb-Nice
Financial Aid: Jordan Grant
Type: Comprehensive **Sex:** Coed **Affiliation:** Free Methodist **Scores:** 97.89% SAT V 400+; 97.9% SAT M 400+; 32.63% ACT 18-23; 49.12% ACT 24-29 **% Accepted:** 93 **Admission Plans:** Early Admission; Early Action **Application Deadline:** February 1 **Application Fee:** $45.00 **H.S. Requirements:** High school diploma required; GED accepted **Costs Per Year:** Application fee: $45. Comprehensive fee: $36,354 includes full-time tuition ($27,450), mandatory fees ($360), and college room and board ($8544). College room only: $4659. Room and board charges vary according to board plan and housing facility. Part-time tuition: $764 per credit. Part-time tuition varies according to course load. **Scholarships:** Available **Calendar System:** Quarter, Summer Session Available **Enrollment:** FT 2,891, PT 125, Grad FT 312, Grad PT 672 **Faculty:** FT 191, PT 160 **Student-Faculty Ratio:** 14:1 **Exams:** SAT I or ACT. **% Receiving Financial Aid:** 67 **% Residing in College-Owned, -Operated, or -Affiliated Housing:** 54 **Final Year or Final Semester Residency Requirement:** Yes **Library Holdings:** 212,247 **Credit Hours For Degree:** 180 credits, Bachelors **ROTC:** Army, Navy, Air Force **Professional Accreditation:** AACSB, ABET, AAMFT, AACN, AAFCS, NASM, NCATE, NCCU **Intercollegiate Athletics:** Basketball M & W; Crew M & W; Cross-Country Running M & W; Gymnastics W; Soccer M & W; Track and Field M & W; Volleyball W

SEATTLE UNIVERSITY
902 12th Ave., PO Box 222000
Seattle, WA 98122-1090
Tel: (206)296-6000; Free: 800-426-7123
Admissions: (206)296-2000
Fax: (206)296-5656
E-mail: admissions@seattleu.edu
Web Site: http://www.seattleu.edu/
President/CEO: Fr. Stephen V. Sundborg
Admissions: Melore Nielsen
Financial Aid: Janet Cantelon
Type: Comprehensive **Sex:** Coed **Affiliation:** Roman Catholic **Scores:** 100% SAT V 400+; 100% SAT M 400+; 27.5% ACT 18-23; 51% ACT 24-29 **% Accepted:** 66 **Admission Plans:** Early Action; Deferred Admission **Application Deadline:** Rolling **Application Fee:** $50.00 **H.S. Requirements:** High school diploma required; GED accepted **Costs Per Year:** Application fee: $50. Comprehensive fee: $38,145 includes full-time tuition ($29,340) and college room and board ($8805). College room only: $5473. Full-time tuition varies according to course load. Room and board charges vary according to board plan. Part-time tuition: $652 per credit hour. Part-time tuition varies according to course load. **Scholarships:** Available **Calendar System:** Quarter, Summer Session Available **Enrollment:** FT 4,062, PT 244, Grad FT 1,570, Grad PT 1,875 **Faculty:** FT 435, PT 243 **Student-Faculty Ratio:** 13:1 **Exams:** SAT I or ACT. SAT essay used for admission. SAT essay used as a validity check on application essay. **% Receiving Financial Aid:** 63 **% Residing in College-Owned, -Operated, or -Affiliated Housing:** 39 **Library Holdings:** 258,540 **Credit Hours For Degree:** 180 credit hours, Bachelors **ROTC:** Army, Air Force **Professional Accreditation:** AACSB, ABET, AACN, ABA, AALS, ATS, JRCEDMS, NASPAA, NCATE, NLN, NCCU **Intercollegiate Athletics:** Archery M & W; Baseball M & W; Basketball M & W; Cheerleading M & W; Crew M & W; Cross-Country Running M & W; Golf M & W; Riflery M & W; Skiing (Downhill) M & W; Soccer M & W; Softball W; Swimming and Diving M & W; Track and Field M & W; Volleyball M & W; Water Polo M & W

SHORELINE COMMUNITY COLLEGE
16101 Greenwood Ave. North
Shoreline, WA 98133-5696
Tel: (206)546-4101
Admissions: (206)546-4581
Fax: (206)546-4599
Web Site: http://www.shore.ctc.edu/
President/CEO: Lee Lambert
Admissions: Chris Linebarger
Financial Aid: Ted Haase
Type: Two-Year College **Sex:** Coed **Affiliation:** Washington State Board for Community and Technical Colleges **Admission Plans:** Open Admission **Application Deadline:** Rolling **H.S. Requirements:** High school diploma or equivalent not required **Scholarships:** Available **Calendar System:** Quarter, Summer Session Available **Faculty:** FT 155, PT 260 **Student-Faculty Ratio:** 21:1 **Exams:** Other. **Library Holdings:** 79,554 **Credit Hours For Degree:** 90 credits, Associates **Professional Accreditation:** ADA, AHIMA, NAACLS, NLN, NCCU **Intercollegiate Athletics:** Archery M & W; Baseball M; Basketball M & W; Cross-Country Running M & W; Soccer M & W; Softball W; Tennis M & W; Volleyball W

SKAGIT VALLEY COLLEGE
2405 College Way
Mount Vernon, WA 98273-5899
Tel: (360)416-7600
Fax: (360)416-7890
E-mail: karenmarie.bade@skagit.edu
Web Site: http://www.skagit.edu/
President/CEO: Dr. Gary Tollefson
Admissions: Karen Marie Bade
Type: Two-Year College **Sex:** Coed **Affiliation:** Washington State Board for Community and Technical Colleges **% Accepted:** 60 **Admission Plans:** Open Admission; Deferred Admission **Application Deadline:** Rolling **Application Fee:** $0.00 **H.S. Requirements:** High school diploma or equivalent not required **Scholarships:** Available **Calendar System:** Quarter, Summer Session Available **Student-Faculty Ratio:** 22:1 **% Residing in College-Owned, -Operated, or -Affiliated Housing:** 1 **Library Holdings:** 78,631 **Credit Hours For Degree:** 90 credits, Associates **Professional Accreditation:** ACF, NLN, NCCU **Intercollegiate Athletics:** Baseball M; Basketball M & W; Cross-Country Running M & W; Golf M & W; Soccer M & W; Softball W; Tennis M & W; Volleyball W

SOUTH PUGET SOUND COMMUNITY COLLEGE
2011 Mottman Rd., SW
Olympia, WA 98512-6292
Tel: (360)754-7711
Fax: (360)664-9407
E-mail: lsharp@spcc.ctc.edu
Web Site: http://www.spscc.ctc.edu/
President/CEO: Dr. Gerald Pumphrey
Admissions: Lyn Sharp
Type: Two-Year College **Sex:** Coed **Affiliation:** Washington State Board for

Community and Technical Colleges **% Accepted:** 100 **Admission Plans:** Open Admission; Early Admission; Deferred Admission **Application Deadline:** Rolling **Application Fee:** $0.00 **H.S. Requirements:** High school diploma or equivalent not required. For nursing program: High school diploma required; GED accepted **Costs Per Year:** Application fee: $0. State resident tuition: $2913 full-time, $84 per credit hour part-time. Nonresident tuition: $3390 full-time, $102 per credit hour part-time. Mandatory fees: $113 full-time. Full-time tuition and fees vary according to course load. Part-time tuition varies according to course load. **Scholarships:** Available **Calendar System:** Quarter, Summer Session Available **Enrollment:** FT 3,014, PT 2,603 **Faculty:** FT 95, PT 256 **Student-Faculty Ratio:** 22:1 **Library Holdings:** 70,879 **Credit Hours For Degree:** 90 credits, Associates **ROTC:** Army **Professional Accreditation:** AAMAE, ACF, ADA, NLN, NCCU **Intercollegiate Athletics:** Basketball M & W; Soccer M; Softball W

SOUTH SEATTLE COMMUNITY COLLEGE
6000 16th Ave., SW
Seattle, WA 98106-1499
Tel: (206)764-5300
E-mail: kimmanderb@sccd.ctc.edu
Web Site: http://southseattle.edu/
President/CEO: Gary Oertli
Admissions: Kim Manderbach
Type: Two-Year College **Sex:** Coed **Affiliation:** Seattle Community College District System **Admission Plans:** Open Admission; Early Admission **Application Deadline:** Rolling **Application Fee:** $0.00 **H.S. Requirements:** High school diploma or equivalent not required **Scholarships:** Available **Calendar System:** Quarter, Summer Session Available **Faculty:** FT 75, PT 210 **Library Holdings:** 34,000 **Credit Hours For Degree:** 90 credits, Associates **Professional Accreditation:** ACF, NCCU

SPOKANE COMMUNITY COLLEGE
1810 North Greene St.
Spokane, WA 99217-5399
Tel: (509)533-7000
Admissions: (509)434-5242
Fax: (509)533-8839
E-mail: mlee@ccs.spokane.edu
Web Site: http://www.scc.spokane.edu/
President/CEO: Dr. Joe Dunlap
Admissions: Brenda Burns
Type: Two-Year College **Sex:** Coed **Affiliation:** Washington State Board for Community and Technical Colleges **Admission Plans:** Open Admission; Early Admission; Deferred Admission **Application Deadline:** Rolling **Application Fee:** $15.00 **H.S. Requirements:** High school diploma required; GED accepted **Scholarships:** Available **Calendar System:** Quarter, Summer Session Available **Enrollment:** FT 4,393, PT 2,589 **Faculty:** FT 296, PT 213 **Student-Faculty Ratio:** 14:1 **Library Holdings:** 38,967 **Credit Hours For Degree:** 90 credits, Associates **ROTC:** Army **Professional Accreditation:** ARCEST, AAMAE, ACF, ADA, AHIMA, AOA, CARC, JRCECT, NLN, NCCU **Intercollegiate Athletics:** Baseball M; Basketball M & W; Cross-Country Running M & W; Soccer M & W; Softball W; Tennis M & W; Track and Field M & W; Volleyball W

SPOKANE FALLS COMMUNITY COLLEGE
3410 West Fort George Wright Dr.
Spokane, WA 99224-5288
Tel: (509)533-3500; Free: 888-509-7944
Admissions: (509)533-3401
Fax: (509)533-3433
Web Site: http://www.spokanefalls.edu/
President/CEO: Mark Palek, EdD
Type: Two-Year College **Sex:** Coed **Affiliation:** State Board for Washington Community and Technical Colleges **Admission Plans:** Open Admission; Early Admission; Deferred Admission **Application Deadline:** Rolling **Application Fee:** $15.00 **H.S. Requirements:** High school diploma required; GED accepted **Scholarships:** Available **Calendar System:** Quarter, Summer Session Available **Enrollment:** FT 3,974, PT 1,684 **Faculty:** FT 164, PT 381 **Student-Faculty Ratio:** 27:1 **Library Holdings:** 58,000 **Credit Hours For Degree:** 90 credits, Associates **ROTC:** Army **Professional Accreditation:** APTA, NCCU **Intercollegiate Athletics:** Baseball M; Basketball M & W; Cross-Country Running M & W; Soccer M & W; Softball W; Tennis M & W; Track and Field M & W; Volleyball W

TACOMA COMMUNITY COLLEGE
6501 South 19th St.
Tacoma, WA 98466
Tel: (253)566-5000
Admissions: (253)566-5325
Fax: (253)566-5376
Web Site: http://www.tacomacc.edu/
President/CEO: Dr. Pamela Transue
Type: Two-Year College **Sex:** Coed **Affiliation:** Washington State Board for Community and Technical Colleges **Admission Plans:** Open Admission; Early Admission **Application Deadline:** Rolling **H.S. Requirements:** High school diploma or equivalent not required. For allied health, law enforcement, nursing programs: High school diploma required; GED accepted **Costs Per Year:** State resident tuition: $2711 full-time, $83.75 per credit part-time. Nonresident tuition: $7895 full-time, $255.75 per credit part-time. Mandatory fees: $116 full-time, $2.25 per credit part-time, $15 per term part-time. Full-time tuition and fees vary according to course load. Part-time tuition and fees vary according to course load. **Scholarships:** Available **Calendar System:** Quarter, Summer Session Available **Student-Faculty Ratio:** 21:1 **Credit Hours For Degree:** 90 credits, Associates **ROTC:** Army **Professional Accreditation:** AHIMA, CARC, JRCERT, JRCEMT, NLN, NCCU **Intercollegiate Athletics:** Baseball M; Basketball M & W; Golf M & W; Soccer M & W; Volleyball W

TRINITY LUTHERAN COLLEGE
4221 228th Ave., SE
Issaquah, WA 98029-9299
Tel: (425)249-4800; Free: 800-843-5659
Admissions: (425)961-5512
Fax: (425)392-0404
E-mail: admissn@lbi.edu
Web Site: http://www.tlc.edu/
President/CEO: Dr. John M. Stamm
Admissions: Pamela Renn
Financial Aid: Susan Dalgleish
Type: Four-Year College **Sex:** Coed **Affiliation:** Lutheran **% Accepted:** 51 **Admission Plans:** Early Admission; Deferred Admission **Application Deadline:** September 15 **Application Fee:** $30.00 **H.S. Requirements:** High school diploma required; GED accepted **Scholarships:** Available **Calendar System:** Quarter, Summer Session Not available **Faculty:** FT 13, PT 15 **Exams:** SAT I or ACT. **Library Holdings:** 31,000 **Credit Hours For Degree:** 90 credits, Associates; 180 credits, Bachelors **Professional Accreditation:** NCCU

UNIVERSITY OF PHOENIX—EASTERN WASHINGTON CAMPUS
8775 East Mission Ave.
Spokane Valley, WA 99212-2531
Tel: (509)327-2443; Free: 800-228-7240
Admissions: (480)557-6151
E-mail: audra.mcquarie@phoenix.edu
Web Site: http://www.phoenix.edu/
President/CEO: William Pepicello
Admissions: Audra McQuarie
Type: Comprehensive **Sex:** Coed **Admission Plans:** Open Admission; Deferred Admission **Application Deadline:** Rolling **Application Fee:** $45.00 **H.S. Requirements:** High school diploma required; GED accepted **Costs Per Year:** Application fee: $45. Tuition: $11,625 full-time. Full-time tuition varies according to course level and course load. **Scholarships:** Available **Calendar System:** Continuous, Summer Session Not available **Enrollment:** FT 37 **Faculty:** FT 5, PT 38 **Student-Faculty Ratio:** 9:1 **Regional Accreditation:** North Central Association of Colleges and Schools **Credit Hours For Degree:** 60 credits, Associates; 120 credits, Bachelors

UNIVERSITY OF PHOENIX—WASHINGTON CAMPUS
7100 Fort Dent Way, Ste. 100
Seattle, WA 98188-7500
Tel: (206)268-5800; Free: 800-228-7240
Admissions: (480)557-3303
Fax: (206)241-8848
E-mail: evelyn.gaskin@phoenix.edu
Web Site: http://www.phoenix.edu/
President/CEO: William Pepicello
Admissions: Evelyn Gaskin
Type: Comprehensive **Sex:** Coed **Admission Plans:** Open Admission;

Deferred Admission **Application Deadline:** Rolling **Application Fee:** $0.00 **H.S. Requirements:** High school diploma required; GED accepted **Costs Per Year:** Application fee: $0. Tuition: $12,525 full-time. Full-time tuition varies according to course level and course load. **Scholarships:** Available **Calendar System:** Continuous, Summer Session Not available **Enrollment:** FT 572 **Faculty:** FT 14, PT 145 **Regional Accreditation:** North Central Association of Colleges and Schools **Credit Hours For Degree:** 60 credits, Associates; 120 credits, Bachelors

UNIVERSITY OF PUGET SOUND
1500 North Warner St.
Tacoma, WA 98416
Tel: (253)879-3100; Free: 800-396-7191
Admissions: (253)879-3211
Fax: (253)879-3500
E-mail: admission@ups.edu
Web Site: http://www.ups.edu/
President/CEO: Dr. Ronald R. Thomas
Admissions: Dr. George Mills
Financial Aid: Maggie A. Mittuch
Type: Comprehensive **Sex:** Coed **Scores:** 99.67% SAT V 400+; 99.83% SAT M 400+; 12.63% ACT 18-23; 57.8% ACT 24-29 **% Accepted:** 63 **Admission Plans:** Early Admission; Early Decision Plan; Deferred Admission **Application Deadline:** January 15 **Application Fee:** $50.00 **H.S. Requirements:** High school diploma required; GED accepted **Costs Per Year:** Application fee: $50. Comprehensive fee: $46,875 includes full-time tuition ($37,030), mandatory fees ($195), and college room and board ($9650). College room only: $5390. Full-time tuition and fees vary according to course load. Room and board charges vary according to board plan and housing facility. Part-time tuition: $4670 per unit. Part-time tuition varies according to course load. **Scholarships:** Available **Calendar System:** Semester, Summer Session Available **Enrollment:** FT 2,585, PT 22, Grad FT 211, Grad PT 83 **Faculty:** FT 226, PT 51 **Student-Faculty Ratio:** 12:1 **Exams:** SAT I or ACT. **% Receiving Financial Aid:** 64 **% Residing in College-Owned, -Operated, or -Affiliated Housing:** 59 **Final Year or Final Semester Residency Requirement:** Yes **Library Holdings:** 423,352 **Credit Hours For Degree:** 32 units, Bachelors **ROTC:** Army **Professional Accreditation:** AOTA, APTA, NASM, NCATE, NCCU **Intercollegiate Athletics:** Baseball M; Basketball M & W; Cheerleading M & W; Crew M & W; Cross-Country Running M & W; Fencing M & W; Football M; Golf M & W; Ice Hockey M & W; Lacrosse M & W; Rugby M; Sailing M & W; Skiing (Downhill) M & W; Soccer M & W; Softball W; Swimming and Diving M & W; Tennis M & W; Track and Field M & W; Volleyball W

UNIVERSITY OF WASHINGTON
Seattle, WA 98195
Tel: (206)543-2100
Admissions: (206)543-9686
Web Site: http://www.washington.edu/
President/CEO: Dr. Mark Emmert
Admissions: Emily Leggio
Type: University **Sex:** Coed **Scores:** 99% SAT V 400+; 100% SAT M 400+; 19% ACT 18-23; 53% ACT 24-29 **% Accepted:** 58 **Admission Plans:** Preferred Admission; Early Admission **Application Deadline:** January 15 **Application Fee:** $60.00 **H.S. Requirements:** High school diploma or equivalent not required **Costs Per Year:** Application fee: $60. State resident tuition: $7125 full-time. Nonresident tuition: $23,800 full-time. Mandatory fees: $567 full-time. Full-time tuition and fees vary according to course load. College room and board: $7800. Room and board charges vary according to board plan and housing facility. **Scholarships:** Available **Calendar System:** Quarter, Summer Session Available **Enrollment:** FT 28,094, PT 4,624, Grad FT 10,478, Grad PT 2,747 **Faculty:** FT 3,046, PT 706 **Exams:** SAT I or ACT. ACT essay used for admission. SAT essay used for admission. **% Receiving Financial Aid:** 37 **% Residing in College-Owned, -Operated, or -Affiliated Housing:** 23 **Library Holdings:** 5,820,229 **Credit Hours For Degree:** 180 credits, Bachelors **ROTC:** Army, Navy, Air Force **Professional Accreditation:** AACSB, ABET, ACPhE, ACEJMC, AACN, ABA, ACNM, ACCE, ADA, ADtA, AHIMA, ACSP, ALA, AOTA, APTA, APA, ASLA, ASLHA, AALS, ACEHSA CEPH, CSWE, LCMEAMA, NAACLS, NAAB, NASM, NASPAA, NCOPE, NCATE, NLN, NCCU, SAF **Intercollegiate Athletics:** Baseball M; Basketball M & W; Cheerleading M & W; Crew M & W; Cross-Country Running M & W; Football M; Golf M & W; Gymnastics W; Soccer M & W; Softball W; Tennis M & W; Track and Field M & W; Volleyball W

UNIVERSITY OF WASHINGTON, BOTHELL
18115 Campus Way NE
Bothell, WA 98011-8246
Tel: (425)352-5000
E-mail: freshmen@uwb.edu
Web Site: http://www.uwb.edu/
President/CEO: Dr. Kenyon Chan
Admissions: Lindsey Wille
Type: Comprehensive **Sex:** Coed **Affiliation:** University of Washington **Scores:** 85% SAT V 400+; 95% SAT M 400+; 54% ACT 18-23; 18% ACT 24-29 **% Accepted:** 77 **Admission Plans:** Early Admission; Deferred Admission **Application Deadline:** January 15 **Application Fee:** $60.00 **H.S. Requirements:** High school diploma or equivalent not required **Costs Per Year:** Application fee: $60. One-time mandatory fee: $250. State resident tuition: $7125 full-time. Nonresident tuition: $23,800 full-time. Mandatory fees: $450 full-time. Full-time tuition and fees vary according to course load. **Enrollment:** FT 1,565, PT 805, Grad FT 204, Grad PT 246 **Faculty:** FT 96, PT 49 **Student-Faculty Ratio:** 19:1 **Exams:** SAT I or ACT. SAT essay used for admission. **% Residing in College-Owned, -Operated, or -Affiliated Housing:** 2 **Final Year or Final Semester Residency Requirement:** Yes **Library Holdings:** 95,403 **Credit Hours For Degree:** 180 credits, Bachelors **ROTC:** Army, Air Force **Professional Accreditation:** NCCU

UNIVERSITY OF WASHINGTON, TACOMA
1900 Commerce St.
Tacoma, WA 98402-3100
Tel: (253)692-4000; Free: 800-736-7750
Admissions: (253)692-4742
E-mail: fionaj@u.washington.edu
Web Site: http://www.tacoma.washington.edu/
President/CEO: Dr. Patricia Spakes
Admissions: Fiona Johnson
Financial Aid: Shari King
Type: Comprehensive **Sex:** Coed **Affiliation:** University of Washington **Scores:** 86.9% SAT V 400+; 91% SAT M 400+; 59% ACT 18-23; 23% ACT 24-29 **% Accepted:** 31 **Admission Plans:** Early Decision Plan; Deferred Admission **Application Deadline:** March 1 **Application Fee:** $60.00 **H.S. Requirements:** High school diploma required; GED accepted **Costs Per Year:** Application fee: $60. State resident tuition: $7653 full-time, $255 per credit part-time. Nonresident tuition: $24,328 full-time, $811 per credit part-time. Full-time tuition varies according to course load. Part-time tuition varies according to course load. College room only: $8949. Room charges vary according to housing facility. **Scholarships:** Available **Calendar System:** Quarter, Summer Session Available **Enrollment:** FT 2,006, PT 562, Grad FT 207, Grad PT 336 **Faculty:** FT 139, PT 52 **Student-Faculty Ratio:** 16:1 **Exams:** SAT I or ACT. **% Residing in College-Owned, -Operated, or -Affiliated Housing:** 1 **Final Year or Final Semester Residency Requirement:** No **Library Holdings:** 7,549,756 **Credit Hours For Degree:** 180 units, Bachelors **ROTC:** Army, Navy, Air Force **Professional Accreditation:** NCCU

WALLA WALLA COMMUNITY COLLEGE
500 Tausick Way
Walla Walla, WA 99362-9267
Tel: (509)522-2500; Free: 877-992-9922
Fax: (509)527-3361
Web Site: http://www.wwcc.edu/home/
President/CEO: Steven L. VanAusdle
Type: Two-Year College **Sex:** Coed **Affiliation:** Washington State Board for Community and Technical Colleges **Admission Plans:** Open Admission **Application Deadline:** Rolling **Application Fee:** $40.00 **H.S. Requirements:** High school diploma or equivalent not required. For nursing program: High school diploma required; GED accepted **Scholarships:** Available **Calendar System:** Quarter, Summer Session Available **Student-Faculty Ratio:** 17:1 **Credit Hours For Degree:** 93 credits, Associates **Professional Accreditation:** ABET, NLN, NCCU **Intercollegiate Athletics:** Baseball M; Basketball M & W; Golf M & W; Soccer M & W; Softball W; Volleyball W

WALLA WALLA UNIVERSITY
204 South College Ave.
College Place, WA 99324-1198
Tel: (509)527-2615; Free: 800-541-8900
Admissions: (509)527-2327
Fax: (509)527-2397

E-mail: dallas@wallawalla.edu
Web Site: http://www.wallawalla.edu/
President/CEO: Dr. John McVay
Admissions: Dallas Weis
Financial Aid: Nancy Caldera
Type: Comprehensive **Sex:** Coed **Affiliation:** Seventh-day Adventist **% Accepted:** 98 **Admission Plans:** Early Decision Plan; Deferred Admission **Application Deadline:** Rolling **Application Fee:** $40.00 **H.S. Requirements:** High school diploma required; GED accepted **Scholarships:** Available **Calendar System:** Quarter, Summer Session Available **Enrollment:** FT 1,468, PT 95 **Faculty:** FT 117, PT 88 **Student-Faculty Ratio:** 13:1 **Exams:** SAT I or ACT. **% Receiving Financial Aid:** 70 **% Residing in College-Owned, -Operated, or -Affiliated Housing:** 63 **Library Holdings:** 273,266 **Credit Hours For Degree:** 96 quarter hours, Associates; 192 quarter hours, Bachelors **Professional Accreditation:** ABET, ACBSP, CSWE, NASM, NLN, NCCU **Intercollegiate Athletics:** Basketball M & W; Golf M; Ice Hockey M; Soccer M; Softball W; Volleyball M & W

WASHINGTON STATE UNIVERSITY
Pullman, WA 99164
Tel: (509)335-3564; Free: 888-468-6978
E-mail: admiss2@wsu.edu
Web Site: http://www.wsu.edu/
President/CEO: Elson S. Floyd
Admissions: Wendy Peterson
Financial Aid: Mike Whaley
Type: University **Sex:** Coed **Scores:** 96.3% SAT V 400+; 97.9% SAT M 400+; 46.5% ACT 18-23; 41.1% ACT 24-29 **% Accepted:** 76 **Application Deadline:** January 31 **Application Fee:** $50.00 **H.S. Requirements:** High school diploma required; GED accepted **Costs Per Year:** Application fee: $50. State resident tuition: $7088 full-time, $380 per credit hour part-time. Nonresident tuition: $18,164 full-time, $934 per credit hour part-time. Mandatory fees: $1401 full-time. Full-time tuition and fees vary according to location and reciprocity agreements. Part-time tuition varies according to course load, location, and reciprocity agreements. College room and board: $8886. College room only: $4852. Room and board charges vary according to board plan, housing facility, and location. **Scholarships:** Available **Calendar System:** Semester, Summer Session Available **Enrollment:** FT 18,712, PT 3,014, Grad FT 3,036, Grad PT 1,339 **Faculty:** FT 1,151, PT 475 **Student-Faculty Ratio:** 15:1 **Exams:** SAT I or ACT. **% Receiving Financial Aid:** 49 **% Residing in College-Owned, -Operated, or -Affiliated Housing:** 35 **Final Year or Final Semester Residency Requirement:** No **Library Holdings:** 2,283,449 **Credit Hours For Degree:** 120 credits, Bachelors **ROTC:** Army, Navy, Air Force **Professional Accreditation:** AACSB, ABET, ACPhE, AACN, ACCE, ADtA, APA, ASLA, ASLHA, AVMA, FIDER, JRCEPAT, NAAB, NASM, NCATE, NLN, NCCU, SAF **Intercollegiate Athletics:** Baseball M; Basketball M & W; Bowling M & W; Cheerleading M & W; Crew M & W; Cross-Country Running M & W; Equestrian Sports M & W; Fencing M & W; Football M; Golf M & W; Gymnastics M & W; Ice Hockey M; Lacrosse M & W; Rugby M & W; Sailing M & W; Skiing (Cross-Country) M & W; Skiing (Downhill) M & W; Soccer M & W; Softball W; Swimming and Diving W; Tennis M & W; Track and Field M & W; Ultimate Frisbee M & W; Volleyball M & W; Water Polo M & W

WENATCHEE VALLEY COLLEGE
1300 Fifth St.
Wenatchee, WA 98801-1799
Tel: (509)682-6800
Admissions: (509)682-6836
Fax: (509)664-2511
E-mail: cescobedo@wvc.edu
Web Site: http://www.wvc.edu/
President/CEO: Jim Richardson
Admissions: Cecilia Escobedo
Type: Two-Year College **Sex:** Coed **Affiliation:** Washington State Board for Community and Technical Colleges **% Accepted:** 100 **Admission Plans:** Open Admission; Early Admission; Deferred Admission **Application Deadline:** Rolling **Application Fee:** $25.00 **H.S. Requirements:** High school diploma or equivalent not required. For allied health programs: High school diploma required; GED accepted **Scholarships:** Available **Calendar System:** Quarter, Summer Session Available **Enrollment:** FT 2,095, PT 1,409 **Library Holdings:** 32,000 **Credit Hours For Degree:** 90 credits, Associates **Professional Accreditation:** JRCERT, NAACLS, NLN, NCCU **Intercollegiate Athletics:** Baseball M; Basketball M & W; Soccer M & W; Softball W

WESTERN WASHINGTON UNIVERSITY
516 High St.
Bellingham, WA 98225-5996
Tel: (360)650-3000
Admissions: (360)650-3440
E-mail: admit@wwu.edu
Web Site: http://www.wwu.edu/
President/CEO: Bruce Sheppard
Admissions: Karen Copetas
Financial Aid: Fidele Dent
Type: Comprehensive **Sex:** Coed **Scores:** 97.74% SAT V 400+; 98.46% SAT M 400+; 38.81% ACT 18-23; 47.71% ACT 24-29 **% Accepted:** 73 **Admission Plans:** Deferred Admission **Application Deadline:** March 1 **Application Fee:** $50.00 **H.S. Requirements:** High school diploma required; GED accepted **Costs Per Year:** Application fee: $50. State resident tuition: $5397 full-time. Nonresident tuition: $16,428 full-time. Mandatory fees: $762 full-time. Full-time tuition and fees vary according to course load and location. College room and board: $8393. Room and board charges vary according to board plan and housing facility. **Scholarships:** Available **Calendar System:** Quarter, Summer Session Available **Enrollment:** FT 12,313, PT 1,083, Grad FT 678, Grad PT 501 **Faculty:** FT 498, PT 232 **Student-Faculty Ratio:** 19:1 **Exams:** SAT I or ACT. ACT essay not being used. SAT essay not being used. **% Receiving Financial Aid:** 41 **% Residing in College-Owned, -Operated, or -Affiliated Housing:** 32 **Library Holdings:** 1,419,810 **Credit Hours For Degree:** 180 quarter hours, Bachelors **Professional Accreditation:** AACSB, ABET, ACA, ASLHA, CORE, NASAD, NASM, NCATE, NRPA, NCCU **Intercollegiate Athletics:** Basketball M & W; Cheerleading M & W; Crew M & W; Cross-Country Running M & W; Golf M & W; Soccer M & W; Softball W; Track and Field M & W; Volleyball W

WHATCOM COMMUNITY COLLEGE
237 West Kellogg Rd.
Bellingham, WA 98226-8003
Tel: (360)676-2170
Fax: (360)676-2171
E-mail: admit@whatcom.ctc.edu
Web Site: http://www.whatcom.ctc.edu/
President/CEO: Dr. Kathi Hiyane-Brown
Type: Two-Year College **Sex:** Coed **Affiliation:** Washington State Board for Community and Technical Colleges **Admission Plans:** Open Admission **Application Deadline:** Rolling **Application Fee:** $0.00 **H.S. Requirements:** High school diploma or equivalent not required. For financial aid applicants, international students: High school diploma required; GED accepted **Costs Per Year:** Application fee: $0. State resident tuition: $3105 full-time, $87 per credit hour part-time. Nonresident tuition: $8325 full-time, $259 per credit hour part-time. Full-time tuition varies according to course load. Part-time tuition varies according to course load. **Scholarships:** Available **Calendar System:** Quarter, Summer Session Available **Faculty:** FT 75, PT 150 **Library Holdings:** 14,680 **Credit Hours For Degree:** 90 quarter hours, Associates **Professional Accreditation:** AAMAE, APTA, NCCU **Intercollegiate Athletics:** Basketball M & W; Cross-Country Running M & W; Soccer M & W; Volleyball W

WHITMAN COLLEGE
345 Boyer Ave.
Walla Walla, WA 99362-2083
Tel: (509)527-5111; Free: 877-462-9448
Admissions: (509)527-5176
Fax: (509)527-4967
E-mail: admission@whitman.edu
Web Site: http://www.whitman.edu/
President/CEO: Dr. George Bridges
Admissions: Tony Cabasco
Financial Aid: Tyson Harlow
Type: Four-Year College **Sex:** Coed **Scores:** 99.66% SAT V 400+; 99.66% SAT M 400+; 1.98% ACT 18-23; 37.62% ACT 24-29 **% Accepted:** 44 **Admission Plans:** Early Decision Plan; Deferred Admission **Application Deadline:** January 15 **Application Fee:** $50.00 **H.S. Requirements:** High school diploma required; GED accepted **Costs Per Year:** Application fee: $50. Comprehensive fee: $48,490 includes full-time tuition ($38,450), mandatory fees ($320), and college room and board ($9720). College room only: $4480. Room and board charges vary according to board plan and housing facility. Part-time tuition: $1602 per credit hour. **Scholarships:** Available **Calendar System:** Semester, Summer Session Not available **Enroll-**

ment: FT 1,483, PT 32 **Faculty:** FT 130, PT 56 **Student-Faculty Ratio:** 10:1 **Exams:** SAT I or ACT. **% Receiving Financial Aid:** 44 **% Residing in College-Owned, -Operated, or -Affiliated Housing:** 62 **Library Holdings:** 395,841 **Credit Hours For Degree:** 124 credits, Bachelors **Professional Accreditation:** NCCU **Intercollegiate Athletics:** Baseball M; Basketball M & W; Cross-Country Running M & W; Fencing M & W; Golf M & W; Ice Hockey M; Lacrosse M & W; Rugby M & W; Skiing (Cross-Country) M & W; Skiing (Downhill) M & W; Soccer M & W; Softball M & W; Swimming and Diving M & W; Tennis M & W; Track and Field M & W; Ultimate Frisbee M & W; Volleyball M & W

WHITWORTH UNIVERSITY
300 West Hawthorne Rd.
Spokane, WA 99251-0001
Tel: (509)777-1000; Free: 800-533-4668
Admissions: (509)777-4348
Fax: (509)777-3773
E-mail: admission@whitworth.edu
Web Site: http://www.whitworth.edu/
President/CEO: Dr. William P. Robinson
Admissions: Marianne Hansen
Financial Aid: Wendy Z. Olson
Type: Comprehensive **Sex:** Coed **Affiliation:** Presbyterian **Scores:** 100% SAT V 400+; 100% SAT M 400+; 15% ACT 18-23; 64% ACT 24-29 **% Accepted:** 49 **Admission Plans:** Early Admission; Early Action; Deferred Admission **Application Deadline:** March 1 **Application Fee:** $0.00 **H.S. Requirements:** High school diploma required; GED accepted **Scholarships:** Available **Calendar System:** 4-1-4, Summer Session Available **Enrollment:** FT 2,048, PT 283 **Faculty:** FT 123, PT 171 **Student-Faculty Ratio:** 13:1 **Exams:** SAT I or ACT. **% Receiving Financial Aid:** 71 **% Residing in College-Owned, -Operated, or -Affiliated Housing:** 63 **Library Holdings:** 17,982 **Credit Hours For Degree:** 130 credits, Bachelors **ROTC:** Army **Professional Accreditation:** JRCEPAT, NASM, NCATE, NLN, NCCU **Intercollegiate Athletics:** Baseball M; Basketball M & W; Cross-Country Running M & W; Football M; Golf M & W; Soccer M & W; Softball W; Swimming and Diving M & W; Tennis M & W; Track and Field M & W; Volleyball W

YAKIMA VALLEY COMMUNITY COLLEGE
PO Box 22520
Yakima, WA 98907-2520
Tel: (509)574-4600
Admissions: (509)574-4702
Fax: (509)574-6860
E-mail: admis@yvcc.edu
Web Site: http://www.yvcc.edu/Pages/default.aspx/
President/CEO: Dr. Linda Kaminski
Admissions: Denise Anderson
Type: Two-Year College **Sex:** Coed **Affiliation:** Washington State Board for Community and Technical Colleges **Admission Plans:** Open Admission; Deferred Admission **Application Deadline:** September 12 **Application Fee:** $20.00 **H.S. Requirements:** High school diploma required; GED accepted. For nursing, dental hygiene, radiological technology, allied health programs: High school diploma required; GED accepted **Costs Per Year:** Application fee: $20. State resident tuition: $2925 full-time, $81 per credit hour part-time. Nonresident tuition: $3315 full-time, $94 per credit hour part-time. Mandatory fees: $308 full-time, $8 per credit hour part-time. Full-time tuition and fees vary according to course load. Part-time tuition and fees vary according to course load. College room only: $3150. Room charges vary according to housing facility. **Scholarships:** Available **Calendar System:** Quarter, Summer Session Available **Enrollment:** FT 2,586, PT 1,675 **Faculty:** FT 109, PT 220 **Student-Faculty Ratio:** 20:1 **Exams:** Other. **Library Holdings:** 31,716 **Credit Hours For Degree:** 90 credits, Associates **Professional Accreditation:** ADA, JRCERT, NLN, NCCU **Intercollegiate Athletics:** Baseball M; Basketball M & W; Soccer W; Softball W; Volleyball W; Wrestling M

ALDERSON-BROADDUS COLLEGE
1 College Hill Dr.
Philippi, WV 26416
Tel: (304)457-1700; Free: 800-263-1549
Fax: (304)457-6239
E-mail: admissions@ab.edu
Web Site: http://www.ab.edu/
President/CEO: Dr. J. Michael Clyburn
Admissions: Kimberly N. Klaus
Financial Aid: Brian Weingart
Type: Comprehensive **Sex:** Coed **Affiliation:** American Baptist Churches in the U.S.A. **Scores:** 93% SAT V 400+; 84% SAT M 400+; 57% ACT 18-23; 23% ACT 24-29 **% Accepted:** 74 **Admission Plans:** Early Decision Plan; Deferred Admission **Application Deadline:** Rolling **Application Fee:** $25.00 **H.S. Requirements:** High school diploma required; GED accepted **Costs Per Year:** Application fee: $25. Comprehensive fee: $28,656 includes full-time tuition ($21,444), mandatory fees ($210), and college room and board ($7002). College room only: $3408. Full-time tuition and fees vary according to program and student level. Room and board charges vary according to housing facility. Part-time tuition: $715 per credit hour. Part-time mandatory fees: $52.50 per term. Part-time tuition and fees vary according to program and student level. **Scholarships:** Available **Calendar System:** Semester, Summer Session Available **Enrollment:** FT 566, PT 26, Grad FT 107, Grad PT 12 **Faculty:** FT 59, PT 30 **Student-Faculty Ratio:** 10:1 **Exams:** SAT I and SAT II or ACT. **% Receiving Financial Aid:** 92 **% Residing in College-Owned, -Operated, or -Affiliated Housing:** 64 **Final Year or Final Semester Residency Requirement:** Yes **Library Holdings:** 60,000 **Regional Accreditation:** North Central Association of Colleges and Schools **Credit Hours For Degree:** 64 credit hours, Associates; 128 credit hours, Bachelors **Professional Accreditation:** NCATE, NLN **Intercollegiate Athletics:** Baseball M; Basketball M & W; Cross-Country Running M & W; Soccer M & W; Softball W; Track and Field M & W; Volleyball W

AMERICAN PUBLIC UNIVERSITY SYSTEM
111 West Congress St.
Charles Town, WV 25414
Tel: 877-755-2787
Admissions: 877-468-6268
E-mail: info@apus.edu
Web Site: http://www.apus.edu/
President/CEO: Wallace Boston
Admissions: Terry Grant
Type: Comprehensive **Sex:** Coed **Affiliation:** American Military University/ American Public University **% Accepted:** 100 **Admission Plans:** Open Admission; Deferred Admission **Application Deadline:** Rolling **Application Fee:** $0.00 **H.S. Requirements:** High school diploma required; GED accepted **Costs Per Year:** Application fee: $0. Tuition: $6000 full-time, $250 per credit hour part-time. **Calendar System:** Miscellaneous, Summer Session Not available **Enrollment:** FT 4,660, PT 18,967, Grad FT 788, Grad PT 6,916 **Faculty:** FT 255, PT 746 **Final Year or Final Semester Residency Requirement:** No **Regional Accreditation:** North Central Association of Colleges and Schools **Credit Hours For Degree:** 61 semester hours, Associates; 121 semester hours, Bachelors **Professional Accreditation:** DETC

APPALACHIAN BIBLE COLLEGE
PO Box ABC
Bradley, WV 25818
Tel: (304)877-6428; Free: 800-678-9ABC
E-mail: admissions2@abc.edu
Web Site: http://www.abc.edu/
President/CEO: Dr. Daniel L. Anderson
Admissions: Ashley Siders
Financial Aid: Cindi Turner
Type: Comprehensive **Sex:** Coed **Affiliation:** nondenominational **Scores:** 92% SAT V 400+; 79% SAT M 400+; 46% ACT 18-23; 38% ACT 24-29 **% Accepted:** 62 **Application Deadline:** Rolling **Application Fee:** $20.00 **H.S. Requirements:** High school diploma required; GED accepted **Costs Per Year:** Application fee: $20. Comprehensive fee: $15,690 includes full-time tuition ($8770), mandatory fees ($1520), and college room and board ($5400). Full-time tuition and fees vary according to program. Room and board charges vary according to housing facility. Part-time tuition: $365 per credit hour. Part-time mandatory fees: $550 per term. Part-time tuition and fees vary according to program. **Scholarships:** Available **Calendar System:** Semester, Summer Session Available **Enrollment:** FT 209, PT 49, Grad FT 10 **Faculty:** FT 11, PT 7 **Student-Faculty Ratio:** 17:1 **Exams:** SAT I or ACT. **% Receiving Financial Aid:** 60 **% Residing in College-Owned, -Operated, or -Affiliated Housing:** 95 **Library Holdings:** 44,944 **Regional Accreditation:** North Central Association of Colleges and Schools **Credit Hours For Degree:** 63 credit hours, Associates; 126 credit hours, Bachelors **Professional Accreditation:** ABHE **Intercollegiate Athletics:** Basketball M & W; Soccer M; Volleyball W

BETHANY COLLEGE
Main St.
Bethany, WV 26032
Tel: (304)829-7000; Free: 800-922-7611
Admissions: (304)829-7611
Fax: (304)829-7142
E-mail: admission@bethanywv.edu
Web Site: http://www.bethanywv.edu/
President/CEO: Dr. Scott D. Miller
Admissions: Karina Dayich
Financial Aid: Karina Dayich
Type: Four-Year College **Sex:** Coed **Affiliation:** Christian Church (Disciples of Christ) **Scores:** 78.39% SAT V 400+; 76.99% SAT M 400+; 51.05% ACT 18-23; 24.21% ACT 24-29 **% Accepted:** 78 **Admission Plans:** Deferred Admission **Application Deadline:** Rolling **Application Fee:** $0.00 **H.S. Requirements:** High school diploma required; GED accepted **Costs Per Year:** Application fee: $0. Comprehensive fee: $30,165 includes full-time tuition ($20,565), mandatory fees ($900), and college room and board ($8700). Room and board charges vary according to housing facility. Part-time tuition: $650 per credit hour. **Scholarships:** Available **Calendar System:** 4-1-4, Summer Session Not available **Enrollment:** FT 820, PT 10 **Faculty:** FT 49, PT 31 **Student-Faculty Ratio:** 14:1 **Exams:** SAT I or ACT. SAT essay used for admission. ACT essay used in place of application essay. SAT essay used in place of application essay. SAT essay used for placement. ACT essay not being used. SAT essay not being used. **% Receiving Financial Aid:** 85 **% Residing in College-Owned, -Operated, or -Affiliated Housing:** 85 **Library Holdings:** 123,352 **Regional Accreditation:** North Central Association of Colleges and Schools **Credit Hours For**

Degree: 128 semester hours, Bachelors **Professional Accreditation:** CSWE, NCATE **Intercollegiate Athletics:** Baseball M; Basketball M & W; Cross-Country Running M & W; Football M; Golf M & W; Soccer M & W; Softball W; Swimming and Diving M & W; Tennis M & W; Track and Field M & W; Volleyball W

BLUE RIDGE COMMUNITY AND TECHNICAL COLLEGE

400 West Stephen St.
Martinsburg, WV 25401
Tel: (304)260-4380
Fax: (304)260-4376
E-mail: bneal@blueridgectc.edu
Web Site: http://www.blueridgectc.edu/
President/CEO: Dr. Peter G. Checkovich
Admissions: Brenda K. Neal

Type: Two-Year College **Sex:** Coed **Scores:** 100% SAT V 400+; 32.88% ACT 18-23; 1.37% ACT 24-29 **Admission Plans:** Open Admission; Deferred Admission **Application Fee:** $25.00 **H.S. Requirements:** High school diploma required; GED accepted **Costs Per Year:** Application fee: $25. State resident tuition: $3072 full-time, $128 per credit hour part-time. Nonresident tuition: $5520 full-time, $230 per credit hour part-time. Full-time tuition varies according to course load and program. Part-time tuition varies according to course load and program. **Enrollment:** FT 922, PT 2,500 **Faculty:** FT 34, PT 72 **Student-Faculty Ratio:** 29:1 **Exams:** SAT I and SAT II or ACT. **Final Year or Final Semester Residency Requirement:** Yes **Regional Accreditation:** North Central Association of Colleges and Schools **Credit Hours For Degree:** 60 credits, Associates

BLUEFIELD STATE COLLEGE

219 Rock St.
Bluefield, WV 24701-2198
Tel: (304)327-4000; Free: 800-654-7798
Admissions: (304)327-4067
Fax: (304)327-7747
E-mail: bscadmit@bluefieldstate.edu
Web Site: http://www.bluefieldstate.edu/
President/CEO: Dr. Albert Walker
Admissions: Kenneth Mandeville
Financial Aid: Tom Ilse

Type: Four-Year College **Sex:** Coed **Affiliation:** West Virginia Higher Education Policy Commission **Scores:** 80% SAT V 400+; 64% SAT M 400+; 50% ACT 18-23; 8% ACT 24-29 **% Accepted:** 79 **Admission Plans:** Early Admission; Deferred Admission **Application Deadline:** Rolling **Application Fee:** $0.00 **H.S. Requirements:** High school diploma required; GED accepted **Costs Per Year:** Application fee: $0. State resident tuition: $4596 full-time, $192 per credit hour part-time. Nonresident tuition: $9000 full-time, $375 per credit hour part-time. **Scholarships:** Available **Calendar System:** Semester, Summer Session Available **Enrollment:** FT 1,599, PT 390 **Faculty:** FT 79, PT 70 **Student-Faculty Ratio:** 17:1 **Exams:** SAT I or ACT. **% Receiving Financial Aid:** 67 **Regional Accreditation:** North Central Association of Colleges and Schools **Credit Hours For Degree:** 64 semester hours, Associates; 128 semester hours, Bachelors **Professional Accreditation:** ABET, AACN, ACBSP, JRCERT, NCATE, NLN **Intercollegiate Athletics:** Baseball M; Basketball M & W; Cheerleading W; Cross-Country Running M & W; Golf M; Softball W; Tennis M & W

COMMUNITY & TECHNICAL COLLEGE AT WEST VIRGINIA UNIVERSITY INSTITUTE OF TECHNOLOGY

405 Fayette Pike
Montgomery, WV 25136
Tel: (304)442-3149; Free: 888-554-8324
Admissions: (304)734-6601
Web Site: http://ctc.wvutech.edu/
President/CEO: Beverly Jo Harris
Admissions: Lisa Graham

Type: Two-Year College **Sex:** Coed **Admission Plans:** Open Admission **Regional Accreditation:** North Central Association of Colleges and Schools

CONCORD UNIVERSITY

Vermillion St., PO Box 1000
Athens, WV 24712-1000
Tel: (304)384-3115; Free: 888-384-5249
Admissions: (304)384-5316
Fax: (304)384-9044
E-mail: admissions@concord.edu
Web Site: http://www.concord.edu/
President/CEO: Dr. Gregory F. Aloia
Admissions: Kent Gamble
Financial Aid: Lisa Spencer

Type: Comprehensive **Sex:** Coed **Affiliation:** State College System of West Virginia **Scores:** 85% SAT V 400+; 88% SAT M 400+; 60% ACT 18-23; 22% ACT 24-29 **% Accepted:** 60 **Admission Plans:** Early Admission; Early Decision Plan **Application Deadline:** Rolling **Application Fee:** $0.00 **H.S. Requirements:** High school diploma required; GED accepted **Costs Per Year:** Application fee: $0. State resident tuition: $4974 full-time, $207 per credit hour part-time. Nonresident tuition: $11,050 full-time, $460 per credit hour part-time. Full-time tuition varies according to course load. Part-time tuition varies according to course load. College room and board: $6766. College room only: $3446. **Scholarships:** Available **Calendar System:** Semester, Summer Session Available **Enrollment:** FT 2,346, PT 466, Grad FT 1, Grad PT 134 **Faculty:** FT 111, PT 88 **Student-Faculty Ratio:** 18:1 **Exams:** ACT, SAT I or ACT. SAT essay used for placement. **% Receiving Financial Aid:** 69 **% Residing in College-Owned, -Operated, or -Affiliated Housing:** 39 **Library Holdings:** 150,151 **Regional Accreditation:** North Central Association of Colleges and Schools **Credit Hours For Degree:** 128 semester hours, Bachelors **Professional Accreditation:** CSWE, NCATE **Intercollegiate Athletics:** Baseball M; Basketball M & W; Cheerleading M & W; Cross-Country Running M & W; Football M; Golf M; Soccer W; Tennis M & W; Track and Field M & W; Volleyball W

DAVIS & ELKINS COLLEGE

100 Campus Dr.
Elkins, WV 26241-3996
Tel: (304)637-1900; Free: 800-624-3157
Admissions: (304)637-1974
Fax: (304)637-1800
E-mail: admiss@davisandelkins.edu
Web Site: http://www.davisandelkins.edu/
President/CEO: Dr. G. Thomas Mann
Admissions: Reneé Heckel
Financial Aid: Susan M. George

Type: Four-Year College **Sex:** Coed **Affiliation:** Presbyterian **Scores:** 86.3% SAT V 400+; 77% SAT M 400+; 48.2% ACT 18-23; 19% ACT 24-29 **% Accepted:** 75 **Admission Plans:** Early Admission; Deferred Admission **Application Deadline:** Rolling **Application Fee:** $35.00 **H.S. Requirements:** High school diploma required; GED accepted **Scholarships:** Available **Calendar System:** 4-1-4, Summer Session Available **Enrollment:** FT 568, PT 72 **Faculty:** FT 44, PT 20 **Student-Faculty Ratio:** 10:1 **Exams:** SAT I or ACT. **% Receiving Financial Aid:** 77 **% Residing in College-Owned, -Operated, or -Affiliated Housing:** 49 **Library Holdings:** 226,705 **Regional Accreditation:** North Central Association of Colleges and Schools **Credit Hours For Degree:** 62 credit hours, Associates; 124 credit hours, Bachelors **Professional Accreditation:** NAST, NLN **Intercollegiate Athletics:** Baseball M; Basketball M & W; Cross-Country Running M & W; Golf M; Skiing (Downhill) M & W; Soccer M & W; Softball W; Volleyball W

EASTERN WEST VIRGINIA COMMUNITY AND TECHNICAL COLLEGE

HC 65 Box 402
Moorefield, WV 26836
Tel: (304)434-8000; Free: 877-982-2322
Web Site: http://www.eastern.wvnet.edu/
President/CEO: Robert Sisk
Admissions: Sharon Bungard

Type: Two-Year College **Sex:** Coed **% Accepted:** 100 **Calendar System:** Semester **Enrollment:** FT 71, PT 715 **Faculty:** FT 1, PT 36 **Student-Faculty Ratio:** 24:1 **Regional Accreditation:** North Central Association of Colleges and Schools

EVEREST INSTITUTE

5514 Big Tyler Rd.
Cross Lanes, WV 25313-1390
Tel: (304)776-6290; Free: 888-741-4271
Web Site: http://www.everest.edu/
President/CEO: Aimee Switzer

Type: Two-Year College **Sex:** Coed **Affiliation:** Corinthian Colleges, Inc. **Admission Plans:** Deferred Admission **Application Deadline:** Rolling **H.S. Requirements:** High school diploma required; GED accepted **Scholar-**

ships: Available **Calendar System:** Quarter, Summer Session Not available **Credit Hours For Degree:** 15 units, Associates **Professional Accreditation:** ACCSCT

FAIRMONT STATE UNIVERSITY
1201 Locust Ave.
Fairmont, WV 26554
Tel: (304)367-4000; Free: 800-641-5678
Admissions: (304)367-4892
Fax: (304)367-4789
E-mail: admit@fairmontstate.edu
Web Site: http://www.fairmontstate.edu/
President/CEO: Dr. Daniel Bradley
Admissions: Steve Leadman
Financial Aid: Cynthia K. Hudok
Type: Comprehensive **Sex:** Coed **Affiliation:** State College System of West Virginia **Scores:** 80% SAT V 400+; 85.5% SAT M 400+; 62.2% ACT 18-23; 17.9% ACT 24-29 **% Accepted:** 61 **Application Deadline:** Rolling **Application Fee:** $0.00 **H.S. Requirements:** High school diploma required; GED accepted **Costs Per Year:** Application fee: $0. State resident tuition: $5172 full-time, $210 per credit hour part-time. Nonresident tuition: $10,904 full-time, $442 per credit hour part-time. Mandatory fees: $200 full-time. Full-time tuition and fees vary according to degree level and location. Part-time tuition varies according to course load, degree level, and location. College room and board: $6900. College room only: $3300. Room and board charges vary according to board plan and housing facility. **Scholarships:** Available **Calendar System:** Semester, Summer Session Available **Enrollment:** FT 3,652, PT 571, Grad FT 118, Grad PT 231 **Faculty:** FT 165, PT 169 **Student-Faculty Ratio:** 17:1 **Exams:** SAT I or ACT. **% Receiving Financial Aid:** 67 **% Residing in College-Owned, -Operated, or -Affiliated Housing:** 21 **Library Holdings:** 280,000 **Regional Accreditation:** North Central Association of Colleges and Schools **Credit Hours For Degree:** 64 credits, Associates; 128 credits, Bachelors **ROTC:** Army **Professional Accreditation:** ABET, AACN, AAFCS, ACBSP, NCATE **Intercollegiate Athletics:** Baseball M; Basketball M & W; Cross-Country Running M & W; Football M; Golf M & W; Softball W; Swimming and Diving M & W; Tennis M & W; Volleyball W

GLENVILLE STATE COLLEGE
200 High St.
Glenville, WV 26351-1200
Tel: (304)462-7361
Admissions: (304)462-4128
Fax: (304)462-8619
E-mail: tommy.oldaker@glenville.edu
Web Site: http://www.glenville.edu/
President/CEO: Dr. Peter B. Barr
Admissions: Tommy Oldaker
Financial Aid: Karen Lay
Type: Four-Year College **Sex:** Coed **Affiliation:** West Virginia Higher Education Policy Commission **Scores:** 57% SAT V 400+; 63% SAT M 400+; 54% ACT 18-23; 13% ACT 24-29 **% Accepted:** 100 **Admission Plans:** Open Admission; Preferred Admission; Deferred Admission **Application Deadline:** Rolling **Application Fee:** $10.00 **H.S. Requirements:** High school diploma required; GED accepted **Costs Per Year:** Application fee: $10. State resident tuition: $4888 full-time, $203.67 per credit hour part-time. Nonresident tuition: $11,702 full-time, $487.58 per credit hour part-time. Part-time tuition varies according to course load. College room and board: $6460. College room only: $3210. Room and board charges vary according to housing facility. **Scholarships:** Available **Calendar System:** Semester, Summer Session Available **Enrollment:** FT 1,156, PT 565 **Faculty:** FT 61, PT 41 **Student-Faculty Ratio:** 18:1 **Exams:** SAT I or ACT. ACT essay not being used. SAT essay not being used. **% Receiving Financial Aid:** 82 **% Residing in College-Owned, -Operated, or -Affiliated Housing:** 33 **Library Holdings:** 116,220 **Regional Accreditation:** North Central Association of Colleges and Schools **Credit Hours For Degree:** 64 credit hours, Associates; 128 credit hours, Bachelors **Professional Accreditation:** NCATE **Intercollegiate Athletics:** Basketball M & W; Cross-Country Running M & W; Football M; Golf M & W; Softball W; Track and Field M & W; Volleyball W

HUNTINGTON JUNIOR COLLEGE
900 Fifth Ave.
Huntington, WV 25701-2004
Tel: (304)697-7550
Fax: (304)697-7554
Web Site: http://www.huntingtonjuniorcollege.com/
President/CEO: Carolyn Smith
Admissions: James Garrett
Type: Two-Year College **Sex:** Coed **Admission Plans:** Open Admission **Application Deadline:** Rolling **Application Fee:** $0.00 **H.S. Requirements:** High school diploma required; GED accepted **Scholarships:** Available **Calendar System:** Quarter, Summer Session Available **Library Holdings:** 1,900 **Regional Accreditation:** North Central Association of Colleges and Schools **Credit Hours For Degree:** 108 credits, Associates **Professional Accreditation:** AAMAE

ITT TECHNICAL INSTITUTE
5183 US Route 60
Bldg. 1, Ste. 40
Huntington, WV 25705
Tel: (304)733-8700; Free: 800-224-4695
Web Site: http://www.itt-tech.edu/
President/CEO: Gina Chapman
Type: Two-Year College **Sex:** Coed **Affiliation:** ITT Educational Services, Inc. **Calendar System:** Quarter **Professional Accreditation:** ACICS

KANAWHA VALLEY COMMUNITY AND TECHNICAL COLLEGE
Thomas W. Cole, Jr., Complex
PO Box 1000
Institute, WV 25112
Tel: (304)766-3118; Free: 800-987-2112
Admissions: (304)766-5765
E-mail: castosb@wvstateu.edu
Web Site: http://www.wvsctc.edu/
President/CEO: Dr. Joseph Badgley
Admissions: Bryce Casto
Type: Two-Year College **Sex:** Coed **Affiliation:** West Council for Community and Technical College Education **% Accepted:** 63 **Costs Per Year:** State resident tuition: $2956 full-time, $121 per credit hour part-time. Nonresident tuition: $8638 full-time, $353 per credit hour part-time. Full-time tuition varies according to class time, course level, course load, degree level, and program. Part-time tuition varies according to course load and degree level. College room and board: $6070. College room only: $2850. Room and board charges vary according to board plan and housing facility. **Enrollment:** FT 1,064, PT 653 **Faculty:** FT 35, PT 52 **Exams:** ACT. **Library Holdings:** 221,184 **Regional Accreditation:** North Central Association of Colleges and Schools **Professional Accreditation:** JRCNMT

MARSHALL UNIVERSITY
One John Marshall Dr.
Huntington, WV 25755
Tel: (304)696-3170
Admissions: 800-642-3499
Fax: (304)696-3135
E-mail: admissions@marshall.edu
Web Site: http://www.marshall.edu/
President/CEO: Dr. Stephen J. Kopp
Admissions: Dr. Tammy Johnson
Financial Aid: Kathy Bialk
Type: University **Sex:** Coed **Affiliation:** University System of West Virginia **Scores:** 88.36% SAT M 400+; 56% ACT 18-23; 32% ACT 24-29 **% Accepted:** 86 **Admission Plans:** Deferred Admission **Application Deadline:** Rolling **Application Fee:** $30.00 **H.S. Requirements:** High school diploma required; GED accepted **Costs Per Year:** Application fee: $30. State resident tuition: $4319 full-time, $180.25 per credit hour part-time. Nonresident tuition: $11,565 full-time, $482.25 per credit hour part-time. Mandatory fees: $917 full-time, $38.50 per credit hour part-time. Full-time tuition and fees vary according to degree level, location, program, and reciprocity agreements. Part-time tuition and fees vary according to course load, degree level, location, program, and reciprocity agreements. College room and board: $7556. College room only: $4474. Room and board charges vary according to board plan and housing facility. **Scholarships:** Available **Calendar System:** Semester, Summer Session Available **Enrollment:** FT 8,043, PT 1,649, Grad FT 1,778, Grad PT 2,306 **Faculty:** FT 478, PT 269 **Student-Faculty Ratio:** 19:1 **Exams:** SAT I or ACT. ACT essay not being used. SAT essay not being used. **% Receiving Financial Aid:** 62 **Library Holdings:** 1,543,571 **Regional Accreditation:** North Central As-

sociation of Colleges and Schools **Credit Hours For Degree:** 69 semester hours, Associates; 128 semester hours, Bachelors **ROTC:** Army **Professional Accreditation:** AACSB, ABET, ACEJMC, AAFCS, AANA, ADtA, AHIMA, APTA, ASLHA, ACBSP, CSWE, JRCEPAT, LCMEAMA, NAACLS, NASM, NCATE, NLN, NRPA **Intercollegiate Athletics:** Baseball M; Basketball M & W; Cross-Country Running M & W; Football M; Golf M & W; Lacrosse M; Rugby M & W; Soccer M & W; Softball W; Swimming and Diving W; Tennis W; Track and Field M & W; Volleyball W

MOUNTAIN STATE COLLEGE
1508 Spring St.
Parkersburg, WV 26101-3993
Tel: (304)485-5487; Free: 800-841-0201
Fax: (304)485-3524
E-mail: jsutton@msc.edu
Web Site: http://www.msc.edu/
President/CEO: Judith K. Sutton
Admissions: Judith Sutton
Type: Two-Year College **Sex:** Coed **H.S. Requirements:** High school diploma required; GED accepted **Scholarships:** Available **Calendar System:** Quarter **Enrollment:** FT 166 **Faculty:** FT 7, PT 4 **Student-Faculty Ratio:** 17:1 **Exams:** Other. **Final Year or Final Semester Residency Requirement:** No **Professional Accreditation:** ACICS

MOUNTAIN STATE UNIVERSITY
Box 9003
Beckley, WV 25802-9003
Tel: (304)253-7351; Free: 800-766-6067
Admissions: (304)929-1433
Fax: (304)253-5072
E-mail: gomsu@mountainstate.edu
Web Site: http://www.mountainstate.edu/
President/CEO: Dr. Charles H. Polk
Admissions: Darlene Brown
Financial Aid: Lynn Whitteker
Type: Comprehensive **Sex:** Coed **Scores:** 42% ACT 18-23; 10% ACT 24-29 **% Accepted:** 100 **Admission Plans:** Open Admission; Early Admission; Deferred Admission **Application Deadline:** Rolling **Application Fee:** $25.00 **H.S. Requirements:** High school diploma required; GED accepted **Costs Per Year:** Application fee: $25. Comprehensive fee: $14,816 includes full-time tuition ($6450), mandatory fees ($2250), and college room and board ($6116). College room only: $3000. Full-time tuition and fees vary according to course load, degree level, location, and program. Room and board charges vary according to board plan. Part-time tuition: $215 per credit hour. Part-time mandatory fees: $75 per credit hour. Part-time tuition and fees vary according to course load, degree level, location, and program. **Scholarships:** Available **Calendar System:** Semester, Summer Session Available **Enrollment:** FT 3,753, PT 1,490, Grad FT 657, Grad PT 51 **Faculty:** FT 97, PT 335 **Student-Faculty Ratio:** 14:1 **Exams:** ACT, SAT I or ACT, SAT I, SAT II. SAT essay used for placement. ACT essay not being used. **% Receiving Financial Aid:** 50 **% Residing in College-Owned, -Operated, or -Affiliated Housing:** 4 **Library Holdings:** 121,378 **Regional Accreditation:** North Central Association of Colleges and Schools **Credit Hours For Degree:** 64 credit hours, Associates; 120 credit hours, Bachelors **Professional Accreditation:** AAMAE, AANA, AOTA, APTA, CARC, CSWE, NLN **Intercollegiate Athletics:** Basketball M; Cheerleading M & W; Cross-Country Running M & W; Soccer M & W; Track and Field M & W; Volleyball W

MOUNTWEST COMMUNITY & TECHNICAL COLLEGE
One John Marshall Dr.
Huntington, WV 25755
Tel: (304)696-6282
Admissions: (304)696-3160
E-mail: admissions@marshall.edu
Web Site: http://www.mctc.edu/
President/CEO: Dr. Keith J. Cotroneo
Admissions: Dr. Tammy Johnson
Type: Two-Year College **Sex:** Coed **Affiliation:** Community and Technical College System of West Virginia **Scores:** 43.5% SAT V 400+; 22% SAT M 400+; 33% ACT 18-23; 3% ACT 24-29 **% Accepted:** 100 **Admission Plans:** Open Admission; Deferred Admission **Application Deadline:** Rolling **Application Fee:** $30.00 **H.S. Requirements:** High school diploma required; GED accepted **Costs Per Year:** Application fee: $30. State resident tuition: $2856 full-time, $119 per credit hour part-time. Nonresident tuition: $8160 full-time, $340.20 per credit hour part-time. Full-time tuition varies according to reciprocity agreements. Part-time tuition varies according to reciprocity agreements. College room and board: $7556. College room only: $4474. Room and board charges vary according to board plan and housing facility. **Calendar System:** Semester, Summer Session Available **Enrollment:** FT 1,400, PT 1,134 **Faculty:** FT 49, PT 107 **Student-Faculty Ratio:** 21:1 **Library Holdings:** 1,610,460 **Regional Accreditation:** North Central Association of Colleges and Schools **Credit Hours For Degree:** 64 credits, Associates **ROTC:** Army **Professional Accreditation:** AAMAE

NEW RIVER COMMUNITY AND TECHNICAL COLLEGE
167 Dye Dr.
Beckley, WV 25801
Tel: (304)255-5821
Admissions: (304)929-6736
Web Site: http://www.newriver.edu/
President/CEO: Dr. Ted Spring
Admissions: Michael Palm
Type: Two-Year College **Sex:** Coed **Regional Accreditation:** North Central Association of Colleges and Schools

OHIO VALLEY UNIVERSITY
One Campus View Dr.
Vienna, WV 26105-8000
Tel: (304)865-6000; Free: 877-446-8668
Admissions: (304)865-6200
Fax: (304)865-6001
E-mail: admissions@ovu.edu
Web Site: http://www.ovu.edu/
President/CEO: Dr. Keith Stotts
Admissions: Valerie Wright
Financial Aid: Summer Cook Boggess
Type: Comprehensive **Sex:** Coed **Affiliation:** Church of Christ **Scores:** 90% SAT V 400+; 91% SAT M 400+; 58% ACT 18-23; 23% ACT 24-29 **% Accepted:** 57 **Admission Plans:** Early Admission; Deferred Admission **Application Deadline:** August 15 **Application Fee:** $20.00 **H.S. Requirements:** High school diploma required; GED accepted **Costs Per Year:** Application fee: $20. One-time mandatory fee: $60. Comprehensive fee: $23,876 includes full-time tuition ($15,688), mandatory fees ($1512), and college room and board ($6676). Full-time tuition and fees vary according to course load. Room and board charges vary according to board plan and housing facility. Part-time tuition: $525 per credit hour. Part-time tuition varies according to course load. **Scholarships:** Available **Calendar System:** Semester, Summer Session Available **Enrollment:** FT 415, PT 64, Grad FT 9, Grad PT 13 **Faculty:** FT 23, PT 52 **Student-Faculty Ratio:** 11:1 **Exams:** SAT I or ACT. ACT essay used for placement. **% Receiving Financial Aid:** 77 **% Residing in College-Owned, -Operated, or -Affiliated Housing:** 48 **Library Holdings:** 34,000 **Regional Accreditation:** North Central Association of Colleges and Schools **Credit Hours For Degree:** 64 semester hours, Associates; 128 semester hours, Bachelors **ROTC:** Air Force **Intercollegiate Athletics:** Baseball M; Basketball M & W; Cross-Country Running M & W; Golf M & W; Lacrosse M; Soccer M & W; Softball W; Volleyball W; Wrestling M

PIERPONT COMMUNITY & TECHNICAL COLLEGE OF FAIRMONT STATE UNIVERSITY
1201 Locust Ave.
Fairmont, WV 26554
Tel: (304)367-4892; Free: 800-641-5678
Fax: (304)367-4692
Web Site: http://www.fairmontstate.edu/
President/CEO: Blair Montgomery
Admissions: Steve Leadman
Type: Two-Year College **Sex:** Coed **Affiliation:** Fairmont State College **% Accepted:** 92 **Admission Plans:** Open Admission; Deferred Admission **Application Deadline:** Rolling **Application Fee:** $0.00 **H.S. Requirements:** High school diploma required; GED accepted **Calendar System:** Semester, Summer Session Available **Enrollment:** FT 1,672, PT 1,180 **Faculty:** FT 232, PT 263 **Student-Faculty Ratio:** 18:1 **Exams:** SAT I or ACT. **% Residing in College-Owned, -Operated, or -Affiliated Housing:** 12 **Regional Accreditation:** North Central Association of Colleges and Schools **Professional Accreditation:** ACF, AHIMA, APTA, NAACLS, NLN

POTOMAC STATE COLLEGE OF WEST VIRGINIA UNIVERSITY
101 Fort Ave.
Keyser, WV 26726-2698
Tel: (304)788-6800; Free: 800-262-7332
Admissions: (304)788-6820
Fax: (304)788-6939
E-mail: go2psc@mail.wvu.edu
Web Site: http://www.potomacstatecollege.edu/
President/CEO: Dr. Kerry S. Odell
Admissions: Beth Little
Type: Two-Year College **Sex:** Coed **Affiliation:** West Virginia Higher Education Policy Commission **Scores:** 72% SAT V 400+; 66% SAT M 400+; 50% ACT 18-23; 9% ACT 24-29 **Admission Plans:** Open Admission; Early Admission **Application Deadline:** Rolling **Application Fee:** $0.00 **H.S. Requirements:** High school diploma required; GED accepted **Scholarships:** Available **Calendar System:** Semester, Summer Session Available **Enrollment:** FT 1,344, PT 466 **Faculty:** FT 41, PT 46 **Student-Faculty Ratio:** 27:1 **Exams:** SAT I or ACT. **Library Holdings:** 44,197 **Regional Accreditation:** North Central Association of Colleges and Schools **Credit Hours For Degree:** 62 credit hours, Associates **Intercollegiate Athletics:** Baseball M; Basketball M & W; Golf M & W; Soccer M & W; Softball W; Volleyball W

SALEM INTERNATIONAL UNIVERSITY
223 West Main St., PO Box 500
Salem, WV 26426-0500
Tel: (304)782-5011; Free: 800-283-4562
Admissions: (304)326-1359
E-mail: admissions@salemiu.edu
Web Site: http://www.salemu.edu/
President/CEO: J. William Brooks
Admissions: Gina Cossey
Financial Aid: Pat Zinsmeister
Type: Comprehensive **Sex:** Coed **Admission Plans:** Deferred Admission **Application Deadline:** Rolling **Application Fee:** $25.00 **H.S. Requirements:** High school diploma required; GED accepted **Scholarships:** Available **Calendar System:** Miscellaneous, Summer Session Not available **Faculty:** FT 13, PT 3 **Student-Faculty Ratio:** 13:1 **Exams:** SAT I or ACT. **% Receiving Financial Aid:** 35 **% Residing in College-Owned, -Operated, or -Affiliated Housing:** 70 **Library Holdings:** 106,991 **Regional Accreditation:** North Central Association of Colleges and Schools **Credit Hours For Degree:** 64 credit hours, Associates; 128 credit hours, Bachelors **Professional Accreditation:** ACBSP **Intercollegiate Athletics:** Baseball M; Basketball M & W; Cheerleading M & W; Golf M; Gymnastics W; Ice Hockey M; Soccer M & W; Softball W; Swimming and Diving M & W; Tennis M; Volleyball W; Water Polo M & W

SHEPHERD UNIVERSITY
PO Box 5000
Shepherdstown, WV 25443
Tel: (304)876-5000; Free: 800-344-5231
Admissions: (304)876-5212
Fax: (304)876-5165
E-mail: admissions@shepherd.edu
Web Site: http://www.shepherd.edu/
President/CEO: Dr. Suzanne Shipley
Admissions: Randall Friend
Financial Aid: Sandra Oerly-Bennett
Type: Comprehensive **Sex:** Coed **Affiliation:** West Virginia Higher Education Policy Commission **Scores:** 97.84% SAT V 400+; 95.69% SAT M 400+; 64.73% ACT 18-23; 29.21% ACT 24-29 **% Accepted:** 94 **Admission Plans:** Early Admission; Early Action; Deferred Admission **Application Deadline:** Rolling **Application Fee:** $45.00 **H.S. Requirements:** High school diploma required; GED accepted **Costs Per Year:** Application fee: $45. State resident tuition: $5234 full-time, $214 per credit hour part-time. Nonresident tuition: $13,574 full-time, $561 per credit hour part-time. Full-time tuition varies according to program and reciprocity agreements. Part-time tuition varies according to program. College room and board: $7228. Room and board charges vary according to board plan and housing facility. **Scholarships:** Available **Calendar System:** Semester, Summer Session Available **Enrollment:** FT 3,301, PT 801, Grad FT 50, Grad PT 104 **Faculty:** FT 124, PT 210 **Student-Faculty Ratio:** 19:1 **Exams:** SAT I or ACT. **% Receiving Financial Aid:** 50 **% Residing in College-Owned, -Operated, or -Affiliated Housing:** 34 **Final Year or Final Semester Residency Requirement:** Yes **Library Holdings:** 169,899 **Regional Accreditation:** North Central Association of Colleges and Schools **Credit Hours For Degree:** 128 semester hours, Bachelors **ROTC:** Air Force **Professional Accreditation:** CSWE, NASM, NCATE, NLN **Intercollegiate Athletics:** Baseball M; Basketball M & W; Football M; Golf M; Lacrosse W; Soccer M & W; Softball W; Tennis M & W; Volleyball W

SOUTHERN WEST VIRGINIA COMMUNITY AND TECHNICAL COLLEGE
Dempsey Branch Rd., PO Box 2900
Mount Gay, WV 25637-2900
Tel: (304)792-7160
Admissions: (304)896-7420
Fax: (304)792-7096
E-mail: admissions@southern.wvnet.edu
Web Site: http://southernwv.edu/
President/CEO: Joanne Tomblin
Admissions: Roy Simmons
Type: Two-Year College **Sex:** Coed **Affiliation:** State College System of West Virginia **% Accepted:** 100 **Admission Plans:** Open Admission; Early Admission; Deferred Admission **Application Deadline:** Rolling **Application Fee:** $0.00 **H.S. Requirements:** High school diploma required; GED accepted **Costs Per Year:** Application fee: $0. State resident tuition: $2102 full-time, $88 per credit hour part-time. Nonresident tuition: $6916 full-time, $284 per credit hour part-time. Full-time tuition varies according to program. Part-time tuition varies according to course load and program. **Scholarships:** Available **Calendar System:** Semester, Summer Session Available **Enrollment:** FT 1,192, PT 708 **Faculty:** FT 66, PT 105 **Student-Faculty Ratio:** 20:1 **Library Holdings:** 66,400 **Regional Accreditation:** North Central Association of Colleges and Schools **Credit Hours For Degree:** 63 semester hours, Associates **Professional Accreditation:** ARCEST, JRCERT, NAACLS, NLN

STRAYER UNIVERSITY - TEAYS VALLEY CAMPUS
100 Corporate Center Dr.
Scott Depot, WV 25560
Tel: (304)760-1700
Fax: (304)757-1430
Web Site: http://www.strayer.edu/teays_valley/
Type: Comprehensive **Sex:** Coed **Application Fee:** $50.00 **Costs Per Year:** Application fee: $50. **Regional Accreditation:** Middle State Association of Colleges and Schools

UNIVERSITY OF CHARLESTON
2300 MacCorkle Ave., SE
Charleston, WV 25304-1099
Tel: (304)357-4800; Free: 800-995-GOUC
Admissions: (304)357-4750
Fax: (304)357-4781
E-mail: admissions@ucwv.edu
Web Site: http://www.ucwv.edu/
President/CEO: Dr. Edwin H. Welch
Admissions: Alan Liebrecht
Financial Aid: Janet M. Ruge
Type: Comprehensive **Sex:** Coed **Scores:** 84% SAT V 400+; 93% SAT M 400+; 52% ACT 18-23; 33% ACT 24-29 **% Accepted:** 79 **Admission Plans:** Early Admission; Deferred Admission **Application Deadline:** Rolling **Application Fee:** $25.00 **H.S. Requirements:** High school diploma required; GED accepted **Costs Per Year:** Application fee: $25. Comprehensive fee: $32,700 includes full-time tuition ($24,000) and college room and board ($8700). College room only: $4750. Room and board charges vary according to board plan and housing facility. Part-time tuition: $400 per credit hour. Part-time mandatory fees: $75 per term. Part-time tuition and fees vary according to program. **Scholarships:** Available **Calendar System:** Semester, Summer Session Available **Enrollment:** FT 981, PT 31, Grad FT 378, Grad PT 6 **Faculty:** FT 86, PT 34 **Student-Faculty Ratio:** 14:1 **Exams:** SAT I or ACT. ACT essay not being used. SAT essay not being used. **% Receiving Financial Aid:** 81 **% Residing in College-Owned, -Operated, or -Affiliated Housing:** 59 **Library Holdings:** 164,457 **Regional Accreditation:** North Central Association of Colleges and Schools **Credit Hours For Degree:** 60 credit hours, Associates; 120 credit hours, Bachelors **ROTC:** Army **Professional Accreditation:** ACPhE, CARC, JRCERT, JRCEPAT, NCATE, NLN **Intercollegiate Athletics:** Baseball M; Basketball M & W; Cheerleading W; Crew M & W; Cross-Country Running M & W; Football M;

Golf M; Soccer M & W; Softball W; Swimming and Diving M & W; Tennis M & W; Track and Field M & W; Volleyball W

VALLEY COLLEGE OF TECHNOLOGY (BECKLEY)
330 Harper Park Dr.
Beckley, WV 25801
Tel: (304)252-9547
Fax: (304)252-1694
Web Site: http://www.vct.edu/
President/CEO: Beth Gardner
Type: Two-Year College **Sex:** Coed

VALLEY COLLEGE OF TECHNOLOGY (MARTINSBURG)
287 Aikens Center
Martinsburg, WV 25404
Tel: (304)263-0979
Fax: (304)263-2413
E-mail: gkennedy@vct.edu
Web Site: http://www.vct.edu/
President/CEO: Rob Evans
Admissions: Gail Kennedy
Type: Two-Year College **Sex:** Coed **Calendar System:** Continuous **Enrollment:** FT 47 **Faculty:** FT 4, PT 2 **Student-Faculty Ratio:** 14:1 **Professional Accreditation:** ACICS

VALLEY COLLEGE OF TECHNOLOGY (PRINCETON)
616 Harrison St.
Princeton, WV 24740
Tel: (304)425-2323
Fax: (304)428-5890
Web Site: http://www.vct.edu/
President/CEO: Sonya Davis
Type: Two-Year College **Sex:** Coed

WEST LIBERTY UNIVERSITY
PO Box 295
West Liberty, WV 26074
Tel: (304)336-5000; Free: 800-732-6204
Admissions: (304)336-8078
Fax: (304)336-8285
E-mail: wladmsn1@westliberty.edu
Web Site: http://www.westliberty.edu/
President/CEO: Robin Capehart
Admissions: Stephanie North
Financial Aid: Scott A. Cook
Type: Comprehensive **Sex:** Coed **Affiliation:** West Virginia Higher Education Policy Commission **Scores:** 74% SAT V 400+; 67.9% SAT M 400+; 55.9% ACT 18-23; 19.4% ACT 24-29 **% Accepted:** 79 **Application Deadline:** Rolling **Application Fee:** $0.00 **H.S. Requirements:** High school diploma required; GED accepted **Costs Per Year:** Application fee: $0. One-time mandatory fee: $100. State resident tuition: $4880 full-time, $203 per credit hour part-time. Nonresident tuition: $11,950 full-time, $498 per credit hour part-time. College room and board: $6870. Room and board charges vary according to board plan and housing facility. **Scholarships:** Available **Calendar System:** Semester, Summer Session Available **Enrollment:** FT 2,266, PT 331, Grad FT 37, Grad PT 11 **Faculty:** FT 114, PT 88 **Student-Faculty Ratio:** 17:1 **Exams:** SAT I or ACT. **% Receiving Financial Aid:** 67 **% Residing in College-Owned, -Operated, or -Affiliated Housing:** 45 **Library Holdings:** 194,715 **Regional Accreditation:** North Central Association of Colleges and Schools **Professional Accreditation:** ADA, NAACLS, NASM, NCATE, NLN **Intercollegiate Athletics:** Baseball M; Basketball M & W; Cross-Country Running M & W; Football M; Golf M & W; Softball W; Tennis M & W; Track and Field M & W; Volleyball W; Wrestling M

WEST VIRGINIA BUSINESS COLLEGE (NUTTER FORT)
116 Pennsylvania Ave.
Nutter Fort, WV 26301
Tel: (304)624-7695
Fax: (304)622-2149
E-mail: info@wvbc.edu
Web Site: http://www.wvbc.edu/
President/CEO: Gary Gorby
Admissions: Robert Wright
Type: Two-Year College **Sex:** Coed **Application Fee:** $50.00 **Costs Per Year:** Application fee: $50. One-time mandatory fee: $150. Tuition: $9000 full-time. **Professional Accreditation:** ACICS

WEST VIRGINIA BUSINESS COLLEGE (WHEELING)
1052 Main St.
Wheeling, WV 26003
Tel: (304)232-0361
Fax: (304)232-0363
E-mail: wvbcwheeling@stratuswave.net
Web Site: http://www.wvbc.edu/
President/CEO: Karen D. Shaw
Admissions: Karen D. Shaw
Financial Aid: Karen D. Shaw
Type: Two-Year College **Sex:** Coed **% Accepted:** 100 **Application Fee:** $50.00 **H.S. Requirements:** High school diploma required; GED accepted **Scholarships:** Available **Calendar System:** Quarter **Faculty:** FT 0, PT 10 **Student-Faculty Ratio:** 6:1 **Professional Accreditation:** ACICS

WEST VIRGINIA JUNIOR COLLEGE (BRIDGEPORT)
176 Thompson Dr.
Bridgeport, WV 26330
Tel: (304)363-8824; Free: 800-470-5627
Admissions: (304)842-4007
E-mail: admissions@wvjcinfo.net
Web Site: http://www.wvjcinfo.net/
President/CEO: Sharron Stevens
Type: Two-Year College **Sex:** Coed **Admission Plans:** Open Admission **Application Deadline:** Rolling **H.S. Requirements:** High school diploma required; GED accepted **Scholarships:** Available **Calendar System:** Quarter, Summer Session Available **Student-Faculty Ratio:** 23:1 **Credit Hours For Degree:** 98 quarter hours, Associates **Professional Accreditation:** ACICS

WEST VIRGINIA JUNIOR COLLEGE (CHARLESTON)
1000 Virginia St. East
Charleston, WV 25301-2817
Tel: (304)345-2820; Free: 800-924-5208
Web Site: http://www.wvjc.edu/
President/CEO: Bonnie Shumate Landon
Type: Two-Year College **Sex:** Coed **Admission Plans:** Open Admission **Application Deadline:** Rolling **H.S. Requirements:** High school diploma required; GED accepted **Calendar System:** Quarter, Summer Session Available **Student-Faculty Ratio:** 17:1 **Credit Hours For Degree:** 90 quarter hours, Associates **Professional Accreditation:** ACICS

WEST VIRGINIA JUNIOR COLLEGE (MORGANTOWN)
148 Willey St.
Morgantown, WV 26505-5521
Tel: (304)296-8282
Web Site: http://www.wvjcmorgantown.edu/
President/CEO: Patricia Callen
Type: Two-Year College **Sex:** Coed **Admission Plans:** Open Admission **Application Deadline:** Rolling **Application Fee:** $25.00 **H.S. Requirements:** High school diploma required; GED accepted **Calendar System:** Quarter **Student-Faculty Ratio:** 32:1 **Credit Hours For Degree:** 92 quarter hours, Associates **Professional Accreditation:** ACICS

WEST VIRGINIA NORTHERN COMMUNITY COLLEGE
1704 Market St.
Wheeling, WV 26003-3699
Tel: (304)233-5900
Admissions: (304)214-8838
Fax: (304)233-5900
E-mail: rmccray@northern.wvnet.edu
Web Site: http://www.wvncc.edu/
President/CEO: Dr. Martin J. Olshinsky
Admissions: Richard McCray
Financial Aid: Janet M. Fike
Type: Two-Year College **Sex:** Coed **Scores:** 77.8% SAT V 400+; 77.8% SAT M 400+; 53.4% ACT 18-23; 6.8% ACT 24-29 **Admission Plans:** Open Admission; Early Admission; Deferred Admission **Application Deadline:** Rolling **Application Fee:** $0.00 **H.S. Requirements:** High school diploma required; GED accepted **Costs Per Year:** Application fee: $0. State resident tuition: $1968 full-time, $82 per credit hour part-time. Nonresident tuition:

$6870 full-time, $270 per credit hour part-time. Mandatory fees: $390 full-time, $15 per credit hour part-time, $15 per term part-time. Full-time tuition and fees vary according to course load and program. Part-time tuition and fees vary according to course load and program. **Scholarships:** Available **Calendar System:** Semester, Summer Session Available **Enrollment:** FT 1,590, PT 1,560 **Faculty:** FT 62, PT 161 **Student-Faculty Ratio:** 14:1 **Exams:** SAT I or ACT. **Final Year or Final Semester Residency Requirement:** No **Library Holdings:** 36,650 **Regional Accreditation:** North Central Association of Colleges and Schools **Credit Hours For Degree:** 60 credit hours, Associates **Professional Accreditation:** ARCEST, ACF, AHIMA, CARC, NAACLS, NLN

WEST VIRGINIA STATE UNIVERSITY
PO Box 1000
Institute, WV 25112-1000
Tel: (304)766-3000; Free: 800-987-2112
Admissions: (304)766-3033
Fax: (304)766-4158
E-mail: jacksoc@wvstateu.edu
Web Site: http://www.wvstateu.edu/
President/CEO: Dr. Hazo W. Carter, Jr.
Admissions: Christopher D. Jackson
Financial Aid: Mary Blizzard
Type: Comprehensive **Sex:** Coed **Affiliation:** State College System of West Virginia **Admission Plans:** Early Admission **Application Deadline:** August 11 **Application Fee:** $0.00 **H.S. Requirements:** High school diploma required; GED accepted **Scholarships:** Available **Calendar System:** Semester, Summer Session Available **Enrollment:** FT 2,021, PT 1,933, Grad FT 41, Grad PT 8 **Student-Faculty Ratio:** 19:1 **Exams:** SAT I or ACT, SAT I. **% Residing in College-Owned, -Operated, or -Affiliated Housing:** 7 **Regional Accreditation:** North Central Association of Colleges and Schools **Credit Hours For Degree:** 120 semester hours, Bachelors **ROTC:** Army **Professional Accreditation:** ABET, CSWE, NCATE, NRPA **Intercollegiate Athletics:** Baseball M; Basketball M & W; Cross-Country Running M & W; Football M; Golf W; Softball W; Tennis M & W; Track and Field M & W; Volleyball W

WEST VIRGINIA UNIVERSITY
University Ave.
Morgantown, WV 26506
Tel: (304)293-0111; Free: 800-344-9881
Admissions: (304)293-2124
Fax: (304)293-3080
E-mail: go2wvu@mail.wvu.edu
Web Site: http://www.wvu.edu/
President/CEO: Dr. James P. Clements
Admissions: Kim Guynn
Financial Aid: Kaye Widney
Type: University **Sex:** Coed **Affiliation:** West Virginia Higher Education Policy Commission **Scores:** 95.59% SAT V 400+; 97.27% SAT M 400+; 51.83% ACT 18-23; 34.82% ACT 24-29 **% Accepted:** 88 **Admission Plans:** Preferred Admission; Early Admission; Deferred Admission **Application Deadline:** August 1 **Application Fee:** $25.00 **H.S. Requirements:** High school diploma required; GED accepted **Costs Per Year:** Application fee: $25. State resident tuition: $5304 full-time, $221 per credit hour part-time. Nonresident tuition: $16,402 full-time, $683 per credit hour part-time. Full-time tuition varies according to location, program, and reciprocity agreements. Part-time tuition varies according to course load, location, program, and reciprocity agreements. College room and board: $7770. Room and board charges vary according to board plan, housing facility, and location. **Scholarships:** Available **Calendar System:** Semester, Summer Session Available **Enrollment:** FT 20,260, PT 1,460, Grad FT 4,639, Grad PT 2,539 **Faculty:** FT 935, PT 300 **Student-Faculty Ratio:** 23:1 **Exams:** SAT I or ACT. ACT essay not being used. SAT essay not being used. **% Receiving Financial Aid:** 49 **% Residing in College-Owned, -Operated, or -Affiliated Housing:** 24 **Final Year or Final Semester Residency Requirement:** No **Library Holdings:** 1,622,266 **Regional Accreditation:** North Central Association of Colleges and Schools **Credit Hours For Degree:** 128 credit hours, Bachelors **ROTC:** Army, Air Force **Professional Accreditation:** AACSB, ABET, ACPhE, ACEJMC, AACN, ABA, ACA, ADA, ADtA, AOTA, APTA, APA, ASLA, ASLHA, ACIPE, AALS, FIDER, CEPH, CORE, CSWE JRCEPAT, LCMEAMA, NAACLS, NASAD, NASM, NASPAA, NAST, NCATE, NRPA, SAF **Intercollegiate Athletics:** Baseball M; Basketball M & W; Cheerleading M & W; Crew W; Cross-Country Running W; Football M; Gymnastics W; Riflery M & W; Soccer M & W; Swimming and Diving M & W; Tennis W; Track and Field W; Volleyball W; Wrestling M

WEST VIRGINIA UNIVERSITY INSTITUTE OF TECHNOLOGY
405 Fayette Pike
Montgomery, WV 25136
Tel: (304)442-3071; Free: 888-554-8324
Admissions: (304)981-6240
Fax: (304)442-3097
E-mail: Reeta.Piirala-Skoglund@mail.wvu.edu
Web Site: http://www.wvutech.edu/
President/CEO: Dr. Scott Hurst
Admissions: Reeta Piirala-Skoglund
Financial Aid: Nina M. Morton
Type: Comprehensive **Sex:** Coed **Affiliation:** University System of West Virginia **Scores:** 66% SAT V 400+; 78% SAT M 400+; 56% ACT 18-23; 20% ACT 24-29 **Admission Plans:** Early Admission **Application Deadline:** Rolling **H.S. Requirements:** High school diploma required; GED accepted **Costs Per Year:** State resident tuition: $4460 full-time, $217 per credit hour part-time. Nonresident tuition: $13,090 full-time, $555 per credit hour part-time. Mandatory fees: $352 full-time. Full-time tuition and fees vary according to program. Part-time tuition varies according to course load and program. College room and board: $8028. College room only: $4928. Room and board charges vary according to board plan and housing facility. **Scholarships:** Available **Calendar System:** Semester, Summer Session Available **Enrollment:** FT 1,006, PT 238 **Faculty:** FT 75, PT 36 **Student-Faculty Ratio:** 14:1 **Exams:** Other, SAT I or ACT. ACT essay not being used. SAT essay not being used. **% Receiving Financial Aid:** 54 **% Residing in College-Owned, -Operated, or -Affiliated Housing:** 25 **Final Year or Final Semester Residency Requirement:** Yes **Library Holdings:** 166,292 **Regional Accreditation:** North Central Association of Colleges and Schools **Credit Hours For Degree:** 128 semester hours, Bachelors **ROTC:** Army **Professional Accreditation:** ABET, ADA, CARC **Intercollegiate Athletics:** Baseball M; Basketball M & W; Cheerleading M & W; Cross-Country Running M & W; Football M; Golf M; Soccer M & W; Softball W; Volleyball W; Wrestling M

WEST VIRGINIA UNIVERSITY AT PARKERSBURG
300 Campus Dr.
Parkersburg, WV 26104
Tel: (304)424-8000
E-mail: violet.mosser@mail.wvu.edu
Web Site: http://www.wvup.edu/
President/CEO: Marie Foster Gnage
Admissions: Violet Mosser
Type: Two-Year College **Sex:** Coed **Affiliation:** West Virginia University **Scores:** 53% ACT 18-23; 10% ACT 24-29 **% Accepted:** 100 **Admission Plans:** Open Admission; Early Admission; Deferred Admission **Application Deadline:** Rolling **Application Fee:** $0.00 **H.S. Requirements:** High school diploma required; GED accepted **Calendar System:** Semester, Summer Session Available **Enrollment:** FT 2,216, PT 1,668 **Faculty:** FT 88, PT 145 **Student-Faculty Ratio:** 20:1 **Library Holdings:** 50,000 **Regional Accreditation:** North Central Association of Colleges and Schools **Credit Hours For Degree:** 64 credit hours, Associates; 128 credit hours, Bachelors **Professional Accreditation:** NCATE, NLN

WEST VIRGINIA WESLEYAN COLLEGE
59 College Ave.
Buckhannon, WV 26201
Tel: (304)473-8000; Free: 800-722-9933
Admissions: (304)473-8510
Fax: (304)472-2571
E-mail: admission@wvwc.edu
Web Site: http://www.wvwc.edu/
President/CEO: Dr. Pamela Balch
Admissions: John Waltz
Financial Aid: Susan George
Type: Comprehensive **Sex:** Coed **Affiliation:** United Methodist Church **Scores:** 83.84% SAT V 400+; 84.85% SAT M 400+; 46% ACT 18-23; 37% ACT 24-29 **% Accepted:** 81 **Admission Plans:** Deferred Admission **Application Fee:** $35.00 **H.S. Requirements:** High school diploma required; GED accepted **Costs Per Year:** Application fee: $35. Comprehensive fee: $31,120 includes full-time tuition ($23,130), mandatory fees ($850), and college room and board ($7140). Full-time tuition and fees vary according to

course load. Room and board charges vary according to board plan and housing facility. **Scholarships:** Available **Calendar System:** Semester, Summer Session Available **Enrollment:** FT 1,321, PT 35, Grad FT 52, Grad PT 8 **Faculty:** FT 75, PT 81 **Student-Faculty Ratio:** 13:1 **Exams:** SAT I or ACT, SAT II. ACT essay used for placement. SAT essay used for placement. **% Receiving Financial Aid:** 76 **% Residing in College-Owned, -Operated, or -Affiliated Housing:** 79 **Library Holdings:** 130,000 **Regional Accreditation:** North Central Association of Colleges and Schools **Credit Hours For Degree:** 120 credit hours, Bachelors **Professional Accreditation:** AAFCS, JRCEPAT, NASM, NCATE, NLN **Intercollegiate Athletics:** Baseball M; Basketball M & W; Cheerleading M & W; Cross-Country Running M & W; Football M; Golf M & W; Lacrosse M & W; Skiing (Downhill) M & W; Soccer M & W; Softball W; Swimming and Diving M & W; Tennis M & W; Track and Field M & W; Volleyball W

WHEELING JESUIT UNIVERSITY
316 Washington Ave.
Wheeling, WV 26003-6295
Tel: (304)243-2000; Free: 800-624-6992
Admissions: (304)243-2425
Fax: (304)243-2397
E-mail: bloy@wju.edu
Web Site: http://www.wju.edu/
President/CEO: Sr. Francis Thrailkill
Admissions: Beth Loy
Financial Aid: Christie Tomczyk

Type: Comprehensive **Sex:** Coed **Affiliation:** Roman Catholic (Jesuit) **Scores:** 98% SAT V 400+; 92% SAT M 400+; 52% ACT 18-23; 40% ACT 24-29 **% Accepted:** 74 **Admission Plans:** Early Admission; Deferred Admission **Application Deadline:** Rolling **Application Fee:** $25.00 **H.S. Requirements:** High school diploma required; GED accepted **Costs Per Year:** Application fee: $25. Tuition: $23,590 full-time, $655 per hour part-time. Mandatory fees: $800 full-time. **Scholarships:** Available **Calendar System:** Semester, Summer Session Available **Enrollment:** FT 900, PT 186, Grad FT 122, Grad PT 153 **Faculty:** FT 72, PT 73 **Student-Faculty Ratio:** 11:1 **Exams:** SAT I or ACT. **% Receiving Financial Aid:** 80 **% Residing in College-Owned, -Operated, or -Affiliated Housing:** 78 **Library Holdings:** 148,117 **Regional Accreditation:** North Central Association of Colleges and Schools **Credit Hours For Degree:** 120 credit hours, Bachelors **Professional Accreditation:** AACN, APTA, ACBSP, CARC, JRCNMT **Intercollegiate Athletics:** Baseball M; Basketball M & W; Cheerleading M & W; Cross-Country Running M & W; Golf M & W; Lacrosse M; Soccer M & W; Softball W; Swimming and Diving M & W; Track and Field M & W; Volleyball W

ALVERNO COLLEGE
3400 South 43rd St., PO Box 343922
Milwaukee, WI 53234-3922
Tel: (414)382-6000; Free: 800-933-3401
Admissions: (414)382-6103
Fax: (414)382-6354
E-mail: admissions@alverno.edu
Web Site: http://www.alverno.edu/
President/CEO: Dr. Mary Meehan
Admissions: Holly Schwoerer
Financial Aid: Dan Goyette
Type: Comprehensive **Affiliation:** Roman Catholic **Scores:** 60% ACT 18-23; 13% ACT 24-29 **% Accepted:** 85 **Admission Plans:** Deferred Admission **Application Deadline:** Rolling **Application Fee:** $20.00 **H.S. Requirements:** High school diploma required; GED accepted **Scholarships:** Available **Calendar System:** Semester, Summer Session Available **Enrollment:** FT 1,720, PT 667, Grad FT 239, Grad PT 189 **Faculty:** FT 118, PT 137 **Student-Faculty Ratio:** 13:1 **Exams:** SAT I or ACT. ACT essay not being used. SAT essay not being used. **% Receiving Financial Aid:** 83 **% Residing in College-Owned, -Operated, or -Affiliated Housing:** 9 **Final Year or Final Semester Residency Requirement:** No **Library Holdings:** 106,372 **Regional Accreditation:** North Central Association of Colleges and Schools **Credit Hours For Degree:** 60 credits, Associates; 120 credits, Bachelors **ROTC:** Army, Air Force **Professional Accreditation:** AACN, NASM, NCATE **Intercollegiate Athletics:** Basketball W; Cross-Country Running W; Soccer W; Softball W; Tennis W; Volleyball W

BELLIN COLLEGE
3201 Eaton Rd.
Green Bay, WI 54305
Tel: (920)433-3560; Free: 800-236-8707
Admissions: (920)433-6699
Fax: (920)433-7416
E-mail: admissio@bcon.edu
Web Site: http://www.bellincollege.edu/
President/CEO: V. Jane Muhl
Admissions: Dr. Penny Croghan
Financial Aid: Lena C. Goodman
Type: Comprehensive **Sex:** Coed **Affiliation:** Bellin Health System **Application Deadline:** Rolling **Application Fee:** $30.00 **H.S. Requirements:** High school diploma required; GED accepted **Scholarships:** Available **Calendar System:** Semester, Summer Session Available **Exams:** ACT. **% Receiving Financial Aid:** 48 **Library Holdings:** 7,000 **Regional Accreditation:** North Central Association of Colleges and Schools **Credit Hours For Degree:** 129 credits, Bachelors **ROTC:** Army **Professional Accreditation:** AACN, NLN

BELOIT COLLEGE
700 College St.
Beloit, WI 53511-5596
Tel: (608)363-2000; Free: 800-9-BELOIT
Admissions: (608)363-2500
Fax: (608)363-2075
E-mail: admiss@beloit.edu
Web Site: http://www.beloit.edu/
President/CEO: Dr. Scott Bierman
Admissions: James S. Zielinski
Financial Aid: Jon Urish
Type: Four-Year College **Sex:** Coed **Scores:** 99.34% SAT V 400+; 96.03% SAT M 400+; 18.64% ACT 18-23; 51.82% ACT 24-29 **% Accepted:** 73 **Admission Plans:** Early Admission; Early Action; Deferred Admission **Application Deadline:** January 15 **Application Fee:** $35.00 **H.S. Requirements:** High school diploma required; GED accepted **Costs Per Year:** Application fee: $35. Comprehensive fee: $40,198 includes full-time tuition ($33,138), mandatory fees ($230), and college room and board ($6830). College room only: $3348. Room and board charges vary according to board plan. Part-time tuition: $4142 per course. **Scholarships:** Available **Calendar System:** Semester, Summer Session Available **Enrollment:** FT 1,346, PT 61 **Faculty:** FT 123, PT 12 **Student-Faculty Ratio:** 11:1 **Exams:** SAT I or ACT. ACT essay not being used. SAT essay not being used. **% Receiving Financial Aid:** 64 **% Residing in College-Owned, -Operated, or -Affiliated Housing:** 96 **Library Holdings:** 631,140 **Regional Accreditation:** North Central Association of Colleges and Schools **Credit Hours For Degree:** 31 units, Bachelors **Intercollegiate Athletics:** Baseball M; Basketball M & W; Crew M & W; Cross-Country Running M & W; Fencing M & W; Football M; Golf M; Ice Hockey M & W; Lacrosse M & W; Soccer M & W; Softball W; Swimming and Diving M & W; Tennis M & W; Track and Field M & W; Volleyball W

BLACKHAWK TECHNICAL COLLEGE
PO Box 5009
Janesville, WI 53547-5009
Tel: (608)758-6900; Free: 800-472-0024
Fax: (608)757-9407
Web Site: http://www.blackhawk.edu/
President/CEO: Eric Larson
Admissions: Barbara Erlandson
Type: Two-Year College **Sex:** Coed **Affiliation:** Wisconsin Technical College System **Admission Plans:** Open Admission; Preferred Admission **Application Deadline:** Rolling **Application Fee:** $30.00 **H.S. Requirements:** High school diploma required; GED accepted **Scholarships:** Available **Calendar System:** Semester, Summer Session Available **Library Holdings:** 25,000 **Regional Accreditation:** North Central Association of Colleges and Schools **Credit Hours For Degree:** 65 credits, Associates **Professional Accreditation:** ACF, ADA, APTA, JRCERT, NLN

BRYANT & STRATTON COLLEGE
310 West Wisconsin Ave.
Ste. 500 East
Milwaukee, WI 53202-2608
Tel: (414)276-5200
Web Site: http://www.bryantstratton.edu/
President/CEO: Peter J. Pavone
Admissions: Kristin Weiss
Type: Two-Year College **Sex:** Coed **Affiliation:** Bryant and Stratton College, Inc. **% Accepted:** 89 **Application Deadline:** Rolling **Application Fee:** $0.00 **H.S. Requirements:** High school diploma required; GED accepted **Scholarships:** Available **Calendar System:** Semester, Summer Session Available **Enrollment:** FT 460, PT 368 **Faculty:** FT 19, PT 83 **Student-Faculty Ratio:** 13:1 **Exams:** Other, SAT I or ACT. **Regional Accreditation:** Middle State

Association of Colleges and Schools **Credit Hours For Degree:** 60 semester hours, Associates; 120 semester hours, Bachelors **Professional Accreditation:** AAMAE

BRYANT & STRATTON COLLEGE - WAUWATOSA CAMPUS
10950 W. Potter Rd.
Wauwatosa, WI 53226
Tel: (414)302-7000
Web Site: http://www.bryantstratton.edu/
President/CEO: Pete Pavone
Admissions: Tony Krocak
Type: Four-Year College **Sex:** Coed **Application Deadline:** Rolling **H.S. Requirements:** High school diploma required; GED accepted **Calendar System:** Semester **Enrollment:** FT 930, PT 334 **Student-Faculty Ratio:** 10:1 **Exams:** Other, SAT I or ACT. **Final Year or Final Semester Residency Requirement:** No **Regional Accreditation:** Middle State Association of Colleges and Schools **Credit Hours For Degree:** 60 credits, Associates; 120 credits, Bachelors

CARDINAL STRITCH UNIVERSITY
6801 North Yates Rd.
Milwaukee, WI 53217-3985
Tel: (414)410-4000; Free: 800-347-8822
Admissions: (414)410-4040
Fax: (414)410-4239
E-mail: admityou@stritch.edu
Web Site: http://www.stritch.edu/
President/CEO: Dr. Helen C. Sobehart
Admissions: Kristine Bueno
Type: Comprehensive **Sex:** Coed **Affiliation:** Roman Catholic **Scores:** 93% SAT V 400+; 63% ACT 18-23; 18% ACT 24-29 **% Accepted:** 93 **Admission Plans:** Deferred Admission **Application Deadline:** August 1 **Application Fee:** $25.00 **H.S. Requirements:** High school diploma required; GED accepted **Scholarships:** Available **Calendar System:** Semester, Summer Session Available **Enrollment:** FT 2,857, PT 223 **Faculty:** FT 98, PT 360 **Student-Faculty Ratio:** 16:1 **Exams:** SAT I or ACT. **% Receiving Financial Aid:** 70 **% Residing in College-Owned, -Operated, or -Affiliated Housing:** 5 **Library Holdings:** 124,897 **Regional Accreditation:** North Central Association of Colleges and Schools **Credit Hours For Degree:** 64 credits, Associates; 128 credits, Bachelors **Professional Accreditation:** AACN, ACBSP, NCATE, NLN **Intercollegiate Athletics:** Baseball M; Basketball M & W; Cross-Country Running M & W; Soccer M & W; Softball W; Volleyball M & W

CARROLL UNIVERSITY
100 North East Ave.
Waukesha, WI 53186-5593
Tel: (262)547-1211; Free: 800-CAR-ROLL
Admissions: (262)524-7221
Fax: (262)524-7139
E-mail: info@carrollu.edu
Web Site: http://www.carrollu.edu/
President/CEO: Dr. Douglas N. Hastad
Admissions: James Wiseman
Financial Aid: Dawn Scott
Type: Comprehensive **Sex:** Coed **Affiliation:** Presbyterian **Scores:** 52.9% ACT 18-23; 40% ACT 24-29 **% Accepted:** 73 **Admission Plans:** Deferred Admission **Application Deadline:** Rolling **Application Fee:** $0.00 **H.S. Requirements:** High school diploma required; GED accepted **Costs Per Year:** Application fee: $0. Comprehensive fee: $30,605 includes full-time tuition ($22,470), mandatory fees ($467), and college room and board ($7668). College room only: $3833. Full-time tuition and fees vary according to program. Room and board charges vary according to board plan and housing facility. Part-time tuition: $270 per credit. Part-time tuition varies according to course load and program. **Scholarships:** Available **Calendar System:** Semester, Summer Session Available **Enrollment:** FT 2,632, PT 484, Grad FT 124, Grad PT 163 **Faculty:** FT 118, PT 203 **Student-Faculty Ratio:** 17:1 **Exams:** ACT, SAT I or ACT. **% Receiving Financial Aid:** 80 **% Residing in College-Owned, -Operated, or -Affiliated Housing:** 52 **Library Holdings:** 150,000 **Regional Accreditation:** North Central Association of Colleges and Schools **Credit Hours For Degree:** 128 semester hours, Bachelors **ROTC:** Army, Air Force **Professional Accreditation:** APTA **Intercollegiate Athletics:** Baseball M; Basketball M & W; Cross-Country Running M & W; Football M; Golf M & W; Soccer M & W; Swimming and Diving M & W; Tennis M & W; Track and Field M & W; Volleyball W

CARTHAGE COLLEGE
2001 Alford Park Dr.
Kenosha, WI 53140
Tel: (262)551-8500; Free: 800-351-4058
Admissions: (262)551-6000
Fax: (262)551-5762
E-mail: admissions@carthage.edu
Web Site: http://www.carthage.edu/
President/CEO: Dr. F. Gregory Campbell
Admissions: Bradley J. Andrews
Financial Aid: Vatistas Vatistas
Type: Comprehensive **Sex:** Coed **Affiliation:** Evangelical Lutheran Church in America **Scores:** 99% SAT V 400+; 99% SAT M 400+; 45% ACT 18-23; 44% ACT 24-29 **% Accepted:** 77 **Admission Plans:** Early Admission; Early Action; Deferred Admission **Application Deadline:** Rolling **Application Fee:** $25.00 **H.S. Requirements:** High school diploma required; GED accepted **Costs Per Year:** Application fee: $25. Comprehensive fee: $36,000 includes full-time tuition ($28,250) and college room and board ($7750). Full-time tuition varies according to reciprocity agreements. Room and board charges vary according to board plan and housing facility. Part-time tuition: $400 per credit hour. Part-time tuition varies according to class time. **Scholarships:** Available **Calendar System:** 4-1-4, Summer Session Available **Enrollment:** FT 2,233, PT 427 **Faculty:** FT 137 **Student-Faculty Ratio:** 15:1 **Exams:** SAT I or ACT. **% Receiving Financial Aid:** 75 **% Residing in College-Owned, -Operated, or -Affiliated Housing:** 68 **Library Holdings:** 128,551 **Regional Accreditation:** North Central Association of Colleges and Schools **Credit Hours For Degree:** 138 credit hours, Bachelors **ROTC:** Army, Air Force **Professional Accreditation:** CSWE, NASM **Intercollegiate Athletics:** Baseball M; Basketball M & W; Bowling M & W; Cross-Country Running M & W; Football M; Golf M & W; Ice Hockey M & W; Lacrosse M & W; Soccer M & W; Softball W; Swimming and Diving M & W; Tennis M & W; Track and Field M & W; Volleyball M & W; Water Polo W

CHIPPEWA VALLEY TECHNICAL COLLEGE
620 West Clairemont Ave.
Eau Claire, WI 54701-6162
Tel: (715)833-6307; Free: 800-547-2882
Admissions: (715)833-6200
Fax: (715)833-6470
Web Site: http://www.cvtc.edu/
President/CEO: Bruce Barker
Admissions: Timothy Shepardson
Type: Two-Year College **Sex:** Coed **Affiliation:** Wisconsin Technical College System **Admission Plans:** Open Admission; Early Admission; Deferred Admission **Application Deadline:** Rolling **Application Fee:** $30.00 **H.S. Requirements:** High school diploma required; GED accepted **Costs Per Year:** Application fee: $30. State resident tuition: $101.40 per credit hour part-time. Nonresident tuition: $606.85 per credit hour part-time. Mandatory fees: $5.58 per credit hour part-time. Part-time tuition and fees vary according to course load and program. **Scholarships:** Available **Calendar System:** Semester, Summer Session Available **Faculty:** FT 350, PT 50 **Student-Faculty Ratio:** 12:1 **Library Holdings:** 34,000 **Regional Accreditation:** North Central Association of Colleges and Schools **Credit Hours For Degree:** 70 credits, Associates **Professional Accreditation:** AHIMA, JRCEDMS, JRCERT, NAACLS, NLN

COLLEGE OF MENOMINEE NATION
PO Box 1179
Keshena, WI 54135
Tel: (715)799-5600
Fax: (715)799-1308
Web Site: http://www.menominee.edu/
President/CEO: Verna Fowler
Admissions: Cynthia Norton
Type: Two-Year College **Sex:** Coed **Admission Plans:** Open Admission **Application Deadline:** August 14 **Application Fee:** $10.00 **H.S. Requirements:** High school diploma required; GED accepted **Scholarships:** Available **Calendar System:** Semester **Enrollment:** FT 206, PT 293 **Faculty:** FT 14 **Regional Accreditation:** North Central Association of Colleges and Schools **Credit Hours For Degree:** 62 credits, Associates

COLUMBIA COLLEGE OF NURSING
2121 East Newport Ave.
Milwaukee, WI 53211-2952
Tel: (414)961-3530; Free: 800-321-6265
Admissions: (414)256-1219
E-mail: admiss@mtmary.edu
Web Site: http://www.ccon.edu/
President/CEO: Dr. Jill Winters
Admissions: Amy Dobson
Type: Four-Year College **Sex:** Coed **Scores:** 62% ACT 18-23; 34% ACT 24-29 **% Accepted:** 46 **Application Deadline:** August 1 **Application Fee:** $25.00 **H.S. Requirements:** High school diploma required; GED accepted **Costs Per Year:** Application fee: $25. Comprehensive fee: $25,550 includes full-time tuition ($19,950), mandatory fees ($1000), and college room and board ($4600). College room only: $3600. Room and board charges vary according to board plan, housing facility, location, and student level. Part-time tuition: $590 per credit. Part-time mandatory fees: $50 per credit. Part-time tuition and fees vary according to program. **Calendar System:** Semester, Summer Session Available **Enrollment:** FT 243, PT 17 **Faculty:** FT 18, PT 2 **Student-Faculty Ratio:** 13:1 **Exams:** SAT I or ACT. **% Residing in College-Owned, -Operated, or -Affiliated Housing:** 5 **Regional Accreditation:** North Central Association of Colleges and Schools **Credit Hours For Degree:** 131 credits, Bachelors **Professional Accreditation:** NLN

CONCORDIA UNIVERSITY WISCONSIN
12800 North Lake Shore Dr.
Mequon, WI 53097-2402
Tel: (262)243-5700; Free: 888-628-9472
Fax: (262)243-4351
E-mail: admission@cuw.edu
Web Site: http://www.cuw.edu/
President/CEO: Patrick Ferry
Admissions: Julie Schroeder
Financial Aid: Steven P. Taylor
Type: Comprehensive **Sex:** Coed **Affiliation:** Lutheran Church–Missouri Synod; Concordia University System **Scores:** 58.9% ACT 18-23; 32.2% ACT 24-29 **% Accepted:** 64 **Application Deadline:** August 15 **Application Fee:** $35.00 **H.S. Requirements:** High school diploma required; GED accepted **Costs Per Year:** Application fee: $35. Comprehensive fee: $28,986 includes full-time tuition ($20,896), mandatory fees ($100), and college room and board ($7990). Full-time tuition and fees vary according to program. Room and board charges vary according to board plan. Part-time tuition: $870 per credit hour. Part-time tuition varies according to program. Tuition guaranteed not to increase for student's term of enrollment. **Scholarships:** Available **Calendar System:** 4-1-4, Summer Session Available **Enrollment:** FT 2,330, PT 1,757, Grad FT 2,262, Grad PT 829 **Faculty:** FT 110, PT 150 **Student-Faculty Ratio:** 12:1 **Exams:** ACT. **% Receiving Financial Aid:** 81 **% Residing in College-Owned, -Operated, or -Affiliated Housing:** 63 **Regional Accreditation:** North Central Association of Colleges and Schools **Credit Hours For Degree:** 126 credit hours, Bachelors **Professional Accreditation:** AACN, AOTA, APTA, CSWE **Intercollegiate Athletics:** Baseball M; Basketball M & W; Cross-Country Running M & W; Football M; Golf M & W; Soccer M & W; Softball W; Tennis M & W; Track and Field M & W; Volleyball W; Wrestling M

DEVRY UNIVERSITY (MILWAUKEE)
411 East Wisconsin Ave.
Ste. 300
Milwaukee, WI 53202
Tel: (414)278-7677
Fax: (414)278-0137
Web Site: http://www.devry.edu/
President/CEO: David George
Type: Comprehensive **Sex:** Coed **Affiliation:** DeVry University **Admission Plans:** Deferred Admission **Application Deadline:** Rolling **Application Fee:** $50.00 **H.S. Requirements:** High school diploma required; GED accepted **Costs Per Year:** Application fee: $50. Tuition: $14,080 full-time, $550 per credit hour part-time. **Scholarships:** Available **Calendar System:** Semester, Summer Session Available **Enrollment:** FT 35, PT 93, Grad FT 5, Grad PT 80 **Faculty:** FT 1, PT 28 **Student-Faculty Ratio:** 9:1 **Exams:** ACT essay used for admission. SAT essay used for admission. ACT essay used for placement. SAT essay used for placement. **% Receiving Financial Aid:** 75 **Regional Accreditation:** North Central Association of Colleges and Schools **Credit Hours For Degree:** 122 credits, Bachelors

DEVRY UNIVERSITY (WAUKESHA)
N14 W23833 Stone Ridge Dr., Ste. 450
Waukesha, WI 53188-1157
Tel: (262)347-2911
Web Site: http://www.devry.edu/
Type: Comprehensive **Sex:** Coed **Calendar System:** Semester **Regional Accreditation:** North Central Association of Colleges and Schools

EDGEWOOD COLLEGE
1000 Edgewood College Dr.
Madison, WI 53711-1997
Tel: (608)663-4861; Free: 800-444-4861
Admissions: (608)663-2294
Fax: (608)663-3291
E-mail: admissions@edgewood.edu
Web Site: http://www.edgewood.edu/
President/CEO: Dr. Daniel Carey
Admissions: Christine Benedict
Financial Aid: Kari Gribble
Type: Comprehensive **Sex:** Coed **Affiliation:** Roman Catholic **Scores:** 100% SAT V 400+; 83% SAT M 400+; 59.5% ACT 18-23; 32% ACT 24-29 **% Accepted:** 72 **Admission Plans:** Deferred Admission **Application Deadline:** August 14 **Application Fee:** $25.00 **H.S. Requirements:** High school diploma required; GED accepted. Current high school students can take classes through Youth Options without completion of their HS diploma. **Costs Per Year:** Application fee: $25. Comprehensive fee: $28,276 includes full-time tuition ($21,042) and college room and board ($7234). College room only: $3606. Full-time tuition varies according to degree level. Room and board charges vary according to housing facility. Part-time tuition: $662 per credit. Part-time tuition varies according to course load and degree level. **Scholarships:** Available **Calendar System:** Semester, Summer Session Available **Enrollment:** FT 1,514, PT 374, Grad FT 92, Grad PT 569 **Faculty:** FT 108, PT 197 **Student-Faculty Ratio:** 11:1 **Exams:** SAT I or ACT. ACT essay not being used. SAT essay not being used. **% Receiving Financial Aid:** 76 **% Residing in College-Owned, -Operated, or -Affiliated Housing:** 30 **Library Holdings:** 107,873 **Regional Accreditation:** North Central Association of Colleges and Schools **Credit Hours For Degree:** 60 credits, Associates; 120 credits, Bachelors **ROTC:** Army **Professional Accreditation:** AACN, ACBSP, NCATE **Intercollegiate Athletics:** Baseball M; Basketball M & W; Cross-Country Running M & W; Golf M & W; Soccer M & W; Softball W; Tennis M & W; Track and Field M & W; Volleyball W

FOX VALLEY TECHNICAL COLLEGE
1825 North Bluemound, PO Box 2277
Appleton, WI 54912-2277
Tel: (920)735-5600; Free: 800-735-3882
Admissions: (920)735-5643
Fax: (920)735-2582
Web Site: http://www.fvtc.edu/
President/CEO: Dr. Susan A May
Financial Aid: Mary Moede
Type: Two-Year College **Sex:** Coed **Affiliation:** Wisconsin Technical College System **Admission Plans:** Open Admission; Early Admission; Deferred Admission **Application Deadline:** Rolling **Application Fee:** $30.00 **H.S. Requirements:** High school diploma required; GED accepted **Costs Per Year:** Application fee: $30. State resident tuition: $3042 full-time. Nonresident tuition: $4563 full-time. **Scholarships:** Available **Calendar System:** Semester, Summer Session Available **Enrollment:** FT 3,080, PT 7,164 **Faculty:** FT 292, PT 575 **Student-Faculty Ratio:** 13:1 **Library Holdings:** 43,307 **Regional Accreditation:** North Central Association of Colleges and Schools **Credit Hours For Degree:** 60 credits, Associates **Professional Accreditation:** ACF, ADA, AOTA, NLN **Intercollegiate Athletics:** Basketball M & W; Volleyball M & W

GATEWAY TECHNICAL COLLEGE
3520 30th Ave.
Kenosha, WI 53144-1690
Tel: (262)564-2200
Fax: (262)564-2201
E-mail: admissions@gtc.edu
Web Site: http://www.gtc.edu/

President/CEO: Bryan Albrecht
Admissions: Susan Roberts
Financial Aid: Janice L. Riutta
Type: Two-Year College **Sex:** Coed **Affiliation:** Wisconsin Technical College System **% Accepted:** 85 **Admission Plans:** Open Admission; Early Admission; Deferred Admission **Application Deadline:** Rolling **Application Fee:** $30.00 **H.S. Requirements:** High school diploma or equivalent not required. For court reporting, health occupations, law enforcement/police sciences programs: High school diploma required; GED accepted **Scholarships:** Available **Calendar System:** Semester, Summer Session Available **Enrollment:** FT 1,304, PT 5,512 **Faculty:** FT 257, PT 325 **Library Holdings:** 45,433 **Regional Accreditation:** North Central Association of Colleges and Schools **Credit Hours For Degree:** 64 credits, Associates **Professional Accreditation:** ARCEST, ADA, AHIMA, APTA, NLN

HERZING UNIVERSITY
5218 East Terrace Dr.
Madison, WI 53718
Tel: (608)249-6611; Free: 800-582-1227
Fax: (608)249-8593
E-mail: info@msn.herzing.edu
Web Site: http://www.herzing.edu/madison/
President/CEO: Donald G. Madelung
Admissions: Matthew Schneider
Type: Four-Year College **Sex:** Coed **Affiliation:** Herzing Institutes, Inc. **Admission Plans:** Open Admission **Application Deadline:** Rolling **Application Fee:** $0.00 **H.S. Requirements:** High school diploma required; GED accepted **Scholarships:** Available **Calendar System:** Semester **Faculty:** FT 28, PT 20 **Library Holdings:** 1,500 **Regional Accreditation:** North Central Association of Colleges and Schools **Credit Hours For Degree:** 60 credits, Associates; 123 credits, Bachelors **Professional Accreditation:** ACCSCT

ITT TECHNICAL INSTITUTE (GREEN BAY)
470 Security Blvd.
Green Bay, WI 54313
Tel: (920)662-9000; Free: 888-884-3626
Web Site: http://www.itt-tech.edu/
President/CEO: Michael Kranzusch
Type: Two-Year College **Sex:** Coed **Affiliation:** ITT Educational Services, Inc. **H.S. Requirements:** High school diploma required; GED accepted **Scholarships:** Available **Calendar System:** Quarter, Summer Session Not available **Credit Hours For Degree:** 96 credit hours, Associates; 180 credit hours, Bachelors **Professional Accreditation:** ACICS

ITT TECHNICAL INSTITUTE (GREENFIELD)
6300 West Layton Ave.
Greenfield, WI 53220-4612
Tel: (414)282-9494
Web Site: http://www.itt-tech.edu/
President/CEO: Jaravis Racine
Type: Two-Year College **Sex:** Coed **Affiliation:** ITT Educational Services, Inc. **H.S. Requirements:** High school diploma required; GED accepted **Scholarships:** Available **Calendar System:** Quarter, Summer Session Not available **Professional Accreditation:** ACICS

ITT TECHNICAL INSTITUTE (MADISON)
2450 Rimrock Rd., Ste. 100
Madison, WI 53713
Tel: (608)288-6301
Admissions: (608)288-6301
Web Site: http://www.itt-tech.edu/
President/CEO: William Vinson
Type: Two-Year College **Sex:** Coed **Affiliation:** ITT Educational Services, Inc.

LAC COURTE OREILLES OJIBWA COMMUNITY COLLEGE
13466 West Trepania Rd.
Hayward, WI 54843-2181
Tel: (715)634-4790; Free: 888-526-6221
Web Site: http://www.lco.edu/
President/CEO: Danielle Hornett
Admissions: Annette Wiggins
Type: Two-Year College **Sex:** Coed **% Accepted:** 100 **Admission Plans:** Open Admission; Early Admission **Application Deadline:** Rolling **Application Fee:** $10.00 **H.S. Requirements:** High school diploma required; GED accepted. For senior citizens, those who demonstrate ability to benefit from program: High school diploma required; GED not accepted **Costs Per Year:** Application fee: $10. One-time mandatory fee: $10. State resident tuition: $3360 full-time, $140 per credit part-time. Nonresident tuition: $3360 full-time, $140 per credit part-time. Mandatory fees: $30 full-time, $140 per credit part-time, $140. Full-time tuition and fees vary according to class time, course level, course load, degree level, location, program, reciprocity agreements, and student level. Part-time tuition and fees vary according to class time, course level, course load, degree level, location, program, reciprocity agreements, and student level. **Scholarships:** Available **Calendar System:** Semester, Summer Session Not available **Enrollment:** FT 341, PT 220 **Faculty:** FT 15, PT 55 **Student-Faculty Ratio:** 15:1 **Exams:** Other. **Final Year or Final Semester Residency Requirement:** No **Library Holdings:** 25,267 **Regional Accreditation:** North Central Association of Colleges and Schools **Credit Hours For Degree:** 64 semester hours, Associates **Professional Accreditation:** AAMAE

LAKELAND COLLEGE
PO Box 359
Sheboygan, WI 53082-0359
Tel: (920)565-1000
Admissions: (920)565-1007
Fax: (920)565-1206
E-mail: admissions@lakeland.edu
Web Site: http://www.lakeland.edu/
President/CEO: Dr. Stephen A. Gould
Admissions: Nick Spaeth
Financial Aid: Patty Taylor
Type: Comprehensive **Sex:** Coed **Affiliation:** United Church of Christ **Scores:** 63% ACT 18-23; 20% ACT 24-29 **% Accepted:** 77 **Admission Plans:** Deferred Admission **Application Deadline:** Rolling **Application Fee:** $0.00 **H.S. Requirements:** High school diploma required; GED accepted **Costs Per Year:** Application fee: $0. Comprehensive fee: $26,656 includes full-time tuition ($19,640) and college room and board ($7016). Part-time tuition: $657 per credit. Tuition guaranteed not to increase for student's term of enrollment. **Scholarships:** Available **Calendar System:** Miscellaneous, Summer Session Available **Enrollment:** FT 1,060, PT 1,957, Grad FT 142, Grad PT 773 **Faculty:** FT 57, PT 14 **Student-Faculty Ratio:** 17:1 **Exams:** SAT I or ACT. **% Receiving Financial Aid:** 80 **% Residing in College-Owned, -Operated, or -Affiliated Housing:** 67 **Library Holdings:** 57,216 **Regional Accreditation:** North Central Association of Colleges and Schools **Credit Hours For Degree:** 120 credits, Bachelors **Professional Accreditation:** TEAC **Intercollegiate Athletics:** Baseball M; Basketball M & W; Cross-Country Running M & W; Football M; Golf M & W; Soccer M & W; Softball W; Tennis M & W; Track and Field M & W; Volleyball M & W; Wrestling M

LAKESHORE TECHNICAL COLLEGE
1290 North Ave.
Cleveland, WI 53015-1414
Tel: (920)693-1000; Free: 888-GO TO LTC
Fax: (920)693-1363
Web Site: http://www.gotoltc.com/
President/CEO: Dr. Michael Lanser
Type: Two-Year College **Sex:** Coed **Affiliation:** Wisconsin Technical College System **% Accepted:** 51 **Admission Plans:** Open Admission; Early Admission; Deferred Admission **Application Deadline:** Rolling **Application Fee:** $30.00 **H.S. Requirements:** High school diploma required; GED accepted **Costs Per Year:** Application fee: $30. State resident tuition: $101.40 per credit part-time. Nonresident tuition: $606.85 per credit part-time. Mandatory fees: $4 per credit part-time. Part-time tuition and fees vary according to course load, program, and reciprocity agreements. **Scholarships:** Available **Calendar System:** Semester, Summer Session Available **Enrollment:** FT 702, PT 2,087 **Faculty:** FT 99, PT 130 **Student-Faculty Ratio:** 14:1 **Exams:** Other, SAT I or ACT. **Library Holdings:** 15,749 **Regional Accreditation:** North Central Association of Colleges and Schools **Credit Hours For Degree:** 64 credits, Associates **Professional Accreditation:** ADA, JRCERT, NLN

LAWRENCE UNIVERSITY
711 East Boldt Way
Appleton, WI 54911

Tel: (920)832-7000; Free: 800-227-0982
Admissions: (920)832-6500
Fax: (920)832-6606
E-mail: excel@lawrence.edu
Web Site: http://www.lawrence.edu/
President/CEO: Dr. Jill Beck
Admissions: Steven T. Syverson
Financial Aid: Sara Beth Holman
Type: Four-Year College **Sex:** Coed **Scores:** 99% SAT V 400+; 100% SAT M 400+; 5% ACT 18-23; 54% ACT 24-29 **% Accepted:** 69 **Admission Plans:** Early Admission; Early Action; Early Decision Plan; Deferred Admission **Application Deadline:** January 15 **Application Fee:** $40.00 **H.S. Requirements:** High school diploma required; GED not accepted **Costs Per Year:** Application fee: $40. Comprehensive fee: $41,649 includes full-time tuition ($34,326), mandatory fees ($270), and college room and board ($7053). Room and board charges vary according to board plan. **Scholarships:** Available **Calendar System:** Trimester, Summer Session Not available **Enrollment:** FT 1,433, PT 62 **Faculty:** FT 157, PT 32 **Student-Faculty Ratio:** 9:1 **Exams:** ACT essay not being used. SAT essay not being used. **% Receiving Financial Aid:** 60 **% Residing in College-Owned, -Operated, or -Affiliated Housing:** 98 **Library Holdings:** 659,425 **Regional Accreditation:** North Central Association of Colleges and Schools **Credit Hours For Degree:** 36 courses, Bachelors **Professional Accreditation:** NASM **Intercollegiate Athletics:** Baseball M; Basketball M & W; Crew M & W; Cross-Country Running M & W; Fencing M & W; Football M; Golf M; Ice Hockey M & W; Soccer M & W; Softball W; Swimming and Diving M & W; Tennis M & W; Track and Field M & W; Ultimate Frisbee M & W; Volleyball M & W

MADISON AREA TECHNICAL COLLEGE
3550 Anderson St.
Madison, WI 53704-2599
Tel: (608)246-6100; Free: 800-322-6282
Fax: (608)246-6880
Web Site: http://www.matcmadison.edu/matc/
President/CEO: Bettsey Barhorst
Admissions: Maureen Menendez
Type: Two-Year College **Sex:** Coed **Affiliation:** Wisconsin Technical College System **Admission Plans:** Open Admission; Preferred Admission; Early Admission **Application Deadline:** July 1 **Application Fee:** $25.00 **H.S. Requirements:** High school diploma or equivalent not required. For health occupations programs: High school diploma required; GED accepted **Scholarships:** Available **Calendar System:** Semester, Summer Session Available **Faculty:** FT 393, PT 1,488 **Exams:** ACT. **Library Holdings:** 66,000 **Regional Accreditation:** North Central Association of Colleges and Schools **Credit Hours For Degree:** 64 credits, Associates **Professional Accreditation:** ACF, ADA, AOTA, AOA, CARC, JRCERT, NAACLS, NLN **Intercollegiate Athletics:** Baseball M; Basketball M & W; Bowling M & W; Cross-Country Running M & W; Softball W; Tennis M & W; Track and Field M & W; Volleyball M & W; Wrestling M

MADISON MEDIA INSTITUTE
2702 Agriculture Dr.
Madison, WI 53718
Tel: (608)663-2000; Free: 800-236-4997
Fax: (608)442-0141
Web Site: http://www.madisonmedia.edu/
President/CEO: Christopher Hutchings
Admissions: Chris K. Hutchings
Type: Two-Year College **Sex:** Coed **Application Deadline:** Rolling **Application Fee:** $30.00 **Costs Per Year:** Application fee: $30. Tuition: $14,100 full-time, $470 per credit hour part-time. Full-time tuition varies according to class time, course level, course load, degree level, program, and student level. Part-time tuition varies according to class time. Tuition guaranteed not to increase for student's term of enrollment. **Faculty:** FT 20, PT 2 **Professional Accreditation:** ACCSCT

MARANATHA BAPTIST BIBLE COLLEGE
745 West Main St.
Watertown, WI 53094
Tel: (920)261-9300; Free: 800-622-2947
Admissions: (920)206-2327
Fax: (920)261-9109
E-mail: admissions@mbbc.edu
Web Site: http://www.mbbc.edu/
President/CEO: Dr. Marty Marriott
Admissions: Dr. James Harrison
Financial Aid: Bruce Roth
Type: Comprehensive **Sex:** Coed **Affiliation:** Baptist **Scores:** 100% SAT V 400+; 45% ACT 18-23; 40% ACT 24-29 **% Accepted:** 50 **Admission Plans:** Preferred Admission **Application Deadline:** Rolling **Application Fee:** $50.00 **H.S. Requirements:** High school diploma required; GED accepted **Costs Per Year:** Application fee: $50. Comprehensive fee: $17,840 includes full-time tuition ($10,500), mandatory fees ($1050), and college room and board ($6290). Full-time tuition and fees vary according to course load. Part-time tuition: $437 per credit hour. Part-time tuition varies according to course load. **Scholarships:** Available **Calendar System:** Semester, Summer Session Available **Enrollment:** FT 737, PT 52, Grad FT 25, Grad PT 45 **Faculty:** FT 46, PT 33 **Student-Faculty Ratio:** 15:1 **Exams:** SAT I or ACT. ACT essay not being used. SAT essay not being used. **% Receiving Financial Aid:** 71 **% Residing in College-Owned, -Operated, or -Affiliated Housing:** 72 **Final Year or Final Semester Residency Requirement:** Yes **Library Holdings:** 122,251 **Regional Accreditation:** North Central Association of Colleges and Schools **Credit Hours For Degree:** 64 semester hours, Associates; 128 semester hours, Bachelors **ROTC:** Army, Air Force **Intercollegiate Athletics:** Baseball M; Basketball M & W; Cross-Country Running M & W; Football M; Soccer M & W; Softball W; Volleyball W; Wrestling M

MARIAN UNIVERSITY
45 South National Ave.
Fond du Lac, WI 54935-4699
Tel: (920)923-7600
Admissions: 800-262-7426
Fax: (920)923-8755
E-mail: admit@marianuniversity.edu
Web Site: http://www.marianuniversity.edu/
President/CEO: Sr. Mary Mollison, CSA
Admissions: Shannon LaLuzerne
Financial Aid: Pam Warren
Type: Comprehensive **Sex:** Coed **Affiliation:** Roman Catholic **Scores:** 50% ACT 18-23; 16% ACT 24-29 **% Accepted:** 83 **Admission Plans:** Deferred Admission **Application Deadline:** Rolling **Application Fee:** $20.00 **H.S. Requirements:** High school diploma required; GED accepted **Costs Per Year:** Application fee: $20. One-time mandatory fee: $100. Comprehensive fee: $26,540 includes full-time tuition ($20,550), mandatory fees ($350), and college room and board ($5640). College room only: $3910. Full-time tuition and fees vary according to class time, course load, degree level, and program. Room and board charges vary according to board plan and housing facility. Part-time tuition: $315 per credit. Part-time mandatory fees: $80 per term. Part-time tuition and fees vary according to class time, course load, degree level, and program. **Scholarships:** Available **Calendar System:** Semester, Summer Session Available **Enrollment:** FT 1,492, PT 493, Grad FT 78, Grad PT 778 **Faculty:** FT 84, PT 202 **Student-Faculty Ratio:** 13:1 **Exams:** SAT I or ACT. **% Receiving Financial Aid:** 84 **% Residing in College-Owned, -Operated, or -Affiliated Housing:** 33 **Final Year or Final Semester Residency Requirement:** No **Library Holdings:** 116,270 **Regional Accreditation:** North Central Association of Colleges and Schools **Credit Hours For Degree:** 128 credits, Bachelors **ROTC:** Army **Professional Accreditation:** AACN, CSWE, NCATE, NLN **Intercollegiate Athletics:** Baseball M; Basketball M & W; Cross-Country Running M & W; Golf M & W; Ice Hockey M & W; Soccer M & W; Softball W; Tennis M & W; Volleyball W

MARQUETTE UNIVERSITY
PO Box 1881
Milwaukee, WI 53201-1881
Tel: (414)288-7250; Free: 800-222-6544
Admissions: (414)288-7004
E-mail: admissions@marquette.edu
Web Site: http://www.marquette.edu/
President/CEO: Rev. Robert A. Wild, SJ
Admissions: Robert Blust
Financial Aid: Susan Teerink
Type: University **Sex:** Coed **Affiliation:** Roman Catholic (Jesuit) **Scores:** 98.7% SAT V 400+; 99.79% SAT M 400+; 15.22% ACT 18-23; 57.92% ACT 24-29 **% Accepted:** 66 **Admission Plans:** Deferred Admission **Application Deadline:** December 1 **Application Fee:** $30.00 **H.S. Requirements:** High

school diploma required; GED accepted **Costs Per Year:** Application fee: $30. Tuition: $30,040 full-time, $875 per credit part-time. Mandatory fees: $422 full-time. Full-time tuition and fees vary according to course load and program. Part-time tuition varies according to program. **Scholarships:** Available **Calendar System:** Semester, Summer Session Available **Enrollment:** FT 7,693, PT 388, Grad FT 2,050, Grad PT 1,558 **Faculty:** FT 627, PT 483 **Student-Faculty Ratio:** 14:1 **Exams:** SAT I or ACT. ACT essay used for admission. SAT essay used for admission. **% Receiving Financial Aid:** 60 **% Residing in College-Owned, -Operated, or -Affiliated Housing:** 54 **Regional Accreditation:** North Central Association of Colleges and Schools **Credit Hours For Degree:** 128 credits, Bachelors **ROTC:** Army, Navy, Air Force **Professional Accreditation:** AACSB, ABET, ACEJMC, AACN, ABA, ACNM, ADA, APTA, APA, ASLHA, AALS, NAACLS, NCATE, NLN **Intercollegiate Athletics:** Baseball M; Basketball M & W; Cheerleading M & W; Crew M & W; Cross-Country Running M & W; Fencing M & W; Football M; Golf M; Lacrosse M; Rugby M & W; Skiing (Downhill) M & W; Soccer M & W; Softball W; Swimming and Diving M & W; Tennis M & W; Track and Field M & W; Volleyball M & W

MID-STATE TECHNICAL COLLEGE
500 32nd St. North
Wisconsin Rapids, WI 54494-5599
Tel: (715)422-5300
Admissions: (715)422-5500
Fax: (715)422-5345
Web Site: http://www.mstc.edu/
President/CEO: John Clark
Admissions: Carole Prochnow
Type: Two-Year College **Sex:** Coed **Affiliation:** Wisconsin Technical College System **% Accepted:** 95 **Admission Plans:** Open Admission; Early Admission; Deferred Admission **Application Deadline:** Rolling **Application Fee:** $25.00 **H.S. Requirements:** High school diploma required; GED accepted **Scholarships:** Available **Calendar System:** Semester, Summer Session Available **Faculty:** FT 200, PT 100 **Library Holdings:** 20,148 **Regional Accreditation:** North Central Association of Colleges and Schools **Credit Hours For Degree:** 64 credits, Associates **Professional Accreditation:** CARC, NLN **Intercollegiate Athletics:** Basketball M & W; Bowling M & W; Golf M; Volleyball W

MILWAUKEE AREA TECHNICAL COLLEGE
700 West State St.
Milwaukee, WI 53233-1443
Tel: (414)297-6600
Admissions: (414)297-6595
Fax: (414)297-7990
E-mail: adamss4@matc.edu
Web Site: http://www.matc.edu/
President/CEO: Dr. Michael Burke
Admissions: Sarah Adams
Type: Two-Year College **Sex:** Coed **Affiliation:** Wisconsin Technical College System **% Accepted:** 51 **Admission Plans:** Open Admission **Application Deadline:** Rolling **Application Fee:** $30.00 **H.S. Requirements:** High school diploma required; GED accepted **Costs Per Year:** Application fee: $30. State resident tuition: $3042 full-time, $113 per credit hour part-time. Nonresident tuition: $7292 full-time, $164 per credit hour part-time. Mandatory fees: $395 full-time. Full-time tuition and fees vary according to course level and degree level. Part-time tuition varies according to course level and degree level. **Scholarships:** Available **Calendar System:** Semester, Summer Session Available **Enrollment:** FT 7,048, PT 13,167 **Faculty:** FT 580, PT 771 **Student-Faculty Ratio:** 14:1 **Exams:** Other. **Final Year or Final Semester Residency Requirement:** No **Library Holdings:** 90,000 **Regional Accreditation:** North Central Association of Colleges and Schools **Credit Hours For Degree:** 68 credits, Associates **Professional Accreditation:** ARCEST, ABFSE, ACF, ADA, AOTA, APTA, COptA, CARC, JRCECT, JRCERT, NAACLS, NLN **Intercollegiate Athletics:** Baseball M; Basketball M & W; Golf M & W; Soccer M; Volleyball W

MILWAUKEE INSTITUTE OF ART AND DESIGN
273 East Erie St.
Milwaukee, WI 53202-6003
Tel: (414)276-7889; Free: 888-749-MIAD
Admissions: (414)847-3200
Fax: (414)291-8077
E-mail: admissions@miad.edu
Web Site: http://www.miad.edu/
President/CEO: Neil Hoffman
Admissions: Stacey Steinberg
Financial Aid: Lloyd Mueller
Type: Four-Year College **Sex:** Coed **Scores:** 56% ACT 18-23; 23% ACT 24-29 **% Accepted:** 82 **Admission Plans:** Deferred Admission **Application Deadline:** Rolling **Application Fee:** $25.00 **H.S. Requirements:** High school diploma required; GED accepted **Scholarships:** Available **Calendar System:** Semester, Summer Session Available **Enrollment:** FT 606, PT 39 **Faculty:** FT 34, PT 95 **Student-Faculty Ratio:** 10:1 **% Receiving Financial Aid:** 86 **% Residing in College-Owned, -Operated, or -Affiliated Housing:** 23 **Library Holdings:** 23,000 **Regional Accreditation:** North Central Association of Colleges and Schools **Credit Hours For Degree:** 123 credits, Bachelors **Professional Accreditation:** NASAD

MILWAUKEE SCHOOL OF ENGINEERING
1025 North Broadway
Milwaukee, WI 53202-3109
Tel: (414)277-7300; Free: 800-332-6763
Admissions: (414)277-6761
Fax: (414)277-7475
E-mail: grennier@msoe.edu
Web Site: http://www.msoe.edu/
President/CEO: Dr. Hermann Viets
Admissions: Dana-Marie Grennier
Financial Aid: Steve Midthun
Type: Comprehensive **Sex:** Coed **Scores:** 100% SAT V 400+; 21% ACT 18-23; 62% ACT 24-29 **% Accepted:** 67 **Admission Plans:** Deferred Admission **Application Deadline:** Rolling **Application Fee:** $25.00 **H.S. Requirements:** High school diploma required; GED accepted **Costs Per Year:** Application fee: $25. Comprehensive fee: $36,951 includes full-time tuition ($29,520) and college room and board ($7431). College room only: $4737. Room and board charges vary according to board plan and housing facility. Part-time tuition: $513 per quarter hour. Part-time tuition varies according to course load. **Scholarships:** Available **Calendar System:** Quarter, Summer Session Available **Enrollment:** FT 2,246, PT 192, Grad FT 25, Grad PT 185 **Faculty:** FT 132, PT 119 **Student-Faculty Ratio:** 14:1 **Exams:** SAT I or ACT. ACT essay not being used. SAT essay not being used. **% Receiving Financial Aid:** 83 **% Residing in College-Owned, -Operated, or -Affiliated Housing:** 40 **Final Year or Final Semester Residency Requirement:** No **Library Holdings:** 84,325 **Regional Accreditation:** North Central Association of Colleges and Schools **Credit Hours For Degree:** 198 quarter hours, Bachelors **ROTC:** Army, Navy, Air Force **Professional Accreditation:** ABET, ACPE, AACN, ACCE **Intercollegiate Athletics:** Baseball M; Basketball M & W; Cheerleading M & W; Crew M; Cross-Country Running M & W; Golf M & W; Ice Hockey M; Lacrosse M; Soccer M & W; Softball W; Tennis M & W; Track and Field M & W; Volleyball M & W; Wrestling M

MORAINE PARK TECHNICAL COLLEGE
235 North National Ave., PO Box 1940
Fond du Lac, WI 54936-1940
Tel: (920)922-8611
Admissions: (920)924-3200
Fax: (920)924-2471
E-mail: kjarvis@morainepark.edu
Web Site: http://www.morainepark.edu/
President/CEO: Dr. Gayle Hytrek
Admissions: Karen Jarvis
Type: Two-Year College **Sex:** Coed **Affiliation:** Wisconsin Technical College System **Admission Plans:** Open Admission; Deferred Admission **Application Deadline:** Rolling **Application Fee:** $30.00 **H.S. Requirements:** High school diploma required; GED accepted **Scholarships:** Available **Calendar System:** Semester, Summer Session Available **Enrollment:** FT 1,691, PT 6,775 **Faculty:** FT 155, PT 250 **Student-Faculty Ratio:** 14:1 **Exams:** ACT, Other. ACT essay not being used. SAT essay not being used. **Library Holdings:** 41,737 **Regional Accreditation:** North Central Association of Colleges and Schools **Credit Hours For Degree:** 62 credits, Associates **Professional Accreditation:** ACF, AHIMA, NLN

MOUNT MARY COLLEGE
2900 North Menomonee River Parkway
Milwaukee, WI 53222-4597
Tel: (414)258-4810
Fax: (414)256-1224

E-mail: admiss@mtmary.edu
Web Site: http://www.mtmary.edu/
President/CEO: Eileen Schwalbach
Admissions: Mary Ellen Strieter
Financial Aid: Debra Duff
Type: Comprehensive **Affiliation:** Roman Catholic **Scores:** 48% ACT 18-23; 9% ACT 24-29 **% Accepted:** 50 **Admission Plans:** Deferred Admission **Application Deadline:** Rolling **Application Fee:** $25.00 **H.S. Requirements:** High school diploma required; GED accepted **Costs Per Year:** Application fee: $25. Comprehensive fee: $29,616 includes full-time tuition ($21,668), mandatory fees ($450), and college room and board ($7498). Full-time tuition and fees vary according to degree level and program. Room and board charges vary according to board plan. Part-time tuition: $648 per credit hour. Part-time mandatory fees: $120 per term. Part-time tuition and fees vary according to course load, degree level, and program. **Scholarships:** Available **Calendar System:** Semester, Summer Session Available **Enrollment:** FT 921, PT 520, Grad FT 336, Grad PT 148 **Student-Faculty Ratio:** 13:1 **Exams:** SAT I or ACT. ACT essay not being used. SAT essay not being used. **% Receiving Financial Aid:** 85 **% Residing in College-Owned, -Operated, or -Affiliated Housing:** 15 **Final Year or Final Semester Residency Requirement:** Yes **Library Holdings:** 692,734 **Regional Accreditation:** North Central Association of Colleges and Schools **Credit Hours For Degree:** 128 credits, Bachelors **ROTC:** Army, Air Force **Professional Accreditation:** ADtA, AOTA, FIDER, CSWE, NLN **Intercollegiate Athletics:** Basketball W; Cross-Country Running W; Soccer W; Softball W; Tennis W; Volleyball W

NICOLET AREA TECHNICAL COLLEGE
Box 518
Rhinelander, WI 54501-0518
Tel: (715)365-4410
Admissions: (715)365-4451
Fax: (715)365-4445
E-mail: inquire@nicoletcollege.edu
Web Site: http://www.nicoletcollege.edu/
President/CEO: Dr. Adrian Lorbetske
Admissions: Susan Kordula
Type: Two-Year College **Sex:** Coed **Affiliation:** Wisconsin Technical College System **Admission Plans:** Open Admission; Preferred Admission; Early Admission **Application Deadline:** Rolling **Application Fee:** $30.00 **H.S. Requirements:** High school diploma required; GED accepted **Scholarships:** Available **Calendar System:** Semester, Summer Session Available **Student-Faculty Ratio:** 16:1 **Exams:** ACT, Other. **Library Holdings:** 38,369 **Regional Accreditation:** North Central Association of Colleges and Schools **Credit Hours For Degree:** 64 credit hours, Associates **Professional Accreditation:** NLN **Intercollegiate Athletics:** Golf M & W

NORTHCENTRAL TECHNICAL COLLEGE
1000 West Campus Dr.
Wausau, WI 54401-1899
Tel: (715)675-3331
Fax: (715)675-9776
Web Site: http://www.ntc.edu/
President/CEO: Dr. Lori Weyers
Admissions: Carolyn Michalski
Type: Two-Year College **Sex:** Coed **Affiliation:** Wisconsin Technical College System **Admission Plans:** Open Admission; Preferred Admission; Early Admission; Deferred Admission **Application Deadline:** Rolling **Application Fee:** $30.00 **H.S. Requirements:** High school diploma required; GED accepted **Scholarships:** Available **Calendar System:** Semester, Summer Session Available **Library Holdings:** 30,000 **Regional Accreditation:** North Central Association of Colleges and Schools **Credit Hours For Degree:** 64 credits, Associates **Professional Accreditation:** ADA, JRCERT, NLN

NORTHEAST WISCONSIN TECHNICAL COLLEGE
2740 W Mason St., PO Box 19042
Green Bay, WI 54307-9042
Tel: (920)498-5400; Free: 800-422-6982
E-mail: heather.hill@nwtc.edu
Web Site: http://www.nwtc.edu/
President/CEO: H. Jeffery Rafn
Admissions: Heather Hill
Type: Two-Year College **Sex:** Coed **Affiliation:** Wisconsin Technical College System **Admission Plans:** Preferred Admission; Early Admission **Application Deadline:** Rolling **Application Fee:** $30.00 **H.S. Requirements:** High school diploma required; GED accepted **Scholarships:** Available **Calendar System:** Semester, Summer Session Available **Library Holdings:** 22,250 **Regional Accreditation:** North Central Association of Colleges and Schools **Credit Hours For Degree:** 64 credits, Associates **Professional Accreditation:** ABET, ADA, AHIMA, APTA, CARC, NAACLS, NLN

NORTHLAND COLLEGE
1411 Ellis Ave.
Ashland, WI 54806-3925
Tel: (715)682-1699; Free: 800-753-1040
Admissions: (715)682-1257
Fax: (715)682-1258
E-mail: admit@northland.edu
Web Site: http://www.northland.edu/
President/CEO: Dr. James Peterson
Admissions: Ralph Stewart
Financial Aid: Debora L. Milanowski
Type: Four-Year College **Sex:** Coed **Affiliation:** United Church of Christ **Scores:** 100% SAT V 400+; 100% SAT M 400+; 41% ACT 18-23; 45% ACT 24-29 **% Accepted:** 79 **Admission Plans:** Deferred Admission **Application Deadline:** Rolling **Application Fee:** $0.00 **H.S. Requirements:** High school diploma required; GED accepted **Costs Per Year:** Application fee: $0. Comprehensive fee: $32,171 includes full-time tuition ($24,500), mandatory fees ($741), and college room and board ($6930). College room only: $2850. Full-time tuition and fees vary according to course level. Room and board charges vary according to board plan and housing facility. **Scholarships:** Available **Calendar System:** Miscellaneous, Summer Session Available **Enrollment:** FT 565, PT 37, Grad PT 10 **Student-Faculty Ratio:** 12:1 **Exams:** SAT I or ACT. ACT essay not being used. SAT essay not being used. **% Receiving Financial Aid:** 80 **% Residing in College-Owned, -Operated, or -Affiliated Housing:** 64 **Library Holdings:** 77,000 **Regional Accreditation:** North Central Association of Colleges and Schools **Credit Hours For Degree:** 124 credits, Bachelors **Intercollegiate Athletics:** Baseball M; Basketball M & W; Cross-Country Running M & W; Ice Hockey M; Soccer M & W; Softball W; Volleyball W

RASMUSSEN COLLEGE GREEN BAY
940 South Taylor St.
Ste. 100
Green Bay, WI 54303
Tel: (920)593-8400; Free: 888-201-9144
Web Site: http://www.rasmussen.edu/
President/CEO: Scott Borley
Type: Two-Year College **Sex:** Coed **Costs Per Year:** Tuition: $365 per credit part-time. Part-time tuition varies according to course load and program. **Regional Accreditation:** North Central Association of Colleges and Schools

RIPON COLLEGE
300 Seward St., PO Box 248
Ripon, WI 54971
Tel: (920)748-8115; Free: 800-947-4766
Admissions: (920)748-8114
Fax: (920)748-7243
E-mail: adminfo@ripon.edu
Web Site: http://www.ripon.edu/
President/CEO: Dr. David C. Joyce
Financial Aid: Steven M. Schuetz
Type: Four-Year College **Sex:** Coed **Scores:** 93% SAT V 400+; 94% SAT M 400+; 39% ACT 18-23; 43% ACT 24-29 **% Accepted:** 79 **Admission Plans:** Deferred Admission **Application Deadline:** Rolling **Application Fee:** $30.00 **H.S. Requirements:** High school diploma required; GED accepted **Costs Per Year:** Application fee: $30. Comprehensive fee: $32,715 includes full-time tuition ($25,170), mandatory fees ($275), and college room and board ($7270). College room only: $3790. Part-time tuition: $900 per credit. **Scholarships:** Available **Calendar System:** Semester, Summer Session Not available **Enrollment:** FT 1,047, PT 18 **Faculty:** FT 60, PT 32 **Student-Faculty Ratio:** 15:1 **Exams:** SAT I or ACT. ACT essay not being used. SAT essay not being used. **% Receiving Financial Aid:** 85 **% Residing in College-Owned, -Operated, or -Affiliated Housing:** 88 **Final Year or Final Semester Residency Requirement:** No **Library Holdings:** 173,259 **Regional Accreditation:** North Central Association of Colleges and Schools **Credit Hours For Degree:** 124 credits, Bachelors **ROTC:** Army **Intercollegiate Athletics:** Baseball M; Basketball M & W; Cheerleading M & W;

Cross-Country Running M & W; Football M; Golf M & W; Rugby M & W; Soccer M & W; Softball W; Swimming and Diving M & W; Tennis M & W; Track and Field M & W; Volleyball W

ST. NORBERT COLLEGE
100 Grant St.
De Pere, WI 54115-2099
Tel: (920)337-3181; Free: 800-236-4878
Admissions: (920)403-3005
Fax: (920)403-4088
E-mail: admit@snc.edu
Web Site: http://www.snc.edu/
President/CEO: Thomas J. Kunkel
Admissions: Bridget O'Connor
Financial Aid: Jeffrey A. Zahn
Type: Comprehensive **Sex:** Coed **Affiliation:** Roman Catholic **Scores:** 46% ACT 18-23; 44% ACT 24-29 **% Accepted:** 83 **Admission Plans:** Preferred Admission; Deferred Admission **Application Deadline:** Rolling **Application Fee:** $25.00 **H.S. Requirements:** High school diploma required; GED accepted **Costs Per Year:** Application fee: $25. Comprehensive fee: $34,024 includes full-time tuition ($26,522), mandatory fees ($450), and college room and board ($7052). College room only: $3694. Full-time tuition and fees vary according to course load. Room and board charges vary according to board plan, housing facility, and student level. Part-time tuition: $829 per credit. Part-time tuition varies according to course load. **Scholarships:** Available **Calendar System:** Semester, Summer Session Available **Enrollment:** FT 2,041, PT 72, Grad PT 62 **Faculty:** FT 134, PT 49 **Student-Faculty Ratio:** 14:1 **Exams:** SAT I or ACT. **% Receiving Financial Aid:** 68 **% Residing in College-Owned, -Operated, or -Affiliated Housing:** 76 **Final Year or Final Semester Residency Requirement:** Yes **Library Holdings:** 230,595 **Regional Accreditation:** North Central Association of Colleges and Schools **Credit Hours For Degree:** 32 courses, Bachelors **ROTC:** Army **Intercollegiate Athletics:** Baseball M; Basketball M & W; Cross-Country Running M & W; Football M; Golf M & W; Ice Hockey M & W; Soccer M & W; Softball W; Tennis M & W; Track and Field M & W; Volleyball W

SILVER LAKE COLLEGE
2406 South Alverno Rd.
Manitowoc, WI 54220-9319
Tel: (920)684-6691
Admissions: (920)686-6199
Fax: (920)684-7082
E-mail: admslc@silver.sl.edu
Web Site: http://www.sl.edu/
President/CEO: Dr. George Arnold
Admissions: Matthew Thielen
Financial Aid: Michelle Leider
Type: Comprehensive **Sex:** Coed **Affiliation:** Roman Catholic **Scores:** 46% ACT 18-23; 19% ACT 24-29 **% Accepted:** 74 **Admission Plans:** Deferred Admission **Application Deadline:** August 1 **Application Fee:** $50.00 **H.S. Requirements:** High school diploma required; GED accepted **Costs Per Year:** Application fee: $50. Comprehensive fee: $27,880 includes full-time tuition ($20,950), mandatory fees ($230), and college room and board ($6700). College room only: $4800. Full-time tuition and fees vary according to location, program, and reciprocity agreements. Room and board charges vary according to board plan and housing facility. Part-time tuition: $625 per credit. Part-time mandatory fees: $60 per term. Part-time tuition and fees vary according to course load, location, and program. **Scholarships:** Available **Calendar System:** Semester, Summer Session Available **Enrollment:** FT 190, PT 317, Grad FT 14, Grad PT 183 **Faculty:** FT 39, PT 78 **Student-Faculty Ratio:** 6:1 **Exams:** SAT I or ACT. ACT essay used for advising. ACT essay used for placement. **% Receiving Financial Aid:** 85 **% Residing in College-Owned, -Operated, or -Affiliated Housing:** 35 **Library Holdings:** 62,531 **Regional Accreditation:** North Central Association of Colleges and Schools **Credit Hours For Degree:** 60 credits, Associates; 120 credits, Bachelors **Professional Accreditation:** NASM, NCATE **Intercollegiate Athletics:** Basketball M & W; Cross-Country Running M & W; Golf M & W

SOUTHWEST WISCONSIN TECHNICAL COLLEGE
1800 Bronson Blvd.
Fennimore, WI 53809-9778
Tel: (608)822-3262
Admissions: (608)822-2354
Fax: (608)822-6019
E-mail: student-services@swtc.edu
Web Site: http://www.swtc.edu/
President/CEO: Dr. Karen R. Knox
Type: Two-Year College **Sex:** Coed **Affiliation:** Wisconsin Technical College System **% Accepted:** 100 **Admission Plans:** Open Admission; Preferred Admission; Early Admission **Application Deadline:** Rolling **Application Fee:** $30.00 **H.S. Requirements:** High school diploma or equivalent not required **Costs Per Year:** Application fee: $30. State resident tuition: $3042 full-time, $101.40 per credit part-time. Nonresident tuition: $4563 full-time, $152.10 per credit part-time. Mandatory fees: $278 full-time. Full-time tuition and fees vary according to course load, degree level, program, and reciprocity agreements. Part-time tuition varies according to course load, degree level, program, and reciprocity agreements. College room and board: $6137. College room only: $3000. Room and board charges vary according to housing facility. **Scholarships:** Available **Calendar System:** Semester, Summer Session Available **Enrollment:** FT 852, PT 2,557 **Faculty:** FT 94, PT 18 **Student-Faculty Ratio:** 18:1 **Exams:** Other. **% Residing in College-Owned, -Operated, or -Affiliated Housing:** 3 **Final Year or Final Semester Residency Requirement:** No **Library Holdings:** 28,000 **Regional Accreditation:** North Central Association of Colleges and Schools **Credit Hours For Degree:** 64 credits, Associates **Professional Accreditation:** NLN **Intercollegiate Athletics:** Golf M & W

UNIVERSITY OF PHOENIX—MADISON CAMPUS
2310 Crossroads Dr., Ste. 3000
Madison, WI 53718-2416
Tel: (608)240-4701
Web Site: http://www.phoenix.edu/
President/CEO: William Pepicello, PhD
Type: Comprehensive **Sex:** Coed **Regional Accreditation:** North Central Association of Colleges and Schools

UNIVERSITY OF PHOENIX—MILWAUKEE CAMPUS
20075 Watertower Blvd.
Brookfield, WI 53045
Tel: (262)785-0608; Free: (866)766-0766
Web Site: http://www.phoenix.edu/
Type: Comprehensive **Sex:** Coed **Regional Accreditation:** North Central Association of Colleges and Schools

UNIVERSITY OF WISCONSIN—BARABOO/SAUK COUNTY
1006 Connie Rd.
Baraboo, WI 53913-1015
Tel: (608)356-8351
Admissions: (608)355-5270
Fax: (608)356-4074
E-mail: booinfo@uwc.edu
Web Site: http://www.baraboo.uwc.edu/
Admissions: Jan Gerlach
Financial Aid: Jo Christianson
Type: Two-Year College **Sex:** Coed **Affiliation:** University of Wisconsin System **Admission Plans:** Preferred Admission; Early Admission; Deferred Admission **Application Deadline:** Rolling **Application Fee:** $35.00 **H.S. Requirements:** High school diploma required; GED accepted **Costs Per Year:** Application fee: $35. One-time mandatory fee: $125. State resident tuition: $4656 full-time, $195.67 per credit hour part-time. Nonresident tuition: $11,637 full-time, $484.86 per credit hour part-time. Part-time tuition varies according to course load. **Scholarships:** Available **Calendar System:** Semester, Summer Session Available **Enrollment:** FT 354, PT 199 **Faculty:** FT 15, PT 27 **Student-Faculty Ratio:** 13:1 **Exams:** ACT, SAT I or ACT. **Library Holdings:** 45,000 **Regional Accreditation:** North Central Association of Colleges and Schools **Credit Hours For Degree:** 60 credits, Associates **Intercollegiate Athletics:** Basketball M; Golf M & W; Soccer M & W; Tennis M & W; Volleyball W

UNIVERSITY OF WISCONSIN—BARRON COUNTY
1800 College Dr.
Rice Lake, WI 54868-2497
Tel: (715)234-8176
Admissions: (715)234-8024
Web Site: http://www.barron.uwc.edu/
Financial Aid: Sheila Wells
Type: Two-Year College **Sex:** Coed **Affiliation:** University of Wisconsin System **Admission Plans:** Deferred Admission **Application Deadline:**

September 15 **Application Fee:** $44.00 **H.S. Requirements:** High school diploma required; GED accepted **Costs Per Year:** Application fee: $44. State resident tuition: $4568 full-time, $190.34 per credit part-time. Nonresident tuition: $11,556 full-time, $481.33 per credit part-time. **Scholarships:** Available **Calendar System:** Semester, Summer Session Available **Exams:** ACT. **Regional Accreditation:** North Central Association of Colleges and Schools **Credit Hours For Degree:** 60 credits, Associates

UNIVERSITY OF WISCONSIN—EAU CLAIRE
PO Box 4004
Eau Claire, WI 54702-4004
Tel: (715)836-2637
Admissions: (715)836-5415
Fax: (715)836-2380
E-mail: admissions@uwec.edu
Web Site: http://www.uwec.edu/
President/CEO: Dr. Brian Levin-Stankevich
Admissions: Kristina Anderson
Financial Aid: Kathleen Sahlhoff
Type: Comprehensive **Sex:** Coed **Affiliation:** University of Wisconsin System **Scores:** 100% SAT V 400+; 97.44% SAT M 400+; 38.11% ACT 18-23; 55.81% ACT 24-29 **% Accepted:** 67 **Admission Plans:** Early Admission **Application Deadline:** Rolling **Application Fee:** $44.00 **H.S. Requirements:** High school diploma required; GED accepted **Costs Per Year:** Application fee: $44. State resident tuition: $5527 full-time, $276 per credit part-time. Nonresident tuition: $13,100 full-time, $592 per credit part-time. Mandatory fees: $1106 full-time, $46 per credit part-time, $2. Full-time tuition and fees vary according to reciprocity agreements. Part-time tuition and fees vary according to reciprocity agreements. College room and board: $5730. College room only: $2830. Room and board charges vary according to board plan and housing facility. **Scholarships:** Available **Calendar System:** Semester, Summer Session Available **Enrollment:** FT 9,802, PT 685, Grad FT 114, Grad PT 445 **Faculty:** FT 410, PT 95 **Student-Faculty Ratio:** 21:1 **Exams:** SAT I or ACT. ACT essay not being used. SAT essay not being used. **% Receiving Financial Aid:** 44 **% Residing in College-Owned, -Operated, or -Affiliated Housing:** 38 **Final Year or Final Semester Residency Requirement:** Yes **Library Holdings:** 944,303 **Regional Accreditation:** North Central Association of Colleges and Schools **Credit Hours For Degree:** 60 credits, Associates; 120 credits, Bachelors **ROTC:** Army **Professional Accreditation:** AACSB, ABET, ACEJMC, AACN, ASLHA, CSWE, NASM **Intercollegiate Athletics:** Basketball M & W; Cross-Country Running M & W; Football M; Golf M & W; Gymnastics W; Ice Hockey M & W; Soccer W; Softball W; Swimming and Diving M & W; Tennis M & W; Track and Field M & W; Volleyball W; Wrestling M

UNIVERSITY OF WISCONSIN—FOND DU LAC
400 University Dr.
Fond du Lac, WI 54935
Tel: (920)929-1100
Admissions: (920)929-1122
E-mail: tom.martin@uwc.edu
Web Site: http://www.fdl.uwc.edu/
President/CEO: Dr. Judy Goldsmith
Admissions: Tom Martin
Financial Aid: Robyn French
Type: Two-Year College **Sex:** Coed **Affiliation:** University of Wisconsin System **Scores:** 73% ACT 18-23; 19% ACT 24-29 **% Accepted:** 85 **Application Deadline:** Rolling **Application Fee:** $35.00 **H.S. Requirements:** High school diploma required; GED accepted **Costs Per Year:** Application fee: $35. State resident tuition: $4268 full-time, $177.83 per credit part-time. Nonresident tuition: $11,578 full-time, $482.42 per credit part-time. Mandatory fees: $163 full-time, $13.60 per credit part-time. Full-time tuition and fees vary according to reciprocity agreements. Part-time tuition and fees vary according to reciprocity agreements. **Scholarships:** Available **Calendar System:** Semester, Summer Session Available **Enrollment:** FT 506, PT 273 **Faculty:** FT 20, PT 17 **Student-Faculty Ratio:** 19:1 **Exams:** SAT I or ACT. **Final Year or Final Semester Residency Requirement:** Yes **Library Holdings:** 41,891 **Regional Accreditation:** North Central Association of Colleges and Schools **Credit Hours For Degree:** 60 credits, Associates **Intercollegiate Athletics:** Basketball M & W; Golf M & W; Soccer M & W; Tennis M & W; Volleyball W

UNIVERSITY OF WISCONSIN—FOX VALLEY
1478 Midway Rd.
Menasha, WI 54952
Tel: (920)832-2600; Free: 888-INFOUWC
Admissions: (920)832-2620
Fax: (920)832-2674
E-mail: foxinfo@uwc.edu
Web Site: http://www.uwfox.uwc.edu/
President/CEO: Dr. James W. Perry
Admissions: Brenda Rickert
Financial Aid: Kathy Gilmore
Type: Two-Year College **Sex:** Coed **Affiliation:** University of Wisconsin System **Admission Plans:** Early Admission **Application Deadline:** Rolling **Application Fee:** $35.00 **H.S. Requirements:** High school diploma required; GED accepted **Costs Per Year:** Application fee: $35. State resident tuition: $4506 full-time. Nonresident tuition: $11,500 full-time. Full-time tuition varies according to course load and reciprocity agreements. **Scholarships:** Available **Calendar System:** Semester, Summer Session Available **Enrollment:** FT 987, PT 760 **Faculty:** FT 31, PT 53 **Exams:** ACT. **Final Year or Final Semester Residency Requirement:** No **Library Holdings:** 29,000 **Regional Accreditation:** North Central Association of Colleges and Schools **Credit Hours For Degree:** 60 credit hours, Associates **Intercollegiate Athletics:** Basketball M & W; Golf M & W; Soccer M & W; Tennis M & W; Volleyball M & W

UNIVERSITY OF WISCONSIN—GREEN BAY
2420 Nicolet Dr.
Green Bay, WI 54311-7001
Tel: (920)465-2000; Free: 888-367-8942
Admissions: (920)465-2111
Fax: (920)465-2032
E-mail: uwgb@uwgb.edu
Web Site: http://www.uwgb.edu/
President/CEO: Thomas K. Harden
Admissions: Pam Harvey-Jacobs
Financial Aid: Ron Ronnenberg
Type: Comprehensive **Sex:** Coed **Affiliation:** University of Wisconsin System **Scores:** 64% ACT 18-23; 31% ACT 24-29 **% Accepted:** 70 **Admission Plans:** Deferred Admission **Application Deadline:** Rolling **Application Fee:** $44.00 **H.S. Requirements:** High school diploma required; GED accepted **Costs Per Year:** Application fee: $44. State resident tuition: $5659 full-time, $236 per credit hour part-time. Nonresident tuition: $13,649 full-time, $569 per credit hour part-time. Mandatory fees: $1250 full-time, $53 per credit hour part-time. Full-time tuition and fees vary according to reciprocity agreements. Part-time tuition and fees vary according to reciprocity agreements. College room and board: $6500. College room only: $3600. Room and board charges vary according to board plan and housing facility. **Scholarships:** Available **Calendar System:** Semester, Summer Session Available **Enrollment:** FT 4,991, PT 1,390, Grad FT 47, Grad PT 236 **Faculty:** FT 189, PT 133 **Student-Faculty Ratio:** 25:1 **Exams:** SAT I or ACT. **% Receiving Financial Aid:** 61 **% Residing in College-Owned, -Operated, or -Affiliated Housing:** 30 **Final Year or Final Semester Residency Requirement:** No **Library Holdings:** 360,795 **Regional Accreditation:** North Central Association of Colleges and Schools **Credit Hours For Degree:** 60 credits, Associates; 120 credits, Bachelors **ROTC:** Army **Professional Accreditation:** ADtA, CSWE, NASM, NLN **Intercollegiate Athletics:** Basketball M & W; Cross-Country Running M & W; Golf M & W; Skiing (Cross-Country) M & W; Soccer M & W; Softball W; Swimming and Diving M & W; Tennis M & W; Volleyball W

UNIVERSITY OF WISCONSIN—LA CROSSE
1725 State St.
La Crosse, WI 54601-3742
Tel: (608)785-8000
Admissions: (608)785-8939
Fax: (608)785-6695
E-mail: admissions@uwlax.edu
Web Site: http://www.uwlax.edu/
President/CEO: Dr. Joe Gow
Admissions: Kathryn Kiefer
Financial Aid: Louise Larson Janke
Type: Comprehensive **Sex:** Coed **Affiliation:** University of Wisconsin System **Scores:** 30.5% ACT 18-23; 64.1% ACT 24-29 **% Accepted:** 69 **Application Deadline:** Rolling **Application Fee:** $44.00 **H.S. Requirements:** High school diploma required; GED accepted **Costs Per Year:** Application fee: $44. State resident tuition: $6425 full-time, $268 per credit hour part-time. Nonresident tuition: $13,998 full-time, $583 per credit hour part-time.

Mandatory fees: $1084 full-time. Full-time tuition and fees vary according to degree level, program, and reciprocity agreements. Part-time tuition varies according to course load, degree level, program, and reciprocity agreements. College room and board: $5630. College room only: $3240. Room and board charges vary according to board plan and housing facility. **Scholarships:** Available **Calendar System:** Semester, Summer Session Available **Enrollment:** FT 8,307, PT 451, Grad FT 423, Grad PT 709 **Faculty:** FT 376, PT 155 **Student-Faculty Ratio:** 21:1 **Exams:** SAT I or ACT. ACT essay not being used. SAT essay not being used. **% Receiving Financial Aid:** 40 **% Residing in College-Owned, -Operated, or -Affiliated Housing:** 34 **Final Year or Final Semester Residency Requirement:** Yes **Library Holdings:** 546,766 **Regional Accreditation:** North Central Association of Colleges and Schools **Credit Hours For Degree:** 60 credits, Associates; 120 credits, Bachelors **ROTC:** Army **Professional Accreditation:** AACSB, AANA, AOTA, APTA, CEPH, JRCERT, JRCEPAT, NAACLS, NASM, NCATE, NRPA **Intercollegiate Athletics:** Baseball M; Basketball M & W; Cross-Country Running M & W; Football M; Gymnastics W; Soccer W; Softball W; Swimming and Diving M & W; Tennis M & W; Track and Field M & W; Volleyball W; Weight Lifting M & W; Wrestling M

UNIVERSITY OF WISCONSIN—MADISON
500 Lincoln Dr.
Madison, WI 53706-1380
Tel: (608)262-1234
Admissions: (608)262-3961
Fax: (608)262-1429
E-mail: onwisconsin@admissions.wisc.edu
Web Site: http://www.wisc.edu/
President/CEO: Carolyn Martin
Type: University **Sex:** Coed **Affiliation:** University of Wisconsin System **Scores:** 99.4% SAT V 400+; 99.9% SAT M 400+; 7.1% ACT 18-23; 57.1% ACT 24-29 **% Accepted:** 57 **Admission Plans:** Deferred Admission **Application Deadline:** February 1 **Application Fee:** $44.00 **H.S. Requirements:** High school diploma required; GED accepted **Costs Per Year:** Application fee: $44. State resident tuition: $7296 full-time, $303.99 per credit hour part-time. Nonresident tuition: $22,045 full-time, $918.56 per credit hour part-time. Mandatory fees: $1018 full-time, $44.25 per credit hour part-time, $44.25. Full-time tuition and fees vary according to program and reciprocity agreements. Part-time tuition and fees vary according to course load, program, and reciprocity agreements. College room and board: $7157. Room and board charges vary according to board plan and housing facility. **Scholarships:** Available **Calendar System:** Semester, Summer Session Available **Enrollment:** FT 27,803, PT 2,540, Grad FT 9,668, Grad PT 2,088 **Faculty:** FT 2,397, PT 441 **Student-Faculty Ratio:** 17:1 **Exams:** SAT I or ACT. ACT essay used for admission. SAT essay used for admission. **% Receiving Financial Aid:** 36 **% Residing in College-Owned, -Operated, or -Affiliated Housing:** 24 **Final Year or Final Semester Residency Requirement:** Yes **Regional Accreditation:** North Central Association of Colleges and Schools **Credit Hours For Degree:** 120 semester hours, Bachelors **ROTC:** Army, Navy, Air Force **Professional Accreditation:** AACSB, ABET, ACPhE, AACN, AAFCS, ABA, ADtA, ACSP, ALA, AOTA, APTA, APA, ASC, ASLA, ASLHA, AVMA, AALS, ACEHSA, FIDER, CORE CSWE, JRCEPAT, LCMEAMA, NAACLS, NASAD, NASM, NAST, SAF **Intercollegiate Athletics:** Basketball M & W; Cheerleading M & W; Cross-Country Running M & W; Football M; Golf M & W; Ice Hockey M & W; Sailing M & W; Soccer M & W; Softball W; Swimming and Diving M & W; Tennis M & W; Track and Field M & W; Ultimate Frisbee M & W; Volleyball W; Water Polo M & W; Wrestling M

UNIVERSITY OF WISCONSIN—MANITOWOC
705 Viebahn St.
Manitowoc, WI 54220-6699
Tel: (920)683-4700
Admissions: (920)683-4707
Fax: (920)683-4776
E-mail: christopher.lewis@uwc.edu
Web Site: http://www.manitowoc.uwc.edu/
President/CEO: Dr. Daniel Campagna
Admissions: Dr. Christopher Lewis
Financial Aid: Cathy Buchner
Type: Two-Year College **Sex:** Coed **Affiliation:** University of Wisconsin System **% Accepted:** 100 **Admission Plans:** Early Admission; Deferred Admission **Application Deadline:** September 1 **Application Fee:** $35.00 **H.S. Requirements:** High school diploma required; GED accepted **Scholarships:** Available **Calendar System:** Semester **Enrollment:** FT 596 **Faculty:** FT 22, PT 18 **Student-Faculty Ratio:** 24:1 **Exams:** SAT I or ACT. **Library Holdings:** 25,750 **Regional Accreditation:** North Central Association of Colleges and Schools **Credit Hours For Degree:** 60 credits, Associates **Intercollegiate Athletics:** Basketball M & W; Golf M & W; Tennis M & W; Volleyball W

UNIVERSITY OF WISCONSIN—MARATHON COUNTY
518 South Seventh Ave.
Wausau, WI 54401-5396
Tel: (715)261-6100; Free: 888-367-8962
Admissions: (715)261-6238
Fax: (715)261-6333
Web Site: http://www.uwmc.uwc.edu/
Admissions: Dr. Nolan Beck
Financial Aid: Kristin Severson
Type: Two-Year College **Sex:** Coed **Affiliation:** University of Wisconsin System **Admission Plans:** Early Admission; Deferred Admission **Application Fee:** $44.00 **H.S. Requirements:** High school diploma required; GED accepted **Costs Per Year:** Application fee: $44. State resident tuition: $4543 full-time, $189.11 per credit part-time. Nonresident tuition: $11,526 full-time, $480.10 per credit part-time. **Scholarships:** Available **Calendar System:** Semester, Summer Session Available **Exams:** ACT. **Regional Accreditation:** North Central Association of Colleges and Schools **Credit Hours For Degree:** 60 credits, Associates **ROTC:** Army

UNIVERSITY OF WISCONSIN—MARINETTE
750 West Bay Shore
Marinette, WI 54143-4299
Tel: (715)735-4300
Admissions: (715)735-4301
E-mail: cynthia.bailey@uwc.edu
Web Site: http://www.uwc.edu/
Admissions: Cynthia M. Bailey
Financial Aid: Cindy Bailey
Type: Two-Year College **Sex:** Coed **Affiliation:** University of Wisconsin System **Admission Plans:** Open Admission **Application Deadline:** Rolling **Application Fee:** $35.00 **H.S. Requirements:** High school diploma required; GED accepted **Costs Per Year:** Application fee: $35. One-time mandatory fee: $60. State resident tuition: $4268 full-time. Nonresident tuition: $11,252 full-time. Mandatory fees: $291 full-time. Full-time tuition and fees vary according to reciprocity agreements. **Scholarships:** Available **Calendar System:** Semester, Summer Session Available **Enrollment:** FT 462 **Faculty:** FT 18, PT 13 **Student-Faculty Ratio:** 15:1 **Exams:** SAT I or ACT. **Library Holdings:** 23,000 **Regional Accreditation:** North Central Association of Colleges and Schools **Credit Hours For Degree:** 60 credits, Associates **Intercollegiate Athletics:** Basketball M & W; Volleyball W

UNIVERSITY OF WISCONSIN—MARSHFIELD/WOOD COUNTY
2000 West 5th St.
Marshfield, WI 54449
Tel: (715)389-6500
Web Site: http://marshfield.uwc.edu/
Admissions: Jeff Meece
Financial Aid: Dawn Messerschmidt
Type: Two-Year College **Sex:** Coed **Affiliation:** University of Wisconsin System **Scores:** 75% ACT 18-23; 15% ACT 24-29 **% Accepted:** 93 **Admission Plans:** Early Admission; Deferred Admission **Application Deadline:** Rolling **Application Fee:** $35.00 **H.S. Requirements:** High school diploma required; GED accepted **Costs Per Year:** Application fee: $35. One-time mandatory fee: $125. State resident tuition: $4268 full-time, $178 per credit hour part-time. Nonresident tuition: $11,252 full-time, $469 per credit hour part-time. Mandatory fees: $170 full-time. Full-time tuition and fees vary according to reciprocity agreements. Part-time tuition varies according to course load. **Scholarships:** Available **Calendar System:** Semester, Summer Session Available **Faculty:** FT 13, PT 23 **Student-Faculty Ratio:** 17:1 **Exams:** SAT I or ACT. **Library Holdings:** 35,000 **Regional Accreditation:** North Central Association of Colleges and Schools **Credit Hours For Degree:** 60 credits, Associates **ROTC:** Army **Intercollegiate Athletics:** Basketball M & W; Golf M & W; Tennis M & W; Volleyball W

UNIVERSITY OF WISCONSIN—MILWAUKEE
PO Box 413
Milwaukee, WI 53201-0413

Tel: (414)229-1122
Admissions: (414)229-4397
Fax: (414)229-6940
E-mail: uwmlook@uwm.edu
Web Site: http://www.uwm.edu/
President/CEO: Carlos E. Santiago
Admissions: Jan Ford
Financial Aid: Jane Hojan-Clark
Type: University **Sex:** Coed **Affiliation:** University of Wisconsin System **Scores:** 90% SAT V 400+; 94.17% SAT M 400+; 56.03% ACT 18-23; 30.42% ACT 24-29 **% Accepted:** 77 **Admission Plans:** Deferred Admission **Application Deadline:** July 1 **Application Fee:** $44.00 **H.S. Requirements:** High school diploma required; GED accepted **Costs Per Year:** Application fee: $44. State resident tuition: $7706 full-time, $321.08 per credit hour part-time. Nonresident tuition: $17,435 full-time, $726.45 per credit hour part-time. Mandatory fees: $816 full-time. Full-time tuition and fees vary according to location, program, and reciprocity agreements. Part-time tuition varies according to course load, location, program, and reciprocity agreements. College room only: $4290. Room charges vary according to housing facility. **Scholarships:** Available **Calendar System:** Semester, Summer Session Available **Enrollment:** FT 21,005, PT 4,199, Grad FT 2,565, Grad PT 2,649 **Faculty:** FT 1,050, PT 557 **Student-Faculty Ratio:** 21:1 **Exams:** Other, SAT I or ACT. ACT essay not being used. SAT essay not being used. **% Receiving Financial Aid:** 56 **% Residing in College-Owned, -Operated, or -Affiliated Housing:** 15 **Library Holdings:** 1,449,333 **Regional Accreditation:** North Central Association of Colleges and Schools **Credit Hours For Degree:** 120 credit hours, Bachelors **ROTC:** Army, Air Force **Professional Accreditation:** AACSB, ABET, AACN, AHIMA, ACSP, ALA, AOTA, APA, ASLHA, CSWE, NAACLS, NAAB, NASM **Intercollegiate Athletics:** Baseball M; Basketball M & W; Cross-Country Running M & W; Soccer M & W; Swimming and Diving M & W; Tennis M & W; Track and Field M & W; Volleyball M & W

UNIVERSITY OF WISCONSIN—OSHKOSH

800 Algoma Blvd.
Oshkosh, WI 54901
Tel: (920)424-1234
Admissions: (920)424-0202
Fax: (920)424-1098
E-mail: oshadmuw@uwosh.edu
Web Site: http://www.uwosh.edu/
President/CEO: Dr. Richard H. Wells
Admissions: Richard Hillman
Financial Aid: Sheila Denney
Type: Comprehensive **Sex:** Coed **Affiliation:** University of Wisconsin System **Scores:** 62% ACT 18-23; 31% ACT 24-29 **% Accepted:** 85 **Admission Plans:** Deferred Admission **Application Deadline:** Rolling **Application Fee:** $35.00 **H.S. Requirements:** High school diploma required; GED accepted **Scholarships:** Available **Calendar System:** Semester, Summer Session Available **Enrollment:** FT 9,242, PT 2,363, Grad FT 193, Grad PT 1,204 **Faculty:** FT 413, PT 195 **Student-Faculty Ratio:** 21:1 **Exams:** Other, SAT I or ACT. **% Receiving Financial Aid:** 46 **% Residing in College-Owned, -Operated, or -Affiliated Housing:** 34 **Library Holdings:** 446,774 **Regional Accreditation:** North Central Association of Colleges and Schools **Credit Hours For Degree:** 60 credits, Associates; 120 credits, Bachelors **ROTC:** Army **Professional Accreditation:** AACSB, ACEJMC, AACN, ACA, CSWE, NASM, NCATE **Intercollegiate Athletics:** Baseball M; Basketball M & W; Cross-Country Running M & W; Football M; Golf W; Gymnastics W; Riflery M & W; Soccer M & W; Softball W; Swimming and Diving M & W; Tennis M & W; Track and Field M & W; Volleyball W; Wrestling M

UNIVERSITY OF WISCONSIN—PARKSIDE

900 Wood Rd., Box 2000
Kenosha, WI 53141-2000
Tel: (262)595-2345
Admissions: (262)595-2454
Fax: (262)595-2630
E-mail: possehl@uwp.edu
Web Site: http://www.uwp.edu/
President/CEO: Dr. Deborah Ford
Admissions: DeAnn Possehl
Financial Aid: Dr. Randall McCready
Type: Comprehensive **Sex:** Coed **Affiliation:** University of Wisconsin System **Scores:** 58% ACT 18-23; 18% ACT 24-29 **% Accepted:** 63 **Application Deadline:** August 1 **Application Fee:** $44.00 **H.S. Requirements:** High school diploma required; GED accepted **Costs Per Year:** Application fee: $44. State resident tuition: $6280 full-time, $223.49 per credit hour part-time. Nonresident tuition: $13,853 full-time, $539.03 per credit hour part-time. Mandatory fees: $916 full-time, $40 per credit hour part-time. Full-time tuition and fees vary according to course load and reciprocity agreements. Part-time tuition and fees vary according to course load. College room and board: $6252. College room only: $3987. Room and board charges vary according to board plan and housing facility. **Scholarships:** Available **Calendar System:** Semester, Summer Session Available **Enrollment:** FT 3,688, PT 1,465, Grad FT 44, Grad PT 106 **Faculty:** FT 175, PT 106 **Student-Faculty Ratio:** 20:1 **Exams:** SAT I or ACT. ACT essay not being used. SAT essay not being used. **% Receiving Financial Aid:** 61 **% Residing in College-Owned, -Operated, or -Affiliated Housing:** 17 **Library Holdings:** 400,000 **Regional Accreditation:** North Central Association of Colleges and Schools **Credit Hours For Degree:** 120 credits, Bachelors **ROTC:** Army **Professional Accreditation:** AACSB **Intercollegiate Athletics:** Baseball M; Basketball M & W; Cross-Country Running M & W; Golf M; Soccer M & W; Softball W; Track and Field M & W; Volleyball W; Wrestling M

UNIVERSITY OF WISCONSIN—PLATTEVILLE

1 University Plaza
Platteville, WI 53818-3099
Tel: (608)342-1491; Free: 800-362-5515
Admissions: (608)342-1125
E-mail: admit@uwplatt.edu
Web Site: http://www.uwplatt.edu/
President/CEO: Dr. Carol Sue Butts
Admissions: Angela Udelhofen
Financial Aid: Elizabeth Tucker
Type: Comprehensive **Sex:** Coed **Affiliation:** University of Wisconsin System **Scores:** 54.08% ACT 18-23; 34.72% ACT 24-29 **% Accepted:** 80 **Admission Plans:** Preferred Admission; Deferred Admission **Application Deadline:** Rolling **Application Fee:** $44.00 **H.S. Requirements:** High school diploma required; GED accepted **Costs Per Year:** Application fee: $44. State resident tuition: $5830 full-time. Nonresident tuition: $13,140 full-time. Mandatory fees: $990 full-time. Full-time tuition and fees vary according to course load, degree level, and reciprocity agreements. College room and board: $5800. College room only: $3100. Room and board charges vary according to board plan. **Scholarships:** Available **Calendar System:** Semester, Summer Session Available **Enrollment:** FT 6,235, PT 624, Grad FT 75, Grad PT 714 **Student-Faculty Ratio:** 20:1 **Exams:** ACT, SAT I or ACT. **% Receiving Financial Aid:** 51 **% Residing in College-Owned, -Operated, or -Affiliated Housing:** 40 **Library Holdings:** 362,247 **Regional Accreditation:** North Central Association of Colleges and Schools **Credit Hours For Degree:** 64 credits, Associates; 120 credits, Bachelors **ROTC:** Army **Professional Accreditation:** ABET, NASM, NCATE, NAIT **Intercollegiate Athletics:** Baseball M; Basketball M & W; Bowling M & W; Cheerleading M & W; Cross-Country Running M & W; Football M; Golf W; Ice Hockey M & W; Lacrosse M & W; Rugby M & W; Soccer M & W; Softball W; Track and Field M & W; Ultimate Frisbee M & W; Volleyball M & W; Wrestling M

UNIVERSITY OF WISCONSIN—RICHLAND

1200 Hwy. 14 West
Richland Center, WI 53581
Tel: (608)647-6186
Admissions: (608)647-8422
Fax: (608)647-6225
E-mail: john.poole@uwc.edu
Web Site: http://richland.uwc.edu/
President/CEO: Dr. Deborah B. Cureton
Admissions: John D. Poole
Financial Aid: Kari Bartels
Type: Two-Year College **Sex:** Coed **Affiliation:** University of Wisconsin System **Application Deadline:** Rolling **Application Fee:** $44.00 **H.S. Requirements:** High school diploma required; GED accepted **Costs Per Year:** Application fee: $44. State resident tuition: $4747 full-time, $198 per credit part-time. Nonresident tuition: $11,731 full-time, $489 per credit part-time. Full-time tuition varies according to reciprocity agreements. Part-time tuition varies according to reciprocity agreements. College room only: $3200. **Scholarships:** Available **Calendar System:** Semester, Summer Session Available **Enrollment:** FT 331, PT 164 **Faculty:** FT 15, PT 16 **Student-**

Faculty Ratio: 17:1 **Exams:** ACT, SAT I or ACT. **Library Holdings:** 40,000 **Regional Accreditation:** North Central Association of Colleges and Schools **Credit Hours For Degree:** 60 credits, Associates **Intercollegiate Athletics:** Basketball M & W; Volleyball W

UNIVERSITY OF WISCONSIN—RIVER FALLS
410 South Third St.
River Falls, WI 54022
Tel: (715)425-3911
Admissions: (715)425-3500
Fax: (715)425-0678
E-mail: admit@uwrf.edu
Web Site: http://www.uwrf.edu/
President/CEO: Dean Van Galen
Admissions: Mark Meydam
Financial Aid: Barbara J. Stinson
Type: Comprehensive **Sex:** Coed **Affiliation:** University of Wisconsin System **Scores:** 100% SAT V 400+; 95.65% SAT M 400+; 60.64% ACT 18-23; 31.12% ACT 24-29 **% Accepted:** 76 **Admission Plans:** Deferred Admission **Application Deadline:** Rolling **Application Fee:** $44.00 **H.S. Requirements:** High school diploma required; GED accepted **Costs Per Year:** Application fee: $44. State resident tuition: $5364 full-time, $446.98 per credit part-time. Nonresident tuition: $13,009 full-time, $1,084.06 per credit part-time. Mandatory fees: $1096 full-time, $257.88 per credit part-time. Full-time tuition and fees vary according to course load, degree level, and reciprocity agreements. Part-time tuition and fees vary according to course load, degree level, and reciprocity agreements. College room and board: $5372. College room only: $3238. Room and board charges vary according to board plan and housing facility. **Scholarships:** Available **Calendar System:** Semester, Summer Session Available **Enrollment:** FT 5,762, PT 460, Grad FT 149, Grad PT 357 **Faculty:** FT 231, PT 112 **Student-Faculty Ratio:** 23:1 **Exams:** ACT, SAT I or ACT. ACT essay not being used. SAT essay not being used. **% Receiving Financial Aid:** 61 **% Residing in College-Owned, -Operated, or -Affiliated Housing:** 38 **Regional Accreditation:** North Central Association of Colleges and Schools **Credit Hours For Degree:** 120 semester credits, Bachelors **ROTC:** Army **Professional Accreditation:** AACSB, ACEJMC, ASLHA, CSWE, NASM, NCATE **Intercollegiate Athletics:** Badminton M & W; Baseball M; Basketball M & W; Cheerleading M; Cross-Country Running M & W; Equestrian Sports M & W; Football M; Golf M & W; Ice Hockey M & W; Lacrosse M & W; Racquetball M & W; Rugby M & W; Soccer M & W; Softball W; Swimming and Diving M & W; Tennis W; Track and Field M & W; Ultimate Frisbee M & W; Volleyball M & W; Weight Lifting M & W

UNIVERSITY OF WISCONSIN—ROCK COUNTY
2909 Kellogg Ave.
Janesville, WI 53546-5699
Tel: (608)758-6565; Free: 888-INFO-UWC
Admissions: (608)758-6523
Fax: (608)758-6564
Web Site: http://rock.uwc.edu/
Financial Aid: Luke Janiak-Fenton
Type: Two-Year College **Sex:** Coed **Affiliation:** University of Wisconsin System **Admission Plans:** Deferred Admission **Application Deadline:** Rolling **Application Fee:** $44.00 **H.S. Requirements:** High school diploma required; GED accepted **Costs Per Year:** Application fee: $44. State resident tuition: $4576 full-time, $190.49 per credit part-time. Nonresident tuition: $11,560 full-time, $481.48 per credit part-time. **Scholarships:** Available **Calendar System:** Semester, Summer Session Available **Exams:** ACT. **Regional Accreditation:** North Central Association of Colleges and Schools **Credit Hours For Degree:** 60 credits, Associates

UNIVERSITY OF WISCONSIN—SHEBOYGAN
One University Dr.
Sheboygan, WI 53081-4789
Tel: (920)459-6600
Admissions: (920)459-6633
Fax: (920)459-6602
Web Site: http://www.sheboygan.uwc.edu/
Financial Aid: Mary Balde
Type: Two-Year College **Sex:** Coed **Affiliation:** University of Wisconsin System **Admission Plans:** Open Admission **Application Deadline:** Rolling **Application Fee:** $44.00 **H.S. Requirements:** High school diploma required; GED accepted **Costs Per Year:** Application fee: $44. State resident tuition: $4547 full-time, $189.28 per credit part-time. Nonresident tuition: $11,530 full-time, $480.27 per credit part-time. Mandatory fees: $2 per term part-time. Full-time tuition varies according to reciprocity agreements. Part-time tuition and fees vary according to reciprocity agreements. **Scholarships:** Available **Calendar System:** Semester, Summer Session Available **Regional Accreditation:** North Central Association of Colleges and Schools **Credit Hours For Degree:** 60 credit hours, Associates

UNIVERSITY OF WISCONSIN—STEVENS POINT
2100 Main St.
Stevens Point, WI 54481-3897
Tel: (715)346-0123
Admissions: (715)346-2441
Fax: (715)346-2561
E-mail: admiss@uwsp.edu
Web Site: http://www.uwsp.edu/
President/CEO: Dr. Mark Nook
Admissions: Catherine Glennon
Financial Aid: Paul Watson
Type: Comprehensive **Sex:** Coed **Affiliation:** University of Wisconsin System **Scores:** 100% SAT V 400+; 55.4% ACT 18-23; 38.7% ACT 24-29 **% Accepted:** 73 **Admission Plans:** Deferred Admission **Application Deadline:** Rolling **Application Fee:** $44.00 **H.S. Requirements:** High school diploma required; GED accepted **Costs Per Year:** Application fee: $44. State resident tuition: $6530 full-time, $272 per credit hour part-time. Nonresident tuition: $14,104 full-time, $587 per credit hour part-time. Mandatory fees: $272 per credit hour part-time. Full-time tuition varies according to course load and reciprocity agreements. Part-time tuition and fees vary according to course load and reciprocity agreements. College room and board: $5612. College room only: $3336. **Scholarships:** Available **Calendar System:** Semester, Summer Session Available **Enrollment:** FT 8,216, PT 488, Grad FT 104, Grad PT 132 **Faculty:** FT 398, PT 85 **Student-Faculty Ratio:** 20:1 **Exams:** SAT I or ACT. ACT essay not being used. SAT essay not being used. **% Receiving Financial Aid:** 49 **% Residing in College-Owned, -Operated, or -Affiliated Housing:** 37 **Library Holdings:** 1,065,315 **Regional Accreditation:** North Central Association of Colleges and Schools **Credit Hours For Degree:** 62 credits, Associates; 120 credits, Bachelors **ROTC:** Army **Professional Accreditation:** ASLHA, FIDER, NAACLS, NASAD, NASD, NASM, NAST, SAF **Intercollegiate Athletics:** Baseball M; Basketball M & W; Cross-Country Running M & W; Football M; Golf W; Ice Hockey M & W; Soccer W; Softball W; Swimming and Diving M & W; Tennis W; Track and Field M & W; Volleyball W; Wrestling M

UNIVERSITY OF WISCONSIN—STOUT
Menomonie, WI 54751
Tel: (715)232-1122
Admissions: (715)232-2639
Fax: (715)232-1667
E-mail: admissions@uwstout.edu
Web Site: http://www.uwstout.edu/
President/CEO: Dr. Charles W. Sorensen
Admissions: Dr. Pamela Holsinger-Fuchs
Financial Aid: Beth M. Boisen
Type: Comprehensive **Sex:** Coed **Affiliation:** University of Wisconsin System **Scores:** 65.2% ACT 18-23; 25.3% ACT 24-29 **% Accepted:** 77 **Application Deadline:** Rolling **Application Fee:** $44.00 **H.S. Requirements:** High school diploma required; GED accepted **Costs Per Year:** Application fee: $44. State resident tuition: $5974 full-time, $199 per credit hour part-time. Nonresident tuition: $13,719 full-time, $457 per credit hour part-time. Mandatory fees: $1847 full-time, $62 per credit hour part-time, $62. Full-time tuition and fees vary according to degree level and reciprocity agreements. Part-time tuition and fees vary according to degree level and reciprocity agreements. College room and board: $5336. College room only: $3200. Room and board charges vary according to board plan and housing facility. **Scholarships:** Available **Calendar System:** 4-1-4, Summer Session Available **Enrollment:** FT 6,802, PT 1,169, Grad FT 300, Grad PT 744 **Faculty:** FT 346, PT 68 **Student-Faculty Ratio:** 20:1 **Exams:** SAT I or ACT. ACT essay not being used. SAT essay not being used. **% Receiving Financial Aid:** 56 **% Residing in College-Owned, -Operated, or -Affiliated Housing:** 40 **Library Holdings:** 229,986 **Regional Accreditation:** North Central Association of Colleges and Schools **Credit Hours For Degree:** 124 credits, Bachelors **ROTC:** Army, Air Force **Professional Accreditation:** ABET, AAMFT, ACCE, ADtA, FIDER, CORE, NASAD, NCATE, NAIT **Intercollegiate Athletics:** Baseball M; Basketball M & W; Cross-Country Running M

& W; Football M; Gymnastics W; Ice Hockey M & W; Soccer M & W; Softball W; Tennis W; Track and Field M & W; Volleyball M & W

UNIVERSITY OF WISCONSIN—SUPERIOR
Belknap and Catlin
PO Box 2000
Superior, WI 54880-4500
Tel: (715)394-8101
Admissions: (715)394-8217
Fax: (715)394-8407
E-mail: admissions@uwsuper.edu
Web Site: http://www.uwsuper.edu/
President/CEO: Dr. Julius E. Erlenbach
Admissions: Tonya Roth
Financial Aid: Tammi Reijo
Type: Comprehensive **Sex:** Coed **Affiliation:** University of Wisconsin System **Scores:** 59% ACT 18-23; 30% ACT 24-29 **% Accepted:** 68 **Admission Plans:** Early Admission; Deferred Admission **Application Deadline:** Rolling **Application Fee:** $44.00 **H.S. Requirements:** High school diploma required; GED accepted **Costs Per Year:** Application fee: $44. State resident tuition: $5571 full-time, $401 per semester hour part-time. Nonresident tuition: $13,144 full-time, $717 per semester hour part-time. Mandatory fees: $1165 full-time. Full-time tuition and fees vary according to course load, program, and reciprocity agreements. Part-time tuition varies according to program and reciprocity agreements. College room and board: $5485. College room only: $2960. Room and board charges vary according to board plan, housing facility, and student level. **Scholarships:** Available **Calendar System:** Semester, Summer Session Available **Enrollment:** FT 2,083, PT 492, Grad FT 77, Grad PT 141 **Faculty:** FT 112, PT 56 **Student-Faculty Ratio:** 18:1 **Exams:** SAT I or ACT. **% Receiving Financial Aid:** 58 **% Residing in College-Owned, -Operated, or -Affiliated Housing:** 24 **Library Holdings:** 190,757 **Regional Accreditation:** North Central Association of Colleges and Schools **Credit Hours For Degree:** 64 credits, Associates; 120 credits, Bachelors **ROTC:** Air Force **Professional Accreditation:** ACA, CSWE, NASM **Intercollegiate Athletics:** Baseball M; Basketball M & W; Cheerleading M & W; Cross-Country Running M & W; Golf W; Ice Hockey M & W; Soccer M & W; Softball W; Track and Field M & W; Volleyball W

UNIVERSITY OF WISCONSIN—WASHINGTON COUNTY
400 University Dr.
West Bend, WI 53095-3699
Tel: (262)335-5200
Admissions: (262)335-5201
Fax: (262)335-5257
E-mail: dan.cibrario@uwc.edu
Web Site: http://www.washington.uwc.edu/
Admissions: Dan Cebrario
Financial Aid: Bonnie Eiring
Type: Two-Year College **Sex:** Coed **Affiliation:** University of Wisconsin System **% Accepted:** 67 **Admission Plans:** Deferred Admission **Application Deadline:** Rolling **Application Fee:** $35.00 **H.S. Requirements:** High school diploma required; GED accepted **Scholarships:** Available **Calendar System:** Semester, Summer Session Available **Enrollment:** FT 663, PT 288 **Faculty:** FT 29, PT 23 **Student-Faculty Ratio:** 21:1 **Exams:** ACT. **Library Holdings:** 46,429 **Regional Accreditation:** North Central Association of Colleges and Schools **Credit Hours For Degree:** 60 credits, Associates **Intercollegiate Athletics:** Basketball M & W; Golf M & W; Soccer M & W; Tennis M & W; Volleyball W

UNIVERSITY OF WISCONSIN—WAUKESHA
1500 North University Dr.
Waukesha, WI 53188-2799
Tel: (414)521-5200
Admissions: (262)521-5200
Fax: (414)521-5491
E-mail: deborah.kusick@uwc.edu
Web Site: http://www.waukesha.uwc.edu/
President/CEO: Dr. Patrick Schmitt
Admissions: Deb Kusick
Financial Aid: Judy Becker
Type: Two-Year College **Sex:** Coed **Affiliation:** University of Wisconsin System **Admission Plans:** Early Admission; Deferred Admission **Application Deadline:** Rolling **Application Fee:** $44.00 **H.S. Requirements:** High school diploma required; GED accepted **Costs Per Year:** Application fee: $44. State resident tuition: $4556 full-time, $191 per credit hour part-time. Nonresident tuition: $11,544 full-time, $482 per credit hour part-time. Full-time tuition varies according to course load and reciprocity agreements. Part-time tuition varies according to course load and reciprocity agreements. **Scholarships:** Available **Calendar System:** Semester, Summer Session Available **Enrollment:** FT 1,161, PT 926 **Faculty:** FT 57, PT 27 **Student-Faculty Ratio:** 25:1 **Exams:** SAT I or ACT. **Final Year or Final Semester Residency Requirement:** No **Library Holdings:** 61,000 **Regional Accreditation:** North Central Association of Colleges and Schools **Credit Hours For Degree:** 60 credits, Associates **Intercollegiate Athletics:** Basketball M & W; Golf M & W; Soccer M & W; Tennis M & W; Volleyball W

UNIVERSITY OF WISCONSIN—WHITEWATER
800 West Main St.
Whitewater, WI 53190-1790
Tel: (262)472-1234
Admissions: (262)472-1440
Fax: (262)472-1515
E-mail: uwwadmit@uww.edu
Web Site: http://www.uww.edu/
President/CEO: Richard J. Telfer
Admissions: Stephen J. McKellips
Financial Aid: Carol Miller
Type: Comprehensive **Sex:** Coed **Affiliation:** University of Wisconsin System **% Accepted:** 69 **Admission Plans:** Deferred Admission **Application Deadline:** Rolling **Application Fee:** $44.00 **H.S. Requirements:** High school diploma required; GED accepted **Costs Per Year:** Application fee: $44. State resident tuition: $5551 full-time, $179 per credit hour part-time. Nonresident tuition: $13,124 full-time, $431 per credit hour part-time. Mandatory fees: $1888 full-time. Full-time tuition and fees vary according to degree level and reciprocity agreements. College room and board: $5028. College room only: $3072. Room and board charges vary according to board plan. **Scholarships:** Available **Calendar System:** Semester, Summer Session Available **Enrollment:** FT 9,117, PT 613, Grad FT 415, Grad PT 994 **Student-Faculty Ratio:** 23:1 **Exams:** ACT, SAT I or ACT. **% Receiving Financial Aid:** 52 **Regional Accreditation:** North Central Association of Colleges and Schools **Credit Hours For Degree:** 60 credits, Associates; 120 credits, Bachelors **ROTC:** Army, Air Force **Professional Accreditation:** AACSB, ACA, ASLHA, CSWE, NASM, NAST, NCATE **Intercollegiate Athletics:** Baseball M; Basketball M & W; Bowling M & W; Cheerleading M & W; Cross-Country Running M & W; Football M; Golf W; Gymnastics W; Ice Hockey M & W; Lacrosse M; Rugby M & W; Soccer M & W; Softball W; Swimming and Diving M & W; Tennis M & W; Track and Field M & W; Volleyball M & W; Weight Lifting M; Wrestling M

VITERBO UNIVERSITY
900 Viterbo Dr.
La Crosse, WI 54601-4797
Tel: (608)796-3000; Free: 800-VIT-ERBO
Admissions: (608)796-3085
Fax: (608)796-3050
E-mail: admission@viterbo.edu
Web Site: http://www.viterbo.edu/
President/CEO: Dr. Richard Artman
Admissions: Wayne Wojciechowski
Financial Aid: Terry Norman
Type: Comprehensive **Sex:** Coed **Affiliation:** Roman Catholic **Scores:** 58% ACT 18-23; 32% ACT 24-29 **% Accepted:** 87 **Admission Plans:** Deferred Admission **Application Deadline:** Rolling **Application Fee:** $25.00 **H.S. Requirements:** High school diploma required; GED accepted **Costs Per Year:** Application fee: $25. Comprehensive fee: $27,820 includes full-time tuition ($20,360), mandatory fees ($490), and college room and board ($6970). College room only: $3120. Room and board charges vary according to board plan and housing facility. Part-time tuition: $600 per credit. Part-time mandatory fees: $15 per credit, $45 per term. **Scholarships:** Available **Calendar System:** Semester, Summer Session Available **Enrollment:** FT 1,633, PT 574, Grad FT 443, Grad PT 632 **Faculty:** FT 112, PT 171 **Student-Faculty Ratio:** 12:1 **Exams:** ACT. **% Receiving Financial Aid:** 80 **% Residing in College-Owned, -Operated, or -Affiliated Housing:** 28 **Final Year or Final Semester Residency Requirement:** No **Library Holdings:** 89,072 **Regional Accreditation:** North Central Association of Colleges and Schools **Credit Hours For Degree:** 62 credits, Associates; 128 credits, Bachelors **ROTC:** Army **Professional Accreditation:** AACN, ADtA,

ACBSP, NASM, NCATE **Intercollegiate Athletics:** Baseball M; Basketball M & W; Bowling M & W; Cross-Country Running M & W; Golf M & W; Soccer M & W; Softball W; Volleyball W

WAUKESHA COUNTY TECHNICAL COLLEGE
800 Main St.
Pewaukee, WI 53072-4601
Tel: (262)691-5566; Free: 888-892-WCTC
Admissions: (262)691-5464
Fax: (262)691-5693
E-mail: kkazda@wctc.edu
Web Site: http://www.wctc.edu/
President/CEO: Dr. Barbara Prindiville
Admissions: Kathleen Kazda
Financial Aid: Timothy K. Jacobson
Type: Two-Year College **Sex:** Coed **Affiliation:** Wisconsin Technical College System **Admission Plans:** Open Admission **Application Deadline:** Rolling **Application Fee:** $30.00 **H.S. Requirements:** High school diploma or equivalent not required **Costs Per Year:** Application fee: $30. State resident tuition: $3042 full-time, $101.40 per credit hour part-time. Nonresident tuition: $18,206 full-time, $606.85 per credit hour part-time. Mandatory fees: $303 full-time, $10.10 per credit hour part-time. Full-time tuition and fees vary according to program. Part-time tuition and fees vary according to program. **Scholarships:** Available **Calendar System:** Semester, Summer Session Available **Enrollment:** FT 2,128, PT 5,478 **Faculty:** FT 190, PT 704 **Regional Accreditation:** North Central Association of Colleges and Schools **Credit Hours For Degree:** 66 credits, Associates **Professional Accreditation:** ARCEST, ACF, ADA, NLN

WESTERN TECHNICAL COLLEGE
304 6th St. North
PO Box C-908
La Crosse, WI 54602-0908
Tel: (608)785-9200; Free: 800-248-9982
Fax: (608)785-9205
E-mail: mildes@wwtc.edu
Web Site: http://www.westerntc.edu/
President/CEO: J. Lee Rasch, EdD
Admissions: Jane Wells
Type: Two-Year College **Sex:** Coed **Affiliation:** Wisconsin Technical College System **% Accepted:** 35 **Admission Plans:** Open Admission; Early Admission **Application Deadline:** Rolling **Application Fee:** $30.00 **H.S. Requirements:** High school diploma required; GED accepted **Costs Per Year:** Application fee: $30. State resident tuition: $3042 full-time, $101.40 per credit part-time. Nonresident tuition: $4563 full-time, $152.10 per credit part-time. Mandatory fees: $70 full-time. Full-time tuition and fees vary according to course level, course load, degree level, and program. Part-time tuition varies according to course level, course load, degree level, and program. **Scholarships:** Available **Calendar System:** Semester, Summer Session Available **Enrollment:** FT 1,910, PT 2,855 **Faculty:** FT 203, PT 685 **Student-Faculty Ratio:** 7:1 **Exams:** ACT, Other. **% Residing in College-Owned, -Operated, or -Affiliated Housing:** 2 **Library Holdings:** 31,243 **Regional Accreditation:** North Central Association of Colleges and Schools **Credit Hours For Degree:** 68 credit hours, Associates **Professional Accreditation:** ADA, AHIMA, AOTA, APTA, CARC, JRCEET, JRCERT, NAACLS, NLN **Intercollegiate Athletics:** Baseball M; Basketball M & W; Volleyball W

WISCONSIN INDIANHEAD TECHNICAL COLLEGE
505 Pine Ridge Dr.
Shell Lake, WI 54871
Tel: (715)468-2815; Free: 800-243-9482
Fax: (715)468-2819
E-mail: Steve.Bitzer@witc.edu
Web Site: http://www.witc.edu/
President/CEO: Dr. Bob Meyer
Admissions: Steve Bitzer
Type: Two-Year College **Sex:** Coed **Affiliation:** Wisconsin Technical College System **Application Deadline:** Rolling **Application Fee:** $30.00 **Costs Per Year:** Application fee: $30. State resident tuition: $3388 full-time. Full-time tuition varies according to course level, course load, degree level, program, and reciprocity agreements. **Calendar System:** Semester **Enrollment:** FT 1,718, PT 2,400 **Faculty:** FT 150, PT 286 **Student-Faculty Ratio:** 10:1 **Regional Accreditation:** North Central Association of Colleges and Schools **Professional Accreditation:** AOTA, NLN

WISCONSIN LUTHERAN COLLEGE
8800 West Bluemound Rd.
Milwaukee, WI 53226-9942
Tel: (414)443-8800; Free: 888-WIS LUTH
Admissions: (414)443-8718
Fax: (414)443-8514
E-mail: meg.wieselmann@wlc.edu
Web Site: http://www.wlc.edu/
President/CEO: Dr. Daniel W. Johnson
Admissions: Meghan Wieselmann
Financial Aid: Linda Loeffel
Type: Four-Year College **Sex:** Coed **Affiliation:** Wisconsin Evangelical Lutheran Synod **Scores:** 41% ACT 18-23; 42% ACT 24-29 **% Accepted:** 76 **Admission Plans:** Deferred Admission **Application Fee:** $20.00 **H.S. Requirements:** High school diploma required; GED accepted **Costs Per Year:** Application fee: $20. Comprehensive fee: $28,630 includes full-time tuition ($21,040), mandatory fees ($140), and college room and board ($7450). College room only: $3950. Room and board charges vary according to board plan, housing facility, and student level. Part-time tuition: $640 per credit. **Scholarships:** Available **Calendar System:** Semester, Summer Session Available **Enrollment:** FT 698, PT 55 **Faculty:** FT 60, PT 36 **Student-Faculty Ratio:** 10:1 **Exams:** Other, SAT I or ACT. **% Receiving Financial Aid:** 75 **% Residing in College-Owned, -Operated, or -Affiliated Housing:** 79 **Library Holdings:** 78,107 **Regional Accreditation:** North Central Association of Colleges and Schools **Credit Hours For Degree:** 128 credits, Bachelors **ROTC:** Army, Navy, Air Force **Intercollegiate Athletics:** Baseball M; Basketball M & W; Cross-Country Running M & W; Football M; Golf M & W; Soccer M & W; Softball W; Tennis M & W; Track and Field M & W; Volleyball W

CASPER COLLEGE
125 College Dr.
Casper, WY 82601-4699
Tel: (307)268-2110; Free: 800-442-2963
Admissions: (307)268-2111
Fax: (307)268-2682
E-mail: kfoltz@caspercollege.edu
Web Site: http://www.caspercollege.edu/
President/CEO: Dr. Walter H. Nolte
Admissions: Kyla Foltz
Type: Two-Year College **Sex:** Coed **Affiliation:** Wyoming Community College Commission **Scores:** 57% SAT V 400+; 72% SAT M 400+; 56% ACT 18-23; 17% ACT 24-29 **% Accepted:** 100 **Admission Plans:** Open Admission; Early Admission **Application Deadline:** August 15 **Application Fee:** $0.00 **H.S. Requirements:** High school diploma required; GED accepted **Costs Per Year:** Application fee: $0. State resident tuition: $1632 full-time, $68 per credit hour part-time. Nonresident tuition: $4896 full-time, $204 per credit hour part-time. Mandatory fees: $216 full-time, $9 per credit hour part-time. Part-time tuition and fees vary according to course load. College room and board: $4160. Room and board charges vary according to board plan and housing facility. **Scholarships:** Available **Calendar System:** Semester, Summer Session Available **Enrollment:** FT 2,078, PT 2,400 **Faculty:** FT 154, PT 103 **Student-Faculty Ratio:** 15:1 **% Residing in College-Owned, -Operated, or -Affiliated Housing:** 15 **Library Holdings:** 124,000 **Regional Accreditation:** North Central Association of Colleges and Schools **Credit Hours For Degree:** 64 credit hours, Associates **Professional Accreditation:** AOTA, JRCERT, NASAD, NASM, NAST, NLN **Intercollegiate Athletics:** Basketball M & W; Cheerleading M & W; Equestrian Sports M & W; Volleyball W

CENTRAL WYOMING COLLEGE
2660 Peck Ave.
Riverton, WY 82501-2273
Tel: (307)855-2000; Free: 800-735-8418
Admissions: (307)855-2119
Fax: (307)855-2092
E-mail: admit@cwc.edu
Web Site: http://www.cwc.edu/
President/CEO: JoAnne McFarland
Admissions: Brenda Barlow
Financial Aid: Jacque Burns
Type: Two-Year College **Sex:** Coed **Affiliation:** Wyoming Community College Commission **Scores:** 73.3% SAT M 400+; 52% ACT 18-23; 18% ACT 24-29 **% Accepted:** 100 **Admission Plans:** Open Admission; Early Admission; Deferred Admission **Application Deadline:** Rolling **Application Fee:** $0.00 **H.S. Requirements:** High school diploma or equivalent not required **Costs Per Year:** Application fee: $0. State resident tuition: $1632 full-time, $68 per credit part-time. Nonresident tuition: $4896 full-time, $204 per credit part-time. Mandatory fees: $504 full-time, $21 per credit part-time. Full-time tuition and fees vary according to course load, program, and reciprocity agreements. Part-time tuition and fees vary according to course load, program, and reciprocity agreements. College room and board: $4085. College room only: $1985. Room and board charges vary according to board plan and housing facility. **Scholarships:** Available **Calendar System:** Semester, Summer Session Available **Enrollment:** FT 934, PT 1,224 **Faculty:** FT 138, PT 100 **Student-Faculty Ratio:** 8:1 **% Residing in College-Owned, -Operated, or -Affiliated Housing:** 10 **Final Year or Final Semester Residency Requirement:** No **Library Holdings:** 54,974 **Regional Accreditation:** North Central Association of Colleges and Schools **Credit Hours For Degree:** 64 credits, Associates **Professional Accreditation:** ARCEST, NLN **Intercollegiate Athletics:** Basketball M & W; Equestrian Sports M & W; Volleyball W

EASTERN WYOMING COLLEGE
3200 West C St.
Torrington, WY 82240-1699
Tel: (307)532-8200; Free: 800-658-3195
Admissions: (307)532-8257
Fax: (307)532-8222
E-mail: rex.cogdill@ewc.wy.edu
Web Site: http://www.ewc.wy.edu/
President/CEO: Dr. Thomas J. Armstrong
Admissions: Dr. Rex Cogdill
Type: Two-Year College **Sex:** Coed **Affiliation:** Wyoming Community College Commission **Admission Plans:** Open Admission; Preferred Admission; Early Admission **Application Deadline:** Rolling **Application Fee:** $0.00 **H.S. Requirements:** High school diploma required; GED accepted **Costs Per Year:** Application fee: $0. State resident tuition: $1632 full-time, $68 per credit hour part-time. Nonresident tuition: $4896 full-time, $204 per credit hour part-time. Mandatory fees: $384 full-time, $16 per credit hour part-time. Full-time tuition and fees vary according to location. Part-time tuition and fees vary according to location. College room and board: $3806. College room only: $1704. Room and board charges vary according to housing facility. **Scholarships:** Available **Calendar System:** Semester, Summer Session Available **Enrollment:** FT 624, PT 767 **Faculty:** FT 47, PT 53 **Student-Faculty Ratio:** 14:1 **Regional Accreditation:** North Central Association of Colleges and Schools **Credit Hours For Degree:** 64 credit hours, Associates

LARAMIE COUNTY COMMUNITY COLLEGE
1400 East College Dr.
Cheyenne, WY 82007-3299
Tel: (307)778-5222
Admissions: (307)778-1117
Fax: (307)778-1399
E-mail: learnmore@lccc.wy.edu
Web Site: http://www.lccc.wy.edu/
President/CEO: Dr. Darrel L. Hammon
Admissions: Holly Allison
Type: Two-Year College **Sex:** Coed **Affiliation:** Wyoming Community College Commission **Scores:** 60% ACT 18-23; 15.2% ACT 24-29 **% Accepted:** 100 **Admission Plans:** Open Admission; Early Admission **Application Deadline:** Rolling **Application Fee:** $20.00 **H.S. Requirements:** High school diploma required; GED accepted **Costs Per Year:** Application fee: $20. One-time mandatory fee: $20. State resident tuition: $1632 full-time, $68 per credit hour part-time. Nonresident tuition: $4896 full-time, $204 per credit hour part-time. Mandatory fees: $840 full-time, $35 per credit hour part-time. Part-time tuition and fees vary according to course load. College room and board: $7140. College room only: $4527. Room and board charges vary according to board plan and housing facility. **Scholarships:** Available **Calendar System:** Semester, Summer Session Available **Enroll-**

ment: FT 2,121, PT 2,784 **Student-Faculty Ratio:** 18:1 **% Residing in College-Owned, -Operated, or -Affiliated Housing:** 4 **Final Year or Final Semester Residency Requirement:** No **Library Holdings:** 56,356 **Regional Accreditation:** North Central Association of Colleges and Schools **Credit Hours For Degree:** 64 credit hours, Associates **ROTC:** Air Force **Professional Accreditation:** ADA, JRCERT, NLN **Intercollegiate Athletics:** Basketball M; Cheerleading M & W; Equestrian Sports M & W; Soccer M & W; Volleyball W

NORTHWEST COLLEGE
231 West 6th St.
Powell, WY 82435-1898
Tel: (307)754-6000; Free: 800-560-4692
Admissions: (307)754-6103
Fax: (307)754-6700
E-mail: west.hernandez@northwestcollege.edu
Web Site: http://www.northwestcollege.edu/
President/CEO: Dr. Paul Prestwich
Admissions: West Hernandez
Financial Aid: Marianne Harrison
Type: Two-Year College **Sex:** Coed **Affiliation:** Wyoming Community College Commission **Admission Plans:** Open Admission **Application Deadline:** Rolling **Application Fee:** $0.00 **H.S. Requirements:** High school diploma required; GED accepted **Costs Per Year:** Application fee: $0. State resident tuition: $2235 full-time, $89 per credit hour part-time. Nonresident tuition: $5499 full-time, $225 per credit hour part-time. Full-time tuition varies according to course load, location, program, and reciprocity agreements. Part-time tuition varies according to location, program, and reciprocity agreements. College room and board: $3916. College room only: $1730. Room and board charges vary according to board plan and housing facility. **Scholarships:** Available **Calendar System:** Semester, Summer Session Available **Enrollment:** FT 1,348, PT 751 **Faculty:** FT 80, PT 72 **Student-Faculty Ratio:** 15:1 **Exams:** Other, SAT I or ACT. ACT essay not being used. SAT essay not being used. **Library Holdings:** 50,100 **Regional Accreditation:** North Central Association of Colleges and Schools **Credit Hours For Degree:** 64 credits, Associates **Professional Accreditation:** NASM, NLN **Intercollegiate Athletics:** Basketball M & W; Equestrian Sports M & W; Soccer M & W; Volleyball W; Wrestling M

SHERIDAN COLLEGE
PO Box 1500
Sheridan, WY 82801-1500
Tel: (307)674-6446; Free: 800-913-9139
Fax: (307)674-7205
E-mail: admissions@sheridan.edu
Web Site: http://www.sheridan.edu/
President/CEO: Dr. Jon Connolly
Admissions: Zane Garstad
Financial Aid: Randy Thompson
Type: Two-Year College **Sex:** Coed **Affiliation:** Wyoming Community College Commission **Admission Plans:** Open Admission; Early Admission; Deferred Admission **Application Deadline:** Rolling **Application Fee:** $0.00 **H.S. Requirements:** High school diploma required; GED accepted **Costs Per Year:** Application fee: $0. State resident tuition: $1632 full-time, $68 per credit hour part-time. Nonresident tuition: $4896 full-time, $204 per credit hour part-time. Mandatory fees: $552 full-time, $23 per credit hour part-time. Full-time tuition and fees vary according to course load, location, program, and reciprocity agreements. Part-time tuition and fees vary according to course load, location, program, and reciprocity agreements. College room and board: $4600. Room and board charges vary according to board plan, housing facility, and location. **Scholarships:** Available **Calendar System:** Semester, Summer Session Available **Enrollment:** FT 1,422, PT 2,508 **Faculty:** FT 92, PT 84 **Student-Faculty Ratio:** 18:1 **% Residing in College-Owned, -Operated, or -Affiliated Housing:** 11 **Final Year or Final Semester Residency Requirement:** No **Library Holdings:** 36,574 **Regional Accreditation:** North Central Association of Colleges and Schools **Credit Hours For Degree:** 64 credit hours, Associates **Professional Accreditation:** ADA, NLN **Intercollegiate Athletics:** Basketball M & W; Cross-Country Running M & W; Volleyball W

UNIVERSITY OF PHOENIX—CHEYENNE CAMPUS
6900 Yellowstone Rd.
Cheyenne, WY 82009
Tel: (307)632-3059
Web Site: http://www.phoenix.edu/
President/CEO: William Pepicello, PhD
Type: Comprehensive **Sex:** Coed **Regional Accreditation:** North Central Association of Colleges and Schools

UNIVERSITY OF WYOMING
1000 East University Ave.
Laramie, WY 82070
Tel: (307)766-1121; Free: 800-342-5996
Admissions: (307)766-5160
Fax: (307)766-2271
E-mail: why-wyo@uwyo.edu
Web Site: http://www.uwyo.edu/
President/CEO: Dr. Thomas Buchanan
Admissions: Aaron Appelhans
Financial Aid: David Gruen
Type: University **Sex:** Coed **Scores:** 95.9% SAT V 400+; 96.3% SAT M 400+; 42.2% ACT 18-23; 45.7% ACT 24-29 **% Accepted:** 96 **Admission Plans:** Deferred Admission **Application Deadline:** August 10 **Application Fee:** $40.00 **H.S. Requirements:** High school diploma required; GED accepted **Costs Per Year:** Application fee: $40. One-time mandatory fee: $100. State resident tuition: $2970 full-time, $99 per credit hour part-time. Nonresident tuition: $11,280 full-time, $376 per credit hour part-time. Mandatory fees: $957 full-time, $239 per term part-time. Full-time tuition and fees vary according to course load, location, and reciprocity agreements. Part-time tuition and fees vary according to course load, location, and reciprocity agreements. College room and board: $8360. College room only: $3612. Room and board charges vary according to board plan and housing facility. **Scholarships:** Available **Calendar System:** Semester, Summer Session Available **Enrollment:** FT 8,128, PT 1,620, Grad FT 1,482, Grad PT 1,197 **Faculty:** FT 730, PT 53 **Student-Faculty Ratio:** 14:1 **Exams:** SAT I or ACT. ACT essay not being used. SAT essay not being used. **% Receiving Financial Aid:** 44 **% Residing in College-Owned, -Operated, or -Affiliated Housing:** 23 **Final Year or Final Semester Residency Requirement:** No **Library Holdings:** 2,971,418 **Regional Accreditation:** North Central Association of Colleges and Schools **Credit Hours For Degree:** 120 semester hours, Bachelors **ROTC:** Army, Air Force **Professional Accreditation:** AACSB, ABET, ACPhE, AACN, AAFCS, ABA, ACA, APA, ASLHA, AALS, CSWE, NASM, NCATE **Intercollegiate Athletics:** Badminton M & W; Baseball M; Basketball M & W; Cheerleading M & W; Cross-Country Running M & W; Equestrian Sports M & W; Fencing M & W; Football M; Golf M & W; Ice Hockey M & W; Lacrosse M & W; Racquetball M & W; Riflery M & W; Rugby M & W; Skiing (Cross-Country) M & W; Skiing (Downhill) M & W; Soccer M & W; Softball W; Swimming and Diving M & W; Tennis W; Track and Field M & W; Ultimate Frisbee M & W; Volleyball W; Wrestling M

WESTERN WYOMING COMMUNITY COLLEGE
PO Box 428
Rock Springs, WY 82902-0428
Tel: (307)382-1600; Free: 800-226-1181
Admissions: (307)382-1647
Fax: (307)382-1636
E-mail: admissions@wwcc.wy.eduadmissions@wwcc.wy.edu
Web Site: http://www.wwcc.wy.edu/
President/CEO: Dr. Karla Leach
Type: Two-Year College **Sex:** Coed **Scores:** 80% ACT 18-23; 10% ACT 24-29 **Admission Plans:** Open Admission; Early Admission; Deferred Admission **Application Deadline:** Rolling **Application Fee:** $0.00 **H.S. Requirements:** High school diploma required; GED accepted **Costs Per Year:** Application fee: $0. Area resident tuition: $84 per credit hour part-time. State resident tuition: $1994 full-time, $118 per credit hour part-time. Nonresident tuition: $5258 full-time, $220 per credit hour part-time. Full-time tuition varies according to reciprocity agreements. Part-time tuition varies according to course load and reciprocity agreements. College room and board: $3837. College room only: $2072. Room and board charges vary according to board plan and housing facility. **Scholarships:** Available **Calendar System:** Semester, Summer Session Available **Enrollment:** FT 1,242, PT 2,878 **Faculty:** FT 71, PT 147 **Student-Faculty Ratio:** 18:1 **% Residing in College-Owned, -Operated, or -Affiliated Housing:** 11 **Library Holdings:** 146,229 **Regional Accreditation:** North Central Association of Colleges and Schools **Credit Hours For Degree:** 64 credit hours, Associates **Professional Accreditation:** CARC, NLN **Intercollegiate Athletics:** Basketball M & W; Cheerleading M & W; Soccer M & W; Volleyball W; Wrestling M

WYOTECH
4373 North Third St.
Laramie, WY 82072-9519
Tel: (307)742-3776; Free: 800-521-7158
Web Site: http://www.wyotech.com/
President/CEO: W. Guy Warpness

Type: Two-Year College **Sex:** Coed **Admission Plans:** Open Admission **Application Deadline:** Rolling **Application Fee:** $100.00 **H.S. Requirements:** High school diploma required; GED accepted **Scholarships:** Available **Calendar System:** Miscellaneous **Student-Faculty Ratio:** 13:1 **Credit Hours For Degree:** 1500 hours, Associates **Professional Accreditation:** ACCSCT

ALBERTA BIBLE COLLEGE
635 Northmount Dr., NW
Calgary, AB, Canada T2K 3J6
Tel: (403)282-2994; Free: 877-542-9492
Fax: (403)282-3084
Web Site: http://www.abc-ca.org/
Type: Four-Year College **Sex:** Coed

ALBERTA COLLEGE OF ART & DESIGN
1407 14 Ave. NW
Calgary, AB, Canada T2N 4R3
Tel: (403)284-7600; Free: 800-251-8290
Admissions: (403)284-7689
E-mail: admissions@acad.ca
Web Site: http://www.acad.ca/
President/CEO: Lance Carlson
Admissions: Joy Borman
Type: Four-Year College **Sex:** Coed **% Accepted:** 46 **Admission Plans:** Early Admission; Early Decision Plan **Application Deadline:** April 1 **Application Fee:** $85.00 **H.S. Requirements:** High school diploma required; GED not accepted. For those granted qualified admission to Artstream program; applicant who is Canadian citizen or resident: High school diploma or equivalent not required. **Costs Per Year:** Application fee: $85. Province resident tuition: $4356 full-time, $145.22 per credit part-time. Canadian resident tuition: $452.97 per credit part-time. Mandatory fees: $805 full-time, $185 per term part-time. Full-time tuition and fees vary according to course load. Part-time tuition and fees vary according to course load. College room and board: $9368. College room only: $5272. Room and board charges vary according to housing facility. International student tuition: $13,589 full-time. **Scholarships:** Available **Calendar System:** Semester, Summer Session Available **Enrollment:** FT 1,079, PT 87 **Faculty:** FT 44, PT 68 **Student-Faculty Ratio:** 17:1 **Library Holdings:** 33,691 **Credit Hours For Degree:** 120 credits, Bachelors **Intercollegiate Athletics:** Baseball W; Basketball M & W; Cross-Country Running M & W; Football M & W; Ice Hockey M & W; Soccer M & W; Volleyball M & W; Wrestling M

AMBROSE UNIVERSITY COLLEGE
630, 833-4th Ave. SW
Calgary, AB, Canada T2P 3T5
Tel: (403)410-2000; Free: 800-461-1222
E-mail: enrolment@ambrose.edu
Web Site: http://www.ambrose.edu/
Type: Comprehensive **Sex:** Coed **Affiliation:** The Christian and Missionary Alliance **Admission Plans:** Open Admission; Early Admission; Deferred Admission **Application Deadline:** Rolling **Application Fee:** $50.00 **H.S. Requirements:** High school diploma required; GED accepted. For applicants 21 or over: High school diploma or equivalent not required **Costs Per Year:** Application fee: $50 Canadian dollars. Tuition, fee, and room and board charges are reported in Canadian dollars. Comprehensive fee: $14,130 includes full-time tuition ($8130), mandatory fees ($510), and college room and board ($5490). Full-time tuition and fees vary according to degree level. Room and board charges vary according to board plan and housing facility. Part-time tuition: $271 per credit hour. Part-time mandatory fees: $5 per credit hour, $12. Part-time tuition and fees vary according to degree level. **Scholarships:** Available **Calendar System:** Semester, Summer Session Available **Student-Faculty Ratio:** 15:1 **Library Holdings:** 65,000 **Credit Hours For Degree:** 94 semester hours, Bachelors **Professional Accreditation:** ABHE, ATS

ATHABASCA UNIVERSITY
1 University Dr.
Athabasca, AB, Canada T9S 3A3
Tel: (780)675-6100; Free: 800-788-9041
Fax: (780)675-6437
E-mail: reginfo@cs.athabascau.ca
Web Site: http://www.athabascau.ca/
President/CEO: Dr. Frits Pannekoek
Financial Aid: Becky Jonasson
Type: Comprehensive **Sex:** Coed **Admission Plans:** Open Admission **Application Deadline:** Rolling **Application Fee:** $60.00 **H.S. Requirements:** High school diploma or equivalent not required **Costs Per Year:** Application fee: $60 Canadian dollars. Tuition and fee charges are reported in Canadian dollars. Province resident tuition: $6100 full-time, $610 per course part-time. Canadian resident tuition: $7150 full-time, $715 per course part-time. Full-time tuition varies according to degree level. Part-time tuition varies according to degree level. International student tuition: $9640 full-time. **Scholarships:** Available **Calendar System:** Continuous, Summer Session Available **Library Holdings:** 178,808 **Regional Accreditation:** Middle State Association of Colleges and Schools **Credit Hours For Degree:** 120 credits, Bachelors

CONCORDIA UNIVERSITY COLLEGE OF ALBERTA
7128 Ada Blvd., NW
Edmonton, AB, Canada T5B 4E4
Tel: (780)479-8481; Free: (866)479-5200
Admissions: (780)479-9220
Fax: (780)474-1933
E-mail: admits@concordia.ab.ca
Web Site: http://www.concordia.ab.ca/
President/CEO: Rev. Gerald S. Krispin
Type: Comprehensive **Sex:** Coed **Affiliation:** Lutheran **% Accepted:** 65 **Admission Plans:** Open Admission; Early Admission **Application Deadline:** June 30 **Application Fee:** $0.00 **H.S. Requirements:** High school diploma required; GED not accepted **Costs Per Year:** Application fee: $0 Canadian dollars. Tuition, fee, and room and board charges are reported in Canadian dollars. Comprehensive fee: $12,139 includes full-time tuition ($6440), mandatory fees ($449), and college room and board ($5250). College room only: $2960. Full-time tuition and fees vary according to class time, course load, degree level, program, and student level. Room and board charges vary according to board plan and housing facility. Part-time tuition: $260 per credit hour. Part-time mandatory fees: $25 per credit hour. Part-time tuition and fees vary according to class time, course load, degree level, program, and student level. International student tuition: $9740 full-time. **Calendar System:** Semester, Summer Session Available **Faculty:** FT 59, PT 94 **Student-Faculty Ratio:** 18:1 **% Residing in College-Owned, -Operated, or -Affiliated Housing:** 3 **Library Holdings:** 89,380 **Credit Hours For Degree:** 120 credits, Bachelors **Intercollegiate Athletics:** Badminton M & W; Basketball M & W; Cross-Country Running M & W; Golf M & W; Ice Hockey M; Soccer M & W; Swimming and Diving M & W

THE KING'S UNIVERSITY COLLEGE
9125 50th St.
Edmonton, AB, Canada T6B 2H3
Tel: (780)465-3500; Free: 800-661-8582
Fax: (780)465-3534
E-mail: admissions@kingsu.ca
Web Site: http://www.kingsu.ca/
President/CEO: Harry Fernhout
Admissions: Glenn Keeler
Financial Aid: Maria Snip
Type: Four-Year College **Sex:** Coed **Affiliation:** interdenominational **% Accepted:** 81 **Application Deadline:** Rolling **Application Fee:** $50.00 **H.S. Requirements:** High school diploma required; GED not accepted **Costs Per Year:** Application fee: $50 Canadian dollars. Tuition, fee, and room and board charges are reported in Canadian dollars. Comprehensive fee: $14,618 includes full-time tuition ($8773), mandatory fees ($455), and college room and board ($5390). College room only: $2840. Full-time tuition and fees vary according to course load. Room and board charges vary according to board plan and housing facility. Part-time tuition: $283 per credit. Part-time mandatory fees: $113.75 per term. Part-time tuition and fees vary according to course load. **Scholarships:** Available **Calendar System:** Miscellaneous, Summer Session Available **Enrollment:** FT 555, PT 41, Grad FT 66 **Faculty:** FT 45, PT 64 **Student-Faculty Ratio:** 12:1 **% Receiving Financial Aid:** 20 **% Residing in College-Owned, -Operated, or -Affiliated Housing:** 36 **Library Holdings:** 112,640 **Credit Hours For Degree:** 93 credits, Bachelors **Intercollegiate Athletics:** Basketball M & W; Soccer M & W; Volleyball M & W

MOUNT ROYAL UNIVERSITY
4825 Mount Royal Gate SW
Calgary, AB, Canada T3E 6K6
Tel: (403)440-6111; Free: 877-440-5001
Admissions: (403)440-5000
Fax: (403)440-5938
Web Site: http://www.mtroyal.ca/
President/CEO: David Marshall, PhD
Type: Four-Year College **Sex:** Coed **Application Fee:** $70.00

PRAIRIE BIBLE INSTITUTE
330 Sixth Ave. North, PO Box 4000
Three Hills, AB, Canada T0M 2N0
Tel: (403)443-5511; Free: 800-661-2425
Fax: (403)443-5540
E-mail: admissions@prairie.edu
Web Site: http://www.prairie.edu/
Admissions: Kevin Kirk
Financial Aid: Doug Johnson
Type: Four-Year College **Sex:** Coed **Affiliation:** interdenominational **Application Deadline:** August 15 **Application Fee:** $35.00 **H.S. Requirements:** High school diploma required; GED accepted **Costs Per Year:** Application fee: $35 Canadian dollars. Tuition, fee, and room and board charges are reported in Canadian dollars. Comprehensive fee: $14,158 includes full-time tuition ($8610), mandatory fees ($448), and college room and board ($5100). College room only: $2300. Full-time tuition and fees vary according to course load and program. Room and board charges vary according to housing facility. Part-time tuition: $359 per credit hour. Part-time tuition varies according to course load and program. **Scholarships:** Available **Calendar System:** Semester, Summer Session Not available **Library Holdings:** 60,745 **Credit Hours For Degree:** 129 credits, Bachelors **Professional Accreditation:** ABHE

ROCKY MOUNTAIN COLLEGE
4039 Brentwood Rd., NW
Calgary, AB, Canada T2L 1L1
Tel: (403)284-5100; Free: 877-YOUnRMC
E-mail: enrolment@rockymountaincollege.ca
Web Site: http://www.rockymountaincollege.ca/
Admissions: Robert Harris
Financial Aid: Duane Erion
Type: Four-Year College **Sex:** Coed **Affiliation:** Missionary Church **Admission Plans:** Deferred Admission **Application Deadline:** Rolling **Application Fee:** $50.00 **H.S. Requirements:** High school diploma required; GED accepted **Scholarships:** Available **Calendar System:** Semester, Summer Session Available **Library Holdings:** 25,280 **Credit Hours For Degree:** 128 semester hours, Bachelors **Professional Accreditation:** ABHE **Intercollegiate Athletics:** Basketball M & W; Ice Hockey M; Soccer M; Volleyball M & W

SOUTHERN ALBERTA INSTITUTE OF TECHNOLOGY
1301 16th Ave. NW
Calgary, AB, Canada T2M 0L4
Tel: (403)284-8110; Free: 877-284-SAIT
Admissions: (403)284-8857
Fax: (403)284-7112
Web Site: http://www.sait.ca/
President/CEO: Irene Lewis
Admissions: Jennifer Bennett
Type: Two-Year College **Sex:** Coed **Admission Plans:** Early Admission; Early Decision Plan **Application Deadline:** Rolling **Application Fee:** $50.00 **H.S. Requirements:** High school diploma required; GED accepted. For most programs require High school diploma.: High school diploma or equivalent not required **Calendar System:** Trimester **Enrollment:** FT 6,954, PT 718 **Library Holdings:** 135,000 **Intercollegiate Athletics:** Basketball M & W; Cross-Country Running M & W; Ice Hockey M & W; Soccer M & W; Volleyball M & W

UNIVERSITY OF ALBERTA
Edmonton, AB, Canada T6G 2E1
Tel: (780)492-3111
Admissions: (780)492-3113
Fax: (780)492-7172
E-mail: registrar@ualberta.ca
Web Site: http://www.ualberta.ca/
President/CEO: Dr. Indira Samarasekera, PhD
Admissions: Patricia Dalton
Financial Aid: Jane Lee
Type: University **Sex:** Coed **Admission Plans:** Preferred Admission; Deferred Admission **Application Deadline:** May 1 **Application Fee:** $0.00 **H.S. Requirements:** High school diploma or equivalent not required **Scholarships:** Available **Calendar System:** Miscellaneous, Summer Session Available **Enrollment:** FT 28,491, PT 1,966, Grad FT 5,745, Grad PT 1,386 **Student-Faculty Ratio:** 21:1 **Exams:** ACT, Other, SAT I or ACT, SAT I and SAT II or ACT, SAT I, SAT II. ACT essay not being used. SAT essay not being used. **Library Holdings:** 9,700,000 **Credit Hours For Degree:** 120 credits, Bachelors **Professional Accreditation:** AACSB, ADA, ALA, LCMEAMA **Intercollegiate Athletics:** Basketball M & W; Cross-Country Running M & W; Field Hockey M & W; Football M; Golf M & W; Gymnastics M & W; Ice Hockey M & W; Rugby W; Skiing (Cross-Country) M & W; Soccer M & W; Swimming and Diving M & W; Tennis M & W; Track and Field M & W; Volleyball M & W; Wrestling M & W

UNIVERSITY OF CALGARY
2500 University Dr., NW
Calgary, AB, Canada T2N 1N4
Tel: (403)220-5110
Admissions: (403)220-3825
Fax: (403)289-1253
E-mail: vandam@ucalgary.ca
Web Site: http://www.ucalgary.ca/
President/CEO: Dr. Harvey P. Weingarten
Admissions: Kim Vandam
Type: University **Sex:** Coed **% Accepted:** 58 **Admission Plans:** Early Admission **Application Deadline:** April 1 **Application Fee:** $130.00 **H.S. Requirements:** High school diploma or equivalent not required **Costs Per Year:** Application fee: $130 Canadian dollars. Tuition, fee, and room and board charges are reported in Canadian dollars. Province resident tuition: $5161 full-time, $516.09 per course part-time. Mandatory fees: $642 full-time, $119.13 per term part-time. College room and board: $7035. College room only: $4435. International student tuition: $17,573 full-time. **Calendar System:** Semester, Summer Session Available **Faculty:** FT 1,731, PT 976 **Student-Faculty Ratio:** 13:1 **Exams:** SAT I, SAT II. **Library Holdings:** 3,318,038 **Credit Hours For Degree:** 15 full-year courses, Bachelors **Professional Accreditation:** AACSB, LCMEAMA **Intercollegiate Athletics:** Basketball M & W; Cross-Country Running M & W; Field Hockey W; Football M; Golf M & W; Ice Hockey M & W; Soccer M & W; Swimming and Diving M & W; Tennis M & W; Track and Field M & W; Volleyball M & W; Wrestling M & W

UNIVERSITY OF LETHBRIDGE
4401 University Dr.
Lethbridge, AB, Canada T1K 3M4
Tel: (403)329-2111
Admissions: (403)320-5700
E-mail: inquiries@uleth.ca
Web Site: http://www.uleth.ca/
President/CEO: Dr. William H. Cade
Admissions: Alice Miller
Type: University **Sex:** Coed **% Accepted:** 56 **Admission Plans:** Early Admission; Early Decision Plan; Deferred Admission **Application Deadline:** June 1 **Application Fee:** $75.00 **H.S. Requirements:** High school diploma required; GED not accepted **Costs Per Year:** Application fee: $75 Canadian dollars. Tuition, fee, and room and board charges are reported in Canadian dollars. Province resident tuition: $4910 full-time, $163.68 per credit hour part-time. Canadian resident tuition: $370.33 per credit hour part-time. Mandatory fees: $649 full-time, $107.95. Full-time tuition and fees vary according to course load. Part-time tuition and fees vary according to course load. College room and board: $6652. College room only: $4262. Room and board charges vary according to board plan and housing facility. International student tuition: $11,110 full-time. **Scholarships:** Available **Calendar System:** Semester, Summer Session Available **Enrollment:** FT 6,876, PT 781, Grad FT 326, Grad PT 226 **Student-Faculty Ratio:** 6:1 **% Residing in College-Owned, -Operated, or -Affiliated Housing:** 10 **Library Holdings:** 573,058 **Credit Hours For Degree:** 40 semester courses, Bachelors **Intercollegiate Athletics:** Cross-Country Running M & W; Ice Hockey M & W; Soccer M & W; Swimming and Diving M & W; Track and Field M & W; Volleyball W

VANGUARD COLLEGE
11617 106 Ave., NW
Edmonton, AB, Canada T5H 0S1
Tel: (780)452-0808
Fax: (780)452-5803
E-mail: tbratton@vanguardcollege.com
Web Site: http://www.vanguardcollege.com/
Admissions: Tim Bratton
Type: Four-Year College **Sex:** Coed **Affiliation:** Pentecostal Assemblies of Canada; Pentecostal Assemblies of Canada (PAOC) **Admission Plans:** Early Decision Plan **Application Deadline:** August 19 **Application Fee:** $50.00 **H.S. Requirements:** High school diploma required; GED accepted **Scholarships:** Available **Calendar System:** Semester, Summer Session Available **Library Holdings:** 23,698 **Credit Hours For Degree:** 133 credits, Bachelors **Professional Accreditation:** ABHE **Intercollegiate Athletics:** Ice Hockey M

BRITISH COLUMBIA INSTITUTE OF TECHNOLOGY
3700 Willingdon Ave.
Burnaby, BC, Canada V5G 3H2
Tel: (604)434-5734
Admissions: (604)432-8496
Fax: (604)278-5363
Web Site: http://www.bcit.ca/
President/CEO: Dr. Don Wright
Admissions: Anna Dosen
Type: Four-Year College **Sex:** Coed **% Accepted:** 44 **Application Fee:** $60.00 **H.S. Requirements:** High school diploma required; GED accepted **Costs Per Year:** Application fee: $60 Canadian dollars. Tuition and fee charges are reported in Canadian dollars. Province resident tuition: $5050 full-time. International student tuition: $16,116 full-time. **Calendar System:** Quarter **Enrollment:** FT 7,120, PT 15,387 **Faculty:** FT 735, PT 624 **Library Holdings:** 169,404

COLUMBIA BIBLE COLLEGE
2940 Clearbrook Rd.
Abbotsford, BC, Canada V2T 2Z8
Tel: (604)853-3358; Free: 800-283-0881
Fax: (604)853-3063
E-mail: aaron.roorda@columbiabc.edu
Web Site: http://www.columbiabc.edu/
President/CEO: Dr. Ron Penner
Admissions: Aaron Roorda
Financial Aid: Adel Klassen
Type: Four-Year College **Sex:** Coed **Affiliation:** Mennonite Brethren **Admission Plans:** Open Admission; Early Admission; Deferred Admission **Application Deadline:** August 15 **Application Fee:** $50.00 **H.S. Requirements:** High school diploma required; GED accepted **Costs Per Year:** Application fee: $50. Tuition: $8550 full-time, $285 per credit hour part-time. Full-time tuition varies according to class time and course load. Part-time tuition varies according to class time and course load. **Scholarships:** Available **Calendar System:** Semester, Summer Session Not available **Faculty:** FT 12, PT 43 **Student-Faculty Ratio:** 17:1 **Library Holdings:** 44,000 **Credit Hours For Degree:** 126 credit hours, Bachelors **Professional Accreditation:** ABHE **Intercollegiate Athletics:** Basketball M & W; Golf M & W; Ice Hockey M; Soccer M & W; Volleyball M & W

EMILY CARR INSTITUTE OF ART DESIGN
1399 Johnston St.
Vancouver, BC, Canada V6H 3R9
Tel: (604)844-3800; Free: 800-832-7788
Fax: (604)844-3801
Web Site: http://www.eciad.ca/
President/CEO: John C. Kerr
Type: Comprehensive **Sex:** Coed **Application Deadline:** January 15 **Application Fee:** $40.00 **Costs Per Year:** Application fee: $40 Canadian dollars. Tuition and fee charges are reported in Canadian dollars. Tuition: $3658 full-time, $365.82 per course part-time. International student tuition: $11,537 full-time.

KWANTLEN POLYTECHNIC UNIVERSITY
12666 72nd Ave.
Surrey, BC, Canada V3W 2M8
Tel: (604)599-2100
Admissions: (604)599-2000
Fax: (604)555-2068
E-mail: admission@kwantlen.ca
Web Site: http://www.kwantlen.ca/
President/CEO: Dr. David Atkinson
Type: Four-Year College **Sex:** Coed **% Accepted:** 41 **Admission Plans:** Open Admission; Preferred Admission; Early Admission; Early Action; Early Decision Plan **Application Deadline:** Rolling **Application Fee:** $40.00 **H.S. Requirements:** High school diploma required; GED accepted. For mature students (19 years or older): High school diploma or equivalent not required **Costs Per Year:** Application fee: $40 Canadian dollars. Tuition and fee charges are reported in Canadian dollars. Province resident tuition: $3564 full-time, $118.80 per credit part-time. Mandatory fees: $565 full-time, $12.67 per credit part-time, $10 per term part-time. Full-time tuition and fees vary according to course load and program. Part-time tuition and fees vary according to course load and program. International student tuition: $12,600 full-time. **Scholarships:** Available **Calendar System:** Semester, Summer Session Available **Enrollment:** FT 7,805, PT 4,803 **Faculty:** FT 485, PT 78 **Student-Faculty Ratio:** 35:1 **Final Year or Final Semester Residency Requirement:** No **Credit Hours For Degree:** 60 credits, Associates; 120 credits, Bachelors **Professional Accreditation:** FIDER **Intercollegiate Athletics:** Badminton M & W; Baseball M & W; Basketball M & W; Golf M & W; Soccer M & W

OKANAGAN COLLEGE
1000 KLO Rd.
Kelowna, BC, Canada V1Y 4X8
Tel: (250)762-5445
E-mail: pgcampo@okanagan.bc.ca
Web Site: http://www.okanagan.bc.ca/
President/CEO: Jim Hamilton
Admissions: Paul Campo
Type: Four-Year College **Sex:** Coed **Affiliation:** Ministry of Advanced Education **% Accepted:** 45 **Admission Plans:** Preferred Admission; Early Admission **Application Fee:** $30.00 **H.S. Requirements:** High school diploma required; GED not accepted. For trades programs: High school diploma required; GED not accepted **Enrollment:** FT 1,598, PT 935 **Student-Faculty Ratio:** 13:1 **Library Holdings:** 112,972 **Intercollegiate Athletics:** Basketball M & W; Soccer M & W; Volleyball M & W

ROYAL ROADS UNIVERSITY
2005 Sooke Rd.
Victoria, BC, Canada V9B 5Y2
Tel: (250)391-2511; Free: 800-788-8028
Fax: (250)391-2522
E-mail: learn.more@royalroads.ca
Web Site: http://www.royalroads.ca/
President/CEO: Allan Cahoon
Type: Two-Year Upper Division **Sex:** Coed **Application Fee:** $102.00 **H.S. Requirements:** High school diploma or equivalent not required **Costs Per Year:** Application fee: $102 Canadian dollars. Tuition and fee charges are reported in Canadian dollars. Province resident tuition: $14,100 full-time. International student tuition: $28,200 full-time. **Calendar System:** Continu-

ous, Summer Session Available **Faculty:** FT 50 **Library Holdings:** 117,326 **Credit Hours For Degree:** 120 credits, Bachelors

SIMON FRASER UNIVERSITY
8888 University Dr.
Burnaby, BC, Canada V5A 1S6
Tel: (604)291-3111
Admissions: (778)782-3498
Fax: (604)291-4969
E-mail: undergraduate-admissions@sfu.ca
Web Site: http://www.sfu.ca/
President/CEO: Dr. Michael Stevenson
Admissions: Louise Legris
Financial Aid: Manoj Bhakthan
Type: University **Sex:** Coed **% Accepted:** 77 **Admission Plans:** Early Admission; Deferred Admission **Application Deadline:** April 30 **Application Fee:** $100.00 **H.S. Requirements:** High school diploma required; GED not accepted **Costs Per Year:** Application fee: $100 Canadian dollars. Tuition, fee, and room and board charges are reported in Canadian dollars. Province resident tuition: $4719 full-time, $157.30 per credit hour part-time. Canadian resident tuition: $490.70 per credit hour part-time. Mandatory fees: $539 full-time, $269.48 per term part-time. Full-time tuition and fees vary according to degree level and program. Part-time tuition and fees vary according to degree level. College room and board: $7464. College room only: $4764. Room and board charges vary according to board plan and housing facility. International student tuition: $14,721 full-time. **Scholarships:** Available **Calendar System:** Trimester, Summer Session Available **Enrollment:** FT 11,762, PT 11,054, Grad FT 3,282, Grad PT 983 **Faculty:** FT 931, PT 11 **Student-Faculty Ratio:** 10:1 **Exams:** SAT I or ACT. **% Residing in College-Owned, -Operated, or -Affiliated Housing:** 9 **Final Year or Final Semester Residency Requirement:** No **Credit Hours For Degree:** 120 credit hours, Bachelors **Professional Accreditation:** AACSB, APA, NCCU **Intercollegiate Athletics:** Basketball M & W; Cross-Country Running M & W; Field Hockey W; Football M; Golf M; Gymnastics M; Soccer M & W; Softball W; Swimming and Diving M & W; Track and Field M & W; Volleyball W; Wrestling M & W

SUMMIT PACIFIC COLLEGE
Box 1700
Abbotsford, BC, Canada V2S 7E7
Tel: (604)853-7491; Free: 800-976-8388
Admissions: (604)851-7225
Fax: (604)853-8951
E-mail: registrar@summitpacific.ca
Web Site: http://www.summitpacific.ca/
Admissions: Melody Deeley
Type: Four-Year College **Sex:** Coed **Affiliation:** Pentecostal Assemblies of Canada **Admission Plans:** Deferred Admission **Application Deadline:** Rolling **Application Fee:** $50.00 **H.S. Requirements:** High school diploma required; GED accepted **Calendar System:** Semester, Summer Session Available **Library Holdings:** 35,409 **Credit Hours For Degree:** 120 credits, Bachelors **Professional Accreditation:** ABHE

THOMPSON RIVERS UNIVERSITY
PO Box 3010, Station Terminal
Kamloops, BC, Canada V2C 5N3
Tel: (250)828-5000
Admissions: (250)828-5008
Fax: (250)828-5086
E-mail: jkeller@tru.ca
Web Site: http://www.tru.ca/
President/CEO: Dr. Roger H. Barnsley
Admissions: Josh Keller
Financial Aid: Gordon Down
Type: Comprehensive **Sex:** Coed **Affiliation:** Ministry of Advanced Education, Province of British Columbia **% Accepted:** 50 **Admission Plans:** Open Admission **Application Deadline:** March 1 **Application Fee:** $25.00 **H.S. Requirements:** High school diploma required; GED accepted. For mature students: High school diploma or equivalent not required **Costs Per Year:** Application fee: $25 Canadian dollars. Tuition, fee, and room only charges are reported in Canadian dollars. Province resident tuition: $3540 full-time, $117.98 per credit hour part-time. Canadian resident tuition: $3540 full-time, $117.98 per credit hour part-time. Mandatory fees: $840 full-time, $20.25 per credit hour part-time, $60.76. Full-time tuition and fees vary according to course load and program. Part-time tuition and fees vary according to course load and program. College room only: $3900. Room charges vary according to housing facility. International student tuition: $13,800 full-time. **Scholarships:** Available **Calendar System:** Semester, Summer Session Available **Faculty:** FT 436, PT 295 **Student-Faculty Ratio:** 12:1 **% Residing in College-Owned, -Operated, or -Affiliated Housing:** 13 **Final Year or Final Semester Residency Requirement:** No **Library Holdings:** 273,900 **Credit Hours For Degree:** 60 credits, Associates; 120 credits, Bachelors **Intercollegiate Athletics:** Badminton M & W; Baseball M; Basketball M & W; Golf M; Ice Hockey M; Soccer M & W; Volleyball M & W

TRINITY WESTERN UNIVERSITY
7600 Glover Rd.
Langley, BC, Canada V2Y 1Y1
Tel: (604)888-7511; Free: 888-468-6898
Fax: (604)513-2061
E-mail: admissions@twu.ca
Web Site: http://www.twu.ca/
Financial Aid: Corwin Koch
Type: Comprehensive **Sex:** Coed **Affiliation:** Evangelical Free Church of America **Admission Plans:** Deferred Admission **Application Deadline:** June 15 **Application Fee:** $40.00 **H.S. Requirements:** High school diploma required; GED accepted **Scholarships:** Available **Calendar System:** Semester, Summer Session Available **Faculty:** FT 77, PT 61 **Student-Faculty Ratio:** 18:1 **Exams:** SAT I or ACT. **Library Holdings:** 190,565 **Credit Hours For Degree:** 122 semester hours, Bachelors **Professional Accreditation:** ACA, ATS **Intercollegiate Athletics:** Basketball M & W; Rugby M; Soccer M & W; Volleyball M & W

THE UNIVERSITY OF BRITISH COLUMBIA
2075 Wesbrook Mall
Vancouver, BC, Canada V6T 1Z1
Tel: (604)822-2211
Admissions: (604)822-8999
Fax: (604)822-3599
Web Site: http://www.ubc.ca/
President/CEO: Stephen J. Toope
Type: University **Sex:** Coed **% Accepted:** 53 **Admission Plans:** Deferred Admission **Application Deadline:** February 28 **Application Fee:** $100.00 **H.S. Requirements:** High school diploma required; GED not accepted **Costs Per Year:** Application fee: $100 Canadian dollars. Tuition, fee, and room and board charges are reported in Canadian dollars. Province resident tuition: $4429 full-time, $147.65 per credit part-time. Canadian resident tuition: $676.86 per credit part-time. Mandatory fees: $725 full-time. Full-time tuition and fees vary according to course load, program, and student level. Part-time tuition varies according to course load, program, and student level. College room and board: $6650. Room and board charges vary according to board plan, housing facility, and location. International student tuition: $20,306 full-time. **Scholarships:** Available **Calendar System:** Miscellaneous, Summer Session Available **Enrollment:** FT 21,628, PT 9,889, Grad FT 11,638, Grad PT 3,516 **Faculty:** FT 2,530 **Student-Faculty Ratio:** 15:1 **Exams:** Other. **% Receiving Financial Aid:** 26 **% Residing in College-Owned, -Operated, or -Affiliated Housing:** 25 **Final Year or Final Semester Residency Requirement:** No **Library Holdings:** 6,420,000 **Credit Hours For Degree:** 120 credits, Bachelors **Professional Accreditation:** AACSB, ACA, ADA, ACSP, ALA, APA, ASLA, LCMEAMA, NCATE **Intercollegiate Athletics:** Baseball M; Basketball M & W; Cheerleading M & W; Crew M & W; Cross-Country Running M & W; Equestrian Sports M & W; Fencing M & W; Field Hockey M & W; Football M; Golf M & W; Ice Hockey M & W; Rock Climbing M & W; Rugby M & W; Skiing (Downhill) M & W; Soccer M & W; Swimming and Diving M & W; Track and Field M & W; Volleyball M & W

THE UNIVERSITY OF BRITISH COLUMBIA—OKANAGAN
3333 University Way
Kelowna, BC, Canada V1V 1V7
Tel: (250)807-8521
Admissions: (250)807-9447
Fax: (250)807-8522
Web Site: http://www.ubc.ca/okanagan/welcome.html
President/CEO: Dr. Doug Owram
Type: University **Sex:** Coed **% Accepted:** 53 **Admission Plans:** Deferred Admission **Application Deadline:** February 28 **Application Fee:** $100.00 **H.S. Requirements:** High school diploma required; GED not accepted

Costs Per Year: Application fee: $100 Canadian dollars. Tuition, fee, and room and board charges are reported in Canadian dollars. Province resident tuition: $4429 full-time, $147.65 per credit part-time. Canadian resident tuition: $676.86 per credit part-time. Mandatory fees: $603 full-time. Full-time tuition and fees vary according to course load, program, and student level. Part-time tuition varies according to course load, program, and student level. College room and board: $5700. Room and board charges vary according to board plan, housing facility, and location. International student tuition: $20,306 full-time. **Enrollment:** FT 4,257, PT 1,213, Grad FT 527, Grad PT 107 **Faculty:** FT 301 **Student-Faculty Ratio:** 14:1 **Exams:** SAT I or ACT. **% Residing in College-Owned, -Operated, or -Affiliated Housing:** 40 **Library Holdings:** 6,420,000 **Credit Hours For Degree:** 120 credits, Bachelors **Intercollegiate Athletics:** Basketball M & W; Soccer M & W; Volleyball M & W

UNIVERSITY OF THE FRASER VALLEY
33844 King Rd.
Abbotsford, BC, Canada V2S 7M8
Tel: (604)504-7441
Fax: (604)855-7614
E-mail: reginfo@ucfv.ca
Web Site: http://www.ufv.ca/
Admissions: Robin Smith
Financial Aid: Carol Ambridge
Type: Comprehensive **Sex:** Coed **Admission Plans:** Open Admission; Deferred Admission **Application Deadline:** January 31 **Application Fee:** $45.00 **H.S. Requirements:** High school diploma or equivalent not required **Scholarships:** Available **Calendar System:** Semester, Summer Session Available **Credit Hours For Degree:** 60 credits, Associates; 120 credits, Bachelors **Intercollegiate Athletics:** Basketball M & W; Soccer M & W

UNIVERSITY OF NORTHERN BRITISH COLUMBIA
3333 University Way
Prince George, BC, Canada V2N 4Z9
Tel: (250)960-5555
Admissions: (250)960-6347
Fax: (250)960-5791
E-mail: registrar-info@unbc.ca
Web Site: http://www.unbc.ca/
President/CEO: Charles Jago
Admissions: Grant Kerr
Financial Aid: Linda Roa
Type: University **Sex:** Coed **% Accepted:** 76 **Admission Plans:** Early Admission; Early Decision Plan **Application Deadline:** March 1 **Application Fee:** $25.00 **H.S. Requirements:** High school diploma required; GED accepted **Scholarships:** Available **Calendar System:** Semester, Summer Session Available **Faculty:** FT 178, PT 204 **Student-Faculty Ratio:** 10:1 **% Residing in College-Owned, -Operated, or -Affiliated Housing:** 16 **Library Holdings:** 310,433 **Credit Hours For Degree:** 120 credits, Bachelors **Intercollegiate Athletics:** Basketball M & W; Skiing (Cross-Country) M & W

UNIVERSITY OF PHOENIX—VANCOUVER CAMPUS
4401 Still Creek Dr., Ste. 200
Burnaby, BC, Canada V5C 6G9
Tel: (604)205-6999; Free: 800-228-7240
Admissions: (480)557-6151
E-mail: audra.mcquarie@phoenix.edu
Web Site: http://www.phoenix.edu/
President/CEO: William Pepicello
Admissions: Audra McQuarie
Type: Comprehensive **Sex:** Coed **Admission Plans:** Open Admission; Deferred Admission **Application Deadline:** Rolling **Application Fee:** $110.00 **H.S. Requirements:** High school diploma required; GED accepted **Costs Per Year:** Application fee: $110. Tuition: $12,180 full-time. Full-time tuition varies according to course level and course load. **Calendar System:** Continuous, Summer Session Not available **Regional Accreditation:** North Central Association of Colleges and Schools **Credit Hours For Degree:** 60 credits, Associates; 120 credits, Bachelors

UNIVERSITY OF VICTORIA
PO Box 1700 STN CSC
Victoria, BC, Canada V8W 2Y2
Tel: (250)721-7211
Admissions: (250)721-8121
Fax: (250)721-6225
E-mail: admit@uvic.ca
Web Site: http://www.uvic.ca/
Admissions: Bruno Rocca
Type: University **Sex:** Coed **% Accepted:** 75 **Admission Plans:** Early Admission; Early Action; Deferred Admission **Application Deadline:** April 30 **Application Fee:** $100.00 **H.S. Requirements:** High school diploma required; GED accepted **Costs Per Year:** Application fee: $100 Canadian dollars. Tuition, fee, and room and board charges are reported in Canadian dollars. Province resident tuition: $4672 full-time, $311.50 per unit part-time. Mandatory fees: $427 full-time. Full-time tuition and fees vary according to program. Part-time tuition varies according to program. College room and board: $7988. Room and board charges vary according to board plan and housing facility. International student tuition: $15,119 full-time. **Scholarships:** Available **Calendar System:** Miscellaneous, Summer Session Available **Enrollment:** FT 10,716, PT 5,866 **Faculty:** FT 721, PT 39 **Student-Faculty Ratio:** 27:1 **Library Holdings:** 1,800,000 **Credit Hours For Degree:** 60 units, Bachelors **Professional Accreditation:** APA **Intercollegiate Athletics:** Basketball M & W; Crew M & W; Cross-Country Running M & W; Field Hockey W; Golf M & W; Rugby M & W; Soccer M & W; Swimming and Diving M & W

VANCOUVER ISLAND UNIVERSITY
900 Fifth St.
Nanaimo, BC, Canada V9R 5S5
Tel: (250)753-3245
Admissions: (250)740-6355
Web Site: http://www.viu.ca/
Admissions: Leslie Peterson
Financial Aid: Karen Stant
Type: Comprehensive **Sex:** Coed **Application Fee:** $30.00 **Scholarships:** Available **Calendar System:** Semester **Professional Accreditation:** ACBSP

BRANDON UNIVERSITY
270 18th St.
Brandon, MB, Canada R7A 6A9
Tel: (204)728-9520
Admissions: (204)727-7352
E-mail: kerr@brandonu.ca
Web Site: http://www.brandonu.ca/
Admissions: Murray Kerr
Type: Comprehensive **Sex:** Coed **% Accepted:** 70 **Admission Plans:** Open Admission; Deferred Admission **Application Deadline:** Rolling **Application Fee:** $60.00 **H.S. Requirements:** High school diploma required; GED accepted **Scholarships:** Available **Calendar System:** Miscellaneous, Summer Session Available **Enrollment:** FT 2,306, PT 1,095 **Faculty:** FT 215, PT 13 **Student-Faculty Ratio:** 11:1 **% Residing in College-Owned, -Operated, or -Affiliated Housing:** 9 **Library Holdings:** 238,816 **Credit Hours For Degree:** 90 credit hours, Bachelors **Intercollegiate Athletics:** Basketball M & W; Volleyball M & W

CANADIAN MENNONITE UNIVERSITY
500 Shaftesbury Blvd.
Winnipeg, MB, Canada R3P 2N2
Tel: (204)487-3300; Free: 877-231-4570
Fax: (204)487-3858
E-mail: cu@cmu.ca
Web Site: http://www.cmu.ca/
President/CEO: Gerald Gerbrandt
Admissions: Abe Bergen
Financial Aid: Gillian Doucet Campbell
Type: Comprehensive **Sex:** Coed **Affiliation:** Mennonite **% Accepted:** 95 **Admission Plans:** Deferred Admission **Application Deadline:** August 28 **Application Fee:** $35.00 **H.S. Requirements:** High school diploma required; GED accepted **Scholarships:** Available **Calendar System:** Semester, Summer Session Not available **Enrollment:** FT 349, PT 83 **Faculty:** FT 23, PT 7 **Student-Faculty Ratio:** 15:1 **% Residing in College-Owned, -Operated, or -Affiliated Housing:** 45 **Library Holdings:** 85,000 **Credit Hours For Degree:** 90 credits, Bachelors **Intercollegiate Athletics:** Basketball M & W; Ice Hockey M; Soccer M & W; Volleyball M & W

COLLEGE UNIVERSITAIRE DE SAINT-BONIFACE
200 Ave. de la Cathèdrale
Saint-Boniface, MB, Canada R2H 0H7
Tel: (204)233-0210
Fax: (204)237-3240
Web Site: http://www.ustboniface.mb.ca/
Type: Comprehensive **Sex:** Coed

PROVIDENCE COLLEGE AND THEOLOGICAL SEMINARY
10 College Crescent
Otterburne, MB, Canada R0A 1G0
Tel: (204)433-7488; Free: 800-668-7768
E-mail: info@prov.ca
Web Site: http://www.prov.ca/
President/CEO: Dr. August Konkel
Admissions: Adrian Enns
Type: Comprehensive **Sex:** Coed **Affiliation:** interdenominational **% Accepted:** 87 **Admission Plans:** Open Admission; Deferred Admission **Application Deadline:** Rolling **Application Fee:** $40.00 **H.S. Requirements:** High school diploma required; GED accepted **Costs Per Year:** Application fee: $40 Canadian dollars. Tuition, fee, and room and board charges are reported in Canadian dollars. Comprehensive fee: $11,830 includes full-time tuition ($6120), mandatory fees ($1140), and college room and board ($4570). Part-time tuition: $218 per credit hour. Part-time mandatory fees: $23 per credit hour. **Calendar System:** Semester, Summer Session Not available **Enrollment:** FT 271, PT 53 **Faculty:** FT 18, PT 32 **Student-Faculty Ratio:** 19:1 **% Residing in College-Owned, -Operated, or -Affiliated Housing:** 65 **Library Holdings:** 71,407 **Credit Hours For Degree:** 96 semester hours, Bachelors **Professional Accreditation:** ABHE, ATS **Intercollegiate Athletics:** Badminton M & W; Basketball M & W; Ice Hockey M; Soccer M & W; Table Tennis M & W; Volleyball M & W

STEINBACH BIBLE COLLEGE
50 PTH 12N
Steinbach, MB, Canada R5G 1T4
Tel: (204)326-6451; Free: 800-230-8478
E-mail: info@sbcollege.ca
Web Site: http://www.sbcollege.ca/
President/CEO: Rob Reimer
Admissions: Kaylene Buhler
Financial Aid: Patrick Martens
Type: Four-Year College **Sex:** Coed **Affiliation:** Mennonite **% Accepted:** 81 **Application Fee:** $50.00 **H.S. Requirements:** High school diploma required; GED accepted **Costs Per Year:** Application fee: $50 Canadian dollars. Tuition, fee, and room and board charges are reported in Canadian dollars. Comprehensive fee: $10,697 includes full-time tuition ($6080), mandatory fees ($297), and college room and board ($4320). Part-time tuition: $190 per credit hour. Part-time mandatory fees: $60 per year. **Scholarships:** Available **Calendar System:** Semester **Enrollment:** FT 94, PT 54 **Faculty:** FT 4, PT 10 **Student-Faculty Ratio:** 18:1 **Professional Accreditation:** ABHE

UNIVERSITY OF MANITOBA
Winnipeg, MB, Canada R3T 2N2
Tel: (204)474-8880
Admissions: (204)474-6382
Web Site: http://www.umanitoba.ca/
Admissions: Peter Dueck
Financial Aid: Jane Lastra
Type: University **Sex:** Coed **Admission Plans:** Early Admission **Application Fee:** $65.00 **H.S. Requirements:** High school diploma required; GED not accepted. For students 21 or over: High school diploma or equivalent not required **Costs Per Year:** Application fee: $65 Canadian dollars. Tuition, fee, and room and board charges are reported in Canadian dollars. Province resident tuition: $2948 full-time. Mandatory fees: $471 full-time. Full-time tuition and fees vary according to course load, program, and reciprocity agreements. College room and board: $7759. College room only: $5511. Room and board charges vary according to board plan and housing facility. International student tuition: $10,319 full-time. **Scholarships:** Available **Calendar System:** Miscellaneous, Summer Session Available **Enrollment:** FT 19,174, PT 4,480, Grad FT 3,039, Grad PT 783 **Library Holdings:** 2,000,000 **Credit Hours For Degree:** 90 credits, Bachelors **Professional**

Accreditation: AACSB, ADA, APA, ASLA, FIDER, LCMEAMA **Intercollegiate Athletics:** Basketball M & W; Cross-Country Running M & W; Field Hockey M & W; Football M & W; Gymnastics M & W; Ice Hockey M & W; Swimming and Diving M & W; Track and Field M & W; Volleyball M & W

THE UNIVERSITY OF WINNIPEG

515 Portage Ave.
Winnipeg, MB, Canada R3B 2E9
Tel: (204)786-7811
Admissions: (204)786-9776
E-mail: admissions@uwinnipeg.ca
Web Site: http://www.uwinnipeg.ca/
President/CEO: Dr. Lloyd Axworthy
Admissions: Colin Russell
Financial Aid: Judy Dyck

Type: Comprehensive **Sex:** Coed **% Accepted:** 75 **Admission Plans:** Early Admission; Deferred Admission **Application Deadline:** August 9 **Application Fee:** $60.00 **H.S. Requirements:** High school diploma required; GED not accepted. For applicants 21 or over: High school diploma required; GED accepted **Scholarships:** Available **Calendar System:** Miscellaneous, Summer Session Available **Enrollment:** FT 6,231, PT 2,775 **Faculty:** FT 270, PT 51 **Student-Faculty Ratio:** 35:1 **% Residing in College-Owned, -Operated, or -Affiliated Housing:** 3 **Library Holdings:** 442,614 **Credit Hours For Degree:** 15 full-year courses, Bachelors **Professional Accreditation:** AAMFT, ATS **Intercollegiate Athletics:** Basketball M & W; Volleyball M & W

WILLIAM AND CATHERINE BOOTH COLLEGE

447 Webb Place
Winnipeg, MB, Canada R3B 2P2
Tel: (204)947-6701; Free: 800-781-6044
Admissions: (204)924-4867
Fax: (204)942-3856
E-mail: cburt@boothcollege.ca
Web Site: http://www.boothcollege.ca/
Admissions: Chantel Burt

Type: Four-Year College **Sex:** Coed **% Accepted:** 71 **Application Deadline:** July 31 **H.S. Requirements:** High school diploma required; GED accepted **Costs Per Year:** Application fee: $0 Canadian dollars. Tuition, fee, and room and board charges are reported in Canadian dollars. Comprehensive fee: $11,380 includes full-time tuition ($7200), mandatory fees ($180), and college room and board ($4000). Part-time tuition: $240 per credit hour. Part-time mandatory fees: $6 per credit hour. **Calendar System:** Semester, Summer Session Available **Faculty:** FT 9, PT 19 **Student-Faculty Ratio:** 9:1 **% Residing in College-Owned, -Operated, or -Affiliated Housing:** 10 **Library Holdings:** 53,000 **Credit Hours For Degree:** 98 credit hours, Bachelors **Professional Accreditation:** ABHE **Intercollegiate Athletics:** Volleyball M & W

New Brunswick

BETHANY BIBLE COLLEGE
26 Western St.
Sussex, NB, Canada E4E 5L2
Tel: (506)432-4400; Free: 888-432-4422
Admissions: (506)432-4422
Fax: (506)432-4425
E-mail: butlerd@bbc.ca
Web Site: http://www.bethany-ca.edu/
President/CEO: Dr. Arthur W. Maxwell
Admissions: Dana Butler
Financial Aid: Ruth Muscroft
Type: Four-Year College **Sex:** Coed **Affiliation:** Wesleyan Church **Scores:** 100% SAT V 400+; 77% SAT M 400+; 66.5% ACT 18-23; 33.5% ACT 24-29 **% Accepted:** 57 **Admission Plans:** Early Admission **Application Deadline:** Rolling **Application Fee:** $20.00 **H.S. Requirements:** High school diploma required; GED accepted **Costs Per Year:** Application fee: $20. Comprehensive fee: $13,650 includes full-time tuition ($8550) and college room and board ($5100). College room only: $2150. Room and board charges vary according to board plan and housing facility. Part-time tuition: $285 per credit hour. **Scholarships:** Available **Calendar System:** Semester, Summer Session Available **Enrollment:** FT 196, PT 7 **Faculty:** FT 11, PT 15 **Student-Faculty Ratio:** 13:1 **Exams:** SAT I or ACT. **% Residing in College-Owned, -Operated, or -Affiliated Housing:** 70 **Library Holdings:** 36,260 **Credit Hours For Degree:** 60 hours, Associates; 134 hours, Bachelors **Professional Accreditation:** ABHE **Intercollegiate Athletics:** Basketball M & W; Ice Hockey M; Soccer M & W; Softball M & W; Volleyball W

CRANDALL UNIVERSITY
Box 6004
Moncton, NB, Canada E1C 9L7
Tel: (506)858-8970; Free: 888-YOU-N-ABU
Fax: (506)858-9694
E-mail: Laura.lutes@crandallu.ca
Web Site: http://www.crandallu.ca/
President/CEO: Dr. Brian D. MacArthur
Admissions: Laura Lutes
Type: Four-Year College **Sex:** Coed **Affiliation:** Baptist; The Council of Christian Colleges and Universities **% Accepted:** 89 **Admission Plans:** Early Admission; Early Decision Plan; Deferred Admission **Application Deadline:** Rolling **Application Fee:** $35.00 **H.S. Requirements:** High school diploma required; GED accepted **Costs Per Year:** Application fee: $35 Canadian dollars. Tuition, fee, and room and board charges are reported in Canadian dollars. Comprehensive fee: $12,965 includes full-time tuition ($6870), mandatory fees ($765), and college room and board ($5330). College room only: $2380. Room and board charges vary according to board plan and housing facility. Part-time tuition: $740 per course. **Scholarships:** Available **Calendar System:** Semester, Summer Session Available **Enrollment:** FT 648, PT 71 **Student-Faculty Ratio:** 17:1 **% Residing in College-Owned, -Operated, or -Affiliated Housing:** 22 **Credit Hours For Degree:** 120 credit hours, Bachelors **Intercollegiate Athletics:** Baseball M; Basketball M & W; Cross-Country Running M & W; Soccer M & W

MERITUS UNIVERSITY
30 Knowledge Park Dr.
Ste. 301
Fredericton, NB, Canada E3C 2R2
Tel: 800-856-3940; Free: 800-856-3940
E-mail: enrolmentinfo@staff.MeritusU.ca
Web Site: http://www.meritusu.ca/
President/CEO: Dr. John Crossley
Admissions: Jaime Gardea
Type: Comprehensive **Sex:** Coed **Admission Plans:** Open Admission **Application Deadline:** Rolling **Application Fee:** $45.00 **H.S. Requirements:** High school diploma required; GED accepted **Costs Per Year:** Application fee: $45 Canadian dollars. Tuition and fee charges are reported in Canadian dollars. Tuition: $8250 full-time, $275 per credit hour part-time. **Faculty:** FT 2, PT 46 **Final Year or Final Semester Residency Requirement:** No **Library Holdings:** 20,000,000 **Credit Hours For Degree:** 120 credits, Bachelors

MOUNT ALLISON UNIVERSITY
65 York St.
Sackville, NB, Canada E4L 1E4
Tel: (506)364-2269
Admissions: (506)364-3294
Fax: (506)364-2272
E-mail: admissions@mta.ca
Web Site: http://www.mta.ca/
President/CEO: Dr. Robert M. Campbell
Admissions: Matt Sheridan-Jonah
Financial Aid: Margaret Ann Esparza-Lee
Type: Comprehensive **Sex:** Coed **% Accepted:** 74 **Admission Plans:** Deferred Admission **Application Deadline:** Rolling **Application Fee:** $50.00 **H.S. Requirements:** High school diploma required; GED accepted **Costs Per Year:** Application fee: $50 Canadian dollars. Tuition, fee, and room and board charges are reported in Canadian dollars. Province resident tuition: $6720 full-time, $672 per course part-time. Canadian resident tuition: $1344 per course part-time. Mandatory fees: $289 full-time, $37.60 per term part-time. Full-time tuition and fees vary according to course load. Part-time tuition and fees vary according to course load. College room and board: $7389. College room only: $3873. Room and board charges vary according to board plan. International student tuition: $13,440 full-time. **Scholarships:** Available **Calendar System:** Miscellaneous, Summer Session Available **Enrollment:** FT 2,398, PT 118, Grad FT 11 **Faculty:** FT 133, PT 31 **Student-Faculty Ratio:** 16:1 **% Residing in College-Owned, -Operated, or -Affiliated Housing:** 50 **Library Holdings:** 400,000 **Credit Hours For Degree:** 120 credits, Bachelors **Intercollegiate Athletics:** Basketball M & W; Football M; Ice Hockey W; Rugby M & W; Soccer M & W; Swimming and Diving M & W

ST. THOMAS UNIVERSITY
51 Dineen Dr.
Fredericton, NB, Canada E3B 5G3
Tel: (506)452-0640
Admissions: (506)452-0532
Fax: (506)450-9615
E-mail: admissions@stu.ca

Web Site: http://www.stu.ca/
President/CEO: Dennis Cochrane
Admissions: Kathryn Monti
Type: Four-Year College **Sex:** Coed **Affiliation:** Roman Catholic **% Accepted:** 84 **Admission Plans:** Early Action **Application Deadline:** August 31 **Application Fee:** $35.00 **H.S. Requirements:** High school diploma required; GED not accepted. For adult learners: High school diploma or equivalent not required **Costs Per Year:** Application fee: $35 Canadian dollars. Tuition, fee, and room and board charges are reported in Canadian dollars. Comprehensive fee: $11,676 includes full-time tuition ($4570), mandatory fees ($306), and college room and board ($6800). Full-time tuition and fees vary according to course load, degree level, and program. Room and board charges vary according to board plan, housing facility, and location. Part-time tuition: $510 per course. Part-time mandatory fees: $31 per course. Part-time tuition and fees vary according to course load. International student tuition: $10,300 full-time. **Calendar System:** Semester, Summer Session Available **Enrollment:** FT 2,182, PT 244, Grad FT 177, Grad PT 23 **Faculty:** FT 108, PT 81 **Student-Faculty Ratio:** 19:1 **Exams:** SAT I. **% Residing in College-Owned, -Operated, or -Affiliated Housing:** 33 **Library Holdings:** 1,224,557 **Credit Hours For Degree:** 120 credit hours, Bachelors **Intercollegiate Athletics:** Basketball M & W; Cross-Country Running M & W; Golf M & W; Ice Hockey M & W; Soccer M & W; Volleyball M & W

UNIVERSITE DE MONCTON
Moncton, NB, Canada E1A 3E9
Tel: (506)858-4000
Admissions: (506)858-4115
Fax: (506)858-4544
E-mail: gallanrm@umoncton.ca
Web Site: http://www.umoncton.ca/
Admissions: Nicole Savois
Financial Aid: Sylvette Dionne-Cormier
Type: Comprehensive **Sex:** Coed **% Accepted:** 86 **Admission Plans:** Deferred Admission **Application Deadline:** June 1 **Application Fee:** $30.00 **H.S. Requirements:** High school diploma required; GED accepted. For education, science, engineering, nutrition, nursing, forestry programs: High school diploma required; GED not accepted **Scholarships:** Available **Calendar System:** Semester, Summer Session Available **Enrollment:** FT 4,540, PT 980 **Faculty:** FT 374, PT 113 **Student-Faculty Ratio:** 12:1 **% Receiving Financial Aid:** 62 **% Residing in College-Owned, -Operated, or -Affiliated Housing:** 15 **Library Holdings:** 789,046 **Credit Hours For Degree:** 126 credits, Bachelors **Intercollegiate Athletics:** Cross-Country Running M & W; Gymnastics W; Ice Hockey M & W; Soccer M & W; Track and Field M & W; Volleyball W

UNIVERSITY OF NEW BRUNSWICK FREDERICTON
PO Box 4400
Fredericton, NB, Canada E3B 5A3
Tel: (506)453-4666
Admissions: (506)453-4865
Fax: (506)453-5016
E-mail: unbfacts@unb.ca
Web Site: http://www.unb.ca/
President/CEO: Dr. Eddy Campbell
Financial Aid: Shelley Clayton
Type: University **Sex:** Coed **% Accepted:** 83 **Admission Plans:** Early Admission; Deferred Admission **Application Deadline:** March 31 **Application Fee:** $45.00 **H.S. Requirements:** High school diploma or equivalent not required **Costs Per Year:** Application fee: $45 Canadian dollars. Tuition and fee charges are reported in Canadian dollars. Province resident tuition: $5482 full-time. Full-time tuition varies according to program. International student tuition: $11,912 full-time. **Scholarships:** Available **Calendar System:** Miscellaneous, Summer Session Available **Enrollment:** FT 8,007, PT 1,272, Grad FT 1,114, Grad PT 534 **Faculty:** FT 625, PT 117 **Student-Faculty Ratio:** 18:1 **Exams:** SAT I. **% Residing in College-Owned, -Operated, or -Affiliated Housing:** 20 **Library Holdings:** 1,272,423 **Professional Accreditation:** APA **Intercollegiate Athletics:** Basketball M & W; Cross-Country Running M & W; Ice Hockey W; Soccer M & W; Swimming and Diving M & W; Volleyball M & W; Wrestling M & W

UNIVERSITY OF NEW BRUNSWICK SAINT JOHN
PO Box 5050
St. John, NB, Canada E2L 4L5
Tel: (506)648-5500; Free: 800-743-5691
Admissions: (506)648-5674
E-mail: apply@unbsj.ca
Web Site: http://www.unb.ca/
Admissions: Sue Ellis Loparco
Financial Aid: Renea Sleep
Type: Comprehensive **Sex:** Coed **Admission Plans:** Early Admission; Deferred Admission **Application Deadline:** Rolling **Application Fee:** $45.00 **H.S. Requirements:** High school diploma required; GED not accepted. For adult students: High school diploma or equivalent not required **Scholarships:** Available **Calendar System:** Miscellaneous, Summer Session Available **Exams:** SAT I. **% Residing in College-Owned, -Operated, or -Affiliated Housing:** 5 **Library Holdings:** 155,500 **Credit Hours For Degree:** 120 credits, Bachelors **Intercollegiate Athletics:** Badminton M & W; Basketball M & W; Crew M & W; Cross-Country Running M & W; Fencing M & W; Ice Hockey M & W; Rugby M & W; Soccer M & W; Volleyball M & W

Nova Scotia

ACADIA UNIVERSITY
Wolfville, NS, Canada B4P 2R6
Tel: (902)542-2201
Admissions: (902)585-1016
Fax: (902)585-1081
E-mail: admissions@acadiau.ca
Web Site: http://www.acadiau.ca/
President/CEO: Raymond Ivany
Admissions: Anne Scott
Financial Aid: Judy Noel- Walsh
Type: Comprehensive **Sex:** Coed **% Accepted:** 36 **Admission Plans:** Deferred Admission **Application Deadline:** July 1 **Application Fee:** $25.00 **H.S. Requirements:** High school diploma required; GED not accepted. For adult students: High school diploma or equivalent not required **Costs Per Year:** Application fee: $25 Canadian dollars. Tuition, fee, and room and board charges are reported in Canadian dollars. One-time mandatory fee: $449. Province resident tuition: $7467 full-time, $890 per course part-time. Canadian resident tuition: $1560 per course part-time. Mandatory fees: $203 full-time, $5 per course part-time. Full-time tuition and fees vary according to course level, course load, degree level, and program. Part-time tuition and fees vary according to course level, course load, degree level, and program. College room and board: $7985. College room only: $4430. Room and board charges vary according to board plan and housing facility. International student tuition: $13,754 full-time. **Scholarships:** Available **Calendar System:** Miscellaneous, Summer Session Available **Enrollment:** FT 2,854, PT 149, Grad FT 114, Grad PT 345 **Faculty:** FT 243, PT 88 **Student-Faculty Ratio:** 10:1 **Exams:** SAT I, SAT II. **Credit Hours For Degree:** 120 credit hours, Bachelors **Professional Accreditation:** ATS **Intercollegiate Athletics:** Baseball M; Basketball M & W; Bowling M; Cheerleading M; Cross-Country Running M & W; Football M; Ice Hockey M & W; Rock Climbing M & W; Soccer M & W; Track and Field M & W; Volleyball W

CAPE BRETON UNIVERSITY
Box 5300
1250 Grand Lake Rd.
Sydney, NS, Canada B1P 6L2
Tel: (902)539-5300; Free: 888-959-9995
Admissions: (902)563-1117
Fax: (902)562-0119
E-mail: brendan_macdonald@cbu.ca
Web Site: http://www.cbu.ca/
President/CEO: H. John Harker
Admissions: Brendan MacDonald
Financial Aid: Bill MacQueen
Type: Comprehensive **Sex:** Coed **% Accepted:** 77 **Admission Plans:** Early Admission; Deferred Admission **Application Deadline:** August 1 **Application Fee:** $35.00 **H.S. Requirements:** High school diploma required; GED accepted **Costs Per Year:** Application fee: $35. One-time mandatory fee: $126. Province resident tuition: $4638 full-time. Canadian resident tuition: $5660 full-time. College room and board: $6560. College room only: $3360. Room and board charges vary according to board plan and housing facility. International student tuition: $11,320 full-time. **Calendar System:** Semester **Faculty:** FT 179, PT 30 **Student-Faculty Ratio:** 15:1 **Final Year or Final Semester Residency Requirement:** No **Library Holdings:** 100,000 **Credit**

Hours For Degree: 90 credits, Associates; 120 credits, Bachelors **Intercollegiate Athletics:** Basketball M & W; Ice Hockey W; Rugby M; Soccer M & W; Volleyball W

DALHOUSIE UNIVERSITY
Halifax, NS, Canada B3H 4R2
Tel: (902)494-2211
Admissions: (902)494-2148
Fax: (902)494-1630
E-mail: admissions@dal.ca
Web Site: http://www.dal.ca/
President/CEO: Dr. Tom Traves
Admissions: Mairead Barry
Type: University **Sex:** Coed **Admission Plans:** Early Admission; Early Decision Plan; Deferred Admission **Application Deadline:** June 1 **Application Fee:** $45.00 **H.S. Requirements:** High school diploma or equivalent not required **Scholarships:** Available **Calendar System:** Semester, Summer Session Available **Enrollment:** FT 9,141, PT 1,391 **Student-Faculty Ratio:** 14:1 **Exams:** SAT I or ACT. **Credit Hours For Degree:** 15 courses, Bachelors **Professional Accreditation:** AACSB, ADA, ALA, APA, ACEHSA, LCMEAMA **Intercollegiate Athletics:** Basketball M & W; Cross-Country Running M & W; Field Hockey W; Ice Hockey M & W; Soccer M & W; Swimming and Diving M & W; Track and Field M & W; Volleyball M & W

MOUNT SAINT VINCENT UNIVERSITY
166 Bedford Hwy.
Halifax, NS, Canada B3M 2J6
Tel: (902)457-6788
Admissions: (902)457-6117
Fax: (902)457-6455
E-mail: admissions@msvu.ca
Web Site: http://www.msvu.ca/
Admissions: Heidi Tattrie
Financial Aid: Frances C. Cody
Type: Comprehensive **Sex:** Coed **% Accepted:** 60 **Admission Plans:** Deferred Admission **Application Deadline:** March 15 **Application Fee:** $30.00 **H.S. Requirements:** High school diploma or equivalent not required. For students out of high school 3 years or more: High school diploma required; GED accepted **Costs Per Year:** Application fee: $30 Canadian dollars. Tuition, fee, and room and board charges are reported in Canadian dollars. Province resident tuition: $5550 full-time, $1110 per unit part-time. Canadian resident tuition: $2169 per unit part-time. Mandatory fees: $790 full-time, $55.45 per unit part-time, $9 per year part-time. Full-time tuition and fees vary according to course level, course load, degree level, location, program, reciprocity agreements, and student level. Part-time tuition and fees vary according to course level, course load, degree level, location, program, reciprocity agreements, and student level. College room and board: $7190. Room and board charges vary according to board plan and housing facility. International student tuition: $10,845 full-time. **Scholarships:** Available **Calendar System:** Miscellaneous, Summer Session Available **Faculty:** FT 149, PT 227 **Student-Faculty Ratio:** 13:1 **% Receiving Financial Aid:** 20 **Library Holdings:** 356,763 **Credit Hours For Degree:** 15 full-year courses, Bachelors **Intercollegiate Athletics:** Badminton M & W; Basketball M & W; Soccer M & W; Volleyball W

NOVA SCOTIA AGRICULTURAL COLLEGE
PO Box 550
Truro, NS, Canada B2N 5E3
Tel: (902)893-6600; Free: 888-700-6722
Admissions: (902)893-8212
E-mail: recruit@nsac.ca
Web Site: http://nsac.ca/
President/CEO: Leslie MacLaren, PhD
Admissions: Elizabeth Johnson
Type: Comprehensive **Sex:** Coed **Affiliation:** Dalhousie University **% Accepted:** 78 **Application Deadline:** August 1 **Application Fee:** $25.00 **H.S. Requirements:** High school diploma required; GED accepted **Costs Per Year:** Application fee: $25. Province resident tuition: $5500 full-time, $550 per course part-time. Canadian resident tuition: $1100 per course part-time. Mandatory fees: $428 full-time, $65 per term part-time. Full-time tuition and fees vary according to course load, degree level, and program. Part-time tuition and fees vary according to course load, degree level, and program. College room and board: $7376. College room only: $3934. Room and board charges vary according to board plan and housing facility. International student tuition: $11,000 full-time. **Scholarships:** Available **Calendar System:** Semester, Summer Session Available **Faculty:** FT 62, PT 18 **Student-Faculty Ratio:** 12:1 **% Residing in College-Owned, -Operated, or -Affiliated Housing:** 50 **Final Year or Final Semester Residency Requirement:** No **Library Holdings:** 23,000 **Credit Hours For Degree:** 40 courses, Bachelors **Intercollegiate Athletics:** Badminton M & W; Basketball M & W; Equestrian Sports M & W; Golf M & W; Rugby M & W; Soccer M & W; Volleyball M & W

NSCAD UNIVERSITY
5163 Duke St.
Halifax, NS, Canada B3J 3J6
Tel: (902)422-7381
Admissions: (902)494-8129
Fax: (902)425-2420
E-mail: admissions@nscad.ca
Web Site: http://www.nscad.ca/
President/CEO: Prof. David B. Smith
Admissions: Terry Bailey
Financial Aid: Bernadette Kehoe
Type: Comprehensive **Sex:** Coed **% Accepted:** 75 **Admission Plans:** Deferred Admission **Application Deadline:** May 15 **Application Fee:** $35.00 **H.S. Requirements:** High school diploma required; GED accepted **Costs Per Year:** Application fee: $35 Canadian dollars. Tuition and fee charges are reported in Canadian dollars. Province resident tuition: $5501 full-time, $687.60 per course part-time. Mandatory fees: $431 full-time, $32.85 per term part-time. Full-time tuition and fees vary according to course load and reciprocity agreements. Part-time tuition and fees vary according to course load and reciprocity agreements. International student tuition: $12,490 full-time. **Scholarships:** Available **Calendar System:** Semester, Summer Session Available **Faculty:** FT 46, PT 68 **Student-Faculty Ratio:** 9:1 **% Residing in College-Owned, -Operated, or -Affiliated Housing:** 10 **Library Holdings:** 32,000 **Credit Hours For Degree:** 120 credits, Bachelors

ST. FRANCIS XAVIER UNIVERSITY
Box 5000
Antigonish, NS, Canada B2G 2W5
Tel: (902)863-3300; Free: 877-867-STFX
Admissions: (902)867-2219
Fax: (902)867-2329
E-mail: mbarry@stfx.ca
Web Site: http://www.stfx.ca/
President/CEO: Dr. Sean E. Riley
Admissions: Sarah Murray
Financial Aid: Heidi Steinitz
Type: Comprehensive **Sex:** Coed **Affiliation:** Roman Catholic **% Accepted:** 82 **Admission Plans:** Early Admission; Early Decision Plan; Deferred Admission **Application Deadline:** Rolling **Application Fee:** $40.00 **H.S. Requirements:** High school diploma required; GED accepted **Scholarships:** Available **Calendar System:** Miscellaneous, Summer Session Available **Enrollment:** FT 2,178, PT 2,176, Grad FT 108, Grad PT 391 **Faculty:** FT 234, PT 66 **Student-Faculty Ratio:** 17:1 **Exams:** SAT I or ACT, SAT II. ACT essay not being used. SAT essay not being used. **% Residing in College-Owned, -Operated, or -Affiliated Housing:** 45 **Library Holdings:** 323,636 **Credit Hours For Degree:** 120 credits, Bachelors **Intercollegiate Athletics:** Baseball M; Basketball M & W; Cheerleading W; Crew M & W; Cross-Country Running M & W; Equestrian Sports W; Field Hockey W; Football M; Ice Hockey M & W; Lacrosse M; Rugby M & W; Soccer M & W; Track and Field M & W; Volleyball W

SAINT MARY'S UNIVERSITY
Halifax, NS, Canada B3H 3C3
Tel: (902)420-5400
Admissions: (902)420-5415
Fax: (902)496-8100
E-mail: greg.ferguson@smu.ca
Web Site: http://www.smu.ca/
Admissions: Greg Ferguson
Financial Aid: Michelle Fougere
Type: Comprehensive **Sex:** Coed **Admission Plans:** Early Action **Application Deadline:** July 1 **Application Fee:** $40.00 **H.S. Requirements:** High school diploma required; GED accepted **Scholarships:** Available **Calendar System:** Semester, Summer Session Available **Library Holdings:** 366,267

Credit Hours For Degree: 15 courses, Bachelors **Professional Accreditation:** AACSB **Intercollegiate Athletics:** Basketball M & W; Cross-Country Running M & W; Field Hockey W; Football M; Ice Hockey M & W; Rugby W; Soccer M & W; Track and Field M & W; Volleyball W

UNIVERSITE SAINTE-ANNE
Church Point, NS, Canada B0W 1M0
Tel: (902)769-2114
Fax: (902)769-2930
E-mail: admission@ustanne.ednet.ns.ca
Web Site: http://www.usainteanne.ca/
Admissions: Blanche Thériault
Financial Aid: Jeannine Boudreau
Type: Four-Year College **Sex:** Coed **% Accepted:** 69 **Application Deadline:** Rolling **Application Fee:** $30.00 **H.S. Requirements:** High school diploma required; GED not accepted. For applicants 22 or over: High school diploma or equivalent not required **Calendar System:** Semester, Summer Session Available **Faculty:** FT 33, PT 8 **% Residing in College-Owned, -Operated, or -Affiliated Housing:** 60 **Library Holdings:** 84,000 **Credit Hours For Degree:** 90 credits, Bachelors **Intercollegiate Athletics:** Badminton M & W; Volleyball M & W

UNIVERSITY OF KING'S COLLEGE
6350 Coburg Rd.
Halifax, NS, Canada B3H 2A1
Tel: (902)422-1271
Fax: (902)423-3357
E-mail: admissions@ukings.ns.ca
Web Site: http://www.ukings.ca/
President/CEO: Dr. William Barker
Admissions: Jill MacBeath
Financial Aid: Tara Buksaitis
Type: Four-Year College **Sex:** Coed **Affiliation:** Dalhousie University **% Accepted:** 78 **Admission Plans:** Early Admission; Early Decision Plan; Deferred Admission **Application Deadline:** March 1 **Application Fee:** $45.00 **H.S. Requirements:** High school diploma or equivalent not required **Costs Per Year:** Application fee: $45 Canadian dollars. Tuition, fee, and room and board charges are reported in Canadian dollars. Province resident tuition: $7207 full-time, $201 per credit hour part-time. Canadian resident tuition: $7207 full-time. Full-time tuition varies according to course load and program. Part-time tuition varies according to course load and program. College room and board: $8410. College room only: $5400. Room and board charges vary according to board plan and housing facility. International student tuition: $14,467 full-time. **Calendar System:** Miscellaneous, Summer Session Available **Enrollment:** FT 1,134, PT 30 **Faculty:** FT 51, PT 2 **Student-Faculty Ratio:** 21:1 **Exams:** SAT I. **% Residing in College-Owned, -Operated, or -Affiliated Housing:** 23 **Library Holdings:** 80,000 **Credit Hours For Degree:** 15 courses, Bachelors **Intercollegiate Athletics:** Badminton M & W; Basketball M & W; Rugby M & W; Soccer M & W; Volleyball M

Prince Edward Island

UNIVERSITY OF PRINCE EDWARD ISLAND
550 University Ave.
Charlottetown, PE, Canada C1A 4P3
Tel: (902)566-0439
Admissions: (902)566-0634
Fax: (902)566-0795
E-mail: dmccardle@upei.ca
Web Site: http://www.upei.ca/
President/CEO: H. Wade MacLauchlan
Admissions: Darcy McCardle
Financial Aid: Belinda Rogers
Type: Comprehensive **Sex:** Coed **% Accepted:** 61 **Admission Plans:** Early Admission **Application Deadline:** August 1 **Application Fee:** $50.00 **H.S. Requirements:** High school diploma required; GED not accepted. For students 22 or over and out of high school at least 2 years can be accepted as mature students: High school diploma or equivalent not required **Scholarships:** Available **Calendar System:** Miscellaneous, Summer Session Available **Enrollment:** FT 2,904, PT 561 **Faculty:** FT 240, PT 190 **Student-Faculty Ratio:** 12:1 **Exams:** SAT I or ACT. **% Residing in College-Owned, -Operated, or -Affiliated Housing:** 14 **Library Holdings:** 402,808 **Credit Hours For Degree:** 120 semester hours, Bachelors **Professional Accreditation:** AVMA **Intercollegiate Athletics:** Basketball M & W; Field Hockey W; Golf M; Ice Hockey M & W; Rugby M & W; Soccer M & W; Volleyball W

MEMORIAL UNIVERSITY OF NEWFOUNDLAND
Elizabeth Ave.
St. John's, NL, Canada A1C 5S7
Tel: (709)737-8000
Admissions: (709)737-3705
Fax: (709)737-4569
E-mail: sturecru@morgan.ucs.mun.ca
Web Site: http://www.mun.ca/
President/CEO: Dr. C. Loomis
Admissions: Marian Abbott
Type: University **Sex:** Coed **Affiliation:** Marine Institute, Sir Wilfred Grenfell College, WRSON, CNS **Admission Plans:** Early Admission; Early Decision Plan; Deferred Admission **Application Deadline:** Rolling **Application Fee:** $40.00 **H.S. Requirements:** High school diploma required; GED not accepted. For mature students (over 21 years), senior citizens: High school diploma or equivalent not required **Costs Per Year:** Application fee: $40. Province resident tuition: $2550 full-time. Mandatory fees: $494 full-time. Full-time tuition and fees vary according to course load and program. College room and board: $5968. College room only: $2174. Room and board charges vary according to board plan, housing facility, and location. International student tuition: $8800 full-time. **Calendar System:** Trimester, Summer Session Available **Enrollment:** FT 12,382, PT 2,323, Grad FT 1,567, Grad PT 1,106 **Faculty:** FT 1,233, PT 36 **Student-Faculty Ratio:** 12:1 **% Residing in College-Owned, -Operated, or -Affiliated Housing:** 10 **Library Holdings:** 1,878,592 **Credit Hours For Degree:** 120 credit hours, Bachelors **Professional Accreditation:** AACSB, LCMEAMA **Intercollegiate Athletics:** Basketball M & W; Cross-Country Running M & W; Soccer M & W; Swimming and Diving M & W; Volleyball M & W; Wrestling M & W

BROCK UNIVERSITY
500 Glenridge Ave.
St. Catharines, ON, Canada L2S 3A1
Tel: (905)688-5550
Fax: (905)988-5488
E-mail: admissns@brocku.ca
Web Site: http://www.brocku.ca/
President/CEO: Dr. Jack N. Lightstone
Admissions: Lynn Thompson-Dovi
Financial Aid: Rico Natale
Type: University **Sex:** Coed **Application Deadline:** April 1 **Application Fee:** $0.00 **H.S. Requirements:** High school diploma required; GED not accepted **Scholarships:** Available **Calendar System:** Miscellaneous, Summer Session Available **Enrollment:** FT 15,949, Grad FT 1,544 **Faculty:** FT 577, PT 0 **Student-Faculty Ratio:** 30:1 **Exams:** SAT I or ACT. **% Residing in College-Owned, -Operated, or -Affiliated Housing:** 14 **Library Holdings:** 769,873 **Credit Hours For Degree:** 15 courses, Bachelors **Professional Accreditation:** AACSB **Intercollegiate Athletics:** Baseball M; Basketball M & W; Cheerleading M & W; Crew M & W; Cross-Country Running M & W; Fencing M & W; Field Hockey W; Ice Hockey M & W; Lacrosse M; Rugby M & W; Soccer M & W; Swimming and Diving M & W; Volleyball W; Wrestling M & W

CARLETON UNIVERSITY
1125 Colonel By Dr.
Ottawa, ON, Canada K1S 5B6
Tel: (613)520-7400
Admissions: (613)520-3663
Fax: (613)520-7455
E-mail: liaison@admissions.carleton.ca
Web Site: http://www.carleton.ca/
Admissions: Jean Mullan
Type: University **Sex:** Coed **% Accepted:** 73 **Admission Plans:** Deferred Admission **Application Deadline:** June 1 **Application Fee:** $85.00 **H.S. Requirements:** High school diploma required; GED not accepted **Calendar System:** Miscellaneous, Summer Session Available **Enrollment:** FT 16,509, PT 4,237 **Faculty:** FT 783, PT 8 **Student-Faculty Ratio:** 26:1 **Exams:** SAT I and SAT II or ACT, SAT I. **% Residing in College-Owned, -Operated, or -Affiliated Housing:** 15 **Library Holdings:** 1,941,340 **Credit Hours For Degree:** 15 full-year courses, Bachelors **Intercollegiate Athletics:** Basketball M & W; Crew M & W; Fencing M & W; Field Hockey W; Football M; Golf M; Ice Hockey M & W; Lacrosse M; Rugby M & W; Skiing (Cross-Country) M & W; Soccer M & W; Swimming and Diving M & W; Volleyball W; Water Polo M & W

CENTENNIAL COLLEGE
PO Box 631, Station 'A'
Scarborough, ON, Canada M1K 5E9
Tel: (416)698-4192; Free: 800-268-4419
Admissions: (416)289-5325
Fax: (416)694-9263
E-mail: success@centennialcollege.ca
Web Site: http://www.centennialcollege.ca/
President/CEO: Ann Buller
Type: Four-Year College **Sex:** Coed **Application Fee:** $95.00

COLLEGE DOMINICAIN DE PHILOSOPHIE ET DE THEOLOGIE
96, Ave. Empress
Ottawa, ON, Canada K1R 7G3
Tel: (613)233-5696
E-mail: registraire@collegedominicain.ca
Web Site: http://www.collegedominicain.ca/
President/CEO: Gabor Csepregi
Admissions: Fr. Herve Tremblay, OP
Financial Aid: Ousmane Diallo
Type: University **Sex:** Coed **Affiliation:** Roman Catholic; Institut de Pastorale **% Accepted:** 100 **Admission Plans:** Deferred Admission **Application Deadline:** June 1 **Application Fee:** $35.00 **H.S. Requirements:** High school diploma required; GED accepted **Costs Per Year:** Application fee: $35 Canadian dollars. Tuition, fee, and room and board charges are reported in Canadian dollars. Comprehensive fee: $10,140 includes full-time tuition ($3420), mandatory fees ($120), and college room and board ($6600). Full-time tuition and fees vary according to degree level. Part-time tuition: $130 per credit. Part-time mandatory fees: $85 per year. Part-time tuition and fees vary according to course load and degree level. International student tuition: $7000 full-time. **Scholarships:** Available **Calendar System:** Semester, Summer Session Available **Enrollment:** FT 57, PT 93, Grad FT 61, Grad PT 5 **Faculty:** FT 22, PT 28 **Student-Faculty Ratio:** 3:1 **% Receiving Financial Aid:** 16 **% Residing in College-Owned, -Operated, or -Affiliated Housing:** 16 **Final Year or Final Semester Residency Requirement:** No **Library Holdings:** 125,000 **Credit Hours For Degree:** 90 credits, Bachelors

EMMANUEL BIBLE COLLEGE
100 Fergus Ave.
Kitchener, ON, Canada N2A 2H2
Tel: (519)894-8900
Fax: (519)894-9430
E-mail: smahon@ebcollege.on.ca
Web Site: http://www.ebcollege.on.ca/
Admissions: Sherry Mahon
Financial Aid: Robert Tees
Type: Four-Year College **Sex:** Coed **Affiliation:** Missionary Church **Admission Plans:** Deferred Admission **Application Deadline:** Rolling **Application Fee:** $100.00 **H.S. Requirements:** High school diploma required; GED accepted **Costs Per Year:** Application fee: $100. Comprehensive fee: $13,705 includes full-time tuition ($8736), mandatory fees ($35), and college room and board ($4934). College room only: $2734. Part-time tuition: $273 per credit. Part-time mandatory fees: $35 per degree program. **Scholarships:** Available **Calendar System:** Semester, Summer Session Available **Library Holdings:** 19,250 **Credit Hours For Degree:** 96 semester hours, Bachelors **Professional Accreditation:** ABHE

HERITAGE BAPTIST COLLEGE AND HERITAGE THEOLOGICAL SEMINARY
175 Holiday Inn Dr.
Cambridge, ON, Canada N3C 3T2
Tel: (519)651-2869
E-mail: mwalther@heritagecollege.net
Web Site: http://www.heritage-theo.edu/
President/CEO: Rev. Marvin R. Brubacher

Admissions: Mark Walther
Type: Comprehensive **Sex:** Coed **Affiliation:** Baptist **% Accepted:** 100 **Admission Plans:** Open Admission; Deferred Admission **Application Deadline:** September 1 **Application Fee:** $50.00 **H.S. Requirements:** High school diploma required; GED accepted **Costs Per Year:** Application fee: $50. One-time mandatory fee: $50. Comprehensive fee: $12,740 includes full-time tuition ($8320), mandatory fees ($100), and college room and board ($4320). College room only: $3420. **Scholarships:** Available **Calendar System:** Miscellaneous, Summer Session Available **Enrollment:** FT 154, PT 37, Grad FT 18, Grad PT 65 **Faculty:** FT 8, PT 28 **Student-Faculty Ratio:** 11:1 **Final Year or Final Semester Residency Requirement:** No **Library Holdings:** 47,243 **Credit Hours For Degree:** 65 credit hours, Associates; 97 credit hours, Bachelors **Professional Accreditation:** ABHE, ATS **Intercollegiate Athletics:** Basketball M & W; Volleyball M & W

LAKEHEAD UNIVERSITY
955 Oliver Rd.
Thunder Bay, ON, Canada P7B 5E1
Tel: (807)343-8110
Admissions: (807)343-8868
Fax: (807)343-8156
E-mail: admissions@lakeheadu.ca
Web Site: http://www.lakeheadu.ca/
President/CEO: Dr. Frederick F. Gilbert
Admissions: Jordana Hughes
Financial Aid: Phyllis Bosnick
Type: Comprehensive **Sex:** Coed **% Accepted:** 76 **Admission Plans:** Early Admission; Deferred Admission **Application Deadline:** September 21 **Application Fee:** $110.00 **H.S. Requirements:** High school diploma required; GED not accepted **Calendar System:** Miscellaneous, Summer Session Available **Enrollment:** FT 5,843, PT 1,296 **Faculty:** FT 304 **Exams:** SAT I or ACT. **% Residing in College-Owned, -Operated, or -Affiliated Housing:** 15 **Library Holdings:** 613,047 **Credit Hours For Degree:** 15 courses, Bachelors **Professional Accreditation:** LCMEAMA **Intercollegiate Athletics:** Basketball M & W; Cross-Country Running M & W; Golf M; Ice Hockey M; Skiing (Cross-Country) M & W; Soccer M & W; Track and Field M & W; Volleyball W; Wrestling M & W

LAURENTIAN UNIVERSITY
935 Ramsey Lake Rd.
Sudbury, ON, Canada P3E 2C6
Tel: (705)675-1151
Fax: (705)675-4840
E-mail: admissions@laurentian.ca
Web Site: http://www.laurentian.ca/
President/CEO: Dominic Giroux
Financial Aid: Diane Bleauparlant
Type: Comprehensive **Sex:** Coed **Admission Plans:** Early Admission **Application Deadline:** April 1 **Application Fee:** $40.00 **H.S. Requirements:** High school diploma required; GED not accepted **Costs Per Year:** Application fee: $40 Canadian dollars. Tuition, fee, and room only charges are reported in Canadian dollars. Province resident tuition: $4894 full-time, $978.80 per course part-time. Mandatory fees: $541 full-time, $36.38 per term part-time. Full-time tuition and fees vary according to program. Part-time tuition and fees vary according to course load. College room only: $3550. Room charges vary according to housing facility. International student tuition: $11,913 full-time. **Scholarships:** Available **Calendar System:** Miscellaneous, Summer Session Available **Credit Hours For Degree:** 90 credits, Bachelors **Professional Accreditation:** LCMEAMA **Intercollegiate Athletics:** Basketball M & W; Cross-Country Running W; Skiing (Downhill) M; Soccer M; Swimming and Diving M & W; Track and Field W; Volleyball M

MASTER'S COLLEGE AND SEMINARY
282 Cummer Ave.
Toronto, ON, Canada M2M 2E7
Tel: (416)482-2224; Free: 800-295-6368
Fax: (416)482-7004
E-mail: flora.anthony@mcs.edu
Web Site: http://www.mcs.edu/
President/CEO: Dr. William Morrow
Admissions: Flora Anthony
Financial Aid: Heather Boudreau
Type: Four-Year College **Sex:** Coed **Affiliation:** Pentecostal **% Accepted:** 95 **Admission Plans:** Deferred Admission **Application Deadline:** August 31 **Application Fee:** $75.00 **H.S. Requirements:** High school diploma required; GED accepted **Costs Per Year:** Application fee: $75. Tuition: $5600 full-time, $175 per credit hour part-time. Mandatory fees: $576 full-time. **Scholarships:** Available **Calendar System:** Semester, Summer Session Available **Faculty:** FT 4, PT 24 **Student-Faculty Ratio:** 11:1 **Final Year or Final Semester Residency Requirement:** No **Library Holdings:** 42,733 **Credit Hours For Degree:** 130 credit hours, Bachelors **Professional Accreditation:** ABHE **Intercollegiate Athletics:** Volleyball W

MCMASTER UNIVERSITY
1280 Main St. West
Hamilton, ON, Canada L8S 4M2
Tel: (905)525-9140
Admissions: (905)525-4600
Fax: (905)527-1105
E-mail: admitmac@mcmaster.ca
Web Site: http://www.mcmaster.ca/
President/CEO: Dr. Peter George
Admissions: Olivia Demerling
Financial Aid: Tracie Long
Type: University **Sex:** Coed **% Accepted:** 68 **Admission Plans:** Deferred Admission **Application Deadline:** June 1 **Application Fee:** $95.00 **H.S. Requirements:** High school diploma required; GED accepted **Calendar System:** Miscellaneous, Summer Session Available **Faculty:** FT 894 **Student-Faculty Ratio:** 25:1 **Exams:** SAT I or ACT. **% Residing in College-Owned, -Operated, or -Affiliated Housing:** 20 **Library Holdings:** 1,735,159 **Credit Hours For Degree:** 90 units, Bachelors **Professional Accreditation:** AACSB, ATS, LCMEAMA, NCATE **Intercollegiate Athletics:** Badminton M & W; Baseball M; Basketball M & W; Cross-Country Running M & W; Fencing M & W; Football M; Golf M & W; Lacrosse M & W; Rugby M & W; Soccer M & W; Squash M & W; Swimming and Diving M & W; Tennis M & W; Track and Field M & W; Volleyball M & W; Water Polo M & W; Wrestling M & W

NER ISRAEL YESHIVA COLLEGE OF TORONTO
8950 Bathurst St.
Thornhill, ON, Canada L4J 8A7
Tel: (905)731-1224
Admissions: Rabbi Y. Kravetz
Type: Comprehensive **Sex:** Men **Affiliation:** Jewish **Application Deadline:** August 15 **Calendar System:** Miscellaneous, Summer Session Available **Library Holdings:** 3,000 **Professional Accreditation:** AARTS

NIPISSING UNIVERSITY
100 College Dr., Box 5002
North Bay, ON, Canada P1B 8L7
Tel: (705)474-3461
Fax: (705)474-1947
E-mail: liaison@nipissingu.ca
Web Site: http://www.nipissingu.ca/
Admissions: Lori-Ann Beckford
Type: Comprehensive **Sex:** Coed **Affiliation:** Ontario Ministry of Training, Colleges and Universities **Admission Plans:** Early Admission; Early Decision Plan **H.S. Requirements:** High school diploma required; GED not accepted **Calendar System:** Semester, Summer Session Available **Exams:** SAT I and SAT II or ACT. **Library Holdings:** 715,494 **Credit Hours For Degree:** 90 credits, Bachelors **Intercollegiate Athletics:** Cross-Country Running M & W; Ice Hockey M; Skiing (Cross-Country) M & W; Soccer M & W; Volleyball M & W

QUEEN'S UNIVERSITY AT KINGSTON
Kingston, ON, Canada K7L 3N6
Tel: (613)533-2000
Admissions: (613)533-2218
Fax: (613)533-6300
E-mail: admission@queensu.ca
Web Site: http://www.queensu.ca/
President/CEO: Dr. Daniel Woolfe
Admissions: Wendy Smith
Financial Aid: Teresa Alm
Type: University **Sex:** Coed **Scores:** 97% SAT V 400+; 99.2% SAT M 400+ **Admission Plans:** Deferred Admission **Application Deadline:** February 1 **Application Fee:** $180.00 **H.S. Requirements:** High school diploma

required; GED not accepted **Costs Per Year:** Application fee: $180 Canadian dollars. Tuition, fee, and room and board charges are reported in Canadian dollars. Province resident tuition: $5005 full-time, $1001 per course part-time. Mandatory fees: $903 full-time, $20 per credit part-time. Full-time tuition and fees vary according to course load, degree level, and program. Part-time tuition and fees vary according to course load, degree level, and program. College room and board: $10,259. College room only: $5737. Room and board charges vary according to board plan. International student tuition: $17,030 full-time. **Scholarships:** Available **Calendar System:** Miscellaneous, Summer Session Available **Enrollment:** FT 13,871, PT 3,507, Grad FT 4,862, Grad PT 361 **Faculty:** FT 1,087, PT 438 **Student-Faculty Ratio:** 15:1 **Exams:** SAT I or ACT. ACT essay not being used. SAT essay not being used. **% Residing in College-Owned, -Operated, or -Affiliated Housing:** 32 **Final Year or Final Semester Residency Requirement:** No **Library Holdings:** 3,509,317 **Credit Hours For Degree:** 15 credits, Bachelors **Professional Accreditation:** AACSB, APA, ATS, LCMEAMA **Intercollegiate Athletics:** Baseball M; Basketball M & W; Cheerleading M & W; Crew M & W; Cross-Country Running M & W; Fencing M & W; Field Hockey W; Football M; Golf M; Gymnastics M & W; Ice Hockey M & W; Lacrosse M & W; Rugby M & W; Sailing M & W; Skiing (Cross-Country) M & W; Skiing (Downhill) M & W; Soccer M & W; Squash M & W; Swimming and Diving M & W; Track and Field M & W; Ultimate Frisbee M; Volleyball M & W; Water Polo M & W; Wrestling M & W

REDEEMER UNIVERSITY COLLEGE
777 Garner Rd. East
Ancaster, ON, Canada L9K 1J4
Tel: (905)648-2131
Admissions: (905)648-2139
Fax: (905)648-2134
E-mail: recruitment@redeemer.ca
Web Site: http://www.redeemer.ca/
President/CEO: Dr. Justin Cooper
Financial Aid: Jeannette Lodewyks
Type: Four-Year College **Sex:** Coed **Affiliation:** interdenominational **Scores:** 36% ACT 18-23; 64% ACT 24-29 **% Accepted:** 81 **Admission Plans:** Preferred Admission; Deferred Admission **Application Deadline:** May 31 **Application Fee:** $40.00 **H.S. Requirements:** High school diploma required; GED accepted. For adult students: High school diploma or equivalent not required **Costs Per Year:** Application fee: $40 Canadian dollars. Tuition, fee, and room and board charges are reported in Canadian dollars. Comprehensive fee: $19,816 includes full-time tuition ($13,212), mandatory fees ($478), and college room and board ($6126). Room and board charges vary according to board plan and housing facility. Part-time tuition: $1326 per course. Part-time mandatory fees: $34.50 per course. **Scholarships:** Available **Calendar System:** Semester, Summer Session Available **Enrollment:** FT 811, PT 107 **Faculty:** FT 53, PT 36 **Student-Faculty Ratio:** 13:1 **Exams:** SAT I or ACT. **% Residing in College-Owned, -Operated, or -Affiliated Housing:** 48 **Final Year or Final Semester Residency Requirement:** Yes **Library Holdings:** 117,404 **Credit Hours For Degree:** 40 courses, Bachelors **Intercollegiate Athletics:** Basketball M & W; Cross-Country Running M & W; Soccer M & W; Ultimate Frisbee M & W; Volleyball M & W

ROYAL MILITARY COLLEGE OF CANADA
PO Box 17000, Station Forces
Kingston, ON, Canada K7K 7B4
Tel: (613)541-6000
Fax: (613)542-3565
E-mail: liaison@rmc.ca
Web Site: http://www.rmc.ca/
President/CEO: Dr. Joel Sokolsky
Admissions: Lt. Col. Rod McDonald
Financial Aid: Sophie Pepin
Type: Comprehensive **Sex:** Coed **Affiliation:** Council of Ontario Universities **% Accepted:** 40 **Admission Plans:** Open Admission; Early Decision Plan **Application Deadline:** January 15 **Application Fee:** $0.00 **H.S. Requirements:** High school diploma required; GED accepted **Scholarships:** Available **Calendar System:** Miscellaneous, Summer Session Not available **% Residing in College-Owned, -Operated, or -Affiliated Housing:** 90 **Library Holdings:** 300,000 **Credit Hours For Degree:** 40 credits, Bachelors **Intercollegiate Athletics:** Basketball M & W; Cross-Country Running M & W; Fencing M & W; Ice Hockey M; Rock Climbing M; Rugby M; Soccer M & W; Volleyball M & W

RYERSON UNIVERSITY
350 Victoria St.
Toronto, ON, Canada M5B 2K3
Tel: (416)979-5000
Admissions: (416)979-5080
E-mail: inquire@ryerson.ca
Web Site: http://www.ryerson.ca/
Admissions: Michelle Beaton
Financial Aid: Carole Scrase
Type: Comprehensive **Sex:** Coed **Application Deadline:** February 1 **Application Fee:** $65.00 **H.S. Requirements:** High school diploma required; GED not accepted **Costs Per Year:** Application fee: $65 Canadian dollars. Tuition and fee charges are reported in Canadian dollars. Province resident tuition: $4983 full-time. Full-time tuition varies according to course load, degree level, and program. International student tuition: $15,390 full-time. **Scholarships:** Available **Calendar System:** Miscellaneous, Summer Session Available **Faculty:** FT 744, PT 211 **% Residing in College-Owned, -Operated, or -Affiliated Housing:** 3 **Library Holdings:** 487,361 **Professional Accreditation:** FIDER **Intercollegiate Athletics:** Badminton M & W; Basketball M & W; Crew M & W; Fencing M & W; Ice Hockey M & W; Soccer M & W; Volleyball M & W

SAINT PAUL UNIVERSITY
223 Main St.
Ottawa, ON, Canada K1S 1C4
Tel: (613)236-1393; Free: 800-637-6859
Fax: (613)782-3033
E-mail: admission@ustpaul.ca
Web Site: http://www.ustpaul.ca/
Type: University **Sex:** Coed **Affiliation:** University of Ottawa **Admission Plans:** Deferred Admission **Application Fee:** $35.00 **H.S. Requirements:** High school diploma required; GED not accepted **Costs Per Year:** Application fee: $35. Province resident tuition: $3930 full-time, $535 per unit part-time. International student tuition: $8420 full-time. **Calendar System:** Miscellaneous, Summer Session Available **Student-Faculty Ratio:** 12:1 **Exams:** SAT I. **Credit Hours For Degree:** 90 credits, Bachelors

TRENT UNIVERSITY
1600 West Bank Dr.
Peterborough, ON, Canada K9J 7B8
Tel: (705)748-1011
Admissions: (705)748-1215
Fax: (705)748-1629
E-mail: leaders@trentu.ca
Web Site: http://www.trentu.ca/
President/CEO: Dr. Steven Franklin
Admissions: Lois Fleming
Financial Aid: Alice Sutton
Type: University **Sex:** Coed **% Accepted:** 20 **Admission Plans:** Deferred Admission **Application Deadline:** June 1 **Application Fee:** $115.00 **H.S. Requirements:** High school diploma required; GED accepted **Costs Per Year:** Application fee: $115 Canadian dollars. Tuition, fee, and room and board charges are reported in Canadian dollars. Province resident tuition: $4989 full-time, $998 per course part-time. Mandatory fees: $2348 full-time, $122 per year part-time. Full-time tuition and fees vary according to location and student level. Part-time tuition and fees vary according to course load and student level. College room and board: $9854. Room and board charges vary according to board plan, housing facility, and location. International student tuition: $13,684 full-time. **Calendar System:** Miscellaneous, Summer Session Available **Enrollment:** FT 6,104, PT 1,308, Grad FT 345, Grad PT 60 **Faculty:** FT 256, PT 187 **Student-Faculty Ratio:** 20:1 **% Residing in College-Owned, -Operated, or -Affiliated Housing:** 17 **Final Year or Final Semester Residency Requirement:** No **Library Holdings:** 740,653 **Credit Hours For Degree:** 15 courses, Bachelors **Intercollegiate Athletics:** Basketball M & W; Crew M & W; Cross-Country Running M & W; Fencing M & W; Field Hockey W; Golf M & W; Rugby M & W; Skiing (Cross-Country) M & W; Soccer M & W; Squash M & W; Swimming and Diving M & W; Volleyball M & W

TYNDALE UNIVERSITY COLLEGE & SEMINARY
25 Ballyconnor Ct.
Toronto, ON, Canada M2M 4B3
Tel: (416)226-6380
Admissions: (416)218-6757

Fax: (416)226-4210
E-mail: admissions@tydale.ca
Web Site: http://www.tyndale.ca/
President/CEO: Dr. Brian C. Stiller
Admissions: Tricia McKenley
Financial Aid: Janis Ruff
Type: Comprehensive **Sex:** Coed **Affiliation:** interdenominational **% Accepted:** 53 **Admission Plans:** Deferred Admission **Application Deadline:** August 15 **Application Fee:** $50.00 **H.S. Requirements:** High school diploma required; GED accepted. For mature student category: High school diploma or equivalent not required **Scholarships:** Available **Calendar System:** Semester, Summer Session Available **Enrollment:** FT 348, PT 131 **Faculty:** FT 54 **Student-Faculty Ratio:** 23:1 **% Residing in College-Owned, -Operated, or -Affiliated Housing:** 30 **Library Holdings:** 65,013 **Credit Hours For Degree:** 90 credit hours, Bachelors **Professional Accreditation:** ABHE, ATS **Intercollegiate Athletics:** Basketball M & W; Ice Hockey M; Ultimate Frisbee M & W; Volleyball M & W

UNIVERSITY OF GUELPH
Guelph, ON, Canada N1G 2W1
Tel: (519)824-4120
E-mail: usainfo@registrar.uoguelph.ca
Web Site: http://www.uoguelph.ca/
President/CEO: Dr. Alastair Summerlee
Admissions: Mary Haggarty
Type: University **Sex:** Coed **% Accepted:** 73 **Admission Plans:** Early Admission **Application Deadline:** March 1 **Application Fee:** $105.00 **H.S. Requirements:** High school diploma or equivalent not required **Costs Per Year:** Application fee: $105. **Scholarships:** Available **Calendar System:** Trimester, Summer Session Available **Faculty:** FT 869 **Student-Faculty Ratio:** 22:1 **Exams:** SAT I or ACT. **% Residing in College-Owned, -Operated, or -Affiliated Housing:** 90 **Credit Hours For Degree:** 30 courses, Bachelors **Professional Accreditation:** AAMFT, ASLA, AVMA **Intercollegiate Athletics:** Baseball M; Basketball M & W; Crew M & W; Cross-Country Running M & W; Field Hockey W; Football M; Golf M & W; Ice Hockey M & W; Lacrosse M & W; Rugby M & W; Skiing (Cross-Country) M & W; Soccer M & W; Swimming and Diving M & W; Track and Field M & W; Volleyball M & W; Wrestling M & W

UNIVERSITY OF OTTAWA
550 Cumberland St.
Ottawa, ON, Canada K1N 6N5
Tel: (613)562-5700
Admissions: (613)562-5800
E-mail: cpharand@uottawa.ca
Web Site: http://www.uottawa.ca/
President/CEO: Allan Rock
Admissions: Caroline Pharand
Financial Aid: Diane Gameiro-Sutton
Type: University **Sex:** Coed **Affiliation:** Saint-Paul University (Ottawa, Ontario) **% Accepted:** 61 **Admission Plans:** Early Admission; Deferred Admission **Application Deadline:** June 1 **Application Fee:** $165.00 **H.S. Requirements:** High school diploma required; GED not accepted. For adult applicants to arts and social science programs: High school diploma or equivalent not required **Costs Per Year:** Application fee: $165 Canadian dollars. Tuition, fee, and room and board charges are reported in Canadian dollars. Province resident tuition: $4964 full-time. Canadian resident tuition: $196.77 per credit part-time. Mandatory fees: $619 full-time, $108 per term part-time. Full-time tuition and fees vary according to program and student level. Part-time tuition and fees vary according to program and student level. College room and board: $6212. College room only: $4212. Room and board charges vary according to board plan and housing facility. International student tuition: $15,134 full-time. **Scholarships:** Available **Calendar System:** Semester, Summer Session Available **Enrollment:** FT 26,816, PT 5,814, Grad FT 4,010, Grad PT 1,282 **Faculty:** FT 1,257, PT 831 **Student-Faculty Ratio:** 23:1 **Exams:** Other. **% Residing in College-Owned, -Operated, or -Affiliated Housing:** 8 **Library Holdings:** 3,277,219 **Credit Hours For Degree:** 90 credits, Bachelors **Professional Accreditation:** AACSB, APA, ACEHSA, LCMEAMA, NRPA **Intercollegiate Athletics:** Badminton M & W; Baseball M & W; Basketball M & W; Cheerleading M & W; Crew M & W; Cross-Country Running M & W; Equestrian Sports M & W; Fencing M & W; Football M; Golf M & W; Ice Hockey M & W; Rugby W; Soccer M & W; Swimming and Diving M & W; Track and Field M & W; Ultimate Frisbee M & W; Volleyball M & W; Water Polo M & W

UNIVERSITY OF TORONTO
Toronto, ON, Canada M5S 1A1
Tel: (416)978-2011
Admissions: (416)978-2190
E-mail: admissions.help@utoronto.ca
Web Site: http://www.utoronto.ca/uoft.html
President/CEO: David Naylor
Type: University **Sex:** Coed **% Accepted:** 71 **Admission Plans:** Preferred Admission; Deferred Admission **Application Deadline:** March 1 **Application Fee:** $115.00 **H.S. Requirements:** High school diploma or equivalent not required **Costs Per Year:** Application fee: $115 Canadian dollars. Tuition, fee, and room and board charges are reported in Canadian dollars. Province resident tuition: $4991 full-time. Canadian resident tuition: $4991 full-time. Mandatory fees: $1000 full-time. Full-time tuition and fees vary according to course level, course load, and program. College room and board: $11,500. College room only: $6500. Room and board charges vary according to board plan, housing facility, and location. International student tuition: $21,344 full-time. **Calendar System:** Miscellaneous, Summer Session Available **Enrollment:** FT 55,939, PT 7,110, Grad FT 12,849, Grad PT 2,001 **Faculty:** FT 2,757, PT 323 **Student-Faculty Ratio:** 24:1 **Exams:** SAT I and SAT II or ACT. **% Residing in College-Owned, -Operated, or -Affiliated Housing:** 15 **Final Year or Final Semester Residency Requirement:** No **Library Holdings:** 13,439,497 **Credit Hours For Degree:** 20 courses, Bachelors **Professional Accreditation:** AACSB, ARCMI, ADA, ALA, APTA, APA, ASLA, ATS, ACEHSA, LCMEAMA **Intercollegiate Athletics:** Archery M & W; Badminton M & W; Basketball M & W; Crew M; Cross-Country Running M & W; Fencing M & W; Field Hockey W; Football M; Golf M; Gymnastics M & W; Ice Hockey M & W; Rugby M; Skiing (Cross-Country) M & W; Skiing (Downhill) M & W; Soccer M & W; Squash M & W; Swimming and Diving M & W; Tennis M & W; Track and Field M & W; Volleyball M & W; Wrestling M

UNIVERSITY OF WATERLOO
200 University Ave. West
Waterloo, ON, Canada N2L 3G1
Tel: (519)888-4567
Fax: (519)746-2882
E-mail: registrar@uwaterloo.ca
Web Site: http://www.uwaterloo.ca/
President/CEO: Prof. David Johnston
Admissions: Nancy Weiner
Financial Aid: Maureen Jones
Type: University **Sex:** Coed **% Accepted:** 58 **Admission Plans:** Early Admission; Deferred Admission **Application Deadline:** March 31 **Application Fee:** $105.00 **H.S. Requirements:** High school diploma required; GED accepted **Costs Per Year:** Application fee: $105. **Scholarships:** Available **Calendar System:** Trimester, Summer Session Available **Enrollment:** FT 22,330, PT 946, Grad FT 3,246, Grad PT 684 **Faculty:** FT 987, PT 784 **Exams:** SAT I or ACT, SAT II. **Library Holdings:** 7,500,000 **Credit Hours For Degree:** 30 term courses, Bachelors **Professional Accreditation:** AOA, APA **Intercollegiate Athletics:** Badminton M & W; Baseball M; Basketball M & W; Cheerleading M & W; Cross-Country Running M & W; Field Hockey W; Football M; Golf M & W; Ice Hockey M & W; Rugby M & W; Skiing (Cross-Country) M & W; Soccer M & W; Squash M; Swimming and Diving M & W; Tennis M & W; Track and Field M & W; Volleyball M & W

THE UNIVERSITY OF WESTERN ONTARIO
London, ON, Canada N6A 5B8
Tel: (519)661-2111
Admissions: (519)661-2100
E-mail: reg-admissions@uwo.ca
Web Site: http://www.uwo.ca/
President/CEO: Dr. Amit Chakma
Financial Aid: Dorothy Cochrane
Type: University **Sex:** Coed **Affiliation:** Brescia University College, Huron University College, King's University College **% Accepted:** 54 **Admission Plans:** Deferred Admission **Application Deadline:** June 1 **Application Fee:** $120.00 **H.S. Requirements:** High school diploma required; GED not accepted **Costs Per Year:** Application fee: $120 Canadian dollars. Tuition, fee, and room and board charges are reported in Canadian dollars. Province resident tuition: $4937 full-time, $987 per course part-time. Canadian resident tuition: $2930 per course part-time. Mandatory fees: $937 full-time, $131 per course part-time. Full-time tuition and fees vary according to program. Part-time tuition and fees vary according to course load, location,

and program. College room and board: $8440. College room only: $5185. Room and board charges vary according to board plan, housing facility, and location. International student tuition: $14,650 full-time. full academic year considered September 1 to April 30th. Full-time students usually complete 5.0 credits per academic year, which may constitute 5 - 10 courses. **Scholarships:** Available **Calendar System:** Miscellaneous, Summer Session Available **Enrollment:** FT 21,344, PT 2,698, Grad FT 4,434, Grad PT 509 **Faculty:** FT 1,374 **Student-Faculty Ratio:** 20:1 **Exams:** SAT I or ACT. **% Residing in College-Owned, -Operated, or -Affiliated Housing:** 19 **Library Holdings:** 3,644,679 **Credit Hours For Degree:** 15 courses, Bachelors **Professional Accreditation:** ADA, ALA, APTA, APA, ATS, LCMEAMA **Intercollegiate Athletics:** Badminton M & W; Baseball M; Basketball M & W; Cheerleading M & W; Crew M & W; Cross-Country Running M & W; Equestrian Sports M & W; Fencing M & W; Field Hockey W; Football M; Golf M & W; Ice Hockey M & W; Lacrosse M & W; Rugby M & W; Soccer M & W; Softball W; Squash M & W; Swimming and Diving M & W; Tennis M & W; Track and Field M & W; Volleyball M & W; Water Polo M; Wrestling M & W

UNIVERSITY OF WINDSOR

401 Sunset Ave.
Windsor, ON, Canada N9B 3P4
Tel: (519)253-3000
Fax: (519)973-7050
E-mail: registr@uwindsor.ca
Web Site: http://www.uwindsor.ca/
President/CEO: Dr. Alan Wildeman
Admissions: Charlene Yates
Financial Aid: Gillian Baxter

Type: University **Sex:** Coed **% Accepted:** 78 **Admission Plans:** Early Admission **Application Deadline:** Rolling **Application Fee:** $60.00 **H.S. Requirements:** High school diploma required; GED accepted **Costs Per Year:** Application fee: $60 Canadian dollars. Tuition, fee, and room and board charges are reported in Canadian dollars. Province resident tuition: $5662 full-time, $732 per course part-time. Canadian resident tuition: $1945 per course part-time. Full-time tuition varies according to course load, degree level, location, and program. Part-time tuition varies according to course load, degree level, location, and program. College room and board: $8185. College room only: $4834. Room and board charges vary according to board plan and housing facility. International student tuition: $15,199 full-time. Required fees vary by program. **Scholarships:** Available **Calendar System:** Semester, Summer Session Available **Enrollment:** FT 10,560, PT 3,060 **Faculty:** FT 524, PT 347 **Student-Faculty Ratio:** 21:1 **Exams:** SAT I or ACT, SAT I and SAT II or ACT, SAT II. **% Residing in College-Owned, -Operated, or -Affiliated Housing:** 13 **Library Holdings:** 2,776,724 **Credit Hours For Degree:** 30 courses, Bachelors **Professional Accreditation:** APA **Intercollegiate Athletics:** Basketball M & W; Cheerleading M & W; Cross-Country Running M & W; Football M; Golf M & W; Ice Hockey M & W; Rugby M & W; Soccer M & W; Softball W; Track and Field M & W; Volleyball M & W

WILFRID LAURIER UNIVERSITY

75 University Ave. West
Waterloo, ON, Canada N2L 3C5
Tel: (519)884-1970
Admissions: (519)884-0710
Fax: (519)884-8826
E-mail: admissions@wlu.ca
Web Site: http://www.wlu.ca/
President/CEO: Dr. Max Blouw
Admissions: Lois Wood
Financial Aid: Ruth MacNeil

Type: Comprehensive **Sex:** Coed **% Accepted:** 68 **Admission Plans:** Early Admission; Early Decision Plan; Deferred Admission **Application Deadline:** May 1 **Application Fee:** $115.00 **H.S. Requirements:** High school diploma required; GED not accepted **Costs Per Year:** Application fee: $115 Canadian dollars. Tuition, fee, and room and board charges are reported in Canadian dollars. Province resident tuition: $4989 full-time, $1,119 per credit part-time. Mandatory fees: $964 full-time, $127.64 per credit part-time, $203 per year part-time. Full-time tuition and fees vary according to course load, degree level, program, and student level. Part-time tuition and fees vary according to course load, degree level, program, and student level. College room and board: $7929. College room only: $4341. Room and board charges vary according to board plan, housing facility, and location. International student tuition: $17,971 full-time. **Scholarships:** Available **Calendar System:** Semester, Summer Session Available **Enrollment:** FT 13,194, PT 2,005, Grad FT 832, Grad PT 623 **Faculty:** FT 497 **Student-Faculty Ratio:** 25:1 **Exams:** SAT I or ACT. **% Residing in College-Owned, -Operated, or -Affiliated Housing:** 24 **Library Holdings:** 1,039,042 **Credit Hours For Degree:** 15 courses, Bachelors **Professional Accreditation:** AACSB, ATS **Intercollegiate Athletics:** Baseball M; Basketball M & W; Cheerleading M & W; Cross-Country Running M & W; Football M; Golf M; Ice Hockey M & W; Lacrosse W; Rugby M & W; Soccer M & W; Swimming and Diving M & W; Volleyball M & W

YORK UNIVERSITY

4700 Keele St.
Toronto, ON, Canada M3J 1P3
Tel: (416)736-2100
Fax: (416)736-5741
E-mail: aburkett@yorku.ca
Web Site: http://www.yorku.ca/
President/CEO: Mamdouh Shoukri
Admissions: Amber Holliday

Type: University **Sex:** Coed **Admission Plans:** Preferred Admission; Deferred Admission **Application Deadline:** February 1 **Application Fee:** $210.00 **H.S. Requirements:** High school diploma required; GED not accepted. For mature applicants: High school diploma or equivalent not required **Costs Per Year:** Application fee: $210 Canadian dollars. Tuition, fee, and room and board charges are reported in Canadian dollars. Province resident tuition: $5761 full-time. Full-time tuition varies according to course load and program. College room and board: $7250. College room only: $4250. Room and board charges vary according to board plan and housing facility. International student tuition: $15,761 full-time. **Scholarships:** Available **Calendar System:** Semester, Summer Session Available **Enrollment:** FT 39,720, PT 7,342, Grad FT 3,963, Grad PT 2,180 **Faculty:** FT 1,465, PT 1,033 **Student-Faculty Ratio:** 19:1 **Exams:** SAT I or ACT. **Library Holdings:** 6,500,000 **Credit Hours For Degree:** 15 courses, Bachelors **Professional Accreditation:** APA **Intercollegiate Athletics:** Badminton M & W; Basketball M & W; Cross-Country Running M & W; Field Hockey W; Football M; Ice Hockey M & W; Rugby W; Soccer M & W; Swimming and Diving M & W; Tennis M & W; Track and Field M & W; Volleyball M & W; Water Polo M & W

BISHOP'S UNIVERSITY
2600 College St.
Sherbrooke, QC, Canada J1M 0C8
Tel: (819)822-9600; Free: 877-822-8200
Fax: (819)822-9661
E-mail: recruitment@ubishops.ca
Web Site: http://www.ubishops.ca/
President/CEO: Michael Goldbloom
Admissions: Jacqueline Belleau
Type: Comprehensive **Sex:** Coed **Affiliation:** Association of Universities and Colleges of Canada (AUCC) **Scores:** 100% SAT V 400+; 100% SAT M 400+; 70% ACT 18-23; 25% ACT 24-29 **Admission Plans:** Early Admission; Early Action; Early Decision Plan; Deferred Admission **Application Deadline:** March 1 **Application Fee:** $60.00 **H.S. Requirements:** High school diploma required; GED not accepted. For some adult students: High school diploma or equivalent not required **Costs Per Year:** Application fee: $60 Canadian dollars. Tuition, fee, and room and board charges are reported in Canadian dollars. Province resident tuition: $1868 full-time, $62.27 per credit part-time. Canadian resident tuition: $5378 full-time, $179.28 per credit part-time. Mandatory fees: $1015 full-time. Full-time tuition and fees vary according to course load, program, reciprocity agreements, and student level. Part-time tuition varies according to course load, program, and student level. College room and board: $6900. Room and board charges vary according to board plan and housing facility. International student tuition: $13,000 full-time. **Scholarships:** Available **Calendar System:** Semester, Summer Session Available **Enrollment:** FT 1,854, PT 425, Grad FT 32 **Faculty:** FT 125, PT 65 **Student-Faculty Ratio:** 16:1 **Exams:** SAT I or ACT. **% Residing in College-Owned, -Operated, or -Affiliated Housing:** 30 **Library Holdings:** 366,807 **Credit Hours For Degree:** 93 credits, Bachelors **Intercollegiate Athletics:** Basketball M & W; Field Hockey W; Football M; Golf M; Ice Hockey W; Lacrosse M & W; Rock Climbing M & W; Skiing (Downhill) M & W; Soccer W; Volleyball W

CONCORDIA UNIVERSITY
1455 de Maisonneuve Blvd. West
Montréal, QC, Canada H3G 1M8
Tel: (514)848-2424
Fax: (514)848-2621
E-mail: fargnoli@alcor.concordia.ca
Web Site: http://www.concordia.ca/
President/CEO: Dr. Judith Woodsworth
Admissions: Assunta Fargnoli
Type: University **Sex:** Coed **Affiliation:** Quebec University Network **% Accepted:** 69 **Admission Plans:** Early Action; Deferred Admission **Application Deadline:** March 1 **Application Fee:** $90.00 **H.S. Requirements:** High school diploma required; GED not accepted. For Canadian applicants 21 or over and out of high school at least 2 years (Mature entry): High school diploma required; GED not accepted **Costs Per Year:** Application fee: $90 Canadian dollars. Tuition, fee, and room and board charges are reported in Canadian dollars. Province resident tuition: $2068 full-time, $68.93 per credit part-time. Canadian resident tuition: $5668 full-time, $188.92 per credit part-time. Mandatory fees: $1175 full-time, $37.67 per credit part-time, $22.50 per term part-time. Full-time tuition and fees vary according to course load and program. Part-time tuition and fees vary according to course load and program. College room and board: $8084. Room and board charges vary according to board plan, housing facility, and location. International student tuition: $14,462 full-time. **Scholarships:** Available **Calendar System:** Semester, Summer Session Available **Enrollment:** FT 18,736, PT 10,043, Grad FT 3,480, Grad PT 1,336 **Faculty:** FT 952, PT 1,006 **Student-Faculty Ratio:** 20:1 **% Residing in College-Owned, -Operated, or -Affiliated Housing:** 2 **Final Year or Final Semester Residency Requirement:** Yes **Credit Hours For Degree:** 90 credits, Bachelors **Professional Accreditation:** AACSB, APA **Intercollegiate Athletics:** Baseball M; Basketball M & W; Cross-Country Running M & W; Football M; Golf M; Ice Hockey M & W; Rugby M & W; Skiing (Downhill) M & W; Soccer M & W; Wrestling M & W

HEC MONTREAL
3000, chemin de la Cte-Sainte-Catherine
Montréal, QC, Canada H3T 2A7
Tel: (514)340-6000
Admissions: (514)340-6151
Fax: (514)340-5640
E-mail: admission.info@hec.ca
Web Site: http://www.hec.ca/
President/CEO: Michel Patry
Admissions: Yolaine Martineau
Financial Aid: Mariam Ladha
Type: Comprehensive **Sex:** Coed **Affiliation:** Universite de Montreal **% Accepted:** 63 **Admission Plans:** Deferred Admission **Application Deadline:** March 1 **Application Fee:** $77.00 **H.S. Requirements:** High school diploma or equivalent not required **Costs Per Year:** Application fee: $77 Canadian dollars. Tuition, fee, and room only charges are reported in Canadian dollars. Province resident tuition: $1968 full-time, $65.60 per credit part-time. Canadian resident tuition: $5501 full-time, $183.36 per credit part-time. Mandatory fees: $962 full-time, $26.95 per credit part-time, $69.39 per term part-time. Full-time tuition and fees vary according to program. Part-time tuition and fees vary according to program. College room only: $3197. Room charges vary according to housing facility. International student tuition: $15,016 full-time. **Scholarships:** Available **Calendar System:** Trimester, Summer Session Available **Enrollment:** FT 4,730, PT 4,907, Grad FT 1,419, Grad PT 1,611 **Faculty:** FT 270, PT 329 **Student-Faculty Ratio:** 23:1 **% Receiving Financial Aid:** 21 **Final Year or Final Semester Residency Requirement:** No **Library Holdings:** 383,938 **Credit Hours For Degree:** 90 credits, Bachelors **Professional Accreditation:** AACSB

MCGILL UNIVERSITY
845 Sherbrooke St. West
Montréal, QC, Canada H3A 2T5
Tel: (514)398-4455
Admissions: (514)398-3910
Fax: (514)398-4193
E-mail: admissions@mcgill.ca
Web Site: http://www.mcgill.ca/
President/CEO: Heather Munroe-Blum
Financial Aid: Judy Stymest
Type: University **Sex:** Coed **Scores:** 100% SAT V 400+; 100% SAT M 400+; 1.26% ACT 18-23; 38.66% ACT 24-29 **% Accepted:** 54 **Admission Plans:** Deferred Admission **Application Deadline:** January 15 **Application Fee:** $85.00 **H.S. Requirements:** High school diploma required; GED not accepted **Costs Per Year:** Application fee: $85 Canadian dollars. Tuition, fee, and room and board charges are reported in Canadian dollars. Province

resident tuition: $1968 full-time, $65.60 per credit part-time. Canadian resident tuition: $5500 full-time, $183.34 per credit part-time. Mandatory fees: $1500 full-time. Full-time tuition and fees vary according to class time, course load, degree level, location, program, and student level. Part-time tuition varies according to class time, course load, degree level, location, program, and student level. College room and board: $11,000. College room only: $7300. Room and board charges vary according to board plan, housing facility, and location. International student tuition: $13,965 full-time. **Scholarships:** Available **Calendar System:** Semester, Summer Session Available **Enrollment:** FT 18,722, PT 3,801 **Faculty:** FT 1,689, PT 867 **Student-Faculty Ratio:** 16:1 **Exams:** SAT I and SAT II or ACT. **% Residing in College-Owned, -Operated, or -Affiliated Housing:** 12 **Library Holdings:** 4,236,684 **Credit Hours For Degree:** 120 credits, Bachelors **Professional Accreditation:** ADA, ALA, APA, ATS, LCMEAMA **Intercollegiate Athletics:** Badminton M & W; Baseball M; Basketball M & W; Cheerleading M & W; Crew M & W; Cross-Country Running M & W; Fencing M & W; Field Hockey W; Football M; Golf M & W; Ice Hockey M & W; Lacrosse M & W; Rugby M & W; Sailing M & W; Skiing (Cross-Country) M & W; Skiing (Downhill) M & W; Soccer M & W; Squash M & W; Swimming and Diving M & W; Tennis M & W; Track and Field M & W; Ultimate Frisbee M & W; Volleyball M & W; Wrestling M & W

TELE-UNIVERSITE
455, rue de l'Église
C.P. 4800, succ. Terminus
Québec, QC, Canada G1K 9H5
Tel: (418)657-2262
Fax: (418)657-2094
Web Site: http://www.teluq.uquebec.ca/
Admissions: Louise Bertrand
Type: Comprehensive **Sex:** Coed **Affiliation:** Université du Québec **% Accepted:** 100 **Admission Plans:** Open Admission **Application Deadline:** Rolling **Application Fee:** $30.00 **H.S. Requirements:** High school diploma required; GED not accepted **Calendar System:** Trimester, Summer Session Available **Faculty:** FT 36, PT 0 **Library Holdings:** 12,567 **Credit Hours For Degree:** 90 credits, Bachelors

UNIVERSITE LAVAL
C.P. 2208, succursale Terminus
Québec, QC, Canada G1K 7P4
Tel: (418)656-3333; Free: 877-785-2825
Admissions: (418)656-2764
Fax: (418)656-2809
E-mail: info@dap.ulaval.ca
Web Site: http://www.ulaval.ca/
Type: University **Sex:** Coed **% Accepted:** 63 **Application Deadline:** March 1 **Application Fee:** $30.00 **H.S. Requirements:** High school diploma required; GED accepted **Calendar System:** Trimester, Summer Session Available **Enrollment:** FT 19,938, PT 7,971 **Faculty:** FT 1,380, PT 76 **Student-Faculty Ratio:** 7:1 **% Residing in College-Owned, -Operated, or -Affiliated Housing:** 7 **Library Holdings:** 3,000,000 **Credit Hours For Degree:** 90 credits, Bachelors **Professional Accreditation:** AACSB, ADA, LCMEAMA **Intercollegiate Athletics:** Badminton M & W; Baseball M; Basketball M & W; Cross-Country Running M & W; Football M; Golf M & W; Gymnastics M & W; Skiing (Downhill) M & W; Soccer M & W; Swimming and Diving M & W; Track and Field M & W; Volleyball M & W

UNIVERSITE DE MONTREAL
CP 6128, Succursale Centre-ville
Montréal, QC, Canada H3C 3J7
Tel: (514)343-6111
Admissions: (514)343-2214
Fax: (514)343-5788
E-mail: pierre.chenard@umontreal.ca
Web Site: http://www.umontreal.ca/
Admissions: Pierre Chenard
Financial Aid: Sylvianne Latour
Type: University **Sex:** Coed **Affiliation:** L'Ecole Polytechnique de Montrèal, HEC Montrèal **Application Deadline:** March 1 **Application Fee:** $50.00 **Scholarships:** Available **Calendar System:** Trimester, Summer Session Available **Enrollment:** FT 26,671, PT 14,779 **Library Holdings:** 4,000,000 **Credit Hours For Degree:** 90 credits, Bachelors **Professional Accreditation:** ADA, ACSP, ALA, AOA, ASLA, AVMA, ACEHSA, LCMEAMA **Intercollegiate Athletics:** Badminton M & W; Skiing (Downhill) M & W; Soccer M & W; Swimming and Diving M & W; Volleyball M & W

UNIVERSITE DU QUEBEC EN ABITIBI-TEMISCAMINGUE
445 Blvd. de l'Université
Rouyn-Noranda, QC, Canada J9X 5E4
Tel: (819)762-0971
Fax: (819)797-4727
E-mail: micheline.chevalier@uqat.uquebec.ca
Web Site: http://www.uqat.ca/
Admissions: Monique Fay
Type: Comprehensive **Sex:** Coed **Affiliation:** Université du Québec **Admission Plans:** Open Admission **Application Deadline:** Rolling **Application Fee:** $30.00 **H.S. Requirements:** High school diploma required; GED not accepted **Calendar System:** Trimester, Summer Session Available **Faculty:** FT 71, PT 88 **Library Holdings:** 135,882 **Credit Hours For Degree:** 90 credits, Bachelors

UNIVERSITE DU QUEBEC ACHICOUTIMI
555, Blvd. de L'Université
Chicoutimi, QC, Canada G7H 2B1
Tel: (418)545-5011
Admissions: (418)545-5005
Fax: (418)545-5012
E-mail: czoccast@uqac.uquebec.ca
Web Site: http://www.uqac.ca/
Admissions: Claudio Zoccastello
Financial Aid: Marie-Claude Bergeron
Type: University **Sex:** Coed **Affiliation:** Université du Québec **Admission Plans:** Open Admission **Application Deadline:** March 1 **H.S. Requirements:** High school diploma required; GED not accepted **Scholarships:** Available **Calendar System:** Trimester, Summer Session Available **Faculty:** FT 221, PT 173 **Library Holdings:** 689,214 **Credit Hours For Degree:** 90 credits, Bachelors **Intercollegiate Athletics:** Badminton M & W; Cross-Country Running M & W; Soccer W; Volleyball M & W

UNIVERSITE DU QUEBEC, ECOLE DE TECHNOLOGIE SUPERIEURE
1100, rue Notre Dame Ouest
Montréal, QC, Canada H3C 1K3
Tel: (514)396-8800
Admissions: (514)396-8885
Fax: (514)289-8950
E-mail: admission@ets.mtl.ca
Web Site: http://www.etsmtl.ca/
Admissions: Francine Gamache
Type: Comprehensive **Sex:** Coed **Affiliation:** Université du Québec **% Accepted:** 88 **Admission Plans:** Open Admission **Application Deadline:** March 1 **Application Fee:** $30.00 **H.S. Requirements:** High school diploma required; GED not accepted **Scholarships:** Available **Calendar System:** Trimester, Summer Session Available **Enrollment:** FT 2,763, PT 1,091 **Faculty:** FT 119, PT 162 **Library Holdings:** 44,195 **Credit Hours For Degree:** 114 credits, Bachelors **Intercollegiate Athletics:** Rugby M

UNIVERSITE DU QUEBEC AMONTREAL
CP 8888, Succursale Centre-ville
Montréal, QC, Canada H3C 3P8
Tel: (514)987-3000
Admissions: (514)987-3132
Fax: (514)987-7728
E-mail: admission@uqam.ca
Web Site: http://www.uqam.ca/
Admissions: Lucille Boisselle-Roy
Type: University **Sex:** Coed **Affiliation:** Université du Québec **Admission Plans:** Open Admission **Application Deadline:** March 1 **H.S. Requirements:** High school diploma required; GED not accepted **Calendar System:** Trimester, Summer Session Available **Faculty:** FT 993, PT 2,011 **Library Holdings:** 2,300,000 **Credit Hours For Degree:** 90 credits, Bachelors

UNIVERSITE DU QUEBEC EN OUTAOUAIS
Case Postale 1250, Succursale Hull
Gatineau, QC, Canada J8X 3X7
Tel: (819)595-3900; Free: 800-567-1283
E-mail: registraire@uqo.ca
Web Site: http://www.uqo.ca/

President/CEO: Jean Vaillancourt
Type: University **Sex:** Coed **Affiliation:** Université du Québec **Admission Plans:** Open Admission **Application Fee:** $60.00 **H.S. Requirements:** High school diploma or equivalent not required **Costs Per Year:** Application fee: $60. Province resident tuition: $2660 full-time, $68.93 per credit part-time. Canadian resident tuition: $6259 full-time. Full-time tuition varies according to course load, degree level, program, and reciprocity agreements. Part-time tuition varies according to course load, degree level, and program. College room only: $5112. Room charges vary according to housing facility. International student tuition: $15,017 full-time. **Calendar System:** Trimester, Summer Session Available **Library Holdings:** 230,910 **Credit Hours For Degree:** 90 credits, Bachelors

UNIVERSITE DU QUEBEC ARIMOUSKI
300, Allee des Ursulines, CP 3300
Rimouski, QC, Canada G5L 3A1
Tel: (418)723-1986
Admissions: (418)724-1433
Fax: (418)724-1525
E-mail: philippe_horth@uqar.uquebec.ca
Web Site: http://www.uqar.ca/
Admissions: Marie Saint Laurent
Type: Comprehensive **Sex:** Coed **Affiliation:** Université du Québec **% Accepted:** 99 **Admission Plans:** Open Admission **Application Deadline:** March 1 **H.S. Requirements:** High school diploma required; GED not accepted **Calendar System:** Trimester, Summer Session Available **Faculty:** FT 168, PT 156 **Library Holdings:** 263,142 **Credit Hours For Degree:** 90 credits, Bachelors **Intercollegiate Athletics:** Badminton M & W; Cross-Country Running M & W; Skiing (Downhill) M & W

UNIVERSITE DU QUEBEC ATROIS-RIVIERES
3351 blvd des Forges, Case post 500
Trois-Rivières, QC, Canada G9A 5H7
Tel: (819)376-5011; Free: 800-365-0922
Fax: (819)376-5210
E-mail: registraire@uqtr.ca
Web Site: http://www.uqtr.ca/
Admissions: Jean Bois
Type: University **Sex:** Coed **Affiliation:** Université du Québec **Admission Plans:** Open Admission **Application Deadline:** March 1 **Application Fee:** $30.00 **H.S. Requirements:** High school diploma required; GED not accepted **Calendar System:** Trimester, Summer Session Available **Faculty:** FT 317, PT 413 **Library Holdings:** 464,338 **Credit Hours For Degree:** 90 credits, Bachelors **Intercollegiate Athletics:** Badminton M & W; Cross-Country Running M; Ice Hockey M & W; Soccer M & W; Swimming and Diving M & W; Track and Field M & W

UNIVERSITE DE SHERBROOKE
Sherbrooke, QC, Canada J1K 2R1
Tel: (819)821-8000
Admissions: (819)821-7687
Fax: (819)821-7966
Web Site: http://www.usherbrooke.ca/
Admissions: Lisa Bedard or Valerie Bergeron
Financial Aid: Gilles Godin
Type: University **Sex:** Coed **% Accepted:** 68 **Admission Plans:** Preferred Admission; Early Admission **Application Deadline:** March 1 **Application Fee:** $70.00 **H.S. Requirements:** High school diploma required; GED not accepted **Scholarships:** Available **Calendar System:** Miscellaneous, Summer Session Available **Enrollment:** FT 10,222, PT 4,215 **Faculty:** FT 882, PT 449 **Library Holdings:** 1,200,000 **Credit Hours For Degree:** 90 credits, Bachelors **Professional Accreditation:** LCMEAMA **Intercollegiate Athletics:** Badminton M & W; Football M; Soccer M & W; Swimming and Diving M & W; Track and Field M & W; Volleyball M & W

BRIERCREST COLLEGE
510 College Dr.
Caronport, SK, Canada S0H 0S0
Tel: (306)756-3200
Fax: (306)756-5500
E-mail: enrollment@briercrest.ca
Web Site: http://www.briercrest.ca/
Admissions: Mike Benallick
Financial Aid: Joan Ballantyne
Type: Four-Year College **Sex:** Coed **Affiliation:** interdenominational; Briercrest Family of Schools **Admission Plans:** Open Admission; Preferred Admission; Early Admission; Deferred Admission **Application Deadline:** August 15 **Application Fee:** $35.00 **H.S. Requirements:** High school diploma required; GED accepted **Scholarships:** Available **Calendar System:** Semester, Summer Session Available **Enrollment:** FT 507, PT 134 **Faculty:** FT 22, PT 34 **Student-Faculty Ratio:** 16:1 **% Residing in College-Owned, -Operated, or -Affiliated Housing:** 75 **Library Holdings:** 76,000 **Credit Hours For Degree:** 126 semester hours, Bachelors **Professional Accreditation:** ABHE **Intercollegiate Athletics:** Basketball M & W; Ice Hockey M; Soccer M & W; Volleyball M & W

ESTON COLLEGE
730 1st St. E.
Box 579
Eston, SK, Canada S0L 1A0
Tel: (306)962-3621; Free: 888-440-3424
Fax: (306)962-3810
Web Site: http://www.estoncollege.ca/
Type: Four-Year College **Sex:** Coed

HORIZON COLLEGE & SEMINARY
1303 Jackson Ave.
Saskatoon, SK, Canada S7H 2M9
Tel: (306)374-6655; Free: 877-374.6655
Fax: (306)373-6968
E-mail: admissions@horizon.edu
Web Site: http://www.horizon.edu/
President/CEO: Rev. Mark Emde
Admissions: Shannon Olson
Financial Aid: Lila Wegner
Type: Four-Year College **Sex:** Coed **Affiliation:** Pentecostal Assemblies of Canada; University of Saskatchewan **% Accepted:** 100 **Admission Plans:** Deferred Admission **Application Deadline:** September 15 **Application Fee:** $50.00 **H.S. Requirements:** High school diploma required; GED accepted **Costs Per Year:** Application fee: $50 Canadian dollars. Tuition, fee, and room and board charges are reported in Canadian dollars. Comprehensive fee: $11,650 includes full-time tuition ($5760), mandatory fees ($890), and college room and board ($5000). Full-time tuition and fees vary according to course load and program. Part-time tuition: $180 per credit hour. Part-time mandatory fees: $370 per year. Part-time tuition and fees vary according to course load and program. **Scholarships:** Available **Calendar System:** Semester, Summer Session Not available **Enrollment:** FT 51, PT 10 **Faculty:** FT 1, PT 11 **Student-Faculty Ratio:** 11:1 **% Residing in College-Owned, -Operated, or -Affiliated Housing:** 0 **Final Year or Final Semester Residency Requirement:** No **Credit Hours For Degree:** 128 credit hours, Bachelors **Professional Accreditation:** ABHE

UNIVERSITY OF REGINA
3737 Wascana Parkway
Regina, SK, Canada S4S 0A2
Tel: (306)585-4111; Free: 800-664-4756
Admissions: (306)585-4942
Fax: (306)585-5203
E-mail: admissions@uregina.ca
Web Site: http://www.uregina.ca/
President/CEO: Dr. Vianne Timmons
Admissions: Susan Husum
Financial Aid: Myrna Handziuk
Type: University **Sex:** Coed **% Accepted:** 88 **Admission Plans:** Preferred Admission; Early Admission; Early Action; Deferred Admission **Application Deadline:** July 1 **Application Fee:** $90.00 **H.S. Requirements:** High school diploma or equivalent not required. For a high school diploma is not required for mature students (21 years of age or older): High school diploma or equivalent not required **Costs Per Year:** Application fee: $90 Canadian dollars. Tuition, fee, and room and board charges are reported in Canadian dollars. Province resident tuition: $4690 full-time, $140 per credit hour part-time. Canadian resident tuition: $140 per credit hour part-time. Mandatory fees: $369 full-time, $128 per term part-time. Full-time tuition and fees vary according to course load and program. Part-time tuition and fees vary according to course load and program. College room and board: $7772. College room only: $5272. Room and board charges vary according to board plan and housing facility. International student tuition: $11,410 full-time. **Scholarships:** Available **Calendar System:** Semester, Summer Session Available **Enrollment:** FT 7,943, PT 2,445, Grad FT 674, Grad PT 528 **Faculty:** FT 529, PT 0 **Student-Faculty Ratio:** 17:1 **Exams:** SAT I or ACT, SAT II. ACT essay not being used. SAT essay not being used. **% Residing in College-Owned, -Operated, or -Affiliated Housing:** 10 **Final Year or Final Semester Residency Requirement:** No **Library Holdings:** 1,056,665 **Credit Hours For Degree:** 120 credit hours, Bachelors **Intercollegiate Athletics:** Basketball M & W; Cross-Country Running M & W; Football M; Ice Hockey M & W; Soccer W; Swimming and Diving M & W; Track and Field M & W; Volleyball M & W; Wrestling M & W

UNIVERSITY OF SASKATCHEWAN
105 Administration Place
Saskatoon, SK, Canada S7N 5A2
Tel: (306)966-4343
Admissions: (306)966-5788
Fax: (306)966-7026
E-mail: admissions@usask.ca
Web Site: http://www.usask.ca/
President/CEO: Peter MacKinnon
Type: University **Sex:** Coed **% Accepted:** 80 **Admission Plans:** Preferred Admission; Early Admission; Early Action **Application Deadline:** May 1 **Application Fee:** $90.00 **H.S. Requirements:** High school diploma required; GED not accepted. For Special (Mature) Admission, Transition Program: High school diploma or equivalent not required **Costs Per Year:** Application fee: $90 Canadian dollars. Tuition, fee, and room and board charges are reported in Canadian dollars. Province resident tuition: $6240 full-time,

$150.38 per credit part-time. Mandatory fees: $695 full-time. Full-time tuition and fees vary according to course load, degree level, location, and program. Part-time tuition varies according to course load, degree level, location, and program. College room and board: $7221. Room and board charges vary according to board plan, housing facility, and location. International student tuition: $19,110 full-time. **Scholarships:** Available **Calendar System:** Miscellaneous, Summer Session Available **Faculty:** FT 1,074 **Student-Faculty Ratio:** 16:1 **Library Holdings:** 2,020,000 **Credit Hours For Degree:** 120 credit units, Bachelors **Professional Accreditation:** ADA, APA, AVMA, LCMEAMA **Intercollegiate Athletics:** Basketball M & W; Cross-Country Running M & W; Football M; Ice Hockey M & W; Soccer M & W; Track and Field M & W; Volleyball M & W; Wrestling M & W

WESTERN CHRISTIAN COLLEGE
100-4400 4th Ave.
Regina, SK, Canada S4T 0H8
Tel: (306)545-1515
E-mail: registrar@westernchristian.ca
Web Site: http://www.westernchristian.ca/
Admissions: Pamela Stonehouse
Financial Aid: Dwight Muller
Type: Four-Year College **Sex:** Coed **Affiliation:** Church of Christ **Application Fee:** $50.00 **H.S. Requirements:** High school diploma required; GED accepted **Costs Per Year:** Application fee: $50 Canadian dollars. Tuition, fee, and room and board charges are reported in Canadian dollars. One-time mandatory fee: $50. Comprehensive fee: $11,975 includes full-time tuition ($6675), mandatory fees ($500), and college room and board ($4800). Full-time tuition and fees vary according to course load. Part-time tuition: $235 per credit hour. Part-time mandatory fees: $200 per term. Part-time tuition and fees vary according to course load. **Calendar System:** Semester **Professional Accreditation:** ABHE

Index of Intercollegiate Athletics

M = Men; W = Women

Archery

Atlantic Cape Community College *New Jersey* M & W
Barnard College *New York* W
City College of San Francisco *California* W
Columbia University *New York* M & W
Columbia University, School of General Studies *New York* W
Diné College *Arizona* M & W
Kenyon College *Ohio* M & W
North Dakota State University *North Dakota* M & W
Penn State University Park *Pennsylvania* M & W
Stanford University *California* M & W
Texas A&M University *Texas* W
United States Air Force Academy *Colorado* M & W
The University of Alabama in Huntsville *Alabama* M & W
University of Hawaii at Manoa *Hawaii* M
University of New Hampshire *New Hampshire* M & W
University of Rio Grande *Ohio* M
University of Southern California *California* M & W
The University of Texas at Austin *Texas* M & W
University of Toronto *Ontario* M & W
Yale University *Connecticut* M & W

Badminton

Albright College *Pennsylvania* W
Baylor University *Texas* M & W
Boston University *Massachusetts* M & W
Bryant University *Rhode Island* M & W
Bryn Athyn College of the New Church *Pennsylvania* M & W
Bryn Mawr College *Pennsylvania* W
California State University, Long Beach *California* M & W
Carleton College *Minnesota* M & W
Carnegie Mellon University *Pennsylvania* W
Claremont McKenna College *California* M & W
Colby College *Maine* M & W
The College of Wooster *Ohio* M & W
Columbia University *New York* M & W
Columbia University, School of General Studies *New York* M & W
Concordia University College of Alberta *Alberta* M & W
Cooper Union for the Advancement of Science and Art *New York* M & W
Dartmouth College *New Hampshire* M & W
Dickinson State University *North Dakota* M & W
McGill University *Quebec* M & W
McMaster University *Ontario* M & W
Mission College *California* M & W
Mount Saint Vincent University *Nova Scotia* M & W
Mt. San Antonio College *California* W
North Carolina State University *North Carolina* M & W
Nova Scotia Agricultural College *Nova Scotia* M & W
Penn State University Park *Pennsylvania* M & W
Providence College and Theological Seminary *Manitoba* M & W
Rensselaer Polytechnic Institute *New York* M & W
Rice University *Texas* M & W
Ryerson University *Ontario* M & W
Saint Louis University *Missouri* M & W
San Jose State University *California* M & W
Southwestern College *Kansas* M & W
Swarthmore College *Pennsylvania* M & W
Syracuse University *New York* M & W
Thompson Rivers University *British Columbia* M & W
Towson University *Maryland* M & W
Université Laval *Quebec* M & W
Université de Montréal *Quebec* M & W
Université du Québec àChicoutimi *Quebec* M & W
Université du Québec àRimouski *Quebec* M & W
Université du Québec àTrois-Rivières *Quebec* M & W
Université Sainte-Anne *Nova Scotia* M & W
Université de Sherbrooke *Quebec* M & W
The University of Alabama in Huntsville *Alabama* M & W
University of California, Santa Cruz *California* M & W
University of Hartford *Connecticut* M & W
University of Idaho *Idaho* M & W
University of King's College *Nova Scotia* M & W
University of Maryland, Baltimore County *Maryland* M & W
University of New Brunswick Saint John *New Brunswick* M & W
University of New Hampshire *New Hampshire* M & W
University of Ottawa *Ontario* M & W
University of Rochester *New York* M & W
University of Southern California *California* M & W
The University of Tennessee *Tennessee* M & W
The University of Texas at Austin *Texas* M & W
University of Toronto *Ontario* M & W
University of Waterloo *Ontario* M & W
The University of Western Ontario *Ontario* M & W
University of Wisconsin–River Falls *Wisconsin* M & W
University of Wyoming *Wyoming* M & W
York University *Ontario* M & W

Baseball

Abilene Christian University *Texas* M
Abraham Baldwin Agricultural College *Georgia* M
Academy of Art University *California* M
Acadia University *Nova Scotia* M
Adelphi University *New York* M
Adirondack Community College *New York* M
Adrian College *Michigan* M
Alabama Agricultural and Mechanical University *Alabama* M
Albany State University *Georgia* M
Alberta College of Art & Design *Alberta* W
Albertus Magnus College *Connecticut* M
Albion College *Michigan* M
Albright College *Pennsylvania* M
Alcorn State University *Mississippi* M
Alderson-Broaddus College *West Virginia* M
Alice Lloyd College *Kentucky* M
Allan Hancock College *California* M
Allegany College of Maryland *Maryland* M
American River College *California* M
Amherst College *Massachusetts* M
Ancilla College *Indiana* M
Anderson University *South Carolina* M
Anderson University *Indiana* M
Andrew College *Georgia* M
Angelina College *Texas* M
Angelo State University *Texas* M
Anna Maria College *Massachusetts* M
Anne Arundel Community College *Maryland* M
Anoka-Ramsey Community College *Minnesota* M
Anoka-Ramsey Community College, Cambridge Campus *Minnesota* M
Antelope Valley College *California* M
Appalachian State University *North Carolina* M
Aquinas College *Michigan* M
Arkansas Tech University *Arkansas* M
Armstrong Atlantic State University *Georgia* M
The Art Institute of Boston at Lesley University *Massachusetts* M
Asbury University *Kentucky* M
Ashford University *Iowa* M
Ashland University *Ohio* M
Assumption College *Massachusetts* M
Atlanta Christian College *Georgia* M
Auburn University *Alabama* M
Auburn University Montgomery *Alabama* M
Augsburg College *Minnesota* M

Augusta State University *Georgia* M
Augustana College *South Dakota* M
Augustana College *Illinois* M
Aurora University *Illinois* M
Austin College *Texas* M
Austin Peay State University *Tennessee* M
Averett University *Virginia* M
Avila University *Missouri* M
Azusa Pacific University *California* M
Babson College *Massachusetts* M
Baker University *Kansas* M
Bakersfield College *California* M
Baldwin-Wallace College *Ohio* M
Ball State University *Indiana* M & W
Baptist Bible College of Pennsylvania *Pennsylvania* M
Barry University *Florida* M
Barstow College *California* M
Barton College *North Carolina* M
Barton County Community College *Kansas* M
Bates College *Maine* M
Baton Rouge Community College *Louisiana* M
Baylor University *Texas* M
Becker College *Massachusetts* M
Belhaven University *Mississippi* M
Bellarmine University *Kentucky* M
Bellevue College *Washington* M
Bellevue University *Nebraska* M
Belmont Abbey College *North Carolina* M
Belmont University *Tennessee* M
Beloit College *Wisconsin* M
Bemidji State University *Minnesota* M
Benedict College *South Carolina* M
Benedictine College *Kansas* M
Benedictine University *Illinois* M
Bentley University *Massachusetts* M
Berea College *Kentucky* M
Bergen Community College *New Jersey* M
Bernard M. Baruch College of the City University of New York *New York* M
Berry College *Georgia* M
Bethany College *West Virginia* M
Bethany College *Kansas* M
Bethany Lutheran College *Minnesota* M
Bethany University *California* M
Bethel College *Indiana* M
Bethel University *Tennessee* M
Bethel University *Minnesota* M
Bethune-Cookman University *Florida* M
Bevill State Community College *Alabama* M
Big Bend Community College *Washington* M
Biola University *California* M
Birmingham-Southern College *Alabama* M
Bishop State Community College *Alabama* M
Bismarck State College *North Dakota* M
Black Hawk College *Illinois* M
Blackburn College *Illinois* M
Blessing-Rieman College of Nursing *Illinois* M & W
Blinn College *Texas* M
Bloomfield College *New Jersey* M
Bloomsburg University of Pennsylvania *Pennsylvania* M
Blue Mountain College *Mississippi* M
Blue Mountain Community College *Oregon* M
Blue Ridge Community College *North Carolina* M
Bluefield College *Virginia* M
Bluefield State College *West Virginia* M
Bluffton University *Ohio* M
Borough of Manhattan Community College of the City University of New York *New York* M
Bossier Parish Community College *Louisiana* M
Boston College *Massachusetts* M
Boston University *Massachusetts* M
Bowdoin College *Maine* M
Bowling Green State University *Ohio* M
Bradley University *Illinois* M
Brandeis University *Massachusetts* M
Brescia University *Kentucky* M
Brevard College *North Carolina* M
Brevard Community College *Florida* M
Brewton-Parker College *Georgia* M
Briar Cliff University *Iowa* M
Briarcliffe College *New York* M
Bridgewater College *Virginia* M
Bridgewater State College *Massachusetts* M
Brigham Young University *Utah* M
Brock University *Ontario* M
Bronx Community College of the City University of New York *New York* M
Brookdale Community College *New Jersey* M
Broome Community College *New York* M
Broward College *Florida* M
Brown University *Rhode Island* M
Bryan College *Tennessee* M
Bryant University *Rhode Island* M
Bucknell University *Pennsylvania* M
Bucks County Community College *Pennsylvania* M
Buena Vista University *Iowa* M
Buffalo State College, State University of New York *New York* M
Bunker Hill Community College *Massachusetts* M
Burlington County College *New Jersey* M
Butler Community College *Kansas* M
Butler County Community College *Pennsylvania* M
Butler University *Indiana* M
Butte College *California* M
Cabrillo College *California* M
Caldwell College *New Jersey* M
California Baptist University *California* M
California Institute of Technology *California* M
California Lutheran University *California* M
California Polytechnic State University, San Luis Obispo *California* M
California State Polytechnic University, Pomona *California* M
California State University, Chico *California* M
California State University, Dominguez Hills *California* M
California State University, East Bay *California* M
California State University, Fresno *California* M
California State University, Fullerton *California* M
California State University, Los Angeles *California* M
California State University, Monterey Bay *California* M
California State University, Northridge *California* M
California State University, Sacramento *California* M
California State University, San Bernardino *California* M
California State University, San Marcos *California* M
California State University, Stanislaus *California* M
California University of Pennsylvania *Pennsylvania* M
Calumet College of Saint Joseph *Indiana* M
Calvin College *Michigan* M
Camden County College *New Jersey* M
Cameron University *Oklahoma* M
Campbell University *North Carolina* M
Campbellsville University *Kentucky* M
Cañada College *California* M
Canisius College *New York* M
Capital University *Ohio* M
Cardinal Stritch University *Wisconsin* M
Carl Albert State College *Oklahoma* M
Carl Sandburg College *Illinois* M
Carleton College *Minnesota* M
Carnegie Mellon University *Pennsylvania* M
Carroll University *Wisconsin* M
Carson-Newman College *Tennessee* M
Carthage College *Wisconsin* M
Case Western Reserve University *Ohio* M
Castleton State College *Vermont* M
Catawba College *North Carolina* M
Catawba Valley Community College *North Carolina* M
The Catholic University of America *District of Columbia* M
Cecil College *Maryland* M
Cedar Valley College *Texas* M
Cedarville University *Ohio* M
Centenary College *New Jersey* M
Centenary College of Louisiana *Louisiana* M
Central Alabama Community College *Alabama* M
Central Arizona College *Arizona* M
Central Baptist College *Arkansas* M & W
Central Christian College of Kansas *Kansas* M
Central College *Iowa* M
Central Connecticut State University *Connecticut* M
Central Florida Community College *Florida* M
Central Lakes College *Minnesota* M
Central Maine Community College *Maine* M
Central Methodist University *Missouri* M
Central Michigan University *Michigan* M
Central Ohio Technical College *Ohio* M
Central Washington University *Washington* M
Centralia College *Washington* M
Centre College *Kentucky* M
Cerritos College *California* M
Cerro Coso Community College *California* M
Chabot College *California* M
Chaffey College *California* M
Chapman University *California* M
Charleston Southern University *South Carolina* M
Chattahoochee Valley Community College *Alabama* M
Chattanooga State Community College *Tennessee* M
Chemeketa Community College *Oregon* M
Chesapeake College *Maryland* M
Chestnut Hill College *Pennsylvania* M
Chicago State University *Illinois* M
Chipola College *Florida* M
Chowan University *North Carolina* M
Christendom College *Virginia* M
Christian Brothers University *Tennessee* M
Christopher Newport University *Virginia* M
Cincinnati Christian University *Ohio* M
Cisco College *Texas* M
The Citadel, The Military College of South Carolina *South Carolina* M
Citrus College *California* M
City College of the City University of New York *New York* M
City Colleges of Chicago, Harry S. Truman College *Illinois* M
City Colleges of Chicago, Olive-Harvey College *Illinois* M
Clackamas Community College *Oregon* M
Claflin University *South Carolina* M & W
Claremont McKenna College *California* M
Clarendon College *Texas* M
Clarion University of Pennsylvania *Pennsylvania* M
Clark Atlanta University *Georgia* M
Clark College *Washington* M
Clark University *Massachusetts* M
Clarke College *Iowa* M
Clarkson University *New York* M
Clearwater Christian College *Florida* M
Clemson University *South Carolina* M
Cleveland State Community College *Tennessee* M
Cleveland State University *Ohio* M
Clinton Community College *New York* M
Cloud County Community College *Kansas* M
Coahoma Community College *Mississippi* M
Coastal Carolina University *South Carolina* M
Cochise College *Arizona* M
Coe College *Iowa* M
Coffeyville Community College *Kansas* M
Coker College *South Carolina* M
Colby College *Maine* M
Colby Community College *Kansas* M
Colby-Sawyer College *New Hampshire* M
Colgate University *New York* M
The College at Brockport, State University of New York *New York* M
College of the Canyons *California* M
College of Charleston *South Carolina* M
College of the Desert *California* M
College of DuPage *Illinois* M
College of the Holy Cross *Massachusetts* M
The College of Idaho *Idaho* M
College of Lake County *Illinois* M
College of Mount St. Joseph *Ohio* M
College of Mount Saint Vincent *New York* M
The College of New Jersey *New Jersey* M
College of the Ozarks *Missouri* M
College of the Redwoods *California* M
The College of Saint Rose *New York* M
The College of St. Scholastica *Minnesota* M
College of the Sequoias *California* M

M = Men; W = Women

M = Men; W = Women

College of the Siskiyous *California* M
College of Southern Idaho *Idaho* M
College of Southern Maryland *Maryland* M
College of Southern Nevada *Nevada* M
College of Staten Island of the City University of
New York *New York* M
The College of William and Mary *Virginia* M
The College of Wooster *Ohio* M
The Colorado College *Colorado* M
Colorado Northwestern Community College
Colorado M
Colorado School of Mines *Colorado* M
Colorado State University *Colorado* M
Colorado State University–Pueblo *Colorado* M
Columbia Basin College *Washington* M
Island* M
Concord University *West Virginia* M
Concordia College *Minnesota* M
Concordia College–New York *New York* M
Concordia University *Quebec* M
Concordia University *Oregon* M
Concordia University *Michigan* M
Concordia University *California* M
Concordia University Chicago *Illinois* M
Concordia University, Nebraska *Nebraska* M
Concordia University, St. Paul *Minnesota* M
Concordia University Texas *Texas* M
Concordia University Wisconsin *Wisconsin* M
Connecticut College *Connecticut* M
Connors State College *Oklahoma* M
Contra Costa College *California* M
Copiah-Lincoln Community College *Mississippi* M
Coppin State University *Maryland* M
Corban University *Oregon* M
Cornell College *Iowa* M
Cornell University *New York* M
Corning Community College *New York* M
Cosumnes River College *California* M
County College of Morris *New Jersey* M
Covenant College *Georgia* M
Cowley County Community College and Area
Vocational–Technical School *Kansas* M
Crandall University *New Brunswick* M
Creighton University *Nebraska* M
Crossroads College *Minnesota* M
Crowder College *Missouri* M
Crown College *Minnesota* M
Cuesta College *California* M
Culver-Stockton College *Missouri* M
Cumberland County College *New Jersey* M
Cumberland University *Tennessee* M
Curry College *Massachusetts* M
Cuyahoga Community College *Ohio* M
Cypress College *California* M
Dakota College at Bottineau *North Dakota* M
Dakota County Technical College *Minnesota* M
Dakota State University *South Dakota* M
Dakota Wesleyan University *South Dakota* M
Dallas Baptist University *Texas* M
Dana College *Nebraska* M
Daniel Webster College *New Hampshire* M
Danville Area Community College *Illinois* M
Dartmouth College *New Hampshire* M
Darton College *Georgia* M
Davidson College *North Carolina* M
Davis & Elkins College *West Virginia* M
Dawson Community College *Montana* M
Daytona State College *Florida* M

De Anza College *California* M
Dean College *Massachusetts* M
Defiance College *Ohio* M
Delaware County Community College
Pennsylvania M
Delaware State University *Delaware* M
Delaware Technical & Community College, Jack F.
Owens Campus *Delaware* M
Delaware Valley College *Pennsylvania* M
Delgado Community College *Louisiana* M
Delta State University *Mississippi* M
Denison University *Ohio* M
DePauw University *Indiana* M
Dixie State College of Utah *Utah* M
Doane College *Nebraska* M
Dodge City Community College *Kansas* M
Dominican College *New York* M
Dominican University *Illinois* M
Dordt College *Iowa* M
Dowling College *New York* M
Drew University *New Jersey* M
Drury University *Missouri* M
D'Youville College *New York* M
Earlham College *Indiana* M
East Carolina University *North Carolina* M
Eastern Kentucky University *Kentucky* M
Eastern Mennonite University *Virginia* M
Eastern Michigan University *Michigan* M
Eastern Nazarene College *Massachusetts* M
Eastern New Mexico University *New Mexico* M
Eastern Oklahoma State College *Oklahoma* M
Eastern University *Pennsylvania* M
Eastfield College *Texas* M
Ecclesia College *Arkansas* M
Eckerd College *Florida* M
Edgewood College *Wisconsin* M
Edmonds Community College *Washington* M
El Camino College *California* M
El Paso Community College *Texas* M
Elgin Community College *Illinois* M
Elizabeth City State University *North Carolina* M
Elizabethtown College *Pennsylvania* M
Ellsworth Community College *Iowa* M
Elmhurst College *Illinois* M
Elms College *Massachusetts* M
Elon University *North Carolina* M
Embry-Riddle Aeronautical University *Florida* M
Emerson College *Massachusetts* M
Emmanuel College *Georgia* M
Emory & Henry College *Virginia* M
Emory University *Georgia* M
Emporia State University *Kansas* M
Endicott College *Massachusetts* M
Enterprise State Community College *Alabama* M
Erie Community College *New York* M
Erie Community College, North Campus *New
York* M
Erie Community College, South Campus *New
York* M
Erskine College *South Carolina* M
Eugenio María de Hostos Community College of the
City University of New York *New York* M
Eureka College *Illinois* M
Evangel University *Missouri* M
Everett Community College *Washington* M

Fairfield University *Connecticut* M
Fairleigh Dickinson University, College at Florham
New Jersey M
Fairleigh Dickinson University, Metropolitan Campus
New Jersey M
Fairmont State University *West Virginia* M
Farmingdale State College *New York* M
Faulkner University *Alabama* M
Feather River College *California* M
Felician College *New Jersey* M
Ferrum College *Virginia* M
Finger Lakes Community College *New York* M
Finlandia University *Michigan* M
Fisher College *Massachusetts* M
Fitchburg State College *Massachusetts* M
Flagler College *Florida* M
Florida Agricultural and Mechanical University
Florida M
Florida Atlantic University *Florida* M
Florida Gulf Coast University *Florida* M
Florida Institute of Technology *Florida* M
Florida International University *Florida* M
Florida Memorial University *Florida* M
Florida Southern College *Florida* M
Florida State College at Jacksonville *Florida* M
Florida State University *Florida* M
Fontbonne University *Missouri* M
Fordham University *New York* M
Fort Hays State University *Kansas* M
Fort Lewis College *Colorado* M
Fort Scott Community College *Kansas* M
Framingham State College *Massachusetts* M
Francis Marion University *South Carolina* M
Franciscan University of Steubenville *Ohio* M
Frank Phillips College *Texas* M
Franklin College *Indiana* M
Franklin & Marshall College *Pennsylvania* M
Friends University *Kansas* M
Frostburg State University *Maryland* M
Fulton-Montgomery Community College *New
York* M
Furman University *South Carolina* M
Gadsden State Community College *Alabama* M
Gallaudet University *District of Columbia* M
Galveston College *Texas* M
Gannon University *Pennsylvania* M
Garden City Community College *Kansas* M
Gardner-Webb University *North Carolina* M
Garrett College *Maryland* M
Gateway Community College *Connecticut* M
Genesee Community College *New York* M
Geneva College *Pennsylvania* M
George C. Wallace Community College *Alabama* M
George Corley Wallace State Community College
Alabama M
George Fox University *Oregon* M
George Mason University *Virginia* M
The George Washington University *District of
Columbia* M
Georgetown College *Kentucky* M
Georgetown University *District of Columbia* M
Georgia College & State University *Georgia* M
Georgia Institute of Technology *Georgia* M
Georgia Perimeter College *Georgia* M
Georgia Southern University *Georgia* M
Georgia Southwestern State University *Georgia* M
Georgia State University *Georgia* M
Gettysburg College *Pennsylvania* M
Glen Oaks Community College *Michigan* M
Glendale Community College *California* M
Glendale Community College *Arizona* M
Globe Institute of Technology *New York* M
Gloucester County College *New Jersey* M
Golden West College *California* M
Gonzaga University *Washington* M
Gordon College *Massachusetts* M
Gordon College *Georgia* M
Goshen College *Indiana* M

Grace College *Indiana* M
Graceland University *Iowa* M
Grambling State University *Louisiana* M
Grand Canyon University *Arizona* M
Grand Rapids Community College *Michigan* M
Grand Valley State University *Michigan* M
Grand View University *Iowa* M
Grays Harbor College *Washington* M
Grayson County College *Texas* M
Green River Community College *Washington* M
Greensboro College *North Carolina* M
Greenville College *Illinois* M
Grinnell College *Iowa* M
Grossmont College *California* M
Grove City College *Pennsylvania* M
Guilford College *North Carolina* M
Guilford Technical Community College *North Carolina* M
Gulf Coast Community College *Florida* M
Gustavus Adolphus College *Minnesota* M
Gwynedd-Mercy College *Pennsylvania* M
Hagerstown Community College *Maryland* M
Hamilton College *New York* M
Hamline University *Minnesota* M
Hampden-Sydney College *Virginia* M
Hannibal-LaGrange College *Missouri* M
Hanover College *Indiana* M
Hardin-Simmons University *Texas* M
Harding University *Arkansas* M
Harford Community College *Maryland* M
Harper College *Illinois* M
Harris-Stowe State University *Missouri* M
Hartnell College *California* M
Harvard University *Massachusetts* M
Harvey Mudd College *California* M
Hastings College *Nebraska* M
Haverford College *Pennsylvania* M
Hawai'i Pacific University *Hawaii* M
Heartland Community College *Illinois* M
Heidelberg University *Ohio* M
Henderson State University *Arkansas* M
Hendrix College *Arkansas* M
Henry Ford Community College *Michigan* M
Herkimer County Community College *New York* M
Hesston College *Kansas* M
Hibbing Community College *Minnesota* M
High Point University *North Carolina* M
Highland Community College *Kansas* M
Highland Community College *Illinois* M
Hilbert College *New York* M
Hill College of the Hill Junior College District *Texas* M
Hillsborough Community College *Florida* M
Hillsdale College *Michigan* M
Hillsdale Free Will Baptist College *Oklahoma* M
Hinds Community College *Mississippi* M
Hiram College *Ohio* M
Hofstra University *New York* M
Holmes Community College *Mississippi* M
Holyoke Community College *Massachusetts* M
Hope College *Michigan* M
Houston Baptist University *Texas* M
Howard College *Texas* M
Howard Payne University *Texas* M
Howard University *District of Columbia* M & W
Huntingdon College *Alabama* M
Huntington University *Indiana* M
Husson University *Maine* M
Huston-Tillotson University *Texas* M
Hutchinson Community College and Area Vocational School *Kansas* M
Illinois Central College *Illinois* M
Illinois College *Illinois* M
Illinois Eastern Community Colleges, Lincoln Trail College *Illinois* M
Illinois Eastern Community Colleges, Olney Central College *Illinois* M
Illinois Eastern Community Colleges, Wabash Valley College *Illinois* M
Illinois Institute of Technology *Illinois* M
Illinois State University *Illinois* M
Illinois Valley Community College *Illinois* M
Illinois Wesleyan University *Illinois* M
Imperial Valley College *California* M
Independence Community College *Kansas* M
Indian Hills Community College *Iowa* M
Indian River State College *Florida* M
Indiana State University *Indiana* M
Indiana Tech *Indiana* M
Indiana University Bloomington *Indiana* M
Indiana University Northwest *Indiana* M
Indiana University of Pennsylvania *Pennsylvania* M
Indiana University Southeast *Indiana* M
Indiana University–Purdue University Fort Wayne *Indiana* M
Indiana Wesleyan University *Indiana* M
Inter American University of Puerto Rico, Aguadilla Campus *Puerto Rico* M
Inter American University of Puerto Rico, Arecibo Campus *Puerto Rico* M
Inter American University of Puerto Rico, Bayamón Campus *Puerto Rico* M
Inter American University of Puerto Rico, Guayama Campus *Puerto Rico* M
Inter American University of Puerto Rico, Ponce Campus *Puerto Rico* M & W
Inter American University of Puerto Rico, San Germán Campus *Puerto Rico* M
Iona College *New York* M
Iowa Central Community College *Iowa* M
Iowa Lakes Community College *Iowa* M
Iowa Wesleyan College *Iowa* M
Iowa Western Community College *Iowa* M
Itasca Community College *Minnesota* M
Ithaca College *New York* M
Jackson Community College *Michigan* M
Jackson State Community College *Tennessee* M
Jackson State University *Mississippi* M
Jacksonville State University *Alabama* M
Jacksonville University *Florida* M
James A. Rhodes State College *Ohio* M
James H. Faulkner State Community College *Alabama* M
James Madison University *Virginia* M
Jamestown College *North Dakota* M
Jamestown Community College *New York* M
Jarvis Christian College *Texas* M
Jefferson College *Missouri* M
Jefferson Community College *New York* M
Jefferson Davis Community College *Alabama* M
Jefferson State Community College *Alabama* M
John A. Logan College *Illinois* M
John Carroll University *Ohio* M
John Jay College of Criminal Justice of the City University of New York *New York* M
John Wood Community College *Illinois* M
The Johns Hopkins University *Maryland* M
Johnson Bible College *Tennessee* M
Johnson County Community College *Kansas* M
Johnson & Wales University *Rhode Island* M
Johnson & Wales University *Colorado* M
Jones County Junior College *Mississippi* M
Judson University *Illinois* M
Juniata College *Pennsylvania* M
Kalamazoo College *Michigan* M
Kalamazoo Valley Community College *Michigan* M
Kankakee Community College *Illinois* M
Kansas City Kansas Community College *Kansas* M
Kansas State University *Kansas* M
Kansas Wesleyan University *Kansas* M
Kaskaskia College *Illinois* M
Kean University *New Jersey* M
Keene State College *New Hampshire* M
Kellogg Community College *Michigan* M
Kennesaw State University *Georgia* M
Kent State University *Ohio* M
Kentucky State University *Kentucky* M
Kentucky Wesleyan College *Kentucky* M
Kenyon College *Ohio* M
Keuka College *New York* M
Keystone College *Pennsylvania* M
King College *Tennessee* M
King's College *Pennsylvania* M
Kingsborough Community College of the City University of New York *New York* M
Kirkwood Community College *Iowa* M
Kishwaukee College *Illinois* M
Knox College *Illinois* M
Kutztown University of Pennsylvania *Pennsylvania* M
Kwantlen Polytechnic University *British Columbia* M & W
La Roche College *Pennsylvania* M
La Salle University *Pennsylvania* M
La Sierra University *California* M
Labette Community College *Kansas* M
Lackawanna College *Pennsylvania* M
Lafayette College *Pennsylvania* M
LaGrange College *Georgia* M
Lake Erie College *Ohio* M
Lake Forest College *Illinois* M
Lake Land College *Illinois* M
Lake Michigan College *Michigan* M
Lake-Sumter Community College *Florida* M
Lakeland College *Wisconsin* M
Lakeland Community College *Ohio* M
Lamar Community College *Colorado* M
Lamar University *Texas* M
Lambuth University *Tennessee* M
Lancaster Bible College & Graduate School *Pennsylvania* M
Lander University *South Carolina* M
Landmark College *Vermont* M
Lane College *Tennessee* M
Lane Community College *Oregon* M
Laney College *California* M
Laredo Community College *Texas* M
Lasell College *Massachusetts* M
Lawrence University *Wisconsin* M
Le Moyne College *New York* M
Lebanon Valley College *Pennsylvania* M
Lee University *Tennessee* M
Lehigh Carbon Community College *Pennsylvania* M
Lehigh University *Pennsylvania* M
Lehman College of the City University of New York *New York* M
LeMoyne-Owen College *Tennessee* M
Lenoir Community College *North Carolina* M
Lenoir-Rhyne University *North Carolina* M
Lesley University *Massachusetts* M
LeTourneau University *Texas* M
Lewis & Clark College *Oregon* M
Lewis and Clark Community College *Illinois* M
Lewis-Clark State College *Idaho* M
Lewis University *Illinois* M
Liberty University *Virginia* M
Limestone College *South Carolina* M
Lincoln Christian University *Illinois* M
Lincoln College *Illinois* M
Lincoln Land Community College *Illinois* M
Lincoln Memorial University *Tennessee* M
Lincoln University *Pennsylvania* M
Lincoln University *Missouri* M
Lindenwood University *Missouri* M
Lindsey Wilson College *Kentucky* M
Linfield College *Oregon* M
Linn-Benton Community College *Oregon* M
Lipscomb University *Tennessee* M
Lock Haven University of Pennsylvania *Pennsylvania* M
Lon Morris College *Texas* M
Long Beach City College *California* M
Long Island University, Brooklyn Campus *New York* M
Long Island University, C.W. Post Campus *New York* M
Longwood University *Virginia* M
Loras College *Iowa* M
Los Angeles Harbor College *California* M
Los Angeles Pierce College *California* M
Los Angeles Valley College *California* M
Los Medanos College *California* M
Louisburg College *North Carolina* M
Louisiana College *Louisiana* M
Louisiana State University and Agricultural and Mechanical College *Louisiana* M
Louisiana State University at Eunice *Louisiana* M
Louisiana State University in Shreveport *Louisiana* M
Louisiana Tech University *Louisiana* M
Lower Columbia College *Washington* M
Loyola Marymount University *California* M

M = Men; W = Women

Loyola University New Orleans *Louisiana* M
Lubbock Christian University *Texas* M
Lurleen B. Wallace Community College *Alabama* M
Luther College *Iowa* M
Luzerne County Community College *Pennsylvania* M
Lynchburg College *Virginia* M
Lyndon State College *Vermont* M
Lyon College *Arkansas* M
Macalester College *Minnesota* M
MacMurray College *Illinois* M
Macomb Community College *Michigan* M
Madison Area Technical College *Wisconsin* M
Madonna University *Michigan* M
Malone University *Ohio* M
Manchester College *Indiana* M
Manchester Community College *Connecticut* M
Manhattan Christian College *Kansas* M
Manhattan College *New York* M
Manhattanville College *New York* M
Mansfield University of Pennsylvania *Pennsylvania* M
Maranatha Baptist Bible College *Wisconsin* M
Marian University *Wisconsin* M
Marian University *Indiana* M
Marietta College *Ohio* M
Marist College *New York* M
Marquette University *Wisconsin* M
Mars Hill College *North Carolina* M
Marshall University *West Virginia* M
Marshalltown Community College *Iowa* M
Martin Luther College *Minnesota* M
Martin Methodist College *Tennessee* M
Maryville College *Tennessee* M
Maryville University of Saint Louis *Missouri* M
Marywood University *Pennsylvania* M
Massachusetts Bay Community College *Massachusetts* M
Massachusetts College of Liberal Arts *Massachusetts* M
Massachusetts Institute of Technology *Massachusetts* M
Massachusetts Maritime Academy *Massachusetts* M
Massasoit Community College *Massachusetts* M
The Master's College and Seminary *California* M
Mayville State University *North Dakota* M
McDaniel College *Maryland* M
McGill University *Quebec* M
McHenry County College *Illinois* M
McKendree University *Illinois* M
McLennan Community College *Texas* M
McMaster University *Ontario* M
McMurry University *Texas* M
McNeese State University *Louisiana* M
Medaille College *New York* M
Mendocino College *California* M
Menlo College *California* M
Merced College *California* M
Mercer County Community College *New Jersey* M
Mercer University *Georgia* M
Mercy College *New York* M
Mercyhurst College *Pennsylvania* M
Meridian Community College *Mississippi* M
Merrimack College *Massachusetts* M
Mesa Community College *Arizona* M
Mesa State College *Colorado* M
Mesabi Range Community and Technical College *Minnesota* M
Messiah College *Pennsylvania* M
Methodist University *North Carolina* M
Metropolitan Community College–Longview *Missouri* M
Metropolitan Community College–Maple Woods *Missouri* M
Metropolitan State College of Denver *Colorado* M
Miami Dade College *Florida* M
Miami University *Ohio* M & W
Miami University Hamilton *Ohio* M
Miami University–Middletown Campus *Ohio* M
Michigan State University *Michigan* M
Mid-America Christian University *Oklahoma* M
Mid-Continent University *Kentucky* M
Mid-Plains Community College *Nebraska* M
MidAmerica Nazarene University *Kansas* M
Middle Georgia College *Georgia* M
Middle Tennessee State University *Tennessee* M
Middlebury College *Vermont* M
Middlesex County College *New Jersey* M
Midland Lutheran College *Nebraska* M
Miles College *Alabama* M
Miles Community College *Montana* M
Millersville University of Pennsylvania *Pennsylvania* M
Milligan College *Tennessee* M
Millikin University *Illinois* M
Millsaps College *Mississippi* M
Milwaukee Area Technical College *Wisconsin* M
Milwaukee School of Engineering *Wisconsin* M
Mineral Area College *Missouri* M
Minnesota State Community and Technical College *Minnesota* M
Minnesota State University Mankato *Minnesota* M
Minnesota West Community and Technical College *Minnesota* M
Minot State University *North Dakota* M
Misericordia University *Pennsylvania* M
Mission College *California* M
Mississippi College *Mississippi* M
Mississippi Delta Community College *Mississippi* M
Mississippi Gulf Coast Community College *Mississippi* M
Mississippi State University *Mississippi* M
Mississippi Valley State University *Mississippi* M
Missouri Baptist University *Missouri* M
Missouri Southern State University *Missouri* M
Missouri State University *Missouri* M
Missouri University of Science and Technology *Missouri* M
Missouri Valley College *Missouri* M
Missouri Western State University *Missouri* M
Mitchell College *Connecticut* M
Modesto Junior College *California* M
Mohawk Valley Community College *New York* M
Molloy College *New York* M
Monmouth College *Illinois* M
Monmouth University *New Jersey* M
Monroe College (Bronx) *New York* M
Monroe College (New Rochelle) *New York* M
Monroe Community College *New York* M
Montana State University Billings *Montana* M
Montclair State University *New Jersey* M
Monterey Peninsula College *California* M
Montgomery College *Maryland* M
Montgomery County Community College *Pennsylvania* M
Montreat College *North Carolina* M
Moorpark College *California* M
Moraine Valley Community College *Illinois* M
Moravian College *Pennsylvania* M
Morehead State University *Kentucky* M
Morningside College *Iowa* M
Morris College *South Carolina* M
Morton College *Illinois* M
Motlow State Community College *Tennessee* M
Mott Community College *Michigan* M
Mount Aloysius College *Pennsylvania* M
Mt. Hood Community College *Oregon* M
Mount Ida College *Massachusetts* M
Mount Marty College *South Dakota* M
Mount Mercy College *Iowa* M
Mount Olive College *North Carolina* M
Mount Saint Mary College *New York* M
Mount St. Mary's University *Maryland* M
Mt. San Antonio College *California* M
Mt. San Jacinto College *California* M
Mount Vernon Nazarene University *Ohio* M
Muhlenberg College *Pennsylvania* M
Murray State College *Oklahoma* M
Murray State University *Kentucky* M
Muscatine Community College *Iowa* M
Muskegon Community College *Michigan* M
Muskingum University *Ohio* M
Napa Valley College *California* M
Nassau Community College *New York* M
Navarro College *Texas* M
Nebraska Wesleyan University *Nebraska* M
Neosho County Community College *Kansas* M
Neumann University *Pennsylvania* M
New England College *New Hampshire* M
New Jersey City University *New Jersey* M
New Jersey Institute of Technology *New Jersey* M
New Mexico Highlands University *New Mexico* M
New Mexico Junior College *New Mexico* M
New Mexico Military Institute *New Mexico* M
New Mexico State University *New Mexico* M
New York Institute of Technology *New York* M
New York University *New York* M
Newberry College *South Carolina* M
Newbury College *Massachusetts* M
Newman University *Kansas* M
NHTI, Concord's Community College *New Hampshire* M
Niagara County Community College *New York* M
Niagara University *New York* M
Nicholls State University *Louisiana* M
Nichols College *Massachusetts* M
Norfolk State University *Virginia* M
North Arkansas College *Arkansas* M
North Carolina Agricultural and Technical State University *North Carolina* M
North Carolina Central University *North Carolina* M
North Carolina State University *North Carolina* M
North Carolina Wesleyan College *North Carolina* M
North Central College *Illinois* M
North Central Missouri College *Missouri* M
North Central Texas College *Texas* M
North Central University *Minnesota* M
North Dakota State University *North Dakota* M
North Georgia College & State University *Georgia* M
North Greenville University *South Carolina* M
North Iowa Area Community College *Iowa* M
North Lake College *Texas* M
North Park University *Illinois* M
Northampton Community College *Pennsylvania* M
Northeast Mississippi Community College *Mississippi* M
Northeast Texas Community College *Texas* M
Northeastern Junior College *Colorado* M
Northeastern Oklahoma Agricultural and Mechanical College *Oklahoma* M
Northeastern State University *Oklahoma* M
Northeastern University *Massachusetts* M
Northern Essex Community College *Massachusetts* M
Northern Illinois University *Illinois* M
Northern Kentucky University *Kentucky* M
Northern Oklahoma College *Oklahoma* M
Northern State University *South Dakota* M
Northland College *Wisconsin* M
Northland Community and Technical College–Thief River Falls *Minnesota* M
Northwest Florida State College *Florida* M
Northwest Mississippi Community College *Mississippi* M
Northwest Missouri State University *Missouri* M
Northwest Nazarene University *Idaho* M
Northwest-Shoals Community College *Alabama* M
Northwestern College *Minnesota* M
Northwestern College *Iowa* M
Northwestern Oklahoma State University *Oklahoma* M
Northwestern State University of Louisiana *Louisiana* M
Northwestern University *Illinois* M
Northwood University *Michigan* M
Northwood University, Florida Campus *Florida* M
Northwood University, Texas Campus *Texas* M
Norwich University *Vermont* M
Notre Dame College *Ohio* M
Nova Southeastern University *Florida* M
Oakland City University *Indiana* M
Oakland University *Michigan* M
Oakton Community College *Illinois* M
Oberlin College *Ohio* M
Occidental College *California* M
Ocean County College *New Jersey* M
Odessa College *Texas* M
Oglethorpe University *Georgia* M
Ohio Christian University *Ohio* M
Ohio Dominican University *Ohio* M

M = Men; W = Women

Ohio Northern University *Ohio* M
The Ohio State University *Ohio* M
The Ohio State University at Lima *Ohio* M
Ohio University *Ohio* M
Ohio University–Zanesville *Ohio* M
Ohio Valley University *West Virginia* M
Ohio Wesleyan University *Ohio* M
Ohlone College *California* M
Oklahoma Baptist University *Oklahoma* M
Oklahoma Christian University *Oklahoma* M
Oklahoma City University *Oklahoma* M
Oklahoma Panhandle State University *Oklahoma* M
Oklahoma Wesleyan University *Oklahoma* M
Old Dominion University *Virginia* M
Olivet College *Michigan* M
Olivet Nazarene University *Illinois* M
Olympic College *Washington* M
Onondaga Community College *New York* M
Oral Roberts University *Oklahoma* M
Orange Coast College *California* M
Orange County Community College *New York* M
Oregon Institute of Technology *Oregon* M
Oregon State University *Oregon* M
Otero Junior College *Colorado* M
Ottawa University *Kansas* M
Otterbein University *Ohio* M
Ouachita Baptist University *Arkansas* M
Our Lady of the Lake University of San Antonio *Texas* M & W
Owens Community College *Ohio* M
Oxnard College *California* M
Pace University *New York* M
Pacific Lutheran University *Washington* M
Pacific University *Oregon* M
Paine College *Georgia* M
Palm Beach Atlantic University *Florida* M
Palm Beach State College *Florida* M
Palomar College *California* M
Panola College *Texas* M
Paradise Valley Community College *Arizona* M
Paris Junior College *Texas* M
Park University *Missouri* M
Parkland College *Illinois* M
Pasadena City College *California* M
Pasco-Hernando Community College *Florida* M
Patten University *California* M
Paul Quinn College *Texas* M
Pearl River Community College *Mississippi* M
Penn State Abington *Pennsylvania* M
Penn State Altoona *Pennsylvania* M
Penn State Beaver *Pennsylvania* M
Penn State Berks *Pennsylvania* M
Penn State Brandywine *Pennsylvania* M
Penn State Erie, The Behrend College *Pennsylvania* M
Penn State Fayette, The Eberly Campus *Pennsylvania* M
Penn State Greater Allegheny *Pennsylvania* M
Penn State Harrisburg *Pennsylvania* M
Penn State Hazleton *Pennsylvania* M
Penn State Lehigh Valley *Pennsylvania* M
Penn State New Kensington *Pennsylvania* M
Penn State University Park *Pennsylvania* M
Penn State Wilkes-Barre *Pennsylvania* M
Penn State Worthington Scranton *Pennsylvania* M
Pennsylvania College of Technology *Pennsylvania* M
Pensacola Junior College *Florida* M
Pepperdine University *California* M
Peru State College *Nebraska* M
Pfeiffer University *North Carolina* M
Philadelphia Biblical University *Pennsylvania* M
Philadelphia University *Pennsylvania* M
Phoenix College *Arizona* M
Piedmont College *Georgia* M
Pierce College at Puyallup *Washington* M
Pikeville College *Kentucky* M
Pima Community College *Arizona* M
Pitt Community College *North Carolina* M
Pittsburg State University *Kansas* M
Pitzer College *California* M
Plymouth State University *New Hampshire* M
Point Loma Nazarene University *California* M
Point Park University *Pennsylvania* M
Polk State College *Florida* M
Polytechnic Institute of NYU *New York* M
Pomona College *California* M
Porterville College *California* M
Portland State University *Oregon* M
Post University *Connecticut* M
Potomac State College of West Virginia University *West Virginia* M
Prairie State College *Illinois* M
Prairie View A&M University *Texas* M
Pratt Community College *Kansas* M
Presbyterian College *South Carolina* M
Presentation College *South Dakota* M
Prince George's Community College *Maryland* M
Princeton University *New Jersey* M
Principia College *Illinois* M
Purchase College, State University of New York *New York* M & W
Purdue University *Indiana* M
Purdue University North Central *Indiana* M
Queens College of the City University of New York *New York* M
Queen's University at Kingston *Ontario* M
Queensborough Community College of the City University of New York *New York* M
Quincy University *Illinois* M
Quinnipiac University *Connecticut* M
Radford University *Virginia* M
Ramapo College of New Jersey *New Jersey* M
Randolph-Macon College *Virginia* M
Ranger College *Texas* M
Raritan Valley Community College *New Jersey* M
Redlands Community College *Oklahoma* M
Reedley College *California* M
Regis University *Colorado* M
Reinhardt University *Georgia* M
Rend Lake College *Illinois* M
Rensselaer Polytechnic Institute *New York* M & W
Research College of Nursing *Missouri* M
Rhode Island College *Rhode Island* M
Rhodes College *Tennessee* M
Rice University *Texas* M
The Richard Stockton College of New Jersey *New Jersey* M
Richland College *Texas* M
Rider University *New Jersey* M
Ridgewater College *Minnesota* M
Rio Hondo College *California* M
Ripon College *Wisconsin* M
Riverland Community College *Minnesota* M
Riverside Community College District *California* M
Rivier College *New Hampshire* M
Roane State Community College *Tennessee* M
Roanoke College *Virginia* M
Robert Morris University *Pennsylvania* M
Robert Morris University Illinois *Illinois* M
Rochester College *Michigan* M
Rochester Community and Technical College *Minnesota* M
Rochester Institute of Technology *New York* M
Rock Valley College *Illinois* M
Rockford College *Illinois* M
Rockhurst University *Missouri* M
Rockingham Community College *North Carolina* M
Rockland Community College *New York* M
Roger Williams University *Rhode Island* M
Rogers State University *Oklahoma* M
Rollins College *Florida* M
Roosevelt University *Illinois* M
Rose-Hulman Institute of Technology *Indiana* M
Rose State College *Oklahoma* M
Rowan University *New Jersey* M
Roxbury Community College *Massachusetts* M
Rust College *Mississippi* M
Rutgers, The State University of New Jersey, Camden *New Jersey* M
Rutgers, The State University of New Jersey, New Brunswick *New Jersey* M
Rutgers, The State University of New Jersey, Newark *New Jersey* M
Sacramento City College *California* M
Sacred Heart University *Connecticut* M
Saddleback College *California* M
Saginaw Valley State University *Michigan* M
St. Ambrose University *Iowa* M
St. Andrews Presbyterian College *North Carolina* M
Saint Anselm College *New Hampshire* M
Saint Augustine's College *North Carolina* M
St. Bonaventure University *New York* M
St. Catharine College *Kentucky* M
Saint Charles Community College *Missouri* M
St. Clair County Community College *Michigan* M
St. Cloud State University *Minnesota* M
St. Cloud Technical College *Minnesota* M
St. Edward's University *Texas* M
St. Francis Xavier University *Nova Scotia* M
St. Gregory's University *Oklahoma* M
St. John Fisher College *New York* M
St. Johns River Community College *Florida* M
St. John's University *New York* M
Saint John's University *Minnesota* M
Saint Joseph's College *Indiana* M
Saint Joseph's College of Maine *Maine* M
Saint Joseph's University *Pennsylvania* M
St. Lawrence University *New York* M
Saint Leo University *Florida* M
St. Louis Christian College *Missouri* M
St. Louis Community College at Florissant Valley *Missouri* M
St. Louis Community College at Meramec *Missouri* M
Saint Louis University *Missouri* M
Saint Martin's University *Washington* M
Saint Mary's College of California *California* M
St. Mary's College of Maryland *Maryland* M
St. Mary's University *Texas* M
Saint Mary's University of Minnesota *Minnesota* M
Saint Michael's College *Vermont* M
St. Norbert College *Wisconsin* M
St. Olaf College *Minnesota* M
Saint Paul's College *Virginia* M
Saint Peter's College *New Jersey* M
St. Petersburg College *Florida* M
St. Thomas Aquinas College *New York* M
St. Thomas University *Florida* M
Saint Vincent College *Pennsylvania* M
Saint Xavier University *Illinois* M
Salem Community College *New Jersey* M
Salem International University *West Virginia* M
Salem State College *Massachusetts* M
Salisbury University *Maryland* M
Salt Lake Community College *Utah* M
Salve Regina University *Rhode Island* M
Sam Houston State University *Texas* M
Samford University *Alabama* M
San Diego Christian College *California* M
San Diego City College *California* M
San Diego Mesa College *California* M
San Diego State University *California* M
San Francisco State University *California* M
San Jacinto College District *Texas* M
San Joaquin Delta College *California* M
San Jose City College *California* M
San Jose State University *California* M
Santa Ana College *California* M
Santa Barbara City College *California* M
Santa Clara University *California* M
Santa Fe College *Florida* M
Santa Rosa Junior College *California* M
Sauk Valley Community College *Illinois* M
Savannah College of Art and Design *Georgia* M
Savannah State University *Georgia* M
Schenectady County Community College *New York* M
Schreiner University *Texas* M
Scottsdale Community College *Arizona* M
Seattle University *Washington* M & W
Seminole State College *Oklahoma* M
Seminole State College of Florida *Florida* M
Seton Hall University *New Jersey* M
Seton Hill University *Pennsylvania* M
Sewanee: The University of the South *Tennessee* M
Seward County Community College *Kansas* M
Shasta College *California* M
Shaw University *North Carolina* M
Shawnee Community College *Illinois* M
Shawnee State University *Ohio* M

M = Men; W = Women

Shelton State Community College *Alabama* M
Shenandoah University *Virginia* M
Shepherd University *West Virginia* M
Shippensburg University of Pennsylvania *Pennsylvania* M
Shoreline Community College *Washington* M
Shorter University *Georgia* M
Siena College *New York* M
Siena Heights University *Michigan* M
Sierra College *California* M
Simpson College *Iowa* M
Simpson University *California* M
Sinclair Community College *Ohio* M
Skagit Valley College *Washington* M
Skidmore College *New York* M
Skyline College *California* M
Slippery Rock University of Pennsylvania *Pennsylvania* M
Snead State Community College *Alabama* M
Solano Community College *California* M
Sonoma State University *California* M
South Dakota State University *South Dakota* M
South Florida Community College *Florida* M
South Georgia College *Georgia* M
South Mountain Community College *Arizona* M
South Suburban College *Illinois* M
Southeast Missouri State University *Missouri* M
Southeastern Community College *North Carolina* M
Southeastern Community College *Iowa* M
Southeastern Illinois College *Illinois* M
Southeastern Louisiana University *Louisiana* M
Southeastern Oklahoma State University *Oklahoma* M
Southeastern University *Florida* M
Southern Arkansas University–Magnolia *Arkansas* M
Southern Connecticut State University *Connecticut* M
Southern Illinois University Carbondale *Illinois* M
Southern Illinois University Edwardsville *Illinois* M
Southern Maine Community College *Maine* M
Southern Methodist University *Texas* M
Southern Nazarene University *Oklahoma* M
Southern New Hampshire University *New Hampshire* M
Southern Polytechnic State University *Georgia* M
Southern State Community College *Ohio* M
Southern University and Agricultural and Mechanical College *Louisiana* M
Southern Utah University *Utah* M
Southern Vermont College *Vermont* M
Southern Virginia University *Virginia* M
Southern Wesleyan University *South Carolina* M
Southwest Baptist University *Missouri* M
Southwest Minnesota State University *Minnesota* M
Southwest Mississippi Community College *Mississippi* M
Southwestern Assemblies of God University *Texas* M
Southwestern College *California* M
Southwestern Community College *Iowa* M
Southwestern Illinois College *Illinois* M
Southwestern Oklahoma State University *Oklahoma* M
Southwestern Oregon Community College *Oregon* M
Southwestern University *Texas* M
Spalding University *Kentucky* M
Spartanburg Methodist College *South Carolina* M
Spokane Community College *Washington* M
Spokane Falls Community College *Washington* M
Spoon River College *Illinois* M
Spring Arbor University *Michigan* M
Spring Hill College *Alabama* M
Springfield College *Massachusetts* M
Springfield College in Illinois *Illinois* M
Stanford University *California* M
Stanly Community College *North Carolina* M
State College of Florida Manatee-Sarasota *Florida* M
State University of New York at Binghamton *New York* M
State University of New York College of Agriculture and Technology at Cobleskill *New York* M
State University of New York College at Cortland *New York* M
State University of New York College at Geneseo *New York* M & W
State University of New York College at Old Westbury *New York* M
State University of New York College at Oneonta *New York* M
State University of New York College of Technology at Alfred *New York* M
State University of New York College of Technology at Canton *New York* M
State University of New York at Fredonia *New York* M
State University of New York Institute of Technology *New York* M
State University of New York Maritime College *New York* M
State University of New York at New Paltz *New York* M
State University of New York at Oswego *New York* M
State University of New York at Plattsburgh *New York* M
Stephen F. Austin State University *Texas* M
Sterling College *Kansas* M
Stetson University *Florida* M
Stevens Institute of Technology *New Jersey* M
Stevenson University *Maryland* M
Stillman College *Alabama* M
Stonehill College *Massachusetts* M
Stony Brook University, State University of New York *New York* M
Suffolk County Community College *New York* M
Suffolk University *Massachusetts* M
Sul Ross State University *Texas* M
Surry Community College *North Carolina* M
Susquehanna University *Pennsylvania* M
Sussex County Community College *New Jersey* M
Swarthmore College *Pennsylvania* M
Syracuse University *New York* M & W
Tabor College *Kansas* M
Tacoma Community College *Washington* M
Taft College *California* M
Tallahassee Community College *Florida* M
Tarleton State University *Texas* M
Taylor University *Indiana* M
Temple College *Texas* M
Temple University *Pennsylvania* M
Tennessee Technological University *Tennessee* M
Tennessee Temple University *Tennessee* M
Tennessee Wesleyan College *Tennessee* M
Texarkana College *Texas* M
Texas A&M International University *Texas* M & W
Texas A&M University *Texas* M
Texas A&M University–Corpus Christi *Texas* M
Texas A&M University–Kingsville *Texas* M
Texas Christian University *Texas* M
Texas College *Texas* M
Texas Lutheran University *Texas* M
Texas Southern University *Texas* M
Texas Southmost College *Texas* M
Texas State University–San Marcos *Texas* M
Texas Tech University *Texas* M
Texas Wesleyan University *Texas* M
Thiel College *Pennsylvania* M
Thomas College *Maine* M
Thomas More College *Kentucky* M
Thomas University *Georgia* M
Thompson Rivers University *British Columbia* M
Three Rivers Community College *Missouri* M
Tiffin University *Ohio* M
Toccoa Falls College *Georgia* M
Tompkins Cortland Community College *New York* M
Towson University *Maryland* M
Transylvania University *Kentucky* M
Treasure Valley Community College *Oregon* M
Trevecca Nazarene University *Tennessee* M
Trine University *Indiana* M
Trinidad State Junior College *Colorado* M
Trinity Bible College *North Dakota* M
Trinity Christian College *Illinois* M
Trinity College *Connecticut* M
Trinity International University *Illinois* M
Trinity University *Texas* M
Triton College *Illinois* M
Troy University *Alabama* M
Truett-McConnell College *Georgia* M
Truman State University *Missouri* M
Tufts University *Massachusetts* M
Tulane University *Louisiana* M
Tusculum College *Tennessee* M
Tuskegee University *Alabama* M
Tyler Junior College *Texas* M
Ulster County Community College *New York* M
Union College *New York* M
Union College *Kentucky* M
Union County College *New Jersey* M
Union University *Tennessee* M
United States Air Force Academy *Colorado* M
United States Coast Guard Academy *Connecticut* M
United States Merchant Marine Academy *New York* M
United States Military Academy *New York* M
United States Naval Academy *Maryland* M
Université Laval *Quebec* M
The University of Akron *Ohio* M
The University of Alabama *Alabama* M
The University of Alabama at Birmingham *Alabama* M
The University of Alabama in Huntsville *Alabama* M
University at Albany, State University of New York *New York* M
The University of Arizona *Arizona* M
University of Arkansas *Arkansas* M
University of Arkansas at Fort Smith *Arkansas* M
University of Arkansas at Little Rock *Arkansas* M
University of Arkansas at Monticello *Arkansas* M
University of Arkansas at Pine Bluff *Arkansas* M
University of Bridgeport *Connecticut* M
The University of British Columbia *British Columbia* M
University at Buffalo, the State University of New York *New York* M
University of California, Berkeley *California* M
University of California, Davis *California* M
University of California, Irvine *California* M
University of California, Los Angeles *California* M
University of California, Riverside *California* M
University of California, San Diego *California* M
University of California, Santa Barbara *California* M
University of California, Santa Cruz *California* M & W
University of Central Arkansas *Arkansas* M
University of Central Florida *Florida* M
University of Central Missouri *Missouri* M
University of Central Oklahoma *Oklahoma* M
University of Charleston *West Virginia* M
University of Chicago *Illinois* M
University of Cincinnati *Ohio* M
University of Cincinnati Clermont College *Ohio* M
University of Colorado at Boulder *Colorado* M
University of Colorado at Colorado Springs *Colorado* M
University of Connecticut *Connecticut* M
University of the Cumberlands *Kentucky* M
University of Dallas *Texas* M
University of Dayton *Ohio* M
University of Delaware *Delaware* M
University of Denver *Colorado* M
University of Dubuque *Iowa* M
University of Evansville *Indiana* M
The University of Findlay *Ohio* M
University of Florida *Florida* M
University of Georgia *Georgia* M
University of Guelph *Ontario* M
University of Hartford *Connecticut* M
University of Hawaii at Hilo *Hawaii* M
University of Hawaii at Manoa *Hawaii* M
University of Houston *Texas* M
University of Idaho *Idaho* M
University of Illinois at Chicago *Illinois* M
University of Illinois at Springfield *Illinois* M
University of Illinois at Urbana–Champaign *Illinois* M
University of the Incarnate Word *Texas* M

M = Men; W = Women

University of Indianapolis *Indiana* M
The University of Iowa *Iowa* M
The University of Kansas *Kansas* M
University of Kentucky *Kentucky* M
University of La Verne *California* M
University of Louisiana at Lafayette *Louisiana* M
University of Louisiana at Monroe *Louisiana* M
University of Louisville *Kentucky* M
University of Maine *Maine* M
University of Maine at Farmington *Maine* M
University of Maine at Presque Isle *Maine* M
University of Mary *North Dakota* M
University of Mary Hardin-Baylor *Texas* M
University of Mary Washington *Virginia* M
University of Maryland, Baltimore County *Maryland* M
University of Maryland, College Park *Maryland* M
University of Maryland Eastern Shore *Maryland* M
University of Massachusetts Amherst *Massachusetts* M
University of Massachusetts Boston *Massachusetts* M
University of Massachusetts Dartmouth *Massachusetts* M
University of Massachusetts Lowell *Massachusetts* M
University of Memphis *Tennessee* M
University of Miami *Florida* M
University of Michigan *Michigan* M
University of Minnesota, Crookston *Minnesota* M
University of Minnesota, Duluth *Minnesota* M
University of Minnesota, Morris *Minnesota* M
University of Minnesota, Twin Cities Campus *Minnesota* M
University of Mississippi *Mississippi* M
University of Missouri *Missouri* M
University of Missouri–St. Louis *Missouri* M
University of Mobile *Alabama* M
The University of Montana *Montana* M
University of Montevallo *Alabama* M
University of Mount Union *Ohio* M
University of Nebraska at Kearney *Nebraska* M
University of Nebraska at Omaha *Nebraska* M
University of Nebraska–Lincoln *Nebraska* M
University of Nevada, Las Vegas *Nevada* M
University of Nevada, Reno *Nevada* M
University of New Hampshire *New Hampshire* M
University of New Haven *Connecticut* M
University of New Mexico *New Mexico* M
University of New Orleans *Louisiana* M
University of North Alabama *Alabama* M
The University of North Carolina at Asheville *North Carolina* M
The University of North Carolina at Chapel Hill *North Carolina* M
The University of North Carolina at Charlotte *North Carolina* M
The University of North Carolina at Greensboro *North Carolina* M
The University of North Carolina at Pembroke *North Carolina* M
The University of North Carolina Wilmington *North Carolina* M
University of North Dakota *North Dakota* M
University of North Florida *Florida* M
University of North Texas *Texas* M
University of Northern Colorado *Colorado* M
University of Notre Dame *Indiana* M
University of Oklahoma *Oklahoma* M
University of Oregon *Oregon* M
University of Ottawa *Ontario* M & W
University of the Ozarks *Arkansas* M
University of the Pacific *California* M
University of Pennsylvania *Pennsylvania* M
University of Pittsburgh *Pennsylvania* M
University of Pittsburgh at Bradford *Pennsylvania* M
University of Pittsburgh at Greensburg *Pennsylvania* M
University of Pittsburgh at Johnstown *Pennsylvania* M
University of Portland *Oregon* M
University of Puerto Rico, Aguadilla University College *Puerto Rico* M
University of Puerto Rico at Arecibo *Puerto Rico* M
University of Puerto Rico at Bayamón *Puerto Rico* M
University of Puerto Rico at Humacao *Puerto Rico* M
University of Puerto Rico, Mayagüez Campus *Puerto Rico* M
University of Puerto Rico at Ponce *Puerto Rico* M
University of Puerto Rico, Río Piedras *Puerto Rico* M
University of Puget Sound *Washington* M
University of Redlands *California* M
University of Rhode Island *Rhode Island* M
University of Richmond *Virginia* M
University of Rio Grande *Ohio* M
University of Rochester *New York* M
University of Saint Francis *Indiana* M
University of St. Francis *Illinois* M
University of Saint Mary *Kansas* M
University of St. Thomas *Texas* M
University of St. Thomas *Minnesota* M
University of San Diego *California* M
University of San Francisco *California* M
University of Science and Arts of Oklahoma *Oklahoma* M
University of the Sciences in Philadelphia *Pennsylvania* M
The University of Scranton *Pennsylvania* M
University of Sioux Falls *South Dakota* M
University of South Alabama *Alabama* M
University of South Carolina *South Carolina* M
University of South Carolina Aiken *South Carolina* M
University of South Carolina Beaufort *South Carolina* M
University of South Carolina Lancaster *South Carolina* M
University of South Carolina Salkehatchie *South Carolina* M
University of South Carolina Upstate *South Carolina* M
University of South Florida *Florida* M
University of Southern California *California* M
University of Southern Indiana *Indiana* M
University of Southern Maine *Maine* M
University of Southern Mississippi *Mississippi* M
University of the Southwest *New Mexico* M
The University of Tampa *Florida* M
The University of Tennessee *Tennessee* M
The University of Tennessee at Martin *Tennessee* M
The University of Texas at Arlington *Texas* M
The University of Texas at Austin *Texas* M
The University of Texas at Brownsville *Texas* M
The University of Texas at Dallas *Texas* M
The University of Texas of the Permian Basin *Texas* M
The University of Texas at San Antonio *Texas* M
The University of Texas at Tyler *Texas* M
The University of Texas–Pan American *Texas* M
The University of Toledo *Ohio* M
University of Utah *Utah* M
University of Virginia *Virginia* M
The University of Virginia's College at Wise *Virginia* M
University of Washington *Washington* M
University of Waterloo *Ontario* M
The University of West Alabama *Alabama* M
University of West Florida *Florida* M
University of West Georgia *Georgia* M
The University of Western Ontario *Ontario* M
University of Wisconsin–La Crosse *Wisconsin* M
University of Wisconsin–Milwaukee *Wisconsin* M
University of Wisconsin–Oshkosh *Wisconsin* M
University of Wisconsin–Parkside *Wisconsin* M
University of Wisconsin–Platteville *Wisconsin* M
University of Wisconsin–River Falls *Wisconsin* M
University of Wisconsin–Stevens Point *Wisconsin* M
University of Wisconsin–Stout *Wisconsin* M
University of Wisconsin–Superior *Wisconsin* M
University of Wisconsin–Whitewater *Wisconsin* M
University of Wyoming *Wyoming* M
Upper Iowa University *Iowa* M
Urbana University *Ohio* M
Ursinus College *Pennsylvania* M
Utah State University *Utah* M
Utah State University–College of Eastern Utah *Utah* M
Utah Valley University *Utah* M
Utica College *New York* M
Valdosta State University *Georgia* M
Valley City State University *North Dakota* M
Valley Forge Christian College *Pennsylvania* M
Valparaiso University *Indiana* M
Vanderbilt University *Tennessee* M
Vanguard University of Southern California *California* M
Vassar College *New York* M
Ventura College *California* M
Vermilion Community College *Minnesota* M
Vermont Technical College *Vermont* M
Vernon College *Texas* M
Victor Valley College *California* M
Villanova University *Pennsylvania* M
Vincennes University *Indiana* M
Virginia Commonwealth University *Virginia* M
Virginia Intermont College *Virginia* M
Virginia Military Institute *Virginia* M
Virginia Polytechnic Institute and State University *Virginia* M
Virginia State University *Virginia* M
Virginia Wesleyan College *Virginia* M
Viterbo University *Wisconsin* M
Volunteer State Community College *Tennessee* M
Voorhees College *South Carolina* M
Wabash College *Indiana* M
Wagner College *New York* M
Wake Forest University *North Carolina* M
Waldorf College *Iowa* M
Walla Walla Community College *Washington* M
Wallace State Community College *Alabama* M
Walsh University *Ohio* M
Walters State Community College *Tennessee* M
Warner University *Florida* M
Wartburg College *Iowa* M
Washburn University *Kansas* M
Washington Adventist University *Maryland* M
Washington College *Maryland* M
Washington & Jefferson College *Pennsylvania* M
Washington and Lee University *Virginia* M
Washington State University *Washington* M
Washington University in St. Louis *Missouri* M
Waubonsee Community College *Illinois* M
Wayland Baptist University *Texas* M
Wayne State College *Nebraska* M
Wayne State University *Michigan* M
Waynesburg University *Pennsylvania* M
Weatherford College *Texas* M
Webber International University *Florida* M
Weber State University *Utah* M
Webster University *Missouri* M
Wenatchee Valley College *Washington* M
Wentworth Institute of Technology *Massachusetts* M
Wesley College *Delaware* M
Wesleyan University *Connecticut* M
West Chester University of Pennsylvania *Pennsylvania* M
West Hills Community College *California* M
West Liberty University *West Virginia* M
West Texas A&M University *Texas* M
West Virginia State University *West Virginia* M
West Virginia University *West Virginia* M
West Virginia University Institute of Technology *West Virginia* M
West Virginia Wesleyan College *West Virginia* M
Westchester Community College *New York* M
Western Carolina University *North Carolina* M
Western Connecticut State University *Connecticut* M
Western Illinois University *Illinois* M
Western Kentucky University *Kentucky* M
Western Michigan University *Michigan* M
Western Nebraska Community College *Nebraska* M
Western Nevada College *Nevada* M
Western New England College *Massachusetts* M
Western Oklahoma State College *Oklahoma* M
Western Oregon University *Oregon* M

M = Men; W = Women

Western State College of Colorado *Colorado* M
Western Technical College *Wisconsin* M
Western Texas College *Texas* M
Westfield State College *Massachusetts* M
Westminster College *Pennsylvania* M
Westminster College *Missouri* M
Westmont College *California* M
Westmoreland County Community College *Pennsylvania* M
Wharton County Junior College *Texas* M
Wheaton College *Massachusetts* M
Wheaton College *Illinois* M
Wheeling Jesuit University *West Virginia* M
Whitman College *Washington* M
Whittier College *California* M
Whitworth University *Washington* M
Wichita State University *Kansas* M
Widener University *Pennsylvania* M
Wiley College *Texas* M
Wilfrid Laurier University *Ontario* M
Wilkes Community College *North Carolina* M
Wilkes University *Pennsylvania* M
Willamette University *Oregon* M
William Carey University *Mississippi* M
William Jewell College *Missouri* M
William Paterson University of New Jersey *New Jersey* M
William Penn University *Iowa* M
William Woods University *Missouri* M
Williams Baptist College *Arkansas* M
Williams College *Massachusetts* M
The Williamson Free School of Mechanical Trades *Pennsylvania* M
Williston State College *North Dakota* M
Wilmington College *Ohio* M
Wilmington University *Delaware* M
Wingate University *North Carolina* M
Winona State University *Minnesota* M
Winthrop University *South Carolina* M
Wisconsin Lutheran College *Wisconsin* M
Wittenberg University *Ohio* M
Wofford College *South Carolina* M
Worcester Polytechnic Institute *Massachusetts* M
Worcester State College *Massachusetts* M
Wright State University *Ohio* M
Xavier University *Ohio* M
Yakima Valley Community College *Washington* M
Yale University *Connecticut* M
Yavapai College *Arizona* M
Yeshiva University *New York* M
York College *Nebraska* M
York College of the City University of New York *New York* M & W
York College of Pennsylvania *Pennsylvania* M
Young Harris College *Georgia* M
Youngstown State University *Ohio* M
Yuba College *California* M
Zane State College *Ohio* M

Basketball

Abilene Christian University *Texas* M & W
Academy of Art University *California* M & W
Acadia University *Nova Scotia* M & W
Adams State College *Colorado* M & W
Adelphi University *New York* M & W
Adirondack Community College *New York* M & W
Adrian College *Michigan* M & W
Agnes Scott College *Georgia* W
AIB College of Business *Iowa* W
Aiken Technical College *South Carolina* M
Alabama Agricultural and Mechanical University *Alabama* M & W
Alabama Southern Community College *Alabama* M & W
Alabama State University *Alabama* M & W
Albany College of Pharmacy and Health Sciences *New York* M & W
Albany State University *Georgia* M & W
Alberta College of Art & Design *Alberta* M & W
Albertus Magnus College *Connecticut* M & W
Albion College *Michigan* M & W
Albright College *Pennsylvania* M & W
Alcorn State University *Mississippi* M & W
Alderson-Broaddus College *West Virginia* M & W
Alfred University *New York* M & W
Alice Lloyd College *Kentucky* M & W
Allan Hancock College *California* M & W
Allegany College of Maryland *Maryland* M & W
Allegheny College *Pennsylvania* M & W
Allen Community College *Kansas* M & W
Allen University *South Carolina* M & W
Alma College *Michigan* M & W
Alpena Community College *Michigan* M & W
Alvernia University *Pennsylvania* M & W
Alverno College *Wisconsin* W
American International College *Massachusetts* M & W
American River College *California* M & W
American University *District of Columbia* M & W
American University of Puerto Rico *Puerto Rico* M & W
Amherst College *Massachusetts* M & W
Ancilla College *Indiana* M & W
Anderson University *South Carolina* M & W
Anderson University *Indiana* M & W
Andrew College *Georgia* W
Angelina College *Texas* M & W
Angelo State University *Texas* M & W
Anna Maria College *Massachusetts* M & W
Anne Arundel Community College *Maryland* M & W
Anoka-Ramsey Community College *Minnesota* M & W
Anoka-Ramsey Community College, Cambridge Campus *Minnesota* M & W
Antelope Valley College *California* M & W
Appalachian Bible College *West Virginia* M & W
Appalachian State University *North Carolina* M & W
Aquinas College *Michigan* M & W
Arcadia University *Pennsylvania* M & W
Arizona State University *Arizona* M & W
Arizona Western College *Arizona* M & W
Arkansas Baptist College *Arkansas* M & W
Arkansas State University - Jonesboro *Arkansas* M & W
Arkansas Tech University *Arkansas* M & W
Armstrong Atlantic State University *Georgia* M & W
The Art Institute of Boston at Lesley University *Massachusetts* M & W
Asbury University *Kentucky* M & W
Ashford University *Iowa* M & W
Ashland University *Ohio* M & W
Assumption College *Massachusetts* M & W
Atlanta Christian College *Georgia* M & W
Atlanta Metropolitan College *Georgia* M & W
Atlantic Cape Community College *New Jersey* M
Auburn University *Alabama* M & W
Auburn University Montgomery *Alabama* M & W
Augsburg College *Minnesota* M & W
Augusta State University *Georgia* M & W
Augustana College *South Dakota* M & W
Augustana College *Illinois* M & W
Aurora University *Illinois* M & W
Austin College *Texas* M & W
Austin Peay State University *Tennessee* M & W
Ave Maria University *Florida* M & W
Averett University *Virginia* M & W
Avila University *Missouri* M & W
Azusa Pacific University *California* M & W
Babson College *Massachusetts* M & W
Baker University *Kansas* M & W
Bakersfield College *California* M & W
Baldwin-Wallace College *Ohio* M & W
Ball State University *Indiana* M & W
Baltimore City Community College *Maryland* M & W
Baptist Bible College *Missouri* M & W
Baptist Bible College of Pennsylvania *Pennsylvania* M & W
Barclay College *Kansas* M & W
Bard College *New York* M & W
Bard College at Simon's Rock *Massachusetts* M & W
Barnard College *New York* W
Barry University *Florida* M & W
Barstow College *California* M
Barton College *North Carolina* M & W
Barton County Community College *Kansas* M & W
Bates College *Maine* M & W
Bay Path College *Massachusetts* W
Bayamón Central University *Puerto Rico* M
Baylor University *Texas* M & W
Becker College *Massachusetts* M & W
Belhaven University *Mississippi* M & W
Bellarmine University *Kentucky* M & W
Bellevue College *Washington* M & W
Bellevue University *Nebraska* M
Belmont Abbey College *North Carolina* M & W
Belmont University *Tennessee* M & W
Beloit College *Wisconsin* M & W
Bemidji State University *Minnesota* M & W
Benedict College *South Carolina* M & W
Benedictine College *Kansas* M & W
Benedictine University *Illinois* M & W
Bennett College for Women *North Carolina* W
Bennington College *Vermont* M & W
Bentley University *Massachusetts* M & W
Berea College *Kentucky* M & W
Bergen Community College *New Jersey* M & W
Bernard M. Baruch College of the City University of New York *New York* M & W
Berry College *Georgia* M & W
Bethany Bible College *New Brunswick* M & W
Bethany College *West Virginia* M & W
Bethany College *Kansas* M & W
Bethany Lutheran College *Minnesota* M & W
Bethany University *California* M & W
Bethel College *Kansas* M & W
Bethel College *Indiana* M & W
Bethel University *Tennessee* M & W
Bethel University *Minnesota* M & W
Bethune-Cookman University *Florida* M & W
Bevill State Community College *Alabama* M
Big Bend Community College *Washington* M & W
Biola University *California* M & W
Birmingham-Southern College *Alabama* M & W
Bishop State Community College *Alabama* M & W
Bishop's University *Quebec* M & W
Bismarck State College *North Dakota* M & W
Black Hawk College *Illinois* M & W
Black Hills State University *South Dakota* M & W
Blackburn College *Illinois* M & W
Blessing-Rieman College of Nursing *Illinois* M & W
Blinn College *Texas* M & W
Bloomfield College *New Jersey* M & W
Bloomsburg University of Pennsylvania *Pennsylvania* M & W
Blue Mountain College *Mississippi* M & W
Blue Mountain Community College *Oregon* M & W
Bluefield College *Virginia* M & W
Bluefield State College *West Virginia* M & W
Bluffton University *Ohio* M & W
Boise State University *Idaho* M & W
Borough of Manhattan Community College of the City University of New York *New York* M & W
Bossier Parish Community College *Louisiana* M
Boston College *Massachusetts* M & W
Boston University *Massachusetts* M & W
Bowdoin College *Maine* M & W
Bowie State University *Maryland* M & W
Bowling Green State University *Ohio* M & W
Bradley University *Illinois* M & W
Brandeis University *Massachusetts* M & W
Brandon University *Manitoba* M & W
Brenau University *Georgia* W
Brescia University *Kentucky* M & W
Brevard College *North Carolina* M & W
Brevard Community College *Florida* M & W
Brewton-Parker College *Georgia* M & W
Briar Cliff University *Iowa* M & W
Bridgewater College *Virginia* M & W
Bridgewater State College *Massachusetts* M & W
Briercrest College *Saskatchewan* M & W
Brigham Young University *Utah* M & W
Brigham Young University–Hawaii *Hawaii* M & W
Brock University *Ontario* M & W
Bronx Community College of the City University of New York *New York* M
Brookdale Community College *New Jersey* M & W
Brooklyn College of the City University of New York *New York* M & W
Broome Community College *New York* M & W
Broward College *Florida* M & W

M = Men; W = Women

Brown University *Rhode Island* M & W
Brunswick Community College *North Carolina* M & W
Bryan College *Tennessee* M & W
Bryant University *Rhode Island* M & W
Bryn Mawr College *Pennsylvania* W
Bucknell University *Pennsylvania* M & W
Bucks County Community College *Pennsylvania* M
Buena Vista University *Iowa* M & W
Buffalo State College, State University of New York *New York* M & W
Bunker Hill Community College *Massachusetts* M & W
Burlington County College *New Jersey* M & W
Butler Community College *Kansas* M & W
Butler County Community College *Pennsylvania* M
Butler University *Indiana* M & W
Butte College *California* M & W
Cabrillo College *California* M & W
Cabrini College *Pennsylvania* M & W
Caldwell College *New Jersey* M & W
Caldwell Community College and Technical Institute *North Carolina* M & W
California Baptist University *California* M & W
California Institute of Technology *California* M & W
California Lutheran University *California* M & W
California Maritime Academy *California* M & W
California Polytechnic State University, San Luis Obispo *California* M & W
California State Polytechnic University, Pomona *California* M & W
California State University, Bakersfield *California* M
California State University, Chico *California* M & W
California State University, Dominguez Hills *California* M & W
California State University, East Bay *California* M & W
California State University, Fresno *California* M & W
California State University, Fullerton *California* M & W
California State University, Long Beach *California* M & W
California State University, Los Angeles *California* M & W
California State University, Monterey Bay *California* M & W
California State University, Northridge *California* M & W
California State University, Sacramento *California* M & W
California State University, San Bernardino *California* M & W
California State University, Stanislaus *California* M & W
California University of Pennsylvania *Pennsylvania* M & W
Calumet College of Saint Joseph *Indiana* M & W
Calvary Bible College and Theological Seminary *Missouri* M & W
Calvin College *Michigan* M & W
Camden County College *New Jersey* M & W
Cameron University *Oklahoma* M & W
Campbell University *North Carolina* M & W
Campbellsville University *Kentucky* M & W
Canadian Mennonite University *Manitoba* M & W
Canisius College *New York* M & W
Cape Breton University *Nova Scotia* M & W
Cape Fear Community College *North Carolina* M
Capital University *Ohio* M & W
Cardinal Stritch University *Wisconsin* M & W
Caribbean University *Puerto Rico* M & W
Carl Albert State College *Oklahoma* M & W
Carl Sandburg College *Illinois* M & W
Carleton College *Minnesota* M & W
Carleton University *Ontario* M & W
Carlow University *Pennsylvania* W
Carnegie Mellon University *Pennsylvania* M & W
Carroll College *Montana* M & W
Carroll University *Wisconsin* M & W
Carson-Newman College *Tennessee* M & W
Carthage College *Wisconsin* M & W
Carver Bible College *Georgia* M
Case Western Reserve University *Ohio* M & W
Casper College *Wyoming* M & W
Castleton State College *Vermont* M & W
Catawba College *North Carolina* M & W
Catawba Valley Community College *North Carolina* M & W
The Catholic University of America *District of Columbia* M & W
Cayuga County Community College *New York* M & W
Cazenovia College *New York* M & W
Cecil College *Maryland* M & W
Cedar Crest College *Pennsylvania* W
Cedar Valley College *Texas* M
Cedarville University *Ohio* M & W
Centenary College *New Jersey* M & W
Centenary College of Louisiana *Louisiana* M & W
Central Arizona College *Arizona* M & W
Central Baptist College *Arkansas* M & W
Central Carolina Community College *North Carolina* M & W
Central Christian College of the Bible *Missouri* M & W
Central Christian College of Kansas *Kansas* M & W
Central College *Iowa* M & W
Central Community College–Columbus Campus *Nebraska* M
Central Connecticut State University *Connecticut* M & W
Central Florida Community College *Florida* M & W
Central Lakes College *Minnesota* M & W
Central Maine Community College *Maine* M & W
Central Methodist University *Missouri* M & W
Central Michigan University *Michigan* M & W
Central Ohio Technical College *Ohio* M & W
Central Pennsylvania College *Pennsylvania* M & W
Central State University *Ohio* M & W
Central Washington University *Washington* M & W
Central Wyoming College *Wyoming* M & W
Centralia College *Washington* M & W
Centre College *Kentucky* M & W
Cerritos College *California* M & W
Cerro Coso Community College *California* W
Chabot College *California* M & W
Chadron State College *Nebraska* M & W
Chaffey College *California* M & W
Chaminade University of Honolulu *Hawaii* M
Chapman University *California* M & W
Charleston Southern University *South Carolina* M & W
Chatham University *Pennsylvania* W
Chattanooga State Community College *Tennessee* M & W
Chemeketa Community College *Oregon* M & W
Chesapeake College *Maryland* M & W
Chestnut Hill College *Pennsylvania* M & W
Cheyney University of Pennsylvania *Pennsylvania* M & W
Chicago State University *Illinois* M & W
Chipola College *Florida* M & W
Chowan University *North Carolina* M & W
Christendom College *Virginia* M & W
Christian Brothers University *Tennessee* M & W
Christopher Newport University *Virginia* M & W
Cincinnati Christian University *Ohio* M & W
Cincinnati State Technical and Community College *Ohio* M & W
Cisco College *Texas* W
The Citadel, The Military College of South Carolina *South Carolina* M
Citrus College *California* M & W
City College of the City University of New York *New York* M & W
City College of San Francisco *California* M
City Colleges of Chicago, Harry S. Truman College *Illinois* M & W
City Colleges of Chicago, Kennedy-King College *Illinois* M & W
City Colleges of Chicago, Malcolm X College *Illinois* M & W
City Colleges of Chicago, Olive-Harvey College *Illinois* M
City Colleges of Chicago, Richard J. Daley College *Illinois* M & W
City Colleges of Chicago, Wilbur Wright College *Illinois* M & W
Clackamas Community College *Oregon* M & W
Claflin University *South Carolina* M & W
Claremont McKenna College *California* M & W
Clarendon College *Texas* M & W
Clarion University of Pennsylvania *Pennsylvania* M & W
Clark Atlanta University *Georgia* M & W
Clark College *Washington* M & W
Clark State Community College *Ohio* M & W
Clark University *Massachusetts* M & W
Clarke College *Iowa* M & W
Clarkson University *New York* M & W
Clayton State University *Georgia* M & W
Clearwater Christian College *Florida* M & W
Clemson University *South Carolina* M & W
Cleveland State Community College *Tennessee* M & W
Cleveland State University *Ohio* M & W
Clinton Community College *New York* M & W
Clinton Community College *Iowa* M
Cloud County Community College *Kansas* M & W
Coahoma Community College *Mississippi* M & W
Coastal Bend College *Texas* M
Coastal Carolina University *South Carolina* M & W
Cochise College *Arizona* M & W
Coe College *Iowa* M & W
Coffeyville Community College *Kansas* M & W
Coker College *South Carolina* M & W
Colby College *Maine* M & W
Colby Community College *Kansas* M & W
Colby-Sawyer College *New Hampshire* M & W
Colgate University *New York* M & W
College of Alameda *California* M & W
The College at Brockport, State University of New York *New York* M & W
College of the Canyons *California* M & W
College of Charleston *South Carolina* M & W
College of Coastal Georgia *Georgia* M
College of the Desert *California* M & W
College of DuPage *Illinois* M & W
College of the Holy Cross *Massachusetts* M & W
The College of Idaho *Idaho* M & W
College of Lake County *Illinois* M & W
College of Marin *California* M & W
College of Mount St. Joseph *Ohio* M & W
College of Mount Saint Vincent *New York* M & W
The College of New Jersey *New Jersey* M & W
The College of New Rochelle *New York* W
College of Notre Dame of Maryland *Maryland* W
College of the Ozarks *Missouri* M & W
College of the Redwoods *California* M & W
College of Saint Benedict *Minnesota* W
College of Saint Elizabeth *New Jersey* W
College of St. Joseph *Vermont* M & W
College of Saint Mary *Nebraska* W
The College of Saint Rose *New York* M & W
The College of St. Scholastica *Minnesota* M & W
College of San Mateo *California* M & W
College of the Sequoias *California* M & W
College of the Siskiyous *California* M & W
College of Southern Idaho *Idaho* M & W
College of Southern Maryland *Maryland* M & W
College of Staten Island of the City University of New York *New York* M & W
The College of William and Mary *Virginia* M & W
The College of Wooster *Ohio* M & W
Collin County Community College District *Texas* M & W
Colorado Christian University *Colorado* M & W
The Colorado College *Colorado* M & W
Colorado Northwestern Community College *Colorado* M & W
Colorado School of Mines *Colorado* M & W
Colorado State University *Colorado* M & W
Colorado State University–Pueblo *Colorado* M & W
Columbia Basin College *Washington* M & W
Columbia Bible College *British Columbia* M & W
Columbia College *South Carolina* W
Columbia College *Missouri* M & W
Columbia College *California* M
Columbia College Chicago *Illinois* M
Columbia-Greene Community College *New York* M

M = Men; W = Women

Columbia State Community College *Tennessee* M & W
Columbia University *New York* M & W
Columbia University, School of General Studies *New York* M & W
Columbus State Community College *Ohio* M & W
Columbus State University *Georgia* M & W
Community College of Allegheny County *Pennsylvania* M & W
The Community College of Baltimore County *Maryland* M & W
Community College of Beaver County *Pennsylvania* M
Community College of Philadelphia *Pennsylvania* M & W
Community College of Rhode Island *Rhode Island* M & W
Concord University *West Virginia* M & W
Concordia College *Minnesota* M & W
Concordia College–New York *New York* M & W
Concordia University *Quebec* M & W
Concordia University *Oregon* M & W
Concordia University *Michigan* M & W
Concordia University *California* M & W
Concordia University Chicago *Illinois* M & W
Concordia University College of Alberta *Alberta* M & W
Concordia University, Nebraska *Nebraska* M & W
Concordia University, St. Paul *Minnesota* M & W
Concordia University Texas *Texas* M & W
Concordia University Wisconsin *Wisconsin* M & W
Connecticut College *Connecticut* M & W
Connors State College *Oklahoma* M & W
Contra Costa College *California* M & W
Converse College *South Carolina* W
Cooper Union for the Advancement of Science and Art *New York* M & W
Copiah-Lincoln Community College *Mississippi* M & W
Coppin State University *Maryland* M & W
Corban University *Oregon* M & W
Cornell College *Iowa* M & W
Cornell University *New York* M & W
Cornerstone University *Michigan* M & W
Corning Community College *New York* M & W
Cosumnes River College *California* M & W
Cottey College *Missouri* W
County College of Morris *New Jersey* M & W
Covenant College *Georgia* M & W
Cowley County Community College and Area Vocational–Technical School *Kansas* M & W
Crandall University *New Brunswick* M & W
Creighton University *Nebraska* M & W
Crossroads College *Minnesota* M & W
Crowder College *Missouri* W
Crown College *Minnesota* M & W
Cuesta College *California* M & W
The Culinary Institute of America *New York* M & W
Culver-Stockton College *Missouri* M & W
Cumberland County College *New Jersey* M & W
Cumberland University *Tennessee* M & W
Curry College *Massachusetts* M & W
Cuyahoga Community College *Ohio* M
Cuyamaca College *California* M & W
Cypress College *California* M & W
Dabney S. Lancaster Community College *Virginia* M
Daemen College *New York* M & W
Dakota College at Bottineau *North Dakota* M & W
Dakota State University *South Dakota* M & W
Dakota Wesleyan University *South Dakota* M & W
Dalhousie University *Nova Scotia* M & W
Dallas Baptist University *Texas* M
Dallas Christian College *Texas* M & W
Dalton State College *Georgia* M & W
Dana College *Nebraska* M & W
Daniel Webster College *New Hampshire* M & W
Danville Area Community College *Illinois* M & W
Dartmouth College *New Hampshire* M & W
Darton College *Georgia* W
Davenport University *Michigan* M & W
Davidson College *North Carolina* M & W
Davis College *New York* M & W
Davis & Elkins College *West Virginia* M & W
Dawson Community College *Montana* M & W
Daytona State College *Florida* M & W
De Anza College *California* M & W
Dean College *Massachusetts* M & W
Defiance College *Ohio* M & W
Delaware County Community College *Pennsylvania* M & W
Delaware State University *Delaware* M & W
Delaware Technical & Community College, Stanton/Wilmington Campus *Delaware* M & W
Delaware Valley College *Pennsylvania* M & W
Delgado Community College *Louisiana* M & W
Delta College *Michigan* M & W
Delta State University *Mississippi* M & W
Denison University *Ohio* M & W
Denmark Technical College *South Carolina* M & W
DePaul University *Illinois* M & W
DePauw University *Indiana* M & W
Des Moines Area Community College *Iowa* M & W
DeSales University *Pennsylvania* M & W
Diablo Valley College *California* M & W
Dickinson College *Pennsylvania* M & W
Dickinson State University *North Dakota* M & W
Dillard University *Louisiana* M & W
Dixie State College of Utah *Utah* M & W
Doane College *Nebraska* M & W
Dodge City Community College *Kansas* M & W
Dominican College *New York* M & W
Dominican University *Illinois* M & W
Dominican University of California *California* M & W
Dordt College *Iowa* M & W
Dowling College *New York* M & W
Drake University *Iowa* M & W
Drew University *New Jersey* M & W
Drexel University *Pennsylvania* M & W
Drury University *Missouri* M & W
Duke University *North Carolina* M & W
Duquesne University *Pennsylvania* M & W
Dutchess Community College *New York* M & W
Dyersburg State Community College *Tennessee* M & W
D'Youville College *New York* M & W
Earlham College *Indiana* M & W
East Carolina University *North Carolina* M & W
East Central Community College *Mississippi* M & W
East Central University *Oklahoma* M & W
East Los Angeles College *California* M & W
East Mississippi Community College *Mississippi* M & W
East Stroudsburg University of Pennsylvania *Pennsylvania* M & W
East Tennessee State University *Tennessee* M & W
East Texas Baptist University *Texas* M & W
East-West University *Illinois* M
Eastern Arizona College *Arizona* M & W
Eastern Connecticut State University *Connecticut* M & W
Eastern Gateway Community College *Ohio* M & W
Eastern Illinois University *Illinois* M & W
Eastern Kentucky University *Kentucky* M & W
Eastern Maine Community College *Maine* M & W
Eastern Mennonite University *Virginia* M & W
Eastern Michigan University *Michigan* M & W
Eastern Nazarene College *Massachusetts* M & W
Eastern New Mexico University *New Mexico* M & W
Eastern Oklahoma State College *Oklahoma* M & W
Eastern Oregon University *Oregon* M & W
Eastern University *Pennsylvania* M & W
Eastern Washington University *Washington* M & W
Eastfield College *Texas* M
Ecclesia College *Arkansas* M & W
Eckerd College *Florida* M & W
Edgewood College *Wisconsin* M & W
Edinboro University of Pennsylvania *Pennsylvania* M & W
Edison State Community College *Ohio* M & W
Edmonds Community College *Washington* M & W
Edward Waters College *Florida* M & W
El Camino College *California* M & W
Elgin Community College *Illinois* M & W
Elizabeth City State University *North Carolina* M & W
Elizabethtown College *Pennsylvania* M & W
Ellsworth Community College *Iowa* M & W
Elmhurst College *Illinois* M & W
Elmira College *New York* M & W
Elms College *Massachusetts* M & W
Elon University *North Carolina* M & W
Embry-Riddle Aeronautical University *Florida* M
Emerson College *Massachusetts* M & W
Emmanuel College *Massachusetts* M & W
Emmanuel College *Georgia* M & W
Emmaus Bible College *Iowa* M & W
Emory & Henry College *Virginia* M & W
Emory University *Georgia* M & W
Emory University, Oxford College *Georgia* M
Emporia State University *Kansas* M & W
Endicott College *Massachusetts* M & W
Enterprise State Community College *Alabama* M & W
Erie Community College *New York* M & W
Erie Community College, North Campus *New York* M & W
Erie Community College, South Campus *New York* M & W
Erskine College *South Carolina* M & W
Essex County College *New Jersey* M & W
Eugene Bible College *Oregon* M
Eugenio María de Hostos Community College of the City University of New York *New York* M & W
Eureka College *Illinois* M & W
Evangel University *Missouri* M & W
Everett Community College *Washington* M & W
The Evergreen State College *Washington* M & W
Fairfield University *Connecticut* M & W
Fairleigh Dickinson University, College at Florham *New Jersey* M & W
Fairleigh Dickinson University, Metropolitan Campus *New Jersey* M & W
Fairmont State University *West Virginia* M & W
Faith Baptist Bible College and Theological Seminary *Iowa* M & W
Farmingdale State College *New York* M & W
Fashion Institute of Technology *New York* M
Faulkner University *Alabama* M & W
Fayetteville State University *North Carolina* M
Feather River College *California* M & W
Felician College *New Jersey* M & W
Ferris State University *Michigan* M & W
Ferrum College *Virginia* M & W
Finger Lakes Community College *New York* M & W
Finlandia University *Michigan* M & W
Fisher College *Massachusetts* M & W
Fisk University *Tennessee* M & W
Fitchburg State College *Massachusetts* M & W
Flagler College *Florida* M & W
Florida Agricultural and Mechanical University *Florida* M & W
Florida Atlantic University *Florida* M & W
Florida College *Florida* M
Florida Gulf Coast University *Florida* M & W
Florida Institute of Technology *Florida* M & W
Florida International University *Florida* M & W
Florida Memorial University *Florida* M & W
Florida Southern College *Florida* M & W
Florida State College at Jacksonville *Florida* M & W
Florida State University *Florida* M & W
Fontbonne University *Missouri* M & W
Foothill College *California* M & W
Fordham University *New York* M & W
Fort Belknap College *Montana* M & W
Fort Berthold Community College *North Dakota* M & W
Fort Hays State University *Kansas* M & W
Fort Lewis College *Colorado* M & W
Fort Scott Community College *Kansas* M & W
Fort Valley State University *Georgia* M & W
Fox Valley Technical College *Wisconsin* M & W
Framingham State College *Massachusetts* M & W
Francis Marion University *South Carolina* M & W
Franciscan University of Steubenville *Ohio* M & W
Frank Phillips College *Texas* M & W
Franklin College *Indiana* M & W
Franklin & Marshall College *Pennsylvania* M & W
Franklin Pierce University *New Hampshire* M & W
Frederick Community College *Maryland* M & W

M = Men; W = Women

Free Will Baptist Bible College *Tennessee* M & W
Freed-Hardeman University *Tennessee* M & W
Fresno City College *California* M & W
Fresno Pacific University *California* M & W
Friends University *Kansas* M & W
Frostburg State University *Maryland* M & W
Fullerton College *California* M & W
Fulton-Montgomery Community College *New York* M & W
Furman University *South Carolina* M & W
Gadsden State Community College *Alabama* M & W
Gallaudet University *District of Columbia* M & W
Gannon University *Pennsylvania* M & W
Garden City Community College *Kansas* M & W
Gardner-Webb University *North Carolina* M & W
Garrett College *Maryland* M & W
Gateway Community College *Connecticut* M & W
Gavilan College *California* M & W
Genesee Community College *New York* M & W
Geneva College *Pennsylvania* M & W
George Corley Wallace State Community College *Alabama* M
George Fox University *Oregon* M & W
George Mason University *Virginia* M & W
The George Washington University *District of Columbia* M & W
Georgetown College *Kentucky* M & W
Georgetown University *District of Columbia* M & W
Georgia College & State University *Georgia* M & W
Georgia Institute of Technology *Georgia* M & W
Georgia Perimeter College *Georgia* M & W
Georgia Southern University *Georgia* M & W
Georgia Southwestern State University *Georgia* M & W
Georgia State University *Georgia* M & W
Georgian Court University *New Jersey* W
Gettysburg College *Pennsylvania* M & W
Glen Oaks Community College *Michigan* M & W
Glendale Community College *California* M & W
Glendale Community College *Arizona* M & W
Glenville State College *West Virginia* M & W
Globe Institute of Technology *New York* M & W
Gloucester County College *New Jersey* M & W
Gogebic Community College *Michigan* M & W
Goldey-Beacom College *Delaware* M & W
Gonzaga University *Washington* M & W
Gordon College *Massachusetts* M & W
Goshen College *Indiana* M & W
Goucher College *Maryland* M & W
Grace Bible College *Michigan* M & W
Grace College *Indiana* M & W
Grace University *Nebraska* M & W
Graceland University *Iowa* M & W
Grambling State University *Louisiana* M & W
Grand Canyon University *Arizona* M & W
Grand Rapids Community College *Michigan* M & W
Grand Valley State University *Michigan* M & W
Grand View University *Iowa* M & W
Grays Harbor College *Washington* M & W
Grayson County College *Texas* M & W
Great Lakes Christian College *Michigan* M & W
Green Mountain College *Vermont* M & W
Green River Community College *Washington* M & W
Greensboro College *North Carolina* M & W
Greenville College *Illinois* M & W
Grinnell College *Iowa* M & W
Grossmont College *California* M & W
Grove City College *Pennsylvania* M & W
Guilford College *North Carolina* M & W
Guilford Technical Community College *North Carolina* M & W
Gulf Coast Community College *Florida* M & W
Gustavus Adolphus College *Minnesota* M & W
Gwynedd-Mercy College *Pennsylvania* M & W
Hagerstown Community College *Maryland* M & W
Hamilton College *New York* M & W
Hamline University *Minnesota* M & W
Hampden-Sydney College *Virginia* M
Hampshire College *Massachusetts* M & W
Hampton University *Virginia* M & W
Hannibal-LaGrange College *Missouri* M & W
Hanover College *Indiana* M & W
Harcum College *Pennsylvania* M & W
Hardin-Simmons University *Texas* M & W
Harding University *Arkansas* M & W
Harford Community College *Maryland* M & W
Harper College *Illinois* M & W
Harris-Stowe State University *Missouri* M & W
Harrisburg Area Community College *Pennsylvania* M & W
Hartnell College *California* M & W
Hartwick College *New York* M & W
Harvard University *Massachusetts* M & W
Harvey Mudd College *California* M & W
Haskell Indian Nations University *Kansas* M & W
Hastings College *Nebraska* M & W
Haverford College *Pennsylvania* M & W
Hawai'i Pacific University *Hawaii* M & W
Heidelberg University *Ohio* M & W
Henderson State University *Arkansas* M & W
Hendrix College *Arkansas* M & W
Henry Ford Community College *Michigan* M & W
Heritage Baptist College and Heritage Theological Seminary *Ontario* M & W
Herkimer County Community College *New York* M & W
Hesston College *Kansas* M & W
Hibbing Community College *Minnesota* M & W
High Point University *North Carolina* M & W
Highland Community College *Kansas* M & W
Highland Community College *Illinois* M & W
Highline Community College *Washington* M & W
Hilbert College *New York* M & W
Hill College of the Hill Junior College District *Texas* M & W
Hillsborough Community College *Florida* M & W
Hillsdale College *Michigan* M & W
Hillsdale Free Will Baptist College *Oklahoma* M & W
Hinds Community College *Mississippi* M & W
Hiram College *Ohio* M & W
Hobart and William Smith Colleges *New York* M & W
Hofstra University *New York* M & W
Hollins University *Virginia* W
Holmes Community College *Mississippi* M & W
Holy Cross College *Indiana* M
Holy Family University *Pennsylvania* M & W
Holy Names University *California* M & W
Holyoke Community College *Massachusetts* M & W
Hood College *Maryland* M & W
Hope College *Michigan* M & W
Hope International University *California* M & W
Houghton College *New York* M & W
Houston Baptist University *Texas* M & W
Howard College *Texas* M & W
Howard Community College *Maryland* M & W
Howard Payne University *Texas* M & W
Howard University *District of Columbia* M & W
Hudson Valley Community College *New York* M & W
Humboldt State University *California* M & W
Hunter College of the City University of New York *New York* M & W
Huntingdon College *Alabama* M & W
Huntington University *Indiana* M & W
Husson University *Maine* M & W
Huston-Tillotson University *Texas* M & W
Hutchinson Community College and Area Vocational School *Kansas* M & W
Idaho State University *Idaho* M & W
Illinois Central College *Illinois* M & W
Illinois Eastern Community Colleges, Lincoln Trail College *Illinois* M & W
Illinois Eastern Community Colleges, Olney Central College *Illinois* M & W
Illinois Eastern Community Colleges, Wabash Valley College *Illinois* M & W
Illinois State University *Illinois* M & W
Illinois Valley Community College *Illinois* M & W
Illinois Wesleyan University *Illinois* M & W
Immaculata University *Pennsylvania* W
Imperial Valley College *California* M & W
Independence Community College *Kansas* M & W
Indian Hills Community College *Iowa* M
Indian River State College *Florida* M & W
Indiana State University *Indiana* M & W
Indiana Tech *Indiana* M & W
Indiana University Bloomington *Indiana* M & W
Indiana University East *Indiana* M
Indiana University Northwest *Indiana* M & W
Indiana University of Pennsylvania *Pennsylvania* M & W
Indiana University South Bend *Indiana* M & W
Indiana University Southeast *Indiana* M & W
Indiana University–Purdue University Fort Wayne *Indiana* M & W
Indiana University–Purdue University Indianapolis *Indiana* M & W
Indiana Wesleyan University *Indiana* M & W
Inter American University of Puerto Rico, Aguadilla Campus *Puerto Rico* M & W
Inter American University of Puerto Rico, Arecibo Campus *Puerto Rico* M & W
Inter American University of Puerto Rico, Barranquitas Campus *Puerto Rico* M & W
Inter American University of Puerto Rico, Bayamón Campus *Puerto Rico* M & W
Inter American University of Puerto Rico, Guayama Campus *Puerto Rico* M & W
Inter American University of Puerto Rico, San Germán Campus *Puerto Rico* M & W
Iona College *New York* M & W
Iowa Central Community College *Iowa* M & W
Iowa Lakes Community College *Iowa* M & W
Iowa State University of Science and Technology *Iowa* M & W
Iowa Wesleyan College *Iowa* M & W
Iowa Western Community College *Iowa* M & W
Irvine Valley College *California* M & W
Itasca Community College *Minnesota* M & W
Itawamba Community College *Mississippi* M & W
Ithaca College *New York* M & W
Jackson Community College *Michigan* M & W
Jackson State Community College *Tennessee* M & W
Jackson State University *Mississippi* M & W
Jacksonville College *Texas* M & W
Jacksonville State University *Alabama* M & W
Jacksonville University *Florida* M & W
James A. Rhodes State College *Ohio* M & W
James H. Faulkner State Community College *Alabama* M & W
James Madison University *Virginia* M & W
Jamestown College *North Dakota* M & W
Jamestown Community College *New York* M & W
Jarvis Christian College *Texas* M & W
Jefferson College *Missouri* W
Jefferson College of Health Sciences *Virginia* M
Jefferson Community College *New York* M & W
Jefferson Davis Community College *Alabama* M
John A. Logan College *Illinois* M & W
John Brown University *Arkansas* M & W
John Carroll University *Ohio* M & W
John Jay College of Criminal Justice of the City University of New York *New York* M & W
John Wood Community College *Illinois* M & W
The Johns Hopkins University *Maryland* M & W
Johnson Bible College *Tennessee* M & W
Johnson C. Smith University *North Carolina* M & W
Johnson College *Pennsylvania* M & W
Johnson County Community College *Kansas* M & W
Johnson State College *Vermont* M & W
Johnson & Wales University *Rhode Island* M & W
Johnson & Wales University *Colorado* M & W
Joliet Junior College *Illinois* M & W
Jones County Junior College *Mississippi* M & W
Judson College *Alabama* W
Judson University *Illinois* M & W
Juniata College *Pennsylvania* M & W
Kalamazoo College *Michigan* M & W
Kalamazoo Valley Community College *Michigan* M & W
Kankakee Community College *Illinois* M & W
Kansas City Kansas Community College *Kansas* M & W
Kansas State University *Kansas* M & W
Kansas Wesleyan University *Kansas* M & W
Kaskaskia College *Illinois* M & W

M = Men; W = Women

Kean University *New Jersey* M & W
Keene State College *New Hampshire* M & W
Kellogg Community College *Michigan* M & W
Kennesaw State University *Georgia* M & W
Kent State University *Ohio* M & W
Kentucky Christian University *Kentucky* M & W
Kentucky State University *Kentucky* M & W
Kentucky Wesleyan College *Kentucky* M & W
Kenyon College *Ohio* M & W
Keuka College *New York* M & W
Keystone College *Pennsylvania* M & W
Kilgore College *Texas* M & W
King College *Tennessee* M & W
King's College *Pennsylvania* M & W
The King's University College *Alberta* M & W
Kingsborough Community College of the City University of *New York* M & W
Kirkwood Community College *Iowa* M & W
Kirtland Community College *Michigan* M & W
Kishwaukee College *Illinois* M & W
Knox College *Illinois* M & W
Kutztown University of Pennsylvania *Pennsylvania* M & W
Kuyper College *Michigan* M & W
Kwantlen Polytechnic University *British Columbia* M & W
La Roche College *Pennsylvania* M & W
La Salle University *Pennsylvania* M & W
La Sierra University *California* M & W
Labette Community College *Kansas* M & W
Lackawanna College *Pennsylvania* M & W
Lafayette College *Pennsylvania* M & W
LaGrange College *Georgia* M & W
Lake Erie College *Ohio* M & W
Lake Forest College *Illinois* M & W
Lake Land College *Illinois* M & W
Lake Michigan College *Michigan* M & W
Lake Region State College *North Dakota* M & W
Lake Superior State University *Michigan* M & W
Lakehead University *Ontario* M & W
Lakeland College *Wisconsin* M & W
Lakeland Community College *Ohio* M & W
Lamar Community College *Colorado* M
Lamar University *Texas* M & W
Lambuth University *Tennessee* M & W
Lancaster Bible College & Graduate School *Pennsylvania* M & W
Lander University *South Carolina* M & W
Landmark College *Vermont* M & W
Lane College *Tennessee* M & W
Lane Community College *Oregon* M & W
Langston University *Oklahoma* M & W
Lansing Community College *Michigan* M & W
Laramie County Community College *Wyoming* M
Lasell College *Massachusetts* M & W
Lassen Community College District *California* M & W
Laurentian University *Ontario* M & W
Lawrence University *Wisconsin* M & W
Lawson State Community College *Alabama* M & W
Le Moyne College *New York* M & W
Lebanon Valley College *Pennsylvania* M & W
Lee College *Texas* M
Lee University *Tennessee* M & W
Lees-McRae College *North Carolina* M & W
Lehigh Carbon Community College *Pennsylvania* M & W
Lehigh University *Pennsylvania* M & W
Lehman College of the City University of New York *New York* M & W
LeMoyne-Owen College *Tennessee* M & W
Lenoir Community College *North Carolina* M
Lenoir-Rhyne University *North Carolina* M & W
Lesley University *Massachusetts* M & W
LeTourneau University *Texas* M & W
Lewis & Clark College *Oregon* M & W
Lewis and Clark Community College *Illinois* M & W
Lewis-Clark State College *Idaho* M & W
Lewis University *Illinois* M & W
Liberty University *Virginia* M & W
Limestone College *South Carolina* M & W
Lincoln Christian University *Illinois* M & W
Lincoln College *Illinois* M & W
Lincoln Land Community College *Illinois* M & W
Lincoln Memorial University *Tennessee* M & W
Lincoln University *Pennsylvania* M & W
Lincoln University *Missouri* M & W
Lindenwood University *Missouri* M & W
Lindsey Wilson College *Kentucky* M & W
Linfield College *Oregon* M & W
Linn-Benton Community College *Oregon* M & W
Lipscomb University *Tennessee* M & W
Little Big Horn College *Montana* M & W
Livingstone College *North Carolina* M & W
Lock Haven University of Pennsylvania *Pennsylvania* M & W
Logan University–College of Chiropractic *Missouri* M & W
Lon Morris College *Texas* M & W
Long Beach City College *California* M & W
Long Island University, Brooklyn Campus *New York* M & W
Long Island University, C.W. Post Campus *New York* M & W
Longwood University *Virginia* M & W
Loras College *Iowa* M & W
Los Angeles City College *California* M
Los Angeles Harbor College *California* M
Los Angeles Pierce College *California* W
Los Angeles Southwest College *California* M & W
Los Angeles Trade-Technical College *California* M & W
Los Angeles Valley College *California* M & W
Los Medanos College *California* M & W
Louisburg College *North Carolina* M & W
Louisiana College *Louisiana* M & W
Louisiana State University and Agricultural and Mechanical College *Louisiana* M & W
Louisiana State University at Eunice *Louisiana* W
Louisiana State University in Shreveport *Louisiana* M & W
Louisiana Tech University *Louisiana* M & W
Lourdes College *Ohio* M
Lower Columbia College *Washington* M & W
Loyola Marymount University *California* M & W
Loyola University Chicago *Illinois* M & W
Loyola University Maryland *Maryland* M & W
Loyola University New Orleans *Louisiana* M & W
Lubbock Christian University *Texas* M & W
Lurleen B. Wallace Community College *Alabama* M & W
Luther College *Iowa* M & W
Luzerne County Community College *Pennsylvania* M & W
Lycoming College *Pennsylvania* M & W
Lynchburg College *Virginia* M & W
Lyndon State College *Vermont* M & W
Lyon College *Arkansas* M & W
Macalester College *Minnesota* M & W
MacMurray College *Illinois* M & W
Macomb Community College *Michigan* M
Madison Area Technical College *Wisconsin* M & W
Madonna University *Michigan* M & W
Maine Maritime Academy *Maine* M & W
Malone University *Ohio* M & W
Manchester College *Indiana* M & W
Manchester Community College *New Hampshire* M
Manchester Community College *Connecticut* M & W
Manhattan Christian College *Kansas* M & W
Manhattan College *New York* M & W
Manhattanville College *New York* M & W
Manor College *Pennsylvania* M & W
Mansfield University of Pennsylvania *Pennsylvania* M & W
Maranatha Baptist Bible College *Wisconsin* M & W
Marian University *Wisconsin* M & W
Marian University *Indiana* M & W
Marietta College *Ohio* M & W
Marion Technical College *Ohio* M & W
Marist College *New York* M & W
Marquette University *Wisconsin* M & W
Mars Hill College *North Carolina* M & W
Marshall University *West Virginia* M & W
Marshalltown Community College *Iowa* M & W
Martin Luther College *Minnesota* M & W
Martin Methodist College *Tennessee* M & W
Mary Baldwin College *Virginia* W
Marygrove College *Michigan* M & W
Marymount University *Virginia* M & W
Maryville College *Tennessee* M & W
Maryville University of Saint Louis *Missouri* M & W
Marywood University *Pennsylvania* M & W
Massachusetts Bay Community College *Massachusetts* M & W
Massachusetts College of Liberal Arts *Massachusetts* M & W
Massachusetts Institute of Technology *Massachusetts* M & W
Massasoit Community College *Massachusetts* M & W
The Master's College and Seminary *California* M & W
Mayland Community College *North Carolina* M
Mayville State University *North Dakota* M & W
McDaniel College *Maryland* M & W
McGill University *Quebec* M & W
McHenry County College *Illinois* M & W
McKendree University *Illinois* M & W
McLennan Community College *Texas* M & W
McMaster University *Ontario* M & W
McMurry University *Texas* M & W
McNeese State University *Louisiana* M & W
McPherson College *Kansas* M & W
Medaille College *New York* M & W
Medgar Evers College of the City University of New York *New York* M & W
Memorial University of Newfoundland *Newfoundland and Labrador* M & W
Mendocino College *California* M & W
Menlo College *California* M & W
Merced College *California* M & W
Mercer County Community College *New Jersey* M & W
Mercer University *Georgia* M & W
Mercy College *New York* M & W
Mercyhurst College *Pennsylvania* M & W
Meredith College *North Carolina* W
Meridian Community College *Mississippi* M & W
Merrimack College *Massachusetts* M & W
Merritt College *California* M & W
Mesa Community College *Arizona* M & W
Mesa State College *Colorado* M & W
Mesabi Range Community and Technical College *Minnesota* M & W
Messiah College *Pennsylvania* M & W
Methodist University *North Carolina* M & W
Metropolitan Community College–Penn Valley *Missouri* M & W
Metropolitan State College of Denver *Colorado* M & W
Miami Dade College *Florida* M & W
Miami University *Ohio* M & W
Miami University Hamilton *Ohio* M & W
Miami University–Middletown Campus *Ohio* M & W
Michigan State University *Michigan* M & W
Michigan Technological University *Michigan* M & W
Mid-America Christian University *Oklahoma* M & W
Mid-Atlantic Christian University *North Carolina* M & W
Mid-Continent University *Kentucky* M & W
Mid-Plains Community College *Nebraska* M & W
Mid-State Technical College *Wisconsin* M & W
MidAmerica Nazarene University *Kansas* M & W
Middle Georgia College *Georgia* M & W
Middle Tennessee State University *Tennessee* M & W
Middlebury College *Vermont* M & W
Middlesex County College *New Jersey* M & W
Midland Lutheran College *Nebraska* M & W
Midway College *Kentucky* W
Midwestern State University *Texas* M & W
Miles College *Alabama* M & W
Miles Community College *Montana* M & W
Millersville University of Pennsylvania *Pennsylvania* M & W
Milligan College *Tennessee* M & W
Millikin University *Illinois* M & W
Millsaps College *Mississippi* M & W
Milwaukee Area Technical College *Wisconsin* M & W

M = Men; W = Women

Milwaukee School of Engineering *Wisconsin* M & W
Mineral Area College *Missouri* M & W
Minnesota State Community and Technical College *Minnesota* M & W
Minnesota State University Mankato *Minnesota* M & W
Minnesota State University Moorhead *Minnesota* M & W
Minnesota West Community and Technical College *Minnesota* M & W
Minot State University *North Dakota* M & W
MiraCosta College *California* M
Misericordia University *Pennsylvania* M & W
Mission College *California* W
Mississippi College *Mississippi* M & W
Mississippi Delta Community College *Mississippi* M & W
Mississippi Gulf Coast Community College *Mississippi* M & W
Mississippi State University *Mississippi* M & W
Mississippi Valley State University *Mississippi* M & W
Missouri Baptist University *Missouri* M & W
Missouri Southern State University *Missouri* M & W
Missouri State University *Missouri* M & W
Missouri State University–West Plains *Missouri* M
Missouri University of Science and Technology *Missouri* M & W
Missouri Valley College *Missouri* M & W
Missouri Western State University *Missouri* M & W
Mitchell College *Connecticut* M & W
Moberly Area Community College *Missouri* M & W
Modesto Junior College *California* M & W
Mohawk Valley Community College *New York* M & W
Molloy College *New York* M & W
Monmouth College *Illinois* M & W
Monmouth University *New Jersey* M & W
Monroe College (Bronx) *New York* M & W
Monroe College (New Rochelle) *New York* M & W
Monroe Community College *New York* M & W
Montana State University *Montana* M & W
Montana State University Billings *Montana* M & W
Montana State University–Northern *Montana* M & W
Montana Tech of The University of Montana *Montana* M & W
Montclair State University *New Jersey* M & W
Monterey Peninsula College *California* M
Montgomery College *Maryland* M
Montgomery County Community College *Pennsylvania* M & W
Montreat College *North Carolina* M & W
Moody Bible Institute *Illinois* M & W
Moorpark College *California* M & W
Moraine Valley Community College *Illinois* M & W
Moravian College *Pennsylvania* M & W
Morehead State University *Kentucky* M & W
Morehouse College *Georgia* M
Morgan State University *Maryland* M & W
Morningside College *Iowa* M & W
Morris College *South Carolina* M & W
Morton College *Illinois* M & W
Motlow State Community College *Tennessee* M & W
Mott Community College *Michigan* M & W
Mount Allison University *New Brunswick* M & W
Mount Aloysius College *Pennsylvania* M & W
Mount Holyoke College *Massachusetts* W
Mt. Hood Community College *Oregon* M & W
Mount Ida College *Massachusetts* M & W
Mount Marty College *South Dakota* M & W
Mount Mary College *Wisconsin* W
Mount Mercy College *Iowa* M & W
Mount Olive College *North Carolina* M & W
Mount Saint Mary College *New York* M & W
Mount St. Mary's University *Maryland* M & W
Mount Saint Vincent University *Nova Scotia* M & W
Mt. San Antonio College *California* M & W
Mt. San Jacinto College *California* M & W
Mount Vernon Nazarene University *Ohio* M & W
Mountain State University *West Virginia* M
Muhlenberg College *Pennsylvania* M & W
Multnomah University *Oregon* M
Murray State College *Oklahoma* M & W
Murray State University *Kentucky* M & W
Muskegon Community College *Michigan* M & W
Muskingum University *Ohio* M & W
Napa Valley College *California* M & W
Nassau Community College *New York* M & W
Navarro College *Texas* M
Nazareth College of Rochester *New York* M & W
Nebraska Christian College *Nebraska* M & W
Nebraska College of Technical Agriculture *Nebraska* M & W
Nebraska Wesleyan University *Nebraska* M & W
Neosho County Community College *Kansas* M & W
Neumann University *Pennsylvania* M & W
New England College *New Hampshire* M & W
New Jersey City University *New Jersey* M & W
New Jersey Institute of Technology *New Jersey* M & W
New Mexico Highlands University *New Mexico* M & W
New Mexico Junior College *New Mexico* M & W
New Mexico Military Institute *New Mexico* M
New Mexico State University *New Mexico* M & W
New York City College of Technology of the City University of New York *New York* M & W
New York Institute of Technology *New York* M & W
New York University *New York* M & W
Newberry College *South Carolina* M & W
Newbury College *Massachusetts* M & W
Newman University *Kansas* M & W
NHTI, Concord's Community College *New Hampshire* M & W
Niagara County Community College *New York* M & W
Niagara University *New York* M & W
Nicholls State University *Louisiana* M & W
Nichols College *Massachusetts* M & W
Norfolk State University *Virginia* M & W
North Arkansas College *Arkansas* M & W
North Carolina Agricultural and Technical State University *North Carolina* M & W
North Carolina Central University *North Carolina* M & W
North Carolina State University *North Carolina* M & W
North Carolina Wesleyan College *North Carolina* M & W
North Central College *Illinois* M & W
North Central Missouri College *Missouri* M & W
North Central University *Minnesota* M & W
North Country Community College *New York* M & W
North Dakota State College of Science *North Dakota* M & W
North Dakota State University *North Dakota* M & W
North Georgia College & State University *Georgia* M & W
North Greenville University *South Carolina* M & W
North Idaho College *Idaho* M & W
North Iowa Area Community College *Iowa* M & W
North Lake College *Texas* M
North Park University *Illinois* M & W
North Seattle Community College *Washington* M & W
Northampton Community College *Pennsylvania* M & W
Northeast Community College *Nebraska* M & W
Northeast Mississippi Community College *Mississippi* M & W
Northeastern Junior College *Colorado* M & W
Northeastern Oklahoma Agricultural and Mechanical College *Oklahoma* M & W
Northeastern State University *Oklahoma* M & W
Northeastern University *Massachusetts* M & W
Northern Arizona University *Arizona* M & W
Northern Essex Community College *Massachusetts* M & W
Northern Illinois University *Illinois* M & W
Northern Kentucky University *Kentucky* M & W
Northern Oklahoma College *Oklahoma* M & W
Northern State University *South Dakota* M & W
Northland College *Wisconsin* M & W
Northland Community and Technical College–Thief River Falls *Minnesota* M & W
Northwest Christian University *Oregon* M & W
Northwest College *Wyoming* M & W
Northwest Florida State College *Florida* M & W
Northwest Indian College *Washington* M & W
Northwest Mississippi Community College *Mississippi* M & W
Northwest Missouri State University *Missouri* M & W
Northwest Nazarene University *Idaho* M & W
Northwest-Shoals Community College *Alabama* M & W
Northwest University *Washington* M & W
Northwestern College *Minnesota* M & W
Northwestern College *Iowa* M & W
Northwestern Oklahoma State University *Oklahoma* M & W
Northwestern State University of Louisiana *Louisiana* M & W
Northwestern University *Illinois* M & W
Northwood University *Michigan* M & W
Northwood University, Florida Campus *Florida* M & W
Norwich University *Vermont* M & W
Notre Dame College *Ohio* M & W
Notre Dame de Namur University *California* M & W
Nova Scotia Agricultural College *Nova Scotia* M & W
Nova Southeastern University *Florida* M & W
Oak Hills Christian College *Minnesota* M
Oakland City University *Indiana* M & W
Oakland Community College *Michigan* M & W
Oakland University *Michigan* M & W
Oakton Community College *Illinois* M & W
Oakwood University *Alabama* M & W
Oberlin College *Ohio* M & W
Occidental College *California* M & W
Ocean County College *New Jersey* M & W
Odessa College *Texas* M & W
Oglethorpe University *Georgia* M & W
Ohio Christian University *Ohio* M & W
Ohio Dominican University *Ohio* M & W
Ohio Northern University *Ohio* M & W
The Ohio State University *Ohio* M & W
The Ohio State University at Lima *Ohio* M & W
The Ohio State University at Marion *Ohio* M
Ohio University *Ohio* M & W
Ohio University–Eastern *Ohio* M & W
Ohio University–Zanesville *Ohio* M & W
Ohio Valley University *West Virginia* M & W
Ohio Wesleyan University *Ohio* M & W
Ohlone College *California* M & W
Okanagan College *British Columbia* M & W
Oklahoma Baptist University *Oklahoma* M & W
Oklahoma Christian University *Oklahoma* M & W
Oklahoma City University *Oklahoma* M & W
Oklahoma Panhandle State University *Oklahoma* M & W
Oklahoma Wesleyan University *Oklahoma* M & W
Old Dominion University *Virginia* M & W
Olivet College *Michigan* M & W
Olivet Nazarene University *Illinois* M & W
Olympic College *Washington* M & W
Onondaga Community College *New York* M & W
Oral Roberts University *Oklahoma* M & W
Orange Coast College *California* M & W
Orange County Community College *New York* M & W
Oregon Institute of Technology *Oregon* M & W
Oregon State University *Oregon* M & W
Otero Junior College *Colorado* M & W
Ottawa University *Kansas* M & W
Otterbein University *Ohio* M & W
Ouachita Baptist University *Arkansas* M & W
Owens Community College *Ohio* M & W
Oxnard College *California* M & W
Ozark Christian College *Missouri* M & W
Pace University *New York* M & W
Pacific Lutheran University *Washington* M & W
Pacific Union College *California* M & W
Pacific University *Oregon* M & W
Paine College *Georgia* M & W
Palm Beach Atlantic University *Florida* M & W

M = Men; W = Women

Palm Beach State College *Florida* M & W
Palomar College *California* M & W
Panola College *Texas* M & W
Paris Junior College *Texas* M & W
Park University *Missouri* M & W
Parkland College *Illinois* M & W
Pasadena City College *California* M & W
Pasco-Hernando Community College *Florida* M
Passaic County Community College *New Jersey* M & W
Patrick Henry College *Virginia* M & W
Paul Quinn College *Texas* M & W
Paul Smith's College *New York* M & W
Peace College *North Carolina* W
Pearl River Community College *Mississippi* M & W
Peninsula College *Washington* M & W
Penn State Abington *Pennsylvania* M & W
Penn State Altoona *Pennsylvania* M & W
Penn State Beaver *Pennsylvania* M
Penn State Berks *Pennsylvania* M & W
Penn State Brandywine *Pennsylvania* M & W
Penn State DuBois *Pennsylvania* M
Penn State Erie, The Behrend College *Pennsylvania* M & W
Penn State Fayette, The Eberly Campus *Pennsylvania* M
Penn State Greater Allegheny *Pennsylvania* M
Penn State Harrisburg *Pennsylvania* M & W
Penn State Hazleton *Pennsylvania* M & W
Penn State Lehigh Valley *Pennsylvania* M & W
Penn State Mont Alto *Pennsylvania* M & W
Penn State New Kensington *Pennsylvania* M & W
Penn State Schuylkill *Pennsylvania* M
Penn State University Park *Pennsylvania* M & W
Penn State Wilkes-Barre *Pennsylvania* M
Penn State Worthington Scranton *Pennsylvania* M & W
Pennsylvania College of Technology *Pennsylvania* M & W
Pensacola Junior College *Florida* M & W
Pepperdine University *California* M & W
Peru State College *Nebraska* M & W
Pfeiffer University *North Carolina* M & W
Philadelphia Biblical University *Pennsylvania* M & W
Philadelphia University *Pennsylvania* M & W
Philander Smith College *Arkansas* M & W
Phoenix College *Arizona* M & W
Piedmont Baptist College and Graduate School *North Carolina* M & W
Piedmont College *Georgia* M & W
Pierce College at Puyallup *Washington* M & W
Pikeville College *Kentucky* M & W
Pima Community College *Arizona* M & W
Pine Manor College *Massachusetts* W
Pitt Community College *North Carolina* M
Pittsburg State University *Kansas* M & W
Pitzer College *California* M & W
Plymouth State University *New Hampshire* M & W
Point Loma Nazarene University *California* M & W
Point Park University *Pennsylvania* M & W
Polk State College *Florida* M
Polytechnic Institute of NYU *New York* M & W
Polytechnic University of Puerto Rico *Puerto Rico* M & W
Pomona College *California* M & W
Pontifical Catholic University of Puerto Rico *Puerto Rico* M
Porterville College *California* M & W
Portland Community College *Oregon* M & W
Portland State University *Oregon* M & W
Post University *Connecticut* M & W
Potomac State College of West Virginia University *West Virginia* M & W
Prairie State College *Illinois* M & W
Prairie View A&M University *Texas* M & W
Pratt Community College *Kansas* M & W
Pratt Institute *New York* M
Presbyterian College *South Carolina* M & W
Presentation College *South Dakota* M & W
Prince George's Community College *Maryland* M & W
Princeton University *New Jersey* M & W
Principia College *Illinois* M & W
Providence College *Rhode Island* M & W
Providence College and Theological Seminary *Manitoba* M & W
Purchase College, State University of New York *New York* M & W
Purdue University *Indiana* M & W
Purdue University Calumet *Indiana* M & W
Purdue University North Central *Indiana* M
Queens College of the City University of New York *New York* M & W
Queens University of Charlotte *North Carolina* M & W
Queen's University at Kingston *Ontario* M & W
Queensborough Community College of the City University of New York *New York* M & W
Quincy University *Illinois* M & W
Quinnipiac University *Connecticut* M & W
Quinsigamond Community College *Massachusetts* M & W
Radford University *Virginia* M & W
Rainy River Community College *Minnesota* M & W
Ramapo College of New Jersey *New Jersey* M & W
Randolph College *Virginia* M & W
Randolph-Macon College *Virginia* M & W
Ranger College *Texas* M & W
Raritan Valley Community College *New Jersey* M & W
Reading Area Community College *Pennsylvania* M & W
Redeemer University College *Ontario* M & W
Redlands Community College *Oklahoma* M & W
Reed College *Oregon* M
Reedley College *California* M & W
Regis College *Massachusetts* M & W
Regis University *Colorado* M & W
Reinhardt University *Georgia* M & W
Rend Lake College *Illinois* M & W
Rensselaer Polytechnic Institute *New York* M & W
Research College of Nursing *Missouri* M & W
Rhode Island College *Rhode Island* M & W
Rhodes College *Tennessee* M & W
Rice University *Texas* M & W
The Richard Stockton College of New Jersey *New Jersey* M & W
Richland College *Texas* M
Rider University *New Jersey* M & W
Ridgewater College *Minnesota* M & W
Rio Hondo College *California* M & W
Ripon College *Wisconsin* M & W
Riverland Community College *Minnesota* M & W
Riverside Community College District *California* M & W
Rivier College *New Hampshire* M & W
Roane State Community College *Tennessee* M & W
Roanoke College *Virginia* M & W
Robert Morris University *Pennsylvania* M & W
Robert Morris University Illinois *Illinois* M & W
Roberts Wesleyan College *New York* M & W
Rochester College *Michigan* M & W
Rochester Community and Technical College *Minnesota* M & W
Rochester Institute of Technology *New York* M & W
Rock Valley College *Illinois* M & W
Rockford College *Illinois* M & W
Rockhurst University *Missouri* M & W
Rockingham Community College *North Carolina* M
Rockland Community College *New York* M & W
Rocky Mountain College *Alberta* M & W
Rocky Mountain College *Montana* M & W
Roger Williams University *Rhode Island* M & W
Rogers State University *Oklahoma* M & W
Rollins College *Florida* M & W
Roosevelt University *Illinois* M & W
Rose-Hulman Institute of Technology *Indiana* M & W
Rose State College *Oklahoma* M & W
Rosemont College *Pennsylvania* M & W
Rowan University *New Jersey* M & W
Roxbury Community College *Massachusetts* M & W
Royal Military College of Canada *Ontario* M & W
Russell Sage College *New York* W
Rust College *Mississippi* M & W
Rutgers, The State University of New Jersey, Camden *New Jersey* M & W
Rutgers, The State University of New Jersey, New Brunswick *New Jersey* M & W
Rutgers, The State University of New Jersey, Newark *New Jersey* M & W
Ryerson University *Ontario* M & W
Sacramento City College *California* M & W
Sacred Heart University *Connecticut* M & W
Saddleback College *California* M & W
Sage College of Albany *New York* M & W
Saginaw Valley State University *Michigan* M & W
St. Ambrose University *Iowa* M & W
St. Andrews Presbyterian College *North Carolina* M & W
Saint Anselm College *New Hampshire* M & W
Saint Augustine's College *North Carolina* M & W
St. Bonaventure University *New York* M & W
St. Catharine College *Kentucky* M & W
St. Catherine University *Minnesota* W
St. Clair County Community College *Michigan* M & W
St. Cloud State University *Minnesota* M & W
St. Cloud Technical College *Minnesota* M & W
St. Edward's University *Texas* M & W
St. Francis College *New York* M & W
Saint Francis University *Pennsylvania* M & W
St. Francis Xavier University *Nova Scotia* M & W
St. Gregory's University *Oklahoma* M & W
St. John Fisher College *New York* M & W
St. Johns River Community College *Florida* M
St. John's University *New York* M & W
Saint John's University *Minnesota* M
Saint Joseph College *Connecticut* W
Saint Joseph's College *Indiana* M & W
St. Joseph's College, Long Island Campus *New York* M & W
Saint Joseph's College of Maine *Maine* M & W
St. Joseph's College, New York *New York* M & W
Saint Joseph's University *Pennsylvania* M & W
St. Lawrence University *New York* M & W
Saint Leo University *Florida* M & W
St. Louis Christian College *Missouri* M & W
St. Louis College of Pharmacy *Missouri* M & W
St. Louis Community College at Florissant Valley *Missouri* M & W
St. Louis Community College at Forest Park *Missouri* M & W
St. Louis Community College at Meramec *Missouri* M & W
Saint Louis University *Missouri* M & W
Saint Martin's University *Washington* M & W
Saint Mary-of-the-Woods College *Indiana* W
Saint Mary's College *Indiana* W
Saint Mary's College of California *California* M & W
St. Mary's College of Maryland *Maryland* M & W
Saint Mary's University *Nova Scotia* M & W
St. Mary's University *Texas* M & W
Saint Mary's University of Minnesota *Minnesota* M & W
Saint Michael's College *Vermont* M & W
St. Norbert College *Wisconsin* M & W
St. Olaf College *Minnesota* M & W
Saint Paul's College *Virginia* M & W
Saint Peter's College *New Jersey* M & W
St. Petersburg College *Florida* M & W
St. Thomas Aquinas College *New York* M & W
St. Thomas University *New Brunswick* M & W
Saint Vincent College *Pennsylvania* M & W
Saint Xavier University *Illinois* M
Salem College *North Carolina* W
Salem Community College *New Jersey* M & W
Salem International University *West Virginia* M & W
Salem State College *Massachusetts* M & W
Salisbury University *Maryland* M & W
Salt Lake Community College *Utah* M & W
Salve Regina University *Rhode Island* M & W
Sam Houston State University *Texas* M & W
Samford University *Alabama* M & W
San Bernardino Valley College *California* M & W
San Diego Christian College *California* M & W
San Diego City College *California* M & W
San Diego Mesa College *California* M & W

M = Men; W = Women

San Diego Miramar College *California* M
San Diego State University *California* M & W
San Francisco State University *California* M & W
San Jacinto College District *Texas* M
San Joaquin Delta College *California* M & W
San Jose City College *California* M & W
San Jose State University *California* M & W
Sandhills Community College *North Carolina* M
Santa Ana College *California* M & W
Santa Barbara City College *California* M & W
Santa Clara University *California* M & W
Santa Fe College *Florida* M & W
Santa Monica College *California* M & W
Santa Rosa Junior College *California* M & W
Sarah Lawrence College *New York* M
Sauk Valley Community College *Illinois* M & W
Savannah State University *Georgia* M & W
Schenectady County Community College *New York* M & W
Schoolcraft College *Michigan* M & W
Schreiner University *Texas* M & W
Scottsdale Community College *Arizona* M & W
Scripps College *California* W
Seattle Pacific University *Washington* M & W
Seattle University *Washington* M & W
Seminole State College *Oklahoma* M & W
Seton Hall University *New Jersey* M & W
Seton Hill University *Pennsylvania* M & W
Sewanee: The University of the South *Tennessee* M & W
Seward County Community College *Kansas* M & W
Shasta College *California* M & W
Shaw University *North Carolina* M & W
Shawnee Community College *Illinois* M & W
Shawnee State University *Ohio* M & W
Shelton State Community College *Alabama* M & W
Shenandoah University *Virginia* M & W
Shepherd University *West Virginia* M & W
Sheridan College *Wyoming* M & W
Shippensburg University of Pennsylvania *Pennsylvania* M & W
Shoreline Community College *Washington* M & W
Shorter University *Georgia* M & W
Siena College *New York* M & W
Siena Heights University *Michigan* M & W
Sierra College *California* M & W
Silver Lake College *Wisconsin* M & W
Simmons College *Massachusetts* W
Simon Fraser University *British Columbia* M & W
Simpson College *Iowa* M & W
Simpson University *California* M & W
Sinclair Community College *Ohio* M & W
Sitting Bull College *North Dakota* M & W
Skagit Valley College *Washington* M & W
Skidmore College *New York* M & W
Skyline College *California* M
Slippery Rock University of Pennsylvania *Pennsylvania* M & W
Smith College *Massachusetts* W
Snead State Community College *Alabama* M & W
Snow College *Utah* M & W
Solano Community College *California* M & W
Sonoma State University *California* M & W
South Carolina State University *South Carolina* M & W
South Dakota School of Mines and Technology *South Dakota* M & W
South Dakota State University *South Dakota* M & W
South Mountain Community College *Arizona* M & W
South Plains College *Texas* M & W
South Puget Sound Community College *Washington* M & W
South Suburban College *Illinois* M & W
Southeast Community College, Beatrice Campus *Nebraska* M & W
Southeast Missouri State University *Missouri* M & W
Southeastern Bible College *Alabama* M
Southeastern Community College *Iowa* M
Southeastern Illinois College *Illinois* M & W
Southeastern Louisiana University *Louisiana* M & W
Southeastern Oklahoma State University *Oklahoma* M & W
Southeastern University *Florida* M & W
Southern Alberta Institute of Technology *Alberta* M & W
Southern Arkansas University–Magnolia *Arkansas* M & W
Southern Baptist Theological Seminary *Kentucky* M
Southern Connecticut State University *Connecticut* M & W
Southern Illinois University Carbondale *Illinois* M & W
Southern Illinois University Edwardsville *Illinois* M & W
Southern Maine Community College *Maine* M
Southern Methodist University *Texas* M & W
Southern Nazarene University *Oklahoma* M & W
Southern New Hampshire University *New Hampshire* M & W
Southern Oregon University *Oregon* M & W
Southern Polytechnic State University *Georgia* M & W
Southern State Community College *Ohio* M & W
Southern University and Agricultural and Mechanical College *Louisiana* M & W
Southern University at New Orleans *Louisiana* M & W
Southern University at Shreveport *Louisiana* M & W
Southern Utah University *Utah* M & W
Southern Vermont College *Vermont* M & W
Southern Virginia University *Virginia* M & W
Southern Wesleyan University *South Carolina* M & W
Southwest Baptist University *Missouri* M & W
Southwest Minnesota State University *Minnesota* M & W
Southwest Mississippi Community College *Mississippi* M & W
Southwest Texas Junior College *Texas* M & W
Southwestern Assemblies of God University *Texas* M & W
Southwestern Christian College *Texas* M & W
Southwestern Christian University *Oklahoma* M
Southwestern College *Kansas* M & W
Southwestern College *California* M & W
Southwestern College *Arizona* M & W
Southwestern Community College *Iowa* M & W
Southwestern Illinois College *Illinois* M & W
Southwestern Oklahoma State University *Oklahoma* M & W
Southwestern Oregon Community College *Oregon* M & W
Southwestern University *Texas* M & W
Spalding University *Kentucky* M & W
Spartanburg Methodist College *South Carolina* M & W
Spelman College *Georgia* W
Spokane Community College *Washington* M & W
Spokane Falls Community College *Washington* M & W
Spoon River College *Illinois* M & W
Spring Arbor University *Michigan* M & W
Spring Hill College *Alabama* M & W
Springfield College *Massachusetts* M & W
Springfield Technical Community College *Massachusetts* M & W
Stanford University *California* M & W
State College of Florida Manatee-Sarasota *Florida* M
State Fair Community College *Missouri* M & W
State University of New York at Binghamton *New York* M & W
State University of New York College of Agriculture and Technology at Cobleskill *New York* M & W
State University of New York College of Agriculture and Technology at Morrisville *New York* M & W
State University of New York College at Cortland *New York* M & W
State University of New York College at Geneseo *New York* M & W
State University of New York College at Old Westbury *New York* M & W
State University of New York College at Oneonta *New York* M & W
State University of New York College at Potsdam *New York* M & W
State University of New York College of Technology at Alfred *New York* M & W
State University of New York College of Technology at Canton *New York* M & W
State University of New York College of Technology at Delhi *New York* M & W
State University of New York at Fredonia *New York* M & W
State University of New York Institute of Technology *New York* M & W
State University of New York Maritime College *New York* M & W
State University of New York at New Paltz *New York* M & W
State University of New York at Oswego *New York* M & W
State University of New York at Plattsburgh *New York* M & W
Stephen F. Austin State University *Texas* M & W
Stephens College *Missouri* W
Sterling College *Kansas* M & W
Stetson University *Florida* M & W
Stevens Institute of Technology *New Jersey* M & W
Stevenson University *Maryland* M & W
Stillman College *Alabama* M & W
Stonehill College *Massachusetts* M & W
Stony Brook University, State University of New York *New York* M & W
Suffolk County Community College *New York* M & W
Suffolk University *Massachusetts* M & W
Sul Ross State University *Texas* M & W
Sullivan County Community College *New York* M & W
Surry Community College *North Carolina* M
Susquehanna University *Pennsylvania* M & W
Sussex County Community College *New Jersey* M
Swarthmore College *Pennsylvania* M & W
Syracuse University *New York* M & W
Tabor College *Kansas* M & W
Tacoma Community College *Washington* M & W
Taft College *California* W
Tallahassee Community College *Florida* M & W
Tarleton State University *Texas* M & W
Taylor University *Indiana* M & W
TCI–The College of Technology *New York* M & W
Temple Baptist College *Ohio* M & W
Temple College *Texas* M & W
Temple University *Pennsylvania* M & W
Tennessee State University *Tennessee* M & W
Tennessee Technological University *Tennessee* M & W
Tennessee Temple University *Tennessee* M & W
Tennessee Wesleyan College *Tennessee* M & W
Texas A&M International University *Texas* M & W
Texas A&M University *Texas* M & W
Texas A&M University–Commerce *Texas* M & W
Texas A&M University–Corpus Christi *Texas* M & W
Texas A&M University–Kingsville *Texas* M & W
Texas Christian University *Texas* M & W
Texas College *Texas* M & W
Texas Lutheran University *Texas* M & W
Texas Southern University *Texas* M & W
Texas State University–San Marcos *Texas* M & W
Texas Tech University *Texas* M & W
Texas Wesleyan University *Texas* M & W
Texas Woman's University *Texas* W
Thaddeus Stevens College of Technology *Pennsylvania* M
Thiel College *Pennsylvania* M & W
Thomas College *Maine* M & W
Thomas More College *Kentucky* M & W
Thompson Rivers University *British Columbia* M & W
Three Rivers Community College *Missouri* M & W
Tiffin University *Ohio* M & W
Toccoa Falls College *Georgia* M & W
Tompkins Cortland Community College *New York* M & W
Tougaloo College *Mississippi* M & W

M = Men; W = Women

M = Men; W = Women

University of Puerto Rico at Ponce *Puerto Rico* M & W
University of Puerto Rico, Río Piedras *Puerto Rico* M & W
University of Puerto Rico at Utuado *Puerto Rico* M & W
University of Puget Sound *Washington* M & W
University of Redlands *California* M & W
University of Regina *Saskatchewan* M & W
University of Rhode Island *Rhode Island* M & W
University of Richmond *Virginia* M & W
University of Rio Grande *Ohio* M & W
University of Rochester *New York* M & W
University of the Sacred Heart *Puerto Rico* M & W
University of Saint Francis *Indiana* M & W
University of St. Francis *Illinois* M & W
University of Saint Mary *Kansas* M & W
University of St. Thomas *Texas* M
University of St. Thomas *Minnesota* M & W
University of San Diego *California* M & W
University of San Francisco *California* M & W
University of Saskatchewan *Saskatchewan* M & W
University of Science and Arts of Oklahoma *Oklahoma* M & W
University of the Sciences in Philadelphia *Pennsylvania* M & W
The University of Scranton *Pennsylvania* M & W
University of Sioux Falls *South Dakota* M & W
University of South Alabama *Alabama* M & W
University of South Carolina *South Carolina* M & W
University of South Carolina Aiken *South Carolina* M & W
University of South Carolina Salkehatchie *South Carolina* M
University of South Carolina Upstate *South Carolina* M & W
The University of South Dakota *South Dakota* M & W
University of South Florida *Florida* M & W
University of Southern California *California* M & W
University of Southern Indiana *Indiana* M & W
University of Southern Maine *Maine* M & W
University of Southern Mississippi *Mississippi* M & W
University of the Southwest *New Mexico* M & W
The University of Tampa *Florida* M & W
The University of Tennessee *Tennessee* M & W
The University of Tennessee at Chattanooga *Tennessee* M & W
The University of Tennessee at Martin *Tennessee* M & W
The University of Texas at Arlington *Texas* M & W
The University of Texas at Austin *Texas* M & W
The University of Texas at Dallas *Texas* M & W
The University of Texas at El Paso *Texas* M & W
The University of Texas of the Permian Basin *Texas* M & W
The University of Texas at San Antonio *Texas* M & W
The University of Texas at Tyler *Texas* M & W
The University of Texas–Pan American *Texas* M & W
The University of Toledo *Ohio* M & W
University of Toronto *Ontario* M & W
University of Tulsa *Oklahoma* M & W
University of Utah *Utah* M & W
University of Vermont *Vermont* M & W
University of Victoria *British Columbia* M & W
University of the Virgin Islands *United States Virgin Islands* M & W
University of Virginia *Virginia* M & W
The University of Virginia's College at Wise *Virginia* M & W
University of Washington *Washington* M & W
University of Waterloo *Ontario* M & W
The University of West Alabama *Alabama* M & W
University of West Florida *Florida* M & W
University of West Georgia *Georgia* M & W
The University of Western Ontario *Ontario* M & W
University of Windsor *Ontario* M & W
The University of Winnipeg *Manitoba* M & W
University of Wisconsin–Baraboo/Sauk County *Wisconsin* M
University of Wisconsin–Eau Claire *Wisconsin* M & W
University of Wisconsin–Fond du Lac *Wisconsin* M & W
University of Wisconsin–Fox Valley *Wisconsin* M & W
University of Wisconsin–Green Bay *Wisconsin* M & W
University of Wisconsin–La Crosse *Wisconsin* M & W
University of Wisconsin–Madison *Wisconsin* M & W
University of Wisconsin–Manitowoc *Wisconsin* M & W
University of Wisconsin–Marinette *Wisconsin* M & W
University of Wisconsin–Marshfield/Wood County *Wisconsin* M & W
University of Wisconsin–Milwaukee *Wisconsin* M & W
University of Wisconsin–Oshkosh *Wisconsin* M & W
University of Wisconsin–Parkside *Wisconsin* M & W
University of Wisconsin–Platteville *Wisconsin* M & W
University of Wisconsin–Richland *Wisconsin* M & W
University of Wisconsin–River Falls *Wisconsin* M & W
University of Wisconsin–Stevens Point *Wisconsin* M & W
University of Wisconsin–Stout *Wisconsin* M & W
University of Wisconsin–Superior *Wisconsin* M & W
University of Wisconsin–Washington County *Wisconsin* M & W
University of Wisconsin–Waukesha *Wisconsin* M & W
University of Wisconsin–Whitewater *Wisconsin* M & W
University of Wyoming *Wyoming* M & W
Upper Iowa University *Iowa* M & W
Urbana University *Ohio* M & W
Ursinus College *Pennsylvania* M & W
Ursuline College *Ohio* W
Utah State University *Utah* M & W
Utah State University–College of Eastern Utah *Utah* M & W
Utah Valley University *Utah* M & W
Utica College *New York* M & W
Valdosta State University *Georgia* M & W
Valley City State University *North Dakota* M & W
Valley Forge Christian College *Pennsylvania* M & W
Valley Forge Military College *Pennsylvania* M
Valparaiso University *Indiana* M & W
Vanderbilt University *Tennessee* M & W
Vanguard University of Southern California *California* M & W
Vassar College *New York* M & W
Ventura College *California* M & W
Vermilion Community College *Minnesota* M & W
Vermont Technical College *Vermont* M & W
Victor Valley College *California* M & W
Villanova University *Pennsylvania* M & W
Vincennes University *Indiana* M & W
Virginia Commonwealth University *Virginia* M & W
Virginia Intermont College *Virginia* M & W
Virginia Military Institute *Virginia* M
Virginia Polytechnic Institute and State University *Virginia* M
Virginia State University *Virginia* M & W
Virginia Union University *Virginia* M & W
Virginia University of Lynchburg *Virginia* M & W
Virginia Wesleyan College *Virginia* M & W
Viterbo University *Wisconsin* M & W
Volunteer State Community College *Tennessee* M & W
Voorhees College *South Carolina* M & W
Wabash College *Indiana* M
Wagner College *New York* M & W
Wake Forest University *North Carolina* M & W
Waldorf College *Iowa* M & W
Walla Walla Community College *Washington* M & W
Walla Walla University *Washington* M & W
Wallace State Community College *Alabama* M & W
Walsh University *Ohio* M & W
Walters State Community College *Tennessee* M & W
Warner Pacific College *Oregon* M & W
Warner University *Florida* M & W
Warren Wilson College *North Carolina* M & W
Wartburg College *Iowa* M & W
Washburn University *Kansas* M & W
Washington Adventist University *Maryland* M & W
Washington Bible College *Maryland* M & W
Washington College *Maryland* M & W
Washington & Jefferson College *Pennsylvania* M & W
Washington and Lee University *Virginia* M & W
Washington State University *Washington* M & W
Washington University in St. Louis *Missouri* M & W
Waubonsee Community College *Illinois* M & W
Waycross College *Georgia* M
Wayland Baptist University *Texas* M & W
Wayne County Community College District *Michigan* M & W
Wayne State College *Nebraska* M & W
Wayne State University *Michigan* M & W
Waynesburg University *Pennsylvania* M & W
Weatherford College *Texas* M & W
Webb Institute *New York* M & W
Webber International University *Florida* M & W
Weber State University *Utah* M & W
Webster University *Missouri* M & W
Wellesley College *Massachusetts* W
Wells College *New York* M & W
Wenatchee Valley College *Washington* M & W
Wentworth Institute of Technology *Massachusetts* M & W
Wesley College *Delaware* M & W
Wesleyan College *Georgia* W
Wesleyan University *Connecticut* M & W
West Chester University of Pennsylvania *Pennsylvania* M & W
West Hills Community College *California* M
West Liberty University *West Virginia* M & W
West Los Angeles College *California* M
West Texas A&M University *Texas* M & W
West Valley College *California* M & W
West Virginia State University *West Virginia* M & W
West Virginia University *West Virginia* M & W
West Virginia University Institute of Technology *West Virginia* M & W
West Virginia Wesleyan College *West Virginia* M & W
Westchester Community College *New York* M & W
Western Carolina University *North Carolina* M & W
Western Connecticut State University *Connecticut* M & W
Western Illinois University *Illinois* M & W
Western Kentucky University *Kentucky* M & W
Western Michigan University *Michigan* M & W
Western Nebraska Community College *Nebraska* M & W
Western New England College *Massachusetts* M & W
Western New Mexico University *New Mexico* M & W
Western Oklahoma State College *Oklahoma* M & W
Western Oregon University *Oregon* M & W
Western State College of Colorado *Colorado* M & W
Western Technical College *Wisconsin* M & W
Western Washington University *Washington* M & W
Western Wyoming Community College *Wyoming* M & W
Westfield State College *Massachusetts* M & W
Westminster College *Utah* M & W
Westminster College *Pennsylvania* M & W
Westminster College *Missouri* M & W
Westmont College *California* M & W
Westmoreland County Community College *Pennsylvania* M & W
Whatcom Community College *Washington* M & W
Wheaton College *Massachusetts* M & W
Wheaton College *Illinois* M & W

M = Men; W = Women

Bowling

Cheerleading

M = Men; W = Women
Widener University *Pennsylvania* M & W
Wilberforce University *Ohio* M & W
Wiley College *Texas* M & W
Wilfrid Laurier University *Ontario* M & W
Wilkes Community College *North Carolina* M & W
Wilkes University *Pennsylvania* M & W
Willamette University *Oregon* M & W
William Carey University *Mississippi* M & W
William Jessup University *California* M & W
William Jewell College *Missouri* M & W
William Paterson University of New Jersey *New Jersey* M & W
William Penn University *Iowa* M & W
Wright State University, Lake Campus *Ohio* M & W
Xavier University *Ohio* M & W
Xavier University of Louisiana *Louisiana* M & W
Yavapai College *Arizona* M & W
Yeshiva University *New York* M & W
York College *Nebraska* M & W
York University *Ontario* M & W
Youngstown State University *Ohio* M & W
Yuba College *California* M & W
Zane State College *Ohio* M & W

Acadia University *Nova Scotia* M
Adelphi University *New York* W
Marist College *New York* M & W
Martin Methodist College *Tennessee* M & W
McKendree University *Illinois* M & W
Medaille College *New York* W
Merced College *California* M & W
Mid-State Technical College *Wisconsin* M & W
Stephen F. Austin State University *Texas* W
Stonehill College *Massachusetts* M & W
Suffolk County Community College *New York* M & W
Syracuse University *New York* M & W

Acadia University *Nova Scotia* M
AIB College of Business *Iowa* M & W
Alabama State University *Alabama* M & W
Albany State University *Georgia* W
Albion College *Michigan* M & W
Albright College *Pennsylvania* M & W
Alice Lloyd College *Kentucky* W
Allegheny College *Pennsylvania* M & W
Allen Community College *Kansas* M & W

Ancilla College *Indiana* M & W
Anderson University *South Carolina* W
Arkansas Baptist College *Arkansas* W
Arkansas Tech University *Arkansas* M & W
Armstrong Atlantic State University *Georgia* M & W
Atlanta Metropolitan College *Georgia* M & W
Auburn University Montgomery *Alabama* M & W
Augustana College *South Dakota* W
Augustana College *Illinois* M & W
Austin College *Texas* M & W
Austin Peay State University *Tennessee* M & W
Avila University *Missouri* W
Babson College *Massachusetts* W
Baker University *Kansas* M & W
Ball State University *Indiana* M & W
Baptist Bible College of Pennsylvania *Pennsylvania* W
Barclay College *Kansas* M & W
Bard College at Simon's Rock *Massachusetts* M & W
Barton County Community College *Kansas* M & W
Becker College *Massachusetts* M & W
Belmont Abbey College *North Carolina* M & W
Benedict College *South Carolina* W
Benedictine College *Kansas* M & W
Bernard M. Baruch College of the City University of New York *New York* M & W
Bethel College *Indiana* M & W
Bethel University *Tennessee* M & W
Bethune-Cookman University *Florida* W
Biola University *California* W
Birmingham-Southern College *Alabama* M & W
Blackburn College *Illinois* M & W
Blinn College *Texas* M & W
Bloomsburg University of Pennsylvania *Pennsylvania* M & W
Bluefield State College *West Virginia* W
Boston College *Massachusetts* M & W
Boston University *Massachusetts* M & W
Bradley University *Illinois* M & W
Brevard College *North Carolina* W
Brewton-Parker College *Georgia* M & W
Bridgewater College *Virginia* M & W
Brigham Young University *Utah* M & W
Brock University *Ontario* M & W
Bryant University *Rhode Island* M & W
Bucknell University *Pennsylvania* M & W
Buffalo State College, State University of New York *New York* W
California Baptist University *California* M & W
California Lutheran University *California* M & W
California State University, Sacramento *California* M & W
California State University, Stanislaus *California* M & W
California University of Pennsylvania *Pennsylvania* M & W
Campbell University *North Carolina* W
Campbellsville University *Kentucky* M & W
Cape Fear Community College *North Carolina* M & W
Carnegie Mellon University *Pennsylvania* M & W
Carroll College *Montana* M & W
Case Western Reserve University *Ohio* M & W
Casper College *Wyoming* M & W
Castleton State College *Vermont* M & W
Catawba College *North Carolina* M & W
Cazenovia College *New York* M & W
Cecil College *Maryland* W
Centenary College *New Jersey* W
Centenary College of Louisiana *Louisiana* M & W
Central Christian College of Kansas *Kansas* M & W
Central State University *Ohio* M & W
Central Washington University *Washington* M & W
Centre College *Kentucky* W
Chapman University *California* M & W
Charleston Southern University *South Carolina* M & W
Chowan University *North Carolina* M & W
Christopher Newport University *Virginia* M & W
Cisco College *Texas* M & W
Claremont McKenna College *California* M & W
Clarendon College *Texas* M & W
Clarke College *Iowa* W
Clayton State University *Georgia* W
Clemson University *South Carolina* M & W
Cleveland State University *Ohio* M & W
Clinton Community College *Iowa* M & W
Coahoma Community College *Mississippi* W
Coastal Carolina University *South Carolina* M & W
Coe College *Iowa* W
Colby Community College *Kansas* M & W
Colgate University *New York* M & W
College of Charleston *South Carolina* M & W
College of DuPage *Illinois* M & W
College of Mount St. Joseph *Ohio* W
College of Mount Saint Vincent *New York* W
College of the Ozarks *Missouri* M & W
College of Southern Idaho *Idaho* M & W
College of Staten Island of the City University of New York *New York* M & W
The College of Wooster *Ohio* W
Colorado State University–Pueblo *Colorado* M & W
Community College of Philadelphia *Pennsylvania* W
Concord University *West Virginia* M & W
Concordia College *Minnesota* W
Concordia University Chicago *Illinois* M & W
Converse College *South Carolina* W
Culver-Stockton College *Missouri* M & W
Cumberland University *Tennessee* M & W
Dakota State University *South Dakota* M & W
Dakota Wesleyan University *South Dakota* M & W
Dartmouth College *New Hampshire* M & W
Davenport University *Michigan* W
Delaware State University *Delaware* W
Delaware Valley College *Pennsylvania* W
Delta State University *Mississippi* M & W
Denmark Technical College *South Carolina* W
DePauw University *Indiana* M & W
Dickinson College *Pennsylvania* M & W
Dickinson State University *North Dakota* M & W
Drake University *Iowa* M & W
Drury University *Missouri* M & W
Duquesne University *Pennsylvania* M & W
Dyersburg State Community College *Tennessee* W
D'Youville College *New York* W
Earlham College *Indiana* W
East Central University *Oklahoma* M & W
East Los Angeles College *California* W
East Mississippi Community College *Mississippi* W
Eastern Connecticut State University *Connecticut* W
Eastern Kentucky University *Kentucky* M & W
Elizabeth City State University *North Carolina* W
Elizabethtown College *Pennsylvania* M & W
Elmira College *New York* W
Elon University *North Carolina* M & W
Embry-Riddle Aeronautical University *Florida* M & W
Emory University *Georgia* M & W
Emporia State University *Kansas* M & W
Endicott College *Massachusetts* W
Enterprise State Community College *Alabama* M & W
Erie Community College *New York* W
Erie Community College, North Campus *New York* W
Erie Community College, South Campus *New York* W
Fairfield University *Connecticut* M & W
Fashion Institute of Technology *New York* W
Faulkner University *Alabama* M & W
Fayetteville State University *North Carolina* M & W
Ferrum College *Virginia* M & W
Florida Agricultural and Mechanical University *Florida* M & W
Florida Atlantic University *Florida* M & W
Florida College *Florida* W
Florida Gulf Coast University *Florida* W
Florida Southern College *Florida* W
Florida State University *Florida* M & W
Fontbonne University *Missouri* W
Fordham University *New York* M & W
Fort Lewis College *Colorado* M & W
Freed-Hardeman University *Tennessee* M & W
Fresno Pacific University *California* W
Friends University *Kansas* M & W
Furman University *South Carolina* M & W
Gannon University *Pennsylvania* M & W
Garden City Community College *Kansas* M & W
Gardner-Webb University *North Carolina* M & W
George Mason University *Virginia* M & W
Georgetown College *Kentucky* W
Georgia College & State University *Georgia* M & W
Georgia Institute of Technology *Georgia* M & W
Georgia Southern University *Georgia* M & W
Gettysburg College *Pennsylvania* M & W
Gogebic Community College *Michigan* M & W
Grace College *Indiana* M & W
Grand Valley State University *Michigan* M & W
Greensboro College *North Carolina* M & W
Grove City College *Pennsylvania* W
Gulf Coast Community College *Florida* M & W
Gwynedd-Mercy College *Pennsylvania* W
Hamline University *Minnesota* W
Hannibal-LaGrange College *Missouri* M & W
Hardin-Simmons University *Texas* M & W
Harding University *Arkansas* W
Harford Community College *Maryland* M & W
Harris-Stowe State University *Missouri* M & W
Hartwick College *New York* W
Haskell Indian Nations University *Kansas* M & W
Hastings College *Nebraska* W
Hawai'i Pacific University *Hawaii* M & W
Hiram College *Ohio* M & W
Holy Family University *Pennsylvania* W
Hope College *Michigan* M & W
Hope International University *California* M & W
Houston Baptist University *Texas* M & W
Howard College *Texas* M & W
Humboldt State University *California* W
Hutchinson Community College and Area Vocational School *Kansas* M & W
Illinois College *Illinois* W
Illinois Wesleyan University *Illinois* M & W
Independence Community College *Kansas* M & W
Indiana Tech *Indiana* M & W
Indiana University East *Indiana* W
Indiana University Southeast *Indiana* W
Indiana Wesleyan University *Indiana* M & W
Inter American University of Puerto Rico, Aguadilla Campus *Puerto Rico* M & W
Inter American University of Puerto Rico, Arecibo Campus *Puerto Rico* M & W
James Madison University *Virginia* M & W
Jamestown Community College *New York* W
Jarvis Christian College *Texas* W
Jefferson College *Missouri* M & W
John Carroll University *Ohio* W
Johnson Bible College *Tennessee* M & W
Johnson C. Smith University *North Carolina* W
Johnson & Wales University *Colorado* M & W
Judson University *Illinois* W
Kansas Wesleyan University *Kansas* M & W
Kaskaskia College *Illinois* M & W
Kennesaw State University *Georgia* W
Kentucky Christian University *Kentucky* W
Kentucky State University *Kentucky* W
Kentucky Wesleyan College *Kentucky* M & W
Kilgore College *Texas* M & W
King College *Tennessee* M & W
King's College *Pennsylvania* M & W
Kutztown University of Pennsylvania *Pennsylvania* W
Labette Community College *Kansas* W
Lackawanna College *Pennsylvania* W
LaGrange College *Georgia* M & W
Lake Forest College *Illinois* M & W
Lake Land College *Illinois* W
Lamar University *Texas* M & W
Lane College *Tennessee* W
Laramie County Community College *Wyoming* M & W
Lee University *Tennessee* M & W
Lehigh University *Pennsylvania* M & W
Lenoir-Rhyne University *North Carolina* M & W
Lewis University *Illinois* M & W
Liberty University *Virginia* M & W
Lincoln Christian University *Illinois* M & W
Lindenwood University *Missouri* M & W
Lindsey Wilson College *Kentucky* M & W

M = Men; W = Women

Lon Morris College *Texas* M & W
Louisiana College *Louisiana* M & W
Louisiana State University and Agricultural and Mechanical College *Louisiana* M & W
Loyola Marymount University *California* M & W
Loyola University Chicago *Illinois* M & W
Loyola University New Orleans *Louisiana* M & W
Lubbock Christian University *Texas* M & W
Lycoming College *Pennsylvania* M & W
Lynchburg College *Virginia* M & W
MacMurray College *Illinois* M & W
Malone University *Ohio* M & W
Manchester College *Indiana* M & W
Manhattan College *New York* M & W
Marian University *Indiana* M & W
Marietta College *Ohio* W
Marist College *New York* M & W
Marquette University *Wisconsin* M & W
Mars Hill College *North Carolina* M & W
Marshalltown Community College *Iowa* M & W
Martin Methodist College *Tennessee* W
Maryville College *Tennessee* M & W
Marywood University *Pennsylvania* M & W
Massachusetts Institute of Technology *Massachusetts* M & W
McGill University *Quebec* M & W
McKendree University *Illinois* M & W
McPherson College *Kansas* M & W
Meridian Community College *Mississippi* W
Merrimack College *Massachusetts* W
Methodist University *North Carolina* M & W
Metropolitan State College of Denver *Colorado* M & W
Miami University Hamilton *Ohio* W
Michigan State University *Michigan* M & W
MidAmerica Nazarene University *Kansas* M & W
Middle Tennessee State University *Tennessee* M & W
Midwestern State University *Texas* M & W
Miles College *Alabama* W
Millersville University of Pennsylvania *Pennsylvania* W
Millikin University *Illinois* M & W
Milwaukee School of Engineering *Wisconsin* M & W
Minnesota State University Mankato *Minnesota* M & W
Minnesota West Community and Technical College *Minnesota* M & W
Minot State University *North Dakota* W
Misericordia University *Pennsylvania* W
Mississippi College *Mississippi* W
Mississippi State University *Mississippi* M & W
Missouri Valley College *Missouri* M & W
Moberly Area Community College *Missouri* M & W
Montana State University *Montana* M & W
Moravian College *Pennsylvania* W
Morgan State University *Maryland* W
Mount Ida College *Massachusetts* M & W
Mount Olive College *North Carolina* W
Mount St. Mary's University *Maryland* W
Mt. San Antonio College *California* M & W
Mountain State University *West Virginia* M & W
Muhlenberg College *Pennsylvania* M & W
Murray State University *Kentucky* M & W
Nassau Community College *New York* M & W
Nebraska Wesleyan University *Nebraska* W
New York University *New York* M & W
Newberry College *South Carolina* W
North Carolina State University *North Carolina* M & W
North Central College *Illinois* W
North Dakota State University *North Dakota* M & W
North Georgia College & State University *Georgia* W
North Greenville University *South Carolina* M & W
North Idaho College *Idaho* M & W
North Lake College *Texas* W
Northeast Community College *Nebraska* W
Northeastern Oklahoma Agricultural and Mechanical College *Oklahoma* M & W
Northern Arizona University *Arizona* M & W
Northern Kentucky University *Kentucky* M & W
Northwest Missouri State University *Missouri* M & W
Northwest Nazarene University *Idaho* W
Northwest-Shoals Community College *Alabama* M & W
Northwestern Oklahoma State University *Oklahoma* M & W
Northwestern University *Illinois* M & W
Northwood University *Michigan* M & W
Nova Southeastern University *Florida* W
Oakland City University *Indiana* W
Oberlin College *Ohio* W
Occidental College *California* W
Ohio Dominican University *Ohio* M & W
The Ohio State University *Ohio* M & W
The Ohio State University at Marion *Ohio* W
Ohio University *Ohio* M & W
Oklahoma City University *Oklahoma* M & W
Oklahoma Panhandle State University *Oklahoma* W
Olivet Nazarene University *Illinois* M & W
Otterbein University *Ohio* M & W
Ouachita Baptist University *Arkansas* M & W
Ozark Christian College *Missouri* M & W
Pacific Lutheran University *Washington* M & W
Palm Beach Atlantic University *Florida* M & W
Penn State Berks *Pennsylvania* M & W
Penn State Erie, The Behrend College *Pennsylvania* M & W
Penn State Hazleton *Pennsylvania* M & W
Penn State Lehigh Valley *Pennsylvania* M & W
Penn State Mont Alto *Pennsylvania* M & W
Penn State New Kensington *Pennsylvania* M & W
Penn State University Park *Pennsylvania* M & W
Penn State Worthington Scranton *Pennsylvania* M & W
Pepperdine University *California* M & W
Peru State College *Nebraska* M & W
Pfeiffer University *North Carolina* M & W
Pikeville College *Kentucky* M & W
Pima Community College *Arizona* W
Pittsburg State University *Kansas* M & W
Plymouth State University *New Hampshire* M & W
Pratt Community College *Kansas* W
Presbyterian College *South Carolina* M & W
Providence College *Rhode Island* W
Purdue University North Central *Indiana* M & W
Queens University of Charlotte *North Carolina* M
Queen's University at Kingston *Ontario* M & W
Quincy University *Illinois* M & W
Regis College *Massachusetts* M & W
Rhodes College *Tennessee* W
Rice University *Texas* M & W
The Richard Stockton College of New Jersey *New Jersey* M & W
Rider University *New Jersey* M & W
Ripon College *Wisconsin* M & W
Rivier College *New Hampshire* M & W
Roane State Community College *Tennessee* W
Robert Morris University *Pennsylvania* M & W
Robert Morris University Illinois *Illinois* M & W
Rochester Institute of Technology *New York* M & W
Rocky Mountain College *Montana* W
Roger Williams University *Rhode Island* W
Rogers State University *Oklahoma* M & W
Rust College *Mississippi* M & W
Sacred Heart University *Connecticut* W
Saginaw Valley State University *Michigan* M & W
St. Ambrose University *Iowa* M & W
Saint Anselm College *New Hampshire* W
St. Bonaventure University *New York* M & W
St. Cloud State University *Minnesota* M & W
St. Francis Xavier University *Nova Scotia* W
St. Gregory's University *Oklahoma* M & W
Saint Joseph's College *Indiana* M & W
Saint Joseph's College of Maine *Maine* M & W
Saint Joseph's University *Pennsylvania* M & W
St. Mary's University *Texas* M & W
Saint Michael's College *Vermont* M & W
Saint Vincent College *Pennsylvania* M & W
Salem International University *West Virginia* M & W
Salt Lake Community College *Utah* M & W
San Jacinto College District *Texas* M
San Jose State University *California* M & W
Savannah College of Art and Design *Georgia* M & W
Savannah State University *Georgia* M & W
Seattle University *Washington* M & W
Shawnee Community College *Illinois* M & W
Shelton State Community College *Alabama* M & W
Shorter University *Georgia* M & W
Siena College *New York* W
Simpson College *Iowa* M & W
Slippery Rock University of Pennsylvania *Pennsylvania* M & W
South Dakota State University *South Dakota* M & W
Southeast Missouri State University *Missouri* M & W
Southeastern University *Florida* M & W
Southern Connecticut State University *Connecticut* M & W
Southern Illinois University Carbondale *Illinois* M & W
Southern Methodist University *Texas* M & W
Southern Nazarene University *Oklahoma* M & W
Southern New Hampshire University *New Hampshire* M & W
Southern Polytechnic State University *Georgia* M & W
Southern Virginia University *Virginia* M & W
Southern Wesleyan University *South Carolina* M & W
Southwest Baptist University *Missouri* M & W
Southwestern College *Kansas* M & W
Southwestern Oklahoma State University *Oklahoma* M & W
Southwestern Oregon Community College *Oregon* M & W
Stanford University *California* M & W
State University of New York at Binghamton *New York* M & W
State University of New York College of Agriculture and Technology at Cobleskill *New York* M & W
State University of New York College at Geneseo *New York* M & W
State University of New York College at Oneonta *New York* W
State University of New York at Fredonia *New York* M & W
Stevenson University *Maryland* M & W
Stonehill College *Massachusetts* M & W
Sul Ross State University *Texas* M & W
Sullivan County Community College *New York* W
Susquehanna University *Pennsylvania* M & W
Syracuse University *New York* M & W
Tabor College *Kansas* M & W
Tarleton State University *Texas* M & W
Temple University *Pennsylvania* M & W
Tennessee Technological University *Tennessee* M & W
Tennessee Wesleyan College *Tennessee* M & W
Texas A&M University–Commerce *Texas* M & W
Texas College *Texas* M & W
Texas State University–San Marcos *Texas* M & W
Thiel College *Pennsylvania* M & W
Three Rivers Community College *Missouri* M & W
Tiffin University *Ohio* M & W
Towson University *Maryland* M & W
Transylvania University *Kentucky* M & W
Trinity Valley Community College *Texas* M & W
Truman State University *Missouri* M & W
Tusculum College *Tennessee* W
Union College *New York* M & W
Union College *Kentucky* M & W
Union University *Tennessee* W
United States Air Force Academy *Colorado* M & W
United States Military Academy *New York* M & W
United States Naval Academy *Maryland* M & W
The University of Akron *Ohio* M & W
The University of Akron–Wayne College *Ohio* W
The University of Alabama *Alabama* M & W
The University of Alabama in Huntsville *Alabama* M & W
The University of British Columbia *British Columbia* M & W
University of Central Arkansas *Arkansas* M & W
University of Central Florida *Florida* M & W

M = Men; W = Women

University of Charleston *West Virginia* W
University of Cincinnati *Ohio* M & W
University of the Cumberlands *Kentucky* M & W
University of Dayton *Ohio* M & W
University of Delaware *Delaware* M & W
The University of Findlay *Ohio* M & W
University of Great Falls *Montana* M & W
University of Hawaii at Manoa *Hawaii* M & W
University of Illinois at Springfield *Illinois* W
University of Illinois at Urbana–Champaign *Illinois* M & W
University of Louisiana at Monroe *Louisiana* M & W
University of Louisville *Kentucky* M & W
University of Maine *Maine* M & W
University of Mary Washington *Virginia* M & W
University of Maryland, College Park *Maryland* W
University of Maryland Eastern Shore *Maryland* M & W
University of Massachusetts Dartmouth *Massachusetts* W
University of Memphis *Tennessee* M & W
University of Miami *Florida* M & W
University of Michigan *Michigan* M & W
University of Michigan–Dearborn *Michigan* M & W
University of Minnesota, Duluth *Minnesota* W
University of Mississippi *Mississippi* M & W
University of Missouri *Missouri* M & W
University of Missouri–Kansas City *Missouri* W
University of Missouri–St. Louis *Missouri* W
University of Mobile *Alabama* W
University of Mount Union *Ohio* W
University of Nevada, Las Vegas *Nevada* M & W
University of Nevada, Reno *Nevada* M & W
University of New Haven *Connecticut* M & W
The University of North Carolina at Asheville *North Carolina* M & W
The University of North Carolina at Charlotte *North Carolina* M & W
The University of North Carolina at Pembroke *North Carolina* M & W
The University of North Carolina Wilmington *North Carolina* M & W
University of Ottawa *Ontario* M & W
University of the Ozarks *Arkansas* M & W
University of Pittsburgh at Johnstown *Pennsylvania* W
University of Puerto Rico at Bayamón *Puerto Rico* M & W
University of Puerto Rico at Humacao *Puerto Rico* M & W
University of Puget Sound *Washington* M & W
University of Rhode Island *Rhode Island* M & W
University of Richmond *Virginia* W
University of Saint Francis *Indiana* M & W
University of St. Francis *Illinois* W
University of St. Thomas *Texas* M & W
University of Science and Arts of Oklahoma *Oklahoma* M & W
University of Sioux Falls *South Dakota* W
University of South Carolina Aiken *South Carolina* M & W
University of Southern California *California* W
University of Southern Indiana *Indiana* M & W
University of Southern Maine *Maine* M & W
University of Southern Mississippi *Mississippi* M & W
The University of Tennessee *Tennessee* M & W
The University of Tennessee at Martin *Tennessee* W
The University of Texas of the Permian Basin *Texas* M & W
The University of Texas at Tyler *Texas* M & W
University of Utah *Utah* M & W
University of Vermont *Vermont* M & W
University of the Virgin Islands *United States Virgin Islands* W
University of Washington *Washington* M & W
University of Waterloo *Ontario* M & W
University of West Georgia *Georgia* M & W
The University of Western Ontario *Ontario* M & W
University of Windsor *Ontario* M & W
University of Wisconsin–Madison *Wisconsin* M & W
University of Wisconsin–Platteville *Wisconsin* M & W
University of Wisconsin–River Falls *Wisconsin* M
University of Wisconsin–Superior *Wisconsin* M & W
University of Wisconsin–Whitewater *Wisconsin* M & W
University of Wyoming *Wyoming* M & W
Ventura College *California* M & W
Villanova University *Pennsylvania* M & W
Virginia State University *Virginia* M & W
Virginia Wesleyan College *Virginia* W
Waldorf College *Iowa* W
Walsh University *Ohio* W
Warner University *Florida* M & W
Wartburg College *Iowa* W
Washburn University *Kansas* M & W
Washington College *Maryland* W
Washington & Jefferson College *Pennsylvania* M & W
Washington and Lee University *Virginia* M & W
Washington State University *Washington* M & W
Wayland Baptist University *Texas* M & W
Wayne State College *Nebraska* M & W
Weatherford College *Texas* M & W
Weber State University *Utah* M & W
West Chester University of Pennsylvania *Pennsylvania* W
West Virginia University *West Virginia* M & W
West Virginia University Institute of Technology *West Virginia* M & W
West Virginia Wesleyan College *West Virginia* M & W
Western Connecticut State University *Connecticut* W
Western Kentucky University *Kentucky* M & W
Western New Mexico University *New Mexico* M & W
Western State College of Colorado *Colorado* M & W
Western Washington University *Washington* M & W
Western Wyoming Community College *Wyoming* M & W
Westfield State College *Massachusetts* M & W
Wheaton College *Illinois* W
Wheeling Jesuit University *West Virginia* M & W
Wichita State University *Kansas* M & W
Widener University *Pennsylvania* W
Wiley College *Texas* M & W
Wilfrid Laurier University *Ontario* M & W
William Carey University *Mississippi* M & W
William Jewell College *Missouri* M & W
William Paterson University of New Jersey *New Jersey* M & W
William Penn University *Iowa* M & W
Winston-Salem State University *North Carolina* M
Winthrop University *South Carolina* M & W
Wofford College *South Carolina* W
Xavier University *Ohio* M & W
York College of Pennsylvania *Pennsylvania* W

Crew

Allegheny College *Pennsylvania* M & W
Amherst College *Massachusetts* M & W
Assumption College *Massachusetts* W
Barnard College *New York* W
Barry University *Florida* W
Bates College *Maine* M & W
Baylor University *Texas* M & W
Beloit College *Wisconsin* M & W
Boston College *Massachusetts* W
Boston University *Massachusetts* M & W
Bowdoin College *Maine* M & W
Brandeis University *Massachusetts* M
Brenau University *Georgia* W
Brock University *Ontario* M & W
Brown University *Rhode Island* M & W
Bryn Mawr College *Pennsylvania* W
Bucknell University *Pennsylvania* M & W
Butler University *Indiana* M & W
California Maritime Academy *California* M & W
California State University, Long Beach *California* M & W
California State University, Sacramento *California* M & W
Calvin College *Michigan* M & W
Carleton College *Minnesota* M & W
Carleton University *Ontario* M & W
Carlow University *Pennsylvania* W
Carnegie Mellon University *Pennsylvania* M & W
Case Western Reserve University *Ohio* M & W
Cazenovia College *New York* M & W
Chapman University *California* M & W
Chatham University *Pennsylvania* W
Clark University *Massachusetts* M & W
Clemson University *South Carolina* M & W
Colby College *Maine* M & W
Colgate University *New York* M & W
College of the Holy Cross *Massachusetts* M & W
College of Saint Benedict *Minnesota* W
Colorado State University *Colorado* M & W
Columbia University *New York* M & W
Columbia University, School of General Studies *New York* M & W
Connecticut College *Connecticut* M & W
Cornell University *New York* M & W
Creighton University *Nebraska* W
Dartmouth College *New Hampshire* M & W
Davidson College *North Carolina* M & W
Denison University *Ohio* M
DePauw University *Indiana* M & W
Dowling College *New York* M & W
Drake University *Iowa* W
Drexel University *Pennsylvania* M & W
Duke University *North Carolina* M & W
Duquesne University *Pennsylvania* M & W
Eastern Michigan University *Michigan* W
Emory University *Georgia* M & W
Endicott College *Massachusetts* M & W
The Evergreen State College *Washington* M & W
Fairfield University *Connecticut* M & W
Florida Institute of Technology *Florida* W
Fordham University *New York* M & W
Franklin & Marshall College *Pennsylvania* M & W
Franklin Pierce University *New Hampshire* M & W
Furman University *South Carolina* M & W
George Mason University *Virginia* W
The George Washington University *District of Columbia* M & W
Georgetown University *District of Columbia* M & W
Gonzaga University *Washington* M & W
Grand Valley State University *Michigan* M & W
Hamilton College *New York* M & W
Hampden-Sydney College *Virginia* M
Harvard University *Massachusetts* M & W
Haverford College *Pennsylvania* M & W
Hobart and William Smith Colleges *New York* M & W
Holy Cross College *Indiana* M & W
Humboldt State University *California* M & W
Indiana University Bloomington *Indiana* W
Iona College *New York* M & W
Ithaca College *New York* M & W
Jacksonville University *Florida* M & W
John Carroll University *Ohio* M & W
Kansas State University *Kansas* W
La Salle University *Pennsylvania* M & W
Lafayette College *Pennsylvania* M & W
Lawrence University *Wisconsin* M & W
Lehigh University *Pennsylvania* M & W
Lewis & Clark College *Oregon* M & W
Long Island University, C.W. Post Campus *New York* M & W
Loyola Marymount University *California* M & W
Loyola University Maryland *Maryland* M & W
Lycoming College *Pennsylvania* M & W
Macalester College *Minnesota* M & W
Manhattan College *New York* M & W
Marietta College *Ohio* M & W
Marist College *New York* M & W
Marquette University *Wisconsin* M & W
Massachusetts Institute of Technology *Massachusetts* M & W
Massachusetts Maritime Academy *Massachusetts* M & W
McGill University *Quebec* M & W
Mercyhurst College *Pennsylvania* M & W
Michigan State University *Michigan* W
Mills College *California* W
Milwaukee School of Engineering *Wisconsin* M
Mount Holyoke College *Massachusetts* W

M = Men; W = Women

Murray State University *Kentucky* M & W
New York University *New York* M & W
North Carolina State University *North Carolina* M & W
Northeastern University *Massachusetts* M & W
Northern Michigan University *Michigan* M & W
Nova Southeastern University *Florida* W
Oklahoma City University *Oklahoma* M & W
Old Dominion University *Virginia* M & W
Orange Coast College *California* M & W
Oregon State University *Oregon* M & W
Pacific Lutheran University *Washington* M & W
Pepperdine University *California* M & W
Princeton University *New Jersey* M & W
Queen's University at Kingston *Ontario* M & W
Rensselaer Polytechnic Institute *New York* M & W
Rice University *Texas* M & W
The Richard Stockton College of New Jersey *New Jersey* W
Robert Morris University *Pennsylvania* W
Robert Morris University Illinois *Illinois* W
Rochester Institute of Technology *New York* M & W
Roger Williams University *Rhode Island* M & W
Rollins College *Florida* M & W
Rutgers, The State University of New Jersey, Camden *New Jersey* M & W
Rutgers, The State University of New Jersey, New Brunswick *New Jersey* M & W
Ryerson University *Ontario* M & W
Sacred Heart University *Connecticut* W
St. Cloud State University *Minnesota* M & W
St. Francis Xavier University *Nova Scotia* M & W
St. John's College *Maryland* M & W
Saint John's University *Minnesota* M
Saint Joseph's University *Pennsylvania* M & W
St. Lawrence University *New York* M & W
Saint Louis University *Missouri* M & W
Saint Mary's College of California *California* M & W
St. Mary's College of Maryland *Maryland* M & W
San Diego State University *California* W
Santa Clara University *California* M & W
Sarah Lawrence College *New York* M & W
Seattle Pacific University *Washington* M & W
Seattle University *Washington* M & W
Sewanee: The University of the South *Tennessee* M & W
Simmons College *Massachusetts* W
Skidmore College *New York* M & W
Smith College *Massachusetts* W
Southern Methodist University *Texas* W
Stanford University *California* M & W
State University of New York College at Geneseo *New York* M & W
State University of New York Maritime College *New York* W
State University of New York at Oswego *New York* M & W
Stetson University *Florida* M & W
Susquehanna University *Pennsylvania* M & W
Syracuse University *New York* M & W
Temple University *Pennsylvania* M & W
Texas A&M University at Galveston *Texas* M & W
Trent University *Ontario* M & W
Trinity College *Connecticut* M & W
Tufts University *Massachusetts* M & W
Tulane University *Louisiana* M & W
Union College *New York* M & W
United States Coast Guard Academy *Connecticut* M & W
United States Merchant Marine Academy *New York* M & W
United States Military Academy *New York* M & W
United States Naval Academy *Maryland* M & W
The University of Alabama *Alabama* W
The University of Alabama in Huntsville *Alabama* M & W
University at Albany, State University of New York *New York* M & W
The University of British Columbia *British Columbia* M & W
University at Buffalo, the State University of New York *New York* W
University of California, Berkeley *California* M & W
University of California, Davis *California* W
University of California, Los Angeles *California* W
University of California, San Diego *California* M & W
University of California, Santa Barbara *California* M & W
University of Central Florida *Florida* W
University of Charleston *West Virginia* M & W
University of Colorado at Boulder *Colorado* M & W
University of Connecticut *Connecticut* W
University of Dayton *Ohio* W
University of Delaware *Delaware* M & W
University of Guelph *Ontario* M & W
The University of Iowa *Iowa* M & W
The University of Kansas *Kansas* W
University of Louisville *Kentucky* W
University of Maine *Maine* W
University of Mary Washington *Virginia* M & W
University of Maryland, Baltimore County *Maryland* M & W
University of Massachusetts Amherst *Massachusetts* W
University of Massachusetts Lowell *Massachusetts* M & W
University of Miami *Florida* M
University of Michigan *Michigan* M
University of Minnesota, Duluth *Minnesota* M & W
The University of Montana *Montana* M & W
University of Nebraska–Lincoln *Nebraska* M & W
University of New Brunswick Saint John *New Brunswick* M & W
University of New Hampshire *New Hampshire* M & W
The University of North Carolina at Chapel Hill *North Carolina* W
University of Notre Dame *Indiana* W
University of Oklahoma *Oklahoma* W
University of Ottawa *Ontario* M & W
University of Pennsylvania *Pennsylvania* M & W
University of Puget Sound *Washington* M & W
University of Rhode Island *Rhode Island* M & W
University of Richmond *Virginia* M & W
University of Rochester *New York* M & W
University of St. Thomas *Minnesota* M & W
University of San Diego *California* M & W
The University of Scranton *Pennsylvania* M & W
University of Southern California *California* M & W
The University of Tampa *Florida* W
The University of Tennessee *Tennessee* M & W
The University of Texas at Austin *Texas* M & W
University of Toronto *Ontario* M
University of Tulsa *Oklahoma* W
University of Vermont *Vermont* M & W
University of Victoria *British Columbia* M & W
University of Virginia *Virginia* W
University of Washington *Washington* M & W
The University of Western Ontario *Ontario* M & W
Vassar College *New York* M & W
Villanova University *Pennsylvania* M & W
Wabash College *Indiana* M
Washington College *Maryland* M & W
Washington State University *Washington* M & W
Washington University in St. Louis *Missouri* M & W
Wellesley College *Massachusetts* W
Wentworth Institute of Technology *Massachusetts* M & W
Wesleyan University *Connecticut* M & W
West Virginia University *West Virginia* W
Western Washington University *Washington* M & W
Wheaton College *Illinois* M & W
Willamette University *Oregon* M & W
Williams College *Massachusetts* M & W
Wittenberg University *Ohio* M & W
Worcester Polytechnic Institute *Massachusetts* M & W
Worcester State College *Massachusetts* W
Xavier University *Ohio* M & W
Yale University *Connecticut* M & W

Cross-Country Running

Abilene Christian University *Texas* M & W
Academy of Art University *California* M & W
Acadia University *Nova Scotia* M & W
Adams State College *Colorado* M & W
Adelphi University *New York* M & W
Adrian College *Michigan* M & W
Alabama Agricultural and Mechanical University *Alabama* M & W
Alabama State University *Alabama* M & W
Albany State University *Georgia* M & W
Alberta College of Art & Design *Alberta* M & W
Albertus Magnus College *Connecticut* M & W
Albion College *Michigan* M & W
Albright College *Pennsylvania* M & W
Alcorn State University *Mississippi* M & W
Alderson-Broaddus College *West Virginia* M & W
Alfred University *New York* M & W
Allan Hancock College *California* M & W
Allegheny College *Pennsylvania* M & W
Allen Community College *Kansas* M & W
Allen University *South Carolina* M & W
Alma College *Michigan* M & W
Alvernia University *Pennsylvania* M & W
Alverno College *Wisconsin* W
American International College *Massachusetts* M & W
American River College *California* M & W
American University *District of Columbia* M & W
Amherst College *Massachusetts* M & W
Anderson University *South Carolina* M & W
Anderson University *Indiana* M & W
Andrew College *Georgia* M & W
Angelo State University *Texas* M & W
Anna Maria College *Massachusetts* M
Anne Arundel Community College *Maryland* M & W
Antelope Valley College *California* M & W
Appalachian State University *North Carolina* M & W
Aquinas College *Michigan* M & W
Arizona State University *Arizona* M & W
Arkansas State University - Jonesboro *Arkansas* M & W
Arkansas Tech University *Arkansas* W
The Art Institute of Boston at Lesley University *Massachusetts* M & W
Asbury University *Kentucky* M & W
Ashford University *Iowa* M & W
Ashland University *Ohio* M & W
Assumption College *Massachusetts* M & W
Auburn University *Alabama* M & W
Augsburg College *Minnesota* M & W
Augusta State University *Georgia* M & W
Augustana College *South Dakota* M & W
Augustana College *Illinois* M & W
Aurora University *Illinois* M & W
Austin Peay State University *Tennessee* M & W
Averett University *Virginia* M & W
Avila University *Missouri* M & W
Azusa Pacific University *California* M & W
Babson College *Massachusetts* M & W
Baker University *Kansas* M & W
Bakersfield College *California* M & W
Baldwin-Wallace College *Ohio* M & W
Ball State University *Indiana* M & W
Baltimore City Community College *Maryland* M & W
Baptist Bible College of Pennsylvania *Pennsylvania* M & W
Bard College *New York* M & W
Bard College at Simon's Rock *Massachusetts* M & W
Barnard College *New York* W
Barton College *North Carolina* M & W
Barton County Community College *Kansas* M & W
Bates College *Maine* M & W
Bay Path College *Massachusetts* W
Bayamón Central University *Puerto Rico* M & W
Baylor University *Texas* M & W
Belhaven University *Mississippi* M & W
Bellarmine University *Kentucky* M & W
Bellevue College *Washington* M & W
Belmont Abbey College *North Carolina* M & W
Belmont University *Tennessee* M & W
Beloit College *Wisconsin* M & W
Bemidji State University *Minnesota* W
Benedictine College *Kansas* M & W
Benedictine University *Illinois* M & W
Bentley University *Massachusetts* M & W
Berea College *Kentucky* M & W
Bergen Community College *New Jersey* M & W

M = Men; W = Women

Bernard M. Baruch College of the City University of New York *New York* M & W
Berry College *Georgia* M & W
Bethany College *West Virginia* M & W
Bethany College *Kansas* M & W
Bethany Lutheran College *Minnesota* M & W
Bethany University *California* M & W
Bethel College *Kansas* M & W
Bethel College *Indiana* M & W
Bethel University *Tennessee* M & W
Bethel University *Minnesota* M & W
Bethune-Cookman University *Florida* M & W
Bevill State Community College *Alabama* W
Biola University *California* M & W
Birmingham-Southern College *Alabama* M & W
Black Hills State University *South Dakota* M & W
Blackburn College *Illinois* M & W
Bloomfield College *New Jersey* M & W
Bloomsburg University of Pennsylvania *Pennsylvania* M & W
Blue Mountain College *Mississippi* M & W
Bluefield College *Virginia* M & W
Bluefield State College *West Virginia* M & W
Bluffton University *Ohio* M & W
Boise State University *Idaho* M & W
Boston College *Massachusetts* M & W
Boston University *Massachusetts* M & W
Bowdoin College *Maine* M & W
Bowie State University *Maryland* M & W
Bowling Green State University *Ohio* M & W
Bradley University *Illinois* M & W
Brandeis University *Massachusetts* M & W
Brenau University *Georgia* W
Brescia University *Kentucky* M & W
Brevard College *North Carolina* M & W
Briar Cliff University *Iowa* M & W
Bridgewater College *Virginia* M & W
Bridgewater State College *Massachusetts* M & W
Brigham Young University *Utah* M & W
Brigham Young University–Hawaii *Hawaii* M & W
Brock University *Ontario* M & W
Bronx Community College of the City University of New York *New York* M & W
Brooklyn College of the City University of New York *New York* M & W
Broome Community College *New York* M & W
Brown University *Rhode Island* M & W
Bryan College *Tennessee* M & W
Bryant University *Rhode Island* M & W
Bryn Mawr College *Pennsylvania* W
Bucknell University *Pennsylvania* M & W
Buena Vista University *Iowa* M & W
Buffalo State College, State University of New York *New York* M & W
Butler Community College *Kansas* M & W
Butler University *Indiana* M & W
Butte College *California* M & W
Cabrillo College *California* M & W
Cabrini College *Pennsylvania* M & W
Caldwell College *New Jersey* W
California Baptist University *California* M & W
California Institute of Technology *California* M & W
California Lutheran University *California* M & W
California Polytechnic State University, San Luis Obispo *California* M & W
California State Polytechnic University, Pomona *California* M & W
California State University, Chico *California* M & W
California State University, Dominguez Hills *California* W
California State University, East Bay *California* M & W
California State University, Fresno *California* M & W
California State University, Fullerton *California* M & W
California State University, Long Beach *California* M & W
California State University, Los Angeles *California* W
California State University, Monterey Bay *California* M & W
California State University, Northridge *California* M & W
California State University, Sacramento *California* M & W
California State University, San Bernardino *California* W
California State University, San Marcos *California* M & W
California State University, Stanislaus *California* M & W
California University of Pennsylvania *Pennsylvania* M & W
Calumet College of Saint Joseph *Indiana* M & W
Calvin College *Michigan* M & W
Cameron University *Oklahoma* M
Campbell University *North Carolina* M & W
Campbellsville University *Kentucky* M & W
Canisius College *New York* M & W
Capital University *Ohio* M & W
Cardinal Stritch University *Wisconsin* M & W
Caribbean University *Puerto Rico* M & W
Carleton College *Minnesota* M & W
Carnegie Mellon University *Pennsylvania* M & W
Carroll College *Montana* M & W
Carroll University *Wisconsin* M & W
Carson-Newman College *Tennessee* M & W
Carthage College *Wisconsin* M & W
Case Western Reserve University *Ohio* M & W
Castleton State College *Vermont* M & W
Catawba College *North Carolina* M & W
The Catholic University of America *District of Columbia* M & W
Cazenovia College *New York* M
Cedar Crest College *Pennsylvania* W
Cedarville University *Ohio* M & W
Centenary College *New Jersey* M & W
Centenary College of Louisiana *Louisiana* M & W
Central Arizona College *Arizona* M & W
Central Baptist College *Arkansas* M & W
Central College *Iowa* M & W
Central Connecticut State University *Connecticut* M & W
Central Methodist University *Missouri* M & W
Central Michigan University *Michigan* M & W
Central State University *Ohio* M & W
Central Washington University *Washington* M & W
Centre College *Kentucky* M & W
Cerritos College *California* M & W
Chabot College *California* M & W
Chaminade University of Honolulu *Hawaii* M & W
Chapman University *California* M & W
Charleston Southern University *South Carolina* M & W
Chatham University *Pennsylvania* W
Chemeketa Community College *Oregon* M & W
Chestnut Hill College *Pennsylvania* M & W
Cheyney University of Pennsylvania *Pennsylvania* M & W
Chicago State University *Illinois* M & W
Christian Brothers University *Tennessee* M & W
Christopher Newport University *Virginia* M & W
Cincinnati Christian University *Ohio* M & W
The Citadel, The Military College of South Carolina *South Carolina* M & W
Citrus College *California* M & W
City College of the City University of New York *New York* M & W
City College of San Francisco *California* M & W
City Colleges of Chicago, Malcolm X College *Illinois* M
Clackamas Community College *Oregon* M & W
Claflin University *South Carolina* M & W
Claremont McKenna College *California* M & W
Clarendon College *Texas* M & W
Clarion University of Pennsylvania *Pennsylvania* W
Clark Atlanta University *Georgia* M & W
Clark College *Washington* M & W
Clark University *Massachusetts* M & W
Clarke College *Iowa* M & W
Clarkson University *New York* M & W
Clayton State University *Georgia* M & W
Clemson University *South Carolina* M & W
Cleveland State University *Ohio* W
Cloud County Community College *Kansas* M & W
Coastal Carolina University *South Carolina* M & W
Coe College *Iowa* M & W
Coffeyville Community College *Kansas* M & W
Coker College *South Carolina* M & W
Colby College *Maine* M & W
Colby Community College *Kansas* M & W
Colby-Sawyer College *New Hampshire* M & W
Colgate University *New York* M & W
The College at Brockport, State University of New York *New York* M & W
College of the Canyons *California* M & W
College of Charleston *South Carolina* M & W
College of the Desert *California* M & W
College of DuPage *Illinois* M & W
College of the Holy Cross *Massachusetts* M & W
The College of Idaho *Idaho* M & W
College of Lake County *Illinois* M & W
College of Marin *California* M & W
College of Mount St. Joseph *Ohio* M & W
College of Mount Saint Vincent *New York* M & W
The College of New Jersey *New Jersey* M & W
The College of New Rochelle *New York* W
College of the Redwoods *California* M & W
College of Saint Benedict *Minnesota* W
College of St. Joseph *Vermont* M & W
College of Saint Mary *Nebraska* W
The College of Saint Rose *New York* M & W
The College of St. Scholastica *Minnesota* M & W
College of San Mateo *California* M & W
College of the Sequoias *California* M & W
College of the Siskiyous *California* M & W
College of Staten Island of the City University of New York *New York* M & W
The College of William and Mary *Virginia* M & W
The College of Wooster *Ohio* M & W
Colorado Christian University *Colorado* M & W
The Colorado College *Colorado* M & W
Colorado Northwestern Community College *Colorado* W
Colorado School of Mines *Colorado* M & W
Colorado State University *Colorado* M & W
Colorado State University–Pueblo *Colorado* W
Columbia College *California* M & W
Columbia University *New York* M & W
Columbia University, School of General Studies *New York* M & W
Columbus State Community College *Ohio* M & W
Columbus State University *Georgia* M & W
Community College of Philadelphia *Pennsylvania* M & W
Community College of Rhode Island *Rhode Island* M & W
Concord University *West Virginia* M & W
Concordia College *Minnesota* M & W
Concordia College–New York *New York* M & W
Concordia University *Quebec* M & W
Concordia University *Oregon* M & W
Concordia University *Michigan* M & W
Concordia University *California* M & W
Concordia University Chicago *Illinois* M & W
Concordia University College of Alberta *Alberta* M & W
Concordia University, Nebraska *Nebraska* M & W
Concordia University, St. Paul *Minnesota* M & W
Concordia University Texas *Texas* M & W
Concordia University Wisconsin *Wisconsin* M & W
Connecticut College *Connecticut* M & W
Contra Costa College *California* M & W
Converse College *South Carolina* W
Cooper Union for the Advancement of Science and Art *New York* M & W
Coppin State University *Maryland* M & W
Corban University *Oregon* M & W
Cornell College *Iowa* M & W
Cornell University *New York* M & W
Cornerstone University *Michigan* M & W
Covenant College *Georgia* M & W
Cowley County Community College and Area Vocational–Technical School *Kansas* M & W
Crandall University *New Brunswick* M & W
Creighton University *Nebraska* M & W
Crown College *Minnesota* M & W
Cuesta College *California* M & W
Culver-Stockton College *Missouri* M & W
Curry College *Massachusetts* W
Cuyahoga Community College *Ohio* M & W

M = Men; W = Women

Cuyamaca College *California* M & W
Daemen College *New York* M & W
Dakota State University *South Dakota* M & W
Dakota Wesleyan University *South Dakota* M & W
Dalhousie University *Nova Scotia* M & W
Dallas Baptist University *Texas* M & W
Dana College *Nebraska* M & W
Daniel Webster College *New Hampshire* M & W
Danville Area Community College *Illinois* M & W
Dartmouth College *New Hampshire* M & W
Darton College *Georgia* M & W
Davenport University *Michigan* M & W
Davidson College *North Carolina* M & W
Davis & Elkins College *West Virginia* M & W
De Anza College *California* M & W
Defiance College *Ohio* M & W
Delaware State University *Delaware* M & W
Delaware Valley College *Pennsylvania* M & W
Delta State University *Mississippi* W
Denison University *Ohio* M & W
DePaul University *Illinois* M & W
DePauw University *Indiana* M & W
Des Moines Area Community College *Iowa* W
DeSales University *Pennsylvania* M & W
Diablo Valley College *California* M & W
Dickinson College *Pennsylvania* M & W
Dickinson State University *North Dakota* M & W
Dillard University *Louisiana* M & W
Diné College *Arizona* M & W
Doane College *Nebraska* M & W
Dodge City Community College *Kansas* M & W
Dominican College *New York* W
Dominican University *Illinois* M & W
Dordt College *Iowa* M & W
Dowling College *New York* M & W
Drake University *Iowa* M & W
Drew University *New Jersey* M & W
Drury University *Missouri* M & W
Duke University *North Carolina* M & W
Duquesne University *Pennsylvania* M & W
D'Youville College *New York* M & W
Earlham College *Indiana* M & W
East Carolina University *North Carolina* M & W
East Central University *Oklahoma* M & W
East Los Angeles College *California* M & W
East Stroudsburg University of Pennsylvania *Pennsylvania* M & W
East Tennessee State University *Tennessee* M & W
East Texas Baptist University *Texas* M & W
Eastern Connecticut State University *Connecticut* M & W
Eastern Illinois University *Illinois* M & W
Eastern Kentucky University *Kentucky* M & W
Eastern Mennonite University *Virginia* M & W
Eastern Michigan University *Michigan* M & W
Eastern Nazarene College *Massachusetts* M & W
Eastern New Mexico University *New Mexico* M & W
Eastern Oregon University *Oregon* M & W
Eastern Washington University *Washington* M & W
Edgewood College *Wisconsin* M & W
Edinboro University of Pennsylvania *Pennsylvania* M & W
El Camino College *California* M & W
Elgin Community College *Illinois* M & W
Elizabeth City State University *North Carolina* M & W
Elizabethtown College *Pennsylvania* M & W
Elmhurst College *Illinois* M & W
Elms College *Massachusetts* M & W
Elon University *North Carolina* M & W
Embry-Riddle Aeronautical University *Florida* M & W
Emerson College *Massachusetts* M & W
Emmanuel College *Massachusetts* M & W
Emory & Henry College *Virginia* M & W
Emory University *Georgia* M & W
Emporia State University *Kansas* M & W
Endicott College *Massachusetts* M & W
Erie Community College *New York* M & W
Erie Community College, North Campus *New York* M & W
Erie Community College, South Campus *New York* M & W

Erskine College *South Carolina* M & W
Essex County College *New Jersey* M & W
Evangel University *Missouri* M & W
Everett Community College *Washington* M & W
The Evergreen State College *Washington* M & W
Fairfield University *Connecticut* M & W
Fairleigh Dickinson University, College at Florham *New Jersey* M & W
Fairleigh Dickinson University, Metropolitan Campus *New Jersey* M & W
Fairmont State University *West Virginia* M & W
Faith Baptist Bible College and Theological Seminary *Iowa* M & W
Farmingdale State College *New York* M & W
Fashion Institute of Technology *New York* M & W
Fayetteville State University *North Carolina* M & W
Felician College *New Jersey* M & W
Ferris State University *Michigan* M & W
Ferrum College *Virginia* M & W
Finger Lakes Community College *New York* M & W
Finlandia University *Michigan* M & W
Fitchburg State College *Massachusetts* M & W
Flagler College *Florida* M & W
Flathead Valley Community College *Montana* M & W
Florida Agricultural and Mechanical University *Florida* M & W
Florida Atlantic University *Florida* M & W
Florida College *Florida* M & W
Florida Gulf Coast University *Florida* M & W
Florida Institute of Technology *Florida* M & W
Florida International University *Florida* M & W
Florida Memorial University *Florida* M & W
Florida Southern College *Florida* M & W
Florida State University *Florida* M & W
Fontbonne University *Missouri* M & W
Fordham University *New York* M & W
Fort Belknap College *Montana* M & W
Fort Berthold Community College *North Dakota* M & W
Fort Hays State University *Kansas* M & W
Fort Lewis College *Colorado* M & W
Framingham State College *Massachusetts* M & W
Francis Marion University *South Carolina* M & W
Franciscan University of Steubenville *Ohio* M & W
Franklin College *Indiana* M & W
Franklin & Marshall College *Pennsylvania* M & W
Franklin Pierce University *New Hampshire* M & W
Fresno City College *California* M & W
Fresno Pacific University *California* M & W
Friends University *Kansas* M & W
Frostburg State University *Maryland* M & W
Fullerton College *California* M & W
Furman University *South Carolina* M & W
Gadsden State Community College *Alabama* W
Gallaudet University *District of Columbia* M & W
Gannon University *Pennsylvania* M & W
Garden City Community College *Kansas* M & W
Gardner-Webb University *North Carolina* M & W
GateWay Community College *Arizona* M & W
Genesee Community College *New York* M & W
Geneva College *Pennsylvania* M & W
George Fox University *Oregon* M & W
George Mason University *Virginia* M & W
The George Washington University *District of Columbia* M & W
Georgetown College *Kentucky* M & W
Georgetown University *District of Columbia* M & W
Georgia College & State University *Georgia* M & W
Georgia Institute of Technology *Georgia* M & W
Georgia Southern University *Georgia* W
Georgia State University *Georgia* M & W
Georgian Court University *New Jersey* W
Gettysburg College *Pennsylvania* M & W
Glendale Community College *California* M & W
Glendale Community College *Arizona* M & W
Glenville State College *West Virginia* M & W
Globe Institute of Technology *New York* M & W
Gloucester County College *New Jersey* M & W
Golden West College *California* M & W
Goldey-Beacom College *Delaware* M & W
Gonzaga University *Washington* M & W
Gordon College *Massachusetts* M & W
Goshen College *Indiana* M & W

Goucher College *Maryland* M & W
Grace College *Indiana* M & W
Graceland University *Iowa* M & W
Grambling State University *Louisiana* M & W
Grand Canyon University *Arizona* M
Grand Valley State University *Michigan* M & W
Grand View University *Iowa* M & W
Green Mountain College *Vermont* M & W
Greensboro College *North Carolina* M & W
Greenville College *Illinois* M & W
Grinnell College *Iowa* M & W
Grossmont College *California* M
Grove City College *Pennsylvania* M & W
Guilford College *North Carolina* M & W
Gustavus Adolphus College *Minnesota* M & W
Gwynedd-Mercy College *Pennsylvania* M & W
Hagerstown Community College *Maryland* M & W
Hamilton College *New York* M & W
Hamline University *Minnesota* M & W
Hampden-Sydney College *Virginia* M
Hampton University *Virginia* M & W
Hannibal-LaGrange College *Missouri* M & W
Hanover College *Indiana* M & W
Hardin-Simmons University *Texas* M & W
Harding University *Arkansas* M & W
Harford Community College *Maryland* M & W
Harper College *Illinois* M & W
Hartnell College *California* M & W
Hartwick College *New York* M & W
Harvard University *Massachusetts* M & W
Harvey Mudd College *California* M & W
Haskell Indian Nations University *Kansas* M & W
Hastings College *Nebraska* M & W
Haverford College *Pennsylvania* M & W
Hawai'i Pacific University *Hawaii* M & W
Heidelberg University *Ohio* M & W
Henderson State University *Arkansas* M & W
Hendrix College *Arkansas* M & W
Herkimer County Community College *New York* M & W
High Point University *North Carolina* M & W
Highland Community College *Kansas* M & W
Highline Community College *Washington* M & W
Hilbert College *New York* M & W
Hinds Community College *Mississippi* M
Hiram College *Ohio* M & W
Hobart and William Smith Colleges *New York* M & W
Hofstra University *New York* M & W
Holy Cross College *Indiana* M & W
Holy Family University *Pennsylvania* M & W
Holy Names University *California* M & W
Hood College *Maryland* M & W
Hope College *Michigan* M & W
Houghton College *New York* M & W
Houston Baptist University *Texas* M & W
Howard Community College *Maryland* M & W
Howard Payne University *Texas* M & W
Howard University *District of Columbia* M & W
Hudson Valley Community College *New York* M & W
Humboldt State University *California* M & W
Hunter College of the City University of New York *New York* M & W
Huntingdon College *Alabama* M & W
Huntington University *Indiana* M & W
Huston-Tillotson University *Texas* W
Hutchinson Community College and Area Vocational School *Kansas* M & W
Idaho State University *Idaho* M & W
Illinois College *Illinois* M & W
Illinois Institute of Technology *Illinois* M & W
Illinois State University *Illinois* M & W
Illinois Wesleyan University *Illinois* M & W
Immaculata University *Pennsylvania* W
Indiana State University *Indiana* M & W
Indiana Tech *Indiana* M & W
Indiana University Bloomington *Indiana* M & W
Indiana University East *Indiana* M & W
Indiana University of Pennsylvania *Pennsylvania* M & W
Indiana University–Purdue University Fort Wayne *Indiana* M & W

M = Men; W = Women

Indiana University–Purdue University Indianapolis *Indiana* M & W
Indiana Wesleyan University *Indiana* M & W
Inter American University of Puerto Rico, Aguadilla Campus *Puerto Rico* M & W
Inter American University of Puerto Rico, Barranquitas Campus *Puerto Rico* M & W
Inter American University of Puerto Rico, Bayamón Campus *Puerto Rico* M & W
Inter American University of Puerto Rico, Guayama Campus *Puerto Rico* M & W
Inter American University of Puerto Rico, Ponce Campus *Puerto Rico* M & W
Inter American University of Puerto Rico, San Germán Campus *Puerto Rico* M & W
Iona College *New York* M & W
Iowa Central Community College *Iowa* M & W
Iowa Lakes Community College *Iowa* M & W
Iowa State University of Science and Technology *Iowa* M & W
Iowa Wesleyan College *Iowa* M & W
Irvine Valley College *California* M & W
Ithaca College *New York* M & W
Jackson Community College *Michigan* M & W
Jackson State University *Mississippi* M & W
Jacksonville State University *Alabama* M & W
Jacksonville University *Florida* M & W
James Madison University *Virginia* W
Jamestown College *North Dakota* M & W
Jamestown Community College *New York* M & W
Jefferson College of Health Sciences *Virginia* M & W
John Carroll University *Ohio* M & W
John Jay College of Criminal Justice of the City University of New York *New York* M & W
The Johns Hopkins University *Maryland* M & W
Johnson Bible College *Tennessee* M & W
Johnson C. Smith University *North Carolina* M & W
Johnson College *Pennsylvania* M & W
Johnson County Community College *Kansas* M & W
Johnson State College *Vermont* M & W
Johnson & Wales University *Rhode Island* M & W
Judson University *Illinois* M & W
Juniata College *Pennsylvania* M & W
Kalamazoo College *Michigan* M & W
Kansas City Kansas Community College *Kansas* M & W
Kansas State University *Kansas* M & W
Kansas Wesleyan University *Kansas* M & W
Keene State College *New Hampshire* M & W
Kennesaw State University *Georgia* M & W
Kent State University *Ohio* M & W
Kentucky Christian University *Kentucky* M & W
Kentucky State University *Kentucky* M & W
Kentucky Wesleyan College *Kentucky* M & W
Kenyon College *Ohio* M & W
Keuka College *New York* M & W
Keystone College *Pennsylvania* M & W
King College *Tennessee* M & W
King's College *Pennsylvania* M & W
Kirtland Community College *Michigan* M & W
Knox College *Illinois* M & W
Kutztown University of Pennsylvania *Pennsylvania* M & W
La Roche College *Pennsylvania* M & W
La Salle University *Pennsylvania* M & W
Lackawanna College *Pennsylvania* M & W
Lafayette College *Pennsylvania* M & W
LaGrange College *Georgia* M & W
Lake Erie College *Ohio* M & W
Lake Forest College *Illinois* M & W
Lake Superior State University *Michigan* M & W
Lakehead University *Ontario* M & W
Lakeland College *Wisconsin* M & W
Lamar Community College *Colorado* W
Lamar University *Texas* M & W
Lander University *South Carolina* W
Landmark College *Vermont* M & W
Lane College *Tennessee* M & W
Lane Community College *Oregon* M & W
Lansing Community College *Michigan* M & W
Las Positas College *California* M & W
Lasell College *Massachusetts* M & W
Lassen Community College District *California* M & W
Laurentian University *Ontario* W
Lawrence University *Wisconsin* M & W
Lawson State Community College *Alabama* M
Le Moyne College *New York* M & W
Lebanon Valley College *Pennsylvania* M & W
Lee University *Tennessee* M & W
Lees-McRae College *North Carolina* M & W
Lehigh University *Pennsylvania* M & W
Lehman College of the City University of New York *New York* M & W
LeMoyne-Owen College *Tennessee* M & W
Lenoir-Rhyne University *North Carolina* M & W
Lesley University *Massachusetts* M & W
LeTourneau University *Texas* M & W
Lewis & Clark College *Oregon* M & W
Lewis-Clark State College *Idaho* M & W
Lewis University *Illinois* M & W
Liberty University *Virginia* M & W
Limestone College *South Carolina* M & W
Lincoln Christian University *Illinois* M & W
Lincoln Memorial University *Tennessee* M & W
Lincoln University *Pennsylvania* M & W
Lincoln University *Missouri* W
Lindenwood University *Missouri* M & W
Lindsey Wilson College *Kentucky* M & W
Linfield College *Oregon* M & W
Lipscomb University *Tennessee* M & W
Livingstone College *North Carolina* M & W
Lock Haven University of Pennsylvania *Pennsylvania* M & W
Lon Morris College *Texas* M & W
Long Beach City College *California* M & W
Long Island University, Brooklyn Campus *New York* M & W
Long Island University, C.W. Post Campus *New York* M & W
Longwood University *Virginia* M & W
Loras College *Iowa* M & W
Los Angeles City College *California* M
Los Angeles Southwest College *California* M & W
Los Angeles Trade-Technical College *California* M & W
Los Angeles Valley College *California* M & W
Louisiana College *Louisiana* W
Louisiana State University and Agricultural and Mechanical College *Louisiana* M & W
Louisiana Tech University *Louisiana* M & W
Loyola Marymount University *California* M & W
Loyola University Chicago *Illinois* M & W
Loyola University Maryland *Maryland* M & W
Loyola University New Orleans *Louisiana* M & W
Lubbock Christian University *Texas* M & W
Luther College *Iowa* M & W
Luzerne County Community College *Pennsylvania* M & W
Lycoming College *Pennsylvania* M & W
Lynchburg College *Virginia* M & W
Lyndon State College *Vermont* M & W
Lyon College *Arkansas* M & W
Macalester College *Minnesota* M & W
Macomb Community College *Michigan* M & W
Madison Area Technical College *Wisconsin* M & W
Madonna University *Michigan* M & W
Maine Maritime Academy *Maine* M & W
Malone University *Ohio* M & W
Manchester College *Indiana* M & W
Manhattan College *New York* M & W
Mansfield University of Pennsylvania *Pennsylvania* M & W
Maranatha Baptist Bible College *Wisconsin* M & W
Marian University *Wisconsin* M & W
Marian University *Indiana* M & W
Marietta College *Ohio* M & W
Marist College *New York* M & W
Marquette University *Wisconsin* M & W
Mars Hill College *North Carolina* M & W
Marshall University *West Virginia* M & W
Martin Luther College *Minnesota* M & W
Mary Baldwin College *Virginia* W
Marymount University *Virginia* M & W
Maryville College *Tennessee* M & W
Maryville University of Saint Louis *Missouri* M & W
Marywood University *Pennsylvania* M & W
Massachusetts Bay Community College *Massachusetts* M & W
Massachusetts College of Liberal Arts *Massachusetts* M & W
Massachusetts Institute of Technology *Massachusetts* M & W
Massachusetts Maritime Academy *Massachusetts* M & W
The Master's College and Seminary *California* M & W
McDaniel College *Maryland* M & W
McGill University *Quebec* M & W
McKendree University *Illinois* M & W
McMaster University *Ontario* M & W
McMurry University *Texas* M & W
McNeese State University *Louisiana* M & W
McPherson College *Kansas* M & W
Medaille College *New York* M & W
Medgar Evers College of the City University of New York *New York* M & W
Memorial University of Newfoundland *Newfoundland and Labrador* M & W
Menlo College *California* M & W
Merced College *California* M
Mercer University *Georgia* M & W
Mercy College *New York* M & W
Mercyhurst College *Pennsylvania* M & W
Meredith College *North Carolina* W
Meridian Community College *Mississippi* M & W
Merrimack College *Massachusetts* M & W
Merritt College *California* M & W
Mesa Community College *Arizona* M
Mesa State College *Colorado* W
Messiah College *Pennsylvania* M & W
Methodist University *North Carolina* M & W
Metropolitan Community College–Longview *Missouri* W
Miami University *Ohio* M & W
Michigan State University *Michigan* M & W
Michigan Technological University *Michigan* M & W
Middle Tennessee State University *Tennessee* M & W
Middlebury College *Vermont* M & W
Middlesex County College *New Jersey* M & W
Midland Lutheran College *Nebraska* M & W
Midwestern State University *Texas* W
Miles College *Alabama* M
Millersville University of Pennsylvania *Pennsylvania* M & W
Milligan College *Tennessee* M & W
Millikin University *Illinois* M & W
Mills College *California* W
Millsaps College *Mississippi* M & W
Milwaukee School of Engineering *Wisconsin* M & W
Minnesota State University Mankato *Minnesota* M & W
Minnesota State University Moorhead *Minnesota* M & W
Minot State University *North Dakota* M & W
MiraCosta College *California* M & W
Misericordia University *Pennsylvania* M & W
Mississippi College *Mississippi* M & W
Mississippi State University *Mississippi* M & W
Mississippi Valley State University *Mississippi* M & W
Missouri Baptist University *Missouri* M & W
Missouri Southern State University *Missouri* M & W
Missouri State University *Missouri* W
Missouri University of Science and Technology *Missouri* M & W
Missouri Valley College *Missouri* M & W
Mitchell College *Connecticut* M & W
Modesto Junior College *California* M & W
Mohawk Valley Community College *New York* M & W
Molloy College *New York* M & W
Monmouth College *Illinois* M & W
Monmouth University *New Jersey* M & W
Montana State University *Montana* M & W
Montana State University Billings *Montana* M & W
Monterey Peninsula College *California* M & W
Montgomery College *Maryland* M & W

M = Men; W = Women

Montreat College *North Carolina* M & W
Moorpark College *California* M & W
Moraine Valley Community College *Illinois* M & W
Moravian College *Pennsylvania* M & W
Morehead State University *Kentucky* M & W
Morehouse College *Georgia* M
Morgan State University *Maryland* M & W
Morningside College *Iowa* M & W
Morris College *South Carolina* M & W
Morton College *Illinois* M & W
Mott Community College *Michigan* M & W
Mount Aloysius College *Pennsylvania* M & W
Mount Holyoke College *Massachusetts* W
Mt. Hood Community College *Oregon* M & W
Mount Ida College *Massachusetts* M & W
Mount Marty College *South Dakota* M & W
Mount Mary College *Wisconsin* W
Mount Mercy College *Iowa* M & W
Mount Olive College *North Carolina* M & W
Mount Saint Mary College *New York* M & W
Mount St. Mary's University *Maryland* M & W
Mt. San Antonio College *California* M & W
Mount Vernon Nazarene University *Ohio* M & W
Mountain State University *West Virginia* M & W
Muhlenberg College *Pennsylvania* M & W
Murray State University *Kentucky* M & W
Muskingum University *Ohio* M & W
Napa Valley College *California* M & W
Nassau Community College *New York* M & W
Nazareth College of Rochester *New York* M & W
Nebraska Wesleyan University *Nebraska* M & W
Neosho County Community College *Kansas* M & W
Neumann University *Pennsylvania* M & W
New England College *New Hampshire* M & W
New Jersey City University *New Jersey* W
New Jersey Institute of Technology *New Jersey* M & W
New Mexico Highlands University *New Mexico* M & W
New Mexico State University *New Mexico* M & W
New York City College of Technology of the City University of New York *New York* M & W
New York Institute of Technology *New York* M & W
New York University *New York* M & W
Newberry College *South Carolina* M & W
Newbury College *Massachusetts* M & W
Newman University *Kansas* M & W
Niagara University *New York* M & W
Nicholls State University *Louisiana* M & W
Nipissing University *Ontario* M & W
North Carolina Agricultural and Technical State University *North Carolina* M & W
North Carolina Central University *North Carolina* M & W
North Carolina State University *North Carolina* M & W
North Central College *Illinois* M & W
North Central University *Minnesota* M & W
North Dakota State University *North Dakota* M & W
North Georgia College & State University *Georgia* M & W
North Greenville University *South Carolina* M & W
North Iowa Area Community College *Iowa* M & W
North Park University *Illinois* M & W
Northeastern University *Massachusetts* M & W
Northern Arizona University *Arizona* M & W
Northern Essex Community College *Massachusetts* M & W
Northern Illinois University *Illinois* W
Northern Kentucky University *Kentucky* M & W
Northern Michigan University *Michigan* W
Northern State University *South Dakota* M & W
Northland College *Wisconsin* M & W
Northwest Christian University *Oregon* M & W
Northwest Missouri State University *Missouri* M & W
Northwest Nazarene University *Idaho* M & W
Northwest University *Washington* M & W
Northwestern College *Minnesota* M & W
Northwestern College *Iowa* M & W
Northwestern Oklahoma State University *Oklahoma* M & W
Northwestern State University of Louisiana *Louisiana* M & W
Northwestern University *Illinois* W
Northwood University *Michigan* M & W
Northwood University, Texas Campus *Texas* M & W
Norwich University *Vermont* M & W
Notre Dame College *Ohio* M & W
Notre Dame de Namur University *California* M & W
Nova Southeastern University *Florida* M & W
Oakland City University *Indiana* M & W
Oakland Community College *Michigan* M & W
Oakland University *Michigan* M & W
Oakton Community College *Illinois* M & W
Oberlin College *Ohio* M & W
Occidental College *California* M & W
Ocean County College *New Jersey* M & W
Odessa College *Texas* M & W
Oglethorpe University *Georgia* M & W
Ohio Dominican University *Ohio* M & W
Ohio Northern University *Ohio* M & W
The Ohio State University *Ohio* M & W
Ohio University *Ohio* M & W
Ohio Valley University *West Virginia* M & W
Ohio Wesleyan University *Ohio* M & W
Oklahoma Baptist University *Oklahoma* M & W
Oklahoma Christian University *Oklahoma* M & W
Oklahoma Panhandle State University *Oklahoma* M & W
Oklahoma Wesleyan University *Oklahoma* M & W
Old Dominion University *Virginia* M & W
Olivet College *Michigan* M & W
Olivet Nazarene University *Illinois* M & W
Olympic College *Washington* M & W
Oral Roberts University *Oklahoma* M & W
Orange Coast College *California* M & W
Oregon Institute of Technology *Oregon* M & W
Ottawa University *Kansas* M & W
Otterbein University *Ohio* M & W
Ouachita Baptist University *Arkansas* W
Our Lady of the Lake University of San Antonio *Texas* M & W
Oxnard College *California* M & W
Pace University *New York* M & W
Pacific Lutheran University *Washington* M & W
Pacific Union College *California* M & W
Pacific University *Oregon* M & W
Paine College *Georgia* M & W
Palm Beach Atlantic University *Florida* M & W
Palo Alto College *Texas* M & W
Paradise Valley Community College *Arizona* M & W
Park University *Missouri* M & W
Pasadena City College *California* M & W
Pasco-Hernando Community College *Florida* W
Paul Smith's College *New York* M & W
Peace College *North Carolina* W
Penn State Altoona *Pennsylvania* M & W
Penn State Berks *Pennsylvania* M & W
Penn State DuBois *Pennsylvania* M & W
Penn State Erie, The Behrend College *Pennsylvania* M & W
Penn State Harrisburg *Pennsylvania* M & W
Penn State Lehigh Valley *Pennsylvania* M & W
Penn State Mont Alto *Pennsylvania* M & W
Penn State Schuylkill *Pennsylvania* M & W
Penn State University Park *Pennsylvania* M & W
Penn State Wilkes-Barre *Pennsylvania* M & W
Penn State Worthington Scranton *Pennsylvania* M & W
Pennsylvania College of Technology *Pennsylvania* M & W
Pepperdine University *California* M & W
Peru State College *Nebraska* W
Pfeiffer University *North Carolina* M & W
Phoenix College *Arizona* M & W
Piedmont College *Georgia* M & W
Pikeville College *Kentucky* M & W
Pima Community College *Arizona* M & W
Pine Manor College *Massachusetts* W
Pittsburg State University *Kansas* M & W
Pitzer College *California* M & W
Point Loma Nazarene University *California* M & W
Point Park University *Pennsylvania* M & W
Polytechnic Institute of NYU *New York* M & W
Polytechnic University of Puerto Rico *Puerto Rico* M & W
Pomona College *California* M & W
Pontifical Catholic University of Puerto Rico *Puerto Rico* M & W
Portland State University *Oregon* M & W
Post University *Connecticut* M & W
Prairie View A&M University *Texas* M & W
Pratt Community College *Kansas* M & W
Pratt Institute *New York* M & W
Presbyterian College *South Carolina* M & W
Presentation College *South Dakota* M & W
Princeton University *New Jersey* M & W
Principia College *Illinois* M & W
Providence College *Rhode Island* M & W
Purchase College, State University of New York *New York* M & W
Purdue University *Indiana* M & W
Queens College of the City University of New York *New York* M & W
Queens University of Charlotte *North Carolina* M & W
Queen's University at Kingston *Ontario* M & W
Queensborough Community College of the City University of New York *New York* M & W
Quinnipiac University *Connecticut* M & W
Radford University *Virginia* M & W
Ramapo College of New Jersey *New Jersey* M & W
Randolph College *Virginia* M & W
Ranger College *Texas* M & W
Redeemer University College *Ontario* M & W
Reinhardt University *Georgia* M & W
Rend Lake College *Illinois* M
Rensselaer Polytechnic Institute *New York* M & W
Rhode Island College *Rhode Island* M & W
Rhodes College *Tennessee* M & W
Rice University *Texas* M & W
The Richard Stockton College of New Jersey *New Jersey* M & W
Rider University *New Jersey* M & W
Rio Hondo College *California* M & W
Ripon College *Wisconsin* M & W
Riverside Community College District *California* M & W
Rivier College *New Hampshire* M & W
Roanoke College *Virginia* M & W
Robert Morris University Illinois *Illinois* M & W
Roberts Wesleyan College *New York* M & W
Rochester Institute of Technology *New York* M & W
Rocky Mountain College *Montana* M & W
Roger Williams University *Rhode Island* M & W
Rollins College *Florida* M & W
Roosevelt University *Illinois* M & W
Rose-Hulman Institute of Technology *Indiana* M & W
Rosemont College *Pennsylvania* M & W
Rowan University *New Jersey* M & W
Royal Military College of Canada *Ontario* M & W
Rust College *Mississippi* M & W
Rutgers, The State University of New Jersey, Camden *New Jersey* W
Rutgers, The State University of New Jersey, New Brunswick *New Jersey* M & W
Rutgers, The State University of New Jersey, Newark *New Jersey* M & W
Sacramento City College *California* M & W
Sacred Heart University *Connecticut* M & W
Saddleback College *California* M & W
Saginaw Valley State University *Michigan* M & W
St. Ambrose University *Iowa* M & W
St. Andrews Presbyterian College *North Carolina* M & W
Saint Anselm College *New Hampshire* M & W
Saint Augustine's College *North Carolina* M & W
St. Bonaventure University *New York* M & W
St. Catherine University *Minnesota* W
St. Cloud State University *Minnesota* M & W
St. Francis College *New York* M & W
Saint Francis University *Pennsylvania* M & W
St. Francis Xavier University *Nova Scotia* M & W
St. John's University *New York* W
Saint John's University *Minnesota* M
Saint Joseph College *Connecticut* W
Saint Joseph's College *Indiana* M & W
St. Joseph's College, Long Island Campus *New York* M & W

M = Men; W = Women

Saint Joseph's College of Maine *Maine* M & W
St. Joseph's College, New York *New York* M & W
Saint Joseph's University *Pennsylvania* M & W
St. Lawrence University *New York* M & W
Saint Leo University *Florida* M & W
St. Louis Christian College *Missouri* W
St. Louis College of Pharmacy *Missouri* M & W
St. Louis Community College at Florissant Valley *Missouri* M & W
Saint Louis University *Missouri* M & W
Saint Martin's University *Washington* M & W
Saint Mary-of-the-Woods College *Indiana* W
Saint Mary's College *Indiana* W
Saint Mary's College of California *California* M & W
St. Mary's College of Maryland *Maryland* M & W
Saint Mary's University *Nova Scotia* M & W
St. Mary's University *Texas* W
Saint Mary's University of Minnesota *Minnesota* M & W
Saint Michael's College *Vermont* M & W
St. Norbert College *Wisconsin* M & W
St. Olaf College *Minnesota* M & W
Saint Paul's College *Virginia* M & W
Saint Peter's College *New Jersey* M & W
St. Thomas Aquinas College *New York* M & W
St. Thomas University *New Brunswick* M & W
St. Thomas University *Florida* M & W
Saint Vincent College *Pennsylvania* M & W
Saint Xavier University *Illinois* W
Salem College *North Carolina* W
Salem State College *Massachusetts* M & W
Salisbury University *Maryland* M & W
Salve Regina University *Rhode Island* M & W
Sam Houston State University *Texas* M & W
Samford University *Alabama* M & W
San Bernardino Valley College *California* M & W
San Diego Christian College *California* M & W
San Diego City College *California* M & W
San Diego Mesa College *California* M & W
San Diego State University *California* W
San Francisco State University *California* M & W
San Joaquin Delta College *California* M & W
San Jose City College *California* M & W
San Jose State University *California* M & W
Santa Ana College *California* M & W
Santa Barbara City College *California* M & W
Santa Clara University *California* M & W
Santa Monica College *California* M & W
Santa Rosa Junior College *California* M & W
Sarah Lawrence College *New York* M & W
Sauk Valley Community College *Illinois* M & W
Savannah College of Art and Design *Georgia* M & W
Savannah State University *Georgia* M & W
Schoolcraft College *Michigan* W
Schreiner University *Texas* M & W
Scottsdale Community College *Arizona* M & W
Scripps College *California* W
Seattle Pacific University *Washington* M & W
Seattle University *Washington* M & W
Seton Hill University *Pennsylvania* M & W
Sewanee: The University of the South *Tennessee* M & W
Shasta College *California* M & W
Shaw University *North Carolina* M & W
Shawnee State University *Ohio* M & W
Shenandoah University *Virginia* M & W
Sheridan College *Wyoming* M & W
Shippensburg University of Pennsylvania *Pennsylvania* M & W
Shoreline Community College *Washington* M & W
Shorter University *Georgia* M & W
Siena College *New York* M & W
Siena Heights University *Michigan* M & W
Silver Lake College *Wisconsin* M & W
Simon Fraser University *British Columbia* M & W
Simpson College *Iowa* M & W
Simpson University *California* M & W
Skagit Valley College *Washington* M & W
Skyline College *California* M & W
Slippery Rock University of Pennsylvania *Pennsylvania* M & W
Smith College *Massachusetts* W
Soka University of America *California* M & W
Sonoma State University *California* M
South Carolina State University *South Carolina* M & W
South Dakota School of Mines and Technology *South Dakota* M & W
South Dakota State University *South Dakota* M & W
South Plains College *Texas* M & W
Southeast Missouri State University *Missouri* M & W
Southeastern Louisiana University *Louisiana* M & W
Southeastern Oklahoma State University *Oklahoma* W
Southern Alberta Institute of Technology *Alberta* M & W
Southern Arkansas University–Magnolia *Arkansas* M & W
Southern Connecticut State University *Connecticut* M & W
Southern Illinois University Carbondale *Illinois* M & W
Southern Illinois University Edwardsville *Illinois* M & W
Southern Methodist University *Texas* W
Southern Nazarene University *Oklahoma* M & W
Southern New Hampshire University *New Hampshire* M & W
Southern Oregon University *Oregon* M & W
Southern University and Agricultural and Mechanical College *Louisiana* M
Southern University at New Orleans *Louisiana* M & W
Southern Utah University *Utah* M & W
Southern Vermont College *Vermont* M & W
Southern Virginia University *Virginia* M & W
Southern Wesleyan University *South Carolina* M & W
Southwest Baptist University *Missouri* M & W
Southwestern College *Kansas* M & W
Southwestern College *California* M & W
Southwestern Oklahoma State University *Oklahoma* W
Southwestern Oregon Community College *Oregon* M & W
Southwestern University *Texas* M & W
Spalding University *Kentucky* M & W
Spartanburg Methodist College *South Carolina* M & W
Spelman College *Georgia* W
Spokane Community College *Washington* M & W
Spokane Falls Community College *Washington* M & W
Spring Arbor University *Michigan* M & W
Spring Hill College *Alabama* M & W
Springfield College *Massachusetts* M & W
Stanford University *California* M & W
State University of New York at Binghamton *New York* M & W
State University of New York College of Agriculture and Technology at Cobleskill *New York* M & W
State University of New York College at Cortland *New York* M & W
State University of New York College of Environmental Science and Forestry *New York* M & W
State University of New York College at Geneseo *New York* M & W
State University of New York College at Old Westbury *New York* M & W
State University of New York College at Oneonta *New York* M & W
State University of New York College at Potsdam *New York* M & W
State University of New York College of Technology at Alfred *New York* M & W
State University of New York College of Technology at Canton *New York* M & W
State University of New York College of Technology at Delhi *New York* M & W
State University of New York at Fredonia *New York* M & W
State University of New York Institute of Technology *New York* W
State University of New York Maritime College *New York* M & W
State University of New York at New Paltz *New York* M & W
State University of New York at Oswego *New York* M & W
State University of New York at Plattsburgh *New York* M & W
Stephen F. Austin State University *Texas* M & W
Stephens College *Missouri* W
Sterling College *Kansas* M & W
Stetson University *Florida* M & W
Stevens Institute of Technology *New Jersey* M & W
Stevenson University *Maryland* M & W
Stillman College *Alabama* M & W
Stonehill College *Massachusetts* M & W
Stony Brook University, State University of New York *New York* M & W
Suffolk County Community College *New York* M & W
Suffolk University *Massachusetts* M & W
Sul Ross State University *Texas* M & W
Sullivan County Community College *New York* M & W
Susquehanna University *Pennsylvania* M & W
Swarthmore College *Pennsylvania* M & W
Syracuse University *New York* M & W
Tabor College *Kansas* M & W
Tarleton State University *Texas* M & W
Taylor University *Indiana* M & W
Temple University *Pennsylvania* M & W
Tennessee State University *Tennessee* M & W
Tennessee Technological University *Tennessee* M & W
Tennessee Wesleyan College *Tennessee* M & W
Texas A&M International University *Texas* M & W
Texas A&M University *Texas* M & W
Texas A&M University–Commerce *Texas* M & W
Texas A&M University–Corpus Christi *Texas* M & W
Texas A&M University–Kingsville *Texas* M & W
Texas Christian University *Texas* M & W
Texas Lutheran University *Texas* M & W
Texas Southern University *Texas* M & W
Texas State University–San Marcos *Texas* M & W
Texas Tech University *Texas* M & W
Thaddeus Stevens College of Technology *Pennsylvania* M
Thiel College *Pennsylvania* M & W
Thomas More College *Kentucky* M & W
Tiffin University *Ohio* M & W
Tougaloo College *Mississippi* M & W
Towson University *Maryland* M & W
Transylvania University *Kentucky* M & W
Treasure Valley Community College *Oregon* M & W
Trent University *Ontario* M & W
Trine University *Indiana* M & W
Trinity Christian College *Illinois* M & W
Trinity College *Connecticut* M & W
Trinity University *Texas* M & W
Troy University *Alabama* M & W
Truett-McConnell College *Georgia* M & W
Truman State University *Missouri* M & W
Tufts University *Massachusetts* M & W
Tulane University *Louisiana* M & W
Tusculum College *Tennessee* M & W
Tuskegee University *Alabama* M & W
Union College *New York* M & W
Union College *Kentucky* M & W
Union University *Tennessee* M & W
United States Air Force Academy *Colorado* M & W
United States Coast Guard Academy *Connecticut* M & W
United States Merchant Marine Academy *New York* M & W
United States Military Academy *New York* M & W
United States Naval Academy *Maryland* M & W
United Tribes Technical College *North Dakota* M & W
Unity College *Maine* M & W
Université Laval *Quebec* M & W
Université de Moncton *New Brunswick* M & W
Université du Québec àChicoutimi *Quebec* M & W
Université du Québec àRimouski *Quebec* M & W
Université du Québec àTrois-Rivières *Quebec* M

M = Men; W = Women

The University of Akron *Ohio* M & W
The University of Alabama *Alabama* M & W
The University of Alabama at Birmingham *Alabama* W
The University of Alabama in Huntsville *Alabama* M & W
University of Alaska Anchorage *Alaska* M & W
University of Alaska Fairbanks *Alaska* M & W
University at Albany, State University of New York *New York* M & W
University of Alberta *Alberta* M & W
The University of Arizona *Arizona* M & W
University of Arkansas *Arkansas* M & W
University of Arkansas at Fort Smith *Arkansas* M & W
University of Arkansas at Little Rock *Arkansas* M & W
University of Arkansas at Monticello *Arkansas* W
University of Arkansas at Pine Bluff *Arkansas* M & W
University of Bridgeport *Connecticut* M & W
The University of British Columbia *British Columbia* M & W
University at Buffalo, the State University of New York *New York* M & W
University of Calgary *Alberta* M & W
University of California, Berkeley *California* M & W
University of California, Davis *California* M & W
University of California, Irvine *California* M & W
University of California, Los Angeles *California* M & W
University of California, Riverside *California* M & W
University of California, San Diego *California* M & W
University of California, Santa Barbara *California* M & W
University of California, Santa Cruz *California* M & W
University of Central Arkansas *Arkansas* M & W
University of Central Florida *Florida* M & W
University of Central Missouri *Missouri* M & W
University of Central Oklahoma *Oklahoma* M & W
University of Charleston *West Virginia* M & W
University of Chicago *Illinois* M & W
University of Cincinnati *Ohio* M & W
University of Colorado at Boulder *Colorado* M & W
University of Colorado at Colorado Springs *Colorado* M & W
University of Connecticut *Connecticut* M & W
University of the Cumberlands *Kentucky* M & W
University of Dallas *Texas* M & W
University of Dayton *Ohio* M & W
University of Delaware *Delaware* M & W
University of Denver *Colorado* M & W
University of Detroit Mercy *Michigan* M & W
University of Dubuque *Iowa* M & W
University of Evansville *Indiana* M & W
The University of Findlay *Ohio* M & W
University of Florida *Florida* M & W
University of Georgia *Georgia* M & W
University of Great Falls *Montana* M & W
University of Guelph *Ontario* M & W
University of Hartford *Connecticut* M & W
University of Hawaii at Hilo *Hawaii* M & W
University of Hawaii at Manoa *Hawaii* W
University of Houston *Texas* M & W
University of Idaho *Idaho* M & W
University of Illinois at Chicago *Illinois* M & W
University of Illinois at Urbana–Champaign *Illinois* M & W
University of the Incarnate Word *Texas* M & W
University of Indianapolis *Indiana* M & W
The University of Iowa *Iowa* M & W
The University of Kansas *Kansas* M & W
University of Kentucky *Kentucky* M & W
University of La Verne *California* M & W
University of Lethbridge *Alberta* M & W
University of Louisiana at Lafayette *Louisiana* M & W
University of Louisiana at Monroe *Louisiana* M & W
University of Louisville *Kentucky* M & W
University of Maine *Maine* M & W
University of Maine at Farmington *Maine* M & W
University of Maine at Machias *Maine* M & W
University of Maine at Presque Isle *Maine* M & W
University of Manitoba *Manitoba* M & W
University of Mary *North Dakota* M & W
University of Mary Washington *Virginia* M & W
University of Maryland, Baltimore County *Maryland* M & W
University of Maryland, College Park *Maryland* M & W
University of Maryland Eastern Shore *Maryland* M & W
University of Massachusetts Amherst *Massachusetts* M & W
University of Massachusetts Boston *Massachusetts* M & W
University of Massachusetts Dartmouth *Massachusetts* M & W
University of Massachusetts Lowell *Massachusetts* M & W
University of Memphis *Tennessee* M & W
University of Miami *Florida* M & W
University of Michigan *Michigan* M & W
University of Michigan–Dearborn *Michigan* M & W
University of Minnesota, Duluth *Minnesota* M & W
University of Minnesota, Morris *Minnesota* M & W
University of Minnesota, Twin Cities Campus *Minnesota* M & W
University of Mississippi *Mississippi* M & W
University of Missouri *Missouri* M & W
University of Missouri–Kansas City *Missouri* M & W
University of Mobile *Alabama* M & W
The University of Montana *Montana* M & W
University of Mount Union *Ohio* M & W
University of Nebraska at Kearney *Nebraska* M & W
University of Nebraska at Omaha *Nebraska* W
University of Nebraska–Lincoln *Nebraska* M & W
University of Nevada, Las Vegas *Nevada* W
University of Nevada, Reno *Nevada* W
University of New Brunswick Fredericton *New Brunswick* M & W
University of New Brunswick Saint John *New Brunswick* M & W
University of New England *Maine* M & W
University of New Hampshire *New Hampshire* M & W
University of New Haven *Connecticut* M & W
University of New Mexico *New Mexico* M & W
University of North Alabama *Alabama* M & W
The University of North Carolina at Asheville *North Carolina* M & W
The University of North Carolina at Chapel Hill *North Carolina* M & W
The University of North Carolina at Charlotte *North Carolina* M & W
The University of North Carolina at Greensboro *North Carolina* M & W
The University of North Carolina at Pembroke *North Carolina* M & W
The University of North Carolina Wilmington *North Carolina* M & W
University of North Dakota *North Dakota* M & W
University of North Florida *Florida* M & W
University of North Texas *Texas* M & W
University of Northern Colorado *Colorado* W
University of Northern Iowa *Iowa* M & W
University of Notre Dame *Indiana* M & W
University of Oklahoma *Oklahoma* M & W
University of Oregon *Oregon* M & W
University of Ottawa *Ontario* M & W
University of the Ozarks *Arkansas* M & W
University of the Pacific *California* W
University of Pennsylvania *Pennsylvania* M & W
University of Pittsburgh *Pennsylvania* M & W
University of Pittsburgh at Bradford *Pennsylvania* M & W
University of Pittsburgh at Greensburg *Pennsylvania* M & W
University of Pittsburgh at Johnstown *Pennsylvania* W
University of Portland *Oregon* M & W
University of Puerto Rico, Aguadilla University College *Puerto Rico* M & W
University of Puerto Rico at Arecibo *Puerto Rico* M & W
University of Puerto Rico at Bayamón *Puerto Rico* M & W
University of Puerto Rico at Carolina *Puerto Rico* M & W
University of Puerto Rico, Cayey University College *Puerto Rico* M & W
University of Puerto Rico at Humacao *Puerto Rico* M & W
University of Puerto Rico, Mayagüez Campus *Puerto Rico* M & W
University of Puerto Rico at Ponce *Puerto Rico* M & W
University of Puerto Rico, Río Piedras *Puerto Rico* M & W
University of Puerto Rico at Utuado *Puerto Rico* M & W
University of Puget Sound *Washington* M & W
University of Redlands *California* M & W
University of Regina *Saskatchewan* M & W
University of Rhode Island *Rhode Island* M & W
University of Richmond *Virginia* M & W
University of Rio Grande *Ohio* M & W
University of Rochester *New York* M & W
University of Saint Francis *Indiana* M & W
University of St. Francis *Illinois* M & W
University of St. Thomas *Minnesota* M & W
University of San Diego *California* M & W
University of San Francisco *California* M & W
University of Saskatchewan *Saskatchewan* M & W
University of the Sciences in Philadelphia *Pennsylvania* M & W
The University of Scranton *Pennsylvania* M & W
University of Sioux Falls *South Dakota* M & W
University of South Alabama *Alabama* M & W
University of South Carolina *South Carolina* W
University of South Carolina Aiken *South Carolina* W
University of South Carolina Beaufort *South Carolina* M & W
University of South Carolina Upstate *South Carolina* M & W
The University of South Dakota *South Dakota* M & W
University of South Florida *Florida* M & W
University of Southern California *California* M & W
University of Southern Indiana *Indiana* M & W
University of Southern Maine *Maine* M & W
University of Southern Mississippi *Mississippi* W
University of the Southwest *New Mexico* M & W
The University of Tampa *Florida* M & W
The University of Tennessee *Tennessee* M & W
The University of Tennessee at Chattanooga *Tennessee* M & W
The University of Tennessee at Martin *Tennessee* M & W
The University of Texas at Arlington *Texas* M & W
The University of Texas at Austin *Texas* M & W
The University of Texas at Dallas *Texas* M & W
The University of Texas at El Paso *Texas* M & W
The University of Texas of the Permian Basin *Texas* M & W
The University of Texas at San Antonio *Texas* M & W
The University of Texas at Tyler *Texas* M & W
The University of Texas–Pan American *Texas* M & W
The University of Toledo *Ohio* M & W
University of Toronto *Ontario* M & W
University of Tulsa *Oklahoma* M & W
University of Utah *Utah* W
University of Vermont *Vermont* M & W
University of Victoria *British Columbia* M & W
University of the Virgin Islands *United States Virgin Islands* M & W
University of Virginia *Virginia* M & W
The University of Virginia's College at Wise *Virginia* M & W
University of Washington *Washington* M & W
University of Waterloo *Ontario* M & W
The University of West Alabama *Alabama* M & W
University of West Florida *Florida* M & W
University of West Georgia *Georgia* M & W
The University of Western Ontario *Ontario* M & W
University of Windsor *Ontario* M & W

M = Men; W = Women

Equestrian Sports
Casper College *Wyoming* M & W
Castleton State College *Vermont* M & W
Cazenovia College *New York* M & W
Goucher College *Maryland* M & W
Hartwick College *New York* W
Hillsdale College *Michigan* W
Hiram College *Ohio* M & W
Hobart and William Smith Colleges *New York* M & W
Hollins University *Virginia* W
Hood College *Maryland* M & W
Johnson & Wales University *Rhode Island* M & W
Judson College *Alabama* W
Juniata College *Pennsylvania* M & W
Kenyon College *Ohio* M & W
Kutztown University of Pennsylvania *Pennsylvania* M & W
Lafayette College *Pennsylvania* M & W
Lamar Community College *Colorado* M & W
Landmark College *Vermont* M & W
Laramie County Community College *Wyoming* M & W
Lawson State Community College *Alabama* M
Lehigh University *Pennsylvania* M & W
Liberty University *Virginia* W
Long Island University, C.W. Post Campus *New York* M & W
Longwood University *Virginia* M & W

M = Men; W = Women

Lycoming College *Pennsylvania* M & W
Lynchburg College *Virginia* W
Marist College *New York* M & W
Maryville College *Tennessee* M & W
Merced College *California* M & W
Miami University *Ohio* M & W
Michigan State University *Michigan* M & W
Middle Tennessee State University *Tennessee* M & W
Midway College *Kentucky* W
Mississippi College *Mississippi* W
Missouri State University *Missouri* M & W
Mitchell Technical Institute *South Dakota* M & W
Molloy College *New York* W
Moravian College *Pennsylvania* M & W
Morehead State University *Kentucky* M & W
Mount Holyoke College *Massachusetts* W
Mount Ida College *Massachusetts* W
Mount St. Mary's University *Maryland* M & W
Murray State University *Kentucky* M & W
Nassau Community College *New York* M & W
National American University (Rapid City) *South Dakota* M & W
Nazareth College of Rochester *New York* M & W
New Mexico State University *New Mexico* M & W
New York University *New York* M & W
North Carolina State University *North Carolina* M & W
North Central Texas College *Texas* M & W
North Georgia College & State University *Georgia* M & W
Northeastern Junior College *Colorado* M & W
Northwest College *Wyoming* M & W
Northwest Mississippi Community College *Mississippi* M & W
Nova Scotia Agricultural College *Nova Scotia* M & W
Oberlin College *Ohio* M & W
Ohio Wesleyan University *Ohio* M & W
Oklahoma Panhandle State University *Oklahoma* W
Otterbein University *Ohio* M & W
Pace University *New York* W
Penn State University Park *Pennsylvania* M & W
Post University *Connecticut* M & W
Randolph College *Virginia* M & W
Rensselaer Polytechnic Institute *New York* M & W
Rice University *Texas* M & W
Rochester Institute of Technology *New York* M & W
Rocky Mountain College *Montana* M & W
Roger Williams University *Rhode Island* M & W
Sacred Heart University *Connecticut* W
Saginaw Valley State University *Michigan* M & W
St. Andrews Presbyterian College *North Carolina* M & W
St. Cloud State University *Minnesota* M & W
St. Francis Xavier University *Nova Scotia* W
St. Lawrence University *New York* M & W
Saint Louis University *Missouri* M & W
Saint Mary-of-the-Woods College *Indiana* W
Saint Mary's College *Indiana* W
St. Mary's College of Maryland *Maryland* M & W
Saint Vincent College *Pennsylvania* M & W
Salve Regina University *Rhode Island* M & W
Sam Houston State University *Texas* M & W
Sarah Lawrence College *New York* M & W
Savannah College of Art and Design *Georgia* M & W
Seton Hill University *Pennsylvania* M & W
Sewanee: The University of the South *Tennessee* M & W
Siena College *New York* M & W
Sierra Nevada College *Nevada* M & W
Skidmore College *New York* W
Slippery Rock University of Pennsylvania *Pennsylvania* M & W
Smith College *Massachusetts* W
South Dakota State University *South Dakota* W
South Plains College *Texas* M & W
Southern Methodist University *Texas* W
Southwest Texas Junior College *Texas* M & W
Southwestern Oklahoma State University *Oklahoma* M & W
Stanford University *California* M & W
State University of New York College of Agriculture and Technology at Morrisville *New York* M & W
State University of New York College at Geneseo *New York* W
State University of New York College at Potsdam *New York* M & W
State University of New York at New Paltz *New York* W
Stephen F. Austin State University *Texas* W
Stevens Institute of Technology *New Jersey* W
Stonehill College *Massachusetts* W
Susquehanna University *Pennsylvania* M & W
Sweet Briar College *Virginia* W
Syracuse University *New York* M & W
Texas A&M University *Texas* W
Texas A&M University–Kingsville *Texas* M & W
Texas Christian University *Texas* W
Texas State University–San Marcos *Texas* M & W
Tiffin University *Ohio* M & W
Towson University *Maryland* M & W
Trinity College *Connecticut* M & W
Truman State University *Missouri* M & W
United States Air Force Academy *Colorado* M & W
United States Military Academy *New York* M & W
The University of British Columbia *British Columbia* M & W
University of California, Santa Barbara *California* M & W
University of California, Santa Cruz *California* M & W
University of Colorado at Boulder *Colorado* M & W
University of Delaware *Delaware* M & W
University of Denver *Colorado* M & W
The University of Findlay *Ohio* W
University of Georgia *Georgia* W
University of Great Falls *Montana* M & W
University of Mary Washington *Virginia* M & W
University of Massachusetts Dartmouth *Massachusetts* W
University of Minnesota, Crookston *Minnesota* W
The University of Montana *Montana* M & W
The University of Montana Western *Montana* M & W
University of Ottawa *Ontario* M & W
University of Rhode Island *Rhode Island* M & W
University of Richmond *Virginia* M & W
University of Rochester *New York* M & W
University of San Diego *California* W
The University of Scranton *Pennsylvania* M & W
University of South Carolina *South Carolina* W
University of Southern California *California* M & W
The University of Tennessee *Tennessee* M & W
The University of Tennessee at Martin *Tennessee* W
University of Vermont *Vermont* M & W
The University of Western Ontario *Ontario* M & W
University of Wisconsin–River Falls *Wisconsin* M & W
University of Wyoming *Wyoming* M & W
Utah State University *Utah* M & W
Valley Forge Military College *Pennsylvania* M
Vernon College *Texas* M & W
Villanova University *Pennsylvania* W
Virginia Intermont College *Virginia* M & W
Washington College *Maryland* M & W
Washington and Lee University *Virginia* W
Washington State University *Washington* M & W
Washington University in St. Louis *Missouri* M & W
Weatherford College *Texas* M & W
Wesleyan College *Georgia* W
Wesleyan University *Connecticut* M & W
West Chester University of Pennsylvania *Pennsylvania* M & W
West Hills Community College *California* M & W
West Texas A&M University *Texas* M & W
Western Carolina University *North Carolina* M & W
Western Nevada College *Nevada* M & W
Western Oklahoma State College *Oklahoma* M & W
Westfield State College *Massachusetts* M & W
Westminster College *Pennsylvania* M & W
Westmont College *California* M
Williams College *Massachusetts* M & W
Xavier University *Ohio* M & W
Yale University *Connecticut* M & W

Fencing

Allegheny College *Pennsylvania* M & W
Amherst College *Massachusetts* M & W
Ball State University *Indiana* M & W
Bard College at Simon's Rock *Massachusetts* M & W
Barnard College *New York* W
Bates College *Maine* M & W
Baylor University *Texas* M & W
Beloit College *Wisconsin* M & W
Boston College *Massachusetts* M & W
Boston University *Massachusetts* M & W
Bowdoin College *Maine* M & W
Brandeis University *Massachusetts* M & W
Brock University *Ontario* M & W
Brown University *Rhode Island* M & W
Buffalo State College, State University of New York *New York* M
California Institute of Technology *California* M & W
California State University, Long Beach *California* M & W
California University of Pennsylvania *Pennsylvania* M & W
Carleton College *Minnesota* M & W
Carleton University *Ontario* M & W
Carnegie Mellon University *Pennsylvania* M & W
Case Western Reserve University *Ohio* M & W
Central Connecticut State University *Connecticut* M & W
Central Washington University *Washington* M & W
City College of the City University of New York *New York* W
City College of San Francisco *California* W
Clark College *Washington* M & W
Clemson University *South Carolina* M & W
Cleveland State University *Ohio* M & W
Colby College *Maine* M & W
Colgate University *New York* M & W
Columbia University *New York* M & W
Columbia University, School of General Studies *New York* M & W
Cornell University *New York* W
Dartmouth College *New Hampshire* M & W
Davidson College *North Carolina* M & W
Dickinson College *Pennsylvania* M & W
Drew University *New Jersey* M & W
Duke University *North Carolina* M & W
Emory University *Georgia* M & W
Fairleigh Dickinson University, Metropolitan Campus *New Jersey* W
Fort Lewis College *Colorado* M & W
Furman University *South Carolina* M & W
Georgia Southern University *Georgia* M & W
Hampden-Sydney College *Virginia* M
Hampshire College *Massachusetts* M & W
Harvard University *Massachusetts* M & W
Haverford College *Pennsylvania* M & W
Hollins University *Virginia* W
Hunter College of the City University of New York *New York* M & W
The Johns Hopkins University *Maryland* M & W
Kenyon College *Ohio* M & W
Lafayette College *Pennsylvania* M & W
Lake Forest College *Illinois* M & W
Lawrence University *Wisconsin* M & W
Lehigh University *Pennsylvania* M & W
Lycoming College *Pennsylvania* M & W
Macalester College *Minnesota* M & W
Marist College *New York* M & W
Marquette University *Wisconsin* M & W
Massachusetts Institute of Technology *Massachusetts* M & W
McGill University *Quebec* M & W
McMaster University *Ontario* M & W
Miami University *Ohio* M & W
Michigan Technological University *Michigan* M & W
Midwestern State University *Texas* M & W
New Jersey Institute of Technology *New Jersey* M & W
New Mexico Military Institute *New Mexico* M & W
New York University *New York* M & W

M = Men; W = Women

North Carolina State University *North Carolina* M & W
Northwestern University *Illinois* W
Norwich University *Vermont* M & W
Oberlin College *Ohio* M & W
The Ohio State University *Ohio* M & W
Old Dominion University *Virginia* M & W
Palm Beach Atlantic University *Florida* M & W
Penn State University Park *Pennsylvania* M & W
Princeton University *New Jersey* M & W
Queens College of the City University of New York *New York* W
Queen's University at Kingston *Ontario* M & W
Reed College *Oregon* M & W
Rensselaer Polytechnic Institute *New York* M & W
Rice University *Texas* M & W
Rochester Institute of Technology *New York* M & W
Royal Military College of Canada *Ontario* M & W
Rutgers, The State University of New Jersey, New Brunswick *New Jersey* M & W
Ryerson University *Ontario* M & W
Sacred Heart University *Connecticut* M & W
St. John's College *New Mexico* M & W
St. John's College *Maryland* M & W
St. John's University *New York* M & W
Saint Louis University *Missouri* M & W
St. Mary's College of Maryland *Maryland* M & W
Saint Vincent College *Pennsylvania* M & W
San Joaquin Delta College *California* M & W
Savannah College of Art and Design *Georgia* M & W
Scripps College *California* W
Sewanee: The University of the South *Tennessee* M & W
Southern Methodist University *Texas* M & W
Stanford University *California* M & W
State University of New York College at Geneseo *New York* M & W
State University of New York College at Oneonta *New York* M & W
State University of New York at New Paltz *New York* M & W
Stevens Institute of Technology *New Jersey* M & W
Swarthmore College *Pennsylvania* M & W
Sweet Briar College *Virginia* W
Temple University *Pennsylvania* W
Texas State University–San Marcos *Texas* M & W
Trent University *Ontario* M & W
Trinity College *Connecticut* M & W
Trinity University *Texas* M & W
Tufts University *Massachusetts* W
Union College *New York* M & W
United States Air Force Academy *Colorado* M & W
United States Military Academy *New York* M & W
United States Naval Academy *Maryland* M & W
The University of British Columbia *British Columbia* M & W
University of California, San Diego *California* M & W
University of California, Santa Barbara *California* M & W
University of California, Santa Cruz *California* M & W
University of Colorado at Boulder *Colorado* M & W
University of Detroit Mercy *Michigan* M & W
University of Maryland, Baltimore County *Maryland* M & W
University of Mississippi *Mississippi* M & W
The University of Montana *Montana* M & W
University of Nebraska–Lincoln *Nebraska* M & W
University of New Brunswick Saint John *New Brunswick* M & W
University of New Hampshire *New Hampshire* M & W
The University of North Carolina at Chapel Hill *North Carolina* M & W
University of North Texas *Texas* M & W
University of Notre Dame *Indiana* M & W
University of Ottawa *Ontario* M & W
University of Pennsylvania *Pennsylvania* M & W
University of Puget Sound *Washington* M & W
University of Richmond *Virginia* M & W
University of St. Thomas *Texas* M & W
University of South Alabama *Alabama* M & W
University of Southern California *California* M & W
The University of Tennessee *Tennessee* M & W
The University of Texas at Austin *Texas* M & W
University of Toronto *Ontario* M & W
University of Vermont *Vermont* M & W
The University of Western Ontario *Ontario* M & W
University of Wyoming *Wyoming* M & W
Vassar College *New York* M & W
Washington and Lee University *Virginia* M & W
Washington State University *Washington* M & W
Washington University in St. Louis *Missouri* M & W
Wayne State University *Michigan* M & W
Weber State University *Utah* M & W
Wellesley College *Massachusetts* W
West Chester University of Pennsylvania *Pennsylvania* M & W
Western Carolina University *North Carolina* M & W
Whitman College *Washington* M & W
Winona State University *Minnesota* M & W
Winthrop University *South Carolina* M & W
Xavier University *Ohio* M & W
Yale University *Connecticut* M & W
Yeshiva University *New York* M & W

Field Hockey

Adelphi University *New York* W
Albright College *Pennsylvania* W
Alvernia University *Pennsylvania* W
American International College *Massachusetts* W
American University *District of Columbia* W
Amherst College *Massachusetts* W
Anna Maria College *Massachusetts* W
Appalachian State University *North Carolina* W
Arcadia University *Pennsylvania* W
Assumption College *Massachusetts* W
Babson College *Massachusetts* W
Ball State University *Indiana* W
Barnard College *New York* W
Bates College *Maine* W
Bay Path College *Massachusetts* W
Becker College *Massachusetts* W
Bellarmine University *Kentucky* W
Bentley University *Massachusetts* W
Bishop's University *Quebec* W
Bloomsburg University of Pennsylvania *Pennsylvania* W
Boston College *Massachusetts* W
Boston University *Massachusetts* W
Bowdoin College *Maine* W
Brandeis University *Massachusetts* W
Bridgewater College *Virginia* W
Bridgewater State College *Massachusetts* W
Brock University *Ontario* W
Brown University *Rhode Island* W
Bryant University *Rhode Island* W
Bryn Mawr College *Pennsylvania* W
Bucknell University *Pennsylvania* W
Cabrini College *Pennsylvania* W
California State University, Chico *California* W
Carleton College *Minnesota* W
Carleton University *Ontario* W
Castleton State College *Vermont* W
The Catholic University of America *District of Columbia* W
Cedar Crest College *Pennsylvania* W
Central Michigan University *Michigan* W
Centre College *Kentucky* W
Christopher Newport University *Virginia* W
Clark University *Massachusetts* W
Clemson University *South Carolina* M & W
Colby College *Maine* W
Colby-Sawyer College *New Hampshire* W
Colgate University *New York* W
The College at Brockport, State University of New York *New York* W
College of the Holy Cross *Massachusetts* W
The College of New Jersey *New Jersey* W
College of Notre Dame of Maryland *Maryland* W
The College of William and Mary *Virginia* W
The College of Wooster *Ohio* W
The Colorado College *Colorado* M & W
Colorado State University *Colorado* M & W
Columbia University *New York* W
Columbia University, School of General Studies *New York* W
Connecticut College *Connecticut* W
Cornell University *New York* W
Dalhousie University *Nova Scotia* W
Daniel Webster College *New Hampshire* W
Dartmouth College *New Hampshire* W
Davidson College *North Carolina* W
Delaware Valley College *Pennsylvania* W
Denison University *Ohio* W
DePauw University *Indiana* W
DeSales University *Pennsylvania* W
Dickinson College *Pennsylvania* W
Drew University *New Jersey* W
Drexel University *Pennsylvania* W
Duke University *North Carolina* M & W
Earlham College *Indiana* W
East Stroudsburg University of Pennsylvania *Pennsylvania* W
Eastern Connecticut State University *Connecticut* W
Eastern Mennonite University *Virginia* W
Eastern University *Pennsylvania* W
Elizabethtown College *Pennsylvania* W
Elmira College *New York* W
Elms College *Massachusetts* W
Elon University *North Carolina* W
Emory University *Georgia* W
Endicott College *Massachusetts* W
Fairfield University *Connecticut* W
Fairleigh Dickinson University, College at Florham *New Jersey* W
Fitchburg State College *Massachusetts* W
Fontbonne University *Missouri* W
Framingham State College *Massachusetts* W
Franklin & Marshall College *Pennsylvania* W
Franklin Pierce University *New Hampshire* W
Frostburg State University *Maryland* W
Georgetown University *District of Columbia* W
Gettysburg College *Pennsylvania* W
Gordon College *Massachusetts* W
Goucher College *Maryland* W
Gwynedd-Mercy College *Pennsylvania* W
Hamilton College *New York* W
Hartwick College *New York* W
Harvard University *Massachusetts* W
Haverford College *Pennsylvania* W
Hendrix College *Arkansas* W
Hobart and William Smith Colleges *New York* W
Hofstra University *New York* W
Hood College *Maryland* W
Houghton College *New York* W
Husson University *Maine* W
Immaculata University *Pennsylvania* W
Indiana University Bloomington *Indiana* W
Indiana University of Pennsylvania *Pennsylvania* W
Ithaca College *New York* W
James Madison University *Virginia* W
John Carroll University *Ohio* W
The Johns Hopkins University *Maryland* W
Juniata College *Pennsylvania* W
Kean University *New Jersey* W
Keene State College *New Hampshire* W
Kent State University *Ohio* W
Kenyon College *Ohio* W
Keystone College *Pennsylvania* W
King's College *Pennsylvania* W
Kutztown University of Pennsylvania *Pennsylvania* W
La Salle University *Pennsylvania* W
Lafayette College *Pennsylvania* W
Lasell College *Massachusetts* W
Lebanon Valley College *Pennsylvania* W
Lehigh University *Pennsylvania* W
Liberty University *Virginia* W
Limestone College *South Carolina* W
Lindenwood University *Missouri* W
Lock Haven University of Pennsylvania *Pennsylvania* W
Long Island University, C.W. Post Campus *New York* W
Longwood University *Virginia* W
Lynchburg College *Virginia* W
Manhattanville College *New York* W

M = Men; W = Women

Football

M = Men; W = Women
McDaniel College *Maryland* W
McGill University *Quebec* W
Mercyhurst College *Pennsylvania* W
Michigan State University *Michigan* W
Middlebury College *Vermont* W
Middlesex County College *New Jersey* W
St. Bonaventure University *New York* W
Saint Francis University *Pennsylvania* W
St. Francis Xavier University *Nova Scotia* W
Saint Joseph's College of Maine *Maine* W
Wellesley College *Massachusetts* W
Wells College *New York* W
Wesley College *Delaware* W

Abilene Christian University *Texas* M
Acadia University *Nova Scotia* M
Adams State College *Colorado* M
Adrian College *Michigan* M
Alabama Agricultural and Mechanical University *Alabama* M
Alabama State University *Alabama* M
Albany State University *Georgia* M
Alberta College of Art & Design *Alberta* M & W
Albion College *Michigan* M
Albright College *Pennsylvania* M
Alcorn State University *Mississippi* M
Alfred University *New York* M
Allan Hancock College *California* M
Allegheny College *Pennsylvania* M
Arizona Western College *Arizona* M
Arkansas Baptist College *Arkansas* M
Arkansas State University - Jonesboro *Arkansas* M
Arkansas Tech University *Arkansas* M
Ashland University *Ohio* M
Assumption College *Massachusetts* M
Auburn University *Alabama* M
Augsburg College *Minnesota* M
Augustana College *South Dakota* M
Augustana College *Illinois* M
Aurora University *Illinois* M

M = Men; W = Women

M = Men; W = Women

Northwestern College *Iowa* M
Northwestern Oklahoma State University *Oklahoma* M
Northwestern State University of Louisiana *Louisiana* M
Northwestern University *Illinois* M
Northwood University *Michigan* M
Norwich University *Vermont* M
Oberlin College *Ohio* M
Occidental College *California* M
Ohio Dominican University *Ohio* M
Ohio Northern University *Ohio* M
The Ohio State University *Ohio* M
Ohio University *Ohio* M
Ohio Wesleyan University *Ohio* M
Oklahoma Panhandle State University *Oklahoma* M
Old Dominion University *Virginia* M
Olivet College *Michigan* M
Olivet Nazarene University *Illinois* M
Orange Coast College *California* M
Oregon State University *Oregon* M
Ottawa University *Kansas* M
Otterbein University *Ohio* M
Ouachita Baptist University *Arkansas* M
Pace University *New York* M
Pacific Lutheran University *Washington* M
Palomar College *California* M
Pasadena City College *California* M
Pearl River Community College *Mississippi* M
Penn State Lehigh Valley *Pennsylvania* M
Penn State University Park *Pennsylvania* M
Peru State College *Nebraska* M
Phoenix College *Arizona* M
Pikeville College *Kentucky* M
Pima Community College *Arizona* M
Pittsburg State University *Kansas* M
Pitzer College *California* M
Plymouth State University *New Hampshire* M
Pomona College *California* M
Portland State University *Oregon* M
Prairie State College *Illinois* M
Prairie View A&M University *Texas* M
Presbyterian College *South Carolina* M
Princeton University *New Jersey* M
Purdue University *Indiana* M
Queen's University at Kingston *Ontario* M
Quincy University *Illinois* M
Randolph-Macon College *Virginia* M
Ranger College *Texas* M
Reedley College *California* M
Rhodes College *Tennessee* M
Rice University *Texas* M
Ridgewater College *Minnesota* M
Ripon College *Wisconsin* M
Riverside Community College District *California* M
Robert Morris University *Pennsylvania* M
Rochester Community and Technical College *Minnesota* M
Rock Valley College *Illinois* M
Rockford College *Illinois* M
Rocky Mountain College *Montana* M
Rose-Hulman Institute of Technology *Indiana* M
Rowan University *New Jersey* M
Rutgers, The State University of New Jersey, New Brunswick *New Jersey* M
Sacramento City College *California* M
Sacred Heart University *Connecticut* M
Saddleback College *California* M
Saginaw Valley State University *Michigan* M
St. Ambrose University *Iowa* M
Saint Anselm College *New Hampshire* M
Saint Augustine's College *North Carolina* M
St. Cloud State University *Minnesota* M
Saint Francis University *Pennsylvania* M
St. Francis Xavier University *Nova Scotia* M
St. John Fisher College *New York* M
Saint John's University *Minnesota* M
Saint Joseph's College *Indiana* M
St. Lawrence University *New York* M
Saint Mary's University *Nova Scotia* M
St. Norbert College *Wisconsin* M
St. Olaf College *Minnesota* M
Saint Paul's College *Virginia* M
Saint Xavier University *Illinois* M

Salisbury University *Maryland* M
Salve Regina University *Rhode Island* M
Sam Houston State University *Texas* M
Samford University *Alabama* M
San Bernardino Valley College *California* M
San Diego City College *California* M
San Diego Mesa College *California* M
San Diego State University *California* M
San Joaquin Delta College *California* M
San Jose City College *California* M
San Jose State University *California* M
Santa Ana College *California* M
Santa Barbara City College *California* M
Santa Monica College *California* M
Santa Rosa Junior College *California* M
Savannah State University *Georgia* M
Scottsdale Community College *Arizona* M
Seton Hill University *Pennsylvania* M
Sewanee: The University of the South *Tennessee* M
Shasta College *California* M
Shaw University *North Carolina* M
Shenandoah University *Virginia* M
Shepherd University *West Virginia* M
Shippensburg University of Pennsylvania *Pennsylvania* M
Shorter University *Georgia* M
Sierra College *California* M
Simon Fraser University *British Columbia* M
Simpson College *Iowa* M
Slippery Rock University of Pennsylvania *Pennsylvania* M
Snow College *Utah* M
Solano Community College *California* M
South Carolina State University *South Carolina* M
South Dakota School of Mines and Technology *South Dakota* M
South Dakota State University *South Dakota* M
Southeast Missouri State University *Missouri* M
Southeastern Louisiana University *Louisiana* M
Southeastern Oklahoma State University *Oklahoma* M
Southern Arkansas University–Magnolia *Arkansas* M
Southern Connecticut State University *Connecticut* M
Southern Illinois University Carbondale *Illinois* M
Southern Methodist University *Texas* M
Southern Nazarene University *Oklahoma* M
Southern Oregon University *Oregon* M
Southern University and Agricultural and Mechanical College *Louisiana* M
Southern Utah University *Utah* M
Southern Virginia University *Virginia* M
Southwest Baptist University *Missouri* M
Southwest Minnesota State University *Minnesota* M
Southwest Mississippi Community College *Mississippi* M
Southwestern Assemblies of God University *Texas* M
Southwestern College *Kansas* M
Southwestern College *California* M
Southwestern Oklahoma State University *Oklahoma* M
Springfield College *Massachusetts* M
Stanford University *California* M
State University of New York College of Agriculture and Technology at Morrisville *New York* M
State University of New York College at Cortland *New York* M & W
State University of New York College of Technology at Alfred *New York* M
State University of New York Maritime College *New York* M
Stephen F. Austin State University *Texas* M
Sterling College *Kansas* M
Stillman College *Alabama* M
Stonehill College *Massachusetts* M
Stony Brook University, State University of New York *New York* M
Sul Ross State University *Texas* M
Susquehanna University *Pennsylvania* M
Syracuse University *New York* M
Tabor College *Kansas* M

Tarleton State University *Texas* M
Taylor University *Indiana* M
Temple University *Pennsylvania* M
Tennessee State University *Tennessee* M
Tennessee Technological University *Tennessee* M
Texas A&M University *Texas* M
Texas A&M University–Commerce *Texas* M
Texas A&M University–Kingsville *Texas* M
Texas Christian University *Texas* M
Texas College *Texas* M
Texas Lutheran University *Texas* M
Texas Southern University *Texas* M
Texas State University–San Marcos *Texas* M
Texas Tech University *Texas* M
Thaddeus Stevens College of Technology *Pennsylvania* M
Thiel College *Pennsylvania* M
Thomas More College *Kentucky* M
Tiffin University *Ohio* M
Towson University *Maryland* M
Trine University *Indiana* M
Trinity Bible College *North Dakota* M
Trinity College *Connecticut* M
Trinity International University *Illinois* M
Trinity University *Texas* M
Trinity Valley Community College *Texas* M
Troy University *Alabama* M
Truman State University *Missouri* M
Tufts University *Massachusetts* M
Tulane University *Louisiana* M
Tusculum College *Tennessee* M
Tuskegee University *Alabama* M
Tyler Junior College *Texas* M
Union College *New York* M
Union College *Kentucky* M
United States Air Force Academy *Colorado* M
United States Coast Guard Academy *Connecticut* M
United States Merchant Marine Academy *New York* M
United States Military Academy *New York* M
United States Naval Academy *Maryland* M
Université Laval *Quebec* M
Université de Sherbrooke *Quebec* M
The University of Akron *Ohio* M
The University of Alabama *Alabama* M
The University of Alabama at Birmingham *Alabama* M
University at Albany, State University of New York *New York* M
University of Alberta *Alberta* M
The University of Arizona *Arizona* M
University of Arkansas *Arkansas* M
University of Arkansas at Monticello *Arkansas* M
University of Arkansas at Pine Bluff *Arkansas* M
The University of British Columbia *British Columbia* M
University at Buffalo, the State University of New York *New York* M
University of Calgary *Alberta* M
University of California, Berkeley *California* M
University of California, Davis *California* M
University of California, Los Angeles *California* M
University of Central Arkansas *Arkansas* M
University of Central Florida *Florida* M
University of Central Missouri *Missouri* M
University of Central Oklahoma *Oklahoma* M
University of Charleston *West Virginia* M
University of Chicago *Illinois* M
University of Cincinnati *Ohio* M
University of Colorado at Boulder *Colorado* M
University of Connecticut *Connecticut* M
University of the Cumberlands *Kentucky* M
University of Dayton *Ohio* M
University of Delaware *Delaware* M
University of Dubuque *Iowa* M
The University of Findlay *Ohio* M
University of Florida *Florida* M
University of Georgia *Georgia* M
University of Guelph *Ontario* M
University of Hawaii at Manoa *Hawaii* M
University of Houston *Texas* M & W
University of Idaho *Idaho* M

M = Men; W = Women

University of Illinois at Urbana–Champaign *Illinois* M
University of the Incarnate Word *Texas* M
University of Indianapolis *Indiana* M
The University of Iowa *Iowa* M
The University of Kansas *Kansas* M
University of Kentucky *Kentucky* M
University of La Verne *California* M
University of Louisiana at Lafayette *Louisiana* M
University of Louisiana at Monroe *Louisiana* M
University of Louisville *Kentucky* M
University of Maine *Maine* M
University of Manitoba *Manitoba* M & W
University of Mary *North Dakota* M
University of Mary Hardin-Baylor *Texas* M
University of Maryland, College Park *Maryland* M
University of Massachusetts Amherst *Massachusetts* M
University of Massachusetts Dartmouth *Massachusetts* M
University of Memphis *Tennessee* M
University of Miami *Florida* M
University of Michigan *Michigan* M
University of Minnesota, Crookston *Minnesota* M
University of Minnesota, Duluth *Minnesota* M
University of Minnesota, Morris *Minnesota* M
University of Minnesota, Twin Cities Campus *Minnesota* M
University of Mississippi *Mississippi* M
University of Missouri *Missouri* M
The University of Montana *Montana* M
The University of Montana Western *Montana* M
University of Mount Union *Ohio* M
University of Nebraska at Kearney *Nebraska* M
University of Nebraska at Omaha *Nebraska* M
University of Nebraska–Lincoln *Nebraska* M
University of Nevada, Las Vegas *Nevada* M
University of Nevada, Reno *Nevada* M
University of New Hampshire *New Hampshire* M
University of New Haven *Connecticut* M
University of New Mexico *New Mexico* M
University of North Alabama *Alabama* M
The University of North Carolina at Chapel Hill *North Carolina* M
The University of North Carolina at Pembroke *North Carolina* M
University of North Dakota *North Dakota* M
University of North Texas *Texas* M
University of Northern Colorado *Colorado* M
University of Northern Iowa *Iowa* M
University of Notre Dame *Indiana* M
University of Oklahoma *Oklahoma* M
University of Oregon *Oregon* M
University of Ottawa *Ontario* M
University of Pennsylvania *Pennsylvania* M
University of Pittsburgh *Pennsylvania* M
University of Puget Sound *Washington* M
University of Redlands *California* M
University of Regina *Saskatchewan* M
University of Rhode Island *Rhode Island* M
University of Richmond *Virginia* M
University of Rochester *New York* M
University of Saint Francis *Indiana* M
University of St. Francis *Illinois* M
University of Saint Mary *Kansas* M
University of St. Thomas *Minnesota* M
University of San Diego *California* M
University of Saskatchewan *Saskatchewan* M
University of Sioux Falls *South Dakota* M
University of South Alabama *Alabama* M
University of South Carolina *South Carolina* M
The University of South Dakota *South Dakota* M
University of South Florida *Florida* M
University of Southern California *California* M
University of Southern Mississippi *Mississippi* M & W
The University of Tennessee *Tennessee* M
The University of Tennessee at Chattanooga *Tennessee* M
The University of Tennessee at Martin *Tennessee* M
The University of Texas at Austin *Texas* M
The University of Texas at El Paso *Texas* M
The University of Toledo *Ohio* M
University of Toronto *Ontario* M
University of Tulsa *Oklahoma* M
University of Utah *Utah* M
University of Virginia *Virginia* M
The University of Virginia's College at Wise *Virginia* M
University of Washington *Washington* M
University of Waterloo *Ontario* M
The University of West Alabama *Alabama* M
University of West Georgia *Georgia* M
The University of Western Ontario *Ontario* M
University of Windsor *Ontario* M
University of Wisconsin–Eau Claire *Wisconsin* M
University of Wisconsin–La Crosse *Wisconsin* M
University of Wisconsin–Madison *Wisconsin* M
University of Wisconsin–Oshkosh *Wisconsin* M
University of Wisconsin–Platteville *Wisconsin* M
University of Wisconsin–River Falls *Wisconsin* M
University of Wisconsin–Stevens Point *Wisconsin* M
University of Wisconsin–Stout *Wisconsin* M
University of Wisconsin–Whitewater *Wisconsin* M
University of Wyoming *Wyoming* M
Upper Iowa University *Iowa* M
Urbana University *Ohio* M
Ursinus College *Pennsylvania* M
Utah State University *Utah* M
Utica College *New York* M
Valdosta State University *Georgia* M
Valley City State University *North Dakota* M
Valley Forge Military College *Pennsylvania* M
Valparaiso University *Indiana* M
Vanderbilt University *Tennessee* M
Ventura College *California* M
Vermilion Community College *Minnesota* M
Victor Valley College *California* M
Villanova University *Pennsylvania* M
Virginia Military Institute *Virginia* M
Virginia Polytechnic Institute and State University *Virginia* M
Virginia State University *Virginia* M
Virginia Union University *Virginia* M
Wabash College *Indiana* M
Wagner College *New York* M
Wake Forest University *North Carolina* M
Waldorf College *Iowa* M
Walsh University *Ohio* M
Wartburg College *Iowa* M
Washburn University *Kansas* M
Washington & Jefferson College *Pennsylvania* M
Washington and Lee University *Virginia* M
Washington State University *Washington* M
Washington University in St. Louis *Missouri* M
Wayne State College *Nebraska* M
Wayne State University *Michigan* M
Waynesburg University *Pennsylvania* M
Webber International University *Florida* M
Weber State University *Utah* M
Wesley College *Delaware* M
Wesleyan University *Connecticut* M
West Chester University of Pennsylvania *Pennsylvania* M
West Hills Community College *California* M
West Liberty University *West Virginia* M
West Los Angeles College *California* M
West Texas A&M University *Texas* M
West Valley College *California* M
West Virginia State University *West Virginia* M
West Virginia University *West Virginia* M
West Virginia University Institute of Technology *West Virginia* M
West Virginia Wesleyan College *West Virginia* M
Western Carolina University *North Carolina* M
Western Connecticut State University *Connecticut* M
Western Illinois University *Illinois* M
Western Kentucky University *Kentucky* M
Western Michigan University *Michigan* M
Western New England College *Massachusetts* M
Western New Mexico University *New Mexico* M
Western Oregon University *Oregon* M
Western State College of Colorado *Colorado* M
Westfield State College *Massachusetts* M
Westminster College *Pennsylvania* M
Westminster College *Missouri* M
Wheaton College *Illinois* M
Whittier College *California* M
Whitworth University *Washington* M
Widener University *Pennsylvania* M
Wilfrid Laurier University *Ontario* M
Wilkes University *Pennsylvania* M
Willamette University *Oregon* M
William Jewell College *Missouri* M
William Paterson University of New Jersey *New Jersey* M
William Penn University *Iowa* M
Williams College *Massachusetts* M
The Williamson Free School of Mechanical Trades *Pennsylvania* M
Wilmington College *Ohio* M
Wingate University *North Carolina* M
Winona State University *Minnesota* M
Winston-Salem State University *North Carolina* M
Wisconsin Lutheran College *Wisconsin* M
Wittenberg University *Ohio* M
Wofford College *South Carolina* M
Worcester Polytechnic Institute *Massachusetts* M
Worcester State College *Massachusetts* M
Xavier University *Ohio* M
Yale University *Connecticut* M
York University *Ontario* M
Youngstown State University *Ohio* M
Yuba College *California* M

Golf

Abilene Christian University *Texas* M
Abraham Baldwin Agricultural College *Georgia* M
Academy of Art University *California* M & W
Adams State College *Colorado* M & W
Adelphi University *New York* M
Adirondack Community College *New York* M
Adrian College *Michigan* M & W
AIB College of Business *Iowa* M & W
Alabama Agricultural and Mechanical University *Alabama* M
Alabama State University *Alabama* M & W
Albion College *Michigan* M & W
Albright College *Pennsylvania* M
Alcorn State University *Mississippi* M & W
Alice Lloyd College *Kentucky* M & W
Allan Hancock College *California* M
Allegheny College *Pennsylvania* M & W
Allen Community College *Kansas* M
Allen University *South Carolina* M & W
Alma College *Michigan* M & W
Alpena Community College *Michigan* M
Alvernia University *Pennsylvania* M & W
American International College *Massachusetts* M
American River College *California* M & W
Amherst College *Massachusetts* M & W
Ancilla College *Indiana* M & W
Anderson University *South Carolina* M & W
Anderson University *Indiana* M & W
Andrew College *Georgia* M & W
Anna Maria College *Massachusetts* M
Anne Arundel Community College *Maryland* M
Appalachian State University *North Carolina* M & W
Aquinas College *Michigan* M & W
Arcadia University *Pennsylvania* M & W
Arizona State University *Arizona* M & W
Arkansas State University - Jonesboro *Arkansas* M & W
Arkansas Tech University *Arkansas* M
Armstrong Atlantic State University *Georgia* M & W
Ashford University *Iowa* M & W
Ashland University *Ohio* M & W
Assumption College *Massachusetts* M
Auburn University *Alabama* M & W
Augsburg College *Minnesota* M & W
Augustana College *South Dakota* M & W
Augustana College *Illinois* M & W
Aurora University *Illinois* M & W
Austin Peay State University *Tennessee* M & W
Ave Maria University *Florida* M
Averett University *Virginia* M
Avila University *Missouri* M & W
Azusa Pacific University *California* M
Babson College *Massachusetts* M

M = Men; W = Women

Baker University *Kansas* M & W
Bakersfield College *California* M
Baldwin-Wallace College *Ohio* M & W
Ball State University *Indiana* M & W
Baptist Bible College of Pennsylvania *Pennsylvania* M
The Baptist College of Florida *Florida* M
Barnard College *New York* W
Barry University *Florida* M & W
Barton College *North Carolina* M
Barton County Community College *Kansas* M & W
Bates College *Maine* M & W
Baylor University *Texas* M & W
Becker College *Massachusetts* M
Belhaven University *Mississippi* M & W
Bellarmine University *Kentucky* M & W
Bellevue College *Washington* M
Belmont Abbey College *North Carolina* M & W
Belmont University *Tennessee* M & W
Beloit College *Wisconsin* M
Bemidji State University *Minnesota* M & W
Benedict College *South Carolina* M
Benedictine College *Kansas* M & W
Benedictine University *Illinois* M & W
Bentley University *Massachusetts* M
Berea College *Kentucky* M
Bergen Community College *New Jersey* M
Berry College *Georgia* M & W
Bethany College *West Virginia* M & W
Bethany College *Kansas* M
Bethany Lutheran College *Minnesota* M & W
Bethel College *Kansas* M & W
Bethel College *Indiana* M & W
Bethel University *Tennessee* M & W
Bethel University *Minnesota* M & W
Bethune-Cookman University *Florida* M & W
Biola University *California* M & W
Birmingham-Southern College *Alabama* M & W
Bishop's University *Quebec* M
Bismarck State College *North Dakota* M & W
Black Hawk College *Illinois* M
Black Hills State University *South Dakota* W
Blackburn College *Illinois* M
Blue Mountain College *Mississippi* M
Bluefield College *Virginia* M
Bluefield State College *West Virginia* M
Boise State University *Idaho* M & W
Boston College *Massachusetts* M & W
Boston University *Massachusetts* M & W
Bowdoin College *Maine* M & W
Bowling Green State University *Ohio* M & W
Bradley University *Illinois* M & W
Brandeis University *Massachusetts* M
Brescia University *Kentucky* M & W
Brevard College *North Carolina* M & W
Brevard Community College *Florida* M
Briar Cliff University *Iowa* M & W
Bridgewater College *Virginia* M
Brigham Young University *Utah* M & W
Brigham Young University–Hawaii *Hawaii* M
Brookdale Community College *New Jersey* M
Broome Community College *New York* M
Brown University *Rhode Island* M & W
Brunswick Community College *North Carolina* M
Bryant University *Rhode Island* M
Bucknell University *Pennsylvania* M & W
Bucks County Community College *Pennsylvania* M & W
Buena Vista University *Iowa* M & W
Bunker Hill Community College *Massachusetts* M & W
Burlington County College *New Jersey* M & W
Butler County Community College *Pennsylvania* M & W
Butler University *Indiana* M & W
Butte College *California* M & W
Cabrillo College *California* M & W
Cabrini College *Pennsylvania* M
Caldwell College *New Jersey* M
Caldwell Community College and Technical Institute *North Carolina* M
California Baptist University *California* M & W
California Lutheran University *California* M
California Maritime Academy *California* M & W
California Polytechnic State University, San Luis Obispo *California* M & W
California State University, Bakersfield *California* M
California State University, Chico *California* M & W
California State University, Dominguez Hills *California* M
California State University, Fresno *California* M & W
California State University, Fullerton *California* M & W
California State University, Long Beach *California* M & W
California State University, Monterey Bay *California* M & W
California State University, Northridge *California* M
California State University, Sacramento *California* M & W
California State University, San Bernardino *California* M
California State University, San Marcos *California* M & W
California State University, Stanislaus *California* M
California University of Pennsylvania *Pennsylvania* M & W
Calumet College of Saint Joseph *Indiana* M & W
Calvin College *Michigan* M & W
Camden County College *New Jersey* M
Cameron University *Oklahoma* M & W
Campbell University *North Carolina* M & W
Campbellsville University *Kentucky* M & W
Canisius College *New York* M
Cape Fear Community College *North Carolina* M & W
Capital University *Ohio* M & W
Carleton College *Minnesota* M & W
Carleton University *Ontario* M
Carnegie Mellon University *Pennsylvania* M
Carroll College *Montana* M & W
Carroll University *Wisconsin* M & W
Carson-Newman College *Tennessee* M
Carthage College *Wisconsin* M & W
Castleton State College *Vermont* M
Catawba College *North Carolina* M & W
Cazenovia College *New York* M
Cedarville University *Ohio* M
Centenary College *New Jersey* M
Centenary College of Louisiana *Louisiana* M & W
Central Alabama Community College *Alabama* M
Central Baptist College *Arkansas* M & W
Central Carolina Community College *North Carolina* M & W
Central Christian College of the Bible *Missouri* M & W
Central Christian College of Kansas *Kansas* M & W
Central College *Iowa* M & W
Central Community College–Columbus Campus *Nebraska* M
Central Connecticut State University *Connecticut* M & W
Central Lakes College *Minnesota* M & W
Central Oregon Community College *Oregon* M & W
Central Pennsylvania College *Pennsylvania* M & W
Central State University *Ohio* M & W
Central Washington University *Washington* M & W
Centralia College *Washington* W
Centre College *Kentucky* M & W
Century College *Minnesota* M & W
Cerritos College *California* M
Chabot College *California* M
Chadron State College *Nebraska* W
Chaminade University of Honolulu *Hawaii* M & W
Chapman University *California* M
Charleston Southern University *South Carolina* M & W
Chestnut Hill College *Pennsylvania* M & W
Chicago State University *Illinois* M & W
Chowan University *North Carolina* M
Christendom College *Virginia* M & W
Christian Brothers University *Tennessee* M & W
Christopher Newport University *Virginia* M
Cincinnati Christian University *Ohio* M
Cincinnati State Technical and Community College *Ohio* M & W
The Citadel, The Military College of South Carolina *South Carolina* W
Citrus College *California* M & W
City College of San Francisco *California* M
Claremont McKenna College *California* M
Clarion University of Pennsylvania *Pennsylvania* M
Clarke College *Iowa* M & W
Clarkson University *New York* M
Clayton State University *Georgia* M
Clearwater Christian College *Florida* M & W
Clemson University *South Carolina* M
Cleveland State University *Ohio* M & W
Coastal Carolina University *South Carolina* M & W
Coe College *Iowa* M & W
Coffeyville Community College *Kansas* M
Coker College *South Carolina* M
Colby College *Maine* M & W
Colby Community College *Kansas* M & W
Colby-Sawyer College *New Hampshire* M & W
Colgate University *New York* M & W
College of the Canyons *California* M & W
College of Charleston *South Carolina* M & W
College of the Desert *California* M & W
College of DuPage *Illinois* M
College of the Holy Cross *Massachusetts* M & W
The College of Idaho *Idaho* M & W
College of Lake County *Illinois* M
College of Marin *California* M & W
College of Mount St. Joseph *Ohio* M & W
College of the Redwoods *California* M
College of Saint Benedict *Minnesota* W
The College of Saint Rose *New York* M
College of San Mateo *California* M
College of the Sequoias *California* M
College of Southern Maryland *Maryland* M
The College of William and Mary *Virginia* M & W
The College of Wooster *Ohio* M & W
Colorado Christian University *Colorado* M
Colorado School of Mines *Colorado* M
Colorado State University *Colorado* M & W
Colorado State University–Pueblo *Colorado* M & W
Columbia Basin College *Washington* M & W
Columbia Bible College *British Columbia* M & W
Columbia University *New York* M
Columbia University, School of General Studies *New York* M
Columbus State Community College *Ohio* M
Columbus State University *Georgia* M & W
Community College of Allegheny County *Pennsylvania* M & W
Community College of Rhode Island *Rhode Island* M & W
Concord University *West Virginia* M
Concordia College *Minnesota* M & W
Concordia University *Quebec* M
Concordia University *Oregon* M & W
Concordia University *Michigan* M & W
Concordia University Chicago *Illinois* M
Concordia University College of Alberta *Alberta* M & W
Concordia University, Nebraska *Nebraska* M & W
Concordia University, St. Paul *Minnesota* M & W
Concordia University Texas *Texas* M & W
Concordia University Wisconsin *Wisconsin* M & W
Copiah-Lincoln Community College *Mississippi* M & W
Corban University *Oregon* M & W
Cornell College *Iowa* M & W
Cornell University *New York* M
Cornerstone University *Michigan* M & W
Corning Community College *New York* M & W
County College of Morris *New Jersey* M
Covenant College *Georgia* M & W
Creighton University *Nebraska* M & W
Crossroads College *Minnesota* M & W
Crown College *Minnesota* M
Culver-Stockton College *Missouri* M & W
Cumberland University *Tennessee* M & W
Cuyamaca College *California* M
Cypress College *California* M & W
Daemen College *New York* M
Dakota Wesleyan University *South Dakota* M & W
Dallas Baptist University *Texas* M & W
Dalton State College *Georgia* W

M = Men; W = Women

Dana College *Nebraska* W
Daniel Webster College *New Hampshire* M & W
Danville Area Community College *Illinois* M
Dartmouth College *New Hampshire* M & W
Darton College *Georgia* M
Davenport University *Michigan* M & W
Davidson College *North Carolina* M
Davis & Elkins College *West Virginia* M
Daytona State College *Florida* W
De Anza College *California* M & W
Dean College *Massachusetts* M
Defiance College *Ohio* M & W
Delaware County Community College *Pennsylvania* M & W
Delaware Technical & Community College, Jack F. Owens Campus *Delaware* M
Delaware Valley College *Pennsylvania* M
Delta State University *Mississippi* M
Denison University *Ohio* M
DePaul University *Illinois* M
DePauw University *Indiana* M & W
Des Moines Area Community College *Iowa* M & W
DeSales University *Pennsylvania* M
Dickinson College *Pennsylvania* M & W
Dickinson State University *North Dakota* M & W
Dixie State College of Utah *Utah* M
Doane College *Nebraska* M & W
Dodge City Community College *Kansas* M
Dominican College *New York* M
Dominican University *Illinois* M
Dominican University of California *California* M & W
Dordt College *Iowa* M & W
Dowling College *New York* M
Drake University *Iowa* M & W
Drexel University *Pennsylvania* M
Drury University *Missouri* M & W
Duke University *North Carolina* M & W
Dutchess Community College *New York* M
D'Youville College *New York* M & W
East Carolina University *North Carolina* M & W
East Central Community College *Mississippi* M & W
East Central University *Oklahoma* M & W
East Mississippi Community College *Mississippi* M
East Stroudsburg University of Pennsylvania *Pennsylvania* W
East Tennessee State University *Tennessee* M & W
Eastern Arizona College *Arizona* M & W
Eastern Illinois University *Illinois* M & W
Eastern Kentucky University *Kentucky* M & W
Eastern Maine Community College *Maine* M
Eastern Michigan University *Michigan* M & W
Eastern University *Pennsylvania* M
Eastern Washington University *Washington* W
Eastfield College *Texas* M
Eckerd College *Florida* M & W
Edgewood College *Wisconsin* M & W
Edmonds Community College *Washington* M & W
El Camino College *California* M
Elgin Community College *Illinois* M
Elizabeth City State University *North Carolina* M
Elizabethtown College *Pennsylvania* M
Ellsworth Community College *Iowa* M & W
Elmhurst College *Illinois* M & W
Elmira College *New York* M & W
Elms College *Massachusetts* M
Elon University *North Carolina* M & W
Embry-Riddle Aeronautical University *Florida* M & W
Emerson College *Massachusetts* M & W
Emmanuel College *Massachusetts* M
Emory & Henry College *Virginia* M
Emory University *Georgia* M
Endicott College *Massachusetts* M & W
Erie Community College *New York* M & W
Erie Community College, North Campus *New York* M & W
Erie Community College, South Campus *New York* M & W
Erskine College *South Carolina* M & W
Eureka College *Illinois* M
Evangel University *Missouri* M & W
Fairfield University *Connecticut* M & W
Fairleigh Dickinson University, College at Florham *New Jersey* M
Fairleigh Dickinson University, Metropolitan Campus *New Jersey* M & W
Fairmont State University *West Virginia* M & W
Farmingdale State College *New York* M
Faulkner University *Alabama* M & W
Fayetteville State University *North Carolina* M
Ferris State University *Michigan* M & W
Ferrum College *Virginia* M
Flagler College *Florida* M & W
Florida Agricultural and Mechanical University *Florida* M & W
Florida Atlantic University *Florida* M & W
Florida Gulf Coast University *Florida* M & W
Florida Institute of Technology *Florida* M & W
Florida International University *Florida* W
Florida Southern College *Florida* M & W
Florida State University *Florida* M & W
Fontbonne University *Missouri* M & W
Foothill College *California* M & W
Fordham University *New York* M
Fort Hays State University *Kansas* M
Fort Lewis College *Colorado* M
Fort Valley State University *Georgia* M
Francis Marion University *South Carolina* M
Frank Phillips College *Texas* M
Franklin College *Indiana* M & W
Franklin & Marshall College *Pennsylvania* M & W
Franklin Pierce University *New Hampshire* M
Frederick Community College *Maryland* M & W
Fresno City College *California* M & W
Friends University *Kansas* M
Fullerton College *California* M & W
Furman University *South Carolina* M & W
Gannon University *Pennsylvania* M & W
Gardner-Webb University *North Carolina* M & W
Garrett College *Maryland* M
GateWay Community College *Arizona* M & W
Gavilan College *California* M
Genesee Community College *New York* M & W
George Fox University *Oregon* M & W
George Mason University *Virginia* M
The George Washington University *District of Columbia* M
Georgetown College *Kentucky* M & W
Georgetown University *District of Columbia* M
Georgia College & State University *Georgia* M
Georgia Institute of Technology *Georgia* M
Georgia Southern University *Georgia* M
Georgia Southwestern State University *Georgia* M
Georgia State University *Georgia* M & W
Gettysburg College *Pennsylvania* M & W
Glen Oaks Community College *Michigan* M
Glendale Community College *Arizona* M
Glenville State College *West Virginia* M & W
Goldey-Beacom College *Delaware* M & W
Gonzaga University *Washington* M & W
Gordon College *Massachusetts* M & W
Goshen College *Indiana* M
Grace College *Indiana* M
Graceland University *Iowa* M & W
Grambling State University *Louisiana* M & W
Grand Canyon University *Arizona* M & W
Grand Rapids Community College *Michigan* M
Grand Valley State University *Michigan* M & W
Grand View University *Iowa* M & W
Grays Harbor College *Washington* M & W
Green Mountain College *Vermont* M
Green River Community College *Washington* M & W
Greensboro College *North Carolina* M
Grinnell College *Iowa* M & W
Grossmont College *California* M
Grove City College *Pennsylvania* M & W
Guilford College *North Carolina* M
Gustavus Adolphus College *Minnesota* M & W
Gwynedd-Mercy College *Pennsylvania* M
Hagerstown Community College *Maryland* M & W
Hamilton College *New York* M & W
Hampden-Sydney College *Virginia* M
Hampton University *Virginia* M & W
Hannibal-LaGrange College *Missouri* M & W
Hanover College *Indiana* M & W
Hardin-Simmons University *Texas* M & W
Harding University *Arkansas* M & W
Harford Community College *Maryland* M
Hartnell College *California* M
Harvard University *Massachusetts* M & W
Harvey Mudd College *California* M
Haskell Indian Nations University *Kansas* M
Hastings College *Nebraska* M & W
Haverford College *Pennsylvania* M & W
Hawai'i Pacific University *Hawaii* M
Heidelberg University *Ohio* M & W
Henderson State University *Arkansas* M & W
Hendrix College *Arkansas* M & W
Henry Ford Community College *Michigan* M
Hibbing Community College *Minnesota* M & W
High Point University *North Carolina* M
Highland Community College *Illinois* M & W
Hilbert College *New York* M & W
Hill College of the Hill Junior College District *Texas* M
Hinds Community College *Mississippi* M
Hiram College *Ohio* M & W
Hobart and William Smith Colleges *New York* M & W
Hofstra University *New York* M & W
Hollins University *Virginia* W
Holmes Community College *Mississippi* M
Holy Family University *Pennsylvania* M
Holy Names University *California* M
Holyoke Community College *Massachusetts* M & W
Hood College *Maryland* M & W
Hope College *Michigan* M & W
Houston Baptist University *Texas* M & W
Hudson Valley Community College *New York* M & W
Huntingdon College *Alabama* M & W
Huntington University *Indiana* M
Husson University *Maine* M & W
Hutchinson Community College and Area Vocational School *Kansas* M
Idaho State University *Idaho* W
Illinois Central College *Illinois* M & W
Illinois College *Illinois* M & W
Illinois State University *Illinois* M & W
Illinois Valley Community College *Illinois* M
Illinois Wesleyan University *Illinois* M & W
Indian Hills Community College *Iowa* M
Indiana State University *Indiana* W
Indiana Tech *Indiana* M & W
Indiana University Bloomington *Indiana* M & W
Indiana University East *Indiana* M & W
Indiana University of Pennsylvania *Pennsylvania* M
Indiana University–Purdue University Fort Wayne *Indiana* M & W
Indiana University–Purdue University Indianapolis *Indiana* M & W
Indiana Wesleyan University *Indiana* M
Iona College *New York* M
Iowa Central Community College *Iowa* M & W
Iowa Lakes Community College *Iowa* M & W
Iowa State University of Science and Technology *Iowa* M & W
Iowa Wesleyan College *Iowa* M & W
Iowa Western Community College *Iowa* M & W
Itawamba Community College *Mississippi* M
Ithaca College *New York* W
Jackson Community College *Michigan* M & W
Jackson State University *Mississippi* M & W
Jacksonville State University *Alabama* M & W
Jacksonville University *Florida* M & W
James A. Rhodes State College *Ohio* M
James H. Faulkner State Community College *Alabama* M
James Madison University *Virginia* M & W
Jamestown College *North Dakota* M & W
Jamestown Community College *New York* M
John A. Logan College *Illinois* M & W
John Brown University *Arkansas* M
John Carroll University *Ohio* M & W
John Wood Community College *Illinois* M
Johnson C. Smith University *North Carolina* M & W
Johnson College *Pennsylvania* M & W
Johnson County Community College *Kansas* M
Johnson State College *Vermont* M

M = Men; W = Women

Johnson & Wales University *Rhode Island* M & W
Johnson & Wales University *Colorado* M
Johnston Community College *North Carolina* M & W
Joliet Junior College *Illinois* M
Jones County Junior College *Mississippi* M
Judson University *Illinois* M & W
Juniata College *Pennsylvania* M & W
Kalamazoo College *Michigan* M & W
Kalamazoo Valley Community College *Michigan* M
Kansas City Kansas Community College *Kansas* M
Kansas State University *Kansas* M & W
Kansas Wesleyan University *Kansas* M & W
Kaskaskia College *Illinois* M & W
Kennesaw State University *Georgia* M & W
Kent State University *Ohio* M & W
Kentucky State University *Kentucky* M
Kentucky Wesleyan College *Kentucky* M & W
Kenyon College *Ohio* M
Keuka College *New York* W
Keystone College *Pennsylvania* M
King College *Tennessee* M & W
King's College *Pennsylvania* M
Kirkwood Community College *Iowa* M
Kirtland Community College *Michigan* M & W
Knox College *Illinois* M & W
Kutztown University of Pennsylvania *Pennsylvania* W
Kwantlen Polytechnic University *British Columbia* M & W
La Roche College *Pennsylvania* M
La Salle University *Pennsylvania* M & W
La Sierra University *California* M
Lackawanna College *Pennsylvania* M & W
Lafayette College *Pennsylvania* M
LaGrange College *Georgia* M
Lake Erie College *Ohio* M & W
Lake Forest College *Illinois* M & W
Lake Superior State University *Michigan* M & W
Lakehead University *Ontario* M
Lakeland College *Wisconsin* M & W
Lakeland Community College *Ohio* M
Lamar Community College *Colorado* M
Lamar University *Texas* M & W
Lambuth University *Tennessee* M
Lander University *South Carolina* M
Laney College *California* M
Lansing Community College *Michigan* M
Lassen Community College District *California* M & W
Lawrence University *Wisconsin* M
Le Moyne College *New York* M & W
Lebanon Valley College *Pennsylvania* M
Lee University *Tennessee* M
Lees-McRae College *North Carolina* M
Lehigh Carbon Community College *Pennsylvania* M & W
Lehigh University *Pennsylvania* M & W
LeMoyne-Owen College *Tennessee* M & W
Lenoir-Rhyne University *North Carolina* M & W
LeTourneau University *Texas* M & W
Lewis & Clark College *Oregon* M & W
Lewis and Clark Community College *Illinois* M
Lewis-Clark State College *Idaho* M & W
Lewis University *Illinois* M & W
Liberty University *Virginia* M
Limestone College *South Carolina* M & W
Lincoln College *Illinois* M & W
Lincoln Memorial University *Tennessee* M & W
Lincoln University *Missouri* M & W
Lindenwood University *Missouri* M & W
Lindsey Wilson College *Kentucky* M & W
Linfield College *Oregon* M & W
Lipscomb University *Tennessee* M & W
Logan University–College of Chiropractic *Missouri* M
Lon Morris College *Texas* M & W
Long Beach City College *California* M & W
Long Island University, Brooklyn Campus *New York* M & W
Longwood University *Virginia* M & W
Loras College *Iowa* M & W
Louisburg College *North Carolina* M & W
Louisiana College *Louisiana* M
Louisiana State University and Agricultural and Mechanical College *Louisiana* M & W
Louisiana Tech University *Louisiana* M
Lourdes College *Ohio* M & W
Loyola Marymount University *California* M
Loyola University Chicago *Illinois* M & W
Loyola University Maryland *Maryland* M
Loyola University New Orleans *Louisiana* M & W
Lubbock Christian University *Texas* M & W
Luther College *Iowa* M & W
Luzerne County Community College *Pennsylvania* M & W
Lycoming College *Pennsylvania* M & W
Lynchburg College *Virginia* M
Lyon College *Arkansas* M & W
Macalester College *Minnesota* M & W
MacMurray College *Illinois* M & W
Madonna University *Michigan* M & W
Malone University *Ohio* M & W
Manchester College *Indiana* M & W
Manhattan College *New York* M
Manhattanville College *New York* M
Marian University *Wisconsin* M & W
Marian University *Indiana* M & W
Marion Military Institute *Alabama* M & W
Marion Technical College *Ohio* M & W
Marquette University *Wisconsin* M
Mars Hill College *North Carolina* M & W
Marshall University *West Virginia* M & W
Marshalltown Community College *Iowa* M & W
Martin Luther College *Minnesota* M
Martin Methodist College *Tennessee* M & W
Marymount College, Palos Verdes, California *California* M & W
Marymount University *Virginia* M
Maryville College *Tennessee* M & W
Maryville University of Saint Louis *Missouri* M & W
Marywood University *Pennsylvania* M & W
Massachusetts Bay Community College *Massachusetts* M & W
Massachusetts College of Liberal Arts *Massachusetts* M
Massachusetts Institute of Technology *Massachusetts* M & W
The Master's College and Seminary *California* M
McDaniel College *Maryland* M & W
McGill University *Quebec* M & W
McKendree University *Illinois* M & W
McLennan Community College *Texas* M & W
McMaster University *Ontario* M & W
McMurry University *Texas* M & W
McNeese State University *Louisiana* M & W
Medaille College *New York* M
Menlo College *California* M
Merced College *California* M & W
Mercer County Community College *New Jersey* M & W
Mercer University *Georgia* M & W
Mercyhurst College *Pennsylvania* M & W
Meridian Community College *Mississippi* M
Mesa Community College *Arizona* M & W
Mesa State College *Colorado* W
Messiah College *Pennsylvania* M
Methodist University *North Carolina* M & W
Metropolitan State College of Denver *Colorado* M & W
Miami University *Ohio* M
Miami University Hamilton *Ohio* M
Miami University–Middletown Campus *Ohio* M & W
Michigan State University *Michigan* M & W
Mid-America Christian University *Oklahoma* M
Mid-Plains Community College *Nebraska* M
Mid-State Technical College *Wisconsin* M
Middle Tennessee State University *Tennessee* M
Middlebury College *Vermont* M & W
Middlesex County College *New Jersey* M & W
Midland Lutheran College *Nebraska* M & W
Midwestern State University *Texas* M & W
Miles Community College *Montana* M & W
Millersville University of Pennsylvania *Pennsylvania* M
Milligan College *Tennessee* M
Millikin University *Illinois* M & W
Millsaps College *Mississippi* M & W
Milwaukee Area Technical College *Wisconsin* M & W
Milwaukee School of Engineering *Wisconsin* M & W
Minnesota State Community and Technical College *Minnesota* M & W
Minnesota State University Mankato *Minnesota* M & W
Minnesota State University Moorhead *Minnesota* M & W
Minnesota West Community and Technical College *Minnesota* M & W
Minot State University *North Dakota* M & W
Misericordia University *Pennsylvania* M
Mississippi College *Mississippi* M
Mississippi Delta Community College *Mississippi* M
Mississippi Gulf Coast Community College *Mississippi* M
Mississippi State University *Mississippi* M & W
Mississippi Valley State University *Mississippi* M & W
Missouri Baptist University *Missouri* M & W
Missouri Southern State University *Missouri* M
Missouri State University *Missouri* M & W
Missouri Valley College *Missouri* M & W
Missouri Western State University *Missouri* M & W
Mitchell College *Connecticut* M & W
Modesto Junior College *California* M
Mohawk Valley Community College *New York* M & W
Monmouth College *Illinois* M & W
Monmouth University *New Jersey* M & W
Monroe Community College *New York* M
Montana State University *Montana* W
Montana State University Billings *Montana* M & W
Montana State University–Northern *Montana* W
Montana Tech of The University of Montana *Montana* M & W
Montclair State University *New Jersey* M & W
Monterey Peninsula College *California* M & W
Montgomery College *Maryland* M
Montreat College *North Carolina* M
Moorpark College *California* M & W
Moraine Valley Community College *Illinois* M
Moravian College *Pennsylvania* M & W
Morehead State University *Kentucky* M
Morningside College *Iowa* M & W
Morris College *South Carolina* M
Mott Community College *Michigan* M
Mount Aloysius College *Pennsylvania* M & W
Mount Holyoke College *Massachusetts* W
Mount Marty College *South Dakota* M & W
Mount Mercy College *Iowa* M & W
Mount Olive College *North Carolina* M
Mount St. Mary's University *Maryland* M & W
Mt. San Antonio College *California* M & W
Mt. San Jacinto College *California* M
Mount Vernon Nazarene University *Ohio* M
Muhlenberg College *Pennsylvania* M & W
Murray State University *Kentucky* M & W
Muskegon Community College *Michigan* M & W
Muskingum University *Ohio* M & W
Nassau Community College *New York* M & W
Nazareth College of Rochester *New York* M & W
Nebraska College of Technical Agriculture *Nebraska* M
Nebraska Wesleyan University *Nebraska* M & W
Neumann University *Pennsylvania* M
New Mexico Institute of Mining and Technology *New Mexico* M & W
New Mexico Junior College *New Mexico* M
New Mexico Military Institute *New Mexico* M
New Mexico State University *New Mexico* M & W
New York University *New York* M & W
Newberry College *South Carolina* M & W
Newbury College *Massachusetts* M & W
Newman University *Kansas* M & W
Niagara County Community College *New York* M & W
Niagara University *New York* M & W
Nicholls State University *Louisiana* M & W
Nichols College *Massachusetts* M
Nicolet Area Technical College *Wisconsin* M & W

M = Men; W = Women

North Carolina Central University *North Carolina* M & W
North Carolina State University *North Carolina* M & W
North Carolina Wesleyan College *North Carolina* M
North Central College *Illinois* M & W
North Central University *Minnesota* M
North Dakota State University *North Dakota* M & W
North Greenville University *South Carolina* M & W
North Iowa Area Community College *Iowa* M & W
North Park University *Illinois* M & W
Northampton Community College *Pennsylvania* M & W
Northeast Mississippi Community College *Mississippi* M
Northeastern Oklahoma Agricultural and Mechanical College *Oklahoma* M
Northeastern State University *Oklahoma* M & W
Northern Arizona University *Arizona* W
Northern Illinois University *Illinois* M & W
Northern Kentucky University *Kentucky* M & W
Northern Maine Community College *Maine* M & W
Northern Michigan University *Michigan* M
Northern State University *South Dakota* M & W
Northwest Christian University *Oregon* M & W
Northwest Mississippi Community College *Mississippi* M
Northwest Missouri State University *Missouri* W
Northwest Nazarene University *Idaho* M
Northwestern College *Minnesota* M & W
Northwestern College *Iowa* M & W
Northwestern Oklahoma State University *Oklahoma* M & W
Northwestern University *Illinois* M & W
Northwood University *Michigan* M & W
Northwood University, Florida Campus *Florida* M & W
Northwood University, Texas Campus *Texas* M & W
Notre Dame College *Ohio* M & W
Notre Dame de Namur University *California* M
Nova Scotia Agricultural College *Nova Scotia* M & W
Nova Southeastern University *Florida* M & W
Oakland City University *Indiana* M & W
Oakland Community College *Michigan* M
Oakland University *Michigan* M & W
Oberlin College *Ohio* M & W
Occidental College *California* M & W
Ocean County College *New Jersey* M & W
Odessa College *Texas* M
Oglethorpe University *Georgia* M & W
Ohio Christian University *Ohio* M
Ohio Dominican University *Ohio* M & W
Ohio Northern University *Ohio* M & W
The Ohio State University *Ohio* M & W
Ohio University *Ohio* M & W
Ohio University–Zanesville *Ohio* M & W
Ohio Valley University *West Virginia* M & W
Ohio Wesleyan University *Ohio* M
Oklahoma Baptist University *Oklahoma* M & W
Oklahoma Christian University *Oklahoma* M
Oklahoma City University *Oklahoma* M & W
Oklahoma Panhandle State University *Oklahoma* M & W
Oklahoma Wesleyan University *Oklahoma* M
Old Dominion University *Virginia* M & W
Olivet College *Michigan* M & W
Olivet Nazarene University *Illinois* M
Olympic College *Washington* M & W
Oral Roberts University *Oklahoma* M & W
Orange Coast College *California* M & W
Orange County Community College *New York* M & W
Oregon State University *Oregon* M & W
Otero Junior College *Colorado* M & W
Ottawa University *Kansas* M
Otterbein University *Ohio* M & W
Ouachita Baptist University *Arkansas* M & W
Our Lady of the Lake University of San Antonio *Texas* M & W
Pace University *New York* M
Pacific Lutheran University *Washington* M & W
Pacific University *Oregon* M & W
Paine College *Georgia* M
Palomar College *California* M
Paradise Valley Community College *Arizona* M & W
Paris Junior College *Texas* M
Park University *Missouri* W
Parkland College *Illinois* M
Pearl River Community College *Mississippi* M & W
Penn State Abington *Pennsylvania* M
Penn State Altoona *Pennsylvania* M & W
Penn State Berks *Pennsylvania* M
Penn State DuBois *Pennsylvania* M & W
Penn State Erie, The Behrend College *Pennsylvania* M & W
Penn State Harrisburg *Pennsylvania* M & W
Penn State Lehigh Valley *Pennsylvania* M & W
Penn State Mont Alto *Pennsylvania* M & W
Penn State New Kensington *Pennsylvania* M & W
Penn State Schuylkill *Pennsylvania* M
Penn State University Park *Pennsylvania* M & W
Penn State Wilkes-Barre *Pennsylvania* M & W
Pennsylvania College of Technology *Pennsylvania* M & W
Pepperdine University *California* M & W
Peru State College *Nebraska* W
Pfeiffer University *North Carolina* M & W
Philadelphia Biblical University *Pennsylvania* M
Philadelphia University *Pennsylvania* M
Phoenix College *Arizona* M & W
Piedmont College *Georgia* M & W
Pikeville College *Kentucky* M & W
Pima Community College *Arizona* M & W
Pitt Community College *North Carolina* M
Pittsburg State University *Kansas* M
Pitzer College *California* M
Point Loma Nazarene University *California* M
Point Park University *Pennsylvania* M & W
Pomona College *California* M & W
Portland State University *Oregon* M & W
Post University *Connecticut* M
Potomac State College of West Virginia University *West Virginia* M & W
Prairie State College *Illinois* M & W
Prairie View A&M University *Texas* M & W
Pratt Community College *Kansas* M & W
Presbyterian College *South Carolina* M & W
Presentation College *South Dakota* M & W
Prince George's Community College *Maryland* M
Princeton University *New Jersey* M & W
Providence College *Rhode Island* M & W
Purchase College, State University of New York *New York* M
Purdue University *Indiana* M & W
Queens College of the City University of New York *New York* M
Queens University of Charlotte *North Carolina* M & W
Queen's University at Kingston *Ontario* M
Quincy University *Illinois* M & W
Quinnipiac University *Connecticut* M
Radford University *Virginia* M & W
Randolph-Macon College *Virginia* M
Ranger College *Texas* M
Reedley College *California* M
Regis University *Colorado* M & W
Reinhardt University *Georgia* M
Rend Lake College *Illinois* M & W
Rensselaer Polytechnic Institute *New York* M
Research College of Nursing *Missouri* M & W
Rhode Island College *Rhode Island* M
Rhodes College *Tennessee* M & W
Rice University *Texas* M
Rider University *New Jersey* M
Ripon College *Wisconsin* M & W
Riverland Community College *Minnesota* M & W
Riverside Community College District *California* M
Rivier College *New Hampshire* M & W
Roanoke College *Virginia* M & W
Robert Morris University *Pennsylvania* M & W
Robert Morris University Illinois *Illinois* M & W
Roberts Wesleyan College *New York* M & W
Rochester College *Michigan* M
Rochester Community and Technical College *Minnesota* M & W
Rock Valley College *Illinois* M
Rockford College *Illinois* M & W
Rockhurst University *Missouri* M & W
Rockingham Community College *North Carolina* M & W
Rockland Community College *New York* M
Rocky Mountain College *Montana* M & W
Rogers State University *Oklahoma* M & W
Rollins College *Florida* M & W
Rose-Hulman Institute of Technology *Indiana* M & W
Rosemont College *Pennsylvania* M
Rutgers, The State University of New Jersey, Camden *New Jersey* M
Rutgers, The State University of New Jersey, New Brunswick *New Jersey* M & W
Sacramento City College *California* M & W
Sacred Heart University *Connecticut* M & W
Saddleback College *California* M & W
Sage College of Albany *New York* M
Saginaw Valley State University *Michigan* M
St. Ambrose University *Iowa* M & W
St. Andrews Presbyterian College *North Carolina* M & W
Saint Anselm College *New Hampshire* M
Saint Augustine's College *North Carolina* M
St. Bonaventure University *New York* M
St. Clair County Community College *Michigan* M
St. Cloud State University *Minnesota* M & W
St. Edward's University *Texas* M & W
St. Francis College *New York* M & W
Saint Francis University *Pennsylvania* M & W
St. John Fisher College *New York* M & W
St. John's University *New York* M & W
Saint John's University *Minnesota* M
Saint Joseph's College *Indiana* M & W
Saint Joseph's College of Maine *Maine* M
Saint Joseph's University *Pennsylvania* M
St. Lawrence University *New York* M & W
Saint Leo University *Florida* M & W
Saint Louis University *Missouri* M & W
Saint Martin's University *Washington* M & W
Saint Mary-of-the-Woods College *Indiana* W
Saint Mary's College *Indiana* W
Saint Mary's College of California *California* M
St. Mary's College of Maryland *Maryland* M & W
St. Mary's University *Texas* M & W
Saint Mary's University of Minnesota *Minnesota* M & W
Saint Michael's College *Vermont* M
St. Norbert College *Wisconsin* M & W
St. Olaf College *Minnesota* M & W
Saint Paul's College *Virginia* M & W
Saint Peter's College *New Jersey* M
St. Thomas Aquinas College *New York* M & W
St. Thomas University *New Brunswick* M & W
St. Thomas University *Florida* M & W
Saint Vincent College *Pennsylvania* M & W
Saint Xavier University *Illinois* M
Salem International University *West Virginia* M
Salem State College *Massachusetts* M
Sam Houston State University *Texas* M & W
Samford University *Alabama* M & W
San Bernardino Valley College *California* M
San Diego City College *California* M & W
San Diego State University *California* M & W
San Jacinto College District *Texas* M
San Joaquin Delta College *California* M & W
San Jose City College *California* M
San Jose State University *California* M & W
Sandhills Community College *North Carolina* M & W
Santa Ana College *California* M
Santa Barbara City College *California* M & W
Santa Clara University *California* M & W
Santa Rosa Junior College *California* M
Savannah College of Art and Design *Georgia* M & W
Savannah State University *Georgia* M & W
Schoolcraft College *Michigan* M & W
Schreiner University *Texas* M & W
Scott Community College *Iowa* M & W
Scottsdale Community College *Arizona* M & W
Scripps College *California* W
Seattle University *Washington* M & W
Seminole State College *Oklahoma* M & W

M = Men; W = Women

Seminole State College of Florida *Florida* W
Seton Hall University *New Jersey* M & W
Seton Hill University *Pennsylvania* W
Sewanee: The University of the South *Tennessee* M & W
Shasta College *California* M & W
Shaw University *North Carolina* M
Shawnee Community College *Illinois* M & W
Shawnee State University *Ohio* M
Shenandoah University *Virginia* M
Shepherd University *West Virginia* M
Shorter University *Georgia* M & W
Siena College *New York* M & W
Siena Heights University *Michigan* M & W
Sierra College *California* M & W
Silver Lake College *Wisconsin* M & W
Simon Fraser University *British Columbia* M
Simpson College *Iowa* M & W
Simpson University *California* M & W
Sinclair Community College *Ohio* M
Skagit Valley College *Washington* M & W
Skidmore College *New York* M
Slippery Rock University of Pennsylvania *Pennsylvania* M & W
Sonoma State University *California* M & W
South Carolina State University *South Carolina* M & W
South Dakota School of Mines and Technology *South Dakota* M & W
South Dakota State University *South Dakota* M & W
South Mountain Community College *Arizona* M & W
Southeast Community College, Beatrice Campus *Nebraska* M
Southeastern Louisiana University *Louisiana* M
Southeastern University *Florida* M
Southern Arkansas University–Magnolia *Arkansas* M
Southern Illinois University Carbondale *Illinois* M & W
Southern Illinois University Edwardsville *Illinois* M & W
Southern Maine Community College *Maine* M & W
Southern Methodist University *Texas* M & W
Southern Nazarene University *Oklahoma* M & W
Southern New Hampshire University *New Hampshire* M
Southern University and Agricultural and Mechanical College *Louisiana* M & W
Southern Utah University *Utah* M
Southern Virginia University *Virginia* M & W
Southern Wesleyan University *South Carolina* M
Southwest Baptist University *Missouri* M
Southwest Minnesota State University *Minnesota* W
Southwest Wisconsin Technical College *Wisconsin* M & W
Southwestern Christian University *Oklahoma* M
Southwestern College *Kansas* M & W
Southwestern Oklahoma State University *Oklahoma* M & W
Southwestern Oregon Community College *Oregon* M & W
Southwestern University *Texas* M & W
Spalding University *Kentucky* M & W
Spartanburg Methodist College *South Carolina* M & W
Spelman College *Georgia* W
Spring Arbor University *Michigan* M
Spring Hill College *Alabama* M & W
Springfield College *Massachusetts* M
Springfield College in Illinois *Illinois* M
Springfield Technical Community College *Massachusetts* M
Stanford University *California* M & W
State University of New York at Binghamton *New York* M
State University of New York College of Agriculture and Technology at Cobleskill *New York* M & W
State University of New York College at Cortland *New York* W
State University of New York College of Environmental Science and Forestry *New York* M & W
State University of New York College at Old Westbury *New York* M
State University of New York College at Potsdam *New York* M
State University of New York College of Technology at Delhi *New York* M & W
State University of New York Institute of Technology *New York* M & W
State University of New York at Oswego *New York* M & W
Stephen F. Austin State University *Texas* M & W
Sterling College *Kansas* M & W
Stetson University *Florida* M & W
Stevens Institute of Technology *New Jersey* M
Stevenson University *Maryland* M & W
Stonehill College *Massachusetts* M & W
Suffolk County Community College *New York* M & W
Suffolk University *Massachusetts* M
Sullivan County Community College *New York* M
Susquehanna University *Pennsylvania* M & W
Swarthmore College *Pennsylvania* M
Tabor College *Kansas* M & W
Tacoma Community College *Washington* M & W
Talladega College *Alabama* M
Tarleton State University *Texas* W
Taylor University *Indiana* M
Temple University *Pennsylvania* M
Tennessee State University *Tennessee* M
Tennessee Technological University *Tennessee* M & W
Tennessee Wesleyan College *Tennessee* M & W
Texas A&M International University *Texas* M & W
Texas A&M University *Texas* M & W
Texas A&M University–Commerce *Texas* M & W
Texas A&M University–Corpus Christi *Texas* W
Texas Christian University *Texas* M & W
Texas Lutheran University *Texas* M & W
Texas Southern University *Texas* M
Texas Southmost College *Texas* M & W
Texas State University–San Marcos *Texas* M & W
Texas Tech University *Texas* M & W
Texas Wesleyan University *Texas* M
Thiel College *Pennsylvania* M & W
Thomas College *Maine* M
Thomas More College *Kentucky* M & W
Thomas University *Georgia* M & W
Thompson Rivers University *British Columbia* M
Tiffin University *Ohio* M & W
Toccoa Falls College *Georgia* M & W
Tompkins Cortland Community College *New York* M & W
Tougaloo College *Mississippi* M
Towson University *Maryland* M & W
Transylvania University *Kentucky* M & W
Trent University *Ontario* M & W
Trevecca Nazarene University *Tennessee* M & W
Tri-County Technical College *South Carolina* M
Trine University *Indiana* M & W
Trinidad State Junior College *Colorado* M & W
Trinity Bible College *North Dakota* M
Trinity College *Connecticut* M
Trinity University *Texas* M & W
Troy University *Alabama* M & W
Truett-McConnell College *Georgia* M & W
Truman State University *Missouri* M & W
Tufts University *Massachusetts* M
Tulane University *Louisiana* W
Tusculum College *Tennessee* M & W
Tuskegee University *Alabama* M
Tyler Junior College *Texas* M & W
Ulster County Community College *New York* M
Union College *New York* M & W
Union College *Kentucky* M & W
Union County College *New Jersey* M & W
Union University *Tennessee* M
United States Air Force Academy *Colorado* M
United States Coast Guard Academy *Connecticut* M & W
United States Merchant Marine Academy *New York* M & W
United States Military Academy *New York* M
United States Naval Academy *Maryland* M
Université Laval *Quebec* M & W
The University of Akron *Ohio* M & W
The University of Akron–Wayne College *Ohio* M
The University of Alabama *Alabama* M & W
The University of Alabama at Birmingham *Alabama* M & W
University at Albany, State University of New York *New York* W
University of Alberta *Alberta* M & W
The University of Arizona *Arizona* M & W
University of Arkansas *Arkansas* M & W
University of Arkansas at Fort Smith *Arkansas* M & W
University of Arkansas at Little Rock *Arkansas* M & W
University of Arkansas at Monticello *Arkansas* M
University of Arkansas at Pine Bluff *Arkansas* M
The University of British Columbia *British Columbia* M & W
University of Calgary *Alberta* M & W
University of California, Berkeley *California* M & W
University of California, Davis *California* M & W
University of California, Irvine *California* M & W
University of California, Los Angeles *California* M & W
University of California, Riverside *California* M & W
University of California, San Diego *California* M
University of California, Santa Barbara *California* M
University of California, Santa Cruz *California* W
University of Central Arkansas *Arkansas* M & W
University of Central Florida *Florida* M & W
University of Central Missouri *Missouri* M
University of Central Oklahoma *Oklahoma* M & W
University of Charleston *West Virginia* M
University of Cincinnati *Ohio* M & W
University of Cincinnati Clermont College *Ohio* M
University of Colorado at Boulder *Colorado* M & W
University of Colorado at Colorado Springs *Colorado* M
University of Connecticut *Connecticut* M
University of the Cumberlands *Kentucky* M & W
University of Dallas *Texas* M
University of Dayton *Ohio* M & W
University of Delaware *Delaware* M
University of Denver *Colorado* M & W
University of Detroit Mercy *Michigan* M & W
University of the District of Columbia *District of Columbia* M
University of Dubuque *Iowa* M & W
University of Evansville *Indiana* M & W
The University of Findlay *Ohio* M & W
University of Florida *Florida* M & W
University of Georgia *Georgia* M & W
University of Great Falls *Montana* M & W
University of Guelph *Ontario* M & W
University of Hartford *Connecticut* M & W
University of Hawaii at Hilo *Hawaii* M
University of Hawaii at Manoa *Hawaii* M & W
University of Houston *Texas* M
University of Idaho *Idaho* M & W
University of Illinois at Springfield *Illinois* M & W
University of Illinois at Urbana–Champaign *Illinois* M & W
University of the Incarnate Word *Texas* M & W
University of Indianapolis *Indiana* M & W
The University of Iowa *Iowa* M & W
The University of Kansas *Kansas* M & W
University of Kentucky *Kentucky* M & W
University of La Verne *California* M
University of Louisiana at Lafayette *Louisiana* M
University of Louisiana at Monroe *Louisiana* M & W
University of Louisville *Kentucky* M & W
University of Maine at Augusta *Maine* M & W
University of Maine at Farmington *Maine* M
University of Maine at Fort Kent *Maine* M & W
University of Maine at Presque Isle *Maine* M
University of Mary *North Dakota* M & W
University of Mary Hardin-Baylor *Texas* M & W
University of Maryland, College Park *Maryland* M & W
University of Massachusetts Dartmouth *Massachusetts* M

M = Men; W = Women

University of Memphis *Tennessee* M & W
University of Miami *Florida* W
University of Michigan *Michigan* M & W
University of Minnesota, Crookston *Minnesota* M & W
University of Minnesota, Morris *Minnesota* M & W
University of Minnesota, Twin Cities Campus *Minnesota* M & W
University of Mississippi *Mississippi* M & W
University of Missouri *Missouri* M & W
University of Missouri–Kansas City *Missouri* M & W
University of Missouri–St. Louis *Missouri* M & W
University of Mobile *Alabama* M & W
The University of Montana *Montana* W
The University of Montana Western *Montana* M & W
University of Montevallo *Alabama* M & W
University of Mount Union *Ohio* M & W
University of Nebraska at Kearney *Nebraska* M & W
University of Nebraska at Omaha *Nebraska* W
University of Nebraska–Lincoln *Nebraska* M & W
University of Nevada, Las Vegas *Nevada* M
University of Nevada, Reno *Nevada* M & W
University of New England *Maine* M
University of New Hampshire *New Hampshire* M & W
University of New Haven *Connecticut* M
University of New Mexico *New Mexico* M & W
University of New Orleans *Louisiana* M
University of North Alabama *Alabama* M
The University of North Carolina at Chapel Hill *North Carolina* M & W
The University of North Carolina at Charlotte *North Carolina* M
The University of North Carolina at Greensboro *North Carolina* M & W
The University of North Carolina at Pembroke *North Carolina* M & W
The University of North Carolina Wilmington *North Carolina* M & W
University of North Dakota *North Dakota* M & W
University of North Florida *Florida* M
University of North Texas *Texas* M & W
University of Northern Colorado *Colorado* M & W
University of Northern Iowa *Iowa* M & W
University of Notre Dame *Indiana* M & W
University of Oklahoma *Oklahoma* M & W
University of Oregon *Oregon* M & W
University of Ottawa *Ontario* M & W
University of the Pacific *California* M
University of Pennsylvania *Pennsylvania* M & W
University of Pittsburgh at Bradford *Pennsylvania* M & W
University of Pittsburgh at Greensburg *Pennsylvania* M & W
University of Pittsburgh at Johnstown *Pennsylvania* M & W
University of Portland *Oregon* M & W
University of Prince Edward Island *Prince Edward Island* M
University of Puget Sound *Washington* M & W
University of Redlands *California* M & W
University of Rhode Island *Rhode Island* M
University of Richmond *Virginia* M & W
University of Rochester *New York* M
University of Saint Francis *Indiana* M & W
University of St. Francis *Illinois* M & W
University of St. Thomas *Minnesota* M & W
University of San Diego *California* M
University of San Francisco *California* M & W
University of the Sciences in Philadelphia *Pennsylvania* M & W
The University of Scranton *Pennsylvania* M
University of Sioux Falls *South Dakota* M & W
University of South Alabama *Alabama* M & W
University of South Carolina *South Carolina* M & W
University of South Carolina Aiken *South Carolina* M
University of South Carolina Beaufort *South Carolina* M & W
University of South Carolina Lancaster *South Carolina* M
University of South Carolina Upstate *South Carolina* M & W
The University of South Dakota *South Dakota* M & W
University of South Florida *Florida* M & W
University of Southern California *California* M & W
University of Southern Indiana *Indiana* M & W
University of Southern Maine *Maine* M & W
University of Southern Mississippi *Mississippi* M & W
University of the Southwest *New Mexico* M & W
The University of Tampa *Florida* M
The University of Tennessee *Tennessee* M & W
The University of Tennessee at Chattanooga *Tennessee* M & W
The University of Tennessee at Martin *Tennessee* M
The University of Texas at Arlington *Texas* M
The University of Texas at Austin *Texas* M & W
The University of Texas at Brownsville *Texas* M & W
The University of Texas at Dallas *Texas* M & W
The University of Texas at El Paso *Texas* M
The University of Texas at San Antonio *Texas* M
The University of Texas at Tyler *Texas* M & W
The University of Texas–Pan American *Texas* M & W
The University of Toledo *Ohio* M & W
University of Toronto *Ontario* M
University of Tulsa *Oklahoma* M & W
University of Utah *Utah* M
University of Victoria *British Columbia* M & W
University of Virginia *Virginia* M & W
The University of Virginia's College at Wise *Virginia* M & W
University of Washington *Washington* M & W
University of Waterloo *Ontario* M & W
University of West Florida *Florida* M
University of West Georgia *Georgia* M & W
The University of Western Ontario *Ontario* M & W
University of Windsor *Ontario* M & W
University of Wisconsin–Baraboo/Sauk County *Wisconsin* M & W
University of Wisconsin–Eau Claire *Wisconsin* M & W
University of Wisconsin–Fond du Lac *Wisconsin* M & W
University of Wisconsin–Fox Valley *Wisconsin* M & W
University of Wisconsin–Green Bay *Wisconsin* M & W
University of Wisconsin–Madison *Wisconsin* M & W
University of Wisconsin–Manitowoc *Wisconsin* M & W
University of Wisconsin–Marshfield/Wood County *Wisconsin* M & W
University of Wisconsin–Oshkosh *Wisconsin* W
University of Wisconsin–Parkside *Wisconsin* M
University of Wisconsin–Platteville *Wisconsin* W
University of Wisconsin–River Falls *Wisconsin* M & W
University of Wisconsin–Stevens Point *Wisconsin* W
University of Wisconsin–Superior *Wisconsin* W
University of Wisconsin–Washington County *Wisconsin* M & W
University of Wisconsin–Waukesha *Wisconsin* M & W
University of Wisconsin–Whitewater *Wisconsin* W
University of Wyoming *Wyoming* M & W
Upper Iowa University *Iowa* M & W
Urbana University *Ohio* M & W
Ursinus College *Pennsylvania* M & W
Ursuline College *Ohio* W
Utah State University *Utah* M
Utah Valley University *Utah* M & W
Utica College *New York* M & W
Valdosta State University *Georgia* M
Valley Forge Military College *Pennsylvania* M
Valparaiso University *Indiana* M & W
Vanderbilt University *Tennessee* M & W
Vassar College *New York* W
Ventura College *California* M
Vermont Technical College *Vermont* M & W
Victor Valley College *California* M
Villanova University *Pennsylvania* M
Vincennes University *Indiana* M
Virginia Commonwealth University *Virginia* M
Virginia Intermont College *Virginia* M
Virginia Military Institute *Virginia* M
Virginia Polytechnic Institute and State University *Virginia* M
Virginia State University *Virginia* M & W
Virginia Union University *Virginia* M
Virginia Wesleyan College *Virginia* M
Viterbo University *Wisconsin* M & W
Wabash College *Indiana* M
Wagner College *New York* M & W
Wake Forest University *North Carolina* M & W
Waldorf College *Iowa* M & W
Walla Walla Community College *Washington* M & W
Walla Walla University *Washington* M
Wallace State Community College *Alabama* M
Walsh University *Ohio* M & W
Walters State Community College *Tennessee* M
Warner Pacific College *Oregon* M & W
Warner University *Florida* M & W
Wartburg College *Iowa* M & W
Washburn University *Kansas* M
Washington & Jefferson College *Pennsylvania* M & W
Washington and Lee University *Virginia* M
Washington State University *Washington* M & W
Washington University in St. Louis *Missouri* M & W
Waubonsee Community College *Illinois* M
Wayland Baptist University *Texas* M & W
Wayne County Community College District *Michigan* M
Wayne State College *Nebraska* M & W
Wayne State University *Michigan* M
Waynesburg University *Pennsylvania* M & W
Webber International University *Florida* M & W
Weber State University *Utah* M & W
Webster University *Missouri* M
Wellesley College *Massachusetts* W
Wells College *New York* M & W
Wentworth Institute of Technology *Massachusetts* M
Wesley College *Delaware* M & W
Wesleyan University *Connecticut* M
West Chester University of Pennsylvania *Pennsylvania* M & W
West Liberty University *West Virginia* M & W
West Los Angeles College *California* M
West Texas A&M University *Texas* M & W
West Valley College *California* M
West Virginia State University *West Virginia* W
West Virginia University Institute of Technology *West Virginia* M
West Virginia Wesleyan College *West Virginia* M & W
Westchester Community College *New York* M
Western Carolina University *North Carolina* M & W
Western Illinois University *Illinois* M & W
Western Kentucky University *Kentucky* M & W
Western Michigan University *Michigan* W
Western New England College *Massachusetts* M
Western New Mexico University *New Mexico* M & W
Western Oklahoma State College *Oklahoma* M & W
Western Washington University *Washington* M & W
Westfield State College *Massachusetts* M & W
Westminster College *Utah* M & W
Westminster College *Pennsylvania* M & W
Westminster College *Missouri* M & W
Westmoreland County Community College *Pennsylvania* M & W
Wheaton College *Illinois* M & W
Wheeling Jesuit University *West Virginia* M & W
Whitman College *Washington* M & W
Whittier College *California* M
Whitworth University *Washington* M & W
Wichita State University *Kansas* M & W
Widener University *Pennsylvania* M
Wilfrid Laurier University *Ontario* M
Wilkes University *Pennsylvania* M

M = Men; W = Women

Willamette University *Oregon* M & W
William Carey University *Mississippi* M
William Jewell College *Missouri* M & W
William Paterson University of New Jersey *New Jersey* M
William Penn University *Iowa* M & W
William Woods University *Missouri* M & W
Williams Baptist College *Arkansas* M
Williams College *Massachusetts* M & W
Wilmington College *Ohio* M & W
Wingate University *North Carolina* M & W
Winona State University *Minnesota* M & W
Winston-Salem State University *North Carolina* M
Winthrop University *South Carolina* M & W
Wisconsin Lutheran College *Wisconsin* M & W
Wittenberg University *Ohio* M & W
Wofford College *South Carolina* M & W
Worcester State College *Massachusetts* M
Wright State University *Ohio* M
Xavier University *Ohio* M & W
Yale University *Connecticut* M & W
Yeshiva University *New York* M
York College of Pennsylvania *Pennsylvania* M
York County Community College *Maine* M
Young Harris College *Georgia* M & W
Youngstown State University *Ohio* M & W
Zane State College *Ohio* M & W

Gymnastics

Arizona State University *Arizona* W
Auburn University *Alabama* W
Ball State University *Indiana* W
Baylor University *Texas* M & W
Boise State University *Idaho* W
Boston University *Massachusetts* M & W
Bowling Green State University *Ohio* W
Brigham Young University *Utah* W
Brown University *Rhode Island* W
California State University, Fullerton *California* W
California State University, Sacramento *California* W
Carleton College *Minnesota* W
Centenary College of Louisiana *Louisiana* W
Central Michigan University *Michigan* W
City College of San Francisco *California* W
The College at Brockport, State University of New York *New York* W
The College of William and Mary *Virginia* M & W
Columbia University, School of General Studies *New York* W
Cornell University *New York* W
Dartmouth College *New Hampshire* M & W
Eastern Michigan University *Michigan* W
El Camino College *California* W
Emory University *Georgia* M & W
The George Washington University *District of Columbia* W
Gustavus Adolphus College *Minnesota* W
Hamline University *Minnesota* W
Hunter College of the City University of New York *New York* W
Illinois State University *Illinois* W
Iowa State University of Science and Technology *Iowa* W
Ithaca College *New York* W
Kent State University *Ohio* W
Los Angeles City College *California* M
Louisiana State University and Agricultural and Mechanical College *Louisiana* W
Massachusetts Institute of Technology *Massachusetts* M & W
Miami University *Ohio* M & W
Michigan State University *Michigan* W
Modesto Junior College *California* W
NHTI, Concord's Community College *New Hampshire* M & W
North Carolina State University *North Carolina* W
Northern Illinois University *Illinois* W
The Ohio State University *Ohio* M & W
Oregon State University *Oregon* W
Penn State University Park *Pennsylvania* M & W
Queen's University at Kingston *Ontario* M & W
Redlands Community College *Oklahoma* W
Rhode Island College *Rhode Island* W
Rutgers, The State University of New Jersey, New Brunswick *New Jersey* W
Saginaw Valley State University *Michigan* M & W
Saint Mary's College *Indiana* W
Salem International University *West Virginia* W
San Jose State University *California* W
Seattle Pacific University *Washington* W
Simon Fraser University *British Columbia* M
Slippery Rock University of Pennsylvania *Pennsylvania* W
Southeast Missouri State University *Missouri* W
Southern Connecticut State University *Connecticut* W
Southern Utah University *Utah* W
Springfield College *Massachusetts* M & W
Stanford University *California* M & W
State University of New York College at Cortland *New York* W
Syracuse University *New York* M & W
Temple University *Pennsylvania* M & W
Texas State University–San Marcos *Texas* M & W
Texas Woman's University *Texas* W
Towson University *Maryland* W
Tulane University *Louisiana* M & W
United States Air Force Academy *Colorado* M & W
United States Military Academy *New York* M
United States Naval Academy *Maryland* M & W
Université Laval *Quebec* M & W
Université de Moncton *New Brunswick* W
The University of Alabama *Alabama* W
University of Alaska Anchorage *Alaska* W
University of Alberta *Alberta* M & W
The University of Arizona *Arizona* W
University of Arkansas *Arkansas* W
University of Bridgeport *Connecticut* W
University of California, Berkeley *California* M & W
University of California, Davis *California* W
University of California, Los Angeles *California* W
University of California, Santa Barbara *California* M & W
University of Denver *Colorado* W
University of Florida *Florida* W
University of Georgia *Georgia* W
University of Idaho *Idaho* M & W
University of Illinois at Chicago *Illinois* M & W
University of Illinois at Urbana–Champaign *Illinois* M & W
The University of Iowa *Iowa* M & W
University of Kentucky *Kentucky* W
University of Manitoba *Manitoba* M & W
University of Maryland, College Park *Maryland* W
University of Michigan *Michigan* M & W
University of Minnesota, Twin Cities Campus *Minnesota* M & W
University of Missouri *Missouri* W
The University of Montana *Montana* W
University of Nebraska–Lincoln *Nebraska* M & W
University of New Hampshire *New Hampshire* W
The University of North Carolina at Chapel Hill *North Carolina* W
University of Oklahoma *Oklahoma* M & W
University of Oregon *Oregon* W
University of Pennsylvania *Pennsylvania* W
University of Pittsburgh *Pennsylvania* W
University of Richmond *Virginia* M & W
The University of Tennessee *Tennessee* M & W
The University of Texas at Austin *Texas* M & W
University of Toronto *Ontario* M & W
University of Utah *Utah* W
University of Vermont *Vermont* M & W
University of Washington *Washington* W
University of Wisconsin–Eau Claire *Wisconsin* W
University of Wisconsin–La Crosse *Wisconsin* W
University of Wisconsin–Oshkosh *Wisconsin* W
University of Wisconsin–Stout *Wisconsin* W
University of Wisconsin–Whitewater *Wisconsin* W
Ursinus College *Pennsylvania* W
Utah State University *Utah* W
Washington State University *Washington* M & W
Washington University in St. Louis *Missouri* M & W
West Chester University of Pennsylvania *Pennsylvania* W
West Virginia University *West Virginia* W
Western Michigan University *Michigan* W
Wilson College *Pennsylvania* W
Winona State University *Minnesota* W
Xavier University *Ohio* M & W
Yale University *Connecticut* W

Ice Hockey

Acadia University *Nova Scotia* M & W
Adrian College *Michigan* M & W
Alberta College of Art & Design *Alberta* M & W
Allegheny College *Pennsylvania* M
American International College *Massachusetts* M
Amherst College *Massachusetts* M & W
Assumption College *Massachusetts* M
Augsburg College *Minnesota* M & W
Babson College *Massachusetts* M & W
Barnard College *New York* W
Bates College *Maine* M & W
Baylor University *Texas* M
Becker College *Massachusetts* M
Beloit College *Wisconsin* M & W
Bemidji State University *Minnesota* M & W
Bentley University *Massachusetts* M
Bethany Bible College *New Brunswick* M
Bethel University *Minnesota* M & W
Bishop's University *Quebec* W
Bloomsburg University of Pennsylvania *Pennsylvania* M
Boston College *Massachusetts* M & W
Boston University *Massachusetts* M & W
Bowdoin College *Maine* M & W
Bowling Green State University *Ohio* M
Briercrest College *Saskatchewan* M
Brock University *Ontario* M & W
Broome Community College *New York* M
Brown University *Rhode Island* M & W
Bryant University *Rhode Island* M
Bryn Athyn College of the New Church *Pennsylvania* M
Bucknell University *Pennsylvania* M
Buffalo State College, State University of New York *New York* M & W
Butler University *Indiana* M
California Institute of Technology *California* M
California State University, Sacramento *California* M
Calvin College *Michigan* M
Canadian Mennonite University *Manitoba* M
Canisius College *New York* M
Cape Breton University *Nova Scotia* W
Carleton College *Minnesota* M & W
Carleton University *Ontario* M & W
Carnegie Mellon University *Pennsylvania* M & W
Carthage College *Wisconsin* M & W
Case Western Reserve University *Ohio* M & W
Castleton State College *Vermont* M & W
Central Washington University *Washington* M & W
Chatham University *Pennsylvania* W
The Citadel, The Military College of South Carolina *South Carolina* M & W
Clarkson University *New York* M & W
Clemson University *South Carolina* M & W
Colby College *Maine* M & W
Colby-Sawyer College *New Hampshire* M & W
Colgate University *New York* M & W
The College at Brockport, State University of New York *New York* M
College of the Canyons *California* M
College of the Holy Cross *Massachusetts* M & W
College of Saint Benedict *Minnesota* W
The College of St. Scholastica *Minnesota* M & W
The Colorado College *Colorado* M & W
Colorado School of Mines *Colorado* M & W
Colorado State University *Colorado* M & W
Colorado State University–Pueblo *Colorado* M
Columbia Bible College *British Columbia* M
Columbia University *New York* W
Columbia University, School of General Studies *New York* M & W
Community College of Allegheny County *Pennsylvania* M
Concordia College *Minnesota* M & W
Concordia University *Quebec* M & W
Concordia University College of Alberta *Alberta* M
Connecticut College *Connecticut* M & W

M = Men; W = Women

Cornell University *New York* M & W
County College of Morris *New Jersey* M
Curry College *Massachusetts* M
Dakota College at Bottineau *North Dakota* M
Dalhousie University *Nova Scotia* M & W
Daniel Webster College *New Hampshire* M & W
Dartmouth College *New Hampshire* M & W
Davenport University *Michigan* M
Denison University *Ohio* M
Dickinson College *Pennsylvania* M
Dordt College *Iowa* M
Duke University *North Carolina* M & W
Duquesne University *Pennsylvania* M
Edinboro University of Pennsylvania *Pennsylvania* M
Elmira College *New York* M & W
Emerson College *Massachusetts* M
Emory University *Georgia* M
Endicott College *Massachusetts* M & W
Erie Community College *New York* M
Erie Community College, North Campus *New York* M
Erie Community College, South Campus *New York* M
Fairfield University *Connecticut* M & W
Farmingdale State College *New York* M
Ferris State University *Michigan* M
Finlandia University *Michigan* M & W
Fitchburg State College *Massachusetts* M
Fordham University *New York* M
Fort Lewis College *Colorado* M & W
Framingham State College *Massachusetts* M
Franklin & Marshall College *Pennsylvania* M
Franklin Pierce University *New Hampshire* M
Furman University *South Carolina* M
Georgetown University *District of Columbia* M
Georgia Institute of Technology *Georgia* M
Gettysburg College *Pennsylvania* M
Grand Valley State University *Michigan* M
Gustavus Adolphus College *Minnesota* M & W
Hamilton College *New York* M & W
Hamline University *Minnesota* M & W
Hartwick College *New York* M
Harvard University *Massachusetts* M & W
Hillsdale College *Michigan* M
Hobart and William Smith Colleges *New York* M & W
Hope College *Michigan* M
Jackson Community College *Michigan* M
John Carroll University *Ohio* M
Johnson & Wales University *Rhode Island* M
Kennebec Valley Community College *Maine* M & W
Kettering University *Michigan* M
Kutztown University of Pennsylvania *Pennsylvania* M
Lafayette College *Pennsylvania* M
Lake Forest College *Illinois* M & W
Lake Superior State University *Michigan* M
Lakehead University *Ontario* M
Lawrence University *Wisconsin* M & W
Lebanon Valley College *Pennsylvania* M
Lehigh University *Pennsylvania* M
Liberty University *Virginia* M
Lindenwood University *Missouri* M & W
Loras College *Iowa* M
Loyola University New Orleans *Louisiana* M & W
Macalester College *Minnesota* M & W
Manhattanville College *New York* M & W
Marian University *Wisconsin* M & W
Marist College *New York* M
Massachusetts Institute of Technology *Massachusetts* M & W
McGill University *Quebec* M & W
McKendree University *Illinois* M
Mercyhurst College *Pennsylvania* M & W
Merrimack College *Massachusetts* M
Mesa State College *Colorado* M
Methodist University *North Carolina* M
Metropolitan State College of Denver *Colorado* M
Miami University *Ohio* M & W
Michigan State University *Michigan* M & W
Michigan Technological University *Michigan* M & W
Middlebury College *Vermont* M & W
Milwaukee School of Engineering *Wisconsin* M
Minnesota State University Mankato *Minnesota* M & W
Minot State University *North Dakota* M
Missouri State University *Missouri* M
Mohawk Valley Community College *New York* M
Monmouth University *New Jersey* M
Monroe Community College *New York* M
Moravian College *Pennsylvania* M & W
Mount Allison University *New Brunswick* W
Mount St. Mary's University *Maryland* M
Neumann University *Pennsylvania* M & W
New England College *New Hampshire* M & W
New Jersey Institute of Technology *New Jersey* M
New York University *New York* M
Niagara University *New York* M & W
Nichols College *Massachusetts* M & W
Nipissing University *Ontario* M
North Carolina State University *North Carolina* M & W
North Country Community College *New York* M
North Dakota State University *North Dakota* M
Northeastern University *Massachusetts* M & W
Northern Michigan University *Michigan* M & W
Northland College *Wisconsin* M
Northwestern College *Minnesota* M
Norwich University *Vermont* M & W
Oakland University *Michigan* M
Oberlin College *Ohio* M & W
The Ohio State University *Ohio* M & W
Ohio University *Ohio* M
Ohio Wesleyan University *Ohio* M & W
Old Dominion University *Virginia* M & W
Otterbein University *Ohio* W
Penn State Erie, The Behrend College *Pennsylvania* M
Penn State Lehigh Valley *Pennsylvania* M & W
Penn State University Park *Pennsylvania* M & W
Plymouth State University *New Hampshire* M & W
Princeton University *New Jersey* M & W
Providence College *Rhode Island* M & W
Providence College and Theological Seminary *Manitoba* M
Queen's University at Kingston *Ontario* M & W
Quinnipiac University *Connecticut* M & W
Rensselaer Polytechnic Institute *New York* M & W
Roanoke College *Virginia* M
Robert Morris University *Pennsylvania* M & W
Robert Morris University Illinois *Illinois* M & W
Rochester Institute of Technology *New York* M & W
Rocky Mountain College *Alberta* M
Royal Military College of Canada *Ontario* M
Ryerson University *Ontario* M & W
Sacred Heart University *Connecticut* M & W
Saginaw Valley State University *Michigan* M
Saint Anselm College *New Hampshire* M & W
St. Catherine University *Minnesota* W
St. Cloud State University *Minnesota* M & W
St. Francis Xavier University *Nova Scotia* M & W
Saint John's University *Minnesota* M
Saint Joseph's College of Maine *Maine* M & W
St. Lawrence University *New York* M & W
Saint Louis University *Missouri* M
Saint Mary's University *Nova Scotia* M & W
Saint Mary's University of Minnesota *Minnesota* M & W
Saint Michael's College *Vermont* M & W
St. Norbert College *Wisconsin* M & W
St. Olaf College *Minnesota* M & W
St. Thomas University *New Brunswick* M & W
Saint Vincent College *Pennsylvania* M
Salem International University *West Virginia* M
Salem State College *Massachusetts* M
Salve Regina University *Rhode Island* M & W
San Jose State University *California* M & W
Santa Rosa Junior College *California* M
Seton Hall University *New Jersey* M
Siena College *New York* M
Skidmore College *New York* M
Slippery Rock University of Pennsylvania *Pennsylvania* M & W
South Dakota State University *South Dakota* M & W
Southern Alberta Institute of Technology *Alberta* M & W
Southern Methodist University *Texas* M
Southern New Hampshire University *New Hampshire* M
Stanford University *California* M
State University of New York College of Agriculture and Technology at Morrisville *New York* M
State University of New York College at Cortland *New York* M & W
State University of New York College at Geneseo *New York* M & W
State University of New York College at Oneonta *New York* M
State University of New York College at Potsdam *New York* M & W
State University of New York College of Technology at Canton *New York* M
State University of New York at Fredonia *New York* M
State University of New York Maritime College *New York* M
State University of New York at New Paltz *New York* M
State University of New York at Oswego *New York* M
State University of New York at Plattsburgh *New York* M & W
Stonehill College *Massachusetts* M
Suffolk University *Massachusetts* M
Swarthmore College *Pennsylvania* M & W
Syracuse University *New York* M & W
Thompson Rivers University *British Columbia* M
Trinity College *Connecticut* M & W
Tufts University *Massachusetts* M
Tulane University *Louisiana* M & W
Tyndale University College & Seminary *Ontario* M
Union College *New York* M & W
United States Air Force Academy *Colorado* M
United States Coast Guard Academy *Connecticut* M
United States Merchant Marine Academy *New York* M
United States Military Academy *New York* M
United States Naval Academy *Maryland* M
Université de Moncton *New Brunswick* M & W
Université du Québec àTrois-Rivières *Quebec* M & W
The University of Alabama in Huntsville *Alabama* M
University of Alaska Anchorage *Alaska* M
University of Alaska Fairbanks *Alaska* M
University of Alberta *Alberta* M & W
The University of Arizona *Arizona* M
The University of British Columbia *British Columbia* M & W
University of Calgary *Alberta* M & W
University of Colorado at Boulder *Colorado* M & W
University of Connecticut *Connecticut* M & W
University of Delaware *Delaware* M
University of Denver *Colorado* M & W
University of Guelph *Ontario* M & W
University of Idaho *Idaho* M
The University of Iowa *Iowa* M
The University of Kansas *Kansas* M
University of Lethbridge *Alberta* M & W
University of Maine *Maine* M & W
University of Maine at Farmington *Maine* M
University of Manitoba *Manitoba* M & W
University of Maryland, Baltimore County *Maryland* M
University of Massachusetts Amherst *Massachusetts* M
University of Massachusetts Boston *Massachusetts* M
University of Massachusetts Dartmouth *Massachusetts* M
University of Massachusetts Lowell *Massachusetts* M
University of Michigan *Michigan* M
University of Michigan–Dearborn *Michigan* M
University of Minnesota, Duluth *Minnesota* M & W
University of Minnesota, Twin Cities Campus *Minnesota* M & W
University of Mississippi *Mississippi* M
University of Missouri–St. Louis *Missouri* M
The University of Montana *Montana* M & W

M = Men; W = Women

University of Nebraska at Omaha *Nebraska* M
University of New Brunswick Fredericton *New Brunswick* W
University of New Brunswick Saint John *New Brunswick* M & W
University of New Hampshire *New Hampshire* M & W
University of North Dakota *North Dakota* M & W
University of North Texas *Texas* M
University of Northern Colorado *Colorado* M
University of Notre Dame *Indiana* M
University of Ottawa *Ontario* M & W
University of Prince Edward Island *Prince Edward Island* M & W
University of Puget Sound *Washington* M & W
University of Regina *Saskatchewan* M & W
University of Rhode Island *Rhode Island* M & W
University of Richmond *Virginia* M
University of Rochester *New York* M & W
University of St. Thomas *Minnesota* M & W
University of Saskatchewan *Saskatchewan* M & W
The University of Scranton *Pennsylvania* M
University of Southern California *California* M & W
University of Southern Indiana *Indiana* M
University of Southern Maine *Maine* M & W
The University of Tennessee *Tennessee* M
The University of Texas at Austin *Texas* M
University of Toronto *Ontario* M & W
University of Vermont *Vermont* M & W
University of Waterloo *Ontario* M & W
The University of Western Ontario *Ontario* M & W
University of Windsor *Ontario* M & W
University of Wisconsin–Eau Claire *Wisconsin* M & W
University of Wisconsin–Madison *Wisconsin* M & W
University of Wisconsin–Platteville *Wisconsin* M & W
University of Wisconsin–River Falls *Wisconsin* M & W
University of Wisconsin–Stevens Point *Wisconsin* M & W
University of Wisconsin–Stout *Wisconsin* M & W
University of Wisconsin–Superior *Wisconsin* M & W
University of Wisconsin–Whitewater *Wisconsin* M & W
University of Wyoming *Wyoming* M & W
Utah State University *Utah* M
Utica College *New York* M & W
Vanguard College *Alberta* M
Villanova University *Pennsylvania* M & W
Wagner College *New York* M
Walla Walla University *Washington* M
Washington College *Maryland* M
Washington and Lee University *Virginia* M & W
Washington State University *Washington* M
Washington University in St. Louis *Missouri* M
Wayne State University *Michigan* W
Weber State University *Utah* M
Wentworth Institute of Technology *Massachusetts* M
Wesleyan University *Connecticut* M & W
West Chester University of Pennsylvania *Pennsylvania* M & W
Western Michigan University *Michigan* M
Western New England College *Massachusetts* M
Western State College of Colorado *Colorado* M
Westfield State College *Massachusetts* M
Wheaton College *Illinois* M
White Mountains Community College *New Hampshire* M & W
Whitman College *Washington* M
Wilfrid Laurier University *Ontario* M & W
William Paterson University of New Jersey *New Jersey* M
Williams College *Massachusetts* M & W
Worcester State College *Massachusetts* M
Xavier University *Ohio* M & W
Yale University *Connecticut* M & W
York University *Ontario* M & W

Lacrosse

Adelphi University *New York* M & W
Adrian College *Michigan* M & W
Agnes Scott College *Georgia* W
Albright College *Pennsylvania* M & W
Alfred University *New York* M & W
Allegheny College *Pennsylvania* W
Alvernia University *Pennsylvania* M & W
American International College *Massachusetts* M & W
American University *District of Columbia* W
Amherst College *Massachusetts* M & W
Anna Maria College *Massachusetts* M & W
Anne Arundel Community College *Maryland* M & W
Aquinas College *Michigan* M & W
Arcadia University *Pennsylvania* W
Assumption College *Massachusetts* M & W
Augustana College *Illinois* M & W
Aurora University *Illinois* M
Babson College *Massachusetts* M & W
Ball State University *Indiana* M & W
Barnard College *New York* W
Bates College *Maine* M & W
Baylor University *Texas* M & W
Becker College *Massachusetts* M & W
Bellarmine University *Kentucky* M
Belmont Abbey College *North Carolina* M & W
Beloit College *Wisconsin* M & W
Bentley University *Massachusetts* M & W
Berry College *Georgia* M & W
Birmingham-Southern College *Alabama* M & W
Bishop's University *Quebec* M & W
Bloomsburg University of Pennsylvania *Pennsylvania* W
Boston College *Massachusetts* W
Boston University *Massachusetts* M & W
Bowdoin College *Maine* M & W
Brandeis University *Massachusetts* M & W
Briarcliffe College *New York* M
Bridgewater College *Virginia* M & W
Bridgewater State College *Massachusetts* M & W
Brigham Young University *Utah* M
Brock University *Ontario* M
Broome Community College *New York* M
Brown University *Rhode Island* M & W
Bryant University *Rhode Island* M & W
Bryn Athyn College of the New Church *Pennsylvania* M
Bryn Mawr College *Pennsylvania* W
Bucknell University *Pennsylvania* M & W
Buffalo State College, State University of New York *New York* M & W
Cabrini College *Pennsylvania* M & W
California State University, Fresno *California* W
California State University, Sacramento *California* M & W
Calvin College *Michigan* M & W
Canisius College *New York* M & W
Carleton College *Minnesota* M & W
Carleton University *Ontario* M
Carnegie Mellon University *Pennsylvania* M & W
Carthage College *Wisconsin* M & W
Castleton State College *Vermont* M & W
Catawba College *North Carolina* M
The Catholic University of America *District of Columbia* M & W
Cayuga County Community College *New York* M & W
Cazenovia College *New York* M & W
Cedar Crest College *Pennsylvania* W
Centenary College *New Jersey* M & W
Central Connecticut State University *Connecticut* M & W
Chapman University *California* M & W
Chestnut Hill College *Pennsylvania* M & W
Christopher Newport University *Virginia* M & W
The Citadel, The Military College of South Carolina *South Carolina* M & W
City College of the City University of New York *New York* M
Claremont McKenna College *California* M & W
Clark University *Massachusetts* M
Clarkson University *New York* M & W
Clemson University *South Carolina* M & W
Colby College *Maine* M & W
Colby-Sawyer College *New Hampshire* W
Colgate University *New York* M & W
The College at Brockport, State University of New York *New York* M & W
College of the Holy Cross *Massachusetts* M & W
College of Mount St. Joseph *Ohio* M & W
College of Mount Saint Vincent *New York* M & W
The College of New Jersey *New Jersey* W
College of Notre Dame of Maryland *Maryland* W
College of Saint Benedict *Minnesota* W
The College of William and Mary *Virginia* W
The College of Wooster *Ohio* M & W
The Colorado College *Colorado* M & W
Colorado School of Mines *Colorado* M
Colorado State University *Colorado* M & W
Columbia College Chicago *Illinois* M
Columbia University *New York* M & W
Columbia University, School of General Studies *New York* M
The Community College of Baltimore County *Maryland* M & W
Concordia University *California* M
Connecticut College *Connecticut* M & W
Converse College *South Carolina* W
Cornell College *Iowa* M & W
Cornell University *New York* M & W
Curry College *Massachusetts* M & W
Daniel Webster College *New Hampshire* M & W
Dartmouth College *New Hampshire* M & W
Davenport University *Michigan* M & W
Davidson College *North Carolina* W
Dean College *Massachusetts* M & W
Delaware Technical & Community College, Terry Campus *Delaware* M
Denison University *Ohio* M & W
DeSales University *Pennsylvania* M & W
Dickinson College *Pennsylvania* M & W
Dominican College *New York* M & W
Dominican University of California *California* M
Dordt College *Iowa* M
Dowling College *New York* M & W
Drew University *New Jersey* M & W
Drexel University *Pennsylvania* M & W
Duke University *North Carolina* M & W
Duquesne University *Pennsylvania* W
Earlham College *Indiana* M & W
East Stroudsburg University of Pennsylvania *Pennsylvania* W
Eastern Connecticut State University *Connecticut* M & W
Eastern Nazarene College *Massachusetts* M
Eastern University *Pennsylvania* M & W
Edinboro University of Pennsylvania *Pennsylvania* W
Elizabethtown College *Pennsylvania* M & W
Elmira College *New York* M & W
Elms College *Massachusetts* W
Elon University *North Carolina* M & W
Emerson College *Massachusetts* M & W
Emmanuel College *Massachusetts* W
Emory University *Georgia* M & W
Endicott College *Massachusetts* M & W
Erie Community College *New York* W
Erie Community College, North Campus *New York* W
Erie Community College, South Campus *New York* W
Erskine College *South Carolina* W
Fairfield University *Connecticut* M & W
Fairleigh Dickinson University, College at Florham *New Jersey* M & W
Farmingdale State College *New York* M & W
Ferrum College *Virginia* W
Finger Lakes Community College *New York* M
Fitchburg State College *Massachusetts* W
Flagler College *Florida* M
Florida Southern College *Florida* M
Fontbonne University *Missouri* M & W
Fordham University *New York* M & W
Fort Lewis College *Colorado* M & W
Framingham State College *Massachusetts* W
Franklin & Marshall College *Pennsylvania* M & W
Franklin Pierce University *New Hampshire* M & W
Frostburg State University *Maryland* M & W
Furman University *South Carolina* M & W
Gannon University *Pennsylvania* W

M = Men; W = Women

Genesee Community College *New York* M
George Mason University *Virginia* W
Georgetown University *District of Columbia* M & W
Georgia Institute of Technology *Georgia* M & W
Georgia Southern University *Georgia* M
Georgian Court University *New Jersey* W
Gettysburg College *Pennsylvania* M & W
Gordon College *Massachusetts* M & W
Goucher College *Maryland* M & W
Grand Canyon University *Arizona* M
Green Mountain College *Vermont* M & W
Greensboro College *North Carolina* M & W
Guilford College *North Carolina* M & W
Gustavus Adolphus College *Minnesota* M
Gwynedd-Mercy College *Pennsylvania* M & W
Hamilton College *New York* M & W
Hamline University *Minnesota* W
Hampden-Sydney College *Virginia* M
Hanover College *Indiana* M
Harding University *Arkansas* M
Harford Community College *Maryland* M & W
Hartwick College *New York* M & W
Harvard University *Massachusetts* M & W
Harvey Mudd College *California* W
Haverford College *Pennsylvania* M & W
Hendrix College *Arkansas* M
Herkimer County Community College *New York* M & W
Hillsdale College *Michigan* M
Hobart and William Smith Colleges *New York* M & W
Hofstra University *New York* M & W
Hollins University *Virginia* W
Holy Cross College *Indiana* M
Holy Family University *Pennsylvania* W
Hood College *Maryland* M & W
Hope College *Michigan* M & W
Howard Community College *Maryland* M & W
Howard University *District of Columbia* W
Hudson Valley Community College *New York* M
Humboldt State University *California* M
Husson University *Maine* M & W
Illinois Wesleyan University *Illinois* M
Immaculata University *Pennsylvania* W
Indiana University of Pennsylvania *Pennsylvania* W
Iona College *New York* W
Ithaca College *New York* M & W
James Madison University *Virginia* W
Jefferson Community College *New York* M & W
John Carroll University *Ohio* M & W
The Johns Hopkins University *Maryland* M & W
Johnson State College *Vermont* W
Juniata College *Pennsylvania* M
Kean University *New Jersey* M & W
Keene State College *New Hampshire* M & W
Kenyon College *Ohio* M & W
Keuka College *New York* M & W
King's College *Pennsylvania* M & W
Kutztown University of Pennsylvania *Pennsylvania* M & W
La Roche College *Pennsylvania* M
La Salle University *Pennsylvania* W
Lafayette College *Pennsylvania* M & W
LaGrange College *Georgia* W
Lake Erie College *Ohio* M & W
Lake Forest College *Illinois* M
Lancaster Bible College & Graduate School *Pennsylvania* W
Lasell College *Massachusetts* M & W
Le Moyne College *New York* M & W
Lebanon Valley College *Pennsylvania* M & W
Lees-McRae College *North Carolina* M & W
Lehigh University *Pennsylvania* M & W
Lewis & Clark College *Oregon* M & W
Liberty University *Virginia* M
Limestone College *South Carolina* M & W
Lindenwood University *Missouri* M & W
Linfield College *Oregon* W
Lock Haven University of Pennsylvania *Pennsylvania* W
Long Island University, Brooklyn Campus *New York* W
Long Island University, C.W. Post Campus *New York* M & W

Longwood University *Virginia* W
Loyola University Maryland *Maryland* M & W
Loyola University New Orleans *Louisiana* M
Lycoming College *Pennsylvania* M & W
Lynchburg College *Virginia* M & W
Lyndon State College *Vermont* M
Maine Maritime Academy *Maine* M
Manhattan College *New York* M & W
Manhattanville College *New York* M & W
Marietta College *Ohio* M
Marist College *New York* M & W
Marquette University *Wisconsin* M
Mars Hill College *North Carolina* M
Marshall University *West Virginia* M
Marymount University *Virginia* M & W
Marywood University *Pennsylvania* M & W
Massachusetts Institute of Technology *Massachusetts* M & W
Massachusetts Maritime Academy *Massachusetts* M
McDaniel College *Maryland* M & W
McGill University *Quebec* M & W
McMaster University *Ontario* M & W
Medaille College *New York* M & W
Mercer University *Georgia* M & W
Mercy College *New York* M & W
Mercyhurst College *Pennsylvania* M & W
Merrimack College *Massachusetts* M & W
Messiah College *Pennsylvania* M & W
Methodist University *North Carolina* M & W
Miami University *Ohio* M & W
Michigan State University *Michigan* M & W
Middlebury College *Vermont* M & W
Millersville University of Pennsylvania *Pennsylvania* W
Millsaps College *Mississippi* M & W
Milwaukee School of Engineering *Wisconsin* M
Misericordia University *Pennsylvania* M & W
Missouri Baptist University *Missouri* M & W
Missouri State University *Missouri* M
Mitchell College *Connecticut* M
Mohawk Valley Community College *New York* M
Molloy College *New York* M & W
Monmouth University *New Jersey* W
Monroe Community College *New York* M
Montclair State University *New Jersey* M & W
Montgomery College *Maryland* M
Moravian College *Pennsylvania* M & W
Mount Holyoke College *Massachusetts* W
Mount Ida College *Massachusetts* M & W
Mount Saint Mary College *New York* M & W
Mount St. Mary's University *Maryland* M & W
Muhlenberg College *Pennsylvania* M & W
Nassau Community College *New York* M & W
Nazareth College of Rochester *New York* M & W
Neumann University *Pennsylvania* M & W
New England College *New Hampshire* M & W
New York Institute of Technology *New York* M
New York University *New York* M & W
Niagara County Community College *New York* M & W
Niagara University *New York* M & W
Nichols College *Massachusetts* M & W
North Carolina State University *North Carolina* M & W
North Central College *Illinois* W
North Dakota State University *North Dakota* M
Northern Michigan University *Michigan* M
Northwestern University *Illinois* W
Norwich University *Vermont* M
Notre Dame de Namur University *California* M
Oberlin College *Ohio* M & W
Occidental College *California* M & W
Oglethorpe University *Georgia* M
The Ohio State University *Ohio* M & W
Ohio Valley University *West Virginia* M
Ohio Wesleyan University *Ohio* M & W
Old Dominion University *Virginia* M & W
Onondaga Community College *New York* M & W
Otterbein University *Ohio* M
Pace University *New York* M
Pacific Lutheran University *Washington* M & W
Pacific University *Oregon* W
Palm Beach Atlantic University *Florida* M & W

Penn State Erie, The Behrend College *Pennsylvania* M
Penn State University Park *Pennsylvania* M & W
Pepperdine University *California* M
Pfeiffer University *North Carolina* M & W
Philadelphia University *Pennsylvania* W
Pine Manor College *Massachusetts* W
Pitzer College *California* W
Plymouth State University *New Hampshire* M & W
Pomona College *California* W
Presbyterian College *South Carolina* M & W
Princeton University *New Jersey* M & W
Providence College *Rhode Island* M
Queens College of the City University of New York *New York* W
Queens University of Charlotte *North Carolina* M & W
Queen's University at Kingston *Ontario* M & W
Quinnipiac University *Connecticut* M & W
Ramapo College of New Jersey *New Jersey* W
Randolph College *Virginia* M & W
Randolph-Macon College *Virginia* M & W
Regis College *Massachusetts* M & W
Regis University *Colorado* W
Reinhardt University *Georgia* M & W
Rensselaer Polytechnic Institute *New York* M & W
Rhode Island College *Rhode Island* W
Rhodes College *Tennessee* M & W
Rice University *Texas* M & W
The Richard Stockton College of New Jersey *New Jersey* M
Roanoke College *Virginia* M & W
Robert Morris University *Pennsylvania* M & W
Robert Morris University Illinois *Illinois* W
Rochester Institute of Technology *New York* M & W
Roger Williams University *Rhode Island* M & W
Rollins College *Florida* M & W
Rosemont College *Pennsylvania* M & W
Rowan University *New Jersey* W
Russell Sage College *New York* W
Rutgers, The State University of New Jersey, Camden *New Jersey* W
Rutgers, The State University of New Jersey, New Brunswick *New Jersey* M & W
Sacred Heart University *Connecticut* M & W
Sage College of Albany *New York* W
Saginaw Valley State University *Michigan* M & W
St. Andrews Presbyterian College *North Carolina* M & W
Saint Anselm College *New Hampshire* M & W
St. Bonaventure University *New York* M & W
Saint Francis University *Pennsylvania* W
St. Francis Xavier University *Nova Scotia* M
St. John Fisher College *New York* M & W
St. John's University *New York* M
Saint John's University *Minnesota* M
Saint Joseph College *Connecticut* W
Saint Joseph's University *Pennsylvania* M & W
St. Lawrence University *New York* M & W
Saint Leo University *Florida* M
Saint Louis University *Missouri* M & W
Saint Mary's College of California *California* M & W
St. Mary's College of Maryland *Maryland* M & W
Saint Michael's College *Vermont* M & W
St. Thomas Aquinas College *New York* W
Saint Vincent College *Pennsylvania* M & W
Salem State College *Massachusetts* M
Salisbury University *Maryland* M & W
Salve Regina University *Rhode Island* M & W
Sam Houston State University *Texas* M
Savannah College of Art and Design *Georgia* W
Scripps College *California* W
Seton Hill University *Pennsylvania* M & W
Sewanee: The University of the South *Tennessee* M & W
Shenandoah University *Virginia* M & W
Shepherd University *West Virginia* W
Shippensburg University of Pennsylvania *Pennsylvania* W
Siena College *New York* M & W
Siena Heights University *Michigan* M
Simmons College *Massachusetts* W
Skidmore College *New York* M & W

M = Men; W = Women

Slippery Rock University of Pennsylvania *Pennsylvania* M & W
Smith College *Massachusetts* W
Southern Connecticut State University *Connecticut* W
Southern Methodist University *Texas* M
Southern New Hampshire University *New Hampshire* M & W
Southern Virginia University *Virginia* M & W
Southwestern University *Texas* M
Springfield College *Massachusetts* M & W
Springfield Technical Community College *Massachusetts* W
Stanford University *California* M & W
State University of New York at Binghamton *New York* M & W
State University of New York College of Agriculture and Technology at Cobleskill *New York* M
State University of New York College of Agriculture and Technology at Morrisville *New York* M & W
State University of New York College at Cortland *New York* M & W
State University of New York College at Geneseo *New York* M & W
State University of New York College at Oneonta *New York* M & W
State University of New York College at Potsdam *New York* M & W
State University of New York College of Technology at Alfred *New York* M
State University of New York College of Technology at Delhi *New York* M
State University of New York at Fredonia *New York* W
State University of New York Institute of Technology *New York* M
State University of New York Maritime College *New York* M & W
State University of New York at New Paltz *New York* M & W
State University of New York at Oswego *New York* M & W
State University of New York at Plattsburgh *New York* M
Stevens Institute of Technology *New Jersey* M & W
Stevenson University *Maryland* M & W
Stonehill College *Massachusetts* M & W
Stony Brook University, State University of New York *New York* M & W
Suffolk County Community College *New York* M
Susquehanna University *Pennsylvania* M & W
Swarthmore College *Pennsylvania* M & W
Sweet Briar College *Virginia* W
Syracuse University *New York* M & W
Temple University *Pennsylvania* W
Tennessee Wesleyan College *Tennessee* M
Texas A&M University at Galveston *Texas* M
Texas State University–San Marcos *Texas* M & W
Thiel College *Pennsylvania* M & W
Thomas College *Maine* M & W
Tiffin University *Ohio* W
Tompkins Cortland Community College *New York* M
Towson University *Maryland* M & W
Trine University *Indiana* M & W
Trinity College *Connecticut* M & W
Trinity University *Texas* M & W
Trinity (Washington) University *District of Columbia* W
Truman State University *Missouri* W
Tufts University *Massachusetts* M & W
Tulane University *Louisiana* M & W
Union College *New York* M & W
United States Air Force Academy *Colorado* M & W
United States Coast Guard Academy *Connecticut* M & W
United States Merchant Marine Academy *New York* M
United States Military Academy *New York* M & W
United States Naval Academy *Maryland* M & W
University at Albany, State University of New York *New York* M & W
The University of Arizona *Arizona* M & W
University of Bridgeport *Connecticut* W
University of California, Berkeley *California* W
University of California, Davis *California* W
University of California, Santa Barbara *California* M & W
University of California, Santa Cruz *California* M & W
University of Cincinnati *Ohio* W
University of Colorado at Boulder *Colorado* M & W
University of Connecticut *Connecticut* W
University of Dallas *Texas* M & W
University of Delaware *Delaware* M & W
University of Denver *Colorado* M & W
University of Florida *Florida* W
University of Guelph *Ontario* M & W
University of Hartford *Connecticut* M
The University of Iowa *Iowa* M & W
University of Louisville *Kentucky* W
University of Maine at Farmington *Maine* M & W
University of Maine at Machias *Maine* M & W
University of Mary Washington *Virginia* M & W
University of Maryland, Baltimore County *Maryland* M & W
University of Maryland, College Park *Maryland* M & W
University of Massachusetts Amherst *Massachusetts* M & W
University of Massachusetts Boston *Massachusetts* M
University of Massachusetts Dartmouth *Massachusetts* M & W
University of Minnesota, Duluth *Minnesota* M & W
University of Mississippi *Mississippi* M & W
The University of Montana *Montana* M & W
University of New England *Maine* M & W
University of New Hampshire *New Hampshire* M & W
University of New Haven *Connecticut* W
The University of North Carolina at Chapel Hill *North Carolina* M & W
University of North Texas *Texas* M & W
University of Northern Colorado *Colorado* M
University of Notre Dame *Indiana* M & W
University of Oregon *Oregon* W
University of Pennsylvania *Pennsylvania* M & W
University of Puget Sound *Washington* M & W
University of Redlands *California* W
University of Rhode Island *Rhode Island* M & W
University of Richmond *Virginia* M & W
University of Rochester *New York* M & W
University of St. Thomas *Minnesota* M & W
University of San Diego *California* M & W
The University of Scranton *Pennsylvania* M & W
University of Southern California *California* M & W
University of Southern Indiana *Indiana* M
University of Southern Maine *Maine* M & W
The University of Tennessee *Tennessee* M & W
The University of Texas at Austin *Texas* M & W
University of Vermont *Vermont* M & W
University of Virginia *Virginia* M & W
The University of Western Ontario *Ontario* M & W
University of Wisconsin–Platteville *Wisconsin* M & W
University of Wisconsin–River Falls *Wisconsin* M & W
University of Wisconsin–Whitewater *Wisconsin* M
University of Wyoming *Wyoming* M & W
Ursinus College *Pennsylvania* M & W
Utica College *New York* M & W
Valley Forge Military College *Pennsylvania* M
Vanderbilt University *Tennessee* W
Vassar College *New York* M & W
Villanova University *Pennsylvania* M & W
Virginia Military Institute *Virginia* M
Virginia Polytechnic Institute and State University *Virginia* W
Virginia Wesleyan College *Virginia* M & W
Wabash College *Indiana* M
Wagner College *New York* M & W
Washington College *Maryland* M & W
Washington & Jefferson College *Pennsylvania* M & W
Washington and Lee University *Virginia* M & W
Washington State University *Washington* M & W
Washington University in St. Louis *Missouri* M & W
Waynesburg University *Pennsylvania* W
Weber State University *Utah* M & W
Wellesley College *Massachusetts* W
Wells College *New York* M & W
Wentworth Institute of Technology *Massachusetts* M
Wesley College *Delaware* M & W
Wesleyan University *Connecticut* M & W
West Chester University of Pennsylvania *Pennsylvania* M & W
West Virginia Wesleyan College *West Virginia* M & W
Western Connecticut State University *Connecticut* M & W
Western New England College *Massachusetts* M & W
Western State College of Colorado *Colorado* M & W
Westfield State College *Massachusetts* M & W
Westminster College *Utah* M & W
Westmont College *California* W
Wheaton College *Massachusetts* M & W
Wheaton College *Illinois* M & W
Wheeling Jesuit University *West Virginia* M
Wheelock College *Massachusetts* M & W
Whitman College *Washington* M & W
Whittier College *California* M & W
Widener University *Pennsylvania* M & W
Wilfrid Laurier University *Ontario* W
Wilkes University *Pennsylvania* W
Willamette University *Oregon* M
Williams College *Massachusetts* M & W
The Williamson Free School of Mechanical Trades *Pennsylvania* M
Wilson College *Pennsylvania* W
Wingate University *North Carolina* M
Winthrop University *South Carolina* M & W
Wittenberg University *Ohio* M & W
Worcester State College *Massachusetts* W
Xavier University *Ohio* M & W
Yale University *Connecticut* M & W
York College of Pennsylvania *Pennsylvania* M & W

Racquetball

Ball State University *Indiana* M & W
Bard College at Simon's Rock *Massachusetts* M & W
Baylor University *Texas* M & W
Brigham Young University *Utah* M & W
Bryant University *Rhode Island* M & W
California State University, Chico *California* M & W
California State University, Sacramento *California* M & W
Carnegie Mellon University *Pennsylvania* M & W
Columbia University *New York* M & W
Columbia University, School of General Studies *New York* M & W
Duke University *North Carolina* M & W
Eastern Illinois University *Illinois* M & W
Graceland University *Iowa* M & W
Lehman College of the City University of New York *New York* M & W
Loyola University New Orleans *Louisiana* M & W
Michigan State University *Michigan* M & W
Michigan Technological University *Michigan* M & W
Missouri State University *Missouri* M & W
Nichols College *Massachusetts* M & W
North Carolina State University *North Carolina* M & W
Providence College *Rhode Island* M & W
Rensselaer Polytechnic Institute *New York* M & W
Saint Louis University *Missouri* M & W
Slippery Rock University of Pennsylvania *Pennsylvania* M & W
Stanford University *California* M & W
State University of New York College at Cortland *New York* M & W
State University of New York at New Paltz *New York* M & W
United States Air Force Academy *Colorado* M & W
University of Colorado at Boulder *Colorado* M & W
University of Denver *Colorado* M & W
University of Florida *Florida* M & W
University of Hartford *Connecticut* M & W

M = Men; W = Women

University of Louisiana at Monroe *Louisiana* M & W
University of Memphis *Tennessee* M & W
The University of North Carolina at Chapel Hill *North Carolina* M & W
University of North Texas *Texas* M & W
University of Southern California *California* M & W
The University of Texas at Austin *Texas* M & W
University of Wisconsin–River Falls *Wisconsin* M & W
University of Wyoming *Wyoming* M & W
Weber State University *Utah* M & W
Xavier University *Ohio* M & W

Riflery

Austin Peay State University *Tennessee* W
Bethel University *Tennessee* M & W
Birmingham-Southern College *Alabama* W
Bowdoin College *Maine* M & W
The Citadel, The Military College of South Carolina *South Carolina* M & W
Clemson University *South Carolina* M & W
College of Saint Benedict *Minnesota* W
Columbia University *New York* M & W
Columbus State University *Georgia* M & W
Denison University *Ohio* M & W
Georgia Military College *Georgia* M & W
Hampden-Sydney College *Virginia* M
Hillsdale College *Michigan* M & W
Jacksonville State University *Alabama* M & W
Lassen Community College District *California* M & W
Lindenwood University *Missouri* M & W
Massachusetts Institute of Technology *Massachusetts* M & W
Massachusetts Maritime Academy *Massachusetts* M & W
Mercer University *Georgia* M
Michigan Technological University *Michigan* M & W
Morehead State University *Kentucky* M & W
Murray State University *Kentucky* M & W
New Mexico Military Institute *New Mexico* M & W
North Carolina State University *North Carolina* M & W
North Dakota State University *North Dakota* M & W
North Georgia College & State University *Georgia* M & W
Norwich University *Vermont* M & W
The Ohio State University *Ohio* M & W
Rensselaer Polytechnic Institute *New York* M & W
Rice University *Texas* M & W
Rose-Hulman Institute of Technology *Indiana* M & W
Saint John's University *Minnesota* M
Sam Houston State University *Texas* M & W
Seattle University *Washington* M & W
State University of New York Maritime College *New York* M & W
Syracuse University *New York* M & W
Tennessee Technological University *Tennessee* M & W
Texas Christian University *Texas* W
Trinity University *Texas* M & W
Tuskegee University *Alabama* M & W
United States Air Force Academy *Colorado* M & W
United States Coast Guard Academy *Connecticut* M & W
United States Military Academy *New York* M & W
United States Naval Academy *Maryland* M & W
The University of Akron *Ohio* M & W
The University of Alabama at Birmingham *Alabama* M & W
University of Alaska Fairbanks *Alaska* M & W
University of Alaska Southeast *Alaska* M & W
University of Idaho *Idaho* M & W
University of Kentucky *Kentucky* M & W
University of Memphis *Tennessee* M & W
University of Mississippi *Mississippi* W
University of Missouri–Kansas City *Missouri* M & W
University of Nebraska–Lincoln *Nebraska* W
University of Nevada, Reno *Nevada* M & W
University of New Hampshire *New Hampshire* M & W
University of the Sciences in Philadelphia *Pennsylvania* M & W
The University of Tennessee at Martin *Tennessee* M & W
The University of Texas at El Paso *Texas* M & W
University of Wisconsin–Oshkosh *Wisconsin* M & W
University of Wyoming *Wyoming* M & W
Valley Forge Military College *Pennsylvania* M
Virginia Military Institute *Virginia* M & W
Wentworth Institute of Technology *Massachusetts* M & W
West Virginia University *West Virginia* M & W
Western Kentucky University *Kentucky* M & W
Wofford College *South Carolina* M & W
Yale University *Connecticut* M & W

Rock Climbing

Acadia University *Nova Scotia* M & W
Ball State University *Indiana* M & W
Bishop's University *Quebec* M & W
Bucknell University *Pennsylvania* M & W
Calvin College *Michigan* M & W
Emory University *Georgia* M & W
Fort Lewis College *Colorado* M & W
Hobart and William Smith Colleges *New York* M & W
Keene State College *New Hampshire* M & W
Lake Forest College *Illinois* M & W
Landmark College *Vermont* M & W
Macalester College *Minnesota* M & W
Northeastern State University *Oklahoma* M & W
Old Dominion University *Virginia* M & W
Royal Military College of Canada *Ontario* M
St. Cloud State University *Minnesota* M & W
St. Mary's College of Maryland *Maryland* M & W
Scripps College *California* W
United States Air Force Academy *Colorado* M & W
United States Military Academy *New York* M & W
University at Albany, State University of New York *New York* M & W
The University of Arizona *Arizona* M & W
The University of British Columbia *British Columbia* M & W
University of Central Missouri *Missouri* M & W
University of Minnesota, Duluth *Minnesota* M & W
University of New Hampshire *New Hampshire* M & W
University of North Texas *Texas* M
University of San Diego *California* M
University of Southern California *California* M & W
Western Carolina University *North Carolina* M & W
Western New Mexico University *New Mexico* M & W
Western State College of Colorado *Colorado* M & W
Yale University *Connecticut* M & W

Rugby

Albright College *Pennsylvania* M & W
Allegheny College *Pennsylvania* M & W
Amherst College *Massachusetts* M & W
Augustana College *South Dakota* W
Babson College *Massachusetts* M & W
Ball State University *Indiana* M & W
Barnard College *New York* W
Bates College *Maine* M & W
Baylor University *Texas* M & W
Boston University *Massachusetts* M & W
Bowdoin College *Maine* M & W
Brandeis University *Massachusetts* M & W
Brigham Young University *Utah* M
Brock University *Ontario* M & W
Brown University *Rhode Island* M & W
Bryant University *Rhode Island* M & W
Bucknell University *Pennsylvania* M & W
Buffalo State College, State University of New York *New York* M & W
Butler University *Indiana* M
California Institute of Technology *California* M
California Maritime Academy *California* M
California State University, Chico *California* M
California State University, Long Beach *California* M
California State University, Sacramento *California* M
Calvin College *Michigan* M
Canisius College *New York* M
Cape Breton University *Nova Scotia* M
Carleton College *Minnesota* M & W
Carleton University *Ontario* M & W
Carnegie Mellon University *Pennsylvania* M & W
Castleton State College *Vermont* M & W
Central Washington University *Washington* M & W
The Citadel, The Military College of South Carolina *South Carolina* M & W
Claremont McKenna College *California* M & W
Clemson University *South Carolina* M & W
Colby College *Maine* M & W
Colby-Sawyer College *New Hampshire* M & W
Colgate University *New York* M & W
College of Saint Benedict *Minnesota* W
The College of Wooster *Ohio* M & W
The Colorado College *Colorado* M & W
Colorado School of Mines *Colorado* M & W
Colorado State University *Colorado* M & W
Columbia University *New York* M & W
Columbia University, School of General Studies *New York* M & W
Concordia College *Minnesota* M & W
Concordia University *Quebec* M & W
Connecticut College *Connecticut* W
Coppin State University *Maryland* M
Dartmouth College *New Hampshire* M & W
Davenport University *Michigan* M
Davidson College *North Carolina* M
Denison University *Ohio* M & W
DePauw University *Indiana* M
Drew University *New Jersey* M & W
Duke University *North Carolina* M & W
Earlham College *Indiana* W
Eastern Illinois University *Illinois* M & W
Elon University *North Carolina* M & W
Emory University *Georgia* M & W
Fairfield University *Connecticut* M & W
Florida State University *Florida* M & W
Fordham University *New York* M & W
Fort Lewis College *Colorado* M & W
Franciscan University of Steubenville *Ohio* M
Franklin & Marshall College *Pennsylvania* M & W
Furman University *South Carolina* M & W
Georgetown University *District of Columbia* M & W
Georgia Institute of Technology *Georgia* M
Georgia Southern University *Georgia* M & W
Gettysburg College *Pennsylvania* M & W
Grand Valley State University *Michigan* M & W
Guilford College *North Carolina* M & W
Gustavus Adolphus College *Minnesota* M & W
Hampden-Sydney College *Virginia* M
Harding University *Arkansas* M
Hartwick College *New York* M
Haverford College *Pennsylvania* M
Hiram College *Ohio* M & W
Hobart and William Smith Colleges *New York* M & W
John Carroll University *Ohio* M & W
Juniata College *Pennsylvania* M & W
Kenyon College *Ohio* M & W
Kutztown University of Pennsylvania *Pennsylvania* M & W
Lafayette College *Pennsylvania* M & W
Lake Forest College *Illinois* M & W
Lee University *Tennessee* M & W
Lehigh University *Pennsylvania* M & W
Longwood University *Virginia* M & W
Loras College *Iowa* M
Loyola University New Orleans *Louisiana* M
Macalester College *Minnesota* M & W
Manhattan College *New York* M
Marion Technical College *Ohio* M
Marist College *New York* M & W
Marquette University *Wisconsin* M & W
Marshall University *West Virginia* M & W
Massachusetts Institute of Technology *Massachusetts* M & W
McGill University *Quebec* M & W
McMaster University *Ontario* M & W
Miami University *Ohio* M & W
Michigan State University *Michigan* M & W
Molloy College *New York* M & W

M = Men; W = Women

Mount Allison University *New Brunswick* M & W
Mount St. Mary's University *Maryland* M & W
New Mexico Institute of Mining and Technology *New Mexico* M & W
Nichols College *Massachusetts* M & W
North Carolina State University *North Carolina* M & W
North Dakota State University *North Dakota* M & W
Northern Michigan University *Michigan* M & W
Norwich University *Vermont* M & W
Nova Scotia Agricultural College *Nova Scotia* M & W
Oberlin College *Ohio* M & W
Occidental College *California* M & W
Ohio Wesleyan University *Ohio* M & W
Old Dominion University *Virginia* M
Palmer College of Chiropractic *Iowa* M & W
Penn State University Park *Pennsylvania* M & W
Pepperdine University *California* M
Providence College *Rhode Island* M & W
Queen's University at Kingston *Ontario* M & W
Reed College *Oregon* M & W
Rensselaer Polytechnic Institute *New York* M & W
Rhodes College *Tennessee* M
Rice University *Texas* M & W
Ripon College *Wisconsin* M & W
Roger Williams University *Rhode Island* M
Royal Military College of Canada *Ontario* M
Saginaw Valley State University *Michigan* M & W
St. Andrews Presbyterian College *North Carolina* M & W
St. Bonaventure University *New York* M & W
St. Francis Xavier University *Nova Scotia* M & W
Saint John's University *Minnesota* M
Saint Louis University *Missouri* M & W
Saint Mary's College of California *California* M & W
St. Mary's College of Maryland *Maryland* M & W
Saint Mary's University *Nova Scotia* W
St. Mary's University *Texas* M
Saint Michael's College *Vermont* M & W
Salve Regina University *Rhode Island* M
Sam Houston State University *Texas* M
San Jose State University *California* M
Santa Rosa Junior College *California* M
Scripps College *California* W
Seton Hall University *New Jersey* M
Sewanee: The University of the South *Tennessee* M
Siena College *New York* M & W
Slippery Rock University of Pennsylvania *Pennsylvania* M & W
South Dakota State University *South Dakota* M & W
Southern Connecticut State University *Connecticut* M & W
Southern Methodist University *Texas* M & W
Southern Vermont College *Vermont* M & W
Stanford University *California* M & W
State University of New York College at Cortland *New York* M & W
State University of New York College at Geneseo *New York* M & W
State University of New York College at Oneonta *New York* M & W
State University of New York College at Potsdam *New York* W
State University of New York at New Paltz *New York* M & W
Stonehill College *Massachusetts* M & W
Susquehanna University *Pennsylvania* M & W
Swarthmore College *Pennsylvania* M & W
Syracuse University *New York* M & W
Texas State University–San Marcos *Texas* M & W
Thomas Jefferson University *Pennsylvania* M
Towson University *Maryland* M & W
Trent University *Ontario* M & W
Trinity College *Connecticut* M & W
Trinity Western University *British Columbia* M
Truman State University *Missouri* M & W
Tulane University *Louisiana* M
Union College *New York* M & W
United States Air Force Academy *Colorado* M & W
United States Coast Guard Academy *Connecticut* M & W
United States Merchant Marine Academy *New York* M
United States Military Academy *New York* M & W
United States Naval Academy *Maryland* M & W
Université du Québec, École de technologie supérieure *Quebec* M
University of Alberta *Alberta* W
The University of British Columbia *British Columbia* M & W
University of California, Berkeley *California* M
University of California, Santa Barbara *California* M
University of California, Santa Cruz *California* M & W
University of Colorado at Boulder *Colorado* M & W
University of Delaware *Delaware* W
University of Guelph *Ontario* M & W
University of Hartford *Connecticut* M & W
University of Idaho *Idaho* M & W
The University of Iowa *Iowa* M & W
The University of Kansas *Kansas* M
University of King's College *Nova Scotia* M & W
University of Mary Washington *Virginia* M & W
University of Maryland, Baltimore County *Maryland* M & W
University of Massachusetts Dartmouth *Massachusetts* M & W
University of Michigan–Dearborn *Michigan* M
University of Minnesota, Duluth *Minnesota* M & W
University of Mississippi *Mississippi* M
The University of Montana *Montana* M & W
University of New Brunswick Saint John *New Brunswick* M & W
University of New Hampshire *New Hampshire* M & W
University of Northern Colorado *Colorado* M & W
University of Ottawa *Ontario* W
University of Portland *Oregon* M
University of Prince Edward Island *Prince Edward Island* M & W
University of Puget Sound *Washington* M
University of Rhode Island *Rhode Island* M & W
University of Richmond *Virginia* M & W
University of Rochester *New York* M & W
University of St. Thomas *Texas* M
University of San Diego *California* M & W
The University of Scranton *Pennsylvania* M & W
University of Southern California *California* M & W
University of Southern Indiana *Indiana* M & W
The University of Tennessee *Tennessee* M & W
The University of Texas at Austin *Texas* M & W
University of Toronto *Ontario* M
University of Utah *Utah* M
University of Vermont *Vermont* M & W
University of Victoria *British Columbia* M & W
University of Waterloo *Ontario* M & W
The University of Western Ontario *Ontario* M & W
University of Windsor *Ontario* M & W
University of Wisconsin–Platteville *Wisconsin* M & W
University of Wisconsin–River Falls *Wisconsin* M & W
University of Wisconsin–Whitewater *Wisconsin* M & W
University of Wyoming *Wyoming* M & W
Ursinus College *Pennsylvania* M & W
Utah State University *Utah* M & W
Vassar College *New York* M & W
Wabash College *Indiana* M
Washington College *Maryland* M & W
Washington and Lee University *Virginia* M
Washington State University *Washington* M & W
Washington University in St. Louis *Missouri* M & W
Wayne State College *Nebraska* M & W
Weber State University *Utah* M & W
Wellesley College *Massachusetts* W
Wentworth Institute of Technology *Massachusetts* M & W
Wesleyan University *Connecticut* M & W
West Chester University of Pennsylvania *Pennsylvania* M & W
Western Carolina University *North Carolina* M
Western State College of Colorado *Colorado* M & W
Westmont College *California* M
Whitman College *Washington* M & W
Wilfrid Laurier University *Ontario* M & W
Williams College *Massachusetts* M & W
Winona State University *Minnesota* M & W
Winthrop University *South Carolina* M
Wittenberg University *Ohio* M & W
Xavier University *Ohio* M & W
Yale University *Connecticut* M & W
York University *Ontario* W

Sailing

Amherst College *Massachusetts* M & W
Barnard College *New York* W
Bates College *Maine* M & W
Baylor University *Texas* M & W
Boston College *Massachusetts* M & W
Boston University *Massachusetts* M & W
Bowdoin College *Maine* M & W
Brandeis University *Massachusetts* M & W
Brown University *Rhode Island* M & W
California Maritime Academy *California* M & W
California State University, Long Beach *California* M & W
California State University, Monterey Bay *California* M & W
Carleton College *Minnesota* M & W
Chapman University *California* M & W
Christopher Newport University *Virginia* M & W
Clemson University *South Carolina* M & W
Colby College *Maine* M & W
Colgate University *New York* M & W
College of Charleston *South Carolina* M & W
Columbia University, School of General Studies *New York* M & W
Connecticut College *Connecticut* M & W
Dartmouth College *New Hampshire* M & W
Davidson College *North Carolina* M & W
Denison University *Ohio* M & W
Duke University *North Carolina* M & W
Eckerd College *Florida* M & W
Emory University *Georgia* M & W
Endicott College *Massachusetts* M & W
Fairfield University *Connecticut* M & W
Fordham University *New York* M & W
Georgetown University *District of Columbia* M & W
Grand Valley State University *Michigan* M & W
Hampton University *Virginia* M & W
Harvard University *Massachusetts* M & W
Hiram College *Ohio* M & W
Hobart and William Smith Colleges *New York* M & W
Hope College *Michigan* M & W
John Carroll University *Ohio* M & W
Johnson & Wales University *Rhode Island* M & W
Kenyon College *Ohio* M & W
Lake Forest College *Illinois* M & W
Loyola University New Orleans *Louisiana* M & W
Maine Maritime Academy *Maine* M & W
Massachusetts Institute of Technology *Massachusetts* M & W
Massachusetts Maritime Academy *Massachusetts* M & W
McGill University *Quebec* M & W
Miami University *Ohio* M & W
Michigan State University *Michigan* M & W
Mitchell College *Connecticut* M & W
Monmouth University *New Jersey* M & W
New College of Florida *Florida* M & W
North Carolina State University *North Carolina* M & W
Norwich University *Vermont* M & W
Ohio Wesleyan University *Ohio* M & W
Old Dominion University *Virginia* M & W
Pepperdine University *California* M & W
Providence College *Rhode Island* M & W
Queen's University at Kingston *Ontario* M & W
Rensselaer Polytechnic Institute *New York* M & W
Rice University *Texas* M & W
Robert Morris University Illinois *Illinois* M & W
Roger Williams University *Rhode Island* M & W
Rollins College *Florida* M & W
St. Mary's College of Maryland *Maryland* M & W
Salve Regina University *Rhode Island* M & W
San Jose State University *California* M & W

M = Men; W = Women

Stanford University *California* M & W
Syracuse University *New York* M & W
Texas A&M University at Galveston *Texas* M & W
Trinity College *Connecticut* M & W
Tufts University *Massachusetts* M & W
Tulane University *Louisiana* M & W
United States Coast Guard Academy *Connecticut* M & W
United States Merchant Marine Academy *New York* M & W
United States Military Academy *New York* M & W
United States Naval Academy *Maryland* M & W
University of California, Irvine *California* M & W
University of California, Santa Barbara *California* M & W
University of Delaware *Delaware* M & W
University of Hawaii at Manoa *Hawaii* M & W
The University of Iowa *Iowa* M & W
University of Maryland, Baltimore County *Maryland* M & W
University of New Hampshire *New Hampshire* M & W
University of North Texas *Texas* M & W
University of Puget Sound *Washington* M & W
University of Rhode Island *Rhode Island* M & W
University of Southern Maine *Maine* M & W
The University of Tennessee *Tennessee* M & W
The University of Texas at Austin *Texas* M & W
University of Vermont *Vermont* M & W
University of Wisconsin–Madison *Wisconsin* M & W
Villanova University *Pennsylvania* M & W
Wabash College *Indiana* M
Washington College *Maryland* M & W
Washington State University *Washington* M & W
Washington University in St. Louis *Missouri* M & W
Webb Institute *New York* M & W
Wellesley College *Massachusetts* W
Wesleyan University *Connecticut* M & W
Williams College *Massachusetts* M & W
Yale University *Connecticut* M & W

Skiing (Cross-Country)

Bates College *Maine* M & W
Bowdoin College *Maine* M & W
Buffalo State College, State University of New York *New York* M & W
Carleton College *Minnesota* M & W
Carleton University *Ontario* M & W
Clarkson University *New York* M & W
Colby College *Maine* M & W
College of Saint Benedict *Minnesota* W
The College of St. Scholastica *Minnesota* M & W
Columbia University *New York* M & W
Connecticut College *Connecticut* M & W
Dartmouth College *New Hampshire* M & W
Duke University *North Carolina* M & W
Eastern Oregon University *Oregon* M & W
Fort Lewis College *Colorado* M & W
Gonzaga University *Washington* M & W
Gustavus Adolphus College *Minnesota* M & W
Harvard University *Massachusetts* M & W
John Carroll University *Ohio* M & W
Lake Tahoe Community College *California* M & W
Lakehead University *Ontario* M & W
Macalester College *Minnesota* M & W
Marywood University *Pennsylvania* M & W
McGill University *Quebec* M & W
Michigan State University *Michigan* M & W
Michigan Technological University *Michigan* M & W
Middlebury College *Vermont* M & W
Montana State University *Montana* M & W
Nipissing University *Ontario* M & W
Northern Michigan University *Michigan* M & W
Norwich University *Vermont* M & W
Paul Smith's College *New York* M & W
Queen's University at Kingston *Ontario* M & W
Rensselaer Polytechnic Institute *New York* M & W
St. Cloud State University *Minnesota* M & W
Saint John's University *Minnesota* M
St. Lawrence University *New York* M & W
Saint Michael's College *Vermont* M & W
St. Olaf College *Minnesota* M & W
State University of New York at New Paltz *New York* M & W
Trent University *Ontario* M & W
United States Air Force Academy *Colorado* M & W
United States Military Academy *New York* M & W
University of Alaska Anchorage *Alaska* M & W
University of Alaska Fairbanks *Alaska* M & W
University of Alberta *Alberta* M & W
University of Colorado at Boulder *Colorado* M & W
University of Denver *Colorado* M & W
University of Guelph *Ontario* M & W
University of Idaho *Idaho* M & W
University of Maine at Fort Kent *Maine* M & W
University of Minnesota, Duluth *Minnesota* M & W
University of Nevada, Reno *Nevada* M & W
University of New Hampshire *New Hampshire* M & W
University of New Mexico *New Mexico* M & W
University of Northern British Columbia *British Columbia* M & W
University of Toronto *Ontario* M & W
University of Utah *Utah* M & W
University of Vermont *Vermont* M & W
University of Waterloo *Ontario* M & W
University of Wisconsin–Green Bay *Wisconsin* M & W
University of Wyoming *Wyoming* M & W
Washington and Lee University *Virginia* M & W
Washington State University *Washington* M & W
Wesleyan University *Connecticut* M & W
Western State College of Colorado *Colorado* M & W
Whitman College *Washington* M & W
Williams College *Massachusetts* M & W
Yale University *Connecticut* M & W

Skiing (Downhill)

Alfred University *New York* M & W
Amherst College *Massachusetts* M & W
Babson College *Massachusetts* M & W
Barnard College *New York* W
Bates College *Maine* M & W
Bishop's University *Quebec* M & W
Boston College *Massachusetts* M & W
Boston University *Massachusetts* M & W
Bowdoin College *Maine* M & W
Brandeis University *Massachusetts* M & W
Brown University *Rhode Island* M & W
Bucknell University *Pennsylvania* M & W
Buffalo State College, State University of New York *New York* M & W
California State University, Long Beach *California* M & W
California State University, Sacramento *California* M & W
Carleton College *Minnesota* M & W
Castleton State College *Vermont* M & W
The Citadel, The Military College of South Carolina *South Carolina* M & W
Claremont McKenna College *California* M & W
Clarkson University *New York* M & W
Colby College *Maine* M & W
Colby-Sawyer College *New Hampshire* M & W
Colgate University *New York* M & W
The College of Idaho *Idaho* M & W
The Colorado College *Colorado* M & W
Colorado Mountain College, Alpine Campus *Colorado* M & W
Colorado School of Mines *Colorado* M & W
Colorado State University *Colorado* M & W
Columbia University *New York* M & W
Columbia University, School of General Studies *New York* M & W
Concordia University *Quebec* M & W
Connecticut College *Connecticut* M & W
Dartmouth College *New Hampshire* M & W
Davis & Elkins College *West Virginia* M & W
Denison University *Ohio* M & W
Dickinson College *Pennsylvania* M & W
Duke University *North Carolina* M & W
Eastern Nazarene College *Massachusetts* M
Eastern Oregon University *Oregon* M & W
Fairfield University *Connecticut* M & W
Fort Lewis College *Colorado* M & W
Garrett College *Maryland* M & W
Gonzaga University *Washington* M & W
Grand Valley State University *Michigan* M & W
Green Mountain College *Vermont* M & W
Harvard University *Massachusetts* M & W
Hobart and William Smith Colleges *New York* M & W
Holyoke Community College *Massachusetts* M & W
John Carroll University *Ohio* M & W
Keene State College *New Hampshire* M & W
Kutztown University of Pennsylvania *Pennsylvania* M & W
Lafayette College *Pennsylvania* M & W
Laurentian University *Ontario* M
Lehigh University *Pennsylvania* M & W
Loras College *Iowa* M
Manchester Community College *New Hampshire* M & W
Marist College *New York* M & W
Marquette University *Wisconsin* M & W
McGill University *Quebec* M & W
Michigan State University *Michigan* M & W
Michigan Technological University *Michigan* M & W
Middlebury College *Vermont* M & W
Montana State University *Montana* M & W
North Carolina State University *North Carolina* M & W
Northern Michigan University *Michigan* M & W
Norwich University *Vermont* M & W
Penn State Erie, The Behrend College *Pennsylvania* M & W
Penn State Lehigh Valley *Pennsylvania* M & W
Penn State University Park *Pennsylvania* M & W
Plymouth State University *New Hampshire* M & W
Queen's University at Kingston *Ontario* M & W
Rochester Institute of Technology *New York* M & W
Rocky Mountain College *Montana* M & W
Saint Anselm College *New Hampshire* M & W
St. Cloud State University *Minnesota* M & W
St. Lawrence University *New York* M & W
Saint Mary's College *Indiana* W
Saint Michael's College *Vermont* M & W
St. Olaf College *Minnesota* M & W
Scripps College *California* W
Seattle University *Washington* M & W
Sierra Nevada College *Nevada* M & W
Slippery Rock University of Pennsylvania *Pennsylvania* M & W
Smith College *Massachusetts* W
Southern Oregon University *Oregon* M & W
Stanford University *California* M & W
State University of New York College at Geneseo *New York* M & W
Syracuse University *New York* M & W
Trinity College *Connecticut* M & W
United States Air Force Academy *Colorado* M & W
United States Military Academy *New York* M & W
United States Naval Academy *Maryland* M & W
Université Laval *Quebec* M & W
Université de Montréal *Quebec* M & W
Université du Québec àRimouski *Quebec* M & W
University of Alaska Anchorage *Alaska* M & W
The University of British Columbia *British Columbia* M & W
University of California, Santa Barbara *California* M & W
University of Colorado at Boulder *Colorado* M & W
University of Denver *Colorado* M & W
University of Idaho *Idaho* M & W
University of Maine at Fort Kent *Maine* M & W
University of Maryland, Baltimore County *Maryland* M & W
University of Minnesota, Duluth *Minnesota* M & W
The University of Montana *Montana* M & W
University of Nevada, Reno *Nevada* M & W
University of New Hampshire *New Hampshire* M & W
University of New Mexico *New Mexico* M & W
University of Puget Sound *Washington* M & W
University of Rhode Island *Rhode Island* M & W
University of Rochester *New York* M & W
University of St. Thomas *Minnesota* M & W
The University of Scranton *Pennsylvania* M & W
University of Southern California *California* M & W
The University of Tennessee *Tennessee* M & W
University of Toronto *Ontario* M & W

M = Men; W = Women

University of Utah *Utah* M & W
University of Vermont *Vermont* M & W
University of Wyoming *Wyoming* M & W
Villanova University *Pennsylvania* M & W
Washington State University *Washington* M & W
Weber State University *Utah* M & W
Wellesley College *Massachusetts* W
Wesleyan University *Connecticut* M & W
West Chester University of Pennsylvania *Pennsylvania* M & W
West Virginia Wesleyan College *West Virginia* M & W
Western State College of Colorado *Colorado* M & W
Westminster College *Utah* M & W
Whitman College *Washington* M & W
William Paterson University of New Jersey *New Jersey* M & W
Williams College *Massachusetts* M & W
Winona State University *Minnesota* M & W
Worcester State College *Massachusetts* M & W
Yale University *Connecticut* M & W

Soccer

Abilene Christian University *Texas* W
Abraham Baldwin Agricultural College *Georgia* W
Academy of Art University *California* M & W
Acadia University *Nova Scotia* M & W
Adams State College *Colorado* M & W
Adelphi University *New York* M & W
Adirondack Community College *New York* M
Adrian College *Michigan* M & W
Agnes Scott College *Georgia* W
Alabama Agricultural and Mechanical University *Alabama* M
Alabama State University *Alabama* W
Albany College of Pharmacy and Health Sciences *New York* M & W
Alberta College of Art & Design *Alberta* M & W
Albertus Magnus College *Connecticut* M & W
Albion College *Michigan* M & W
Albright College *Pennsylvania* M & W
Alcorn State University *Mississippi* W
Alderson-Broaddus College *West Virginia* M & W
Alfred University *New York* M & W
Allan Hancock College *California* M & W
Allegany College of Maryland *Maryland* M & W
Allegheny College *Pennsylvania* M & W
Allen Community College *Kansas* M & W
Alma College *Michigan* M & W
Alvernia University *Pennsylvania* M & W
Alverno College *Wisconsin* W
American International College *Massachusetts* M & W
American River College *California* M & W
American University *District of Columbia* M & W
Amherst College *Massachusetts* M & W
Ancilla College *Indiana* M
Anderson University *South Carolina* M & W
Anderson University *Indiana* M & W
Andrew College *Georgia* M & W
Angelo State University *Texas* W
Anna Maria College *Massachusetts* M & W
Anne Arundel Community College *Maryland* M & W
Anoka-Ramsey Community College *Minnesota* M & W
Anoka-Ramsey Community College, Cambridge Campus *Minnesota* M & W
Antelope Valley College *California* W
Appalachian Bible College *West Virginia* M
Appalachian State University *North Carolina* M & W
Aquinas College *Michigan* M & W
Arcadia University *Pennsylvania* M & W
Arizona State University *Arizona* W
Arizona Western College *Arizona* M
Arkansas State University - Jonesboro *Arkansas* W
The Art Institute of Boston at Lesley University *Massachusetts* M & W
Asbury University *Kentucky* M & W
Ashford University *Iowa* M & W
Ashland University *Ohio* M & W
Assumption College *Massachusetts* M & W
Atlanta Christian College *Georgia* M & W
Auburn University *Alabama* W
Auburn University Montgomery *Alabama* M & W
Augsburg College *Minnesota* M & W
Augustana College *South Dakota* M & W
Augustana College *Illinois* M & W
Aurora University *Illinois* M & W
Austin College *Texas* M & W
Austin Peay State University *Tennessee* W
Ave Maria University *Florida* M & W
Averett University *Virginia* M & W
Avila University *Missouri* M & W
Azusa Pacific University *California* M & W
Babson College *Massachusetts* M & W
Baker University *Kansas* M & W
Bakersfield College *California* W
Baldwin-Wallace College *Ohio* M & W
Ball State University *Indiana* M & W
Baptist Bible College *Missouri* M
Baptist Bible College of Pennsylvania *Pennsylvania* M & W
Barclay College *Kansas* M
Bard College *New York* M & W
Bard College at Simon's Rock *Massachusetts* M & W
Barnard College *New York* W
Barry University *Florida* M & W
Barton College *North Carolina* M & W
Barton County Community College *Kansas* M & W
Bates College *Maine* M & W
Bay Path College *Massachusetts* W
Baylor University *Texas* M & W
Becker College *Massachusetts* M & W
Belhaven University *Mississippi* M & W
Bellarmine University *Kentucky* M & W
Bellevue College *Washington* M
Bellevue University *Nebraska* M & W
Belmont Abbey College *North Carolina* M & W
Belmont University *Tennessee* M & W
Beloit College *Wisconsin* M & W
Bemidji State University *Minnesota* W
Benedictine College *Kansas* M & W
Benedictine University *Illinois* M & W
Benjamin Franklin Institute of Technology *Massachusetts* M
Bennington College *Vermont* M & W
Bentley University *Massachusetts* M & W
Berea College *Kentucky* M & W
Bergen Community College *New Jersey* M & W
Bernard M. Baruch College of the City University of New York *New York* M
Berry College *Georgia* M & W
Bethany Bible College *New Brunswick* M & W
Bethany College *West Virginia* M & W
Bethany College *Kansas* M & W
Bethany Lutheran College *Minnesota* M & W
Bethany University *California* M & W
Bethel College *Kansas* M & W
Bethel College *Indiana* M & W
Bethel University *Tennessee* M & W
Bethel University *Minnesota* M & W
Biola University *California* M & W
Birmingham-Southern College *Alabama* M & W
Bishop's University *Quebec* W
Blackburn College *Illinois* M & W
Blessing-Rieman College of Nursing *Illinois* M & W
Bloomfield College *New Jersey* M & W
Bloomsburg University of Pennsylvania *Pennsylvania* M & W
Bluefield College *Virginia* M & W
Bluffton University *Ohio* M & W
Boise State University *Idaho* W
Borough of Manhattan Community College of the City University of New York *New York* M
Bossier Parish Community College *Louisiana* W
Boston College *Massachusetts* M & W
Boston University *Massachusetts* M & W
Bowdoin College *Maine* M & W
Bowling Green State University *Ohio* M & W
Bradley University *Illinois* M
Brandeis University *Massachusetts* W
Brenau University *Georgia* W
Brescia University *Kentucky* M & W
Brevard College *North Carolina* M & W
Brewton-Parker College *Georgia* M & W
Briar Cliff University *Iowa* M & W
Briarcliffe College *New York* W
Bridgewater College *Virginia* M & W
Bridgewater State College *Massachusetts* M & W
Briercrest College *Saskatchewan* M & W
Brigham Young University *Utah* M & W
Brigham Young University–Hawaii *Hawaii* M & W
Brock University *Ontario* M & W
Bronx Community College of the City University of New York *New York* M
Brookdale Community College *New Jersey* M & W
Brooklyn College of the City University of New York *New York* M
Broome Community College *New York* M & W
Broward College *Florida* W
Brown University *Rhode Island* M & W
Bryan College *Tennessee* M & W
Bryant & Stratton College - Syracuse Campus *New York* M & W
Bryant University *Rhode Island* M & W
Bryn Athyn College of the New Church *Pennsylvania* M
Bryn Mawr College *Pennsylvania* W
Bucknell University *Pennsylvania* M & W
Bucks County Community College *Pennsylvania* M & W
Buena Vista University *Iowa* M & W
Buffalo State College, State University of New York *New York* M & W
Bunker Hill Community College *Massachusetts* M & W
Burlington County College *New Jersey* M & W
Butler Community College *Kansas* W
Butler University *Indiana* M & W
Butte College *California* W
Cabrillo College *California* M & W
Cabrini College *Pennsylvania* M & W
Caldwell College *New Jersey* M & W
California Baptist University *California* M & W
California Institute of Technology *California* M & W
California Lutheran University *California* M & W
California Maritime Academy *California* M
California Polytechnic State University, San Luis Obispo *California* M & W
California State Polytechnic University, Pomona *California* M & W
California State University, Bakersfield *California* M
California State University, Chico *California* M & W
California State University, Dominguez Hills *California* M & W
California State University, East Bay *California* M & W
California State University, Fresno *California* W
California State University, Fullerton *California* M & W
California State University, Long Beach *California* M & W
California State University, Los Angeles *California* M & W
California State University, Monterey Bay *California* M & W
California State University, Northridge *California* M
California State University, Sacramento *California* M & W
California State University, San Bernardino *California* M & W
California State University, San Marcos *California* M & W
California State University, Stanislaus *California* M & W
California University of Pennsylvania *Pennsylvania* M & W
Calumet College of Saint Joseph *Indiana* M & W
Calvary Bible College and Theological Seminary *Missouri* M
Calvin College *Michigan* M & W
Camden County College *New Jersey* M & W
Campbell University *North Carolina* M & W
Campbellsville University *Kentucky* M & W
Canadian Mennonite University *Manitoba* M & W
Canisius College *New York* M & W
Cape Breton University *Nova Scotia* M & W
Cape Fear Community College *North Carolina* M & W
Capital University *Ohio* M & W

M = Men; W = Women

Cardinal Stritch University *Wisconsin* M & W
Carleton College *Minnesota* M & W
Carleton University *Ontario* M & W
Carlow University *Pennsylvania* W
Carnegie Mellon University *Pennsylvania* M & W
Carroll College *Montana* W
Carroll University *Wisconsin* M & W
Carson-Newman College *Tennessee* M & W
Carthage College *Wisconsin* M & W
Case Western Reserve University *Ohio* M & W
Castleton State College *Vermont* M & W
Catawba College *North Carolina* M & W
The Catholic University of America *District of Columbia* M & W
Cayuga County Community College *New York* M & W
Cazenovia College *New York* M & W
Cecil College *Maryland* W
Cedar Crest College *Pennsylvania* W
Cedar Valley College *Texas* W
Cedarville University *Ohio* M & W
Centenary College *New Jersey* M & W
Centenary College of Louisiana *Louisiana* M & W
Central Christian College of Kansas *Kansas* M & W
Central College *Iowa* M & W
Central Connecticut State University *Connecticut* M & W
Central Maine Community College *Maine* M & W
Central Methodist University *Missouri* M & W
Central Michigan University *Michigan* W
Central Washington University *Washington* M & W
Centre College *Kentucky* M & W
Century College *Minnesota* M & W
Cerritos College *California* M
Chabot College *California* M & W
Chaffey College *California* M & W
Chapman University *California* M & W
Charleston Southern University *South Carolina* W
Chatham University *Pennsylvania* W
Chesapeake College *Maryland* M & W
Chestnut Hill College *Pennsylvania* M & W
Chowan University *North Carolina* M & W
Christendom College *Virginia* M & W
Christian Brothers University *Tennessee* M & W
Christopher Newport University *Virginia* M & W
Cincinnati Christian University *Ohio* M & W
Cincinnati State Technical and Community College *Ohio* M & W
Cisco College *Texas* M
Citrus College *California* M & W
City College of the City University of New York *New York* M & W
City College of San Francisco *California* M
City Colleges of Chicago, Kennedy-King College *Illinois* M
City Colleges of Chicago, Richard J. Daley College *Illinois* M & W
Clackamas Community College *Oregon* W
Claremont McKenna College *California* M & W
Clark College *Washington* M & W
Clark University *Massachusetts* M & W
Clarke College *Iowa* M & W
Clarkson University *New York* M & W
Clayton State University *Georgia* M & W
Clearwater Christian College *Florida* M & W
Clemson University *South Carolina* M & W
Cleveland State University *Ohio* M & W
Clinton Community College *New York* M & W
Clinton Community College *Iowa* M & W
Cloud County Community College *Kansas* M & W
Coastal Carolina University *South Carolina* M & W
Cochise College *Arizona* W
Coe College *Iowa* M & W
Coker College *South Carolina* M & W
Colby College *Maine* M & W
Colby-Sawyer College *New Hampshire* M & W
Colgate University *New York* M & W
The College at Brockport, State University of New York *New York* M & W
College of the Canyons *California* M & W
College of Charleston *South Carolina* M & W
College of the Desert *California* M
College of DuPage *Illinois* M & W
College of the Holy Cross *Massachusetts* M & W
The College of Idaho *Idaho* M & W
College of Lake County *Illinois* M & W
College of Marin *California* M & W
College of Mount St. Joseph *Ohio* M & W
College of Mount Saint Vincent *New York* M & W
The College of New Jersey *New Jersey* M & W
College of Notre Dame of Maryland *Maryland* W
College of the Redwoods *California* W
College of Saint Benedict *Minnesota* W
College of Saint Elizabeth *New Jersey* W
College of St. Joseph *Vermont* M & W
College of Saint Mary *Nebraska* W
The College of Saint Rose *New York* M & W
The College of St. Scholastica *Minnesota* M & W
College of San Mateo *California* W
College of the Sequoias *California* W
College of Southern Maryland *Maryland* M & W
College of Staten Island of the City University of New York *New York* M & W
College of The Albemarle *North Carolina* M
The College of William and Mary *Virginia* M & W
The College of Wooster *Ohio* M & W
Colorado Christian University *Colorado* M & W
The Colorado College *Colorado* M & W
Colorado Mountain College *Colorado* M & W
Colorado School of Mines *Colorado* M & W
Colorado State University *Colorado* M & W
Colorado State University–Pueblo *Colorado* M & W
Columbia Basin College *Washington* M & W
Columbia Bible College *British Columbia* M & W
Columbia College *South Carolina* W
Columbia College *Missouri* M
Columbia-Greene Community College *New York* M & W
Columbia University *New York* M & W
Columbia University, School of General Studies *New York* M & W
Columbus State Community College *Ohio* M
Columbus State University *Georgia* W
The Community College of Baltimore County *Maryland* M & W
Community College of Philadelphia *Pennsylvania* M
Community College of Rhode Island *Rhode Island* M & W
Concord University *West Virginia* W
Concordia College *Minnesota* M & W
Concordia College–New York *New York* M & W
Concordia University *Quebec* M & W
Concordia University *Oregon* M & W
Concordia University *Michigan* M & W
Concordia University *California* M & W
Concordia University Chicago *Illinois* M & W
Concordia University College of Alberta *Alberta* M & W
Concordia University, Nebraska *Nebraska* M & W
Concordia University, St. Paul *Minnesota* W
Concordia University Texas *Texas* M & W
Concordia University Wisconsin *Wisconsin* M & W
Connecticut College *Connecticut* M & W
Converse College *South Carolina* W
Cooper Union for the Advancement of Science and Art *New York* M & W
Corban University *Oregon* M & W
Cornell College *Iowa* M & W
Cornell University *New York* M & W
Cornerstone University *Michigan* M & W
Corning Community College *New York* M & W
Cosumnes River College *California* M & W
County College of Morris *New Jersey* M & W
Covenant College *Georgia* M & W
Cowley County Community College and Area Vocational–Technical School *Kansas* M & W
Crandall University *New Brunswick* M & W
Creighton University *Nebraska* M & W
Crowder College *Missouri* M
Crown College *Minnesota* M & W
Cuesta College *California* W
The Culinary Institute of America *New York* M & W
Culver-Stockton College *Missouri* M & W
Cumberland University *Tennessee* M & W
Curry College *Massachusetts* M & W
Cuyahoga Community College *Ohio* M
Cuyamaca College *California* M & W
Cypress College *California* M & W
Daemen College *New York* M & W
Dakota County Technical College *Minnesota* M & W
Dalhousie University *Nova Scotia* M & W
Dallas Baptist University *Texas* W
Dallas Christian College *Texas* M & W
Dana College *Nebraska* M & W
Daniel Webster College *New Hampshire* M & W
Danville Area Community College *Illinois* M
Dartmouth College *New Hampshire* M & W
Darton College *Georgia* M & W
Davenport University *Michigan* M & W
Davidson College *North Carolina* M & W
Davis College *New York* M & W
Davis & Elkins College *West Virginia* M & W
De Anza College *California* M & W
Dean College *Massachusetts* M & W
Defiance College *Ohio* M & W
Delaware County Community College *Pennsylvania* M
Delaware State University *Delaware* W
Delaware Technical & Community College, Stanton/Wilmington Campus *Delaware* M
Delaware Technical & Community College, Terry Campus *Delaware* M & W
Delaware Valley College *Pennsylvania* M & W
Delta College *Michigan* M
Delta State University *Mississippi* M & W
Denison University *Ohio* M & W
DePaul University *Illinois* M & W
DePauw University *Indiana* M & W
DeSales University *Pennsylvania* M & W
Diablo Valley College *California* W
Dickinson College *Pennsylvania* M & W
Dixie State College of Utah *Utah* M & W
Doane College *Nebraska* M & W
Dominican College *New York* M & W
Dominican University *Illinois* M & W
Dominican University of California *California* M & W
Dordt College *Iowa* M & W
Dowling College *New York* M & W
Drake University *Iowa* M & W
Drew University *New Jersey* M & W
Drexel University *Pennsylvania* M & W
Drury University *Missouri* M & W
Duke University *North Carolina* M & W
Duquesne University *Pennsylvania* M & W
Dutchess Community College *New York* M & W
D'Youville College *New York* M & W
Earlham College *Indiana* M & W
East Carolina University *North Carolina* M & W
East Central College *Missouri* M
East Central Community College *Mississippi* M & W
East Central University *Oklahoma* W
East Los Angeles College *California* M & W
East Mississippi Community College *Mississippi* M & W
East Stroudsburg University of Pennsylvania *Pennsylvania* M & W
East Tennessee State University *Tennessee* M & W
East Texas Baptist University *Texas* M & W
Eastern Connecticut State University *Connecticut* M & W
Eastern Illinois University *Illinois* M & W
Eastern Mennonite University *Virginia* M & W
Eastern Michigan University *Michigan* W
Eastern Nazarene College *Massachusetts* M & W
Eastern New Mexico University *New Mexico* W
Eastern Oregon University *Oregon* W
Eastern University *Pennsylvania* M & W
Eastern Washington University *Washington* W
Eastfield College *Texas* W
Eckerd College *Florida* M & W
Edgewood College *Wisconsin* M & W
Edinboro University of Pennsylvania *Pennsylvania* W
Edmonds Community College *Washington* M & W
El Camino College *California* M
Elgin Community College *Illinois* M & W
Elizabethtown College *Pennsylvania* M & W
Elmhurst College *Illinois* M & W
Elmira College *New York* M & W
Elms College *Massachusetts* M & W

M = Men; W = Women

Elon University *North Carolina* M & W
Embry-Riddle Aeronautical University *Florida* M & W
Emerson College *Massachusetts* M & W
Emmanuel College *Massachusetts* M & W
Emmanuel College *Georgia* M & W
Emory & Henry College *Virginia* M & W
Emory University *Georgia* M & W
Emory University, Oxford College *Georgia* W
Emporia State University *Kansas* W
Endicott College *Massachusetts* M & W
Erie Community College *New York* M & W
Erie Community College, North Campus *New York* M & W
Erie Community College, South Campus *New York* M & W
Erskine College *South Carolina* M & W
Essex County College *New Jersey* M
Eugene Bible College *Oregon* M & W
Everett Community College *Washington* M & W
The Evergreen State College *Washington* M & W
Evergreen Valley College *California* M
Fairfield University *Connecticut* M & W
Fairleigh Dickinson University, College at Florham *New Jersey* M & W
Fairleigh Dickinson University, Metropolitan Campus *New Jersey* M & W
Faith Baptist Bible College and Theological Seminary *Iowa* M & W
Farmingdale State College *New York* M & W
Faulkner University *Alabama* M & W
Feather River College *California* M & W
Felician College *New Jersey* M & W
Ferris State University *Michigan* M & W
Ferrum College *Virginia* M & W
Finger Lakes Community College *New York* M & W
Finlandia University *Michigan* M & W
Fisher College *Massachusetts* M & W
Fitchburg State College *Massachusetts* M & W
Flagler College *Florida* M & W
Flathead Valley Community College *Montana* M & W
Florida Atlantic University *Florida* M & W
Florida Gulf Coast University *Florida* M & W
Florida Institute of Technology *Florida* M & W
Florida International University *Florida* M & W
Florida Southern College *Florida* M & W
Florida State University *Florida* M & W
Fontbonne University *Missouri* M & W
Foothill College *California* M & W
Fordham University *New York* M & W
Fort Lewis College *Colorado* M & W
Framingham State College *Massachusetts* M & W
Francis Marion University *South Carolina* M & W
Franciscan University of Steubenville *Ohio* M & W
Franklin College *Indiana* M & W
Franklin & Marshall College *Pennsylvania* M & W
Franklin Pierce University *New Hampshire* M & W
Franklin W. Olin College of Engineering *Massachusetts* M & W
Frederick Community College *Maryland* M & W
Freed-Hardeman University *Tennessee* M & W
Fresno City College *California* M & W
Fresno Pacific University *California* M & W
Friends University *Kansas* M & W
Frostburg State University *Maryland* M & W
Fullerton College *California* M
Fulton-Montgomery Community College *New York* M & W
Furman University *South Carolina* M & W
Gallaudet University *District of Columbia* M & W
Gannon University *Pennsylvania* M & W
Garden City Community College *Kansas* M & W
Gardner-Webb University *North Carolina* M & W
Gateway Community College *Connecticut* M
Gavilan College *California* M & W
Genesee Community College *New York* M & W
Geneva College *Pennsylvania* M & W
George Fox University *Oregon* M & W
George Mason University *Virginia* M & W
The George Washington University *District of Columbia* M & W
Georgetown College *Kentucky* M & W
Georgetown University *District of Columbia* M & W
Georgia College & State University *Georgia* W
Georgia Institute of Technology *Georgia* M & W
Georgia Perimeter College *Georgia* M & W
Georgia Southern University *Georgia* M & W
Georgia Southwestern State University *Georgia* M & W
Georgia State University *Georgia* M & W
Georgian Court University *New Jersey* W
Gettysburg College *Pennsylvania* M & W
Glendale Community College *California* M & W
Glendale Community College *Arizona* M & W
Globe Institute of Technology *New York* M
Gloucester County College *New Jersey* M & W
Golden West College *California* M & W
Goldey-Beacom College *Delaware* M & W
Gonzaga University *Washington* M & W
Gordon College *Massachusetts* M & W
Gordon College *Georgia* M & W
Goshen College *Indiana* M & W
Goucher College *Maryland* M & W
Grace Bible College *Michigan* M
Grace College *Indiana* M & W
Grace University *Nebraska* M
Graceland University *Iowa* M & W
Grand Canyon University *Arizona* M & W
Grand Valley State University *Michigan* M & W
Grand View University *Iowa* M & W
Great Lakes Christian College *Michigan* M
Green Mountain College *Vermont* M & W
Green River Community College *Washington* W
Greensboro College *North Carolina* M & W
Greenville College *Illinois* M & W
Grinnell College *Iowa* M & W
Grossmont College *California* W
Grove City College *Pennsylvania* M & W
Guilford College *North Carolina* M & W
Gustavus Adolphus College *Minnesota* M & W
Gwynedd-Mercy College *Pennsylvania* M & W
Hagerstown Community College *Maryland* M & W
Hamilton College *New York* M & W
Hamline University *Minnesota* M & W
Hampden-Sydney College *Virginia* M
Hampshire College *Massachusetts* M & W
Hannibal-LaGrange College *Missouri* M & W
Hanover College *Indiana* M & W
Hardin-Simmons University *Texas* M & W
Harding University *Arkansas* M & W
Harford Community College *Maryland* M & W
Harper College *Illinois* M & W
Harris-Stowe State University *Missouri* M & W
Harrisburg Area Community College *Pennsylvania* M
Hartnell College *California* M & W
Hartwick College *New York* M & W
Harvard University *Massachusetts* M & W
Harvey Mudd College *California* M & W
Hastings College *Nebraska* M & W
Haverford College *Pennsylvania* M & W
Hawai'i Pacific University *Hawaii* M & W
Heartland Community College *Illinois* M & W
Heidelberg University *Ohio* M & W
Hendrix College *Arkansas* M & W
Herkimer County Community College *New York* M & W
Hesston College *Kansas* M & W
High Point University *North Carolina* M & W
Highline Community College *Washington* M & W
Hilbert College *New York* M & W
Hill College of the Hill Junior College District *Texas* M & W
Hillsdale College *Michigan* M & W
Hillsdale Free Will Baptist College *Oklahoma* M
Hinds Community College *Mississippi* M & W
Hiram College *Ohio* M & W
Hobart and William Smith Colleges *New York* M & W
Hofstra University *New York* M & W
Hollins University *Virginia* W
Holmes Community College *Mississippi* M
Holy Cross College *Indiana* M & W
Holy Family University *Pennsylvania* M & W
Holy Names University *California* M & W
Holyoke Community College *Massachusetts* M & W
Hood College *Maryland* M & W
Hope College *Michigan* M & W
Hope International University *California* M & W
Houghton College *New York* M & W
Houston Baptist University *Texas* M & W
Howard Community College *Maryland* M & W
Howard Payne University *Texas* M & W
Howard University *District of Columbia* M
Hudson Valley Community College *New York* M
Humboldt State University *California* M & W
Hunter College of the City University of New York *New York* M
Huntingdon College *Alabama* M & W
Huntington University *Indiana* M & W
Husson University *Maine* M & W
Huston-Tillotson University *Texas* M & W
Hutchinson Community College and Area Vocational School *Kansas* W
Idaho State University *Idaho* W
Illinois Central College *Illinois* M & W
Illinois College *Illinois* M & W
Illinois Institute of Technology *Illinois* M & W
Illinois State University *Illinois* W
Illinois Wesleyan University *Illinois* M & W
Immaculata University *Pennsylvania* W
Imperial Valley College *California* M & W
Indiana State University *Indiana* W
Indiana Tech *Indiana* M & W
Indiana University Bloomington *Indiana* M & W
Indiana University of Pennsylvania *Pennsylvania* W
Indiana University–Purdue University Fort Wayne *Indiana* M & W
Indiana University–Purdue University Indianapolis *Indiana* M & W
Indiana Wesleyan University *Indiana* M & W
Inter American University of Puerto Rico, Aguadilla Campus *Puerto Rico* M
Inter American University of Puerto Rico, San Germán Campus *Puerto Rico* M
Iona College *New York* M & W
Iowa Central Community College *Iowa* M & W
Iowa Lakes Community College *Iowa* M & W
Iowa State University of Science and Technology *Iowa* W
Iowa Wesleyan College *Iowa* M & W
Irvine Valley College *California* M & W
Ithaca College *New York* M & W
Jackson Community College *Michigan* M & W
Jackson State University *Mississippi* W
Jacksonville State University *Alabama* W
Jacksonville University *Florida* M & W
James Madison University *Virginia* M & W
Jamestown College *North Dakota* M & W
Jamestown Community College *New York* M & W
Jefferson College *Missouri* M
Jefferson Community College *New York* M & W
John Brown University *Arkansas* M & W
John Carroll University *Ohio* M & W
John Jay College of Criminal Justice of the City University of New York *New York* M & W
The Johns Hopkins University *Maryland* M & W
Johnson Bible College *Tennessee* M & W
Johnson County Community College *Kansas* M & W
Johnson State College *Vermont* M & W
Johnson & Wales University *Rhode Island* M & W
Johnson & Wales University *Colorado* M
Jones County Junior College *Mississippi* M & W
Judson College *Alabama* W
Judson University *Illinois* M & W
Juniata College *Pennsylvania* M & W
Kalamazoo College *Michigan* M & W
Kankakee Community College *Illinois* M
Kansas City Kansas Community College *Kansas* M
Kansas Wesleyan University *Kansas* M & W
Kaskaskia College *Illinois* M & W
Kean University *New Jersey* M & W
Keene State College *New Hampshire* M & W
Kellogg Community College *Michigan* M
Kennesaw State University *Georgia* M & W
Kent State University *Ohio* W
Kentucky Christian University *Kentucky* M & W
Kentucky Wesleyan College *Kentucky* M & W
Kenyon College *Ohio* M & W
Keuka College *New York* M & W

M = Men; W = Women

Keystone College *Pennsylvania* M & W
King College *Tennessee* M & W
King's College *Pennsylvania* M & W
The King's University College *Alberta* M & W
Kingsborough Community College of the City University of New York *New York* M
Kirkwood Community College *Iowa* M & W
Kishwaukee College *Illinois* M
Knox College *Illinois* M & W
Kutztown University of Pennsylvania *Pennsylvania* M & W
Kuyper College *Michigan* M
Kwantlen Polytechnic University *British Columbia* M & W
La Roche College *Pennsylvania* M & W
La Salle University *Pennsylvania* M & W
La Sierra University *California* M & W
Lackawanna College *Pennsylvania* W
Lafayette College *Pennsylvania* M & W
LaGrange College *Georgia* M & W
Lake Erie College *Ohio* M & W
Lake Forest College *Illinois* M & W
Lakehead University *Ontario* M & W
Lakeland College *Wisconsin* M & W
Lakeland Community College *Ohio* M
Lamar University *Texas* W
Lambuth University *Tennessee* M & W
Lancaster Bible College & Graduate School *Pennsylvania* M & W
Lander University *South Carolina* M & W
Landmark College *Vermont* M & W
Lane Community College *Oregon* W
Laramie County Community College *Wyoming* M & W
Las Positas College *California* M & W
Lasell College *Massachusetts* M & W
Laurentian University *Ontario* M
Lawrence University *Wisconsin* M & W
Le Moyne College *New York* M & W
Lebanon Valley College *Pennsylvania* M & W
Lee University *Tennessee* M & W
Lees-McRae College *North Carolina* M & W
Lehigh Carbon Community College *Pennsylvania* M
Lehigh University *Pennsylvania* M & W
Lehman College of the City University of New York *New York* M & W
Lenoir-Rhyne University *North Carolina* M & W
Lesley University *Massachusetts* M & W
LeTourneau University *Texas* M & W
Lewis & Clark College *Oregon* M & W
Lewis and Clark Community College *Illinois* M & W
Lewis University *Illinois* M & W
Liberty University *Virginia* M & W
Limestone College *South Carolina* M & W
Lincoln Christian University *Illinois* M & W
Lincoln College *Illinois* M & W
Lincoln Land Community College *Illinois* M
Lincoln Memorial University *Tennessee* M & W
Lincoln University *Pennsylvania* M & W
Lindenwood University *Missouri* M & W
Lindsey Wilson College *Kentucky* M & W
Linfield College *Oregon* M & W
Lipscomb University *Tennessee* M & W
Lock Haven University of Pennsylvania *Pennsylvania* M & W
Logan University–College of Chiropractic *Missouri* M
Lon Morris College *Texas* M & W
Long Beach City College *California* M & W
Long Island University, Brooklyn Campus *New York* M & W
Long Island University, C.W. Post Campus *New York* M & W
Longwood University *Virginia* M & W
Loras College *Iowa* M & W
Los Angeles Harbor College *California* M & W
Los Angeles Valley College *California* W
Los Medanos College *California* M
Louisburg College *North Carolina* M & W
Louisiana College *Louisiana* M & W
Louisiana State University and Agricultural and Mechanical College *Louisiana* W
Louisiana State University in Shreveport *Louisiana* W
Loyola Marymount University *California* M & W
Loyola University Chicago *Illinois* M & W
Loyola University Maryland *Maryland* M & W
Loyola University New Orleans *Louisiana* M & W
Luther College *Iowa* M & W
Luzerne County Community College *Pennsylvania* M & W
Lycoming College *Pennsylvania* M & W
Lynchburg College *Virginia* M & W
Lyndon State College *Vermont* M & W
Lyon College *Arkansas* M & W
Macalester College *Minnesota* M & W
MacMurray College *Illinois* M & W
Macomb Community College *Michigan* M
Madonna University *Michigan* M & W
Maharishi University of Management *Iowa* M & W
Maine Maritime Academy *Maine* M & W
Malone University *Ohio* M & W
Manchester College *Indiana* M & W
Manchester Community College *New Hampshire* M & W
Manchester Community College *Connecticut* M & W
Manhattan Christian College *Kansas* M & W
Manhattan College *New York* M & W
Manhattanville College *New York* M & W
Manor College *Pennsylvania* M & W
Mansfield University of Pennsylvania *Pennsylvania* W
Maranatha Baptist Bible College *Wisconsin* M & W
Marian University *Wisconsin* M & W
Marian University *Indiana* M & W
Marietta College *Ohio* M & W
Marion Military Institute *Alabama* M & W
Marist College *New York* M & W
Marlboro College *Vermont* M & W
Marquette University *Wisconsin* M & W
Mars Hill College *North Carolina* M & W
Marshall University *West Virginia* M & W
Marshalltown Community College *Iowa* M & W
Martin Luther College *Minnesota* M & W
Martin Methodist College *Tennessee* M & W
Mary Baldwin College *Virginia* W
Marymount College, Palos Verdes, California *California* M
Marymount University *Virginia* M & W
Maryville College *Tennessee* M & W
Maryville University of Saint Louis *Missouri* M & W
Marywood University *Pennsylvania* M & W
Massachusetts Bay Community College *Massachusetts* M & W
Massachusetts College of Liberal Arts *Massachusetts* M & W
Massachusetts Institute of Technology *Massachusetts* M & W
Massachusetts Maritime Academy *Massachusetts* M
Massasoit Community College *Massachusetts* M & W
The Master's College and Seminary *California* M & W
McDaniel College *Maryland* M & W
McGill University *Quebec* M & W
McHenry County College *Illinois* M
McKendree University *Illinois* M & W
McMaster University *Ontario* M & W
McMurry University *Texas* M & W
McNeese State University *Louisiana* W
McPherson College *Kansas* M & W
Medaille College *New York* M & W
Medgar Evers College of the City University of New York *New York* M & W
Memorial University of Newfoundland *Newfoundland and Labrador* M & W
Mendocino College *California* W
Menlo College *California* M & W
Merced College *California* M
Mercer County Community College *New Jersey* M & W
Mercer University *Georgia* M & W
Mercy College *New York* M & W
Mercyhurst College *Pennsylvania* M & W
Meredith College *North Carolina* W
Meridian Community College *Mississippi* M
Merrimack College *Massachusetts* M & W
Mesa Community College *Arizona* M & W
Mesa State College *Colorado* M & W
Messiah College *Pennsylvania* M & W
Methodist University *North Carolina* M & W
Metropolitan Community College–Blue River *Missouri* M & W
Metropolitan Community College–Maple Woods *Missouri* M & W
Metropolitan State College of Denver *Colorado* M & W
Miami University *Ohio* M & W
Michigan State University *Michigan* M & W
Michigan Technological University *Michigan* M & W
Mid-America Christian University *Oklahoma* M & W
Mid-Continent University *Kentucky* M
MidAmerica Nazarene University *Kansas* M & W
Middle Georgia College *Georgia* M & W
Middle Tennessee State University *Tennessee* W
Middlebury College *Vermont* M & W
Middlesex County College *New Jersey* M & W
Midland Lutheran College *Nebraska* M & W
Midway College *Kentucky* W
Midwestern State University *Texas* M & W
Millersville University of Pennsylvania *Pennsylvania* M & W
Milligan College *Tennessee* M & W
Millikin University *Illinois* M & W
Mills College *California* W
Millsaps College *Mississippi* M & W
Milwaukee Area Technical College *Wisconsin* M
Milwaukee School of Engineering *Wisconsin* M & W
Minnesota State University Mankato *Minnesota* W
Minnesota State University Moorhead *Minnesota* W
MiraCosta College *California* W
Misericordia University *Pennsylvania* M & W
Mission College *California* M & W
Mississippi College *Mississippi* M & W
Mississippi Delta Community College *Mississippi* M
Mississippi Gulf Coast Community College *Mississippi* M & W
Mississippi State University *Mississippi* W
Missouri Baptist University *Missouri* M & W
Missouri Southern State University *Missouri* M & W
Missouri State University *Missouri* M & W
Missouri University of Science and Technology *Missouri* M & W
Missouri Valley College *Missouri* M & W
Missouri Western State University *Missouri* W
Mitchell College *Connecticut* M & W
Modesto Junior College *California* M & W
Mohawk Valley Community College *New York* M & W
Molloy College *New York* M & W
Monmouth College *Illinois* M & W
Monmouth University *New Jersey* M & W
Monroe College (Bronx) *New York* M
Monroe College (New Rochelle) *New York* M
Monroe Community College *New York* M & W
Montana State University Billings *Montana* M & W
Montclair State University *New Jersey* M & W
Montgomery College *Maryland* M & W
Montgomery County Community College *Pennsylvania* M & W
Montreat College *North Carolina* M & W
Moody Bible Institute *Illinois* M
Moorpark College *California* M & W
Moraine Valley Community College *Illinois* M & W
Moravian College *Pennsylvania* M & W
Morehead State University *Kentucky* W
Morningside College *Iowa* M & W
Morton College *Illinois* M
Mount Allison University *New Brunswick* M & W
Mount Aloysius College *Pennsylvania* M & W
Mount Holyoke College *Massachusetts* W
Mount Ida College *Massachusetts* M & W
Mount Marty College *South Dakota* M & W
Mount Mary College *Wisconsin* W
Mount Mercy College *Iowa* M & W
Mount Olive College *North Carolina* M & W
Mount Saint Mary College *New York* M & W
Mount St. Mary's University *Maryland* M & W
Mount Saint Vincent University *Nova Scotia* M & W

M = Men; W = Women

Mt. San Antonio College *California* M & W
Mt. San Jacinto College *California* W
Mount Vernon Nazarene University *Ohio* M & W
Mountain State University *West Virginia* M & W
Muhlenberg College *Pennsylvania* M & W
Murray State University *Kentucky* W
Muskingum University *Ohio* M & W
Napa Valley College *California* M
Nashua Community College *New Hampshire* M & W
Nassau Community College *New York* M & W
Navarro College *Texas* W
Nazareth College of Rochester *New York* M & W
Nebraska Christian College *Nebraska* M
Nebraska Wesleyan University *Nebraska* M & W
Neumann University *Pennsylvania* M & W
New England College *New Hampshire* M & W
New Jersey City University *New Jersey* M & W
New Jersey Institute of Technology *New Jersey* M & W
New Mexico Highlands University *New Mexico* W
New Mexico Institute of Mining and Technology *New Mexico* M & W
New York City College of Technology of the City University of New York *New York* M
New York Institute of Technology *New York* M & W
New York University *New York* M & W
Newberry College *South Carolina* M & W
Newbury College *Massachusetts* M & W
Newman University *Kansas* M & W
NHTI, Concord's Community College *New Hampshire* M & W
Niagara County Community College *New York* M & W
Niagara University *New York* M & W
Nicholls State University *Louisiana* W
Nichols College *Massachusetts* M & W
Nipissing University *Ontario* M & W
North Carolina State University *North Carolina* M & W
North Carolina Wesleyan College *North Carolina* M & W
North Central College *Illinois* M & W
North Central University *Minnesota* M & W
North Country Community College *New York* M & W
North Dakota State University *North Dakota* M & W
North Georgia College & State University *Georgia* M & W
North Greenville University *South Carolina* M & W
North Idaho College *Idaho* M & W
North Iowa Area Community College *Iowa* M
North Park University *Illinois* M & W
Northampton Community College *Pennsylvania* M
Northeastern Oklahoma Agricultural and Mechanical College *Oklahoma* M & W
Northeastern State University *Oklahoma* M & W
Northeastern University *Massachusetts* M & W
Northern Arizona University *Arizona* W
Northern Illinois University *Illinois* M & W
Northern Kentucky University *Kentucky* M & W
Northern Maine Community College *Maine* M & W
Northern Michigan University *Michigan* M & W
Northern Oklahoma College *Oklahoma* M & W
Northern State University *South Dakota* W
Northland College *Wisconsin* M & W
Northwest Christian University *Oregon* M & W
Northwest College *Wyoming* M & W
Northwest Missouri State University *Missouri* W
Northwest Nazarene University *Idaho* M & W
Northwest University *Washington* M & W
Northwestern College *Minnesota* M & W
Northwestern College *Iowa* M & W
Northwestern Oklahoma State University *Oklahoma* W
Northwestern State University of Louisiana *Louisiana* W
Northwestern University *Illinois* M & W
Northwood University *Michigan* M & W
Northwood University, Florida Campus *Florida* M & W
Northwood University, Texas Campus *Texas* M & W
Norwich University *Vermont* M & W
Notre Dame College *Ohio* M & W
Notre Dame de Namur University *California* M & W
Nova Scotia Agricultural College *Nova Scotia* M & W
Nova Southeastern University *Florida* M & W
Oakland City University *Indiana* M & W
Oakland Community College *Michigan* M
Oakland University *Michigan* M & W
Oakton Community College *Illinois* M & W
Oberlin College *Ohio* M & W
Occidental College *California* M & W
Ocean County College *New Jersey* M & W
Oglethorpe University *Georgia* M & W
Ohio Christian University *Ohio* M
Ohio Dominican University *Ohio* M & W
Ohio Northern University *Ohio* M & W
The Ohio State University *Ohio* M & W
The Ohio State University at Marion *Ohio* M
The Ohio State University–Mansfield Campus *Ohio* M & W
Ohio University *Ohio* W
Ohio Valley University *West Virginia* M & W
Ohio Wesleyan University *Ohio* M & W
Ohlone College *California* M & W
Okanagan College *British Columbia* M & W
Oklahoma Baptist University *Oklahoma* M & W
Oklahoma Christian University *Oklahoma* M & W
Oklahoma City University *Oklahoma* M & W
Oklahoma Panhandle State University *Oklahoma* M & W
Oklahoma Wesleyan University *Oklahoma* M & W
Old Dominion University *Virginia* M & W
Olivet College *Michigan* M & W
Olivet Nazarene University *Illinois* M & W
Olympic College *Washington* M & W
Oral Roberts University *Oklahoma* M & W
Orange Coast College *California* M & W
Orange County Community College *New York* M & W
Oregon Institute of Technology *Oregon* W
Oregon State University *Oregon* M & W
Otero Junior College *Colorado* M
Ottawa University *Kansas* M & W
Otterbein University *Ohio* M & W
Ouachita Baptist University *Arkansas* M & W
Our Lady of the Lake University of San Antonio *Texas* M & W
Owens Community College *Ohio* M
Oxnard College *California* M & W
Ozark Christian College *Missouri* M
Pace University *New York* W
Pacific Lutheran University *Washington* M & W
Pacific University *Oregon* M & W
Palm Beach Atlantic University *Florida* M & W
Palomar College *California* M & W
Paradise Valley Community College *Arizona* M & W
Park University *Missouri* M & W
Parkland College *Illinois* M & W
Pasadena City College *California* M & W
Passaic County Community College *New Jersey* M
Patrick Henry College *Virginia* M & W
Paul Quinn College *Texas* M & W
Paul Smith's College *New York* M & W
Peace College *North Carolina* W
Pearl River Community College *Mississippi* M & W
Peninsula College *Washington* M
Penn State Abington *Pennsylvania* M & W
Penn State Altoona *Pennsylvania* M & W
Penn State Berks *Pennsylvania* M & W
Penn State Brandywine *Pennsylvania* M & W
Penn State Erie, The Behrend College *Pennsylvania* M & W
Penn State Harrisburg *Pennsylvania* M & W
Penn State Hazleton *Pennsylvania* M
Penn State Lehigh Valley *Pennsylvania* M & W
Penn State Mont Alto *Pennsylvania* M & W
Penn State Schuylkill *Pennsylvania* M
Penn State University Park *Pennsylvania* M & W
Penn State Wilkes-Barre *Pennsylvania* M & W
Penn State Worthington Scranton *Pennsylvania* M
Pennsylvania College of Technology *Pennsylvania* M & W
Pepperdine University *California* M & W
Pfeiffer University *North Carolina* M & W
Philadelphia Biblical University *Pennsylvania* M & W
Philadelphia University *Pennsylvania* M & W
Phoenix College *Arizona* M & W
Piedmont Baptist College and Graduate School *North Carolina* M
Piedmont College *Georgia* M & W
Pierce College at Puyallup *Washington* M
Pikeville College *Kentucky* M & W
Pima Community College *Arizona* M & W
Pine Manor College *Massachusetts* W
Pitzer College *California* M & W
Plymouth State University *New Hampshire* M & W
Point Loma Nazarene University *California* M & W
Point Park University *Pennsylvania* M
Polk State College *Florida* W
Polytechnic Institute of NYU *New York* M & W
Polytechnic University of Puerto Rico *Puerto Rico* M
Pomona College *California* M & W
Porterville College *California* M & W
Portland State University *Oregon* W
Post University *Connecticut* M & W
Potomac State College of West Virginia University *West Virginia* M & W
Prairie State College *Illinois* M & W
Prairie View A&M University *Texas* W
Pratt Institute *New York* M & W
Presbyterian College *South Carolina* M & W
Presentation College *South Dakota* M & W
Prince George's Community College *Maryland* M & W
Princeton University *New Jersey* M & W
Principia College *Illinois* M & W
Providence College *Rhode Island* M & W
Providence College and Theological Seminary *Manitoba* M & W
Purchase College, State University of New York *New York* M & W
Purdue University *Indiana* W
Queens College of the City University of New York *New York* M & W
Queens University of Charlotte *North Carolina* M & W
Queen's University at Kingston *Ontario* M & W
Queensborough Community College of the City University of New York *New York* M
Quincy University *Illinois* M & W
Quinnipiac University *Connecticut* M & W
Radford University *Virginia* M & W
Ramapo College of New Jersey *New Jersey* M & W
Randolph College *Virginia* M & W
Randolph-Macon College *Virginia* M & W
Raritan Valley Community College *New Jersey* M
Reading Area Community College *Pennsylvania* M & W
Redeemer University College *Ontario* M & W
Reed College *Oregon* M & W
Regis College *Massachusetts* M & W
Regis University *Colorado* M & W
Reinhardt University *Georgia* M & W
Rensselaer Polytechnic Institute *New York* M & W
Research College of Nursing *Missouri* M & W
Rhode Island College *Rhode Island* M & W
Rhodes College *Tennessee* M & W
Rice University *Texas* M & W
The Richard Stockton College of New Jersey *New Jersey* M & W
Richland College *Texas* M & W
Rider University *New Jersey* M & W
Ridgewater College *Minnesota* M
Ripon College *Wisconsin* M & W
Riverside Community College District *California* M & W
Rivier College *New Hampshire* M & W
Roanoke College *Virginia* M & W
Robert Morris University *Pennsylvania* M & W
Robert Morris University Illinois *Illinois* M & W
Roberts Wesleyan College *New York* M & W
Rochester College *Michigan* M & W
Rochester Community and Technical College *Minnesota* W
Rochester Institute of Technology *New York* M & W

M = Men; W = Women

Rockford College *Illinois* M & W
Rockhurst University *Missouri* M & W
Rockland Community College *New York* M & W
Rocky Mountain College *Alberta* M
Rocky Mountain College *Montana* M & W
Roger Williams University *Rhode Island* M & W
Rogers State University *Oklahoma* M & W
Rollins College *Florida* M & W
Rose-Hulman Institute of Technology *Indiana* M & W
Rose State College *Oklahoma* W
Rosemont College *Pennsylvania* M
Rowan University *New Jersey* M & W
Roxbury Community College *Massachusetts* M & W
Royal Military College of Canada *Ontario* M & W
Russell Sage College *New York* W
Rutgers, The State University of New Jersey, Camden *New Jersey* M & W
Rutgers, The State University of New Jersey, New Brunswick *New Jersey* M & W
Rutgers, The State University of New Jersey, Newark *New Jersey* M & W
Ryerson University *Ontario* M & W
Sacramento City College *California* W
Sacred Heart University *Connecticut* M & W
Sage College of Albany *New York* M & W
Saginaw Valley State University *Michigan* M & W
St. Ambrose University *Iowa* M & W
St. Andrews Presbyterian College *North Carolina* M & W
Saint Anselm College *New Hampshire* M & W
St. Bonaventure University *New York* M & W
St. Catherine University *Minnesota* W
Saint Charles Community College *Missouri* M & W
St. Cloud State University *Minnesota* M & W
St. Edward's University *Texas* M & W
St. Francis College *New York* M
Saint Francis University *Pennsylvania* M & W
St. Francis Xavier University *Nova Scotia* M & W
St. Gregory's University *Oklahoma* M & W
St. John Fisher College *New York* M & W
St. John's University *New York* M & W
Saint John's University *Minnesota* M
Saint Joseph College *Connecticut* W
Saint Joseph's College *Indiana* M & W
Saint Joseph's College of Maine *Maine* M & W
Saint Joseph's University *Pennsylvania* M & W
St. Lawrence University *New York* M & W
Saint Leo University *Florida* M & W
St. Louis Community College at Florissant Valley *Missouri* M & W
St. Louis Community College at Forest Park *Missouri* M & W
St. Louis Community College at Meramec *Missouri* M & W
Saint Louis University *Missouri* M & W
Saint Martin's University *Washington* M & W
Saint Mary-of-the-Woods College *Indiana* W
Saint Mary's College *Indiana* W
Saint Mary's College of California *California* M & W
St. Mary's College of Maryland *Maryland* M & W
Saint Mary's University *Nova Scotia* M & W
St. Mary's University *Texas* M & W
Saint Mary's University of Minnesota *Minnesota* M & W
Saint Michael's College *Vermont* M & W
St. Norbert College *Wisconsin* M & W
St. Olaf College *Minnesota* M & W
Saint Peter's College *New Jersey* M & W
St. Thomas Aquinas College *New York* M & W
St. Thomas University *New Brunswick* M & W
St. Thomas University *Florida* M & W
Saint Vincent College *Pennsylvania* M & W
Saint Xavier University *Illinois* M & W
Salem College *North Carolina* W
Salem International University *West Virginia* M & W
Salem State College *Massachusetts* M & W
Salisbury University *Maryland* M & W
Salt Lake Community College *Utah* M & W
Salve Regina University *Rhode Island* M & W
Sam Houston State University *Texas* M & W
Samford University *Alabama* M & W
San Bernardino Valley College *California* M & W
San Diego Christian College *California* M & W
San Diego City College *California* M & W
San Diego Mesa College *California* M & W
San Diego State University *California* M & W
San Francisco State University *California* M & W
San Jacinto College District *Texas* M & W
San Joaquin Delta College *California* M & W
San Jose State University *California* M & W
Santa Ana College *California* M
Santa Barbara City College *California* M & W
Santa Clara University *California* M & W
Santa Monica College *California* W
Santa Rosa Junior College *California* M & W
Sarah Lawrence College *New York* M
Savannah College of Art and Design *Georgia* M & W
Schoolcraft College *Michigan* M & W
Schreiner University *Texas* M & W
Scott Community College *Iowa* M & W
Scottsdale Community College *Arizona* M & W
Scripps College *California* W
Seattle Pacific University *Washington* M & W
Seattle University *Washington* M & W
Seton Hall University *New Jersey* M & W
Seton Hill University *Pennsylvania* M & W
Sewanee: The University of the South *Tennessee* M & W
Shasta College *California* M & W
Shawnee State University *Ohio* M & W
Shelton State Community College *Alabama* W
Shenandoah University *Virginia* M & W
Shepherd University *West Virginia* M & W
Shippensburg University of Pennsylvania *Pennsylvania* M & W
Shoreline Community College *Washington* M & W
Shorter University *Georgia* M & W
Siena College *New York* M & W
Siena Heights University *Michigan* M & W
Sierra College *California* W
Simmons College *Massachusetts* W
Simon Fraser University *British Columbia* M & W
Simpson College *Iowa* M & W
Simpson University *California* M & W
Skagit Valley College *Washington* M & W
Skidmore College *New York* M & W
Skyline College *California* M
Slippery Rock University of Pennsylvania *Pennsylvania* M & W
Smith College *Massachusetts* W
Soka University of America *California* M & W
Sonoma State University *California* M & W
South Carolina State University *South Carolina* W
South Dakota State University *South Dakota* M & W
South Georgia College *Georgia* M
South Mountain Community College *Arizona* M
South Puget Sound Community College *Washington* M
South Suburban College *Illinois* M & W
Southeast Missouri State University *Missouri* W
Southeastern Louisiana University *Louisiana* W
Southeastern University *Florida* M & W
Southern Alberta Institute of Technology *Alberta* M & W
Southern Connecticut State University *Connecticut* M & W
Southern Illinois University Edwardsville *Illinois* M & W
Southern Maine Community College *Maine* M & W
Southern Methodist University *Texas* M & W
Southern Nazarene University *Oklahoma* M & W
Southern New Hampshire University *New Hampshire* M & W
Southern Oregon University *Oregon* W
Southern Polytechnic State University *Georgia* M
Southern State Community College *Ohio* M
Southern Vermont College *Vermont* M & W
Southern Virginia University *Virginia* M & W
Southern Wesleyan University *South Carolina* M & W
Southwest Baptist University *Missouri* M & W
Southwest Minnesota State University *Minnesota* W
Southwest Mississippi Community College *Mississippi* M & W
Southwestern Assemblies of God University *Texas* M & W
Southwestern Christian University *Oklahoma* M
Southwestern College *Kansas* M & W
Southwestern College *California* M & W
Southwestern College *Arizona* M
Southwestern Illinois College *Illinois* M
Southwestern Oklahoma State University *Oklahoma* W
Southwestern Oregon Community College *Oregon* M & W
Southwestern University *Texas* M & W
Spalding University *Kentucky* M & W
Spartanburg Methodist College *South Carolina* M & W
Spelman College *Georgia* W
Spokane Community College *Washington* M & W
Spokane Falls Community College *Washington* M & W
Spring Arbor University *Michigan* M & W
Spring Hill College *Alabama* M & W
Springfield College *Massachusetts* M & W
Springfield College in Illinois *Illinois* M & W
Springfield Technical Community College *Massachusetts* M & W
Stanford University *California* M & W
State University of New York at Binghamton *New York* M & W
State University of New York College of Agriculture and Technology at Cobleskill *New York* M & W
State University of New York College of Agriculture and Technology at Morrisville *New York* M & W
State University of New York College at Cortland *New York* M & W
State University of New York College of Environmental Science and Forestry *New York* M & W
State University of New York College at Geneseo *New York* M & W
State University of New York College at Old Westbury *New York* M
State University of New York College at Oneonta *New York* M & W
State University of New York College at Potsdam *New York* M & W
State University of New York College of Technology at Alfred *New York* M & W
State University of New York College of Technology at Canton *New York* M & W
State University of New York College of Technology at Delhi *New York* M & W
State University of New York at Fredonia *New York* M & W
State University of New York Institute of Technology *New York* M & W
State University of New York Maritime College *New York* M & W
State University of New York at New Paltz *New York* M & W
State University of New York at Oswego *New York* M & W
State University of New York at Plattsburgh *New York* M & W
Stephen F. Austin State University *Texas* W
Sterling College *Kansas* M & W
Stetson University *Florida* M & W
Stevens Institute of Technology *New Jersey* M & W
Stevenson University *Maryland* M & W
Stonehill College *Massachusetts* M & W
Stony Brook University, State University of New York *New York* M & W
Suffolk County Community College *New York* M
Suffolk University *Massachusetts* M
Susquehanna University *Pennsylvania* M & W
Sussex County Community College *New Jersey* M & W
Swarthmore College *Pennsylvania* M & W
Sweet Briar College *Virginia* W
Syracuse University *New York* M & W
Tabor College *Kansas* M & W
Tacoma Community College *Washington* M & W
Taft College *California* M

M = Men; W = Women

Taylor University *Indiana* M & W
Temple University *Pennsylvania* M & W
Tennessee Technological University *Tennessee* W
Tennessee Temple University *Tennessee* M
Tennessee Wesleyan College *Tennessee* M & W
Texas A&M International University *Texas* M & W
Texas A&M University *Texas* W
Texas A&M University–Commerce *Texas* W
Texas Christian University *Texas* W
Texas College *Texas* M & W
Texas Lutheran University *Texas* M & W
Texas Southern University *Texas* M & W
Texas Southmost College *Texas* M & W
Texas State University–San Marcos *Texas* M & W
Texas Tech University *Texas* W
Texas Wesleyan University *Texas* M & W
Texas Woman's University *Texas* W
Thiel College *Pennsylvania* M & W
Thomas College *Maine* M & W
Thomas More College *Kentucky* M & W
Thomas University *Georgia* M & W
Thompson Rivers University *British Columbia* M & W
Tiffin University *Ohio* M & W
Toccoa Falls College *Georgia* M & W
Tompkins Cortland Community College *New York* M & W
Towson University *Maryland* M & W
Transylvania University *Kentucky* M & W
Treasure Valley Community College *Oregon* M & W
Trent University *Ontario* M & W
Trevecca Nazarene University *Tennessee* M & W
Tri-County Technical College *South Carolina* M
Trine University *Indiana* M & W
Trinity Christian College *Illinois* M & W
Trinity College *Connecticut* M & W
Trinity International University *Illinois* M & W
Trinity University *Texas* M & W
Trinity (Washington) University *District of Columbia* W
Trinity Western University *British Columbia* M & W
Triton College *Illinois* M
Troy University *Alabama* W
Truett-McConnell College *Georgia* M & W
Truman State University *Missouri* M & W
Tufts University *Massachusetts* M & W
Tulane University *Louisiana* M & W
Tusculum College *Tennessee* M & W
Tuskegee University *Alabama* M
Tyler Junior College *Texas* M
Ulster County Community College *New York* M
Union College *New York* M & W
Union College *Kentucky* M & W
Union County College *New Jersey* M
Union University *Tennessee* M & W
United States Air Force Academy *Colorado* M & W
United States Coast Guard Academy *Connecticut* M & W
United States Merchant Marine Academy *New York* M
United States Military Academy *New York* M & W
United States Naval Academy *Maryland* M & W
Unity College *Maine* M
Université Laval *Quebec* M & W
Université de Moncton *New Brunswick* M & W
Université de Montréal *Quebec* M & W
Université du Québec àChicoutimi *Quebec* W
Université du Québec àTrois-Rivières *Quebec* M & W
Université de Sherbrooke *Quebec* M & W
The University of Akron *Ohio* M & W
The University of Alabama *Alabama* W
The University of Alabama at Birmingham *Alabama* M & W
The University of Alabama in Huntsville *Alabama* M & W
University at Albany, State University of New York *New York* M & W
University of Alberta *Alberta* M & W
The University of Arizona *Arizona* M & W
University of Arkansas *Arkansas* W
University of Arkansas at Little Rock *Arkansas* W
University of Bridgeport *Connecticut* M & W
The University of British Columbia *British Columbia* M & W
The University of British Columbia–Okanagan *British Columbia* M & W
University at Buffalo, the State University of New York *New York* M & W
University of Calgary *Alberta* M & W
University of California, Berkeley *California* M & W
University of California, Davis *California* M & W
University of California, Irvine *California* M & W
University of California, Los Angeles *California* M & W
University of California, Riverside *California* M & W
University of California, San Diego *California* M & W
University of California, Santa Barbara *California* M & W
University of California, Santa Cruz *California* M & W
University of Central Arkansas *Arkansas* M & W
University of Central Florida *Florida* M & W
University of Central Missouri *Missouri* M & W
University of Central Oklahoma *Oklahoma* W
University of Charleston *West Virginia* M & W
University of Chicago *Illinois* M & W
University of Cincinnati *Ohio* M & W
University of Colorado at Boulder *Colorado* M & W
University of Colorado at Colorado Springs *Colorado* M & W
University of Connecticut *Connecticut* M & W
University of the Cumberlands *Kentucky* M & W
University of Dallas *Texas* M & W
University of Dayton *Ohio* M & W
University of Delaware *Delaware* M & W
University of Denver *Colorado* M & W
University of Detroit Mercy *Michigan* M & W
University of the District of Columbia *District of Columbia* M
University of Dubuque *Iowa* M & W
University of Evansville *Indiana* M & W
The University of Findlay *Ohio* M & W
University of Florida *Florida* M & W
University of the Fraser Valley *British Columbia* M & W
University of Georgia *Georgia* W
University of Great Falls *Montana* M & W
University of Guelph *Ontario* M & W
University of Hartford *Connecticut* M & W
University of Hawaii at Manoa *Hawaii* W
University of Houston *Texas* W
University of Idaho *Idaho* M & W
University of Illinois at Chicago *Illinois* M
University of Illinois at Springfield *Illinois* M & W
University of Illinois at Urbana–Champaign *Illinois* W
University of the Incarnate Word *Texas* M & W
University of Indianapolis *Indiana* M & W
The University of Iowa *Iowa* M & W
The University of Kansas *Kansas* W
University of Kentucky *Kentucky* M & W
University of King's College *Nova Scotia* M & W
University of La Verne *California* M & W
University of Lethbridge *Alberta* M & W
University of Louisiana at Lafayette *Louisiana* W
University of Louisiana at Monroe *Louisiana* M & W
University of Louisville *Kentucky* M & W
University of Maine *Maine* W
University of Maine at Augusta *Maine* W
University of Maine at Farmington *Maine* M & W
University of Maine at Fort Kent *Maine* M & W
University of Maine at Machias *Maine* M & W
University of Maine at Presque Isle *Maine* M & W
University of Mary *North Dakota* M & W
University of Mary Hardin-Baylor *Texas* M & W
University of Mary Washington *Virginia* M & W
University of Maryland, Baltimore County *Maryland* M & W
University of Maryland, College Park *Maryland* M & W
University of Massachusetts Amherst *Massachusetts* M & W
University of Massachusetts Boston *Massachusetts* M & W
University of Massachusetts Dartmouth *Massachusetts* M & W
University of Massachusetts Lowell *Massachusetts* M
University of Memphis *Tennessee* M & W
University of Miami *Florida* W
University of Michigan *Michigan* M & W
University of Michigan–Dearborn *Michigan* M & W
University of Minnesota, Crookston *Minnesota* W
University of Minnesota, Duluth *Minnesota* M & W
University of Minnesota, Morris *Minnesota* M & W
University of Minnesota, Twin Cities Campus *Minnesota* W
University of Mississippi *Mississippi* M & W
University of Missouri *Missouri* W
University of Missouri–Kansas City *Missouri* M
University of Missouri–St. Louis *Missouri* M & W
University of Mobile *Alabama* M & W
The University of Montana *Montana* W
University of Montevallo *Alabama* M & W
University of Mount Union *Ohio* M & W
University of Nebraska at Kearney *Nebraska* W
University of Nebraska at Omaha *Nebraska* M & W
University of Nebraska–Lincoln *Nebraska* W
University of Nevada, Las Vegas *Nevada* M & W
University of Nevada, Reno *Nevada* W
University of New Brunswick Fredericton *New Brunswick* M & W
University of New Brunswick Saint John *New Brunswick* M & W
University of New England *Maine* M & W
University of New Hampshire *New Hampshire* M & W
University of New Haven *Connecticut* M & W
University of New Mexico *New Mexico* M & W
University of North Alabama *Alabama* W
The University of North Carolina at Asheville *North Carolina* M & W
The University of North Carolina at Chapel Hill *North Carolina* M & W
The University of North Carolina at Charlotte *North Carolina* M & W
The University of North Carolina at Greensboro *North Carolina* M & W
The University of North Carolina at Pembroke *North Carolina* M & W
The University of North Carolina Wilmington *North Carolina* M & W
University of North Dakota *North Dakota* W
University of North Florida *Florida* M & W
University of North Texas *Texas* M & W
University of Northern Colorado *Colorado* M & W
University of Northern Iowa *Iowa* W
University of Notre Dame *Indiana* M & W
University of Oklahoma *Oklahoma* W
University of Oregon *Oregon* W
University of Ottawa *Ontario* M & W
University of the Ozarks *Arkansas* M & W
University of the Pacific *California* W
University of Pennsylvania *Pennsylvania* M & W
University of Pittsburgh *Pennsylvania* M & W
University of Pittsburgh at Bradford *Pennsylvania* M & W
University of Pittsburgh at Greensburg *Pennsylvania* M & W
University of Pittsburgh at Johnstown *Pennsylvania* M & W
University of Portland *Oregon* M & W
University of Prince Edward Island *Prince Edward Island* M & W
University of Puerto Rico, Cayey University College *Puerto Rico* M
University of Puerto Rico, Mayagüez Campus *Puerto Rico* M
University of Puerto Rico, Río Piedras *Puerto Rico* M
University of Puget Sound *Washington* M & W
University of Redlands *California* M & W
University of Regina *Saskatchewan* W
University of Rhode Island *Rhode Island* M & W
University of Richmond *Virginia* M & W
University of Rio Grande *Ohio* M & W
University of Rochester *New York* M & W
University of Saint Francis *Indiana* M & W

M = Men; W = Women

University of St. Francis *Illinois* M & W
University of Saint Mary *Kansas* M & W
University of St. Thomas *Texas* M & W
University of St. Thomas *Minnesota* M & W
University of San Diego *California* M & W
University of San Francisco *California* M & W
University of Saskatchewan *Saskatchewan* M & W
University of Science and Arts of Oklahoma *Oklahoma* M & W
The University of Scranton *Pennsylvania* M & W
University of Sioux Falls *South Dakota* M & W
University of South Alabama *Alabama* W
University of South Carolina *South Carolina* M & W
University of South Carolina Aiken *South Carolina* M & W
University of South Carolina Lancaster *South Carolina* W
University of South Carolina Salkehatchie *South Carolina* M & W
University of South Carolina Upstate *South Carolina* M & W
The University of South Dakota *South Dakota* W
University of South Florida *Florida* M & W
University of Southern California *California* M & W
University of Southern Indiana *Indiana* M & W
University of Southern Maine *Maine* M & W
University of Southern Mississippi *Mississippi* W
University of the Southwest *New Mexico* M & W
The University of Tampa *Florida* M & W
The University of Tennessee *Tennessee* M & W
The University of Tennessee at Chattanooga *Tennessee* W
The University of Tennessee at Martin *Tennessee* W
The University of Texas at Austin *Texas* M & W
The University of Texas at Brownsville *Texas* M & W
The University of Texas at Dallas *Texas* M & W
The University of Texas of the Permian Basin *Texas* M & W
The University of Texas at Tyler *Texas* M & W
The University of Toledo *Ohio* W
University of Toronto *Ontario* M & W
University of Tulsa *Oklahoma* M & W
University of Utah *Utah* W
University of Vermont *Vermont* M & W
University of Victoria *British Columbia* M & W
University of Virginia *Virginia* M & W
University of Washington *Washington* M & W
University of Waterloo *Ontario* M & W
University of West Florida *Florida* M & W
University of West Georgia *Georgia* W
The University of Western Ontario *Ontario* M & W
University of Windsor *Ontario* M & W
University of Wisconsin–Baraboo/Sauk County *Wisconsin* M & W
University of Wisconsin–Eau Claire *Wisconsin* W
University of Wisconsin–Fond du Lac *Wisconsin* M & W
University of Wisconsin–Fox Valley *Wisconsin* M & W
University of Wisconsin–Green Bay *Wisconsin* M & W
University of Wisconsin–La Crosse *Wisconsin* W
University of Wisconsin–Madison *Wisconsin* M & W
University of Wisconsin–Milwaukee *Wisconsin* M & W
University of Wisconsin–Oshkosh *Wisconsin* M & W
University of Wisconsin–Parkside *Wisconsin* M & W
University of Wisconsin–Platteville *Wisconsin* M & W
University of Wisconsin–River Falls *Wisconsin* M & W
University of Wisconsin–Stevens Point *Wisconsin* W
University of Wisconsin–Stout *Wisconsin* M & W
University of Wisconsin–Superior *Wisconsin* M & W
University of Wisconsin–Washington County *Wisconsin* M & W
University of Wisconsin–Waukesha *Wisconsin* M & W
University of Wisconsin–Whitewater *Wisconsin* M & W
University of Wyoming *Wyoming* M & W
Upper Iowa University *Iowa* M & W
Urbana University *Ohio* M & W
Ursinus College *Pennsylvania* M & W
Ursuline College *Ohio* W
Utah State University *Utah* M & W
Utah Valley University *Utah* W
Utica College *New York* M & W
Valley Forge Christian College *Pennsylvania* M & W
Valley Forge Military College *Pennsylvania* M
Valparaiso University *Indiana* M & W
Vanderbilt University *Tennessee* W
Vanguard University of Southern California *California* M & W
Vassar College *New York* M & W
Ventura College *California* W
Vermont Technical College *Vermont* M & W
Victor Valley College *California* M & W
Villanova University *Pennsylvania* M & W
Virginia Commonwealth University *Virginia* M & W
Virginia Intermont College *Virginia* M
Virginia Military Institute *Virginia* M
Virginia Polytechnic Institute and State University *Virginia* M & W
Virginia Wesleyan College *Virginia* M & W
Viterbo University *Wisconsin* M & W
Wabash College *Indiana* M
Wagner College *New York* W
Wake Forest University *North Carolina* M & W
Waldorf College *Iowa* M & W
Walla Walla Community College *Washington* M & W
Walla Walla University *Washington* M
Wallace State Community College *Alabama* M & W
Walsh University *Ohio* M & W
Warner Pacific College *Oregon* M & W
Warner University *Florida* M & W
Warren Wilson College *North Carolina* M & W
Wartburg College *Iowa* M & W
Washburn University *Kansas* W
Washington Adventist University *Maryland* M & W
Washington College *Maryland* M & W
Washington & Jefferson College *Pennsylvania* M & W
Washington and Lee University *Virginia* M & W
Washington State University *Washington* M & W
Washington University in St. Louis *Missouri* M & W
Waubonsee Community College *Illinois* M
Wayland Baptist University *Texas* M & W
Wayne State College *Nebraska* M & W
Waynesburg University *Pennsylvania* M & W
Webb Institute *New York* M & W
Webber International University *Florida* M & W
Weber State University *Utah* M & W
Webster University *Missouri* M & W
Wellesley College *Massachusetts* W
Wells College *New York* M & W
Wenatchee Valley College *Washington* M & W
Wentworth Institute of Technology *Massachusetts* M & W
Wesley College *Delaware* M & W
Wesleyan College *Georgia* W
Wesleyan University *Connecticut* M & W
West Chester University of Pennsylvania *Pennsylvania* M & W
West Texas A&M University *Texas* M & W
West Valley College *California* M
West Virginia University *West Virginia* M & W
West Virginia University Institute of Technology *West Virginia* M & W
West Virginia Wesleyan College *West Virginia* M & W
Westchester Community College *New York* M
Western Carolina University *North Carolina* W
Western Connecticut State University *Connecticut* M & W
Western Illinois University *Illinois* M & W
Western Michigan University *Michigan* M & W
Western Nebraska Community College *Nebraska* M & W
Western Nevada College *Nevada* W
Western New England College *Massachusetts* M & W
Western Oregon University *Oregon* W
Western State College of Colorado *Colorado* M & W
Western Washington University *Washington* M & W
Western Wyoming Community College *Wyoming* M & W
Westfield State College *Massachusetts* M & W
Westminster College *Utah* M & W
Westminster College *Pennsylvania* M & W
Westminster College *Missouri* M & W
Westmont College *California* M & W
Whatcom Community College *Washington* M & W
Wheaton College *Massachusetts* M & W
Wheaton College *Illinois* M & W
Wheeling Jesuit University *West Virginia* M & W
Wheelock College *Massachusetts* M & W
White Mountains Community College *New Hampshire* M & W
Whitman College *Washington* M & W
Whittier College *California* M & W
Whitworth University *Washington* M & W
Widener University *Pennsylvania* M & W
Wilfrid Laurier University *Ontario* M & W
Wilkes University *Pennsylvania* M & W
Willamette University *Oregon* M & W
William Carey University *Mississippi* M & W
William Jessup University *California* M & W
William Jewell College *Missouri* M & W
William Paterson University of New Jersey *New Jersey* M & W
William Penn University *Iowa* M & W
William Woods University *Missouri* M & W
Williams Baptist College *Arkansas* M & W
Williams College *Massachusetts* M & W
The Williamson Free School of Mechanical Trades *Pennsylvania* M
Wilmington College *Ohio* M & W
Wilson College *Pennsylvania* W
Wingate University *North Carolina* M & W
Winona State University *Minnesota* M & W
Winthrop University *South Carolina* M
Wisconsin Lutheran College *Wisconsin* M & W
Wittenberg University *Ohio* M & W
Wofford College *South Carolina* M & W
Worcester Polytechnic Institute *Massachusetts* M & W
Worcester State College *Massachusetts* M & W
Wright State University *Ohio* M & W
Xavier University *Ohio* M & W
Yakima Valley Community College *Washington* W
Yale University *Connecticut* M & W
Yavapai College *Arizona* M
Yeshiva University *New York* M & W
York College *Nebraska* M & W
York College of the City University of New York *New York* M
York College of Pennsylvania *Pennsylvania* M & W
York University *Ontario* M & W
Young Harris College *Georgia* M & W
Youngstown State University *Ohio* W
Yuba College *California* M & W

Softball

Abilene Christian University *Texas* W
Abraham Baldwin Agricultural College *Georgia* W
Academy of Art University *California* W
Adams State College *Colorado* W
Adelphi University *New York* W
Adirondack Community College *New York* W
Adrian College *Michigan* W
Agnes Scott College *Georgia* W
Alabama Southern Community College *Alabama* W
Alabama State University *Alabama* W
Albany State University *Georgia* W
Albertus Magnus College *Connecticut* W
Albion College *Michigan* W
Albright College *Pennsylvania* W
Alcorn State University *Mississippi* W
Alderson-Broaddus College *West Virginia* W
Alfred University *New York* W
Alice Lloyd College *Kentucky* W
Allan Hancock College *California* W

M = Men; W = Women

Allegany College of Maryland *Maryland* W
Allegheny College *Pennsylvania* W
Allen Community College *Kansas* W
Alma College *Michigan* W
Alpena Community College *Michigan* W
Alvernia University *Pennsylvania* W
Alverno College *Wisconsin* W
Alvin Community College *Texas* W
American International College *Massachusetts* W
American River College *California* W
Amherst College *Massachusetts* W
Ancilla College *Indiana* W
Anderson University *South Carolina* W
Anderson University *Indiana* W
Andrew College *Georgia* W
Angelo State University *Texas* W
Anna Maria College *Massachusetts* W
Anne Arundel Community College *Maryland* W
Anoka-Ramsey Community College *Minnesota* W
Anoka-Ramsey Community College, Cambridge Campus *Minnesota* W
Antelope Valley College *California* W
Appalachian State University *North Carolina* W
Aquinas College *Michigan* W
Arcadia University *Pennsylvania* W
Arizona State University *Arizona* W
Arizona Western College *Arizona* W
Arkansas Tech University *Arkansas* W
Armstrong Atlantic State University *Georgia* W
The Art Institute of Boston at Lesley University *Massachusetts* W
Asbury University *Kentucky* W
Ashford University *Iowa* W
Ashland University *Ohio* M & W
Assumption College *Massachusetts* W
Auburn University *Alabama* W
Auburn University Montgomery *Alabama* W
Augsburg College *Minnesota* W
Augusta State University *Georgia* W
Augustana College *South Dakota* W
Augustana College *Illinois* W
Aurora University *Illinois* W
Austin College *Texas* W
Austin Peay State University *Tennessee* W
Averett University *Virginia* W
Avila University *Missouri* W
Azusa Pacific University *California* W
Babson College *Massachusetts* W
Baker University *Kansas* W
Bakersfield College *California* W
Baldwin-Wallace College *Ohio* W
Ball State University *Indiana* W
Baptist Bible College of Pennsylvania *Pennsylvania* W
Barnard College *New York* W
Barry University *Florida* W
Barton College *North Carolina* W
Barton County Community College *Kansas* W
Bates College *Maine* W
Bay Path College *Massachusetts* W
Baylor University *Texas* W
Becker College *Massachusetts* W
Belhaven University *Mississippi* W
Bellarmine University *Kentucky* W
Bellevue College *Washington* W
Bellevue University *Nebraska* W
Belmont Abbey College *North Carolina* W
Belmont University *Tennessee* W
Beloit College *Wisconsin* W
Bemidji State University *Minnesota* W
Benedict College *South Carolina* W
Benedictine College *Kansas* W
Benedictine University *Illinois* W
Bentley University *Massachusetts* W
Berea College *Kentucky* W
Bergen Community College *New Jersey* W
Bernard M. Baruch College of the City University of New York *New York* W
Berry College *Georgia* W
Bethany Bible College *New Brunswick* M & W
Bethany College *West Virginia* W
Bethany College *Kansas* W
Bethany Lutheran College *Minnesota* W
Bethany University *California* W
Bethel College *Indiana* W
Bethel University *Tennessee* W
Bethel University *Minnesota* W
Bethune-Cookman University *Florida* W
Bevill State Community College *Alabama* W
Big Bend Community College *Washington* W
Biola University *California* W
Birmingham-Southern College *Alabama* W
Bishop State Community College *Alabama* W
Black Hawk College *Illinois* W
Blackburn College *Illinois* W
Blinn College *Texas* W
Bloomfield College *New Jersey* W
Bloomsburg University of Pennsylvania *Pennsylvania* W
Blue Mountain College *Mississippi* W
Blue Mountain Community College *Oregon* W
Bluefield College *Virginia* W
Bluefield State College *West Virginia* W
Bluffton University *Ohio* W
Boise State University *Idaho* W
Bossier Parish Community College *Louisiana* W
Boston College *Massachusetts* W
Boston University *Massachusetts* W
Bowdoin College *Maine* W
Bowie State University *Maryland* W
Bowling Green State University *Ohio* W
Bradley University *Illinois* M & W
Brandeis University *Massachusetts* W
Brenau University *Georgia* W
Brescia University *Kentucky* W
Brevard College *North Carolina* W
Brevard Community College *Florida* W
Brewton-Parker College *Georgia* W
Briar Cliff University *Iowa* W
Briarcliffe College *New York* W
Bridgewater College *Virginia* W
Bridgewater State College *Massachusetts* W
Brigham Young University *Utah* W
Brigham Young University–Hawaii *Hawaii* W
Brookdale Community College *New Jersey* W
Brooklyn College of the City University of New York *New York* W
Broome Community College *New York* W
Broward College *Florida* W
Brown University *Rhode Island* W
Brunswick Community College *North Carolina* W
Bryant University *Rhode Island* W
Bucknell University *Pennsylvania* W
Buena Vista University *Iowa* W
Buffalo State College, State University of New York *New York* W
Bunker Hill Community College *Massachusetts* W
Burlington County College *New Jersey* W
Butler Community College *Kansas* W
Butler County Community College *Pennsylvania* W
Butler University *Indiana* W
Butte College *California* W
Cabrillo College *California* W
Cabrini College *Pennsylvania* W
Caldwell College *New Jersey* W
California Baptist University *California* W
California Lutheran University *California* W
California Polytechnic State University, San Luis Obispo *California* W
California State University, Bakersfield *California* W
California State University, Chico *California* W
California State University, Dominguez Hills *California* W
California State University, East Bay *California* W
California State University, Fresno *California* W
California State University, Fullerton *California* W
California State University, Long Beach *California* W
California State University, Monterey Bay *California* W
California State University, Northridge *California* W
California State University, Sacramento *California* W
California State University, San Bernardino *California* W
California State University, Stanislaus *California* W
California University of Pennsylvania *Pennsylvania* W
Calumet College of Saint Joseph *Indiana* W
Calvin College *Michigan* W
Camden County College *New Jersey* W
Cameron University *Oklahoma* W
Campbell University *North Carolina* W
Campbellsville University *Kentucky* W
Canisius College *New York* W
Capital University *Ohio* W
Cardinal Stritch University *Wisconsin* W
Carl Albert State College *Oklahoma* M
Carleton College *Minnesota* W
Carlow University *Pennsylvania* W
Carnegie Mellon University *Pennsylvania* W
Carson-Newman College *Tennessee* W
Carthage College *Wisconsin* W
Case Western Reserve University *Ohio* W
Castleton State College *Vermont* W
Catawba College *North Carolina* W
The Catholic University of America *District of Columbia* W
Cazenovia College *New York* W
Cecil College *Maryland* W
Cedar Crest College *Pennsylvania* W
Cedarville University *Ohio* W
Centenary College *New Jersey* W
Centenary College of Louisiana *Louisiana* W
Central Alabama Community College *Alabama* W
Central Arizona College *Arizona* W
Central Baptist College *Arkansas* W
Central Carolina Community College *North Carolina* W
Central Christian College of Kansas *Kansas* W
Central College *Iowa* W
Central Community College–Columbus Campus *Nebraska* W
Central Connecticut State University *Connecticut* W
Central Florida Community College *Florida* W
Central Lakes College *Minnesota* W
Central Maine Community College *Maine* W
Central Methodist University *Missouri* W
Central Michigan University *Michigan* W
Central Ohio Technical College *Ohio* W
Central Washington University *Washington* W
Centralia College *Washington* W
Centre College *Kentucky* W
Cerritos College *California* W
Chabot College *California* W
Chaffey College *California* W
Chaminade University of Honolulu *Hawaii* W
Chapman University *California* W
Charleston Southern University *South Carolina* W
Chatham University *Pennsylvania* W
Chattahoochee Valley Community College *Alabama* W
Chattanooga State Community College *Tennessee* W
Chesapeake College *Maryland* W
Chestnut Hill College *Pennsylvania* W
Chipola College *Florida* W
Chowan University *North Carolina* W
Christian Brothers University *Tennessee* W
Christopher Newport University *Virginia* W
Cisco College *Texas* W
Citrus College *California* W
City College of the City University of New York *New York* W
Clackamas Community College *Oregon* W
Claflin University *South Carolina* W
Claremont McKenna College *California* W
Clarendon College *Texas* W
Clarion University of Pennsylvania *Pennsylvania* W
Clark Atlanta University *Georgia* W
Clark College *Washington* W
Clark State Community College *Ohio* W
Clark University *Massachusetts* W
Clarke College *Iowa* W
Clearwater Christian College *Florida* W
Clemson University *South Carolina* W
Cleveland State Community College *Tennessee* W
Cleveland State University *Ohio* W
Clinton Community College *New York* W
Clinton Community College *Iowa* W
Cloud County Community College *Kansas* W
Coahoma Community College *Mississippi* W

M = Men; W = Women

Coastal Carolina University *South Carolina* W
Coe College *Iowa* W
Coffeyville Community College *Kansas* W
Coker College *South Carolina* W
Colby College *Maine* W
Colby Community College *Kansas* W
Colby-Sawyer College *New Hampshire* W
Colgate University *New York* W
The College at Brockport, State University of New York *New York* W
College of the Canyons *California* W
College of Charleston *South Carolina* W
College of Coastal Georgia *Georgia* W
College of the Desert *California* W
College of DuPage *Illinois* W
College of the Holy Cross *Massachusetts* W
The College of Idaho *Idaho* W
College of Lake County *Illinois* W
College of Mount St. Joseph *Ohio* W
College of Mount Saint Vincent *New York* W
The College of New Jersey *New Jersey* W
The College of New Rochelle *New York* W
College of Notre Dame of Maryland *Maryland* W
College of the Redwoods *California* W
College of Saint Benedict *Minnesota* W
College of Saint Elizabeth *New Jersey* W
College of Saint Mary *Nebraska* W
The College of Saint Rose *New York* W
The College of St. Scholastica *Minnesota* W
College of the Sequoias *California* W
College of the Siskiyous *California* W
College of Southern Idaho *Idaho* W
College of Southern Maryland *Maryland* W
College of Staten Island of the City University of New York *New York* W
The College of Wooster *Ohio* W
Colorado Northwestern Community College *Colorado* W
Colorado School of Mines *Colorado* W
Colorado State University *Colorado* W
Colorado State University–Pueblo *Colorado* W
Columbia College *South Carolina* W
Columbia College *Missouri* W
Columbia-Greene Community College *New York* W
Columbia State Community College *Tennessee* W
Columbia University *New York* W
Columbus State Community College *Ohio* W
Columbus State University *Georgia* W
Community College of Allegheny County *Pennsylvania* W
The Community College of Baltimore County *Maryland* W
Community College of Beaver County *Pennsylvania* W
Community College of Philadelphia *Pennsylvania* W
Community College of Rhode Island *Rhode Island* W
Concordia College *Minnesota* W
Concordia College–New York *New York* W
Concordia University *Oregon* W
Concordia University *Michigan* W
Concordia University *California* W
Concordia University Chicago *Illinois* W
Concordia University, Nebraska *Nebraska* W
Concordia University, St. Paul *Minnesota* W
Concordia University Texas *Texas* W
Concordia University Wisconsin *Wisconsin* W
Connors State College *Oklahoma* W
Contra Costa College *California* W
Copiah-Lincoln Community College *Mississippi* W
Coppin State University *Maryland* W
Corban University *Oregon* W
Cornell College *Iowa* W
Cornell University *New York* W
Cornerstone University *Michigan* W
Corning Community College *New York* W
Cosumnes River College *California* W
Cottey College *Missouri* W
County College of Morris *New Jersey* W
Covenant College *Georgia* W
Cowley County Community College and Area Vocational–Technical School *Kansas* W
Creighton University *Nebraska* W
Crossroads College *Minnesota* W
Crown College *Minnesota* W
Cuesta College *California* W
Culver-Stockton College *Missouri* W
Cumberland County College *New Jersey* W
Cumberland University *Tennessee* W
Curry College *Massachusetts* W
Cuyahoga Community College *Ohio* W
Cypress College *California* W
Dakota College at Bottineau *North Dakota* W
Dakota County Technical College *Minnesota* W
Dakota State University *South Dakota* W
Dakota Wesleyan University *South Dakota* W
Dalton State College *Georgia* M & W
Dana College *Nebraska* W
Daniel Webster College *New Hampshire* W
Danville Area Community College *Illinois* W
Dartmouth College *New Hampshire* W
Darton College *Georgia* W
Davis & Elkins College *West Virginia* W
Dawson Community College *Montana* W
Daytona State College *Florida* W
De Anza College *California* W
Dean College *Massachusetts* W
Defiance College *Ohio* W
Delaware County Community College *Pennsylvania* W
Delaware State University *Delaware* W
Delaware Technical & Community College, Jack F. Owens Campus *Delaware* W
Delaware Technical & Community College, Stanton/Wilmington Campus *Delaware* W
Delaware Technical & Community College, Terry Campus *Delaware* W
Delaware Valley College *Pennsylvania* W
Delta College *Michigan* W
Delta State University *Mississippi* W
Denison University *Ohio* W
DePaul University *Illinois* W
DePauw University *Indiana* W
DeSales University *Pennsylvania* W
Diablo Valley College *California* W
Dickinson College *Pennsylvania* W
Dickinson State University *North Dakota* W
Dillard University *Louisiana* W
Dixie State College of Utah *Utah* W
Doane College *Nebraska* W
Dodge City Community College *Kansas* W
Dominican College *New York* W
Dominican University *Illinois* W
Dominican University of California *California* W
Dordt College *Iowa* W
Dowling College *New York* W
Drake University *Iowa* W
Drew University *New Jersey* W
Drexel University *Pennsylvania* W
Drury University *Missouri* W
Duke University *North Carolina* M & W
Dutchess Community College *New York* W
Dyersburg State Community College *Tennessee* W
D'Youville College *New York* W
East Carolina University *North Carolina* W
East Central College *Missouri* W
East Central Community College *Mississippi* W
East Central University *Oklahoma* W
East Los Angeles College *California* W
East Mississippi Community College *Mississippi* W
East Stroudsburg University of Pennsylvania *Pennsylvania* W
East Tennessee State University *Tennessee* W
East Texas Baptist University *Texas* W
Eastern Arizona College *Arizona* W
Eastern Connecticut State University *Connecticut* W
Eastern Illinois University *Illinois* W
Eastern Kentucky University *Kentucky* W
Eastern Mennonite University *Virginia* W
Eastern Michigan University *Michigan* W
Eastern Nazarene College *Massachusetts* W
Eastern New Mexico University *New Mexico* W
Eastern Oklahoma State College *Oklahoma* W
Eastern University *Pennsylvania* W
Eckerd College *Florida* W
Edgewood College *Wisconsin* W
Edinboro University of Pennsylvania *Pennsylvania* W
Edmonds Community College *Washington* W
El Paso Community College *Texas* W
Elgin Community College *Illinois* W
Elizabeth City State University *North Carolina* W
Elizabethtown College *Pennsylvania* W
Ellsworth Community College *Iowa* W
Elmhurst College *Illinois* W
Elmira College *New York* W
Elms College *Massachusetts* W
Elon University *North Carolina* W
Emerson College *Massachusetts* W
Emmanuel College *Massachusetts* W
Emmanuel College *Georgia* W
Emory & Henry College *Virginia* W
Emory University *Georgia* W
Emporia State University *Kansas* W
Endicott College *Massachusetts* W
Enterprise State Community College *Alabama* W
Erie Community College *New York* W
Erie Community College, North Campus *New York* W
Erie Community College, South Campus *New York* W
Erskine College *South Carolina* W
Eureka College *Illinois* W
Evangel University *Missouri* W
Everett Community College *Washington* W
Fairfield University *Connecticut* W
Fairleigh Dickinson University, College at Florham *New Jersey* W
Fairleigh Dickinson University, Metropolitan Campus *New Jersey* W
Fairmont State University *West Virginia* W
Farmingdale State College *New York* W
Faulkner University *Alabama* W
Fayetteville State University *North Carolina* W
Feather River College *California* W
Felician College *New Jersey* W
Ferris State University *Michigan* W
Ferrum College *Virginia* W
Finger Lakes Community College *New York* W
Finlandia University *Michigan* W
Fisher College *Massachusetts* W
Fitchburg State College *Massachusetts* W
Flagler College *Florida* W
Florida Agricultural and Mechanical University *Florida* W
Florida Atlantic University *Florida* W
Florida Gulf Coast University *Florida* W
Florida Institute of Technology *Florida* W
Florida International University *Florida* W
Florida Southern College *Florida* W
Florida State College at Jacksonville *Florida* W
Florida State University *Florida* W
Fontbonne University *Missouri* W
Foothill College *California* W
Fordham University *New York* W
Fort Hays State University *Kansas* W
Fort Lewis College *Colorado* W
Fort Scott Community College *Kansas* W
Framingham State College *Massachusetts* W
Francis Marion University *South Carolina* W
Franciscan University of Steubenville *Ohio* W
Frank Phillips College *Texas* W
Franklin College *Indiana* W
Franklin & Marshall College *Pennsylvania* W
Franklin Pierce University *New Hampshire* W
Frederick Community College *Maryland* W
Freed-Hardeman University *Tennessee* W
Fresno City College *California* W
Friends University *Kansas* W
Frostburg State University *Maryland* W
Fulton-Montgomery Community College *New York* W
Furman University *South Carolina* W
Gadsden State Community College *Alabama* W
Gallaudet University *District of Columbia* W
Galveston College *Texas* W
Gannon University *Pennsylvania* W
Garden City Community College *Kansas* W
Gardner-Webb University *North Carolina* W
Gateway Community College *Connecticut* W

M = Men; W = Women

M = Men; W = Women

Lindenwood University *Missouri* W
Lindsey Wilson College *Kentucky* W
Linfield College *Oregon* W
Lipscomb University *Tennessee* W
Livingstone College *North Carolina* W
Lock Haven University of Pennsylvania *Pennsylvania* W
Lon Morris College *Texas* W
Long Beach City College *California* W
Long Island University, Brooklyn Campus *New York* W
Long Island University, C.W. Post Campus *New York* W
Longwood University *Virginia* W
Loras College *Iowa* W
Los Angeles Harbor College *California* W
Los Angeles Pierce College *California* W
Los Angeles Valley College *California* W
Los Medanos College *California* W
Louisburg College *North Carolina* W
Louisiana College *Louisiana* W
Louisiana State University and Agricultural and Mechanical College *Louisiana* W
Louisiana Tech University *Louisiana* W
Loyola Marymount University *California* W
Loyola University Chicago *Illinois* W
Lubbock Christian University *Texas* W
Lurleen B. Wallace Community College *Alabama* W
Luther College *Iowa* W
Luzerne County Community College *Pennsylvania* W
Lycoming College *Pennsylvania* W
Lynchburg College *Virginia* W
Lyndon State College *Vermont* W
Lyon College *Arkansas* W
Macalester College *Minnesota* W
MacMurray College *Illinois* W
Macomb Community College *Michigan* W
Madison Area Technical College *Wisconsin* W
Madonna University *Michigan* W
Maine Maritime Academy *Maine* W
Malone University *Ohio* W
Manchester College *Indiana* W
Manchester Community College *Connecticut* W
Manhattan College *New York* W
Manhattanville College *New York* W
Mansfield University of Pennsylvania *Pennsylvania* W
Maranatha Baptist Bible College *Wisconsin* W
Marian University *Wisconsin* W
Marian University *Indiana* W
Marietta College *Ohio* W
Marion Technical College *Ohio* W
Marist College *New York* W
Marquette University *Wisconsin* W
Mars Hill College *North Carolina* W
Marshall University *West Virginia* W
Marshalltown Community College *Iowa* W
Martin Luther College *Minnesota* W
Martin Methodist College *Tennessee* W
Mary Baldwin College *Virginia* W
Maryville College *Tennessee* W
Maryville University of Saint Louis *Missouri* W
Marywood University *Pennsylvania* W
Massachusetts Bay Community College *Massachusetts* W
Massachusetts College of Liberal Arts *Massachusetts* W
Massachusetts Institute of Technology *Massachusetts* W
Massachusetts Maritime Academy *Massachusetts* W
Massasoit Community College *Massachusetts* W
Mayville State University *North Dakota* W
McDaniel College *Maryland* W
McHenry County College *Illinois* W
McKendree University *Illinois* W
McLennan Community College *Texas* W
McNeese State University *Louisiana* W
McPherson College *Kansas* W
Medaille College *New York* W
Menlo College *California* W
Merced College *California* W
Mercer County Community College *New Jersey* W
Mercer University *Georgia* W
Mercy College *New York* W
Mercyhurst College *Pennsylvania* W
Meredith College *North Carolina* W
Meridian Community College *Mississippi* W
Merrimack College *Massachusetts* W
Mesa Community College *Arizona* W
Mesa State College *Colorado* W
Mesabi Range Community and Technical College *Minnesota* W
Messiah College *Pennsylvania* W
Methodist University *North Carolina* W
Metropolitan Community College–Maple Woods *Missouri* W
Metropolitan State College of Denver *Colorado* W
Miami Dade College *Florida* W
Miami University *Ohio* M & W
Miami University Hamilton *Ohio* W
Miami University–Middletown Campus *Ohio* W
Michigan State University *Michigan* W
Mid-America Christian University *Oklahoma* W
Mid-America College of Funeral Service *Indiana* M & W
Mid-Continent University *Kentucky* W
Mid-Plains Community College *Nebraska* W
MidAmerica Nazarene University *Kansas* W
Middle Georgia College *Georgia* W
Middle Tennessee State University *Tennessee* W
Middlebury College *Vermont* W
Middlesex County College *New Jersey* W
Midland Lutheran College *Nebraska* W
Midway College *Kentucky* W
Midwestern State University *Texas* W
Miles College *Alabama* W
Millersville University of Pennsylvania *Pennsylvania* W
Milligan College *Tennessee* W
Millikin University *Illinois* W
Millsaps College *Mississippi* W
Milwaukee School of Engineering *Wisconsin* W
Minnesota State Community and Technical College *Minnesota* W
Minnesota State University Mankato *Minnesota* W
Minnesota State University Moorhead *Minnesota* W
Minnesota West Community and Technical College *Minnesota* W
Minot State University *North Dakota* W
Misericordia University *Pennsylvania* W
Mission College *California* W
Mississippi College *Mississippi* W
Mississippi Gulf Coast Community College *Mississippi* W
Mississippi State University *Mississippi* W
Mississippi Valley State University *Mississippi* W
Missouri Baptist University *Missouri* W
Missouri Southern State University *Missouri* W
Missouri State University *Missouri* W
Missouri University of Science and Technology *Missouri* W
Missouri Valley College *Missouri* W
Missouri Western State University *Missouri* W
Mitchell College *Connecticut* W
Modesto Junior College *California* W
Mohawk Valley Community College *New York* W
Molloy College *New York* W
Monmouth College *Illinois* W
Monmouth University *New Jersey* W
Monroe College (Bronx) *New York* W
Monroe College (New Rochelle) *New York* W
Monroe Community College *New York* W
Montana State University Billings *Montana* W
Montclair State University *New Jersey* W
Monterey Peninsula College *California* W
Montgomery College *Maryland* W
Montgomery County Community College *Pennsylvania* W
Montreat College *North Carolina* W
Moorpark College *California* W
Moraine Valley Community College *Illinois* W
Moravian College *Pennsylvania* W
Morehead State University *Kentucky* W
Morgan State University *Maryland* W
Morningside College *Iowa* W
Morris College *South Carolina* W
Morton College *Illinois* W
Motlow State Community College *Tennessee* W
Mott Community College *Michigan* W
Mount Aloysius College *Pennsylvania* W
Mt. Hood Community College *Oregon* W
Mount Ida College *Massachusetts* W
Mount Marty College *South Dakota* W
Mount Mary College *Wisconsin* W
Mount Mercy College *Iowa* W
Mount Olive College *North Carolina* W
Mount Saint Mary College *New York* W
Mount St. Mary's University *Maryland* W
Mt. San Antonio College *California* W
Mt. San Jacinto College *California* W
Mount Vernon Nazarene University *Ohio* W
Muhlenberg College *Pennsylvania* W
Murray State College *Oklahoma* W
Murray State University *Kentucky* W
Muscatine Community College *Iowa* W
Muskegon Community College *Michigan* W
Muskingum University *Ohio* W
Napa Valley College *California* W
Nassau Community College *New York* W
Navarro College *Texas* W
Nazareth College of Rochester *New York* W
Nebraska Wesleyan University *Nebraska* W
Neosho County Community College *Kansas* W
Neumann University *Pennsylvania* W
New England College *New Hampshire* W
New Jersey City University *New Jersey* W
New Mexico Highlands University *New Mexico* W
New Mexico State University *New Mexico* W
New York City College of Technology of the City University of New York *New York* W
New York Institute of Technology *New York* W
New York University *New York* W
Newberry College *South Carolina* W
Newbury College *Massachusetts* W
Newman University *Kansas* W
NHTI, Concord's Community College *New Hampshire* W
Niagara County Community College *New York* W
Niagara University *New York* W
Nicholls State University *Louisiana* W
Nichols College *Massachusetts* W
Norfolk State University *Virginia* W
North Arkansas College *Arkansas* W
North Carolina Agricultural and Technical State University *North Carolina* W
North Carolina Central University *North Carolina* W
North Carolina State University *North Carolina* W
North Carolina Wesleyan College *North Carolina* W
North Central College *Illinois* W
North Central Missouri College *Missouri* W
North Central University *Minnesota* W
North Country Community College *New York* W
North Dakota State College of Science *North Dakota* W
North Dakota State University *North Dakota* W
North Georgia College & State University *Georgia* W
North Greenville University *South Carolina* W
North Idaho College *Idaho* W
North Iowa Area Community College *Iowa* W
North Park University *Illinois* W
Northampton Community College *Pennsylvania* W
Northeast Mississippi Community College *Mississippi* W
Northeast Texas Community College *Texas* W
Northeastern Oklahoma Agricultural and Mechanical College *Oklahoma* W
Northeastern State University *Oklahoma* W
Northern Illinois University *Illinois* W
Northern Kentucky University *Kentucky* W
Northern Oklahoma College *Oklahoma* W
Northern State University *South Dakota* W
Northland College *Wisconsin* W
Northland Community and Technical College–Thief River Falls *Minnesota* W
Northwest Christian University *Oregon* W
Northwest Florida State College *Florida* W
Northwest Mississippi Community College *Mississippi* W
Northwest Missouri State University *Missouri* W

M = Men; W = Women

Northwest Nazarene University *Idaho* W
Northwest-Shoals Community College *Alabama* W
Northwestern College *Minnesota* W
Northwestern College *Iowa* W
Northwestern Oklahoma State University *Oklahoma* W
Northwestern State University of Louisiana *Louisiana* W
Northwestern University *Illinois* W
Northwood University *Michigan* W
Northwood University, Florida Campus *Florida* W
Northwood University, Texas Campus *Texas* W
Norwich University *Vermont* W
Notre Dame College *Ohio* W
Notre Dame de Namur University *California* W
Nova Southeastern University *Florida* W
Oakland City University *Indiana* W
Oakland Community College *Michigan* W
Oakland University *Michigan* W
Oakton Community College *Illinois* W
Oberlin College *Ohio* W
Occidental College *California* W
Ocean County College *New Jersey* W
Odessa College *Texas* W
Ohio Christian University *Ohio* W
Ohio Dominican University *Ohio* W
Ohio Northern University *Ohio* W
The Ohio State University *Ohio* W
The Ohio State University at Marion *Ohio* M & W
Ohio University *Ohio* W
Ohio University–Zanesville *Ohio* W
Ohio Valley University *West Virginia* W
Ohio Wesleyan University *Ohio* W
Ohlone College *California* W
Oklahoma Baptist University *Oklahoma* W
Oklahoma Christian University *Oklahoma* W
Oklahoma City University *Oklahoma* W
Oklahoma Panhandle State University *Oklahoma* W
Old Dominion University *Virginia* W
Olivet College *Michigan* W
Olivet Nazarene University *Illinois* W
Olympic College *Washington* W
Onondaga Community College *New York* W
Orange Coast College *California* W
Orange County Community College *New York* W
Oregon Institute of Technology *Oregon* W
Oregon State University *Oregon* W
Otero Junior College *Colorado* W
Ottawa University *Kansas* W
Otterbein University *Ohio* W
Ouachita Baptist University *Arkansas* W
Owens Community College *Ohio* W
Oxnard College *California* W
Pace University *New York* W
Pacific Lutheran University *Washington* W
Pacific University *Oregon* W
Paine College *Georgia* W
Palm Beach Atlantic University *Florida* W
Palm Beach State College *Florida* W
Palomar College *California* W
Paradise Valley Community College *Arizona* W
Paris Junior College *Texas* W
Park University *Missouri* W
Parkland College *Illinois* W
Pasadena City College *California* W
Pasco-Hernando Community College *Florida* W
Patten University *California* W
Peace College *North Carolina* W
Pearl River Community College *Mississippi* W
Peninsula College *Washington* W
Penn State Abington *Pennsylvania* W
Penn State Altoona *Pennsylvania* W
Penn State Beaver *Pennsylvania* M & W
Penn State Berks *Pennsylvania* W
Penn State Erie, The Behrend College *Pennsylvania* W
Penn State Fayette, The Eberly Campus *Pennsylvania* W
Penn State Greater Allegheny *Pennsylvania* W
Penn State Harrisburg *Pennsylvania* W
Penn State Hazleton *Pennsylvania* W
Penn State Mont Alto *Pennsylvania* W
Penn State New Kensington *Pennsylvania* W
Penn State Schuylkill *Pennsylvania* W
Penn State University Park *Pennsylvania* W
Penn State Worthington Scranton *Pennsylvania* W
Pennsylvania College of Technology *Pennsylvania* W
Pensacola Junior College *Florida* W
Peru State College *Nebraska* W
Pfeiffer University *North Carolina* W
Philadelphia Biblical University *Pennsylvania* W
Philadelphia University *Pennsylvania* W
Phoenix College *Arizona* W
Piedmont College *Georgia* W
Pierce College at Puyallup *Washington* W
Pikeville College *Kentucky* W
Pima Community College *Arizona* W
Pine Manor College *Massachusetts* W
Pitt Community College *North Carolina* W
Pittsburg State University *Kansas* W
Pitzer College *California* W
Plymouth State University *New Hampshire* W
Point Loma Nazarene University *California* W
Point Park University *Pennsylvania* W
Polk State College *Florida* W
Polytechnic Institute of NYU *New York* W
Polytechnic University of Puerto Rico *Puerto Rico* M & W
Pomona College *California* W
Porterville College *California* W
Portland State University *Oregon* W
Post University *Connecticut* W
Potomac State College of West Virginia University *West Virginia* W
Prairie State College *Illinois* M & W
Prairie View A&M University *Texas* W
Pratt Community College *Kansas* W
Presbyterian College *South Carolina* W
Presentation College *South Dakota* W
Prince George's Community College *Maryland* W
Princeton University *New Jersey* W
Principia College *Illinois* W
Providence College *Rhode Island* W
Purchase College, State University of New York *New York* M & W
Purdue University *Indiana* W
Purdue University North Central *Indiana* W
Queens College of the City University of New York *New York* W
Queens University of Charlotte *North Carolina* W
Queensborough Community College of the City University of New York *New York* W
Quincy University *Illinois* W
Quinnipiac University *Connecticut* W
Quinsigamond Community College *Massachusetts* W
Radford University *Virginia* W
Rainy River Community College *Minnesota* W
Ramapo College of New Jersey *New Jersey* W
Randolph College *Virginia* W
Randolph-Macon College *Virginia* W
Ranger College *Texas* W
Raritan Valley Community College *New Jersey* W
Reedley College *California* W
Regis College *Massachusetts* W
Regis University *Colorado* W
Reinhardt University *Georgia* W
Rend Lake College *Illinois* W
Rensselaer Polytechnic Institute *New York* W
Research College of Nursing *Missouri* W
Rhode Island College *Rhode Island* W
Rhodes College *Tennessee* W
Rice University *Texas* W
The Richard Stockton College of New Jersey *New Jersey* W
Rider University *New Jersey* W
Ridgewater College *Minnesota* W
Rio Hondo College *California* W
Ripon College *Wisconsin* W
Riverland Community College *Minnesota* W
Riverside Community College District *California* W
Rivier College *New Hampshire* W
Roane State Community College *Tennessee* W
Roanoke College *Virginia* W
Robert Morris University *Pennsylvania* W
Robert Morris University Illinois *Illinois* W
Rochester College *Michigan* W
Rochester Community and Technical College *Minnesota* W
Rochester Institute of Technology *New York* W
Rock Valley College *Illinois* W
Rockford College *Illinois* W
Rockhurst University *Missouri* W
Rockingham Community College *North Carolina* W
Rockland Community College *New York* W
Roger Williams University *Rhode Island* W
Rogers State University *Oklahoma* W
Rollins College *Florida* W
Rose-Hulman Institute of Technology *Indiana* W
Rosemont College *Pennsylvania* W
Rowan University *New Jersey* W
Russell Sage College *New York* W
Rutgers, The State University of New Jersey, Camden *New Jersey* W
Rutgers, The State University of New Jersey, New Brunswick *New Jersey* W
Sacramento City College *California* W
Sacred Heart University *Connecticut* W
Saddleback College *California* W
Sage College of Albany *New York* W
Saginaw Valley State University *Michigan* W
St. Ambrose University *Iowa* W
St. Andrews Presbyterian College *North Carolina* W
Saint Anselm College *New Hampshire* W
Saint Augustine's College *North Carolina* W
St. Bonaventure University *New York* W
St. Catharine College *Kentucky* W
St. Catherine University *Minnesota* W
Saint Charles Community College *Missouri* W
St. Clair County Community College *Michigan* W
St. Cloud State University *Minnesota* W
St. Cloud Technical College *Minnesota* W
St. Edward's University *Texas* W
Saint Francis University *Pennsylvania* W
St. Gregory's University *Oklahoma* W
St. John Fisher College *New York* W
St. Johns River Community College *Florida* W
St. John's University *New York* W
Saint Joseph College *Connecticut* W
Saint Joseph's College *Indiana* W
St. Joseph's College, Long Island Campus *New York* W
Saint Joseph's College of Maine *Maine* W
St. Joseph's College, New York *New York* W
Saint Joseph's University *Pennsylvania* W
St. Lawrence University *New York* W
Saint Leo University *Florida* W
St. Louis Community College at Florissant Valley *Missouri* W
St. Louis Community College at Forest Park *Missouri* W
St. Louis Community College at Meramec *Missouri* W
Saint Louis University *Missouri* W
Saint Martin's University *Washington* W
Saint Mary-of-the-Woods College *Indiana* W
Saint Mary's College *Indiana* W
Saint Mary's College of California *California* W
St. Mary's University *Texas* W
Saint Mary's University of Minnesota *Minnesota* W
Saint Michael's College *Vermont* W
St. Norbert College *Wisconsin* W
St. Olaf College *Minnesota* W
Saint Paul's College *Virginia* W
Saint Peter's College *New Jersey* W
St. Petersburg College *Florida* W
St. Thomas Aquinas College *New York* W
St. Thomas University *Florida* W
Saint Vincent College *Pennsylvania* W
Saint Xavier University *Illinois* W
Salem Community College *New Jersey* W
Salem International University *West Virginia* W
Salem State College *Massachusetts* W
Salisbury University *Maryland* W
Salt Lake Community College *Utah* W
Salve Regina University *Rhode Island* W
Sam Houston State University *Texas* M & W
Samford University *Alabama* W
San Diego City College *California* W
San Diego Mesa College *California* W

M = Men; W = Women

M = Men; W = Women

University of Central Oklahoma *Oklahoma* W
University of Charleston *West Virginia* W
University of Chicago *Illinois* W
University of Cincinnati Clermont College *Ohio* W
University of Colorado at Boulder *Colorado* W
University of Colorado at Colorado Springs *Colorado* W
University of Connecticut *Connecticut* W
University of the Cumberlands *Kentucky* M & W
University of Dallas *Texas* W
University of Dayton *Ohio* W
University of Delaware *Delaware* W
University of Denver *Colorado* W
University of Detroit Mercy *Michigan* W
University of Dubuque *Iowa* W
University of Evansville *Indiana* W
The University of Findlay *Ohio* W
University of Florida *Florida* W
University of Georgia *Georgia* W
University of Great Falls *Montana* W
University of Hartford *Connecticut* W
University of Hawaii at Hilo *Hawaii* W
University of Hawaii at Manoa *Hawaii* W
University of Houston *Texas* W
University of Illinois at Chicago *Illinois* W
University of Illinois at Springfield *Illinois* W
University of Illinois at Urbana–Champaign *Illinois* W
University of the Incarnate Word *Texas* W
University of Indianapolis *Indiana* W
The University of Iowa *Iowa* W
The University of Kansas *Kansas* W
University of Kentucky *Kentucky* W
University of La Verne *California* W
University of Louisiana at Lafayette *Louisiana* W
University of Louisiana at Monroe *Louisiana* W
University of Louisville *Kentucky* W
University of Maine *Maine* W
University of Maine at Farmington *Maine* W
University of Maine at Presque Isle *Maine* W
University of Mary *North Dakota* W
University of Mary Hardin-Baylor *Texas* W
University of Mary Washington *Virginia* W
University of Maryland, Baltimore County *Maryland* W
University of Maryland, College Park *Maryland* W
University of Maryland Eastern Shore *Maryland* W
University of Massachusetts Amherst *Massachusetts* W
University of Massachusetts Boston *Massachusetts* W
University of Massachusetts Dartmouth *Massachusetts* W
University of Memphis *Tennessee* W
University of Michigan *Michigan* W
University of Michigan–Dearborn *Michigan* W
University of Minnesota, Crookston *Minnesota* W
University of Minnesota, Duluth *Minnesota* W
University of Minnesota, Morris *Minnesota* W
University of Minnesota, Twin Cities Campus *Minnesota* W
University of Mississippi *Mississippi* W
University of Missouri *Missouri* W
University of Missouri–Kansas City *Missouri* W
University of Missouri–St. Louis *Missouri* W
University of Mobile *Alabama* W
University of Mount Union *Ohio* W
University of Nebraska at Kearney *Nebraska* W
University of Nebraska at Omaha *Nebraska* W
University of Nebraska–Lincoln *Nebraska* W
University of Nevada, Las Vegas *Nevada* W
University of Nevada, Reno *Nevada* W
University of New England *Maine* W
University of New Hampshire *New Hampshire* W
University of New Haven *Connecticut* W
University of New Mexico *New Mexico* W
University of North Alabama *Alabama* W
The University of North Carolina at Chapel Hill *North Carolina* W
The University of North Carolina at Charlotte *North Carolina* W
The University of North Carolina at Greensboro *North Carolina* W
The University of North Carolina at Pembroke *North Carolina* W
The University of North Carolina Wilmington *North Carolina* W
University of North Dakota *North Dakota* W
University of North Florida *Florida* W
University of North Texas *Texas* M & W
University of Northern Colorado *Colorado* W
University of Northern Iowa *Iowa* W
University of Notre Dame *Indiana* W
University of Oklahoma *Oklahoma* W
University of Oregon *Oregon* W
University of the Ozarks *Arkansas* W
University of the Pacific *California* W
University of Pennsylvania *Pennsylvania* W
University of Pittsburgh *Pennsylvania* W
University of Pittsburgh at Bradford *Pennsylvania* W
University of Pittsburgh at Greensburg *Pennsylvania* W
University of Puerto Rico, Aguadilla University College *Puerto Rico* W
University of Puerto Rico at Arecibo *Puerto Rico* W
University of Puerto Rico at Bayamón *Puerto Rico* W
University of Puerto Rico, Cayey University College *Puerto Rico* M & W
University of Puerto Rico at Humacao *Puerto Rico* W
University of Puerto Rico, Mayagüez Campus *Puerto Rico* W
University of Puerto Rico, Río Piedras *Puerto Rico* M & W
University of Puerto Rico at Utuado *Puerto Rico* M & W
University of Puget Sound *Washington* W
University of Redlands *California* W
University of Rhode Island *Rhode Island* W
University of Rio Grande *Ohio* W
University of Rochester *New York* W
University of Saint Francis *Indiana* W
University of St. Francis *Illinois* W
University of Saint Mary *Kansas* W
University of St. Thomas *Minnesota* W
University of San Diego *California* W
University of San Francisco *California* M & W
University of Science and Arts of Oklahoma *Oklahoma* W
University of the Sciences in Philadelphia *Pennsylvania* W
The University of Scranton *Pennsylvania* W
University of Sioux Falls *South Dakota* W
University of South Carolina *South Carolina* W
University of South Carolina Aiken *South Carolina* W
University of South Carolina Salkehatchie *South Carolina* W
University of South Carolina Upstate *South Carolina* W
The University of South Dakota *South Dakota* W
University of South Florida *Florida* W
University of Southern California *California* W
University of Southern Indiana *Indiana* W
University of Southern Maine *Maine* W
University of Southern Mississippi *Mississippi* W
University of the Southwest *New Mexico* W
The University of Tampa *Florida* W
The University of Tennessee *Tennessee* W
The University of Tennessee at Chattanooga *Tennessee* W
The University of Tennessee at Martin *Tennessee* W
The University of Texas at Arlington *Texas* M
The University of Texas at Austin *Texas* W
The University of Texas at Dallas *Texas* W
The University of Texas of the Permian Basin *Texas* W
The University of Texas at San Antonio *Texas* W
The University of Toledo *Ohio* W
University of Tulsa *Oklahoma* W
University of Utah *Utah* W
University of Virginia *Virginia* W
The University of Virginia's College at Wise *Virginia* W
University of Washington *Washington* W
The University of West Alabama *Alabama* W
University of West Florida *Florida* W
University of West Georgia *Georgia* W
The University of Western Ontario *Ontario* W
University of Windsor *Ontario* W
University of Wisconsin–Eau Claire *Wisconsin* W
University of Wisconsin–Green Bay *Wisconsin* W
University of Wisconsin–La Crosse *Wisconsin* W
University of Wisconsin–Madison *Wisconsin* W
University of Wisconsin–Oshkosh *Wisconsin* W
University of Wisconsin–Parkside *Wisconsin* W
University of Wisconsin–Platteville *Wisconsin* W
University of Wisconsin–River Falls *Wisconsin* W
University of Wisconsin–Stevens Point *Wisconsin* W
University of Wisconsin–Stout *Wisconsin* W
University of Wisconsin–Superior *Wisconsin* W
University of Wisconsin–Whitewater *Wisconsin* W
University of Wyoming *Wyoming* W
Upper Iowa University *Iowa* W
Urbana University *Ohio* W
Ursinus College *Pennsylvania* W
Ursuline College *Ohio* W
Utah State University *Utah* W
Utah Valley University *Utah* W
Utica College *New York* W
Valdosta State University *Georgia* W
Valley City State University *North Dakota* W
Valparaiso University *Indiana* W
Vanguard University of Southern California *California* W
Ventura College *California* W
Vermilion Community College *Minnesota* W
Vermont Technical College *Vermont* W
Vernon College *Texas* W
Victor Valley College *California* W
Villanova University *Pennsylvania* W
Virginia Intermont College *Virginia* W
Virginia State University *Virginia* W
Virginia Union University *Virginia* W
Virginia Wesleyan College *Virginia* W
Viterbo University *Wisconsin* W
Volunteer State Community College *Tennessee* W
Voorhees College *South Carolina* W
Wagner College *New York* W
Waldorf College *Iowa* W
Walla Walla Community College *Washington* W
Walla Walla University *Washington* W
Wallace State Community College *Alabama* W
Walsh University *Ohio* W
Walters State Community College *Tennessee* W
Warner University *Florida* W
Wartburg College *Iowa* W
Washburn University *Kansas* W
Washington Adventist University *Maryland* W
Washington College *Maryland* W
Washington & Jefferson College *Pennsylvania* W
Washington and Lee University *Virginia* W
Washington State University *Washington* W
Washington University in St. Louis *Missouri* W
Waubonsee Community College *Illinois* W
Waycross College *Georgia* W
Wayne State College *Nebraska* W
Wayne State University *Michigan* W
Waynesburg University *Pennsylvania* W
Webber International University *Florida* W
Weber State University *Utah* W
Webster University *Missouri* W
Wellesley College *Massachusetts* W
Wells College *New York* W
Wenatchee Valley College *Washington* W
Wentworth Institute of Technology *Massachusetts* W
Wesley College *Delaware* W
Wesleyan College *Georgia* W
Wesleyan University *Connecticut* W
West Chester University of Pennsylvania *Pennsylvania* W
West Hills Community College *California* W
West Liberty University *West Virginia* W
West Texas A&M University *Texas* W
West Virginia State University *West Virginia* W

M = Men; W = Women

West Virginia University Institute of Technology *West Virginia* W
West Virginia Wesleyan College *West Virginia* W
Westchester Community College *New York* W
Western Carolina University *North Carolina* W
Western Connecticut State University *Connecticut* W
Western Illinois University *Illinois* W
Western Kentucky University *Kentucky* W
Western Michigan University *Michigan* W
Western Nebraska Community College *Nebraska* W
Western New England College *Massachusetts* W
Western New Mexico University *New Mexico* W
Western Oklahoma State College *Oklahoma* W
Western Oregon University *Oregon* W
Western Texas College *Texas* W
Western Washington University *Washington* W
Westfield State College *Massachusetts* W
Westminster College *Pennsylvania* W
Westminster College *Missouri* M & W
Westmoreland County Community College *Pennsylvania* W
Wheaton College *Massachusetts* W
Wheaton College *Illinois* W
Wheeling Jesuit University *West Virginia* W
Wheelock College *Massachusetts* W
Whitman College *Washington* M & W
Whittier College *California* W
Whitworth University *Washington* W
Wichita State University *Kansas* W
Widener University *Pennsylvania* W
Wilkes University *Pennsylvania* W
Willamette University *Oregon* W
William Carey University *Mississippi* W
William Jessup University *California* W
William Jewell College *Missouri* W
William Paterson University of New Jersey *New Jersey* W
William Penn University *Iowa* W
William Woods University *Missouri* W
Williams Baptist College *Arkansas* W
Williams College *Massachusetts* W
Wilmington College *Ohio* W
Wilmington University *Delaware* W
Wilson College *Pennsylvania* W
Wingate University *North Carolina* W
Winona State University *Minnesota* W
Winston-Salem State University *North Carolina* M & W
Winthrop University *South Carolina* W
Wisconsin Lutheran College *Wisconsin* W
Wittenberg University *Ohio* W
Worcester Polytechnic Institute *Massachusetts* W
Worcester State College *Massachusetts* W
Wright State University *Ohio* W
Xavier University *Ohio* M & W
Yakima Valley Community College *Washington* W
Yale University *Connecticut* W
Yavapai College *Arizona* W
York College *Nebraska* W
York College of the City University of New York *New York* W
York College of Pennsylvania *Pennsylvania* W
Young Harris College *Georgia* W
Youngstown State University *Ohio* W
Yuba College *California* W

Squash

Amherst College *Massachusetts* M & W
Bard College *New York* M
Barnard College *New York* W
Bates College *Maine* M & W
Bowdoin College *Maine* M & W
Brandeis University *Massachusetts* M
Brown University *Rhode Island* M & W
Bryant University *Rhode Island* M & W
Carnegie Mellon University *Pennsylvania* M & W
Colby College *Maine* M & W
Colgate University *New York* M & W
Columbia University *New York* M & W
Columbia University, School of General Studies *New York* M & W
Connecticut College *Connecticut* M & W
Cornell University *New York* M & W
Dartmouth College *New Hampshire* M & W
Denison University *Ohio* M & W
Dickinson College *Pennsylvania* M & W
Duke University *North Carolina* M & W
Fordham University *New York* M
Franklin & Marshall College *Pennsylvania* M & W
Hamilton College *New York* M & W
Harvard University *Massachusetts* M & W
Haverford College *Pennsylvania* M & W
Hobart and William Smith Colleges *New York* M & W
Kenyon College *Ohio* M & W
Lafayette College *Pennsylvania* M
Massachusetts Institute of Technology *Massachusetts* M
McGill University *Quebec* M & W
McMaster University *Ontario* M & W
Metropolitan State College of Denver *Colorado* M & W
Michigan Technological University *Michigan* M & W
Middlebury College *Vermont* W
Mount Holyoke College *Massachusetts* W
Princeton University *New Jersey* M & W
Queen's University at Kingston *Ontario* M & W
Reed College *Oregon* M & W
Rensselaer Polytechnic Institute *New York* M & W
St. Lawrence University *New York* M & W
Smith College *Massachusetts* W
Southeastern Community College *North Carolina* W
Stanford University *California* M & W
State University of New York at New Paltz *New York* W
Swarthmore College *Pennsylvania* M & W
Syracuse University *New York* M & W
Trent University *Ontario* M & W
Trinity College *Connecticut* M & W
Tufts University *Massachusetts* M & W
United States Air Force Academy *Colorado* M & W
United States Naval Academy *Maryland* M
University of Hartford *Connecticut* M & W
University of Pennsylvania *Pennsylvania* M & W
University of Richmond *Virginia* M & W
University of Rochester *New York* M
University of Southern California *California* M & W
University of Toronto *Ontario* M & W
University of Waterloo *Ontario* M
The University of Western Ontario *Ontario* M & W
Vassar College *New York* M & W
Wellesley College *Massachusetts* W
Wesleyan University *Connecticut* M & W
Williams College *Massachusetts* M & W
Yale University *Connecticut* M & W

Swimming and Diving

Adams State College *Colorado* W
Adelphi University *New York* M & W
Albion College *Michigan* M & W
Albright College *Pennsylvania* M & W
Alfred University *New York* M & W
Allegheny College *Pennsylvania* M & W
Alma College *Michigan* M & W
American River College *California* M & W
American University *District of Columbia* M & W
American University of Puerto Rico *Puerto Rico* M & W
Amherst College *Massachusetts* M & W
Arcadia University *Pennsylvania* M & W
Arizona State University *Arizona* M & W
Asbury University *Kentucky* M & W
Ashland University *Ohio* M & W
Assumption College *Massachusetts* W
Auburn University *Alabama* M & W
Augsburg College *Minnesota* W
Augustana College *Illinois* M & W
Austin College *Texas* M & W
Babson College *Massachusetts* M & W
Baldwin-Wallace College *Ohio* M & W
Ball State University *Indiana* M & W
Bard College at Simon's Rock *Massachusetts* M & W
Barnard College *New York* W
Bates College *Maine* M & W
Bayamón Central University *Puerto Rico* M & W
Bellarmine University *Kentucky* M & W
Beloit College *Wisconsin* M & W
Bentley University *Massachusetts* M & W
Berea College *Kentucky* M & W
Bernard M. Baruch College of the City University of New York *New York* M & W
Berry College *Georgia* M & W
Bethany College *West Virginia* M & W
Biola University *California* M & W
Bloomsburg University of Pennsylvania *Pennsylvania* M & W
Boston College *Massachusetts* M & W
Boston University *Massachusetts* M & W
Bowdoin College *Maine* M & W
Bowling Green State University *Ohio* W
Brandeis University *Massachusetts* M & W
Brenau University *Georgia* W
Bridgewater College *Virginia* W
Bridgewater State College *Massachusetts* M & W
Brigham Young University *Utah* M & W
Brock University *Ontario* M & W
Brooklyn College of the City University of New York *New York* M & W
Broward College *Florida* M & W
Brown University *Rhode Island* M & W
Bryant University *Rhode Island* M & W
Bryn Mawr College *Pennsylvania* W
Bucknell University *Pennsylvania* M & W
Buffalo State College, State University of New York *New York* M & W
Butler University *Indiana* W
Cabrillo College *California* M & W
Cabrini College *Pennsylvania* M & W
California Baptist University *California* M & W
California Institute of Technology *California* M & W
California Lutheran University *California* M & W
California Polytechnic State University, San Luis Obispo *California* M & W
California State University, Bakersfield *California* M & W
California State University, East Bay *California* W
California State University, Fresno *California* W
California State University, Northridge *California* M & W
California State University, San Bernardino *California* M & W
California University of Pennsylvania *Pennsylvania* W
Calvin College *Michigan* M & W
Campbell University *North Carolina* W
Campbellsville University *Kentucky* W
Canisius College *New York* M & W
Carleton College *Minnesota* M & W
Carleton University *Ontario* M & W
Carnegie Mellon University *Pennsylvania* M & W
Carroll University *Wisconsin* M & W
Carthage College *Wisconsin* M & W
Case Western Reserve University *Ohio* M & W
Catawba College *North Carolina* M & W
The Catholic University of America *District of Columbia* M & W
Centenary College of Louisiana *Louisiana* M & W
Central Connecticut State University *Connecticut* W
Centre College *Kentucky* M & W
Cerritos College *California* M & W
Chabot College *California* M & W
Chaffey College *California* M & W
Chapman University *California* M & W
Chatham University *Pennsylvania* W
Citrus College *California* M & W
City College of San Francisco *California* M
Claremont McKenna College *California* M & W
Clarion University of Pennsylvania *Pennsylvania* M & W
Clark University *Massachusetts* M & W
Clarkson University *New York* M & W
Clemson University *South Carolina* M & W
Cleveland State University *Ohio* M & W
Coe College *Iowa* M & W
Colby College *Maine* M & W
Colby-Sawyer College *New Hampshire* M & W
Colgate University *New York* M & W
The College at Brockport, State University of New York *New York* M & W

M = Men; W = Women

College of the Canyons *California* M & W
College of Charleston *South Carolina* M & W
College of DuPage *Illinois* M & W
College of the Holy Cross *Massachusetts* M & W
The College of Idaho *Idaho* M & W
College of Marin *California* M & W
College of Mount Saint Vincent *New York* W
The College of New Jersey *New Jersey* M & W
The College of New Rochelle *New York* W
College of Notre Dame of Maryland *Maryland* W
College of Saint Benedict *Minnesota* W
College of Saint Elizabeth *New Jersey* W
College of Saint Mary *Nebraska* W
The College of Saint Rose *New York* M & W
College of the Sequoias *California* M & W
College of Staten Island of the City University of New York *New York* M & W
The College of William and Mary *Virginia* M & W
The College of Wooster *Ohio* M & W
The Colorado College *Colorado* M & W
Colorado School of Mines *Colorado* M & W
Colorado State University *Colorado* W
Columbia University *New York* M & W
Columbia University, School of General Studies *New York* M & W
Concordia College *Minnesota* W
Concordia University *California* M & W
Concordia University College of Alberta *Alberta* M & W
Connecticut College *Connecticut* M & W
Converse College *South Carolina* W
Cornell University *New York* M & W
Cosumnes River College *California* M & W
Cuesta College *California* M & W
Cypress College *California* M & W
Dalhousie University *Nova Scotia* M & W
Dartmouth College *New Hampshire* M & W
Darton College *Georgia* M & W
Davidson College *North Carolina* M & W
Daytona State College *Florida* M & W
De Anza College *California* M & W
Delta State University *Mississippi* M & W
Denison University *Ohio* M & W
DePauw University *Indiana* M & W
Diablo Valley College *California* M & W
Dickinson College *Pennsylvania* M & W
Drew University *New Jersey* M & W
Drexel University *Pennsylvania* M & W
Drury University *Missouri* M & W
Duke University *North Carolina* M & W
Duquesne University *Pennsylvania* W
East Carolina University *North Carolina* M & W
East Stroudsburg University of Pennsylvania *Pennsylvania* W
Eastern Connecticut State University *Connecticut* W
Eastern Illinois University *Illinois* M & W
Eastern Michigan University *Michigan* M & W
Edinboro University of Pennsylvania *Pennsylvania* M & W
El Camino College *California* M & W
Elizabethtown College *Pennsylvania* M & W
Elms College *Massachusetts* M & W
Elon University *North Carolina* M & W
Emory University *Georgia* M & W
Erie Community College *New York* M & W
Erie Community College, North Campus *New York* M & W
Erie Community College, South Campus *New York* M & W
Eureka College *Illinois* M & W
Fairfield University *Connecticut* M & W
Fairleigh Dickinson University, College at Florham *New Jersey* M & W
Fairmont State University *West Virginia* M & W
Fashion Institute of Technology *New York* M & W
Florida Agricultural and Mechanical University *Florida* M & W
Florida Atlantic University *Florida* M & W
Florida Gulf Coast University *Florida* W
Florida International University *Florida* W
Florida Southern College *Florida* M & W
Florida State University *Florida* M & W
Foothill College *California* M & W
Fordham University *New York* M & W
Franklin & Marshall College *Pennsylvania* M & W
Fresno Pacific University *California* M & W
Frostburg State University *Maryland* M & W
Fullerton College *California* M & W
Furman University *South Carolina* M & W
Gallaudet University *District of Columbia* M & W
Gannon University *Pennsylvania* M & W
Gardner-Webb University *North Carolina* M & W
Genesee Community College *New York* M & W
George Mason University *Virginia* M & W
The George Washington University *District of Columbia* M & W
Georgetown University *District of Columbia* M & W
Georgia Institute of Technology *Georgia* M & W
Georgia Southern University *Georgia* W
Gettysburg College *Pennsylvania* M & W
Golden West College *California* M & W
Gordon College *Massachusetts* M & W
Goucher College *Maryland* M & W
Graceland University *Iowa* M & W
Grand Canyon University *Arizona* M & W
Grand Rapids Community College *Michigan* M & W
Grand Valley State University *Michigan* M & W
Greensboro College *North Carolina* W
Grinnell College *Iowa* M & W
Grossmont College *California* M & W
Grove City College *Pennsylvania* M & W
Guilford College *North Carolina* W
Gustavus Adolphus College *Minnesota* M & W
Hamilton College *New York* M & W
Hamline University *Minnesota* M & W
Hannibal-LaGrange College *Missouri* M & W
Hartnell College *California* M & W
Hartwick College *New York* M & W
Harvard University *Massachusetts* M & W
Harvey Mudd College *California* M & W
Henderson State University *Arkansas* M & W
Hendrix College *Arkansas* M & W
Herkimer County Community College *New York* M & W
Hillsdale College *Michigan* W
Hiram College *Ohio* M & W
Hobart and William Smith Colleges *New York* W
Hollins University *Virginia* W
Hood College *Maryland* M & W
Hope College *Michigan* M & W
Howard University *District of Columbia* M & W
Hunter College of the City University of New York *New York* W
Husson University *Maine* W
Illinois College *Illinois* M & W
Illinois Institute of Technology *Illinois* M & W
Illinois State University *Illinois* W
Illinois Wesleyan University *Illinois* M & W
Indian River State College *Florida* M & W
Indiana University Bloomington *Indiana* M & W
Indiana University of Pennsylvania *Pennsylvania* M & W
Indiana University–Purdue University Indianapolis *Indiana* M & W
Inter American University of Puerto Rico, Bayamón Campus *Puerto Rico* M & W
Inter American University of Puerto Rico, Guayama Campus *Puerto Rico* M
Inter American University of Puerto Rico, San Germán Campus *Puerto Rico* M & W
Iona College *New York* M & W
Iowa State University of Science and Technology *Iowa* M & W
Ithaca College *New York* M & W
James Madison University *Virginia* W
Jamestown Community College *New York* M & W
John Carroll University *Ohio* M & W
John Jay College of Criminal Justice of the City University of New York *New York* W
The Johns Hopkins University *Maryland* M & W
Juniata College *Pennsylvania* W
Kalamazoo College *Michigan* M & W
Keene State College *New Hampshire* M & W
Kenyon College *Ohio* M & W
Keuka College *New York* W
King College *Tennessee* M & W
King's College *Pennsylvania* M & W
Knox College *Illinois* M & W
Kutztown University of Pennsylvania *Pennsylvania* W
La Salle University *Pennsylvania* M & W
Lafayette College *Pennsylvania* M & W
LaGrange College *Georgia* M & W
Lake Forest College *Illinois* M & W
Laurentian University *Ontario* M & W
Lawrence University *Wisconsin* M & W
Le Moyne College *New York* M & W
Lebanon Valley College *Pennsylvania* M & W
Lehigh University *Pennsylvania* M & W
Lehman College of the City University of New York *New York* M & W
Lenoir-Rhyne University *North Carolina* W
Lewis & Clark College *Oregon* M & W
Lewis University *Illinois* M & W
Limestone College *South Carolina* M & W
Lincoln College *Illinois* M & W
Lindenwood University *Missouri* M & W
Lindsey Wilson College *Kentucky* M & W
Linfield College *Oregon* M & W
Lock Haven University of Pennsylvania *Pennsylvania* W
Long Beach City College *California* M & W
Long Island University, C.W. Post Campus *New York* W
Longwood University *Virginia* M & W
Loras College *Iowa* M & W
Los Angeles Pierce College *California* M & W
Los Angeles Valley College *California* M & W
Louisiana State University and Agricultural and Mechanical College *Louisiana* M & W
Loyola Marymount University *California* W
Loyola University Maryland *Maryland* M & W
Loyola University New Orleans *Louisiana* M & W
Luther College *Iowa* M & W
Lycoming College *Pennsylvania* M & W
Macalester College *Minnesota* M & W
MacMurray College *Illinois* M & W
Malone University *Ohio* M & W
Manhattan College *New York* W
Manhattanville College *New York* W
Mansfield University of Pennsylvania *Pennsylvania* W
Marist College *New York* M & W
Marquette University *Wisconsin* M & W
Mars Hill College *North Carolina* M & W
Marshall University *West Virginia* W
Mary Baldwin College *Virginia* W
Marymount University *Virginia* M & W
Maryville College *Tennessee* M & W
Marywood University *Pennsylvania* M & W
Massachusetts Institute of Technology *Massachusetts* M & W
McDaniel College *Maryland* M & W
McGill University *Quebec* M & W
McMaster University *Ontario* M & W
McMurry University *Texas* M & W
Memorial University of Newfoundland *Newfoundland and Labrador* M & W
Merced College *California* M & W
Messiah College *Pennsylvania* M & W
Metropolitan State College of Denver *Colorado* M & W
Miami University *Ohio* M & W
Michigan State University *Michigan* M & W
Michigan Technological University *Michigan* M & W
Middlebury College *Vermont* M & W
Millersville University of Pennsylvania *Pennsylvania* W
Milligan College *Tennessee* M & W
Millikin University *Illinois* M & W
Mills College *California* W
Minnesota State University Mankato *Minnesota* M & W
Minnesota State University Moorhead *Minnesota* W
Misericordia University *Pennsylvania* M & W
Missouri State University *Missouri* M & W
Missouri University of Science and Technology *Missouri* M
Modesto Junior College *California* M & W
Monmouth College *Illinois* M & W
Monroe Community College *New York* M & W

M = Men; W = Women

Montclair State University *New Jersey* M & W
Monterey Peninsula College *California* M & W
Morningside College *Iowa* M & W
Mount Allison University *New Brunswick* M & W
Mount Holyoke College *Massachusetts* W
Mount Saint Mary College *New York* M & W
Mount St. Mary's University *Maryland* W
Mt. San Antonio College *California* M & W
Napa Valley College *California* M & W
Nazareth College of Rochester *New York* M & W
New Jersey Institute of Technology *New Jersey* M & W
New Mexico State University *New Mexico* W
New York University *New York* M & W
Niagara University *New York* M & W
North Carolina Agricultural and Technical State University *North Carolina* W
North Carolina State University *North Carolina* M & W
North Central College *Illinois* M & W
North Lake College *Texas* M & W
Northeastern University *Massachusetts* W
Northern Arizona University *Arizona* W
Northern Illinois University *Illinois* M & W
Northern State University *South Dakota* W
Northwestern University *Illinois* M & W
Norwich University *Vermont* M & W
Nova Southeastern University *Florida* M & W
Oakland University *Michigan* M & W
Oberlin College *Ohio* M & W
Occidental College *California* M & W
Ocean County College *New Jersey* M & W
Ohio Northern University *Ohio* M & W
The Ohio State University *Ohio* M & W
Ohio University *Ohio* W
Ohio Wesleyan University *Ohio* M & W
Ohlone College *California* M & W
Old Dominion University *Virginia* M & W
Olivet College *Michigan* M & W
Orange Coast College *California* M & W
Oregon State University *Oregon* W
Ouachita Baptist University *Arkansas* M & W
Pace University *New York* M & W
Pacific Lutheran University *Washington* M & W
Pacific University *Oregon* M & W
Palo Alto College *Texas* M & W
Palomar College *California* M & W
Pasadena City College *California* M & W
Penn State Altoona *Pennsylvania* M & W
Penn State Erie, The Behrend College *Pennsylvania* M & W
Penn State University Park *Pennsylvania* M & W
Pepperdine University *California* W
Pfeiffer University *North Carolina* M & W
Pitzer College *California* M & W
Plymouth State University *New Hampshire* W
Pomona College *California* M & W
Pontifical Catholic University of Puerto Rico *Puerto Rico* M & W
Princeton University *New Jersey* M & W
Principia College *Illinois* M & W
Providence College *Rhode Island* M & W
Purchase College, State University of New York *New York* W
Purdue University *Indiana* M & W
Queens College of the City University of New York *New York* M & W
Queen's University at Kingston *Ontario* M & W
Radford University *Virginia* W
Ramapo College of New Jersey *New Jersey* M & W
Randolph-Macon College *Virginia* W
Regis College *Massachusetts* M & W
Rensselaer Polytechnic Institute *New York* M & W
Rhodes College *Tennessee* M & W
Rice University *Texas* W
Rider University *New Jersey* M & W
Rio Hondo College *California* M & W
Ripon College *Wisconsin* M & W
Riverside Community College District *California* M & W
Robert Morris University Illinois *Illinois* W
Rochester Institute of Technology *New York* M & W
Roger Williams University *Rhode Island* M & W
Rollins College *Florida* M & W
Rose-Hulman Institute of Technology *Indiana* M & W
Rowan University *New Jersey* M & W
Rutgers, The State University of New Jersey, New Brunswick *New Jersey* M & W
Sacramento City College *California* M & W
Sacred Heart University *Connecticut* W
Saddleback College *California* M & W
St. Bonaventure University *New York* M & W
St. Catherine University *Minnesota* W
St. Cloud State University *Minnesota* M & W
St. Francis College *New York* M & W
Saint Francis University *Pennsylvania* M & W
Saint John's University *Minnesota* M
Saint Joseph College *Connecticut* W
St. Lawrence University *New York* M & W
Saint Leo University *Florida* M & W
Saint Louis University *Missouri* M & W
Saint Mary's College *Indiana* W
St. Mary's College of Maryland *Maryland* M & W
Saint Mary's University of Minnesota *Minnesota* M & W
Saint Michael's College *Vermont* M & W
St. Olaf College *Minnesota* M & W
Saint Peter's College *New Jersey* M & W
Saint Vincent College *Pennsylvania* M & W
Salem College *North Carolina* W
Salem International University *West Virginia* M & W
Salisbury University *Maryland* M & W
San Diego Mesa College *California* M & W
San Diego State University *California* W
San Joaquin Delta College *California* M & W
San Jose State University *California* W
Santa Ana College *California* M
Santa Monica College *California* M & W
Santa Rosa Junior College *California* M & W
Sarah Lawrence College *New York* W
Savannah College of Art and Design *Georgia* M & W
Scripps College *California* W
Seattle University *Washington* M & W
Seton Hall University *New Jersey* M & W
Sewanee: The University of the South *Tennessee* M & W
Shasta College *California* M & W
Shippensburg University of Pennsylvania *Pennsylvania* M & W
Siena College *New York* W
Sierra College *California* M & W
Simmons College *Massachusetts* W
Simon Fraser University *British Columbia* M & W
Simpson College *Iowa* M & W
Skidmore College *New York* M & W
Slippery Rock University of Pennsylvania *Pennsylvania* M & W
Smith College *Massachusetts* W
Soka University of America *California* M & W
Solano Community College *California* M & W
South Dakota State University *South Dakota* M & W
Southern Connecticut State University *Connecticut* M & W
Southern Illinois University Carbondale *Illinois* M & W
Southern Methodist University *Texas* M & W
Southwestern College *Kansas* M & W
Southwestern College *California* M & W
Southwestern University *Texas* M & W
Springfield College *Massachusetts* M & W
Stanford University *California* M & W
State University of New York at Binghamton *New York* M & W
State University of New York College of Agriculture and Technology at Cobleskill *New York* M & W
State University of New York College of Agriculture and Technology at Morrisville *New York* M & W
State University of New York College at Cortland *New York* M & W
State University of New York College at Geneseo *New York* M & W
State University of New York College at Old Westbury *New York* M & W
State University of New York College at Oneonta *New York* M & W
State University of New York College at Potsdam *New York* M & W
State University of New York College of Technology at Alfred *New York* M & W
State University of New York College of Technology at Delhi *New York* M & W
State University of New York at Fredonia *New York* M & W
State University of New York Maritime College *New York* M & W
State University of New York at New Paltz *New York* M & W
State University of New York at Oswego *New York* M & W
Stephens College *Missouri* W
Stevens Institute of Technology *New Jersey* M & W
Stony Brook University, State University of New York *New York* M & W
Suffolk County Community College *New York* M & W
Susquehanna University *Pennsylvania* M & W
Swarthmore College *Pennsylvania* M & W
Sweet Briar College *Virginia* W
Syracuse University *New York* M & W
Texas A&M University *Texas* M & W
Texas Christian University *Texas* M & W
Towson University *Maryland* M & W
Transylvania University *Kentucky* M & W
Trent University *Ontario* M & W
Trinity College *Connecticut* M & W
Trinity University *Texas* M & W
Trinity (Washington) University *District of Columbia* W
Truman State University *Missouri* M & W
Tufts University *Massachusetts* M & W
Tulane University *Louisiana* M & W
Union College *New York* M & W
Union College *Kentucky* M & W
United States Air Force Academy *Colorado* M & W
United States Coast Guard Academy *Connecticut* M & W
United States Merchant Marine Academy *New York* M & W
United States Military Academy *New York* M & W
United States Naval Academy *Maryland* M & W
Université Laval *Quebec* M & W
Université de Montréal *Quebec* M & W
Université du Québec àTrois-Rivières *Quebec* M & W
Université de Sherbrooke *Quebec* M & W
The University of Akron *Ohio* W
The University of Alabama *Alabama* M & W
University of Alberta *Alberta* M & W
The University of Arizona *Arizona* M & W
University of Arkansas *Arkansas* W
University of Arkansas at Little Rock *Arkansas* W
University of Bridgeport *Connecticut* M & W
The University of British Columbia *British Columbia* M & W
University at Buffalo, the State University of New York *New York* M & W
University of Calgary *Alberta* M & W
University of California, Berkeley *California* M & W
University of California, Davis *California* M & W
University of California, Los Angeles *California* W
University of California, San Diego *California* M & W
University of California, Santa Barbara *California* M & W
University of California, Santa Cruz *California* M & W
University of Charleston *West Virginia* M & W
University of Chicago *Illinois* M & W
University of Cincinnati *Ohio* M & W
University of Colorado at Boulder *Colorado* M & W
University of Connecticut *Connecticut* M & W
University of the Cumberlands *Kentucky* M & W
University of Delaware *Delaware* M & W
University of Denver *Colorado* M & W
University of Evansville *Indiana* M & W
The University of Findlay *Ohio* M & W
University of Florida *Florida* M & W

M = Men; W = Women

University of Georgia *Georgia* M & W
University of Guelph *Ontario* M & W
University of Hawaii at Manoa *Hawaii* M & W
University of Houston *Texas* W
University of Illinois at Chicago *Illinois* M & W
University of Illinois at Urbana–Champaign *Illinois* W
University of the Incarnate Word *Texas* M & W
University of Indianapolis *Indiana* M & W
The University of Iowa *Iowa* M & W
The University of Kansas *Kansas* W
University of Kentucky *Kentucky* M & W
University of La Verne *California* M & W
University of Lethbridge *Alberta* M & W
University of Louisiana at Monroe *Louisiana* M & W
University of Louisville *Kentucky* M & W
University of Maine *Maine* M & W
University of Manitoba *Manitoba* M & W
University of Mary Washington *Virginia* M & W
University of Maryland, Baltimore County *Maryland* M & W
University of Maryland, College Park *Maryland* M & W
University of Massachusetts Amherst *Massachusetts* M & W
University of Massachusetts Dartmouth *Massachusetts* M & W
University of Massachusetts Lowell *Massachusetts* M
University of Memphis *Tennessee* M & W
University of Miami *Florida* W
University of Michigan *Michigan* M & W
University of Minnesota, Duluth *Minnesota* M & W
University of Minnesota, Morris *Minnesota* W
University of Minnesota, Twin Cities Campus *Minnesota* M & W
University of Missouri *Missouri* M & W
University of Mount Union *Ohio* M & W
University of Nebraska at Kearney *Nebraska* W
University of Nebraska at Omaha *Nebraska* W
University of Nebraska–Lincoln *Nebraska* W
University of Nevada, Las Vegas *Nevada* M & W
University of Nevada, Reno *Nevada* W
University of New Brunswick Fredericton *New Brunswick* M & W
University of New England *Maine* W
University of New Hampshire *New Hampshire* W
University of New Mexico *New Mexico* W
University of New Orleans *Louisiana* M & W
The University of North Carolina at Chapel Hill *North Carolina* M & W
The University of North Carolina Wilmington *North Carolina* M & W
University of North Dakota *North Dakota* M & W
University of North Florida *Florida* W
University of North Texas *Texas* M & W
University of Northern Colorado *Colorado* W
University of Northern Iowa *Iowa* W
University of Notre Dame *Indiana* M & W
University of Ottawa *Ontario* M & W
University of the Pacific *California* M & W
University of Pennsylvania *Pennsylvania* M & W
University of Pittsburgh *Pennsylvania* M & W
University of Pittsburgh at Bradford *Pennsylvania* M & W
University of Puerto Rico, Aguadilla University College *Puerto Rico* M & W
University of Puerto Rico at Arecibo *Puerto Rico* M & W
University of Puerto Rico at Bayamón *Puerto Rico* M & W
University of Puerto Rico, Cayey University College *Puerto Rico* M & W
University of Puerto Rico at Humacao *Puerto Rico* M & W
University of Puerto Rico, Mayagüez Campus *Puerto Rico* M & W
University of Puerto Rico, Río Piedras *Puerto Rico* M & W
University of Puget Sound *Washington* M & W
University of Redlands *California* M & W
University of Regina *Saskatchewan* M & W
University of Rhode Island *Rhode Island* W
University of Richmond *Virginia* M & W
University of Rochester *New York* M & W
University of the Sacred Heart *Puerto Rico* M & W
University of St. Thomas *Minnesota* M & W
University of San Diego *California* W
The University of Scranton *Pennsylvania* M & W
University of South Carolina *South Carolina* M & W
The University of South Dakota *South Dakota* M & W
University of Southern California *California* M & W
The University of Tampa *Florida* M & W
The University of Tennessee *Tennessee* M & W
The University of Texas at Austin *Texas* M & W
The University of Texas of the Permian Basin *Texas* M & W
The University of Toledo *Ohio* W
University of Toronto *Ontario* M & W
University of Utah *Utah* M & W
University of Vermont *Vermont* W
University of Victoria *British Columbia* M & W
University of the Virgin Islands *United States Virgin Islands* M & W
University of Virginia *Virginia* M & W
University of Waterloo *Ontario* M & W
The University of Western Ontario *Ontario* M & W
University of Wisconsin–Eau Claire *Wisconsin* M & W
University of Wisconsin–Green Bay *Wisconsin* M & W
University of Wisconsin–La Crosse *Wisconsin* M & W
University of Wisconsin–Madison *Wisconsin* M & W
University of Wisconsin–Milwaukee *Wisconsin* M & W
University of Wisconsin–Oshkosh *Wisconsin* M & W
University of Wisconsin–River Falls *Wisconsin* M & W
University of Wisconsin–Stevens Point *Wisconsin* M & W
University of Wisconsin–Whitewater *Wisconsin* M & W
University of Wyoming *Wyoming* M & W
Ursinus College *Pennsylvania* M & W
Ursuline College *Ohio* W
Utica College *New York* M & W
Valparaiso University *Indiana* M & W
Vanguard University of Southern California *California* M & W
Vassar College *New York* M & W
Ventura College *California* M & W
Villanova University *Pennsylvania* M & W
Vincennes University *Indiana* M & W
Virginia Military Institute *Virginia* M
Virginia Polytechnic Institute and State University *Virginia* M & W
Wabash College *Indiana* M
Wagner College *New York* W
Warren Wilson College *North Carolina* M & W
Washington College *Maryland* M & W
Washington & Jefferson College *Pennsylvania* M & W
Washington and Lee University *Virginia* M & W
Washington State University *Washington* W
Washington University in St. Louis *Missouri* M & W
Wayne State University *Michigan* M & W
Weber State University *Utah* M & W
Webster University *Missouri* M & W
Wellesley College *Massachusetts* W
Wells College *New York* M & W
Wesleyan University *Connecticut* M & W
West Chester University of Pennsylvania *Pennsylvania* M & W
West Valley College *California* M & W
West Virginia University *West Virginia* M & W
West Virginia Wesleyan College *West Virginia* M & W
Western Carolina University *North Carolina* M & W
Western Connecticut State University *Connecticut* W
Western Illinois University *Illinois* M & W
Western Kentucky University *Kentucky* M & W
Western New England College *Massachusetts* W
Westfield State College *Massachusetts* W
Westminster College *Pennsylvania* M & W
Wheaton College *Massachusetts* M & W
Wheaton College *Illinois* M & W
Wheeling Jesuit University *West Virginia* M & W
Whitman College *Washington* M & W
Whittier College *California* M & W
Whitworth University *Washington* M & W
Wichita State University *Kansas* M & W
Widener University *Pennsylvania* M & W
Wilfrid Laurier University *Ontario* M & W
Willamette University *Oregon* M & W
William Paterson University of New Jersey *New Jersey* M & W
Williams College *Massachusetts* M & W
Wilmington College *Ohio* M & W
Wingate University *North Carolina* M & W
Wittenberg University *Ohio* M & W
Worcester Polytechnic Institute *Massachusetts* M & W
Wright State University *Ohio* M & W
Xavier University *Ohio* M & W
Yale University *Connecticut* M & W
York College of the City University of New York *New York* M & W
York College of Pennsylvania *Pennsylvania* M & W
York University *Ontario* M & W
Youngstown State University *Ohio* W

Table Tennis

Allegheny College *Pennsylvania* M & W
Birmingham-Southern College *Alabama* M & W
Bryant University *Rhode Island* M & W
California State University, Long Beach *California* M
Caribbean University *Puerto Rico* M & W
Colgate University *New York* M & W
Columbia University *New York* M & W
Columbia University, School of General Studies *New York* M & W
Community College of Allegheny County *Pennsylvania* M & W
Dalton State College *Georgia* M & W
Dartmouth College *New Hampshire* M & W
Duke University *North Carolina* M & W
Fashion Institute of Technology *New York* M & W
Florida State University *Florida* M & W
Hiram College *Ohio* M & W
Inter American University of Puerto Rico, Aguadilla Campus *Puerto Rico* M & W
Inter American University of Puerto Rico, Barranquitas Campus *Puerto Rico* M & W
Inter American University of Puerto Rico, Bayamón Campus *Puerto Rico* M & W
Inter American University of Puerto Rico, Ponce Campus *Puerto Rico* M & W
Inter American University of Puerto Rico, San Germán Campus *Puerto Rico* M & W
Lake Forest College *Illinois* M & W
Lehman College of the City University of New York *New York* M & W
Lindenwood University *Missouri* M & W
Massachusetts Institute of Technology *Massachusetts* M & W
Michigan Technological University *Michigan* M & W
Mississippi College *Mississippi* M & W
North Carolina State University *North Carolina* M & W
Northwestern Polytechnic University *California* M
Penn State University Park *Pennsylvania* M
Polytechnic University of Puerto Rico *Puerto Rico* M & W
Pontifical Catholic University of Puerto Rico *Puerto Rico* M & W
Providence College and Theological Seminary *Manitoba* M & W
Queens College of the City University of New York *New York* M & W
Rensselaer Polytechnic Institute *New York* M & W
Saint Louis University *Missouri* M & W
Texas Wesleyan University *Texas* M
Universidad Metropolitana *Puerto Rico* M & W
The University of Alabama in Huntsville *Alabama* M & W
University of California, Santa Cruz *California* M & W

M = Men; W = Women

University of Idaho *Idaho* M & W
The University of Iowa *Iowa* M & W
University of Missouri–St. Louis *Missouri* M & W
University of Puerto Rico, Aguadilla University College *Puerto Rico* M
University of Puerto Rico at Bayamón *Puerto Rico* M & W
University of Puerto Rico, Cayey University College *Puerto Rico* M
University of Puerto Rico at Ponce *Puerto Rico* M & W
University of Puerto Rico, Río Piedras *Puerto Rico* M & W
University of Puerto Rico at Utuado *Puerto Rico* M & W
University of Southern California *California* M & W
University of Utah *Utah* M & W
University of Vermont *Vermont* M & W
University of the Virgin Islands *United States Virgin Islands* M & W
Washington University in St. Louis *Missouri* M & W
Yale University *Connecticut* M & W

Tennis

Abilene Christian University *Texas* M & W
Abraham Baldwin Agricultural College *Georgia* M & W
Academy of Art University *California* W
Adelphi University *New York* M & W
Adirondack Community College *New York* M
Adrian College *Michigan* M & W
Agnes Scott College *Georgia* W
Alabama Agricultural and Mechanical University *Alabama* M & W
Alabama State University *Alabama* M & W
Albany State University *Georgia* W
Albertus Magnus College *Connecticut* M & W
Albion College *Michigan* M & W
Albright College *Pennsylvania* M & W
Alcorn State University *Mississippi* M & W
Alfred University *New York* M & W
Allan Hancock College *California* M & W
Allegany College of Maryland *Maryland* M & W
Allegheny College *Pennsylvania* M & W
Alma College *Michigan* M & W
Alvernia University *Pennsylvania* M & W
Alverno College *Wisconsin* W
American International College *Massachusetts* M & W
American River College *California* M & W
Amherst College *Massachusetts* M & W
Anderson University *South Carolina* M & W
Anderson University *Indiana* M & W
Anna Maria College *Massachusetts* M & W
Antelope Valley College *California* W
Appalachian State University *North Carolina* M & W
Aquinas College *Michigan* M & W
Arcadia University *Pennsylvania* M & W
Arizona State University *Arizona* W
Arkansas State University - Jonesboro *Arkansas* W
Arkansas Tech University *Arkansas* W
Armstrong Atlantic State University *Georgia* M & W
Asbury University *Kentucky* M & W
Ashland University *Ohio* M & W
Assumption College *Massachusetts* M & W
Auburn University *Alabama* M & W
Auburn University Montgomery *Alabama* M & W
Augusta State University *Georgia* M & W
Augustana College *South Dakota* M & W
Augustana College *Illinois* M & W
Aurora University *Illinois* M & W
Austin College *Texas* M & W
Austin Peay State University *Tennessee* M & W
Averett University *Virginia* M & W
Azusa Pacific University *California* M
Babson College *Massachusetts* M & W
Baker University *Kansas* M & W
Bakersfield College *California* M & W
Baldwin-Wallace College *Ohio* M & W
Ball State University *Indiana* M & W
Baptist Bible College of Pennsylvania *Pennsylvania* W
Barclay College *Kansas* M & W
Bard College *New York* M & W
Barnard College *New York* W
Barry University *Florida* M & W
Barton College *North Carolina* M & W
Barton County Community College *Kansas* M & W
Bates College *Maine* M & W
Bay Path College *Massachusetts* W
Baylor University *Texas* M & W
Becker College *Massachusetts* M & W
Belhaven University *Mississippi* M & W
Bellarmine University *Kentucky* M & W
Bellevue College *Washington* W
Belmont Abbey College *North Carolina* M & W
Belmont University *Tennessee* M & W
Beloit College *Wisconsin* M & W
Bemidji State University *Minnesota* W
Benedict College *South Carolina* M
Benedictine University *Illinois* W
Bentley University *Massachusetts* M & W
Berea College *Kentucky* M & W
Bergen Community College *New Jersey* M & W
Bernard M. Baruch College of the City University of New York *New York* M & W
Berry College *Georgia* M & W
Bethany College *West Virginia* M & W
Bethany College *Kansas* M & W
Bethany Lutheran College *Minnesota* M & W
Bethel College *Kansas* M & W
Bethel College *Indiana* M & W
Bethel University *Tennessee* M & W
Bethel University *Minnesota* M & W
Bethune-Cookman University *Florida* M & W
Biola University *California* M & W
Birmingham-Southern College *Alabama* M & W
Bismarck State College *North Dakota* M & W
Blackburn College *Illinois* W
Bloomfield College *New Jersey* M
Bloomsburg University of Pennsylvania *Pennsylvania* M & W
Bluefield College *Virginia* M & W
Bluefield State College *West Virginia* M & W
Boise State University *Idaho* M & W
Boston College *Massachusetts* M & W
Boston University *Massachusetts* M & W
Bowdoin College *Maine* M & W
Bowie State University *Maryland* W
Bowling Green State University *Ohio* W
Bradley University *Illinois* M & W
Brandeis University *Massachusetts* M & W
Brenau University *Georgia* W
Brevard College *North Carolina* M & W
Briar Cliff University *Iowa* M & W
Bridgewater College *Virginia* M & W
Bridgewater State College *Massachusetts* M & W
Brigham Young University *Utah* M & W
Brigham Young University–Hawaii *Hawaii* M & W
Brookdale Community College *New Jersey* M & W
Brookhaven College *Texas* M & W
Brooklyn College of the City University of New York *New York* M & W
Broome Community College *New York* M & W
Broward College *Florida* W
Brown University *Rhode Island* M & W
Bryant University *Rhode Island* M & W
Bryn Mawr College *Pennsylvania* W
Bucknell University *Pennsylvania* M & W
Bucks County Community College *Pennsylvania* M & W
Buena Vista University *Iowa* M & W
Buffalo State College, State University of New York *New York* W
Butler Community College *Kansas* M & W
Butler University *Indiana* M & W
Cabrillo College *California* M & W
Cabrini College *Pennsylvania* M & W
Caldwell College *New Jersey* M & W
California Institute of Technology *California* M & W
California Lutheran University *California* M & W
California Polytechnic State University, San Luis Obispo *California* M & W
California State Polytechnic University, Pomona *California* M & W
California State University, Bakersfield *California* W
California State University, Chico *California* M & W
California State University, Fresno *California* M & W
California State University, Fullerton *California* W
California State University, Long Beach *California* W
California State University, Los Angeles *California* W
California State University, Northridge *California* W
California State University, Sacramento *California* M & W
California State University, San Bernardino *California* W
California State University, Stanislaus *California* W
California University of Pennsylvania *Pennsylvania* W
Calumet College of Saint Joseph *Indiana* M & W
Calvin College *Michigan* M & W
Cameron University *Oklahoma* M & W
Campbell University *North Carolina* M & W
Campbellsville University *Kentucky* M & W
Capital University *Ohio* M & W
Carleton College *Minnesota* M & W
Carlow University *Pennsylvania* W
Carnegie Mellon University *Pennsylvania* M & W
Carroll University *Wisconsin* M & W
Carson-Newman College *Tennessee* M & W
Carthage College *Wisconsin* M & W
Case Western Reserve University *Ohio* M & W
Castleton State College *Vermont* M & W
Catawba College *North Carolina* M & W
The Catholic University of America *District of Columbia* M & W
Cecil College *Maryland* W
Cedar Crest College *Pennsylvania* W
Cedarville University *Ohio* M & W
Centenary College of Louisiana *Louisiana* M & W
Central Alabama Community College *Alabama* M & W
Central Christian College of the Bible *Missouri* M & W
Central Christian College of Kansas *Kansas* M & W
Central College *Iowa* M & W
Central Florida Community College *Florida* W
Central State University *Ohio* M & W
Centre College *Kentucky* M & W
Cerritos College *California* M & W
Chabot College *California* M & W
Chaffey College *California* M & W
Chaminade University of Honolulu *Hawaii* M & W
Chapman University *California* M & W
Charleston Southern University *South Carolina* M & W
Chatham University *Pennsylvania* W
Chesapeake College *Maryland* M & W
Chestnut Hill College *Pennsylvania* M & W
Chicago State University *Illinois* M & W
Chowan University *North Carolina* M & W
Christian Brothers University *Tennessee* M & W
Christopher Newport University *Virginia* M & W
The Citadel, The Military College of South Carolina *South Carolina* M
Citrus College *California* M & W
City College of the City University of New York *New York* M & W
City College of San Francisco *California* M & W
City Colleges of Chicago, Harry S. Truman College *Illinois* M & W
Claremont McKenna College *California* M & W
Clarion University of Pennsylvania *Pennsylvania* W
Clark Atlanta University *Georgia* W
Clark University *Massachusetts* M & W
Clarke College *Iowa* W
Clayton State University *Georgia* W
Clemson University *South Carolina* M & W
Cleveland State University *Ohio* M & W
Cloud County Community College *Kansas* M & W
Coastal Carolina University *South Carolina* M & W
Coe College *Iowa* M & W
Coker College *South Carolina* M & W
Colby College *Maine* M & W
Colby-Sawyer College *New Hampshire* M & W
Colgate University *New York* M & W
The College at Brockport, State University of New York *New York* W

M = Men; W = Women

College of Charleston *South Carolina* M & W
College of the Desert *California* M & W
College of DuPage *Illinois* M & W
College of the Holy Cross *Massachusetts* M & W
The College of Idaho *Idaho* M & W
College of Lake County *Illinois* M & W
College of Marin *California* M & W
College of Mount St. Joseph *Ohio* M & W
College of Mount Saint Vincent *New York* M & W
The College of New Jersey *New Jersey* M & W
The College of New Rochelle *New York* W
College of Notre Dame of Maryland *Maryland* W
College of Saint Benedict *Minnesota* W
College of Saint Elizabeth *New Jersey* W
The College of Saint Rose *New York* W
The College of St. Scholastica *Minnesota* M & W
College of San Mateo *California* W
College of the Sequoias *California* M & W
College of Southern Maryland *Maryland* M
College of Staten Island of the City University of New York *New York* M & W
The College of William and Mary *Virginia* M & W
The College of Wooster *Ohio* M & W
Collin County Community College District *Texas* M & W
Colorado Christian University *Colorado* M & W
The Colorado College *Colorado* M & W
Colorado State University *Colorado* M & W
Colorado State University–Pueblo *Colorado* M & W
Columbia College *South Carolina* W
Columbia College *California* M & W
Columbia University *New York* M & W
Columbia University, School of General Studies *New York* M & W
Columbus State University *Georgia* M & W
Community College of Allegheny County *Pennsylvania* M & W
Community College of Beaver County *Pennsylvania* M & W
Community College of Philadelphia *Pennsylvania* M & W
Community College of Rhode Island *Rhode Island* M & W
Concord University *West Virginia* M & W
Concordia College *Minnesota* M & W
Concordia College–New York *New York* M & W
Concordia University *California* M & W
Concordia University Chicago *Illinois* M & W
Concordia University, Nebraska *Nebraska* M & W
Concordia University Texas *Texas* M & W
Concordia University Wisconsin *Wisconsin* M & W
Connecticut College *Connecticut* M & W
Converse College *South Carolina* W
Cooper Union for the Advancement of Science and Art *New York* M & W
Copiah-Lincoln Community College *Mississippi* M & W
Coppin State University *Maryland* M & W
Cornell College *Iowa* M & W
Cornell University *New York* M & W
Cosumnes River College *California* M & W
County College of Morris *New Jersey* M
Covenant College *Georgia* M & W
Cowley County Community College and Area Vocational–Technical School *Kansas* M & W
Creighton University *Nebraska* M & W
Crossroads College *Minnesota* M & W
Cuesta College *California* W
The Culinary Institute of America *New York* M & W
Cumberland University *Tennessee* M & W
Curry College *Massachusetts* M & W
Cuyamaca College *California* W
Cypress College *California* M & W
Dallas Baptist University *Texas* M & W
Dalton State College *Georgia* M & W
Dartmouth College *New Hampshire* M & W
Davidson College *North Carolina* M & W
De Anza College *California* M & W
Defiance College *Ohio* M & W
Delaware County Community College *Pennsylvania* M & W
Delaware State University *Delaware* M & W
Delta State University *Mississippi* M & W
Denison University *Ohio* M & W
DePaul University *Illinois* M & W
DePauw University *Indiana* M & W
DeSales University *Pennsylvania* M & W
Diablo Valley College *California* M & W
Dickinson College *Pennsylvania* M & W
Dixie State College of Utah *Utah* W
Doane College *Nebraska* M & W
Dominican University *Illinois* M & W
Dominican University of California *California* W
Dowling College *New York* M & W
Drake University *Iowa* M & W
Drew University *New Jersey* M & W
Drexel University *Pennsylvania* M & W
Drury University *Missouri* M & W
Duke University *North Carolina* M & W
Duquesne University *Pennsylvania* M & W
Dutchess Community College *New York* M & W
D'Youville College *New York* M & W
Earlham College *Indiana* M & W
East Carolina University *North Carolina* M & W
East Central Community College *Mississippi* M & W
East Central University *Oklahoma* M & W
East Stroudsburg University of Pennsylvania *Pennsylvania* M & W
East Tennessee State University *Tennessee* M & W
Eastern Illinois University *Illinois* M & W
Eastern Kentucky University *Kentucky* M & W
Eastern Michigan University *Michigan* W
Eastern Nazarene College *Massachusetts* M & W
Eastern Washington University *Washington* M & W
Eastfield College *Texas* M & W
Eckerd College *Florida* M & W
Edgewood College *Wisconsin* M & W
Edward Waters College *Florida* M & W
El Camino College *California* M & W
Elgin Community College *Illinois* M & W
Elizabeth City State University *North Carolina* W
Elizabethtown College *Pennsylvania* M & W
Elmhurst College *Illinois* M & W
Elmira College *New York* M & W
Elon University *North Carolina* M & W
Embry-Riddle Aeronautical University *Florida* M & W
Emerson College *Massachusetts* M & W
Emmanuel College *Massachusetts* W
Emmanuel College *Georgia* M & W
Emory & Henry College *Virginia* M & W
Emory University *Georgia* M & W
Emory University, Oxford College *Georgia* M & W
Emporia State University *Kansas* M & W
Endicott College *Massachusetts* M & W
Erskine College *South Carolina* M & W
Eureka College *Illinois* M & W
Evangel University *Missouri* M & W
Fairfield University *Connecticut* M & W
Fairleigh Dickinson University, College at Florham *New Jersey* M & W
Fairleigh Dickinson University, Metropolitan Campus *New Jersey* M & W
Fairmont State University *West Virginia* M & W
Farmingdale State College *New York* M & W
Fashion Institute of Technology *New York* W
Fayetteville State University *North Carolina* W
Ferris State University *Michigan* M & W
Ferrum College *Virginia* M & W
Flagler College *Florida* M & W
Florida Agricultural and Mechanical University *Florida* M & W
Florida Atlantic University *Florida* M & W
Florida Gulf Coast University *Florida* M & W
Florida Institute of Technology *Florida* M & W
Florida International University *Florida* W
Florida Southern College *Florida* M & W
Florida State College at Jacksonville *Florida* W
Florida State University *Florida* M & W
Fontbonne University *Missouri* M & W
Foothill College *California* M
Fordham University *New York* M & W
Fort Hays State University *Kansas* W
Fort Valley State University *Georgia* M & W
Francis Marion University *South Carolina* M & W
Franciscan University of Steubenville *Ohio* M & W
Franklin College *Indiana* M & W
Franklin & Marshall College *Pennsylvania* M & W
Franklin Pierce University *New Hampshire* M & W
Fresno City College *California* M & W
Fresno Pacific University *California* M & W
Friends University *Kansas* M & W
Frostburg State University *Maryland* M & W
Fullerton College *California* M & W
Furman University *South Carolina* M & W
Gadsden State Community College *Alabama* M
Gallaudet University *District of Columbia* M
Gardner-Webb University *North Carolina* M & W
GateWay Community College *Arizona* M & W
Gavilan College *California* M
Geneva College *Pennsylvania* W
George Fox University *Oregon* M & W
George Mason University *Virginia* M & W
The George Washington University *District of Columbia* M & W
Georgetown College *Kentucky* M & W
Georgetown University *District of Columbia* M & W
Georgia College & State University *Georgia* M & W
Georgia Institute of Technology *Georgia* M & W
Georgia Perimeter College *Georgia* W
Georgia Southern University *Georgia* M & W
Georgia Southwestern State University *Georgia* M & W
Georgia State University *Georgia* M & W
Georgian Court University *New Jersey* W
Gettysburg College *Pennsylvania* M & W
Glendale Community College *California* M & W
Glendale Community College *Arizona* M & W
Gloucester County College *New Jersey* M & W
Goldey-Beacom College *Delaware* W
Gonzaga University *Washington* M & W
Gordon College *Massachusetts* M & W
Gordon College *Georgia* W
Goshen College *Indiana* M & W
Goucher College *Maryland* M & W
Grace College *Indiana* M & W
Graceland University *Iowa* M & W
Grambling State University *Louisiana* M & W
Grand Canyon University *Arizona* W
Grand Rapids Community College *Michigan* M & W
Grand Valley State University *Michigan* M & W
Green Mountain College *Vermont* M
Green River Community College *Washington* M & W
Greensboro College *North Carolina* M & W
Greenville College *Illinois* M & W
Grinnell College *Iowa* M & W
Grossmont College *California* M & W
Grove City College *Pennsylvania* M & W
Guilford College *North Carolina* M & W
Gustavus Adolphus College *Minnesota* M & W
Gwynedd-Mercy College *Pennsylvania* M & W
Hamilton College *New York* M & W
Hamline University *Minnesota* M & W
Hampden-Sydney College *Virginia* M
Hampton University *Virginia* M & W
Hanover College *Indiana* M & W
Hardin-Simmons University *Texas* M & W
Harding University *Arkansas* M & W
Harford Community College *Maryland* M & W
Harrisburg Area Community College *Pennsylvania* M & W
Hartnell College *California* M & W
Hartwick College *New York* M & W
Harvard University *Massachusetts* M & W
Harvey Mudd College *California* M & W
Hastings College *Nebraska* M & W
Haverford College *Pennsylvania* M & W
Hawai'i Pacific University *Hawaii* M & W
Heidelberg University *Ohio* M & W
Henderson State University *Arkansas* M & W
Hendrix College *Arkansas* M & W
Henry Ford Community College *Michigan* W
Herkimer County Community College *New York* M & W
Hesston College *Kansas* M & W
High Point University *North Carolina* M & W
Hillsborough Community College *Florida* W
Hinds Community College *Mississippi* M & W
Hiram College *Ohio* M & W

M = Men; W = Women

Hobart and William Smith Colleges *New York* M & W
Hofstra University *New York* M & W
Hollins University *Virginia* W
Holmes Community College *Mississippi* W
Holy Family University *Pennsylvania* W
Hood College *Maryland* M & W
Hope College *Michigan* M & W
Hope International University *California* M & W
Howard Payne University *Texas* M & W
Howard University *District of Columbia* M & W
Hudson Valley Community College *New York* M & W
Hunter College of the City University of New York *New York* M & W
Huntingdon College *Alabama* M & W
Huntington University *Indiana* M & W
Idaho State University *Idaho* M & W
Illinois College *Illinois* M & W
Illinois Eastern Community Colleges, Wabash Valley College *Illinois* M
Illinois State University *Illinois* M & W
Illinois Valley Community College *Illinois* M & W
Illinois Wesleyan University *Illinois* M & W
Immaculata University *Pennsylvania* W
Imperial Valley College *California* M & W
Independence Community College *Kansas* M & W
Indiana University Bloomington *Indiana* M & W
Indiana University East *Indiana* M & W
Indiana University of Pennsylvania *Pennsylvania* W
Indiana University Southeast *Indiana* M & W
Indiana University–Purdue University Fort Wayne *Indiana* M & W
Indiana University–Purdue University Indianapolis *Indiana* M & W
Indiana Wesleyan University *Indiana* M & W
Inter American University of Puerto Rico, Aguadilla Campus *Puerto Rico* M & W
Inter American University of Puerto Rico, Barranquitas Campus *Puerto Rico* M & W
Inter American University of Puerto Rico, San Germán Campus *Puerto Rico* M & W
Iowa State University of Science and Technology *Iowa* W
Irvine Valley College *California* M & W
Itawamba Community College *Mississippi* M & W
Ithaca College *New York* M & W
Jackson State University *Mississippi* M & W
Jacksonville State University *Alabama* M & W
Jacksonville University *Florida* M & W
James H. Faulkner State Community College *Alabama* M & W
James Madison University *Virginia* M & W
Jefferson College of Health Sciences *Virginia* M & W
John Brown University *Arkansas* M & W
John Carroll University *Ohio* M & W
John Jay College of Criminal Justice of the City University of New York *New York* M & W
The Johns Hopkins University *Maryland* M & W
Johnson C. Smith University *North Carolina* M & W
Johnson County Community College *Kansas* M & W
Johnson State College *Vermont* M & W
Johnson & Wales University *Rhode Island* M & W
Johnson & Wales University *Colorado* M & W
Joliet Junior College *Illinois* M & W
Jones County Junior College *Mississippi* M & W
Judson College *Alabama* W
Judson University *Illinois* M & W
Juniata College *Pennsylvania* M & W
Kalamazoo College *Michigan* M & W
Kalamazoo Valley Community College *Michigan* W
Kansas State University *Kansas* W
Kansas Wesleyan University *Kansas* M & W
Kaskaskia College *Illinois* M
Kean University *New Jersey* W
Kennesaw State University *Georgia* M & W
Kentucky Wesleyan College *Kentucky* W
Kenyon College *Ohio* M & W
Keystone College *Pennsylvania* M & W
King College *Tennessee* M & W
King's College *Pennsylvania* M & W
Kingsborough Community College of the City University of New York *New York* M & W
Knox College *Illinois* M & W
Kutztown University of Pennsylvania *Pennsylvania* M & W
La Roche College *Pennsylvania* W
La Salle University *Pennsylvania* M & W
La Sierra University *California* M & W
Labette Community College *Kansas* W
Lafayette College *Pennsylvania* M & W
LaGrange College *Georgia* M & W
Lake Erie College *Ohio* M & W
Lake Forest College *Illinois* M & W
Lake Land College *Illinois* M & W
Lake Superior State University *Michigan* M & W
Lakeland College *Wisconsin* M & W
Lamar University *Texas* M & W
Lambuth University *Tennessee* M & W
Lander University *South Carolina* M & W
Lane College *Tennessee* M & W
Laredo Community College *Texas* M & W
Lawrence University *Wisconsin* M & W
Le Moyne College *New York* M & W
Lebanon Valley College *Pennsylvania* M & W
Lee College *Texas* W
Lee University *Tennessee* M & W
Lees-McRae College *North Carolina* M & W
Lehigh University *Pennsylvania* M & W
Lehman College of the City University of New York *New York* M & W
LeMoyne-Owen College *Tennessee* M & W
Lenoir-Rhyne University *North Carolina* M & W
LeTourneau University *Texas* M & W
Lewis & Clark College *Oregon* M & W
Lewis and Clark Community College *Illinois* M & W
Lewis-Clark State College *Idaho* M & W
Lewis University *Illinois* M & W
Liberty University *Virginia* M & W
Limestone College *South Carolina* M & W
Lincoln College *Illinois* M & W
Lincoln Memorial University *Tennessee* M & W
Lincoln University *Pennsylvania* M & W
Lincoln University *Missouri* W
Lindenwood University *Missouri* M & W
Lindsey Wilson College *Kentucky* M & W
Linfield College *Oregon* M & W
Lipscomb University *Tennessee* M & W
Livingstone College *North Carolina* W
Logan University–College of Chiropractic *Missouri* M
Long Beach City College *California* M & W
Long Island University, Brooklyn Campus *New York* W
Long Island University, C.W. Post Campus *New York* W
Longwood University *Virginia* M & W
Loras College *Iowa* M & W
Los Angeles Pierce College *California* M & W
Los Angeles Trade-Technical College *California* M
Louisiana College *Louisiana* W
Louisiana State University and Agricultural and Mechanical College *Louisiana* M & W
Louisiana Tech University *Louisiana* W
Loyola Marymount University *California* M & W
Loyola University Maryland *Maryland* M & W
Loyola University New Orleans *Louisiana* M & W
Luther College *Iowa* M & W
Lycoming College *Pennsylvania* M & W
Lynchburg College *Virginia* M & W
Lyndon State College *Vermont* M & W
Macalester College *Minnesota* M & W
Madison Area Technical College *Wisconsin* M & W
Malone University *Ohio* M & W
Manchester College *Indiana* M & W
Manhattan College *New York* M & W
Manhattanville College *New York* M & W
Marian University *Wisconsin* M & W
Marian University *Indiana* M & W
Marietta College *Ohio* M & W
Marion Military Institute *Alabama* M & W
Marist College *New York* M & W
Marquette University *Wisconsin* M & W
Mars Hill College *North Carolina* M & W
Marshall University *West Virginia* W
Martin Luther College *Minnesota* M & W
Martin Methodist College *Tennessee* M & W
Mary Baldwin College *Virginia* W
Marymount College, Palos Verdes, California *California* M & W
Maryville College *Tennessee* M & W
Maryville University of Saint Louis *Missouri* M & W
Marywood University *Pennsylvania* M & W
Massachusetts Bay Community College *Massachusetts* M & W
Massachusetts College of Liberal Arts *Massachusetts* W
Massachusetts Institute of Technology *Massachusetts* M & W
The Master's College and Seminary *California* W
McDaniel College *Maryland* M & W
McDowell Technical Community College *North Carolina* M
McGill University *Quebec* M & W
McHenry County College *Illinois* M & W
McKendree University *Illinois* M & W
McMaster University *Ontario* M & W
McMurry University *Texas* M & W
McNeese State University *Louisiana* W
McPherson College *Kansas* M & W
Medgar Evers College of the City University of New York *New York* W
Merced College *California* M & W
Mercer County Community College *New Jersey* M & W
Mercer University *Georgia* M & W
Mercy College *New York* M
Mercyhurst College *Pennsylvania* M & W
Meredith College *North Carolina* W
Meridian Community College *Mississippi* M & W
Merrimack College *Massachusetts* M & W
Mesa Community College *Arizona* M & W
Mesa State College *Colorado* M & W
Messiah College *Pennsylvania* M & W
Methodist University *North Carolina* M & W
Metropolitan State College of Denver *Colorado* M & W
Miami University *Ohio* M & W
Miami University Hamilton *Ohio* M & W
Miami University–Middletown Campus *Ohio* M & W
Michigan State University *Michigan* M & W
Michigan Technological University *Michigan* M & W
Middle Tennessee State University *Tennessee* M & W
Middlebury College *Vermont* M & W
Middlesex County College *New Jersey* M & W
Midland Lutheran College *Nebraska* M & W
Midway College *Kentucky* W
Midwestern State University *Texas* M & W
Millersville University of Pennsylvania *Pennsylvania* M & W
Milligan College *Tennessee* M & W
Millikin University *Illinois* W
Mills College *California* W
Millsaps College *Mississippi* M & W
Milwaukee School of Engineering *Wisconsin* M & W
Minnesota State University Mankato *Minnesota* M & W
Minnesota State University Moorhead *Minnesota* W
Misericordia University *Pennsylvania* M & W
Mission College *California* M & W
Mississippi College *Mississippi* M & W
Mississippi Delta Community College *Mississippi* M & W
Mississippi Gulf Coast Community College *Mississippi* M & W
Mississippi State University *Mississippi* M & W
Mississippi Valley State University *Mississippi* M & W
Missouri Baptist University *Missouri* M & W
Missouri Southern State University *Missouri* W
Missouri Valley College *Missouri* M & W
Missouri Western State University *Missouri* W
Modesto Junior College *California* M & W
Mohawk Valley Community College *New York* M & W
Molloy College *New York* W
Monmouth College *Illinois* M & W

M = Men; W = Women

Monmouth University *New Jersey* M & W
Monroe Community College *New York* M & W
Montana State University *Montana* M & W
Montana State University Billings *Montana* M & W
Monterey Peninsula College *California* M & W
Montgomery College *Maryland* M & W
Montreat College *North Carolina* M & W
Moraine Valley Community College *Illinois* M & W
Moravian College *Pennsylvania* M & W
Morehead State University *Kentucky* M & W
Morehouse College *Georgia* M
Morgan State University *Maryland* M & W
Morningside College *Iowa* M & W
Morris College *South Carolina* M & W
Mount Holyoke College *Massachusetts* W
Mount Ida College *Massachusetts* W
Mount Mary College *Wisconsin* W
Mount Olive College *North Carolina* M & W
Mount Saint Mary College *New York* M & W
Mount St. Mary's University *Maryland* M & W
Mt. San Antonio College *California* M & W
Mt. San Jacinto College *California* M & W
Muhlenberg College *Pennsylvania* M & W
Murray State University *Kentucky* M & W
Muskegon Community College *Michigan* M & W
Muskingum University *Ohio* M & W
Napa Valley College *California* M & W
Nassau Community College *New York* M & W
Nazareth College of Rochester *New York* M & W
Nebraska Wesleyan University *Nebraska* M & W
Neumann University *Pennsylvania* M & W
New Jersey Institute of Technology *New Jersey* M & W
New Mexico Military Institute *New Mexico* M & W
New Mexico State University *New Mexico* M & W
New York City College of Technology of the City University of New York *New York* M & W
New York University *New York* M & W
Newberry College *South Carolina* M & W
Newbury College *Massachusetts* M & W
Newman University *Kansas* M & W
Niagara University *New York* M & W
Nicholls State University *Louisiana* M & W
Nichols College *Massachusetts* M & W
Norfolk State University *Virginia* M & W
North Carolina Agricultural and Technical State University *North Carolina* M & W
North Carolina Central University *North Carolina* M & W
North Carolina State University *North Carolina* M & W
North Carolina Wesleyan College *North Carolina* M & W
North Central College *Illinois* M & W
North Central Texas College *Texas* W
North Central University *Minnesota* M & W
North Georgia College & State University *Georgia* M & W
North Greenville University *South Carolina* M & W
Northampton Community College *Pennsylvania* M & W
Northeast Mississippi Community College *Mississippi* M & W
Northeastern State University *Oklahoma* W
Northern Arizona University *Arizona* M & W
Northern Illinois University *Illinois* M & W
Northern Kentucky University *Kentucky* M & W
Northern State University *South Dakota* M & W
Northwest Mississippi Community College *Mississippi* M & W
Northwest Missouri State University *Missouri* M & W
Northwestern College *Minnesota* M & W
Northwestern College *Iowa* M & W
Northwestern State University of Louisiana *Louisiana* W
Northwestern University *Illinois* M & W
Northwood University *Michigan* M & W
Northwood University, Florida Campus *Florida* M & W
Norwich University *Vermont* M & W
Notre Dame College *Ohio* M
Notre Dame de Namur University *California* W
Nova Southeastern University *Florida* W

Oakland City University *Indiana* M & W
Oakland Community College *Michigan* W
Oakland University *Michigan* W
Oakton Community College *Illinois* M & W
Oberlin College *Ohio* M & W
Occidental College *California* M & W
Ocean County College *New Jersey* M & W
Oglethorpe University *Georgia* M & W
Ohio Dominican University *Ohio* M & W
Ohio Northern University *Ohio* M & W
The Ohio State University *Ohio* M & W
Ohio University–Zanesville *Ohio* M & W
Ohio Wesleyan University *Ohio* M & W
Ohlone College *California* M & W
Oklahoma Baptist University *Oklahoma* M & W
Oklahoma Christian University *Oklahoma* M & W
Oklahoma Wesleyan University *Oklahoma* M & W
Old Dominion University *Virginia* M & W
Olivet College *Michigan* W
Olivet Nazarene University *Illinois* M & W
Onondaga Community College *New York* M & W
Oral Roberts University *Oklahoma* M & W
Orange Coast College *California* M & W
Orange County Community College *New York* M & W
Otterbein University *Ohio* M & W
Ouachita Baptist University *Arkansas* M & W
Our Lady of the Lake University of San Antonio *Texas* M & W
Pace University *New York* M & W
Pacific Lutheran University *Washington* M & W
Pacific University *Oregon* M & W
Palm Beach Atlantic University *Florida* M & W
Palomar College *California* M & W
Paradise Valley Community College *Arizona* M & W
Pasadena City College *California* M & W
Peace College *North Carolina* W
Pearl River Community College *Mississippi* M & W
Penn State Abington *Pennsylvania* M & W
Penn State Altoona *Pennsylvania* M & W
Penn State Berks *Pennsylvania* M & W
Penn State Brandywine *Pennsylvania* M & W
Penn State Erie, The Behrend College *Pennsylvania* M & W
Penn State Harrisburg *Pennsylvania* M & W
Penn State Hazleton *Pennsylvania* M & W
Penn State Lehigh Valley *Pennsylvania* M & W
Penn State Mont Alto *Pennsylvania* M & W
Penn State University Park *Pennsylvania* M & W
Pennsylvania College of Technology *Pennsylvania* M & W
Pepperdine University *California* M & W
Pfeiffer University *North Carolina* M & W
Philadelphia Biblical University *Pennsylvania* W
Philadelphia University *Pennsylvania* M & W
Phoenix College *Arizona* M & W
Piedmont College *Georgia* M & W
Pikeville College *Kentucky* M & W
Pima Community College *Arizona* M & W
Pine Manor College *Massachusetts* W
Pitzer College *California* M & W
Plymouth State University *New Hampshire* W
Point Loma Nazarene University *California* M & W
Polytechnic Institute of NYU *New York* M & W
Polytechnic University of Puerto Rico *Puerto Rico* M & W
Pomona College *California* M & W
Pontifical Catholic University of Puerto Rico *Puerto Rico* M & W
Porterville College *California* M & W
Portland State University *Oregon* M & W
Prairie State College *Illinois* W
Prairie View A&M University *Texas* M & W
Pratt Institute *New York* M & W
Presbyterian College *South Carolina* M & W
Prince George's Community College *Maryland* M & W
Princeton University *New Jersey* M & W
Principia College *Illinois* M & W
Providence College *Rhode Island* W
Purdue University *Indiana* M & W
Queens College of the City University of New York *New York* M & W

Queens University of Charlotte *North Carolina* M & W
Queensborough Community College of the City University of New York *New York* M & W
Quincy University *Illinois* M & W
Quinnipiac University *Connecticut* M & W
Radford University *Virginia* M & W
Ramapo College of New Jersey *New Jersey* M & W
Randolph College *Virginia* M & W
Randolph-Macon College *Virginia* M & W
Reedley College *California* M & W
Regis College *Massachusetts* W
Reinhardt University *Georgia* M & W
Rend Lake College *Illinois* W
Rensselaer Polytechnic Institute *New York* M & W
Research College of Nursing *Missouri* M & W
Rhode Island College *Rhode Island* M & W
Rhodes College *Tennessee* M & W
Rice University *Texas* M & W
The Richard Stockton College of New Jersey *New Jersey* W
Rider University *New Jersey* M & W
Rio Hondo College *California* M & W
Ripon College *Wisconsin* M & W
Riverside Community College District *California* M & W
Roanoke College *Virginia* M & W
Robert Morris University *Pennsylvania* M & W
Robert Morris University Illinois *Illinois* W
Roberts Wesleyan College *New York* M & W
Rochester Institute of Technology *New York* M & W
Rock Valley College *Illinois* M & W
Rockford College *Illinois* M & W
Rockhurst University *Missouri* M & W
Rockland Community College *New York* M & W
Roger Williams University *Rhode Island* M & W
Rollins College *Florida* M & W
Roosevelt University *Illinois* M & W
Rose-Hulman Institute of Technology *Indiana* M & W
Rosemont College *Pennsylvania* M & W
Rowan University *New Jersey* M & W
Roxbury Community College *Massachusetts* M & W
Russell Sage College *New York* W
Rust College *Mississippi* M & W
Rutgers, The State University of New Jersey, New Brunswick *New Jersey* M & W
Rutgers, The State University of New Jersey, Newark *New Jersey* M & W
Sacramento City College *California* M & W
Sacred Heart University *Connecticut* M & W
Saddleback College *California* M & W
Sage College of Albany *New York* M & W
Saginaw Valley State University *Michigan* M & W
St. Ambrose University *Iowa* M & W
St. Andrews Presbyterian College *North Carolina* M & W
Saint Anselm College *New Hampshire* M & W
Saint Augustine's College *North Carolina* M & W
St. Bonaventure University *New York* M & W
St. Catherine University *Minnesota* W
St. Cloud State University *Minnesota* M & W
St. Edward's University *Texas* M & W
St. Francis College *New York* M & W
Saint Francis University *Pennsylvania* M & W
St. John Fisher College *New York* M & W
St. John's University *New York* M & W
Saint John's University *Minnesota* M
Saint Joseph College *Connecticut* W
Saint Joseph's College *Indiana* M & W
Saint Joseph's University *Pennsylvania* M & W
St. Lawrence University *New York* M & W
Saint Leo University *Florida* M & W
Saint Louis University *Missouri* M & W
Saint Mary's College *Indiana* W
Saint Mary's College of California *California* M & W
St. Mary's College of Maryland *Maryland* M & W
St. Mary's University *Texas* M & W
Saint Mary's University of Minnesota *Minnesota* M & W
Saint Michael's College *Vermont* M & W
St. Norbert College *Wisconsin* M & W

M = Men; W = Women

St. Olaf College *Minnesota* M & W
Saint Paul's College *Virginia* M & W
Saint Peter's College *New Jersey* M & W
St. Thomas Aquinas College *New York* M & W
St. Thomas University *Florida* M & W
Saint Vincent College *Pennsylvania* M & W
Salem College *North Carolina* W
Salem Community College *New Jersey* M & W
Salem International University *West Virginia* M
Salem State College *Massachusetts* M & W
Salisbury University *Maryland* M & W
Salve Regina University *Rhode Island* M & W
Sam Houston State University *Texas* M & W
Samford University *Alabama* M & W
San Bernardino Valley College *California* M & W
San Diego City College *California* M & W
San Diego Mesa College *California* M & W
San Diego State University *California* M & W
San Jacinto College District *Texas* M & W
San Joaquin Delta College *California* M & W
San Jose State University *California* W
Santa Ana College *California* M & W
Santa Barbara City College *California* M & W
Santa Clara University *California* M & W
Santa Monica College *California* W
Santa Rosa Junior College *California* M & W
Sarah Lawrence College *New York* M & W
Sauk Valley Community College *Illinois* M & W
Savannah College of Art and Design *Georgia* M & W
Savannah State University *Georgia* W
Schreiner University *Texas* M & W
Scottsdale Community College *Arizona* M & W
Scripps College *California* W
Seton Hall University *New Jersey* W
Seton Hill University *Pennsylvania* W
Sewanee: The University of the South *Tennessee* M & W
Seward County Community College *Kansas* M & W
Shasta College *California* M & W
Shaw University *North Carolina* M & W
Shawnee State University *Ohio* W
Shenandoah University *Virginia* M & W
Shepherd University *West Virginia* M & W
Shippensburg University of Pennsylvania *Pennsylvania* W
Shoreline Community College *Washington* M & W
Shorter University *Georgia* M & W
Siena College *New York* M & W
Sierra College *California* M & W
Simmons College *Massachusetts* W
Simpson College *Iowa* M & W
Sinclair Community College *Ohio* M & W
Skagit Valley College *Washington* M & W
Skidmore College *New York* M & W
Slippery Rock University of Pennsylvania *Pennsylvania* M & W
Smith College *Massachusetts* W
Snead State Community College *Alabama* W
Sonoma State University *California* M & W
South Carolina State University *South Carolina* M & W
South Dakota School of Mines and Technology *South Dakota* M
South Dakota State University *South Dakota* M & W
South Florida Community College *Florida* W
Southeast Missouri State University *Missouri* W
Southeastern Louisiana University *Louisiana* W
Southeastern Oklahoma State University *Oklahoma* M & W
Southeastern University *Florida* W
Southern Arkansas University–Magnolia *Arkansas* W
Southern Illinois University Carbondale *Illinois* M & W
Southern Illinois University Edwardsville *Illinois* M & W
Southern Methodist University *Texas* M & W
Southern Nazarene University *Oklahoma* M & W
Southern New Hampshire University *New Hampshire* M & W
Southern Oregon University *Oregon* W
Southern University and Agricultural and Mechanical College *Louisiana* M & W
Southern Utah University *Utah* W
Southern Virginia University *Virginia* M & W
Southwest Baptist University *Missouri* M & W
Southwest Minnesota State University *Minnesota* W
Southwest Mississippi Community College *Mississippi* M & W
Southwestern College *Kansas* M & W
Southwestern College *California* M & W
Southwestern Illinois College *Illinois* M & W
Southwestern University *Texas* M & W
Spartanburg Methodist College *South Carolina* M & W
Spelman College *Georgia* W
Spokane Community College *Washington* M & W
Spokane Falls Community College *Washington* M & W
Spring Arbor University *Michigan* M & W
Spring Hill College *Alabama* M & W
Springfield College *Massachusetts* M & W
Stanford University *California* M & W
State University of New York at Binghamton *New York* M & W
State University of New York College of Agriculture and Technology at Cobleskill *New York* M & W
State University of New York College of Agriculture and Technology at Morrisville *New York* W
State University of New York College at Cortland *New York* W
State University of New York College at Geneseo *New York* M & W
State University of New York College at Oneonta *New York* M & W
State University of New York College at Potsdam *New York* W
State University of New York College of Technology at Delhi *New York* M & W
State University of New York at Fredonia *New York* M & W
State University of New York at New Paltz *New York* M & W
State University of New York at Oswego *New York* M & W
State University of New York at Plattsburgh *New York* W
Stephen F. Austin State University *Texas* W
Stephens College *Missouri* W
Sterling College *Kansas* M & W
Stetson University *Florida* M & W
Stevens Institute of Technology *New Jersey* M & W
Stevenson University *Maryland* M & W
Stillman College *Alabama* M & W
Stonehill College *Massachusetts* M & W
Stony Brook University, State University of New York *New York* M & W
Suffolk County Community College *New York* M & W
Suffolk University *Massachusetts* M & W
Sul Ross State University *Texas* M & W
Susquehanna University *Pennsylvania* M & W
Swarthmore College *Pennsylvania* M & W
Sweet Briar College *Virginia* W
Syracuse University *New York* M & W
Tabor College *Kansas* M & W
Talladega College *Alabama* W
Tarleton State University *Texas* W
Taylor University *Indiana* M & W
Temple College *Texas* M & W
Temple University *Pennsylvania* M & W
Tennessee State University *Tennessee* M & W
Tennessee Technological University *Tennessee* M & W
Tennessee Wesleyan College *Tennessee* M & W
Texas A&M University *Texas* M & W
Texas A&M University–Corpus Christi *Texas* M & W
Texas Christian University *Texas* M & W
Texas Lutheran University *Texas* M & W
Texas Southern University *Texas* M & W
Texas State University–San Marcos *Texas* M & W
Texas Tech University *Texas* M & W
Thomas College *Maine* M
Thomas More College *Kentucky* M & W
Tiffin University *Ohio* M & W
Towson University *Maryland* M & W
Transylvania University *Kentucky* M & W
Treasure Valley Community College *Oregon* M & W
Trine University *Indiana* M & W
Trinity College *Connecticut* M & W
Trinity University *Texas* M & W
Trinity (Washington) University *District of Columbia* W
Troy University *Alabama* M & W
Truman State University *Missouri* M & W
Tufts University *Massachusetts* M & W
Tulane University *Louisiana* M & W
Tusculum College *Tennessee* M & W
Tuskegee University *Alabama* M & W
Tyler Junior College *Texas* M & W
Ulster County Community College *New York* M
Union College *New York* M & W
Union College *Kentucky* M & W
United States Coast Guard Academy *Connecticut* M & W
United States Merchant Marine Academy *New York* M & W
United States Military Academy *New York* M & W
United States Naval Academy *Maryland* M & W
Universidad Metropolitana *Puerto Rico* M & W
The University of Akron *Ohio* W
The University of Alabama *Alabama* M & W
The University of Alabama at Birmingham *Alabama* M & W
The University of Alabama in Huntsville *Alabama* M & W
University at Albany, State University of New York *New York* W
University of Alberta *Alberta* M & W
The University of Arizona *Arizona* M & W
University of Arkansas *Arkansas* M & W
University of Arkansas at Fort Smith *Arkansas* M & W
University of Arkansas at Little Rock *Arkansas* M & W
University of Arkansas at Monticello *Arkansas* W
University at Buffalo, the State University of New York *New York* M & W
University of Calgary *Alberta* M & W
University of California, Berkeley *California* M & W
University of California, Davis *California* M & W
University of California, Irvine *California* M & W
University of California, Los Angeles *California* M & W
University of California, Riverside *California* M & W
University of California, San Diego *California* M & W
University of California, Santa Barbara *California* M & W
University of California, Santa Cruz *California* M & W
University of Central Arkansas *Arkansas* W
University of Central Florida *Florida* M & W
University of Central Oklahoma *Oklahoma* M & W
University of Charleston *West Virginia* M & W
University of Chicago *Illinois* M & W
University of Cincinnati *Ohio* W
University of Colorado at Boulder *Colorado* M & W
University of Connecticut *Connecticut* M & W
University of the Cumberlands *Kentucky* M & W
University of Dayton *Ohio* M & W
University of Delaware *Delaware* M & W
University of Denver *Colorado* M & W
University of Detroit Mercy *Michigan* W
University of the District of Columbia *District of Columbia* M & W
University of Dubuque *Iowa* M & W
University of Evansville *Indiana* W
The University of Findlay *Ohio* M & W
University of Florida *Florida* M & W
University of Georgia *Georgia* M & W
University of Hartford *Connecticut* M & W
University of Hawaii at Hilo *Hawaii* M & W
University of Hawaii at Manoa *Hawaii* M & W
University of Houston *Texas* W
University of Idaho *Idaho* M & W
University of Illinois at Chicago *Illinois* M & W
University of Illinois at Springfield *Illinois* M & W

M = Men; W = Women

M = Men; W = Women

West Liberty University *West Virginia* M & W
West Valley College *California* M & W
West Virginia State University *West Virginia* M & W
West Virginia University *West Virginia* W
West Virginia Wesleyan College *West Virginia* M & W
Western Carolina University *North Carolina* M & W
Western Connecticut State University *Connecticut* M & W
Western Illinois University *Illinois* M & W
Western Kentucky University *Kentucky* M & W
Western Michigan University *Michigan* M & W
Western New England College *Massachusetts* M & W
Western New Mexico University *New Mexico* M & W
Westminster College *Pennsylvania* M & W
Westminster College *Missouri* M & W
Westmont College *California* M & W
Wheaton College *Massachusetts* M & W
Wheaton College *Illinois* M & W
Wheelock College *Massachusetts* M
Whitman College *Washington* M & W
Whittier College *California* M & W
Whitworth University *Washington* M & W
Wichita State University *Kansas* M & W
Widener University *Pennsylvania* M & W
Wilkes University *Pennsylvania* M & W
Willamette University *Oregon* M & W
William Jewell College *Missouri* M & W
Williams College *Massachusetts* M & W
Wilmington College *Ohio* M & W
Wilson College *Pennsylvania* W
Wingate University *North Carolina* M & W
Winona State University *Minnesota* W
Winston-Salem State University *North Carolina* M & W
Winthrop University *South Carolina* M & W
Wisconsin Lutheran College *Wisconsin* M & W
Wittenberg University *Ohio* M & W
Wofford College *South Carolina* M & W
Worcester State College *Massachusetts* W
Wright State University *Ohio* M & W
Xavier University *Ohio* M & W
Xavier University of Louisiana *Louisiana* M & W
Yale University *Connecticut* M & W
Yeshiva University *New York* M & W
York College of the City University of New York *New York* M
York College of Pennsylvania *Pennsylvania* M & W
York University *Ontario* M & W
Young Harris College *Georgia* M & W
Youngstown State University *Ohio* M & W
Yuba College *California* M & W

Track and Field

Abilene Christian University *Texas* M & W
Academy of Art University *California* M & W
Acadia University *Nova Scotia* M & W
Adams State College *Colorado* M & W
Adelphi University *New York* M & W
Adrian College *Michigan* M & W
Alabama Agricultural and Mechanical University *Alabama* M & W
Alabama State University *Alabama* M & W
Albany State University *Georgia* M & W
Albion College *Michigan* M & W
Albright College *Pennsylvania* M & W
Alcorn State University *Mississippi* M & W
Alderson-Broaddus College *West Virginia* M & W
Alfred University *New York* M & W
Allan Hancock College *California* M & W
Allegheny College *Pennsylvania* M & W
Allen Community College *Kansas* M & W
Allen University *South Carolina* M & W
Alma College *Michigan* M & W
Alvernia University *Pennsylvania* M & W
American River College *California* M & W
American University *District of Columbia* M & W
American University of Puerto Rico *Puerto Rico* M & W
Amherst College *Massachusetts* M & W
Anderson University *South Carolina* M & W
Anderson University *Indiana* M & W
Angelo State University *Texas* M & W
Antelope Valley College *California* M & W
Appalachian State University *North Carolina* M & W
Aquinas College *Michigan* M & W
Arizona State University *Arizona* M & W
Arkansas State University - Jonesboro *Arkansas* M & W
Ashford University *Iowa* M & W
Ashland University *Ohio* M & W
Assumption College *Massachusetts* M & W
Auburn University *Alabama* M & W
Augsburg College *Minnesota* M & W
Augustana College *South Dakota* M & W
Augustana College *Illinois* M & W
Aurora University *Illinois* M & W
Austin Peay State University *Tennessee* W
Azusa Pacific University *California* M & W
Babson College *Massachusetts* M & W
Baker University *Kansas* M & W
Bakersfield College *California* M & W
Baldwin-Wallace College *Ohio* M & W
Ball State University *Indiana* W
Baltimore City Community College *Maryland* M & W
Baptist Bible College of Pennsylvania *Pennsylvania* M & W
Bard College *New York* M & W
Barnard College *New York* W
Barton County Community College *Kansas* M & W
Bates College *Maine* M & W
Bayamón Central University *Puerto Rico* M & W
Baylor University *Texas* M & W
Bellarmine University *Kentucky* M & W
Bellevue College *Washington* M & W
Belmont Abbey College *North Carolina* M & W
Belmont University *Tennessee* M & W
Beloit College *Wisconsin* M & W
Bemidji State University *Minnesota* M & W
Benedict College *South Carolina* M
Benedictine College *Kansas* M & W
Benedictine University *Illinois* M & W
Bentley University *Massachusetts* M & W
Berea College *Kentucky* M & W
Bergen Community College *New Jersey* M & W
Bethany College *West Virginia* M & W
Bethany College *Kansas* M & W
Bethany Lutheran College *Minnesota* M & W
Bethel College *Kansas* M & W
Bethel College *Indiana* M & W
Bethel University *Tennessee* M & W
Bethel University *Minnesota* M & W
Bethune-Cookman University *Florida* M & W
Bevill State Community College *Alabama* W
Biola University *California* M & W
Birmingham-Southern College *Alabama* M & W
Black Hills State University *South Dakota* M & W
Bloomsburg University of Pennsylvania *Pennsylvania* M & W
Bluffton University *Ohio* M & W
Boise State University *Idaho* M & W
Boston College *Massachusetts* M & W
Boston University *Massachusetts* M & W
Bowdoin College *Maine* M & W
Bowie State University *Maryland* M & W
Bowling Green State University *Ohio* W
Bradley University *Illinois* W
Brandeis University *Massachusetts* M & W
Brescia University *Kentucky* M & W
Brevard College *North Carolina* M & W
Briar Cliff University *Iowa* M & W
Briarcliffe College *New York* M & W
Bridgewater College *Virginia* M & W
Bridgewater State College *Massachusetts* M & W
Brigham Young University *Utah* M & W
Bronx Community College of the City University of New York *New York* M & W
Brooklyn College of the City University of New York *New York* M & W
Brown University *Rhode Island* M & W
Bryan College *Tennessee* M & W
Bryant University *Rhode Island* M & W
Bryn Mawr College *Pennsylvania* W
Bucknell University *Pennsylvania* M & W
Buena Vista University *Iowa* M & W
Buffalo State College, State University of New York *New York* M & W
Butler Community College *Kansas* M & W
Butler University *Indiana* M & W
Butte College *California* M & W
Cabrillo College *California* M & W
Cabrini College *Pennsylvania* M & W
California Institute of Technology *California* M & W
California Lutheran University *California* M & W
California Polytechnic State University, San Luis Obispo *California* M & W
California State Polytechnic University, Pomona *California* M & W
California State University, Bakersfield *California* M & W
California State University, Chico *California* M & W
California State University, Dominguez Hills *California* W
California State University, Fresno *California* M & W
California State University, Fullerton *California* M & W
California State University, Long Beach *California* M & W
California State University, Los Angeles *California* M & W
California State University, Northridge *California* M & W
California State University, Sacramento *California* M & W
California State University, San Marcos *California* M & W
California State University, Stanislaus *California* M & W
California University of Pennsylvania *Pennsylvania* M & W
Calumet College of Saint Joseph *Indiana* M & W
Calvin College *Michigan* M & W
Campbell University *North Carolina* M & W
Campbellsville University *Kentucky* M & W
Capital University *Ohio* M & W
Caribbean University *Puerto Rico* M & W
Carleton College *Minnesota* M & W
Carnegie Mellon University *Pennsylvania* M & W
Carroll University *Wisconsin* M & W
Carson-Newman College *Tennessee* M & W
Carthage College *Wisconsin* M & W
Case Western Reserve University *Ohio* M & W
The Catholic University of America *District of Columbia* M & W
Cedar Crest College *Pennsylvania* W
Cedarville University *Ohio* M & W
Central Arizona College *Arizona* M & W
Central College *Iowa* M & W
Central Connecticut State University *Connecticut* M & W
Central Methodist University *Missouri* M & W
Central Michigan University *Michigan* M & W
Central State University *Ohio* M & W
Central Washington University *Washington* M & W
Centre College *Kentucky* M & W
Cerritos College *California* M & W
Chabot College *California* M & W
Chadron State College *Nebraska* M & W
Chaffey College *California* M & W
Chapman University *California* W
Charleston Southern University *South Carolina* M & W
Chemeketa Community College *Oregon* M & W
Cheyney University of Pennsylvania *Pennsylvania* M & W
Chicago State University *Illinois* M & W
Christopher Newport University *Virginia* M & W
The Citadel, The Military College of South Carolina *South Carolina* M & W
Citrus College *California* M & W
City College of the City University of New York *New York* M & W
City College of San Francisco *California* M & W
City Colleges of Chicago, Kennedy-King College *Illinois* M & W
Clackamas Community College *Oregon* M & W
Claflin University *South Carolina* M & W
Claremont McKenna College *California* M & W

M = Men; W = Women

Clarion University of Pennsylvania *Pennsylvania* W
Clark Atlanta University *Georgia* M & W
Clark College *Washington* M & W
Clarke College *Iowa* M & W
Clayton State University *Georgia* M & W
Clemson University *South Carolina* M & W
Cleveland State University *Ohio* W
Cloud County Community College *Kansas* M & W
Coastal Carolina University *South Carolina* M & W
Coe College *Iowa* M & W
Coffeyville Community College *Kansas* M & W
Colby College *Maine* M & W
Colby Community College *Kansas* M & W
Colby-Sawyer College *New Hampshire* M & W
Colgate University *New York* M & W
The College at Brockport, State University of New York *New York* M & W
College of the Canyons *California* M & W
College of Charleston *South Carolina* W
College of the Desert *California* M & W
College of DuPage *Illinois* M & W
College of the Holy Cross *Massachusetts* M & W
The College of Idaho *Idaho* M & W
College of Marin *California* M & W
College of Mount St. Joseph *Ohio* M & W
College of Mount Saint Vincent *New York* W
The College of New Jersey *New Jersey* M & W
College of the Redwoods *California* M & W
College of Saint Benedict *Minnesota* W
The College of Saint Rose *New York* M & W
The College of St. Scholastica *Minnesota* M & W
College of San Mateo *California* M & W
College of the Sequoias *California* M & W
College of the Siskiyous *California* M & W
The College of William and Mary *Virginia* M & W
The College of Wooster *Ohio* M & W
The Colorado College *Colorado* M & W
Colorado School of Mines *Colorado* M & W
Colorado State University *Colorado* M & W
Colorado State University–Pueblo *Colorado* W
Columbia University *New York* M & W
Columbia University, School of General Studies *New York* M & W
Columbus State Community College *Ohio* M & W
The Community College of Baltimore County *Maryland* W
Community College of Philadelphia *Pennsylvania* M & W
Community College of Rhode Island *Rhode Island* M & W
Concord University *West Virginia* M & W
Concordia College *Minnesota* M & W
Concordia University *Oregon* M & W
Concordia University *California* M & W
Concordia University Chicago *Illinois* M & W
Concordia University, Nebraska *Nebraska* M & W
Concordia University, St. Paul *Minnesota* M & W
Concordia University Wisconsin *Wisconsin* M & W
Connecticut College *Connecticut* M & W
Contra Costa College *California* M & W
Copiah-Lincoln Community College *Mississippi* M
Coppin State University *Maryland* M & W
Corban University *Oregon* M & W
Cornell College *Iowa* M & W
Cornell University *New York* M & W
Cornerstone University *Michigan* M & W
Cosumnes River College *California* M & W
Cowley County Community College and Area Vocational–Technical School *Kansas* M & W
Cuesta College *California* M & W
Culver-Stockton College *Missouri* M & W
Cumberland County College *New Jersey* M
Cuyamaca College *California* M & W
Dakota State University *South Dakota* M & W
Dakota Wesleyan University *South Dakota* M & W
Dalhousie University *Nova Scotia* M & W
Dallas Baptist University *Texas* M & W
Dana College *Nebraska* M & W
Dartmouth College *New Hampshire* M & W
Davenport University *Michigan* M & W
Davidson College *North Carolina* M & W
De Anza College *California* M & W
Defiance College *Ohio* M & W
Delaware State University *Delaware* M & W
Delaware Valley College *Pennsylvania* M & W
Delgado Community College *Louisiana* W
Denison University *Ohio* M & W
DePaul University *Illinois* M & W
DePauw University *Indiana* M & W
DeSales University *Pennsylvania* M & W
Diablo Valley College *California* M & W
Dickinson College *Pennsylvania* M & W
Dickinson State University *North Dakota* M & W
Dillard University *Louisiana* M & W
Doane College *Nebraska* M & W
Dominican College *New York* M & W
Dordt College *Iowa* M & W
Drake University *Iowa* M & W
Drury University *Missouri* M & W
Duke University *North Carolina* M & W
Duquesne University *Pennsylvania* M & W
Earlham College *Indiana* M & W
East Carolina University *North Carolina* M & W
East Central University *Oklahoma* M & W
East Los Angeles College *California* M & W
East Stroudsburg University of Pennsylvania *Pennsylvania* M & W
East Tennessee State University *Tennessee* M & W
Eastern Connecticut State University *Connecticut* M & W
Eastern Illinois University *Illinois* M & W
Eastern Kentucky University *Kentucky* M & W
Eastern Mennonite University *Virginia* M & W
Eastern Michigan University *Michigan* M & W
Eastern New Mexico University *New Mexico* M & W
Eastern Oregon University *Oregon* M & W
Eastern Washington University *Washington* M & W
Edgewood College *Wisconsin* M & W
Edinboro University of Pennsylvania *Pennsylvania* M & W
Edward Waters College *Florida* M & W
El Camino College *California* M & W
El Paso Community College *Texas* M & W
Elizabethtown College *Pennsylvania* M & W
Ellsworth Community College *Iowa* M & W
Elmhurst College *Illinois* M & W
Elon University *North Carolina* W
Embry-Riddle Aeronautical University *Florida* M & W
Emerson College *Massachusetts* W
Emmanuel College *Massachusetts* M & W
Emory University *Georgia* M & W
Emporia State University *Kansas* M & W
Erie Community College *New York* M & W
Erie Community College, North Campus *New York* M & W
Erie Community College, South Campus *New York* M & W
Essex County College *New Jersey* M & W
Evangel University *Missouri* M & W
The Evergreen State College *Washington* M & W
Fairfield University *Connecticut* M & W
Fairleigh Dickinson University, Metropolitan Campus *New Jersey* M & W
Faith Baptist Bible College and Theological Seminary *Iowa* M
Farmingdale State College *New York* M & W
Felician College *New Jersey* M & W
Ferris State University *Michigan* M & W
Finger Lakes Community College *New York* M & W
Fitchburg State College *Massachusetts* M & W
Florida Agricultural and Mechanical University *Florida* M & W
Florida Atlantic University *Florida* W
Florida International University *Florida* M & W
Florida Memorial University *Florida* M & W
Florida Southern College *Florida* M & W
Florida State University *Florida* M & W
Fontbonne University *Missouri* M & W
Fordham University *New York* M & W
Fort Hays State University *Kansas* M & W
Fort Scott Community College *Kansas* M & W
Fort Valley State University *Georgia* M & W
Francis Marion University *South Carolina* M & W
Franciscan University of Steubenville *Ohio* M & W
Franklin College *Indiana* M & W
Franklin & Marshall College *Pennsylvania* M & W
Fresno City College *California* M & W
Fresno Pacific University *California* M & W
Friends University *Kansas* M & W
Frostburg State University *Maryland* M & W
Fullerton College *California* M & W
Furman University *South Carolina* M & W
Gallaudet University *District of Columbia* M & W
Garden City Community College *Kansas* M & W
Gardner-Webb University *North Carolina* M & W
Geneva College *Pennsylvania* M & W
George Fox University *Oregon* M & W
George Mason University *Virginia* M & W
Georgetown College *Kentucky* M & W
Georgetown University *District of Columbia* M & W
Georgia Institute of Technology *Georgia* M & W
Georgia Southern University *Georgia* W
Georgia State University *Georgia* M & W
Georgian Court University *New Jersey* W
Gettysburg College *Pennsylvania* M & W
Glen Oaks Community College *Michigan* M & W
Glendale Community College *California* M & W
Glendale Community College *Arizona* M & W
Glenville State College *West Virginia* M & W
Globe Institute of Technology *New York* M & W
Gloucester County College *New Jersey* M & W
Golden West College *California* M & W
Gonzaga University *Washington* M & W
Gordon College *Massachusetts* M & W
Goshen College *Indiana* M & W
Goucher College *Maryland* M & W
Grace College *Indiana* M & W
Graceland University *Iowa* M & W
Grambling State University *Louisiana* M & W
Grand Rapids Community College *Michigan* M
Grand Valley State University *Michigan* M & W
Grand View University *Iowa* M & W
Greenville College *Illinois* M & W
Grinnell College *Iowa* M & W
Grossmont College *California* M
Grove City College *Pennsylvania* M & W
Gustavus Adolphus College *Minnesota* M & W
Gwynedd-Mercy College *Pennsylvania* M & W
Hagerstown Community College *Maryland* M & W
Hamilton College *New York* M & W
Hamline University *Minnesota* M & W
Hampton University *Virginia* M & W
Hannibal-LaGrange College *Missouri* M & W
Hanover College *Indiana* M & W
Harcum College *Pennsylvania* M & W
Hardin-Simmons University *Texas* M & W
Harding University *Arkansas* M & W
Harper College *Illinois* M & W
Hartnell College *California* M & W
Harvard University *Massachusetts* M & W
Harvey Mudd College *California* M & W
Haskell Indian Nations University *Kansas* M & W
Hastings College *Nebraska* M & W
Haverford College *Pennsylvania* M & W
Heidelberg University *Ohio* M & W
Hendrix College *Arkansas* M & W
Henry Ford Community College *Michigan* M
Herkimer County Community College *New York* M & W
High Point University *North Carolina* M & W
Highland Community College *Kansas* M & W
Highline Community College *Washington* M & W
Hillsdale College *Michigan* M & W
Hinds Community College *Mississippi* M & W
Hiram College *Ohio* M & W
Holy Family University *Pennsylvania* M & W
Hood College *Maryland* M & W
Hope College *Michigan* M & W
Houghton College *New York* M & W
Houston Baptist University *Texas* M & W
Howard Community College *Maryland* M & W
Howard University *District of Columbia* M & W
Hudson Valley Community College *New York* M & W
Humboldt State University *California* M & W
Hunter College of the City University of New York *New York* M & W
Huntington University *Indiana* M & W
Huston-Tillotson University *Texas* M & W

M = Men; W = Women

Hutchinson Community College and Area Vocational School *Kansas* M & W
Idaho State University *Idaho* M & W
Illinois College *Illinois* M & W
Illinois State University *Illinois* M & W
Illinois Wesleyan University *Illinois* M & W
Independence Community College *Kansas* M & W
Indiana State University *Indiana* M & W
Indiana Tech *Indiana* M & W
Indiana University Bloomington *Indiana* M & W
Indiana University East *Indiana* M & W
Indiana University of Pennsylvania *Pennsylvania* M & W
Indiana University–Purdue University Fort Wayne *Indiana* W
Indiana Wesleyan University *Indiana* M & W
Inter American University of Puerto Rico, Aguadilla Campus *Puerto Rico* M & W
Inter American University of Puerto Rico, Arecibo Campus *Puerto Rico* M & W
Inter American University of Puerto Rico, Barranquitas Campus *Puerto Rico* M & W
Inter American University of Puerto Rico, Bayamón Campus *Puerto Rico* M & W
Inter American University of Puerto Rico, Ponce Campus *Puerto Rico* M & W
Inter American University of Puerto Rico, San Germán Campus *Puerto Rico* M & W
Iona College *New York* M & W
Iowa State University of Science and Technology *Iowa* M & W
Iowa Wesleyan College *Iowa* M & W
Iowa Western Community College *Iowa* M & W
Itawamba Community College *Mississippi* M
Ithaca College *New York* M & W
Jackson State University *Mississippi* M & W
Jacksonville University *Florida* W
James Madison University *Virginia* W
Jamestown College *North Dakota* M & W
John Carroll University *Ohio* M & W
The Johns Hopkins University *Maryland* M & W
Johnson C. Smith University *North Carolina* M & W
Johnson County Community College *Kansas* M & W
Jones County Junior College *Mississippi* M
Judson University *Illinois* M & W
Juniata College *Pennsylvania* M & W
Kansas City Kansas Community College *Kansas* M & W
Kansas State University *Kansas* M & W
Kansas Wesleyan University *Kansas* M & W
Kean University *New Jersey* M & W
Keene State College *New Hampshire* M & W
Kennesaw State University *Georgia* M & W
Kent State University *Ohio* M & W
Kentucky State University *Kentucky* M & W
Kenyon College *Ohio* M & W
Keuka College *New York* M
Keystone College *Pennsylvania* M & W
King College *Tennessee* M & W
Kingsborough Community College of the City University of New York *New York* M & W
Knox College *Illinois* M & W
Kutztown University of Pennsylvania *Pennsylvania* M & W
La Salle University *Pennsylvania* M & W
Lafayette College *Pennsylvania* M & W
Lake Erie College *Ohio* M & W
Lake Forest College *Illinois* M & W
Lake Superior State University *Michigan* M & W
Lakehead University *Ontario* M & W
Lakeland College *Wisconsin* M & W
Lamar University *Texas* M & W
Lane College *Tennessee* M & W
Lane Community College *Oregon* M & W
Langston University *Oklahoma* M & W
Lansing Community College *Michigan* M & W
Lasell College *Massachusetts* M & W
Lassen Community College District *California* M & W
Laurentian University *Ontario* W
Lawrence University *Wisconsin* M & W
Lebanon Valley College *Pennsylvania* M & W
Lees-McRae College *North Carolina* M & W
Lehigh University *Pennsylvania* M & W
Lehman College of the City University of New York *New York* M & W
Lenoir-Rhyne University *North Carolina* M & W
Lewis & Clark College *Oregon* M & W
Lewis University *Illinois* M & W
Liberty University *Virginia* M & W
Limestone College *South Carolina* M & W
Lincoln University *Pennsylvania* M & W
Lincoln University *Missouri* M & W
Lindenwood University *Missouri* M & W
Lindsey Wilson College *Kentucky* M & W
Linfield College *Oregon* M & W
Livingstone College *North Carolina* M & W
Lock Haven University of Pennsylvania *Pennsylvania* M & W
Long Beach City College *California* M & W
Long Island University, Brooklyn Campus *New York* M & W
Longwood University *Virginia* M & W
Loras College *Iowa* M & W
Los Angeles City College *California* M & W
Los Angeles Southwest College *California* M & W
Los Angeles Trade-Technical College *California* M & W
Los Angeles Valley College *California* M & W
Louisiana State University and Agricultural and Mechanical College *Louisiana* M & W
Louisiana Tech University *Louisiana* M & W
Loyola Marymount University *California* M & W
Loyola University Chicago *Illinois* M & W
Loyola University Maryland *Maryland* M & W
Loyola University New Orleans *Louisiana* M & W
Lubbock Christian University *Texas* M & W
Luther College *Iowa* M & W
Lynchburg College *Virginia* M & W
Macalester College *Minnesota* M & W
Macomb Community College *Michigan* M & W
Madison Area Technical College *Wisconsin* M & W
Malone University *Ohio* M & W
Manchester College *Indiana* M & W
Manhattan College *New York* M & W
Mansfield University of Pennsylvania *Pennsylvania* M & W
Marian University *Indiana* M & W
Marietta College *Ohio* M & W
Marist College *New York* M & W
Marquette University *Wisconsin* M & W
Mars Hill College *North Carolina* M & W
Marshall University *West Virginia* M & W
Martin Luther College *Minnesota* M & W
Maryville University of Saint Louis *Missouri* M & W
Marywood University *Pennsylvania* M & W
Massachusetts Institute of Technology *Massachusetts* M & W
Massachusetts Maritime Academy *Massachusetts* M & W
The Master's College and Seminary *California* M & W
McDaniel College *Maryland* M & W
McGill University *Quebec* M & W
McKendree University *Illinois* M & W
McMaster University *Ontario* M & W
McMurry University *Texas* M & W
McNeese State University *Louisiana* M & W
McPherson College *Kansas* M & W
Medgar Evers College of the City University of New York *New York* M & W
Merced College *California* M & W
Mercer County Community College *New Jersey* M & W
Mercy College *New York* M & W
Meridian Community College *Mississippi* M & W
Merrimack College *Massachusetts* M & W
Merritt College *California* M & W
Mesa Community College *Arizona* M & W
Mesa State College *Colorado* W
Messiah College *Pennsylvania* M & W
Methodist University *North Carolina* M & W
Metropolitan State College of Denver *Colorado* M & W
Miami University *Ohio* M & W
Michigan State University *Michigan* M & W
Michigan Technological University *Michigan* M & W
Middle Tennessee State University *Tennessee* M & W
Middlebury College *Vermont* M & W
Middlesex County College *New Jersey* M & W
Midland Lutheran College *Nebraska* M & W
Midway College *Kentucky* W
Miles College *Alabama* M
Millersville University of Pennsylvania *Pennsylvania* M & W
Millikin University *Illinois* M & W
Millsaps College *Mississippi* M & W
Milwaukee School of Engineering *Wisconsin* M & W
Minnesota State University Mankato *Minnesota* M & W
Minnesota State University Moorhead *Minnesota* M & W
Minot State University *North Dakota* M & W
MiraCosta College *California* W
Misericordia University *Pennsylvania* M & W
Mississippi College *Mississippi* M & W
Mississippi Delta Community College *Mississippi* M
Mississippi Gulf Coast Community College *Mississippi* M
Mississippi State University *Mississippi* M & W
Mississippi Valley State University *Mississippi* M & W
Missouri Baptist University *Missouri* M & W
Missouri Southern State University *Missouri* M & W
Missouri State University *Missouri* W
Missouri University of Science and Technology *Missouri* M & W
Missouri Valley College *Missouri* M & W
Modesto Junior College *California* M & W
Mohawk Valley Community College *New York* M & W
Molloy College *New York* M & W
Monmouth College *Illinois* M & W
Monmouth University *New Jersey* M & W
Monroe College (Bronx) *New York* M & W
Montana State University *Montana* M & W
Montclair State University *New Jersey* M & W
Monterey Peninsula College *California* M & W
Montgomery College *Maryland* M & W
Moorpark College *California* M & W
Moravian College *Pennsylvania* M & W
Morehead State University *Kentucky* M & W
Morehouse College *Georgia* M
Morgan State University *Maryland* M & W
Morningside College *Iowa* M & W
Morris College *South Carolina* M & W
Mount Holyoke College *Massachusetts* W
Mt. Hood Community College *Oregon* M & W
Mount Marty College *South Dakota* M & W
Mount Mercy College *Iowa* M & W
Mount St. Mary's University *Maryland* M & W
Mt. San Antonio College *California* M & W
Mountain State University *West Virginia* M & W
Muhlenberg College *Pennsylvania* M & W
Murray State University *Kentucky* M & W
Muskingum University *Ohio* M & W
Nassau Community College *New York* M & W
Nazareth College of Rochester *New York* M & W
Nebraska Wesleyan University *Nebraska* M & W
Neosho County Community College *Kansas* M
New Jersey City University *New Jersey* M & W
New Jersey Institute of Technology *New Jersey* M & W
New Mexico Highlands University *New Mexico* M & W
New Mexico Military Institute *New Mexico* M
New Mexico State University *New Mexico* W
New York City College of Technology of the City University of New York *New York* M & W
New York University *New York* M & W
Nicholls State University *Louisiana* M & W
Nichols College *Massachusetts* M & W
Norfolk State University *Virginia* M & W
North Carolina Agricultural and Technical State University *North Carolina* M & W
North Carolina Central University *North Carolina* M & W
North Carolina State University *North Carolina* M & W

M = Men; W = Women

North Central College *Illinois* M & W
North Central University *Minnesota* M & W
North Dakota State University *North Dakota* M & W
North Georgia College & State University *Georgia* M & W
North Iowa Area Community College *Iowa* M & W
North Park University *Illinois* M & W
Northeastern University *Massachusetts* M & W
Northern Arizona University *Arizona* M & W
Northern Michigan University *Michigan* M & W
Northern State University *South Dakota* M & W
Northwest Christian University *Oregon* M & W
Northwest Missouri State University *Missouri* M & W
Northwest Nazarene University *Idaho* M & W
Northwest University *Washington* M & W
Northwestern College *Minnesota* M & W
Northwestern College *Iowa* M & W
Northwestern State University of Louisiana *Louisiana* M & W
Northwood University *Michigan* M & W
Northwood University, Texas Campus *Texas* M & W
Norwich University *Vermont* M & W
Notre Dame College *Ohio* M & W
Nova Southeastern University *Florida* M
Oakland Community College *Michigan* M & W
Oakland University *Michigan* M & W
Oakton Community College *Illinois* M & W
Oberlin College *Ohio* M & W
Occidental College *California* M & W
Oglethorpe University *Georgia* M & W
Ohio Northern University *Ohio* M & W
The Ohio State University *Ohio* M & W
Ohio University *Ohio* W
Ohio Wesleyan University *Ohio* M & W
Oklahoma Baptist University *Oklahoma* M & W
Oklahoma Christian University *Oklahoma* M & W
Oklahoma City University *Oklahoma* M & W
Oklahoma Wesleyan University *Oklahoma* M & W
Olivet College *Michigan* M & W
Olivet Nazarene University *Illinois* M & W
Oral Roberts University *Oklahoma* M & W
Orange Coast College *California* M & W
Oregon Institute of Technology *Oregon* M & W
Ottawa University *Kansas* M & W
Otterbein University *Ohio* M & W
Oxnard College *California* M & W
Pace University *New York* M & W
Pacific Lutheran University *Washington* M & W
Pacific University *Oregon* M & W
Paine College *Georgia* M & W
Palo Alto College *Texas* M & W
Palomar College *California* M & W
Paradise Valley Community College *Arizona* M & W
Park University *Missouri* M & W
Pasadena City College *California* M & W
Paul Quinn College *Texas* M & W
Penn State Erie, The Behrend College *Pennsylvania* M & W
Penn State University Park *Pennsylvania* M & W
Phoenix College *Arizona* M & W
Pima Community College *Arizona* M & W
Pittsburg State University *Kansas* M & W
Pitzer College *California* M & W
Point Loma Nazarene University *California* M & W
Polytechnic Institute of NYU *New York* M & W
Polytechnic University of Puerto Rico *Puerto Rico* M & W
Pomona College *California* M & W
Pontifical Catholic University of Puerto Rico *Puerto Rico* M & W
Portland State University *Oregon* M & W
Prairie View A&M University *Texas* M & W
Pratt Community College *Kansas* M & W
Pratt Institute *New York* M & W
Princeton University *New Jersey* M & W
Principia College *Illinois* M & W
Providence College *Rhode Island* M & W
Purdue University *Indiana* M & W
Queens College of the City University of New York *New York* M & W
Queen's University at Kingston *Ontario* M & W
Queensborough Community College of the City University of New York *New York* M & W
Quinnipiac University *Connecticut* W
Radford University *Virginia* M & W
Ramapo College of New Jersey *New Jersey* M & W
Ranger College *Texas* M & W
Reedley College *California* M & W
Regis College *Massachusetts* M & W
Rend Lake College *Illinois* M & W
Rensselaer Polytechnic Institute *New York* M & W
Rhode Island College *Rhode Island* M & W
Rhodes College *Tennessee* M & W
Rice University *Texas* M & W
The Richard Stockton College of New Jersey *New Jersey* M & W
Rider University *New Jersey* M & W
Ripon College *Wisconsin* M & W
Riverside Community College District *California* M & W
Roanoke College *Virginia* M & W
Robert Morris University *Pennsylvania* M & W
Robert Morris University Illinois *Illinois* W
Roberts Wesleyan College *New York* M & W
Rochester Institute of Technology *New York* M & W
Roger Williams University *Rhode Island* M & W
Rose-Hulman Institute of Technology *Indiana* M & W
Rowan University *New Jersey* M & W
Rust College *Mississippi* M & W
Rutgers, The State University of New Jersey, Camden *New Jersey* M & W
Rutgers, The State University of New Jersey, New Brunswick *New Jersey* M & W
Rutgers, The State University of New Jersey, Newark *New Jersey* M
Sacramento City College *California* M & W
Sacred Heart University *Connecticut* M & W
Saddleback College *California* M & W
Saginaw Valley State University *Michigan* M & W
St. Ambrose University *Iowa* M & W
Saint Augustine's College *North Carolina* M & W
St. Catherine University *Minnesota* W
St. Cloud State University *Minnesota* M & W
St. Francis College *New York* M & W
Saint Francis University *Pennsylvania* M & W
St. Francis Xavier University *Nova Scotia* M & W
St. John's University *New York* W
Saint John's University *Minnesota* M
Saint Joseph's College *Indiana* M & W
Saint Joseph's University *Pennsylvania* M & W
St. Lawrence University *New York* M & W
St. Louis Community College at Florissant Valley *Missouri* M & W
Saint Louis University *Missouri* M & W
Saint Martin's University *Washington* M & W
Saint Mary's University *Nova Scotia* M & W
Saint Mary's University of Minnesota *Minnesota* M & W
St. Norbert College *Wisconsin* M & W
St. Olaf College *Minnesota* M & W
Saint Paul's College *Virginia* M & W
Saint Peter's College *New Jersey* M & W
Saint Vincent College *Pennsylvania* M
Salem State College *Massachusetts* M & W
Salisbury University *Maryland* M & W
Salve Regina University *Rhode Island* W
Sam Houston State University *Texas* M & W
Samford University *Alabama* M & W
San Bernardino Valley College *California* M & W
San Diego City College *California* M & W
San Diego Mesa College *California* M & W
San Diego State University *California* W
San Francisco State University *California* W
San Joaquin Delta College *California* M & W
San Jose City College *California* M & W
Santa Ana College *California* M & W
Santa Barbara City College *California* M & W
Santa Clara University *California* M & W
Santa Monica College *California* M & W
Santa Rosa Junior College *California* M & W
Savannah State University *Georgia* M & W
Scottsdale Community College *Arizona* M & W
Scripps College *California* W
Seattle Pacific University *Washington* M & W
Seattle University *Washington* M & W
Seton Hill University *Pennsylvania* M & W
Sewanee: The University of the South *Tennessee* M & W
Shasta College *California* M & W
Shaw University *North Carolina* M & W
Shippensburg University of Pennsylvania *Pennsylvania* M & W
Shorter University *Georgia* M & W
Siena College *New York* M & W
Siena Heights University *Michigan* M & W
Simon Fraser University *British Columbia* M & W
Simpson College *Iowa* M & W
Skyline College *California* M & W
Slippery Rock University of Pennsylvania *Pennsylvania* M & W
Smith College *Massachusetts* W
Soka University of America *California* M & W
South Carolina State University *South Carolina* M & W
South Dakota School of Mines and Technology *South Dakota* M & W
South Dakota State University *South Dakota* M & W
South Plains College *Texas* M & W
Southeast Missouri State University *Missouri* M & W
Southeastern Louisiana University *Louisiana* M & W
Southern Arkansas University–Magnolia *Arkansas* M & W
Southern Connecticut State University *Connecticut* M & W
Southern Illinois University Carbondale *Illinois* M & W
Southern Illinois University Edwardsville *Illinois* M & W
Southern Methodist University *Texas* W
Southern Nazarene University *Oklahoma* M & W
Southern Oregon University *Oregon* M & W
Southern University and Agricultural and Mechanical College *Louisiana* M & W
Southern University at New Orleans *Louisiana* M & W
Southern Utah University *Utah* M & W
Southern Vermont College *Vermont* M & W
Southern Virginia University *Virginia* M & W
Southwest Baptist University *Missouri* M & W
Southwest Mississippi Community College *Mississippi* M & W
Southwestern Christian College *Texas* M & W
Southwestern Christian University *Oklahoma* M & W
Southwestern College *Kansas* M & W
Southwestern College *California* M & W
Southwestern Oregon Community College *Oregon* M & W
Spelman College *Georgia* W
Spokane Community College *Washington* M & W
Spokane Falls Community College *Washington* M & W
Spoon River College *Illinois* M & W
Spring Arbor University *Michigan* M & W
Springfield College *Massachusetts* M & W
Stanford University *California* M & W
State University of New York at Binghamton *New York* M & W
State University of New York College of Agriculture and Technology at Cobleskill *New York* M & W
State University of New York College of Agriculture and Technology at Morrisville *New York* M & W
State University of New York College at Cortland *New York* M & W
State University of New York College at Geneseo *New York* M & W
State University of New York College at Oneonta *New York* M & W
State University of New York College at Potsdam *New York* M & W
State University of New York College of Technology at Alfred *New York* M & W
State University of New York College of Technology at Delhi *New York* M & W
State University of New York at Fredonia *New York* M & W

M = Men; W = Women

State University of New York at New Paltz *New York* M & W
State University of New York at Oswego *New York* M & W
State University of New York at Plattsburgh *New York* M & W
Stephen F. Austin State University *Texas* M & W
Sterling College *Kansas* M & W
Stevens Institute of Technology *New Jersey* M & W
Stevenson University *Maryland* M & W
Stillman College *Alabama* M & W
Stonehill College *Massachusetts* M & W
Stony Brook University, State University of New York *New York* M & W
Suffolk County Community College *New York* M & W
Sul Ross State University *Texas* M & W
Susquehanna University *Pennsylvania* M & W
Swarthmore College *Pennsylvania* M & W
Syracuse University *New York* M & W
Tabor College *Kansas* M & W
Tarleton State University *Texas* M & W
Taylor University *Indiana* M & W
Temple University *Pennsylvania* M & W
Tennessee State University *Tennessee* M & W
Tennessee Technological University *Tennessee* W
Texas A&M University *Texas* M & W
Texas A&M University–Commerce *Texas* M & W
Texas A&M University–Corpus Christi *Texas* M & W
Texas A&M University–Kingsville *Texas* M & W
Texas Christian University *Texas* M & W
Texas College *Texas* M & W
Texas Lutheran University *Texas* W
Texas Southern University *Texas* M & W
Texas State University–San Marcos *Texas* M & W
Texas Tech University *Texas* M & W
Thaddeus Stevens College of Technology *Pennsylvania* M
Thiel College *Pennsylvania* M & W
Tiffin University *Ohio* M & W
Towson University *Maryland* M & W
Transylvania University *Kentucky* M & W
Treasure Valley Community College *Oregon* M & W
Trine University *Indiana* M & W
Trinity Baptist College *Florida* M
Trinity Bible College *North Dakota* M & W
Trinity Christian College *Illinois* M & W
Trinity College *Connecticut* M & W
Trinity International University *Illinois* M & W
Trinity University *Texas* M & W
Troy University *Alabama* M & W
Truman State University *Missouri* M & W
Tufts University *Massachusetts* M & W
Tulane University *Louisiana* M & W
Tuskegee University *Alabama* M & W
Union College *New York* M & W
Union College *Kentucky* M & W
Union University *Tennessee* M & W
United States Air Force Academy *Colorado* M & W
United States Coast Guard Academy *Connecticut* M & W
United States Merchant Marine Academy *New York* M & W
United States Military Academy *New York* M & W
United States Naval Academy *Maryland* M & W
Universidad Metropolitana *Puerto Rico* M & W
Université Laval *Quebec* M & W
Université de Moncton *New Brunswick* M & W
Université du Québec àTrois-Rivières *Quebec* M & W
Université de Sherbrooke *Quebec* M & W
The University of Akron *Ohio* M & W
The University of Alabama *Alabama* M & W
The University of Alabama at Birmingham *Alabama* W
The University of Alabama in Huntsville *Alabama* M & W
University of Alaska Anchorage *Alaska* M & W
University at Albany, State University of New York *New York* M & W
University of Alberta *Alberta* M & W
The University of Arizona *Arizona* M & W
University of Arkansas *Arkansas* M & W
University of Arkansas at Little Rock *Arkansas* M & W
University of Arkansas at Pine Bluff *Arkansas* M & W
The University of British Columbia *British Columbia* M & W
University at Buffalo, the State University of New York *New York* M & W
University of Calgary *Alberta* M & W
University of California, Berkeley *California* M & W
University of California, Davis *California* M & W
University of California, Irvine *California* M & W
University of California, Los Angeles *California* M & W
University of California, Riverside *California* M & W
University of California, San Diego *California* M & W
University of California, Santa Barbara *California* M & W
University of California, Santa Cruz *California* M & W
University of Central Arkansas *Arkansas* M & W
University of Central Florida *Florida* W
University of Central Missouri *Missouri* M & W
University of Charleston *West Virginia* M & W
University of Chicago *Illinois* M & W
University of Cincinnati *Ohio* M & W
University of Colorado at Boulder *Colorado* M & W
University of Colorado at Colorado Springs *Colorado* M & W
University of Connecticut *Connecticut* M & W
University of the Cumberlands *Kentucky* M & W
University of Dallas *Texas* M & W
University of Dayton *Ohio* W
University of Delaware *Delaware* M & W
University of Detroit Mercy *Michigan* M & W
University of the District of Columbia *District of Columbia* M & W
University of Dubuque *Iowa* M & W
The University of Findlay *Ohio* M & W
University of Florida *Florida* M & W
University of Georgia *Georgia* M & W
University of Great Falls *Montana* M & W
University of Guelph *Ontario* M & W
University of Hartford *Connecticut* M & W
University of Hawaii at Manoa *Hawaii* W
University of Houston *Texas* M & W
University of Idaho *Idaho* M & W
University of Illinois at Chicago *Illinois* M & W
University of Illinois at Urbana–Champaign *Illinois* M & W
University of the Incarnate Word *Texas* M & W
University of Indianapolis *Indiana* M & W
The University of Iowa *Iowa* M & W
The University of Kansas *Kansas* M & W
University of Kentucky *Kentucky* M & W
University of La Verne *California* M & W
University of Lethbridge *Alberta* M & W
University of Louisiana at Lafayette *Louisiana* M & W
University of Louisiana at Monroe *Louisiana* M & W
University of Louisville *Kentucky* M & W
University of Maine *Maine* M & W
University of Manitoba *Manitoba* M & W
University of Mary *North Dakota* M & W
University of Mary Washington *Virginia* M & W
University of Maryland, Baltimore County *Maryland* M & W
University of Maryland, College Park *Maryland* M & W
University of Maryland Eastern Shore *Maryland* M & W
University of Massachusetts Amherst *Massachusetts* M & W
University of Massachusetts Boston *Massachusetts* M & W
University of Massachusetts Dartmouth *Massachusetts* M & W
University of Massachusetts Lowell *Massachusetts* M & W
University of Memphis *Tennessee* M & W
University of Miami *Florida* M & W
University of Michigan *Michigan* M & W
University of Minnesota, Duluth *Minnesota* M & W
University of Minnesota, Morris *Minnesota* M & W
University of Minnesota, Twin Cities Campus *Minnesota* M & W
University of Mississippi *Mississippi* M & W
University of Missouri *Missouri* M & W
University of Missouri–Kansas City *Missouri* M & W
University of Mobile *Alabama* M & W
The University of Montana *Montana* M & W
University of Mount Union *Ohio* M & W
University of Nebraska at Kearney *Nebraska* M & W
University of Nebraska–Lincoln *Nebraska* M & W
University of Nevada, Las Vegas *Nevada* W
University of Nevada, Reno *Nevada* W
University of New Hampshire *New Hampshire* M & W
University of New Haven *Connecticut* M & W
University of New Mexico *New Mexico* M & W
The University of North Carolina at Asheville *North Carolina* M & W
The University of North Carolina at Chapel Hill *North Carolina* M & W
The University of North Carolina at Charlotte *North Carolina* M & W
The University of North Carolina at Pembroke *North Carolina* M & W
The University of North Carolina Wilmington *North Carolina* M & W
University of North Dakota *North Dakota* M & W
University of North Florida *Florida* M & W
University of North Texas *Texas* M & W
University of Northern Colorado *Colorado* M & W
University of Northern Iowa *Iowa* M & W
University of Notre Dame *Indiana* M & W
University of Oklahoma *Oklahoma* M & W
University of Oregon *Oregon* M & W
University of Ottawa *Ontario* M & W
University of Pennsylvania *Pennsylvania* M & W
University of Pittsburgh *Pennsylvania* M & W
University of Pittsburgh at Johnstown *Pennsylvania* W
University of Portland *Oregon* M & W
University of Puerto Rico, Aguadilla University College *Puerto Rico* M & W
University of Puerto Rico at Arecibo *Puerto Rico* M & W
University of Puerto Rico at Bayamón *Puerto Rico* M & W
University of Puerto Rico at Carolina *Puerto Rico* M & W
University of Puerto Rico, Cayey University College *Puerto Rico* M & W
University of Puerto Rico at Humacao *Puerto Rico* M & W
University of Puerto Rico, Mayagüez Campus *Puerto Rico* M & W
University of Puerto Rico at Ponce *Puerto Rico* M & W
University of Puerto Rico, Río Piedras *Puerto Rico* M & W
University of Puerto Rico at Utuado *Puerto Rico* M & W
University of Puget Sound *Washington* M & W
University of Redlands *California* M & W
University of Regina *Saskatchewan* M & W
University of Rhode Island *Rhode Island* M & W
University of Richmond *Virginia* M & W
University of Rio Grande *Ohio* M & W
University of Rochester *New York* M & W
University of the Sacred Heart *Puerto Rico* M & W
University of Saint Francis *Indiana* M & W
University of St. Francis *Illinois* M & W
University of St. Thomas *Minnesota* M & W
University of San Diego *California* W
University of San Francisco *California* M & W
University of Saskatchewan *Saskatchewan* M & W
The University of Scranton *Pennsylvania* M & W
University of Sioux Falls *South Dakota* M & W
University of South Alabama *Alabama* M & W
University of South Carolina *South Carolina* M & W
University of South Carolina Beaufort *South Carolina* M & W
University of South Carolina Upstate *South Carolina* M & W

M = Men; W = Women

The University of South Dakota *South Dakota* M & W
University of South Florida *Florida* M & W
University of Southern California *California* M & W
University of Southern Maine *Maine* M & W
University of Southern Mississippi *Mississippi* M & W
University of the Southwest *New Mexico* M & W
The University of Tennessee *Tennessee* M & W
The University of Tennessee at Chattanooga *Tennessee* M & W
The University of Texas at Arlington *Texas* M & W
The University of Texas at Austin *Texas* M & W
The University of Texas at El Paso *Texas* M & W
The University of Texas at San Antonio *Texas* M & W
The University of Texas at Tyler *Texas* M & W
The University of Texas–Pan American *Texas* M & W
The University of Toledo *Ohio* W
University of Toronto *Ontario* M & W
University of Tulsa *Oklahoma* M & W
University of Utah *Utah* W
University of Vermont *Vermont* M & W
University of the Virgin Islands *United States Virgin Islands* M & W
University of Virginia *Virginia* M & W
The University of Virginia's College at Wise *Virginia* M & W
University of Washington *Washington* M & W
University of Waterloo *Ontario* M & W
University of West Florida *Florida* W
The University of Western Ontario *Ontario* M & W
University of Windsor *Ontario* M & W
University of Wisconsin–Eau Claire *Wisconsin* M & W
University of Wisconsin–La Crosse *Wisconsin* M & W
University of Wisconsin–Madison *Wisconsin* M & W
University of Wisconsin–Milwaukee *Wisconsin* M & W
University of Wisconsin–Oshkosh *Wisconsin* M & W
University of Wisconsin–Parkside *Wisconsin* M & W
University of Wisconsin–Platteville *Wisconsin* M & W
University of Wisconsin–River Falls *Wisconsin* M & W
University of Wisconsin–Stevens Point *Wisconsin* M & W
University of Wisconsin–Stout *Wisconsin* M & W
University of Wisconsin–Superior *Wisconsin* M & W
University of Wisconsin–Whitewater *Wisconsin* M & W
University of Wyoming *Wyoming* M & W
Ursinus College *Pennsylvania* M & W
Ursuline College *Ohio* W
Utah State University *Utah* M & W
Utah Valley University *Utah* M & W
Valley City State University *North Dakota* M & W
Valparaiso University *Indiana* M & W
Vanderbilt University *Tennessee* W
Vanguard University of Southern California *California* M & W
Vassar College *New York* M & W
Ventura College *California* M & W
Victor Valley College *California* M & W
Villanova University *Pennsylvania* M & W
Vincennes University *Indiana* M & W
Virginia Commonwealth University *Virginia* M & W
Virginia Military Institute *Virginia* M & W
Virginia Polytechnic Institute and State University *Virginia* M & W
Virginia State University *Virginia* M & W
Virginia Union University *Virginia* M & W
Virginia Wesleyan College *Virginia* M & W
Voorhees College *South Carolina* M & W
Wabash College *Indiana* M
Wagner College *New York* M & W
Wake Forest University *North Carolina* M & W
Wallace State Community College *Alabama* M & W
Walsh University *Ohio* M & W
Warner Pacific College *Oregon* M & W
Warner University *Florida* M & W
Wartburg College *Iowa* M & W
Washington Adventist University *Maryland* M & W
Washington & Jefferson College *Pennsylvania* M & W
Washington and Lee University *Virginia* M & W
Washington State University *Washington* M & W
Washington University in St. Louis *Missouri* M & W
Wayland Baptist University *Texas* M & W
Wayne County Community College District *Michigan* M
Wayne State College *Nebraska* M & W
Waynesburg University *Pennsylvania* M & W
Webber International University *Florida* M & W
Weber State University *Utah* M & W
Webster University *Missouri* M & W
Wellesley College *Massachusetts* W
Wentworth Military Academy and College *Missouri* M & W
Wesleyan University *Connecticut* M & W
West Chester University of Pennsylvania *Pennsylvania* M & W
West Liberty University *West Virginia* M & W
West Los Angeles College *California* M & W
West Valley College *California* M
West Virginia State University *West Virginia* M & W
West Virginia University *West Virginia* W
West Virginia Wesleyan College *West Virginia* M & W
Western Carolina University *North Carolina* M & W
Western Illinois University *Illinois* M & W
Western Kentucky University *Kentucky* M & W
Western Michigan University *Michigan* W
Western Oregon University *Oregon* M & W
Western State College of Colorado *Colorado* M & W
Western Washington University *Washington* M & W
Westfield State College *Massachusetts* M & W
Westminster College *Pennsylvania* M & W
Westminster College *Missouri* M & W
Westmont College *California* M & W
Wheaton College *Massachusetts* M & W
Wheaton College *Illinois* M & W
Wheeling Jesuit University *West Virginia* M & W
Whitman College *Washington* M & W
Whittier College *California* M & W
Whitworth University *Washington* M & W
Wichita State University *Kansas* M & W
Widener University *Pennsylvania* M & W
Wiley College *Texas* M & W
Willamette University *Oregon* M & W
William Jewell College *Missouri* M & W
William Penn University *Iowa* M & W
William Woods University *Missouri* M & W
Williams College *Massachusetts* M & W
Wilmington College *Ohio* M & W
Winona State University *Minnesota* W
Winthrop University *South Carolina* M & W
Wisconsin Lutheran College *Wisconsin* M & W
Wittenberg University *Ohio* M & W
Wofford College *South Carolina* M & W
Worcester Polytechnic Institute *Massachusetts* M & W
Worcester State College *Massachusetts* M & W
Wright State University *Ohio* W
Xavier University *Ohio* M & W
Yale University *Connecticut* M & W
York College *Nebraska* M & W
York College of the City University of New York *New York* M & W
York College of Pennsylvania *Pennsylvania* M & W
York University *Ontario* M & W
Youngstown State University *Ohio* M & W
Yuba College *California* M & W

Ultimate Frisbee

Allegheny College *Pennsylvania* M & W
Amherst College *Massachusetts* M & W
Augustana College *Illinois* M & W
Ball State University *Indiana* M & W
Bates College *Maine* M & W
Beulah Heights University *Georgia* M & W
Boston University *Massachusetts* M & W
Bowdoin College *Maine* M & W
Bryant University *Rhode Island* M & W
Bucknell University *Pennsylvania* M & W
California State University, Chico *California* M
Calvin College *Michigan* M & W
Carleton College *Minnesota* M & W
Carnegie Mellon University *Pennsylvania* M & W
Case Western Reserve University *Ohio* M & W
Clemson University *South Carolina* M & W
Colby College *Maine* M & W
College of Saint Benedict *Minnesota* W
The College of Wooster *Ohio* M & W
The Colorado College *Colorado* M & W
Colorado School of Mines *Colorado* M & W
Colorado State University *Colorado* M & W
Columbia University *New York* M & W
Connecticut College *Connecticut* M & W
Corcoran College of Art and Design *District of Columbia* M & W
Dartmouth College *New Hampshire* M & W
Davidson College *North Carolina* M & W
Dickinson College *Pennsylvania* M & W
Duke University *North Carolina* M & W
Earlham College *Indiana* M & W
Eastern Illinois University *Illinois* M & W
Elon University *North Carolina* M & W
Emory University *Georgia* M & W
Fordham University *New York* M & W
Fort Lewis College *Colorado* M & W
Franklin & Marshall College *Pennsylvania* M & W
Franklin W. Olin College of Engineering *Massachusetts* M & W
Furman University *South Carolina* M & W
Georgetown University *District of Columbia* M & W
Georgia Southern University *Georgia* M & W
Graceland University *Iowa* M & W
Gustavus Adolphus College *Minnesota* M & W
Hampden-Sydney College *Virginia* M
Hampshire College *Massachusetts* M & W
Harding University *Arkansas* M & W
Haverford College *Pennsylvania* M & W
Hiram College *Ohio* M & W
Hobart and William Smith Colleges *New York* M & W
Hope International University *California* M & W
Illinois Wesleyan University *Illinois* M & W
John Carroll University *Ohio* M
Juniata College *Pennsylvania* M & W
Kennesaw State University *Georgia* M
Kenyon College *Ohio* M & W
Kutztown University of Pennsylvania *Pennsylvania* M & W
Laguna College of Art & Design *California* M & W
Lake Forest College *Illinois* M & W
Lawrence University *Wisconsin* M & W
Loyola University New Orleans *Louisiana* M & W
Lycoming College *Pennsylvania* M & W
Macalester College *Minnesota* M & W
Maharishi University of Management *Iowa* M & W
Maryville College *Tennessee* M & W
Massachusetts Institute of Technology *Massachusetts* M & W
McGill University *Quebec* M & W
Miami University *Ohio* M & W
Midwives College of Utah *Utah* M & W
Missouri State University *Missouri* M & W
National American University (Rapid City) *South Dakota* M & W
New York University *New York* M & W
North Carolina State University *North Carolina* M & W
Northern Michigan University *Michigan* M & W
Oberlin College *Ohio* M & W
Occidental College *California* M & W
Ohio University–Zanesville *Ohio* M & W
Ohio Wesleyan University *Ohio* M & W
Pacific Lutheran University *Washington* M & W
Pomona College *California* M & W
Queen's University at Kingston *Ontario* M
Rabbinical College of America *New Jersey* M
Redeemer University College *Ontario* M & W
Rensselaer Polytechnic Institute *New York* M & W
Rice University *Texas* M & W
Rochester Institute of Technology *New York* M & W
Saginaw Valley State University *Michigan* M & W

M = Men; W = Women

St. Cloud State University *Minnesota* M & W
Saint John's University *Minnesota* M
St. Louis Christian College *Missouri* M & W
Saint Louis University *Missouri* M & W
Saint Luke's College *Missouri* M & W
Saint Mary's College *Indiana* W
St. Mary's College of Maryland *Maryland* M & W
Scripps College *California* W
Slippery Rock University of Pennsylvania *Pennsylvania* M & W
Southern Connecticut State University *Connecticut* M & W
Southern University at New Orleans *Louisiana* M & W
Stanford University *California* M & W
State University of New York College at Geneseo *New York* M & W
State University of New York at New Paltz *New York* M & W
Stonehill College *Massachusetts* M & W
Swarthmore College *Pennsylvania* M & W
Texas State University–San Marcos *Texas* M & W
Towson University *Maryland* M & W
Trinity College *Connecticut* M & W
Truman State University *Missouri* M & W
Tyndale University College & Seminary *Ontario* M & W
Union College *New York* M & W
United States Air Force Academy *Colorado* M & W
University of Arkansas for Medical Sciences *Arkansas* M & W
University of California, Santa Barbara *California* M & W
University of California, Santa Cruz *California* M & W
University of Colorado at Boulder *Colorado* M & W
University of Florida *Florida* M & W
University of Idaho *Idaho* M & W
The University of Iowa *Iowa* M & W
The University of Kansas *Kansas* M & W
University of Maine at Farmington *Maine* M & W
University of Maryland, Baltimore County *Maryland* M & W
University of Michigan–Dearborn *Michigan* M
University of Minnesota, Duluth *Minnesota* M & W
The University of Montana *Montana* M & W
University of New Hampshire *New Hampshire* M & W
The University of North Carolina at Chapel Hill *North Carolina* M & W
University of North Texas *Texas* M & W
University of Ottawa *Ontario* M & W
University of Rhode Island *Rhode Island* M
University of Richmond *Virginia* M & W
University of Rochester *New York* M & W
University of the Sacred Heart *Puerto Rico* M & W
University of St. Thomas *Texas* M & W
University of San Diego *California* M & W
University of Southern California *California* M & W
The University of Tennessee *Tennessee* M & W
The University of Texas Medical Branch *Texas* M & W
University of Vermont *Vermont* M & W
University of Wisconsin–Madison *Wisconsin* M & W
University of Wisconsin–Platteville *Wisconsin* M & W
University of Wisconsin–River Falls *Wisconsin* M & W
University of Wyoming *Wyoming* M & W
Vassar College *New York* M & W
Virginia Polytechnic Institute and State University *Virginia* M & W
Washington and Lee University *Virginia* M & W
Washington State University *Washington* M & W
Washington University in St. Louis *Missouri* M & W
Wellesley College *Massachusetts* W
Western Carolina University *North Carolina* M & W
Westwood College–Atlanta Northlake *Georgia* M & W
Whitman College *Washington* M & W
Winona State University *Minnesota* M & W
Xavier University *Ohio* M & W
Yale University *Connecticut* M & W

Volleyball

Abilene Christian University *Texas* W
Academy of Art University *California* W
Acadia University *Nova Scotia* W
Adams State College *Colorado* W
Adelphi University *New York* W
Adirondack Community College *New York* W
Adrian College *Michigan* W
Agnes Scott College *Georgia* W
Alabama Agricultural and Mechanical University *Alabama* W
Alabama State University *Alabama* W
Albany State University *Georgia* W
Alberta College of Art & Design *Alberta* M & W
Albertus Magnus College *Connecticut* M & W
Albion College *Michigan* M & W
Albright College *Pennsylvania* W
Alcorn State University *Mississippi* W
Alderson-Broaddus College *West Virginia* W
Alfred University *New York* W
Allan Hancock College *California* W
Allegany College of Maryland *Maryland* W
Allegheny College *Pennsylvania* M & W
Allen Community College *Kansas* W
Allen University *South Carolina* W
Alma College *Michigan* W
Alpena Community College *Michigan* W
Alvernia University *Pennsylvania* W
Alverno College *Wisconsin* W
American International College *Massachusetts* W
American River College *California* W
American University *District of Columbia* W
American University of Puerto Rico *Puerto Rico* M & W
Amherst College *Massachusetts* M & W
Ancilla College *Indiana* W
Anderson University *South Carolina* W
Anderson University *Indiana* W
Angelo State University *Texas* W
Anna Maria College *Massachusetts* W
Anne Arundel Community College *Maryland* W
Anoka-Ramsey Community College *Minnesota* W
Anoka-Ramsey Community College, Cambridge Campus *Minnesota* W
Antelope Valley College *California* W
Appalachian Bible College *West Virginia* W
Appalachian State University *North Carolina* W
Aquinas College *Michigan* W
Arcadia University *Pennsylvania* W
Arizona State University *Arizona* W
Arizona Western College *Arizona* W
Arkansas State University - Jonesboro *Arkansas* W
Arkansas Tech University *Arkansas* W
Armstrong Atlantic State University *Georgia* W
The Art Institute of Boston at Lesley University *Massachusetts* M & W
Asbury University *Kentucky* W
Ashford University *Iowa* W
Ashland University *Ohio* W
Assumption College *Massachusetts* W
Atlanta Christian College *Georgia* W
Auburn University *Alabama* W
Augsburg College *Minnesota* W
Augusta State University *Georgia* W
Augustana College *South Dakota* W
Augustana College *Illinois* M & W
Aurora University *Illinois* W
Austin College *Texas* W
Austin Peay State University *Tennessee* W
Ave Maria University *Florida* W
Averett University *Virginia* W
Avila University *Missouri* W
Azusa Pacific University *California* M & W
Babson College *Massachusetts* W
Baker University *Kansas* W
Bakersfield College *California* W
Baldwin-Wallace College *Ohio* W
Ball State University *Indiana* M & W
Baptist Bible College *Missouri* W
Baptist Bible College of Pennsylvania *Pennsylvania* W
The Baptist College of Florida *Florida* W
Barclay College *Kansas* W
Bard College *New York* M & W
Barnard College *New York* W
Barry University *Florida* W
Barstow College *California* W
Barton College *North Carolina* W
Barton County Community College *Kansas* W
Bates College *Maine* M & W
Bay Path College *Massachusetts* W
Bayamón Central University *Puerto Rico* M & W
Baylor University *Texas* M & W
Becker College *Massachusetts* W
Belhaven University *Mississippi* W
Bellarmine University *Kentucky* W
Bellevue College *Washington* W
Bellevue University *Nebraska* W
Belmont Abbey College *North Carolina* W
Belmont University *Tennessee* W
Beloit College *Wisconsin* W
Bemidji State University *Minnesota* W
Benedict College *South Carolina* W
Benedictine College *Kansas* W
Benedictine University *Illinois* W
Bentley University *Massachusetts* W
Berea College *Kentucky* W
Bergen Community College *New Jersey* W
Bernard M. Baruch College of the City University of New York *New York* M & W
Berry College *Georgia* W
Bethany Bible College *New Brunswick* W
Bethany College *West Virginia* W
Bethany College *Kansas* W
Bethany Lutheran College *Minnesota* W
Bethany University *California* W
Bethel College *Kansas* W
Bethel College *Indiana* W
Bethel University *Tennessee* W
Bethel University *Minnesota* M & W
Bethune-Cookman University *Florida* W
Beulah Heights University *Georgia* M & W
Big Bend Community College *Washington* W
Biola University *California* W
Birmingham-Southern College *Alabama* W
Bishop's University *Quebec* W
Bismarck State College *North Dakota* W
Black Hawk College *Illinois* W
Black Hills State University *South Dakota* W
Blackburn College *Illinois* W
Blessing-Rieman College of Nursing *Illinois* M & W
Blinn College *Texas* W
Bloomfield College *New Jersey* W
Bloomsburg University of Pennsylvania *Pennsylvania* M & W
Blue Mountain Community College *Oregon* W
Blue Ridge Community College *North Carolina* W
Bluefield College *Virginia* W
Bluffton University *Ohio* W
Boise State University *Idaho* W
Boston College *Massachusetts* W
Boston University *Massachusetts* M & W
Bowdoin College *Maine* M & W
Bowie State University *Maryland* W
Bowling Green State University *Ohio* W
Bradley University *Illinois* W
Brandeis University *Massachusetts* W
Brandon University *Manitoba* M & W
Brenau University *Georgia* W
Brescia University *Kentucky* W
Brevard College *North Carolina* W
Brevard Community College *Florida* W
Brewton-Parker College *Georgia* W
Briar Cliff University *Iowa* W
Bridgewater College *Virginia* W
Bridgewater State College *Massachusetts* W
Briercrest College *Saskatchewan* M & W
Brigham Young University *Utah* M & W
Brigham Young University–Hawaii *Hawaii* W
Brock University *Ontario* W
Bronx Community College of the City University of New York *New York* W
Brookhaven College *Texas* W
Brooklyn College of the City University of New York *New York* M & W
Broome Community College *New York* W
Broward College *Florida* W
Brown University *Rhode Island* M & W

M = Men; W = Women

Bryan College *Tennessee* W
Bryant University *Rhode Island* M & W
Bryn Athyn College of the New Church *Pennsylvania* W
Bryn Mawr College *Pennsylvania* W
Bucknell University *Pennsylvania* M & W
Bucks County Community College *Pennsylvania* W
Buena Vista University *Iowa* W
Buffalo State College, State University of New York *New York* M & W
Butler Community College *Kansas* W
Butler County Community College *Pennsylvania* W
Butler University *Indiana* W
Butte College *California* W
Cabrillo College *California* M & W
Cabrini College *Pennsylvania* W
Caldwell Community College and Technical Institute *North Carolina* W
California Baptist University *California* M & W
California Institute of Technology *California* M & W
California Lutheran University *California* W
California Maritime Academy *California* W
California Polytechnic State University, San Luis Obispo *California* W
California State Polytechnic University, Pomona *California* W
California State University, Bakersfield *California* W
California State University, Chico *California* W
California State University, Dominguez Hills *California* W
California State University, East Bay *California* W
California State University, Fresno *California* W
California State University, Fullerton *California* W
California State University, Long Beach *California* M & W
California State University, Los Angeles *California* W
California State University, Monterey Bay *California* W
California State University, Northridge *California* M & W
California State University, Sacramento *California* M & W
California State University, San Bernardino *California* W
California State University, Stanislaus *California* W
California University of Pennsylvania *Pennsylvania* M & W
Calumet College of Saint Joseph *Indiana* W
Calvary Bible College and Theological Seminary *Missouri* W
Calvin College *Michigan* M & W
Cameron University *Oklahoma* W
Campbell University *North Carolina* W
Campbellsville University *Kentucky* W
Canadian Mennonite University *Manitoba* M & W
Canisius College *New York* M & W
Cape Breton University *Nova Scotia* W
Cape Fear Community College *North Carolina* M & W
Capital University *Ohio* W
Cardinal Stritch University *Wisconsin* M & W
Caribbean University *Puerto Rico* M & W
Carl Sandburg College *Illinois* W
Carleton College *Minnesota* M & W
Carleton University *Ontario* W
Carlow University *Pennsylvania* W
Carnegie Mellon University *Pennsylvania* M & W
Carroll College *Montana* W
Carroll University *Wisconsin* W
Carson-Newman College *Tennessee* W
Carthage College *Wisconsin* M & W
Case Western Reserve University *Ohio* M & W
Casper College *Wyoming* W
Castleton State College *Vermont* W
Catawba College *North Carolina* W
Catawba Valley Community College *North Carolina* W
The Catholic University of America *District of Columbia* W
Cazenovia College *New York* W
Cecil College *Maryland* W
Cedar Crest College *Pennsylvania* W
Cedar Valley College *Texas* W
Cedarville University *Ohio* W
Centenary College *New Jersey* W
Centenary College of Louisiana *Louisiana* W
Central Alabama Community College *Alabama* W
Central Baptist College *Arkansas* W
Central Carolina Community College *North Carolina* W
Central Christian College of the Bible *Missouri* W
Central Christian College of Kansas *Kansas* W
Central College *Iowa* W
Central Community College–Columbus Campus *Nebraska* W
Central Connecticut State University *Connecticut* W
Central Lakes College *Minnesota* W
Central Methodist University *Missouri* W
Central Michigan University *Michigan* W
Central Ohio Technical College *Ohio* M & W
Central State University *Ohio* W
Central Washington University *Washington* W
Central Wyoming College *Wyoming* W
Centralia College *Washington* W
Centre College *Kentucky* W
Cerritos College *California* W
Chabot College *California* W
Chadron State College *Nebraska* W
Chaffey College *California* W
Chaminade University of Honolulu *Hawaii* W
Chapman University *California* W
Charleston Southern University *South Carolina* W
Chatham University *Pennsylvania* W
Chemeketa Community College *Oregon* W
Chesapeake College *Maryland* W
Chestnut Hill College *Pennsylvania* W
Cheyney University of Pennsylvania *Pennsylvania* W
Chicago State University *Illinois* W
Chowan University *North Carolina* W
Christendom College *Virginia* W
Christian Brothers University *Tennessee* W
Christopher Newport University *Virginia* W
Cincinnati Christian University *Ohio* W
Cisco College *Texas* W
The Citadel, The Military College of South Carolina *South Carolina* W
Citrus College *California* W
City College of the City University of New York *New York* W
City College of San Francisco *California* M & W
City Colleges of Chicago, Olive-Harvey College *Illinois* W
Clackamas Community College *Oregon* W
Claflin University *South Carolina* W
Claremont McKenna College *California* M & W
Clarendon College *Texas* W
Clarion University of Pennsylvania *Pennsylvania* W
Clark Atlanta University *Georgia* W
Clark College *Washington* W
Clark State Community College *Ohio* W
Clark University *Massachusetts* W
Clarke College *Iowa* M & W
Clarkson University *New York* W
Clearwater Christian College *Florida* W
Clemson University *South Carolina* M & W
Cleveland State University *Ohio* W
Clinton Community College *Iowa* W
Cloud County Community College *Kansas* W
Coastal Bend College *Texas* W
Coastal Carolina University *South Carolina* W
Coe College *Iowa* W
Coffeyville Community College *Kansas* W
Coker College *South Carolina* W
Colby College *Maine* M & W
Colby Community College *Kansas* W
Colby-Sawyer College *New Hampshire* W
Colgate University *New York* M & W
The College at Brockport, State University of New York *New York* W
College of the Canyons *California* W
College of Charleston *South Carolina* W
College of the Desert *California* W
College of DuPage *Illinois* W
College of the Holy Cross *Massachusetts* W
The College of Idaho *Idaho* W
College of Lake County *Illinois* W
College of Marin *California* M & W
College of Mount St. Joseph *Ohio* M & W
College of Mount Saint Vincent *New York* M & W
The College of New Rochelle *New York* W
College of Notre Dame of Maryland *Maryland* W
College of the Ozarks *Missouri* W
College of the Redwoods *California* W
College of Saint Benedict *Minnesota* W
College of Saint Elizabeth *New Jersey* W
College of Saint Mary *Nebraska* W
The College of Saint Rose *New York* W
The College of St. Scholastica *Minnesota* W
College of the Sequoias *California* W
College of the Siskiyous *California* W
College of Southern Idaho *Idaho* M & W
College of Southern Maryland *Maryland* W
College of Staten Island of the City University of New York *New York* W
The College of William and Mary *Virginia* W
The College of Wooster *Ohio* M & W
Collin County Community College District *Texas* W
Colorado Christian University *Colorado* W
The Colorado College *Colorado* M & W
Colorado School of Mines *Colorado* M & W
Colorado State University *Colorado* W
Colorado State University–Pueblo *Colorado* W
Columbia Basin College *Washington* W
Columbia Bible College *British Columbia* M & W
Columbia College *South Carolina* W
Columbia College *Missouri* W
Columbia College *California* W
Columbia University *New York* M & W
Columbia University, School of General Studies *New York* W
Columbus State Community College *Ohio* W
Community College of Allegheny County *Pennsylvania* W
The Community College of Baltimore County *Maryland* W
Community College of Beaver County *Pennsylvania* W
Community College of Philadelphia *Pennsylvania* M & W
Community College of Rhode Island *Rhode Island* W
Concord University *West Virginia* W
Concordia College *Minnesota* M & W
Concordia College–New York *New York* W
Concordia University *Oregon* W
Concordia University *Michigan* W
Concordia University *California* W
Concordia University Chicago *Illinois* W
Concordia University, Nebraska *Nebraska* W
Concordia University, St. Paul *Minnesota* W
Concordia University Texas *Texas* W
Concordia University Wisconsin *Wisconsin* W
Connecticut College *Connecticut* M & W
Contra Costa College *California* W
Converse College *South Carolina* W
Cooper Union for the Advancement of Science and Art *New York* M & W
Coppin State University *Maryland* W
Corban University *Oregon* W
Corcoran College of Art and Design *District of Columbia* M & W
Cornell College *Iowa* M & W
Cornell University *New York* W
Cornerstone University *Michigan* W
Corning Community College *New York* W
Cosumnes River College *California* W
Cottey College *Missouri* W
Covenant College *Georgia* W
Cowley County Community College and Area Vocational–Technical School *Kansas* W
Creighton University *Nebraska* W
Crossroads College *Minnesota* M & W
Crown College *Minnesota* W
Cuesta College *California* W
Culver-Stockton College *Missouri* W
Cumberland University *Tennessee* W
Cuyamaca College *California* W
Cypress College *California* W
Daemen College *New York* W
Dakota College at Bottineau *North Dakota* W

M = Men; W = Women

Dakota State University *South Dakota* W
Dakota Wesleyan University *South Dakota* W
Dalhousie University *Nova Scotia* M & W
Dallas Baptist University *Texas* W
Dallas Christian College *Texas* W
Dalton State College *Georgia* M & W
Dana College *Nebraska* W
Daniel Webster College *New Hampshire* M & W
Danville Area Community College *Illinois* W
Dartmouth College *New Hampshire* M & W
Davenport University *Michigan* W
Davidson College *North Carolina* W
Davis & Elkins College *West Virginia* W
De Anza College *California* M & W
Dean College *Massachusetts* W
Defiance College *Ohio* W
Delaware County Community College *Pennsylvania* W
Delaware State University *Delaware* W
Delaware Valley College *Pennsylvania* W
Delta College *Michigan* W
Denison University *Ohio* W
DePaul University *Illinois* W
DePauw University *Indiana* W
Des Moines Area Community College *Iowa* W
DeSales University *Pennsylvania* W
Diablo Valley College *California* W
Dickinson College *Pennsylvania* M & W
Dickinson State University *North Dakota* W
Dillard University *Louisiana* W
Dixie State College of Utah *Utah* W
Doane College *Nebraska* W
Dodge City Community College *Kansas* W
Dominican College *New York* W
Dominican University *Illinois* M & W
Dominican University of California *California* W
Dordt College *Iowa* W
Dowling College *New York* W
Drake University *Iowa* W
Drury University *Missouri* W
Duke University *North Carolina* M & W
Duquesne University *Pennsylvania* W
Dutchess Community College *New York* W
D'Youville College *New York* M & W
Earlham College *Indiana* M & W
East Carolina University *North Carolina* W
East Central College *Missouri* W
East Central University *Oklahoma* W
East Los Angeles College *California* W
East Stroudsburg University of Pennsylvania *Pennsylvania* W
East Tennessee State University *Tennessee* W
East Texas Baptist University *Texas* W
Eastern Arizona College *Arizona* W
Eastern Connecticut State University *Connecticut* W
Eastern Illinois University *Illinois* M & W
Eastern Kentucky University *Kentucky* W
Eastern Mennonite University *Virginia* M & W
Eastern Michigan University *Michigan* W
Eastern Nazarene College *Massachusetts* M & W
Eastern New Mexico University *New Mexico* W
Eastern Oregon University *Oregon* W
Eastern University *Pennsylvania* W
Eastern Washington University *Washington* W
Eastfield College *Texas* M & W
Eckerd College *Florida* M & W
Edgewood College *Wisconsin* W
Edinboro University of Pennsylvania *Pennsylvania* W
Edison State Community College *Ohio* W
Edmonds Community College *Washington* W
El Camino College *California* M & W
Elgin Community College *Illinois* W
Elizabeth City State University *North Carolina* W
Elizabethtown College *Pennsylvania* M & W
Ellsworth Community College *Iowa* W
Elmhurst College *Illinois* W
Elmira College *New York* M & W
Elms College *Massachusetts* M & W
Elon University *North Carolina* W
Embry-Riddle Aeronautical University *Florida* W
Embry-Riddle Aeronautical University *Arizona* W
Emerson College *Massachusetts* M & W
Emmanuel College *Massachusetts* M & W
Emory & Henry College *Virginia* W
Emory University *Georgia* M & W
Emporia State University *Kansas* W
Endicott College *Massachusetts* M & W
Erie Community College *New York* W
Erie Community College, North Campus *New York* W
Erie Community College, South Campus *New York* W
Erskine College *South Carolina* W
Eugene Bible College *Oregon* M & W
Eugenio María de Hostos Community College of the City University of New York *New York* W
Eureka College *Illinois* W
Evangel University *Missouri* W
Everett Community College *Washington* W
The Evergreen State College *Washington* W
Fairfield University *Connecticut* M & W
Fairleigh Dickinson University, College at Florham *New Jersey* W
Fairleigh Dickinson University, Metropolitan Campus *New Jersey* W
Fairmont State University *West Virginia* W
Faith Baptist Bible College and Theological Seminary *Iowa* W
Farmingdale State College *New York* W
Fashion Institute of Technology *New York* W
Faulkner University *Alabama* W
Fayetteville State University *North Carolina* W
Ferris State University *Michigan* W
Ferrum College *Virginia* W
Finger Lakes Community College *New York* W
Finlandia University *Michigan* W
Flagler College *Florida* M & W
Florida Agricultural and Mechanical University *Florida* W
Florida Atlantic University *Florida* W
Florida College *Florida* W
Florida Gulf Coast University *Florida* W
Florida Institute of Technology *Florida* W
Florida International University *Florida* W
Florida Memorial University *Florida* M & W
Florida Southern College *Florida* M & W
Florida State College at Jacksonville *Florida* W
Florida State University *Florida* M & W
Fontbonne University *Missouri* M & W
Foothill College *California* W
Fordham University *New York* W
Fort Belknap College *Montana* M & W
Fort Hays State University *Kansas* W
Fort Lewis College *Colorado* W
Fort Scott Community College *Kansas* W
Fort Valley State University *Georgia* W
Fox Valley Technical College *Wisconsin* M & W
Framingham State College *Massachusetts* W
Francis Marion University *South Carolina* W
Franciscan University of Steubenville *Ohio* W
Frank Phillips College *Texas* W
Franklin College *Indiana* W
Franklin & Marshall College *Pennsylvania* M & W
Franklin Pierce University *New Hampshire* W
Frederick Community College *Maryland* W
Freed-Hardeman University *Tennessee* W
Fresno City College *California* W
Fresno Pacific University *California* M & W
Friends University *Kansas* W
Frostburg State University *Maryland* W
Fullerton College *California* W
Fulton-Montgomery Community College *New York* W
Furman University *South Carolina* W
Gadsden State Community College *Alabama* W
Gallaudet University *District of Columbia* W
Galveston College *Texas* W
Gannon University *Pennsylvania* W
Garden City Community College *Kansas* W
Gardner-Webb University *North Carolina* W
Garrett College *Maryland* W
Gavilan College *California* W
Genesee Community College *New York* M & W
Geneva College *Pennsylvania* M & W
George Fox University *Oregon* W
George Mason University *Virginia* M & W
The George Washington University *District of Columbia* W
Georgetown College *Kentucky* W
Georgetown University *District of Columbia* M & W
Georgia Institute of Technology *Georgia* W
Georgia Southern University *Georgia* W
Georgia State University *Georgia* W
Georgian Court University *New Jersey* W
Gettysburg College *Pennsylvania* W
Glendale Community College *California* W
Glendale Community College *Arizona* W
Glenville State College *West Virginia* W
Globe Institute of Technology *New York* W
Golden West College *California* M & W
Goldey-Beacom College *Delaware* W
Gonzaga University *Washington* W
Gordon College *Massachusetts* W
Goshen College *Indiana* W
Goucher College *Maryland* W
Grace Bible College *Michigan* W
Grace College *Indiana* W
Grace University *Nebraska* W
Graceland University *Iowa* M & W
Grambling State University *Louisiana* W
Grand Canyon University *Arizona* W
Grand Rapids Community College *Michigan* W
Grand Valley State University *Michigan* M & W
Grand View University *Iowa* W
Great Lakes Christian College *Michigan* W
Green Mountain College *Vermont* W
Green River Community College *Washington* W
Greensboro College *North Carolina* W
Greenville College *Illinois* W
Grinnell College *Iowa* W
Grossmont College *California* M & W
Grove City College *Pennsylvania* W
Guilford College *North Carolina* W
Guilford Technical Community College *North Carolina* W
Gulf Coast Community College *Florida* W
Gustavus Adolphus College *Minnesota* M & W
Gwynedd-Mercy College *Pennsylvania* W
Hagerstown Community College *Maryland* W
Hamilton College *New York* M & W
Hamline University *Minnesota* W
Hampton University *Virginia* W
Hannibal-LaGrange College *Missouri* M & W
Hanover College *Indiana* W
Harcum College *Pennsylvania* W
Hardin-Simmons University *Texas* W
Harding University *Arkansas* W
Harford Community College *Maryland* W
Harper College *Illinois* W
Harris-Stowe State University *Missouri* W
Hartnell College *California* W
Hartwick College *New York* W
Harvard University *Massachusetts* M & W
Harvey Mudd College *California* W
Haskell Indian Nations University *Kansas* W
Hastings College *Nebraska* W
Haverford College *Pennsylvania* M & W
Hawai'i Pacific University *Hawaii* W
Heidelberg University *Ohio* M & W
Henderson State University *Arkansas* W
Hendrix College *Arkansas* W
Henry Ford Community College *Michigan* W
Heritage Baptist College and Heritage Theological Seminary *Ontario* M & W
Herkimer County Community College *New York* W
Hesston College *Kansas* W
Hibbing Community College *Minnesota* W
High Point University *North Carolina* W
Highland Community College *Kansas* W
Highland Community College *Illinois* W
Highline Community College *Washington* W
Hilbert College *New York* M & W
Hill College of the Hill Junior College District *Texas* W
Hillsborough Community College *Florida* W
Hillsdale College *Michigan* W
Hillsdale Free Will Baptist College *Oklahoma* W
Hiram College *Ohio* M & W
Hofstra University *New York* W
Holy Family University *Pennsylvania* W

M = Men; W = Women

M = Men; W = Women

Marist College *New York* M & W
Marquette University *Wisconsin* M & W
Mars Hill College *North Carolina* W
Marshall University *West Virginia* W
Marshalltown Community College *Iowa* W
Martin Luther College *Minnesota* W
Martin Methodist College *Tennessee* W
Mary Baldwin College *Virginia* W
Marymount University *Virginia* W
Maryville College *Tennessee* W
Maryville University of Saint Louis *Missouri* W
Marywood University *Pennsylvania* W
Massachusetts Bay Community College *Massachusetts* W
Massachusetts Institute of Technology *Massachusetts* M & W
Massachusetts Maritime Academy *Massachusetts* W
Master's College and Seminary *Ontario* W
The Master's College and Seminary *California* W
Mayland Community College *North Carolina* W
Mayville State University *North Dakota* W
McDaniel College *Maryland* W
McGill University *Quebec* M & W
McHenry County College *Illinois* W
McKendree University *Illinois* W
McMaster University *Ontario* M & W
McMurry University *Texas* W
McNeese State University *Louisiana* W
McPherson College *Kansas* W
Medaille College *New York* M & W
Medgar Evers College of the City University of New York *New York* M & W
Memorial University of Newfoundland *Newfoundland and Labrador* M & W
Mendocino College *California* W
Menlo College *California* W
Merced College *California* W
Mercer University *Georgia* W
Mercy College *New York* W
Mercyhurst College *Pennsylvania* W
Meredith College *North Carolina* W
Merrimack College *Massachusetts* M & W
Mesa Community College *Arizona* W
Mesa State College *Colorado* W
Mesabi Range Community and Technical College *Minnesota* W
Messiah College *Pennsylvania* W
Methodist University *North Carolina* W
Metropolitan Community College–Longview *Missouri* W
Metropolitan State College of Denver *Colorado* W
Miami Dade College *Florida* W
Miami University *Ohio* M & W
Miami University Hamilton *Ohio* W
Miami University–Middletown Campus *Ohio* W
Michigan State University *Michigan* M & W
Michigan Technological University *Michigan* W
Mid-America Christian University *Oklahoma* W
Mid-Atlantic Christian University *North Carolina* W
Mid-Continent University *Kentucky* W
Mid-Plains Community College *Nebraska* W
Mid-State Technical College *Wisconsin* W
MidAmerica Nazarene University *Kansas* W
Middle Tennessee State University *Tennessee* W
Middlebury College *Vermont* W
Midland Lutheran College *Nebraska* W
Midway College *Kentucky* W
Midwestern State University *Texas* W
Midwives College of Utah *Utah* M & W
Millersville University of Pennsylvania *Pennsylvania* W
Milligan College *Tennessee* W
Millikin University *Illinois* W
Mills College *California* W
Millsaps College *Mississippi* W
Milwaukee Area Technical College *Wisconsin* W
Milwaukee School of Engineering *Wisconsin* M & W
Mineral Area College *Missouri* W
Minnesota State Community and Technical College *Minnesota* W
Minnesota State University Mankato *Minnesota* W
Minnesota State University Moorhead *Minnesota* W
Minnesota West Community and Technical College *Minnesota* W
Minot State University *North Dakota* W
Misericordia University *Pennsylvania* W
Mississippi College *Mississippi* W
Mississippi State University *Mississippi* W
Missouri Baptist University *Missouri* M & W
Missouri Southern State University *Missouri* W
Missouri State University *Missouri* M & W
Missouri State University–West Plains *Missouri* W
Missouri University of Science and Technology *Missouri* W
Missouri Valley College *Missouri* M & W
Missouri Western State University *Missouri* W
Mitchell College *Connecticut* W
Modesto Junior College *California* W
Mohawk Valley Community College *New York* W
Molloy College *New York* W
Monmouth College *Illinois* W
Monroe College (Bronx) *New York* W
Monroe College (New Rochelle) *New York* W
Monroe Community College *New York* W
Montana State University *Montana* W
Montana State University Billings *Montana* W
Montana State University–Northern *Montana* W
Montana Tech of The University of Montana *Montana* W
Montclair State University *New Jersey* W
Monterey Peninsula College *California* W
Montgomery College *Maryland* M & W
Montreat College *North Carolina* W
Moody Bible Institute *Illinois* M & W
Moorpark College *California* M & W
Moraine Valley Community College *Illinois* W
Moravian College *Pennsylvania* W
Morehead State University *Kentucky* W
Morgan State University *Maryland* W
Morningside College *Iowa* W
Morris College *South Carolina* W
Morton College *Illinois* W
Mott Community College *Michigan* W
Mount Aloysius College *Pennsylvania* W
Mount Holyoke College *Massachusetts* W
Mt. Hood Community College *Oregon* W
Mount Ida College *Massachusetts* M & W
Mount Marty College *South Dakota* W
Mount Mary College *Wisconsin* W
Mount Mercy College *Iowa* W
Mount Olive College *North Carolina* M & W
Mount Saint Mary College *New York* W
Mount Saint Vincent University *Nova Scotia* W
Mt. San Antonio College *California* M & W
Mt. San Jacinto College *California* W
Mount Vernon Nazarene University *Ohio* W
Mountain State University *West Virginia* W
Muhlenberg College *Pennsylvania* W
Multnomah University *Oregon* W
Murray State University *Kentucky* W
Muskegon Community College *Michigan* W
Muskingum University *Ohio* W
Napa Valley College *California* W
Nassau Community College *New York* W
National American University (Rapid City) *South Dakota* M & W
Navarro College *Texas* W
Nazareth College of Rochester *New York* M & W
Nebraska Christian College *Nebraska* W
Nebraska Wesleyan University *Nebraska* W
Neosho County Community College *Kansas* W
Neumann University *Pennsylvania* W
New Jersey City University *New Jersey* M & W
New Jersey Institute of Technology *New Jersey* M & W
New Mexico Highlands University *New Mexico* W
New Mexico Military Institute *New Mexico* W
New Mexico State University *New Mexico* W
New York City College of Technology of the City University of New York *New York* M & W
New York Institute of Technology *New York* W
New York University *New York* M & W
Newberry College *South Carolina* W
Newbury College *Massachusetts* M & W
Newman University *Kansas* W
NHTI, Concord's Community College *New Hampshire* M & W
Niagara County Community College *New York* W
Niagara University *New York* W
Nicholls State University *Louisiana* W
Nichols College *Massachusetts* M & W
Nipissing University *Ontario* M & W
Norfolk State University *Virginia* W
North Carolina Agricultural and Technical State University *North Carolina* W
North Carolina Central University *North Carolina* W
North Carolina State University *North Carolina* M & W
North Carolina Wesleyan College *North Carolina* W
North Central College *Illinois* W
North Central Texas College *Texas* W
North Central University *Minnesota* W
North Country Community College *New York* W
North Dakota State College of Science *North Dakota* W
North Dakota State University *North Dakota* M & W
North Greenville University *South Carolina* W
North Idaho College *Idaho* W
North Iowa Area Community College *Iowa* W
North Lake College *Texas* W
North Park University *Illinois* W
Northampton Community College *Pennsylvania* M & W
Northeastern Junior College *Colorado* W
Northeastern Oklahoma Agricultural and Mechanical College *Oklahoma* W
Northeastern University *Massachusetts* W
Northern Arizona University *Arizona* W
Northern Essex Community College *Massachusetts* M & W
Northern Illinois University *Illinois* W
Northern Kentucky University *Kentucky* W
Northern Michigan University *Michigan* W
Northern Oklahoma College *Oklahoma* M & W
Northern State University *South Dakota* W
Northland College *Wisconsin* W
Northland Community and Technical College–Thief River Falls *Minnesota* W
Northwest Christian University *Oregon* W
Northwest College *Wyoming* W
Northwest Missouri State University *Missouri* W
Northwest Nazarene University *Idaho* W
Northwest-Shoals Community College *Alabama* W
Northwest University *Washington* W
Northwestern College *Minnesota* M & W
Northwestern College *Iowa* W
Northwestern State University of Louisiana *Louisiana* W
Northwestern University *Illinois* W
Northwood University *Michigan* W
Northwood University, Florida Campus *Florida* W
Norwich University *Vermont* M & W
Notre Dame College *Ohio* W
Notre Dame de Namur University *California* W
Nova Scotia Agricultural College *Nova Scotia* M & W
Nova Southeastern University *Florida* W
Oak Hills Christian College *Minnesota* W
Oakland City University *Indiana* W
Oakland Community College *Michigan* W
Oakland University *Michigan* W
Oakton Community College *Illinois* W
Oberlin College *Ohio* M & W
Occidental College *California* W
Oglethorpe University *Georgia* W
Ohio Christian University *Ohio* W
Ohio Dominican University *Ohio* W
Ohio Northern University *Ohio* M & W
The Ohio State University *Ohio* M & W
The Ohio State University at Lima *Ohio* M & W
The Ohio State University at Marion *Ohio* W
Ohio University *Ohio* W
Ohio University–Eastern *Ohio* W
Ohio University–Zanesville *Ohio* M & W
Ohio Valley University *West Virginia* W
Ohio Wesleyan University *Ohio* M & W
Ohlone College *California* M & W
Okanagan College *British Columbia* M & W

M = Men; W = Women

Oklahoma Panhandle State University *Oklahoma* W
Oklahoma Wesleyan University *Oklahoma* W
Olivet College *Michigan* W
Olivet Nazarene University *Illinois* W
Olympic College *Washington* W
Onondaga Community College *New York* W
Oral Roberts University *Oklahoma* W
Orange Coast College *California* W
Orange County Community College *New York* W
Oregon Institute of Technology *Oregon* W
Oregon State University *Oregon* W
Otero Junior College *Colorado* W
Ottawa University *Kansas* W
Otterbein University *Ohio* W
Ouachita Baptist University *Arkansas* W
Our Lady of the Lake University of San Antonio *Texas* W
Owens Community College *Ohio* W
Oxnard College *California* W
Ozark Christian College *Missouri* W
Pace University *New York* W
Pacific Lutheran University *Washington* M & W
Pacific Union College *California* M & W
Pacific University *Oregon* W
Paine College *Georgia* W
Palm Beach Atlantic University *Florida* W
Palm Beach State College *Florida* M & W
Palomar College *California* M & W
Panola College *Texas* W
Paris Junior College *Texas* W
Park University *Missouri* M & W
Parkland College *Illinois* W
Pasadena City College *California* W
Pasco-Hernando Community College *Florida* W
Passaic County Community College *New Jersey* W
Paul Smith's College *New York* W
Peace College *North Carolina* W
Penn State Abington *Pennsylvania* W
Penn State Beaver *Pennsylvania* W
Penn State Berks *Pennsylvania* W
Penn State Brandywine *Pennsylvania* W
Penn State DuBois *Pennsylvania* W
Penn State Erie, The Behrend College *Pennsylvania* M & W
Penn State Fayette, The Eberly Campus *Pennsylvania* W
Penn State Greater Allegheny *Pennsylvania* W
Penn State Harrisburg *Pennsylvania* W
Penn State Hazleton *Pennsylvania* M & W
Penn State Lehigh Valley *Pennsylvania* M & W
Penn State Mont Alto *Pennsylvania* W
Penn State New Kensington *Pennsylvania* W
Penn State Schuylkill *Pennsylvania* W
Penn State University Park *Pennsylvania* M & W
Penn State Wilkes-Barre *Pennsylvania* W
Penn State Worthington Scranton *Pennsylvania* W
Pennsylvania College of Technology *Pennsylvania* M & W
Pensacola Junior College *Florida* W
Pepperdine University *California* M & W
Peru State College *Nebraska* W
Pfeiffer University *North Carolina* W
Philadelphia Biblical University *Pennsylvania* M & W
Philadelphia University *Pennsylvania* W
Philander Smith College *Arkansas* W
Phoenix College *Arizona* W
Piedmont Baptist College and Graduate School *North Carolina* W
Piedmont College *Georgia* W
Pierce College at Puyallup *Washington* W
Pikeville College *Kentucky* W
Pima Community College *Arizona* W
Pine Manor College *Massachusetts* W
Pitt Community College *North Carolina* W
Pittsburg State University *Kansas* W
Pitzer College *California* W
Plymouth State University *New Hampshire* M & W
Point Loma Nazarene University *California* W
Point Park University *Pennsylvania* W
Polk State College *Florida* W
Polytechnic Institute of NYU *New York* M & W
Polytechnic University of Puerto Rico *Puerto Rico* M & W
Pomona College *California* M & W
Pontifical Catholic University of Puerto Rico *Puerto Rico* M & W
Porterville College *California* W
Portland State University *Oregon* W
Post University *Connecticut* W
Potomac State College of West Virginia University *West Virginia* W
Prairie View A&M University *Texas* W
Pratt Community College *Kansas* W
Pratt Institute *New York* W
Presbyterian College *South Carolina* W
Presentation College *South Dakota* W
Prince George's Community College *Maryland* W
Princeton University *New Jersey* M & W
Principia College *Illinois* W
Providence College *Rhode Island* M & W
Providence College and Theological Seminary *Manitoba* M & W
Purchase College, State University of New York *New York* M & W
Purdue University *Indiana* W
Purdue University North Central *Indiana* W
Queens College of the City University of New York *New York* W
Queens University of Charlotte *North Carolina* W
Queen's University at Kingston *Ontario* M & W
Queensborough Community College of the City University of New York *New York* M & W
Quincy University *Illinois* M & W
Quinnipiac University *Connecticut* W
Rabbinical College of America *New Jersey* M
Radford University *Virginia* W
Rainy River Community College *Minnesota* W
Ramapo College of New Jersey *New Jersey* M & W
Randolph College *Virginia* W
Randolph-Macon College *Virginia* W
Redeemer University College *Ontario* M & W
Redlands Community College *Oklahoma* W
Reedley College *California* W
Regis College *Massachusetts* M & W
Regis University *Colorado* W
Reinhardt University *Georgia* W
Rend Lake College *Illinois* W
Rensselaer Polytechnic Institute *New York* M & W
Research College of Nursing *Missouri* W
Rhode Island College *Rhode Island* W
Rhodes College *Tennessee* W
Rice University *Texas* M & W
The Richard Stockton College of New Jersey *New Jersey* W
Richland College *Texas* W
Rider University *New Jersey* W
Ridgewater College *Minnesota* W
Rio Hondo College *California* W
Ripon College *Wisconsin* W
Riverland Community College *Minnesota* W
Riverside Community College District *California* W
Rivier College *New Hampshire* M & W
Roanoke College *Virginia* M & W
Robert Morris University *Pennsylvania* W
Robert Morris University Illinois *Illinois* M & W
Roberts Wesleyan College *New York* W
Rochester College *Michigan* W
Rochester Community and Technical College *Minnesota* W
Rochester Institute of Technology *New York* M & W
Rock Valley College *Illinois* W
Rockford College *Illinois* M & W
Rockhurst University *Missouri* W
Rockingham Community College *North Carolina* W
Rockland Community College *New York* W
Rocky Mountain College *Alberta* M & W
Rocky Mountain College *Montana* W
Roger Williams University *Rhode Island* M & W
Rollins College *Florida* W
Rose-Hulman Institute of Technology *Indiana* W
Rosemont College *Pennsylvania* W
Rowan University *New Jersey* W
Royal Military College of Canada *Ontario* M & W
Russell Sage College *New York* W
Rutgers, The State University of New Jersey, Camden *New Jersey* W
Rutgers, The State University of New Jersey, New Brunswick *New Jersey* W
Rutgers, The State University of New Jersey, Newark *New Jersey* M & W
Ryerson University *Ontario* M & W
Sacramento City College *California* W
Sacred Heart University *Connecticut* M & W
Saddleback College *California* W
Sage College of Albany *New York* M & W
Saginaw Valley State University *Michigan* W
St. Ambrose University *Iowa* M & W
St. Andrews Presbyterian College *North Carolina* W
Saint Anselm College *New Hampshire* W
Saint Augustine's College *North Carolina* W
St. Catherine University *Minnesota* W
St. Clair County Community College *Michigan* W
St. Cloud State University *Minnesota* M & W
St. Cloud Technical College *Minnesota* W
St. Edward's University *Texas* W
St. Francis College *New York* W
Saint Francis University *Pennsylvania* M & W
St. Francis Xavier University *Nova Scotia* W
St. Gregory's University *Oklahoma* W
St. John Fisher College *New York* W
St. Johns River Community College *Florida* W
St. John's University *New York* W
Saint John's University *Minnesota* M
Saint Joseph College *Connecticut* W
Saint Joseph's College *Indiana* W
St. Joseph's College, Long Island Campus *New York* M & W
Saint Joseph's College of Maine *Maine* W
St. Joseph's College, New York *New York* M & W
St. Lawrence University *New York* W
Saint Leo University *Florida* W
St. Louis Christian College *Missouri* W
St. Louis College of Pharmacy *Missouri* W
St. Louis Community College at Florissant Valley *Missouri* W
St. Louis Community College at Meramec *Missouri* W
Saint Louis University *Missouri* M & W
Saint Luke's College *Missouri* M & W
Saint Martin's University *Washington* W
Saint Mary's College *Indiana* W
Saint Mary's College of California *California* M & W
St. Mary's College of Maryland *Maryland* W
Saint Mary's University *Nova Scotia* W
St. Mary's University *Texas* W
Saint Mary's University of Minnesota *Minnesota* W
Saint Michael's College *Vermont* W
St. Norbert College *Wisconsin* W
St. Olaf College *Minnesota* W
Saint Paul's College *Virginia* M & W
Saint Peter's College *New Jersey* W
St. Petersburg College *Florida* W
St. Thomas Aquinas College *New York* W
St. Thomas University *New Brunswick* M & W
St. Thomas University *Florida* W
Saint Vincent College *Pennsylvania* W
Saint Xavier University *Illinois* W
Salem College *North Carolina* W
Salem International University *West Virginia* W
Salem State College *Massachusetts* W
Salisbury University *Maryland* W
Salt Lake Community College *Utah* W
Salve Regina University *Rhode Island* W
Sam Houston State University *Texas* W
Samford University *Alabama* W
San Bernardino Valley College *California* W
San Diego Christian College *California* W
San Diego City College *California* M & W
San Diego Mesa College *California* M & W
San Diego State University *California* W
San Francisco State University *California* W
San Jacinto College District *Texas* W
San Joaquin Delta College *California* W
San Jose City College *California* W
San Jose State University *California* M & W
Sandhills Community College *North Carolina* W
Santa Ana College *California* W
Santa Barbara City College *California* M & W

M = Men; W = Women

M = Men; W = Women

University at Albany, State University of New York *New York* W
University of Alberta *Alberta* M & W
The University of Arizona *Arizona* M & W
University of Arkansas *Arkansas* W
University of Arkansas at Fort Smith *Arkansas* W
University of Arkansas at Little Rock *Arkansas* W
University of Arkansas for Medical Sciences *Arkansas* M & W
University of Arkansas at Pine Bluff *Arkansas* W
University of Bridgeport *Connecticut* W
The University of British Columbia *British Columbia* M & W
The University of British Columbia–Okanagan *British Columbia* M & W
University at Buffalo, the State University of New York *New York* W
University of Calgary *Alberta* M & W
University of California, Berkeley *California* W
University of California, Davis *California* W
University of California, Irvine *California* M & W
University of California, Los Angeles *California* M & W
University of California, Riverside *California* W
University of California, San Diego *California* M & W
University of California, Santa Barbara *California* M & W
University of California, Santa Cruz *California* M & W
University of Central Arkansas *Arkansas* W
University of Central Florida *Florida* W
University of Central Missouri *Missouri* W
University of Central Oklahoma *Oklahoma* W
University of Charleston *West Virginia* W
University of Chicago *Illinois* W
University of Cincinnati *Ohio* W
University of Cincinnati Clermont College *Ohio* W
University of Colorado at Boulder *Colorado* M & W
University of Colorado at Colorado Springs *Colorado* M & W
University of Connecticut *Connecticut* W
University of the Cumberlands *Kentucky* W
University of Dallas *Texas* W
University of Dayton *Ohio* W
University of Delaware *Delaware* W
University of Denver *Colorado* W
University of the District of Columbia *District of Columbia* W
University of Dubuque *Iowa* W
University of Evansville *Indiana* W
The University of Findlay *Ohio* W
University of Florida *Florida* M & W
University of Georgia *Georgia* W
University of Great Falls *Montana* W
University of Guelph *Ontario* M & W
University of Hartford *Connecticut* M & W
University of Hawaii at Hilo *Hawaii* W
University of Hawaii at Manoa *Hawaii* M & W
University of Houston *Texas* W
University of Idaho *Idaho* W
University of Illinois at Chicago *Illinois* W
University of Illinois at Springfield *Illinois* W
University of Illinois at Urbana–Champaign *Illinois* W
University of the Incarnate Word *Texas* W
University of Indianapolis *Indiana* W
The University of Iowa *Iowa* M & W
The University of Kansas *Kansas* W
University of Kentucky *Kentucky* W
University of King's College *Nova Scotia* M
University of La Verne *California* W
University of Lethbridge *Alberta* W
University of Louisiana at Lafayette *Louisiana* W
University of Louisiana at Monroe *Louisiana* M & W
University of Louisville *Kentucky* W
University of Maine at Farmington *Maine* W
University of Maine at Fort Kent *Maine* W
University of Maine at Machias *Maine* W
University of Maine at Presque Isle *Maine* W
University of Manitoba *Manitoba* M & W
University of Mary *North Dakota* W
University of Mary Hardin-Baylor *Texas* W
University of Mary Washington *Virginia* M & W
University of Maryland, Baltimore County *Maryland* M & W
University of Maryland, College Park *Maryland* W
University of Maryland Eastern Shore *Maryland* W
University of Massachusetts Boston *Massachusetts* W
University of Massachusetts Dartmouth *Massachusetts* W
University of Massachusetts Lowell *Massachusetts* W
University of Memphis *Tennessee* W
University of Miami *Florida* W
University of Michigan *Michigan* W
University of Michigan–Dearborn *Michigan* W
University of Minnesota, Crookston *Minnesota* W
University of Minnesota, Duluth *Minnesota* M & W
University of Minnesota, Morris *Minnesota* W
University of Minnesota, Twin Cities Campus *Minnesota* W
University of Mississippi *Mississippi* M & W
University of Missouri *Missouri* W
University of Missouri–Kansas City *Missouri* W
University of Missouri–St. Louis *Missouri* W
University of Mobile *Alabama* W
The University of Montana *Montana* W
The University of Montana Western *Montana* W
University of Montevallo *Alabama* W
University of Mount Union *Ohio* W
University of Nebraska at Kearney *Nebraska* W
University of Nebraska at Omaha *Nebraska* W
University of Nebraska–Lincoln *Nebraska* W
University of Nevada, Las Vegas *Nevada* W
University of Nevada, Reno *Nevada* W
University of New Brunswick Fredericton *New Brunswick* M & W
University of New Brunswick Saint John *New Brunswick* M & W
University of New England *Maine* W
University of New Hampshire *New Hampshire* M & W
University of New Haven *Connecticut* M & W
University of New Mexico *New Mexico* W
University of New Orleans *Louisiana* W
University of North Alabama *Alabama* W
The University of North Carolina at Asheville *North Carolina* W
The University of North Carolina at Chapel Hill *North Carolina* M & W
The University of North Carolina at Charlotte *North Carolina* W
The University of North Carolina at Greensboro *North Carolina* W
The University of North Carolina at Pembroke *North Carolina* W
The University of North Carolina Wilmington *North Carolina* W
University of North Dakota *North Dakota* W
University of North Florida *Florida* W
University of North Texas *Texas* W
University of Northern Colorado *Colorado* W
University of Northern Iowa *Iowa* W
University of Notre Dame *Indiana* W
University of Oklahoma *Oklahoma* W
University of Oregon *Oregon* W
University of Ottawa *Ontario* M & W
University of the Pacific *California* M & W
University of Pennsylvania *Pennsylvania* W
University of Pittsburgh *Pennsylvania* W
University of Pittsburgh at Bradford *Pennsylvania* W
University of Pittsburgh at Greensburg *Pennsylvania* W
University of Pittsburgh at Johnstown *Pennsylvania* W
University of Portland *Oregon* W
University of Prince Edward Island *Prince Edward Island* W
University of Puerto Rico at Arecibo *Puerto Rico* M & W
University of Puerto Rico at Bayamón *Puerto Rico* M & W
University of Puerto Rico at Carolina *Puerto Rico* M & W
University of Puerto Rico, Cayey University College *Puerto Rico* M & W
University of Puerto Rico at Humacao *Puerto Rico* M & W
University of Puerto Rico, Mayagüez Campus *Puerto Rico* M & W
University of Puerto Rico at Ponce *Puerto Rico* M & W
University of Puerto Rico, Río Piedras *Puerto Rico* M & W
University of Puerto Rico at Utuado *Puerto Rico* M & W
University of Puget Sound *Washington* W
University of Redlands *California* W
University of Regina *Saskatchewan* M & W
University of Rhode Island *Rhode Island* M & W
University of Richmond *Virginia* M & W
University of Rio Grande *Ohio* W
University of Rochester *New York* M & W
University of the Sacred Heart *Puerto Rico* M & W
University of Saint Francis *Indiana* W
University of St. Francis *Illinois* W
University of Saint Mary *Kansas* W
University of St. Thomas *Texas* W
University of St. Thomas *Minnesota* W
University of San Diego *California* M & W
University of San Francisco *California* M & W
University of Saskatchewan *Saskatchewan* M & W
University of the Sciences in Philadelphia *Pennsylvania* W
The University of Scranton *Pennsylvania* M & W
University of Sioux Falls *South Dakota* W
University of South Alabama *Alabama* W
University of South Carolina *South Carolina* W
University of South Carolina Aiken *South Carolina* W
University of South Carolina Salkehatchie *South Carolina* W
University of South Carolina Upstate *South Carolina* W
The University of South Dakota *South Dakota* W
University of South Florida *Florida* W
University of Southern California *California* M & W
University of Southern Indiana *Indiana* W
University of Southern Maine *Maine* W
University of Southern Mississippi *Mississippi* W
The University of Tampa *Florida* W
The University of Tennessee *Tennessee* M & W
The University of Tennessee at Chattanooga *Tennessee* W
The University of Tennessee at Martin *Tennessee* W
The University of Texas at Arlington *Texas* W
The University of Texas at Austin *Texas* M & W
The University of Texas at Brownsville *Texas* W
The University of Texas at Dallas *Texas* W
The University of Texas at El Paso *Texas* W
The University of Texas Medical Branch *Texas* M & W
The University of Texas of the Permian Basin *Texas* W
The University of Texas at San Antonio *Texas* W
The University of Texas at Tyler *Texas* W
The University of Texas–Pan American *Texas* W
The University of Toledo *Ohio* W
University of Toronto *Ontario* M & W
University of Tulsa *Oklahoma* W
University of Utah *Utah* W
University of Vermont *Vermont* M & W
University of the Virgin Islands *United States Virgin Islands* M
University of Virginia *Virginia* W
The University of Virginia's College at Wise *Virginia* W
University of Washington *Washington* W
University of Waterloo *Ontario* M & W
The University of West Alabama *Alabama* W
University of West Florida *Florida* W
University of West Georgia *Georgia* W
The University of Western Ontario *Ontario* M & W
University of Windsor *Ontario* M & W
The University of Winnipeg *Manitoba* M & W
University of Wisconsin–Baraboo/Sauk County *Wisconsin* W

M = Men; W = Women

University of Wisconsin–Eau Claire *Wisconsin* W
University of Wisconsin–Fond du Lac *Wisconsin* W
University of Wisconsin–Fox Valley *Wisconsin* M & W
University of Wisconsin–Green Bay *Wisconsin* W
University of Wisconsin–La Crosse *Wisconsin* W
University of Wisconsin–Madison *Wisconsin* W
University of Wisconsin–Manitowoc *Wisconsin* W
University of Wisconsin–Marinette *Wisconsin* W
University of Wisconsin–Marshfield/Wood County *Wisconsin* W
University of Wisconsin–Milwaukee *Wisconsin* M & W
University of Wisconsin–Oshkosh *Wisconsin* W
University of Wisconsin–Parkside *Wisconsin* W
University of Wisconsin–Platteville *Wisconsin* M & W
University of Wisconsin–Richland *Wisconsin* W
University of Wisconsin–River Falls *Wisconsin* M & W
University of Wisconsin–Stevens Point *Wisconsin* W
University of Wisconsin–Stout *Wisconsin* M & W
University of Wisconsin–Superior *Wisconsin* W
University of Wisconsin–Washington County *Wisconsin* W
University of Wisconsin–Waukesha *Wisconsin* W
University of Wisconsin–Whitewater *Wisconsin* M & W
University of Wyoming *Wyoming* W
Upper Iowa University *Iowa* W
Urbana University *Ohio* W
Ursinus College *Pennsylvania* W
Ursuline College *Ohio* W
Utah State University *Utah* M & W
Utah State University–College of Eastern Utah *Utah* W
Utah Valley University *Utah* W
Utica College *New York* W
Valdosta State University *Georgia* W
Valley City State University *North Dakota* W
Valley Forge Christian College *Pennsylvania* W
Valparaiso University *Indiana* W
Vanguard University of Southern California *California* W
Vassar College *New York* M & W
Ventura College *California* W
Vermilion Community College *Minnesota* W
Vernon College *Texas* W
Victor Valley College *California* W
Villanova University *Pennsylvania* M & W
Vincennes University *Indiana* W
Virginia Commonwealth University *Virginia* W
Virginia Intermont College *Virginia* W
Virginia Polytechnic Institute and State University *Virginia* W
Virginia State University *Virginia* W
Virginia Union University *Virginia* W
Virginia Wesleyan College *Virginia* W
Viterbo University *Wisconsin* W
Voorhees College *South Carolina* W
Wake Forest University *North Carolina* W
Waldorf College *Iowa* W
Walla Walla Community College *Washington* W
Walla Walla University *Washington* M & W
Wallace State Community College *Alabama* W
Walsh University *Ohio* W
Warner Pacific College *Oregon* W
Warner University *Florida* W
Wartburg College *Iowa* W
Washburn University *Kansas* W
Washington Bible College *Maryland* W
Washington College *Maryland* W
Washington & Jefferson College *Pennsylvania* W
Washington and Lee University *Virginia* M & W
Washington State University *Washington* M & W
Washington University in St. Louis *Missouri* M & W
Waubonsee Community College *Illinois* W
Wayland Baptist University *Texas* W
Wayne County Community College District *Michigan* W
Wayne State College *Nebraska* W
Wayne State University *Michigan* W
Waynesburg University *Pennsylvania* W
Webb Institute *New York* M & W
Webber International University *Florida* M & W
Weber State University *Utah* W
Webster University *Missouri* W
Wellesley College *Massachusetts* W
Wentworth Institute of Technology *Massachusetts* M & W
Wesleyan College *Georgia* W
Wesleyan University *Connecticut* M & W
West Chester University of Pennsylvania *Pennsylvania* M & W
West Hills Community College *California* W
West Liberty University *West Virginia* W
West Los Angeles College *California* W
West Texas A&M University *Texas* W
West Valley College *California* M & W
West Virginia State University *West Virginia* W
West Virginia University *West Virginia* W
West Virginia University Institute of Technology *West Virginia* W
West Virginia Wesleyan College *West Virginia* W
Westchester Community College *New York* W
Western Carolina University *North Carolina* W
Western Connecticut State University *Connecticut* W
Western Illinois University *Illinois* W
Western Kentucky University *Kentucky* W
Western Michigan University *Michigan* W
Western Nebraska Community College *Nebraska* W
Western New England College *Massachusetts* W
Western New Mexico University *New Mexico* W
Western Oregon University *Oregon* W
Western State College of Colorado *Colorado* M & W
Western Technical College *Wisconsin* W
Western Washington University *Washington* W
Western Wyoming Community College *Wyoming* W
Westfield State College *Massachusetts* W
Westminster College *Utah* W
Westminster College *Pennsylvania* W
Westminster College *Missouri* W
Westmont College *California* M & W
Westmoreland County Community College *Pennsylvania* W
Westwood College–Atlanta Northlake *Georgia* M & W
Wharton County Junior College *Texas* W
Whatcom Community College *Washington* W
Wheaton College *Massachusetts* W
Wheaton College *Illinois* M & W
Wheeling Jesuit University *West Virginia* W
Whitman College *Washington* M & W
Whittier College *California* W
Whitworth University *Washington* W
Wichita State University *Kansas* M & W
Widener University *Pennsylvania* W
Wiley College *Texas* W
Wilfrid Laurier University *Ontario* M & W
Wilkes Community College *North Carolina* W
Wilkes University *Pennsylvania* W
Willamette University *Oregon* W
William and Catherine Booth College *Manitoba* M & W
William Jessup University *California* W
William Jewell College *Missouri* W
William Paterson University of New Jersey *New Jersey* W
William Penn University *Iowa* W
William Woods University *Missouri* M & W
Williams Baptist College *Arkansas* W
Williams College *Massachusetts* M & W
Williston State College *North Dakota* W
Wilmington College *Ohio* W
Wilmington University *Delaware* W
Wingate University *North Carolina* W
Winona State University *Minnesota* M & W
Winston-Salem State University *North Carolina* W
Winthrop University *South Carolina* W
Wisconsin Lutheran College *Wisconsin* W
Wittenberg University *Ohio* M & W
Wofford College *South Carolina* W
Worcester Polytechnic Institute *Massachusetts* W
Worcester State College *Massachusetts* M & W
Wright State University *Ohio* W
Xavier University *Ohio* M & W
Yakima Valley Community College *Washington* W
Yale University *Connecticut* M & W
Yavapai College *Arizona* W
Yeshiva University *New York* M
York College *Nebraska* W
York College of the City University of New York *New York* M & W
York College of Pennsylvania *Pennsylvania* M & W
York University *Ontario* M & W
Youngstown State University *Ohio* W
Yuba College *California* W

Water Polo

American River College *California* M & W
Amherst College *Massachusetts* M & W
Arizona State University *Arizona* W
Ball State University *Indiana* M & W
Bates College *Maine* M & W
Baylor University *Texas* M & W
Boston University *Massachusetts* W
Bowdoin College *Maine* M & W
Bridgewater State College *Massachusetts* M & W
Brown University *Rhode Island* M & W
Bucknell University *Pennsylvania* M & W
Cabrillo College *California* M & W
California Baptist University *California* M & W
California Institute of Technology *California* M & W
California Lutheran University *California* M & W
California Maritime Academy *California* M & W
California State University, Bakersfield *California* W
California State University, Chico *California* M & W
California State University, East Bay *California* W
California State University, Long Beach *California* M & W
California State University, Monterey Bay *California* W
California State University, San Bernardino *California* M & W
Carleton College *Minnesota* M & W
Carleton University *Ontario* M & W
Carnegie Mellon University *Pennsylvania* M & W
Carthage College *Wisconsin* W
Central Washington University *Washington* M & W
Cerritos College *California* M
Chabot College *California* W
Chaffey College *California* M & W
Chaminade University of Honolulu *Hawaii* M
Chapman University *California* M & W
Chatham University *Pennsylvania* W
Citrus College *California* M & W
City College of San Francisco *California* M
Claremont McKenna College *California* M & W
Colby College *Maine* M & W
Colgate University *New York* M & W
College of Marin *California* M & W
College of the Sequoias *California* M
Colorado State University *Colorado* M & W
Columbia University *New York* M & W
Columbia University, School of General Studies *New York* M & W
Concordia University *California* M & W
Connecticut College *Connecticut* M & W
Cosumnes River College *California* M & W
Cuesta College *California* M & W
Cypress College *California* M & W
Dartmouth College *New Hampshire* M & W
De Anza College *California* M
Diablo Valley College *California* M & W
Duke University *North Carolina* M & W
El Camino College *California* M
Emory University *Georgia* M & W
Foothill College *California* M & W
Fordham University *New York* M
Fresno Pacific University *California* M & W
Fullerton College *California* M
Gannon University *Pennsylvania* M & W
The George Washington University *District of Columbia* M
Georgetown University *District of Columbia* M
Golden West College *California* M & W
Grand Valley State University *Michigan* M & W
Grossmont College *California* M & W

M = Men; W = Women

Grove City College *Pennsylvania* W
Hamilton College *New York* M & W
Hartnell College *California* M
Hartwick College *New York* M & W
Harvard University *Massachusetts* M & W
Harvey Mudd College *California* M & W
Illinois Wesleyan University *Illinois* M
Indiana University Bloomington *Indiana* W
Iona College *New York* M & W
The Johns Hopkins University *Maryland* M
Lake Forest College *Illinois* M & W
Lehman College of the City University of New York *New York* M
Lindenwood University *Missouri* M & W
Long Beach City College *California* M & W
Loras College *Iowa* M
Los Angeles Pierce College *California* M
Los Angeles Valley College *California* M & W
Loyola Marymount University *California* M & W
Lycoming College *Pennsylvania* M & W
Macalester College *Minnesota* M & W
Marist College *New York* W
Massachusetts Institute of Technology *Massachusetts* M & W
McMaster University *Ontario* M & W
Merced College *California* M
Mercyhurst College *Pennsylvania* M & W
Miami University *Ohio* M & W
Michigan State University *Michigan* M & W
Michigan Technological University *Michigan* M & W
Modesto Junior College *California* M & W
Mt. San Antonio College *California* M & W
North Carolina State University *North Carolina* M & W
Oberlin College *Ohio* M & W
Occidental College *California* M & W
Ohlone College *California* M
Orange Coast College *California* M & W
Palomar College *California* M & W
Pasadena City College *California* M
Penn State Erie, The Behrend College *Pennsylvania* M & W
Penn State University Park *Pennsylvania* M & W
Pepperdine University *California* M & W
Pitzer College *California* M & W
Pomona College *California* M & W
Princeton University *New Jersey* M & W
Queens College of the City University of New York *New York* M
Queen's University at Kingston *Ontario* M & W
Rensselaer Polytechnic Institute *New York* M & W
Rice University *Texas* M & W
Rio Hondo College *California* M & W
Riverside Community College District *California* M & W
Rochester Institute of Technology *New York* M & W
Sacramento City College *California* W
Saddleback College *California* M & W
St. Francis College *New York* M & W
Saint John's University *Minnesota* M
Saint Louis University *Missouri* M
Saint Mary's College *Indiana* W
Saint Mary's College of California *California* M & W
Salem International University *West Virginia* M & W
San Diego Mesa College *California* M & W
San Diego Miramar College *California* M & W
San Diego State University *California* W
San Joaquin Delta College *California* M & W
San Jose State University *California* W
Santa Ana College *California* M
Santa Clara University *California* M & W
Santa Monica College *California* M & W
Santa Rosa Junior College *California* M & W
Scripps College *California* W
Seattle University *Washington* M & W
Siena College *New York* W
Sierra College *California* M & W
Slippery Rock University of Pennsylvania *Pennsylvania* M
Soka University of America *California* M & W
Solano Community College *California* M & W
Sonoma State University *California* W
Southwestern College *California* M & W
Stanford University *California* M & W
State University of New York College at Geneseo *New York* M & W
Swarthmore College *Pennsylvania* M & W
Syracuse University *New York* M & W
Texas State University–San Marcos *Texas* M & W
Trinity College *Connecticut* M & W
Trinity University *Texas* M & W
Tulane University *Louisiana* M & W
United States Air Force Academy *Colorado* M & W
United States Coast Guard Academy *Connecticut* M
United States Military Academy *New York* M
United States Naval Academy *Maryland* M
University of California, Berkeley *California* M & W
University of California, Davis *California* M & W
University of California, Irvine *California* M & W
University of California, Los Angeles *California* M & W
University of California, San Diego *California* M & W
University of California, Santa Barbara *California* M & W
University of California, Santa Cruz *California* M & W
University of Colorado at Boulder *Colorado* M & W
University of Denver *Colorado* M & W
The University of Findlay *Ohio* M & W
University of Hawaii at Manoa *Hawaii* W
University of La Verne *California* M & W
University of Maryland, College Park *Maryland* W
University of Michigan *Michigan* W
The University of North Carolina at Chapel Hill *North Carolina* M & W
University of Ottawa *Ontario* M & W
University of the Pacific *California* M & W
University of Puerto Rico, Mayagüez Campus *Puerto Rico* M
University of Puerto Rico, Río Piedras *Puerto Rico* M & W
University of Redlands *California* M & W
University of Richmond *Virginia* M & W
University of Rochester *New York* M & W
University of Southern California *California* M & W
The University of Tennessee *Tennessee* M & W
The University of Texas at Austin *Texas* M & W
University of Vermont *Vermont* M & W
The University of Western Ontario *Ontario* M
University of Wisconsin–Madison *Wisconsin* M & W
Utica College *New York* W
Ventura College *California* M & W
Villanova University *Pennsylvania* M & W
Wabash College *Indiana* M
Wagner College *New York* W
Washington College *Maryland* M & W
Washington & Jefferson College *Pennsylvania* M & W
Washington State University *Washington* M & W
Washington University in St. Louis *Missouri* M & W
Weber State University *Utah* M & W
Wesleyan University *Connecticut* M
West Chester University of Pennsylvania *Pennsylvania* W
West Valley College *California* M
Wheaton College *Illinois* M & W
Whittier College *California* M & W
Williams College *Massachusetts* M & W
Worcester Polytechnic Institute *Massachusetts* M & W
Xavier University *Ohio* M & W
Yale University *Connecticut* M & W
York University *Ontario* M & W

Weight Lifting

American University of Puerto Rico *Puerto Rico* M
Bayamón Central University *Puerto Rico* M & W
Bucknell University *Pennsylvania* M & W
Caribbean University *Puerto Rico* M & W
Clemson University *South Carolina* M & W
Davidson College *North Carolina* M & W
Emory University *Georgia* M & W
Furman University *South Carolina* M & W
Inter American University of Puerto Rico, Aguadilla Campus *Puerto Rico* M & W
Inter American University of Puerto Rico, Barranquitas Campus *Puerto Rico* M & W
Inter American University of Puerto Rico, Bayamón Campus *Puerto Rico* M
Inter American University of Puerto Rico, Ponce Campus *Puerto Rico* M & W
Inter American University of Puerto Rico, San Germán Campus *Puerto Rico* M
Lafayette College *Pennsylvania* M & W
Lindenwood University *Missouri* M & W
Louisiana Tech University *Louisiana* M & W
Miami University *Ohio* M & W
Norwich University *Vermont* M & W
Penn State University Park *Pennsylvania* M & W
Pontifical Catholic University of Puerto Rico *Puerto Rico* M & W
Rensselaer Polytechnic Institute *New York* M & W
Texas State University–San Marcos *Texas* M & W
Truman State University *Missouri* M & W
United States Air Force Academy *Colorado* M & W
United States Military Academy *New York* M & W
United States Naval Academy *Maryland* M & W
Universidad Metropolitana *Puerto Rico* M & W
University of Louisiana at Monroe *Louisiana* M & W
University of Puerto Rico, Aguadilla University College *Puerto Rico* M & W
University of Puerto Rico at Arecibo *Puerto Rico* M & W
University of Puerto Rico at Bayamón *Puerto Rico* M & W
University of Puerto Rico, Cayey University College *Puerto Rico* M & W
University of Puerto Rico at Humacao *Puerto Rico* M & W
University of Puerto Rico at Ponce *Puerto Rico* M & W
University of Puerto Rico, Río Piedras *Puerto Rico* M & W
University of Puerto Rico at Utuado *Puerto Rico* M & W
University of the Sacred Heart *Puerto Rico* M & W
The University of Texas at Austin *Texas* M & W
University of Wisconsin–La Crosse *Wisconsin* M & W
University of Wisconsin–River Falls *Wisconsin* M & W
University of Wisconsin–Whitewater *Wisconsin* M

Wrestling

Adams State College *Colorado* M
Alberta College of Art & Design *Alberta* M
American International College *Massachusetts* M
American University *District of Columbia* M
Amherst College *Massachusetts* M & W
Anderson University *South Carolina* M
Appalachian State University *North Carolina* M
Arizona State University *Arizona* M
Ashland University *Ohio* M
Augsburg College *Minnesota* M
Augustana College *South Dakota* M
Augustana College *Illinois* M
Baker University *Kansas* M
Bakersfield College *California* M
Baldwin-Wallace College *Ohio* M
Ball State University *Indiana* M
Baylor University *Texas* M
Belmont Abbey College *North Carolina* M
Bergen Community College *New Jersey* M
Bloomsburg University of Pennsylvania *Pennsylvania* M
Boise State University *Idaho* M
Boston University *Massachusetts* M
Briar Cliff University *Iowa* M
Bridgewater State College *Massachusetts* M
Brock University *Ontario* M & W
Broward College *Florida* M
Brown University *Rhode Island* M
Bryant University *Rhode Island* M
Bucknell University *Pennsylvania* M
Buena Vista University *Iowa* M
Cabrillo College *California* M
California Baptist University *California* M
California Polytechnic State University, San Luis Obispo *California* M

M = Men; W = Women

M = Men; W = Women

Southern Vermont College *Vermont* M
Southern Virginia University *Virginia* M
Southwest Minnesota State University *Minnesota* M
Southwestern Oregon Community College *Oregon* M
Spartanburg Methodist College *South Carolina* M
Springfield College *Massachusetts* M
Springfield Technical Community College *Massachusetts* M
Stanford University *California* M
State University of New York at Binghamton *New York* M
State University of New York College of Agriculture and Technology at Morrisville *New York* M
State University of New York College at Cortland *New York* M
State University of New York College at Oneonta *New York* M
State University of New York College of Technology at Alfred *New York* M
State University of New York College of Technology at Delhi *New York* M
State University of New York at Oswego *New York* M
Stevens Institute of Technology *New Jersey* M
Syracuse University *New York* M
Texas State University–San Marcos *Texas* M & W
Thaddeus Stevens College of Technology *Pennsylvania* M
Thiel College *Pennsylvania* M
Towson University *Maryland* M
Trine University *Indiana* M
Trinity Bible College *North Dakota* M
Trinity College *Connecticut* M
Triton College *Illinois* M
Truman State University *Missouri* M
United States Air Force Academy *Colorado* M
United States Coast Guard Academy *Connecticut* M
United States Merchant Marine Academy *New York* M
United States Military Academy *New York* M
United States Naval Academy *Maryland* M
University of Alberta *Alberta* M & W
The University of Arizona *Arizona* M
University at Buffalo, the State University of New York *New York* M
University of Calgary *Alberta* M & W
University of California, Davis *California* M
University of Central Missouri *Missouri* M
University of Central Oklahoma *Oklahoma* M
University of Chicago *Illinois* M
University of Colorado at Boulder *Colorado* M
University of the Cumberlands *Kentucky* M & W
University of Delaware *Delaware* M
University of Dubuque *Iowa* M
The University of Findlay *Ohio* M
University of Great Falls *Montana* M
University of Guelph *Ontario* M & W
University of Illinois at Urbana–Champaign *Illinois* M
University of Indianapolis *Indiana* M
The University of Iowa *Iowa* M
University of Mary *North Dakota* M
University of Maryland, Baltimore County *Maryland* M
University of Maryland, College Park *Maryland* M
University of Maryland Eastern Shore *Maryland* M
University of Michigan *Michigan* M
University of Minnesota, Twin Cities Campus *Minnesota* M
University of Missouri *Missouri* M
University of Mount Union *Ohio* M
University of Nebraska at Kearney *Nebraska* M
University of Nebraska at Omaha *Nebraska* M
University of Nebraska–Lincoln *Nebraska* M
University of New Brunswick Fredericton *New Brunswick* M & W
University of New Hampshire *New Hampshire* M
The University of North Carolina at Chapel Hill *North Carolina* M
The University of North Carolina at Greensboro *North Carolina* M
The University of North Carolina at Pembroke *North Carolina* M
University of Northern Colorado *Colorado* M
University of Northern Iowa *Iowa* M
University of Oklahoma *Oklahoma* M
University of Pennsylvania *Pennsylvania* M
University of Pittsburgh *Pennsylvania* M
University of Pittsburgh at Johnstown *Pennsylvania* M
University of Puerto Rico at Arecibo *Puerto Rico* M
University of Puerto Rico at Bayamón *Puerto Rico* M
University of Puerto Rico, Cayey University College *Puerto Rico* M
University of Puerto Rico at Humacao *Puerto Rico* M
University of Puerto Rico, Mayagüez Campus *Puerto Rico* M
University of Puerto Rico, Río Piedras *Puerto Rico* M & W
University of Regina *Saskatchewan* M & W
University of Rhode Island *Rhode Island* M
University of Saskatchewan *Saskatchewan* M & W
The University of Scranton *Pennsylvania* M
University of Southern California *California* M
University of Southern Indiana *Indiana* M
University of Southern Maine *Maine* M
The University of Tennessee at Chattanooga *Tennessee* M
The University of Texas at Austin *Texas* M & W
University of Toronto *Ontario* M
University of Virginia *Virginia* M
The University of Western Ontario *Ontario* M & W
University of Wisconsin–Eau Claire *Wisconsin* M
University of Wisconsin–La Crosse *Wisconsin* M
University of Wisconsin–Madison *Wisconsin* M
University of Wisconsin–Oshkosh *Wisconsin* M
University of Wisconsin–Parkside *Wisconsin* M
University of Wisconsin–Platteville *Wisconsin* M
University of Wisconsin–Stevens Point *Wisconsin* M
University of Wisconsin–Whitewater *Wisconsin* M
University of Wyoming *Wyoming* M
Upper Iowa University *Iowa* M
Ursinus College *Pennsylvania* M
Utah Valley University *Utah* M
Valley Forge Military College *Pennsylvania* M
Victor Valley College *California* M
Virginia Military Institute *Virginia* M
Wabash College *Indiana* M
Waldorf College *Iowa* M
Wartburg College *Iowa* M
Washington & Jefferson College *Pennsylvania* M
Washington and Lee University *Virginia* M
Waubonsee Community College *Illinois* M
Wayne State College *Nebraska* M
Waynesburg University *Pennsylvania* M
Wentworth Military Academy and College *Missouri* M
Wesleyan University *Connecticut* M
West Liberty University *West Virginia* M
West Valley College *California* M
West Virginia University *West Virginia* M
West Virginia University Institute of Technology *West Virginia* M
Western Carolina University *North Carolina* M
Western New England College *Massachusetts* M
Western State College of Colorado *Colorado* M & W
Western Wyoming Community College *Wyoming* M
Wheaton College *Illinois* M
Wilkes University *Pennsylvania* M
William Penn University *Iowa* M
Williams College *Massachusetts* M
The Williamson Free School of Mechanical Trades *Pennsylvania* M
Wilmington College *Ohio* M
Winona State University *Minnesota* M
Worcester Polytechnic Institute *Massachusetts* M
Yakima Valley Community College *Washington* M
Yale University *Connecticut* M
Yeshiva University *New York* M
York College *Nebraska* M
York College of Pennsylvania *Pennsylvania* M

M = Men; W = Women

Index of Professional Accreditations

AACSB International-The Association to Advance Collegiate Schools of Busin (AACSB)

Abilene Christian University *Texas*
Adelphi University *New York*
Alfred University *New York*
American University *District of Columbia*
Appalachian State University *North Carolina*
Arizona State University *Arizona*
Arkansas State University - Jonesboro *Arkansas*
Arkansas Tech University *Arkansas*
Auburn University *Alabama*
Auburn University Montgomery *Alabama*
Augusta State University *Georgia*
Babson College *Massachusetts*
Ball State University *Indiana*
Barry University *Florida*
Baylor University *Texas*
Bellarmine University *Kentucky*
Belmont University *Tennessee*
Bentley University *Massachusetts*
Bernard M. Baruch College of the City University of New York *New York*
Berry College *Georgia*
Birmingham-Southern College *Alabama*
Bloomsburg University of Pennsylvania *Pennsylvania*
Boise State University *Idaho*
Boston College *Massachusetts*
Boston University *Massachusetts*
Bowling Green State University *Ohio*
Bradley University *Illinois*
Brandeis University *Massachusetts*
Brigham Young University *Utah*
Brock University *Ontario*
Bryant University *Rhode Island*
Butler University *Indiana*
California Polytechnic State University, San Luis Obispo *California*
California State Polytechnic University, Pomona *California*
California State University, Bakersfield *California*
California State University, Chico *California*
California State University, East Bay *California*
California State University, Fresno *California*
California State University, Fullerton *California*
California State University, Long Beach *California*
California State University, Los Angeles *California*
California State University, Northridge *California*
California State University, Sacramento *California*
California State University, San Bernardino *California*
California State University, Stanislaus *California*
Canisius College *New York*
Carnegie Mellon University *Pennsylvania*
Case Western Reserve University *Ohio*
Central Michigan University *Michigan*
Chapman University *California*
The Citadel, The Military College of South Carolina *South Carolina*
Clarion University of Pennsylvania *Pennsylvania*
Clark Atlanta University *Georgia*
Clark University *Massachusetts*
Clarkson University *New York*
Clayton State University *Georgia*
Clemson University *South Carolina*
Cleveland State University *Ohio*
Coastal Carolina University *South Carolina*
The College at Brockport, State University of New York *New York*
College of Charleston *South Carolina*
The College of New Jersey *New Jersey*
The College of William and Mary *Virginia*
Colorado State University *Colorado*
Colorado State University–Pueblo *Colorado*
Columbia University *New York*
Columbus State University *Georgia*
Concordia University *Quebec*
Cornell University *New York*
Creighton University *Nebraska*
Dalhousie University *Nova Scotia*
Dartmouth College *New Hampshire*
Delaware State University *Delaware*
DePaul University *Illinois*
Drake University *Iowa*
Drexel University *Pennsylvania*
Duke University *North Carolina*
Duquesne University *Pennsylvania*
East Carolina University *North Carolina*
East Tennessee State University *Tennessee*
Eastern Illinois University *Illinois*
Eastern Kentucky University *Kentucky*
Eastern Michigan University *Michigan*
Eastern Washington University *Washington*
Elon University *North Carolina*
Emory University *Georgia*
Emporia State University *Kansas*
Fairfield University *Connecticut*
Fairleigh Dickinson University, College at Florham *New Jersey*
Fairleigh Dickinson University, Metropolitan Campus *New Jersey*
Fayetteville State University *North Carolina*
Florida Atlantic University *Florida*
Florida Gulf Coast University *Florida*
Florida International University *Florida*
Florida State University *Florida*
Fordham University *New York*
Fort Lewis College *Colorado*
Francis Marion University *South Carolina*
Frostburg State University *Maryland*
George Mason University *Virginia*
The George Washington University *District of Columbia*
Georgetown University *District of Columbia*
Georgia College & State University *Georgia*
Georgia Institute of Technology *Georgia*
Georgia Southern University *Georgia*
Georgia Southwestern State University *Georgia*
Georgia State University *Georgia*
Gonzaga University *Washington*
Grambling State University *Louisiana*
Grand Valley State University *Michigan*
Harvard University *Massachusetts*
HEC Montreal *Quebec*
Henderson State University *Arkansas*
Hofstra University *New York*
Howard University *District of Columbia*
Idaho State University *Idaho*
Illinois Institute of Technology *Illinois*
Illinois State University *Illinois*
Indiana State University *Indiana*
Indiana University Bloomington *Indiana*
Indiana University Kokomo *Indiana*
Indiana University Northwest *Indiana*
Indiana University of Pennsylvania *Pennsylvania*
Indiana University South Bend *Indiana*
Indiana University Southeast *Indiana*
Indiana University–Purdue University Fort Wayne *Indiana*
Indiana University–Purdue University Indianapolis *Indiana*
Iona College *New York*
Iowa State University of Science and Technology *Iowa*
Ithaca College *New York*
Jackson State University *Mississippi*
Jacksonville State University *Alabama*
James Madison University *Virginia*
John Carroll University *Ohio*
Kansas State University *Kansas*
Kennesaw State University *Georgia*
Kent State University *Ohio*
King's College *Pennsylvania*
La Salle University *Pennsylvania*
Lamar University *Texas*
Lander University *South Carolina*
Le Moyne College *New York*
Lehigh University *Pennsylvania*
Long Island University, C.W. Post Campus *New York*
Longwood University *Virginia*
Louisiana State University and Agricultural and Mechanical College *Louisiana*
Louisiana State University in Shreveport *Louisiana*
Louisiana Tech University *Louisiana*
Loyola Marymount University *California*
Loyola University Chicago *Illinois*
Loyola University Maryland *Maryland*
Loyola University New Orleans *Louisiana*
Manhattan College *New York*
Marist College *New York*
Marquette University *Wisconsin*
Marshall University *West Virginia*
Massachusetts Institute of Technology *Massachusetts*
McMaster University *Ontario*
McNeese State University *Louisiana*
Memorial University of Newfoundland *Newfoundland and Labrador*
Mercer University *Georgia*
Miami University *Ohio*
Michigan State University *Michigan*
Michigan Technological University *Michigan*
Middle Tennessee State University *Tennessee*
Millsaps College *Mississippi*
Minnesota State University Mankato *Minnesota*
Mississippi State University *Mississippi*
Missouri State University *Missouri*
Monmouth University *New Jersey*
Montana State University *Montana*

Montclair State University *New Jersey*
Morehead State University *Kentucky*
Morehouse College *Georgia*
Morgan State University *Maryland*
Murray State University *Kentucky*
New Jersey Institute of Technology *New Jersey*
New Mexico State University *New Mexico*
New York University *New York*
Niagara University *New York*
Nicholls State University *Louisiana*
Norfolk State University *Virginia*
North Carolina Agricultural and Technical State University *North Carolina*
North Carolina Central University *North Carolina*
North Carolina State University *North Carolina*
North Dakota State University *North Dakota*
Northeastern University *Massachusetts*
Northern Arizona University *Arizona*
Northern Illinois University *Illinois*
Northern Kentucky University *Kentucky*
Northern Michigan University *Michigan*
Northwestern State University of Louisiana *Louisiana*
Northwestern University *Illinois*
Oakland University *Michigan*
Ohio Northern University *Ohio*
The Ohio State University *Ohio*
Ohio University *Ohio*
Oklahoma State University *Oklahoma*
Old Dominion University *Virginia*
Oregon State University *Oregon*
Ouachita Baptist University *Arkansas*
Pace University *New York*
Pacific Lutheran University *Washington*
Penn State Erie, The Behrend College *Pennsylvania*
Penn State Harrisburg *Pennsylvania*
Penn State University Park *Pennsylvania*
Pepperdine University *California*
Pittsburg State University *Kansas*
Portland State University *Oregon*
Prairie View A&M University *Texas*
Purdue University *Indiana*
Queens University of Charlotte *North Carolina*
Queen's University at Kingston *Ontario*
Quinnipiac University *Connecticut*
Radford University *Virginia*
Rensselaer Polytechnic Institute *New York*
Rice University *Texas*
Rider University *New Jersey*
Robert Morris University *Pennsylvania*
Rochester Institute of Technology *New York*
Rockhurst University *Missouri*
Rollins College *Florida*
Rowan University *New Jersey*
Rutgers, The State University of New Jersey, Camden *New Jersey*
Rutgers, The State University of New Jersey, Newark *New Jersey*
Sacred Heart University *Connecticut*
Saginaw Valley State University *Michigan*
St. Bonaventure University *New York*
St. Cloud State University *Minnesota*
St. John Fisher College *New York*
St. John's University *New York*
Saint Joseph's University *Pennsylvania*
Saint Louis University *Missouri*
Saint Mary's University *Nova Scotia*
St. Mary's University *Texas*
Salisbury University *Maryland*
Sam Houston State University *Texas*
Samford University *Alabama*
San Diego State University *California*
San Francisco State University *California*
San Jose State University *California*
Santa Clara University *California*
Savannah State University *Georgia*
Seattle Pacific University *Washington*
Seattle University *Washington*
Seton Hall University *New Jersey*
Shenandoah University *Virginia*
Shippensburg University of Pennsylvania *Pennsylvania*
Simon Fraser University *British Columbia*
Sonoma State University *California*
South Carolina State University *South Carolina*
Southeast Missouri State University *Missouri*
Southeastern Louisiana University *Louisiana*
Southeastern Oklahoma State University *Oklahoma*
Southern Illinois University Carbondale *Illinois*
Southern Illinois University Edwardsville *Illinois*
Southern Methodist University *Texas*
Southern University and Agricultural and Mechanical College *Louisiana*
Southern Utah University *Utah*
Stanford University *California*
State University of New York at Binghamton *New York*
State University of New York College at Geneseo *New York*
State University of New York Institute of Technology *New York*
State University of New York at Oswego *New York*
State University of New York at Plattsburgh *New York*
Stephen F. Austin State University *Texas*
Stetson University *Florida*
Suffolk University *Massachusetts*
Susquehanna University *Pennsylvania*
Syracuse University *New York*
Temple University *Pennsylvania*
Tennessee State University *Tennessee*
Tennessee Technological University *Tennessee*
Texas A&M International University *Texas*
Texas A&M University *Texas*
Texas A&M University–Commerce *Texas*
Texas A&M University–Corpus Christi *Texas*
Texas Christian University *Texas*
Texas Southern University *Texas*
Texas State University–San Marcos *Texas*
Texas Tech University *Texas*
Towson University *Maryland*
Trinity University *Texas*
Truman State University *Missouri*
Tulane University *Louisiana*
Tuskegee University *Alabama*
United States Air Force Academy *Colorado*
Université Laval *Quebec*
The University of Akron *Ohio*
The University of Alabama *Alabama*
The University of Alabama at Birmingham *Alabama*
The University of Alabama in Huntsville *Alabama*
University of Alaska Anchorage *Alaska*
University of Alaska Fairbanks *Alaska*
University at Albany, State University of New York *New York*
University of Alberta *Alberta*
The University of Arizona *Arizona*
University of Arkansas *Arkansas*
University of Arkansas at Little Rock *Arkansas*
University of Baltimore *Maryland*
The University of British Columbia *British Columbia*
University at Buffalo, the State University of New York *New York*
University of Calgary *Alberta*
University of California, Berkeley *California*
University of California, Davis *California*
University of California, Irvine *California*
University of California, Los Angeles *California*
University of California, Riverside *California*
University of Central Arkansas *Arkansas*
University of Central Florida *Florida*
University of Central Missouri *Missouri*
University of Chicago *Illinois*
University of Cincinnati *Ohio*
University of Colorado at Boulder *Colorado*
University of Colorado at Colorado Springs *Colorado*
University of Colorado Denver *Colorado*
University of Connecticut *Connecticut*
University of Dayton *Ohio*
University of Delaware *Delaware*
University of Denver *Colorado*
University of Detroit Mercy *Michigan*
University of Evansville *Indiana*
University of Florida *Florida*
University of Georgia *Georgia*
University of Hartford *Connecticut*
University of Hawaii at Manoa *Hawaii*
University of Houston *Texas*
University of Houston–Clear Lake *Texas*
University of Houston–Downtown *Texas*
University of Houston–Victoria *Texas*
University of Idaho *Idaho*
University of Illinois at Chicago *Illinois*
University of Illinois at Springfield *Illinois*
University of Illinois at Urbana–Champaign *Illinois*
The University of Iowa *Iowa*
The University of Kansas *Kansas*
University of Kentucky *Kentucky*
University of Louisiana at Lafayette *Louisiana*
University of Louisiana at Monroe *Louisiana*
University of Louisville *Kentucky*
University of Maine *Maine*
University of Manitoba *Manitoba*
University of Maryland, College Park *Maryland*
University of Massachusetts Amherst *Massachusetts*
University of Massachusetts Boston *Massachusetts*
University of Massachusetts Dartmouth *Massachusetts*
University of Massachusetts Lowell *Massachusetts*
University of Memphis *Tennessee*
University of Miami *Florida*
University of Michigan *Michigan*
University of Michigan–Dearborn *Michigan*
University of Michigan–Flint *Michigan*
University of Minnesota, Duluth *Minnesota*
University of Minnesota, Twin Cities Campus *Minnesota*
University of Mississippi *Mississippi*
University of Missouri *Missouri*
University of Missouri–Kansas City *Missouri*
University of Missouri–St. Louis *Missouri*
The University of Montana *Montana*
University of Montevallo *Alabama*
University of Nebraska at Kearney *Nebraska*
University of Nebraska at Omaha *Nebraska*
University of Nebraska–Lincoln *Nebraska*
University of Nevada, Las Vegas *Nevada*
University of Nevada, Reno *Nevada*
University of New Hampshire *New Hampshire*
University of New Mexico *New Mexico*
University of New Orleans *Louisiana*
The University of North Carolina at Chapel Hill *North Carolina*
The University of North Carolina at Charlotte *North Carolina*
The University of North Carolina at Greensboro *North Carolina*
The University of North Carolina Wilmington *North Carolina*
University of North Dakota *North Dakota*
University of North Florida *Florida*
University of North Texas *Texas*
University of Northern Colorado *Colorado*
University of Northern Iowa *Iowa*
University of Notre Dame *Indiana*
University of Oklahoma *Oklahoma*
University of Oregon *Oregon*
University of Ottawa *Ontario*
University of the Pacific *California*
University of Pennsylvania *Pennsylvania*
University of Pittsburgh *Pennsylvania*
University of Portland *Oregon*
University of Rhode Island *Rhode Island*
University of Richmond *Virginia*
University of Rochester *New York*
University of San Diego *California*
University of San Francisco *California*
The University of Scranton *Pennsylvania*
University of South Alabama *Alabama*
University of South Carolina *South Carolina*
University of South Carolina Aiken *South Carolina*
University of South Carolina Upstate *South Carolina*
The University of South Dakota *South Dakota*
University of South Florida *Florida*
University of Southern California *California*
University of Southern Indiana *Indiana*
University of Southern Maine *Maine*
University of Southern Mississippi *Mississippi*
The University of Tampa *Florida*
The University of Tennessee *Tennessee*
The University of Tennessee at Chattanooga *Tennessee*
The University of Tennessee at Martin *Tennessee*
The University of Texas at Arlington *Texas*
The University of Texas at Austin *Texas*
The University of Texas at Dallas *Texas*

Accreditation Board for Engineering and Technology, Inc. (ABET)

Kent State University at Tuscarawas *Ohio*
Kettering University *Michigan*
Lafayette College *Pennsylvania*
Lake Superior State University *Michigan*
Lakeland Community College *Ohio*
Lamar University *Texas*
Lawrence Technological University *Michigan*
Lehigh University *Pennsylvania*
LeTourneau University *Texas*
Louisiana State University and Agricultural and Mechanical College *Louisiana*
Louisiana State University in Shreveport *Louisiana*
Louisiana Tech University *Louisiana*
Loyola Marymount University *California*
Loyola University Maryland *Maryland*
Maine Maritime Academy *Maine*
Manhattan College *New York*
Marietta College *Ohio*
Marquette University *Wisconsin*
Marshall University *West Virginia*
Massachusetts Institute of Technology *Massachusetts*
McNeese State University *Louisiana*
Mercer University *Georgia*
Merrimack College *Massachusetts*
Messiah College *Pennsylvania*
Metropolitan State College of Denver *Colorado*
Miami University *Ohio*
Michigan State University *Michigan*
Michigan Technological University *Michigan*
Middle Tennessee State University *Tennessee*
Middlesex County College *New Jersey*
Midlands Technical College *South Carolina*
Midwestern State University *Texas*
Millersville University of Pennsylvania *Pennsylvania*
Milwaukee School of Engineering *Wisconsin*
Minnesota State University Mankato *Minnesota*
Mississippi State University *Mississippi*
Missouri Southern State University *Missouri*
Missouri State University *Missouri*
Missouri University of Science and Technology *Missouri*
Missouri Western State University *Missouri*
Mohawk Valley Community College *New York*
Monroe Community College *New York*
Montana State University *Montana*
Montana State University–Northern *Montana*
Montana Tech of The University of Montana *Montana*
Montclair State University *New Jersey*
Morgan State University *Maryland*
Morrison Institute of Technology *Illinois*
Murray State University *Kentucky*
Nashua Community College *New Hampshire*
Nashville State Technical Community College *Tennessee*
Nassau Community College *New York*
Naugatuck Valley Community College *Connecticut*
New England Institute of Technology *Rhode Island*
New Jersey Institute of Technology *New Jersey*
New Mexico Institute of Mining and Technology *New Mexico*
New Mexico State University *New Mexico*
New York City College of Technology of the City University of New York *New York*
New York Institute of Technology *New York*
NHTI, Concord's Community College *New Hampshire*
Nicholls State University *Louisiana*
Norfolk State University *Virginia*
North Carolina Agricultural and Technical State University *North Carolina*
North Carolina State University *North Carolina*
North Dakota State University *North Dakota*
Northeast Wisconsin Technical College *Wisconsin*
Northeastern University *Massachusetts*
Northern Arizona University *Arizona*
Northern Illinois University *Illinois*
Northern Kentucky University *Kentucky*
Northwest State Community College *Ohio*
Northwestern State University of Louisiana *Louisiana*
Northwestern University *Illinois*
Norwich University *Vermont*
Oakland University *Michigan*
Ohio Northern University *Ohio*
The Ohio State University *Ohio*
Ohio University *Ohio*
Oklahoma Christian University *Oklahoma*
Oklahoma State University *Oklahoma*
Old Dominion University *Virginia*
Olivet Nazarene University *Illinois*
Onondaga Community College *New York*
Oral Roberts University *Oklahoma*
Orangeburg-Calhoun Technical College *South Carolina*
Oregon Institute of Technology *Oregon*
Oregon State University *Oregon*
Owens Community College *Ohio*
Pace University *New York*
Pacific Lutheran University *Washington*
Paul Smith's College *New York*
Pellissippi State Technical Community College *Tennessee*
Penn State Altoona *Pennsylvania*
Penn State Beaver *Pennsylvania*
Penn State Berks *Pennsylvania*
Penn State DuBois *Pennsylvania*
Penn State Erie, The Behrend College *Pennsylvania*
Penn State Fayette, The Eberly Campus *Pennsylvania*
Penn State Harrisburg *Pennsylvania*
Penn State Hazleton *Pennsylvania*
Penn State New Kensington *Pennsylvania*
Penn State Schuylkill *Pennsylvania*
Penn State Shenango *Pennsylvania*
Penn State University Park *Pennsylvania*
Penn State Wilkes-Barre *Pennsylvania*
Penn State Worthington Scranton *Pennsylvania*
Penn State York *Pennsylvania*
Pennsylvania College of Technology *Pennsylvania*
Philadelphia University *Pennsylvania*
Piedmont Technical College *South Carolina*
Pittsburg State University *Kansas*
Point Park University *Pennsylvania*
Polytechnic Institute of NYU *New York*
Polytechnic University of Puerto Rico *Puerto Rico*
Portland State University *Oregon*
Prairie View A&M University *Texas*
Prince George's Community College *Maryland*
Princeton University *New Jersey*
Purdue University *Indiana*
Purdue University Calumet *Indiana*
Purdue University North Central *Indiana*
Queensborough Community College of the City University of New York *New York*
Radford University *Virginia*
Rensselaer Polytechnic Institute *New York*
Rice University *Texas*
Robert Morris University *Pennsylvania*
Rochester Institute of Technology *New York*
Roger Williams University *Rhode Island*
Rose-Hulman Institute of Technology *Indiana*
Rowan University *New Jersey*
Rutgers, The State University of New Jersey, New Brunswick *New Jersey*
Saginaw Valley State University *Michigan*
St. Ambrose University *Iowa*
St. Cloud State University *Minnesota*
Saint Louis University *Missouri*
Saint Martin's University *Washington*
St. Mary's University *Texas*
San Diego State University *California*
San Francisco State University *California*
San Jose State University *California*
San Juan College *New Mexico*
Santa Clara University *California*
Savannah State University *Georgia*
Savannah Technical College *Georgia*
Seattle Pacific University *Washington*
Seattle University *Washington*
Sinclair Community College *Ohio*
South Carolina State University *South Carolina*
South Dakota School of Mines and Technology *South Dakota*
South Dakota State University *South Dakota*
Southeast Missouri State University *Missouri*
Southeastern Louisiana University *Louisiana*
Southern Connecticut State University *Connecticut*
Southern Illinois University Carbondale *Illinois*
Southern Illinois University Edwardsville *Illinois*
Southern Methodist University *Texas*
Southern Polytechnic State University *Georgia*
Southern University and Agricultural and Mechanical College *Louisiana*
Southwest Tennessee Community College *Tennessee*
Southwestern Oklahoma State University *Oklahoma*
Spartanburg Community College *South Carolina*
Stanford University *California*
Stark State College of Technology *Ohio*
State University of New York at Binghamton *New York*
State University of New York College of Agriculture and Technology at Morrisville *New York*
State University of New York College of Environmental Science & Forestry, Ranger School *New York*
State University of New York College of Environmental Science and Forestry *New York*
State University of New York College of Technology at Alfred *New York*
State University of New York College of Technology at Canton *New York*
State University of New York Institute of Technology *New York*
State University of New York Maritime College *New York*
State University of New York at New Paltz *New York*
Stephen F. Austin State University *Texas*
Stevens Institute of Technology *New Jersey*
Stony Brook University, State University of New York *New York*
Swarthmore College *Pennsylvania*
Syracuse University *New York*
TCI–The College of Technology *New York*
Temple University *Pennsylvania*
Tennessee State University *Tennessee*
Tennessee Technological University *Tennessee*
Texas A&M University *Texas*
Texas A&M University at Galveston *Texas*
Texas A&M University–Corpus Christi *Texas*
Texas A&M University–Kingsville *Texas*
Texas Christian University *Texas*
Texas Southern University *Texas*
Texas State University–San Marcos *Texas*
Texas Tech University *Texas*
Three Rivers Community College *Connecticut*
Towson University *Maryland*
Tri-County Technical College *South Carolina*
Trident Technical College *South Carolina*
Trine University *Indiana*
Trinidad State Junior College *Colorado*
Trinity College *Connecticut*
Trinity University *Texas*
Tufts University *Massachusetts*
Tulane University *Louisiana*
Tuskegee University *Alabama*
Union College *New York*
United States Air Force Academy *Colorado*
United States Coast Guard Academy *Connecticut*
United States Merchant Marine Academy *New York*
United States Military Academy *New York*
United States Naval Academy *Maryland*
The University of Akron *Ohio*
The University of Alabama *Alabama*
The University of Alabama at Birmingham *Alabama*
The University of Alabama in Huntsville *Alabama*
University of Alaska Anchorage *Alaska*
University of Alaska Fairbanks *Alaska*
The University of Arizona *Arizona*
University of Arkansas *Arkansas*
University of Arkansas at Little Rock *Arkansas*
University of Bridgeport *Connecticut*
University at Buffalo, the State University of New York *New York*
University of California, Berkeley *California*
University of California, Davis *California*
University of California, Irvine *California*
University of California, Los Angeles *California*
University of California, Riverside *California*
University of California, San Diego *California*
University of California, Santa Barbara *California*
University of California, Santa Cruz *California*
University of Central Florida *Florida*
University of Central Missouri *Missouri*
University of Cincinnati *Ohio*
University of Colorado at Boulder *Colorado*

University of Colorado at Colorado Springs *Colorado*
University of Colorado Denver *Colorado*
University of Connecticut *Connecticut*
University of Dayton *Ohio*
University of Delaware *Delaware*
University of Denver *Colorado*
University of Detroit Mercy *Michigan*
University of the District of Columbia *District of Columbia*
University of Evansville *Indiana*
University of Florida *Florida*
University of Georgia *Georgia*
University of Hartford *Connecticut*
University of Hawaii at Manoa *Hawaii*
University of Houston *Texas*
University of Houston–Clear Lake *Texas*
University of Houston–Downtown *Texas*
University of Idaho *Idaho*
University of Illinois at Chicago *Illinois*
University of Illinois at Urbana–Champaign *Illinois*
The University of Iowa *Iowa*
The University of Kansas *Kansas*
University of Kentucky *Kentucky*
University of Louisiana at Lafayette *Louisiana*
University of Louisiana at Monroe *Louisiana*
University of Louisville *Kentucky*
University of Maine *Maine*
University of Maryland, Baltimore County *Maryland*
University of Maryland, College Park *Maryland*
University of Massachusetts Amherst *Massachusetts*
University of Massachusetts Dartmouth *Massachusetts*
University of Massachusetts Lowell *Massachusetts*
University of Memphis *Tennessee*
University of Miami *Florida*
University of Michigan *Michigan*
University of Michigan–Dearborn *Michigan*
University of Minnesota, Duluth *Minnesota*
University of Minnesota, Twin Cities Campus *Minnesota*
University of Mississippi *Mississippi*
University of Missouri *Missouri*
University of Missouri–St. Louis *Missouri*
The University of Montana *Montana*
University of Nebraska at Omaha *Nebraska*
University of Nebraska–Lincoln *Nebraska*
University of Nevada, Las Vegas *Nevada*
University of Nevada, Reno *Nevada*
University of New Hampshire *New Hampshire*
University of New Haven *Connecticut*
University of New Mexico *New Mexico*
University of New Orleans *Louisiana*
University of North Alabama *Alabama*
The University of North Carolina at Chapel Hill *North Carolina*
The University of North Carolina at Charlotte *North Carolina*
The University of North Carolina at Greensboro *North Carolina*
University of North Dakota *North Dakota*
University of North Florida *Florida*
University of North Texas *Texas*
University of Notre Dame *Indiana*
University of Oklahoma *Oklahoma*
University of Oklahoma Health Sciences Center *Oklahoma*
University of the Pacific *California*
University of Pennsylvania *Pennsylvania*
University of Pittsburgh *Pennsylvania*
University of Pittsburgh at Johnstown *Pennsylvania*
University of Portland *Oregon*
University of Puerto Rico, Mayagüez Campus *Puerto Rico*
University of Rhode Island *Rhode Island*
University of Rochester *New York*
University of St. Thomas *Minnesota*
University of San Diego *California*
The University of Scranton *Pennsylvania*
University of South Alabama *Alabama*
University of South Carolina *South Carolina*
University of South Carolina Upstate *South Carolina*
University of South Florida *Florida*
University of Southern California *California*
University of Southern Indiana *Indiana*
University of Southern Maine *Maine*
University of Southern Mississippi *Mississippi*
The University of Tennessee *Tennessee*
The University of Tennessee at Chattanooga *Tennessee*
The University of Tennessee at Martin *Tennessee*
The University of Texas at Arlington *Texas*
The University of Texas at Austin *Texas*
The University of Texas at Dallas *Texas*
The University of Texas at El Paso *Texas*
The University of Texas Health Science Center at Houston *Texas*
The University of Texas at San Antonio *Texas*
The University of Texas at Tyler *Texas*
The University of Texas–Pan American *Texas*
The University of Toledo *Ohio*
University of Tulsa *Oklahoma*
University of Utah *Utah*
University of Vermont *Vermont*
University of Virginia *Virginia*
University of Washington *Washington*
University of West Georgia *Georgia*
University of Wisconsin–Eau Claire *Wisconsin*
University of Wisconsin–Madison *Wisconsin*
University of Wisconsin–Milwaukee *Wisconsin*
University of Wisconsin–Platteville *Wisconsin*
University of Wisconsin–Stout *Wisconsin*
University of Wyoming *Wyoming*
Utah State University *Utah*
Utah Valley University *Utah*
Valparaiso University *Indiana*
Vanderbilt University *Tennessee*
Vaughn College of Aeronautics and Technology *New York*
Vermont Technical College *Vermont*
Villanova University *Pennsylvania*
Virginia Commonwealth University *Virginia*
Virginia Military Institute *Virginia*
Virginia Polytechnic Institute and State University *Virginia*
Virginia State University *Virginia*
Wake Technical Community College *North Carolina*
Walla Walla Community College *Washington*
Walla Walla University *Washington*
Washington State University *Washington*
Washington University in St. Louis *Missouri*
Wayne State University *Michigan*
Webb Institute *New York*
Weber State University *Utah*
Wentworth Institute of Technology *Massachusetts*
West Virginia State University *West Virginia*
West Virginia University *West Virginia*
West Virginia University Institute of Technology *West Virginia*
Western Carolina University *North Carolina*
Western Kentucky University *Kentucky*
Western Michigan University *Michigan*
Western New England College *Massachusetts*
Western Washington University *Washington*
Wichita State University *Kansas*
Widener University *Pennsylvania*
Wilkes University *Pennsylvania*
Winona State University *Minnesota*
Winston-Salem State University *North Carolina*
Winthrop University *South Carolina*
Worcester Polytechnic Institute *Massachusetts*
Wright State University *Ohio*
Yale University *Connecticut*
York College of Pennsylvania *Pennsylvania*
York Technical College *South Carolina*
Youngstown State University *Ohio*
Zane State College *Ohio*

Accreditation Commission for Acupuncture and Oriental Medicine (NACSCAO)

Bastyr University *Washington*
Mercy College *New York*
New York College of Health Professions *New York*
Swedish Institute, College of Health Sciences *New York*
University of Bridgeport *Connecticut*

Accreditation Committee for Perfusion Education (ACPE)

Barry University *Florida*
Drexel University *Pennsylvania*
Medical University of South Carolina *South Carolina*
Milwaukee School of Engineering *Wisconsin*
Northeastern University *Massachusetts*
The Ohio State University *Ohio*
Rush University *Illinois*
State University of New York Upstate Medical University *New York*
University of Nebraska Medical Center *Nebraska*

Accreditation Council for Pharmacy Education (ACPhE)

Albany College of Pharmacy and Health Sciences *New York*
Auburn University *Alabama*
Belmont University *Tennessee*
Butler University *Indiana*
Campbell University *North Carolina*
Creighton University *Nebraska*
Drake University *Iowa*
Duquesne University *Pennsylvania*
Ferris State University *Michigan*
Florida Agricultural and Mechanical University *Florida*
Hampton University *Virginia*
Harding University *Arkansas*
Howard University *District of Columbia*
Idaho State University *Idaho*
Lipscomb University *Tennessee*
Loma Linda University *California*
Long Island University, Brooklyn Campus *New York*
Massachusetts College of Pharmacy and Health Sciences *Massachusetts*
Medical University of South Carolina *South Carolina*
Mercer University *Georgia*
North Dakota State University *North Dakota*
Northeastern University *Massachusetts*
Nova Southeastern University *Florida*
Ohio Northern University *Ohio*
The Ohio State University *Ohio*
Oregon State University *Oregon*
Pacific University *Oregon*
Palm Beach Atlantic University *Florida*
Purdue University *Indiana*
Rutgers, The State University of New Jersey, New Brunswick *New Jersey*
St. John Fisher College *New York*
St. John's University *New York*
St. Louis College of Pharmacy *Missouri*
Samford University *Alabama*
Shenandoah University *Virginia*
South Dakota State University *South Dakota*
South University *Georgia*
Southern Illinois University Edwardsville *Illinois*
Southwestern Oklahoma State University *Oklahoma*
Temple University *Pennsylvania*
Texas Southern University *Texas*
Thomas Jefferson University *Pennsylvania*
The University of Arizona *Arizona*
University of Arkansas for Medical Sciences *Arkansas*
University at Buffalo, the State University of New York *New York*
University of California, San Diego *California*
University of Charleston *West Virginia*
University of Cincinnati *Ohio*
University of Colorado Denver *Colorado*
University of Connecticut *Connecticut*
The University of Findlay *Ohio*
University of Florida *Florida*
University of Georgia *Georgia*
University of Houston *Texas*
University of Illinois at Chicago *Illinois*
University of the Incarnate Word *Texas*
The University of Iowa *Iowa*
The University of Kansas *Kansas*
University of Kentucky *Kentucky*
University of Louisiana at Monroe *Louisiana*
University of Michigan *Michigan*
University of Minnesota, Twin Cities Campus *Minnesota*
University of Mississippi *Mississippi*

University of Missouri–Kansas City *Missouri*
The University of Montana *Montana*
University of Nebraska Medical Center *Nebraska*
University of New Mexico *New Mexico*
The University of North Carolina at Chapel Hill *North Carolina*
University of Oklahoma Health Sciences Center *Oklahoma*
University of the Pacific *California*
University of Pittsburgh *Pennsylvania*
University of Puerto Rico, Medical Sciences Campus *Puerto Rico*
University of Rhode Island *Rhode Island*
University of the Sciences in Philadelphia *Pennsylvania*
University of South Carolina *South Carolina*
University of Southern California *California*
The University of Texas at Austin *Texas*
The University of Toledo *Ohio*
University of Utah *Utah*
University of Washington *Washington*
University of Wisconsin–Madison *Wisconsin*
University of Wyoming *Wyoming*
Virginia Commonwealth University *Virginia*
Washington State University *Washington*
Wayne State University *Michigan*
West Virginia University *West Virginia*
Wilkes University *Pennsylvania*
Wingate University *North Carolina*
Xavier University of Louisiana *Louisiana*

Accreditation Review Committee on Education for the Anesthesiologist Assis (ARCAA)

Case Western Reserve University *Ohio*
Emory University *Georgia*

Accreditation Review Committee on Education in Surgical Technology (ARCEST)

Amarillo College *Texas*
Ashland Community and Technical College *Kentucky*
Augusta Technical College *Georgia*
Austin Community College *Texas*
Baker College of Cadillac *Michigan*
Baker College of Clinton Township *Michigan*
Baker College of Flint *Michigan*
Baker College of Jackson *Michigan*
Baker College of Muskegon *Michigan*
Baker College of Port Huron *Michigan*
Baltimore City Community College *Maryland*
Bismarck State College *North Dakota*
Bunker Hill Community College *Massachusetts*
Cabarrus College of Health Sciences *North Carolina*
Career Technical College *Louisiana*
Central Florida Institute *Florida*
Central Ohio Technical College *Ohio*
Central Wyoming College *Wyoming*
Cincinnati State Technical and Community College *Ohio*
City Colleges of Chicago, Malcolm X College *Illinois*
Coastal Carolina Community College *North Carolina*
Columbus State Community College *Ohio*
Columbus Technical College *Georgia*
Community College of Allegheny County *Pennsylvania*
Community College of Denver *Colorado*
Cuyahoga Community College *Ohio*
Del Mar College *Texas*
Delaware County Community College *Pennsylvania*
Delta College *Michigan*
East Central Community College *Mississippi*
Eastern Idaho Technical College *Idaho*
El Paso Community College *Texas*
Everest Institute (Hialeah) *Florida*
Everest Institute (Miami) *Florida*
Frederick Community College *Maryland*
Gateway Technical College *Wisconsin*
Griffin Technical College *Georgia*
Henry Ford Community College *Michigan*
Holmes Community College *Mississippi*
Itawamba Community College *Mississippi*
Ivy Tech Community College–Central Indiana *Indiana*
Ivy Tech Community College–Columbus *Indiana*
Ivy Tech Community College–East Central *Indiana*
Ivy Tech Community College–Lafayette *Indiana*
Ivy Tech Community College–Northwest *Indiana*
Ivy Tech Community College–Southwest *Indiana*
Ivy Tech Community College–Wabash Valley *Indiana*
James H. Faulkner State Community College *Alabama*
Kilgore College *Texas*
Kirkwood Community College *Iowa*
Lakeland Community College *Ohio*
Lamar State College–Port Arthur *Texas*
Loma Linda University *California*
Lorain County Community College *Ohio*
Luzerne County Community College *Pennsylvania*
Macomb Community College *Michigan*
Manchester Community College *New Hampshire*
Manchester Community College *Connecticut*
Mercy College of Health Sciences *Iowa*
Milwaukee Area Technical College *Wisconsin*
Montgomery College *Maryland*
Mount Aloysius College *Pennsylvania*
Mt. Hood Community College *Oregon*
Nassau Community College *New York*
New England Institute of Technology *Rhode Island*
Niagara County Community College *New York*
North Arkansas College *Arkansas*
Northwest Technical College *Minnesota*
Odessa College *Texas*
Our Lady of the Lake College *Louisiana*
Owens Community College *Ohio*
Parkland College *Illinois*
Pearl River Community College *Mississippi*
Presentation College *South Dakota*
Renton Technical College *Washington*
Richland Community College *Illinois*
Rochester Community and Technical College *Minnesota*
St. Cloud Technical College *Minnesota*
San Joaquin Valley College (Visalia) *California*
Seward County Community College *Kansas*
Sinclair Community College *Ohio*
Skyline College *California*
Southeast Arkansas College *Arkansas*
Southeast Community College, Lincoln Campus *Nebraska*
Southern University at Shreveport *Louisiana*
Southern West Virginia Community and Technical College *West Virginia*
Southwestern College *California*
Spokane Community College *Washington*
Springfield Technical Community College *Massachusetts*
Stevens-Henager College *Utah*
Trinity Valley Community College *Texas*
Trocaire College *New York*
Tyler Junior College *Texas*
The University of Akron *Ohio*
University of Arkansas at Fort Smith *Arkansas*
University of Arkansas for Medical Sciences *Arkansas*
University of Saint Francis *Indiana*
Vincennes University *Indiana*
Waukesha County Technical College *Wisconsin*
Wayne County Community College District *Michigan*
West Virginia Northern Community College *West Virginia*
Wichita Area Technical College *Kansas*

Accreditation Review Committee for the Medical Illustrator (ARCMI)

The Johns Hopkins University *Maryland*
Medical College of Georgia *Georgia*
University of Illinois at Chicago *Illinois*
University of Michigan *Michigan*
The University of Texas Southwestern Medical Center at Dallas *Texas*
University of Toronto *Ontario*

Accrediting Bureau of Health Education Schools (ABHES)

The Academy of Health Care Professions *Texas*
Allied College *Missouri*
Anthem College Aurora *Colorado*
Apollo College *Washington*
Apollo College–Boise *Idaho*
Apollo College–Phoenix *Arizona*
Apollo College–Tri-City, Inc. *Arizona*
Apollo College–Tucson, Inc. *Arizona*
Apollo College–Westside, Inc. *Arizona*
Arizona College of Allied Health *Arizona*
Bay State College *Massachusetts*
Brown Mackie College–Merrillville *Indiana*
Brown Mackie College–Michigan City *Indiana*
The Bryman School of Arizona *Arizona*
Central Florida Institute *Florida*
CollegeAmerica–Flagstaff *Arizona*
Colorado Technical University North Kansas City *Missouri*
Community Care College *Oklahoma*
Everest Institute (Fort Lauderdale) *Florida*
Everest Institute (Hialeah) *Florida*
Everest Institute (Miami) *Florida*
Everest Institute (Miami) *Florida*
IntelliTec Medical Institute *Colorado*
Keiser University *Florida*
MedVance Institute *Florida*
Midwest Institute (Earth City) *Missouri*
Pima Medical Institute *Washington*
Pima Medical Institute *New Mexico*
Pima Medical Institute *Nevada*
Pima Medical Institute *Colorado*
Pima Medical Institute *California*
Pima Medical Institute (Mesa) *Arizona*
Pima Medical Institute (Tucson) *Arizona*
Professional Skills Institute *Ohio*
Sanford-Brown College (Hazelwood) *Missouri*
Sanford-Brown Institute (Jacksonville) *Florida*
Southwestern Oklahoma State University at Sayre *Oklahoma*

Accrediting Commission of Career Schools and Colleges (ACCSCT)

American Academy of Art *Illinois*
Anthem College Aurora *Colorado*
Antonelli College *Ohio*
Antonelli College (Hattiesburg) *Mississippi*
Antonelli College (Jackson) *Mississippi*
Antonelli Institute *Pennsylvania*
Arizona Automotive Institute *Arizona*
The Art Center Design College *Arizona*
The Art Institute of California–Inland Empire *California*
The Art Institute of California–San Diego *California*
The Art Institute of Cincinnati *Ohio*
The Art Institute of Las Vegas *Nevada*
The Art Institute of Salt Lake City *Utah*
The Art Institute of York–Pennsylvania *Pennsylvania*
ATI Career Training Center (Fort Lauderdale) *Florida*
ATI Career Training Center (Oakland Park) *Florida*
ATI College of Health *Florida*
ATI Technical Training Center *Texas*
Aviation Institute of Maintenance–Indianapolis *Indiana*
Aviation Institute of Maintenance–Kansas City *Missouri*
Aviation Institute of Maintenance–Manassas *Virginia*
Aviation Institute of Maintenance–Virginia Beach *Virginia*
Baton Rouge School of Computers *Louisiana*
Bel–Rea Institute of Animal Technology *Colorado*
Berks Technical Institute *Pennsylvania*
Bidwell Training Center *Pennsylvania*
Boulder College of Massage Therapy *Colorado*
Brown College *Minnesota*
Brown Mackie College–Hopkinsville *Kentucky*
Brown Mackie College–Louisville *Kentucky*
Bryan College *California*
The Bryman School of Arizona *Arizona*
Business Informatics Center, Inc. *New York*
California College *California*
California Culinary Academy *California*
Career College of Northern Nevada *Nevada*
Career Training Academy (Monroeville) *Pennsylvania*
Career Training Academy (New Kensington) *Pennsylvania*
Career Training Academy (Pittsburgh) *Pennsylvania*
Centro de Estudios Multidisciplinarios *Puerto Rico*
Centura College (Chesapeake) *Virginia*

Accrediting Council on Education in Journalism and Mass Communications (ACEJMC)

Indiana University Bloomington *Indiana*
Iona College *New York*
Iowa State University of Science and Technology *Iowa*
Jackson State University *Mississippi*
Kansas State University *Kansas*
Kent State University *Ohio*
Louisiana State University and Agricultural and Mechanical College *Louisiana*
Marquette University *Wisconsin*
Marshall University *West Virginia*
Michigan State University *Michigan*
Middle Tennessee State University *Tennessee*
Murray State University *Kentucky*
New Mexico State University *New Mexico*
New York University *New York*
Nicholls State University *Louisiana*
Norfolk State University *Virginia*
Northwestern State University of Louisiana *Louisiana*
Northwestern University *Illinois*
Ohio University *Ohio*
Oklahoma State University *Oklahoma*
Penn State University Park *Pennsylvania*
St. Cloud State University *Minnesota*
San Francisco State University *California*
San Jose State University *California*
South Dakota State University *South Dakota*
Southern Illinois University Carbondale *Illinois*
Southern Illinois University Edwardsville *Illinois*
Southern University and Agricultural and Mechanical College *Louisiana*
Syracuse University *New York*
Temple University *Pennsylvania*
Texas A&M University *Texas*
Texas Christian University *Texas*
Texas State University–San Marcos *Texas*
Texas Tech University *Texas*
The University of Alabama *Alabama*
University of Alaska Anchorage *Alaska*
University of Alaska Fairbanks *Alaska*
The University of Arizona *Arizona*
University of Arkansas *Arkansas*
University of California, Berkeley *California*
University of Colorado at Boulder *Colorado*
University of Connecticut *Connecticut*
University of Florida *Florida*
University of Georgia *Georgia*
University of Hawaii at Manoa *Hawaii*
University of Illinois at Urbana–Champaign *Illinois*
The University of Iowa *Iowa*
The University of Kansas *Kansas*
University of Kentucky *Kentucky*
University of Louisiana at Lafayette *Louisiana*
University of Louisiana at Monroe *Louisiana*
University of Maryland, College Park *Maryland*
University of Memphis *Tennessee*
University of Miami *Florida*
University of Minnesota, Twin Cities Campus *Minnesota*
University of Mississippi *Mississippi*
University of Missouri *Missouri*
The University of Montana *Montana*
University of Nebraska–Lincoln *Nebraska*
University of Nevada, Reno *Nevada*
The University of North Carolina at Chapel Hill *North Carolina*
University of North Texas *Texas*
University of Oklahoma *Oklahoma*
University of Oregon *Oregon*
University of South Carolina *South Carolina*
The University of South Dakota *South Dakota*
University of South Florida *Florida*
University of Southern California *California*
University of Southern Mississippi *Mississippi*
The University of Tennessee *Tennessee*
The University of Tennessee at Chattanooga *Tennessee*
The University of Tennessee at Martin *Tennessee*
The University of Texas at Austin *Texas*
University of Utah *Utah*
University of Washington *Washington*
University of Wisconsin–Eau Claire *Wisconsin*
University of Wisconsin–Oshkosh *Wisconsin*
University of Wisconsin–River Falls *Wisconsin*
Virginia Commonwealth University *Virginia*
Washington and Lee University *Virginia*
West Virginia University *West Virginia*
Western Kentucky University *Kentucky*
Winthrop University *South Carolina*

Accrediting Council for Independent Colleges and Schools (ACICS)

Academy of Art University *California*
Academy College *Minnesota*
Academy of Court Reporting (Cleveland) *Ohio*
The Art Institute of California–Hollywood *California*
The Art Institute of California–Los Angeles *California*
The Art Institute of California–Orange County *California*
The Art Institute of California–Sacramento *California*
The Art Institute of California–San Francisco *California*
The Art Institute of California–Sunnyvale *California*
The Art Institute of Charlotte *North Carolina*
The Art Institute of Colorado *Colorado*
The Art Institute of Fort Lauderdale *Florida*
The Art Institute of Indianapolis *Indiana*
The Art Institute of New York City *New York*
The Art Institute of Philadelphia *Pennsylvania*
The Art Institute of Phoenix *Arizona*
The Art Institute of Pittsburgh *Pennsylvania*
The Art Institutes International Minnesota *Minnesota*
ASA Institute, The College of Advanced Technology *New York*
Atlantic College *Puerto Rico*
ATS Institute of Technology *Ohio*
Beal College *Maine*
Beckfield College *Kentucky*
Bradford School *Pennsylvania*
Bradford School *Ohio*
Brookline College *New Mexico*
Brookline College (Phoenix) *Arizona*
Brookline College (Tempe) *Arizona*
Brookline College (Tucson) *Arizona*
Brooks Institute *California*
Brown Mackie College–Akron *Ohio*
Brown Mackie College–Cincinnati *Ohio*
Brown Mackie College–Findlay *Ohio*
Brown Mackie College–Fort Wayne *Indiana*
Brown Mackie College–Hopkinsville *Kentucky*
Brown Mackie College–Louisville *Kentucky*
Brown Mackie College–Merrillville *Indiana*
Brown Mackie College–Michigan City *Indiana*
Brown Mackie College–North Canton *Ohio*
Brown Mackie College–Northern Kentucky *Kentucky*
Brown Mackie College–South Bend *Indiana*
Brown Mackie College–Tucson *Arizona*
California Miramar University *California*
Cambria-Rowe Business College (Indiana) *Pennsylvania*
Cambria-Rowe Business College (Johnstown) *Pennsylvania*
Camelot College *Louisiana*
Charter College *Alaska*
City College (Casselberry) *Florida*
City College (Fort Lauderdale) *Florida*
City College (Gainesville) *Florida*
City College (Miami) *Florida*
Coleman University (San Diego) *California*
Coleman University (San Marcos) *California*
College of Court Reporting *Indiana*
The College of Office Technology *Illinois*
Colorado Heights University *Colorado*
Colorado Technical University North Kansas City *Missouri*
Columbia College (Caguas) *Puerto Rico*
Columbia College (Yauco) *Puerto Rico*
Consolidated School of Business (Lancaster) *Pennsylvania*
Consolidated School of Business (York) *Pennsylvania*
Court Reporting Institute of Dallas *Texas*
Court Reporting Institute of Houston *Texas*
Daymar College (Bowling Green) *Kentucky*
Daymar College (Chillicothe) *Ohio*
Daymar College (Jackson) *Ohio*
Daymar College (Lancaster) *Ohio*
Daymar College (Louisville) *Kentucky*
Daymar College (Owensboro) *Kentucky*
Daymar Institute (Clarksville) *Tennessee*
Daymar Institute (Nashville) *Tennessee*
Delta School of Business & Technology *Louisiana*
Denver Academy of Court Reporting *Colorado*
Design Institute of San Diego *California*
Douglas Education Center *Pennsylvania*
DuBois Business College *Pennsylvania*
Duluth Business University *Minnesota*
EDP College of Puerto Rico, Inc. *Puerto Rico*
EDP College of Puerto Rico–San Sebastian *Puerto Rico*
Elmira Business Institute *New York*
Empire College *California*
Erie Business Center, Main *Pennsylvania*
Erie Business Center, South *Pennsylvania*
Everest College *Washington*
Everest College *Virginia*
Everest College *Utah*
Everest College *Oregon*
Everest College *Missouri*
Everest College *Arizona*
Everest College (Arlington) *Texas*
Everest College (Aurora) *Colorado*
Everest College (Colorado Springs) *Colorado*
Everest College (Dallas) *Texas*
Everest College (Denver) *Colorado*
Everest Institute *Pennsylvania*
Everest Institute *New York*
Everest University (Clearwater) *Florida*
Everest University (Jacksonville) *Florida*
Everest University (Lakeland) *Florida*
Everest University (Melbourne) *Florida*
Everest University (Orange Park) *Florida*
Everest University (Orlando) *Florida*
Everest University (Orlando) *Florida*
Everest University (Pompano Beach) *Florida*
Everest University (Tampa) *Florida*
Everest University (Tampa) *Florida*
Fashion Careers College *California*
Florida Career College *Florida*
Florida Technical College (Auburndale) *Florida*
Florida Technical College (DeLand) *Florida*
Florida Technical College (Jacksonville) *Florida*
Florida Technical College (Orlando) *Florida*
Forrest Junior College *South Carolina*
Fortis College–Ravenna *Ohio*
Fox College *Illinois*
Gallipolis Career College *Ohio*
Gem City College *Illinois*
Globe Institute of Technology *New York*
Globe University *Minnesota*
Goodwin College *Connecticut*
Gulf Coast College *Florida*
Harrison College *Ohio*
Harrison College (Anderson) *Indiana*
Harrison College (Columbus) *Indiana*
Harrison College (Elkhart) *Indiana*
Harrison College (Evansville) *Indiana*
Harrison College (Fort Wayne) *Indiana*
Harrison College (Indianapolis) *Indiana*
Harrison College (Indianapolis) *Indiana*
Harrison College (Indianapolis) *Indiana*
Harrison College (Lafayette) *Indiana*
Harrison College (Muncie) *Indiana*
Harrison College (Terre Haute) *Indiana*
Herzing College *Louisiana*
Herzing College *Florida*
Herzing University *Georgia*
Hickey College *Missouri*
Hondros College *Ohio*
Huertas Junior College *Puerto Rico*
Humacao Community College *Puerto Rico*
Institute of Business & Medical Careers *Colorado*
International Academy of Design & Technology *Illinois*
International Academy of Design & Technology *Florida*
International Business College (Fort Wayne) *Indiana*
International Business College (Indianapolis) *Indiana*
International Technological University *California*
ITT Technical Institute *West Virginia*
ITT Technical Institute *Utah*
ITT Technical Institute *Oregon*
ITT Technical Institute *New Mexico*
ITT Technical Institute *Nevada*
ITT Technical Institute *Nebraska*
ITT Technical Institute *Mississippi*

American Academy for Liberal Education (AALE)

American Association of Blood Banks (AABB)

University of Illinois at Chicago *Illinois*
The University of Texas Health Science Center at San Antonio *Texas*

American Association of Colleges of Nursing (AACN)

Abilene Christian University *Texas*
Adelphi University *New York*
Allen College *Iowa*
Alvernia University *Pennsylvania*
Alverno College *Wisconsin*
American International College *Massachusetts*
Arizona State University *Arizona*
Armstrong Atlantic State University *Georgia*
Ashland University *Ohio*
Auburn University Montgomery *Alabama*
Augsburg College *Minnesota*
Augustana College *South Dakota*
Aurora University *Illinois*
Avila University *Missouri*
Azusa Pacific University *California*
Baker University *Kansas*
Ball State University *Indiana*
Baptist College of Health Sciences *Tennessee*
Barry University *Florida*
Baylor University *Texas*
Bellarmine University *Kentucky*
Bellin College *Wisconsin*
Belmont University *Tennessee*
Bemidji State University *Minnesota*
Berea College *Kentucky*
Bethel College *Kansas*
Bethel University *Minnesota*
Blessing-Rieman College of Nursing *Illinois*
Bloomfield College *New Jersey*
Bloomsburg University of Pennsylvania *Pennsylvania*
Bluefield State College *West Virginia*
Boston College *Massachusetts*
Brigham Young University *Utah*
Cabarrus College of Health Sciences *North Carolina*
California Baptist University *California*
California State University, Bakersfield *California*
California State University, Chico *California*
California State University, Dominguez Hills *California*
California State University, Fresno *California*
California State University, Fullerton *California*
California State University, Long Beach *California*
California State University, Los Angeles *California*
California State University, Northridge *California*
California State University, Sacramento *California*
California State University, San Bernardino *California*
California State University, Stanislaus *California*
California University of Pennsylvania *Pennsylvania*
Capital University *Ohio*
Cardinal Stritch University *Wisconsin*
Carlow University *Pennsylvania*
Carroll College *Montana*
Carson-Newman College *Tennessee*
The Catholic University of America *District of Columbia*
Cedarville University *Ohio*
Central Connecticut State University *Connecticut*
Chatham University *Pennsylvania*
Christopher Newport University *Virginia*
Clarke College *Iowa*
Clayton State University *Georgia*
Clemson University *South Carolina*
Cleveland State University *Ohio*
Coe College *Iowa*
Colby-Sawyer College *New Hampshire*
The College at Brockport, State University of New York *New York*
College of Mount St. Joseph *Ohio*
College of Mount Saint Vincent *New York*
The College of New Jersey *New Jersey*
The College of New Rochelle *New York*
College of Saint Benedict *Minnesota*
The College of St. Scholastica *Minnesota*
Columbia University *New York*
Concordia College *Minnesota*
Concordia University Wisconsin *Wisconsin*
Cox College of Nursing and Health Sciences *Missouri*
Creighton University *Nebraska*
Curry College *Massachusetts*
Delaware State University *Delaware*
Delta State University *Mississippi*
DePaul University *Illinois*
Dominican College *New York*
Dominican University of California *California*
Drexel University *Pennsylvania*
Duke University *North Carolina*
Duquesne University *Pennsylvania*
D'Youville College *New York*
East Tennessee State University *Tennessee*
East Texas Baptist University *Texas*
Eastern Kentucky University *Kentucky*
Eastern Michigan University *Michigan*
Eastern University *Pennsylvania*
Eastern Washington University *Washington*
Edgewood College *Wisconsin*
Edinboro University of Pennsylvania *Pennsylvania*
Elmhurst College *Illinois*
Elms College *Massachusetts*
Emory University *Georgia*
Fairfield University *Connecticut*
Fairleigh Dickinson University, Metropolitan Campus *New Jersey*
Fairmont State University *West Virginia*
Fayetteville State University *North Carolina*
Felician College *New Jersey*
Fitchburg State College *Massachusetts*
Florida Atlantic University *Florida*
Florida Gulf Coast University *Florida*
Florida International University *Florida*
Florida Southern College *Florida*
Florida State University *Florida*
Fort Hays State University *Kansas*
Gannon University *Pennsylvania*
George Mason University *Virginia*
Georgetown University *District of Columbia*
Georgia Southern University *Georgia*
Georgia State University *Georgia*
Goldfarb School of Nursing at Barnes-Jewish College *Missouri*
Gonzaga University *Washington*
Goshen College *Indiana*
Graceland University *Iowa*
Grand Canyon University *Arizona*
Grand Valley State University *Michigan*
Grand View University *Iowa*
Gustavus Adolphus College *Minnesota*
Hampton University *Virginia*
Hardin-Simmons University *Texas*
Hartwick College *New York*
Holy Family University *Pennsylvania*
Holy Names University *California*
Howard University *District of Columbia*
Humboldt State University *California*
Hunter College of the City University of New York *New York*
Husson University *Maine*
Idaho State University *Idaho*
Illinois State University *Illinois*
Illinois Wesleyan University *Illinois*
Immaculata University *Pennsylvania*
Indiana University Kokomo *Indiana*
Indiana University Northwest *Indiana*
Indiana University of Pennsylvania *Pennsylvania*
Indiana University South Bend *Indiana*
Indiana University Southeast *Indiana*
Indiana University–Purdue University Indianapolis *Indiana*
Indiana Wesleyan University *Indiana*
Jacksonville State University *Alabama*
Jacksonville University *Florida*
James Madison University *Virginia*
Jefferson College of Health Sciences *Virginia*
The Johns Hopkins University *Maryland*
Kennesaw State University *Georgia*
Kent State University *Ohio*
King College *Tennessee*
La Salle University *Pennsylvania*
Lakeview College of Nursing *Illinois*
Le Moyne College *New York*
Lees-McRae College *North Carolina*
Lehman College of the City University of New York *New York*
Lewis-Clark State College *Idaho*
Lewis University *Illinois*
Liberty University *Virginia*
Loma Linda University *California*
Long Island University, Brooklyn Campus *New York*
Long Island University, C.W. Post Campus *New York*
Louisiana College *Louisiana*
Louisiana State University Health Sciences Center *Louisiana*
Lourdes College *Ohio*
Loyola University Chicago *Illinois*
Luther College *Iowa*
Lynchburg College *Virginia*
MacMurray College *Illinois*
Madonna University *Michigan*
Malone University *Ohio*
Marian University *Wisconsin*
Marquette University *Wisconsin*
Marymount University *Virginia*
Maryville University of Saint Louis *Missouri*
McKendree University *Illinois*
McMurry University *Texas*
McNeese State University *Louisiana*
Medical College of Georgia *Georgia*
Medical University of South Carolina *South Carolina*
Mercer University *Georgia*
Mercy College *New York*
Mercy College of Health Sciences *Iowa*
Mesa State College *Colorado*
Messiah College *Pennsylvania*
Metropolitan State University *Minnesota*
Michigan State University *Michigan*
MidAmerica Nazarene University *Kansas*
Middle Tennessee State University *Tennessee*
Midwestern State University *Texas*
Milligan College *Tennessee*
Millikin University *Illinois*
Milwaukee School of Engineering *Wisconsin*
Minnesota State University Mankato *Minnesota*
Minnesota State University Moorhead *Minnesota*
Misericordia University *Pennsylvania*
Mississippi University for Women *Mississippi*
Missouri State University *Missouri*
Missouri Western State University *Missouri*
Molloy College *New York*
Monmouth University *New Jersey*
Montana State University *Montana*
Moravian College *Pennsylvania*
Mount Carmel College of Nursing *Ohio*
Mount Mercy College *Iowa*
Mount Saint Mary College *New York*
Mount St. Mary's College *California*
Murray State University *Kentucky*
National University *California*
Nazareth College of Rochester *New York*
Nebraska Methodist College *Nebraska*
New Mexico State University *New Mexico*
New York University *New York*
Newman University *Kansas*
Nicholls State University *Louisiana*
North Dakota State University *North Dakota*
North Park University *Illinois*
Northeastern University *Massachusetts*
Northern Arizona University *Arizona*
Northern Illinois University *Illinois*
Northern Michigan University *Michigan*
Northwest Nazarene University *Idaho*
Northwest University *Washington*
Northwestern State University of Louisiana *Louisiana*
Norwich University *Vermont*
Nova Southeastern University *Florida*
Oakland University *Michigan*
The Ohio State University *Ohio*
Ohio University *Ohio*
Oklahoma Wesleyan University *Oklahoma*
Old Dominion University *Virginia*
Olivet Nazarene University *Illinois*
Oregon Health & Science University *Oregon*
Otterbein University *Ohio*
Pace University *New York*
Pacific Lutheran University *Washington*
Penn State University Park *Pennsylvania*
Pittsburg State University *Kansas*
Point Loma Nazarene University *California*
Prairie View A&M University *Texas*

Purdue University *Indiana*
Queens University of Charlotte *North Carolina*
Radford University *Virginia*
Regis University *Colorado*
Research College of Nursing *Missouri*
Rhode Island College *Rhode Island*
The Richard Stockton College of New Jersey *New Jersey*
Robert Morris University *Pennsylvania*
Roberts Wesleyan College *New York*
Rush University *Illinois*
Rutgers, The State University of New Jersey, Camden *New Jersey*
Rutgers, The State University of New Jersey, Newark *New Jersey*
Sacred Heart University *Connecticut*
Saginaw Valley State University *Michigan*
St. Ambrose University *Iowa*
Saint Anselm College *New Hampshire*
Saint Anthony College of Nursing *Illinois*
Saint Francis University *Pennsylvania*
St. John Fisher College *New York*
Saint John's University *Minnesota*
Saint Joseph College *Connecticut*
Saint Joseph's College of Maine *Maine*
Saint Louis University *Missouri*
Saint Luke's College *Missouri*
Saint Mary's College of California *California*
St. Olaf College *Minnesota*
Saint Peter's College *New Jersey*
Saint Xavier University *Illinois*
Salem State College *Massachusetts*
Salisbury University *Maryland*
Samford University *Alabama*
Samuel Merritt University *California*
San Diego State University *California*
San Francisco State University *California*
San Jose State University *California*
Seattle Pacific University *Washington*
Seattle University *Washington*
Seton Hall University *New Jersey*
Shenandoah University *Virginia*
Simmons College *Massachusetts*
South Dakota State University *South Dakota*
Southeast Missouri State University *Missouri*
Southeastern Louisiana University *Louisiana*
Southern Connecticut State University *Connecticut*
Southern Illinois University Edwardsville *Illinois*
Southern Nazarene University *Oklahoma*
Southern University and Agricultural and Mechanical College *Louisiana*
Southwestern College *Kansas*
Spalding University *Kentucky*
Spring Arbor University *Michigan*
Spring Hill College *Alabama*
State University of New York at Binghamton *New York*
State University of New York Downstate Medical Center *New York*
State University of New York Institute of Technology *New York*
State University of New York at New Paltz *New York*
State University of New York at Plattsburgh *New York*
State University of New York Upstate Medical University *New York*
Stony Brook University, State University of New York *New York*
Tabor College *Kansas*
Tarleton State University *Texas*
Temple University *Pennsylvania*
Tennessee Technological University *Tennessee*
Tennessee Wesleyan College *Tennessee*
Texas A&M University–Corpus Christi *Texas*
Texas A&M University–Texarkana *Texas*
Texas Christian University *Texas*
Texas Woman's University *Texas*
Thomas Edison State College *New Jersey*
Thomas Jefferson University *Pennsylvania*
Towson University *Maryland*
Trinity Christian College *Illinois*
Truman State University *Missouri*
Union College *Nebraska*
Union University *Tennessee*
Universidad del Turabo *Puerto Rico*
The University of Akron *Ohio*
The University of Alabama *Alabama*
The University of Alabama at Birmingham *Alabama*
The University of Alabama in Huntsville *Alabama*
The University of Arizona *Arizona*
University of Arkansas *Arkansas*
University of Arkansas for Medical Sciences *Arkansas*
University at Buffalo, the State University of New York *New York*
University of California, Los Angeles *California*
University of Central Arkansas *Arkansas*
University of Central Florida *Florida*
University of Central Missouri *Missouri*
University of Cincinnati *Ohio*
University of Colorado at Colorado Springs *Colorado*
University of Colorado Denver *Colorado*
University of Connecticut *Connecticut*
University of Delaware *Delaware*
University of Detroit Mercy *Michigan*
University of Florida *Florida*
University of Hartford *Connecticut*
University of Hawaii at Manoa *Hawaii*
University of Illinois at Chicago *Illinois*
University of the Incarnate Word *Texas*
University of Indianapolis *Indiana*
The University of Iowa *Iowa*
The University of Kansas *Kansas*
University of Kentucky *Kentucky*
University of Louisiana at Lafayette *Louisiana*
University of Louisiana at Monroe *Louisiana*
University of Louisville *Kentucky*
University of Maine *Maine*
University of Maine at Fort Kent *Maine*
University of Mary *North Dakota*
University of Mary Hardin-Baylor *Texas*
University of Massachusetts Amherst *Massachusetts*
University of Massachusetts Boston *Massachusetts*
University of Massachusetts Lowell *Massachusetts*
University of Memphis *Tennessee*
University of Miami *Florida*
University of Michigan *Michigan*
University of Michigan–Flint *Michigan*
University of Minnesota, Twin Cities Campus *Minnesota*
University of Mississippi Medical Center *Mississippi*
University of Missouri *Missouri*
University of Missouri–Kansas City *Missouri*
University of Missouri–St. Louis *Missouri*
University of Mobile *Alabama*
University of Nebraska Medical Center *Nebraska*
University of Nevada, Las Vegas *Nevada*
University of Nevada, Reno *Nevada*
University of New Hampshire *New Hampshire*
University of New Mexico *New Mexico*
University of North Alabama *Alabama*
The University of North Carolina at Chapel Hill *North Carolina*
The University of North Carolina at Charlotte *North Carolina*
The University of North Carolina at Greensboro *North Carolina*
The University of North Carolina at Pembroke *North Carolina*
The University of North Carolina Wilmington *North Carolina*
University of North Dakota *North Dakota*
University of North Florida *Florida*
University of Northern Colorado *Colorado*
University of Pennsylvania *Pennsylvania*
University of Phoenix *Arizona*
University of Pittsburgh *Pennsylvania*
University of Portland *Oregon*
University of Puerto Rico, Medical Sciences Campus *Puerto Rico*
University of Rhode Island *Rhode Island*
University of Rochester *New York*
University of Saint Francis *Indiana*
University of St. Francis *Illinois*
University of San Diego *California*
University of San Francisco *California*
The University of Scranton *Pennsylvania*
University of South Alabama *Alabama*
University of South Carolina *South Carolina*
University of South Florida *Florida*
University of Southern California *California*
University of Southern Indiana *Indiana*
University of Southern Maine *Maine*
University of Southern Mississippi *Mississippi*
The University of Tennessee *Tennessee*
The University of Tennessee at Chattanooga *Tennessee*
The University of Texas at Arlington *Texas*
The University of Texas at Austin *Texas*
The University of Texas at El Paso *Texas*
The University of Texas Health Science Center at Houston *Texas*
The University of Texas Health Science Center at San Antonio *Texas*
The University of Texas Medical Branch *Texas*
The University of Texas at San Antonio *Texas*
The University of Texas at Tyler *Texas*
The University of Texas–Pan American *Texas*
The University of Toledo *Ohio*
University of Utah *Utah*
University of Vermont *Vermont*
University of Virginia *Virginia*
The University of Virginia's College at Wise *Virginia*
University of Washington *Washington*
University of West Florida *Florida*
University of West Georgia *Georgia*
University of Wisconsin–Eau Claire *Wisconsin*
University of Wisconsin–Madison *Wisconsin*
University of Wisconsin–Milwaukee *Wisconsin*
University of Wisconsin–Oshkosh *Wisconsin*
University of Wyoming *Wyoming*
Ursuline College *Ohio*
Valdosta State University *Georgia*
Valparaiso University *Indiana*
Villanova University *Pennsylvania*
Viterbo University *Wisconsin*
Walden University *Minnesota*
Washburn University *Kansas*
Washington State University *Washington*
Wayne State University *Michigan*
Waynesburg University *Pennsylvania*
West Chester University of Pennsylvania *Pennsylvania*
West Suburban College of Nursing *Illinois*
West Texas A&M University *Texas*
West Virginia University *West Virginia*
Western Carolina University *North Carolina*
Western Connecticut State University *Connecticut*
Western Kentucky University *Kentucky*
Western Michigan University *Michigan*
Westminster College *Utah*
Wheeling Jesuit University *West Virginia*
Wichita State University *Kansas*
Widener University *Pennsylvania*
Wilkes University *Pennsylvania*
William Carey University *Mississippi*
William Jewell College *Missouri*
William Paterson University of New Jersey *New Jersey*
Wilmington University *Delaware*
Winona State University *Minnesota*
Winston-Salem State University *North Carolina*
Worcester State College *Massachusetts*
Wright State University *Ohio*
Xavier University *Ohio*
Yale University *Connecticut*
York College of Pennsylvania *Pennsylvania*

American Association of Family and Consumer Sciences (AAFCS)

Abilene Christian University *Texas*
Alabama Agricultural and Mechanical University *Alabama*
Alcorn State University *Mississippi*
Appalachian State University *North Carolina*
Ashland University *Ohio*
Auburn University *Alabama*
Ball State University *Indiana*
Baylor University *Texas*
Berea College *Kentucky*
Berry College *Georgia*
Bowling Green State University *Ohio*
Bradley University *Illinois*
California State University, Fresno *California*
California State University, Long Beach *California*
California State University, Northridge *California*

Carson-Newman College *Tennessee*
Chadron State College *Nebraska*
College of Saint Elizabeth *New Jersey*
Colorado State University *Colorado*
Concordia College *Minnesota*
Cornell University *New York*
Delta State University *Mississippi*
East Carolina University *North Carolina*
East Tennessee State University *Tennessee*
Eastern Illinois University *Illinois*
Eastern Kentucky University *Kentucky*
Eastern New Mexico University *New Mexico*
Fairmont State University *West Virginia*
Florida State University *Florida*
Fontbonne University *Missouri*
Fort Valley State University *Georgia*
Framingham State College *Massachusetts*
Georgia Southern University *Georgia*
Harding University *Arkansas*
Henderson State University *Arkansas*
Illinois State University *Illinois*
Indiana State University *Indiana*
Indiana University of Pennsylvania *Pennsylvania*
Iowa State University of Science and Technology *Iowa*
Jacksonville State University *Alabama*
Kansas State University *Kansas*
Lamar University *Texas*
Liberty University *Virginia*
Louisiana State University and Agricultural and Mechanical College *Louisiana*
Louisiana Tech University *Louisiana*
Marshall University *West Virginia*
Marygrove College *Michigan*
Marywood University *Pennsylvania*
The Master's College and Seminary *California*
McNeese State University *Louisiana*
Mercyhurst College *Pennsylvania*
Meredith College *North Carolina*
Michigan State University *Michigan*
Middle Tennessee State University *Tennessee*
Mississippi College *Mississippi*
Mississippi State University *Mississippi*
Missouri State University *Missouri*
Montana State University *Montana*
Montclair State University *New Jersey*
Morehead State University *Kentucky*
Murray State University *Kentucky*
New Mexico State University *New Mexico*
Nicholls State University *Louisiana*
North Carolina Agricultural and Technical State University *North Carolina*
North Carolina Central University *North Carolina*
North Dakota State University *North Dakota*
Northern Illinois University *Illinois*
Northwest Missouri State University *Missouri*
Northwestern State University of Louisiana *Louisiana*
The Ohio State University *Ohio*
Ohio University *Ohio*
Olivet Nazarene University *Illinois*
Oregon State University *Oregon*
Ouachita Baptist University *Arkansas*
Pittsburg State University *Kansas*
Point Loma Nazarene University *California*
Purdue University *Indiana*
Queens College of the City University of New York *New York*
Saint Joseph College *Connecticut*
St. Olaf College *Minnesota*
Sam Houston State University *Texas*
Samford University *Alabama*
San Francisco State University *California*
Seattle Pacific University *Washington*
Seton Hill University *Pennsylvania*
South Carolina State University *South Carolina*
South Dakota State University *South Dakota*
Southern University and Agricultural and Mechanical College *Louisiana*
Southern Utah University *Utah*
State University of New York College at Oneonta *New York*
Stephen F. Austin State University *Texas*
Tarleton State University *Texas*
Tennessee State University *Tennessee*
Tennessee Technological University *Tennessee*
Texas A&M University *Texas*
Texas State University–San Marcos *Texas*
Texas Tech University *Texas*
Texas Woman's University *Texas*
Tuskegee University *Alabama*
The University of Akron *Ohio*
The University of Alabama *Alabama*
The University of Arizona *Arizona*
University of Arkansas *Arkansas*
University of Arkansas at Pine Bluff *Arkansas*
University of Central Arkansas *Arkansas*
University of Central Missouri *Missouri*
University of Florida *Florida*
University of Georgia *Georgia*
University of Idaho *Idaho*
University of Kentucky *Kentucky*
University of Louisiana at Lafayette *Louisiana*
University of Louisiana at Monroe *Louisiana*
University of Maryland Eastern Shore *Maryland*
University of Massachusetts Amherst *Massachusetts*
University of Memphis *Tennessee*
University of Mississippi *Mississippi*
University of Missouri *Missouri*
University of Montevallo *Alabama*
University of Nebraska at Kearney *Nebraska*
University of Nebraska–Lincoln *Nebraska*
University of New Mexico *New Mexico*
University of North Alabama *Alabama*
The University of North Carolina at Greensboro *North Carolina*
University of North Texas *Texas*
University of Northern Iowa *Iowa*
University of Southern Mississippi *Mississippi*
The University of Tennessee *Tennessee*
The University of Tennessee at Martin *Tennessee*
University of Wisconsin–Madison *Wisconsin*
University of Wyoming *Wyoming*
Virginia Polytechnic Institute and State University *Virginia*
Wayne State College *Nebraska*
West Virginia Wesleyan College *West Virginia*
Western Carolina University *North Carolina*
Western Illinois University *Illinois*
Western Kentucky University *Kentucky*
Western Michigan University *Michigan*
Youngstown State University *Ohio*

American Association for Marriage and Family Therapy (AAMFT)

Abilene Christian University *Texas*
Alliant International University *California*
Appalachian State University *North Carolina*
Auburn University *Alabama*
Brigham Young University *Utah*
Central Connecticut State University *Connecticut*
Chapman University *California*
Colorado State University *Colorado*
Converse College *South Carolina*
Drexel University *Pennsylvania*
East Carolina University *North Carolina*
Fairfield University *Connecticut*
Florida State University *Florida*
Friends University *Kansas*
Gonzaga University *Washington*
Harding University *Arkansas*
Indiana State University *Indiana*
Iona College *New York*
Iowa State University of Science and Technology *Iowa*
Kansas State University *Kansas*
Loma Linda University *California*
Mercer University *Georgia*
Michigan State University *Michigan*
North Dakota State University *North Dakota*
Northern Illinois University *Illinois*
Northwestern University *Illinois*
Nova Southeastern University *Florida*
The Ohio State University *Ohio*
Oklahoma State University *Oklahoma*
Pacific Lutheran University *Washington*
Purdue University *Indiana*
Purdue University Calumet *Indiana*
St. Cloud State University *Minnesota*
Saint Joseph College *Connecticut*
St. Mary's University *Texas*
Seattle Pacific University *Washington*
Seton Hall University *New Jersey*
Seton Hill University *Pennsylvania*
Southern Connecticut State University *Connecticut*
Syracuse University *New York*
Texas Tech University *Texas*
The University of Akron *Ohio*
University of Connecticut *Connecticut*
University of Georgia *Georgia*
University of Guelph *Ontario*
University of Houston–Clear Lake *Texas*
University of Kentucky *Kentucky*
University of Louisiana at Monroe *Louisiana*
University of Louisville *Kentucky*
University of Maryland, College Park *Maryland*
University of Massachusetts Boston *Massachusetts*
University of Minnesota, Twin Cities Campus *Minnesota*
University of Nebraska–Lincoln *Nebraska*
University of Nevada, Las Vegas *Nevada*
University of New Hampshire *New Hampshire*
University of Rhode Island *Rhode Island*
University of Rochester *New York*
University of San Diego *California*
University of Southern Mississippi *Mississippi*
The University of Winnipeg *Manitoba*
University of Wisconsin–Stout *Wisconsin*
Utah State University *Utah*
Valdosta State University *Georgia*
Virginia Polytechnic Institute and State University *Virginia*

American Association of Medical Assistants' Endowment (AAMAE)

Alpena Community College *Michigan*
Argosy University, Twin Cities *Minnesota*
Arkansas Tech University *Arkansas*
ASA Institute, The College of Advanced Technology *New York*
Baker College of Auburn Hills *Michigan*
Baker College of Cadillac *Michigan*
Baker College of Clinton Township *Michigan*
Baker College of Flint *Michigan*
Baker College of Jackson *Michigan*
Baker College of Muskegon *Michigan*
Baker College of Owosso *Michigan*
Baker College of Port Huron *Michigan*
Beal College *Maine*
Belmont Technical College *Ohio*
Bergen Community College *New Jersey*
Berks Technical Institute *Pennsylvania*
Bossier Parish Community College *Louisiana*
Broome Community College *New York*
Brown Mackie College–Akron *Ohio*
Brown Mackie College–Cincinnati *Ohio*
Brown Mackie College–South Bend *Indiana*
Bryant & Stratton College *Wisconsin*
Bryant & Stratton College - Albany Campus *New York*
Bryant & Stratton College - Buffalo Campus *New York*
Bryant & Stratton College - Greece Campus *New York*
Bryant & Stratton College - Henrietta Campus *New York*
Bryant & Stratton College - Syracuse Campus *New York*
The Bryman School of Arizona *Arizona*
Bucks County Community College *Pennsylvania*
Cabrillo College *California*
Capital Community College *Connecticut*
Career Training Academy (Monroeville) *Pennsylvania*
Career Training Academy (New Kensington) *Pennsylvania*
Central Community College–Hastings Campus *Nebraska*
Central Pennsylvania College *Pennsylvania*
Central Piedmont Community College *North Carolina*
Chabot College *California*
Charles Drew University of Medicine and Science *California*
Cincinnati State Technical and Community College *Ohio*
Cisco College *Texas*

American Association of Nurse Anesthetists (AANA)

Rush University *Illinois*
Saint Joseph's University *Pennsylvania*
Saint Mary's University of Minnesota *Minnesota*
Samford University *Alabama*
Samuel Merritt University *California*
Southern Connecticut State University *Connecticut*
Southern Illinois University Edwardsville *Illinois*
State University of New York Downstate Medical Center *New York*
Texas Christian University *Texas*
Texas Wesleyan University *Texas*
Thomas Jefferson University *Pennsylvania*
Union University *Tennessee*
The University of Akron *Ohio*
The University of Alabama at Birmingham *Alabama*
University at Buffalo, the State University of New York *New York*
University of Cincinnati *Ohio*
University of Detroit Mercy *Michigan*
The University of Iowa *Iowa*
The University of Kansas *Kansas*
University of Miami *Florida*
University of Michigan–Flint *Michigan*
University of Minnesota, Twin Cities Campus *Minnesota*
University of Missouri–Kansas City *Missouri*
University of New England *Maine*
The University of North Carolina at Charlotte *North Carolina*
The University of North Carolina at Greensboro *North Carolina*
University of North Dakota *North Dakota*
University of North Florida *Florida*
University of Pennsylvania *Pennsylvania*
University of Pittsburgh *Pennsylvania*
University of Puerto Rico, Medical Sciences Campus *Puerto Rico*
The University of Scranton *Pennsylvania*
University of South Carolina *South Carolina*
University of South Florida *Florida*
University of Southern California *California*
The University of Tennessee *Tennessee*
The University of Tennessee at Chattanooga *Tennessee*
The University of Texas Health Science Center at Houston *Texas*
University of Wisconsin–La Crosse *Wisconsin*
Villanova University *Pennsylvania*
Virginia Commonwealth University *Virginia*
Wake Forest University *North Carolina*
Wayne State University *Michigan*
Webster University *Missouri*
Western Carolina University *North Carolina*
Westminster College *Utah*
Xavier University of Louisiana *Louisiana*
York College of Pennsylvania *Pennsylvania*
Youngstown State University *Ohio*

American Bar Association (ABA)

American University *District of Columbia*
Arizona State University *Arizona*
Barry University *Florida*
Baylor University *Texas*
Boston College *Massachusetts*
Boston University *Massachusetts*
Brigham Young University *Utah*
Campbell University *North Carolina*
Capital University *Ohio*
Case Western Reserve University *Ohio*
The Catholic University of America *District of Columbia*
Chapman University *California*
Cleveland State University *Ohio*
The College of William and Mary *Virginia*
Columbia University *New York*
Cornell University *New York*
Creighton University *Nebraska*
DePaul University *Illinois*
Drake University *Iowa*
Duke University *North Carolina*
Duquesne University *Pennsylvania*
Elon University *North Carolina*
Emory University *Georgia*
Faulkner University *Alabama*
Florida Agricultural and Mechanical University *Florida*
Florida International University *Florida*
Florida State University *Florida*
Fordham University *New York*
George Mason University *Virginia*
The George Washington University *District of Columbia*
Georgetown University *District of Columbia*
Georgia State University *Georgia*
Golden Gate University *California*
Gonzaga University *Washington*
Hamline University *Minnesota*
Harvard University *Massachusetts*
Hofstra University *New York*
Howard University *District of Columbia*
Illinois Institute of Technology *Illinois*
Indiana University Bloomington *Indiana*
Indiana University–Purdue University Indianapolis *Indiana*
Inter American University of Puerto Rico, Metropolitan Campus *Puerto Rico*
Lewis & Clark College *Oregon*
Liberty University *Virginia*
Louisiana State University and Agricultural and Mechanical College *Louisiana*
Loyola Marymount University *California*
Loyola University Chicago *Illinois*
Loyola University New Orleans *Louisiana*
Marquette University *Wisconsin*
Mercer University *Georgia*
Mississippi College *Mississippi*
New York University *New York*
North Carolina Central University *North Carolina*
Northeastern University *Massachusetts*
Northern Illinois University *Illinois*
Northern Kentucky University *Kentucky*
Northwestern University *Illinois*
Nova Southeastern University *Florida*
Ohio Northern University *Ohio*
The Ohio State University *Ohio*
Oklahoma City University *Oklahoma*
Pace University *New York*
Pepperdine University *California*
Pontifical Catholic University of Puerto Rico *Puerto Rico*
Quinnipiac University *Connecticut*
Regent University *Virginia*
Roger Williams University *Rhode Island*
Rutgers, The State University of New Jersey, Camden *New Jersey*
Rutgers, The State University of New Jersey, Newark *New Jersey*
St. John's University *New York*
Saint Louis University *Missouri*
St. Mary's University *Texas*
St. Thomas University *Florida*
Samford University *Alabama*
Santa Clara University *California*
Seattle University *Washington*
Seton Hall University *New Jersey*
Southern Illinois University Carbondale *Illinois*
Southern Methodist University *Texas*
Southern University and Agricultural and Mechanical College *Louisiana*
Stanford University *California*
Stetson University *Florida*
Suffolk University *Massachusetts*
Syracuse University *New York*
Temple University *Pennsylvania*
Texas Southern University *Texas*
Texas Tech University *Texas*
Texas Wesleyan University *Texas*
Touro College *New York*
Tulane University *Louisiana*
The University of Akron *Ohio*
The University of Alabama *Alabama*
The University of Arizona *Arizona*
University of Arkansas *Arkansas*
University of Arkansas at Little Rock *Arkansas*
University of Baltimore *Maryland*
University at Buffalo, the State University of New York *New York*
University of California, Berkeley *California*
University of California, Davis *California*
University of California, Los Angeles *California*
University of Chicago *Illinois*
University of Cincinnati *Ohio*
University of Colorado at Boulder *Colorado*
University of Connecticut *Connecticut*
University of Dayton *Ohio*
University of Denver *Colorado*
University of Detroit Mercy *Michigan*
University of the District of Columbia *District of Columbia*
University of Florida *Florida*
University of Georgia *Georgia*
University of Hawaii at Manoa *Hawaii*
University of Houston *Texas*
University of Idaho *Idaho*
University of Illinois at Urbana–Champaign *Illinois*
The University of Iowa *Iowa*
The University of Kansas *Kansas*
University of Kentucky *Kentucky*
University of La Verne *California*
University of Louisville *Kentucky*
University of Memphis *Tennessee*
University of Miami *Florida*
University of Michigan *Michigan*
University of Minnesota, Twin Cities Campus *Minnesota*
University of Mississippi *Mississippi*
University of Missouri *Missouri*
University of Missouri–Kansas City *Missouri*
The University of Montana *Montana*
University of Nebraska–Lincoln *Nebraska*
University of Nevada, Las Vegas *Nevada*
University of New Mexico *New Mexico*
The University of North Carolina at Chapel Hill *North Carolina*
University of North Dakota *North Dakota*
University of Notre Dame *Indiana*
University of Oklahoma *Oklahoma*
University of Oregon *Oregon*
University of the Pacific *California*
University of Pennsylvania *Pennsylvania*
University of Pittsburgh *Pennsylvania*
University of Puerto Rico, Río Piedras *Puerto Rico*
University of Richmond *Virginia*
University of St. Thomas *Minnesota*
University of San Diego *California*
University of San Francisco *California*
University of South Carolina *South Carolina*
The University of South Dakota *South Dakota*
University of Southern California *California*
University of Southern Maine *Maine*
The University of Tennessee *Tennessee*
The University of Texas at Austin *Texas*
The University of Toledo *Ohio*
University of Tulsa *Oklahoma*
University of Utah *Utah*
University of Virginia *Virginia*
University of Washington *Washington*
University of Wisconsin–Madison *Wisconsin*
University of Wyoming *Wyoming*
Valparaiso University *Indiana*
Vanderbilt University *Tennessee*
Villanova University *Pennsylvania*
Wake Forest University *North Carolina*
Washburn University *Kansas*
Washington and Lee University *Virginia*
Washington University in St. Louis *Missouri*
Wayne State University *Michigan*
West Virginia University *West Virginia*
Western New England College *Massachusetts*
Whittier College *California*
Widener University *Pennsylvania*
Willamette University *Oregon*
Yale University *Connecticut*
Yeshiva University *New York*

American Board of Funeral Service Education (ABFSE)

Amarillo College *Texas*
American Academy McAllister Institute of Funeral Service *New York*
American River College *California*
Arapahoe Community College *Colorado*
Arkansas State University–Mountain Home *Arkansas*
Bishop State Community College *Alabama*
Carl Sandburg College *Illinois*
Cincinnati College of Mortuary Science *Ohio*
City Colleges of Chicago, Malcolm X College *Illinois*

Commonwealth Institute of Funeral Service *Texas*
The Community College of Baltimore County *Maryland*
Cypress College *California*
Dallas Institute of Funeral Service *Texas*
Delgado Community College *Louisiana*
East Mississippi Community College *Mississippi*
Fayetteville Technical Community College *North Carolina*
Florida State College at Jacksonville *Florida*
Gupton-Jones College of Funeral Service *Georgia*
Hudson Valley Community College *New York*
Jefferson State Community College *Alabama*
John A. Gupton College *Tennessee*
John Tyler Community College *Virginia*
Kansas City Kansas Community College *Kansas*
Lincoln College of New England (Southington) *Connecticut*
Mercer County Community College *New Jersey*
Mesa Community College *Arizona*
Miami Dade College *Florida*
Mid-America College of Funeral Service *Indiana*
Milwaukee Area Technical College *Wisconsin*
Mississippi Gulf Coast Community College *Mississippi*
Mt. Hood Community College *Oregon*
Mount Ida College *Massachusetts*
Nassau Community College *New York*
Norfolk State University *Virginia*
Northampton Community College *Pennsylvania*
Northwest Mississippi Community College *Mississippi*
Ogeechee Technical College *Georgia*
Piedmont Technical College *South Carolina*
Pittsburgh Institute of Mortuary Science, Incorporated *Pennsylvania*
St. Louis Community College at Forest Park *Missouri*
St. Petersburg College *Florida*
San Antonio College *Texas*
Simmons Institute of Funeral Service *New York*
Southern Illinois University Carbondale *Illinois*
State University of New York College of Technology at Canton *New York*
University of Arkansas Community College at Hope *Arkansas*
University of Central Oklahoma *Oklahoma*
University of the District of Columbia *District of Columbia*
University of Minnesota, Twin Cities Campus *Minnesota*
Vincennes University *Indiana*
Wayne State University *Michigan*
Worsham College of Mortuary Science *Illinois*

American College of Nurse-Midwives (ACNM)

Boston University *Massachusetts*
California State University, Fullerton *California*
Case Western Reserve University *Ohio*
Charles Drew University of Medicine and Science *California*
Columbia University *New York*
East Carolina University *North Carolina*
Emory University *Georgia*
Georgetown University *District of Columbia*
Marquette University *Wisconsin*
Medical University of South Carolina *South Carolina*
New York University *New York*
The Ohio State University *Ohio*
Oregon Health & Science University *Oregon*
Philadelphia University *Pennsylvania*
San Diego State University *California*
Shenandoah University *Virginia*
State University of New York Downstate Medical Center *New York*
Stony Brook University, State University of New York *New York*
University of Cincinnati *Ohio*
University of Colorado Denver *Colorado*
University of Florida *Florida*
University of Illinois at Chicago *Illinois*
University of Indianapolis *Indiana*
The University of Kansas *Kansas*
University of Miami *Florida*
University of Michigan *Michigan*
University of Minnesota, Twin Cities Campus *Minnesota*
University of New Mexico *New Mexico*
University of Pennsylvania *Pennsylvania*
University of Puerto Rico, Medical Sciences Campus *Puerto Rico*
University of Rhode Island *Rhode Island*
The University of Texas at El Paso *Texas*
The University of Texas Medical Branch *Texas*
The University of Texas Southwestern Medical Center at Dallas *Texas*
University of Utah *Utah*
University of Washington *Washington*
Vanderbilt University *Tennessee*
Wayne State University *Michigan*
Yale University *Connecticut*

American Council for Construction Education (ACCE)

Arizona State University *Arizona*
Auburn University *Alabama*
Boise State University *Idaho*
Bowling Green State University *Ohio*
Bradley University *Illinois*
Brigham Young University *Utah*
California Polytechnic State University, San Luis Obispo *California*
California State University, Chico *California*
California State University, Fresno *California*
California State University, Sacramento *California*
Central Connecticut State University *Connecticut*
Central New Mexico Community College *New Mexico*
Central Washington University *Washington*
Cincinnati State Technical and Community College *Ohio*
Clemson University *South Carolina*
Colorado State University *Colorado*
Columbus State Community College *Ohio*
East Carolina University *North Carolina*
Eastern Kentucky University *Kentucky*
Eastern Michigan University *Michigan*
Ferris State University *Michigan*
Florida International University *Florida*
Georgia Institute of Technology *Georgia*
Georgia Southern University *Georgia*
Hudson Valley Community College *New York*
Indiana State University *Indiana*
Jefferson State Community College *Alabama*
John A. Logan College *Illinois*
John Brown University *Arkansas*
Kansas State University *Kansas*
Louisiana State University and Agricultural and Mechanical College *Louisiana*
Michigan State University *Michigan*
Milwaukee School of Engineering *Wisconsin*
Minnesota State University Moorhead *Minnesota*
North Carolina Agricultural and Technical State University *North Carolina*
North Dakota State University *North Dakota*
North Lake College *Texas*
Northern Arizona University *Arizona*
Northern Kentucky University *Kentucky*
Oregon State University *Oregon*
Purdue University *Indiana*
Roger Williams University *Rhode Island*
Santa Fe College *Florida*
Southern Illinois University Edwardsville *Illinois*
Southern Polytechnic State University *Georgia*
State University of New York College of Technology at Alfred *New York*
State University of New York College of Technology at Delhi *New York*
Texas A&M University *Texas*
University of Arkansas at Little Rock *Arkansas*
University of Central Missouri *Missouri*
University of Cincinnati *Ohio*
University of Florida *Florida*
University of Louisiana at Monroe *Louisiana*
University of Maryland Eastern Shore *Maryland*
University of Nebraska–Lincoln *Nebraska*
University of Nevada, Las Vegas *Nevada*
University of New Mexico *New Mexico*
University of North Florida *Florida*
University of Oklahoma *Oklahoma*
University of Southern Mississippi *Mississippi*
University of Washington *Washington*
University of Wisconsin–Stout *Wisconsin*
Virginia Polytechnic Institute and State University *Virginia*
Washington State University *Washington*
Wentworth Institute of Technology *Massachusetts*

American Counseling Association (ACA)

Adams State College *Colorado*
Andrews University *Michigan*
Appalachian State University *North Carolina*
Argosy University, Schaumburg *Illinois*
Arizona State University *Arizona*
Arkansas State University - Jonesboro *Arkansas*
Auburn University *Alabama*
Augusta State University *Georgia*
Ball State University *Indiana*
Barry University *Florida*
Boise State University *Idaho*
Bradley University *Illinois*
Bridgewater State College *Massachusetts*
Brigham Young University *Utah*
Butler University *Indiana*
California Polytechnic State University, San Luis Obispo *California*
California State University, Fresno *California*
California State University, Fullerton *California*
California State University, Los Angeles *California*
California State University, Northridge *California*
California State University, Sacramento *California*
California University of Pennsylvania *Pennsylvania*
Canisius College *New York*
Capella University *Minnesota*
Central Washington University *Washington*
Chicago State University *Illinois*
The Citadel, The Military College of South Carolina *South Carolina*
Clemson University *South Carolina*
Cleveland State University *Ohio*
The College at Brockport, State University of New York *New York*
The College of New Jersey *New Jersey*
The College of William and Mary *Virginia*
Colorado State University *Colorado*
Columbus State University *Georgia*
Concordia University Chicago *Illinois*
Delta State University *Mississippi*
Duquesne University *Pennsylvania*
East Tennessee State University *Tennessee*
Eastern Illinois University *Illinois*
Eastern Kentucky University *Kentucky*
Eastern Mennonite University *Virginia*
Eastern Michigan University *Michigan*
Eastern Washington University *Washington*
Edinboro University of Pennsylvania *Pennsylvania*
Emporia State University *Kansas*
Fairfield University *Connecticut*
Florida Atlantic University *Florida*
Florida Gulf Coast University *Florida*
Florida International University *Florida*
Florida State University *Florida*
Gallaudet University *District of Columbia*
Gannon University *Pennsylvania*
Gardner-Webb University *North Carolina*
Geneva College *Pennsylvania*
The George Washington University *District of Columbia*
Georgia Southern University *Georgia*
Georgia State University *Georgia*
Gonzaga University *Washington*
Governors State University *Illinois*
Grace College *Indiana*
Henderson State University *Arkansas*
Idaho State University *Idaho*
Illinois State University *Illinois*
Indiana State University *Indiana*
Indiana University Bloomington *Indiana*
Indiana University of Pennsylvania *Pennsylvania*
Indiana University South Bend *Indiana*
Indiana Wesleyan University *Indiana*
Jackson State University *Mississippi*
James Madison University *Virginia*
John Carroll University *Ohio*
Kansas State University *Kansas*
Kean University *New Jersey*

Kent State University *Ohio*
Lehman College of the City University of New York *New York*
Lindsey Wilson College *Kentucky*
Long Island University, C.W. Post Campus *New York*
Louisiana State University and Agricultural and Mechanical College *Louisiana*
Loyola University Maryland *Maryland*
Loyola University New Orleans *Louisiana*
Lynchburg College *Virginia*
Marymount University *Virginia*
Marywood University *Pennsylvania*
Middle Tennessee State University *Tennessee*
Minnesota State University Mankato *Minnesota*
Minnesota State University Moorhead *Minnesota*
Mississippi College *Mississippi*
Mississippi State University *Mississippi*
Monmouth University *New Jersey*
Montana State University *Montana*
Murray State University *Kentucky*
New Mexico State University *New Mexico*
North Carolina Agricultural and Technical State University *North Carolina*
North Carolina Central University *North Carolina*
North Carolina State University *North Carolina*
North Dakota State University *North Dakota*
Northeastern Illinois University *Illinois*
Northern Arizona University *Arizona*
Northern Illinois University *Illinois*
Northwest Nazarene University *Idaho*
Northwestern State University of Louisiana *Louisiana*
Oakland University *Michigan*
Ohio University *Ohio*
Old Dominion University *Virginia*
Oregon State University *Oregon*
Our Lady of Holy Cross College *Louisiana*
Penn State University Park *Pennsylvania*
Pittsburg State University *Kansas*
Plymouth State University *New Hampshire*
Portland State University *Oregon*
Purdue University *Indiana*
Radford University *Virginia*
Regent University *Virginia*
Regis University *Colorado*
Rider University *New Jersey*
Rollins College *Florida*
Roosevelt University *Illinois*
St. Bonaventure University *New York*
St. Cloud State University *Minnesota*
St. John Fisher College *New York*
St. John's University *New York*
St. Mary's University *Texas*
San Francisco State University *California*
Shippensburg University of Pennsylvania *Pennsylvania*
Slippery Rock University of Pennsylvania *Pennsylvania*
Sonoma State University *California*
South Carolina State University *South Carolina*
South Dakota State University *South Dakota*
Southeast Missouri State University *Missouri*
Southeastern Louisiana University *Louisiana*
Southern Connecticut State University *Connecticut*
Southern Illinois University Carbondale *Illinois*
Southern University and Agricultural and Mechanical College *Louisiana*
State University of New York at Plattsburgh *New York*
Stephen F. Austin State University *Texas*
Stetson University *Florida*
Syracuse University *New York*
Texas A&M University–Commerce *Texas*
Texas A&M University–Corpus Christi *Texas*
Texas State University–San Marcos *Texas*
Texas Tech University *Texas*
Texas Woman's University *Texas*
Trinity Western University *British Columbia*
Troy University *Alabama*
Truman State University *Missouri*
The University of Akron *Ohio*
The University of Alabama *Alabama*
University of Arkansas *Arkansas*
The University of British Columbia *British Columbia*
University of Central Florida *Florida*
University of Cincinnati *Ohio*
University of Colorado at Colorado Springs *Colorado*
University of Colorado Denver *Colorado*
University of Connecticut *Connecticut*
University of Detroit Mercy *Michigan*
University of Florida *Florida*
University of Georgia *Georgia*
University of Hawaii at Manoa *Hawaii*
University of Idaho *Idaho*
University of Illinois at Springfield *Illinois*
The University of Iowa *Iowa*
University of Louisiana at Monroe *Louisiana*
University of Maryland, College Park *Maryland*
University of Memphis *Tennessee*
University of Minnesota, Duluth *Minnesota*
University of Mississippi *Mississippi*
University of Missouri–St. Louis *Missouri*
The University of Montana *Montana*
University of Montevallo *Alabama*
University of Nebraska at Kearney *Nebraska*
University of Nebraska at Omaha *Nebraska*
University of Nevada, Las Vegas *Nevada*
University of Nevada, Reno *Nevada*
University of New Mexico *New Mexico*
University of New Orleans *Louisiana*
University of North Alabama *Alabama*
The University of North Carolina at Chapel Hill *North Carolina*
The University of North Carolina at Charlotte *North Carolina*
The University of North Carolina at Greensboro *North Carolina*
University of North Florida *Florida*
University of North Texas *Texas*
University of Northern Colorado *Colorado*
University of Northern Iowa *Iowa*
University of Phoenix–Phoenix Campus *Arizona*
University of Phoenix–Southern Arizona Campus *Arizona*
University of Phoenix–Utah Campus *Utah*
University of Pittsburgh *Pennsylvania*
University of Rochester *New York*
The University of Scranton *Pennsylvania*
University of South Carolina *South Carolina*
The University of South Dakota *South Dakota*
University of South Florida *Florida*
University of Southern Maine *Maine*
University of Southern Mississippi *Mississippi*
The University of Tennessee *Tennessee*
The University of Tennessee at Chattanooga *Tennessee*
The University of Toledo *Ohio*
University of Vermont *Vermont*
University of Virginia *Virginia*
University of West Georgia *Georgia*
University of Wisconsin–Oshkosh *Wisconsin*
University of Wisconsin–Superior *Wisconsin*
University of Wisconsin–Whitewater *Wisconsin*
University of Wyoming *Wyoming*
Vanderbilt University *Tennessee*
Virginia Commonwealth University *Virginia*
Virginia Polytechnic Institute and State University *Virginia*
Wake Forest University *North Carolina*
Walsh University *Ohio*
Wayne State University *Michigan*
West Chester University of Pennsylvania *Pennsylvania*
West Virginia University *West Virginia*
Western Carolina University *North Carolina*
Western Connecticut State University *Connecticut*
Western Illinois University *Illinois*
Western Kentucky University *Kentucky*
Western Michigan University *Michigan*
Western Washington University *Washington*
William Paterson University of New Jersey *New Jersey*
Wilmington University *Delaware*
Winona State University *Minnesota*
Winthrop University *South Carolina*
Wright State University *Ohio*
Xavier University *Ohio*
Youngstown State University *Ohio*

American Culinary Federation, Inc. (ACF)

Anne Arundel Community College *Maryland*
The Art Institute of Atlanta *Georgia*
The Art Institute of Colorado *Colorado*
The Art Institute of Dallas *Texas*
The Art Institute of Fort Lauderdale *Florida*
The Art Institute of Houston *Texas*
The Art Institute of New York City *New York*
The Art Institute of Philadelphia *Pennsylvania*
The Art Institute of Seattle *Washington*
The Art Institutes International Minnesota *Minnesota*
Austin Community College *Texas*
Baker College of Muskegon *Michigan*
Bellingham Technical College *Washington*
Bishop State Community College *Alabama*
Blackhawk Technical College *Wisconsin*
Boise State University *Idaho*
Bossier Parish Community College *Louisiana*
California Culinary Academy *California*
Central New Mexico Community College *New Mexico*
Central Oregon Community College *Oregon*
Chattahoochee Technical College *Georgia*
Cincinnati State Technical and Community College *Ohio*
City College of San Francisco *California*
College of DuPage *Illinois*
College of Southern Nevada *Nevada*
Columbia College *California*
Columbus State Community College *Ohio*
Cuyahoga Community College *Ohio*
Del Mar College *Texas*
Delgado Community College *Louisiana*
Des Moines Area Community College *Iowa*
Diablo Valley College *California*
Elgin Community College *Illinois*
Florida Culinary Institute *Florida*
Florida State College at Jacksonville *Florida*
Fox Valley Technical College *Wisconsin*
Grand Rapids Community College *Michigan*
Greenville Technical College *South Carolina*
Guilford Technical Community College *North Carolina*
Gulf Coast Community College *Florida*
Hennepin Technical College *Minnesota*
Henry Ford Community College *Michigan*
Hillsborough Community College *Florida*
Hocking College *Ohio*
Horry-Georgetown Technical College *South Carolina*
Hudson County Community College *New Jersey*
Idaho State University *Idaho*
The Illinois Institute of Art–Chicago *Illinois*
Indian Hills Community College *Iowa*
Indiana University of Pennsylvania *Pennsylvania*
Iowa Western Community College *Iowa*
Ivy Tech Community College–Central Indiana *Indiana*
Ivy Tech Community College–North Central *Indiana*
Ivy Tech Community College–Northeast *Indiana*
Ivy Tech Community College–Northwest *Indiana*
James H. Faulkner State Community College *Alabama*
Jefferson Community and Technical College *Kentucky*
Jefferson State Community College *Alabama*
Johnson County Community College *Kansas*
Joliet Junior College *Illinois*
Kapiolani Community College *Hawaii*
Kendall College *Illinois*
Kirkwood Community College *Iowa*
Lake Washington Technical College *Washington*
Lamar University *Texas*
Le Cordon Bleu College of Culinary Arts in Chicago *Illinois*
Leeward Community College *Hawaii*
Los Angeles Trade-Technical College *California*
Macomb Community College *Michigan*
Madison Area Technical College *Wisconsin*
Manchester Community College *Connecticut*
Maui Community College *Hawaii*
Metropolitan Community College *Nebraska*
Milwaukee Area Technical College *Wisconsin*
Monroe County Community College *Michigan*
Moraine Park Technical College *Wisconsin*
New York Institute of Technology *New York*

American Dental Association (ADA)

Marquette University *Wisconsin*
Marshalltown Community College *Iowa*
Martin Community College *North Carolina*
Massachusetts College of Pharmacy and Health Sciences *Massachusetts*
Massasoit Community College *Massachusetts*
Maui Community College *Hawaii*
McGill University *Quebec*
Medical College of Georgia *Georgia*
Medical University of South Carolina *South Carolina*
Meridian Community College *Mississippi*
Metropolitan Community College *Nebraska*
Metropolitan Community College–Penn Valley *Missouri*
Miami Dade College *Florida*
Mid-Plains Community College *Nebraska*
Middle Georgia Technical College *Georgia*
Middlesex Community College *Massachusetts*
Middlesex County College *New Jersey*
Midlands Technical College *South Carolina*
Midwestern State University *Texas*
Milwaukee Area Technical College *Wisconsin*
Minneapolis Community and Technical College *Minnesota*
Minnesota State University Mankato *Minnesota*
Minnesota West Community and Technical College *Minnesota*
Mississippi Delta Community College *Mississippi*
Missouri College *Missouri*
Missouri Southern State University *Missouri*
Modesto Junior College *California*
Monroe Community College *New York*
Montana State University–Great Falls College of Technology *Montana*
Monterey Peninsula College *California*
Montgomery County Community College *Pennsylvania*
Mott Community College *Michigan*
Mt. Hood Community College *Oregon*
Mount Ida College *Massachusetts*
New York City College of Technology of the City University of New York *New York*
New York University *New York*
NHTI, Concord's Community College *New Hampshire*
Normandale Community College *Minnesota*
North Dakota State College of Science *North Dakota*
Northampton Community College *Pennsylvania*
Northcentral Technical College *Wisconsin*
Northeast Mississippi Community College *Mississippi*
Northeast State Technical Community College *Tennessee*
Northeast Wisconsin Technical College *Wisconsin*
Northern Arizona University *Arizona*
Northern Essex Community College *Massachusetts*
Northern Virginia Community College *Virginia*
Northwest Florida State College *Florida*
Northwest Technical College *Minnesota*
Northwestern Michigan College *Michigan*
Nova Southeastern University *Florida*
Oakland Community College *Michigan*
Ogeechee Technical College *Georgia*
The Ohio State University *Ohio*
Old Dominion University *Virginia*
Onondaga Community College *New York*
Orange Coast College *California*
Orange County Community College *New York*
Oregon Health & Science University *Oregon*
Oregon Institute of Technology *Oregon*
Owens Community College *Ohio*
Oxnard College *California*
Ozarks Technical Community College *Missouri*
Palm Beach State College *Florida*
Palomar College *California*
Parkland College *Illinois*
Pasadena City College *California*
Pasco-Hernando Community College *Florida*
Pearl River Community College *Mississippi*
Pennsylvania College of Technology *Pennsylvania*
Pensacola Junior College *Florida*
Phoenix College *Arizona*
Pierce College at Puyallup *Washington*
Pikes Peak Community College *Colorado*
Pima Community College *Arizona*
Portland Community College *Oregon*
Prairie State College *Illinois*
Provo College *Utah*
Pueblo Community College *Colorado*
Pulaski Technical College *Arkansas*
Quinsigamond Community College *Massachusetts*
Renton Technical College *Washington*
Rio Salado College *Arizona*
Riverside Community College District *California*
Roane State Community College *Tennessee*
Rochester Community and Technical College *Minnesota*
Rock Valley College *Illinois*
Rose State College *Oklahoma*
Rowan-Cabarrus Community College *North Carolina*
Sacramento City College *California*
St. Cloud Technical College *Minnesota*
St. Louis Community College at Forest Park *Missouri*
St. Petersburg College *Florida*
Salish Kootenai College *Montana*
Salt Lake Community College *Utah*
San Antonio College *Texas*
San Diego Mesa College *California*
San Joaquin Valley College (Visalia) *California*
San Jose City College *California*
San Juan College *New Mexico*
Santa Fe College *Florida*
Santa Fe Community College *New Mexico*
Santa Rosa Junior College *California*
Savannah Technical College *Georgia*
Scott Community College *Iowa*
Shasta College *California*
Shawnee State University *Ohio*
Sheridan College *Wyoming*
Shoreline Community College *Washington*
Sinclair Community College *Ohio*
South Central College *Minnesota*
South Florida Community College *Florida*
South Puget Sound Community College *Washington*
Southeast Community College, Lincoln Campus *Nebraska*
Southern Illinois University Carbondale *Illinois*
Southern Illinois University Edwardsville *Illinois*
Southern University at Shreveport *Louisiana*
Southwestern College *California*
Spartanburg Community College *South Carolina*
Spokane Community College *Washington*
Springfield Technical Community College *Massachusetts*
Stark State College of Technology *Ohio*
State College of Florida Manatee-Sarasota *Florida*
State Fair Community College *Missouri*
Stony Brook University, State University of New York *New York*
Taft College *California*
Tallahassee Community College *Florida*
Tarrant County College District *Texas*
Temple College *Texas*
Temple University *Pennsylvania*
Tennessee State University *Tennessee*
Texas A&M Health Science Center *Texas*
Texas State Technical College Harlingen *Texas*
Texas State Technical College Waco *Texas*
Texas Woman's University *Texas*
Tri-County Technical College *South Carolina*
Trident Technical College *South Carolina*
Truckee Meadows Community College *Nevada*
Tufts University *Massachusetts*
Tulsa Community College *Oklahoma*
Tunxis Community College *Connecticut*
Tyler Junior College *Texas*
Université Laval *Quebec*
Université de Montréal *Quebec*
The University of Alabama at Birmingham *Alabama*
University of Alaska Anchorage *Alaska*
University of Alberta *Alberta*
University of Arkansas at Fort Smith *Arkansas*
University of Arkansas for Medical Sciences *Arkansas*
University of Bridgeport *Connecticut*
The University of British Columbia *British Columbia*
University at Buffalo, the State University of New York *New York*
University of California, Los Angeles *California*
University of Cincinnati Raymond Walters College *Ohio*
University of Colorado Denver *Colorado*
University of Detroit Mercy *Michigan*
University of Florida *Florida*
University of Hawaii at Manoa *Hawaii*
University of Illinois at Chicago *Illinois*
The University of Iowa *Iowa*
University of Kentucky *Kentucky*
University of Louisiana at Monroe *Louisiana*
University of Louisville *Kentucky*
University of Maine at Augusta *Maine*
University of Manitoba *Manitoba*
University of Michigan *Michigan*
University of Minnesota, Twin Cities Campus *Minnesota*
University of Mississippi Medical Center *Mississippi*
University of Missouri–Kansas City *Missouri*
University of Nebraska Medical Center *Nebraska*
University of Nebraska–Lincoln *Nebraska*
University of Nevada, Las Vegas *Nevada*
University of New England *Maine*
University of New Haven *Connecticut*
University of New Mexico *New Mexico*
University of New Mexico–Gallup *New Mexico*
The University of North Carolina at Chapel Hill *North Carolina*
University of Oklahoma Health Sciences Center *Oklahoma*
University of the Pacific *California*
University of Pennsylvania *Pennsylvania*
University of Pittsburgh *Pennsylvania*
University of Puerto Rico, Medical Sciences Campus *Puerto Rico*
University of Saskatchewan *Saskatchewan*
The University of South Dakota *South Dakota*
University of Southern California *California*
University of Southern Indiana *Indiana*
The University of Texas Health Science Center at Houston *Texas*
The University of Texas Health Science Center at San Antonio *Texas*
University of Toronto *Ontario*
University of Vermont *Vermont*
University of Washington *Washington*
The University of Western Ontario *Ontario*
Utah Valley University *Utah*
Valdosta State University *Georgia*
Valdosta Technical College *Georgia*
Valencia Community College *Florida*
Vet Tech Institute *Pennsylvania*
Virginia Commonwealth University *Virginia*
Virginia Western Community College *Virginia*
Volunteer State Community College *Tennessee*
Wake Technical Community College *North Carolina*
Wallace State Community College *Alabama*
Washtenaw Community College *Michigan*
Waukesha County Technical College *Wisconsin*
Wayne Community College *North Carolina*
Wayne County Community College District *Michigan*
Weber State University *Utah*
West Kentucky Community and Technical College *Kentucky*
West Liberty University *West Virginia*
West Los Angeles College *California*
West Virginia University *West Virginia*
West Virginia University Institute of Technology *West Virginia*
Western Iowa Tech Community College *Iowa*
Western Kentucky University *Kentucky*
Western Piedmont Community College *North Carolina*
Western Technical College *Wisconsin*
Westmoreland County Community College *Pennsylvania*
Wharton County Junior College *Texas*
Wichita Area Technical College *Kansas*
Wichita State University *Kansas*
Wilkes Community College *North Carolina*
Wytheville Community College *Virginia*
Yakima Valley Community College *Washington*
York Technical College *South Carolina*
Youngstown State University *Ohio*

American Dietetic Association (ADtA)

Alcorn State University *Mississippi*
Andrews University *Michigan*
Appalachian State University *North Carolina*
Ball State University *Indiana*
Bastyr University *Washington*
Baylor University *Texas*
Benedictine University *Illinois*
Boston University *Massachusetts*
Bowling Green State University *Ohio*
Brigham Young University *Utah*
Brooklyn College of the City University of New York *New York*
Buffalo State College, State University of New York *New York*
California State Polytechnic University, Pomona *California*
California State University, Chico *California*
California State University, Fresno *California*
California State University, Long Beach *California*
California State University, Los Angeles *California*
California State University, Northridge *California*
California State University, Sacramento *California*
Case Western Reserve University *Ohio*
Central Michigan University *Michigan*
Central Washington University *Washington*
Clemson University *South Carolina*
College of Saint Benedict *Minnesota*
College of Saint Elizabeth *New Jersey*
Colorado State University *Colorado*
Concordia College *Minnesota*
Cornell University *New York*
Delta State University *Mississippi*
D'Youville College *New York*
East Carolina University *North Carolina*
East Tennessee State University *Tennessee*
Eastern Illinois University *Illinois*
Eastern Kentucky University *Kentucky*
Eastern Michigan University *Michigan*
Edinboro University of Pennsylvania *Pennsylvania*
Emory University *Georgia*
Florida International University *Florida*
Florida State University *Florida*
Framingham State College *Massachusetts*
Gannon University *Pennsylvania*
Georgia State University *Georgia*
Goldfarb School of Nursing at Barnes-Jewish College *Missouri*
Harvard University *Massachusetts*
Howard University *District of Columbia*
Hunter College of the City University of New York *New York*
Idaho State University *Idaho*
Illinois State University *Illinois*
Immaculata University *Pennsylvania*
Indiana State University *Indiana*
Indiana University of Pennsylvania *Pennsylvania*
Indiana University–Purdue University Indianapolis *Indiana*
Iowa State University of Science and Technology *Iowa*
James Madison University *Virginia*
The Johns Hopkins University *Maryland*
Kansas State University *Kansas*
Keene State College *New Hampshire*
Kent State University *Ohio*
La Salle University *Pennsylvania*
Lamar University *Texas*
Lehman College of the City University of New York *New York*
Life University *Georgia*
Lipscomb University *Tennessee*
Loma Linda University *California*
Long Island University, C.W. Post Campus *New York*
Louisiana State University and Agricultural and Mechanical College *Louisiana*
Louisiana Tech University *Louisiana*
Loyola University Chicago *Illinois*
Marshall University *West Virginia*
Marywood University *Pennsylvania*
McNeese State University *Louisiana*
Medical University of South Carolina *South Carolina*
Mercyhurst College *Pennsylvania*
Meredith College *North Carolina*
Michigan State University *Michigan*
Mississippi State University *Mississippi*
Montclair State University *New Jersey*
Morehead State University *Kentucky*
Mount Carmel College of Nursing *Ohio*
Mount Marty College *South Dakota*
Mount Mary College *Wisconsin*
Murray State University *Kentucky*
New York Institute of Technology *New York*
New York University *New York*
Nicholls State University *Louisiana*
North Carolina Central University *North Carolina*
North Dakota State University *North Dakota*
Northern Illinois University *Illinois*
Oakwood University *Alabama*
The Ohio State University *Ohio*
Oklahoma State University *Oklahoma*
Oregon Health & Science University *Oregon*
Penn State University Park *Pennsylvania*
Prairie View A&M University *Texas*
Purdue University *Indiana*
Queens College of the City University of New York *New York*
Radford University *Virginia*
Rush University *Illinois*
Saint Joseph College *Connecticut*
Saint Louis University *Missouri*
Sam Houston State University *Texas*
San Diego State University *California*
San Francisco State University *California*
San Jose State University *California*
Seton Hill University *Pennsylvania*
Simmons College *Massachusetts*
Southeast Missouri State University *Missouri*
Southern Illinois University Carbondale *Illinois*
Southern University and Agricultural and Mechanical College *Louisiana*
State University of New York College at Oneonta *New York*
Stephen F. Austin State University *Texas*
Stony Brook University, State University of New York *New York*
Syracuse University *New York*
Texas A&M University *Texas*
Texas A&M University–Kingsville *Texas*
Texas Christian University *Texas*
Texas State University–San Marcos *Texas*
Texas Tech University *Texas*
Texas Woman's University *Texas*
Tufts University *Massachusetts*
Tulane University *Louisiana*
The University of Akron *Ohio*
The University of Alabama *Alabama*
The University of Alabama at Birmingham *Alabama*
University of Alaska Anchorage *Alaska*
The University of Arizona *Arizona*
University of Arkansas for Medical Sciences *Arkansas*
University at Buffalo, the State University of New York *New York*
University of California, Berkeley *California*
University of California, Davis *California*
University of California, Los Angeles *California*
University of Central Arkansas *Arkansas*
University of Central Oklahoma *Oklahoma*
University of Cincinnati *Ohio*
University of Connecticut *Connecticut*
University of Delaware *Delaware*
University of Florida *Florida*
University of Georgia *Georgia*
University of Houston *Texas*
University of Idaho *Idaho*
University of Illinois at Chicago *Illinois*
University of Illinois at Urbana–Champaign *Illinois*
University of the Incarnate Word *Texas*
The University of Iowa *Iowa*
The University of Kansas *Kansas*
University of Kentucky *Kentucky*
University of Louisiana at Lafayette *Louisiana*
University of Maine *Maine*
University of Maryland, College Park *Maryland*
University of Maryland Eastern Shore *Maryland*
University of Massachusetts Amherst *Massachusetts*
University of Memphis *Tennessee*
University of Michigan *Michigan*
University of Minnesota, Twin Cities Campus *Minnesota*
University of Missouri *Missouri*
University of Nebraska Medical Center *Nebraska*
University of Nebraska–Lincoln *Nebraska*
University of Nevada, Reno *Nevada*
University of New Hampshire *New Hampshire*
University of New Mexico *New Mexico*
The University of North Carolina at Chapel Hill *North Carolina*
The University of North Carolina at Greensboro *North Carolina*
University of North Dakota *North Dakota*
University of North Florida *Florida*
University of Northern Colorado *Colorado*
University of Oklahoma Health Sciences Center *Oklahoma*
University of Pittsburgh *Pennsylvania*
University of Puerto Rico, Medical Sciences Campus *Puerto Rico*
University of Rhode Island *Rhode Island*
The University of South Dakota *South Dakota*
University of Southern California *California*
University of Southern Mississippi *Mississippi*
The University of Tennessee *Tennessee*
The University of Tennessee at Martin *Tennessee*
The University of Texas at Austin *Texas*
The University of Texas Health Science Center at Houston *Texas*
The University of Texas Southwestern Medical Center at Dallas *Texas*
The University of Texas–Pan American *Texas*
University of Utah *Utah*
University of Virginia *Virginia*
University of Washington *Washington*
University of Wisconsin–Green Bay *Wisconsin*
University of Wisconsin–Madison *Wisconsin*
University of Wisconsin–Stout *Wisconsin*
Utah State University *Utah*
Vanderbilt University *Tennessee*
Virginia Commonwealth University *Virginia*
Virginia Polytechnic Institute and State University *Virginia*
Virginia State University *Virginia*
Viterbo University *Wisconsin*
Washington State University *Washington*
Wayne State University *Michigan*
West Virginia University *West Virginia*
Western Carolina University *North Carolina*
Western Michigan University *Michigan*
Winthrop University *South Carolina*
Yale University *Connecticut*
Youngstown State University *Ohio*

American Health Information Management Association (AHIMA)

Adirondack Community College *New York*
Arapahoe Community College *Colorado*
Arkansas Tech University *Arkansas*
Baker College of Clinton Township *Michigan*
Baker College of Flint *Michigan*
Baker College of Jackson *Michigan*
Baker College of Muskegon *Michigan*
Baltimore City Community College *Maryland*
Bishop State Community College *Alabama*
Boise State University *Idaho*
Borough of Manhattan Community College of the City University of New York *New York*
Bowling Green State University–Firelands College *Ohio*
Bristol Community College *Massachusetts*
Broome Community College *New York*
Broward College *Florida*
Brunswick Community College *North Carolina*
Burlington County College *New Jersey*
Catawba Valley Community College *North Carolina*
Central Community College–Hastings Campus *Nebraska*
Central Oregon Community College *Oregon*
Central Piedmont Community College *North Carolina*
Chabot College *California*
Charles Drew University of Medicine and Science *California*
Chattanooga State Community College *Tennessee*
Chicago State University *Illinois*

Chippewa Valley Technical College *Wisconsin*
Cincinnati State Technical and Community College *Ohio*
City College of San Francisco *California*
Clark Atlanta University *Georgia*
Coastal Bend College *Texas*
College of DuPage *Illinois*
College of Lake County *Illinois*
College of Saint Mary *Nebraska*
The College of St. Scholastica *Minnesota*
College of Southern Nevada *Nevada*
Columbus State Community College *Ohio*
Community College of Allegheny County *Pennsylvania*
Community College of Philadelphia *Pennsylvania*
Cosumnes River College *California*
Cuyahoga Community College *Ohio*
Cypress College *California*
Dakota State University *South Dakota*
Darton College *Georgia*
Davidson County Community College *North Carolina*
Daytona State College *Florida*
Del Mar College *Texas*
Delgado Community College *Louisiana*
Duquesne University *Pennsylvania*
East Carolina University *North Carolina*
East Central University *Oklahoma*
East Los Angeles College *California*
Eastern Kentucky University *Kentucky*
Edgecombe Community College *North Carolina*
El Paso Community College *Texas*
Erie Community College, North Campus *New York*
Ferris State University *Michigan*
Fisher College *Massachusetts*
Florence-Darlington Technical College *South Carolina*
Florida Agricultural and Mechanical University *Florida*
Florida International University *Florida*
Florida State College at Jacksonville *Florida*
Fresno City College *California*
Gateway Technical College *Wisconsin*
Gogebic Community College *Michigan*
Greenville Technical College *South Carolina*
Gwynedd-Mercy College *Pennsylvania*
Henry Ford Community College *Michigan*
Hinds Community College *Mississippi*
Hocking College *Ohio*
Hodges University *Florida*
Houston Community College System *Texas*
Howard College *Texas*
Hudson County Community College *New Jersey*
Huertas Junior College *Puerto Rico*
Hutchinson Community College and Area Vocational School *Kansas*
Idaho State University *Idaho*
Illinois State University *Illinois*
Indian Hills Community College *Iowa*
Indian River State College *Florida*
Indiana University Northwest *Indiana*
Indiana University–Purdue University Fort Wayne *Indiana*
Indiana University–Purdue University Indianapolis *Indiana*
Inter American University of Puerto Rico, San Germán Campus *Puerto Rico*
Itawamba Community College *Mississippi*
John A. Logan College *Illinois*
Kaplan University, Hagerstown Campus *Maryland*
Kean University *New Jersey*
Kennebec Valley Community College *Maine*
Kirkwood Community College *Iowa*
Labouré College *Massachusetts*
Lake-Sumter Community College *Florida*
Lamar Institute of Technology *Texas*
Lee College *Texas*
Lehigh Carbon Community College *Pennsylvania*
Lincoln College of New England (Southington) *Connecticut*
Loma Linda University *California*
Lonestar College–North Harris *Texas*
Long Island University, C.W. Post Campus *New York*
Louisiana Tech University *Louisiana*
Macon State College *Georgia*
Marshall University *West Virginia*
McLennan Community College *Texas*
Medical College of Georgia *Georgia*
Mercy College of Northwest Ohio *Ohio*
Meridian Community College *Mississippi*
Metropolitan Community College–Penn Valley *Missouri*
Miami Dade College *Florida*
Midland College *Texas*
Midlands Technical College *South Carolina*
Missouri Western State University *Missouri*
Mohawk Valley Community College *New York*
Molloy College *New York*
Monroe College (Bronx) *New York*
Monroe Community College *New York*
Montana State University–Great Falls College of Technology *Montana*
Montgomery College *Maryland*
Moraine Park Technical College *Wisconsin*
Moraine Valley Community College *Illinois*
Mountain View College *Texas*
Nashua Community College *New Hampshire*
National College (Louisville) *Kentucky*
National Park Community College *Arkansas*
North Dakota State College of Science *North Dakota*
Northeast Iowa Community College *Iowa*
Northeast Wisconsin Technical College *Wisconsin*
Northeastern University *Massachusetts*
Northern Essex Community College *Massachusetts*
Northern Virginia Community College *Virginia*
Northwest Iowa Community College *Iowa*
Northwest Technical College *Minnesota*
Northwestern College *Illinois*
Oakton Community College *Illinois*
The Ohio State University *Ohio*
Onondaga Community College *New York*
Ozarks Technical Community College *Missouri*
Panola College *Texas*
Passaic County Community College *New Jersey*
Pensacola Junior College *Florida*
Phoenix College *Arizona*
Pierpont Community & Technical College of Fairmont State University *West Virginia*
Pitt Community College *North Carolina*
Polk State College *Florida*
Portland Community College *Oregon*
Prince George's Community College *Maryland*
Rasmussen College Eagan *Minnesota*
Rasmussen College Eden Prairie *Minnesota*
Rasmussen College Mankato *Minnesota*
Rasmussen College St. Cloud *Minnesota*
Regis University *Colorado*
Rend Lake College *Illinois*
Ridgewater College *Minnesota*
Roane State Community College *Tennessee*
Rochester Community and Technical College *Minnesota*
Rockland Community College *New York*
Rose State College *Oklahoma*
Saint Charles Community College *Missouri*
Saint Louis University *Missouri*
St. Petersburg College *Florida*
St. Philip's College *Texas*
San Diego Mesa College *California*
San Juan College *New Mexico*
Santa Barbara City College *California*
Santa Fe College *Florida*
Schoolcraft College *Michigan*
Shawnee Community College *Illinois*
Shoreline Community College *Washington*
Sinclair Community College *Ohio*
South Hills School of Business & Technology (State College) *Pennsylvania*
South Piedmont Community College *North Carolina*
South Plains College *Texas*
South Texas College *Texas*
Southeastern Illinois College *Illinois*
Southern University at Shreveport *Louisiana*
Southwestern Community College *North Carolina*
Southwestern Illinois College *Illinois*
Southwestern Oklahoma State University *Oklahoma*
Spokane Community College *Washington*
Stark State College of Technology *Ohio*
State University of New York College of Technology at Alfred *New York*
State University of New York Institute of Technology *New York*
Stephens College *Missouri*
Suffolk County Community College *New York*
Tacoma Community College *Washington*
Tarrant County College District *Texas*
Temple University *Pennsylvania*
Tennessee State University *Tennessee*
Texas Southern University *Texas*
Texas State Technical College Harlingen *Texas*
Texas State University–San Marcos *Texas*
Tidewater Community College *Virginia*
Trocaire College *New York*
Tulsa Community College *Oklahoma*
Tyler Junior College *Texas*
United Tribes Technical College *North Dakota*
Universidad Adventista de las Antillas *Puerto Rico*
Universidad del Este *Puerto Rico*
The University of Alabama at Birmingham *Alabama*
University of Alaska Southeast, Sitka Campus *Alaska*
University of Central Florida *Florida*
University of Illinois at Chicago *Illinois*
The University of Kansas *Kansas*
University of Louisiana at Lafayette *Louisiana*
University of Maine *Maine*
University of Mississippi Medical Center *Mississippi*
University of New Mexico–Gallup *New Mexico*
University of Pittsburgh *Pennsylvania*
University of Puerto Rico, Medical Sciences Campus *Puerto Rico*
University of Washington *Washington*
University of Wisconsin–Milwaukee *Wisconsin*
Vernon College *Texas*
Vincennes University *Indiana*
Volunteer State Community College *Tennessee*
Wallace State Community College *Alabama*
Washburn University *Kansas*
Weber State University *Utah*
West Virginia Northern Community College *West Virginia*
Western Carolina University *North Carolina*
Western Kentucky University *Kentucky*
Western Nebraska Community College *Nebraska*
Western Technical College *Wisconsin*
Wharton County Junior College *Texas*

American Institute of Certified Planners/Association of Collegiate Schools of (ACSP)

Alabama Agricultural and Mechanical University *Alabama*
Arizona State University *Arizona*
Auburn University *Alabama*
Ball State University *Indiana*
California Polytechnic State University, San Luis Obispo *California*
California State Polytechnic University, Pomona *California*
Clemson University *South Carolina*
Cleveland State University *Ohio*
Columbia University *New York*
Cornell University *New York*
East Carolina University *North Carolina*
Eastern Michigan University *Michigan*
Eastern Washington University *Washington*
Florida Atlantic University *Florida*
Florida State University *Florida*
Georgia Institute of Technology *Georgia*
Harvard University *Massachusetts*
Hunter College of the City University of New York *New York*
Iowa State University of Science and Technology *Iowa*
Jackson State University *Mississippi*
Kansas State University *Kansas*
Massachusetts Institute of Technology *Massachusetts*
Michigan State University *Michigan*
Missouri State University *Missouri*
Morgan State University *Maryland*
New York University *New York*
The Ohio State University *Ohio*
Portland State University *Oregon*
Pratt Institute *New York*

Rutgers, The State University of New Jersey, New Brunswick *New Jersey*
San Jose State University *California*
Texas A&M University *Texas*
Texas Southern University *Texas*
Tufts University *Massachusetts*
Université de Montréal *Quebec*
University at Albany, State University of New York *New York*
The University of Arizona *Arizona*
The University of British Columbia *British Columbia*
University at Buffalo, the State University of New York *New York*
University of California, Berkeley *California*
University of California, Irvine *California*
University of California, Los Angeles *California*
University of Cincinnati *Ohio*
University of Colorado Denver *Colorado*
University of Florida *Florida*
University of Hawaii at Manoa *Hawaii*
University of Illinois at Chicago *Illinois*
University of Illinois at Urbana–Champaign *Illinois*
The University of Iowa *Iowa*
The University of Kansas *Kansas*
University of Louisville *Kentucky*
University of Maryland, College Park *Maryland*
University of Massachusetts Amherst *Massachusetts*
University of Memphis *Tennessee*
University of Michigan *Michigan*
University of Minnesota, Twin Cities Campus *Minnesota*
University of Nebraska–Lincoln *Nebraska*
University of New Mexico *New Mexico*
University of New Orleans *Louisiana*
The University of North Carolina at Chapel Hill *North Carolina*
University of Oklahoma *Oklahoma*
University of Oregon *Oregon*
University of Pennsylvania *Pennsylvania*
University of Puerto Rico, Río Piedras *Puerto Rico*
University of Rhode Island *Rhode Island*
University of Southern California *California*
The University of Tennessee *Tennessee*
The University of Texas at Arlington *Texas*
The University of Texas at Austin *Texas*
University of Utah *Utah*
University of Virginia *Virginia*
University of Washington *Washington*
University of Wisconsin–Madison *Wisconsin*
University of Wisconsin–Milwaukee *Wisconsin*
Virginia Commonwealth University *Virginia*
Virginia Polytechnic Institute and State University *Virginia*
Wayne State University *Michigan*

American Library Association (ALA)

The Catholic University of America *District of Columbia*
Clarion University of Pennsylvania *Pennsylvania*
Clark Atlanta University *Georgia*
Dalhousie University *Nova Scotia*
Dominican University *Illinois*
Drexel University *Pennsylvania*
Emporia State University *Kansas*
Florida State University *Florida*
Indiana University Bloomington *Indiana*
Kent State University *Ohio*
Long Island University, C.W. Post Campus *New York*
Louisiana State University and Agricultural and Mechanical College *Louisiana*
McGill University *Quebec*
North Carolina Central University *North Carolina*
Pratt Institute *New York*
Queens College of the City University of New York *New York*
Rutgers, The State University of New Jersey, New Brunswick *New Jersey*
St. John's University *New York*
San Jose State University *California*
Simmons College *Massachusetts*
Southern Connecticut State University *Connecticut*
Syracuse University *New York*
Texas Woman's University *Texas*
Université de Montréal *Quebec*
The University of Alabama *Alabama*
University at Albany, State University of New York *New York*
University of Alberta *Alberta*
The University of Arizona *Arizona*
The University of British Columbia *British Columbia*
University at Buffalo, the State University of New York *New York*
University of California, Los Angeles *California*
University of Denver *Colorado*
University of Hawaii at Manoa *Hawaii*
University of Illinois at Urbana–Champaign *Illinois*
The University of Iowa *Iowa*
University of Kentucky *Kentucky*
University of Maryland, College Park *Maryland*
University of Michigan *Michigan*
University of Missouri *Missouri*
The University of North Carolina at Chapel Hill *North Carolina*
The University of North Carolina at Greensboro *North Carolina*
University of North Texas *Texas*
University of Oklahoma *Oklahoma*
University of Pittsburgh *Pennsylvania*
University of Puerto Rico, Río Piedras *Puerto Rico*
University of Rhode Island *Rhode Island*
University of South Carolina *South Carolina*
University of South Florida *Florida*
University of Southern Mississippi *Mississippi*
The University of Tennessee *Tennessee*
The University of Texas at Austin *Texas*
University of Toronto *Ontario*
University of Washington *Washington*
The University of Western Ontario *Ontario*
University of Wisconsin–Madison *Wisconsin*
University of Wisconsin–Milwaukee *Wisconsin*
Valdosta State University *Georgia*
Wayne State University *Michigan*

American Occupational Therapy Association (AOTA)

Alabama State University *Alabama*
Allegany College of Maryland *Maryland*
Alvernia University *Pennsylvania*
Amarillo College *Texas*
American International College *Massachusetts*
Anoka Technical College *Minnesota*
Atlantic Cape Community College *New Jersey*
Augusta Technical College *Georgia*
Austin Community College *Texas*
Baker College of Muskegon *Michigan*
Barry University *Florida*
Bay Path College *Massachusetts*
Belmont University *Tennessee*
Boston University *Massachusetts*
Brenau University *Georgia*
Bristol Community College *Massachusetts*
Brown Mackie College–Fort Wayne *Indiana*
Brown Mackie College–South Bend *Indiana*
Cabarrus College of Health Sciences *North Carolina*
California State University, Dominguez Hills *California*
Cape Fear Community College *North Carolina*
Casper College *Wyoming*
Chatham University *Pennsylvania*
Chicago State University *Illinois*
Cincinnati State Technical and Community College *Ohio*
City Colleges of Chicago, Wilbur Wright College *Illinois*
Cleveland State University *Ohio*
College of Saint Mary *Nebraska*
The College of St. Scholastica *Minnesota*
College of Southern Nevada *Nevada*
Colorado State University *Colorado*
Columbia University *New York*
Community College of Allegheny County *Pennsylvania*
The Community College of Baltimore County *Maryland*
Community College of Rhode Island *Rhode Island*
Concordia University Wisconsin *Wisconsin*
Creighton University *Nebraska*
Cuyahoga Community College *Ohio*
Darton College *Georgia*
Daytona State College *Florida*
Del Mar College *Texas*
Delaware Technical & Community College, Jack F. Owens Campus *Delaware*
Delaware Technical & Community College, Stanton/Wilmington Campus *Delaware*
Delgado Community College *Louisiana*
Dominican College *New York*
Dominican University of California *California*
Duquesne University *Pennsylvania*
Durham Technical Community College *North Carolina*
D'Youville College *New York*
East Carolina University *North Carolina*
Eastern Kentucky University *Kentucky*
Eastern Michigan University *Michigan*
Eastern New Mexico University–Roswell *New Mexico*
Eastern Washington University *Washington*
Elizabethtown College *Pennsylvania*
Erie Community College, North Campus *New York*
Fiorello H. LaGuardia Community College of the City University of New York *New York*
Florida Agricultural and Mechanical University *Florida*
Florida Gulf Coast University *Florida*
Florida Hospital College of Health Sciences *Florida*
Florida International University *Florida*
Fox Valley Technical College *Wisconsin*
Gannon University *Pennsylvania*
Genesee Community College *New York*
Governors State University *Illinois*
Grand Rapids Community College *Michigan*
Grand Valley State University *Michigan*
Green River Community College *Washington*
Greenville Technical College *South Carolina*
Grossmont College *California*
Herkimer County Community College *New York*
Holmes Community College *Mississippi*
Housatonic Community College *Connecticut*
Houston Community College System *Texas*
Howard University *District of Columbia*
Husson University *Maine*
Idaho State University *Idaho*
Illinois Central College *Illinois*
Indiana University–Purdue University Indianapolis *Indiana*
Ithaca College *New York*
James A. Rhodes State College *Ohio*
James Madison University *Virginia*
Jamestown Community College *New York*
Jefferson College of Health Sciences *Virginia*
Jefferson Community and Technical College *Kentucky*
John A. Logan College *Illinois*
Kapiolani Community College *Hawaii*
Kaplan Career Institute, ICM Campus *Pennsylvania*
Kean University *New Jersey*
Keiser University *Florida*
Kennebec Valley Community College *Maine*
Kent State University at East Liverpool *Ohio*
Keuka College *New York*
Kirkwood Community College *Iowa*
Lake Area Technical Institute *South Dakota*
Lake Michigan College *Michigan*
Laredo Community College *Texas*
Lehigh Carbon Community College *Pennsylvania*
Lenoir-Rhyne University *North Carolina*
Lewis and Clark Community College *Illinois*
Lincoln College of New England (Southington) *Connecticut*
Lincoln Land Community College *Illinois*
Loma Linda University *California*
Lonestar College–Kingwood *Texas*
Lonestar College–Tomball *Texas*
Long Island University, Brooklyn Campus *New York*
Louisiana State University Health Sciences Center *Louisiana*
Macomb Community College *Michigan*
Madison Area Technical College *Wisconsin*
Madisonville Community College *Kentucky*
Manchester Community College *Connecticut*
Maria College *New York*
Maryville University of Saint Louis *Missouri*
Medical College of Georgia *Georgia*
Medical University of South Carolina *South Carolina*
Mercy College *New York*

Metropolitan Community College–Penn Valley *Missouri*
Middle Georgia College *Georgia*
Milligan College *Tennessee*
Milwaukee Area Technical College *Wisconsin*
Misericordia University *Pennsylvania*
Mott Community College *Michigan*
Mount Aloysius College *Pennsylvania*
Mount Mary College *Wisconsin*
Mountain State University *West Virginia*
Murray State University *Kentucky*
Nashua Community College *New Hampshire*
Nashville State Technical Community College *Tennessee*
Navarro College *Texas*
New England Institute of Technology *Rhode Island*
New York Institute of Technology *New York*
New York University *New York*
North Dakota State College of Science *North Dakota*
North Shore Community College *Massachusetts*
Nova Southeastern University *Florida*
The Ohio State University *Ohio*
Oklahoma City Community College *Oklahoma*
Orange County Community College *New York*
Owens Community College *Ohio*
Ozarks Technical Community College *Missouri*
Pacific University *Oregon*
Panola College *Texas*
Parkland College *Illinois*
Pearl River Community College *Mississippi*
Penn State Berks *Pennsylvania*
Penn State DuBois *Pennsylvania*
Penn State Mont Alto *Pennsylvania*
Pennsylvania College of Technology *Pennsylvania*
Philadelphia University *Pennsylvania*
Pitt Community College *North Carolina*
Polk State College *Florida*
Pueblo Community College *Colorado*
Quinnipiac University *Connecticut*
Quinsigamond Community College *Massachusetts*
Rend Lake College *Illinois*
The Richard Stockton College of New Jersey *New Jersey*
Roane State Community College *Tennessee*
Rockhurst University *Missouri*
Rockland Community College *New York*
Rush University *Illinois*
Russell Sage College *New York*
Sacramento City College *California*
Sacred Heart University *Connecticut*
Saginaw Valley State University *Michigan*
St. Ambrose University *Iowa*
St. Catherine University *Minnesota*
Saint Charles Community College *Missouri*
Saint Francis University *Pennsylvania*
St. Louis Community College at Meramec *Missouri*
Saint Louis University *Missouri*
St. Philip's College *Texas*
Salem State College *Massachusetts*
Salt Lake Community College *Utah*
Samuel Merritt University *California*
San Francisco Conservatory of Music *California*
San Jose State University *California*
Santa Ana College *California*
Seton Hall University *New Jersey*
Shawnee Community College *Illinois*
Shawnee State University *Ohio*
Shenandoah University *Virginia*
Sinclair Community College *Ohio*
South Arkansas Community College *Arkansas*
South College *Tennessee*
South Suburban College *Illinois*
South Texas College *Texas*
Southeastern Illinois College *Illinois*
Southwestern Oklahoma State University at Sayre *Oklahoma*
Spalding University *Kentucky*
Springfield College *Massachusetts*
Springfield Technical Community College *Massachusetts*
Stark State College of Technology *Ohio*
State College of Florida Manatee-Sarasota *Florida*
State University of New York College of Technology at Canton *New York*
State University of New York Downstate Medical Center *New York*
Stony Brook University, State University of New York *New York*
Suffolk County Community College *New York*
Temple University *Pennsylvania*
Tennessee State University *Tennessee*
Texas Woman's University *Texas*
Thomas Jefferson University *Pennsylvania*
Tidewater Community College *Virginia*
Touro College *New York*
Towson University *Maryland*
Trident Technical College *South Carolina*
Tufts University *Massachusetts*
Tulsa Community College *Oklahoma*
Tuskegee University *Alabama*
The University of Alabama at Birmingham *Alabama*
University at Buffalo, the State University of New York *New York*
University of Central Arkansas *Arkansas*
The University of Findlay *Ohio*
University of Florida *Florida*
University of Hartford *Connecticut*
University of Illinois at Chicago *Illinois*
University of Indianapolis *Indiana*
The University of Kansas *Kansas*
University of Kentucky *Kentucky*
University of Louisiana at Monroe *Louisiana*
University of Mary *North Dakota*
University of Minnesota, Twin Cities Campus *Minnesota*
University of Mississippi Medical Center *Mississippi*
University of Missouri *Missouri*
University of New England *Maine*
University of New Hampshire *New Hampshire*
University of New Mexico *New Mexico*
The University of North Carolina at Chapel Hill *North Carolina*
University of North Dakota *North Dakota*
University of Oklahoma Health Sciences Center *Oklahoma*
University of Pittsburgh *Pennsylvania*
University of Puerto Rico at Humacao *Puerto Rico*
University of Puerto Rico, Medical Sciences Campus *Puerto Rico*
University of Puget Sound *Washington*
University of Saint Francis *Indiana*
University of the Sciences in Philadelphia *Pennsylvania*
The University of Scranton *Pennsylvania*
University of South Alabama *Alabama*
The University of South Dakota *South Dakota*
University of Southern California *California*
University of Southern Indiana *Indiana*
University of Southern Maine *Maine*
The University of Texas at El Paso *Texas*
The University of Texas Health Science Center at San Antonio *Texas*
The University of Texas Medical Branch *Texas*
The University of Texas–Pan American *Texas*
The University of Toledo *Ohio*
University of Utah *Utah*
University of Washington *Washington*
University of Wisconsin–La Crosse *Wisconsin*
University of Wisconsin–Madison *Wisconsin*
University of Wisconsin–Milwaukee *Wisconsin*
Utica College *New York*
Virginia Commonwealth University *Virginia*
Wallace State Community College *Alabama*
Washington University in St. Louis *Missouri*
Wayne County Community College District *Michigan*
Wayne State University *Michigan*
West Virginia University *West Virginia*
Western Career College (San Leandro) *California*
Western Kentucky University *Kentucky*
Western Michigan University *Michigan*
Western New Mexico University *New Mexico*
Western Technical College *Wisconsin*
Winston-Salem State University *North Carolina*
Wisconsin Indianhead Technical College *Wisconsin*
Worcester State College *Massachusetts*
Xavier University *Ohio*
York College of the City University of New York *New York*
Zane State College *Ohio*

American Optometric Association (AOA)

Ferris State University *Michigan*
Indiana University Bloomington *Indiana*
Madison Area Technical College *Wisconsin*
Northeastern State University *Oklahoma*
Nova Southeastern University *Florida*
The Ohio State University *Ohio*
Pacific University *Oregon*
Spokane Community College *Washington*
Université de Montréal *Quebec*
The University of Alabama at Birmingham *Alabama*
University of California, Berkeley *California*
University of Houston *Texas*
University of the Incarnate Word *Texas*
University of Missouri–St. Louis *Missouri*
University of Waterloo *Ontario*

American Osteopathic Association (AOsA)

Lincoln Memorial University *Tennessee*
Michigan State University *Michigan*
New York Institute of Technology *New York*
Nova Southeastern University *Florida*
Ohio University *Ohio*
Pikeville College *Kentucky*
University of New England *Maine*

American Physical Therapy Association (APTA)

Alabama State University *Alabama*
Allegany College of Maryland *Maryland*
Amarillo College *Texas*
American International College *Massachusetts*
Andrews University *Michigan*
Angelo State University *Texas*
Anne Arundel Community College *Maryland*
Anoka-Ramsey Community College *Minnesota*
Arapahoe Community College *Colorado*
Arcadia University *Pennsylvania*
Arkansas State University - Jonesboro *Arkansas*
Armstrong Atlantic State University *Georgia*
Athens Technical College *Georgia*
Atlantic Cape Community College *New Jersey*
Austin Community College *Texas*
Azusa Pacific University *California*
Baker College of Flint *Michigan*
Baker College of Muskegon *Michigan*
Baltimore City Community College *Maryland*
Bay State College *Massachusetts*
Baylor University *Texas*
Becker College *Massachusetts*
Bellarmine University *Kentucky*
Belmont University *Tennessee*
Bergen Community College *New Jersey*
Berkshire Community College *Massachusetts*
Bishop State Community College *Alabama*
Black Hawk College *Illinois*
Blackhawk Technical College *Wisconsin*
Blinn College *Texas*
Bossier Parish Community College *Louisiana*
Boston University *Massachusetts*
Bowling Green State University *Ohio*
Bradley University *Illinois*
Broome Community College *New York*
Broward College *Florida*
Brown Mackie College–South Bend *Indiana*
Butler County Community College *Pennsylvania*
California State University, Fresno *California*
California State University, Long Beach *California*
California State University, Northridge *California*
California State University, Sacramento *California*
California University of Pennsylvania *Pennsylvania*
Capital Community College *Connecticut*
Carl Albert State College *Oklahoma*
Carroll Community College *Maryland*
Carroll University *Wisconsin*
Central Florida Community College *Florida*
Central Michigan University *Michigan*
Central Pennsylvania College *Pennsylvania*
Central Piedmont Community College *North Carolina*
Cerritos College *California*
Chapman University *California*
Chatham University *Pennsylvania*

Southwest Tennessee Community College *Tennessee*
Southwestern Community College *North Carolina*
Southwestern Illinois College *Illinois*
Southwestern Oklahoma State University *Oklahoma*
Spokane Falls Community College *Washington*
Springfield College *Massachusetts*
Springfield Technical Community College *Massachusetts*
Stark State College of Technology *Ohio*
State College of Florida Manatee-Sarasota *Florida*
State University of New York College of Technology at Canton *New York*
State University of New York Downstate Medical Center *New York*
State University of New York Upstate Medical University *New York*
Stony Brook University, State University of New York *New York*
Suffolk County Community College *New York*
Tarrant County College District *Texas*
Temple University *Pennsylvania*
Tennessee State University *Tennessee*
Texas State University–San Marcos *Texas*
Texas Woman's University *Texas*
Thomas Jefferson University *Pennsylvania*
Touro College *New York*
Trident Technical College *South Carolina*
Tulsa Community College *Oklahoma*
Tunxis Community College *Connecticut*
Union County College *New Jersey*
The University of Alabama at Birmingham *Alabama*
University at Buffalo, the State University of New York *New York*
University of Central Arkansas *Arkansas*
University of Central Florida *Florida*
University of Cincinnati *Ohio*
University of Colorado Denver *Colorado*
University of Connecticut *Connecticut*
University of Delaware *Delaware*
University of Evansville *Indiana*
The University of Findlay *Ohio*
University of Florida *Florida*
University of Hartford *Connecticut*
University of Illinois at Chicago *Illinois*
University of Indianapolis *Indiana*
The University of Iowa *Iowa*
The University of Kansas *Kansas*
University of Kentucky *Kentucky*
University of Louisville *Kentucky*
University of Mary *North Dakota*
University of Maryland Eastern Shore *Maryland*
University of Massachusetts Lowell *Massachusetts*
University of Miami *Florida*
University of Michigan–Flint *Michigan*
University of Minnesota, Twin Cities Campus *Minnesota*
University of Mississippi Medical Center *Mississippi*
University of Missouri *Missouri*
University of Mobile *Alabama*
The University of Montana *Montana*
University of Nebraska Medical Center *Nebraska*
University of Nevada, Las Vegas *Nevada*
University of New England *Maine*
University of New Mexico *New Mexico*
The University of North Carolina at Chapel Hill *North Carolina*
University of North Dakota *North Dakota*
University of North Florida *Florida*
University of Oklahoma Health Sciences Center *Oklahoma*
University of the Pacific *California*
University of Pittsburgh *Pennsylvania*
University of Pittsburgh at Titusville *Pennsylvania*
University of Puerto Rico at Humacao *Puerto Rico*
University of Puerto Rico, Medical Sciences Campus *Puerto Rico*
University of Puerto Rico at Ponce *Puerto Rico*
University of Puget Sound *Washington*
University of Rhode Island *Rhode Island*
University of Saint Francis *Indiana*
University of the Sciences in Philadelphia *Pennsylvania*
The University of Scranton *Pennsylvania*
University of South Alabama *Alabama*
University of South Carolina *South Carolina*
The University of South Dakota *South Dakota*
University of South Florida *Florida*
University of Southern California *California*
The University of Tennessee at Chattanooga *Tennessee*
The University of Texas at El Paso *Texas*
The University of Texas Health Science Center at San Antonio *Texas*
The University of Texas Medical Branch *Texas*
The University of Texas Southwestern Medical Center at Dallas *Texas*
The University of Toledo *Ohio*
University of Toronto *Ontario*
University of Utah *Utah*
University of Vermont *Vermont*
University of Washington *Washington*
The University of Western Ontario *Ontario*
University of Wisconsin–La Crosse *Wisconsin*
University of Wisconsin–Madison *Wisconsin*
Utica College *New York*
Villa Maria College of Buffalo *New York*
Vincennes University *Indiana*
Virginia Commonwealth University *Virginia*
Volunteer State Community College *Tennessee*
Wallace State Community College *Alabama*
Walsh University *Ohio*
Walters State Community College *Tennessee*
Washburn University *Kansas*
Washington State Community College *Ohio*
Washington University in St. Louis *Missouri*
Wayne State University *Michigan*
West Kentucky Community and Technical College *Kentucky*
West Virginia University *West Virginia*
Western Carolina University *North Carolina*
Western Iowa Tech Community College *Iowa*
Western Technical College *Wisconsin*
Wharton County Junior College *Texas*
Whatcom Community College *Washington*
Wheeling Jesuit University *West Virginia*
Wichita State University *Kansas*
Widener University *Pennsylvania*
Williston State College *North Dakota*
Winston-Salem State University *North Carolina*
Wytheville Community College *Virginia*
Youngstown State University *Ohio*
Zane State College *Ohio*

American Podiatric Medical Association (APMA)

Barry University *Florida*
Temple University *Pennsylvania*

American Psychological Association (APA)

Adelphi University *New York*
Alfred University *New York*
American University *District of Columbia*
Appalachian State University *North Carolina*
Argosy University, Atlanta *Georgia*
Argosy University, Chicago *Illinois*
Argosy University, Hawai'i *Hawaii*
Argosy University, Phoenix *Arizona*
Argosy University, San Francisco Bay Area *California*
Argosy University, Schaumburg *Illinois*
Argosy University, Tampa *Florida*
Argosy University, Washington DC *Virginia*
Arizona State University *Arizona*
Auburn University *Alabama*
Azusa Pacific University *California*
Ball State University *Indiana*
Baylor University *Texas*
Biola University *California*
Boston College *Massachusetts*
Boston University *Massachusetts*
Bowling Green State University *Ohio*
Brigham Young University *Utah*
Brown University *Rhode Island*
Butler University *Indiana*
California Institute of Integral Studies *California*
California State University, Long Beach *California*
Carlos Albizu University *Puerto Rico*
Carlos Albizu University, Miami Campus *Florida*
Case Western Reserve University *Ohio*
The Catholic University of America *District of Columbia*
Central Michigan University *Michigan*
City College of the City University of New York *New York*
Clark University *Massachusetts*
The College of William and Mary *Virginia*
Colorado State University *Colorado*
Concordia University *Quebec*
Dalhousie University *Nova Scotia*
Dartmouth College *New Hampshire*
DePaul University *Illinois*
Drexel University *Pennsylvania*
Duke University *North Carolina*
Duquesne University *Pennsylvania*
Emory University *Georgia*
Fairleigh Dickinson University, Metropolitan Campus *New Jersey*
Florida Institute of Technology *Florida*
Florida State University *Florida*
Fordham University *New York*
Gallaudet University *District of Columbia*
George Fox University *Oregon*
George Mason University *Virginia*
The George Washington University *District of Columbia*
Georgia State University *Georgia*
Grand Valley State University *Michigan*
Harvard University *Massachusetts*
Hofstra University *New York*
Howard University *District of Columbia*
Idaho State University *Idaho*
Illinois Institute of Technology *Illinois*
Illinois State University *Illinois*
Immaculata University *Pennsylvania*
Indiana State University *Indiana*
Indiana University Bloomington *Indiana*
Indiana University of Pennsylvania *Pennsylvania*
Indiana University–Purdue University Indianapolis *Indiana*
Iowa State University of Science and Technology *Iowa*
Jackson State University *Mississippi*
James Madison University *Virginia*
John F. Kennedy University *California*
The Johns Hopkins University *Maryland*
Kansas State University *Kansas*
Kent State University *Ohio*
La Salle University *Pennsylvania*
Lehigh University *Pennsylvania*
Loma Linda University *California*
Long Island University, Brooklyn Campus *New York*
Long Island University, C.W. Post Campus *New York*
Louisiana State University and Agricultural and Mechanical College *Louisiana*
Louisiana State University Health Sciences Center *Louisiana*
Louisiana Tech University *Louisiana*
Loyola University Chicago *Illinois*
Loyola University Maryland *Maryland*
Marquette University *Wisconsin*
McGill University *Quebec*
Medical College of Georgia *Georgia*
Medical University of South Carolina *South Carolina*
Metropolitan State College of Denver *Colorado*
Miami University *Ohio*
Michigan State University *Michigan*
Mississippi State University *Mississippi*
Montana State University *Montana*
New Mexico State University *New Mexico*
New York University *New York*
Norfolk State University *Virginia*
North Carolina State University *North Carolina*
Northeastern University *Massachusetts*
Northern Illinois University *Illinois*
Northwestern University *Illinois*
Nova Southeastern University *Florida*
The Ohio State University *Ohio*
Ohio University *Ohio*
Oklahoma State University *Oklahoma*
Old Dominion University *Virginia*
Oregon Health & Science University *Oregon*
Our Lady of the Lake University of San Antonio *Texas*
Pace University *New York*

Pacific University *Oregon*
Penn State University Park *Pennsylvania*
Purdue University *Indiana*
Queen's University at Kingston *Ontario*
Regent University *Virginia*
Roosevelt University *Illinois*
Rutgers, The State University of New Jersey, New Brunswick *New Jersey*
St. John's University *New York*
Saint Louis University *Missouri*
San Diego State University *California*
Seton Hall University *New Jersey*
Simon Fraser University *British Columbia*
Southern Illinois University Carbondale *Illinois*
Spalding University *Kentucky*
Stanford University *California*
State University of New York at Binghamton *New York*
State University of New York Upstate Medical University *New York*
Stony Brook University, State University of New York *New York*
Suffolk University *Massachusetts*
Syracuse University *New York*
Temple University *Pennsylvania*
Tennessee State University *Tennessee*
Texas A&M University *Texas*
Texas State University–San Marcos *Texas*
Texas Tech University *Texas*
Texas Woman's University *Texas*
Towson University *Maryland*
Tufts University *Massachusetts*
Tulane University *Louisiana*
The University of Akron *Ohio*
The University of Alabama *Alabama*
The University of Alabama at Birmingham *Alabama*
University at Albany, State University of New York *New York*
The University of Arizona *Arizona*
University of Arkansas *Arkansas*
University of Arkansas for Medical Sciences *Arkansas*
The University of British Columbia *British Columbia*
University at Buffalo, the State University of New York *New York*
University of California, Berkeley *California*
University of California, Davis *California*
University of California, Irvine *California*
University of California, Los Angeles *California*
University of California, San Diego *California*
University of California, Santa Barbara *California*
University of California, Santa Cruz *California*
University of Central Florida *Florida*
University of Chicago *Illinois*
University of Cincinnati *Ohio*
University of Colorado at Boulder *Colorado*
University of Connecticut *Connecticut*
University of Delaware *Delaware*
University of Denver *Colorado*
University of Detroit Mercy *Michigan*
University of Florida *Florida*
University of Georgia *Georgia*
University of Hartford *Connecticut*
University of Hawaii at Manoa *Hawaii*
University of Houston *Texas*
University of Illinois at Chicago *Illinois*
University of Illinois at Urbana–Champaign *Illinois*
University of Indianapolis *Indiana*
The University of Iowa *Iowa*
The University of Kansas *Kansas*
University of Kentucky *Kentucky*
University of La Verne *California*
University of Louisville *Kentucky*
University of Maine *Maine*
University of Manitoba *Manitoba*
University of Maryland, Baltimore County *Maryland*
University of Maryland, College Park *Maryland*
University of Massachusetts Amherst *Massachusetts*
University of Massachusetts Boston *Massachusetts*
University of Memphis *Tennessee*
University of Miami *Florida*
University of Michigan *Michigan*
University of Minnesota, Twin Cities Campus *Minnesota*
University of Mississippi *Mississippi*
University of Mississippi Medical Center *Mississippi*
University of Missouri *Missouri*
University of Missouri–Kansas City *Missouri*
University of Missouri–St. Louis *Missouri*
The University of Montana *Montana*
University of Nebraska–Lincoln *Nebraska*
University of Nevada, Reno *Nevada*
University of New Brunswick Fredericton *New Brunswick*
University of New Hampshire *New Hampshire*
University of New Mexico *New Mexico*
The University of North Carolina at Chapel Hill *North Carolina*
The University of North Carolina at Charlotte *North Carolina*
The University of North Carolina at Greensboro *North Carolina*
University of North Dakota *North Dakota*
University of North Texas *Texas*
University of Northern Colorado *Colorado*
University of Notre Dame *Indiana*
University of Oklahoma *Oklahoma*
University of Oklahoma Health Sciences Center *Oklahoma*
University of Oregon *Oregon*
University of Ottawa *Ontario*
University of Pennsylvania *Pennsylvania*
University of Pittsburgh *Pennsylvania*
University of Rhode Island *Rhode Island*
University of Rochester *New York*
University of St. Thomas *Minnesota*
University of San Diego *California*
University of Saskatchewan *Saskatchewan*
University of South Carolina *South Carolina*
The University of South Dakota *South Dakota*
University of South Florida *Florida*
University of Southern California *California*
University of Southern Mississippi *Mississippi*
The University of Tennessee *Tennessee*
The University of Texas at Austin *Texas*
The University of Texas Health Science Center at Houston *Texas*
The University of Texas Health Science Center at San Antonio *Texas*
The University of Texas Medical Branch *Texas*
The University of Texas Southwestern Medical Center at Dallas *Texas*
The University of Toledo *Ohio*
University of Toronto *Ontario*
University of Tulsa *Oklahoma*
University of Utah *Utah*
University of Vermont *Vermont*
University of Victoria *British Columbia*
University of Virginia *Virginia*
University of Washington *Washington*
University of Waterloo *Ontario*
The University of Western Ontario *Ontario*
University of Windsor *Ontario*
University of Wisconsin–Madison *Wisconsin*
University of Wisconsin–Milwaukee *Wisconsin*
University of Wyoming *Wyoming*
Utah State University *Utah*
Vanderbilt University *Tennessee*
Virginia Commonwealth University *Virginia*
Virginia Polytechnic Institute and State University *Virginia*
Washington State University *Washington*
Washington University in St. Louis *Missouri*
Wayne State University *Michigan*
West Virginia University *West Virginia*
Western Michigan University *Michigan*
Wheaton College *Illinois*
Wichita State University *Kansas*
Widener University *Pennsylvania*
Wright State University *Ohio*
Xavier University *Ohio*
Yale University *Connecticut*
Yeshiva University *New York*
York University *Ontario*

American Society of Cytopathology (ASC)

Albany College of Pharmacy and Health Sciences *New York*
Bellarmine University *Kentucky*
Eastern Kentucky University *Kentucky*
Goldfarb School of Nursing at Barnes-Jewish College *Missouri*
Indiana University–Purdue University Indianapolis *Indiana*
Loma Linda University *California*
Medical University of South Carolina *South Carolina*
Nicholls State University *Louisiana*
Oakland University *Michigan*
Old Dominion University *Virginia*
State University of New York Upstate Medical University *New York*
Stony Brook University, State University of New York *New York*
Thomas Jefferson University *Pennsylvania*
The University of Akron *Ohio*
The University of Alabama at Birmingham *Alabama*
University of Arkansas for Medical Sciences *Arkansas*
University of California, Los Angeles *California*
The University of Kansas *Kansas*
University of Mississippi Medical Center *Mississippi*
University of North Dakota *North Dakota*
The University of Texas Health Science Center at Houston *Texas*
University of Utah *Utah*
University of Vermont *Vermont*
University of Wisconsin–Madison *Wisconsin*
Wayne State University *Michigan*

American Society of Landscape Architects (ASLA)

Arizona State University *Arizona*
Auburn University *Alabama*
Ball State University *Indiana*
California Polytechnic State University, San Luis Obispo *California*
California State Polytechnic University, Pomona *California*
Chatham University *Pennsylvania*
City College of the City University of New York *New York*
Clemson University *South Carolina*
Colorado State University *Colorado*
Cornell University *New York*
Florida International University *Florida*
Harvard University *Massachusetts*
Iowa State University of Science and Technology *Iowa*
Kansas State University *Kansas*
Louisiana State University and Agricultural and Mechanical College *Louisiana*
Michigan State University *Michigan*
Mississippi State University *Mississippi*
Morgan State University *Maryland*
North Carolina Agricultural and Technical State University *North Carolina*
North Carolina State University *North Carolina*
North Dakota State University *North Dakota*
The Ohio State University *Ohio*
Oklahoma State University *Oklahoma*
Penn State University Park *Pennsylvania*
Purdue University *Indiana*
Rhode Island School of Design *Rhode Island*
Rutgers, The State University of New Jersey, New Brunswick *New Jersey*
State University of New York College of Environmental Science and Forestry *New York*
Temple University *Pennsylvania*
Texas A&M University *Texas*
Texas Tech University *Texas*
Université de Montréal *Quebec*
The University of Arizona *Arizona*
University of Arkansas *Arkansas*
The University of British Columbia *British Columbia*
University of California, Berkeley *California*
University of California, Davis *California*
University of Colorado Denver *Colorado*
University of Connecticut *Connecticut*
University of Florida *Florida*
University of Georgia *Georgia*
University of Guelph *Ontario*
University of Idaho *Idaho*
University of Illinois at Urbana–Champaign *Illinois*
University of Kentucky *Kentucky*
University of Manitoba *Manitoba*
University of Maryland, College Park *Maryland*

University of Massachusetts Amherst *Massachusetts*
University of Michigan *Michigan*
University of Minnesota, Twin Cities Campus *Minnesota*
University of Nevada, Las Vegas *Nevada*
University of New Mexico *New Mexico*
University of Oklahoma *Oklahoma*
University of Oregon *Oregon*
University of Pennsylvania *Pennsylvania*
University of Rhode Island *Rhode Island*
The University of Texas at Arlington *Texas*
University of Toronto *Ontario*
University of Virginia *Virginia*
University of Washington *Washington*
University of Wisconsin–Madison *Wisconsin*
Utah State University *Utah*
Virginia Polytechnic Institute and State University *Virginia*
Washington State University *Washington*
West Virginia University *West Virginia*

American Speech-Language-Hearing Association (ASLHA)

Abilene Christian University *Texas*
Adelphi University *New York*
Alabama Agricultural and Mechanical University *Alabama*
Appalachian State University *North Carolina*
Arizona State University *Arizona*
Arkansas State University - Jonesboro *Arkansas*
Auburn University *Alabama*
Ball State University *Indiana*
Baylor University *Texas*
Bloomsburg University of Pennsylvania *Pennsylvania*
Boston University *Massachusetts*
Bowling Green State University *Ohio*
Brigham Young University *Utah*
Brooklyn College of the City University of New York *New York*
Buffalo State College, State University of New York *New York*
California State University, Chico *California*
California State University, East Bay *California*
California State University, Fresno *California*
California State University, Fullerton *California*
California State University, Long Beach *California*
California State University, Los Angeles *California*
California State University, Northridge *California*
California State University, Sacramento *California*
California University of Pennsylvania *Pennsylvania*
Case Western Reserve University *Ohio*
Central Michigan University *Michigan*
Clarion University of Pennsylvania *Pennsylvania*
Cleveland State University *Ohio*
The College of New Jersey *New Jersey*
The College of Saint Rose *New York*
Duquesne University *Pennsylvania*
East Carolina University *North Carolina*
East Stroudsburg University of Pennsylvania *Pennsylvania*
East Tennessee State University *Tennessee*
Eastern Illinois University *Illinois*
Eastern Kentucky University *Kentucky*
Eastern Michigan University *Michigan*
Eastern New Mexico University *New Mexico*
Eastern Washington University *Washington*
Edinboro University of Pennsylvania *Pennsylvania*
Emerson College *Massachusetts*
Florida Atlantic University *Florida*
Florida International University *Florida*
Florida State University *Florida*
Fontbonne University *Missouri*
Fort Hays State University *Kansas*
Gallaudet University *District of Columbia*
The George Washington University *District of Columbia*
Georgia State University *Georgia*
Governors State University *Illinois*
Hampton University *Virginia*
Hofstra University *New York*
Howard University *District of Columbia*
Hunter College of the City University of New York *New York*
Idaho State University *Idaho*
Illinois State University *Illinois*
Indiana State University *Indiana*
Indiana University Bloomington *Indiana*
Indiana University of Pennsylvania *Pennsylvania*
Ithaca College *New York*
Jackson State University *Mississippi*
James Madison University *Virginia*
Kansas State University *Kansas*
Kean University *New Jersey*
Kent State University *Ohio*
La Salle University *Pennsylvania*
Lamar University *Texas*
Lehman College of the City University of New York *New York*
Loma Linda University *California*
Long Island University, Brooklyn Campus *New York*
Long Island University, C.W. Post Campus *New York*
Louisiana State University and Agricultural and Mechanical College *Louisiana*
Louisiana State University Health Sciences Center *Louisiana*
Louisiana Tech University *Louisiana*
Loyola University Maryland *Maryland*
Marquette University *Wisconsin*
Marshall University *West Virginia*
Marywood University *Pennsylvania*
Medical University of South Carolina *South Carolina*
Mercy College *New York*
Miami University *Ohio*
Michigan State University *Michigan*
Minnesota State University Mankato *Minnesota*
Minnesota State University Moorhead *Minnesota*
Minot State University *North Dakota*
Misericordia University *Pennsylvania*
Mississippi University for Women *Mississippi*
Missouri State University *Missouri*
Montclair State University *New Jersey*
Murray State University *Kentucky*
Nazareth College of Rochester *New York*
New Mexico State University *New Mexico*
New York University *New York*
North Carolina Central University *North Carolina*
Northeastern State University *Oklahoma*
Northeastern University *Massachusetts*
Northern Arizona University *Arizona*
Northern Illinois University *Illinois*
Northern Michigan University *Michigan*
Northwestern University *Illinois*
Nova Southeastern University *Florida*
The Ohio State University *Ohio*
Ohio University *Ohio*
Oklahoma State University *Oklahoma*
Old Dominion University *Virginia*
Our Lady of the Lake University of San Antonio *Texas*
Penn State University Park *Pennsylvania*
Portland State University *Oregon*
Purdue University *Indiana*
Queens College of the City University of New York *New York*
Radford University *Virginia*
Rockhurst University *Missouri*
Rush University *Illinois*
St. Cloud State University *Minnesota*
St. John's University *New York*
Saint Louis University *Missouri*
Saint Xavier University *Illinois*
San Diego State University *California*
San Francisco State University *California*
San Jose State University *California*
Seton Hall University *New Jersey*
South Carolina State University *South Carolina*
Southeast Missouri State University *Missouri*
Southeastern Louisiana University *Louisiana*
Southern Connecticut State University *Connecticut*
Southern Illinois University Carbondale *Illinois*
Southern Illinois University Edwardsville *Illinois*
Southern University and Agricultural and Mechanical College *Louisiana*
State University of New York College at Geneseo *New York*
State University of New York at Fredonia *New York*
State University of New York at New Paltz *New York*
State University of New York at Plattsburgh *New York*
Stephen F. Austin State University *Texas*
Syracuse University *New York*
Temple University *Pennsylvania*
Tennessee State University *Tennessee*
Texas A&M University–Kingsville *Texas*
Texas Christian University *Texas*
Texas State University–San Marcos *Texas*
Texas Tech University *Texas*
Texas Woman's University *Texas*
Touro College *New York*
Towson University *Maryland*
Truman State University *Missouri*
The University of Akron *Ohio*
The University of Alabama *Alabama*
The University of Arizona *Arizona*
University of Arkansas *Arkansas*
University of Arkansas at Little Rock *Arkansas*
University at Buffalo, the State University of New York *New York*
University of California, San Diego *California*
University of Central Arkansas *Arkansas*
University of Central Florida *Florida*
University of Central Missouri *Missouri*
University of Central Oklahoma *Oklahoma*
University of Cincinnati *Ohio*
University of Colorado at Boulder *Colorado*
University of Connecticut *Connecticut*
University of the District of Columbia *District of Columbia*
University of Florida *Florida*
University of Georgia *Georgia*
University of Hawaii at Manoa *Hawaii*
University of Houston *Texas*
University of Illinois at Urbana–Champaign *Illinois*
The University of Iowa *Iowa*
The University of Kansas *Kansas*
University of Kentucky *Kentucky*
University of Louisiana at Lafayette *Louisiana*
University of Louisiana at Monroe *Louisiana*
University of Louisville *Kentucky*
University of Maine *Maine*
University of Maryland, College Park *Maryland*
University of Massachusetts Amherst *Massachusetts*
University of Memphis *Tennessee*
University of Minnesota, Duluth *Minnesota*
University of Minnesota, Twin Cities Campus *Minnesota*
University of Mississippi *Mississippi*
University of Missouri *Missouri*
University of Montevallo *Alabama*
University of Nebraska at Kearney *Nebraska*
University of Nebraska at Omaha *Nebraska*
University of Nebraska–Lincoln *Nebraska*
University of Nevada, Reno *Nevada*
University of New Hampshire *New Hampshire*
University of New Mexico *New Mexico*
The University of North Carolina at Chapel Hill *North Carolina*
The University of North Carolina at Greensboro *North Carolina*
University of North Dakota *North Dakota*
University of North Texas *Texas*
University of Northern Colorado *Colorado*
University of Northern Iowa *Iowa*
University of Oklahoma Health Sciences Center *Oklahoma*
University of Oregon *Oregon*
University of the Pacific *California*
University of Pittsburgh *Pennsylvania*
University of Puerto Rico, Medical Sciences Campus *Puerto Rico*
University of Redlands *California*
University of Rhode Island *Rhode Island*
University of South Alabama *Alabama*
University of South Carolina *South Carolina*
The University of South Dakota *South Dakota*
University of South Florida *Florida*
University of Southern Mississippi *Mississippi*
The University of Tennessee *Tennessee*
The University of Texas at Austin *Texas*
The University of Texas at Dallas *Texas*
The University of Texas at El Paso *Texas*
The University of Texas–Pan American *Texas*
The University of Toledo *Ohio*
University of Tulsa *Oklahoma*

University of Utah *Utah*
University of Vermont *Vermont*
University of Virginia *Virginia*
University of Washington *Washington*
University of Wisconsin–Eau Claire *Wisconsin*
University of Wisconsin–Madison *Wisconsin*
University of Wisconsin–Milwaukee *Wisconsin*
University of Wisconsin–River Falls *Wisconsin*
University of Wisconsin–Stevens Point *Wisconsin*
University of Wisconsin–Whitewater *Wisconsin*
University of Wyoming *Wyoming*
Utah State University *Utah*
Valdosta State University *Georgia*
Vanderbilt University *Tennessee*
Washington State University *Washington*
Washington University in St. Louis *Missouri*
Wayne State University *Michigan*
West Chester University of Pennsylvania *Pennsylvania*
West Texas A&M University *Texas*
West Virginia University *West Virginia*
Western Carolina University *North Carolina*
Western Illinois University *Illinois*
Western Kentucky University *Kentucky*
Western Michigan University *Michigan*
Western Washington University *Washington*
Wichita State University *Kansas*
William Paterson University of New Jersey *New Jersey*
Worcester State College *Massachusetts*

American Veterinary Medical Association (AVMA)

Auburn University *Alabama*
Colorado State University *Colorado*
Cornell University *New York*
Iowa State University of Science and Technology *Iowa*
Kansas State University *Kansas*
Louisiana State University and Agricultural and Mechanical College *Louisiana*
Michigan State University *Michigan*
Mississippi State University *Mississippi*
North Carolina State University *North Carolina*
The Ohio State University *Ohio*
Oklahoma State University *Oklahoma*
Oregon State University *Oregon*
Purdue University *Indiana*
Texas A&M University *Texas*
Tufts University *Massachusetts*
Tuskegee University *Alabama*
Université de Montréal *Quebec*
University of California, Davis *California*
University of Florida *Florida*
University of Georgia *Georgia*
University of Guelph *Ontario*
University of Illinois at Urbana–Champaign *Illinois*
University of Maryland, College Park *Maryland*
University of Minnesota, Twin Cities Campus *Minnesota*
University of Missouri *Missouri*
University of Pennsylvania *Pennsylvania*
University of Prince Edward Island *Prince Edward Island*
University of Saskatchewan *Saskatchewan*
The University of Tennessee *Tennessee*
University of Wisconsin–Madison *Wisconsin*
Vet Tech Institute at Bradford School *Ohio*
Vet Tech Institute at Fox College *Illinois*
Vet Tech Institute at Hickey College *Missouri*
Vet Tech Institute at International Business College (Indianapolis) *Indiana*
Vet Tech Institute at International Business College (Fort Wayne) *Indiana*
Virginia Polytechnic Institute and State University *Virginia*
Washington State University *Washington*

Association of Advanced Rabbinical and Talmudic Schools (AARTS)

Bais Binyomin Academy *Connecticut*
Beis Medrash Heichal Dovid *New York*
Beth HaMedrash Shaarei Yosher Institute *New York*
Beth Hatalmud Rabbinical College *New York*
Beth Medrash Govoha *New Jersey*
Central Yeshiva Tomchei Tmimim-Lubavitch *New York*
Darkei Noam Rabbinical College *New York*
Kehilath Yakov Rabbinical Seminary *New York*
Kol Yaakov Torah Center *New York*
Machzikei Hadath Rabbinical College *New York*
Mesivta of Eastern Parkway–Yeshiva Zichron Meilech *New York*
Mesivta Tifereth Jerusalem of America *New York*
Mesivta Torah Vodaath Rabbinical Seminary *New York*
Mirrer Yeshiva *New York*
Ner Israel Rabbinical College *Maryland*
Ner Israel Yeshiva College of Toronto *Ontario*
Ohr Hameir Theological Seminary *New York*
Ohr Somayach/Joseph Tanenbaum Educational Center *New York*
Rabbi Jacob Joseph School *New Jersey*
Rabbinical Academy Mesivta Rabbi Chaim Berlin *New York*
Rabbinical College of America *New Jersey*
Rabbinical College Beth Shraga *New York*
Rabbinical College Bobover Yeshiva B'nei Zion *New York*
Rabbinical College Ch'san Sofer *New York*
Rabbinical College of Long Island *New York*
Rabbinical College of Ohr Shimon Yisroel *New York*
Rabbinical College of Telshe *Ohio*
Rabbinical Seminary Adas Yereim *New York*
Rabbinical Seminary of America *New York*
Rabbinical Seminary M'kor Chaim *New York*
Sh'or Yoshuv Rabbinical College *New York*
Talmudic College of Florida *Florida*
Talmudical Academy of New Jersey *New Jersey*
Talmudical Institute of Upstate New York *New York*
Talmudical Seminary Oholei Torah *New York*
Talmudical Yeshiva of Philadelphia *Pennsylvania*
Telshe Yeshiva–Chicago *Illinois*
Torah Temimah Talmudical Seminary *New York*
United Talmudical Seminary *New York*
U.T.A. Mesivta of Kiryas Joel *New York*
Yeshiva Beth Moshe *Pennsylvania*
Yeshiva College of the Nation's Capital *Maryland*
Yeshiva Derech Chaim *New York*
Yeshiva D'Monsey Rabbinical College *New York*
Yeshiva Gedolah of Greater Detroit *Michigan*
Yeshiva Gedolah Imrei Yosef D'Spinka *New York*
Yeshiva Gedolah Rabbinical College *Florida*
Yeshiva Karlin Stolin Rabbinical Institute *New York*
Yeshiva and Kolel Bais Medrash Elyon *New York*
Yeshiva and Kollel Harbotzas Torah *New York*
Yeshiva of Nitra Rabbinical College *New York*
Yeshiva Ohr Elchonon Chabad/West Coast Talmudical Seminary *California*
Yeshiva Shaar Hatorah Talmudic Research Institute *New York*
Yeshiva Shaarei Torah of Rockland *New York*
Yeshiva of the Telshe Alumni *New York*
Yeshiva Toras Chaim Talmudical Seminary *Colorado*
Yeshivas Novominsk *New York*
Yeshivat Mikdash Melech *New York*
Yeshivath Viznitz *New York*
Yeshivath Zichron Moshe *New York*

Association of American Law Schools (AALS)

American University *District of Columbia*
Arizona State University *Arizona*
Baylor University *Texas*
Boston College *Massachusetts*
Boston University *Massachusetts*
Brigham Young University *Utah*
Capital University *Ohio*
Case Western Reserve University *Ohio*
The Catholic University of America *District of Columbia*
Cleveland State University *Ohio*
The College of William and Mary *Virginia*
Columbia University *New York*
Cornell University *New York*
Creighton University *Nebraska*
DePaul University *Illinois*
Drake University *Iowa*
Duke University *North Carolina*
Duquesne University *Pennsylvania*
Emory University *Georgia*
Florida State University *Florida*
Fordham University *New York*
George Mason University *Virginia*
The George Washington University *District of Columbia*
Georgetown University *District of Columbia*
Georgia State University *Georgia*
Golden Gate University *California*
Gonzaga University *Washington*
Hamline University *Minnesota*
Harvard University *Massachusetts*
Hofstra University *New York*
Howard University *District of Columbia*
Illinois Institute of Technology *Illinois*
Lewis & Clark College *Oregon*
Louisiana State University and Agricultural and Mechanical College *Louisiana*
Loyola Marymount University *California*
Loyola University Chicago *Illinois*
Loyola University New Orleans *Louisiana*
Marquette University *Wisconsin*
Mercer University *Georgia*
Mississippi College *Mississippi*
New York University *New York*
Northeastern University *Massachusetts*
Northern Illinois University *Illinois*
Northern Kentucky University *Kentucky*
Northwestern University *Illinois*
Nova Southeastern University *Florida*
Ohio Northern University *Ohio*
The Ohio State University *Ohio*
Oklahoma City University *Oklahoma*
Pace University *New York*
Pepperdine University *California*
Quinnipiac University *Connecticut*
Rutgers, The State University of New Jersey, Camden *New Jersey*
Rutgers, The State University of New Jersey, Newark *New Jersey*
St. John's University *New York*
Saint Louis University *Missouri*
St. Mary's University *Texas*
St. Thomas University *Florida*
Samford University *Alabama*
Santa Clara University *California*
Seattle University *Washington*
Seton Hall University *New Jersey*
Southern Illinois University Carbondale *Illinois*
Southern Methodist University *Texas*
Stanford University *California*
Stetson University *Florida*
Suffolk University *Massachusetts*
Syracuse University *New York*
Temple University *Pennsylvania*
Texas Tech University *Texas*
Touro College *New York*
Tulane University *Louisiana*
The University of Akron *Ohio*
The University of Alabama *Alabama*
The University of Arizona *Arizona*
University of Arkansas *Arkansas*
University of Arkansas at Little Rock *Arkansas*
University of Baltimore *Maryland*
University at Buffalo, the State University of New York *New York*
University of California, Berkeley *California*
University of California, Davis *California*
University of California, Los Angeles *California*
University of Chicago *Illinois*
University of Cincinnati *Ohio*
University of Colorado at Boulder *Colorado*
University of Connecticut *Connecticut*
University of Dayton *Ohio*
University of Denver *Colorado*
University of Detroit Mercy *Michigan*
University of Florida *Florida*
University of Georgia *Georgia*
University of Hawaii at Manoa *Hawaii*
University of Houston *Texas*
University of Idaho *Idaho*
University of Illinois at Urbana–Champaign *Illinois*
The University of Iowa *Iowa*
The University of Kansas *Kansas*
University of Kentucky *Kentucky*
University of Louisville *Kentucky*
University of Maine *Maine*

University of Memphis *Tennessee*
University of Miami *Florida*
University of Michigan *Michigan*
University of Minnesota, Twin Cities Campus *Minnesota*
University of Mississippi *Mississippi*
University of Missouri *Missouri*
University of Missouri–Kansas City *Missouri*
The University of Montana *Montana*
University of Nebraska–Lincoln *Nebraska*
University of Nevada, Las Vegas *Nevada*
University of New Mexico *New Mexico*
The University of North Carolina at Chapel Hill *North Carolina*
University of North Dakota *North Dakota*
University of Notre Dame *Indiana*
University of Oklahoma *Oklahoma*
University of Oregon *Oregon*
University of the Pacific *California*
University of Pennsylvania *Pennsylvania*
University of Pittsburgh *Pennsylvania*
University of Puerto Rico, Río Piedras *Puerto Rico*
University of Richmond *Virginia*
University of San Diego *California*
University of San Francisco *California*
University of South Carolina *South Carolina*
The University of South Dakota *South Dakota*
University of Southern California *California*
The University of Tennessee *Tennessee*
The University of Texas at Austin *Texas*
The University of Toledo *Ohio*
University of Tulsa *Oklahoma*
University of Utah *Utah*
University of Virginia *Virginia*
University of Washington *Washington*
University of Wisconsin–Madison *Wisconsin*
University of Wyoming *Wyoming*
Valparaiso University *Indiana*
Vanderbilt University *Tennessee*
Villanova University *Pennsylvania*
Wake Forest University *North Carolina*
Washburn University *Kansas*
Washington and Lee University *Virginia*
Washington University in St. Louis *Missouri*
Wayne State University *Michigan*
West Virginia University *West Virginia*
Western New England College *Massachusetts*
Whittier College *California*
Widener University *Pennsylvania*
Willamette University *Oregon*
Yale University *Connecticut*
Yeshiva University *New York*

Association for Biblical Higher Education (ABHE)

Alaska Bible College *Alaska*
Allegheny Wesleyan College *Ohio*
Ambrose University College *Alberta*
American Baptist College of American Baptist Theological Seminary *Tennessee*
Appalachian Bible College *West Virginia*
Arlington Baptist College *Texas*
Baptist Bible College *Missouri*
Baptist Bible College of Pennsylvania *Pennsylvania*
Baptist University of the Americas *Texas*
Barclay College *Kansas*
Bethany Bible College *New Brunswick*
Bethesda Christian University *California*
Beulah Heights University *Georgia*
Boise Bible College *Idaho*
Briercrest College *Saskatchewan*
Calvary Bible College and Theological Seminary *Missouri*
Carolina Christian College *North Carolina*
Carver Bible College *Georgia*
Central Bible College *Missouri*
Central Christian College of the Bible *Missouri*
Cincinnati Christian University *Ohio*
Clear Creek Baptist Bible College *Kentucky*
Colegio Pentecostal Mizpa *Puerto Rico*
College of Biblical Studies–Houston *Texas*
Columbia Bible College *British Columbia*
Columbia International University *South Carolina*
Crossroads Bible College *Indiana*
Crossroads College *Minnesota*
Dallas Christian College *Texas*
Davis College *New York*
Ecclesia College *Arkansas*
Emmanuel Bible College *Ontario*
Emmanuel Bible College *California*
Emmaus Bible College *Iowa*
Eugene Bible College *Oregon*
Faith Baptist Bible College and Theological Seminary *Iowa*
Florida Christian College *Florida*
Free Will Baptist Bible College *Tennessee*
God's Bible School and College *Ohio*
Grace Bible College *Michigan*
Grace University *Nebraska*
Great Lakes Christian College *Michigan*
Heritage Baptist College and Heritage Theological Seminary *Ontario*
Heritage Christian University *Alabama*
Hobe Sound Bible College *Florida*
Horizon College & Seminary *Saskatchewan*
John Wesley College *North Carolina*
Johnson Bible College *Tennessee*
Kentucky Mountain Bible College *Kentucky*
The King's College and Seminary *California*
Kuyper College *Michigan*
Lancaster Bible College & Graduate School *Pennsylvania*
Life Pacific College *California*
Lincoln Christian University *Illinois*
Manhattan Christian College *Kansas*
Master's College and Seminary *Ontario*
Mid-Atlantic Christian University *North Carolina*
Moody Bible Institute *Illinois*
Multnomah University *Oregon*
Nazarene Bible College *Colorado*
Nebraska Christian College *Nebraska*
Oak Hills Christian College *Minnesota*
Ohio Christian University *Ohio*
Ozark Christian College *Missouri*
Philadelphia Biblical University *Pennsylvania*
Prairie Bible Institute *Alberta*
Providence College and Theological Seminary *Manitoba*
Rio Grande Bible Institute *Texas*
Rocky Mountain College *Alberta*
Rosedale Bible College *Ohio*
St. Louis Christian College *Missouri*
School of Urban Missions *California*
Somerset Christian College *New Jersey*
Southeastern Baptist College *Mississippi*
Southeastern Bible College *Alabama*
Steinbach Bible College *Manitoba*
Summit Pacific College *British Columbia*
Toccoa Falls College *Georgia*
Tri-State Bible College *Ohio*
Trinity Bible College *North Dakota*
Trinity College of Florida *Florida*
Tyndale University College & Seminary *Ontario*
Universidad Teológica del Caribe *Puerto Rico*
Vanguard College *Alberta*
Washington Bible College *Maryland*
Western Christian College *Saskatchewan*
William and Catherine Booth College *Manitoba*
William Jessup University *California*
Williamson Christian College *Tennessee*
Zion Bible College *Massachusetts*

Association for Clinical Pastoral Education, Inc. (ACIPE)

Anderson University *Indiana*
Baylor University *Texas*
Boston University *Massachusetts*
Drew University *New Jersey*
Duke University *North Carolina*
Eastern Mennonite University *Virginia*
Eastern University *Pennsylvania*
Emory University *Georgia*
Gardner-Webb University *North Carolina*
George Fox University *Oregon*
Georgetown University *District of Columbia*
Gonzaga University *Washington*
Harvard University *Massachusetts*
Howard University *District of Columbia*
Indiana University–Purdue University Indianapolis *Indiana*
The Jewish Theological Seminary *New York*
The Johns Hopkins University *Maryland*
Liberty University *Virginia*
Loma Linda University *California*
Loyola University Chicago *Illinois*
Mount Angel Seminary *Oregon*
New Orleans Baptist Theological Seminary *Louisiana*
New York University *New York*
The Ohio State University *Ohio*
Regent University *Virginia*
Rush University *Illinois*
Sacred Heart Major Seminary *Michigan*
St. John's University *New York*
Saint Louis University *Missouri*
Seton Hall University *New Jersey*
Sewanee: The University of the South *Tennessee*
Southeastern Baptist Theological Seminary *North Carolina*
Southern Baptist Theological Seminary *Kentucky*
Southern Methodist University *Texas*
Stanford University *California*
Texas Christian University *Texas*
Thomas Jefferson University *Pennsylvania*
The University of Alabama at Birmingham *Alabama*
University of Arkansas for Medical Sciences *Arkansas*
University of California, Davis *California*
University of California, Los Angeles *California*
University of Chicago *Illinois*
University of Dubuque *Iowa*
The University of Iowa *Iowa*
University of Kentucky *Kentucky*
University of Louisville *Kentucky*
University of Minnesota, Twin Cities Campus *Minnesota*
The University of North Carolina at Chapel Hill *North Carolina*
University of Notre Dame *Indiana*
University of Oklahoma Health Sciences Center *Oklahoma*
University of Pennsylvania *Pennsylvania*
University of Rochester *New York*
University of St. Thomas *Texas*
University of St. Thomas *Minnesota*
The University of Tennessee *Tennessee*
The University of Texas Health Science Center at Houston *Texas*
University of Virginia *Virginia*
Vanderbilt University *Tennessee*
Virginia Commonwealth University *Virginia*
Virginia Union University *Virginia*
Wake Forest University *North Carolina*
Washington University in St. Louis *Missouri*
West Virginia University *West Virginia*
Yale University *Connecticut*

Association of Collegiate Business Schools and Programs (ACBSP)

Abilene Christian University *Texas*
Aiken Technical College *South Carolina*
Alabama State University *Alabama*
Albany State University *Georgia*
Alpena Community College *Michigan*
Alvernia University *Pennsylvania*
Anderson University *South Carolina*
Anderson University *Indiana*
Angelo State University *Texas*
Arcadia University *Pennsylvania*
Argosy University, Chicago *Illinois*
Arkansas Northeastern College *Arkansas*
Ashland Community and Technical College *Kentucky*
Ashland University *Ohio*
Athens State University *Alabama*
Athens Technical College *Georgia*
Atlanta Metropolitan College *Georgia*
Augsburg College *Minnesota*
Aurora University *Illinois*
Baker University *Kansas*
Baltimore City Community College *Maryland*
Berkeley College *New Jersey*
Biola University *California*
Bishop State Community College *Alabama*
Bluefield State College *West Virginia*
Bowie State University *Maryland*
Bronx Community College of the City University of New York *New York*

Bucks County Community College *Pennsylvania*
Butler County Community College *Pennsylvania*
Caldwell College *New Jersey*
California Baptist University *California*
California State University, Dominguez Hills *California*
Cameron University *Oklahoma*
Campbell University *North Carolina*
Capital University *Ohio*
Cardinal Stritch University *Wisconsin*
Carlos Albizu University, Miami Campus *Florida*
Catawba Valley Community College *North Carolina*
Central Carolina Technical College *South Carolina*
Central Maine Community College *Maine*
Central New Mexico Community College *New Mexico*
Chadron State College *Nebraska*
Chattahoochee Technical College *Georgia*
City Colleges of Chicago, Harold Washington College *Illinois*
City Colleges of Chicago, Wilbur Wright College *Illinois*
Claflin University *South Carolina*
College of Mount Saint Vincent *New York*
The College of Saint Rose *New York*
College of Southern Maryland *Maryland*
Colorado Technical University Colorado Springs *Colorado*
Columbus State Community College *Ohio*
Community College of Rhode Island *Rhode Island*
Concordia University, St. Paul *Minnesota*
Cossatot Community College of the University of Arkansas *Arkansas*
County College of Morris *New Jersey*
Cumberland University *Tennessee*
Cuyahoga Community College *Ohio*
Dakota State University *South Dakota*
Dallas Baptist University *Texas*
Dana College *Nebraska*
Delaware Technical & Community College, Jack F. Owens Campus *Delaware*
Delaware Technical & Community College, Stanton/Wilmington Campus *Delaware*
Delaware Technical & Community College, Terry Campus *Delaware*
Delgado Community College *Louisiana*
Delta State University *Mississippi*
Denmark Technical College *South Carolina*
DeSales University *Pennsylvania*
Doane College *Nebraska*
Dominican University *Illinois*
Doña Ana Branch Community College *New Mexico*
Drury University *Missouri*
East Arkansas Community College *Arkansas*
East Central University *Oklahoma*
Eastern New Mexico University *New Mexico*
Edgewood College *Wisconsin*
Edinboro University of Pennsylvania *Pennsylvania*
Elizabethtown College *Pennsylvania*
Embry-Riddle Aeronautical University *Florida*
Embry-Riddle Aeronautical University Worldwide *Florida*
Erie Community College *New York*
Fairmont State University *West Virginia*
Ferris State University *Michigan*
Fisk University *Tennessee*
Florence-Darlington Technical College *South Carolina*
Florida Memorial University *Florida*
Florida State College at Jacksonville *Florida*
Fontbonne University *Missouri*
Freed-Hardeman University *Tennessee*
Gadsden State Community College *Alabama*
Gainesville State College *Georgia*
Gallaudet University *District of Columbia*
Gannon University *Pennsylvania*
Gardner-Webb University *North Carolina*
Geneva College *Pennsylvania*
George Fox University *Oregon*
Georgia Southwestern State University *Georgia*
Georgian Court University *New Jersey*
Goldey-Beacom College *Delaware*
Governors State University *Illinois*
Grand Canyon University *Arizona*
Greenville Technical College *South Carolina*
Hardin-Simmons University *Texas*
Harding University *Arkansas*
Harper College *Illinois*
Harris-Stowe State University *Missouri*
Harrisburg Area Community College *Pennsylvania*
Henry Ford Community College *Michigan*
High Point University *North Carolina*
Hocking College *Ohio*
Holy Family University *Pennsylvania*
Holyoke Community College *Massachusetts*
Hood College *Maryland*
Horry-Georgetown Technical College *South Carolina*
Houston Baptist University *Texas*
Indiana University East *Indiana*
Ivy Tech Community College–Bloomington *Indiana*
Ivy Tech Community College–Central Indiana *Indiana*
Ivy Tech Community College–Columbus *Indiana*
Ivy Tech Community College–East Central *Indiana*
Ivy Tech Community College–Kokomo *Indiana*
Ivy Tech Community College–Lafayette *Indiana*
Ivy Tech Community College–North Central *Indiana*
Ivy Tech Community College–Northeast *Indiana*
Ivy Tech Community College–Northwest *Indiana*
Ivy Tech Community College–Richmond *Indiana*
Ivy Tech Community College–Southeast *Indiana*
Ivy Tech Community College–Southern Indiana *Indiana*
Ivy Tech Community College–Southwest *Indiana*
Ivy Tech Community College–Wabash Valley *Indiana*
Jackson Community College *Michigan*
Jackson State Community College *Tennessee*
James A. Rhodes State College *Ohio*
Jarvis Christian College *Texas*
Jefferson State Community College *Alabama*
Johnson C. Smith University *North Carolina*
Johnson County Community College *Kansas*
Joliet Junior College *Illinois*
Jones County Junior College *Mississippi*
Kansas City Kansas Community College *Kansas*
Kennebec Valley Community College *Maine*
Kent State University at Ashtabula *Ohio*
Kent State University at East Liverpool *Ohio*
Kent State University at Geauga *Ohio*
Kent State University at Salem *Ohio*
Kent State University at Trumbull *Ohio*
Kent State University at Tuscarawas *Ohio*
Kentucky State University *Kentucky*
Kettering University *Michigan*
La Roche College *Pennsylvania*
LaGrange College *Georgia*
Lamar State College–Port Arthur *Texas*
Lambuth University *Tennessee*
Langston University *Oklahoma*
Lawrence Technological University *Michigan*
Lawson State Community College *Alabama*
Lebanon Valley College *Pennsylvania*
Lehigh Carbon Community College *Pennsylvania*
Lenoir-Rhyne University *North Carolina*
Lewis University *Illinois*
LIM College *New York*
Lincoln Memorial University *Tennessee*
Lincoln University *Missouri*
Lindenwood University *Missouri*
Lipscomb University *Tennessee*
Louisiana College *Louisiana*
Lycoming College *Pennsylvania*
Lynchburg College *Virginia*
Manchester Community College *New Hampshire*
Marshall University *West Virginia*
Marymount University *Virginia*
Maryville University of Saint Louis *Missouri*
Marywood University *Pennsylvania*
McHenry County College *Illinois*
Medgar Evers College of the City University of New York *New York*
Mercy College *New York*
Methodist University *North Carolina*
Metropolitan Community College *Nebraska*
Midlands Technical College *South Carolina*
Midwestern State University *Texas*
Millersville University of Pennsylvania *Pennsylvania*
Millikin University *Illinois*
Mississippi College *Mississippi*
Mississippi University for Women *Mississippi*
Mississippi Valley State University *Mississippi*
Missouri Southern State University *Missouri*
Morehead State University *Kentucky*
Motlow State Community College *Tennessee*
Mount Vernon Nazarene University *Ohio*
Nashville State Technical Community College *Tennessee*
National Park Community College *Arkansas*
Nebraska Wesleyan University *Nebraska*
New Jersey City University *New Jersey*
New Mexico Highlands University *New Mexico*
North Carolina Central University *North Carolina*
North Central State College *Ohio*
North Georgia College & State University *Georgia*
North Hennepin Community College *Minnesota*
Northampton Community College *Pennsylvania*
Northeast State Technical Community College *Tennessee*
Northeastern State University *Oklahoma*
Northern Arizona University *Arizona*
Northern Maine Community College *Maine*
Northern New Mexico College *New Mexico*
Northern Oklahoma College *Oklahoma*
Northwest Missouri State University *Missouri*
Northwest Nazarene University *Idaho*
Northwest State Community College *Ohio*
Northwest University *Washington*
Northwestern College *Minnesota*
Northwestern College *Illinois*
Northwestern Michigan College *Michigan*
Norwich University *Vermont*
Notre Dame de Namur University *California*
Oakwood University *Alabama*
Ohio Dominican University *Ohio*
Oklahoma Baptist University *Oklahoma*
Oklahoma Christian University *Oklahoma*
Oklahoma City University *Oklahoma*
Oral Roberts University *Oklahoma*
Orange County Community College *New York*
Orangeburg-Calhoun Technical College *South Carolina*
Our Lady of the Lake University of San Antonio *Texas*
Owens Community College *Ohio*
Paine College *Georgia*
Peirce College *Pennsylvania*
Pellissippi State Technical Community College *Tennessee*
Philander Smith College *Arkansas*
Phillips Community College of the University of Arkansas *Arkansas*
Piedmont College *Georgia*
Piedmont Technical College *South Carolina*
Plymouth State University *New Hampshire*
Point Loma Nazarene University *California*
Pontifical Catholic University of Puerto Rico *Puerto Rico*
Pratt Community College *Kansas*
Presbyterian College *South Carolina*
Purdue University North Central *Indiana*
Queens University of Charlotte *North Carolina*
Queensborough Community College of the City University of New York *New York*
Reid State Technical College *Alabama*
Rivier College *New Hampshire*
Roanoke College *Virginia*
Roosevelt University *Illinois*
St. Ambrose University *Iowa*
Saint Vincent College *Pennsylvania*
Saint Xavier University *Illinois*
Salem International University *West Virginia*
Salt Lake Community College *Utah*
San Juan College *New Mexico*
Schenectady County Community College *New York*
Shawnee State University *Ohio*
Sinclair Community College *Ohio*
Slippery Rock University of Pennsylvania *Pennsylvania*
South Suburban College *Illinois*
South University *South Carolina*
South University *Georgia*
South University *Alabama*
South University (Royal Palm Beach) *Florida*
Southeast Community College, Beatrice Campus *Nebraska*
Southeast Community College, Lincoln Campus *Nebraska*

Southeast Community College, Milford Campus *Nebraska*
Southeastern Oklahoma State University *Oklahoma*
Southern Nazarene University *Oklahoma*
Southern New Hampshire University *New Hampshire*
Southern Polytechnic State University *Georgia*
Southern Utah University *Utah*
Southwest Baptist University *Missouri*
Southwest Tennessee Community College *Tennessee*
Southwestern Illinois College *Illinois*
Southwestern Oklahoma State University *Oklahoma*
Spartanburg Community College *South Carolina*
Spring Hill College *Alabama*
State University of New York College of Agriculture and Technology at Morrisville *New York*
Sul Ross State University *Texas*
Sullivan County Community College *New York*
Tarleton State University *Texas*
Taylor University *Indiana*
Technical College of the Lowcountry *South Carolina*
Texas A&M University–Kingsville *Texas*
Texas Lutheran University *Texas*
Texas Wesleyan University *Texas*
Three Rivers Community College *Missouri*
Three Rivers Community College *Connecticut*
Tiffin University *Ohio*
Tri-County Technical College *South Carolina*
Trident Technical College *South Carolina*
Trinity Christian College *Illinois*
Troy University *Alabama*
The University of Akron–Wayne College *Ohio*
University of Bridgeport *Connecticut*
University of Central Oklahoma *Oklahoma*
University of Dallas *Texas*
University of the District of Columbia *District of Columbia*
University of the Incarnate Word *Texas*
University of Indianapolis *Indiana*
University of Mobile *Alabama*
University of North Alabama *Alabama*
University of Northwestern Ohio *Ohio*
University of Phoenix *Arizona*
University of Saint Francis *Indiana*
University of St. Francis *Illinois*
University of St. Thomas *Texas*
University of South Carolina Lancaster *South Carolina*
University of the Virgin Islands *United States Virgin Islands*
The University of West Alabama *Alabama*
Vancouver Island University *British Columbia*
Vincennes University *Indiana*
Virginia Union University *Virginia*
Virginia Western Community College *Virginia*
Viterbo University *Wisconsin*
Volunteer State Community College *Tennessee*
Voorhees College *South Carolina*
Wagner College *New York*
Walla Walla University *Washington*
Walters State Community College *Tennessee*
West Texas A&M University *Texas*
Western New Mexico University *New Mexico*
Westminster College *Utah*
Wheeling Jesuit University *West Virginia*
Wilkes University *Pennsylvania*
Williamsburg Technical College *South Carolina*
Wingate University *North Carolina*
Woodbury University *California*
Xavier University of Louisiana *Louisiana*
York College of Pennsylvania *Pennsylvania*
York Technical College *South Carolina*

The Association of Technology, Management, and Applied Engineering (NAIT)

Alcorn State University *Mississippi*
Bowling Green State University *Ohio*
Butler County Community College *Pennsylvania*
California Polytechnic State University, San Luis Obispo *California*
California State University, Chico *California*
Central Connecticut State University *Connecticut*
Cleveland State Community College *Tennessee*
College of the Redwoods *California*
Crowder College *Missouri*
Delgado Community College *Louisiana*
East Carolina University *North Carolina*
Eastern Illinois University *Illinois*
Eastern Kentucky University *Kentucky*
Eastern Michigan University *Michigan*
Elaine P. Nunez Community College *Louisiana*
Elizabeth City State University *North Carolina*
Georgia Southern University *Georgia*
Illinois State University *Illinois*
Indiana State University *Indiana*
Iowa State University of Science and Technology *Iowa*
Ivy Tech Community College–Central Indiana *Indiana*
Ivy Tech Community College–Lafayette *Indiana*
Ivy Tech Community College–Northeast *Indiana*
Ivy Tech Community College–Richmond *Indiana*
Ivy Tech Community College–Southern Indiana *Indiana*
Ivy Tech Community College–Southwest *Indiana*
Ivy Tech Community College–Wabash Valley *Indiana*
Jackson State Community College *Tennessee*
Jackson State University *Mississippi*
Jacksonville State University *Alabama*
Kean University *New Jersey*
Linn State Technical College *Missouri*
Middle Tennessee State University *Tennessee*
Millersville University of Pennsylvania *Pennsylvania*
Minnesota State University Moorhead *Minnesota*
Missouri State University *Missouri*
Moberly Area Community College *Missouri*
Morehead State University *Kentucky*
Norfolk State University *Virginia*
North Carolina Agricultural and Technical State University *North Carolina*
Northeast State Technical Community College *Tennessee*
Northern Illinois University *Illinois*
Northern Michigan University *Michigan*
Ozarks Technical Community College *Missouri*
Purdue University *Indiana*
San Jose State University *California*
Sinclair Community College *Ohio*
Southeast Missouri State University *Missouri*
Southeastern Louisiana University *Louisiana*
Southern Illinois University Carbondale *Illinois*
Southern University at Shreveport *Louisiana*
State Fair Community College *Missouri*
Tennessee Technological University *Tennessee*
Texas A&M University–Commerce *Texas*
Texas A&M University–Kingsville *Texas*
Texas Southern University *Texas*
University of Arkansas at Pine Bluff *Arkansas*
University at Buffalo, the State University of New York *New York*
University of Central Missouri *Missouri*
University of Louisiana at Lafayette *Louisiana*
University of Nebraska at Kearney *Nebraska*
University of North Dakota *North Dakota*
University of Northern Iowa *Iowa*
University of Southern Maine *Maine*
The University of Texas at Tyler *Texas*
University of Wisconsin–Platteville *Wisconsin*
University of Wisconsin–Stout *Wisconsin*
Walters State Community College *Tennessee*
Western Kentucky University *Kentucky*

Association of Theological Schools in the United States and Canada (ATS)

Abilene Christian University *Texas*
Acadia University *Nova Scotia*
Ambrose University College *Alberta*
Amridge University *Alabama*
Anderson University *Indiana*
Andrews University *Michigan*
Ashland University *Ohio*
Azusa Pacific University *California*
Baptist Missionary Association Theological Seminary *Texas*
Barry University *Florida*
Baylor University *Texas*
Biola University *California*
Boston College *Massachusetts*
Boston University *Massachusetts*
Campbell University *North Carolina*
The Catholic University of America *District of Columbia*
Cincinnati Christian University *Ohio*
Columbia International University *South Carolina*
Delta State University *Mississippi*
Drew University *New Jersey*
Duke University *North Carolina*
Eastern Mennonite University *Virginia*
Eastern University *Pennsylvania*
Emory University *Georgia*
Gardner-Webb University *North Carolina*
George Fox University *Oregon*
Gonzaga University *Washington*
Hardin-Simmons University *Texas*
Harvard University *Massachusetts*
Heritage Baptist College and Heritage Theological Seminary *Ontario*
Howard University *District of Columbia*
La Sierra University *California*
Lipscomb University *Tennessee*
Loyola Marymount University *California*
Loyola University Chicago *Illinois*
McGill University *Quebec*
McMaster University *Ontario*
Mercer University *Georgia*
Mount Angel Seminary *Oregon*
Mount St. Mary's University *Maryland*
Multnomah University *Oregon*
New Orleans Baptist Theological Seminary *Louisiana*
Oakland City University *Indiana*
Oral Roberts University *Oklahoma*
Pontifical College Josephinum *Ohio*
Providence College and Theological Seminary *Manitoba*
Queen's University at Kingston *Ontario*
Regent University *Virginia*
Sacred Heart Major Seminary *Michigan*
St. Charles Borromeo Seminary, Overbrook *Pennsylvania*
Saint John's University *Minnesota*
Samford University *Alabama*
Seattle University *Washington*
Seton Hall University *New Jersey*
Sewanee: The University of the South *Tennessee*
Shaw University *North Carolina*
Southeastern Baptist Theological Seminary *North Carolina*
Southern Baptist Theological Seminary *Kentucky*
Southern Methodist University *Texas*
Texas Christian University *Texas*
Trinity International University *Illinois*
Trinity Western University *British Columbia*
Tyndale University College & Seminary *Ontario*
University of Chicago *Illinois*
University of Dubuque *Iowa*
University of Notre Dame *Indiana*
University of St. Thomas *Texas*
University of St. Thomas *Minnesota*
University of Toronto *Ontario*
The University of Western Ontario *Ontario*
The University of Winnipeg *Manitoba*
Vanderbilt University *Tennessee*
Virginia Union University *Virginia*
Wake Forest University *North Carolina*
Wilfrid Laurier University *Ontario*
Yale University *Connecticut*

Aviation Accreditation Board International (CAA)

Auburn University *Alabama*
Daniel Webster College *New Hampshire*
Embry-Riddle Aeronautical University *Florida*
Embry-Riddle Aeronautical University *Arizona*
Florida Institute of Technology *Florida*
Hampton University *Virginia*
Louisiana Tech University *Louisiana*
Mercer County Community College *New Jersey*
Middle Tennessee State University *Tennessee*
North Shore Community College *Massachusetts*
Purdue University *Indiana*
St. Cloud State University *Minnesota*
Saint Louis University *Missouri*
University of Central Missouri *Missouri*
University of Nebraska at Omaha *Nebraska*

University of North Dakota *North Dakota*
Western Michigan University *Michigan*

Commission on Accreditation of Healthcare Management Education (ACEHSA)

Arizona State University *Arizona*
Armstrong Atlantic State University *Georgia*
Baylor University *Texas*
Bernard M. Baruch College of the City University of New York *New York*
Boston University *Massachusetts*
California State University, Long Beach *California*
Columbia University *New York*
Cornell University *New York*
Dalhousie University *Nova Scotia*
Duke University *North Carolina*
Florida International University *Florida*
The George Washington University *District of Columbia*
Georgia State University *Georgia*
Governors State University *Illinois*
Indiana University–Purdue University Indianapolis *Indiana*
The Johns Hopkins University *Maryland*
King's College *Pennsylvania*
Marymount University *Virginia*
Medical University of South Carolina *South Carolina*
New York University *New York*
Northwestern University *Illinois*
The Ohio State University *Ohio*
Penn State University Park *Pennsylvania*
Rush University *Illinois*
Saint Louis University *Missouri*
San Diego State University *California*
Simmons College *Massachusetts*
Temple University *Pennsylvania*
Texas State University–San Marcos *Texas*
Texas Tech University *Texas*
Texas Woman's University *Texas*
Trinity University *Texas*
Tulane University *Louisiana*
Université de Montréal *Quebec*
The University of Alabama at Birmingham *Alabama*
University of Arkansas at Little Rock *Arkansas*
University of California, Berkeley *California*
University of California, Los Angeles *California*
University of Central Florida *Florida*
University of Colorado Denver *Colorado*
University of Florida *Florida*
University of Houston–Clear Lake *Texas*
The University of Iowa *Iowa*
The University of Kansas *Kansas*
University of Kentucky *Kentucky*
University of Memphis *Tennessee*
University of Miami *Florida*
University of Michigan *Michigan*
University of Minnesota, Twin Cities Campus *Minnesota*
University of Missouri *Missouri*
The University of North Carolina at Chapel Hill *North Carolina*
The University of North Carolina at Charlotte *North Carolina*
University of Oklahoma Health Sciences Center *Oklahoma*
University of Ottawa *Ontario*
University of Pennsylvania *Pennsylvania*
University of Pittsburgh *Pennsylvania*
University of Puerto Rico, Medical Sciences Campus *Puerto Rico*
University of St. Thomas *Minnesota*
The University of Scranton *Pennsylvania*
University of South Carolina *South Carolina*
University of Southern California *California*
University of Southern Maine *Maine*
University of Toronto *Ontario*
University of Washington *Washington*
University of Wisconsin–Madison *Wisconsin*
Virginia Commonwealth University *Virginia*
Washington University in St. Louis *Missouri*
Widener University *Pennsylvania*
Xavier University *Ohio*
Yale University *Connecticut*

Commission on Opticianry Accreditation (COptA)

Camden County College *New Jersey*
College of Southern Nevada *Nevada*
DeKalb Technical College *Georgia*
Durham Technical Community College *North Carolina*
El Paso Community College *Texas*
Erie Community College *New York*
Essex County College *New Jersey*
Hillsborough Community College *Florida*
Holyoke Community College *Massachusetts*
Indiana University Bloomington *Indiana*
J. Sargeant Reynolds Community College *Virginia*
Miami Dade College *Florida*
Middlesex Community College *Connecticut*
Milwaukee Area Technical College *Wisconsin*
New York City College of Technology of the City University of New York *New York*
Ogeechee Technical College *Georgia*
Raritan Valley Community College *New Jersey*
Roane State Community College *Tennessee*
Seattle Central Community College *Washington*
Southwestern Indian Polytechnic Institute *New Mexico*
Tyler Junior College *Texas*

Committee on Accreditation of Education Programs in Kinesiotherapy (CAEPK)

California State University, Long Beach *California*
Norfolk State University *Virginia*
San Diego State University *California*
Shaw University *North Carolina*
University of Southern Mississippi *Mississippi*
The University of Toledo *Ohio*

Committee on Accreditation for Respiratory Care (CARC)

Allegany College of Maryland *Maryland*
Alvin Community College *Texas*
Amarillo College *Texas*
American River College *California*
Angelina College *Texas*
Apollo College–Phoenix *Arizona*
Apollo College–Tri-City, Inc. *Arizona*
Armstrong Atlantic State University *Georgia*
Ashland Community and Technical College *Kentucky*
Athens Technical College *Georgia*
ATI College of Health *Florida*
Augusta Technical College *Georgia*
Baltimore City Community College *Maryland*
Baptist College of Health Sciences *Tennessee*
Bellarmine University *Kentucky*
Bergen Community College *New Jersey*
Berkshire Community College *Massachusetts*
Black River Technical College *Arkansas*
Bluegrass Community and Technical College *Kentucky*
Boise State University *Idaho*
Borough of Manhattan Community College of the City University of New York *New York*
Bossier Parish Community College *Louisiana*
Bowling Green State University *Ohio*
Bowling Green Technical College *Kentucky*
Brevard Community College *Florida*
Brookdale Community College *New Jersey*
Broward College *Florida*
Butte College *California*
Carteret Community College *North Carolina*
Catawba Valley Community College *North Carolina*
Central New Mexico Community College *New Mexico*
Central Piedmont Community College *North Carolina*
Champlain College *Vermont*
Chattanooga State Community College *Tennessee*
Cincinnati State Technical and Community College *Ohio*
College of DuPage *Illinois*
College of Southern Nevada *Nevada*
Collin County Community College District *Texas*
Columbia State Community College *Tennessee*
Columbus State Community College *Ohio*
Community College of Allegheny County *Pennsylvania*
Community College of Aurora *Colorado*
The Community College of Baltimore County *Maryland*
Community College of Philadelphia *Pennsylvania*
Community College of Rhode Island *Rhode Island*
Concorde Career Institute *Missouri*
Concorde Career Institute *California*
Copiah-Lincoln Community College–Natchez Campus *Mississippi*
Crafton Hills College *California*
Cuyahoga Community College *Ohio*
Dakota State University *South Dakota*
Darton College *Georgia*
Daytona State College *Florida*
Del Mar College *Texas*
Delaware County Community College *Pennsylvania*
Delaware Technical & Community College, Jack F. Owens Campus *Delaware*
Delaware Technical & Community College, Stanton/Wilmington Campus *Delaware*
Delgado Community College *Louisiana*
Delta College *Michigan*
Des Moines Area Community College *Iowa*
Doña Ana Branch Community College *New Mexico*
Durham Technical Community College *North Carolina*
East Los Angeles College *California*
East Tennessee State University *Tennessee*
Eastern Gateway Community College *Ohio*
Eastern New Mexico University–Roswell *New Mexico*
Edgecombe Community College *North Carolina*
Edison State College *Florida*
El Camino College *California*
El Centro College *Texas*
El Paso Community College *Texas*
Erie Community College, North Campus *New York*
Fayetteville Technical Community College *North Carolina*
Ferris State University *Michigan*
Florence-Darlington Technical College *South Carolina*
Florida Agricultural and Mechanical University *Florida*
Florida State College at Jacksonville *Florida*
Foothill College *California*
Forsyth Technical Community College *North Carolina*
Frederick Community College *Maryland*
Fresno City College *California*
Front Range Community College *Colorado*
Gannon University *Pennsylvania*
GateWay Community College *Arizona*
Genesee Community College *New York*
George C. Wallace Community College *Alabama*
Georgia State University *Georgia*
Gloucester County College *New Jersey*
Greenville Technical College *South Carolina*
Grossmont College *California*
Gulf Coast Community College *Florida*
Gwinnett Technical College *Georgia*
Gwynedd-Mercy College *Pennsylvania*
Hannibal-LaGrange College *Missouri*
Harrisburg Area Community College *Pennsylvania*
Hawkeye Community College *Iowa*
Henry Ford Community College *Michigan*
Highline Community College *Washington*
Hillsborough Community College *Florida*
Hinds Community College *Mississippi*
Houston Community College System *Texas*
Hudson Valley Community College *New York*
Illinois Central College *Illinois*
Independence University *Utah*
Indian River State College *Florida*
Indiana University Northwest *Indiana*
Indiana University of Pennsylvania *Pennsylvania*
Indiana University–Purdue University Indianapolis *Indiana*
Itawamba Community College *Mississippi*
Ivy Tech Community College–Central Indiana *Indiana*
Ivy Tech Community College–Lafayette *Indiana*
Ivy Tech Community College–Northeast *Indiana*
Ivy Tech Community College–Northwest *Indiana*

J. Sargeant Reynolds Community College *Virginia*
Jackson State Community College *Tennessee*
James A. Rhodes State College *Ohio*
Jefferson College of Health Sciences *Virginia*
Jefferson Community and Technical College *Kentucky*
Johnson County Community College *Kansas*
Kalamazoo Valley Community College *Michigan*
Kankakee Community College *Illinois*
Kansas City Kansas Community College *Kansas*
Kapiolani Community College *Hawaii*
Kaplan College, Phoenix Campus *Arizona*
Kaskaskia College *Illinois*
Kennebec Valley Community College *Maine*
Kettering College of Medical Arts *Ohio*
Kirkwood Community College *Iowa*
Labette Community College *Kansas*
Lake Superior College *Minnesota*
Lakeland Community College *Ohio*
Lamar Institute of Technology *Texas*
Lane Community College *Oregon*
Lincoln Land Community College *Illinois*
Loma Linda University *California*
Lonestar College–Kingwood *Texas*
Long Island University, Brooklyn Campus *New York*
Los Angeles Valley College *California*
Louisiana State University at Eunice *Louisiana*
Louisiana State University Health Sciences Center *Louisiana*
Macomb Community College *Michigan*
Macon State College *Georgia*
Madison Area Technical College *Wisconsin*
Madisonville Community College *Kentucky*
Manchester Community College *Connecticut*
Mansfield University of Pennsylvania *Pennsylvania*
Marygrove College *Michigan*
Massachusetts Bay Community College *Massachusetts*
Massasoit Community College *Massachusetts*
Maysville Community and Technical College (Maysville) *Kentucky*
Maysville Community and Technical College (Morehead) *Kentucky*
McLennan Community College *Texas*
Medical College of Georgia *Georgia*
Metropolitan Community College *Nebraska*
Miami Dade College *Florida*
Mid-State Technical College *Wisconsin*
Midland College *Texas*
Midlands Technical College *South Carolina*
Midwestern State University *Texas*
Millersville University of Pennsylvania *Pennsylvania*
Milwaukee Area Technical College *Wisconsin*
Mississippi Gulf Coast Community College *Mississippi*
Missouri Southern State University *Missouri*
Modesto Junior College *California*
Mohawk Valley Community College *New York*
Molloy College *New York*
Monroe County Community College *Michigan*
Montana State University–Great Falls College of Technology *Montana*
Moraine Valley Community College *Illinois*
Morehead State University *Kentucky*
Mott Community College *Michigan*
Mt. Hood Community College *Oregon*
Mt. San Antonio College *California*
Mountain Empire Community College *Virginia*
Mountain State University *West Virginia*
Muskegon Community College *Michigan*
Napa Valley College *California*
Nashua Community College *New Hampshire*
Nassau Community College *New York*
National-Louis University *Illinois*
Naugatuck Valley Community College *Connecticut*
Nebraska Methodist College *Nebraska*
Newman University *Kansas*
Nicholls State University *Louisiana*
North Central State College *Ohio*
North Dakota State University *North Dakota*
North Shore Community College *Massachusetts*
Northeast Iowa Community College *Iowa*
Northeast Mississippi Community College *Mississippi*
Northeast Wisconsin Technical College *Wisconsin*
Northeastern University *Massachusetts*
Northern Essex Community College *Massachusetts*
Northern Kentucky University *Kentucky*
Northern Virginia Community College *Virginia*
NorthWest Arkansas Community College *Arkansas*
Northwest Mississippi Community College *Mississippi*
Northwest Technical College *Minnesota*
Norwalk Community College *Connecticut*
Oakland Community College *Michigan*
Odessa College *Texas*
The Ohio State University *Ohio*
Ohlone College *California*
Oklahoma City Community College *Oklahoma*
Onondaga Community College *New York*
Orange Coast College *California*
Our Lady of Holy Cross College *Louisiana*
Ozarks Technical Community College *Missouri*
Palm Beach State College *Florida*
Parkland College *Illinois*
Passaic County Community College *New Jersey*
Pearl River Community College *Mississippi*
Pensacola Junior College *Florida*
Piedmont Technical College *South Carolina*
Pima Community College *Arizona*
Pima Medical Institute *Colorado*
Pima Medical Institute (Mesa) *Arizona*
Pima Medical Institute (Tucson) *Arizona*
Pitt Community College *North Carolina*
Prince George's Community College *Maryland*
Pueblo Community College *Colorado*
Pulaski Technical College *Arkansas*
Quinnipiac University *Connecticut*
Quinsigamond Community College *Massachusetts*
Reading Area Community College *Pennsylvania*
Roane State Community College *Tennessee*
Robeson Community College *North Carolina*
Rochester Community and Technical College *Minnesota*
Rock Valley College *Illinois*
Rogue Community College *Oregon*
Rose State College *Oklahoma*
St. Augustine College *Illinois*
St. Louis Community College at Forest Park *Missouri*
Saint Paul College–A Community & Technical College *Minnesota*
St. Petersburg College *Florida*
St. Philip's College *Texas*
Salisbury University *Maryland*
San Joaquin Valley College (Visalia) *California*
Sandhills Community College *North Carolina*
Sanford-Brown College (Fenton) *Missouri*
Sanford-Brown Institute–Pittsburgh *Pennsylvania*
Santa Fe College *Florida*
Santa Monica College *California*
Seattle Central Community College *Washington*
Seminole State College of Florida *Florida*
Seward County Community College *Kansas*
Shawnee State University *Ohio*
Shelton State Community College *Alabama*
Shenandoah University *Virginia*
Sinclair Community College *Ohio*
Skyline College *California*
South Plains College *Texas*
Southeast Community College, Lincoln Campus *Nebraska*
Southeast Kentucky Community and Technical College *Kentucky*
Southern Illinois University Carbondale *Illinois*
Southern Maine Community College *Maine*
Southern University at Shreveport *Louisiana*
Southwest Georgia Technical College *Georgia*
Southwest Virginia Community College *Virginia*
Southwestern Community College *North Carolina*
Southwestern Illinois College *Illinois*
Spartanburg Community College *South Carolina*
Spokane Community College *Washington*
Springfield Technical Community College *Massachusetts*
Stanly Community College *North Carolina*
Stark State College of Technology *Ohio*
State College of Florida Manatee-Sarasota *Florida*
State University of New York Upstate Medical University *New York*
Stony Brook University, State University of New York *New York*
Tacoma Community College *Washington*
Tallahassee Community College *Florida*
Tarrant County College District *Texas*
Temple College *Texas*
Tennessee State University *Tennessee*
Texas Southern University *Texas*
Texas Southmost College *Texas*
Texas State University–San Marcos *Texas*
Tidewater Community College *Virginia*
Trident Technical College *South Carolina*
Triton College *Illinois*
Tulsa Community College *Oklahoma*
Tyler Junior College *Texas*
Union County College *New Jersey*
Universidad Adventista de las Antillas *Puerto Rico*
The University of Akron *Ohio*
The University of Alabama at Birmingham *Alabama*
University of Arkansas Community College at Hope *Arkansas*
University of Arkansas for Medical Sciences *Arkansas*
University of Central Florida *Florida*
University of Charleston *West Virginia*
University of the District of Columbia *District of Columbia*
University of Hartford *Connecticut*
The University of Kansas *Kansas*
University of Mary *North Dakota*
University of Missouri *Missouri*
The University of Montana *Montana*
University of Pittsburgh at Johnstown *Pennsylvania*
University of South Alabama *Alabama*
University of Southern Indiana *Indiana*
The University of Texas Health Science Center at San Antonio *Texas*
The University of Texas Medical Branch *Texas*
The University of Toledo *Ohio*
Valencia Community College *Florida*
Victor Valley College *California*
Victoria College *Texas*
Vincennes University *Indiana*
Volunteer State Community College *Tennessee*
Wallace State Community College *Alabama*
Walters State Community College *Tennessee*
Washburn University *Kansas*
Washington Adventist University *Maryland*
Washington State Community College *Ohio*
Wayne County Community College District *Michigan*
Weatherford College *Texas*
Weber State University *Utah*
West Chester University of Pennsylvania *Pennsylvania*
West Virginia Northern Community College *West Virginia*
West Virginia University Institute of Technology *West Virginia*
Westchester Community College *New York*
Western Technical College *Wisconsin*
Western Wyoming Community College *Wyoming*
Wheeling Jesuit University *West Virginia*
York College of Pennsylvania *Pennsylvania*
Youngstown State University *Ohio*

Council on Chiropractic Education (CCE)

Cleveland Chiropractic College–Kansas City Campus *Kansas*
Cleveland Chiropractic College–Los Angeles Campus *California*
D'Youville College *New York*
Life University *Georgia*
Logan University–College of Chiropractic *Missouri*
Palmer College of Chiropractic *Iowa*
University of Bridgeport *Connecticut*

Council on Education for Public Health (CEPH)

Arizona State University *Arizona*
Armstrong Atlantic State University *Georgia*
Boston University *Massachusetts*
Bowling Green State University *Ohio*
Brooklyn College of the City University of New York *New York*
Brown University *Rhode Island*
California State University, Fresno *California*
California State University, Long Beach *California*

California State University, Northridge *California*
Cleveland State University *Ohio*
Columbia University *New York*
Dartmouth College *New Hampshire*
Drexel University *Pennsylvania*
East Stroudsburg University of Pennsylvania *Pennsylvania*
East Tennessee State University *Tennessee*
Emory University *Georgia*
Florida Agricultural and Mechanical University *Florida*
Florida International University *Florida*
The George Washington University *District of Columbia*
Harvard University *Massachusetts*
Hunter College of the City University of New York *New York*
Idaho State University *Idaho*
Indiana University Bloomington *Indiana*
Indiana University–Purdue University Indianapolis *Indiana*
The Johns Hopkins University *Maryland*
Kent State University *Ohio*
Loma Linda University *California*
Louisiana State University Health Sciences Center *Louisiana*
Morgan State University *Maryland*
New Jersey Institute of Technology *New Jersey*
New Mexico State University *New Mexico*
New York University *New York*
Northern Arizona University *Arizona*
Northern Illinois University *Illinois*
Northwestern University *Illinois*
Nova Southeastern University *Florida*
The Ohio State University *Ohio*
Old Dominion University *Virginia*
Oregon Health & Science University *Oregon*
Oregon State University *Oregon*
Portland State University *Oregon*
Saint Louis University *Missouri*
San Diego State University *California*
San Francisco State University *California*
San Jose State University *California*
Southern Connecticut State University *Connecticut*
Temple University *Pennsylvania*
Texas A&M Health Science Center *Texas*
Tufts University *Massachusetts*
Tulane University *Louisiana*
The University of Akron *Ohio*
The University of Alabama at Birmingham *Alabama*
University at Albany, State University of New York *New York*
The University of Arizona *Arizona*
University of Arkansas for Medical Sciences *Arkansas*
University of California, Berkeley *California*
University of California, Los Angeles *California*
University of Hawaii at Manoa *Hawaii*
University of Illinois at Chicago *Illinois*
The University of Iowa *Iowa*
The University of Kansas *Kansas*
University of Maryland, College Park *Maryland*
University of Massachusetts Amherst *Massachusetts*
University of Miami *Florida*
University of Michigan *Michigan*
University of Minnesota, Twin Cities Campus *Minnesota*
University of Nebraska Medical Center *Nebraska*
University of Nebraska at Omaha *Nebraska*
University of New Mexico *New Mexico*
The University of North Carolina at Chapel Hill *North Carolina*
The University of North Carolina at Greensboro *North Carolina*
University of Northern Colorado *Colorado*
University of Oklahoma Health Sciences Center *Oklahoma*
University of Pittsburgh *Pennsylvania*
University of Puerto Rico, Medical Sciences Campus *Puerto Rico*
University of Rochester *New York*
University of South Carolina *South Carolina*
University of South Florida *Florida*
University of Southern California *California*
University of Southern Mississippi *Mississippi*
The University of Tennessee *Tennessee*
The University of Texas Health Science Center at Houston *Texas*
The University of Texas Medical Branch *Texas*
The University of Toledo *Ohio*
University of Utah *Utah*
University of Washington *Washington*
University of Wisconsin–La Crosse *Wisconsin*
Virginia Commonwealth University *Virginia*
West Chester University of Pennsylvania *Pennsylvania*
West Virginia University *West Virginia*
Western Kentucky University *Kentucky*
Wichita State University *Kansas*
Yale University *Connecticut*
Youngstown State University *Ohio*

Council for Interior Design Accreditation (FIDER)

Academy of Art University *California*
American InterContinental University Buckhead Campus *Georgia*
Arizona State University *Arizona*
The Art Center Design College *Arizona*
The Art Institute of Atlanta *Georgia*
The Art Institute of Dallas *Texas*
Auburn University *Alabama*
Boston Architectural College *Massachusetts*
Brenau University *Georgia*
Brigham Young University–Idaho *Idaho*
Buffalo State College, State University of New York *New York*
California College of the Arts *California*
California State University, Fresno *California*
California State University, Northridge *California*
California State University, Sacramento *California*
Colorado State University *Colorado*
Columbus College of Art & Design *Ohio*
Cornell University *New York*
Dakota County Technical College *Minnesota*
Design Institute of San Diego *California*
Drexel University *Pennsylvania*
East Carolina University *North Carolina*
Eastern Michigan University *Michigan*
El Centro College *Texas*
Endicott College *Massachusetts*
Fashion Institute of Technology *New York*
Florida State University *Florida*
The George Washington University *District of Columbia*
Georgia Southern University *Georgia*
Harrington College of Design *Illinois*
The Illinois Institute of Art–Chicago *Illinois*
The Illinois Institute of Art–Schaumburg *Illinois*
Illinois State University *Illinois*
Indiana University Bloomington *Indiana*
Interior Designers Institute *California*
International Academy of Design & Technology *Illinois*
International Academy of Design & Technology *Florida*
Iowa State University of Science and Technology *Iowa*
James Madison University *Virginia*
Kansas State University *Kansas*
Kean University *New Jersey*
Kent State University *Ohio*
Kwantlen Polytechnic University *British Columbia*
La Roche College *Pennsylvania*
Lawrence Technological University *Michigan*
Louisiana State University and Agricultural and Mechanical College *Louisiana*
Louisiana Tech University *Louisiana*
Marymount University *Virginia*
Maryville University of Saint Louis *Missouri*
Meredith College *North Carolina*
Miami University *Ohio*
Michigan State University *Michigan*
Middle Tennessee State University *Tennessee*
Mississippi State University *Mississippi*
Moore College of Art & Design *Pennsylvania*
Mount Ida College *Massachusetts*
Mount Mary College *Wisconsin*
New York Institute of Technology *New York*
New York School of Interior Design *New York*
Newbury College *Massachusetts*
North Dakota State University *North Dakota*
The Ohio State University *Ohio*
Ohio University *Ohio*
Oklahoma State University *Oklahoma*
O'More College of Design *Tennessee*
Philadelphia University *Pennsylvania*
Pratt Institute *New York*
Purdue University *Indiana*
Ringling College of Art and Design *Florida*
Rochester Institute of Technology *New York*
Rocky Mountain College of Art Design *Colorado*
Ryerson University *Ontario*
Samford University *Alabama*
School of Visual Arts *New York*
Southern Illinois University Carbondale *Illinois*
Stephen F. Austin State University *Texas*
Suffolk University *Massachusetts*
Syracuse University *New York*
Texas Christian University *Texas*
Texas State University–San Marcos *Texas*
Texas Tech University *Texas*
The University of Akron *Ohio*
The University of Alabama *Alabama*
University of Arkansas *Arkansas*
University of California, Berkeley *California*
University of California, Los Angeles *California*
University of Central Oklahoma *Oklahoma*
University of Cincinnati *Ohio*
University of Florida *Florida*
University of Georgia *Georgia*
University of Kentucky *Kentucky*
University of Louisiana at Lafayette *Louisiana*
University of Louisville *Kentucky*
University of Manitoba *Manitoba*
University of Memphis *Tennessee*
University of Minnesota, Twin Cities Campus *Minnesota*
University of Missouri *Missouri*
University of Nebraska–Lincoln *Nebraska*
University of Nevada, Las Vegas *Nevada*
The University of North Carolina at Greensboro *North Carolina*
University of North Texas *Texas*
University of Oklahoma *Oklahoma*
University of Oregon *Oregon*
University of Southern Mississippi *Mississippi*
The University of Tennessee *Tennessee*
The University of Tennessee at Chattanooga *Tennessee*
The University of Texas at Arlington *Texas*
The University of Texas at Austin *Texas*
The University of Texas at San Antonio *Texas*
University of Wisconsin–Madison *Wisconsin*
University of Wisconsin–Stevens Point *Wisconsin*
University of Wisconsin–Stout *Wisconsin*
Utah State University *Utah*
Virginia Commonwealth University *Virginia*
Virginia Polytechnic Institute and State University *Virginia*
Washington State University *Washington*
Watkins College of Art, Design, & Film *Tennessee*
Wentworth Institute of Technology *Massachusetts*
West Valley College *California*
West Virginia University *West Virginia*
Western Carolina University *North Carolina*
Western Michigan University *Michigan*
Winthrop University *South Carolina*
Woodbury University *California*

Council on Occupational Education (COE)

Albany Technical College *Georgia*
Altamaha Technical College *Georgia*
Ashland Community and Technical College *Kentucky*
Atlanta Technical College *Georgia*
Aviation & Electronic Schools of America *California*
Big Sandy Community and Technical College *Kentucky*
Bowling Green Technical College *Kentucky*
Brown Mackie College–Atlanta *Georgia*
Cameron College *Louisiana*
Career Technical College *Louisiana*
Center for Advanced Legal Studies *Texas*
Central Georgia Technical College *Georgia*
College of Business and Technology *Florida*

Computer Career Center *Texas*
Concorde Career College *Tennessee*
East Central Technical College *Georgia*
Elizabethtown Community and Technical College *Kentucky*
Flint Hills Technical College *Kansas*
Flint River Technical College *Georgia*
Florida Culinary Institute *Florida*
Gateway Community and Technical College *Kentucky*
Georgia Northwestern Technical College *Georgia*
Griffin Technical College *Georgia*
H. Councill Trenholm State Technical College *Alabama*
Heart of Georgia Technical College *Georgia*
Interactive College of Technology *Georgia*
J. F. Drake State Technical College *Alabama*
Kaplan Career Institute, Nashville Campus *Tennessee*
Kaplan College, Arlington *Texas*
Kaplan College, Dallas *Texas*
Lanier Technical College *Georgia*
Lincoln College of Technology *Florida*
Louisiana Technical College *Louisiana*
Louisiana Technical College–Florida Parishes Campus *Louisiana*
Louisiana Technical College–Northeast Louisiana Campus *Louisiana*
Louisiana Technical College–Young Memorial Campus *Louisiana*
Maysville Community and Technical College (Morehead) *Kentucky*
Medical Careers Institute (Newport News) *Virginia*
Medical Careers Institute (Richmond) *Virginia*
Medical Careers Institute (Virginia Beach) *Virginia*
MedVance Institute *Tennessee*
MedVance Institute *Louisiana*
MedVance Institute *Florida*
Middle Georgia Technical College *Georgia*
Morrison Institute of Technology *Illinois*
Moultrie Technical College *Georgia*
North Central Institute *Tennessee*
North Georgia Technical College *Georgia*
Northeast Kansas Technical Center of Highland Community College *Kansas*
Northwest Kansas Technical College *Kansas*
Ogeechee Technical College *Georgia*
Okefenokee Technical College *Georgia*
Owensboro Community and Technical College *Kentucky*
Reid State Technical College *Alabama*
Sandersville Technical College *Georgia*
School of Communication Arts *North Carolina*
Somerset Community College *Kentucky*
South Georgia Technical College *Georgia*
Southeastern Technical College *Georgia*
Southwest Georgia Technical College *Georgia*
Stratford University (Falls Church) *Virginia*
Texas Culinary Academy *Texas*
Valdosta Technical College *Georgia*
West Georgia Technical College *Georgia*
West Kentucky Community and Technical College *Kentucky*
Wichita Area Technical College *Kansas*

Council on Rehabilitation Education (CORE)

Alabama Agricultural and Mechanical University *Alabama*
Arkansas State University - Jonesboro *Arkansas*
Assumption College *Massachusetts*
Auburn University *Alabama*
Ball State University *Indiana*
Boston University *Massachusetts*
Bowling Green State University *Ohio*
California State University, Fresno *California*
California State University, Los Angeles *California*
California State University, Sacramento *California*
California State University, San Bernardino *California*
Coppin State University *Maryland*
Drake University *Iowa*
East Carolina University *North Carolina*
East Central University *Oklahoma*
Edinboro University of Pennsylvania *Pennsylvania*
Emporia State University *Kansas*
Florida State University *Florida*
Fort Valley State University *Georgia*
The George Washington University *District of Columbia*
Georgia State University *Georgia*
Hofstra University *New York*
Hunter College of the City University of New York *New York*
Illinois Institute of Technology *Illinois*
Jackson State University *Mississippi*
Kent State University *Ohio*
Langston University *Oklahoma*
Louisiana State University Health Sciences Center *Louisiana*
Maryville University of Saint Louis *Missouri*
Michigan State University *Michigan*
Minnesota State University Mankato *Minnesota*
Mississippi State University *Mississippi*
Montana State University Billings *Montana*
New York University *New York*
Northeastern University *Massachusetts*
Northern Illinois University *Illinois*
The Ohio State University *Ohio*
Ohio University *Ohio*
Penn State University Park *Pennsylvania*
Portland State University *Oregon*
St. Cloud State University *Minnesota*
St. John's University *New York*
Salve Regina University *Rhode Island*
San Diego State University *California*
San Francisco State University *California*
South Carolina State University *South Carolina*
Southern Illinois University Carbondale *Illinois*
Southern University and Agricultural and Mechanical College *Louisiana*
Springfield College *Massachusetts*
Stephen F. Austin State University *Texas*
Syracuse University *New York*
Thomas University *Georgia*
Troy University *Alabama*
The University of Alabama *Alabama*
The University of Alabama at Birmingham *Alabama*
University at Albany, State University of New York *New York*
The University of Arizona *Arizona*
University of Arkansas *Arkansas*
University of Arkansas at Little Rock *Arkansas*
University at Buffalo, the State University of New York *New York*
University of Florida *Florida*
University of Hawaii at Manoa *Hawaii*
University of Idaho *Idaho*
University of Illinois at Urbana–Champaign *Illinois*
The University of Iowa *Iowa*
University of Kentucky *Kentucky*
University of Maryland, College Park *Maryland*
University of Maryland Eastern Shore *Maryland*
University of Massachusetts Boston *Massachusetts*
University of Memphis *Tennessee*
University of Missouri *Missouri*
The University of North Carolina at Chapel Hill *North Carolina*
University of North Florida *Florida*
University of North Texas *Texas*
University of Northern Colorado *Colorado*
University of Pittsburgh *Pennsylvania*
University of Puerto Rico, Río Piedras *Puerto Rico*
The University of Scranton *Pennsylvania*
University of South Carolina *South Carolina*
University of South Florida *Florida*
University of Southern Maine *Maine*
The University of Tennessee *Tennessee*
The University of Texas at Austin *Texas*
The University of Texas Southwestern Medical Center at Dallas *Texas*
The University of Texas–Pan American *Texas*
University of Wisconsin–Madison *Wisconsin*
University of Wisconsin–Stout *Wisconsin*
Utah State University *Utah*
Virginia Commonwealth University *Virginia*
Wayne State University *Michigan*
West Virginia University *West Virginia*
Western Michigan University *Michigan*
Western Oregon University *Oregon*
Western Washington University *Washington*
Winston-Salem State University *North Carolina*
Wright State University *Ohio*

Council on Social Work Education (CSWE)

Abilene Christian University *Texas*
Adelphi University *New York*
Alabama Agricultural and Mechanical University *Alabama*
Alabama State University *Alabama*
Albany State University *Georgia*
Alvernia University *Pennsylvania*
Anderson University *Indiana*
Andrews University *Michigan*
Anna Maria College *Massachusetts*
Appalachian State University *North Carolina*
Arizona State University *Arizona*
Arkansas State University - Jonesboro *Arkansas*
Ashland University *Ohio*
Atlantic Union College *Massachusetts*
Auburn University *Alabama*
Augsburg College *Minnesota*
Augustana College *South Dakota*
Aurora University *Illinois*
Austin Peay State University *Tennessee*
Avila University *Missouri*
Azusa Pacific University *California*
Ball State University *Indiana*
Barry University *Florida*
Barton College *North Carolina*
Baylor University *Texas*
Belmont University *Tennessee*
Bemidji State University *Minnesota*
Benedict College *South Carolina*
Bennett College for Women *North Carolina*
Bethany College *West Virginia*
Bethany College *Kansas*
Bethel College *Kansas*
Bethel University *Minnesota*
Bloomsburg University of Pennsylvania *Pennsylvania*
Bluffton University *Ohio*
Boise State University *Idaho*
Boston College *Massachusetts*
Boston University *Massachusetts*
Bowie State University *Maryland*
Bowling Green State University *Ohio*
Bradley University *Illinois*
Brescia University *Kentucky*
Briar Cliff University *Iowa*
Bridgewater State College *Massachusetts*
Brigham Young University *Utah*
Brigham Young University–Hawaii *Hawaii*
Bryn Mawr College *Pennsylvania*
Buena Vista University *Iowa*
Buffalo State College, State University of New York *New York*
Cabrini College *Pennsylvania*
California State University, Bakersfield *California*
California State University, Chico *California*
California State University, Dominguez Hills *California*
California State University, East Bay *California*
California State University, Fresno *California*
California State University, Fullerton *California*
California State University, Long Beach *California*
California State University, Los Angeles *California*
California State University, Northridge *California*
California State University, Sacramento *California*
California State University, San Bernardino *California*
California State University, Stanislaus *California*
California University of Pennsylvania *Pennsylvania*
Calvin College *Michigan*
Campbell University *North Carolina*
Campbellsville University *Kentucky*
Capital University *Ohio*
Carlow University *Pennsylvania*
Carthage College *Wisconsin*
Case Western Reserve University *Ohio*
Castleton State College *Vermont*
The Catholic University of America *District of Columbia*
Cedar Crest College *Pennsylvania*
Cedarville University *Ohio*
Central Connecticut State University *Connecticut*
Central Michigan University *Michigan*

Slippery Rock University of Pennsylvania *Pennsylvania*
Smith College *Massachusetts*
South Carolina State University *South Carolina*
Southeast Missouri State University *Missouri*
Southeastern Louisiana University *Louisiana*
Southern Adventist University *Tennessee*
Southern Arkansas University–Magnolia *Arkansas*
Southern Connecticut State University *Connecticut*
Southern Illinois University Carbondale *Illinois*
Southern Illinois University Edwardsville *Illinois*
Southern University and Agricultural and Mechanical College *Louisiana*
Southern University at New Orleans *Louisiana*
Southwest Minnesota State University *Minnesota*
Southwestern Adventist University *Texas*
Southwestern Oklahoma State University *Oklahoma*
Spalding University *Kentucky*
Spring Arbor University *Michigan*
Springfield College *Massachusetts*
State University of New York at Binghamton *New York*
State University of New York at Fredonia *New York*
State University of New York at Plattsburgh *New York*
Stephen F. Austin State University *Texas*
Stony Brook University, State University of New York *New York*
Syracuse University *New York*
Talladega College *Alabama*
Tarleton State University *Texas*
Taylor University *Indiana*
Temple University *Pennsylvania*
Tennessee State University *Tennessee*
Texas A&M University–Commerce *Texas*
Texas A&M University–Kingsville *Texas*
Texas Christian University *Texas*
Texas Southern University *Texas*
Texas State University–San Marcos *Texas*
Texas Tech University *Texas*
Texas Woman's University *Texas*
Troy University *Alabama*
Tulane University *Louisiana*
Tuskegee University *Alabama*
Union University *Tennessee*
The University of Akron *Ohio*
The University of Alabama *Alabama*
The University of Alabama at Birmingham *Alabama*
University of Alaska Anchorage *Alaska*
University of Alaska Fairbanks *Alaska*
University at Albany, State University of New York *New York*
University of Arkansas *Arkansas*
University of Arkansas at Little Rock *Arkansas*
University of Arkansas at Monticello *Arkansas*
University of Arkansas at Pine Bluff *Arkansas*
University at Buffalo, the State University of New York *New York*
University of California, Berkeley *California*
University of California, Los Angeles *California*
University of Central Florida *Florida*
University of Central Missouri *Missouri*
University of Chicago *Illinois*
University of Cincinnati *Ohio*
University of Connecticut *Connecticut*
University of Denver *Colorado*
University of Detroit Mercy *Michigan*
University of the District of Columbia *District of Columbia*
The University of Findlay *Ohio*
University of Georgia *Georgia*
University of Guam *Guam*
University of Hawaii at Manoa *Hawaii*
University of Houston *Texas*
University of Illinois at Chicago *Illinois*
University of Illinois at Springfield *Illinois*
University of Illinois at Urbana–Champaign *Illinois*
University of Indianapolis *Indiana*
The University of Iowa *Iowa*
The University of Kansas *Kansas*
University of Kentucky *Kentucky*
University of Louisiana at Monroe *Louisiana*
University of Louisville *Kentucky*
University of Maine *Maine*
University of Maine at Presque Isle *Maine*
University of Mary *North Dakota*
University of Mary Hardin-Baylor *Texas*
University of Maryland, Baltimore County *Maryland*
University of Memphis *Tennessee*
University of Michigan *Michigan*
University of Michigan–Flint *Michigan*
University of Minnesota, Duluth *Minnesota*
University of Minnesota, Twin Cities Campus *Minnesota*
University of Mississippi *Mississippi*
University of Missouri *Missouri*
University of Missouri–Kansas City *Missouri*
University of Missouri–St. Louis *Missouri*
The University of Montana *Montana*
University of Montevallo *Alabama*
University of Nebraska at Kearney *Nebraska*
University of Nebraska at Omaha *Nebraska*
University of Nevada, Las Vegas *Nevada*
University of Nevada, Reno *Nevada*
University of New England *Maine*
University of New Hampshire *New Hampshire*
University of North Alabama *Alabama*
The University of North Carolina at Chapel Hill *North Carolina*
The University of North Carolina at Charlotte *North Carolina*
The University of North Carolina at Greensboro *North Carolina*
The University of North Carolina at Pembroke *North Carolina*
The University of North Carolina Wilmington *North Carolina*
University of North Dakota *North Dakota*
University of North Texas *Texas*
University of Northern Iowa *Iowa*
University of Oklahoma *Oklahoma*
University of Pennsylvania *Pennsylvania*
University of Pittsburgh *Pennsylvania*
University of Puerto Rico at Humacao *Puerto Rico*
University of Puerto Rico, Río Piedras *Puerto Rico*
University of Rio Grande *Ohio*
University of the Sacred Heart *Puerto Rico*
University of Saint Francis *Indiana*
University of St. Francis *Illinois*
University of St. Thomas *Minnesota*
University of Sioux Falls *South Dakota*
University of South Carolina *South Carolina*
The University of South Dakota *South Dakota*
University of South Florida *Florida*
University of Southern California *California*
University of Southern Indiana *Indiana*
University of Southern Maine *Maine*
University of Southern Mississippi *Mississippi*
The University of Tennessee *Tennessee*
The University of Tennessee at Chattanooga *Tennessee*
The University of Tennessee at Martin *Tennessee*
The University of Texas at Arlington *Texas*
The University of Texas at Austin *Texas*
The University of Texas at El Paso *Texas*
The University of Texas at San Antonio *Texas*
The University of Texas–Pan American *Texas*
The University of Toledo *Ohio*
University of Utah *Utah*
University of Vermont *Vermont*
University of Washington *Washington*
University of West Florida *Florida*
University of Wisconsin–Eau Claire *Wisconsin*
University of Wisconsin–Green Bay *Wisconsin*
University of Wisconsin–Madison *Wisconsin*
University of Wisconsin–Milwaukee *Wisconsin*
University of Wisconsin–Oshkosh *Wisconsin*
University of Wisconsin–River Falls *Wisconsin*
University of Wisconsin–Superior *Wisconsin*
University of Wisconsin–Whitewater *Wisconsin*
University of Wyoming *Wyoming*
Ursuline College *Ohio*
Utah State University *Utah*
Valdosta State University *Georgia*
Valparaiso University *Indiana*
Virginia Commonwealth University *Virginia*
Virginia Intermont College *Virginia*
Virginia Union University *Virginia*
Walla Walla University *Washington*
Warren Wilson College *North Carolina*
Wartburg College *Iowa*
Washburn University *Kansas*
Washington University in St. Louis *Missouri*
Wayne State University *Michigan*
Weber State University *Utah*
West Chester University of Pennsylvania *Pennsylvania*
West Texas A&M University *Texas*
West Virginia State University *West Virginia*
West Virginia University *West Virginia*
Western Carolina University *North Carolina*
Western Connecticut State University *Connecticut*
Western Illinois University *Illinois*
Western Kentucky University *Kentucky*
Western Michigan University *Michigan*
Western New England College *Massachusetts*
Western New Mexico University *New Mexico*
Westfield State College *Massachusetts*
Wheelock College *Massachusetts*
Whittier College *California*
Wichita State University *Kansas*
Widener University *Pennsylvania*
William Woods University *Missouri*
Winona State University *Minnesota*
Winthrop University *South Carolina*
Wright State University *Ohio*
Xavier University *Ohio*
Yeshiva University *New York*
York College of the City University of New York *New York*
Youngstown State University *Ohio*

Distance Education and Training Council (DETC)

Allied American University *California*
American College of Technology *Missouri*
American Public University System *West Virginia*
Andrew Jackson University *Alabama*
Applied Professional Training, Inc. *California*
Ashworth College *Georgia*
Aspen University *Colorado*
California National University for Advanced Studies *California*
City Vision College *Missouri*
Cleveland Institute of Electronics *Ohio*
College of the Humanities and Sciences, Harrison Middleton University *Arizona*
Columbia Southern University *Alabama*
Dunlap-Stone University *Arizona*
Global University *Missouri*
Grantham University *Missouri*
Griggs University *Maryland*
Henley-Putnam University *California*
Huntington College of Health Sciences *Tennessee*
Independence University *Utah*
INSTE Bible College *Iowa*
National Paralegal College *Arizona*
The Paralegal Institute, Inc. *Arizona*
Penn Foster Career School *Pennsylvania*
Penn Foster College *Arizona*
Sessions College for Professional Design *Arizona*
Southwest University *Louisiana*
Universidad FLET *Florida*
University of Management and Technology *Virginia*
Western Governors University *Utah*
World College *Virginia*

Joint Commission on Allied Health Personnel in Ophthalmology (JCAHPO)

Emory University *Georgia*
Lakeland Community College *Ohio*
Louisiana State University Health Sciences Center *Louisiana*
Old Dominion University *Virginia*
Portland Community College *Oregon*
Pueblo Community College *Colorado*
Triton College *Illinois*

Joint Review Committee on Education in Cardiovascular Technology (JRCECT)

Augusta Technical College *Georgia*
Edison State College *Florida*
El Centro College *Texas*
Geneva College *Pennsylvania*
Grossmont College *California*
Gwynedd-Mercy College *Pennsylvania*

Milwaukee Area Technical College *Wisconsin*
Orange Coast College *California*
Southeast Technical Institute *South Dakota*
Spokane Community College *Washington*
The University of Toledo *Ohio*

Joint Review Committee on Education in Diagnostic Medical Sonography (JRCEDMS)

Austin Community College *Texas*
Baptist College of Health Sciences *Tennessee*
Bellevue College *Washington*
Bergen Community College *New Jersey*
Boise State University *Idaho*
Broward College *Florida*
Bunker Hill Community College *Massachusetts*
Caldwell Community College and Technical Institute *North Carolina*
Central Ohio Technical College *Ohio*
Chippewa Valley Technical College *Wisconsin*
College of Southern Nevada *Nevada*
Community College of Allegheny County *Pennsylvania*
Cuyahoga Community College *Ohio*
Del Mar College *Texas*
Delaware Technical & Community College, Stanton/Wilmington Campus *Delaware*
Delta College *Michigan*
El Centro College *Texas*
Florida Hospital College of Health Sciences *Florida*
Forsyth Technical Community College *North Carolina*
The George Washington University *District of Columbia*
Gloucester County College *New Jersey*
Hillsborough Community College *Florida*
Jackson Community College *Michigan*
Keiser University *Florida*
Kettering College of Medical Arts *Ohio*
Lorain County Community College *Ohio*
Medical College of Georgia *Georgia*
Mercy College of Health Sciences *Iowa*
Miami Dade College *Florida*
Middlesex Community College *Massachusetts*
Nebraska Methodist College *Nebraska*
New York University *New York*
Oakland Community College *Michigan*
Orange Coast College *California*
Owens Community College *Ohio*
Pitt Community College *North Carolina*
Rochester Institute of Technology *New York*
St. Catherine University *Minnesota*
Sanford-Brown Institute–Pittsburgh *Pennsylvania*
Seattle University *Washington*
Springfield Technical Community College *Massachusetts*
State University of New York Downstate Medical Center *New York*
Thomas Jefferson University *Pennsylvania*
Triton College *Illinois*
Tyler Junior College *Texas*
University of Nebraska Medical Center *Nebraska*
University of Oklahoma Health Sciences Center *Oklahoma*
Valencia Community College *Florida*
Wallace State Community College *Alabama*

Joint Review Committee on Education in Electroneurodiagnostic Technology (JRCEET)

Kirkwood Community College *Iowa*
Labouré College *Massachusetts*
Niagara County Community College *New York*
Orange Coast College *California*
Scott Community College *Iowa*
Southwestern Community College *North Carolina*
Western Technical College *Wisconsin*

Joint Review Committee on Education in Radiologic Technology (JRCERT)

Aims Community College *Colorado*
Albany Technical College *Georgia*
Allegany College of Maryland *Maryland*
Allen College *Iowa*
Amarillo College *Texas*
Angelina College *Texas*
Anne Arundel Community College *Maryland*
Apollo College *Washington*
Argosy University, Twin Cities *Minnesota*
Arkansas State University - Jonesboro *Arkansas*
Armstrong Atlantic State University *Georgia*
Asheville-Buncombe Technical Community College *North Carolina*
Athens Technical College *Georgia*
Austin Community College *Texas*
Avila University *Missouri*
Bacone College *Oklahoma*
Baker College of Jackson *Michigan*
Baker College of Owosso *Michigan*
Bakersfield College *California*
Ball State University *Indiana*
Bellevue College *Washington*
Bergen Community College *New Jersey*
Blackhawk Technical College *Wisconsin*
Blinn College *Texas*
Bluefield State College *West Virginia*
Boise State University *Idaho*
Brevard Community College *Florida*
Bronx Community College of the City University of New York *New York*
Brookdale Community College *New Jersey*
Broome Community College *New York*
Bunker Hill Community College *Massachusetts*
Cabrillo College *California*
Caldwell Community College and Technical Institute *North Carolina*
California State University, Long Beach *California*
California State University, Northridge *California*
Cañada College *California*
Capital Community College *Connecticut*
Carl Sandburg College *Illinois*
Carteret Community College *North Carolina*
Casper College *Wyoming*
Central Ohio Technical College *Ohio*
Central Virginia Community College *Virginia*
Chaffey College *California*
Champlain College *Vermont*
Charles Drew University of Medicine and Science *California*
Chesapeake College *Maryland*
Chippewa Valley Technical College *Wisconsin*
City College of San Francisco *California*
City Colleges of Chicago, Malcolm X College *Illinois*
City Colleges of Chicago, Wilbur Wright College *Illinois*
Clarkson College *Nebraska*
Cleveland Community College *North Carolina*
Clovis Community College *New Mexico*
College of Coastal Georgia *Georgia*
College of DuPage *Illinois*
College of Lake County *Illinois*
Colorado Technical University North Kansas City *Missouri*
Columbia State Community College *Tennessee*
Columbus State Community College *Ohio*
Community College of Allegheny County *Pennsylvania*
The Community College of Baltimore County *Maryland*
Community College of Denver *Colorado*
Community College of Philadelphia *Pennsylvania*
Community College of Rhode Island *Rhode Island*
Copiah-Lincoln Community College *Mississippi*
County College of Morris *New Jersey*
Cumberland County College *New Jersey*
Cuyahoga Community College *Ohio*
Cypress College *California*
Del Mar College *Texas*
Delaware Technical & Community College, Jack F. Owens Campus *Delaware*
Delaware Technical & Community College, Stanton/Wilmington Campus *Delaware*
Delgado Community College *Louisiana*
Delta College *Michigan*
Doña Ana Branch Community College *New Mexico*
East Tennessee State University *Tennessee*
Eastern Gateway Community College *Ohio*
Eastern Maine Community College *Maine*
Edgecombe Community College *North Carolina*
Edison State College *Florida*
El Camino College *California*
El Centro College *Texas*
Emory University *Georgia*
Erie Community College *New York*
Essex County College *New Jersey*
Eugenio María de Hostos Community College of the City University of New York *New York*
Fayetteville Technical Community College *North Carolina*
Ferris State University *Michigan*
Florence-Darlington Technical College *South Carolina*
Florida Hospital College of Health Sciences *Florida*
Foothill College *California*
Forsyth Technical Community College *North Carolina*
Fort Hays State University *Kansas*
Fresno City College *California*
Gadsden State Community College *Alabama*
Galveston College *Texas*
Gannon University *Pennsylvania*
Gateway Community College *Connecticut*
GateWay Community College *Arizona*
George C. Wallace Community College *Alabama*
Goldfarb School of Nursing at Barnes-Jewish College *Missouri*
Grand Rapids Community College *Michigan*
Greenville Technical College *South Carolina*
Gulf Coast Community College *Florida*
Gwinnett Technical College *Georgia*
Gwynedd-Mercy College *Pennsylvania*
Hagerstown Community College *Maryland*
Hazard Community and Technical College *Kentucky*
Hillsborough Community College *Florida*
Hinds Community College *Mississippi*
Holy Family University *Pennsylvania*
Holyoke Community College *Massachusetts*
Horry-Georgetown Technical College *South Carolina*
Houston Community College System *Texas*
Howard University *District of Columbia*
Hudson Valley Community College *New York*
Hutchinson Community College and Area Vocational School *Kansas*
Illinois Central College *Illinois*
Illinois Eastern Community Colleges, Olney Central College *Illinois*
Indian Hills Community College *Iowa*
Indian River State College *Florida*
Indiana University Northwest *Indiana*
Indiana University South Bend *Indiana*
Indiana University–Purdue University Indianapolis *Indiana*
Iowa Central Community College *Iowa*
Itawamba Community College *Mississippi*
Ivy Tech Community College–Central Indiana *Indiana*
Ivy Tech Community College–Wabash Valley *Indiana*
Jackson State Community College *Tennessee*
James A. Rhodes State College *Ohio*
Jefferson State Community College *Alabama*
Johnston Community College *North Carolina*
Jones County Junior College *Mississippi*
Kapiolani Community College *Hawaii*
Kaskaskia College *Illinois*
Keiser University *Florida*
Kellogg Community College *Michigan*
Kent State University at Salem *Ohio*
Kettering College of Medical Arts *Ohio*
Kilgore College *Texas*
Kishwaukee College *Illinois*
Labette Community College *Kansas*
Labouré College *Massachusetts*
Lake Michigan College *Michigan*
Lakeland Community College *Ohio*
Lakeshore Technical College *Wisconsin*
Lamar University *Texas*
Lansing Community College *Michigan*
Laramie County Community College *Wyoming*
Laredo Community College *Texas*
Lincoln Land Community College *Illinois*
Loma Linda University *California*
Long Beach City College *California*
Long Island University, C.W. Post Campus *New York*
Lorain County Community College *Ohio*
Los Angeles City College *California*

Louisiana State University at Eunice *Louisiana*
Madison Area Technical College *Wisconsin*
Mansfield University of Pennsylvania *Pennsylvania*
Marion Technical College *Ohio*
Marygrove College *Michigan*
Massachusetts Bay Community College *Massachusetts*
Massasoit Community College *Massachusetts*
McLennan Community College *Texas*
McNeese State University *Louisiana*
Medical College of Georgia *Georgia*
Merced College *California*
Mercer County Community College *New Jersey*
Mercy College of Northwest Ohio *Ohio*
Meridian Community College *Mississippi*
Merritt College *California*
Mesa State College *Colorado*
Metropolitan Community College–Penn Valley *Missouri*
Miami Dade College *Florida*
Mid Michigan Community College *Michigan*
Middlesex Community College *Massachusetts*
Middlesex Community College *Connecticut*
Middlesex County College *New Jersey*
Midland College *Texas*
Midlands Technical College *South Carolina*
Milwaukee Area Technical College *Wisconsin*
Misericordia University *Pennsylvania*
Mississippi Delta Community College *Mississippi*
Mississippi Gulf Coast Community College *Mississippi*
Missouri Southern State University *Missouri*
Monroe Community College *New York*
Moorpark College *California*
Moraine Valley Community College *Illinois*
Morehead State University *Kentucky*
Mt. San Antonio College *California*
Nassau Community College *New York*
National-Louis University *Illinois*
National Park Community College *Arkansas*
Naugatuck Valley Community College *Connecticut*
New York City College of Technology of the City University of New York *New York*
Newman University *Kansas*
NHTI, Concord's Community College *New Hampshire*
Niagara County Community College *New York*
North Arkansas College *Arkansas*
North Central State College *Ohio*
North Country Community College *New York*
North Shore Community College *Massachusetts*
Northampton Community College *Pennsylvania*
Northcentral Technical College *Wisconsin*
Northeast Mississippi Community College *Mississippi*
Northern Essex Community College *Massachusetts*
Northern Kentucky University *Kentucky*
Northern New Mexico College *New Mexico*
Northwest Technical College *Minnesota*
Northwestern State University of Louisiana *Louisiana*
Oakland Community College *Michigan*
Odessa College *Texas*
Orange Coast College *California*
Orangeburg-Calhoun Technical College *South Carolina*
Oregon Health & Science University *Oregon*
Oregon Institute of Technology *Oregon*
Our Lady of the Lake College *Louisiana*
Owens Community College *Ohio*
Owensboro Community and Technical College *Kentucky*
Palm Beach State College *Florida*
Parkland College *Illinois*
Pasadena City College *California*
Passaic County Community College *New Jersey*
Pearl River Community College *Mississippi*
Penn State New Kensington *Pennsylvania*
Penn State Schuylkill *Pennsylvania*
Pennsylvania College of Technology *Pennsylvania*
Pensacola Junior College *Florida*
Piedmont Technical College *South Carolina*
Pima Community College *Arizona*
Pima Medical Institute *Washington*
Pima Medical Institute *New Mexico*
Pima Medical Institute *Colorado*
Pima Medical Institute (Mesa) *Arizona*
Pima Medical Institute (Tucson) *Arizona*
Pitt Community College *North Carolina*
Polk State College *Florida*
Portland Community College *Oregon*
Presentation College *South Dakota*
Prince George's Community College *Maryland*
Quinnipiac University *Connecticut*
Quinsigamond Community College *Massachusetts*
Riverland Community College *Minnesota*
Roane State Community College *Tennessee*
Robert Morris University *Pennsylvania*
Rose State College *Oklahoma*
Rowan-Cabarrus Community College *North Carolina*
St. Louis Community College at Forest Park *Missouri*
St. Philip's College *Texas*
Salt Lake Community College *Utah*
Sandhills Community College *North Carolina*
Sanford-Brown College (Fenton) *Missouri*
Sanford-Brown Institute–Pittsburgh *Pennsylvania*
Santa Barbara City College *California*
Santa Fe College *Florida*
Santa Rosa Junior College *California*
Sauk Valley Community College *Illinois*
Scott Community College *Iowa*
Shawnee State University *Ohio*
Sinclair Community College *Ohio*
South Arkansas Community College *Arkansas*
South Plains College *Texas*
South Suburban College *Illinois*
Southeast Arkansas College *Arkansas*
Southeast Community College, Lincoln Campus *Nebraska*
Southern Maine Community College *Maine*
Southern Union State Community College *Alabama*
Southern University at Shreveport *Louisiana*
Southern West Virginia Community and Technical College *West Virginia*
Southwest Tennessee Community College *Tennessee*
Southwest Virginia Community College *Virginia*
Southwestern Community College *North Carolina*
Southwestern Illinois College *Illinois*
Southwestern Oklahoma State University at Sayre *Oklahoma*
Spartanburg Community College *South Carolina*
Springfield Technical Community College *Massachusetts*
State College of Florida Manatee-Sarasota *Florida*
State University of New York Upstate Medical University *New York*
Tacoma Community College *Washington*
Tarrant County College District *Texas*
Texas Southmost College *Texas*
Texas State University–San Marcos *Texas*
Thomas Jefferson University *Pennsylvania*
Tidewater Community College *Virginia*
Trident Technical College *South Carolina*
Triton College *Illinois*
Trocaire College *New York*
Truckee Meadows Community College *Nevada*
Tulsa Community College *Oklahoma*
Tyler Junior College *Texas*
Universidad Central del Caribe *Puerto Rico*
The University of Alabama at Birmingham *Alabama*
University of Arkansas at Fort Smith *Arkansas*
University of Arkansas for Medical Sciences *Arkansas*
University of Central Florida *Florida*
University of Charleston *West Virginia*
University of Cincinnati Raymond Walters College *Ohio*
University of the District of Columbia *District of Columbia*
University of Hartford *Connecticut*
University of Louisiana at Monroe *Louisiana*
University of Louisville *Kentucky*
University of Michigan–Flint *Michigan*
University of Missouri *Missouri*
University of Nebraska Medical Center *Nebraska*
The University of North Carolina at Chapel Hill *North Carolina*
University of Oklahoma Health Sciences Center *Oklahoma*
University of Puerto Rico, Medical Sciences Campus *Puerto Rico*
University of Saint Francis *Indiana*
University of Southern Indiana *Indiana*
The University of Texas at Brownsville *Texas*
The University of Texas Health Science Center at Houston *Texas*
University of Wisconsin–La Crosse *Wisconsin*
Valdosta Technical College *Georgia*
Valencia Community College *Florida*
Vance-Granville Community College *North Carolina*
Virginia Commonwealth University *Virginia*
Virginia Highlands Community College *Virginia*
Virginia Western Community College *Virginia*
Volunteer State Community College *Tennessee*
Wake Technical Community College *North Carolina*
Wallace State Community College *Alabama*
Washburn University *Kansas*
Washtenaw Community College *Michigan*
Wayne State University *Michigan*
Wenatchee Valley College *Washington*
Westchester Community College *New York*
Western Oklahoma State College *Oklahoma*
Western Technical College *Wisconsin*
Wharton County Junior College *Texas*
Wor-Wic Community College *Maryland*
Xavier University *Ohio*
Yakima Valley Community College *Washington*
York Technical College *South Carolina*
Yuba College *California*
Zane State College *Ohio*

Joint Review Committee on Educational Programs in Athletic Training (JRCEPAT)

Alvernia University *Pennsylvania*
Anderson University *Indiana*
Appalachian State University *North Carolina*
Arkansas State University - Jonesboro *Arkansas*
Augustana College *South Dakota*
Azusa Pacific University *California*
Ball State University *Indiana*
Barry University *Florida*
Bethel University *Minnesota*
Boise State University *Idaho*
Boston University *Massachusetts*
Bridgewater State College *Massachusetts*
Brigham Young University *Utah*
California State University, Fresno *California*
California State University, Fullerton *California*
California State University, Northridge *California*
California State University, Sacramento *California*
California University of Pennsylvania *Pennsylvania*
Campbell University *North Carolina*
Canisius College *New York*
Capital University *Ohio*
Castleton State College *Vermont*
Catawba College *North Carolina*
Central Connecticut State University *Connecticut*
Central Methodist University *Missouri*
Central Michigan University *Michigan*
Colby-Sawyer College *New Hampshire*
The College at Brockport, State University of New York *New York*
College of Charleston *South Carolina*
Dakota Wesleyan University *South Dakota*
DePauw University *Indiana*
Duquesne University *Pennsylvania*
East Carolina University *North Carolina*
East Stroudsburg University of Pennsylvania *Pennsylvania*
Eastern Illinois University *Illinois*
Eastern Kentucky University *Kentucky*
Eastern Michigan University *Michigan*
Elon University *North Carolina*
Emory & Henry College *Virginia*
Emporia State University *Kansas*
Endicott College *Massachusetts*
Florida Southern College *Florida*
Fort Lewis College *Colorado*
George Fox University *Oregon*
The George Washington University *District of Columbia*
Georgia Southern University *Georgia*
Grand Valley State University *Michigan*
Gustavus Adolphus College *Minnesota*

High Point University *North Carolina*
Hofstra University *New York*
Hope College *Michigan*
Illinois State University *Illinois*
Indiana State University *Indiana*
Indiana University Bloomington *Indiana*
Indiana University of Pennsylvania *Pennsylvania*
Iowa State University of Science and Technology *Iowa*
Ithaca College *New York*
James Madison University *Virginia*
Kansas State University *Kansas*
Kean University *New Jersey*
Keene State College *New Hampshire*
King's College *Pennsylvania*
Lasell College *Massachusetts*
Lenoir-Rhyne University *North Carolina*
Lincoln Memorial University *Tennessee*
Linfield College *Oregon*
Lipscomb University *Tennessee*
Lock Haven University of Pennsylvania *Pennsylvania*
Longwood University *Virginia*
Manchester College *Indiana*
Marietta College *Ohio*
Mars Hill College *North Carolina*
Marshall University *West Virginia*
Mercyhurst College *Pennsylvania*
Merrimack College *Massachusetts*
Messiah College *Pennsylvania*
Methodist University *North Carolina*
Miami University *Ohio*
Minnesota State University Mankato *Minnesota*
Missouri State University *Missouri*
New Mexico State University *New Mexico*
North Dakota State University *North Dakota*
Northeastern University *Massachusetts*
Northern Illinois University *Illinois*
Ohio Northern University *Ohio*
Ohio University *Ohio*
Oklahoma State University *Oklahoma*
Oregon State University *Oregon*
Otterbein University *Ohio*
Park University *Missouri*
Penn State University Park *Pennsylvania*
Plymouth State University *New Hampshire*
Purdue University *Indiana*
Roanoke College *Virginia*
Rowan University *New Jersey*
Sacred Heart University *Connecticut*
Salem State College *Massachusetts*
Salisbury University *Maryland*
Samford University *Alabama*
San Diego State University *California*
San Jose State University *California*
Slippery Rock University of Pennsylvania *Pennsylvania*
South Dakota State University *South Dakota*
Southeast Missouri State University *Missouri*
Southern Connecticut State University *Connecticut*
Southern Illinois University Carbondale *Illinois*
Southwestern University *Texas*
Springfield College *Massachusetts*
State University of New York College at Cortland *New York*
Stetson University *Florida*
Temple University *Pennsylvania*
Texas Christian University *Texas*
Texas State University–San Marcos *Texas*
Towson University *Maryland*
Troy University *Alabama*
Truman State University *Missouri*
The University of Alabama *Alabama*
University of Central Florida *Florida*
University of Charleston *West Virginia*
University of Cincinnati *Ohio*
University of Delaware *Delaware*
University of Florida *Florida*
University of Georgia *Georgia*
University of Illinois at Urbana–Champaign *Illinois*
University of Indianapolis *Indiana*
The University of Iowa *Iowa*
University of Mary *North Dakota*
The University of Montana *Montana*
University of Mount Union *Ohio*
University of Nebraska at Kearney *Nebraska*
University of Nebraska at Omaha *Nebraska*
University of Nevada, Las Vegas *Nevada*
University of New Hampshire *New Hampshire*
University of New Mexico *New Mexico*
The University of North Carolina at Chapel Hill *North Carolina*
University of North Dakota *North Dakota*
University of North Florida *Florida*
University of Northern Colorado *Colorado*
University of Northern Iowa *Iowa*
University of Pittsburgh *Pennsylvania*
University of South Carolina *South Carolina*
University of Southern Maine *Maine*
University of Southern Mississippi *Mississippi*
The University of Toledo *Ohio*
University of Tulsa *Oklahoma*
University of Utah *Utah*
University of Vermont *Vermont*
The University of West Alabama *Alabama*
University of Wisconsin–La Crosse *Wisconsin*
University of Wisconsin–Madison *Wisconsin*
Valdosta State University *Georgia*
Vanguard University of Southern California *California*
Washington State University *Washington*
Waynesburg University *Pennsylvania*
West Chester University of Pennsylvania *Pennsylvania*
West Virginia University *West Virginia*
West Virginia Wesleyan College *West Virginia*
Western Illinois University *Illinois*
Westfield State College *Massachusetts*
Whitworth University *Washington*
William Paterson University of New Jersey *New Jersey*
Wilmington College *Ohio*
Wingate University *North Carolina*
Winona State University *Minnesota*
Wright State University *Ohio*
Xavier University *Ohio*

Joint Review Committee on Educational Programs for the EMT-Paramedic (JRCEMT)

Austin Community College *Texas*
Bismarck State College *North Dakota*
Borough of Manhattan Community College of the City University of New York *New York*
Brevard Community College *Florida*
Broward College *Florida*
Capital Community College *Connecticut*
Catawba Valley Community College *North Carolina*
Central Florida Community College *Florida*
Central Washington University *Washington*
Century College *Minnesota*
Chemeketa Community College *Oregon*
Columbia Basin College *Washington*
Columbia College *California*
Columbia State Community College *Tennessee*
Columbus State Community College *Ohio*
Crafton Hills College *California*
Creighton University *Nebraska*
Daytona State College *Florida*
Delaware Technical & Community College, Terry Campus *Delaware*
Delgado Community College *Louisiana*
Dixie State College of Utah *Utah*
Doña Ana Branch Community College *New Mexico*
Eastern Kentucky University *Kentucky*
Eastern New Mexico University–Roswell *New Mexico*
Edison State College *Florida*
Florida State College at Jacksonville *Florida*
Gadsden State Community College *Alabama*
Galveston College *Texas*
George C. Wallace Community College *Alabama*
Greenville Technical College *South Carolina*
Gulf Coast Community College *Florida*
Harrisburg Area Community College *Pennsylvania*
Hillsborough Community College *Florida*
Holmes Community College *Mississippi*
Houston Community College System *Texas*
Hudson Valley Community College *New York*
Indian River State College *Florida*
Ivy Tech Community College–Southwest *Indiana*
Jackson State Community College *Tennessee*
Jefferson College of Health Sciences *Virginia*
Johnson County Community College *Kansas*
Jones County Junior College *Mississippi*
Lake City Community College *Florida*
Lansing Community College *Michigan*
Lee College *Texas*
Lurleen B. Wallace Community College *Alabama*
Miami Dade College *Florida*
Mississippi Gulf Coast Community College *Mississippi*
Monroe Community College *New York*
NHTI, Concord's Community College *New Hampshire*
Nicholls State University *Louisiana*
Northeast Alabama Community College *Alabama*
Northern Virginia Community College *Virginia*
NorthWest Arkansas Community College *Arkansas*
Oklahoma City Community College *Oklahoma*
Palm Beach State College *Florida*
Pasco-Hernando Community College *Florida*
Pennsylvania College of Technology *Pennsylvania*
Pensacola Junior College *Florida*
Polk State College *Florida*
Pueblo Community College *Colorado*
St. Petersburg College *Florida*
Santa Fe College *Florida*
Seminole State College of Florida *Florida*
Southern Union State Community College *Alabama*
Tacoma Community College *Washington*
Tallahassee Community College *Florida*
Texas Tech University *Texas*
Tidewater Community College *Virginia*
The University of Alabama at Birmingham *Alabama*
University of Arkansas for Medical Sciences *Arkansas*
University of Maryland, Baltimore County *Maryland*
University of New Mexico *New Mexico*
University of Pittsburgh *Pennsylvania*
University of South Alabama *Alabama*
The University of Texas Health Science Center at San Antonio *Texas*
Valencia Community College *Florida*
Volunteer State Community College *Tennessee*
Wallace State Community College *Alabama*
Weber State University *Utah*
Western Carolina University *North Carolina*
Youngstown State University *Ohio*

Joint Review Committee on Educational Programs in Nuclear Medicine Technology (JRCNMT)

Amarillo College *Texas*
Baptist College of Health Sciences *Tennessee*
Bronx Community College of the City University of New York *New York*
Broward College *Florida*
Caldwell Community College and Technical Institute *North Carolina*
Cedar Crest College *Pennsylvania*
Community College of Allegheny County *Pennsylvania*
Cuyahoga Community College *Ohio*
Delaware Technical & Community College, Stanton/Wilmington Campus *Delaware*
Ferris State University *Michigan*
Florida Hospital College of Health Sciences *Florida*
Forsyth Technical Community College *North Carolina*
Galveston College *Texas*
Gateway Community College *Connecticut*
Gloucester County College *New Jersey*
Hillsborough Community College *Florida*
Houston Community College System *Texas*
Indiana University–Purdue University Indianapolis *Indiana*
Kanawha Valley Community and Technical College *West Virginia*
Kent State University at Salem *Ohio*
Massachusetts College of Pharmacy and Health Sciences *Massachusetts*
Medical College of Georgia *Georgia*
Molloy College *New York*
Old Dominion University *Virginia*
Prince George's Community College *Maryland*
Rochester Institute of Technology *New York*
Saint Louis University *Missouri*

Saint Mary's University of Minnesota *Minnesota*
Salem State College *Massachusetts*
Santa Fe College *Florida*
Southeast Technical Institute *South Dakota*
Springfield Technical Community College *Massachusetts*
Triton College *Illinois*
The University of Alabama at Birmingham *Alabama*
University of Arkansas for Medical Sciences *Arkansas*
University at Buffalo, the State University of New York *New York*
University of Cincinnati *Ohio*
The University of Findlay *Ohio*
University of the Incarnate Word *Texas*
The University of Iowa *Iowa*
University of Missouri *Missouri*
University of Nebraska Medical Center *Nebraska*
University of Nevada, Las Vegas *Nevada*
University of Oklahoma Health Sciences Center *Oklahoma*
University of Puerto Rico, Medical Sciences Campus *Puerto Rico*
The University of Tennessee *Tennessee*
University of Vermont *Vermont*
Vanderbilt University *Tennessee*
Virginia Commonwealth University *Virginia*
Wheeling Jesuit University *West Virginia*
Worcester State College *Massachusetts*

Liaison Committee on Medical Education/American Medical Association (LCMEAMA)

Boston University *Massachusetts*
Brown University *Rhode Island*
Case Western Reserve University *Ohio*
Columbia University *New York*
Creighton University *Nebraska*
Dalhousie University *Nova Scotia*
Dartmouth College *New Hampshire*
Drexel University *Pennsylvania*
Duke University *North Carolina*
East Carolina University *North Carolina*
East Tennessee State University *Tennessee*
Emory University *Georgia*
Florida State University *Florida*
The George Washington University *District of Columbia*
Georgetown University *District of Columbia*
Harvard University *Massachusetts*
Howard University *District of Columbia*
Indiana University–Purdue University Indianapolis *Indiana*
The Johns Hopkins University *Maryland*
Lakehead University *Ontario*
Laurentian University *Ontario*
Loma Linda University *California*
Louisiana State University Health Sciences Center *Louisiana*
Louisiana State University in Shreveport *Louisiana*
Loyola University Chicago *Illinois*
Marshall University *West Virginia*
McGill University *Quebec*
McMaster University *Ontario*
Medical College of Georgia *Georgia*
Medical University of South Carolina *South Carolina*
Memorial University of Newfoundland *Newfoundland and Labrador*
Mercer University *Georgia*
Michigan State University *Michigan*
New York University *New York*
Northwestern University *Illinois*
The Ohio State University *Ohio*
Oregon Health & Science University *Oregon*
Queen's University at Kingston *Ontario*
Rush University *Illinois*
Saint Louis University *Missouri*
Southern Illinois University Carbondale *Illinois*
Stanford University *California*
State University of New York Downstate Medical Center *New York*
State University of New York Upstate Medical University *New York*
Stony Brook University, State University of New York *New York*
Temple University *Pennsylvania*
Texas A&M Health Science Center *Texas*
Thomas Jefferson University *Pennsylvania*
Tufts University *Massachusetts*
Tulane University *Louisiana*
Universidad Central del Caribe *Puerto Rico*
Université Laval *Quebec*
Université de Montréal *Quebec*
Université de Sherbrooke *Quebec*
The University of Alabama at Birmingham *Alabama*
University of Alberta *Alberta*
The University of Arizona *Arizona*
University of Arkansas for Medical Sciences *Arkansas*
The University of British Columbia *British Columbia*
University at Buffalo, the State University of New York *New York*
University of Calgary *Alberta*
University of California, Davis *California*
University of California, Irvine *California*
University of California, Los Angeles *California*
University of California, San Diego *California*
University of Chicago *Illinois*
University of Cincinnati *Ohio*
University of Colorado Denver *Colorado*
University of Florida *Florida*
University of Hawaii at Manoa *Hawaii*
University of Illinois at Chicago *Illinois*
The University of Iowa *Iowa*
The University of Kansas *Kansas*
University of Kentucky *Kentucky*
University of Louisville *Kentucky*
University of Manitoba *Manitoba*
University of Miami *Florida*
University of Michigan *Michigan*
University of Minnesota, Duluth *Minnesota*
University of Minnesota, Twin Cities Campus *Minnesota*
University of Mississippi Medical Center *Mississippi*
University of Missouri *Missouri*
University of Missouri–Kansas City *Missouri*
University of Nebraska Medical Center *Nebraska*
University of Nevada, Reno *Nevada*
University of New Mexico *New Mexico*
The University of North Carolina at Chapel Hill *North Carolina*
University of North Dakota *North Dakota*
University of Oklahoma Health Sciences Center *Oklahoma*
University of Ottawa *Ontario*
University of Pennsylvania *Pennsylvania*
University of Pittsburgh *Pennsylvania*
University of Puerto Rico, Medical Sciences Campus *Puerto Rico*
University of Rochester *New York*
University of Saskatchewan *Saskatchewan*
University of South Alabama *Alabama*
University of South Carolina *South Carolina*
The University of South Dakota *South Dakota*
University of South Florida *Florida*
University of Southern California *California*
The University of Texas Health Science Center at Houston *Texas*
The University of Texas Health Science Center at San Antonio *Texas*
The University of Texas Medical Branch *Texas*
The University of Texas Southwestern Medical Center at Dallas *Texas*
The University of Toledo *Ohio*
University of Toronto *Ontario*
University of Utah *Utah*
University of Vermont *Vermont*
University of Virginia *Virginia*
University of Washington *Washington*
The University of Western Ontario *Ontario*
University of Wisconsin–Madison *Wisconsin*
Vanderbilt University *Tennessee*
Virginia Commonwealth University *Virginia*
Wake Forest University *North Carolina*
Washington University in St. Louis *Missouri*
Wayne State University *Michigan*
West Virginia University *West Virginia*
Wright State University *Ohio*
Yale University *Connecticut*
Yeshiva University *New York*

Midwifery Education Accreditation Council (MEAC)

Birthingway College of Midwifery *Oregon*
The Florida School of Midwifery *Florida*
Miami Dade College *Florida*
Midwives College of Utah *Utah*
National College of Midwifery *New Mexico*

Montessori Accreditation Council for Teacher Education (MACTE)

Barry University *Florida*
Brevard Community College *Florida*
Chaminade University of Honolulu *Hawaii*
Chestnut Hill College *Pennsylvania*
Contra Costa College *California*
Fort Valley State University *Georgia*
Indiana University South Bend *Indiana*
Lander University *South Carolina*
Lonestar College–North Harris *Texas*
New York University *New York*
Oklahoma City University *Oklahoma*
Palm Beach State College *Florida*
Saint Mary's College of California *California*
Three Rivers Community College *Connecticut*
Tidewater Community College *Virginia*
Xavier University *Ohio*

National Accrediting Agency for Clinical Laboratory Sciences (NAACLS)

Alamance Community College *North Carolina*
Alexandria Technical College *Minnesota*
Allegany College of Maryland *Maryland*
Amarillo College *Texas*
Andrews University *Michigan*
Arapahoe Community College *Colorado*
Argosy University, Twin Cities *Minnesota*
Arizona State University *Arizona*
Arkansas State University - Jonesboro *Arkansas*
Arkansas State University–Beebe *Arkansas*
Armstrong Atlantic State University *Georgia*
Asheville-Buncombe Technical Community College *North Carolina*
Auburn University Montgomery *Alabama*
Austin Community College *Texas*
Austin Peay State University *Tennessee*
Baker College of Owosso *Michigan*
Barton County Community College *Kansas*
Beaufort County Community College *North Carolina*
Bellarmine University *Kentucky*
Bergen Community College *New Jersey*
Bevill State Community College *Alabama*
Bismarck State College *North Dakota*
Bowling Green State University *Ohio*
Brevard Community College *Florida*
Brigham Young University *Utah*
Bristol Community College *Massachusetts*
Broome Community College *New York*
California State University, Dominguez Hills *California*
Camden County College *New Jersey*
Carolinas College of Health Sciences *North Carolina*
Central Community College–Hastings Campus *Nebraska*
Central Georgia Technical College *Georgia*
Central Maine Community College *Maine*
Central New Mexico Community College *New Mexico*
Central Piedmont Community College *North Carolina*
Central Texas College *Texas*
Central Virginia Community College *Virginia*
Chippewa Valley Technical College *Wisconsin*
Cincinnati State Technical and Community College *Ohio*
Clark State Community College *Ohio*
Clinton Community College *New York*
Clover Park Technical College *Washington*
Coastal Carolina Community College *North Carolina*
College of Coastal Georgia *Georgia*
College of Southern Nevada *Nevada*
Columbus State Community College *Ohio*
Community College of Allegheny County *Pennsylvania*
Community College of Philadelphia *Pennsylvania*

Community College of Rhode Island *Rhode Island*
Copiah-Lincoln Community College *Mississippi*
Dalton State College *Georgia*
Darton College *Georgia*
Davidson County Community College *North Carolina*
DeKalb Technical College *Georgia*
Del Mar College *Texas*
Delaware Technical & Community College, Jack F. Owens Campus *Delaware*
Delaware Technical & Community College, Stanton/Wilmington Campus *Delaware*
Delgado Community College *Louisiana*
Des Moines Area Community College *Iowa*
Dutchess Community College *New York*
East Carolina University *North Carolina*
East Tennessee State University *Tennessee*
Eastern Gateway Community College *Ohio*
Eastern Kentucky University *Kentucky*
Eastern Michigan University *Michigan*
El Centro College *Texas*
El Paso Community College *Texas*
Elgin Community College *Illinois*
Erie Community College, North Campus *New York*
Farmingdale State College *New York*
Felician College *New Jersey*
Ferris State University *Michigan*
Fitchburg State College *Massachusetts*
Florence-Darlington Technical College *South Carolina*
Florida Gulf Coast University *Florida*
Florida State College at Jacksonville *Florida*
Gadsden State Community College *Alabama*
The George Washington University *District of Columbia*
Goldfarb School of Nursing at Barnes-Jewish College *Missouri*
Grand Valley State University *Michigan*
Grayson County College *Texas*
Greenville Technical College *South Carolina*
Halifax Community College *North Carolina*
Harcum College *Pennsylvania*
Harford Community College *Maryland*
Harrisburg Area Community College *Pennsylvania*
Hartnell College *California*
Hawkeye Community College *Iowa*
Hazard Community and Technical College *Kentucky*
Henderson Community College *Kentucky*
Hibbing Community College *Minnesota*
Hinds Community College *Mississippi*
Housatonic Community College *Connecticut*
Houston Community College System *Texas*
Idaho State University *Idaho*
Illinois Central College *Illinois*
Illinois State University *Illinois*
Indian River State College *Florida*
Indiana University Northwest *Indiana*
Indiana University–Purdue University Indianapolis *Indiana*
Inter American University of Puerto Rico, Metropolitan Campus *Puerto Rico*
Inter American University of Puerto Rico, San Germán Campus *Puerto Rico*
Iowa Central Community College *Iowa*
Ivy Tech Community College–North Central *Indiana*
Ivy Tech Community College–Wabash Valley *Indiana*
J. Sargeant Reynolds Community College *Virginia*
Jackson State Community College *Tennessee*
Jefferson State Community College *Alabama*
John A. Logan College *Illinois*
Kankakee Community College *Illinois*
Kapiolani Community College *Hawaii*
Keiser University *Florida*
Kellogg Community College *Michigan*
Kilgore College *Texas*
Lake Area Technical Institute *South Dakota*
Lake City Community College *Florida*
Lake Superior College *Minnesota*
Lakeland Community College *Ohio*
Lamar State College–Orange *Texas*
Lanier Technical College *Georgia*
Lansing Community College *Michigan*
Laredo Community College *Texas*
Lincoln Memorial University *Tennessee*
Loma Linda University *California*
Long Island University, C.W. Post Campus *New York*
Lorain County Community College *Ohio*
Louisiana State University at Alexandria *Louisiana*
Louisiana State University Health Sciences Center *Louisiana*
Madison Area Technical College *Wisconsin*
Manchester Community College *Connecticut*
Marion Technical College *Ohio*
Marist College *New York*
Marquette University *Wisconsin*
Marshall University *West Virginia*
McLennan Community College *Texas*
McNeese State University *Louisiana*
Medical College of Georgia *Georgia*
MedVance Institute *Tennessee*
MedVance Institute *Louisiana*
Mercer County Community College *New Jersey*
Mercy College of Northwest Ohio *Ohio*
Meridian Community College *Mississippi*
Miami Dade College *Florida*
Michigan State University *Michigan*
Mid-Plains Community College *Nebraska*
Middlesex County College *New Jersey*
Midlands Technical College *South Carolina*
Milwaukee Area Technical College *Wisconsin*
Minnesota State Community and Technical College *Minnesota*
Minnesota West Community and Technical College *Minnesota*
Mississippi Delta Community College *Mississippi*
Mississippi Gulf Coast Community College *Mississippi*
Mitchell Technical Institute *South Dakota*
Montgomery County Community College *Pennsylvania*
Morgan State University *Maryland*
Mt. San Antonio College *California*
Nashua Community College *New Hampshire*
National Park Community College *Arkansas*
Navarro College *Texas*
Neumann University *Pennsylvania*
New Mexico State University–Alamogordo *New Mexico*
Norfolk State University *Virginia*
North Arkansas College *Arkansas*
North Georgia Technical College *Georgia*
North Hennepin Community College *Minnesota*
Northeast Mississippi Community College *Mississippi*
Northeast State Technical Community College *Tennessee*
Northeast Wisconsin Technical College *Wisconsin*
Northeastern Oklahoma Agricultural and Mechanical College *Oklahoma*
Northeastern University *Massachusetts*
Northern Illinois University *Illinois*
Northern Michigan University *Michigan*
Northern Virginia Community College *Virginia*
Northwest Technical College *Minnesota*
Oakton Community College *Illinois*
Odessa College *Texas*
The Ohio State University *Ohio*
Okefenokee Technical College *Georgia*
Old Dominion University *Virginia*
Orange County Community College *New York*
Orangeburg-Calhoun Technical College *South Carolina*
Oregon Health & Science University *Oregon*
Oregon Institute of Technology *Oregon*
Our Lady of the Lake College *Louisiana*
Pearl River Community College *Mississippi*
Penn State Hazleton *Pennsylvania*
Penn State New Kensington *Pennsylvania*
Phillips Community College of the University of Arkansas *Arkansas*
Pierpont Community & Technical College of Fairmont State University *West Virginia*
Pikeville College *Kentucky*
Pontifical Catholic University of Puerto Rico *Puerto Rico*
Portland Community College *Oregon*
Presentation College *South Dakota*
Quinnipiac University *Connecticut*
Reading Area Community College *Pennsylvania*
Rend Lake College *Illinois*
Rose State College *Oklahoma*
Rush University *Illinois*
St. Louis Community College at Forest Park *Missouri*
Saint Louis University *Missouri*
Saint Paul College–A Community & Technical College *Minnesota*
St. Petersburg College *Florida*
St. Philip's College *Texas*
Salisbury University *Maryland*
Salt Lake Community College *Utah*
San Francisco State University *California*
Sandhills Community College *North Carolina*
Seminole State College *Oklahoma*
Seward County Community College *Kansas*
Shawnee Community College *Illinois*
Shawnee State University *Ohio*
Shoreline Community College *Washington*
Somerset Community College *Kentucky*
South Arkansas Community College *Arkansas*
South Central College *Minnesota*
Southeast Community College, Lincoln Campus *Nebraska*
Southeast Kentucky Community and Technical College *Kentucky*
Southeastern Community College *North Carolina*
Southeastern Illinois College *Illinois*
Southern Illinois University Carbondale *Illinois*
Southern Illinois University Edwardsville *Illinois*
Southern University at Shreveport *Louisiana*
Southern West Virginia Community and Technical College *West Virginia*
Southwest Georgia Technical College *Georgia*
Southwest Tennessee Community College *Tennessee*
Southwestern Community College *North Carolina*
Southwestern Illinois College *Illinois*
Spartanburg Community College *South Carolina*
Springfield Technical Community College *Massachusetts*
Stark State College of Technology *Ohio*
State University of New York College of Agriculture and Technology at Cobleskill *New York*
State University of New York Upstate Medical University *New York*
Stevenson University *Maryland*
Stony Brook University, State University of New York *New York*
Tarleton State University *Texas*
Temple College *Texas*
Tennessee State University *Tennessee*
Texas A&M University–Corpus Christi *Texas*
Texas Southern University *Texas*
Texas Southmost College *Texas*
Texas State University–San Marcos *Texas*
Thomas Jefferson University *Pennsylvania*
Thomas Nelson Community College *Virginia*
Three Rivers Community College *Missouri*
Tri-County Technical College *South Carolina*
Trident Technical College *South Carolina*
Tulsa Community College *Oklahoma*
Tuskegee University *Alabama*
Tyler Junior College *Texas*
The University of Alabama at Birmingham *Alabama*
University of Alaska Anchorage *Alaska*
The University of Arizona *Arizona*
University of Arkansas for Medical Sciences *Arkansas*
University at Buffalo, the State University of New York *New York*
University of California, Davis *California*
University of California, Irvine *California*
University of Central Florida *Florida*
University of Cincinnati *Ohio*
University of Connecticut *Connecticut*
University of Delaware *Delaware*
University of Hartford *Connecticut*
University of Hawaii at Manoa *Hawaii*
University of Illinois at Springfield *Illinois*
The University of Iowa *Iowa*
The University of Kansas *Kansas*
University of Kentucky *Kentucky*
University of Maine at Augusta *Maine*
University of Maine at Presque Isle *Maine*
University of Massachusetts Dartmouth *Massachusetts*

University of Massachusetts Lowell *Massachusetts*
University of Minnesota, Twin Cities Campus *Minnesota*
University of Mississippi Medical Center *Mississippi*
University of Nebraska Medical Center *Nebraska*
University of Nevada, Las Vegas *Nevada*
University of New Hampshire *New Hampshire*
University of New Mexico *New Mexico*
University of New Mexico–Gallup *New Mexico*
The University of North Carolina at Chapel Hill *North Carolina*
University of North Dakota *North Dakota*
University of Puerto Rico, Medical Sciences Campus *Puerto Rico*
University of Rio Grande *Ohio*
University of the Sacred Heart *Puerto Rico*
University of South Alabama *Alabama*
University of Southern Mississippi *Mississippi*
The University of Tennessee *Tennessee*
The University of Texas at El Paso *Texas*
The University of Texas Health Science Center at Houston *Texas*
The University of Texas Health Science Center at San Antonio *Texas*
The University of Texas Medical Branch *Texas*
The University of Texas Southwestern Medical Center at Dallas *Texas*
The University of Texas–Pan American *Texas*
University of Utah *Utah*
University of Vermont *Vermont*
University of Washington *Washington*
University of West Florida *Florida*
University of Wisconsin–La Crosse *Wisconsin*
University of Wisconsin–Madison *Wisconsin*
University of Wisconsin–Milwaukee *Wisconsin*
University of Wisconsin–Stevens Point *Wisconsin*
Valdosta Technical College *Georgia*
Vanderbilt University *Tennessee*
Victoria College *Texas*
Virginia Commonwealth University *Virginia*
Wake Forest University *North Carolina*
Wake Technical Community College *North Carolina*
Wallace State Community College *Alabama*
Washington State Community College *Ohio*
Wayne State University *Michigan*
Weber State University *Utah*
Wenatchee Valley College *Washington*
West Liberty University *West Virginia*
West Virginia Northern Community College *West Virginia*
West Virginia University *West Virginia*
Western Carolina University *North Carolina*
Western Piedmont Community College *North Carolina*
Western Technical College *Wisconsin*
Wichita Area Technical College *Kansas*
Wichita State University *Kansas*
Winston-Salem State University *North Carolina*
Wright State University *Ohio*
Wytheville Community College *Virginia*
York Technical College *South Carolina*
Youngstown State University *Ohio*
Zane State College *Ohio*

National Architectural Accrediting Board, Inc. (NAAB)

Arizona State University *Arizona*
Auburn University *Alabama*
Ball State University *Indiana*
Boston Architectural College *Massachusetts*
California College of the Arts *California*
California Polytechnic State University, San Luis Obispo *California*
California State Polytechnic University, Pomona *California*
Carnegie Mellon University *Pennsylvania*
The Catholic University of America *District of Columbia*
City College of the City University of New York *New York*
Clemson University *South Carolina*
Columbia University *New York*
Cooper Union for the Advancement of Science and Art *New York*
Cornell University *New York*
Drexel University *Pennsylvania*
Drury University *Missouri*
Florida Agricultural and Mechanical University *Florida*
Georgia Institute of Technology *Georgia*
Hampton University *Virginia*
Harvard University *Massachusetts*
Howard University *District of Columbia*
Illinois Institute of Technology *Illinois*
Iowa State University of Science and Technology *Iowa*
Kansas State University *Kansas*
Kent State University *Ohio*
Lawrence Technological University *Michigan*
Louisiana State University and Agricultural and Mechanical College *Louisiana*
Louisiana Tech University *Louisiana*
Massachusetts Institute of Technology *Massachusetts*
Miami University *Ohio*
Mississippi State University *Mississippi*
Montana State University *Montana*
Morgan State University *Maryland*
New Jersey Institute of Technology *New Jersey*
New York Institute of Technology *New York*
Newschool of Architecture & Design *California*
North Carolina State University *North Carolina*
North Dakota State University *North Dakota*
Norwich University *Vermont*
The Ohio State University *Ohio*
Oklahoma State University *Oklahoma*
Parsons The New School for Design *New York*
Penn State University Park *Pennsylvania*
Philadelphia University *Pennsylvania*
Pratt Institute *New York*
Princeton University *New Jersey*
Rensselaer Polytechnic Institute *New York*
Rhode Island School of Design *Rhode Island*
Rice University *Texas*
Roger Williams University *Rhode Island*
Savannah College of Art and Design *Georgia*
Southern California Institute of Architecture *California*
Southern Polytechnic State University *Georgia*
Syracuse University *New York*
Temple University *Pennsylvania*
Texas A&M University *Texas*
Texas Tech University *Texas*
Tulane University *Louisiana*
Tuskegee University *Alabama*
The University of Arizona *Arizona*
University of Arkansas *Arkansas*
University at Buffalo, the State University of New York *New York*
University of California, Berkeley *California*
University of California, Los Angeles *California*
University of Cincinnati *Ohio*
University of Colorado Denver *Colorado*
University of Detroit Mercy *Michigan*
University of the District of Columbia *District of Columbia*
University of Florida *Florida*
University of Hawaii at Manoa *Hawaii*
University of Houston *Texas*
University of Idaho *Idaho*
University of Illinois at Chicago *Illinois*
University of Illinois at Urbana–Champaign *Illinois*
The University of Kansas *Kansas*
University of Kentucky *Kentucky*
University of Louisiana at Lafayette *Louisiana*
University of Maryland, College Park *Maryland*
University of Miami *Florida*
University of Michigan *Michigan*
University of Minnesota, Twin Cities Campus *Minnesota*
University of Nebraska–Lincoln *Nebraska*
University of Nevada, Las Vegas *Nevada*
University of New Mexico *New Mexico*
The University of North Carolina at Charlotte *North Carolina*
University of Notre Dame *Indiana*
University of Oklahoma *Oklahoma*
University of Oregon *Oregon*
University of Pennsylvania *Pennsylvania*
University of Puerto Rico, Río Piedras *Puerto Rico*
University of South Florida *Florida*
University of Southern California *California*
The University of Tennessee *Tennessee*
The University of Texas at Arlington *Texas*
The University of Texas at Austin *Texas*
University of Utah *Utah*
University of Virginia *Virginia*
University of Washington *Washington*
University of Wisconsin–Milwaukee *Wisconsin*
Virginia Polytechnic Institute and State University *Virginia*
Washington State University *Washington*
Washington University in St. Louis *Missouri*
Wentworth Institute of Technology *Massachusetts*
Woodbury University *California*
Yale University *Connecticut*

National Association of Nurse Practitioners in Women's Health (NANPWH)

Emory University *Georgia*
The University of Texas Southwestern Medical Center at Dallas *Texas*

National Association of Schools of Art and Design (NASAD)

Academy of Art University *California*
Alfred University *New York*
Appalachian State University *North Carolina*
Arcadia University *Pennsylvania*
Arizona State University *Arizona*
Arkansas State University - Jonesboro *Arkansas*
Art Academy of Cincinnati *Ohio*
Art Center College of Design *California*
The Art Institute of Boston at Lesley University *Massachusetts*
Auburn University *Alabama*
Augusta State University *Georgia*
Austin Peay State University *Tennessee*
Azusa Pacific University *California*
Ball State University *Indiana*
Belhaven University *Mississippi*
Biola University *California*
Boise State University *Idaho*
Bowling Green State University *Ohio*
Bradley University *Illinois*
Brigham Young University *Utah*
Bucks County Community College *Pennsylvania*
Buffalo State College, State University of New York *New York*
California College of the Arts *California*
California Institute of the Arts *California*
California Polytechnic State University, San Luis Obispo *California*
California State Polytechnic University, Pomona *California*
California State University, Chico *California*
California State University, East Bay *California*
California State University, Fullerton *California*
California State University, Long Beach *California*
California State University, Los Angeles *California*
California State University, Northridge *California*
California State University, Sacramento *California*
California State University, San Bernardino *California*
California State University, Stanislaus *California*
Carnegie Mellon University *Pennsylvania*
Carson-Newman College *Tennessee*
Casper College *Wyoming*
Central Michigan University *Michigan*
Clarion University of Pennsylvania *Pennsylvania*
Clemson University *South Carolina*
The Cleveland Institute of Art *Ohio*
Coastal Carolina University *South Carolina*
College for Creative Studies *Michigan*
The College of Saint Rose *New York*
Columbia College *South Carolina*
Columbus College of Art & Design *Ohio*
Columbus State University *Georgia*
Cooper Union for the Advancement of Science and Art *New York*
Corcoran College of Art and Design *District of Columbia*
Cornish College of the Arts *Washington*
Del Mar College *Texas*
Delta State University *Mississippi*
Drake University *Iowa*
Drexel University *Pennsylvania*
East Carolina University *North Carolina*

East Tennessee State University *Tennessee*
Eastern Illinois University *Illinois*
Edinboro University of Pennsylvania *Pennsylvania*
Emporia State University *Kansas*
Fashion Institute of Technology *New York*
Ferris State University *Michigan*
FIDM/The Fashion Institute of Design & Merchandising, Los Angeles Campus *California*
FIDM/The Fashion Institute of Design & Merchandising, Orange County Campus *California*
FIDM/The Fashion Institute of Design & Merchandising, San Francisco Campus *California*
FIDM/The Fashion Institute of Design & Merchandising, San Diego Campus *California*
Florida International University *Florida*
Florida State University *Florida*
Francis Marion University *South Carolina*
Georgia Southern University *Georgia*
Georgia State University *Georgia*
Grand Valley State University *Michigan*
Harrington College of Design *Illinois*
Hartwick College *New York*
Hope College *Michigan*
Howard University *District of Columbia*
Humboldt State University *California*
Illinois State University *Illinois*
Indiana State University *Indiana*
Indiana University Bloomington *Indiana*
Indiana University of Pennsylvania *Pennsylvania*
Indiana University–Purdue University Indianapolis *Indiana*
Institute of American Indian Arts *New Mexico*
Jackson State University *Mississippi*
Jacksonville State University *Alabama*
James Madison University *Virginia*
Kansas City Art Institute *Missouri*
Kansas State University *Kansas*
Kean University *New Jersey*
Kennesaw State University *Georgia*
Kent State University *Ohio*
Kutztown University of Pennsylvania *Pennsylvania*
La Roche College *Pennsylvania*
Laguna College of Art & Design *California*
Lander University *South Carolina*
Lawrence Technological University *Michigan*
Louisiana State University and Agricultural and Mechanical College *Louisiana*
Louisiana Tech University *Louisiana*
Loyola Marymount University *California*
Lyme Academy College of Fine Arts *Connecticut*
Maine College of Art *Maine*
Maryland Institute College of Art *Maryland*
Maryville University of Saint Louis *Missouri*
Marywood University *Pennsylvania*
Massachusetts College of Art and Design *Massachusetts*
Memphis College of Art *Tennessee*
Messiah College *Pennsylvania*
Metropolitan State College of Denver *Colorado*
Miami University *Ohio*
Millersville University of Pennsylvania *Pennsylvania*
Milwaukee Institute of Art and Design *Wisconsin*
Minneapolis College of Art and Design *Minnesota*
Minnesota State University Mankato *Minnesota*
Minnesota State University Moorhead *Minnesota*
Mississippi State University *Mississippi*
Mississippi University for Women *Mississippi*
Mississippi Valley State University *Mississippi*
Montana State University *Montana*
Montana State University Billings *Montana*
Montclair State University *New Jersey*
Montserrat College of Art *Massachusetts*
Moore College of Art & Design *Pennsylvania*
Mount Ida College *Massachusetts*
Murray State University *Kentucky*
New Hampshire Institute of Art *New Hampshire*
New Jersey City University *New Jersey*
New World School of the Arts *Florida*
New York School of Interior Design *New York*
Nicholls State University *Louisiana*
North Carolina State University *North Carolina*
North Dakota State University *North Dakota*
Northern Illinois University *Illinois*
Northwestern State University of Louisiana *Louisiana*
The Ohio State University *Ohio*
Ohio University *Ohio*
Old Dominion University *Virginia*
Oregon College of Art & Craft *Oregon*
Otis College of Art and Design *California*
Pacific Northwest College of Art *Oregon*
Parsons The New School for Design *New York*
Penn State University Park *Pennsylvania*
Pennsylvania College of Art & Design *Pennsylvania*
Philadelphia University *Pennsylvania*
Portland State University *Oregon*
Pratt Institute *New York*
Purchase College, State University of New York *New York*
Purdue University *Indiana*
Rhode Island College *Rhode Island*
Rhode Island School of Design *Rhode Island*
Ringling College of Art and Design *Florida*
Roberts Wesleyan College *New York*
Rochester Institute of Technology *New York*
Rocky Mountain College of Art Design *Colorado*
Rowan University *New Jersey*
Russell Sage College *New York*
Sage College of Albany *New York*
St. Cloud State University *Minnesota*
St. Louis Community College at Florissant Valley *Missouri*
St. Louis Community College at Meramec *Missouri*
Saint Mary's College *Indiana*
Salem State College *Massachusetts*
Salve Regina University *Rhode Island*
San Diego State University *California*
San Francisco Art Institute *California*
San Francisco State University *California*
San Jose State University *California*
School of the Art Institute of Chicago *Illinois*
School of the Museum of Fine Arts, Boston *Massachusetts*
School of Visual Arts *New York*
Siena Heights University *Michigan*
Sinclair Community College *Ohio*
Skidmore College *New York*
Sonoma State University *California*
Southern Illinois University Carbondale *Illinois*
Southern Methodist University *Texas*
Southern Utah University *Utah*
State University of New York at New Paltz *New York*
State University of New York at Oswego *New York*
Stephen F. Austin State University *Texas*
Suffolk University *Massachusetts*
Syracuse University *New York*
Temple University *Pennsylvania*
Tennessee State University *Tennessee*
Tennessee Technological University *Tennessee*
Texas Christian University *Texas*
Texas Tech University *Texas*
Union University *Tennessee*
The University of Akron *Ohio*
The University of Alabama *Alabama*
The University of Alabama at Birmingham *Alabama*
University of Alaska Anchorage *Alaska*
The University of Arizona *Arizona*
University of Arkansas at Little Rock *Arkansas*
University of Arkansas at Pine Bluff *Arkansas*
The University of the Arts *Pennsylvania*
University of Bridgeport *Connecticut*
University at Buffalo, the State University of New York *New York*
University of Central Arkansas *Arkansas*
University of Central Missouri *Missouri*
University of Cincinnati *Ohio*
University of Connecticut *Connecticut*
University of Denver *Colorado*
University of Florida *Florida*
University of Georgia *Georgia*
University of Hartford *Connecticut*
University of Idaho *Idaho*
University of Illinois at Chicago *Illinois*
University of Illinois at Urbana–Champaign *Illinois*
University of Indianapolis *Indiana*
The University of Kansas *Kansas*
University of Kentucky *Kentucky*
University of Louisiana at Lafayette *Louisiana*
University of Massachusetts Dartmouth *Massachusetts*
University of Massachusetts Lowell *Massachusetts*
University of Memphis *Tennessee*
University of Michigan *Michigan*
University of Mississippi *Mississippi*
The University of Montana *Montana*
University of Montevallo *Alabama*
University of Nebraska at Omaha *Nebraska*
University of Nebraska–Lincoln *Nebraska*
University of Nevada, Las Vegas *Nevada*
University of New Orleans *Louisiana*
University of North Alabama *Alabama*
University of North Dakota *North Dakota*
University of North Texas *Texas*
University of Northern Iowa *Iowa*
University of Notre Dame *Indiana*
University of Oregon *Oregon*
University of the Pacific *California*
University of Saint Francis *Indiana*
University of South Alabama *Alabama*
University of South Carolina *South Carolina*
The University of South Dakota *South Dakota*
University of South Florida *Florida*
University of Southern Maine *Maine*
University of Southern Mississippi *Mississippi*
The University of Tennessee *Tennessee*
The University of Tennessee at Chattanooga *Tennessee*
The University of Texas at Arlington *Texas*
The University of Texas at Austin *Texas*
The University of Texas at San Antonio *Texas*
The University of Toledo *Ohio*
University of West Georgia *Georgia*
University of Wisconsin–Madison *Wisconsin*
University of Wisconsin–Stevens Point *Wisconsin*
University of Wisconsin–Stout *Wisconsin*
Valdosta State University *Georgia*
Vincennes University *Indiana*
Virginia Commonwealth University *Virginia*
Virginia Polytechnic Institute and State University *Virginia*
Virginia State University *Virginia*
Washburn University *Kansas*
Washington University in St. Louis *Missouri*
Watkins College of Art, Design, & Film *Tennessee*
West Virginia University *West Virginia*
Western Kentucky University *Kentucky*
Western Michigan University *Michigan*
Western Washington University *Washington*
William Paterson University of New Jersey *New Jersey*
Winthrop University *South Carolina*
Youngstown State University *Ohio*

National Association of Schools of Dance (NASD)

Barnard College *New York*
Brigham Young University *Utah*
Butler University *Indiana*
California Institute of the Arts *California*
California State University, Fullerton *California*
California State University, Long Beach *California*
The College at Brockport, State University of New York *New York*
Columbia College *South Carolina*
Florida State University *Florida*
Fordham University *New York*
Hope College *Michigan*
Jacksonville University *Florida*
James Madison University *Virginia*
Kent State University *Ohio*
Loyola Marymount University *California*
Montclair State University *New Jersey*
New World School of the Arts *Florida*
Oakland University *Michigan*
The Ohio State University *Ohio*
Ohio University *Ohio*
Point Park University *Pennsylvania*
Rutgers, The State University of New Jersey, New Brunswick *New Jersey*
St. Olaf College *Minnesota*
San Jose State University *California*
Slippery Rock University of Pennsylvania *Pennsylvania*
Southern Methodist University *Texas*
Temple University *Pennsylvania*
Texas Woman's University *Texas*
Towson University *Maryland*
The University of Akron *Ohio*

The University of Alabama *Alabama*
The University of Arizona *Arizona*
University of California, Santa Barbara *California*
University of Cincinnati *Ohio*
University of Hartford *Connecticut*
University of Illinois at Urbana–Champaign *Illinois*
University of Michigan *Michigan*
University of Minnesota, Twin Cities Campus *Minnesota*
University of New Mexico *New Mexico*
The University of North Carolina at Greensboro *North Carolina*
University of Southern Mississippi *Mississippi*
The University of Texas at Austin *Texas*
University of Utah *Utah*
University of Wisconsin–Stevens Point *Wisconsin*
Virginia Commonwealth University *Virginia*
Wayne State University *Michigan*
Western Michigan University *Michigan*
Wichita State University *Kansas*
Winthrop University *South Carolina*

National Association of Schools of Music (NASM)

Abilene Christian University *Texas*
Adams State College *Colorado*
Alabama State University *Alabama*
Albion College *Michigan*
Alcorn State University *Mississippi*
Alma College *Michigan*
Alverno College *Wisconsin*
Amarillo College *Texas*
American University *District of Columbia*
Anderson University *South Carolina*
Anderson University *Indiana*
Andrews University *Michigan*
Angelo State University *Texas*
Anna Maria College *Massachusetts*
Appalachian State University *North Carolina*
Arizona State University *Arizona*
Arkansas State University - Jonesboro *Arkansas*
Arkansas Tech University *Arkansas*
Armstrong Atlantic State University *Georgia*
Asbury University *Kentucky*
Ashland University *Ohio*
Atlantic Union College *Massachusetts*
Auburn University *Alabama*
Augsburg College *Minnesota*
Augusta State University *Georgia*
Augustana College *South Dakota*
Augustana College *Illinois*
Austin Peay State University *Tennessee*
Azusa Pacific University *California*
Baker University *Kansas*
Baldwin-Wallace College *Ohio*
Ball State University *Indiana*
The Baptist College of Florida *Florida*
Baylor University *Texas*
Belhaven University *Mississippi*
Belmont University *Tennessee*
Bemidji State University *Minnesota*
Benedictine College *Kansas*
Berry College *Georgia*
Bethany College *Kansas*
Biola University *California*
Birmingham-Southern College *Alabama*
Black Hills State University *South Dakota*
Bluffton University *Ohio*
Boise State University *Idaho*
The Boston Conservatory *Massachusetts*
Boston University *Massachusetts*
Bowling Green State University *Ohio*
Bradley University *Illinois*
Brevard College *North Carolina*
Brewton-Parker College *Georgia*
Brigham Young University *Utah*
Brigham Young University–Idaho *Idaho*
Broward College *Florida*
Bucknell University *Pennsylvania*
Bucks County Community College *Pennsylvania*
Butler University *Indiana*
California Baptist University *California*
California Institute of the Arts *California*
California Polytechnic State University, San Luis Obispo *California*
California State University, Chico *California*
California State University, Dominguez Hills *California*
California State University, East Bay *California*
California State University, Fresno *California*
California State University, Fullerton *California*
California State University, Long Beach *California*
California State University, Los Angeles *California*
California State University, Northridge *California*
California State University, Sacramento *California*
California State University, San Bernardino *California*
California State University, Stanislaus *California*
Calvin College *Michigan*
Cameron University *Oklahoma*
Campbellsville University *Kentucky*
Capital University *Ohio*
Carnegie Mellon University *Pennsylvania*
Carson-Newman College *Tennessee*
Carthage College *Wisconsin*
Case Western Reserve University *Ohio*
Casper College *Wyoming*
The Catholic University of America *District of Columbia*
Centenary College of Louisiana *Louisiana*
Central College *Iowa*
Central Connecticut State University *Connecticut*
Central Methodist University *Missouri*
Central Michigan University *Michigan*
Central State University *Ohio*
Central Washington University *Washington*
Chapman University *California*
Charleston Southern University *South Carolina*
Chicago State University *Illinois*
Chowan University *North Carolina*
Christopher Newport University *Virginia*
Clarion University of Pennsylvania *Pennsylvania*
Clarke College *Iowa*
Cleveland Institute of Music *Ohio*
Cleveland State University *Ohio*
Coe College *Iowa*
Coker College *South Carolina*
The Colburn School Conservatory of Music *California*
College of Charleston *South Carolina*
College of Mount St. Joseph *Ohio*
The College of New Jersey *New Jersey*
College of Saint Benedict *Minnesota*
The College of Saint Rose *New York*
The College of Wooster *Ohio*
Colorado State University *Colorado*
Colorado State University–Pueblo *Colorado*
Columbia College *South Carolina*
Columbus State University *Georgia*
The Community College of Baltimore County *Maryland*
Concordia College *Minnesota*
Concordia University Chicago *Illinois*
Concordia University, Nebraska *Nebraska*
Converse College *South Carolina*
Cornerstone University *Michigan*
Cottey College *Missouri*
Culver-Stockton College *Missouri*
Curtis Institute of Music *Pennsylvania*
Dallas Baptist University *Texas*
Del Mar College *Texas*
Delta State University *Mississippi*
DePaul University *Illinois*
DePauw University *Indiana*
Drake University *Iowa*
Drury University *Missouri*
Duquesne University *Pennsylvania*
East Carolina University *North Carolina*
East Central University *Oklahoma*
East Tennessee State University *Tennessee*
East Texas Baptist University *Texas*
Eastern Illinois University *Illinois*
Eastern Kentucky University *Kentucky*
Eastern Michigan University *Michigan*
Eastern New Mexico University *New Mexico*
Eastern Washington University *Washington*
Edinboro University of Pennsylvania *Pennsylvania*
Elizabethtown College *Pennsylvania*
Emory University *Georgia*
Emporia State University *Kansas*
Evangel University *Missouri*
Fisk University *Tennessee*
Florida Atlantic University *Florida*
Florida International University *Florida*
Florida State University *Florida*
Fort Hays State University *Kansas*
Fort Lewis College *Colorado*
Friends University *Kansas*
Furman University *South Carolina*
Gardner-Webb University *North Carolina*
George Fox University *Oregon*
George Mason University *Virginia*
The George Washington University *District of Columbia*
Georgia College & State University *Georgia*
Georgia Southern University *Georgia*
Georgia State University *Georgia*
Gordon College *Massachusetts*
Grace College *Indiana*
Grambling State University *Louisiana*
Grand Rapids Community College *Michigan*
Grand Valley State University *Michigan*
Greensboro College *North Carolina*
Gustavus Adolphus College *Minnesota*
Hamline University *Minnesota*
Hampton University *Virginia*
Hardin-Simmons University *Texas*
Harding University *Arkansas*
Harper College *Illinois*
Hartwick College *New York*
Hastings College *Nebraska*
Heidelberg University *Ohio*
Henderson State University *Arkansas*
Hendrix College *Arkansas*
Hiram College *Ohio*
Holyoke Community College *Massachusetts*
Hope College *Michigan*
Houghton College *New York*
Howard Payne University *Texas*
Howard University *District of Columbia*
Humboldt State University *California*
Huntingdon College *Alabama*
Huntington University *Indiana*
Idaho State University *Idaho*
Illinois Central College *Illinois*
Illinois State University *Illinois*
Illinois Wesleyan University *Illinois*
Immaculata University *Pennsylvania*
Indiana State University *Indiana*
Indiana University Bloomington *Indiana*
Indiana University of Pennsylvania *Pennsylvania*
Indiana University–Purdue University Fort Wayne *Indiana*
Indiana Wesleyan University *Indiana*
Iowa State University of Science and Technology *Iowa*
Ithaca College *New York*
Jackson State University *Mississippi*
Jacksonville State University *Alabama*
Jacksonville University *Florida*
James Madison University *Virginia*
The Johns Hopkins University *Maryland*
Joliet Junior College *Illinois*
Judson College *Alabama*
Kansas State University *Kansas*
Kean University *New Jersey*
Keene State College *New Hampshire*
Kennesaw State University *Georgia*
Kent State University *Ohio*
Kentucky State University *Kentucky*
Kutztown University of Pennsylvania *Pennsylvania*
La Sierra University *California*
Lamar University *Texas*
Lander University *South Carolina*
Lawrence University *Wisconsin*
Lebanon Valley College *Pennsylvania*
Lee University *Tennessee*
Limestone College *South Carolina*
Lincoln University *Missouri*
Linfield College *Oregon*
Lipscomb University *Tennessee*
Longwood University *Virginia*
Louisiana State University and Agricultural and Mechanical College *Louisiana*
Louisiana Tech University *Louisiana*
Loyola Marymount University *California*
Loyola University New Orleans *Louisiana*
Luther College *Iowa*

University of Mobile *Alabama*
The University of Montana *Montana*
University of Montevallo *Alabama*
University of Mount Union *Ohio*
University of Nebraska at Kearney *Nebraska*
University of Nebraska at Omaha *Nebraska*
University of Nebraska–Lincoln *Nebraska*
University of Nevada, Las Vegas *Nevada*
University of Nevada, Reno *Nevada*
University of New Hampshire *New Hampshire*
University of New Mexico *New Mexico*
University of New Orleans *Louisiana*
University of North Alabama *Alabama*
The University of North Carolina at Greensboro *North Carolina*
The University of North Carolina at Pembroke *North Carolina*
The University of North Carolina Wilmington *North Carolina*
University of North Dakota *North Dakota*
University of North Florida *Florida*
University of North Texas *Texas*
University of Northern Colorado *Colorado*
University of Northern Iowa *Iowa*
University of Oklahoma *Oklahoma*
University of Oregon *Oregon*
University of the Pacific *California*
University of Portland *Oregon*
University of Puget Sound *Washington*
University of Redlands *California*
University of Rhode Island *Rhode Island*
University of Richmond *Virginia*
University of Rochester *New York*
University of St. Thomas *Minnesota*
University of Science and Arts of Oklahoma *Oklahoma*
University of South Alabama *Alabama*
University of South Carolina *South Carolina*
The University of South Dakota *South Dakota*
University of South Florida *Florida*
University of Southern California *California*
University of Southern Maine *Maine*
University of Southern Mississippi *Mississippi*
The University of Tampa *Florida*
The University of Tennessee *Tennessee*
The University of Tennessee at Chattanooga *Tennessee*
The University of Tennessee at Martin *Tennessee*
The University of Texas at Arlington *Texas*
The University of Texas at Austin *Texas*
The University of Texas at El Paso *Texas*
The University of Texas at San Antonio *Texas*
The University of Toledo *Ohio*
University of Tulsa *Oklahoma*
University of Utah *Utah*
University of Washington *Washington*
University of West Florida *Florida*
University of West Georgia *Georgia*
University of Wisconsin–Eau Claire *Wisconsin*
University of Wisconsin–Green Bay *Wisconsin*
University of Wisconsin–La Crosse *Wisconsin*
University of Wisconsin–Madison *Wisconsin*
University of Wisconsin–Milwaukee *Wisconsin*
University of Wisconsin–Oshkosh *Wisconsin*
University of Wisconsin–Platteville *Wisconsin*
University of Wisconsin–River Falls *Wisconsin*
University of Wisconsin–Stevens Point *Wisconsin*
University of Wisconsin–Superior *Wisconsin*
University of Wisconsin–Whitewater *Wisconsin*
University of Wyoming *Wyoming*
Utah State University *Utah*
Valdosta State University *Georgia*
Valley City State University *North Dakota*
Valparaiso University *Indiana*
Vanderbilt University *Tennessee*
VanderCook College of Music *Illinois*
Virginia Commonwealth University *Virginia*
Virginia State University *Virginia*
Viterbo University *Wisconsin*
Walla Walla University *Washington*
Wartburg College *Iowa*
Washburn University *Kansas*
Washington State University *Washington*
Wayland Baptist University *Texas*
Wayne State University *Michigan*
Weber State University *Utah*
Webster University *Missouri*
Wesleyan College *Georgia*
West Chester University of Pennsylvania *Pennsylvania*
West Liberty University *West Virginia*
West Texas A&M University *Texas*
West Virginia University *West Virginia*
West Virginia Wesleyan College *West Virginia*
Western Carolina University *North Carolina*
Western Connecticut State University *Connecticut*
Western Illinois University *Illinois*
Western Kentucky University *Kentucky*
Western Michigan University *Michigan*
Western Oregon University *Oregon*
Western State College of Colorado *Colorado*
Western Washington University *Washington*
Westminster College *Pennsylvania*
Wheaton College *Illinois*
Whitworth University *Washington*
Wichita State University *Kansas*
Willamette University *Oregon*
William Carey University *Mississippi*
William Jewell College *Missouri*
William Paterson University of New Jersey *New Jersey*
Wingate University *North Carolina*
Winona State University *Minnesota*
Winston-Salem State University *North Carolina*
Winthrop University *South Carolina*
Wittenberg University *Ohio*
Wright State University *Ohio*
Xavier University of Louisiana *Louisiana*
Yale University *Connecticut*
Young Harris College *Georgia*
Youngstown State University *Ohio*

National Association of Schools of Public Affairs and Administration (NASPAA)

Albany State University *Georgia*
American University *District of Columbia*
Appalachian State University *North Carolina*
Arizona State University *Arizona*
Arkansas State University - Jonesboro *Arkansas*
Auburn University *Alabama*
Auburn University Montgomery *Alabama*
Bernard M. Baruch College of the City University of New York *New York*
Boise State University *Idaho*
Bridgewater State College *Massachusetts*
Brigham Young University *Utah*
California State Polytechnic University, Pomona *California*
California State University, Bakersfield *California*
California State University, Chico *California*
California State University, Dominguez Hills *California*
California State University, East Bay *California*
California State University, Fresno *California*
California State University, Fullerton *California*
California State University, Long Beach *California*
California State University, Los Angeles *California*
California State University, San Bernardino *California*
California State University, Stanislaus *California*
Carnegie Mellon University *Pennsylvania*
Clark Atlanta University *Georgia*
Cleveland State University *Ohio*
The College at Brockport, State University of New York *New York*
College of Charleston *South Carolina*
DePaul University *Illinois*
East Carolina University *North Carolina*
Eastern Kentucky University *Kentucky*
Eastern Michigan University *Michigan*
Florida Atlantic University *Florida*
Florida Gulf Coast University *Florida*
Florida International University *Florida*
Florida State University *Florida*
George Mason University *Virginia*
The George Washington University *District of Columbia*
Georgia College & State University *Georgia*
Georgia Southern University *Georgia*
Georgia State University *Georgia*
Governors State University *Illinois*
Grambling State University *Louisiana*
Grand Valley State University *Michigan*
Harvard University *Massachusetts*
Howard University *District of Columbia*
Indiana University Bloomington *Indiana*
Indiana University Northwest *Indiana*
Indiana University South Bend *Indiana*
Indiana University–Purdue University Fort Wayne *Indiana*
Indiana University–Purdue University Indianapolis *Indiana*
Iowa State University of Science and Technology *Iowa*
Jackson State University *Mississippi*
John Jay College of Criminal Justice of the City University of New York *New York*
Kansas State University *Kansas*
Kean University *New Jersey*
Kennesaw State University *Georgia*
Kent State University *Ohio*
Kentucky State University *Kentucky*
Long Island University, Brooklyn Campus *New York*
Long Island University, C.W. Post Campus *New York*
Michigan State University *Michigan*
Mississippi State University *Mississippi*
Missouri State University *Missouri*
New Mexico State University *New Mexico*
New York University *New York*
North Carolina State University *North Carolina*
Northeastern University *Massachusetts*
Northern Illinois University *Illinois*
Northern Kentucky University *Kentucky*
Oakland University *Michigan*
The Ohio State University *Ohio*
Old Dominion University *Virginia*
Penn State Harrisburg *Pennsylvania*
Portland State University *Oregon*
Rutgers, The State University of New Jersey, Camden *New Jersey*
Rutgers, The State University of New Jersey, Newark *New Jersey*
Saint Louis University *Missouri*
San Diego State University *California*
San Francisco State University *California*
San Jose State University *California*
Savannah State University *Georgia*
Seattle University *Washington*
Seton Hall University *New Jersey*
Southern Illinois University Carbondale *Illinois*
Southern Illinois University Edwardsville *Illinois*
Southern University and Agricultural and Mechanical College *Louisiana*
State University of New York at Binghamton *New York*
Suffolk University *Massachusetts*
Syracuse University *New York*
Tennessee State University *Tennessee*
Texas A&M University *Texas*
Texas State University–San Marcos *Texas*
Texas Tech University *Texas*
Troy University *Alabama*
The University of Akron *Ohio*
The University of Alabama at Birmingham *Alabama*
University at Albany, State University of New York *New York*
The University of Arizona *Arizona*
University of Arkansas at Little Rock *Arkansas*
University of Baltimore *Maryland*
University of Central Florida *Florida*
University of Colorado at Colorado Springs *Colorado*
University of Colorado Denver *Colorado*
University of Connecticut *Connecticut*
University of Dayton *Ohio*
University of Delaware *Delaware*
University of Georgia *Georgia*
University of Illinois at Chicago *Illinois*
University of Illinois at Springfield *Illinois*
The University of Kansas *Kansas*
University of Kentucky *Kentucky*
University of La Verne *California*
University of Louisville *Kentucky*
University of Maine *Maine*
University of Maryland, Baltimore County *Maryland*
University of Maryland, College Park *Maryland*

University of Memphis *Tennessee*
University of Minnesota, Twin Cities Campus *Minnesota*
University of Missouri *Missouri*
University of Missouri–Kansas City *Missouri*
University of Missouri–St. Louis *Missouri*
University of Nebraska at Omaha *Nebraska*
University of Nevada, Las Vegas *Nevada*
University of New Mexico *New Mexico*
The University of North Carolina at Chapel Hill *North Carolina*
The University of North Carolina at Charlotte *North Carolina*
The University of North Carolina at Greensboro *North Carolina*
The University of North Carolina Wilmington *North Carolina*
University of North Dakota *North Dakota*
University of North Florida *Florida*
University of North Texas *Texas*
University of Oregon *Oregon*
University of Pittsburgh *Pennsylvania*
University of South Carolina *South Carolina*
The University of South Dakota *South Dakota*
University of South Florida *Florida*
University of Southern California *California*
University of Southern Maine *Maine*
The University of Tennessee *Tennessee*
The University of Tennessee at Chattanooga *Tennessee*
The University of Texas at Arlington *Texas*
The University of Texas at Austin *Texas*
The University of Texas at Dallas *Texas*
The University of Texas at El Paso *Texas*
The University of Texas at San Antonio *Texas*
The University of Toledo *Ohio*
University of Utah *Utah*
University of Washington *Washington*
University of West Florida *Florida*
University of West Georgia *Georgia*
Valdosta State University *Georgia*
Virginia Commonwealth University *Virginia*
Virginia Polytechnic Institute and State University *Virginia*
Wayne State University *Michigan*
West Virginia University *West Virginia*
Western Michigan University *Michigan*
Wichita State University *Kansas*
Willamette University *Oregon*
Wright State University *Ohio*

National Association of Schools of Theatre (NAST)

American Academy of Dramatic Arts *New York*
American Academy of Dramatic Arts *California*
Appalachian State University *North Carolina*
Auburn University *Alabama*
Ball State University *Indiana*
Baylor University *Texas*
Boise State University *Idaho*
Bowling Green State University *Ohio*
Bradley University *Illinois*
Brigham Young University *Utah*
Butler University *Indiana*
California Institute of the Arts *California*
California State University, Dominguez Hills *California*
California State University, Fresno *California*
California State University, Fullerton *California*
California State University, Long Beach *California*
California State University, Northridge *California*
California State University, Sacramento *California*
California State University, San Bernardino *California*
California State University, Stanislaus *California*
Casper College *Wyoming*
College of the Holy Cross *Massachusetts*
Columbus State University *Georgia*
The Community College of Baltimore County *Maryland*
Dartmouth College *New Hampshire*
Davis & Elkins College *West Virginia*
Del Mar College *Texas*
Florida International University *Florida*
Florida State University *Florida*
Francis Marion University *South Carolina*
Grambling State University *Louisiana*
Hope College *Michigan*
Howard University *District of Columbia*
Humboldt State University *California*
Illinois State University *Illinois*
Indiana University Bloomington *Indiana*
Indiana University of Pennsylvania *Pennsylvania*
Ithaca College *New York*
Jacksonville State University *Alabama*
James Madison University *Virginia*
Kansas State University *Kansas*
KD Studio *Texas*
Kean University *New Jersey*
Kennesaw State University *Georgia*
Kent State University *Ohio*
Lander University *South Carolina*
Lehigh University *Pennsylvania*
Longwood University *Virginia*
Louisiana State University and Agricultural and Mechanical College *Louisiana*
Loyola Marymount University *California*
Loyola University Chicago *Illinois*
Mars Hill College *North Carolina*
Miami University *Ohio*
Missouri State University *Missouri*
Montclair State University *New Jersey*
New World School of the Arts *Florida*
North Carolina Agricultural and Technical State University *North Carolina*
North Carolina Central University *North Carolina*
North Dakota State University *North Dakota*
Northern Illinois University *Illinois*
Northwestern State University of Louisiana *Louisiana*
Northwestern University *Illinois*
Oakland University *Michigan*
The Ohio State University *Ohio*
Ohio University *Ohio*
Oklahoma State University *Oklahoma*
Old Dominion University *Virginia*
Otterbein University *Ohio*
Penn State University Park *Pennsylvania*
Portland State University *Oregon*
Purdue University *Indiana*
Radford University *Virginia*
Rowan University *New Jersey*
St. Cloud State University *Minnesota*
St. Olaf College *Minnesota*
Salem State College *Massachusetts*
San Diego State University *California*
San Francisco State University *California*
San Jose State University *California*
Southern Illinois University Carbondale *Illinois*
Southern Methodist University *Texas*
State University of New York at Fredonia *New York*
State University of New York at New Paltz *New York*
Stephen F. Austin State University *Texas*
Temple University *Pennsylvania*
Texas Tech University *Texas*
Towson University *Maryland*
The University of Alabama *Alabama*
The University of Arizona *Arizona*
University of Arkansas at Little Rock *Arkansas*
University of California, Los Angeles *California*
University of Central Arkansas *Arkansas*
University of Cincinnati *Ohio*
University of Connecticut *Connecticut*
University of Florida *Florida*
University of Georgia *Georgia*
University of Illinois at Urbana–Champaign *Illinois*
University of the Incarnate Word *Texas*
The University of Iowa *Iowa*
University of Louisville *Kentucky*
University of Maryland, College Park *Maryland*
University of Memphis *Tennessee*
University of Minnesota, Twin Cities Campus *Minnesota*
University of Mississippi *Mississippi*
University of Missouri–Kansas City *Missouri*
The University of Montana *Montana*
University of Nebraska–Lincoln *Nebraska*
University of Nevada, Las Vegas *Nevada*
University of New Mexico *New Mexico*
University of New Orleans *Louisiana*
The University of North Carolina at Greensboro *North Carolina*
University of North Dakota *North Dakota*
University of Oklahoma *Oklahoma*
University of Pittsburgh *Pennsylvania*
University of Portland *Oregon*
University of South Carolina *South Carolina*
The University of South Dakota *South Dakota*
University of South Florida *Florida*
University of Southern Mississippi *Mississippi*
The University of Texas at Austin *Texas*
The University of Texas–Pan American *Texas*
University of Virginia *Virginia*
University of West Georgia *Georgia*
University of Wisconsin–Madison *Wisconsin*
University of Wisconsin–Stevens Point *Wisconsin*
University of Wisconsin–Whitewater *Wisconsin*
Valdosta State University *Georgia*
Vincennes University *Indiana*
Virginia Commonwealth University *Virginia*
Virginia Polytechnic Institute and State University *Virginia*
Wayne State University *Michigan*
West Virginia University *West Virginia*
Western Illinois University *Illinois*
Western Michigan University *Michigan*
Winona State University *Minnesota*
Winthrop University *South Carolina*
Youngstown State University *Ohio*

National Commission on Orthotic and Prosthetic Education (NCOPE)

California State University, Dominguez Hills *California*
The University of Texas Southwestern Medical Center at Dallas *Texas*
University of Washington *Washington*

National Council for Accreditation of Teacher Education (NCATE)

Adelphi University *New York*
Alabama Agricultural and Mechanical University *Alabama*
Alabama State University *Alabama*
Alaska Pacific University *Alaska*
Albany State University *Georgia*
Alcorn State University *Mississippi*
Alderson-Broaddus College *West Virginia*
Alverno College *Wisconsin*
American University *District of Columbia*
Anderson University *South Carolina*
Anderson University *Indiana*
Andrews University *Michigan*
Angelo State University *Texas*
Antioch University McGregor *Ohio*
Appalachian State University *North Carolina*
Arkansas State University - Jonesboro *Arkansas*
Arkansas Tech University *Arkansas*
Armstrong Atlantic State University *Georgia*
Asbury University *Kentucky*
Ashland University *Ohio*
Athens State University *Alabama*
Atlanta Christian College *Georgia*
Auburn University *Alabama*
Auburn University Montgomery *Alabama*
Augsburg College *Minnesota*
Augusta State University *Georgia*
Augustana College *South Dakota*
Augustana College *Illinois*
Aurora University *Illinois*
Austin Peay State University *Tennessee*
Azusa Pacific University *California*
Baker University *Kansas*
Baldwin-Wallace College *Ohio*
Ball State University *Indiana*
Barton College *North Carolina*
Baylor University *Texas*
Bellarmine University *Kentucky*
Belmont Abbey College *North Carolina*
Belmont University *Tennessee*
Bemidji State University *Minnesota*
Benedict College *South Carolina*
Benedictine College *Kansas*
Bennett College for Women *North Carolina*
Berea College *Kentucky*
Berry College *Georgia*
Bethany College *West Virginia*
Bethany College *Kansas*

Bethel College *Indiana*
Bethune-Cookman University *Florida*
Birmingham-Southern College *Alabama*
Black Hills State University *South Dakota*
Bloomsburg University of Pennsylvania *Pennsylvania*
Bluefield State College *West Virginia*
Bluffton University *Ohio*
Boise State University *Idaho*
Boston College *Massachusetts*
Bowie State University *Maryland*
Bowling Green State University *Ohio*
Bradley University *Illinois*
Brenau University *Georgia*
Bridgewater State College *Massachusetts*
Brigham Young University *Utah*
Brooklyn College of the City University of New York *New York*
Buffalo State College, State University of New York *New York*
Butler University *Indiana*
California Lutheran University *California*
California State University, Bakersfield *California*
California State University, Chico *California*
California State University, Dominguez Hills *California*
California State University, East Bay *California*
California State University, Fresno *California*
California State University, Fullerton *California*
California State University, Long Beach *California*
California State University, Los Angeles *California*
California State University, Monterey Bay *California*
California State University, Northridge *California*
California State University, San Bernardino *California*
California State University, San Marcos *California*
California State University, Stanislaus *California*
California University of Pennsylvania *Pennsylvania*
Calvin College *Michigan*
Cameron University *Oklahoma*
Campbell University *North Carolina*
Campbellsville University *Kentucky*
Canisius College *New York*
Capella University *Minnesota*
Capital University *Ohio*
Cardinal Stritch University *Wisconsin*
Carson-Newman College *Tennessee*
Catawba College *North Carolina*
The Catholic University of America *District of Columbia*
Centenary College of Louisiana *Louisiana*
Central Connecticut State University *Connecticut*
Central Michigan University *Michigan*
Central State University *Ohio*
Central Washington University *Washington*
Chadron State College *Nebraska*
Charleston Southern University *South Carolina*
Cheyney University of Pennsylvania *Pennsylvania*
Chicago State University *Illinois*
Chowan University *North Carolina*
The Citadel, The Military College of South Carolina *South Carolina*
City College of the City University of New York *New York*
Claflin University *South Carolina*
Clarion University of Pennsylvania *Pennsylvania*
Clark Atlanta University *Georgia*
Clayton State University *Georgia*
Clemson University *South Carolina*
Cleveland State University *Ohio*
Coastal Carolina University *South Carolina*
The College at Brockport, State University of New York *New York*
College of Charleston *South Carolina*
The College of New Jersey *New Jersey*
College of Notre Dame of Maryland *Maryland*
College of Saint Benedict *Minnesota*
The College of Saint Rose *New York*
College of Staten Island of the City University of New York *New York*
The College of William and Mary *Virginia*
Colorado State University *Colorado*
Columbia College *South Carolina*
Columbus State University *Georgia*
Concord University *West Virginia*
Concordia University *Michigan*
Concordia University Chicago *Illinois*
Concordia University, Nebraska *Nebraska*
Concordia University, St. Paul *Minnesota*
Converse College *South Carolina*
Coppin State University *Maryland*
Creighton University *Nebraska*
Cumberland University *Tennessee*
Dakota State University *South Dakota*
Dana College *Nebraska*
Davidson College *North Carolina*
Defiance College *Ohio*
Delaware State University *Delaware*
Delta State University *Mississippi*
DePaul University *Illinois*
DePauw University *Indiana*
Dickinson State University *North Dakota*
Dillard University *Louisiana*
Doane College *Nebraska*
Dominican University *Illinois*
Dowling College *New York*
Drury University *Missouri*
Duke University *North Carolina*
Duquesne University *Pennsylvania*
East Carolina University *North Carolina*
East Central University *Oklahoma*
East Stroudsburg University of Pennsylvania *Pennsylvania*
East Tennessee State University *Tennessee*
Eastern Connecticut State University *Connecticut*
Eastern Illinois University *Illinois*
Eastern Kentucky University *Kentucky*
Eastern Mennonite University *Virginia*
Eastern Michigan University *Michigan*
Eastern New Mexico University *New Mexico*
Eastern Washington University *Washington*
Edgewood College *Wisconsin*
Edinboro University of Pennsylvania *Pennsylvania*
Elizabeth City State University *North Carolina*
Elmhurst College *Illinois*
Elon University *North Carolina*
Emory University *Georgia*
Emporia State University *Kansas*
Evangel University *Missouri*
Fairfield University *Connecticut*
Fairmont State University *West Virginia*
Fayetteville State University *North Carolina*
Fitchburg State College *Massachusetts*
Five Towns College *New York*
Florida Agricultural and Mechanical University *Florida*
Florida Atlantic University *Florida*
Florida International University *Florida*
Florida Memorial University *Florida*
Florida State University *Florida*
Fontbonne University *Missouri*
Fordham University *New York*
Fort Hays State University *Kansas*
Fort Valley State University *Georgia*
Francis Marion University *South Carolina*
Franciscan University of Steubenville *Ohio*
Franklin College *Indiana*
Freed-Hardeman University *Tennessee*
Friends University *Kansas*
Frostburg State University *Maryland*
Furman University *South Carolina*
Gallaudet University *District of Columbia*
Gardner-Webb University *North Carolina*
George Fox University *Oregon*
George Mason University *Virginia*
The George Washington University *District of Columbia*
Georgetown College *Kentucky*
Georgia College & State University *Georgia*
Georgia Southern University *Georgia*
Georgia Southwestern State University *Georgia*
Georgia State University *Georgia*
Glenville State College *West Virginia*
Gonzaga University *Washington*
Goshen College *Indiana*
Governors State University *Illinois*
Grace College *Indiana*
Graceland University *Iowa*
Grambling State University *Louisiana*
Grand Valley State University *Michigan*
Greensboro College *North Carolina*
Guilford College *North Carolina*
Gustavus Adolphus College *Minnesota*
Hamline University *Minnesota*
Hampton University *Virginia*
Hanover College *Indiana*
Harding University *Arkansas*
Harris-Stowe State University *Missouri*
Hastings College *Nebraska*
Heidelberg University *Ohio*
Henderson State University *Arkansas*
Hendrix College *Arkansas*
High Point University *North Carolina*
Hofstra University *New York*
Hope College *Michigan*
Howard University *District of Columbia*
Hunter College of the City University of New York *New York*
Huntington University *Indiana*
Idaho State University *Idaho*
Illinois State University *Illinois*
Indiana State University *Indiana*
Indiana University Bloomington *Indiana*
Indiana University East *Indiana*
Indiana University Kokomo *Indiana*
Indiana University Northwest *Indiana*
Indiana University of Pennsylvania *Pennsylvania*
Indiana University South Bend *Indiana*
Indiana University Southeast *Indiana*
Indiana University–Purdue University Fort Wayne *Indiana*
Indiana Wesleyan University *Indiana*
Iona College *New York*
Jackson State University *Mississippi*
Jacksonville State University *Alabama*
James Madison University *Virginia*
John Brown University *Arkansas*
John Carroll University *Ohio*
The Johns Hopkins University *Maryland*
Johnson C. Smith University *North Carolina*
Jones International University *Colorado*
Kansas State University *Kansas*
Kansas Wesleyan University *Kansas*
Kean University *New Jersey*
Keene State College *New Hampshire*
Kennesaw State University *Georgia*
Kent State University *Ohio*
Kentucky State University *Kentucky*
King's College *Pennsylvania*
Kutztown University of Pennsylvania *Pennsylvania*
LaGrange College *Georgia*
Lamar University *Texas*
Lander University *South Carolina*
Langston University *Oklahoma*
Lee University *Tennessee*
Lees-McRae College *North Carolina*
Lehman College of the City University of New York *New York*
LeMoyne-Owen College *Tennessee*
Lenoir-Rhyne University *North Carolina*
Lewis & Clark College *Oregon*
Lewis University *Illinois*
Liberty University *Virginia*
Lincoln University *Missouri*
Lipscomb University *Tennessee*
Livingstone College *North Carolina*
Lock Haven University of Pennsylvania *Pennsylvania*
Longwood University *Virginia*
Louisiana State University and Agricultural and Mechanical College *Louisiana*
Louisiana State University in Shreveport *Louisiana*
Louisiana Tech University *Louisiana*
Loyola Marymount University *California*
Loyola University Chicago *Illinois*
Loyola University Maryland *Maryland*
Luther College *Iowa*
Lyon College *Arkansas*
Madonna University *Michigan*
Malone University *Ohio*
Manchester College *Indiana*
Manhattanville College *New York*
Mansfield University of Pennsylvania *Pennsylvania*
Marian University *Wisconsin*
Marian University *Indiana*
Marietta College *Ohio*
Marquette University *Wisconsin*
Mars Hill College *North Carolina*

University of Maryland, College Park *Maryland*
University of Maryland Eastern Shore *Maryland*
University of Massachusetts Amherst *Massachusetts*
University of Massachusetts Boston *Massachusetts*
University of Massachusetts Lowell *Massachusetts*
University of Memphis *Tennessee*
University of Miami *Florida*
University of Minnesota, Duluth *Minnesota*
University of Minnesota, Morris *Minnesota*
University of Minnesota, Twin Cities Campus *Minnesota*
University of Mississippi *Mississippi*
University of Missouri *Missouri*
University of Missouri–Kansas City *Missouri*
University of Missouri–St. Louis *Missouri*
The University of Montana *Montana*
The University of Montana Western *Montana*
University of Montevallo *Alabama*
University of Nebraska at Kearney *Nebraska*
University of Nebraska at Omaha *Nebraska*
University of Nebraska–Lincoln *Nebraska*
University of Nevada, Las Vegas *Nevada*
University of Nevada, Reno *Nevada*
University of New Mexico *New Mexico*
University of New Orleans *Louisiana*
University of North Alabama *Alabama*
The University of North Carolina at Asheville *North Carolina*
The University of North Carolina at Chapel Hill *North Carolina*
The University of North Carolina at Charlotte *North Carolina*
The University of North Carolina at Greensboro *North Carolina*
The University of North Carolina at Pembroke *North Carolina*
The University of North Carolina Wilmington *North Carolina*
University of North Dakota *North Dakota*
University of North Florida *Florida*
University of North Texas *Texas*
University of Northern Colorado *Colorado*
University of Oklahoma *Oklahoma*
University of the Ozarks *Arkansas*
University of the Pacific *California*
University of Portland *Oregon*
University of Puerto Rico, Mayagüez Campus *Puerto Rico*
University of Puerto Rico, Río Piedras *Puerto Rico*
University of Puget Sound *Washington*
University of Rhode Island *Rhode Island*
University of Rio Grande *Ohio*
University of Rochester *New York*
University of Saint Francis *Indiana*
University of St. Francis *Illinois*
University of Saint Mary *Kansas*
University of St. Thomas *Minnesota*
University of San Diego *California*
University of Science and Arts of Oklahoma *Oklahoma*
The University of Scranton *Pennsylvania*
University of Sioux Falls *South Dakota*
University of South Alabama *Alabama*
University of South Carolina *South Carolina*
University of South Carolina Aiken *South Carolina*
University of South Carolina Upstate *South Carolina*
The University of South Dakota *South Dakota*
University of South Florida *Florida*
University of Southern Indiana *Indiana*
University of Southern Maine *Maine*
University of Southern Mississippi *Mississippi*
The University of Tennessee *Tennessee*
The University of Tennessee at Chattanooga *Tennessee*
The University of Tennessee at Martin *Tennessee*
The University of Texas at Arlington *Texas*
The University of Texas of the Permian Basin *Texas*
The University of Toledo *Ohio*
University of Tulsa *Oklahoma*
University of Vermont *Vermont*
University of Virginia *Virginia*
University of Washington *Washington*
The University of West Alabama *Alabama*
University of West Florida *Florida*
University of West Georgia *Georgia*
University of Wisconsin–La Crosse *Wisconsin*
University of Wisconsin–Oshkosh *Wisconsin*
University of Wisconsin–Platteville *Wisconsin*
University of Wisconsin–River Falls *Wisconsin*
University of Wisconsin–Stout *Wisconsin*
University of Wisconsin–Whitewater *Wisconsin*
University of Wyoming *Wyoming*
Ursuline College *Ohio*
Utah State University *Utah*
Valdosta State University *Georgia*
Valley City State University *North Dakota*
Valparaiso University *Indiana*
Vanderbilt University *Tennessee*
Virginia Commonwealth University *Virginia*
Virginia Polytechnic Institute and State University *Virginia*
Virginia State University *Virginia*
Virginia Union University *Virginia*
Viterbo University *Wisconsin*
Wabash College *Indiana*
Wagner College *New York*
Wake Forest University *North Carolina*
Walsh University *Ohio*
Warren Wilson College *North Carolina*
Wartburg College *Iowa*
Washburn University *Kansas*
Washington State University *Washington*
Washington University in St. Louis *Missouri*
Wayne State College *Nebraska*
Weber State University *Utah*
Webster University *Missouri*
Wesley College *Delaware*
West Chester University of Pennsylvania *Pennsylvania*
West Liberty University *West Virginia*
West Virginia State University *West Virginia*
West Virginia University *West Virginia*
West Virginia University at Parkersburg *West Virginia*
West Virginia Wesleyan College *West Virginia*
Western Carolina University *North Carolina*
Western Connecticut State University *Connecticut*
Western Governors University *Utah*
Western Illinois University *Illinois*
Western Kentucky University *Kentucky*
Western Michigan University *Michigan*
Western New Mexico University *New Mexico*
Western Oregon University *Oregon*
Western Washington University *Washington*
Westfield State College *Massachusetts*
Wheaton College *Illinois*
Wheelock College *Massachusetts*
Whitworth University *Washington*
Wichita State University *Kansas*
Willamette University *Oregon*
William Paterson University of New Jersey *New Jersey*
Williams Baptist College *Arkansas*
Wilmington University *Delaware*
Wingate University *North Carolina*
Winona State University *Minnesota*
Winston-Salem State University *North Carolina*
Winthrop University *South Carolina*
Wittenberg University *Ohio*
Wright State University *Ohio*
Xavier University of Louisiana *Louisiana*
Youngstown State University *Ohio*

National League for Nursing (NLN)

Abraham Baldwin Agricultural College *Georgia*
Adelphi University *New York*
Adirondack Community College *New York*
Albany State University *Georgia*
Alcorn State University *Mississippi*
Alderson-Broaddus College *West Virginia*
Allegany College of Maryland *Maryland*
Allen College *Iowa*
Alvernia University *Pennsylvania*
Alvin Community College *Texas*
Amarillo College *Texas*
American International College *Massachusetts*
Anderson University *Indiana*
Andrews University *Michigan*
Angelo State University *Texas*
Anna Maria College *Massachusetts*
Anne Arundel Community College *Maryland*
Anoka-Ramsey Community College *Minnesota*
Aquinas College *Tennessee*
Arizona State University *Arizona*
Arizona Western College *Arizona*
Arkansas Northeastern College *Arkansas*
Arkansas State University - Jonesboro *Arkansas*
Arkansas Tech University *Arkansas*
Armstrong Atlantic State University *Georgia*
Ashland Community and Technical College *Kentucky*
Athens Technical College *Georgia*
Atlantic Cape Community College *New Jersey*
Atlantic Union College *Massachusetts*
Auburn University *Alabama*
Augsburg College *Minnesota*
Augusta State University *Georgia*
Austin Community College *Texas*
Austin Peay State University *Tennessee*
Azusa Pacific University *California*
Bacone College *Oklahoma*
Baker University *Kansas*
Ball State University *Indiana*
Baltimore City Community College *Maryland*
Barton College *North Carolina*
Barton County Community College *Kansas*
Becker College *Massachusetts*
Bellarmine University *Kentucky*
Bellevue College *Washington*
Bellin College *Wisconsin*
Bemidji State University *Minnesota*
Benedictine University *Illinois*
Berea College *Kentucky*
Bergen Community College *New Jersey*
Berkshire Community College *Massachusetts*
Bethel College *Indiana*
Bethel University *Minnesota*
Bethune-Cookman University *Florida*
Bevill State Community College *Alabama*
Biola University *California*
Bishop State Community College *Alabama*
Black Hawk College *Illinois*
Blackhawk Technical College *Wisconsin*
Blessing-Rieman College of Nursing *Illinois*
Blinn College *Texas*
Blue Ridge Community College *Virginia*
Bluefield State College *West Virginia*
Bluegrass Community and Technical College *Kentucky*
Boise State University *Idaho*
Borough of Manhattan Community College of the City University of New York *New York*
Bowie State University *Maryland*
Bradley University *Illinois*
Brenau University *Georgia*
Briar Cliff University *Iowa*
Brigham Young University *Utah*
Brigham Young University–Idaho *Idaho*
Bristol Community College *Massachusetts*
Bronx Community College of the City University of New York *New York*
Brookdale Community College *New Jersey*
Broome Community College *New York*
Broward College *Florida*
Bucks County Community College *Pennsylvania*
Bunker Hill Community College *Massachusetts*
Burlington County College *New Jersey*
Butler Community College *Kansas*
Butler County Community College *Pennsylvania*
Cabarrus College of Health Sciences *North Carolina*
Calhoun Community College *Alabama*
California State University, Bakersfield *California*
California State University, Chico *California*
California State University, Dominguez Hills *California*
California State University, East Bay *California*
California State University, Fresno *California*
California State University, Fullerton *California*
California State University, Los Angeles *California*
California State University, San Bernardino *California*
California State University, Stanislaus *California*
California University of Pennsylvania *Pennsylvania*
Calvin College *Michigan*
Cape Cod Community College *Massachusetts*
Cape Fear Community College *North Carolina*
Capital Community College *Connecticut*

Henry Ford Community College *Michigan*
Hesston College *Kansas*
Highline Community College *Washington*
Hillsborough Community College *Florida*
Hinds Community College *Mississippi*
Hocking College *Ohio*
Holmes Community College *Mississippi*
Holy Family University *Pennsylvania*
Holy Names University *California*
Holyoke Community College *Massachusetts*
Hope College *Michigan*
Hopkinsville Community College *Kentucky*
Horry-Georgetown Technical College *South Carolina*
Houston Baptist University *Texas*
Howard College *Texas*
Howard Community College *Maryland*
Howard University *District of Columbia*
Hudson Valley Community College *New York*
Husson University *Maine*
Hutchinson Community College and Area Vocational School *Kansas*
Illinois Central College *Illinois*
Illinois Eastern Community Colleges, Frontier Community College *Illinois*
Illinois Eastern Community Colleges, Lincoln Trail College *Illinois*
Illinois Eastern Community Colleges, Olney Central College *Illinois*
Illinois Eastern Community Colleges, Wabash Valley College *Illinois*
Illinois State University *Illinois*
Illinois Valley Community College *Illinois*
Immaculata University *Pennsylvania*
Indian River State College *Florida*
Indiana State University *Indiana*
Indiana University Bloomington *Indiana*
Indiana University East *Indiana*
Indiana University Kokomo *Indiana*
Indiana University Northwest *Indiana*
Indiana University South Bend *Indiana*
Indiana University–Purdue University Fort Wayne *Indiana*
Indiana University–Purdue University Indianapolis *Indiana*
Inter American University of Puerto Rico, Arecibo Campus *Puerto Rico*
Inter American University of Puerto Rico, Metropolitan Campus *Puerto Rico*
Inver Hills Community College *Minnesota*
Iowa Central Community College *Iowa*
Iowa Wesleyan College *Iowa*
Itawamba Community College *Mississippi*
Ivy Tech Community College–Bloomington *Indiana*
Ivy Tech Community College–Central Indiana *Indiana*
Ivy Tech Community College–Lafayette *Indiana*
Ivy Tech Community College–North Central *Indiana*
Ivy Tech Community College–Richmond *Indiana*
Ivy Tech Community College–Southwest *Indiana*
J. Sargeant Reynolds Community College *Virginia*
Jackson State Community College *Tennessee*
Jacksonville University *Florida*
James A. Rhodes State College *Ohio*
Jamestown College *North Dakota*
Jamestown Community College *New York*
Jefferson College of Health Sciences *Virginia*
Jefferson Community College *New York*
Jefferson Community and Technical College *Kentucky*
Jefferson Davis Community College *Alabama*
Jefferson State Community College *Alabama*
John Tyler Community College *Virginia*
The Johns Hopkins University *Maryland*
Johnson County Community College *Kansas*
Joliet Junior College *Illinois*
Jones County Junior College *Mississippi*
Kansas City Kansas Community College *Kansas*
Kansas Wesleyan University *Kansas*
Kapiolani Community College *Hawaii*
Kaskaskia College *Illinois*
Kauai Community College *Hawaii*
Kean University *New Jersey*
Kennebec Valley Community College *Maine*
Kennesaw State University *Georgia*
Kent State University at Ashtabula *Ohio*
Kent State University at East Liverpool *Ohio*
Kent State University at Tuscarawas *Ohio*
Kentucky State University *Kentucky*
Kettering College of Medical Arts *Ohio*
Keuka College *New York*
Kilgore College *Texas*
Kingsborough Community College of the City University of New York *New York*
Kutztown University of Pennsylvania *Pennsylvania*
La Roche College *Pennsylvania*
La Salle University *Pennsylvania*
Labette Community College *Kansas*
Labouré College *Massachusetts*
LaGrange College *Georgia*
Lake City Community College *Florida*
Lake Land College *Illinois*
Lake Michigan College *Michigan*
Lake Superior State University *Michigan*
Lakeland Community College *Ohio*
Lakeshore Technical College *Wisconsin*
Lakeview College of Nursing *Illinois*
Lamar University *Texas*
Lander University *South Carolina*
Lane Community College *Oregon*
Langston University *Oklahoma*
Lansing Community College *Michigan*
Laramie County Community College *Wyoming*
Laredo Community College *Texas*
Lawson State Community College *Alabama*
Lee College *Texas*
Lehigh Carbon Community College *Pennsylvania*
Lehman College of the City University of New York *New York*
Lenoir-Rhyne University *North Carolina*
Lewis and Clark Community College *Illinois*
Lewis University *Illinois*
Liberty University *Virginia*
Lincoln Land Community College *Illinois*
Lincoln Memorial University *Tennessee*
Lincoln University *Missouri*
Linfield College *Oregon*
Linn-Benton Community College *Oregon*
Lock Haven University of Pennsylvania *Pennsylvania*
Lonestar College–North Harris *Texas*
Long Beach City College *California*
Long Island College Hospital School of Nursing *New York*
Long Island University, C.W. Post Campus *New York*
Lorain County Community College *Ohio*
Los Angeles Harbor College *California*
Los Angeles Pierce College *California*
Los Angeles Trade-Technical College *California*
Los Angeles Valley College *California*
Louisiana College *Louisiana*
Louisiana State University at Alexandria *Louisiana*
Louisiana State University at Eunice *Louisiana*
Louisiana Tech University *Louisiana*
Lourdes College *Ohio*
Lower Columbia College *Washington*
Loyola University Chicago *Illinois*
Loyola University New Orleans *Louisiana*
Lubbock Christian University *Texas*
Luzerne County Community College *Pennsylvania*
Lynchburg College *Virginia*
Macomb Community College *Michigan*
Macon State College *Georgia*
Madison Area Technical College *Wisconsin*
Madisonville Community College *Kentucky*
Madonna University *Michigan*
Malone University *Ohio*
Manchester Community College *New Hampshire*
Manhattan Area Technical College *Kansas*
Mansfield University of Pennsylvania *Pennsylvania*
Maria College *New York*
Marian University *Wisconsin*
Marian University *Indiana*
Marion Technical College *Ohio*
Marquette University *Wisconsin*
Marshall University *West Virginia*
Marymount University *Virginia*
Maryville University of Saint Louis *Missouri*
Marywood University *Pennsylvania*
Massachusetts Bay Community College *Massachusetts*
Massachusetts College of Pharmacy and Health Sciences *Massachusetts*
Massasoit Community College *Massachusetts*
Maui Community College *Hawaii*
McKendree University *Illinois*
McLennan Community College *Texas*
McNeese State University *Louisiana*
Medcenter One College of Nursing *North Dakota*
Medgar Evers College of the City University of New York *New York*
Medical College of Georgia *Georgia*
Medical University of South Carolina *South Carolina*
Mercer County Community College *New Jersey*
Mercy College of Health Sciences *Iowa*
Mercy College of Northwest Ohio *Ohio*
Mercyhurst College *Pennsylvania*
Meridian Community College *Mississippi*
Mesa Community College *Arizona*
Metropolitan Community College *Nebraska*
Metropolitan Community College–Penn Valley *Missouri*
Metropolitan State College of Denver *Colorado*
Metropolitan State University *Minnesota*
Miami Dade College *Florida*
Miami University *Ohio*
Miami University Hamilton *Ohio*
Miami University–Middletown Campus *Ohio*
Mid-State Technical College *Wisconsin*
MidAmerica Nazarene University *Kansas*
Middle Georgia College *Georgia*
Middle Tennessee State University *Tennessee*
Middlesex Community College *Massachusetts*
Middlesex County College *New Jersey*
Midland College *Texas*
Midland Lutheran College *Nebraska*
Midlands Technical College *South Carolina*
Midway College *Kentucky*
Midwestern State University *Texas*
Miles Community College *Montana*
Millersville University of Pennsylvania *Pennsylvania*
Millikin University *Illinois*
Milwaukee Area Technical College *Wisconsin*
Minneapolis Community and Technical College *Minnesota*
Minnesota State University Mankato *Minnesota*
Minnesota State University Moorhead *Minnesota*
Minnesota West Community and Technical College *Minnesota*
Minot State University *North Dakota*
Misericordia University *Pennsylvania*
Mississippi College *Mississippi*
Mississippi Delta Community College *Mississippi*
Mississippi Gulf Coast Community College *Mississippi*
Mississippi University for Women *Mississippi*
Missouri Southern State University *Missouri*
Missouri State University *Missouri*
Missouri Western State University *Missouri*
Mohawk Valley Community College *New York*
Monroe Community College *New York*
Monroe County Community College *Michigan*
Montana State University–Northern *Montana*
Monterey Peninsula College *California*
Montgomery County Community College *Pennsylvania*
Moorpark College *California*
Moraine Park Technical College *Wisconsin*
Moraine Valley Community College *Illinois*
Morehead State University *Kentucky*
Morningside College *Iowa*
Motlow State Community College *Tennessee*
Mott Community College *Michigan*
Mount Aloysius College *Pennsylvania*
Mount Carmel College of Nursing *Ohio*
Mt. Hood Community College *Oregon*
Mount Marty College *South Dakota*
Mount Mary College *Wisconsin*
Mount Wachusett Community College *Massachusetts*
Mountain Empire Community College *Virginia*
Mountain State University *West Virginia*
Murray State College *Oklahoma*
Murray State University *Kentucky*
Nashua Community College *New Hampshire*
Nassau Community College *New York*
National Park Community College *Arkansas*

Southwest Virginia Community College *Virginia*
Southwest Wisconsin Technical College *Wisconsin*
Southwestern Adventist University *Texas*
Southwestern College *Kansas*
Southwestern College *California*
Southwestern Illinois College *Illinois*
Southwestern Oklahoma State University *Oklahoma*
Spalding University *Kentucky*
Spokane Community College *Washington*
Springfield Technical Community College *Massachusetts*
Stark State College of Technology *Ohio*
State College of Florida Manatee-Sarasota *Florida*
State University of New York College of Agriculture and Technology at Morrisville *New York*
State University of New York College of Technology at Alfred *New York*
State University of New York College of Technology at Canton *New York*
State University of New York College of Technology at Delhi *New York*
State University of New York Downstate Medical Center *New York*
State University of New York Institute of Technology *New York*
State University of New York at Plattsburgh *New York*
State University of New York Upstate Medical University *New York*
Stephen F. Austin State University *Texas*
Stevenson University *Maryland*
Suffolk County Community College *New York*
Sullivan County Community College *New York*
Syracuse University *New York*
Tacoma Community College *Washington*
Tarrant County College District *Texas*
Technical College of the Lowcountry *South Carolina*
Temple College *Texas*
Tennessee State University *Tennessee*
Tennessee Technological University *Tennessee*
Texarkana College *Texas*
Texas A&M International University *Texas*
Texas Southmost College *Texas*
Texas Woman's University *Texas*
Thomas Edison State College *New Jersey*
Thomas More College *Kentucky*
Thomas Nelson Community College *Virginia*
Thomas University *Georgia*
Three Rivers Community College *Missouri*
Three Rivers Community College *Connecticut*
Tidewater Community College *Virginia*
Tompkins Cortland Community College *New York*
Tri-County Technical College *South Carolina*
Trident Technical College *South Carolina*
Trinity Christian College *Illinois*
Trinity Valley Community College *Texas*
Triton College *Illinois*
Trocaire College *New York*
Troy University *Alabama*
Truckee Meadows Community College *Nevada*
Truman State University *Missouri*
Tulsa Community College *Oklahoma*
Tuskegee University *Alabama*
Ulster County Community College *New York*
Umpqua Community College *Oregon*
Union County College *New Jersey*
Universidad Adventista de las Antillas *Puerto Rico*
Universidad Metropolitana *Puerto Rico*
The University of Akron *Ohio*
The University of Alabama in Huntsville *Alabama*
University of Alaska Anchorage *Alaska*
The University of Arizona *Arizona*
University of Arkansas *Arkansas*
University of Arkansas Community College at Batesville *Arkansas*
University of Arkansas at Fort Smith *Arkansas*
University of Arkansas at Little Rock *Arkansas*
University of Arkansas for Medical Sciences *Arkansas*
University of Arkansas at Monticello *Arkansas*
University of Arkansas at Pine Bluff *Arkansas*
University of California, Los Angeles *California*
University of Central Arkansas *Arkansas*
University of Central Florida *Florida*
University of Central Missouri *Missouri*
University of Central Oklahoma *Oklahoma*
University of Charleston *West Virginia*
University of Cincinnati Raymond Walters College *Ohio*
University of Colorado at Colorado Springs *Colorado*
University of Colorado Denver *Colorado*
University of Connecticut *Connecticut*
University of Delaware *Delaware*
University of Detroit Mercy *Michigan*
University of the District of Columbia *District of Columbia*
University of Evansville *Indiana*
University of Guam *Guam*
University of Hartford *Connecticut*
University of Hawaii at Hilo *Hawaii*
University of Hawaii at Manoa *Hawaii*
University of Indianapolis *Indiana*
University of Kentucky *Kentucky*
University of Louisiana at Lafayette *Louisiana*
University of Maine at Augusta *Maine*
University of Maine at Fort Kent *Maine*
University of Mary *North Dakota*
University of Mary Hardin-Baylor *Texas*
University of Massachusetts Dartmouth *Massachusetts*
University of Memphis *Tennessee*
University of Miami *Florida*
University of Michigan–Flint *Michigan*
University of Minnesota, Twin Cities Campus *Minnesota*
University of Mississippi Medical Center *Mississippi*
University of Mobile *Alabama*
University of Nevada, Las Vegas *Nevada*
University of New England *Maine*
University of New Mexico–Gallup *New Mexico*
University of North Alabama *Alabama*
The University of North Carolina at Chapel Hill *North Carolina*
The University of North Carolina at Greensboro *North Carolina*
The University of North Carolina Wilmington *North Carolina*
University of North Florida *Florida*
University of Northern Colorado *Colorado*
University of Oklahoma Health Sciences Center *Oklahoma*
University of Pennsylvania *Pennsylvania*
University of Phoenix *Arizona*
University of Phoenix–Atlanta Campus *Georgia*
University of Phoenix–Bay Area Campus *California*
University of Phoenix–Central Florida Campus *Florida*
University of Phoenix–Denver Campus *Colorado*
University of Phoenix–Detroit Campus *Michigan*
University of Phoenix–Hawaii Campus *Hawaii*
University of Phoenix–Louisiana Campus *Louisiana*
University of Phoenix–Metro Detroit Campus *Michigan*
University of Phoenix–New Mexico Campus *New Mexico*
University of Phoenix–North Florida Campus *Florida*
University of Phoenix–Phoenix Campus *Arizona*
University of Phoenix–Sacramento Valley Campus *California*
University of Phoenix–San Diego Campus *California*
University of Phoenix–South Florida Campus *Florida*
University of Phoenix–Southern Arizona Campus *Arizona*
University of Phoenix–Southern California Campus *California*
University of Phoenix–Southern Colorado Campus *Colorado*
University of Phoenix–Utah Campus *Utah*
University of Phoenix–West Florida Campus *Florida*
University of Phoenix–West Michigan Campus *Michigan*
University of Pittsburgh at Bradford *Pennsylvania*
University of Portland *Oregon*
University of Puerto Rico at Arecibo *Puerto Rico*
University of Puerto Rico at Humacao *Puerto Rico*
University of Puerto Rico, Mayagüez Campus *Puerto Rico*
University of Puerto Rico, Medical Sciences Campus *Puerto Rico*
University of Rio Grande *Ohio*
University of Rochester *New York*
University of the Sacred Heart *Puerto Rico*
University of Saint Francis *Indiana*
University of St. Francis *Illinois*
University of San Francisco *California*
University of South Carolina Aiken *South Carolina*
University of South Carolina Lancaster *South Carolina*
University of South Carolina Upstate *South Carolina*
The University of South Dakota *South Dakota*
University of South Florida *Florida*
University of Southern Maine *Maine*
University of Southern Mississippi *Mississippi*
The University of Tampa *Florida*
The University of Tennessee *Tennessee*
The University of Tennessee at Martin *Tennessee*
The University of Texas at Arlington *Texas*
The University of Texas at Brownsville *Texas*
The University of Texas Health Science Center at Houston *Texas*
The University of Texas Medical Branch *Texas*
The University of Texas at Tyler *Texas*
The University of Toledo *Ohio*
University of Tulsa *Oklahoma*
University of Vermont *Vermont*
University of the Virgin Islands *United States Virgin Islands*
University of Virginia *Virginia*
University of Washington *Washington*
The University of West Alabama *Alabama*
University of West Florida *Florida*
University of West Georgia *Georgia*
University of Wisconsin–Green Bay *Wisconsin*
Utah State University–College of Eastern Utah *Utah*
Utah Valley University *Utah*
Utica College *New York*
Valdosta State University *Georgia*
Valencia Community College *Florida*
Vanderbilt University *Tennessee*
Vermont Technical College *Vermont*
Victoria College *Texas*
Villanova University *Pennsylvania*
Vincennes University *Indiana*
Virginia Commonwealth University *Virginia*
Virginia Highlands Community College *Virginia*
Virginia Western Community College *Virginia*
Wagner College *New York*
Walla Walla Community College *Washington*
Walla Walla University *Washington*
Wallace State Community College *Alabama*
Walsh University *Ohio*
Walters State Community College *Tennessee*
Washington Adventist University *Maryland*
Washington State University *Washington*
Washtenaw Community College *Michigan*
Waukesha County Technical College *Wisconsin*
Wayne State University *Michigan*
Waynesburg University *Pennsylvania*
Weber State University *Utah*
Webster University *Missouri*
Wenatchee Valley College *Washington*
Wesley College *Delaware*
West Chester University of Pennsylvania *Pennsylvania*
West Kentucky Community and Technical College *Kentucky*
West Liberty University *West Virginia*
West Suburban College of Nursing *Illinois*
West Virginia Northern Community College *West Virginia*
West Virginia University at Parkersburg *West Virginia*
West Virginia Wesleyan College *West Virginia*
Western Connecticut State University *Connecticut*
Western Iowa Tech Community College *Iowa*
Western Kentucky University *Kentucky*
Western Michigan University *Michigan*
Western Nevada College *Nevada*
Western New Mexico University *New Mexico*
Western Oklahoma State College *Oklahoma*
Western Piedmont Community College *North Carolina*
Western Technical College *Wisconsin*
Western Wyoming Community College *Wyoming*
Whitworth University *Washington*
Widener University *Pennsylvania*
William Carey University *Mississippi*

Wilmington University *Delaware*
Winona State University *Minnesota*
Winston-Salem State University *North Carolina*
Wisconsin Indianhead Technical College *Wisconsin*
Worcester State College *Massachusetts*
Wright State University *Ohio*
Wytheville Community College *Virginia*
Yakima Valley Community College *Washington*
Yale University *Connecticut*
Yavapai College *Arizona*
York College of the City University of New York *New York*
York College of Pennsylvania *Pennsylvania*
York Technical College *South Carolina*
Youngstown State University *Ohio*

National Recreation and Park Association (NRPA)

Appalachian State University *North Carolina*
Arizona State University *Arizona*
Arkansas Tech University *Arkansas*
Aurora University *Illinois*
Bowling Green State University *Ohio*
Brigham Young University *Utah*
California Polytechnic State University, San Luis Obispo *California*
California State University, Chico *California*
California State University, Fresno *California*
California State University, Long Beach *California*
California State University, Northridge *California*
California State University, Sacramento *California*
Central Michigan University *Michigan*
Clemson University *South Carolina*
The College at Brockport, State University of New York *New York*
Colorado State University *Colorado*
East Carolina University *North Carolina*
East Stroudsburg University of Pennsylvania *Pennsylvania*
Eastern Illinois University *Illinois*
Eastern Kentucky University *Kentucky*
Eastern Michigan University *Michigan*
Eastern Washington University *Washington*
Ferris State University *Michigan*
Ferrum College *Virginia*
Florida International University *Florida*
Florida State University *Florida*
Frostburg State University *Maryland*
Gallaudet University *District of Columbia*
Georgia Southern University *Georgia*
Grambling State University *Louisiana*
Green Mountain College *Vermont*
Illinois State University *Illinois*
Indiana State University *Indiana*
Indiana University Bloomington *Indiana*
Ithaca College *New York*
Kansas State University *Kansas*
Kent State University *Ohio*
Lincoln University *Pennsylvania*
Longwood University *Virginia*
Lyndon State College *Vermont*
Marshall University *West Virginia*
Metropolitan State College of Denver *Colorado*
Michigan State University *Michigan*
Middle Tennessee State University *Tennessee*
Minnesota State University Mankato *Minnesota*
Missouri State University *Missouri*
Montclair State University *New Jersey*
North Carolina Central University *North Carolina*
North Carolina State University *North Carolina*
Northern Arizona University *Arizona*
Ohio University *Ohio*
Oklahoma State University *Oklahoma*
Old Dominion University *Virginia*
Radford University *Virginia*
San Diego State University *California*
San Francisco State University *California*
San Jose State University *California*
Slippery Rock University of Pennsylvania *Pennsylvania*
Southeast Missouri State University *Missouri*
Southern Illinois University Carbondale *Illinois*
Springfield College *Massachusetts*
State University of New York College at Cortland *New York*
Temple University *Pennsylvania*
Texas A&M University *Texas*
Texas State University–San Marcos *Texas*
University of Arkansas *Arkansas*
University of Florida *Florida*
University of Georgia *Georgia*
University of Idaho *Idaho*
University of Illinois at Urbana–Champaign *Illinois*
The University of Iowa *Iowa*
University of Maine at Machias *Maine*
University of Maine at Presque Isle *Maine*
University of Minnesota, Twin Cities Campus *Minnesota*
University of Mississippi *Mississippi*
University of Missouri *Missouri*
The University of Montana *Montana*
University of New Hampshire *New Hampshire*
The University of North Carolina at Chapel Hill *North Carolina*
The University of North Carolina at Greensboro *North Carolina*
The University of North Carolina Wilmington *North Carolina*
University of North Texas *Texas*
University of Northern Iowa *Iowa*
University of Ottawa *Ontario*
University of St. Francis *Illinois*
University of Southern Mississippi *Mississippi*
The University of Tennessee *Tennessee*
The University of Toledo *Ohio*
University of Utah *Utah*
University of Wisconsin–La Crosse *Wisconsin*
Utah State University *Utah*
Virginia Commonwealth University *Virginia*
Virginia Wesleyan College *Virginia*
West Virginia State University *West Virginia*
West Virginia University *West Virginia*
Western Illinois University *Illinois*
Western Kentucky University *Kentucky*
Western Washington University *Washington*
Winston-Salem State University *North Carolina*
York College of Pennsylvania *Pennsylvania*

New York State Board of Regents (NYSBR)

American Academy of Dramatic Arts *New York*
Bramson ORT College *New York*
Globe Institute of Technology *New York*
Holy Trinity Orthodox Seminary *New York*
Institute of Design and Construction *New York*
The King's College *New York*
New York Career Institute *New York*
TCI–The College of Technology *New York*
Utica School of Commerce *New York*
Wood Tobe–Coburn School *New York*

Northwest Commission on Colleges and Universities (NCCU)

Alaska Pacific University *Alaska*
The Art Institute of Portland *Oregon*
The Art Institute of Seattle *Washington*
Bastyr University *Washington*
Bates Technical College *Washington*
Bellevue College *Washington*
Bellingham Technical College *Washington*
Big Bend Community College *Washington*
Blackfeet Community College *Montana*
Blue Mountain Community College *Oregon*
Boise State University *Idaho*
Brigham Young University *Utah*
Brigham Young University–Idaho *Idaho*
Carroll College *Montana*
Cascadia Community College *Washington*
Central Oregon Community College *Oregon*
Central Washington University *Washington*
Centralia College *Washington*
Chemeketa Community College *Oregon*
Chief Dull Knife College *Montana*
City University of Seattle *Washington*
Clackamas Community College *Oregon*
Clark College *Washington*
Clatsop Community College *Oregon*
Clover Park Technical College *Washington*
The College of Idaho *Idaho*
College of Southern Idaho *Idaho*
College of Southern Nevada *Nevada*
Columbia Basin College *Washington*
Columbia Gorge Community College *Oregon*
Concordia University *Oregon*
Corban University *Oregon*
Cornish College of the Arts *Washington*
Dawson Community College *Montana*
Dixie State College of Utah *Utah*
Eastern Idaho Technical College *Idaho*
Eastern Oregon University *Oregon*
Eastern Washington University *Washington*
Edmonds Community College *Washington*
Eugene Bible College *Oregon*
Everett Community College *Washington*
The Evergreen State College *Washington*
Flathead Valley Community College *Montana*
Fort Belknap College *Montana*
Fort Peck Community College *Montana*
George Fox University *Oregon*
Gonzaga University *Washington*
Grays Harbor College *Washington*
Great Basin College *Nevada*
Green River Community College *Washington*
Heritage University *Washington*
Highline Community College *Washington*
Idaho State University *Idaho*
Ilisagvik College *Alaska*
Klamath Community College *Oregon*
Lake Washington Technical College *Washington*
Lane Community College *Oregon*
LDS Business College *Utah*
Lewis & Clark College *Oregon*
Lewis-Clark State College *Idaho*
Linfield College *Oregon*
Linn-Benton Community College *Oregon*
Little Big Horn College *Montana*
Lower Columbia College *Washington*
Marylhurst University *Oregon*
Miles Community College *Montana*
Montana State University *Montana*
Montana State University Billings *Montana*
Montana State University–Great Falls College of Technology *Montana*
Montana State University–Northern *Montana*
Montana Tech of The University of Montana *Montana*
Mount Angel Seminary *Oregon*
Mt. Hood Community College *Oregon*
Multnomah University *Oregon*
Nevada State College at Henderson *Nevada*
North Idaho College *Idaho*
North Seattle Community College *Washington*
Northwest Christian University *Oregon*
Northwest Indian College *Washington*
Northwest Nazarene University *Idaho*
Northwest University *Washington*
Olympic College *Washington*
Oregon College of Art & Craft *Oregon*
Oregon Health & Science University *Oregon*
Oregon Institute of Technology *Oregon*
Oregon State University *Oregon*
Oregon State University–Cascades *Oregon*
Pacific Lutheran University *Washington*
Pacific Northwest College of Art *Oregon*
Pacific University *Oregon*
Peninsula College *Washington*
Pierce College at Puyallup *Washington*
Portland Community College *Oregon*
Portland State University *Oregon*
Reed College *Oregon*
Renton Technical College *Washington*
Rocky Mountain College *Montana*
Rogue Community College *Oregon*
Saint Martin's University *Washington*
Salish Kootenai College *Montana*
Salt Lake Community College *Utah*
Seattle Central Community College *Washington*
Seattle Pacific University *Washington*
Seattle University *Washington*
Shoreline Community College *Washington*
Sierra Nevada College *Nevada*
Simon Fraser University *British Columbia*
Skagit Valley College *Washington*
Snow College *Utah*
South Puget Sound Community College *Washington*
South Seattle Community College *Washington*
Southern Oregon University *Oregon*
Southern Utah University *Utah*

Southwestern Oregon Community College *Oregon*
Spokane Community College *Washington*
Spokane Falls Community College *Washington*
Stone Child College *Montana*
Tacoma Community College *Washington*
Tillamook Bay Community College *Oregon*
Treasure Valley Community College *Oregon*
Trinity Lutheran College *Washington*
Truckee Meadows Community College *Nevada*
Umpqua Community College *Oregon*
University of Alaska Anchorage *Alaska*
University of Alaska Anchorage, Kenai Peninsula College *Alaska*
University of Alaska Anchorage, Kodiak College *Alaska*
University of Alaska Anchorage, Matanuska-Susitna College *Alaska*
University of Alaska Fairbanks *Alaska*
University of Alaska, Prince William Sound Community College *Alaska*
University of Alaska Southeast *Alaska*
University of Alaska Southeast, Ketchikan Campus *Alaska*
University of Alaska Southeast, Sitka Campus *Alaska*
University of Great Falls *Montana*
University of Idaho *Idaho*
The University of Montana *Montana*
The University of Montana Western *Montana*
The University of Montana–Helena College of Technology *Montana*
University of Nevada, Las Vegas *Nevada*
University of Nevada, Reno *Nevada*
University of Oregon *Oregon*
University of Portland *Oregon*
University of Puget Sound *Washington*
University of Utah *Utah*
University of Washington *Washington*
University of Washington, Bothell *Washington*
University of Washington, Tacoma *Washington*
Utah State University *Utah*
Utah State University–College of Eastern Utah *Utah*
Utah Valley University *Utah*
Walla Walla Community College *Washington*
Walla Walla University *Washington*
Warner Pacific College *Oregon*
Washington State University *Washington*
Weber State University *Utah*
Wenatchee Valley College *Washington*
Western Governors University *Utah*
Western Nevada College *Nevada*
Western Oregon University *Oregon*
Western Washington University *Washington*
Westminster College *Utah*
Whatcom Community College *Washington*
Whitman College *Washington*
Whitworth University *Washington*
Willamette University *Oregon*
Yakima Valley Community College *Washington*

Society of American Foresters (SAF)

Alabama Agricultural and Mechanical University *Alabama*
Auburn University *Alabama*
California Polytechnic State University, San Luis Obispo *California*
Clemson University *South Carolina*
Colorado State University *Colorado*
Duke University *North Carolina*
Humboldt State University *California*
Iowa State University of Science and Technology *Iowa*
Louisiana State University and Agricultural and Mechanical College *Louisiana*
Louisiana Tech University *Louisiana*
Michigan State University *Michigan*
Michigan Technological University *Michigan*
Mississippi State University *Mississippi*
North Carolina State University *North Carolina*
Northern Arizona University *Arizona*
The Ohio State University *Ohio*
Oklahoma State University *Oklahoma*
Oregon State University *Oregon*
Penn State University Park *Pennsylvania*
Purdue University *Indiana*
Southern Illinois University Carbondale *Illinois*
State University of New York College of Environmental Science & Forestry, Ranger School *New York*
State University of New York College of Environmental Science and Forestry *New York*
Stephen F. Austin State University *Texas*
Texas A&M University *Texas*
University of Alaska Fairbanks *Alaska*
University of Arkansas at Monticello *Arkansas*
University of California, Berkeley *California*
University of Florida *Florida*
University of Georgia *Georgia*
University of Idaho *Idaho*
University of Illinois at Urbana–Champaign *Illinois*
University of Kentucky *Kentucky*
University of Maine *Maine*
University of Massachusetts Amherst *Massachusetts*
University of Michigan *Michigan*
University of Minnesota, Twin Cities Campus *Minnesota*
University of Missouri *Missouri*
The University of Montana *Montana*
University of New Hampshire *New Hampshire*
The University of Tennessee *Tennessee*
University of Vermont *Vermont*
University of Washington *Washington*
University of Wisconsin–Madison *Wisconsin*
University of Wisconsin–Stevens Point *Wisconsin*
Utah State University *Utah*
Virginia Polytechnic Institute and State University *Virginia*
Washington State University *Washington*
West Virginia University *West Virginia*
Yale University *Connecticut*

Teacher Education Accreditation Council (TEAC)

Adams State College *Colorado*
Alfred University *New York*
Aquinas College *Michigan*
Bard College *New York*
Bethel University *Minnesota*
Boston College *Massachusetts*
Brigham Young University *Utah*
Buena Vista University *Iowa*
Caldwell College *New Jersey*
Calvin College *Michigan*
Cambridge College *Massachusetts*
Case Western Reserve University *Ohio*
Centenary College *New Jersey*
Central Michigan University *Michigan*
Chapman University *California*
Colgate University *New York*
College of Mount St. Joseph *Ohio*
College of Mount Saint Vincent *New York*
The College of St. Scholastica *Minnesota*
Colorado State University *Colorado*
Colorado State University–Pueblo *Colorado*
Dominican College *New York*
Dordt College *Iowa*
Fairleigh Dickinson University, Metropolitan Campus *New Jersey*
Felician College *New Jersey*
Ferris State University *Michigan*
Florida Atlantic University *Florida*
Georgian Court University *New Jersey*
Hofstra University *New York*
Hollins University *Virginia*
Holy Family University *Pennsylvania*
Lakeland College *Wisconsin*
Le Moyne College *New York*
Lee University *Tennessee*
Lesley University *Massachusetts*
Lindenwood University *Missouri*
Long Island University, Brooklyn Campus *New York*
Long Island University, C.W. Post Campus *New York*
Lourdes College *Ohio*
Manhattan College *New York*
Mary Baldwin College *Virginia*
Marygrove College *Michigan*
Medaille College *New York*
Michigan State University *Michigan*
Michigan Technological University *Michigan*
Misericordia University *Pennsylvania*
Montana State University *Montana*
Nazareth College of Rochester *New York*
New Jersey City University *New Jersey*
New York University *New York*
Oakland University *Michigan*
Oberlin College *Ohio*
Olivet College *Michigan*
Regis University *Colorado*
Rice University *Texas*
Robert Morris University *Pennsylvania*
Rochester Institute of Technology *New York*
Rockhurst University *Missouri*
Rutgers, The State University of New Jersey, New Brunswick *New Jersey*
St. Ambrose University *Iowa*
Saint Francis University *Pennsylvania*
St. John's University *New York*
St. Lawrence University *New York*
Saint Martin's University *Washington*
Saint Peter's College *New Jersey*
Seton Hill University *Pennsylvania*
Shenandoah University *Virginia*
Siena Heights University *Michigan*
Southern Utah University *Utah*
Spring Arbor University *Michigan*
State University of New York at Binghamton *New York*
State University of New York Empire State College *New York*
State University of New York at Plattsburgh *New York*
Sweet Briar College *Virginia*
Temple University *Pennsylvania*
Tulane University *Louisiana*
University at Albany, State University of New York *New York*
University at Buffalo, the State University of New York *New York*
University of Detroit Mercy *Michigan*
The University of Findlay *Ohio*
University of Houston–Victoria *Texas*
University of Massachusetts Boston *Massachusetts*
University of Michigan *Michigan*
University of Michigan–Dearborn *Michigan*
University of Missouri *Missouri*
University of Nebraska–Lincoln *Nebraska*
University of New Hampshire *New Hampshire*
University of Phoenix *Arizona*
University of Pittsburgh *Pennsylvania*
University of St. Thomas *Texas*
University of Southern Maine *Maine*
The University of Texas at Tyler *Texas*
University of Tulsa *Oklahoma*
University of Utah *Utah*
University of Virginia *Virginia*
Utah State University *Utah*
Utah Valley University *Utah*
Utica College *New York*
Wayne State College *Nebraska*
Wayne State University *Michigan*
Westminster College *Utah*
Wilmington College *Ohio*
Xavier University *Ohio*

Transnational Association of Christian Colleges and Schools (TACCS)

Apex School of Theology *North Carolina*
Bethesda Christian University *California*
Beulah Heights University *Georgia*
Boston Baptist College *Massachusetts*
California Christian College *California*
Christian Life College *Illinois*
Clinton Junior College *South Carolina*
Community Christian College *California*
Epic Bible College *California*
Gutenberg College *Oregon*
Heritage Bible College *North Carolina*
Hillsdale Free Will Baptist College *Oklahoma*
International Baptist College *Arizona*
The King's College and Seminary *California*
Liberty University *Virginia*
Luther Rice University *Georgia*
Maple Springs Baptist Bible College and Seminary *Maryland*
Messenger College *Missouri*
Midwest University *Missouri*

New Life Theological Seminary *North Carolina*
New Saint Andrews College *Idaho*
Pacific Islands University *Guam*
Patrick Henry College *Virginia*
Piedmont Baptist College and Graduate School *North Carolina*
San Diego Christian College *California*
Shasta Bible College *California*
Southern California Seminary *California*
Southern Methodist College *South Carolina*
Temple Baptist College *Ohio*
Tennessee Temple University *Tennessee*
Trinity Baptist College *Florida*
Virginia University of Lynchburg *Virginia*
Williamson Christian College *Tennessee*

Index of U.S. Colleges

Index of U.S. Colleges

Index of Canadian Colleges